POLITICAL SCIENCE ABSTRACTS

1989

Annual Supplement

In three volumes
Volume 1

POLITICAL SCIENCE ABSTRACTS
(Formerly The Universal Reference System, Political Science, Government, and Public Policy Series)

Volume   I   *International Affairs (Second Edition)*

Volume   II   *Legislative Process, Representation, and Decision Making*

Volume   III   *Bibliography of Bibliographies in Political Science, Government, and Public Policy*

Volume   IV   *Administrative Management: Public and Private Bureaucracy*

Volume   V   *Current Events and Problems of Modern Society*

Volume   VI   *Public Opinion, Mass Behavior, and Political Psychology*

Volume   VII   *Law, Jurisprudence, and Judicial Process*

Volume   VIII   *Economic Regulation, Business, and Government*

Volume   IX   *Public Policy and the Management of Science*

Volume   X   *Comparative Government and Cultures*

1967 Annual Supplement   *1978 Annual Supplement*

1968 Annual Supplement   *1979 Annual Supplement*

1969 Annual Supplement   *1980 Annual Supplement*

1970 Annual Supplement   *1981 Annual Supplement*

1971 Annual Supplement   *1982 Annual Supplement*

1972 Annual Supplement   *1983 Annual Supplement*

1973 Annual Supplement   *1984 Annual Supplement*

1974 Annual Supplement   *1985 Annual Supplement*

1975 Annual Supplement   *1986 Annual Supplement*

1976 Annual Supplement   *1987 Annual Supplement*

1977 Annual Supplement   *1988 Annual Supplement*

1989 Annual Supplement

POLITICAL SCIENCE ABSTRACTS

1989

Annual Supplement

In three volumes

Volume 1

Compiled by the staff of
IFI/Plenum Data Company

SPRINGER SCIENCE+BUSINESS MEDIA, LLC

Political Science Abstracts is a continuation of the
Political Science, Government, and Public Policy Series of
The Universal Reference System, consisting of the ten volumes
listed facing the title page of this volume and annual
supplements published from 1967 to 1986.

Library of Congress Catalog Card Number 78-6367

ISBN 978-1-4615-7621-1   ISBN 978-1-4615-7619-8 (eBook)
DOI 10.1007/978-1-4615-7619-8

© 1990 Springer Science+Business Media New York
Originally published by IFI/Plenum Data Company New York in 1990

PREFACE

The 1989 Supplement of *Political Science Abstracts* contains 10,000 carefully prepared abstracts of materials from public affairs magazines, major newspapers, professional journals, and books devoted to politics and political analysis. The organization of the preceding volumes has been retained intact, as has the recently added list of subdisciplinary descriptors. Users of earlier volumes will be on familiar ground, while those new to *Political Science Abstracts* will find the instructions on page ix easy to master.

CONTENTS

HOW TO USE THIS SUPPLEMENT

Three simple steps are all that are needed to introduce the user to this easily accessible indexing system.

STEP 1: Turn to the Index of Terms and locate as many terms as possible which deal with your subject. If you are interested in coverage of a more generic nature, you may instead turn to the next page, where key descriptors are listed which are associated with the major subject areas in political science and with their subdivisions. Note that the index includes methodological as well as topical terms. Numerical listings (e.g., 24TH/PAR/C) are located at the end of the alphabetical listing.

STEP 2: Turn to the Bibliographic Index and look up the terms which you found in Step 1. The list of indexing terms below each entry indicates the key terms chosen to describe that entry. Scan the entries to determine which apply to your topic, jotting down the page and item numbers of entries that fit your needs. Follow this same procedure with all indexing terms which relate to your subject. The bibliographic entry includes the author, title, indexing terms, the page on which the full citation and the abstract appear, and the item number of the entry.

STEP 3: Turn to the page and find the item number which you found in Step 2. This will give you a short abstract of the article or book. Abstracts are arranged alphabetically by author. Unsigned entries have been placed at the front of the alphabetical listing. A full author index can be found in Volume 3.

POLITICAL SCIENCE
SUBDISCIPLINARY DESCRIPTORS

I. Foreign and Cross-National Political Institutions and Behavior
    Code: FOR/CROS

1. Analyses of particular systems or subsystems
    Code: (e.g., USSR, CHINA, GREAT/BRIT)
2. Decision-making processes
    Code: DECISION
3. Elites and their oppositions
    Code: ELITES, OPPOSITION
4. Mass participation and communications
    Code: PARTICIPAT, COMMUNICAT
5. Parties, mass movements, secondary associations
    Code: POL/PARTY, POL/MVMNT, VOL/ASSN
6. Political development and modernization
    Code: POL/DEVEL, MODERNIZE
7. Politics of planning
    Code: PLANNING
8. Values, ideologies, belief systems, political culture
    Code: ALL/VALS, IDEOLOGY, BELIEF/SYS, POL/CULTUR

II. International Law, Organization, and Politics
     Code: INT/POL

9. International law
    Code: INT/LAW
10. International organization and administration
    Code: INT/ORG
11. International politics
    Code: INT/REL

III. Methodology
      Code: METHODOLGY

12. Computer techniques
    Code: COMPUTER
13. Content analysis
    Code: CON/ANAL
14. Epistemology and philosophy of science
    Code: EPIST, PHILOS/SCI
15. Experimental design
    Code: EXPER/DES

16. Field data collection
    Code: CASE/STUDY
17. Measurement and index construction
    Code: MEASURE, INDEX
18. Model building
    Code: MODEL
19. Statistical analysis
    Code: STATISTICS
20. Survey design and analysis
    Code: SURVEY, DATA/COMP

IV. Political Stability, Instability, and Change
     Code: POL/BEHAV, POL/PSYCH, POL/SOGY

21. Cultural modification and diffusion
    Code: CULTR/MOD
22. Personality and motivation
    Code: PERSONALTY, MOTIVATE
23. Political leadership and recruitment
    Code: LEADERSHIP, RECRUITMNT
24. Political socialization
    Code: SOCIALZATN
25. Revolution and violence
    Code: REVOLUTION, VIOLENCE
26. Schools and political education
    Code: SCHOOL, POL/ED
27. Social and economic stratification
    Code: SOC/STRATA, SOC/STRUCT, SOC/STATUS, SOCIO/ECON

V. Political Theory
    Code: POL/THEORY

28. Systems of political ideas in history
    Code: BELIEF/SYS
29. Ideology systems
    Code: IDEOLOGY
30. Political philosophy (general)
    Code: POL/PHILOS
31. Methodological and analytical systems
    Code: METH/CNCPT

INDEX OF TERMS

DESCRIPTOR	FREQUENCY	PAGE
COMMON/LAW ...COMMON LAW; SEE ALSO LAW, ENGLSH/LAW	1	892
COMMON/MKT ...COMMON MARKET	3	892
COMMONWLTH ...BRITISH COMMONWEALTH OF NATIONS; SEE ALSO APPROPRIATE NATIONS	15	892
COMMUN/DEV ...COMMUNITY DEVELOPMENT; SEE ALSO URBAN/RNWL, MUNICIPAL, NEIGHBOR	15	892
COMMUNAL ...COMMUNALISM, COMMUNAL VIOLENCE	2	893
COMMUNES ...COMMUNES	1	893
COMMUNICA ...COMMUNICATIONS	22	893
COMMUNICATION, MASS ...SEE MASS/MEDIA, TV, PRESS, COM/INDUS		
COMMUNICATION, PERSONAL ...SEE PERSON/REL		
COMMUNICATIONS INDUSTRY ...SEE COM/INDUS, TV, PRESS, MASS/MEDIA		
COMMUNICATIONS SATELLITE ...SEE COMSAT		
COMMUNISM ...COMMUNISM	136	894
COMMUNISM ...SEE MARXISM		
COMMUNIST CHINA ...SEE CHINA/COM		
COMMUNIST ECONOMIC ORGANIZATION ...SEE COMECON		
COMMUNIST INFORMATION BUREAU ...SEE COMINFORM		
COMMUNIST PARTY ...SEE COMMUNST/P, MARXISM, POL/PARTY		
COMMUNIST THIRD INTERNATIONAL ...SEE COMINTERN		
COMMUNITY ...SEE NEIGHBOR		
COMMUNITY ACTION PROJECT ...SEE CAP		
COMMUNITY DEVELOPMENT ...SEE COMMUN/DEV		
COMMUNST/P ...COMMUNIST PARTY (ALL NATIONS); SEE ALSO MARXISM, POL/PARTY	367	897
COMORO/IS ...COMORO ISLANDS	2	905
COMP/ANAL ...COMPARATIVE ANALYSIS	6	905
COMPANY, LARGE ...SEE LARGE/CO		
COMPANY, SMALL ...SEE SMALL/CO		
COMPARISON OF ALTERNATIVE POLICIES ...SEE METH/COMP		
COMPARISON OF GOVERNMENTS ...SEE GOVT/COMP		
COMPARISON OF GROUPS ...SEE GROUP/COMP		
COMPARISON OF IDEAS ...SEE IDEA/COMP		
COMPARISON OF INDIVIDUALS ...SEE PERS/COMP		
COMPARISON OF NATIONS ...SEE NAT/COMP		
COMPETENCE ...SEE SKILL, KNOWLEDGE		
COMPULSORY NATIONAL SERVICE ...SEE NATL/SERV		
COMPUTER ...COMPUTER TECHNIQUES AND TECHNOLOGY; SEE ALSO INFO/RTRVL	14	905
COMTE/A ...AUGUST COMTE	1	906
CON/ANAL ...QUANTITATIVE CONTENT ANALYSIS	1	906
CONFED ...CONFEDERATE STATES OF AMERICA	1	906
CONFEDERATION OF CHRISTIAN TRADE UNIONISTS ...SEE CLASC		
CONFER ...CONFERENCES; SEE ALSO GP/DELIB	2	906
CONFERENCES ...SEE CONFER, GP/DELIB		
CONFIDENCE, PERSONAL ...SEE SUPEGO		
CONFLICT ...CONFLICT	96	906
CONFLICT/I ...CONFLICT OF INTEREST	2	908
CONFLICT, MILITARY ...SEE WAR, FORCES, COERCION AND SPECIFIC CONFLICTS		
CONFLICT, PERSONAL ...SEE PERSON/REL, ROLE		
CONFORMITY ...SEE CONSENSUS, DOMINATION		
CONFUCIUS ...CONFUCIUS	3	908
CONGO ...PEOPLE'S REPUBLIC OF THE CONGO; SEE ALSO AFRICA/W	2	908
CONGRESS ...CONGRESS (ALL NATIONS); SEE ALSO LEGISLATUR, HOUSE/REP, SENATE, GP/DELIB	156	909
CONGRESS OF INDUSTRIAL ORGANIZATIONS ...SEE CIO		
CONGRESS OF RACIAL EQUALITY ...SEE CORE		
CONGRESS OF VIENNA ...SEE CON/VIENNA		
CONGRESS/P ...CONGRESS PARTY (ALL NATIONS); SEE ALSO POL/PARTY	23	912
CONNECTICT ...CONNECTICUT	3	913
CONSCIENCE ...SEE SUPEGO		
CONSCN/OBJ ...CONSCIENTIOUS OBJECTION TO WAR AND KILLING	1	913
CONSCRIPTN ...CONSCRIPTION, SEE ALSO SELEC/SERV, DRAFT	7	913
CONSENSUS ...CONSENSUS	2	913
CONSERV/P ...CONSERVATIVE PARTY (ALL NATIONS); SEE ALSO POL/PARTY, CONSERVE	15	913
CONSERVATISM ...SEE CONSERVE		
CONSERVATIVE PARTY (ALL NATIONS) ...SEE CONSERV/P, POL/PARTY, CONSERVE		
CONSERVATN ...CONSERVATION	10	914
CONSERVE ...CONSERVATISM AND CONSERVATIVES	77	914
CONSOLDATN ...POLITICAL, ECONOMIC, OR SOCIAL CONSOLIDATION OR INTEGRATION OF SUB-NATIONAL GROUPS, ENTITIES, STATES OR THEIR POLITICAL SUBDIVISIONS; SEE ALSO NATL/INTEG, UNIFICATN	2	916
CONSTITNCY ...CONSTITUENCY	2	916
CONSTITUENCY ...SEE REPRESENT		
CONSTITUTN ...CONSTITUTIONS; FOR U.S. CONSTITUTION, SEE ALSO SPECIFIC AMENDMENTS (E.G. AMEND/I)	103	916
CONSTN/CNV ...CONSTITUTIONAL CONVENTION	3	918
CONSULT ...CONSULTANTS	6	918
CONSUMER ...CONSUMER AFFAIRS	12	919
CONSUMER PRICE INDEX ...SEE CPI		
CONTAIN ...CONTAINMENT	11	919
CONTAINMENT ...SEE STRATEGY		
CONTENT ANALYSIS ...SEE CON/ANAL, DOC/ANAL		
CONTINENTAL SHELF ...SEE CONT/SHELF		
CONTRACT ...CONTRACTS, CONTRACT ADMINISTRATORS; SEE ALSO AGREEMENT	1	919
CONTRAS ...CONTRAS; SEE ALSO NICARAGUA	15	919
CONTROL ...CONTROL OF HUMAN GROUP OPERATIONS	2	920
CONTROLLED DIRECT OBSERVATION ...SEE CONT/OBS		
CONVENTION ...SEE PARTY/CONV, POL/PARTY, GP/DELIB, CONFER		
CONVERTIBILITY ...SEE GOLD, SILVER		
COOP/FED ...COOPERATIVE FEDERALISM	1	920
COOPERATION ...SEE AGREEMENT		
COOPERATIVE ...SEE VOL/ASSN, COOPERATVE, COOP/FED, ECO/TACTIC		
COOPERATIVE ECONOMY ...SEE COOPERATVE		
COOPERATIVE FEDERALISM ...SEE COOP/FED		
COOPERATVE ...COOPERATIVE ECONOMY, UNDERTAKINGS; SEE ALSO ECO/TACTIC	7	920
COORDINATION ...SEE CENTRAL		
COPYRIGHT ...COPYRIGHT	1	920
CORN/LAWS ...CORN LAWS	1	920
CORONATIONS ...SEE INAUGURATE, KING		
CORPORATION ...SEE LARGE/CO, SMALL/CO, INDUSTRY, MULTI/CORP		
CORPORATSM ...CORPORATISM	14	920
CORRECTION ...CORRECTIONS	10	921
CORRECTIONAL INSTITUTION ...SEE PUBL/INST, PRISON		
CORRESPONDENCE ...SEE WRITING, BIOGRAPHY, AUTOBIOG		
CORRUPTION ...CORRUPTION OF AND ILLEGAL INFLUENCE OVER DECISION-MAKERS; SEE ALSO BOSSISM	71	921
COST ...ECONOMIC VALUE; SEE ALSO PROFIT, PRICE	4	922
COSTA/RICA ...COSTA RICA; SEE ALSO CENTRAL/AM, LATIN/AMER	12	923
COUNCIL OF ECONOMIC ADVISORS ...SEE CEA, CONSULT, GP/DELIB, ECO/TACTIC, ECONOMICS		
COUNCIL OF STATE ...SEE CONSULT		
COUNCIL-MANAGER SYSTEM OF LOCAL GOVERNMENT ...SEE COUNCL/MGR, LOCAL/GOVT		
COUNCL/EUR ...COUNCIL OF EUROPE	3	923
COUNCL/MGR ...COUNCIL-MANAGER SYSTEM OF LOCAL GOVERNMENT; SEE ALSO LOCAL/GOVT, MUNICIPAL	1	923
COUNT/REV ...COUNTER-REVOLUTION; SEE ALSO REVOLUTION	1	923
COUNTIES ...SEE LOCAL/GOVT		
COUP ...COUP D'ETAT; SEE ALSO REVOLUTION	27	923
COURAGE ...SEE DRIVE		
COURT MARTIAL ...SEE CT/MARTIAL		
COURT OF APPEALS ...SEE CT/APPEALS		
COURT OF MAN ...SEE COURT/MAN		
COURT SYSTEMS ...SEE CT/SYSTEM, SUPREME/CT, CT/APPEALS, DIST/COURT, JUVNL/CT, ADJUDICATN		
COVERT ...COVERT ACTIVITIES, INCLUDING SECRET GOVERNMENT OPERATIONS, SUCH AS THE IRAN-CONTRA ARMS DEAL	12	924
CPI ...CONSUMER PRICE INDEX	1	924
CREATE ...CREATIVE PROCESSES	2	924
CREDIT ...CREDIT	2	924
CRIME ...CRIME	22	924
CRIME/ORG ...ORGANIZED CRIME	1	925
CRIMINAL LAW ...SEE CRIMNL/LAW		
CRIMINL ...CRIMINAL	3	925
CRIMNL/LAW ...CRIMINAL LAW; SEE ALSO LAW	14	925
CRISIS/INT ...CRISIS INTERVENTION, (ALL TYPES)	5	925
CRITICAL/T ...CRITICAL THEORY	2	925
CROATIA ...CROATIA	1	926
CROSS-CULTURAL COMPARISON ...SEE CULTR/COMP		
CROSS-NATIONAL COMPARISON ...SEE NAT/COMP		
CROSS-PRESSURES ...SEE ROLE		
CT/SYSTEM ...COURT SYSTEM; SEE ALSO SUPREME/CT, CT/APPEALS, DIST/COURT, JUVNL/CT, ADJUDICATN	26	926
CUBA ...CUBA	60	926
CUBN/MISSL ...CUBAN MISSILE CRISIS	8	928
CULT ...CULTS OR CULTISM; SEE ALSO EXTREMISM	1	928
CULT/EXCHG ...CULTURAL EXCHANGE; SEE ALSO CULTURE, INT/REL	7	928
CULTR/COMP ...COMPARISON OF CULTURES; SEE ALSO CULTURE, NAT/COMP	9	928
CULTS ...SEE SECT		
CULTUR/REV ...CULTURAL REVOLUTION	4	928
CULTURAL ASSIMILATION ...SEE ASSIMILATN, GROUP/REL, INGP/REL		
CULTURAL COMPARISONS ...SEE CULTR/COMP, CULTURE, NAT/COMP		
CULTURAL DIFFERENCES ...SEE CULTR/COMP		
CULTURAL EXCHANGE ...SEE CULT/EXCHG, CULTURE, INT/REL		
CULTURAL INTEGRATION ...SEE ASSIMILATN, GROUP/REL, INGP/REL		
CULTURAL REVOLUTION IN CHINA ...SEE CULTUR/REV		
CULTURE ...CULTURAL PATTERNS; FOR POLITICAL CULTURE SEE POL/CULTUR	50	929
CURRENCY ...NATURE OF CURRENCY AND MONIES IN USE	4	930
CUSTOMS BUREAU ...SEE BUR/CUSTOM		
CWLTH ...COMMONWEALTH, EXCEPT BRITISH COMMONWEALTH	2	930
CYBERNETIC ...CYBERNETICS; SEE ALSO FEEDBACK, SIMULATION, CONTROL	1	930
CYCLES ...SEE TIME/SEQ		

DESCRIPTOR	FREQUENCY	PAGE
UDALL/M ...MORRIS UDALL	1	1666
UGANDA ...UGANDA; SEE ALSO AFRICA/E	11	1666
UK ...UNITED KINGDOM	8	1667
UKRAINE ...UKRAINE	10	1667
ULSTER ...ULSTER	2	1667
UN ...UNITED NATIONS; SEE ALSO INT/ORG, INT/REL	94	1667
UNCTAD ...UNITED NATIONS COMMISSION ON TRADE, AID, AND DEVELOPMENT	1	1669
UNDERDEVELOPED COUNTRIES ...SEE ECO/UNDEV, POL/DEVEL AND SPECIFIC NATIONS		
UNESCO ...UNITED NATIONS EDUCATIONAL, SCIENTIFIC, AND CULTURAL ORGANIZATION; SEE ALSO UN, INT/ORG	2	1669
UNIFICATN ...UNIFICATION OR REUNIFICATION OF SOVEREIGN GEOGRAPHIC-POLITICAL ENTITIES; SEE ALSO POL/DEVEL, ECO/INTEG AND SPECIFIC NATIONS. FOR UNIFICATION AT OTHER LEVELS, SEE NATL/INTEG, CONSOLDATN	6	1670
UNIFORM NARCOTIC DRUG ACT ...SEE NARCO/ACT		
UNION ...UNION	14	1670
UNION AFRICAINE ET MALGACHE, ALSO OCAM ...SEE UAM		
UNION LABOR PARTY ...SEE UN/LABOR/P, LABOR, POL/PARTY		
UNION OF CENTRAL AFRICAN STATES ...SEE UEAC		
UNION OF SOUTH AFRICA ...SEE SOUTH/AFR		
UNION OF SOVIET SOCIALIST REPUBLICS ...SEE USSR		
UNION PARTY ...SEE UNION/P		
UNIONS ...SEE LABOR		
UNITED ARAB EMIRATES ...SEE UAE		
UNITED ARAB REPUBLIC ...SEE EGYPT, SYRIA		
UNITED AUTO WORKERS ...SEE UAW		
UNITED FARM WORKERS ...SEE MIGRANT/WK, LABOR, CHAVEZ/C, AGRICULTUR		
UNITED KINGDOM ...SEE UK, COMMONWLTH		
UNITED MINE WORKERS ...SEE UMW		
UNITED NATIONS ...SEE UN		
UNITED NATIONS ATOMIC ENERGY AUTHORITY ...SEE AEA		
UNITED NATIONS COMMISSION ON TRADE, AID, AND DEVELOPMENT.... SEE UNCTAD		
UNITED NATIONS CONFERENCE ON THE APPLICATION OF SCIENCE AND TECHNOLOGY FOR THE BENEFIT OF THE LESS-DEVELOPED AREAS ... SEE UNCSAT, UN		
UNITED NATIONS DEVELOPMENT PROGRAM ...SEE UNDP, UN		
UNITED NATIONS ECONOMIC AND SOCIAL COUNCIL ...SEE ECOSOC		
UNITED NATIONS EDUCATIONAL, SCIENTIFIC, AND CULTURAL ORGANIZATION ...SEE UNESCO		
UNITED NATIONS EMERGENCY FORCE ...SEE UNEF, UN		
UNITED NATIONS GENERAL ASSEMBLY ...SEE GEN/ASSEM, UN		
UNITED NATIONS INDUSTRIAL DEVELOPMENT ORGANIZATION ...SEE UNIDO, UN		
UNITED NATIONS INTERNATIONAL LAW COMMISSION ...SEE ILC		
UNITED NATIONS RELIEF AND REHABILITATION AGENCY ...SEE UNRRA, UN, REHABILITN, AGENCIES		
UNITED NATIONS RELIEF AND WORKS AGENCY ...SEE UNRWA, UN, AGENCIES		
UNITED NATIONS SECRETARY GENERAL ...SEE UN/SEC/GEN, UN		
UNITED NATIONS SECURITY COUNCIL ...SEE SECUR/COUN		
UNITED NATIONS SPECIAL FUND ...SEE UNSF, UN		
UNITED STATES ...SEE PRE/AMER, PRE/US/AM, USA-45, USA+45, US/WEST, US/EAST, US/NORTH, US/SOUTH, US/MIDWEST, AND SPECIFIC STATES AND CITIES		
UNIVERSAL ...UNIVERSAL TO MAN	2	1671
UNIVERSITIES ...SEE HIGHER/ED		
UNRWA ...UNITED NATIONS RELIEF AND WORKS AGENCY	1	1671
URBAN ...URBAN, IN ANY CONTEXT	61	1671
URBAN/PROB ...URBAN PROBLEMS	11	1672
URBAN/RNWL ...URBAN RENEWAL; SEE ALSO COMMUN/DEV, MUNICIPAL, TOWN/PLAN	7	1673
URBAN/STUD ...URBAN STUDIES	1	1673
URBANIZATN ...URBANIZATION; SEE ALSO MUNICIPAL	7	1673
URUGUAY ...URUGUAY; SEE ALSO SOUTH/AMER, LATIN/AMER	10	1673
US AGENCY FOR INTERNATIONAL DEVELOPMENT ...SEE US/AID		
US ARMS CONTROL AND DISARMAMENT AGENCY ...SEE ACD		
US ATOMIC ENERGY COMMISSION ...SEE AEC		
US ATTORNEY GENERAL ...SEE ATTRNY/GEN		
US BUREAU OF ELECTIONS ...SEE BUR/ELECT		
US BUREAU OF INDIAN AFFAIRS ...SEE BUR/INDIAN		
US BUREAU OF PRISONS ...SEE BUR/PRISON		
US BUREAU OF RECLAMATION ...SEE BUR/RECLAM		
US BUREAU OF STANDARDS ...SEE BUR/STNDRD		
US BUREAU OF THE BUDGET ...SEE BUR/BUDGET		
US CENTRAL INTELLIGENCE AGENCY ...SEE CIA		
US CIVIL AERONAUTICS BOARD ...SEE CAB		
US COUNCIL OF ECONOMIC ADVISERS ...SEE CEA		
US CUSTOMS BUREAU ...SEE BUR/CUSTOM		
US DEPARTMENT OF AGRICULTURE ...SEE DEPT/AGRI		
US DEPARTMENT OF COMMERCE ...SEE DEPT/COM		
US DEPARTMENT OF DEFENSE ...SEE DEPT/DEFEN		
US DEPARTMENT OF HEALTH, EDUCATION, AND WELFARE ...SEE DEPT/HEW		
US DEPARTMENT OF HOUSING AND URBAN DEVELOPMENT ...SEE DEPT/HUD		
US DEPARTMENT OF JUSTICE ...SEE DEPT/JUST		
US DEPARTMENT OF LABOR AND INDUSTRY ...SEE DEPT/LABOR		
US DEPARTMENT OF STATE ...SEE DEPT/STATE		
US DEPARTMENT OF THE INTERIOR ...SEE DEPT/INTER		
US DEPARTMENT OF THE TREASURY ...SEE DEPT/TREAS		
US DEPARTMENT OF TRANSPORATION ...SEE DEPT/TRANS		
US DEPARTMENT OF WAR ...SEE DEPT/WAR		
US FEDERAL AVIATION AGENCY ...SEE FAA		
US FEDERAL BUREAU OF INVESTIGATION ...SEE FBI		
US FEDERAL COMMUNICATIONS COMMISSION ...SEE FCC		
US FEDERAL COUNCIL FOR SCIENCE AND TECHNOLOGY ...SEE FEDSCI/TEC		
US FEDERAL ENERGY ADMINISTRATION ...SEE FEA		
US FEDERAL HOUSING ADMINISTRATION ...SEE FHA		
US FEDERAL OPEN MARKET COMMITTEE ...SEE FED/OPNMKT		
US FEDERAL POWER COMMISSION ...SEE FPC		
US FEDERAL RESERVE SYSTEM ...SEE FED/RESERV		
US FEDERAL TRADE COMMISSION ...SEE FTC		
US FOOD AND AGRICULTURAL ORGANIZATION ...SEE FAO		
US FOOD AND DRUG ASSOCIATION ...SEE FDA		
US GENERAL ACCOUNTING OFFICE ...SEE GAO		
US HOUSE COMMITTEE ON UNAMERICAN ACTIVITIES ...SEE HUAC		
US HOUSE OF REPRESENTATIVES ...SEE HOUSE/REP		
US HOUSE RULES COMMITTEE ...SEE RULES/COMM		
US INFORMATION AGENCY ...SEE USIA		
US INTERNAL REVENUE SERVICE ...SEE IRS		
US INTERNATIONAL COOPERATION ADMINISTRATION ...SEE ICA		
US INTERSTATE COMMERCE COMMISSION ...SEE ICC		
US NATIONAL AERONAUTICS AND SPACE ADMINISTRATION ...SEE NASA		
US NATIONAL SECURITY AGENCY ...SEE NSA, NATL/SECUR		
US OFFICE OF DIRECT FOREIGN INVESTMENTS ...SEE OFDI		
US OFFICE OF ECONOMIC OPPORTUNITY ...SEE OEO		
US OFFICE OF EDUCATION ...SEE OFF/EDUCN, DEPT/HEW		
US OFFICE OF EMERGENCY PLANNING ...SEE OEP		
US OFFICE OF FOOD FOR PEACE ...SEE FOOD/PEACE		
US OFFICE OF MANAGEMENT AND BUDGET ...SEE OMB		
US OFFICE OF PRICE ADMINISTRATION ...SEE OPA		
US OFFICE OF WAR INFORMATION ...SEE OWI		
US PATENT OFFICE ...SEE PATENT/OFF		
US PEACE CORPS ...SEE PEACE/CORP		
US SECRETARY OF STATE ...SEE SEC/STATE		
US SECURITIES AND EXCHANGE COMMISSION ...SEE SEC/EXCHNG		
US SENATE ...SEE SENATE		
US SENATE COMMITTEE ON BANKING AND CURRENCY ...SEE BANK/CUR/C, CURRENCY, BANKING, SENATE		
US SENATE COMMITTEE ON FOREIGN RELATIONS ...SEE FOREIGNREL		
US SENATE SCIENCE ADVISORY COMMISSION ...SEE SCI/ADVSR		
US SMALL BUSINESS ADMINISTRATION ...SEE SBA		
US SOUTH ...SEE SOUTH/US		
US/AID ...UNITED STATES AGENCY FOR INTERNATIONAL DEVELOPMENT; SEE ALSO FOR/AID	1	1675
USA+45 ...UNITED STATES, 1945 TO PRESENT; SEE ALSO SPECIFIC TOPICS	1791	1675
USA-45 ...UNITED STATES PRIOR TO 1945; SEE ALSO SPECIFIC TOPICS	91	1715
USIA ...UNITED STATES INFORMATION AGENCY	2	1718
USIS ...SEE USIA		
USSR ...UNION OF SOVIET SOCIALIST REPUBLICS; SEE ALSO RUSSIA	990	1718
UTAH ...UTAH	1	1740
UTIL/TH ...UTILITY THEORY	1	1740
UTILITARN ...UTILITARIANISM	1	1740
UTOPIA ...ENVISIONED GENERAL SOCIAL CONDITIONS; SEE ALSO STEREOTYPE	3	1740
UTTAR/PRAD ...UTTAR PRADESH, INDIA; SEE ALSO INDIA	3	1740
VALIDITY (AS CONCEPT) ...SEE METH/CNCPT		
VALUE-ADDED TAX ...SEE TAX/STRUCT, TAX		
VALUE-FREE THOUGHT ...SEE OBJECTIVE		
VALUES ...CONCERNS ALL VALUES	9	1740
VANUATA ...VANUATA; SEE ALSO ASIA/PAC, PACIFIC	2	1741
VARGAS/J ...JORGE B. VARGAS	1	1741
VATICAN ...VATICAN; SEE ALSO POPE, CATHOLIC	6	1741
VEBLEN/T ...THORSTEIN VEBLEN	2	1741
VENETIAN REPUBLIC ...SEE VENICE		
VENEZUELA ...VENEZUELA; SEE ALSO SOUTH/AMER, LATIN/AMER	12	1741
VERMONT ...VERMONT	2	1741
VERSAILLES ...VERSAILLES, FRANCE	1	1741
VET ...VETERANS	2	1741
VETO ...VETO	3	1741
VICE/PRES ...VICE-PRESIDENT (ALL NATIONS); SEE ALSO EXEC/STRUC	1	1741
VICTIM ...VICTIM, VICTIMOLOGY	1	1742
VIDEO/TAPE ...VIDEO TAPE	1	1742
VIENNA ...VIENNA, AUSTRIA	4	1742
VIET MINH ...SEE VIETNAM, GUERRILLA, COLONIAL		
VIETNAM ...VIETNAM; SEE ALSO VIETNAM/N, VIETNAM/S, S/EASTASIA, VIETNM/WAR	60	1742
VIETNAM SUMMER (1967 ANTI-WAR ORGANIZATION) ...SEE		

ABSTRACTS OF DOCUMENTS
IN THIS SUPPLEMENT

00001
    "CON CON" BATTLES EXPECTED IN 13 STATES
CHURCH AND STATE, 42(2) (FEB 89), 13 (37)-14 (38).
    THE CITIZENS TO PROTECT THE CONSTITUTION COALITION
EXPECTS ACTIVITY ON BEHALF OF A NATIONAL CONSTITUTIONAL
CONVENTION IN 13 STATES IN 1989. SPURRED BY THE NATIONAL
TAXPAYERS UNION AND OTHER ANTI-TAX RADICALS, THE CONVENTION
DRIVE CLAIMS TO SEEK A NATIONAL GATHERING ONLY TO ADD A
BALANCED BUDGET AMENDMENT TO THE CONSTITUTION. BUT EXPERTS
SAY A CONVENTION COULD NOT BE LIMITED TO ONE TOPIC.

00002
    "DUAL RECOGNITION" NOT ACCEPTABLE
BEIJING REVIEW, 32(43) (OCT 89), 14.
    THE GOVERNMENT OF THE PEOPLE'S REPUBLIC OF CHINA IS THE
ONLY LEGITIMATE CHINESE GOVERNMENT AND TAIWAN IS AN
INALIENABLE PART OF CHINA'S TERRITORY. THIS IS CHINA'S
UNSWERVING POSITION ON THE QUESTION OF ONE CHINA OR TWO.
CHINA OPPOSES THE IDEA OF COUNTRIES THAT HAVE DIPLOMATIC
RELATIONS WITH IT ALSO TRYING TO ESTABLISH DIPLOMATIC
RELATIONS WITH TAIWAN AND CONDUCTING EXCHANGES OF A
GOVERNMENTAL NATURE WITH THE TAIWANESE. HOWEVER, CHINA DOES
NOT TAKE EXCEPTION TO OTHER COUNTRIES' ECONOMIC EXCHANGES OF
A NON-GOVERNMENTAL NATURE WITH TAIWAN.

00003
    "DUAL RECOGNITION" WILL GET NOWHERE
BEIJING REVIEW, 32(33) (AUG 89), 14.
    ON JULY 19, 1989, GRENADA ANNOUNCED IT HAD ESTABLISHED
DIPLOMATIC RELATIONS WITH TAIWAN IN VIOLATION OF THE
PRINCIPLES ARTICULATED IN THE COMMUNIQUE ESTABLISHING
DIPLOMATIC RELATIONS WITH CHINA IN 1985. THIS INCIDENT IS
ANOTHER STEP TAKEN BY TAIWANESE AUTHORITIES TO PROMOTE THEIR
"ELASTIC DIPLOMACY" IN DEFIANCE OF THE DESIRE OF THE CHINESE
PEOPLE ON BOTH SIDES OF THE TAIWAN STRAITS.

00004
    "INTERNATIONALIZATION" OF HK QUESTION OPPOSED
BEIJING REVIEW, 32(45) (NOV 89), 9.
    CHINESE PREMIER LI PENG HAS SAID THAT IT IS FUTILE TO
PRESSURE THE CHINESE GOVERNMENT ON THE HONG KONG QUESTION.
HE EMPHASIZED THAT CHINA AND BRITAIN HAVE ALREADY REACHED AN
AGREEMENT AND THAT ARGUMENTS ATTEMPTING TO EXERT PRESSURE ON
THE CHINESE GOVERNMENT BY CITING "POPULAR WILL," "CONFIDENCE,
" OR "INTERNATIONALIZATION" ARE USELESS.

00005
    "NO" TO TAIWAN'S ELASTIC DIPLOMACY
BEIJING REVIEW, 32(1) (JAN 89), 10-11.
    IN DOING THEIR UTMOST TO PUSH THEIR SO-CALLED "ELASTIC
DIPLOMACY," THE TAIWANESE AUTHORITIES ARE ACTUALLY TRYING TO
CREATE TWO CHINAS OR ONE CHINA AND ONE TAIWAN. BUT THE
MAINLAND CHINESE GOVERNMENT IS UNALTERABLY OPPOSED TO THE
CONCEPT.

00006
    "PRACTICAL ECUMENISM" BRINGS CATHOLICS, EVANGELICALS
TOGETHER FOR POLITICS
CHURCH AND STATE, 42(3) (MAR 89), 17 (65).
    WHILE THE DRIVE FOR ECUMENICAL ACTION AMONG MAINSTREAM
PROTESTANTS AND CATHOLICS SEEMS TO HAVE PEAKED, A NEW KIND
OF ECUMENISM BETWEEN TRADITIONALIST CATHOLICS AND
EVANGELICAL PROTESTANTS IS GROWING RAPIDLY. THE INCREASINGLY
MILITANT ANTI-ABORTION MOVEMENT HAS DRAWN TOGETHER THE TWO
TRADITIONALLY HOSTILE BRANCHES OF CHRISTIANITY. IN RECENT
YEARS, THE TWO GROUPS HAVE JOINED FORCES AT EVERY LEVEL OF
SOCIAL ACTION, FROM GRASSROOTS PROTESTS TO LOBBYING CONGRESS
FOR CHANGES IN PUBLIC POLICY.

00007
    "THE COUP WAS A CON TRICK"
NEW AFRICAN, (267) (DEC 89), 22-23.
    A COUP IN SUDAN ON JUNE BY GENERAL OMER HASSAN EL BESHIR
HAS MEANT IMPRISONMENT FOR ALL PREVIOUS PARTY LEADERS, AND
OPPOSITION FORCES. UMMA PARTY LEADER AND EX-PRIME MINISTER
SADIQ EL MAHDI AND HIS ENTIRE CABINET, EXCEPT THE EX-
MINISTER OF THE INTERIOR, MUBAREK EL FADIL, ARE ALL
IMPRISONED. THEY ARE AWAITING CHARGES WHICH MAY LEAD TO THE
DEATH PENALTY.

00008
    "TIBETAN INDEPENDENCE"--FACT OR FICTION?
BEIJING REVIEW, 32(7-8) (FEB 89), 25-30.
    IN THIS ARTICLE, THE AUTHOR STUDIES SEVERAL ISSUES IN
TIBETAN HISTORY AND EXAMINES CLAIMS TO TIBETAN INDEPENDENCE.
THE ARGUMENT THAT TIBET IS LEGITIMATELY PART OF CHINA IS
STRONGLY ENDORSED.

00009
    "VERBAL VIOLENCE" AND THE FIRST AMENDMENT
CHURCH AND STATE, 42(4) (APR 89), 11 (83).
    THE DIFFERENCE BETWEEN VERBAL VIOLENCE AND REAL VIOLENCE
IS CLEAR AND THE DISTINCTIONS SHOULD NOT BE MINIMIZED. IT
DOES NO CREDIT TO THE CONCEPT OF RELIGIOUS LIBERTY FOR
AMERICANS TO SHRINK FROM DEFENDING THE PRINCIPLES OF FREE
SPEECH AND CHURCH-STATE SEPARATION THAT HAVE MADE THE UNITED
STATES THE FREEST NATION IN WORLD HISTORY. ALL RELIGIOUS AND
POLITICAL LEADERS SHOULD JOIN FORCES IN CLEARLY AND
UNAMBIGUOUSLY DEFENDING THE ABSOLUTE RIGHT TO COMMENT ON
RELIGION OR POLITICS WITHOUT FEAR OF GOVERNMENT ACTION OR
INDIVIDUAL VIOLENCE. THE MORE CONTROVERSIAL THE COMMENT, THE
MORE IT NEEDS UNIFIED PROTECTION.

00010
    A BARRIER TO ANARCHY
SOUTH, (104) (JUN 89), 8.
    AGAINST ALL ODDS, THE URUGUAY ROUND SURVIVED ITS FIRST
MAJOR CRISIS. WHEN TRADE MINISTERS LOCKED HORNS AT THE
REVIEW CONFERENCE IN MONTREAL IN DECEMBER 1988, IT APPEARED
THAT DIFFERENCES WERE UNBRIDGEABLE AND THAT THE NEGOTIATIONS
TO REDUCE WORLD TRADE BARRIERS WOULD BE BROUGHT PREMATURELY
TO AN END. BUT ENOUGH COMMON GROUND HAS BEEN ESTABLISHED IN APRIL
1989 TO GET THE SHOW BACK ON THE ROAD.

00011
    A CALL FOR UNITY AGAINST TURMOIL
BEIJING REVIEW, 32(18) (MAY 89), 13.
    THE PEOPLE'S DAILY, THE OFFICIAL ORGAN OF THE CHINESE
COMMUNIST PARTY CENTRAL COMMITTEE, HAS PUBLISHED AN
EDITORIAL URGING THE PEOPLE TO TAKE A FIRM STAND AGAINST
PUBLIC DISTURBANCES. THE EDITORIAL WAS PROMPTED BY VIOLENCE
DURING THE MOURNING PERIOD FOR FORMER PARTY GENERAL
SECRETARY HU YAOBANG, WHO DIED ON APRIL 15, 1989. IN BEIJING,
A HANDFUL OF INDIVIDUALS FABRICATED RUMORS AGAINST THE
PARTY AND INCITED PEOPLE TO SHOUT REACTIONARY SLOGANS AND TO
ATTEMPT TO STORM COMMUNIST PARTY HEADQUARTERS.

00012
    A CHRONICLE OF EVENTS 1920-1988 IN NAGORNO-KARABAKH
GLASNOST, (16-18) (JAN 89), 11-17.
    THIS CHRONOLOGY OF EVENTS OUTLINES MAJOR HAPPENINGS IN
THE HISTORY OF NAGORNO-KARABAKH FROM THE ESTABLISHMENT OF
SOVIET POWER IN AZERBAIJAN, NAGORNO-KARABAKH, NAKHICHEVAN,
AND ARMENIA IN 1920 TO THE ETHNIC STRIFE OF THE LATE 1980'S.

00013
    A CLIMATE FOR NEGOTIATIONS?
AFRICA REPORT, 34(6) (NOV 89), 27-29.
    THIS IS AN EDITED TRANSCRIPT OF TWO PRESENTATIONS ON THE
QUESTION OF WHETHER THE WHITE SOUTH AFRICAN LEADERSHIP IS
CREATING A CLIMATE FOR NEGOTIATIONS WITH THE BLACK MAJORITY.
THE PRESENTATIONS HERE GIVEN BY THABO MBEKI, DIRECTOR OF THE
INTERNATIONAL DEPARTMENT OF THE AFRICAN NATIONAL CONGRESS,
AND WILLY ESTERHUYSE, A PROFESSOR OF POLITICAL PHILOSOPHY AT
THE UNIVERSITY OF STELLENBOSCH AND AN ADVISOR TO THE
GOVERNMENT OF PRESIDENT F.W. DEKLERK.

00014
    A CONVERSATION WITH MELISSA WELLS
AFRICA REPORT, 34(2) (MAR 89), 20.
    MELISSA WELLS IS THE AMERICAN AMBASSADOR IN MAPUTO. IN
THIS ARTICLE, SHE DISCUSSES THE EVOLUTION OF US-MOZAMBICAN
RELATIONS, PROSPECTS FOR AMERICAN NON-LETHAL MILITARY AID TO
MOZAMBIQUE, RIGHT-WING SUPPORT FOR RENAMO, AND PRESIDENT
CHISSANO'S DIALOGUE WITH SOUTH AFRICA.

00015
    A CRUCIAL TRANSITION
SOUTH, (102) (APR 89), 9.
    ARGENTINE PRESIDENT RAUL ALFONSIN'S MOST FUNDAMENTAL
SUCCESS LIES IN THE FACT THAT. DESPITE RUMBLINGS OF COUPS
AND REBELLIONS, HE COMPLETED HIS TERM. DEMOCRACY IS NOW PART
OF THE ARGENTINE NATIONAL MENTALITY, AND THE MAJOR POLITICAL
PARTIES HAVE AGREED THAT A CONTEST AMONG THEMSELVES IS
PREFERABLE TO ALLOWING THE MILITARY A CHANCE TO REGAIN POWER.

00016
    A DREAM COMPELS US: VOICES OF SALVADORAN WOMEN
SOUTH END PRESS, BOSTON, MA, 1989, .
    THIS ANTHOLOGY INCLUDES INTERVIEWS AND ARTICLES BY AND
ABOUT WOMEN INVOLVED IN THE POPULAR AND REVOLUTIONARY
MOVEMENTS OF EL SALVADOR. THE WOMEN SPEAK ABOUT THE EVENTS
AND CONDITIONS THAT HAVE LED MANY OF THEM INTO POLITICAL
ACTIVISM.

00017
    A LOOK AT CHINA'S ETHNIC MINORITIES
CHINA RECONSTRUCTS, XXXVIII(12) (DEC 89), 14.
    OFFICIAL CHINESE POLICY ON MINORITIES CALLS FOR NATIONAL
UNITY AND EQUALITY AMONG ALL ETHNIC GROUPS. OPPRESSION OR
DISCRIMINATION BY THE MAJORITY IS FORBIDDEN. ACCORDING TO
THE CONSTITUTION OF THE PEOPLE'S REPUBLIC OF CHINA, REGIONAL
NATIONAL AUTONOMY IS GRANTED TO ALL AREAS WHERE MINORITY
NATIONALITIES LIVE IN COMPACT COMMUNITIES. THE CONSTITUTION
ALSO STIPULATES THAT EVERY MINORITY NATIONALITY HAS THE
FREEDOM TO USE AND DEVELOP ITS OWN LANGUAGE.

00018
A MOVE TO POISON SINO-U.S. TIES
BEIJING REVIEW, 32(50) (DEC 89), 13-14.
SOME MEMBERS OF THE U.S. CONGRESS ARE ATTEMPTING TO
EXERT PRESSURE ON CHINA THROUGH ECONOMIC AND POLITICAL
SANCTIONS, WANTONLY INTERFERING IN CHINA'S INTERNAL AFFAIRS
AND UNDERMINING SINO-AMERICAN RELATIONS. THESE CONGRESSIONAL
ACTIONS ARE ANOTHER SERIOUS BLOW TO SINO-AMERICAN TIES AND
ARE HASTENING THE DETERIORATION OF THE RELATIONSHIP. THE
RECENT PASSAGE OF AN EMERGENCY CHINESE IMMIGRATION RELIEF
ACT BY THE CONGRESS RUNS COUNTER TO INTERNATIONAL NORMS AND
DAMAGES NORMAL EDUCATIONAL EXCHANGE BETWEEN THE TWO
COUNTRIES.

00019
A NEW WAVE OF UNEMPLOYMENT
CHINA NEWS ANALYSIS, (1392) (SEP 89), 1-9.
THE CHINESE UNEMPLOYMENT RATE WILL REACH AT LEAST FOUR
PERCENT IN 1989. THE 1978 REFORM WAS SUCCESSFUL IN PROVIDING
NEW JOBS FOR MILLIONS OF WORKERS, BUT NOW IT HAS RUN ITS
COURSE AND THERE IS NO EASY SOLUTION AT HAND. THE
UNEMPLOYMENT PROBLEM REPRESENTS A POTENTIAL THREAT TO THE
SOCIAL ORDER AND PRESENTS BASIC, UNTRACTABLE QUESTIONS ABOUT
THE PRIVILEGES OF THE CITIES AND OF THE STATE ENTERPRISES—
QUESTIONS THAT HAVE BEEN TABOO FOR SEVERAL DECADES AND FOR
WHICH THE PRESENT LEADERSHIP MAY HAVE LITTLE TIME.

00020
A PROPOSAL FOR POLITICAL REFORM
JAPAN ECHO, XVI(3) (AUT 89), 22-24.
ON MAY 19, 1989, IN RESPONSE TO THE RECRUIT SCANDAL, THE
RULING LIBERAL DEMOCRATIC PARTY UNVEILED A PLAN TO CLEAN UP
JAPANESE POLITICS AND THE MANAGEMENT OF THE NATIONAL DIET.
THIS ARTICLE SUMMARIZES THE REFORM PROGRAM, WHICH INCLUDES
THE ESTABLISHMENT OF POLITICAL REFORM HEADQUARTERS IN BOTH
THE PARTY AND THE DIET TO WORK WITH THE GOVERNMENT'S
ELECTION SYSTEM COUNCIL TO IMPLEMENT CHANGES.

00021
A RACE AGAINST TIME
AUSTRIA TODAY, (3) (1989), 9-12.
THE NEGOTIATIONS ON CONVENTIONAL ARMED FORCES IN EUROPE
ARE MAKING CONCRETE PROGRESS IN A FRACTION OF THE TIME IT
TOOK THE MBFR TALKS TO GRIND INTO A STALEMATE ON THE
QUESTION OF HOW TO COUNT THE MILITARY PERSONNEL IN NATO AND
THE WARSAW PACT. BUT THERE STILL REMAINS A GOOD DEAL OF
SCEPTICISM AROUND THE NEGOTIATING TABLE. THERE IS NO LONGER
ANY SUBSTANTIAL DOUBT THAT BOTH SIDES ARE GENUINELY SERIOUS
ABOUT DISARMAMENT, BUT THERE IS CONCERN AS TO WHETHER THE
REFORMERS IN EASTERN EUROPE HAVE THE STAMINA TO SEE IT
THROUGH, IN VIEW OF THE INTERNAL DIFFICULTIES THEY ARE
EXPERIENCING.

00022
A SKEPTICAL VIEW
MACLEAN'S (CANADA'S NEWS MAGAZINE), 102(11) (MAR 89), 22.
BISHOP DESMOND TUTU DECLARED HIS SKEPTICISM ABOUT THE
NATIONAL PARTY'S PROPOSED REFORMS. HE ARGUES THAT THE
BULWARK OF APARTHEID, THE RACE CLASSIFICATION ACT, REMAINS
INTACT AND THAT THE OTHER REFORMS ARE PERIPHERAL AND HOLLOW.
HE IS GUARDEDLY POSITIVE ABOUT THE DEVELOPMENTS IN NAMIBIA
AND FEELS THAT NAMIBIAN INDEPENDENCE WILL INCREASE PRESSURE
ON SOUTH AFRICA TO ELIMINATE APARTHEID.

00023
A SYMPOSIUM: IS THIS ANY WAY TO PICK A PRESIDENT?
BROOKINGS REVIEW, 7(2) (SPR 89), 24-33.
A NUMBER OF POLITICAL EXPERTS DISCUSS THE 1988
PRESIDENTIAL CAMPAIGN, FOCUSING ON THE QUESTION: WHAT SINGLE
ASPECT OF THE PRESIDENTIAL ELECTION PROCESS DID YOU FIND
MOST DISTURBING IN 1988 AND HOW WOULD YOU SET ABOUT
CORRECTING IT?

00024
A TROUBLED REVOLUTION
MACLEAN'S (CANADA'S NEWS MAGAZINE), 102(30) (JUL 89),
27-28.
ON JULY 19, 1979, THE SANDINISTA REGIME ASSUMED POWER IN
NICARAGUA AND WON THE HEARTS OF MUCH OF THE FREE WORLD WITH
PROMISES OF A "NEW JERUSALEM" OF DEMOCRACY AND SOCIAL
JUSTICE. CELEBRATING THE REVOLUTION'S TEN YEAR MARK WITH A
NEW WAVE OF PROPAGANDA, THE SANDINISTAS ARE ATTEMPTING TO
BRIDGE THE GAP BETWEEN DREAMS AND REALITY. THE NATION IS IN
POLITICAL WOES ON THE "IMPERIALIST WAR OF AGGRESSION," THE
REGIME'S BASE OF SUPPORT IS RAPIDLY SHRINKING.

00025
A VOTE OF CONFIDENCE
COMMONWEAL, CXVI(17) (OCT 89), 516-517.
UNDER PRESSURE FROM CONGRESS, THE BUSH ADMINISTRATION
HAS SCRAPPED ITS PLAN TO USE NATIONAL ENDOWMENT FOR
DEMOCRACY FUNDS TO SUPPORT POLITICAL PARTIES IN NICARAGUA.
INSTEAD, IT WILL FUNNEL CAMPAIGN FUNDS THROUGH THE US AGENCY
FOR INTERNATIONAL DEVELOPMENT AND ADHERE TO THE STIPULATIONS

OF NICARAGUA'S SUPREME ELECTORAL COUNCIL.

00026
A ZONE OF TRUST AND SECURITY FOR CENTRAL EUROPE
INFORMATION BULLETIN, 26(21-22) (NOV 88), 8-9.
THIS ARTICLE IS THE TEXT OF THE DOCUMENT IN WHICH THE
JOINT WORKING GROUP OF THE SOCIAL DEMOCRATIC PARTY OF
GERMANY AND THE SOCIALIST UNITY PARTY OF GERMANY PRESENT
THEIR PROPOSAL FOR A ZONE OF CONFIDENCE AND SECURITY IN
CENTRAL EUROPE.

00027
ABC BILL ADVANCES TO SENATE FLOOR, DESPITE CHURCH-STATE
CONFLICTS
CHURCH AND STATE, 42(4) (APR 89), 12 (84)-13 (85).
PASSAGE OF THE ACT FOR BETTER CHILD CARE SERVICES WAS
BLOCKED IN 1988 PRIMARILY BECAUSE OF A DISPUTE OVER THE
INVOLVEMENT OF CHURCH-RELATED DAY CARE CENTERS. IN MID-MARCH
1989 THE BILL MOVED ONE STEP CLOSER TO CONGRESSIONAL
APPROVAL WHEN THE SENATE LABOR AND HUMAN RESOURCES COMMITTEE
APPROVED NEW CHURCH-STATE PROVISIONS AND VOTED TO RECOMMEND
THE MEASURE TO THE FULL SENATE.

00028
ABORTION: ATTITUDES ON ABORTION LITTLE CHANGED SINCE
SUPREME COURT'S 1973 RULING
GALLUP REPORT, (281) (FEB 89), 16-23.
THE 1988 PRESIDENTIAL CAMPAIGN HAS AGAIN FOCUSED PUBLIC
ATTENTION ON THE ABORTION ISSUE. THE DEMOCRATIC PLATFORM
SUPPORTS THE WOMAN'S RIGHT TO CHOOSE ABORTION, WHILE THE GOP
CALLS FOR A CONSTITUTIONAL AMENDMENT THAT WOULD BAN MOST
ABORTIONS. PUBLIC OPINION ON THE ISSUE HAS REMAINED
VIRTUALLY UNCHANGED SINCE THE SUPREME COURT'S LANDMARK 1973
DECISION.

00029
ACTIVISTS PROMOTE CALIFORNIA REFERENDUM ON SCHOOL PRAYER
CHURCH AND STATE, 42(8) (SEP 89), 15 (183)-16 (184).
A CALIFORNIA WOMAN HAS LAUNCHED A GRASSROOTS EFFORT TO
AMEND THE STATE'S CONSTITUTION TO ALLOW STATE-SPONSORED
MOMENTS FOR PRAYER IN THE PUBLIC SCHOOLS. HER PROPOSAL WOULD
ALSO ALLOW THE LORD'S PRAYER TO BE RECITED AT GRADUATION
CEREMONIES, PLAYS, AND ASSEMBLIES. SHE BELIEVES THE PLAN IS
CONSTITUTIONAL BECAUSE IT FORBIDS SCHOOL PERSONNEL FROM
ADVISING OR TEACHING THEIR OWN FORM OF PRAYER.

00030
ADDENDA TO PARTY LEADERS' PROFILES
BEIJING REVIEW, 32(29) (JUL 89), 23-24.
THIS ARTICLE OFFERS BIOGRAPHICAL INFORMATION ON LI PENG,
QIAO SHI, AND YAO YILIN, FOCUSING ON THEIR QUALIFICATIONS
FOR LEADERSHIP IN THE CHINESE COMMUNIST PARTY.

00031
ADDRESS BY GEORGE BUSH AT THE JOINT MEETING OF THE SEJM
AND THE SENATE OF THE POLISH PEOPLE'S REPUBLIC
CONTEMPORARY POLAND, XXII(8) (1989), 31-36.
IN THIS SPEECH TO THE POLISH PARLIAMENT, U.S. PRESIDENT
GEORGE BUSH DISCUSSED THE STATUS OF U.S.-POLISH RELATIONS
AND THE PROCESS OF CHANGE THAT POLAND HAS EMBARKED UPON.

00032
ADDRESS BY MIECZYSLAW F. RAKOWSKI AT A MEETING WITH PARTY
ACTIVISTS, WROCLAW, JUNE 15, 1989
CONTEMPORARY POLAND, XXII(7) (1989), 32-37.
THE FIRST ROUND OF THE JUNE 1989 ELECTIONS TO THE POLISH
PARLIAMENT WAS A VICTORY FOR THE OPPOSITION RUNNING AGAINST
THE POLISH UNITED WORKERS' PARTY. THE DEFEAT WAS DUE TO
REACTION TO PAST FAILURES, TO THE MANNER OF GOVERNING,
DISSATISFACTION WITH LIVING CONDITIONS, AND PUBLIC
DISAPPOINTMENT OVER BROKEN PROMISES.

00033
AFGHANISTAN: SOVIET OCCUPATION AND WITHDRAWAL
DEPARTMENT OF STATE BULLETIN (US FOREIGN POLICY), 89(2144)
(MAR 89). 72-90.
THE AUTHOR REVIEWS THE AFGHANISTAN SITUATION IN 1988,
INCLUDING THE GENEVA NEGOTIATIONS, GORBACHEV'S POLICIES, THE
MILITARY SITUATION, POLITICAL DEVELOPMENTS, AND THE SEARCH
FOR POLITICAL SOLUTION.

00034
AGRICULTURE TAKES TOP PRIORITY
BEIJING REVIEW, 32(50) (DEC 89), 10-11.
THE CHINESE GOVERNMENT WILL MAKE AGRICULTURE A TOP
PRIORITY IN THE DEVELOPMENT OF ITS NATIONAL ECONOMY AND WILL
SPEED UP THE COMPREHENSIVE DEVELOPMENT OF AGRICULTURE. THE
CHINESE COMMUNIST PARTY'S FUNDAMENTAL PRINCIPLES FOR RURAL
AREAS INCLUDE ITS POLICY ON THE HOUSEHOLD CONTRACT SYSTEM IN
PRODUCTION AND THE POLICY OF ENCOURAGING SOME FARMERS TO
PROSPER BEFORE OTHERS. THE STATE COUNCIL HAS LAUNCHED A
COMPREHENSIVE DEVELOPMENT PROJECT TO IMPROVE AGRICULTURAL
PRODUCTION IN THE SONGLIAO PLAIN; THE BASIN OF THE
HEILONGJIANG, #WUSULIJIANG, AND SONGHUAJIANG RIVERS; AND THE

PLAIN DRAINED BY THE YELLOW, HUAI, AND HAI RIVERS.

00035
AID AND THE MARKETPLACE
MULTINATIONAL MONITOR, 11(10) (OCT 89), 6.
FOR THE LAST 45 YEARS, THE UNITED STATES HAS SPENT TENS
OF BILLIONS OF TAX DOLLARS TO INSTITUTE AND MAINTAIN AN
INTERNATIONAL ECONOMIC ORDER CONDUCIVE TO CORPORATE
INTERESTS, OFTEN IN CONTRAVENTION OF THE HUMAN RIGHTS ITS
LEADERS ESPOUSE. THIS SITUATION HAS BEEN EXACERBATED IN THE
1980'S BY THE ENSHRINEMENT OF PRIVATIZATION AS THE
PREVAILING SHIBBOLETH GUIDING U.S. POLICY.

00036
AID TO DEVELOPING COUNTRIES
SURVEY OF CURRENT AFFAIRS, 19(12) (DEC 89), 461-464.
MINISTER FOR OVERSEAS DEVELOPMENT LYNDA CHALKER
ENUMERATED THE PRIORITIES FOR BRITAIN'S FOREIGN AID PROGRAM
IN THE COMING DECADE IN A SPEECH BEFORE THE PARLIAMENTARY
GROUP ON OVERSEAS DEVELOPMENT ON NOVEMBER 8, 1989. INCREASES
IN BRITAIN'S AID BUDGET, INCLUDING ITS CONTRIBUTIONS # TO
INTERNATIONAL BODIES AND VOLUNTARY ORGANIZATIONS, WERE
ANNOUNCED.

00037
ALLIANCE OF FREE DEMOCRATS: SOCIO-LIBERAL OPPOSITION IN
TODAY'S HUNGARY
WORLD AFFAIRS, 151(4) (1989), 165-179.
POLITICAL CHANGE IN HUNGARY IS HERALDED BY THE BIRTH OF
COMPETING POLITICAL GROUPS AND BY THE REBIRTH OF THE PARTIES
OF THE SHORT-LIVED DEMOCRATIC PERIOD OF 1945-47. THE ARTICLE
EXAMINES THE ALLIANCE OF FREE DEMOCRATS (AFD) AS A
SIGNIFICANT EXAMPLE OF THE NEW POLITICAL ORGANIZATIONS WHICH
ARE DEMANDING FREE ELECTIONS AND OTHER REFORMS. THE ADF IS
CHARACTERIZED BY THREE WORDS: OPPOSITION, EUROPEAN, AND
RADICAL. THE ARTICLE ANALYZES SPECIFIC ORGANIZATION
CHARACTERISTICS AND GOALS. THE ADF ADVOCATES REFORMS IN THE
CURRENT BALANCE OF POWER, OF OWNERSHIP, AND OF HUNGARIAN
FOREIGN POLICY.

00038
AMERICAN CATHOLICS AND SEPARATION: A BICENTENNIAL APPEAL
CHURCH AND STATE, 42(10) (NOV 89), 11 (227).
MOST AMERICAN CATHOLICS HOLD A DEEP APPRECIATION FOR THE
PRINCIPLES OF RELIGIOUS LIBERTY EMBODIED IN THE FIRST
AMENDMENT, AND MORE NEEDS TO BE DONE TO ENLIST THE AID OF
CATHOLICS IN DEFENDING THOSE PRINCIPLES. HISTORICALLY, THE
CATHOLIC HIERARCHY TOOK A STRONG STAND SUPPORTING THE
SEPARATION OF CHURCH AND STATE. BUT RECENTLY, DUE TO THE
EXPENSE OF OPERATING A PAROCHIAL SCHOOL SYSTEM AND THE LURE
OF POLITICAL POWER, CATHOLIC BISHOPS HAVE ADOPTED AN
ACCOMMODATIONIST STANCE THAT ALLOWS FOR NONPREFERENTIAL
GOVERNMENT AID TO RELIGION. THEY HAVE ALSO ASKED POLITICIANS
TO WRITE THE CHURCH'S RELIGIOUS DOGMA ON ABORTION INTO CIVIL
LAW.

00039
AMERICANS DIVIDED?
CHURCH AND STATE, 42(6) (JUN 89), 14 (134).
THE AUTHOR NOTES THREE RECENT EXAMPLES OF NEGATIVE
POLITICAL ACTIVITY BY RELIGIOUS GROUPS THAT SUPPORT PUBLIC
SUBSIDIES TO PRIVATE RELIGIOUS EDUCATION. HE STATES THAT
THESE ACTIVITIES ARE UNFORTUNATE AND UNHEALTHY IN A NATION
THAT SEEKS TO UPHOLD THE CONSTITUTIONAL SEPARATION OF CHURCH
AND STATE.

00040
AMERICANS UNITED PROTESTS VATICAN-U.S. TIES AS NEW
AMBASSADOR WINS CONFIRMATION
CHURCH AND STATE, 42(8) (SEP 89), 18 (186).
THE BAPTIST JOINT COMMITTEE ON PUBLIC AFFAIRS AND
AMERICANS UNITED FOR SEPARATION OF CHURCH AND STATE HAVE
URGED THE CONGRESS TO RE-EXAMINE THE CONSTITUTIONALITY OF U.
S.-VATICAN TIES. DESPITE THE PROTEST FROM THE TWO GROUPS,
THE SENATE ACTED TO CONFIRM THE NOMINATION OF THOMAS P.
MELADY AS AMBASSADOR TO THE HOLY SEE IN AUGUST 1989.

00041
AN APPEAL TO SCHOLARS, CREATIVE ARTISTS, JOURNALISTS
GLASNOST, (16-18) (JAN 89), 21-22.
THIS STATEMENT ISSUED BY THE COLLECTIVE OF THE INSTITUTE
OF PHILOSOPHY AND LAW REPORTS MASS DEMONSTRATIONS IN YEREVAN
CONCERNING THE REUNIFICATION OF KARABAKH WITH SOVIET ARMENIA.
IT ALSO REVIEWS THE BIASED REPORTING OF THE DEMONSTRATIONS
BY THE SOVIET PRESS AND THE REACTION OF THE AZERBAIJANIS WHO
LIVE IN ARMENIA.

00042
AN ENERGY POLICY WITH A FUTURE
MULTINATIONAL MONITOR, 10(1-2) (JAN 89), 5-6.
IT IS DISTURBING THAT TEN YEARS AFTER THE THREE MILE
ISLAND ACCIDENT THE NUCLEAR POWER INDUSTRY IS ANTICIPATING A
RESURRECTION. THE INDUSTRY HOPES THAT NUCLEAR POWER CAN BE
SOLD TO THE PUBLIC AS THE SOLUTION TO THE PROBLEM OF GLOBAL

WARMING. SENATOR TIM WIRTH HAS PROPOSED, IN HIS
COMPREHENSIVE GLOBAL WARMING LEGISLATION, FUNDING FOR
RESEARCH ON NUCLEAR POWER AS AN OPTION FOR SOLVING PROBLEMS
CAUSED BY FOSSIL FUELS. THE WIRTH LEGISLATION SUGGESTS THAT
REPLACING OILAND COAL-GENERATED ELECTRICITY WITH NUCLEAR-
GENERATED ELECTRICITY MIGHT REDUCE CARBON DIOXIDE EMISSIONS
AND, THEREFORE, SLOW GLOBAL WARMING. BUT THERE ARE SAFER,
LESS COSTLY, AND MORE EFFICIENT OPTIONS TO ATTACK THE GLOBAL
WARMING PROBLEM.

00043
AN HISTORICAL REFERENCE: HOW NAGORNO-KARABAKH BECAME A
PROBLEM
GLASNOST, (16-18) (JAN 89), 18-19, 33.
THE NATIONAL TERRITORIAL BOUNDARIES AND ADMINISTRATIVE
DIVISIONS IN THE CAUCASUS WERE DRAWN DURING THE 1920'S. IT
WAS AN UNSETTLED TIME OF POLITICAL DOUBLE-DEALING, TERRORIST
ACTIVITY, FOREIGN INTERVENTION, AND NATIONALIST REGIMES.
TODAY, MANY DISTRICTS WITH HUNDREDS OF THOUSANDS OF
ARMENIANS ARE INCORPORATED INTO SOVIET AZERBAIJAN. THESE
ARMENIANS ARE ARTIFICIALLY CUT OFF FROM WHAT SHOULD BE
COMMON ECONOMIC-CULTURAL DEVELOPMENT WITH THE ARMENIAN
REPUBLIC. THIS ARTICLE DISCUSSES THE HISTORIC BACKGROUNDS OF
THE PROVINCES DIRECTLY LINKED TO ARMENIA, SUCH AS
NAKHICHEVAN AND NAGORNO-KARABAKH, AS WELL AS THE DISTRICTS
OF DASHKESAN, SHAUMYAN, KHANLAR, AND KEDABEG.

00044
AN UNWANTED INHERITANCE
SOUTH, (104) (JUN 89), 9.
PRIME MINISTER BHUTTO'S PROBLEMS ARE LARGELY INHERITED
AND NOT OF HER OWN CREATION; THE AFGHAN WAR AND THE PERILOUS
STATE OF PAKISTAN'S ECONOMY ARE JUST TWO OF THE MOST
IMPORTANT. THE PROBLEM WITH THE GREATEST POTENTIAL TO ERODE
HER POWER TO GOVERN EFFECTIVELY IS THE AFGHAN WAR. BUT THE
DECISION TO END PAKISTAN'S INVOLVEMENT OR ESCALATE IT DOES
NOT REST WITH BHUTTO ALONE. THERE MUST BE AN INTERNATIONAL
COMMITMENT TO END THE FIGHTING AND PREVENT IT FROM BECOMING
A LARGER, REGIONAL CONFLICT.

00045
ANC INTERNATIONAL
SECHABA, 23(10) (OCT 89), 19.
THIS ARTICLE REPORTS ON THE EXPELLING OF SOUTH AFRICAN
MAYORS FROM THE ANNUAL CONGRESS OF THE WORLD CONFERENCE OF
MAYORS BECAUSE OF APARTHEID ISSUES; YORK UNIVERSITY, THE
FIRST CANADIAN INSTITUTION TO HONOR NELSON MANDELA; AND
DENMART BEING HOST TO ANC.

00046
ANC INTERNATIONAL: KEEP RADIO FREEDOM ON THE AIR
SECHABA, 23(9) (SEP 89), 5.
BROADCAST FOR RADIO FREEDOM, A DUTCH SUPPORT GROUP IS
CAMPAIGNING FOR FUNDS THAT WOULD MAKE A HIGH-POWERED SHORT-
WAVE RADIO TRANSMITTER POSSIBLE. CURRENT BROADCASTS OF ANC
RADIO FREEDOM ARE BEING JAMMED BY THE SOUTH AFRICAN
GOVERNMENT. THE ARTICLE APPLAUDS THE ACTIVITIES OF BROADCAST
FOR RADIO FREEDOM AND CALLS FOR INCREASED INTERNATIONAL
SUPPORT.

00047
ANGLO-IRISH AGREEMENT
SURVEY OF CURRENT AFFAIRS, 19(6) (JUN 89), 219-221.
FOLLOWING A JOINT REVIEW OF THE INTERGOVERNMENTAL
CONFERENCE SET UP UNDER THE 1985 ANGLO-IRISH AGREEMENT,
BRITIAN AND THE IRISH REPUBLIC HAVE REAFFIRMED THEIR FULL
COMMITMENT TO THE PROVISIONS OF THE AGREEMENT.

00048
ANGOLA/NAMIBIA ACCORDS
DEPARTMENT OF STATE BULLETIN (US FOREIGN POLICY), 89(2143)
(FEB 89), 10-16.
THIS REPORT ON THE ANGOLA/NAMIBIA ACCORDS INCLUDES THE
TEXTS OF THE AGREEMENT OF DEC. 22, 1988, AND STATEMENTS BY
PRESIDENT REAGAN AND ASSISTANT SECRETARY CROCKER OF THE US
STATE DEPARTMENT.

00049
ANOTHER SHOT IN THE DARK
SOUTH, (107) (SEP 89), 8-9.
MEXICO IS BEING VIEWED AS THE TEST CASE FOR THE BRADY
PLAN FOR REDUCING THIRD WORLD DEBT. UNDER THIS PLAN, THE
INTERNATIONAL MONETARY FUND, THE WORLD BANK, AND JAPAN ARE
PUTTING UP ABOUT US$30 BILLION TO FACILITATE DEBT BUY-BACKS
BY DEVELOPING COUNTRIES AND TO PROVIDE COLLATERAL AND
GUARANTEES FOR THE LOWER-VALUE OR LOWER-INTEREST BONDS
OFFERED TO BANKS IN EXCHANGE FOR EXISTING LOANS.

00050
ANTI-CHINA CLAMOUR CANNOT INTIMIDATE CHINESE PEOPLE
BEIJING REVIEW, 32(29) (JUL 89), 18-19.
THE COUNTER-REVOLUTIONARY RIOT IN BEIJING WAS PLANNED
AND ENGINEERED BY A SMALL NUMBER OF PEOPLE WHO ARE HOSTILE
TOWARDS THE COMMUNIST PARTY AND THE SOCIALIST SYSTEM. IN

ORDER TO SAFEGUARD THE REPUBLIC AND THE GOVERNMENT AND TO PRESERVE THE VICTORIOUS RESULTS OF CHINA'S CONSTRUCTION AND REFORM, THE CHINESE GOVERNMENT RESOLUTELY TOOK THE NECESSARY STEPS TO QUELL THE REVOLT. AFTER BEING BRIEFED ABOUT THE RIOT AND LEARNING THE TRUTH, MANY FOREIGN FRIENDS HAVE COME TO UNDERSTAND THE GOVERNMENT'S STEPS IN PUTTING DOWN THE DEMONSTRATIONS. BUT SOME MEMBERS OF THE U.S. CONGRESS, WHO ARE HOSTILE TOWARDS CHINA AND SOCIALISM, ALWAYS CHOOSE TO IGNORE FACTS AND THE TRUTH.

00051
ANTI-COMMUNIST VIGILANTES IN THE PHILIPPINES
AVAILABLE FROM NTIS, NO. AD-A199 631/3/GAR, JUN 13 88, 110.
THIS STUDY EXAMINED THE CONDITIONS WHICH BROUGHT ABOUT THE ORGANIZATION AND GROWTH OF ANTI-COMMUNIST VIGILANTES, AND THEIR IMPACT ON THE COUNTERINSURGENCY EFFORT AND SOCIETY IN THE PHILIPPINES. THE ANALYSIS AIMED AT DETERMINING A SUITABLE ROLE FOR ANTI-COMMUNIST VIGILANTES IN A COMPREHENSIVE COUNTERINSURGENCY PROGRAM AND THEIR FUTURE ROLE IN A POST-INSURGENCY PHILIPPINE SOCIETY. MOREOVER, THE RESEARCH WAS ALSO DIRECTED AT DEFINING THE ROLE OF GOVERNMENT OR ANY OF ITS AGENCIES IN THE ANTI-COMMUNIST VIGILANTE MOVEMENTS IN THE PHILIPPINES. THIS WAS REINFORCED BY A SURVEY ADMINISTERED TO ALL ARMED FORCES OF THE PHILIPPINES OFFICERS AND ENLISTED PERSONNEL ATTENDING TRAINING IN THE CONTINENTAL U.S. SERVICE SCHOOLS. THE STUDY FINDS THAT THE POLITICO PSYCHOLOGICAL IMPACTS, VOID OF AN IDEOLOGY, OF VIGILANTISM TO A NATION MENACED BY A VIOLENCE PRONE INSURGENT MOVEMENT MORE THAN OUTWEIGHS THE PORTENT OF ANARCHY THAT MAY RESULT FROM THE EXISTENCE OF POPULAR MILITIAS, UN-REGULATED BY GOVERNMENT.

00052
ANTS AND THE GREAT WALL
COMMONWEAL, CXVI(12) (JUN 89), 356.
CHINA MADE A NECESSARY AND FATEFUL DECISION A DECADE AGO WHEN IT OPTED FOR MORE DIVERSIFIED, RAPID ECONOMIC DEVELOPMENT. DESPITE THE REPRESSION OF THE STUDENT DEMOSTRATIONS IN 1989, CHINA WILL BE FORCED TO CHANGE, DUE TO THE LIBERALIZING IN THE SOVIET UNION AND CHINA'S CONTACT WITH THE MARKET ECONOMIES OF OTHER MAJOR PACIFIC NATIONS. COMMERCIAL, CULTURAL, EDUCATIONAL, AND POLITICAL CONTACTS WILL CONTINUE TO EXERT TREMENDOUS PRESSURE ON CHINA FOR POLITICAL REFORM.

00053
APARTHEID CHANGES ITS CLOTHES
SECHABA, 23(8) (AUG 89), 1.
MANY OBSERVERS VIEW F.W. DE KLERK AS A BETTER REFORMIST THAN SOUTH AFRICA'S CURRENT LEADER, P.W. BOTHA. HOWEVER, DEMOCRATIC ORGANIZATIONS IN SOUTH AFRICA (SUCH AS THE UNITED DEMOCRATIC FRONT) REFUSE TO CONSIDER DE KLERK'S PLEA TO WAIT ANOTHER FIVE YEARS FOR REFORM. AS LONG AS DE KLERK AND HIS PARTY CONTINUE TO REJECT MAJORITY RULE AND FUNDAMENTAL CHANGE, THE STRUGGLE FOR FREEDOM IN SOUTH AFRICA WILL CONTINUE ALONG PRESENT LINES.

00054
APPEAL BY THE USSR SUPREME SOVIET TO THE U.S. CONGRESS ON THE QUESTION OF A MORATORIUM ON NUCLEAR EXPLOSIONS AND TERMINATION OF NUCLEAR TESTS
REPRINTS FROM THE SOVIET PRESS, 49(7) (OCT 89), 43-44.
IN APPEALING TO THE U.S. CONGRESS THE USSR SUPREME SOVIET STATES THAT THE USSR IS PREPARED TO ANNOUNCE ANY DAY AND HOUR, ON THE BASIS OF RECIPROCITY, A MORATORIUM ON ALL NUCLEAR EXPLOSIONS, WHICH COULD BE A PROLOGUE TO CONCLUDING A VERIFIABLE AGREEMENT ON A COMPREHENSIVE NUCLEAR TEST BAN. THE SOVIETS PROPOSE TO DISCUSS THIS ISSUE AT A MEETING BETWEEN SOVIET AND U.S. PARLIAMENTARIANS, WHICH COULD BE HELD IN MOSCOW OR WASHINGTON IN THE NEAR FUTURE.

00055
ARENA TAKES THE HELM
CENTRAL AMERICA BULLETIN, 8(11) (OCT 89), 1-3, 6-8.
EVENTS IN EL SALVADOR SINCE THE NATIONAL REPUBLICAN ALLIANCE (ARENA) CAME TO POWER INDICATE THAT THE NEW GOVERNMENT IS PERFORMING A DELICATE BALANCING ACT BETWEEN THE WISHES OF PARTY HARDLINERS AND THE MILITARY, ON THE ONE HAND, AND EFFORTS TO MAINTAIN AN IMAGE OF LEGITIMACY, ON THE OTHER. WHILE EXTRALEGAL REPRESSION IS CLEARLY ON THE RISE, ARENA'S TACTICS REFLECT A MARKED SAVVY WITH REGARD TO EL SALVADOR'S CHANGED POLITICAL LANDSCAPE. FOR THE MOMENT AT LEAST, PURSUING A TOTAL WAR STRATEGY AGAINST THE FMLN AND EL SALVADOR'S POPULAR MOVMENT SEEMS TO HAVE BEEN RULED OUT. INSTEAD THE NEW GOVERNMENT IS TAKING STEPS TO LEGALIZE REPRESSION, LARGELY THROUGH LEGISLATIVE REFORMS, WHILE ASSUMING A POSTURE OF WILLINGNESS TO TALK WITH THE REBEL FORCES.

00056
ASSISTANCE FOR POLAND AND HUNGARY
DEPARTMENT OF STATE BULLETIN (US FOREIGN POLICY), 89(2153) (DEC 89), 39-40.
THE BUSH ADMINISTRATION IS COMMITTED TO PROVIDING A COMPREHENSIVE PACKAGE OF ASSISTANCE TO SUPPORT THE ECONOMIC AND POLITICAL REGENERATION IN POLAND AND HUNGARY. THE UNITED STATES NEEDS TO PLAY A LEADING ROLE IN DEVELOPING A CONCERTED WESTERN APPROACH TO POLAND'S ECONOMIC RECOVERY.

00057
ATTEMPT TO KILL TEKERE
NEW AFRICAN, (267) (DEC 89), 20.
1990 IS A CRUCIAL YEAR FOR ZIMBABWE. ZIMBABWEANS WILL GO TO THE POLLS FOR THE THIRD TIME SINCE INDEPENDENCE TO VOTE FOR THE GOVERNMENT OF THEIR CHOICE. EDGAR TEKERE IS CHALLENGING THE RULING PARTY IN THIS ELECTION. TEKERE'S PARTY IS CALLED THE ZIMBABWE UNITY MOVEMENT. ORDINARY ZIMBABWEANS SEEM TO HAVE LOST INTEREST IN POLITICS. THEY COMPLAIN OF HIGH TAXATION, UNEMPLOYMENT, CORRUPTION AMONG TOP GOVERNMENT OFFICIALS AND PRICE HIKES. EVEN IN LIGHT OF THIS PUBLIC APATHY AND SEVERAL ATTEMPTS TO ASSASSINATE HIM, TEKERE IS CONFIDENT THAT HIS PARTY WILL GAIN POWER IN 1990.

00058
AUTONOMY FOR THE MINORITY NATIONALITIES OF CHINA
CHINA NEWS ANALYSIS, (1391) (AUG 89), 1-9.
THE MINORITY NATIONALITIES POLICY OF THE PEOPLE'S REPUBLIC OF CHINA (PRC) IN THE PAST HAS APPEARED BOTH INGENIOUS AND CLUMSY, REFLECTING AT DIFFERENT PERIODS THE INTERNAL STRUGGLE WITHIN THE CHINESE COMMUNIST PARTY BETWEEN THE RIGHTISTS AND THE ULTRA-LEFTISTS. SINCE THE FOUNDING OF THE STATE, THE QUARREL HAS ALWAYS BEEN CENTRED ON HOW TO UNDERSTAND THE FUNDAMENTAL AXIOM OF THE COUNTRY: "THE PEOPLE'S REPUBLIC OF CHINA IS A UNIFIED MULTINATIONAL STATE, " A SENTENCE WHICH MANY CHINESE ANTHROPOLOGISTS STILL FEEL NECESSARY TO USE TODAY AS AN INTRODUCTION TO ANY SUBJECT DEALING WITH ETHNIC MINORITIES.

00059
BAJA ELECTION A "POLITICAL TEST"
MEXICO-UNITED STATES REPORT, II(8) (MAY 89), 3.
THE SECOND STATE ELECTION IN BAJA IS BEING LABELED A "TRUE TEST FOR MEXICAN DEMOCRACY," AND OF PRESIDENT SALINAS' CAMPAIGN PLEDGE TO ACCEPT DEMOCRACY AS A FACT OF MODERN LIFE. HIS INSTITUTIONAL REVOLUTIONARY PARTY (PRI) HAS NEVER PERMITTED AN OPPOSITION CANDIDATE TO WIN A STATE GOVERNORSHIP IN ALL ITS 60-YEAR RULE OF MEXICO. OPPOSITION CANDIDATES ARE PREPARED FOR PRI TACTICS OF FRAUD, REPRESSION AND MEDIA CONTROL DESPITE PRI ASSURANCES OF FAIR PLAY.

00060
BASIC CONTRADICTIONS OF CAPITALISM
BEIJING REVIEW, 32(19) (MAY 89), 18-22.
THE AUTHOR, WHO IS DIRECTOR OF THE WORLD ECONOMIC AND POLITICAL RESEARCH INSTITUTE OF THE CHINA ACADEMY OF SOCIAL SCIENCES, ANALYZES THE VARIOUS CONTRADICTIONS OF MODERN CAPITALISM AS THEY OCCUR WITHIN A COUNTRY AND IN THE WORLD AS A WHOLE. HE EMPHASIZES THAT THE BASIC CONTRADICTIONS OF CAPITALISM EXERCISE A DESTRUCTIVE INFLUENCE, ON THE ONE HAND, AND PROMOTE SOCIAL DEVELOPMENT, ON THE OTHER. MODERN CAPITALISM IS NOW IN THE STAGE OF STATE MONOPOLY CAPITALISM.

00061
BEFORE THEY SAT DOWN AT THE ROUND TABLE
CONTEMPORARY POLAND, XXII(3) (1989), 12-21.
THE ROUND TABLE MEETING BEGAN FEB. 6, 1989, AT THE PALACE OF THE COUNCIL OF MINISTERS IN WARSAW. PARTICIPANTS BEGAN THEIR DELIBERATIONS CONVINCED THAT THE REASON FOR CALLING THE ROUND TABLE WAS THE RENEWAL OF THE POLISH REPUBLIC IN THE NAME OF NATIONAL AND STATE INTERESTS AND WITH A SENSE OF RESPONSIBILITY FOR DECISIONS ON CRUCIAL ISSUES FOR POLAND AND THE POLISH PEOPLE. THIS ARTICLE PRESENTS THE BACKGROUND TO THE HISTORIC ROUND TABLE MEETING.

00062
BEHIND THE "PETTY ACTION" OF SOME AMERICANS
BEIJING REVIEW, 32(15) (APR 89), 40.
ACCORDING TO CHINESE FOREIGN MINISTER QIAN QICHEN, THERE ARE SOME PEOPLE IN THE UNITED STATES WHO LIKE TO SUPPORT CHINESE DISSIDENTS BUT THIS KIND OF "PETTY ACTION" IS UNFAVORABLE FOR THE FURTHER DEVELOPMENT OF SINO-AMERICAN RELATIONS.

00063
BENAZIR BHUTTO VISITS CHINA
BEIJING REVIEW, 32(7-8) (FEB 89), 10-11.
PAKISTANI PRIME MINISTER BENAZIR BHUTTO AND CHINESE PREMIER LI PENG EXCHANGED VIEWS ON A WIDE RANGE OF BILATERAL AND INTERNATIONAL ISSUES DURING TALKS IN FEBRUARY 1989. DURING BHUTTO'S VISIT, TWO AGREEMENTS WERE SIGNED: ONE ON THE RECIPROCAL ENCOURAGEMENT AND PROTECTION OF INVESTMENTS AND THE OTHER EXTENDING AN EXISTING TRADE PROTOCOL TO 1990.

00064
BIOGRAPHICAL NOTES
CONTEMPORARY POLAND, XXII(8) (1989), 13-17.
THIS ARTICLE CONTAINS SHORT BIOGRAPHICAL SKETCHES OF POLISH LEADERS, INCLUDING WOJCIECH JARUZELSKI, MIKOLAJ

KOZAKIEWICZ, TADEUSZ FISZBACH, TERES KATARZYNA DOBIELINSKA-ELISZEWSKA, OLGA KRZYZANKOWSKA, ANDRZEJ STELMA-CHOWSKI, ZOFIA KURATOWSKA, JOZEF SLISZ, AND ANDRZEJ WIELOWIEYSKI.

00065
BIOGRAPHICAL NOTES
CONTEMPORARY POLAND, XXII(9) (1989), 16-21.
THIS ARTICLE PROFILES THE FOLLOWING POLISH LEADERS: PRIME MINISTER TADEUSZ MAZOWIECKI, MIECZYSLAW F. RAKOWSKI, MANFRED GORYHODA, JANUSZ KUBASIEWICZ, LESZEK MILLER, MAREK KROL, WLODZIMIERZ NATORF, MARCIN SWIECICKI, AND SLAWOMIR WIATR.

00066
BIOGRAPHICAL NOTES: MEMBERS OF PUWP CC POLITICAL BUREAU
CONTEMPORARY POLAND, XXII(1) (1989), 24-30.
THIS ARTICLE PRESENTS BRIEF PROFILES OF THE NEW PARTY LEADERS ELECTED AT THE TENTH PLENUM OF THE POLISH UNITED WORKERS' PARTY CC. THEY INCLUDE STANISLAW CIOSEK, KAZIMIERZ CYPRYNIAK, IWONA LUBOWSKA, ZBIGNIEW MICHALEK, WIKTOR PYRKOSZ, GABRIELA REMBISZ, JANUSZ REYKOWSKI, ZDZISLAW SWIATEK, ZDZISLAW BALICKI, MAREK HOLDAKOWSKI, ZBIGNIEW SOBOTKA, ZYGMUNT CZARZASTY, LESZEK MILLER, AND MARIAN STEPIEN.

00067
BRAINSTORMS
FREE CHINA REVIEW, 39(10) (OCT 89), 1.
THE EVENTS OF JUNE 1989 EMPHASIZED AN ATTITUDE TOWARD MODERNIZATION IN MAINLAND CHINA THAT IS FAR DIFFERENT FROM TAIWAN'S. MAINLAND LEADERS HAVE TENACIOUSLY ADHERED TO THE IDEA THAT LONG-TERM ECONOMIC REFORMS CAN OCCUR WITHOUT MAJOR SHIFTS IN THE SOCIAL AND POLITICAL ENVIRONMENT. CHINESE STUDENTS ARE EXPECTED TO USE THEIR NEWLY-ACQUIRED TECHNICAL SKILLS BUT TO WASH THEIR MINDS OF ANY LIBERAL IDEAS, SUCH AS INDIVIDUAL FREEDOMS OR DEMOCRATIC POLITICAL FORMS.

00068
BRAZIL: ENSURE THE STABILITY OF THE GOVERNMENT AND THE SOVEREIGNTY OF THE CONSTITUENT NATIONAL CONGRESS
INFORMATION BULLETIN, 25/26(1-2) (JAN 88), 21.
THE BRAZILIAN COMMUNIST PARTY REITERATES THAT THE STABILITY OF THE SARNEY GOVERNMENT IS A PRINCIPAL ELEMENT OF THE TRANSITIONAL PERIOD AND THAT IT IS TO GUARANTEE THE ATMOSPHERE OF FREEDOM WHICH NOW EXISTS IN BRAZIL. IT IS ALSO ESSENTIAL FOR CONTINUED DEMOCRATIZATION. IN ORDER TO PRESERVE THIS ATMOSPHERE OF DEMOCRACY AND TO CHANGE THE CURRENT ECONOMIC POLICY WHICH RUNS COUNTER TO THE INTERESTS OF THE WORKING PEOPLE AND, IN MANY RESPECTS, TO NATIONAL INTERESTS, THE GOVERNMENT MUST INVARIABLY ACT THROUGH NEGOTIATION INSTEAD OF CONFRONTATION AND RELY ON THE NATION'S MOBILIZATION AND ON THE POWER OF THE WORKING MASSES.

00069
BRIDGING THE ECONOMIC GAP
BEIJING REVIEW, 32(5) (JAN 89), 20-27.
A DECADE HAS PASSED SINCE THE REPUBLIC OF CHINA INITIATED ITS PROGRAM OF ECONOMIC REFORM AND OPENING TO THE OUTSIDE WORLD. THIS ARTICLE COMPARES CHINA'S ECONOMIC PERFORMANCE WITH OTHER COUNTRIES AROUND THE GLOBE, IN ORDER TO ASSESS THE ACHIEVEMENTS AND PROBLEMS OF THE CHINESE PROGRAM.

00070
BRITAIN AND THE COMMONWEALTH
SURVEY OF CURRENT AFFAIRS, 19(5) (MAY 89), 182-184.
BRITAIN'S ROLE IN THE COMMONWEALTH AND THE PROBLEMS FACING THE ORGANISATION WERE THE SUBJECTS OF A SPEECH BY THE FOREIGN AND COMMONWEALTH SECRETARY, SIR GEOFFREY HOWE, TO THE COMMONWEALTH PRESS UNION IN LONDON ON 24 APRIL 1989. THE COMMONWEALTH IS "A BROAD CHURCH", SIR GEOFFREY SAID, EACH MEMBER STATE HAVING "SOMETHING DISTINCTIVE, SOMETHING DIFFERENT TO CONTRIBUTE". BUT ALL SHARE A COMMITMENT TO THE DECLARATION OF COMMONWEALTH PRINCIPLES SET OUT BY THE HEADS OF GOVERNMENT AT THEIR MEETING IN 1971: THE PROMOTION OF REPRESENTATIVE INSTITUTIONS AND GUARANTEES OF FREEDOM UNDER THE LAW; FIGHTING RACIAL DISCRIMINATION; NARROWING THE GAP BETWEEN RICH AND POOR; AND FOSTERING INTERNATIONAL CO-OPERATION IN THE CAUSE OF PEACE, TOLERANCE, JUSTICE AND DEVELOPMENT.

00071
BRITAIN'S REFUGEE POLICY
SURVEY OF CURRENT AFFAIRS, 19(2) (FEB 89), 51-52.
THE PRINCIPLES BEHIND BRITAIN'S REFUGEE POLICY WERE OUTLINED IN A SPEECH BY TIMOTHY RENTON, MINISTER OF STATE AT THE HOME OFFICE, IN JANUARY 1989. EARLIER, IN DECEMBER 1988, BRITAIN ANNOUNCED THAT IT WOULD BE PREPARED IN PRINCIPLE TO ACCEPT A FURTHER 1,000 VIETNAMESE REFUGEES HELD IN CAMPS IN HONG KONG PROVIDED THAT OTHER COUNTRIES MADE COMMENSURATE CONTRIBUTIONS.

00072
BRITAIN'S RELATIONS WITH CHINA
SURVEY OF CURRENT AFFAIRS, 19(6) (JUN 89), 232-234.
BRITAIN HAS JOINED OTHER GOVERNMENTS IN DEPLORING THE VIOLENT SUPPRESSION BY UNITS OF THE CHINESE PEOPLE'S LIBERATION ARMY OF PEACEFUL AND POPULAR DEMONSTRATIONS IN PEKING IN JUNE 1989. BRITIAN HAS ANNOUNCED THE SUSPENSION OF ALL SCHEDULED MINISTERIAL EXCHANGES WITH THE PEOPLE'S REPUBLIC OF CHINA AND OF ALL HIGH-LEVEL MILITARY CONTACTS AND A BAN ON ALL ARMS SALES.

00073
BRITAIN'S RELATIONS WITH IRAN
SURVEY OF CURRENT AFFAIRS, 19(3) (MAR 89), 92-94.
IRAN HAS BROKEN OFF DIPLOMATIC RELATIONS WITH BRITAIN AND THE GOVERNMENT IS ORDERING A NUMBER OF IRANIANS TO LEAVE BRITAIN. THE MOVES FOLLOW A DISPUTE OVER STATEMENTS BY AYATOLLAH KHOMEINI CALLING FOR THE DEATH OF THE BRITISH AUTHOR SALMAN RUSHDIE BECAUSE OF PASSAGES IN HIS NOVEL "THE SATANIC VERSES" THAT ARE CONSIDERED OFFENSIVE TO ISLAM.

00074
BRITISH FOREIGN POLICY
SURVEY OF CURRENT AFFAIRS, 19(10) (OCT 89), 371-373.
IN A SPEECH TO THE UNITED NATIONS GENERAL ASSEMBLY ON SEPTEMBER 27, 1989, BRITISH FOREIGN AND COMMONWEALTH SECRETARY JOHN MAJOR DISCUSSED THE SERIOUS PROBLEMS FACING THE INTERNATIONAL COMMUNITY AND THE ROLE OF THE UN IN RESOLVING THEM. MAJOR COMMENTED ON EAST-WEST RELATIONS, SOUTHERN AFRICA, THE MIDDLE EAST, THE VIETNAMESE BOAT PEOPLE, HONG KONG, DRUG TRAFFICKING, AND ENVIRONMENTAL PROBLEMS.

00075
BRITISH-ARGENTINE RELATIONS
SURVEY OF CURRENT AFFAIRS, 19(11) (NOV 89), 422-423.
FOLLOWING A MEETING IN OCTOBER 1989, BRITAIN AND ARGENTINA AGREED TO ESTABLISH CONSULAR RELATIONS AND TO RESUME AIR AND MARITIME COMMUNICATIONS. BUT A JOINT STATEMENT STRESSED THAT NOTHING IN THE CONDUCT OR CONTENT OF THE MEETING SHOULD BE INTERPRETED AS A CHANGE IN THE POSITION OF EITHER GOVERNMENT REGARDING SOVEREIGNTY OR TERRITORIAL AND MARITIME JURISDICTION OVER THE FALKLAND ISLANDS, SOUTH GEORGIA, OR THE SOUTH SANDWICH ISLANDS.

00076
BUDAPEST REFORM CIRCLE PLATFORM
WORLD AFFAIRS, 151(4) (1989), 203-207.
THE "REFORM CIRCLE" OF THE HUNGARIAN SOCIALIST WORKERS PARTY (MSZMP) DECLARES ITS PLATFORMS AND GOALS. THE ARTICLE IS AN EXCERPT OF THE GROUP'S PLATFORM. IT INCLUDES THE CIRCLE'S VIEW OF PAST ATTEMPTS TO IMPLEMENT STALINIST OR UTOPIAN MODELS OF SOCIALISM AS WELL AS A DENUNCIATION OF THE REPRESSION HUNGARY'S OCTOBER, 1956 MOVEMENT. IT OUTLINES THE FUTURE ROLE OF THE MSZMP AS A UNITED, LEFT-WING, REFORM-ORIENTED PARTY. IT CONCLUDES WITH AN ANALYSIS OF THE MEASURES NECESSARY TO FACILITATE A PEACEFUL TRANSITION INTO DEMOCRACY AND A CONSTITUTIONAL STATE.

00077
BUSH RECOMMENDS AID FOR PRIVATE SCHOOLS, WAFFLES ON TAX CREDITS
CHURCH AND STATE, 42(5) (MAY 89), 14 (110).
IN APRIL 1989, PRESIDENT BUSH UNVEILED AN EDUCATIONAL INITIATIVE THAT HAS BEEN CRITICIZED BECAUSE OF ITS PROVISIONS TO AWARD PUBLIC FUNDS TO PRIVATE SCHOOLS. BUSH'S PROPOSAL, THE EDUCATIONAL EXCELLENCE ACT OF 1989, INCLUDES PLANS TO GIVE CASH AWARDS TO "OUTSTANDING" PUBLIC AND PRIVATE SCHOOLS AND TEACHERS. ALTHOUGH THE BILL STIPULATES THAT RELIGIOUS SCHOOLS MAY NOT USE THE GRANTS FOR "RELIGIOUS INSTRUCTION OR FOR OTHER SECTARIAN PURPOSES," CRITICS FEAR THAT THE PLAN WOULD BE IMPOSSIBLE TO MONITOR AND WOULD LEAD TO CHURCH-STATE ENTANGLEMENT. ONLY DAYS BEFORE BUSH ANNOUNCED THIS BILL, HE SAID THAT HE HAS NO PLANS TO PUSH FOR TUITION TAX CREDITS FOR PRIVATE SCHOOLS.

00078
CALIFORNIA BISHOP ASSAILS PUBLIC SCHOOL "MONOPOLY," CALLS FOR PAROCHIAID
CHURCH AND STATE, 42(10) (NOV 89), 14 (230)-15 (231).
SACRAMENTO BISHOP FRANCIS A. QUINN HAS STATED THAT PUBLIC SCHOOLS ENJOY A FINANCIAL MONOPOLY AND THAT PARENTS OF CATHOLIC SCHOOL STUDENTS DESERVE A TAX REBATE FOR EDUCATIONAL EXPENSES. HE ADVOCATED VOUCHERS, TUITION TAX CREDITS, TEXTBOOK LOANS, AND SPECIAL TAX ARRANGEMENTS TO TREAT "ALL FAMILIES EQUITABLY."

00079
CALIFORNIANS WANT TOUGHER BORDER RESTRICTIONS
MEXICO-UNITED STATES REPORT, II(9) (JUN 89), 4.
A RECENT POLL REVEALS THAT TWO OUT OF THREE CALIFORNIANS FAVOR REPLACING CURRENT BORDER FENCING WITH A FENCE THAT CANNOT BE EASILY CLIMBED OR DESTROYED. THE POLL IS A REFLECTION OF AN INCREASING FRUSTRATION OF THE STATE'S POPULATION WITH THEIR ELECTED OFFICIALS AND THE MANNER IN WHICH ILLEGAL IMMIGRATION AND NARCOTICS SMUGGLING IS BEING DEALT WITH.

00080
CALLS FOR DEMOCRATIZATION IN THE GDR
EAST EUROPEAN REPORTER, 3(4) (SPR 89), 29-30.
THE ARTICLE IS COMPRISED OF A TEXT WRITTEN BY A
COALITION OF PEACE ACTIVISTS AND CHURCH GROUPS. IT CALLS ON
PARISH WORK GROUPS, CHRISTIAN, AND OTHER "INITIATIVE" GROUPS,
TO STEP FORWARD IN PROMOTING DEMOCRATIZATION AND OPENNESS.
IT DECLARES THAT ONLY THROUGH THE GUARANTEE OF CIVIL
FREEDOMS AND INDIVIDUAL HUMAN RIGHTS CAN SOCIALISM SURVIVE
AND THRIVE.

00081
CAMBODIA
SURVEY OF CURRENT AFFAIRS, 19(9) (SEP 89), 344-345.
AN INTERNATIONAL CONFERENCE ON CAMBODIA, WHICH BEGAN IN
PARIS ON 30 JULY, HAS SUSPENDED ON 29 AUGUST 1989 BECAUSE OF
DIFFERENCES BETWEEN THE FOUR CAMBODIAN FACTIONS. BRITAIN'S
VIEWS OF THE SITUATION IN CAMBODIA WERE SET OUT BY THE
FOREIGN AND COMMONWEALTH SECRETARY, JOHN MAJOR, IN A SPEECH
AT THE OPENING SESSION OF THE CONFERENCE. A STATEMENT WAS
MADE AT THE END OF THE CONFERENCE BY LORD BRABAZON OF TARA,
MINISTER OF STATE AT THE FOREIGN AND COMMONWEALTH OFFICE.

00082
CAN SALINAS GOVERN WITHOUT MEXICO CITY?
MEXICO-UNITED STATES REPORT, II(8) (MAY 89), 7.
THE FACT THAT MEXICO CITY, THE NATION'S CAPITAL AND
CENTER OF INDUSTRY, FINANCE, CULTURE, EDUCATION AND
COMMUNICATION, IS OVERWHELMINGLY IN THE HAND OF HIS
OPPOSITION WILL PSYCHOLOGICALLY HANDICAP PRESIDENT SALINAS
WITH THE KNOWLEDGE THAT HE IS SURROUNDED BY A CITIZENRY THAT
OPPOSES HIM. IF THE COMBINED OPPOSITION WISHES TO CHALLENGE
SALINAS ON A KEY ISSUE AND CALLS A DEMONSTRATION OR STRIKE,
IT CAN COUNT ON THE LARGE MAJORITY OF MEXICO CITY'S
INHABITANTS FOR SUPPORT, CONCEIVABLY PARALYZING THE CAPITAL

00083
CAN THE ECONOMIC ORDER BE RECTIFIED?
CHINA NEWS ANALYSIS, (1385) (MAY 89), 1-9.
THE FIRST STAGE OF CHINA'S PROGRAM TO IMPROVE AND
RECTIFY THE ECONOMY HAS BEEN COMPLETED, BUT ITS ACHIEVEMENTS
ARE DUBIOUS. THE STUDENT DEMONSTRATIONS IN BEIJING AND OTHER
PARTS OF THE COUNTRY HAVE ALREADY GIVEN THE LEADERSHIP ONE
VERDICT ON THE SUCCESS OF THEIR REFORMS. THE PROBLEM IS
COMPLEX AND IS AS MUCH POLITICAL AS ECONOMIC, EVEN THOUGH
THE ECONOMIC SITUATION IS A FACT OF LIFE AND AFFECTS THE
POPULATION DIRECTLY.

00084
CANADA: ON THE PARTY
INFORMATION BULLETIN, 26(23-24) (DEC 88), 7-12.
THIS ARTICLE DESCRIBES THE OUTCOME OF THE 27TH
CONVENTION OF THE COMMUNIST PARTY OF CANADA. FOCUS IS ON THE
POLITICAL RESOLUTION ADOPTED BY THE CONVENTION: THIS
RESOLUTION OUTLINES THE PARTY'S PRINCIPAL TASKS IN DOMESTIC
AND FOREIGN POLICY FOR THE COMING DECADE.

00085
CAPITALISM AND THE ENVIRONMENT
MONTHLY REVIEW, 41(2) (JUN 89), 1-10.
THE ARTICLE OUTLINES THE EVER INCREASING ENVIRONMENTAL
PROBLEMS THAT THE HUMAN RACE IS FACING. IT POINTS TO
CAPITALISM AS A MAJOR CAUSE OF THE CURRENT ENVIRONMENTAL
DEGRADATION AND WARNS THAT NOTHING SHORT OF A COMPLETE
ABANDONMENT OF CAPITALISM WILL BE ABLE TO REVERSE THE
CURRENT TRENDS OF ENVIRONMENTAL CHANGE.

00086
CARNAGE CONTROL
COMMONWEAL, CXVI(7) (APR 89), 195-196.
CALIFORNIA'S PLAYGROUND MASSACRE SEEMS FINALLY TO HAVE
GALVANIZED THE PUBLIC AND POLITICIANS TO ACTION ON CARNAGE
CONTROL, IF NOT YET ON GUN CONTROL.

00087
CATHOLIC BISHOPS ACCUSE U.S. OF "CONTRACEPTIVE
IMPERIALISM" OVERSEAS
CHURCH AND STATE, 42(1) (JAN 89), 15.
AT A VATICAN MEETING ON BIRTH CONTROL, ROMAN CATHOLIC
BISHOPS ACCUSED THE UNITED STATES AND OTHER WEALTHY NATIONS
OF IMPOSING POPULATION CONTROLS ON DEVELOPING COUNTRIES AS A
CONDITION OF RECEIVING AID. THE BISHOPS CALLED THE PRACTICE
"CONTRACEPTIVE IMPERIALISM" AND CLAIMED THAT DEVELOPMENT
FUNDS ARE OFTEN CONTINGENT ON MASSIVE PROGRAMS OF
CONTRACEPTION AND STERILIZATION.

00088
CATHOLIC HIERARCHY PRESSURES BUSH ON TUITION TAX CREDITS
CHURCH AND STATE, 42(7) (JUL 89), 14 (158)-15 (159).
IN MARCH 1989, PRESIDENT BUSH SAID THAT THE COUNTRY
CANNOT AFFORD TO IMPLEMENT A SYSTEM OF TUITION TAX CREDITS
AND THAT PARENTS WHO CHOOSE PRIVATE SCHOOL EDUCATION SHOULD
EXPECT TO PAY FOR IT. FOLLOWING HIS STATEMENT, A COALITION
OF ROMAN CATHOLIC EDUCATION LEADERS ASKED HIM TO CLARIFY HIS
STAND ON TUITION TAX CREDITS AND CITED THE ROLE CATHOLICS
PLAYED IN HIS ELECTION. BUSH THEN MET WITH PAROCHIAID
LOBBYISTS AND REASSURED THEM OF HIS SUPPORT.

00089
CATHOLIC POLITICIANS MUST VOTE AGAINST ABORTION, SAYS L.A.
ARCHBISHOP
CHURCH AND STATE, 42(8) (SEP 89), 16 (184)-17 (185).
CATHOLICS HOLDING PUBLIC OFFICE HAVE A MORAL OBLIGATION
TO WORK FOR LAWS BANNING ABORTION, ACCORDING TO ARCHBISHOP
ROGER M. MAHONY OF LOS ANGELES. MAHONY SAID THAT "THERE IS
NO SUCH THING AS A CATHOLIC PRO-CHOICE ELECTED OR APPOINTED
OFFICIAL."

00090
CENSORSHIP IN CAMERON
NEW AFRICAN, (258) (MAR 89), 31.
THOUGH PRESIDENT BIYA PROMISED A MORE OPEN SOCIETY WHEN
HE CAME TO POWER IN 1982, THE MONOLITHIC CAMEROON
BUREAUCRACY STILL STIFLES EARNEST MEDIA INQUIRY. THE
GOVERNMENT BANS MATERIAL THAT IS EMBARRASSING TO ITSELF AND
STIFLES PUBLICATIONS THAT ATTACK ITS FRIENDS IN HIGH PLACES.

00091
CHANGES IN THE SFRY CONSTITUTION
YUGOSLAV SURVEY, XXX(1) (1989), 3-38.
THIS ARTICLE SUMMARIZES AMENDMENTS IX-XLVIII TO THE SFRY
CONSTITUTION, WHICH WAS ADOPTED IN 1974. THE NEW AMENDMENTS
WERE PROMULGATED BY THE SFRY ASSEMBLY FEDERAL CHAMBER ON
NOVEMBER 25, 1988.

00092
CHAPTER FIVE: A BORDER ADRIFT: ORIGINS OF THE IRAQ - IRAN
WAR; THE LONG SHADOW
TRANSACTION PUBLISHERS, NEW BRUNSWICK, NJ, 1989, 65-90.
THIS CHAPTER EXPLAINS ASPECTS OF THE IRAQ - IRAN
CONFLICT. GENERAL HOSTILITY BETWEEN ARABS VERSUS IRANIANS;
PAN-ARABISTS VERSUS PAN-ISLAMISTS; SEMITES VERSUS ARYANS,
AND SUNNIS VERSUS SHI'IS IS EXPLORED FEARS OF A SHI'L
REBELLION AND THE SHAFT AL - 'ARAB AND OTHER TERRITORIAL
DISPUTES ARE DETAILED. THE IMPERIAL AND INDEPENDENT PERIODS
AND OTHER DISPUTES, AS WELL AS GEOGRAPHY AND ECONOMICS EACH
AS FACTORS OF THE IRAQ - IRAN WAR.

00093
CHARITIES LEGISLATION
SURVEY OF CURRENT AFFAIRS, 19(7) (JUL 89), 257-260.
GOVERNMENT PROPOSALS TO REFORM CHARITY LAW IN ENGLAND
AND WALES HAVE BEEN SET OUT IN A WHITE PAPER PUBLISHED ON 16
MAY 1989. THE MEASURES ARE DESIGNED TO GIVE THE CHARITY
COMMISSION, WHICH ADVISES AND REGULATES CHARITIES, NEW
POWERS TO DEAL WITH FRAUD AND MISMANAGEMENT, TO INCREASE THE
PUBLIC ACCOUNTABILITY OF CHARITIES AND TO PLACE GREATER
RESPONSIBILITY ON TRUSTEES. AT THE SAME TIME, AN EFFICIENCY
SCRUTINY OF GOVERNMENT FUNDING OF THE VOLUNTARY SECTOR HAS
BEEN ANNOUNCED.

00094
CHEMICAL WEAPONS
SURVEY OF CURRENT AFFAIRS, 19(1) (JAN 89), 10-12.
THE CONCLUDING DECLARATION OF THE JANUARY 1989 CHEMICAL
WEAPONS CONFERENCE IN PARIS EXPRESSED A DETERMINATION TO
PREVENT ANY RECOURSE TO CHEMICAL WEAPONS BY COMPLETELY
ELIMINATING THEM. GREAT BRITAIN, WHICH HAS BEEN ACTIVE FOR
MANY YEARS IN NEGOTIATIONS ON CHEMICAL WEAPONS, WELCOMED THE
SUCCESSFUL CONCLUSION OF THE CONFERENCE AND ENDORSED ITS
RECOMMENDATIONS.

00095
CHEMICAL WEAPONS AND NUCLEAR NON-PROLIFERATION
SURVEY OF CURRENT AFFAIRS, 19(7) (JUL 89), 263-264.
BRITAIN'S VIEWS ON THE NEED FOR A BAN ON CHEMICAL
WEAPONS AND ON THE NON-PROLIFERATION OF NUCLEAR WEAPONS WERE
EXPRESSED IN A SPEECH BY WILLIAM WALDEGRAVE, MINISTER OF
STATE AT THE FOREIGN AND COMMONWEALTH OFFICE, AT THE
COFERENCE ON DISARMAMENT AT GENEVA IN JUNE 1989. A BRITISH
PAPER ON PRACTICE CHALLENGE INSPECTIONS OF MILITARY
FACILITIES HAS ALSO TABLED.

00096
CHIEF OF GENERAL STAFF SPELLS OUT DEFENSIVE AIMS OF SOVIET
MILITARY DOCRINE AT MEETING WITH ELECTORATE
REPRINTS FROM THE SOVIET PRESS, 48(6) (MAR 89), 38-42.
THE SOVIET MILITARY POLICY IS UNDERGOING PERESTROIKA
ALONG WITH POLITICAL AND ECONOMIC POLICIES. IN AN ADDRESS TO
THE ELECTORATE, COL-GEN. MIKHAIL MOISEYEV DISCUSSED THE
GROWING CONSENSUS BEHIND SHIFTING TO A DEFENSIVE MILITARY
DOCTRINE. HE POINTS TO THE REDUCTION IN NUCLEAR WEAPONS AND
THE UNILATERAL TROOP REDUCTION OF THE SOVIET ARMED FORCES AS
WELL AS THE SOVIET WITHDRAWAL FROM AFGHANISTAN AS EXAMPLES
OF THE NEW POSTURE OF THE SOVIET MILITARY. HE ALSO OUTLINES
SOME OF THE ORGANIZATIONAL AND LOGISTICAL RESTRUCTURING THAT
IS CURRENTLY TAKING PLACE.

00097
CHILD WELFARE
SURVEY OF CURRENT AFFAIRS, 19(5) (MAY 89), 207-210.
GREAT BRITAIN'S PROPOSED CHILDREN BILL WILL REFORM THE
EXISTING LAW ON CHILD CARE AND FAMILY SERVICES AND THE
EMERGENCY PROTECTION OF CHILDREN IN ENGLAND AND WALES. ITS
GOAL IS TO INTEGRATE THE PRIVATE AND PUBLIC LAW RELATING TO
CHILDREN INTO A SINGLE RATIONALISED SYSTEM. IN ADDITION, NEW
GOVERNMENT INITIATIVES ON CHILD CARE PROVISION AND THE FIRST
GRANT ALLOCATIONS TO LOCAL AUTHORITIES FOR STAFF TRAINING IN
PRACTICE AND MANAGEMENT IN CHILD CARE UNDER A NEW SEVEN
MILLION POUND TRAINING SUPPORT PROGRAM HAVE BEEN ANNOUNCED.

00098
CHILE: ALL THE EFFORTS INTO THE FIGHT AGAINST THE
DICTATORSHIP
INFORMATION BULLETIN, 26(21-22) (NOV 88), 10-11.
THIS ARTICLE DESCRIBES THE ATTEMPTS UNDERTAKEN OF THE
COMMUNIST PARTY OF CHILE TO EXAMINE THE DEVELOPMENT OF THE
MULTI-FACETED STRUGGLE AGAINST THE PINOCHET DICTATORSHIP AND
ESPECIALLY TO ANALYZE THE QUESTION OF THE PLEBISCITE.

00099
CHINA AND INDIA FOR A NEW INTERNATIONAL ORDER
BEIJING REVIEW, 32(44) (OCT 89), 7, 9.
CHINESE VICE-PREMIER WU XUEQIAN AND INDIAN EXTERNAL
AFFAIRS MINISTER NARASIMHA RAO EXCHANGED VIEWS ON BILATERAL
RELATIONS AND INTERNATIONAL PROBLEMS AT A MEETING ON OCTOBER
12, 1989. THE TWO LEADERS AGREED THAT THEIR COUNTRIES WISH
TO WORK TOGETHER TO HELP ESTABLISH A NEW INTERNATIONAL
POLITICAL AND ECONOMIC ORDER.

00100
CHINA DROPS THE CURTAIN
SOUTH, (105) (JUL 89), 8-9.
FRIENDS OF CHINA ARE DEEPLY DISTRESSED AND DISTURBED BY
THE TIANANMEN SQUARE MASSACRE. THE CHINESE PEOPLE HAD BEEN
MOVING TOWARD A MORE OPEN SOCIETY WHERE AUTHORITY IS
ACCOUNTABLE AND FUNDAMENTAL RIGHTS AND FREEDOMS GUARANTEED.
THE ARMY ACTION SHOWED THAT THE POSTPONEMENT OF POLITICAL
REFORM, WHILE ECONOMIC REFORM AND THE INTRODUCTION OF
PRIVATE ENTERPRISE PROCEEDED APACE, HAD CREATED SEVERE
CONTRADICTIONS. CLEARLY, REFORM HAS BEEN SET BACK SEVERAL
YEARS AS A CONSEQUENCE OF THE DECISION TO CHOOSE REPRESSION
RATHER THAN CONCESSION.

00101
CHINA HOPES TO FURTHER COOPERATE WITH ADB
BEIJING REVIEW, 32(45) (NOV 89), 12.
ON OCTOBER 24, 1989, CHINESE PREMIER LI PENG STATED THAT
CHINA HOPES TO MAINTAIN AND EXPAND ITS COOPERATION WITH THE
ASIAN DEVELOPMENT BANK. LI SAID THAT CHINA WILL CONTINUE TO
RELY PRIMARILY ON ITS OWN RESOURCES FOR ECONOMIC DEVELOPMENT
BUT WILL NOT CLOSE THE COUNTRY TO THE OUTSIDE WORLD. HE ALSO
DECLARED THAT CHINA'S BASIC POLICIES GOVERNING ITS FOREIGN
RELATIONS REMAIN UNCHANGED.

00102
CHINA MEETS ECONOMIC CHALLENGES
BEIJING REVIEW, 32(43) (OCT 89), 7, 9.
ON OCTOBER 10, 1989, CHINESE PREMIER LI PENG MET WITH
PAUL VICTOR OBENG OF GHANA. LI TOLD OBENG THAT THE POLITICAL
SITUATION IN CHINA HAS STABILIZED BUT THE COUNTRY IS FACING
SOME TEMPORARY ECONOMIC DIFFICULTIES. LI SPOKE FAVORABLY OF
THE GHANAIAN GOVERNMENT'S POLICY OF POSITIVE NEUTRALITY AND
NONALIGNMENT, OF OPPOSING POWER POLITICS, AND OF DEDICATING
ITSELF TO STRENGTHENING AFRICAN SOLIDARITY.

00103
CHINA NOT TO YIELD TO FOREIGN PRESSURE
BEIJING REVIEW, 32(27) (JUL 89), 9.
ON JUNE 21, 1989, CHINESE PREMIER LI PENG REITERATED
THAT CHINA WILL NOT YIELD TO ANY FORM OF FOREIGN PRESSURE,
AND HE FEELS OPTIMISTIC AND CONFIDENT ON THE FUTURE OF THE
NATION.

00104
CHINA PROTESTS U.S. CONGRESS BILL
BEIJING REVIEW, 32(48) (NOV 89), 11.
THE CHINESE GOVERNMENT HAS LODGED A STRONG PROTEST
AGAINST THE UNITED STATES GOVERNMENT AFTER THE HOUSE OF
REPRESENTATIVES AND THE SENATE ADOPTED AN AMENDMENT ON
SANCTIONS AGAINST CHINA. THE ACTION ADOPTED BY THE US
CONGRESS IS BASED ON FALSE REPORTS AND RUMOURS, AND THUS
GRAVELY DAMAGES SINO-US RELATIONS.

00105
CHINA REJECTS U.S. PROTEST
BEIJING REVIEW, 32(29) (JUL 89), 12-13.
ON JULY 6, 1989, CHINESE ASSISTANT FOREIGN MINISTER LIU
HUAQUI MET THE U.S. AMBASSADOR TO CHINA AND HANDED HIM A
NOTE STATING THAT THE FOREIGN MINISTRY "CATEGORICALLY
REJECTS THE U.S. EMBASSY'S GROUNDLESS ACCUSATION AND STRONG
PROTEST AGAINST THE CHINESE GOVERNMENT" CONTAINED IN A NOTE

FROM THE AMERICAN EMBASSY DATED JULY 3, 1989. THE EXCHANGE
GREW OUT OF A CHARGE THAT CHINESE TROOPS HAD DELIBERATELY
FIRED AT THE FOREIGN DIPLOMATS' COMPOUND DURING THE VIOLENCE
IN BEIJING IN JUNE 1989.

00106
CHINA STICKS TO "ONE CHINA" POLICY
BEIJING REVIEW, 32(46) (NOV 89), 15-16.
THE GOVERNMENT OF THE PEOPLE'S REPUBLIC OF CHINA
SUSPENDED DIPLOMATIC RELATIONS WITH BELIZE ON OCTOBER 23,
1989. THIS STEP WAS TAKEN BECAUSE BELIZE HAD EARLIER
ESTABLISHED DIPLOMATIC RELATIONS WITH TAIWAN. THE CHINESE
GOVERNMENT HAS REPEATEDLY DECLARED THAT THERE IS ONLY ONE
CHINA, THAT THE PEOPLE'S REPUBLIC OF CHINA IS THE SOLE
LEGITIMATE GOVERNMENT REPRESENTING ALL OF CHINA, AND THAT
TAIWAN IS AN INALIENABLE PART OF CHINA.

00107
CHINA STICKS TO HK, MACAO POLICY
BEIJING REVIEW, 32(27) (JUL 89), 10.
JI PENGFEI, DIRECTOR OF THE HONG KONG AND MACAO AFFAIRS
OFFICE UNDER THE STATE COUNCIL, ON BEHALF OF THE CHINESE
GOVERNMENT, SOLEMNLY DECLARED THAT THE CHINESE GOVERNMENT'S
POLICIES TOWARDS HONG KONG AND MACAO, WHICH HAVE BEEN
FORMULATED IN LINE WITH THE CONCEPTION OF "ONE COUNTRY, TWO
SYSTEMS," WOULD NOT CHANGE FOLLOWING THE POLITICAL TURMOIL
IN BEIJING IN 1989.

00108
CHINA SUSPENDS DIPLOMATIC RELATIONS WITH GRENADA
BEIJING REVIEW, 32(33) (AUG 89), 11.
THE ESTABLISHMENT OF "DIPLOMATIC RELATIONS" BETWEEN
GRENADA AND TAIWAN IS A "DUAL RECOGNITION" PLOT AIMED AT
SPLITTING CHINA. TO DEFEND ITS PRINCIPLES, CHINA HAS SEVERED
DIPLOMATIC RELATIONS WITH GRENADA.

00109
CHINA SUSPENDS TIES WITH BELIZE
BEIJING REVIEW, 32(45) (NOV 89), 11.
ON OCTOBER 11, 1989, THE GOVERNMENT OF BELIZE
ESTABLISHED DIPLOMATIC RELATIONS WITH TAIWAN. IN DOING SO,
BELIZE NEGATED THE JOINT COMMUNIQUE ESTABLISHING DIPLOMATIC
RELATIONS BETWEEN IT AND THE PEOPLE'S REPUBLIC OF CHINA.

00110
CHINA, AFRICA AFFIRM BONDS
BEIJING REVIEW, 32(6) (FEB 89), 10.
CHINESE PRESIDENT YANG SHANGKUN MET WITH MALIAN
PRESIDENT MOUSSA TRAORE ON JANUARY 25, 1989. AT A MEETING
BETWEEN TRAORE AND PREMIER LI PING, DISCUSSIONS FOCUSED ON
THE DEBT PROBLEMS CONFRONTING AFRICA. LI POINTED OUT THAT
THE INTERNATIONAL DEBT QUESTION IS NOT A SIMPLE ONE OF
RELATIONS BETWEEN THE DEBTOR AND CREDITOR NATIONS. HE STATED
THAT ECONOMIC RELATIONS BETWEEN THE DEVELOPING AND DEVELOPED
COUNTRIES ARE BASED ON THE EXCHANGE OF UNEQUAL VALUES AND
THIS EXCHANGE HAS MADE THE RICH RICHER WHILE THE POOR HAVE
BECOME POORER.

00111
CHINA, THAILAND SHARE VIEWS ON KAMPUCHEAN ISSUE
BEIJING REVIEW, 32(45) (NOV 89), 9-10.
ON OCTOBER 26, 1989, DENG XIAOPING EXCHANGED VIEWS ON
KAMPUCHEA WITH THE PRIME MINISTER OF THAILAND, CHATICHAI
CHOONHAVAN. DENG SAID THAT THERE ARE TWO ESSENTIAL STEPS TO
SOLVING THE KAMPUCHEAN QUESTION: VIETNAM MUST COMPLETELY
WITHDRAW ITS TROOPS AND A FOUR-PARTY PROVISIONAL COALITION
GOVERNMENT HEADED BY PRINCE NORODOM SIHANOUK MUST BE
ESTABLISHED.

00112
CHINA'S DIPLOMATS MEET IN BEIJING
BEIJING REVIEW, 32(30) (JUL 89), 7.
CHINESE COMMUNIST PARTY LEADER JIANG ZEMIN AND PREMIER
LI PENG CALLED FOR CHINESE DIPLOMATS TO WORK WITH VIGILANCE
IN REGARDS TO THE COMPLICATED POLITICAL STRUGGLES IN THE
WORLD COMMUNITY. AT A WEEK-LONG MEETING OF CHINESE
DIPLOMATIC ENVOYS TO OTHER COUNTRIES, THE LEADERS ALSO
BRIEFED THEM ABOUT THE DOMESTIC POLITICAL AND ECONOMIC
SITUATION AND REITERATED CHINA'S FOREIGN POLICY.

00113
CHINA'S FIVE STEPS TO PEACE IN MIDDLE EAST
BEIJING REVIEW, 32(42) (OCT 89), 10-11.
IN OCTOBER 1989, CHINESE PREMIER LI PENG OFFERED A FIVE-
POINT PROPOSAL TO BRING PEACE TO THE MIDDLE EAST. THE PLAN
INCLUDES (1) A POLITICAL SETTLEMENT OF THE MIDEAST PROBLEM
WITHOUT USING MILITARY FORCE; (2) AN INTERNATIONAL MIDDLE
EAST PEACE CONFERENCE PRESIDED OVER BY THE UNITED NATIONS
AND ATTENDED BY ALL PERMANENT MEMBERS OF THE UN SECURITY
COUNCIL AND OTHER CONCERNED PARTIES; (3) DIALOGUES OF
VARIOUS FORMS IN THE MIDEAST, INCLUDING DIRECT TALKS BETWEEN
ISRAEL AND THE PLO; (4) A WITHDRAWAL OF TROOPS BY ISRAEL
FROM THE OCCUPIED TERRITORIES, WHILE ENSURING THE SECURITY
OF ISRAEL; AND (5) ALLOWING THE PALESTINIAN AND ISRAELI

PEOPLE TO COEXIST PEACEFULLY, WITH THE STATES OF PALESTINE AND ISRAEL RECOGNIZING EACH OTHER.

00114
CHINA'S FOREIGN TRADE POLICY REMAINS UNCHANGED
BEIJING REVIEW, 32(30) (JUL 89), 17-19.
IN THIS INTERVIEW, THE DIRECTOR OF THE DEPARTMENT OF POLICIES AND STRUCTURAL REFORM UNDER THE MINISTRY OF FOREIGN ECONOMIC RELATIONS AND TRADE ANSWERS QUESTIONS ABOUT CHINA'S OPEN TRADE POLICY AND THE SAFETY OF FOREIGN BUSINESSMEN IN THE WAKE OF THE POLITICAL VIOLENCE IN BEIJING IN JUNE 1989. HE EMPHASIZES THAT CHINA'S REFORM POLICIES WILL CONTINUE AND DECLARES THAT ECONOMIC SANCTIONS BY OTHER COUNTRIES ARE "UNJUST AND SHORT-SIGHTED."

00115
CHINA'S INTERNAL AFFAIRS BROOK NO INTERFERENCE
BEIJING REVIEW, 32(31) (JUL 89), 14-15.
LEADERS AT THE 1989 SUMMIT OF THE SEVEN LEADING INDUSTRIALIZED NATIONS IN PARIS IGNORED THE REALITIES IN CHINA AND MADE JUDGMENTS ON CHINESE AFFAIRS BASED ON THEIR OWN VALUES. THEY MADE UNWARRANTED CHARGES AGAINST CHINA AND DENOUNCED ITS HANDLING OF THE POLITICAL TURMOIL IN BEIJING AS A "VIOLENT SUPPRESSION" OF HUMAN RIGHTS. THESE GROUNDLESS CHARGES, WHICH REPRESENT GROSS INTERFERENCE IN CHINA'S INTERNAL AFFAIRS, ARE UNACCEPTABLE TO THE CHINESE GOVERNMENT AND PEOPLE.

00116
CHINA'S POLICY TOWARDS THE DALAI LAMA
BEIJING REVIEW, 32(10) (MAR 89), 30-31.
THIS ARTICLE COMPARES THE DIVERGENT VIEWS OF THE CHINESE GOVERNMENT AND THE DALAI LAMA CONCERNING THE SITUATION IN TIBET. THE DALAI LAMA'S "NEW PROPOSAL" AND THE CONCEPT OF A GREATER TIBERTAN AUTONOMOUS REGION ARE ALSO ANALYZED.

00117
CHINA'S POSITION ON ARMS TRANSFER
BEIJING REVIEW, 32(22) (MAY 89), 17-18.
CHINESE AMBASSADOR FOR DISARMAMENT FAN GUOXIANG MADE A NINE-POINT STATEMENT ON THE QUESTION OF INTERNATIONAL ARMS TRANSFER TO THE UNITED NATIONS DISARMAMENT COMMISSION ON MAY 11, 1989. HIS POINTS INCLUDED THE FOLLOWING: THE TRANSFER OF ARMS MUST SERVE TO SAFEGUARD THE INDEPENDENCE, SOVEREIGNTY, AND TERRITORIAL INTEGRITY OF THE STATES CONCERNED; INTERNATIONAL ARMS TRANSFERS SHOULD HELP THE PEOPLE IN THEIR JUST STRUGGLES AGAINST COLONIAL DOMINATION, FOREIGN AGGRESSION, AND OCCUPATION; THE QUESTION OF INTERNATIONAL ARMS TRANSFER SHOULD BE ADDRESSED IN CONJUNCTION WITH REDUCING INTERNATIONAL TENSIONS, REMOVING REGIONAL CONFLICTS, AND CHECKING THE ARMS RACE.

00118
CHINESE COMMUNIST CAN'T REPRESS RELIGIOUS SPIRIT
ASIAN OUTLOOK, 24(3) (MAY 89), 18.
THE RELIGIOUS SPIRIT IN MANKIND CAN NEVER BE TOTALLY SUPPRESSED. BUT COMMUNISTS AROUND THE WORLD HAVE NEVER ABSORBED THIS SIMPLE TRUTH. PERHAPS NOWHERE IS THIS FACT SO SELF-EVIDENT AS IN COMMUNIST CHINA, WHERE THE RESURGENCE OF CHRISTIANITY IS CHALLENGING COMMUNISM AND COMMUNIST LEADERS ALIKE

00119
CHINESE LEADER MEETS INDIAN GUESTS
BEIJING REVIEW, 32(29) (JUL 89), 11.
IN A JULY 1989 MEETING WITH INDIAN LEADERS, JIANG ZEMIN COFIRMED THAT CHINA WILL NOT CHANGE ITS POLICIES BECAUSE OF THE RECENT POLITICAL TURMOIL IN BEIJING. HE ALSO STATED THAT IT IS FUTILE FOR OTHER COUNTRIES TO ATTEMPT TO FORCE CHINA TO SUBMIT THROUGH ECONOMIC SANCTIONS, BECAUSE THE CHINESE PEOPLE WOULD NEVER YIELD TO OUTSIDE PRESSURE. THE INDIAN DELEGATION WAS IN CHINA TO ATTEND THE FIRST MEETING OF THE JOINT WORKING GROUP ON THE SINO-INDIAN BOUNDARY QUESTION.

00120
CHINESE LEADERS AND DENG MEET U.S. ENVOY
BEIJING REVIEW, 32(51) (DEC 89), 7, 9.
CHINESE LEADER DENG XIAOPING MET WITH BRENT SCOWCROFT, SPECIAL ENVOY OR PRESIDENT GEORGE BUSH, IN DECEMBER 1989. DENG STATED THAT, ALTHOUGH THERE ARE CURRENTLY SOME PROBLEMS BETWEEN CHINA AND THE USA, THE TWO COUNTRIES' RELATIONS SHOULD EVENTUALLY IMPROVE. SCOWCROFT REPLIED THAT THE USA IS READY TO COOPERATE WITH CHINA TO PROMOTE BETTER RELATIONS. SCOWCROFT ALSO MET WITH OTHER CHINESE LEADERS, INCLUDING JIANG ZEMIN AND PREMIER LI PENG.

00121
CHINESE LEADERS MEET NYERERE
BEIJING REVIEW, 32(49) (DEC 89), 10-11.
CHINESE PRESIDENT YANG SHANGKUN MET WITH JULIUS NYERERE, CHAIRMAN OF THE TANZANIAN REVOLUTIONARY PARTY, IN NOVEMBER 1989. SHANGKUN REITERATED CHINA'S COMMITMENT TO ITS POLICY OF OPENING TO THE OUTSIDE WORLD AND DEPLORED THE ECONOMIC SANCTIONS THAT SOME WESTERN COUNTRIES HAVE IMPOSED AGAINST CHINA. NYERERE STATED THAT THE THIRD WORLD NATIONS MUST PRACTICE SELF-RELIANCE, INTENSIFY UNITY AND COOPERATION AMONG THEMSELVES, AND PURSUE DIALOGUE WITH THE INDUSTRIALIZED WORLD.

00122
CHRISTIAN DEMOCRATS FAIL TO CONSOLIDATE POWER
CENTRAL AMERICA BULLETIN, 8(12) (NOV 89), 1-3, 6-8.
THE GOVERNMENT OF VINICIO CEREZO IS FACING ITS MOST SERIOUS POLITICAL CRISIS SINCE TAKING OFFICE. THE PAST THREE MONTHS HAVE WITNESSED A WAVE OF POLITICAL VIOLENCE, INCLUDING THE ASSASSINATION OF CHRISTIAN DEMOCRATIC LEADER DANILO BARILLAS AND THE DISAPPEARANCE OF SEVERAL STUDENT LEADERS. AT THE HEART OF THE CRISIS IS THE WIDESPREAD PERCEPTION THAT THE GOVERNMENT HAS BECOME INCREASINGLY UNRESPONSIVE TO THE DEMANDS OF ALL SECTORS.

00123
CHURCH-STATE LAW IS CONFUSED, CONFUSING, SAYS JUSTICE SCALIA
CHURCH AND STATE, 42(11) (DEC 89), 13 (253).
SUPREME COURT ASSOCIATE JUSTICE ANTONIN SCALIA HAS SAID THAT NO AREA OF COURT DOCTRINE IS "MORE CONFUSED OR CONFUSING" THAT THE LAW GOVERNING THE SEPARATION OF CHURCH AND STATE. HE ALSO STATED THAT THE COURT IS "NOT EVEN ON THE ROAD TO SOME CONSISTENCY" REGARDING THE ISSUE.

00124
CHURCH-STATE SEPARATION: IN HOT WATER
CHURCH AND STATE, 42(8) (SEP 89), 13 (181).
THE 1989 SESSION OF THE U.S. SUPREME COURT SERVED AS A REMINDER THAT THE CONSTITUTIONAL RULES GOVERNING THE RELATIONSHIP BETWEEN CHURCH AND STATE COULD SOON BE CHANGED BY JUDICIAL FIAT. CHIEF JUSTICE WILLIAM REHNQUIST, WHO HAS CANDIDLY EXPRESSED HIS CONTEMPT FOR THE WALL OF SEPARATION BETWEEN CHURCH AND STATE, NOW HAS THREE ALLIES WHO GENERALLY VOTE WITH HIM ON MATTERS PERTAINING TO THE NO-ESTABLISHMENT CLAUSE.

00125
CHURCH-STATE TERMS OF ABC BILL CREATE NEW DISPUTE
CHURCH AND STATE, 42(7) (JUL 89), 12 (156)-13 (157).
IN JUNE 1989, THE U.S. SENATE BEGAN DEBATE ON THE ACT FOR BETTER CHILD CARE SERVICES (ABC). IN LATE MAY, THE U.S. CATHOLIC CONFERENCE HAD RENEGED ON AN AGREEMENT TO ACCEPT COMPROMISE CHURCH-STATE LANGUAGE THAT WOULD EASE PASSAGE OF ABC. INSTEAD, THE USCC ENDORSED AN AMENDMENT THAT WOULD ALLOW FEDERAL AID FOR SECTARIAN CHILD CARE.

00126
CLINIC VOTE COSTS VIRGINIA POLITICAN HOLY COMMUNION
CHURCH AND STATE, 42(3) (MAR 89), 18 (66)-19 (67).
AN ALEXANDRIA, VIRGINIA, CITY COUNCIL MEMBER SAYS A PRIEST REFUSED TO GIVE HIM COMMUNION BECAUSE HE VOTED IN FAVOR OF A HEALTH CLINIC THAT DISTRIBUTES BIRTH CONTROL DEVICES. THE INCIDENT ILLUSTRATES THE AMERICAN CATHOLIC HIERARCHY'S INCREASINGLY HARD-LINE STANCE ON ABORTION AND BIRTH CONTROL, WHICH IRONICALLY COMES AT A TIME WHEN BISHOPS AROUND THE WORLD SEEM TO BE RELAXING THEIRS.

00127
COLUMN
ENCOUNTER, LXXIII(1) (JUN 89), 27-29.
IN GORBACHEV'S MIND DETENTE AND DISARMAMENT ARE LINKED WITH ECONOMIC PROSPERITY AND ENVIRONMENTAL IMPROVEMENTS. THE SOVIET UNION CANNOT REALLY AFFORD AN INTENSE COLD WAR. COUPLED WITH ELECTIONS IN THE USSR AND SIGNS OF CHANGE IN AT LEAST TWO EASTERN EUROPEAN SATELLITES, GORBACHEV'S PRONOUNCEMENTS MAKE IT HARD NOT TO FEEL THAT A NEW EPOCH MAY BE PRECARIOUSLY AT HAND.

00128
COMING OF AGE
INDIA TODAY, XIV(2) (JAN 89), 22-24.
IN DECEMBER 1988, THE LEADERS OF THE SEVEN NATIONS BELONGING TO THE SOUTH ASIAN ASSOCIATION FOR REGIONAL COOPERATION MET FOR THE FOURTH TIME. THE SUMMIT SAW THE ORGANIZATION FLOWER INTO A USEFUL DIPLOMATIC FORUM AND INDICATED THAT, EVEN THOUGH DISCORDS CONTINUE, THE ORGANIZATION HAS BEGUN MOVING TOWARDS REAL COOPERATION.

00129
COMMONWEALTH HEADS OF GOVERNMENT MEETING
SURVEY OF CURRENT AFFAIRS, 19(11) (NOV 89), 409-422.
THE MOST RECENT IN THE SERIES OF BIENNIAL COMMONWEALTH HEADS OF GOVERNMENT MEETINGS WAS HELD IN KUALA LUMPUR, MALAYSIA, FROM 18 TO 24 OCTOBER 1989. IN ADDITION TO A FINAL COMMUNIQUE, THE MEETING ISSUED STATEMENTS ON SOUTHERN AFRICA, THE ENVIRONMENT, AND COMMONWEALTH FUNCTIONAL CO-OPERATION. A SEPARATE STATEMENT ON SOUTHERN AFRICA WAS ISSUED BY THE BRITISH GOVERNMENT. BRITAIN WAS REPRESENTED AT THE MEETING BY THE PRIME MINISTER, MARGARET THATCHER, ACCOMPANIED BY THE FOREIGN AND COMMONWEALTH SECRETARY, JOHN MAJOR.

00130
    COMMUNIQUE OF FIFTH PLENARY SESSION OF 13TH CPC CENTRAL
    COMMITTEE
BEIJING REVIEW, 32(47) (NOV 89), 15-23.
    THE FIFTH PLENARY SESSION OF THE 13TH CENTRAL COMMITTEE
OF THE COMMUNIST PARTY OF CHINA WAS HELD IN BEIJING IN
NOVEMBER 1989. THE SESSION DELIBERATED AND ADOPTED THE CPC
CENTRAL COMMITTEE'S DECISION TO FURTHER IMPROVE THE ECONOMIC
ENVIRONMENT, CORRECT THE ECONOMIC ORDER, AND DEEPEN THE
REFORM EFFORT. IT ALSO ACCEPTED DENG XIAOPING'S RESIGNATION
FROM HIS PARTY POST AS CHAIRMAN OF THE CPC CENTRAL COMMITTEE
MILITARY COMMISSION.

00131
    COMMUNIQUE OF THE FOURTH PLENARY SESSION OF THE 13TH CPC
    CENTRAL COMMITTEE
BEIJING REVIEW, 32(27) (JUL 89), 13-14.
    THE FOURTH PLENARY SESSION OF THE 13TH CPC CENTRAL
COMMITTEE WAS CONVENED IN BEIJING ON JUNE 23 AND 24, 1989.
THE DELEGATES CONCLUDED THAT A VERY SMALL NUMBER OF PEOPLE
TOOK ADVANTAGE OF STUDENT UNREST TO STIR UP PLANNED,
ORGANIZED, AND PREMEDITATED POLITICAL TURMOIL IN BEIJING AND
SOME OTHER PLACES, WHICH LATER DEVELOPED INTO A COUNTER-
REVOLUTIONARY REBELLION. IN THIS POLITICAL STRUGGLE, THE
POLICY DECISIONS AND MAJOR MEASURES TAKEN BY THE PARTY
CENTRAL COMMITTEE WERE NECESSARY AND WON THE SUPPORT OF THE
WHOLE PARTY AND THE PEOPLE. ZHAO ZIYANG MADE THE MISTAKE OF
SUPPORTING THE TURMOIL AND SPLITTING THE PARTY AND MUST
ACCEPT RESPONSIBILITY FOR THE DEVELOPMENT OF THE TURMOIL.

00132
    COMMUNIQUE OF THE MEETING OF THE POLITICAL CONSULTATIVE
    COMMITTEE OF THE WARSAW TREATY STATES
REPRINTS FROM THE SOVIET PRESS, 49(5) (SEP 89), 26-32.
    A MEETING OF THE POLITICAL CONSULTATIVE COMMITTEE OF THE
COUNTRIES PARTICIPANTS IN THE WARSAW TREATY OF FRIENDSHIP,
COOPERATION AND MUTUAL ASSISTANCE WAS HELD IN BUCHAREST ON
JULY 7-8, 1889. THE PARTICIPANTS OF THE MEETING EXCHANGED
VIEWS ON THE EVOLVING INTERNATIONAL SITUATION AND DISCUSSED
MAIN AREAS OF INTERACTION AMONG THE ALLIED STATES IN THE
INTERESTS OF PEACE AND STABILITY IN EUROPE, DISARMAMENT, AND
INCREASING INTERNATIONAL DIALOGUE AND COOPERATION.

00133
    COMMUNIST PARTY OF CHINA PUSHES PARTY HYGIENE
BEIJING REVIEW, 32(5) (JAN 89), 9.
    AT A DECEMBER 1988 MEETING, THE SECRETARIAT OF THE CPC
CENTRAL COMMITTEE STRESSED THAT THE PARTY AND THE GOVERNMENT
MUST KEEP PARTY MEMBERS AND STATE ORGANIZATIONS CLEAN AND
HONEST. THE SECRETARIAT POINTED OUT THAT SOME PEOPLE ABUSE
THEIR POWER TO INDUCE BRIBES AND EMBEZZLE PUBLIC MONEY,
ALTHOUGH THE MAJORITY OF PARTY MEMBERS AND CADRES ARE
UPRIGHT IN THEIR BEHAVIOR. EFFECTIVE MEASURES MUST BE TAKEN
TO ELIMINATE CORRUPTION.

00134
    COMMUNIST PARTY OF THE PHILIPPINES (CPP) AND THE NEW
    PEOPLE'S ARMY (NPA)
AVAILABLE FROM NTIS, NO. AD-A206 651/2/GAR, DEC 88, 44.
    THIS BIBLIOGRAPHY PROVIDES A COMPREHENSIVE COLLECTION OF
REFERENCES ON THE PHILIPPINES. SPECIAL EMPHASIS HAS BEEN
PLACED ON THE SELECTION OF SOURCES DEALING WITH THE
COMMUNIST PARTY OF THE PHILIPPINES (CPP) AND THE NEW
PEOPLE'S ARMY (NPA). THESE ARTICLES HAVE BEEN SPECIFICALLY
SELECTED TO PROVIDE THE MILITARY PLANNER/ANALYST WITH AN
ACCURATE ASSESSMENT OF THE SCOPE AND NATURE OF THE
INSURGENCY IN THE PHILIPPINES AS WELL AS THE RAMIFICATIONS
OF THAT INSURGENCY FOR THE MILITARY OPTIONS FACING THE
UNITED STATES IN THE PACIFIC BASIN.

00135
    CONCLUDING REMARKS AT THE CENTRAL COMMITTEE PLENUM
REPRINTS FROM THE SOVIET PRESS, 49(10) (NOV 89), 32-37.
    THIS IS A TEXT OF THE CONCLUDING REMARKS THAT MIKHAIL
GORBACHEV, GENERAL SECRETARY OF THE SOVIET COMMUNIST PARTY
CENTRAL COMMITTEE, MADE AT THE PARTY'S PLENUM ON SEPTEMBER
20, 1989. HE BRIEFLY SUMS UP THE RESULTS OF MATTERS
SUBMITTED TO THE CURRENT PLENUM. HE DISCUSSES THE NEW POLICY
ON THE NATIONALITIES QUESTION, THE CONSOLIDATION OF
SOVEREIGNTY OF THE REPUBLICS, AND FEDERALISM AND HUMAN
RIGHTS.

00136
    CONGRESS (1) EDGES AHEAD
INDIA TODAY, 14(16) (AUG 89), 22-28.
    THE LATEST MARG-INDIA TODAY OPINION POLL SHOWS CONGRESS
(1) MARGINALLY IMPROVING ITS PERFORMANCE. IT REPORTS THAT
UNLESS SOMETHING GOES DRASTICALLY WRONG, ONLY A COMBINED
OPPOSITION CAN STOP RAJIV GANDHI FROM RETURNING TO POWER. IT
ALSO NOTES THE SWING IN FAVOR OF THE BJP IN THE HINDU-
SPEAKING BELT. IT SHOWS CONGRESS (1) STRENGTH IN LOK SABHA
AND ILLUSTRATES GANDHI'S SWAYING POPULARITY. IT EXPLORES
QUESTIONS SUCH AS WILL THE OPPOSITION BE ABLE TO FORM A
GOVERNMENT, UNSTABLE OPPOSITION, AWARENESS OF SCHEMES, MIXED

REACTIONS AND IMPLEMENTATION DOUBTS.

00137
    CONGRESS AND PRAYER: TURNING UP THE VOLUME?
CHURCH AND STATE, 42(6) (JUN 89), 13 (133).
    REP. WILLIAM DANNEMEYER IS A CONSERVATIVE CALIFORNIA
CONGRESSMAN WHO OPPOSES THE SUPREME COURT'S 1962 DECISION
BARRING SCHOOL-SPONSORED PRAYERS AND BELIEVES SCHOOL BOARDS
SHOULD BE ALLOWED TO SET ASIDE TIME FOR VOCAL OR SILENT
PRAYER BY STUDENTS. DANNEMEYER CITES A BOOK BY EVANGELIST
DAVID BARTON WHO CLAIMS THAT STATISTICS "PROVE" THAT
AMERICAN CREATIVITY, FAMILY STABILITY, MORALITY, ACHIEVEMENT,
AND INDUSTRIAL PRODUCTION HAVE DECLINED AS A RESULT OF THE
SUPREME COURT'S PRAYER DECISION.

00138
    CONGRESS: EIGHT IN TEN AMERICANS OPPOSE CONGRESSIONAL PAY
    RAISE
GALLUP REPORT, (281) (FEB 89), 6-8.
    THE VAST MAJORITY OF AMERICANS FEEL MEMBERS OF CONGRESS
DON'T DESERVE A $45,000 PAY RAISE. OPPOSITION TO THE
INCREASE MAY REFLECT THE GENERALLY LOW PUBLIC ESTEEM IN
WHICH CONGRESS IS HELD.

00139
    CONSERVATIVES TO FIGHT IN NORTHERN IRELAND
CONSTITUTIONAL REFORM QUARTERLY REVIEW, 4(3) (FAL 89), 3.
    THE LONG CAMPAIGN BY ACTIVISTS WITHIN THE BRITISH
CONSERVATIVE PARTY TO GAIN FULL RECOGNITION AND AFFILIATION
FOR LOCAL ASSOCIATIONS IN NORTHERN IRELAND ENDED IN A
DECISIVE VICTORY. FOR THE FIRST TIME, AT THE NEXT GENERAL
ELECTION, THERE ARE EXPECTED TO BE CONSERVATIVE, AS WELL AS
TRADITIONAL ALLIED UNIONIST PARTY CANDIDATES STANDING IN ALL
OF NORTHERN IRELAND'S 17 CONSTITUENCIES.

00140
    CONSIDER THE WALL
COMMONWEAL, CXVI(21) (DEC 89), 659-660.
    BY BRINGING DOWN THE BERLIN WALL, THE EAST GERMANS
CONFIRMED THEIR GOVERNMENT IN AN ACCELERATED PACE OF
POLITICAL REFORM. MOREOVER, BY REFUSING TO STOP THE EVENTS
IN THE MILITARILY STRATEGIC EAST GERMANY, MIKHAIL GORBACHEV
ONCE AGAIN CONFIRMED A LIMITED AUTONOMY FOR THE EVOLUTION
OF EASTERN EUROPE. BUT THE BREACHING OF THE WALL SHOULD NOT
BE INFUSED WITH MORE MEANING THAN IT CAN REALISTICALLY BEAR.
IT IS A BEGINNING, NOT AN OUTCOME. THE EAST GERMANS MUST
STILL CONSTRUCT A GENUINE POLITICAL CULTURE AND A
FUNCTIONING PLURALISTIC DEMOCRACY.

00141
    CONSTRUCTION OF THE CHINESE LEGAL SYSTEM
BEIJING REVIEW, 32(44) (OCT 89), 17-20.
    SINCE 1949 CHINA'S SOCIALIST LEGAL SYSTEM HAS GONE
THROUGH FOUR STAGES: ESTABLISHMENT, INITIAL DEVELOPMENT,
DESTRUCTION, AND RAPID ADVANCEMENT. BEGINNING IN 1979, THE
NATIONAL PEOPLE'S CONGRESS AND ITS STANDING COMMITTEE HAVE
ENACTED, REVISED, AND SUPPLEMENTED A TOTAL OF 147 LAWS AND
REGULATIONS COVERING VARIOUS ASPECTS OF STATE AND SOCIAL
LIFE. A SOCIALIST LEGAL SYSTEM WITH CHINESE CHARACTERISTICS
HAS TAKEN SHAPE. THE JUDICIARY HAS BEEN STRENGTHENED AND THE
PEOPLE'S SENSE OF RESPONSIBILITY TO THE LAW HAS BEEN
ENHANCED AFTER YEARS OF NATIONWIDE PUBLICITY AND EDUCATION
ABOUT THE LEGAL SYSTEM.

00142
    CONTRARY TO AFRICAN PEOPLE'S INTERESTS
INFORMATION BULLETIN, 27(3-4) (FEB 89), 11-12.
    THERE MUST BE FUNDAMENTAL CHANGE IN THE CONTENT AND
CHARACTER OF COOPERATION, INCLUDING MILITARY COOPERATION,
BETWEEN FRANCE AND AFRICAN COUNTRIES, TOWARDS WHICH IT HAS
GREAT RESPONSIBILITIES STEMMING, IN PARTICULAR, FROM THE
COLONIALIST PAST OF OUR COUNTRY. SUCH COOPERATION OF A NEW
TYPE COULD BECOME AN EFFECTIVE FACTOR OF SHAPING NEW
INTERNATIONAL RELATIONS THAT WOULD PRECLUDE ANY INEQUALITY
OR UNEQUAL RELATIONS AND MAKE IT POSSIBLE REALLY TO ADVANCE
TOWARDS THE NEW INTERNATIONAL ECONOMIC, POLITICAL AND SOCIAL
ORDER.

00143
    CONVENTIONAL FORCES IN EUROPE
SURVEY OF CURRENT AFFAIRS, 19(3) (MAR 89), 90-92.
    PROPOSALS FROM THE COUNTRIES OF THE NORTH ATLANTIC
TREATY ORGANIZATION (NATO) COVERING CONVENTIONAL ARMS
REDUCTIONS AND CONFIDENCE-BUILDING MEASURES WERE OUTLINED BY
THE FOREIGN AND COMMONWEALTH SECRETARY, SIR GEOFFREY HOWE,
AT THE CONFERENCE ON CONVENTIONAL FORCES IN EUROPE IN VIENNA
IN MARCH 1989. THIS ARTICLE SUMMARIZES THOSE PROPOSALS.

00144
    CONVENTIONAL FORCES IN EUROPE: A NATO ANALYSIS
NATO'S SIXTEEN NATIONS, 34(1) (1989), 85-89.
    THIS NATO REPORT CONTAINS THE ALLIANCE'S OWN ASSESSMENT
OF THE STRENGTHS OF THE ARMED FORCES BELONGING TO THE
COUNTRIES OF THE NORTH ATLANTIC ALLIANCE AND THOSE OF THE

WARSAW TREATY ORGANIZATION. THE REPORT INCLUDES FIGURES ON
GROUND FORCES AND AIRCRAFT, BUT NOT ON NAVAL FORCES, AND ARE
INTENDED TO SERVE AS BACKGROUND TO THE NEGOTIATIONS ON
CONVENTIONAL ARMS CONTROL WITHIN THE FRAMEWORK OF THE
CONFERENCE ON SECURITY AND COOPERATION IN EUROPE.

00145
CORPORATE MERGER LEGISLATION
CONGRESSIONAL DIGEST, 68(3) (MAR 89), 67-73.
THE ARTICLE REVIEWS FEDERAL SECURITIES AND MERGER LAWS,
THE ROLE OF THE SECURITIES AND EXCHANGE COMMISSION, AND
RECENT CONGRESSIONAL ACTION ON CORPORATE MERGER LEGISLATION.

00146
CORRALLING PRICES: MAIN TASK OF 1989
BEIJING REVIEW, 32(4) (JAN 89), 9-10.
CHINA'S CENTRAL AUTHORITIES ARE DETERMINED TO CORRAL
PRICE HIKES AND INFLATION AND DOUSE THE OVERHEATED GROWTH
RATE. ALL THESE ARE BELIEVED TO HARM THE COUNTTRY'S ECONOMY
AND REFORM. ACCORDING TO A STATE COUNCIL SPOKESMAN, THIS
YEAR'S INFLATION WILL BE 3-5 PERCENTAGE POINTS LOWER THAN
LAST YEAR'S. AND A HASTY DEFLATION WILL NOT BE GOOD FOR THE
COUNTRY.

00147
COSTA RICA: A STEADY POLICY FOR LEFT UNITY
INFORMATION BULLETIN, 26(19-20) (OCT 88), 30.
THIS ARTICLE DESCRIBES AN AGREEMENT BETWEEN THE COSTA
RICAN PEOPLE'S PARTY (PPC), THE DEMOCRATIC BROAD FRONT (FAD)
AND THE POPULAR VANGUARD PARTY OF COSTA RICA (PVP) TO JOIN
FORCES IN ELECTION CAMPAIGN POLICY. ALL THE THREE PARTIES
WANT TO LAY THE FOUNDATION NECESSARY FOR JOINT EFFORTS TO
ENLIST OTHER POLITICAL FORCES ON A BASIS OF EQUALITY. THIS
IMPLIES THAT OTHER POLITICAL FORCES CAN PARTICIPATE WITH
EQUAL RIGHT IN WORKING OUT THE ELECTION PROGRAM AND TACTICS,
IN NOMINATING THE CANDIDATES AND IN ALL THE AFFAIRS OF THE
COALITION.

00148
COUNTER-REVOLUTIONARY RIOT QUELLED
BEIJING REVIEW, 32(24-25) (JUN 89), 9.
ON JUNE 5, 1989, THE CENTRAL COMMITTEE OF THE COMMUNIST
PARTY OF CHINA (CPC) AND THE STATE COUNCIL ISSUED A JOINT
MESSAGE TO ALL PARTY MEMBERS AND THE PUBLIC, SAYING THAT THE
CHINESE CAPITAL WAS IN A CRITICAL STATE DUE TO THE SHOCKING
COUNTER-REVOLUTIONARY RIOT INSTIGATED BY A HANDFUL OF
PROTESTORS WITH ULTERIOR MOTIVES. THE RIOT WAS AIMED AT
NEGATING THE LEADERSHIP OF THE COMMUNIST PARTY, DESTROYING
THE SOCIALIST SYSTEM, AND OVERTHROWING THE PEOPLE'S REPUBLIC.
DUE TO THESE CIRCUMSTANCES, THE PEOPLE'S LIBERATION ARMY
WAS COMPELLED TO TAKE ACTION.

00149
COUNTING THE COST
CHINA NEWS ANALYSIS, (1390) (AUG 89), 1-10.
RECESSION IS THE ORDER OF THE DAY IN CHINA. FOLLOWING
SEVERAL YEARS OF "OVERHEATING," THE ECONOMY IS SLOWING DOWN
AND IDEOLOGICAL POT-HOLES LITTER THE WAY. THE STATE'S
CAMPAIGNS AGAINST CORRUPTION AND TAX EVASION ARE SIGNS THAT
THE AIMS OF THE REFORM ARE BEING RE-THOUGHT, WITH THE
IMMEDIATE GOAL OF FILLING THE STATE COFFERS. ADVERSE
ECONOMIC CONDITIONS HAVE COMBINED WITH THE OFFENSIVE AGAINST
FORMER PARTY LEADER ZHAO ZIYANG TO PROVIDE FERTILE GROUND
FOR HALF-MORAL, HALF-IDEOLOGICAL ACCUSATIONS AND SERMONS.

00150
CPC CENTRAL COMMITTEE HOLDS PLENUM
BEIJING REVIEW, 32(27) (JUL 89), 7.
AT A CPC CENTRAL COMMITTEE PLENUM RECENTLY HELD IN
BEIJING, PARTY GENERAL SECRETARY ZHAO ZIYANG WAS DISMISSED
FROM ALL HIS LEADING POSTS IN THE PARTY FOR SUPPORTING THE
TURMOIL AND SPLITTING THE PARTY. A PARTIAL ADJUSTMENT IN THE
PARTY'S LEADERSHIP WAS MADE, WITH JIANG ZEMIN, FORMER PARTY
CHIEF OF SHANGHAI, AS THE NEW PARTY GENERAL SECRETARY. THE
SESSION ALSO REAFFIRMED THAT ALL THE FUNDAMENTAL POLICIES
ADOPTED SINCE THE THIRD PLENARY SESSION OF THE 11TH PARTY
CENTRAL COMMITTEE WILL CONTINUE.

00151
CPC TO BOOST IDEOLOGICAL WORK
BEIJING REVIEW, 32(31) (JUL 89), 9.
AT A JULY 1989 MEETING, THE LEADERS OF THE COMMUNIST
PARTY OF CHINA STRESSED THE IMPORTANCE OF STRENGTHENING
PROPAGANDA AND IDEOLOGICAL WORK FOLLOWING THE POLITICAL
VIOLENCE IN BEIJING. LI PENG AND LI RUIHUAN SAID THAT THE
TASK OF IDEOLOGICAL AND POLITICAL WORK IS TO PROPAGATE THE
SPIRIT OF THE FOURTH PLENARY SESSION OF THE CPC'S 13TH
CENTRAL COMMITTEE AND THE RECENT SPEECHES MADE BY DENG
XIAOPING, TO UNIFY THE THINKING OF THE WHOLE PARTY AND THE
PEOPLE, AND TO ENHANCE EDUCATION IN ADHERING TO THE FOUR
CARDINAL PRINCIPLES AND OPPOSING BOURGEOIS LIBERALIZATION.

00152
CPC VOWS TO END CORRUPTION

BEIJING REVIEW, 32(32) (AUG 89), 9.
THE COMMUNIST PARTY OF CHINA HAS ADOPTED NEW MEASURES TO
FIGHT OFFICIAL CORRUPTION. THE STATE COUNCIL HAS SET SEVEN
GOALS REGARDING CORRUPTION: CLEAN UP COMPANIES WITH A FOCUS
ON CLOSING THE EXCESSIVE COMMERCIAL, FOREIGN TRADE,
MATERIALS SUPPLY, AND FINANCIAL FIRMS; STOP CHILDREN OF
SENIOR OFFICIALS FROM ENGAGING IN COMMERCIAL ACTIVITIES;
CANCEL THE SPECIAL SUPPLY OF FOODSTUFFS TO LEADING OFFICIALS;
ALLOT CARS STRICTLY IN LINE WITH RELEVANT STIPULATIONS AND
STOP THE IMPORT OF SEDANS; STRICTLY FORBID USING PUBLIC
FUNDS FOR ENTERTAINING AND GIFT-GIVING; STRICTLY LIMIT
OFFICIAL VISITS TO FOREIGN COUNTRIES; AND SEVERELY PUNISH
CORRUPTION, BRIBE-TAKING, AND PROFITEERING.

00153
CPSU CENTRAL COMMITTEE STATEMENT ON EVENTS IN THE BALTIC
REPUBLICS
REPRINTS FROM THE SOVIET PRESS, 49(9) (NOV 89), 26-32.
THIS ARTICLE IS A CALL FROM THE COMMUNIST PARTY TO THE
BALTIC REPUBLICS TO "PRESERVE THE SINGLE FAMILY OF SOVIET
PEOPLES AND THE UNITY OF THE COMMUNIST PARTY OF THE SOVIET
UNION." IT VOICES ITS CONCERN THAT LITHUANIA, LATVIA AND
ESTONIA HAVE BEEN TAKING ADVANTAGE OF PERESTROIKA" TO
INTRODUCE AN UNHEALTHY ASPECT INTO THE DEVELOPMENT OF EVENTS.

00154
CRACKDOWN ON CORRUPTION CONTINUES
BEIJING REVIEW, 42(29) (JUL 89), 11-12.
AS PART OF THE CHINESE GOVERNMENT'S CRACKDOWN ON
CORRUPTION, THE PEOPLE'S PROCURATORATE OF ZHEJIANG PROVINCE
CHARGED 162 COMMUNIST PARTY MEMBERS AND GOVERNMENT OFFICIALS
WITH CORRUPTION OR BRIBERY AND DISCIPLINED THEM IN THE FIRST
FOUR MONTHS OF 1989. OF THESE, SEVENTEEN CASES INVOLVED HIGH-
RANKING OFFICIALS IN IMPORTANT POSITIONS.

00155
CRIMPING THE ACCORDS
COMMONWEAL, CXVI(8) (APR 89), 227-228.
PRESIDENT BUSH'S UNILATERAL DECISION TO MAINTAIN 11,000
CONTRAS IN HONDURAS THROUGH FEBRUARY 1990 ECHOES THE
UNSPOKEN CLAIM THAT THE USA HAS THE RIGHT TO ORDER THE
POLITICS OF NICARAGUA. HIS PLAN MAY SEEM REASONABLE IN LIGHT
OF LONGSTANDING US POLICY INTERESTS, BUT IT SUBTLY
CONTRADICTS THE ADMINISTRATION'S HIGH-SOUNDING PRAISE FOR
THE ESQUIPULAS II ACCORDS.

00156
CRISIS IN THE MAKING?
CENTRAL AMERICA BULLETIN, 8(2) (JAN 89), 5-6.
EL SALVADOR MAY PRESENT THE BUSH ADMINISTRATION WITH ITS
FIRST MAJOR FOREIGN POLICY CRISIS. EL SALVADOR IS ENTERING A
NEW POLITICAL AND MILITARY ERA THAT WILL BE QUALITATIVELY
DIFFERENT FROM THE RECENT PAST. THIS IS PRIMARILY DUE TO THE
APPARENT STRENGTH OF THE FMLN, WHICH HAS BEGUN A POWERFUL
OFFENSIVE WITH A NEW FOCUS ON URBAN AREAS. THE FMLN
OFFENSIVE, THE COLLAPSE OF BOTH THE CHRISTIAN DEMOCRATIC
PARTY AND THE MILITARY'S COUNTERINSURGENCY PROJECT, AND
INCREASING HUMAN RIGHTS VIOLATIONS COULD SOON CONFRONT THE
BUSH ADMINISTRATION WITH A MAJOR POLITICAL AND MILITARY
CRISIS IN EL SALVADOR.

00157
CROWING BEFORE SUNRISE
COMMONWEAL, CXVI(12) (JUN 89), 355-356.
AT HIS FIRST NATO SUMMIT, GEORGE BUSH PROPOSED A
NEGOTIATING POSTURE FOR THE WESTERN ALLIANCE THAT CALLS FOR
EARLY, SUBSTANTIAL, BILATERAL REDUCTIONS IN CONVENTIONAL
FORCES ON THE EUROPEAN FRONT AS A PRECONDITION FOR TALKS
AIMED AT PARTIAL ELIMINATION OF SHORT-RANGE NUCLEAR MISSILES.
BUSH'S PROPOSAL WILL ENABLE THE ALLIANCE TO POSTPONE THE
FUNDAMENTAL CHOICE OF A FUTURE POLITICAL/STRATEGIC COURSE
FOR NATO.

00158
CSCE FOLLOW-UP MEETING HELD IN VIENNA
DEPARTMENT OF STATE BULLETIN (US FOREIGN POLICY), 89(2144)
(MAR 89), 21-54.
A MEETING OF THE CONFERENCE ON SECURITY AND COOPERATION
IN EUROPE WAS HELD IN VIENNA FROM NOVEMBER 1986 TO JANUARY
1989. THIS REPORT INCLUDES THE TEXT OF THE CONFERENCE'S
CONCLUDING STATEMENT AND US SECRETARY OF STATE SHULTZ'S
ADDRESS AT THE CLOSING SESSION.

00159
CUBAN SUBVERSION IN LATIN AMERICA
ASIAN OUTLOOK, 24(3) (MAY 89), 32.
FIDEL CASTRO IS NO FRIEND OF GLASNOST AND PERESTROIKA.
HE CANNOT BEAR TO BETRAY HIS REVOLUTIONARY IDEAS, AND HE
CONTINUES TO ENTERTAIN TERRORIST AND SUBVERSIVE AMBITIONS
THROUGHOUT THE LATIN AMERICAN CONTINENT. IN URUGUAY, THE
CUBANS HAVE BEEN ENCOURAGING LOCAL POLITICAL ACTIVISTS TO
UNDERTAKE TERRORIST ATTACKS. CUBAN SUBVERSION HAS ALSO BEEN
SUSPECTED IN VENEZUELA, CHILE, ARGENTINA, AND COLOMBIA.

00160
    CUE FOR DEMOCRACY
    NEW AFRICAN, (APR 88), 20-22.
        THIS ARTICLE REPORTS ON A MUCH NEEDED FRESH START AS
    RECENT ELECTIONS WERE KENYA'S CUE (QUEUE) FOR DEMOCRACY. IT
    DESCRIBES HOW THE NEW QUEUEING SYSTEM OVERCAME THE PROBLEM
    OF VIOLENCE ASSOCIATED WITH PAST ELECTION CAMPAIGNS. THE
    AMAZING RESULTS OF THE MILLIONS OF VOTES AND THE RELEASED
    DETAINEES ARE EXPLORED.

00161
    CURRENT ECONOMIC POLICY PAYS OFF
    BEIJING REVIEW, 32(37) (SEP 89), 9-10.
        CHINA'S ECONOMIC RETRENCHMENT HAS ACHIEVED CONSIDERABLE
    RESULTS. CHINA'S OUTPUT OF SUMMER GRAIN CROPS HIT A RECORD
    HIGH IN 1989, AND THE SOWING AREA FOR FALL CROPS SHOWED A
    SUBSTANTIAL INCREASE. THE OVERHEATED ECONOMY HAS COOLED DOWN
    DUE TO THE ENFORCEMENT OF MONETARY AUSTERITY MEASURES AND
    POLICIES ADOPTED TO CORRECT PROBLEMS WITH THE ECONOMIC
    STRUCTURE.

00162
    CYPRUS: THE HEART OF THE MATTER
    MIDDLE EAST INTERNATIONAL, (349) (APR 89), 19-20.
        THE CRUX OF THE CYPRUS SITUATION IS A CONFLICT BETWEEN
    THE TURKISH CYPRIOT DETERMINATION NEVER AGAIN TO BE
    SUBJECTED TO DOMINATION BY THE GREEK CYRPRIOTS AND THE GREEK
    CYPRIOT DETERMINATION TO KEEP THE DOOR OPEN TO BRINGING THE
    WHOLE ISLAND AGAIN UNDER GREEK CONTROL. IT MAY BE THAT GREEK
    CYPRIOTS HAVE ABANDONED VIOLENCE AS A MEANS OF SECURING
    THEIR ENDS, BUT THAT DOES NOT MEAN THAT THEY HAVE ABANDONED
    HOPE OF ACHIEVING THEIR GOAL BY OTHER MEANS.

00163
    CZECHOSLOVAKIA: INTERVIEW GIVEN BY MILOS JAKES, GENERAL
    SECRETARY OF THE CC OF THE CP OF CZECHOSLOVAKIA TO "LE
    FIGARO"
    INFORMATION BULLETIN, 27 (MAR 89), 20-22.
        JAKES ANSWERS QUESTIONS ABOUT ECONOMIC REFORM IN
    CZECHOSLOVAKIA, POLITICAL REFORM, NEW STRUCTURES FOR THE
    CMEA, ARMS CONTROL, OPPOSITION WITHIN CZECHOSLOVAKIA, THE
    RELATIONSHIP BETWEEN THE REFORMS OF DUBCEK AND GORBACHEV,
    AND THE NEED TO REASSES COMMUNIST HISTORY IN CZECHOSLOVAKIA.

00164
    CZECHOSLOVAKIA: INTRODUCTION "HAVEL NA HRAD!"
    EAST EUROPEAN REPORTER, 4(1) (WIN 89), 37.
        THE ARTICLE BRIEFLY EXAMINES THE CHANGES THAT HAVE TAKEN
    PLACE IN CZECHOSLOVAKIA IN THE LAST MONTHS OF 1989. LIKE
    MUCH OF EASTERN EUROPE, POPULAR DISSATISFACTION AND UNREST
    LED TO THE TOPPLING OF COMMUNIST REGIMES. CZECHOSLOVAKIA IS
    DIFFERENT ONLY THAT THE CHANGES TOOK PLACE AT AN EVEN FASTER
    RATE THAN IN OTHER NATIONS OF EAST EUROPE. THE NATION NOW
    FACES SIGNIFICANT CHALLENGES AND CHOICES AS 36 POLITICAL
    PARTIES VIE FOR POWER IN THE APPROACHING FREE ELECTIONS.

00165
    DEATH PENALTY: PUBLIC SUPPORT FOR DEATH PENALTY IS HIGHEST
    IN GALLUP ANNALS
    GALLUP REPORT, (280) (JAN 89), 27-29.
        THE 1988 PRESIDENTIAL CAMPAIGN FOCUSED ATTENTION ON
    CAPITAL PUNISHMENT. USING THE WILLIE HORTON FURLOUGH CASE
    AND MICHAEL DUKAKIS' OPPOSITION TO THE DEATH PENALTY AS
    SYMBOLS OF SOFTNESS ON CRIME, GEORGE BUSH MADE THE DEATH
    PENALTY ONE OF THE CAMPAIGN'S CENTRAL ISSUES. PUBLIC SUPPORT
    FOR THE DEATH PENALTY IS AT THE HIGHEST POINT RECORDED IN
    MORE THAN 50 YEARS OF SCIENTIFIC POLLING, WITH ALMOST EIGHT
    IN 10 AMERICANS FAVORING THE EXECUTION OF PERSONS CONVICTED
    OF MURDER.

00166
    DECEIT WITHOUT PARALLEL
    SOUTH, (103) (MAY 89), 8-9.
        THE SOUTH AFRICAN FOREIGN MINISTER HAS ACCUSED SWAPO OF
    TAKING UNFAIR ADVANTAGE OF THE CEASE-FIRE TO DISPATCH ARMED
    GUERRILLAS INTO NORTHERN NAMIBIA. BUT UN OBSERVERS WHO WERE
    SENT TO INVESTIGATE THE INCIDENT STATED THAT THE GUERRILLAS
    ENGAGED IN NO SUBVERSIVE ACTIVITY, ATTACKED NO INSTALLATION,
    AND COMMITTED NO ACT OF VIOLENCE. ALL THEY DID WAS ANNOUNCE
    THEIR PRESENCE, WHICH SO INFURIATED SOUTH AFRICA THAT IT
    DECIDED TO UNLEASH ITS MONSTROUS WAR MACHINE.

00167
    DEFEND PERESTROIKA, DEFEND DEMOCRACY
    REPRINTS FROM THE SOVIET PRESS, 48(11-12) (JUN 89), 21-23.
        DEMOCRACY NOT ONLY BROADENS RIGHTS BUT ALSO REQUIRES
    GREATER RESPONSIBILITY, DISCIPLINE AND ORDER. THE DECREE OF
    THE USSR SUPREME SOVIET PRESIDIUM "ON AMENDMENTS TO THE USSR
    LAW 'ON CRIMINAL RESPONSIBILITY FOR STATE CRIMES' AND SOME
    OTHER LEGISLATIVE ACTS OF THE USSR" WILL SERVE AS A BASIS
    FOR BRINGING TO ACCOUNT THOSE WHOSE ACTIONS ARE AIMED AT
    UNDERMINING THE SOVIET STATE AND SOCIAL SYSTEM, AND
    CONSTITUTE CRIME AGAINST THE STATE, VIOLATE NATIONAL AND
    RACIAL EQUALITY, INSULT OR DISCREDIT STATE BODIES AND PUBLIC

ORGANIZATIONS.

00168
    DEMOCRACY MUST FIT CHINA'S REALITY
    BEIJING REVIEW, 32(32) (AUG 89), 39-40.
        ALTHOUGH MANY COLLEGE STUDENTS HAVE CHANTED SLOGANS
    ESPOUSING DEMOCRACY IN RECENT YEARS, FEW CAN SAY EXACTLY
    WHAT KIND OF DEMOCRACY THEY WANT. DEMOCRACY IN CAPITALIST
    SOCIETIES HAS ALWAYS BEEN RESTRICTED BY CAPITAL OR PROPERTY,
    AND THE EXERCISE OF DEMOCRATIC RIGHTS IS NOT ALLOWED TO
    ENCROACH ON THE CAPITALIST SYSTEM. SOCIALIST DEMOCRACY, ON
    THE OTHER HAND, STRIVES TO MAKE THE PEOPLE THEIR OWN MASTERS.
    ALTHOUGH CHINA HAS A LONG WAY TO GO TO PERFECT ITS
    DEMOCRATIC SYSTEM, THE CHINESE PEOPLE ALREADY ENJOY
    EXTENSIVE DEMOCRACY AND FREEDOM.

00169
    DEMOCRACY NOW - "THESES FOR A DEMOCRATIC TRANSFORMATION IN
    THE GDR"
    ACROSS FRONTIERS, 5(3) (FAL 89), 5-6.
        AS THE CRISIS IN THE GDR CONTINUED TO UNFOLD, A NUMBER
    OF LONG-TIME INDEPENDENT ACTIVISTS CAME TOGETHER TO FOUND
    THE INFORMAL CITIZEN'S ASSOCIATION "DEMOCRACY NOW." THIS
    ARTICLE DESCRIBES THE PRELIMINARY "THESES" WHICH WERE ISSUED
    AS AN AID FOR FURTHER DISCUSSION. IT DETAILS THE WAY TO GO
    FROM AUTHORITARIAN STATE TO REPUBLIC. IT FAVORS GOING FROM
    NATIONALIZATION TO SOCIALIZATION AS THE MEANS OF PRODUCTION,
    AND FROM EXPLOITATION AND POLUTION OF THE ENVIRONMENT TO A
    LASTING COEXISTENCE WITH NATURE.

00170
    DEMOCRACY ON THE UPSWING
    REPRINTS FROM THE SOVIET PRESS, 48(6) (MAR 89), 43-45.
        IN AN INTERVIEW WITH PRAVDA, CENTRAL ELECTORAL
    COMMISSION CHAIRMAN, VLADIMIR ORLOV DISCUSSES THE ONGOING
    ELECTION CAMPAIGN IN THE SOVIET UNION. HE OUTLINES THE
    SUCCESSFUL NOMINATION PROCESS THAT HAS ALREADY TAKEN PLACE
    AND THE CHALLENGES THAT LIE AHEAD WITH REGARDS TO THE
    APPROACHING ELECTIONS. HE ALSO DISCUSSES SOME OF THE
    VIOLATIONS OF THE ELECTIONS ACT THAT HAS TAKEN PLACE.

00171
    DEMONSTRATION LAW APPROVED
    BEIJING REVIEW, 32(46) (NOV 89), 7.
        CHINA'S FIRST LAW ON MASS RALLIES AND DEMONSTRATIONS HAS
    BEEN ADOPTED BY THE NATIONAL PEOPLE'S CONGRESS AND WENT INTO
    EFFECT OCTOBER 31, 1989. THE LAW DEALS WITH APPLICATIONS FOR
    HOLDING RALLIES, THE PROCEDURES FOR CONDUCTING RALLIES AND
    DEMONSTRATIONS, AND THE LEGAL LIABILITIES OF DEMONSTRATORS.
    ITS OBJECTIVE IS TO PROTECT THE LEGAL RIGHTS TO GATHER,
    PARADE, AND DEMONSTRATE WHILE SAFEGUARDING SOCIAL STABILITY
    AND PUBLIC ORDER.

00172
    DEMONSTRATIONS IN CHINA
    DEPARTMENT OF STATE BULLETIN (US FOREIGN POLICY), 89(2149)
    (AUG 89), 75-77.
        THIS REPORT ON THE DEMONSTRATIONS IN CHINA INCLUDES
    STATEMENTS ISSUED BY THE WHITE HOUSE AND THE STATE
    DEPARTMENT IN MAY AND JUNE 1989.

00173
    DEMYSTIFYING THE WORKING OF THE E.C.
    EUROPE, (291) (NOV 89), 38-40.
        THE ARTICLE EXAMINES THE GOALS AND INSTITUTIONS OF THE
    EUROPEAN COMMUNITY. ITS GOALS ARE PRIMARILY ECONOMIC AND ARE
    DESIGNED TO PROMOTE GROWTH AND INTEGRATION. ITS INSTITUTIONS
    ARE POLITICAL IN NATURE AND INCLUDE THE EUROPEAN COMMISSION,
    THE COUNCIL OF MINISTERS, THE EUROPEAN PARLIAMENT, AND THE
    COURT OF JUSTICE. THE ARTICLE EXAMINES THE LEGISLATIVE
    PROCESS AND HOW IT IS AFFECTED BY EACH OF THE PRINCIPAL
    INSTITUTIONS.

00174
    DENG HAILS ARMYMEN
    BEIJING REVIEW, 32(24-25) (JUN 89), 7.
        DENG XIAOPING, CHAIRMAN OF THE CENTRAL MILITARY
    COMMISSION, MET SENIOR COMMANDERS FROM THE MARTIAL LAW
    ENFORCEMENT TROOPS ON JUNE 9, 1989. IN A SPEECH TO THE
    COMMANDERS, DENG SHOWED HOW THE RECENT COUNTERREVOLUTIONARY
    RIOT HAD COME ABOUT AND WHAT IT HAD TRIED TO ACHIEVE. HE
    HIGHLY PRAISED THE CONTRIBUTIONS MADE BY THE PEOPLE'S
    LIBERATION ARMY IN PUTTING IT DOWN. HE REAFFIRMED THE
    CORRECTNESS OF ALL THE POLICIES PURSUED SINCE 1978.

00175
    DENG MEETS HENRY KISSINGER
    BEIJING REVIEW, 32(47) (NOV 89), 6.
        DENG XIAOPING MET FORMER U.S. SECRETARY OF STATE HENRY
    KISSINGER IN BEIJING ON NOV. 10, 1989, A DAY AFTER DENG'S
    RETIREMENT FROM HIS LAST COMMUNIST PARTY POST. KISSINGER
    ALSO MET WITH CHINESE FOREIGN MINISTER QIAN QICHEN, JIANG
    ZEMIN, LI PENG, AND HANG SHANGKUN. QIAN SAID THAT CHINA HAS
    WORKED VERY HARD TO PROTECT SINO-U.S. RELATIONS AND THAT HE

EXPECTS THE U.S. GOVERNMENT TO TAKE THE INITIATIVE IN
SMOOTHING THE STRAINED RELATIONS DUE TO THE TIANANMEN SQUARE
EPISODE.

00176
DENG MEETS LAST FOREIGN GUESTS OFFICIALLY
BEIJING REVIEW, 32(48) (NOV 89), 9-10.
JUST-RETIRED CHINESE SENIOR LEADER DENG XIAOPING MET A
JAPANESE BUSINESS DELEGATION ON NOVEMBER 13, 1989, THE LAST
GROUP OF GUESTS HE SAID HE WOULD MEET OFFICIALLY. TO
PRACTISE TRUE RETIREMENT, HE SAID HE WOULD NO LONGER MEET
VISITORS IN THE NAME OF THE COLLECTIVE, THE PARTY, OR THE
STATE.

00177
DENG ON HANDLING INTERNATIONAL RELATIONS
BEIJING REVIEW, 32(40) (OCT 89), 5-6.
ON SEPT. 19, 1989, WHILE MEETING WITH JAPANESE LEADER
MASAYOSHI ITO, DENG XIAOPING DECLARED THAT THE FIVE
PRINCIPLES OF PEACEFUL COEXISTENCE SHOULD BE THE GUIDELINE
FOR SETTLING INTERNATIONAL POLITICAL AND ECONOMIC PROBLEMS.
DENG ALSO TOLD ITO THAT NO MATTER WHAT HAPPENS IN THE WORLD,
THE FRIENDSHIP BETWEEN CHINA AND JAPAN MUST NOT CHANGE.

00178
DENG RETIRES, JIANG APPOINTED MILITARY CHIEF
BEIJING REVIEW, 32(47) (NOV 89), 5-6.
ON NOVEMBER 9, 1989, THE COMMUNIST PARTY OF CHINA
ENDORSED DENG XIAOPING'S RESIGNATION FROM HIS LAST PARTY
POST AS CHAIRMAN OF THE CPC CENTRAL COMMITTEE MILITARY
COMMISSION. THE PLENARY SESSION APPROVED THE APPOINTMENT OF
JIANG ZEMIN AS THE NEW CHAIRMAN OF THE MILITARY COMMISSION.
IT ALSO DECIDED ON FURTHER ECONOMIC REVAMPING AND REFORMS IN
CHINA.

00179
DENG URGES PLA TO STAY LOYAL
BEIJING REVIEW, 32(48) (NOV 89), 7, 9.
UNDER ITS NEW LEADERSHIP, THE CHINESE PEOPLE'S
LIBERATION ARMY WILL CONTINUE TO FOLLOW THE THEORY AND
PRINCIPLES ON ARMY-BUILDING LAID DOWN BY DENG XIAOPING. IT
WILL CONTINUE TO PUSH FORWARD WITH ITS REVOLUTIONIZATION,
MODERNIZATION, AND REGULARIZATION. DENG RECENTLY URGED THE
PLA TO CONTRIBUTE MORE TO SAFEGUARDING THE INDEPENDENCE AND
SOVEREIGNTY OF CHINA, THE COUNTRY'S SOCIALIST CONSTRUCTION,
AND THE PRINCIPLES AND POLICIES FORMULATED SINCE THE THIRD
PLENARY SESSION OF THE ELEVENTH CPC CENTRAL COMMITTEE.

00180
DENG XIAOPING ON UPHOLDING THE FOUR CARDINAL PRINCIPLES
AND COMBATING BOURGEOIS LIBERALIZATION
BEIJING REVIEW, 32(29) (JUL 89), 20-23.
THE FOUR CARDINAL PRINCIPLES PROCLAIMED BY DENG XIAOPING
IN 1979 ARE AS FOLLOWS: KEEP TO THE SOCIALIST ROAD, UPHOLD
THE DICTATORSHIP OF THE PROLETARIAT, UPHOLD THE LEADERSHIP
OF THE COMMUNIST PARTY, AND UPHOLD MARXISM-LENINISM AND MAO
ZEDONG THOUGHT. BECAUSE THESE FOUR PRINCIPLES HAVE NOT BEEN
EFFECTIVELY IMPLEMENTED, THE TREND TOWARD BOURGEOIS
LIBERALIZATION HAS GAINED A HOLD IN SOME PLACES AND AMONG
SOME PEOPLE IN CHINA. THIS WAS A MAJOR CAUSE OF THE
POLITICAL TURMOIL IN BEIJING AND OTHER CHINESE CITIES IN
1989.

00181
DENG'S TALKS ON QUELLING REBELLION IN BEIJING
BEIJING REVIEW, 32(28) (JUL 89), 18-21.
AT A JUNE 9, 1989, MEETING WITH COMMANDERS OF THE
MARTIAL LAW ENFORCEMENT TROOPS, DENG XIAOPING DISCUSSED THE
RECENT REBELLION IN BEIJING. HE SAID THAT THE REBELLION HAD
TO COME SOONER OR LATER, BECAUSE IT WAS THE PRODUCT OF THE
INTERNATIONAL AND DOMESTIC POLITICAL CLIMATE. HE STATED THAT
"IT WAS JUST A MATTER OF TIME AND SCALE." HE CLAIMED THAT,
ALTHOUGH SOME COMRADES DO NOT UNDERSTAND WHAT HAPPENED, THEY
WILL EVENTUALLY UNDERSTAND AND SUPPORT THE DECISION OF THE
CENTRAL COMMITTEE.

00182
DEVELOPING THE ECONOMY IN A SUSTAINED, STABLE, AND
HARMONIOUS WAY
BEIJING REVIEW, 32(49) (DEC 89), 17-22.
IN THIS ADDRESS TO THE FIFTH PLENUM OF THE THIRTEENTH
CPC CENTRAL COMMITTEE, CPC GENERAL SECRETARY JIANG ZEMIN
SUMMARIZED THE DELIBERATIONS OF THE PLENARY SESSION. HE ALSO
SURVEYED THE CHINESE ECONOMIC SITUATION AND EXPLAINED THE
NEED FOR STRAIGHTENING OUT THE ECONOMIC ORDER AND DEEPENING
REFORM EFFORTS.

00183
DEVELOPING THE PRIVATE SECTOR: A CHALLENGE FOR THE WORLD
BANK GROUP
AVAILABLE FROM NTIS, NO. PB89-217798/GAR, 1989, 50.
THE REVIEW GROUP'S REPORT CONSIDERS HOW THE PRIVATE
SECTOR CAN CONTRIBUTE TO ECONOMIC GROWTH IN DEVELOPING
COUNTRIES AND HOW GOVERNMENTS CAN REFORM THEIR POLICIES AND

INTERVENTIONS TO GIVE THE PRIVATE SECTOR GREATER SCOPE. THE
REPORT ALSO PROVIDES AN OVERVIEW OF THE WORLD BANK GROUP'S
EXPERIENCE WITH PRIVATE SECTOR DEVELOPMENT, FORMULATES A
STRATEGY FOR THE FUTURE, AND RECOMMENDS WAYS TO EXPAND AND
IMPROVE THE EFFORTS OF EACH MEMBER OF THE WORLD BANK GROUP.
THE RECOMMENDATIONS OF THE REPORT FORMED THE BASIS FOR AN
ACTION PROGRAM, WHICH THE BANK GROUP'S MANAGEMENT HAS
ADOPTED TO EXPAND AND FOCUS ITS SUPPORT OF PRIVATE SECTOR
DEVELOPMENT IN PRIORITY AREAS.

00184
DISARMAMENT FOR DEVELOPMENT
INFORMATION BULLETIN, 25/26(1-2) (JAN 88), 7-8.
THIS JOINT STATEMENT BY THE CPSU-SDPG WORKING GROUP SETS
FORTS THE OPERATING PRINCIPLE THAT A SCALING DOWN OF ARMS
SPENDING IS AN IMPORTANT STEP TO END THE ARMS RACE AND ITS
ESCALATING PERILS, TO THE BENEFIT OF HUMANITY. APPRECIABLE
ENROADS INTO THE MILITARY BUDGETS COULD BE A VITAL MOVE IN
SETTING UP A SYSTEM OF COMPREHENSIVE INTERNATIONAL SECURITY.

00185
DISSATISFACTION WITH WASHINGTON ON THE RISE; BUSH
"HONEYMOON" WITH PUBLIC MAY BE OVER
GALLUP REPORT, (284) (MAY 89), 9-15.
IN INCREASING NUMBERS, AMERICANS ARE BEING TURNED OFF BY
WHAT'S HAPPENING IN WASHINGTON. A NEW GALLUP POLL REVEALS
THAT FEWER AMERICANS HOLD FAVORABLE OPINIONS OF THE
PRESIDENT, THE VICE PRESIDENT, CONGRESS, AND THE SUPREME
COURT THAN IN THE RECENT PAST. THE PRESIDENT'S APPROVAL
RATINGS HAVE BEGUN TO SLIP AS CRITICISM HAS RISEN REGARDING
HIS ABILITY TO COMMUNICATE HIS POLICIES AND PLANS. HOUSE
SPEAKER JIM WRIGHT'S TROUBLES APPEAR TO HAVE TAKEN A TOLL ON
THE IMAGE OF CONGRESS. EVEN THE SUPREME COURT HAS NOT
ESCAPED THE RECENT DECLINE IN PUBLIC CONFIDENCE IN
WASHINGTON INSTITUTIONS.

00186
DISSIDENT EDITOR SAYS PERESTROIKA SUFFERS ECONOMIC
CREDITABILITY GAP
GLASNOST, II(4) (SEP 89), 36-39.
THE SOVIET LEADERSHIP HAS ABANDONED THE CAUSE OF REFORM.
THE LEADERS CONTINUE TO TALK ABOUT GLASNOST AND PERESTROIKA,
WHILE IN REALITY TRYING TO STIFLE REAL DEMOCRATIZATION AND
PREVENT ANY ECONOMIC REFORM. THE SOVIET LEADERSHIP
UNDERSTANDS QUITE CLEARLY THAT THE MOVEMENT TO REFORM THE
COUNTRY IS OUT OF CONTROL AND THAT IT REPRESENTS A THREAT TO
THE PARTY'S RULE. YET PUBLIC REPUDIATION OF REFORM IS
INEXPEDIENT FOR MIKHAIL GORBACHEV AND HIS GOVERNMENT. HE
DOES NOT WANT TO ADMIT PUBLICLY THAT HIS COURSE HAS BEEN
UNSUCCESSFUL, AND HE WANTS TO CONTINUE TO RECEIVE WESTERN
CREDITS AND LOANS. THUS, WHILE CONTINUING TO TALK ABOUT
GLASNOST AND PERESTROIKA IN THE WEST, HE IS INTRODUCING LAWS
TO COMBAT DEMOCRATIZATION.

00187
DO EVERYTHING TO ENSURE A REAL TURNABOUT IN WORLD POLITICS
TO STRENGTHENING PEACE
INFORMATION BULLETIN, 27 (JAN 89), 8-9.
A REGULAR MEETING OF THE FOREIGN MINISTERS COMMITTEE OF
THE MEMBER STATES OF THE WARSAW TREATY OF FRIENDSHIP,
COOPERATION AND MUTUAL ASSISTANCE TOOK PLACE IN BUDAPEST ON
OCTOBER 28 AND 29, 1988. THE MINISTERS EXAMINED THE
SITUATION IN EUROPE AND THE WORLD, NOTING THE CONTINUING
RELEVANCE OF THE APPRAISALS OF THE STATE AND PROSPECTS OF
INTERNATIONAL RELATIONS GIVEN AT THE MEETING OF THE
POLITICAL CONSULTATIVE COMMITTEE IN WARSAW IN JULY 1988. THE
WARSAW TREATY MEMBER STATES WILL CONTINUE DOING EVERYTHING
IN THEIR POWER TO ENSURE A REAL TURNABOUT IN WORLD POLITICS
TO STRENGTHENING PEACE, BRINGING ABOUT DISARMAMENT, AND
LAUNCHING EXTENSIVE, MUTUALLY BENEFICIAL COOPERATION ON THE
BASIS OF EQUALITY, RESPECT FOR INDEPENDENCE AND SOVEREIGNTY,
NON-INTERFERENCE IN INTERNAL AFFAIRS AND ALL THE OTHER
GENERALLY RECOGNIZED PRINCIPLES AND RULES OF INTERNATIONAL
LAW. THE MEETING ADOPTED A STATEMENT ON CONFIDENCE AND
SECURITY-BUILDING MEASURES AND DISARMAMENT IN EUROPE.

00188
DOCTORED DATA
COMMONWEAL, CXVI(11) (JUN 89), 325.
AN ADMINISTRATION SPOKESMAN HAS CONCEDED THAT THE OFFICE
OF MANAGEMENT AND BUDGET ALTERED THE WORDS AND CONCLUSIONS
OF DR. JAMES E. HANSEN'S TESTIMONY ON THE GREENHOUSE EFFECT
SCHEDULED TO BE DELIVERED TO CONGRESS. UNBEKNOWNST TO TO
HANSEN, HIS ASSESSMENT OF GLOBAL WARMING TRENDS WAS
REWRITTEN TO SUBSTANTIATE CONCLUSIONS DICTATED BY THE WHITE
HOUSE'S GO SLOW, FREE MARKET INSPIRED APPROACH TO POLLUTION
CONTAINMENT.

00189
DOCUMENT RELATING TO DISARMAMENT: ADDRESS BY GENERAL
SECRETARY MIKHAIL GORBACHEV AT THE FORTY-THIRD SESSION OF
THE GENERAL ASSEMBLY, 7 DECEMBER 1988 (EXCERPTS)
DISARMAMENT, XII(1) (WIN 89), 117-121.
IN THIS SPEECH, MIKHAIL GORBACHEV DECLARED THAT THE

WORLD IS WITNESSING THE EMERGENCE OF A NEW HISTORIC REALITY:
A TURNING AWAY FROM THE PRINCIPLE OF SUPER-ARMAMENT TO THE
PRINCIPLE OF REASONABLE DEFENSE SUFFICIENCY. HE ALSO STATED
THAT THE SOVIET UNION HAD DECIDED TO REDUCE ITS ARMED FORCES
BY 500,000 MEN.

00190
    DODD, HATCH JOIN FORCES TO PROMOTE CHILD CARE BILLS
    CHURCH AND STATE, 42(3) (MAR 89), 14 (62)-15 (63).
    A CHILD CARE BILL PROPOSED BY SEN. CHRISTOPHER DODD
WOULD AUTHORIZE APPROXIMATELY $2.5 BILLION IN PUBLIC FUNDS
TO SUBSIDIZE CHILD CARE THROUGH PARENTAL VOUCHERS AND DIRECT
FUNDING OF CHILD CARE AGENCIES, INCLUDING THOSE THAT ARE
CHURCH-AFFILIATED. ALTHOUGH MOST OF THE BILL'S CONGRESSIONAL
SUPPORT CAME FROM DEMOCRATS IN 1988, CONSERVATIVE REPUBLICAN
ORRIN HATCH HAS SIGNED AS A CO-SPONSOR. DODD AND HATCH HAVE
ALSO AGREED TO INTRODUCE A SECOND CHILD CARE BILL THAT
EMPHASIZES TAX CREDITS AS A FUNDING MECHANISM. CHURCH-STATE
ISSUES AND FIRST AMENDMENT QUESTIONS REMAIN A PROBLEM IN
CRAFTING CHILD CARE LEGISLATION.

00191
    DOES UGANDA REALLY WANT DEMOCRACY?
    NEW AFRICAN, (256) (JAN 89), 22.
    WHILE MANY GROUPS WANT TO RESTORE DEMOCRACY IN UGANDA,
THERE IS NO AGREEMENT ABOUT HOW TO DO IT. THE MONARCHISTS,
THE DEMOCRATIC PARTY, AND CURRENT PRESIDENT MUSEVENI HAVE
DIFFERENT IDEAS ABOUT HOW THE GOVERNMENT SHOULD BE
STRUCTURED WHEN MUSEVENI'S TERM ENDS.

00192
    DR ZWANE VICTIMISED
    NEW AFRICAN, (266) (NOV 89), 19.
    THIS ARTICLE REPORTS ON ILL TREATMENT GIVEN TO DR.
AMBROSE ZWANE, SWAZILAND'S FIRST DOCTOR OF MEDICINE. IT
REPORTS ON POLICE HARASSMENT AND THE FAILURE OF KING SOBHUZA
TO PROTECT HIM AS LONG AS DR. ZWANE REFRAINED FROM
PARTICIPATION IN PUBLIC POLITICAL ACTIVITY.

00193
    DRAFT LAW OPENS FOR DISCUSSION
    BEIJING REVIEW, 32(29) (JUL 89), 9-10.
    TO PERMIT PUBLIC DISCUSSION, THE STANDING COMMITTEE OF
THE NATIONAL PEOPLE'S CONGRESS HAS DECIDED TO PUBLISH ITS
DRAFT LAW ON DEMONSTRATIONS BEFORE FORMALLY ENACTING IT.
WHILE ENSURING THE RIGHTS OF CITIZENS TO HOLD RALLIES AND
DEMONSTRATIONS, THE DRAFT STIPULATES THAT CITIZENS
EXERCISING THE RIGHT TO DEMONSTRATE SHALL NOT IMPINGE UPON
THE INTERESTS OF THE STATE OR SOCIETY OR ON THE LEGITIMATE
FREEDOM AND RIGHTS OF OTHER CITIZENS. IT ALSO STATES THAT
PROTESTORS WILL NOT BE ALLOWED TO FLAUNT THE BASIC
PRINCIPLES OF THE CONSTITUTION OR GO AGAINST THE LEADERSHIP
OF THE CHINESE COMMUNIST PARTY OR THE SOCIALIST SYSTEM.

00194
    DRAFT PROGRAMME OF DEMOCRATIC AWAKENING
    EAST EUROPEAN REPORTER, 4(1) (WIN 89), 22.
    THE ARTICLE CONTAINS EXTRACTS FORM A DRAFT PROGRAM OF
DEMOCRATIC AWAKENING--SOCIAL AND ECOLOGICAL, AND EAST GERMAN
REFORM GROUP. IT CALLS FOR SUCH POLITICAL REFORMS AS
SEPARATION OF STATE AND PARTY(IES), DEVELOPMENT OF A FREE
PUBLIC SPHERE, PUBLIC EXPRESSION OF THE WILL OF THE
POPULATION, AND AN ECOLOGICAL RESTRUCTURING OF THE
INDUSTRIAL SOCIETY. DEMOCRATIC AWAKENING DOES NOT REJECT
SOCIALISM OUTRIGHT, IT MERELY CRITICIZES MANY OF THE
FEATURES OF THE EXISTING SOCIALISM. ITS ULTIMATE GOAL IS THE
CREATION OF A DEMOCRATIC, SOCIALLY JUST, AND ECOLOGICAL
SOCIETY.

00195
    E.C. CITIZENS ELECT NEW EUROPEAN PARLIAMENT
    EUROPE, 288 (JUL 89), 24.
    FOR THE THIRD TIME IN ITS HISTORY, CITIZENS FROM THE E.C.
'S 12 MEMBER STATES DIRECTLY ELECTED A NEW EUROPEAN
PARLIAMENT BETWEEN JUNE 15 AND 18. AT 56 PERCENT, OVERALL
VOTER TURNOUT WAS LOW. THE SOCIALISTS WERE RETURNED AS THE
LARGEST PARTY IN THE 518-MEMBER PARLIAMENT, AND THE GREENS
ALMOST DOUBLED THEIR NUMBER OF SEATS. THE CENTER-RIGHT
PARTIES, A MAJORITY BLOC IN THE PREVIOUS PARLIAMENT, DID
RELATIVELY POORLY, CEDING THEIR POSITION TO A NEW CENTER-
LEFT MAJORITY COMPOSED OF SOCIALISTS, GREENS, AND COMMUNISTS,
WITH A COMBINED TOTAL OF 261 SEATS, AN ABSOLUTE MAJORITY OF
TWO SEATS. ON THE WHOLE, THE NEW PARLIAMENT IS EXPECTED TO
URGE CAUTION ON ENVIRONMENT AND SOCIAL GROUNDS ABOUT A
DEREGULATED MARKET.

00196
    EAST ASIA, THE PACIFIC, AND THE US: AN ECONOMIC PARTNERSHIP
    DEPARTMENT OF STATE BULLETIN (US FOREIGN POLICY), 89(2145)
    (APR 89), 33-37.
    EAST ASIAN ECONOMIC SUCCESS HAS BEEN ACCOMPANIED BY THE
GROWTH OF DEMOCRACY IN THE REGION. THE ECONOMIC AND
POLITICAL PROGRESS HAS BEEN BUTTRESSED BY BILATERAL MILITARY
ARRANGEMENTS WITH THE USA, WHICH PROVIDE SECURITY AND

STABILITY IN THE REGION. THE ECONOMIC AND POLITICAL
DEVELOPMENT WILL PROBABLY GIVE THE EAST ASIAN REGION A
GREATER ROLE IN WORLD AFFAIRS IN THE COMING DECADES.

00197
    EAST GERMANS GO WEST
    COMMONWEAL, CXVI(19) (NOV 89), 580-581.
    AFTER TRYING TO CRUSH POLITICAL PROTESTS IN LEIPZIG AND
DRESDEN, THE EAST GERMAN POLITBURO HAS REVERSED ITSELF. IT
HAS EMBARKED ON A CRITICAL SELF-EXAMINATION AND HAS PUBLICLY
CALLED FOR A DISCUSSION OF "THE BASIC QUESTIONS" OF POLITICS
AND SOCIETY.

00198
    EAST-WEST RELATIONS
    SURVEY OF CURRENT AFFAIRS, 19(10) (OCT 89), 373-376.
    PROGRESS IN SOVIET INTERNAL REFORMS, HUMANS RIGHTS
QUESTIONS, ARMS CONTROL, AND BILATERAL RELATIONS WERE
DISCUSSED IN TALKS IN MOSCOW BETWEEN THE PRIME MINISTER, MRS
MARGARET THATCHER, AND THE SOVIET PRESIDENT, MR MIKHAIL
GORBACHEV, ON 23 SEPTEMBER 1989.

00199
    EAST-WEST RELATIONS
    SURVEY OF CURRENT AFFAIRS, 19(12) (DEC 89), 453-456.
    BRITAIN HAS WELCOMED MOVES TOWARDS DEMOCRACY IN THE
GERMAN DEMOCRATIC REPUBLIC AND CZECHOSLOVAKIA, WHERE
COMMUNIST GOVERNMENTS HAVE BEEN REPLACED BY COALITION
GOVERNMENTS COMMITTED TO THE HOLDING OF FREE ELECTIONS IN
1990. THESE CHANGES, RESULTING FROM WIDE POPULAR DEMANDS FOR
RADICAL REFORMS, WERE DISCUSSED AT A NUMBER OF INTERNATIONAL
MEETINGS IN NOVEMBER AND DECEMBER 1989.

00200
    ECONOMIC AND SCIENTIFIC AFFAIRS: AUTUMN STATEMENT
    SURVEY OF CURRENT AFFAIRS, 19(12) (DEC 89), 465-468.
    TIGHT CONTROL OF PUBLIC EXPENDITURES COMBINED WITH
INCREASES IN SPENDING IN PRIORITY AREAS WERE THE KEY
ELEMENTS IN THE AUTUMN STATEMENT, WHICH WAS PRESENTED BY
CHANCELLOR OF THE EXCHEQUER JOHN MAJOR TO THE HOUSE OF
COMMONS ON NOVEMBER 15, 1989. A SLOWER RATE OF ECONOMIC
GROWTH, WHICH REACHED UNSUSTAINABLE LEVELS IN 1987 AND 1988,
AND AN IMPROVEMENT IN THE CURRENT ACCOUNT OF THE BALANCE OF
PAYMENTS WERE FORECAST FOR 1990.

00201
    ECONOMIC ASSISTANCE
    LINK, 22(2) (MAY 89), 3-6.
    THE ARTICLE EXAMINES THE ECONOMIC ASSISTANCE RENDERED TO
ISRAEL BY VARIOUS COUNTRIES. IT FOLLOWS THE HISTORY OF AID
TO ISRAEL BEGINING WITH THE ASSISTANCE GIVEN BY GREAT
BRITAIN, FRANCE AND THROUGH WEST GERMAN REPARATIONS. IT ALSO
TRACES THE INCREASE OF AID FROM WORLDWIDE JEWISH GROUPS AND
FROM THE US GOVERNMENT. AS ISRAEL'S ECONOMIC WOES INCREASED,
SO DID THE AMOUNT OF AID REQUIRED. THE US WAS THE MAJOR
ACTOR THAT MOVED IN TO FILL THE GAP. AT ONE POINT IN TIME,
THE US GOVERNMENT ACTUALLY BAILED OUT THE ISRAELI TREASURY.
THE END RESULT IS THAT THE HIGH STANDARD OF LIVING IN ISRAEL
IS SOMEWHAT ILLUSIONARY BECAUSE IT IS DEPENDENT ON OUTSIDE
SOURCES.

00202
    ECONOMIC PROGRESS TO GAIN A NEW QUALITY
    REPRINTS FROM THE SOVIET PRESS, 48(5) (MAR 89), 8-22.
    THE ARTICLE DISCUSSES THE CURRENT FIVE YEAR PLAN AND THE
PIVOTAL IMPORTANCE OF 1989 TO THE SUCCESS OF THE SOVIET
ECONOMIC REFORMS. IT ASSESSES THE IMPORTANCE OF ECONOMIC
REFORM GOING HAND IN HAND WITH POLITICAL REFORM AND ANALYZES
THE CHALLENGES THAT THE SOVIET ECONOMIC PLANNERS FACE. IT
CONCLUDES THAT A NEW QUALITY OF ECONOMIC PROGRESS IS A
NECESSARY PREREQUISITE FOR LONG-TERM SUCCESS.

00203
    ECONOMIC STRUCTURAL IMBALANCE: ITS CAUSES AND CORRECTIVES
    BEIJING REVIEW, 32(36) (SEP 89), 22-28.
    BASED ON FACTS AND FIGURES FOR 1978-88 PROVIDED BY
CHINA'S STATE STATISTICAL BUREAU, THIS ARTICLE OUTLINES THE
CAUSES OF ECONOMIC STRUCTURAL IMBALANCE AND PROPOSES
MEASURES FOR ITS REMEDY. IT STRESSES THE IMPORTANCE OF
READJUSTING THE ECONOMIC STRUCTURE IN THE CURRENT EFFORT TO
IMPROVE THE ECONOMIC ENVIRONMENT AND STRAIGHTEN OUT THE
ECONOMIC ORDER.

00204
    ECUADOR: ORIENTATION FOR THE NEAR FUTURE
    INFORMATION BULLETIN, 26(21-22) (NOV 88), 11-12.
    THE COMMUNIST PARTY OF ECUADOR HERE ESTABLISHES ITS FOUR-
PART CRITERIA FOR DEFINING ITS POLICY ON ACCESSION TO POWER
OF THE NEW GOVERNMENT.

00205
    EFFORTS TOWARD A CAMBODIAN SETTLEMENT
    DEPARTMENT OF STATE BULLETIN (US FOREIGN POLICY), 89(2143)
    (FEB 89), 65-68.

THIS REPORT ON EFFORTS TOWARD A CAMBODIAN SETTLEMENT INCLUDES THE TEXT OF UN GENERAL ASSEMBLY RESOLUTION 4319 OF NOV. 3, 1989, AND A STATEMENT BY THE US PERMANENT REPRESENTATIVE TO THE UN, VERNON A. WALTERS.

00206
EGYPT: "LEFT" COMPLEXION OF THE RULING REGIME
INFORMATION BULLETIN, 25/26(1-2) (JAN 88), 23-24.
THIS STATEMENT OF THE SECRETARIAT OF THE EGYPTIAN COMMUNIST PARTY DENOUNCES EGYPT'S RULING REGIME, WHICH, IN ACCEPTING THE INTERNATIONAL MONETARY FUND (IMF) TERMS, IS ADVANCING THE INTERESTS OF EGYPTIAN BIG BOURGEOISIE AT THE EXPENSE OF THE WORKING CLASS. THE TERMS WILL ONLY WORSEN EGYPT'S ECONOMIC CRISIS WHICH, COMBINED WITH THE TRADE DEFICIT AND THE DROP IN EXPORTS/GROWTH IN IMPORTS, REVEALS ITSELF IN A HUGE STATE BUDGET DEFICIT.

00207
EL SALVADOR: THE BATTLE FOR DEMOCRACY
DEPARTMENT OF STATE BULLETIN (US FOREIGN POLICY), 89(2142) (JAN 89), 44-49.
AT THE END OF 1988, THE QUESTION FOR EL SALVADOR IS HOW TO CONTINUE ITS DEMOCRATIC EXPERIMENT. EXTREMIST FORCES ARE DECLINING IN NUMBERS, BUT THEIR BEHAVIOR STILL REFLECTS THE POLITICS AND PASSIONS OF A DECADE AGO. THE VIOLENT RIGHT REMAINS ISOLATED OUTSIDE THE SYSTEM, THE ARMED LEFT STILL ATTEMPTS TO ADVANCE ITS AGENDA BY DRIVING THE SALVADORAN PEOPLE TO REVOLUTIONARY DESPAIR.

00208
ELECTIONS TO THE SEJM AND THE SENATE
CONTEMPORARY POLAND, XXII(7) (1989), 10.
ELECTIONS TO THE SEJM AND THE SENATE WERE HELD IN POLAND ON JUNE 4 AND 18, 1989. THIS ARTICLE EXPLAINS THE ELECTION PROCEDURES AND THE RESULTS OF THE FIRST ROUND OF VOTING.

00209
ELECTIONS, 1984-88: FIGHTING ON MULTIPLE FRONTS
CENTRAL AMERICA BULLETIN, 8(10) (SEP 89), 4-7.
THIS ARTICLE DISCUSSES ELECTIONS AND THE DEVELOPMENT OF THE POLITICAL SYSTEM IN NICARAGUA SINCE THE 1979 REVOLUTION. IT FOCUSES ON NICARAGUAN EFFORTS TO WRITE A CONSTITUTION AND INSTITUTIONALIZE NONVIOLENT POLITICAL DISCOURSE IN THE MIDST OF THE U.S.-FINANCED CONTRA WAR.

00210
EMBARGO POLITICS
MULTINATIONAL MONITOR, 11(12) (DEC 89), 6.
A MELANGE OF ELEMENTS MAKES UP POSTWAR U.S. POLICY TOWARD THE THIRD WORLD. MOST SIGNIFICANT AMONG THEM ARE ANTI-COMMUNIST IDEOLOGY, ECONOMIC PRIORITIES, COLD WAR ELECTIONEERING, AND GEOPOLITICS OR NATIONAL SECURITY. BENEATH THE RHETORICAL POSTURING, THESE FACTORS ARE THE REAL MOTIVATIONAL FORCES SHAPING U.S. FOREIGN POLICY. IT'S TIME TO IDENTIFY THE REAL U.S. POLICY OBJECTIVES IN NICARAGUA AND UNDERSTAND HOW A CONTINUATION OF THE EMBARGO IS RELATED TO THEM.

00211
END APARTHEID EXECUTIONS
SECHABA, 23(12) (DEC 89), 15.
THIS ARTICLE IS AN ASSESSMENT OF THE SITUATION IN SOUTH AFRICAN APARTHEID POLICY IN REGARDS TO EXECUTIONS. IT RECOUNTS THE CATEGORIES OF THE 74 PATRIOTS UNDER SENTENCE OF DEATH AND CONCLUDES THAT THERE CAN BE NO SERIOUS TALK ABOUT RECONCILIATION WHEN PEOPLE CONTINUE TO BE HANGED.

00212
END OF A POLITICAL ERA?
JAPAN ECHO, XVI(4) (WIN 89), 6-8.
THE AUTHOR DISCUSSES THE JAPANESE PUBLIC'S CHANGING ATTITUDES TOWARD THE LIBERAL DEMOCRATIC PARTY AND THE WHOLE POLITICAL SCENE FOLLOWING THE RECRUIT INFLUENCE-PEDDLING SCANDAL AND THE SEX SCANDAL INVOLVING PRIME MINISTER UNO SOUSUKE.

00213
END THE WAR AND TERROR
INFORMATION BULLETIN, 26(13-14) (JUL 88), 15.
THE COMMUNIST AND DEMOCRATIC PARTIES OF ARAB COUNTRIES STATE HERE THEIR INTENTION TO INTENSIFY THE STRUGGLE FOR TERMINATING THE IRAQ-IRAN WAR ON THE BASIS OF UN SECURITY COUNCIL RESOLUTION 598, ON A FAIR BASIS THAT MEETS THE COMMON INTERESTS OF BOTH PEOPLES, ON THE BASIS OF RESPECT FOR THE SOVEREIGNTY AND TERRITORIAL INTEGRITY OF THE TWO COUNTRIES, ON THE BASIS OF STRUGGLE AGAINST IMPERIALISM AND ZIONISM.

00214
ENLARGING THE CLOTH
COMMONWEAL, CXVI(15) (SEP 89), 451-452.
TWO YEARS AFTER OSCAR ARIAS SANCHEZ'S INITIAL EFFORT AT ESQUIPULAS, GUATEMALA, THE REGIONAL PEACE MAKING PROCESS INAUGURATED THERE CONTINUES WITH GREATER SERIOUSNESS AND

SPECIFICITY. THE TELA ACCORD SETS OUT NOT ONLY TO CREATE A MEANS OF DISBANDING AND RESETTLING THE NICARAGUAN CONTRAS BUT TO ESTABLISH WAYS OF SOLVING OTHER REGIONAL CONFLICTS AND OF PROMOTING INTRAREGIONAL TRADE.

00215
ENTERPRISES: FORMS, ORGANIZATION, SELF-MANAGEMENT, AND MANAGEMENT
YUGOSLAV SURVEY, XXX(3) (1989), 27-58.
CONSTITUTIONAL CHANGES IN YUGOSLAVIA'S SOCIO-ECONOMIC SYSTEM HAVE CONSIDERABLY INCREASED THE OPERATING SPACE FOR ECONOMIC LAWS. THE CONCEPT OF OWNERSHIP AND THE POSITION OF ECONOMIC ENTITIES HAVE BEEN MODIFIED. THE PRINCIPLE OF SELF-ORGANIZATION HAS BEEN AFFIRMED, THEREBY PROVIDING AN IMPORTANT PART OF THE CONDITIONS FOR ENTREPRENEURSHIP, WHICH IS THE BASIC CONCEPT BEHIND A MARKET ECONOMY. POSSIBILITIES HAVE OPENED UP FOR INDIVIDUAL ENTREPRENEURIAL INITIATIVE REGARDLESS OF THE ORGANIZATIONAL FORM OF THE ENTERPRISE.

00216
ENTERPRISES: WILL THE REFORM STAY?
CHINA NEWS ANALYSIS, (1396) (NOV 89), 1-9.
IN AUGUST 1989, PREMIER LI PENG ANNOUNCED A THREE-YEAR ECONOMIC PROGRAM DESIGNED TO CURB INFLATION AND CORRECT STRUCTURAL IMBALANCES IN CHINA'S ECONOMY. HE STATED THAT THE MANAGEMENT CONTRACT SYSTEM, UNDER ATTACK IN SOME INFLUENTIAL SECTORS OF THE STATE COUNCIL, WOULD NOT BE ALTERED. PENG'S REPORT REFERRED TO THE "BASIC IDEAS OF THE 1991-1995 EIGHTH FIVE-YEAR PLAN" WHICH WAS DRAFTED BY THE STATE PLANNING COMMISSION. THIS DOCUMENT IS SAID TO EMPHASIZE SECTORAL/VERTICAL DEVELOPMENT AND A FULL-SCALE RE-CENTRALIZATION OF ECONOMIC POWER, INCLUDING TAXATION. IF THIS PROGRAM WERE FULLY ENDORSED, IT WOULD BE DIFFICULT NOT TO ALTER THE CONTRACT SYSTEM TO SOME EXTENT.

00217
ENVIRONMENTAL CHALLENGES THAT LIE AHEAD
AMERICAN CITY AND COUNTY, 104(5) (MAY 89), 62-66.
LEE THOMAS, THE FORMER ADMINISTRATOR OF THE U.S. ENVIRONMENTAL PROTECTION AGENCY, ANSWERS QUESTIONS ABOUT THE ROLE OF LOCAL GOVERNMENT IN MANAGING AND GUARDING THE ENVIRONMENT. THE INTERVIEW INCLUDES QUESTIONS ABOUT THE PROSPECTS FOR MORE FEDERAL LEGISLATION AND FUNDING TO HELP COMMUNITIES DEAL WITH THEIR WASTE PROBLEMS.

00218
EURO ELECTIONS: CONSTITUTIONAL PROPOSALS
CONSTITUTIONAL REFORM QUARTERLY REVIEW, 4(2) (SUM 89), 2.
OF THE PARTIES WHO FOUGHT THE 1989 EUROPEAN PARLIAMENTARY ELECTION IN GREAT BRITAIN, ONLY THE MANIFESTOS OF THE DEMOCRATS, THE GREENS, THE SNP, AND THE SDP CONTAINED MAJOR CONSTITUTIONAL CHANGES. THE CONSERVATIVE AND LABOUR PARTIES BOTH ARGUED AGAINST THE GIVING OF GREATER POWERS TO THE EUROPEAN PARLIAMENT. THE MINORITY PARTIES ALL SAW DEVOLUTION OF POWER TO THE REGIONS WITHIN THE SUPRANATIONAL EUROPEAN COMMUNITY GOVERNMENT FRAMEWORK AS A MEANS OF INCREASING LOCAL DEMOCRATIC PARTICIPATION AND ACCOUNTABILITY.

00219
EUROPE NEEDS POLITICAL CHANGE
CONSTITUTIONAL REFORM QUARTERLY REVIEW, 4(2) (SUM 89), 4.
THE ARTICLE ARGUES THAT THE DELORS PLAN FOR MONETARY UNION IN EUROPE WILL FAIL WITHOUT A CONCOMITANT GROWTH IN THE STRENGTH OF EUROPE'S DEMOCRATIC POLITICAL INSTITUTIONS. FURTHERMORE, IF THE EUROPEAN COMMUNITY CONTINUES ITS DRIVE TO ESTABLISH SUPRANATIONAL POLICIES IN ECONOMIC, ENVIRONMENTAL, MONETARY AND EVEN "FOREIGN" AFFAIRS, THERE MUST ALSO BE POLITICAL AND INSTITUTIONAL CHANGE TO MATCH. THE UNAVOIDABLE CONCLUSION IS THAT CONSTITUTIONAL THEORY, PERHAPS EVEN FEDERALIST THEORY, IS A NECESSARY PRECONDITION TO THE PROPOSED POLITICAL CHANGES IN EUROPE.

00220
EUROPEAN COMMUNITY
SURVEY OF CURRENT AFFAIRS, 19(6) (JUN 89), 231-232.
GREAT BRITAIN'S MINISTER OF STATE FOR FOREIGN AND COMMONWEALTH AFFAIRS, LYNDA CHALKER, HAS OUTLINED BRITAIN'S VIEW OF THE EUROPEAN COMMUNITY'S ROLE IN "A WIDER EUROPE." CHALKER REVIEWED SOME OF THE POST-WAR ACCOMPLISHMENTS AND STEPS TOWARD GREATER EUROPEAN UNITY. SHE ALSO OFFERED SOME OBSERVATIONS ON CHANGES IN THE SOVIET UNION AND EASTERN EUROPE AND THEIR IMPLICATIONS.

00221
EUROPEAN COUNCIL
SURVEY OF CURRENT AFFAIRS, 19(12) (DEC 89), 457-459.
THE EUROPEAN COUNCIL MET IN STRASBOURG IN DECEMBER 1989. THE FOUR MAIN ISSUES UNDER DISCUSSION HERE THE COMPLETION OF THE SINGLE EUROPEAN MARKET, MONETARY UNION, THE SOCIAL CHARTER, AND EVENTS IN EASTERN EUROPE. THIS ACCOUNT OF THE MEETING INCLUDES A SUMMARY OF BRITISH PRIME MINISTER THATCHER'S VIEWS ON THESE ISSUES.

00222
EUROPEAN ECONOMIC AND MONETARY UNION
SURVEY OF CURRENT AFFAIRS, 19(11) (NOV 89), 408-409.
A MARKET-BASED AND EVOLUTIONARY APPROACH TO EUROPEAN
ECONOMIC AND MONETARY UNION HAS BEEN PUT FORWARD BY THE
CHANCELLOR OF THE EXCHEQUER, JOHN MAJOR. THIS REFLECTS THE
BRITISH GOVERNMENT'S PREFERENCE FOR A PARTNERSHIP OF
INDIVIDUAL EUROPEAN MEMBER STATES RATHER THAN A FEDERATION.

00223
EUROPEAN ELECTIONS: ITALIAN VOTE AND POSITION
ITALIAN JOURNAL, III(2-3) (1989), 14-15.
MOST RULING PARTIES SUFFERED SETBACKS IN THE EURO-
ELECTIONS OF JUNE 1989. THE BROAD AGREEMENT ON ECONOMIC
POLICY AMONG MOST MAINSTREAM PARTIES MEAN THAT PROTEST VOTES
HAD TO SEEK OUT EXTREME, ANTI-ESTABLISHMENT PARTIES. HENCE,
THE GAINS FOR THE FAR RIGHT IN FRANCE, WEST GERMANY, AND
BELGIUM; FOR THE COMMUNISTS IN ITALY, SPAIN, AND PORTUGAL;
AND FOR THE GREENS ALMOST EVERYWHERE.

00224
EUROPEAN MILITARY BALANCE
WORLD MARXIST REVIEW, 32(4) (APR 89), 20-23.
IN JANUARY, 1989 THE COMMITTEE OF THE MINISTERS OF
DEFENSE OF THE WARSAW TREATY MEMBER STATES PUBLISHED A
STATEMENT "ON THE RELATIVE STRENGTH OF THE ARMED FORCES AND
ARMAMENTS OF THE WARSAW TREATY ORGANISATION AND THE NORTH
ATLANTIC TREATY ORGANISATION IN EUROPE AND ADJACENT WATER
AREAS". GENERAL OF THE ARMY DOBRI DZHUROV, A MEMBER OF THE
POLITICAL BUREAU OF THE CC OF THE BULGARIAN COMMUNIST PARTY
AND MINISTER OF NATIONAL DEFENCE OF BULGARIA, OFFERS HIS
ASSESSMENT OF THE DOCUMENT. AS HE EXPLAINS, THE NEW DOCTRINE
IS DEFENSIVE: THE WTO COUNTRIES HAVE PLEDGED NEVER UNDER ANY
CIRCUMSTANCES TO LAUNCH MILITARY OPERATIONS AGAINST ANY
STATE OR ALLIANCE OF STATES SAVE IN RESPONSE TO AN ARMED
ATTACK, AND TO REFRAIN FROM THE FIRST USE OF NUCLEAR WEAPONS.
THE PRIORITY IS TO MAKE WAR IMPOSSIBLE.

00225
EUROPEAN MONETARY ISSUES
SURVEY OF CURRENT AFFAIRS, 19(2) (FEB 89), 49-51.
A FREE-MARKET APPROACH TO THE SINGLE EUROPEAN MARKET WAS
ADVOCATED BY THE CHANCELLOR OF THE EXCHEQUER, NIGEL LAWSON,
IN A SPEECH IN LONDON ON 25 JANUARY 1989. HE REJECTED THE
IDEA OF TAX HARMONISATION, WHICH WAS NOT A PRECONDITION FOR
THE SINGLE MARKET, AND CONFIRMED THAT BRITAIN WOULD NOT JOIN
THE EXCHANGE RATE MECHANISM OF THE EUROPEAN MONETARY SYSTEM
UNTIL THE TIME WAS RIGHT. FULL ECONOMIC AND MONETARY UNION,
MR LAWSON WARNED, IS NOT CONSISTENT WITH SOVEREIGNTY IN
FISCAL AND MONETARY POLICIES.

00226
EUROPEAN SECURITY NEGOTIATIONS OPEN IN VIENNA
DEPARTMENT OF STATE BULLETIN (US FOREIGN POLICY), 89(2146)
(MAY 89), 33-36.
SEPARATE NEGOTIATIONS ON CONVENTIONAL ARMED FORCES IN
EUROPE AND ON CONFIDENCE AND SECURITY-BUILDING MEASURES
OPENED IN VIENNA ON MARCH 9, 1989. THIS REPORT INCLUDES A
STATEMENT BY THE HEAD OF THE US DELEGATION TO THE
CONVENTIONAL ARMED FORCES NEGOTIATIONS, THE TEXT OF THE
WESTERN POSITION PAPER ON CONVENTIONAL FORCES IN EUROPE, AND
A STATEMENT BY THE HEAD OF THE US DELEGATION TO THE
CONFIDENCE AND SECURITY-BUILDING TALKS.

00227
EXTENDING THE RIGHT OF REFUGE
SOUTH, (106) (AUG 89), 9.
THE WORLD NEEDS A NEW INTERNATIONAL CONSENSUS ON HOW TO
HANDLE ITS REFUGEE PROBLEM. WHEN THE UN REFUGEE CONVENTION
OF 1951 WAS DRAFTED, THERE WERE ABOUT TWO MILLION REFUGEES
IN THE WORLD. TODAY THERE ARE MORE THAN TEN MILLION, MOST
FROM THE THIRD WORLD. THE SIZE OF THE PROBLEM REQUIRES A
REDEFINITION OF "REFUGEE" AND A RECONSIDERATION OF THE
IMPACT OF REFUGEES ON HOST COUNTRIES.

00228
EXTERNAL AFFAIRS AND DEFENCE: BRITAIN'S DEFENCE POLICY
SURVEY OF CURRENT AFFAIRS, 19(5) (MAY 89), 172-180.
THE NEED FOR THE NORTH ATLANTIC TREATY ORGANISATION TO
MAINTAIN FIRM DEFENCES WHILE ALSO MAKING THE MOST OF THE
OPPORTUNITIES CREATED BY THE IMPROVED EAST-WEST ATMOSPHERE
IS ONE OF THE MAIN POINTS IN THE 1989 DEFENCE WHITE PAPER,
PUBLISHED IN MAY 1989. THE DEFENCE BUDGET FOR 1989-90 IS 20,
143 MILLION POUNDS, WHICH AS A PERCENTAGE OF GROSS DOMESTIC
PRODUCT IS THE HIGHEST IN THE ALLIANCE AFTER THE UNITED
STATES AND GREECE.

00229
EXTERNAL AFFAIRS AND DEFENCE: BRITISH-SOVIET RELATIONS
SURVEY OF CURRENT AFFAIRS, 19(4) (APR 89), 129-130.
PRIME MINISTER MARGARET THATCHER AND SOVIET PRESIDENT
MIKHAIL GORBACHEV DISCUSSED EAST-WEST RELATIONS, ARMS
CONTROL, AND REGIONAL PROBLEMS DURING THE PRESIDENT'S
OFFICIAL VISIT TO BRITAIN IN APRIL 1989. THEY ALSO SIGNED

SEVERAL AGREEMENTS INVOLVING TRADE AND INWARD INVESTMENT
PROTECTION AND AID TO ARMENIA.

00230
EXTERNAL AFFAIRS AND DEFENCE: CONFERENCE ON SECURITY AND
COOPERATION IN EUROPE
SURVEY OF CURRENT AFFAIRS, 19(2) (FEB 89), 43-49.
THE NEED TO KEEP UP THE PRESSURE FOR IMPROVEMENTS IN
HUMAN RIGHTS AND SECURITY IN EUROPE HAS BEEN EMPHASISED BY
BRITAIN FOLLOWING THE SIGNING BY 35 EUROPEAN AND NORTH
AMERICAN STATES OF THE CONCLUDING DOCUMENT AT THE END OF THE
VIENNA CONFERENCE ON SECURITY AND CO-OPERATION IN EUROPE IN
JANUARY 1989. IN THE SAME MONTH, A BRITISH GOVERNMENT
STATEMENT REVIEWED HUMAN RIGHTS IN THE SOVIET UNION AND
EASTERN EUROPE DURING THE LAST SIX MONTHS OF 1988.

00231
EXTERNAL AFFAIRS AND DEFENCE: POLAND
SURVEY OF CURRENT AFFAIRS, 19(9) (SEP 89), 343-344.
BRITAIN HAS WELCOMED THE EMERGENCE OF A NEW GOVERNMENT
IN POLAND, FOLLOWING THE ELECTION BY THE POLISH PARLIAMENT
ON 21 AUGUST 1989 OF A LEADING MEMBER OF THE INDEPENDENT
TRADE UNION SOLIDARITY, TADEUSZ MAZOWIECKI, AS PRIME
MINISTER.

00232
EXTRADITION AND TERRORISM
SURVEY OF CURRENT AFFAIRS, 19(1) (JAN 89), 7-9.
BRITAIN HAS EXPRESSED ITS CONCERN AT THE REFUSAL OF
BELGIUM AND THE REPUBLIC OF IRELAND TO ALLOW PATRICK RYAN, A
FORMER ROMAN CATHOLIC PRIEST FROM IRELAND, TO BE EXTRADITED
TO BRITAIN, WHERE HE IS WANTED ON CHARGES RELATED TO
TERRORISM. THE GOVERNMENT HAS ALSO CALLED FOR CLOSER CO-
OPERATION BETWEEN MEMBERS OF THE EUROPEAN COMMUNITY ON THE
EXTRADITION OF SUSPECTED TERRORISTS.

00233
EYEWITNESS ACCOUNTS OF THE CLEARING OF TIANANMEN SQUARE
BEIJING REVIEW, 32(43) (OCT 89), 30-33.
MISINFORMATION SPREAD BY WESTERN, TAIWAN, AND HONG KONG
PRESS OF A "TIANANMEN MASSACRE" HAS BEEN REFUTED BY THE
FACTS, AND MORE AND MORE PEOPLE HAVE BEGUN TO UNDERSTAND THE
REAL SITUATION. IN THIS REPORT, HUNGER STRIKERS AND DOCTORS
GIVE EYEWITNESS ACCOUNTS OF THE ARMY'S OPERATION TO CLEAR
THE TIANANMEN SQUARE ON JUNE 4, 1989.

00234
FACING SOUTH
COMMONWEAL, CXVI(4) (FEB 89), 99-100.
THE BUSH ADMINISTRATION HAS A REMARKABLE, HISTORTI
OPPORTUNITY IN CENTRAL AMERICA. IT SHOULD BECOME AN ENGAGED,
RESPECTFUL, AND DISCIPLINED NEGOTIATOR WITH ALL COUNTRIES IN
THE REGION. THIS WOULD MEAN DIRECT NEGOTIATIONS WITH THE
GOVERNMENT OF NICARAGUA AND BELATED, GENUINE SUPPORT FOR THE
ARAIS ACCORD.

00235
FACING THE ELECTIONS
CENTRAL AMERICA BULLETIN, 8(9) (AUG 89), 4-6.
HONDURAS' 1989 ELECTION WILL BE THE THIRD GENERAL
ELECTION SINCE THE END OF DIRECT MILITARY RULE AND APPEARS
TO INDICATE THAT THE FRAGILE DEMOCRACY ESTABLISHED UNDER THE
REAGAN ADMINISTRATION HAS FIRMLY TAKEN ROOT. BUT THE
HONDURANS WILL BE ELECTING CANDIDATES WHO WILL HAVE LITTLE
CONTROL OVER THE DESTINY OF THEIR NATION. SINCE 1980, U.S.
MILITARY AND ECONOMIC AID HAS CONTRIBUTED TO AN
UNPRECEDENTED MILITARIZATION OF HONDURAN SOCIETY, WHILE
OBSCURING DEEP STRUCTURAL PROBLEMS, SUCH AS FOREIGN DEBT AND
AGRARIAN REFORM. THE PRESENCE OF U.S. AND CONTRA TROOPS HAS
CAUSED WIDESPREAD SOCIAL DISLOCATION AND WORSENING POLITICAL
VIOLENCE. SOLUTIONS TO THESE CRISES, AND THE DETERMINATION
OF HONDURAS' DOMESTIC AND INTERNATIONAL PRIORITIES,
ULTIMATELY LIE IN WASHINGTON.

00236
FARM FALLACIES
SOUTH, (110) (DEC 89), 8-9.
THE UNITED STATES' PROPOSALS FOR REFORMING WORLD
AGRICULTURE HAVE SET OFF A PREDICTABLE FURORE. IN ALL BUT
NAME, THE PROPOSALS ARE A REPACKAGING OF IDEAS WASHINGTON
HAS LONG BEEN PUSHING AS THE "ZERO OPTION." THEY CALL FOR AN
END TO ALL EXPORT SUBSIDIES IN FIVE YEARS AND THE CONVERSION
OF ALL OTHER NON-TARIFF BARRIERS AND PRICE SUPPORTS INTO
TARIFFS, PRIOR TO PHASING THEM OUT OVER A TEN-YEAR PERIOD.
THE EUROPEAN COMMUNITY HAS ATTACKED THE PROPOSALS AS A
"POLITICALLY IMPOSSIBLE" DEMAND FOR THE ABOLITION OR ITS OWN
AGRICULTURAL POLICY.

00237
FAX MAY RESCUE MISSING VOTES
CAMPAIGNS AND ELECTIONS, 10(4) (DEC 89), 10.
IF BUREAUCRACY DOESN'T GET IN THE WAY, SOME SIX MILLION
MILITARY AND CIVILIAN VOTERS STATIONED OVERSEAS MAY CAST
THEIR NEXT PRESIDENTIAL VOTES BY FAX MACHINE. FAX USE WOULD

ELIMINATE THE TIME PROBLEM IN OVERSEAS VOTING. CURRENTLY, A
COMBINATION OF APPLICATION DEADLINES AND FOREIGN POSTAL
SERVICE DELAYS ROUTINELY CONSPIRE TO SUBVERT LONG-DISTANCE
DEMOCRACY.

00238
    FEDERAL GOVERNMENT: BROAD CONSENSUS FAVORS ITEM VETO,
    BALANCED BUDGET AMENDMENT; INCREASED MAJORITY SEES BUDGET
    DEFICIT AS A "VERY SERIOUS" PROBLEM
    GALLUP REPORT, (281) (FEB 89), 2-5.
    A RECENT GALLUP POLL FOUND BETTER THAN 2-TO-1 PUBLIC
BACKING FOR A CONSTITUTIONAL AMENDMENT REQUIRING THE FEDERAL
GOVERNMENT TO BALANCE ITS BUDGET EACH YEAR. THE SURVEY ALSO
REVEALED THAT THE PUBLIC SUPPORTS THE LINE ITEM VETO BY
ALMOST 3-TO-1. SIXTY-THREE PERCENT CHARACTERIZE THE FEDERAL
BUDGET DEFICIT AS A "VERY SERIOUS" PROBLEM. DEMOCRATS AND
INDEPENDENTS ARE SLIGHTLY MORE INCLINED THAN REPUBLICANS TO
FEEL THIS WAY ABOUT THE DEFICIT.

00239
    FEDERALISM AND THE CONSTITUTION: A SYMPOSIUM ON "GARCIA"
    AVAILABLE FROM NTIS, NO. PB89-150643/GAR, JUL 87, 88.
    THE DECISION OF THE U.S. SUPREME COURT IN GARCIA V. SAN
ANTONIO METROPOLITAN TRANSIT AUTHORITY (1985) HAS REFOCUSED
NATIONAL ATTENTION ON THE LEGAL AND POLITICAL PARAMETERS OF
AMERICAN FEDERALISM. TO EXPLORE THE IMPACT OF GARCIA ON
FEDERALISM AND THE CONSTITUTION, A SYMPOSIUM OF LEGAL AND
POLITICAL SCHOLARS IN APRIL 1986 WAS CONVENED. THE VOLUME
CONSISTS OF THE PAPERS FROM THAT SYMPOSIUM, INCLUDING: (1)
AN INTELLECTUAL CRISIS IN AMERICAN FEDERALISM: THE MEANING
OF GARCIA; (2) THE COURT'S ROLE IN CONGRESSIONAL FEDERALISM:
A PLAY WITH (AT LEAST) THREE ACTS; (3) FEDERALISM AS A
SUBJECT OF INTERPRETATION; (4) GARCIA, CONSTITUTIONAL RULE,
AND THE CENTRAL-GOVERNMENT TRAP; (5) THE CONTEMPORARY
SUPREME COURT AND FEDERALISM: SYMPOSIUM DISCUSSION; AND (6)
FEDERALISM AND CONSTITUTION MAKING.

00240
    FEDERATION OF YOUNG DEMOCRATS DECLARATION OF POLITICAL
    PROGRAM AND CHRONOLOGY
    WORLD AFFAIRS, 151(4) (1989), 170-176.
    THE ARTICLE EXAMINES THE FEDERATION OF YOUNG DEMOCRATS
(FIDESZ), A HUNGARIAN YOUTH ORGANIZATION. IT OUTLINES THE
GROUP'S GROWTH AND ACTIVITIES BEGINNING WITH ITS FORMATION
ON MARCH 30, 1988 AND ENDING WITH ITS RECENT ACTIVITIES. THE
ARTICLE ALSO OUTLINES THE AIMS OF THE GROUP WHICH INCLUDE: A
GUARANTEE OF FREEDOM, DEMOCRACY, AND HUMAN RIGHTS.

00241
    FINANCIAL REGULATION OF FOREIGN TRANSACTION
    REPRINTS FROM THE SOVIET PRESS, 48(11-12) (JUN 89), 24-30.
    THE REGULATION WHICH REGULATES THE TRANSFER OF FOREIGN
EXCHANGE TO THE ACCOUNTS OF PUBLIC AND COOPERATIVE SECTOR
OPERATORS IS SET FORTH IN THIS ARTICLE. THE REGULATION WAS
ENDORSED BY THE USSR FOREIGN ECONOMIC BANK IN COMPLIANCE
WITH RESOLUTION NO. 1405 PASSED BY THE USSR COUNCIL OF
MINISTER ON DECEMBER 2, 1988. ALSO SET FORTH IN THIS ARTICLE
IS THE REGULATION COVERING RUBLE SETTLEMENTS AND TRANS
RELATIVE TO EXPORT AND IMPORTS BY PUBLIC AND COOPERATIVE
SECTOR OPERATORS AND PARTNERS IN RESEARCH AND CO-PRODUCTION
PROGRAMS WITH FOREIGN INVOLVEMENT.

00242
    FINDING NEW WAYS TO FUND PUBLIC WORKS
    AMERICAN CITY AND COUNTY, 104(2) (FEB 89), 44-50.
    THE FEDERAL GOVERNMENT HAS CUT FUNDING FOR MUNICIPAL
WORKS PROJECTS DURING THE PAST SEVERAL YEARS. TAXPAYERS HAVE
ALSO BEEN HESITANT TO FUND BADLY NEEDED FACILITIES. THIS HAS
LED TO CREATIVE SOLUTIONS TO THE PROBLEM: USING ROAD IMPACT
FEES TO FINANCE OFF-SITE INFRASTRUCTURE, USING RESOURCE
RECOVERY PLANTS TO SUPPLY LOW-COST ENERGY, RECOVERING
SANITARY LAND-FILL GAS, AND PRIVATIZING WASTE-WATER
TREATMENT.

00243
    FIREARMS: FEDERAL BAN ON ASSAULT GUNS BACKED BY LARGE
    MAJORITY
    GALLUP REPORT, (282-283) (MAR 89), 2-6.
    ALMOST THREE-FOURTHS OF THE AMERICAN PEOPLE FAVOR
FEDERAL LEGISLATION BANNING THE MANUFACTURE, SALE, AND
POSSESSION OF SEMI-AUTOMATIC ASSAULT GUNS. A SURVEY ALSO
FOUND OVERWHELMING SUPPORT FOR FEDERAL LEGISLATION BANNING
THE MANUFACTURE, SALE, AND PRIVATE POSSESSION OF CHEAP
HANDGUNS (SATURDAY NIGHT SPECIALS) AND OF PLASTIC GUNS THAT
ARE INVISIBLE TO METAL DETECTORS.

00244
    FLAG DESECRATION LEGISLATION
    CONGRESSIONAL DIGEST, 68(8-9) (AUG 89), 193-201.
    THE ARTICLE INCLUDES A SUMMARY OF RECENT CONGRESSIONAL
ACTION REGARDING FLAG DESECRATION LEGISLATION ALONG WITH A
REVIEW OF THE COURT CASE AND SUPREME COURT DECISION THAT
PROMPTED THE RECENT CONTROVERSY.

00245
    FOR A STABLE AND SAFE EUROPE, FREE FROM NUCLEAR AND
    CHEMICALS WEAPONS, FOR A SUBSTANTIAL REDUCTION OF ARMED
    FORCES, ARAMENTS AND MILITARY SPENDING
    REPRINTS FROM THE SOVIET PRESS, 49(5) (SEP 89), 33-43.
    A MEETING OF THE POLITICAL CONSULTATIVE COMMITTEE OF THE
COUNTRIES PARTICIPANTS IN THE WARSAW TREATY OF FRIENDSHIP,
COOPERATION AND MUTUAL ASSISTANCE HAS HELD IN BUCHAREST ON
JULY 7-8, 1989. THIS REPORT OF THE MEETING STATES THAT THE
WARSAW TREATY MEMBER COUNTRIES REGARD THE CONSOLIDATION OF
PEACE, THE ELIMINATION OF THE THREAT OF WAR TO HUMANKIND AND
THE DEVELOPMENT OF EXTENSIVE MUTUALLY BENEFICIAL
INTERNATIONAL COOPERATION AS THE SUPREME GOAL OF THEIR
FOREIGN POLICY. THEY INTEND TO CONTINUE THEIR EFFORTS TO
FURTHER COMPREHENSIVE AND EQUAL SECURITY. THE WARSAW TREATY
MEMBERS COUNTRIES REGARD THE TERMINATION OF THE ARMS RACE
THE ACHIEVEMENT OF DISARMAMENT AS THE CHIEF TASKS OF THE
PRESENT TIMES.

00246
    FOREIGN AFFAIRS IN THE SUPREME SOVIET OF THE USSR
    INTERNATIONAL AFFAIRS (MOSCOW), (10) (OCT 89), 14-33.
    THIS ARTICLE REPORTS ON THE SESSION OF THE COMMITTEE ON
INTERNATIONAL AFFAIRS OF THE USSR SUPREME SOVIET HELD ON
JULY 21, 1989. PARTICIPANTS INCLUDED ALEXANDER DZASOKHOV,
ACTING CHAIRMAN OF THE COMMITTEE, AND VLADIMIR PETROVSKY,
DEPUTY FOREIGN MINISTER.

00247
    FOREIGN DIRECT INVESTMENT IN A GLOBAL ECONOMY
    DEPARTMENT OF STATE BULLETIN (US FOREIGN POLICY), 89(2147)
    (JUN 89), 32-34.
    THE AUTHOR SUMMARIZES THE PRINCIPLES GOVERNING UNITED
STATES POLICY TOWARD FOREIGN INVESTMENT.

00248
    FOREIGN INVESTMENTS
    YUGOSLAV SURVEY, XXX(3) (1989), 59-70.
    CHANGES IN THE YUGOSLAV CONSTITUTION INITIATED A RADICAL
MODIFICATION PROCESS IN THE CONDITIONS FOR FOREIGN
INVESTMENTS. AMENDMENT XV TO THE YUGOSLAV CONSTITUTION
ENABLES FOREIGN LEGAL ENTITIES TOGETHER WITH DOMESTIC LEGAL
ENTITIES TO ESTABLISH MIXED ENTERPRISES AS WELL AS THEIR OWN
ENTERPRISES. THEREBY, THE CONCEPT OF OWNERSHIP THROUGH
FOREIGN INVESTMENTS HAS ALSO BEEN ACCEPTED IN YUGOSLAVIA,
ALONG WITH CONSIDERABLE BROADENING OF THE ACTIVITIES IN
WHICH FOREIGNERS CAN INVEST. INSTITUTIONAL CONDITIONS HAVE
BEEN CREATED FOR A HIGHLY LIBERAL REGIME OF FOREIGN
INVESTMENTS.

00249
    FOREIGN MINISTER QIAN ASSESSES WORLD SITUATION
    BEIJING REVIEW, 32(37) (SEP 89), 12-13.
    THIS ARTICLE SUMMARIZES REMARKS MADE BY CHINESE FOREIGN
MINISTER QIAN QICHEN REGARDING INTERNATIONAL AFFAIRS AND
CHINA'S FOREIGN POLICY.

00250
    FORMAL INVESTIGATION INTO THE CIRCUMSTANCES SURROUNDING
    THE DOWNING OF IRAN AIR FLIGHT 655 ON 3 JULY 1988
    AVAILABLE FROM NTIS, NO. AD-A203577/GAR, AUG 88, 69.
    THE DOWNING OF CIVILIAN IRAN AIR FLIGHT 655 ON 3 JULY
WAS A TRAGIC AND REGRETTABLE ACCIDENT AND, AS IS SO OFTEN
THE CASE IN A COMBAT ENVIRONMENT, THERE WERE A NUMBER OF
CONTRIBUTING FACTORS. IT IS IMPORTANT TO PUT THE EVENTS OF
THAT DAY IN THE LOCAL CONTEXT. THE U.S. GOVERNMENT COMMITTED
NAVAL FORCES TO THE CONVOYING OF AMERICAN FLAG TANKERS IN
THE SPRING OF 1987. FROM THE ONSET, THE ADMINISTRATION
EMPHASIZED THAT WHILE OUR FORCES COULD ACHIEVE THIS MISSION,
IT WOULD INVOLVE RISKS AND UNCERTAINTIES. THIS PREDICTION
WAS BORNE OUT BY SEVERAL INCIDENTS, E.G., THE INDISCRIMINATE
LAYING OF IRANIAN MINES, THE BRIDGETON EXPLOSION, THE STARK
TRAGEDY, THE SAMUEL B. ROBERTS STRIKING A MINE, THE CAPTURE
OF THE IRAN AJAR, IRANIAN FIRING ON U.S. HELOS, AND THE
INCIDENTS OF APRIL 18 WHEN IRANIAN SHIPS AND AIRCRAFT
ATTEMPTED TO DAMAGE U.S. UNITS. THROUGHOUT THIS PERIOD AND
ESPECIALLY IN THE WAKE OF THE ABOVE EVENTS, THE GOVERNMENT
OF IRAN ISSUED INFLAMMATORY STATEMENTS THREATENING
RETALIATION AGAINST AMERICAN PERSONNEL AND INTERESTS.
REINFORCING THE HIGH LEVEL OF TENSION, BOTH BAGHDAD AND
TEHERAN HAVE CONTINUED TO ATTACK UNARMED MERCHANT SHIPS, THE
FORMER WITH AIRCRAFT AND THE LATTER WITH SMALL BOATS, SHIPS
AND AIRCRAFT. IRANIAN ASSAULTS HAVE BEEN LARGELY
CONCENTRATED IN THE SOUTHERN GULF AND ON OCCASION HAVE TAKEN
PLACE IN THE PRESENCE OF FOREIGN WARSHIPS.

00251
    FORMER KMT PERSONNEL WON'T BE PROSECUTED
    BEIJING REVIEW, 32(39) (SEP 89), 11-12.
    THE CHINESE GOVERNMENT HAS ANNOUNCED THAT CHINESE PEOPLE
NOW LIVING IN TAIWAN WHO COMMITTED OFFENSES ON THE MAINLAND
AFTER THE FOUNDING OF THE PEOPLE'S REPUBLIC OF CHINA AND
BEFORE THE ESTABLISHMENT OF LOCAL PEOPLE'S GOVERNMENTS ARE
NO LONGER SUBJECT TO PROSECUTION. THE ANNOUNCEMENT WAS

INTENDED TO REASSURE FORMER KUOMINTANG MILITARY AND
GOVERNMENT PERSONNEL LIVING ABROAD WHO STILL HAVE MISGIVINGS
ABOUT VISITING THEIR RELATIVES OR SIGHTSEEING IN MAINLAND
CHINA.

00252
    FORUMS ON FIGHTING LIBERALIZATION
    BEIJING REVIEW, 32(32) (AUG 89), 12-13.
    THE DEBATE THAT HAS BEEN GOING ON DURING THE PAST DECADE
IN CHINA IS, IN ESSENCE, A STRUGGLE BETWEEN THOSE WHO
PROMOTE THE FOUR CARDINAL PRINCIPLES AND THOSE WHO OPPOSE
THEM WHILE ADVOCATING BOURGEOIS LIBERALIZATION. THE
BOURGEOIS LIBERALIZATION FALLACY HAS POISONED PEOPLE'S MINDS
AND ENDANGERED THE SECURITY OF THE SOCIALIST STATE.

00253
    FOUNDING STATEMENT OF THE DEMOCRATIC TRADE UNION OF
    SCIENTIFIC WORKERS
    WORLD AFFAIRS, 151(4) (1989), 177-178.
    THE ARTICLE IS A TRANSLATION OF THE FOUNDING STATEMENT
OF THE DEMOCRATIC TRADE UNION OF SCIENTIFIC WORKERS, A
HUNGARIAN OPPOSITION GROUP. THE TERM "SCIENTIFIC WORKERS" IS
USED IN A BROAD SENSE TO ENCOMPASS ALL MANNER OF
PROFESSIONALS WHOSE WORK REQUIRES HIGHER EDUCATION. THE
STATEMENT EMPHASIZES THE ORGANIZATION'S SOLIDARITY AND ITS
DESIRE TO GUARANTEE THE RIGHT TO WORK AND IMPROVEMENT OF
LIVING CONDITIONS.

00254
    FOUR HUNDRED ARRESTS FOLLOW RIOTS
    BEIJING REVIEW, 32(26) (JUN 89), 12.
    IN JUNE 1989, POLICE AND MARTIAL LAW TROOPS ARRESTED 400
PERSONS FOR COMMITTING COUNTER-REVOLUTIONARY CRIMES. SOME
WERE ACCUSED OF BEING LEADERS OF OUTLAWED ORGANIZATIONS,
SUCH AS THE BEIJING COLLEGE STUDENTS' AUTONOMOUS FEDERATION
AND THE BEIJING WORKERS' AUTONOMOUS FEDERATION, WHICH HAD
INSTIGATED THE COUNTER-REVOLUTIONARY RIOT IN BEIJING.

00255
    FRANCE: WE SUPPORT PERESTROIKA FIRMLY AND RESOLUTELY
    INFORMATION BULLETIN, 27 (MAR 89), 25-26.
    IN THIS INTERVIEW, GEORGES MARCHAIS ANSWERS QUESTIONS
ABOUT FRANCE'S SOCIAL PROBLEMS, ITS SOCIALIST GOVERNMENT,
THE COMMUNIST ROLE IN FRANCE'S MUNICIPAL GOVERNMENTS, AND
THE FRENCH COMMUNIST STAND ON GORBACHEV'S REFORMS IN THE
SOVIET UNION.

00256
    FREEDOM AND WORLD PROSPERITY
    DEPARTMENT OF STATE BULLETIN (US FOREIGN POLICY), 89(2153)
    (DEC 89), 8-10.
    IN A SPEECH BEFORE THE WORLD BANK/INTERNATIONAL MONETARY
FUND'S 1989 ANNUAL MEETING, PRESIDENT GEORGE BUSH STATED
THAT ECONOMIC AND POLITICAL FREEDOM ARE INSEPARABLE
COMPANIONS ON THE ROAD TO NATIONAL PROSPERITY. HE ALSO
DISCUSSED THE NEED FOR COORDINATING ECONOMIC POLICIES TO
HELP PROVIDE SUSTAINED GROWTH WITH LOW INFLATION, REDUCED
TRADE IMBALANCES, AND GREATER STABILITY IN EXCHANGE MARKETS.
HE STATED THAT THE URUGUAY ROUND OFFERS A TREMENDOUS
OPPORTUNITY TO ADVANCE WORLD TRADE.

00257
    FREEDOM TO KUTLU AND SARGIN
    INFORMATION BULLETIN, 26(19-20) (OCT 88), 26-27.
    THIS JOINT STATEMENT BY 28 EUROPEAN COMMUNIST PARTIES
CONDEMNS THE PERSECUTION AND TRIAL OF TURKISH COMMUNIST
LEADERS KUTLU AND SARGIN, WHO AFTER THEIR RETURN FROM EXILE
TO SET UP A LEGAL UNITED COMMUNIST PARTY IN TURKEY, WERE
ARRESTED AND TORTURED AS SUBVERSIVES.

00258
    FSX COPRODUCTION PROHIBITION DISAPROVED BY PRESIDENT
    DEPARTMENT OF STATE BULLETIN (US FOREIGN POLICY), 89(2151)
    (OCT 89), 32.
    ON JULY 31, 1989, PRESIDENT BUSH REFUSED TO APPROVE A
JOINT CONGRESSIONAL RESOLUTION THAT WOULD HAVE PROHIBITED
THE EXPORT OF CERTAIN TECHNOLOGY, DEFENSE ARTICLES, AND
DEFENSE SERVICES IN CONNECTION WITH THE CO-DEVELOPMENT AND
CO-PRODUCTION OF THE FSX AIRCRAFT WITH JAPAN. HE STATED THAT
THE RESOLUTION WAS NOT NEEDED TO PROTECT THE INTERESTS OF
THE USA AND WAS NOT CONSISTENT WITH THE REQUIREMENTS OF THE
ARMS EXPORT CONTROL ACT. HE ALSO ARGUED THAT THE RESOLUTION
WOULD UNCONSTITUTIONALLY INFRINGE ON THE POWERS OF THE
EXECUTIVE BRANCH OF GOVERNMENT.

00259
    FUNDAMENTAL CHANGES IN PERSPECTIVE
    FREE CHINA REVIEW, 39(7) (JUL 89), 1-3.
    THE TAIWANESE GOVERNMENT IS AWARE OF CHANGES IN THE
OVERSEAS CHINESE POPULATION, BUT SOME IMPORTANT LEGAL AND
EMOTIONAL HURDLES MUST BE OVERCOME BEFORE IT CAN ADOPT MORE
REALISTIC POLICIES TO COPE WITH THEM. HISTORICALLY, TAIWAN
HAS ACCEPTED THE JUS SANGUINIS PRINCIPLE OF CITIZENSHIP, AS
WELL AS THE PRACTICE OF DUAL NATIONALITY. THE TAIWANESE

CONSTITUTION STIPULATES THAT ALL OF THE CENTRAL
REPRESENTATIVE BODIES MUST HAVE A CERTAIN NUMBER OF
DELEGATES FROM OVERSEAS CHINESE COMMUNITIES. BUT IT IS NOT
CLEAR WHETHER ONLY CHINESE WHO RETAIN ACTIVE TAIWANESE
CITIZENSHIP ARE ELIGIBLE OR IF ALL ETHNIC CHINESE, EVEN
THOSE WITH FOREIGN CITIZENSHIP, ARE INCLUDED.

00260
    GANDHI'S AWAY GAME
    SOUTH, (100) (FEB 89), 5.
    THE AUTHOR DISCUSSES THE SIGNIFICANCE OF INDIAN PRIME
MINISTER GANDHI'S VISITS TO PAKISTAN AND CHINA IN DECEMBER
1988.

00261
    GATT: INTERNATIONAL TRADE 1987-88 VOLUME 1 AND VOLUME 2
    AVAILABLE FROM NTIS, NO. PB89-154009/GAR, 1988, 225.
    TABLE OF CONTENTS: VOLUME I; THE REPORT IN BRIEF;
DEVELOPMENTS IN WORLD MERCHANDISE TRADE; TRADE TRENDS IN
AGRICULTURE; TRADE POLICY IN AN EVOLVING GLOBAL ECONOMY;
APPENDIX TABLES; VOLUME II: WORLD MERCHANDISE TRADE; TRADE
BY PRODUCT; MERCHANDISE TRADE BY AREA; MERCHANDISE TRADE BY
REGION; ABBREVIATIONS AND SYMBOLS; LIST OF TABLES AND CHARTS;
APPENDIX I; APPENDIX II.

00262
    GBAGBO FREED
    NEW AFRICAN, 261 (JUN 89), 19-20.
    THE COTE D'IVOIRE'S REPUTATION FOR PEACEFULNESS, WHICH
TENDED TO ENCOURAGE A "LAISSEY-FAIRE" ATTITUDE, PROVIDES AN
IDEAL OPPORTUNITY FOR SUBVERSIVES TO OPERATE. THIS ARTICLE
FOCUSES ON THE DETENTION AND ARREST OF PROFESSOR LAURENT
GBAGBO AND COLONEL LAMINE FADIKA, AND EXAMINES WHETHER THE
COUNTRY'S SECURITY FORCES, RUN MAINLY BY FOREIGNERS, ARE OUT
OF CONTROL.

00263
    GONE WITH THE WIND
    COMMONWEAL, CXVI(3) (FEB 89), 68-69.
    THE SECRET OF RANOLD REAGAN'S SUCCESS, BOTH AS AN ACTOR
AND A POLITICIAN, WAS HIS ABILITY TO PLAY TO HIS AUDIENCE.
HE KNEW HOW TO PLEASE. AND WHEN HE DID NOT PLEASE, HE WAS
HURT. HE NEVER FORGAVE THE CRITICS OF HIS MOVIES OR THE
NEGATIVE VOICES RAISED IN THE PRESS OVER HIS POLITICAL
DECISIONS.

00264
    GOODBYE TO THE '80S: A DISMAL DECADE
    CHURCH AND STATE, 42(11) (DEC 89), 12 (252).
    THE AUTHOR REVIEWS SOME OF THE MAJOR VICTORIES AND
DEFEATS FOR CHURCH-STATE SEPARATION IN THE UNITED STATES
DURING THE 1980'S.

00265
    GOVERNMENT ACTION ON AIDS
    SURVEY OF CURRENT AFFAIRS, 19(12) (DEC 89), 480-481.
    THE BRITISH GOVERNMENT ANNOUNCED ADDITIONAL OFFICIAL
MEASURES TO MONITOR THE SPREAD OF AIDS AND HELP THOSE
AFFECTED BY THE VIRUS IN NOVEMBER 1989. THESE INCLUDED A
GRANT OF 19 MILLION POUNDS TO HELP AFFECTED HAEMOPHILIACS,
GRANTS TO VOLUNTARY HEALTH ORGANIZATIONS, AND INTRODUCTION
OF ANONYMOUS BLOOD TESTING FOR HIV INFECTION, BEGINNING IN
1990. GOVERNMENT STATISTICS SHOW A STEADY INCREASE IN THE
INCIDENCE OF AIDS IN INTRAVENOUS DRUG USERS AND
HETEROSEXUALS.

00266
    GUN CONTROL: NINE IN TEN FAVOR SEVEN-DAY WAITING PERIOD
    BEFORE HANDGUN PURCHASE
    GALLUP REPORT, (280) (JAN 89), 25-26.
    NINETY-ONE PERCENT OF THE AMERICAN PUBLIC SUPPORTS
PROPOSED FEDERAL LEGISLATION REQUIRING A SEVEN-DAY WAITING
PERIOD BEFORE A HANDGUN COULD BE PURCHASED. OVERWHELMING
SUPPORT FOR THE LAW IS FOUND IN ALL MAJOR POPULATION GROUPS,
INCLUDING HANDGUN OWNERS. THE VIEWS OF REPUBLICANS,
DEMOCRATS, AND INDEPENDENTS ARE REMARKABLY SIMILAR, WITH
LARGE MAJORITIES OF ALL POLITICAL PERSUASIONS BACKING GUN
CONTROL MEASURES.

00267
    GUYANA: WORKING PEOPLE'S PARTY
    INFORMATION BULLETIN, 27 (JAN 89), 10-12.
    THE 23RD CONGRESS OF THE PEOPLE'S PROGRESSIVE PARTY OF
GUYANA ISSUED A POLITICAL RESOLUTION CALLING FOR NUCLEAR
DISARMAMENT, SOLIDARITY AMONG DEVELOPING COUNTRIES, AND A
DEMOCRATIC POLITICAL SOLUTION TO GUYANA'S PROBLEMS.

00268
    HAINAN'S DOOR KEEPS OPEN
    BEIJING REVIEW, 32(31) (JUL 89), 10-11.
    ON JULY 18, 1989, THE SECRETARY OF THE HAINAN PROVINCIAL
COMMITTEE OF THE CHINESE COMMUNIST PARTY SAID THAT THE
HAINAN SPECIAL ECONOMIC ZONE WILL RESOLUTELY STICK TO ITS
ECONOMIC REFORM AND THE POLICY OF OPENING TO THE OUTSIDE

WORLD. HE ADDED THAT THE ESTABLISHMENT OF THE SPECIAL
ECONOMIC ZONE IS AN IMPORTANT PART OF THE DEVELOPMENT
STRATEGY FOR COASTAL AREAS ADOPTED BY THE PARTY CENTRAL
COMMITTEE. THE CENTRAL GOVERNMENT'S POLICIES TOWARD HAINAN
WILL NOT BE CHANGED AND THE LEGISLATIVE POWER GRANTED TO THE
PROVINCE WILL REMAIN INTACT.

00269
    HAMMERING HAMAD
    NEW AFRICAN, (APR 88), 17-18.
    THIS ARTICLE REPORTS ON THE FALL OF THE CHIEF MINISTER
OF ZANZIBAR, SELF SHARIFF HAMAD, BY OLD WAASISA OPPONENTS.
IT EXPLORES THE PROBLEMS CREATED BY THE FACT OF HAMAD'S
PEMBAN ORGIN, HIS FALL AND DESCRIBES NYERERE'S ROLE IN IT.

00270
    HANDSHAKE, BUT NO EMBRACE
    SOUTH, (106) (AUG 89), 8-9.
    THE TASK OF REACHING NATIONAL RECONCILIATION IN ANGOLA
IS TO BE ENTRUSTED TO A COMMISSION HEADED BY ZAIRE'S
PRESIDENT MOBUTU SESE SEKO WITH DELEGATES FROM THE ANGOLAN
GOVERNMENT AND UNITA. THE COMMISSION HAS A NUMBER OF
PROBLEMS TO SOLVE, BUT THE PRIMARY DILEMMA IS DETERMINING
THE FUTURE ROLE OF JONAS SAVIMBI. ZAMBIAN PRESIDENT KENNETH
KAUNDA HAS SUGGESTED TEMPORARY EXILE BUT SAVIMBI SAYS HE HAS
NO INTENTION OF LEAVING ANGOLA.

00271
    HE'S WONDERFUL, HE'S SUPERMAN
    MEXICO-UNITED STATES REPORT, II(6) (FEB 89), 2-3.
    US POLITICAL COMMENTATORS HAVE HASTILY AND PREMATURELY
MADE MEXICAN PRESIDENT CARLOS SALINAS A HERO. BUT ONLY TIME
WILL TELL IF SALINAS CAN SOLVE MEXICO'S PROBLEMS. PREMATURE
PRAISE CAN ONLY MISLEAD PUBLIC OPINION AND ILL PREPARE IT TO
FACE REALITY IF SALINAS' POLICIES GO AWRY.

00272
    HERITAGE FOUNDATION, RADICAL RIGHT PUSH EDUCATION CHANGES
    CHURCH AND STATE, 42(21) (FEB 89), 12 (36)-13 (37).
    THE HERITAGE FOUNDATION AND OTHER PUBLIC SCHOOL CRITICS
ARE PRESSURING THE BUSH ADMINISTRATION TO PROMOTE VOUCHERS
AND OTHER RADICAL REMEDIES FOR THE NATION'S EDUCATION
PROBLEMS. THE HERITAGE FOUNDATION'S POLITICAL BLUEPRINT,
"MANDATE FOR LEADERSHIP III: POLICY STRATEGIES FOR THE
1990'S," DEMANDS THAT THE ADMINISTRATION INITIATE A COMPLETE
RESTRUCTURING OF THE EDUCATIONAL SYSTEM. TAX CREDITS AND
VOUCHERS TO BENEFIT PRIVATE SCHOOLS ARE ADVOCATED.

00273
    HONDURANS PRESSURE U.S. OVER CONTRAS
    CENTRAL AMERICA BULLETIN, 8(2) (JAN 89), 4.
    DESPITE GEORGE BUSH'S PLEDGE TO CONTINUE U.S. SUPPORT
FOR THE CONTRAS, MANY HONDURANS SEE THE END OF THE CONTRA
WAR AS IMMINENT. NEWSPAPERS AND SOME OFFICIALS NOW REGULARLY
REFER TO THE "DEFEATED CONTRAS," AND SOME OBSERVERS BELIEVE
HONDURAS IS ALREADY FASHIONING A POST-CONTRA POLICY. EVENTS
SINCE OCTOBER 1988 SUGGEST THAT HONDURAS HAS PLACED THIS
ISSUE AND WHAT TO DO WITH THE THOUSANDS OF REFUGEES AT THE
TOP OF THE AGENDA IN ITS RELATIONS WITH THE USA.

00274
    HONESTY VS. CORRUPTION
    CHINA RECONSTRUCTS, XXXVIII(11) (NOV 89), 5.
    THE CHINESE GOVERNMENT AND THE COMMUNIST PARTY ARE
DETERMINED TO ELIMINATE THE SERIOUS PROBLEM OF CORRUPTION.
THEIR EFFORTS ARE CLOSELY RELATED TO THE POLITICAL PROTESTS
IN BEIJING IN THE SPRING OF 1989. ONE REASON FOR THE
DEMONSTRATIONS WAS PUBLIC DISGUST WITH THE CORRUPT PRACTICES
THAT PERVADE THE POLITICAL, ECONOMIC, AND CULTURAL LIFE OF
CHINESE SOCIETY. SOME CITIZENS HAVE LOST FAITH IN THE
GOVERNMENT'S DESIRE AND ABILITY TO SOLVE THIS PROBLEM.

00275
    HONG KONG
    SURVEY OF CURRENT AFFAIRS, 19(7) (JUL 89), 267-270.
    BRITAIN'S COMMITMENT TO THE FUTURE OF HONG KONG AND THE
NEED FOR THE PEOPLE'S REPUBLIC OF CHINA TO IMPLEMENT THE
1984 JOINT DECLARATION WERE EMPHSISED BY THE FOREIGN AND
COMMONWEALTH SECRETARY, SIR GEOFFREY HOWE, IN A SPEECH
DURING A VISIT TO HONG KONG IN JULY 1989. ON THE QUESTION OF
THE RIGHT OF ABODE FOR HONG KONG CITIZENS IN BRITAIN, SIR
GEOFFREY SAID THAT THE BRITISH PARLIAMENT COULD NOT BE
PURSUADED TO SUPPORT AN OPEN-ENDED SCHEME ALLOWING SEVERAL
MILLION PEOPLE TO SETTLE THERE.

00276
    HONG KONG POLICY REMAINS UNCHANGED
    BEIJING REVIEW, 32(51) (DEC 89), 12.
    CHINA'S POLICY OF "ONE COUNTRY, TWO SYSTEMS" WILL NOT BE
CHANGED. THE CHINESE GOVERNMENT WILL WORK HARD TO STRICTLY
IMPLEMENT THE SINO-BRITISH JOINT DECLARATION ON THE QUESTION
OF HONG KONG AND TO FORMULATE A BASIC LAW THAT ENSURES HONG
KONG'S STABILITY AND PROSPERITY.

00277
    HOW FOI WORKS IN AUSTRALIA, CANADA, AND NZ
    CONSTITUTIONAL REFORM QUARTERLY REVIEW, 4(2) (SUM 89), 1.
    ALTHOUGH FREEDOM OF INFORMATION LEGISLATION, WHICH WAS
INTRODUCED IN AUSTRALIA, NEW ZEALAND, AND CANADA IN 1982,
HAS NOT REALIZED ITS SUPPORTERS' MOST AMBITIOUS OBJECTIVES--
FOR EXAMPLE INCREASED PARTICIPATION IN GOVERNMENT DECISION-
MAKING--NEITHER HAS IT FULFILLED ITS OPPONENTS' WORST FEARS.
AN ANALYSIS OF THE CHANGES RESULTING FROM SUCH LEGISLATION
REVEALS LITTLE POLITICAL IMPACT. HOWEVER, THE PUBLIC REMAINS
STRONGLY IN FAVOR OF MAINTAINING FREEDOM OF INFORMATION
LEGISLATION. THE LACK OF PUBLIC USE OF FOI LEGISLATION IS
DUE TO THE EXEMPTIONS ALLOWED UNDER THE ACTS, AND TO THE
LENGTH OF TIME REQUIRED TO OBTAIN INFORMATION.

00278
    HUMAN RIGHTS IN CUBA: AN UPDATE
    DEPARTMENT OF STATE BULLETIN (US FOREIGN POLICY), 89(2145)
    (APR 89), 59-62.
    SINCE HE CAME TO POWER IN 1959, FIDEL CASTRO HAS SOUGHT
TO SUBORDINATE ALL ASPECTS OF CUBAN LIFE TO THE IDEALS AND
AIMS OF THE REVOLUTION. THE CURRENT CONSTITUTION STATES THAT
CIVIL LIBERTIES MAY NOT BE EXERCISED "CONTRARY TO THE
DECISION OF THE CUBAN PEOPLE TO BUILD SOCIALISM AND
COMMUNISM." ALTHOUGH THE CUBAN GOVERNMENT PAYS LIP SERVICE
TO CIVIL LIBERTIES AND HUMAN RIGHTS, IT SUBORDINATES THEM TO
ITS OWN AIMS AND HAS BECOME ONE OF THE WORST HUMAN RIGHTS
VIOLATORS IN THE WESTERN HEMISPHERE.

00279
    HUNGARIAN SOCIALIST PARTY MANIFESTO
    WORLD AFFAIRS, 151(4) (1989), 224-225.
    THE REFORM WING OF THE HUNGARIAN SOCIALIST WORKERS PARTY
VOTED TO DISSOLVE ITSELF AND CREATE A NEW PARTY. ALTHOUGH
COMMUNIST PARTIES HAVE FREQUENTLY CHANGED THEIR NAMES FOR
TACTICAL AND COSMETIC REASONS, THE NEW HUNGARIAN SOCIALIST
PARTY TOOK EXTRAORDINARY STEPS TO SEPARATE ITSELF FROM THE
RULING COMMUNISTS. ITS MANIFESTO DENOUNCES ALL FORMS OF
STALINISM AND UPHOLDS SUCH VALUES AS DEMOCRACY, FREEDOM, AND
GENUINE COLLECTIVITY. THE RESULT IS THAT THE NEW HUNGARIAN
SOCIALIST PARTY RESEMBLES THE SOCIALIST PARTIES OF THE
DEMOCRATIC WORLD RATHER THAN THE RULING PARTIES OF THE
COMMUNIST WORLD.

00280
    HUNGARY: POLICY FOR RENEWAL
    INFORMATION BULLETIN, 27 (JAN 89), 13-14.
    A PLENARY MEETING OF THE CENTRAL COMMITTEE OF THE
HUNGARIAN SOCIALIST WORKERS' PARTY (HSWP) WAS HELD IN
BUDAPEST ON NOVEMBER 1-2, 1988. IT DISCUSSED AND PASSED
RESOLUTIONS ON TWO MAJOR QUESTIONS: (A) PARTY TASKS IN THE
LIGHT OF THE INTERNAL POLITICAL SITUATION; AND (B) THE
DEVELOPMENT OF THE NATIONAL ECONOMY IN 1988 AND THE BASIC
GUIDELINES AND TOOLS OF ECONOMIC POLICY FOR 1989-1990.

00281
    IDEOLOGY AND POLITICAL WORK: TOUGH WORDS, DEAF EARS
    CHINA NEWS ANALYSIS, (1395) (OCT 89), 1-9.
    BELEAGUERED BY UNCERTAINTIES OVER ECONOMIC POLICY AND
THE FUTURE OF REFORM, THE COMMUNIST PARTY OF CHINA IS NOW
CONCEDING PAST FAILURES ON THE PROPAGANDA FRONT. THE PARTY
ADMITS THAT IT HAS LOST GROUND OVER THE YEARS, ALLOWING
DOUBTS ABOUT THE MERITS OF SOCIALISM TO BECOME ENTRENCHED IN
THE MINDS OF THE PEOPLE. BOURGEOIS-LIBERAL IDEAS WERE AT THE
ROOT OF SUCH DOUBTS AND WERE COMPOUNDED BY LAX IDEOLOGICAL
SCHOLARSHIP. UNFORTUNATELY, THESE SAME IDEAS SEEPED INTO THE
THINKING UNDERLYING PARTS OF THE REFORM PROGRAM. THAT IS WHY
REFORM AND OPENING WILL CONTINUE, BUT ONLY SUCH REFORM AND
OPENING AS ARE CONSISTENT WITH THE FOUR BASIC PRINCIPLES:
THE SUPERIORITY OF THE SOCIALIST SYSTEM, THE DEMOCRATIC
DICTATORSHIP OF OF THE PEOPLE, THE LEADERSHIP OF THE
COMMUNIST PARTY, AND THE PRIMACY OF MARXIST-LENINIST-MAOIST
THOUGHT.

00282
    IMMIGRATION REFORM
    CONGRESSIONAL DIGEST, 68(10) (OCT 89), 225-235.
    THIS ARTICLE SUMMARIZES THE 1986 IMMIGRATION ACT, TRENDS
IN IMMIGRATION, AND RECENT ACTION IN CONGRESS REGARDING
IMMIGRATION LEGISLATION.

00283
    IMPACT OF THE INDUSTRIAL POLICIES OF DEVELOPED COUNTRIES
    ON DEVELOPING COUNTRIES
    AVAILABLE FROM NTIS, NO. PB89-211668/GAR, MAY 89, 101.
    THE PAPER LOOKS AT THE INDUSTRIAL POLICIES OF INDUSTRIAL
COUNTRIES IN TERMS OF HOW THEY MAY AFFECT TRADE FLOWS IN A
BROAD SENSE AND, IN PARTICULAR, THE TRADE OF DEVELOPING
COUNTRIES. THE FOCUS, THEREFORE, IS LARGELY ON THE MORE
DEFENSIVE ASPECTS OF SUCH POLICIES. IN PREPARATION FOR THE
STUDY, THE STAFF HELD DISCUSSIONS WITH AUTHORITIES IN
AUSTRALIA, CANADA, FRANCE, THE FEDERAL REPUBLIC OF GERMANY,
JAPAN, THE REPUBLIC OF KOREA, MEXICO, NEW ZEALAND, SINGAPORE,
THE UNITED KINGDOM, AND THE UNITED STATES. DISCUSSIONS WERE

ALSO HELD WITH OFFICIALS FROM THE SECRETARIATS OF THE GROUP OF AFRICAN, CARIBBEAN, AND PACIFIC STATES, THE EUROPEAN FREE TRADE ASSOCIATION, THE EUROPEAN COMMUNITIES, THE GENERAL AGREEMENT ON TARIFFS AND TRADE, THE ORGANIZATION FOR ECONOMIC CO-OPERATION AND DEVELOPMENT, AND THE UNITED NATIONS CONFERENCE ON TRADE AND DEVELOPMENT. EXTENSIVE USE HAS BEEN MADE OF THE PUBLICATIONS OF A NUMBER OF THESE ORGANIZATIONS. SECTIONS EXAMINE THE REASONS FOR INDUSTRIAL POLICIES IN INDUSTRIAL COUNTRIES, THE RANGE AND STATUS OF THESE POLICIES, THE EFFECTS OF THESE POLICIES, WITH PARTICULAR REFERENCE TO DEVELOPING COUNTRIES, AND TRADE TRENDS. THE FINAL SECTION DRAWS SOME PRELIMINARY CONCLUSIONS.

00284
    IMPARTIAL CHOICES--SELECTING THE SELECT COMMITTEE
PARLIAMENTARIAN, 70(2) (APR 89), 77-82.
    THE AUTHOR DISCUSSES THE EVOLVING ROLE OF THE DEPARTMENTAL SELECT COMMITTEE OF THE BRITISH HOUSE OF COMMONS, WHICH HAS BECOME A POWERFUL INSTRUMENT FOR PARLIAMENTARY SCRUTINY OF THE EXECUTIVE. WHEN THE COMMONS AGREED IN JUNE 1979 TO ESTABLISH THESE FOURTEEN COMMITTEES, POWER WAS REMOVED FROM THE PART WHIPS. SINCE THIS TIME, THE SELECT COMMITTEES HAVE BECOME SO POWERFUL, THAT THE COMMITTEE OF SELECTION FOUND ITS ACTIVITIES BEING DEBATED ON THE FLOOR OF THE HOUSE AND IN PUBLIC AFTER THE 1983 AND 1987 ELECTIONS. THE AUTHOR DISCUSSES BIPARTISANSHIP, ALTERNATIVE DEFINITIONS OF THE COMMITTEE OF SELECTIONS' ROLE, AND POSSIBLE SCENARIOS WHICH MIGHT BE REALIZED IN ORDER TO REESTABLISH AND CREATE A BALANCE AMONG DIFFERING PARTY'S INTERESTS.

00285
    IMPORTANT ROLE OF THE CPPCC REITERATED
BEIJING REVIEW, 32(43) (OCT 89), 7.
    CHINA'S NON-COMMUNIST PARTIES ARE NOT PART OF THE GOVERNMENT NOR IN OPPOSITION TO IT BUT ARE FRIENDLY TO THE COMMUNIST PARTY AND COOPERATE WITH IT. NON-COMMUNIST PARTIES PARTICIPATE IN THE MANAGEMENT OF STATE AFFAIRS AND INVOLVE THEMSELVES IN POLICY-MAKING ON MAJOR POLITICAL AND SOCIAL ISSUES THROUGH CONSULTATION.

00286
    IN THE NAME OF "CLEAN" LEADERSHIP
CHINA NEWS ANALYSIS, (1387) (JUN 89), 1-2.
    THE AUTHOR CONDEMNS THE USE OF FORCE IN PUTTING DOWN POLITICAL DEMONSTRATIONS IN TIANANMEN SQUARE IN JUNE 1989 AND REGRETS THAT THE SLAUGHTER HAS SILENCED THE YOUNGER GENERATION OF PARTY INTELLECTUALS AND PROFESSIONALS.

00287
    IN THE SPIRIT OF THE TIMES
INFORMATION BULLETIN, 26(23-24) (DEC 88), 13-14.
    AT THE THIRD MEETING OF SOUTH AMERICAN COMMUNIST PARTIES THE PARTICIPANTS RECTERATED THEIR BELIEF THAT THE ECONOMIC REMEDIES APPLIED BY MANY GOVERNMENTS HAVE ONLY SERVED TO CONFIRM THAT THE LATIN AMERICAN FOREIGN BEBT IS UNREPAYABLE. THE PARTICIPANTS URGE THE ESTABLISHMENT OF A NEW INTERNATIONAL ECONOMIC ORDER WHICH WOULD PROVIDE FOR AN AUTHENTIC INTEGRATION AS AN ESSENTIAL PRE-CONDITION FOR INDEPENDENT ECONOMIC DEVELOPMENT OF THE REGION.

00288
    INDIA-BANGLADESH: STRUGGLE FOR DEMOCRACY
INFORMATION BULLETIN, 27 (JAN 89), 20.
    THIS ARTICLE SUMMARIZES THE RESULTS OF AN AUGUST 1988 MEETING BETWEEN DELEGATIONS FROM THE COMMUNIST PARTIES OF INDIA AND BANGLADESH. THE TWO GROUPS EXCHANGED VIEWS ON THE OUTSTANDING ISSUES BETWEEN BOTH COUNTRIES. THEY HELD THAT THE PROBLEMS BETWEEN THE TWO NATIONS SHOULD BE SOLVED IN A SPIRIT OF NEIGHBORLINESS, MUTUAL TRUST, AND UNDERSTANDING.

00289
    INDIA: FOR A LEFT - DEMOCRATIC SECULAR FRONT
INFORMATION BULLETIN, 26(19-20) (OCT 88), 14-15.
    THIS ARTICLE HIGHLIGHTS THE ISSUES DISCUSSED AND RESOLVED AT A SITTING OF THE NATURAL COUNCIL OF THE COMMUNIST PARTY OF INDIA. FOREMOST ON THE AGENDA WAS AN EVALUATION OF INDIA - USA RELATIONS, AND OF EFFORTS TO CREATE A FAVORABLE ATMOSPHERE FOR ECONOMIC AND CULTURAL RELATIONS BETWEEN THE TWO COUNTRIES.

00290
    INDIA: IN PREPARATION FOR THE CONGRESS
INFORMATION BULLETIN, 27 (MAR 89), 7-9.
    THIS IS A REPORT ON A MEETING OF THE NATIONAL COUNCIL OF THE CP INDIA ON OCTOBER 12-15, 1989. THE COUNCIL ADOPTED RESOLUTIONS ON SEVERAL ISSUES, INCLUDING COMMUNAL PROBLEMS, POSITIVE TRENDS IN INTERNATIONAL RELATIONS, INDIA'S RELATIONS WITH HER NEIGHBORS, THE NEED TO SUPPORT PERESTROIKA, AND DEVELOPMENTS IN INDIA'S BOURGEOIS OPPOSITION PARTIES.

00291
    INDIAN RIGHTS IN THE NEW BRAZILIAN CONSTITUTION

CULTURAL SURVIVAL QUARTERLY, 13(1) (1989), 6-12.
    IN JUNE 1988, BRAZIL'S NATIONAL CONSTITUENT ASSEMBLY VOTED TO ACCEPT THE CHAPTER OF THE NEW BRAZILIAN CONSTITUTION REFERRING TO THE INDIANS. THIS CHAPTER COMPLEMENTS OTHER ISOLATED DISPOSITIONS VOTED ON EARLIER. ALTHOUGH THE ASSEMBLY DID NOT ADOPT THE PROPOSALS SUBMITTED BY THE UNION OF INDIAN NATIONS AND SEVERAL HUMAN RIGHTS ORGANIZATIONS, THE VOTE WAS A GREAT VICTORY BECAUSE THE NEW CONSTITUTION CONTAINS FUNDAMENTAL GUARANTEES FOR THE INDIGENOUS PEOPLE OF BRAZIL.

00292
    INDO-CHINESE REFUGEES: INTERNATIONAL CONFERENCE
SURVEY OF CURRENT AFFAIRS, 19(7) (JUL 89), 265-267.
    THE NEED FOR VIETNAM TO STEM THE OUTFLOW OF ITS POPULATION AND TO EASE THE BURDEN ON AREAS OF FIRST ASYLUM LIKE HONG KONG HAS EMPHASISED BY THE FOREIGN AND COMMONWEALTH SECRETARY, SIR GEOFFREY HOWE, IN A SPEECH TO THE INTERNATIONAL CONFERENCE ON INDO-CHINESE REFUGEES IN GENEVA ON 13 JUNE 1989.

00293
    INDOCHINESE REFUGEES CONFERENCE HELD IN GENEVA
DEPARTMENT OF STATE BULLETIN (US FOREIGN POLICY), 89(2151) (OCT 89), 69-73.
    AN INTERNATIONAL CONFERENCE ON INDOCHINESE REFUGEES WAS HELD IN GENEVA IN JUNE 1989. THIS REPORT ON THE MEETING INCLUDES A STATEMENT BY THE UNITED STATES' DEPUTY SECRETARY OF STATE, LAWRENCE S. EAGLEBURGER, AND THE TEXTS OF THE DRAFT DECLARATION AND COMPREHENSIVE PLAN OF ACTION ADOPTED AT THE CONFERENCE.

00294
    INDUSTRIAL RELATIONS
SURVEY OF CURRENT AFFAIRS, 19(4) (APR 89), 151-152.
    GOVERNMENT PROPOSALS FOR FURTHER REFORMS IN INDUSTRIAL RELATIONS, INCLUDING MEASURES ON THE PRE-ENTRY CLOSED SHOP, WERE SET OUT IN A GREEN PAPER PUBLISHED ON 20 MARCH 1989. THE GREEN PAPER SAYS THAT THE GOVERNMENT HAS GIVEN HIGH PRIORITY TO A PROGRAMME OF STEP-BY-STEP REFORM OF INDUSTRIAL RELATIONS AND TRADE UNION LAW, A MAJOR PURPOSE OF WHICH HAS BEEN TO REMOVE UNNECESSARY BARRIERS TO JOBS. THE REMOVAL OF BARRIERS TO ECONOMIC EFFICIENCY HAS MADE AN IMPORTANT CONTRIBUTION TO THE IMPROVEMENT IN EMPLOYMENT, WITH A SUBSTANTIAL INCREASE IN THE WORKFORCE IN EMPLOYMENT AND A CONSIDERABLE DECLINE IN UNEMPLOYMENT. HOWEVER, IT IS ESSENTIAL TO CONTINUE THE SEARCH FOR GREATER FLEXIBILITY AND TO EXAMINE OBSTACLES TO THE GROWTH OF JOBS WHICH STILL REMAIN, AND THE GOVERNMENT HAS TO ENSURE THAT THE LEGAL FRAMEWORK FOR INDUSTRIAL RELATIONS IS ADAPTED TO THE NEEDS OF THE 1990S.

00295
    INDUSTRIAL RESEARCH AND DEVELOPMENT
SURVEY OF CURRENT AFFAIRS, 19(6) (JUN 89), 236-237.
    IN A SPEECH ON 9 MAY 1989 THE PARLIAMENTARY UNDERSECRETARY OF STATE FOR INDUSTRY AND CONSUMER AFFAIRS, ERIC FORTH, ENCOURAGED BRITISH COMPANIES TO DEVOTE MORE RESOURCES TO RESEARCH AND DEVELOPMENT. HE OUTLINED GOVERNMENT POLICY ON THE SUPPORT OF INDUSTRIAL RESEARCH AND STRESSED THE IMPORTANCE OF THE APPROACHING SINGLE EUROPEAN MARKET.

00296
    INFORMATION TECHNOLOGY POLICY
SURVEY OF CURRENT AFFAIRS, 19(4) (APR 89), 153-156.
    THE BRITISH GOVERNMENT HAS PUBLISHED A WHITE PAPER IN REPLY TO THE HOUSE OF COMMONS TRADE AND INDUSTRY SELECT COMMITTEE'S REPORT ON INFORMATION TECHNOLOGY, WHICH ARGUED THAT THE THATCHER GOVERNMENT HAD NO STRATEGY FOR INFORMATION TECHNOLOGY AND HAD FAILED TO COORDINATE THE VARIOUS ASPECTS OF THE FIELD. THE WHITE PAPER OUTLINES THE GOVERNMENT'S FIVE MAJOR POLICY OBJECTIVES REGARDING INFORMATION TECHNOLOGY.

00297
    INTENSIFICATION OF PARTY CONSOLIDATION URGED
BEIJING REVIEW, 32(36) (SEP 89), 9-10.
    AT A NATIONAL MEETING ATTENDED BY DIRECTORS OF VARIOUS ORGANIZATIONAL DEPARTMENTS OF THE CHINESE COMMUNIST PARTY, GENERAL SECRETARY JIANG ZEMIN CALLED ON LOCAL PARTY COMMITTEES AT ALL LEVELS TO CONCENTRATE THEIR ATTENTION ON STRENGTHENING PARTY BUILDING. HE REITERATED THE NECESSITY TO PUNISH THE CORRUPT WITHIN THE PARTY.

00298
    INTERETHNIC RELATIONS IN THE USSR
INTERNATIONAL AFFAIRS (MOSCOW), (11) (NOV 89), 74-78.
    THE AUTHOR LOOKS AT HOW THE CONCEPTS OF "INTERNATIONAL" AND "INTERETHNIC" HAVE BEEN INTERPRETED IN SOVIET NATIONAL LIFE. HE ALSO CONSIDERS THE PAST AND PRESENT STATE OF INTERETHNIC RELATIONS IN THE SOVIET UNION.

00299
    INTERNATIONAL CONFERENCE ON CAMBODIA HELD IN PARIS

DEPARTMENT OF STATE BULLETIN (US FOREIGN POLICY), 89(2151)
(OCT 89), 25-26.
    AN INTERNATIONAL CONFERENCE ON CAMBODIA WAS HELD IN
PARIS IN JULY AND AUGUST 1989. THIS REPORT ON THE CONFERENCE
INCLUDES A STATEMENT PREPARED FOR DELIVERY BY SECRETARY OF
STATE JAMES BAKER AND THE TEST OF THE STATEMENT ISSUED AT
THE CONCLUSION OF THE CONFERENCE.

00300
    INTERNATIONAL ENERGY AGENCY MINISTERS MEET IN PARIS
DEPARTMENT OF STATE BULLETIN (US FOREIGN POLICY), 89(2150)
(SEP 89), 83-86.
    THE INTERNATIONAL ENERGY AGENCY (IEA) MET IN MINISTERIAL
SESSION IN PARIS IN MAY 1989. THE MINISTERS CALLED ATTENTION
TO TWO ASPECTS OF THE CURRENT ENERGY SITUATION THAT ARE
CAUSE FOR DEEP CONCERN: GROWING WORLDWIDE OIL CONSUMPTION
AND THE ENVIRONMENTAL IMPACT OF ENERGY SUPPLY AND
CONSUMPTION. THE MINISTERS ENDORSED POLICIES TO DEAL WITH
THE CHALLENGES THESE ENERGY CONCERNS WILL GENERATE IN THE
FUTURE.

00301
    INTERNATIONAL SIGNIFICANCE OF PERESTROIKA IN THE USSR
INFORMATION BULLETIN, 26(21-22) (NOV 88), 13-14.
    THE COMMUNIST PARTY OF URUGUAY BELIEVES THAT THE
PROCESSES IN COMMUNIST MOVEMENT SHOULD BE REGARDED IN THE
LIGHT OF THE PERESTROIKA. WHAT IS BEING DONE IN THE USSR HAS
WORLD-WIDE REPERCUSSIONS. APPLYING THIS PROCESS TO THE
URUGUYAN MOVEMENT, ONE HAS TO REACH THE CONCLUSION THAT THE
CLIMATE OF VIGOR AND RENEWAL BEING ASSERTED IN THE SOCIALIST
CAMP AND RESONATING THROUGHOUT THE WORLD IS IN ACCORD WITH
THE INTERNATIONAL COMMUNIST MOVEMENT, NOTABLY, THE LATIN
AMERICAN MOVEMENT. THE CPSU HAS DECLARED THAT THERE IS NO
LEADER-PARTY, THERE IS NO HEGEMONY, BUT THERE SHOULD BE NO
GLORIFICATION OR SELF-ISOLATION OF EACH PARTY.

00302
    INTERNATIONAL SOLIDARITY WITH PRISONERS
EAST EUROPEAN REPORTER, 3(4) (SPR 89), 72-73.
    ALTHOUGH NOT AS NEWSWORTHY AS IN PREVIOUS YEARS,
MOVEMENTS AIMING TO ENCOURAGE THE RELEASE OF POLITICAL
PRISONERS IN EASTERN EUROPE ARE STILL ACTIVE. THE ARTICLE
INCLUDES SEVERAL LETTERS SENT BY REPRESENTATIVES OF SUCH
MOVEMENTS TO AUTHORITIES IN CZECHOSLOVAKIA AND HUNGARY. THE
LETTERS DEMAND THE RELEASE OF SUCH FIGURES AS PLAYWRIGHT
VACLAV JAVEL, EDITOR, FRANTISEK STAREK, AND ACTIVIST PETR
CIBULKA.

00303
    INTERVIEW WITH PARTY PRESIDIUM
WORLD AFFAIRS, 151(4) (1989), 192-202.
    THE ARTICLE IS AN INTERVIEW WITH THE NEWLY CREATED
HUNGARIAN SOCIALIST WORKERS PARTY PRESIDIUM. THE FOUR-MEMBER
ORGANIZATION IS COMPOSED PRIMARILY OF WELL-KNOWN REFORMERS.
THEY DISCUSS THE ROLE AND STRUCTURE OF THE PRESIDIUM AND THE
FUTURE COURSE OF HUNGARY'S POLITICAL AND ECONOMIC SYSTEM.
THEY DECLARE THAT ALTHOUGH THERE IS DISAGREEMENT OVER
SPECIFIC REFORMS, THE PRESIDIUM IS IN AGREEMENT ON THE
FUNDAMENTAL ISSUES AND IN THEIR DESIRE FOR DEMOCRATIC
SOCIALISM.

00304
    IRAN AND THE GULF ARABS
MIDDLE EAST REPORT, 19(156) (JAN 89), 23-24.
    WITHIN WEEKS OF IRAN'S ACCEPTANCE OF A CEASEFIRE,
PERCEPTIONS OF THE TEHERAN REGIME ON THE ARAB SIDE OF THE
GULF UNDERWENT A RADICAL TRANSFORMATION. GOVERNMENTS IN
KUWAIT, RIYADH, AND BAHRAIN PLEDGED TO FORGET PAST CLASHES,
RESTORE FULL DIPLOMATIC TIES, AND LAUNCH A NEW ERA OF
POLITICAL COOPERATION. BUT MANY SHI'I SYMPATHIZERS SAW THE
FINAL COLLAPSE OF A REVOLUTIONARY IDEAL, THE DEFEAT OF A NEW
PATRON, AND THE ECLIPSE OF A BEACON.

00305
    IRAN: STOP BARBARIC REPRESSION OF POLITICAL PRISONERS
INFORMATION BULLETIN, 26(19-20) (OCT 88), 29.
    IN THIS STATEMENT THE TUDEH PARTY OF IRAN DENOUNCES THE
EXECUTION BY IRANIAN AUTHORITIES OF FOUR IRANIAN POLITICAL
PRISONERS. THE PARTY LAUNCHES AN URGENT APPEAL TO CONDEMN
THIS CRIMINAL ACT AND OTHER PERSECUTIONS OF POLITICAL
PRISONERS IN IRAN.

00306
    IRAN: STOP THE EXECUTIONS, SAVE THE POLITICAL PRISONERS
INFORMATION BULLETIN, 27(3-4) (FEB 89), 20.
    THIS PRESS RELEASE OF THE CENTRAL COMMITTEE OF THE TUDEH
PARTY OF IRAN INCLUDES A PARTIAL LIST OF PARTY MEMBERS WHO
HAVE FALLEN VICTIM TO THE IRANIAN REGIME'S "CLEARING - UP"
OPERATION IN THE PRISONS. THE TUDEH PARTY OF IRAN CALLS ON
ALL INDIVIDUALS, INSTITUTIONS, AND POLITICAL ORGANIZATION TO
LAUNCH A MASS CAMPAIGN IN PROTEST AGAINST IRANIAN DISREGARD
FOR HUMAN RIGHTS.

00307
    IRAN: THE BLOODY WAR MUST NOT BECOME A BLOODY PEACE
INFORMATION BULLETIN, 26(23-24) (DEC 88), 21-22.
    THIS STATEMENT BY THE TUDEH PARTY OF IRAN CHARACTERIZES
THE POLICIES OF THE IRANIAN AND IRAQI REGIMES AS POLICIES OF
REPRESSIONS, PERSECUTION, AND EXECUTION. THE STATEMENT
DESCRIBES AND OFFERS EXAMPLES OF THE ATROCIOUS CRIMES BEING
PERPETRATED AGAINST POLITICAL PRISONERS AND OPPOSITION
PARTIES.

00308
    IRANIAN VISIT BOOSTS TIES
BEIJING REVIEW, 32(21) (MAY 89), 11.
    CHINESE LEADER DENG XIAOPING HAS CALLED ON THIRD WORLD
COUNTRIES TO TAKE ADVANTAGE OF THE CURRENT RELAXED WORLD
SITUATION TO STIMULATE ECONOMIC DEVELOPMENT. DENG SAID THAT
THIRD WORLD COUNTRIES SHOULD UNITE AND REFRAIN FROM WASTING
THEIR RESOURCES ON DISPUTES. IN TALKS WITH IRANIAN LEADERS
IN MAY 1989, DENG AND CHINESE PRESIDENT YANG SHANGKUN
EXPRESSED THE HOPE THAT IRAN AND IRAQ WOULD FULLY COMPLY
WITH RESOLUTION 598 OF THE UNITED NATIONS SECURITY COUNCIL.
DENG ALSO EXPRESSED HOPES FOR GREATER STABILITY AND PEACE IN
THE MIDDLE EAST IN GENERAL.

00309
    ISRAEL, THE WEST BANK, AND GAZA: TOWARD A SOLUTION
NEW OUTLOOK, 32(5 (291)) (MAY 89), 38-43.
    THIS ARTICLE REPRINTS A BOOKLET PUBLISHED BY TEL AVIV
UNIVERSITY'S JAFFEE CENTER FOR STRATEGIC STUDIES. IT
INCLUDES A SUMMARY OF ISRAEL'S OPTIONS FOR PEACE, A
DESCRIPTION OF THE STATUS QUO, A DISCUSSION OF AUTONOMY IN
THE OCCUPIED TERRITORIES, AND RELATED MATERIAL. IT ALSO
PRESENTS IDEAS DEVELOPED BY THE JAFFEE CENTER EXPERTS FOR
MOVING ISRAEL AND THE PALESTINIANS TOWARD A SOLUTION THAT
DOES NOT NEGATE THE POSSIBILITY OF A PALESTINIAN STATE BUT
DOES NOT COMMIT ISRAEL TO THAT IN ADVANCE.

00310
    ISRAELI ELECTIONS: OPTICAL ILLUSION
MIDDLE EAST INTERNATIONAL, (346) (MAR 89), 11-13.
    THE LIKUD'S SUCCESS IN THE FEBRUARY 1989 ELECTIONS DID
NOT EXPAND ITS ACHIEVEMENTS IN THE NOVEMBER 1988 GENERAL
ELECTION. AT MOST, THE FEBRUARY RESULTS MERELY CONFIRMED
THAT THE LIKUD ENJOYS THE ALLEGIANCE OF ONE-THIRD OF THE
ELECTORATE. EVEN THOUGH THE LIKUD'S TRIUMPH WAS SOMETHING OF
AN OPTICAL ILLUSION, THAT DID NOT SOFTEN THE BLOW TO LABOUR,
AND THERE WERE RENEWED CALLS FOR A LEADERSHIP SHAKE-UP IN
THE LABOUR PARTY.

00311
    IT'S TIME FOR REHABILITATION
GLASNOST, II(2) (MAR 89), 57-58.
    THE SOVIET GOVERNMENT IS ADOPTING MERE HALF-MEASURES.
THE RESULT IS AN OBLIQUE EXONERATION OF ARBITRARY RULE
COMBINED WITH A SEMI-EXONERATION OF ITS VICTIMS. THE PEOPLE
ARE DEMANDING JUSTICE, WHICH MEANS THE UNCONDITIONAL
RESTORATION OF ALL RIGHTS. WHAT'S NEEDED IS BASIC LAW. BUT
THERE IS NONE. THE BUREAUCRACY FUNCTIONS AS BEFORE, WITH THE
SAME PEOPLE AND THE SAME TABLES OF ORGANIZATION CONSTITUTING
A CEMENT WEIGHT ON THE BACK OF SOCIETY.

00312
    JAPAN AS A CHALLENGE ON THE WORLD MARKET
AUSTRIA TODAY, (4) (1989), 23.
    DURING 1988, AUSTRIAN EXPORTS TO JAPAN INCREASED BY 25
PERCENT WHILE JAPANESE EXPORTS TO AUSTRIA GREW BY 29 PERCENT.
THE GAP IN THE TRADE DEFICIT BETWEEN AUSTRIA AND JAPAN
WIDENED STILL FURTHER DURING THE FIRST FIVE MONTHS OF 1989.
AN OFFICIAL VISIT BY THE AUSTRIAN FEDERAL CHANCELLOR TO
JAPAN IN OCTOBER 1989 PROVIDED A NUMBER OF POSITIVE IMPULSES
BETWEEN THE TWO GOVERNMENT, BECAUSE THE POLITICAL TALKS WERE
FOLLOWED BY INTENSIVE ECONOMIC DISCUSSIONS. THE JAPANESE
SHOWED CONSIDERABLE INTEREST IN AUSTRIA'S INTERNATIONAL
ECONOMIC POSITION, WITH SPECIAL REFERENCE TO HER RELATIONS
WITH THE EUROPEAN COMMUNITY AND WITH EASTERN EUROPE.

00313
    JIANG REITERATES PARTY'S POLICIES
BEIJING REVIEW, 32(28) (JUL 89), 7, 9.
    JIANG ZEMIN, THE NEWLY-ELECTED PARTY GENERAL SECRETARY,
GAVE A TALK ON QUESTIONS OF POPULAR CONCERN AT A JUNE 1989
FORUM ATTENDED BY LEADERS OF CHINA'S DEMOCRATIC PARTIES AND
NON-PARTY FIGURES. HE REITERATED THAT CHINA'S OVERALL POLICY
OF REFORM AND OPENING TO THE OUTSIDE WORLD WOULD NEVER
CHANGE. HE SAID THAT LEADERS AT ALL LEVELS MUST CONCENTRATE
ON ECONOMIC CONSTRUCTION WHILE CONTINUING TO QUELL THE
COUNTER-REVOLUTIONARY REBELLION AND STABILIZING THE
SITUATION.

00314
    JOINT SOVIET - JAPANESE COMMUNIQUE
REPRINTS FROM THE SOVIET PRESS, 48(3) (FEB 89), 23-27.
    PROCEEDING FROM THE RESULT OF THE EARLIER HELD 11TH
MEETING OF THE SOVIET-JAPANESE AND JAPANESE-SOVIET

COMMITTEES FOR ECONOMIC COOPERATION AND OF THE SOVIET-JAPANESE INTERGOVERNMENTAL CONSULTATIONS ON COMMERCIAL AND ECONOMIC PROBLEMS, THE MINISTERS OF THESE TWO COUNTRIES AT A RECENT VISIT BY EDWARD SHEVARDNAZE TO JAPAN EXPRESSED READINESS TO GO ON PROMOTING THE EXPANSION OF COMMERCIAL AND ECONOMIC RELATIONS BETWEEN THE USSR AND JAPAN ON THE BASIS OF MUTUAL BENEFIT AND WITH DUE REGARD FOR THE ECONOMIC REFORM IN THE SOVIET UNION AND FOR STRUCTURAL CHANGES IN JAPANESE ECONOMY.

00315
    JOINT SOVIET-AMERICAN STATEMENT ON CHEMICAL WEAPONS
    REPRINTS FROM THE SOVIET PRESS, 49(11/12) (DEC 89), 13-14.
    DURING A MEETING IN WYOMING, SEPEMBER 22-23 SOVIET FOREIGN MINISTER SHEVARDNADZE AND U.S. SECRETARY BAKER REAFFIRMED THE TWO COUNTRIES DETERMINATION TO STRIVE FOR THE PROHIBITION OF CHEMICAL WEAPONS AND THE DESTRUCTION OF ALL THEIR STOCKPILES ON THE BASIS OF A COMPREHENSIVE, EFFECTIVELY, VERIFIABLE AND TRULY GLOBAL PLAN. THIS REPORT DETAILS VERIFICATION TESTS AND DATA EXCHANGE PLANS, PROCEDURES FOR CONDUCTING CHALLENGE INSPECTIONS, AND WELCOMES AUSTRALIA'S CONVOCATION HELD ON THE SAME SUBJECT.

00316
    JOINT USSR-FRG STATEMENT
    REPRINTS FROM THE SOVIET PRESS, 49(4) (AUG 89), 50-54.
    THIS IS A REPORT ON NEW POLITICAL THINKING BY THE USSR AND THE FRG FOR THE FUTURE. IT CONCERNS HUMAN RIGHTS, PEACE, NUCLEAR AND CONVENTIONAL WAR, INTERNATIONAL LAW, COOPERATION IN ALL FIELDS. THE ENVIRONMENT, POVERTY, TERRORISM AND EPIDEMICS. THIS NEW POLICY WILL HEAL THE WOUNDS OF THE PAST WITH UNDERSTANDING AND RECONCILIATION AND WILL HELP BUILD A BETTER FUTURE TOGETHER.

00317
    JORDAN: A FRANK AND DEMOCRATIC DIALOGUE NECESSARY
    INFORMATION BULLETIN, 26(23-24) (DEC 88), 22-23.
    THIS STATEMENT BY THE JORDANIAN COMMUNIST PARTY URGES DISSOLUTION OF THE OLD JORDANIAN PARLIAMENT, WITH ITS TARNISHED REPUTATION; REPEAL OF THE PRESENT REACTIONARY ELECTROAL LAW; AND, THE ADOPTION OF A NEW DEMOCRATIC LAW WITH SUBSEQUENT ELECTIONS TO THE NATIONAL ASSEMBLY FREE OF DISCRIMINATION IN THE ELECTION AND NOMINATION PROCESS.

00318
    JOURNALS OF THE LEAGUE OF COMMUNISTS OF YUGOSLAVIA
    YUGOSLAV SURVEY, XXX(1) (1989), 123-130.
    THE SOCIAL RESEARCH CENTER OF THE LEAGUE OF COMMUNISTS OF YUGOSLAVIA CENTRAL COMMITTEE ORGANIZED A STUDY OF THE LEAGUE'S JOURNALS. THE RESEARCHERS STUDIED FIFTEEN JOURNALS. THEIR GOALS WERE TO GAIN INSIGHT INTO THE POSITION OF THE LEAGUE'S JOURNALS, THEIR CONCEPT, THE ORIENTATION OF THEIR SUBJECT MATTER, THE AUTHORS, AND THE EDITORS.

00319
    JUDICIAL ACTIVISTS HAVE EXPANDED FIRST AMENDMENT RIGHTS TOO FAR, SAYS BORK
    CHURCH AND STATE, 42(1) (JAN 89), 13-14.
    ACCORDING TO ROBERT H. BORK, LIBERAL THINKING IN THE COURT SYSTEM HAS LED FEDERAL JUDGES TO EXPAND THE INTERPRETATION OF THE FIRST AMENDMENT, BRINGING ITS RELIGIOUS CLAUSES INTO CONFLICT WITH ONE ANOTHER. HE STATED THAT BECAUSE OF THIS, RELIGIOUS GROUPS CANNOT RECEIVE NON-PREFERENTIAL AID FROM THE GOVERNMENT AND CHURCHES ARE NOT ALLOWED TO DISPLAY SECTARIAN SYMBOLS IN PUBLIC.

00320
    KAMPUCHEA'S PROBLEMS ARE CLOSE TO RESOLUTION
    REPRINTS FROM THE SOVIET PRESS, 48(11-12) (JUN 89), 43-47.
    THE COUNTRIES WHICH PARTICIPATED IN THE JAKARTA MEETING HAVE ASSUMED AN OBLIGATION NOT TO RENDER MILITARY AID TO THE KAMPUCHEAN SIDES IMMEDIATELY FOLLOWING THE WITHDRAWAL OF THE VIETNAMESE TROOPS. THESE OBLIGATIONS FORM A RELIABLE BASIS FOR SETTLEMENT. ANY VIOLATIONS OF THEM WOULD AGGRAVATE THE SITUATION, CREATE CONDITIONS FOR RETURN OF THE POL POT GENOCIDE REGIME TO KAMPUCHEA, CAUSE A NEW CIVIL WAR, AND ENCROACH ON KAMPUCHEA'S SOVEREIGNTY AND ON THE PEACEFUL LIFE OF THE KAMPUCHEAN PEOPLE.

00321
    KAUNDA'S REVENGE
    NEW AFRICAN, (OCT 89), 19-20.
    THIS ARTICLE REPORTS ON THE CURRENT SITUATION IN ZAMBIA. IT ADDRESSES THE ECONOMIC WOES OF THE COUNTRY AND DESCRIBES PROCEDURES BY THE ZAMBIAN GOVERNMENT WHICH HAVE PERSECUTED JUNIOR DOCTORS WHILE AT THE SAME TIME GOVERNMENT LEADERS HAVE ENRICHED THEMSELVES.

00322
    KENYA TAPS A WEALTH OF PARLIAMENTARY EXPERIENCE
    PARLIAMENTARIAN, 70(3) (JUL 89), 162-164.
    THE AUTHOR EXAMINES THE LONG TRADITION WITHIN THE KENYAN NATIONAL ASSEMBLY OF PLACING EXPERIENCED PARLIAMENTARY VETERANS IN KEY HOUSE POSITIONS, WHICH WAS UPHELD IN THE MARCH 1988 GENERAL ELECTIONS WHEN VACANCIES IN THE SPEAKERSHIP OF THE HOUSE WERE DECIDED UPON. THE ROLE OF THE SPEAKER IS HIGHLIGHTED. WITH LEADERSHIP CHANGES WHICH OCCURRED SINCE 1970 EXAMINED.

00323
    KENYA: A COFFIN FULL OF DRUGS
    NEW AFRICAN, (269) (DEC 89), 14-15.
    DRUG SMUGGLERS IN KENYA ARE ROBBING THE GOVERNMENT IN LARGE QUANTITIES. MOST OF THE DRUGS ARE STOLEN FROM KENYAN HOSPITALS AND ARE SOLD ON THE STREETS OF THE COUNTRY. IT IS A THRIVING BUSINESS AND THE OPERATORS FIND IT WELL WORTH TAKING THE RISK. THE SITUATION IS THAT MOST GOVERNMENT HOSPITALS GO WITHOUT ESSENTIAL DRUGS AND GAUZE, THESE ARE READILY AVAILABLE ON THE STREETS AND IN PRIVATE HOSPITALS.

00324
    KENYA: THE ROLE OF WOMEN IN ECONOMIC DEVELOPMENT
    AVAILABLE FROM NTIS, NO. PB89-209522/GAR, 1989, 198.
    SINCE INDEPENDENCE IN 1963, KENYA HAS BEEN WORKING TO MAKE WOMEN ACTIVE PARTNERS IN THE DEVELOPMENT OF ITS ECONOMY. IT HAS INTEGRATED WOMEN INTO THE DEVELOPMENT PROCESS BY CAREFUL DESIGN OF MAINSTREAM PROGRAMS, RATHER THAN BY INSTITUTING SEPARATE PROGRAMS FOR WOMEN, THUS BENEFITING WOMEN ALONG WITH THE ENTIRE POPULATION. ITS EFFORTS TO ASSIST WOMEN CONSTITUTE AN INTEGRAL ASPECT FOR THE OVERALL POLICY FRAMEWORK. THE REPORT CONCERNS WOMEN IN KENYA GENERALLY, BUT IT FOCUSES ESPECIALLY ON RURAL WOMEN IN FOUR SECTORS: AGRICULTURE, EDUCATION, HEALTH, AND WATER. IT ASSESSES WOMEN'S CONTRIBUTIONS, ANALYZES PROMISING APPROACHES, AND SUGGESTS WAYS TO EXTEND KENYAN EFFORTS TO INCLUDE WOMEN IN DEVELOPMENT. IN SO DOING, IT IS MEANT TO CONTRIBUTE TO THE INTERNATIONAL ANALYTIC BASE FOR POLICY AND PROGRAM PLANNING AND TO PROVIDE FOOD FOR THOUGHT ON PRACTICAL APPROACHES.

00325
    KILOWATTS FOR THE NEXT CENTURY
    CHINA NEWS ANALYSIS, (1378) (FEB 89), 1-10.
    ELECTRICITY SHORTAGES ARE UNIVERSAL IN CHINA, WHERE INDUSTRIES FUNCTION WELL BELOW THEIR MAXIMUM CAPACITY DUE TO LACK OF POWER. ELECTRICITY IS THE TOP PRIORITY OF THE NEW MINISTRY OF ENERGY, WHICH WAS ESTABLISHED IN 1988. AT THE NATIONAL LEVEL, CONFIDENCE IN CHINA'S COAL, OIL, AND HYDROELECTRIC RESOURCES HAS WANTED. SOME EXPERTS ARGUE THAT NUCLEAR GENERATION IS AN URGENT NECESSITY TO SATISFY BOTH SHORT- AND LONG-TERM NEEDS.

00326
    KOLO'S CONVERSION
    NEW AFRICAN, (266) (NOV 89), 22.
    THIS ARTICLE REPORTS ON THE REASONS FOR MAJOR OKELLO KOLO, FORMER MEMBER OF THE NATIONAL RESISTANCE COUNCIL AND THE NRA HIGH COMMAND, DEFECTION IN 1988, IT EXPLORES DETAILED EVIDENCE OF GENOCIDE IN GULU, KITGUM, LIRA, AND APEC.

00327
    LABOUR'S CONSTITUTIONAL REFORM PROPOSALS
    CONSTITUTIONAL REFORM QUARTERLY REVIEW, 4(2) (SUM 89), 3.
    THE ARTICLE EXAMINES THE CONSTITUTIONAL REFORMS PROPOSED BY BRITAIN'S LABOUR PARTY. THEY INCLUDE: REFORM OF PARLIAMENT, THE CREATION OF REGIONAL AND NATIONAL ASSEMBLIES, FREEDOM OF INFORMATION LEGISLATION, AND SCRUTINY OF THE SECURITY SERVICES, THE PARTY DISMISSES THE IDEA OF AN INTRODUCTION OF A BILL OF RIGHTS.

00328
    LAND POLICY
    YUGOSLAV SURVEY, XXX(1) (1989), 79-92.
    LAND POLICY IS A CENTRAL FACTOR IN SOLVING THE AGRARIAN QUESTION IN YUGOSLAVIA. SOCIO-ECONOMIC RELATIONS IN AGRICULTURE ARE STRONGLY REFLECTED IN THE LEGAL PROVISIONS AND OTHER MEASURES GOVERNING LAND MANAGEMENT. DUE TO THE OWNERSHIP STRUCTURE OF YUGOSLAVIAN AGRICULTURE AND THE ABANDONMENT OF THE STALINIST MODEL OF COLLECTIVIZATION, LAND POLICY CONSTITUTES A VERY INTRICATE SOCIO-ECONOMIC, SOCIAL, AND POLITICAL ISSUE.

00329
    LANGUAGE RIGHTS ON THE NICARAGUAN ATLANTIC COAST
    CULTURAL SURVIVAL QUARTERLY, 13(3) (1989), 7-10.
    THE EDUCATIONAL AND RESEARCH PROGRAMS INVOLVING FOUR INDIGENOUS LANGUAGES IN NICARAGUA ARE DUE IN LARGE MEASURE TO A CONSTRUCTIVE, EXEMPLARY STRUGGLE TO RESOLVE AN IMPORTANT AND COMPLEX CONTRADICTION INHERENT IN THE BUILDING OF A REVOLUTIONARY SOCIETY DEVOTED TO BRINGING JUSTICE TO THE PEOPLE OF AN ETHNICALLY DIVERSE NATION. THE CONTRADICTION OCCURS WHEN THE INTERESTS OF THE NATION AND THE INTERESTS OF LOCAL ETHNIC COMMUNITIES CONFLICT. THE INSTRUMENT THAT HAS RESULTED FROM THIS CONFLICT IS THE AUTONOMY PROJECT, A MODEL OF POLITICAL CONSTRUCTION BUILT BY THOSE PARTICIPATING IN THE PROCESS OF STRUGGLE. THE AUTONOMY PROJECT AFFECTS VIRTUALLY EVERY ASPECT OF THE LIVES OF THE

PEOPLES OF THE ATLANTIC COAST, INCLUDING EDUCATION, LAND RIGHTS, HEALTH, SUBSISTENCE, AND LANGUAGE.

00330
LAOTIAN LEADER VISITS CHINA
BEIJING REVIEW, 32(42) (OCT 89), 11-12.
ON OCTOBER 7, 1989, DENG XIAOPING STATED THAT CHINA WOULD AGREE TO A PROPOSAL FROM VIETNAM FOR A NORMALIZATION OF RELATIONS ON THE CONDITION THAT VIETNAM WITHDRAW ALL ITS TROOPS FROM KAMPUCHEA. DENG POINTED OUT THAT CHINA HAS NORMALIZED ITS RELATIONS WITH THE SOVIET UNION AND IMPROVED ITS RELATIONS WITH LAOS, LEAVING ONLY VIETNAM.

00331
LEADERSHIP FOR AMERICA: REBUILDING THE PUBLIC SERVICE
AVAILABLE FROM NTIS, NO. PB89-180368/GAR, 1989, 72.
THE NATIONAL COMMISSION ON THE PUBLIC SERVICE WAS FORMED IN 1987 WITH AN AGENDA TO EXPLORE WHAT WAS VIEWED AS A QUIET CRISIS IN GOVERNMENT. TOO MANY OF THE BEST OF THE NATION'S SENIOR EXECUTIVES ARE READY TO LEAVE GOVERNMENT AND NOT ENOUGH OF ITS MOST TALENTED YOUNG PEOPLE ARE WILLING TO JOIN. IT WAS THE COMMISSION'S TASK TO MAKE RECOMMENDATIONS THAT WOULD RESULT IN THE REBUILDING OF AN EFFECTIVE, PRINCIPLED, AND ENERGETIC PUBLIC SERVICE. ALTHOUGH THE COMMISSION CONCENTRATED ON THE QUALITY AND PERFORMANCE AT THE SENIOR ADMINISTRATIVE AND PROFESSIONAL LEVELS OF THE FEDERAL GOVERNMENT, A NUMBER OF ITS BROAD RECOMMENDATIONS ARE ALSO RELEVANT FOR OTHER PARTS AND LEVELS OF GOVERNMENT.

00332
LEADING ROLE OF WORKING CLASS REAFFIRMED
BEIJING REVIEW, 32(32) (AUG 89), 11-12.
THE COMMUNIST PARTY IS THE VANGUARD OF THE WORKING CLASS AND THE TRADE UNIONS ARE A MASS ORGANIZATION OF THE WORKERS. THEREFORE, TRADE UNIONS MUST CONDUCT THEIR ACTIVITIES UNDER THE LEADERSHIP OF THE COMMUNIST PARTY AND ALSO WORK INDEPENDENTLY ACCORDING TO THEIR CONSITUTIONS. THE TRADE UNIONS SHOULD BECOME A COMMUNIST UNIVERSITY FOR THE MASSES OF WORKERS TO CONDUCT IDEOLOGICAL EDUCATION TO STRIVE FOR THE PROMOTION OF SOCIALIST AND PATRIOTIC EDUCATION AND TO MAKE ARDUOUS EFFORTS COMBAT THE INFLUENCE OF BOURGEOIS LIBERALIZATION.

00333
LEBANON: RESTORE THE COUNTRY'S UNITY
INFORMATION BULLETIN, 26(23-24) (DEC 88), 24-25.
THE LEBANESE COMMUNIST PARTY CALLS FOR THE ORGANIZATION OF A LEBANESE MOVEMENT FOR UNITY AND LIBERATION. WITHIN THIS MOVEMENT ALL THE FORCES WOULD UNITE WHICH ARE ANXIOUS TO FIGHT STEADFASTLY FOR THE UNIFICATION OF LEBANON, FOR ITS LIBERATION FROM THE FASCIST RULE AND ISRAELI AGGRESSION. WITHIN THIS MOVEMENT A POLITICAL, DEMOCRATIC AND INFORMATIONAL ACTIVITY, DIVERSE FORMS OF POPULAR AND TRADE UNION ACTIONS WOULD BE ORGANIZED WHICH WOULD MERGE INTO THE MAINSTREAM OF STRUGGLE FOR UNITY AND LIBERATION. WITHIN THIS MOVEMENT MILITARY UNDERTAKINGS OF LIBERATION STRUGGLE, MEASURES TO COUNTERACT THE FASCIST REPRESSION, THE MILITARY DICTATORSHIP AND THE PLANS FOR RESUMING THE CIVIL WAR WOULD BE PREPARED AND CARRIED OUT.

00334
LEBANON: THE THREAT OF DISMEMBERMENT
INFORMATION BULLETIN, 27 (JAN 89), 25-26.
THIS IS A REPORT OF A PRESS CONFERENCE HELD BY NADIM ABDEL AL-SAMAD, THE DEPUTY GENERAL SECRETARY OF THE LEBANESE COMMUNIST PARTY CENTRAL COMMITTEE, AND SHARIF FAYAD, THE DEPUTY CHAIRMAN AND CENTRAL COMMITTEE SECRETARY OF THE PROGRESSIVE SOCIALIST PARTY OF LEBANON. THEY DISCUSSED EFFORTS TO CARRY OUT THE 1982 PLAN, THE DANGER OF ANTI-UPRISING AND ANTI-SYRIAN ATTITUDES, AND THE THREAT OF DIVISION IN LEBANON.

00335
LECH WALESA'S SPEECH AT THE INAUGURATION OF THE ROUND TABLE
CONTEMPORARY POLAND, XXII(3) (1989), 43-46.
THE ROUND TABLE IS A SPECIAL MOMENT AND MUCH DEPENDS ON IT. DELIBERATIONS ARE BEGINNING IN THE SPOTLIGHT, WHILE THERE IS SADNESS AND FEAR OF POVERTY IN THE STREETS. THE ROUND TABLE DELEGATES ARE UTTERING GRAND WORDS, BUT WHAT POLAND NEEDS ARE FACTS, BOLD DECISIONS, AND WISE AND ENERGETIC ACTION. THE ROAD AHEAD IS LONG AND BUMPY. THE RESULTS OF REFORM EFFORTS ARE UNCERTAIN. IT IS NECESSARY TO EXTRICATE POLAND FROM INERTIA, AND THE POLES FROM THEIR SENSE OF HOPELESSNESS.

00336
LEONID LUBMAN: THE STORY OF A POLITICAL PRISONER
GLASNOST, (16-18) (JAN 89), 55.
IN HIS WORK FOR SOVIET SCIENTIFIC AND INDUSTRIAL INSTITUTIONS, LEONID YAKOVLEVICH LUBMAN CAME FACE TO FACE WITH THE VICES OF THE SYSTEM, THE LIES, AND THE CAREERISM PERVASIVE AT EVERY LEVEL OF SOCIETY. HE COULD NOT RECONCILE HIMSELF WITH THESE THINGS. IN A MANUSCRIPT THAT HE INTENDED TO SMUGGLE OUT TO THE WEST, LUBMAN EXPLAINED HIS ATTITUDES TOWARD THE SYSTEM AND THE BEHAVIOR OF SOVIET TOWARD THE SYSTEM AND THE BEHAVIOR OF SOVIET OFFICIALS. WHEN HIS MANUSCRIPT FELL INTO THE HANDS OF SOVIET OFFICIALS, HE WAS IMPRISONED ON CHARGES OF ESPIONAGE. TODAY, DESPITE THE EXONERATION OF SOME POLITICAL PRISONERS, LUBMAN REMAINS INCARCERATED ON ONE OF THE ISLANDS OF THE PERM GULAG.

00337
LESSONS OF THE 1988 ELECTIONS
MONTHLY REVIEW, 40(9) (FEB 89), 1-9..
THE 1988 UNITED STATES CAMPAIGNS AND THE ELECTIONS REMAINED FIRMLY ANCHORED WITHIN THIS MAINSTREAM CONSENSUS; AND THE OUTCOME, A REPUBLICAN PRESIDENT AND A DEMOCRATIC CONGRESS, CONTINUES WHAT HAS BY NOW COME TO BE CONSIDERED AS A WELL ESTABLISHED TRADITION. IT IS IMPORTANT TO UNDERSTAND THAT THIS SHARING OF POWER REFLETS A DEEPLY ROOTED REALITY. THE PARTIES HAVE THE SAME PURPOSE, TO PRESERVE CAPITALISM AND SERVE THE INTERESTS OF ITS RULING CLASS, BUT THEY GO ABOUT IT SOMEWHAT DIFFERENTLY. GENERALLY SPEAKING THE REPUBLICANS APPEAL TO THE UPPER HALF OF THE INCOME DISTRIBUTION AND THE DEMOCRATS TO THE LOWER HALF. THEY ARE ENGAGED IN A COMMON ENTERPRISE WHICH, HOWEVER, REQUIRES A DIVISION OF LABOR FOR ITS SUCCESSFUL MANAGEMENT. IT IS THEREFORE FITTING AND FOR THE MOST PART SATISFACTORY TO BOTH PARTIES THAT THEY SHOULD SHARE THE REWARDS.

00338
LI PENG MEETS WITH STUDENT LEADERS
BEIJING REVIEW, 32(22) (MAY 89), 20-21, 27-28.
THIS ARTICLE RECOUNTS A MEETING BETWEEN CHINESE PREMIER LI PENG AND REPRESENTATIVES OF STRIKING STUDENTS ON MAY 18, 1989, THE SIXTH DAY OF THE HUNGER STRIKE THAT ESCALATED INTO THE TIANANMEN SQUARE MASSACRE.

00339
LI PENG ON CURRENT DOMESTIC AND INTERNATIONAL POLICIES
BEIJING REVIEW, 32(42) (OCT 89), 18-21.
IN HIS SPEECH AT THE RECEPTION MARKING THE 40TH ANNIVERSARY OF THE FOUNDING OF THE PEOPLE'S REPUBLIC OF CHINA, PREMIER LI PENG TALKED ABOUT QUESTIONS OF COMMON CONCERN. WHILE REAFFIRMING THAT CHINA'S REFORM AND OPEN POLICY WILL REMAIN UNCHANGED, LI SAID THE COUNTRY'S REFORM AND OPENING UP IS BASED ON THE PREREQUISITE OF THE FOUR CARDINAL PRINCIPLES AND IS INTENDED FOR THE DEVELOPMENT AND IMPROVEMENT OF THE SOCIALIST SYSTEM. ALTHOUGH THEY WILL CAUSE THE COUNTRY TEMPORARY DIFFICULTIES, THE ECONOMIC SANCTIONS IMPOSED ON CHINA BY SOME WESTERN COUNTRIES WILL STIMULATE THE CHINESE PEOPLE'S SPIRIT OF SELF-RELIANCE.

00340
LI PENG ON DOMESTIC AND WORLD ISSUES
BEIJING REVIEW, 32(49) (DEC 89), 12-14.
ACCORDING TO CHINESE PREMIER LI PENG, CHINA'S TOP PRIORITY IS DEVELOPING ITS ECONOMY. A THREE-PHASE DEVELOPMENT PLAN HAS BEEN ADOPTED, WITH THE INITIAL PHASE OF MODERNIZATION TO BE COMPLETED BY THE END OF THIS CENTURY. BECAUSE THE POLITICAL TURMOIL IN THE SPRING OF 1989 THREATENED CHINA'S SECURITY AND THE FUTURE OF ITS SOCIALIST SYSTEM, IT WAS NECESSARY TO CHECK THE REBELLION. THE PROPRIETY OF THIS WILL BECOME CLEARER IN THE FUTURE, ACCORDING TO LI.

00341
LI PENG SCORES TOKYO TOUCHDOWN
BEIJING REVIEW, 32(17) (APR 89), 10-11.
CHINESE PREMIER LI PENG VISITED JAPAN IN APRIL 1989 AS PART OF CHINA'S POLICY OF DEVELOPING FRIENDLY, MUTUALLY BENEFICIAL TIES WITH JAPAN. LI PENG AND JAPANESE PRIME MINISTER NOBORU TAKESHITA EXCHANGED VIEWS ON ISSUES OF COMMON CONCERN.

00342
LI PUTS NEW GENERATION IN FOCUS
BEIJING REVIEW, 32(38) (SEP 89), 10-12.
CHINESE PREMIER LI PENG HAS STATED THAT IT IS NECESSARY TO TRAIN YOUTH TO CHERISH LOFTY IDEALS AND TO NOURISH WITHIN THEM A SENSE OF MORALITY AND DISCIPLINE WHILE THEY DEVELOP INTELLECTUALLY, IN ORDER TO ENSURE CHINA'S PROSPERITY. HE ALSO SAID THAT NURTURING AND EDUCATING INFANTS, CHILDREN, AND TEENAGERS IS A SOCIAL ISSUE THAT INVOLVES EVERY FAMILY AND IS DIRECTLY RELATED TO THE PEOPLE'S INTERESTS. PROPAGANDA SHOULD SPREAD THREE AREAS OF KNOWLEDGE: QUALITY BREEDING, CHILD NURTURING, AND EDUCATION.

00343
LI STRESSES STABLE ECONOMY
BEIJING REVIEW, 32(35) (AUG 89), 7, 9.
ACCORDING TO CHINESE PREMIER LI PENG, STABLE PRICES TOP THE LIST OF CHINA'S ECONOMIC GOALS FOR THE LAST HALF OF 1989. OTHER MAJOR GOALS ARE THE ACHIEVEMENT OF A GOOD HARVEST AND THE REDUCTION OF IMBALANCES IN SUPPLY AND DEMAND.

00344
LI URGES AN ORDERLY ECONOMY

BEIJING REVIEW, 32(34) (AUG 89), 5.
ON AUGUST 9, 1989, CHINESE PREMIER LI PENG DECLARED THAT
THE PURPOSE OF ECONOMIC RECTIFICATION IS TO CREATE BETTER
CONDITIONS FOR REFORM AND CHINA'S OPENING TO THE OUTSIDE
WORLD. HE SET THREE GOALS FOR IMPROVING THE ECONOMIC
ENVIRONMENT IN 1989: STABILIZING PRICES, STRIVING FOR A GOOD
HARVEST, AND EASING CONTRADICTIONS IN SUPPLY AND DEMAND IN
THE MARKETPLACE.

00345
LI WRAPS UP SOUTH ASIAN TOUR
BEIJING REVIEW, 32(48) (NOV 89), 10-11.
DURING AN OFFICIAL VISIT TO PAKISTAN, CHINESE PREMIER LI
PENG DECLARED THAT CHINA WOULD NOT CHANGE ITS POLITICAL AND
ECONOMIC SYSTEM JUST BECAUSE OF THE CHANGES TAKING PLACE IN
EASTERN EUROPE. HE STATED THAT CHINA WAS ADOPTING A WAIT-AND-
SEE ATTITUDE ON THE QUESTION OF WHETHER THE CHANGES IN EAST
GERMANY ARE GOOD OR BAD. HE ALSO DISCUSSED CHINESE RELATIONS
WITH THE USA, SINO-INDIAN TIES, THE SITUATION IN AFGHANISTAN,
AND PROSPECTS FOR KAMPUCHEA.

00346
LI: CHINESE GOVERNMENT "STABLE AND ABLE"
BEIJING REVIEW, 32(23) (JUN 89), 9-10.
ON MAY 25, 1989, PREMIER LI PENG STATED THAT HIS
GOVERNMENT WAS STABLE, CAPABLE OF FULFILLING ITS DUTIES, AND
COULD SOLVE THE CURRENT PROBLEMS RAISED BY THE TURMOIL IN
BEIJING. HE SAID THAT MARTIAL LAW HAD BEEN IMPOSED IN SOME
PARTS OF BEIJING AS A WARNING AND AS A SAFETY MEASURE TO
PROTECT LIVES AND PROPERTY.

00347
LIFESCAPE: CHRISTIAN DEMOCRATS IN POLAND
POLISH PERSPECTIVES, XXXII(2) (1989), 70.
IN FEBRUARY 1989, IT WAS ANNOUNCED THAT THE POLISH
CHRISTIAN DEMOCRAT LABOUR PARTY, WHICH HAD BEEN INACTIVE FOR
FORTY YEARS, HAD BEEN REACTIVATED. IN ITS INAUGURAL
DECLARATION, THE PARTY EXPRESSED ITS SUPPORT FOR LECH
WALESA'S EFFORTS TO HAVE SOLIDARITY LEGALIZED AS A TRADE
UNION UNENCUMBERED WITH THE ROLE OF A SUBSTITUTE POLITICAL
PARTY. THE DECLARATION ALSO STATED THAT THE PARTY OPPOSED
THE RULING COALITION AND WOULD WORK FOR FULL POLITICAL
DEMOCRACY IN POLAND.

00348
LIFTING THE VEIL IN PAKISTAN
SOUTH, (99) (JAN 89), 5.
THE DECEMBER 1988 ELECTION IN PAKISTAN PROVED THAT THE
PAKISTANIS HAVE EMBRACED THE DEMOCRATIC OPTION WITH GREAT
ENTHUSIASM AND COMMITMENT. THE POOR, UNEDUCATED VOTER ACTED
WITH GREAT PERCEPTION, REJECTING A WHOLE GENERATION OF AGED
POLITICIANS AND DEFEATING FOUR FORMER COMMANDERS-IN-CHIEF.
THE ELECTION SENT A CLEAR MESSAGE THAT THE PEOPLE WANT
MILITARY OFFICERS OUT OF POLITICS. IT ALSO MARKED THE END OF
ZIA'S SELF-SERVING PROGRAM OF ISLAMIZATION.

00349
LOME IV NEGOTIATIONS
SURVEY OF CURRENT AFFAIRS, 19(3) (MAR 89), 96-97.
BRITAIN'S AIMS IN THE CURRENT RENEGOTIATION OF THE LOME
CONVENTION (WHICH GOVERNS TRADING ARRANGEMENTS BETWEEN THE
EUROPEAN COMMUNITY AND DEVELOPING COUNTRIES IN AFRICA, THE
CARIBBEAN AND THE PACIFIC) WERE SET OUT BY THE MINISTER FOR
OVERSEAS DEVELOPMENT, CHRISTOPHER PATTEN, IN A SPEECH IN
LONDON ON 9 FEBRUARY 1989.

00350
LOOKING AHEAD TO A SOCIALIST AMERICA
POLITICAL AFFAIRS, 68(12) (DEC 89), 2-4.
THIS ARTICLE TRACES THE HISTORY OF THE COMMUNIST PARTY,
USA SINCE IT WAS ESTABLISHED IN CHICAGO ON SEPTEMBER 1, 1919.
IT RECOUNTS PARTY INVOLVEMENT DURING WWI, THE DEPRESSION,
WWII, MCCARTHYISM, CAPITALISM AND THE FARM CRISIS. IT
EXPLORES THE GOALS AND ACCOMPLISHMENTS OF THE PAST 70 YEARS
AND LOOKS AHEAD TO THE FUTURE.

00351
LOUISIANA PAROCHIAID: MODEL FOR DISASTER
CHURCH AND STATE, 42(9) (OCT 89), 11 (203).
ADVOCATES OF PAROCHIAL SCHOOL AID FREQUENTLY TOUT
LOUISIANA AS A "MODEL" BECAUSE THE STATE LEGISLATURE HAS
PROBABLY GIVEN NON-PUBLIC SCHOOLS MORE TAX DOLLARS PER
CAPITA THAN ANY OTHER STATE IN THE UNION. BUT EVEN A
PERFUNCTORY GLANCE AT THE LOUISIANA "SUCCESS STORY" REVEALS
AN UNPLEASANT TRUTH. AID TO PRIVATE SCHOOLS IN LOUISIANA HAS
EXACTED A HIGH PRICE, NAMELY THE EVISCERATION OF CHURCH-
STATE SEPARATION AND THE DECIMATION OF THE STATE'S PUBLIC
SCHOOL SYSTEM. LOUISIANA HAS THE HIGHEST DROP-OUT RATE IN
THE NATION, AND NEARLY 50 PERCENT OF ITS HIGH SCHOOL
GRADUATES WHO ENTER COLLEGE NEED REMEDIAL EDUCATION.

00352
MADDOX DISCUSSES DAY CARE, TUITION TAX CREDITS WITH BUSH
AT WHITE HOUSE
CHURCH AND STATE, 42(6) (JUN 89), 15 (135)-16 (136).
ALTHOUGH PRESIDENT BUSH HAS STATED THAT HE BELIEVES
STRONGLY IN THE SEPARATION OF CHURCH AND STATE, HE HAS ALSO
INDICATED THAT HE SUPPORTS PERMITTING SECTARIAN DAY CARE
CENTERS TO PARTICIPATE IN GOVERNMENT SUBSIDY PROGRAMS.

00353
MAINLAND-TAIWAN TRADE RELATIONS
BEIJING REVIEW, 32(21) (MAY 89), 38.
TAIWANESE BUSINESSMEN ARE SHOWING ENTHUSIASM FOR
INVESTING ON THE CHINESE MAINLAND. IN THE PAST, PRODUCTS
FROM THE MAINLAND OFTEN COMPETED WITH PRODUCTS FROM TAIWAN
IN THE INTERNATIONAL MARKET. WITH THE DEVELOPMENT OF TRADE
CONTACTS AND WITH THE INCREASING NUMBER OF FACTORIES SET UP
BY THE TAIWANESE ON THE MAINLAND, THIS COMPETITIVE
RELATIONSHIP IS TURNING INTO A COOPERATIVE ONE.

00354
MAINLAND'S TAIWAN POLICY UNCHANGED
BEIJING REVIEW, 32(50) (DEC 89), 43.
IN NOVEMBER 1989, AN OFFICIAL OF THE MINISTRY OF FOREIGN
ECONOMIC RELATIONS AND TRADE RESTATED THE MAINLAND'S POLICY
ON ECONOMIC AND TRADE RELATIONS WITH TAIWAN, EMPHASIZING
THAT THE POLICY WOULD NOT BE CHANGED. HIS SPEECH WAS
DIRECTED TOWARDS THE NEWSPAPERS AND MAGAZINES WHICH HAD
REPORTED THAT THE MAINLAND AUTHORITIES WERE ADOPTING TIGHTER
MEASURES TOWARD TAIWAN AND WOULD PROHIBIT TAIWAN-FUNDED
ENTERPRISES ON THE MAINLAND FROM IMPORTING RAW MATERIALS
FROM TAIWAN, THEREBY FORCING TAIWANESE BUSINESSMEN TO
WITHDRAW THEIR INVESTMENTS AND GIVE THEIR ENTERPRISES TO THE
MAINLAND.

00355
MAJOR ISSUES IN THE 101ST CONGRESS
CRS REVEIW, 10(1) (JAN 89), 15-24.
THIS ARTICLE LISTS AND BRIEFLY SUMMARIZES 22 MAJOR
ISSUES FACING THE 101ST CONGRESS, INCLUDING AIDS, ARMS
CONTROL, CAMPAIGN FINANCING, CHILD CARE, DEFENSE SPENDING,
DRUG CONTROL, GLOBAL CLIMATE CHANGE, AND WASTE MANAGEMENT.

00356
MAJOR PARTIES PIN HOPES ON LOCAL ELECTIONS
MEXICO-UNITED STATES REPORT, II(7) (APR 89), 7-8.
THE 1989 STATE AND MUNICIPAL ELECTIONS WILL BE AN
IMPORTANT BAROMETER IN MEXICAN POLITICS. THE RULING
INSTITUTIONAL REVOLUTIONARY PARTY MUST REBOUND AFTER ITS
DECLINING SHOWING IN 1988. ON THE OTHER HAND, THE OPPOSITION
NEEDS TO FORCE ELECTORAL REFORMS THAT WILL PRODUCE A TRUE
SHOWING OF ITS STRENGTH AMONG VOTERS.

00357
MANLEY'S UPHILL TASK
SOUTH, (101) (MAR 89), 5.
MICHAEL MANLEY, THE PEOPLE'S NATIONAL PARTY CANDIDATE,
HAS BEEN ELECTED PRIME MINISTER OF JAMAICA FOR THE THIRD
TIME. MANLEY'S FOCUS CONTINUES TO BE PEOPLE, PRODUCTION, AND
PARTICIPATION. THE VERDICT OF THE ELECTORATE WAS NOT BASED
SIMPLY ON ITS EXPECTATION OF A BETTER ECONOMIC DEAL. THE
PEOPLE DECIDED THAT MANLEY'S PROGRAM AND ALIGNMENT CAME
CLOSER TO RECOGNIZING THEIR POLITICAL ASPIRATIONS.

00358
MANY COLOURS IN THIS PALETTE
CONTEMPORARY POLAND, XXII(5) (1989), 15-17.
THE POLITICAL PLURALISM OF POLAND APPEARS TO HAVE BECOME
A PERMANENT PART OF THE LANDSCAPE. AMONG THE MANY ORGANIZED
POLITICAL GROUPS THAT HAVE SPRUNG UP ARE THE SOCIAL
DEMOCRATS, THE LIBERAL SOCIALISTS, THE CHRISTIAN SOCIALISTS,
THE CHRISTIAN LIBERALS, AND THE ENLIGHTENED CONSERVATIVES.
THIS PLURALITY OF INITIATIVES PROVES THAT THE ATTEMPT TO
CREATE A POLITICALLY UNIFORM SOCIETY IN POLAND HAS BEEN
ABORTIVE AND THAT THE PEOPLE WISH TO SPEAK WITH THEIR OWN
VOICES. THE EVOLUTION OCCURRING WITHIN THE COUNTRY'S
OFFICIAL POLITICAL STRUCTURES IS EQUALLY INTERESTING.

00359
MASSES IN REVOLT AGAINST STIFLING AUTHORITARIAN GRIP
FAR EASTERN ECONOMIC REVIEW, 141(34) (AUG 88), 12-13.
ALTHOUGH A MORE POPULAR FIGURE THAN RECENTLY RESIGNED
SEIN LWIN MAY PLACATE THE BURMESE POPULACE FOR A TIME, IT IS
CLEAR THAT MANY BURMESE ARE INSISTING ON POLITICAL
LIBERALIZATION AS A NECESSARY STEP TO SERIOUS ECONOMIC
CHANGE. GIVEN THE POLITICAL UNCERTAINTY IN BURMA, IT IS
DIFFICULT TO FORECAST THE TYPES OF CHANGES THAT MIGHT BE
IMPLEMENTED. IT IS POSSIBLE THAT A ONE-PARTY SYSTEM THAT
GURANTEES ECONOMIC REFORMS COULD BE IN BURMA'S FUTURE.

00360
MAYORS CONFERENCE ADOPTS "POSITIVE AGENDA"
AMERICAN CITY AND COUNTY, 104(8) (AUG 89), 20-21.
THE 1989 U.S. CONFERENCE OF MAYORS FOCUSED ON THE WAR
AGAINST DRUGS AND OTHER SOCIAL ISSUES. THE GROUP ADOPTED
FIFTY POLICY POSITIONS, INCLUDING RESOLUTIONS CALLING FOR A
MAJOR EXPANSION OF THE WAR ON DRUGS, SUPPORT AMENDMENTS TO

THE CLEAN AIR ACT, AND COMPETITION IN CABLE TELEVISION
MARKETING AND FRANCHISING.

00361
      MEDIA MUST SERVE PEOPLE, SOCIALISM--JIANG
      BEIJING REVIEW, 32(50) (DEC 89), 7, 9.
      JIANG ZEMIN, GENERAL SECRETARY OF THE CENTRAL COMMITTEE
OF THE CPC, HAS STATED THAT CHINESE JOURNALISM MUST SERVE
THE PEOPLE AND SOCIALISM. HE SAID THAT CHINESE JOURNALISTS
SHOULD PUBLICIZE THE PARTY'S BASIC LINE, THE PARTY'S
THEORIES FOR BUILDING SOCIALISM WITH CHINESE CHARACTERISTICS,
AND THE ACHIEVEMENTS OF CHINA'S REFORMS AND MODERNIZATION
EFFORTS.

00362
      MIDDLE EAST: ARAB-ISRAEL DISPUTE
      SURVEY OF CURRENT AFFAIRS, 19(1) (JAN 89), 12-14.
      BRITAIN AND THE EUROPEAN COMMUNITY HAVE WELCOMED THE
RECENT DECISIONS OF THE PALESTINE NATIONAL COUNCIL AND
PALESTINE LIBERATION ORGANISATION RENOUNCING TERRORISM AND
RECOGNISING THE STATE OF ISRAEL. MR WILLIAM WALDEGRAVE,
MINISTER OF STATE AT THE FOREIGN AND COMMONWEALTH OFFICE,
HAS HAD TALKS WITH MR YASSER ARAFAT, THE CHAIRMAN OF THE
PALESTINE LIBERATION ORGANISATION.

00363
      MIKHAIL GORBACHEV MEETS ICFTU LEADERS
      INFORMATION BULLETIN, 25/26(1-2) (JAN 88), 4-6.
      THIS ARTICLE DESCRIBES THE RESULTS OF GORBACHEV'S
MEETING WITH REPRESENTATIVES OF THE INTERNATIONAL
CONFEDERATION OF FREE TRADE UNIONS. GORBACHEV PARTICULARLY
SINGLED OUT FOR DISCUSSION THE CORRECTION BETWEEN
DISARMAMENT AND DEVELOPMENT. HE CALLED FOR A SERIOUS
EVALUATION OF THE SQUANDERING OF RESOURCES ON ARMAMENTS AT A
TIME WHEN MORE THAN ONE BILLION PEOPLE LIVED IN POVERTY.

00364
      MIKHAIL GORBACHEV'S CLOSING REMARKS TO THE CONGRESS OF
      PEOPLE'S DEPUTIES OF THE USSR
      REPRINTS FROM THE SOVIET PRESS, 49(4) (AUG 89), 11-26.
      MIKHAIL GORBACHEV CONCLUDES THAT THIS PARTICULAR
CONGRESS HAS TAKEN THEM TO A NEW STAGE IN DEVELOPMENT OF
DEMOCRACY AND GLASTNOST AND PERESTROIKA IN THE COUNTRY. HE
ADDRESSES THE NEED FOR THE PRINCIPLE OF PLURALISM OF
OPINIONS TO BE IMPLEMENTED. HE CALLS FOR THE NEED FOR QUEST,
FOR ORIGINALITY IN DECISIONS, FOR A BREAKTHROUGH IN THINKING,
IN SCIENCE AND PRACTICE.

00365
      MIKHAIL GORBACHEV'S MESSAGE TO THE NON-ALIGNED SUMMIT
      REPRINTS FROM THE SOVIET PRESS, 49(10) (NOV 89), 44-45.
      MIKHAIL GORBACHEV'S MESSAGE TO THE NON-ALIGNED SUMMIT
STATED THAT THE SOVIET UNION IS OPEN FOR DIALOGUE AND
INTERACTION WITH EACH OF THE NON-ALIGNED STATES AND WITH THE
MOVEMENT AS A WHOLE, HE ADDRESSES THE BUILDING OF A NEW
INTERNATIONAL ORDER, THE SETTLEMENT OF REGIONAL CONFLICTS,
BUILDING A WORLD FREE OF NUCLEAR WEAPONS & AGRESSION, AND
THE PROBLEMS OF UNDER DEVELOPMENT.

00366
      MILITARIZATION: AN ATTACK ON THE ENVIRONMENT
      INFORMATION BULLETIN, 27(3-4) (FEB 89), 11.
      NANISVIK, NEAR THE NORTH END OF BAFFIN ISLAND, IS THE
EASTERN ENTRANCE TO THE PASSAGE BETWEEN THE ATLANTIC AND
PACIFIC. IT THE PROPOSED SITE FOR A PERMANENT MILITARY BASE.
THE BASE WILL BE OPEN WITHIN FIVE YEARS, AND NO COST FOR THE
PROJECT HAS BEEN REVEALED. IT WILL BE USED TO TRAIN SOLDIERS
AND TEST EQUIPMENT FOR ARCTIC WARFARE. MILITARIZATION COULD
HAVE DISASTROUS EFFECTS ON THE NORTHERN ENVRONMENT. MANY
ACTIVITIES WITHIN THE REGION HAVE PROFOUND EFFECTS ON LOCAL
BIOLOGICAL SYSTEMS. INDUSTRIALIZATION AND OTHER ACTIVITIES
FAR TO THE SOUTH ARE NOW AFFECTING THE NORTH.

00367
      MILITARY ASSISTANCE
      LINK, 22(2) (MAY 89), 6-7.
      THE ARTICLE EXAMINES THE MILITARY ASSISTANCE RENDERED TO
THE STATE OF ISRAEL WITH EMPHASIS ON MILITARY ASSISTANCE
COMING FROM THE US. IT OUTLINES THE SHIFT FROM LOANS AND
SALES TO OUTRIGHT GRANTS, AND DOCUMENTS THE INCREASING
AMOUNT OF MATERIAL GRANTED TO ISRAEL. US AID TO ISRAEL NOW
NUMBERS IN BILLIONS OF DOLLARS. IT ALSO DISCUSSES SEVERAL
PROPOSED PLANS OF MILITARY COOPERATION BETWEEN THE US AND
ISRAEL AND ANALYZES THE PROGRAMS' COST EFFECTIVENESS.

00368
      MILITARY IN THE WAR ON DRUGS: A SELECTED BIBLIOGRAPHY
      AVAILABLE FROM NTIS, NO. AD-A199 699/0/GAR, JUN 88, 13.
      RECENTLY THERE HAS BEEN SUBSTANTIAL CONTROVERSY OVER THE
UNITED STATES MILITARY'S ROLE IN THE DRUG WAR. UNDER
LEGISLATION PASSED IN 1981, THE DEPARTMENT OF DEFENSE NOW
ASSISTS CIVILIAN LAW ENFORCEMENT AGENCIES IN THEIR FIGHT TO
COMBAT ILLEGAL DRUG TRAFFICKING BY LENDING MILITARY
EQUIPMENT AND FACILITIES, THROUGH INTELLIGENCE SHARING, AND

BY PROVIDING EXPERT TRAINING AND ADVICE TO CIVILIANS. THE
USE OF MILITARY PERSONNEL IS ALSO CONTRIBUTING TO THE ANTI-
DRUG EFFORT AND IS PROBABLY THE MOST SENSITIVE AREA OF
CONSIDERATION. CLEARLY, SOME POLICYMAKERS SEE THE DRUG
PROBLEM AS A THREAT TO THE ECONOMIC, SOCIAL, AND NATIONAL
SECURITY OF OUR COUNTRY AND LOOK TO THE MILITARY FOR
ASSISTANCE AND COOPERATION. HOWEVER, OTHERS THINK THAT
PROVIDING MILITARY ASSISTANCE TO CIVIL AUTHORITIES WILL
INTERFERE WITH THE PRIMARY MISSION OF THE DEPARTMENT OF
DEFENSE--MILITARY PREPAREDNESS. TO ASSIST RESEARCHERS IN A
BETTER UNDERSTANDING OF HOW THE ARMED SERVICES ARE INVOLVED
IN THE DRUG WAR, THE US ARMY WAR COLLEGE LIBRARY PRESENTS
THE MILITARY IN THE WAR ON DRUGS: A SELECTED BIBLIOGRAPHY.
THIS LISTING OF BOOKS, DOCUMENTS, AND PERIODICAL AND
NEWSPAPER ARTICLES PROVIDES VARIOUS VIEWPOINTS FROM
MATERIALS PUBLISHED DURING THE PAST FIVE YEARS WHICH ARE
READILY AVAILABLE IN THE USAWC LIBRARY COLLECTION. KEYWORDS:
LAW ENFORCEMENT.

00369
      MINIMUM WAGE LEGISLATION
      CONGRESSIONAL DIGEST, 68(5) (MAY 89), 131-137.
      THIS ARTICLE REVIEWS THE EVOLUTION OF US MINIMUM WAGE
LEGISLATION, AN ECONOMIC IMPACT STUDY ON THE EFFECT OF
MINIMUM WAGE LAWS, AND RECENT CONGRESSIONAL ACTION ON
MINIMUM WAGE.

00370
      MORAL MAJORITY TO DISBAND THIS AUGUST, SAYS FALWELL
      CHURCH AND STATE, 42(7) (JUL 89), 13 (157).
      THE REV. JERRY FALWELL HAS ANNOUNCED THAT THE MORAL
MAJORITY, THE ORGANIZATION THAT SPEARHEADED THE GROWTH OF
THE RELIGIOUS RIGHT FOR A DECADE, WILL CLOSE IN AUGUST 1989.
FALWELL STATED THAT THE ORGANIZATION HAS ACCOMPLISHED ITS
GOALS AND IS NO LONGER NEEDED. SOME OBSERVERS NOTED THAT THE
GROUP'S POLITICAL POWER HAD PEAKED AND THAT THE LAST THREE
YEARS HAD BEEN ITS LEAST SUCCESSFUL FOR FUNDRAISING.

00371
      MOSCOW TRIES OUT DEMOCRACY
      BEIJING REVIEW, 32(28) (JUL 89), 16-17.
      THE PRIMARY TASK FACING THE FIRST CONGRESS OF PEOPLE'S
DEPUTIES IS TO ESTABLISH A SOVIET UNION RULED BY LAW WITH
THE CONGRESS AND THE SUPREME SOVIET AS THE LEADING
LEGISLATIVE BODIES, IN ORDER TO SAFEGUARD DEMOCRATIZATION,
GLASNOST, AND THE DIVERSITY OF OPINION. AT THE CONGRESS'
OPENING CEREMONY, GORBACHEV SAID THAT REFORM HAS MET WITH
SETBACKS AND HAS ENTERED ITS MOST DIFFICULT PERIOD BUT THE
GOVERNMENT HAS CONTROL OF THE SITUATION.

00372
      MOZAMBIQUE: FOCUS ON THE NATIONAL INTERESTS
      INFORMATION BULLETIN, 27 (JAN 89), 14-16.
      THIS IS A REPORT ON THE FRELIMO PARTY NATIONAL
CONFERENCE HELD IN JULY 1988 AT MAPUTU. CONFERENCE DELEGATES
DISCUSSED ECONOMIC PROBLEMS. AT THE CENTRAL COMMITTEE
MEETING, PRESIDENT JOAQUIN CHISSANO STATED THAT MOZAMBIQUE
REMAINS COMMITTED TO SOCIALIST DEVELOPMENT AND TO RAISING
THE STANDARD OF LIVING IN MOZAMBIQUE WHILE ELIMINATING
INEQUALITY AND EXPLOITATION.

00373
      MULTI-PARTY COOPERATION CONTINUES
      BEIJING REVIEW, 32(38) (SEP 89), 10.
      CHINA WILL NOT CHANGE ITS SYSTEM OF MULTI-PARTY
COOPERATION. THE POLITICAL TURMOIL OF 1989 TESTED THE
RELATIONSHIP BETWEEN THE CPC AND THE NON-COMMUNIST PARTIES,
BUT THE FOUNDATION OF MULTI-PARTY COOPERATION WITHSTOOD THE
TEST. THE FUTURE FOR FURTHER COOPERATION IS BRIGHT.

00374
      MUSEVENI BREAKS HIS PLEDGE
      NEW AFRICAN, (267) (DEC 89), 17.
      WHEN PRESIDENT MUSEVENI OF UGANDA CAME INTO POWER IN
1986 HE PLEDGED TO RESTORE DEMOCRATIC GOVERNMENT IN 1990. HE
HAS EXTENDED HIS GOVERNMENT ANOTHER FIVE YEARS. THE UGANDA
PARLIAMENT GAVE ITS SUPPORT, BUT THE PEOPLE ARE NOT SO
TRUSTING. GROUPS SUCH AS THE DEMOCRATIC PARTY, THE DP
MOBILISERS GROUP, AND THE BAGANDA TRADITIONALISTS ARE
BITTERLY DISSAPOINTED. THESE GROUPS SAY THAT THE GOVERNMENT
HAS MADE EMPTY PROMISES ABOUT CROP FINACE, EDUCATION AND
HEALTH.

00375
      MUSLIMS IN BRITAIN
      SURVEY OF CURRENT AFFAIRS, 19(9) (SEP 89), 361-362.
      IN A LETTER ADDRESSED TO SEVERAL OF THE LEADING MEMBERS
OF THE BRITISH MUSLIM COMMUNITY, THE MINISTER OF STATE AT
THE HOME OFFICE, JOHN PATTEN, HAS SET OUT THE GOVERNMENT'S
THINKING ON RACE RELATIONS IN BRITAIN. IN IT HE STRESSES THE
IMPORTANCE OF INTEGRATION, OR ACTIVE PARTICIPATION, BY
ETHNIC MINORITY GROUPS IN THE MAINSTREAM OF BRITISH LIFE.

00376
MWINYA'S DILEMMA
NEW AFRICAN, 261 (JUN 89), 20-21.
PRESIDENT MWINYI OF TANZANIA HAS BEEN TRYING TO
STRENGTHEN HIS POSITION BY SACKING ENEMIES AND BY PROMOTING
FRIENDS TO HIGH OFFICE, BUT HIS CHOICES MAY HAVE
INADVERTANTLY WEAKENED HIS POSITION. THIS ARTICLE EXAMINES
WHETHER HE HAS TILTED THE BALANCE TOO FAR TOWARDS MOSLEM
FUNDAMENTALISTS.

00377
MYSTERY MAN MAKHOHA, AGENT OR DISSIDENT?
NEW AFRICAN, (OCT 89), 42.
THIS ARTICLE EXPLORES THE POLICE RECORD OF FATHER SAMWEL
MAKHOHA SINCE 1980. HE HAS A HISTORY OF BEING CHARGED WITH
CRIMES AND THEN BEING CLEARED AND RELEASED. HE HAS RECENTLY
RETURNED TO KENYA FROM NORWAY AS A DISSIDENT CLAIMING THAT
THE AMNESTY GRANTED BY PRESIDENT MOI HAD NOTHING TO DO WITH
HIS RETURN. MANY UNANSWERED QUESTIONS ABOUT MA ARE RAISED IN
THIS ARTICLE.

00378
NAMING THE GOOD, THE BAD AND THE UGLY OF A NATION
FAR EASTERN ECONOMIC REVIEW, 141(38) (SEP 88), 51,53.
IN AN EFFORT TO IDENTIFY THE "STRENGTHS AND WEAKNESSES
OF CHARACTER" OF THE PHILIPPINE PEOPLE, AND TO FORMULATE
MEASURES TO SOLVE THE NATION'S ILLS AND STRENGTHEN THE
NATION'S MORAL FIBRE, THE GOVERNMENT AUTHORIZED AN INVENTORY
OF EXPERTS IN THE FIELDS OF PSYCHIATRY, PSYCHOLOGY,
SOCIOLOGY, AND OTHER SOCIAL SCIENCES TO DETERMINE THE
CHARACTERISTICS OF THE PHILIPPINE POPULACE. THE RESULT WAS
"THE MORAL RECOVERY PROGRAM: BUILDING A PEOPLE--BUILDING A
NATION" A REPORT THAT LISTS THE STRENGTHS AND WEAKNESSES OF
THE PEOPLE AND SUGGESTS REMEDIES FOR THE SOCIAL ILLS LISTED.
SUCH A REPORT IS UTOPIAN AT BEST, AND SUFFERS FROM SEVERAL
MAJOR FLAWS, BUT AT THE SAME TIME IS ADMIRABLE IN ITS
ATTEMPT TO FORCE A "FILIPINO IDENTITY."

00379
NATIONAL HEALTH SERVICE
SURVEY OF CURRENT AFFAIRS, 19(2) (FEB 89), 70-74.
THE GOVERNMENT HAS PROPOSED A MAJOR PROGRAMME OF REFORM
FOR THE NATIONAL HEALTH SERVICE WHICH IS INTENDED TO GIVE
PATIENTS BETTER HEALTH CARE AND GREATER CHOICE AND TO OFFER
GREATER SATISFACTION TO THOSE WORKING IN THE SERVICE. THE
REFORMS (WHICH WOULD BE INTRODUCED IN THREE MAIN PHASES
DURING 1989, 1990, AND 1991) ARE DESIGNED TO OFFER PATIENTS
A NEW DEAL, WITH MORE CHOICE, HIGH STANDARDS, AND BETTER
QUALITY. IF IMPLEMENTED, THEY WOULD ENABLE THE SERVICE TO
CONTINUE TO BE OPEN TO ALL REGARDLESS OF INCOME AND TO BE
FINANCED MAINLY OUT OF GENERAL TAXATION. THE GOVERNMENT HAS
ALSO ISSUED EIGHT WORKING PAPERS EXPLAINING IN DETAIL HOW
MAJOR ASPECTS OF THE PROPOSALS ARE TO BE IMPLEMENTED.

00380
NATO AND EUROPEAN SECURITY
SURVEY OF CURRENT AFFAIRS, 19(5) (MAY 89), 180-182.
THE FUTURE OF THE NORTH ATLANTIC ALLIANCE AND THE ROLE
OF WESTERN EUROPE WERE AMONG THE ISSUES ADDRESSED BY THE
BRITISH FOREIGN AND COMMONWEALTH SECRETARY, SIR GEOFFREY
HOWE, IN A SPEECH ON APRIL 11, 1989. GEOFFREY SAID THAT NATO
WOULD REMAIN THE BEDROCK OF WESTERN EUROPE'S SECURITY. HE
ENUMERATED SEVERAL CHALLENGES FOR THE FUTURE, INCLUDING THE
PRACTICAL PROBLEM OF HOW TO STRENGTHEN MILITARY COOPERATION
AND GET THE MOST VALUE FOR THE DEFENSE DOLLAR, THE
INTELLECTUAL CHALLENGE OF HOW TO CONTRIBUTE GREATER INPUT
INTO ARMS CONTROL, AND THE PUBLIC RELATIONS CHALLENGE OF
EXPLAINING THE NEED FOR DETERRENCE WHEN EAST-WEST RELATIONS
ARE IMPROVING.

00381
NATO DEFENSE PLANNING COMMITTEE MEETS IN BRUSSELS
DEPARTMENT OF STATE BULLETIN (US FOREIGN POLICY), 89(2143)
(FEB 89), 42-43.
THE DEFENSE MINISTERS OF THE NORTH ATLANTIC TREATY
ORGANIZATION MET IN BRUSSELS IN DECEMBER 1988. THIS REPORT
REPRINTS THE TEXT OF THE FINAL COMMUNIQUE ISSUED BY THE
MINISTERS.

00382
NATO DEFENSE PLANNING COMMITTEE MEETS IN BRUSSELS
DEPARTMENT OF STATE BULLETIN (US FOREIGN POLICY), 89(2149)
(AUG 89), 77-79.
THIS REPORT ON THE JUNE 1989 MEETING OF THE NATO DEFENSE
MINISTERS REPRINTS THE TEXT OF THE FINAL COMMUNIQUE ISSUED
BY THE MINISTERS.

00383
NEBRASKA, KENTUCKY, OREGON FACE PAROCHIAID CAMPAIGNS
CHURCH AND STATE, 42(10) (NOV 89), 13 (229).
LEGISLATORS IN NEBRASKA, KENTUCKY, AND OREGON ARE FACING
NEW DRIVES FOR PAROCHIAID. TWO OF THE PROPOSALS WOULD
INVOLVE TAX CREDITS FOR PARENTS WHO PAY PAROCHIAL OR PRIVATE
SCHOOL TUITION. THE THIRD PLAN FOCUSES ON PROMOTING PUBLIC
SCHOOL CHOICE, WHICH WOULD EVENTUALLY BE EXPANDED TO
ENCOMPASS PRIVATE SCHOOLS.

00384
NEITHER FREE NOR FAIR ELECTIONS IN NAMIBIA
SECHABA, 23(10) (OCT 89), 9-13.
THIS ARTICLE REPORTS ON THE ELECTIONS IN NAMIBIA WHERE
THE FUTURE CONSTITUTION IS AT STAKE. IT ADDRESSES A
SITUATION WHERE PRETORIA SUPERVISES AND CONTROLS THE
ELECTORAL PROCESS. WHERE THE BALLOT IS NOT SECRET BUT THE
COUNT IS, AND VOTERS ARE DISQUALIFIED IN SECRET, FAILURE FOR
THE ELECTIONS IS PREDICTED AS PRETORIA PLANS FOR FUTURE
DESTABILISATION.

00385
NEW POLITICAL PERSPECTIVE IN THE MAKING
CONTEMPORARY POLAND, XXII(2) (1989), 19-21.
ANXIOUS AND HOPEFUL POLES ARE AWAITING THE OUTCOME OF
PRIME MINISTER RAKOWSKI'S REFORM DRIVE. THEY ARE ALSO
AWAITING THE CONCOMITANT FORMATION OF THE NEW POLITICAL
PANORAMA THAT HAS RECEIVED A STRONG IMPULSE FROM THE THESES,
MEETINGS, AND RESOLUTIONS OF THE TENTH PLENUM OF THE POLISH
UNITED WORKERS' PARTY CC. MORE ATTENTION THAN EVER BEFORE IS
BEING GIVEN TO WHAT THE COALITION PARTIES SAY.

00386
NEW SOVIET CUSTOMS RULES NARROW GAP WITH GATT
REPRINTS FROM THE SOVIET PRESS, 48(10) (MAY 89), 43.
IN NEW CONDITIONS OF DECENTRALIZATION OF SOVIET FOREIGN
ECONOMIC RELATIONS THE CUSTOMS SERVICE CANNOT CONFINE ITS
FUNCTIONS TO EXERCISING CONTROL OVER THE LUGGAGE OF SOVIET
AND FOREIGN CITIZENS. IT SHOULD ALSO BECOME A MECHANISM
REGULATING FOREIGN TRADE. THIS CAN BE ACHIEVED ONLY THROUGH
THE CREATION OF A CUSTOMS AND TARIFF SYSTEM THAT WOULD
INCLUDE AN EFFECTIVE CUSTOMS TARIFF, STATE NON-TARIFF
REGULATIONS AND STATE CUSTOMS STATISTICS. THESE THREE
ELEMENTS SHOULD BE BASED ON A CLASSIFICATION OF GOODS
UNDERSTANDABLE TO THE SOVIET UNION'S FOREIGN TRADE PARTNERS.
THIS IS WHY MEASURES TO INTRODUCE A BALANCED CODING SYSTEM
OF GOODS ACCEPTED IN MOST COUNTRIES ARE NOW BEING WORKED OUT.

00387
NEW ZEALAND: SOCIAL ISSUES IN FOCUS
INFORMATION BULLETIN, 25/26(1-2) (JAN 88), 20.
THE PLENARY MEETING OF THE SOCIALIST UNITY PARTY OF NEW
ZEALAND FOCUSED ON THE ISSUES OF SOCIAL POLICY, ESPECIALLY
UNEMPLOYMENT; ECONOMIC DEVELOPMENT; THE ACCIDENT
COMPENSATION CORPORATION; HOUSING; AND HEALTH. THE MEETING
SCRUTINIZED THE PARTY'S ROLE IN DIRECTING AND FORMULATING
POLICY IN THESE AREAS.

00388
NEWS CONFERENCE IN JACKSON HOLE, WYOMING
REPRINTS FROM THE SOVIET PRESS, 49(10) (NOV 89), 38-43.
EDUARD SHEVARDNADZE AND U.S. SECRETARY OF STATE JAMES
BAKER CONDUCTED TALKS IN JACKSON HOLE, WYOMING. THEIR
RESULTS WERE SUMMED UP AT A NEWS CONFERENCE THERE BY
SHEVARDNADZE. HE REPORTED THAT THE TALKS MARKED A NEW STAGE
IN SOVIET-U.S. DIALOGUE, HE BRIEFLY OUTLINED THE ISSUES THAT
WERE CONSIDERED, WHICH INCLUDED DISARMAMENT, CHEMICAL
WEAPONS AND REGIONAL PROBLEMS. HE CONCLUDED THAT THE TALKS
WERE SUCCESSFUL.

00389
NICARAGUAN ELECTIONS: CHALLENGE TO SANDINISTAS AND U.S.
CENTRAL AMERICA BULLETIN, 8(9) (AUG 89), 1-3, 7-8.
IN NICARAGUA, THE CONTRAS ARE WIDELY DISMISSED AS
IRRELEVANT DUE TO THEIR BATTLEFIELD DEFEATS AND DIPLOMATIC
FAILURES. SINCE MID-1988, THE DEBATE WITHIN NICARAGUA HAS
CENTERED ON THE ECONOMIC CRISIS AND THE UPCOMING ELECTION.
OVER THE LAST FEW MONTHS, THE BUSH ADMINISTRATION SEEMS TO
HAVE GRADUALLY AWAKENED TO THIS SHIFTING REALITY. ALTHOUGH
THE BUSH ADMINISTRATION HAS NOT ABANDONED THE CONTRAS, IT
SEEMS TO BE TAKING THE ELECTION SERIOUSLY AND HOPES TO PLAY
A DECISIVE ROLE IN IT THROUGH FINANCIAL ASSISTANCE, TRAINING,
AND TECHNICAL ADVICE TO THE OPPOSITION CAMPAIGN.

00390
NIGERIA'S UNEASY SULTAN
NEW AFRICAN, (257) (FEB 89), 22.
ALHAJI IBRAHMIN DASUKI, THE MILLIONAIRE PRINCE WHO WAS
INSTALLED AS THE 18TH SULTAN OF SOKOTO CALIPHATE IN NOVEMBER
1988, SEEMS TO HAVE WEATHERED THE STORM OF VIOLENCE AND
CONTROVERSY SURROUNDING HIS SELECTION TO THE MOST POWERFUL
TRADITIONAL THRONE IN NIGERIA. BUT HE HAS YET TO WIN THE
TRADITIONAL AWE AND REVERENCE ENJOYED BY HIS PREDECESSOR,
SIR ABUBAKAR III.

00391
NO CHANGE IN REFORM AND OPEN POLICY
CHINA RECONSTRUCTS, XXXVIII(9) (SEP 89), 5.
DUE TO THE EVENTS IN BEIJING IN THE SPRING OF 1989, SOME
CHINESE ARE WORRIED THAT THE NATIONAL POLICY OF REFORM AND
OPENING TO THE OUTSIDE WORLD WILL BE ABANDONED, THAT THERE

WILL BE A RETROGRESSION. BUT DENG XIAOPING HAS DECLARED THAT THE POLITICAL LINE, POLICIES, AND PRINCIPLES PURSUED FOR THE LAST DECADE (INCLUDING THE ADHERENCE TO SOCIALISM, REFORM, AND THE OPEN POLICY) WERE ALL CORRECT AND WILL REMAIN UNCHANGED.

00392
NO CHANGE IN REFORM POLICY--DENG
BEIJING REVIEW, 32(39) (SEP 89), 9.
DENG XIAOPING HAS STRESSED THAT CHINA WILL NOT CHANGE ITS POLICIES FORMULATED DURING A DECADE OF REFORM AND OPENING UP TO THE OUTSIDE WORLD. HE HAS ALSO STATED THAT THE UNREST IN THE SPRING OF 1989 TAUGHT CHINESE LEADERS A MAJOR LESSON. HE ATTRIBUTED THE POLITICAL TURMOIL TO THE FACT THAT SOME LEADERS DID NOT PAY ENOUGH ATTENTION TO IDEOLOGICAL AND POLITICAL DEVELOPMENTS AND ALSO RELAXED THEIR STANCE AGAINST GOVERNMENT CORRUPTION.

00393
NORTH ATLANTIC COUNCIL SESSION HELD IN BRUSSELS
DEPARTMENT OF STATE BULLETIN (US FOREIGN POLICY), 89(2143) (FEB 89), 43-50.
THE SEMI-ANNUAL SESSION OF THE NORTH ATLANTIC COUNCIL MINISTERIAL MEETING WAS HELD IN BRUSSELS IN DECEMBER 1988. THIS REPORT INCLUDES THE TEXTS OF A STATEMENT ON CONVENTIONAL ARMS CONTROL, THE MINISTERS' FINAL COMMUNIQUE, EXTRACTS FROM THE MINUTES OF THE MEETING, AND REMARKS BY US SECRETARY OF STATE SHULTZ.

00394
NORTH ATLANTIC TREATY ORGANISATION SUMMIT MEETING
SURVEY OF CURRENT AFFAIRS, 19(6) (JUN 89), 222-230.
AT A SUMMIT MEETING IN BRUSSELS ON 29 AND 30 MAY 1989, HEADS OF GOVERNMENT OF THE 16 MEMBERS OF THE NORTH ATLANTIC TREATY ORGANISATION ADOPTED A STRATEGY FOR THE CONDUCT OF FUTURE EAST-WEST RELATIONS, INCLUDING NEW PROPOSALS ON CONVENTIONAL ARMS CONTROL. FURTHER, THEY AGREED THAT IN 1992 THE INTRODUCTION AND DEPLOYMENT OF SHORT-RANGE NUCLEAR WEAPONS TO REPLACE THE LANCE MISSILE WOULD BE ADDRESSED. THEY ALSO AGREED TO NEGOTIATE WITH THE WARSAW PACT ON A PARTIAL REDUCTION OF SHORT-RANGE NUCLEAR FORCES.

00395
NORWAY AFTER THE SUMMIT: INTERVIEW WITH THE MINISTER OF DEFENCE
NATO'S SIXTEEN NATIONS, 34(4) (AUG 89), 29-30, 32-34, 36.
NORWAY STANDS FIRM WITHIN THE COHERENT ALLIANCE POLICY THAT EMERGED FROM THE NATO SUMMIT MEETING. ALTHOUGH ITS ENTRY INTO THE WESTERN EUROPEAN UNION IS NOT ENVISAGED AT THE MOMENT, NORWAY REMAINS A VITAL PART OF THE EUROPEAN PILLAR. MINISTER OF DEFENCE JOHAN JORGEN HOLST CONSIDERS THE RECENT DEVELOPMENTS IN EAST-WEST RELATIONS TO BE POSITIVE BUT HE IS ALSO AWARE OF THE LARGE SOVIET FORCES STATIONED IN THE NORTH.

00396
NOT ONLY SOVIET TANKS CRUSLED THE PROGUE SPRING
NEW POLITICS, 11(2) (WIN 89), 55-65.
THIS ARTICLE PROVIDES A CHRONOLOGY OF THE SOVIET INVASION OF CZECHOSLOVAKIA IN 1968 AND OFFERS AN INTERVIEW WITH J AROSLAV SABATA, A GOVERNMENT MEMBER OF THE CZECH COMMUNIST PARTY IN 1968. SABATA PROVIDES RARE DETAILS OF THE CZECH LEADERSHIP'S STEP - BY - STEP CHOICES WHICH ENSURED THE SUCCESS OF THE KREMLIN.

00397
NPC MEETING FOCUSES ON REBELLION
BEIJING REVIEW, 32(29) (JUL 89), 7, 9.
THE EIGHTH MEETING OF THE STANDING COMMITTEE OF THE SEVENTH NATIONAL PEOPLE'S CONGRESS CLOSED JULY 5, 1989, WITH A RESOLUTION EXPRESSING SATISFACTION WITH THE GOVERNMENT'S ACTIONS TO QUELL THE COUNTER-REVOLUTIONARY REBELLION IN BEIJING IN JUNE. THE RESOLUTION ALSO ASKED THE STATE COUNCIL TO CONTINUE IMPROVING THE ECONOMIC ORDER, TO DEEPEN THE REFORM, AND TO STRESS THE POLICY OF OPENING TO THE OUTSIDE WORLD. THE MEETING DECIDED TO DISMISS ZHAO ZIYANG FROM HIS POST AS VICE-CHAIRMAN OF THE STATE CENTRAL MILITARY COMMISSION.

00398
NPC MESSAGE TO TAIWAN COMPARTRIOTS
BEIJING REVIEW, 32(2) (JAN 89), 10.
TAIWAN'S SEPARATION FROM THE MOTHERLAND IS ARTIFICIAL AND CONTRARY TO ALL NATIONAL INTERESTS AND ASPIRATIONS. THIS STATE OF AFFAIRS MUST NOT BE ALLOWED TO CONTINUE. EARLY REUNIFICATION OF CHINA IS NOT ONLY THE COMMON DESIRE OF ALL CHINESE PEOPLE, BUT THE COMMON WISH OF ALL PEACE-LOVING PEOPLES AND COUNTRIES. THE WORLD IN GENERAL RECOGNIZES ONLY ONE CHINA, WITH THE GOVERNMENT OF THE PEOPLE'S REPUBLIC OF CHINA AS ITS SOLE LEGAL GOVERNMENT.

00399
NPC, CPPCC PROTEST AGAINST U.S. SANCTIONS
BEIJING REVIEW, 32(49) (DEC 89), 9.
THE FOREIGN AFFAIRS COMMITTEE OF CHINA'S NATIONAL PEOPLE'S CONGRESS AND THE CHINESE PEOPLE'S POLITICAL CONSULTATIVE CONFERENCE HAVE ISSUED STATEMENTS CENSURING AN AMENDMENT ON SANCTIONS ADOPTED BY THE U.S. CONGRESS. THE CHINESE GROUPS VIEW THE ECONOMIC SANCTIONS AGAINST CHINA AS INTERFERENCE IN ITS INTERNAL AFFAIRS AND HAVE WARNED THAT THEY WILL POISON SINO-AMERICAN RELATIONS.

00400
NUCLEAR AND SPACE TALKS OPEN ROUND 11
DEPARTMENT OF STATE BULLETIN (US FOREIGN POLICY), 89(2149) (AUG 89), 73-74.
THE BUSH ADMINISTRATION'S GOALS FOR ROUND 11 OF THE NUCLEAR AND SPACE TALKS (NST) IS TO ACHIEVE VERIFIABLE AGREEMENTS THAT IMPROVE AMERICAN SECURITY WHILE ENHANCING STABILITY AND REDUCING THE RISK OF WAR. IN THE STRATEGIC ARMS REDUCTION TALKS, THE US EMPHASIS IS ON CREATING A MORE STABLE NUCLEAR BALANCE AND STRENGTHENING DETERRENCE. THE UNITED STATES IS PURSUING COMPLEMANTARY GOALS IN THE DEFENSE AND SPACE TALKS, SEEKING AN AGREEMENT ON A COOPERATIVE TRANSITION TO A MORE STABLE NUCLEAR BALANCE THAT RELIES INCREASINGLY ON DEFENSES.

00401
NUCLEAR POWER AND ELECTRICITY PRIVATISATION
SURVEY OF CURRENT AFFAIRS, 19(12) (DEC 89), 473.
THE THATCHER GOVERNMENT HAS DECIDED THAT NUCLEAR POWER STATIONS IN GREAT BRITAIN WILL REMAIN IN THE PUBLIC SECTOR AFTER THE PRIVATISATION OF THE ELECTRICITY SUPPLY INDUSTRY. GOVERNMENT CALCULATIONS REVEALED THAT THE COSTS OF NUCLEAR POWER AFTER PRIVATISATION WOULD BE HIGHER THAN THOSE OF POWER FROM FOSSIL-FUELED GENERATING STATIONS AND THIS LED TO THE DECISION THAT THE MAGNOX STATIONS WOULD REMAIN UNDER GOVERNMENT CONTROL. THE GOVERNMENT'S GOALS ARE TO PRESERVE THE STRATEGIC ROLE OF NUCLEAR POWER, MAINTAIN DIVERSITY OF SUPPLY, AVOID TOO MUCH RELIANCE ON A SINGLE FUEL, AND OBTAIN THE BENEFITS OF ENVIRONMENTALLY CLEAN NUCLEAR ENERGY.

00402
OBSTACLES TO INSTITUTIONAL DEVELOPMENT IN HAITI
INDIAN JOURNAL OF POLITICAL SCIENCE, L(3) (JUL 89), 409-437.
FOUR FACTORS SIGNIFICANTLY CONDITION POSSIBILITIES FOR INSTITUTIONAL DEVELOPMENT IN HAITI: (1) A LARGE POPULATION AND LABOR FORCE GROWTH; (2) AGRICULTURAL STAGNATION; (3) LANGUAGE DUALISM; AND (4) THE RIGIDITY OF THE ADMINISTRATIVE STRUCTURES. AGRICULTURE IS THE KEY SOURCE OF ECONOMIC GROWTH POTENTIAL. LANGUAGE IS A KEY FACTOR SINCE COMMUNICATION AND THE EXCHANGE OF INFORMATION ARE INDISPENSABLE FOR THE TRANSMISSION OF NEW TECHNOLOGY. THE PUBLIC BUREAUCRACY IS A MAJOR ACTOR, BOTH IN DEFINING DEVELOPMENT POLICY AND IN CARRYING IT OUT.

00403
OCCUPATIONAL HEALTH LEGISLATION
CONGRESSIONAL DIGEST, 68(4) (APR 89), 98-104.
THE ARTICLE REVIEWS FACTORS INVOLVED IN OCCUPATIONAL HEALTH LEGISLATION AND RECENT ACTION REGARDING SUCH LEGISLATION IN CONGRESS.

00404
OECD COUNCIL MINISTERIAL HELD IN PARIS
DEPARTMENT OF STATE BULLETIN (US FOREIGN POLICY), 89(2150) (SEP 89), 78-83.
THE ANNUAL COUNCIL OF THE ORGANIZATION FOR ECONOMIC COOPERATION AND DEVELOPMENT WAS HELD IN PARIS IN MAY AND JUNE 1989. THE MINISTERS DISCUSSED WAYS TO MAINTAIN SOLID, BALANCED ECONOMIC GROWTH WHILE REDUCING UNSUSTAINABLY LARGE EXTERNAL IMBALANCES. IMPROVING LIVING STANDARDS BY CREATING NEW JOBS AND BUSINESS OPPORTUNITIES, PROVIDING ADEQUATE SUPPORT FOR DEVELOPING NATIONS TO STRENGTHEN THEIR ECONOMIES, AND REMAINING VIGILANT AGAINST INFLATION.

00405
OFFICIAL SECRETS BILL
SURVEY OF CURRENT AFFAIRS, 19(1) (JAN 89), 4-6.
THE PROPOSED CHANGES TO GREAT BRITAIN'S OFFICIAL SECRETS ACT WOULD CREATE TWO OFFENSES OF DISCLOSING INFORMATION RELATING TO SECURITY OR INTELLIGENCE. THE FIRST WOULD APPLY TO MEMBERS AND FORMER MEMBERS OF THE SECURITY AND INTELLIGENCE SERVICES, PROHIBITING THEM FROM DISCLOSING INFORMATION RELATING TO, OR PURPORTING TO RELATE TO, SECURITY OR INTELLIGENCE MATTERS. THE SECOND OFFENSE REGARDS ANY OTHER CROWN SERVANT OR GOVERNMENT CONTRACTOR WHO DISCLOSES, WITHOUT LAWFUL AUTHORITY, INFORMATION THAT WOULD BE LIKELY TO DAMAGE THE WORK OF THE SECURITY AND INTELLIGENCE SERVICES.

00406
ON BIRDS AND CAGES: THE CHINESE FINANCIAL SYSTEM
CHINA NEWS ANALYSIS, (1398) (DEC 89), 1-9.
DESPITE ALL THE POLICY AND PROPAGANDA EFFORTS, THERE REMAINS A CONSTITUENCY WITHIN THE COMMUNIST PARTY OF CHINA THAT IS NOT CONVINCED OF THE NEED FOR THE RECENT ECONOMIC

STRIGENCY IMPOSED BY THE CENTRAL GOVERNMENT. IT IS STILL UNCLEAR WHICH OF THE TWO MAIN FORCES WILL DETERMINE THE DIRECTION OF FUTURE ECONOMIC CHANGE: THE CENTRALIZING OR THE CENTRIFUGAL FORCES. ALTHOUGH THE CONSERVATIVE WING HAS BEEN GAINING STEADILY WITHIN THE PARTY, THE REFORMERS HAVE SO FAR HELD THEIR GROUND.

00407
    ON THE BRINK OF INSURRECTION
    CENTRAL AMERICA BULLETIN, 8(4) (MAR 89), 1-3, 7-8.
    BOTH THE DYNAMICS OF THE UNFOLDING SITUATION IN EL SALVADOR AND CURRENT CONDITIONS SUGGEST THAT THE CONFRONTATION THERE MAY DRAMATICALLY ESCALATE. THERE ARE TWO KEY VARIABLES IN THE CURRENT SITUATION: HAS THE FARABUNDO MARTI NATIONAL LIBERATION FRONT ALREADY LAUNCHED A MAJOR OFFENSIVE? WILL ITS ELECTORAL PROPOSAL BE ACCEPTED BY THE UNITED STATES, THE SALVADORAN ARMED FORCES, AND THE GOVERNMENT? A THIRD UNKNOWN IS THE IMPACT OF THE UPCOMING ELECTIONS.

00408
    ON THE EUROPEAN SCENE
    INTERNATIONAL AFFAIRS (MOSCOW), (9) (SEP 89), 122-125.
    A SENSE OF EUROPEAN COMMUNITY IS CLEARLY GAINING STRENGTH IN WHAT HAS FOR DECADES BEEN A CONTINENT OF ESTRANGEMENT AND CONFRONTATION BETWEEN THE TWO SOCIO-POLITICAL SYSTEMS. THERE ARE REAL OPPORTUNITIES FOR OVERCOMING BARRIERS CREATED BY STALINISM AND BY THE COLD WAR. THE LAST FEW WEEKS HAVE BEEN A KIND OF LANDMARK IN THE MOVEMENT TOWARD GREATER EUROPEAN HARMONY, AS MIKHAIL GORBACHEV'S TRIPS TO WEST GERMANY AND FRANCE HAVE REVEALED THAT SOVIET REFORMS ARE GENERALLY APPLAUDED IN WESTERN EUROPE.

00409
    ON THE JAPANESE THREAT: AN INTERVIEW WITH CHALMERS JOHNSON
    MULTINATIONAL MONITOR, 11(11) (NOV 89), 18-21.
    THE JAPANESE THREAT TO AMERICA IS IN SOME WAYS A SELF-INFLICTED WOUND. AND THE PROBLEM IS NOT GOING TO GO AWAY BY HARASSING JAPAN. IT BASICALLY IS CAUSED BY INCOMPETENCE IN THE AMERICAN GOVERNMENT.

00410
    ON THE RELATIVE STRENGTH OF THE ARMED FORCES AND ARMAMENTS OF THE WTO AND NATO IN EUROPE AND ADJACENT WATER AREAS
    REPRINTS FROM THE SOVIET PRESS, 48(5) (MAR 89), 5-7.
    IN VIEW OF THE CURRENT TREND TOWARDS ARMS CONTROL AND DISARMAMENT IN EUROPE, THE ARTICLE SEEKS TO DETERMINE THE RELATIVE STRENGTHS AND WEAKNESSES OF NATO AND WARSAW PACT FORCES. IT ENGAGES IN A WEAPON BY WEAPON ANALYSIS OF GROUND, AIR, AND NAVAL FORCES. IT CONCLUDES THAT ALTHOUGH THERE ARE SIGNIFICANT IMBALANCES IN INDIVIDUAL WEAPONS CATAGORIES, THERE IS AN OVERALL ROUGH DEGREE OF PARITY. NEITHER SIDE HAS ENOUGH SUPERIORITY TO ENGAGE IN A SURPRISE CONVENTIONAL ATTACK. THE ARTICLE CONCLUDES THAT LARGE SCALE REDUCTIONS ON BOTH SIDES WOULD INCREASE STABILITY AND REDUCE THE RISK OF CONFLICT EVEN MORE.

00411
    ON THE RIGHTS OF TRADE UNIONS
    REPRINTS FROM THE SOVIET PRESS, 49(1) (JUL 89), 12-19.
    STEPAN SHALAYEV, CHAIRMAN OF THE ALL-UNION CENTRAL COUNCIL OF TRADE UNIONS IN THE USSR, DISCUSSES THE DRAFT LAW: "ON THE RIGHTS OF TRADE UNIONS OF THE USSR." HE OUTLINES ITS MAJOR PROVISIONS AND DISCUSSES ITS IMPLICATIONS FOR THE FUTURE OF THE TRADE UNION MOVEMENT. SOME OF THE PROVISIONS ARE AIMED AT ENHANCING THE PROTECTIVE ROLE OF TRADE UNIONS, OTHERS DEAL WITH THE FIELD OF PRICE SETTING; STILL OTHERS GRANT TRADE UNIONS THE RIGHT TO WORK STOPPAGE IN SPECIAL CASES.

00412
    ON THE WAY TO DEMOCRACY
    CONTEMPORARY POLAND, XXII(8) (1989), 18-21.
    THE AUTHOR SUMMARIZES INTERVIEWS WITH POLISH PRESIDENT WOJCIECH JARUZELSKI AND WITH THE FIRST SECRETARY OF THE POLISH UNITED WORKERS' PARTY CC, MIECZYSLAW F. RAKOWSKI. THE TWO MEN DISCUSS CURRENT ISSUES, INCLUDING POLAND'S ECONOMIC DEVELOPMENT AND REFORM EFFORTS.

00413
    ONE STEP FORWARD
    FAR EASTERN ECONOMIC REVIEW, 142(52) (DEC 89), 45.
    THE EUROPEAN COMMUNITY UNVEILED A CAUTIOUS BLUEPRINT FOR REFORMING WORLDWIDE FARM TRADE. A PROPOSAL FOR A COMMUNITY-WIDE QUOTA ON JAPANESE CARS WAS REJECTED IN FAVOR OF A VOLUNTARY-RESTRAIN ARRANGEMENT UNDER WHICH TOKYO IS TO MODERATE CAR EXPORTS TO THE COMMUNITY. BOTH STEPS ARE SEEN AS POSITIVE STEPS TOWARDS TRADE LIBERALIZATION.

00414
    ONE TRAIN, SINGLE TRACK
    SOUTH, (101) (MAR 89), 4.
    THE NEED TO ADOPT A MORE RATIONAL ALLOCATION OF GLOBAL

RESOURCES TO REFLECT THE PROSPECTS OF DISARMAMENT AND PEACE REMAINS UNEXPLORED. THE QUESTION IS HOW TO ELIMINATE WAR, GIVEN MANKIND'S CONGENITAL INCLINATION TOWARD AGGRESSION. AS A FIRST STEP, EVERY NATION SHOULD ABANDON TRADITIONAL DOCTRINES OF NATIONAL SECURITY. THE THREAT IS NOT FROM ONE'S NEIGHBORS. THE REAL PREDATORS ARE POVERTY, INEQUALITY, AND EXPLOITATION.

00415
    ONLY THE BEGINNING
    SOUTH, (109) (NOV 89), 9.
    MOST WESTERN OBSERVERS THINK THAT LIBERALISM HAS FINALLY VANQUISHED RELIGION, AUTHORITARIANISM, AND COMMUNISM. IN FACT, WHEREVER OBSCURANTISM AND AUTHORITARIANISM HAVE YIELDED GROUND, IT HAS BEEN THROUGH THE STRUGGLE OF THE MASSES RESPONDING TO THE IRRESISTIBLE FORCE OF THE DEMOCRATIC TRUTH -- THE ETHOS OF LIBERTY AND EQUALITY—NOT BECAUSE OF THE SUPERIORITY OF THE WESTERN LIBERAL SYSTEM.

00416
    OPINIONS ABOUT THE GOVERNMENT: A PUBLIC OPINION POLLING CENTRE SURVEY
    CONTEMPORARY POLAND, XXII(2) (1989), 13.
    A NOVEMBER 1988 SURVEY BY THE PUBLIC OPINION POLLING CENTRE REVEALED THAT THE RAKOWSKI GOVERNMENT WAS FAVORED BY MORE THAN TWICE AS MANY RESPONDENTS AS THOSE WHO APPROVED OF MESSNER IN AUGUST 1988. IN THE PAST, POLLS HAD SHOWN RAKOWSKI TO BE A CONTROVERSIAL FIGURE. BETWEEN DECEMBER 1985 AND AUGUST 1988, SURVEYS REVEALED THAT HE HAD MORE DETRACTORS THAN SUPPORTERS. BUT SYMPATHY TOWARDS HIM INCREASED WITH HIS APPOINTMENT TO THE POST OF PRIME MINISTER, AND IN NOVEMBER HE RANKED ALONGSIDE WILCZEK AS THE MOST POPULAR POLITICIAN IN POLAND.

00417
    OPTIMIZATION: REFORM OR NOT?
    BEIJING REVIEW, 32(9) (FEB 89), 12-13.
    UNDER CHINA'S CURRENT OPTIMUM ORGANIZATION PRACTICE, THE EXCESS FAT IN THE FORM OF LESS TALENTED AND LESS VITAL WORKERS IS BEING TRIMMED FROM THE WORKING PLACE. BUT IN SOME CASES, ESPECIALLY THOSE INVOLVING TEACHERS, THIS PRACTICE IS BEING ABUSED, BRINGING INTO QUESTION THE STATUS OF THE PEOPLE'S CONSTITUTIONALLY GUARANTEED RIGHT TO WORK.

00418
    OUTLINE ECONOMIC PROGRAMME: MAIN ASSUMPTIONS AND DIRECTIONS
    CONTEMPORARY POLAND, XXII(11-12) (1989), 30-42.
    THE POLISH ECONOMY REQUIRES FUNDAMENTAL CHANGES AND A MARKET SYSTEM AKIN TO THOSE FOUND IN THE INDUSTRIALLY-DEVELOPED COUNTRIES. THIS MUST BE ACHIEVED QUICKLY THROUGH RADICAL ACTION, SO THAT THE TRANSITIONAL STAGE, WHICH WILL BE HARD ON THE PEOPLE, CAN BE AS SHORT AS POSSIBLE. THE SURFACE-ONLY REFORMS OF THE 1980'S DID NOT WORK. WITHOUT FUNDAMENTAL CHANGE, POLAND WILL CONTINUE TO SINK INTO GENERAL INCAPACITY AND PERMANENT ECONOMIC CRISIS.

00419
    OUTLINES OF A NEW WORLD OF FREEDOM
    DEPARTMENT OF STATE BULLETIN (US FOREIGN POLICY), 89(2152) (NOV 89), 27-31.
    IN THIS ADDRESS TO THE UNITED NATIONS GENERAL ASSEMBLY IN SEPTEMBER 1989, PRESIDENT GEORGE BUSH DISCUSSED ECONOMIC GROWTH, THE WORLD ENVIRONMENT, ARMS CONTROL, AND THE U.S. CHEMICAL WEAPONS INITIATIVE.

00420
    OVERSEAS CHINESE AFFAIRS HIGH ON AGENDA
    BEIJING REVIEW, 32(52) (DEC 89), 9-10.
    OVERSEAS CHINESE AFFAIRS HAVE ALWAYS BEEN HIGH ON THE AGENDA OF BOTH THE COMMUNIST PARTY OF CHINA AND THE GOVERNMENT. DURING THE CULTURAL REVOLUTION, THE GOVERNMENT PERSECUTED CITIZENS WHO HAD OVERSEAS RELATIONS, BUT THAT WAS A MISTAKE AND IS NO LONGER THE POLICY. WITH THE RISE OF CHINA'S INTERNATIONAL ROLE AND ITS SOCIALIST MODERNIZATION, CHINA NEEDS A BETTER UNDERSTANDING OF THE OUTSIDE WORLD AND VICE VERSA. OVERSEAS CHINESE AND THEIR RELATIVES CAN HELP THE PEOPLE OF THE WORLD TO UNDERSTAND CHINA.

00421
    OVERVIEW: GLOBAL CHALLENGES
    CRS REVIEW, 10(7) (AUG 89), 1-2.
    THE THREAT OF GLOBAL CLIMATE CHANGE IS ONE OF THE MOST PERVASIVE AND POTENTIALLY DISRUPTIVE OF THE ENVIRONMENTAL ISSUES FACING THE WORLD. MEASURABLE INCREASES IN CONCENTRATIONS OF SOME ATMOSPHERIC GASES HAVE LED TO A CONSENSUS AMONG SCIENTISTS THAT DRAMATIC CHANGES IN CLIMATE ARE POSSIBLE THROUGH ENHANCEMENT OF THE GREENHOUSE EFFECT. THIS RAISES A WIDE ARRAY OF POLICY ISSUES, INCLUDING THE POTENTIAL FOR INTERNATIONAL AGREEMENTS TO STIMULATE COOPERATION AND COORDINATED ACTION. OTHER AREAS WHERE U.S. POLICY MAKERS FACE THE NEED TO DEAL WITH ISSUES THAT HAVE CRITICAL INTERNATIONAL DIMENSIONS INCLUDE THE THREAT TO THE WORLD'S OCEANS FROM POLLUTION AND THE THREAT OF TROPICAL DEFORESTATION.

00422
PALESTINE AND ISRAEL IN THE US ARENA
MIDDLE EAST REPORT, 19(158) (MAY 89), 4-5.
THE AMERICAN POLICY OF TALKING WITH THE PLO IS DESIGNED
TO ACHIEVE WHAT THE POLICY OF BOYCOTTING FAILED TO
ACCOMPLISH: TO END THE INTIFADA THROUGH A COMBINATION OF
ISRAELI REPRESSION AND VAGUE PROMISES TO ADDRESS LEGITIMATE
PALESTINIAN RIGHTS. ONLY IF THE BUSH ADMINISTRATION IS
CONVINCED THAT THE UPRISING CANNOT BE CRUSHED OR BARGAINED
AWAY AND THAT IT IS MORE THREATENING TO AMERICAN REGIONAL
INTERESTS THAN A NEGOTIATED SETTLEMENT WILL WASHINGTON
SERIOUSLY PRESS ISRAEL TO WITHDRAW FROM THE OCCUPIED
TERRITORIES AND NEGOTIATE WITH THE PLO.

00423
PANAMA ELECTIONS
DEPARTMENT OF STATE BULLETIN (US FOREIGN POLICY), 89(2148)
(JUL 89), 66-72.
THIS REPORT ON PANAMA'S 1989 ELECTIONS INCLUDES
STATEMENTS BY PRESIDENT BUSH AND THE US STATE DEPARTMENT
DETAILING THE NORIEGA REGIME'S CAPAIGN TO SABOTAGE THE
ELECTIONS AND REMAIN IN POWER.

00424
PANAMA: UPHOLD THE PEOPLE'S GAINS
INFORMATION BULLETIN, 26(23-24) (DEC 88), 15-17.
THIS MANIFESTS OF THE PEOPLE'S PARTY OF PANAMA URGES THE
PANAMANIAN PEOPLE TO BE THE PROTAGONIST OF THE CHANGES
AFFECTING PANAMA, NOT MERE COOPERATIVES IN UNITED STATES'
FALSE CAMPAIGNS OF "DEMOCRATIZATION AND MORAL IMPROVEMENT."

00425
PARAGUAY: IN THE VANGUARD OF THE STRUGGLE AGAINST THE
DICTATORSHIP
INFORMATION BULLETIN, 25/26(1-2) (JAN 88), 15-17.
THIS ARTICLE IS A SUMMARY OF THE DECISIONS AND
CONCLUSIONS OF THE PLENARY MEETING OF THE PARAGUAYAN
COMMUNIST PARTY. THE PARTY SINGLES OUT THE NEED FOR A
UNIFIED LEFT ALLIANCE IF EFFORTS TO SET UP A NATIONAL ANTI-
DICTATORSHIP FRONT ARE TO BE SUCCESSFUL.

00426
PARAGUAY: STRENGTHEN LINKS WITH THE MASSES
INFORMATION BULLETIN, 26(21-22) (NOV 88), 12-13.
IT WAS STRESSED AT THE PLENARY MEETING OF THE PARAGUAYAN
COMMUNIST PARTY THAT THANKS TO THE REVOLUTIONARY TURN IN THE
POLITICAL, ECONOMIC, SOCIAL AND CULTURAL LIFE OF THE USSR, A
STEP HAS BEEN TAKEN TOWARD THE SOLUTION OF THE PRINCIPAL
ISSUE FACED BY HUMANITY IN OUR TIMES, OF DEFENDING WORLD
PEACE THROUGH EXPANDING TIES AND STRENGTHENING FRIENDSHIP
BETWEEN ALL NATIONS AND PEOPLES, IRRESPECTIVE OF THE WAY OF
THINKING AND THE SOCIAL SYSTEMS.

00427
PARAGUAY'S SLIM CHANCE
SOUTH, (103) (MAY 89), 9.
GEN. ANDRES RODRIGUEZ, WHO OUSTED GEN. ALFREDO
STROESSNER IN A BLOODY COUP, HAS PROMISED PARAGUAY MULTI-
PARTY ELECTIONS AND A NEW ERA OF RESPECT FOR HUMAN RIGHTS
AND PRESS FREEDOM. SEVERAL PARTIES HAVE NOMINATED CANDIDATES
FOR THE MAY 1989 ELECTIONS, BUT RODRIGUEZ IS EXPECTED TO WIN
AS THE CANDIDATE OF THE FASCISTIC COLORADO PARTY, WHICH
STROESSNER USED AS A PROPAGANDA MACHINE DURING HIS RULE.

00428
PART ONE: RE-READING THE LATIN AMERICAN CRISIS LATIN
AMERICA: CRISIS AND PERPLEXITY
DEVELOPMENT DIALOGUE, (1) (1989), 7-16.
THE ARTICLE EXAMINES THE LATIN AMERICA "CRISIS".
ALTHOUGH THERE IS A GENERAL AGREEMENT THAT LATIN AMERICA IS
IN A STATE OF CRISIS, THERE IS LITTLE AGREEMENT ON THE
CAUSES AND EVEN LESS ON THE SOLUTIONS TO THE CHALLENGES THAT
LATIN AMERICA FACES. THE ARTICLE SEEKS TO ANALYZE THE
ECONOMIC POLICIES OF DEVELOPMENTALISM AND NEO-LIBERAL
MONETARISM AND WHY THESE POLICIES HAVE NOT EXPERIENCED THE
FULL SUCCESS THAT WAS INITIALLY EXPECTED.

00429
PARTNERS, NOT ENEMIES
FREE CHINA REVIEW, 39(4) (APR 89), 1.
EVEN THOUGH FRICTIONS EXIST BETWEEN THE USA AND TAIWAN,
THERE IS GENERAL CONSENSUS BETWEEN THE TWO ABOUT THE NEED
FOR FURTHER LIBERALIZATION AND INTERNATIONALIZATION OF THE
LOCAL ECONOMY. BUT THE TWO DISAGREE ABOUT THE PACE OF
REACHING IT. TAIWAN IS EXPERIENCING SWEEPING TRANSFORMATIONS
IN BOTH POLITICAL AND ECONOMIC AREAS IN A DRASTICALLY
TELESCOPED PERIOD OF TIME. SOLVING TRADE FRICTIONS REMAINS
ONE OF THE GOVERNMENT'S HIGHEST PRIORITIES, AND COOPERATING
WITH THE USA TO SOLVE TRADE PROBLEMS IS IMPORTANT BUT WILL
TAKE TIME.

00430
PARTY STILL BACKS INTELLECTUALS
BEIJING REVIEW, 32(33) (AUG 89), 10.
SINCE THE COMMUNIST PARTY'S MODERNIZATION GOAL AND THE
POLICIES ADOPTED BY THE THIRD PLENARY SESSION OF THE 11TH
CENTRAL COMMITTEE OF THE PARTY HAVE NOT CHANGED, THE PARTY'S
POLICY TOWARDS INTELLECTUALS WAS NOT AFFECTED BY THE
POLITICAL TURMOIL OF JUNE 1989. MOST CHINESE INTELLECTUALS
ARE TRUSTWORTHY BECAUSE THEY HAVE UNDERGONE LONG-TERM
EDUCATION BY THE PARTY AND MANY TESTS IN THE COURSE OF
SOCIALIST REVOLUTION AND CONSTRUCTION. THE VERY FEW
INTELLECTUALS WHO OPPOSE THE PARTY AND PEOPLE ARE NOT
REPRESENTATIVE OF THE INTELLIGENTSIA.

00431
PEACE AND RELIEF IN SUDAN
DEPARTMENT OF STATE BULLETIN (US FOREIGN POLICY), 89(2145)
(APR 89), 24-26.
THE SAD REALITY IS THAT STARVATION IN SUDAN WILL ALMOST
CERTAINLY NOT END UNTIL THE CIVIL WAR ENDS. THE USA HAS
CALLED ON THE SUDANESE GOVERNMENT AND THE SUDANESE PEOPLE'S
LIBERATION ARMY TO AGREE TO AN EARLY CEASE-FIRE TO PROMOTE
PEACE AND ALLOW INTERNATIONAL RELIEF AID TO REACH THOSE IN
NEED.

00432
PEACE AT LAST?
NEW AFRICAN, 261 (JUN 89), 9-11.
THE SUDAN IS AT THE MOST CRUCIAL CROSSROADS OF ITS
EXISTENCE AS AN INDEPENDENT STATE. PEACE WITH JOHN GARANG'S
SPLA WILL MEAN A NEW BEGINNING; CONTINUED WAR WILL MEAN
INEVITABLE DISINTEGRATION. THIS ARTICLE EXAMINES THE ROOT
CAUSES OF THE WAR WITH A FOCUS ON THE HUMAN SITUATION IN THE
SOUTH - THE STATUS SOUTHERN SUDANESE AS SECOND-CLASS
CITIZENS IN THEIR OWN COUNTRY.

00433
PEACE TO THE LAND OF KARABAKH
REPRINTS FROM THE SOVIET PRESS, 48(4) (FEB 89), 38-45.
THROUGHOUT THE PAST YEAR INTER-ETHNIC STRIFE CONTINUED
TO GROW MORE AND MORE ACUTE, AND DEVELOPED INTO OPEN CLASHES
IN THE LAST MONTHS OF THE YEAR. MORE THAN 200,000 PEOPLE
BOTH FROM ARMENIA AND AZERBAIJAN WERE COMPELLED TO LEAVE
THEIR HOMES, JOBS, LIVING PLACES AND CULTIVATED LANDS.
BRIGHT AND CAPABLE PEOPLE, GOOD NEIGHBORS, WERE EXPELLED
JUST FOR BELONGING TO A DIFFERENT NATIONALITY. INJUSTICE AND
EVEN CRUELTY PREVAILED OVER REASON AND TOOK ROOT AMONG THE
PEOPLE. TO STOP THE ORGY OF VIOLENCE, RIGID MEASURES HAD TO
BE TAKEN, AND A STATE OF EMERGENCY HAD TO BE INTRODUCED IN
NUMBER OF REGIONS. THIS ARTICLE DESCRIBES THE IMPACT OF A
SPECIFIC FORCED MEASURE -- THE ESTABLISHMENT OF A COMMITTEE
FOR SPECIAL GOVERNMENT IN NAGORNO-KARABAKH WHICH IS BASED ON
A MUTUALLY ACCEPTABLE COMPROMISE.

00434
PEACE TO THE PERSIAN GRIEF
INFORMATION BULLETIN, 26(21-22) (NOV 88), 7-8.
HOPES HAVE AT LAST APPEARED FOR AN END TO THE SENSELESS
IRAN-IRAQ WAR THANKS TO THE EFFORTS OF ALL PROGRESSIVE
FORCES OF THE WORLD, THE INTERNATIONAL PUBLIC, THE UNITED
NATIONS ORGANIZATION, ITS SECRETARY GENERAL, AND THE UN
SECURITY COUNCIL. THROUGHOUT THE CONFLICT, ALL COMMUNIST
PARTIES OF THE WORLD HAVE CONSISTENTLY INSISTED ON ENDING
THE BLOODSHED AND IMMEDIATELY STARTING THE ELIMINATION OF
ITS POLITICAL, SOCIAL AND ECONOMIC CONSEQUENCES. THE
DOCUMENTS AND MATERIAL IN THIS ARTICLE PROVIDE COMPELLING
EVIDENCE, AND INCLUDE MESSAGES OF HOPE FROM THE COMMUNIST
PARTIES OF IRAN AND IRAQ.

00435
PEKING MADNESS, TAIPEI REACTION
ASIAN OUTLOOK, 24(3) (MAY 89), 5.
ONLY HOURS AFTER PEKING UNLEASED A REIGN OF TERROR UPON
ITS OWN CITIZENS WHO WERE DEMANDING MORE FREEDOM, TAIPEI
CONDEMNED THE CHINESE COMMUNIST REGIME. TAIWAN'S PRESIDENT
LEE TENG-HUI ISSUED A STERN STATEMENT, CONDEMNING THE
MASSACRE OF UNARMED PRO-DEMOCRACY STUDENT PROTESTORS AS AN
"ACT OF MADNESS" AND DEMANDING AN IMMEDIATE HALT TO THE
BRUTAL CRACKDOWN.

00436
PERESTROIKA-88: A FAMOUS POLITICAL DISCUSSION CLUB SPEAKS
OUT ON NAGORNO-KARABAKH
GLASNOST, (16-18) (JAN 89), 9-10.
THE NATIONALITY ISSUE IS OF UTMOST IMPORTANCE FOR THE
SOVIET UNION. THE USSR INCLUDES PEOPLES OF DIFFERING
CULTURAL TRADITIONS AND OF DIVERSE POLITICAL, ECONOMIC, AND
SOCIAL EXPERIENCES. IN MANY CASES, THESE PEOPLES WERE NOT
BROUGHT TOGETHER IN A PEACEFUL, PAINLESS WAY. THUS, IT WAS
INEVITABLE THAT NUMEROUS PROBLEMS WOULD DEVELOP AMONG THE
NATIONALITIES. THESE PROBLEMS WERE EXACERBATED BY JOSEPH
STALIN'S POLICIES, WHICH TO A LARGE EXTENT CONTINUED THE
TRADITIONS OF IMPERIAL RUSSIA. THE TREATMENT OF NAGORNO-
KARABAKH IS ONE OF THE MANY EXAMPLES OF THE SORT OF ETHNIC
CRISS-CROSSING THAT STALIN AND HIS HENCHMEN EMPLOYED TO
DIVIDE AND RULE THEIR SUBJECT PEOPLES.

00437
PERMANENT U.S. BASES?
CENTRAL AMERICA BULLETIN, 8(3) (FEB 89), 4-5.
IN SEPTEMBER 1988, IT WAS REVEALED THAT HONDURAN
MILITARY OFFICIALS WERE CONDUCTING SECRET NEGOTIATIONS WITH
THE UNITED STATES REGARDING PERMANENT U.S. MILITARY BASES ON
HONDURAN SOIL. THE NEGOTIATIONS REVOLVED AROUND PROTOCOL III,
AN AMENDMENT TO THE 1954 MUTUAL SECURITY TREATY BETWEEN THE
USA AND HONDURAS. UNDER THE PROTOCOL TERMS, THE USA WOULD BE
ABLE TO BUILD PERMANENT MILITARY INSTALLATIONS. THE
STRUCTURES WOULD BE HONDURAN PROPERTY, BUT THE UNITED STATES
WOULD HAVE THE RIGHT TO USE THEM INDEFINITELY. WHILE THE
BASES WOULD BE NOMINALLY UNDER HONDURAN CONTROL, THE TROOPS
OCCUPYING THE BASES WOULD BE UNDER U.S. COMMAND.

00438
PERSPECTIVES ON NATION BUILDING IN LOW-DENSITY, HIGH-
PROBABILITY CONFLICTS
MILITARY REVIEW, LXIX(2) (FEB 89), 29-52.
AT THE LOW-INTENSITY END OF THE CONFLICT SPECTRUM, THE
UNITED STATES FACES UNIQUE AND VARYING DEMANDS IN MEETING
ITS NATIONAL AND REGIONAL SECURITY RESPONSIBILITIES.
NATIONAL AND MILITARY STRATEGIES ARE DEVELOPED AND REVISED
IN A CONTINUOUS EFFORT TO COUNTER THREATS TO PEACE AND
STABILITY. IN LATIN AMERICA, A NEW SOUTHCOM STRATEGY IS
PRODUCING VERY POSITIVE RESULTS. A "COMBINED ARMS TEAM FOR
LIC," COMPOSED OF ENGINEERS, MEDICS, PUBLIC AFFAIRS
SPECIALISTS AND OTHER COMBAT SUPPORT AND SERVICE SUPPORT
ASSETS FROM BOTH ACTIVE AND RESERVE COMPONENTS, IS LEADING
IN THIS FIGHT. THESE PERSPECTIVES DESCRIBE EARLY SUCCESSES
AND PROBLEM AREAS ENCOUNTERED IN IMPLEMENTING THIS STRATEGY.

00439
PHILADELPHIA ARCHBISHOP LECTURES PRESIDENT BUSH ON
PAROCHIAID
CHURCH AND STATE, 42(6) (JUN 89), 18 (138)-19 (139).
CATHOLIC ARCHBISHOP ANTHONY J. BEVILACQUA OF
PHILADELPHIA HAS ASKED PRESIDENT GEORGE BUSH TO SUPPORT
PAROCHIAL SCHOOL AID BECAUSE OF POLITICAL SUPPORT HE
RECEIVED FROM PENNSYLVANIA CATHOLICS DURING THE 1988
ELECTION. BECAUSE BUSH HAS WAFFLED ON THE ISSUE OF TUITION
TAX CREDITS FOR PRIVATE SCHOOLS, PENNSYLVANIA'S CATHOLIC
BISHOPS HAVE SAID THAT THEY ARE UNCLEAR CONCERNING BUSH'S
STANCE ON THE ISSUE. BEVILACQUA, SPEAKING ON BEHALF OF THE
BISHOPS, ALSO ASKED BUSH TO CLARIFY HIS POSITION. A WHITE
HOUSE SPOKESMAN SAID THAT BUSH SUPPORTS THE TAX CREDITS BUT
BUDGET CONSTRAINTS PREVENT THEIR IMPLEMENTATION.

00440
PHILIPPINES: EXPOSE CARP'S DECEPTIVE FEATURES! CONTINUE
THE STRUGGLE FOR AGRARIAN REFORM!
INFORMATION BULLETIN, 26(21-22) (NOV 88), 26-27.
THIS STATEMENT OF THE PHILIPPINE COMMUNIST PARTY
CONDEMNS THE COMPREHENSIVE AGRARIAN REFORM PROGRAM AS A
VICTORY FOR LANDOWNERS AND FOR AGRIBUSINESS INTERESTS AND A
DEFEAT FOR THE RURAL POOR OF THE PHILIPPINES.

00441
POGROMS AGAINST NORTHERNERS
NEW AFRICAN, (266) (NOV 89), 20.
THIS ARTICLE REPORTS ON PERSECUTION OF NORTHERN
MALAWIANS BY BANDA'S REGIME. IT EXPLORES THIS AS A
CONTINUATION OF THE VICTIMISATION OF NORTHERNER'S THAT BEGAN
TWO DECADES AGO. IT EXAMINES THE INCREASED SUFFERING OF THE
NORTHERNERS.

00442
POINTS OF MUTUAL ADVANTAGE: PERESTROIKA AND AMERICAN
FOREIGN POLICY
DEPARTMENT OF STATE BULLETIN (US FOREIGN POLICY), 89(2153)
(DEC 89), 10-14.
PERESTROIKA PROMISES SOVIET ACTIONS MORE ADVANTAGEOUS TO
U.S. INTERESTS THAN PAST SOVIET POLICIES HAVE. THE TASK IS
TO SEARCH CREATIVELY FOR THOSE POINTS OF MUTUAL AMERICAN-
SOVIET ADVANTAGE THAT MAY BE POSSIBLE DUE TO PERESTROIKA.
BUT THE UNITED STATES MUST MAINTAIN A DEFENSE BUDGET
COMMENSURATE WITH ITS SECURITY REQUIREMENTS AND MUST BE
VIGILANT AND URGE MOSCOW TOWARD COOPERATIVE BEHAVIOR ACROSS
THE FULL RANGE OF AMERICAN-SOVIET RELATIONS.

00443
POLAND HAS FINALLY GOT A PRIME MINISTER DETERMINED TO GO A
LONG WAY
CONTEMPORARY POLAND, XXII(4) (1989), 16-18.
IN THIS INTERVIEW, COUNT EDWARD RACZYNSKI DISCUSSES THE
ACTIVITIES OF POLISH EMIGRES AND THE POLONIA SOCIETY.
RACZYNSKI, WHO SERVED AS PRESIDENT OF THE POLISH GOVERNMENT
IN EXILE FROM 1979 TO 1986, ANSWERS QUESTIONS ABOUT THE
NORMALIZATION OF RELATIONS BETWEEN PCLES LIVING ABROAD AND
THE POLISH AUTHORITIES UNDER THE FOREIGN MINISTRY OF RADEUSZ
OLECHOWSKI.

00444
POLAND IN THE EUROPEAN ECONOMIC COMMUNITY
CONTEMPORARY POLAND, XXII(9) (1989), 22-24.
IN THIS INTERVIEW, THE DIRECTOR OF THE INSTITUTE OF
BASIC TECHNICAL PROBLEMS OF THE POLISH ACADEMY OF SCIENCES
ANSWERS QUESTIONS ABOUT THE POSSIBILITY OF POLAND JOINING
THE EUROPEAN COMMON MARKET, THE TECHNOLOGICAL COLLAPSE IN
POLAND, THE STATE OF POLISH INDUSTRY, AND RELATED MATTERS.

00445
POLAND'S PRECIPECE
COMMONWEAL, CXVI(16) (SEP 89), 483-484.
SOLIDARITY'S SUCCESS IN BREAKING THE COMMUNIST PARTY'S
MONOPOLY OVER THE POLISH GOVERNMENT SHOULD BE CELEBRATED.
THE POLISH GENIUS FOR POLITICAL PERSISTENCE HAS TRIUMPHED.
BUT THE SORRY STATE OF THE POLISH ECONOMY WILL SORELY TEST
THEIR ACHIEVEMENT.

00446
POLICY ON TAIWAN UNCHANGED
BEIJING REVIEW, 32(28) (JUL 89), 12.
ON JUNE 26, 1989, A STATE COUNCIL OFFICIAL STATED THAT
THE CHINESE COMMUNIST PARTY AND GOVERNMENT WILL NOT CHANGE
THE BASIC NATIONAL POLICY ON THE SOLUTION OF THE TAIWAN
QUESTION--NAMELY, "PEACEFUL REUNIFICATION AND ONE COUNTRY,
TWO SYSTEMS." IN LINE WITH THIS POLICY, THE CHINESE
GOVERNMENT WILL CONTINUE TO GUARANTEE THE PERSONAL SAFETY
AND PROTECT THE PROPERTY AND LEGITIMATE RIGHTS AND INTERESTS
OF TAIWANESE COMPATRIOTS WHO VISIT, TOUR, OR DO BUSINESS ON
THE MAINLAND. IT WILL ALSO CONTINUE TO PROMOTE TRADE,
NAVIGATION, COMMUNICATIONS, AND EXCHANGES BETWEEN THE TWO
SIDES OF THE TAIWAN STRAIT.

00447
POLICY POSITIONS AND CONCLUSIONS OF THE PRESIDENCY OF THE
SPRY ON THE STATUTE OF INTERCOMMUNAL AND INTERREPUBLICAN
RELATIONS AND CASES OF NATIONALISM
YUGOSLAV SURVEY, XXX(4) (1989), 55-58.
ON NOVEMBER 8, 1989, THE PRESIDENCY OF THE SFRY
CONSIDERED THE PROBLEMS CONCERNING THE RELATIONS AMONG THE
NATIONAL GROUPS LIVING IN YUGOSLAVIA AND NATIONALIST
ACTIVITIES THAT THREATEN THE CONSTITUTIONALLY GUARANTEED
ORDER. THE PRESIDENCY ADOPTED A POLICY REGARDING THE
SITUATION THAT STATES THAT RESOLUTE STEPS MUST BE TAKEN TO
STOP THE DETERIORATION IN INTERCOMMUNAL AND INTER-REPUBLICAN
RELATIONS. IT ALSO DECLARES THAT IT IS IMPERATIVE TO CREATE
A CLIMATE THAT WILL FOSTER A CONSTRUCTIVE DIALOGUE AND THE
REMOVAL OF MISTRUST AND INTOLERANCE IN RELATIONS BETWEEN THE
NATIONAL GROUPS AND REPUBLICS.

00448
POLISH DIPLOMACY: OPENNESS AND REALISM
CONTEMPORARY POLAND, XXII(1) (1989), 31-32.
POLAND'S FOREIGN MINISTER TADEUSCZ OLECHOWSKI HAS
DECLARED THAT OPENNESS IS A CHARCTERISTIC TRAIT IN POLISH
RELATIONS WITH THE WORLD AND CURRENT CONDITIONS ARE
PARTICULARLY FAVORABLE FOR CONTINUING THAT POLICY. TODAY
POLISH FOREIGN POLICY PIVOTS ON SUPPORT FOR THE PROCESS OF
REFORM AND DEVELOPMENT IN POLAND. POLAND IS ATTEMPTING TO
OVERCOME ITS FEELINGS OF HISTORIC FATALISM DUE TO ITS
GEOGRAPHIC LOCATION AND TO EMBRACE POSITIVE THINKING AND
BENEFIT FROM ITS POSITION IN THE CENTER OF EUROPE, WHERE
EAST MEETS WEST.

00449
POLITICAL STATEMENT OF FATH'S FIFTH CONGRESS
NEW OUTLOOK, 32(9-10 (295-296)) (SEP 89), 47-49.
THE FIFTH CONGRESS OF THE FATH MOVEMENT CONVENED IN
TUNISIA IN AUGUST 1989. THE DELIBERATIONS DEALT IN-DEPTH
WITH THE PROBLEMS FACING THE PALESTINIAN PEOPLE IN RELATION
TO THEIR NATIONAL CAUSE. THE CONGRESS ADOPTED IMPORTANT
RESOLUTIONS CONCERNING THE INTIFADA AND WAYS OF SUPPORTING
IT. IT STRESSED THAT THE INTIFADA REPRESENTS THE EPITOME OF
PERSEVERANCE AND DETERMINATION AND IS A TURNING POINT IN THE
STRUGGLE AGAINST THE ISRAELI OCCUPATION.

00450
POLYCENTRISM REVISITED
ROUND TABLE, (311) (JUL 89), 262-2664.
TODAY THE FRONT OF SOCIALIST CONSTRUCTION IN THE
COUNTRIES WHERE THE COMMUNISTS ARE THE PARTY IN POWER IS SO
VAST, COMPRISING A THIRD OF HUMANITY, THAT EVEN FOR THIS
PART SOVIET MODEL CANNOT AND SHOULD NOT ANY LONGER BE
OBLIGATORY. IN THE REST OF THE WORLD THERE ARE COUNTRIES
WHERE IT IS HOPED TO ACHIEVE SOCIALISM WITHOUT COMMUNISTS
NECESSARILY BEING THE RULING PARTY. IN OTHERS THE ASVANCE
TOWARDS SOCIALISM IS AN OBJECTIVE WHICH DRAWS TOGETHER
VARIOUS MOVEMENTS WHICH HAVE NOT YET REACHED ANY MUTUAL
AGREEMENT OR EVEN UNDERSTANDING. THE WHOLE SYSTEM IS
BECOMING POLYCENTRIC, AND EVEN IN THE COMMUNIST MOVEMENT
ITSELF IT IS NOT A SINGLE GUIDE, BUT RATHER OF PROGRESS
WHICH IS ACHIEVED BY FOLLOWING PATHS WHICH ARE OFTEN
DIFFERENT. ALL POLITICAL SYSTEMS HAVE TO ACCEPT OR ADJUST TO
GENERATIONAL CHANGE, COMMUNIST JUST AS INESCAPABLY AS THE

LIBERAL CONSTITUTIONAL REGIMES. THE PRESENT-DAY COMMUNIST
WORLD IS A VERY SUBSTANTIAL PORTION OF HUMANITY.
POLYCENTRISM IN THE SOCIALIST WORLD IS PART OF THE VOLATILE
POLYCENTRISM OF THE CONTEMPORY WORLD.

00451
    POSITIVE REPORTING BY MEDIA STRESSED
    BEIJING REVIEW, 32(49) (DEC 89), 9-10.
    LI RUIHUAN, A SENIOR OFFICIAL WITH THE COMMUNIST PARTY
OF CHINA, HAS DECLARED THAT THE MASS MEDIA SHOULD ADHERE TO
THE PRINCIPLE OF PUBLICIZING POSITIVE MATTERS FIRST. HE
STATED THAT THIS IS THE MOST IMPORTANT GUIDELINE FOR
SOCIALIST MASS MEDIA REPORTING. THE MEDIA SHOULD REFLECT THE
MAINSTREAM OF SOCIAL LIFE TO ENCOURAGE THE PUBLIC IN ITS
MARCH TOWARD SOCIALISM AND TO CREATE PUBLIC OPINION THAT IS
CONDUCIVE TO POLITICAL STABILITY.

00452
    POST-ELECTION TENSION BUILDS
    CENTRAL AMERICA BULLETIN, 8(6) (MAY 89), 1-3, 7.
    THE SITUATION IN EL SALVADOR REMAINS VERY TENSE, WITH
GROWING REPRESSION AND RISING CONFRONTATIONS BETWEEN THE
STATE AND THE FMLN. THE ARENA PARTY'S ELECTORAL VICTORIES
HAVE INCREASED THE LEVEL OF POLITICAL POLARIZATION. WHILE
THE SPECIFIC DIRECTION EVENTS WILL TAKE IS UNKNOWN, IT
DEPENDS HEAVILY ON TWO FACTORS. THE FIRST IS THE ABILITY OF
THE FMLN TO PRESSURE THE REGIME AND FORCE IT TO NEGOTIATE A
RESOLUTION TO THE CONFLICT. THE SECOND IS THE ABILITY OF
ARENA'S LEADERSHIP AND ELEMENTS OF THE ARMED FORCES TO
LAUNCH A "QUICK WAR" AGAINST THE FMLN AND ITS SUPPORTERS.
DESPITE THE UNCERTAINTIES, U.S. POLICY WILL PROBABLY
CONTINUE ON ITS CURRENT COURSE. EVEN IF ARENA AND THE ARMY
SIGNIFICANTLY ESCALATE THE CONFLICT, THE BUSH ADMINISTRATION
IS LIKELY TO CONTINUE TO SUPPORT THEM.

00453
    PREMIER LI OUTLINES CURRENT TASKS
    BEIJING REVIEW, 32(26) (JUN 89), 9-10.
    CHINESE PREMIER LI PENG HAS CALLED FOR EFFORTS TO UNIFY
THE PEOPLE'S THINKING ON THE BASIS OF A SPEECH BY DENG
XIAOPING TO THE COMMANDERS OF THE MARTIAL LAW ENFORCEMENT
TROOPS ON JUNE 9, 1989. LI SAID THAT DENG'S SPEECH OFFERED A
PROFOUND ANALYSIS OF THE CAUSE AND NATURE OF THE COUNTER-
REVOLUTIONARY REBELLION AND THE PROPRIETY OF THE MEASURES
THE GOVERNMENT ADOPTED TO DEAL WITH IT. LI ALSO PRAISED THE
ROLE PLAYED BY THE MARTIAL LAW ENFORCEMENT TROOPS DURING THE
INCIDENT.

00454
    PREMIER LI'S REMARKS IN JAPAN
    BEIJING REVIEW, 32(18) (MAY 89), 14-15.
    DURING AN OFFICIAL VISIT TO JAPAN IN APRIL 1989, PREMIER
LI PENG DISCUSSED MAJOR DOMESTIC AND INTERNATIONAL ISSUES,
INCLUDING SINO-JAPANESE RELATIONS, JOINT SINO-JAPANESE
BUSINESS VENTURES, STABILITY IN CHINA, AND SINO-SOVIET
RELATIONS.

00455
    PREMIERS COME, PREMIERS GO
    NEW AFRICAN, (264) (SEP 89), .
    THIS REPORT EXAMINES THE PROCESS OF PREMIERS COMING AND
GOING AT THE BEHEST OF THE KING, TOTALLY, IN SWIZILAND. THE
FORMER POLICE CHIEF, SOTSHA, HAS BEEN SUDDENLY DISMISSED AND
A FORMER TRADES UNIONIST, OBED, HAS BEEN APPOINTED IN HIS
PLACE. THE MYSTERIES OF THE SWAZILAND SYSTEM ARE EXPLORED AS
THE PATTERN OF CHOICE FOR THE LAST SIX PRIME MINISTERS IS
DETAILED. THE REQUIREMENTS ARE LISTED AND DESCRIBED

00456
    PREREQUISITES AND PRINCIPLES FOR ARMS CONTROL
    DEPARTMENT OF STATE BULLETIN (US FOREIGN POLICY), 89(2153)
    (DEC 89), 14-20.
    OVER THE LAST FORTY YEARS, ARMS CONTROL HAS PLAYED A
LIMITED ROLE IN SHAPING THE U.S.-SOVIET SECURITY
RELATIONSHIP BECAUSE THE POLITICAL DIFFERENCES WERE SIMPLY
TOO WIDE TO ALLOW ENDURING AND SUBSTANTIAL PROGRESS. NOW
PERESTROIKA COULD, IN PART, LIFT THE SHADOW. THE POLITICAL
PREREQUISITE FOR ENDURING AND STRATEGICALLY SIGNIFICANT ARMS
CONTROL MAY FINALLY BE MATERIALIZING.

00457
    PRESIDENT BUSH VISITS EUROPE
    DEPARTMENT OF STATE BULLETIN (US FOREIGN POLICY), 89(2150)
    (SEP 89), 22-53.
    PRESIDENT BUSH VISITED POLAND, HUNGARY, FRANCE, AND THE
NETHERLANDS IN JULY 1989. THIS ACCOUNT OF THE TRIP INCLUDES
STATEMENTS DELIVERED BY THE PRESIDENT AND ACTION PLANS
PROPOSED FOR POLAND AND HUNGARY.

00458
    PRESIDENT MEETS WITH EGYPTIAN PRESIDENT
    DEPARTMENT OF STATE BULLETIN (US FOREIGN POLICY), 89(2153)
    (DEC 89), 45-46.
    FOLLOWING A MEETING BETWEEN PRESIDENT BUSH AND EGYPTIAN

PRESIDENT MUBARAK, SECRETARY OF STATE BAKER HELD A NEWS
BRIEFING TO DISCUSS THE TALKS. HE DISCUSSED THE EGYPTIAN TEN-
POINT PLAN FOR RESOLVING THE ISRAELI-PALESTINIAN PROBLEM,
THE PLO RESPONSE TO THE TEN POINTS, REPORTS THAT ISRAEL
PLANS TO RESETTLE SOVIET JEWS ON THE WEST BANK, AND RELATED
TOPICS.

00459
    PRESIDENT ROH TAE WOO'S SPECIAL ADDRESS CONCERNING
    NATIONAL UNIFICATION, SEPTEMBER 11, 1989
    KOREA OBSERVER, XX(4) (WIN 89), 537-548.
    IN THIS SPEECH, SOUTH KOREAN PRESIDENT ROH TAE WOO
OUTLINES HIS POLICY ON THE REUNIFICATION OF KOREA AND
DECLARES THAT KOREANS MUST NOT ALLOW THE PAINFUL SEPARATION
TO CONTINUE INTO THE NEXT CENTURY.

00460
    PRESIDENT TAMBO ON NEGOTIATIONS
    SECHABA, 23(8) (AUG 89), 2-4.
    THE ARTICLE CONTAINS EXTRACTS FROM AFRICAN NATIONAL
CONGRESS PRESIDENT OLIVER TAMBO'S STATEMENT TO THE ORDINARY
CONGRESS OF THE SOCIALIST INTERNATIONAL IN STOCKHOLM ON 20
JUNE 1989. TAMBO CRITICIZES THE SOUTH AFRICAN GOVERNMENT FOR
ITS CONTINUING THREATS TOWARDS NAMIBIA AND FOR ITS COMPLETE
LACK OF FUNDAMENTAL REFORM. TAMBO MAINTAINS THE ANC POSITION
THAT APARTHEID CANNOT BE REFORMED, ONLY ABOLISHED. IN
ADDITION, NEGOTIATIONS WITH PRETORIA ARE POSSIBLE ONLY AFTER
THE LIFTING OF THE STATE OF EMERGENCY, THE RELEASE OF
POLITICAL PRISONERS, AND THE LIFTING OF RESTRICTIONS ON ALL
POLITICAL ORGANIZATIONS.

00461
    PRESIDENT VISITS EUROPE; ATTENDS NORTH ATLANTIC COUNCIL
    MEETING
    DEPARTMENT OF STATE BULLETIN (US FOREIGN POLICY), 89(2149)
    (AUG 89), 11-45.
    THIS ARTICLE REPORTS ON PRESIDENT BUSH'S VISIT TO ITALY,
THE VATICAN, BELGIUM, WEST GERMANY, AND THE UNITED KINGDOM
IN MAY AND JUNE 1989. IT INCLUDES STATEMENTS DELIVERED BY
BUSH DURING THE TRIP.

00462
    PRESIDENT'S TRIP TO JAPAN, CHINA, AND SOUTH KOREA
    DEPARTMENT OF STATE BULLETIN (US FOREIGN POLICY), 89(2146)
    (MAY 89), 1-22.
    THIS ARTICLE REVIEWS THE HIGHLIGHTS OF PRESIDENT BUSH'S
TRIP TO ASIA IN FEBRUARY 1989. THE PRESIDENT VISITED CHINA,
SOUTH KOREA, AND JAPAN, WHERE HE ATTENDED THE FUNERAL OF
EMPEROR HIROHITO.

00463
    PRESS CONFERENCE OF WOJCIECH JARUZELSKI, PUWP CC FIRST
    SECRETARY, FOLLOWING TENTH PARTY PLENUM
    CONTEMPORARY POLAND, XXII(2) (1989), 37-48.
    THE TENTH PUWP CC PLENUM WAS DEVOTED ABOVE ALL TO INTRA-
PARTY MATTERS: THE STYLE OF WORK, THE REORGANIZATION OF
STRUCTURES, ACCURACY IN FORECASTING, AND EFFECTIVENESS IN
ACTION. IN ADDITION, THE PLENUM SOUGHT TO ANSWER MANY
QUESTIONS CURRENTLY PLAGUING POLISH SOCIETY, PARTICULARLY
ITS EMPLOYEE GROUPS.

00464
    PRETORIA'S MIXED SIGNALS
    COMMONWEAL, CXVI(22) (DEC 89), 692-693.
    THE SIGNALS FROM F.W. DEKLERK'S GOVERNMENT ARE MIXED. ON
THE ONE HAND, THE GOVERNMENT IS CONSULTING WITH WALTER
SISULU AND NELSON MANDELA ABOUT HOW TO PROCEED TOWARD THE
END OF APARTHEID AND THE CONTINUING OFFICIAL STATE OF
EMERGENCY. BUT OTHER EVENTS AND NON-EVENTS SUGGEST THAT
LITTLE, IF ANYTHING, HAS CHANGED IN SOUTH AFRICA.

00465
    PRIORITY TO POLITICAL MEANS
    INTERNATIONAL AFFAIRS (MOSCOW), (8) (AUG 89), 60-62.
    SOVIET NATIONAL SECURITY MUST BE ENSURED PRIMARILY BY
POLITICAL MEANS, AS PART OF UNIVERSAL AND EQUAL
INTERNATIONAL SECURITY, BUILDING ON THE PRESTIGE AND
POSSIBILITIES OF THE UNITED NATIONS. NUCLEAR WEAPONS MUST BE
ELIMINATED THROUGH NEGOTIATIONS AIMED AT BRINGING
DISARMAMENT AND LIMITING THE DEFENSE POTENTIAL OF THE STATE
TO THE LEVEL OF REASONABLE SUFFICIENCY. THE THREAT OR USE OF
FORCE AS A MEANS OF ACHIEVING POLITICAL, ECONOMIC, OR OTHER
OBJECTIVES IS IMPERMISSIBLE. DIALOGUE AND NEGOTIATIONS,
DIRECTED TOWARDS ESTABLISHING A BALANCE OF INTERESTS, SHOULD
BE THE ONLY METHOD OF SOLVING INTERNATIONAL PROBLEMS AND
SETTLING CONFLICTS. THE SOVIET ECONOMY SHOULD ORGANICALLY
JOIN THE WORLD ECONOMY ON MUTUALLY BENEFICIAL AND EQUAL
TERMS.

00466
    PRIVATE INTENTIONS
    SOUTH, (102) (APR 89), 11.
    IN THIS INTERVIEW, CROWN PRINCE HASSAN OF JORDAN
DISCUSSES PLANS FOR A REVIVAL OF ARAB ECONOMIC INTEGRATION,

REGIONAL DEVELOPMENT PROGRAMS, JORDAN'S AUSTERITY POLICY, AND MEASURES TO DEVELOP JORDAN'S ENERGY RESOURCES.

00467
PRIVATISATION OF THE ELECTRICITY SUPPLY INDUSTRY
SURVEY OF CURRENT AFFAIRS, 19(1) (JAN 89), 16-19.
GREAT BRITAIN'S PROPOSED ELECTRICITY BILL WOULD RESTRUCTURE AND OFFER FOR PRIVATE SALE THE ELECTRICAL SUPPLY INDUSTRY IN ENGLAND, WALES, AND SCOTLAND. THE BILL ENVISIONS A NATIONAL GRID OF DISTRIBUTION COMPANIES AND ESTABLISHES THE FRAMEWORK FOR A REGULATORY SYSTEM TO OVERSEE THE OPERATIONS.

00468
PRIVATISATION: HAS AUSTRALIA CAUGHT THE BRITISH "DISEASE"?
WORLD TRADE UNION MOVEMENT, 1 (1988), 27-28.
THIS ARTICLE STUDIES THE THATCHER APPROACH TO GOVERNING THE UNITED KINGDOM THROUGH PRIVATIZATION, AND CONCLUDES THAT PRIVATIZATION HAS CAUSED LOSS OF JOBS AND WAGES AND ENCOURAGES THE MISUSE OF PUBLIC FUNDS BY CONTRACTORS. THE DECISION OF THE AUSTRALIAN GOVERNMENT TO CONSIDER PRIVATIZATION OF ASSETS IS ANALYSED. ITS EFFECT ON THE ECONOMY APPEARS TO BE A NEGATIVE ONE.

00469
PRIVATIZATION BIBLIOGRAPHY, SPRING 1989
AVAILABLE FROM NTIS, NO. PB89-182075/GAR, SPR 89, 65.
THE OFFICE OF PRIVATIZATION HAS UPDATED ITS BIBLIOGRAPHY OF BOOKS, ARTICLES AND GOVERNMENT DOCUMENTS RELATING TO PRIVATIZATION. IT IS ARRANGED ALPHABETICALLY; HOWEVER, ARTICLES WITH UNLISTED AUTHORS APPEAR FIRST. IN ADDITION TO THE COMPREHENSIVE LIST, THE BIBLIOGRAPHY MAY BE OBTAINED BY SUBJECT AREA. SUBJECTS AVAILABLE ARE: POSTAL SERVICE; PRISONS; WELFARE; GENERAL PRIVATIZATION; PRIVATIZATION IN LESSER DEVELOPED COUNTRIES; PRIVATIZATION IN THE UNITED KINGDOM; CONTRACTING OUT; ASSET SALES; ENVIRONMENTAL ISSUES; EDUCATION; INFRASTRUCTURE; INTERNATIONAL PRIVATIZATION INITIATIVES; PUBLIC-PRIVATE PARTNERSHIPS; AIR AND SPACE; URBAN PUBLIC SERVICES; AND MEDICAL SERVICES.

00470
PROFILES OF THE PARTY'S LEADERS
BEIJING REVIEW, 32(28) (JUL 89), 21-25.
THIS COLLECTION OF BRIEF BIOGRAPHIES PROFILES CHINESE COMMUNIST PARTY LEADERS, INCLUDING LI PENG, JIANG ZEMIN, QIAO SHI. YAO YILIN, SONG PING, AND LI RUIHUAN.

00471
PROGRAM OF THE DEMOCRATIC TRADE UNION OF SCIENTIFIC WORKERS
WORLD AFFAIRS, 151(4) (1989), 179-183.
THE DEMOCRATIC TRADE UNION OF SCIENTIFIC WORKERS, A HUNGARIAN OPPOSITION GROUP, OUTLINE THEIR POLICIES AND OBJECTIVES. CENTRAL TO THE ORGANIZATION'S IDEOLOGY IS A REJECTION OF THE CURRENT GOVERNMENT MONOPOLY ON SCIENTIFIC KNOWLEDGE AND EMPLOYMENT. THE ARTICLE OUTLINES PROGRAMS DESIGNED TO SAFEGUARD THE INTERESTS OF PROFESSIONALS WORKING IN SCIENCE IN A TWELVE POINT EDUCATIONAL AND SCIENCE POLICY.

00472
PROGRAM OF THE HUNGARIAN DEMOCRATIC FORUM
WORLD AFFAIRS, 151(4) (1989), 159-164.
AMONG THE NUMEROUS POLITICAL SOCIETIES WITH DEMOCRATIC PHILOSOPHIES THAT HAVE ARISEN IN HUNGARY, THE LARGEST AND ONE OF THE MOST PROMINENT IS THE HUNGARIAN DEMOCRATIC FORUM (HDF). THE ARTICLE EXAMINES THE COMPOSITION AND GOALS OF THE ORGANIZATION. IT OUTLINES THE POLITICAL AND ECONOMIC REFORMS PROPOSED BY THE HDF AS WELL AS FOREING POLICY OBJECTIVES. HDF POLICY IS LARGELY INFLUENCED BY A BELIEF IN FUNDAMENTAL HUMAN RIGHTS, THE ESTABLISHMENT OF A WELFARE SOCIETY, AND THE SPIRIT OF NATIONAL DEMOCRATIC TRADITIONS.

00473
PROGRAMME FOR THE NEW SESSION
SURVEY OF CURRENT AFFAIRS, 19(12) (DEC 89), 448-450.
THE QUEEN'S SPEECH ON THE OPENING OF THE NEW SESSION OF PARLIAMENT - THE THIRD SESSION OF THE FIFTIETH PARLIAMENT OF THE UNITED KINGDOM - WAS FIFTIETH PARLIAMENT OF THE UNITED KINGDOM - WAS DELIVERED IN THE HOUSE OF LORDS ON 21 NOVEMBER 1989 TO MEMBERS OF BOTH HOUSES. AMONG THE LEGISLATION WHICH THE GOVERNMENT PROPOSES TO INTRODUCE ARE MEASURES TO STREGTHEN CO-OPERATION BETWEEN BRITAIN AND OTHER COUNTRIES IN THE INVESTIGATION OF CRIME; TO IMPROVE THE ADMINISTRATION OF CIVIL JUSTICE AND TO INCREASE CHOICE IN THE PROVISION OF LEGAL SERVICES; TO SAFEGUARD STANDARDS OF FOOD SAFETY; TO MAKE AVAILABLE NEW POWERS TO CONTROL POLLUTION AND WASTE; TO PROVIDE FOR A WIDER CHOICE OF BROADCASTING SERVICES, STRENGTHEN THE OVERSIGHT OF PROGRAMME STANDARDS AND REFORM INDEPENDENT TELEVISION AND RADIO; TO IMPROVE THE NATIONAL HEALTH SERVICE AND THE MANAGEMENT OF COMMUNITY CARE; AND TO INSTITUTE A LEGAL FRAMEWORK FOR SCIENTIFIC DEVELOPMENTS CONCERNING HUMAN FERTILISATION AND EMBRYOLOGY.

00474
PROGRAMME OF ECONOMIC POLICY MEASURES FOR 1989

YUGOSLAV SURVEY, XXX(2) (1989), 21-50.
THE PROGRAMME OF ECONOMIC POLICY MEASURES CONSTITUTES A COMPREHENSIVE, CONSISTENT CONCEPT OF YUGOSLAVIA'S NEW ECONOMIC SYSTEM AND ITS NEW ECONOMIC AND DEVELOPMENT POLICIES. IT ALSO INCLUDES MEASURES ALREADY UNDERTAKEN BY THE FEDERAL EXECUTIVE COUNCIL AS WELL AS MEASURES AND ACTIVITIES AT VARIOUS STAGES OF PREPARATION. THE PROGRAMME OF MEASURES IS BASED ON THE REFORM OF THE ECONOMIC SYSTEM, WHICH CREATES THE PREREQUISITES FOR THE COMPLETION OF THE INTEGRAL MARKET AND THE IMPLEMENTATION OF THE NEW DEVELOPMENT ORIENTATION.

00475
PROPOSALS TO TRIM AID TO ELDERLY MEET WITH STIFF PUBLIC OPPOSITION
GALLUP REPORT, (284) (MAY 89), 16-21.
ANY ATTEMPT TO IMPOSE INCREASED TAXES OR A MEANS TEST ON AFFLUENT SOCIAL SECURITY RECIPIENTS OR TO FURTHER LIMIT MEDICARE BENEFITS WOULD RUN INTO A SOLID WALL OF PUBLIC OPPOSITION, ALTHOUGH EVEN MODEST CUTS IN THESE PROGRAMS WOULD MAKE A BIG DENT IN THE FEDERAL DEFICIT.

00476
PUBLIC EXPECTATIONS FOR BUSH PRESIDENCY: PEACE, PROSPERITY, AND HIGHER TAXES
GALLUP REPORT, (280) (JAN 89), 9-11.
THE AMERICAN PEOPLE HAVE MIXED EXPECTATIONS FOR PRESIDENT BUSH'S ADMINISTRATION. THEY ARE MOST OPTIMISTIC THAT BUSH WILL KEEP TWO CAMPAIGN PROMISES THAT CONTRIBUTED IMPORTANTLY TO THE ELECTION VICTORY: KEEPING THE USA OUT OF WAR AND KEEPING IT PROSPEROUS. THEY ARE MUCH LESS SANGUINE ABOUT BUSH'S CAPACITY TO IMPROVE THE LOT OF MINORITIES AND THE POOR, LOWER THE CRIME RATE, AND REDUCE THE FEDERAL BUDGET DEFICIT.

00477
PUBLIC EXPENDITURE PLANS
SURVEY OF CURRENT AFFAIRS, 19(2) (FEB 89), 54-58.
GREAT BRITAIN'S PUBLIC EXPENDITURE WHITE PAPER, PUBLISHED IN JANUARY 1989, ESTIMATED THAT TOTAL PUBLIC EXPENDITURES WOULD REACH 153,400 MILLION POUNDS FOR 1988-89. SOCIAL SECURITY, HEALTH, DEFENSE, EDUCATION, AND SCIENCE WERE IDENTIFIED AS THE MAJOR SPENDING AREAS.

00478
PUBLIC GIVES BUSH HIGH RATINGS FOR SOVIET RELATIONS, FOREIGN POLICY
GALLUP REPORT, (282-283) (MAR 89), 13-15.
THE AMERICAN PEOPLE GIVE PRESIDENT BUSH HIGHER MARKS FOR HIS HANDLING OF SOVIET RELATIONS AND FOREIGN POLICY THAN FOR HIS OTHER UNDERTAKINGS. APPROVAL LEVELS ARE 70 PERCENT FOR BUSH'S HANDLING OF RELATIONS WITH THE USSR, 52 PERCENT FOR DOMESTIC ECONOMIC POLICY, 48 PERCENT FOR THE DRUG EPIDEMIC, AND 37 PERCENT FOR THE CENTRAL AMERICAN SITUATION.

00479
PUBLIC GROWS MORE OPTIMISTIC IN PERCEPTIONS OF BUSH PRESIDENCY
GALLUP REPORT, (281) (FEB 89), 11-13.
THE AMERICAN PEOPLE HAVE MIXED EXPECTATIONS FOR PRESIDENT BUSH'S ADMINISTRATION, BUT CONFIDENCE HAS GROWN SINCE NOVEMBER 1988 THAT HE WILL BE ABLE TO FULFILL MANY OF HIS CAMPAIGN PROMISES. DEMOCRATS REMAIN MORE SKEPTICAL THAN REPUBLICANS ABOUT BUSH'S ABILITY TO MEET THE CHALLENGES. BUT THE HARSH VIEWS DEMOCRATS EXPRESS IN THE POST-ELECTION POLL HAVE SOFTENED.

00480
PUBLIC SUPPORT OF THE ARTS
REPORT FROM THE INSTITUTE FOR PHILOSOPHY AND PUBLIC POLICY, 9(4) (FAL 89), 1-5.
AT THE EYE OF THE STORM OVER PUBLIC FUNDING FOR THE ARTS STANDS THE NATIONAL ENDOWMENT FOR THE ARTS. FOR SOME PUBLIC OFFICIALS, THE QUESTION IS WHETHER THE GOVERNMENT SHOULD BE FUNDING OBSCENE OR MORALLY-REPREHENSIBLE ART. FOR OTHERS, THE QUESTION IS ONE OF CENSORSHIP AND FREEDOM OF EXPRESSION.

00481
PUSH AND PULL IN THE DRUGS WAR
SOUTH, (108) (OCT 89), 9.
THE ASSASSINATION OF A YOUNG COLOMBIAN SENATOR AND PRESIDENTIAL CANDIDATE, AT THE HANDS OF THE DRUG MAFIA, HAS PRODUCED DETERMINATION AND RESOLVE AMONG LATIN AMERICA'S POLITICAL LEADERS. THIS GIVES SOME CAUSE FOR OPTIMISM THAT VICTORY MIGHT YET BE ACHIEVED AGAINST AN INTERNATIONAL CRIMINAL CLASS THAT HAS BECOME INCREASINGLY VIOLENT AND IMMORAL. BUT THE WAR WITHIN COUNTRIES PLAGUED BY COCAINE AND HEROIN PRODUCTION MUST NOT BE WAGED BY US TROOPS OR USED AS A PRETEXT FOR US FORCES TO EXTEND THEIR OPERATIONS IN CENTRAL AMERICA AND THE ANDEAN COUNTRIES.

00482
PUWP CENTRAL COMMITTEE'S POSITION ON THE FORMATION OF A NEW GOVERNMENT AND THE CURRENT POLITICAL SITUATION

CONTEMPORARY POLAND, XXII(9) (1989), 36-37.
POLAND CAN ONLY BE LED OUT OF ITS PRESENT CRISIS THROUGH EVOLUTIONARY, CONSISTENT REFORMS BY A GOVERNMENT WITH ALL POLITICAL FORCES REPRESENTED IN THE SEJM. SHORT-LIVED ALLIANCES CANNOT REPLACE A GRAND COALITION GOVERNMENT. THE LEADERSHIP OF THE DEPUTY CLUBS OF THE UNITED PEASANT PARTY AND DEMOCRATIC PARTY HAVE VIOLATED THE ACCORD ON THE ARRANGEMENT OF POLITICAL FORCES IN THE SEJM BY CONSENTING TO A COALITION WITHOUT THE POLISH UNITED WORKER'S PARTY. EMBARKING ON THE ROAD TO CONFRONTATION WITH THE PUWP CANNOT SERVE THE COUNTRY'S BEST INTERESTS.

00483
QIAN ON SINO-AFRICAN TIES
BEIJING REVIEW, 32(49) (DEC 89), 14-15.
IN THIS INTERVIEW, CHINESE FOREIGN MINISTER QIAN QICHEN DISCUSSES HIS 1989 VISIT TO SIX SOUTHERN AFRICAN NATIONS, THE CONTRIBUTIONS SINO-AFRICAN COOPERATION HAS MADE TO INTERNATIONAL PEACE AND DEVELOPMENT, AND THE FUTURE OF SINO-AFRICAN RELATIONS IN THE COMING DECADE.

00484
QUESTIONS OF INTEREST ABOUT CHINA
BEIJING REVIEW, 32(44) (OCT 89), 12-14.
IN THIS INTERVIEW, STATE COUNCIL SPOKESMAN YUAN MU ANSWERS QUESTIONS ABOUT CHINA'S ECONOMIC PROBLEMS, DESTABILIZING POLITICAL FACTORS, INTERNATIONAL ISOLATION, SINO-JAPANESE TIES, AND TAIWAN'S "ELASTIC DIPLOMACY."

00485
REACTIONS TO AMERICAN REVISIONISM
JAPAN ECHO, XVI(4) (WIN 89), 50-51.
THE REVISIONIST VIEW OF JAPAN, PROPOUNDED MAINLY BY AMERICANS, IS BOTH INTRIGUING AND DISTURBING. JAPAN WAS PREVIOUSLY SEEN AS A FULL-FLEDGED MEMBER OF THE FREE WORLD AND AN IMPORTANT PARTNER OF THE UNITED STATES WITHIN THE FRAMEWORK OF THE EAST-WEST CONFRONTATION. NOW THAT THE SOVIET THREAT IS RECEDING, THE JAPANESE CHALLENGE SEEMS TO BE GROWING. THE CONCLUSION MANY PEOPLE HAVE REACHED IS THAT JAPAN DID NOT PLAY BY THE RULES OF CAPITALISM IN ACHIEVING ITS ECONOMIC SUCCESS. MOREOVER, JAPAN'S POLITICAL AND ECONOMIC SYSTEMS ARE FAR DIFFERENT FROM THEIR WESTERN COUNTERPARTS. THEREFORE, SOMETHING MUST BE DONE TO REIN IN THIS ECONOMIC GIANT.

00486
REAGAN RECEIVES HIGHEST FINAL APPROVAL RATING SINCE FRANKLIN ROOSEVELT
GALLUP REPORT, (280) (JAN 89), 12-15.
RONALD REAGAN ENDED HIS TERM IN OFFICE WITH THE HIGHEST APPROVAL RATING OF ANY PRESIDENT SINCE FRANKLIN ROOSEVELT. SIXTY-THREE PERCENT OF THOSE POLLED APPROVED OF THE JOB REAGAN DID AS PRESIDENT, COMPARED WITH 66 PERCENT FOR ROOSEVELT.

00487
REBUILDING AMERICA
MULTINATIONAL MONITOR, 10(5) (MAY 89), 18-20.
REBUILD AMERICA IS A PUBLIC POLICY ORGANIZATION COMMITTED TO DEVELOPING INITIATIVES TO INCREASE PRODUCTIVE INVESTMENT IN THE UNITED STATES. ONE OF ITS MAIN MESSAGES IS THAT THE FAILURE OF AMERICA'S STRATEGIC INDUSTRIES WILL PRODUCE GENERATIONS OF ECONOMIC, POLITICAL, AND SOCIAL DECLINE. THE AVERAGE AMERICAN DOES NOT EVEN BEGIN TO UNDERSTAND THE CURRENT SERIOUS ECONOMIC CRISIS AND, THEREFORE, THE POLITICAL AND SOCIAL CRISES THAT AWAIT THE USA IN THE NEXT 20 YEARS.

00488
RECOVERY HOPES OVER A BARREL
SOUTH, (99) (JAN 89), 19.
THE ECONOMIC EUPHORIA THAT FOLLOWED THE CEASEFIRE IN THE GULF IS UNLIKELY TO CARRY OVER INTO 1989. THERE MAY BE NO WAR IN THE GULF, BUT THERE IS ALSO NO PEACE. THIS AND FEAR OF A DROP IN OIL PRICES HAVE DAMPENED HOPE FOR A POST-WAR BOOM. THE OIL-RICH COUNTRIES ARE IN FOR ANOTHER YEAR OF BELT-TIGHTENING. THE DEBT-STRICKEN COUNTRIES IN NORTH AFRICA AND THE LEVANT WILL KNOW REAL HARDSHIP. AS AUSTERITY MEASURES PRESS UPON THE POOR, GOVERNMENTS WILL HAVE TO WEIGH THEIR FINANCIAL OBLIGATIONS AGAINST THE NEED FOR POLITICAL STABILITY.

00489
REFORM OF THE PARTY: PRECONDITION OF SUCCESS OF THE STRATEGY OF RENEWAL AND REFORM
CONTEMPORARY POLAND, XXII(1) (1989), 40-45.
FUNDAMENTAL CHANGES IN THE POLISH UNITED WORKERS' PARTY ARE A MUST. THREE AREAS MUST BE SUBJECTED TO ESPECIALLY DETAILED, CRITICAL EVALUATION: (1) THE MAIN POINTS OF REFERENCE THAT DETERMINE THE IDEOLOGICAL AND POLITICAL IDENTITY OF THE PARTY; (2) THE PLACE AND THE ROLE OF THE PARTY IN THE STATE AND SOCIETY IN CONDITIONS OF FAR-REACHING REFORM OF THE SYSTEM OF AUTHORITY AND GOVERNING AND DEEP TRANSFORMATION IN PRODUCTION RELATIONS; AND (3) THE INTERNAL

ORGANIZATION OF THE PARTY, THE STRUCTURES, AND METHODS OF ITS ACTIVITY.

00490
REFORMS CRACK "IRON RICE BOWL"
BEIJING REVIEW, 32(1) (JAN 89), 12-14.
REFORMS IN CHINA'S LABOR, WAGE, AND INSURANCE SYSTEMS HAVE PRODUCED A NEW LOOK IN CHINA'S ENTERPRISE MANAGEMENT SYSTEM AND BOOSTED THE DEVELOPMENT OF THE SOCIALIST COMMODITY ECONOMY. IN ORDER TO INVIGORATE THE LETHARGIC LIFETIME EMPLOYMENT SYSTEM, MORE THAN 26,000 STATE-OWNED ENTERPRISES HAVE REORGANIZED THEIR PERMANENT WORK FORCES AND WILL TRIM SURPLUS LABOR. THIS REFORM IN EMPLOYMENT PRACTICES HAS SHAKEN THE TRADITION OF LIFETIME EMPLOYMENT, CALLED THE "IRON RICE BOWL."

00491
RELATION BETWEEN SOCIALISM AND CAPITALISM IN POLAND
CONTEMPORARY POLAND, XXII(10) (1989), 8-21.
THE SEVENTH ANNUAL MEETING OF PARTICIPANTS IN THE OPINION RESEARCH WORKSHOP OF THE PUBLIC OPINION POLLING CENTRE WAS HELD IN JADWISIN, POLAND, IN THE SPRING OF 1989. THIS ARTICLE REVIEWS THE GROUP'S DISCUSSIONS ON THE RELATIONSHIP BETWEEN SOCIALISM AND CAPITALISM IN POLAND. THE PARTICIPANTS CONSIDERED THE QUESTIONS OF WHAT CAPITALISM IS, WHAT CAN BE TAKEN FROM IT, WHICH OF ITS ELEMENTS POLAND SHOULD ACCEPT AND ABSORB, AND WHICH ELEMENTS SHOULD BE AVOIDED.

00492
RELATIONS BETWEEN BRITAIN AND ARGENTINA
SURVEY OF CURRENT AFFAIRS, 19(9) (SEP 89), 345-346.
FOLLOWING TALKS BETWEEN BRITISH AND ARGENTINE REPRESENTATIVES IN NEW YORK IN AUGUST 1989, BRITAIN AND ARGENTINA HAVE AGREED TO MEET IN MADRID TO DISCUSS A NUMBER OF PRACTICAL ISSUES IN THE HOPE THAT THIS WILL LEAD TO MORE NORMAL RELATIONS BETWEEN THE TWO COUNTRIES.

00493
RELATIONS BETWEEN YUGOSLAVIA AND VIETNAM
YUGOSLAV SURVEY, XXX(3) (1989), 139-150.
RELATIONS BETWEEN YUGOSLAVIA AND THE SOCIALIST REPUBLIC OF VIETNAM (PREVIOUSLY THE DEMOCRATIC REPUBLIC OF VIETNAM) HAVE BEEN CHARACTERIZED BY A RATHER MODEST DEGREE OF COOPERATION IN THE POLITICAL, ECONOMIC, CULTURAL AND OTHER FIELDS. AND EVEN THIS COOPERATION, SUCH AS IT IS, HAS HAD ITS UPS AND DOWNS. THE REASONS FOR THIS ARE NOT MERELY OF AN OBJECTIVE CHARACTER (THE GEOGRAPHICAL REMOTENESS OF THE COUNTRIES FROM ONE ANOTHER, THE LONG YEARS OF FIGHTING IN THE WAR OF LIBERATION AND DEFENCE WAGED IN VIETNAM, OR THE EXTREMELY LIMITED EXPORT-IMPORT CAPACITY OF THAT COUNTRY). OTHER FACTORS HAVE BEEN POLITICAL AND IDEOLOGICAL DIFFERENCES BETWEEN THE TWO COUNTRIES, INCLUDING DIFFERENT VIEWS ON THE KEY PROBLEMS OF SOCIALISM AND THE PRINCIPLES ON WHICH COOPERATION BETWEEN SOCIALIST COUNTRIES SHOULD BE BASED, VIETNAM'S FOREIGN POLICY PRIORITIES, AND DIFFERENCES IN POSITIONS ON MAJOR INTERNATIONAL PROBLEMS AND IN INTERPRETATION OF THE GOALS AND PRINCIPLES OF THE NON-ALIGNED MOVEMENT.

00494
REPORT BY A HUNGARIAN SOCIALIST WORKERS PARTY CENTRAL COMMITTEE WORKING COMMITTEE ON THE PAST FOUR DECADES (ABRIDGED)
WORLD AFFAIRS, 151(4) (1989), 184-191.
THE ARTICLE PRESENTS A HISTORICAL ANALYSIS OF HUNGARY'S PAST FOUR DECADES FROM A COMMUNIST VIEWPOINT. THE HUNGARIAN SOCIALIST WORKERS PARTY CENTRAL COMMITTEE DIVIDES HUNGARIAN HISTORY INTO SEVERAL PERIODS: THE SYSTEM OF PEOPLE'S DEMOCRACY FROM 1944-1947; CHANGES IN 1947-1948 AND THE EARLY 1950S; THE POPULAR UPRISING IN OCTOBER 1956; ATTEMPTS AT RENEWING SOCIALISM; ECONOMIC REFORM; AND THE CRISIS THAT HAS EMERGED AS REFORM BREAKS DOWN 1973-1988. THE PARTY EMPHASIZES ITS ROLE IN ESTABLISHING SIGNIFICANT REFORMS AND BLAMES THE INTERNATIONAL ECONOMY FOR THEIR FAILURE.

00495
REPORT BY NIKOLAI RYZHKOV TO THE FIRST SESSION OF THE USSR SUPREME SOVIET
REPRINTS FROM THE SOVIET PRESS, 49(4) (AUG 89), 27-35.
NIKOLAI RYZHKOV ENUMERATES THE TASKS SET FORTH BY THE CONGRESS OF PEOPLE'S DEPUTIES. THEY ARE: TO TAKE THE COUNTRY OUT OF THE ECONOMIC DOLDRUMS WITHIN A SHORT PERIOD OF TIME, RADICALLY TRANSFORM THE STATE POLITICAL SYSTEM, CREATE CONDITIONS FOR A STEADY GROWTH OF THE SOVIET PEOPLE'S WELFARE, AND OF CULTURAL ENRICHMENT OF THE INDIVIDUAL. HE DETAILS THE EXISTING STRUCTURE OF ECONOMIC MANAGEMENT IN ORDER TO DETERMINE WHAT ORGANIZATIONAL STRUCTURE OF STATE ADMINISTRATION CAN OBJECTIVELY MEET THE NEW REQUIREMENTS MADE OF IT.

00496
REPORT ON NATIONALITY POLICY TO THE CPSU CENTRAL COMMITTEE
REPRINTS FROM THE SOVIET PRESS, 49(10) (NOV 89), 5-31.

MIKHAIL GORBACHEV ADVISES THE CPSU THAT THE NEED FOR COMPREHENSIVE PROFOUND CHANGES IS LONG OVERDUE IN ETHNIC RELATIONS. HE SUGGESTS THAT THE HISTORY OF THE USSR NEEDS TO BE VIEWED FROM AN OBJECTIVE STANDPOINTTHAT TO IDEALIZE THE PAST AND TO PRESENT IT IN ROSY COLORS ALONE ARE FUTILE AND UNACCEPTABLE. THE PARTY IS FOR FULLY RESTORING HISTORICAL TRUTH, AND GORBACHEV DISCLOSES INJUSTICES AND LAWLESS ACTS AGAINST SOME ETHNIC GROUPS IN THE PAST. THE USSR SHOULD DO EVERYTHING POSSIBLE TO RESTORE FLOUTED RIGHTS OF ETHNIC GROUPS, GORBACHEV STATES.

00497
REPRESENTATION OF THE PEOPLE BILL
SURVEY OF CURRENT AFFAIRS, 19(7) (JUL 89), 255-257.
A BILL TO EXTEND THE FRANCHISE FOR BRITISH CITIZENS LIVING ABROAD AND TO SET A NEW LIMIT ON CANDIDATES' EXPENSES AT PARLIAMENTARY BY-ELECTIONS RECEIVED A SECOND READING IN THE HOUSE OF COMMONS ON 29 JUNE 1989. IT IS ESTIMATED THAT THE PROPOSED LEGISLATION, WHICH WOULD APPLY TO PARLIAMENTARY ELECTIONS AND ELECTIONS TO THE EUROPEAN PARLIAMENT THROUGHOUT BRITAIN, WOULD ENFRANCHISE A FURTHER TWO MILLION OVERSEAS VOTERS. IN ADDITION, A REVIEW OF CANDIDATES' EXPENSES AT BOTH GENERAL ELECTIONS AND PARLIAMENTARY BY-ELECTIONS HAS BEEN ANNOUNCED.

00498
RESEARCH AND DEVELOPMENT
SURVEY OF CURRENT AFFAIRS, 19(12) (DEC 89), 475-477.
THE BRITISH GOVERNMENT'S ANNUAL REVIEW OF RESEARCH AND DEVELOPMENT SHOWS THAT GOVERNMENT RESEARCH SPENDING REPRESENTED 4.2 PERCENT OF TOTAL CENTRAL GOVERNMENT EXPENDITURE IN 1987-88 AND TOTALED APPROXIMATELY 4,600 MILLION POUNDS, ABOUT THE SAME AS IN 1986-87. MEASURED ACCORDING TO INTERNATIONAL DEFINITIONS, BRITAIN'S TOTAL RESEARCH AND DEVELOPMENT EXPENDITURE IN 1987 WAS APPROXIMATELY 9,500 MILLION POUNDS, WHICH WAS ABOUT SIX PERCENT GREATER THAN IN 1986 AND REPRESENTED 2.3 PERCENT OF THE GROSS DOMESTIC PRODUCT.

00499
RESOLUTION OF THE CONGRESS OF PEOPLE'S DEPUTIES OF THE UNION OF SOVIET SOCIALIST REPUBLICS
REPRINTS FROM THE SOVIET PRESS, 49(5) (SEP 89), 5-25.
THIS ARTICLE ADDRESSES GUIDELINES FOR DOMESTIC AND FOREIGN POLICY OF THE.USSR. IT STATES THAT THE PROCESS OF DEEP RESTRUCTURING OF ALL ASPECTS OF LIFE IN SOCIETY, IS DESIGNED TO LEAD THE COUNTRY OUT OF THE PROFOUND CRISIS IN WHICH IT FOUND ITSELF IN THE EARLY EIGHTIES, MAKES A COMPLETE BREAK WITH EVERYTHING THAT HAMPERS ITS PROGRESS, GIVES SOCIALISM A MODERN IMAGE AND OPENS FOR SOVIET SOCIETY NEW PROSPECTS FOR SOCIAL PROGRESS.

00500
RESOLUTION OF THE TENTH PLENUM OF PUWP CC
CONTEMPORARY POLAND, XXII(2) (1989), 28-33.
CONTINUATION OF THE RENEWAL OF SOCIALISM REQUIRES PROFOUND REFORM WITHIN THE POLISH UNITED WORKERS' PARTY. THE ROAD TO MODERNIZED SOCIALISM LEADS THROUGH MATERIALIZATION OF THE PARTY'S BASIC OBJECTIVES IN THE SOCIO-ECONOMIC, POLITICAL, AND SPIRITUAL LIFE OF THE NATION. THESE GOALS INCLUDE HUMANISM, THE WELFARE OF MAN, HIS NEEDS AND ASPIRATIONS; EFFICIENT WELL ORGANIZED WORK TO PROVIDE THE BASIC SOURCE OF MAN'S SELF-REALIZATION AND MAINTENANCE; SOCIAL JUSTICE; DEMOCRACY; FREEDOM CONCEIVED AS THE CREATION OF ROOM FOR INITIATIVE, ASPIRATIONS, AND ACTION IN THE ECONOMIC, POLITICAL, SCIENTIFIC, AND CULTURAL SPHERES; PATRIOTISM; AND INTERNATIONALISM EXPRESSED THROUGH TIES WITH THE FORCES OF PROGRESS, DEMOCRACY, AND SOCIALISM.

00501
RESTRUCTURING THE WORK OF THE PARTY - TODAY'S VITAL TASK
REPRINTS FROM THE SOVIET PRESS, 49(6) (SEP 89), 7-40.
THIS IS A REPORT BY MIKHAIL GORBACHEV TO THE CENTRAL COMMITTEE OF THE CPSU AT A MEETING HELD TO DISCUSS CURRENT PROBLEMS CONNECTED WITH THE ACTIVITY OF THE PARTY DURING THE PRESENT PHASE OF PERESTROIKA. THIS IS DONE IN CONTEXT OF THE CURRENT POLITICAL SITUATION IN RUSSIA. HE REVIEWS THE CONGRESS OF PEOPLE'S DEPUTIES, ANALYZES THE CORRELATION OF SOCIAL FORCES, THE STATUS OF PERESTROIKA, AND REANALYZES THE FUNCTIONS AND THE ROLE OF THE PARTY IN SOCIETY AND DETERMINES ITS COORDINATES IN THE POLITICAL SYSTEM OF RENEWING SOCIALISM. HE ALSO ADDRESSES THE RECENT ELECTION CAMPAIGN, TRADE UNION, THE KOMOSOMOL, THE MEDIA, COOPERATIVES AND DEMOCRATIZATION OF THE PARTY.

00502
RETREATING UNDER LEFTIST PRESSURE
MEXICO-UNITED STATES REPORT, II(9) (JUN 89), 3.
AFTER TAKING THE UNPRECEDENTED STEP OF BACKING ON OAS RESOLUTION CONDEMNING PANAMA'S GENERAL NORIEGA, MEXICO SEEMS TO BE HAVING SECOND THOUGHTS. A GROUP OF LEFTIST MEMBERS OF THE CHAMBER OF DEPUTIES ORGANIZED A SIT IN IN THE DEPARTMENT OF FOREIGN RELATIONS AND DEMANDED THAT MEXICO CHANGE ITS STAND TOWARDS PANAMA. ALTHOUGH MEXICO HAS NOT COMPLETELY

RETREATED FROM THEIR ORIGINAL POSITION, SIGNS THAT THEY WOULD ACCEPT THE CURRENT STATE OF AFFIRS ARE ON THE INCREASE.

00503
REVENGE OF THE BUREAUCRATS?
GLASNOST, II(3) (MAY 89), 19-20.
VASILY SELYUNIN, A LEADING SOVIET ECONOMIST, SAYS THAT THE BIGGEST DISAPPOINTMENT OF 1988 WAS THE UNRESPONSIVE ECONOMY. AND HE DOES NOT EXPECT IMPROVEMENT IN 1989. SELYUNIN SEES A POSSIBLE SCENARIO IN WHICH CONSERVATIVE REVANCHISTS SUCCEED IN ROUSING THE SO-CALLED "SILENT MAJORITY" WITH SUCH SLOGANS AS "JUST DISTRIBUTION" AND "IT'S TIME FOR HARSH ORDER." IN THIS EVENTUALITY, THE SOVIET ECONOMY WOULD SWIFTLY COLLAPSE.

00504
REVISITING SOVIET ECONOMIC PERFORMANCE UNDER GLASNOST: IMPLICATIONS FOR CIA ESTIMATES
AVAILABLE FROM NTIS, NO. PB88-928 105/GAR, SEP 88, 31.
THE PAPER ASSESSES THE IMPLICATIONS OF RECENT GLASNOST-INSPIRED CRITIQUES OF THE USSR'S OFFICIAL ECONOMIC STATISTICS FOR CIA'S ESTIMATES OF SOVIET ECONOMIC PERFORMANCE. THE CIA ESTIMATES, ALTHOUGH PREDICATED ON THE BELIEF THAT MOSCOW'S MACROECONOMIC MEASURES ARE UNRELIABLE, ARE BASED ON A VARIETY OF OFFICIAL SOVIET DATA. IN PARTICULAR, THE PAPER FOCUSES ON WHAT THE RECENT CRITICISMS HAVE TO TELL US ABOUT THE ACCURACY OF CIA'S ESTIMATES OF THE GROWTH AND STRUCTURE OF SOVIET GROSS NATIONAL PRODUCT.

00505
RIGHT TO LIFE CLAIMS RIGHT TO AIR WAS CENSORED
CAMPAIGNS AND ELECTIONS, 10(4) (DEC 89), 7.
THE NATIONAL RIGHT TO LIFE COMMITTEE, WHOSE ENDORSEMENT WAS VIRTUALLY IGNORED BY REPUBLICAN CANDIDATE MARSHALL COLEMAN IN VIRGINIA'S 1989 GUBERNATORIAL CAMPAIGN, CLAIMS ITS ANTI-ABORTION, PRO-COLEMAN ADS WERE SNUBBED BY MAJOR MEDIA OUTLETS. THE ORGANIZATION SAYS EIGHT VIRGINIA AND WASHINGTON, D.C., TELEVISION STATIONS REFUSED TO AIR ITS 30-SECOND COMMERCIALS.

00506
RIGHTS, FREEDOMS AND COOPERATION
WORLD MARXIST REVIEW, 32(8) (AUG 89), 15-19.
"HUMAN RIGHTS IN A SOCIALIST STATE" WAS THE THEME OF AN INTERNATIONAL ROUNDTABLE WITH SENIOR UN OFFICIALS AND JURISTS FROM EASTERN EUROPE. THIS ARTICLE IS A SLIGHTLY ABRIDGED RECORD OF THIS DISCUSSION. COVERED IS HUMAN RIGHTS AND ITS RELATION TO A SOCIALIST RULE-OF-LAW STATE FOR SOME OF THE EAST EUROPEAN COUNTRIES. IT IS CONCLUDED THAT THE ONLY ACCEPTABLE APPROACH TO HUMANITARIAN ISSUES IN EAST-WEST RELATIONS IS ONE THAT IS CONSTRUCTIVE RATHER THAN CONFRONTATIONAL.

00507
ROC BUILDS OWN JET FIGHTER AS USA STOPS DELIVERY
ASIAN OUTLOOK, 24(3) (MAY 89), 25.
TAIWAN HAS PRODUCED A PROTOTYPE OF ITS FIRST HOME-GROWN JET FIGHTER. TAIWAN IS PLANNING TO MASS PRODUCE THE AIRCRAFT, WHICH WAS DESIGNED AND INITIATED AFTER THE UNITED STATES FROZE ITS WEAPON DELIVERIES TO THE ISLAND. THE FIGHTER WILL ENABLE TAIWAN TO MAINTAIN AIR SUPREMACY OVER THE TAIWAN STRAITS, WHICH SEPARATE THE ISLAND FROM THE CHINESE MAINLAND.

00508
ROCK AND RESISTANCE: "RESIST THE LIES AND SPEAK THE TRUTH"
ACROSS FRONTIERS, 5(2) (SUM 89), 23.
THIS ARTICLE IS AN INTERVIEW WITH MEMBERS OF THE POZNAN BAND. POZNAN MEANS "PARADISE OF IRON BARS" WHICH IS A SUBTLE PLAY ON A POLISH WORD WHICH MEANS "LAND OF THE SOVIETS." THE ARTICLE EXAMINES THE BAND MEMBERS ATTITUDES ABOUT LIFE IN POLAND, HOPELESSNESS OF THE YOUTH IN POLAND, CENSORSHIP, FAITH, SOLIDARITY, AND AN INDIVIDUAL'S RELATIONSHIP IN SOCIETY.

00509
RORAIMA, BRAZIL: A DEATH WARNING
CULTURAL SURVIVAL QUARTERLY, 13(4) (1989), 59-67.
THE YANOMAMI (OR YANOMAMO) INDIANS IN RORAIMA ARE THREATENED WITH CULTURAL AND PHYSICAL EXTINCTION DUE TO THE BRAZILIAN CONSTITUTION'S FAILURE TO GUARANTEE THEIR RIGHTS. A TYPICAL PROBLEM IS FOUND IN THE VILLAGE AT PAAPIU, WHERE THE BRAZILIAN AIR FORCE HAS BUILT A RUNWAY. NO MILITARY PERSONNEL ARE STATIONED THERE, BUT SOME 1,000 GOLD PROSPECTORS HAVE INVADED THE AREA AND ARE DECIMATING THE YANOMAMI IN THE REGION. THERE IS NO OFFICIAL CONTROL, NO PRESENCE OF ANY AUTHORITY, AND NO POLICE PATROL. THE INTRUDERS ARE POISONING THE RIVER AND DESTROYING THE FORESTS.

00510
ROUGH RIDE FOR RAWLINGS
NEW AFRICAN, (267) (DEC 89), 9-11.
ON DECEMBER 31, 1989, JERRY RAWLINGS, HEAD OF THE GOVERNMENT IN GHANA, CELEBRATED EIGHT YEARS OF HOLDING THAT POSITION. AFTER A LONG PERIOD OF COMPARITAVE STABILITY,

RUMORS WERE SURFACING THAT ALL WAS NOT WELL FOR RAWLINGS.
THE GOVERNMENT HAD BOXED ITSELF INTO A CORNER FROM WHICH IT
WILL BE DIFFICULT TO ESCAPE. THE DISSENTION CAME FROM THE
INSIDE OF THE TOP LEVEL OF GOVERNMENT, AND EVERY INDICATION
POINTED TO A SERIOUS SPLIT. THIS ARTICLE DISCUSSES THE
CENTRAL CHARACTERS IN THE GHANA SITUATION, ALONG WITH THEIR
POSSIBLE MOTIVES. IT CONCLUDES WITH A BRIEF DISCUSSION OF
RAWLINGS' OPTIONS.

00511
    RULES OF THE HUNGARIAN SOCIALIST PARTY
WORLD AFFAIRS, 151(4) (1989), 226-227.
    THE ARTICLE IS A PUBLICATION OF THE NEWLY CREATED
HUNGARIAN SOCIALIST PARTY. IT OUTLINES THE GOALS OF THE
PARTY, ITS NATURE, AND THE BASIC PRINCIPLES OF ITS OPERATION.
THESE BASIC PRINCIPLES INCLUDE: VOLUNTARY POLITICAL
ACTIVITY, FREEDOM OF CONSCIENCE, DEMOCRACY, SOLIDARITY,
TOLERANCE, OPENNESS, AND THE ASSERTION OF COMMON WILL.

00512
    RUMOURS AND THE TRUTH
BEIJING REVIEW, 32(37) (SEP 89), 20-26.
    THE TIANANMAN SQUARE INCIDENT HAS EMBELLISHED BY THE
MEDIA IN SOME WESTERN COUNTRIES, IN HONG KONG, AND IN TAIWAN
AND PARTICULARLY BY THE VOICE OF AMERICA. THIS ARTICLE LISTS
SOME OF THE WIDESPREAD, INCENDIARY RUMORS THAT CONTRIBUTED
TO THE TURMOIL AND REFUTES THEM WITH THE TRUTH.

00513
    RURAL ENTERPRISES IN CHINA: TOO MANY, TOO SOON?
CHINA NEWS ANALYSIS, (1380) (MAR 89), 1-9.
    DESPITE A STAGGERING NUMBER OF BANKRUPTCIES, RURAL
ENTERPRISES ARE BLOSSOMING IN CHINA. THE ORIGINAL PURPOSE OF
THE RURAL ENTERPRISES WAS TWOFOLD: TO ABSORB THE SURPLUS OF
THE AGRICULTURAL WORKFORCE AND TO GEAR PRODUCTION TOWARDS
CONSUMER GOODS. BECAUSE OF ITS SUCCESS, THE RURAL ENTERPRISE
SYSTEM HAS OUTGROWN ITS ORIGINAL MANDATE AND IS NOW BEING
PROPOSED AS A MODEL FOR THE REST OF CHINA'S INDUSTRIES. BUT
IT IS QUESTIONABLE HOW SUCH A MODEL CAN BE APPLIED IN THE
PRESENT STAGE OF THE RESTRUCTURING OF THE ECONOMY. THE RURAL
ENTERPRISE SYSTEM IS KNOWN FOR ITS SUPPLE DECISION-MAKING
AND ITS ADHERENCE TO LAISSEZ-FAIRE PHILOSOPHY. IT WOULD BE
DIFFICULT TO RECONCILE THESE TWO MAJOR CHARACTERISTICS WITH
THE ONGOING "CONTROL AND RECTIFY" CAMPAIGN WITHOUT BEING
CONFUSED AS TO THE REAL INTENTION OF THE CENTRAL ECONOMIC
POLICY.

00514
    SA REFORM RECOGNIZED
SOUTH AFRICA FOUNDATION REVIEW, 15(11) (NOV 89), 4.
    AN EDITORIAL COMMENT FROM THE FINANCIAL TIMES OF LONDON
PRAISED SOUTH AFRICA'S PRESIDENT DE KLERK'S REFORMS AND THE
OVERALL CHANGES TAKING PLACE IN SOUTH AFRICA. THE RELEASE OF
EIGHT POLITICAL PRISONERS INCLUDING WAKTER SISULU, SECOND
ONLY TO NELSON MANDELA, THE RELAXATION OF EMERGENCY LAWS,
THE INCREASING RESTRAINT EXERCISED BY THE POLICE, AND THE
PRELIMINARY INDIRECT CONTACTS BETWEEN THE RULING GOVERNMENT
AND ANTI-APARTHEID GROUPS SUCH AS THE AFRICAN NATIONAL
CONGRESS ARE ALL ENCOURAGING SIGNS.

00515
    SA REFORM RECOGNIZED: SUNDAY STAR
SOUTH AFRICA FOUNDATION REVIEW, 15(11) (NOV 89), 5.
    THE NEWSPAPER SUNDAY STAR DECLARED THAT THE RELEASE OF
EIGHT BLACK LEADERS FROM SOUTH AFRICAN PRISON HAS SPREAD
MORE OPTIMISM THROUGHOUT THE COUNTRY THAN PEOPLE CAN
REMEMBER FOR DECADES. ALTHOUGH THE ROAD TO FULL-SCALE
NEGOTIATIONS WILL BE LONG AND TRYING, OBSERVERS ARE BECOMING
INCREASINGLY OPTIMISTIC ABOUT THE ULTIMATE OUTCOME.

00516
    SA REFORM RECOGNIZED: TRANSVALER
SOUTH AFRICA FOUNDATION REVIEW, 15(11) (NOV 89), 5.
    THE SOUTH AFRICAN NEWSPAPER HAILED SUCH REFORMS AS THE
DECISION THAT PEACEFUL MASS DEMONSTRATIONS WILL BE ALLOWED,
AND THE RELEASE OF EIGHT BLACK LEADERS FROM PRISON WITH
PRAISE AND HOPE. SUCH REFORMS INCREASE THE LIKELIHOOD OF
NEGOTIATIONS AND A PEACEFUL TRANSITION AWAY FROM APARTHEID.
IN ADDITION, THE REFORMS MAKE IT POSSIBLE FOR FRIENDLY
FOREIGN NATIONS TO CONTINUE TO DEFEND THEIR STANCE AGAINST
SANCTIONS AND BOYCOTTS.

00517
    SALIM'S CHALLENGE FOR THE OAU
NEW AFRICAN, 263 (AUG 89), 24.
    THIS IS A REPORT ON TANZANIA'S DEPUTY PREMIER AND
DEFENCE MINISTER, SALIM AHMED SALIM'S DECISION TO LEAVE
NATIONAL POLITICS TO SEEK THE PRESTIGIOUS POST OF SECRETARY-
GENERAL OF THE ORGANISATION OF AFRICAN UNITY (OAU). IT
TRACES HIS RISE TO POLITICAL PROMINENCE AND THEN HIS DECLINE,
LEAVING HIM A FRUSTRATED AND AN INCREASINGLY ISOLATED MAN.
HIS CHANCES OF BEATING THE INCUMBENT OAU SECRETARY GENERAL
ARE EXPLORED, AS WELL AS FUTURE POLITICAL POSSIBILITIES.

00518
    SALINAS, ASPE BLOW HOT AND COLD
MEXICO-UNITED STATES REPORT, II(8) (MAY 89), 1.
    PRESIDENT CARLOS SALINAS DE GORTARI TOLD MEXICAN
INDUSTRIALISTS IN MID-APRIL THAT A SOLUTION TO MEXICO'S DEBT
PROBLEM "IS IN SIGHT." HIS OPTIMISM WAS BASED ON THE
ANNOUNCEMENT, THE DAY BEFORE, THAT MEXICO HAD SIGNED A
LETTER OF INTENT WITH THE INTERNATIONAL MONETARY FUND FOR
"GROWTH WITHOUT NEW ECONOMIC ADJUSTMENTS." SCARCELY THREE
WEEKS LATER, MEXICAN TREASURY SECRETARY PEDRO ASPE WAS
EXPRESSING CONCERN THAT "THERE IS STILL NO AGREEMENT" WITH
MORE THAN 300 U.S. COMMERCIAL BANKS, ACCORDING TO AN
AMERICAN BANKER WHO HAD MET WITH HIM IN WASHINGTON. MEXICO
OWES THE BANKS $60 BILLION, OR 60 PER CENT OF ITS TOTAL
FOREIGN DEBT OF ABOUT $100 BILLION AS CALCULATED BY ASPE.
NEITHER OFFICIAL DEALT WITH TWO OTHER WHOLLY INTERNAL
SOURCES OF REVENUE THAT ARE READILY AVAILABLE: SAVING
ENORMOUS SUBSIDIES TO STATE-OWNED COMPANIES BY PRIVATIZING
THEM, AND INDUCING THE REPATRIATION OF CAPITAL ABROAD BY
PROVIDING INCENTIVES.

00519
    SALUTE TO IMAGINATIVE ECONOMIC DEVELOPMENT PROGRAMS
AVAILABLE FROM NTIS, NO. PB89-224059/GAR, JUL 89, 130.
    IN COMMUNITIES ACROSS THE NATION, LOCAL LEADERS ARE
DISCOVERING NEW WAYS TO SPUR ECONOMIC DEVELOPMENT. THE
HANDBOOK LISTS MORE THAN 45 EXAMPLES OF NEW BUSINESSES,
DEVELOPMENT AND INNOVATIVE PRACTICES WHICH HAVE HELPED TO
CREATE OR RETAIN JOBS. EACH HAS ENABLED LOCAL COMMUNITIES TO
BE MORE FLEXIBLE AND INNOVATIVE IN THEIR APPROACH TO
ECONOMIC DEVELOPMENT. THE EXAMPLES WERE SELECTED FROM A
NATIONAL COMPETITION AND A SERIES OF REGIONAL CONFERENCES ON
THE SUBJECTS OF BUSINESS RETENTION, COMMERCIAL REDEVELOPMENT,
COMMUNITY DEVELOPMENT, CREATIVE FINANCE, ENTREPRENEURSHIP,
EXPORT PROMOTION, MARKETING FOR BUSINESS RECRUITMENT,
MINORITY ENTERPRISE DEVELOPMENT AND TECHNOLOGY TRANSFER.

00520
    SAVE EL SALVADOR
COMMONWEAL, CXVI(21) (DEC 89), 660-661.
    FOR A DECADE, SAN SALVADOR HAS BEEN A DIVIDED CITY IN A
DIVIDED LAND. THE INTENSE NOVEMBER 1989 OFFENSIVE BY THE
FMLN GUERRILLAS AND THE MASSIVE COUNTER-ATTACK BY THE
SALVADORAN MILITARY MERELY CONFIRMED WHAT SALVADORANS
ALREADY KNEW: THE COUNTRY IS RULED BY THE GUN AND DIVIDED BY
WALLS OF THE MIND.

00521
    SAVINGS AND LOAN LEGISLATION
CONGRESSIONAL DIGEST, 68(6-7) (JUN 89), 163-169.
    THE ARTICLE SURVEYS THE EVOLUTION OF US BANKING
LEGISLATION, THE FEDERAL AGENCIES INVOLVED, THE ORIGINS OF
THE SAVINGS AND LOAN CRISIS, AND RECENT CONGRESSIONAL ACTION
ON THE CRISIS.

00522
    SCOWCROFT'S VISIT SEEN AS "CONSTRUCTIVE"
BEIJING REVIEW, 32(52) (DEC 89), 13.
    CHINESE GOVERNMENT SPOKESMAN JIN GUIHUA DESCRIBED THE
VISIT OF U.S. PRESIDENTIAL ENVOY BRENT SCOWCROFT AS
"CONSTRUCTIVE AND USEFUL." ALTHOUGH THE TALKS BETWEEN
SCOWCROFT AND CHINESE LEADERS DID NOT SOLVE ALL THE PROBLEMS
IN SINO-AMERICAN RELATIONS, BOTH SIDES AGREED THAT THEY HAVE
MAJOR MUTUAL INTERESTS ON A WIDE RANGE OF ISSUES.

00523
    SCRAMBLE FOR THE PRESIDENCY
NEW AFRICAN, (264) (SEP 89), 11.
    THIS REPORT GIVES A BRIEF DESCRIPTION OF THOSE WHO WANT
TO BECOME THE NEXT CIVILIAN PRESIDENT OF NIGERIA. TWENTY-
EIGHT NAMES ARE LISTED AS POSSIBLE CANDIDATES WITH THE MOST
EXTENSIVE DESCRIPTIONS GIVEN OF ALHAJI BALARABE MUSA, DR.
TOKUNBO AWOLOWO, AND CHIEF EMMANUEL IWUANYANWU.

00524
    SCRUTINY OF EUROPEAN LEGISLATION
CONSTITUTIONAL REFORM QUARTERLY REVIEW, 4(3) (FAL 89), 1.
    THE BRITISH GOVERNMENT HAS BEEN CRITICIZED BY THE
COMMONS SELECT COMMITTEE ON EUROPEAN LEGISLATION FOR NOT
ALLOWING MEMBERS OF PARLIAMENT TO DEBATE THE DELORS
COMMITTEE'S PROPOSALS FOR ECONOMIC AND MONETARY UNION BEFORE
CRUCIAL DECISIONS ON THE CONTROVERSIAL PROPOSALS WERE TAKEN
BY THE EUROPEAN COUNCIL IN JUNE. ALTHOUGH NATIONAL
PARLIAMENT HAVE NO FORMAL STANDING IN THE EUROPEAN COMMUNITY
(EC) LEGISLATIVE PROCESS, THE QUALITY OF COMMONS SCRUTINY OF
EC LEGISLATION IS CURRENTLY BEING EXAMINED. THERE IS GROWING
CONCERN THAT TOO MUCH EC LEGISLATION IS GOING THROUGH THE
HOUSE WITHOUT PROPER SCRUTINY AND DEBATE.

00525
    SEARCH FOR AFRICAN VALUES
NEW AFRICAN, (258) (MAR 89), 28-29.
    THE BANNING OF TWO MAGAZINES IN KENYA SPARKED A MAJOR
CONTROVERSY REGARDING DRESS, CUSTOMS, AND MORALITY IN AFRICA.

KENYA'S MINISTRY OF NATIONAL GUIDANCE AND POLITICAL AFFAIRS
BANNED ONE OF THE TWO FOR PUBLISHING A PHOTOGRAPH OF NAKED
GIRLS DANCING BEFORE KING MSWATI OF SWAZILAND. BUT SOME
KENYANS DEFENDED THE DANCE AS PART OF TRADITIONAL AFRICAN
CULTURE AND COMMENDED MSWATI FOR WEARING SKINS WHEN
APPROPRIATE WHILE SOME AFRICAN LEADERS HAVE ABANDONED
TRADITIONAL GARB.

00526
SECOND SESSION OF THE SEVENTH NPC ENDS
BEIJING REVIEW, 32(16) (APR 89), 9-10.
THE ERA OF UNANIMOUS VOTING IN CHINA'S PARLIAMENT ENDED,
POSSIBLY FOREVER, ON APRIL 4, 1989, WHEN THE ASSEMBLY
MANAGED TO PASS A BILL THAT AUTHORIZED SPECIAL LEGISLATIVE
RIGHTS FOR SHENZHEN'S LEGISLATURE DESPITE THE FACT THAT A
LARGE NUMBER OF DELEGATES EITHER VOTED AGAINST IT OR
ABSTAINED. HAVING A "LOYAL OPPOSITION" IS UNIQUE IN THE
NATIONAL PEOPLE'S CONGRESS AND INDICATES FURTHER PROGRESS
TOWARDS CHINA'S FORMATION OF A POLITICAL DEMOCRACY.

00527
SECREATARY'S TRIP TO MOSCOW AND NATO
DEPARTMENT OF STATE BULLETIN (US FOREIGN POLICY), 89(2148)
(JUL 89), 29-36.
SECRETARY OF STATE BAKER VISITED HELSINKI, MOSCOW, AND
BRUSSELS IN MAY 1989. THIS REPORT ON THE TRIP INCLUDES
BAKER'S REMARKS ON HUMNAN RIGHTS AND REFUSENIKS, INTERVIEWS,
AND EXCERPTS FROM PRESS CONFERENCES WITH SOVIET JOURNALISTS.

00528
SECRETARY MEETS WITH SOVIET FOREIGN MINISTER
DEPARTMENT OF STATE BULLETIN (US FOREIGN POLICY), 89(2146)
(MAY 89), 59-60.
SECRETARY OF STATE JAMES BAKER MET WITH SOVIET FOREIGN
MINISTER SHEVARDNADZE IN VIENNA ON MARCH 7, 1989. THIS
REPORT ON THAT MEETING INCLUDES REMARKS BY SECRETARY BAKER
AND A QUESTION-AND-ANSWER SESSION WITH REPORTERS THAT
FOLLOWED THE MEETING.

00529
SECRETARY VISITS JAPAN, BRUNEI, AND OMAN
DEPARTMENT OF STATE BULLETIN (US FOREIGN POLICY), 89(2150)
(SEP 89), 56-62.
IN JULY 1989, SECRETARY OF STATE BAKER VISITED JAPAN,
OMAN, AND BRUNEI TO PARTICIPATE IN THE ASEAN POST-
MINISTERIAL CONFERENCE. THIS REPORT ON THE TRIP INCLUDES
BAKER'S ADDRESS BEFORE A SPECIAL PUBLIC SESSION OF THE
MULTILATERAL ASSISTANCE INITIATIVE PLEDGING CONFERENCE FOR
THE PHILIPPINES AND STATEMENTS MADE AT THE ASEAN
POSTERMINISTERIAL CONFERENCE.

00530
SECRETARY'S NEWS BRIEFINGS IN NEW YORK
DEPARTMENT OF STATE BULLETIN (US FOREIGN POLICY), 89(2152)
(NOV 89), 31-43.
IN NEWS BRIEFINGS HELD IN SEPTEMBER 1989, SECRETARY OF
STATE BAKER DISCUSSED EGYPT'S STANCE ON THE MIDEAST
SITUATION, THE DEVELOPMENTS IN PANAMA, U.S. RELATIONS WITH
THE USSR, AND ARMS CONTROL, INCLUDING CHEMICAL WEAPONS.

00531
SECTORAL TARGETING: A TOOL FOR STRENGTHENING STATE AND
LOCAL ECONOMIES
AVAILABLE FROM NTIS, NO. PB89-160303/GAR, JUN 87, 33.
STEELMAKING IN CHICAGO AND FOOD PROCESSING AND FURNITURE
MANUFACTURING IN THE NORTHERN TIER OF MASSACHUSETTS ARE TWO
INDUSTRIES EXAMINED IN THE REPORT OF LOCALITIES WHICH HAVE
TARGETED EXISTING FIRMS FOR GROWTH. IT EXAMINES SECTORAL
TARGETING OF THIS TYPE, WHICH IT LABELS A 'NEW BREED' OF
POLICIES GEARED TO PARTICULAR INDUSTRIES AND REPRESENTING
STRATEGIC PLANNING FOR GROWTH. WORKING WITH EXISTING
INDUSTRIES HOLDS MORE PROMISE FOR GROWTH THAN STRATEGIES TO
ATTRACT NEW FIRMS WITH OFFERS OF TAX FORGIVENESS, LOW COST
INFRASTRUCTURE AND LOANS. AS STATES AND LOCAL COMMUNITIES
REDUCE THEIR DEPENDENCE ON THE FEDERAL GOVERNMENT FOR
ASSISTANCE TO GENERATE JOBS, MORE ATTENTION MUST BE FOCUSED
ON HELPING EXISTING FIRMS AND ATTRACTING ALLIED INDUSTRIES.

00532
SECURITY COUNCIL ADOPTS RESOLUTION ON CENTRAL AMERICAN
PEACE
DEPARTMENT OF STATE BULLETIN (US FOREIGN POLICY), 89(2151)
(OCT 89), 73-74.
THIS ARTICLE CONTAINS THE TEXT OF A UNITED NATIONS
SECURITY COUNCIL RESOLUTION REGARDING PEACE IN CENTRAL
AMERICA ADOPTED ON JULY 27, 1989 AND A STATEMENT BY THE
UNITED STATES' ACTING PERMANENT REPRESENTATIVE TO THE UNITED
NATIONS, HERBERT S. OKUN.

00533
SELECTED ASPECTS OF THE ECONOMIC SITUATION AND THE
INHERENT CONCLUSIONS
CONTEMPORARY POLAND, XXII(1) (1989), 46-53.
THE INFORMATION PRESENTED TO THE TENTH PLENUM OF THE

PUWP CC CONCERNING THE ECONOMIC SITUATION IN 1988 POINTS TO
THE COMPLEX NATURE OF ECONOMIC PROBLEMS IN POLAND. USING THE
GAUGE OF PRODUCTION GROWTH RATES, THE RESULTS ATTAINED IN
1988 COULD BE VIEWED AS SATISFACTORY BECAUSE THE COUNTRY
EXPERIENCED GROWTH IN INDUSTRIAL OUTPUT, PRODUCTIVITY,
EXPORTS, AND INVESTMENT. BUT THERE IS ANOTHER SIDE TO THE
COIN. IN AREAS THAT ARE CONCERNED MOST HEAVILY WITH
SATISFYING THE WANTS OF THE WORKING PEOPLE, THERE IS NOT
ONLY A LACK OF IMPROVEMENT; THE THREAT IS LOOMING EVER
LARGER. THE AREAS OF HOUSING, INFLATION, AND THE MARKET
REMAIN REASONS FOR CONCERN.

00534
SEN. HATFIELD OPPOSES "CHRISTIAN NATION" VIEW OF THE
UNITED STATES
CHURCH AND STATE, 42(4) (APR 89), 14 (86).
U.S. SENATOR MARK O. HATFIELD HAS STATED THAT THE UNITED
STATES HAS NEVER MEANT TO BE A "CHRISTIAN NATION." THE
REPUBLICAN FROM OREGON ALSO DECLARED THAT THE USA WAS
INTENDED TO BE PLURALISTIC AND THAT CIVIL RELIGION REDUCES
THE GOD OF THE BIBLE TO A TRIBAL GOD OF CULTURE.

00535
SENATOR CRITICIZED FOR PUSHING "NEW AGE" COMMISSION
CHURCH AND STATE, 42(7) (JUL 89), 16 (160).
A PLAN BY SENATOR CLAIBORNE PELL TO STUDY HUMAN
POTENTIAL HAS APPARENTLY BEEN SCUTTLED AFTER BOTH
CONSERVATIVE AND LIBERAL CRITICS RAISED CHURCH-STATE
CONCERNS ABOUT IT. CONSERVATIVE CHRISTIAN CRITICS SAID THE
MEASURE ENDORSED NEW AGE BELIEFS, WHICH ARE OFTEN LINKED TO
EASTERN RELIGIONS. CIVIL LIBERTARIANS STATED THAT THE PLAN
WAS VAGUE AND CARRIED THE POTENTIAL FOR CHURCH-STATE ABUSES.

00536
SENATOR HELMS ACCEPTS MONEY FROM MOON
CHURCH AND STATE, 42(10) (NOV 89), 14 (230).
IN 1988 SENATOR JESSE HELMS ACCEPTED $10,000 IN SPEAKING
FEES FROM AN ORGANIZATION AFFILIATED WITH THE REV. SUN MYUNG
MOON. THE MONEY CAME FROM THE AMERICAN LEADERSHIP CONFERENCE
(ALC), WHICH IS AFFILIATED WITH CAUSA, THE POLITICAL ARM OF
MOON'S UNIFICATION CHURCH. OTHER CONSERVATIVE POLITICAL
LEADERS WHO HAVE ADDRESSED THE ALC INCLUDE ORRIN HATCH OF
UTAH, PETE WILSON OF CALIFORNIA, AND JACK KEMP OF NEW YORK.

00537
SHEVARDNADZE INTERVIEWED BY TIME MAGAZINE
REPRINTS FROM THE SOVIET PRESS, 49(1) (JUL 89), 20-26.
THE ARTICLE CONSISTS OF THE FULL TEXT OF THE INTERVIEW
OF SOVIET FOREIGN MINISTER EDUARD SHEVARDNADZE BY TIME
MAGAZINE. THE FOREIGN MINISTER DISCUSSES THE "NEW WAY OF
POLITICAL THINKING" THAT IS TRANSFORMING THE USSR AND ITS
IMPLICATIONS FOR SOVIET FOREIGN POLICY. HE SPECIFICALLY
ADDRESSES FUTURE SOVIET-US RELATIONS, SINO-SOVIET RELATIONS,
AFGHANISTAN, ARMS CONTROL, EUROPE, AND THE NATIONAL TENSIONS
WITHIN THE SOVIET UNION.

00538
SHEVARDNADZE-BAKER JOINT STATEMENT
REPRINTS FROM THE SOVIET PRESS, 49(11/12) (DEC 89), 5-12.
THE MINISTER OF FOREIGN AFFAIRS OF THE USSR, EDUARD
SHEVARDNADZE, AND THE U.S. SECRETARY OF STATE, JAMES BAKER,
ON SEPTEMBER 22-23 HELD TALKS AT JACKSON HOLE, WYOMING TO
DISCUSS THE ENTIRE RANGE OF SOVIET-AMERICAN RELATIONS. BOTH
SIGNED A SERIES OF SPECIFIC AGREEMENTS IN SOME AREAS AND
DEFINED SOME NEW FIELDS OF ACTION. AREAS DISCUSSED HERE ARMS
CONTROL AND DISARMAMENT, REGIONAL ISSUES, AFGHANISTAN, HUMAN
RIGHTS, HUMANITARIAN ISSUES AND, FINALLY, BILATERAL AND
INTERNATIONAL ISSUES.

00539
SHOULD A CONSTITUTIONAL AMENDMENT TO PREVENT FLAG
DESECRATION BE APPROVED?
CONGRESSIONAL DIGEST, 68(8-9) (AUG 89), 202-223.
THE ARGUMENTS FOR AND AGAINST A CONSTITUTIONAL AMENDMENT
TO PREVENT FLAG DESECRATION ARE PRESENTED BY THE HONORABLE
ROBERT BORK, A REPRESENTATIVE OF THE AMERICAN LEGION, WALTER
DELLINGER, LAURENCE TRIBE, JAMES H. WARNER, AND SENATORS
MICHEL, WARNER, GRAMM, KERREY, AND METZENBAUM.

00540
SHOULD CONGRESS ADOPT THE "HIGH RISK OCCUPATIONAL DISEASE
NOTIFICATION AND PREVENTION ACT OF 1987"?
CONGRESSIONAL DIGEST, 68(4) (APR 89), 106-125.
ARGUMENTS FOR AND AGAINST THE HIGH RISK OCCUPATIONAL
DISEASE NOTIFICATION AND PREVENTION ACT OF 1987 ARE
PRESENTED BY SENATORS KENNEDY, STAFFORD, METZENBAUM,
DURENBERGER, BREAUX, HATCH, BOSCHWITZ, SIMPSON, KASTEN, AND
MCCONNELL.

00541
SHOULD PRESIDENT BUSH'S MINIMUM WAGE PROPOSAL BE ADOPTED?
CONGRESSIONAL DIGEST, 68(5) (MAY 89), 138-149.
ADOPTION OF PRESIDENT BUSH'S MINIMUM WAGE PROPOSAL IS
DEBATED BY REPRESENTATIVES MICHEL, GOODLING, GREEN, BARLETT,

COOPER, HAWKINS, CLAY, MURPHY, HOYER, AND MARTINEZ.

00542
SHOULD THE CONGRESS ADOPT THE "ACID DEPOSITION CONTROL ACT OF 1987"?
CONGRESSIONAL DIGEST, 68(2) (FEB 89), 56-61.
THE PROS AND CONS OF THE ACID DEPOSITION CONTROL ACT OF 1987 ARE PRESENTED BY CONGRESSMAN SIKORSKI AND REPRESENTATIVES OF THE NATIONAL CLEAN AIR COALITION, THE NATIONAL COAL ASSOCIATION, AND THE NATIONAL ENVIRONMENTAL DEVELOPMENT ASSOCIATION.

00543
SHOULD THE CONGRESS ADOPT THE "CLEAN AIR ACT AMENDMENTS OF 1987"?
CONGRESSIONAL DIGEST, 68(2) (FEB 89), 42-49.
ADOPTION OF THE CLEAN AIR ACT AMENDMENTS OF 1987 IS DEBATED BY THE AMERICAN AUTOMOBILE ASSOCIATION, THE RENEWABLE FUELS ASSOCIATION, THE ENVIRONMENTAL PROTECTION AGENCY, AND THE AMERICAN PETROLEUM INSTITUTE.

00544
SHOULD THE CONGRESS ADOPT THE "FINANCIAL INSTITUTIONS REFORM, RECOVERY, AND ENFORCEMENT ACT OF 1989"?
CONGRESSIONAL DIGEST, 68(6-7) (JUN 89), 170-191.
THE FINANCIAL INSTITUTIONS REFORM, RECOVERY, AND ENFORCEMENT ACT OF 1989 IS DEBATED BY SENATORS GARN, RICGLE, SANFORD, BOND, MIKULSKI, HOLLINGS, METZENBAUM, BRADLEY, CONRAD, AND KERREY.

00545
SHOULD THE CONGRESS ADOPT THE "TENDER OFFER DISCLOSURE AND FAIRNESS ACT OF 1987"?
CONGRESSIONAL DIGEST, 68(3) (MAR 89), 74-87.
THE ARTICLE INCLUDES STATEMENTS ON THE TENDER OFFER DISCLOSURE AND FAIRNESS ACT OF 1987 MADE BY SENATORS PROXMIRE, SARBANES, SASSER, GARN, ARMSTRONG, AND GRAMM.

00546
SHOULD THE CONGRESS ADOPT THE "TEXTILE AND APPAREL TRADE ACT OF 1987?"
CONGRESSIONAL DIGEST, 68(1) (JAN 89), 10-31.
CONGRESSIONAL DEBATE ON THE TEXTILE AND APPAREL TRADE ACT IS SUMMARIZED WITH STATEMENTS BY SENATORS THURMOND, HOLLINGS, PACKWOOD, BINGAMAN, AND ADAMS AND REPRESENTATIVES QUILLEN, TALLON, HEFNER, SPRATT, CRANE, LAFALCE, AND BONKER.

00547
SHOULD THE HOUSE-PASSED WAGE PROPOSAL BE ENACTED?
CONGRESSIONAL DIGEST, 68(5) (MAY 89), 150-159.
REPRESENTATIVES WEISS, GARCIA, COYNE, KENNELLY, ENGLE, FRENZEL, TAUKE, DREIER, SMITH, AND HEFLEY DEBATE WHETHER THE HOUSE OF REPRESENTATIVES' MINIMUM WAGE PROPOSAL SHOULD BE ENACTED.

00548
SHOULD THE SENATE- PASSED IMMIGRATION ACT OF 1989 BE APPROVED?
CONGRESSIONAL DIGEST, 68(10) (OCT 89), 236-255.
THE PROS AND CONS OF THE SENATE'S IMMIGRATION ACT OF 1989 ARE DISCUSSED BY SENATORS KENNEDY, SIMPSON, SIMON, GRAMM, SANFORD, ADAMS, BYRD, CRANSTON, HELMS, BUMPERS, CONRAD, AND MILKULSKI.

00549
SINO-CUBAN TIES ENTER NEW ERA
BEIJING REVIEW, 32(5) (JAN 89), 15.
CUBAN FOREIGN MINISTER ISIDORO MALMIERCA PEOLI VISITED BEIJING IN JANUARY 1989, BECOMING THE FIRST CUBAN FOREIGN MINISTER TO ENTER CHINA IN 29 YEARS. BOTH CUBA AND CHINA REGARDED THE VISIT AS A SIGN OF IMPROVEMENT AND DEVELOPMENT IN RELATIONS BETWEEN THE TWO COUNTRIES.

00550
SINO-LIBERIAN TIES CUT
BEIJING REVIEW, 32(43) (OCT 89), 9-10.
ON OCTOBER 10, 1989, THE CHINESE GOVERNMENT ANNOUNCED THAT IT HAD SUSPENDED DIPLOMATIC RELATIONS WITH LIBERIA BECAUSE THE AFRICAN NATION HAD RE-ESTABLISHED DIPLOMATIC RELATIONS WITH TAIWAN.

00551
SINO-SOVIET FURTHER COOPERATION
BEIJING REVIEW, 32(39) (SEP 89), 10-11.
THE CHAIRMAN OF THE CHINESE NATIONAL PEOPLE'S CONGRESS STANDING COMMITTEE HAS STATED THAT STRENGTHENING SINO-SOVIET COOPERATION IS CONDUCIVE NOT ONLY TO WORLD PEACE BUT ALSO TO THE DEVELOPMENT AND CONSTRUCTION OF THE TWO COUNTRIES. HE POINTED OUT THAT BOTH CHINA AND THE USSR ARE UNDERTAKING REFORMS IN ALL AREAS, AND EXCHANGING KNOWLEDGE AND EXPERIENCES COULD PROMOTE THE ADVANCE OF SOCIALISM.

00552
SINO-SOVIET JOINT COMMUNIQUE
BEIJING REVIEW, 32(32) (MAY 89), 15-17.
MIKHAIL GORBACHEV PAID AN OFFICIAL VISIT TO THE PEOPLE'S REPUBLIC OF CHINA IN MAY 1989. GORBACHEV AND DENG XIAOPING EXCHANGED VIEWS ON SINO-SOVIET RELATIONS AND INTERNATIONAL ISSUES OF MUTUAL INTEREST. BOTH EXPRESSED READINESS TO RESOLVE ALL DISPUTES BETWEEN THE TWO COUNTRIES THROUGH PEACEFUL NEGOTIATIONS. THEY ALSO HAD AN IN-DEPTH EXCHANGE OF VIEWS ON THE SETTLEMENT OF THE KAMPUCHEAN QUESTION.

00553
SINO-SOVIET RELATIONS: NORMALIZED AT LAST
CHINA RECONSTRUCTS, XXXVIII(8) (AUG 89), 29-31.
IN MAY 1989, SOVIET PRESIDENT MIKHAIL GORBACHEV VISITED CHINA AND MET WITH DENG XIAOPING. A JOINT STATEMENT ANNOUNCED THAT THIS MEETING MARKED THE NORMALIZATION OF RELATIONS BETWEEN THE TWO COUNTRIES AND THE TWO COMMUNIST PARTIES, ENDING MORE THAN 30 YEARS OF ESTRANGEMENT AND HOSTILITY.

00554
SINO-SOVIET TRADE BOOMS
BEIJING REVIEW, 32(5) (JAN 89), 40, 42.
WITH THE IMPROVEMENT IN SINO-SOVIET RELATIONS OVER THE LAST DECADE, TRADE BETWEEN THE TWO COUNTRIES HAS INCREASED DRAMATICALLY. CHINA NOW ACCOUNTS FOR THREE PERCENT OF THE SOVIET UNION'S FOREIGN TRADE, AND PROSPECTS FOR THE FUTURE ARE BRIGHT. THE FOUNDATIONS FOR THIS SINO-SOVIET ECONOMIC COOPERATION WERE LAID IN TWO AGREEMENTS SIGNED IN 1985.

00555
SINO-U.S. CHRONOLOGY (1971-1988)
BEIJING REVIEW, 32(2) (JAN 89), 35.
THE EVOLUTION OF CONTEMPORARY SINO-AMERICAN RELATIONS IS TRACED THROUGH BRIEF SUMMARIES BEGINNING WITH RICHARD NIXON'S 1971 ANNOUNCEMENT THAT HENRY KISSINGER HAD PAID A SECRET VISIT TO BEIJING AND ENDING WITH CHINA'S AGREEMENT TO ACCEPT THE PEACE CORPS IN 1988.

00556
SISTERS IN A TURF WAR
SOUTH, (102) (APR 89), 8.
THE WORLD BANK, THE PREMIER DEVELOPMENT AGENCY, AND THE IMF, THE CAPITALIST SYSTEM'S CHIEF FIREFIGHTER, ARE HAVING A ROW. IT AMOUNTS TO A BATTLE FOR TURF, BROUGHT TO A HEAD BY THE FAILURE TO RESOLVE THE THIRD WORLD DEBT CRISIS AND RESTORE SUSTAINABLE ECONOMIC GROWTH TO LARGE AREAS OF THE GLOBE. THE CURRENT ROW IS OVER WHICH AGENCY WILL PLAY THE LEAD ROLE IN THE NEXT ACT OF THIS EVOLVING DRAMA.

00557
SOCIAL SECURITY BILL
SURVEY OF CURRENT AFFAIRS, 19(1) (JAN 89), 29-30.
THE SOCIAL SECURITY BILL RECEIVED ITS SECOND READING IN THE HOUSE OF COMMONONS ON 10 JANUARY 1989. IT MAIN PROVISIONS AIM TO ENSURE THAT PEOPLE SEEKING UNEMPLOYMENT BENEFIT TAKE ACTIVE STEPS TO FIND WORK; TO CHANGE THE RULES UNDER WHICH AN UNEMPLOYED PERSON IS CONSIDERED TO HAVE GOOD CAUSE FOR TURNING DOWN A JOB; AND TO INCREASE BO THE AGE LIMIT FOR RECEIPT OF MOBILITY ALLOWANCE. THE BILL IS ALSO DESIGNED TO BRING BRITISH LAW INTO LINE WITH THE EUROPEAN COMMUNITY DIRECTIVE ON EQUAL TREATMENT FOR MEN AND WOMEN IN OCCUPATIONAL PENSION SCHEMES. MEASURES PROPOSED IN THE BILL WOULD REDUCE PUBLIC EXPENDITURE BY ABOUT 100 MILLION POUNDS BETWEEN 1989 AND 1990.

00558
SOCIAL SECURITY: THE TRUST FUND RESERVE ACCUMULATION, THE ECONOMY AND THE FEDERAL BUDGET
AVAILABLE FROM NTIS, NO. AD-A204 168/9/GAR, JAN 19 89, 58.
THIS GAO REPORT DISCUSSES THE CURRENT FINANCING PLAN FOR THE SOCIAL SECURITY TRUST FUNDS, AS WELL AS THE FUNDS' RELATIONSHIP TO THE FEDERAL BUDGET AND THE LONG-TERM HEALTH OF THE ECONOMY. GAO ALSO DISCUSSES POLICY OPTIONS WITH RESPECTS TO THE SCHEDULED ACCUMULATION OF TRUST FUND RESERVES. THIS DOCUMENT SUMMARIZES GAO'S ANALYSIS AND CONCLUSIONS WHICH ARE BASED ON A REVIEW OF MAJOR STUDIES, SOCIAL SECURITY PROJECTIONS AND DISCUSSIONS WITH EXPERTS. DETAILS OF THE ANALYSIS ARE PRESENTED IN THE APPENDIXES. IN 1988, THREE MAJOR CONGRESSIONAL COMMITTEES HELD HEARINGS TO RECEIVE EXPERT TESTIMONY ON THE IMPLICATIONS OF RESERVE ACCUMULATION AND POSSIBLE POLICY RESPONSES. IN ADDITION, TWO EXPERT SEMINARS WERE HELD TO DISCUSS THE RESULTS OF TECHNICAL STUDIES COMMISSIONED BY THE PUBLIC MEMBERS OF THE BOARD OF TRUSTEES OF THE OLD-AGE, SURVIVORS' AND DISABILITY INSURANCE (OASD) PROGRAM. THESE STUDIES EXPLORED ECONOMIC, FINANCIAL, AND BUDGET POLICY IMPLICATIONS OF THE ACCUMULATION OF LARGE RESERVES. THE FOCUS OF SOCIAL SECURITY PROGRAM DEBATES HAS CHANGED, AWAY FROM THREATENED INSOLVENCY IN THE 1970S AND EARLY 1980S AND TOWARD THE ACCUMULATING SURPLUSES.

00559
SOLDIERS GET TOP JOBS
NEW AFRICAN, (260) (MAY 89), 23-24.

PRESIDENT KAUNDA HAS DISMISSED HIS PRIME MINISTER AND
APPOINTED GENERAL MALIMBA MASHEKE TO THE POST. KAUNDA HAS
AWARDED DIPLOMATIC AND POLITICAL JOBS TO A NUMBER OF
MILITARY OFFICERS, NOT ONLY AS A REWARD FOR THEIR LOYALTY
BUT ALSO AS A CHECK AGAINST THEIR HIDDEN POLITICAL AMBITIONS.

00560
SOS FOR EXILE CAPITAL
SOUTH, (110) (DEC 89), 23.
SOCIALIST SOUTH YEMEN HAS SWALLOWED ITS PRIDE AND
LAUNCHED AN APPEAL TO THE PRIVATE SECTOR, ESPECIALLY WEATHY
EXPATRIATES, TO RAISE FUNDS TO REVITALIZE ITS AILING ECONOMY.
THE IDEA IS TO CASH IN ON THE CLAN LOYALTIES THAT BIND
EXPATRIATES TO THEIR COMMUNITIES OF ORIGIN, GIVE THEM AN
OPPORTUNITY TO PROVIDE EMPLOYMENT FOR FAMILY MEMBERS STILL
LIVING IN YEMEN, AND DISTRIBUTE PROFITS LOCALLY.

00561
SOUTH AFRICA'S DEBT CRISIS
SECHABA, 23(10) (OCT 89), 14-18.
THIS ARTICLE EXPLORES THE FINANCIAL AND ECONOMIC CRISIS
THAT THE SOUTH AFRICAN REGIME IS IN WHICH IS BROUGHT ABOUT
BY THE STRUGGLE WITHIN THE COUNTRY AND PRESSURE FOR
SANCTIONS AND DIS INVESTMENT OVERSEAS. IT PROVIDES A
BACKGROUND TO THE NO DEBT CAMPAIGN AND PROVIDES AN INSIGHT
INTO THE STATE OF THE SOUTH AFRICAN ECONOMY.

00562
SOUTHERN AFRICA
SURVEY OF CURRENT AFFAIRS, 19(4) (APR 89), 130-131.
DURING A VISIT TO SOUTHERN AFRICA IN MARCH 1989, PRIME
MINISTER MARGARET THATCHER REAFFIRMED BRITAIN'S SUPPORT FOR
THE UNITED NATIONS PLAN FOR NAMIBIAN INDEPENDENCE. SHE ALSO
CONDEMNED THE APARTHEID SYSTEM IN SOUTH AFRICA AND STRESSED
THE NEED TO STIMULATE AND RESPOND TO GENUINE CHANGE THERE.

00563
SOVIET CHAMBER OF COMMERCE AND INDUSTRY: CHANGES UNDER WAY
REPRINTS FROM THE SOVIET PRESS, 48(11-12) (JUN 89), 31-33.
ON JANUARY 15, 1989 THE USSR CHAMBER OF COMMERCE AND
INDUSTRY AND ITS AGENCIES SWITCHED TO SELF-FINANCING
ARRANGEMENTS. WITH THIS CHANGE CAME NEW FUNCTIONS FOR THE
CHAMBER, WHICH INCLUDE: PARTICIPATING IN DRAFTING AND
IMPLEMENTING PLANS TO BOOST EXPORT POTENTIAL ON THE REGIONAL
LEVEL; SUPERVISION OF THE ACTIVITY OF ASSOCIATIONS FOR
BUSINESS COOPERATION WITH FOREIGN STATES, REGIONS, AND
SECTORAL ASSOCIATIONS; ASSISTING SOVIET FACTORIES IN
ESTABLISHING OF DIRECT COOPERATION LINKS WITH THEIR
COUNTERPARTS IN CMEA COUNTRIES; AND SEARCHING FOR PARTNERS
IN INDUSTRIALIZED AND DEVELOPING COUNTRIES.

00564
SOVIET GOVERNMENT'S STATEMENT ON TROOPS WITHDRAWAL
REPRINTS FROM THE SOVIET PRESS, 48(6) (MAR 89), 28-29.
THE SOVIET WITHDRAWAL FROM AFGHANISTAN IS COMPLETE;
THERE IS NOT A SINGLE SOVIET SOLDIER LEFT IN THE COUNTRY.
AFGHANISTAN'S FUTURE WILL LARGELY DEPEND ON THE OTHER
PARTIES TO THE GENEVA AGREEMENTS WILL FOLLOW THE EXAMPLE OF
THE USSR AND THE REPUBLIC OF AFGHANISTAN IN EXERCISING
RESTRAINT AND RESPONSIBLY WORKING FOR PEACE. THE UN ALSO HAS
A LARGE ROLE IN THE FUTURE OF AFGHANISTAN AS PROBLEMS SUCH
AS THE LARGE NUMBER OF REFUGEES AND CONTINUED VIOLENCE WILL
NEED TO BE CONFRONTED AND OVERCOME.

00565
SOVIET POLICY BREAK INTO "GLASNOST" OFFICE
GLASNOST, I1(2) (MAR 89), 4-5.
ON MAY 9, 1988, KGB AND MILITIAMEN RAIDED THE EDITORIAL
OFFICE OF "GLASNOST" MAGAZINE. THE EDITOR AND ALL WORKERS
WERE ARRESTED. THE BUILDING WAS SEARCHED. SOME PROPERTY WAS
STOLEN AND OTHER PROPERTY HAS REMOVED OR PLACED "IN SAFE
KEEPING."

00566
SOVIET UNION: AMERICANS ARE SYMPATHETIC TO SOVIET REFORMS
BUT EQUIVOCAL ABOUT U.S. ASSISTANCE
GALLUP REPORT, (280) (JAN 89), 18-19.
THE AMERICAN PEOPLE ARE GENERALLY SYMPATHETIC TO THE
CHANGES IN THE SOVIET UNION UNDER GORBACHEV, AND A LARGE
MAJORITY FEELS THESE REFORMS HAVE IMPROVED THE CHANCES FOR
PEACE IN THAT PART OF THE WORLD. BUT AMERICANS ARE EQUIVOCAL
ABOUT THE EXTENT TO WHICH PRESIDENT BUSH SHOULD HELP
GORBACHEV REVIVE THE SOVIET ECONOMY, EVEN THOUGH MOST FAVOR
EXPANDED TRADE BETWEEN THE TWO NATIONS.

00567
SOVIET-CHINESE JOINT COMMUNIQUE
REPRINTS FROM THE SOVIET PRESS, 49(2) (JUL 89), 7-11.
THE COMMUNIQUE IS ON THE RESULTS OF SOVIET LEADER
MIKHAIL GORBACHEV'S OFFICIAL VISIT TO THE PEOPLE'S REPUBLIC
OF CHINA. ISSUES COVERED INCLUDED FUTURE RELATIONS -- THEIR
PROCESS AND IMPLICATIONS, ARMS CONTROL, THE KAMPUCHEAN
CONFLICT, BORDER DISPUTES, COMMUNIST PARTY RELATIONS, THE
"TAIWAN" ISSUE, INTERNATIONAL ORGANIZATIONS, AND FURTHER

DIALOGUE, EXCHANGE OF INFORMATION AND TRADE.

00568
SPAIN: THE LEFT RESPONSE -- A STRONG COMMUNIST PARTY
INFORMATION BULLETIN, 26(13-14) (JUL 88), 6-7.
THIS ARTICLE DESCRIBES SOME OF THE RESOLUTIONS ADOPTED
AT THE 12TH CONGRESS OF THE COMMUNIST PARTY OF SPAIN.
FOREMOST AMONG THE ISSUES ADDRESSED WERE THE PALESTENIAN
ISSUED, THE PLIGHT OF POLITICAL PRISONERS, THE FUTURE FOR
AGRICULTURAL DAY LABORERS AND THE FATE OF SOUTH AFRICA.

00569
SPEECH DELIVERED BY PRIME MINISTER TADEUSZ MAZOWIECKI AT
THE MEETING OF THE SEJM ON SEPTEMBER 12, 1989
CONTEMPORARY POLAND, XXII(10) (1989), 40-53.
POLAND FACES TWO PRINCIPAL PROBLEMS: THE POLITICAL
RESTRUCTURING OF THE STATE AND SAVING THE COUNTRY FROM
ECONOMIC CATASTROPHE. IT WILL BE EXTREMELY DIFFICULT TO
RECONCILE AND FULFILL THESE TWO GOALS. THE NEW GOVERNMENT
THAT WILL WORK TO BUILD DEMOCRACY IN POLAND MAY FALL IN THE
FACE OF ECONOMIC COLLAPSE. BUT DEMOCRATIC INSTITUTIONS ARE
USELESS UNLESS MAJOR CHANGES OCCUR IN EVERYDAY LIFE.

00570
SPOKESMAN ON CURRENT SITUATION
BEIJING REVIEW, 32(27) (JUL 89), 15-18.
ON JUNE 17, 1989, YUAN MU, THE SPOKESMAN FOR THE CHINESE
STATE COUNCIL, DECLARED THAT MOST OF THE CHINESE PEOPLE
SUPPORT THE LEADERSHIP OF THE COMMUNIST PARTY AND DO NOT
WANT TO SEE THE GOVERNMENT SUBVERTED. HE ALSO STATED THAT NO
ONE WAS SHOT DOWN OR CRUSHED WHEN THE PLA TROOPS MARCHED
INTO TIANANMEN SQUARE TO ENFORCE MARTIAL LAW AND THAT THE
STUDENTS WITHDREW PEACEFULLY.

00571
SPORT FOR PEOPLE WITH DISABILITIES
SURVEY OF CURRENT AFFAIRS, 19(9) (SEP 89), 359-361.
THE GOVERNMENT HAS PUBLISHED A MAJOR REPORT CALLING FOR
A REORGANIZATION OF THE STRUCTURE OF SPORT FOR PEOPLE WITH
DISABILITIES, UNDER WHICH DISABLED SPORTSMEN AND WOMEN WOULD
BE INTEGRATED INTO ABLE-BODIED SPORT AND THE GOVERNING
BODIES OF SPORT WOULD ASSUME RESPONSIBILITY FOR ALL
PARTICIPANTS IN THEIR SPORT - WHETHER ABLE-BODIED OR
DISABLED.

00572
SRI LANKA: ACCORD ON RESOLVING THE TAMIL ISSUE
INFORMATION BULLETIN, 25/26(1-2) (JAN 88), 24-25.
THIS STATEMENT OF THE COMMUNIST PARTY OF SRI LANKA
FOCUSES ON THE INDO-SRI LANKA ACCORD AS A WELCOME, IF
BELATED SOLUTION TO A PROBLEM OF INTERNATIONAL SECURITY AND
HARMONY. THE PARTY SUPPORTS THE ACCORD AND URGES ITS
IMMEDIATE IMPLEMENTATION WITHOUT VACILLATION OR RETREAT.

00573
STANCE OF THE CENTRAL COMMITTEE ON POLITICAL PLURALISM AND
TRADE UNION PLURALISM
CONTEMPORARY POLAND, XXII(2) (1989), 34-36.
THE CENTRAL COMMITTEE OF THE POLISH UNITED WORKERS'
PARTY BELIEVES IT TO BE NECESSARY TO ESTABLISH A NEW FORMULA
FOR SHAPING POLITICAL PLURALISM. THE FORMULA SHOULD REFLECT
THE DIFFERENTIATION AND MULTITUDE OF INTERESTS AS WELL AS
THE POLITICAL ORIENTATIONS AND CONVICTIONS OF INDIVIDUAL
GROUPS AND STRATA OF SOCIETY AND SHOULD BE CONDUCTIVE TO
SOLVING CONTRADICTIONS AND DISPUTES WITHOUT HARMING THE
SUPREME VALUES OF THE NATION.

00574
STATE-CHURCH
POLISH PERSPECTIVES, XXXII(3) (1989), 14-18.
KAZIMIERZ BARCIKOWSKI, DEPUTY CHAIRMAN OF THE COUNCIL OF
STATE, PLAYED A MAJOR ROLE IN THE ENACTMENT OF NEW POLISH
LAWS REGARDING THE QUESTION OF CHURCH-STATE RELATIONS. IN
THIS INTERVIEW, BARCIKOWSKI DISCUSSES POLAND'S NEW LAWS
GRANTING RELIGIOUS FREEDOM AND ENABLING THE CHURCH TO OPEN A
RANGE OF INSTITUTIONS, INCLUDING SCHOOLS AND HOSPITALS.

00575
STATEMENT BY ANTE MARKOVIC IN THE ASSEMBLY OF THE SFRY ON
THE OCCASION OF HIS ELECTION TO THE OFFICE OF PRESIDENT OF
THE FEDERAL EXECUTIVE COUNCIL
YUGOSLAV SURVEY, XXX(1) (1989), 39-66.
ON MARCH 16, 1989, THE FEDERAL CHAMBER AND THE CHAMBER
OF REPUBLICS OF THE ASSEMBLY OF YUGOSLAVIA ELECTED ANTE
MARKOVIC TO BE PRESIDENT OF THE NEW FEDERAL EXECUTIVE
COUNCIL. MARKOVIC STATED THAT YUGOSLAVIA MUST SEEK THE
SOLUTION TO ITS PROBLEMS IN REFORMS. IN A COMMITMENT TO AN
INTEGRAL MARKET, IN THE INDEPENDENCE OF ECONOMIC ENTITIES
AND THEIR RIGHT TO ECONOMIC DECISION-MAKING, AND IN
DEVELOPMENT INVOLVING OPENING TO THE WORLD AND INTEGRATION
IN ITS PROCESSES.

00576
STATEMENT BY ANTE MARKOVIC, PRESIDENT OF THE FEDERAL

EXECUTIVE COUNCIL, IN THE ASSEMBLY OF THE SFR YUGOSLAVIA
YUGOSLAV SURVEY, XXX(3) (1989), 3-26.
IN THIS STATEMENT TO THE SFRY ASSEMBLY, PRESIDENT ANTE
MARKOVIC REVIEWED THE RESULTS OF YUGOSLAVIA'S ECONOMIC
POLICY AND OFFERED PROPOSALS FOR CURBING INFLATION.

00577
STATEMENT BY PRESIDENT OF THE FEDERAL EXECUTIVE COUNCIL
ANTE MARKOVIC GIVEN IN THE SFRY ASSEMBLY ON THE PROGRAMME
OF ECONOMIC REFORMS AND ECONOMIC POLICY MEASURES IN 1989
YUGOSLAV SURVEY, XXX(4) (1989), 29-54.
IN THIS SPEECH TO THE SFRY ASSEMBLY ON DECEMBER 18, 1989,
ANTE MARKOVIC REVIEWS YUGOSLAVIA'S ECONOMIC ACCOMPLISHMENTS
OVER THE PRECEDING NINE-MONTH PERIOD AND OUTLINES SHORT- AND
LONG-TERM PLANS FOR ECONOMIC REFORM.

00578
STATEMENT BY THE DEFENCE MINISTERS' COMMITTEE OF THE
STATES-PARTIES TO THE WARSAW TREATY: "ON THE NUMERICAL
RATIO OF THE ARMED FORCES AND ARMAMENTS OF THE WARSAW
TREATY AND THE NORTH ATLANTIC PACT IN EUROPE AND ADJOINING
BASINS"
CONTEMPORARY POLAND, XXII(3) (1989), 50-59.
THE DEFENCE MINISTERS' COMMITTEE OF THE STATES-PARTIES
TO THE WARSAW TREATY ENDORSES THE CAUSE OF STRENGTHENING
INTERNATIONAL PEACE, SECURITY, AND CONFIDENCE AS EVIDENCED
BY UNILATERAL SOVIET MOVES TO REDUCE SOVIET ARMED FORCES AND
ARMAMENTS IN EUROPE. THE COMMITTEE BELIEVES THAT IT IS OF
UTMOST IMPORTANCE TO PREVENT WAR, HALT THE RACE IN NUCLEAR
AND CONVENTIONAL ARMS, AND MOVE TOWARD GRADUAL DISARMAMENT.
THE ARMED FORCES OF NATO AND THE WARSAW PACT SHOULD BE
SUFFICIENT FOR DEFENSE BUT SHOULD NOT POSSESS THE MEANS TO
MOUNT A SURPRISE ATTACK ON THE OTHER SIDE.

00579
STATEMENT BY THE SOVIET AFRO-ASIAN SOLIDARITY COMMITTEE
SECHABA, 23(5) (MAY 89), 5.
THE STATEMENT REAFFIRMS THE POSITION OF THE SOVIET UNION
WITH REGARDS TO SOUTH AFRICA. DESPITE CLAIMS BY THE MASS
MEDIA OF THE WEST, THE USSR REMAINS COMMITTED TO THE FIGHT
AGAINST APARTHEID AND IS STILL MAINTAINING FRIENDLY
RELATIONS WITH THE ANC. THE USSR ALSO CONFIRMS ITS READINESS
TO DEVELOP RELATIONS WITH ALL FORCES IN SOUTH AFRICA WHICH
ARE AGAINST APARTHEID.

00580
STATEMENT BY THE WARSAW TREATY MEMBER STATES ON TACTICAL
NUCLEAR WEAPONS IN EUROPE
REPRINTS FROM THE SOVIET PRESS, 48(11-12) (JUN 89), 52-54.
THE WARSAW TREATY MEMBER STATES EXPRESS THEIR
DETERMINATION TO DO EVERYTHING IN THEIR POWER TO SECURE
PROGRESS AT TALKS THAT HAVE STARTED ON CONVENTIONAL ARMED
FORCES IN EUROPE. IN THIS CONNECTION THE WARSAW TREATY
MEMBER STATES SUGGEST TO THE MEMBER STATES OF NATO OPENING
SEPARATE TALKS ON TACTICAL NUCLEAR ARMS IN EUROPE, INCLUDING
THE NUCLEAR COMPONENTS OF DUAL-PURPOSE SYSTEMS, IN THE NEAR
FUTURE.

00581
STATISTICS FOR 1988 SOCIO-ECONOMIC DEVELOPMENT
BEIJING REVIEW, 32(10) (MAR 89), I-VIII.
IN 1988, CHINA'S NATIONAL ECONOMY DEVELOPED AMIDST A
DRIVE TO DEEPEN ITS REFORMS AND ACCELERATE OPENING UP TO THE
OUTSIDE WORLD. THE ANNUAL GROSS NATIONAL PRODUCT INCREASED
11.2 PERCENT OVER 1987, WHILE NATIONAL INCOME GREW 11.4
PERCENT. THE MAJOR ECONOMIC PROBLEMS WERE OVERHEATED DEMAND,
A SHARPENING OF THE CONTRADICTION BETWEEN SUPPLY AND DEMAND
AND OF THE STRUCTURAL CONTRADICTIONS, PRICE HIKES, AND
INFLATION.

00582
STOP ESCALATION OF THE HOSTILITIES
INFORMATION BULLETIN, 26(13-14) (JUL 88), 4-5.
THIS STATEMENT BY THE IRAQI COMMUNIST PARTY, THE
PEOPLE'S PARTY OF IRAN, AND COMMUNIST AND WORKERS' PARTIES
OF TURKEY CONDEMNS ANY ESCALATION OF MILITARY OPERATIONS IN
THE PERSIAN GULF BY U.S. IMPERIALIST FORCES.

00583
STOPPING TOXIC TRADE
MULTINATIONAL MONITOR, 10(7-8) (JUL 89), 6.
THE USA AND OTHER INDUSTRIALIZED NATIONS ARE USING THE
THIRD WORLD AS A DUMPING GROUND FOR HAZARDOUS CHEMICALS AND
WASTE. PRODUCERS OF THESE DANGEROUS MATERIALS WANT TO FOCUS
INTERNATIONAL DEBATE ON STRONGER EXPORT REGULATION OF
HAZARDOUS SUBSTANCES AND PRIOR INFORMED CONSENT. BUT AN
OUTRIGHT BAN IS IN ORDER. AT PRESENT, THE EPA IS RESPONSIBLE
FOR MONITORING THE EXPORT OF HAZARDOUS CHEMICALS FROM THE
USA, BUT A GAO REPORT HAS FOUND THE EPA DEFICIENT IN ITS
OVERSIGHT.

00584
STRONG MEASURES DECLARED TO CURB "TURMOIL"
BEIJING REVIEW, 32(22) (MAY 89), 19-20.

THIS ARTICLE REPRINTS EXCERPTS FROM A SPEECH BY PREMIER
LI PENG CALLING FOR RESOLUTE AND POWERFUL MEASURES TO CURB
TURMOIL AND RESTORE ORDER IN BEIJING. SPEAKING ON MAY 19,
1989, TO THE PARTY, GOVERNMENT, AND ARMY CADRES, HE SAID
THAT A HANDFUL OF DISSIDENTS HAD STIRRED UP UNREST BECAUSE
THEIR POLITICAL GOALS WERE UNOBTAINABLE THROUGH DEMOCRATIC
AND LEGAL CHANNELS.

00585
STUDENT DEMOS SHAKE BEIJING
BEIJING REVIEW, 32(19) (MAY 89), 9-10.
OFFICIALS FROM THE STATE COUNCIL AND THE BEIJING
MUNICIPALITY SAT DOWN WITH STUDENTS FROM 16 COLLEGES ON
APRIL 29, 1989, TO ENGAGE IN THE FIRST DIALOGUE SINCE THE
STUDENT UNREST STARTED IN BEIJING. THEIR DISCUSSIONS
CENTERED AROUND PUBLIC CORRUPTION, PROBLEMS IN EDUCATION,
OBJECTIVE REPORTING IN THE PRESS, AND THE STUDENT STRIKES.

00586
STUDENT RIOTS
NEW AFRICAN, (JAN 88), 28.
THIS ARTICLE REPORTS ON THE BOYCOTTS, STORMY MEETINGS
AND RIOTS WHICH HAVE CLOSED DOWN THE UNIVERSITY OF NAIROBI.
IT EXAMINES THE ROLE OF THE STUDENTS UNION AS BEING
ADVERSARIAL TO THE GOVERNMENT OF KENYA.

00587
STUDENTS RETURN TO CLASSES
BEIJING REVIEW, 32(20) (MAY 89), 10-11.
ON MAY 4, 1989, STUDENTS ORGANIZERS DECLARED AN END TO
THEIR BOYCOTT OF CLASSES AND CALLED ON ALL STRIKING STUDENTS
IN BEIJING TO RETURN TO SCHOOL. AT THE SAME TIME, THEY
REPEATED THEIR DEMAND FOR TALKS WITH STATE LEADERS. ON THE
SAME DAY, GENERAL SECRETARY ZHAO ZIYANG SAID THAT THE
STUDENTS WHO HAD STAGED THE DEMONSTRATIONS DID NOT
FUNDAMENTALLY OPPOSE THE CHINESE POLITICAL SYSTEM BUT WANTED
TO SEE THE ERRORS OF THE PARTY AND THE GOVERNMENT CORRECTED.

00588
SUMMIT OF THE ARCH
DEPARTMENT OF STATE BULLETIN (US FOREIGN POLICY), 89(2150)
(SEP 89), 1-21.
PRESIDENT BUSH ATTENDED THE 15TH ECONOMIC SUMMIT OF THE
INDUSTRIALIZED NATIONS IN PARIS IN JULY 1989. THIS REPORT ON
THE SUMMIT INCLUDES POLITICAL AND ECONOMIC DECLARATIONS
ISSUED AT THE MEETINGS.

00589
SUPPORT FOR EACH OTHER'S FREEDOM
EAST EUROPEAN REPORTER, 3(4) (SPR 89), 73.
THE ARTICLE EXAMINES THE SOLIDARITY THAT AROSE FROM THE
REPRESSION OF DEMONSTRATIONS ION PRAGUE IN AUGUST AND
OCTOBER, 1988, AND JANUARY, 1989. GROUPS FROM HUNGARY, THE
USSR, YUGOSLAVIA, AND POLAND ALL EXPRESSED THEIR CONCERN AND
SOLIDARITY WITH THEIR CZECHOSLOVAKIAN COUNTERPARTS.

00590
SYNCHING ECONOMIC, POLITICAL REFORMS
BEIJING REVIEW, 32(52) (DEC 89), 10-11.
PREMIER LI PENG HAS DECLARED THAT THE REFORM OF CHINA'S
POLITICAL STRUCTURE SHOULD OCCUR SIMULTANEOUSLY WITH
ECONOMIC REFORM. HE ADDED THAT POLITICAL RESTRUCTURING
SHOULD BE CARRIED OUT IN A MANNER CONDUCIVE TO THE STABILITY
AND PROSPERITY OF THE COUNTRY, WITHOUT CAUSING SOCIAL
DISTURBANCES. LIKE ECONOMIC REFORM, POLITICAL CHANGE SHOULD
PROCEED FROM CHINA'S ACTUAL CONDITIONS WITH A VIEW TOWARD
MOBILIZING THE INITIATIVE OF THE PEOPLE AND INSPIRING THEM
TO WORK WHOLEHEARTEDLY AND WITH FULL CONFIDENCE FOR THE
REALIZATION OF THE FOUR MODERNIZATIONS.

00591
TAIWAN: WHAT COURSE TO FOLLOW?
BEIJING REVIEW, 32(7-8) (FEB 89), 53.
RELATIONS BETWEEN MAINLAND CHINA AND TAIWAN IMPROVED IN
1988, BUT SOME PEOPLE BELIEVE THAT THE DOOR IS OPENING TOO
SLOWLY. IN AUGUST 1988, TAIWAN INDEPENDENCE ADVOCATES
BRAZENLY DEMANDED THAT TAIWAN BE ESTABLISHED AS AN NEW AND
INDEPENDENT NATION. IN ADDITION, SOME TAIWANESE GOVERNMENT
OFFICIALS SPEAK OF "ELASTIC DIPLOMACY" AND "DUAL RECOGNITION,
" BOTH OF WHICH ARE UNACCEPTABLE TO THE MAINLAND LEADERSHIP.

00592
TAKEOVER WARS
SOUTH, (106) (AUG 89), 27-28.
UNITED ENGINEERS (MALAYSIA) IS CONSTRUCTING A US$1.48
BILLION EXPRESSWAY PROJECT ACROSS PENINSULAR MALAYSIA AND
WILL COLLECT THE TOLLS ON THE HIGHWAY FOR 30 YEARS AFTER
COMPLETION. CRITICS CHARGE THAT THE PRIVATIZATION OF THE
EXPRESSWAY, WHICH COULD HAVE BEEN BUILT BY THE MALAYSIAN
HIGHWAY AUTHORITY, IS SIMPLY AN ATTEMPT TO PROP UP UMNO'S
AILING FINANCES AND PROVIDE THE PARTY WITH A LONG-TERM
SOURCE OF INCOME, SINCE UNITED ENGINEERS' LARGEST
SHAREHOLDER IS A COMPANY CONTROLLED BY UMNO.

00593
    TALK AND MORE TALK
    FAR EASTERN ECONOMIC REVIEW, 141(37) (SEP 88), 17-18.
    THE RECENT SINO-SOVIET TALKS ON THE CAMBODIAN CONFLICT
FAILED TO PRODUCE A MAJOR BREAKTHROUGH IN RELATIONS AND NO
SUMMIT WAS ANNOUNCED. MOSCOW HAS BEEN A LONG-TIME SUPPORTER
OF VIETNAM'S OCCUPATION OF CAMBODIA, WHILE PEKING HAS BACKED
ANTI-HANOI KHMER ROUGE RESISTANCE FORCES. THE FACT THAT THE
TWO SIDES HAVE AGREED TO PURSUE DIALOGUE IS ENCOURAGING, BUT
THERE IS MUCH CONFLICT TO BE OVERCOME ON THE ROAD TO PEACE
IN SOUTHEAST ASIA.

00594
    TALKING: PREMIER AND THE MINISTER
    CONTEMPORARY POLAND, XXII(11-12) (1989), 17-22.
    THIS ARTICLE REPRINTS EXTENSIVE EXCERPTS FROM TWO
INTERVIEWS BY POLISH GOVERNMENT OFFICIALS. IN ONE INTERVIEW,
PRIME MINISTER TADEUSZ MAZOWIECKI ANSWERS QUESTIONS ABOUT
RECENT CHANGES IN THE POLISH GOVERNMENT AND THE ROLE OF THE
COMMUNISTS. IN THE SECOND INTERVIEW, FOREIGN MINISTER
KRZYSZTOF SKUBISZEWSKI ANSWERS QUESTIONS POSED BY A SPANISH
WEEKLY.

00595
    TASMANIA-BICAMERALISM AND CONSTITUTIONAL REFORM
    PARLIAMENTARIAN, 70(3) (JUL 89), 140-145.
    THE AUTHOR PROVIDES AN OVERVIEW OF BICAMERALISM AND
CONSTITUTIONAL REFORM IN THE ISLAND STATE OF THE AUSTRALIAN
FEDERATION KNOWN AS TASMANIA. BACKGROUND INFORMATION IS
PROVIDED ON THE BICAMERAL PARLIAMENTS, WHICH INCLUDES THE
LEGISLATIVE COUNCIL AND THE HOUSE OF ASSEMBLY, AS WELL AS
AMENDMENTS TO THE CONSTITUTION WHICH HAVE OCCURRED SINCE
INDEPENDENCE IN THE MID-1850S. REFORM WHICH OCCURRED IN THE
MID-1920S IS HIGHLIGHTED, ALONG WITH THE ESTABLISHMENT IN
NOVEMBER 1981 OF A THREE-PERSON ROYAL COMMISSION ON THE
CONSTITUTION. A BILL WHICH WOULD AFFECT THE BALANCE OF POWER
BETWEEN THE TWO NATIONAL BODIES CONCERNING FINANCIAL AFFAIRS
IS DEBATED AND PLANS FOR A 1990 REFERENDUM ON THIS BILL ARE
PRESENTED.

00596
    TAXES: TAX REFORM FAILS TO CONVINCE
    GALLUP REPORT, (282-283) (MAR 89), 21-24.
    AMERICANS DOUBT THAT THE TAX REFORM ACT OF 1986 MADE THE
SYSTEM FAIRER AND THEY ARE CONCERNED THAT TAXES WILL
ACTUALLY INCREASE BY THE END OF 1989. DESPITE THE BUSH
ADMINISTRATION'S CONTINUED ASSURANCES THAT THERE WILL BE NO
NEW TAXES, FULLY THREE-QUARTERS OF AMERICANS EXPECT TAXES TO
INCREASE.

00597
    TECHNOLOGY TRANSFER: CONSTRAINTS PERCEIVED BY FEDERAL
        LABORATORY AND AGENCY OFFICIALS
    AVAILABLE FROM NTIS, NO. N89-20874/8/GAR, MAR 88, 25.
    FEDERAL LABORATORY AND AGENCY OFFICIALS WERE INTERVIEWED
TO IDENTIFY CONSTRAINTS TO TRANSFERRING TECHNOLOGY FROM
FEDERAL LABS TO U.S. BUSINESSES. FOLLOWING ARE FOUR MAJOR
CONSTRAINTS WHICH WERE IDENTIFIED BY SEVERAL LABS: (1) WHILE
RECENT CHANGES IN THE LAW ALLOW FEDERAL LABS TO PATENT AND
EXCLUSIVELY LICENSE INVENTIONS, FEDERAL COMPUTER SOFTWARE IS
PUBLICLY DISSEMINATED, THUS BUSINESSES DO NOT HAVE AN
INCENTIVE TO FULLY DEVELOP AND MARKET IT: (2) BECAUSE
FEDERAL LABS GENERALLY CANNOT CONDUCT PROPRIETARY RESEARCH
AND THEREFORE COMPETITORS CAN OBTAIN ACCESS TO RESEARCH
RESULTS, BUSINESSES ARE LESS INCLINED TO ENTER INTO
COLLABORATIVE RESEARCH EFFORTS; (3) THE REQUIREMENT THAT
SEVERAL OF THE DOE'S CONTRATOR OPERATED LABS MUST REQUEST
THE DEPARTMENT TO WAIVE ITS TITLE RIGHTS TO INVENTIONS THAT
THEY MAKE CAUSES UNCERTAINTY AND DELAY AND REDUCES INDUSTRY
INTEREST IN GETTING INVOLVED: AND (4) FEDERAL LABS, IN THEIR
EFFORTS TO BE FAIR IN PROVIDING BUSINESSES OPPORTUNITIES TO
COLLOBORATE ON RESEARCH, MAY INSTITUTE BIRTH DENSOME AND
TIME CONSUMING PROCEDURES THAT INHIBIT INDUSTRY
PARTICIPATION.

00598
    TELA ACCORDS: CONTRA DEMOBILIZATION?
    CENTRAL AMERICA BULLETIN, 8(10) (SEP 89), 1-3, 8.
    THE TELA ACCORD IS ANOTHER CONCRETE STEP IN REGIONAL
DIPLOMATIC EFFORTS TO END THE CONTRA WAR AGAINST NICARAGUA.
WITHOUT IMPOSING ADDITIONAL CONDITIONS ON NICARAGUA, IT
CALLS FOR THE IMMEDIATE DEMOBILIZATION OF THE CONTRAS. BUT
IT MAY NOT YET SIGNAL THE DEATH KNELL OF THE CONTRAS. WHILE
IT IMPOSES NEW POLITICAL CONSTRAINTS ON THE UNITED STATES,
IT LACKS ANY MECHANISM TO COMPEL THE CONTRAS TO DISARM AND
LEAVE HONDURAS. THE CONTRAS THEMSELVES HAVE DENOUNCED THE
ACCORD AND PROMISED TO CONTINUE FIGHTING INSIDE NICARGUA.

00599
    TEN BIG EVENTS IN RELATIONS ACROSS THE STRAITS
    BEIJING REVIEW, 32(2) (JAN 89), 11-12.
    THIS IS A CHRONOLOGY OF TEN MAJOR EVENTS IN RELATIONS
BETWEEN COMMUNIST CHINA AND TAIWAN IN THE DECADE BEGINNING
IN 1979, WHEN THE STANDING COMMITTEE OF THE NATIONAL

PEOPLE'S CONGRESS PUBLISHED ITS MESSAGE TO COMPATRIOTS IN
TAIWAN.

00600
    TEXT OF BUSH'S ASSEMBLY SPEECH
    KOREA OBSERVER, XX(1) (SPR 89), 131-136.
    IN THIS SPEECH TO THE SOUTH KOREAN ASSEMBLY, U.S.
PRESIDENT GEORGE BUSH PRAISED THE SOUTH KOREANS FOR THEIR
ECONOMIC AND DIPLOMATIC ACHIEVEMENTS IN THE RECENT PAST. HE
PLEDGED THAT AMERICAN ARMED FORCES WILL REMAIN IN SOUTH
KOREA AS LONG AS THEY ARE NEEDED TO HELP MAINTAIN THE PEACE
AND SECURITY OF NORTHEAST ASIA.

00601
    TEXT OF THE JOINT USSR-USA STATEMENT FOLLOWING THE SUMMIT
        MEETING IN MOSCOW, 29 MAY - 2 JUNE 1988
    AVAILABLE FROM NTIS, NO. DE88704456/GAR, JUN 88, 10.
    THE DOCUMENT REPRODUCES THE TEXT OF THE JOINT USSRUSA
STATEMENT FOLLOWING THE SUMMIT MEETING BETWEEN THE PRESIDENT
OF THE UNITED STATES, RONALD W. REAGAN AND THE GENERAL
SECRETARY OF THE CENTRAL COMMITTEE OF THE COMMUNIST PARTY OF
THE SOVIET UNION, MIKHAIL S. GORBACHEV, HELD IN MOSCOW
BETWEEN MAY 29 - JUNE 2, 1988. IT REFERS TO THE ARMS CONTROL
(INCLUDING NUCLEAR WEAPONS), HUMAN RIGHTS AND HUMANITARIAN
CONCERNS, REGIONAL ISSUES, BILATERAL AFFAIRS AND FURTHER
MEETINGS.

00602
    THAT'S WHERE ALL THE MONEY GOES
    SOUTH, (100) (FEB 89), 16-17.
    THE LAST 25 YEARS WITNESSED A DRAMATIC WIDENING IN THE
GAP BETWEEN THE RICH AND THE POOR. ONLY ASIA SHOWS ANY SIGNS
OF BEING ABLE TO CATCH UP WITH THE PROSPEROUS WORLD LEADERS
AND, AT PRESENT RATES, THIS WILL TAKE NEARLY 250 YEARS.
AFRICA AND LATIN AMERICA WILL CONTINUE TO FALL BEHIND.

00603
    THE AGE OF VULNERABILITY: EISENHOWER AND THE NATIONAL
        INSECURITY STATE
    AMERICAN HISTORICAL REVIEW, 94(4) (OCT 89), 963-989.
    ENOUGH MATERIAL HAS BECOME AVAILABLE DURING THE PAST FEW
YEARS TO ALLOW A RELATIVELY THOROUGH RECONSTRUCTION OF THE
MANNER IN WHICH AMERICAN POLICY MAKERS, MOST NOTABLY IN THE
ADMINISTRATION OF DWIGHT D. EISENHOWER, TACKLED THE PROBLEMS
THAT HAVE VEXED AMERICAN NATIONAL SECURITY PLANNING SINCE
THE 1950'S: HOW TO INTEGRATE NUCLEAR WEAPONS INTO OVERALL
DEFENSE STRATEGY, HOW TO DEFEND THE USA AGAINST AN OPPONENT
ARMED WITH SUCH WEAPONS, AND HOW TO BALANCE ECONOMIC HEALTH
AGAINST MILITARY STRENGTH.

00604
    THE AGE-OLD APPEAL OF EVIL
    GLASNOST, II(2) (MAR 89), 33-35.
    ANTI-SEMITISM FLOURISHES IN THE SOVIET UNION. MEMBERS OF
SUCH GROUPS AS ZHIDAM AND PAMYAT ADD A PATRIOTIC APPEAL TO
THEIR DIATRIBES AGAINST SOVIET JEWS. THESE GROUPS DECRY
ZIONISM AS THE GREATEST OBSTACLE TO MUTUAL UNDERSTANDING
AMONG NATIONS AND A THREAT TO WORLD PEACE.

00605
    THE ANSWER FROM BAKU
    GLASNOST, (16-18) (JAN 89), 29, 33.
    THIS ARTICLE SUMMARIZES A BAKU TELEVISION PROGRAM IN
WHICH SOVIET EXPERTS DISCUSSED THE STATUS OF THE AZERBAIJANI
PEOPLE IN THE SOVIET UNION AND THE ETHNIC STRIFE INVOLVING
THEM.

00606
    THE BUDGET
    SURVEY OF CURRENT AFFAIRS, 19(4) (APR 89), 134-141.
    THIS ARTICLE SUMMARIZES THE MAJOR BUDGET PROPOSALS FOR
1989-90. A MAIN FEATURE OF THE BUDGET, AS PRESENTED BY THE
CHANCELLOR OF THE EXCHEQUER ON MARCH 14, 1989, IS THE REFORM
OF EMPLOYEES' NATIONAL INSURANCE CONTRIBUTIONS. THE BUDGET
ALSO PROVIDES FOR RAISING THE PROFIT LIMITS FOR CORPORATION
TAX AND CONTAINS ADDITIONAL MEASURES TO ENCOURAGE SHARE
OWNERSHIP. SOME SLOWING IN THE RATE OF ECONOMIC GROWTH IS
FORECAST FOR 1989-90, AND LARGE REPAYMENTS OF PUBLIC SECTOR
DEBT ARE PLANNED.

00607
    THE CHINESE STATE: FICTION AND REALITY
    CHINA NEWS ANALYSIS, (1389) (JUL 89), 1-9.
    AS THE POLITICAL CRISIS THAT FOLLOWED THE DEATH OF HU
YAOBANG UNFOLDED IN THE SPRING OF 1989 IN FRONT OF AN
ASTONISHED WORLD AUDIENCE, INCONSISTENCIES IN OFFICIAL
PRONOUNCEMENTS AND ACTIONS WERE PLENTIFUL--OFTEN VERGING ON
THE RIDICULOUS, THE INCOMPETENT, OR THE UNTRUTHFUL, OR ALL
OF THESE AT THE SAME TIME.

00608
    THE CIVIL SERVICE AND THE POLICY OF ADMINISTRATIVE
        MODERNIZATION IN FRANCE
    INTERNATIONAL REVIEW OF ADMINISTRATIVE SCIENCES, 55(3)

(OCT 89), 445-466.

ROUBAN, L. THE PROSPECT OF ADMINISTRATIVE REFORM IS
BECOMING A PRIORITY TO THE FRENCH GOVERNMENT. THE PURPOSE OF
THIS ARTICLE IS TO EXAMINE THE RECENT REORGANIZATION OF THE
ARTICULATION BETWEEN THE EFFICIENCY/EFFECTIVENESS IMPERATIVE
AND THE MANAGEMENT OF THE CIVIL SERVICE SEEN AS A SINGULAR
SOCIO-OCCUPATIONAL ENVIRONMENT. A CIVIL SERVICE POLICY IS
NOT THE SAME THING AS A POLICY OF ADMINISTRATIVE
MODERNIZATION, NOR DO THE TWO NECESSARILY MERGE TOGETHER.
THE FRENCH SOLUTION IS AIMED AT ACHIEVING FULL PARTICIPATION
BY CIVIL SERVANTS IN ADMINISTRATIVE MODERNIZATION, SEEKS TO
PRESERVE THE CIVIL SERVICE AS A SEPARATE SOCIAL ENTITY. THE
CHIEF DIFFICULTY LIES IN THE FACT THAT THAT SOCIAL ENTITY IS
COMPOSED OF MANY REPRESENTATIONAL WORLDS: THE CIVIL SERVICE
HAS NEITHER THE SAME RESOURCES NOR THE SAME INTERESTS AS
LOCAL GOVERNMENT PERSONNEL OR PUBLIC CORPORATIONS.

00609
    THE CLEAN AIR ACT
    CONGRESSIONAL DIGEST, 68(2) (FEB 89), 35-41.
        THE EVOLUTION OF US CLEAN AIR LEGISLATION, AN ACID RAIN
    REPORT, AND RECENT CONGRESSIONAL ACTION ON CLEAN AIR LAWS
    ARE REVIEWED.

00610
    THE CMEA COUNTRIES COLLECTIVE CONCEPT
    FOREIGN TRADE, 10 (1988), 2.
        THIS ARTICLE DEFINES THE CMEA COUNTRIES COLLECTIVE
    CONCEPT AS A BASIS FOR COORDINATING ECONOMIC POLICIES IN
    AREAS PERTAINING TO THE COOPERATION OF PARTICIPATING
    COUNTRIES. NEW FORMS AND METHODS TO BUILD AND STRENGTHEN
    DIRECT TIES ARE ENCOURAGED APPROVED PRO OSALS ARE EXAMINED.

00611
    THE ECONOMY: ECONOMIC FREEDOMS
    POLISH PERSPECTIVES, XXXII(1) (1989), 56-59.
        IN DECEMBER 1988, THE SEJM PASSED A LAW ON ENTERPRISE
    AND A LAW ON JOINT VENTURES, WHICH WILL RADICALLY ALTER THE
    POLISH ECONOMIC SYSTEM. THE ENTERPRISE LAW INTRODUCES
    COMPLETE FREEDOM OF ECONOMIC ACTIVITY, REGARDLESS OF THE
    FORM OF OWNERSHIP, AND GIVES THE PRIVATE SECTOR EQUAL STATUS
    WITH THE PUBLIC. THE LAW ON JOINT VENTURES REMOVES THE
    REQUIREMENT THAT POLISH EQUITY MUST BE AT LEAST FIFTY-ONE
    PERCENT OF JOINT VENTURES AND OPENS THE WAY FOR OPERATIONS
    IN WHICH THE WHOLE OF THE SHARE CAPITAL IS HELD BY FOREIGN
    INVESTORS.

00612
    THE ECONOMY: THE ROUND TABLE BILL
    POLISH PERSPECTIVES, XXXII(3) (1989), 56-60.
        THE ACCORDS CONCLUDED AT THE ROUND TABLE OUTLINE 253
    GOALS FOR THE POLISH ECONOMY. VIRTUALLY ALL OF THE GOALS ARE
    THINGS THAT NOBODY WOULD QUESTION. THEY COVER A WIDE RANGE
    OF PROBLEMS, BUT THEY HAVE ONE FEATURE IN COMMON: THEY WILL
    COST MONEY. THIS HAS SET ECONOMISTS TO WRINGING THEIR HANDS
    BECAUSE THE STATE OF THE ECONOMY IN THE FIRST MONTHS OF 1989
    OFFERS LITTLE HOPE THAT EVEN A FRACTION OF THE ECONOMIC
    GOALS CAN BE MET.

00613
    THE EFFICACY OF SYMMETRY
    SOUTH, (99) (JAN 89), 4.
        IF THERE IS ROOM FOR HOPE IN NAMIBIA, IT IS NOT BECAUSE
    SOUTH AFRICA HAS CHANGED BUT BECAUSE IT CANNOT CONTINUE TO
    COUNT ON THE SUPPORT OF POWERFUL WESTERN STATES TO ASSIST IT
    IN EVADING THE DIRECTIVE OF THE INTERNATIONAL COMMUNITY AND
    BECAUSE THE SOVIET UNION IS NO LONGER BEING DELIBERATELY
    EXCLUDED FROM THE REGIONAL PEACE SETTLEMENT IN SOUTHERN
    AFRICA.

00614
    THE EGYPTIAN TEN-POINT PLAN
    NEW OUTLOOK, 32(9-10 (295-296)) (SEP 89), 50.
        EGYPTIAN PRESIDENT HOSNI MUBARAK'S TEN-POINT INITIATIVE,
    AIMED AT CLARIFYING THE MAY 1989 PEACE PLAN OF THE ISRAELI
    GOVERNMENT AND LAYING THE GROUND-WORK FOR PALESTINIAN
    PARTICIPATION, HAS RECENTLY BEEN THE FOCUS OF POLITICAL
    ACTIVITY IN ISRAEL AND ABROAD. THIS ARTICLE REPRINTS THE
    ORIGINAL TEXT OF THE EGYPTIAN CONDITIONS FOR HOLDING
    ELECTIONS IN THE OCCUPIED TERRITORIES.

00615
    THE ELECTION
    POLISH PERSPECTIVES, XXXII(3) (1989), 5-9.
        THE JUNE 1989 PARLIAMENTARY ELECTIONS WERE THE FINAL ACT
    IN A COMPLEX SERIES OF DEVELOPMENTS AIMED AT REMODELING THE
    POLISH POLITICAL SYSTEM AND GOVERNMENT. THE POLITICAL
    OVERHAUL WAS NEEDED TO STRENGTHEN THE STATE AND ENABLE IT TO
    CARRY OUT PROFOUND REFORMS. THE NEW POLITICAL SYSTEM
    INCLUDES PARTICIPATION BY OPPOSITION PARTIES, SUCH AS
    SOLIDARITY. WITHOUT SUCH PARTICIPATION, THE NEW POLITICAL
    SYSTEM WOULD NOT BE ACCEPTED BY THE SEGMENTS OF SOCIETY THAT
    HAD BEEN ALIENATED UNDER THE OLD SYSTEM.

00616
    THE EUROPEAN COMMUNITY'S PROGRAM FOR A SINGLE MARKET IN
    1992
    DEPARTMENT OF STATE BULLETIN (US FOREIGN POLICY), 89(2142)
    (JAN 89), 23-28.
        IN AN ENVIRONMENT OF INCREASED ECONOMIC INTERDEPENDENCE,
    THE 12 MEMBER STATES OF THE EUROPEAN COMMUNITY ARE WORKING
    TO REMOVE BARRIERS TO THE MOVEMENT OF GOODS, SERVICES,
    CAPITAL, AND LABOR. IF ALL GOES AS PLANNED, THE EUROPEAN
    COMMUNITY WILL BECOME A SINGLE MARKET OF MORE THAN 320
    MILLION CONSUMERS BY JANUARY 1, 1993.

00617
    THE EUROPEAN MONETARY SYSTEM: TEN YEARS OF PROGRESS IN
    MONETARY COOPERATION
    EUROPE, (285) (APR 89), 23, 47.
        THE ARTICLE EXAMINES THE PERFORMANCE OF THE EUROPEAN
    MONETARY SYSTEM (EMS) OVER THE PAST 10 YEARS. IT OUTLINES
    THREE PHASES IN THE DEVELOPMENT OF THE EMS AND THE ECONOMIC
    BENEFITS TO THE NATIONS INVOLVED. IT CONCLUDES THAT THE EMS
    HAS PROMOTED LOWER INFLATION AND MORE STABLE EXCHANGE RATES,
    WHICH FOSTER ECONOMIC GROWTH. THE EMS HAS BEEN A DRIVING
    FORCE BEHIND THE GENERAL CONVERGENCE OF ECONOMIC POLICY AND
    PERFORMANCE AMONG ITS MEMBERS AND WILL MAKE A MAJOR
    CONTRIBUTION TO THE CREATION OF THE SINGLE MARKET.

00618
    THE FEDERAL GOVERNMENT: FIFTY-EIGHT PERCENT APPROVE BUSH'S
    JOB PERFORMANCE; ONE-FOURTH UNDECIDED
    GALLUP REPORT, (284) (MAY 89), 7-8.
        AFTER THREE MONTHS IN OFFICE, PRESIDENT BUSH HAS FAR
    MORE BOOSTERS (58 PERCENT) THAN DETRACTORS (16 PERCENT). BUT
    ONE AMERICAN IN FOUR (26 PERCENT) IS WILLING OR UNABLE TO
    JUDGE THE PRESIDENT'S JOB PERFORMANCE, FUELING CRITICISM
    THAT HIS ADMINISTRATION LACKS A CLEAR SENSE OF PURPOSE.

00619
    THE FORTY-NINTH GOVERNMENT
    ITALIAN JOURNAL, III(2-3) (1989), 24-25.
        ON JULY 21, 1989, THE FORTY-NINTH POSTWAR ITALIAN
    GOVERNMENT HAS SWORN IN. THE NEW GOVERNMENT IS LED BY GIULIO
    ANDREOTTI AND DOMINATED BY THE CHRISTIAN DEMOCRATIC PARTY.
    OTHER PARTIES REPRESENTED IN THE COALITION GOVERNMENT ARE
    THE SOCIALISTS, THE REPUBLICANS, THE LIBERALS, AND THE
    SOCIAL DEMOCRATS.

00620
    THE FREE TRADE AREA
    LINK, 22(2) (MAY 89), 12.
        THE ARTICLE DISCUSSES THE FREE TRADE AREA AGREEMENT
    BETWEEN THE US AND ISRAEL THAT WAS COMPLETED IN 1985. IT
    ANALYZES THE IMPLICATIONS OF THE AGREEMENT AND SOME POSSIBLE
    CONSEQUENCES WHICH INCLUDE THE POSSIBILITY OF ISRAEL
    BECOMING A FUNNEL FOR CHEAP TEXTILES MANUFACTURED IN THE
    MIDDLE EAST AND AFRICA. THE POSSIBILITY OF ISRAEL ACTING AS
    A GO-BETWEEN FOR CIRCUMVENTING UN SANCTIONS AGAINST SOUTH
    AFRICA. IS ALSO DISCUSSED

00621
    THE FUTURE OF ECONOMIC AND MONETARY UNION DOMINATES E.C.
    SUMMIT
    EUROPE, 288 (JUL 89), 22-23.
        AT THE EUROPEAN COMMUNITY'S SUMMIT MEETING IN JUNE 1989,
    LEADERS REACHED A COMPROMISE ON THE BEGINNING OF THE FIRST
    STAGE OF ECONOMIC AND MONETARY UNION. DISCUSSION REVOLVED
    AROUND THE DELORS COMMITTEE'S REPORT ON ECONOMIC UNION THAT
    HAS ADOPTED BY THE E.C.'S CENTRAL BANK GOVERNORS AND FIVE
    OUTSIDE EXPERTS. LEADERS ALSO DISCUSSED SOCIAL CHARTER,
    ENVIRONMENT, THIRD WORLD DEBT AND INTERNATIONAL RELATIONS.

00622
    THE FUTURE OF FURTHER EDUCATION
    SURVEY OF CURRENT AFFAIRS, 19(3) (MAR 89), 112-113.
        IN A RECENT SPEECH, THE SECRETARY OF STATE FOR EDUCATION
    AND SCIENCE, KENNETH BAKER, OUTLINED PLANS FOR THE REFORM OF
    FURTHER EDUCATION AS PART OF THE GOVERNMENT'S STRATEGY FOR
    MEETING EMPLOYERS' REQUIREMENTS FOR SKILLED STAFF INTO THE
    NEXT CENTURY. HE SAID THAT THE NUMBER OF YOUNG PEOPLE
    ENGAGED IN FURTHER EDUCATION SHOULD BE EXPANDED AND THAT
    EVERYONE OUGHT IN FUTURE TO RECEIVE SYSTEMATIC EDUCATION OR
    TRAINING UP TO THE AGE OF 19.

00623
    THE FUTURE OF LOCAL GOVERNMENT
    SURVEY OF CURRENT AFFAIRS, 19(12) (DEC 89). 450-451.
        IN A SPEECH ON THE FUTURE OF LOCAL GOVERNMENT, SECRETARY
    OF STATE FOR THE ENVIRONMENT CHRISTOPHER PATTEN SPOKE OF THE
    NEED FOR STABILITY AND CONSOLIDATION FOLLOWING THE MAJOR
    CHANGES EXPERIENCED IN RECENT YEARS. HE CONSIDERS THAT A NEW
    DIALOGUE TO IMPROVE CO-OPERATION AND PARTNERSHIP BETWEEN
    CENTRAL AND LOCAL GOVERNMENT WOULD HELP TO ACHIEVE THIS AND
    WOULD BE IN THE INTERESTS OF ALL LOCAL COMMUNITIES.

00624
THE GENEVA ACCORDS ON AFGHANISTAN
INTERNATIONAL AFFAIRS (MOSCOW), (7) (JUL 89), 65-69.
THIS ARTICLE SUMMARIZES THE PROVISIONS OF THE APRIL 1988 GENEVA ACCORDS ON AFGHANISTAN IN ORDER TO PROVIDE A CLEAR PICTURE OF HOW THE AGREEMENTS ARE WORKING AND WHO OR WHAT IS RESPONSIBLE FOR THE FACT THAT SOME PROVISIONS HAVE NOT BEEN IMPLEMENTED.

00625
THE GLOBAL ENVIRONMENT
SURVEY OF CURRENT AFFAIRS, 19(6) (JUN 89), 240-241.
BRITAIN HAS CALLED FOR THE URGENT CONSIDERATION OF A FRAMEWORK CONVENTION ON CLIMATE CHANGE AND FOR INCREASED RESOURCES TO STRENGTHEN THE UNITED NATIONS ENVIRONMENT PROGRAMME. THE GOVERNMENT FAVOURS USING EXISTING BILATERAL AND MULTILATERAL AID CHANNELS TO ASSIST DEVELOPING COUNTRIES TO ADOPT TECHNOLOGIES FREE OF CHLOROFLUOROCARBONS.

00626
THE GLOBAL ENVIRONMENT
SURVEY OF CURRENT AFFAIRS, 19(11) (NOV 89), 427-430.
IN A WIDE-RANGING SPEECH CONCERNING GLOBAL ENVIRONMENTAL ISSUES, GIVEN TO THE UNITED NATIONS GENERAL ASSEMBLY IN NEW YORK ON 8 NOVEMBER 1989, PRIME MINISTER MARGARET THATCHER ANNOUNCED THAT BRITAIN WOULD BE ESTABLISHING A NEW CENTRE FOR THE PREDICTION OF CLIMATE CHANGE. SHE CALLED FOR A CONVENTION ON GLOBAL CLIMATE CHANGE TO BE SET UP BY 1992 AND ALSO FOR ONE ON THE CONSERVATION OF PLANT AND ANIMAL LIFE. BRITAIN WILL GIVE 100 MILLION POUNDS IN AID TO HELP MANAGE AND PRESERVE THE TROPICAL FORESTS. OTHER BRITISH ENVIRONMENTAL ASSISTANCE WAS OUTLINED BY THE MINISTER FOR OVERSEAS DEVELOPMENT, LYNDA CHALKER, IN A SPEECH EARLIER IN THE MONTH. BRITAIN HAS ALSO SUPPORTED MEASURES TO SAFEGUARD THE ANTARCTIC ENVIRONMENT.

00627
THE GOOD HUMOR MAN
CAMPAIGNS AND ELECTIONS, 10(2) (AUG 89), 22-27.
IN THIS INTERVIEW, POLITICAL SPEECH WRITER BOB ORBEN DISCUSSES THE IMPORTANCE OF HUMOR TO POLITICIANS AND CAMPAIGNS.

00628
THE HOLE IN THE OZONE LOGIC
SOUTH, (102) (APR 89), 9.
DEVELOPING COUNTRIES DO NOT DOUBT THAT PRESERVING THE ENVIRONMENT IS A GLOBAL ISSUE THAT REQUIRES GLOBAL SOLUTIONS. BUT THEY ARE WORRIED ABOUT THE UNEVEN SHARING BETWEEN THE UNDEVELOPED COUNTRIES AND THE INDUSTRIALIZED WORLD OF THE COSTS AND BENEFITS OF SOUND ECOLOGICAL PRACTICES.

00629
THE HUMAN DRAMA OF NAGORNO-KARABAKH
GLASNOST, (16-18) (JAN 89), 23-25.
THIS ARTICLE RECOUNTS INCIDENTS OF ETHNIC STRIFE IN ARMENIA IN EARLY 1988 AND REPORTS ON OFFICIAL SOVIET REACTION TO THE PROBLEM.

00630
THE INDIVIDUALLY OWNED ECONOMY
BEIJING REVIEW, 32(9) (FEB 89), 27-28.
CHINA HAS PERMITTED INDIVIDUALLY-OWNED AND HOUSEHOLD BUSINESSES SINCE 1978. SINCE THEN, THIS SECTOR OF THE ECONOMY HAS REGISTERED RAPID GROWTH IN BOTH RURAL AND URBAN AREAS, LARGELY IN INDUSTRIAL AND COMMERCIAL ENTERPRISES. THIS ARTICLE PRESENTS STATISTICS CHARTING THE EXPANSION OF CHINA'S INDIVIDUALLY-OWNED ECONOMY AND ITS EFFECT ON THE OVERALL ECONOMIC PICTURE.

00631
THE INVISIBLE MAN
COMMONWEAL, CXVI(10) (MAY 89), 291-292.
THE AUTHOR REVIEWS THE BUSH ADMINISTRATION'S POLICY RESPONSE TO THE WEST GERMAN INTEREST IN EAST-WEST NEGOTIATIONS OVER SHORT-RANGE MISSILES AND OTHER GORBACHEV INITIATIVES.

00632
THE ISRAELI VETO EXPOSED
SOUTH, (99) (JAN 89), 4-5.
ISRAEL BRUSQUELY AND CONTEMPTUOUSLY DISMISSED THE PALESTINE NATIONAL COUNCIL'S DECLARATION OF A PALESTINIAN STATE AND ITS INVITATION TO NEGOTIATIONS FOR A PEACEFUL SETTLEMENT. THE PLO HAS ACCEPTED UN RESOLUTIONS 242 AND 338, AND IT HAS EXPLICITLY RENOUNCED TERRORISM AS AN INSTRUMENT OF POLICY IN ITS LIBERATION STRUGGLE. ISRAEL'S RELUCTANCE TO BEGIN NEGOTIATIONS EXPOSES THOSE EARLIER ISRAELI DEMANDS AS A TACTIC TO STALL ITS WITHDRAWAL FROM THE OCCUPIED TERRITORIES. WHILE ISRAEL'S POLITICAL LEADERS ARE TRYING TO CREATE A WORKABLE COALITION GOVERNMENT AT HOME, TIME AND PATIENCE ARE RUNNING OUT IN PALESTINE.

00633
THE JAPANESE RED ARMY
DEPARTMENT OF STATE BULLETIN (US FOREIGN POLICY), 89(2152) (NOV 89), 64-65.
THE JAPANESE RED ARMY SUPPORTS A WORLDWIDE MARXIST-LENINIST REVOLUTION, USING TERRORISM AS ITS MAIN WEAPON. THE JRA HAS LONG IDENTIFIED ITSELF WITH RADICAL PALESTINIAN MOVEMENTS, ESPECIALLY THE POPULAR FRONT FOR THE LIBERATION OF PALESTINE, AND IS BELIEVED TO BE AFFILIATED WITH THE JAPANESE ANTI-WAR DEMOCRATIC FRONT. THE JRA'S GOALS FOR ITS NATIVE JAPAN INCLUDE UNITING LEFTIST ANARCHIST ORGANIZATIONS, ENDING THE IMPERIAL SYSTEM, OPPOSING JAPANESE IMPERIALISM, AND ESTABLISHING A PEOPLE'S REPUBLIC. IN RECENT YEARS, THE JRA HAS BEEN LINKED WITH LIBYA, WHICH APPEARS TO PROVIDE IT WITH FINANCIAL AID AND OTHER ASSISTANCE.

00634
THE JEWISH LOBBY
LINK, 22(2) (MAY 89), 2-3.
THE ARTICLE OUTLINES THE GROWTH OF THE JEWISH LOBBY THAT GENERALLY REPRESENTED THE MOST HAWKISH ISRAELI VIEWS. IT DOCUMENTS THE CORRESPONDING RISE IN US AID TO ISRAEL. US AID TO ISRAEL HAS GRADUALLY INCREASED OVER THE 1950'S AND 1960'S, AND SKYROCKETED IN THE 70'S AND 80'S. THE TYPE OF AID HAS ALSO CHANGED FROM BEING PRIMARILY ECONOMIC TO PRIMARILY MILITARY AID..

00635
THE LAST HURRAH
CAMPAIGNS AND ELECTIONS, 10(2) (AUG 89), 31-37.
THE LAST THIRD OF A CENTURY HAS SEEN A STEADY DECLINE IN THE POWER OF THE POLITICAL MACHINE, BUT A FEW OLD-STYLE POLITICAL BOSSES STILL SURVIVE. THEY CONTINUE TO OPERATE IN MUCH THE SAME WAY AS THEY OR THEIR PREDECESSORS DID A GENERATION AGO. THEY USE EITHER PATRONAGE OR THE POWERS AND PERQUISITES OF OFFICE TO DELIVER THE VOTE AND KEEP THEIR SUPPORTERS IN LINE. THEY OPERATE IN MIDDLE OR LOW-INCOME AREAS DEPENDENT ON GOVERNMENT LARGESS.

00636
THE LESSONS OF PERESTROIKA
SOUTH, (100) (FEB 89), 4.
MIKHAIL GORBACHEV'S ADDRESS TO THE 43RD SESSION OF THE UN GENERAL ASSEMBLY IN DECEMBER 1988 DEMANDS ATTENTION AT ALL LEVELS, PARTICULARLY IN THE THIRD WORLD. STRATEGIC AND ECONOMIC ISSUES CAN NO LONGER BE TREATED AS NATIONAL OR REGIONAL BECAUSE THEY HAVE ACQUIRED A GLOBAL DIMENSION. NOR IS IT POSSIBLE TO RETAIN A CLOSED SOCIETY: NO STATE CAN NOW DEVELOP NORMALLY OUTSIDE THE WORLD ECONOMY, WHICH IS BECOMING A SINGLE ORGANISM. THE WIDENING GAP BETWEEN THE DEVELOPED AND UNDEVELOPED COUNTRIES IS BECOMING A SERIOUS GLOBAL THREAT: HENCE, THE NEED TO SEARCH FOR A FUNDAMENTALLY NEW TYPE OF INDUSTRIAL PROGRESS.

00637
THE LOGIC OF U.S. GEOPOLITICS: AN INTERVIEW WITH GABRIEL KOLKO
MULTINATIONAL MONITOR, 10(9) (SEP 89), 27-31.
IN THIS INTERVIEW, GABRIEL KOLKO DISCUSSES THE FACTORS THAT HAVE SHAPED THE PATTERN OF U.S. INTERVENTION IN THE THIRD WORLD, THE INTERRELATION BETWEEN U.S. ECONOMIC INTERESTS AND FOREIGN POLICY, THE CHALLENGE TO U.S. POWER IN LATIN AMERICA, AND RELATED TOPICS.

00638
THE LONGER MARCH
COMMONWEAL, CXVI(9) (MAY 89), 259-260.
THE 300,000 MARCHERS IN WASHINGTON ON APRIL 9. 1989, RANKED WITH THE LARGEST DEMONSTRATIONS IN THE NATION'S HISTORY. THE NUMBERS PROVED THAT A WOMAN'S RIGHT TO ABORTION CAN SUMMON AS GREAT A POLITICAL RESPONSE AS SECURING THE CIVIL RIGHTS OF BLACKS OR ENDING THE WAR IN VIETNAM. THEY ALSO DEMONSTRATED THAT, AMONG ALL THE CAUSES ASSOCIATED WITH MOVEMENT FOR WOMEN'S RIGHTS, ABORTION STILL HAS THE GREATEST DRAWING POWER.

00639
THE MAKING OF A GENERAL SECRETARY
CHINA NEWS ANALYSIS, (1394) (OCT 89), 1-9.
IN JUNE 1989, JIANG ZEMIN WAS APPOINTED HEAD OF THE COMMUNIST PARTY OF CHINA. ZEMIN, WHO HAS GRADUALLY AND PATIENTLY CLIMBED THE LADDER OF POWER, IS THE FIRST PARTY GENERAL SECRETARY TO HAVE HAD LITTLE PART IN THE WAR OF LIBERATION AND TO HAVE BEEN CHOSEN FOR HIS RECORD OF SERVICE TO THE "NEW CHINA." THE NEW LEADER MUST SHOW HIS CAPACITY FOR LEADERSHIP IN ORDER TO OVERCOME RESISTANCE AND OPPOSITION WITHIN THE CENTRAL COMMITTEE.

00640
THE MIDDLE EAST: DECISION TO OPEN TALKS WITH PLO ENDORSED BY LARGE MAJORITY
GALLUP REPORT, (280) (JAN 89), 20-24.
A LARGE MAJORITY OF AMERICANS ENDORSE THE UNITED STATES' RECENT DECISION TO INITIATE TALKS WITH THE PLO, AND MOST

BELIEVE NEGOTIATIONS WITH THE PLO WILL IMPROVE THE CHANCES
FOR PEACE IN THE MIDDLE EAST.

00641
    THE NATIONALITIES POLICY OF THE PARTY IN PRESENT-DAY
    CONDITIONS (CPSU PLATFORM)
    REPRINTS FROM THE SOVIET PRESS, 49(8) (OCT 89), 5-23.
        IN ACCORDANCE WITH THE RESOLUTION OF THE POLITBURO OF
    THE CPSU CENTRAL COMMITTEE, THIS ARTICLE PRESENTS THE CPSU'S
    DRAFT PROGRAM - THE NATIONALITIES POLICY OF THE PARTY IN
    PRESENT - DAY CONDITIONS - WHICH WAS TO BE DISCUSSED AT THE
    COMING CENTRAL COMMITTEE'S PLENARY MEETING ON INTER-ETHNIC
    RELATIONS. IT DISCUSSES THE INHERITED LEGACY OF THE SOVIET
    UNION AND IDENTIFIES WAYS TO RESTRUCTURE THE SOVIET
    FEDERATION TO MAKE IT A FULL-FLEDGED ENTITY. EXAMINED ARE
    METHODS WITH WHICH TO ENHANCE THE ROLE AND LEGAL STATUS OF
    AUTONOMOUS STRUCTURES. IT CONCLUDES WITH AN EXAMINATION OF
    THE IDEOLOGICAL AND THEORETICAL ASPECT OF THE NATIONALITIES
    QUESTION.

00642
    THE NEW SOCIAL PLANNING SYSTEM
    YUGOSLAV SURVEY, XXX(2) (1989), 51-62.
        YUGOSLAVIA'S NEW ECONOMIC SYSTEM MARKS A RADICAL TURNING
    POINT IN THE PLANNING SYSTEM IN THAT ORGANIZATIONS OF
    ASSOCIATED LABOUR (OAL) IN ECONOMIC AND SOCIAL ACTIVITIES,
    OTHER SELF-MANAGEMENT ORGANIZATIONS AND COMMUNITIES, AND
    SOCIO-POLITICAL COMMUNITIES (PLANNING ENTITIES) WILL
    INDEPENDENTLY PLAN THEIR WORK AND DEVELOPMENT IN CONJUNCTION
    WITH THEIR INTERESTS, WHICH ARE ESTABLISHED ON A SELF-
    MANAGEMENT BASIS. DUE TO THE REDUCED ROLE OF THE STATE IN
    THE PLANNING SYSTEM, PLANNING ENTITIES WILL DRAFT THEIR OWN
    DEVELOPMENT PLANS AND BE DIRECTLY RESPONSIBLE FOR THEIR
    EXECUTION.

00643
    THE NEXT GOLD RUSH?
    CAMPAIGNS AND ELECTIONS, 10(3) (OCT 89), 16.
        AMONG THE EARLY CONTENDERS IN CALIFORNIA'S GUBERNATORIAL
    RACE, A SECONDARY CONTEST HAS DEVELOPED OVER ENDORSEMENTS OF
    POTENTIALLY LUCRATIVE BALLOT INITIATIVES TO BYPASS THE
    FINANCE RESTRICTIONS OF PROPOSITION 73. WHILE INDIVIDUAL
    CONTRIBUTIONS TO A CANIDATE ARE LIMITED TO $1,000, THERE IS
    NO SPENDING LIMIT ON INITIATIVES. THEREFORE, CANDIDATES ARE
    SCRAMBLING TO ADOPT BALLOT INITIATIVES ALREADY IN
    CIRCULATION AND, IN SOME CASES, TO CREATE THEIR OWN
    INITIATIVES.

00644
    THE PAN-EUROPEAN IDEA
    AUSTRIA TODAY, (2) (1989), 26-28.
        JUST OVER SIX DECADES AGO, A MOVEMENT WITH A
    BREATHTAKING GOAL SPREAD THROUGHOUT EUROPE. AFTER WORLD WAR
    I HAD COST TEN MILLION LIVES AND BROUGHT MISERY TO COUNTLESS
    MILLIONS, THE CONTINENT WHERE THE WAR HAD STARTED AND WHERE
    FAR-REACHING STRUCTURAL CHANGES RESULTED, WOULD FINALLY BE
    BROUGHT TO A STATE OF PEACEFUL COOPERATION BY MEANS OF A
    EUROPEAN UNION. EUROPE'S BEST POLITICAL, ECONOMIC, AND
    SCIENTIFIC MINDS WORKED ON THE IDEA. IT WAS SUCCESSFUL ONLY
    ON THE SECOND ATTEMPT, AFTER WORLD WAR II. BUT THE FACT
    REMAINS THAT THE FIRST DRESS REHEARSAL FOR EVENTS AFTER 1945
    CONCEIVED A EUROPEAN COMMON MARKET AS EARLY AS THE 1930'S.
    NOW WHEN THE TALK IS OF A "COMMON EUROPEAN HOUSE," IT IS
    IMPORTANT TO REMEMBER THAT EAST AND WEST WERE UNITED IN
    JOINTLY GIVING BIRTH TO THE IDEA.

00645
    THE PARTY AND THE SOVIETS
    REPRINTS FROM THE SOVIET PRESS, 49(7) (OCT 89), 14-15.
        THE COMMUNIST PARTY SHAPES POLICY AND IMPLEMENTS IT
    THROUGH THE SOVIETS, AND IS MAKING ITS FIRST STEPS IN
    DELEGATING POWER TO THE SOVIETS. THIS ARTICLE DESCRIBES SOME
    OF THE IMPEDIMENTS TO THE IMPLEMENTATION OF THIS DELEGATION
    OF POWER. IT DEFINES THE ROLE OF THE PARTY AS BEING
    ABSOLUTELY NECESSARY TO THE POLITICAL SYSTEM OF SOCIALISM,
    AND DESCRIBES HOW IMPORTANT IT IS THAT THE PARTY AND THE
    SOVIETS BACK UP THEIR AUTHORITY WITH PRACTICAL WORK AND MAKE
    PROGRESS.

00646
    THE PERILS OF PANAMA
    COMMONWEAL, CXVI(11) (JUN 89), 323-325.
        THE MOMENT TO START ON THE LONG ROAD TO DEMOCRACY IN
    PANAMA IS NOT THE DAY AFTER NORIEGA LEAVES, BUT TODAY. AND
    THE SUREST PATH LIES IN ALLOWING AND ENCOURAGING THE
    PANAMANIAN PEOPLE TO FIND THEIR WAY TO BRING ABOUT NEEDED
    CHANGE. THE OUSTER OF NORIEGA AND THE ACCESSION TO OFFICE OF
    DULY ELECTED LEADERS ARE THE OBVIOUS AND ESSENTIAL FIRST
    STEPS. BUT OTHER PROBLEMS LIE AHEAD. AN ORGANIZED
    INTERNATIONAL DRUG CARTEL LURKS IN THE BACKGROUND,
    COLLECTIVELY MORE POWERFUL AND HARDER TO OUST THAN NORIEGA.
    THE COUNTRY, ONCE PROSPEROUS, IS GRADUALLY SINKING INTO
    IMPOVERISHMENT--EXACERBATED BY THE ECONOMIC SANCTIONS THE U.
    S. APPLIED LAST YEAR TO SQUEEZE OUT NORIEGA.

00647
    THE PHONY WAR
    COMMONWEAL, CXVI(17) (OCT 89), 515-516.
        BUSH'S COMPREHENSIVE, FOUR-PRONGED STRATEGY AGAINST
    DRUGS IS SO IMBALANCED AND GROSSLY UNDERFUNDED THAT IT
    LEAVES THE NATION IN DOUBT AS TO THE PRESIDENT'S COMPETENCE
    AND SERIOUSNESS.

00648
    THE POLITICS OF EVASION
    COMMONWEAL, CXVI(19) (NOV 89), 579-580.
        THE VISCERAL ANTIPATHY AMONG AMERICANS TO GOVERNMENT
    INTERFERENCE IN THEIR LIVES LIES DEEP IN THE NATIONAL PSYCHE.
    THIS NEUROSIS HAS WELL NOURISHED DURING THE ANTI-ABORTION
    REAGAN ADMINISTRATION, AND NOW HAS BEEN GIVEN REAL VITALITY
    IN THE IMAGE OF A WOMAN FORCED TO BEAR A CHILD THROUGH THE
    POLITICAL POWER OF JESSE HELMS AND HIS ALLIES. BUT REAL
    DEBATE ON THE ABORTION ISSUE IS LACKING, AS POLITICIANS SEEM
    INTENT ON EVADING THE PROBLEM.

00649
    THE PRESIDENCY: CONFIDENCE IN BUSH LARGELY UNSHAKEN BY
    PROBLEMS FACING ADMINISTRATION
    GALLUP REPORT, (282-283) (MAR 89), 9-12.
        DESPITE THE TOWER CONTROVERSY AND CRITICISM THAT THE
    BUSH ADMINISTRATION IS ADRIFT, THE PRESIDENT CONTINUES TO
    ENJOY A LARGE MEASURE OF PUBLIC CONFIDENCE. MORE THAN 63
    PERCENT APPROVE OF BUSH'S PERFORMANCE IN OFFICE WHILE ONLY
    13 PERCENT DISAPPROVE AND 24 PERCENT ARE UNDECIDED.

00650
    THE PRESIDENCY: MAJORITY APPROVES BUSH'S FIRST WEEK BUT
    RECORD NUMBER ARE UNDECIDED
    GALLUP REPORT, (281) (FEB 89), 9-10.
        PRESIDENT BUSH HAS BEGUN HIS PRESIDENCY WITH THE
    APPROVAL OF A THIN MAJORITY OF THE AMERICAN PEOPLE. HIGH
    LEVELS OF UNCERTAINTY ARE CHARACTERISTIC OF EARLY SURVEYS OF
    INCOMING PRESIDENTS, BUT AN EXCEPTIONALLY LARGE NUMBER (43
    PERCENT) HAVE NOT YET FORMED OPINIONS ABOUT BUSH.

00651
    THE PRIVATELY-RUN ENTERPRISES
    CHINA NEWS ANALYSIS, (1382) (APR 89), 1-10.
        BY DEFINITION, A CHINESE PRIVATELY-RUN ENTERPRISE (PRE)
    IS A "LUCRATIVE ORGANIZATION IN WHICH ASSETS ARE PRIVATELY
    OWNED" AND CAPITAL "HIRES A LABOR FORCE OF EIGHT OR MORE."
    IN 1988, A CONSTITUTIONAL AMENDMENT GRANTED LEGITIMACY TO
    THE PRE'S. CHINA'S PRIVATE ENTREPRENEURS UNDERSTAND THAT THE
    GOVERNMENT NEEDS NOT ROCKEFELLERS BUT ONLY PRIVATE MANAGERS
    TO HELP THE ECONOMY ACROSS THE FIRST STAGE OF SOCIALISM.
    PRE'S ARE STRONGER IN RURAL AREAS THAN IN THE CITIES, AND IN
    A FEW REGIONS THEY HAVE DRASTICALLY MODIFIED THE LOCAL
    ECONOMIES.

00652
    THE PROGRAMME OF ACTION
    INTERNATIONAL AFFAIRS (MOSCOW), (2) (FEB 89), 62-65.
        PROFOUND QUALITATIVE CHANGES HAVE BEEN EFFECTED IN
    SOVIET FOREIGN POLICY. THESE CHANGES REFLECT NEW POLITICAL
    THINKING, REJECTION OF DOGMATISM, AND SOBER ANALYSIS, BASED
    ON COMMON SENSE, OF WHAT REALLY HELPS TO SAFEGUARD PEACE AND
    SECURITY. TENSIONS HAVE EASED, AND CONFRONTATION HAS
    DECREASED. THE PHILOSOPHY OF PEACEFUL COEXISTENCE HAS BEEN
    FILLED WITH NEW CONTENT AND COEXISTENCE IS NO LONGER
    REGARDED AS A "SPECIFIC FORM OF CLASS STRUGGLE."

00653
    THE PROSPECTS OF POLITICAL DEVELOPMENT
    CHINA NEWS ANALYSIS, (1399) (DEC 89), 4-9.
        THE AUTHOR CONSIDERS THE WRITING OF WANG HUNING ON
    CHINESE POLITICAL DEVELOPMENT. TO JUSTIFY HIS VIEW THAT THE
    BASIC GOAL OF CHINA'S POLITICAL DEVELOPMENT IS "SOCIALIST
    HIGH-DEGREE DEMOCRACY," WANG HUNING DOES NOT QUOTE MARX OR
    DENG XIAOPING BUT REFERS TO THE PROGRESS OF CHINESE HISTORY
    AND THE EXPERIENCE OF MANKIND, WHICH SHOW THAT "ANY HUMAN
    COMMUNITY, WHATEVER ITS CONDITION" IS ON ITS WAY TO
    DEMOCRACY.

00654
    THE PURGE
    NEW AFRICAN, (OCT 89), 17.
        THIS ARTICLE DESCRIBES THE METHODS OF NEW GOVERNMENT
    LEADER, BESHIR, AND HIS CABINET TO PURGE SUDAN OF
    UNDERSIRABLES. INSPIRED BY FUNDAMENTALIST ISLAMIC VIEWS, THE
    GOVERNMENT IS FORCIBLY PERSECUTING ANYONE ASSOCIATED WITH
    EITHER PROSTITUTION OR ALCOHOLIC DRINKS. THE ARTICLE
    SUGGESTS A BETTER APPROACH TO SOLVING THESE PROBLEMS

00655
    THE REFORM GAME: CORRUPTION
    CHINA NEWS ANALYSIS, (1393) (SEP 89), 1-9.
        ONCE AGAIN, THE CHINESE PROPAGANDA MACHINE HAS ANNOUNCED
    A MASSIVE EFFORT "ONCE AND FOR ALL" TO ELIMINATE THE CORRUPT

ELEMENTS IN THE CHINESE COMMUNIST PARTY AND THE GOVERNMENT. IN ADDITION TO THE FEAR OF POPULAR REJECTION, THE PARTY CONSERVATIVES HAVE OTHER GOOD REASONS TO FOCUS ON CORRUPTION; IT IS A READY-MADE, ACCEPTABLE PRETEXT TO EXPLAIN THE CHANGE IN POLICY ORIENTATION. NOW THAT THE PREVIOUS LEADERSHIP HAS BEEN PUSHED ASIDE, THE CAMPAIGN AGAINST CORRUPTION CAN BE USED TO "EXPOSE" KEY ADMINISTRATORS AND MANAGERS IDENTIFIED WITH THE LOSERS IN THE POWER STRUGGLE.

00656
THE REQUIREMENTS FOR STABLE COEXISTENCE IN SOVIET-U.S. RELATIONS
INTERNATIONAL AFFAIRS (MOSCOW), (1) (JAN 89), 133-142.
THIS ARTICLE REPRINTS A REPORT PREPARED BY THE INSTITUTE OF THE UNITED STATES AND CANADA OF THE USSR ACADEMY OF SCIENCES AND THE AMERICAN COMMITTEE ON U.S.-SOVIET RELATIONS. THE REPORT RECOMMENDS MEASURES NECESSARY TO ACHIEVE AND SUSTAIN A CONDITION OF STABLE COEXISTENCE IN U.S.-SOVIET AFFAIRS.

00657
THE RESURGENCE OF THE SMALLHOLDERS PARTY
EAST EUROPEAN REPORTER, 3(4) (SPR 89), 15-16.
IN 1945, THE HUNGARIAN SMALLHOLDERS PARTY WON 57% OF THE POPULAR VOTE AND HELD THE POSTS OF PRESIDENT AND PRIME MINISTER. HOWEVER, THE PARTY SLIPPED INTO OBLIVION WHEN THE COMMUNISTS SEIZED POWER. THE ARTICLE OUTLINES THE GUIDING PRINCIPLES OF REVIVED PARTY INCLUDING PARTY POLICY WITH REGARDS TO NATIONAL INTERESTS, FOREIGN POLICY, FOREIGN TRADE, DEMOCRATIC TRANSFORMATION OF HUNGARY, ECONOMIC ORGANIZATION, THE WELFARE SYSTEM, AND PROTECTION OF THE ENVIRONMENT.

00658
THE ROLE AND LIMITS OF THE MODERN STATE
CONSTITUTIONAL REFORM QUARTERLY REVIEW, 4(3) (FAL 89), 4.
THE ISSUE OF THE ROLE AND LIMITS OF THE STATE IN MODERN SOCIETY IS AS AN IMPORTANT QUESTION IN LONDON AS IN BUDAPEST. CONSERVATIVES, LIBERALS, AND COMMUNISTS ALL FACE THE SAME PARADOX: THE STATE IS LESS POTENT THAN WAS HOPED, BUT NO LESS NECESSARY. IN BRITAIN, THE ABSENCE OF CHECKS AND BALANCES HAS ALLOWED AN IMPATIENT ADMINISTRATION TO GATHER POWER TO ITSELF. CONSIDERATION OF THE APPROPRIATE ROLE FOR THE STATE OFTEN SUFFERS FROM THE LACK OF ANY THEORETICAL OR CONSTITUTIONAL BASIS FOR DISCUSSION.

00659
THE ROOTS OF HUNGER: POWER AND POLITICS IN THE PHILIPPINES
MULTINATIONAL MONITOR, 11(10) (OCT 89), 17-20.
PEOPLE GO HUNGRY NOT BECAUSE THERE IS AN INADEQUATE SUPPLY OF FOOD BUT BECAUSE THEY ARE POOR. THE POOR DO NOT HAVE CONTROL OF LAND OR RESOURCES. IN VIRTUALLY EVERY COUNTRY WHERE PEOPLE GO HUNGRY, ENOUGH FOOD IS AVAILABLE. BUT POOR PEOPLE DO NOT HAVE THE POWER TO LAY CLAIM TO IT.

00660
THE STATE OF THE ENVIRONMENT AND ENVIRONMENTAL POLICY
YUGOSLAV SURVEY, XXX(2) (1989), 117-136.
THE FEDERAL CONFERENCE OF THE SOCIALIST ALLIANCE OF THE WORKING PEOPLE OF YUGOSLAVIA REVIEWED ENVIRONMENTAL ISSUES AT A MEETING ON MAY 23, 1989. ITS COORDINATING COMMITTEE FOR THE ENVIRONMENT, LANDSCAPING, HOUSING, AND PUBLIC UTILITIES PRESENTED A REPORT ON THE STATE OF THE ENVIRONMENT AND ENVIRONMENTAL POLICY IN YUGOSLAVIA. THIS ARTICLE INCLUDES AN ABBREVIATED VERSION OF THE REPORT.

00661
THE STRUGGLE FOR DEMOCRACY AND THE WAY FORWARD
INFORMATION BULLETIN, 26(23-24) (DEC 88), 20-21.
THIS ARTICLE IS THE TEXT OF A DECLARATION OF DIALOGUE AMONG REPRESENTATIVES OF PROGRESSIVE AND REVOLUTIONARY PARTIES OF THE CARIBBEAN AND CENTRAL AMERICA. THE PARTICIPANTS IN THE DIALOGUE FOCUS ON THE REVITALIZATION OF SOCIALISM AND ON THE ISSUE OF SOLIDARITY IN THE REGION.

00662
THE TEXTILE AND APPAREL TRADE ACT
CONGRESSIONAL DIGEST, 68(1) (JAN 89), 1-9.
THIS ARTICLE DISCUSSES THE EVOLUTION OF US TRADE LAWS, THE US TRADE BALANCE, THE AMERICAN TEXTILE INDUSTRY, AND RECENT CONGRESSIONAL ACTION REGARDING TEXTILE AND APPAREL TRADE LEGISLATION.

00663
THE U.S. AND THE U.N.: THE HERITAGE FOUNDATION POINT OF VIEW (AN INTERVIEW WITH MARK FRANZ)
MULTINATIONAL MONITOR, 10(7-8) (JUL 89), 28-31.
IN THIS INTERVIEW, THE POLICY ANALYST FOR THE HERITAGE FOUNDATION'S UNITED NATIONS ASSESSMENT PROJECT ANSWERS QUESTIONS ABOUT THE PROJECT AND ABOUT THE UNITED STATES' ROLE IN THE UNITED NATIONS, AS CONCEIVED BY THE HERITAGE FOUNDATION.

00664
THE UNDERSIDE OF PARADISE

SOUTH, (109) (NOV 89), 8.
DESPITE ITS HEALTH OF RESOURCES, BRAZIL IS INHABITED BY A POPULATION ENDURING SOCIAL CONDITIONS AMONG THE WORST IN THE WORLD. BRAZIL'S NEW PRESIDENT WILL BE ELECTED WITH THE VOTES OF THOSE WHO SUFFER POVERTY AND WANT TO SEE BRAZIL CHANGED. BUT HE WILL ALSO SERVE VOTERS WHO WANT TO CLING TO THEIR PRIVILEGES AND ARE RELUCTANT TO MAKE THE SACRIFICES NEEDED FOR SIGNIFICANT CHANGE.

00665
THE VOLKER COMMISSION SUMMARY
BUREAUCRAT, 18(2) (SUM 89), 60-62.
THE CENTRAL MESSAGE OF THE REPORT OF THE COMMISSION ON PUBLIC SERVICE IS THAT A RENEWED SENSE OF COMMITMENT BY ALL AMERICANS TO THE HIGHEST TRADITIONS OF THE PUBLIC SERVICE IS URGENTLY NEEDED. THE MULTIPLE CHALLENGES THRUST UPON THE AMERICAN GOVERNMENT AS THE 21ST CENTURY APPROACHES CAN ONLY REINFORCE THE POINT. YET THERE IS EVIDENCE ON ALL SIDES OF AN EROSION OF PERFORMANCE AND MORALE ACROSS GOVERNMENT IN THE USA.

00666
THE WAR ON DRUGS: IS IT TIME TO SURRENDER?
REPORT FROM THE INSTITUTE FOR PHILOSOPHY AND PUBLIC POLICY, 9(2-3) (SPR 89), 1-5.
WHATEVER THE STRENGTH OF THE VARIOUS ARGUMENTS FOR THE LEGALIZATION OF DRUGS, A SOBER COST-BENEFIT ANALYSIS THAT PAYS HEED TO THE TERRIBLE COSTS BROUGHT BY THE UNITED STATES' NATIONAL WAR ON DRUGS SEEMS TO SUPPORT SOME DEGREE OF DECRIMINALIZATION. IN THE END, THE BEST WAR ON DRUGS MAY BE TO REVIVE AND OVERHAUL THE OLD WAR ON POVERTY: TO TAKE THE RESOURCES AND ENERGY MARSHALED IN THE WAR ON DRUGS AND DIRECT THEM INSTEAD TO PROGRAMS DESIGNED TO COMBAT THE ENTRENCHED HOPELESSNESS THAT MAKES DRUG USE SO TRAGICALLY APPEALING.

00667
THE WAR WITHIN
INDIA TODAY, XIV(12) (JUN 89), 14-29.
IN ONE BLOODY SWEEP, THE MASSACRE OF PROTESTING STUDENTS IN CHINA HAS DESTROYED THE GAINS OF A DECADE OF MODERNIZATION. THIS ARTICLE DESCRIBES HOW, AFTER PARTIALLY OPENING OUT TO THE REST OF THE WORLD AND GETTING OVER THE BRUTALITIES OF THE CULTURAL REVOLUTION, CHINA SEEMS TO BE HEADING FOR ANOTHER PERIOD OF ISOLATION AND INTERNAL STRIFE.

00668
THE WINTER WAR: DOCUMENTS ON SOVIET-FINNISH RELATIONS IN 1939-1940
INTERNATIONAL AFFAIRS (MOSCOW), (9) (SEP 89), 49-71.
DOCUMENTS FROM THE USSR FOREIGN POLICY ARCHIVES RECENTLY MADE PUBLIC FOR THE FIRST TIME PROVIDE AN OUTLINE OF THE SOVIET-FINNISH TALKS IN THE SPRING AND AUTUMN OF 1939. THE FAILURE OF THESE TALKS ULTIMATELY LED TO HOSTILITIES BETWEEN THE TWO COUNTRIES. DOCUMENTS FROM THE ARCHIVES ALSO RECOUNT THE NEGOTIATIONS ON CONCLUDING THE PEACE TREATY OF MARCH 1940.

00669
THE WITTENBERG THESES ON SOCIAL RENEWEL
EAST EUROPEAN REPORTER, 3(4) (SPR 89), 30-31.
CONTINUING IN THE TRADITION OF MARTIN LUTHER WHO STATED "THE TIME FOR SILENCE IS PAST; THE TIME FOR DIALOGUE HAS COME," A CHURCH ASSEMBLY IN WITTENBERG PUBLISHES A SERIES OF THESES ON THE TOPIC OF SOCIAL RENEWAL. THESE 20 POINTS DEAL WITH SUCH ISSUES AS SOCIAL APATHY, DISARMAMENT, PROTECTING THE ENVIRONMENT, AND THE PROBLEMS CONFRONTED BY CENTRALIZED SOCIALISM.

00670
THE WORLD IS INDIVISBILE AND INTERDEPENDENT
INFORMATION BULLETIN, 26(21-22) (NOV 88), 18-21.
THIS STATEMENT OF THE CENTRAL COMMITTEE POLITICAL BUREAU OF THE LEBANESE COMMUNIST PARTY NOTES THAT THE SOVIET LEADERSHIP'S FIRM AND PRINCIPLED STAND ON THE ARABISRAELI CONFLICT, WHICH IS ROOTED IN THE PROBLEM OF THE PALESTINIAN PEOPLE (A STAND REAFFIRMED AT THE MOSCOW SUMMIT) AND THE SOVIET LEADERSHIP'S DESIRE TO PUT ON THE SUMMIT AGENDA THE PROBLEM OF LEBANON, IN PARTICULAR THE QUESTION OF THE ISRAELI OCCUPATION OF A PART OF ITS TERRITORY, WHICH HAS NOT ACCEPTED BY THE U.S. SIDE, EARNED THE HIGH APPRECIATION AND RESPECT OF THE LEBANESE COMMUNISTS AND PATRIOTS, OF THE ENTIRE LEBANESE PEOPLE, OF ALL THE ARAB PEOPLES AND THEIR PATRIOTIC AND PROGRESSIVE FORCES.

00671
THE WYOMING MINISTERIAL
DEPARTMENT OF STATE BULLETIN (US FOREIGN POLICY), 89(2152) (NOV 89), 1-26.
IN SEPTEMBER 1989, SOVIET FOREIGN MINISTER EDUARD A. SHEVARDNADZE MET WITH PRESIDENT BUSH IN WASHINGTON AND THEN ACCOMPANIED SECRETARY OF STATE BAKER TO WYOMING FOR A MINISTERIAL SESSION. THIS ACCOUNT OF THE VISIT INCLUDES REMARKS MADE BY BAKER AND SHEVARDNADZE, THE TEXTS OF THE

JOINT STATEMENTS ISSUED DURING THE TRIP, AND THE TEXTS OF AGREEMENTS SIGNED BY THE REPRESENTATIVES OF THE USA AND THE USSR.

00672
  THIRD REPORT ON CYPRUS
  DEPARTMENT OF STATE BULLETIN (US FOREIGN POLICY), 89(2153) (DEC 89), 41.
  IN THIS REPORT TO CONGRESS, PRESIDENT GEORGE BUSH NOTES THAT THE NEGOTIATING PROCESS ON CYPRUS UNDER THE AUSPICES OF THE UN SECRETARY GENERAL CONTINUED IN JUNE 1989 AND WERE ADJOURNED ON JUNE 29. AS OF MID-SEPTEMBER 1989 THE TALKS HAD NOT RECONVENED DUE TO A CONTROVERSY OVER THE STATUS AND CONTENT OF THE DRAFT OUTLINE FOR FUTURE TALKS. PRESIDENT BUSH ALSO STATES THAT HE HAS STRESSED THE UNITED STATES' CONTINUED SUPPORT FOR UN EFFORTS TO HIGH-RANKING OFFICIALS IN TURKEY, GREECE, AND CYPRUS.

00673
  THRIFT POLICY HOLDS INFLATION
  BEIJING REVIEW, 32(14) (APR 89), 10.
  FINANCE MINISTER WANG BINGQIAN HAS DECLARED THAT BOTH CENTRAL AND LOCAL GOVERNMENTS MUST BALANCE THEIR BOOKS TO ELIMINATE STATE DEFICITS. OVERALL, WANG SAID THAT THE 1989 BUDGET WILL PURSUE A POLICY OF FINANCIAL RETRENCHMENT, CURB THE DEMAND FOR FUNDS, REDUCE EXPENDITURES, AND CONTROL DEFICITS.

00674
  THRIFTS ON THE SLIDE
  COMMONWEAL, CXVI(1) (JAN 89), 3-4.
  THE REAL CRISIS IN THE SAVINGS AND LOAN INDUSTRY BEGAN WITH FEDERAL DEREGULATION IN 1982. IT WAS NOURISHED BY THE INADEQUATE SUPERVISION OF THE FEDERAL HOME LOAN BANK BOARD.

00675
  TIBET 30 YEARS AGO AND NOW: "MILLIONS OF SERFS HAVE STOOD UP"
  CHINA RECONSTRUCTS, XXXVIII(4) (APR 89), 5.
  THE YEAR 1989 MARKS THE 30TH ANNIVERSARY OF THE SUPPRESSION OF THE ARMED REBELLION IN TIBET LED BY UPPER CLASS SERF-OWNERS AND OTHER COUNTERREVOLUTIONARIES. THE CONFLICT BROUGHT THE BEGINNINGS OF DEMOCRATIC REFORM AND FREEDOM TO THE OVERWHELMINGLY MAJORITY OF THE TIBETAN POPULATION, WHO HAD BEEN SERFS OR HOUSEHOLD SLAVES UNDER THE OLD REGIME.

00676
  TIBET: HUMAN RIGHT AND RELIGION
  BEIJING REVIEW, 32(9) (FEB 89), 28-31.
  USING A QUESTION AND ANSWER FORMAT, THIS ARTICLE PRESENTS THE OFFICIAL CHINESE RESPONSE TO QUESTIONS ABOUT TIBETAN POLITICAL PRISONERS, HUMAN RIGHTS, RACIAL DISCRIMINATION, RELIGION, AND EDUCATION.

00677
  TIES THAT BLIND
  COMMONWEAL, CXVI(18) (OCT 89), 547-548.
  THE AUTHOR DISCUSSES TWO RECENT ISSUES THAT ILLUSTRATE THE CURRENT STATUS OF US-ISRAELI RELATIONS: SAUDI ARABIA'S PROPOSED PURCHASE OF BATTLEFIELD TANKS FROM GENERAL DYNAMICS AND ISRAELI POLICY ON SOVIET JEWISH EMIGRANTS.

00678
  TIME TO TAKE A DEEP BREATH
  SOUTH, (105) (JUL 89), 9.
  THE AYATOLLAH RUHOLLAH KHOMEINI WAS ONE OF THOSE RARE INDIVIDUALS WHO TRANSFORM THE ESTABLISHED ORDER. KHOMEINI DERIVED HIS REVOLUTIONARY IDEOLOGY FROM ISLAM AND USED ISLAMIC PRINCIPLES TO MOBILIZE THE PEOPLE. HE ASSUMED THAT ONCE THE PEOPLE HAD TRIUMPHED, THEIR EXPECTATIONS AND FERVOR COULD BE RECAST IN FAMILIAR MOULDS OF THE PAST. THE RESULT HAS REGIMENTATION AND THE REPLACEMENT OF DYNASTIC RULE BY CLERICAL AUTHORITY. THE REVOLUTIONARY SYMBOLS BECAME SUBSTITUTES FOR POLICIES AND THE PEOPLE WERE KEPT IN A CONSTANT STATE OF ANGER AND FRENZY TO MAINTAIN THE ILLUSION OF THE REVOLUTION.

00679
  TIME TO TRADE
  MULTINATIONAL MONITOR, 10(4) (APR 89), 5.
  AS MANY CRITICS HAVE POINTED OUT, CUBA IS NOT THE REVOLUTIONARY PARADISE THAT LEFTISTS ENVISIONED WHEN CASTRO FIRST TOOK OFFICE. BUT POST-REVOLUTIONARY CUBA HAS ACHIEVED A NUMBER OF IMPRESSIVE ACCOMPLISHMENTS, INCLUDING ELIMINATING HUNGER AND IMPROVING LITERACY AND MEDICAL CARE. U.S. POLICY TOWARD CUBA HAS FAILED, AND CASTRO HAS INDICATED THAT HE WANTS TO NORMALIZE RELATIONS WITH THE U.S. THE BUSH ADMINISTRATION FEELS A NEED TO MAINTAIN ITS HARD-LINE STAND AGAINST THE COMMUNIST THREAT IN THE WESTERN HEMISPHERE, BUT AMERICAN BUSINESSES WANT TO TRADE WITH AND PROFIT FROM CUBA. BUSH MUST ALSO CONFRONT THE FACT THAT HIS FEAR OF LOSING FACE IS DETRACTING FROM HIS ABILITY TO WIELD POWER IN THE REGION.

00680
  TIME TO TRUST BUST
  MULTINATIONAL MONITOR, 11(11) (NOV 89), 6.
  CORPORATE MERGERS STRENGTHEN CORPORATE CONTROL AND POWER. CORPORATE CONCENTRATION HAS INCREASED IN RECENT YEARS IN PART AS A RESULT OF THE FAILURE OF THE REAGAN AND BUSH ADMINISTRATIONS TO ENFORCE ANTITRUST LAWS. UNDER REAGAN, THE STAFF OF THE JUSTICE DEPARTMENT'S ANTITRUST DIVISION WAS CUT BY MORE THAN ONE-THIRD. BUSH'S ANTITRUST REGULATORS COULD DO A GREAT DEAL MORE THAN REAGAN OFFICIALS DID AND STILL NOT ADEQUATELY ADDRESS THE CURRENT MONOPOLY MADNESS. THE REGULATORY APPARATUS IN THIS COUNTRY WAS DEVASTATED BY THE REAGAN PRESIDENCY. IT MUST BE STRENGTHENED AND REBUILT THROUGH LEGISLATION AND WITH INCREASED ALLOCATION OF RESOURCES TO THE APPROPRIATE AGENCIES.

00681
  TOO MANY ABORTIONS
  COMMONWEAL, 66(14) (AUG 89), 419-420.
  THE AUTHOR WARNS THAT THE SUPREME COURT'S DECISION IN WEBSTER V. REPRODUCTIVE HEALTH SERVICES DID NOT DISMANTLE ROE V. WADE.

00682
  TOP PARTY LEADERS ANSWER QUESTIONS AT PRESS CONFERENCE
  BEIJING REVIEW, 32(40) (OCT 89), 15-18.
  THIS ARTICLE QUOTES EXTENSIVELY FROM A PRESS CONFERENCE GIVEN ON SEPT. 26, 1989, BY CPC OFFICIALS JIANG ZEMIN, LI PENG, QIAO SHI, YAO YILIN, SONG PING, AND LI RUIHUAN. TOPICS INCLUDE THE JUNE COUNTER-REVOLUTIONARY REBELLION, CHINA'S REFORM POLICY, AND THE CHINESE LEGAL SYSTEM.

00683
  TOWARD A NEW IMAGE OF SOCIALISM
  REPRINTS FROM THE SOVIET PRESS, 49(11/12) (DEC 89), 19-23.
  THIS ARTICLE EXPLORES THE TWO SOCIAL SYSTEMS THAT THE WORLD HAS BEEN DIVIDED INTO FOR MORE THAN SEVEN DECADES - SOCIALISM AND CAPITALISM. IT DESCRIBES HUMANKIND'S SOCIAL ASCENT FROM CAPITALISM TO SOCIALISM WITH A NUMBER OF FUNDAMENTALLY NEW CHARACTERISTICS OF TODAY. IT SEES THE TRANSITION FROM CAPITALISM AS A MANY-SIDED PROCESS WHICH LASTS FOR MANY DECADES IT ALSO SEES THE STATE AS THE MOST IMPORTANT INSTITUTE IN THE FORSEEABLE FUTURE OF THE POLITICAL SYSTEM OF THE NEW SOCIETY. IT DEFINES THE URGENT TASK OF COMMUNISTS TO PROVIDE A HISTORIC PERSPECTIVE TO MAINTAIN AND CONFIRM THE VANGUARD ROLE OF THE PARTY IN THE CONDITIONS OF DEMOCRATIC PLURALISM WITHOUT CLAIMING A MONOPOLY ON POLITICAL POWER.

00684
  TOWARDS NATIONAL COALITION
  CONTEMPORARY POLAND, XXII(3) (1989), 27-30.
  HOW POLES WILL LIVE IN THE NEAR, AND MORE DISTANT, FUTURE DEPENDS ON THE SOCIAL CONSENSUS THEY ARE STRIVING TO ACHIEVE NOW. THE CONSENSUS WILL DETERMINE WHICH POLITICAL AND ECONOMIC MODEL IS ADOPTED TO TACKLE THE CRISIS SITUATION. ALTHOUGH VIEWS ON HOW TO ARRIVE AT SUCH A CONSENSUS DIFFER, ALL SIDES GENERALLY CONCUR THAT THIS CONSENSUS IS INDISPENSABLE.

00685
  TOWER NOMINATION: MAJORITY OPPOSES TOWER CONFIRMATION
  GALLUP REPORT, (282-283) (MAR 89), 16-20.
  OPPOSITION TO JOHN TOWER'S CONFIRMATION AS SECRETARY OF DEFENSE OUTWEIGHS SUPPORT BY A 3-TO-1 RATIO. THOSE OPPOSING CONFIRMATION CITE HIS REPORTED DRINKING PROBLEM AND DEALINGS WITH DEFENSE CONTRACTORS.

00686
  TRIPLE PLAY
  COMMONWEAL, CXVI(19) (NOV 89), 581-582.
  THE AUTHOR CRITIQUES STATEMENTS ISSUED BY THE US CATHOLIC BISHOPS ON THE MIDDLE EAST CONFLICT, AIDS, AND THIRD WORLD DEBT.

00687
  TROOPS ORDERED TO RESTORE ORDER
  BEIJING REVIEW, 32(24-25) (JUN 89), 9-10.
  ON JUNE 3, 1989, THE PEOPLE'S LIBERATION ARMY ISSUED PUBLIC NOTICES STATING THAT THE PLA WOULD IMPOSE MARTIAL LAW IN PARTS OF BEIJING AND GIVING THE PUBLIC INSTRUCTIONS NOT TO INTERFERE WITH WITH THE TROOPS. THE PLA ALSO ISSUED AN ANNOUNCEMENT STATING THAT A SERIOUS POLITICAL STRUGGLE WAS UNDERWAY CONCERNING THE FUTURE AND DESTINY OF THE STATE AND THE NATION.

00688
  TRUE FRIENDS AND FALSE
  COMMONWEAL, CXVI(12) (JUN 89), 357.
  SECRETARY OF STATE JAMES BAKER CALLED ON THE ISRAELIS TO LAY ASIDE "THE UNREALISTIC VISION OF A GREATER ISRAEL" IN A SPEECH TO THE AMERICAN ISRAEL PUBLIC AFFAIRS COMMITTEE. HE ALSO CALLED ON THE PALESTINIANS TO AMEND THE PALESTINE

NATIONAL CONVENANT AND TRANSFORM THE VIOLENCE OF THE
INTIFADA INTO A DIALOGUE OF POLITICS AND DIPLOMACY.

00689
TURMOIL WON'T CLOSE OPEN DOOR
BEIJING REVIEW, 32(26) (JUN 89), 10-11.
THE CHINESE MINISTER OF FOREIGN ECONOMIC RELATIONS AND
TRADE HAS DECLARED THAT THE COUNTRY'S OPEN POLICY WILL
CONTINUE DESPITE THE COUNTER-REVOLUTIONARY REVOLT THAT
OCCURRED IN JUNE 1989. HE SAID THAT CHINA WILL CONTINUE TO
DEVELOP ECONOMIC AND TRADE RELATIONS WITH FOREIGN COUNTRIES.
HE ACCUSED SOME FOREIGN GOVERNMENTS OF BEING SHORT-SIGHTED
AND BASING THEIR ACTIONS ON RUMORS RATHER THAN FACTS BECAUSE
THEY HALTED LOANS AND SUSPENDED TECHNOLOGY TRANSFERS AFTER
THE TURMOIL IN JUNE.

00690
TURNING OFF THE GAS
COMMONWEAL, CXVI(18) (OCT 89), 548-549.
AS LONG AS THE SUPERPOWERS INSIST ON ENHANCING THEIR
CHEMICAL WEAPON STOCKPILES—AS THE U.S. IS NOW DOING WITH ITS
BINARY PRODUCTTION—THE REST OF THE WORLD WILL HARDLY BE
CONVINCED THAT THEY SHOULD GIVE UP THEIR QUEST FOR SUCH
WEAPONS; AND THE RISKS OF CHEMICAL TERRORISM WILL THEREBY
INCREASE. TO ASSURE THE WORLD COMMUNITY OF HIS SERIOUSNESS,
PRESIDENT BUSH SHOULD NOT ONLY CALL FOR THE ABOLITION OF ALL
CHEMICAL WEAPONS; HE SHOULD IMMEDIATELY CEASE THE PRODUCTION
OF FURTHER BINARY WEAPONS.

00691
U.S. ARMS CONTROL INITIATIVES
DEPARTMENT OF STATE BULLETIN (US FOREIGN POLICY), 88(2134
(MAY 88), 26-30.
THE ARTICLE OUTLINES THE NUMEROUS ARMS CONTROL
INITIATIVES THAT HAVE BEEN INTRODUCED BY THE US. THEY
INCLUDE THE INF TREATY, INITIATIVES WITH REGARDS TO DEFENSE
AND SPACE ISSUES, NUCLEAR TESTING, NUCLEAR RISK REDUCTION
CENTERS, NUCLEAR NONPROLIFERATION, CHEMICAL WEAPONS,
DISARMAMENT IN EUROPE, MUTUAL AND BALANCED FORCE REDUCTIONS,
AND CONVENTIONAL STABILITY TALKS.

00692
U.S. ARMY ENTERS DRUG WAR
MEXICO-UNITED STATES REPORT, 111(2) (NOV 89), 8.
MEXICAN GOVERNMENT WARNED THAT THE U.S. DECISION TO
EMPLOY ITS ARMED FORCES TO HELP FIGHT DRUG SMUGGLING FROM
MEXICO INTO THE U.S. WILL HAVE "NEGATIVE CONSEQUENCES" ON
BILATERAL RELATIONS. MEXICAN PRESIDENT CARLOS SALINAS DE
GORTARI ALSO REJECTED THE POSSIBILITY OF ANY JOINT MILITARY
ACTION ON MEXICAN SOIL AGAINST NARCOTICS TRAFFICKERS.
ALARMED BY THE GROWING RATE OF DOMESTIC DRUG USE, SALINAS
HAS APPROVED STEPPED UP EFFORTS AGAINST NARCOTICS
TRAFFICKING WITHIN MEXICO. HOWEVER, HE REMAINS ADAMANT IN
HIS CRITICISM OF THE U.S. DECISION.

00693
U.S. ATTEMPTS TO EXPLOIT HURRICANE JOAN
CENTRAL AMERICA BULLETIN, 8(2) (JAN 89), 1-3, 6-8.
ON OCTOBER 22, 1988, NICARAGUA WAS DEVASTED BY HURRICANE
JOAN. IN ITS WAKE, THE STORM LEFT NICARAGUA FACING EPIDEMICS,
STARVATION, AND ECONOMIC COLLAPSE. THE UNITED STATES AND
ITS CONTRA ALLIES CALLED ON THE WORLD TO DENY NICARAGUA
RELIEF AID AS A MEANS OF INSOLATING THE SANDINISTAS INSIDE
NICARAGUA. BUT THE QUICK AND EFFECTIVE MEASURES TAKEN BY THE
SANDINISTAS, BOTH BEFORE AND AFTER THE STORM, COUPLED WITH
THE U.S. POSITION HAVE STRENGTHENED THE SANDINISTAS'
STANDING WITH THE NICARAGUAN PEOPLE.

00694
U.S. CONGRESS' BILL REFUTED
BEIJING REVIEW, 32(31) (JUL 89), 10.
IN A STATEMENT ISSUED JULY 19, 1989, THE FOREIGN AFFAIRS
COMMITTEE OF CHINA'S NATIONAL PEOPLE'S CONGRESS EXPRESSED
INDIGNATION OVER THE U.S. CONGRESS' INTERFERENCE IN CHINA'S
INTERNAL AFFAIRS. IT OBJECTED TO LANGUAGE IN AN AMERICAN
CONGRESSIONAL AMENDMENT THAT CALLED THE 1989 REBELLION A
"PRO-DEMOCRACY MOVEMENT" AND TERMED THE LEADERS "PEACEFUL
PRO-DEMOCRACY DEMONSTRATORS." THE STATEMENT WARNED THAT U.S.
CONGRESSIONAL ACTIONS TO INTERFERE IN INTERNAL CHINESE
AFFAIRS COULD HARM U.S.-SINO RELATIONS.

00695
U.S. DENIES VISA TO PLO LEADER ARAFAT
DEPARTMENT OF STATE BULLETIN (US FOREIGN POLICY), 89(2143)
(FEB 89), 53.
THE UN HEADQUARTERS AGREEMENT OBLIGATES THE USA TO
PROVIDE CERTAIN RIGHTS OF ENTRY, TRANSIT, AND RESIDENCE TO
PERSONS INVITED TO UN HEADQUARTERS IN NEW YORK. BUT THE US
GOVERNMENT RETAINED THE AUTHORITY TO BAR THE ENTRY OF ALIENS
"IN ORDER TO SAFEGUARD ITS OWN SECURITY." IN THIS REGARD, US
LAW EXCLUDES MEMBERS OF THE PLO ENTRY INTO THE USA BY VIRTUE
OF THEIR AFFILIATION WITH AN ORGANIZATION THAT ENGAGES IN
TERRORISM.

00696
U.S. INTERFERENCE PROTESTED
BEIJING REVIEW, 32(24-25) (JUN 89), 11-13.
ON JUNE 7, 1989, THE CHINESE GOVERNMENT EXPRESSED "ITS
PROFOUND REGRET" THAT THE USA HAD SUSPENDED ALL U.S. ARMS
SALES TO CHINA AT THE GOVERNMENTAL LEVEL AND CANCELED VISITS
BETWEEN MILITARY LEADERS OF THE TWO COUNTRIES. THE CHINESE
FOREIGN MINISTRY STATED THAT WASHINGTON HAD TAKEN UNILATERAL
ACTION THAT WOULD CAUSE THE DETERIORATION OF RELATIONS AND
WAS ATTEMPTING TO EXERT PRESSURE UPON THE CHINESE GOVERNMENT
IN A COMPLETELY UNACCEPTABLE MANNER.

00697
U.S. MUST TAKE STEPS TO PATCH UP SINO-U.S. RIFT
BEIJING REVIEW, 32(46) (NOV 89), 9-10.
CHINA'S SENIOR LEADER DENG XIAOPING MET WITH FORMER US
PRESIDENT RICHARD NIXON, WHO WAS ON HIS SIXTH VISIT TO CHINA.
DENG SAID CHINA HOPES THE TWO COUNTRIES "WILL SOLVE AS SOON
AS POSSIBLE THE PROBLEMS IN THEIR RELATIONS AND WILL CREATE
A SOUND BASIS ON WHICH TO PROMOTE FUTURE TIES. HOWEVER, IT
IS UP TO THE UNITED STATES TO TAKE THE INITIATIVE."

00698
U.S. OPENS DIALOGUE WITH PLO
DEPARTMENT OF STATE BULLETIN (US FOREIGN POLICY), 89(2143)
(FEB 89), 51-53.
THIS REPORT ON THE OPENING OF A DIALOGUE BETWEEN THE USA
AND THE PLO CONTAINS A STATEMENT ISSUED BY PRESIDENT REAGAN,
A STATEMENT BY THE SECRETARY OF STATE, AND REMARKS BY THE
SECRETARY IN RESPONSE TO QUESTIONS FROM THE PRESS.

00699
U.S. RELATIONS WITH KOREA
DEPARTMENT OF STATE BULLETIN (US FOREIGN POLICY), 89(2151)
(OCT 89), 30-31.
UNITED STATES POLICY TOWARD THE REPUBLIC OF KOREA RESTS
ON THREE INTERDEPENDENT COMPONENTS: SECURITY, DEMOCRACY, AND
ECONOMIC PARTNERSHIP. US-SOUTH KOREAN DEFENSE ARRANGEMENTS
ARE THE KEY ELEMENT IN THE AMERICAN STRATEGIC POSTURE IN
NORTHEAST ASIA. IN RECENT YEARS, GROWING ANTI-AMERICANISM
HAS STRAINED THE TRADITIONAL FRIENDSHIP. THE CONTINUED
PRESENCE OF AMERICAN TROOPS ON KOREAN SOIL HAS BECOME A
POINT OF CONTENTION, WHILE CHANGES IN THE ECONOMIC
RELATIONSHIP ARE REDEFINING THE OVERALL NATURE OF THE
RELATIONS.

00700
U.S. SUPPORT FOR DEMOCRACY AND PEACE IN CENTRAL AMERICA
DEPARTMENT OF STATE BULLETIN (US FOREIGN POLICY), 89(2147)
(JUN 89), 55-59.
AT A WHITE HOUSE NEWS BRIEFING ON MARCH 24, 1989, A
BIPARTISAN ACCORD ARTICULATING UNITED STATES SUPPORT FOR
PEACE, SECURITY, AND CONTINUED DEMOCRATIZATION IN CENTRAL
AMERICA WAS ANNOUNCE. THE ACCORD CALLS FOR THE ESTABLISHMENT
OF OPEN, REPRESENTATIVE GOVERNMENT IN NICARAGUA; AN END TO
NICARAGUAN ASSESTANCE TO SUBVERSIVE GROUPS IN NEIGHBORING
COUNTRIES; AND A HALT TO SOVIET-BLOC MILITARY AID THAT
IMPINGES OF REGIONAL SECURITY.

00701
U.S. TRADE OBJECTIVES IN THE URUGUAY ROUND
DEPARTMENT OF STATE BULLETIN (US FOREIGN POLICY), 89(2143)
(FEB 89), 35-37.
THE CURRENT ROUND OF MULTILATERAL TRADE NEGOTIATIONS IS
VITAL TO THE FUTURE WELL-BEING OF THE UNITED STATES AND THE
GLOBAL ECONOMY. THE MAJOR AMERICAN GOALS IN THE URUGUAY
ROUND ARE TRADE LIBERALIZATION EXTENDING GATT COVERAGE TO
MAJOR NEW AREAS AND RENEWAL OF THE GATT SYSTEM OF
INTERNATIONAL RULES THROUGH TIMELY AND EFFICIENT ENFORCEMENT.

00702
U.S.-MEXICO BINATIONAL COMMISSION MEETS IN MEXICO CITY
DEPARTMENT OF STATE BULLETIN (US FOREIGN POLICY), 89(2151)
(OCT 89), 76-84.
ON ANY GIVEN DAY, US-MEXICAN RELATIONS ARE A DYNAMIC MIX
OF COOPERATION AND CHALLENGE; GROWING STRATEGIC, COMMERCIAL,
FINANCIAL, AND DEMOGRAPHIC INTERDEPENDENCE; AND CULTURAL
EXCHANGE. THE US AND MEXICAN GOVERNMENTS SHARE COMMON
INTERESTS IN PROTECTING AND PROMOTING SECURITY, PROSPERITY,
AND DEMOCRACY IN THE HEMISPHERE AND THROUGHOUT THE WORLD.

00703
U.S.-SOVIET RELATIONS: A DISCUSSION OF PERESTROIKA AND
ECONOMIC REFORM
DEPARTMENT OF STATE BULLETIN (US FOREIGN POLICY), 89(2153)
(DEC 89). 20-26.
IT WOULD BE A MISTAKE TO ANALYZE PERESTROIKA AS SIMPLY
AN ECONOMIC PHENOMENON. THE COURSE SET BY GORBACHEV INVOLVES
CHANGES IN THE POLITICAL STRUCTURE, IDEOLOGY, LEGAL
PRACTICES, AND POPULAR ATTITUDES, AS WELL AS THE ECONOMY.
PERESTROIKA COULD ALSO HAVE FAR-REACHING IMPLICATIONS FOR
SOVIET FOREIGN POLICY, INCLUDING RELATIONS WITH THE UNITED
STATES.

07700-07713   POLITICAL SCIENCE ABSTRACTS

INDEBTEDNESS - TO THE TUNE OF $45 BILLION AS PART OF THE GLOBAL PATTERN OF THIRD WORLD DEPENDENCE RATHER THAN AS A UNIQUE PHENOMENON. MUBARAK HAS COME TO ADVOCATE A UNITED STAND ON THE PART OF DEBTOR NATIONS, AND TO THIS END TABLED A JOINT PROPOSAL WITH VENEZUELA, MEXICO AND INDONESIA AT THE PARIS BICENTENARY CELEBRATIONS. ON THE HOME FRONT, TALK OF PRIVATISING EGYPT'S COLOSSALLY INEFFICIENT PUBLIC SECTOR, OR AT LEAST PARTS OF IT, MUST WARM THE HEARTS OF AID DONORS WHO FOR YEARS HAVE BEEN TEARING THEIR HAIR OUT OVER THE OBSTINACY OF WHAT HAS COME TO BE KNOWN AS THE NASSERIST LOBBY, IE THOSE WHO REGARD THE DISMANTLING OF THE BLOATED STATE AS AN ACT OF TREASON.

07700 RODENBECK, M.
MUBARAKS TEN POINTS
MIDDLE EAST INTERNATIONAL, (359) (SEP 89), 3.
EGYPTIAN PRESIDENT HUSNI MUBARAK'S ANNOUNCEMENT OF TEN CLARIFYING POINTS DESIGNED TO FOSTER DIRECT PALESTINIAN-ISRAELI TALKS HAS CAUSED A FLURRY OF DIPLOMATIC ACTIVITY. ALTHOUGH MANY PALESTINIAN AND ISRAELI REPRESENTATIVES HAVE MET IN EGYPT TO DISCUSS OPTIONS, THEY HAVE MAINTAINED AN OFFICIAL SILENCE ON THE POSSIBLE OUTCOMES. ALTHOUGH SOME OBSERVERS FEEL THAT THE EGYPTIAN ANNOUNCEMENT MAY CAUSE ISRAEL TO SHAKE OFF ITS DIPLOMATIC LETHARGY, MANY FEEL THAT ISRAEL'S REJECTION OF THE "TEN POINTS" IS A FOREGONE CONCLUSION.

07701 RODENBECK, M.
SLAPS AND WIRE TAPS
MIDDLE EAST INTERNATIONAL, (345) (MAR 89), 16.
WHEN MINISTER OF INTERIOR ZAKI BADR WAS CALLED TO DEFEND HIS GOVERNMENT AGAINST CHARGES OF POLICE BRUTALITY, OBSERVERS ANTICIPATED A STORMY SESSION IN EGYPT'S PARLIAMENT. BUT THE OPPOSITION'S IMPATIENCE WITH HIS BLUSTERY SPEECH GAVE WAY TO FURIOUS INDIGNATION WHEN HE PLAYED COMPROMISING RECORDINGS OF OPPOSITION POLITICIANS. THE OUTRAGED OPPOSITION CLAIMED THE EAVESDROPPING WAS AN UNCONSTITUTIONAL INFRINGEMENT OF PARLIAMENTARY IMMUNITY.

07702 RODENBECK, M.
THE FRUITS OF CASABLANCA
MIDDLE EAST INTERNATIONAL, 352 (JUN 89), 5.
THE MOST IMMEDIATE AND DIRECT BONUS OF THE CASABLANCA SUMMIT HAS BEEN THE DRAMATIC IMPROVEMENT IN TIES WITH WHAT IS NOW FREQUENTLY REFERRED TO IN THE CAIRO PRESS AS "SISTERLY LIBYA". FOLLOWING A 13 YEAR HIATUS, THE REOPENING OF THE COUNTRIES' BORDER HAS BROUGHT AN ALMOST TANGIBLE RELEASE OF PRESSURE ON A CROWDED EGYPT, HEMMED IN IN RECENT YEARS BY STRIFE IN ADJACENT NATIONS. IN THE FIRST WEEK OF USE, A REPORTED 10,000 TRAVELLERS CROSSED THE NEWLY OPENED LAND BORDER. ALREADY, DAILY FLIGHTS FLY BETWEEN CAIRO, TRIPOLI AND BENGHAZI, SHORT-CIRCUITING THE TORTUOUS ROUTES THROUGH ATHENS AND MALTA THAT THE 200,000 EGYTIANS RESIDENT IN LIBYA HAVE HAD TO ENDURE FOR THE PAST DECADE.

07703 RODENBECK, M.
THE PLO IN CAIRO
MIDDLE EAST INTERNATIONAL, (363) (NOV 89), 8.
A RECENT MEETING OF THE PLO'S EXECUTIVE COMMITTEE IN CAIRO STIRRED UP MUCH SPECULATION, BUT GARNERED LITTLE OR NO SIGNIFICANT RESULTS. MOST OBSERVERS FEEL THAT THE PALESTINIANS ARE UNLIKELY TO ACCEPT THE US-SPONSORED BAKER PLAN; YASSER ARAFAT DECLARED THAT THE SOLE AIM OF THE US PEACE PLAN IS TO BUT TIME FOR THE SHAMIR GOVERNMENT. MEANWHILE, EGYPT FACES SOME INTERNAL PROBLEMS INCLUDING A GROWING ISLAMIC TREND. STRAINS IN RELATIONS WITH IRAQ ARE ALSO BECOMING EVIDENT.

07704 RODENBECK, M.
WARMING EGYPTIAN HEARTS
MIDDLE EAST INTERNATIONAL, (345) (MAR 89), 5-6.
IN A GESTURE THAT MARKED THE THAWING OF SOVIET-EGYPTIAN TIES, FOREIGN MINISTER SHEVARDNADZE VISITED EGYPT AND EXPRESSED "IDENTICAL VIEWS" WITH THE EGYPTIANS AND THE PALESTINIANS. IN A RELATED DEVELOPMENT, AN AMERICAN-BROKERED AGREEMENT RESULTED IN ISRAEL'S CEDING TABA BACK TO EGYPT.

07705 RODINA, C.
SOCIALIST-CAPITALIST JOINT VENTURES
FOREIGN TRADE, 10 (1988), 13-16.
THIS ARTICLE REPORTS ON JOINT VENTURES BETWEEN CMEA AND CAPITALIST COUNTRIES SINCE 1970. LEGISLATION IN MANY CMEA COUNTRIES WHICH PRESCRIBES BASIC PRINCIPLES OF JOINT VENTURE PERFORMANCE IS EXPLORED. OPERATIONS IN CHINA, HUNGARY, POLAND, KOREA, BULGARIA, ROMANIA AND CZECHOSLOVAKIA ARE EXPLORED. SOME OF THE DIFFICULTIES ARE NOTED.

07706 RODMAN, P. W.
IS THE COLD WAR OVER?
WILSON QUARTERLY, XIII(1) (JAN 89), 39-42.
WHILE MUCH HAS CHANGED IN EAST-WEST RELATIONS UNDER GOVBACHEV AND THE WEST SHOULD TAKE ADVANTAGE OF THE NEW OPPORTUNITIES TO SETTLE SOME OUTSTANDING ISSUES AND SCALE DOWN THE MILITARY DANGER, THE WEST SHOULD ALSO BE AWARE OF

THE CONTINUTIES THAT REMAIN IN SOVIET POLICY AND THE PERSISTENCE OF EAST-WEST COMPETITION IN AREAS THAT HAVE NOT BEEN BLESSED WITH DIPLOMATIC SOLUTIONS. FOREMOST AMONG THESE IS EUROPE. LIKE HIS PREDECESSORS, GORBACHEV HAS CONTINUED THE POLITICAL WARFARE AGAINST NATO COHESION AND NATO STRATEGIES WHILE REJECTING THE WESTERN CALL TO TEAR DOWN THE BERLIN WALL AND END THE ARTIFICIAL DIVISION OF THE CONTINENT. MOREOVER, IN NICARAGUA, THE SOVIETS CONTINUE TO PROVIDE A SUBSTANTIAL FLOW OF ARMS TO THE SANDINISTA MILITARY.

07707 RODMAN, S.
HAITI'S PROSPECTS UNDER PROSPER AVRIL
NEW LEADER, LXXII(13) (SEP 89), 5-7.
THE ARTICLE EXAMINES THE ATTITUDES AND POLICIES OF HAITI'S "INTERIM LEADER," PROSPER ARVIL. ARVIL SEEMS TO BE ONE OF THE RARE CASES OF A "BAD MAN TURNED GOOD." AN ADVISER TO THE TYRANNICAL DUVALIER DYNASTY FOR MANY YEARS, ARVIL WAS RUMORED TO KNOW MORE ABOUT THE DICTATORS' PERSONAL FINANCES THAN THEY DID. HOWEVER, AFTER BECOMING PRESIDENT IN A COUP INSTIGATED BY NONCOMISSIONED OFFICERS, ARVIL SEEMS DETERMINED TO GUARANTEE FREE ELECTIONS AND ECONOMIC REFORM.

07708 RODMAN, S.
LITTLE PRIEST, BIG GENERAL
NATIONAL REVIEW, XLI(18) (SEP 89), 24-25.
HAITI'S CLIMB FROM THE DEPTHS OF STAGNATION IN THE THREE YEARS OF COUPS AND COUNTER -- COUPS THAT FOLLOWED THE OUSTER OF THE DUVALIER DYNASTY HAS BEEN FAIRFULLY SLOW. BUT LAW AND ORDER NOW REIGNS IN THE STREETS WITH NO MILITARY PRESENCE, AND THE IMPROVEMENT IN THE POLITICAL CLIMATE SINCE THE TERM OF PRESIDENT PROSPER AVRIL IS MURACULOUS.

07709 RODMAN, S.
THE DILEMMA IN PUERTO RICO
NEW LEADER, LXXII(6) (MAR 89), 3-5.
AN INDEPENDENCE PLEBISCITE IS TENTATIVELY SCHEDULED FOR PUERTO RICO IN 1990 AND THE QUESTION OF STATEHOOD HAS MONOPOLIZED THE PUERTO RICAN PRESS FOR SEVERAL MONTHS. BY DECLARING THAT HE FAVORS GIVING THE PUERTO RICANS THE STATUS THEY CHOOSE, GEORGE BUSH HAS FIRED UP THE PRO-STATEHOOD FORCES. BUT GOVERNOR RAFAEL HERNANDEZ COLON SUPPORTS AN "ENHANCED COMMONWEALTH" AS THE ISLAND'S BEST OPTION.

07710 RODRIGO, N.
"THE DISCONTINUANCE OF ALL TEST EXPLOSIONS OF NUCLEAR WEAPONS FOR ALL TIME . . ."
DISARMAMENT, XII(2) (SUM 89), 109-116.
WHEN THE USA, THE UNITED KINGDOM, AND THE SOVIET UNION SIGNED THE TREATY BANNING NUCLEAR WEAPONS TESTS IN THE ATMOSPHERE, IN OUTER SPACE, AND UNDER WATER, THEY PROCLAIMED THAT THEIR PRINCIPAL AIM WAS "THE SPEEDIEST POSSIBLE ACHIEVEMENT OF AN AGREEMENT ON GENERAL AND COMPLETE DISARMAMENT UNDER STRICT INTERNATIONAL CONTROL." THEY ALSO SOUGHT "THE DISCONTINUANCE OF ALL TEST EXPLOSIONS OF NUCLEAR WEAPONS FOR ALL TIME." BUT PROGRESS TOWARD THESE GOALS HAS BEEN LIMITED, DESPITE INTERNATIONAL PRESSURE EXERTED THROUGH THE UNITED NATIONS, THE CONFERENCE ON DISARMAMENT, AND OTHER MULTILATERAL FORUMS, SUCH AS THE MOVEMENT OF NONALIGNED COUNTRIES.

07711 RODRIGUEZ, C.R.
CUBA: TRYING TO PAY THE DEBT IS A POLITICAL ERROR
INFORMATION BULLETIN, 26(19-20) (OCT 88), 27-29.
THIS ARTICLE IS THE TEXT OF A SPEED ON EXTERNAL DEBT DELIVERED BY RODRIOUEZ TO THE THIRD WORLD FOUNDATION. RODRIOUEZ NOTES THAT THE MAIN CONCLUSION THAT SHOULD BE DRAWN IN THE LIGHT OF THE EXPERIENCE OF MANY YEARS OF FUTILE EFFORTS AND THE STEADILY WORSENING LATIN AMERICAN DEBT SITUATION IS TO ADMIT THAT THE ATTEMPTS TO NEGOTIATE SEPARATELY ARE STERILE AND NEGATIVE. IT IS NECESSARY TO WORK OUT A JOINT APPROACH, AND NOT ONLY A LATIN AMERICAN ONE, BUT ONE THAT IS COMMON TO ALL THE DEBTOR COUNTRIES. CONSIDERING THAT THE CREDITORS HAVE THEIR OWN CLUB, THE DEBTORS SHOULD, AT LEAST, HAVE THEIR GROUP TO ELABORATE JOINT SOLUTIONS.

07712 RODRIGUEZ, E.
UNITY AND STRUGGLE IN THE POLICY OF ALLIANCES
WORLD MARXIST REVIEW, 32(9) (SEP 89), 78-81.
THIS ARTICLE REPORTS ON PREPARATIONS FOR THE UPCOMING GENERAL ELECTIONS IN URUGUAY. IT DETAILS THE COMMUNIST PARTY PRIORITY TO UNITE ALL SOCIAL GROUPS, PARTIES AND PUBLIC MOVEMENTS IN ORDER TO RID THE COUNTRY OF ITS DEPENDENCE ON FOREIGN POWERS AND TO CREATE THE CONDITIONS FOR THE FREE DEVELOPMENT OF URUGUAY. SINCE PRACTICE SHOWS THAT UNITY NEVER OCCURS SPONTANEOUSLY, THE NEED TO ACCURATELY DEFINE THE THEORETICAL BASIS AND PRACTICAL FOUNDATIONS OF THE POLICY OF ALLIANCES IS DETAILED. THE FACTORS INVOLVED IN DEVELOPING THIS ALLIANCE ARE EXPLORED.

07713 ROE, E.M.
UNCOMMON GROUNDS FOR COMMONS MANAGEMENT: MAKING SENSE OF LIVESTOCK RANGELAND PROJECTS SOUTH OF THE SAHARA
DISSERTATION ABSTRACTS INTERNATIONAL, 49(11) (MAY 89), 3502-A.

INFORMATION BULLETIN, 27 (MAR 89), 17-20.
THIS STATEMENT ISSUED BY THE CPSU CENTRAL COMMITTEE
REVIEWS THE PROGRESS MADE IN THE FIRST YEARS OF PERESTROIKA
AND SUMMARIZES THE PARTY'S KEY GOALS FOR THE NEAR FUTURE.

00720
VACLAV HAVEL: CARD ON THE TABLE
EAST EUROPEAN REPORTER, 3(4) (SPR 89), 54-55.
THE ARTICLE ARGUES THAT 1988 WAS IMPORTANT FOR
CZECHOSLOVAKIA; ALTHOUGH MAJOR POLITICAL CHANGE DID NOT TAKE
PLACE, CITIZENS BEGAN TO VISIBLY DEMONSTRATE THEIR
DISSATISFACTION WITH THE STATUS QUO. THE TABOO SURROUNDING
THE LEADING ROLE IS BREAKING AND INDEPENDENT ACTIVISTS ARE
GAINING IN REPUTATION AND INFLUENCE. ALTHOUGH EVENTS OF 1988
WILL NOT NECESSARILY DETERMINE THE FUTURE COURSE OF
CZECHOSLOVAKIA, THEY DO SIGNIFY THE INCREASED PROBABILITY OF
CONSIDERABLE CHANGE.

00721
VENEZUELA: THE AGGRESSION AGAINST PANAMA IS AGGRESSION
AGAINST VENEZUELA
INFORMATION BULLETIN, 26(13-14) (JUL 88), 14.
THE IMMEDIATE PROBLEM CONFRONTING THE PEOPLE OF PANAMA
IS TO ASSURE THEIR NATIONAL INDEPENDENCE AND TO WRECK THE
PLANS OF REAGAN WITH RESPECT TO THE FUTURE OF THE CANAL. IN
EFFECT, ONE WITNESSES THE INTENTION TO ANNUAL IN PRACTICE
THE TORRIJOSCARTER ACCORDS THROUGH ALL KINDS OF MANEUVERS
AND PROVOCATIONS, WHICH REAGAN HAS FIXED AS THE CENTRAL
OBJECTIVE OF HIS CENTRAL AMERICAN POLICY SINCE HE CAME TO
THE WHITE HOUSE. BEHIND THE MASQUERADE OF A SUPPOSED FIGHT
AGAINST DRUG TRAFFICKING, IN THIS CASE IN PANAMA, ATTEMPS
ARE BEING MADE TO CONCEAL THE TRADITIONAL DESIGNS OF
DOMINATION AND EXPLOITATION ALWAYS PRESENT IN THE POLICY OF
THE U.S. STATE DEPARTMENT TOWARD THE LATIN AMERICAN AND
CARIBBEAN COUNTRIES.

00722
VETERANS SPEAK OF THE DIPLOMATIC SERVICE
INTERNATIONAL AFFAIRS (MOSCOW), (10) (OCT 89), 130-141.
THIS IS A TRANSCRIPT OF A DISCUSSION OF SOVIET FOREIGN
POLICY, PAST AND PRESENT, BY ELEVEN SOVIET DIPLOMATS. THEY
EXPLAIN HOW FOREIGN POLICY DECISIONS WERE MADE IN THE PAST
AND HOW THE SOVIET FOREIGN POLICY STANCE IS CHANGING.

00723
VICE PRESIDENTIAL RUMPUS
NEW AFRICAN, (260) (MAY 89), 24-25.
KENYA'S VICE PRESIDENT JOSEPHAT KARANJA HAS BEEN HIT
WITH A BATTERY OF UNSUBSTANTIATED ACCUSATIONS AGAINST HIM BY
HIS POLITICAL OPPONENTS. IN A SYSTEMATIC CAMPAIGN,
POLITICANS FROM KARANJA'S HOME DISTRICT HAVE ACCUSED HIM OF
FANNING TRIBAL SENTIMENTS AND BEHAVING LIKE A "SMALL GOD."
LEADING THE CAMPAIGN IS ARTHUR MAGUGU, THE MINISTER FOR
MANPOWER DEVELOPMENT AND EMPLOYMENT.

00724
VISIT OF ITALIAN PRESIDENT
DEPARTMENT OF STATE BULLETIN (US FOREIGN POLICY), 89(2153)
(DEC 89), 42-44.
PRESIDENT FRANCESCO COSSIGA OF THE ITALIAN REPUBLIC MADE
A STATE VISIT TO THE UNITED STATES IN OCTOBER 1989 TO MEET
WITH PRESIDENT BUSH AND OTHER GOVERNMENT OFFICIALS. THIS
ARTICLE REPRINTS REMARKS MADE BY THE TWO PRESIDENTS ON
OCTOBER 11, 1989.

00725
VISIT OF MEXICAN PRESIDENT SALINAS
DEPARTMENT OF STATE BULLETIN (US FOREIGN POLICY), 89(2153)
(DEC 89), 1-7.
PRESIDENT CARLOS SALINAS DE GORTARI OF THE UNITED
MEXICAN STATES MADE A STATE VISIT TO THE USA IN OCTOBER 1989
TO MEET WITH PRESIDENT GEORGE BUSH AND OTHER OFFICIALS. THIS
ACCOUNT OF THE VISIT INCLUDES REMARKS MADE BY BOTH
PRESIDENTS AT THE WELCOMING CEREMONY, AT THE AGREEMENTS'
SIGNING CEREMONY, AND AT THE STATE DINNER.

00726
VOA REPORT CALLED "NONSENSE"
BEIJING REVIEW, 32(3) (JAN 89), 9.
ON JANUARY 6, 1989, VOICE OF AMERICA (VOA) REPORTED A
CLAIM BY SOME AFRICAN STUDENTS THAT CHINESE AUTHORITIES HAD
IMPOSED NEW RESTRICTIONS ON THEIR SOCIAL ACTIVITIES. THE
PRESIDENT OF HEHAI UNIVERSITY CRITICIZED SUCH VOA REPORTS AS
"PURELY FICTITIOUS" AND "SHEER NONSENSE." HE STATED THAT
PERSONS WITH ULTERIOR MOTIVES WERE TRYING TO STIR UP RACIAL
CONFLICT IN ORDER TO DISRUPT THE FRIENDLY RELATIONS BETWEEN
CHINA AND THE AFRICAN COUNTRIES.

00727
VOTES THAT DO NOT COUNT
SOUTH, (108) (OCT 89), 8.
THE RESULTS OF SOUTH AFRICA'S ELECTORIAL FARCE DO NOT
REVEAL ANY CHANGE OF HEART AMONG THE WHITES. THE NEW
PRESIDENT, F.W. DEKLERK, IS A HARDENED CONSERVATIVE

AFRIKANER. THE NATIONAL PARTY WILL USE ITS MANDATE NOT TO
DISMANTLE APARTHEID BUT TO MAKE IT APPEAR LESS HIDEOUS.

00728
WAR OF THE BURNING IVORY
NEW AFRICAN, (264) (SEP 89), 24-25.
THIS ARTICLE EXAMINES THE DECLARED WAR BETWEEN ZIMBABWE
AND KENYA OVER THE IVORY TRADE. ACCUSATIONS MADE BY
ZIMBABWEANS THAT THE KENYANS WERE PAID BY THE UNITED STATES
TO BURN 12 TONS OF IVORY ARE EXPLORED. THAT THIS HAS BEEN
DENIED BY THE NATIONAL WILDLIFE MANAGEMENT SERVICES,
ALTHOUGH THE KENYA GOVERNMENT HAS NOT DENIED IT, IS EXPLORED.
STRATEGIES TO COMBAT POACHING ARE DESCRIBED, AND THE
DIFFERENCES IN POLICIES CONCERNING THE IVORY TRADE IN
VARIOUS COUNTRIES ARE EXPLAINED.

00729
WARSAW TREATY COUNTRIES' ADDRESS TO NATO COUNTRIES
REPRINTS FROM THE SOVIET PRESS, 49(2) (JUL 89), 40-43.
THE ARTICLE RECOUNTS THE ADDRESS OF THE WARSAW TREATY
COUNTRIES TO NATO COUNTRIES ON THE EVE OF THEIR SUMMIT. THEY
CALLED UPON NATO TO EVALUATE NEW REALITIES OF THE WORLD AND
TO TAKE ADVANTAGE OF THE CHANCE TO OVERCOME THE CONSEQUENCES
OF THE COLD WAR. THEY OUTLINE A NEW CONCEPT OF SECURITY
BASED ON THE CONSTANT LOWERING OF MILITARY CONFRONTATION AND
ARMS REDUCTION UNTIL THE MENACE OF AN OUTBREAK OF WAR IS
ELIMINATED. THEY ALSO DISCUSSED SPECIFIC ARMS REDUCTION
PROPOSALS AND THE DEVELOPMENT OF COOPERATION IN OTHER AREAS
OF INTERNATIONAL RELATIONS.

00730
WARSAW TREATY FOREIGN MINISTERS COMMITTEE COMMUNIQUE
REPRINTS FROM THE SOVIET PRESS, 48(11-12) (JUN 89), 48-51.
THE COMMITTEE OF THE FOREIGN MINISTERS OF THE STATES
PARTICIPATING IN THE WARSAW TREATY OF FRIENDSHIP,
COOPERATION AND MUTUAL ASSISTANCE HELD A REGULAR MEETING IN
BERLIN ON APRIL 11-12, 1989. THE MINISTERS WERE SATISFIED TO
NOTE PROGRESS IN STRENGTHENING PEACE AND DISARMAMENT, WHICH
OFFERS FAVORABLE OPPORTUNITIES FOR BROADENING COOPERATION
AMONG STATES AND PEOPLES. THEY STATED AT THE SAME TIME THAT
THE WORLD SITUATION REMAINS COMPLICATED AND CONTRADICTORY.
THE WARSAW TREATY MEMBERCOUNTRIES ARE FULLY RESOLVED TO
CONTINUE A POLICY OF FUNDAMENTALLY IMPROVING THE SITUATION
IN EUROPE AND THE WORLD AND EXPECT OTHER STATES TO SHOW THE
REQUIRED CONSTRUCTIVE ATTITUDES AND REALISM

00731
WASHINGTON'S LOST CAUSE
SOUTH, (110) (DEC 89), 9.
WITH SOUTHERN AFRICAN POLITICS UNDERGOING PROFOUND
CHANGE AND THE ANGOLAN GOVERNMENT MOVING FORWARD WITH MARKET-
ORIENTED ECONOMIC REFORM, IT IS TIME FOR WASHINGTON TO
REASSESS ITS POLICY OF MILITARY SUPPORT FOR JONAS SAVIMBIS
UNITA REBELS. IT IS BECOMING CLEAR THAT GEORGE BUSH WOULD
LIKE TO EXTRICATE THE USA FROM ANGOLA, BUT HE DARE NOT LEAVE
SAVIMBI OUT IN THE COLD, FOR FEAR OF ANGERING HIS
CONSERVATIVE SUPPORTERS IN THE REPUBLICAN PARTY. IN ANGOLA,
AMERICAN DOMESTIC CONCERNS HAVE DICTATED US MOVES AND
SUPPORT FOR SAVIMBI REMAINS MORE AN ASSET THAN A LIABILITY
FOR BUSH.

00732
WHAT SHOULD A LAW-GOVERNED STATE BE?
SOVIET REVIEW, 30(5) (SEP 89), 3-17.
THIS ARTICLE IS BASED ON A ROUNDTABLE DISCUSSION ON THE
FEATURES OF THE SOCIALIST LAW-GOVERNED STATE. THE
PARTICIPANTS ACKNOWLEDGED THAT A REVOLUTION OF CONSCIOUSNESS
WILL BE REQUIRED FOR THE IDEA TO TAKE ROOT THAT THE LAW IS
NOT A TOOL OF THE STATE, BUT THAT THE STATE IS SUBORDINATE
TO THE LAW. THE PARTICIPANTS ALSO DISCUSSED THE APPROPRIATE
ROLES AND RELATIONSHIPS OF STATE, PARTY, AND SOCIETY.

00733
WHERE THE FRENCH GOVERNMENT WANTS TO LEAD SINO-FRENCH
RELATIONS
BEIJING REVIEW, 32(41) (OCT 89), 9-10.
YAN JIAQI, WU'ER KAIXI, AND OTHER LEADERS OF THE 1989
COUNTER-REVOLUTIONARY REBELLION HAVE FLED ABROAD TO CONTINUE
THEIR ACTIVITIES AGAINST THE CHINESE GOVERNMENT. THESE
"CRIMINALS" WHO ARE ACTIVELY PLOTTING TO SUBVERT THE
GOVERNMENT ARE BEING OPENLY SUPPORTED BY FRANCE. THE FRENCH
GOVERNMENT HAS TURNED A DEAF EAR TO REPEATED PROTESTS FROM
CHINESE OFFICIALS AND ALLOWED THE EXILES TO LAUNCH THE
"FEDERATION FOR DEMOCRACY IN CHINA." IN DOING SO, THE FRENCH
GOVERNMENT VIOLATED INTERNATIONAL LAW AND THE UNITED NATIONS
CHARTER.

00734
WHO WILL BELL THE KHMER CAT?
SOUTH, (107) (SEP 89), 9.
FOR A LASTING PEACE IN CAMBODIA, THE KHMER ROUGE MUST BE
PREVENTED FROM RESTORING ITS GENOCIDAL REGIME. GIVEN ITS
RECORD, THE KHMER ROUGE IS UNLIKELY TO BE AN ELECTORAL
THREAT AND WILL PROBABLY CONTINUE ATTEMPTS TO SEIZE

BATTAMBANG AND INSTALL A GOVERNMENT-IN-OPPOSITION. TO
PREVENT THIS, CHINA MUST DENY IT MILITARY HARDWARE AND
THAILAND MUST CUT OFF THE SUPPLY ROUTES.

00735
WHY CHINA SHOULD NOT INTRODUCE THE TRIPARTITE POLITICAL
SYSTEM
BEIJING REVIEW, 32(45) (NOV 89), 40, 42.
DIFFERENT ECONOMIC BASES DEMAND DIFFERENT SUPER-
STRUCTURES. IN CAPITALIST COUNTRIES, PRIVATE OWNERSHIP GIVES
BIRTH TO THE POLITICAL SYSTEM OF THREE CONSTITUTIONAL POWERS.
CHINA'S ECONOMY REVOLVES AROUND THE SOCIALIST OWNERSHIP OF
PRODUCTION. EVEN THOUGH THE REFORM OF THE CHINESE ECONOMIC
SYSTEM HAS ALLOWED THE DEVELOPMENT OF DIFFERENT FORMS OF
ECONOMIC OWNERSHIP, THE POSITION OF SOCIALIST OWNERSHIP AS
THE CENTRAL ECONOMIC FACT HAS REMAINED AND WILL REMAIN
UNCHANGED. IN CHINA, THE REALITY OF SOCIALIST OWNERSHIP OF
THE MEANS OF PRODUCTION DEMANDS THE ESTABLISHMENT OF A
SOCIALIST POLITICAL SYSTEM. SUCH SOCIALIST OWNERSHIP DOES
NOT PERMIT CHINA TO COPY THE BOURGEOIS POWER-SHARING SYSTEM.

00736
WOMEN AND PEACE
NEW OUTLOOK, 32(6-7 (292-293)) (JUN 89), 30-33.
THIS IS AN EDITED VERSION OF THE PROCEEDINGS AT A
WORKSHOP ON "WOMEN AND PEACE," HELD IN MARCH 1989. THE FIVE
ISRAELI AND PALESTINIAN PANELISTS CONSIDERED SUCH QUESTIONS
AS: DO WOMEN HAVE A SPECIAL ROLE TO PLAY IN THE PEACE
PROCESS? DO THEY BRING TO BEAR DIFFERENT EXPERIENCES AND
PERCEPTIONS THAT MIGHT CONTRIBUTE TO A PEACEFUL RESOLUTION
OF THE ARAB-ISRAELI CONFLICT?

00737
WORLD BANK LINK STILL EXISTS
BEIJING REVIEW, 32(28) (JUL 89), 11.
FOLLOWING THE TIANANMEN SQUARE VIOLENCE, A TOP FINANCE
OFFICIAL EXPRESSED THE HOPE THAT CHINA'S COOPERATION WITH
THE WORLD BANK WILL CONTINUE, UNHINDERED BY POLITICAL ISSUES.
HE SAID THAT THERE IS NO TRUTH TO THE RUMORS THAT THE WORLD
BANK HAS CLOSED ITS BEIJING OFFICE AND DECIDED TO STOP
GRANTING CHINA NEW LOANS, ALTHOUGH SOME COUNTRIES DID
PRESSURE THE BANK TO SUSPEND DISCUSSIONS ON LOANS AND THE
BANK RESPONDED BY POSTPONING DECISIONS ON SOME PROJECTS.

00738
WORLD DEBT TABLES 1988-89
AVAILABLE FROM NTIS, NO. PB89-153472/GAR, 1988, 580.
THE 1988-89 EDITION OF THE WORLD DEBT TABLES COMES IN
THREE VOLUMES. VOLUME 1 CONTAINS ANALYSIS AND COMMENTARY ON
RECENT DEVELOPMENTS IN INTERNATIONAL LENDING TO THE
DEVELOPING COUNTRIES, TOGETHER WITH SUMMARY DEBT DATA TABLES
FOR ALL COUNTRIES, FOR SELECTED REGIONS, AND FOR OTHER
GROUPS, VOLUMES II AND III CONTAIN STATISTICAL TABLES
SHOWING THE EXTERNAL DEBT OF THE 111 COUNTRIES REPORT PUBLIC
AND PUBLICLY GUARANTEED DEBT UNDER THE WORLD BANK'S DEBTOR
REPORTING SYSTEM

00739
WORLD ECONOMY IN TRANSITION: THE URBAN EXPLOSION
FINANCE AND DEVELOPMENT, 26(4) (DEC 89), 47.
THIS REPORT IS ON TOTAL AND URBAN POPULATION GROWTH IN
THE WORLD AND SELECTED REGIONS, 1970-2000 (IN MILLIONS), AND
ALSO ON 25 MEGA CITIES (IN MILLIONS) THROUGHOUT THE WORLD.
THE SOURCE OF INFORMATION IS FROM "THE PROSPECTS OF WORLD
URBANIZATION", NEW YORK: UNITED NATIONS, 1987.

00740
YUAN MU ON FANG AND TURMOIL PROBLEMS
BEIJING REVIEW, 32(35) (AUG 89), 9-10.
ON AUGUST 16, 1989, YUAN MU DECLARED THAT THE SOLUTION
TO THE FANG LIZHI PROBLEM LIES WITH THE U.S. GOVERNMENT,
SINCE FANG HAS TAKEN REFUGE IN THE AMERICAN EMBASSY IN
BEIJING. YUAN STATED THAT THE UNITED STATES HAS INTERFERED
IN CHINA'S INTERNAL AFFAIRS BY SHELTERING FANG, WHO HAS AN
INSTIGATOR OF THE DEMONSTRATIONS IN TIANANMEN SQUARE. HE
ALSO SAID THAT THE CHINESE GOVERNMENT WILL NOT FORCIBLY
REMOVE FANG FROM THE EMBASSY BUT WILL BLOCK ANY U.S. ATTEMPT
TO MOVE FANG TO A NEUTRAL COUNTRY.

00741
YUGOSLAV-TURKISH RELATIONS, 1976-1988
YUGOSLAV SURVEY, XXX(4) (1989), 133-152.
RELATIONS BETWEEN YUGOSLAVIA AND TURKEY CONTINUED TO BE
GOOD AND STABLE FROM 1976 TO 1988. TURKEY'S MEMBERSHIP IN
NATO AND YUGOSLAVIA'S ADHERENCE TO THE NON-ALIGNED MOVEMENT
HAVE NOT IMPEDED COOPERATION BETWEEN THE TWO COUNTRIES.
THERE ARE NO SERIOUS UNRESOLVED ISSUES BETWEEN THE TWO, AND
BOTH SIDES HAVE A STAKE IN PROMOTING BILATERAL COOPERATION.

00742
YUGOSLAVIA: THE FAILURE OF "DEMOCRATIC" COMMUNISM
FREEDOM HOUSE, NEW YORK, NY, 1988, 88.
THIS BOOK IS BASED ON A 1987 CONFERENCE WHERE 14 EMIGRES
AND DISSIDENTS FROM YUGOSLAVIA DISCUSSED THE CRISIS IN THEIR

HOMELAND. IT DESCRIBES THE POLITICAL, ECONOMIC, AND ETHNIC
SITUATION IN A COUNTRY THAT SEEMS TO BE ON THE BRINK OF
COLLAPSE.

00743
YUGOSLAVIA'S PARTICIPATION AT THE NINTH CONFERENCE OF
HEADS OF STATE OR GOVERNMENT OF NON-ALIGNED COUNTRIES
YUGOSLAV SURVEY, XXX(4) (1989), 123-132.
THIS IS A REPORT ON THE NINTH CONFERENCE OF HEADS OF
STATE OR GOVERNMENT OF NON-ALIGNED COUNTRIES IN SEPTEMBER
1989. THE REPORT INCLUDES BASIC DATA ON THE CONFERENCE, A
LIST OF PARTICIPATING COUNTRIES. MESSAGES SENT TO THE
CONFERENCE, AND AN OUTLINE OF THE MAIN CONFERENCE TOPICS.

00744
YUGOSLOVIA: MENDING THE SOCIAL SITUATION IN THE COUNTRY
INFORMATION BULLETIN, 27(3-4) (FEB 89), 14-17.
THIS ARTICLE DETAILS THE SIXTEEN POINT RESOLUTION
ADOPTED BY THE LEAGUE OF COMMUNISTS OF YUGOSLAVIA (LCY)
DESIGNED TO OVERCOME THE UNFAVORABLE POLITICAL, ECONOMIC,
AND SOCIAL SITUATION IN THAT COUNTRY.

00745
ZHAO REVISITS DPRK
BEIJING REVIEW, 32(19) (MAY 89), 10.
ZHAO ZIYANG VISITED THE DEMOCRATIC PEOPLE'S REPUBLIC OF
KOREA IN APRIL 1989 TO IMPROVE UNDERSTANDING, FRIENDSHIP,
AND COOPERATION BETWEEN THE TWO COUNTRIES. ZHAO REAFFIRMED
CHINA'S SUPPORT FOR THE KOREAN PEOPLE'S QUEST FOR THE
PEACEFUL REUNIFICATION OF THEIR COUNTRY. HE ALSO STATED THAT
THE COMMUNIST PARTY OF CHINA WILL CONTINUE ITS PEACEFUL AND
INDEPENDENT FOREIGN POLICY, WILL SAFEGUARD CHINA'S
SOVEREIGNTY AND SAFETY, WILL SUPPORT THE JUST CAUSES OF
OTHER NATIONS, AND WILL STRIVE FOR A LONG-TERM PEACEFUL
INTERNATIONAL ENVIRONMENT.

00746
1989: A YEAR OF DECISION?
CENTRAL AMERICA BULLETIN, 8(5) (APR 89), 1-3, 7-8.
THE YEAR 1988 MARKED THE ABSOLUTE FAILURE OF THE REAGAN
ADMINISTRATION'S FOREIGN POLICY IN EL SALVADOR. THE
SALVADORANS IDENTIFY THE CHRISTIAN DEMOCRATS AND PRESIDENT
DUARTE WITH THE PROLONGATION OF THE CONFLICT, THE KILLINGS,
THE BOMBINGS, AND THE DEPOPULATION. THE SO-CALLED
"DEMOCRACY" THAT REAGAN TRIED TO SELL IN EL SALVADOR
PRODUCED POLITICAL AND ECONOMIC CRISIS. IT IS UNLIKELY THAT
THE 1989 ELECTIONS WILL RESOLUTE THE SALVADORAN CRISIS
BECAUSE THE PEOPLE HAVE BECOME DISENCHANTED WITH THE
ELECTORAL PROCESS AND THE POLITICAL PARTIES.

00747
24,000 OFFICIALS REPORTED FOR IRREGULARITIES
BEIJING REVIEW, 32(5) (JAN 89), 13.
IN THE LAST HALF OF 1988, MORE THAN 24,000 CHINESE
COMMUNIST PARTY AND GOVERNMENT OFFICIALS, INCLUDING 17 AT
MINISTERIAL AND PROVINCIAL LEVELS, WERE REPORTED FOR
COMMITTING CRIMES. THE OFFICIALS WERE REPORTED FOR
EMBEZZLEMENT, BRIBERY, TAX EVASION, PROFITEERING,
SPECULATION, AND VIOLATING THE DEMOCRATIC RIGHTS OF CITIZENS

00748 A.D.M. WALKER
OBLIGATIONS OF GRATITUDE AND POLITICAL OBLIGATION
PHILOSOPHY AND PUBLIC AFFAIRS, 18(4) (FAL 89), 359-364.
THIS ARTICLE IS A REJOINDER TO GEORGE KLOSKOS REPLY TO A.
D.M. WALKER'S ATTEMPT TO SHOW THAT POLITICAL OBLIGATION IS
AN OBLIGATION OF GRATITUDE. IT CONCENTRATES ON THE OBJECTION
THAT OBLIGATIONS OF GRATITUDE ARE NOT STRONG ENOUGH TO
PROVIDE THE FOUNDATIONS FOR POLITICAL OBLIGATION AND DEFENDS
ORIGINAL POSITION.

00749 AARON, H.J.; BOSWORTH, B.P.; BURTLESS, G.
CAN AMERICA AFFORD TO GROW OLD?
THE BROOKINGS INSTITUTION, WASHINGTON, D.C., 1989, .
THIS BOOK ADDRESSES QUESTIONS ABOUT THE STATUS AND
FUTURE OF THE SOCIAL SECURITY SYSTEM IN THE US. IT CONCLUDES
THAT WORKERS IN THE FUTURE WILL HAVE TO SUPPORT PRESENT
COSTS. IT FINDS THAT IF NATIONAL SAVINGS IS INCREASED THE
ADDED INCOME WILL OFFSET MOST OF THE ADDED COSTS OF THE
BENEFITS. THE AUTHORS URGE THAT INCREASED SOCIAL SECURITY
SURPLUSES BE USED NOT TO OFFSET DEFICITS IN OTHER PARTS OF
THE FEDERAL BUDGET BUT TO RAISE NATIONAL SAVING.

00750 AARON, H.J.; BOSWORTH, B.P.; BURTLESS, G.
POLICY OPTIONS; CAN AMERICA AFFORD TO GROW OLD?
THE BROOKINGS INSTITUTION, WASHINGTON, D.C., 1989, 115-126.
THE ACCUMULATION OF LARGE OASDHI RESERVES RAISES A
NUMBER OF QUESTIONS INVOLVING BOTH POLITICS AND ECONOMICS
THAT THIS CHAPTER OF THE BOOK ADDRESSES, TWO ISSUES ARISE:
1) THE PRIVATIZING OF SOCIAL SECURITY AND 2) THE OFFICIAL
BUDGET. THIS CHAPTER ALSO SUMMARIZES THE MAJOR LESSONS OF
THE ANALYSIS OF THE SOCIAL SECURITY SITUATION.

00751 ABASA-NYARKO, C.
THE ECONOMIC PERFORMANCE OF CIVILIAN AND MILITARY REGIMES:

GHANA, 1957-1985
DISSERTATION ABSTRACTS INTERNATIONAL, 49(9) (MAR 89),
2792-A.
    GHANA PROVIDES AN EXCELLENT OPPORTUNITY TO COMPARE
MILITARY AND CIVILIAN REGIMES BECAUSE IT HAS EXPERIENCED A
SUCCESSION OF SEVEN CIVILIAN AND MILITARY GOVERNMENTS SINCE
INDEPENDENCE. IN THIS DISSERTATION, THE AUTHOR COMPARES THE
ECONOMIC POLICIES AND PERFORMANCE OF GHANA'S REGIMES FROM
1957 TO 1985.

00752 ABBASI, S.M.; HOLLMAN, K.W.; MURREY, J.H. JR.
    ISLAMIC ECONOMICS: FOUNDATIONS AND PRACTICES
INTERNATIONAL JOURNAL OF SOCIAL ECONOMICS, 16(5) (1989),
5-17.
    RECENT EVENTS IN THE ISLAMIC WORLD HAVE CAPTURED THE
ATTENTION OF THE GENERAL PUBLIC IN THE WEST TO AN
UNPRECEDENTED DEGREE. MANY OF THESE EVENTS ARE WIDELY
MISUNDERSTOOD OR MISCONSTRUED. THIS COULD BE ATTRIBUTED TO
THE IGNORANCE OF WESTERNERS CONCERNING THINGS ISLAMIC,
INCLUDING THE CULTURE, ART, GEOGRAPHY, HISTORY AND POLITICS
OF ISLAMIC COUNTRIES AS WELL AS THE PRECEPTS AND CONDITIONS
OF THE ISLAMIC RELIGION. WESTERNERS OFTEN FAIL TO COMPREHEND
THE UNSHAKEABLE CONVICTION THAT MUSLIMS HAVE IN THE
SUPERIORITY OF THEIR RELIGION; THE ISLAMIC BELIEF THAT THERE
IS BUT ONE GOD WHO IS THE SOLE CREATOR AND RULER OF THE
DESTINY OF MEN; THE BELIEF IN THE NECESSITY FOR MANIFEST
ACTS OF COMMON WORSHIP AND DEVOTIONAL REQUIREMENTS FOR THE
ISLAMIC FAITHFUL; AND THE BELIEF THAT CONSCIENTIOUS
APPLICATION OF THE SACRED LAW OF ISLAM IS NOT ONLY NECESSARY
FOR ONE'S ULTIMATE SALVATION AND DELIVERANCE BUT ALSO FOR
THE FULFILMENT OF HUMAN EXISTENCE ON EARTH. TO THE MUSLIM
FAITHFUL, A MERE INTELLECTUAL GRASP OF THE RELIGION IS NOT
SUFFICIENT; THANKS MUST BE RENDERED AND OBEDIENCE MUST BE
SHOWN IN THE MOST PROFOUND MANNER.

00753 ABDI, N. I.
    WHY SIYAD IS SLIPPING
NEW AFRICAN, (257) (FEB 89), 31.
    THERE ARE THREE MAIN REASONS WHY THE SOMALIA NATIONAL
MOVEMENT TOOK UP ARMS AND PLUNGED THE COUNTRY INTO A BLOODY
WAR. THE REBELS ARE PROTESTING GENERAL SIYAD BARRE'S
POLICIES OF TRIBAL INJUSTICE, HIS HUMAN RIGHTS VIOLATIONS,
AND HIS ECONOMIC MISMANAGEMENT.

00754 ABDUL-RAHMAN, Y.
    TRADE WITH IRAQ: AN EMERGING MARKET
AMERICAN-ARAB AFFAIRS, (28) (SPR 89), 38-41.
    THE ARTICLE EXAMINES THE POST-WAR TRADE SITUATION FOR
THE REPUBLIC OF IRAQ. CESSATION OF HOSTILITIES AND
NORMALIZATION OF RELATIONS WITH THE US AND OTHER NATIONS
HAVE RESULTED IN AN INCREASE IN TRADE AND AN INCREASE IN
DEVELOPMENT ASSISTANCE BEING EXTENDED BY INTERNATIONAL
COUNTRIES. THE ARTICLE ANALYZES SOME OF THE CHALLENGES THAT
IRAQ WILL HAVE TO CONFRONT IF THEY ARE TO CONTINUE ON THE
PATH OF ECONOMIC DEVELOPMENT AND INTERNATIONAL TRADE.

00755 ABDULWAHID, A.A.
    COMPUNICATION AND NATIONAL SECURITY
DISSERTATION ABSTRACTS INTERNATIONAL, 50(6) (DEC 89),
1792-A.
    THE AUTHOR ARGUES THAT COMPUNICATION IS A DOUBLE-EDGED
SWORD THAT CAN BOTH HINDER AND ENHANCE THE NATIONAL SECURITY
OF A COUNTRY. HE USES SAUDI ARABIA AS AN EXAMPLE OF THE
UTILIZATION OF COMPUNICATION FOR THE CREATION AND
MAINTENANCE OF ADEQUATE CONDITIONS OF NATIONAL SECURITY. HE
CONTENDS THAT THE DEVELOPMENT OF TOO MANY COMPUNICATION
SYSTEMS IN SAUDI ARABIA OVER THE PAST DECADE IS REACHING THE
POINT WHERE THE MERE COEXISTENCE OF SO MANY SYSTEMS MAY BE
COUNTER-PRODUCTIVE BECAUSE IT MAY IMPEDE FURTHER DEVELOPMENT
AND NATIONAL SECURITY.

00756 ABE, M.A.
    UNDERCURRENTS OF FRUSTRATION AND ROLES OF "GAIATSU" IN
JAPAN: EMERGING DIVISION IN ECONOMIC STRATA AND THE
UNIFICATION OF LABOR MOVEMENT
ASIAN PROFILE, 17(5) (OCT 89), 397-406.
    A DIVISION IN ECONOMIC STRATA IS NOW EMERGING IN JAPAN.
FOR THE FIRST TIME, JAPAN'S BOOMING ECONOMY HAS CREATED A
NEW RICH AND A NEW POOR. THE EMERGING UNDERCURRENT OF
FRUSTRATION, WHICH IS STARTING TO UNDERMINE BASIC JAPANESE
ATTITUDES, PRESENTS A THREAT TO THE RULING LIBERAL
DEMOCRATIC PARTY AND COULD EVENTUALLY AFFECT THE HARMONY AND
SOCIAL FABRIC OF JAPANESE SOCIETY.

00757 ABEDIN, N.
    THE POLITICS OF SEPARATISM: SOME REFLECTIONS AND QUESTIONS
ROUND TABLE, (310) (APR 89), 223-236.
    THE ARTICLE EXPLORES THE CENTRIFUGAL TENDENCIES THAT
HAVE BEEN A PROMINENT CHARACTERISTIC OF MANY NEW STATES AND
EVEN SOME OLD STATES IN THE WEST. IT AIMS TO EXAMINE THE
MULTIDIMENSIONAL RAMIFICATIONS OF THIS ASPECT OF POLITICS IN
BOTH DEVELOPED AND DEVELOPING SOCIETIES. IT SEEKS TO DEFINE
SEPARATISM AND ITS OBJECTIVES AND SOME OF THE POLITICAL
DILEMMAS IT CREATES.

00758 ABEL, C.
    THE CRISIS OF LIBERALISM IN COLUMBIA
CONTEMPORARY REVIEW, 225(1482) (JUL 89), 1-8.
    THE ARTICLE EXAMINES THE CURRENT SOCIAL, POLITICAL, AND
ECONOMIC SITUATION IN COLUMBIA. THE TWO-PARTY SYSTEM OF
LIBERALS AND CONSERVATIVES HAS PROVED HIGHLY DURABLE AND,
ALTHOUGH, LIBERAL PARTIES HAVE BEEN SUCCESSFUL IN PROMOTING
ECONOMIC DIVERSIFICATION AND GROWTH, THE CURRENT LIBERAL
ADMINISTRATION IS FACED WITH SIGNIFICANT CHALLENGES. THESE
INCLUDE: ORGANIZED VIOLENCE IN THE FORM OF LEFT-WING
GUERRILLAS, RIGHT-WING PARAMILITARY DEATH SQUADS, AND
NARCOTERRORIST GROUPS. THE LIBERAL GOVERNMENT ALSO FACES
LEGITIMATE POLITICAL OPPOSITION AND INCREASING PUBLIC
DISSATISFACTION WITH LIBERALISM'S INHERENT AMBIGUITIES.

00759 ABELL, J.D.
    THE IMPACT OF DEMAND MANAGEMENT POLICIES ON BLACK VS.
WHITE EMPLOYMENT
REVIEW OF BLACK POLITICAL ECONOMY, 18(2) (FAL 89), 43-60.
    THIS ARTICLE USES VECTOR AUTOREGRESSION ANALYSIS TO
EXAMINE THE RELATIVE IMPACTS ON BLACK AND WHITE EMPLOYMENT
GROWTH OF MONETARY AND FISCAL ACTIONS. IT WAS FOUND THAT THE
EMPLOYMENT RESPONSES TO ANTICIPATED POLICY ACTIONS, WHILE
SIGNIFICANT, WERE GENERALLY SHORT-LIVED, WITH THE EXCEPTION
OF THE EFFECTS OF ANTICIPATED MONEY GROWTH ON WHITE
EMPLOYMENT. THE INFLUENCES OF UNANTICIPATED POLICY CHANGES
ARE OF A LONGER DURATION. THE PREDOMINANT FINDING IN WHICH
BLACK EMPLOYMENT GROWTH RESPONDED DIFFERENTLY FROM WHITE
EMPLOYMENT GROWTH WAS IN RESPONSE TO A MONETARY SHOCK. THE
BLACK EMPLOYMENT RESPONSE WAS SHARPLY NEGATIVE WHILE THE
WHITE EMPLOYMENT RESPONSE WAS A GRADUAL INCREASE OVER NINE
QUARTERS. THE RESULTS INDICATE THAT THIS DIFFERENCE OCCURRED
ONLY DURING THE 1980S AND NOT IN THE 1970S AND SUGGESTS THAT
THE EFFECTS OF BANK FAILURES AND CREDIT RATIONING DURING
THIS PERIOD MAY HAVE SIGNIFICANTLY HURT MINORITY EMPLOYMENT
OPPORTUNITIES.

00760 ABENTE, D.
    FOREIGN CAPITAL, ECONOMIC ELITES, AND THE STATE IN
PARAGUAY DURING THE LIBERAL REPUBLIC (1870-1936)
JOURNAL OF LATIN AMERICAN STUDIES, 21(1) (FEB 89), 61-88.
    THE AUTHOR STUDIES THE INTERRELATION BETWEEN FOREIGN
ECONOMIC DEPENDENCE, THE EMERGING NATIVE ECONOMIC ELITE, AND
THE STATE. HE BEGINS BY TRACING THE CHANGING NATURE OF
DEPENDENCE AND THE ROLE PLAYED BY FOREIGN COMPANIES IN
PARAGUAY. HE ANALYZES THE SHIFTING ECONOMIC BASIS OF
DOMESTIC HEGEMONY CHARACTERIZED BY THE DISPLACEMENT OF THE
LANDED OLIGARCHY BY THE MERCANTILE ELITE. FINALLY, HE
EXPLORES THE STRATEGIES ARTICULATED BY THE STATE TO DEAL
WITH THESE DIFFERENT FORMS OF DEPENDENCE AND THE POWERFUL
MERCANTILE ELITE.

00761 ABERBACH, J.D.; ROCKMAN, B.A.
    MANDATES OR MANDARINS? CONTROL AND DISCRETION IN THE
MODERN ADMINISTRATIVE STATE
PUBLIC ADMINISTRATION REVIEW, 48(2) (MAR 88), 606-612.
    THIS PAPER ADDRESSES THE STRUGGLE BETWEEN POLITICAL
CONTROL AND ADMINISTRATIVE DISCRETION, THE "MANDARIN"
PERSPECTIVE, THAT A PROFESSIONALIZED BUREAUCRACY ELEVATES
THE EFFECTIVENESS OF GOVERNMENT IS DISCUSSED. THE
INTELLECTUAL JUSTIFICATION OF POLITICAL COMMAND AND THE
PRESIDENTIAL ROLE IN THE ADMINISTRATIVE PROCESS IS EXAMINED.
COLLECTIVE RATIONALITY AND INDIVIDUAL RATIONALITY ARE
CONTRASTED.

00762 ABERBACH, J.D.; ROCKMAN, B.A.
    ON THE RISE, TRANSFORMATION, AND DECLINE OF ANALYSIS IN
THE US GOVERNMENT
GOVERNANCE, 2(3) (JUL 89), 293-315.
    THIS ARTICLE RAISES A NUMBER OF QUESTIONS ABOUT THE
RELATIONSHIP BETWEEN POLICY ANALYSIS AND POLICYMAKING IN
GOVERNMENT. IT SEEKS FOR THE FACTORS THAT CONDITION THE
SUPPLY OF ANALYSIS AND ITS USES IN DECISIONS, AND FOR WHAT
CONDITIONS THE EMPLOYMENT OF SPECIFIC FORMS OF POLICY
ANALYSIS. THE LOGIC IN THE EXPOSITION PROCEEDS BY EXAMINING
CRITERIA FOR POLICYMAKING IN GOVERNMENT AND THE ROLE OF
ANALYSIS AMONG THOSE CRITERIA, BY EXAMINING BROADLY
CONDITIONS THAT PROMOTE ANALYSIS AND ITS PROBABLE USE, BY
EXAMINING MODES OF, AND JUSTIFICATIONS FOR, ANALYSIS, AND BY
LOOKING AT THE RELATIONSHIP BETWEEN ANALYTIC USE AND
POLITICAL GOALS PARTICULARLY WITHIN THE CONTEXT OF HIGH
GOVERNMENTAL RELATIVE RESOURCE SCARCITY (STRONG BUDGET
CONSTRAINT).

00763 ABEYSINGHE, A.; VIVEKANANDA, F.
    ECONOMICS OF SOUTH PACIFIC COUNTRIES: COLONIAL HANGOVERS--
DEPENDENCY AND CHALLENGES TO ECONOMIC DEVELOPMENT
SCANDINAVIAN JOURNAL OF DEVELOPMENT ALTERNATIVES, VIII(1)
(MAR 89), 167-206.
    THE ARTICLE ANALYZES THE POTENTIAL FOR ECONOMIC
DEVELOPMENT IN THE VAST AND DIVERSE PACIFIC ISLANDS REGION.
IT EXAMINES GEOGRAPHY, CULTURE, AND POLITICAL CLIMATE TO
ESTABLISH A FRAMEWORK IN WHICH TO DISCUSS ECONOMIC

STRATEGIES. IT DISCUSSES RESOURCES, MANPOWER, AND THE
CURRENT TRADING SITUATION IN MICRONESIA, MELANESIA, AND
POLYNESIA. IT CONCLUDES WITH THE FUTURE ECONOMIC PROSPECTS
FOR THE PACIFIC ISLANDS REGION IN LIGHT OF CURRENT POLICIES.

00764 ABEYSINGHE, A.; VIVEKANANDA, F.
THE AFTERMATH OF THE INDO-SRI LANKA PEACE ACCORD AND THE
ROLE OF THE INDIAN PEACE KEEPING FORCE IN SRI LANKA
SCANDINAVIAN JOURNAL OF DEVELOPMENT ALTERNATIVES, 8(4)
(DEC 89), 123-138.
JULY 29, 1987 SAW THE SIGNING OF THE INDO-SRI LANKA
PEACE ACCORD AND THE FIRST VISIT OF RAJIV GANDHI TO SRI
LANKA AS THE INDIAN PRIME MINISTER. THE ACCORD PROVIDED THAT
THE SRI LANKAN GOVERNMENT COULD CALL UPON THE INDIAN
GOVERNMENT TO RENDER MILITARY ASSISTANCE TO INSURE THE
IMPLEMENTATION OF THE AGREEMENT. THIS ARTICLE TRACES THE
EVENTS BOTH LEADING UP TO THE NEED FOR THE ACCORD AND EVENTS
FOLLOWING IT. IT OFFERS THE STANDARD ARGUMENTS FOR
JUSTIFYING MILITARY OPERATIONS. THE PROSPECTS FOR PEACE IN
SRI LANKA AND IMPLICATIONS ARE GIVEN. IT CONCLUDES WITH A
TEXT OF THE PROVISIONS OF THE ACCORD.

00765 ABIDI, S.M.
SOCIAL CHANGE AND THE POLITICS OF RELIGION IN PAKISTAN
DISSERTATION ABSTRACTS INTERNATIONAL, 50(1) (JUL 89),
244-A.
THIS STUDY PROVIDES AN ANALYSIS OF THE ISLAMIZATION
PROGRAM OF THE DECEASED PRESIDENT OF PAKISTAN, ZIA-UL-HAQ.
IT IS ARGUED THAT NEITHER CONVENTIONAL MAINSTREAM POLITICAL
APPROACHES NOR RECENT NEO-MARXIST APPROACHES ARE ADEQUATE TO
THE TASKS OF UNDERSTANDING SOCIAL CHANGE AND POLITICS OF
RELIGION IN PAKISTAN. RATHER, THE EFFORT IS MADE TO
INTEGRATE THESE INTO AN ANALYSIS WHICH TRACES AND EXPLAINS A
STRUGGLE FOR AUTHORITY BETWEEN A NUMBER OF COMPETING
DISCOURSES: RELIGIOUS, STRATEGIC, DEVELOPMENTAL AND
POLITICAL.

00766 ABIDIN, S.Z.
REGIONALIZATION AND DEVELOPMENT PERFORMANCE IN INDONESIA
DISSERTATION ABSTRACTS INTERNATIONAL, 50(3) (SEP 89),
788-A.
USING KATZ' DEVELOPMENT ACTION SYSTEM WITH MODIFICATIONS
FOR INDONESIA, THE AUTHOR STUDIES THE IMPACT OF REGIONAL
ORGANIZATION AND MANAGEMENT OF DEVELOPMENT AND REGIONAL
DEVELOPMENT PERFORMANCES. HE USES TWO MAIN INDICATORS FOR
OPERATIONALIZING REGIONALIZATION: (1) THE PRIORITY GIVEN TO
REGIONAL DEVELOPMENT BY THE CENTRAL GOVERNMENT AND (2) THE
DEGREE OF REGIONAL AUTONOMY OR DECENTRALIZATION AS EXPRESSED
IN THE ROLE THE REGION PLAYS IN DEVELOPMENT DECISION-MAKING.

00767 ABIR, M.
SAUDI-SOVIET RELATIONS AND THE IRAN-IRAQ WAR
MIDDLE EAST REVIEW, XXII(1) (FAL 89), 10-16.
THE AUTHOR REVIEWS THE HISTORY OF RELATIONS BETWEEN THE
SOVIET UNION AND SAUDI ARABIA, FROM 1924 THROUGH THE TIME OF
THE IRAN-IRAQ WAR.

00768 ABIZADEH, S.; YOUSEFI, M.
GOVERNMENT DEFICITS AND INFLATION
JOURNAL OF SOCIAL, POLITICAL AND ECONOMIC STUDIES, 13(4)
(WIN 88), 395-404.
GIVEN THE CONTROVERSY CONCERNING THE IMPACT OF DEFICITS
ON THE RATE OF INFLATION, THE MAIN THRUST OF THIS PAPER IS
TO RE-EXAMINE THE EMPIRICAL EVIDENCE BY USING ALTERNATIVE
MEASURES OF GOVERNMENT DEFICITS. A MODEL, USING DEFICIT
MEASURES SUGGESTED BY EISNER AND OTHERS, IS PRESENTED TO
INVESTIGATE THE LINK BETWEEN DEFICITS AND INFLATION.

00769 ABNEY, G.
LOBBYING BY INSIDERS: PARALLELS OF STATE AGENCIES AND
INTEREST GROUPS
PUBLIC ADMINISTRATION REVIEW, 48(5) (SEP 88), 911-917.
IN THIS ARTICLE PARALLELS ARE DRAWN BETWEEN LEGISLATIVE
LOBBYING AND THAT OF PRIVATE SECTOR GROUPS. IN MANY RESPECTS,
LOBBYING BY STATE AGENCIES IS SIMILAR TO THAT OF INTEREST
GROUPS. INDEED, THEIR LOBBYING IS OFTEN COORDINATED. EVEN SO,
THE ROLE AND TECHNIQUES OF THE TWO DO DIFFER. BESIDES THE
LITERATURE ON LOBBYING, THE DATABASE FOR THIS ARTICLE
CONSISTS OF A SERIES OF IN-DEPTH INTERVIEWS CONDUCTED BY THE
AUTHOR IN 1987 WITH OFFICIALS OF 13 MAJOR STATE AGENCIES AND
WITH OTHERS INVOLVED IN THE LEGISLATIVE PROCESS IN GEORGIA.3
QUOTATIONS FROM THESE IN-DEPTH INTERVIEWS ARE USED IN THE
TEXT AND ARE PRESENTED IN A FASHION TO PROTECT THE IDENTITY
OF THE INTERVIEWEES. ALSO, RESPONSES FROM A MAIL SURVEY OF
LEGISLATORS ARE USED TO CONFIRM INFORMATION GAINED FROM THE
INTERVIEWS.

00770 ABOIMOV, I.; GORINOVICH, G.; ILYINSKY, I.; KLEPATSKY, L.;
KOLIKOV, N.; KRASNOV, L.; OSADCHUK, Y.; SHVETSOVA, S.;
SOLOVYEV, V.; YAGODOVSKY, L.
THE SOCIALIST COMMUNITY: DEMOCRATISATION AND RENEWAL
INTERNATIONAL AFFAIRS (MOSCOW), (1) (JAN 89), 123-132.
THE SOCIALIST COMMUNITY IS AN INFLUENTIAL, AUTHORITATIVE
COMPONENT OF THE WORLD COMMUNITY. IT HAS REGISTERED MANY

SUCCESSES OF HISTORIC SIGNIFICANCE AND HAS PROVED THE
POSSIBILITY OF ESTABLISHING A SOCIAL SYSTEM FREE OF
EXPLOITATION AND OPPRESSION AND EQUAL TO THE DIFFICULT
PROBLEMS OF DEVELOPMENT. A KEY LINE OF SOVIET FOREIGN POLICY
IS TO STRENGTH SOCIALISM AND RAISE ITS PRESTIGE AND ROLE IN
THE WORLD. THUS, RELATIONS BETWEEN THE SOVIET UNION AND THE
SOCIALIST COUNTRIES OF EUROPE ARE AN IMPORTANT ELEMENT IN
FURTHERING WORLD SOCIALISM.

00771 ABRAHAM, K.
THE MISSING MILLIONS
SOUTH, (110) (DEC 89), 131.
A NEW SYNDROME OF PRIVATIZATION IS SPREADING IN AFRICA
AS ONE GOVERNMENT AFTER ANOTHER SHIFTS THE BURDEN OF
FINANCING EDUCATION TO PARENTS, GUARDIANS, AND STUDENTS. THE
SHOCK OF AUSTERITY IS MOSTLY BEING FELT IN THE HIGHER
ECHELONS OF EDUCATION, BUT EDUCATION AT LOWER LEVELS IS NOT
EXEMPT. THE CUTBACKS IN SPENDING ARE CAUSING DECLINING
SCHOOL ENROLLMENTS IN A NUMBER OF COUNTRIES.

00772 ABRAHAM, N.
HUMAN RIGHTS BRIEFING (SYRIA)
MIDDLE EAST REPORT, 19(5) (SEP 89), 37-38.
AN AMNESTY INTERNATIONAL REPORT REVEALS THAT TORTURE IS
A REGULAR EXPERIENCE FOR THOUSANDS OF POLITICAL PRISONERS IN
SYRIA. NOT ONLY HAS THE NUMBER OF INCIDENTS INCREASED, BUT
THE METHODS OF TORTURE HAVE ALSO DIVERSIFIED. THE REPORT
LISTS 38 DIFFERENT TYPES OF TORTURE AS COMPARED TO 23 IN
1983. THE ARTICLE EXAMINES SEVERAL OF THE GRUESOME TORTURE
DEVICES COMMONLY FOUND IN SYRIA.

00773 ABRAHAMSE, L.G.
AGM 1989
SOUTH AFRICA FOUNDATION REVIEW, 15(3) (MAR 89), 1-2.
SOUTH AFRICA CAN EXPECT A CONTINUED FOREIGN CONCERN WITH
ITS DOMESTIC AFFAIRS. THE REAL ISSUE WILL BE WHETHER THAT
INVOLVEMENT ASSISTS PROGRESS TOWARD PEACE, PROSPERITY, AND
JUSTICE IN SOUTH AFRICA. THIS WILL DEPEND ON THE EXTENT TO
WHICH SOUTH AFRICANS ENGAGE IN CREATING A BETTER SOCIETY AND
ARE PERCEIVED TO BE DOING SO.

00774 ABRAM, M.
CSCE CONFERENCE ON THE HUMAN DIMENSION
DEPARTMENT OF STATE BULLETIN (US FOREIGN POLICY), 89(2150)
(SEP 89), 88-90.
DESPITE RECENT PROGRESS IN HUMAN RIGHTS, NONCOMPLIANCE
WITH THE HELSINKI, MADRID, AND VIENNA DOCUMENTS ON HUMAN
RIGHTS CONTINUES. COMPLIANCE WITH HELSINKI'S HUMAN DIMENSION
COMMITMENTS CANNOT BE ACHIEVED OVERNIGHT, BUT CONSIDERABLE
IMPROVEMENTS HAVE OCCURED IN SOME COUNTRIES.

00775 ABRAM, M.B.
U.S. POLICY AND THE U.N.: MULTILATERALISM WITH A MORAL FACE
FREEDOM AT ISSUE, (106) (JAN 89), 4-8.
SINCE THE MID-1960'S, WITH THE PROLIFERATION OF MEMBER
STATES, THE UNITED NATIONS HAS INCREASINGLY TURNED AGAINST
THE WEST AND THE UNITED STATES. IN 1987, THE UNITED NATIONS'
NON-DEMOCRATIC AND ANTI-DEMOCRATIC MAJORITY VOTED ALONGSIDE
THE USSR NEARLY 85 PERCENT OF THE TIME. IN RECENT YEARS, THE
USA HAS BEEN BEEN APPALLED BY POLITICIZATION THROUGHOUT THE
U.N. SYSTEM AND, IN PARTICULAR, THE SECRETARIAT. U.S. FUNDS
HAVE BEEN WITHHELD FROM THE U.N. NOT OUT OF MALICE OR AS A
DEMONSTRATION OF AMERICAN HOSTILITY TOWARD IT BUT RATHER AS
A MEANS OF PROJECTING FAITH IN THE INHERENT WORTH OF THE U.N.
AND IN THE LEGACY OF ITS MANDATE.

00776 ABRAMOWITZ, A.I.
CAMPAIGN SPENDING IN U.S. SENATE ELECTIONS
LEGISLATIVE STUDIES QUARTERLY, 14(4) (NOV 89), 487-508.
THE SKYROCKETING COST OF U.S. SENATE CAMPAIGNS HAS LED
TO PROPOSALS TO LIMIT CANDIDATES' SPENDING. REPUBLICAN
OPPOSITION TO SPENDING LIMITS HAS BEEN BASED ON THE BELIEF
THAT SUCH LIMITS WOULD ADVERSELY AFFECT THE MINORITY PARTY,
SINCE ITS CHALLENGERS WOULD NEED TO SPEND MORE THAN THE
ALLOWABLE LIMIT IN ORDER TO OVERCOME THE ELECTORAL ADVANTAGE
ENJOYED BY DEMOCRATIC INCUMBENTS. HOWEVER, VERY FEW GOP
CHALLENGERS IN 1986 OR 1988 REACHED THE SPENDING CEILINGS
WHICH HAVE BEEN PROPOSED IN RECENT REFORM LEGISLATION. IN
GENERAL, REPUBLICAN CHALLENGERS HAVE HAD DIFFICULTY RAISING
ADEQUATE CAMPAIGN WAR CHESTS, EVEN IN YEARS SUCH AS 1984
WHEN GOP PROSPECTS APPEARED PROMISING. IN THE LONG RUN,
SPENDING LIMITS MIGHT WORK TO THE ADVANTAGE OF THE
REPUBLICAN PARTY BY CAUSING SENATE CANDIDATES TO RELY MORE
HEAVILY ON INDEPENDENT EXPENDITURES AND INDIRECT FINANCIAL
SUPPORT FROM PARTY COMMITTEES.

00777 ABRAMOWITZ, A.I.
VIABILITY, ELECTABILITY, AND CANDIDATE CHOICE IN A
PRESIDENTIAL PRIMARY ELECTION: A TEST OF COMPETING MODELS
THE JOURNAL OF POLITICS, 51(4) (NOV 89), 977-992.
USING DATA FROM AN EXIT POLL, THIS PAPER TESTS THREE
MODELS OF VOTER DECISION MAKING IN A PRESIDENTIAL PRIMARY: A
SIMPLE CANDIDATE PREFERENCE MODEL, A BANDWAGON MODEL, AND AN
EXPECTED UTILITY MODEL. FOR BOTH REPUBLICAN AND WHITE

DEMOCRATIC PRIMARY VOTERS, THE DATA SUPPORT THE EXPECTED
UTILITY MODEL. IN CHOOSING A CANDIDATE FOR THEIR PARTY'S
NOMINATION, REPUBLICAN AND DEMOCRATIC PRIMARY VOTERS WEIGHED
ELECTABILITY IN ADDITION TO THEIR GENERAL EVALUATIONS OF THE
CANDIDATES. OPINIONS ABOUT ELECTABILITY WERE, IN TURN,
STRONGLY INFLUENCED BY PERCEPTIONS OF CANDIDATES' NOMINATION
PROSPECTS. THUS, VIABILITY HAD AN IMPORTANT, BUT INDIRECT,
INFLUENCE ON VOTER DECISION MAKING.

00778 ABRAMS, B.
    NERVOUSLY AWAITING 1997
    REASON, 20(8) (JAN 89), 32-35.
        THE CITIZENS OF HONG KONG NERVOUSLY AWAIT THE TRANSFER
    OF THEIR TERRITORY TO THE CHINESE COMMUNISTS IN 1997,
    FEARING THE RUIN OF THEIR SUCCESSFUL ECONOMY. WHAT ACTUALLY
    HAPPENS MAY DEPEND ON THE COURSE OF FREE-MARKET REFORMS IN
    MAINLAND CHINA.

00779 ABRAMS, E.
    ARE THE CONTRAS FINISHED?
    NATIONAL REVIEW, XLI(4) (MAR 89), 30-31.
        THE CONTRAS HAVE NOT DISPERSED AND THEY ARE NOT
    DEMORALIZED, BUT THEY ARE WAITING FOR NEWS FROM WASHINGTON.
    FACED WITH VICIOUS ATTACKS FROM U.S. ENEMIES, CUT OFF BY
    CONGRESS, AND CONFRONTED WITH CONTINUED SOVIET AID ARRIVING
    IN MANAGUA, THE CONTRAS HAVE SIMPLY HUNKERED DOWN FOR THE
    LONGER HAUL.

00780 ABRAMS, E.
    THE DEAL IN CENTRAL AMERICA
    COMMENTARY, 87(5) (MAY 89), 29-32.
        THE AUTHOR REVIEWS RONALD REAGAN'S POLICY IN CENTRAL
    AMERICA AND THE PEACE PLAN ADOPTED AT THE ESQUIPULAS SUMMIT.

00781 ABRAMS, R.M.
    THE U.S. MILITARY AND HIGHER EDUCATION: A BRIEF HISTORY
    PHILADELPHIA: ANLS OF AMER ACMY OF POLITICAL AND SOC
    SCIENCE, (502) (MAR 89), 15-28.
        FROM ALMOST UNNOTICED BEGINNINGS IN THE MORRILL LAND-
    GRANT COLLEGE ACT OF 1862, THE MILITARY-UNIVERSITY
    RELATIONSHIP HAS, SINCE 1940, BECOME A MAJOR FEATURE OF
    AMERICAN SOCIETY. PUTTING HIGHER EDUCATION TO THE SERVICE OF
    PUBLIC PRIORITIES HAS LONGER AND STRONGER ROOTS IN THE
    AMERICAN TRADITION THAN DOES THE IDEAL OF THE UNIVERSITY AS
    A SANCTUARY FOR INDEPENDENT, CRITICAL SCHOLARSHIP AND
    DISINTERESTED PURSUIT OF LEARNING FOR ITS OWN SAKE.
    IRONICALLY, THE UNIVERSITY GAINED ITS PRINCIPAL CLAIM TO
    EMINENCE IN THE AMERICAN MAINSTREAM ONLY IN THE EARLY
    THENTIETH CENTURY WHEN MUCH OF THE NATION'S ELITE CAME TO
    RESPECT THE IDEAL OF AUTONOMOUS, DISINTERESTED RESEARCH AND
    TEACHING WITHIN AN ACADEMIC SANCTUARY. ALTHOUGH THE IDEAL
    CONTINUED TO BE HONORED AS WORTHY, ITS APPROXIMATION TO
    REALITY FADED EGREGIOUSLY AFTER 1940. ITS VERY IMPORTANCE
    FOR THE ACHIEVEMENT OF PUBLIC PRIORITIES, MOST CONSPICUOUSLY
    FOR NATIONAL DEFENSE, LED THE UNIVERSITY TO ACCEPT
    INDUCEMENTS AND CONSTRAINTS THAT PULLED IT NOTABLY AWAY FROM
    ITS BRIEFLY ASSUMED MISSION AS A PROTECTED REFUGE FOR THE
    DISPASSIONATE AND CRITICAL STUDY OF SCIENCE AND SOCIETY.

00782 ABRAMSON, G.
    SAHARAN STATESMANSHIP
    AFRICA REPORT, 34(2) (MAR 89), 52-55.
        AFTER MORE THAN A DECADE, THE WAR THAT HAS SPLIT AFRICAN
    STATES INTO TWO CAMPS AND LED TO MOROCCO'S WITHDRAWAL FROM
    THE ORGANIZATION OF AFRICAN UNITY MAY BE AT A TURNING POINT.
    THE POLISARIO FRONT AND THE MOROCCAN GOVERNMENT ARE ENGAGED
    IN DIPLOMATIC EFFORTS THAT MAY PROMPT A REFERENDUM TO
    DETERMINE THE FATE OF THE DISPUTED WESTERN SAHARA.

00783 ABRAMSON, P.R.
    GENERATIONAL REPLACEMENT, ETHNIC CHANGE, AND PARTISAN
    SUPPORT IN ISRAEL
    THE JOURNAL OF POLITICS, 51(3) (AUG 89), 545-574.
        A TIME-SERIES COHORT ANALYSIS OF ISRAELI ELECTION
    SURVEYS CONDUCTED BETWEEN 1969 AND 1984 IS USED TO ESTIMATE
    THE IMPACT OF GENERATIONAL REPLACEMENT AND ETHNIC CHANGE ON
    THE BALANCE OF PARTISAN FORCES. THE ANALYSIS DEMONSTRATES
    THAT TWO CLOSELY RELATED LONG-TERM CHANGES MADE A MAJOR
    CONTRIBUTION TO THE DECLINE OF THE LABOR ALIGNMENT: THE
    GROWING NUMBER OF JEWS OF ASIAN AND AFRICAN ORIGINS, A
    CHANGE THAT RESULTED FROM GENERATIONAL REPLACEMENT, AND THE
    REPLACEMENT OF VOTERS WHO ENTERED THE ELECTORATE DURING A
    PERIOD OF DOMINANCE BY MAPAI (ISRAEL WORKERS' PARTY) WITH
    VOTERS WHO ENTERED THE ELECTORATE AFTER HERUT (FREEDOM
    PARTY) BEGAN TO EMERGE AS A MAJOR POLITICAL CHALLENGE.

00784 ABRAMSON, P.R.; CLAGGETT, W.
    RACE-RELATED DIFFERENCES IN SELF-REPORTED AND VALIDATED
    TURNOUT IN 1986
    THE JOURNAL OF POLITICS, 51(2) (MAY 89), 397-408.
        BLACK AMERICANS ARE LESS LIKELY TO PARTICIPATE IN
    POLITICS THAN WHITE AMERICANS ARE, BUT MANY STUDENTS OF
    POLITICAL PARTICIPATION HAVE ARGUED THAT THESE DIFFERENCES
    RESULT SOLELY FROM RACIAL DIFFERENCES IN SOCIOECONOMIC

STATUS. THE AUTHOR QUESTION THESE CONCLUSIONS BY ANALYZING
THE 1964, 1976, 1978, 1980, AND 1984 VOTE VALIDATION STUDIES
IN WHICH LOCAL REGISTRATION AND VOTING RECORDS WERE USED TO
MEASURE ELECTORAL PARTICIPATION. WHEN PARTICIPATION WAS
MEASURED BY THE VOTE VALIDATION STUDIES, RACIAL DIFFERENCES
WERE REDUCED AFTER CONTROLS WERE INTRODUCED, BUT WHITES WERE
STILL MORE LIKELY TO VOTE THAN BLACKS. THE 1986 SURVEY
RESEARCH CENTER-CENTER FOR POLITICAL STUDIES (SRC-CPS) VOTE
VALIDATION STUDY IS USED TO UPDATE THE FINDINGS. THE RESULTS
ARE CONSISTENT WITH PREVIOUS ANALYSES. THE 1986 STUDY DOES
NOT CONFIRM THE FINDING OF U.S. CENSUS BUREAU SURVEY THAT
YOUNG BLACKS WERE MORE LIKELY TO VOTE THAN YOUNG WHITES.
HOWEVER, THESE ANALYSES DO SUPPORT THE BASIC FINDING OF THE
BUREAU THAT RACIAL DIFFERENCES IN ELECTORAL PARTICIPATION
HAVE DECLINED.

00785 ABUELNOUR, A.G.M.
    FOREIGN AID, ECONOMIC DEVELOPMENT, AND THE INDEBTEDNESS
    PROBLEM, WITH SPECIAL REFERENCE TO THE SUDAN
    DISSERTATION ABSTRACTS INTERNATIONAL, 49(8) (FEB 89),
    2313-A.
        THE AUTHOR STUDIES THE ROLE OF FOREIGN AID IN ECONOMIC
    DEVELOPMENT, WITH SPECIAL REFERENCE TO THE SUDAN. HE
    CONSIDERS THREE MAJOR ASPECTS OF THE QUESTION: (1) A REVIEW
    OF THE LITERATURE AND THE RELEVANT CONTROVERSIES, (2) THE
    ROLE OF AID IN THE SUDAN'S DEVELOPMENT, AND (3) THE DEBT
    PROGRAM OF DEVELOPING COUNTRIES.

00786 ABUKHALIL, A.
    THE POLITICS OF SECTARIAN ETHNICITY: SEGMENTATION IN
    LEBANESE SOCIETY
    DISSERTATION ABSTRACTS INTERNATIONAL, 49(12) (JUN 89),
    3855-A.
        THE AUTHOR STUDIES THE NATURE AND IMPACT OF CLEAVAGES IN
    LEBANESE SOCIETY ALONG WITH THE ORIGINS AND EVOLUTION OF
    SEGMENTED GROUPS IN CONTEMPORARY LEBANON. HE EXAMINES THE
    FOUNDATIONS OF THE LEBANESE POLITICAL SYSTEM AS IT EXISTED
    BEFORE THE WAR, BOTH IN PRACTICE AND IN THE TEXTS OF THE
    CONSTITUTION AND THE NATIONAL PACT.

00787 ACAREL, S.
    THE ALLIANCE'S DEFENCE INDUSTRY AND TURKEY
    NATO'S SIXTEEN NATIONS, 34(6) (OCT 89), 74-75 (SPECIAL
    SECTION).
        TURKEY NEEDS TO EQUIP ITS ARMED FORCES AND MODERNIZE ITS
    DEFENCE INDUSTRY WHILE, AT THE SAME TIME, MODERNIZING ITS
    ECONOMIC STRUCTURE. THIS IS A LARGE BURDEN, AND TURKEY
    BELIEVES THAT ITS ALLIES SHOULD SHARE THE LOAD. NATO NATIONS
    WITH ADVANCED DEFENCE INDUSTRIES HAVE HELPED TURKEY IN THE
    PAST AND ARE EXPECTED TO DO SO IN THE FUTURE.

00788 ADALJA, S.K.
    MOI BIDS TO PLUG THE LEAKING SHIP OF STATE
    SOUTH, (104) (JUN 89), 29-30.
        IN THE NICK OF TIME KEYNA HAS SECURED OFFICIAL FOREIGN
    AID AND DEBT WRITE-OFFS TO HELP OFFSET THE CRIPPLING EFFECTS
    OF CONTINUING DISINVESTMENT BY THE TRANSNATIONALS. THE
    EXODUS HAS BEEN FUELLED BY FEARS OF POLITICAL INSTABILITY
    STIRRED UP BY THE DECLINE OF KENYA'S ECONOMIC PERFORMANCE.

00789 ADAMANY, D.
    WISCONSIN GOV. LUCEY: SUCCESSFUL HANDS-OFF MANAGEMENT
    JOURNAL OF STATE GOVERNMENT, 62(4) (JUL 89), 140-146.
        PATRICK J. LUCEY CAME TO THE WISCONSIN GOVERNORSHIP AS A
    SUCCESSFUL BUSINESSMAN AND POLITICAL ORGANIZER WHO HAD
    REVITALIZED THE WISCONSIN DEMOCRATIC PARTY. BUT DURING HIS
    YEARS AS GOVERNOR, HE WAS NOT THE HANDS-ON MANAGER OF STATE
    GOVERNMENT THAT MANY EXPECTED. THE REASONS LAY IN A SERIES
    OF IMPORTANT STRUCTURAL CHANGES IN WISCONSIN'S GOVERNORSHIP,
    IN LUCEY'S COMMITMENT TO POLICY INNOVATION, IN HIS
    WILLINGNESS TO DELEGATE AUTHORITY TO MEMBERS OF HIS CABINET,
    TO THE CHARACTER OF THE CABINET AND EXECUTIVE OFFICE STAFF
    LUCEY ASSEMBLED, AND TO THE QUALITY AND EFFECTIVENESS OF
    WISCONSIN'S CIVIL SERVICE BUREAUCRACY. LUCEY'S STYLE
    EMPHASIZED WIDE DELEGATION TO AGENCIES CONTROLLED BY
    GUBERNATORIAL APPOINTEES, WITH CLOSE SCRUTINY RESERVED FOR
    AGENCIES BEYOND THE GOVERNOR'S DIRECT ADMINISTRATIVE CONTROL.

00790 ADAMOLEKUN, L; AYO, S.
    THE EVOLUTION OF THE NIGERIAN FEDERAL ADMINISTRATION SYSTEM
    PUBLIUS: THE JOURNAL OF FEDERALISM, 19(1) (WIN 89),
    157-176.
        THIS ARTICLE REVIEWS THE MAJOR CONSEQUENCES FOR THE
    EVOLUTION OF NIGERIA'S PUBLIC ADMINISTRATION OF THE PROCESS
    BY WHICH THE "LOOSE" MODEL OF FEDERALISM ADOPTED IN 1954 WAS
    TRANSFORMED INTO ONE IN WHICH THE NATIONAL GOVERNMENT BECAME
    DOMINANT FROM 1966 ONWARDS. TO ILLUSTRATE HOW THIS
    DEVELOPMENT AFFECTED THE EMERGING PUBLIC ADMINISTRATION
    SYSTEM, TWO BROAD THEMES ARE EXAMINED: (1) THE STRUCTURE,
    ORGANIZATION, AND FUNCTIONING OF THE FEDERAL AND SUBNATIONAL
    UNITS AND (2) ISSUES IN INTERGOVERNMENTAL RELATIONS, NOTABLY
    THE ALLOCATION OF JURISDICTIONAL POWERS, FISCAL FEDERALISM,
    PUBLIC PERSONNEL ADMINISTRATION, AND LOCAL GOVERNMENTS. THE
    CONCLUSION POINTS OUT SOME OF THE KEY ISSUES THAT ARE LIKELY

TO DOMINATE THE NIGERIAN FEDERAL SYSTEM DURING THE NEXT DECADE.

00791 ADAMS, A.P. JR.
IRAN'S THREATS AGAINST AUTHOR
DEPARTMENT OF STATE BULLETIN (US FOREIGN POLICY), 89(2146) (MAY 89), 78-80.
THE AUTHOR, WHO IS THE BUSH ADMINISTRATION'S ACTING COORDINATOR FOR COUNTER-TERRORISM, REVIEWS THE CONTROVERSY GENERATED BY IRAN'S THREATS AGAINST SALMAN RUSHDIE. HE STATES THAT THE US GOVERNMENT WILL DO WHATEVER IT CAN TO PROTECT THE FREEDOM OF EXPRESSION AND THAT THE RUSHDIE AFFAIR IS AN EXTREMELY COMPLEX SITUATION BECAUSE IT STRIKES VERY SENSITIVE POLITICAL AND RELIGIOUS NERVES.

00792 ADAMS, D.
DISARMAMENT: IDEOLOGY AND TASKS
POLITICAL AFFAIRS, LXVIII(6) (JUN 89), 28-30.
THE ARTICLE EXAMINES THE NEW CHALLENGE PRESENTED TO HUMANITY IN GENERAL AND TO MARXIST-LENINIST IDEOLOGY IN PARTICULAR BY THE THREAT OF NUCLEAR WAR. THE POSSIBILITY OF WORLD DESTRUCTION HAS CAUSED A "HISTORICAL SPEEDUP" IN WHICH COMMUNISTS MUST NOT WAIT FOR THE ARRIVAL OF WORLD SOCIALISM TO SOLVE THE PROBLEM, BUT MUST TAKE ACTIVE MEASURES TO SOLVE THE PROBLEM WITHIN EXISTING SYSTEMS AND CONDITIONS. THE ARTICLE ALSO OUTLINES THE CHALLENGES OF "SYNERGIZING" OR INTERLOCKING THE CLASS AND DISARMMAMENT STRUGGLE AND PRESENTS SUGGESTIONS FOR THE COMMUNIST PARTY TO ACCOMPLISH THESE GOALS.

00793 ADAMS, D.
PALESTINIANS IN HONDURAS: SUCCESS BREEDS RESENTMENT
MIDDLE EAST INTERNATIONAL, (341) (JAN 89), 19-20.
THE STORY OF PALESTINIAN MIGRATION TO HONDURAS IS A PARABLE OF THE CHALLENGES OF AN IMMIGRANT COMMUNITY SEEKING ASSIMILATION IN A FOREIGN LAND. THE PALESTINIAN SETTLERS HAVE ENORMOUS WEALTH BY HONDURAN STANDARDS, AND IN COMMERCIAL-INDUSTRIAL TERMS, THEY DOMINATE THE COUNTRY. BUT THEIR ECONOMIC SUCCESS HAS AROUSED RESENTMENT AMONG THE INDIAN AND LATIN COMMUNITIES. IN THE PAST, THE PALESTINIANS HAVE STAYED OUT OF HONDURAN POLITICS, BUT THERE ARE SIGNS THAT THIS IS CHANGING.

00794 ADAMS, F.G.
THE MACROECONOMIC IMPACTS OF INCREASING THE MINIUM WAGE
JOURNAL OF POLICY MODELING, 11(1) (SUM 89), 179-189.
THE ADJUSTMENT OF THE U.S. MINIMUM WAGE TO MAKE UP THE EROSION RESULTING FROM INFLATION HAS AROUSED CONTROVERSY ABOUT THE QUANTITATIVE EFFECTS OF THE MINIMUM WAGE ON EMPLOYMENT AND INFLATION. THIS ARTICLE EXAMINES THE DIMENSIONS OF THIS IMPACT THROUGH ANALYSIS OF THE PAST EXPERIENCE AND THROUGH MACRO-MODEL SIMULATION. THE PAPER CONCLUDES THAT IN THE FRAMEWORK OF CURRENT ECONOMIC CONDITIONS—A SLUGGISH ECONOMY BUT RELATIVELY STRONG LABOR MARKETS, PARTICULARLY FOR LOW WAGE WORKERSADJUSTMENT OF THE MINIMUM WAGE WOULD INCUR ONLY SMALL INFLATIONARY AND EMPLOYMENT COSTS.

00795 ADAMS, G.; CAIN, S.
DEFENSE DILEMMAS IN THE 1990'S
INTERNATIONAL SECURITY, 13(4) (SPR 89), 5-15.
THE ARTICLE EXAMINES THE EVENTS THAT HAVE LED UP TO THE DILEMMAS THAT THE NEW ADMINISTRATION FACES WITH REGARDS TO DEFENSE. DUE THE DEFENSE DEPARTMENT'S LACK OF FISCAL RESTRAINT, THERE IS NOW A SIGNIFICANT GAP BETWEEN PLANNED SYSTEMS AND THE RESOURCES NECESSARY TO IMPLEMENT THEM. CONTINUING ON THE PRESENT COURSE WILL LEAD TO BUDGETARY CHAOS AND MILITARY DISORGANIZATION. THE NEW ADMINISTRATION CAN PROVIDE ADAQUATE MILITARY SECURITY WITHIN BUDGETARY RESTRAINTS ONLY BY MAKING POLITICALLY DIFFICULT DECISIONS WHICH INVOLVE A FUNDAMENTAL RETINKING OF DEFENSE PRIORITIES, PROGRAMS, AND POLICIES.

00796 ADAMS, J.D.; KENNY, L., W.
THE RETENTION OF STATE GOVERNORS
PUBLIC CHOICE, 62(1) (JUL 89), 1-14.
THE PAPER DEVELOPS A MEASURE OF PERFORMANCE BY STATE ECONOMIES THAT IS SPECIFIC TO PARTICULAR ADMINISTRATIONS OF GOVERNORS OF THOSE STATES. BY CARRYING OUT SUCH A MEASUREMENT, AND BY CONTRASTING THE STATISTICAL INFLUENCE ON REELECTION CHANCES OF ECONOMIC PERFORMANCE DURING THE GOVERNOR'S TENURE WITH THE STATISTICAL INFLUENCES OF NATIONAL ECONOMIC CONDITIONS AND THE COATTAIL EFFECTS EMPHASIZED BY OTHER WRITERS, THE AUTHORS SEEK TO FURTHER CLARIFY THE DEGREE OF ACCOUNTABILITY. THEY FIND SUPPORT FOR A MODEL OF ELECTORAL ACCOUNTABILITY, IN WHICH GOVERNORS ARE POWERFUL IN STATE GOVERNMENTS AND STATE GOVERNMENTS HAVE THE ABILITY TO DIFFERENTIALLY TAX FIXED FACTORS RELATIVE TO NEIGHBORING STATES.

00797 ADAMS, J.R.
THE BIG FIX
AMERICAN SPECTATOR, 22(3) (MAR 89), 21-24.
THE SAVINGS AND LOAN DEBACLE IS NO LONGER THE PRODUCT OF REGIONAL RECESSION, OR DECLINING OIL PRICES. THE DEREGULATIONS OF THE EARLY 1980S PLAYED A ROLE, BUT NOT NECESSARILY THE ONE ARGUED BY REAGAN'S CRITICS. THE ROOT CAUSE IS THE ONE SINGLED OUT BY THE REGULATORS - FRAUD AND MISMANAGEMENT. AS CONGRESS SCURRIES AND POSTURES ON THE THRIFT CRISIS, YOU MAY EXPECT A GREAT DEAL OF INDIGNATION ABOUT EVERYTHING BUT ITS REAL CAUSE, THE POLITICIZATION OF FEDERAL SUPERVISION. THE UNDERPAID, UNDERTRAINED EXAMINERS WILL BE SCAPEGOATS, EVEN THOUGH THEIR HANDS WERE TIED BY CONGRESS.

00798 ADAMS, J.S.
CHANGE AND CONTINUITY IN SOVIET CENTRAL AMERICAN POLICY
PROBLEMS OF COMMUNISM, XXXVIII(2-3) (MAR 89), 112-120.
GORBACHEV'S NEW THINKING HAS INTRODUCED PERCEPTIBLE CHANGES IN SOVIET POLICY TOWARD CENTRAL AMERICA AND THE CARIBBEAN: NOTABLY, A NEW SOVIET RELUCTANCE TO CONTINUE PROVIDING MILITARY AND ECONOMIC SUPPORT TO CLIENTS IN THE REGION AT PREVIOUS LEVELS, SIGNS OF PRESSURE FROM MOSCOW ON CLIENT STATES AND MOVEMENTS TO SETTLE REGIONAL CONFLICTS BY POLITICAL RATHER THAN MILITARY MEANS, AND SOME EFFORTS BY THE USSR TO PLAY DOWN IDEOLOGY IN RELATIONS WITH STATES AND PARTIES OF THE REGION. WHILE THIS NEW POSTURE MAY OFFER A WINDOW OF OPPORTUNITY FOR REGIONAL STATES TO RESOLVE THEIR DIFFERENCES LESS BURDENED BY EAST-WEST ISSUES, THE SOVIET UNION CONTINUES TO SEEK POWER AND INFLUENCE IN THE REGION, NOT LEAST OF ALL BY PURSUING TRADITIONAL LINES OF BEHAVIOR, INCLUDING SUPPORT FOR GROUPS PURSUING SOCIAL REVOLUTION BY VIOLENT MEANS, PROVISION OF CONSIDERABLE AMOUNTS OF MILITARY, ECONOMIC, AND POLITICAL ASSISTANCE TO MAJOR CLIENT STATES, AND THE MOUNTING OF VIRULENT IDEOLOGICAL ATTACKS AND DISINFORMATION CAMPAIGNS AIMED AT THE UNITED STATES.

00799 ADAMS, L.E.
EUROPEAN SECURITY NEGOTIATIONS AND NATIONAL STRATEGY: U.S. AND SOVIET NEGOTIATING PATTERNS TOWARD A EUROPEAN SECURITY REGIME
DISSERTATION ABSTRACTS INTERNATIONAL, 50(1) (JUL 89), 249-A.
THE AUTHOR REVIEWS THREE SETS OF NEGOTIATIONS THAT CONSTITUTE THE CONTINUOUS PURSUIT OF A USA-USSR EUROPEAN SECURITY REGIME: THE GENEVA TALKS OF 1955, THE SURPRISE ATTACK TALKS OF 1958, AND THE MUTUAL AND BALANCED FORCE REDUCTION TALKS AND THE CONFERENCE ON COOPERATION AND SECURITY IN EUROPE OF THE 1970'S AND 1980'S. THE USA AND THE USSR HAVE USED THESE SECURITY NEGOTIATIONS NOT FOR ACCOMMODATION OF THE OTHER'S SECURITY INTERESTS OR FOR THE ALTERATION OF THE POST-WAR MILITARY STAND-OFF; RATHER EACH HAS USED THESE TALKS TO ATTEMPT TO REQUIRE THE OTHER TO ACCEPT THE PATTERNS OF SECURITY IT HAS ACHIEVED AS A RESULT OF ITS DOMINANT POSITION IN EUROPE.

00800 ADAMS, M.
AMERICA, ZIONISM, AND THE PROSPECTS FOR PEACE
JOURNAL OF PALESTINE STUDIES, 19(1) (FAL 89), 32-45.
THE DIVERSITY OF OPINION REGARDING A PEACEFUL SETTLEMENT IN PALESTINE IS OFFERED IN THIS ARTICLE. ARGUMENTS TO JUSTIFY BOTH AN OPTIMISTIC AND A PESSIMISTIC CONCLUSION TO THIS CONFLICT ARE PRESENTED. THE HISTORY OF THE ARAB-ISRAELI PROBLEM IS EXPLORED AND IT IS CONCLUDED THAT WITHOUT THE LIES, ZIONISM COULD NOT HAVE PROSPERED AS IT DID, AND THAT THE PATTERN OF DECEPTION HAS LONG SINCE BECOME A HABIT, ONE WHICH HAS BROUGHT OUTWARD SUCCESS AT THE COST OF INWARD, PSYCHOLOGICAL, CONFUSION. IT ALSO CONCLUDES THAT IT IS THE UNITED STATES, MORE THAN ANYONE ELSE, THAT IS PREVENTING A SOLUTION TO THE CONFLICT.

00801 ADAMS, M.
PRESS RESTRICTIONS IN PALESTINE
MIDDLE EAST INTERNATIONAL, (358) (SEP 89), 20.
THE ARTICLE SUMMARIZES A REPORT ENTITLED JOURNALISM UNDER OCCUPATION WHICH EXAMINES THE EFFECT OF ISRAEL'S USE OF MILITARY EMERGENCY LAWS ON THE PALESTINIAN PRESS. IT CONCLUDES ISRAEL'S RESTRICTION OF PALESTINIAN PRESS IS NOT A RESULT OF THE INTIFADA, BUT A CAUSE. IN FACT, THE INTIFADA STANDS AS UNDENIABLE PROOF THAT ISRAELI CENSORSHIP, DONE OSTENSIBLY IN THE NAME OF KEEPING THE PEACE AND PREVENTING UPRISING, IS COUNTERPRODUCTIVE.

00802 ADAMS, M.L.
THERE'S NO PLACE LIKE HOME: ON THE PLACE OF IDENTITY IN FEMINIST POLITICS
FEMINIST REVIEW, (31) (SPR 89), 22-33.
THE AUTHOR CONSIDERS THE ISSUE OF IDENTITY POLITICS AND WHETHER PARTICULAR VARIETIES OF IDENTITY POLITICS ARE APPROPRIATE IN PARTICULAR POLITICAL SITUATIONS. SHE ENDEAVORS TO ASCERTAIN WHAT IS AND IS NOT POSSIBLE USING A POLITICAL STRATEGY INFUSED WITH THE CONCEPTS OF IDENTITY AND PERSONAL EXPERIENCE.

00803 ADAMS, P.
FAMILY POLICY AND LABOR MIGRATION IN EAST AND WEST GERMANY
SOCIAL SERVICE REVIEW, 63(2) (JUN 89), 245-263.
FACED WITH IMMEDIATE LABOR SHORTAGES AND LOW BIRTH RATES,

GOVERNMENTS OF FOREIGN STATES HAVE ATTEMPTED TO REGULATE
THEIR LABOR SUPPLIES BY PREVENTING EMIGRATION OF WORKERS AND
CHILDREN, IMPORTING "GUEST WORKERS," SUPPORTING CHILD
REARING THROUGH SPECIAL SOCIAL PROVISIONS, OR ENCOURAGING
THE EMPLOYMENT OF WOMEN. THE CASE OF THE TWO GERMAN STATES
IS EXAMINED FOR THE LIGHT IT CASTS ON THE CAPACITY OF STATES
TO MANAGE THE REPRODUCTION OF THEIR LABOR FORCES OR TO
ENFORCE THE INTERGENERATIONAL CONTRACT ON WHICH THE WELFARE
STATE DEPENDS, THROUGH SOCIAL POLICY.

00804 ADAMSON, W.L.
FASCISM AND CULTURE: AVANT-GARDES AND SECULAR RELIGION IN
THE ITALIAN CASE
JOURNAL OF CONTEMPORARY HISTORY, 24(3) (JUL 89), 411-435.
THE AUTHOR PROBES THE POSSIBILITIES FOR AN "INTERNAL"
APPROACH TO ITALIAN FASCISM BY CONSIDERING THE WAY THAT
APPROACH HAS BEEN DEVELOPED TO DATE IN THE STUDY OF EUROPEAN
FASCISM GENERALLY. HE DOES NOT SEEK TO CONTRIBUTE TO PRIMARY
RESEARCH ABOUT THE RELATIONSHIP IN QUESTION, NOR DOES HE
ATTEMPT TO OFFER EXTENSIVE EVIDENCE FOR THE ARGUMENTS ABOUT
THAT RELATIONSHIP. RATHER, HIS GOAL IS TO SHED LIGHT ON THE
ORGANIZING PRINCIPLES OR PERSPECTIVES OF THE EXISTING
RESEARCH, TO SUBJECT THEM TO CRITICAL SCRUTINY, AND TO ARGUE
FOR A NEW DIRECTION IN RESEARCH.

00805 ADDIS, E.
WOMEN'S LIBERATION AND THE LAW ON SEXUAL VIOLENCE: THE
ITALIAN FEMINIST DEBATE
SOCIALIST REVIEW, 19(4) (OCT 89), 105-128.
THE ARTICLE EXAMINES THE ITALIAN FEMINIST MOVEMENT WITH
REGARDS TO RECENT MOVEMENTS AIMED AT CHANGING ITALY'S SEXUAL
VIOLENCE LAWS AS WELL AS THE LARGER CONTEXT OF VARIOUS
MOVEMENTS AND CAUSES IN THE PAST TWO IT CONCLUDES THAT
CONFLICT OVER SEXUAL VIOLENCE LAWS HAS SHARPLY ILLUMINATED
THE DIFFERENCES BETWEEN VARIOUS FACTIONS IN ITALY'S WOMEN'S
MOVEMENTS. IT CONCLUDES THAT IN THE FUTURE IT WILL BE
IMPOSSIBLE TO SPEAK OF THE WOMEN'S MOVEMENT AS ONE SINGLE
ACTOR WITH A SINGLE AGENDA.

00806 ADELMAN, I.; ROLAND-HOLST, D.W.; SARRIS, A.; YELDAN, E.
OPTIMAL ADJUSTMENT TO TRADE SHOCKS UNDER ALTERNATIVE
DEVELOPMENT STRATEGIES
JOURNAL OF POLICY MODELING, 11(4) (WIN 89), 451-505.
THE TECHNIQUES OF STOCHASTIC CONTROL ARE APPLIED TO A
CGE MODEL OF TURKEY TO COMPARE THE ROBUSTNESS OF ALTERNATIVE
DEVELOPMENT STRATEGIES TO DISRUPTIONS LIKE THE 1979 OIL
SHOCK. THE USE OF INSTRUMENTS AND THE EXTENT OF DEVIATION OF
STATE VARIABLES FROM THEIR TARGET VALUES ARE COMPARED UNDER
THREE DIFFERENT OBJECTIVE FUNCTIONS (GROWTH, STABILIZATION
OR EQUALITY) AND THREE DIFFERENT DEVELOPMENT STRATEGIES
(EXPORT EXPANSION, AGRICULTURAL DEVELOPMENT LED
INDUSTRALIZATION, OR IMPORT-SUBSTITUTION). THE RESULTS ARE
SENSITIVE TO BOTH DEVELOPMENT STRATEGIES AND OBJECTIVES.

00807 ADEN, J. B.
OIL AND POLITICS IN INDONESIA, 1945 TO 1980 (VOLUMES I AND
II)
DISSERTATION ABSTRACTS INTERNATIONAL, 49(8) (FEB 89),
2372-A.
THE AUTHOR ANALYZES CHANGES IN THE DISTRIBUTION OF OIL-
GENERATED INCOME AND CONTROL OF OIL PRODUCTION BETWEEN THE
GOVERNMENT OF INDONESIA AND FOREIGN OIL COMPANIES IN
INDONESIA FROM 1945 TO 1980. SHE EXAMINES THE HYPOTHESIS
THAT, WHEN INDONESIA'S GAINS IN INCOME AND CONTROL PRECEDED
OR LAGGED BEHIND THOSE OF OTHER OIL-PRODUCING COUNTRIES, THE
CAUSE WAS AN INTERNAL FACTOR - NAMELY, THE DEGREE OF
CONCENTRATION OF POWER IN THE NATIONAL-LEVEL GOVERNMENT.

00808 ADENIJI, O.
AFRICAN POLITICAL, MILITARY, AND ECONOMIC AFFAIRS IN THEIR
RELATIONSHIP TO SECURITY, DISARMAMENT, AND CONFIDENCE-
BUILDING
DISARMAMENT. XII(1) (WIN 89), 51-67.
AFRICA'S SITUATION CALLS FOR GREAT IMAGINATION IN THE
PURSUIT OF CONTINENTAL SELF-RELIANCE. WHILE ABIDING BY ITS
CHARTER PLEDGE OF NON-INTERFERENCE IN THE INTERNAL AFFAIRS
OF MEMBER STATES, THE OAU CAN AT LEAST APPEAL TO ITS MEMBERS
TO PUT THEIR INTERNAL POLITICAL SITUATIONS IN ORDER GREATER
ATTENTION MUST BE PAID TO THE DEVELOPMENT OF CRISIS
MANAGEMENT, CONFLICT RESOLUTION, AND CONFIDENCE-BUILDING
MEASURES IN AFRICA. PEACE-MAKING AND PEACE-KEEPING
CAPACITIES MUST BE DEVELOPED THROUGH IMAGINATIVE MEASURES.
CONSIDERATION SHOULD BE GIVEN TO CONFIDENCE-BUILDING
MEASURES THAT WOULD REDUCE MILITARY RIVALRY, AND SUBREGIONAL
AND REGIONAL STEPS FOR ECONOMIC INTEGRATION SHOULD BE
HASTENED.

00809 ADEWOLE, M.F.
EXPLORING THE EXPORT POTENTIALS OF DEVELOPING COUNTRIES:
CAN INDIVIDUALIZED GOODS MAKE A DIFFERENCE
DISSERTATION ABSTRACTS INTERNATIONAL, 50(1) (JUL 89),
253-A.
THE AUTHOR INVESTIGATES WHETHER THE EXPORT OF
INDIVIDUALIZED GOODS HAS THE POTENTIAL FOR CONTRIBUTING TO

THE FINANCING OF DEVELOPMENT EXPENDITURES IN LESS DEVELOPED
COUNTRIES. TRADE IMBALANCES BETWEEN LESS DEVELOPED AND
DEVELOPED COUNTRIES HAVE TRADITIONALLY BEEN ADDRESSED
THROUGH EXTERNAL FINANCES, INCLUDING LOANS, INVESTMENT, AND
GRANTS-IN-AID. THIS DISSERTATION SUGGESTS THAT THE MORE
RESPONSIVE EARNINGS FROM HANDICRAFTS AND TOURISM ARE TO THE
INCOMES OF DEVELOPED COUNTRIES, THE MORE SUCH PRODUCTS CAN
CONTRIBUTE TO THIRD WORLD NATIONAL ECONOMICS AND THE LESS
DEPENDENT ON EXTERNAL SOURCES OF FINANCE THE LESS DEVELOPED
COUNTRIES WILL BECOME.

00810 ADIE, W.A.C.
THE LONG MARCH TO THE MARKET
ENCOUNTER, LXXIII(4) (NOV 89), 16-25.
THE MOST SURPRISING THING ABOUT CHINA'S MASSACRE IN JUNE
1989 WAS THE NUMBER OF PEOPLE WHO WERE SURPRISED BY IT. ONCE
DENG XIAOPING AND HIS CRONIES HAD DEFINED THE SITUATION AS
"TURMOIL," THE RESPONSE WAS PREDICTABLE. BUT THE "WINNERS"
IN THE SPRING'S EVENTS HAVE LOST BOTH HEGEMONY AND DAO, THAT
ALL-IMPORTANT MORAL INFLUENCE AND SOURCE OF POWER FOR
CHINESE LEADERSHIP. ON THE OTHER HAND, THE OUTLOOK FOR THE
PEOPLE OF CHINA IS GOOD, PROVIDED THAT THE SITUATION IS
PROPERLY UNDERSTOOD AND HANDLED, ESPECIALLY AS REGARDS THE
SECURITY OF HONG KONG AND ITS INHABITANTS. CHINA HAS
IRREVERSIBLY BECOME PART OF THE GLOBAL, BORDERLESS MARKET OF
GOODS, FUNDS, AND INFORMATION. DAILY IT BECOMES MORE CLOSELY
LINKED TO (AND MORE LIKE) TAIWAN, SOUTH KOREA, JAPAN, HONG
KONG, SINGAPORE, AND CHINATOWNS AROUND THE WORLD.

00811 ADLER, G.
WHAT'S GOOD FOR GENERAL MOTORS? BLACK WORKER'S RESPONSE TO
DISINVESTMENT, OCTOBER-NOVEMBER 1986
JOURNAL OF SOUTHERN AFRICAN STUDIES, 15(3) (APR 89),
415-439.
THIS ARTICLE STUDIES THE SITUATION IN SOUTH AFRICA
RESULTING FROM THE GM WORKERS DISPUTATION OVER THE COMPANY'S
DISINVESTMENT STRATEGY. THE CASE IS CLOSLY EXAMINED WITH THE
BACKGROUND OF CRISIS IN THE MOTOR INDUSTRY, THE EXISTENCE OF
SANCTIONS, THE DISINVESTMENT AND THE STRIKING OF THE WORKERS.
THE CASE OF THE DEFEATED WORKERS CHALLENGES OTHER UNIONS TO
DEVELOP MORE EFFECTIVE STRATEGIES TO COPE WITH NEW
CONDITIONS FOLLOWING THE PASSAGE OF SANCTIONS.

00812 ADONIS, A.
GREAT BRITIAN
ELECTORAL STUDIES, 8(3) (DEC 89), 262-269.
THIS ARTICLE EXAMINES THE RESULTS OF THE 1989 ELECTION
FOR BRITIAN'S 78 SEATS IN THE EUROPEAN PARLIAMENT. THE THREE
WEEK CAMPAIGN IS REPLAYED AND AN ANALYSIS OF THE ELECTION IS
PRESENTED WITH TABLES. IT CONCLUDES THAT SO FAR AS THE
VOTING IS CONCERNED, THE ONLY CONCLUSION WHICH CAN BE
REACHED WITH ANY CONFIDENCE IS THAT THE 1989 EURO-ELECTION
WAS HIGHLY INCONCLUSIVE.

00813 ADRIASOLA, C.
CHILE: U.S. EMBARGO
THIRD WORLD WEEK, 8(4) (MAR 89), 26-27.
THE UNITED STATES' FIVE-DAY BAN ON CHILEAN FRUIT BRUISED
BILATERAL RELATIONS, BUT NO PERMANENT DAMAGE IS THOUGHT
LIKELY. THE BRIEF EMBARGO, WHICH WAS IMPOSED AFTER U.S.
INSPECTORS FOUND TRACE AMOUNTS OF CYANIDE IN A GRAPE
SHIPMENT, DISRUPTED CHILE'S ECONOMY AND AWAKENED ANTI-YANKEE
FEELINGS. EVEN THE MOST CHARITABLE CHILEANS REGARDED THE U.S.
BAN AS AN OVERREACTION.

00814 ADVISORY COMMISSION ON INTERGOVERNMENTAL RELATIONS
CHANGING PUBLIC ATTITUDES ON GOVERNMENTS AND TAXES, 1988
AVAILABLE FROM NTIS, NO. PB89-149033/GAR, 1988, 84.
MAJOR FINDINGS FROM THE U.S. ADVISORY COMMISSION ON
INTERGOVERNMENTAL RELATIONS JUNE 1988 POLL ON CHANGING
PUBLIC ATTITUDES ON GOVERNMENT AND TAXES ARE PRESENTED. THE
FINDINGS INCLUDE: THE PUBLIC WAS EVENLY DIVIDED OVER WHETHER
IT GETS THE MOST FOR ITS MONEY FROM THE FEDERAL GOVERNMENT,
STATE GOVERNMENT, OR LOCAL GOVERNMENT. FOR THE TENTH
STRAIGHT YEAR, THE FEDERAL INCOME TAX WAS RATED AS THE WORST
(LEAST FAIR) TAX. RESPONDENTS WERE ALSO ASKED A NEW SERIES
OF QUESTIONS ABOUT THE EFFICIENCY OF THE FEDERAL, STATE, AND
LOCAL GOVERNMENTS. JUST OVER HALF OF THOSE SURVEYED WERE NOT
AWARE THAT THEIR STATE HAS ITS OWN CONSTITUTION. THE PUBLIC
HAS ALMOST EVENLY DIVIDED ABOUT THE WISDOM OF SPENDING STATE
AND LOCAL FUNDS ABROAD TO PROMOTE INTERNATIONAL TRADE. A 59%
MAJORITY SAID THAT IT IS IMPROPER FOR CITY COUNCILS TO PASS
FOREIGN POLICY RESOLUTIONS. A PLURALITY OF RESPONDENTS (36%)
GAVE ROADS AND BRIDGES A GRADE OF 'C' ON THEIR PERFORMANCE,
AND ANOTHER 27% GRADED THEM AT 'B'.

00815 AFRAZ, S.
THE JUNAGADH AFFAIR AND THE HYDERABAD CASE
ROUND TABLE, 309 (JAN 89), 101-106.
THE QUESTION OF THE ACCESSION OF THE THREE PRINCELY
STATES OF JUNAGADH, HYDERABAD AND KASHMIR WAS THE CAUSE OF
MUCH FRICTION BETWEEN PAKISTAN AND INDIA AT THE TIME OF
PARTITION. IN THE BRITISH POSITION DURING THE DEBATES
LEADING UP TO THE PASSAGE OF THE INDIAN INDEPENDENCE ACT,

THERE WERE STRONG EXHORTATION THAT EACH OF THESE STATES SHOULD ACCEDE TO EITHER INDIA OR PAKISTAN AND NOT ATTEMPT SEPARATE EXISTENCE AS A LONG RANGE PROPOSITION. THIS ARTICLE DESCRIBES THE DIPLOMATIC EFFORTS MADE TO PEACEFULLY RESOLVE ACCESSION RESENTMENTS WHICH DEVELOPED OVER CHOICE AND ETHNOLOGICAL/GEOGOPHICAL CONSIDERATIONS.

00816 AFTERGOOD, S.
TOWARDS A BAN ON NUCLEAR POWER IN EARTH ORBIT
SPACE POLICY, 5(1) (FEB 89), 25-40.
TO DATE THE USA HAS LAUNCHED 23 SPACE NUCLEAR POWER SYSTEMS, AND THE USSR MORE THAN 30. ABOUT 15% OF ALL NUCLEARPOWERED SPACECRAFT HAVE SUFFERED ACCIDENTS, LAUNCH ABORTS OR OTHER FAILURES. BEYOND THE ENVIRONMENTAL HAZARDS OF SUCH INCIDENTS, THE PRIMARY APPLICATIONS OF NUCLEAR POWER IN ORBIT ARE THEMSELVES A PROVOCATION AND A THREAT. THE LARGE NUCLEAR POWER SOURCES NOW UNDER DEVELOPMENT WILL EXACERBATE THESE ENVIRONMENTAL AND STRATEGIC RISKS. THE AUTHOR ARGUES IN FAVOUR OF THE BAN ON NUCLEAR POWER IN ORBIT PROPOSED BY THE FEDERATION OF AMERICAN SCIENTISTS AND THE COMMITTEE OF SOVIET SCIENTISTS AGAINST THE NUCLEAR THREAT.

00817 AGANBEGYAN, A.
PHASED ACCELERATION
WORLD MARXIST REVIEW, 31(1) (JAN 88), 103-113.
THE IMMEDIATE TASK OF PERESTROIKA IS TO BREAK UP THE MECHANISM, WHICH TOOK SHAPE IN THE PAST AND WHICH HAS ACTED AS A BRAKE ON OUR GROWTH, AND TO REPLACE IT WITH A MECHANISM OF ACCELERATION. WHAT IS EVEN MORE IMPORTANT IS TO GIVE GROWTH A NEW QUALITY AND TO BRING ABOUT A RADICAL CHANGE IN ITS CONTENT, SOURCES AND ORIENTATION. THE ACCELERATION IS TO RENOVATE SOVIET ECONOMY AND TO BOOST IT TO A LEVEL AT WHICH ALL THE ADVANTAGES OF SOCIALISM ARE MORE AMPLY IN EVIDENCE. THE IDEA IS TO CARRY THE ECONOMY TO THE MOST FORWARD LINE, TO ATTAIN THE WORLD'S HIGHEST PRODUCTIVITY OF SOCIAL LABOUR AND PRODUCT QUALITY AND TO IMPROVE THE SOVIET PEOPLE'S WELL BEING.

00818 AGNELLI, G.
THE EUROPE OF 1992
FOREIGN AFFAIRS, 68(4) (FAL 89), 61-70.
THE CURRENT UNITY OF WESTERN EUROPE IS NOT SO MUCH THE RESULT OF A UTOPIAN DREAM AS IT IS THE POLITICAL RECOGNITION OF ECONOMIC REALITY: THE REALITY OF GLOBAL MARKETS, THE REALITY OF ECONOMIC INTERDEPENDENCE, AND THE REALITY OF COMPETITIVE PRESSURES. THE ERECTION OF A SINGLE EUROPEAN MARKET IN 1992 WILL NOT LEAD TO DISUNITY DUE TO NATIONAL AND LOCAL POLITICAL PRESSURES NOR WILL IT CREATE A "FORTRESS EUROPE" THAT WILL CLOSE EUROPEAN TRADE TO OUTSIDERS.

00819 AGRANOFF, R.; PATTAKOS, A.N.
MANAGEMENT OF HUMAN SERVICES IN LOCAL GOVERNMENTS: A NATIONAL SURVEY
STATE AND LOCAL GOVERNMENT REVIEW, 21(2) (SPR 89), 74-83.
THIS PAPER EXAMINES THE CURRENT ROLES OF LOCAL GENERAL-PURPOSE GOVERNMENTS IN ADMINISTERING HUMAN SERVICES. IT IS BASED ON A SURVEY OF MULTIPLE TYPES OF JURISDICTIONAL INVOLVEMENTS IN SERVICES TO THE ELDERLY, CHILDREN AND YOUTH, PERSONS WITH DISABILITIES, AND THE GENERAL POPULATION, AS WELL AS VARIOUS ASPECTS OF HUMAN SERVICES PLANNING AND MANAGEMENT PRACTICES, INCLUDING THE EXTENT TO WHICH CITIES AND COUNTIES HAVE WORKED WITH OTHER GOVERNMENTS AND NONGOVERNMENTAL ENTITIES WHEN DEALING WITH HUMAN PROBLEMS. ALTHOUGH RARELY FIRST-LINE OPERATORS OF HUMAN SERVICES, LOCAL GOVERNMENTS ARE INVOLVED IN A HOST OF ARRANGEMENTS WITH OTHER GOVERNMENTS AND AGENCIES, IN ORDER TO RESPOND TO THE SOCIAL PROBLEMS IN THEIR MIDST. THIS PRESENTS A NEED FOR KINDS OF MANAGEMENT THAT DIFFER FROM THE SINGLE-ORGANIZATION SERVICE DELIVERY APPROACH. EMERGING MANAGEMENT CHALLENGES SUGGESTED BY THE SURVEY ARE DISCUSSED.

00820 AGRON, L.
A LANDMARK GATHERING
MIDSTREAM, XXXV(4) (MAY 89), 26-32.
THE DELEGATES AT THE FIRST INTERNATIONAL JEWISH FEMINIST CONFERENCE AGREED THAT THROUGH SUBSEQUENT CONTACT AND COALITION-BUILDING JEWISH FEMINISTS WILL ENHANCE THEIR PROSPECTS FOR SUCCESSFULLY ENACTING THEIR SOCIAL AND POLITICAL AGENDA. ONE OF THE ISSUES THAT PROMPTED THE MOST SPIRITED DISCUSSION AT THE CONFERENCE WAS HOW TO ACHIEVE PEACE BETWEEN ISRAELIS AND PALESTINIANS.

00821 AGUDA, A.S.
CRISIS, REPRESSION AND THE PROSPECTS FOR DEMOCRACY IN NIGERIA
SCANDINAVIAN JOURNAL OF DEVELOPMENT ALTERNATIVES, 8(4) (DEC 89), 107-122.
THIS ARTICLE LAYS THE BACKGROUND TO THE REBELLION IN NIGERIA AGAINST THE IMF AFTER WHICH THE UPRISING ITSELF IS DOCUMENTED. THE PROGNOSIS OF THESE MILITANT PROTESTS AGAINST OPPRESSION AND WHAT THEY PORTEND FOR THE TRANSITION TO DEMOCRACY ARE/ALSO EXAMINED. IT ARGUES THAT SAP AND OTHER IMF POLICIES BEING IMPLEMENTED IN NIGERIA HAVE STRUCTURED THE FUTURE OF DEMOCRACY. IT ILLUSTRATES THAT THE SAME

GOVERNMENT WHICH PROFESSES A TRANSITION TO DEMOCRACY IS, THROUGH PROSCRIPTIONS AND SIMILAR EXCESSES IN TOTAL DISREGARD FOR THE CONSTITUTION AND THE COURTS, ERODING THE VERY FOUNDATIONS FOR DEMOCRACY.

00822 AGUILAR, F.V. JR.
THE PHILIPPINE PEASANT AS CAPITALIST: BEYOND THE CATEGORIES OF IDEAL-TYPICAL CAPITALISM
JOURNAL OF PEASANT STUDIES, 17(1) (OCT 89), 41-67.
AS ELSEWHERE, MARXIST DISCUSSIONS ABOUT THE PEASANTRY IN THE PHILIPPINES HAVE ALSO BEEN INFORMED BY 'ARTICULATION THEORY' WHICH RENDERS IT DIFFICULT TO CONCEIVE OF PEASANTS AS FULL PARTICIPANTS IN THE CAPITALIST LABOUR PROCESS EITHER AS 'CAPITALISTS' OR 'PROLETARIANS'. THIS CONCEPTUAL DIFFICULTY IS TRACED TO IDEAL-TYPICAL PRESUPPOSITIONS ABOUT CAPITALISM AND ITS 'STANDARD' FORM OF PRODUCTIVE RELATIONS. THE CONVENTIONAL CATEGORIES OF MARXISM THUS BECOME INADEQUATE IN ANALYSING SOCIETIES IN THE WORLD-CAPITALIST PERIPHERY. HOWEVER, THE METHODOLOGY OF HISTORICAL MATERIALISM IS RELEVANT IN ILLUMINATING THE CAPITALIST NATURE OF TENANCY AS WELL AS THE MULTIPLE RELATIONS OF EXPLOITATION OBSERVABLE IN SMALL-SCALE RICE FARMING IN THE PHILIPPINES.

00823 AGURSKY, M.
PILGRIMAGE OF TRUTH
MIDSTREAM, XXXV(9) (DEC 89), 23-25.
RECENT DEVELOPMENTS IN THE SOVIET UNION AND EASTERN EUROPE HAVE DEMONSTRATED THE BANKRUPTCY OF WESTERN SOVIET STUDIES. THE MAJORITY OF BOOKS AND MYRIADS OF ARTICLES ON THE USSR AND THE COMMUNIST BLOC HAVE BECOME OBSOLETE AND EVEN HARMFUL.

00824 AGURSKY, M.
SOVIET DISINFORMATION AND FORGERIES
INTERNATIONAL JOURNAL ON WORLD PEACE, VI(I) (JAN 89), 13-30.
THE ARTICLE ANALYZES THE USE OF FORGERIES BY THE SOVIET SECRET POLICE. EXAMPLES INCLUDE FAKED CONSPIRACIES WHOSE REAL PURPOSE WAS TO TRAP GENUINE CONSPIRATORS AND TO PENETRATE WHITE EMIGRATION AND FOREIGN INTELLIGENCE IN ORDER TO PARALYZE THEM, FORGED CONSPIRACIES AGAINST OPPOSITION WITHIN THE PARTY, AND FAKED DEFECTIONS OF TWO SOVIET DIPLOMATS AND THE WORKS THEY PUBLISHED ON JOSEF STALIN. IN SPITE OF THEIR OBVIOUS CRUDENESS, SOVIET FORGERIES WERE ACCEPTED IN THE WEST AND TRANSLATED INTO MANY LANGUAGES. SIGNIFICANT EXAMPLES OF FORGERY INCLUDE THE OMNIPOTENT MONARCHIST CONSPIRACY TREST, AND THE PUBLICATION OF LITIVINOV'S DIARIES BY ANDRE DEUSTCH IN 1955.

00825 AGYEMANG BADU, O.O.
THE AKAN SYSTEM OF GOVERNMENT AND ITS CONTRIBUTION TO THE MODERN GOVERNMENT OF GHANA
DISSERTATION ABSTRACTS INTERNATIONAL, 50(1) (JUL 89), 253-A.
THE AUTHOR STUDIES THE AKAN SYSTEM OF GOVERNMENT AND ITS CONTRIBUTION TO THE MODERN GOVERNMENT OF GHANA. HE EXAMINES THE GOVERNMENT OF AN AKAN STATE (OMAN) IN PRE-COLONIAL DAYS, THE EARLY HISTORICAL CONTACTS AND RELATIONS BETWEEN THE BRITISH AND THE NATIVES LEADING TO THE INSTITUTION OF THE PAX BRITANNICA OVER THE TERRITORY, THE CONSTITUTIONAL GOVERNMENTS OF GHANA SINCE INDEPENDENCE, AND THE MILITARY REGIMES THAT HAVE RULED GHANA SINCE 1966.

00826 AHAMED, E.
REGIONAL UNDERSTANDING THROUGH ECONOMIC AND SOCIO-CULTURAL INTERACTION: THE CASE OF SAARC
SOUTH ASIA JOURNAL, 2(3) (JAN 89), 233-250.
THE PAPER ANALYZES THE PROSPECTS OF SOUTH ASIAN REGIONAL COOPERATION WITH EMPHASIS ON ECONOMIC AND CULTURAL COOPERATION. IT FOCUSES ON THE SOUTH ASIAN ASSOCIATION FOR REGIONAL COOPERATION (SAARC), AN ORGANIZATION THAT IS THE ATTEMPTING TO INCREASE ECONOMIC AND CULTURAL COOPERATION, WHILE AT THE SAME TIME ADMITTING TO POLITICAL DIFFERENCES BETWEEN THE NATIONS INVOLVED. TO ANALYZE THE SAARC'S POTENTIAL FOR SUCCESS, THE ARTICLE EXAMINES THE ROLE OF POLITICAL HARMONY IN SOUTH ASIA, THE EXISTING REGIONAL MILLIEU AND THE INTERNATIONAL POWER EQUATION, AND THE PRESENT PATTERN OF LEADERSHIP, IN SOUTH ASIA.

00827 AHEARN, R.J.
A MORE OPEN JAPANESE MARKET?
CRS REVEIW, 10(6) (JUL 89), 3-5.
JAPAN HAS A LONG WAY TO GO TO REACH ITS POTENTIAL AS A MAJOR IMPORTER OF MANUFACTURED GOODS RELATIVE TO THE SIZE OF ITS ECONOMY. FOR THIS TO HAPPEN, A MAZE OF BARRIERS TO IMPORTS WILL HAVE TO BE REDUCED OR ELIMINATED. A MUCH MORE OPEN JAPANESE MARKET AND AN END TO ITS CLOSED MARKET IMAGE WILL REQUIRE CONSIDERABLE POLITICAL LEADERSHIP FROM THE GOVERNMENT IN TOKYO.

00828 AHEARN, R.J.
A MORE UNIFIED EUROPE AND THE ALLIANCE
CRS REVEIW, 10(4) (APR 89), 23-24.

DRIVEN BY THE 1992 PLAN FOR THE CREATION OF A TRULY
UNIFIED EUROPEAN MARKET, U.S. RELATIONS WITH ITS EUROPEAN
ALLIES ARE ENTERING A HISTORIC CROSSROADS. WHILE ATTENTION
HAS FOCUSED PRIMARILY ON THE IMPLICATIONS FOR U.S. ECONOMIC
INTERESTS, THE STAKES FOR OTHER ALLIANCE RELATIONS ARE ALSO
ENORMOUS. THE 1992 PLAN REPRESENTS A NEW VISION OF A SELF-
ASSURED, MORE ASSERTIVE EUROPE. HOW FAR AND HOW FAST EUROPE
TRANSFORMS ITSELF IN THE YEARS AHEAD COULD FUNDAMENTALLY
INFLUENCE AND EVEN TOTALLY RESHAPE U.S.-EUROPEAN RELATIONS.
A MORE UNIFIED EUROPE COULD CREATE BOTH OPPORTUNITIES AND
THREATS TO LONGSTANDING POLITICAL, MILITARY, AND ECONOMIC
RELATIONSHIPS WITHIN NATO.

00829 AHEARNE, J.
FIXING THE NATION'S NUCLEAR WEAPONS REACTORS
TECHNOLOGY REVIEW, 92(5) (JUL 89), 24-29.
THE ARTICLE ANALYZES THE INCREASING PROBLEMS OF SAFETY
WITH REAGRDS TO THE AGING NUCLEAR WEAPONS PLANTS OF THE US.
THE PROBLEMS OF ANTIQUATED EQUIPMENT AND NEGLIGENCE ARE
SIGNIFICANT AND ALTHOUGH NEW OVERSIGHT GROUPS HAVE BEEN
ESTABLISHED TO ANALYZE THE PROBLEM, IT IS EXPECTED THAT LONG-
TERM SOLUTIONS WILL NOT BE FORTHCOMING FOR YEARS.

00830 AHMAD, A.A.
THE IMPACT OF INFORMATION CHANGE UPON CONGRESSIONAL
APPROPRIATIONS DELIBERATION
DISSERTATION ABSTRACTS INTERNATIONAL, 50(3) (SEP 89),
788-A.
THIS STUDY TESTED THE IMPACT OF INFORMATION CHANGE,
REPRESENTED BY REFORM IN THE BUDGETARY SYSTEM, ON
CONGRESSIONAL BEHAVIOR. IT FOCUSED ON THE HOUSE
APPROPRIATIONS SUBCOMMITTEES BECAUSE OF THEIR LARGE ROLE IN
BUDGETARY MATTERS AND THE IMPACT OF THE SUBCOMMITTEES'
DECISION-MAKING PROCESSES ON THEIR MEMBERS' BEHAVIOR.

00831 AHMAD, E.; BUTTERFIELD, J.; CHOMSKY, N.; DOYON, D.;
HURHITZ, D.; RYAN, S.; ZOGBY, J.
MIDDLE EAST PEACE PRIORITIES IN THE US
MIDDLE EAST REPORT, 19(158) (MAY 89), 6-11.
THE AUTHORS ENUMERATE THE ISSUES THAT MUST BE SETTLED IN
THE MIDDLE EAST AND DISCUSS RECENT AMERICAN DIPLOMATIC MOVES
THERE.

00832 AHMAD, M.
MULTILATERAL AND BILATERAL APPROACHES TO DISARMAMENT
DISARMAMENT, XII(3) (AUT 89), 35-39.
THERE IS SUBSTANCE IN THE ASSERTION THAT, IN CONCRETE
TERMS, BILATERAL AND/OR OTHER RESTRICTED FORUMS ARE
PROVIDING MORE EFFICIENT MECHANISMS FOR CONCLUDING ARMS
CONTROL AND DISARMAMENT AGREEMENTS THAN THE UNITED NATIONS.
BUT THIS SHOULD BE NEITHER UNEXPECTED NOR DISAPPOINTING. THE
MULTILATERAL APPROACH IS NOT IN COMPETITION WITH THE
BILATERAL OR VICE VERSA. THE ONE DOES NOT CONTRADICT THE
OTHER. THEY ARE NOT MUTUALLY EXCLUSIVE. THE MULTILATERALISM
THAT THE UN FACILITATES IS THE INDISPENSABLE ADJUNCT OF
BILATERALISM. THERE IS A COMPLEX INTERACTION BETWEEN THEM
THAT SHOULD LEAD TO A MUTUALLY SUPPORTIVE RELATIONSHIP. BOTH
ARE RELEVANT AND BOTH CONTRIBUTE TO AN ENVIRONMENT FROM
WHICH THE TWO APPROACHES, TOGETHER OR SEPARATELY, CAN DERIVE
BENEFIT. AT A GIVEN PERIOD IN TIME, THE MULTILATERAL
APPROACH MAY HAVE GREATER RELEVANCE, BUT EACH IS NECESSARY.

00833 AHMANN, R.
THE GERMAN TREATIES WITH ESTONIA AND LATVIA OF 7 JUNE 1939:
BARGAINING PLOY OR AN ALTERNATIVE FOR GERMAN-SOVIET
UNDERSTANDING?
JOURNAL OF BALTIC STUDIES, XX(4) (WIN 89), 337-364.
HISTORIANS HAVE TENDED TO NEGLECT THE GERMAN NON-
AGGRESSION PACTS WITH ESTONIA AND LATVIA OF JUNE 1939, WHICH
HERE CONCLUDED TWO MONTHS BEFORE THE GERMAN-SOVIET PACT. A
CLOSE LOOK AT THE BACKGROUND OF GERMANY'S TREATY OFFERS TO
LATVIA AND ESTONIA REFUTES THE INTERPRETATION THAT THEY WERE
AN ANSWER TO ROOSEVELT'S ADDRESS OF APRIL 15, 1939, OR THAT
THEY WERE A DIPLOMATIC MOVE TOWARD MOSCOW. ANALYSIS
UNDERLINES THAT THEY WERE, IN FACT, WHAT THEY FIRST APPEARED
TO BE: THE EXPRESSION OF A SPECIAL GERMAN POLICY TOWARDS THE
BALTIC STATES IN THE SPECIFIC SITUATION OF THE SPRING AND
SUMMER OF 1939. THE TREATY NEGOTIATIONS FORMED PART OF
GERMAN EFFORTS TO SECURE, ECONOMICALLY AND MILITARILY, THE
LOCALIZATION OF AN ATTACK ON POLAND WITHOUT AN UNDERSTANDING
WITH THE USSR.

00834 AHMED, A.S.
IDENTITY AND IDEOLOGY IN PAKISTAN: AN INTERVIEW
THIRD WORLD QUARTERLY, 11(4) (OCT 89), 54 - 69.
THIS ARTICLE IS AN INTERVIEW OF AKBAR S. AHMED BY SHAHID
QADIR. IT COVERS THE RESILENCE OF RACE AND RELIGION IN THE
COMMUNAL POLITICS OF SOUTH ASIA, ISLAMIC UNIVERSALISM,
FORMER GENERAL ZIA, BENAZIR, THE HEALING OF ETHNIC DIVIDES
IN PAKISTAN, PUNJABI DOMINANCE, THE MILITARY, PROVINCIAL
DEMANDS FOR AUTONOMY, THE FUTURE OF KARACHI, AND THE
RESOLUTION OF PAKISTAN'S ETHNIC QUAGMIRE AND THE PREVENTION
OF AN IMPLOSION OF PAKISTAN SOCIETY.

00835 AHMED, F.
A POLITICAL FARCE
INDIA TODAY, XIV(1) (JAN 89), 36-37.
IN BIHAR, THE SIMMERING TENSION BETWEEN GOVERNOR GOVIND
NARAIN SINGH, ASSEMBLY SPEAKER SHIV CHANDA JHA, FORMER CHIEF
MINISTER JAGANNATH MISHRA, AND CHIEF MINISTER BHAGHAT JHA
AZAD ERUPTED WITH POLITICAL SAVAGERY IN EARLY 1989. SINGH
SAID THAT IT WAS DIFFICULT TO WORK WITH AZAD WHILE THE CHIEF
MINISTER COMPLAINED THAT HE COULD NOT FUNCTION WITH SINGH
AND JHA IN THEIR POSITIONS.

00836 AHMED, F.
DARJEELING: LOSING GROUND
INDIA TODAY, XIV(11) (JUN 89), 25.
RAJIV GANDHI IS CONVINCED THAT THE CONGRESS (I), DESPITE
ITS FORTY PERCENT OF THE VOTES IN THE LAST ASSEMBLY POLL, IS
AS GOOD AS DEAD IN WEST BENGAL. HIS RECENT VISIT TO
DARJEELING DEMONSTRATED THAT HE IS IN A MOOD TO DESERT THIS
CONSTITUENCY.

00837 AHMED, F.
DEATH BY POLITICS
INDIA TODAY, XIV(8) (MAY 89), 24-26.
POLITICAL VIOLENCE AND GUTTER POLITICS ARE BECOMING A
WAY OF LIFE IN WEST BENGAL, WHERE SEVERAL CONGRESS (I) PARTY
WORKERS HAVE BEEN KILLED BY MARXISTS. MANY CONGRESS (I)
MEMBERS INSIST THAT THE MARXISTS HAVE A SYSTEMATIC PLAN TO
ELIMINATE ALL THEIR ACTIVE WORKERS.

00838 AHMED, F.; MENON, R.; RATTAN, K.
DIALECTICAL WARS
INDIA TODAY, XIV(8) (APR 89), 31-33.
TWENTY-FIVE YEARS AFTER THE THE COMMUNIST PARTY OF INDIA
SPLIT INTO TWO ORGANIZATIONS, FEAR AND SUSPICION CONTINUE TO
CLOUD UNITY EFFORTS BETWEEN THE CPI (M) AND THE CPI. UNITY
HAS BEEN A TOP PRIORITY FOR THE CPI FOR SOME TIME, BUT THE
MARXISTS CONTINUE TO WAVER ON THE ISSUE.

00839 AHMED, F.
MONSOON OF DISCONTENT
INDIA TODAY, 14(15) (AUG 89), 30-32.
THIS IS A REPORT ON ASSAM CHIEF MINISTER, PRAFULLA KUMAR
MAHANTA'S, FIGHT TO KEEP HIS GRIP ON HIS PARTY AND THE STATE,
SINCE AFTER ONLY THREE YEARS IN POWER, AGITATIONS,
DISSIDENCE AND SCANDALS RUN RIFE. IT EXAMINES CHARGES MADE
BY HIM THAT CONGRESS (1) AND HIS OWN PARTY DISSIDENTS, THE
ASOM GANA PARISHAD, ARE THREATS TO HIS GOVERNMENT. IT
DETAILS THE LATEST PROBLEM, THE RETURN OF FORMER CONGRESS
(1) CHIEF MINISTER, HITESWAR SAIKIA, TO ACTIVE POLITICS.

00840 AHMED, F.
TEMPORARY REPRIEVE
INDIA TODAY, XIV(3) (FEB 89), 30-32.
BHAGHAT JHA AZAD, THE MAN HAND-PICKED BY PRIME MINISTER
RAJIV GANDHI AS BIHAR'S CHIEF MINISTER, HAS BEEN UNDER SIEGE
FROM DISSIDENTS. AFTER MUCH VACILLATION, THE CENTRE HAS
ANNOUNCED THAT IT WILL NOT REPLACE AZAD. IT WAS DECIDED THAT
DUMPING AZAD WOULD ENCOURAGE DISSIDENCE ELSEWHERE,
PARTICULARLY IN GUJARAT AND RAJASTHAN.

00841 AHMED, F.; GUPTA, U.S.
THE OLD GUARD RETURNS
INDIA TODAY, XIV(6) (MAR 89), 18-20.
JAGANNATH PAHADIA HAS BEEN CHOSEN AS THE NEW GOVERNOR OF
BIHAR, JAGANNATH MISHRA IS THE NEW PRESIDENT OF THE BIHAR
PRADESH CONGRESS (I) COMMITTEE, AND SATYENDRA NARAIN SINHA
IS THE NEW CHIEF MINISTER. EVEN BEFORE SINHA COULD BE SWORN
IN, SOME LEGISLATORS QUESTIONED THE SAGACITY OF HIS CHOICE.

00842 AHMED, N.
GOVERNMENT POLITICS AND VILLAGE REFORM IN BANGLADESH: A
NOTE ON ALTERNATIVE APPROACHES
INTERNATIONAL REVIEW OF ADMINISTRATIVE SCIENCES, 55(3)
(SEP 89), 493-516.
THIS ARTICLE EXAMINES THE PROBLEM OF EXTENDING
GOVERNMENT POLITICS TO THE PERIPHERY IN INDIA. IT IDENTIFIES
THREE DIFFERENT APPROACHES: BUREAUCRATIC, DEMOCRATIC AND
PARTY POLITICAL. EACH OF THESE THREE APPRACHES PROVIDES FOR
DISTINCTIVE STRUCTURES AND RULES AND HAS ITS OWN STYLE OF
OPERATION. YET THEY ARE NOT MUTUALLY EXCLUSIVE, NOR DOES ONE
ALWAYS OPERATE INDEPENDENTLY OF THE OTHER. INDEED, ONE CAN
SEE THAT THE NATIONAL GOVERNMENT HAS SIMULTANEOUSLY FOLLOWED
MORE THAN ONE APPROACH SINCE THE 1920S, ALTHOUGH THE EXTENT
TO WHICH PRIORITY IS GIVEN TO ONE OR THE OTHER DEPENDS
MAINLY ON ITS IDEOLOGY AND INTEREST, AND SPORADICALLY ON
LOCAL REACTIONS AND RESPONSIVENESS. IN CONCLUSION, THE
RATIONALE OF PARTISANSHIP IN VILLAGE GOVERNMENT FAR
OUTWEIGHS ITS LIMITATIONS. BESIDES MAKING VILLAGE GOVERNMENT
MORE REPRESENTATIVEAND ACCOUNTABLE, PARTISANSHIP CAN HELP
PROMOTE ALTERNATIVE POLICY IDEAS ON VILLAGE REFORM AND
CHANGE.

00843 AHO, J.A.
OUT OF HATE: A SOCIOLOGY OF DEFECTION FROM NEO-NAZISM

CURRENT RESEARCH ON PEACE AND VIOLENCE, 11(4) (1988),
159-168.
    PEACE IS NOT ACHIEVABLE WITHOUT COMING TO GRIPS WITH ITS
CONTRADICTION, HATRED. THIS ARTICLE PRESENTS A STUDY OF
INDIVIDUALS WHOSE LIVES, ONCE DEVOTED TO HATRED, HAVE COME
TO PEACE WITH THEIR ONE-TIME ANTAGONISTS. ITS OBJECTIVE IS
TO ANALYZE SOCIOLOGICALLY THE CONDITIONS OF THEIR
CONVERSIONS AND SO TO ADD A PROPOSITION TO THE GENERAL
THEORY OF PEACE. THE PEOPLE STUDIED ARE: TOMMY TARRANTS,
GREG WITHROW, CLINTON SIPES, TOMMY ROLLINS JOYCE BENEDICT,
AND JOHN LUFKIN. THE CONCLUSION IS THAT IT WOULD BE A
MISTAKE TO VIEW INVOLVEMENT IN NEO-NAZISM AS NECESSARILY
ENDURING. IN GENERAL, A SIGNIFICANT OTHER, WILLING TO
ESTABLISH TIES WITH SOMEONE WHO HATES, IS REQUIRED TO HELP
THAT PERSON MOVE AWAY FROM HIS HATRED.

00844 AHSAN, S.A.; CHAKMA, B.
    PROBLEMS OF NATIONAL INTEGRATION IN BANGLADESH: THE
    CHITTAGONG HILL TRACTS
    ASIAN SURVEY, 29(10) (OCT 89), 959-970.
    IN RECENT YEARS, STRUGGLES FOR SELF-DETERMINATION IN THE
DEVELOPED AND UNDERDEVELOPED WORLD HAVE PRODUCED DOUBTS
ABOUT THE APPLICABILITY OF CERTAIN ASSUMPTIONS REGARDING
NATIONAL INTEGRATION/DISINTEGRATION. GENERALLY, MARXISTS
HAVE ASSUMED THAT CLASS STRUGGLES BETWEEN THE CAPITALIST AND
WORKING CLASSES WOULD REPLACE CONFLICTS DERIVED FROM
CULTURAL DIFFERENCES. SUCH CONFLICT WOULD NOT SEEK TO
PRODUCE SECESSION BUT TO REPLACE THE RULING CLASSES OR ALTER
THEIR POLICIES AND ORIENTATIONS. LIBERALS HAVE ASSUMED THAT
SOCIAL MOBILIZATION AND COMMUNICATION WOULD WEAKEN
PRIMORDIAL TIES SUCH AS LINGUISTIC AND/OR RELIGIOUS
AFFINITIES, AND WOULD FOSTER NATIONAL INTEGRATION. BUT SUCH
ASSUMPTIONS HAVE BEEN NULLIFIED BY RECENT ETHNIC CONFLICTS
THAT IN SOME CASES HAVE LED TO OUTRIGHT SECESSION. THE
TRIBAL INSURGENCY IN THE CHITTAGONG HILL TRACTS OF
BANGLADESH IS AN INTERESTING EXAMPLE OF A STRUGGLE FOR SELF-
DETERMINATION. THIS ARTICLE ANALYZES THE THEORETICAL AND
EMPIRICAL ASPECTS OF THIS STRUGGLE FOR AUTONOMY.

00845 AI, V.V.
    VIETNAM: ANOTHER CRISIS OF COMMUNISM
    FREEDOM AT ISSUE, (111) (NOV 89), 26-29.
    SINCE 1975, WHATEVER ATTENTION VIETNAM HAS DRAWN IN THE
USA HAS BEEN PRIMARILY DUE TO THE EXODUS OF THE BOAT PEOPLE.
RELATIVELY LITTLE HAS BEEN HEARD ABOUT THE SITUATION INSIDE
VIETNAM. BUT THE CONTINUING GRAVE VIOLATIONS OF HUMAN RIGHTS
IN VIETNAM CRY OUT FOR INTERNATIONAL ATTENTION. AND THE
SIGNS OF GROWING POLITICAL OPPOSITION AND DEEPENING
ECONOMIC CRISIS INDICATE THAT IN VIETNAM, AS IN OTHER
COMMUNIST REGIMES, COMMUNISM IS IN CRISIS AND BEREFT OF
POPULAR LEGITIMACY.

00846 AICHINGER, W.
    WHAT ACTUALLY IS NEUTRALITY?
    AUSTRIA TODAY, (3) (1989), 13-15.
    THE TERM "NEUTRAL" REQUIRES A CLEAR DEFINITION BECAUSE
IT IS OFTEN MISUNDERSTOOD, MISINTERPRETED, OR CONFUSED WITH
"NEUTRALIST" AND "NEUTRALIZED." THE DUTIES AND COMMITMENTS
INVOLVED IN THE STATUS OF NEUTRALITY WERE LAID DOWN IN A
1907 HAGUE CONVENTION. THIS ARTICLE EXPLAINS HOW EUROPE'S
NEUTRAL STATES CAME TO BE THAT WAY AND WHY AUSTRIA'S
NEUTRALITY WAS NOT ARTICULATED IN THE 1955 STATE TREATY NOR
GUARANTEED BY ANY FOREIGN POWER BUT WAS DECLARED BY THE
AUSTRIAN PARLIAMENT AS A SOVEREIGN ACT AND ENSHRINED IN A
CONSTITUTIONAL LAW.

00847 AIMER, P.
    TRAVELLING TOGETHER: PARTY IDENTIFICATION AND VOTING IN
    THE NEW ZEALAND GENERAL ELECTION OF 1987
    ELECTORAL STUDIES, 8(2) (AUG 89), 131-142.
    NEW ZEALAND HAS BEEN EXPERIENCING A PERIOD OF ELECTORAL
INSTABILITY, WHICH HAS INVOLVED CONSIDERABLE VOTE CHANGING
IN RESPONSE TO THE PRESENCE OF EPHEMERAL OR FLUCTUATING
THIRD PARTIES, AND TO THE RADICAL POLICIES OF THE FOURTH
LABOUR GOVERNMENT. IN THESE CIRCUMSTANCES, ONE WOULD EXPECT
TO SEE EVIDENCE OF PARTISAN DEALIGNMENT IN THE FORM OF A
LOOSENING OF THE RELATIONSHIP BETWEEN ELECTORS' PARTY
IDENTIFICATIONS AND THEIR VOTES. HOWEVER, DATA FROM A POST-
ELECTION SURVEY DO NOT BEAR THIS OUT. RATHER, RATES OF
IDENTIFICATION HAVE REMAINED HIGH AND IN A PERIOD OF
POLITICAL FLUX IDENTIFICATIONS AND VOTES HAVE REMAINED
COUPLED TOGETHER, IN A MANNER THAT SUGGESTS THAT THE
RELATIONSHIP BETWEEN THEM IS STRONGLY RECIPROCAL.

00848 AIRD, P.
    WHOSE WOODS ARE THEY?
    POLICY OPTIONS, 10(3) (APR 89), 35-36.
    THE FOREST INDUSTRY REPRESENTS A MAJOR SECTOR IN THE
CANADIAN ECONOMY AND AN ANNUAL TRADE BALANCE GREATER THAN
THAT IN AGRICULTURE, FISHERIES AND MINING COMBINED. MOST OF
THIS TRADE IS WITH THE UNITED STATES, SO THE IMPACT OF THE
FREE TRADE AGREEMENT WILL BE KEENLY FELT IN THIS SECTOR. THE
FTA REPRESENTS A SERIOUS THREAT TO THE INDUSTRY. IN THE
FIRST PLACE, THE EXPORT ASSISTANCE NOW PROVIDED BY MANY

PROVINCES WILL PROBABLY BE DEFINED AS A "COUNTERVAILABLE
SUBSIDY," WHICH WILL RESULT IN A TARIFF AGAINST PRODUCTS. IN
THE SECOND PLACE, REGIONAL DEVELOPMENT PROGRAMS GENERALLY
HAVE ALREADY BEEN DEFINED AS COUNTERVAILABLE BY THE
AMERICANS IN THE SOFTWOOD LUMBER CASE AND, UNLESS A RIDER IS
ADDED TO THE AGREEMENT, ALL SUCH PROGRAMS ARE IN DANGER.

00849 AIRHART, M.
    VIOLENCE AGAINST GAYS AND LESBIANS ON THE RISE
    SOJOURNERS, 18(9) (OCT 89), 12.
    THIS ARTICLE EXAMINES A 40-PAGE REPORT, TITLED "ANTI-GAY
VIOLENCE: VICTIMIZATION AND DEFAMATION IN 1988" WHICH BREAKS
DOWN THE STATISTICS TO REVEAL A BATTLEFIELD OF OFTEN-
CONCEALED BIGOTRY SCARRING THE NATION FROM MAINE TO HAWAII.
IT SUGGESTS THAT THE LEVELS OF VIOLENCE NOTED IN THE STUDY
ARE BUT A FRACTION OF THE REAL CRISIS THAT HAS CONTINUED
UNABATED THROUGHOUT THE 1980S. REV. DON EASTMAN, A PASTOR OF
THE UNIVERSAL FELLOWSHIP OF METROPOLITAN COMMUNITY CHURCHES,
STATES THAT THE BEST PLACE TO START TO DEAL EFFECTIVELY WITH
THE PROBLEM OF VIOLENCE AGAINST GAYS AND LESBIANS IS IN THE
CHURCHES.

00850 AIRIKYAN, P.
    SOLVING NATIONALITY PROBLEMS: SOME WORDS OF DEMOCRATIC
    WISDOM
    GLASNOST, (16-18) (JAN 89), 7-8.
    THE SOVIET UNION HAS AS MANY PROBLEMS AS IT HAS
NATIONALITIES. THE PROBLEMS PERCEIVED BY NATIONALITIES ARE
TO A LARGE EXTENT DETERMINED BY THEIR LEVEL OF NATIONAL SELF-
AWARENESS RATHER THAN BY THEIR CONCRETE HISTORICAL
CIRCUMSTANCES.

00851 AITMATOV, T.
    SOME REFLECTIONS ON THE PROBLEMS OF NATIONAL CULTURES IN
    THE USSR
    PLURAL SOCIETIES, 18(2) (MAR 89), 92-94.
    THE RUSSIAN LANGUAGE IS UNDOUBTEDLY A GREAT ONE, BUT
EFFORTS TO PROVE ITS GREATNESS YET AGAIN, IS LIKE TRYING TO
FORCE AN OPEN DOOR. IT IS A GREAT LANGUAGE, BUT THIS DOES
NOT IMPLY THAT THE INTERNAL LAWS OF OTHER NATIONAL LANGUAGES
CAN BE IGNORED IN AN EFFORT TO INCORPORATE WHAT CANNOT BE
INCORPORATED. A PEOPLE'S PROMISE OF IMMORTALITY IS ROOTED IN
ITS LANGUAGE. ALL PEOPLE HOLD THEIR OWN LANGUAGE IN HIGH
ESTEEM AND EACH ONE OF US OWES IT TO OUR OWN PEOPLE - FROM
WHOM WE ORIGINATE AND WHO GAVE US OUR GREATEST RICHNESS, OUR
LANGUAGE - TO WATCH OVER ITS PURITY AND ENRICH IT.

00852 AIZENBERG, E.
    BUENOS AIRES UPDATE: THE CHALLENGES OF DEMOCRACY
    MIDSTREAM, XXXV(3) (APR 89), 43-45.
    LIKE THEIR FELLOW CITIZENS, ARGENTINA'S JEWS ARE
LEARNING THAT DEMOCRACY IS NOT A PANACEA FOR EVERY ILL.
AFTER YEARS OF DICTATORSHIP AND WHAT WAS EUPHEMISTICALLY
KNOWN AS "EL PROCESO DE REORGANIZACION NACIONAL," ARGENTINES
EXPECTED THAT FREEDOM WOULD BRING BOTH PEACE AND PROSPERITY.
THE HOPES PLACED IN PRESIDENT RAUL ALFONSIN WERE SO GREAT
THAT REALITY WAS BOUND TO FALL SHORT OF THE IDEA. DESPITE
THE ACHIEVEMENTS OF THE ALFONSIN ADMINISTRATION, ARGENTINA
SUFFERS FROM ECONOMIC PROBLEMS, OVERWHELMING DEBT, COUP
ATTEMPTS, AND A GENERAL FEELING THAT ALFONSIN'S PARTY DID
NOT DELIVER ENOUGH. DESPITE ITS SHORTCOMINGS, ALFONSIN'S
DEMOCRATIC RESTORATION DID PRODUCE BENEFITS FOR ARGENTINE
JEWS, WHO WERE OFTEN THE VICTIMS OF "EL PROCESO."

00853 AJU, A.
    REINDUSTRIALIZATION AND GOVERNMENT INDUSTRIAL RESEARCH
    INSTITUTES IN AN INERT ECONOMY
    DISSERTATION ABSTRACTS INTERNATIONAL, 50(4) (OCT 89),
    1085-A.
    THE AUTHOR STUDIES THE PERFORMANCE OF NIGERIA'S
INDUSTRIAL RESEARCH INSTITUTES OVER THE LAST 40 YEARS. HE
CONTENDS THAT THE DORMANT SELECTION ENVIRONMENT LACKS
SUFFICIENTLY PROVOCATIVE AND INTEGRATIVE INNOVATION POLICIES,
AND THE EXISTENCE OF INCOHERENT, OFTEN INCOMPATIBLE
POLICIES HAS ALIENATED THE INDUSTRIAL RESEARCH INSTITUTES
FROM THE MANUFACTURING SECTOR. THE RESEARCH AND DEVELOPMENT
CAPACITY OF THE INSTITUTES HAS BEEN WEAKENED TO THE EXTENT
THAT THE GOVERNMENT, THE NIGERIAN PUBLIC, AND MANUFACTURING
FIRMS APPEAR TO HAVE LOST CONFIDENCE IN THE GOVERNMENT
INSTITUTES.

00854 AKBAR, M.
    REVOLUTION AND COUNTERREVOLUTION IN AFGHANISTAN
    JOURNAL OF CONTEMPORARY ASIA, 18(4) (1988), 458-472.
    THE CHANGES REVOLUTIONARIES SEEK ARE NOT LIMITED TO
RULING CIRCLES, BUT HAVE AN IMPACT BEYOND THAT. THE
TRANSFORMATION OF SOCIETY AND SUBSTITUTION OF NEW STRUCTURES
FOR OLD ONES INVOLVES AN IMPACT ON THE COMMUNITY; CULTURAL
VALUES AND INSTITUTIONS THAT LIE BENEATH GOVERNMENT AND
REGIME. IN CASE REVOLUTIONARIES FAIL TO ACCOMPLISH THOSE
CHANGES, THE REVOLUTION TURNS INTO A ABORTIVE CASE," AND
PROVOKES COUNTERREVOLUTION. THIS ARTICLE IS AN ATTEMPT TO
ANALYZE THE NATURE OF SUCH A REVOLUTION: THE SAUR REVOLUTION
IN AFGHANISTAN, WHERE THE REVOLUTIONARIES, AFTER SEIZING

POWER BROUGHT RAPID REFORMS TO CHANGE THE POLITICAL AND
SOCIAL STRUCTURE OF SOCIETY INTO A CENTRALIZED SOCIALIST
STATE. THE CHANGES REVOLUTIONARIES SOUGHT COULD NOT BE
ACCOMPLISHED AND ALIENATED A MAJORITY OF THE AFGHAN PEOPLE
FROM THE GOVERNMENT AND LED TO FULL-FLEDGED
COUNTERREVOLUTION AGAINST THE RULING REVOLUTIONARY
GOVERNMENT.

00855 AKBAR, M.
    REVOLUTIONARY CHANGES AND SOCIAL RESISTANCE IN AFGHANISTAN
ASIAN PROFILE, 17(3) (JUN 89), 271-282.
    THE AUTHOR EXAMINES THE NATURE OF REVOLUTIONARY CHANGES
AND THE PROBLEM OF ACHIEVING THEM IN AFGHANISTAN. AFTER
SEIZING POWER IN THE AFGHAN REVOLUTION OF 1978, THE PEOPLE'S
DEMOCRATIC PARTY OF AFGHANISTAN (PDPA) INTRODUCED RAPID
REFORMS TO CHANGE THE POLITICAL AND SOCIAL STRUCTURE OF
AFGHAN SOCIETY INTO A CENTRALIZED SOCIALIST STATE. BUT THE
TRANSFORMATION ENVISIONED BY THE REVOLUTIONARIES COULD NOT
BE ACHIEVED. THIS ALIENATED A MAJORITY OF THE AFGHAN PEOPLE
FROM THE GOVERNMENT AND LED TO A FULL-FLEDGED COUNTER-
REVOLUTION AGAINST THE RULING PDPA REGIME.

00856 AKBARI, A.H.
    THE BENEFITS OF IMMIGRANTS TO CANADA: EVIDENCE ON TAX AND
    PUBLIC SERVICES
CANADIAN REVIEW OF SOCIOLOGY AND ANTHROPOLOGY, 15(4) (DEC
89), 424-435.
    THE LIFE-CYCLE THEORY IMPLICATION THAT IMMIGRANTS, BEING
YOUNG AT THE TIME OF ARRIVAL, SHOULD BENEFIT THE NATIVE-BORN
POPULATION IN A TAX-TRANSFER SYSTEM IS ANALYSED FOR CANADA.
MICRODATA FROM THE 1981 CANADIAN CENSUS OF POPULATION ARE
USED. CONSUMPTION OF MAJOR PUBLIC SERVICES AND PAYMENT OF
MAJOR TAXES BY THE AVERAGE IMMIGRANT AND NON-IMMIGRANT
HOUSEHOLDS ARE CONSIDERED. IT IS OBSERVED THAT EVEN AFTER
THEY HAVE STAYED FOR 35 YEARS IN CANADA, IMMIGRANT
HOUSEHOLDS ARE A SOURCE OF PUBLIC FUND TRANSFERS TO NON-
IMMIGRANTS. THIS CONFIRMS THE LIFE-CYCLE NET BENEFIT
HYPOTHESIS. IMPLICATIONS FOR PUBLIC POLICY WITH RESPECT TO
IMMIGRATION POLICY ARE SUGGESTED.

00857 AKEF, M.A.
    THE ECONOMICS OF DEVELOPMENT ASSISTANCE: THE EGYPTIAN CASE
DISSERTATION ABSTRACTS INTERNATIONAL, 49(8) (FEB 89),
2314-A.
    THE AUTHOR STUDIES THE QUESTION OF WHETHER OFFICIAL
ECONOMIC ASSISTANCE BENEFITS DEVELOPING COUNTRIES AND,
SPECIFICALLY, EGYPT. THE AMERICAN ECONOMIC SUPPORT PROGRAM
IS EXAMINED IN THREE MAJOR EGYPTIAN SECTORS: AGRICULTURE,
INDUSTRY, AND HUMAN SERVICES. THE AUTHOR FINDS THAT THE AID
HAD SOME POSITIVE IMPACTS ON THE EGYPTIAN ECONOMY BUT NOT AS
GREAT AS EXPECTED.

00858 AKEHURST, J.
    NATO AND EUROPE: PRACTICAL ISSUES AND MILITARY INTERESTS
RUSI JOURNAL, 134(1) (SPR 89), 9-14.
    THE AUTHOR CONSIDERS THE GORBACHEV EFFECT IN
INTERNATIONAL RELATIONS, THE EAST-WEST MILITARY EQUATION,
ARMS CONTROL, AND DEFENSE BURDEN-SHARING BETWEEN THE USA AND
NATO.

00859 AKHALWAYA, A.
    THE RED HERRING FACTOR
AFRICA REPORT, 34(1) (JAN 89), 13-15.
    THE SOUTH AFRICAN GOVERNMENT'S RECENT DIPLOMATIC
INITIATIVES IN SOUTHERN AFRICA, AS WELL AS THE RELEASES FROM
JAIL OF SELECTED POLITICAL PRISONERS, MAY HAVE IMPROVED ITS
IMAGE IN WORLD OPINION. BUT BLACK SOUTH AFRICANS, SKEPTICAL
OF THE MOTIVATIONS BEHIND THESE MOVES, CAUTION THAT FURTHER
PUBLIC RELATIONS GAMBITS CAN BE EXPECTED IN 1989--
REPRESENTING YET ANOTHER MEANS OF FORESTALLING FUNDAMENTAL
STEPS TOWARD DISMANTLING APARTHEID.

00860 AKINRINADE, O.
    AFRICA AND THE COMMONWEALTH, 1960-80
ROUND TABLE, 309 (JAN 89), 33-53.
    THE PURPOSE OF THIS PAPER IS TO ANALYSE THE IMPACT ON
THE FOREIGN POLICIES OF AFRICAN STATES, OF THEIR
PARTICIPATION IN THE COMMONWEALTH. IN THE LATTER PART OF THE
PAPER, SOME GENERAL QUESTIONS THAT AROSE IN THE PROCESS ARE
DISCUSSED. IN PARTICULAR, CONSIDERATION IS GIVEN TO (I) THE
GENERAL IMPLICATIONS OF THE COMMONWEALTH FOR AFRICAN FOREIGN
POLICY, AND (II) THE ROLE OF INTERNATIONAL ORGANIZATION
GENERALLY AS INSTRUMENTS OF POLICY FOR DEVELOPING STATES.

00861 AKSYUCHITS, V.
    AS GORBACHEV SITS ON THE KREMLIN WALL, IS HE POSITIONED
    FOR A PRATFALL?
GLASNOST, II(2) (MAR 89), 67-69.
    PERESTROIKA IS CLEARLY BOGGING DOWN AT ITS VERY
INCEPTION, WITHOUT EVER GETTING A CHANCE TO ACCELERATE. THE
PLAN FOR 1988 AND ITS EXTENSION FOR 1989 STIPULATE AN
INCREASE OF CENTRALLY-DETERMINED INDICATORS, WHICH IS
CONTRARY TO THE LOGIC OF REFORM. THE ONLY COMMITTED SUPPORT
FOR GORBACHEV'S POLICIES FROM THE INTELLIGENTSIA IN THE

MAJOR CITIES. GLASNOST RINGS RESONANTLY ONLY IN THE CENTRAL
PRESS. THE MASS MEDIA OUTSIDE MOSCOW IS ALMOST ENTIRELY IN
THE HANDS OF CONSERVATIVES OPPOSED TO REFORM.

00862 AKSYUCHITS, V.
    THE WEST IS NOT THE BEST
GLASNOST, II(2) (MAR 89), 22-25.
    THE WEST MANIFESTS AN INNER SYMPATHY FOR COMMUNIST
IDEALS AND AN INSTINCTIVE HOSTILITY TO RUSSIA.
"COMMUNOPHILIA" AND "RUSSOPHOBIA" SPRING FROM THE SAME
SOURCE--THE SPIRITUAL ILLNESS OF THE WEST. THE WEST LACKS
THE WILL TO OPPOSE COMMUNISM BECAUSE IT DOES NOT WANT TO
ADMIT THE EXISTENCE OF RADICAL EVIL.

00863 AKSYUCHITS, V.
    WITH MALICE TOWARDS ALL AND CHARITY TO ONE
GLASNOST, II(3) (MAY 89), 24, 29.
    SOVIET NATIONALITIES SUFFER FROM LACK OF UNDERSTANDING
AMONG THEMSELVES AND CALLOUSNESS TOWARD ONE ANOTHER'S
PROBLEMS. EACH ETHNIC GROUP IS CONCERNED ONLY WITH ITS OWN
PROBLEMS AND REGARDS SOME OTHER NATION AS THE SOURCE OF ITS
DIFFICULTIES. TO JUSTIFY THIS APPROACH, DISPUTATIOUS PARTIES
FALSIFY HISTORY AND GIVE THEIR OWN INTERPRETATION TO CURRENT
EVENTS. WHEN NATIONALIST PARTISANS RECALL THE PAST, THEY
JUSTIFY THEIR VIEWS BY LEVELLING ACCUSATIONS AGAINST THEIR
OPPONENTS. THE RESULT IS MUTUAL MISUNDERSTANDING ENDING IN
MALICE TOWARDS ALL AND CHARITY TO ONESELF.

00864 AKUNWAFOR, D.D.
    THE POLITICS OF TAX REFORM IN THE UNITED STATES (1980-86)
DISSERTATION ABSTRACTS INTERNATIONAL, 50(6) (DEC 89),
1798-A.
    THE AUTHOR REVIEWS THE DEBATES OVER TAXATION FROM THE
NEW DEAL TO THE 1986 TAX REFORM ACT. HE EXPLORES THREE MAIN
ISSUES: (1) THE LEGISLATIVE PROCESS AND THE NATURE OF THE
TAX REFORMS BETWEEN 1980 AND 1986, (2) THE IMPACT OF THE
1981 TAX REFORM ON ECONOMIC GROWTH AND EQUITY AND THE
POTENTIAL IMPACT OF THE 1986 TAX REFORM, AND (3) THE ROLE OF
POLITICAL ACTION COMMITTEES IN THE 1986 TAX REFORM.

00865 AL-AWAJI, I.
    BUREAUCRACY AND DEVELOPMENT IN SAUDI ARABIA: THE CASE OF
    LOCAL ADMINISTRATION
JOURNAL OF ASIAN AND AFRICAN STUDIES, XXIV(1-2) (1989),
49-61.
    THIS PAPER EXAMINES THE ROLE OF THE SAUDI BUREAUCRACY IN
DEVELOPMENT BY FOCUSSING ON LOCAL ADMINISTRATION. IT POINTS
TO SEVERAL SHORTCOMINGS OF THE SAUDI LOCAL ADMINISTRATIVE
SYSTEM, INCLUDING DIVERSE ORGANIZATIONAL STRUCTURES, LOW
EDUCATIONS QUALIFICATIONS OF LOCAL PUBLIC OFFICIALS,
IMBALANCE BETWEEN THE EXECUTIVE AUTHORITY AND THE ASSIGNED
RESPONSIBILITIES OF LOCAL AGENCIES, A HIGH DEGREE OF
DUPLICATION, AND LACK OF CO-ORDINATION OF SERVICES. ALL OF
THESE CONSTITUTE SERIOUS OBSTACLES TO THE SAUDI LOCAL
ADMINISTRATION PLAYING AN EFFECTIVE ROLE IN PROMOTING SOCIO-
ECONOMIC AND POLITICAL DEVELOPMENT. DESPITE THESE
SHORTCOMINGS, HOWEVER, THE SAUDI LOCAL ADMINISTRATIVE SYSTEM
HAS BEEN ACTIVE IN THE DYNAMIC DEVELOPMENT OF THE SAUDI
KINGDOM. THIS ACTIVE ROLE HAS BEEN STRENGTHENED BY NATIONAL
DEVELOPMENT PLANS WHICH EMPHASIZE THE DEVELOPMENT OF THE
KINGDOM'S GEOGRAPHIC REGIONS THROUGH THE ESTABLISHMENT OF
REGIONAL DEVELOPMENT CENTRES.

00866 AL-BAHRANI, K.M.
    FACTORS INFLUENCING RULING ELITES' POLICIES ON POLITICAL
    PARTICIPATION IN THE STATE OF KUWAIT
DISSERTATION ABSTRACTS INTERNATIONAL, 49(7) (JAN 89),
1944-A.
    RULING ELITES POLICIES TOWARD POLITICAL PARTICIPATION
ARE DETERMINED BY SEVERAL FACTORS, BOTH INTERNAL AND
EXTERNAL IN NATURE. THIS STUDY EXAMINES THE POSITIONAL OR
RULING ELITE IN KUWAIT AND POLICIES ON POLITICAL
PARTICIPATION.

00867 AL-CHALABI, F.J.
    THE CAUSES AND THE IMPLICATIONS FOR OPEC OF THE OIL PRICE
    DECLINE OF 1986
OPEC REVIEW, 12(1) (SPR 88), 1-16.
    THIS PAPER IS BASED ON A CHAPTER OF A BOOK BY THE AUTHOR
ENTITLED "THE THIRD OIL SHOCK: CAUSES AND IMPLICATIONS OF
THE OIL PRICE DECLINE OF 1986" AND REFLECTS HIS PERSONAL
VIEWS. IT EXAMINES EARLIER PRICING POLICIES WHICH RESULTING
IN SELF DEFEAT. IT CONTINUES BY DESCRIBING THREE
DEVELOPMENTS WHICH OCCURRED AS A RESULT: 1) A DECLINE OF
ENERGY CONSUMPTION, 2) A CHANGE IN THE WORLD ENERGY
STRUCTURE, AND 3) LESS PURCHASE OF OPEC OIL.

00868 AL-GHABRA, S.N.
    PALESTINIANS IN KUWAIT: THE FAMILY AND THE POLITICS OF
    SURVIVAL
DISSERTATION ABSTRACTS INTERNATIONAL, 50(3) (SEP 89),
786-A.
    THE AUTHOR STUDIES THE SOCIAL, OCCUPATIONAL, CULTURAL,
AND POLITICAL BEHAVIOR OF TWO STRATA OF PALESTINIANS (THE

INTELLIGENTSIA AND THE PEASANTRY) WHO SETTLED IN KUWAIT BETWEEN 1948 AND THE EARLY 1950'S. THIS DISCUSSION SETS THE STAGE FOR EXPLORING THE ROLE OF THE FAMILY IN KUWAIT AS A FUNCTIONAL UNIT OF ECONOMIC, POLITICAL, NATIONAL, AND SOCIAL SURVIVAL.

00869 AL-GHAITH, M.A.
THE INTERRELATIONSHIP BETWEEN PERFORMANCE APPRAISAL AND ORGANIZATIONAL EFFECTIVENESS: A PARADIGM THEORY OF EMPLOYEE APPRAISAL IN PUBLIC ADMINISTRATION
DISSERTATION ABSTRACTS INTERNATIONAL, 49(9) (MAR 89), 2800-A.
USING A MULTI-DIMENSIONAL STRATEGY AND AN EXPLORATORY/DEVELOPMENTAL/ EXPERIMENTAL/ACTION TYPE OF RESEARCH, THIS STUDY FINDS AND BUILDS THE LINK BETWEEN THREE ESSENTIAL, INTERRELATED CONCEPTS: PERFORMANCE APPRAISAL, ORGANIZATIONAL EFFECTIVENESS, AND THE PARADIGM OF PUBLIC ADMINISTRATION.

00870 AL-HARITHI, T.A.
MOROCCAN POLICY TOWARDS THE UNITED STATES: A STUDY IN MOROCCAN SOCIETY UNDER THE IMPACT OF WESTERN PENETRATION, 1830-1912
DISSERTATION ABSTRACTS INTERNATIONAL, 49(3) (SEP 88), 612-A.
THE RELATIONS BETWEEN THE US AND MOROCCO DURING THE PERIOD 1830-1912 ARE ANALYZED WITH EMPHASIS ON THE UNDERLYING MOTIVATIONS OF BOTH NATIONS. MOROCCO WAS EAGER TO GAIN US AID IN FENDING OFF PENETRATION BY EUROPEAN POWERS. BOTH INTERNAL AND EXTERNAL FACTORS ARE ANALYZED AND THEIR IMPACT ON OVERALL RELATIONS ARE ASSESSED.

00871 AL-HUMAIDHI, B.
TWENTY-EIGHT YEARS OF DEVELOPMENT COOPERATION: THE KUWAIT FUND FOR ARAB ECONOMIC DEVELOPMENT
AMERICAN-ARAB AFFAIRS, (31) (WIN 89), 11-14.
THIS ARTICLE OFFERS HIGHLIGHTS OF THE AID EFFORTS BY THE KUWAIT FUND IN DEVELOPMENT COOPERATION OVER THE LAST TWENTY-EIGHT YEARS WHICH REPRESENTS ONLY PART OF THE COLLECTIVE EFFORT OF AID-GIVING BY THE STATE OF KUWAIT. THE MAGNITUDE OF TOTAL CONCESSIONAL RESOURCES TRANSFERRED BY KUWAIT REVEALS AN IMPRESSIVE RECORD OF AID PERFORMANCE BY ANY STANDARD. IT CONCLUDES THAT THE KUWAIT FUND IS THERE TO STAY AND WILL CONTINUE TO PURSUE ITS DEVELOPMENT COOPERATION WITH KEEN INTEREST AND CONCERTED EFFORTS.

00872 AL-JEBARIN, A. I.
THE UNITED STATES-EGYPTIAN RELATIONS, 1945-1958
DISSERTATION ABSTRACTS INTERNATIONAL, 49(8) (FEB 89), 2363-A.
THIS STUDY OF AMERICAN-EGYPTIAN RELATIONS DEMONSTRATES THE WAYS IN WHICH U.S. POLICYMAKERS OF THE TRUMAN AND EISENHOWER ADMINISTRATIONS ATTEMPTED TO ENHANCE AMERICAN INFLUENCE IN THE ARAB MIDDLE EAST. AMERICAN STRATEGY WAS DESIGNED TO CONTAIN ALLEGED SOVIET PENETRATION, PROVIDE AID TO PRO-WESTERN ARAB REGIMES, AND PROMOTE PEACE IN THE REGION WHILE PROTECTING ISRAEL.

00873 AL-JOMAIH, I. A.
THE USE OF THE QUR'AN IN POLITICAL ARGUMENT: A STUDY OF EARLY ISLAMIC PARTIES
DISSERTATION ABSTRACTS INTERNATIONAL, 49(8) (FEB 89), 2362-A.
THE AUTHOR STUDIES THE USE OF THE QUR'AN IN EARLY POLITICAL ARGUMENT FROM ALI IBN ABI TALIB TO ABD AL-MALIK IBN MARWAN. HE FINDS THE MOST IMPORTANT ISSUES EXPRESSED IN QUR'ANIC TERMS TO BE POLITICAL AUTHORITY, GOD'S ASSISTANCE, GOD'S POWER OVER EVENTS, GOD'S PRESCRIBED PUNISHMENTS, COLLECTIVE PUNISHMENT, AND THE QUESTION OF WHETHER IT IS LAWFUL TO SHED THE BLOOD OF MUSLIMS.

00874 AL-KHALIFA, M.B.M.
BAHRAIN: READY AND WAITING FOR AMERICAN BUSINESS
AMERICAN-ARAB AFFAIRS, (30) (FAL 89), 18-21.
THIS IS AN ADDRESS BY THE MINISTER OF FOREIGN AFFAIRS OF THE STATE OF BAHRAIN DELIVERED IN WASHINGTON D.C. ON AUGUST 1, 1989. HE TALKS ABOUT ECONOMIC DEVELOPMENT IN BAHRAIN AND ALSO EXPLAINS THEIR OUTLOOK FOR DEVELOPMENT IN THE FUTURE. HE INCLUDES INDUSTRY, BANKING, AND THE GULF COOPERATION COUNCIL IN HIS ASSESSMENT OF THE GENERAL ECONOMIC DEVELOPMENT, AND TALKS ABOUT FUTURE INDUSTRIAL PLANS. HE INVITES THE AUDIENCE (OUTSTANDING BUSINESS LEADERS) TO PARTICIPATE WITH BAHRAIN IN THEIR ECONOMIC DEVELOPMENT.

00875 AL-MASRI, T.
AMMAN IS READY FOR COOPERATION
INTERNATIONAL AFFAIRS (MOSCOW), (8) (AUG 89), 14-16.
THE SOVIET UNION INVARIABLY ENJOYS GREAT PRESTIGE WITH THE JORDANIAN PEOPLE AND THE ARABS AS A WHOLE. THE SOVIETS HAVE CONSISTENTLY SUPPORTED THE LEGITIMATE DEMANDS OF THE PALESTINIANS AND HAVE REPEATEDLY SHOWN THEMSELVES TO BE A STEADFAST FRIEND OF THE ARABS. THE SOVIET UNION HAS NEVER STOPPED WORKING FOR THE REALIZATION OF ITS MIDEAST INITIATIVES, WHICH REPRESENT A FORCEFUL MANIFESTATION OF

POLITICAL REALISM.

00876 AL-OTAIBI, A.S.
BUREAUCRACY AND THE CHALLENGES OF REGIONAL DISPARITY: THE CASE OF SAUDI ARABIA
DISSERTATION ABSTRACTS INTERNATIONAL, 50(1) (JUL 89), 253-A.
SAUDI ARABIA'S FIVE REGIONS SUFFER FROM MAJOR REGIONAL IMBALANCES, WITH DISPARITY BETWEEN URBAN AND RURAL AREAS IN GENERAL. THIS DISSERTATION SURVEYS THE ROLE OF BUREAUCRACY IN DEALING WITH THIS PROBLEM. FIRST, THE STUDY ANALYZES THE POLICIES THAT HAVE BEEN INITIATED TO TACKLE THE PROBLEM. THEN IT ASSESSES THE CONDITIONS OF THE REGIONS AS OF THE MID-1980'S. IT CONCLUDES THAT THE BUREAUCRACY HAS BEEN INCAPABLE OF DEALING WITH THE ISSUE IN AN EFFECTIVE WAY, BECAUSE THE BUREAUCRACY HAS REDEFINED THE PROBLEM AND SIMPLIFIED IT IN ORDER TO HANDLE IT IN A UNIVERSAL, ROUTINE FASHION.

00877 AL-QAQ, Z.M.
THE IRAQ-IRAN WAR, 1980-OCTOBER 1983, WITH PARTICULAR REFERENCE TO POLITICAL AND DIPLOMATIC EFFORTS TO TERMINATE THE CONFLICT
DISSERTATION ABSTRACTS INTERNATIONAL, 50(6) (DEC 89), 1792-A.
THE AUTHOR IDENTIFIES THE CAUSES OF THE IRAN-IRAQ WAR AND EVALUATES SEVERAL HYPOTHESES REGARDING THE MOTIVATIONS OF THE TWO COUNTRIES. HE ALSO REVIEWS EFFORTS AT POLITICAL MEDIATION OF THE CONFLICT AND THE ROLE OF SYRIA IN THE PROBLEM.

00878 AL-RASHED, A.
THE GOALS OF OUR FRONT
WORLD MARXIST REVIEW, 32(11) (NOV 89), 66-67.
THE AUTHOR EXAMINES WHAT HE CONSIDER TO BE A CLOSE LINK BETWEEN THE ENDING OF THE IRAN-IRAQ WAR AND THE SIGNING OF THE GENEVA ACCORDS ON AFGOANESTAN. THE CESSATION OF HOSTILITIES HAS HAD A BENEFICIAL EFFECT ON BAHRAIN AND ON THE SITUATION IN THE GULF AND ARAB PENINSULA AS A WHOLE.

00879 AL-SAAD, M.A.
DETERMINANTS OF THE TIME-PATTERN OF GOVERNMENT SPENDING IN DEVELOPING COUNTRIES: THE CASE OF IRAQ
DISSERTATION ABSTRACTS INTERNATIONAL, 49(9) (MAR 89), 2792-A.
THE AUTHOR EXAMINES THE ECONOMIC AND SOCIO-POLITICAL FACTORS DETERMING THE GROWTH PATTERN OF PUBLIC SPENDING IN IRAQ. HE CONCLUDES THAT, GENERALLY, DEFENSE SPENDING HAS BEEN RATED A TOP PRIORITY DUE TO POLITICAL FACTORS, ECONOMIC SERVICES HAVE BEEN SENSITIVE TO CHANGES IN GOVERNMENT REVENUE, AND SOCIAL SERVICES HAVE BEEN DETERMINED LARGELY BY CHANGES IN THE POPULATION STRUCTURE.

00880 AL-SAGRI, S.H.
BRITAIN AND THE ARAB EMIRATES, 1820-1956: A DOCUMENTARY STUDY
DISSERTATION ABSTRACTS INTERNATIONAL, 50(1) (JUL 89), 249-A.
BRITISH POLICY TOWARDS THE TRUCIAL STATES FROM 1820 TO 1956 CAN BE DIVIDED INTO TWO STAGES. DURING THE FIRST PERIOD (1820-1945), BRITAIN CONCENTRATED ON MAINTAINING ITS INTERESTS AND REFRAINED FROM INTERFERING IN THE INTERNAL AFFAIRS OF THE EMIRATES EXCEPT WHEN BRITISH INTERESTS WERE THREATENED. FROM 1945 TO 1956, BRITAIN FOLLOWED A NEW POLICY AIMED AT DEVELOPING THE SOCIAL, ECONOMIC, AND POLITICAL CONDITIONS IN THE EMIRATES. IN 1952, BRITAIN MANAGED FOR THE FIRST TIME TO UNIFY THE SHEIKHS IN A TRUCIAL STATES COUNCIL TO HELP CARRY OUT THE BRITISH DEVELOPMENT PROGRAM. THIS POLICY PRODUCED A LEGAL SYSTEM, FORMAL EDUCATION, AN ADMINISTRATIVE SYSTEM, AND STABLE ECONOMIC RESOURCES.

00881 AL-SAMER, B.
HUMAN RIGHTS AND GLOBAL SECURITY
WORLD MARXIST REVIEW, 32(8) (JUL 89), 43-46.
THIS ARTICLE EXPLORES WHAT IS NEEDED TO CREATE A FAVORABLE ATMOSPHERE FOR THE HUMANIZATION OF INTERNATIONAL RELATIONS AND A STEADY ADVANCE TOWARDS UNIVERSAL PEACE AND SECURITY. IT GIVES THE HISTORICAL BACKGROUND OF HUMAN RIGHTS INCLUDING THE FRENCH REVOLUTION AND THE UN. UNIVERSAL DECLARATION OF HUMAN RIGHTS. EXAMINED ARE GOVERNMENTS AND REGIMES WHICH VIOLATE HUMAN RIGHTS. IT CALLS FOR BROAD SOLIDARITY, JOINT EFFORTS, AND AN AWARENESS OF HUMAN WORTH TO PUT AN END TO ENCROACHMENTS ON PERSONAL LIFE AND FREEDOMS.

00882 AL-SHAMSIE, S.D.
ADMINISTRATIVE ECLECTICISM
DISSERTATION ABSTRACTS INTERNATIONAL, 50(5) (NOV 89), 1429-A.
ADMINISTRATIVE ELECTICISM REFERS TO THE TENDENCY TO SELECT SPECIFIC CONCEPTS FROM OTHER FIELDS AND THEN AGGREGATE THEM AS PRINCIPLES IN PUBLIC ADMINISTRATION THEORY. THIS DISSERTATION FOCUSES ON HOW CONCEPTS FROM POLITICAL SCIENCE, PSYCHOLOGY, SOCIOLOGY, AND PHILOSOPHY HAVE BEEN ADOPTED IN PUBLIC ADMINISTRATION.

00883 ALAGAPPA, M.
THE MAJOR POWERS AND SOUTHEAST ASIA
INTERNATIONAL JOURNAL, XLIV(3) (SUM 89), 541-597.
MAJOR POWER RELATIONS IN THE ASIA-PACIFIC REGION ARE IN
THE MIDST OF CHANGE. THE EXTENT OF THESE CHANGES AND THEIR
IMPACT ON SOUTHEAST ASIA IS THE FOCUS OF THIS PAPER. THE
PAPER FIRST EXPLORES THE PERCEPTIONS, POLICIES, AND ISSUES
IN THE RELATIONS OF THE MAJOR POWERS WITH THE COUNTRIES OF
THE REGION. IT THEN EXAMINES RECENT DEVELOPMENTS IN SOVIET-
AMERICAN, SINOSOVIET, AND SINO-AMERICAN RELATIONS AND THEIR
IMPLICATIONS FOR SOUTHEAST ASIA. FINALLY, THE IMPLICATIONS
OF THESE DEVELOPMENTS FOR REGIONAL STRATEGIES TO MANAGE
RELATIONS WITH THE MAJOR POWERS ARE DISCUSSED.

00884 ALAGIAH, G.; FISH, J.; GEORGE, M.; VIDAL-HALL, J.
A RISING TIDE OF POPULISM
SOUTH, (99) (JAN 89), 32-34.
POLITICAL SUCCESSION MAY BE MOVING AWAY FROM THE WHIMS
OF ARMY GENERALS AND THE OBSTINACY OF INCUMBENTS. IN 1989,
EIGHT LATIN AMERICAN STATES WILL GO TO THE POLLS, A SIGN OF
HOW FAR THE REGION HAS COME SINCE THE DAYS OF DIRTY WARS AND
JUNTAS. IN SOME OF THESE STATES, VICTORIES WILL BE WON ON A
TIDE OF POPULISM. IN ASIA, PEOPLE'S POWER HAS BEGUN TO SPILL
OVER FROM THE PHILLIPINES INTO OTHER COUNTRIES BUT HAS YET
TO WORK ITS WAY THROUGH THE REGION. WITH MOST OF THE MIDDLE
EAST RULED BY THE MILITARY OR FAMILY DYNASTIES, CHANGE OF
GOVERNMENT THROUGH ELECTION IS NOT AN OPTION. IN AFRICA, THE
POLITICS OF THE POST-COLONIAL ERA OFTEN CENTERED AROUND THE
CREATION OF A NATIONAL IDENTITY, BUT THIS IS NOW GIVING WAY
TO THE POLITICS OF ECONOMIC MANAGEMENT.

00885 ALAGIAH, G.
PATIENTS IN NEED OF INTENSIVE CARE
SOUTH, (99) (JAN 89), 18.
MOST OF THE 28 AFRICAN GOVERNMENTS ENGAGED IN ECONOMIC
REFORM PROGRAMS WILL SOON BE FACING QUESTIONS ABOUT WHETHER
ADJUSTMENT IS WORKING FOR THEM. MEANWHILE, THE AFRICAN DEBT
OUTLOOK IS NOT IMPROVING. THE WORLD'S SEVEN LARGEST
INDUSTRIALIZED COUNTRIES HAVE ACCEPTED IN PRINCIPLE THAT
AFRICA'S DEBT MAY HAVE TO BE REPAID AT LOWER THAN MARKET
INTEREST RATES OR CANCELLED ALTOGETHER. BUT AFRICA'S 17
POOREST COUNTRIES WILL BENEFIT ONLY AFTER THEY HAVE
SATISFIED THE PARIS CLUB, WHERE OFFICIAL DEBT TO WESTERN
COUNTRIES IS NEGOTIATED, THAT THEY ARE PURSUING ECONOMIC
ADJUSTMENT PROGRAMS WITH THE REQUIRED VIGOR.

00886 ALAGIAH, G.
21ST-CENTURY BLUEPRINT
SOUTH, (100) (FEB 89), 22-23.
IN A FAR-REACHING ATTEMPT TO PLOT AFRICA'S LONG-TERM
ECONOMIC RECOVERY AND SET THE CONTINENT ON A DEVELOPMENT
PATH FOR THE COMING CENTURY, WORLD BANK OFFICIALS AND
AFRICAN POLICY-MAKERS ARE THRASHING OUT A JOINT STRATEGY. A
WORLD BANK STUDY STATES THAT A RADICAL SHIFT IN DEVELOPMENT
STRATEGY IS REQUIRED IF AFRICA IS TO AVOID A NIGHTMARE
SCENARIO. POLICIES THAT BENEFIT AFRICA'S CHAUFFEUR-DRIVEN
CLASSES MUST GIVE WAY TO PROGRAMS THAT MOTIVATE AND OPEN
DOORS FOR THE CONTINENT'S HIDDEN ENTREPRENEURS.

00887 ALAILIMA, P.J.
THE IMPACT OF PUBLIC POLICY ON THE POOR IN SRI LANKA: A
STUDY OF POLICIES RELATING TO INCOMES, ASSETS, AND LIVING
STANDARDS AND THEIR EFFECTS ON THE POOR
DISSERTATION ABSTRACTS INTERNATIONAL, 50(2) (AUG 89),
539-A.
DESPITE THEIR DECLINING REAL INCOME, THE POOR IN SRI
LANKA HAVE EXPERIENCED CONTINUED IMPROVEMENT IN CERTAIN
SECTORS. THE IMPROVEMENT IS MOST MARKED IN EDUCATION AND, TO
A LESSER EXTENT, IN HEALTH CARE. WHERE ACCESS TO SERVICES IS
DETERMINED BY THE ABILITY TO PAY--AS IN HOUSING, WATER
SUPPLY, AND SANITATION SERVICES--CAPABILITIES ARE CLOSELY
DETERMINED BY ENTITLEMENTS. THE PUBLIC ASSET DISTRIBUTION
PROGRAM, PARTICULARLY OF LAND, CLEARLY BENEFITED THE POOR
AND TO SOME EXTENT CUSHIONED THE EFFECT OF DECLINING INCOME.

00888 ALAM, M.
THE SOUTH KOREAN 'MIRACLE': EXAMINING THE MIX OF
GOVERNMENT AND MARKETS
JOURNAL OF DEVELOPING AREAS, 23(2) (JAN 89), 233-258.
THE MAIN OBJECTIVE OF THE ARTICLE IS TO ATTEMPT AN
EVALUATION OF THIS DOMINANT NEOCLASSICAL READING OF THE
KOREAN EXPERIENCE DURING THE 1960'S AND 1970'S. IT EXAMINES
THE EXTENT WHICH THE POLICIES EMPLOYED BY KOREA OPERATED
THROUGH THE MARKET OR CIRCUMVENTED IT, AND ALSO WHETHER THE
STRUCTURE OF INCENTIVES RESULTING FROM THESE POLICIES WAS
NEUTRAL OR BIASED. IT ALSO DISCUSSES THE LINKS BETWEEN
ECONOMIC POLICIES AND KOREA'S GROWTH PERFORMANCE. IT ALSO
EXPLORES THE EXTRAECONOMIC FACTORS IN KOREA THAT CONDITIONED
THE SUCCESS OF HER POLICIES.

00889 ALAN, R.
AN ANGLO-SPANISH NIGHTMARE
NEW LEADER, LXXII(17) (NOV 89), 10-11.
ALTHOUGH RELATIONS BETWEEN SPAIN AND GREAT BRITAIN ARE
CORDIAL ENOUGH ON A DIPLOMATIC LEVEL, THE COMMON PEOPLE
OFTEN DO NOT SEE EYE TO EYE. A SIGNIFICANT CAUSE OF THIS
ENMITY IS THE LESS THAN CIVILIZED BEHAVIOR OF AN INCREASING
NUMBER OF BRITISH TOURISTS IN SPAIN. ALTHOUGH THE ACTUAL
PERCENTAGE OF MISBEHAVING TOURISTS IS QUITE SMALL, IT IS
LARGE ENOUGH TO BE PAINFULLY VISIBLE.

00890 ALAPURO, R.
STATE AND REVOLUTION IN FINLAND
UNIVERSITY OF CALIFORNIA PRESS, BERKELEY, CA, 1988, 320.
THE AUTHOR SEARCHES FOR THE DECISIVE FACTORS SHAPING
20TH CENTURY POLITICS IN SMALL COUNTRIES THAT ARE
ECONOMICALLY AND POLITICALLY DEPENDENT ON BIG COUNTRIES. HE
FOCUSES ON FINLAND AND ITS POLITICAL, SOCIAL, AND ECONOMIC
HISTORY SINCE 1809.

00891 ALAVI, H. (ED.); HARRISS, J. (ED.)
SOUTH ASIA
MONTHLY REVIEW PRESS, NEW YORK, NY, 1989, 288.
THE CONTRIBUTORS ATTEMPT TO PRESENT A COHERENT VIEW OF
SOUTH ASIAN SOCIETY AS A HISTORICALLY DEVELOPING TOTALITY OF
RELATIONS. THUS THEY REJECT AN APPROACH THAT ARGUES THAT A
"TRADITIONAL" INDIA IS BEING CHANGED BY FORCES OF
"MODERNIZATION", AND, WHILE ACKNOWLEDGING THE IMPORTANCE OF
THE IDEOLOGIES OF THE SOUTH ASIAN PEOPLE THEMSELVES, THEY DO
NOT ACCEPT THE CULTURALIST PREMISE OF THOSE SOCIOLOGICAL
INTERPRETATIONS THAT MAINTAIN THAT CASTE AND RELIGION MAKE
SOUTH ASIA ESSENTIALLY DIFFERENT FROM OTHER REGIONS. THEIR
APPROACH IS A HISTORICAL ONE, ASSIGNING CAUSAL PRIMACY TO
NEITHER ECONOMICS NOR POLITICS NOR IDEOLOGY, RECOGNIZING THE
ORGANIC UNITY OF SOCIAL STRUCTURES AND PROCESSES.

00892 ALAWNAH, A.K.
THE IMPACT OF THE INTIFADA ON THE PALESTINIAN AND ISRAELI
ECONOMIES
NEW OUTLOOK, 32(11-12 (297-298)) (NOV 89), 20-23.
THE PALESTINIAN PEOPLE'S INTIFADA IS CREATING A NEW
POLITICAL, ECONOMIC AND SOCIAL REALITY IN THE OCCUPIED
TERRITORIES. THIS PAPER AIMS AT EXPLORING IN DETAIL THE PRE-
INTIFADA ECONOMIC RELATIONS BETWEEN THE OCCUPIED TERRITORIES
AND ISRAEL, IN ORDER TO EXPLORE THE IMPACT OF THE INTIFADA
AND THE ISRAELI COUNTERMEASURES ON THE PALESTINIAN AND
ISRAELI ECONOMIES.

00893 ALBANO, T.
THE YOUNG COMMUNIST LEAGUE: CHOICE OF A NEW GENERATION
POLITICAL AFFAIRS, LXVIII(6) (JUN 89), 11-15.
THE ARTICLE RECOUNTS THE EVENTS SURROUNDING THE FIRST
NATIONAL CONFERENCE OF THE YOUNG COMMUNIST LEAGUE USA. THE
CONFERENCE BROUGHT YCL MEMBERS FROM ACROSS THE US AS WELL AS
FROM CANADA, IRAN, EL SALVADOR, AND SOUTH AFRICA. THE
ARTICLE OUTLINED THE INCREASING SUPPORT AND INCREASING
MILITANCY OF THE ORGANIZATION AND RECOUNTS SOME OF THE
RECENT ACTIVITIES OF THE GROUP.

00894 ALBISHI, M.F.
ARAB GULF COOPERATION COUNCIL
AVAILABLE FROM NTIS, NO. AD-A202 042/8/GAR, APR 88, 34.
MANY PEOPLE INCLUDING THE U.S.A. BELIEVE THE GULF
COOPERATION COUNCIL, GCC, IS A VERY IMPORTANT PART OF THE
MIDDLE EAST AND ITS STABILITY IS A MAJOR ISSUE. THIS PAPER
WILL ATTEMPT TO ANSWER THE QUESTION, 'DO THE GCC COUNTRIES
HAVE A COMMON INTEREST WITH THE U.S.A. AND WHY IS ITS
STABILITY SO IMPORTANT TO THE WEST.'.

00895 ALBRIGHT, D.E.
THE USSR AND THE THIRD WORLD IN THE 1980'S
PROBLEMS OF COMMUNISM, XXXVIII(2-3) (MAR 89), 50-70.
IN THE LAST DECADE, THE NUMBER OF DISTINCT SOVIET
SCHOOLS OF THOUGHT CONCERNING WHAT POLICY THE USSR SHOULD
PURSUE TOWARD THE THIRD WORLD HAS MULTIPLIED SIGNIFICANTLY.
TO THOS WHO WOULD SUPPORT "REVOLUTIONARY-DEMOCRATIC" AND/OR
RADICAL MILITARY REGIMES HAVE BEEN ADDED THOSE WHO ADVOCATE
SOME ACCEPTANCE OF THE ATTRACTION THAT CAPITALISM HAS FOR
EMERGENT THIRD WORLD GOVERNMENTS OR WHO SEE THE SOVIET
UNION'S INTERESTS TO LIE IN DEALING WITH THE THIRD WORLD AS
PART OF AN ECONOMICALLY INTERDEPENDENT WORLD ECONOMY. THE
TOP SOVIET LEADERSHIP, IN CONTRAST WITH EARLIER PERIODS, HAS
NOT ENDORSED A SINGLE SCHOOL OF THOUGHT EXCLUSIVELY, BUT
RATHER HAS COMBINED ELEMENTS OF THE POLICY PRESCRIPTIONS OF
ALL OF THE CONTENDING SCHOOLS, THE MIX VARYING SUBSTANTIALLY
FROM REGION TO REGION.

00896 ALBRITTON, R.
IMPACTS OF INTERGOVERNMENTAL FINANCIAL INCENTIVES ON STATE
WELFARE POLICYMAKING AND INTERSTATE EQUITY
PUBLIUS: THE JOURNAL OF FEDERALISM, 19(2) (SPR 89),
127-142.
WELFARE POLICY IN THE UNITED STATES IS STRONGLY
INFLUENCED BY INTERGOVERNMENTAL FACTORS. THIS ANALYSIS
TRACES THE EFFECTS OF FEDERAL FINANCIAL INCENTIVES ON STATE
WELFARE POLICY DECISIONS ACROSS PROGRAMS AND EXAMINES HOW
CHANGES IN FEDERAL INCENTIVES AFFECT STATE POLICY CHOICES
OVER TIME. THE DATA INDICATE THAT HIGHER LEVELS OF FEDERAL

PARTICIPATION ARE ASSOCIATED WITH SUBSTANTIAL REDUCTIONS IN VARIANCE OF WELFARE GRANTS AMONG THE STATES AND WITH HIGHER LEVELS OF INTERSTATE EQUITY. THESE FINDINGS IMPLY THAT SIGNIFICANT SHIFTS IN WELFARE OUTPUTS WOULD RESULT FROM A DEVOLUTION OF RESPONSIBILITY FOR WELFARE TO THE STATES.

00897 ALDOUS, J.
WHAT IF INFLATION RETURNS?
SOCIETY, 26(2) (SEP 89), 76-82.
INFLATION HAS BECOME A CHRONIC DANGER FOR DEVELOPED COUNTRIES. THE UNITED STATES HAS EXPERIENCED A FUNDAMENTAL SHIFT IN ITS ECONOMY IN THE LAST EIGHT YEARS THAT SUGGESTS IT MAY BE IN FOR A PERIOD OF HIGHER INFLATION RATES. THE U.S. NO LONGER ENJOYS FOREIGN-TRADE SURPLUSES, BUT IS ON THE SHORT END WITH TRADING PARTNERS. CITIZENS ARE SAVING LESS AND CONSUMING MORE, SO THAT LARGE FEDERAL DEFICITS RESULTING FROM TAX CUTS AND CONTINUED HIGH FEDERAL SPENDING HAVE HAD TO BE FINANCED OUTSIDE THE U.S. BORDERS. THE UNITED STATES HAS LOST ITS POSITION AS THE WORLD'S LARGEST CREDITOR NATION AND, INSTEAD, HAS BECOME ITS LARGEST DEBTOR NATION. AS A CONSEQUENCE, THE VALUE OF THE DOLLAR IS UNDER DOWNWARD PRESSURE, AND INFLATION AGAIN MAY BECOME A CENTRAL POLITICAL ISSUE. POSSIBLE INFLATION-FIGHTING STRATEGIES LARGELY FOCUS ON EASING THE COSTS OF DEFLATING THE ECONOMY TO HOUSEHOLDS WITH JOB HOLDERS. WHEN MAKING INFLATION-CONTROL STRATEGIES, POLICYMAKERS MUST KEEP INFLATION AND FORIEGN CREDITORS COMPARATIVELY QUIESCENT WHILE STRENGHENING THE ECONOMY.

00898 ALDRICH, J.H.; BORGIDA, E.; SULLIVAN, J.L.
FOREIGN AFFAIRS AND ISSUE VOTING: DO PRESIDENTIAL CANDIDATES "WALTZ BEFORE A BLIND AUDIENCE?"
AMERICAN POLITICAL SCIENCE REVIEW, 83(1) (MAR 89), 123-142.
WHILE CANDIDATES REGULARLY SPEND MUCH TIME AND EFFORT CAMPAIGNING ON FOREIGN AND DEFENSE POLICIES, THE THRUST OF PREVAILING SCHOLARLY OPINION IS THAT VOTERS POSSESS LITTLE INFORMATION AND WEAK ATTITUDES ON THESE ISSUES, WHICH THEREFORE HAVE NEGLIGIBLE IMPACT ON THEIR VOTING BEHAVIOR. THIS ESSAY ARGUES THAT PUBLIC ATTITUDES ON FOREIGN AND DEFENSE POLICIES ARE AVAILABLE AND COGNITIVELY ACCESSIBLE, THAT THE PUBLIC HAS PERCEIVED CLEAR DIFFERENCES BETWEEN THE CANDIDATES ON THESE ISSUES IN RECENT ELECTIONS, AND THAT THESE ISSUES HAVE AFFECTED THE PUBLIC'S VOTE CHOICES. DATA INDICATE THAT THESE CONCLUSIONS ARE APPROPRIATE FOR FOREIGN AFFAIRS ISSUES AND DOMESTIC ISSUES.

00899 ALDRIDGE, D.P.
AFRICAN-AMERICAN WOMEN IN THE ECONOMIC MARKETPLACE: A CONTINUING STRUGGLE
JOURNAL OF BLACK STUDIES, 20(2) (DEC 89), 129-154.
THIS ARTICLE ATTEMPTS TO EXAMINE THE ECONOMIC STATUS OF AFRICAN-AMERICAN WOMEN IN AMERICA. IT EXAMINES THEIR OCCUPATIONAL STATUS, EDUCATIONAL ATTAINMENT, EARNINGS, AND LEVEL OF BUSINESS OWNERSHIP SINCE 1910 TO DETERMINE TO WHAT EXTENT THEY HAVE "MADE IT" IN THE ECONOMIC MARKETPLACE AND TO WHAT EXTENT THE STRUGGLE CONTINUES. EACH OF THESE VARIABLES ARE ASSESSED IN TERMS OF THE DISTRIBUTION OF ALL WOMEN WHO ARE INVOLVED IN THE WORLD OF WORK OUTSIDE OF THE HOME. FURTHERMORE, SOME SPECIAL ISSUES CONFRONTING AFRICANAMERICAN WOMEN ARE PRESENTED.

00900 ALESINA, A.; ROSENTHAL, H.
PARTISAN CYCLES IN CONGRESSIONAL ELECTIONS AND THE MACROECONOMY
AMERICAN POLITICAL SCIENCE REVIEW, 83(2) (JUN 89), 373-398.
IN THE POSTWAR UNITED STATES THE PRESIDENT'S PARTY HAS ALWAYS DONE WORSE IN THE MIDTERM CONGRESSIONAL ELECTIONS THAN IN THE PREVIOUS CONGRESSIONAL ELECTION. REPUBLICAN ADMINISTRATIONS EXHIBIT BELOW-AVERAGE, AND DEMOCRATIC ADMINISTRATIONS ABOVE-AVERAGE, ECONOMIC GROWTH IN THE FIRST HALF OF EACH TERM, WHEREAS IN THE LATTER HALVES THE TWO SEE EQUAL GROWTH. A RATIONAL EXPECTATIONS MODEL IS CONSISTENT WITH THESE TWO REGULARITIES. IN PRESIDENTIAL ELECTIONS, VOTERS CHOOSE BETWEEN TWO POLARIZED CANDIDATES. THEY THEN USE MIDTERM ELECTIONS TO COUNTERBALANCE THE PRESIDENT'S POLICIES BY STRENGTHENING THE OPPOSITION IN CONGRESS. SINCE PRESIDENTS OF DIFFERENT PARTIES ARE ASSOCIATED WITH DIFFERENT POLICIES, THE MODEL PREDICTS A (SPURIOUS) CORRELATION BETWEEN THE STATE OF THE ECONOMY AND ELECTIONS. THE PREDICTIONS CONTRAST WITH THOSE OF RETROSPECTIVE VOTING MODELS, IN WHICH VOTERS REWARD THE INCUMBENT IF THE ECONOMY IS DOING WELL BEFORE THE ELECTION. THE MODEL PERFORMS EMPIRICALLY AT LEAST AS WELL AS, AND OFTEN BETTER THAN, ALTERNATIVE MODELS.

00901 ALEXANDER, A.; WRIGLEY, C.
THE DECLINE OF LOCAL GOVERNMENT
CONTEMPORARY RECORD, 2(6) (SUM 89), 2-8.
AN OVERVIEW OF THE CHANGING FORTUNES OF BRITISH LOCAL GOVERNMENT SINCE WORLD WAR II IS FOLLOWED BY A LOOK AT "HUNG" COUNTY COUNCILS, WHICH HAVE BECOME THE NORM INSTEAD OF THE EXCEPTION.

00902 ALEXANDER, D.
MEXICO BUSINESSMEN FILE INJUNCTIONS AGAINST TAX
MEXICO-UNITED STATES REPORT, II(6) (FEB 89), 1,6.
OUTRAGED BY THE SALINAS GOVERNMENT'S NEW TAX ON THE NET WORTH OF PRIVATE COMPANIES, MEXICAN BUSINESSMEN HAVE FILED INJUNCTIONS TO HAVE THE TAX DECLARED ILLEGAL. THE 1988 LEFTIST PRESIDENTIAL CANDIDATE, CUAUHTEMOC CARDENAS, ALSO OPPOSES THE TAX BECAUSE IT IS A BLOW TO THE PRODUCTIVE CAPACITY OF SMALL AND MEDIUM ENTERPRISES.

00903 ALEXANDER, F.
CLASS CONSCIOUS FORCES, ECONOMIC STRUGGLES, AND CONDITIONS AMONG AFRICAN AMERICANS
POLITICAL AFFAIRS, LXVIII(4) (APR 89), 31-33.
THE CURRENT DEBATE AMONG COMMUNIST AND LEFT FORCES ON WHETHER OR NOT TO PLACE MAJOR EMPHASIS ON WORK INSIDE THE DEMOCRATIC PARTY IS ERECTING AN ARTIFICIAL WALL BETWEEN ECONOMIC STRUGGLES, ON ONE HAND, AND OTHER DEMOCRATIC QUESTIONS (INCLUDING THE STRUGGLE FOR ATTAINING FULL LEGAL, POLITICAL, SOCIAL, AND ECONOMIC EQUALITY FOR AFRICAN AMERICANS), ON THE OTHER. THE ARGUMENTS INDICATE THAT CLASS-CONSCIOUS FORCES HAVE UNDERSTOOD THEIR ROLE IN ECONOMIC STRUGGLES BUT HAVE MISUNDERSTOOD THEIR ROLE IN DEMOCRATIC STRUGGLES.

00904 ALEXANDER, J.
DILLON'S RULE UNDER THE BURGER COURT: THE MUNICIPAL LIABILITY CASES
PUBLIUS: THE JOURNAL OF FEDERALISM, 18(1) (WIN 88), 127-140.
THE ARTICLE EXAMINES THE ISSUE OF TORT LIABILITY OF MUNICIPALITIES UNDER THE BURGER COURT. IT EXPLORES THE BACKGROUND OF THE ISSUE INCLUDING THE 1943 PARKER V. BROWN OF THE US SUPREME COURT. IT ALSO EXAMINES MANY OF THE LEGAL ISSUES SUCH AS MUNICIPALITIES AS PUBLIC ACTORS, THE DOCTRINE OF EXPRESSED POWERS, AND THE INTERSTICES OF STATE LAW. THE ARTICLE CONCLUDES THAT ALTHOUGH THE BURGER COURT RULED THAT MUNICIPALITIES ARE NOT AUTOMATICALLY IMMUNIZED FROM TORT LIABILITY, IT FAILED TO ADDRESS THE FUNDAMENTAL QUESTION OF WHETHER MUNICIPALITIES AS PUBLIC ACTORS SHOULD BE LIABLE TO PRIVATE DAMAGES IN THE COURSE OF THEIR PUBLIC FUNCTIONS.

00905 ALEXANDER, J.D.
THE POLITICAL ECONOMY OF TAX-BASED INCOMES POLICY: WEALTH EFFECTS OF POST KEYNESIAN TIP
JOURNAL OF ECONOMIC ISSUES, 23(1) (MAR 89), 135-146.
THIS ANALYSIS APPLIES THREE POLITICAL ECONOMIC CRITERIA TO EVALUATE TIP: EFFICIENCY, EQUITY AND "DEMOCRACY" - THE EXTENT TO WHICH ECONOMIC AGENTS PARTICIPATE IN DECISIONS THAT HAVE AN IMPACT UPON THEM (SEE (BOWLES AND EDWARDS 1985, CHAP. 2)). TO PROVIDE A SHARP AND PROVOCATIVE FOCUS ON THE REDISTRIBUTIVE WEALTH EFFECTS OF TIP, THIS ARTICLE ASKS UNDER WHAT CONDITIONS THE TRADITIONAL HOSTILITY OF LABOR ORGANIZATIONS AND THE WORKING POOR TO TIP WOULD BE RATIONAL. THE DEFINES THE SALIENT FEATURES OF A GROWTH-GENERATING TIP, AND TRACES WEALTH EFFECTS THAT MIGHT REASONABLY EVOKE CHARGES OF UNJUST REDISTRIBUTION. NOT ONLY DO QUESTIONS OF EQUITY EMERGE, BUT ALSO ISSUES OF DEMOCRACY ARISE IN AREAS OF CONSUMER SOVEREIGNTY AND ACCESS TO CREDIT, AND THE ISSUE OF MACROECONOMIC EFFICIENCY EMERGES IN THE COMBINATION OF TIP AND DEMAND STIMULUS. THE ARTICLE CONCLUDES BY MENTIONING SOME POSSIBLE CONDITIONS NECESSARY FOR TIP TO SUCCEED, INCLUDING SOCIAL POLICIES THAT WAGE-DEPENDENT AND POORER HOUSEHOLDS MIGHT ACCEPT AS COMPENSATION FOR TIP REDISTRIBUTION.

00906 ALEXEYEVA, L.
IN THE AGE OF GLASNOST: NATIONALIST MOVEMENTS IN THE USSR
NEW POLITICS, 11(2) (WIN 89), 133-147.
THE CALLS FOR GLASNOST AND DEMOCRATIZATION PROMOTED BY THE PRESENT SOVIET LEADERSHIP HAVE INEVITABLY STIMULATED DEMAND FROM BELOW FOR THE RESOLUTION OF LONG-STANDING GRIEVANCES. THE RESPONSE TO THESE DEMANDS REVEALS THAT THIS LEADERSHIP IS DEVOID OF ANY "NEW THINKING" ABOUT NATIONALITY POLICY, AN AREA OF PRIMARY IMPORTANCE FOR A MULTI-NATIONAL STATE. THE GORBACHEV GOVERNMENT HAS MADE NO ATTEMPT TO RESOLVE A SINGLE ONE OF THE NUMEROUS NATIONALITY PROBLEMS, FOCUSING ONLY ON THOSE WHICH ESCALATE INTO OPEN CONFLICT. THE OCCURRENCE OF THESE CONFLICTS DETERMINES THE SEQUENCE IN WHICH THEY ARE DEALT WITH BY THE SOVIET LEADERSHIP. ONLY INITIATIVES FROM BELOW OR THE ACTIONS OF THE LOWER CLASSES FORCES THE GOVERNMENT TO COME TO GRIPS WITH THE NATIONALITIES PROBLEM. EVEN THEN, INSTEAD OF SEARCHING FOR SOLUTIONS, THE AUTHORITIES TRY TO EXTINGUISH OPEN CONFLICT BY FORCING THE AGGRIEVED TO ACCEPT AN INTOLERABLE SITUATION.

00907 ALGABBANI, F.M.
IN-SERVICE TRAINING NEEDS ASSESSMENT IN SAUDI ARABIA: PRESENT AND FUTURE
DISSERTATION ABSTRACTS INTERNATIONAL, 50(3) (SEP 89), 788-A.
THE GOALS OF THIS STUDY HERE TO UNDERSTAND THE CURRENT IN-SERVICE TRAINING NEEDS ASSESSMENT IN SAUDI ARABIA AND TO UNDERSTAND THE APPLICABILITY OF DIFFERENT NEEDS ASSESSMENT TECHNIQUES IN THE SAUDI ORGANIZATIONAL CONTEXT. THE AUTHOR SURVEYED INSTITUTE OF PUBLIC ADMINISTRATION POLICY MAKERS,

IPA TRAINERS, GOVERNMENT TRAINING MANAGERS, GOVERNMENT LINE
MANAGERS, AND PUBLIC EMPLOYEES.

00908 ALI SHAH, S. M.
    PAKISTAN AND THE GULF WAR
    SOUTH ASIA JOURNAL, 2(4) (APR 89), 435-442.
        PREDOMINANTLY A MUSLIM STATE, SHARING COMMON BORDERS
    WITH IRAN; AND HAVING A HOST OF ECONOMIC AND STRATEGIC TIES
    WITH THE ARAB STATES, PAKISTAN HAD A GREAT DEAL AT STAKE IN
    GULF WAR. IT MAY BE NOTED THAT THE GULF WAR WHICH FOLLOWED
    THE IRANIAN REVOLUTION IN FEBRUARY 1979, AND THE SOVIET
    INVASION OF AFGHANISTAN IN DECEMBER OF THE SAME YEAR, HAD
    BROUGHT NEW OPPORTUNITIES AND RAISED NEW RISKS FOR
    PAKISTAN'S MILITARY RULER, LATE GENERAL ZIA-UL-HAQ, WHO IN
    APRIL 1979 EXECUTED CHARISMATIC ZULFIQAR ALI BHUTTO, THE
    ELECTED PRIME MINISTER OF PAKISTAN. THIS ARTICLE PURPORTS TO
    EXAMINE GENERAL ZIA'S DILEMMA AND THE COURSE HE CAREFULLY
    CHARTED DURING THE GULF WAR. FOR UNDERSTANDING GENERAL ZIA'S
    DIFFICULTIES ARISING OUT OF THE GULF CONFLICT, AND HIS
    RESPONSE TO IT, THE ARTICLE DEALS BRIEFLY WITH THE ORIGINS
    OF THE GULF WAR.

00909 ALI, S.
    A LAW UNTO HIMSELF
    FAR EASTERN ECONOMIC REVIEW, 141(35) (SEP 88), 19-21.
        THE ARTICLE EXAMINES THE TENURE AS PRESIDENT OF PAKISTAN
    OF THE LATE ZIA-UL HAQ. IT OUTLINES THE COUP D'ETAT IN WHICH
    ZIA ASSUMED POWER AND HIS PROGRESSION FROM BEGINING AS AN
    INTERNATIONAL PARIAH BECAUSE OF THE EXECUTION OF ZULFIKAR
    ALI BHUTTO AND OTHER HARSH REPRESSIVE MEASURES, TO A
    SIGNIFICANT FIGURE ON THE WORLD SCENE. ZIA'S ABILITY TO TAKE
    ADVANTAGE OF OPPORTUNITY WAS ONE OUTSTANDING TRAIT THAT HE
    POSSESSED: HE SAW THE SOVIET INVASION OF AFGHANISTAN AS A
    GREAT OPPORTUNITY TO ACQUIRE A LARGE AMOUNT OF AID FROM THE
    WEST AS WELL AS INTERNATIONAL RECOGNITION.

00910 ALI, S.
    A NUDGE FOR NORMALISATION
    FAR EASTERN ECONOMIC REVIEW, 141(37) (SEP 88), 24.
        THE PLANNED VISIT OF INDIAN PRIME MINISTER RAJIV GANDHI
    TO CHINA IS A SIGNIFICANT BREAKTHROUGH IN SINO-INDIAN
    RELATIONS. THE VISIT WILL GIVE A POLITICAL PUSH TO THE
    PROCESS OF NORMALIZATION AND TO THE SEARCH FOR A FORMULA TO
    THE LONG-STANDING BORDER DISPUTE. A SERIES OF LOW-KEY
    MINISTERIAL AND OTHER VISITS TO CHINA OVER THE PAST TWO
    YEARS HAVE LED UP TO THE MEETING OF LEADERS. ALTHOUGH THE
    TWO NATIONS MIGHT ANNOUNCE A SET OF AGREED PRINCIPLES FOR
    RESOLVIN THE HIMALAYAN BORDER DISPUTE, THE SETTLEMENT OF THE
    ISSUE ITSELF IS CONSIDERED A LONG-TERM PROSPECT.

00911 ALI, S.
    COMMENT AT YOUR PERIL
    FAR EASTERN ECONOMIC REVIEW, 141(37) (SEP 88), 18.
        INDIA'S PROUD REPUTATION OF HAVING THE FREEST PRESS IN
    THE THIRD WORLD IS UNDER THE WORST ASSAULT SINCE THE MEDIA
    CURBS OF 1975. THE LOWER HOUSE OF PARLIAMENT PASSED A BILL
    DEFINING DEFAMATION AND PRESCRIBING A MANDATORY JAIL
    SENTENCE. THE UPROAR WAS IMMEDIATE AND FURIOUS AND THE
    GOVERNMENT WAS FORCED TO RETREAT AT LEAST TEMPORARILY.

00912 ALI, S.
    NO WINNERS, ONE LOSER
    FAR EASTERN ECONOMIC REVIEW, 141(36) (SEP 88), 26-27.
        THE SIGNING OF TWO AGREEMENTS WITH THE COMMUNIST STATE
    GOVERNMENT OF WEST BENGAL AND THE CENTRAL GOVERNMENT IN NEW
    DELHI BY THE GURKHA NATIONAL LIBERATION FRONT (GNLF) ENDED
    TWO YEARS OF VIOLENCE AS THE GNLF STRUGGLED FOR A SPEARATE
    STATE. ALTHOUGH IT APPEARS THAT NONE OF THE PARTIES OF
    INVOLVED HAVE COME OUT AHEAD, OBSERVERS AGREE THAT THE
    CENTRAL GOVERNMENT HAS LOST CREDIBILITY WITH BOTH THE
    BENGALIS AND GURKHAS.

00913 ALI, S.
    PROPAGANDA BARRAGE
    FAR EASTERN ECONOMIC REVIEW, 142(51) (DEC 89), 23.
        INDIA'S CONSTRUCTION OF A BARRAGE ON THE JHELUM RIVER AT
    WULAR IN KASHMIR HAS CAUSED A MAJOR DOMESTIC POLITICAL ROW
    IN PAKISTAN. PRESSURE FROM PUNJAB CHIEF MINISTER NAWAZ
    SHARIF HAS CAUSED THE PAKISTAN PEOPLE'S PARTY (PPP) TO MAKE
    SEVERAL SPECTACULAR SOMERSAULTS ON SEEMINGLY IRREVOCABLE
    STANDS ON THE ISSUE. ALTHOUGH PAKISTAN DOES HAVE A LEGAL
    CASE AGAINST INDIA (THE INDUS BASIN TREATY AWARDED THE
    JHELUM TO PAKISTAN), INDIA IS CURRENTLY WILLING TO CONCEDE
    MORE TO PAKISTAN IN EXCHANGE FOR PERMISSION TO BUILD THE
    BARRAGE THAN PAKISTAN COULD EVER HOPE TO GAIN THROUGH
    ARBITRATION. HOWEVER, IF REGIONAL PRESSURE FROM PUNJAB
    CONTINUES, ISLAMABAD MAY BE FORCED TO OPT FOR ARBITRATION.

00914 ALI, S.
    REFORM AT THE ROOTS
    FAR EASTERN ECONOMIC REVIEW, 146(51) (DEC 89), 52.
        IN ITS FIRST YEAR IN POWER IN PAKISTAN, BENAZIR BHUTTO'S
    GOVERNMENT HAS SPENT MUCH ENERGY TRYING TO LAY THE POLITICAL,
    ADMINISTRATIVE, AND PHYSICAL FOUNDATIONS FOR PRIVATE

INVESTMENT-LED GROWTH. BHUTTO CLAIMS THESE EFFORTS ARE
BEGINNING TO SHOW DIVIDENDS. ALTHOUGH THE FIGURES SHE CITES
HAVE YET TO BE CONFIRMED, THEY BODE WELL FOR BHUTTO'S
ATTEMPTS TO ENCOURAGE PRIVATE INVESTMENT. OBSERVERS STATE
THAT THE MOST IMPORTANT REFORM THAT REMAINS TO BE
IMPLEMENTED IS STOCK MARKET REGULATION.

00915 ALI, S.
    RENEGING ON REVOLUTION
    FAR EASTERN ECONOMIC REVIEW, 141(38) (SEP 88), 38-39.
        COMMUNISTS WORLDWIDE HAVE BEEN THROWN INTO IDEOLOGICAL
    DISARRAY BY THE SOVIET UNION'S NEW POLICIES OF GLASNOST AND
    PERESTROIKA. THEIR TRADITIONAL RALLYING CRY FOR CLASS
    STRUGGLE AND AGAINST IMPERIALISM AND CAPITALISM IS IN DANGER
    OF BEING NEUTRALIZIED AS THE WORLD MOVEMENT PONDERS THE
    IMPLICATIONS OF THE SOVIET'S REFORMS. COMMUNIST PARTIES IN
    INDIA WERE NO EXCEPTION, BUT THE COMMUNIST PART OF INDIA-
    MARXIST HAS OPENLY DECLARED ITS ANNOYANCE WITH THE SOVIET
    CHANGES AND HAVE DRAFTED A DOCUMENT WHICH CRITICIZES THE
    SOVIETS ON SEVERAL COUNTS AND FAULTS THEM FOR HAVING A
    "FAULTY VIEW OF THE WORLD SITUATION."

00916 ALI, S.
    TALKING WITH THE TRIBALS
    FAR EASTERN ECONOMIC REVIEW, 141(35) (SEP 88), 32, 34.
        INDIA'S GOVERNMENT ANNOUCED THAT IT HAD LIFTED THEN BAN
    ON THE TRIPURA NATIONAL VOLUNTEERS (TNV) AND HAD REACHED AN
    AGREEMENT WITH THE INSURGENTS TO END THE CONFLICT WITHIN A
    MONTH. THE FLIGHT OF MANY OF THE TNV TO BANGLADESH HAS LONG
    BEEN A POINT OF CONFLICT BETWEEN THE TWO NATIONS.

00917 ALI, S.
    THE CREDIBILITY FACTOR
    FAR EASTERN ECONOMIC REVIEW, 141(35) (SEP 88), 30-31.
        INDIAN PRIME MINISTER RAJIV GANDHI IS AT THE LOWEST
    POINT IN HIS POLITICAL CAREER AND THERE ARE DOUBTS THAT
    CONGRESS CAN ARREST THE DECLINE OF THE RULING PARTY. HOWEVER,
    GANDHI REMAINS OPTIMISTIC, BELIEVING IN THE CYCLICAL THEORY
    OF INDIAN POLITICS WHICH INDICATES THAT AFTER A LOW POINT IN
    THE FOURTH YEAR OF A TERM, AN INCUMBENT PRIME MINISTER WILL
    EXPERIENCE AN UPSWING IN POPULARITY IN THE FOLLOWING YEAR.
    HOWEVER, CYCLES MAY NOT BE ENOUGH TO SAVE GANDHI WHO IS
    PERCEIVED BY MANY IN INDIA TO BE AN INEFFECTUAL RULER WITH
    LITTLE CONCEPT OF THE CRISES THAT FACE INDIA.

00918 ALI, S.
    TOGETHER, YET APART
    FAR EASTERN ECONOMIC REVIEW, 141(35) (SEP 88), 31.
        THE ANNOUNCEMENT OF THE CREATION OF A NATIONAL FRONT
    ALLIANCE OF SOME OF THE OPPOSITION PARTIES IN INDIA RAISES
    SOME OLD QUESTIONS ABOUT OPPOSITION POLITICS IN INDIA. MOST
    OBSERVERS BELIEVE THAT THE OPPOSITION COULD HAVE BROKEN THE
    RULE OF THE CONGRESS PARTY WHICH EXTENDS BACK TO 1947 MANY
    TIMES IF IT WEREN'T FOR THE INTERNAL STRIFE AND SECTARIAN
    CLASHES THAT SPLIT ANY ATTEMPTS AT OPPOSITION ALLIANCE. THE
    NATIONAL FRONT SEEMS TO BE NO EXCEPTION AS IT IS STILL
    DIFFICULT TO DECIDE WHETHER THEIR COMMON ANTIPATHY TO THE
    RULING CONGRESS IS STRONGER THAN THEIR MUTUAL ANTAGONISM.

00919 ALI, T.
    PEACE IN CAMBODIA
    AVAILABLE FROM NTIS, NO. ADA207 265/0/GAR, MAR 89, 58.
        THIS STUDY WILL EXAMINE THE CASES OF THE CONFLICT IN
    CAMBODIA AND BRIEFLY DISCUSS THE PRESENT INITIATIVES FOR
    PEACE. THE ADVANTAGES AND DISADVANTAGES OF EACH INITIATIVE
    ARE EXPLORED. IN CONCLUSION, THE BEST OPTION AVAILABLE FOR
    PEACE IN CAMBODIA WILL BE PRESENTED.

00920 ALIBONI, R.
    EUROPEAN SECURITY AND OUT-OF-NATO AREA CRISES
    INTERNATIONAL SPECTATOR, XXIII(2) (APR 88), 90-97.
        SINCE THE END OF THE SEVENTIES, WESTERN EUROPEAN NATIONS
    HAVE, EITHER ALONE OR TOGETHER WITH THE US, REPEATEDLY
    INTERVENED IN CRISES OUTSIDE OF THE NATO AREA. THE MEANING
    AND THE IMPLICATIONS OF THIS DEVELOPMENT ARE THE OBJECT OF
    DEBATE BOTH IN MULTILATERAL WESTERN INSTITUTIONS AND IN
    INDIVIDUAL COUNTRIES.

00921 ALIOTO, M.F.
    INCREMENTAL AND NON-INCREMENTAL POLITICAL CHANGE PATTERNS:
    COMPARISONS OF ELEVEN HELLENIC, LATIN EUROPEAN, AND LATIN
    AMERICAN PARLIAMENTARY AND PRESIDENTIAL SYSTEMS (1922-1987)
    DISSERTATION ABSTRACTS INTERNATIONAL, 50(6) (DEC 89),
    1784-A.
        THE AUTHOR DISTINGUISHES BETWEEN THE MOST COMMON SETS OF
    INCREMENTAL AND NON-INCREMENTAL PATTERNS OF POLITICAL CHANGE
    IN ARGENTINA, CHILE, COLOMBIA, CYPRUS, GREECE, ITALY, THE
    PHILIPPINES, PORTUGAL, SPAIN, URUGUAY, AND VENZUELA. CHANGE-
    PATTERN CHARACTERISTICS ARE IDENTIFIED, EXPLAINED, AND
    COMPARED. SUCH FACTORS AS PARTY ALIGNMENT, COALITION
    CONFLICT, AND EXTRA-PARLIAMENTARY GROUP PARTICIPATION ARE
    CONSIDERED.

00922 ALLCOCK, J.B.
IN PRAISE OF CHAUVINISM: RHETORICS OF NATIONALISM IN
YUGOSLAV POLITICS
THIRD WORLD QUARTERLY, 11(4) (OCT 89), 208-222.
THE PURPOSE OF THIS ARTICLE IS TO EXPLORE
DISPASSIONATELY THE SOCIOLOGICAL SIGNIFICANCE OF NATIONALISM
IN YUGOSLAVIA. THE TITLE POINTS TO A BASIC RE-EVALUATION OF
THIS PROBLEM. THEORIES OF NATIONALISM, AND NATIONALISM AS
POLITICAL 'RHETORIC' AND THE FAILURE OF POLITICAL RHETORIC
IN YUGOSLAVIA ARE, EACH IN TURN, EXAMINED. THE DIVERSITY OF
YUGOSLAV 'NATIONALISMS' IS DETAILED. THE CONCLUSION IS THAT
BY ITS FAILURE TO INSTITUTIONALISE A COMMON RHETORIC BASED
UPON SOCIALISM, THE YUGOSLAV REGIME HAS KEPT ALIVE THE
POSSIBILITY OF ALTERNATIVE RHETORICS.

00923 ALLEN, C.L.
THE MYSTERIES OF RU-486
AMERICAN SPECTATOR, (OCT 89), 17-20.
THIS ARTICLE EXPLORES THE ABORTION PILL, RU-486, WHICH
IS FAR FROM A DO-IT-YOURSELF ABORTION FIX, AS MANY
OPTIMISTIC PEOPLE WOULD LIKE TO THINK IT IS. IT DETAILS THE
WAY RU-486 WORKS. THE SIDE EFFECTS AND RESERVATIONS THAT
SOME MEMBERS OF THE MEDICAL PROFESSION HAVE EXPRESSED, IT
EXAMINES THE POLITICAL IMPLICATIONS AS THE U.S. GOVERNMENT
AND FEMINIST AND POPULATION CONTROL GROUPS GRAPLE WITH THE
FACT THAT THE ABORTION PILL IS CAUGHT IN THE GOVERNMENT'S
REGULATORY MACHINERY.

00924 ALLEN, C.S.
CORPORATION AND REGIONAL ECONOMIC POLICIES IN THE FEDERAL
REPUBLIC OF GERMANY: THE "MESO" POLITICS OF INDUSTRIAL
ADJUSTMENT
PUBLIUS: THE JOURNAL OF FEDERALISM, 19(4) (FAL 89),
147-164.
THIS ARTICLE EXAMINES CORPORATIST THEORY (BUSINESS,
LABOR, GOVERNMENT INTERACTION) IN THE CONTEXT OF REGIONAL
GOVERNMENTS AND ECONOMIC POLICY IN THE FEDERAL REPUBLIC OF
GERMANY. WEST GERMAN REGIONAL GOVERNMENTS, FAR MORE THAN THE
FEDERAL GOVERNMENT, HAVE ACTED TO SHAPE INDUSTRIAL
ADJUSTMENT AND ENHANCE INTERNATIONAL COMPETITIVENESS.
CORPORATIST THEORY IS ANALYZED IN THE CONTEXT OF ITS
EVOLUTION FROM A MACRO TO A MESO VARIANT, WHICH ATTEMPTS TO
ADDRESS SECTORAND REGION-SPECIFIC FORMS OF ECONOMIC
DISLOCATION. THE NEW MESO-CORPORATIST APPROACH IS FOUND
INSUFFICIENT BECAUSE IT LOOKS ONLY AT PRIVATE INTERESTS AND
NEGLECTS THE REGIONAL POLITICS OF INDUSTRIAL ADJUSTMENT. THE
VERY DIFFERENT "MESO-POLITICAL" PATTERNS OF ADJUSTMENT ARE
EXAMINED HERE IN A SYNTHETIC REVIEW OF RECENT RESEARCH ON
ECONOMIC POLICYMAKING IN BADEN-WURTTEMBERG, BAVARIA, AND
NORTH-RHINE WESTPHALIA. MESO-CORPORATISM MAY STILL PROVE
USEFUL THEORETICALLY, BUT ONLY IF IT INCLUDES THE ROLE OF
REGIONAL GOVERNMENTS.

00925 ALLEN, D.
ANTIWAR ASIAN SCHOLARS AND THE VIETNAM/INDOCHINA WAR
BULLETIN OF CONCERNED ASIAN SCHOLARS, 21(2-4) (APR 89),
112-134.
THIS ARTICLE IS A REVIEW OF THOUGHTS, FEELINGS AND
COMMITMENTS AND EXPECTATIONS OF VARIOUS ASIAN SCHOLARS IN
THE 60S AND 70S AND MORE RECENTLY, THE RESULTS OF A
QUESTIONNAIRE SENT TO ANTIWAR AND ANTI-IMPERIALIST ASIAN
SCHOLARS. IT DESCRIBES SOME OF THE ISSUES FACED BY ASIAN
SCHOLARS DURING THE TIME PERIOD OF THE VIETNAM WAR. IT
BRIEFLY INTERVIEWS: NGO VINH LONG, CHRISTINE WHITE, GARETH
PORTER, NINA ADAMS, NOAM CHOMSKY, EDWARD FRIEDMAN, SANDY
STURDEVANT, FELICIA OLDFATHER, MARK SELDON, ELAINE EMLING,
JAMES MORRELL, MARTHA WINNACKER, AND KATHLEEN GOUGH.

00926 ALLEN, E.
BAZIL: INDIANS AND THE NEW CONSTITUTION
THIRD WORLD QUARTERLY, 11(4) (OCT 89), 148-165.
THIS ARTICLE ADDRESSES ETHNICITY IN BRAZIL WITH SPECIAL
EMPHASIS ON BRAZIL'S INDIAN POPULATION. INDIANS AND
LEGISLATION ARE DISCUSSED AS WELL AS THE CONSTITUENT
ASSEMBLY AND THE 1988 CONSTITUTION. PRESSURES AND
CONTRADICTIONS ARE EXPLORED AND ALSO, THE MILITARY AND CALHA
NORTE.

00927 ALLEN, G.
THE PAIN OF POVERTY: AMERICA
MACLEAN'S (CANADA'S NEWS MAGAZINE), 102(26) (JUL 89), 39.
THE ARTICLE ANALYZES THE WELFARE SYSTEM OF THE US
THROUGH THE EYES OF A SINGLE MOTHER IN MAINE. TO MANY, THE
US SYSTEM OF WELFARE IS A FRUSTRATING PATCHWORK OF SUBSIDIES,
FOOD STAMPS AND MEDICAL COVERAGE. PEOPLE ON WELFARE HAVE
DIFFICULTY ESCAPING DUE TO THE IMMEDIATE LOSS OF BENEFITS
SUCH AS HEALTH INSURANCE UPON THE ACQUISITION OF AN, OFTEN
LOW-PAYING, JOB. ROUGHLY HALF OF ALL AMERICANS FEEL THAT A
GAURANTEED MINIMUM INCOME FOR EVERYONE IS AN ABSOLUTE RIGHT

00928 ALLEN, G.
THE PAIN OF PROVERTY: CANADA
MACLEAN'S (CANADA'S NEWS MAGAZINE), 102(26) (JUL 89), 38.
THE ARTICLES USES AN EXAMPLE OF A SINGLE MOTHER IN NOVA
SCOTIA TO ILLUSTRATE THE WORKINGS OF THE CANADIAN WELFARE
SYSTEM. NOVIA SCOTIA OPERATES ON A TWO-TIER SYSTEM OF
WELFARE THAT SOME ARGUE "PROMOTES INEQUITY." NEW WELFARE
APPLICANTS MUST FIRST SEEK BENEFITS FROM THE LOCAL
GOVERNMENT AND CAN RECEIVE THE HIGHER BENEFITS OF THE SECOND-
TIER PROGRAM ONLY AFTER SIX MONTHS. ALTHOUGH A SINGNIFICANT
NUMBER OF CANADIANS DEEM SOCIAL PROGRAMS TO BE AN "ABSOLUTE"
RIGHT, MANY FEEL ASHMED AND STIGMATIZED UPON ACCEPT
GOVERNMENT HELP.

00929 ALLEN, M. P.; BROYLES, P.
CLASS HEGEMONY AND POLITICAL FINANCE: PRESIDENTIAL
CAMPAIGN CONTRIBUTIONS OF WEALTHY CAPITALIST FAMILIES
AMERICAN SOCIOLOGICAL REVIEW, 54(2) (APR 89), 275-287.
THIS RESEARCH EXAMINES THE CAMPAIGN CONTRIBUTIONS OF 629
MEMBERS OF 100 WEALTHY CAPITALIST FAMILIES TO THE
PRESIDENTIAL CAMPAIGN OF 1972, THE LAST CAMPAIGN CONDUCTED
WITHOUT ANY LIMITS ON INDIVIDUAL CONTRIBUTIONS. THE ANALYSIS
REVEALS THAT ROUGHLY HALF OF THE MEMBERS OF THESE FAMILIES
CONTRIBUTED LITTLE OR NOTHING TO THIS PRESIDENTIAL CAMPAIGN,
BUT OTHER FAMILY MEMBERS WERE OFTEN MAJOR CONTRIBUTORS.
FAMILY MEMBERS WHO WERE MOST VISIBLE AS CORPORATE DIRECTORS
OR FOUNDATION TRUSTEES OR WHO WERE LISTED IN "WHO'S WHO IN
AMERICA" CONTRIBUTED THE MOST TO THIS CAMPAIGN. IN ADDITION,
WEALTHY ENTREPRENEURS CONTRIBUTED MORE TO THE CAMPAIGN THAN
MEMBERS OF SUBSEQUENT GENERATIONS OF WEALTHY CAPITALIST
FAMILIES. MEMBERS OF WEALTHY JEWISH AND SOUTHERN FAMILIES
CONTRIBUTED SLIGHTLY MORE TO THE REPUBLICAN PARTY THAN THE
DEMOCRATIC PARTY, BUT THEY CONTRIBUTED MUCH MORE TO THE
DEMOCRATIC PARTY THAN DID THE MEMBERS OF OTHER WEALTHY
CAPITALIST FAMILIES. IN ADDITION, THE MEMBERS OF FAMILIES
THAT WERE MAJOR STOCKHOLDERS IN OIL COMPANIES OR COMPANIES
WITH LARGE GOVERNMENT CONTACTS CONTRIBUTED MORE TO THE
CAMPAIGN THAN DID THE MEMBERS OF OTHER WEALTHY CAPITALIST
FAMILIES. CONVERSELY, THE MEMBERS OF FAMILIES THAT WERE
MAJOR STOCKHOLDERS IN MEDIA COMPANIES CONTRIBUTED RELATIVELY
LITTLE TO THIS CAMPAIGN.

00930 ALLEN, R. L.; BROWN, R. E.; DAWSON, M. C.
A SCHEMA-BASED APPROACH TO MODELING AN AFRICAN-AMERICAN
RACIAL BELIEF SYSTEM
AMERICAN POLITICAL SCIENCE REVIEW, 83(2) (JUN 89), 421-442.
THE AUTHORS USE A COGNITIVE SCHEMA-BASED APPROACH TO
MODEL AN AFRICAN-AMERICAN RACIAL BELIEF SYSTEM, SHOWING THE
CONTENT OF RACIAL BELIEF SYSTEMS IN A NATIONAL SAMPLE TO BE
ASSOCIATED WITH THE INDIVIDUAL'S DEGREE OF SOCIOECONOMIC
STATUS, RELIGIOSITY, AND EXPOSURE TO BLACK MEDIA. AFRICAN-
AMERICANS WITH A HIGHER SOCIOECONOMIC STATUS ARE LESS
SUPPORTIVE OF BLACK POLITICAL AUTONOMY AND THEY FEEL MORE
DISTANT FROM BLACK MASSES AND BLACK ELITES THAN DO THOSE OF
LOWER SOCIOECONOMIC STATUS. RELIGIOSITY, WHILE UNRELATED TO
BLACK AUTONOMY, STRENGTHENS CLOSENESS TO BLACK MASSES AND
BLACK ELITES. BLACK TELEVISION-AND, TO A MUCH LESSER DEGREE,
BLACK PRINT MEDIA-HAS A CONSISTENT IMPACT ON THE RACIAL
BELIEF SYSTEM.

00931 ALLEN, V.
THE LIMITS AND MEANING OF DETENTE IN EUROPE
PEACE AND THE SCIENCES, 1 (1989), 24-30.
NOT ALL THE CONSEQUENCES OF THE INF AGREEMENT HAVE BEEN
POSITIVE. PEOPLE ARE ASSUMING THAT THE MOMENTUM FOR
DISARMAMENT CAN BE MAINTAINED WITHOUT THEIR OWN
PARTICIPATION AND WITHOUT, THEREFORE, PUTTING PRESSURE ON
THEIR RESPECTIVE GOVERNMENTS. THIS IS A MISTAKEN ASSUMPTION.
WHEN CAPITALIST GOVERNMENTS ARE LEFT WITHOUT PUBLIC PRESSURE
THEY PROTECT THE IMMEDIATE INTERESTS OF CAPITALISM. THIS
NEGATIVE CONSEQUENCE OF THE INF AGREEMENT HAS ENABLED THE
AGREEMENT TO BE UNDERMINED. FURTHERMORE, IT HAS TAKEN THE
PRESSURE OFF WESTERN GOVERNMENTS TO PROCEED TO THE NEXT
STAGE, NAMELY THE 50 PER CENT REDUCTION IN THE STOCKPILE OF
STRATEGIC WEAPONS.

00932 ALLEY, R.S.
RELIGIOUS FREEDOM ON CAPITOL HILL: CONGRESS' CHECKERED PAST
CHURCH AND STATE, 42(11) (DEC 89), 8 (248)-11 (251).
THE AUTHOR REVIEWS SOME OF THE MORE SIGNIFICANT EVENTS
IN U.S. CONGRESSIONAL HISTORY THAT RELATE DIRECTLY TO THE
RELIGION CLAUSES OF THE FIRST AMENDMENT TO THE CONSTITUTION.

00933 ALLISON, W.
HOW TO WIN AN ELECTION
NATIONAL REVIEW, XLI(19) (OCT 89), 24.
THE AUTHOR WARNS THAT THE GOP WILL CONTINUE TO LOSE
ELECTIONS UNLESS IT GETS ITS MIND OFF WASHINGTON AND ONTO
LOCAL ISSUES. ONLY WITH A PLATFORM THAT SQUARELY ADDRESSES
THE PUBLIC'S ALARM ABOUT DETERIORATING SOCIAL CONDITIONS CAN
REPUBLICAN CANDIDATES FACE THE VOTERS WITH A MESSAGE THAT
MAKES SENSE WHERE IT COUNTS: AT HOME.

00934 ALLSOP, D.T.
THE DYNAMIC NATURE OF PARTY IDENTIFICATION DURING A
PRESIDENTIAL CAMPAIGN
DISSERTATION ABSTRACTS INTERNATIONAL, 49(9) (MAR 89),
2792-A.

POLITICAL PARTY AFFILIATION IS MORE RESPONSIVE AND DYNAMIC THAN PREVIOUSLY DEMONSTRATED. INTERVIEWS CONDUCTED DURING THE LAST FIVE MONTHS OF THE 1984 PRESIDENTIAL CAMPAIGN DEMONSTRATE THAT PARTY AFFILIATION RESPONDS TO THE CONTINUOUS ACTION, DECISIONS, AND EVENTS OF A POLITICAL CAMPAIGN. ELECTION-YEAR EFFECTS AND CAMPAIGN EFFECTS BOTH EXERT A CONSIDERABLE INFLUENCE ON PARTY IDENTIFICATION.

00935 ALLYN, B.; BLIGHT, J.; WELCH, D.
ESSENCE OF REVISION: MOSCOW, HAVANA, AND THE CUBAN MISSILE CRISIS
INTERNATIONAL SECURITY, 14(3) (WIN 90), 136-172.
ALTHOUGH INFORMATION ABOUT THE AMERICAN SIDE OF THE CUBAN MISSILE CRISIS IS PLENTIFUL, BOTH CUBA AND THE SOVIET UNION HAVE CLOSELY GUARDED THE HISTORIES OF THEIR SIDES OF THE EVENT. HOWEVER, GLASNOST HAS LED TO AN INCREASING AMOUNT OF INFORMATION BECOMING ACCESSIBLE. THE ARTICLE DRAWS ON EVIDENCE AND TESTIMONY PRESENTED IN A TRIPARITE CONFERENCE IN MOSCOW IN JANUARY 1989, AN EARLIER US-SOVIET CONFERENCE IN CAMBRIDGE, MASSACHUSETTS, AND IN SUPPLEMENTAL INTERVIEWS TO DEMONSTRATE SOME OF THE NEW LIGHT THAT HAS BEEN SHED ON THE SOVIET AND CUBAN SIDES OF THE CRISIS. TOPICS THAT ARE MORE FULLY ILLUMINATED INCLUDE: SOVIET MOTIVES FOR DEPLOYING MISSILES TO CUBA; THE MEANING, SIGNIFICANCE, AND PERCEPTIONS OF AMERICAN MILITARY ACTIVITIES AND COVERT OPERATIONS IN 1962; THE GENESIS, TERMS, AND CONDUCT OF THE MISSILE DEPLOYMENT; THE OPERATIONAL STATUS OF THE MISSILES; AND THE ACUTE TENSIONS IN SOVIET-CUBAN RELATIONS IMMEDIATELY FOLLOWING RESOLUTION OF THE CRISIS.

00936 ALLYN, B.; BROWN, S.; FISHER, R.: ISRAELYAN, V.; PERESYPKIN, V.; RICIGLIANO, R.; SHUSTOV, V.; STEPANOV, A.
THE ART OF DIPLOMATIC NEGOTIATING
INTERNATIONAL AFFAIRS (MOSCOW), (9) (SEP 89), 148-156.
THIS IS A TRANSCRIPT OF A DISCUSSION ON THE PROBLEMS OF DIPLOMATIC NEGOTIATIONS. THE DISCUSSION PANEL INCLUDED AMERICAN POLITICAL EXPERTS FROM HARVARD UNIVERSITY AND SOVIET SCHOLARS AND DIPLOMATS.

00937 ALMOND, G.A.
REVIEW ARTICLE: THE INTERNATIONAL-NATIONAL CONNECTION
BRITISH JOURNAL OF POLITICAL SCIENCE, 19(2) (APR 89), 237-259.
ONE OF THE POSITIVE CONTRIBUTIONS ATTRIBUTED TO THE DEPENDENCY MOVEMENT IS ITS STRESS ON THE IMPORTANCE OF THE INTERNATIONAL CONTEXT IN THE EXPLANATION OF INTERNAL POLITICS AND POLITICAL DEVELOPMENT. THE DEPENDENCY WRITERS REJECTED THE DEVELOPMENT RESEARCH OF THE 1950'S AND THE 1960'S ON THE GROUNDS THAT IT FAILED TO CONSIDER THE CONSTRAINTS IMPOSED ON THIRD WORLD DEVELOPMENT BY THE CONTEXT OF INTERNATIONAL CAPITALISM, WHICH PENETRATED, CONTROLLED, AND DISTORTED THE POLITICAL ECONOMIES OF THOSE COUNTRIES. THESE CONSTRAINTS WERE VIEWED AS SO COMPLETE AS TO REDUCE INTERNAL VARIABLES TO INSIGNIFICANCE. THIS POSITION IS NO LONGER SERIOUSLY ADVANCED, BUT THE DEPENDENCY MOVEMENT IS CREDITED WITH HAVING TURNED DEVELOPMENT STUDIES AROUND BY BRINGING THE INTERNATIONAL DIMENSION INTO THE DEVELOPMENT PICTURE.

00938 ALOKI, A.
RURAL DEVELOPMENT IN SUB-SAHARAN AFRICA: A DIFFERENT VIEW OF POLITICAL AND ADMINISTRATIVE DECENTRALIZATION
INTERNATIONAL REVIEW OF ADMINISTRATIVE SCIENCES, 55(3) (SEP 89), 401-432.
THE APPROACH TO THE PROBLEM OF THIRD WORLD DEVELOPMENT HAS UNDERGONE RADICAL CHANGES IN RECENT DECADES. THE WORLD BANK EMPHASIZES THE NEED FOR DEVELOPING COUNTRIES TO PURSUE INTERNAL POLICY REFORMS, UNDERLINING THE VALUE OF DECENTRALIZED DECISION-MAKING: FOR EXPANDING THE POWERS OF REGIONAL AND LOCAL GOVERNMENT MAKES IT EASIER TO DEVOLVE RESPONSIBILITY OF RURAL ENTITIES. DEVELOPMENTAL ACTIONS, ECONOMIC AND SOCIAL PROJECTS WOULD HAVE CONCRETE EFFECTS AT LOCAL LEVEL THROUGH COMMUNITY INVOLVEMENT. DECENTRALIZATION OF THIS ORDER WOULD CERTAINLY NOT WEAKEN EITHER THE STATE OR CENTRAL ADMINISTRATION. IT WOULD STRENGTHEN BOTH SO THAT RESPONSIBILITIES WOULD BE SHARED BETWEEN NATIONAL AND LOCAL LEADERS, RATHER THAN BEING CONCENTRATED IN THE CENTER.

00939 ALOZIE, N.O.
WOMEN AND MINORITIES IN THE JUDICIARY: AN EMPIRICAL EXAMINATION OF THE CAUSES AND CONSEQUENCES OF VARIATIONS AMONG THE STATES
DISSERTATION ABSTRACTS INTERNATIONAL, 50(6) (DEC 89), 1785-A.
THIS STUDY EXPLORES THE RELATIONSHIP BETWEEN JUDICIAL SELECTION METHODS IN THE AMERICAN STATES AND THE NUMBER OF WOMEN, BLACKS, AND HISPANICS HOLDING JUDICIAL OFFICE. THE RESULTS INDICATE THAT THE INFLUENCE OF JUDICIAL SELECTION METHODS ON THE ACHIEVEMENT OF JUDICIAL OFFICE HAS BEEN OVERSTATED. THEY ALSO SHOW THAT THE RELATIONSHIP BETWEEN SELECTION METHODS AND FEMALE AND ETHNIC MINORITY REPRESENTATION IS MORE COMPLEX THAN PREVIOUSLY THOUGHT.

00940 ALSHAYEJI, A.K.
DEMOCRATIZATION IN KUWAIT: THE NATIONAL ASSEMBLY AS A STRATEGY FOR POLITICAL SURVIVAL
DISSERTATION ABSTRACTS INTERNATIONAL, 49(8) (FEB 89), 2373-A.
THE HYBRID KUWAITI POLITICAL SYSTEM COMBINES A POWERFUL HEREDITARY RULE WITH A LIMITED DEMOCRATIC PRACTICE EMBODIED BY THE NATIONAL ASSEMBLY, WHICH DEVELOPED AS PART OF A STRATEGY TO LESSEN AND CONTAIN KUWAIT'S ACUTE VULNERABILITY. THIS STUDY CHRONICLES THE RISE AND DEMISE OF THE NATIONAL ASSEMBLY, CONCENTRATING ON ITS ROLE, STRUCTURE, LEGITIMACY, AND MECHANISMS AS WELL AS ITS RELEVANCE AND OVERALL CONTRIBUTION TO THE KUWAITI POLITICAL SYSTEM.

00941 ALSHIED, M.Y.M.
THE GULF COOPERATION COUNCIL: A MODEL OF A REGIONAL INTERNATIONAL REGIME
DISSERTATION ABSTRACTS INTERNATIONAL, 49(8) (FEB 89), 2380-A.
THE AUTHOR DEVELOPS A MODEL TO STUDY INTERNATIONAL REGIMES AND USES IT TO INCORPORATE MINOR STATES INTO THE THEORY OF THE INTERNATIONAL SYSTEM. HE UTILIZES THE GULF COOPERATION COUNCIL TO OPERATIONALIZE THE DEVELOPED MODEL.

00942 ALTAMIRANO, B.
FOLLOWING THE SPIRIT AND LETTER OF THE ACCORD
WORLD MARXIST REVIEW, 31(12) (DEC 88), 10-13.
DESPITE ALL IMPERIALIST FORAYS, THE NICARGUAN PEOPLE ARE DEFENDING THEIR REVOLUTION SUCCESSFULLY. ALTHOUGH THEY HAD TO PAY A HIGH PRICE FOR IT, THE DEFEAT OF THE CONTRAS IS, STRATEGICALLY, A FACT. IT IS NOW TIME TO SECURE PEACE WHICH IS ESSENTIAL TO THE IMPLEMENTATION OF ECONOMIC PROGRAMMES, TO FULL EMPLOYMENT AND TO HIGHER LIVING STANDARDS AND, IN THE LONG TERM, TO A TRANSITION TO SOCIALISM. IN THIS CONNECTION THE SANDINIST NATIONAL LIBERATION FRONT HAS CLEARLY OUTLINED TWO MAJOR POLITICAL TASKS--PEACE AND ECONOMIC DEVELOPMENT. THE FORMER IS AN ESSENTIAL CONDITION OF THE LATTER.

00943 ALTENBURG, W.
DEFENSIVE ALLIANCE IN A NUCLEAR WORLD
NATO'S SIXTEEN NATIONS, 34(7) (DEC 89), 17-20, 23.
THE NEW ATMOSPHERE IN EAST-WEST RELATIONS INDUCES OPTIMISM FOR THE FUTURE. NEVERTHELESS, THIS SHOULD BE TINGED BY CAUTION - THE SOVIET POTENTIAL FOR AGGRESSION EXISTS, WHATEVER THE STATED INTENTIONS. FOR NATO, POSSESSION OF NUCLEAR WEAPONS NOT ONLY DOES NOT REPRESENT A DANGER OF NUCLEAR WAR BUT, FAR MORE COMPREHENSIVELY, IS A MEANS TO DETER ALL WAR. AT THE SAME TIME ARMS CONTROL CAN LEAD TO STABILITY BY CREATING FORCE SYMMETRY AT LOWER LEVELS.

00944 ALTERMAN, E.
WHO IS GEORGE, WHAT IS HE?
SOUTH, (99) (JAN 89), 27.
THE KEY UNANSWERED QUESTION FOR THE BUSH ADMINISTRATION IS "WHO IS GEORGE?" OBSERVERS ARE WAITING TO SEE IF BUSH, AS PRESIDENT, WILL REVERT TO HIS MODERATE, TRILATERALIST PAST OR HAS HE CONVERTED TO THE FIRE-BREATHING REAGANITE RELIGION?

00945 ALTHAUS, R.R.
AN ADMINSTRATIVE ANALYSIS OF RELATIONSHIPS BETWEEN THE DEPARTMENTS OF AGRICULTURE AND STATE: STUDIES IN CONFLICT AND NETWORK THEORIES
DISSERTATION ABSTRACTS INTERNATIONAL, 49(7) (JAN 89), 1953-A.
THIS INQUIRY EXAMINES ADMINSTRATIVE INTERACTION BETWEEN THE DEPARTMENTS OF AGRICULTURE AND STATE ON ISSUES OF U.S. INTERNATIONAL AGRICULTURAL POLICY. THE CASE STUDY METHOD IS USED TO INVESTIGATE CONDITIONS OF CONFLICT AND COOPERATION BETWEEN THE TWO DEPARTMENTS. BOTH ROUTINE AND NON-ROUTINE CASES WERE SELECTED, REPRESENTING SITUATIONS WHERE FOREIGN POLICY AND DOMESTIC AGRICULTURAL POLICY OBJECTIVES MIGHT LOGICALLY BE OPPOSED.

00946 ALTHUMDALI, L.
CONFLICT IN SRI LANKA AND PERCEPTIONS OF THE U.S. ROLE
SCANDINAVIAN JOURNAL OF DEVELOPMENT ALTERNATIVES, 8(3) (SEP 89), 79-90.
THE MINISTER FOR NATIONAL SECURITY AFFAIRS FOR THE GOVERNMENT OF SRI LANKA DELIVERED THIS SPEECH AT AN UNIVERSITY IN THE U.S. AND DEALS WITH THE PRESENT SITUATION IN SRI LANKA WITH ALL ITS COMPLEXITIES AND THEN ADDRESSES ATTENTION TO THE RELATIONSHIP BETWEEN SRI LANKA AND THE UNITED STATES. HE DETAILS THE BASIC FACTORS THAT UNDERLINE THE CURRENT SOCI-ECONOMIC AND POLITICAL SITUATION DESCRIBED AS LOW INCOME BUT AHEAD IN SOCIAL TERMS OF OTHER DEVELOPING COUNTRIES OF LIKE INCOME. HE DESCRIBES THEIR BELIEF IN DEMOCRATIC METHODS, PRINCIPLES, AND THEIR PLURALISTIC SOCIETY. MAJORITY VERSUS MINORITY ISSUES ARE EXAMINED. THE SIMILARITY BETWEEN SRI LANKA AND THE U.S. IS NOTED, AS WELL AS BILATERAL TRADE RELATIONS AND U.S. DEVELOPMENT ASSISTANCE. REGIONAL GROUPINGS AND THE NEED FOR CONTINUING U.S. SUPPORT IS NOTED.

00947 ALTMAN, E.; MINOWA, Y.
    ANALYZING RISKS, RETURNS AND POTENTIAL INTEREST IN THE US
    HIGH YIELD CORPORATE DEBT MARKET FOR JAPANESE INVESTORS
    JAPAN AND THE WORLD ECONOMY, 1(2) (MAR 89), 163-186.
    THE HIGH YIELD BOND MARKET HAS BEEN GROWING IMPRESSIVELY
    SINCE THE EARLY 1980S AND ESPECIALLY IN THE LAST FIVE YEARS
    (1984-1988), DURING WHICH OVER $120 BILLION OF NEW DEBT HAS
    BEEN ISSUED. THESE NON-INVESTMENT-GREAT, STRAIGHT-DEBT
    SECURITIES HAVE PROVIDED INVESTORS, PRIMARILY U.S. FINANCIAL
    INSTITUTIONS, WITH SIGNIFICANT RETURN SPREADS OVER RISK-FREE
    AND INVESTMENT GRADE BONDS. IT SHOULD BE NOTED, HOWEVER,
    THAT THESE HIGH COUPON, STRAIGHT (NON-CONVERTIBLE) BONDS
    HAVE NOT ALWAYS RETURNED POSITIVE SPREADS, ESPECIALLY IN
    PERIODS OF DECREASING INTEREST RATES WHEN RETURNS ON LONG-
    TERM GOVERNMENT BOND WERE HIGHER, E.G., IN THE 1984-1986
    PERIOD. THE PURPOSE OF THIS PAPER IS TO ANALYZE THE
    POTENTIAL INVOLVEMENT OF JAPANESE INVESTORS IN THE HIGH
    YIELD BOND MARKET AND TO SIMULATE JAPANESE INVESTOR
    PERFORMANCE.

00948 ALTMAN, I., (ED.); ZUBE, E., (ED.)
    PUBLIC PLACES AND SPACES
    BLENUM PRESS, NEW YORK, NY, 1989, 316.
    PUBLIC PLACES AND SPACES COMPRISE A MULTITUDE OF MAN-
    MADE AND NATURAL SETTINGS, INCLUDING URBAN STREETS, PLAZAS
    AND SQUARES, MALLS, PARKS, AQUATIC ENVIRONMENTS, NATIONAL
    PARKS, AND FORESTS, AND WILDERNESS AREAS. THE IMPORTANCE OF
    THESE PUBLIC SETTINGS IS HIGHLIGHTED BY DIFFICULT QUESTIONS
    OF ACCESS, CONTROL, AND MANAGEMENT; UNIQUE NEEDS AND
    PROBLEMS OF DIFFERENT USERS; AND THE DRAMATIC RESHAPING OF
    THESE ENVIRONMENTS THAT HAS OCCURRED AND WILL CONTINUE TO
    OCCUR IN THE FUTURE. THE ISSUES ADDRESSED IN THE CHAPTERS OF
    PUBLIC PLACES AND SPACES COVER A BROAD ARRAY OF THEMES,
    RESEARCH TOPICS, AND DESIGN ISSUES CONCERNING PUBLIC PLACES
    AND SPACES IN URBAN, SUBURBAN, RURAL, AND WILDERNESS
    SETTINGS.

00949 ALTSHULER, A.
    MASSACHUSETTS GOV. SARGENT: SARGE IN CHARGE
    JOURNAL OF STATE GOVERNMENT, 62(4) (JUL 89), 153-160.
    AS A REPUBLICAN IN A STATE THAT WAS OVERWHELMINGLY
    DEMOCRATIC, GOV. FRANK SARGENT NEVER HAD THE OPTION OF A
    PARTISAN LEADERSHIP STYLE. HE MIGHT HAVE SOUGHT A COALITION
    WITH CONSERVATIVE DEMOCRATS AND INDEPENDENTS, BUT HE CHOSE
    THE OPPOSITE COURSE. DECIDING TO REACH OUT TOWARD LIBERAL
    RATHER THAN CONSERVATIVE DEMOCRATS AND INDEPENDENTS, SARGENT
    WAS IN CONSTANT TENSION WITH THE CONSERVATIVES WHO
    INCREASINGLY DOMINATED HIS PARTY.

00950 ALUKO, O.
    BRITAIN AND THE CONFLICT IN SOUTHERN AFRICA
    ROUND TABLE, 309 (JAN 89), 54-64.
    IRRESPECTIVE OF WHAT HAPPENS IN SOUTH AFRICA, BRITAIN
    WILL STRIVE TO PROTECT AND DEFEND ITS NATIONAL INTERESTS
    THERE. FURTHERMORE, IT IS NOT LIKELY THAT THE UK WILL EVER
    SUPPORT THE IMPOSITION OF MANDATORY SANCTIONS AGAINST SOUTH
    AFRICA. IN ACTUAL FACT, GIVEN THE PARLOUS STATE OF AFRICAN
    ECONOMIES, THEIR POLITICAL FRAGILITY AND MILITARY WEAKNESS,
    BRITAIN IS LIKELY TO WATER DOWN SOME OF THE LIMITED
    SANCTIONS ALREADY IMPOSED. ALREADY THE THATCHER GOVERNMENT
    HAS VIOLATED THE GLENEAGLES AGREEMENT ON SPORTING LINKS WITH
    SOUTH AFRICA AS WELL AS OTHER SANCTIONS.

00951 ALVARADO, K.A.H.
    SEXUAL HARASSMENT: IMPLEMENTATION OF FEDERAL POLICY
    DISSERTATION ABSTRACTS INTERNATIONAL, 50(3) (SEP 89),
    788-A.
    THE AUTHOR SURVEYS THE IMPLEMENTATION OF TITLE VII OF
    THE CIVIL RIGHTS ACT OF 1964, AS IT CONCERNS DISCRIMINATION
    ON THE BASIS OF SEX AS OUTLINED IN THE "US EQUAL EMPLOYMENT
    OPPORTUNITY COMMISSION'S GUIDELINES ON DISCRIMINATION
    BECAUSE OF SEX." SHE SEEKS TO DETERMINE THE LEVEL OF
    UNDERSTANDING AND IMPLEMENTATION OF THE LAW IN THE PUBLIC
    SECTOR.

00952 ALVAREZ, R.R.
    LATIN AMERICA: CHANGES IN THE OFFING
    WORLD MARXIST REVIEW, 32(7) (JUL 89), 20-23.
    THIS ARTICLE ADDRESSES THE SITUATION OF LATIN AMERICAN
    TODAY WHICH IS MARKED BY ECONOMIC CRISIS, EXTERNAL DEBT,
    SOCIAL AND POLITICAL INSTABILITY. AMERICAN POLICY IN THIS
    AREA OF THE WORLD IS ANALYZED. CENTRAL AMERICA, CUBA, CHILI,
    PERU, VENEZUELA, MEXICO AND ARGENTINA ARE EACH EXAMINED. IT
    CONCLUDES THAT THERE CAN BE NO DEVELOPMENT WITHOUT PEACE,
    BUT THERE WILL BE NO PEACE WITHOUT DEVELOPMENT.

00953 ALVES, D.
    THE CHARGING NEW ZEALAND DEFENSE POSTURE
    ASIAN SURVEY, XXIX(4) (APR 89), 363-381.
    NEW ZEALAND'S HISTORICAL ISOLATION IS SOMETIMES
    OVERLOOKED BY PEOPLE IN THE NORTHERN HEMISPHERE, AND THE
    ACTIONS OF THE LANGE GOVERNMENT AND NEW ZEALANDERS'
    REACTIONS HAVE SURPRISED MEMBERS OF THE WESTERN ALLIANCE WHO
    FIND IT HARD TO UNDERSTAND THE PREOCCUPATION WITH NUCLEAR

WAR, THE PRIME MINISTER'S TERGIVERSATIONS, AND THE DEGREE OF
PUBLIC SUPPORT FOR POLICIES THAT HAVE UNDERMINED WESTERN
SOLIDARITY. BUT THERE ARE PRECEDENTS IN THE COUNTRY'S
HISTORY FOR SURPRISING LEGISLATION AND ACCEPTANCE BY THE
PEOPLE, AND NEW ZEALAND'S DEVELOPING EMPHASIS ON THE SOUTH
PACIFIC REGION IS LINKED TO A GROWING APPRECIATION OF THE
ANCIENT MAORI TRADITION OF BELONGING TO THE REGION. MOREOVER,
BEHIND TODAY'S ATTITUDES LIE THE MEMORY OF THE MUSHROOM
CLOUD THAT RESULTED FROM FRENCH ATMOSPHERIC TESTING IN THE
1960S AND A MOUNTING FRUSTRATION AT THE GROWTH OF THE
SUPERPOWERS' NUCLEAR STOCKPILES. THIS ARTICLE TRACE THE
CHANGES IN GOVERNMENT POSTURE IN THE PAST FEW YEARS AND
NOTES THE MANY DIFFERENT ATTITUDES TOWARD DEFENSE IN NEW
ZEALAND.

00954 AMBROSIUS, M.M.
    THE EFFECTIVENESS OF STATE ECONOMIC DEVELOPMENT POLICIES:
    A TIME-SERIES ANALYSIS
    WESTERN POLITICAL QUARTERLY, 42(3) (SEP 89), 283-300.
    THIS STUDY EXAMINES THE EFFECTS OF EIGHT STATE ECONOMIC
    DEVELOPMENT POLICIES ON MEASURES OF STATE ECONOMIC HEALTH,
    ON UNEMPLOYMENT RATES, AND ON MANUFACTURING VALUE ADDED.
    USING AN INTERRUPTED TIME-SERIES REGRESSION ANALYSIS, THESE
    POLICIES ARE SEEN AS HAVING NO DISCERNIBLE EFFECT ON THESE
    INDICATORS. REASONS FOR THE CONTINUED ADOPTION OF THESE
    POLICIES, DESPITE THEIR LACK OF EFFECT, ARE THEN SUGGESTED:
    REASONS SUCH AS THE PRESSURES OF BUSINESS INTERESTS ON SUB-
    NATIONAL UNITS IN A FEDERAL SYSTEM.

00955 AMBROSIUS, M.M.
    THE ROLE OF OCCUPATIONAL INTERESTS IN STATE ECONOMIC
    DEVELOPMENT POLICY MAKING
    WESTERN POLITICAL QUARTERLY, 42(1) (MAR 89), 53-68.
    DESPITE EVIDENCE THAT STATE ECONOMIC DEVELOPMENT
    POLICIES HAVE LITTLE EFFECT ON THE HEALTH OF STATE ECONOMIES,
    STATE POLICY-MAKERS HAVE CONTINUED TO ADOPT THEM. MANCUR
    OLSON'S RECENT VOLUME DEALING WITH DISTRIBUTIONAL COALITIONS,
    COUPLED WITH THE WORK OF CHARLES LINDBLOM ON THE ROLE OF
    BUSINESS INTERESTS IN DEMOCRACIES, SUGGESTS AN EXPLANATION.
    PERHAPS THE ADOPTION OF STATE ECONOMIC DEVELOPMENT POLICIES,
    PARTICULARLY THOSE WHICH GIVE BENEFITS DIRECTLY TO
    BUSINESSES, CONSTITUTE A POLITICAL MECHANISM BY WHICH
    OLSON'S DISTRIBUTIONAL COALITIONS SEEK TO REDISTRIBUTE
    BENEFITS WITHIN THE STATE ECONOMY. THIS THEORETICAL APPROACH
    INFORMS THIS STUDY OF FORTY-EIGHT STATES OVER A FOURTEEN-
    YEAR TIME PERIOD. USING A NEW MEASURE OF OCCUPATIONAL
    INTEREST STRENGTH IN THE STATES, THE ANALYSIS TESTS THE
    HYPOTHESIS THAT STATES WITH GREATER INTEREST STRENGTH SCORES
    WILL ADOPT MORE ECONOMIC DEVELOPMENT POLICIES AND WILL BE
    ESPECIALLY LIKELY TO ADOPT POLICIES WHICH BENEFIT BUSINESS
    DIRECTLY. THIS EXPLANATION IS SUPPORTED BY THE ANALYSIS

00956 AMER, M.; NICKELS, I.
    THE CONGRESS: FROM QUILL TO SCREEN
    CRS REVEIH, 10(2) (FEB 89), 30-32.
    IN 200 YEARS, THE REPORTING OF CONGRESSIONAL PROCEEDINGS
    HAS PROGRESSED FROM NOTATIONS OF ACTIONS IN THE HOUSE AND
    SENATE JOURNALS, RECONSTRUCTIVE ABSTRACTS OF FLOOR
    PROCEEDINGS, AND LENGTHY WRITTEN ACCOUNTS OF DEBATES TO LIVE
    TELEVISION COVERAGE OF HOUSE AND SENATE SESSIONS THAT REACH
    SOME 39 MILLION AMERICAN HOUSEHOLDS.

00957 AMIDEI, N.
    FIGHTING OR FRIENDLY?
    COMMONWEAL, CXVI(1) (JAN 89), 5-6.
    THE 101ST CONGRESS MUST DEAL WITH A GROWING LIST OF
    POLITICALLY SENSITIVE DOMESTIC POLICY CRISES: SAVINGS AND
    LOAN BANKRUPTICIES, HOUSING, LONG-TERM PATIENT CARE, CHILD
    CARE, AND SOCIAL SECURITY. LOOMING OVER EVERYTHING IS THE
    DEFICIT AND COMPLICATING ALL OTHER TASKS ARE UNRESOLVED
    QUESTIONS OF ETHICS AND CAMPAIGN FINANCING

00958 AMIEL, B.
    FEMINISM HITS MIDDLE AGE
    NATIONAL REVIEW, 62(22) (NOV 89), 23 - 25.
    THIS ARTICLE REPORTS ON THE CURRENT STATUS OF FEMINISM.
    IT DESCRIBES THE EVOLUTION OF THOUGHT WHICH HAS DEVELOPED
    OVER THE LAST THIRTY YEARS. EXPLORED ARE: THE EARLY THINKING
    THAT MALE PROTECTIVENESS WAS PATRONIZING, AND, THE PRESENT
    SITUATION WHERE WOMEN NOW SEEK THE COMFORTING EMBRACE OF THE
    PATERNAL STATE."

00959 AMIEL, B.
    THEY'VE COME A LONG WAY, MAGGIE
    MACLEAN'S (CANADA'S NEWS MAGAZINE), 102(3) (JAN 89), 10.
    MARGARET THATCHER HAS COME A LONG WAY IN CURING THE
    "BRITISH DISEASE" OF ECONOMIC MALAISE. IN ADDITION, SHE HAS
    DONE WHAT MARXISM COULD NEVER ACHIEVE: MADE THE UPPER
    CLASSES IRRELEVANT WITHOUT BLOODSHED. HOWEVER, THE ISSUE OF
    THATCHER'S INFLUENCE ON FEMINISM IN BRITAIN IS A THORNY ONE.
    SHE FREQUENTLY ESPOUSES THE ROLE OF WOMEN AS MOTHERS AND
    HOMEMAKERS, BUT HER OWN LIFE APTLY ILLUSTRATES THE
    SUPERWOMAN MYTH.

00960 AMIN, H.A.
THE JUDGE'S HOME: A ONE-ACT PLAY
MIDDLE EASTERN STUDIES, 25(1) (JAN 89), 23-30.
HUSEIN AMIN PUBLISHED THIS PLAY ON THE OCCASION OF THE
1987 ATTEMPT BY GUNMEN OF A MILITANT ISLAMIC ORGANIZATION TO
ASSASSINATE IN CAIRO THE GOVERNMENT MINISTER HASAN ABU BASHA.
HUSEIN AMIN'S WRITING ON ISLAMIC TOPICS NOT ONLY SHOWS HIS
MASTERY OF THE ARABIC LANGUAGE BUT IS ALSO MARKED BY AN
IMPRESSIVE USE OF ISLAMIC SOURCES, AND AN EXTRAORDINARILY
ERUDITE DISCUSSION OF ISLAMIC LAW. HIS CRITIQUE OF THE MORE
RECENT MILITANT ISLAMIC ORGANIZATIONS IS VERY MUCH IN
ISLAMIC TERMS, BUT CHARACTERIZED BY AN OPEN CRITICAL
APPROACH AND A STRICT RESPECT FOR THE TRUTH. HIS WORK, IN
GENERAL, IS REFRESHING FOR ITS INTELLECTUAL INTEGRITY, AND
ITS INVITATION OF OPEN, TOLERANT DEBATE.

00961 AMIN, N.
ECONOMIC EMERGENCY MEASURES FAIL TO TAKE HOLD
AFRICAN BUSINESS, (DEC 88), 22-23.
THIS ARTICLE EXAMINES SIERRA LEONE PRESIDENT, JOSEPH
MOMOH'S ATTEMPTS TO BRING ABOUT ECONOMIC REFORM FOR HIS
COUNTRY. IT REVIEWS THE MEASURES IMPLEMENTED IN MOMOH'S
ECONOMIC STATE OF EMERGENCY, AND CONCLUDES THAT AFTER A
BRIEFLY PROMISING START, THAT THE EMERGENCY REGULATIONS SEEM
TO BE FAILING.

00962 AMIN, S.
EUROCENTRISM
MONTHLY REVIEW PRESS, NEW YORK, NY, 1989, 144.
AMIN ARGUES THAT MUCH OF THE PRECAPITALIST WORLD WAS
ORGANIZED AND UNIFIED AROUND A TRIBUTARY SYSTEM OF
PRODUCTION, IN WHICH THE ISLAMIC ORIENT PROVIDED THE
INTELLECTUAL AND STRUCTURAL CENTER AND FEUDAL EUROPE FORMED
THE PERIPHERY. CAPITALISM AROSE IN EUROPE BECAUSE OF THE
FLEXIBILITY EUROPE ENJOYED AS A RESULT OF ITS PERIPHERAL
POSITION WITHIN THE PRECAPITALIST WORLD, NOT BECAUSE OF ANY
PRESUMED EUROPEAN SUPERIORITY. AMIN ADDRESSES A BROAD SET OF
CONCERNS, RANGING FROM THE IDEOLOGICAL NATURE OF SCHOLASTIC
METAPHYSICS TO THE "ASIAN REGIONAL TRIBUTARY SYSTEM" FORMED
BY CHINA AND JAPAN TO THE MEANINGS AND SHORTCOMINGS OF
CONTEMPORARY ISLAMIC FUNDAMENTALISM.

00963 AMIN, S.
PEACE, NATIONAL AND REGIONAL SECURITY AND DEVELOPMENT:
SOME REFLECTIONS ON THE AFRICAN EXPERIENCE
ALTERNATIVES, XIV(2) (APR 89), 215-229.
THE IDEOLOGY OF ETHNICITY IS IN LARGE MEASURE A BY-
PRODUCT OF THE IDEOLOGIZATION OF THE NATION, AND SO PROVIDES
ONLY A DEFORMED, SOMETIMES MYTHICAL, PICTURE OF REALITY.
THUS, IT IS NOT ETHNOCENTRIC ATAVISM WHICH COMPELS PEOPLE TO
MISAPPREHEND REALITIES OTHER THAN THOSE OF THE COMMUNITIES
TO WHICH THEY BELONG. NOR DOES SOME OTHER KIND OF AUTOCRATIC
ATAVISM CONSTRAIN THE RULERS TO MANIPULATE "ETHNIC SATANS"
AS THE "CAUSES" OF SUCH CONFLICTS. RATHER, THE WEAKNESS OF
PERIPHERAL SOCIETY AS A WHOLE, AND PARTICULARLY ITS RULING
CLASSES, MUST BE CONSIDERED.

00964 AMIN, S.
SOCIALISM AND THE DEMANDS OF DEVELOPMENT
WORLD MARXIST REVIEW, 32(5) (MAY 89), 36-39.
STAGE-BY-STAGE, THE FOREMOST CONTRADICTION OF THE MODERN
WORLD (THE EFFECT OF THE CONTINUED ACCUMULATION OF CAPITAL)
IS BECOMING INCREASINGLY AGGRAVATED. THE WORLDWIDE EXPANSION
OF CAPITAL EXACERBATES RATHER THAN ALLEVIATES THE CONFLICT
BETWEEN THE CENTRE AND THE PERIPHERY OF CAPITALISM. IF THE
DEVELOPING NATIONS CANNOT RESPOND TO THIS CRISIS EFFECTIVELY,
IF THE PROGRESSIVE FORCES OF THE DEVELOPED COUNTRIES ALLOW
THEMSELVES TO BE PUSHED ASIDE AND TOE THE LINE OF BIG
CAPITAL, THE WORLD WILL LAPSE DEEPER INTO BARBARISM. THE
CHOICE IS BETWEEN SOCIALISM AND BARBARISM. BUT WHILE
CLASSICAL MARXISM MAINTAINED THAT THE TRANSITION TO
SOCIALISM DEPENDS ON THE TRIUMPHANT STRUGGLE OF THE WORKING
CLASS IN THE INDUSTRIALLY DEVELOPED COUNTRIES, TODAY THIS
PATH APPEARS LONGER AND MORE ARDUOUS, PASSING THROUGH THE
NATIONAL POPULAR REVOLUTION ON THE PERIPHERY IN ANTICIPATION
OF A TIME WHEN, THANKS TO THEIR OWN GAINS, THE NATIONS OF
THE WEST HELP CREATE CONDITIONS NECESSARY FOR GLOBAL RENEWAL.

00965 AMINA, P.
PURGE ON RUMOUR MONGERS
NEW AFRICAN, (258) (MAR 89), 27.
KENYA'S PRESIDENT ARAP MOI HAS WARNED AGAINST RUMOUR-
MONGERING AND ASKED LEADERS TO VERIFY ANY STATEMENTS THEY
MAKE ON ISSUES. HE FEELS LOOSE TALK DAMAGES KENYA'S
INTERNATIONAL REPUTATION AND HAS AN ADVERSE EFFECT ON
FOREIGN INVESTMENT.

00966 AMIT, M.
DIMINISHING THE THREAT
IDF JOURNAL, (18) (FAL 89), 8-10.
THIS ARTICLE EXPLORES INTELLIGENCE AND THE WAR AGAINST
TERRORISM AND IS WRITTEN BY A RETIRED MAJOR GENERAL WHO
SERVED A DIRECTOR OF IDF MILITARY INTELLIGENCE IN ISRAEL.
THE RANGE OF MEASURES TO USE AGAINST A PARTICULAR TERRORIST

THREAT IS EXPLORED AND INTELLIGENCE AS THE MOST CRUTIAL
WEAPON AGAINST TERRORISM IS EXPLAINED. ANTI-TERRORIST
PLANNING AND THE DECISION MAKING PROCESS ARE DETAILED.

00967 AMJAD, M.
ASPECTS OF FISCAL FEDERALISM IN PAKISTAN: AN EMPIRICAL
STUDY OF THE ALLOCATIVE, REVENUE MOBILIZATION, AND EQUITY
EFFECTS OF FEDERAL FISCAL TRANSFERS IN PAKISTAN
DISSERTATION ABSTRACTS INTERNATIONAL, 50(3) (SEP 89),
789-A.
THERE IS EVIDENCE THAT THE PRESENT SCHEME OF FEDERAL
FISCAL TRANSFERS IN PAKISTAN MAY BE PRODUCING EFFECTS
CONTRARY TO THE OBJECTIVES OF THE NATIONAL POLICY PLANNERS.
THE INSTITUTIONS ENTRUSTED WITH FISCAL ROLES, NOTABLY THE
NATIONAL FINANCE COMMISSION, NEED TO BE RESTRUCTURED TO
PERFORM THEIR DUTIES MORE EFFECTIVELY. THERE IS A PRESSING
NEED TO REDEFINE THE ROLES OF THE PLANNING COMMISSION AND
THE FEDERAL MINISTRY OF FINANCE.

00968 AMJAD, M.
SHI'ISM AND REVOLUTION IN IRAN
JOURNAL OF CHURCH & STATE, 31(1) (WIN 89), 35-54.
THE AUTHOR STUDIES THE IMPACT OF ISLAM ON THE IRANIAN
REVOLUTION. HE INVESTIGATES THE DEVELOPMENT OF SHI'ISM,
SOCIOECONOMIC FACTORS THAT MADE THE MOLLAHS AN IMPORTANT
POLITICAL FACTOR, AND THE DOMINATION OF THE REVOLUTION BY
THE MOLLAHS.

00969 AMR, Z.A.
THE INTIFADA: CAUSES AND FACTORS OF CONTINUITY
NEW OUTLOOK, 32(11-12 (297-298)) (NOV 89), 7-11.
THE ROOT CAUSES OF THE INTIFADA ARE EMBEDDED IN TWENTY
YEARS OF ISRAELI OCCUPATION AND ISRAELI POLICIES AIMED AT
UNDERMINING THE ECONOMIC AND NATIONAL EXISTENCE OF THE
PALESTINIANS IN THEIR OWN LAND. ISRAEL HAS CONFISCATED ARAB
LAND AND LAUNCHED AN AGGRESSIVE SETTLEMENT POLICY THAT HAS
LEFT THE WEST BANK AND GAZA FRAGMENTED, BOTH GEOGRAPHICALLY
AND DEMOGRAPHICALLY. ISRAEL HAS CONTINUOUSLY DENIED
PALESTINIAN NATIONAL ASPIRATIONS, SELF-DETERMINATION, AND
INDEPENDENCE.

00970 AMUZEGAR, J.
THE NEW BOGEYMAN: FOREIGN DIRECT INVESTMENT
SAIS REVIEW, 9(2) (SUM 89), 101-110.
THE AUTHOR HERE PUTS THE RECENT ALARM SET OFF BY
INCREASED LEVELS OF FOREIGN DIRECT INVESTMENT INTO
HISTORICAL AND CURRENT PERSPECTIVE. THE ARTICLE COMPARES AND
CONTRASTS THE INVESTMENTS OF FOREIGNERS IN THE UNITED STATES
WITH AMERICAN STRATEGIES ABROAD, PROVIDING STATISTICS AND
THEORIES AS TO WHY SUCH A PANIC HAS ENSUED FROM THE CAPITAL
HILL COMMITTEE MEMBER TO THE MIDDLE AMERICAN AUTO WORKER.

00971 ANANIEV, D.
REFLECTING ON THE CONCEPT OF THE PARTY
WORLD MARXIST REVIEW, 31(2) (FEB 88), 89-92.
THE BULGARIAN COMMUNIST PARTY CAN RESOLVE NEW PROBLEMS
SUCCESSFULLY IF IT IS ITSELF IN UNINTERRUPTED DEVELOPMENT,
FREE OF THE 'INFALLIBILITY' COMPLEX, CRITICALLY ASSESSES THE
RESULTS THAT HAVE BEEN ATTAINED, AND CLEARLY SEES WHAT HAS
TO BE DONE. LIKE OTHER ORGANISATIONS, THE PARTY HAS ITS
SHARE OF MISCONCEPTIONS, VACILLATION, DOUBTS, HESITANT MOVES,
UTOPIAN NOTIONS AND ILLUSIONS. THE CONCLUSIONS IT MAKES ARE
NOT A PRIORI TRUTHS. DEDUCED FROM PRACTICE, THEY ARE
CONSTANTLY CHECKED AND COMPARED AGAINST IT. AND ONLY THOSE
THAT WITHSTAND THIS RIGOROUS TEST CAN CLAIM TO BE UNIVERSAL.

00972 ANCHORDOGUY.
THE PUBLIC CORPORATION: A POTENT JAPANESE POLICY WEAPON
POLITICAL SCIENCE QUARTERLY, 103(4) (WIN 89), 707-724.
JAPAN, LIKE OTHER INDUSTRIALIZED NATIONS, HAS USED
PUBLIC CORPORATIONS TO PROVIDE IMPORTANT PUBLIC SERVICES,
SUCH AS RAILROADS AND AIRLINES. BUT THE BUREAUCRACY HAS ALSO
USED AN ARRAY OF PUBLIC CORPORATIONS AS OPERATING ARMS OF
SPECIFIC MINISTRIES TO SERVE THEIR PURPOSES. SOME HAVE BEEN
KEY PLAYERS IN JAPAN'S EFFORTS TO TARGET STRATEGIC
INDUSTRIES. ANALYSIS OF HOW THE JAPAN ELECTRONIC COMPUTER
COMPANY WAS ESTABLISHED AND HOW IT INFLUENCES THE DEMAND,
SUPPLY, PRICE, AND SOPHISTICATION OF DOMESTIC COMPUTERS
OFFERS NEW INSIGHT INTO JAPAN'S GOVERNMENT-BUSINESS
RELATIONSHIP.

00973 ANDERSON, A.B.
THE CHANGING SITUATION OF ETHNOLINGUISTIC MINORITIES ALONG
THE YUGOSLAVIAN FRONTIER
CANADIAN REVIEW OF STUDIES IN NATIONALISM, XVI(1-2) (1989),
263-275.
COMPLEX ETHNIC HETEROGENEITY CHARACTERIZES THE
INTERNATIONAL FRONTIER BETWEEN YUGOSLAVIA AND ITS NEIGHBORS.
THE POLITICAL INSTABILITY OF THESE FRONTIER AREAS IS RELATED
TO ETHNIC MINORITY DEMANDS. THE ETHNO-NATIONALISM OF THE
DIVERSE MINORITIES WITHIN YUGOSLAVIA COUNTERBALANCES THE
NATIONALISM OR SUB-NATIONALISM OF THE DOMINANT SERBS, CROATS,
AND SLOVENES, IF NOT THE EMERGENCE OF AN EFFECTIVE PAN-
YUGOSLAVIAN NATIONALISM. MOREOVER, THE FAILURE OF ARBITRARY

POLITICAL BOUNDARIES TO COINCIDE WITH ETHNIC TERRITORIALITY HAS GREATLY COMPLICATED YUGOSLAVIA'S RELATIONS WITH ITS NEIGHBORS.

00974 ANDERSON, D.
INFRASTRUCTURE PRICING POLICIES AND THE PUBLIC REVENUE IN AFRICAN COUNTRIES
WORLD DEVELOPMENT, 17(4) (APR 89), 525-542.
THE PAPER SHOWS THAT THE PUBLIC REVENUE CONSTRAINT ON ECONOMICALLY AND SOCIALLY DESIRABLE PROGRAMS IN AFRICA COULD BE GREATLY RELAXED THROUGH THE ADOPTION OF COST-REFLECTING PRICING POLICIES FOR PHYSICAL INFRASTRUCTURE SERVICES - ROADS AND DRAINAGE, WATER AND SEWERAGE, ELECTRICITY, AND TELECOMMUNICATIONS. CURRENTLY, THE PRICES OF INFRASTRUCTURE SERVICES ARE FREQUENTLY BELOW BOTH ECONOMIC COSTS AND WHAT IS NEEDED TO FINANCE INVESTMENT, OPERATING AND MAINTENANCE EXPENDITURES. THE SERVICES GENERATE POOR FINANCIAL RETURNS AND ABSORB MUCH PUBLIC FINANCE, WHEN IN PRACTICE THEY ARE CAPABLE OF EARNING APPRECIABLE SURPLUSES. THE PAPER DISCUSSES THE BENEFITS OF REFORMING INFRASTRUCTURE PRICING POLICIES, THE INSTITUTIONAL AND OTHER DIFFICULTIES OF BRINGING REFORMS INTO EFFECT, AND FINALLY MAKES SOME PROPOSALS. ALTHOUGH MUCH OF THE ANALYSIS RELATES TO AFRICA, SEVERAL OF ITS FINDINGS APPLY MORE GENERALLY.

00975 ANDERSON, G.M.
THE BUTCHER, THE BAKER, AND THE POLICY-MAKER: ADAM SMITH ON PUBLIC CHOICE, WITH A REPLY BY STIGLER
HISTORY OF POLITICAL ECONOMY, 21(4) (WIN 89), 641-660.
STIGLER'S MAIN THESIS ARTICULATES THE VIEW THAT SMITH FAILED TO EXTEND ECONOMIC ANALYSIS TO POLITICAL AFFAIRS AND CONSEQUENTLY "THE WEALTH OF NATIONS" HAS LITTLE TO OFFER IN THE WAY OF WHAT IS NOWADAYS TERMED "PUBLIC CHOICE THEORY." IN THIS ESSAY, THE AUTHOR CHALLENGES THIS INTERPRETATION. HE ARGUES THAT, CONTRARY TO STIGLER, SMITH APPLIED THE PRINCIPLES OF ECONOMICS TO POLITICS VIGOROUSLY AND CONSISTENTLY. HE FREQUENTLY EMPLOYED THE MODEL OF RATIONAL AND SELF-INTERESTED BEHAVIOR TO EXPLAIN BOTH THE ORIGIN AND CONSEQUENCES OF POLITICAL POLICIES. MOREOVER, PUBLIC CHOICE WAS ONE OF SMITH'S MAJOR ANALYTICAL INTERESTS.

00976 ANDERSON, P.
ROBERTO UNGER AND THE POLITICS OF EMPOWERMENT
NEW LEFT REVIEW, (173) (JAN 89), 93-108.
BASED UPON PHILOSOPHICAL ANTHROPOLOGY, A THEORY OF FORMATIVE CONTEXT IN HISTORY, AND A GENEALOGY OF THE MODERN WORLD, ROBERTO UNGER'S POLITICAL THEORY IS ESSENTIALLY CONCEIVED AS A RADICAL POLITICAL ALTERNATIVE TO BOTH MARXISM AND SOCIAL DEMOCRACY. IN THIS ESSAY, THE AUTHOR WEIGHS THE THEORETICAL CLAIMS OF UNGER'S WORK AND CRITICALLY EXAMINES THE MAIN LINES OF ITS PROGRAMMATIC AGENDA.

00977 ANDERTON, C.H.
ARMS RACE MODELING: PROBLEMS AND PROSPECTS
JOURNAL OF CONFLICT RESOLUTION, 33(2) (JUN 89), 346-367.
ARMS RACE MODELING BEGAN WITH THE WORK OF LEWIS F. RICHARDSON PRIOR TO THE OUTBREAK OF WORLD WAR I. IT WAS NOT UNTIL ANATOL RAPOPORT'S ARTICLE IN 1957 AND RICHARDSON'S POSTHUMOUS ARMS AND INSECURITY (1960) THAT ARMS RACE MODELING BECAME WELL KNOWN. SINCE THEN THERE HAS BEEN A PROLIFERATION OF ARMS RACE MODELS IN JOURNALS AND BOOKS ACROSS MANY DISCIPLINES. DESPITE THIS PROLIFERATION, THERE ARE SOME FUNDAMENTAL METHODOLOGICAL PROBLEMS ASSOCIATED WITH RICHARDSON-TYPE MODELS AND THE ARMS RACE MODELING ENTERPRISE IN GENERAL. THE AUTHORS DISCUSS THESE METHODOLOGICAL PROBLEMS AND OFFER SOME SUGGESTIONS ON WHERE ARMS RACE MODELERS SHOULD CONCENTRATE THEIR RESEARCH EFFORTS.

00978 ANDEWEG, R.
INSTITUTIONAL CONSERVATISM IN THE NETHERLANDS: PROPOSALS FOR AND RESISTANCE TO CHANGE
WEST EUROPEAN POLITICS, 12(1) (JAN 89), 42-60.
TO A CONSIDERABLE EXTENT THE INSTITUTIONAL FRAMEWORK OF DUTCH POLITICS HAS BEEN IMPOSED FROM ABROAD, OR HAS BEEN SHAPED UNDER THE INFLUENCE OF INTERNATIONAL EVENTS. GIVEN THIS LACK OF A DOMESTIC PEDIGREE, IT IS SURPRISING THAT THE INSTITUTIONS HAVE NEVER BEEN CHALLENGED SUCCESSFULLY. THE MOST RECENT ATTEMPT AT INSTITUTIONAL REVISION TOOK PLACE IN THE 1960S AND 1970S. CRITICISM OF THE TENUOUS LINK BETWEEN VOTERS, THE FORMATION OF GOVERNMENTS, AND THE POLICYMAKING PROCESS GAVE RISE TO VARIOUS PROPOSALS FOR POLITICAL REFORM AND ADMINISTRATIVE REORGANISATION. DESPITE POPULAR SUPPORT THE MOVEMENT FOR DEMOCRATIC REFORM RAN AGROUND. THIS REMARKABLE INSTITUTIONAL CONSERVATISM IS ATTRIBUTED TO THE FACT THAT THE PROPOSALS WOULD HAVE WEAKENED THE POSITION OF THE ESTABLISHED NATIONAL PARTY ORGANISATIONS, AND TO THE DYNAMICS OF POLITICAL ATTENTION.

00979 ANDONI, L.
AN ALARMING SCENARIO
MIDDLE EAST INTERNATIONAL, (351) (MAY 89), 5.
THE ISRAELI PEACE PROPOSAL WAS APPARENTLY CRAFTED IN SUCH A WAY AS TO BE ENTIRELY UNACCEPTABLE TO THE PLO. FURTHERMORE, ITS IMPLEMENTATION WOULD UNDERMINE EVEN THE

MOST MODERATE AND COMPROMISING RESPONSE THE PALESTINIANS COULD OFFER. MANY SEE THE PROPOSAL SIMPLY AS A PLOY BY THE US AND ISRAEL TO BUY TIME AND AVOID AN INTERNATIONAL PEACE CONFERENCE THAT IS PROPOSED BY THE PLO.

00980 ANDONI, L.
ARAB COOPERATION COUNCIL: ALLAYING FEARS
MIDDLE EAST INTERNATIONAL, (344) (FEB 89), 8.
THE FORMATION OF THE ARAB COOPERATION COUNCIL REFLECTS THE TREND TOWARD SUB-REGIONAL ARAB COMMUNITIES, SUCH AS THE GULF COOPERATION COUNCIL. ALTHOUGH IT IS TOO EARLY TO ASSESS THE POLITICAL AND ECONOMIC IMPLICATIONS OF THE NEW COUNCIL, INDICATIONS ARE THAT THE ARAB COUNTRIES, DISILLUSIONED WITH PROSPECTS FOR REAL ARAB UNITY, HAVE SETTLED FOR WHAT IS OFFICIALLY PERCEIVED AS A MORE REALISTIC FORM OF INTER-ARAB COOPERATION.

00981 ANDONI, L.
ARAFAT AND HUSSEIN
MIDDLE EAST INTERNATIONAL, (357) (AUG 89), 12.
JORDAN'S INCREASING MONETARY DIFFICULTIES WERE ALLEVIATED SOMEWHAT BY THE REOPENING OF THE PALESTINE NATIONAL FUND (PNF). THE MOVE WILL AID JORDAN BY INCREASING CIRCULATION OF THE JORDANIAN DINAR INSIDE THE WEST BANK AND JORDAN AS WELL AS DECREASING FOREIGN SPECULATION. THE MOVE ALSO BROUGHT ABOUT A SIGNIFICANT IMPROVEMENT IN JORDANIAN-PALESTINIAN RELATIONS.

00982 ANDONI, L.
ARAFAT TAKES A STAND
MIDDLE EAST INTERNATIONAL, 356 (AUG 89), 7-8.
ON THE EVE OF THE FIFTH FATAH CONGRESS PLO CHAIRMAN YASSER ARAFAT HAS TAKEN AN UNUSUALLY HARD LINE ON BOTH THE ISRAELI PROPOSALS FOR ELECTIONS IN THE OCCUPIED TERRITORIES AND THE AMERICAN ATTITUDE TO THEM. THE PLO LEADERS HAVE CONCLUDED THAT DESPITE THE SIGNIFICANCE OF THE AMERICAN-PALESTINIAN DIALOGUE, IT HAS BEEN A DIALOGUE BETWEEN THE DEAF. EVEN WORSE, THERE IS A GROWING FEELING AMONG SENIOR PLO LEADERS THAT WASHINGTON IS EXPLOITING THE DIALOGUE TO ALLOW THE ISRAELIS TIME TO CRUSH THE INTIFADA - A VIEW ALSO TAKEN BY JORDAN. IN ARAFAT'S VIEW THE US WAS COMPLYING WITH AN ISRAELI "REQUEST" TO GIVE IT SIX MONTHS TO END THE UPRISING.

00983 ANDONI, L.
CHALKING UP THE PLUSES
MIDDLE EAST INTERNATIONAL, (345) (MAR 89), 6-7.
MOSCOW'S PEACE DRIVE IN THE MIDDLE EAST HAS GIVEN THE PLO WHAT IT WAS WAITING FOR-A PRACTICAL SOVIET ATTEMPT TO BREAK THE AMERICAN MONOPOLY ON BROKERING PEACEFUL SETTLEMENTS. THE PLO BELIEVES THAT SOVIET MINISTER SHEVARDNADZE'S MISSION TO THE MIDEAST LED TO SOME GAINS BY DIRECTLY CHALLENGING WASHINGTON TO JOIN THE INTERNATIONAL PEACE CONFERENCE BANDWAGON, BY WARNING THAT TEL AVIV MIGHT FACE DIPLOMATIC ISOLATION BY REFUSING TO TALK TO THE PLO, AND BY ENDORSING THE NEED FOR A COORDINATION MEETING BETWEEN SYRIA, EGYPT, THE PLO, AND JORDAN.

00984 ANDONI, L.
CONFLICTING PRIORITIES
MIDDLE EAST INTERNATIONAL, (347) (MAR 89), 8-9.
ALTHOUGH THE BUSH ADMINISTRATION HAS INDICATED A NEW SERIOUSNESS IN AMERICA'S DEALINGS WITH THE PLO, IT PROBABLY LACKS THE WILL TO SOLVE THE PALESTINIAN QUESTION, ACCORDING TO THE PLO LEADERSHIP. THE PLO LEADERS FEAR THAT THE USA IS MERELY PLAYING FOR TIME AND TRYING TO KEEP ITS OPTIONS OPEN IN THE HOPE THAT IT CAN PRESSURE THE ARABS TO STOP THE INTIFADA.

00985 ANDONI, L.
CRITICISM OF THE BOSS
MIDDLE EAST INTERNATIONAL, (350) (MAY 89), 5.
DURING HIS HISTORIC VISIT TO PARIS IN MAY 1989, YASSER ARAFAT MADE STATEMENTS THAT SPARKED CONTROVERSY AMONG PALESTINIAN LEADERS, MANIFESTING ONCE AGAIN THE LACK OF COORDINATION AMONG PALESTINIAN FACTIONS AND ARAFAT'S INSISTENCE ON DEFYING THE PLO LEADERSHIP'S MILITANT ATTITUDE.

00986 ANDONI, L.
JORDAN AND SYRIA
MIDDLE EAST INTERNATIONAL, (358) (SEP 89), 8-9.
RELATIONS BETWEEN JORDAN AND SYRIA CONTINUE TO DETERIORATE AS THE TWO NATIONS REFUSE TO SEE EYE TO EYE OVER THE LEBANON CONFLICT. JORDAN IN NO UNCERTAIN TERMS WARNED AGAINST THE INTERNATIONALIZATION OF THE CONFLICT, THE RESULT OF WHICH MIGHT BE A PARTITION OF LEBANON. FEARING THE DOMINO EFFECT THAT SUCH A PARTITION MIGHT HAVE, JORDAN HAS GIVEN TACIT APPROVAL TO IRAQ'S MILITARY AID TO THE FORCES OF GENERAL MICHEL AOUN.

00987 ANDONI, L.
JORDAN FREES POLITICAL PRISONERS
MIDDLE EAST INTERNATIONAL, (358) (SEP 89), 9-10.
JORDAN'S NEW GOVERNMENT OF SHARIF ZAID BIN SHAKIR HAS

RECENTLY TAKEN A SERIES OF STEPS IN RESPONSE TO POPULAR
DEMANDS FOR POLITICAL AND ECONOMIC REFORMS. THE LATEST STEP
WAS THE RELEASE OF 60 POLITICAL DETAINEES ARRESTED LAST
APRIL. SCANT HOURS AFTER THEIR RELEASE SEVERAL OF THE EX-
PRISONER DECLARED THEIR CANDIDACY IN JORDAN'S UPCOMING
ELECTIONS. SOME OBSERVERS STILL FEAR THAT FULL POLITICAL
PARTICIPATION WILL NOT BE ALLOWED, BUT AS OF YET, THE
CAMPAIGNS FOR JORDAN'S FIRST FREE ELECTIONS IN 37 YEARS ARE
UNHINDERED AND MOVING ON SCHEDULE.

00988 ANDONI, L.
       JORDAN: A "NATIONAL CHARTER"
       MIDDLE EAST INTERNATIONAL, (354) (JUL 89), 12.
          JORDANIAN LEADERS ARE CURRENTLY ENGAGED IN DRAWING UP A
       NATIONAL CHARTER THAT WILL DEFINE AND REGULATE POLITICAL
       FREEDOMS AND POPULAR PARTICIPATION. THE IDEA OF A CHARTER
       RESPONDS TO THE GROWING POPULAR DEMAND, STRIDENTLY EXPRESSED
       DURING RECENT RIOTS THAT SWEPT THE NATION, FOR BROADER
       POPULAR PARTICIPATION AND DEMOCRATIC REFORMS. ALTHOUGH THE
       CHARTER IS LIKELY TO ALLOW THE FORMATION OF POLITICAL
       PARTIES, THEY ARE LIKELY TO BE RESTRICTED TO THOSE THAT ARE
       SUPPORTIVE OF MONARCHY AND THOSE THAT DO NOT HAVE
       EXTRANATIONAL TIES.

00989 ANDONI, L.
       JORDAN: NEW ERA FOR THE PRESS?
       MIDDLE EAST INTERNATIONAL, (351) (MAY 89), 12.
          THE INTERIM GOVERNMENT OF JORDAN HAS LIFTED RESTRICTIONS
       ON THE PRESS THAT WERE PLACED IN A CRACK-DOWN BY THE RIFAI
       GOVERNMENT. THE INTERIM GOVERNMENT ALSO RESTORED THE
       AUTHORITY OF JORDAN'S CENTRAL BANK. THESE TWO MOVES WERE
       SEEN AS ESSENTIAL IF POPULAR CONFIDENCE IN THE GOVERNMENT
       WAS TO BE RESTORED.

00990 ANDONI, L.
       JORDAN: NO CHANGE AT THE TOP
       MIDDLE EAST INTERNATIONAL, (341) (JAN 89), 14.
          JORDAN'S PRIME MINISTER ZAID AL-RIFAI RESHUFFLED HIS
       CABINET IN DECEMBER 1988. THE CABINET CHANGES WERE
       ACCOMPANIED BY CHANGES IN KEY PALACE POSTS, INVOLVING THREE
       OF THE KING'S CLOSEST ADVISORS. THE RESHUFFLE HAS SEEN AS
       ANOTHER STEP IN JORDAN'S DISENGAGEMENT FROM THE WEST BANK
       AND A BOOST IN THE STATUS OF PRIME MINISTER ZAID.

00991 ANDONI, L.
       JORDAN: POOR PROGNOSIS
       MIDDLE EAST INTERNATIONAL, 352 (JUN 89), 10-11.
          THE NEW JORDANIAN GOVERNMENT IS SAID TO BE WORKING TO
       IDENTIFY WAYS OF CUTTING EXPENDITURE WITHOUT HURTING THE
       GROWING NUMBERS OF LOW-INCOME FAMILIES. BUT EVEN WITH A
       BALANCED PROGRAMME GEARED AT MINIMISING THE HARDSHIP FOR
       THESE GROUPS, ECONOMISTS ARGUE THAT FOREIGN AND ARAB GRANTS
       ARE BADLY NEEDED TO SALVAGE THE JORDANIAN ECONOMY. IRAQ,
       OMAN AND KUWAIT ARE SAID TO HAVE PLEDGED $120M IN GRANTS AND
       KUWAIT ALSO OFFERED TO SUPPLY $40M WORTH OF CRUDE OIL. BUT
       ACCORDING TO AVAILABLE INFORMATION THE DEAL WITH THE IMF IS
       BASED ON THE ASSUMPTION OF RECEIVING $400M IN ARAB AID.

00992 ANDONI, L.
       JORDAN: THE KING AS COORDINATOR
       MIDDLE EAST INTERNATIONAL, (343) (FEB 89), 11-12.
          KING HUSSEIN HAS BEEN ACTIVELY PURSUING TWO
       COMPLIMENTARY GOALS. ON ONE HAND, HE HAS INTENSIFIED HIS
       EFFORTS TO CLEAR INTER-ARAB DIFFERENCES, PAVING THE WAY TO
       CONVENING AN ARAB SUMMIT. ON THE OTHER, HE IS PUSHING THE
       IDEA OF FORMING A REGIONAL FOUR-MEMBER ECONOMIC COOPERATION
       COMMUNITY, WHICH WOULD BE OPEN TO PARTICIPATION BY OTHER
       ARAB COUNTRIES. THE MOVES REFLECT THE OFFICIAL JORDANIAN
       VIEW OF ITS ROLE IN THE PALESTINIAN QUESTION AND IN THE ARAB
       WORLD.

00993 ANDONI, L.
       JORDAN: THE TASKS AHEAD
       MIDDLE EAST INTERNATIONAL, (350) (MAY 89), 10-11.
          DESPITE THE NEWLY-APPOINTED INTERIM GOVERNMENT OF FIELD MARSHAL
       ZAID BIN SHAKIR MUST BRING JORDANIANS TO TERMS WITH THE HARD
       REALITY OF LIVING IN A COUNTRY THAT HAS SCANT NATURAL
       RESOURCES TO DEVELOP. AS THE RIOTS AND DEMANDS VOICED BY THE
       PROTESTORS SHOW, THE JORDANIANS ARE MORE LIKELY TO COOPERATE
       IF THE GOVERNMENT ENDORSES A PROGRAM OF SUBSTANTIAL ECONOMIC
       AND POLITICAL REFORMS.

00994 ANDONI, L.
       JORDAN'S ELECTION CAMPAIGN
       MIDDLE EAST INTERNATIONAL, (359) (SEP 89), 11.
          AS CAMPAIGNING FOR JORDAN'S FIRST GENERAL ELECTIONS GETS
       UNDER WAY, THE SCOPE AND NATURE OF PUBLIC INVOLVEMENT IS
       INCREASING TO UNPRECEDENTED HIGHS. PUBLIC DEBATE INVOLVING
       SENSITIVE ISSUES SUCH AS THE BREAK WITH THE WEST BANK, THE
       PEACE PROCESS, ECONOMIC CORRUPTION, AND THE POWER OF
       SECURITY SERVICES HAS BECOME INCREASINGLY WIDESPREAD AND
       OUTSPOKEN. THERE IS ALSO STRONG PRESSURE TO END THE CURBS ON
       POLITICAL FREEDOMS AND TO ENGAGE IN ELECTORAL REFORM.

00995 ANDONI, L.
       JORDAN'S ELECTION PROGRESS
       MIDDLE EAST INTERNATIONAL, (362) (NOV 89), 8-10.
          THE ARTICLE ANALYZES THE POLITICAL TRENDS THAT HAVE
       SURFACED IN JORDAN. KING HUSSEIN'S DECISION TO ON MEMBERS OF
       "ILLEGAL GROUPS" TO PARTICIPATE IN GENERAL ELECTIONS HAS
       RESULTED IN SEVERAL POLITICAL MOVEMENT. THE ARTICLE BRIEFLY
       EXAMINES THE ISLAMIC, LEFTIST, ARAB NATIONALIST, LIBERAL,
       AND TRADITIONALIST TRENDS AND ANALYZES THEIR RELATIVE
       STRENGTHS AND WEAKNESSES. FACTIONALISM IS LIKELY TO REDUCE
       THE POWER OF ANY AND ALL OPPOSITION GROUPS.

00996 ANDONI, L.
       JORDAN'S ELECTIONS
       MIDDLE EAST INTERNATIONAL, (361) (OCT 89), 11-12.
          MORE THAN A THOUSAND CANDIDATES DESIRING TO PARTICIPATE
       IN JORDAN'S FIRST PARLIAMENTARY ELECTIONS HAVE SUBMITTED
       APPLICATIONS TO JORDANIAN COURTS. THUS FAR, ONLY FIVE HAVE
       BEEN PROHIBITED FROM RUNNING FOR OFFICE. TAKING ADVANTAGE OF
       A 1986 ELECTORAL LAW ALLOWING IT TO DEPRIVE MEMBERS OF
       POLITICAL GROUPS IN THE COUNTRY THE RIGHT TO PARTICIPATE,
       THE GOVERNMENT HAS BARRED THREE JORDANIAN BEDOUINS AND TWO
       SUSPECTED PLO MEMBERS FROM RUNNING. SOME OBSERVERS FEAR
       FURTHER PROHIBITIONS, BUT THE SIGNALS FROM THE GOVERNMENT
       HAVE BEEN MIXED.

00997 ANDONI, L.
       JORDAN'S NEW GOVERNMENT
       MIDDLE EAST INTERNATIONAL, (365) (DEC 89), 8-.
          CHANGE IN JORDAN HAS RIVALED THAT IN EASTERN EUROPE. THE
       NATION IS ENGAGED IN LIBERALIZATION THAT AFFECTS THE ROLE OF
       THE LEGISLATIVE HOUSE AND INTELLIGENCE ORGANIZATIONS.
       HOWEVER, SOME REFORMS HAVE A MORE DIRECT EFFECT ON THE
       PEOPLE OF JORDAN. THEY INCLUDE: THE RELEASE OF POLITICAL
       DETAINEES, THE RETURN OF CONFISCATED PASSPORTS, AND A LIFT
       ON THE TRAVEL BAN PLACED ON MANY JORDANIANS. THE REFORMS ARE
       LARGELY THE WORK OF PRIME MINISTER MADAR BADRAN, A FORMER
       CHIEF OF INTELLIGENCE. HOWEVER, HE STILL FACES A TOUGH
       BATTLE FROM DEPUTIES INSISTING ON A PROGRAM INVOLVING THE
       UNEQUIVOCAL LIFTING OF MARTIAL LAW AND OTHER EMERGENCY
       "DEFENSE REGULATIONS."

00998 ANDONI, L.
       JORDAN'S NEW SPEAKER
       MIDDLE EAST INTERNATIONAL, (364) (DEC 89), 10.
          NEWLY ELECTED PARLIAMENTARY SPEAKER, SULEIMAN ARAR, HAS
       CALLED FOR CONTINUED LIBERALIZATION OF JORDAN'S POLITICAL
       INSTITUTIONS. KING HUSSEIN APPARENTLY IS IN FULL AGREEMENT:
       HE HAS DECLARED HIS INTENTION TO SCALE DOWN THE POWER OF
       JORDAN'S INTELLIGENCE COMMUNITY AND EXTRAORDINARY COURTS.
       EVEN HARD-LINE ISLAMIC FUNDAMENTALIST GROUPS ARE TONING DOWN
       THEIR CRITICISM OF THE REFORMS.

00999 ANDONI, L.
       PALESTINIANS IN POLITICS
       MIDDLE EAST INTERNATIONAL, 356 (AUG 89), 11.
          THE JORDANIAN WING OF THE DEMOCRATIC FRONT FOR THE
       LIBERATION OF PALESTINE (DFLP) HAS ANNOUNCED THE FORMATION
       OF A NEW INDEPENDENT JORDANIAN POLITICAL PARTY ADVOCATING
       FREE PARLIAMENTARY ELECTIONS, THE LIFTING OF RESTRICTIONS ON
       POLITICAL ACTIVITIES AND A REASSESSMENT OF JORDANIAN
       ECONOMIC POLICIES. THE JORDANIAN DEMOCRATIC POPULAR PARTY
       (JDPP) PRESENTED ITSELF AS REPRESENTING BOTH JORDANIANS AND
       PALESTINIANS IN JORDAN IN THE STRUGGLE FOR "DEMOCRACY,
       SOCIAL EQUALITY AND FOSTERING JORDAN'S INDEPENDENCE AND
       SOVEREIGNTY". THE MOVE IS SIGNIFICANT IN VIEW OF THE ONGOING
       SEPARATION BETWEEN THE JORDANIAN OPPOSITION AND THE
       PALESTINIAN ORGANISATIONS IN RESPONSE TO JORDAN'S OFFICIAL
       BREAK WITH THE WEST BANK AND THE DECLARATION OF AN
       INDEPENDENT PALESTINIAN STATE.

01000 ANDONI, L.
       PLO PATIENCE STRETCHED
       MIDDLE EAST INTERNATIONAL, (364) (DEC 89), 7-8.
          DESPITE A FLURRY OF PROPOSALS AND COUNTER-PROPOSALS THAT
       ARE BEING EXCHANGED BETWEEN THE US AND THE PLO, COMPROMISE
       AND AGREEMENT ON KEY ISSUES SEEM NO CLOSER. THE MAIN ISSUES
       AT STAKE ARE THE REPRESENTATIVES IN THE PLANNED ISRAELI-
       PALESTINIAN NEGOTIATIONS. THE US DEMANDS THAT EGYPT CHOOSE
       THE REPRESENTATIVES, AND THE PLO DEMANDS A MORE DIRECT ROLE.
       PROGRESS IS VIRTUALLY UNSEEN AND PLO CHAIRMAN YASSER ARAFAT
       HAS BEEN QUOTED AS STATING PATIENCE HAS ITS LIMITS."

01001 ANDONI, L.
       PLO-US TALKS
       MIDDLE EAST INTERNATIONAL, (357) (AUG 89), 11-12.
          AMERICAN ATTEMPTS TO COMPEL THE PLO TO RECONSIDER THE
       HARD-LINE TONE VOICED BY THE FATAH CONGRESS FAILED
       COMPLETELY IN THE FIFTH SESSION OF US-PLO DIALOGUE. THE PLO
       IS BECOMING INCREASINGLY DISILLUSIONED WITH THE US-TALKS.
       ALTHOUGH THEY ACKNOWLEDGE THAT THE DIALOGUE HAS GIVEN THE
       ORGANIZATION LEGITIMACY AND HAS PROVIDED A "SMALL WINDOW"
       THROUGH WHICH THE PLO CAN ADDRESS AMERICAN PUBLIC OPINION,
       THEY ARE BECOMING AWARE THAT LITTLE SUBSTANTIVE PROGRESS IS

BEING MADE.

01002 ANDONI, L.
    PLO: GAINS AT THE SUMMIT
    MIDDLE EAST INTERNATIONAL, 352 (JUN 89), 5-6.
        THE CASABLANCA SUMMIT'S ENDORSEMENT OF THE PALESTINIAN
    PEACE STRATEGY WAS AN IMPORTANT POLITICAL VICTORY, BUT IN
    VIEW OF THE CURRENT ISRAELI CRACK-DOWN ON THE INTIFADA,
    PROSPECTS FOR A FORESEEABLE BREAKTHROUGH IN THE PEACE
    PROCESS ARE DIMINISHING. THE CASABLANCA RESOLUTIONS ON THE
    PALESTINE ISSUE REMAIN VERY SIGNIFICANT BECAUSE THEY MEAN
    THAT THE PALESTINIAN PEACE STRATEGY HAS VIRTUALLY BECOME THE
    JOINT ARAB NEGOTIATING POSITION, UNDERMINING ISRAELI CLAIMS
    THAT ARAFAT WAS ACTING ON HIS OWN WITHOUT ARAB SUPPORT.

01003 ANDONI, L.
    PLO: GETTING BACK TO BASICS
    MIDDLE EAST INTERNATIONAL, (349) (APR 89), 5-6.
        RECENT STATEMENTS AND ACTIVITIES SUGGEST THAT THERE IS A
    TREND INSIDE THE PLO TO BUY THE AMERICAN IDEA OF "BUILDING
    ON THE PRINCIPLE OF ELECTIONS" IN THE OCCUPIED TERRITORIES.
    SOME WEST BANK LEADERS ARE TRYING TO WIN YASSER ARAFAT'S
    ENDORSEMENT FOR A PACKAGE OF PROPOSALS STARTING WITH A
    PARTIAL ISRAELI WITHDRAWAL, MOVING ON TO THE ELECTION OF
    PALESTINIAN NEGOTIATORS, AND THEN INITIATING PEACE
    NEGOTIATIONS THAT THE PLO WOULD JOIN LATER.

01004 ANDONI, L.
    PLO: SUSPICIONS CONFIRMED
    MIDDLE EAST INTERNATIONAL, 355 (JUL 89), 8.
        NEW CONDITIONS ATTACHED TO THE SO-CALLED ISRAELI PEACE
    PLAN, THE ENSUING INTERNAL CRISIS WHICH THREATENED THE
    FRAGILE ISRAELI COALITION GOVERNMENT AND FINALLY THE PARIS
    DECLARATION BY THE SEVEN MAJOR INDUSTRIAL COUNTRIES
    SUPPORTING THE CONVENING OF AN INTERNATIONAL PEACE
    CONFERENCE, DEALT SERIOUS BLOWS TO YITZHAK SHAMIR'S PROPOSAL
    TO FIND PALESTINIAN NEGOTIATORS FROM INSIDE THE OCCUPIED
    TERRITORIES. YET SHAMIR'S PLAN, ALTHOUGH IN INTENSIVE CARE,
    IS FAR FROM DEAD, AND CERTAINLY WASHINGTON HAS NOT WASHED
    ITS HANDS OF IT. BUT THE PLO LEADERSHIP SAW FOUR ENCOURAGING
    ELEMENTS IN THE DECLARATION: AN INTERNATIONAL CONFERENCE
    BEING RECOGNISED AS THE MOST ACCEPTABLE FRAMEWORK FOR PEACE
    NEGOTIATIONS; THE PRINCIPLE OF LAND FOR PEACE, AS THE BASIS
    FOR ANY PEACEFUL SETTLEMENT; THE AMERICAN ENDORSEMEN OF THE
    DECLARATION, AND THAT ELECTIONS SHOULD BE PART OF A
    COMPREHESIVE PLAN BASED ON A LAND-FOR-PEACE FORMULA.

01005 ANDONI, L.
    REPORT FROM AMMAN
    MIDDLE EAST REPORT, 19(156) (JAN 89), 35-36.
        WHEN KING HUSSAIN ANNOUNCED THAT JORDAN WAS SEVERING ITS
    POLITICAL TIES WITH THE WEST BANK, HE IMPLICITLY
    ACKNOWLEDGED THAT HIS STRATEGY OF 20 YEARS HAD BEEN
    OVERTAKEN BY THE PALESTINIAN UPRISING. THE PALESTINIAN
    REVOLT HAS ASSERTED AN INDEPENDENT POLITICAL IDENTITY WITH
    SUCH CLARITY AND FORCE AS TO MAKE IT IMPOSSIBLE FOR JORDAN
    TO CONTINUE TO CLAIM TO REPRESENT THE OCCUPIED TERRITORIES
    POLITICALLY.

01006 ANDONI, L.
    THE FATAH CONGRESS
    MIDDLE EAST INTERNATIONAL, (357) (AUG 89), 11.
        THE FIFTH FATAH CONGRESS ELECTED YASSER ARAFAT AS
    PRESIDENT OF THE CENTRAL COMMITTEE AND GAVE HIM A
    "QUALIFIED" MANDATE TO PURSUE HIS PEACE STRATEGY. ARAFAT
    SKILLFULLY MANAGED TO DEFUSE MUCH OF THE OPPOSITION TO HIS
    PEACE DIPLOMACY BY PLEDGING COMMITMENT TO ARMED STRUGGLE (IF
    PEACE NEGOTIATIONS FAIL) AND REPEATING CRITICISM OF THE
    AMERICAN POSITION.

01007 ANDONI, L.
    THE FIVE DAYS THAT SHOOK JORDAN
    MIDDLE EAST INTERNATIONAL, (349) (APR 89), 3-4.
        LESS THAN TWO DAYS AFTER THE GOVERNMENT ANNOUNCED PRICE
    INCREASES FOR BASIC COMMODITIES AS PART OF AN ECONOMIC
    REFORM PLAN, PROTESTORS IN MAAN SPARKED JORDAN'S OWN
    INTIFADA. IN THE FOLLOWING FIVE DAYS, THE ACCUMULATION OF
    FRUSTRATIONS ERUPTED IN THE JORDANIAN PEOPLE'S FIRST
    STRIDENT OUTCRY FOR SOCIAL JUSTICE AND DEMOCRACY.

01008 ANDONI, L.
    THE PLO AND THE US
    MIDDLE EAST INTERNATIONAL, (361) (OCT 89), 6-7.
        A MEETING OF PLO LEADERSHIP IN BAGDHAD CONCLUDED WITH
    THE STATEMENT THAT THE DIALOGUE WITH THE US HAS REACHED A
    DEADLOCK AND THE PLO SHOULD EXPLORE OTHER MEANS OF DEALING
    WITH WASHINGTON. ALTHOUGH MANY IN THE PLO LEADERSHIP HAVE
    NOT COMPLETELY ABANDONED YASSER ARAFAT'S ATTEMPT AT
    DIPLOMACY, THE SEARCH FOR NEW ALTERNATIVES HAS ALREADY BEGUN.
    HOWEVER, IT IS UNLIKELY THAT THE PLO WILL RELINQUISH ITS
    SUPPORT FOR THE INTIFADA.

01009 ANDONI, L.
    THE PLO AND THE US: PREPARING FOR TOUGH TALKING

MIDDLE EAST INTERNATIONAL, (346) (MAR 89), 5-6.
        AS THE SECOND ROUND OF THE AMERICAN-PALESTINIAN DIALOGUE
    APPROACHES, THE GAP BETWEEN THE NEGOTIATORS REMAINS WIDE ON
    MOST SUBSTANTIVE AND PROCEDURAL ISSUES. THE PLO IS BRACING
    ITSELF FOR A TOUGH CONFRONTATION WITH THE BUSH
    ADMINISTRATION OVER THE INTIFADA AND ITS RIGHT TO
    PARTICIPATE IN THE PEACE PROCESS AS THE EXCLUSIVE VOICE OF
    THE PALESTINIAN PEOPLE. THE PLO WILL TRY TO PERSUADE
    WASHINGTON TO ADDRESS THE ESCALATION OF ISRAEL'S IRON-FIST
    POLICY AGAINST THE PALESTINIANS.

01010 ANDONI, L.
    THE PLO UNENTHUSIASTIC
    MIDDLE EAST INTERNATIONAL, (359) (SEP 89), 5-6.
        ALTHOUGH EGYPT'S PROPOSALS TO BREAK THE CURRENT
    STALEMATE IN THE PEACE PROCESS MAY BE BENEFICIAL TO THE PLO
    IN THE SHORT TERM, THEY ARE REJECTING MUBARAK'S IDEAS AS
    BEING FUNDAMENTALLY DANGEROUS TO THE BASIS OF THE
    PALESTINIAN PEACE STRATEGY. ALTHOUGH THE MEASURES CERTAINLY
    PUT INCREASED PRESSURE ON ISRAEL TO MAKE SOME IMPORTANT
    CONCESSIONS, PLO LEADERS STATE THAT THE "TEN POINTS" CALL
    FOR MORE CONCESSIONS THAN THE PALESTINIANS ARE WILLING TO
    GIVE.

01011 ANDONI, L.
    THE PLO: "PRESIDENT" ARAFAT UNDER FIRE
    MIDDLE EAST INTERNATIONAL, (348) (APR 89), 9.
        ALTHOUGH NEWLY DESIGNATED PRESIDENT OF PALESTINE, YASSIR
    ARAFAT STILL ENJOYS A GREAT DEAL OF SUPPORT FROM ALL
    PALESTINIAN GROUPS, HE STILL FACES TWO CRUCIAL TESTS:
    REMAINING THE SYMBOL OF THE PALESTINIAN MOVEMENT, AND
    CONTINUING TO DEMONSTRATE HIS DIPLOMATIC SKILLS. SIGNS OF
    INTERNAL DISSENT AND DISSATISFACTION WITH ARAFATS UNILATERAL
    STYLE OF LEADERSHIP AND HIS APARENT COMPROMISING STATEMENTS
    WILL ALSO NEED TO BE DEALT WITH IF ARAFAT IS TO SUCCEED IN
    HIS GOAL OF LEADING THE PALESTINIANS TO FREEDOM AND
    INDEPENDENCE.

01012 ANDONI, L.
    THE PLO: CONTRADICTORY SIGNALS
    MIDDLE EAST INTERNATIONAL, 353 (JUN 89), 6-7.
        AS WAS EXPECTED, THE THIRD ROUND OF THE OFFICIAL
    DIALOGUE BETWEEN THE US AND THE PALESTINE LIBERATION
    ORGANISATION (PLO) FOCUSED ON THE IDEA AND PRE-CONDITIONS OF
    CONDUCTING ELECTIONS IN THE ISRAELI OCCUPIED WEST BANK AND
    GAZA STRIP. THE ISRAELIS AND THE AMERICANS HAVE SUCCEEDED IN
    TURNING THE FOCUS OF THE TALKS AWAY FROM THE CONVENING OF AN
    INTERNATIONAL PEACE CONFERENCE, PROVIDING INTERNATIONAL
    SECURITY FOR THE PALESTINIANS IN THE OCCUPIED TERRITORIES,
    AND PALESTINIAN SELF-DETERMINATION, TO THAT OF THE ELECTIONS
    ISSUE. IN OTHER WORDS, INSTEAD OF CLARIFYING THEIR POSITION
    ON THE THREE ABOVE ISSUES, THE AMERICANS, USING THE ISRAELI
    PROPOSAL FOR ELECTIONS, HAVE THROWN THE BALL INTO THE PLO'S
    COURT.

01013 ANDONI, L.
    THE PLO: SLEEPING ON IT
    MIDDLE EAST INTERNATIONAL, (343) (FEB 89), 9-10.
        THE SUCCESSES ACHIEVED BY PLO CHAIRMAN YASSER ARAFAT IN
    WESTERN EUROPE HAVE BOOSTED THE ORGANIZATION'S PEACE DRIVE
    AND INTERNATIONAL STATUS. BUT ARAFAT HAS YET TO SERIOUSLY
    TACKLE INTERNAL PALESTINIAN DIFFERENCES. A DISAGREEMENT OVER
    TACTICS, WHICH COULD EASILY GROW, EMERGED AFTER ARAFAT'S
    GENEVA PRESS CONFERENCE. THE PFLP AND DFLP FACTIONS BOTH
    SHARPLY CRITICIZED ARAFAT'S STATEMENTS AS CONTRADICTING PNC
    RESOLUTIONS.

01014 ANDONI, L.
    THE PLO: THE PROVISIONAL GOVERNMENT DEBATE
    MIDDLE EAST INTERNATIONAL, (342) (JAN 89), 10-11.
        DESPITE THE CLEAR ENDORSEMENT BY THE 1988 PNC OF A
    PALESTINIAN PROVISIONAL GOVERNMENT, THE ISSUE IS STILL
    SUBJECT TO INTENSE DEBATE INSIDE THE PLO. A MAJOR POINT OF
    DISAGREEMENT IS THE TIMING. THE PFLP BELIEVES THAT IT IS
    PREMATURE FOR THE PLO TO EMBARK ON SUCH A STEP. OTHER
    FACTIONS, INCLUDING THE DFLP AND THE COMMUNISTS, ARGUE THAT
    THE FORMATION OF A PROVISIONAL GOVERNMENT IS AN URGENT
    NECESSITY.

01015 ANDONI, L.
    THE PLO'S RESPONSE: UNDER PRESSURE
    MIDDLE EAST INTERNATIONAL, (365) (DEC 89), 5.
        ON THE SECOND ANNIVERSARY OF THE INTIFADA AND A YEAR
    AFTER THE OPENING OF THE US-PLO DIALOGUE, THE ORGANIZATION
    IS SUFFERING FROM SERIOUS SETBACKS ON THE DIPLOMATIC LEVEL.
    ALTHOUGH THE INTIFADA CONTINUES, THE PLO HAS YET TO FIND A
    WAY TO ESCALATE PALESTINIAN RESISTANCE WITHOUT PROVOKING A
    MASSIVE MILITARY RETRIBUTION. IN ADDITION, EGYPT'S
    ASSUMPTION OF THE ROLE OF PRINCIPAL NEGOTIATOR WITH THE US
    RENDERS THE PLO-US DIALOGUE ALMOST REDUNDANT.

01016 ANDONI, L.
    THE PLO'S SUSPICIONS
    MIDDLE EAST INTERNATIONAL, (360) (OCT 89), 5.

IN SPITE OF CONTINUOUS PUBLICITY AND DIPLOMATIC ACTIVITY, THE PLO REMAINS FAR FROM A REAL SOLUTION TO THE PROBLEMS IN THE OCCUPIED TERRITORIES. ALTHOUGH THE PRINCIPLE OF DIRECT ISRAELI-PALESTINIAN NEGOTIATIONS IS ACCEPTED ON ALL FRONTS, SERIOUS PROCEDURAL AND SUBSTANTIVE OBSTACLES REMAIN. THESE INCLUDE THE ROLE OF SUCH TALKS AND THE MAKEUP OF THE PALESTINIAN DELEGATION.

01017 ANDONIS, L.
THE PLO AND THE US: EXTREME CAUTION
MIDDLE EAST INTERNATIONAL, (341) (JAN 89), 7.
ALTHOUGH THE PLO REGARDS THE AMERICAN DECISION TO OPEN DIALOGUE AS A MAJOR BREAKTHROUGH, PLO LEADERS ARE CAUTIOUS. THEY REALIZE THERE IS A LONG WAY TO GO BEFORE THERE IS ANY REAL CHANGE IN THE AMERICAN POSITION TOWARDS AN INTERNATIONAL PEACE CONFERENCE AND RECOGNITION OF PALESTINIAN NATIONAL RIGHTS.

01018 ANDOVL, L.
JORDAN'S ELECTION
MIDDLE EAST INTERNATIONAL, (363) (NOV 89), 3-4.
JORDAN'S KING HUSSEIN HAS BROUGHT ABOUT SIGNIFICANT REFORM AND CHANGE, UNPRECEDENTED IN THE ARAB WORLD. AFTER 35 YEARS OF POLITICAL SUPPRESSION, HE OVERSAW ELECTIONS THAT WERE COMPLETELY FREE AND FAIR. HUSSEIN AND HIS NATIONA NOW FACE THE CHALLENGE OF TRANSLATING REFORM INTO REALITY, ESPECIALLY ON THE ECONOMIC FRONT. PERHAPS THE LARGEST INTERNAL OBSTACLE IS THE ADVENT OF THE MUSLIM BROTHERHOOD, AN EXTREME POLITICAL GROUP, WHICH GAINED A SURPRISING NUMBER OF SEATS IN THE NOVEMBER ELECTION.

01019 ANDREAS, P.; YOUNGERS, C.
"BUSTING" THE ANDEAN COCAINE INDUSTRY
WORLD POLICY JOURNAL, VI(3) (SUM 89), 529-561.
THE RAPID RISE OF THE INTERNATIONAL COCAINE INDUSTRY IN THE 70S AND 80S HAS FUNDAMENTALLY TRANSFORMED U.S.-LATIN AMERICAN RELATIONS. THIS HAS BEEN MOST APPARENT IN PERU, COLUMBIA, AND BOLIVIA. AS DRUG-RELATED VIOLENCE HAVE ESCALATED IN THE U.S. THE TENDENCY HAS BEEN TO BLAME THE ANDEAN COUNTRIES. THIS ARTICLE DISCUSS THE EVOLUTION OF THE COCAINE INDUSTRY AND ITS IMPACT ON PRODUCER COUNTRIES. THE U.S. POLICY RESPONSE IS DISCUSSED. IDEAS FOR A WORKABLE DRUG POLICY CONCLUDE THE ARTICLE.

01020 ANDREWS, G.A.
AMERICAN LABOR AND THE MEXICAN REVOLUTION
DISSERTATION ABSTRACTS INTERNATIONAL, 49(8) (FEB 89), 2363-A.
THE AUTHOR STUDIES THE PHILOSOPHICAL ASSUMPTIONS THAT GUIDED SAMUEL GOMPERS AND OTHER AFL LEADERS AS THEY RESPONDED TO THE POLITICAL FERMENT OF MEXICAN WORKERS DURING THE REVOLUTION OF 1910. HE PROBES LABOR'S REACTION TO THE BROADER POLITICAL, ECONOMIC, AND STRATEGIC ISSUES RAISED BY THE MEXICAN REVOLUTION AND EXAMINES PROGRESSIVE ERA ATTEMPTS TO FORGE A CORPORATIST CONSENSUS ON CHALLENGES TO U.S. HEGEMONY IN LATIN AMERICA.

01021 ANDREYEV, S.
USSR-ITALY: 40TH ANNIVERSARY OF THE TREATY.
FOREIGN TRADE, 12 (1988), 27-29.
THE USSR-ITALY TREATY ON TRADE AND NAVIGATION HAS BEEN A RELIABLE LEGAL FRAMEWORK FOR EXPANDING MUTUALLY BENEFICIAL BUSINESS TIES AND LATELY FOR INTRODUCING NEW PROMISING FORMS OF USSR-ITALY COOPERATION. THIS ARTICLE TRACES THE 40 YEAR OLD HISTORY OF THE BILATERAL ECONOMIC TIES OF THESE TWO COUNTRIES. THE 16TH SESSION OF THE JOINT COMMISSION ON ECONOMIC, SCIENTIFIC AND TECHNICAL COOPERATION BETWEEN THE USSR AND ITALY WILL BE HELD ON THE 40TH ANNIVERSARY OF THE TREATY.

01022 ANDRIESSEN, F.
CLOSE U.S., E.C. COOPERATION VITAL FOR WORLD TRADE
EUROPE, 284 (MAR 89), 14-15.
BILATERAL AND, EVEN MORE SO, UNILATERAL MEASURES CANNOT PROVIDE AN ADEQUATE ALTERNATIVE TO A REFORMED MULTILATERAL TRADING SYSTEM AND EFFORTS SHOULD BE CONCENTRATED ON ACHIEVING THE LATTER. THE NEW U.S. TRADE ACT CONTINUES TO WORRY THE COMMUNITY BECAUSE IT CONTAINS PROVISIONS THAT RUN COUNTER TO THE GENERAL AGREEMENT ON TARIFFS AND TRADE (GATT) AND CONFIRM A TENDENCY TOWARD UNILATERALISM THAT DOES LITTLE TO ENCOURAGE RESPECT FOR THE GATT. EVEN IF NO ACTION IS TAKEN, THE MERE THREAT OF ACTION FOR WHICH THE TRADE ACT PROVIDES, IS DETRIMENTAL TO THE MULTILATERAL TRADING SYSTEM. THE COMMUNITY WILL, OF COURSE, BE MONITORING CLOSELY THE IMPLEMENTATION OF THELEGISLATION. IT GOES WITHOUT SAYING THAT IT WILL TAKE PROMPT ACTION TO DEFEND ITS RIGHTS IF ITS INTERESTS ARE ADVERSELY AFFECTED.

01023 ANGEL, R.C.
PRIME MINISTERIAL LEADERSHIP IN JAPAN: RECENT CHANGES IN PERSONAL STYLE AND ADMINISTRATIVE ORGANIZATION
PACIFIC AFFAIRS, 61(4) (WIN 89), 583-602.
JAPAN'S CONSTITUTION ASSIGNS CRUCIAL COORDINATION AND LEADER SHIP FUNCTIONS TO THE OFFICE OF PRIME MINISTER. YET INCUMBENTS DURING MOST OF THE POSTWAR PERIOD HAVE BEEN PASSIVE "CONSENSUS ARTICULATORS" RATHER THAN GOAL ARTICULATING AND GOAL PROMOTING ACTIVISTS. A NUMBER OF FACTORS HAVE COMBINED DURING THE LAST SEVERAL YEARS TO CHANGE THE NATURE OF JAPAN'S PRIME MINISTERIAL LEADERSHIP WITH IMPORTANT IMPLICATIONS FOR THE NATIONAL POLICY PROCESSES. THIS PAPER REVIEWS THE TRADITIONAL ROLE OF THE POSTWAR PRIME MINISTER AND THOSE FACTORS THAT HAVE ENCOURAGED MORE AGGRESSIVE PRIME MINISTERIAL INVOLVEMENT IN NATIONAL POLICY FORMULATION AND IMPLEMENTATION. IT FOCUSES UPON YASUHIRO NAKASONE'S RECENT FIVE-YEAR PERFORMANCE, WITH SPECIAL ATTENTION TO THE LONGER-TERM IMPLICATIONS OF CHANGES IN STRUCTURE OF THE CABINET SECRETARIAT MADE IN 1986. THE PAPER CONCLUDES THAT DOMESTIC AND INTERNATIONAL FACTORS WILL CONTINUE TO PRESS JAPAN'S PRIME MINISTERS INTO A MORE ACTIVE ROLE ON THE NATIONAL POLITICAL SCENE.

01024 ANGELI, F.
ITALY TODAY: SOCIAL PICTURE AND TRENDS 1987
AVAILABLE FROM NTIS, NO. PB89-122790/GAR, 1988, 199.
THE DOCUMENT IS A WORKING INSTRUMENT WIDELY USED BY ECONOMISTS, EXECUTIVES AND EXPERTS IN THE VARIOUS SECTORS OF SOCIAL POLICY-MAKING AND ACTION, PROVIDING AS IT DOES A WEALTH OF MATERIAL - STATISTICS, COMMENTS, INTERPRETATIONS AND FORECASTS - RELATING TO THE MAIN TRENDS UNDER WAY IN ITALIAN SOCIETY. THE REPORT CONTAINS AN INTRODUCTORY PART CONTAINING GENERAL REMARKS (A 'WINDOW' LOOKING INTO UNDERLYING TRENDS AND RESPONSE ALL OVER THE COUNTRY); A SECOND PART WHICH TACKLES THE SPECIFIC TRENDS EMERGING IN THE CULTURAL SPHERE AND IN SOCIETY, ESPECIALLY THOSE ACTING AS POINTERS TO THE MOST SIGNIFICANT CHANGES; AND A THIRD PART DEALING WITH THE VARIOUS SECTORS, EXPLORING IN DEPTH, WITH A SOLID SUPPORT OF STATISTICAL DATA, THOSE THINGS THAT HAVE BEEN CHANGING DURING THE COURSE OF THE YEAR IN THE VARIOUS ACTIONS AND BEHAVIORS: RANGING FROM EDUCATION TO THE STRUCTURE OF THE LABOR MARKET, FROM HEALTH TO SOCIAL SECURITY, FROM HOUSING AND REGIONAL PLANNING TO THE GREAT THEMES OF EXPENDITURE AND THE POLES OF SOCIAL POLICY IN GENERAL.

01025 ANGENFORT, J.
"RESPECTABLE" NEO-NAJIAM TODAY
WORLD MARXIST REVIEW, 32(11) (NOV 89), 69-71.
THERE ARE NOW ABOUT 50 NEO-NAJI GROUPS IN THE FEDERAL REPUBLIC OF GERMANY; THEY ENJOY CONSIDERABLE POPULARITY AND OTHER PROFASCIST FORCES INCREASINGLY TAKE THEIR CUE FROM THEM THIS ARTICLE DESCRIBES HOW THE NEO-NAZI PARTIES SERVE AS A RESERVOIR FOR CATCHING THE VOTES OF ELECTORS DISAFFECTED WITH GOVERNMENT POLICY. THEY CONTRIBUTE TO A FURTHER RIGHTWARD SWING IN THE PUBLIC MOOD BY DISSEMINATING THE IDEAS WHICH OTHER RIGHTWING FORCES, INCLUDING THOSE REPRESENTED IN THE GOVERNMENT, SO FAR CANNOT OR DO NOT WANT TO PUBLICLY EXPRESS IN SUCH A FORM. THE USE OR THREAT OF FORCE, TO WHICH THE NEO-NAZIS OFTEN RESORT MAKES IT POSSIBLE TO INTIMIDATE THE MASSES AND TO SPREAD FEAR, WARNING AGAINST PRODEMOCRACY ACTION. FINALLY, THE NEO-NAZIS MIGHT BECOME THE CDU/CSU'S COALITION PARTNER IF IT PROVES IMPOSSIBLE TO FORM OTHER ALLIANCES FOR CONTINUING THE "RIGHTWARD SHIFT".

01026 ANGLIN, D.
CONFLICT IN SUB-SAHARAN AFRICA 1988-1989; CANADA AND REGIONAL CONFLICTS 1988-1989
MONTREAL; ETUDES STRATEGIQUES ET MILITAIRES ETUDES STRATEGIQUES ET MILITAIRES, MONTREAL, QUEBEC, 1989, 110-143.
THE ARTICLE EXAMINES CHANGE AND CONFLICT IN SUB-SAHARAN AFRICA. IT ANALYZES GENERAL POLITICAL AND SOCIO-ECONOMIC TRENDS AS WELL AS PATTERNS OF VIOLENCE. IT ALSO CONCENTRATES ON SPECIFIC POINTS OF CONFLICT INCLUDING: CONFLICTS AROUND THE HORN OF AFRICA, ETHIOPIA, SOMALIA, AND SUDAN; AND CONFLICTS CENTERED AROUND SOUTH AFRICA. THE ARTICLE CONCLUDES WITH AN ANALYSIS OF CANADA'S ROLE AND FOREIGN POLICY IN SUB-SAHARAN AFRICA.

01027 ANGRESANO, J.
THE EVOLUTIONARY -- INSTITUTIONAL APPROACH TO THE STUDY OF COMPARATIVE ECONOMIES
JOURNAL OF ECONOMIC ISSUES, XXIII(2) (JUN 89), 511-517.
THIS BRIEF DESCRIPTION OF THE JAPANESE ECONOMY ILLUSTRATES THE IMPORTANCE OF THE NATION'S HISTORY AND CULTURE IN SHAPING THE ECONOMY'S PRINCIPAL INSTITUTIONS. UNDERSTANDING THE ROOTS AND NATURE OF THE SOCIAL AND POLITICAL STRUCTURES IS ALSO SIGNIFICANT, FOR IT IS THROUGH THESE STRUCTURES THAT WORKING RULES FOR THE ECONOMY ARE ESTABLISHED AND MODIFIED.

01028 ANGUITA, J.
POLITICS - SCIENCE: SUBORDINATION OR EQUALITY?
WORLD MARXIST REVIEW, 32(10) (OCT 89), 41-45.
THIS IS A TRANSCRIPT OF A RECORDED CONVERSATION BETWEEN GENERAL SECRETARY OF THE COMMUNIST PARTY OF SPAIN, JULIO ANGUITA, AND PROFESSOR GRIGORI VODOLAZOV (USSR). IT EXAMINES WHAT OUGHT TO BE THE NORMAL CONNECTIONS BETWEEN POLITICIANS AND SCIENTISTS, AND THE MEANING OF DEMOCRACY IN SCIENCE, IN

POLITICS, AND IN THEIR RELATIONS WITH EACH OTHER. IT DEALS WITH SCIENCE AS HUMANISM, CHOICE AND SCIENTIFIC OPPOSITION, AND SCIENTISTS AND POLITICIANS AS CO-AUTHORS OF A MANIFESTO FOR THE 21ST CENTURY.

01029 ANGUITA, J.
SPAIN: UPHOLDING THE BASIC VALUES OF PEACE AND DEMOCRACY
INFORMATION BULLETIN, 27(3-4) (FEB 89), 26-29.
IN THE EEC THE TENSION BETWEEN THE HIGHLY DEVELOPED AND FOR THAT REASON DOMINANT STATES, AND THE LESS DEVELOPED COUNTRIES WHICH ARE IN A SUBORDINATE POSITION IS AN EXPRESSION OF THE DIALECTICS OF THE CLASS STRUGGLE. WHEN SPEAKING OF THE EUROPEAN ECONOMIC COMMUNITY FROM THE STANDPOINT OF THE LEFT, IT IS NOT RIGHT TO BE GUIDED BY VAGUE REFERENCES TO EURO-ISM -- AND THIS MUST BE CLEAR TO ONE AND ALL -- BUT BY THE CONCRETE ECONOMIC, SOCIAL AND POLITICAL REALITIES, THE GIST OF WHICH IS A CONFLICT BETWEEN THE DOMINANT AND THE DOMINATED. THE COMMUNIST PARTY OF SPAIN DOES NOT CONCEIVE OF EUROPE IN DETACHMENT FROM THE THIRD WORLD, WHICH MAKES UP THREE-QUARTERS OF HUMANKIND. CONTRARY TO THE THEORY OF EUROCENTRISM, THE PARTY BELIEVES THAT A EUROPE OF SOLIDARITY, ONCE IT IS INDEPENDENT, MUST DISPLAY SOLIDARITY WITH THEM IN EVERY SPHERE NOT ONLY ON THE EXTERNAL DEBT PROBLEM, BUT ALSO IN THE ESTABLISHMENT OF A NEW INTERNATIONAL ECONOMIC ORDER.

01030 ANGUITA, J.
WHAT SORT OF EUROPE?
WORLD MARXIST REVIEW, 32(5) (MAY 89), 3-6.
THE IMPLEMENTATION OF THE SINGLE EUROPEAN ACT BY 1992 POSES GRAVE PROBLEMS FOR SPAIN. EVEN THOUGH THIS DOCUMENT SPEAKS OF FREE TRADE, THE FREE MOVEMENT OF CAPITAL AND LABOUR, AND OF SOCIAL PERSPECTIVES, ITS MAIN EMPHASIS IS ON THOSE ASPECTS WHICH WILL BENEFIT CONSERVATIVE ECONOMIC CIRCLES THE MOST. DAILY, THE WORD "EUROPE" IS BEING BANDIED ABOUT ON RADIO, TV AND IN THE PRESS. JUDGING BY THE STATEMENTS FROM THOSE WHO GOVERN US, EUROPEISM IS SYNONYMOUS WITH MODERNITY. BUT WHAT SORT OF EUROPE ARE THEY TALKING ABOUT? THE COMMUNIST PARTY OF SPAIN SUPPORTS GORBACHOV'S CONCEPT OF A "COMMON EUROPEAN HOME". THIS EUROPEAN PHENOMENON IS BEGINNING TO APPEAR FAR BEYOND THE COMMON MARKET BECAUSE OF THE SHEER LOGIC OF ECONOMIC DEVELOPMENT. TODAY, PEOPLE IN VASTLY DIFFERENT PLACES WATCH THE SAME TELEVISION PROGRAMMES OR LISTEN TO THE SAME RADIO STATIONS. MODERN COMMUNICATIONS, THE PRESS AND TOURISM HAVE DRAWN PEOPLE CLOSER TOGETHER, SHORTENED DISTANCES, AND CUT ACROSS BOUNDARIES. THIS IMPLIES THAT, LIKE IT OR NOT, EUROPE WILL ULTIMATELY CONSTITUTE A SINGLE WHOLE.

01031 ANIMASHAUN, T.A.
PUBLIC POLICY IMPACT ON TECHNOLOGY DEVELOPMENT: A COMPARATIVE ANALYSIS OF NIGERIA AND SELECTED NICS
DISSERTATION ABSTRACTS INTERNATIONAL, 50(5) (NOV 89), 1426-A.
THIS STUDY ANALYZES INDUSTRIALIZATION AND TECHNOLOGY DEVELOPMENT IN NIGERIA IN THE PAST THREE DECADES. FOCUSING ON THE IDEOLOGICAL AND POLITICAL FACTORS ASSOCIATED WITH THE POLICIES AND STRATEGIES TOWARDS TECHNOLOGY DEVELOPMENT IN THE CAPITAL GOODS INDUSTRIES, IT DRAWS CONCLUSIONS ABOUT THE IMPACT OF THE GOVERNMENT POLICIES AND STRATEGIES ON PAST DEVELOPMENT AND IDENTIFIES CRITICAL ISSUES FOR FUTURE INDUSTRIAL POLICY. THE OBJECTIVES OF THE STUDY ARE THREE-FOLD: TO ANALYZE THE GENERAL PROBLEMS OF TECHNOLOGICAL AND INDUSTRIAL DEVELOPMENT IN NIGERIA, TO EXAMINE HOW SOME OF THE DEVELOPING COUNTRIES HAVE APPROACHED THE ISSUES OF TECHNOLOGICAL AND INDUSTRIAL DEVELOPMENT AND TO RECOMMEND GENERAL POLICY DIRECTIONS IN WHICH THE NIGERIAN POLICYMAKERS CAN IMPROVE THEIR TECHNOLOGICAL AND INDUSTRIAL DEVELOPMENT.

01032 ANKOMAH, B.
HOW THE HUMAN RIGHTS CONFERENCE WAS QUASHED
NEW AFRICAN, (267) (DEC 89), 11-12.
RELATIONS BETWEEN THE GHANA GOVERNMENT AND THE GHANA BAR ASSOCIATION (GBA) HAS HIT AN ALL TIME LOW AS TENSION BUILDS TO A BREAKING POINT OVER THE GOVERNMENT'S CANCELLATION OF THE 6TH BIENNIAL CONFERENCE OF THE AFRICAN BAR ASSOCIATION WHICH SHOULD HAVE BEEN HELD FROM 17-22 SEPTEMBER 1989. THE THEME WAS HUMAN RIGHTS IN AFRICA. ABOUT 250 DELEGATES FROM 40 COUNTRIES SHOULD HAVE ATTENDED. THE BAR ASSOCIATION SUDDENLY ISSUED A PRESS STATEMENT SAYING THAT THE CONFERENCE HAD BEEN CALLED OFF. THERE WAS NO REASON GIVEN. THIS INCIDENT WAS A GREAT EMBARRASSMENT TO THE GBA. ITS MEMBERS HAD WORKED TIRELESSLY TO GET THE CONFERENCE TO TAKE PLACE IN ACCRA, AND A LOT OF PREPARATION HAD GONE INTO HOSTING THE THE DELEGATES. THE CONFERENCE IS POSTPONED INDEFINITELY.

01033 ANKOMAH, B.
LESSONS OF TIANANMEN SQUARE
NEW AFRICAN, (263) (AUG 89), 15.
THE WRITER LOOKS AT RECENT EVENTS IN CHINA AND COMPARES THEM TO THE AFRICAN COUNTRIES WHICH HAVE BEEN RUN ON NOT TOO DISSIMILAR LINES AS CHINA. HE CONCLUDES THAT SINCE SO FEW AFRICAN LEADERS HAVE CONDEMNED THE KILLINGS IN CHINA IT SHOWS HOW GUILTY THEY FEEL OF REPRESSION AT HOME. HE ALSO

SUGGESTS LESSONS THAT AFRICA CAN LEARN FROM TIANANMEN SQUARE BEFORE IT IS TOO LATE.

01034 ANKOMAH, B.
LIBERIA: WORKERS' LACK OF RIGHTS THREATENS PREFERENTIAL TRADE WITH US
AFRICAN BUSINESS, (FEB 89), 18-19.
THIS ARTICLE REVIEWS LIBERIA'S ACTIONS TO LIMIT WORKERS' RIGHTS TO PARTICIPATE FULLY AND FREELY IN UNION ACTIVITIES. FOR THIS REASON, THE UNITED STATES IS CONSIDERING REMOVING LIBERIA FROM THE GENERALIZED SYSTEM OF TRADE PREFERENCES, WHICH PERMITS DUTY-FREE ENTRY OF PRODUCTS INTO THE UNITED STATES. THE AUTHOR EVALUATES THE ISSUES INVOLVED IN THESE MATTERS.

01035 ANKOMAH, B.
MUGABE'S MISTAKE
NEW AFRICAN, (OCT 89), 25.
THIS ARTICLE DESCRIBES PUBLIC REACTION TO THE WILLOWGATE CAR SCANDAL ESCALATED BECAUSE OF PRESIDENT ROBERT MUGABE'S PARDON OF THE GOVERNMENT OFFICIAL OFFENDERS IN THE SITUATION. WRITER, BAFFOUR ANKOMAH PREDICTS THAT THE GOVERNMENT WILL NOT BE ALLOWED TO GO UNPUNISHED FOR ITS CRIMES.

01036 ANKOMAH, B.
NIGERIAN LIBERALS BID FOR POWER
NEW AFRICAN, (264) (SEP 89), 13,14.
THIS REPORT EXAMINES ONE GROUP OF HOPEFUL ASPIRANTS TO POWER IN NIGERIA -THOSE FROM THE BRAND NEW NIGERIAN LIBERAL MOVEMENT. THE WRITER WITNESSED THE RATHER TENTATIVE LAUNCH OF THE NEW BREED POLITICIANS IN LONDON AND SUGGESTS THAT THEY ARE NO DIFFERENT THAN THE OLD POLITICIANS. DR. ODIDI'S SPEECH IS ANALYSED AS WELL AS THE CONTROVERSIAL SHARIA LAW WHICH HAS BEEN INSERTED INTO NIGERIA'S NEW CONSTITUTION.

01037 ANKOMAH, B.
PRESIDENTS AND PRISONERS
NEW AFRICAN, (256) (JAN 89), 43.
MANY AFRICAN LEADERS HAVE APPALLING HUMAN RIGHTS RECORDS. THIS IS TRUE NOT ONLY OF HIGHLY-PUBLICIZED DICTATORS, SUCH AS MOBUTU AND PIERRE BUYOYA, BUT ALSO OF PRESIDENTS LIKE KENNETH KAUNDA. KAUNDA UNDERSTANDS THE ISSUES AND CALLS HIMSELF A HUMANIST CHRISTIAN. YET HE DETAINS HIS OPPONENTS AND SUPPRESSES HUMAN LIBERTY.

01038 ANKOMAH, B.
RACISM GOES BEYOND CHINA
NEW AFRICAN, (258) (MAR 89), 9.
THE AUTHOR STATES THAT BLACKS, PARTICULARLY AFRICANS, EXPERIENCE SOME DEGREE OF RACISM EVERYWHERE IN THE WORLD. HE SAYS THAT "AFRICA DESERVES TO HIT BACK IN THE STRONGEST OF TERMS." HE BLAMES THE PROBLEM ON AFRICA'S CORRUPT LEADERSHIP.

01039 ANKOMAH, B.
STUDENTS IN FERMENT
NEW AFRICAN, (260) (MAY 89), 9-12.
SINCE THE BEGINNING OF 1989, STUDENTS THROUGHOUT AFRICA HAVE BEEN STAGING PROTESTS, DEMONSTRATIONS, AND RIOTS. THE VIRUS OF DISCONTENT HAS SPREAD TO ZAIRE, THE CONGO, CAMEROON, NIGERIA, BENIN, SENEGAL, SUDAN, AND ZIMBABWE. UNDERLYING THE UPSURGE OF STUDENT PROTEST ARE NOT SIMPLY HIGH SPIRITS AND POLITICAL POSTURING BUT A FUNDAMENTAL REVOLT AGAINST BAD TEACHING, POOR CONDITIONS, UNPAID SCHOLARSHIPS, RISING PRICES, APATHY BY AUTHORITIES, AND GENERAL DETERIORATION OF EDUCATIONAL CONDITIONS.

01040 ANKOMAH, B.
WHO ISN'T AFRAID OF 1992?
NEW AFRICAN, (257) (FEB 89), 25.
THE EEC WILL TURN EUROPE INTO A SINGLE ECONOMIC MARKET IN DECEMBER 1992. SEVERAL COUNTRIES OUTSIDE THE ORGANIZATION ARE FEARFUL THAT EUROPE MIGHT BECOME A PROTECTIONIST FORTRESS DISPENSING ECONOMIC JUSTICE AS IT DEEMS FIT. EVEN INDUSTRIAL LEADERS ARE WORRIED AND ARE DISCUSSING WAYS TO COMBAT THE LOOMING DANGER. ALTHOUGH THE EFFECTS OF 1992 COULD BE DEVASTATING TO AFRICAN ECONOMIES, AFRICA CHARACTERISTICALLY APPEARS TO BE UNCONCERNED.

01041 ANNA, H.J.
THE AGENCY PERSPECTIVE AND THE FUTURE OF LOCAL GOVERNMENT ADMINISTRATION
INTERNATIONAL JOURNAL OF PUBLIC ADMINISTRATION, 12(2) (1989), 251-263.
THIS ESSAY EXPLORES THE APPLICATION OF THE CONCEPT OF THE AGENCY PERSPECTIVE, WHICH WAS DEVELOPED PRIMARILY WITH REFERENCE TO THE NATIONAL GOVERNMENT, TO LOCAL GOVERNMENT AND CONSIDERS THE IMPLICATIONS OF THE AGENCY PERSPECTIVE FOR THE FUTURE ROLE OF LOCAL GOVERNMENT ADMINISTRATION. THE ESSAY CONCLUDES THAT THE CONCEPT OF THE AGENCY PERSPECTIVE FITS LOCAL GOVERNMENTS AS WELL. IF THESE ARGUMENTS MEET WITH WIDESPREAD ACCEPTANCE, THIS SUGGESTS A GROWING, MORE ACTIVE ROLE FOR PUBLIC ADMINISTRATION IN U. S. LOCAL GOVERNMENTS.

01042 ANSAH, J.O.
DETAINEES SECRETLY RELEASED
NEW AFRICAN, (258) (MAR 89), 24-25.
WANTING TO PROJECT A CLEAN HUMAN RIGHTS RECORD ABROAD,
GHANA HAS BEGUN THE SECRET RELEASE OF POLITICAL PRISONERS.
THE GOVERNMENT IS NOT CALLING ATTENTION TO THE RELEASES
BECAUSE IT HAS STATED THAT THERE ARE NO POLITICAL DETAINEES
IN GHANA.

01043 ANTAL, V.
ACHIEVING SUCCESS IN THE GLOBAL ARENA
EUROPE, (290) (NOV 89), 16-17.
THE ARTICLE DISCUSSES CORPORATE LEADERS' CONCLUSION AT
THE NINTH INTERNATIONAL INDUSTRIAL CONFERENCE WITH REGARDS
TO THE FUTURE OF THE GLOBAL MARKETPLACE. THEY EXPRESSED
CONCERN OVER THE AVAILABILITY AND QUALITY OF TRAINED WORKERS;
THE NECESSITY OF A MANAGEMENT POOL WITH AN UNDERSTANDING OF
DIFFERENT CULTURES; AND REGIONAL BARRIERS TO TRADE. THEY
ALSO CONCLUDED THAT THE NEW ERA OF GLOBAL COMPETITIVENESS
WILL FORCE MANAGEMENT TO RESPOND TO DISTINCT MARKET
DIFFERENCES AND INDIVIDUAL MARKET NICHES WITH UNIQUE
PRODUCTS AND IDEAS, AND WITH NEW TALENTS AND SKILLS TO
COMPETE EFFECTIVELY.

01044 ANTHONY, B. JR.
PUTTING AMERICA ON A SOLID FOUNDATION
AMERICAN CITY AND COUNTY, 104(10) (OCT 89), 10.
FROM 1980 TO 1987, FEDERAL AID TO STATES AND CITIES
DECLINED THIRTY-SEVEN PERCENT IN REAL TERMS. UNABLE TO
IGNORE LOCAL INFRASTRUCTURE NEEDS, STATE GOVERNMENTS CURRENT
PROVIDE SEVENTY PERCENT OF ALL INFRASTRUCTURE INVESTMENT,
WHICH GOES PRIMARILY FOR OPERATION AND CONSTRUCTION RATHER
THAN NEW CONSTRUCTION AND REPLACEMENT. TO COVER THIS, MOST
STATE AND LOCAL GOVERNMENTS ARE INCREASING USER FEES,
PROPERTY TAXES, AND LOCAL INCOME TAXES OR DECREASING CAPITAL
SPENDING AND REDUCING WORKFORCES AND SERVICES.

01045 ANTINMO, T.
CAN AFRICA FEED ITSELF: THE NEED FOR A COMPREHENSIVE
APPROACH
WORLD MARXIST REVIEW, 32(9) (SEP 89), 76-77.
THIS ARTICLE ADDRESSES THE NEED FOR A COMPREHENSIVE
APPROACH TO SOLVE THE FOOD SHORTAGE IN AFRICA IN GENERAL, AN
IN NIGERIA IN PARTICULAR. IT EXAMINES FARM PRODUCTION. THE
MARKET SITUATION, GOVERNMENT PROGRAMS AND COOPERATION AMONG
AFRICAN COUNTRIES. IT CONCLUDES THAT AFRICA CAN FEED ITSELF,
GIVEN THE NECESSARY CONDITIONS.

01046 ANTOUN, R.D.
THE IMPACT OF WAR ON THE LEBANESE ADMINISTRATION: A STUDY
IN ADMINISTRATIVE DISRUPTION
DISSERTATION ABSTRACTS INTERNATIONAL, 50(4) (OCT 89),
1085-A.
THIS IS A STUDY OF ADMINISTRATIVE DISRUPTION ARISING OUT
OF THE CIVIL WAR IN LEBANON. IT PROVIDES A FRAMEWORK FOR THE
INVESTIGATION OF THE CONCEPT OF ADMINISTRATIVE DISRUPTION,
WHICH IS UNDERSTOOD AS THE EFFECTS UPON A GIVEN BUREAUCRATIC
SYSTEM OF MASSIVE AND SUDDEN CHANGES IN ITS ENVIRONMENT,
SUCH AS THOSE OCCASIONED BY NATURAL DISASTERS OR BY WAR.

01047 ANYADIKE, O.
MISSILE THREAT
NEW AFRICAN, (264) (SEP 89), 21-22.
THIS ARTICLE REPORTS ON INDICATIONS THAT PRETORIA NOW
POSSESSES THE MEANS TO LAUNCH A MISSILE CAPABLE OF
DELIVERING A NUCLEAR WAR-HEAD TO TARGETS WITHIN ALL
FRONTLINE STATES. THIS IS TEN YEARS AFTER US SATELLITES
RECORDED THE NOTORIOUS "DOUBLE FLASH" OVER SOUTH AFRICAN
TERRITORY IN THE INDIAN OCEAN, WHICH WAS GENERALLY REGARDED
AS CONFIRMATION OF AN ISRAELI-SOUTH AFRICAN AIR-BURST
NUCLEAR TEST. THIS IS NOW CONFIRMED BY PRETORIA ALTHOUGH IT
DENYS ANY INVOLVEMENT WITH ISRAEL. EVIDENCE REFUTING SOUTH
AFRICA'S DISCLAIMER IS EXPLORED, AND IT POINTS TO SOUTH
AFRICA AS THE SLEEPING PARTNER IN SEVERAL MAJOR ISRAELI
WEAPONS PROGRAMS PRETORIA'S ESCALATING DEFENCE BUDGET IN A
TIME OF PEACE IS EXAMINED.

01048 ANYANWU, T.
ABUJA: CONTROVERSY CONTINUES
NEW AFRICAN, (263) (AUG 89), 34.
THIS ARTICLE EXAMINES THE CONTINUING CONTROVERSY OVER
THE NEW CAPITAL, ABUJA, CREATED IN NIGERIA. THE OUTSTANDING
ISSUES ARE DISCUSSED - ITS FEDERAL STATUS, ITS RELIGIOUS
ALIGNMENTS, AND THE ADMINISTRATION OF ITS LAWS. THE
POLARISATION ALONG ETHNIC AND RELIGIOUS LINES IS EXPLORED AS
THE ATTEMPTS BY THE PRESIDENT AND BY THE FORMER CONSTITUENT
ASSEMBLY TO SETTLE THE CONTROVERSY CONTINUE TO FALTER.

01049 ANZAM, S.; TASKER, R.
FAREWELL TO ARMS
FAR EASTERN ECONOMIC REVIEW, 142(50) (DEC 89), 36-37.
THE COMMUNIST PARTY OF MALAYA (CPM) MARKED THE MOST
SIGNIFICANT MILESTONE IN SOUTHEAST ASIAN COMMUNISM IN YEARS
WHEN IT ABANDONED ITS 41-YEAR ARMED STRUGGLE TO OVERTHROW

THE MALAYSIAN GOVERNMENT. WHETHER THE CPM WILL BE A
POLITICAL FORCE IN MALAYSIA REMINS TO BE SEEN. THE EVENT
COULD MARK A NEW ERA OF BILATERAL COOPERATION BETWEEN
MALAYSIA AND THAILAND. BOTH COUNTRIES WERE CRITICAL OF EACH
OTHER FOR HARBORING REVOLUTIONARY GUERRILLA GROUPS
(COMMUNISTS IN THAILAND, AND MUSLIMS IN MALAYSIA).

01050 APPAVOO, P.J.
THE SMALL STATE AS DONOR: CANADIAN AND SWEDISH DEVELOPMENT
ASSISTANCE POLICIES, 1960-1976
DISSERTATION ABSTRACTS INTERNATIONAL, 50(6) (DEC 89),
1792-A.
THE AUTHOR REVIEWS THE DEVELOPMENT ASSISTANCE POLICIES
OF CANADA AND SWEDEN FROM 1960 TO 1976 TO IDENTIFY THE
SIMILARITIES AND DIFFERENCES AND TO EXPLAIN THE POLICY
CHOICES MADE BY EACH STATE. SHE FOCUSES ON FOUR DECISION
AREAS: VOLUME OF AID, CHOICE OF RECIPIENTS, PROJECT/PROGRAM
EMPHASIS, AND TERMS OF ASSISTANCE. SHE CONCLUDES THAT AID
POLICY DECISIONS WERE AFFECTED BY A MIX OF FACTORS RELATED
TO INTERNATIONAL POLITICS, DOMESTIC POLITICS, BUREAUCRATIC
NEEDS, AND HISTORIC CIRCUMSTANCES.

01051 APPELBAUM, R.
THE AFFORDABILTY GAP
SOCIETY, 26(4) (MAY 89), 6-7.
THE AUTHOR DISCUSSES THE UNDERLYING ECONOMIC CAUSES OF
THE INCREASING NUMBER OF HOMELESS PEOPLE IN THE US. THE
PRIMARY CAUSE IS THE "AFFORDABILITY GAP" THAT IS CONTINUALLY
RISING BETWEEN INCOME AND HOUSING COSTS. THIS PHENOMENON
HITS THE LOWER CLASS THE HARDEST BECAUSE AS THEIR INCOMES
DECLINE, THE INCENTIVES TO BUILD LOW INCOME HOUSING DECLINES
AS WELL. THE AUTHOR ADVOCATES FEDERALLY FUNDED, NONPROFIT
HOUSING OF VARIOUS FORMS AS THE BEST SOULTION TO THE PROBLEM.

01052 APPLBAUM, A.I.
KNOWLEDGE AND NEGOTIATION: LEARNING UNDER CONFLICT,
BARGAINING UNDER UNCERTAINTY
DISSERTATION ABSTRACTS INTERNATIONAL, 49(10) (APR 89),
3139-A.
THIS DISSERTATION POSES A PROBLEM IN COLLECTIVE DECISION-
MAKING FOR POLITICAL AND MANAGERIAL ACTORS: WHEN KNOWLEDGE
ABOUT THE VALUE OF CHOICES IS UNCERTAIN, THE INTERESTS OF
PARTIES CONFLICT, AND POWER IS SHARED, HOW DOES ONE LEARN
WHAT ONE WANTS TO DO AS ONE BARGAINS TO GET SOMETHING DONE?
THE PROBLEM IS PRESENTED IN THE FORM OF A STYLIZED
NEGOTIATION EXERCISE. THE US-USSR GRAIN AGREEMENT IS USED TO
ILLUSTRATE HOW LEARNING AFFECTS LEVERAGE.

01053 APPLEGATE, W.R.
BRITISH DEFENSE POLICY: A NEW APPROACH
AVAILABLE FROM NTIS, NO. AD-A203 142/5/GAR, DEC 88, 124.
THIS THESIS TRACES THE DEVELOPMENT OF BRITISH DEFENSE
POLICY AND ITS COMPONENT ORGANIZATIONS FROM THE 14TH CENTURY
UNTIL PRESENT DAY. IN-DEPTH ANALYSIS OF THE ROYAL NAVY, ARMY,
ROYAL AIR FORCE, AND MINISTRY OF DEFENSE IS PROVIDED.
FURTHER, IT COMPARES THE RECORD OF THE THATCHER GOVERNMENTS
CONCERNING BRITISH DEFENSE POLICY WITH THOSE OF PREVIOUS
GOVERNMENTS AND MONARCHS, CONCLUDING THAT MRS. THATCHER'S
TREATMENT OF DEFENSE IS MORE CORRECTLY DESCRIBED AS 'MORE OF
THE SAME' RATHER THAN A 'NEW APPROACH'.

01054 APPLEYARD, R.
MIGRATION AND DEVELOPMENT: MYTHS AND REALITY
INTERNATIONAL MIGRATION REVIEW, 23(3) (FAL 89), 486-499.
RECENT RESEARCH ON THE IMPACT OF LABOR MIGRATION ON THE
SOCIOECONOMIC DEVELOPMENT OF DEVELOPING COUNTRIES HAS
PROVIDED OPPORTUNITY TO TRY AND RESOLVE SOME OF THE LONG-
STANDING POLEMICS THAT HAVE PERVADED THE LITERATURE ON
MIGRATION AND DEVELOPMENT. THIS ARTICLE FOCUSES ON FINDINGS
CONCERNING THE LABOR, REMITTANCE AND SOCIAL IMPACTS OF
EMIGRATION ON COUNTRIES THAT HAVE PARTICIPATED IN LABOR
EMIGRATION. WHILE A GREAT DEAL MORE RESEARCH NEEDS TO BE
DONE, RECENT FINDINGS CONFIRM THAT IN SOME SITUATIONS THE
SHORT-TERM IMPACTS OF LABOR MIGRATION ON SENDING COUNTRIES
HAVE BEEN CONSIDERABLE.

01055 APTHEKER, H.
MARXISM: DEMISE OR RENEWAL?
POLITICAL AFFAIRS, 68(12) (DEC 89), 5-9.
THIS ARTICLE IS BASED ON A LECTURE GIVEN AT THE FIRST
UNITARIAN CHURCH IN LOS ANGELES, OCTOBER 15, 1989. IT
DEFINES MARXISM AND ITS GOALS FOR A NEW WORLD. IT DELVES
INTO THREE AREAS UNSUFFICIENTLY ANALYZED IN MARXISM'S
DEVELOPMENT -- PSYCHOLOGY, NATIONALISM, AND POWER. IT
CONCLUDES THAT MARXISM WILL EXPAND RATHER THAN DIMINISH AND
CALLS FOR A RENEWED REVOLUTIONARY COMMITMENT.

01056 APTHEKER, H.
MYTHS AND REALITIES OF TODAY
INFORMATION BULLETIN, 26(13-14) (JUL 88), 5-6.
THE NATO-WASHINGTON POLICY OF "USING NUCLEAR WEAPONS
FIRST" IS A GLARING CONTRAST TO THE UNILATERAL PLEDGE BY THE
USSR NEVER TO USE NUCLEAR WEAPONS FIRST, UNDER ANY
CIRCUMSTANCES. LET THE U.S. JOIN THE USSR IN THIS PLEDGE.

THAT WOULD GIVE AN ENORMOUS BOOST TO THE CURRENT EFFORT TO
RATIFY THE INF TREATY AND TO EXTEND IT IN A FUTURE SUMMIT BY
AGREEMENT TO DESTROY NOT ONLY SHORTER AND INTERMEDIATE-RANGE
LAND-BASED NUCLEAR WEAPONS, BUT BY BEGINNING THE PROCESS OF
DESTROYING STRATEGIC NUCLEAR WEAPONS ALSO.

01057 APTHEKER, H.
   ON THE BICENTENNIAL OF THE U.S. CONSTITUTION: A MARXIST
   VIEW
   POLITICAL AFFAIRS, LXVIII(4) (APR 89), 18-25.
      THE CONSTITUTION OF THE UNITED STATES REPRESENTS A
   CONSOLIDATION OF THE AMERICAN REVOLUTION. WHILE, ON BALANCE,
   IT DOES REPRESENT A RIGHTWARD TREND FROM THE HIGH POINT OF
   THE REVOLUTION, IT NEVERTHELESS COMPRISES THE ESSENCE OF
   THAT REVOLUTION. BUT THE AMERICAN RULING CLASS TODAY IS
   SEEKING TO THWART THE FORWARD MARCH OF HUMANITY, TO
   UNDERMINE AND VIOLATE THE CONSTITUTION.

01058 APTHEKER, M.
   THE ASSAULT ON HUMAN RIGHTS: THE REAGAN-BUSH SUPREME COURT
   POLITICAL AFFAIRS, LXVIII(11) (NOV 89), 2-7.
      THE ARTICLE FOCUSES ON THE REACTIONARY BLOWS STRUCK BY
   THE SUPREME COURT'S "FOUL FIVE," JUSTICES RHENQUIST, KENNEDY,
   SCALIA, O'CONNOR, AND WHITE, AGAINST RACIALLY AND
   NATIONALLY OPPRESSED PEOPLES AND ALL WOMEN, AS WELL AS THE
   ENTIRE WORKING CLASS. IN THE WORDS OF JUSTICE THURGOOD
   MARSHALL THE COURT HAS "COME FULL CIRCLE" AND IS BACK WHERE
   THEY STARTED SOME THIRTY-FIVE YEARS AGO.

01059 AQENBEGIAN, A.G.
   THE PERESTROIKA IN PRACTICE
   REVIEW OF INTERNATIONAL AFFAIRS, (JAN 88), 20-22.
      IN THIS ARTICLE, THE AUTHOR, ARCHITECT OF THE CURRENT
   CHANGES IN THE SOVIET UNION'S SOCIAL AND ECONOMIC SYSTEM
   INTERPRETS "PERESTROIKA." THE CHANGES AND IMPROVEMENTS ON
   THE BUSINESS INDUSTRIAL, SOCIAL AND POLITICAL FRONTS HAVE
   BEEN PREPARED FOR AND NOW THE STAGE IS SET FOR THE ACTUAL
   WORK TO BEGIN. AS THE OUTLET NOTES, THIS IS THE MOST
   DANGEROUS AND VULNERABLE ASPECT OF PERESTROIKA. VISIBLE
   CHANGES WILL BE NOTICED AND SOMETIMES CHANGE IS A DIFFICULT
   MASTER. BUT WITHOUT ACTION, THE SOVIET UNION WILL NOT EVOLVE.

01060 AQING, S.
   PREDICTING THE FUTURE OF SINO-U.S. RELATIONS
   BEIJING REVIEW, 32(5) (JAN 89), 36-38.
      SOME SCHOLARS BELIEVE THAT THE STRATEGIC FOUNDATION ON
   WHICH SINO-U.S. RELATIONS HAS BUILT HAS BEEN WEAKENED, AND
   THEY PREDICT THAT DIFFERENCES BETWEEN THE TWO COUNTRIES WILL
   INCREASE. AS A RESULT OF THE IMPROVEMENT IN U.S.-SOVIET AND
   SINO-SOVIET RELATIONS, THE SOVIET THREAT TO AMERICAN AND
   CHINESE SECURITY HAS DIMINISHED. THIS COULD INCREASE THE
   COMPLEXITY OF SINO-U.S. RELATIONS, SINCE THE UNITED STATES
   MAY PUT MORE RESTRAINTS ON ITS DEALINGS WITH CHINA BECAUSE
   THE SOVIET FACTOR HAS BECOME LESS IMPORTANT.

01061 AQUINO, B.A.
   DEMOCRACY IN THE PHILIPPINES
   CURRENT HISTORY, 88(537) (APR 89), 181-184, 190, 201-202.
      PRESIDENT AQUINO'S GREATEST ACHIEVEMENTS HAVE BEEN IN
   REDEMOCRATIZATION, PARTICULARLY RESTORING THE BASIC FREEDOMS
   AND CIVIL LIBERITIES OF THE FILIPINOS. BUT SHE FACES MANY
   PROBLEMS, INCLUDING DEMANDS TO END THE PHILIPPINE-AMERICAN
   SPECIAL RELATIONSHIP.

01062 ARAB, M.K.
   THE EFFECT OF THE LEADER'S BELIEF SYSTEM ON FOREIGN POLICY:
   THE CASE OF LIBYA
   DISSERTATION ABSTRACTS INTERNATIONAL, 49(12) (JUN 89),
   3861-A.
      USING LIBYA AS A CASE STUDY, THE AUTHOR CONSIDERS
   WHETHER IT IS POSSIBLE TO FORECAST A STATE'S BEHAVIOR
   THROUGH THE LEADER'S ARTICULATED VALUES. HE FOCUSES ON THE
   EFFECT OF COLONEL QADDAFI'S VALUES ON LIBYAN FOREIGN POLICY
   TOWARD CHAD, ETHIOPIA, AND THE SUDAN. HE FINDS SEVEN MAJOR
   VALUES IN QADDAFI'S WORDS AND ACTIONS: ANTI-IMPERIALISM, PRO-
   ARAB UNITY, ANTI-ISRAEL, PRO-ISLAM, ANTI-COMMUNISM, POWER,
   AND SECURITY. HE CONCLUDES THAT THE RELATIONSHIP BETWEEN
   THESE VALUES AND EVENTS HAS BEEN STRONG, ALTHOUGH IT HAS
   BEEN STRONGER FOR SOME THAN OTHERS.

01063 ARAYA, M.
   ERITREA, 1941-1952, THE FAILURE OF THE EMERGENCE OF THE
   NATION-STATE: TOWARDS A CLARIFICATION OF THE ERITREAN
   QUESTION IN ETHIOPIA
   DISSERTATION ABSTRACTS INTERNATIONAL, 50(5) (NOV 89),
   1420-A.
      THE AUTHOR EXAMINES THE IDEOLOGICAL DEBATE BETWEEN THE
   ETHIOPIAN REGIME AND THE ERITREAN NATIONALISTS. HE ALSO
   ANALYZES THE ROLES AND RELATIONSHIPS OF CLASS, ETHNIC
   IDENTITY, AND ERITREAN NATIONALISM. BY REJECTING THE
   ASSUMPTIONS AND PERSPECTIVES OF BOTH THE ETHIOPIANS AND THE
   ERITREANS, HE REFORMULATES THE ERITREAN PROBLEM AS A CRISIS
   RELATED TO THE PROCESS OF STATE-BUILDING IN THE POLITICAL
   HISTORY OF ETHIOPIA.

01064 ARGERSINGER, P.H.
   THE VALUE OF THE VOTE: POLITICAL REPRESENTATION IN THE
   GILDED AGE
   JOURNAL OF AMERICAN HISTORY, 76(1) (JUN 89), 59-90.
      HISTORIANS OF AMERICAN POLITICS HAVE NEGLECTED THE
   SUBJECT OF REPRESENTATION. THIS ESSAY INVESTIGATES POLITICAL
   REPRESENTATION IN THE GILDED AGE OF AMERICAN HISTORY IN
   ORDER TO SHED LIGHT ON A SUBJECT THAT HAS NOT RECEIVED THE
   SCHOLARLY ATTENTION IT DESERVES.

01065 ARGIOLAS, A.
   PROGRESS THROUGH NONVIOLENCE
   WORLD MARXIST REVIEW, 32(11) (NOV 89), 37-39.
      HURVANIST INTERNATIONAL REPRESENTS THE CONSOLIDATION OF
   AN ALTERNATIVE MOVEMENT WHICH EMERGED ON THE BASIS OF YOUTH
   ORGANIZATION IN LATIN AMERICA AND WESTERN EUROPE IN THE LATE
   1960S AND EARLY 1970'S, THE PERIOD WHEN THE COUNTERCULTURE
   REVOLT OF THE "NEW LEFT" BEGAN TO WANE. IN THIS ARTICLE THE
   PRESIDENT OF HUMANIST INTERNATIONAL EVALUATES THE OBJECTIVES
   OF THE NEW ORGANIZATION AND EXAMINES HOW THEY DIFFER FROM
   OTHER LEFT FORCES.

01066 ARGUELLES, M.D.P.
   NATIONAL SELF-DETERMINATION AND PUERTO RICO, 1809-1948
   DISSERTATION ABSTRACTS INTERNATIONAL, 50(5) (NOV 89),
   1426-A.
      THE AUTHOR DESCRIBES AND ANALYZES THE PROCESS OF
   NATIONAL SELF-DETERMINATION AND DECOLONIZATION IN PUERTO
   RICO UNDER SPANISH AND U.S. RULE. SHE STUDIES THE INTERPLAY
   BETWEEN THE EXERCISE OF COLONIAL DOMINATION AND THE STRUGGLE
   TO ELIMINATE IT, USING A TRI-DIMENSIONAL APPROACH. SHE
   EXAMINES THE SOCIO-POLITICAL CONDITIONS EXISTING IN THE
   METROPOLITAN SOCIETY, THE SOCIO-POLITICAL CONDITIONS
   EXISTING IN A COLONIZED SOCIETY THAT SERVE AS THE BREEDING
   GROUND FOR THE EMERGENCE OF A MOVEMENT FOR DECOLONIZATION
   AND NATIONAL SELF-DETERMINATION, AND THE WIDER CONTEXT OF
   THE PREVALENT INTERNATIONAL SYSTEM AND THE GIVEN
   GEOPOLITICAL AREA.

01067 ARIAN, A.
   A PEOPLE APART: COPING WITH NATIONAL SECURITY PROBLEMS IN
   ISRAEL
   JOURNAL OF CONFLICT RESOLUTION, 33(4) (DEC 89), 605-631.
      ISRAELIS BELIEVE THEIR COUNTRY FACES SERIOUS THREAT AND
   THEY WILL SUCCEED IN OVERCOMING THESE THREATS. THE
   MECHANISMS EMPLOYED FOR DEALING WITH THESE TWO ATTITUDE
   CLUSTERS ARE EXPLORED. BASED ON A NATIONAL SAMPLE (N= 1,116),
   THREE MECHANISMS ARE SHOWN TO DOMINATE: PERCEIVED SUCCESS,
   DENIAL, AND A BELIEF SYSTEM IDENTIFIED AS THE PEOPLE APART
   SYNDROME. THE SYNDROME CONSISTED OF TWO CONSTRUCTS: GOD-AND-
   US, RELATING TO A SPECIAL MYSTICAL RELATION PERCEIVED BY
   MANY BETWEEN GOD, ISRAEL, AND JEWISH HISTORY; AND GO-IT-
   ALONE, DEALING WITH FEELINGS OF ISOLATION AND THE BELIEF
   THAT ULTIMATELY JEWISH DESTINY DEPENDS ON THE JEWS.
   PSYCHOLOGICAL FACTORS WERE SHOWN TO BE MUCH MORE POWERFUL
   THAN DEMOGRAPHIC VARIABLES IN EXPLAINING THESE DISTRIBUTIONS.
   THE WIDELY SHARED SYNDROME CAPTURED THE TONE OF ISRAELI
   POLITICAL DISCOURSE AND THE MINDSET OF A LARGE PORTION OF
   THE POPULATION. ITS DISTRIBUTION AMONG PLACE OF BIRTH GROUPS
   BY POLICY PREFERENCE AND RELIGIOUS OBSERVANCE REVEALED THE
   PERVASIVE NATURE OF THE SYNDROME.

01068 ARISMENDI, R.
   WE LIVE IN A NEW, CHANGED WORLD
   WORLD MARXIST REVIEW, 31(1) (JAN 88), 20-27.
      VETERAN COMMUNISTS KNOW BETTER THAN ANYONE ELSE THAT THE
   ACCOMPLISHMENTS WHICH CHANGED THE ENTIRE WORLD RADICALLY
   ALSO INVOLVED MISTAKES, DEVIATIONS FROM THE CHARTED PATH,
   AND EVEN TRAGEDIES. MIKHAIL GORBACHOV'S SPEECH AT THE 70TH
   ANNIVERSARY CELEBRATIONS PUTS THE PROBLEM INTO A CLEARER AND
   MORE ORDERLY PERSPECTIVE: STALIN'S PERSONALITY CULT
   DRAMATICALLY AFFECTED SOVIET REALITIES AND LED TO
   DIFFERENCES WITHIN THE COMMUNIST MOVEMENT IN OTHER WORDS,
   THERE HAVE BEEN MISTAKES OVER A BROAD RANGE OF ISSUES, BUT
   THE IMPORTANT THING IS THAT IN SUMMING UP THE HISTORICAL
   RECORD, ONLY ONE CONCLUSION IS POSSIBLE -- SOCIALISM HAS
   TRIUMPHED.

01069 ARISMENDI, R.
   WE NEED CHANGES IN OUR OWN RANKS
   WORLD MARXIST REVIEW, 32(2) (FEB 89), 30-35.
      PERESTROIKA IN LATIN AMERICA SIGNIFIES ACTIVE
   INVOLVEMENT IN A POLICY FOR PEACE, THE DRIVE FOR SELF-
   DETERMINATION AND A NEW INTERNATIONAL ECONOMIC ORDER, FOR
   THE MOST UNBIASED TREATMENT OF THE EXTERNAL DEBT PROBLEM,
   AND A GREATER AUTONOMY FOR THE REGION'S COUNTRIES WITH
   REGARD TO THE USA. THUS, IN LINKING PERESTROIKA AND THE
   REALITY OF MODERN LATIN AMERICA ONE SHOULD BEAR IN MIND TWO
   THINGS. THE FIRST REFERS TO THE DIALECTICS OF THE REVOLUTION,
   OF THE DEVELOPMENT OF THE PARTIES, POPULAR FRONTS AND SO
   FORTH. THE SECOND REQUIRES AN ANALYSIS OF LATIN AMERICA'S
   ROLE AS AN EFFECTIVE PLAYER IN THE EFFORTS TO TACKLE THE
   GLOBAL PROBLEMS OF HUMANITY.

01070 ARIZALA, J.
BEYOND TRADITIONAL PARLIAMENTARISM
WORLD MARXIST REVIEW, 32(10) (OCT 89), 74-78.
THIS ARTICLE EXPLORES POPULAR RULE IN THE LIGHT OF NEW
POLITICAL THINKING AS A DIALOGUE UNFOLDING BETWEEN THE
COMMUNISTS AND SOCIAL DEMOCRATS TODAY. LEADERS OF THE MORE
INFLUENTIAL LATIN AMERICAN SOCIAL DEMOCRATIC PARTIES GIVE
THEIR VIES ON DEMOCRACY AND ITS MAJOR PRECONDITIONS. THE
ALSO EXAMINE THE CORRELATION BETWEEN THE ECONOMIC SITUATION
AND THE CULTURAL AND HISTORIC FEATURES OF LATIN AMERICAN
COUNTRIES, AS WELL AS DEMOCRACY AND PRIVATE OWNERSHIP,
POLITICAL PLURALISM, AND PLANS FOR RESTRUCTURING SOCIALIST
THOUGHT IN THOSE COUNTRIES.

01071 ARIZALA, J.
COMBINING DIFFERENT METHODS OF STRUGGLE
WORLD MARXIST REVIEW, 32(5) (MAY 89), 47-50.
THE COLOMBIAN COMMUNIST PARTY HELD ITS 15TH CONGRESS IN
BOGOTA IN DECEMBER 1988, REASSERTING OPENLY AND BOLDLY ITS
DEDICATION TO DEMOCRACY AND PEACE. THE HUNDREDS OF
PHOTOGRAPHS OF ASSASSINATED AND MISSING COMMUNISTS ON THE
WALLS OF THE CONGRESS HALL WERE PROOF OF THE GREAT
SACRIFICES THE VANGUARD OF THE WORKING PEOPLE HAS TO MAKE IN
ITS STRUGGLE. AS THE CONGRESS STRESSED, IT IS IMPORTANT TO
MOVE VIGOROUSLY TO PROMOTE MASS RESISTANCE AND USE THE
PEOPLE'S RIGHT TO LEGITIMATE SELF-DEFENCE AGAINST THE
INHUMAN BRUTALITY OF THE REACTIONARIES. TODAY, THE FOREMOST
TASK IS TO FIGHT FOR THE RIGHT TO LIFE, AND AGAINST
ASSASSINATIONS, TORTURE AND KIDNAPPINGS. A MOVEMENT TO
PROMOTE THOSE NOBLE OBJECTIVES HAS SPREAD ACROSS THE NATION,
COVERING LARGE SECTIONS OF THE POPULATION.

01072 ARJOMAND, S.
HISTORY, STRUCTURE, AND REVOLUTION IN THE SHI'ITE
TRADITION IN CONTEMPORARY IRAN
INTERNATIONAL POLITICAL SCIENCE REVIEW, 10(2) (APR 89),
111-120.
ABSTRACT. THE AIM OF THIS ARTICLE IS TO DRAW THEORETICAL
LESSONS FROM THE CONTEMPORARY TRANSFORMATION OF SHI'ISM BY
EXAMINING THE BEARING OF HISTORY, STRUCTURE AND CULTURAL
TRADITION ON THE CAUSES AND CONSEQUENCES OF THE ISLAMIC
REVOLUTION IN IRAN. IT IS ARGUED THAT THE ISLAMIC REVOLUTION
CAN BE VIEWED AS THE TRADITIONALIZATION OF A MODERNIZING
NATION-STATE, AND AT THE SAME TIME THE MODERNIZATION OF THE
SHI'ITE TRADITION. THIS APPARENTLY PARADOXICAL
CHARACTERIZATION STRONGLY SUGGESTS THAT A WEBERIAN PARADIGM
FOR CULTURALLY SPECIFIC PATTERNS OF SOCIAL CHANGE IS MORE
HELPFUL FOR ITS COMPREHENSION THAN ANY ALTERNATIVE MODEL.

01073 ARKES, H.
MORAL OBTUSENESS IN AMERICA
NATIONAL REVIEW, XLI(11) (JUN 89), 33-36.
THE ARTICLE COMMENTS ON THE RECENT PBS SERIES: ETHICS IN
AMERICA. THE SERIES DEALT WITH THE CONFLICT BETWEEN A
MORALITY OF CONVENTION---MARKED BY PROFESSIONALS CAST IN
"ROLES" -- AND A MORALITY THAT IS CONSTANTLY LOOKING PAST
THE SYSTEM OF ROLES AND APPEALING TO A MORE EXACTING,
UNIVERSAL MORAL STANDARD. THE WILLINGNESS OF JOURNALISTS AND
LAWYERS TO CLING TO THEIR "CODES OF PROFESSIONAL CONDUCT" IN
THE FACE OF CONFLICT WITH AN APPARENTLY "HIGHER" LAW WAS
USED TO ILLUSTRATE THE PROBLEM IN AMERICA.

01074 ARKIN, W.M.
THE BUILDUP THAT WASN'T
BULLETIN OF THE ATOMIC SCIENTISTS, 45(1) (JAN 89), 6-10.
THE AUTHOR REVIEWS THE NUCLEAR MILITARY STRENGTHS,
WEAKNESSES, AND CHANGES IN THE REAGAN YEARS, DURING HIS
FIRST TERM, REAGAN REVISED THE PUBLIC'S PERCEPTION OF THE
UNITED STATES' STRENGTH FROM VULNERABLE TO "WE ARE NUMBER
ONE." THIS NEW PERCEPTION STOPPED SUPPORT FOR GREATER
WEAPONS SPENDING.

01075 ARMACOST, M.
IMPLICATIONS OF GORBACHEV FOR US-SOVIET RELATIONS
JOURNAL OF INTERNATIONAL AFFAIRS, 42(2) (SPR 89), 445-456.
THE REFORMS OF MIKHAIL GORBACHEV ARE PRIMARILY DOMESTIC
AND INTERNAL. HOWEVER, SOME CHANGES IN SOVIET FOREIGN POLICY
HAVE ALSO BEEN MADE TO FACILITATE DOMESTIC REFORM. THESE
INCLUDE A SIZABLE REDUCTION IN MILITARY SPENDING AND A
RELIANCE ON "REASONABLE SUFFICIENCY", A REDUCTION OF THE
INFLUENCE THAT THE MILITARY HAS ON THE POLITICAL
DECISIONMAKING PROCESS AND AN INCREASED RELAINCE ON
POLITICAL SOLUTIONS TO REGIONAL AND INTERNATIONAL PROBLEMS.
THE USSR HAS ALSO PURSUED BETTER RELATIONS WITH A NUMBER OF
NATIONS THAT WERE RELATIVELY NEGLECTED IN THE BREZHNEV ERA.
THE ARTICLE EXAMINES THESE CHANGES AND THEIR IMPLICATIONS
FOR SOVIET-US RELATIONS. IT PLOTS A FUTURE COURSE FOR US
FOREIGN POLICY WITH REGARDS TO THE USSR AND EMPHASIZES THE
USE OF "CREATIVE DIALOGUE" TO CONTINUE THE FAVORABLE
MOMENTUM AND RESOLVE FUTURE PROBLEMS.

01076 ARMACOST, M.H.
MILITARY POWER AND DIPLOMACY: THE REAGAN LEGACY
DEPARTMENT OF STATE BULLETIN (US FOREIGN POLICY), 88(2140)
(NOV 88), 40-44.
THE AUTHOR EXAMINES THE RELATIONSHIP BETWEEN MILITARY
POWER AND DIPLOMACY AND COMES TO SEVERAL CONCLUSIONS. THEY
INCLUDE: 1) THERE IS AN ESSENTIAL RELATIONSHIP BETWEEN
MILITARY STRENGTH AND EFFECTIVE DIPLOMACY. 2) THE REAGAN
ADMINISTRATION HAS RECOGNIZED THIS TRUTH AND BY RESTORING US
MILITARY STRENGTH, HAS ENHANCED THE ABILITY TO EMPLOY FORCES
IN SUPPORT OF US INTERESTS ABROAD. 3) THE RESULTS OF THIS
POLICY HAVE GENERATED SOME IMPORTANT SUCCESSES FOR THE US IN
THE LAST FEW YEARS. 4) A NUMBER OF TRENDS FAVORABLE TO US
INTERESTS COMBINE WITH THIS POLICY TO MAKE A BRIGHT FUTURE.

01077 ARMACOST, M.H.
REGIONAL ISSUES AND US-SOVIET RELATIONS
DEPARTMENT OF STATE BULLETIN (US FOREIGN POLICY), 88(2138)
(SEP 88), 18-23.
THE ARTICLE DISCUSSES THE SIGNIFICANT PROGRESS THAT HAS
BEEN MADE ON SEVERAL REGIONAL ISSUES WITH REGARDS TO US-
SOVIET RELATIONS. IT DISCUSSES THE APPROACH THAT THE REAGAN
ADMINISTRATION HAS UTILIZED TOWARDS REGIONAL ISSUES WHICH
HAS EMPHASIZED MUTUAL RESTRAINT, DIALOGUE, AND NEGOTIATION.
IT USES AS EXAMPLES THE US SUCCESSES IN INFLUENCING THE
SITUATIONS IN AFGHANISTAN, CAMBODIA, AND SOUTHERN AFRICA.

01078 ARMACOST, M.H.
THE UNITED STATES IN THE CHANGING ASIA OF THE 1990'S
DEPARTMENT OF STATE BULLETIN (US FOREIGN POLICY), 88(2138)
(SEP 88), 9-12.
THE ARTICLE EXAMINES MANY OF THE TRENDS THAT ARE
CHANGING AND WILL CONTINUE TO CHANGE ASIA IN THE YEARS AHEAD.
THEY INCLUDE: WORLD ECONOMIC AND FINANCIAL POWER TO
CONTINUE TO MOVE TOWARD THE PACIFIC, INTERNAL STRUCTURAL
ADJUSTMENTS AND ECONOMIC REFORMS OF ASIAN NATIONS, CONTINUED
ECONOMIC GROWTH AND INCREASING POLITICAL STABILITY, A NEW
GENERATION OF LEADERSHIP BY THE TURN OF THE CENTURY, AN
INCREASING TREND TOWARD PLURALISTIC AND DEMOCRATIC POLITICAL
SYSTEMS, AND AN INCREASE OF REGIONAL CONSULTATION AND
COOPERATION AMONG EAST ASIAN NATIONS. THE ARTICLE ASSESSES
THE IMPLICATIONS THAT THESE TRENDS HAVE FOR THE US AND
OFFERS SUGGESTIONS FOR FUTURE US POLICY.

01079 ARMAND, Y.
DEMOCRACY IN HAITI: THE LEGACY OF ANTI-DEMOCRATIC
POLITICAL AND SOCIAL TRADITIONS
INTERNATIONAL JOURNAL OF POLITICS, CULTURE AND SOCIETY,
2(4) (SUM 89), 537-561.
THIS PAPER EXAMINES HAITI'S ENDURING POLITICAL
INSTABILITY IN TERMS OF CULTURAL AND SOCIO-HISTORICAL
VARIABLES. FOLLOWING AN OVERVIEW OF THE MAIN EVENTS OF THE
PAST TWO AND A HALF YEARS, THIS PAPER EXAMINES THE LEGACY OF
HAITI'S POLITICAL AND ECONOMIC PAST, THE IMPACT OF HAITI'S
DUAL CLASS AND STATUS DIFFERENTIATION ON ITS POLITICAL
INSTITUTIONS AND PROCESSES, AND AN ASSORTMENT OF OTHER
OBSTRUCTIONS THAT SERIOUSLY IMPEDE THE ESTABLISHMENT OF
DEMOCRACY IN HAITI.

01080 ARMOUR, D.
EAST GERMANY AFTER HONECKER
WORLD TODAY, 45(12) (DEC 89), 203-204.
FOUR FACTORS ARE AT WORK PUSHING EAST GERMANY TOWARD
REFORM: CHANGE ELSEWHERE IN EASTERN EUROPE, DOMESTIC
PRESSURES PROMPTED BY THE EXAMPLE OF EXTERNAL REFORMS,
PRESSURE FROM WEST GERMANY, AND PRESSURE FROM GORBACHEV. THE
MOST IMMEDIATE IMPACT HAS BEEN FROM THE GROWING PRESSURE AT
HOME. THE PREVIOUSLY INERT PUBLIC HAS BEEN EMBOLDENED AND
GALVANIZED INTO NEW POLITICAL DYNAMISM BY WHAT HAS BEEN
HAPPENING IN POLAND AND HUNGARY. SPONTANEOUS GRASSROOTS
ORGANIZATIONS HAVE SPRUNG UP, COMPOSED OF CITIZENS WHO DO
NOT WANT TO EMIGRATE. THEY WANT TO STAY AND GIVE EAST GERMAN
SOCIALISM A NEW FACE.

01081 ARMSTRONG, A.
BRIDGING THE GAP: INTELLIGENCE AND POLICY
WASHINGTON QUARTERLY, 12(1) (WIN 89), 23-34.
TO A REMARKABLE EXTENT, HIGH-LEVEL OFFICIALS ARE UNAWARE
OF WHAT THE INTELLIGENCE COMMUNITY CAN AND CANNOT DO AND OF
THE TYPE OF GUIDANCE IT NEEDS IF ITS WORK IS TO BE AS USEFUL
FOR POLICY-MAKING AS POSSIBLE. BECAUSE OF INCREASED FUTURE
DEMANDS ON INTELLIGENCE, THE PRESIDENT, HIS KEY AIDES, AND
THE NATIONAL SECURITY COUNCIL (NSC) WILL HAVE TO PAY MUCH
CLOSER ATTENTION TO THE WORKINGS OF THE INTELLIGENCE
COMMUNITY AND THE MEASURES THAT GUIDE IT IF THE GAP BETWEEN
INTELLIGENCE AND POLICY IS TO BE BRIDGED IN THE COMING YEARS.
THIS STRATEGY OF NARROWING THE DISTANCE BETWEEN
INTELLIGENCE AND POLICY HOLDS CERTAIN RISKS FOR THE
INTEGRITY OF THE FORMER. NEVERTHELESS, THESE RISKS MUST BE
RUN.

01082 ARNADE, C.; SHANE, M.; STALLINGS, D.
FOREIGN DEBT, CAPITAL FORMATION AND DEBTOR BEHAVIOR
AVAILABLE FROM NTIS, NO. PB89-231401/GAR, JUL 89, 30.
PROBLEM DEBTOR COUNTRIES, THOSE WITH OVER $10 BILLION IN
EXTERNAL DEBT WHICH HAVE RESCHEDULED THEIR PAYMENTS, USED

THEIR BORROWED FUNDS TO INVEST LESS AND CONSUME MORE THAN A
COMPARABLE GROUP OF DEBTORS WITHOUT REPAYMENT PROBLEMS. THE
PROBLEM DEBTOR COUNTRIES PROBABLY UNDERESTIMATED THE TOTAL
LONGRUN COST OF THEIR SPENDING, LEADING TO THE DEBT CRISES
AMONG DEVELOPING COUNTRIES. THE AUTHORS USED A GENERAL MODEL
OF CONSUMPTION AND INVESTMENT OVER 1974-86 TO DESCRIBE HOW A
LOAN MAY BE ALLOCATED BETWEEN THE TWO.

01083 ARNDT, J.C.
MAINE IN THE NORTHEASTERN BOUNDARY CONTROVERSY: STATES'
RIGHTS IN ANTEBELLUM NEW ENGLAND
NEW ENGLAND QUARTERLY, LXII(2) (JUN 89), 205-223.
THE NORTHEASTERN BOUNDRY DISPUTE PROVIDED A CONVENIENT
PLATFORM FROM WHICH POLITICIANS OF ANY STRIPE COULD DAMN
OPPONENTS AT BOTH THE LOCAL AND NATIONAL LEVELS. POLITICIANS,
IN TURN, WERE DRIVEN BY ECONOMIC MOTIVES, WHICH HELP TO
EXPLAIN WHY MAINE ABANDONED ITS CLAIMS OF STATES' RIGHTS. BY
1842, IT WAS CLEAR THAT GREAT BRITAIN HAS BENT ON HAVING A
ROUTE ALONG THE ST. JOHN AND THAT THE TYLER ADMINISTRATION
WAS EAGER TO SETTLE THE BOUNDARY DISPUTE. DESPERATE TO
REVIVE LAND SALES, EAGER TO LOWER THE STATE DEBT, AND
DETERMINED TO TAP THE TIMBER RESERVES OF THE ST. JOHN, STATE
LEADERS SETTLED FOR THE RIGHT OF NAVIGATION UPON THAT RIVER
AND CONTROL OF THE RICH AROOSTOOK VALLEY.

01084 ARNETT, E.H.
GUNBOAT DIPLOMACY AND THE BOMB: NUCLEAR PROLIFERATION AND
THE U.S. NAVY
DISSERTATION ABSTRACTS INTERNATIONAL, 50(5) (NOV 89),
1427-A.
THE AUTHOR ANALYZES THE EFFECT OF NUCLEAR PROLIFERATION
ON U.S. REGIONAL INTERESTS, FOCUSING ON THE PROSPECTS FOR
NAVAL POWER PROJECTION. HE CONSTRUCTS SCENARIOS THAT TEST
THE RELEVANCE OF PROLIFERANT ARSENALS TO U.S. CAPABILITY AND
WILLINGNESS TO PROTECT ITS INTERESTS IN FUTURE CRISES IN
INDIA, IRAN, AND LIBYA. INDIA IS FOUND UNLIKELY TO THREATEN
U.S. INTERESTS IN SUCH A WAY THAT ITS NUCLEAR ARSENAL MIGHT
MAKE A DIFFERENCE. WHILE IRAN AND LIBYA ARE LIKELY TO HOLD
AMERICAN INTERESTS AT RISK BUT ARE UNLIKELY TO ACQUIRE
NUCLEAR WEAPONS IN THE NEAR FUTURE.

01085 ARNOLD, G.
MARXISM OUT
NEW AFRICAN, (266) (NOV 89), 17.
THIS ARTICLE EXPLORES THE POLITICAL AND ECONOMIC
REPRECUSSIONS OF THE DECISION OF THE FRELIMO FIFTH PARTY
CONGRESS IN MOZAMBIQUE TO DROP MARXISM-LENINISM. IT REPORTS
ON EFFORTS TO TURN TO THE PRIVATE SECTOR AND TO FOREIGN AID
TO REVIVE THE ECONOMY.

01086 ARNOLD, G.
NAMBIA; ECONOMY OF OPPORTUNITY
NEW AFRICAN, (267) (DEC 89), 27.
NAMBIA MUST FACE ITS ECONOMIC FUTURE. THIS BECOME MORE
IMPERATIVE AS THE POLITICAL EXCITEMENT OF ELECTIONS,
CONSTITUTION-MAKING AND INDEPENDENCE ARE FADING. ECONOMIC
OPTIONS ARE LIMITED AND MUST BE CAREFULLY HANDEED. THE
AGRICULTURE SECTOR IS WEAK, AND WILL PRESENT MANY PROBLEMS.
FISHERIES OFFER GOOD LONG-TERM PROSPECTS. THE MANUFACTURING
SECTOR IS BY FAR THE WEAKEST, YET DEPENDING UPON HOW IT IS
HANDLED, IT OFFERS THE GREATEST POSSIBILITIES FOR GROWTH.

01087 ARNOLD, H.
AUSTRIA AND THE EUROPEAN COMMUNITY
AUSSEN POLITIK, 40(4) (1989), 385 - 386.
THIS ARTICLE EXPLORES AUSTRIA'S APPROACH TO THE EUROPEAN
COMMUNITY A ITS APPLICATION FOR FULL MEMBERSHIP IS SUBMITTED
TO BRUSSELS. IT EXANINES THE POLITICAL LINK BETWEEN THE 1955
TREATY ENDING AUSTRIA'S OCCUPATION BY ALLIED TROOPS AND ITS
NEUTRALITY. SOVIET ATTITUDE AND ITS SIGNIFICANCE FOR
AUSTRIAN POLICY IS DETAILED AS WELL AS THE CONDITIONS WHICH
MUST EXIST FOR THE EC TO ACCEPT AUSTRIA AS A MEMBER.

01088 ARNOLD, P. E.
REORGANIZATION AND REGIME IN THE UNITED STATES AND BRITAIN
PUBLIC ADMINISTRATION REVIEW, 48(3) (MAY 88), 726-734.
WHAT IS THE RELATIONSHIP BETWEEN A GOVERNMENTAL REGIME
AND ITS MODE OF PUBLIC ADMINISTRATION?4 THIS ARTICLE PURSUES
A TENTATIVE, PARTIAL ANSWER TO THAT QUESTION BY COMPARING
CASES OF STRUCTURAL ADMINISTRATIVE REFORM IN THE UNITED
STATES AND GREAT BRITAIN DURING THIS CENTURY. THE UNITED
STATES CONSTITUTION CREATES A REGIME OF DISPERSED POWERS AND
OVERLAPPING RESPONSIBILITIES AMONG THE PRESIDENT, CONGRESS,
AND THE JUDICIARY. THE BRITISH CONSTITUTION IS ONE OF
CENTRAL POWER AND SUFFICIENT RESPONSIBILITY LODGED IN
PARLIAMENT AND EXERCISED BY THE CABINET ACTING IN THE
EXECUTIVE CAPACITY. IN THE CONTEXT OF DIFFERENT POLITICAL
REGIMES, ADMINISTRATIVE GOVERNMENT DEVELOPED IN BOTH AMERICA
AND BRITAIN. IN EACH SOCIETY, PROBLEMS OF EFFICIENCY AND
CHANGE WERE RAISED BY THE GROWING SCALE OF THE
ADMINISTRATIVE APPARATUS. THIS ARTICLE ARGUES THAT HOW EACH
SOCIETY DEVELOPED ITS APPROACH TO ADMINISTRATIVE
REORGANIZATION REVEALS WAYS IN WHICH ADMINISTRATION RESPONDS
TO THE CHARACTERISTICS OF THE REGIME WITHIN WHICH IT

OPERATES.5

01089 ARNOLD, P.W.
FUTURE DOMESTIC AND INTERNATIONAL TERRORISM: THE US/A
PERSPECTIVE
TERRORISM, 11(6) (1988), 541-542.
THIS IS A TALK GIVEN AT A CONFERENCE ON TERRORISM BY
PHILIP ARNOLD, CHIEF OF POLICY AND GUIDANCE OF THE U.S.
INFORMATION AGENCY (US/A). HE FOCUSES ON THE
RESPONSIBILITIES OF THE US/A IN THE AREA OF INTERNATIONAL
TERRORISM AS THE AGENCY DEALS WITH FOREIGN PUBLICS WHO, IN
TURN, HAVE THEIR INFLUENCE ON THEIR GOVERNMENTS HE DESCRIBES
THE U.S. GOVERNMENT'S DEALINGS WITH TERRORISM AS SLOW AND
INCREMENTAL. HE TALKS ABOUT POLLING PUBLIC OPINION IN
WESTERN EUROPE AND THE EFFORTS TO DEMYSTIFY THE TERRORIST
ORGANIZATIONS. HE CONCLUDES THAT THIS LOW-INTENSITY WARFARE
IS GOING TO CONTINUE.

01090 ARNOLD, T.C.
POLITICAL THEORY AND LANGUAGE
DISSERTATION ABSTRACTS INTERNATIONAL, 49(12) (JUN 89),
3855-A.
THE RELATIONSHIP OF LANGUAGE TO THE STUDY AND PRACTICE
OF POLITICAL THEORY IS THE SUBJECT OF THIS DISSERTATION.
BUILDING ON THE WITTGENSTEINIAN AND HABERMASIAN SCHOOLS OF
THOUGHT AND ON THE LINGUISTIC PRACTICES OF HOBBES AND
TOCQUEVILLE, STUDY REVEALS THAT LANGUAGE IS CENTRAL TO THE
DISCIPLINE. ITS SIGNIFICANCE IS GROUNDED IN ITS VALUE AS
BOTH A UNIT FOR POLITICAL ANALYSIS AND AS A MEDIUM FOR
POLITICAL PARTICIPATION.

01091 ARNOLD, W.
BUREAUCRATIC POLITICS, STATE CAPACITY, AND TAIWAN'S
AUTOMOBILE INDUSTRIAL POLICY
MODERN CHINA, 15(2) (APR 89), 178-214.
THIS STUDY OF TAIWAN'S AUTOMOTIVE INDUSTRY ATTEMPTS TO
ELUCIDATE THE VARYING DEGREES OF STATE AUTONOMY, CAPACITY,
AND EFFECTIVENESS IN THE FORMULATION AND IMPLEMENTATION OF
DEVELOPMENTAL POLICIES FOR TAIWAN'S INDUSTRIAL ECONOMY. THE
HISTORICAL DEVELOPMENT AND THE INSTITUTIONAL FRAMEWORK OF
TAIWAN'S AUTOMOTIVE INDUSTRY ARE IMPORTANT BECAUSE TAIWAN'S
AUTO INDUSTRIAL POLICY HAS BEEN FAR LESS SUCCESSFUL THAN
SIMILAR STATE POLICIES THAT WERE DEVISED AND IMPLEMENTED FOR
SUCH STRATEGIC INDUSTRIES AS STEEL, ELECTRONICS, AND
PETROCHEMICALS. AN ANALYSIS OF SPECIFIC DEVELOPMENT POLICIES
REVEALS THAT TAIWAN'S AUTO POLICY HAS NOT CONSOLIDATED THE
NUMBER OF AUTO MAKERS NOR HAS IT REDUCED THE INDUSTRY'S
VULNERABILITY TO FOREIGN DEPENDENCE. MOREOVER, IT HAS NOT
GENERATED HIGHER VALUE-ADDED PRODUCTION OR CREATED A DESIRED
MECHANICAL ENGINEERING MULTIPLIER EFFECT TO BENEFIT
TAIWANESE MACHINERY INDUSTRIES IN GENERAL.

01092 ARNON, A.
THE EARLY TOOKE AND RICARDO: A POLITICAL ALLIANCE AND
FIRST SIGNS OF THEORETICAL DISAGREEMENTS
HISTORY OF POLITICAL ECONOMY, 21(1) (SPR 89), 1-14.
THE AUTHOR ANALYZES AND COMPARES TOOKE'S PRE-BANKING
SCHOOL VIEWS WITH THOSE OF RICARDO AND ARGUES THAT TOOKE'S
EARLY VIEWS ON ECONOMIC POLICY WERE VERY SIMILAR TO
RICARDO'S. THEN HE DESCRIBES RICARDO'S AND TOOKE'S
ACTIVITIES IN PROMOTING THE RESUMPTION AND FREE TRADE
THROUGH THE POLITICAL ECONOMY CLUB. HE ALSO COMPARES TOOKE'S
EARLY VIEWS ON MONETARY ISSUES WITH THOSE OF RICARDO, WITH
PARTICULAR REFERENCE TO THE PRICE-SPECIE-FLOW MECHANISM.

01093 ARNSON, C.J.
CONGRESS AND CENTRAL AMERICA: THE SEARCH FOR CONSENSUS
DISSERTATION ABSTRACTS INTERNATIONAL, 49(7) (JAN 89),
1948-A.
THE AUTHOR STUDIES THE CONGRESSIONAL ROLE IN POLICY-
MAKING ON CENTRAL AMERICA FROM 1976 TO 1986, WITH EMPHASIS
ON THE REAGAN ADMINISTRATION.

01094 ARON, L.
WHAT GLASTNOST HAS DESTROYED
COMMENTARY, 88(5) (NOV 89), 30-34.
THIS ARTICLE EXAMINES THE STATE OF SPIRITUAL TURMOIL IN
WHICH SOVIET SOCIETY FINDS ITSELF AND FOR WHICH THERE IS NO
PRECEDENT IN ITS ENTIRE HISTORY. IT FINDS THAT IN
GORBACHEV'S SOVIET UNION, ALMOST EVERY MAJOR LEGITIMIZING
MYTH IS BEING SHATTERED IT EXPLORES THE MYTH OF "SOCIAL
PROTECTION" AND DISCOVERS THAT ALL THE EVILS PLAGUING
CAPITALISM PLAGUE SOVIET SOCIETY AS WELL. IT THEN CONTINUES
ON TO THE MYTH OF WWII, THE GREAT PATRIOTIC WAR, AND THEN TO
THE MYTHS SURROUNDING THE FOUNDING FATHERS OF THE SOVIET
UNION. THE ARTICLE CONCLUDES THAT GLASTNOST HAS DESTROYED
THE LEGITIMACY OF A REFORMED ONE PARTY STATE SOCIALISM AND
THAT NOTHING CAN HOPE TO FILL THIS SPIRITUAL VACUUM, AND
WONDERS WHAT WILL FILL IT?

01095 ARONSFELD, C.C.
PERSPECTIVES OF THE NAZI-SOVIET PACT: HITLER'S AND
NAPOLEON'S DEALINGS WITH RUSSIA
CONTEMPORARY REVIEW, 255(1485) (OCT 89), 193-196.

THIS ARTICLE EXAMINES HISTORY REPEATING ITSELF IN THE
PHASE OF HITLER'S CAREER WHEN COMPARED WITH THAT OF NAPOLEON.
IT TRACES THE AMBITION OF BOTH TO CONQUER THE WORLD AND
HAVING FAILED TO SUBDUE ENGLAND, THEY PURSUED THEIR AMBITION
BY TRYING TO WIN POWER OVER RUSSIA. IT CONCLUDES BY SEEING
THAT HISTORY CAN REPEAT ITSELF ALMOST PREDICTABLY, YET SO
OFTEN IT IS STILL UNEXPECTED.

01096 ARONSFELD, C.C.
THE MALAISE OF BRITISH EXPORTS
CONTEMPORARY REVIEW, 225(1482) (JUL 89), 9-11.
THE ARTICLE EXAMINES THE UNDERLYING CAUSES OF THE LONG-
STANDING "MALAISE" THAT HAS PLAGUED BRITISH ATTEMPTS AT
ESTABLISHING LONG-TERM TRADE RELATIONS WITH OTHER NATIONS.
IT ANALYZES HISTORICAL EVIDENCE THROUGH COMPARISONS WITH
GERMANY AND OTHER EUROPEAN NATIONS. IT CONCLUDES THAT THE
"LINGUISTIC CHAUVINISM" THAT EXISTS IN BRITAIN; MOST BRITISH
SCHOOLS DO NOT PROVIDE THE OPPORTUNITY TO LEARN A FOREIGN
LANGUAGE AND EVEN FEWER AVAIL THEMSELVES OF THE CHANCE. THE
ARTICLE ADVOCATES AN INCREASED EMPHASIS ON THE LEARNING OF
FOREIGN LANGUAGES AND OF ESTABLISHING A MORE VISIBLE
PRESENCE IN OTHER NATIONS.

01097 ARREAZA, A.
DEMOCRACIES IN A CHAOTIC WORLD
FREEDOM AT ISSUE, (108) (MAY 89), 23-25.
MANY PEOPLE STILL FAIL TO REALIZE THAT THE ONLY
POLITICAL STRUCTURE THAT REALLY PROMOTES SOCIAL AND ECONOMIC
WELL-BEING IS A DECENTRALIZED DEMOCRACY. THIS IS THE ONLY
SYSTEM THAT HAS PROVED SUCCESSFUL IN VARIOUS PARTS OF THE
WORLD, MAKING IT POSSIBLE FOR SOME PEOPLE TO BECOME
MATERIALLY AND SPIRITUALLY WELL-BALANCED AND TO CREATE A
PROSPEROUS NATION. IT IS OBVIOUS THAT THE COMMUNITIES THAT
HAVE CHOSEN DECENTRALIZED DEMOCRACY ARE LIVING AND EVOLVING
MUCH BETTER THAN THE REST OF HUMANITY.

01098 ART, R.J.
THE PENTAGON: THE CASE FOR BIENNIAL BUDGETING
POLITICAL SCIENCE QUARTERLY, 104(2) (SUM 89), 193-214.
FOR A LONG TIME, THE DEFENSE DEPARTMENT'S CENTRAL
RESOURCE ALLOCATION MECHANISM (THE PLANNING, PROGRAMMING,
AND BUDGETING SYSTEM INSTITUTED IN 1961) HAS BEEN PLAGUED BY
POOR PLANNING AND INADEQUATE EVALUATION. THESE DEFICIENCIES
HAVE CONTRIBUTED TO DEFECTIVE RESOURCE ALLOCATION AND MUST
BE RECTIFIED IF DEFENSE RESOURCES ARE TO BE ALLOCATED
EFFECTIVELY AND EFFICIENTLY. THEY CAN BE MORE EASILY
RECTIFIED IF THE DEFENSE DEPARTMENT BUDGETS BIENNIALLY
RATHER THAN ANNUALLY.

01099 ARTER, D.
A TALE OF TWO CARLSSONS: THE SWEDISH GENERAL ELECTION OF
1988
PARLIAMENTARY AFFAIRS, 42(1) (JAN 89), 84-101.
THE ARTICLE ANALYZES THE EVENTS THAT LED AFFECTED THE
OUTCOME OF THE 1988 GENERAL ELECTION OF SWEDEN. SIGNIFICANT
AMONG THESE WERE A SCANDAL INVOLVING THE RULING SOCIAL
DEMOCRATIC PARTY AND EBBE CARLSSON, A PRIVATE INVESTIGATOR
WHICH LED TO THE RESIGNATION OF A MINISTER OF JUSTICE, AND
THE ADVENT OF A GREEN COALITION WHICH GARNERED AS MUCH AS
10% IN OPINION POLLS. HOWEVER, THE OUTCOME OF THE ELECTIONS
FAVORED PRIME MINISTER INGVAR CARLSSON AND THE RULING PARTY.
THE GREENS MADE SOME GAINS, BUT THE SOCIAL DEMOCRATS
SOLIDIFIED THEIR POSITION AS THE NATURAL PARTY OF SWEDEN.

01100 ARURI, N.
AMERICA'S TIMID PEACE EFFORTS
MIDDLE EAST INTERNATIONAL, (363) (NOV 89), 1677.
THE ARTICLE EXAMINES SOME OF THE RECENT ATTEMPTS OF THE
BUSH ADMINISTRATION TO "RESOLVE" THE PROBLEM OF THE OCCUPIED
TERRITORIES. IT CONCLUDES THAT BUSH AND BAKER HAVE ATTEMPTED
TO "PLAY IT SAFE" AND HAVE MOVED ONLY WHEN NO OTHER OPTION
WAS EVIDENT. THE RESULT IS A "TIMID" FOREIGN POLICY THAT IS
UNLIKELY TO FACILITATE ANY MORE PROGRESS THAN THAT OF ITS
FORERUNNERS. THE US, ISRAEL, AND THE PALESTINIANS WILL ALL
NEED CONSIDERABLY MORE FLEXIBILITY OF THIS THORNY PROBLEM IS
EVER TO BE SOLVED.

01101 ARURI, N.
REAGAN'S LEGACY TO BUSH
MIDDLE EAST INTERNATIONAL, (343) (FEB 89), 16-18.
THE REAGAN ERA LEFT THE BUSH ADMINISTRATION A LEGACY OF
HOSTILITY TO THE PALESTINIANS. REAGAN SUCCEEDED IN
MARGINALISING THE PALESTINIAN QUESTION THROUGH THE SPECIAL
US-ISRAELI RELATIONSHIP AND HIS ANTI-TERRORIST CAMPAIGN,
WHICH BECAME THE PRINCIPAL IMPEDIMENT TO A POLITICAL
SETTLEMENT UNDER INTERNATIONAL AUSPICES. THE SHULTZ PLAN AND
THE DIALOGUE WITH THE PLO, BOTH IN 1988, CAME LARGELY IN
RESPONSE TO PROFOUND CHANGES IN THE INTERNATIONAL, REGIONAL,
AND LOCAL CONTEXT OF THE PALESTINIAN QUESTION AND THE
PRESSURE ON THE USA TO ADJUST TO THOSE CHANGES.

01102 ARURI, N.
THE UNITED STATES AND PALESTINE: REAGAN'S LEGACY TO BUSH
JOURNAL OF PALESTINE STUDIES, XVIII(3) (SPR 89), 3-21.

THE FIRM COMMITMENT OF GEORGE BUSH TO THE STRATEGIC
ALLIANCE WITH ISRAEL IS NOT LIKELY TO ERODE IN THE NEAR
FUTURE. HIS PARTY'S PLATFORM DURING THE 1988 CAMPAIGN
COMMITS HIM TO OPPOSING THE CREATION OF AN INDEPENDENT
PALESTINIAN STATE, DEEMED AS "INIMICAL TO THE SECURITY
INTERESTS OF ISRAEL, JORDAN, AND THE U.S." SUCH OPPOSITION,
HOWEVER WILL NOT NECESSARILY LEAD THE BUSH ADMINISTRATION TO
STOP THE PALESTINIANS FROM PURSUING THAT OPTION. ALTHOUGH
THE REAGAN PLAN OF 1982 PERCEIVED PEACE AS BEING ACHIEVABLE
NEITHER ON THE BASIS OF THE FORMATION OF AN INDEPENDENT
PALESTINIAN STATE, NOR ON THE BASIS OF ISRAELI SOVEREIGNTY
IN THE WEST BANK AND GAZA, CAMP DAVID, ON THE OTHER HAND,
LEFT BOTH OPTIONS OPEN FOR NEGOTIATIONS. GIVEN THAT THESE
TWO DOCUMENTS CONSTITUTE THE U.S. DIPLOMATIC FRAMEWORK FOR
ADDRESSING THE PALESTINE-ISRAEL CONFLICT, ANY NEW
INITIATIVES BY THE BUSH ADMINISTRATION MAY BE EXPECTED TO
FALL SOMEWHERE ALONG THAT SPECTRUM, WHICH IS CAPABLE OF
ACCOMMODATING THE POST-1988 PALESTINIAN MINIMALIST POSITION
AS WELL AS THE POST-INTIFADAH LIKUD POSITION.

01103 ASANTE, S.K.B.; ASOMBANG, W.W.
AN INDEPENDENT NAMIBIA? THE FUTURE FACING SWAPO
THIRD WORLD QUARTERLY, 11(3) (JUL 89), 1-19.
THE AUTHORS ENUMERATE THE MAIN ECONOMIC AND SOCIO-
POLITICAL CHALLENGES LIKELY TO CONFRONT THE FUTURE NAMIBIAN
GOVERNMENT, WHICH THEY ASSUME WILL BE THE SOUTH WEST AFRICAN
PEOPLES' ORGANIZATION (SWAPO). THE REALITIES OF NAIMBIA'S
POLITICAL AND ECONOMIC STRUCTURE WILL SHARE ITS ECONOMY
AFTER INDEPENDENCE. THE EVOLUTION OF SWAPO'S RELATIONSHIPS
WITH DIFFERENT CLASSES, ETHNIC AND POLITICAL GROUPS,
TRADITIONAL CHIEFS, AND CHURCHES AND ITS ABILITY TO OPERATE
INSIDE NAMIBIA HOLD IMPLICATIONS NOT ONLY FOR THE
INDEPENDENCE AND ELECTORAL PROGRESSES BUT ALSO FOR ITS
HANDLING OF THE SOCIO-ECONOMIC CHALLENGES OF THE IMMEDIATE
POST-INDEPENDENCE PERIOD.

01104 ASCH, M.
WILDLIFE: DEFINING THE ANIMALS OF THE DENE HUNT AND THE
SETTLEMENT OF ABORIGINAL RIGHTS CLAIMS
CANADIAN PUBLIC POLICY--ANALYSE DE POLITIQUES, XV(2) (JUN
89), 205-219.
THIS ARTICLE CONCERNS THE IMPACT OF TERMINOLOGY USED IN
LAND CLAIMS AGREEMENTS ON THE CONCEPTS AND INTERESTS OF
ABORIGINAL PARTIES. SPECIFICALLY, IT EXAMINES HOW WELL THE
WORD 'WILDLIFE' DESCRIBES THE DENE/METIS CONCEPT OF THE
ANIMALS THEY HUNT. IT SUGGESTS THAT ALTERNATIVES EXIST THAT
ARE RECONCILABLE TO EURO-CANADIAN IDEAS AND PROVIDE A BETTER
APPROXIMATION OF DENE/METIS PERCEPTIONS AND INTERESTS IN
THESE ANIMALS THAN DOES THE TERM 'WILDLIFE'. THE ARTICLE
CONCLUDES BY ARGUING THAT THE IMPASSE TO ADOPTING MORE
APPROPRIATE TERMINOLOGY LIES NOT IN FINDING CONCEPTUAL
PARALLELS BUT RATHER IN THE LACK OF POLITICAL WILL ON THE
PART OF CANADIAN GOVERNMENTS TO INCORPORATE SUCH TERMINOLOGY
INTO THESE AGREEMENTS.

01105 ASCHER, W.
ON THE CONVERGENCE OF EFFICIENCY AND EQUITY VIA
NEOCLASSICAL PRESCRIPTIONS
JOURNAL OF INTERAMERICAN STUDIES AND WORLD AFFAIRS, 31(1,
2) (SPR 89), 49-62.
THIS ARTICLE EXPLORES THE POTENTIAL USE OF NEOCLASSICAL
ECONOMIC POLICIES TO ACHIEVE BOTH EQUITY AND EFFECIENCY. IT
SHOWS HOW IMPROVED INTELLIGENCE, PROMOTION, PRESCRIPTION,
INVOCATION, APPLICATION, APPRAISAL AND TERMINATION CAN
IMPROVE THE POSSIBILITY OF PURSUING THE OBJECTIVES OF EQUITY
AND EFFICIENCY THROUGH THE SAME NEOCLASSICAL POLICY
INSTRUMENTS. ASCHERS PRESCRIPTIONS CONTAIN THE POTENTIAL TO
CORRECT PUBLIC POLICY IN A SIGNIFICANT WAY.

01106 ASHFORD, D.E.
DEATH OF A GREAT SURVIVOR: THE MANPOWER SERVICES
COMMISSION IN THE UK
GOVERNANCE, 2(4) (OCT 89), 365-383.
THIS ARTICLE EXPLORES THE MANPOWER SERVICES COMMISSION
(MSC) IN THE UNITED KINGDOM AND CALLS THE MSC SAGA AN "ARCH-
TYPICAL PHENOMENON THAT REVEALS THE PECULIAR FEATURES OF
BRITISH POLICYMAKING". IT OFFERS A HISTORY OF INDUSTRIAL
TRAINING IN ORDER TO UNDERSTAND HOW THE MSC PERMEATED SO
MANY CREVICES OF BRITISH GOVERNMENT AND TRACES ITS GROWTH TO
BECOME A STRANGE COMBINATION OF ADMINISTRATIVE DEFENSIVENESS
AND POLITICAL COMPLACENCY. WEAKNESSES IN BRITISH POLICY-
MAKING ARE EXAMINED.

01107 ASHFORTH, A.
ON THE "NATIVE QUESTION": A READING OF THE GRAND TRADITION
OF COMMISSIONS OF INQUIRY INTO THE "NATIVE QUESTION" IN
TWENTIETH-CENTURY SOUTH AFRICA
DISSERTATION ABSTRACTS INTERNATIONAL, 49(8) (FEB 89),
2417-A.
THE COMMISSION OF INQUIRY HAS BEEN ONE OF THE PRINCIPAL
FORUMS FOR SOLVING THE "NATIVE QUESTION" IN SOUTH AFRICA. IN
THIS DISSERTATION, THE AUTHOR OUTLINES A "GRAND TRADITION"
OF APPOINTING COMMISSIONS OF INQUIRY DURING PERIODS OF
CRISIS AND ARGUES THAT THEY HAVE BEEN USED AS "SCHEMES OF

LEGITIMATION."

01108 ASHKAR, A.
PALESTINIAN AGRICULTURE
MIDDLE EAST INTERNATIONAL, (358) (SEP 89), 18-19.
THE ARTICLE EXAMINES THE EFFECT THAT OVER 20 YEARS OF
ISRAELI OCCUPATION HAS HAD ON AGRICULTURAL OUTPUT IN THE
OCCUPIED TERRITORIES. THE RATE OF CONFISCATION OF LAND,
DESTRUCTION OF CROPS, AND HARASSMENT OF FARMERS HAS
INCREASED DRAMATICALLY WITH THE ADVENT OF THE INTIFADA.
HOWEVER, EVEN MORE DETRIMENTAL TO PALESTINIAN FARMERS ARE
PROHIBITIONS ON EXPORT IMPOSED BY ISRAEL. AGRICULTURAL
COMMITTEES CRATED BY INTIFADA LEADERS HAVE ATTEMPTED TO DEAL
WITH THESE DIFFICULT SITUATIONS THROUGH ORGANIZATION AND
COOPERATION, BUT THE AVERAGE PALESTINIAN FARMER STILL
SUFFERS CONSIDERABLY FROM ISRAEL'S OPPRESSION.

01109 ASHTON, C.
WASHINGTON LISTENS BUT DOES IT HEAR?
PACIFIC DEFENCE REPORTER, 16(3) (SEP 89), 49-50.
THE IDEA OF THE PACIFIC ISLANDS REGION AS A TRANQUIL
AMERICAN LAKE OF LOYAL, PRO-WESTERN ISLAND PEOPLE DIES HARD.
THIS ARTICLE DETAILS THE FEELING OF PACIFIC ISLAND
SPECIALISTS, BOTH AUSTRALIAN AND AMERICAN, THAT WASHINGTON'S
PERCEPTIONS REQUIRE SHARP CORRECTION.

01110 ASIWAJU, A.I.
BORDER REGIONS IN AFRICA: COLLABORATION OR CONFLICT?
DISARMAMENT, XII(1) (WIN 89), 94-103.
INTERNATIONAL EFFORTS HAVE BEEN IMPLEMENTED WITH THE
GOAL OF MAXIMIZING THE POTENTIAL OF BORDER REGIONS IN THE
CAUSE OF PEACE AND DEVELOPMENT IN AFRICA. THE POTENTIAL CAN
BE BEST DEVELOPED BY THE POPULARIZATION OF TRANS-BORDER
COOPERATION POLICY FOR ALL ADJACENT STATES OF THE CONTINENT
AND ITS SUB-REGIONS. ENCOURAGEMENT MUST COME FROM ALL
DIRECTIONS AND AT ALL LEVELS. IN PARTICULAR, THE OAU SHOULD
RESOLVE TO PROMOTE BORDERS IN CONFORMITY WITH THE PRINCIPLE
OF "UTI POSSIDETIS."

01111 ASKIN, S.
THE BUSINESS OF SANCTIONS BUSTING
AFRICA REPORT, 34(1) (JAN 89), 18-20.
ALTHOUGH THE US CONGRESS HAS HOTLY DEBATED ECONOMIC
SANCTIONS AGAINST SOUTH AFRICA, THE REAL IMPACT OF ANY
SANCTIONS DEPENDS ON AN ISSUE RARELY ADDRESSED IN CONGRESS:
WILL THE US CRACK DOWN ON SANCTION BUSTERS? PRETORIA'S
NETWORK OF SECRETIVE TRADE LINKS INVOLVES ECONOMIC PARTNERS
IN NATIONS ACROSS THE POLITICAL SPECTRUM: TAIWAN, ISRAEL,
THE USA, BRITAIN, HOLLAND, AND THE USSR.

01112 ASLANBEIGUI, N.; SUMMERFIELD, G.
IMPACT OF THE RESPONSIBILITY SYSTEM ON WOMEN IN RURAL
CHINA: AN APPLICATION OF SEN'S THEORY OF ENTITLEMENTS
WORLD DEVELOPMENT, 17(3) (MAR 89), 343-350.
IN EARLY 1983, THE CHINESE GOVERNMENT ANNOUNCED A
UNIFORM NATIONAL POLICY OF THE RURAL "RESPONSIBILITY SYSTEM,
" WHICH HAD PREVIOUSLY BEEN LIMITED TO AN EXPERIMENTAL BASIS.
THIS POLICY SUBDIVIDES THE "TEAM" (PREVIOUSLY THE SMALLEST
PRODUCTION UNIT) DOWN TO THE HOUSEHOLD. HOUSEHOLDS CONSIST
OF TENANT FARMERS WHO CONTRACT PLOTS OF LAND FROM THE TEAM
IN EXCHANGE FOR FULFILLING PRODUCTION QUOTAS AND TAXES. THE
REFORMS HAVE LED TO AN ALMOST COMPLETE DECOLLECTIVIZATION OF
CHINESE AGRICULTURE AND TO INCREASES IN PRODUCTIVITY. BUT
ECONOMISTS AND OTHER SOCIAL SCIENTISTS SHARE CONCERNS ABOUT
CERTAIN NEGATIVE TRENDS CREATED BY THE RESPONSIBILITY SYSTEM.
THESE RANGE FROM THE UNEQUAL CHANGE IN INCOMES ACROSS
HOUSEHOLDS AND REGIONS, TO AN UNHEALTHY SHIFT IN EMPHASIS
FROM INVESTMENT TO CONSUMPTION, AND TO THE REINFORCEMENT OF
TRADITIONAL ECONOMIC ARRANGEMENTS THAT DECREASE THE POWER OF
WOMEN.

01113 ASLUND, A.
GORBACHEV'S STRUGGLE FOR ECONOMIC REFORM
JOHN SPIERS PUBLISHING, BRIGHTON, SUSSEX, GB, 1989, 256.
THE AUTHOR EXAMINES THE PRESENT SOVIET REFORM PROCESS,
TRACING ITS ORIGINS TO YURI ANDROPOV'S ACCESSION TO POWER IN
1982. HE INVESTIGATES THE STATE OF THE SOVIET ECONOMY AND
THE REASONS FOR ECONOMIC REFORM. HE ALSO SURVEYS THE STATE
OF SOVIET ECONOMIC SCIENCE AND HOW LEADING SOVIET
POLITICIANS STAND ON ECONOMIC REFORM.

01114 ASLUND, A.
SOVIET AND CHINESE REFORMS: WHY THEY MUST BE DIFFERENT
WORLD TODAY, 45(11) (NOV 89), 188-191.
UNTIL THE MASSACRE IN TIAN AN MEN SQUARE, IT WAS
FASHIONABLE TO PRAISE THE CHINESE REFORM AT THE EXPENSE OF
THE SOVIET REFORM. BUT THE DIFFERENCES IN THE REFORM
ATTEMPTS ARE LARGELY A RESULT OF THE EXISTING CONDITIONS IN
EACH SOCIETY. THUS, THE LEADERS HAVE A MUCH NARROWER RANGE
OF CHOICES THAN IS USUALLY THOUGHT. THEIR POWERS ARE OFTEN
EXAGGERATED, AS THE MYTH OF AN OMNIPOTENT LEADER LINGERS ON
LONG AFTER THE TOTALITARIAN MODEL HAS PROVED INADEQUATE.

01115 ASMAL, K.
JUDGES AND JUSTICE IN SOUTH AFRICA
SECHABA, 23(3) (MAR 89), 19-21.
THE ARTICLE ATTEMPTS TO EXAMINE THE MYTH THAT PREVAILS
AMONG SOME COMMENTATORS THAT THE JUDICIARY IN SOUTH AFRICA
IS STILL A FORCE FOR GOOD, AND THAT THE APARTHEID STATE HAS
GONE SOME WAY TOWARDS MAINTAINING THE NOTION OF JUDICIAL
IMPARTIALITY AND INDEPENDENCE. IT CONCLUDES THAT A REVIEW OF
THE COURT'S RECORD OVER THE PAST DECADE WILL REVEAL THAT AN
IMPARTIAL JUDICIARY IS MERELY A MYTH; THE JUDICIARY OF SOUTH
AFRICA IS RUN IN THE INTERESTS OF A MINORITY AND PROTECTED
BY ITS MONOPOLY OF STATE POWER.

01116 ASMAL, K.
THE ILLEGITIMACY OF APARTHEID
SECHABA, 23(12) (DEC 89), 26-29.
THIS IS AN EXTRACT FROM A PAPER WHICH WAS DELIVERED AT A
LEGAL SEMINAR ORGANIZED BY THE WORLD COUNCIL OF CHURCHES AND
THE SOUTH AFRICAN COUNCIL OF CHURCHES IN HARARE IN SEPTEMBER
1989. IT COVERS THE LACK OF AUTHENTIC REPRESENTATIVES OF THE
PEOPLE OF SOUTH AFRICA; THE CONSEQUENCES OF ILLEGITIMACY;
THE BASIS FOR SANCTIONS; AND THE STATUS OF THE LIBERATION
MOVEMENT. IT CONCLUDES WITH A HUMANISTIC ALTERNATIVE TO
APARTHEID.

01117 ASMTON, W.
BURMA STILL STRUGGLING FOR PEACE AND STABILITY
PACIFIC DEFENCE REPORTER, 16(3) (SEP 89), 18-19.
BURMA'S ECONOMIC PROBLEMS AND INTERNAL POLITICAL UNREST
WILL ENSURE ITS CONTINUING PREOCCUPATION WITH DOMESTIC
AFFAIRS FOR THE FORESEEABLE FUTURE. NOR IS THERE ANY SIGN
THAT OTHER COUNTRIES WISH SIGNIFICANTLY TO INTERFERE IN
BURMA'S AFFAIRS, WHICH SEEM DESTINED TO CONTINUE THEIR
PRESENT TROUBLED COURSE. BURMA CANNOT ALWAYS REMAIN UNDER
THE DOMINATION OF AN ISOLATIONIST MILITARY DICTATORSHIP,
PURSUING BANKRUPT SOCIALIST ECONOMIC POLICIES.

01118 ASOYAN, B.
RUSSIA AND SOUTH AFRICA
INTERNATIONAL AFFAIRS (MOSCOW), (12) (DEC 89), 41-49.
THE MORE IMPENETRABLY THE IRON CURTAIN OF APARTHEID
ISOLATED SOUTH AFRICA FROM THE REST OF THE WORLD, THE
FIERCER BECAME THE ATTACK OF THE RULING REGIME ON COMMUNISM
AND THE SOVIET UNION. SOUTH AFRICAN PROPAGANDA WARNED BOTH
BLACKS AND WHITES THAT COMMUNISM WAS THE GREATEST THREAT TO
THEIR COUNTRY. AT THE SAME TIME, THE TONE AND SCOPE OF
SOVIET PROPAGANDA AGAINST THE SOUTH AFRICAN REGIME EXCEEDED
THE LEVEL OF SOVIET INVOLVEMENT IN THE REGION. STALINISM
ALLOWED THE ADVOCATES OF APARTHEID TO REDUCE SOCIALISM AND
COMMUNISM TO AN EVIL FORCE AND TO JUSTIFY APARTHEID AS A
PROPER RESPONSE TO THE COMMUNIST THREAT.

01119 ASPIN, L.T.; HALL, W.K.
FRIENDS AND NEIGHBORS VOTING IN JUDICIAL RETENTION
ELECTIONS: A RESEARCH NOTE COMPARING TRIAL AND APPELLATE
COURT ELECTIONS
WESTERN POLITICAL QUARTERLY, 42(4) (DEC 89), 587-596.
THE FRIENDS AND NEIGHBORS EFFECT IS EXAMINED IN BOTH
TRIAL COURT AND APPELLATE COURT RETENTION ELECTIONS THAT
TOOK PLACE IN FIVE STATES FROM 1976 THROUGH 1984. FOR BOTH
TYPES OF COURTS NON-HOME COUNTY VOTERS (1) ARE LESS LIKELY
TO VOTE THAN ARE THE HOME COUNTY VOTERS, AND (2) GIVE THE
SAME LEVEL OF SUPPORT TO ALL JUDGES ON THE BALLOT. WHILE
HOME COUNTY VOTERS ARE MORE LIKELY TO VOTE IN RETENTION
ELECTIONS THAN ARE NONHOME COUNTY VOTERS. REGARDLESS OF THE
TYPE OF COURT, HOME COUNTY VOTING BEHAVIOR VARIES FROM ONE
TYPE OF COURT TO ANOTHER. THERE IS A FOUR-POINT HOME COUNTY
ADVANTAGE FOR APPELLATE COURT RETENTION ELECTIONS, BUT NOT
FOR TRIAL COURT ELECTIONS. THE DEGREE OF HOME COUNTY
ADVANTAGE IS FOUND NOT TO BE RELATED TO THE POPULATION OF
THE JUDICIAL DISTRICT. IN ADDITION, WHILE THE FOUR-POINT
HOME COUNTY ADVANTAGE IS SIMILAR TO THAT REPORTED FOR
STATEWIDE PARTISAN ELECTIONS, UNLIKE THE PARTISAN ELECTIONS,
THE DEGREE OF HOME COUNTY ADVANTAGE IS NOT RELATED TO THE
SIZE OF THE HOME COUNTY.

01120 ASSAM, M.A.
BUREAUCRACY AND DEVELOPMENT IN SUDAN
JOURNAL OF ASIAN AND AFRICAN STUDIES, XXIV(1-2) (1989),
28-48.
WITH GOOD EDUCATION AND A RELATIVELY HIGH FUNCTIONAL
CAPABILITY, SUDANESE PUBLIC SERVANTS HAVE HAD THE POTENTIAL
TO PLAY A MAJOR ROLE IN THE POLITICAL AND SOCIO-ECONOMIC
DEVELOPMENT OF THEIR COUNTRY. UNFORTUNATELY, ALL DEVELOPMENT
PLANS SINCE INDEPENDENCE HAVE FAILED TO ACHIEVE THEIR GOALS.
THIS FAILURE HAS CAUSED BY ADMINISTRATIVE INEFFICIENCY AND
OBSOLETE STRUCTURES, BUREAUCRATIC INFIGHTING, AND THE LACK
OF CO-ORDINATION, LEADING TO POOR IMPLEMENTATION AND
EXECUTION OF GOVERNMENT POLICIES.

01121 ASSIRI, A.R.
KUWAIT'S POLITICAL SURVEY IN THE 1980 AND BEYOND: SMALL-
NATION RESPONSE TO REGIONAL PRESSURE
AMERICAN-ARAB AFFAIRS, (30) (FAL 89), 27-35.

THIS ARTICLE ATTEMPTS TO EXPLAIN HOW KUWAIT WAS ABLE TO COPE WITH THE MAIN CHANGES IN THE REGION IN THE LATE 1970S AND 1980S AND TO ANALYZE ITS OPTIONS FOR THE FUTURE. IT EXPLORES THE LONG-RANGE IMPACTS ON THE INTERNAL DYNAMISM OF THE COUNTRY, AND ON ITS BEHAVIOR, OF THE IRAN REVOLUTION AND THE WAR IN THE GULF. IT CONCLUDES THAT IN PURSUING ITS CENTRIST, UNCOMMITTED ROLE, KUWAIT SHOULD AGAIN ATTEMPT TO AVOID BEING DRAGGED INTO INTRAREGIONAL CONFLICTS.

01122 ASTROW, A.
    MAINA WA KINYATTI: A HISTORY OF RESISTANCE
    AFRICA REPORT, 34(4) (JUL 89), 55-58.
        MAINA WA KINYATTI, A FORMER SENIOR LECTURER IN HISTORY
    AT KENYATTA UNIVERSITY, RECENTLY FLED FROM KENYA ONLY A FEW
    MONTHS AFTER HAVING BEEN RELEASED FROM A SIXYEAR PRISON TERM
    FOR ALLEGEDLY POSSESSING A "SEDITIOUS" DOCUMENT. ONE OF THE
    COUNTRY'S LEADING POLITICAL PRISONERS, KINYATTI HAD BEEN
    REPEATEDLY TORTURED BY POLICE IN AN EFFORT TO MAKE HIM
    CONFESS TO MEMBERSHIP IN MWAKENYA, THE CLANDESTINE
    OPPOSITION ORGANIZATION. UPON HIS RELEASE FROM JAIL, HE WAS
    THREATENED WITH RE-ARREST FOR REFUSING TO ASK PRESIDENT
    DANIEL ARAP MOI FOR AN OFFICIAL PARDON AS A CONDITION FOR
    REINSTATEMENT TO HIS PREVIOUS JOB, FORCING HIM TO LEAVE
    KENYA IN SECRET AND SEEK REFUGE IN THE U.S.

01123 ASUMAH, S.N.
    POWER, POLITICS, AND MILITARY REGIMES: ACQUIESCENCE,
    QUIESCENCE, # AND EXIT IN GHANA
    DISSERTATION ABSTRACTS INTERNATIONAL, 49(11) (MAY 89),
    3501-A.
        MILITARY LEADERSHIP MODELS OF GUARDIAN, ARBITRATOR, AND
    DIRECT-RULER TYPE AND THREE DIFFERENT POWER DIMENSIONS ARE
    USED TO ASSESS POLITICAL PARTICIPATION AND THE ROOT CAUSES
    OF ACQUIESENCE, QUIESCENCE, AND EXIT IN GHANA. THE AUTHOR
    ALSO CONSIDERS THE OUTLOOK FOR DEMILITARIZATION AND
    REDEMOCRATIZATION IN THE AFRICAN STATE.

01124 ATENGA, C.N.
    INTERREGIONAL MILITARY TRAINING IN AFRICA AS A CONFIDENCE-
    BUILDING FACTOR
    DISARMAMENT, XII(1) (WIN 89), 73-87.
        THE AUTHOR CONSIDERS THE QUESTION OF WHETHER INTER-
    REGIONAL MILITARY TRAINING IN AFRICA CAN BE A CONFIDENCE-
    BUILDING FACTOR. HE CONCLUDES THAT THERE IS NO DOUBT THAT
    MILITARY TRAINING AND EDUCATION ADAPTED TO THE SINGULAR
    SITUATION OF AFRICA, TO THE NEEDS OF PEACE AS WELL AS THE
    REALITIES OF MODERN TIMES, WOULD GREATLY CONTRIBUTE TO THE
    STRENGTHENING OF CONFIDENCE BETWEEN THE STATES ON THE
    AFRICAN CONTINENT.

01125 ATHEARN, R.A.
    THE CONSTITUTION, TASTE, AND "VIOLENCE OF FACTIONS"
    DISSENT, (SPR 89), 263-265.
        THE CURRENTLY PREVALENT NOTION OF DEMOCRACY AS AN ARENA
    FOR THE UNCONSTRAINED COMBAT OF A PLURALITY OF FACTIONAL
    INTERESTS WAS PRECISELY WHAT JAMES MADISON HOPED THE
    CONSTITUTION WOULD PREVENT. MADISON'S CONCEPTION OF THE
    CONSTITUTION WAS THAT IT WOULD CONTROL WHAT HE CALLED "THE
    VIOLENCE OF FACTIONS" AND ASSURE THE INVIOLABLE MAINTENANCE
    OF THE EQUALITY OF THE PRIVILEGES AND IMMUNITIES OF
    CITIZENSHIP. ALTHOUGH MADISON RECOGNIZED THE UNAVOIDABILITY
    OF FACTIONS, HE EXPECTED THAT THE CONSTITUTION WOULD PROVIDE
    A FRAMEWORK THAT WOULD "BREAK AND CONTROL THE VIOLENCE OF
    FACTIONS."

01126 ATHERTON, C. R.
    THE WELFARE STATE: STILL ON SOLID GROUND
    SOCIAL SERVICE REVIEW, 63(2) (JUN 89), 167-179.
        THE WELFARE STATES OF NORTH AMERICA AND WESTERN EUROPE
    HAVE SEEN SLOWER GROWTH AND EVEN CUTBACKS DURING THE 1970S
    AND 1980S. CRITICS ON THE RIGHT BLAME THE FAULTY IDEOLOGY
    BEHIND "SOCIAL ENGINEERING," THE LEFT POINTS TO THE
    FUNDAMENTAL INCOMPATIBILITY OF THE WELFARE IDEOLOGY WITH
    CAPITALISM. THE AUTHOR ARGUES THAT THE SLOWDOWN IN GROWTH IS
    A DECISION MADE BY THE MIDDLE OF THE POLITICAL SPECTRUM.
    CONSERVATIVE AND MODERATE POLITICAL VICTORIES OF THE PERIOD
    HAVE NOT GIVEN CONSERVATIVES A MANDATE FOR THE DISMANTLEMENT
    OF THE WELFARE STATE. AT THE SAME TIME, THE VOTERS HAVE
    REJECTED THE LEFT'S EXTREME VIEW OF "SUBSTANTIVE EQUALITY."

01127 ATKIN, M.
    THE SURVIVAL OF ISLAM IN SOVIET TAJIKISTAN
    MIDDLE EAST JOURNAL, 43(4) (FAL 89), 605-618.
        THIS ARTICLE CONSIDERS THE SURVIVAL TACTICS OF ISLAM IN
    TAJIKISTAN, THE ONE NON-TURKIC REPUBLIC OF SOVIET CENTRAL
    ASIA. IT SHARES MORE INTIMATELY THAN DO ITS SOVIET NEIGHBORS
    THE PERSIAN HERITAGE THAT PREVAILS TO THE SOUTH. IN ADDITION
    TO DRAWING ON MORE READILY AVAILABLE REFERENCES, THIS STUDY
    BENEFITS PARTICULARLY FROM AN ASSIDUOUS READING OF TAJIK
    SOURCES.

01128 ATKINSON, J.
    MASS COMMUNICATIONS, ECONOMIC LIBERALISATION, AND THE NEW
    MEDIATORS

POLITICAL SCIENCE, 41(2) (DEC 89), 85-108.
    THE NEW INFORMATION TECHNOLOGY HAS HAD PARADOXICAL
CONSEQUENCES. REDUCING THE STATE'S RELIANCE ON TRADITIONAL
STRUCTURES OF POLITICAL INTERMEDIATION AND PROMOTING LESS-
ACCOUNTABLE, MORE COMMERCIALLY-ORIENTED MEDIATORS HAS
CREATED POLITICAL CONDITIONS HIGHLY CONGENIAL TO FREE MARKET
IDEOLOGIES, BUT IT HAS ALSO PUSHED IN THE OPPOSITE DIRECTION:
SUBVERTING THEIR FLIMSY THEORETICAL CLAIMS AND RENDERING
THEIR PRACTICAL IMPLICATIONS MORE REGRESSIVE. MASS
COMMUNICATIONS TECHNOLOGY HAS ERODED THE QUALITY AND
DIMINISHED THE IMPACT OF THOSE KINDS OF LOCAL KNOWLEDGE UPON
WHICH FREE MARKET CHAMPIONS WANT SOCIAL DECISION-MAKING TO
BE BASED. FAR FROM SOCIAL DECISION-MAKING BEING
DECENTRALIZED, IT IS BECOMING INCREASINGLY CENTRALIZED. THE
NEW TECHNOLOGIES HAVE BEEN CONSISTENTLY ASSOCIATED WITH
STRONGLY OLIGARCHICAL TENDENCIES RATHER THEN WITH MORE
DEMOCRATIZATION.

01129 ATKINSON, M.; NIGOL, R.
    SELECTING POLICY INSTRUMENTS: NEO-INSTITUTIONAL AND
    RATIONAL CHOICE INTERPRETATIONS OF AUTOMOBILE INSURANCE IN
    ONTARIO
    CANADIAN JOURNAL OF POLITICAL SCIENCE, XXII(1) (MAR 89),
    107-136.
        ABSTRACT. THE RATIONAL CHOICE MODEL OF POLITICS, WHICH
    CONSTRUES IMPORTANT POLITICAL PROCESSES AS A SERIES OF
    CHOICES TAKEN BY SELF-INTERESTED POLITICAL ACTORS, HAS
    DOMINATED THEORIZING ON THE SUBJECT OF POLICY INSTRUMENTS IN
    CANADA. WHILE USEFUL, THIS APPROACH IS NONETHELESS LIMITED
    BY ITS NARROW CONCEPTION OF RATIONALITY AND ITS INATTENTION
    TO THE CONTEXT OF INSTRUMENT CHOICE. AS AN ALTERNATIVE, THE
    NEO-INSTITUTIONAL APPROACH OFFERS A PERSPECTIVE ON POLITICAL
    CHOICE THAT TAKES BETTER ACCOUNT OF CONTEXTUAL AND
    ORGANIZATIONAL FACTORS. IN THIS ARTICLE, THE LOGIC OF BOTH
    APPROACHES IS USED TO EXPLAIN THE POLICY PROCESS IN THE CASE
    OF AUTOMOBILE INSURANCE IN ONTARIO. THE STUDY CONCLUDES THAT
    IT IS ESSENTIAL THAT RESEARCH STRATEGIES IN THE REALM OF
    INSTRUMENT CHOICE INCORPORATE INSIGHTS FROM THE NEO-
    INSTITUTIONAL APPROACH.

01130 ATKINSON, M.M.; COLEMAN, W.D.
    STRONG STATES AND WEAK STATES: SECTORAL POLICY NETWORKS IN
    ADVANCED CAPITALIST ECONOMIES
    BRITISH JOURNAL OF POLITICAL SCIENCE, 19(1) (JAN 89),
    47-67.
        THE AUTHORS USE THE CONCEPTS OF STATE CAPACITY AND
    SOCIETAL MOBILIZATION TO IDENTIFY SIX IDEAL TYPICAL POLICY
    NETWORKS AT THE SECTORAL LEVEL. THEY ELABORATE ON THE
    ORGANIZATIONAL LOGIC ASSOCIATED WITH THESE POLICY NETWORKS
    BY EXAMINING THEM IN CONJUCTION WITH INDUSTRIAL POLICY.
    AFTER DISTINGUISHING BETWEEN TWO APPROACHES TO INDUSTRIAL
    POLICY (ANTICIPATORY AND REACTIVE), THEY SHOW HOW DIFFERENT
    POLICY NETWORKS EMERGE TO SUPPORT ALTERNATIVE APPROACHES AND
    HOW A DISJUNCTION BETWEEN NETWORKS AND APPROACHES CAN
    PRODUCE POLICY FAILURE.

01131 ATOADE, J.
    THE CULTURE DEBATE IN AFRICA
    BLACK SCHOLAR, 20(3/4) (SUM 89), 2-6.
        THE ARTICLE EXPLORES THE ORIGINS AND DEVELOPMENT OF
    AFRICAN CULTURE. IT OUTLINES THE ROLE THAT ANTI-COLONIALISM
    PLAYED IN STRENGTHENING AFRICAN CULTURE; CULTURE WAS OFTEN
    USED AS A TOOL FOR POLITICAL INDEPENDENCE. THE ARTICLE
    FOLLOWS THE STAGES OF AFRICAN CULTURE (ASSERTION, REJECTION,
    AND APPLICATION) AND CONCLUDES THAT ALTHOUGH CULTURE WAS A
    POWERFUL INSTRUMENT OF DECOLONIZATION, IT NOW REMAINS A TOOL
    OF AUTONOMIST AND SELF-DETERMIST FACTIONS AND CREATES
    NATIONAL UNITY

01132 ATSUSHI, K.
    U.S. PRESSURE: BOON OR BANE?
    JAPAN ECHO, XVI(2) (SUM 89), 60-65.
        THE AUTHOR CONSIDERS AMERICAN PRESSURE ON JAPAN FOR
    TRADE REFORM AND OTHER CHANGES, FOCUSING ON TWO MAJOR ISSUES.
    THE FIRST IS WHETHER THE JAPANESE SHOULD CONTINUE TO
    PASSIVELY ACCEPT EXTERNAL PRESSURE AS A TOOL FOR ACHIEVING
    GRADUAL PROGRESS IN IMPLEMENTING DOMESTIC REFORMS OR WHETHER
    THEY SHOULD INSTEAD SEIZE THE INITIATIVE IN SUCH AREAS AS
    MARKET OPENING AND ECONOMIC RESTRUCTURING. THE SECOND
    QUESTION IS WHETHER U.S. CONGRESSIONAL DEMANDS HAVE, ON THE
    WHOLE, BEEN JUSTIFIED OR WHETHER THEY HAVE BEEN SELF-SERVING
    AND NEEDLESSLY PRODUCED TENSION IN THE JAPANESE-AMERICAN
    RELATIONSHIP.

01133 ATSUSHI, O.
    KAIFY TOSHIKI: PRIME MINISTER BETWINXT AND BETWEEN
    JAPAN QUARTERLY, XXXVI(4) (OCT 89), 368-374.
        AUG. 9, 1989, WHEN THE KAIFU TOSHIKI CABINET CAME INTO
    BEING, WILL BE REMEMBERED IN THE CHRONICLES OF MODERN
    JAPANESE POLITICS. FOR ONLY THE SECOND TIME IN JAPAN'S
    PARLIMANENTARY HISTORY, TWO DIFFERENT CANDIDATES FOR PRIME
    MINISTER WERE NOMINATED BY THE TWO HOUSE OF THE DIET.
    KAIFU'S ELECTION ALLOWED THE RULING LIBERAL DEMOCRATIC PARTY
    TO REMAIN IN POWER, BUT THE SINGLE-PARTY DOMINANCE IS NOT AS

STRONG AS IT WAS BEFORE.

01134 ATTWOOD, D.W.
DOES COMPETITION HELP COOPERATION?
JOURNAL OF DEVELOPMENT STUDIES, 26(1) (OCT 89), 5-27.
CO-OPERATIVE SUGAR FACTORIES IN WESTERN INDIA ARE
ECONOMICALLY SUCCESSFUL EVEN THOUGH RIFE WITH FACTIONAL
POLITICS. SINCE THEY ARE NOT HEAVILY SUBSIDISED, WHAT MAKES
THEM OPERATE EFFICIENTLY? POLITICAL COMPETITION BETWEEN
ELECTED LEADERS OF NEIGHBOURING FACTORIES DRIVES THEM TO
COMPETE ECONOMICALLY. THIS IN TURN DRIVES THEM TO EXPAND,
INNOVATE AND DIVERSIFY PRODUCTION. NOTHING IN THE STANDARD
RHETORIC OF CO-OPERATION EXPLAINS THIS TENDENCY TOWARD
COMPETITIVE RISK-TAKING. LIKEWISE, STANDARD ECONOMIC
THEORIES OF COMPETITION OVERLOOK THE POLITICAL FORCES WHICH
DRIVE THESE INDUSTRIAL LEADERS.

01135 ATTYAS, S.
A VISIT TO THE TOMBS
MIDDLE EAST REPORT, 19(5) (SEP 89), 14.
THE ARTICLE RECOUNTS THE VISIT OF NEVZAT HELVACI, THE
PRESIDENT OF THE TURKISH HUMAN RIGHTS ASSOCIATION, TO THE
"TOMBS" PRISON IN NEW YORK CITY. THE SEEMINGLY GOOD AND
EERIELY QUIET CONDITIONS LED HELVACI TO SUSPECT THAT THE
TOMBS IS NOT A TYPICAL US PRISON. APPARENTLY HIS SUSPICIONS
HAVE SOME JUSTIFICATION; A VISIT, TO RIKERS, ANOTHER NEW
YORK PRISON WITH A MUCH WORSE REPUTATION WAS DENIED BY
AUTHORITIES.

01136 AUCION, P.
MIDDLE MANAGERS--THE CRUCIAL LINK: DISCUSSION SUMMARY
CANADIAN PUBLIC ADMINISTRATION, 32(2) (SUM 89), 187-209.
THE AUTHOR CONSIDERS BROAD ISSUES OF PUBLIC MIDDLE
MANAGEMENT, INCLUDING THE DEFINITION, CHALLENGES, AND
TRAINING AND DEVELOPMENT OF MIDDLE MANAGERS.

01137 AUDI, M.J.
AMBEDKAR'S STRUGGLE FOR UNTOUCHABLES: REFLECTIONS
INDIAN JOURNAL OF POLITICAL SCIENCE, L(3) (JUL 89),
307-320.
AMBEDKAR WAS A THINKER AND AN ACTIVIST WHO GREATLY
INFLUENCED INDIA'S DEVELOPMENT, BUT THE PROBLEM WITH WHICH
HE STRUGGLED CONTINUES TO DEFY SOLUTION. BORN AS AN
UNTOUCHABLE, AMBEDKAR HAD INTIMATE KNOWLEDGE OF THEIR
DISABILITIES, HUMILIATIONS, AND SUFFERINGS, AND HE LABORED
TO LIBERATE THEM FROM BONDAGE. HIS GOAL WAS TO RAISE THEM TO
THEIR RIGHTFUL STATUS IN SOCIETY. AMBEDKAR'S STRUGGLE FOR
CIVIL RIGHTS CAN BE DIVIDED INTO TWO PHASES: THE COLONIAL
PERIOD (1925-1947) AND THE SHARAJ PERIOD (1947-1956).

01138 AUDI, R.
THE SEPARATION OF CHURCH AND STATE AND THE OBLIGATIONS OF
CITIZENSHIP
PHILOSOPHY AND PUBLIC AFFAIRS, 18(3) (SUM 89), 259-296.
THIS ARTICLE APPROACHES THE SEPARATION OF CHURCH AND
STATE FROM A CONCEPTUAL AND MORAL STAND POINT. TWO AIMS ARE
SATISFIED: 1) TO CLARIFY THE TRADITIONAL SEPARATION DOCTRINE,
2) TO ASCERTAIN WHAT RESTRICTIONS ON INDIVIDUAL CONDUCT
SHOULD ACCOMPANY A COMMITMENT TO SEPARATION OF CHURCH AND
STATE.

01139 AUERBACH, Y.
LEGITIMATION FOR TURNING-POINT DECISIONS IN FOREIGN POLICY:
ISRAEL VIS-A-VIS GERMANY 1952 AND EGYPT 1977
REVIEW OF INTERNATIONAL STUDIES, 15(4) (OCT 89), 329-340.
THIS PAPER EXAMINES THE TRANSITION FROM WAR AND CONFLICT
TO PEACE AND COOPERATION IN THE LEGITIMATION OF THE TURNING-
POINT DECISIONS WHICH ENGENIER NORMALIZATION IN RELATIONS
BETWEEN ENEMIES. IT PRESENTS AN ANALYTICAL FRAME WORK WHICH
FACILITATES THE STUDY OF STRATEGIES EMPLOYED BY DECISION
MAKERS IN THEIR EFFORTS TO WIN SUPPORT FOR TURNING-POINT
DECISIONS ENTAILING TRANSITIONS FROM CONFLICT TO PEACE

01140 AUKEN, S.
ON COOPERATION -- FROM THE STANDPOINT OF REALISM
WORLD MARXIST REVIEW, 31(10) (OCT 88), 21-27.
THE SOCIAL DEMOCRATS WERE AND REMAIN THE LARGEST
COMPONENT OF THE LEFT-WING FORCES AND THE MOST INFLUENTIAL
POLITICAL PARTY IN DENMARK (ABOUT 30 PER CENT OF THE VOTES
AT MAY'S EARLY PARLIAMENTARY ELECTIONS). IN THIS ARTICLE, THE
CHAIRMAN OF THE SOCIAL-DEMOCRATIC PARTY OF DENMARK SHARES
HIS THOUGHTS ABOUT THE COUNTRY'S SECURITY POLICY AND ABOUT
THE POTENTIAL FOR INTERACTION BETWEEN THE SUPPORTERS OF
PEACE AND PROGRESS BOTH AT HOME AND INTERNATIONALLY.

01141 AUNG-THWIN, M.
BURMESE DAYS
FOREIGN AFFAIRS, 68(2) (SPR 89), 143-161.
THE 1988 UPRISING AGAINST BURMA'S AUTHORITARIAN REGIME
WAS LONG OVERDUE. BUT IT IS TOO EARLY TO PREDICT WHAT FRUIT
THE SHSORT-LIVED DEMOCRACY MOVEMENT WILL BEAR BECAUSE, FOR
AS LONG AS HE LIVES, NE WIN IS LIKELY TO CONTROL BURMESE
POLITICAL DEVELOPMENTS, NO MATTER WHO IS TITULARLY AT THE
HELM OF GOVERNMENT.

01142 AURANZEB, A.
HOW UGANDA'S FREEDOM TRAIN WAS DERAILED
SOUTH, (107) (SEP 89), 20-21.
WHEN BORDER CLASHES ERUPTED BETWEEN UGANDA AND KENYA IN
1988, THE KENYAN GOVERNMENT IMMEDIATELY BLAMED LIBYAN
INVOLVEMENT. BUT IT HAS BECOME INCREASINGLY EVIDENT THAT THE
ROOT CAUSE IS THE LOSSES INFLICTED ON PRIVATE ROAD TRANSPORT
BUSINESS INTERESTS CLOSE TO THE KENYAN POLITICAL LEADERSHIP.
UGANDAN PRESIDENT YOWERI MUSEVENI'S QUEST FOR ECONOMIC
INDEPENDENCE AND HIS DECISION TO SHIP COFFEE VIA RAILWAYS
INSTEAD OF ROAD HAULAGE COMPANIES HAVE DAMAGED TRANSPORT
BUSINESSES OWNED BY KENYAN CABINET MINISTERS AND
PARLIAMENTARIANS.

01143 AUSTER, L.
THE REGENT'S ROUND TABLE
NATIONAL REVIEW, 61(23) (DEC 89), 18-21.
THIS ARTICLE EXAMINES THE EDUCATIONAL CHALLENGES FACED
BY AMERICAN SCHOOLS AS DECISIONS ABOUT WHAT TO TEACH
MINORITIES IS DISCUSSED. IT ANALYSES NEW YORK STATE'S ANSWER
TO THE EDUCATION CRISIS: MORE "RACIAL SENSITIVITY" IN THE
CURRICULUM. A REPORT, RECENTLY ISSUED BY NEW YORK STATE
COMMISSIONER OF EDUCATION SUGGESTS A CHANGE IN EMPHASIS, A
DISMANTLING OF THE DOMINANT CULTURE.

01144 AUSTIN, R.E.
THE CHANGING POLITICAL ECONOMY OF HOSPITALS: THE EMERGENCE
OF THE "BUSINESS MODEL" HOSPITAL
DISSERTATION ABSTRACTS INTERNATIONAL, 50(5) (NOV 89),
1429-A.
FORCES DEMANDING COST CONTAINMENT ARE NOW FORGING NEW
POLITICAL AND ECONOMIC OPERATING RULES FOR HEALTH CARE
PROVIDERS. THIS DISSERTATION DESCRIBES THE NEW POLITICAL
ECONOMY OF HEALTH CARE AND IDENTIFIES THE CRUCIAL ISSUES
FACED BY HOSPITAL ADMINISTRATORS AND SPECIFIC ACTIONS THEY
ARE TAKING TO ADAPT TO THEIR NEW ENVIRONMENT. EMERGING
PUBLIC POLICY ISSUES ARE DISCUSSED ALONG WITH
RECOMMENDATIONS AS TO HOW POLICY-MAKERS CAN DEAL WITH THEM.

01145 AUYEUNG, P.K.
CHINA'S ECLECTIC THEORY OF TAXATION
CHINA REPORT, 25(2) (APR 89), 121-133.
THIS ARTICLE EXPLORES THE THEORETICAL ISSUES UNDERLYING
THE DEVELOPMENT OF THE CHINESE TAX SYSTEM. IT ADDRESSES
WHETHER CHINA HAS DEVELOPED A THEORY OF TAXATION DURING THE
PROCESS OF ITS TAX EVOLUTION. IT GIVES A BRIEF OVERVIEW OF
SOME BASIC WESTERN THEORIES AND ANALYSES HOW THE CHINESE
APPROACH DIFFERS FROM THAT OF THE WEST. IT CONCLUDES THAT
CHINA MAY LACK A COHERENT PLAN FOR TAX REFORM BECAUSE THE
TAX SYSTEM 'JUST GREW.'

01146 AVERYT, W.F.
QUEBEC'S ECONOMIC DEVELOPMENT POLICIES, 1960-1987: BETWEEN
ETATISME AND PRIVATISATION
AMERICAN REVIEW OF CANADIAN STUDIES, 19(2) (SUM 89),
159-176.
THIS PAPER ATTEMPTS TO INTERPRET THE PAST THREE DECADES
OF SHARP STRUCTURAL CHANGES IN THE ECONOMY OF QUEBEC, IT
FOCUSES ON THREE MAJOR EFFECTS OF THE REVOLUTION TRANQUILLE:
THE RISE OF A GROWTH IDEOLOGY OF SECULAR MODERNIZATION, THE
CREATION OF FRANCOPHONE MANAGERIAL AND SKILLED LABOR FORCES,
AND THE REPOSITIONING OF QUEBEC IN THE GLOBAL MARKET.

01147 AVILA, F.A. JR.
PRUDENCE IN THE STATECRAFT OF EDMUND BURKE
DISSERTATION ABSTRACTS INTERNATIONAL, 50(6) (DEC 89),
1785-A.
THE AUTHOR STUDIES THE CONFLICT BETWEEN PRUDENCE AND
THEORY IN THE POLITICAL THOUGHT OF EDMUND BURKE.

01148 AVNERY, U.
THE INTIFADA: SUBSTANCE AND ILLUSION
NEW OUTLOOK, 32(11-12 (297-298)) (NOV 89), 12-13.
AFTER TWO YEARS OF THE INTIFADA, THE ISRAELI AND
AMERICAN GOVERNMENTS STILL REFUSE TO COME TO GRIPS WITH THE
NEW PALESTINIAN REALITY. IF THIS SITUATION CONTINUES, THERE
COULD BE A DRASTIC UPSURGE IN PALESTINIAN VIOLENCE, MARKING
A NEW CHAPTER IN THE ISRAELI-PALESTINIAN TRAGEDY.

01149 AWASTHI, D.
LENGTHY LEGALESE
INDIA TODAY, XIV(11) (JUN 89), 30-31.
THIS ARTICLE DESCRIBES HOW ALL THE SENSATIONAL ELEMENTS
OF THE SYED MODI MURDER CASE - WHICH AT ONE TIME SEEMED
WOULD AFFECT THE COURSE OF STATE POLIITICS HAVE BEEN
SMOTLERED UNDER REAMS OF LEGALESE. THE CASE HAS COME UP IN
THE COURTS ON 27 DIFFERENT OCASSIONS IN THE PAST NINE MONTH,
WITH NO SIGN OF THE TRIAL ACTUALLY BEGINNING. DESPERATE
HAIRSPLITTING AND MORE ELABORATE DELAY TACTICS ARE LIKELY TO
CONTINUE.

01150 AWASTHI, D.
POLL BY PROXY

INDIA TODAY, XIV(3) (FEB 89), 51-52.
IN THE JANUARY 1989 LOCAL ELECTIONS IN UTTAR PRADESH,
THE MAJOR POLITICAL PARTIES SHIED AWAY OR FOUGHT BY PROXY.
THERE WAS TOO MUCH AT STAKE FOR BOTH THE CONGRESS (I) AND
THE JANATA DAL TO RISK TESTING THE POLITICAL WATERS AT A
TIME WHEN THE COUNTRY WAS POISED AT THE THRESHOLD OF A
GENERAL ELECTION.

01151 AXELGARD, F.
AMERICA'S MINIMALIST APPROACH
MIDDLE EAST INTERNATIONAL, (346) (MAR 89), 3-4.
THE BUSH ADMINISTRATION IS ADOPTING A SLOW, LOW-KEY
APPROACH TO THE MIDEAST, URGING ISRAEL TO CONSIDER STEPS
THAT WOULD EASE TENSIONS IN THE OCCUPIED TERRITORIES AND
PRODUCE AN ENVIRONMENT FOR EVENTUAL, CONSTRUCTIVE ISRAELI-
PALESTINIAN NEGOTIATIONS. TO THIS END, WASHINGTON HAS
PROPOSED THAT ISRAEL CONSIDER RELEASING SOME OF THE
IMPRISONED PALESTINIANS, EASING HARSH SECURITY MEASURES, AND
EASING RESTRICTIONS ON ECONOMIC ACTIVITY IN THE OCCUPIED
TERRITORIES.

01152 AXELGARD, F.
BUSH'S FIRST CRISIS
MIDDLE EAST INTERNATIONAL, 356 (AUG 89), 4-5.
THE PURPORTED HANGING OF LT. COLONEL WILLIAM R HIGGINS,
BY THE ORGANISATION OF THE OPPRESSED ON EARTH, HAS QUICKLY
BECOME A MAJOR FOREIGN POLICY CRISIS FOR THE BUSH
ADMINISTRATION, AND THEIR HOPES AND PLANS TO PRESS FOR AN
END OF HOSTILITY AND BITTERNESS ON SEVERAL FRONTS ACROSS THE
MIDDLE EAST. TO DATE, HIS RESPONSE CAN BE INTERPRETED ON TWO
LEVELS AT LEAST - AS HOPE THAT POLITICAL DIALOGUE MAY YET
FREE THE HOSTAGES, AND AS HOPE THAT THIS PRESIDENT, UNLIKE
HIS TWO IMMEDIATE PREDECESSORS, MIGHT ESCAPE THE PERSONAL
AND POLITICAL NIGHTMARE OF MANIPULATION BY EXTREMISTS
HOLDING AMERICAN HOSTAGES ABROAD.

01153 AXELGARD, F.
DIFFICULTIES FOR BUSH
MIDDLE EAST INTERNATIONAL, (358) (SEP 89), 4-5.
THE UNITED STATES DIALOGUE WITH THE PLO HAS GRINDED DOWN
TO A HALT IN RECENT WEEKS. PLO CHAIRMAN, YASSER ARAFAT, IS
UNDER INTENSE PRESSURE FROM HIS SUPPORTERS TO MAKE NO MORE
CONCESSIONS TO THE US OR ISRAEL. THE US IS EQUALLY UNWILLING
TO MOVE FROM ITS ORIGINAL STANCE. HOWEVER, US-ISRAEL
RELATIONS ARE MARKED BY INCREASING TENSION AS ISRAELI
REPRESSION OF THE INTIFADA BECOMES INCREASINGLY BRUTAL.
HOWEVER, PERHAPS THE MOST IMPORTANT EVENT IN THE ONGOING
NEGOTIATING DRAMA WILL BE THE DECISION TO GRANT A VISA TO
YASSER ARAFAT TO ADDRESS THE UNITED NATIONS. IF THE US
REVERSES ITS EARLIER POSITION AND GRANTS THE VISA TO ARAFAT,
THE PLO CHAIRMAN WILL BE UNDER SIGNIFICANT PRESSURE TO BREAK
THE NEGOTIATIONS OUT OF THE CURRENT IMPASSE.

01154 AXELGARD, F.
IRAQ: THE POSTWAR POLITICAL SETTING
AMERICAN-ARAB AFFAIRS, (28) (SPR 89), 30-37.
THE ARTICLE EXAMINES WHAT PERHAPS WILL BECOME IRAQ'S
MOST INTERESTING AND CRITICAL POLITICAL ERA SINCE THE
REVOLUTION OF 1958. IT OUTLINES THE PRESSURE FELT BY IRAQI
PRESIDENT SADDAM HUSSEIN AND THE RULING BAATH PARTY TO
REFORM IRAQ'S POLITICAL SYSTEM. THIS PRESSURE HAS INCREASED
SINCE THE CESSATION OF THE IRAN-IRAQ WAR. AS OF YET, HUSSEIN
HAS BEEN ABLE TO OUTMANEUVER HIS OPPONENTS AND LITTLE REFORM
HAS TAKEN PLACE. THE ARTICLE EXAMINES THE 1989 NATIONAL-
ASSEMBLY ELECTION AND OTHER EVENTS TO ANALYZE THE FUTURE OF
THE IRAQI POLITICAL SYSTEM. IT CONCLUDES THAT ALTHOUGH
SIGNIFICANT, LONG-TERM REFORM REMAINS UNLIKELY, HUSSEIN WILL
PROBABLY CONCEDE SOMEWHAT TO HIS OPPONENTS' DEMANDS.

01155 AXELGARD, F.
SAUDI ARABIA LOOKS AHEAD
MIDDLE EAST INTERNATIONAL, (346) (MAR 89), 16-17.
THE REGIONAL SECURITY AND POLITICS OF THE GULF ARE
ENTERING A NEW ERA, AS IS EVIDENT IN SAUDI ARABIA.
CONSIDERABLE SAUDI INTEREST HAS BEEN AROUSED BY THE
FORMATION OF THE ARAB COOPERATION COUNCIL. RIYADH'S TIES TO
WASHINGTON REMAIN CENTRAL TO ITS SECURITY, BUT IT IS WIDELY
RECOGNIZED THAT THIS RELATIONSHIP IS LESS "SPECIAL" THAN IT
WAS 10 YEARS AGO.

01156 AXELGARD, F.
SHAMIR IN WASHINGTON: A QUESTION OF NUANCE
MIDDLE EAST INTERNATIONAL, (348) (APR 89), 3-4.
THE ARTICLE ANALYZES THE IMPLICATIONS OF THE VISIT OF
EGYPTIAN PRESIDENT HUSNI MUBARAK AND ISRAELI PRIME MINISTER
YITZHAK SHAMIR TO WASHINGTON D.C. ALTHOUGH SOME DRAMATIC
EVENTS OCCURRED SUCH AS PRESIDENT BUSH'S STATEMENT THAT THE
END OF THE ISRAELI OCCUPATION IS AN AIM OF US POLICY, AND
MUBARAK'S STATEMENT THAT IF SHAMIR IS WILLING TO HOLD
ELECTIONS IN PALESTINE, HE WILL "HELP TO THE MAXIMUM". MOST
ANALYSTS FEEL THAT THE MEETINGS OF LEADERS WAS AT BEST A
SMALL, FIRST STEP IN THE LONG ROAD TO PEACE IN THE MIDEAST
AND A RESOLUTION OF THE PALESTINIAN PROBLEM.

01157 AXELGARD, F.
THE CHALLENGE FACING BUSH
MIDDLE EAST INTERNATIONAL, 352 (JUN 89), 9-10.
THE CURRENT TONE OF THE BUSH ADMINISTRATION'S POSITION
CONVEYS NONE OF THE SENSE OF URGENCY INHERENT IN THE GROWING
VIOLENCE IN THE OCCUPIED TERRITORIES, AND THE GROWING ROLE
OF ISRAELI SETTLERS IN THAT VIOLENCE. BUT NO ONE EXPECTS
WASHINGTON TO REMAIN PERMANENTLY ALOOF FROM THE SUBJECT OF
IRAN. MR BUSH, BEGINNING WITH HIS INAUGURAL SPEECH, HAS
ALREADY LAID OUT SEVERAL HINTS OF HIS OWN INTEREST IN MOVING
TOWARD A MORE NORMAL RELATIONSHIP WITH THE ISLAMIC REPUBLIC.
ALTHOUGH THESE HINTS PREDATED THE RUSHDIE AFFAIR, THEY WERE
REPORTEDLY FED BY A STRONG PERSONAL CONCERN ON THE PART OF
THE PRESIDENT. HENCE FORMULATING AN EFFECTIVE US MIDDLE EAST
POLICY MAY WELL BECOME A "TWO-FRONT" EXERCISE IN THE NOT-TOO-
DISTANT FUTURE - ONE THAT WILL DEMAND ALL OF THE CREDIBILITY
AND CREATIVITY AT MR BUSH'S DISPOSAL.

01158 AXELGARD, F.
THE UNITED STATES: A GROWING SENSE OF URGENCY
MIDDLE EAST INTERNATIONAL, (350) (MAY 89), 9-10.
TIME IS RUNNING SHORT FOR THE PROPOSAL TO ADVANCE THE
MIDDLE EAST PEACE PROCESS BY HOLDING ELECTIONS IN THE WEST
BANK AND GAZA, AND THE BUSH ADMINISTRATION MAY BE
MANOEUVERING TO DO SOMETHING ABOUT IT. SECRETARY OF STATE
BAKER HAS INDICATED THAT THE MIDEAST WILL RECEIVE ATTENTION
DURING HIS VISIT TO MOSCOW IN MAY 1989. IN ADDITION, BAKER
WILL SEND A DELEGATION LED BY DENNIS ROSS TO ISRAEL, JORDAN,
AND EGYPT.

01159 AXELGARD, F.
THE UNITED STATES: THE OUTLOOK FOR BUSH AND BAKER
MIDDLE EAST INTERNATIONAL, (342) (JAN 89), 7-8.
THE AUTHOR CONSIDERS RONALD REAGAN'S POLICY IN THE
MIDEAST AND THE PROSPECTS FOR THE BUSH ADMINISTRATION TO
IMPROVE THE MIDEAST SITUATION.

01160 AXELGARD, F.
US AND RAN: NOT MUCH WORRIED
MIDDLE EAST INTERNATIONAL, (354) (JUL 89), 5-6.
THE US REACTION TO IRANIAN LEADER HASHEMI RAFSANJANI'S
MOSCOW VISIT WAS SURPRISINGLY MUTED. ONLY THE POSSIBILITY OF
SOVIET ARMS TRANSFERS TO IRAN RAISED ANY SIGN OF AGITATION
IN WASHINGTON. THE ONLY EXCEPTION TO THE GENERAL APATHY
TOWARDS IRAN HAS BEEN THE ACTION OF PRESIDENT BUSH. DESPITE
THE WARNINGS FROM THE INTELLIGENCE COMMUNITY THAT ANY
GESTURE OF CONCILIATION WOULD NOT BE TIMELY NOR EFFECTIVE,
PRESIDENT BUSH PURSUED HIS STATED GOAL OF COMPENSATING THE
FAMILIES OF LAST YEAR'S AIRBUS DISASTER.

01161 AXELGARD, F.
WASHINGTON STICKS BY SHAMIR
MIDDLE EAST INTERNATIONAL, (360) (OCT 89), 4-5.
DESPITE WIDESPREAD PUBLIC OPINION IN SUPPORT OF THE
MUBARAK INITIAVE, LEADERS IN WASHINGTON APPEAR TO BE
UNWILLING TO STRONG-ARM ISRAEL INTO ACCEPTING IT. INSTEAD,
THE US REMAINS COMMITTED TO THE SHAMIR PEACE PLAN WHICH
CALLS FOR ELECTIONS IN THE OCCUPIED TERRITORIES. IN ADDITION,
US MILITARY AID TO ISRAEL IS ON THE RISE AS ARE PLANS TO
LEND MILITARY EQUIPMENT AND TO STORE IT IN ISRAEL.

01162 AXELGARD, F. H.
U.S. POLICY TOWARD IRAQ, 1946-1958
DISSERTATION ABSTRACTS INTERNATIONAL, 49(8) (FEB 89),
2381-A.
FROM 1946 TO 1958, AMERICAN POLICY TOWARD IRAQ NEGLECTED
OR UNDERESTIMATED INDIGENOUS POLITICAL SENTIMENT WHILE
EMPHASIZING IRAQ'S POTENTIAL TO HELP CURB SOVIET INFLUENCE
IN THE MIDDLE EAST. BUT THIS STRATEGIC INTEREST BECAME
SECONDARY WHEN IT CONFLICTED WITH US POLICY REGARDING THE
ARAB-ISRAELI SITUATION. DURING THIS TIME, WASHINGTON
VIRTUALLY INSTITUTIONALIZED ITS SECONDARY POSITION IN IRAQ.

01163 AXEN, H.
A SOCIALIST CLASS POSITION AND HUMANITY'S INTERESTS:
PEACEFUL COEXISTENCE TODAY
POLITICAL AFFAIRS, LXVIII(4) (APR 89), 26-30.
BY NATURE, THE CAPITALIST SYSTEM IS UNABLE TO MASTER
GLOBAL PROBLEMS ON ITS OWN. THE NATURE OF THE SOCIALIST
ORDER OF SOCIETY ENABLES IT TO DO SO. BUT AS THINGS STAND
NOW, SOCIALISM ALONE DOES NOT HAVE THE STRENGTH TO ELIMINATE
GLOBAL THREATS. UNDER EXISTING CIRCUMSTANCES, THE PEACEFUL
COEXISTENCE OF SOCIALIST AND CAPITALIST COUNTRIES IS NO
LONGER ONE OF SEVERAL POSSIBILITIES. IT IS THE ONLY WAY.

01164 AXEN, H.
THE IMPERATIVE OF GENERAL HUMAN INTERESTS
WORLD MARXIST REVIEW, 32(4) (APR 89), 5-8.
IN THE EFFORTS TO SOLVE GLOBAL PROBLEMS, ESPECIALLY TO
AVERT A THERMONUCLEAR DISASTER, SOCIALISM HAS LED THE WAY
FOR THE OTHER SOCIAL FORCES AND SYSTEMS, SO ESTABLISHING
ITSELF NOT ONLY AS THE SOCIAL ALTERNATIVE TO CAPITALISM, BUT
ALSO AS THE SAVIOR OF CIVILISATION. THIS IS A MANIFESTATION
OF THE INTERCONNECTION BETWEEN THE SCIENTIFIC AND TECHNICAL

REVOLUTION, AND THE SOCIAL REVOLUTION. SOCIALISM, THE SOCIAL SYSTEM WHOSE VITAL PRINCIPLE IS THE CREATION AND DEFENCE OF PEACE, HAS DONE MOST TO COMPEL IMPERIALISM TO THE LONGEST PERIOD OF PEACE IN OUR CENTURY. SOCIALISM HAS NOW ALSO MANIFESTED ITSELF AS THE SYSTEM WHOSE PROPOSALS FOR COMPREHENSIVE INTERNATIONAL SECURITY AND COOPERATION PAVE THE WAY FOR MANKIND TO SOLVE THE MOST ACUTE PROBLEMS IN A COMMON EFFORT, AND THEREBY FOR SURVIVAL AND FRESH PERSPECTIVES IN SOCIAL DEVELOPMENT.

01165 AYALA, C.J.
    THEORIES OF BIG BUSINESS IN AMERICAN SOCIETY
    CRITICAL SOCIOLOGY, 16(23) (SUM 89), 91-119.
       THIS PAPER EXAMINES THE ROBBER BARON, MANAGERIAL, AND BANK SPHERE APPROACHES TO THE STRUCTURE OF BIG BUSINESS IN THE UNITED STATES. THE ROBBER BARON SCHOOL ARGUES THAT BIG BUSINESS REPRESENTS A HISTORICAL REGRESSION WHICH FEUDALIZED THE ECONOMY; THE MANAGERIAL SCHOOL HAS SEVERAL VARIANTS, ALL OF WHICH ARGUE THAT MANAGERS RULE THE ECONOMY; THE BANK SPHERE SCHOOL ARGUES THAT BANKS RULE THE ECONOMY.

01166 AYANIAN, R.
    NUCLEAR CONSEQUENCES OF THE WELFARE STATE REVISITED: DANGER IN THE DATA
    PUBLIC CHOICE, 61(2) (MAY 89), 167-170.
       THE AUTHOR RE-EXAMINES THE "PARKINSON STRATEGY" OF THE USSR. THE THEORY STATES THAT THE USSR STOCKPILED NUCLEAR WEAPONS AS US FEDERAL NON-DEFENSE BUDGET CLAIMS ON US GNP HAVE RISEN, SINCE SUCH CLAIMS INCREASINGLY PRE-EMPT THE RESOURCES REQUIRED FOR A US STOCKPILING RESPONSE. HOWEVER, THE RELEASE OF MORE RECENT FIGURES BY THE DEPARTMENT OF DEFENSE NECESSITATE A RE-EXAMINATION OF THE THEORY. THE RE-EXAMINATION REVEALS A POSITIVE, BUT NOW STATISTICALLY INSIGNIFICANT RELATION BETWEEN THE SOVIET TO US NUCLEAR FORCE RATIOS AND THE US NON-DEFENSE BUDGET SHARE OF THE GNP. THE AUTHOR STANDS CORRECTED!

01167 AYANIAN, R.
    PERESTROIKA AND ARMS CONTROL
    CONTEMPORARY POLICY ISSUES, VII(1) (JAN 89), 70-74.
       MIKHAIL GORBACHEV'S PERESTROIKA HAS HAD ITS MOST CONSPICUOUS SUCCESS IN RESTRUCTURING U.S.-SOVIET RELATIONS. THE INF TREATY WITH THE UNITED STATES AND THE TALKS NOW UNDER WAY ON A PROSPECTIVE START AGREEMENT ARE MAJOR DEVELOPMENTS IN INTERNATIONAL ARMS CONTROL. BUT SOVIET START PROPOSALS ARE A THREAT TO NUCLEAR DETERRENCE. START REDUCTIONS IN STRATEGIC NUCLEAR WEAPONS WILL DECREASE U.S. SECURITY DANGEROUSLY UNLESS THEY ARE IMPLEMENTED UNDER THE PROTECTIVE UMBRELLA OF A U.S. MISSILE DEFENSE SYSTEM.

01168 AYANIAN, R.
    POLITICAL RISK, NATIONAL DEFENSE AND THE DOLLAR
    ECONOMIC INQUIRY, 26(2) (APR 88), 345-352.
       THIS PAPER PROVIDES EVIDENCE THAT POLITICAL RISK IS A SIGNIFICANT DETERMINANT IN THE REAL U.S. EXCHANGE RATE, AND THUS, BY IMPLICATION, A MAJOR ARGUMENT IN FOREIGN ASSET DEMAND FUNCTIONS. IT ARGUES THAT THE SOVIET MILITARY THREAT TO THE WEST HAS CREATED A POPULATION OF FOREIGN INVESTORS FOR WHOM U.S. MILITARY SECURITY IS A MAJOR DETERMINATE OF THE PROPORTION OF THEIR WEALTH WHICH THEY WISH TO KEEP IN THE U.S. THE REAL TRADE-WEIGHTED DOLLAR AND THE DEFENSE SHARE OF THE GNP IS ANALYSED.

01169 AYISI, R.A.
    THE MOST INNOCENT VICTIMS
    AFRICA REPORT, 34(5) (SEP 89), 59-61.
       SOME 200,000 CHILDREN HAVE BEEN SEPARATED FROM THEIR FAMILIES AS A RESULT OF THE WAR IN MOZAMBIQUE, INCLUDING MANY YOUNGSTERS WHO HAVE BEEN KIDNAPPED BY RENAMO. EFFORTS ARE BEING MADE TO REUNITE THESE CHILDREN WITH THEIR FAMILIES AND REHABILITATE THEM, BUT THEY BEAR DEEP PSYCHOLOGICAL SCARS FROM THEIR WAR EXPERIENCES.

01170 AYKAN, M.B.
    IDEOLOGY AND NATIONAL INTEREST IN TURKISH FOREIGN POLICY TOWARD THE MUSLIM WORLD: 1960-1987
    DISSERTATION ABSTRACTS INTERNATIONAL, 49(11) (MAY 89), 3496-A.
       THE AUTHOR CONSIDERS WHETHER THERE HAS BEEN A DEVIATION FROM THE WESTERN-ORIENTED, SECULAR KEMALIST LINE IN TURKISH FOREIGN POLICY SINCE THE DEATH OF ATATURK. HE CONCLUDES THAT THE IDEOLOGICAL FOUNDATIONS OF THE TURKISH STATE HAVE NOT BEEN BASICALLY CHALLENGED FROM THE DEATH OF ATATURK UNTIL THE PRESENT, EVEN THOUGH THEY HAVE BEEN ADAPTED TO NEW DOMESTIC AND INTERNATIONAL CIRCUMSTANCES AS NECESSITATED BY TURKISH NATIONAL INTERESTS. MOREOVER, TURKEY'S EFFORTS TO DEVELOP ITS RELATIONS WITH THE ISLAMIC WORLD HAVE NOT DEVIATED FROM ATATURK'S FOREIGN POLICY.

01171 AYLEN, L.
    TREASURES OF THE NATION, BURDENS OF THE PEOPLE
    ENCOUNTER, LXXIII(3) (SEP 89), 65-70.
       THERE ARE FOUR MAIN BLACK SOUTH AFRICAN POLITICAL PARTIES--EACH WITH ITS OWN VISION OF A FREE SOUTH AFRICA:

AZAPO, PAC, INKATHA, AND THE ANC-UDF ALLIANCE. THE ANC IS BANNED IN SOUTH AFRICA, BUT THE UDF FOLLOWS THE SAME POLICIES. THE MASS DEMOCRATIC MOVEMENT IS A LOOSE GROUPING OF POLITICAL ORGANIZATIONS FORMED PRIMARILY TO PROTEST THE WHITE ELECTIONS SCHEDULED FOR SEPTEMBER 1989. INKATHA WAS FOUNDED BY ZULUS IN 1975, WITH THE BACKING OF THE ANC, BUT THE TWO ORGANIZATIONS SPLIT IN 1979.

01172 AYOOB, M.
    INDIA IN SOUTH ASIA: THE QUEST FOR REGIONAL PREDOMINANCE
    WORLD POLICY JOURNAL, (WIN 89), 107-133.
       THIS ARTICLE EXPLORES THE IMPORTANCE OF "REGIONAL INFLUENTIALS" LIKE INDIA WHICH CAN BE EXPECTED TO GROW, AND WITH IT INTERNATIONAL CONCERN ABOUT THE POWER THEY EXERCISE. IT EXAMINES NEW DELHI'S MILITARY CAPACITY TO AFFECT OUTCOMES IN SOUTH ASIA AND ALSO ITS POLITICAL WILL TO MOLD THE REGIONAL SECURITY ENVIRONMENT SO AS TO ENHANCE INDIAN POLITICAL AND SECURITY INTERESTS. IT ALSO DETAILS INDIA'S NAVAL BUILDUP; ITS CONSENSUS ON FOREIGN AFFAIRS; AND ITS RELATIONSHIP WITH CHINA, PAKISTAN, SRI LANKA, AND THE UNITED STATES.

01173 AYOOB, M.
    THE THIRD WORLD IN THE SYSTEM OF STATES: ACUTE SCHIZOPHRENIA OR GROWING PAINS?
    INTERNATIONAL STUDIES QUARTERLY, 33(1) (MAR 89), 67-80.
       THIS ARTICLE ATTEMPTS TO LOCATE AND UNDERSTAND THE PLACE OF THIRD WORLD STATES IN THE INTERNATIONAL SYSTEM BOTH IN TERMS OF THEIR COLLECTIVE IMPACT ON THE SYSTEM AS THE "INTRUDER" ELEMENT INTO THE EUROCENTRIC SYSTEM OF STATES AND IN TERMS OF THEIR ROLE AS INDIVIDUAL NEW SOVEREIGN STATES TRYING TO ADJUST TO AN INTERNATIONAL ORDER THAT CAN ONLY BE DEFINED AS AN "ANARCHICAL SOCIETY." IT IS ARGUED THAT AN EXPANDED DEFINITION OF THE CONCEPT OF "SECURITY" IS ESSENTIAL FOR THE CONSTRUCTION OF ANY PARADIGM THAT WOULD HAVE SUFFICIENT POWER TO EXPLAIN WHY THIRD WORLD STATES BEHAVE AS THEY DO WITHIN THE INTERNATIONAL SYSTEM. IT IS ALSO ARGUED THAT THE PRESENT DIFFICULTIES THEY FACE IN ADJUSTING TO THE SYSTEM OF SOVEREIGN STATES IS ANALOGOUS TO THE GROWING PAINS OF ADOLESCENCE RATHER THAN TO THE SCHIZOPHRENIA OF THE DEMENTED.

01174 AYUBI, N.N.
    BUREAUCRACY AND DEVELOPMENT IN EGYPT TODAY
    JOURNAL OF ASIAN AND AFRICAN STUDIES, XXIV(1-2) (1989), 62-78.
       IN SPITE OF THE ADOPTION OF AN OPEN DOOR ECONOMIC POLICY, THE SIZE OF THE EGYPTIAN BUREAUCRACY CONTINUES TO GROW, AND ITS CONTROL FUNCTIONS REMAIN QUITE SIGNIFICANT. THERE IS VERY LITTLE RETRENCHMENT IN THE ECONOMIC ROLE OF THE BUREAUCRACY, ALTHOUGH THAT ROLE IS NOW MUCH LESS INTEGRATED WITH ANY COMPREHENSIVE PLANS FOR NATIONAL DEVELOPMENT. THE MAIN PREFERENCE SEEMS TO BE FOR A JOINT VENTURE FORMULA BETWEEN THE PUBLIC SECTOR AND FOREIGN CAPITAL. THE MOST IMPORTANT CASUALTY OF THIS PRACTICE HAS BEEN THE EGYPTIAN PUBLIC SECTOR ITSELF.

01175 AYYAD, A. A.
    THE POLITICS OF REFORMIST ISLAM: MUHAMMAD ABDUH AND HASAN AL-BANNA
    DISSERTATION ABSTRACTS INTERNATIONAL, 49(8) (FEB 89), 2362-A.
       TO UNDERSTAND THE FOUNDATIONS AND NATURE OF THE MODERN ISLAMIC REFORM MOVEMENT, THE AUTHOR STUDIES THE REFORM PROGRAMS OF MUHAMMAD AB DUH (1849-1905) AND HASAN AL-BANNA (1906-1949). HE FOCUSES ON THE DIVERGENCE OF ABDUH'S AND AL-BANNA'S POSITION ON SOCIOECONOMIC AND POLITICAL ISSUES IN MODERN EGYPT.

01176 AZEL, J.
    ASSESSING THE CARIBBEAN BASIN INITIATIVE: THEORETICAL CONSIDERATIONS AND EMPIRICAL TESTS OF A US FOREIGN ECONOMIC POLICY FORMULATION
    DISSERTATION ABSTRACTS INTERNATIONAL, 50(3) (SEP 89), 786-A.
       IN FEBRUARY 1982, PRESIDENT REAGAN ANNOUNCED THE CARRIBBEAN BASIC INITIATIVE (CBI), WHICH WAS DESIGNED TO ASSIST THE SMALL DEVELOPING COUNTRIES OF THE CARRIBBEAN AND CENTRAL AMERICA. THIS DISSERTATION ASSESSES THE EFFECTIVENESS OF THE CBI IN A SCHOLARLY FASHION AND CONCLUDES THAT IT HAS FAILED.

01177 AZICRI, M.
    COMPARING TWO SOCIAL REVOLUTIONS: THE DYNAMICS OF CHANGE IN CUBA AND NICARAGUA
    JOURNAL OF COMMUNIST STUDIES, 5(4) (DEC 89), 17-39.
       A COMPARATIVE STUDY OF THE CUBAN AND NICARAGUAN REVOLUTIONS REVEALS INTERESTING POLITICAL ISSUES RELATED TO THE DYNAMICS OF THEIR PROCESSES OF POLITICAL AND SOCIO-ECONOMIC CHANGE. DIFFERENCES IN THE TWO REVOLUTIONS IDEOLOGIES AND POLITICAL CULTURES, DIFFERENT TIMING OF THE PROCESS OF INSTITUTIONALIZATION OF THE TWO REVOLUTIONS, CONTRASTING ELECTORAL EXPERIENCES, AND CONSTITUTIONS OF QUITE DISTINCT TYPES HAVE LED TO THE ESTABLISHMENT OF QUITE

DIVERGENT POLITICAL SYSTEMS. WHILE EMANATING FROM VERY SIMILAR HISTORICAL AND GEOGRAPHICAL CONTEXTS AND SHARING SUBSTANTIVE COMMON FEATURES, THE CUBAN AND NICARAGUAN REVOLUTIONS ARE QUITE DIFFERENT, PROVIDING TWO CONTRASTING MODELS OF REVOLUTIONARY CHANGE.

01178 AZIZ, A.
ETHNIC CONFLICT IN SRI LANKA: AN ANALYSIS.
SCANDINAVIAN JOURNAL OF DEVELOPMENT ALTERNATIVES, 8(3) (SEP 89), 111-122.
IN DEALING WITH THE QUESTION OF THE ETHNIC CONFLICT IN SRI LANKA THE ARTICLE BEGINS BY QUOTING THE STATEMENT ON "THE REGISTRATION OF ELECTORS BILL" WHICH HAS PASSED BY SRI LANKA PARLIAMENT IN APRIL 1989. IT THEN EXPLORES THE ETHNIC PROBLEMS RESULTING FROM THE ENTITLEMENT TO RIGHT OF VOTE FOR THE PERSONS OF RECENT INDIAN ORIGIN. THE SOULBURY COMMISSION FOR POLITICAL REFORMS IS EXPLORED IN GREAT DETAIL. IT OBSERVES THAT WHILE THE PROBLEM OF THE TAMILS IS BEING SETTLED, THE QUESTION OF THE MUSLIMS IN THE EASTERN PROVINCES STILL REMAINS TO BE SOLVED.

01179 AZNAM, S.
A QUESTION OF IDENTITY
FAR EASTERN ECONOMIC REVIEW, 141(32) (AUG 88), 31.
THE MALAYSIAN CHINESE ASSOCIATION, THE LARGEST CHINESE POLITICAL PARTY IN THE RULING NATIONAL FRONT COALITION, HAS ALWAYS BEEN A CONSERVATIVE PARTY. BUT TODAY'S SHIFTING POLITICAL AND ECONOMIC DEMANDS REQUIRE A DIFFERENT IDENTITY, ONE THAT THE MCA HAS OF YET FAILED TO CREATE. INSTEAD THEY HAVE BEEN ROCKED BY A RECENT WAVE OF ARRESTS OF FORMER PARTY LEADERS FOR CRIMINAL BREACH OF TRUST.

01180 AZNAM, S.
AN END TO TOLERANCE
FAR EASTERN ECONOMIC REVIEW, 141(37) (SEP 88), 29-30.
MALAYSIA IS PLANNING TO TIGHTEN ITS REFUGEE POLICY THAT HAS BEEN IGNORED SINCE THE 1979 GENEVA CONFERENCE ON REFUGEES. THE POLICY NOW IS THAT ANY REFUGEE WHO LANDS WILL BE DEEMED AN ILLEGAL IMMIGRANT AND DEPORTED. UP TO NOW, MALAYSIA HAS ACCEPTED REFUGEES BECAUSE THE US, CANADA, AND AUSTRALIA HAVE BEEN FAIRLY RECEPTIVE IN RESETTLING REFUGEES FROM MALAYSIAN CAMPS. HOWEVER, THE NUMBER OF ARRIVALS IS NOW ALMOST DOUBLE THE NUMBER OF DEPARTURES.

01181 AZNAM, S.
JUDGEMENT WEEK
FAR EASTERN ECONOMIC REVIEW, 141(33) (AUG 88), 22-23.
MALAYSIAN PRIME MINISTER DATUK SERI MAHATHIR MOHAMAD HAS JUMPED TWO HURDLES CENTERING AROUND MALAYSIA'S COURTS. THE FIRST INVOLVED THE DISMISSAL OF SUPREME COURT LORD PRESIDENT TUN MOHAMED SALLEH ABAS ON FIVE CHARGES OF MISCONDUCT. STATED ONE LEGAL SOURCE: "FROM NOW ON, THE JUDICIARY WILL BE COWED." THE OTHER SUCCESS OF THE PRIME MINISTER INVOLVED THE ORIGINIAL RULING PARTY: UNITED MALAYS NATIONAL ORGANIZATION (UMNO). 11 DISSIDENTS WERE ATTEMPTING TO RESUSCITATE THE PARTY AT THE EXPENSE OF MAHATHIR'S NEW UMNC PARTY. HOWEVER, THE COURTS RULED IN FAVOR OF THE PRIME MINISTER WHO NOW CAN PROCEED WITH THE NEW UMNO AS THE COUNTRY'S DE FACTO RULING PARTY.

01182 AZNAM, S.
OBJECTIONS OVERRULED
FAR EASTERN ECONOMIC REVIEW, 141(29) (JUL 88), 12-13.
IN MALAYSIA THERE IS AN ONGOING STRUGGLE BETWEEN MALAYSIA'S EXECUTIVE AND JUDICIARY. GOVERNMENT MOVES HAVE MET SHARP REACTIONS FROM LAWYERS AND JUDGES. JUDICIAL HEADS HAVE ROLLED AS THE EXECUTIVE, WITH THE APPROVAL OF THE KING, HAS SUSPENDED LORD PRESIDENT TUN MOHAMMED SALLEH ABAS AND FIVE OTHER SUPREME COURT JUDGES. LAWYERS AND JUDGES HAVE RALLIED BEHIND THE SUSPENDED JUDGES AND A COMPLEX SERIES OF CONTEMPT PROCEEDINGS HAVE BEEN INITIATED. THE FUTURE IS STILL UNVERTAIN, BUT THE FIGHT HAS SHARPENED THE EXECUTIVE'S DETERMINATION TO DOMINATE THE COUNTRY'S JUDICIARY.

01183 AZOULAY, K.G.
INACCURATE EQUATIONS: RACISM VS. NATIONALISM
NEW OUTLOOK, 32(3-4 (289-290)) (MAR 89), 38-39.
COMPARING SOUTH AFRICA WITH ISRAEL MAY BE FASHIONABLE, BUT IT IS INVIDIOUS. THE ISRAELI-PALESTINIAN CONFLICT CENTERS AROUND OPPOSING NATIONALITIES, TWO PEOPLES WHO WANT THEIR OWN STATE. SOUTH AFRICA HAS BALKANIZED ITS TERRITORIES, IMPOSING LEGALLY BINDING ETHNIC IDENTITIES ON ITS POPULATION, OVER THE OBJECTIONS OF THE PEOPLE AFFECTED BY THIS DECISION. THE ISRAELI OCCUPATION OF THE WEST BANK AND GAZA IS A DIRECT RESULT OF WARS WITH NEIGHBORING COUNTRIES THAT WANT ISRAEL'S DESTRUCTION. THE QUESTION OF RACISM AS PRACTICED IN SOUTH AFRICA, THEREFORE, IS IRRELEVANT TO ANY DISCUSSION OF ISRAELI BEHAVIOR.

01184 BABA, I.
MOVING TO A LIMITED PLURALISM
EAST EUROPEAN REPORTER, 3(4) (SPR 89), 4-7.
IVAN BABA, CHIEF EDITOR OF THE FIRST HUNGARIAN INDEPENDENT OPPOSITION DAILY NEWSPAPER, RESPONDS TO QUESTIONS ABOUT THE OPPOSITION GROUPS, AND THE FUTURE OF ECONOMIC AND POLITICAL REFORMS IN HUNGARY. HE CONCLUDES THAT ALTHOUGH OPINION POLLS INDICATE A MAJORITY OF HUNGARIANS SUPPORT OPPOSITION GROUPS AND ARE INCREASINGLY OUTSPOKEN IN THEIR CRITICISM OF THE RULING COMMUNIST PARTY, THE COMMUNIST PARTY REMAINS THE SINGLE LARGEST POPULAR GROUP AND STILL WIELDS SIGNIFICANT POWER OUTSIDE OF THE CAPITAL. HE PREDICTS A FUTURE OF "LIMITED PLURALISM," THE SCALE OF WHICH WILL BE DETERMINED BY THE CURRENT ECONOMIC SITUATION.

01185 BABIN, N.
MILITARY SPENDING, ECONOMIC GROWTH, AND THE TIME FACTOR
ARMED FORCES AND SOCIETY, 15(2) (WIN 89), 249-262.
FEW EMPIRICAL ANALYSES OF THE RELATIONSHIP BETWEEN MILITARY EXPENDITURES AND ECONOMIC PERFORMANCE IN LESS-DEVELOPED COUNTRIES INCLUDE THE TIME FACTOR. IT HAS NOT YET BEEN DETERMINED HOW LONG, OR HOW MANY YEARS, IT TAKES FOR MILITARY SPENDING TO HAVE AN EFFECT ON ECONOMIC GROWTH OR WHETHER THE NATURE OF THE RELATIONSHIP CHANGES AS THE TIME LENGTHENS. IN THIS STUDY THE TIME FACTOR IS INCORPORATED INTO THE ANALYSES BY EXAMINING THE RELATIONSHIP BETWEEN EXPENDITURES AND GROWTH AND BY SUCCESSIVELY CHANGING THE NUMBER OF YEARS BETWEEN THE TWO VARIABLES. TWO-WAVE PANEL REGRESSION MODELS ARE EMPLOYED THAT ACCOMMODATE THE ANALYSIS OF RELATIONSHIPS OVER TIME BY MEASURING THE DEPENDENT VARIABLE AT TWO POINTS IN TIME WHILE CONTROLLING FOR ITS INITIAL LEVEL. THE LONGITUDINAL ANALYSES INDICATE THAT AS THE NUMBER OF YEARS BETWEEN MILITARY

01186 BACH, S.
THE NATURE OF CONGRESSIONAL RULES
JOURNAL OF LAW & POLITICS, 5(4) (SUM 89), 725-758.
THIS ESSAY EXPLORES THE NATURE OF CONGRESSIONAL RULES OF PROCEDURE. ARE THESE RULES IMPOSED ON CONGRESS -- AND, THEREFORE, BEYOND CONGRESSIONAL CONTROL -- OR ARE THEY MATTERS FOR THE HOUSE AND SENATE TO DECIDE? CAN CONGRESS BE COMPELLED TO COMPLY WITH ITS OWN RULES, OR IS IT FREE TO WAIVE, SUSPEND, VIOLATE OR IGNORE THEM? DO ALL RULES HAVE THE SAME FORCE AND STANDING, OR ARE SOME RULES MORE CONCLUSIVE AND CONTROLLING THAN OTHERS? ARE THE RULES FIXED DURING THE COURSE OF A TWO-YEAR CONGRESS OR EVEN DURING CONSIDERATION OF INDIVIDUAL BILLS, OR MAY THEY BE ADJUSTED AS CIRCUMSTANCES WARRANT? EVEN IF RULES ARE ENFORCEABLE, ARE THEY ALL ENFORCED WITH THE SAME CONSISTENCY? MOST GENERALLY, TO WHAT EXTENT ARE CONGRESSIONAL RULES CONSTANTS OR VARIABLES IN THE PROCESS OF LEGISLATIVE DECISION-MAKING?

01187 BACH, S.
THE SENATE CONSENSUS FOR CHANGE?
CRS REVEIW, 10(1) (JAN 89), 4-5.
THE RULES AND ADMINISTRATION COMMITTEE'S 1988 REPORT ON SENATE OPERATIONS ADDRESSED SOME OF THE IMPORTANT PROCEDURAL AND OPERATIONAL PROBLEMS FACING THIS CONGRESSIONAL BODY. AFTER REVIEWING THE FINDINGS AND RECOMMENDATIONS OF FOUR PREVIOUS STUDIES COMMISSIONED BY THE SENATE, THE COMMITTEE SELECTED FOUR GENERAL ISSUES FOR ANALYSIS: (1) THE QUESTION OF COMMITTEE JURISDICTIONS, ASSIGNMENTS, AND SCHEDULES; (2) THE DIFFICULTIES AND UNCERTAINTIES OF SCHEDULING BUSINESS ON THE SENATE FLOOR; (3) PROPOSALS FOR IMPOSING GERMANENESS AND OTHER RESTRICTIONS ON FLOOR AMENDMENTS; AND (4) THE FRUSTRATIONS ASSOCIATED WITH THE BUDGET AND APPROPRIATIONS PROCESS. WHILE REFRAINING FROM ENDORSING SPECFIC RULES CHANGES, THE COMMITTEE SELECTED AN ARRAY OF PROPOSALS AS AN AGENDA FOR THE 101ST CONGRESS.

01188 BACHMAN, D.
CHINA'S POLITICS: CONSERVATISM PREVAILS
CURRENT HISTORY, 88(539) (SEP 89), 257-260, 296-297, 320.
THE DECLARATION OF MARTIAL LAW IN BEIJING ON MAY 19 AND THE MILITARY SUPPRESSION OF JUNE 3-4, 1989 WERE THE GOVERNMENT'S ANSWER TO PUBLIC OPINION. THE CRACKDOWN AND THE ENSUING WAVE OF REPRESSION HAVE DELEGITIMIZED THE GOVERNMENT AND THE LEADERSHIP OF THE CHINESE COMMUNIST PARTY (CCP), HAVE GREATLY UNDERCUT THE DECADE OF PROGRESS MADE UNDER ECONOMIC AND OTHER REFORMS, AND HAVE CREATED THE CONDITIONS FOR POWER STRUGGLES WITHIN THE CHINESE LEADERSHIP THAT WILL PROBABLY LAST FOR YEARS.

01189 BACHMAN, D.
THE MINISTRY OF FINANCE AND CHINESE POLITICS
PACIFIC AFFAIRS, 62(2) (SUM 89), 167-187.
THIS PAPER EXAMINES THE ROLE OF THE MINISTRY OF FINANCE IN THE CHINESE POLITICAL PROCESS. FIRST, IT DISCUSSES THE RESOURES, CONSTRAINTS, AND INTERESTS, OF THE MINISTRY OF FINANCE AT THE CENTRAL GOVERNMENT LEVEL. SECOND, IT FOCUSES ON THE ROLES THE MINISTRY OF FINANCE HAS PLAYED OVER TIME IN CHINSE ECONOMIC POLICY MAKING. THESE INCLUDE A PASSIVE SURVIVALIST ROLE; A BUREACRATIC INTEREST GROUP WITHIN THREE DIFFERENT TYPES OF COALITIONS A CONTENDER FOR POWER; AND A RESTORE OF BALANCE. THIRD, THE ROLES THE MINISTRY PLAYS ARE RELATED TO SEVERAL BROAD INDEPENDENT VARIABLES, SUCH AS THE POLITICAL AND ECONOMIC CLIMATES, AND THE DEGREE OF FINIANCIAL CENTRALIZATION AND DECENTRALIZATION. THESE STRUCTURAL VARIABLES ARE MORE EFFECTIVE IN EXPLAINING THE

ROLES OF THE MINISTRY THAN ARE MINISTRY LEADERSHIP VARIABLES.

01190 BACHRACH, E.R.
OIL AND DEVELOPMENT: THE CASE OF AGRICULTURE IN NIGERIA
AND ALGERIA
DISSERTATION ABSTRACTS INTERNATIONAL, 49(11) (MAY 89),
3487-A.
THE AUTHOR PROBES THE RELATIONSHIP BETWEEN THE OIL BOOM
OF THE 1970'S AND DEVELOPMENTAL PROGRESS AND PROSPECTS IN
TWO AFRICAN OPEC STATES, ALGERIA AND NIGERIA. ALGERIA'S
GREATER SUCCESS IN MANAGING ITS OIL ECONOMY SUPPORTS THE
PROMISE OF A MIXED POLITICAL ECONOMY STATE MODEL.

01191 BACHTELL, J.
IDEOLOGY AND TODAY'S YOUTH
POLITICAL AFFAIRS, LXVIII(7) (JUL 89), 28-32.
THE POINT OF DEPARTURE FOR EXAMINING YOUTH THOUGHT
PATTERNS IS ON THE BASIS OF CLASS. YOUTH ITSELF IS A MULTI-
CLASS SOCIAL CATEGORY. SOME QUESTIONS TOUCH MOST OF THE
ENTIRE GENERATION AND HELP TO SHAPE ITS THINKING--THREAT OF
NUCLEAR WAR, ENVIRONMENTAL CATASTROPHE, DRUGS, AIDS, ETC.
HOWEVER, THE VAST MAJORITY OF YOUTH AND STUDENTS ARE WORKING-
CLASS. THEIR OUTLOOK IS NOT ONLY SHAPED BY THE GLOBAL ISSUES
BUT ALSO CLASS ISSUES AND THE CLASS STRUGGLE. THIS
PREDOMINANT WORKINGCLASS COMPOSITION MAKES THE YOUNG
GENERATION, AS A WHOLE, A POTENTIAL ALLY OF THE WORKING
CLASS AND SUSCEPTIBLE TO WORKING-CLASS IDEAS.

01192 BADHWAR, I.; CHAWLA, P.
"I WON'T WRECK OUR UNITY"
INDIA TODAY, 14(15) (AUG 89), 24-25.
THIS IS AN INTERVIEW WITH CHANDRA SHEKHAR WHO IS
CONSIDERED ONE OF THE MAIN BARRIERS TO OPPOSITION UNITY AND
COHESIVE FUNCTIONING OF THE JANATA DAL, AND WHO RECENTLY
BURIED THE HATCHET WITH PARTY PRESIDENT V.P. SINGH. IN THIS
INTERVIEW HE BREAKS HIS SILENCE ON SOME CONTROVERSIAL ISSUES
PLAGUING OPPOSITION POLITICS.

01193 BADHWAR, I.
A NEW CONFIDENCE
INDIA TODAY, XIV(3) (FEB 89), 34-39.
MOST POLITICAL OBSERVERS HAD WRITTEN OFF THE BHARATIYA
JANATA PARTY AS A SPENT FORCE FOLLOWING ITS ISOLATION FROM
NATIONAL OPPOSITION GROUPINGS. BUT INSTEAD OF RETREATING
INTO THE WILDERNESS, THE BJP SEEMS TO BE BOUNCING BACK INTO
THE NATIONAL POLITICAL ARENA DUE TO ELECTORAL SUCCESSES IN
UTTAR PRADESH'S CIVIC ELECTIONS. AND THERE IS A SENSE OF
EUPHORIA WITHIN THE PARTY.

01194 BADHWAR, I.; MUDGAL, V.
ENCOURAGING SIGNALS
INDIA TODAY, XIV(6) (MAR 89), 14-15, 17.
IN MARCH 1989, PRIME MINISTER RAJIV GANDHI DID WHAT
CRITICS OF HIS PUNJAB POLICY HAD LONG URGED HIM TO DO. HE
CURBED RUNAWAY POLICE POWERS AND FREED PRISONERS DETAINED
WITHOUT CHARGES. BUT NO ONE WAS PARTICULARLY EXULTANT
BECAUSE THE CENTRE'S POLICIES IN PUNJAB HAVE SEESAWED
ILLOGICALLY AND FEW OF ITS BELEAGUERED CITIZENS TAKE THE
GOVERNMENT'S PROMISES SERIOUSLY ANY MORE.

01195 BADHWAR, I.
FAROOG UNDER THE GUN: THE ROOTS OF UNREST
INDIA TODAY, XIV(10) (MAY 89), 41-43.
THIS ARTICLE EXAMINES HOW THE CURRENT CRISIS IN KASHMIR
IS DEEPLY ROOTED IN A PAST CHARACTERIZED BY A TORTUROUS WEB
OF INTRIGUE, BLACKMAIL RECONCILATION, DECEPTION AND REVOLT.
CUT OFF FROM THE REST OF THE COUNTRY FOR SIX MONTHS A YEAR
BY HIGH MOUNTAIN RANGES, AND ENSLAVED FOR CERTURIES BY
MUGHALS, PATHANS, SIKHS AND DOGRAS, THE PEOPLE OF KASHMIR
BELIEVE THEY HAVE NEVER BEEN TRULY FREE OR ALLOWED A
DEMOCRATIC VOICE.

01196 BADHWAR, I.; CHAWLA, P.
GUIDING THEIR LOINS
INDIA TODAY, XIV(12) (JUN 89), 34-39.
AS ELECTIONS DRAW NEAR, INDIAN'S CONGRESS (I) IS SETTING
INTO MOTION ITS AWESOME ORGANIZATIONAL MACHINERY WHILE THE
OPPOSITION JANATA DAL CONCENTRATES ON PERSONALIZING THE
CONTEST. THE RULING CONGRESS (I) HAS THE UPPER HAND AT THE
MOMENT, BUT THE OPPOSITION CAMPAIGN IS EXPECTED TO PEAK
CLOSER TO THE ELECTION.

01197 BADHWAR, I.
KASHMIR: VALLEY OF TEARS
INDIA TODAY, XIV(10) (MAY 89), 34-40.
THIS ARTICLE DESCRIBES THE VIOLENCE WHICH ERUPTED
RECENTLY IN THE KASHMIR VALLEY, WHERE A MILITANT SEPARATIST
STRUGGLE HAS BEEN GATHERING STRENGTH FOR THE LAST YEAR. MOST
GRIEVANCES RELATE TO CORRUPTION AND AN INSENSITIVE
ADMINISTRATION. AS THE AUTHOR SHOWS, THE PEOPLE FEEL THEIR
DEMOCRATIC VOICE IS BEING STIFLED BY A MANIPULATIVE CENTRE.

01198 BADHWAR, I.; MERAJ, Z.
ON A SHORT FUSE
INDIA TODAY, XIV(8) (APR 89), 14-15, 17.
THE VIOLENCE IN KASHMIR HAS TURNED INTO A "WAR-LIKE
SITUATION," ADDING ANOTHER DIMENSION TO THE DISCONTENT THERE.
ESPECIALLY TROUBLING ARE THE USE OF AUTOMATIC WEAPONS BY
SECESSIONISTS AND THE GROWING SECESSIONIST SENTIMENT AMONG
YOUTH.

01199 BADHWAR, I.; CHAWLA, P.
R. K. DHAWAN: EYE OF THE STORM
INDIA TODAY, XIV(7) (APR 89), 14-20, 23.
THE RELEASE OF THE THAKKAR COMMISSION REPORT ON THE
MURDER OF MRS INDIRA GANDHI AND THE LEAK THAT PRECEDED IT
WERE SIGNALS OF SERIOUS FIGHTING BETWEEN FACTIONS IN THE
RULING PARTY OF INDIA. MUCH OF THE CONTROVERSY STEMS FROM
THE RETURN OF R. K. DHAWAN, AN EXPERIENCED POLITICIAN AND
FRIEND OF PRIME MINISTER RAJIV GANDHI. DHAWAN HAS RUMORED TO
BE IMPLICATED BY THE COMMISSION REPORT TO BE INVOLVED IN THE
MURDER OF INDIRA GANDHI, BUT APPARENTLY WAS CLEARED AFTER
THE RELEASE OF THE REPORT.

01200 BADHWAR, I.
RETURN OF THE FAITHFUL
INDIA TODAY, XIV(5) (MAR 89), 38-40.
FOUR YEARS AFTER HE WAS UNCERMONIOUSLY DUMPED, R.K.
DHAWAN IS BACK AS A PRIME MINISTERIAL AIDE. MORE THAN
ANYTHING ELSE, HIS APPOINTMENT WITH ITS EMPHASIS ON LOYALTY
INDICATES A CONSCIOUS ATTEMPT BY RAJIV GANDHI TO REVAMP HIS
IMAGE AND IDENTIFY HIMSELF WITH THE PARTY MAINSTREAM.

01201 BADHWAR, I.
STAR-CROSSED
INDIA TODAY, XIV(1) (JAN 89), 42-43.
THE FATES OF RAJIV GANDHI AND VISHWHANTH PRATAP SINGH
MESHED IN 1988. GANDHI LOST SO MUCH GROUND THAT HE WAS
FORCED TO FALL BACK ON WHAT HE HAD PREVIOUSLY REJECTED, AND
HE RESORTED TO REPEATED CABINET RESHUFFLES. ALTHOUGH SINGH
REMAINED THE ONLY OPPOSITION LEADER WITH A NATIONAL IMAGE,
HE RESORTED TO COMPROMISE AND OFTEN AVOIDED CONFRONTATION.

01202 BADHWAR, I.; CHAWLA, P.
THE OPPOSITION: COMING ALIVE
INDIA TODAY, XIV(14) (JUL 89), 14-20.
OPPOSITION PARTIES IN INDIA HAVE COMMONLY BEEN
CHARACTERIZED AS BEING PLAGUED WITH ORGANIZATIONAL PORBLEMS
AND INTRAPARTY STRIFE. HOWEVER, FOR THE TIME BEING THE
OPPOSITION SEEMS TO HAVE SET DIFFERENCES ASIDE AND UNITE
AROUND A COMMON ENEMY: PRIME MINISTER RAJIV GHANDI AND THE
RULING CONGRESS (I) PARTY. LED BY V.P. SINGH AND THE
POWERFUL JANATA DAL PARTY, THE OPPOSITION IS DEMONSTRATING
SURPRISING UNITY AND IS SLOWLY PICKING UP MOMENTUM. EFFORTS
TO DEPICT V.P. SINGH AS A STRONG AND HONEST LEADER AS
OPPOSED TO THE WEAKNESS AND CORRUPTION THAT IS EVIDENT IN
THE RULING PARTY AND EMBODIES IN RAJIV GANDHI IS BEGINNING
TO TAKE ITS TOLL.

01203 BADIE, B.
COMPARATIVE ANALYSIS IN POLITICAL SCIENCE: REQUIEM OR
RESURRECTION?
POLITICAL STUDIES, 37(3) (SEP 89), 340-351.
COMPARATIVE METHOD IN POLITICAL SCIENCE IS CURRENTLY
GOING THROUGH A CRITICAL TIME, PARTICULARLY AFTER THE
FAILURE OF DEVELOPMENTALISM, AND OF THE CLASSICAL PARADIGM
OF COMPARATIVE GOVERNMENT. THIS CRISIS STEMS FROM
QUESTIONING UNIVERSALISM, MONODETERMINISM AND THE
COMPARTMENTALISM BETWEEN POLITICAL SCIENCE SCIENCE AND
HISTORY. NEW PARADIGMS ARE NOW CONCEIVED IN ORDER TO
OVERCOME THIS CRISIS: CULTURALISM, SOCIAL ACTION, HISTORICAL
SOCIOLOGY. CAN THEY BE USED TO CONSTUCT A NEW KIND OF
COMPARISON? CAN THEY DEAL EFFECTIVELY WITH THE NEW OBJECTS
OF COMPARISON WHICH DERIVE FROM THE INCREASING
DIFFERENTIATION OF POLITICAL SITUATIONS AND POLITICAL
PRACTICES THAT WE CURRENTLY OBSERVE?

01204 BADR, G.
THE MIDDLE EAST PEACE PROCESS: AN ISRAELI PERSPECTIVE
AMERICAN-ARAB AFFAIRS, (30) (FAL 89), 81-83.
DR. BADR SUGGESTS THAT THE THEOLOGICAL DIMENTIONS OF THE
CONFLICT IN THE MIDDLE EAST ARE SECONDARY TO THE CORE ISSUES
OF TERRITORY AND IDENTITY. HE ILLUSTRATES THIS BY DESCRIBING
THE POSITION OF ISLAM VIS-A-VIS CHRISTIANITY AND JUDAISM. HE
CONCLUDES THAT SINCE ISLAM'S VIEW OF BOTH JUDAISM AND
CHRISTIANITY IS NOT THAT OF AN ALIEN FAITH THAT THERE IS NO
PROBLEM FOR MUSLIMS IN COEXISTING WITH CHRISTIANITY OR
JUDAISM.

01205 BADZO, G.
WHY ECONOMIC PERESTROIKA IS GOING BANKRUPT
GLASNOST, II(4) (SEP 89), 10-12.
THE AUTHOR POSES THE QUESTION "WHO'S HINDERING
PERESTROIKA?" HE STATES THAT THE ANSWER CAN BE FOUND BY
APPLYING A POLITICAL AXIOM: DEMOCRACY IS HINDERED BY THOSE
WHOM IT THREATENS. AND IT THREATENS THE POWER OF THE
COMMUNIST PARTY. THERE HAS NEVER BEEN A CASE IN HISTORY
WHERE A RULING SOCIAL CLASS SURRENDERED ON ITS OWN

INITIATIVE THE CONTROL OF THE MEANS OF PRODUCTION. TO THE
EXTENT THAT ECONOMIC REFORMS HAVE OCCURRED IN THE SOVIET
UNION, THE COMMUNIST PARTY HAS ACTED UNDER THE COMPULSION OF
NEW HISTORICAL CIRCUMSTANCES AND IS FIGHTING A REARGUARD
ACTION TO SHORE UP ITS SHAKY POSITION.

01206 BAE, K.
    LABOR STRATEGY FOR INDUSTRIALIZATION IN SOUTH KOREA ·
    PACIFIC AFFAIRS, 62(3) (FAL 89), 353-363.
        THE REMARKABLE ECONOMIC GROWTH OF SOUTH KOREA OVER THE
    PAST SEVERAL DECADES IS OFTEN CONSIDERED AN UNUSUAL CASE
    BECAUSE IT DOES NOT FIT NEATLY INTO THE ESTABLISHED PATTERN
    OF DEVELOPMENT. HOWEVER, IT IS NOT UNUSUAL IN THAT IT IS A
    RESULT OF RATIONAL EVALUATION-A PROCESS OF EVALUATION WHICH
    INVOLVED INTERACTION AMONG GOVERNMENT, EMPLOYERS, AND
    EMPLOYEES WHO COLLECTIVELY TOOK NOTE OF SITUATIONS PECULIAR
    TO SOUTH KOREA. A LABOR SHORTAGE WAS OVERCOME BY THE
    SUCCESSFUL LABOR TRAINING PROGRAM AND ITS UNIQUE RECRUITMENT
    SYSTEM-A MIX OF JAPANESE AND WESTERN PRACTICES. KOREAN
    MANAGERS RATIONALLY EVALUATED ALTERNATIVE STRATEGIES AND
    DEVISED A BALANCED SYSTEM THAT LIES SOMEWHERE BETWEEN
    JAPAN'S NENKO (SYSTEM OF SENIORITY) AND THE WEST'S MARKET-
    DRIVEN SYSTEM. THE LABOUR-MANAGEMENT COUNCIL, THE FACTORY
    NEW VILLAGE MOVEMENT, AND THE MILITARY MODEL OF
    ENTREPRENEURIAL IDEOLOGY WERE DEVICES TO SKILLFULLY MANAGE
    THIS NEW LABOR FORCE SYSTEM. WHILE THIS SYSTEM IS A PRODUCT
    OF A RATIONAL DECISION-MAKING POLICY THAT BEARS LOCAL
    SITUATIONS IN MIND IT ALSO DRAWS ON KOREA'S CONFUCIAN
    HERITAGE.

01207 BAE, M.
    PROSPECTS OF INTER-KOREAN MILITARY RELATIONS
    KOREA OBSERVER, XX(1) (SPR 89), 21-38.
        THE AUTHOR ANALYZES THE SIGNIFICANCE OF THE LATEST ARMS
    BUILD-UPS IN SOUTH AND NORTH KOREA, EXAMINES THE NORTH
    KOREANS' COOPERATIVE MILITARY RELATIONSHIP WITH THE SOVIET
    UNION, AND PRESENTS EVIDENCE THAT NORTH KOREA'S CONSPIRACY
    AGAINST THE SOUTH HAS NOT BEEN ABANDONED AND WILL CONTINUE.

01208 BAERWALD, H.H.
    JAPAN'S HOUSE OF COUNCILLORS ELECTION: A MINI-REVOLUTION?
    ASIAN SURVEY, 29(9) (SEP 89), 833-841.
        THE LONG-GOVERNING LIBERAL DEMOCRATIC PARTY (LDP) IN
    JAPAN LOST A NATIONAL ELECTION FOR THE FIRST TIME SINCE IT
    WAS ORGANIZED IN THE FALL OF 1955. IN CONTRAST, THE LONG
    DECLINING JAPAN SOCIALIST PARTY (JSP) WON UNDER THE
    LEADERSHIP OF TAKAKO DOI, THE FIRST WOMAN TO HEAD ONE OF
    JAPAN'S MAJOR POLITICAL PARTIES. THIS ARTICLE LOOKS AT THE
    SITUATIONAL FACTORS THAT SET THE TONE OR MOOD FOR THE
    ELECTION. IT THEN LOOKS AT HOW AND WHERE THE ELECTION WAS
    WON BY THE JSP AND LOST BY THE LDP. THE RESULTS OF THIS WILL
    BE THAT THE LEGISLATIVE PROCESS WILL PROCEED EVEN MORE
    SLOWLY THAN BEFORE, PRESENTING AN UNPRECEDENTED CHALLENGE AT
    HOME AS WELL AS ABROAD, THE ARTICLE CONCLUDES.

01209 BAGEHOT, H.
    FRANCE AND LEBANON: AMATEURISH OPERATION
    MIDDLE EAST INTERNATIONAL, (349) (APR 89), 10-12.
        THE FRENCH GOVERNMENT IS HEAVING A SIGH OF RELIEF THAT
    ITS POORLY CONCEIVED AND EXECUTED HUMANITARIAN MISSION TO
    LEBANON ENDED RELATIVELY WELL. THE SUCCESS HAS NOT
    STRENGTHENED FRANCE'S INFLUENCE IN THE REGION, HOWEVER. IN
    FACT, THE REVERSE IS TRUE DUE TO THE LAST REMNANTS OF FRENCH
    COLONIAL NOSTALGIA, WHICH IS CONCENTRATED IN THE CHRISTIAN
    COMMUNITIES OF LEBANON.

01210 BAGEHOT, H.
    MITTERAND'S GAMBLE THAT PAID OFF
    MIDDLE EAST INTERNATIONAL, (350) (MAY 89), 3-4.
        THE OFFICIAL VISIT OF YASSER ARAFAT TO PARIS REPRESENTED
    A GAMBLE FOR THE FRENCH GOVERNMENT AND FOR PRESIDENT
    MITTERAND. IT PAID OFF AS FRANCE GAINED PRESTIGE AS A
    MEDIATOR IN THE MIDDLE EAST CONFLICT. IT WAS ALSO NOTEWORTHY
    BECAUSE ARAFAT ANNOUNCED THAT THE PALESTINE NATIONAL CHARTER
    WAS "CADUC."

01211 BAGEHOT, H.
    MITTERAND'S INVITATION
    MIDDLE EAST INTERNATIONAL, (348) (APR 89), 9-10.
        THE INVITATION OF FRENCH PRESIDENT FRANCOIS MITTERAND TO
    YASSER ARAFAT TO VISIT PARIS HAS HAD SIGNIFICANT
    REPERCUSSIONS BOTH IN THE EUROPEAN COMMUNITY AND IN THE
    LARGEST JEWISH COMMUNITY IN EUROPE. MOST OF THE REACTION,
    HOWEVER WAS SURPRISINGLY MODERATE. THE VISIT IS NOT LIKELY
    TO TAKE PLACE IN THE NEAR FUTURE DUE TO THE CONFLICT IN
    LEBANON: THE PLIGHT OF LEBANESE CHRISTIANS HAVE BEEN A BIG
    ISSUE IN THE FRENCH MEDIA, AND FOR MITTERAND TO RECEIVE
    ARAFAT WHILE THE CONFLICT CONTINUES WOULD GIVE APPEARANCES
    OF GIVING PALESTINIANS HIGHER PRIORITY THAN LEBANESE
    CHRISTIANS.

01212 BAGGOTT, R.
    REGULATORY REFORM IN BRITAIN: THE CHANGING FACE OF SELF-
    REGULATION

PUBLIC ADMINISTRATION, 67(4) (WIN 89), 435-454.
    SELF-REGULATION HAS BEEN AT THE CENTRE OF A NUMBER OF
PUBLIC AND ACADEMIC DEBATES IN BRITAIN IN RECENT YEARS. THIS
ARTICLE ENQUIRES INTO THE NATURE OF SELF-REGULATION AND
ATTEMPTS TO IMPROVE OUR UNDERSTANDING OF IT IN A NUMBER OF
WAYS: BY ATTEMPTING TO DEFINE SELFREGULATION; BY ASSESSING
CERTAIN TRENDS AND DEVELOPMENTS IN SELF-REGULATORY SYSTEMS;
BY TRYING TO EXPLAIN THESE TRENDS AND DEVELOPMENTS; AND BY
OUTLINING THE IMPLICATIONS OF SELFREGULATION FOR POLICY
MAKING AND PUBLIC ACCOUNTABILITY. THE MAIN CONCLUSION
REACHED IS THAT, FROM A PUBLIC ADMINISTRATION PERSPECTIVE AT
LEAST, CONCERN SHOULD NOT CENTRE UPON WHETHER OR NOT SELF-
REGULATION IS INCREASING OR DECREASING. INSTEAD, THE MAIN
FOCUS SHOULD BE UPON THE ABILITY OF SUCH SYSTEMS TO RESPOND
TO PRESSURES FOR REFORM AND PROVIDE EFFECTIVE REGULATION
WITHIN A BROAD FRAMEWORK OF PUBLIC ACCOUNTABILITY.

01213 BAGLEY, B.M.
    COLUMBIA: THE WRONG STRATEGY
    FOREIGN POLICY, (77) (WIN 89), 154-171.
        THIS ARTICLE REPORTS ON THE PRICE IN BLOOD THAT COLUMBIA
    IS PAYING IN THE INTERNATIONAL WAR ON DRUGS. IT DETAILS
    COLUMBIAN GOVERNMENT EFFORTS TO BOLSTER THE CAMPAIGN AGAINST
    THE DRUG CARTELS AND ITS APPEAL TO THE INTERNATIONAL
    COMMUNITY FOR ECONOMIC AND TECHNICAL SUPPORT. IT EXPLORES
    THE METHODS THAT THE COLUMBIAN TRAFFICKERS HAVE USED TO GAIN
    SUPPORT FROM GRATEFUL FOLLOWINGS, AND ALSO THE COLLAPSE OF
    THE WEAK AND ANTIQUATED JUDICIAL SYSTEM OF THE COLUMBIAN
    GOVERNMENT. IT CONTENDS THAT U.S. POLICY TO AID THE WAR
    EFFORT IS MISGUIDED AND THAT TO SEND TROOPS IN WOULD BE A
    MISTAKE. IT CONCLUDES THAT THE BASIC CHALLENGE FOR U.S.
    POLICYMAKERS IS TO FASHION A BALANCED LONG-RUN STRATEGY THAT
    ADDRESSES BOTH THE DEMAND AND SUPPLY SIDES OF THE EQUATION.

01214 BAHIRI, S.
    ISRAEL'S MILITARY ECONOMY
    NEW OUTLOOK, 32(2 (288)) (FEB 89), 34-35.
        THE AUTHOR FOCUSES ON THE ECONOMIC BACKGROUND OF ISRAELI
    ARMS TRADE, HE BRIEFLY SURVEYS THE KEY ELEMENTS OF ISRAEL'S
    MILITARY ECONOMY, THE GNP AND THE MILITARY BUDGET, MILITARY
    RESEARCH AND DEVELOPMENT, AND THE ROLE OF DEFENSE
    CONTRACTORS IN THE MILITARY INDUSTRIES.

01215 BAHL, S.K.
    CHINA'S FAILURE IN TIBET - PULLS AND PRESSURES OF DOMESTIC
    POLITICS
    CHINA REPORT, 25(3) (JUL 89), 259-290.
        THIS ARTICLE EXPLORES CHINESE SUCCESS IN TIDING OVER A
    SERIOUS SOCIOECONOMIC AND POLITICAL CRISIS IN TIBET TIL
    AFTER 1956. IT THEN EXAMINES THE BEGINNINGS OF PROBLEMS
    CAUSED BY '17 POINT SINO-TIBETAN AGREEMENT' IN 1951. IT
    DETAILS MAO'S STRATEGY, THE SINO-DALAIACCORD AND THE NEED
    FOR REFORM. THE ATTEMPT TO WIN OVER THE DALAI LAMA AND THE
    TIBETAN PEOPLE, DALAI'S FLIGHT TO INDIA AND OTHER MAO
    POLICIES ARE STUDIED. THE FAILURE OF CHINA'S TIBET POLICY IS
    CONCLUDED TO BE CAUSED BY THE NATURE OF POLICIES AND ALSO
    THEIR IMPLEMENTATION AT THE LOWER LEVELS.

01216 BAHL, S.K.
    TRANSNATIONAL CORPORATIONS AND SINO-INDIAN ECONOMIC
    COMPETITION
    CHINA REPORT, 25(1) (JAN 89), 11-38.
        THE ARTICLE EXPLORES THE MEASURES TAKEN BY CHINA AND
    INDIA TO ENCOURAGE INVESTMENT FROM TRANSNATIONAL
    CORPORATIONS (TNC). WITH EMPHASIS ON CHINA, IT OUTLINES THE
    IDEOLOGICAL JUSTIFICATION USED BY DENG XIAOPING AND OTHERS
    TO ALLOW CAPITALIST FOREIGN INVESTMENT WITHIN A SOCIALIST
    REGIME, AND THE SPECIFIC MEASURES THAT BEIJING HAS TAKEN TO
    ENCOURAGE TNC INVESTMENT. IT ALSO EXAMINES MANY OF THE
    PROBLEMS THAT TNCS CONFRONT IN CHINA, PROBLEMS WHICH ARE
    INCREASING THE ATTRACTIVENESS OF INDIA AS A LOCATION FOR
    FUTURE INVESTMENT. THE AUTHOR ANALYZES THE FUTURE
    IMPLICATIONS THAT COMPETITION WOULD HAVE FOR SINO-INDIAN
    RELATIONS AND OFFERS SUGGESTIONS ON OVERCOMING MUTUALLY
    DAMAGING CONFLICTS.

01217 BAHR, S.J.; RICKS, S.S.
    INCREASING THE ECONOMIC WELL-BEING OF SEPARATED, DIVORCED,
    AND WIDOWED WOMEN OVER THE AGE OF THIRTY
    POLICY STUDIES REVIEW, 8(3) (SPR 89), 689-703.
        DATA FROM THE CONTINUOUS LONGITUDINAL MANPOWER SURVEY
    AND THE CURRENT POPULATION SURVEY WERE USED TO ESTIMATE THE
    EFFECTS OF CETA, A GOVERNMENTAL JOBS PROGRAM, ON THE
    ECONOMIC WELL-BEING OF SEPARATED, DIVORCED, AND WIDOWED
    WOMEN OVER AGE THIRTY. AFTER TRAINING, CETA PARTICIPANTS HAD
    INCREASES IN EARNINGS AND TENDED TO HAVE HIGHER EARNINGS
    THAN COMPARABLE CPS RESPONDENTS. PARTICIPANTS IN ON-THE-JOB
    TRAINING AND PUBLIC SERVICE EMPLOYMENT HAD GREATER INCREASES
    THAN PARTICIPANTS IN THE OTHER CETA PROGRAMS. CETA ENROLLEES
    WITH A HIGH SCHOOL DEGREE HAD GREATER INCREASES IN EARNINGS
    THAN THOSE WHO HAD NOT COMPLETED HIGH SCHOOL, WHILE WHITES
    HAD GREATER INCREASES IN EARNINGS THAN NON-WHITES.

01218 BAILEY, P.P.
CONSUMER HEALTH LAW OVERVIEW: COMPETITION SPURS CHANGES
FOR GOOD, ILL
JOURNAL OF STATE GOVERNMENT, 62(3) (MAY 89), 99-101.
FOR THE LAST 15 YEARS, A REVOLUTION HAS BEEN UNDERWAY IN
HEALTH CARE. MANY OF THE DRAMATIC CHANGES CAN BE TRACED TO
DEREGULATION, WHICH HAS SPURRED THE GROWTH OF COMPETITION.
MUCH OF THE DEREGULATION HAS ORIGINATED THROUGH ANTITRUST
LAWSUITS BY THE FEDERAL TRADE COMMISSION AND THE DEPARTMENT
OF JUSTICE. THE NEW COMPETITIVE SPIRIT IN HEALTH CARE IS
EVIDENCED IN THE GROWTH OF FOR-PROFIT HOSPITAL CHAINS,
HEALTH MAINTENANCE ORGANIZATIONS, WALK-IN STORE-FRONT
CLINICS, AND SO FORTH. STATE GOVERNMENTS SHOULD TAKE FULL
ADVANTAGE OF THE BENEFITS RESULTING FROM THE NEW COMPETITIVE
SPIRIT IN HEALTH CARE, BUT THEY MUST ALSO REMAIN WATCHFUL
FOR PROBLEMS THAT CAN RESULT FROM COMPETITION.

01219 BAILIN, F.
EGYPT, LIBYA IMPROVE RELATIONS
BEIJING REVIEW, 32(47) (NOV 89), 12-13.
RELATIONS BETWEEN EGYPT AND LIBYA HAVE IMPROVED
DRAMATICALLY AFTER TWO ROUNDS OF TALKS BETWEEN EGYPTIAN
PRESIDENT HOSNI MUBARAK AND LIBYA'S MUAMMAR GADDAFI. THE
OCTOBER 1989 MEETINGS WERE THE FIRST BETWEEN LEADERS OF THE
TWO COUNTRIES SINCE DIPLOMATIC RELATIONS WERE SERVED IN 1977.
MUBARAK SAID THE TWO COUNTRIES ARE MOVING TOWARDS
NORMALIZING RELATIONS.

01220 BAISSA, L.
FOREIGN POLICY DECISION-MAKING: THE CASE OF ETHIOPIA, 1959-
1981
DISSERTATION ABSTRACTS INTERNATIONAL, 50(1) (JUL 89),
250-A.
THIS STUDY INVESTIGATES FOREIGN POLICY DECISION-MAKING
IN ETHIOPIA BETWEEN 1959 AND 1981 UNDER EMPEROR HAILE
SELASSIE AND LT. COLONEL MENGISTU HAIL MARIAM. USING SIX
FOREIGN POLICY DECISIONS, THE STUDY EXAMINES HOW AND WHY
EMPEROR HAILE SELASSIE'S REGIME REACHED A RAPPROCHEMENT WITH
THE USSR IN 1959, HOSTED THE PAN-AFRICAN SUMMIT CONFERENCE
IN MAY 1963, AND SEVERED DIPLOMATIC TIES WITH ISRAEL IN
1973. SIMILARLY, IT EXAMINES HOW AND WHY THE MILITARY REGIME
OF LT. COLONEL MENGISTU ALIGNED WITH THE USSR IN 1977,
REACHED A RAPPROCHEMENT WITH SUDAN IN 1980, AND JOINED THE
TRIPARTITE PACT WITH LIBYA AND SOUTH YEMEN IN 1981.

01221 BAKER, J.A. III
A NEW PACIFIC PARTNERSHIP: FRAMEWORK FOR THE FUTURE
DEPARTMENT OF STATE BULLETIN (US FOREIGN POLICY), 89(2149)
(AUG 89), 64-66.
IN ASIA, AS IN EUROPE, A NEW ORDER IS TAKIN SHAPE. THE
RITES OF PASSAGE WILL BE PAINFUL, BUT IT IS AN ORDER FULL OF
PROMISE AND HOPE. THE UNITED STATES, WITH ITS REGIONAL
FRIENDS, MUST PLAY A CRUCIAL ROLE IN DESIGNING THE
ARCHITECTURE OF THE NEW ORDER. AMERICAN ENGAGEMENT IN THE
REGION'S POLITICS, COMMERCE, AND SECURITY IS NEEDED TO FORM
A NEW PACIFIC PARTNERSHIP.

01222 BAKER, J.A. III
AFTER THE NATO SUMMIT: CHALLENGES FOR THE WEST IN A
CHANGING WORLD
DEPARTMENT OF STATE BULLETIN (US FOREIGN POLICY), 89(2149)
(AUG 89), 55-60.
PRESIDENT BUSH'S CONVENTIONAL PARITY INITIATIVE PROMISES
TO ACCELERATE A POTENTIALLY HISTORIC CHANGE IN THE BALANCE
OF MILITARY FORCES IN EUROPE. IF ACCEPTED BY THE EAST, IT
WOULD REDUCE THE SIZE OF BOTH NATO AND WARSAW PACT
CONVENTIONAL FORCES. NATO HAS AGREED THAT THE SHORT-RANGE
NUCLEAR FORCES NEGOTIATIONS LEADING TO PARTIAL NUCLEAR
REDUCTIONS WILL BEGIN ONLY AFTER THE IMPLEMENTATION OF A
CONVENTIONAL FORCES AGREEMENT IS UNDERWAY.

01223 BAKER, J.A. III; WROBLESKI, A.B.
CERTIFICATION FOR NARCOTICS SOURCE AND TRANSIT COUNTRIES
DEPARTMENT OF STATE BULLETIN (US FOREIGN POLICY), 89(2146)
(MAY 89), 68-72.
DESPITE DEDICATION BOTH IN THE USA AND ABROAD, THE
INTERNATIONAL WAR ON NARCOTICS IS CLEARLY NOT BEING WON. BUT
THE BUSH ADMINISTRATION HAS PLEDGED THAT NARCOTICS WILL BE A
KEY ELEMENT ON ITS FOREIGN POLICY AGENDA AND THAT COUNTRIES
KNOWN TO BE SOURCES OF ILLEGAL DRUGS WILL BE URGED TO DO
MORE TO END THE DRUG TRADE.

01224 BAKER, J.A. III
CHALLENGES AHEAD FOR NATO AND DEVELOPMENTS IN EAST-WEST
RELATIONS
DEPARTMENT OF STATE BULLETIN (US FOREIGN POLICY), 89(2149)
(AUG 89), 61-64.
IN THIS STATEMENT, SECRETARY OF STATE BAKER DICUSSES
EAST-WEST RELATIONS AND EUROPEAN SECURITY POLICY.

01225 BAKER, J.A. III
NEW HORIZONS IN EUROPE
DEPARTMENT OF STATE BULLETIN (US FOREIGN POLICY), 89(2146)
(MAY 89), 56-59.
THIS ARTICLE REPRINTS SECRETARY OF STATE BAKER'S ADDRESS
AT THE MINISTERIAL MEETING SIGNALING THE OPENING OF TWO NEW
SECURITY NEGOTIATIONS: TALKS ON CONFIDENCE- AND SECURITY-
BUILDING MEASURES AND TALKS ON CONVENTIONAL ARMED FORCES IN
EUROPE. BAKER'S REMARKS INCLUDE HIS VISION OF A NEW EUROPE
BUILT ON FREEDOM.

01226 BAKER, J.A. III
POWER FOR GOOD: AMERICAN FOREIGN POLICY IN THE NEW ERA
DEPARTMENT OF STATE BULLETIN (US FOREIGN POLICY), 89(2147)
(JUN 89), 8-11.
IN THIS SPEECH, THE SECRETARY OF STATE DISCUSSES THE
CHANGES TAKING PLACE IN THE WORLD POLITICAL SITUATION AND
THE ACTIONS THE BUSH ADMINISTRATION HAS TAKEN TO LAY THE
FOUNDATION OF A NEW AMERICAN FOREIGN POLICY TO RESPOND TO
THE CHANGES.

01227 BAKER, J.A. III
PRINCIPLES AND PRAGMATISM: AMERICAN POLICY TOWARD THE
ARABISRAELI CONFLICT
DEPARTMENT OF STATE BULLETIN (US FOREIGN POLICY), 89(2148)
(JUL 89), 24-27.
THE BUSH ADMINISTRATION HAS ADOPTED A POLICY OF
CONTINUITY REGARDING RELATIONS BETWEEN THE UNITED STATES AND
ISRAEL. AMERICAN SUPPORT FOR ISRAEL WILL CONTINUE TO BE THE
FOUNDATION OF THE UNITED STATES' APPROACH TO THE PROBLEMS OF
THE MIDDLE EAST.

01228 BAKER, J.A. III
SECRETARY MEETS WITH NATO ALLIES
DEPARTMENT OF STATE BULLETIN (US FOREIGN POLICY), 89(2145)
(APR 89), 38-42.
SECRETARY OF STATE BAKER MET WITH THE UNITED STATES'
NATO ALLIES IN FEBRUARY 1989. THE MEETINGS REVIEWED THE
CHANGES TAKING PLACE IN EAST-WEST RELATIONS AND PROPOSALS
FOR DISARAMENT.

01229 BAKER, J.A. III
SECRETARY-DESIGNATE'S CONFIRMATION HEARINGS
DEPARTMENT OF STATE BULLETIN (US FOREIGN POLICY), 89(2145)
(APR 89), 10-16.
IN THIS SPEECH, SECRETARY OF STATE DESIGNATE JAMES BAKER
ENUMERATED FIVE TRANSFORMATIONS THAT WILL CHANGE THE WORLD
IN THE COMING DECADE: THE DEMOCRATIC REVOLUTION, THE SPREAD
OF FREE ENTERPRISE, CHANGE IN THE COMMUNIST WORLD,
TECHNOLOGICAL PROGRESS, AND NEW MILITARY TRENDS. THEN HE
OUTLINED HIS APPROACH TO THESE TRANSFORMATIONS.

01230 BAKER, J.A. III
THE CHALLENGE OF CHANGE IN US-SOVIET RELATIONS
DEPARTMENT OF STATE BULLETIN (US FOREIGN POLICY), 89(2148)
(JUL 89), 36-39.
IN THIS ADDRESS, SECRETARY OF STATE BAKER REVIEWED THE
CHANGES OCCURING IN THE SOVIET UNION AND WHAT THEY MEAN FOR
US-SOVIET RELATIONS, INCLUDING ARMS CONTROL.

01231 BAKER, J.A. III
THE INTERNATIONAL AGENDA AND THE FY 1990 BUDGET REQUEST
DEPARTMENT OF STATE BULLETIN (US FOREIGN POLICY), 89(2145)
(APR 89), 16-21.
IN THIS SPEECH, THE SECRETARY OF STATE DISCUSSES THE
MAIN ELEMENTS OF THE BUSH ADMINISTRATION'S FOREIGN POLICY
AND THE BUDGET NEEDED TO SUPPORT THAT POLICY.

01232 BAKER, J.A. III
U.S. AND LATIN AMERICA: A SHARED DESTINY
DEPARTMENT OF STATE BULLETIN (US FOREIGN POLICY), 89(2147)
(JUN 89), 5-8.
THE AMERICAS FACE A CHOICE BETWEEN TWO VERY DIFFERENT
FUTURES. DOWN ONE ROAD LIES A VISION OF FREEDOM, OPPORTUNITY,
AND ECONOMIC DEVELOPMENT. DOWN THE OTHER ROAD LIES A FAILED
VISION OF DICTATORSHIP, STATE CONTROL, AND MISSED
OPPORTUNITY. INTERNATIONAL COOPERATION IS NECESSARY TO
BUILDING THE RIGHT FUTURE. THE USA, LATIN AMERICA, AND THE
CARIBBEAN NEED ONE ANOTHER TODAY AS NEVER BEFORE.

01233 BAKER, J.R.
REPRESENTATION IN STATE LEGISLATURES: AN EMPIRICAL
ANALYSIS OF THE EFFECTS OF LEGISLATIVE PROFESSIONALIZATION,
1953-1983
DISSERTATION ABSTRACTS INTERNATIONAL, 49(7) (JAN 89),
1954-A.
UTILIZING A DUAL METHOD, THE AUTHOR TESTS THE HYPOTHESIS
THAT INCREASED PROFESSIONALIZATION IMPROVES REPRESENTATION
BY: (1) DECREASING THE STATUS GAP BETWEEN LEGISLATORS AND
CONSTITUENTS AND (2) INCREASING THE DIVERSITY OF THE CHAMBER
MEMBERSHIP.

01234 BAKER, J.S.
MAKE PEACE WITH NATURE
WORLD MARXIST REVIEW, 32(12) (DEC 89), 20-21.
GORBACHOV AND HIS COLLEAGUES, LIKE SOME NORTH AMERICANS,
NOW SEE THE RESOURCES AND THE STATE OF NATURE AS CRUCIAL TO
THE CONTINUED EXISTENCE OF THE HUMAN RACE. THIS ARTICLE

TRIES TO PROVE THIS POINT BY EXAMINING RECENT CLAIMS OF
ECOLOGISTS, CLIMATOLOGISTS, AND BIOLOGISTS REGARDING CLIMATE
STABILIZATION AND EARTH REGENERATION.

01235 BAKER, L.
CULTURAL SURVIVAL IMPORTS: MARKETING THE RAIN FOREST
CULTURAL SURVIVAL QUARTERLY, 13(3) (1989), 64-67.
HITH MORE THAN ONE-FIFTH OF BRAZIL'S TROPICAL FORESTS
DESTROYED, A NUMBER OF NATIONS, INTERNATIONAL BODIES, AND
NONGOVERNMENTAL ORGANIZATIONS ALARMED AT THE EFFECTS ON THE
WORLD'S ECOSYSTEM HAVE BEGUN PURSUING VARIOUS STRATEGIES TO
HALT THIS ECOLOGICAL CARNAGE. BUT MOST OF THESE PROPOSALS
ARE NEGATIVE AND ANTAGONISTIC, HIGHLIGHTING THE EVILS OF
DEFORESTATION AND CRITICIZING THE GUILTY GOVERNMENTS. THE
FACT IS THAT DESPERATE CONDITIONS OFTEN LEAD THE POOR TO CUT
THEIR FORESTS AND GOVERNMENT INDEBTEDNESS IS THE MAJOR CAUSE
OF THE GET-RICH-QUICK SCHEMES THAT HAVE SPROUTED IN THE RAIN
FORESTS. AS A POSITIVE ALTERNATIVE, A NUMBER OF RAINFOREST
COMMUNITIES ARE NOW ATTEMPTING TO MAINTAIN THEIR WAY OF LIFE
AND EXPAND THEIR INCOME THROUGH SUSTAINABLE EXTRACTION OF
RESOURCES.

01236 BAKER, L.
SERGIO RAMIREZ'S SANDINO
LATIN AMERICAN PERSPECTIVES, 16(3) (SUM 89), 83-85.
RAMIREZ'S HISTORY OF HIS COUNTRY. PRESENTS A WORLD IN
WHICH PEOPLE MAKE HISTORY, THOUGH OF COURSE THEY DO NOT MAKE
IT IN CIRCUMSTANCES OR WITH RESOURCES OF THEIR UNCONDITIONED
CHOOSING. IT IS A WORLD IN WHICH PEOPLE'S CHOICES DO MAKE A
DIFFERENCEAND TO OTHER PEOPLE'S WELFARE AS WELL AS TO THEIR
DEFINITION OF THEIR PERSONAL ETHICAL IDENTITY. RAMIREZ'S
HISTORY OF HIS PATRIA OFFERS HIS COMPATRIOTS COMPETING
POSSIBILITIES FOR THEIR CHOICE OF SPIRITUAL PADRES, AND HE
PUTS US IN TOUCH WITH THESE FATHERS AT MOMENTS OF CRUCIAL
CHOICE.

01237 BAKER, P.K.
THE AMERICAN CHALLENGE IN SOUTHERN AFRICA
CURRENT HISTORY, 88(538) (MAY 89), 209-212, 245-246.
PRESIDENT BUSH FACES FORMIDABLE CONSTRAINTS AND FRESH
OPPORTUNITIES IN SOUTHERN AFRICA. THE REGION COULD BE A
MAJOR TESTING GROUND FOR HIS ADMINISTRATION, PARTICULARLY
ITS ABILITY TO FORGE A BIPARTISAN FOREIGN POLICY.

01238 BAKER, R.
INSTITUTIONAL INNOVATION, DEVELOPMENT AND ENVIRONMENTAL
MANAGEMENT: AN 'ADMINISTRATIVE TRAP' REVISITED. PART II
PUBLIC ADMINISTRATION AND DEVELOPMENT, 9(2) (APR 89),
159-168.
THE FIRST PART OF THIS ARTICLE (VOL 9, NO. 1) EXAMINED
THE WAYS IN WHICH THE STRUCTURE AND DIVISION OF
RESPONSIBILITIES WITHIN PUBLIC ADMINISTRATIONS OFTEN
RENDERED THEM UNABLE TO PERCEIVE OR COPE WITH BROAD PROBLEMS
OF ENVIRONMENTAL DECLINE. IN THE DEVELOPING WORLD THIS IS
COMPOUNDED BY THE CONTRADICTIONS BETWEEN PRESSURES FOR
ECONOMIC SURVIVAL VERSUS THE LONG-TERM CONSIDERATIONS FOR
SUSTAINABILITY AND CONSERVATION IN THE POLICY ARENA. IN THIS
SECOND PART THE AUTHOR REVIEWS AND EVALUATES FURTHER AREAS
OF ADMINISTRATIVE INNOVATION IN THIS AREA AND CONSIDERS THE
CLIMATE FOR POLICY AND INSTITUTIONAL CHANGE 25 YEARS AFTER
THE STOCKHOLM CONFERENCE. IN CONCLUSION, BASIC PRINCIPLES
GUIDING POLICY FORMULATION, METHODOLOGY AND ADMINISTRATIVE
ORGANIZATION ARE PRESENTED TO ALLOW ADMINISTRATIONS TO GAIN
SOME GROUND IN THE WORSENING ENVIRONMENTAL BALANCE SHEET.

01239 BAKER, R.S.
THE VERSAILLES TREATY AND AFTER
CURRENT HISTORY, 88(534) (JAN 89), 20-23.
THE AUTHOR DISCUSSES THE TRADITIONAL AMERICAN
ISOLATIONISM. PRESIDENT WOODROW WILSON'S LEADERSHIP AFTER
1917, THE UNITED STATES' FAILURE IN THE LEAGUE OF NATIONS,
AND THE GREED AND HASTE THAT LED TO THE VERSAILLES TREATY.

01240 BAKHASH, S.
AFTER THE GULF WAR I: IRAN'S HOME FRONT
WORLD TODAY, 45(3) (MAR 89), 46-48.
DESPITE SOME STRIKING CONTINUITIES ACROSS THE WATERSHED
OF THE IRANIAN REVOLUTION, SIGNIFICANT AND PROFOUND CHANGES
HAVE OCCURRED IN A NUMBER OF AREAS SINCE THE OVERTHROW OF
THE SHAH IN JANUARY 1979. AREAS OF MAJOR CHANGE INCLUDE
TRANSFORMATIONS IN THE RULING ELITES, THE OWNERSHIP OF
PROPERTY AND WEALTH, STATE CONTROL, AND THE CONSTITUTIONAL
STRUCTURE OF THE STATE.

01241 BAKHASH, S.
THE ISLAMIC REPUBLIC OF IRAN, 1979-1989
WILSON QUARTERLY, XIII(4) (AUT 89), 54-62.
THE AUTHOR SURVEYS THE FIRST TEN YEARS OF THE ISLAMIC
REPUBLIC OF IRAN TO SEE HOW A FUNDAMENTALIST THEOCRACY HAS
FARED IN COPING WITH THE PROBLEMS OF EVERYDAY GOVERNANCE. HE
NOTES THAT THE IRANIAN EXPERIMENT IS UNIQUE, ALTHOUGH OTHER
MODERN STATES ALSO ESPOUSE THE CONCEPT OF ISLAMICIZATION.

01242 BAKHASH, S.
THE POLITICS OF LAND, LAW, AND SOCIAL JUSTICE IN IRAN
MIDDLE EAST JOURNAL, 43(2) (SPR 89), 186-201.
IN OCTOBER 1986 THE IRANIAN MAJLIS APPROVED A BILL TO
TRANSFER OWNERSHIP OF SO-CALLED TEMPORARY CULTIVATION
AGRICULTURAL LAND FROM THE OWNERS TO THE CULTIVATORS
ACTUALLY WORKING THE LAND. THE CONTROVERSY REGARDING THIS
LEGISLATION IS USED IN THIS ARTICLE TO ADDRESS A NUMBER OF
OTHER ISSUES THAT HAVE ENGAGED THE ATTENTION OF IRAN'S
LEADERS SINCE THE ISLAMIC REVOLUTION OF 1979. THESE INCLUDE
THE APPLICATION OF ISLAMIC LAW TO MATTERS OF PUBLIC POLICY,
THE MEANS OF REALIZING THE GOAL OF SOCIAL JUSTICE, THE
AUTHORITY OF THE MAJLIS OR THE COUNCIL OF GUARDIANS TO
DECIDE SUCH MATTERS, AND THE ROLE OF THE AYATOLIAH AS THE
LEGITIMATOR OF MAJOR POLICY DECISIONS.

01243 BAKVIS, H.
REGIONAL POLITICS AND POLICY IN THE MULRONEY CABINET, 1984-
88: TOWARDS A THEORY OF THE REGIONAL MINISTER SYSTEM IN
CANADA
CANADIAN PUBLIC POLICY--ANALYSE DE POLITIQUES, XV(2) (JUN
89), 121-134.
IT HAS BEEN CLAIMED THAT THE LAST TRUDEAU CABINET (1980-
84) SAW A REVERSAL IN THE TREND TOWARDS THE DECLINE OF
REGIONAL MINISTERS. THIS ARTICLE ARGUES THAT THIS REVERSAL
WAS NEITHER TEMPORARY NOR UNIQUE. NOT ONLY HAS THE REGIONAL
MINISTER SYSTEM BEEN EVIDENT IN THE POLICIES AND OPERATIONS
OF THE MULRONEY CABINET (1984-88) BUT ITS OVERALL STRENGTH
AND PERSISTENCE HAS PROBABLY BEEN UNDERVALUED. THE SPECIFIC
FORM OF REGIONAL MINISTERIAL INFLUENCE UNDER MULRONEY,
NAMELY THE EMERGENCE OF A LIMITED NUMBER OF REGIONAL FIGURES
EXERCISING SIGNIFICANT INFLUENCE OVER MAJOR PROJECTS, IS
EXAMINED. TO ACCOUNT FOR THE ROLE OF REGIONAL MINISTERS IN
BOTH THE TRUDEAU AND MULRONEY CABINETS, ATTENTION IS DRAWN
TO TWO FACTORS - THE COMPLEXITIES OF THE MODERN
ADMINISTRATIVE STATE AND THE RISE OF MODERN COMPETITIVE
FEDERALISM - IRONICALLY THE SAME FACTORS USUALLY CITED IN
CONNECTION WITH THE DECLINE OF REGIONAL MINISTERS.

01244 BALABAN, A.
ELECTIONS AND LITERATURE IN ISRAEL
MIDSTREAM, XXXV(2) (FEB 89), 34-37.
THE RESULTS OF THE 1988 ELECTIONS IN ISRAEL, IN WHICH
THE RELIGIOUS PARTIES GAINED FIFTY PERCENT MORE VOTES THAN
IN PREVIOUS ELECTIONS, CAUGHT ALMOST EVERYONE BY SURPRISE.
CONSIDERING THE FACT THAT MANY VOTERS WITH A RELIGIOUS
AFFINITY TRADITIONALLY VOTE FOR THE LIKUD PARTY, IT WOULD
SEEM THAT RELIGION IS A MUCH MORE POWERFUL FACTOR IN ISRAEL
THAN POLITICAL EXPERTS HAD EVER GUESSED. BUT ANY OBSERVER
WHO CONCEIVES OF LITERATURE AS A MIRROR OF SOCIETY AND WHO
HAS CAREFULLY READ MODERN ISRAELI FICTION SHOULD NOT HAVE
BEEN SURPRISED. A CLOSE EXAMINATION OF CONTEMPORARY
LITERATURE REVEALS THAT THE YOUNG ISRAELI NOVELISTS DO NOT
DEAL WITH ONLY SECULAR, EXISTENTIAL ISSUES. IN THE WORKS OF
THE MOST PROMINENT ISRAELI WRITERS, ONE FINDS STRONG
OVERTONES OF RELIGIOUS YEARNING.

01245 BALABAN, E.; ALEKSEYEV, B.; ZINOVGEV, N.
USSR-USA: SEARCH FOR PRODUCTIVE COOPERATION
FOREIGN TRADE, 8 (1988), 16-22.
THIS ARTICLE REPORTS ON ATTEMPTS BY THE USSR TO
REVITALIZE A DECREASING TENDENCY OF TRADE TURNOVER WITH THE
UNITED STATES. IT REPORTS ON SPECIFIC PROPOSALS FOR
EXPANDING MUTUALLY BENEFICIAL TRADE AND ECONOMIC RELATIONS
COVERED AT THE 10TH SESSION OF THE JOINT COMMERCIAL
COMMISSION, EXAMINED ARE THE POLITICAL BARRIERS WHICH
OBSTRUCT THE NORMALIZATION OF BILATERAL TRADE, AND SOVIET
CONCERNS THAT TIES BE BASED ON REAL BUSINESS INTERESTS AND
ON PRINCIPLES OF EQUALITY AND NONDISCRIMINATION.

01246 BALABAN, O.
THE POSITIVISTIC NATURE OF THE CRITICAL THEORY
SCIENCE AND SOCIETY, 53(4) (WIN 89), 442-458.
AUTHOR, ODED BALABAN, EXAMINES MARCUSE (CRITICAL THEORY
OF THE FRANKFORT SCHOOL) AND OFFERS A TRENCHANT RE-
EXAMINATION OF THE DICHOTOMY BETWEEN "TRUE" AND "FALSE"
NEEDS, WHICH IS SEEN AS A VEILED FORM OF THE POSITIVIST
"IS"/ "OUGHT" DISTINCTION AND THUS A CONCESSION TO
POSITIVISM. HE USES MARX'S CONCEPT OF CRITIQUE TO OPPOSE THE
CONCEPT OF CRITIQUE IN THE CRITICAL THEORY. HE ALSO GIVES A
CRITIQUE OF THE FETISHISTIC DEFINITION. HE CONCLUDES THAT
THE HUMAN SCIENCES AWAIT A TRUE CRITICAL EXPLANATION OF
SOCIETY.

01247 BALAKHONOV, V.
SOVIET INDIANS: ARE THEY BEGINNING TO HAVE RESERVATIONS?
GLASNOST, II(3) (MAY 89), 25-26, 29.
THE RACIAL AND LINGUISTIC APARTHEID OF YAKUTIA IS A SIGN
OF INTENSIFYING ETHNIC DISCORD, WHICH HAS BECOME A PROBLEM
OF NATIONAL DIMENSIONS IN THE SOVIET UNION. YAKUTS ARE NO
LONGER CONTENT TO BE TREATED AS SILENT AND AMIABLE "LITTLE
BROTHERS." THE ETHNIC RENAISSANCE OF RECENT DECADES AND THE
GROWTH OF NATIONAL SELF-AWARENESS HAVE HAD THEIR EFFECT.
GRADUALLY, THE YAKUTS HAVE BECOME AWARE NOT ONLY OF THEIR

ABSOLUTE SUBJUGATION TO MOSCOW BUT ALSO OF THEIR DE FACTO
SECONDARY DEMOGRAPHIC STATUS IN YAKUTIA. THIS UNPLEASANT
REALIZATION IS ACCOMPANIED BY MOSCOW'S IRREVERSIBLE
EXPLOITATION OF YAKUTIA'S RICH NATURAL RESOURCES, INCLUDING
GOLD, DIAMONDS, AND COAL.

01248 BALAKRISHNAN, N.
MUTED PROTEST
FAR EASTERN ECONOMIC REVIEW, 142(52) (DEC 89), 20.
A PROPOSAL TO NOMINATE MEMBERS OF SINGAPORE'S PARLIAMENT
HAS SPARKED PASSIONATE AND PUBLIC OBJECTIONS FROM THE
NORMALLY DOCILE MPS OF THE RULING PEOPLE'S ACTION PARTY
(PAP). WHILE THE BILL EVENTUALLY PASSED ITS SECOND READING
IN PARLIAMENT, THE DEBATE INDICATED GROWING FACTIONALISM IN
THE PARTY WITH THE EXPECTED TRANSFER OF PRIME MINISTERSHIP
FROM LEE KUAN KEW TO FIRST DEPUTY PRIME MINISTER GOH CHOK
TONG. THE EMERGING FACTIONALISM, ALTHOUGH SMALL BY REGIONAL
STANDARDS, HAS RECEIVED ATTENTION BOTH LOCALLY AND ABROAD,
AND IS LIKELY TO INCREASE AS GOH GRAPPLES FOR POWER WITH THE
ONCE HEIR APPARENT SON OF LEE, TRADE AND INDUSTRY MINISTER
LEE HSIEN LOONG.

01249 BALAWYDER, A.
CANADIAN-SLAVIC CULTURAL NATIONALISM AND THE CANADIAN
GOVERNMENT'S REACTION
CANADIAN REVIEW OF STUDIES IN NATIONALISM, XVI(1-2) (1989),
197-208.
THE AUTHOR SURVEYS SLAVIC IMMIGRATION TO CANADA AND
EXAMINES EVIDENCE OF CULTURAL NATIONALISM AMONG SLAVIC
GROUPS THERE. HE ALSO LOOKS AT THE CANADIAN GOVERNMENT'S
RESPONSE TO THE SITUATION.

01250 BALCAR, L.
A BREAK IN THE CLOUDS: A TWO-WAY STREET
WORLD MARXIST REVIEW, 32(9) (SEP 89), 36-37.
THIS REPORT BY CZECHOSLOVAKIA AMBASSADOR, LADISLAV
BALCAR, ONE OF THE CHIEF NEGOTIATORS IN THE VIENNA TALKS ON
CONVENTIONAL ARMS IN EUROPE, GIVES HIS IMPRESSION OF THE
PROGRESS SO FAR, AND THE PROSPECTS AHEAD. HE FEELS THAT BOTH
SIDES NOW SEEM TO BE SPEAKING A COMMON LANGUAGE ON A NUMBER
OF MAJOR ISSUES AND THAT THIS HAS PAVED THE WAY FOR ADVANCE
TOWARDS THE EARLY CONCLUSION OF A TREATY ON CONVENTIAL ARMED
FORCES IN EUROPE, THE FIRST SUCH TREATY THERE. HE CONCLUDES
THAT THERE ARE DIFFICULTIES WHICH STILL REMAIN TO BE
RESOLVED AND THAT THERE IS STILL WORK TO BE DONE.

01251 BALCEROWKZ,
MEMORANDUM OF THE ECONOMIC REFORM PROGRAMME
EAST EUROPEAN REPORTER, 4(1) (WIN 89), 66-69.
THE MEMORANDUM OUTLINES THE BASIC ECONOMIC RESTRUCTURING
PLAN OF THE GOVERNMENT OF POLAND. IT CONTAINS MEASURES
DEALING WITH MONETARY PRICE STABILIZATION; STRUCTURAL
ADJUSTMENTS INCLUDING IMPROVING THE ENVIRONMENT FOR ECONOMIC
ACTIVITY, PRIVATIZATION OF STATE ENTERPRISES, IMPROVING THE
EFFICIENCY OF PUBLIC SECTOR ENTERPRISES, THE REALLOCATION OF
RESOURCES AMONG SECTORS, AND THE DEVELOPMENT OF A SYSTEM OF
SOCIAL WELFARE SAFEGUARDS; AND OUTLINES THE NEED FOR FOREIGN
ECONOMIC ASSISTANCE AND A REDUCTION OF EXTERNAL DEBT.

01252 BALDAN, T.
MONGOLIA AND THE CMEA COUNTRIES
FOREIGN TRADE, 3 (1988), 5-7.
THIS ARTICLE EXPLORES THE ALL-ROUND COOPERATION WITH THE
CMEA (EAST EUROPEAN ECONOMIC COMMUNITY) AS BEING A POWERFUL
FACTOR IS ASSISTING MONGOLIA'S ACCELERATED SOCIO-ECONOMIC
DEVELOPMENT. IT TRACES THE HISTORY OF MONGOLIA'S INVOLVEMENT
WITH THE CMEA SINCE JOINING IN 1962. IT EXPLORES THE TRADE
GROWTH WHICH STEMS FROM INCREASED EXPORT POTENTIAL.

01253 BALDASSARE, M.
CITIZEN SUPPORT FOR REGIONAL GOVERNMENT IN THE NEW SUBURBIA
URBAN AFFAIRS QUARTERLY, 24(3) (MAR 89), 460-469.
POLITICAL FRAGMENTATION, IN THE FORM OF MANY SMALL
MUNICIPALITIES CHARTING THEIR OWN DESTINIES, IS A
FUNDAMENTAL ATTRIBUTE OF SUBURBAN REGIONS. SCHOLARS ARE
DIVIDED ABOUT THE NEED FOR ADDRESSING FRAGMENTATION THROUGH
NEW REGIONAL-LEVEL GOVERNMENTS. IN ORANGE COUNTY, CALIFORNIA,
WHICH IS A MULTIMUNICIPALITY SUBURBAN REGION STRICKEN WITH
GROWTH AND TRAFFIC PROBLEMS, A REPRESENTATIVE SURVEY OF 1,
008 RESIDENTS INDICATES TWO-TO-ONE OPPOSITION TO MERGING
COUNTY AND CITY GOVERNMENTS INTO ONE COUNTYWIDE AUTHORITY.
SEVERAL FACTORS ARE ASSOCIATED WITH STRONG OPPOSITION TO
MERGING LOCAL GOVERNMENTS; MOST SIGNIFICANT ARE THE DESIRE
TO MAINTAIN CITY POWER AND THE BELIEF THAT THE COUNTY WILL
BECOME A WORSE PLACE TO LIVE IN THE FUTURE. IN SUM, PUBLIC
OPINION IS A SERIOUS OBSTACLE TO REGIONAL-LEVEL AUTHORITY IN
SUBURBIA.

01254 BALDWIN, N.
PRESSURE GROUPS AND THE HOUSE OF LORDS
CONSTITUTIONAL REFORM QUARTERLY REVIEW, 4(2) (SUM 89), 5.
BRITAIN'S HOUSE OF LORDS ENLARGES BOTH THE SIZE AND
SCOPE OF THE PARLIAMENTARY LOBBY AND PROVIDES GROUPS WITH
ANOTHER ACCESS ROUTE TO POWER. IN RECENT YEARS AS A DIRECT

RESULT BOTH OF INCREASED ACTIVITY OF THE MEMBERS AND THEIR
WILLINGNESS TO VOTE AGAINST THE GOVERNMENT, THE HOUSE OF
LORDS HAS TAKEN ON AN INCREASED RELEVANCE FOR PRESSURE
GROUPS. HOWEVER, THE RELATIONSHIP IS NOT ENTIRELY ONE-WAY;
MANY PEERS SPEAK OF THE CONSIDERABLE ASSISTANCE THEY RECEIVE
FROM GROUPS WHEN THE INITIAL APPROACH WAS MADE BY A PEER TO
A GROUP RATHER THAN THE OTHER WAY AROUND.

01255 BALDWIN, P.
THE SCANDINAVIAN ORIGINS OF THE SOCIAL INTERPRETATION OF
THE WELFARE STATE
COMPARATIVE STUDIES IN SOCIETY AND HISTORY, 31(1) (JAN 89),
3-24.
THIS ARTICLE EXAMINES THE ORIGINS OF SCANDINAVIAN SOCIAL
POLICY'S UNIQUE FEATURES. IT ANALYZES THE REASONS WHY
MEASURES HERE WERE UNIVERSALIST, COVERING ALL REGARDLESS OF
SOCIAL CLASS, AND WHY THEY WERE FINANCED SIGNIFICANTLY
THROUGH TAXES, NOT PREMIUMS. IT TAKES PENSION POLICY AS THE
MOST CONVENIENT GATEWAY TO THESE ISSUES. IT CONCLUDES THAT
UNIVERSALISM AND TAX FINANCING HERE NOT THE EXPRESSION IN
TERMS OF WELFARE POLICY OF ANY UNIQUELY NORDIC SENSE OF
SOCIAL SOLIDARITY AND CERTAINLY NOT ONE INSPIRED BY
SOCIALISTS OR WORKERS. INSTEAD, THESE FEATURES WERE THE
RESULT OF NARROW INTEREST DISPUTES FOUGHT OUT BETWEEN THE
RISING RURAL MIDDLE CLASS AND THE ENTRENCHED BUREAUCRATIC
AND URBAN ELITES. IT FOLLOWS THAT THE SOCIAL INTERPRETATION
OF THE WELFARE STATE RESTS ON SHAKY FOUNDATIONS EVEN IN ITS
SCANDINAVIAN REDOUBT.

01256 BALIBAR, E.
RACISM AS UNIVERSALISM
NEW POLITICAL SCIENCE, (FAL 89), 9-22.
THE AUTHOR EXAMINES THE SEMANTICS OF USE OF THE TERM
UNIVERSALISM, AND MAKES SEMANTIC COMPARISONS WITH CERTAIN
OPPOSING CONCEPTS: RACISM, SEXISM, AND NATIONALISM. EACH OF
THESE OPPOSING TERMS FIT INTO THE CATEGORY OF EXISTENCE FROM
WHICH AN INTENTIONAL OR AN EXTENSIONAL VIEWPOINT DIVIDES THE
UNIVERSALITY OF THE HUMAN SPECIES INTO EXCLUSIVE
TRANSHISTORICAL GROUPS. THE IMPACT OF THESE WORDS, AS WELL
AS VARIOUS INTERPRETATIONS ARE DEBATED.

01257 BALILES, G.
US GOVERNORS GET A FIRST-HAND LOOK AT 1992
EUROPE, (289) (SEP 89), 14-15.
THE ARTICLE REPORTS ON THE VISIT OF NINE US STATE
GOVERNORS TO EUROPE. THEY VISITED WITH VARIOUS LEADERS OF
THE EUROPEAN COMMUNITY AND DISCUSSED THE IMPLICATIONS OF THE
SINGLE EUROPEAN ACT. US GOVERNORS ARE BECOMING INCREASINGLY
AWARE OF THE NECESSITY OF ACKNOWLEDGING AND REACTING TO
INTERNATIONAL TRADE REALITIES.

01258 BALL, D.
CONTROLLING THEATRE NUCLEAR WAR
BRITISH JOURNAL OF POLITICAL SCIENCE, 19(3) (JUL 89),
303-327.
THE AUTHOR ADDRESSES ASPECTS OF COMMAND AND CONTROL IN
THE EUROPEAN THEATRE, WHICH HAS A MORE DEVELOPED, EXTENSIVE,
COMPREHENSIVE, SOPHISTICATED, AND PRACTISED C3I (COMMAND,
CONTROL, COMMUNICATIONS, AND INTELLIGENCE) ARCHITECTURE THAN
THAT OF ANY OTHER THEATRE. THE PRIMARY CONCERN IS THE
IMPLICATIONS OF THE COMPLEXITY AND VULNERABILITIES OF THE
THEATRE C3I SYSTEM FOR THE CONTROL OF ESCALATION DURING A
MAJOR CONFLICT. THE AUTHOR ALSO EXPLORES SOME CONNECTIONS
BETWEEN THE THEATRE AND GLOBAL/STRATEGIC C3I SYSTEMS, WHICH
SUGGEST THAT A MAJOR WAR IN EUROPE WOULD GREATLY IMPEDE THE
TRANSITION TO ANY LIMITED OR CONTROLLED STRATEGIC NUCLEAR
EXCHANGE BETWEEN THE USA AND THE USSR.

01259 BALL, J.
AFTER ALBERT AND BALL: THE PROGRESS OF THE EUROPEAN
COMMUNITY
AVAILABLE FROM NTIS, NO. PB89-192819/GAR, AUG 88, 44.
THE PAPER IS DIVIDED INTO THREE MAIN SECTIONS. THE FIRST
REVIEWS THE ALBERT-BALL REPORT, ITS BACKGROUND, THE IDEAS
PRESENTED, AND OFFERS SOME BRIEF OBSERVATIONS AS TO ITS
SIGNIFICANCE. IN THE SECOND SOME CONSIDERATION IS GIVEN TO
MICRO-ECONOMIC DEVELOPMENTS THAT WERE PART OF A MAIN THEME
OF ALBERT-BALL AND WHICH ARE NOW ENCAPSULATED IN THE SYMBOL
OF 1992. THIRDLY THE AUTHORS REVIEW SOME IMPORTANT ASPECTS
OF MACRO-ECONOMIC POLICY AND THE DEVELOPMENT OF MONETARY AND
FISCAL INTEGRATION. FINALLY THERE ARE SOME CONCLUDING
OBSERVATIONS.

01260 BALL, W. R.
INTER-AGENCY COORDINATION AND COMPETITIVE BUREAUS IN THE
IMPLEMENTATION OF DEVELOPMENT ADMINISTRATION PROGRAMS IN
SOUTHERN THAILAND
DISSERTATION ABSTRACTS INTERNATIONAL, 49(8) (FEB 89),
2373-A.
COORDINATION IS A VALUED GOOD/GOAL WITHIN THE THAI
BUREAUCRACY. A HIGH INCIDENCE OF INTER-AGENCY INFORMATION-
TRANSFERS OCCURS DURING THE IMPLEMENTATION PHASE OF
DEVELOPMENT PROGRAMS. INFORMAL RELATIONS PLAY A MAJOR ROLE
IN INTER-AGENCY CONTACT, AND A BUREAUCRACY-WIDE NORM OF

INDIVIDUAL BUREAU SELF-INTEREST STRONGLY AFFECTS BOTH THE
FREQUENCY AND METHOD OF INTER-AGENCY COORDINATION OF
DEVELOPMENT PROGRAMS.

01261 BALOGH, A.
    STABILITY IS ESSENTIAL TO DEVELOPMENT
    WORLD MARXIST REVIEW, 31(11) (NOV 88), 39-42.
        WITHOUT A DRASTIC REDUCTION OF THE MILITARY
    INFRASTRUCTURE, ONE CANNOT EXPECT TO FULLY TAP THE POTENTIAL
    OF NEW THINKING, SINCE ONE CANNOT RULE OUT THE DANGER OF
    RELAPSES INTO OLD-FASHIONED CONCEPTS, METHODS AND
    STEREOTYPES. THE MOST SERIOUS IMPEDIMENT TO STABLE AND
    EFFECTIVE DEVELOPMENT IS ROOTED NOT ONLY IN THE EXISTENCE OF
    THE HUGE MILITARY INDUSTRIES, BUT ALSO IN THE PROFOUND
    ECONOMIC, SOCIAL, POLITICAL AND IDEOLOGICAL CONSEQUENCES OF
    THE LONG DECADES OF CONFRONTATION.

01262 BAMATTRE-MANOUKIAN, P.
    GREAT JUDGES, GREAT LEADERS: KIND TRANSFORMATIONAL
      JUDICIAL LEADERSHIP
    DISSERTATION ABSTRACTS INTERNATIONAL, 50(5) (NOV 89),
    1430-A.
        THIS DISSERTATION SURVEYS THE LEADERSHIP ROLE OF THE
    JUDGE, THE IMPACT OF JUDICIAL DECISIONS AND JUDICIAL
    LEADERSHIP, LEADERSHIP THEORIES, LEADERSHIP STYLES, THE
    TRAINING AND DEVELOPMENT OF KIND TRANSFORMATIONAL JUDICIAL
    LEADERS, AND EXAMPLES OF JUDGES WHO ARE VIEWED AS GREAT
    LEADERS, INCLUDING JOHN MARSHALL, CHARLES EVANS HUGHES, EARL
    WARREN, AND JAMES R. BROWING.

01263 BAMFORD, D.
    ALGERIA: DUMPING "SOCIALISM"
    MIDDLE EAST INTERNATIONAL, (344) (FEB 89), 13-14.
        THE FORM OF ALGERIAN SOCIALISM HAS CHANGED SINCE THE
    HEAVILY-CENTRALIZED BUREAUCRACY, DOMINATED BY THE NATIONAL
    LIBERATION FRONT, FOUND ITSELF UNABLE TO COPE WITH THE WAVE
    OF SOCIAL UNREST THAT ACCOMPANIED THE IMPOSITION OF HEAVY
    AUSTERITY MEASURES IN 1988. SUPPORTED BY THE ARMY, PRESIDENT
    CHADLI BENJADID HAS MOVED TO PURGE THE RULING ELITE OF THE
    OLD GUARD IDEOLOGUES AND INTRODUCE AN ALGERIAN VERSION OF
    GLASNOST.

01264 BAMFORD, D.
    ALGERIA: ON THE WAY TO PLURALISM
    MIDDLE EAST INTERNATIONAL, (345) (MAR 89), 16.
        ALGERIANS WENT TO THE POLLS ON FEB. 23, 1989, TO APPROVE
    A NEW CONSTITUTION THAT OPENS THE WAY TO AN END OF THE ONE-
    PARTY, SOCIALIST STATE. UNDER THE NEW CONSTITUTION,
    INDEPENDENT POLITICAL ASSOCIATIONS WILL BE ALLOWED FOR THE
    FIRST TIME. THESE ARE EXPECTED TO FORM THE BASIS OF A MULTI-
    PARTY SYSTEM.

01265 BAMFORD, D.
    ALGERIA: TOWARDS PLURALISM
    MIDDLE EAST INTERNATIONAL, (354) (JUL 89), 14.
        ALGERIA TOOK ANOTHER STEP TOWARDS INTRODUCING A MULTI-
    PARTY SYSTEM WHEN THE NATIONAL ASSEMBLY VOTED TO ADOPT A NEW
    POLITICAL PARTIES LAW. UNDER ITS PROVISIONS, ASSOCIATIONS OF
    A POLITICAL CHARACTER AND INDEPENDENT OF THE RULING NATIONAL
    LIBERATION FRONT ARE ALLOWED TO APPLY FOR REGISTRATION AND
    COMPETE IN FUTURE NATIONAL ELECTIONS. UP TO 30 GROUPS THAT
    HAVE FORMED BEFORE AND SINCE THE OCTOBER RIOTS ARE EXPECTED
    TO TRY AND BENEFIT FROM THE NEW LEGISLATION. DRAFT LAWS ON
    ELECTORAL CODES AND FREEDOM OF EXPRESSION ARE ALSO BEING
    CONSIDERED.

01266 BAMFORD, D.
    ALGERIA: UNCONVINCING WIN
    MIDDLE EAST INTERNATIONAL, (341) (JAN 89), 16.
        BECAUSE INCUMBENT CHADLI BENJEDID WAS THE ONLY CANDIDATE
    IN ALGERIA'S PRESIDENTIAL ELECTION, THE VOTING SERVED AS AN
    INDICATOR OF POPULAR SUPPORT FOR CHADLI AND HIS POST-OCTOBER
    RIOTS PROGRAM. CHADLI SUFFERED A MORAL DEFEAT, SECURING
    FEWER "YES" VOTES THAN IN ANY PRESIDENTIAL ELECTION SINCE
    ALGERIAN INDEPENDENCE.

01267 BAMFORD, D.
    ASAD GETS AWAY WITH IT
    MIDDLE EAST INTERNATIONAL, 352 (JUN 89), 4-5.
        THE EXTRAORDINARY ARAB SUMMIT THAT BEGAN IN MOROCCO ON
    23 MAY FORMALLY MARKED THE RETURN OF EGYPT TO THE ARAB FOLD
    AFTER THE TEN YEAR "SUSPENSION" THAT FOLLOWED ITS SIGNING OF
    THE CAMP DAVID ACCORDS WITH ISRAEL. THE SUMMIT ALSO SAW THE
    PLO GETTING VIRTUALLY ALL IT ASKED FOR IN TERMS OF ARAB
    SUPPORT FOR YASSER ARAFAT'S DIPLOMATIC INITIATIVES AND A
    FURTHER PROMISE OF FINANCIAL SUPPORT FOR THE INTIFADA. BUT
    THE SUMMIT FAILED IN ITS PRIME OBJECTIVE, TO FIND COMMON
    GROUND ON WHICH TO BUILD A PLAN FOR PEACE IN LEBANON.

01268 BAMFORD, D.
    BACK TO SQUARE ONE
    MIDDLE EAST INTERNATIONAL, 356 (AUG 89), 13-14.
        IN THE DAYS LEADING UP TO THE OAU SUMMIT IN ADDIS ABABA
    IT WAS THE DISPUTE BETWEEN LIBYA AND ITS SOUTHERN NEIGHBOUR
    CHAD THAT DOMINATED THE HEADLINES. FIGHTING BETWEEN THE TWO
    ARMIES STOPPED LAST AUGUST WHEN COLONEL QADHAFI DECLARED
    THAT LIBYA NO LONGER SUPPORTED CHADIAN REBEL GROUPS TRYING
    TO OUST THE REGIME OF PRESIDENT HISSENE HABRE. SINCE THEN,
    LIBYA AND CHAD HAVE EXCHANGED AMBASSADORS. BUT THE ISSUE OF
    WHO OWNS THE AOUZOU STRIP ALONG THEIR JOINT BORDER, OCCUPIED
    BY LIBYA SINCE 1978, HAS CONTINUED TO MAR RELATIONS.

01269 BAMFORD, D.
    BACK WHERE HE STARTED
    MIDDLE EAST INTERNATIONAL, 353 (JUN 89), 11.
        THE POLITICAL HONEYMOON FOR PRESIDENT ZINE EL-ABIDINE
    BEN ALI SEEMS TO BE COMING TO AN END, AS RENEWED TURBULENCE
    INVOLVING THE ISLAMIC FUNDAMENTALIST MOVEMENT COINCIDES WITH
    BAD NEWS ON THE ECONOMIC FRONT. AFTER LAST YEAR'S OPTIMISTIC
    RESULTS, INCLUDING A CURRENT ACCOUNT SURPLUS THANKS TO
    IMPRESSIVE RECEIPTS FROM TOURISM, THE FIRST HALF OF 1989 IS
    SHOWING A DRAMATIC RISE IN IMPORTS DUE TO CONTINUING DROUGHT
    AND WAVERING TOURIST ARRIVALS. A 1989 ECONOMIC GROWTH TARGET
    OF 5.5 PER CENT IS BEING SHARPLY SCALED DOWN.

01270 BAMFORD, D.
    BRITAIN AND THE PLO: QUEUING TO SEE ARAFAT
    MIDDLE EAST INTERNATIONAL, (342) (JAN 89), 5-6.
        ON JANUARY 11, 1989, GERALD KAUFMAN BECAME THE FIRST
    BRITISH OPPOSITION FRONT BENCHER TO MEET YASSER ARAFAT. ON
    JANUARY 13, BRITISH FOREIGN OFFICE MINISTER OF STATE WILLIAM
    WALDEGRAVE ALSO TALKED WITH ARAFAT.

01271 BAMFORD, D.
    HASSAN'S DIPLOMATIC OFFENSIVE
    MIDDLE EAST INTERNATIONAL, 355 (JUL 89), 13-14.
        MOROCCO IS CALLING IN ITS DIPLOMATIC CHIPS, AND KING
    HASSAN HAS DISPATCHED ENVOYS ACROSS THE CONTINENT TO RALLY
    SUPPORT AT LEAST FOR THE FREEZING OF POLISARIO INVOLVEMENT
    IN THE OAU PENDING THE RESULT OF A UN/OAU SPONSORED
    REFERENDUM ON SELF-DETERMINATION IN THE DISPUTED TERRITORY.
    HASSAN HAS ARMED HIMSELF WITH EVIDENCE THAT IT IS MOROCCO,
    RATHER THAN POLISARIO, THAT IS WORKING TOWARDS A PEACEFUL
    SOLUTION TO THE WESTERN SAHARA CONFLICT. NOT ONLY HAS
    MOROCCO EXPRESSED FULL SUPPORT FOR THE REFERENDUM, BUT IT
    HAS HELD UNPRECEDENTED DIRECT TALKS WITH REPRESENTATIVES OF
    POLISARIO. HOWEVER, THOSE TALKS - HELD ON 4 JANUARY AT THE
    KING'S PALACE IN MARRAKECH - DID NOT AMOUNT TO NEGOTIATIONS
    ON A SOLUTION AS PROPOSED BY THE OAU, AND, TO THE CHAGRIN OF
    POLISARIO, THEY HAVE NOT BEEN FOLLOWED UP WITH FURTHER
    MEETINGS.

01272 BAMFORD, D.
    LIBYA: IMAGE PROBLEMS
    MIDDLE EAST INTERNATIONAL, (341) (JAN 89), 12.
        COLONEL QADHAFI'S "OPERATION CHARM," DESIGNED IMPROVE
    HIS IMAGE, HAS BEEN IN FULL SWING FOR SIX MONTHS. BUT HIS
    NEW IMAGE WAS TARNISHED BY ALLEGATIONS THAT A FACTORY AT
    RABA HAS SET TO MASS PRODUCE CHEMICAL WEAPONS. ADDED TO THIS
    WAS SPECULATION THAT THE FATAH REVOLUTIONARY COUNCIL OF ABU
    NIDAL, A RADICAL PALESTINIAN GROUP LINKED TO LIBYA, WAS
    BEHIND THE DESTRUCTION OF PAN AM FLIGHT 103.

01273 BAMFORD, D.
    LIBYA: THE COLONEL EYES SUDAN
    MIDDLE EAST INTERNATIONAL, (346) (MAR 89), 14.
        THE VISIT TO LIBYA BY SUDANESE PRIME MINISTER SADIQ AL-
    MAHDI ON MARCH 7, 1989, CAME WHILE HE WAS UNDER FIRE AT HOME
    FOR DRAWING HIS COUNTRY TOO CLOSE TO COLONEL QAHHAFI,
    JEOPARDIZING SUDAN'S RELATIONSHIP WITH EGYPT.

01274 BAMFORD, D.
    QADAHFI'S ANNIVERSARY PARTY
    MIDDLE EAST INTERNATIONAL, (358) (SEP 89), 11-12.
        THE ARTICLE REPORTS ON LIBYA'S CELEBRATION OF THE
    TWENTIETH ANNIVERSARY OF THE REVOLUTION THAT PUT MU'AMMAR
    QADHAFI IN POWER. THE WIDE RANGE OF HEADS OF STATE THAT
    ATTENDED THE FESTIVITIES WAS DESIGNED TO SHOW HO FAR LIBYA'S
    THREE-YEAR OLD "FRIENDSHIP OFFENSIVE" HAD PROGRESSED. THE
    CELEBRATION WAS HELD A DAY AFTER THE DRAMATIC ANNOUNCEMENT
    THAT LIBYAN AND CHADIAN FOREIGN MINISTERS HAD SIGNED AN
    AGREEMENT ON AN END TO THEIR BORDER DISPUTE OVER THE AOUZOU
    STRIP.

01275 BAMFORD, D.
    SECOND THOUGHTS
    MIDDLE EAST INTERNATIONAL, 356 (AUG 89), 14-15.
        THE LEADERSHIP IN ALGERIA AND TUNISIA, IN THEIR
    DIFFERENT WAYS, HAVE BEEN ADVOCATING SINCE LAST YEAR THE
    REPLACEMENT OF THEIR DE FACTO ONE-PARTY REGIMES WITH
    PLURALIST SYSTEMS IN WHICH OPPOSITION POLITICAL MOVEMENTS
    WOULD BE ALLOWED A FAIR SHOT AT NATIONAL REPRESENTATION.
    WITH NEWLY DESIGNED ELECTORAL POLICIES, ALGERIAN ELECTIONS
    ARE NOW AKIN TO THE TUNISIAN WINNER-TAKES-ALL MODEL, UNDER
    WHICH THE BIGGEST PARTY WHICH IN EACH CASE IS THE RULING
    PARTY, THE ONLY ONE ABLE TO PROPERLY DEVELOP UNTIL NOW -
    WILL CONTINUE TO DOMINATE FOR THE FORESEEABLE FUTURE.

01276 BAMFORD, D.
STRUGGLE IN ALGERIA
MIDDLE EAST INTERNATIONAL, (359) (SEP 89), 10-11.
BEHIND THE SCENES POLITICAL STRUGGLES OVER THE NATURE
AND PACE OF REFORMS IN ALGERIA BECAME APPARENT WITH THE
DISMISSAL OF PRIME MINISTER QASDI MERBAH. THE PRESIDENTIAL
DECREE BLAMED MERBAH FOR DELAYING MANY OF THE POLITICAL AND
ECONOMIC REFORMS THAT WERE PROMISED AFTER THE STREET RIOTS
OF OCTOBER, 1988. MOULOUD HAMROUCHE, THE NEW PRIME MINISTER,
IS VERY MUCH THE PRESIDENT'S MAN, AND THE MAJORITY OF THE
NEW CABINET ARE KNOWN FOR THEIR LOYALTY. THE CHANGE OF
LEADERSHIP RESULTED IN SOME IMMEDIATE REFORMS; TWO KEY
OPPOSITION PARTIES WERE RECOGNIZED WITHIN DAYS OF
HAMROUCHE'S APPOINTMENT.

01277 BAMFORD, D.
THE ARAB SUMMIT: COMPLEX AND THORNY
MIDDLE EAST INTERNATIONAL, (351) (MAY 89), 9.
THE REINTEGRATION OF EGYPT INTO THE ARAB LEAGUE HAD AN
IMPACT ON THE RECENT EMERGENCY SUMMIT AS EGYPT WENT STRAIGHT
TO THE OFFENSIVE, DECLARING THAT IT INTENDED TO TRY TO
RESOLVE THE LEBANON ISSUE AND BEGAN SETTING ITSELF UP AS A
BUFFER AGAINST SYRIAN ENCROACHMENTS ON PLO INTERESTS.
ALTHOUGH HE THREATENED A BOYCOTT OF THE SUMMIT, LIBYA'S
COLONEL QADHAFI WAS CONVINCED TO ATTEND, WHICH HE DID AFTER
HIS OWN FASHION.

01278 BAMFORD, D.
THE MAGHREB: THE DREAM COMES TRUE?
MIDDLE EAST INTERNATIONAL, (345) (MAR 89), 14-15.
A NEW STAGE IN THE MAGHREB UNITY PROCESS WAS DECLARED
FEB. 17, 1989, WHEN FIVE NORTH AFRICAN LEADERS SIGNED A
TREATY ESTABLISHING THE ARAB MAGREB UNION (AMU). THE TREATY
IS PRIMARILY CONCERNED WITH ECONOMIC INTEGRATION AS THE AMU
MEMBERS, WHO ARE DEPENDENT ON TRADE WITH THE EEC, TRY TO
GEAR UP FOR THE CONSEQUENCES OF THE SINGLE EUROPEAN MARKET
IN 1992.

01279 BAMFORD, D.
THE MAGHREB: WHAT DOES "UNION" MEAN?
MIDDLE EAST INTERNATIONAL, (343) (FEB 89), 12-13.
FOLLOWING A MEETING ON JAN. 24, 1989, MOROCCO, ALGERIA,
LIBYA, TUNISIA, AND MAURITANIA ISSUED A STATEMENT CALLING
FOR UNITY. THE COMMUNIQUE CALLED FOR THE ESTABLISHMENT OF
THE "ARAB MAGHREB UNION," ALTHOUGH THERE WAS NO AGREEMENT ON
EXACTLY WHAT THE UNION WILL ENTAIL.

01280 BAMFORD, D.
TUNISIA: CLEAN SWEEP
MIDDLE EAST INTERNATIONAL, (348) (APR 89), 11-12.
THE ELECTIONS IN TUNISIA YIELDED FEW SURPRISES. BEN ALI,
THE CURRENT PRESIDENT, WAS APPROVED AS WERE ALL 141
CANDIDATES OF THE RULING CONSTITUTIONAL DEMOCRATIC RALLY.
THE ONLY SIGNIFICANT OPPOSITION WAS FROM THE ISLAMIC
FUNDAMENTALIST FRONT. MOST OPPOSITION LEADERS AGREED WITH
THE FORMAT AND OUTCOME OF THE ELECTION DUE TO THEIR DECISION
TO ADHERE TO BEN ALI'S NATIONAL PACT WHICH LAYS OUT A
LONGTERM PROGRAM OF POLITICAL AND ECONOMIC REFORMS.

01281 BAMFORD, D.
US AND THE PLO: EDGING FORWARD
MIDDLE EAST INTERNATIONAL, (347) (MAR 89), 8.
IN MARCH 1989, TALKS BETWEEN THE PLO AND THE USA
REOPENED IN CARTHAGE. THE PLO APPEARED TO BE GIVING WAY TO
THE AMERICAN INSISTENCE ON BILATERAL PALESTINIAN-ISRAELI
TALKS BEFORE ANY INTERNATIONAL CONFERENCE. MEANWHILE, THE
USA SEEMED TO SOFTEN TO THE IDEA THAT ONLY THE PLO CAN
REPRESENT THE PALESTINIANS AT THOSE TALKS.

01282 BANDOW, D.
CONGRESSIONAL FODDER
REASON, 20(9) (FEB 89), 48-49.
THE AUTHOR SURVEYS ISSUES FACING CONGRESS AND THE BUSH
ADMINISTRATION: TAXES, SAVINGS AND LOANS, BANKING
DEREGULATION, MINIMUM WAGE, CHILD CARE, PARENTAL LEAVE,
CAMPAIGN FINANCE REFORM, EDUCATION, ENVIRONMENTAL REGULATION,
TAKEOVERS, AND MARKET-ORIENTED INITIATIVES.

01283 BANDOW, D.
WHAT NEXT FOR NATO? GET THE SUPERPOWERS OUT OF EUROPE
REASON, 20(11) (APR 89), 32-36.
THE FORMAL COLLAPSE OF NATO IS NOT IMMINENT BUT THE
ALLIANCE IS INCREASINGLY INCAPABLE OF RESPONDING TO THE
SOVIET CHALLENGE. GORBACHEV HAS MANIPULATED WESTERN EUROPEAN
PERCEPTIONS OF THE SOVIET THREAT AND UNDERMINED NATO'S
COHESION AND SUPPORT FOR NUCLEAR FORCE MODERNIZATION AND
CONVENTIONAL FORCE BUILDUP.

01284 BANDOW, D.
WHAT'S STILL WRONG WITH THE WORLD BANK?
ORBIS, 33(1) (WIN 89), 73-89.
THE ONLY WAY TO BRING GLOBAL ECONOMIC POLICY INTO LINE
WITH REALITY -- THUS PROMOTING DEVELOPMENT AND REDUCING
POVERTY -IS TO REDUCE LENDING. THAT IS THE COURSE PRIVATE

CREDIT TO THIRD WORLD GOVERNMENTS HAS BEEN FOLLOWING SINCE
1981. BUT LOANS FROM MULTILATERAL DEVELOPMENT INSTITUTIONS,
LED BY THE WORLD BANK, ROSE FROM $22.5 BILLION IN 1985 TO
$27.2 BILLION IN 1987. (GOVERNMENT-TO-GOVERNMENT LOANS
INCREASED OVER THE SAME PERIOD, FROM $11.5 BILLION TO $13.4
BILLION). THESE NEW LOANS, TO FINANCE THE INTEREST PAYMENTS
ON OLD DEBT, OBSCURE ECONOMIC REALITY. IT WOULD BE FAR
BETTER TO CUT OFF NEW CREDIT WHILE PROVIDING DEBT RELIEF.
THE ECONOMIC EFFECTS WOULD BE MUCH THE SAME, BUT THE PROCESS
WOULD MORE ACCURATELY REFLECT THE FINANCIAL HEALTH OF BOTH
CREDITORS AND DEBTORS. IT WOULD ALSO STOP PILING DEBT UPON
DEBT.

01285 BANKS, A.J.
FREE SPEECH-THE CONFLICT BETWEEN A MEMBER OF PARLIAMENT'S
FREEDOM OF SPEECH AND CONTEMPT OF COURT
PARLIAMENTARIAN, 70(1) (JAN 89), 21-23.
AN OPPOSITION PARTY MEMBER IN NEW ZEALAND DESCRIBES HIS
CHALLENGE IN THE COURTS TO FIGHT CHARGES OF CONTEMPT OF
COURT FOR COMMENTS HE MADE IN POLITICAL DEBATE OUTSIDE OF
NEW ZEALAND'S PARLIAMENT. CONTEMPT CHARGES WERE FILED
AGAINST THE AUTHOR AND THE BROADCASTING CORPORATION OF NEW
ZEALAND, AS WELL AS AGAINST THE AUTHOR AND WELLINGTON
NEWSPAPERS LTD., ALLEGING THAT STATEMENTS WERE MADE BY THE
AUTHOR, CONCERNING THREE INDIVIDUALS ACCUSED OF THE MURDERS
OF ELDERLY WOMEN AND CHILDREN, WHICH MIGHT PREJUDICE THEIR
TRIALS. THE CONSTITUTIONAL IMPORTANCE OF THE CASE, RULE OF
PARLIAMENTARY PRIVILEGES, AND THE LAWS OF CONTEMPT ARE
ANALYZED, IN RELATION TO THIS SPECIFIC CONFLICT CONCERNING
FREEDOM OF SPEECH IN NEW ZEALAND.

01286 BANKS, J.S.
AGENCY BUDGETS, COST INFORMATION, AND AUDITING
AMERICAN JOURNAL OF POLITICAL SCIENCE, 33(3) (AUG 89),
670-699.
A MODEL OF LEGISLATURE-AGENCY INTERACTION IS ANALYZED
WHERE THE AGENCY POSSESSES AN INFORMATIONAL ADVANTAGE IN
THAT ONLY IT KNOWS THE COST OF ITS SERVICES. THE LEGISLATURE
HAS THE ABILITY TO AUDIT THE AGENCY, WHERE AUDITING IS A
COSTLY MEANS OF VERIFYING THE AGENCY'S INFORMATION. TWO
DIFFERENT PROCEDURES ARE ANALYZED FOR DETERMINING THE
AGENCY'S BUDGET: IN ONE, THE AGENCY MAKES A BUDGET REQUEST,
AFTER WHICH THE LEGISLATURE CAN EITHER ACCEPT THE
REQUEST, OR AUDIT THE AGENCY AND IMPOSE A BUDGET EQUAL TO
THE TRUE COST OF SERVICES. IN THE OTHER PROCEDURE, THE
LEGISLATURE CAN FOLLOW A REQUEST WITH A COUNTERPROPOSAL TO
THE AGENCY, WHICH CAN THEN EITHER ACCEPT OR REJECT. SINCE
UNDER BOTH PROCEDURES AUDITING IS COSTLY, IT WILL BE OPTIMAL
FOR THE LEGISLATURE TO REFRAIN FROM AUDITING A REQUEST IF
THE PERCEIVED BENEFITS DO NOT OUTWEIGH THIS COST. AT ISSUE
IS THE ABILITY OF THE LEGISLATURE TO IMPOSE DISCIPLINE ON
THE AGENCY'S REQUEST AND FINAL BUDGET THROUGH AN OPTIMAL
CHOICE OF AUDIT AND COUNTERPROPOSAL STRATEGIES, THE EXTENT
OF THE INFORMATION TRANSMITTED THROUGH THE AGENCY'S BUDGET
REQUEST, AND THE EFFICIENCY OF THE RESULTING OUTCOMES. A
REFINEMENT OF THE SEQUENTIAL EQUILIBRIUM CONCEPT PROVIDES
THE BEHAVIORAL PREDICTIONS FOR THE PROCEDURES.

01287 BANKS, J.S.
EQUILIBRIUM OUTCOMES IN TWO-STAGE AMENDMENT PROCEDURES
AMERICAN JOURNAL OF POLITICAL SCIENCE, 33(1) (FEB 89),
25-43.
THIS PAPER ANALYZES THE SET OF SOPHISTICATED VOTING
OUTCOMES UNDER THE FOLLOWING TWO-STAGE AMENDMENT PROCEDURE:
THE SET OF ALTERNATIVES IS PARTITIONED INTO TWO SUBSETS; ONE
SUBSET IS VOTED ON VIA AN AMENDMENT PROCEDURE AT THE FIRST
STAGE, FOLLOWED BY THE REMAINING SUBSET AT THE SECOND STAGE.
THE SURVIVING ALTERNATIVES ARE THEN PAIRED AT THE FINAL VOTE.
THIS PROCEDURE IS RELATED TO THAT USED IN CONGRESSIONAL
DECISION MAKING WHEN BOTH A BILL AND A SUBSTITUTE BILL ARE
IN ORDER ON THE FLOOR AND HENCE ARE OPEN TO AMENDMENTS. IT
IS SHOWN THAT IT IS "EASIER" FOR ALTERNATIVES INITIALLY
CONSIDERED AT THE SECOND STAGE TO BE THE OUTCOME OF THE
VOTING GAME THAN THOSE CONSIDERED AT THE FIRST STAGE. THE
SET OF OUTCOMES IS CONTRASTED WITH THAT GENERATED BY THE
(ONE-STAGE) AMENDMENT PROCEDURE AS WELL AS THE CONCEPT OF
THE UNCOVERED SET.

01288 BANKS, J.S.; KIEWIET, D.R.
EXPLAINING PATTERNS OF CANDIDATE COMPETITION IN
CONGRESSIONAL ELECTIONS
AMERICAN JOURNAL OF POLITICAL SCIENCE, 33(4) (NOV 89),
997-1015.
THE LOW PROBABILITY OF DEFEATING INCUMBENT MEMBERS OF
CONGRESS DETERS POTENTIALLY STRONG RIVALS FROM CHALLENGING
THEM. YET ALMOST ALL INCUMBENTS ARE CHALLENGED, USUALLY BY
OPPONENTS WHO LACK PREVIOUS EXPERIENCE IN OFFICE AND RUN
UNDERFINANCED, INEFFECTUAL CAMPAIGNS. BUT IF STRONG
CHALLENGERS ARE DETERRED FROM CHALLENGING INCUMBENTS, WHY
ARE NOT WEAK CHALLENGERS, WHO HAVE EVEN LESS CHANCE OF
UNSEATING AN INCUMBENT? THE MODEL DEVELOPED IN THIS PAPER
INDICATES THAT THERE IS A SIMPLE REASON WHY WEAK CANDIDATES
CHOOSE TO RUN AGAINST INCUMBENTS: THEY DO SO IN ORDER TO
MAXIMIZE THEIR PROBABILITY OF GETTING ELECTED TO CONGRESS.

TOGETHER WITH THE FINDINGS OF PREVIOUS RESEARCHERS, THE
RESULTS OF THIS ANALYSES OF CONGRESSIONAL PRIMARY DATA FROM
1980 THROUGH 1984 PROVIDE STRONG SUPPORT FOR THE MAJOR
HYPOTHESES DERIVED FROM THE MODEL.

01289 BANNAN, T. S.
IBN-TAYMIYYAH'S THEORY OF POLITICAL LEGITIMACY
DISSERTATION ABSTRACTS INTERNATIONAL, 49(8) (FEB 89),
2373-A.
THE AUTHOR ANALYZES THE POLITICAL THOUGHT OF TAQI AD-DIN
AHMMAD IBN-TAY MIYYAH, A MEDIEVAL MUSLIM JURIST, TO SHED
LIGHT ON THE QUESTION OF WHAT CONSTITUTES A LEGITIMATE
POLITICAL AUTHORITY IN MUSLIM SOCIETIES.

01290 BANTZ, D.N.
AN EXAMINATION OF SECTION 1983 LAWSUITS AGAINST STATE AND
LOCAL PUBLIC OFFICIALS
DISSERTATION ABSTRACTS INTERNATIONAL, 50(1) (JUL 89),
254-A.
THE AUTHOR ANALYZES 1279 SECTION 1983 LAWSUITS FILED
AGAINST STATE AND LOCAL GOVERNMENTS AND PUBLIC OFFICIALS TO
DETERMINE WHO IS BEARING THE BURDEN OF THE LAWSUITS, IN
WHICH FUNCTIONAL AREA IS THE BURDEN THE GREATEST, AND WHAT
ARE THE RAMIFICATIONS. HE CONCLUDES THAT GOVERNMENT
OFFICIALS ARE NOT AT SIGNIFICANT RISK TO NEGATIVE OUTCOMES
FROM SECTION 1983 LAWSUITS AS LONG AS THEY OPERATE WITHIN
EXISTING POLICIES, DO NOT GROSSLY VIOLATE CITIZENS' CIVIL
RIGHTS IN BAD FAITH, AND ARE AWARE OF THE BASIC PRINCIPLES
OF CONSTITUTIONALISM AND THE RULE OF LAW.

01291 BAOCHENG, H.
DOES CHINA FACE STAGFLATION?
BEIJING REVIEW, 32(16) (APR 89), 7, 9.
DOES CHINA'S ECONOMIC RECTIFICATION CAMPAIGN RUN THE
RISK OF LEADING TO STAGFLATION? HAN BAOCHENG ARGUES IT WILL
NOT, PROVIDED THE COUNTRY CAN ELIMINATE EXCESSIVE INVESTMENT
IN CAPITAL CONSTRUCTION, RATIONALIZE THE COUNTRY'S ECONOMIC
STRUCTURE, AND STRENGTHEN LAWS COVERING FINANCE AND TAXATION.

01292 BAOLIN, M.
UNITED STATES SEES NO RISK
BEIJING REVIEW, 32(26) (JUN 89), 29-30, 32-33.
ON MAY 15, 1989, AFTER THREE DECADES OF BITTER RIVALRY,
CHINA AND THE SOVIET UNION RESUMED FRIENDLY RELATIONS WITH A
MEETING BETWEEN MIKHAIL GORBACHEV AND CHINESE LEADERS. IF
THE MEETING HAD OCCURRED TEN YEARS EARLIER, IT WOULD HAVE
HAD THE UNITED STATES ON TENTERHOOKS. BUT THE WORLD IS
CHANGING. THE AMERICANS FOUND THEMSELVES QUITE AT EASE WHEN
THE RUSSIANS AND THE CHINESE MET FOR TALKS IN BEIJING. THE
INITIAL AMERICAN REACTIONS TO THE SINO-SOVIET SUMMIT WERE
POSITIVE.

01293 BAOQIN, H.; TONGJUN, N.
BUSH ADMINISTRATION'S SOVIET POLICY
BEIJING REVIEW, 32(24-25) (JUN 89), 14-17.
THE BUSH ADMINISTRATION'S SOVIET POLICY IS SLIGHTLY
DIFFERENT FROM THAT OF THE LATER PERIOD OF THE REAGAN
ADMINISTRATION. IT STRESSES THAT THE USA AND THE SOVIET
UNION HAVE NOT YET ENDED THE COLD WAR AND THE SOVIET UNION
IS STILL THE "MAIN OPPONENT," AND MAINTAINS VIGILANCE
AGAINST SOVIET INTENTIONS. AT THE SAME TIME, IT WILL CO-
OPERATE MORE WITH MOSCOW TO SOLVE SOME OF THE ISSUES THEY
FACE.

01294 BAPUJI, M.
PARADIGMS OF PUBLIC ADMINISTRATION: AN ASSESSMENT
INDIAN JOURNAL OF POLITICAL SCIENCE, L(3) (JUL 89),
389-401.
PUBLIC ADMINISTRATION IS A BROAD, AMORPHOUS COMBINATION
OF THEORY AND PRACTICE. ITS PURPOSE IS TO PROMOTE A SUPERIOR
UNDERSTANDING OF GOVERNMENT AND ITS RELATIONSHIP WITH THE
SOCIETY IT GOVERNS. THIS PAPER ADDRESSES THE PARADIGMS OF
PUBLIC ADMINISTRATION IN ORDER TO UNDERSTAND ITS PRESENT
STATUS.

01295 BAR-HAIM, G.
EASTERN EUROPEAN YOUTH CULTURE: THE WESTERNIZATION OF A
SOCIAL MOVEMENT
INTERNATIONAL JOURNAL OF POLITICS, CULTURE AND SOCIETY,
2(1) (FAL 88), 45-65.
THIS PAPER EXAMINES THE SOCIAL CONTEXTS WHICH FACILITATE
THE ADOPTION OF WESTERN VALUES AND STYLES BY EAST EUROPEAN
YOUTH AND EXPLORES THE IMPLICATIONS OF THIS DEVELOPMENT. IT
FURTHER ATTEMPTS TO ILLUMINATE THE CONTRADICTIONS THAT
UNDERLIE THE COLLECTIVE EXPERIENCE OF YOUTH AND CONSEQUENTLY
ITS PERCEPTION OF THE WEST.

01296 BAR-ON, M.
THE ISRAELI PEACE MOVEMENT AFTER ALGIERS
NEW OUTLOOK, 32(5) (MAY 89), 22-26.
THE PLO'S NEW POLICIES HAVE MOVED IT FARTHER ALONG THE
ROAD TO CONCESSION THAN HAVE THE ELECTED ISRAELI
GOVERNMENTAL BODIES. IT IS PATENTLY CLEAR THAT ISRAEL MUST
TAKE THE NEXT STEP. THE POLITICAL AND MORAL BALL IS IN ITS

COURT.

01297 BAR-TAL, D.; KLAR, Y.; KRUGLANSKI. A.H.
CONFLICT TERMINATION: AN EPISTEMOLOGICAL ANALYSIS OF
INTERNATIONAL CASES
POLITICAL PSYCHOLOGY, 10(2) (JUN 89), 233-255.
INTERNATIONAL CONFLICTS HAVE BEEN PRESENTLY VIEWED IN
TERMS OF THE NOTION OF CONFLICT SCHEMA, DENOTING A BELIEF IN
THE INCOMPATIBILITY OF GOALS HELD BY THE PARTIES. THIS
BELIEF SUBSCRIBES TO THE SAME EPISTEMIC PROCESS WHEREBY ALL
BELIEFS ARE FORMED AND/OR CHANGED. ACCORDING TO THE
EPISTEMOLOGICAL APPROACH, A CONFLICT SITUATION OCCURS WHEN
AT LEAST ONE OF THE PARTIES ACTIVATES THE CONFLICT SCHEMA.
THUS, THE RETENTION OR MODIFICATION OF THE CONFLICT SCHEMA
MAY DETERMINE WHETHER CONFLICT IS MAINTAINED OR TERMINATED.
THE PRESENT APPROACH SUGGESTS TWO MODES OF CONFLICT
TERMINATION: (1) CONFLICT RESOLUTION WHEREBY THE CONFLICT
SCHEMA IS UNFROZEN VIA UNDERMINING THE CONFLICT BELIEF AND
(2) CONFLICT DISSOLUTION WHEREBY THE CONFLICT SCHEMA BECOMES
RELATIVELY INACCESSIBLE. THE EPISTEMIC PROCESSES WHICH
CHARACTERIZE THE TWO MODES OF CONFLICT TERMINATION ARE
DISCUSSED.

01298 BARAM, A.
THE DECLINE OF THE LABOR PARTY
TIKKUN, 4(3) (SEP 89), 55-58.
THIS ARTICLE PROPOSES THAT LABOR IS FAILING IN ITS
EFFORTS TO WIN PUBLIC SUPPORT FOR ITS PEACE POLITICS BECAUSE
IT HAS BEEN UNABLE TO COMMUNICATE A COHERENT POLICY THAT
POSES A SERIOUS ALTERNATIVE TO LIKUD'S WORLDVIEW. IT
SUGGESTS THAT UNLESS IT CAN ARTICULATE SUCH AN ALTERNATIVE,
LABOR MAY FIND ITSELF A MORE SERIOUS LOSER IN FUTURE
ELECTORAL STRUGGLES FOR POWER IT LISTS THE LABOR MEMBERS OF
KNESSET AND WHERE THEY STAND.

01299 BARAM, A.
THE RULING POLITICAL ELITE IN BA'THI IRAQ, 1968-1986: THE
CHANGING FEATURES OF A COLLECTIVE ROLE
INTERNATIONAL JOURNAL OF MIDDLE EAST STUDIES, 21(4) (NOV
89), 447-493.
TO THE CASUAL OBSERVER IRAQ APPEARS TO HAVE BEEN RULED
BY THE SAME POLITICAL ELITE SINCE 1968, BUT CLOSER
EXAMINATION REVEALS THAT ITS LEADERSHIP UNDERWENT IMPORTANT
CHANGES BETWEEN 1968 AND THE MID-1980'S. IN THIS ESSAY, THE
AUTHOR ARGUES THAT THESE CHANGES WERE VERY GRADUAL,
SOMETIMES ALMOST IMPERCEPTIBLE, BUT THE ACCUMULATED EFFECT
WAS CONSIDERABLE. THE CHANGES WERE BROUGHT ABOUT CHIEFLY BY
SADDAM HUSAYN, WHO BECAME PRESIDENT IN 1979 AND WAS A
CENTRAL FIGURE BEFORE THAT, AND BY THOSE WITHIN HIS CLOSE
CIRCLE.

01300 BARAM, H.
POWER-STRUGGLE IN LIKUD
MIDDLE EAST INTERNATIONAL, (365) (DEC 89), 5-7.
THE ARTICLE EXAMINES THE ONGOING CONFLICT WITHIN
ISRAEL'S RULING LIKUD PARTY. ALTHOUGH THE CONFLICT IS OFTEN
DEPICTED IN QUITE SIMPLISTIC TERMS OF TENSION BETWEEN THE
HARD-LINE, RADICAL RIGHT AND MORE MODERATE ELEMENTS, THE
ACTUAL CONFLICT IS MUCH MORE COMPLEX. PRIME MINISTER YITZHAK
SHAMIR HAS HAD DIFFICULTY PLACATING BOTH GROUPS, BUT A
POSTPONEMENT OF US-ISRAEL DIALOGUE, A FORERUNNER OF DIRECT
ISRAEL-PLO NEGOTIATIONS, HAS GRANTED SHAMIR SOME BREATHING
ROOM.

01301 BARAM, H.
SHAMIR KEEPS HIS TAIL UP
MIDDLE EAST INTERNATIONAL, (364) (DEC 89), 6-7.
PRIME MINISTER YITZHAK SHAMIR'S LESS THAN SUCCESSFUL
TRIPS TO EUROPE AND THE US HAVE INCREASED TENSION AND
DISCONTENT IN ISRAEL. NOT ONLY IS HE LOSING GROUND AT HOME,
BUT HIS STANDING IN THE US JEWISH COMMUNITY IS ALSO
DECREASING. THE ARTICLE IDENTIFIES TWO BODIES AS THE ONLY
OBSTACLES TO PEACE IN THE MIDDLE EAST: THE LIKUD CENTRAL
COMMITTEE AND AIPAC, THE ISRAELI LOBBY IN WASHINGTON. SHAMIR
REMAINS CONFIDENT IN HIS ABILITY TO MAINTAIN HIS
REJECTIONIST STANCE.

01302 BARANCZAK, S.
BEFORE THE THAW: THE BEGINNINGS OF DISSENT IN POSTWAR
POLISH LITERATURE (THE CASE OF ADAM WAZYK'S "A POEM FOR
ADULTS")
EASTERN EUROPEAN POLITICS AND SOCIETIES, 3(1) (WIN 89),
3-21.
IN POLAND THE PROCESS OF REVIVAL BEGAN BEFORE THE ACTUAL
THAW OF 1956. THE WORK THAT GAVE IT A DECISIVE PUSH IS
UNDOUBTEDLY "A POEM FOR ADULTS" (POEMAT DLA DOROSTYCH) BY
ADAM WAZYK (1905-1982), PUBLISHED IN THE OFFICIAL LITERARY
WEEKLY NOWA KULTURA ON AUGUST 21,1955. THE STRANGE HISTORY
OF THIS LONG POEM FIRST PUBLISHED IN WARSAW IN THE SUMMER OF
1955 GIVES PERHAPS THE MOST ELOQUENT PICTURE OF A CRUCIAL
MOMENT IN POSTWAR POLAND'S CULTURAL LIFE: THE BIRTH OF
POLITICAL DISSENT IN LITERATURE AFTER MORE THAN SIX YEARS OF
SUFFOCATION BY THE PRINCIPLES OF SOCIALIST REALISM.

01303 BARANOVSKY, V.
PERSPECTIVES OF DISARMAMENT AND DETENTE IN EUROPE AFTER
THE INF TREATY
PEACE AND THE SCIENCES, 1 (1989), 1-9.
THE INF TREATY SEEMS TO BE A USEFUL ARMS CONTROL AND
NEGOTIATING EXPERIENCE IN TERMS OF THE FUTURE DEVELOPMENT OF
POSITIVE TRENDS IN EUROPE. THIS ARTICLE EXAMINES HOW SOME OF
THE ELEMENTS OF THE TREATY, AS WELL AS SOME OF THE
CHARACTERISTICS OF THE POLITICAL PROCESS WHICH RESULTED IN
THE SOVIET-AMERICAN AGREEMENT COULD BE REPRODUCED IN
RELATION WITH OTHER ISSUES OF EUROPEAN SECURITY, THUS
INCREASING THE CHANCES FOR THEIR SUCCESSFUL RESOLUTION.

01304 BARAULIN, A.
USSR-ROMANIA: DEEPENING ECONOMIC TIES
FOREIGN TRADE, 5 (1988), 2-7.
THIS ARTICLE EXAMINES THE STATUS OF ECONOMIC TIES
BETWEEN THE USSR AND ROMANIA. ALTHOUGH TRADE RELATIONS HAVE
BEEN PROGRESSING, THE NEED FOR INVIGORATION OF THE PROCESS
IS ASSESSED. AGREEMENTS BETWEEN THE TWO COUNTRIES AIMED AT
INCREASING TRADE ARE DETAILED AS WELL AS THE AREAS OF
SPECIFIC INDUSTRY CONCERNED, COOPERATION BETWEEN SCIENTISTS
AND RESEARCHERS IS DETAILED AS ONE OF THE DYNAMICALLY
DEVELOPING SPHERES OF SOVIET-ROMANIAN INTERACTION.

01305 BARBER, B.R.
LETTER FROM AMERICA, JUNE 1989
GOVERNMENT AND OPPOSITION, 24(3) (SUM 89), 300-308.
GEORGE BUSH'S LOW-METABOLISM ADMINISTRATION HAS
ANAESTHETIZED BOTH THE MEDIA AND THE CONGRESS. INVISIBILITY
IS AN APPROPRIATE HALLMARK OF THE VICE-PRESIDENCY, BUT BUSH
APPEARS UNABLE TO SHAKE OFF THE INVISIBILITY CLOAK EVEN
THOUGH HE IS NOW PRESIDENT. BUSH'S MOVES HAVE BEEN
OVERSHADOWED IN THE MEDIA BY SCANDALS INVOLVING OLIVER NORTH,
SPEAKER OF THE HOUSE JIM WRIGHT, AND JOHN TOWER.

01306 BARBER, J.
SICK TO DEATH
MACLEAN'S (CANADA'S NEWS MAGAZINE), 102(7) (FEB 89), 32-35.
CANADA'S HOSPITALS ARE INCREASINGLY TAKING BEDS OUT OF
SERVICE, LIMITING THE NUMBERING OF OPERATIONS THEY PERFORM
AND CUTTING BACK OTHER SERVICES AS THE GOVERNMENT BATTLES TO
KEEP DOWN SPIRALING HEALTH CARE COSTS. HIGHER PAY AND
BENEFITS FOR MEDICAL PERSONNEL, THE SOARING COST OF MEDICAL
TECHNOLOGY, AND A GROWING NUMBER OF OLDER CANADIANS ARE
POSSIBLE CAUSES OF THE INCREASED EXPENDITURES. THE MOUNTING
STRAINS ON THE 20-YEAR OLD PUBLICLY FUNDED UNIVERSAL SYSTEM
THAT PROVIDES ONE OF THE WORLD'S HIGHEST STANDARDS OF
MEDICAL CARE ARE BEGINNING TO RAISE THE PROSPECT OF USER
FEES AND DEDUCTIBLES BEING INTRODUCED.

01307 BARBER, S.
WASHINGTON STOPS FIGHTING ITSELF OVER SOUTH AFRICA
SOUTH AFRICA FOUNDATION REVIEW, 15(7) (JUL 89), 1-2.
APARTHEID IN SOUTH AFRICA HAS BEEN ECLIPSED BY EVENTS IN
THE USSR, POLAND, CHINA, AND IRAN. THIS SHIFT OF EMPHASIS,
COMBINED WITH MODEST REFORMS IN SOUTH AFRICA, HAS DECREASED
THE EMPHASIS PLACED ON ECONOMIC SANCTIONS AND OTHER MEASURES
BY THE BUSH ADMINISTRATION AND CONGRESS. BOTH THE U.S. AND
OTHER WESTERN NATIONS ARE BECOMING INCREASINGLY CONFIDENT
THAT MEANINGFUL NEGOTIATIONS LIE NOT TOO FAR IN THE FUTURE.

01308 BARBERO, M.D.
PEACEMAKING: THE BROTHER OF PEACEKEEPING OR A COMBAT
OPERATION
AVAILABLE FROM NTIS, NO. AD-A208 768/2/GAR, FEB 7 89, 54.
THIS PAPER ANALYZES THE DOCTRINAL RELATIONSHIP BETWEEN
PEACEMAKING AND PEACEKEEPING OPERATIONS. SINCE WWII WE HAVE
WITNESSED A RISE IN THE FREQUENCY OF 'LOW-INTENSITY
CONFLICTS' (LIC). TWO TYPES OF OPERATIONS CONDUCTED IN
RESPONSE TO THIS TYPE OF CONFLICT ARE PEACEKEEPING AND
PEACEMAKING OPERATIONS. CURRENT ARMY DOCTRINE FOR LIC, AS
OUTLINED IN FM 100-20, IMPLIES THAT WHILE PEACEMAKING IS
ESSENTIALLY A COMBAT OPERATION, A STRONG RELATIONSHIP EXISTS
BETWEEN PEACEKEEPING AND PEACEMAKING OPERATIONS. AND
PEACEMAKING OPERATIONS CAN SUCCESSFULLY TRANSITION TO
PEACEKEEPING. THIS PAPER BEGINS WITH AN ANALYSIS OF THE
MORAL, CYBEMETIC AND PHYSICAL DOMAINS OF PEACEMAKING AND
PEACEKEEPING IN ORDER TO DETERMINE THE TRUE NATURE OF EACH
OPERATION. THE U.N. MODEL AND THE MULTINATIONAL FORCE AND
OBSERVERS (MFO) SERVE AS THE BASIS FOR THE ANALYSIS OF
PEACEKEEPING. AND THE U.S. EXPERIENCE IN THE DOMINICAN
REPUBLIC IN 1965 AND IN LEBANON IN 1958 AND 1982-84 PROVIDE
THE BASIS FOR THE ANALYSIS OF PEACEMAKING OPERATIONS. ONCE
THE TWO OPERATIONS HAVE BEEN ANALYZED, A DETERMINATION OF
THE COMPATIBILITY OF PEACEMAKING AND PEACEMAKING IS MADE.
THE CONCLUSION OF THIS STUDY IS THAT THE TWO OPERATIONS ARE
FUNDAMENTALLY DIFFERENT. AND, THEREFORE, IT WOULD BE
DANGEROUS TO EXPECT A TACTICAL COMMANDER TO TRANSITION FROM
ONE OPERATION TO THE OTHER SUCCESSFULLY.

01309 BARBIER, E.B.
CASH CROPS, FOOD CROPS, AND SUSTAINABILITY: THE CASE OF
INDONESIA
WORLD DEVELOPMENT, 17(6) (JUN 89), 879-895.
RECENT EVIDENCE SUGGESTS THAT THE MAIN OBSTACLE TO
SUSTAINABLE AGRICULTURAL DEVELOPMENT IS THE FAILURE OF ANY
ECONOMIC POLICY, WHETHER PROMOTING FOOD CROPS OR EXPORTS, TO
ADDRESS ADEQUATELY PROBLEMS OF NATURAL RESOURCE MANAGEMENT.
POLICIES TO ACHIEVE FOOD SELFSUFFICIENCY MAY THEREFORE BE
NEITHER INHERENTLY MORE NOR INHERENTLY LESS ENVIRONMENTALLY
SUSTAINABLE THAN EXPORT-ORIENTED AGRICULTURAL DEVELOPMENT.
INDONESIA SERVES AS A USEFUL ILLUSTRATION, AS THE COUNTRY'S
PURSUIT OF BOTH FOOD SELF-SUFFICIENCY AND EXPORT CROP
PROMOTION STRATEGIES HAS ENCOUNTERED MANY PROBLEMS OF
ENVIRONMENTAL AND RESOURCE DEGRADATION. OVERCOMING THESE
PROBLEMS WILL REQUIRE THE EXPLICIT INTEGRATION OF NATURAL
RESOURCE MANAGEMENT CONCERNS WITHIN THE ECONOMIC POLICY
FRAMEWORK FOR INDONESIAN AGRICULTURE.

01310 BARBIER, E.B.
SUSTAINING AGRICULTURE ON MARGIN LAND: A POLICY FRAMEWORK
ENVIRONMENT, 31(9) (NOV 89), 12-17; 36-40.
THIS ARTICLE EXAMINES THE POVERTY AND LACK OF RESOURCES
WHICH OFTEN DRIVE SMALL-SCALE FARMERS AND PASTORALISTS TO
UNSUSTAINABLE PRACTICES. IT EXPLORES NATIONAL POLICIES THAT
EMPHASIZE LOW-INPUT TECHNOLOGIES, LAND REFORM, AND ECONOMIC
INCENTIVES FOR MARGINAL AGRICULTURALISTS WHICH CAN ENCOURAGE
SUSTAINABLE SYSTEMS. CURRENT POLICY SHORTCOMINGS ARE
DETAILED AS WELL AS THE ROLE OF ECONOMICS.

01311 BARD, M.
FUTURE U.S. MIDDLE EAST POLICY: TWO VIEWS
MIDSTREAM, XXXV(1) (JAN 89), 24-27.
THE BROOKINGS INSTITUTITION AND THE WASHINGTON INSTITUTE
FOR NEAR EAST POLICY HAVE ISSUED REPORTS THAT OFFER
DIFFERING PERSPECTIVES ON THE OPTIONS AVAILABLE TO U.S.
POLICY-MAKERS IN THE MIDEAST. THE BROOKINGS REPORT ADVISES
THE BUSH ADMINISTRATION NOT TO PROMISE MORE THAN CAN BE
DELIVERED AND TO BE ALERT TO NEW OPPORTUNITIES FOR PEACE-
MAKING. THE STUDY ALSO MAKES THE IMPORTANT POINT THAT THE
BUSH ADMINISTRATION MUST ENSURE THAT CONGRESS AND THE PUBLIC
UNDERSTAND AND SHARE ITS OBJECTIVES.

01312 BARD, M.
STABILITY IN THE ARAB WORLD
MIDSTREAM, XXXV(2) (FEB 89), 21-26.
THE EIGHT-YEAR WAR IN THE PERSIAN GULF HELPED PERPETUATE
THE NOTION THAT THE MIDDLE EAST IS AN UNSTABLE REGION. BUT
THE TRUTH IS THAT THE ARAB STATES, WITH THE EXCEPTION OF
LEBANON, HAVE ENJOYED A REMARKABLE DEGREE OF INTERNAL
STABILITY FOR NEARLY TWO DECADES. THIS IS NOT TO SAY THAT
THERE IS A GURANTEE AGAINST UPHEAVAL, BUT THE EVIDENCE
INDICATES THAT ALL OF THE PRESENT ARAB REGIMES SHOULD REMAIN
FIRMLY IN CONTROL FOR THE FORESEEABLE FUTURE. THEREFORE,
AMERICAN POLICY TOWARD THE ARAB WORLD SHOULD BE PREDICATED,
LESS ON FEAR OF INTERNAL UPHEAVAL THAN ON THE CORRESPONDENCE
BETWEEN THE INTERESTS OF THE USA AND THOSE OF THE ARAB
STATES.

01313 BARD, M.
THE WANING THREAT OF ISLAMIC FUNDAMENTALISM
MIDSTREAM, XXXV(3) (APR 89), 7-10.
THE PRINCIPLE AMERICAN FEAR IN THE MIDEAST SINCE 1979
HAS BEEN THAT IRANIAN-INSPIRED FUNDAMENTALISM WOULD SPREAD
TO THE GULF SHEIKDOMS AND OTHER AREAS AND THEREBY THREATEN
ARAB NATIONS FRIENDLY TOWARD THE UNITED STATES. THE STRATEGY
THAT EMERGED TO COUNTER THIS DANGER WAS TO BOLSTER PRO-
WESTERN REGIMES WITH ARMS AND TAKE MEASURES TO INSURE THAT
IRAN WOULD NOT WIN A DECISIVE VICTORY OVER IRAQ. IRONICALLY,
IT HAS NOT BEEN AMERICAN MEASURES THAT HAVE RESTRAINED THE
FUNDAMENTALISTS. RATHER, IT HAS BEEN THE ACTIONS OF THE
ARAB/MUSLIM NATIONS THEMSELVES. IT IS NOW CLEAR THAT THE
ISLAMIC FUNDAMENTALIST MOVEMENT IS ON THE DECLINE AND THE
THREAT TO AMERICAN INTERESTS HAS WANED.

01314 BARD, M.G.
THE EVOLUTION OF ISRAEL'S AFRICA POLICY
MIDDLE EAST REVIEW, XXI(2) (WIN 89), 21-28.
WHILE THERE CAN BE NO DOUBT THAT ISRAELI LEADERS HAVE
ALWAYS HAD PHILANTHROPIC ATTITUDES TOWARD AFRICA, THEIR
PRIMARY INTEREST IN THE CONTINENT HAS RESTED ON THE MORE
TANGIBLE GROUNDS OF REALPOLITIK. JUST AS AFRICA HAS BEEN THE
SCENE OF BATTLES OF INFLUENCE AMONG THE SUPERPOWERS, SO HAS
IT BEEN A BATTLEFIELD BETWEEN ISRAEL AND THE ARABS. EVEN
SMALL AFRICAN NATIONS LIKE TOGO HAVE BEEN PAWNS IN ARAB-
ISRAELI EFFORTS TO GAIN AN ADVANTAGE ON THE CONTINENT.

01315 BARDEHLE, P.
"BLUE HELMUTS" FROM GERMANY? OPPORTUNITIES AND LIMITS OF
UN PEACEKEEPING
AUSSEN POLITIK, 40(4) (1989), 372-384.
THIS ARTICLE ADDRESSES THE TOPIC OF PEACEKEEPING IN
GENERAL, USING THE RECENT DISPATCH OF A UN PEACEKEEPING
FORCE TO SMOOTH NAMIBIA'S TRANSITION INTO INDEPENDENCE AS A
POINT OF DEPARTURE AS THE FEDERAL REPUBLIC OF GERMANY
AGREE'S TO SEND POLICE TO NAMIBIA. IT DESCRIBES THE
EVOLUTION OF PEACEKEEPING AND EXPLORES GERMANY'S TRADITIONAL

REFUSAL TO TAKE PART IN PEACEKEEPING BECAUSE OF THEIR LAWS AGAINST IT.

01316 BARDIS, P.
ETHIOPIA: MENGISTU AND MARXISM
SCANDINAVIAN JOURNAL OF DEVELOPMENT ALTERNATIVES, VIII(1) (MAR 89), 41-46.
THE ARTICLE BRIEFLY EXPLORES THE ABUSES AND ATROCITIES COMMITTED BY MENGISTU IN THE NAME OF SOCIALISM IN ETHIOPIA. IT ALSO ANALYZES THE UNDERLYING REASONS WHY SO MANY OF THE NATIONS IN AFRICA HAVE ADOPTED SOCIALIST SYSTEMS OF GOVERNMENT IN THE FACE OF INCREASING EVIDENCE OF SOCIALISM'S FAILURE TO SOLVE EVEN THE MOST BASIC ECONOMIC PROBLEMS.

01317 BARGERY, S.
COTE D'IVOIRE FALLS ON HARD TIMES
NEW AFRICAN, (258) (MAR 89), 35.
THE REPUBLIC OF COTE D'IVOIRE IS FACING ITS MOST SERIOUS CRISIS YET. FELIX HOUPHOUET-BOIGNY PRESIDED OVER THE "IVORIAN MIRACLE" IN THE 1960'S AND 1970'S. NOW HE IS LEADING A COUNTRY WITH A DETERIORATING ECONOMY AND A HUGE DEBT. THE AGING HOUPHOUET-BIOGNY IS ALSO TRYING TO PREVENT A HARMFUL FIGHT OVER SUCCESSION. TO APPEASE VARIOUS FACTIONS, HE HAS ACCEDED TO CALLS FOR IVORIANIZATION IN THE DOMESTIC ARENA AND HAS OPENED DIPLOMATIC TIES WITH THE USSR.

01318 BARK, D.L.; HARRIES, O.; MILLAR, T.
AIMS, TARGETS, AND INSTRUMENTS; THE RED ORCHESTRA
HOOVER INSTITUTION PRESS, STANFORD, CALIFORNIA, 1989, 15-22.
THIS CHAPTER TRACES THE HISTORY OF DEVELOPMENT IN THE SOUTH PACIFIC AND EXPLORES SOVIET INTENTION TO INTEGRATE THE ASIA-PACIFIC REGION INTO A COMPREHENSIVE SYSTEM OF INTERNATIONAL SECURITY. IT APPEALS TO THE U.S. TO HAVE A POLITE, CARING, WATCHFUL POLICY TO COUNTER SOVIET ACTIVITIES, RATHER THAN CRIES OF PUBLIC ALARM.

01319 BARK, D.L.; HARRIES, O.; WHEELDON, J.
AUSTRALIA'S COMMUNISTS; THE RED ORCHESTRA
HOOVER INSTITUTION PRESS, STANFORD, CA., 1989, 251-256.
THIS CHAPTER EXAMINES THE SEVERAL POLITICAL GROUPS IN AUSTRALIA THAT DESCRIBE THEMSELVES AS COMMUNIST. IT TRACES THE HISTORY OF THE COMMUNIST PARTY IN AUSTRALIA AND TRACKS ITS INFLUENCE DURING THE YEARS SINCE 1920. IT CONCLUDES THAT THERE ARE ORGANIZATIONS AND INDIVIDUALS IN THAT COUNTRY WHO ARE ANXIOUS TO SEE THE WEAKENING OF AUSTRALIA'S ALLIANCE WITH THE UNITED STATES, AND WHO WOULD THEREBY BENEFIT MOSCOW, WHETHER OR NOT THAT OUTCOME WERE INTENDED.

01320 BARK, D.L.; HARRI, O.; KOTOBALAVU, J.
FISHING AS BAIT; THE RED ORCHESTRA
HOOVER INSTITUTION PRESS, STANFORD, CA., 1989, 154-159.
THIS CHAPTER EXPLORES THE IMPACT OF THE THE SIGNING OF FISHERIES ACCESS AGREEMENTS BY THE SOVIET UNION WITH SOUTH PACIFIC NATIONS ON SOVIET PRESENCE IN THE SOUTH PACIFIC REGION. IT DETAILS THE QUESTION OF HOW THE WEST CAN SUPPORT FISHERIES DEVELOPMENT IN THE REGION IN ORDER TO REGAIN GOOD WILL AND SECURE THE WEST'S STRATEGIC AND SECURITY INTERESTS IN THE AREA. IT CONCLUDES THAT THE BEST WAY TO DO THIS WOULD BE A MULTINATIONAL EFFORT BY WESTERN FRIENDS TO HELP THE PACIFIC ISLAND COUNTRIES TO ATTAIN THIS OBJECTIVE.

01321 BARK, D.L.; HARRIES, O.; HENDERSON, G.
HOW FERTILE THE GROUND?; THE RED ORCHESTRA
HOOVER INSTITUTION PRESS, STANFORD, CA., 1989, 215-226.
THIS CHAPTER EXAMINES THE POLITICAL CLIMATE OF AUSTRALIA IN ITS RELATIONSHIP WITH BOTH THE USSR AND THE UNITED STATES. IT DETAILS DETERIORATING SUPPORT OF THE UNITED STATES AND INCREASING INTERACTION WITH RUSSIA BY THE HAWKE LABOR GOVERNMENT. IT DETAILS WHAT IS REFERRED TO AS THE DIBB REPORT WHICH HAS INFLUENCED THINKING ABOUT THE TWO SUPER POWERS. THE LESSONS TO BE LEARNED BY THE ASSESSMENT OF THE PRESENT STATUS OF AUSTRALIA ARE EXAMINED.

01322 BARK, D.L.; EASSON, M.; HARRIES, O.
LABOUR AND THE LEFT IN THE PACIFIC; THE RED ORCHESTRA
HOOVER INSTITUTION PRESS, STANFORD, CA., 1989, 74-118.
THIS CHAPTER ARGUES THAT EVEN THOUGH THE PRO-SOVIET ELEMENTS OF THE NEW ZEALAND AND AUSTRALIAN LABOR MOVEMENTS HAVE DONATED THEMSELVES TO A MAJOR OPPOSITION TO THEIR IDEAS IN THE SOUTHWEST PACIFIC, THE DEGREE OF INFLUENCE AND POPULAR SUPPORT THEY HAVE ACHIEVED IS LIMITED. IT ALSO MAINTAINS THAT THERE IS NO GROUND FOR COMPLACENCY ABOUT THE FOOTHOLD THEY HAVE GAINED IN THE REGION. IT PROPOSES THAT LABOR UNIONS ARE THE BEST-ORGANIZED AND STRONGEST INSTITUTIONS IN MOST PACIFIC COUNTRIES. THIS CHAPTER ATTEMPTS TO CONVEY A LITTLE OF THE DIVERSITY AND COMPLEXITY OF THE PACIFIC LABOR MOVEMENT AND ITS POLITICS.

01323 BARK, D.L.; COLEMAN, P.T.; HARRIES, O.
NEW CALDONIA: A PAWN IN THE EAST-WEST STRUGGLE; THE RED ORCHESTRA
HOOVER INSTITUTION PRESS, STANFORD, CA., 1989, 143-153.
THIS CHAPTER NOTES THE TRANSITION PERIOD OF THE NATIONS OF THE SOUTH PACIFIC AS THEY BEGIN TO IMPACT GLOBAL CONCERNS. IT EXPLORES SOVIET INTEREST IN THE AREA, WITH NEW CALDONIA AS A PRIMARY TARGET. IT EXAMINES THE FRENCH IN NEW CALDONIA AND INDEPENDENCE OR SELF DETERMINATION FOR NEW CALDONIA AND ADDRESSES GOBAL EFECTS OF THE PROBLEMS IN NEW CALDONIA WHICH ARE GAINING AN INTERNATIONAL DIMENSION.

01324 BARK, D.L.; HARRIES, O.; WEST, D.A.
PERCEPTIONS AND OBJECTIVES; THE RED ORCHESTRA
HOOVER INSTITUTION PRESS, STANFORD, CA., 1989, 23-37.
THIS CHAPTER EXAMINES SOVIET POLICY IN THE SOUTHWEST PACIFIC DURING THE 1980S. THREE FACTORS ARE GROUPED IN THREE CATEGORIES: PERCEPTIONS, OPPORTUNITIES, AND RESOURCES. IT DISCUSSES THE IMPORTANCE THAT SOVIET ECONOMIC-POLITICAL POWER IN THE REGION WILL ASSUME, AND THE RESPONSE THAT SOUTH PACIFIC AWARENESS SHOULD ASSUME.

01325 BARK, D.L.; HARRIES, O.; MORGAN, B.
RACE RELATIONS, THE CHURCHES, AND THE PEACE MOVEMENT; THE RED ORCHESTRA
HOOVER INSTITUTION PRESS, STANFORD, CA., 1989, 173-189.
THIS CHAPTER LOOKS AT THREE ASPECTS OF NEW ZEALAND LIFE IN WHICH THE EXTREME LEFT TAKES A CLOSE INTEREST (AND PLAYS AN ACTIVE ROLE: RACE RELATIONS (WHICH ENCOMPASSES THE QUESTIONS OF NATIONAL IDENTITY), THE CHURCHES, AND THE PEACE MOVEMENT. IT ATTEMPTS TO FORECAST THE FUTURE CONFIGURATION OF FORCES PROMOTING INDEPENDENCE, PEACE, SOCIAL JUSTICE AND HUMANITARIAN ENDEAVORS, WITH CHANGE IN NEW ZEALAND AS A CERTAINTY.

01326 BARK, D.L.; DANBY, M.; HARRIES, O.
THE ACCUMULATION OF ASSETS; THE RED ORCHESTRA
HOOVER INSTITUTION PRESS, STANFORD, CA., 1989, 227-238.
THIS CHAPTER DETAILS INCIDENTS IN AUSTRALIA WHICH CUMULATIVELY REPRESENT A PATTERN OF BEHAVIOR AND AN INVESTMENT THAT INDICATES A SERIOUS INTENT BY THE USSR TO INFILTRATE THE REGION AND INFLUENCE ITS POLITICAL LIFE, IT CONTENDS THAT THE INTRODUCTION OF GLASTNOST IN THE USSR HAS NOT MODIFIED EFFORTS BY MOSCOW TO PENETRATE IN INFLUENCE POLITICAL LIFE IN THE SOUTH PACIFIC REGION, AND CONCLUDES THAT IT WOULD BE FOOLISH FOR THE UNITED STATES TO BE FOOLISH ABOUT THE POSSIBLE EFFECTS OF SOVIET ACITIVITIES THERE.

01327 BARK, D.L.; HARRIES, O.; MANNE, R.
THE COMBE AFFAIR AND THE AUSTRALIAN MEDIA; A CASE STUDY IN BIAS; THE RED ORCHESTRA
HOOVER INSTITUTION PRESS, STANFORD, CA., 1989, 257-272.
THIS CHAPTER CONTENDS THAT THE QUESTION OF POLITICAL BIAS IN THE MEDIA CAN BE ADDRESSED OBJECTIVELY IN AUSTRALIA. ITS METHOD IS THE CASE STUDY AND ITS SUBJECT MATTER IS THE COMBE AFFAIR. EXAMINED IN DETAIL ARE THE PERFORMANCES OF THE PUBLICLY FUNDED ABC AND THE QUALITY PRESS OF SIDNEY AND MELBOURNE, IT FOCUSES ON THE SURPRISING AND DISTURBING FACT THAT THE COMBE AFFAIR, AS A VERSION OF THE ANTI-UNITED STATES WORLDVIEW, CAPTURED ALMOST THE ENTIRE JOURNALISTIC WORLD.

01328 BARK, D.L.; HARRIES, O.; JAMIESON, E.
THE DAMAGED MEMORIAL; THE RED ORCHESTRA
HOOVER INSTITUTION PRESS, STANFORD, CA, 1989, 201 - 214.
THIS CHAPTER DEALS WITH THE NATURE OF ANTI - AMERICANISM IN NEW ZEALAND. IT USES THE MEMORIAL COMMEMORATING THE AID OF AMERICAN TROOPS IN DEFENSE OF NEW ZEALAND IN 1942 AS A SYMBOL IN WHICH THE MEMORIAL HAS BEEN DAMAGED AND THEN REPAIRED. IT EXAMINES THE "PEACEMAKING NOW" CONFERENCE, AND ANTI - REAGAN SENTIMENT, AND THE INCREASE OF NATIONALISM IN THE SMALL COUNTRY. IT COUPLES THE FEAR OF NUCLEAR ARMS GROWTH WITH FUTURE POLICY TRENDS. IT CONCLUDES THAT WHILE A RETURN TO THE OLD RELATIONSHIP IS UNCLEAR, THAT THE SYMBOLISM OF THE RECONSTRUCTION OF THE MARINES MEMORIAL SHOULD NOT BE FORGOTTEN.

01329 BARK, D.L.; HARRIES, O.; NEARY, A.J.
THE INFILTRATION OF THE TRADE UNION MOVEMENT; THE RED ORCHESTRA
HOOVER INSTITUTION PRESS, STANFORD, CA., 1989, 190-200.
THIS CHAPTER EXAMINES HOW THE SOVIET UNION THROUGH ONE OF ITS MAIN FRONT ORGANIZATIONS, WFTU (WORLD FEDERATION OF TRADE UNIONS) HAS SUCCESSFULLY INFILTRATED THE NEW ZEALAND TRADE UNION MOVEMENT AND CHANGED ITS DIRECTION. IT ATTEMPTS TO ASSESS THE DEGREE OF INFLUENCE EXERTED BY THE EXTREME LEFT, WHICH NOW DOMINATES THE FEDERATION OF LABOR (NEW ZEALAND). IT CONCLUDES THAT SOVIET INFLUENCE IS CONSIDERABLE AND IS GROWING.

01330 BARK, D.L.; HARRIES, O.; HEGARTY, D.W.
THE LIBYAN CONNECTION; THE RED ORCHESTRA
HOOVER INSTITUTION PRESS, STANFORD, CA., 1989, 119-142.
THIS CHAPTER ADDRESS THE CHANGE IN THE SOUTH PACIFIC IN SECURITY OUTLOOK AS THE SOVIET UNION SHOWS INCREASED INTEREST IN THE REGION. IT EXPLORES LIBYAN INTEREST IN THE SOUTH PACIFIC SINCE 1984, GIVING THE HISTORY OF LIBYAN ACTIVITY THERE. VANTUATU'S POLITICAL DIRECTION AND RELATIONS WITH LIBYA ARE EXPLORED. IT RAISES THE QUESTION OF WHETHER

OR NOT LIBYA IS DO MOSCOW'S BIDDING AND THUS SPARING THE
USSR'S DIRECT INVOLVEMENT WITH RADICAL CAUSES OR MOVEMENTS.

01331 BARK, D.L.; HARRIES, O.; RUBENSTEIN, C.
THE MEDIA; THE RED ORCHESTRA
HOOVER INSTITUTION PRESS, STANFORD, CA., 1989, 239-250.
THIS CHAPTER EXAMINES THE LEFT WING POLITICAL BIAS WHICH
IS EVIDENT IN SECTIONS OF THE AUSTRALIAN MEDIA. IT FOCUSES
ON THE PERFORMANCE OF THE PUBLICLY OWNED RADIO AND
TELEVISION SERVICE, THE ABC; THE HEAVY DEPENDENCE ON AND
PROMOTION OF SO-CALLED EXPERTS WHO CAN BE RELIED ON TO
PROVIDE ANALYSES OR JUDGMENTS HOSTILE TO THE UNITED STATES;
AND THE COVERAGE OF EVENTS IN FIJI DURING 1987.

01332 BARK, D.L.; HARRIES, O.; WHITEHALL, J.
THE NUCLEAR-FREE AND INDEPENDENT MOVEMENT; THE RED
ORCHESTRA
HOOVER INSTITUTION PRESS, STANFORD, CA., 1989, 286.
THIS CHAPTER EXAMINES THE TREND IN THE SOUTH PACIFIC
AWAY FROM AN ATTITUDE OF PRO-WESTERN FRIENDSHIP AND
COOPERATION TOWARD NEUTRALITY, AND IN SOME CASES, OUTRIGHT
HOSTILITY TOWARD THE WEST IN GENERAL AND THE U.S. IN
PARTICULAR. IT IS THE RESULT OF ALMOST TWO DECADES OF
CAREFUL PREPARATION. IT EXPLORES TRADE UNIONS AND THE PEACE
MOVEMENT IN FIJI AND AUSTRALIA, AS WELL AS THE INFLUENCE OF
THE CHURCH. IT CONCLUDES THAT A CLEAR UNDERSTANDING OF THE
NATURE OF THE IDEOLOGICAL STRUGGLE AND ORGANIZATIONAL EFFORT
IS A PREREQUISITE FOR COUNTERING THE PRO-SOVIET FORCES AT
WORK THERE AND THAT NUCLEAR ARMAMENT IS AN ISSUE.

01333 BARK, D.L.; HARRIES. O.
THE RED ORCHESTRA
HOOVER INSTITUTION PRESS. STANFORD, CALIFORNIA, 1989, 271.
THIS BOOK IS ABOUT THE RECENT ACTIVITIES OF THE SOVIET
UNION IN THE SOUTHWEST PACIFIC AND OF THOSE PEOPLE AND
ORGANIZATIONS WHO EITHER WITTINGLY OR UNWITTINGLY MAY SHARE
ITS INTERESTS IN THAT REGION. IT EXPLORES THE POLITICAL
IMPACT THAT A SMALL EXPENDITURE CAN STILL ACHIEVE AND THE
FACT THAT THE SOVIETS CAN CONTINUE TO BE ACTIVE WITHOUT
PROVOKING THE KIND OF HOSTILE REACTION THAT WOULD ENDANGER
THEIR PURSUIT OF DETENTE. THE PURPOSE OF THE BOOK IS TO
INFORM THE UNITED STATES ABOUT SOVIET ACTIVITY IN THE
SOUTHWEST PACIFIC.

01334 BARK, D.L.; HARRIES, O.; JACKSON, K.D.
THE RED ORCHESTRA AND THE U.S. RESPONSE IN THE SOUTH
PACIFIC: AN EXPLORATION OF THE METAPHOR; THE RED ORCHESTRA
HOOVER INSTITUTION PRESS, STANFORD, CALIFORNIA, 1989, 3-14.
THIS CHAPTER SERVES AS AN INTRODUCTION TO THE BOOK TITLE,
"THE RED ORCHESTRA", IT EXPLORES SOVIET INTERESTS IN THE
PACIFIC, POLITICAL THEMES, AND THE OUTLOOK AND U.S. POLICY
REQUIREMENTS. IT UTILIES THE ORCHESTRA METAPHOR AS IT
ASSESSES THE CURRENT SITUATION OF THESE ISLANDS WHILE THE
COLD WAR CONTINUES.

01335 BARK, D.L.; HARRIES, O.; SAUGURU, A.M.
THE U.S. DILEMMA; THE RED ORCHESTRA
HOVER INSTITUTION PRESS, STANFORD, CA., 1989, 160-172.
THIS CHAPTER; ORIGINALLY INTENDED TO LOOK AT HOW U.S.
INTERESTS IN THE SOUTHWESTERN PACIFIC MIGHT BE THREATENED BY
NEW AND EXPANDING SOVIET PRESENCE THERE, CONTENDS THAT U.S.
INTERESTS ARE MORE THREATENED BY ITS OWN ACTIONS THAN BY
THOSE OF THE SOVIET UNION. THEREFORE, IT DISCUSSES ON THE U.
S., RATHER THAN THE SOVIET, PRESENCE. IT EXPRESSES THE VIEWS
OF A PACIFIC ISLANDER. IT ACCUSES THE U.S. OF IGNORING THE
REGION'S EXPRESSED WISHES, INTERESTS, ISSUES, AND CRIES FOR
FAIR PLAY. IT CONCLUDES THAT A U.S. SIGNITURE TO THE
RAROTONGA PROTOCOLS WOULD BE BENEFICIAL TO BOTH SIDES - THAT
THE DILEMMA BELONGS TO THE UNITED STATES, NOT THE SOUTH
PACIFIC.

01336 BARK, D.L.; HARRIES, O.; MCLAY, J.K.
THE VULNERABILITIES AND STRENGTHS OF THE REGION.; THE RED
ORCHESTRA
HOOVER INSTITUTION PRESS, STANFORD, CA., 1989, 38-50.
THIS CHAPTER ADDRESSES THE DIFFERENCES IN PERCEPTION OF
THE SOVIET THREAT IN THE SOUTH PACIFIC. IT DETAILS SOVIET
INTERESTS AND ACTIVITIES IN THE REGION. IT DISCUSSES THE
HISTORY OF NO VIOLENCE, THE WESTERN ORIENTATION, THE LACK OF
A COMMUNIST PARTY, ALSO WESTERN POLICY WHICH HAS CAUSED
FRICTION, THE FEELING OF WESTERN NEGLECT, NEW AND
INEXPERIENCED POLITICAL LEADERS, AND ECONOMIC VULNERABILITY
OF THE ISLANDS. THE ROLE OF AUSTRALIA AND NEW ZEALAND IS
EXPLORED.

01337 BARKAN, J.
SWEDEN: NOT YET PARADISE, BUT ...
DISSENT, (SPR 89), 147-151.
FOR MANY SWEDES, THE WORD "SOCIALISM" CONJURES UP IMAGES
OF PRISON CAMPS AND FOOD LINES. ACTIVITIES IN THE SOCIAL
DEMOCRATIC MOVEMENT EXPRESS SOME OF THE SAME WARINESS, BUT
THEIR POSITION IS MORE COMPLEX. MANY CONSIDER THEMSELVES TO
BE COMMITTED SOCIALISTS, BUT FEW HAVE ANY INTEREST IN WHAT
HAS TRADITIONALLY DEFINED SOCIALISM--PUBLIC OWNERSHIP OF THE
MEANS OF PRODUCTION. THIS AVERSION HAS HISTORICAL AND
GEOPOLITICAL ROOTS BECAUSE SWEDISH SOCIALISTS EARLY ON
JUDGED THE SOVIET EXPERIMENT TO BE A FAILURE. IDENTIFICATION
WITH THAT SYSTEM WAS MADE ALL THE MORE UNAPPEALING BY A
CENTURIES-OLD FEAR OF THE NEIGHBORING RUSSIAN EMPIRE.

01338 BARKER, A.
PLANNING POLICY AND PLANNING RIGHTS
CONSTITUTIONAL REFORM QUARTERLY REVIEW, 4(3) (FAL 89), 5.
THE DECISION OF DEPARTMENT OF THE ENVIRONMENT MINISTER
CHRIS PATTEN TO ORDER A PROPERTY DEVELOPER TO REIMBURSE THE
COSTS OF SEVERAL LOCAL PLANNING AUTHORITIES WHO SUCCESSFULLY
RESISTED THE DEVELOPER'S SCHEME RAISES SOME INTERESTING
QUESTIONS IN THE AREA OF LAND-USE PLANNING AND
CONSTITUTIONAL RIGHTS. UNDER CURRENT BRITISH LAW, THE STATE
MAY IMPOSE CERTAIN POLICY RESTRAINTS AND THE COURTS WILL NOT
CHALLENGE THEIR MERITS SO LONG AS THEY ARE COHERENT,
PRACTICABLE, OR ENFORCEABLE. HOWEVER, PATTEN'S DECISION
RAISES THE QUESTION OF WHETHER A DEVELOPER SHOULD BE FORCED
TO PAY THE LOCAL PLANNING AUTHORITIES' COSTS AFTER AN
INQUIRY BECAUSE THE APPELLATE AUTHORITY THINKS HE SHOULD
HAVE KNOWN IN ADVANCE THAT SUCH A SCHEME COULD NOT HAVE
SUCCEEDED. THE IMPLICATIONS OF PATTEN'S DECISION WILL
PROBABLY NOT BE EVIDENT FOR SOME TIME; BRITISH PLANNING
POLICY IS DETERMINED ON A CASE-BY-CASE BASIS ONLY AFTER OPEN
CHALLENGE AND DEBATE.

01339 BARKER, P.
THE CANADA HEALTH ACT AND THE CABINET DECISION-MAKING
SYSTEM OF PIERRE ELLIOTT TRUDEAU
CANADIAN PUBLIC ADMINISTRATION, 32(1) (SPR 89), 84-103.
THE CABINET DECISION-MAKING SYSTEM OF THE LAST TRUDEAU
GOVERNMENT WAS THE OBJECT OF MUCH CRITICISM. THE SYSTEM
PURPORTEDLY FRAUSTRATED INDIVIDUAL MINISTERS, RELIED
EXCESSIVELY ON CENTRAL AGENCIES, AND MADE POLICY-MAKING
DIFFICULT. BASED ON A STUDY OF THE MANNER IN WHICH THE
FEDERAL GOVERNMENT DEALT WITH THE ISSUE OF DIRECT PATIENT
CHARGES, THIS ARTICLE ARGUES THAT THE FAILINGS OF THE
TRUDEAU DECISION-MAKING SYSTEM WERE EXAGGERATED. INSTEAD OF
BEING SEEN AS A FLAWED ATTEMPT TO STRUCTURE HOW OTTAWA
DECIDES, THE TRUDEAU SYSTEM OF 1980-84 SHOULD BE VIEWED AS
AN IMPORTANT CONTRIBUTION TOWARDS THE DEVELOPMENT OF AN
EFFECTIVE CABINET DECISION-MAKING PROCESS.

01340 BARKLEY, H.J.
STATE AUTONOMY AND THE CRISIS OF IMPORT SUBSTITUTION
COMPARATIVE POLITICAL STUDIES, 22(3) (OCT 89), 291-314.
IMPORT SUBSTITUTING INDUSTRIALIZATION (ISI) STRATEGIES
THAT WERE INSTITUTED WITH GREAT EXPECTATIONS IN LATIN
AMERICA AND ELSEWHERE HAVE NOT PRODUCED THE DESIRED RESULTS.
INSTEAD, ISI HAS BEEN BLAMED FOR GIVING RISE TO INEFFICIENT
ECONOMIC STRUCTURES AND EVEN FOR THE EMERGENCE OF
BUREAUCRATIC AUTHORITARIAN STATES. THIS ARTICLE ARGUES THAT
THE PROBLEMS GENERALLY ATTRIBUTED TO ISI ARE, IN FACT, DUE
TO A LACK OF STATE AUTONOMY. WHAT CAUSES THE LOSS OF
AUTONOMY IS THE EMERGENCE OF POWERFUL AND FIERCELY COMPETING
PRIVATE SECTOR INTERESTS INTENT ON MAXIMIZING THEIR SHARE OF
"ECONOMIC RENTS." THE RESULTING PRIVATE SECTOR-STATE DYNAMIC
HAMPERS THE FORMULATION OF LONG-TERM POLICIES. THE OPERATION
OF THIS DYNAMIC IS DEMONSTRATED THROUGH A CASE STUDY OF
TURKEY IN THE 1970S, WHERE THE STATE, PARALYZED BY PRIVATE
SECTOR COMPETITION, JUST WITNESSED THE COLLAPSE OF ITS
POLITICAL ECONOMY.

01341 BARNDS, H.J.
ASIAN TRIUMPHS AND TRAGEDIES
FREEDOM AT ISSUE, (106) (JAN 89), 12-16.
IN 1988 DEVELOPMENTS REGARDING FREEDOM AND HUMAN RIGHTS
MOVED IN SEVERAL DIRECTIONS IN ASIA, BUT THE MAJOR THRUST
WAS AWAY FROM MILITARY RULE AND AUTHORITARIANISM TOWARD
NATIONAL FREEDOM, CIVILIAN RULE, AND POLITICAL OPENNESS. THE
MOST DRAMATIC EVENTS CAME IN THE SMALLER AND MEDIUM-SIZED
NATIONS: AFGHANISTAN, PAKISTAN, TAIWAN, SOUTH KOREA, AND
THAILAND. BUT ETHNIC VIOLENCE IN SRI LANKA AND THE BRUTAL
SUPPRESSION OF POPULAR OPPOSITION TO THE REGIME IN BURMA
CAST A SHADOW ON THE ASIAN SCENE, AS DID CHINA'S POLITICAL
AND ECONOMIC TROUBLES.

01342 BARNEKOV, T.; RICH, D.
PRIVATISM AND THE LIMITS OF LOCAL ECONOMIC DEVELOPMENT
POLICY
URBAN AFFAIRS QUARTERLY, 25(2) (DEC 89), 212-238.
CONTEMPORARY LOCAL ECONOMIC DEVELOPMENT POLICIES REFLECT
AN UNDERLYING COMMITMENT TO PRIVATISM -- TO ENHANCING AND
ENLARGING THE ROLE OF THE PRIVATE SECTOR IN URBAN
REGENERATION. THIS STUDY CHALLENGES CONVENTIONAL
EXPECTATIONS ABOUT THE BENEFITS OF LOCAL ECONOMIC
DEVELOPMENT POLICIES THAT ARE BASED ON THIS COMMITMENT,
ANALYSIS SUPPORTS A SET OF PROPOSITINS THAT DEFINE COMMON
LIMITATIONS OF THE LOCAL ECONOMIC DEVELOPMENT POLICIES
PURSUED IN THE 1970S AND 1980S. THERE ARE SUCH LIMITATIONS
WHENEVER PRIVATISM IS ACCEPTED AS THE FRAMEWORK FOR URBAN
DEVELOPMENT AND REGENERATION POLICIES.

01343 BARNES, D.A.
THE DYNAMICS OF A PROTEST MOVEMENTS THE FARMERS ALLIANCE
AND THE PEOPLE'S PARTY MOVEMENT IN TEXAS, 1877-1900
DISSERTATION ABSTRACTS INTERNATIONAL, 48(10) (APR 88),
2730-A.
THE DEVELOPMENTAL HISTORY OF THE TAXAS FARMERS ALLIANCE
AND PEOPLE'S PARTY IS EXAMINED AND THE HISTORY IS USED TO
REFLECT UPON BOTH THE PERSPECTIVE GENERALLY USED TO ANALYZE
PROTEST MOVEMENTS: STRUCTURAL STRAIN AND MOBILIZATION, THE
LIMITATIONS OF BOTH THE PERSPECTIVES ARE DISCUSSED AND THE
ADVANTAGES OF THE MOBILIZATION PERSPECTIVE ARE NOTED.

01344 BARNES, F.
BENNETT, THE DRUG CZAR: AN AGENDA
AMERICAN SPECTATOR, 22(4) (APR 89), 14-15.
WILLIAM BENNETT RECOGNIZES THAT THE WAR AGAINST DRUGS IS
WINNABLE, BUT A REAL WAR MUST BE FOUGHT. IF HE MERELY DOES
MORE OF WHAT'S ALREADY BEING DONE TO FIGHT DRUGS, HE WON'T
ACCOMPLISH MUCH. RECOGNIZING THE THREAT POSED BY COLOMBIA'S
DRUGS TO AMERICA'S NATIONAL SECURITY IS ONE NECESSARY STEP.

01345 BARNES, F.
LESSONS OF CAMPAIGN '88
AMERICAN SPECTATOR, 22(1) (JAN 89), 14-16.
THE LESSONS OF THE 1988 ELECTION ISN'T THAT REPUBLICANS
NOW HAVE A ELECTORAL LOCK ON THE PRESIDENCY. ON THE CONTRARY,
THE LESSON IS HOW EASY IT WOULD BE FOR THE RIGHT DEMOCRATIC
PRESIDENTIAL NOMINEE TO WIN THE WHITE HOUSE. MICHAEL DUKAKIS
RAN THE WORST NATIONAL CAMPAIGH OF MODERN TIMES AND GEORGE
BUSH RAN ONE OF THE BEST. DUKAKIS CAME ACROSS AS THE LEAST
LIKABLE POLITICAL FIGURE SINCE THOMAS DEWEY. YET DUKAKIS GOT
46 PERCENT OF THE VOTE IN AN ERA OF REPUBLICAN PEACE AND
PROSPERITY IMAGINE IF DEMOCRATS HAD NOMINATED SOMEONE ELSE -
BILL BRADLEY, SAY, OR LLOYD BENTSEN.

01346 BARNES, F.
SO YOU WANT TO REFORM CONGRESS?
AMERICAN SPECTATOR, 22(9) (SEP 89), 14 - 16.
THE AUTHOR PROPOSE THAT, IN ORDER TO REMIND SENATORS AND
HOUSE MEMBERS WHY THEY WHERE SENT TO CONGRESS,THE AMERICAN
SYSTEM SHOULD CUT BACK ON PACS, THE FRANK, CAMPAIGN STASHES
AND LIFETIME TENURE.

01347 BARNES, J.A.
WHY CABLE COSTS TOO MUCH
WASHINGTON MONTHLY, 21(5) (JUN 89), 12-14, 16-17.
THIS ARTICLE EXPLORES REGULATION BY THE GOVERNMENT OF
CABLE TELEVISION FRANCHISING AND THE RESULTANT MONOPOLY. THE
CABLE COMPANIES AND THE POLITICIANS HAVE CO-OPERATED IN
PRICE GOUGING, BRIBERY, INFLUENCE PEDDLING, AND IN VIOLATION
OF FREE SPEECH WHICH HAS RESULTED IN HIGHER PRICES FOR THE
CONSUMER. THIS ARTICLE ADVOCATES CONGRESS FORBID FRANCHISING
AND ALLOW FREE INTERPRISE TO EXIST.

01348 BARNET, R.
THE CHALLENGE OF CHANGE
SOJOURNERS, 18(6) (JUN 89), 14-18.
ALTHOUGH THE COLD WAR SEEMS TO BE OVER, AND MANY OF THE
CONFLICTS AND PROBLEMS THAT THE US HAS FACED FOR DECADES ARE
BEING RESOLVED, THE US STILL FACES A WIDE ARRAY OF
CHALLENGES IN THE NEXT FEW YEARS. THE AUTHOR DICSUSSES SOME
OF THESE CHALLENGES AND THE MEASURES THAT WILL BE NECESSARY
TO MEET THEM. ISSUES SUCH AS RACISM, DRUGS, AND POVERTY
COFRONT THE US ON THE DOMESTIC LEVEL, AND ON THE
INTERNATIONAL FRONT REGIONAL CONFLICTS STILL ABOUND,
POPULATION, POVERTY, AND ENVIRONMENTAL DEGRADATION LOOM
LARGE, AND THE INSTITUTIONS THAT HAVE PROVIDED THE ENERGY
FOR THE COLD WAR ARE STILL INTACT AND ARMED TO THE TEETH.

01349 BARNETT, M.N.
WAR PREPARATION AND THE RESTRUCTURING OF STATE-SOCIETY
RELATIONS: ISRAEL AND EGYPT IN COMPARATIVE PERSPECTIVE
DISSERTATION ABSTRACTS INTERNATIONAL, 50(5) (NOV 89),
1427-A.
THE AUTHOR PRESENTS A THEORETICAL FRAMEWORK FOR
UNDERSTANDING THE CONNECTION BETWEEN WAR PREPARATION, STATE
POWER, AND THE SUSTAINED MOBILIZATION OF FINANCIAL,
PRODUCTIVE, AND HUMAN RESOURCES BY THE STATE FOR NATIONAL
SECURITY. HE DEMONSTRATES HOW WAR PREPARATION AND ITS
EFFECTS ARE DEPENDENT ON THE PRE-WAR PREPARATION SOCIAL
STRUCTURE AND THE DECISIONS MADE BY GOVERNMENT OFFICIALS. HE
TRACES THE EFFECTS OF WAR PREPARATION ON STATE POWER IN THE
CASES OF ISRAEL (1948-1977) AND EGYPT (1952-1977).

01350 BARON, D.P.
A NONCOOPERATIVE THEORY OF LEGISLATIVE COALITIONS
AMERICAN JOURNAL OF POLITICAL SCIENCE, 33(4) (NOV 89),
1047-1084.
THIS NONCOOPERATIVE THEORY IS BASED ON A MODEL THAT
INCORPORATES AN INSTITUTIONAL STRUCTURE THAT REFLECTS THE
SEQUENTIAL PROCESS OF AGENDA FORMATION AND VOTING IN A
LEGISLATURE THAT HAS THE TASK OF ALLOCATING PARTICULARISTIC
BENEFITS AMONG LEGISLATIVE DISTRICTS. THE THEORY IS INTENDED
TO IDENTIFY THE INCENTIVES FOR THE FORMATION OF PROPOSAL-

COORDINATING COALITIONS AS A FUNCTION OF CHARACTERISTICS OF
THE POLITICAL SYSTEM AND THE RULES THAT GOVERN AGENDA
FORMATION. COALITION PROPOSALS ALLOCATE ALL THE BENEFITS TO
THEIR DISTRICTS, AND WHENEVER THE COALITION HAS DISCIPLINE
OR CONTROLS THE CHAIR, IT WILL BE OF MINIMAL WINNING SIZE
WHEN PROPOSALS ARE GOVERNED BY A CLOSED RULE. WHEN COALITION
DISCIPLINE IS ABSENT AND THE CHAIR IS NEUTRAL, THE COALITION
WILL BE COMPRISED OF APPROXIMATELY 70% OF THE LEGISLATURE. A
LEGISLATIVE RULE THAT ALLOWS AMENDMENTS MAY RESULT IN LARGER
COALITIONS. COALITION COMPOSITION IS ALSO CONSIDERED.

01351 BARON, D.P.; FEREJOHN, J.A.
BARGAINING IN LEGISLATURES
AMERICAN POLITICAL SCIENCE REVIEW, 83(4) (DEC 89),
1181-1206.
BARGAINING IN LEGISLATURES IS CONDUCTED ACCORDING TO
FORMAL RULES SPECIFYING WHO MAY MAKE PROPOSALS AND HOW THEY
WILL BE DECIDED. LEGISLATIVE OUTCOMES DEPEND ON THOSE RULES
AND ON THE STRUCTURE OF THE LEGISLATURE. ALTHOUGH THE SOCIAL
CHOICE LITERATURE PROVIDES THEORIES ABOUT VOTING EQUILIBRIA,
IT DOES NOT ENDOGENIZE THE FORMATION OF THE AGENDA ON WHICH
THE VOTING IS BASED AND RARELY TAKES INTO ACCOUNT THE
INSTITUTIONAL STRUCTURE FOUND IN LEGISLATURES. IN THEORY
MEMBERS OF THE LIGISLATURE ACT NONCOOPERATIVELY IN CHOOSING
STRATEGIES TO SERVE THEIR OWN DISTRICTS, EXPLICITLY TAKING
INTO ACCOUNT THE STRATEGIES MEMBERS ADOPT IN RESPONSE TO THE
SEQUENTIAL NATURE OF PROPOSAL MAKING AND VOTING. THE MODEL
PERMITS THE CHARACTERIZATION OF A LEGISLATIVE EQUILIBRIUM
REFLECTING THE STRUCTURE OF THE LEGISLATURE AND ALSO ALLOWS
CONSIDERATIN OF THE CHOICE OF ELEMENTS OF THAT STRUCTURE IN
A CONTEXT IN WHICH THE STANDARD, INSTITUTION-FREE MODEL OF
SOCIAL CHOICE THEORY YIELDS NO EQUILIBRIUM.

01352 BARRELL, H
DESTABILISATION STRATEGY
NEW AFRICAN, (FEB 88), 9-10.
THIS ARTICLE REPORT ON SOUTH AFRICA'S DESTABILISATION
STRATEGY OF ITS NEIGHBORS AND THROUGHOUT THE WORLD. IT IS A
DEVASTATING INDICTMENT OF THE APARTHEID REGIME IN SOUTH
AFRICA. IT REVEALS THE PLIGHT OF THE HOMELESS BLACKS, THE
USE OF TORTURE ON CHILDREN BY THE POLICE AND THE SYSTEMATIC
SUPPRESSION OF PRESS FREEDOM.

01353 BARRETT, D.M.
THE MYTHOLOGY SURROUNDING LYNDON JOHNSON, HIS ADVISERS,
AND THE 1965 DECISION TO ESCALATE THE VIETNAM WAR
POLITICAL SCIENCE QUARTERLY, 103(4) (WIN 89), 637-664.
A MYTHOLOGY EXISTS REGARDING LYNDON JOHNSON, HIS
WILLINGNESS TO LISTEN TO A VARIETY OF ADVICE ON HANDLING THE
VIETNAM SITUATION IN 1965, AND THE SCOPE OF THE ADVICE HE
RECEIVED BEFORE DECIDING ON ESCALATION. THE MOST IMPORTANT
MYTH IS THAT JOHNSON WAS A "VICTIM OF GROUP THINK." A
SECONDARY, RELATED MYTH CLAIMS THAT JOHNSON'S PERSONALITY
AND EGO WERE SUCH THAT HE WOULD NOT COUNTENANCE THE
EXPRESSION OF CONFLICTING ADVICE THAT MIGHT RAISE THE
POSSIBILITY THAT THE USA WOULD BE WRONG TO INCREASE ITS
MILITARY PRESENCE IN VIETNAM.

01354 BARRETT, T.J.
DRUG WAR DOWN SOUTH: GAINING MORAL ASCENDENCY IN THE
AMERICAS
AVAILABLE FROM NTIS, NO. AD-A207 507/5/GAR, APR 89, 46.
SUPPRESSION OF ILLICIT DRUG TRAFFICKING IN SOURCE AND
TRANSIT COUNTRIES IN THE AMERICAS HAS BEEN AN IMPORTANT PART
OF THE U.S. WAR ON DRUGS. IT IS A PART OF THE WAR WE ARE
LOSING. U.S. SUPPORTED EFFORTS TO BLOCK PRODUCTION AND
SHIPMENT OF ILLICIT DRUGS ARE A FAILURE. DRUG TRAFFICKING IN
THE AMERICAS IS FLOURISHING AND CIA ESTIMATES INDICATE NON-
STOP EXPANSION OF THE COCOA INDUSTRY. THIS STUDY REVIEWS
COUNTER-DRUG PROGRAMS IN OUR HEMISPHERE AND PROPOSES A
REVISED U.S. STRATEGY. TO FORGE A NEW STRATEGY THE STUDY
CONSIDERS CENTERS OF GRAVITY, THE IMPERATIVES OF LOW
INTENSITY CONFLICT, AND THE 'REMARKABLE TRINITY' OF THE
GOVERNMENT, THE COMMANDER AND THE ARMY, AND THE PEOPLE WHICH
ACCORDING TO CLAUSEWITZ DEFINES THE CHARACTER OF ANY 'WAR'.
THE STUDY SUGGESTS U.S. STRATEGIC OBJECTIVES SHOULD
EMPHASIZE SUPPORT FOR DEMOCRACY AND ECONOMIC DEVELOPMENT AND
ELIMINATE CROP ERADICATION AND CERTAIN OTHER ANTI-DRUG
INITIATIVES. A REVAMPED ROLE FOR THE U.S. MILITARY STRESSING
FOREIGN INTERNAL DEFENSE AND NATION BUILDING IS ALSO
PROPOSED. THE OVER-ARCHING GOAL IS TO GAIN MORAL ASCENDENCY
IN THE DRUG WAR IN THE AMERICAS.

01355 BARRID, D.; GIBBINS, R.
PARLIAMENTARY CAREERS IN THE CANADIAN FEDERAL STATE
CANADIAN JOURNAL OF POLITICAL SCIENCE, XXII(1) (MAR 89),
137-146.
THE AUTHORS EXAMINES THE POLITICAL CAREER PATHS FOLLOWED
BY THE 3,803 INDIVIDUAL WHO SERVED IN THE HOUSE OF COMMONS
AND/OR SENATE BETWEEN 1867 AND 1984 INCLUSIVE. GIVEN JOSEPH
SCHLESINGER'S ARGUMENT THAT CAREER PATTERNS SIGNIFICANTLY
AFFECT POLITICAL INTEGRATION IN FEDERAL STATES, PARTICULAR
ATTENTION IS PAID TO THE PROVINCIAL EXPERIENCE OF NATIONAL
PARLIAMENTARIANS, AND TO VARIATIONS IN THAT EXPERIENCE OVER

TIME AND ACROSS REGIONS. THE DATA SHOW THAT NATIONAL
RECRUITMENT FROM PROVINCIAL LEGISLATURES HAS DECLINED OVER
TIME, AND IS PARTICULARLY UNCOMMON IN ONTARIO AND QUEBEC.
OVERALL, THE STRUCTURE OF POLITICAL CAREERS IN CANADA IS
BIFURCATED OTHER THAN INTEGRATED; POLITICIANS DO NOT MOVE
THROUGH THE RANKS BUT RATHER FACE A CHOICE BETWEEN
PROVINCIAL OR NATIONAL CAREERS.

01356 BARRIOS, J.
THE PEOPLE MUST EXPRESS THEIR WILL FREELY
WORLD MARXIST REVIEW, 31(10) (OCT 88), 69-74.
EL SALVADOR'S MARCH 1988 PARLIAMENTARY AND MUNICIPAL
ELECTIONS WERE A FARCE, WITH RIGHT-WING PARTIES THE ONLY
ONES FIELDING CANDIDATES. THE CONTINUING ARMED STRUGGLE, THE
AUTHORITIES' ANTIPEOPLE TERROR, AND THE VIRTUALLY UNPUNISHED
ACTIVITY OF THE NOTORIOUS DEATH SQUADS UTTERLY INVALIDATED
THE POSSIBILITY OF A FREE EXPRESSION OF THE ELECTORATE'S
WILL.

01357 BARRITEAU, E.; CLARKE, R.
GRENADIAN PERCEPTIONS OF THE PEOPLE'S REVOLUTIONARY
GOVERNMENT AND ITS POLICIES
SOCIAL AND ECONOMIC STUDIES, 38(3) (SEP 89), 53-91.
THIS ARTICLE IS A REPORT OF A SURVEY CONDUCTED IN
GRENADA IN 1984 DURING THE CAMPAIGN PERIOD OF THE GENERAL
ELECTION WHICH PROVIDED A SUITABLE CLIMATE FOR SOLICITING
PUBLIC OPINION ON MAJOR QUESTIONS CONCERNING THE PERFORMANCE
OF THE PRG. THE SURVEY TEAM FOUND THAT GRENADIANS WERE
WILLING AND EAGER TO DISCUSS AND CONFRONT THE QUESTION OF
ASSESSING THE GOVERNMENT OF GRENADA LED BY THE LATE MAURICE
BISHOP AND BERNARD COARD OF THE NEW JEWEL MOVEMENT FROM 1979
TO 1983. THE SURVEY SOUGHT TO DISCOVER THE AMOUNT OF POPULAR
SUPPORT ENJOYED BY THE PRG. LEVELS OF SUPPORT SEEM TO BE
RELATED TO EDUCATIONAL ATTAINMENT, AGE AND GENDER, WHETHER
THE PERSONS WERE EMPLOYED OR NOT AFTER THE 1983 INVASION;
CONDITIONS OF LIVING UNDER THE PRG. SPECIFIC PROGRAMMES WERE
SINGLED OUT FROM THE OVER-ALL PLAN FOR APPROVAL, SUCH AS
POPULAR INVOLVEMENT AND PARTICIPATION OF THE PEOPLE. THE
PEOPLE'S PERCEPTIONS OF THE PRG'S ELECTION STRATEGY AND NOT
HOLDING OF ELECTIONS, CHANGING FREEDOM OF SPEECH, THE CUBAN
PRESENCE AND THE COMMUNIST THREAT WERE ALSO POLLED.

01358 BARRON, A.
REFERENDA ON THE PALESTINE QUESTION IN FOUR U.S. CITIES
JOURNAL OF PALESTINE STUDIES, XVIII(4) (SUM 89), 71-83.
THE ARTICLE EXAMINES THE EFFORT OF PRO-PALESTINIAN
GROUPS IN THE U.S. TO INCREASE AWARENESS OF THE PALESTINIAN
ISSUE BY PLACING REFERENDA ON THE BALLOTS OF FOUR U.S.
CITIES. VOTERS IN SAN FRANCISCO AND IN CAMBRIDGE AND NEWTON
(A SUBURB OF BOSTON), MASSACHUSETTS VOTED ON THE QUESTION OF
U.S. SUPPORT FOR PALESTINIAN STATEHOOD WHILE CITIZENS IN
BERKELEY, CALIFORNIA WERE ASKED IF BERKELEY SHOULD ESTABLISH
A SISTER-CITY RELATIONSHIP WITH A PALESTINIAN REFUGEE CAMP.
RESISTANCE FROM ORGANIZED JEWISH COMMUNITIES IN THE FOUR
CITIES HELPED TO DEFEAT THE REFERENDA IN SAN FRANCISCO,
BERKELEY, AND NEWTON. ONLY THE CAMBRIDGE INITIATIVE--THE
ONLY ONE THAT CALLED FOR A CUT IN AID TO ISRAEL--EMERGED
VICTORIOUS.

01359 BARRY, N.P.
THE LIBERAL CONSTITUTION: RATIONAL DESIGN OR EVOLUTION?
CRITICAL REVIEW, 3(2) (SPR 89), 267-282.
THIS ARTICLE EXPLORES THREE REASONS FOR THE LIBERAL
INTEREST IN CONSTITUTIONALISM. THE FIRST IS THAT MODERN
LIBERAL DEMOCRACY HAS PROVED TO BE DISAPPOINTING TO
INDIVIDUALISTS; THE SECOND IS THE CONTEMPORARY ASSOCIATION
BETWEEN LIBERALISM AND SUBJECTIVISM IN ETHICS; AND THIRD,
THE SWITCH IN EMPHASIS FROM IDEAS TO GROUP PROCESSES AS THE
CAUSAL DETERMINANTS OF SOCIAL AND POLITICAL EVENTS. PRESSURE
GROUP POLITICS IS ADDRESSED, AND HAYAKS SOCIAL PHILOSOPHY IS
EXPLORED.

01360 BARSKY, Y.
PALESTINIAN UPRISING IN AMERICA
IDF JOURNAL, (16) (WIN 89), 7-8.
THE AUTHOR LOOKS AT HOW ARAB-AMERICAN ORGANIZATIONS HAVE
ADAPTED THEIR LOBBYING AND PUBLIC RELATIONS STRATEGIES TO
TAKE ADVANTAGE OF THE INTIFADA.

01361 BARTELS, L.M.
PRESIDENTIAL PRIMARIES AND THE DYNAMICS OF PUBLIC CHOICE
PRINCETON UNIVERSITY PRESS, LAWRENCEVILLE, NJ, 1988, 468.
THIS STUDY BLENDS SOPHISTICATED STATISTICAL ANALYSES,
CAMPAIGN ANECDOTES, AND POLITICAL INSIGHT TO EXPLORE ONE OF
AMERICA'S MOST CONTROVERSIAL POLITICAL INSTITUTIONS -- THE
PROCESS BY WHICH MAJOR PARTIES NOMINATE CANDIDATES FOR THE
PRESIDENCY. LARRY BARTELS FOCUSES ON THE NATURE AND IMPACT
OF "MOMENTUM" IN THE CONTEMPORARY NOMINATING SYSTEM. HE
DESCRIBES THE COMPLEX INTERCONNECTIONS AMONG PRIMARY
ELECTION RESULTS, EXPECTATIONS, AND SUBSEQUENT PRIMARY
RESULTS THAT HAVE MADE IT POSSIBLE FOR CANDIDATES LIKE JIMMY
CARTER, GEORGE BUSH, AND GARY HART TO EMERGE FROM RELATIVE
OBSCURITY INTO POLITICAL PROMINENCE IN RECENT NOMINATING
CAMPAIGNS.

01362 BARTELS, L.M.; BROH, C.A.
THE 1988 PRESIDENTIAL PRIMARIES
PUBLIC OPINION QUARTERLY, 53(4) (WIN 89), 563-589.
POLLING IN STATE PRESIDENTIAL PRIMARIES IS, BY
COMPARISON WITH THAT IN GENERAL ELECTIONS, BOTH A NEWER AND
MORE DIFFICULT ART. THE PRIMARY SEASON INVOLVES A MORE
COMPLEX SET OF CONTESTS THAN THE SUBSEQUENT GENERAL ELECTION
CAMPAIGN, MORE CANDIDATES, FEWER VOTERS, A LESS-
KNOWLEDGEABLE AND LESS-COMMITTED PUBLIC, AND HARDER-TO-
UNDERSTAND CAMPAIGN AND ELECTION RULES. IN THIS ARTICLE, THE
AUTHORS DESCRIBE AND ASSESS THE EFFORTS OF THREE PROMINENT
POLLING ORGANIZATIONS IN THE 1988 PRESIDENTIAL PRIMARY
CAMPAIGN: THE GALLUP ORGANIZATION, THE HARRIS POLL, AND THE
CBS NEWS/NEW YORK TIMES COMBINE. THEIR GOAL IS TO USE THE
EXPERIENCES OF THESE ORGANIZATIONS TO ILLUSTRATE SOME OF THE
POSSIBILITIES AND PITFALLS FACING ANY POLLING GROUP IN A
PRESIDENTIAL PRIMARY CAMPAIGN.

01363 BARTHOLOMEW, R.
U.S. EFFORTS AGAINST THE SPREAD OF CHEMICAL WEAPONS
DEPARTMENT OF STATE BULLETIN (US FOREIGN POLICY), 89(2150)
(SEP 89), 74-77.
THE AUTHOR REVIEWS THE PRINCIPAL ELEMENTS OF US POLICY
ON CHEMICAL AND BIOLOGICAL WEAPONS, THE STATUS OF US
CHEMICAL AND BIOLOGICAL WEAPONS SANCTIONS LEGISLATION, AND
THE STATUS OF INTERNATIONAL CHEMICAL WEAPONS NEGOTIATIONS IN
GENEVA.

01364 BARTLES, W.
JAILED FOR SUPPORTING THE INF TREATY
WORLD MARXIST REVIEW, 32(9) (SEP 89), 44-45.
THIS LETTER TO THE MAGAZINE IS A CALL FOR SUPPORT FOR
PEOPLE WHO ARE IMPRISONED FOR THEIR PEACEFUL SUPPORT OF THE
INF TREATY. IT DETAILS THE EXPERIENCES OF SEVERAL
INDIVIDUALS WHO ARE PRESENTLY SERVING SENTENCES FOR
DEMONSTRATING THEIR OPPOSITION TO NUCLEAR WEAPONS. IT
RECOUNTS THEIR EXPERIENCES, THEIR COMMITTMENT TO THEIR
BELIEFS, AND THE RESULTS OF THEIR PEACEFUL DEMONSTRATIONS.

01365 BARTLETT, L.
SECURITY COUP
NEW AFRICAN, (257) (FEB 89), 19, 21.
THE ZIMBABWEAN CENTRAL INTELLIGENCE ORGANIZATION HAS
CRACKED A WELL-ORGANIZED SOUTH AFRICAN SPY-SABOTAGE SQUAD.
THE SPIES WERE INVOLVED IN VIOLENT PLOTS TO ASSASSINATE
MEMBERS OF THE ANC.

01366 BARTLEY, R. L.
HOW REAGANOMICS MADE THE WORLD WORK
NATIONAL REVIEW, XLI(7) (APR 89), 30-34.
THE ARTICLE EXPLORES THE ORIGINS OF REAGANOMINCS AND
ANALYZES ITS RELATIVE SUCCESS OVER THE PAST DECADE. IT ALSO
ASSESSES THE RELATIVE IMPACT OF ECONOMIC PROBLEMS SUCH AS
THE BUDGET AND TRADE DEFICITS AND THE STOCK MARKET CRASH OF
OCTOBER 1987. IT CONCLUDES THAT REAGANOMICS HAS BEEN ABLE TO
WEATHER THESE PROBLEMS AND WILL CONTINUE TO DO SO IF
PRESIDENT BUSH CONTINUES THE TREND.

01367 BARTRA, R.
CULTURE AND POLITICAL POWER IN MEXICO
LATIN AMERICAN PERSPECTIVES, 16(2) (SPR 89), 61-69.
MARXISM IS EXPERIENCING A CRISIS MAINLY BECAUSE OF ITS
DIFFICULTY IN EXPLAINING THE CONDITIONS SURROUNDING THE
CLASS STRUGGLE. ORTHODOX EXPLANATIONS HAD DISCARDED AS
NONESSENTIAL SOME PHENOMENA THAT TODAY EMERGE AS FUNDAMENTAL.
ONE OF THESE PHENOMENA IS THE INFLUENCE OF CULTURE. THE
PAPER DISCUSSES SOME OF THE ELEMENTS OF MEXICAN POLITICAL
CULTURE THAT SHED LIGHT ON THE PROBLEM.

01368 BARTZ. D.
TOXIC WASTE: DUMPING ON LATIN AMERICA
NACLA REPORT ON THE AMERICAS, XXIII(2) (JUL 89), 7-9.
LAX REGULATIONS HAVE TURNED LATIN AMERICA AND THE
CARIBBEAN INTO A CHEAP AND CONVENIENT DUMP FOR HAZARDOUS
WASTE FROM THE UNITED STATES. HOWEVER, SOME GOVERNMENTS IN
THE REGION -- AND SECTORS OF THE POPULATION -- HAVE NOT BEEN
AS COOPERATIVE AS THE WASTE COMPANIES WOULD LIKE. VENEZUELA
HAS SPEARLEADED THE FIGHT FOR A GLOBAL TREATY BANNING ALL
INTERNATIONAL TRAFFIC IN TOXIC TRASH. ON MARCH 22 OF THIS
YEAR, FOLLOWING 18 MONTHS OF NEGOTIATIONS, 105 MEMBERS OF
THE NAIROBI-BASED U.N. ENVIRONMENTAL PROGRAM SIGNED AN
ACCORD WHICH ESTABLISHES SOME CONTROLS OVER TOXIC WASTE
EXPORTS.

01369 BARUAH, S.
INDIGENOUS PEOPLES, CULTURAL SURVIVAL, AND MINORITY POLICY
IN NORTHEAST INDIA
CULTURAL SURVIVAL QUARTERLY, 13(2) (1989), 53-58.
THE SUCCESSFUL POLITICAL INCORPORATION OF DISSENTING
MINORITY GROUPS BY GIVING THEM SIGNIFICANT LEVELS OF
POLITICAL AUTONOMY AND A MAJOR VOICE IN DETERMINING PUBLIC
POLICY IS AN IMPORTANT BUT RELATIVELY UNRECOGNIZED PART OF
THE INDIAN GOVERNMENT'S STRATEGY IN THE NORTHEAST. IT IS

PARTLY THE RESULT OF THE CONTINUATION OF COLONIAL POLICY,
WHICH EMPHASIZED THE PROTECTION OF VULNERABLE INDIGENOUS
PEOPLES FROM THEIR CRAFTIER NEIGHBORS. IT IS ALSO PARTIALLY
THE RESULT OF THE DIFFUSION OF A MODEL OF POLITICAL AUTONOMY
THROUGH CULTURALLY DEFINED STATES THAT WAS DEVELOPED MAINLY
WITH RESPECT TO PENINSULAR INDIA. EVEN THOUGH THE MODEL WAS
THOUGHT TO BEAR LITTLE RELEVANCE TO NORTHEAST INDIA, IT HAS
SHAPED THE POLITICAL IMAGINATION OF THAT REGION'S INDIGENOUS
MINORITIES.

01370 BARUAH, S.
TURMOIL ON THE LEFT: THE SOVIET REFORMS AND INDIAN
COMMUNISTS
SOCIALISM AND DEMOCRACY, (8) (SPR 89), 11-44.
IN THIS ARTICLE SANJIB BARUAH LOOKS AT GLASTNOST FROM
THE POINT OF VIEW OF A COMMUNIST PARTY IN INDIA WHOSE
OPPOSITIONAL POLITICS ARE PROFOUNDLY AFFECTED BY RECENT
CHANGES IN SOVIET POLICY. IT ADDRESSES THE QUESTION FOR
OFFICIALS IN THE COMMUNIST PARTY OF INDIA ABOUT WHAT ASPECTS
OF EXISTING SOCIALISM IN THE USSR CONSTITUTE ADEQUATE POINTS
OF REFERENCE FOR THOSE SUPPORTING THE INTERNATIONAL MOVEMENT.
EXPLORED ARE THE IMPLICATIONS OF GLASTNOST WHICH MANY
INDIAN COMMUNISTS BELIEVE WILL MAKE IT DIFFICULT FOR THEIR
PARTY TO MAINTAIN ITS LEGITIMACY AS A VIABLE OPPOSITION.

01371 BARZUN, J.
IS DEMOCRATIC THEORY FOR EXPORT?
SOCIETY, 26(3) (MAR 89), 16-24.
A PERMANENT WISH OF AMERICAN FOREIGN POLICY HAS BEEN THE
EXPORTING OF DEMOCRACY: CONVINCING OTHER NATIONS OF THE
"ERROR OF THEIR WAYS" AND LEADING THEM ON THE PATH TO
FREEDOM FOR THE PEOPLE. THE ARTICLE GRAPPLES WITH THE
UNDERLYING PROBLEM OF DEFINING DEMOCRACY. IT CONCLUDES THAT
THERE IS VERY LITTLE AGREEMENT ON THE EXACT NATURE OF
DEMOCRACY AND EVEN LESS ON THE MECHANISMS NECESSARY TO
IMPLEMENT IT. IT CONCLUDES THAT DEMOCRACY HAS NO THEORY TO
EXPORT BECAUSE IT IS NOT AN IDEOLOGY BUT A HISTORICAL
DEVELOPMENT. FURTHERMORE, THE CONFLICT BETWEEN DESIRES FOR
EQUALITY AND DESIRES FOR FREEDOM PLACE THE WORLD'S
DEMOCRACIES IN A STATE OF CONSTANT FLUX AND CONFLICT.

01372 BASHEVKIN, S.
FREE TRADE AND CANADIAN FEMINISM: THE CASE OF THE NATIONAL
ACTION COMMITTEE ON THE STATUS OF WOMEN
CANADIAN REVIEW OF SOCIOLOGY AND ANTHROPOLOGY, 15(4) (DEC
89), 363-375.
EXISTING STUDIES OF THE FREE TRADE DEBATE HAVE
OVERLOOKED THE INTERVENTION OF THE NATIONAL ACTION COMMITTEE
ON THE STATUS OF WOMEN (NAC) ON THIS ISSUE. NAC'S
PARTICIPATION REFLECTED AN EXTENSION OF ITS POLICY FOCUS
BEYOND CONVENTIONAL 'WOMEN'S ISSUES,' NOTABLY LEGAL RIGHTS
AND SOCIAL POLICY QUESTIONS, TOWARD AN INTEGRATION OF THESE
CONCERNS WITH BROADER ECONOMIC POLICY. AS WELL, NAC'S
STRATEGY ON THE FREE TRADE QUESTION REPRESENTED A CHANGE
FROM ITS EARLIER EMPHASIS UPON CO-OPERATIVE RELATIONS WITH
THE FEDERAL GOVERNMENT IN ORDER TO OBTAIN REFORMS ON
'WOMEN'S ISSUES.' THIS ARTICLE EXAMINES THE BACKGROUND TO
NAC'S PARTICIPATION IN THE FREE TRADE DEBATE, ITS MAIN
CRITICISMS OF FREE TRADE AND, MOST IMPORTANTLY, THE
POTENTIAL CONSEQUENCES OF THIS POLICY INTERVENTION FOR BOTH
NAC AND THE LARGER CANADIAN WOMEN'S MOVEMENT.

01373 BASKIN, M.A.
THE EVOLUTION OF POLICY COMMUNITIES IN SOCIALIST
YUGOSLAVIA: THE CASE OF WORKER MIGRATION ABROAD
GOVERNANCE, 2(1) (JAN 89), 67-85.
THIS ARTICLE EXAMINES THE EVOLUTION OF A POLICY
COMMUNITY IN SOCIALIST YUGOSLAVIA CONCERNED WITH WORKER
MIGRATION ABROAD FROM THE MID-1960S THROUGH THE MID-1980S TO
ASCERTAIN HOW CLOSELY THEY MATCH THE DEVELOPMENT OF POLICY
COMMUNITIES IN PLURALIST SYSTEMS (WALKER 1974; KINGDON 1984).
IT PROVES THAT POLITICAL AND ECONOMIC REFORMS IN
AUTHORITARIAN SYSTEMS CAN GENERATE A SETTING WHERE
COMMUNITIES OF SPECIALISTS CAN FORM, GAIN AUTONOMY, AND
DEVELOP INFLUENTIAL INTERPRETATIONS OF ISSUES OF PUBLIC
POLICY. IT FURTHER SUGGESTS THAT THE AUTONOMY AND INFLUENCE
OF SUCH COMMUNITIES DEPEND ON CHANGES IN STATE STRUCTURE AND
THE DISPOSITIONS OF GENERALIST POLITICAL ELITES.

01374 BASOM, R.E. JR.
STAKEHOLDERS' FRAMES OF REFERENCE AND THEIR IMPACTS ON
PERFORMANCE ASSESSMENT
DISSERTATION ABSTRACTS INTERNATIONAL, 50(6) (DEC 89),
1798-A.
THE AUTHOR PRESENTS AN APPROACH TO ORGANIZATIONAL
PERFORMANCE ASSESSMENT THAT TAKES THE DIVERSE REALITY OF
PUBLIC SERVICE ORGANIZATIONAL MANAGEMENT INTO ACCOUNT. HE
OFFERS A SOLUTION TO THE PROBLEM OF HOW TO INVOLVE
STAKEHOLDERS IN PARTICIPATORY MANAGEMENT, ASSUMING MULTIPLE
AND COMPETING VALUES. THE PERFORMANCE ASSESSMENT THROUGH
STAKEHOLDERS (PATS) METHODOLOGY TAKES A STEP TOWARD CLOSING
THE GAP BETWEEN TOP-DOWN MANDATED ASSESSMENT CRITERIA AND
THEIR FREQUENT IRRELEVANCE IN DAY-TO-DAY POLICY
IMPLEMENTATION.

01375 BASS, L.
FOR MORE LIVELY TIES BETWEEN THE USSR AND BULGARIA
FOREIGN TRADE, 5 (1988), 6-8.
THIS ARTICLE REPORTS ON THE 27TH CONGRESS OF THE CPSU
AND THE 13TH CONGRESS OF THE BCP WHICH WERE DISCUSSED AT A
JOINT SOVIET-BULGARIAN SYMPOSIUM. THE PROBLEMS OF USSR-
BULGARIAN BILATERAL TRADE WERE EXPLORED AS WELL AS THE NEED
TO REORIENTATE THE EXISTING STRUCTURE OF THE DIVISION OF
LABOUR AND MUTUAL EXCHANGES. THE TRANSITION TO BILATERAL
ECONOMIC COOPERATION AT THE LEVEL OF ECONOMIC ORGANIZATIONS
WAS EXPLORED.

01376 BASSEY, C.O.
RETROSPECTS AND PROSPECTS OF POLITICAL STABILITY IN NIGERIA
AFRICAN STUDIES REVIEW, 32(1) (APR 89), 97-113.
THE AUTHOR ENDEAVORS TO ANALYZE AND COMPREHEND THE
SOCIAL DYNAMICS THAT GENERATE THE PERSISTENT SYNDROME OF
POLITICAL INSTABILITY IN NIGERIA AND, ON THAT BASIS, TO
HAZARD A GUESS ABOUT THE FUTURE OF THE NIGERIAN STATE AS IT
MIGHT BE SHAPED BY SYSTEMATIC CHALLENGES. THE ESSAY BEGINS
WITH A METHODOLOGICAL NOTE BEFORE EXAMINING EXTANT
THEORETICAL PERSPECTIVES ON INSTABILITY AND ORDER IN NIGERIA.

01377 BASTIAT, F.
OUR SECRET DESIRES: WHY WE END UP WITH TRADE BARRIERS
REASON, 20(10) (MAR 89), 36-38.
THE AUTHOR EXAMINES THE ECONOMIC PROPOSITION THAT
ABUNDANCE IS DANGEROUS AND SCARCITY IS ADVANTAGEOUS. HE
CONCLUDES THAT RESTRICTIVE TRADE LAWS LIMIT THE SUPPLY OF
GOODS AND RAISE THEIR PRICES AND, CONSEQUENTLY, FAVOR THE
PRODUCER.

01378 BASU, J.
WHY WE HAVE THE PEOPLE'S TRUST
WORLD MARXIST REVIEW, 32(10) (OCT 89), 56-58.
THIS ARTICLE GIVES THE VIEWS OF THE CHIEF MINISTER OF
WEST BENGAL AS HE DESCRIBES THE ACTIVITY OF THE STATE
GOVERNMENT, THE COMMUNIST'S ROLE IN EXPRESSING THE WILL OF
THE ELECTORATE, AND THE PRESENT STATE OF THE WORLD AND THE
COMMUNIST MOVEMENT. IT EXPLORES THE CPICM) IS ELECTORAL
SUCCESS, THE RELATIONSHIP BETWEEN THE STATE AND THE CENTRAL
GOVERNMENT, ECONOMICS, AND THE PROBLEM OF DEMOCRACY.

01379 BASU, R.
THE POLITICO-ADMINISTRATIVE RELATIONSHIP IN DEVELOPMENT
ADMINISTRATION IN INDIA
INDIAN JOURNAL OF POLITICAL SCIENCE, L(2) (APR 89),
209-220.
THE AUTHOR CONSIDERS THE GENERAL FIELD OF DEVELOPMENT
ADMINISTRATION AND THE POLITICO-ADMINISTRATIVE RELATIONSHIP
IN DEVELOPMENT ADMINISTRATION IN INDIA.

01380 BASZKIEWICZ, J.
FROM THE FRENCH TO CONTEMPORARY REVOLUTIONS
POLISH PERSPECTIVES, XXXII(2) (1989), 27-36.
THE AUTHOR COMPARES AND CONTRASTS THE FRENCH REVOLUTION
WITH CONTEMPORARY MARXIST REVOLUTIONS.

01381 BATES, R.H.
IS LIBERALISM STILL POSSIBLE
NATIONAL REVIEW, 61(25) (DEC 89), 17.
THIS ARTICLE PREDICTS THE DOWNFALL OF LIBERALISM AND
SUGGESTS THAT RARELY HAS A HEGEMONIC FORCE FALLEN SO QUICKLY
FROM THE PINNACLE OF POWER. AMONG THE MANY REASONS SUGGESTED
FOR FALL ARE GIVEN, THIS REPORT HAS ITS OWN THEORY, THE OLD
LIBERALISM WAS POPULAR BECAUSE IT PROVIDED A WAY BY WHICH
GOVERNMENTS COULD USE POLITICAL POWER TO ACHIEVE ECONOMIC
PROSPERITY. BECAUSE OF TODAY'S ECONOMY, INCREASED
GOVERNMENTAL SPENDING THREATENS THE CLASSIC ECONOMIC GOALS
OF LIBERALISM - EMPLOYMENT AND GROWTH. THE DECLINING APPEAL
OF LIBERAL CANDIDATES SUGGESTS THAT THE VOTING PUBLIC
RECOGNIZES THIS FACT.

01382 BATES, S.G.
CHURCH, PRESS, AND AMERICAN SELF-GOVERNMENT
FREEDOM AT ISSUE, (109) (JUL 89), 9-14.
TWO PRIVATE INSTITUTIONS SUBSTANTIALLY SHAPE THE
AMERICAN NATION AND ITS POLITICAL LIFE: THE CHURCH AND THE
PRESS. THEIR CONTRIBUTIONS ARE SUBSTANTIAL, BUT VARIOUS
LEGAL DOCTRINES PREVENT THEM FROM REACHING THEIR FULL
POTENTIALS. IN THIS ARTICLE, THE AUTHOR ANALYZES THE STATUS
OF CHURCH AND PRESS FREEDOMS BASED ON THE INSTITUTIONS' SELF-
GOVERNMENT ROLES. HE ARGUES THAT STRICT SEPARATION DOCTRINES,
WHICH HAVE BEEN FORMULATED OFTEN FOR THE CHURCH AND
OCCASIONALLY FOR THE PRESS, NO LONGER SUFFICE.

01383 BATHURST, R.B.
SOME PROBLEMS IN SOVIET-AMERICAN WAR TERMINATION:
CROSS/CULTURAL ASYMMETRIES
AVAILABLE FROM NTIS, NO. AD-A204 784/3/GAR, SEP 88, 74.
THE ANALYSIS OF THE PROCESS OF WAR TERMINATION CANNOT BE
UNDERSTOOD AS A LOGICAL ONE. CULTURAL PRECONCEPTIONS
HISTORICALLY OVERRIDE LOGIC IN WAR. CULTURAL VALUES MANIFEST

THEMSELVES AS SIGNS AND ARE CONVEYED THROUGH SIGNALS. AN
ENORMOUS PROBLEM IS HOW TO INTERPRET ANOTHER CULTURE'S
SIGNALS. THIS PAPER PRESENTS SOME OF THE MAJOR ASYMMETRIES
IN THEORIES OF WAR AND ITS TERMINATION BETWEEN THE U.S. AND
SOVIET UNION. IT PROVIDES A KIND OF CHECKLIST OF DANGEROUS
MISCONCEPTIONS AND THEIR CONSEQUENCES. APPLYING SOME OF THE
CONCEPTS OF POLITICAL CULTURE TO THE CURRENT STATE OF SOVIET
MILITARY SCIENCE, IT PREDICTS HOW SOVIET MILITARY THOUGHT
WILL BE AFFECTED BY PERESTROYKA. USING THE SAME TECHNIQUES,
IT PROPOSES, FOR PURPOSES OF WAR TERMINATION THE CREATION OF
A SHADOW AMERICAN POLITBURO, A TRAINED GROUP TO MIRROR IMAGE
SOVIET CONCEPTIONS OF AMERICAN POWER.

01384 BATLEY, R.
   LONDON DOCKLANDS: AN ANALYSIS OF POWER RELATIONS BETWEEN
   UDCS AND LOCAL GOVERNMENT
   PUBLIC ADMINISTRATION, 67(2) (SUM 89), 167-188.
      THIS ARTICLE SETS UP A FRAMEWORK FOR EXAMINING THE
   DIFFERENCES AND RELATIONS BETWEEN URBAN DEVELOPMENT
   CORPORATIONS AND LOCAL GOVERNMENT. IT ANALYSES THE INTEREST
   TO WHICH THE TWO SORTS OF BODY ARE RESPONSIVE, THE
   ORGANIZATIONAL STRUCTURES WHICH CONDITION THEIR RELATIONSHIP
   AND THE STYLES OF DECISION-MAKING THROUGH WHICH THEY OPERATE.
   THIS FRAMEWORK IS USED TO ANALYSE THE LONDON DOCKLANDS
   EXPERIENCE WITH THE OBJECTIVE OF DISTINGUISHING THE SPECIAL
   ASPECTS OF THIS CASE FROM THOSE WHICH ARE LIKELY TO BE
   GENERALLY APPLICABLE.

01385 BATPR, F.M.
   MUST WE RETRENCH?
   FOREIGN AFFAIRS, 68(2) (SPR 89), 93-124.
      TO AVOID THE FATE OF OVER-EXTENDED EMPIRES OF THE PAST,
   SOME ANALYSTS SAY THE USA MUST SPEND LESS ON DEFENSE AND
   ADJUST ITS INTERNATIONAL INVOLVEMENTS ACCORDINGLY. THE AIR
   IS FULL OF WARNINGS AGAINST OVERESTIMATING AMERICA'S
   ECONOMIC STRENGTH. BUT, IN FACT, THE USA IS MORE LIKELY TO
   UNDERESTIMATE ITS ECONOMIC PROWESS.

01386 BATTAH, A.M.
   IBN KHALDUN'S PRINCIPLES OF POLITICAL ECONOMY: RUDIMENTS
   OF A NEW SCIENCE
   DISSERTATION ABSTRACTS INTERNATIONAL, 49(11) (MAY 89),
   3496-A.
      IBN KHALDUN'S CONTRIBUTION TO POLITICAL ECONOMY IS
   ORIGINAL AND SO GREAT AS TO QUALIFY HIM FOR THE TITLE
   "FATHER OF POLITICAL ECONOMY." HIS WORK HAS COMMANDED GREAT
   RESPECT FROM WRITERS IN SOCIOLOGY, HISTORY, AND PHILOSOPHY
   AND HAS EXERTED NOTICEABLE INFLUENCE ON ARAB AND MUSLIM
   SCHOLARSHIP. IT REMAINS RELEVANT AND TIMELY TODAY.

01387 BATTLE, J.
   IN SEARCH OF GORBACHEV'S REVOLUTION FROM BELOW
   INTERNATIONAL PERSPECTIVES, XVIII(3) (MAY 89), 7-11.
      DESPITE HIS OWN ADMISSION THAT PREVIOUS REVOLUTIONS FROM
   ABOVE HAD LED TO DEFORMITIES RESULTING IN HIGH
   SOCIOPOLITICAL AND MORAL COSTS, AND DESPITE HIS CALLS FOR
   THE DEMOCRATIZATION OF SOVIET SOCIETY, GORBACHEV HAS HIMSELF
   NOT REFRAINED FROM USING OLD METHODS TO ACCOMPLISH NEW GOALS.
   THE SEPTEMBER 30, 1988, PLENUM IN WHICH MAJOR POLITICAL
   FIGURES SUCH AS ANDREI GROMYKO AND ANATOLY DOBRYNIN WERE
   RETIRED, AND YEGOR LIGACHEV AND VICTOR CHEBRIKOV WERE
   DEMOTED TO POSITIONS OF LESSER AUTHORITY, IS A CASE IN POINT.
   CARRIED OUT IN STRICT SECRECY BEHIND CLOSED DOORS, THESE
   CHANGES HAD LITTLE TO DO WITH GLASNOST OR PERESTROIKA. IN
   TYPICAL, NON-DEMOCRATIC STYLE. THE PUBLIC WAS NOT ASKED FOR
   ITS OPINION, NO RATIONALE FOR THE SHAKEUP WAS GIVEN, AND THE
   MEDIA PROVIDED ONLY MEAGER DETAILS. GORBACHEV'S "REVOLUTION
   FROM BELOW" IS, IN FACT, A CHANGE IN NAME ONLY. THE REALITY
   IS, BUSINESS AS USUAL.

01388 BAUER, M.; HIBBING, J.R.
   WHICH INCUMBENTS LOSE IN HOUSE ELECTIONS: A RESPONSE TO
   JACOBSON'S "THE MARGINALS NEVER VANISHED"
   AMERICAN JOURNAL OF POLITICAL SCIENCE, 33(1) (FEB 89),
   262-271.
      AFTER THE APPEARANCE OF SCORES OF SCHOLARLY WORKS
   ATTEMPTING TO EXPLAIN WHY INCUMBENT MEMBERS OF THE HOUSE OF
   REPRESENTATIVES BECAME SAFER IN THE MID1960S, GARY JACOBSON,
   IN A RECENT (FEBRUARY 1987) ARTICLE IN THIS JOURNAL, CLAIMS
   THAT "COMPETITION FOR HOUSE SEATS HELD BY INCUMBENTS HAS NOT,
   IN FACT, DECLINED." THE CRUX OF JACOBSON'S CASE RESTS AN
   ALLEGED INCREASE IN THE CHANCES OF AN INCUMBENT WINNING BY A
   LARGE MARGIN IN ONE ELECTION AND THEN LOSING THE SEAT TWO
   YEARS LATER. THUS, JACOBSON BELIEVES, "MARGINALITY" NEEDS TO
   BE REDEFINED RATHER THAN MEMORIALIZED. IN THIS RESPONSE WE
   RAISE SOME ADDITIONAL ISSUES RELEVANT TO THE MATTER OF
   INCUMBENT SAFETY. THE PRESENT ANALYSIS OF THE EVIDENCE
   SUGGESTS THERE MAY HAVE BEEN A SLIGHT, TEMPORARY INCREASE IN
   THE LATE 1960S AND EARLY 1970S IN THE CHANCES OF BIG WINNERS
   LOSING THEIR NEXT RACE, BUT CLEARLY INDICATES THAT IN THE
   SIX ELECTIONS SINCE 1974 THE PROPORTION OF BIG WINNERS WHO
   LOSE THE NEXT ELECTION IS VIRTUALLY IDENTICAL TO THE
   PROPORTION IN THE 1950S AND EARLY 1960S. WHAT IS MORE, THOSE
   WHO DO LOSE ALMOST ALWAYS DO SO BECAUSE OF AN ADVERSE

REDISTRICTING OR A MAJOR, PERSONAL SCANDAL. THUS, UNLIKE
JACOBSON, THE AUTHORS CONCLUDE THAT (1) THERE HAS BEEN NO
MEANINGFUL INCREASE IN THE CHANCES OF BIG WINNERS
SUBSEQUENTLY LOSING AND (2) IN RECENT ELECTIONS THE CHANCES
OF A SCANDAL-FREE, UNREDISTRICTED, PREVIOUSLY SAFE INCUMBENT
LOSING ARE PRACTICALLY NIL. THE LEVEL OF COMPETITION IN
CONGRESSIONAL ELECTIONS HAS DECLINED AND SHOULD BE A SOURCE
OF CONCERN TO THOSE WHO VALUE ELECTORAL ACCOUNTABILITY.

01389 BAUGHMAN, C. M.
   AUCTIONING OF QUOTAS: LOTS OF PAIN FOR LITTLE GAIN
   WORLD ECONOMY, 11(3) (SEP 88), 397-416.
      THIS ARTICLE EXAMINES THE ARGUEMENTS PRO AND CON FOR THE
   AUCTIONING OF QUOTAS, ADVOCATES OF AUCTIONING POINT TO
   ECONOMIC THEORY AS EVIDENCE THAT IT COULD RAISE CONSIDERABLE
   REVENUES TO FUND ADJUSTMENTS AND PROMOTO TRADE
   LIBERALIZATION. BUT IN REAL-WORLD CONTEXT, THE IMPACT OF
   AUCTIONING WOULD BE QUITE DIFFERENT FROM WHAT THEORISTS
   PREDICT, IN REALITY, AUCTIONING IS LIKELY TO ACHIEVE THE
   GOALS OF ITS SUPPORTERS ONLY AT GREAT COST TO AMERICAN
   ECONOMY IF AT ALL.

01390 BAUM, D.
   SOUTH AFRICAN SHOWPIECE?
   NEW AFRICAN, (257) (FEB 89), 18.
      THE COMORO GOVERNMENT HAS DENIED THAT IT RECEIVES
   FINANCIAL AID FROM SOUTH AFRICA, BUT EVIDENCE INDICATES THAT
   IT DOES. THE COMOREAN PRESIDENTIAL GUARD SERVES AS THE
   CONDUIT FOR ALL SOUTH AFRICAN AID.

01391 BAUM, D.
   THE COMOROS CONNECTION
   AFRICA REPORT, 34(1) (JAN 89), 49.
      WITH PRECIOUS FEW FRIENDS IN BLACK AFRICA, SOUTH AFRICA
   IS WOOING COMOROS WITH FINANCIAL AID, ALMOST ALL SOUTH
   AFRICAN AID IS FUNNELED THROUGH THE PRESIDENTIAL GUARD,
   GREEN-BERET STORMTROOPERS LED BY A BAND OF FOREIGN
   MERCENARIES WITH A REPUTATION FOR BRUTALITY. THE POWER OF
   THE GUARD IS SAID TO RIVAL THAT OF PRESIDENT AHMED ABDALLAH.

01392 BAUM, D.
   THE WAYWARD SIBLINGS
   AFRICA REPORT, 34(1) (JAN 89), 47-50.
      BOTH MAURITIUS AND MADAGASCAR HAVE ADOPTED THE FREE
   MARKET DOCTRINE OF THE WORLD BANK AND IMF IN THEIR EFFORTS
   TO BOOST ECONOMIC DEVELOPMENT. WHILE THE MAURITIAN ECONOMY
   IS TRYING TO COPE WITH TOO RAPID EXPANSION AND CRITICISM OF
   ITS TRADE WITH SOUTH AFRICA, MADAGASCAR, WHICH SHOULD BE THE
   REGION'S SUPERPOWER, CONTINUES TO STRUGGLE WITH THE LEGACY
   OF A NORTH KOREAN-INSPIRED ECONOMIC MODEL.

01393 BAUM, L.
   COMPARING THE POLICY POSITIONS OF SUPREME COURT JUSTICES
   FROM DIFFERENT PERIODS
   WESTERN POLITICAL QUARTERLY, 42(4) (DEC 89), 509-522.
      ANALYSES OF DECISION MAKING ON THE SUPREME COURT BENEFIT
   FROM COMPARING LARGER NUMBERS OF JUSTICES THAN THE NINE WHO
   SERVE AT A GIVEN TIME. BUT JUSTICES WHO SERVE OVER DIFFERENT
   PERIODS ADDRESS DIFFERENT SETS OF CASES, SO THAT SUCH
   ANALYSES FACE PROBLEMS OF COMPARABILITY. THIS ARTICLE OFFERS
   ONE METHOD TO CONTROL FOR DIFFERENCES IN THE CONTENT OF
   CASES OVER TIME AND THUS TO FACILITATE IDEOLOGICAL
   COMPARISONS AMONG JUSTICES WHOSE CAREERS SPAN DIFFERENT SETS
   OF TERMS. THE METHOD IS USED TO ESTIMATE THE RELATIVE
   SUPPORT FOR CIVIL LIBERTIES OF JUSTICES WHO SERVED DURING
   THE 1946-85 TERMS. THE RESULTS INDICATE THAT THE JUSTICES OF
   THE BURGER COURT WERE MORE FAVORABLE TO CIVIL LIBERTIES,
   RELATIVE TO THEIR PREDECESSORS, THAN SIMPLE PROPORTIONS OF
   VOTES FOR AND AGAINST LITIGANTS WITH CIVIL LIBERTIES CLAIMS
   WOULD INDICATE.

01394 BAUM, P.; DANZIGER, R.
   A REGENERATED PLO? THE PALESTINE NATIONAL COUNCIL'S 1988
   RESOLUTIONS AND THEIR REPERCUSSIONS
   MIDDLE EAST REVIEW, XXII(1) (FAL 89), 17-25.
      ONLY THE COMPLEX COMPOSITE OF WRITTEN DOCUMENTS AND ORAL
   COMMENTARY, OF FORMAL RESOLUTIONS AND SPONTANEOUS MEDIA
   RESPONSES, OF ORGANIZATIONAL CONCESSIONS AND INDIVIDUAL
   ASSESSMENTS, TOGETHER WITH ALL THEIR CONTRADICTIONS AND
   AMBIGUITIES, CAN PRESENT AN ACCURATE PICTURE OF THE CURRENT
   PLO POSTURE. THE ANALYSIS IN THIS ESSAY IS DIRECTED TOWARD
   UNDERSTANDING THE MEANING OF THE ALGIERS RESOLUTIONS. THE
   AUTHORS CONCLUDE THAT, GIVEN ALL THE DISTURBING INDICATIONS,
   IT IS DIFFICULT TO ACCEPT THE PNC'S LATEST RENUNCIATION OF
   TERRORISM AS COMPREHENSIVE AND SERIOUS, LET ALONE
   IRREVOCABLY BINDING.

01395 BAUM, R.
   INTRODUCTION: BEYOND LENINISM? ECONOMIC REFORM AND
   POLITICAL DEVELOPMENT IN POST-MAO CHINA
   STUDIES IN COMPARATIVE COMMUNISM, 22(2/3) (SUM 89),
   111-124.
      THIS ARTICLE IS AN INTRODUCTION TO A SPECIAL DOUBLE
   ISSUE OF STUDIES IN COMPARATIVE COMMUNISM AND CONTAINS

LENGTHY ABSTRACTS OF SCHOLARS WHO EXAMINE IN DEPTH THE VARIOUS FACETS OF THE POST-MAO REFORM MOVEMENT IN CHINA. THE AUTHORS EXPLORE ISSUES RANGING FROM THE LONG TERM MACRO-POLITICAL EVOLUTION OF LENINIST SYSTEMS TO THE SHORT TERM EFFECTS OF PRICE REFORM UPON URBAN INFLATION.

01396 BAUMAN, Z.; RAKOWSKI, M.
TWO VIEWS ON THE LESSONS OF THATCHERISM
EAST EUROPEAN REPORTER, 4(1) (WIN 89), 71-72.
THE ARTICLE PRESENTS TWO WIDELY DIFFERENT VIEWS ON THE APPLICABILITY OF THATCHERITE ECONOMICS TO POLAND. PROFESSOR BAUMAN ARGUES THAT THATCHERISM HAS TORN ENGLAND'S SOCIAL FABRIC AND HAS NOT ACHIEVED ANY REAL ECONOMIC GAINS. HE CONCLUDES THAT THE NATIONAL ENCHANTMENT OF POLES WITH THATCHER IS A "GROSS MISUNDERSTANDING." ON THE OTHER HAND, ECONOMIST JACEK ROSTOWSKI ARGUES THAT THE ECONOMIC SUCCESS OF THATCHERISM HAS BEEN OBVIOUS AND INDISPUTABLE. HE CONCLUDES THAT NATIONS SUCH AS POLAND AND HUNGARY CAN LEARN THE VALUABLE LESSON THAT ECONOMIC PROGRESS IS POSSIBLE AT A PRICE.

01397 BAUMGARTNER, F.R.; WALKER, J.L.
EDUCATIONAL POLICYMAKING AND THE INTEREST GROUP STRUCTURE IN FRANCE AND THE UNITED STATES
COMPARATIVE POLITICS, 21(3) (APR 89), 273-288.
ANY EFFORT TO CHARACTERIZE THE POLICYMAKING PROCESS IN INDUSTRIAL DEMOCRACIES MUST INCLUDE AN ANALYSIS OF BOTH THE ORGANIZATION OF THE STATE AND THE ORGANIZED FACTIONS, PARTIES, AND INTEREST GROUPS THAT SEEK TO INFLUENCE THE STATE. BOTH SIDES OF THE POLICYMAKING EQUATION ARE IMPORTANT DETERMINANTS OF POLICY OUTCOMES, AND EACH INTERACTS WITH THE OTHER TO PRODUCE A DISTINCTIVE NATIONAL SYSTEM OF POLITICS AND POLICYMAKING. THE IMPORTANCE OF THIS OBSERVATION IS CLEARLY ILLUSTRATED WHEN EDUCATIONAL POLICYMAKING IS EXAMINED IN FRANCE AND THE UNITED STATES.

01398 BAUMGARTNER, F.R.
INDEPENDENT AND POLITICIZED POLICY COMMUNITIES: EDUCATION AND NUCLEAR ENERGY IN FRANCE AND IN THE UNITED STATES
GOVERNANCE, 2(1) (JAN 89), 42-66.
A MYRIAD OF POLICY COMMUNITIES SURROUNDING DIFFERENT ISSUES FORM THE ESSENTIAL ARENAS IN WHICH POLICIES ARE MADE IN FRANCE AND IN THE UNITED STATES. THESE POLICY COMMUNITIES ARE OFTEN DOMINATED BY ELITE CIVIL SERVANTS AND A SELECT GROUP OF INTEREST GROUP OR BUSINESS REPRESENTATIVES; HOWEVER, THEY OFTEN INCLUDE A SMALL NUMBER OF ELECTED OFFICIALS WITH PARTICULAR INTEREST IN THE AREA, AS WELL AS A VARIETY OF ACADEMICS AND MEDIA COMMENTATORS. SOME POLICY COMMUNITIES APPEAR TO REVOLVE AROUND PURELY TECHNICAL ISSUES AND ARE RARELY DISCUSSED IN THE NATION'S MEDIA, WHILE OTHERS SEEM CONSTANTLY TO BE THE SUBJECT OF POLITICAL CONTROVERSY AND ELITE-LEVEL DISCUSSION. THIS ARTICLE EXPLAINS WHY SOME POLICY COMMUNITIES ARE MORE INSULATED FROM POLITICS THAN OTHERS. IT FOCUSES ON THE DEGREE OF CONFLICT PRESENT WITHIN THE COMMUNITY OF EXPERTS, ON THE STRATEGIC BEHAVIORS OF THE POLICY MAKERS INVOLVED IN THEM, AND ON THE SUCCESS OR FAILURE OF STRATEGIC EFFORTS TO SHIFT THE VENUE OF A POLICY DEBATE. THE ORGANIZATION OF A POLICY COMMUNITY DETERMINES ITS MEMBERS' ABILITY TO DOMINATE THE POLICY PROCESS AND TO AVOID THE INTRUSION OF NON-SPECIALISTS.

01399 BAUN, M.J.
THE TRADE UNIONS AND THE GREEN MOVEMENT IN THE FEDERAL REPUBLIC OF GERMANY: THE NEW POLITICS AND THE SPLIT WITHIN THE LEFT IN ADVANCED INDUSTRIAL SOCIETY
DISSERTATION ABSTRACTS INTERNATIONAL, 50(5) (NOV 89), 1420-A.
THROUGH A STUDY OF TRADE UNIONS AND THE GREEN MOVEMENT IN WEST GERMANY, THE AUTHOR EXPLORES THE SPLIT WITHIN THE LEFT IN ADVANCED INDUSTRIAL SOCIETIES. HE CONSIDERS THREE HYPOTHESES CONCERNING THE SOURCES OF CONFLICT BETWEEN THE LABOR-MOVEMENT OLD LEFT AND THE POSTINDUSTRIAL NEW LEFT: (1) DISAGREEMENTS OVER THE RELATIVE PRIORITY OF MATERIAL AND NON-MATERIAL POLITICAL GOALS, (2) DIVERGENT POLITICAL-CULTURAL NORMS AND VALUES, AND (3) CONFLICTS BETWEEN ESTABLISHED AND NON-ESTABLISHED POLITICAL GROUPS. THESE HYPOTHESES ARE APPLIED TO RELATIONS BETWEEN THE TRADE UNIONS/OLD LEFT AND THE GREENS/NEW LEFT IN WEST GERMANY.

01400 BAXLEY, H.W.
PERESTROIKA AND GLASNOST: WHERE WILL THEY LEAD
AVAILABLE FROM NTIS, NO. AD-A208 012/5/GAR, APR 89, 41.
THE IMPLEMENTATION OF PERESTROIKA AND GLASNOST BY MIKHAIL GORBACHEV IN 1985 INITIATED A SERIES OF EVENTS WHICH HAVE BEEN AFFECTING GOVERNMENTS AND PEOPLE THROUGHOUT MUCH OF THE WORLD. PEOPLE HAVE BEEN WATCHING THE SOVIET UNION WITH RENEWED INTEREST, AND THE SCOPE AND SPEED OF ACTIONS TAKEN BY MR. GORBACHEV HAVE GENERATED QUESTIONS SUCH AS: WHERE WILL PERESTROIKA AND GLASNOST LEAD. WHAT IMPACT WILL THERE BE AND ON WHOM. WHAT WILL BE THE RESULTS OF THESE INITIATIVES. SHOULD THE UNITED STATES' MILITARY STRATEGY BE CHANGED. THIS STUDY REVIEWS CURRENT U.S. MILITARY STRATEGY, BRIEFLY DESCRIBES THE DEVELOPMENT AND INTENDED PURPOSES OF THE SOVIET PROGRAMS, IDENTIFIES ACHIEVEMENTS AND IMPACTS

WHICH HAVE RESULTED, ATTEMPTS TO PREDICT AND ANALYZE POSSIBLE OUTCOMES, DETERMINES EFFECTS ON U.S. MILITARY STRATEGY, AND POSTULATES REQUIRED CHANGES TO U.S. MILITARY STRATEGY.

01401 BAXTER, C.
THE STRUGGLE FOR DEVELOPMENT IN BANGLADESH
CURRENT HISTORY, 88(542) (DEC 89), 437-440, 442-444.
IN ITS ALMOST 18 YEARS OF INDEPENDENCE, BANGLADESH HAS FAILED TO DEVELOP SIGNIFICANTLY IN THE POLITICAL, ECONOMIC, OR SOCIAL ARENAS. IN 1989, BANGLADESH IS STILL IN THE EARLY STAGES OF POLITICAL DEVELOPMENT; IT HAS SEVERE ECONOMIC LIMITATIONS; ITS SOCIAL DEVELOPMENT IS RESTRICTED BY THE INSTABILITY OF ITS POLITICAL SYSTEM AND THE WEAKNESS OF ITS ECONOMY.

01402 BAYAT, A.
CAPITAL ACCUMULATION, POLITICAL CONTROL AND LABOUR ORGANIZATION IN IRAN, 1965-75
MIDDLE EASTERN STUDIES, 25(2) (APR 89), 198-207.
IN A DISCUSSION OF THE PRE-REVOLUTIONARY IRANIAN LABOUR MOVEMENT BETWEEN 1965-75 TWO GENERAL ASSUMPTIONS PREVAIL. ONE IS THAT INDUSTRIAL LABOUR DID NOT MAKE ANY ATTEMPT TO ORGANIZE ITSELF INTO INDEPENDENT LABOUR UNIONS (TRADE UNIONS, ETC). THE SECOND IS THAT THE FAILURE OF LABOURERS TO ORGANIZE THEMSELVES WAS DUE TO THE POLITICAL REPRESSION UNDER THE SHAH. IN THIS ARTICLE, THE AUTHOR ARGUES: A) ASSUMPTIONS ARE ONLY PARTLY TRUE; B) THAT BY THEMSELVES THEY MISREPRESENT THE POSITION OF IRANIAN LABOUR IN THE DECADE 1965-75, AND C) THAT THE ASSUMPTIONS ARE BASED UPON A PROBLEMATIC THEORETICAL PREMISE WHICH ESTABLISHES A NECESSARY LINK BETWEEN POLITICAL CONDITIONS (FREEDOM CONTROL) AND LABOUR ACTIVITIES (ORGANIZATION/NON-ORGANIZATION). THIS POSTULATES THAT LABOUR ACTIVITIES ARE DETERMINED BY THE POLITICAL CONDITIONS. THE AUTHOR SUGGESTS THAT THE RELATIONSHIP BETWEEN THE TWO IS ONLY CONTINGENT, AND THAT OTHER FACTORS MUST BE SOUGHT TO ACCOUNT FOR THE NATURE OF LABOUR ACTIVITIES. BY DISCUSSING THESE ISSUES THE AUTHOR HOPES TO CAST SOME NEW LIGHT ON THE RECENT HISTORY OF IRANIAN LABOUR.

01403 BAYER, M.
MOSCOW
CONTEMPORARY REVIEW, 254(1480) (MAY 89), 244-247.
THIS ESSAY DESCRIBES THE AUTHOR'S IMPRESSIONS OF MOSCOW AND RUSSIAN CULTURE WHILE HE WAS ON A BUSINESS TRIP TO HELP DESIGN THE CONSTRUCTION OF LEISURE FACILITIES FOR FOREIGN RESIDENTS IN THE CITY. THE AUTHOR EXMINES THE BEGINNING OF A MOVEMENT WHICH SHOULD OPEN UP HALF THE WORLD TO THE OTHER HALF, AFFORDING OPPORTUNITY FOR EXCHANGE OF CULTURE, TRADE AND POLITICAL PERSPECTIVE.

01404 BEALL, J.; HASSIM, S.; TODES, A.
"A BIT ON THE SIDE"? GENDER STRUGGLES IN THE POLITICS OF TRANSFORMATION IN SOUTH AFRICA
FEMINIST REVIEW, (33) (AUT 89), 30-56.
THE WAY IN WHICH POLITICAL ORGANIZATIONS HAVE CONCEPTUALIZED WOMEN'S OPPRESSION AND THEIR ROLE IN STRUGGLE HAS LIMITATIONS. THIS HAS IMPLICATIONS FOR THE WAY IN WHICH WOMEN'S INTERESTS AND NEEDS ARE ADDRESSED IN THE COURSE OF STRUGGLE AND FOR DEVELOPMENT POLICY IN A POST-APARTHEID FUTURE. THIS PAPER IS A CRITIQUE OF THE "WOMAN QUESTION" POSITION THAT HAS BEEN ADOPTED BY THE PROGRESSIVE MOVEMENT IN SOUTH AFRICA. THIS POSITION IS BROADLY BASED ON THE CLASSICAL SOCIALIST POSITION ON WOMEN'S OPPRESSION, NAMELY THAT WOMEN'S OPPRESSION WILL BE ELIMINATED IN THE COURSE OF THE TRANSITION TO SOCIALISM. AS AN ALTERNATIVE, A SOCIALIST-FEMINIST POSITION VIEWS WOMEN'S STRUGGLES AS A LEGITIMATE AND INTEGRAL PART OF BROADER STRUGGLES, WHICH TRANSFORM NOT ONLY THE FORM AND CONTENT OF THOSE STRUGGLES BUT ALSO THE TYPE OF DEVELOPMENT POLICY THAT FLOWS FROM THEM.

01405 BEAMISH, T.
WHAT'S THE BIG IDEA, THEN?
CONTEMPORARY REVIEW, 254(1481) (JUN 89), 315-320.
EVERY SO OFTEN IT BECOMES APPARENT THAT THE WORLD DOES NOT FIT OUR CONCEPTUAL MAPS IN SOME RESPECT; THIS IS NOT, AS A RULE, DUE TO SOME SUDDEN EASILY INDENTIFIABLE CHANGE, BUT TO THE CUMULATIVE EFFECT OF ALL THE CHANGES WHICH HAVE TAKEN PLACE SINCE OUR CURRENT MAPS WERE PREPARED. AT THESE CRITICAL PERIODS, A NEW MAP OF OUR ENVIRONMENT BECOMES NECESSARY SO THAT NEW POLICY OPTIONS CAN BE FOMULATED. IT IS THE AUTHOR'S CONTENTION THAT THE WORLD HAS CHANGED SO MUCH SINCE THE BEGINNING OF THE INDUSTRIAL ERA THAT WE ARE BEING FORCED TO CHANGE OUR PRIMARY SOCIAL OBJECTIVES AS WELL.

01406 BEAN, C.; MUGHAN, A.
LEADERSHIP EFFECTS IN PARLIMENTARY ELECTIONS IN AUSTRALIA AND BRITAIN
AMERICAN POLITICAL SCIENCE REVIEW, 83(4) (DEC 89), 1165-1180.
POLITICAL PARTY LEADERS ARE AN INCREASINGLY INFLUENTIAL ELECTORAL FORCE IN CONTEMPORARY LIBERAL DEMOCRACIES. SAME THEORIZE THAT THEIR APPEAL IS IDIOSYNCRATIC, THAT IS, THAT

THEIR ELECTORAL EFFECT IS A FUNCTION OF THE LEADERSHIP
QUALITIES VOTERS PERCEIVE INDIVIDUAL CANDIDATES AS
POSSESSING. THUS, THE LESS SIMILAR THEIR PERSONALITY
PROFILES, THE MORE THE CHARACTERISTICS INFLUENCING THE VOTE
SHOULD DIFFER FROM ONE LEADER TO ANOTHER. A COMPARISON OF
AUSTRALIA AND BRITAIN FINDS THE OPPOSITE TO BE THE CASE.
DESPITE THE DIVERGENT PROFILES OF PARTY LEADERS, THE PRECISE
CHARACTERISTICS INFLUENCING THE VOTE ARE REMARKABLY SIMILAR
IN THE TWO COUNTRIES. THIS DOES NOT MEAN, HOWEVER, THAT
VARIATION IN THE DISTRIBUTION OF THESE CHARACTERISTICS IS
UNIMPORTANT. IT CAN AFFECT THE BALANCE OF THE PARTY VOTE AND
MAY EVEN HAVE BEEN THE DIFFERENCE BETWEEN VICTORY AND DEFEAT
FOR THE AUSTRALIAN LABOR PARTY IN THE CLOSELY FOUGHT 1987
ELECTION.

01407 BEATTY, K.M.; WALTER, O.
     A GROUP THEORY OF RELIGION AND POLITICS: THE CLERGY AS
     GROUP LEADERS
     WESTERN POLITICAL QUARTERLY, 42(1) (MAR 89), 129-146.
       THIS PAPER USES GROUP THEORY TO EXPLAIN VARIATION IN
     CLERICAL POLITICAL ATTITUDES AND BEHAVIOR. TWO GROUPS ARE
     CITED AS IMPORTANT IN THE EXPLANATION: THE
     LIBERALCONSERVATIVE THEOLOGICAL GROUPS AND RELIGIOUS
     DENOMINATIONAL GROUPS. DATA WERE DERIVED FROM A NATIONAL
     SURVEY OF CLERGY IN NINE DENOMINATIONS. RESULTS SUPPORT THE
     GROUP MODEL.

01408 BEAUMONT, E.
     THE ETHICAL PUBLIC MANAGER
     BUREAUCRAT, 18(1) (SPR 89), 14-16.
       THE LITERATURE ON ETHICS IN PUBLIC ADMINISTRATION
     SUGGESTS THAT THERE ARE THREE MAJOR SCHOOLS OF THOUGHT ON
     THE SUBJECT. THE FIRST ADVOCATES HIRING ETHICAL PERSONS AS
     THE KEY. OTHERS ARE MORE CONCERNED WITH ENSURING ETHICAL
     BEHAVIOR AFTER EMPLOYMENT. THEY FOCUS UPON RULES THAT GOVERN
     EXPENSE ACCOUNTS, OUTSIDE INCOME, USE OF INFORMATION, AND
     CONFLICT OF INTEREST. THE THIRD GROUP IS CONCERNED WITH THE
     ETHICAL PROBLEMS OF HIGH-LEVEL BUREAUCRATS AFTER THEY LEAVE
     GOVERNMENT SERVICE. THIS HAS LED TO LAWS DEALING WITH
     LIMITATIONS ON OUTSIDE EMPLOYMENT RELATED TO WORK INSIDE
     GOVERNMENT.

01409 BEBLER, A.
     YUGOSLAVIA'S POSITION AND POLICIES ON ARMS CONTROL AND
     DISARMAMENT
     INTERNATIONAL SPECTATOR, XXIV(2) (APR 89), 94-101.
       THE AUTHOR SURVEYS YUGSLAVIA'S POLICIES ON ARMS CONTROL
     AND DISARMAMENT AND THE HISTORICAL BACKGROUND UNDERLYING
     THEM.

01410 BECHTOLDT, H.
     A TURNING POINT FOR SOCIALISM: GORBACHEV'S REFORMS PRESS
     EASTERN EUROPE
     AUSSEN POLITIK, 40(3) (1989), 215-231.
       "SOCIALISM IS MERELY A DETOUR FROM CAPITALISM" TO
     CAPITALISM"-THIS CURRENT SLOGAN IS TOO SIMPLE A SUMMARY OF
     THE HIGHLY COMPLEX CHANGES UNDER WAY IN THE SOVIET UNION AND
     THE OTHER SOCIALIST COUNTRIES OF EASTERN EUROPE. AND IT DOES
     NOT EVEN BEGIN TO DESCRIBE THE KEY PROBLEMS ARISING FROM THE
     CONFRONTATION BETWEEN ONE-PARTY STATES AND SOCIETIES
     CLAIMING THEIR RIGHT TO HAVE A VOICE IN DECISION-MAKING AND
     A SHARE OF POWER. DR. HEINRICH BECHTOLDT, THE MANAGING
     EDITOR OF THIS MAGAZINE AND PROFESSOR OF POLITICAL SCIENCE
     AT STUTTGART'S TWO UNIVERSITIES, SEES GORBACHEV'S INDUSTRIAL
     AND AGRICULTURAL REFORMS AS A RENUNCIATION OF SOCIALISM IN
     THE STALINIST MOULD AND AN AFFIRMATION OF FREE-MARKET
     PRINCIPLES. THE OLD SYSTEM'S PRETENSIONS TO BE WORTHY OF
     EMULATION ARE THUS ABANDONED. THE COMMUNIST LEADERS IN
     EASTERN EUROPE KNOW THEIR RESPECTIVE ECONOMIES CANNOT BE
     REHABILITATED WITHOUT MOBILISING THE SUPPORT OF THE PEOPLE;
     HENCE CONCESSIONS TO CONTRARY AND EVEN OPENLY ANTAGONISTIC
     POLITICAL ELEMENTS ARE UNAVOIDABLE. THAT OPENS THEM UP TO
     DEMANDS THAT MULTIPLE VIEWS BE HEARD AND, BY EXTENSION, THAT
     MULTIPLE POLITICAL PARTIES BE ALLOWED AS WELL -- DEMANDS FOR
     DEMOCRACY THAT COULD INCLUDE A TRANSITION OF POWER. HUNGARY
     AND POLAND HAVE TAKEN THE FIRST STEPS IN THIS DIRECTION.
     ROMANIA, THE GERMAN DEMOCRATIC REPUBLIC (GDR) AND BULGARIA
     ARE BALKING SO LONG AS THE OLD GUARD IS NOT FORCED TO STEP
     DOWN. A PARTIAL CHANGING OF THE GUARD HAS BEGUN IN
     CZECHOSLOVAKIA BUT REMAINS IN A TRANSITIONAL PHASE. THERE IS
     TALK OF REFORMS EVERYWHERE BECAUSE THE SITUATION IS
     ADMITTEDLY CATASTROPHIC. FETTERS ON PRIVATE PRODUCTION ARE
     BEING REMOVED OUT OF NECESSITY, BUT STATE OWNERSHIP OF THE
     MEANS OF PRODUCTION AND CENTRAL PLANNING ARE TO REMAIN,
     SERVING AS POLITICAL INSTRUMENTS THAT SECURE THE
     MONOPOLISTIC PARTIES' RIGHT TO EXIST. BUT IF ECONOMIC
     FREEDOMS ARE IMPOSSIBLE WITHOUT POLITICAL FREEDOMS, THEN
     THIS SIDE OF SOCIALISM'S CLAIM TO UNIVERSAL VALIDITY IS
     INVALIDATED TOO. BOTH ECONOMICALLY AND POLITICALLY, IT IS
     THE TURN OF AN ERA FOR SOCIALISM.

01411 BECK, J.; CHEEK, L. JR.
     RECAPTURING THE ENVIRONMENTAL HIGH GROUND
     INTERNATIONAL SOCIAL SCIENCE REVIEW, 64(2) (SPR 89), 76-78.
       THE ENVIRONMENTAL POLICY DEBATES AND PROGRAMS OF THE
     LAST DECADE PRODUCED FEW TANGIBLE RESULTS. SOME RECENT
     CONSERVATIVE AND LIBERAL PROPOSALS TO REFORM THE ENVIRONMENT
     HAVE HAD MUCH INSIGHT TO TRANSMIT, BUT THE POTENTIAL FOR
     POSITIVE CHANGE HAS BEEN REDUCED BY THE LACK OF DISCOURSE
     BETWEEN LIBERALS AND CONSERVATIVES. THIS ESSAY SUGGESTS THAT
     A SYNTHESIS IS POSSIBLE-WHEN ENVIRONMENTAL REFORM IS BASED
     ON A MORE THOROUGH UNDERSTANDING OF ECONOMIC AND
     ADMINISTRATIVE FACTORS.

01412 BECK, J.H.
     THE TREATMENT OF MARITAL STATUS UNDER STATE INCOME TAXES
     STATE AND LOCAL GOVERNMENT REVIEW, 21(2) (SPR 89), 66-73.
       STATES SHOW A WIDE VARIETY OF PRACTICES IN TREATMENT OF
     THE FAMILY UNIT FOR INCOME TAX PURPOSES. THE 11 THAT USE
     COMBINED SEPARATE RETURNS HAVE ACHIEVED MARRIAGE NEUTRALITY
     (EXCEPT FOR THE EFFECTS OF DIFFERENT STANDARD DEDUCTIONS);
     HOWEVER, THESE STATES SHOW WIDE DIFFERENCES IN TAX BURDENS
     ON COUPLES EARNING THE SAME COMBINED INCOME BUT WITH
     DIFFERENT SHARES EARNED BY EACH SPOUSE. THE 10 INCOME-
     SPLITTING STATES, ON THE OTHER HAND, HAVE ACHIEVED
     HORIZONTAL EQUITY AMONG MARRIED COUPLES BUT VIOLATE MARRIAGE
     NEUTRALITY. THOSE STATES WITH TAX STRUCTURES SIMILAR TO THE
     FEDERAL INCOME TAX GIVE MARRIAGE PENALTIES OR BONUSES,
     DEPENDING ON HOW MUCH IS EARNED BY EACH SPOUSE.

01413 BECK, P.J.
     A NEW POLAR FACTOR IN INTERNATIONAL RELATIONS
     WORLD TODAY, 45(4) (APR 89), 65-68.
       TRADITIONALLY THE POLAR REGIONS HAVE BEEN TREATED
     SEPARATELY FROM THE WIDER INTERNATIONAL COMMUNITY DUE TO
     THEIR PHYSICAL CHARACTER, GEOGRAPHIC ISOLATION, AND STATUS
     AS PERIPHERAL REGIONS. BUT RECENTLY THERE HAS BEEN A
     DRAMATIC TRANSFORMATION IN THEIR PERCEIVED SIGNIFICANCE DUE
     TO RESOURCES, THE ENVIRONMENT, AND POLITICAL REASONS,
     INCLUDING THE DESIRE TO ENSURE THAT THE POLAR REGIONS ARE
     MANAGED IN A RESPONSIBLE AND PEACEFUL MANNER IN THE
     INTERESTS OF ALL MANKIND.

01414 BECK, R.J.
     MUNICH'S LESSONS RECONSIDERED
     INTERNATIONAL SECURITY, 14(2) (FAL 89), 161-191.
       TODAY, MOST AMERICAN INTERNATIONAL RELATIONS SCHOLARS
     APPEAR TO ACCEPT THE CONVENTIONAL ACCOUNT OF "MUNICH." IN
     THE LAST TWENTY-FIVE YEARS OR SO, HOWEVER, THE CONSENSUS
     AMONG HISTORIANS ABOUT WHAT HAPPENED IN SEPTEMBER OF 1938
     HAS UNRAVELLED INTO A VARIETY OF DIFFERENT STRANDS, AND THE
     STUDENT OF MUNICH NOW CONFRONTS A BEWILDERING ARRAY OF
     "LESSONS." WHAT IS ONE TO MAKE OF THIS PROLIFERATION OF
     HISTORICAL INTERPRETATIONS? WHERE DID THEY ORIGINATE? WHY
     WERE THEY FIRST PUT FORTH? WITH SO MANY DIFFERENT ACCOUNTS
     OF THE MUNICH CONFERENCE, CAN ANYTHING BE SAID WITH
     CONFIDENCE ABOUT NEVILLE CHAMBERLAIN'S ACTIONS THERE? THIS
     ESSAY WILL FIRST SKETCH THE FIVE-DECADE HISTORIOGRAPHY OF
     MUNICH, DEMONSTRATING HOW AND SUGGESTING WHY ONE
     INTERPRETATION BECAME MANY. NEXT, IT WILL SET OUR FOUR
     CONCLUSIONS ABOUT CHAMBERLAIN'S MUNICH DIPLOMACY THAT
     REFLECT THE MAJORITY OF CONTEMPORARY MUNICH SCHOLARSHIP.
     FINALLY, IT WILL ASSESS THE BROADER IMPLICATIONS OF THE
     MUNICH CONFERENCE FIFTY YEARS AFTER THE OUTBREAK OF THE
     SECOND WORLD WAR.

01415 BECK, R.L.; HUSSEY, D.
     POLITICS, PROPERTY RIGHTS, AND COTTAGE DEVELOPMENT
     CANADIAN PUBLIC POLICY--ANALYSE DE POLITIQUES, XV(1) (MAR
     89), 25-33.
       THIS PAPER EXPLORES RECREATIONAL LAND USE PLANNING
     ISSUES, GIVING SPECIAL ATTENTION TO THE APPLICABILITY OF
     BENEFIT/COST ANALYSIS AND THE ECONMICS OF PROPERTY RIGHTS.
     THE ANALYSIS SUGGESTS THAT THE POLITICAL PROCESS DOES NOT
     FUNCTION AS WELL AS IS OFTEN ASSUMED, AND AN EXPLANATION IS
     OFFERED BASED ON THE PUBLIC CHOICE THEORY OF GOVERNMENT. AN
     ALBERTA PLAN FOR ITS MAJOR WATER-BASED RECREATIONAL
     RESOURCES IS USED TO ILLUSTRATE GENERALIZATIONS ABOUT
     RECREATIONAL LAND USE PLANNING AND POLITICAL PROCESS.

01416 BECKER, D.
     THE WAY THE INTIFADA SHOULD GO
     MIDDLE EAST INTERNATIONAL, (361) (OCT 89), 18-20.
       THE ARTICLE EXAMINES THE IMPLICATIONS OF THE 22 MONTH-
     OLD INTIFADA IN THE OCCUPIED TERRITORIES. IT CONCLUDES THAT
     ALTHOUGH THE MOVEMENT HAS INCREASED PALESTINE'S VISIBILITY,
     MUCH REMAINS TO BE DONE. THE AUTHOR WARNS OF THE DANGERS OF
     INCREASING VIOLENCE; SUCH A MOVE WOULD ONLY PROPEL THE MYTH
     OF ISRAEL SURROUNDED IN A RING OF FOES. INSTEAD,
     PALESTINIANS WOULD SEE MORE PROGRESS AS A RESULT OF
     ATTEMPTING TO DISPEL WIDELY HELD MYTHS OF INSATIABLE
     PALESTINIAN HATRED OF JEWS.

01417 BECKER, E.
     THE PROGRESS OF PEACE IN CAMBODIA
     CURRENT HISTORY, 88(537) (APR 89), 169-172, 200-201.
       GORBACHEV PUBLICLY LAUNCHED AN INTERNATIONAL CAMPAIGN TO
     BREAK THE CAMBODIAN DEADLOCK WITH A SPEECH AT VLADIVOSTOCK

ON JULY 28, 1986. THE INTERNATIONAL COMMUNITY HAS RESPONDED
FAVORABLY BUT IT REMAINS TO BE SEEN WHETHER THE GOOD
INTENTIONS WILL ACTUALLY ACHIEVE PEACE IN CAMBODIA.

01418 BECKER, J.
    IS THERE A CASE FOR TERRORISM?
    ENCOUNTER, LXXII(2) (FEB 89), 19-24.
        THE WORD "TERRORISM" IS USED ALMOST UNIVERSALLY AS A
    PEJORATIVE, BUT THERE IS NO AGREEMENT ON WHAT IT IS. THE PLO
    MAY RENOUNCE TERRORISM AND YET CONTINUE TO BOMB AND MURDER
    BECAUSE SUCH ACTIVITY IS "LEGITIMATE ARMED STRUGGLE." IT IS
    WIDELY AGREED THAT INTERNATIONAL TERRORISM CAN BEST BE
    TACKLED BY INTERNATIONAL COOPERATION, TO WHICH GOVERNMENTS
    EARNESTLY COMMIT THEMSELVES BY WORD AND SIGNATURE. BUT SUCH
    COMMITMENTS ARE OFTEN BREACHED RATHER THAN HONORED.

01419 BECKER, M.E.
    THE RIGHTS OF UNWED PARENTS: FEMINIST APPROACHES
    SOCIAL SERVICE REVIEW, 63(4) (DEC 89), 496-517.
        TRADITIONAL RULES PUNISHED UNWED MOTHERS FOR SEX OUTSIDE
    MARRIAGE BY IGNORING THE CONNECTION BETWEEN ILLEGITIMATE
    CHILDREN AND MEN. THIS ARTICLE APPLIES THREE DIFFERENT
    FEMINIST APPROACHES TO LEGAL CHANGE TO THE QUESTION, SHOULD
    UNWED MOTHERS AND FATHERS OF A NEWBORN INFANT HAVE EQUAL
    RIGHTS WITH RESPECT TO THE CUSTODY-ADOPTION DECISION? FORMAL
    EQUALITY, THE DOMINANT LEGAL APPROACH TO SUCH ISSUES TODAY,
    CAN BE MANIPULATED TO YIELD WHATEVER ANSWER ONE DESIRES, YES,
    OR NO. UNDER THE OTHER TWO FEMINIST APPROACHES TO LEGAL
    CHANGE - THE DOMINANCE APPROACH AND FEMINIST UTILITARIANISM -
    THE ANSWER IS NO, UNWED MOTHERS SHOULD CONTINUE TO CONTROL
    THE CUSTODY-ADOPTION DECISION.

01420 BECKER, U.
    CLASS THEORY AND THE SOCIAL SCIENCES: ERIK OLIN WRIGHT ON
    CLASSES
    POLITICS AND SOCIETY, 17(1) (MAR 89), 67-88.
        THERE IS A CERTAIN SPECIFICITY OF CLASS -- A SPECIFICITY
    OVERLOOKED BY BOTH THE ADHERENTS AND THE CRITICS OF THE
    CENTRALITY OF CLASS. IT STEMS FROM THE STRUCTURAL DYNAMICS
    OF THE RELATIONSHIP BETWEEN CAPITAL AND LABOR. CAPITAL IS
    COMPELLED TO ACCUMULATE, AND LABOR IS PRESSED TO RESIST THE
    "LOGIC OF CAPITAL." THE STRUCTURALLY DYNAMIC CHARACTER OF
    THE CONFLICT BETWEEN LABOR AND CAPITAL RENDERS THE PRESENCE
    OF THIS CONFLICT IN THE HISTORY OF CAPITALISM PLAUSIBLE, AND
    IT DEFINES A SPECIAL QUALITY OF THE RESPECTIVE CLASS
    LOCATIONS AS BASES FOR POLITICO-IDEOLOGICAL ARTICULATION AND
    ACTION. NO A PRIORI EXPLANATORY PRIMACY, HOWEVER, CAN BE
    DEDUCED FROM THIS SPECIFICITY. THEREFORE, ERIK OLIN WRIGHT'S
    VIEW ON THIS ISSUE MUST BE REJECTED. MOREOVER, THE NOTION OF
    OBJECTIVE INTERESTS OF THE WORKING CLASS IN SOCIALISM IS NOT
    TENABLE.

01421 BECKERMAN, C.
    NO TAXATION WITHOUT REPRESENTATION: NONVIOLENT RESISTANCE
    IN BEIT SAHUR
    NEW OUTLOOK, 32(9-10 (295-296)) (SEP 89), 23-26.
        THE PALESTINIAN TOWN OF BEIT SAHUR NEAR BETHLEHEM
    (POPULATION 12,000) IS ENGAGING IN A DIFFERENT KIND OF
    INTIFADA. IT HAS TAKEN UP THE FLAG OF NONVIOLENT CIVIL
    DISOBEDIENCE AGAINST THE ISRAELI OCCUPATION. IN MAY 1988
    SOME BEIT SAHUR RESIDENTS BEGAN REFUSING TO PAY TAXES TO THE
    ISRAELI CIVIL ADMINISTRATION. IN RECENT MONTHS THE
    OCCUPATION AUTHORITIES HAVE BEGUN AN ALL-OUT CAMPAIGN TO
    CRUSH THE BURGEONING TAX RESISTANCE WITH WIDESPREAD RAIDS,
    ARRESTS, CURFEWS, AND THE CONFISCATION OF THREE-QUARTERS OF
    A MILLION DOLLARS IN COMMERCIAL AND PRIVATE PROPERTY. NOTING
    THAT BEIT SAHUR HOPES TO BECOME A MODEL FOR CIVIL
    DISOBEDIENCE THROUGHOUT THE WEST BANK, DEFENSE MINISTER
    YITZHAK RABIN HAS SAID THAT HE WILL BREAK THE BEIT SAHUR TAX
    RESISTANCE AT ALL COSTS, EVEN IF IT MEANS KEEPING THE TOWN
    UNDER CURFEW FOR TWO MONTHS.

01422 BECKWITH, K.
    SNEAKING WOMEN INTO OFFICE: ALTERNATIVE ACCESS TO
    PARLIAMENT IN FRANCE AND ITALY
    WOMEN AND POLITICS, 9(3) (1989), 1-16.
        THIS ARTICLE EMPLOYS THE RESEARCH ON ELECTORAL STRUCTURE
    AND WOMEN'S ACCESS TO OFFICE AS A CONTEXT FOR EXAMINING
    ALTERNATIVE ROUTES FOR WOMEN'S ACCESS TO PARLIAMENTARY SEATS.
    USING THE CASES OF FRANCE (1981) AND ITALY (1983), IT
    FOCUSES ON A PRE-ELECTION STRATEGY FOR REPLACING ELECTED
    MALE NOMINEES WHO ACCEPT SEATS IN OTHER ELECTORAL DISTRICTS
    OR WHO ACCEPT CABINET POSITIONS. POSSIBILITIES FOR THIS TYPE
    OF STRATEGIC NOMINATION OF WOMEN EXIST IN BOTH POLITICAL
    SYSTEMS (THROUGH SUPPLEANT AND SUBENTRATA PROVISIONS). ONLY
    IN ITALY HAVE THESE ALTERNATIVE ROUTES TO PARLIAMENT BEEN
    USED EXTENSIVELY. THE ARTICLE CONCLUDES WITH SPECULATIONS
    ABOUT ELECTORAL SYSTEM RESEARCH AND WOMEN'S ACCESS TO
    NATIONAL ELECTIVE OFFICE.

01423 BECRAFT, C.H.
    WOMEN AND THE MILITARY: BUREAUCRATIC POLICIES AND POLITICS
    BUREAUCRAT, 18(3) (FAL 89), 33-36.
        WHILE INSISTING THAT THEY WON'T STAND FOR WOMEN IN

COMBAT, POLITICIANS IN BOTH POLITICAL PARTIES HAVE
RELUCTANTLY PUSHED THE DEPARTMENT OF DEFENSE TO EXPAND THE
NUMBERS OF AND ROLES FOR MILITARY WOMEN, DUE TO THE
DECLINING POOL OF MALES ELIGIBLE FOR MILITARY SERVICE. DOD
HAS REACTED TO THIS EXTERNAL PRESSURE BY TRYING TO REAFFIRM
THE INSTITUTIONAL CULTURE, VALUES, AND TRADITIONS THAT HAVE
SERVED TO JUSTIFY ITS EXCLUSIONARY PRACTICES.

01424 BEEDY, K.J.
    EXPORT AGRICULTURE AND WORLD HUNGER: THE MAKING OF BAD
    PUBLIC POLICY
    DISSERTATION ABSTRACTS INTERNATIONAL, 50(5) (NOV 89),
    1420-A.
        THERE ARE TWO BODIES OF CONFLICTING THOUGHT ON EXPORT
    CROP PROMOTION POLICIES AND THE ROLE EXPORT AGRICULTURE
    PLAYS IN WORLD HUNGER. ONE BODY ARGUES THAT THE PRODUCTION
    OF EXPORT CROPS CONTRIBUTES TO HUNGER AND POVERTY IN THE
    COUNTRIES WHERE THE PRODUCE ORIGINATES. THE OTHER ARGUES
    THAT WHAT THE PEASANT FARMERS PRODUCE IS NOT AS IMPORTANT AS
    WHAT IS RECEIVED IN THE WAY OF INCOME FROM THE EXPORTS. THIS
    DISSERTATION CONCLUDES THAT EXPORT AGRICULTURE NEGATIVELY
    AFFECTS FOOD CONSUMPTION AMONG THE POOR BUT POSITIVELY
    AFFECTS THE PROCESS OF MODERNIZATION.

01425 BEEGHLEY, L.; DWYER, J.W.
    INCOME TRANSFERS AND INCOME INEQUALITY
    POPULATION RESEARCH AND POLICY REVIEW, 8(2) (MAY 89),
    119-142.
        THIS ARTICLE ATTEMPTS TO ADVANCE UNDERSTANDING OF THE
    IMPACT OF INCOME TRANSFERS ON THE SIZE DISTRIBUTION OF
    INCOME SINCE ABOUT WORLD WAR II. TWO CONTENDING
    INTERPRETATIONS EXIST, WHICH THE AUTHORS LABEL THE
    INEQUALITY REDUCTION AND THE INEQUALITY STABILITY HYPOTHESES,
    RESPECTIVELY. THIS PAPER HELPS TO RESOLVE THE DILEMMA POSED
    BY THESE CONTRADICTORY HYPOTHESES; IT SHOWS THAT THE
    INEQUALITY REDUCTION LITERATURE OMITS INCOME TRANSFERS GOING
    TO THE NONPOOR POPULATION AND PRESENTS EMPIRICAL DATA THAT
    ADDRESSES THIS OMISSION. THE RESULT SUPPORTS THE INEQUALITY
    STABILITY HYPOTHESIS.

01426 BEENSTOCK, M.
    A DEMOCRATIC MODEL OF THE "RENT-SOUGHT" BENEFIT CYCLE
    PUBLIC CHOICE, 63 (1989), 1-14.
        THIS PAPER DISCUSSES THE FACTORS THAT ARE LIKELY TO
    INFLUENCE THE CHOICE BETWEEN THE BANDWAGGON AND PROTEST
    OPTIONS. IN DOING SO IT EXPLAINS WHY IT MIGHT BE THAT
    SOCIETY SOMETIMES PROTESTS AT THE ARBITRARY CONCESSION OF
    BENEFITS WHILE AT OTHER TIMES IT TACITLY OR EVEN ACTIVELY
    CONDONES THEM. IT ALSO EXPLAINS WHY THE CONCESSION OF
    BENEFITS MIGHT SPREAD AND CORRESPONDINGLY WHY THE
    BUREAUCRACY AND TAXATION MIGHT GROW OVER TIME. FOLLOWING ON
    FROM THIS IT CONSIDERS AT WHAT POINT, IF ANY, THE SPREAD OF
    BENEFITS WILL CEASE BECAUSE SOCIETY PREFERS A "REFORM" THAT
    AT ONCE WILL CURTAIL BENEFITS AND REDUCE TAXES. FINALLY, IT
    CONSIDERS THE CONDITIONS UNDER WHICH THIS CYCLE OF RENT-
    SOUGHT BENEFITS MIGHT BE REPEATED.

01427 BEHDAD, S.
    WINNERS AND LOSERS OF THE IRANIAN REVOLUTION: A STUDY IN
    INCOME DISTRIBUTION
    INTERNATIONAL JOURNAL OF MIDDLE EAST STUDIES, 21(3) (AUG
    89), 327-358.
        THE AUTHOR STUDIES CHANGES IN THE INCOME INEQUALITY GAP
    IN POST-REVOLUTIONARY IRAN. SECTION I OF THE PAPER DEALS
    WITH THE EFFECTS OF THE REDISTRIBUTIVE POLICIES OF THE
    ISLAMIC REPUBLIC OF IRAN ON INCOME DISTRIBUTION. SECTION II
    EVALUATES THE IMPACT OF MACROECONOMIC DISTURBANCES, THE
    SUBSEQUENT NORMALIZATION PROCESS, AND THE WAR. SECTION III
    DISCUSSES THE SIZE DISTRIBUTION OF URBAN AND RURAL HOUSEHOLD
    EXPENDITURES FOR 1977 TO 1984. SECTION IV SUMMARIZES THE
    DISTRIBUTION OF HOUSEHOLD EXPENDITURES WITHIN SOME MAJOR
    URBAN SOCIAL GROUPS.

01428 BEI, R.
    NAMIBIA: A KEY STEP TOWARDS INDEPENDENCE
    BEIJING REVIEW, 32(48) (NOV 89), 15-16.
        THE SOUTH WEST AFRICA PEOPLE'S ORGANIZATION WON THE MOST
    VOTES IN NAMIBIA'S PRE-INDEPENDENCE ELECTIONS, BUT DID NOT
    POLL ENOUGH VOTES TO CLAIM TOTAL POWER. BECAUSE SWAPO FAILED
    TO WIN A TWO-THIRDS MAJORITY, IT MUST FORM A COALITION
    GOVERNMENT WITH SIX OTHER PARTIES.

01429 BEI, R.
    UN CALLS FOR VIETNAMESE WITHDRAWAL FROM KAMPUCHEA
    BEIJING REVIEW, 32(49) (DEC 89), 16.
        THE UNITED NATIONS GENERAL ASSEMBLY HAS ADOPTED A
    RESOLUTION CALLING FOR A COMPREHENSIVE POLITICAL SETTLEMENT
    IN KAMPUCHEA WITH A UN-VERIFIED VIETNAMESE WITHDRAWAL FROM
    THE WAR-TORN COUNTRY AND ESTABLISHMENT OF A QUADRIPARTITE
    COALITION GOVERNMENT UNDER THE LEADERSHIP OF PRINCE NORODOM
    SIHANOUK.

01430 BEIER, A.E.; MCELFISH, J.M. JR.
    FEDERAL OVERSIGHT OF ALTERNATIVE BOND SYSTEMS UNDER SMCRA

POLICY STUDIES REVIEW, 9(1) (AUT 89), 132-142.
THE 1977 SURFACE MINING CONTROL AND RECLAMATION ACT
(SMCRA) REQUIRES MINE OPERATORS TO POST RECLAMATION BONDS
BEFORE MINING BEGINS. THE FEDERAL OFFICE OF SURFACE MINING
RECLAMATION AND ENFORCEMENT (OSMRE) HAS APPROVED ALTERNATIVE
BOND SYSTEMS IN SEVEN STATES. THESE SYSTEMS, RATHER THAN
REQUIRING BOND AMOUNTS AT THE FULL COST OF RECLAMATION,
REQUIRE OPERATORS TO SUBMIT ONLY A FLAT RATE, ACREAGE
SPECIFIC BOND. ADDITIONAL RECLAMATION COSTS SHOULD BE
COVERED BY A SUPPLEMENTAL FUND COMPOSED GENERALLY OF PERMIT
FEES, TAXES, OR PENALTIES. IN MANY CASES, ALTERNATIVE BOND
SYSTEMS FAIL TO ENSURE THAT FUNDS WILL BE AVAILABLE TO
RECLAIM COAL MINED LAND IN THE EVENT OF OPERATOR DEFAULT, AS
REQUIRED BY SMCRA. OSMRE NEEDS TO TAKE A MORE ACTIVE ROLE IN
OVERSIGHT OF EXISTING STATE ALTERNATIVE BOND SYSTEMS TO
ENSURE THAT RECLAMATION OCCURS.

01431 BEILER, D.
A SHORT IN THE ELECTRONIC BALLOT BOX
CAMPAIGNS AND ELECTIONS, 10(2) (AUG 89), 39-42.
AS OLD-STYLE VOTE TAMPERING HAS DIMINISHED, ELECTION
EXPERTS HAVE BEEN CALLING ATTENTION TO A NEW DANGER: THE
VULNERABILITY OF COMPUTERIZED VOTING, THE PROCESS BY WHICH
ALMOST TWO-THIRDS OF THE BALLOTS CAST IN THE USA ARE NOW
RECORDED AND TALLIED. TO DATE, NO COURT HAS RULED THAT AN
ELECTION WAS "STOLEN" BY A COMPUTER. BUT THERE IS INCREASING
CONCERN THAT DEFICIENCIES IN COMPUTERIZED VOTING SYSTEMS
HAVE ALREADY HAD AN IMPACT ON SOME CLOSE RACES. AND THERE IS
A WIDESPREAD CONSENSUS THAT FEW JURISDICTIONS HAVE THE
TECHNICAL OR ADMINISTRATIVE CONTROLS TO CATCH OR THWART
ACCIDENTAL OR INTENTIONAL SUBVERSION OF THE VOTING PUBLIC'S
WILL.

01432 BEINART, W.
INTRODUCTION: THE POLITICS OF COLONIA CONSERVATION
JOURNAL OF SOUTHERN AFRICAN STUDIES, 15(2) (JAN 89),
143-162.
THE ARTICLE OUTLINES THE CONFLICTS THAT AROSE WHEN
WESTERN COLONISTS ATTEMPTED TO "CONSERVE" LAND AND RESOURCES
IN AFRICA. IT DEMONSTRATES THE TENSION THAT COLONIZER'S
ATTEMPTS TO ESTABLISH HUNTING AND GAME RESERVES, NATIONAL
PARKS, AND ATTEMPTS TO REDUCE SOIL EROSION AND REHABILITATE
LAND CAUSED AMONG THE NATIVE AFRICAN PEOPLE. IT EXAMINES THE
UNDERLYING CONFLICT OF IDEAS THAT THE PROBLEMS WITH
CONSERVATION DEMONSTRATED.

01433 BEININ, J.
LABOR, CAPITAL, AND THE STATE IN NASSERIST EGYPT, 1952-1961
INTERNATIONAL JOURNAL OF MIDDLE EAST STUDIES, 21(1) (FEB
89), 71-90.
IN THE DECADE BEFORE THE EGYPTIAN MILITARY COUP OF 1952,
AN INCREASINGLY MILITANT WORKERS' MOVEMENT WAS AN IMPORTANT
COMPONENT OF THE SOCIAL AND POLITICAL UPHEAVAL THAT
UNDERMINED THE MONARCHY AND ENDED THE ERA OF BRITISH
COLONIALISM. AFTER THE COUP, THE GOVERNMENT ATTEMPTED TO
DISCOURAGE CONTINUED COLLECTIVE ACTION AMONG THE WORKERS,
EVEN THOUGH THE WORKING CLASS SOCIAL MOVEMENT COULD NOT BE
ABRUPTLY TURNED OFF THE MOMENT THE RCC CAME TO POWER.
NEITHER THE COUP NOR THE CONSOLIDATION OF POWER BY GAMAL
ABDEL NASSER FULLY RESOLVED THE ISSUES THAT HAD OCCUPIED THE
LABOR MOVEMENT UNDER THE MONARCHY. CONSEQUENTLY, UNDER THE
NEW REGIME, THERE WERE MANY MANIFESTATIONS OF CONTINUING
CONFLICT BETWEEN LABOR AND CAPITAL, WITH THE LATTER OFTEN
SUPPORTED BY THE STATE.

01434 BEIT-HALLAHMI, B,
BLACK HEBREWS IN THE PROMISED LAND
MIDDLE EAST REPORT, 19(5) (SEP 89), 36.
THE ARTICLE EXAMINES THE PHENOMENON OF BLACK HEBREWS.
THEY ARE GROUP OF AFRICAN-AMERICANS WHO HAVE SETTLED IN
ISRAEL, WHERE THEIR CONTROVERSIAL PRESENCE HAS FED CHARGES
OF ISRAELI RACISM. THE GROUP CLAIMS DESCENT FROM THE
ORIGINAL ISRAELITES OF THE OLD TESTAMENT AND BELIEVE THAT
THEY ARE DESTINED TO INHERIT THE HOLY LAND. SEVERAL CLASHES
AND EMBARRASSING INCIDENTS HAVE OCCURRED WHEN THE BLACK
HEBREWS HAVE ATTEMPTED TO MOVE TO ISRAEL, WHERE THEIR
IDEOLOGY IS SIMILAR TO, BUT CONFLICTS WITH TRADITIONAL
ISRAELI ZIONISM.

01435 BELIKOVA, G.; SHOKHIN, A.
THE BLACK MARKET: PEOPLE, THINGS, AND FACTS
SOVIET REVIEW, 30(3) (MAY 89), 26-69.
THE AUTHORS DESCRIBE THE SOVIET UNION'S UBIQUITOUS, BUT
LITTLE DISCUSSED, UNDERGROUND ECONOMY. IN THE SOVIET BLACK
MARKET, DECENTRALIZED MECHANISMS OF DECISION-MAKING AND A
SIGNIFICANT REDISTRIBUTION OF INCOME AND RESOURCES HAVE
ALREADY EVOLVED WITHOUT THE BENEFIT OF OFFICIAL POLICY
GUIDANCE.

01436 BELL, D.; CRIDDLE, B.
NO MAJORITY FOR THE PRESIDENT: THE FRENCH LEGISLATIVE
ELECTIONS OF JUNE 1988
PARLIAMENTARY AFFAIRS, 42(1) (JAN 89), 72-83.
THE ARTICLE EXAMINES THE FRENCH LEGISLATIVE ELECTIONS OF

JUNE 1988 AND THEIR IMPLICATIONS. FOR THE FIRST TIME IN THE
THIRTY YEAR HISTORY OF THE FIFTH REPUBLIC A NEWLY-ELECTED
PRESIDENT WAS DENIED THE PARLIAMENTARY MAJORITY HE HAD
REQUESTED AND WAS PRESENTED INSTEAD WITH A HUNG PARLIAMENT.
PRESIDENT FRANCOIS MITTERAND WAS ELECTED BY VIRTUE OF A
PERSONAL POPULARITY THAT TRANSCENDED TRADITIONAL POLITICAL
DIVISIONS. HOWEVER, HIS SOCIALIST PARTY DID NOT ENJOY HIS
WIDESPREAD APPEAL. THE ARTICLE EXAMINES THE IMPLICATIONS OF
THE ELECTIONS FOR THE SOCIALISTS, THE COMMUNISTS, AND THE
RIGHT WING PARTIES.

01437 BELL, D.; CRIDDLE, B.
THE DECLINE OF THE FRENCH COMMUNIST PARTY
BRITISH JOURNAL OF POLITICAL SCIENCE, 19(4) (OCT 89),
515-536.
THE MOST SIGNIFICANT DEVELOPMENT IN FRENCH POLITICS
DURING THE 1980'S HAS BEEN THE DECLINE OF THE COMMUNIST
PARTY. IT HAS LED TO A REASSESSMENT OF THE FRENCH COMMUNIST
PHENOMENON AND CAST RETROSPECTIVE DOUBT ON MUCH OF THE
ANALYSIS OF THE PARTY'S POSTWAR HISTORY. THE DEBATE ABOUT
THE NATURE OF THE COMMUNIST DECLINE IS CLOUDED BY A LACK OF
HARD DATA; WHILE ELECTORAL STATISTICS MAY BE CLEAR,
MEMBERSHIP FIGURES, THE SIZE OF THE CGT, AND THE CIRCULATION
FIGURES FOR PARTY NEWSPAPERS ARE MUCH LESS SO.

01438 BELL, J.
REVOLUTIONARY INSURGENCY: THE THREAT TO THIS GENERATION
WAITING FOR THE FAT LADY TO SING
CONFLICT, 9(3) (1989), 251-270.
AMERICAN POLICYMAKERS HAVE ELEVATED THE FIGHT AGAINST
REVOLUTIONARY INSURGENCY, OR LOW-INTENSITY CONFLICT (LIC),
TO AN ART FORM. ODDLY ENOUGH, THIS HAS OCCURRED WHILE THE
LESSONS OF VIETNAM REMAIN UNLEARNED. AMERICANS STILL INSIST
ON APPLYING CONVENTIONAL SOLUTIONS TO SITUATIONS CALLING FOR
THE UNCONVENTIONAL. IF U.S. POLICYMAKERS CONTINUE TO IGNORE
THE HISTORICAL AND CULTURAL CAUSES OF LIC, THEY ARE DOOMED
TO REPEAT THE MISTAKES MADE IN VIETNAM. THIS ARTICLE DETAILS
THE CAUSES BEHIND REVOLUTIONARY INSURGENCY AND GIVES
PARTICULAR ATTENTION TO THE IRISH EXPERIENCE.

01439 BELLO, W.
CONFRONTING THE BRAVE NEW WORLD ECONOMIC ORDER: TOWARD A
SOUTHERN AGENDA FOR THE 1990S
ALTERNATIVES, XIV(2) (APR 89), 135-167.
THIS PAPER EXPLORES SELECTED DIMENSIONS OF THIS
CONTEMPORARY CRISIS OF ECONOMIC DEVELOPMENT IN THE THIRD
WORLD, FOCUSSING ON THAT VITAL INTERSECTION AND INTERACTION
OF INTERNAL POLICIES AND INTERNATIONAL ECONOMIC TRENDS. THE
FIRST SECTION PROVIDES AN OVERVIEW OF THE EXTENT OF THE
EROSION OF LIVING STANDARDS THROUGHOUT THE SOUTH. THE PAPER
THEN PROCEEDS TO A DISCUSSION OF THE ACTUAL LOSS OF
SOVEREIGNTY THAT HAS ACCOMPANIED THIS PROCESS OF
IMPOVERISHMENT. THE FINAL SECTION DISCUSSES THE VERY REAL
THREAT OF PROTECTIONIST TECHNO-ECONOMIC BLOCS EMERGING IN
THE NEXT DECADE AND SUGGESTS AN OPTION THAT THIRD WORLD
COUNTRIES MAY TAKE, NOT ONLY TO ASSURE THEIR SURVIVAL AS
NATIONAL ECONOMIC ENTITIES BUT ALSO TO EMBARK ON SUSTAINED
DEVELOPMENT IN THE MIDST OF A HARSH INTERNATIONAL ECONOMIC
CLIMATE.

01440 BELLO, W.; ROSENFELD, S.
DRAGONS IN DISTRESS: THE END OF AN ERA FOR SOUTH KOREA AND
TAIWAN
MULTINATIONAL MONITOR, 11(11) (NOV 89), 10-14.
AT A TIME WHEN ECONOMISTS ARE BUSILY ENSHRINING THE
NEWLY INDUSTRIALIZING COUNTRIES MODEL AS THE NEW ORTHODOXY
IN DEVELOPMENT ECONOMICS, THE FORMULA HAS STOPPED WORKING IN
TAIWAN AND SOUTH KOREA. EXPORT-ORIENTED INDUSTRIALIZATION,
AN UNDERVALUED CURRENCY, AND CHEAP LABOR ARE THE CENTRAL
ELEMENTS OF THE NIC FORMULA. BUT ALL THESE ADVANTAGES ARE
BEING SERIOUSLY ERODED BY FAST-MOVING DEVELOPMENTS IN BOTH
THE WORLD ECONOMY AND THE NEWLY INDUSTRIALIZING COUNTRIES
THEMSELVES.

01441 BELLOWS, THOMAS J
SINAPORE IN 1988: THE TRANSITION MOVES FORWARD
ASIAN SURVEY, XXIX(2) (FEB 89), 145-153.
POLITICAL CHANGE WAS GRADUAL, BUT SIGNIFICANT IN
SINGAPORE DURING 1988. THE OVERALL CHANGES SIGNALED A SHIFT
FROM THE OLD GUARD TO THE NEW GUARD. PRIME MINISTER LEE KUAN
KEW HAS DESCRIBED HIS ROLE AS A "GOALKEEPER" AND HAS ALLOWED
MOST DECISIONS TO BE MADE BY SECOND-GENERATION LEADERS AND
EXPECTS TO STEP DOWN FROM OFFICE IN 1989. SINGAPORE'S
ECONOMIC GROWTH CONTINUED, BUT PRESIDENT REAGAN'S REMOVAL OF
SINGAPORE FROM THE GENERALIZED SYSTEM OF PREFERENCE WILL
NECESSITATE ADAPTATION IN THE FUTURE. SINGAPORE CLASHED
DIPLOMATICALLY WITH THE US SEVERAL TIMES OVER THE YEAR, BUT
NO PERMANENT DAMAGE OCCURRED.

01442 BELMAN, D.; HEYWOOD, J. S.
INCENTIVE SCHEMES AND RACIAL WAGE DISCRIMINATION
REVIEW OF BLACK POLITICAL ECOMOMY, 17(1) (SUM 88), 47-56.
THIS ARTICLE TESTS THE CLAIM THAT RACIAL WAGE
DISCRIMINATION IS LESS SEVERE WHEN WORKERS ARE PAID

ACCORDING TO INCENTIVE SCHEMES. THIS CLAIM IS BASED ON THE
DISTINCTION BETWEEN INCENTIVE AND TIME METHODS OF PAYMENT.
THE CONCLUSION IS DRAWN THAT IT IS EASIER FOR MANAGERS TO
DISCRIMINATE WHERE EARNINGS ARE BASED ON PERCEPTIONS OF
EFFORT RATHER THAN ON MORE OBJECTIVE MEASURES OF WORKER
PERFORMANCE.

01443 BELOFF, M.
    1989, A FAREWELL TO ARMS: A REJOINDER
    INTERNATIONAL AFFAIRS, 65(3) (SUM 89), 415-418.
        THIS REJOINDER SUGGESTS THAT SIR MICHAEL HOWARD'S
    COMPARISON OF RECENT HAPPENINGS IN THE SOVIET UNION WITH THE
    REVOLUTION IN FRANCE AND WITH LENIN'S COUP D'ETAT IS HARDLY
    CONVINCING. THE ARTICLE EXPLORES THE SOVIET ONE-PARTY SYSTEM,
    ECONOMICS, GORBACHEV AS A DIPLOMAT AND A PROPAGANDIST, THE
    ALLIANCE, THE GERMAN FACTOR, AND THE NEED FOR THE UNITED
    STATES TO CONCENTRATE ON THEIR OWN HEMISPHERE. IT CONCLUDES
    THAT IT DOES NOT HELP TO PRETEND THAT GORBACHEV WILL PROVIDE
    EVIDENCE OF GENUINE COOPERATION IN SETTLING 'REGIONAL'
    ISSUES, ARMS CONTROL, AND IN REALIZING THAT CHEMICAL AND
    BIOLOGICAL WEAPONS ARE PROBABLY 'UNVERIFIBLE,' EVEN THOUGH
    IT IS HOPED THAT IT WILL HAPPEN.

01444 BELONOGOV, A.; BONDAREVSKY, G.; KHILCHEVSKY, Y.; KOVALEV,
    F.; KREMENYUK, V.; PERFILYEV, V.; PETROVSKY, Y.; PRYAKHIN,
    V.; SAFRONCHUK, V.; TSVETOV, V.; ZAMOSHKIN, Y.; ZINCHENKO,
    V.
    INTERNATIONALISING THE DIALOGUE AND THE NEGOTIATING PROCESS
    INTERNATIONAL AFFAIRS (MOSCOW), (2) (FEB 89), 131-140.
        MANY SPHERES OF SOVIET GOVERNMENT, INCLUDING DIPLOMACY,
    SUFFERED FROM THE PERSONALITY CULT, VOLUNTARISM, AND
    STAGNATION. INSTEAD OF SERVING AS A MEANS OF ASCERTAINING
    AREAS OF AGREEMENT AND ACHIEVING MUTUALLY ACCEPTABLE RESULTS,
    DIPLOMACY VIRTUALLY LOST ITS ESSENCE AND PLAYED THE ROLE OF
    AN AUXILIARY PROPAGANDA MEDIUM. IN THIS SYMPOSIUM, SOVIET
    OFFICIALS DISCUSS THE PAST FALLACIES OF SOVIET DIPLOMACY AND
    THE NEW DIRECTIONS IT IS TAKING.

01445 BELOUS, V.
    SDI: THE PHILOSOPHY OF DOOM
    REPRINTS FROM THE SOVIET PRESS, 48(10) (MAY 89), 15-23.
        THE SOVIET UNION IS PREPARED TO CONTINUE THE DIALOGUE
    WITH THE UNITED STATES IN A SPIRIT OF REALISM, OPENNESS AND
    GOODWILL. IN THE MILITARY FIELD IT IS IMPORTANT, FIRST AND
    FOREMOST, TO CONSISTENTLY ADVANCE TOWARD THE CONCLUSION OF A
    TREATY ON A 50 PERCENT REDUCTION IN STRATEGIC DEFENSE
    WEAPONS WITH THE PRESERVATION OF THE ABM TREATY. HOWEVER,
    SDI REMAINS THE MAIN OBSTACLE ON THIS ROAD. AMERICANS CAN
    HARDLY SUPPOSE THAT THE SOVIET UNION WILL DESTROY LAUNCHING
    SILOS AND UNDERGROUND COMMAND POSTS IN WHICH HUNDREDS OF
    MILLIONS OF RUBLES ARE INVESTED, HAVING NO FIRM GUARANTEES
    AGAINST THE SPREAD OF THE ARMS RACE TO OUTER SPACE. IT IS TO
    BE HOPED THAT THE NEW POLITICAL THINKING AND COMMON SENSE
    WILL TRIUMPH. THEY ARE ABOVE OLD STEREOTYPES AND DOGMAS AND
    WILL PAVE THE WAY FOR GENUINE INTERNATIONAL SECURITY, FOR A
    NUCLEAR WEAPONS-FREE, DURABLE AND NONVIOLENT WORLD.

01446 BEN-MEIR, A.
    BACKGROUND TO A NEW COURSE
    MIDSTREAM, XXXV(2) (FEB 89), 6-11.
        YASIR ARAFAT'S RECOGNITION OF ISRAEL'S RIGHT TO EXIST,
    HIS RENUNCIATION OF VIOLENCE IN ALL FORMS, AND HIS
    ACCEPTANCE OF U.N. RESOLUTIONS 242 AND 338 CONSTITUTE A
    MAJOR TURNING POINT IN RELATIONS IN THE MIDDLE EAST. DURING
    THE PAST 25 YEARS, THE PLO HAS EVOLVED--VERY GRADUALLY AND
    VERY PAINFULLY--FROM A LOOSE ALLIANCE OF TERRORIST
    ORGANIZATIONS INTO A POLITICAL MOVEMENT. THE ISSUE OF A TWO-
    STATE SOLUTION IS NO LONGER A RHETORICAL ONE. IF THE PLO
    ADHERES TO ITS PUBLIC DECLARATIONS REGARDING ISRAEL'S RIGHT
    TO EXIST AND THE RENUNCIATION OF TERRORISM, ISRAEL AND THE U.
    S. WILL EVENTUALLY FIND IT DIFFICULT NOT TO MEET PALESTINIAN
    DEMANDS.

01447 BEN-MEIR, A.
    JERUSALEM IN THE FABRIC OF JEWISH HISTORY
    MIDSTREAM, XXXV(4) (MAY 89), 16-20.
        THE UNIFICATION OF JERUSALEM GAVE SUBSTANCE AND FULL
    MEANING TO THE CONCEPT OF REDEMPTION. ALTHOUGH JERUSALEM IS
    STILL A KEY ELEMENT IN THE ARAB-ISRAELI CONFLICT, ISRAEL'S
    POSITION HAS NEVER BEEN OPEN TO MISINTERPRETATION. JERUSALEM
    WILL REMAIN ISRAEL'S CAPITAL FOREVER, A CITY UNIFIED BY ITS
    HOPES AND DREAMS, WHERE VARIOUS RELIGIOUS GROUPS CAN LIVE
    TOGETHER IN PEACE AND ENJOY FREEDOM OF WORSHIP. TO
    UNDERSTAND WHY ISRAELIS STAND UNITED ON THE QUESTION OF
    JERUSALEM, IT IS NECESSARY TO REVIEW THE HISTORY OF
    JERUSALEM.

01448 BEN-MEIR, A.
    STATEHOOD AND REDEMPTION
    MIDSTREAM, XXXV(3) (APR 89), 38-42.
        THE CONTEMPORARY JEW, WHO SURVIVED THE GERMAN HORRORS OF
    WORLD WAR II AND SAW THE CREATION OF ISRAEL, IS VIVIDLY
    REPRESENTED BY TWO EXTRAORDINARY GENERATIONS. THE FIRST
    GENERATION - THE HEIRS OF THE HOLOCAUST - WITNESSED THE NEAR

DESTRUCTION OF THE JEWISH PEOPLE, AND THE SECOND-THE
GENERATION OF REDEMPTION-IS SYMBOLIZED BY THE ESTABLISHMENT
OF ISRAEL. THE TWO GENERATIONS STAND IN TOTAL CONTRAST: THE
FORMER WAS FILLED WITH UTTER DESPAIR AND HOPELESSNESS, WHILE
THE LATTER WAS IMMERSED IN EXHILARATION AND GLORY.

01449 BEN-MEIR, A.
    TERRITORY AND NATIONAL IDENTITY
    MIDSTREAM, XXXV(1) (JAN 89), 11-14.
        ONE OF THE MAJOR ISSUES THAT CONTINUES TO HAUNT THE
    ISRAELIS AND PALESTINIANS IS THE CORE QUESTION OF NATIONAL
    IDENTITY AS IT RELATES TO A TERRITORIAL SETTLEMENT. ANY
    SOLUTION TO THE ISRAELI-PALESTINIAN CONFLICT WOULD STILL
    LEAVE THE PALESTINIANS DISPERSED WITHIN ISRAEL, THE WEST
    BANK, JORDAN, GAZA, AND VARIOUS OTHER ARAB STATES. THE
    CREATION OF A PALESTINIAN STATE IN THE WEST BANK AND GAZA
    WOULD NOT CHANGE THE CURRENT DEMOGRAPHIC SITUATION OF THE
    PALESTINIANS IN ANY DRAMATIC WAY. BY THE SAME TOKEN, ANY
    FUTURE SOLUTION MUST PROVIDE FOR THE JEWS' AFFINITY TO THE
    LAND OF THEIR ANCESTORS. NO ISRAELI GOVERNMENT COULD EVEN
    CONTEMPLATE THE RETURN OF THE ENTIRE WEST BANK TO THE
    PALESTINIANS AND ABROGATE THE JEWISH RIGHT TO SETTLE IN AT
    LEAST PART OF THESE TERRITORIES. AT ISSUE IS THE VALIDITY OF
    THE ISRAELIS' AND PALESTINIANS' DUAL TERRITORIAL CLAIM AND
    HOW THAT CAN BE RECONCILED WITH THE NEED TO ESTABLISH AND
    MAINTAIN THEIR SEPARATE NATIONAL IDENTITIES.

01450 BEN-MEIR, A.
    THE MIDDLE EAST: A HUMAN RIGHTS TRAGEDY
    MIDSTREAM, XXXV(5) (JUN 89), 6-10.
        IN MOST MIDDLE EASTERN COUNTRIES, FLAGRANT HUMAN RIGHTS
    ABUSES EXIST IN ABUNDANCE BECAUSE SOCIAL DISCORD AND
    ECONOMIC DISLOCATION PERSIST, LACK OF POLITICAL MATURITY IS
    PERVASIVE, AND RELIGIOUS FANATICISM IS EGREGIOUS. THE VAST
    MAJORITY OF COUNTRIES IN THE MIDDLE EAST AND NORTH AFRICA
    CONTINUE TO VIOLATE HUMAN RIGHTS. THESE ABUSES CONTRIBUTE TO
    THE CYCLE OF SOCIAL AND POLITICAL INSTABILITY IN THE REGION.

01451 BEN-RAFAEL, E.
    ISRAEL AS A MULTI-CLEAVAGE SETTING
    PLURAL SOCIETIES, 19(1) (SEP 89), 21-40.
        THE AUTHOR EXAMINES THREE ETHNIC CLEAVAGES WHICH CAPTURE
    THE PUBLIC ARENA IN THE REGION AROUND ISRAEL AND WHICH HE
    SEES AS INHERENTLY BOUND TO THE EVOLUTION OF ISRAELI SOCIETY
    AS IT IS. THESE ARE AS FOLLOWS: 1) THE JEWISH-ARAB DIVISION,
    WHICH CONCERNS AN ARAB MINORITY, MOSTLY SUNNITE MUSLIM, WHO
    REMAINED IN THE COUNTRY WHEN THE JEWISH STATE WAS
    ESTABLISHED IN 1948, 2) THE INTRA-JEWISH RELIGIOUS DIVISION,
    WHICH DIVIDES THAT MAJORITY FROM A RELIGIOUS SECTOR,
    REPRESENTING 20-25% OF THE JEWISH INHABITANTS, WHICH ITSELF
    IS DIVIDED INTO DIVERSE FACTIONS, AND 3) THE CLEAVAGE
    RELATED TO GROUPS OF ORIGIN, GENERALLY CATAGORIZED INTO A
    DOMINANT ASHKENAZI STOCK OF EUROPEAN DESCENT AND AN ORIENTAL
    STRATUM OF NORTH AFRICAN OR MIDDLE EASTERN ORIGIN.

01452 BEN-ZADOK, E.
    DEMAND FOR POWER-SHARING IN ISRAEL
    MIDSTREAM, XXXV(2) (FEB 89), 16-20.
        SINCE THE EARLY 1970'S, THE GROWING PLURALISM OF
    INTERESTS AND THE CLASHES BETWEEN THEM HAVE CHANGED THE
    PATTERN OF DISTRIBUTION OF ECONOMIC RESOURCES AND POLITICAL
    POWER WITHIN ISRAEL. OBSERVERS HAVE FORMED TWO PERSPECTIVES
    TO ANALYZE THESE DEVELOPMENTS WITHIN ISRAELI POLITICS. THE
    FIRST PERSPECTIVE IS OF A SOCIETY DEEPLY DIVIDED BY
    NATIONWIDE SOCIAL TENSIONS AND POLITICAL CLEAVAGES BETWEEN
    ETHNIC, CLASS, RELIGIOUS, AND SECULAR GROUPS. THE ASSUMPTION
    OF THIS PERSPECTIVE IS THAT THE STILL HIGHLY-CENTRALIZED
    SYSTEM IS CHARACTERIZED BY POLITICAL CLEAVAGES ON THE
    NATIONAL LEVEL. THE SECOND PERSPECTIVE EMPHASIZES THE
    DECENTRALIZATION TREND. IT SUGGESTS THAT LOCAL COMMUNITIES
    AND REGIONS WITHIN ISRAEL HAVE BEGUN TO VOCALLY EXPRESS
    THEIR OWN INTERESTS AND DEMONSTRATE INDEPENDENCE FROM THE
    NATIONAL CENTER.

01453 BENDER, G.J.
    PEACEMAKING IN SOUTHERN AFRICA: THE LAUNDA-PRETORIA TUG OF
    WAR
    THIRD WORLD QUARTERLY, 11(2) (APR 89), 15-30.
        IN 1978, SOUTH AFRICA'S SIGNING OF UN SECURITY COUNCIL
    RESOLUTION 435 RAISED EXPECTATIONS THAT PEACE WAS AROUND THE
    CORNER IN SOUTHERN AFRICA. A DECADE LATER, THE SIGNING OF
    THE 1988 ACCORD BY SOUTH AFRICA, ANGOLA, AND CUBA ONCE AGAIN
    RAISED ANTICIPATIONS ABOUT PEACE IN SOUTHERN AFRICA. THIS
    ESSAY REVIEWS WHAT HAPPENED DURING THE DECADE FROM 1978 TO
    1988 AND ASSESSES THE PROSPECTS FOR PEACE.

01454 BENDER, L.
    SEX DISCRIMINATION OR GENDER INEQUALITY?
    FORDHAM LAW REVIEW, 57(6) (MAY 89), 941-954.
        THIS ARTICLE CONTENDS THAT THE ELIMINATION OF SEX
    DISCRIMINATION IN THE LAW PROFESSION IS NOT ENOUGH, THAT
    THERE MUST BE GENDER EQUALITY. IT DEFINES GENDER AS: THE
    CULTURAL/SOCIAL CONSTRUCTION AND ATTRIBUTION OF QUALITIES TO
    DIFFERENT BIOLOGICAL SEXES; THEN STATES THAT THE GOAL MUST

BE TO EMPOWER BOTH GENDERS AND TO ELIMINATE THE
PRIVILEGE/POWER OF ONE GENDER OVER ANOTHER. THE GENDER-BASED
DIFFERENCES ARE EXPLORED AS WELL AS THE FACT THAT THE MALE
NORM OF EXISTING LEGAL INSTITUTIONS IS ACCEPTED AND THAT
WOMEN ARE EXPECTED TO CONFORM TO ITS EXPECTATIONS AND
DEMANDS. THE ARTICLE CONCLUDES THAT IN ORDER TO ACHIEVE
GENDER EQUALITY THAT WOMEN MUST TAKE RESPONSIBILITY.

01455 BENHABIB, S.
ON CONTEMPORARY FEMINIST THEORY
DISSENT, (SUM 89), 366-370.
FEMALE SCHOLARS OF POLITICAL THOUGHT HAVE DOCUMENTED THE
MISOGYNIST ORIGINS OF THE WESTERN TRADITION AND ITS
CONTINUING GENDER BIAS WELL INTO THE ENLIGHTENMENT AND THE
MODERN PERIOD. THEY HAVE GONE FURTHER AND IDENTIFIED THE
GENDER SUBTEXT IN VISIONS OF THE POLITICAL SUBJECT, IN THE
DEFINITION OF THE POLITICAL REALM, AND IN THE LOGIC OF TERMS
LIKE "PARTICIPATION," "AUTONOMY," "CONSENT," AND "RIGHTS."

01456 BENICNOU, M.
THE DEVELOPMENT OF ANGLO-FRENCH RELATIONS IN DEFENSE
EQUIPMENT
RUSI JOURNAL, 134(4) (WIN 89), 55-57.
THE ARTICLE EXAMINES OVERALL TRENDS AND CHANGES IN
BRITISH-FRENCH COOPERATION IN THE AREA OF DEFENSE EQUIPMENT.
PRIOR TO A 1987 COOPERATION ARRANGEMENT THE TWO NATIONS
PURCHASED ONLY SPARE PARTS FROM EACH OTHER. HOWEVER, THE
ARRANGEMENTS WILL EVENTUALLY BE ABLE TO OVERCOME THE PAST
LACK OF COOPERATION AND INTERLINK THE PROCUREMENT ACTIVITIES
OF BOTH NATIONS. THE END RESULT WILL BE A STRONGER, MORE
HOMOGENEOUS EUROPE.

01457 BENN, D.
GLASNOST, DIALOGUE AND EAST-WEST RELATIONS
INTERNATIONAL AFFAIRS, 65(2) (SPR 89), 289-304.
THE ARTICLE EXAMINES THE EFFECTS OF GLASNOST ON EAST-
WEST DIALOGUE. IT CONCLUDES THAT GLASNOST HAS ALREADY
BROUGHT AN ENORMOUS CHANGE TO THE SOVIET INTELLECTUAL
CLIMATE. IT HAS STARTED A PROCESS THAT COULD BE REFERRED TO
AS "DE-ORWELLIANIZATION." WHICH IN ITSELF HAS CHANGED THE
CONTEXT IN WHICH EAST-WEST DISCUSSIONS TAKE PLACE. THE
ARTICLE ARGUES THAT IS IMPOSSIBLE TO UNDERSTAND GLASNOST
FULLY WITHOUT UNDERSTANDING THE SOVIET MEDIA OF THE PAST.
THEREFORE, IT TRACES THE DEVELOPMENT OF THE SOVIET MEDIA AND
ITS ATTEMPTS AT CREATING PROPOAGANDA.

01458 BENN, P.
POLAND IN TRANSITION: A BRITISH VISITOR'S VIEW
CONTEMPORARY REVIEW, 255(1486) (NOV 89), 232-236.
RECENT HAPPENINGS LEAVE ONE TO WONDER WHAT SHAPE
COMMUNISM WILL HAVE TO TAKE IN THE NEXT CENTURY. THIS PAPER
EXPLORES SOME OF THE MOST TALKED ABOUT CHANGES WHICH HAVE
BEEN IN POLAND. IT EXAMINES THE OFFICIAL REBIRTH OF
SOLIDARITY, THE ELECTION CAMPAIGN, AND THE ELECTIONS
THEMSELVES ON JUNE 4TH. ALSO NOTED ARE: THE EFFECT OF
PERESTROIKA AND GLASTNOST; ECONOMICS: THE STRENGTH OF THE
CHURCH; AND THE POSSIBILITY OF THE EMERGENCE OF A POPULAR
NON-COMMUNIST SECULAR FORCE.

01459 BENNAMIA, A.
PALESTINE IN ALGERIAN FOREIGN POLICY, 1962-1978
DISSERTATION ABSTRACTS INTERNATIONAL, 49(7) (JAN 89),
1948-A.
THE AUTHOR TRACES ALGERIAN FOREIGN POLICY ON THE
PALESTINIAN PROBLEM FROM INDEPENDENCE TO THE DEATH OF
PRESIDENT BOUMEDIENE.

01460 BENNETT, G.
THE FRENCH CONNECTION
SOUTH, (101) (MAR 89), 27-28.
AFRICA'S POVERTY IS DRIVING A WEDGE BETWEEN FRANCE AND
ITS FORMER COLONIES THERE. THE OLD CONGENIAL RELATIONSHIP IS
BEING STRAINED BY THE WITHDRAWAL OF FRENCH COMPANIES FROM A
CONTINENT IN ECONOMIC CRISIS. BUT PARIS CONTINUES TO STRESS
CONTINUITY, AND PRESIDENT FRANCOIS MITTERAND HAS TRIED TO
DEMONSTRATE HIS COMMITMENT TO THE REGION BY APPOINTING HIS
SON AS THE KEY PRESIDENTIAL ADVISER ON AFRICAN AFFAIRS.

01461 BENNETT, J.R.
MANAGING CONSENSUS: THE PRESIDENTIAL COMMISSION AS AN
INDICTMENT FOR BUREAUCRATIC POLICY CONTROL
NEW POLITICAL SCIENCE, (FAL 89), 155-178.
THE AUTHOR DEBATES VARIOUS MEASURES WHICH ARE AVAILABLE
TO ENFORCE POLICY CONTROLS OVER THE BUREAUCRACY,
PARTICULARLY IN THE UNITED STATES USE OF PRESIDENTIAL
COMMISSIONS. THIS APPROACH IS CONTRASTED TO THE BRITISH
SYSTEM OF ROYAL COMMISSION INQUIRIES IN THAT PRESIDENTIAL
COMMISSIONS APPEAR TO MORE OFTEN ORIGINATE IN SUPPORT OF
ALREADY ESTABLISHED PROGRAMS THAN DO THEIR BRITISH
COUNTERPARTS. EXAMPLES OF VARIOUS COMMISSION REPORTS WHICH
WERE UNDERTAKEN DURING THE REAGAN ADMINISTRATION ARE
DISCUSSED.

01462 BENNETT, K.M.
FINANCING ECONOMIC GROWTH WITH SPECIAL REFERENCE TO JAMAICA
SOCIAL AND ECONOMIC STUDIES, 38(4) (DEC 89), 95-114.
THIS PAPER ATTEMPTS TO DETERMINE THE LEVEL OF INVESTMENT
REQUIRED TO ACHIEVE A DESIRED TARGET RATE OF GROWTH AND THE
FINANCING NECESSARY FOR THAT LEVEL OF INVESTMENT AN
EXPLORATION IS MADE OF THE MAJOR FACTOR CONSTRAINING GROWTH
OVER THE PAST DECADE IN JAMAICA, NAMELY, THE SHORTAGE OF
FOREIGN EXCHANGE, AND THE MEASURES NEEDED TO ALLEVIATE IT.
THE SECOND SECTION IS CONCERNED WITH THE IDENTIFICATION OF
SECTORAL INVESTMENT PRIORITIES, THE ROLE TO BE PLAYED BY THE
PUBLIC AND PRIVATE SECTORS, AS WELL AS DIRECT INVESTMENT IN
TRYING TO ENSURE THAT GROWTH IS ASSOCIATED WITH STRUCTURAL
CHANGE.

01463 BENNETT, L.L.M.; BENNETT, S.E.
ENDURING GENDER DIFFERENCES IN POLITICAL INTERESTS: THE
IMPACT OF SOCIALIZATION AND POLITICAL DISPOSITIONS
AMERICAN POLITICS QUARTERLY, 17(1) (JAN 89), 105-122.
ALTHOUGH WOMEN NOW VOTE IN NATIONAL ELECTIONS AT THE
SAME RATE AS MEN, THEY ARE STILL LESS POLITICALLY INTERESTED.
USING REGRESSION ANALYSIS AND TWO NEW SCALES TO TAP AN
ORIENTATION TOWARD WOMEN'S PLACE IN THE PUBLIC ARENA
(TRADITIONAL FEMININE ROLE SCALE) AND POLITICAL INTEREST
(POLITICAL APATHY SCALE), THIS ARTICLE SEEKS TO TEST THE
UTILITY OF THE THREE STANDARD EXPLANATIONS FOR WOMEN'S
POLITICAL ORIENTATIONS (SITUATIONAL, STRUCTURAL, AND SEX-
ROLE SOCIALIZATION) IN UNDERSTANDING THE CONTINUING "GENDER
GAP" IN POLITICAL INTEREST. OTHER THAN EDUCATION,
SITUATIONAL AND STRUCTURAL FACTORS ARE FOUND TO HAVE MINIMAL
EXPLANATORY CAPACITY. ASIDE FROM EDUCATION, POLITICAL
DISPOSITIONS FAR OUTSTRIP SITUATIONAL AND STRUCTURAL FACTORS
AS PREDICTORS OF ATTENTIVENESS. STRONGEST SUPPORT FOR THE
IMPACT OF SOCIALIZATION IS PROVIDED BY THE DIFFERENT
PREDICTORS OF INTEREST AMONG DIFFERENT AGE GROUPS. AMONG
WOMEN UNDER 30 EDUCATION IS LESS IMPORTANT AS A PREDICTOR
THAN IS PARTISANSHIP. AMONG WOMEN OVER 45, THE TRADITIONAL
FEMININE ROLE SCALE EMERGES AS AN INCREASINGLY IMPORTANT
PREDICTOR AS THEY AGE.

01464 BENNETT, S.E.
TRENDS IN AMERICANS' POLITICAL INFORMATION, 1967-1987
AMERICAN POLITICS QUARTERLY, 17(4) (OCT 89), 422-435.
THIS STUDY UTILIZES NATIONAL OPINION RESEARCH CENTER
(NORC) SURVEYS IN 1967, 1987, AND 1988, AND SURVEY RESEARCH
CENTER/CENTER FOR POLITICAL STUDIES (SRC/CPS) DATA FROM 1960
TO 1986 TO EXPLORE TRENDS IN AMERICANS' KNOWLEDGE OF PUBLIC
AFFAIRS. NORC AND SRC/CPS DATA INDICATE THAT, DESPITE BEING
BETTER EDUCATED, THE PUBLIC IN THE 1980S IS SLIGHTLY LESS
INFORMED THAN IN THE 1960S. THE PRIMARY CULPRITS FOR
DIMINISHED POLITICAL INFORMATION ARE DIMINUTION IN POLITICAL
INTEREST AND LESSENED RELIANCE ON NEWSPAPERS.

01465 BENOIST, J-M.
THATCHERISM ACROSS THE CHANNEL
NATIONAL REVIEW, 110(21) (NOV 89), 23-25.
THIS ARTICLE REPORTS ON THE EFFORT TO PRESERVE FREE
ENTERPRISE IN A UNIFIED WESTERN EUROPE. IT EXPLORES THE
IDEAS DEVELOPED BY PRIME MINISTER MARGARET THATCHER IN HER
FAMOUS "BRUGES SPEECH," AND ALSO FEARS BY SOME OBSERVERS IN
AMERICA AND ASIA THAT THE "SINGLE MARKET" CREATED IN EUROPE
MIGHT BECOME A FORMIDABLE ECONOMIC POWER DEPLOYING
PROTECTIONIST WEAPONS AGAINST THE OUTSIDE WORLD. CONTENTION
BETWEEN THE THATCHERITE, FREE MARKET, PATRIOTIC EUROPEANS
BLOC AND THE BUREAUCRATIC, SOCIALIST HOMOGENIZERS BLOC AND
ITS IMPLICATIONS ARE ANALYSED.

01466 BENSABAT, R.; BENSABAT, J. N.
CHILEAN PLEBISCITE: EXIT PINOCHET?
INTERNATIONAL PERSPECTIVES, XVIII(1) (JAN 89), 18-21.
THE AUTHORS DISCUSS THE 1988 PLEBISCITE IN CHILE AND
SPECULATE ABOUT WHAT IT MEANS FOR THE FUTURE. THEY WARN THAT
THE STRUGGLE FOR DEMOCRACY HAS JUST BEGUN AND IT WILL BE AN
UPHILL BATTLE.

01467 BENSI, X.
CERTAIN THEORETICAL ISSUES CONCERNING THE SOCIAL REFORMS
IN CHINA
CHINA REPORT, 25(1) (JAN 89), 53-66.
THE ARTICLE EXAMINES MANY OF THE REFORMS THAT CHINA HAS
ATTEMPTED, WITH EMPHASIS ON THE ECONOMIC SPHERE. IT ANALYZES
THE EFFORTS THAT CHINESE LEADERS HAVE MADE TO SYNTHESIZE
CAPITALIST ECONOMIC TOOLS WITHIN A SOCIALIST FRAMEWORK. IT
CONCLUDES THAT IF THE SITUATION OF CHINA IS GENUINELY
UNDERSTOOD AND USED AS A FOUNDATION FOR REFORM, THE CHANCES
FOR SUCCESS ARE HIGH. IT CONCLUDES WITH AN ANALYSIS OF THE
POLITICAL IMPLICATIONS OF CHINA'S ECONOMIC REFORMS.

01468 BENSMAN, J.
THE CRISIS OF CONFIDENCE IN MODERN POLITICS
INTERNATIONAL JOURNAL OF POLITICS, CULTURE AND SOCIETY,
2(1) (FAL 88), 15-35.
ONE OF THE MOST OBVIOUS HYPOTHETICAL REASONS FOR THE
FAILURE OF BELIEF IN SOCIETY, ITS LEADERS AND ITS

INSTITUTIONS IS THAT MODERN POLITICAL AUDIENCES, THE PUBLIC, HAVE PERCEIVED TOO OFTEN THAT THEY ARE THE OBJECTS OF LIES, DECEIT, AND FRAUD, OF UNFULFILLED AND UNFULFILLABLE PROMISES, RIP-OFFS AND POST-ELECTION NEGLECT. THIS HAS BEEN CALLED THE "CRISIS OF CREDIBILITY." IN THIS PAPER, THE AUTHOR EVALUATES STRUCTURAL FACTORS WHICH ACCOUNT FOR THE LOSS OF CREDIBILITY, THE "FAILURE OF LEGITIMACY" AND THE CRISIS OF CONFIDENCE. THE AUTHOR EXAMINES THE EXPECTATIONS THAT CITIZENS PLACE UPON THEIR LEADERSHIP AND INSTITUTIONS, HOW THESE EXPECTATIONS ARE AROUSED, HOW CITIZENS RESPOND TO THE FAILURE OF EXPECTATIONS, AND HOW LEADERS AROUSE AND DEAL WITH BOTH THESE EXPECTANCIES.

01469 BENSON, B.L.
ENFORCEMENT OF PRIVATE PROPERTY RIGHTS IN PRIMITIVE SOCIETIES: LAW WITHOUT GOVERNMENT
JOURNAL OF LIBERTARIAN STUDIES, IX(1) (WIN 89), 1-26.
THIS ESSAY IS DIVIDED INTO SIX SECTIONS. FIRST, THE CONCEPT OF LAW AS DEFINED BY LEGAL SCHOLARS AND ANTHROPOLOGISTS IS EXPLORED. SECONDLY, THE CONCEPT OF GOVERNMENT IS EXAMINED. THE NEXT THREE SECTIONS ARE DEVOTED TO SEPARATE STUDIES OF THREE PRIMITIVE SOCIETIES, IN ORDER TO ESTABLISH THE GENERAL CHARACTER OF PRIVATELY-PRODUCED LEGAL SYSTEMS. THE SIXTH SECTION OFFERS CONCLUDING OBSERVATIONS.

01470 BENSON, B.L.
FURTHER THOUGHTS ON RENT-SEEKING, BUREAUCRATIC OUTPUT, AND THE PRICE OF COMPLEMENTS
PUBLIC CHOICE, 63(3) (DEC 89), 279-282.
THE POINT OF THIS NOTE IS THAT RENT EXTRACTION IN NOT CONDITIONED ON THE ASSUMPTION THAT THE BUREAU IS SOMETHING OTHER THAN A NET-REVENUE MAXIMIZER. ALL THAT IS REQUIRED IS THAT COMPETITION IN THE SUPPLY OF A COMPLEMENT IS LIMITED AS A RESULT OF SUCCESSFUL RENT-SEEKING ACTIVITIES. THUS, EVEN IF INCENTIVES CAN BE PUT IN PLACE TO INDUCE A BUREAU TO ESTABLISH A CAPACITY AND PRICE CONSISTENT WITH NET-REVENUE MAXIMIZATION, BUREAUCRATIC INEFFICIENCY CAN RESULT UNLESS POLITICIANS' PROPENSITY TO MEET THE DEMANDS OF RENT-SEEKERS CAN BE CURBED.

01471 BENSTON, M.
THE POLITICAL ECONOMY OF WOMEN'S LIBERATION
MONTHLY REVIEW, 41(7) (DEC 89), 31-43.
THIS ARTICLE ARGUES THAT THE ROOTS OF THE SECONDARY STATUS OF WOMEN ARE IN FACT ECONOMIC, AND THAT IT CAN BE SHOWN THAT WOMEN AS A GROUP DO INDEED HAVE A DEFINITE RELATION TO THE MEANS OF PRODUCTION, AND THAT THIS IS DIFFERENT FROM THAT OF MEN. IT DEFINES WOMEN AS THAT GROUP OF PEOPLE WHO ARE RESPONSIBLE FOR THE PRODUCTION OF SIMPLE USE-VALUES IN THOSE ACTIVITIES ASSOCIATED WITH THE HOME AND FAMILY, AND SUGGESTS THAT THE MATERIAL BASIS FOR THE INFERIOR STATUS OF WOMEN IS TO BE FOUND IN THIS DEFINITION. IT ADDRESSES THE NEED FOR CONVERTING PRIVATE PRODUCTION OF HOUSEHOLD WORK INTO PUBLIC PRODUCTION. IT ADVOCATES A COMPLETE REORGANIZATION OF THE FAMILY, MOVING THE WORK INTO THE PUBLIC SECTOR AND THAT OTHER STRUCTURES SUBSTITUTE FOR THE NUCLEAR FAMILY.

01472 BENTLEY, M.
IS MRS. THATCHER A CONSERVATIVE?
CONTEMPORARY RECORD, 2(6) (SUM 89), 35-36.
THE THATCHERITES HAVE BEEN ACCUSED OF WANTING TO DESTROY THE CONSERVATIVE PAST. IN FACT, THEY COULD NOT AFFORD THAT. RATHER, THEIR PURPOSE HAS BEEN TO RESCUE, REKINDLE, AND BEND SELECTED CONTINUITIES FROM THE CONSERVATIVE PAST IDENTIFIABLE IN THE LATE 19TH CENTURY AND EVIDENT BETWEEN THE TWO WORLD WARS.

01473 BENTON, T.
MARXISM AND NATURAL LIMITS: AN ECOLOGICAL CRITIQUE AND RECONSTRUCTION
NEW LEFT REVIEW, (178) (NOV 89), 51-86.
MANY ON THE LEFT FIND A SOURCE OF HOPE IN THE REALIGNMENT OF GREEN AND SOCIALIST PERSPECTIVES. BUT IMPORTANT CURRENTS WITHIN GREEN POLITICS AND CULTURE ARE HOSTILE TO SOCIALISM (AS THEY UNDERSTAND IT), WHILE THE RESPONSE OF THE SOCIALIST LEFT TO THE RISE OF ECOLOGICAL POLITICS HAS GENERALLY BEEN DEEPLY AMBIGUOUS. IN THIS ESSAY, THE AUTHOR ENDEAVORS TO (1) DEMONSTRATE THAT THESE TENSIONS AND OPPOSITIONS HAVE DEEP ROOTS IN THE MOST INFLUENTIAL INTELLECTUAL TRADITION ON THE LEFT AND (2) PROVIDE SOME NEW CONCEPTUAL MARKERS THAT COULD PLAY A PART IN FACILITATING THE GROWING RED/GREEN DIALOGUE.

01474 BENZ, A.
INTERGOVERNMENTAL RELATIONS IN THE 1980S
PUBLIUS: THE JOURNAL OF FEDERALISM, 19(4) (FAL 89), 203-220.
INTERGOVERNMENTAL RELATIONS IN WEST GERMAN COOPERATIVE FEDERALISM HAVE OFTEN BEEN CRITICIZED AS INEFFICIENT AND INFLEXIBLE. THE ABOLITION OF JOINT POLICYMAKING AND THE PROMOTION OF DECENTRALIZATION HAVE BEEN RECOMMENDED IN ORDER TO REDUCE INTERDEPENDENCIES BETWEEN GOVERNMENTS AND TO AVOID OVERLOADING CENTRAL POLICYMAKING. SUCH PROPOSALS HAVE USUALLY BEEN PUT FORWARD WITHOUT CONSIDERING THE GOVERNMENTAL COMPLEXITY THAT IMPEDES LARGE-SCALE REFORMS. HOWEVER, A DETAILED ANALYSIS OF FEDERALISM, FOCUSING ON PROCESSES RATHER THAN STRUCTURES AND ON DIFFERENT POLICIES RATHER THAN AGGREGATIONS, REVEALS THAT INTERGOVERNMENTAL RELATIONS IN THE 1980S ARE NOT THE SAME AS THOSE IN THE 1960S OR EARLY 1970S. THE INHERENT DYNAMICS OF INTERGOVERNMENTAL RELATIONS HAVE PRODUCED MANY CHANGES. THESE CHANGES HAVE CONTRIBUTED TO THE OVERALL STABILITY OF WEST GERMAN FEDERALISM BECAUSE THEY HAVE REFLECTED FLEXIBLE ADAPTATIONS OF RELATIONS AMONG FEDERAL, LAND, AND LOCAL GOVERNMENTS TO NEW SOCIOECONOMIC, SOCIOCULTURAL, AND ECOLOGICAL CHALLENGES. HENCE, EVENTS OF THE 1980S PROVIDE AN OCCASION FOR REASSESSING COOPERATIVE FEDERALISM.

01475 BERARDI, G.K.
THE ROLE OF CHURCH AMNESTY ASSISTANCE PROGRAMS IN THE IMPLEMENTATION OF THE 1986 IMMIGRATION REFORM AND CONTROL ACT
JOURNAL OF BORDERLAND STUDIES, IV(2) (FAL 89), 59-69.
THIS ESSAY EXAMINES THE ROLE OF THE CHURCH-SPONSORED QDES IN DEEP EAST TEXAS INVOLVED IN PHASE I OF THE IRCA AMNESTY PROGRAM. SPECIFICALLY, THE REASONS FOR THE INCLUSION OF VOLUNTARY AGENCIES IN THE AMNESTY PROCESS AND THEIR ROLES ARE DESCRIBED. IN ADDITION, PROBLEMS ENCOUNTERED BY THE QDES ARE EXPLORED AND SUGGESTIONS FOR THEIR FUTURE ROLE IN THE DEVELOPMENT AND IMPLEMENTATION OF IMMIGRATION PROGRAMS ARE MADE. CHURCH-SPONSORED AGENCIES WERE SELECTED BECAUSE OF THEIR CENTRAL IMPORTANCE IN PROVIDING COUNSELING TO IMMIGRANTS IN THE DEEP EAST TEXAS AREA. APART FROM IMMIGRATION ATTORNEYS, FEW OTHER RESOURCES EXIST THAT CAN PROVIDE DETAILED INFORMATION ABOUT IRCA.

01476 BERECS, J.
HUNGARY: IN THE INTERESTS OF SOCIALIST CONSTRUCTION
INFORMATION BULLETIN, 27 (MAR 89), 12-13.
THE AUTHOR CALLS FOR RENEWAL WITHIN THE HSWP AND DISCUSSES THE EMERGENCE OF RIVAL POLITICAL ORGANIZATIONS WITHIN HUNGARY.

01477 BEREZHKOV, V.
STALIN'S ERROR OF JUDGEMENT
INTERNATIONAL AFFAIRS (MOSCOW), (9) (SEP 89), 13-26.
THE AUTHOR DISCUSSES WHY STALIN MADE THE FATAL ERROR OF JUDGMENT ABOUT THE TIMING OF HITLER'S INVASION OF THE SOVIET UNION AND, INDEED, ABOUT THE VERY INEVITABILITY OF NAZI AGGRESSION AGAINST THE USSR.

01478 BEREZOWSKI, M.
A VISIT OF IMPORTANCE FAR BEYOND POLAND
CONTEMPORARY POLAND, XXII(8) (1989), 1-2.
U.S. PRESIDENT GEORGE BUSH'S VISIT TO POLAND OPENED A NEW CHAPTER IN POLISH-AMERICAN RELATIONS IN PSYCHOLOGICAL AND SYMBOLIC TERMS, AS WELL AS IN FINANCIAL AND ECONOMIC COOPERATION. THE VISIT ALSO HAD IMPORTANT INTERNATIONAL IMPLICATIONS, BECAUSE IT REFLECTS THE UNITED STATES' ACTIVE EUROPEAN POLICY AND EXPANDS THE HORIZON OF THE POLISH PERCEPTION OF THE WORLD.

01479 BERG, E.
THE LIBERALIZATION OF RICE MARKETING IN MADAGASCAR
WORLD DEVELOPMENT, 17(5) (MAY 89), 719-728.
MADAGASCAR'S EXPERIENCE WITH RICE MARKETING LIBERALIZATION BETWEEN 1985 AND 1988 ILLUSTRATES THE MANY OBSTACLES IN THE WAY OF EFFECTIVE DEREGULATION OF AGRICULTURAL MARKETS: THE RESISTANCE OF AMBIGUOUS REGULATION, CONTINUING LIMITS ON FREE ENTRY, ATTEMPTS AT CARTELIZATION, AND TENACIOUS RESISTANCE OF EXISTING STAKEHOLDERS AND INSTITUTIONS. AT THE SAME TIME, THE EXPERIENCE SHOWS THE ABILITY OF HIGHER PRICES AND FREER MARKETS TO OVERCOME MUCH OF THIS RESISTANCE AND TO STIMULATE PRODUCTION EVEN IN THE PRESENCE OF SO-CALLED STRUCTURAL CONSTRAINTS SUCH AS POOR ROADS, WEAK EXTENSION SERVICES, INADEQUATE CREDIT SYSTEMS, AND INPUT SUPPLY ARRANGEMENTS.

01480 BERGANT, B.
COOPERATION AMONG THE NON-ALIGNED COUNTRIES BROADCASTING ORGANISATIONS.
REVIEW OF INTERNATIONAL AFFAIRS, (JAN 88), 18-20.
IN THE FIELD OF INFORMATION THE DEVELOPED WORLD STILL DICTATES THE VOLUME AND CONTENT OF INFORMATION EXCHANGE. EVEN THE MOST OUTSTANDING EVENTS IN THE DEVELOPING COUNTRIES CAN RARELY COMPETE ON THE WORLD INFORMATION BURSE A MANY OF THE DEVELOPING COUNTRIES HAVE ADOPTED THE TECHNOLOGY OF SATELLITE COMMUNICATION, HOWEVER DUE TO THE HIGH TARIFFS THEY ARE UNABLE TO RECEIVE AND BROADCAST TV SIGNALS EVERY DAY. IN SPITE OF THE UNBELIEVABLY ACCLERATED OPERATIONS, FOR THEM TARIFFS ARE BEING REDUCED TOO SLOWLY. THIS ARTICLE DESCRIBES THE HISTORY AND IMPACT OF THE NON-ALIGNED COUNTRIES BROADCASTING ORGANIZATIONS (BONAC), AND THAT MOVEMENTS' EFFORTS TO PARTICIPATE FULLY IN INFORMATION TECHNOLOGY AND TRANSMISSION.

01481 BERGLUND, S.
THE DECLINE AND FALL OF SWEDISH COMMUNISM?
JOURNAL OF COMMUNIST STUDIES, 5(1) (MAR 89), 83-86.
FROM A NORDIC PERSPECTIVE, THE SWEDISH COMMUNIST PARTY
HAS DONE REMARKABLY WELL, BUT WHEN OBSERVED FROM AN OVERALL
POLITICAL CONTEXT, THE PARTY APPEARS TO BE IN DECLINE. THE
ARTICLE ANALYZES THE REASONS FOR THE DECLINING SUCCESS OF
SWEDISH COMMUNISTS IN VOTER MOBILIZATION AND ELECTORAL
EFFORTS. WORLDWIDE CONFLICT BETWEEN BARIOUS COMMUNIST
MOVEMENTS ARE REFLECTED BY INTERNAL PARTY STRIFE IN SWEDEN.

01482 BERGMAN, T.
PEACE AND DISARMAMENT: SPACE FOR STARS, NOT FOR WARS! (THE
ECONOMIC AND SOCIAL CONSEQUENCES OF THE MILITARISATION OF
SPACE)
WORLD TRADE UNION MOVEMENT, 1 (1988), 7-9.
THIS ARTICLE EXAMINES THE U.S. STRATEGIC DEFENSE
INITIATIVE AND CONCLUDES THAT IT IS AN INTEGRAL PART OF AN
OFFENSIVE SYSTEM. IT INVESTIGATES THE "REAL" COSTS OF STAR
WARS AND CHARGES THAT IT WILL BE A BURDEN FOR ALL COUNTRIES
OF THE WORLD. IT CONTENDS THAT STOCKPILING WEAPONS DOES NOT
GUARANTEE PROSPERITY AND THAT THERE ARE FEW ADVANTAGES FOR
THE CIVILIAN SECTOR.

01483 BERKHOUT, F.
RADIOACTIVE WASTE: INSTITUTIONAL DETERMINANTS OF
MANAGEMENT AND DISPOSAL POLICY IN THREE EUROPEAN COUNTRIES
DISSERTATION ABSTRACTS INTERNATIONAL, 50(6) (DEC 89),
1798-A.
THE AUTHOR REVIEWS THE POLICY AND PRACTICE OF
RADIOACTIVE WASTE MANAGEMENT IN GREAT BRITAIN, SWEDEN, AND
WEST GERMANY. BY COMPARING THE EVOLUTION OF THE POLICY
PROCESS IN THREE COUNTRIES, HE OFFERS A BETTER UNDERSTANDING
OF THE PARTICULAR OPERATIONAL, REGULATORY, AND POLITICAL
FACTORS DETERMINING POLICY IN EACH CASE.

01484 BERLAN, J-P.
THE COMMODIFICATION OF LIFE
MONTHLY REVIEW, 41(7) (DEC 89), 24-30.
THIS ARTICLE EXPLORES THE PRINCIPLE OF THE NON-
PATENTABILITY OF LIVING THINGS. IT TRACES THE JOURNEY OF
GRANTED PATENTS FROM MEDICINE IN 1940 TO PLANTS AND ANIMALS
IN THE 1980S, IT EXAMINES ETHICS, DEMOCRACY AND POLITICAL
CONFRONTATION OF THE PROBLEMS PRESENTED BY THE
"COMMODIFICATION OF LIFE". IT EXAMINES, ALSO, THE
REPERCUSIONS OF A CHANGE OF ATITUDE TOWARD PATENTS AS THE
COURTS PROCEED ON A CASE-BY-CASE BASIS AND ON PURELY
TECHNICAL GROUNDS.

01485 BERMAN, D. R.; MARTIN, L.L.
STATE-LOCAL RELATIONS: AN EXAMINATION OF LOCAL DISCRETION
PUBLIC ADMINISTRATION REVIEW, 48(2) (MAR 88), 637-640.
STATE-LOCAL RELATIONS ARE EXPLORED IN THIS ARTICLE.
DISCRETIONARY MEASUREMENTS HAVE NOT BEEN EXAMINED FOR THEIR
NATURE SIGNIFICANCE OF THEIR INTERRELATIONSHIPS, OR THEIR
UTILITY IN UNDERSTANDING WHAT FACTORS CONDITION THE EXTENT
TO WHICH STATE GOVERNMENTS DELEGATE AUTHORITY TO LOCAL
GOVERNMENTS THUS FAR, THE ARTICLE ATTEMPTS TO FILL THESE
VOIDS IN THE LITERATURE. STATISTICAL ANALYSIS IS USED TO
EXPLORE RELATIONSHIPS BETWEEN COMPONENTS OF CITY AND COUNTY
DISCRETIONARY MEASUREMENTS AND ALSO RELATIONSHIPS BETWEEN
MEASURES AND SELECTED VARIABLES.

01486 BERMAN, P.
THE BAD AND THE HORSE
TIKKUN, 4(1) (JAN 89), 48-49.
RACIAL AND RELIGIOUS BIGOTRY HAS ONCE A TINY ELEMENT IN
BLACK NATIONALIST FRINGE POLITICS. BUT IT HAS GROWN - NOT
ONLY IN REGARD TO JEWS BUT ALSO IN REGARD TO ASIAN-AMERICANS
AND ARAB-AMERICANS. THERE'S REASON TO WORRY THAT JESSE
JACKSON'S POLITICAL SUCCESS ADVANCES THE CAUSE OF THESE
REACTIONARY ELEMENTS AS MUCH AS IT ADVANCES THE CAUSE OF
PROGRESSIVE ELEMENTS.

01487 BERMAN, P.J.
THE ATTORNEY/CLIENT PRIVILEGE AND THE IRS: ASSESSING THE
CURRENCY TRANSACTION REPORTING REGULATIONS
ILLINOIS BAR JOURNAL, 77(10) (JUN 89), 530-536.
THE IRS CASH REPORTING REGULATIONS MAKE NO EXCEPTION FOR
CASH PAYMENT OF LEGAL FEES. THIS ARTICLE WILL DISCUSS THE
TENSION BETWEEN THE REGULATIONS AND AN ATTORNEY'S OBLIGATION
UNDER THE ILLINOIS CODE OF PROFESSIONAL RESPONSIBILITY TO
KEEP CLIENT CONFIDENCES AND SECRETS.

01488 BERMAN, R.
THE FEMINIZATION OF THE U.S. WORKFORCE
MONTHLY REVIEW, 41(6) (NOV 89), 1-11.
THE PURPOSE OF THIS TALK WAS TO SUGGEST THE NEED FOR
REFOCUSSING ATTENTION ON THE NEW ASPECTS OF WOMEN'S POSITION
IN SOCIETY. IT SUGGESTS THAT THE VERY PROCESSES OF ECONOMIC
AND SOCIAL DEVELOPMENT THAT HAVE MADE WOMEN PRIMARILY
REACTIVE TO THE DOMINANT ROLE OF THE MALE, HAVE NOW BECOME
COMPLICIT IN PLACING WOMEN'S STRUGGLE FOR SURVIVAL AT THE
CENTER OF SOCIAL CHANGE, ALSO IT POSES THE NEED FOR A NEW

WOMEN'S-ROLE-CENTERED HISTORICAL MATERIALIST ANALYSIS OF
ADVANCED MONOPOLY CAPITALISM'S RELATIONS OF PRODUCTION IN
THE UNITED STATES TODAY.

01489 BERNHARD, M.H.
THE REBIRTH OF PUBLIC POLITICS IN POLAND: WORKERS AND
INTELLECTUALS IN THE DEMOCRATIC OPPOSITION, 1976-1980
DISSERTATION ABSTRACTS INTERNATIONAL, 49(12) (JUN 89),
3855-A.
USING THE ILLEGAL UNDERGROUND PRESS, THE AUTHOR TRACES
THE DEVELOPMENT OF POLITICAL OPPOSITION IN POLAND FOLLOWING
THE STRIKES OF JUNE 1976 THROUGH A RANGE OF POLITICALLY AND
SOCIALLY DIFFERENTIATED PROTEST MOVEMENTS, MOST PROMINENTLY
THE WORKERS' DEFENSE COMMITTEE AND THE FOUNDING COMMITTES
FOR FREE TRADE UNIONS.

01490 BERNS, W.
FLAG - BURNING AND OTHER MODES OF EXPRESSION
COMMENTARY, 88(4) (OCT 89), 37-41.
THIS ARTICLE EXPLORES HOW FLAG BURNING AND OTHER MODES
OF EXPRESSION ARE TREATED BY THE COURTS IN THEIR
INTERPRETATION OF THE FIRST AMMENDENT. IT INVESTIGATES
FREEDOM OF SPEECH AND POLITICAL EXPRESSION AND DIFFERENCE OF
OPINION, AS WELL AS SELF-EXPRESSION AND SELF-ASSERTION. IT
CONCLUDES THAT LIBELOUS SPEECH IS NOT PROTECTED BY THE FIRST
AMENDMENT, NOR ARE PERJURY, FALSE ADVERTISING OR
CONTEMPTUOUS SPEECH IN A COURTROOM AND THAT THE LIST IS LONG
ENOUGH TO INCLUDE FLAG-BURNING. IT MAKES A DISTINCTION
BETWEEN WHAT PEOPLE CAN SAY AND WHAT PEOPLE CAN DO.

01491 BERNSTEIN, B.J.
CROSSING THE RUBICON: A MISSED OPPORTUNITY TO STOP THE H-
BOMB?
INTERNATIONAL SECURITY, 14(2) (FAL 89), 132-160.
THIS ESSAY ARGUES THAT, BECAUSE OF THE DOMESTIC
POLITICAL CONSENSUS AND THE VIEWS OF THE TRUMAN
ADMINISTRATION ITSELF, THERE WAS NO LIKELIHOOD THAT TRUMAN'S
1952 PROPOSAL TO BAN THERMONUCLEAR TESTING COULD HAVE WON
ACCEPTANCE IN THE UNITED STATES. TO PUT THESE ISSUES IN A
BROAD CONTEXT, THE ESSAY ALSO BRIEFLY DISCUSSES THE 1952-53
PANEL'S GENERAL REPORT FOR REORIENTING AMERICAN NUCLEAR
POLICY, THE RELATIONSHIP OF THESE RECOMMENDATIONS TO THE
1953-54 OPPENHEIMER LOYALTY-SECURITY CASE, AND THE QUESTION
WHETHER THE SOVIET UNION IN 1952-53 MIGHT HAVE ACCEPTED AN
AMERICAN PROPOSAL TO BAR ALL THERMONUCLEAR TESTING. SUCH A
PROPOSAL, THIS ARTICLE CONCLUDES, WOULD HAVE BEEN IN THE
SOVIETS' INTEREST AND MIGHT INDEED HAVE PROVED ACCEPTABLE.

01492 BERNSTEIN, H.
GROWTH OF THE WOMEN'S STRUGGLE
SECHABA, 23(9) (SEP 89), 17-21.
ALTHOUGH WOMEN ARE NOT HIGHLY VISIBLE IN MANY GROUPS AND
ACTIVITIES, THE ROLE OF WOMEN IN STRUGGLES FOR LIBERATION IN
SOUTH AFRICA IS SIGNIFICANT. THE ARTICLE EXAMINES THE
IMPORTANCE OF WOMEN PARTICIPATING IN THE STRUGGLE FOR
FREEDOM, BOTH AS INDEPENDENT ORGANIZATIONS (SUCH AS THE
FEDERATION OF SOUTH AFRICAN WOMEN) AND AS A PART OF LARGER
GROUPS. WOMEN HAVE FOUGHT AND SUFFERED ALONG WITH MEN IN THE
FIGHT AGAINST REPRESSION AND ARE BECOMING INCREASINGLY
PREPARED TO PLAY THEIR FULL PART IN A FEE, NON-SEXIST, NON-
RACIST DEMOCRATIC SOUTH AFRICA.

01493 BERNTS, T.
SANCTIONING RISKY LIFE-STYLES: ATTITUDES TOWARD SOLIDARITY
OR EQUITABLE DISTRIBUTION OF HEALTH CARE
SOCIAL JUSTICE RESEARCH, 2(4) (DEC 88), 249-262.
RISING COSTS OF MEDICAL CARE AND INCREASING KNOWLEDGE
ABOUT BEHAVIOR-RELATED HEALTH RISKS FAVOR THE USE OF THE
EQUITY PRINCIPLE IN HEALTH CARE ALLOCATION. THIS PAPER DEALS
WITH ATTITUDES TO THE QUESTION OF WHETHER OR NOT ONE'S
PAYMENTS SHOULD BE CONTINGENT UPON THE RISKS ONE TAKES. FROM
AN EXPLORATIVE ANALYSIS OF ARGUMENTS ESPOUSED BY LETTER
WRITERS FROM A DUTCH HEALTH MAGAZINE, IT BECOMES APPARENT
THAT EQUITY PLAYS A MAJOR ROLE IN THE RESPONDENTS' VIEWS OF
THE DISTRIBUTION OF HEALTH CARE FACILITIES. NEXT, THE ROLE
OF ATTRIBUTION IN ADOPTING ATTITUDES TOWARD RISKY LIFE-
STYLES IS STUDIED ON THE BASIS OF A SURVEY USING A
REPRESENTATIVE SAMPLE OF DUTCH HOUSEHOLDS. BELIEFS ABOUT THE
INDIVIDUAL ABILITY TO INFLUENCE HEALTH HAVE NO EFFECT ON
RISK SOLIDARITY, WHEREAS BELIEFS ABOUT THE PROPER AMOUNT OF
EFFORT TO AVOID HEALTH RISKS DO HAVE AN EFFECT.

01494 BERRIDGE, G.
DIPLOMACY AND THE ANGOLA/NAMIBIA ACCORDS
INTERNATIONAL AFFAIRS, 65(3) (SUM 89), 463-480.
ON 22 DECEMBER 1988 TWO AGREEMENTS WERE SIGNED IN NEW
YORK WHICH BROUGHT TO AN END OVER TWO DECADES OF FIGHTING IN
SOUTH-WESTERN AFRICA. CERTAIN CHARACTERISTIC PLOYS OF
DIPLOMACY WERE EMPLOYED WITH GREAT SKILL BY THE STATES
CONCERNED WHICH HAVE NOT BEEN GIVEN SUFFICIENT CREDIT IN
HISTORICAL ACCOUNTS OF NEGOTIATIONS OF THIS KIND, FOR THIS
REASON, THIS ARTICLE CONCENTRATES ON THEIR INFLUENCE ON THE
MAKING OF THE ANGOLA/NAMIBIA ACCORDS. THE PROCEDURES
DISCUSSED ARE: MEDIATION; THE LINKAGE OF ISSUES; THE USE OF

SENIOR OFFICIALS IN NEGOTIATIONS: THE CHOICE OF VENUES FOR NEGOTIATION; DEADLINES, SUSTAINING MOMENTUM, AND THE OFFER OF GUARANTEES.

01495 BERRIDGE, G. R.
ENTENTES AND ALLIANCES
REVIEW OF INTERNATIONAL STUDIES, 15(3) (JUL 89), 251-260.
ENTENTES ARE LESS LIKELY THAN ALLIANCES TO DISCHARGE THE DETERRENCE FUNCTION EFFICIENTLY, AND THIS IS AS MUCH BECAUSE THEY ENGENDER LESS PRESSURE ON THE PARTNERS TO FOLLOW UP THEIR COMMITMENTS WITH PRACTICAL MILITARY PREPARATIONS AS BECAUSE OF THE UNCERTAINTY OF THOSE COMMITMENTS THEMSELVES. IN ADDITION, THE AMBIGUITY COMMONLY SURROUNDING THESE COMMITMENTS, THE ELEVATION OF THE IMPLICIT AT THE EXPENSE OF THE EXPLICIT WHICH THEY TEND TO REPRESENT, OFTEN LEADS TO GENUINE CONFUSION BETWEEN THE PARTNERS OR INVITES TENDENTIOUS INTERPRETATION AT TIMES WHEN, FOR OTHER REASONS, RELATIONS MAY BE STRAINED. ENTENTES ALSO ENCOURAGE POLICY DRIFT, MAY FOSTER VESTED INTERESTS WHICH ARE AS ADEPT AT PREVENTING CHANGE AS THE BUREAUCRACIES OF MAJOR MODERN ALLIANCES, AND MAY WELL BE MORE OPEN TO MANIPULATION BY THE DOMINANT POWER--THOUGH WHETHER THIS IS A GOOD OR A BAD THING WILL OBVIOUSLY DEPEND ON THE POLICIES OF THE POWERS INVOLVED. IN SOME CIRCUMSTANCES ENTENTES MAY WELL BE PREFERABLE TO ALLIANCES (AND MAY INDEED BE THE ONLY ALTERNATIVE) BUT IT IS AS WELL THAT THEIR DRAWBACKS BE KEPT CLEARLY IN VIEW.

01496 BERRINGTON, H.
WHEN DOES PERSONALITY MAKE A DIFFERENCE? LORD CHERWELL AND THE AREA BOMBING OF GERMANY
INTERNATIONAL POLITICAL SCIENCE REVIEW, 10(1) (JAN 89), 9-34.
THE AREA BOMBING OF GERMANY IN 1942-43 BRINGS INTO RELIEF SEVERAL IMPORTANT ISSUES THAT ARISE IN THE STUDY OF POLITICAL PSYCHOLOGY. THE AREA BOMBING ISSUE ILLUSTRATES THE IMPORTANCE OF PERSONALITY: WHEN POWERFUL INSTITUTIONAL FORCES ARE IN CONFLICT; WHEN THE SITUATION IS HIGHLY AMBIGUOUS; AND WHEN THE ACTOR HAS SPECIAL ACCESS TO THE ULTIMATE DECISION-MAKERS AND CAN LIMIT ACCESS BY OTHERS. THE POLICY ADVOCATED BY CHURCHILL'S SCIENTIFIC ADVISER, PROFESSOR LINDEMANN (LORD CHERWELL), WAS PARTICULARLY CONGENIAL TO CHERWELL'S TEMPERAMENT. THE CONSEQUENCES OF THE ADOPTION OF THIS POLICY ARE STILL NOT EASY TO ASSESS, THOUGH POST-WAR APPRAISALS TEND TO QUESTION ITS MILITARY EFFECTIVENESS. THE LACK OF ANY AGREED CONCLUSION ABOUT ITS WORTH UNDERLINES THE INHERENT AMBIGUITY OF THE SITUATION CONFRONTING BRITISH POLICY-MAKERS IN 1942, AND THE OPPORTUNITY THIS PROVIDED FOR THE IMPACT OF PERSONALITY.

01497 BERRY, C.J.
LUXURY AND THE POLITICS OF NEED AND DESIRE: THE ROMAN CASE
HISTORY OF POLITICAL THOUGHT, X(4) (WIN 89), 597-613.
DIFFERENT EVALUATIONS OF DESIRE AND DIFFERENT IDENTIFICATIONS OF NEED WILL PRODUCE DIFFERENT CONCEPTIONS OF POLITICAL ORDER. HENCE, IN MODERN THOUGHT, LIBERALISM IS CHARACTERIZED BY ITS WILLINGNESS TO ACCEPT DESIRES AS THE AUTHENTIC VOICE OF INDIVIDUAL PREFERENCE AND BY ITS DISTRUST OF MUCH NEEDS-TALK. CONVERSELY, SOCIALISM IS CHARACTERIZED BY ITS WILLINGNESS TO EXAMINE INDIVIDUAL DESIRES FOR ANY SELF-DECEPTION OR LACK OF AUTHENTICITY AND BY ITS COMMITMENT TO NEEDS AS A BASIC DISTRIBUTIVE PRINCIPLE. THIS PAPER AIMS TO ENCOMPASS THESE TWO DIMENSIONS OF THE ONE 'REALITY' BY EXAMINING SOME ASPECTS OF THE MORALISTIC SPECULATION AS WELL AS SOME INSTANCES OF THE ACTUAL LEGISLATION PASSED.

01498 BERRY, F.S.
IMPACT OF THE 1973 WAR POWERS RESOLUTION ON THE MILITARY
AVAILABLE FROM NTIS, NO. AD-A209 194/0/GAR, APR 7 89, 147.
THE WAR POWERS RESOLUTION WAS PASSED OVER PRESIDENT NIXON'S VETO ON 7 NOVEMBER 1973. SINCE PASSAGE, THAT LEGISLATION HAS GENERATED CONSIDERABLE DEBATE AND CONFLICT BETWEEN THE LEGISLATIVE AND EXECUTIVE BRANCHES OF GOVERNMENT, AS EVERY PRESIDENT SINCE NIXON HAS EXERCISED HIS CONSTITUTIONAL POWERS AS COMMANDER IN CHIEF OF THE ARMED FORCES AND CHIEF ARCHITECT OF AMERICA'S FOREIGN POLICY. BUT THE CONFLICT BETWEEN THE PRESIDENT AND CONGRESS ALSO REFLECTS CONGRESSIONAL SUSPICION OF PRESIDENTIAL WAR-MAKING POWERS, WHICH BEGAN IN THE 19TH CENTURY, GAINED MOMENTUM DURING THE KOREAN WAR, AND CULMINATED IN THE WAR IN VIETNAM BY A CONGRESS THAT IS NO LONGER SATISFIED TO EXERCISE RESTRAINT ON THE PRESIDENT ONLY THROUGH THE POWER OF THE PURSE. CONGRESS ALSO WANTS TO BE CODETERMINANTS OF FOREIGN POLICY, ESPECIALLY WHEN DECISIONS ARE MADE FOR DEPLOYMENT OF MILITARY FORCES. CAUGHT IN THE MIDDLE OF THIS CONTROVERSY IS THE ARMED FORCES OF THE UNITED STATES. THIS PAPER PROVIDES A BRIEF HISTORICAL OVERVIEW OF PRESIDENTIAL WAR-MAKING POWERS, THE DEVELOPMENT OF THE WAR POWERS RESOLUTION, AND EXAMINES THE IMPACTS, BOTH REAL AND PERCEIVED, WHICH THAT RESOLUTION HAS HAD ON MILITARY OPERATIONS SINCE THAT LEGISLATION WAS PASSED. IT ALSO EXAMINES SOME OF THE ETHICAL ISSUES FACING SENIOR MILITARY LEADERS AND MAKES RECOMMENDATIONS FOR THEIR RESPONSE IN THE HEAT OF THE WAR POWERS DEBATE WHENEVER A NATIONAL CRISIS OCCURS.

01499 BERRY, P.
THE ORGANIZATION AND INFLUENCE OF THE CHANCELLORY DURING THE SCHMIDT AND KOHL CHANCELLORSHIPS
GOVERNANCE, 2(3) (JUL 89), 339-355.
THE GERMAN FEDERAL EXECUTIVE CLEARLY DOMINATES THE POLICY MAKING PROCESS. TO EXAMINE THE FUNCTIONING OF THE CHANCELLORY UNDER DIFFERENT CHANCELLORS THIS ARTICLE EMPLOYS AN APPROACH WHICH OFFERS CRITERIA FOR COMPARISON. FOR THAT PURPOSE THIS STUDY ADOPTS THE CONCEPT OF INSTITUTIONALIZATION, DEFINED AS THE DEGREE TO WHICH A POLITICAL BODY EXHIBITS REGULAR PATTERNS OF BEHAVIOR. INSTITUTIONALIZATION NECESSARILY FOCUSES ON VARIATIONS IN ORGANIZATION AND FUNCTION, AND OFFERS CRITERIA FOR MEASURING THESE VARIATIONS. THIS STUDY WILL USE ROGER GILMOUR'S APPLICATION OF THE CONCEPT. GILMOUR OFFERS FOUR CRITERIA WITH WHICH TO MEASURE INSTITUTIONALIZATION: ORGANIZATIONAL COMPLEXITY, BOUNDARIES, SYMBOLIC ATTACHMENT, AND ROUTINIZATION AND ROLE DEVELOPMENT (1975). BEFORE THE CHANCELLORY IS ANALYZED THE ARTICLE FIRST TAKES A LOOK AT THE CHANCELLOR HIMSELF, AND HIS GOALS IN OFFICE. AS THIS STUDY WILL REVEAL, AN ORGANIC LINK EXISTS BETWEEN THE CHANCELLOR'S POLICY GOALS AND LEADERSHIP STYLE AND THE ORGANIZATION AND EFFECTIVENESS OF THE CHANCELLORY.

01500 BERRY, W.D.; LOWERY, D.
CONVERGENCE AND DIVERGENCE IN EMPIRICAL ANALYSES OF FISCAL POLITICS
AMERICAN POLITICS QUARTERLY, 17(4) (OCT 89), 446-475.
IN RECENT YEARS A NUMBER OF SUBLITERATURES ON FISCAL POLITICS HAVE CONVERGED TOWARD A CORE SET OF HYPOTHESIZED EXPLANATORY VARIABLES - REPRESENTING POLITICAL, ECONOMIC, AND SOCIAL CONDITIONS - AND A COMMON MODELING STRATEGY. BUT, RATHER THAN INDICATING A CONSENSUS ABOUT THE NATURE OF DECISION MAKING, THE CONVERGENCE MASKS DIVERGENCE. THIS ARTICLE DESCRIBES THE DEVELOPMENT OF THIS DIVERGENCE IN ASSUMPTIONS IN AN EFFORT TO EVALUATE ITS IMPACT ON EMPIRICAL MODELING EXERCISES. IT CONCLUDES WITH SOME PRESCRIPTIONS FOR DEFINING THE RESEARCH AGENDA FOR THE BUDGETING LITERATURE THROUGH THE 1990S,

01501 BERTHOIN, G.
DEMOCRATIC GROWTH ON GRIDLOCK?
WASHINGTON QUARTERLY, 12(2) (SPR 89), 183-188.
DEMOCRACY MUST RECONCILE ITSELF WITH NATIONAL SOVEREIGNTY WHICH BY NATURE REJECTS OUTSIDE INTERFERENCE WHILE IT HAS TO ACCEPT AND INTEGRATE THE NECESSITY OF INTERNATIONAL COOPERATION. BECAUSE OF THE PRINCIPLE OF GOVERNMENT OF THE PEOPLE, BY THE PEOPLE, FOR THE PEOPLE, A GOVERNMENT MUST ACCEPT CONTACTS, COOPERATION, AND INTEGRATION WITH OTHER PEOPLES WHO HAVE THE SAME DEMANDS OF SOVEREIGNTY. THIS NEW TYPE OF INTERRELATION AND ITS PRACTICAL CONSEQUENCES SEEM CONTRARY TO SOVEREIGNTY. THE CHALLENGE IS SERIOUS BECAUSE APPLYING THE DEMOCRATIC PRINCIPLE TO THE GLOBAL LEVEL CAN BE PERCEIVED AS BETRAYING THE VERY SOVEREIGNTY OF THE PEOPLE, WHO ARE ACCUSTOMED TO EXPRESSING IT EXCLUSIVELY WITHIN THE LIMIT OF NATIONAL BOUNDARIES.

01502 BESANCON, A.
CAN POLAND EVER BE FREE?
COMMENTARY, 87(4) (APR 89), 15-20.
MOBILIZED, THE 40 MILLION POLES WITH THEIR "CRITICAL MASS" COULD TOTTER THE SOVIET EMPIRE. BUT POLAND IS NOT MOBILIZED. RATHER, IT GIVES THE IMPRESSION OF A PRISONER WHOSE CELL HAS BEEN UNBOLTED BUT WHO NEVERTHELESS REMAINS TRANSFIXED AND ALL BUT IMMOVABLE WITHIN. ONE MAJOR FACTOR IS THE APOLITICAL NATURE OF THE ROMAN CATHOLIC CHURCH, AND ANOTHER IS THE LEADERSHIP OF SOLIDARITY.

01503 BESSMERTNY-ANZIMIROV, A.
THE FINE SOVIET ART OF IMPRESSING RONALD REAGAN
GLASNOST, II(2) (MAR 89), 20-21.
THE AUTHOR REPORTS ON A MEETING OF THE FREEDOM OF RELIGION IN THE USSR DISCUSSION CLUB ON MAY 19, 1988. THE MEETING WAS FILMED BY BOTH SOVIET AND AMERICAN TELEVISION, SO THAT IT COULD BE VIEWED LATER BY U.S. PRESIDENT RONALD REAGAN.

01504 BESTUZHEV-LADA, I.
WHAT IS THERE IN STORE FOR US IN THE 21ST CENTURY: THE DESTINY OF SOCIALISM AND CIVILIZATION
INTERNATIONAL AFFAIRS (MOSCOW), (8) (AUG 89), 82-90.
THE IDEOLOGY OF SCIENTIFIC SOCIALISM HAS BEEN THE MOST SIGNIFICANT AND INFLUENTIAL IN WORLD SOCIAL THOUGHT THROUGHOUT THE TWENTIETH CENTURY. AND THERE IS REASON TO BELIEVE THAT WITHOUT CONSISTENTLY AND FULLY REALIZING THE IDEAS OF SCIENTIFIC SOCIALISM AND COMMUNISM, HUMANITY WILL BE UNABLE TO SOLVE TODAY'S GLOBAL PROBLEMS, TO SURVIVE IN THE NEXT CENTURY, OR EVEN TO SURVIVE IN ITS FIRST DECADES. TO UNDERSTAND THIS, IT IS NECESSARY TO DELVE INTO THE ESSENCE OF CONTEMPORARY GLOBAL PROBLEMS.

01505 BETHELL, T.
GOLDEN STATE OPPORTUNITY

NATIONAL REVIEW, 110(21) (NOV 89), 34.
THIS ARTICLE EXAMINES THE EFFECT THAT CALIFORNIA'S
GUBERNATORIAL 1990 RACE WILL HAVE UPON THE CONTROL OF
CONGRESS AFTER 1992. IT EXPLORES THE ISSUES OF POPULATION
GROWTH, ABORTION, PRO-LIFE, AIDS, INSURANCE REGULATION, AND
WELFARE, AND DECLARES THAT THE 1990 ELECTION RESULTS WILL
TURN ON THE TENSIONS BETWEEN CIVIC VIRTUE AND THE
'COMPASSIONATE' STATE.

01506 BETHELL, T.
JIM BAKER: MINISTERING TO THE MEDIA
NATIONAL REVIEW, XLI(8) (MAY 89), 24-27.
THE AUTHOR PROFILES SECRETARY OF STATE JAMES BAKER AND
SUGGESTS THAT HE IS TOO WILLING TO COOPERATE WITH THE MEDIA
AND WITH CONGRESSIONAL DEMOCRATS.

01507 BETHELL, T.
MILLER TIME: REAGAN'S BUDGET BOSS SPEAKS OUT
REASON, 21(1) (MAY 89), 32-37.
PRESIDENT REAGAN'S DIRECTOR OF THE OFFICE OF MANAGEMENT
AND BUDGET, JAMES C MILLER III, SPEAKS ABOUT VARIOUS
ECONOMIC PROBLEMS AND POLICIES IN THE US. HE DISCUSSES THE
DEFICIT, THE GRAMM-RUDMAN LAW, THE BALANCED BUDGET
AMMENDMENT, AND POTENTIAL TAX INCREASES. HE ARGUES THAT
ALTHOUGH GOOD PEOPLE ARE A NECESSITY IN GOVERNMENT, GOOD
RULES ARE EVEN MORE IMPORTANT. HE ALSO DEFENDS PRIVATIZATION
AS AN IDEA WHOSE "TIME HAS COME."

01508 BETHELL, T.
SOCIALISM BY THE TEXTBOOK
NATIONAL REVIEW, XLI(19) (OCT 89), 36-38.
THE AUTHOR EXPLAINS THAT ALTHOUGH THE BEST-SELLING
ECONOMICS TEXTBOOKS STILL TREAT SOCIALISM AS THE IDEAL
SYSTEM AND COMMUNISM AS ITS IMPERFECT EMBODIMENT, A
CHALLENGE IS COMING FROM CONSERVATIVES ECONOMISTS, AND FROM
MIKHAIL GORBACHEV. THIS ARTICLE EXAMINES THE ECONOMIC
POLICIES AND THEORIES PUT FORWARD IN THE CURRENT TOP TEN
ECONOMIC TEXTBOOKS, INCLUDING NUMBER ONE BEST-SELLING
TEXTBOOK ECONOMICS, BY CAMPBELL MCCONNELL.

01509 BETHELL, T.
THE COLONY OF EL SALVADOR
AMERICAN SPECTATOR, 22(5) (MAY 89), 11-13.
THE MOST IMPORTANT TASK FACING THE U.S. TODAY IS
PROMOTING FREEMARKET, PRIVATE-PROPERTY BASED ECONOMIES
ABROAD, PARTICULARLY IN LATIN AMERICA. RECENTLY, HOWEVER,
THE MOST SERIOUS OBSTRUCTION TO SUCH PROGRESS HAS ITSELF
ORIGINATED IN THE U.S. AMERICA INJECTED A POISONOUS DOSE OF
HOMEOPATHIC MEDICINE INTO EL SALVADOR, WITH VERY BAD RESULTS.
THE U.S. ALSO PRESCRIBED ELECTIONS, AND THE GOOD NEWS IS
THAT, IN MARCH, ALFREDO CHRISTIANI'S ARENA PARTY WON THE
PRESIDENTIAL CONTEST. NOW THEY CAN RID THEMSELVES OF THIS
POISON.

01510 BETTO, F.
FAITH AND POLITICS
WORLD MARXIST REVIEW, 32(10) (OCT 89), 53-55.
THIS ARTICLE IS ANSWERS TO QUESTIONS PUT TO FREI BETTO,
A BRAZILIAN CLERGYMAN. IT ADDRESSES WHAT MARXIST IDEAS ARE
ESPECIALLY RELEVANT TO THE FAITH, ATHEISM IN GENERAL, WHAT
CATHOLICISM CAN DO TO OVERCOME CIVILIZATION TODAY IN A
CRISIS, THE WORLD MORAL CLIMATE, NONVIOLENCE, LIBERATION
THEOLOGY AND THE PROCESSES OF DEMOCRATISATION.

01511 BETTS, R.K.
NATO'S MID-LIFE CRISIS
FOREIGN AFFAIRS, 68(2) (SPR 89), 37-52.
THE CHALLENGE FOR NATO NOW IS HOW TO KEEP ITSELF IN
SHAPE WHILE REACTING SENSIBLY TO SOVIETY INITIATIVES.
KEEPING IN SHAPE MEANS AVOIDING DAMAGE TO THE ORGANIZATION'S
MILITARY POSITION. WHICH COULD BE SQUEEZED BETWEEN ZEALOUS
HAWKS FORCING TOO MUCH ATTENTION ON CONTROVERSIAL STRATEGIC
PROBLEMS AND ENTHUSIASTIC DOVES ARGUING THAT EXCESSIVE
DEVOTION TO DETERRENCE OR DEFENSE WILL BLOCK PEACE RATHER
THAN GUARD IT.

01512 BEURY, K.
INTERSTATE TRASH DISPOSAL EXAMINED
AMERICAN CITY AND COUNTY, 104(4) (APR 89), 14.
A BILL HAS BEEN INTRODUCED IN CONGRESS THAT WOULD
PROHIBIT A STATE FROM SHIPPING ITS GARBAGE TO ANOTHER STATE
WITHOUT THE TARGETED JURISDICTION'S CONSENT. STATES CANNOT
REGULATE INTER-STATE COMMERCE, AND COURTS HAVE RULED THAT A
STATE CURRENTLY CANNOT BAN OUT-OF-STATE WASTE. UNDER THE
PROPOSED LEGISLATION, CONGRESS WOULD GIVE STATES THE
AUTHORITY TO REGULATE SOLID WASTE CROSSING THEIR BORDERS AND
STATES WOULD BE ABLE TO REFUSE OUT-OF-STATE SOLID WASTE
WITHOUT VIOLATING THE U.S. CONSTITUTION.

01513 BEURY, K.
REACTIONS MIXED TO BUSH BAILOUT
AMERICAN CITY AND COUNTY, 104(5) (MAY 89), 14.
WHILE THE BUSH ADMINISTRATION IS ATTACKING A PROBLEM THE
FEDERAL GOVERNMENT HAS LONG IGNORED--RESCUING THE NATION'S

INSOLVENT SAVINGS AND LOANS--LOCAL OFFICIALS FEAR AMERICAN
CITIES AND COUNTRIES MAY FOOT THE BILL. BUSH'S BAILOUT PLAN
REVOLVES AROUND THE SALE OF $50 BILLION IN GOVERNMENT BONDS
TO COMPLEMENT THE $40 BILLION COMMITTED BY THE REAGAN
ADMINISTRATION. TAXPAYERS WILL PAY THE INTEREST ON THESE
BONDS. BECAUSE THE BAILOUT IS ESTIMATED TO COST IN THE RANGE
OF $200 BILLION AND BUSH HAS NOT PROPOSED ANY NEW TAXES TO
COVER THE COST, OFFICIALS EXPECT FEDERAL FUNDS FOR LOCAL
GOVERNMENT PROGRAMS MAY PAY INTEREST ON THE BONDS. THE
FEDERAL GOVERNMENT'S ENTRY INTO THE MONEY MARKET MAY PUSH
INTEREST RATES HIGHER, ADDING TO THE COST OF BORROWING BY
LOCAL GOVERNMENTS.

01514 BEVIR, M.
FABIANISM AND THE THEORY OF RENT
HISTORY OF POLITICAL THOUGHT, X(2) (SUM 89), 313-327.
IN THIS ARTICLE THE AUTHOR CENTENDS FIRST THAT THE
LEADING FABIANS HAD DIFFERENT THEORIES OF RENT. SECOND
THATTHESE DIFFERENT THEORIES ARE LINKED TO DIFFERENT REASONS
FOR BEING PARLIAMENTARY GRADUALISTS, DIFFERENT VIEWS OF HOW
TO SECURE PARLIAMENTARY POWER AND DIFFERENT VISIONS OFA
SOCIALIST SOCIETY. THUS, IF THERE IS A DISTINCTIVE FABIAN
SOCIALISM IT DOES NOT REST ON A SHARED THEORY OF RENT. ITS
SOPHISTICATION AND HOW IT FORMED THE BASIS FOR S

01515 BEYME, K.V.
REFORM AND REGIONAL POLICIES IN THE SOVIET UNION
JOURNAL OF COMMUNIST STUDIES, 5(3) (SEP 89), 267-285.
PERESTROIKA HAS BROUGHT NEW APPROACHES TO REGIONAL
POLICY IN THE SOVIET UNION, ALTHOUGH THE TENDENCY FOR
DECENTRALIZATION ON ONE LEVEL TO BE ACCOMPANIED BY
CENTRALIZATION ON ANOTHER LINGERS ON, AS DOES THE MISMATCH
BETWEEN THE IMPERATIVES OF ECONOMIC EFFICIENCY AND THE
DEMANDS FOR AUTONOMY. IN THE PAST, TOC, ECONOMIC EFFICIENCY
HAS BEEN SET ASIDE FOR POLITICAL REASONS. GORBACHEV IS
ATTEMPTING TO CHANGE THIS THROUGH STRENGTHENING LOCAL
LEADERSHIPS. THIS HAS LED TO OPEN CRITICISM OF INDIVIDUAL
REPUBLICS, AND TO A SHAKE-OUT OF PERSONNEL AT REPUBLIC LEVEL
IN FAVOUR OF AN INCREASE AT REGIONAL AND LOCAL LEVEL. THE
DIVERSITY OF DEVELOPMENTAL POLICIES FOLLOWED BY THE
REPUBLICS IN THE PAST IS LIKELY TO GROW. AS FOR THE GAP
BETWEEN RICH AND POOR REGIONS, AN EXAMINATION OF INCOME,
ECONOMIC DEVELOPMENT AND SOCIAL PROVISION YIELDS INTERESTING
DIFFERENTIAL RESULTS.

01516 BEZYMENSKY, L.
HITLER'S PROPOSAL TO LONDON, AUGUST 1939
INTERNATIONAL AFFAIRS (MOSCOW), (9) (SEP 89), 38-48.
THE AUTHOR RECOUNTS A MEETING BETWEEN ADOLF HITLER,
ALBRECHT FORSTER, AND CARL BURCKHARDT ON AUGUST 11, 1939.
BURCKHARDT WAS THE HIGH COMMISSIONER OF THE LEAGUE OF
NATIONS IN THE "FREE CITY" OF DANZIG AND A SWISS DIPLOMAT.
FORSTER WAS THE NAZI GAULEITER OF DANZIG. THE MEETING WAS
VERY IMPORTANT IN UNDERSTANDING THE EXPLOSIVE POLITICAL
SITUATION IN EUROPE IN THE SUMMER AND AUTUMN OF 1939.

01517 BHAGWATI, J.N.
NATION -- STATES IN A INTERNATIONAL FRAMEWORK: AN
ECONOMIST'S PRESPECTIVE
ALTERNATIVES, XIV(2) (APR 89), 231-244.
THE AUTHOR ANALYZES THE POSITION OF THE NATION-STATE IN
THE INTERNATIONAL CONTEXT, FROM THE VIEWPOINT OF HOW
NATIONAL SOVEREIGNTY MUST BE CONSIDERED IN THAT WIDER MILIEU.
FOCUS IS ON THE KEY RESPECTS IN WHICH THE WORLD ECONOMY HAS
WITNESSED INCREASED INTERACTION OR "GLOBALIZATION" AND ON
THE VARIOUS IMPLICATIONS FOR SOVEREIGNTY.

01518 BHATIA, S.; HURTADO, M.E.
BACK TO BASICS
SOUTH, (107) (SEP 89), 101.
INDIA'S UNEVEN DEVELOPMENT, IN WHICH MASS POVERTY
COEXISTS WITH HIGHLY ADVANCED TECHNOLOGIES, IS REFLECTED IN
ITS EDUCATIONAL SYSTEM. SINCE INDEPENDENCE, THE EMPHASIS HAS
BEEN ON CREATING AN EDUCATED ELITE RATHER THAN ON PROVIDING
MASS PRIMARY EDUCATION. EDUCATORS BLAME THE PROBLEM ON THE
FAILURE OF CENTRAL AND STATE GOVERNMENTS TO IMPLEMENT
GRANDIOSE PLANS FOR IMPROVING EDUCATIONAL OPPORTUNITIES.

01519 BHATIA, S.
FIRST SEEDS OF THE CORPORATE CULTURE
SOUTH, (102) (APR 89), 34-35.
RAJIV GANDHI'S WESTERN-ORIENTED REFORMS HAVE PRODUCED A
NEW CORPORATE SCENE IN INDIA. AN UNPRECEDENTED BOOM IN THE
INDIAN STOCK MARKETS HAS BEEN FUELED BY LIBERALIZATION
POLICIES THAT HAVE TRANSFORMED THE FINANCIAL SCENE. NOW
OBSERVERS ARE URGING THE LIFTING OF FOREIGN EXCHANGE
RESTRICTIONS TO COMPLETE THE PROCESS.

01520 BHATIA, S.
INDIGENOUS DEFENCE OF THE REALM
SOUTH, (109) (NOV 89), 81.
IN MAY 1989, INDIA JOINED THE INTERMEDIATE-RANGE
BALLISTIC MISSILE CLUB WHEN IT FIRED AN INDIGENOUSLY
DEVELOPED SURFACE-TO-SURFACE MISSILE WITH A RANGE OF ABOUT 2,

500KM. INDIA'S MISSILE PROGRAM HAS DRAWN CRITICISM FROM WASHINGTON, AND THE CIA CLAIMS THAT THE NEW MISSILE'S MAIN COMPONENTS ARE BASED ON IMPORTED TECHNOLOGY. CIA ANALYSTS HAVE ALSO BEEN REPORTED AS SAYING THAT THE DESIGN RESEMBLES AMERICAN ROCKETS OF THE 1960'S, BUT INDIA DENIES THIS.

01521 BHATIA, V.G.
ASIAN AND PACIFIC DEVELOPING ECONOMIES: PERFORMANCE AND ISSUES
ASIAN DEVELOPMENT REVIEW, 6(1) (1988), 1-21.
THIS ARTICLE REPORTS ON THE DEVELOPMENT OF COUNTRIES IN THE ASIAN AND PACIFIC REGIONIT REVIEWS THEIR PAST ECONOMIC PERFORMANCE AND ASSESSES FUTURE PROSPECTS. UNDER GROWTH PERFORMANCE AND QUALITY OF LIFE THE FOLLOWING CORRELATIONS ARE DETAILED: 1) PERCAPITA INCOME AND LIFE EXPECTANCY, 2) PERCAPITA INCOME AND LITERACY, 3) SECONDARY AND HIGHER EDUCATION, 4) CALORIE SUPPLY AND FOOD PRODUCTION, 5) DEMOGRAPHY AND FERTILITY, AND 6) URBANIZATION.

01522 BHATT, E.
TOWARD EMPOWERMENT
WORLD DEVELOPMENT, 17(7) (JUL 89), 1059-1065.
SOME 94 PERCENT OF WORKING WOMEN IN INDIA ARE SELF-EMPLOYED-AS HOME-BASED WORKERS, PETTY TRADERS, OR PROVIDERS OF OTHER SERVICES AND MANUAL LABOR. THEY ARE UNDERCOUNTED IN OFFICIAL STATISTICS, UNPROTECTED BY LABOR LAWS, WITHOUT ACCESS TO HELTH CARE, SKILLS TRAINING, OR CREDIT. THEIR SITUATION WORSENS AS TRADITIONAL SUPPORT SYSTEMS BREAK DOWN. SEWA - THE SELFEMPLOYED WOMEN'S ASSOCIATION - WAS FORMED AS A TRADE UNION TO GIVE THESE WOMEN POLITICAL VISIBILITY AND POWER OVER THE FORCES THAT CONTROL THEIR LIVES. EACH STAGE OF THE ORGANIZING PROCESS HAS BEEN, AND CONTINUES TO BE, A STRUGGLE. BUT IT IS SUCCEEDING.

01523 BHATT, G.
EUROPE 1992
FINANCE AND DEVELOPMENT, 26(2) (JUN 89), 40-42.
THE ARTICLE EXAMINES THE EFFORTS OF THE EUROPEAN COMMUNITY TO REMOVE ALL EXISTING BARRIERS IMPEDING THE FREE FLOW OF GOODS, SERVICES, CAPITAL, AND LABOR AMONG MEMBER COUNTRIES. IT DISCUSSES THE PROGRESS THAT HAS BEEN MADE ON SEVERAL OF THE PROPOSALS IN THE "WHITE PAPER" INCLUDING PROGRESS IN THE AREAS OF BORDER CONTROLS. TECHNICAL STANDARDS, PUBLIC PROCUREMENT, FREE MOVEMENT OF LABOR, FREE CAPITAL MOBILITY, AND FINANCIAL SERVICES. IT ALSO DISCUSSES SOME OF THE REMAINING OBSTACLES TO FULL ECONOMIC INTEGRATION AS WELL AS THE IMPLICATIONS FOR THE REST OF THE WORLD THAT THESE EFFORTS HAVE.

01524 BHATTACHARYA, D.
GROWTH AND DISTRIBUTION IN INDIA
JOURNAL OF CONTEMPORARY ASIA, 19(2) (1989), 150-166.
IT IS MORE THAN FOUR DECADES SINCE INDIA BECAME INDEPENDENT ON 15 AUGUST, 1947. THE CENTRAL PURPOSE OF THIS ARTICLE IS TO DESCRIBE AND ANALYSE INDIAN ECONOMIC GROWTH AND DISTRIBUTION SINCE INDEPENDENCE. THE FIRST SECTION STARTS WITH DEFINITIONS OF "GROWTH" AND "DISTRIBUTION." A VERY BRIEF DESCRIPTION OF THE OBJECTIVES OF INDIAN ECONOMIC DEVELOPMENT WILL BE MADE, WHILE THE ACHIEVEMENTS OF INDIAN ECONOMY WILL BE CRITICALLY ANALYSED IN SECTION 2. THE PROBLEMS OF DISTRIBUTION WILL BE EXPLAINED IN SECTION 3. FINALLY, SOME OBSERVATIONS, CONCLUSIONS AND POLICY RECOMMENDATIONS WILL BE SUGGESTED IN SECTION 4.

01525 BHATTACHARYA, S.
COMINTERN, M.N. ROY AND THE CHINESE REVOLUTION
CHINA REPORT, 24(4) (OCT 88), 405-418.
DURING THE LAST DECADE OR SO THERE HAS BEEN A SPECIAL EMPHASIS IN THE SOVIET UNION TO DISCREDIT M.N. ROY AND THE CHINESE COMMUNIST PARTY AND TO HOLD THEM RESPONSIBLE FOR THE FIASCO IN CHINA IN THE TWENTIES, AND TO LAUD THE ROLE OF THE SOVIET GOVERNMENT IN ORDER TO COUNTERACT DISILLUSIONMENT AMONG THE COMMUNISTS IN THE COUNTRIES OF ASIA, AFRICA AND LATIN AMERICA ABOUT THE POLICY AND ACTIONS OF THE SOVIET COMMUNIST PARTY AND THE SOVIET GOVERNMENT. THIS ARTICLE IS CONFINED TO THE UNDERSTANDING OF THE POLICY OF THE COMINTERN ON COLONIAL LIBERATION MOVEMENTS, M.N. ROY'S ROLE IN SHAPING IT AND ITS APPLICATION IN CHINA.

01526 BHAVE, A.B.
THE NEWLOOK PLA
CHINA REPORT, 25(2) (APR 89), 161-169.
THIS ARTICLE DEALS WITH THE IMPLEMENTATION OF A RANK SYSTEM IN THE PEOPLE'S LIBERATION ARMY (PLA) SINCE 1939 AND DURING THE KOREAN WAR AND THE SINO-SOVIET WAR. THE ABOLITION OF RANKS OCCURED DURING THE GREAT CULTURAL REVOLUTION AND REINSTATED BY DENG'S REFORM OF THE PLA. IT CONCLUDES THAT REFORM IS INDICATIVE OF THE GREAT TRANSFORMATIONS TAKING PLACE IN ALL SPHERES OF LIFE IN CHINA.

01527 BHAVNANI, K.
COMPLEXITY, ACTIVISM, OPTIMISM: AN INTERVIEW WITH ANGELA Y. DAVIS
FEMINIST REVIEW, (31) (SPR 89), 66-81.

IN THIS INTERVIEW, ANGELA DAVIS DISCUSSES HER MEMBERSHIP IN THE COMMUNIST PARTY, THE POLITICAL STRUGGLES OF THE LATE 1960'S, AND RELATED TOPICS.

01528 BHEENICK, R.; BONKOUNGOU, E.G.; HILL, C.B.; MCFARLAND, E.L.; MOKGETHI, D.N.
SUCCESSFUL DEVELOPMENT IN AFRICA: CASE STUDIES OF PROJECTS, PROGRAMS AND POLICIES
AVAILABLE FROM NTIS, NO. PB89-196810/GAR, MAR 89, 222.
THE COLLECTION OF CASE STUDIES EXAMINES A VARIETY OF SUCCESSFUL DEVELOPMENT PROJECTS, PROGRAMS, OR POLICY ACTIONS UNDERTAKEN IN A NUMBER OF AFRICAN COUNTRIES. EACH STUDY ANALYZES THE PROBLEMS THAT A SPECIFIC DEVELOPMENT ACTIVITY ADDRESSED, THE EXPERIENCE IN CARRYING OUT THE ACTIVITY, THE DEGREE OF SUCCESS, AND POSSIBLE IMPLICATIONS FOR SIMILAR ACTIVITIES IN OTHER SETTINGS. THE FOLLOWING STUDIES ARE PRESENTED: BURKINA FASO: THE PROJECT AGRO-FORESTIER--A CASE STUDY OF AGRICULTURAL RESEARCH AND EXTENSION; WEST AFRICA: THE ONCHOCERCIASIS CONTROL PROGRAM; MALAWI: LESSONS FROM THE GRAVITY-FED PIPED WATER SYSTEM; KENYA: A CASE STUDY OF THE PRODUCTION AND EXPORT OF HORTICULTURAL COMMODITIES; MAURITIUS: A CASE STUDY OF THE EXPORT PROCESSING ZONE; GHANA: ECONOMIC RECOVERY PROGRAM-A CASE STUDY OF STABILIZATION AND STRUCTURAL ADJUSTMENT IN SUB-SAHARAN AFRICA; AND BOTSWANA: MACROECONOMIC MANAGEMENT OF COMMODITY BOOMS, 1975-86.

01529 BHUTANI, V.C.
SOURCES OF FRONTIER STUDIES: THE NORTH-EAST FRONTIER OF INDIA
CHINA REPORT, 24(3) (JUL 88), 299-375.
THE HISTORY OF THE MAKING OF INDIA'S NORTHERN BOUNDARY CAN BE STUDIED FROM THE RECORDS OF THE GOVERNMENT SUPPLEMENTED BY DARY MAKING. IN THIS PAPER AN ATTEMPT IS MADE TO IDENTIFY THE SOURCES AND FACTORS RELEVANT TO THE STUDY OF THE NORTH-EASTERN BOUNDARY OF INDIA. THE BOUNDARY HERE CONSIDERED IS GEOGRAPHICALLY THE BOUNDARY BETWEEN EASTERN TIBET AND THE BRITISH PROVINCES OF ASSAM AND BURMA. EXTRACTS (APPENDIX PART III) ARE SPECIFICALLY SELECTED TO DEMONSTRATE HOW DECISIONS AS TO THE BOUNDARY WHICH LATER BECOME KNOWN AS THE MCMAHON LINE HERE TAKEN.

01530 BHUYAN, B.C.
DISTRICT COUNCIL AND THE STATE GOVENMENT: KARBI ANGLONG DISTRICT COUNCIL AND THE GOVERNMENT OF ASSAM
INDIAN JOURNAL OF POLITICAL SCIENCE, L(2) (APR 89), 221-233.
THE DISTRICT COUNCIL IS AN AUTONOMOUS BODY CREATED UNDER THE PROVISIONS OF THE SIXTH SCHEDULE TO THE CONSTITUTION AND DESIGNED TO WORK WITHIN THE FRAMEWORK OF THE STATE GOVERNMENT. USING THE KARBI ANGLONG DISTRICT COUNCIL OF ASSAM AS A CASE STUDY, THIS PAPER STUDIES THE RELATIONSHIP BETWEEN THE COUNCIL AND THE STATE GOVERNMENT. THE RELATIONS ARE LEGISLATIVE, EXECUTIVE, ADMINISTRATIVE, FINANCIAL, JUDICIAL, AND TECHNICAL IN NATURE.

01531 BIALER, S.
THE DOMESTIC AND INTERNATIONAL SOURCES OF GORBACHEV'S REFORMS
JOURNAL OF INTERNATIONAL AFFAIRS, 42(2) (SPR 89), 283-298.
IN WESTERN WRITINGS ON THE REFORMS OF MIKHAIL GORBACHEV, THERE IS A TENDENCY TO ASCRIBE THESE CHANGES PRIMARILY OR EVEN EXCLUSIVELY TO DOMESTIC FACTORS. THE AUTHOR ARGUES THAT SUCH ANALYSES ARE UNNECESSARILY ONE-SIDED AND SEEKS TO EXAMINE NOT ONLY THE DOMESTIC SOURCES OF SOVIET REFORM, BUT THE INTERNATIONAL SOURCES AS WELL. THE DOMESTIC SOURCES INCLUDE: THE DOMESTIC PERFORMANCE OF THE SOVIET SYSTEM DURING THE BREZHNEV ERA, THE NEW AND NECESSARY CONDITIONS OF SOVIET ECONOMIC GROWTH UNDER CONTEMPORARY CIRCUMSTANCES, AND THE CHANGED NATURE OF SOVIET SOCIETY. INTERNATIONAL FACTORS INCLUDE THE SOVIET LEADERSHIP'S TENDENCY TO EVALUATE THEIR DOMESTIC ACCOMPLISHMENTS AGAINST THE BACKGROUND OF ECONOMIC TRENDS IN THE CAPITALIST WORLD AND THE STRUCTURAL LIMITATIONS IMPOSED BY DECLINING SOVIET CAPABILITIES IN THE GLOBAL ARENA.

01532 BIANCHI, R.
ISLAM AND DEMOCRACY IN EGYPT
CURRENT HISTORY, 88(535) (FEB 89), 93-95, 104.
A MAJOR REASON WHY THE GOVERNMENT OF PRESIDENT HOSNI MUBARAK HAS BEEN SO WILLING TO SEEK AN ACCOMMODATION WITH ITS RELIGIOUS OPPONENTS IS THE REALIZATION THAT THE 'ISLAMIC AWAKENING' IS NOT AN ALIEN AND INHERENTLY SUBVERSIVE FORCE BUT THE CONTINUATION OF LONGSTANDING MOVEMENTS THAT CONTAIN MANY ELEMENTS COMPATIBLE WITH THE DEVELOPMENT OF CAPITALISM AND DEMOCRACY.

01533 BIANCO, W.T.
DOING THE POLITICALLY RIGHT THING: RESULTS, BEHAVIOR, AND VOTE TRADING
THE JOURNAL OF POLITICS, 51(4) (NOV 89), 886-889.
THE CURRENT UNDERSTANDING OF VOTE TRADING ASSUMES LEGISLATORS' PAYOFFS VARY ONLY WITH RESULTS--THE MOTIONS ENACTED OR DEFEATED BY THEIR VOTES. THIS CHARACTERIZATION IS NOT SUPPORTED BY EVIDENCE FROM THE MODERN CONGRESS. THIS

PAPER SPECIFIES A MODEL OF VOTE TRADING IN WHICH
LEGISLATORS' PAYOFFS ARE A FUNCTION OF RESULTS AND VOTING
BEHAVIOR. ANALYSIS OF THIS GAME AMENDS THE STANDARD WISDOM
ABOUT VOTING AND VOTE TRADING IN TWO AREAS: THE EXISTENCE OF
A NONEMPTY CORE, AND THE CONDITIONS UNDER WHICH
SOPHISTICATED VOTING PRODUCES AN OUTCOME IN THE CORE.

01534 BICK, M.M.
THE LIBERAL-COMMUNITARIAN DEBATE: A DEFENCE OF HOLISTIC
INDIVIDUALISM
DISSERTATION ABSTRACTS INTERNATIONAL, 50(1) (JUL 89),
245-A.
THE AUTHOR ANALYZES THE DEBATE BETWEEN CERTAIN LIBERAL
AUTHORS AND A GROUP OF THEIR CRITICS, WHO HAVE BECOME KNOWN
AS "COMMUNITARIANS." SHE STUDIES THE THEORIES OF JOHN RAWLS,
RONALD DWORKIN, CHARLES TAYLOR, MICHAEL SANDEL, MICHAEL
WALZER, AND ALASDAIR MACINTYRE.

01535 BICKERS, K.N.
THE POLITICS OF REGULATORY DESIGN: TELECOMMUNICATIONS
REGULATION IN HISTORICAL AND THEORETICAL PERSPECTIVE
DISSERTATION ABSTRACTS INTERNATIONAL, 49(8) (FEB 89),
2373-A.
THIS DISSERTATION ANALYZES THE POLITICAL PROCESSES
UNDERLYING THE DESIGN OF GOVERNMENT INSTITUTIONS FOR THE
REGULATION OF THE AMERICAN TELECOMMUNICATIONS INDUSTRY
DURING THE PAST CENTURY. THE DEVELOPMENT OF REGULATORY
INSTITUTIONS HAS REQUIRED A REAPPRAISAL OF EARLIER VIEWS
ABOUT THE APPROPRIATE ROLE OF THE STATE IN THE ECONOMY AND A
RENEGOTIATION OF THE EXISTING RELATIONSHIPS BETWEEN THE
COURTS, THE CONGRESS, AND THE EXECUTIVE BRANCH.

01536 BIDDICK, T.V.
DIPLOMATIC RIVALRY IN THE SOUTH PACIFIC: THE PRC AND TAIWAN
ASIAN SURVEY, 29(8) (AUG 89), 800-815.
THIS ARTICLE BRIEFLY EXAMINES THE HISTORICAL BACKGROUND
OF CHINESE IMMIGRATION IN THE SOUTH PACIFIC; THE DIPLOMATIC
RIVALRY BETWEEN BEIJING AND TAIPEI IN THE 1970S AND 1980S,
WITH PARTICULAR REFERENCE TO THE SOLOMON ISLANDS AND FIJI;
AND THE EVOLUTION OF PRC FOREIGN POLICY THEMES DURING THIS
PERIOD. THE PRIMARY THESIS IS THAT BEIJING AND TAIPEI HAVE
BEEN AND REMAIN MOST IMMEDIATELY CONCERNED WITH THEIR
COMPETITION FOR DIPLOMATIC RECOGNITION AND POLITICAL
INFLUENCE IN THE SOUTH PACIFIC AND THAT ECONOMIC MOTIVATIONS
HAVE BEEN A SECONDARY FACTOR. AT THE SAME TIME, THE PRC
VIEWS THE REGION IN A LARGER GEOSTRATEGIC CONTEXT AS AN
ARENA OF CONTENTION BY THE MAJOR POWERS, INCLUDING THE
SOVIET UNION. IN ADDITION TO THE INHERENT GEOGRAPHIC
IMPORTANCE OF THE SOUTH PACIFIC IN TERMS OF MARITIME
STRATEGY BEIJING IS INTERESTED IN ACCESS TO THE REGION'S
FISHERY AND SEABED RESOURCES. IN THE LONG RUN, THE RRC IS
LIKELY TO PLAY A LARGER ROLE AS A MARITIME POWER, RAISING
NEW QUESTIONS FOR THIS REGION OF TRADITIONAL WESTERN
INFLUENCE.

01537 BIDDISS, M.
POLITICAL JUDGMENT IN HISTORICAL PERSPECTIVE: THE EPOCH OF
THE GREAT WAR AS CASE STUDY
GOVERNMENT AND OPPOSITION, 24(4) (AUT 89), 401-412.
THE AUTHOR USES THE CONCEPT OF "UNDERCOMPREHENSION" TO
REVIEW SOME OF THE PRINCIPAL FEATURES OF THE EUROPEAN
EXPERIENCE DURING 1910-1920, A DECADE WHEN THE FRAILTIES OF
JUDGMENT DENOTED BY THE TERM WERE SINGULARLY CATASTGROPHIC
IN THEIR EFFECTS.

01538 BIDDLE, T.D.
HANDLING THE SOVIET THREAT: "PROJECT CONTROL" AND THE
DEBATE ON AMERICAN STRATEGY IN THE EARLY COLD WAR YEARS
JOURNAL OF STRATEGIC STUDIES, 12(3) (SEP 89), 273-302.
BETWEEN 1953 AND 1954 COLONEL RAYMOND S. SLEEPER OF THE
UNITED STATES AIR FORCE HEADED A STUDY AT THE AIR WAR
COLLEGE CALLED "PROJECT CONTROL." PROJECT CONTROL ADVOCATED
A UNIQUE METHOD OF HANDLING THE SOVIET THREAT: TAKING
CONTROL OF SOVIET AIR SPACE AND OFFERING A SERIES OF
ULTIMATA DESIGNED TO RADICALLY CHANGE SOVIET POLITICAL
BEHAVIOR. IF THE SOVIETS RESISTED, THEY WOULD BE EXPOSED TO
INCREASING PRESSURE, WHICH MIGHT CULMINATE IN A LARGE-SCALE
ATOMIC BOMBING CAMPAIGN. THIS ESSAY LOOKS AT WHAT PROJECT
CONTROL REVEALS ABOUT AIR FORCE THOUGHT AND ABOUT THE PERIOD
IN WHICH IT WAS WRITTEN.

01539 BIDDLE, W.J.; STEPHENS, J.D.
DEPENDENT DEVELOPMENT AND FOREIGN POLICY: THE CASE OF
JAMAICA
INTERNATIONAL STUDIES QUARTERLY, 33(4) (DEC 89), 411-434.
DEPENDENCY THEORY CONTENDS THAT THIRD WORLD STATES WHICH
ARE ECONOMICALLY DEPENDENT ON CORE CAPITALIST COUNTRIES WILL
DEVELOP FOREIGN POLICY POSITIONS CONSISTENT WITH THE
INTERESTS OF CORE COUNTRIES. ECONOMIC DEPENDENCE PRODUCES
THIS OUTCOME, IT IS ARGUED, BECAUSE THE STRUCTURES OF
DEPENDENCE PRODUCE ECONOMIC AND POLITICAL ELITES IN THE
PERIPHERAL COUNTRIES WHOSE INTERESTS COINCIDE WITH THOSE OF
MULTINATIONAL CORPORATIONS AND CORE COUNTRY POLITICAL ELITES.
THIS ARTICLE EXAMINES THE CASE OF JAMAICA, WHICH, ALTHOUGH

EXTREMELY DEPENDENT ECONOMICALLY ON THE UNITED STATES, HAS
EXPERIENCED DRAMATIC CHANGES IN ITS FOREIGN POLICY SINCE ITS
INDEPENDENCE IN 1962. THE CAUSES OF THESE CHANGES ARE
EXAMINED BASED ON INTERVIEWS WITH JAMAICAN ELITES IN 1962,
1974, AND 1982, ON HISTORICAL EVIDENCE, AND ON INTERVIEWS
WITH AMERICAN POLICY MAKERS AND ALUMINUM COMPANY EXECUTIVES.
THE EVIDENCE SHOWS THAT THOUGH THE JAMAICAN BUSINESS ELITE
STRONGLY FAVORED A VERY PRO-U.S. FOREIGN POLICY THROUGHOUT
THE PERIOD, A LARGE SEGMENT OF THE POLITICAL ELITE
AFFILIATED WITH MICHAEL MANLEY'S PEOPLE'S NATIONAL PARTY
MOVED TO A MILITANTLY THIRD WORLD-ORIENTED POSITION THAT
INCLUDED A MAJOR OFFENSIVE AGAINST THE ALUMINUM
MULTINATIONALS WHEN THE PARTY WAS IN POWER IN THE 1970S. IT
IS ARGUED THAT THIS POLICY CHANGE WAS A DIRECT PRODUCT OF
THE CONTRADICTORY OUTCOMES OF JAMAICA'S SUCCESSFUL PURSUIT
OF A DEPENDENT DEVELOPMENT ECONOMIC STRATEGY IN THE 1950S
AND 1960S, AND THAT SUCH CHALLENGES TO CORE COUNTRY ECONOMIC
INTERESTS IN FOREIGN POLICY ARE AN INHERENT FEATURE OF
DEPENDENT WHICH IS LIKELY TO APPEAR IN OTHER CASES OF
SUCCESSFUL DEPENDENT DEVELOPMENT.

01540 BIEHL, J.
GODDESS MYTHOLOGY IN ECOLOGICAL POLITICS
NEW POLITICS, 11(2) (WIN 89), 84-105.
A NUMBER OF GREENS SEEM TO BE TAKING A DESPAIRING
RECOURSE TO THEISM IN ITS VARIOUS FORMS. RITUALS AND
MEDITATIONS DOT THE AGENDAS OF MANY GREEN, ECOFEMINIST, AND
BIOREGIONAL CONFERENCES. THERE, ACTIVISTS WHO WISH TO
DEVELOP A MOVEMENT TO HALT THE DESTRUCTION OF THE BIOSPHERE
MAY ENCOUNTER THE WORSHIP OF A GODDESS; IN CONTRAST TO A
DEATH-DEALING, ECOCIDAL CULTURE, THEY ARE ASKED TO SEE "LIFE
AND THE WORLD" AS "IMMANENT DIVINITY." A MORAL AND HEALTHY
ECOLOGY MOVEMENT MUST RETAIN ITS REALISM AS WELL AS ITS
IDEALISM, IN THE BEST SENSE OF THE WORD. SUCH A MOVEMENT
SURELY MUST PROVIDE SOCIETY WITH A NEW ECOLOGICAL
SENSIBILITY, BUT NOT ONE THAT IS STRUCTURED AROUND ILLUSION.
A MYSTICAL TENDENCY THAT INDULGES OUR FANTASIES AND SUBTLY
RENDERS US CAPTIVE TO COMMODIFIED SOCIETY MAY EVENTUALLY,
DESPITE ITS GOOD INTENTIONS, DEPRIVE US BOTH OF OUR FREEDOM
AS INDIVIDUALS AND OF OUR ACTIVISM AS SOCIAL BEINGS.

01541 BIENEFELD, M.
THE LESSONS OF HISTORY AND THE DEVELOPING WORLD
MONTHLY REVIEW, 41(3) (JUL 89), 9-41.
THIS PAPER USES KARL POLANYI'S "THE GREAT TRANSFORMATION
AS A REFERENCE TO ADDRESS THE ISSUES DISCUSSED. THE PREMISE
IS POLANYI'S THESIS THAT THE CONCEPT OF THE SELF REGULATING
MARKET IS A DANGEROUS MYTH, AND THAT THE MARKET IS A
WONDERFUL SERVANT BUT A DISASTROUS MASTER. THIS PAPER
CONSIDERS THE PROCESS BY WHICH THESE ALREADY LEARNED LESSONS
WERE FORGOTTEN. IT ASSESSES BOTH THE REAL AND THE
IDEOLOGICAL CHANGES THAT COMBINED TO REVIVE THE MYTH OF THE
SELF REGULATING MARKET.

01542 BIENEN, H.; KAPUR, D.; PARKS, J.; RIEDINGER, J.
DECENTRALIZATION IN NEPAL: PRESPECTIVES OF LOCAL
DEVELOPMENT OFFICERS
INTERNATIONAL REVIEW OF ADMINISTRATIVE SCIENCES, 55(3)
(SEP 89), 433-444.
THE GOVERNMENT IN NEPAL HAS PUT FORWARD MANY NEW
DECENTRALIZATION REFORMS IN THE 1980S. THIS ARTICLE IS THE
ANAYLISES OF A SURVEY CONDUCTED ON MANY CRITICALLY PLACED
LOCAL DEVELOPMENT OFFICERS (LDO) IN NEPAL. THE LDOS ARE LINE
REPRESENATIVES OF A CENTRAL MINISTRY. THEIR RESPONSIBILITIES
INCLUDE, CO-ORDINATING DEVELOPMENT IN THE DISTRICTS OF NEPAL,
WORK WITH ELECTED DISTRICT PANCHANAYATS AND ASSEMBLIES ON
BUDGET, PLANNING AND PROJECT IMPLEMENTATION. THIS ARTICLE
DISCUSSES DECENTRALIZATION IN NEPAL FROM THE LDOS POINT OF
VIEW THEN CONCLUDES THAT THEY HAVE UNREALISTIC EXPECTATIONS.
THE PLANNING PROCEDURES ARE TOO COMPLEX AND DEMANDING GIVEN
THE RESOURCES IN THE NEPALI CONTEXT.

01543 BIENEN, H.; WATERBURY, J.
THE POLITICAL ECONOMY OF PRIVATIZATION IN DEVELOPING
COUNTRIES
WORLD DEVELOPMENT, 17(5) (MAY 89), 617-632.
PRIVATIZATION IN LDCS REFERS TO THE SALE OR LEASING OF
ASSETS IN WHICH THE STATE HAS A MAJORITY INTEREST AND THE
CONTRACTING OUT OF PUBLICLY PROVIDED SERVICES. PRIVATIZATION
IS IN PART A RESPONSE TO THE NEED FOR FISCAL AUSTERITY. ITS
PACE AND SCOPE WILL BE DETERMINED IMPORTANTLY BY THE WAY IN
WHICH THE PUBLIC SECTOR WAS BUILT. PRIVATIZATION IS EASIER
TO IMPLEMENT THAN HAS BEEN SUPPOSED BECAUSE ITS AUSTERITY
AND EQUITY COSTS ARE RELATIVELY SMALL COMPARED TO THOSE OF
BROADER STRUCTURAL ADJUSTMENT PROCESSES IN WHICH IT IS
COMMONLY SITUATED. HOWEVER, THE PAYOFFS FROM PRIVATIZATION
ARE RELATIVELY SMALL TOO. THERE IS HIGH OPPORTUNITY COST IN
TIME AND MANAGEMENT FOR THE COMPLICATED TASK OF PREPARING
PUBLIC ASSETS FOR SALE. CAPITAL MARKET THINNESS
CHARACTERIZES LDCS, AND "POPULAR CAPITALISM" DOES NOT APPEAR
TO BE A REALISTIC OPTION. IN LDCS, PRIVATIZATION IS LIKELY
TO BE ENTANGLED IN REGIONAL AND ETHNIC CONFLICTS. THESE MAY
BE AS CONSEQUENTIAL FOR FORMULATING AND IMPLEMENTING
PROGRAMS AS ARE THE CRITICAL COALITIONS THAT FORM BETWEEN

ECONOMIC SECTORS SUCH AS CAPITAL AND LABOR OR IMPORTERS AND EXPORTERS.

01544 BIENEN, H.; VANDEWALLE, N.
TIME AND POWER IN AFRICA
AMERICAN POLITICAL SCIENCE REVIEW, 83(1) (MAR 89), 19-34.
BOTH RAPID LEADERSHIP TURNOVER AND REMARKABLY DURABLE
LEADERS CAN BE FOUND IN AFRICAN SYSTEMS OF PERSONAL RULE. IN
ORDER TO EXPLAIN DIFFERENCES IN TIME IN POWER AMONG AFRICAN
LEADERS, THE AUTHORS EMPLOY LIFE TABLES ANALYSIS AND HAZARD
MODELS. THEY FIND THAT THE RISK OF LOSING POWER IS A
DECREASING FUNCTION OF TIME THAT IS LITTLE AFFECTED BY
COUNTRY OR LEADER PARTICULARITIES. THE BEST PREDICTOR OF
WHETHER A LEADER WILL LOSE POWER IN ANY GIVEN PERIOD IS THE
LENGTH OF RULE UP TO THAT POINT.

01545 BIENVENUE, R.M.
LANGUAGE POLITICS AND SOCIAL DIVISIONS IN MANITOBA
AMERICAN REVIEW OF CANADIAN STUDIES, 19(2) (SUM 89),
187-202.
THIS ARTICLE BEGINS WITH AN OVERVIEW OF FRENCH-LANGUAGE
RIGHTS IN MANITOBA. THE CENTRAL FOCUS IS HOW THE ISSUES OF
POWER AND LEGITIMATION WERE REFLECTED IN MANITOBA IN 1983-84,
AND HOW VARIOUS SEGMENTS OF THE POPULATION EXPRESSED THEIR
POSITION ON BILINGUALISM. THE ANALYSIS INCLUDES A DISCUSSION
OF TWO MAJOR CONTROVERSIES: CONFLICTING VIEWS CONCERNING THE
SOURCE OF LEGITIMATION FOR A TWO-LANGUAGE POLICY, AND
MINORITY RIGHTS AN THE QUESTION OF POWER. IT IDENTIFIES THE
ROLE OF REGIONALISM AND PREJUDICES IN THE LANGUAGE DEBATE.

01546 BIERMAN, J.; ERASMUS, C.; LOWTHER, W.; SILVER, E.;
WILSON-SMITH, A.
A GLIMPSE OF GREATER PEACE
MACLEAN'S (CANADA'S NEWS MAGAZINE), 102(4) (JAN 89), 34-36.
GEORGE BUSH WILL FACE A LESS MENACING WORLD THAN THE ONE
PRESIDENT RONALD REAGAN FACED IN 1981. UNLIKE THE COLD WAR
CONFRONTATION THAT CHARACTERIZED INTERNATIONAL RELATIONS IN
1981, PRAGMATISM AND CONFLICT RESOLUTION MARK THE CURRENT
TREND TOWARDS INCREASED PEACE. ALTHOUGH TROUBLE SPOTS REMAIN
(PARTICULARLY THE MIDDLE EAST), THE OVERALL INTERNATIONAL
CLIMATE IS MUCH LESS TENSE DUE TO A VARIETY OF FACTORS.
THESE INCLUDE PROGRESS TOWARDS CONFLICT RESOLUTION IN ANGOLA,
AFGHANISTAN, KAMPUCHEA, AND OTHER AREAS; SOVIET ARMS
REDUCTION OVERTURES; AND AN OVERALL WARMING OF RELATIONS
BETWEEN THE US, USSR, AND CHINA.

01547 BIERMAN, J.
FIGHTING BACK
MACLEAN'S (CANADA'S NEWS MAGAZINE), 102(10) (MAR 89), 20.
AGAINST THE ADVICE OF HER SUPPORTERS, WINNIE MANDELA
BATTLED BACK AGAINST HER DETRACTORS. SHE CONDEMNED THOSE WHO
HAD CONDEMNED HER FOR CONDONING--OR PERHAPS EVEN ENCOURAGING-
-THE VIOLENT ACTIONS OF HER BODYGUARDS. ALTHOUGH THE DETAILS
SURROUNDING THE DEATH OF 14-YEAR OLD STOMPIE MOEKETSI MAY
NEVER BE KNOWN, IT IS CLEAR THAT THE AFFAIR HAS CAUSED
INCREASE DIVISION AMONG BLACK FACTIONS.

01548 BIERMAN, J.; DRAKE, C.; LEWIS, P.; LOWTHOL, W.; NEMETH, M.;
SILVER, E.; WILSON-SMITH, A.
GUNNING FOR GADHAFI
MACLEAN'S (CANADA'S NEWS MAGAZINE), 120(3) (JAN 89), 18-19.
FOR THE FOURTH TIME SINCE HE TOOK OFFICE IN JANUARY,
1981, RONALD REAGAN'S COLD WAR AGAINST LIBYAN LEADER MUMMAR
GADHAFI FLARED INTO OPEN CONFLICT AS U.S. JETS SHOT DOWN TWO
LIBYAN WARPLANES OVER THE MEDITERRANEAN. MANY OBSERVERS LINK
THE ATTACK TO FEARS OF A LIBYAN FACTORY THAT WASHINGTON
ALLEGES WAS BUILT TO MASS-PRODUCE CHEMICAL WEAPONS. OTHERS
SEE THE ACTION AS A REACTION TO THE DECEMBER 21 BOMBING OF
PAN AM FLIGHT 103, IN WHICH A PALESTINIAN TERRORIST GROUP
KNOWN TO BE SUPPORTED BY GHADAFI IS A PRIME SUSPECT.
WHATEVER THE MOTIVATION, MANY NATIONS RANGING FROM THE USSR
TO SAUDI ARABIA HAVE DENOUNCED THE U.S. ACTION. SOME
OBSERVERS SEE A POSSIBLE SOURING OF INTERNATIONAL RELATIONS
DUE TO THE INCIDENT.

01549 BIERMAN, J.; HOUSE, R.
MURDER IN THE AMAZON
MACLEAN'S (CANADA'S NEWS MAGAZINE), 102(2) (JAN 89), 21.
FOR YEARS THE CATTLE BARONS OF BARZIL'S REMOTE WESTERN
AMAZONIA HAVE ACKNOWLEDGED ONLY THE LAW OF THE FRONTIER.
THROUGH VIOLENCE AND CORRUPTION THEY HAVE LEVELLED VAST
TRACTS OF RAIN FOREST AND OFTEN HAVE MURDERED ANYONE WHO
STOOD IN THEIR WAY. HOWEVER, THE MURDER OF THEIR MOST
PROMINENT OPPONENT, PEASANT UNION LEADER FRANCISCO MENDES,
THE CATTLE BARONS MAY HAVE GONE TOO FAR. MENDES'S FIGHT HAD
MADE HIM AN INTERNATIONALLY KNOWN FIGURE AMONG
ENVIRONMENTALISTS, AND THE ASSASSINATION SPARKED A WAVE OF
PROTEST THAT, OBSERVERS SAY, MAY AT LAST FORCE THE BRAZILIAN
GOVERNMENT TO REIN IN THE CATTLEMEN AND TRY TO PRESERVE THE
RAPIDLY DWINDLING AMAZON FOREST.

01550 BIERMAN, J.
POISED FOR CHANGE
MACLEAN'S (CANADA'S NEWS MAGAZINE), 102(11) (MAR 89),
18-21.
SOUTH AFRICA--FROM MINORITY WHITE GOVERNMENT TO BLACK
RESISTANCE--SEEMS TO BE IN A STATE OF POLITICAL FLUX
UNPARALLELED SINCE 1948. RULING NATIONAL PARTY LEADER
FREDERICK DE KLERK DECLARED THAT WHITE DOMINATION SHOULD BE
DONE AWAY WITH. BLACK AFRICAN LEADERS DECRIED THE ACTIONS OF
IMPORTANT SYMBOL WINNIE MANDELA. TALK OF REFORM IS THICK IN
THE AIR, BUT MANY MAINTAIN A GUARDED SKEPTICISM. FEARING A
CONSERVATIVE BACKLASH, THE GOVERNMENT REMAINS HESITANT TO
END THE STATE OF EMERGENCY AND REPEAL RACIAL LAWS. HOWEVER,
MOST OBSERVERS VIEW SOUTH AFRICA'S FUTURE WITH OPTIMISM.

01551 BIERMAN, J.; KURLANSKT, M.
POLLING IN PARADISE
MACLEAN'S (CANADA'S NEWS MAGAZINE), 102(6) (FEB 89), 20.
JAMAICA PREPARES FOR A GENERAL ELECTION AND HOPES NOT TO
REPEAT THE CARNAGE THAT FOLLOWED THE ELECTION OF 1980 THAT
CLAIMED THE LIVES OF 500 TO 700 PEOPLE. PRIME MINISTER
EDWARD SEAGA'S JAMAICA LABOUR PARTY AND OPPOSITION LEADER
MICHAEL MANLEY'S PEOPLE'S NATIONAL PARTY HAVE SIGNED AN
ACCORD WHICH RENOUNCES VIOLENCE AND THE TWO LEADERS HAVE MET
TO REAFFIRM THAT PLEDGE. ALTHOUGH THE OUTCOME OF THE
ELECTIONS IS STILL ANYONE'S GUESS, BOTH SIDES WANT PEACEFUL
ELECTIONS SO AS NOT TO DIMINISH THE ECONOMIC BENEFITS OF
JAMAICA'S TOURIST SEASON.

01552 BIERMAN, J.; SILVER, E.
RUNNING OUT OF ANSWERS
MACLEAN'S (CANADA'S NEWS MAGAZINE), 102(6) (FEB 89), 24.
ISRAEL'S LEADERS APPEAR TO BE SUGGESTING THAT THEY ARE
RUNNING OUT OF IDEAS AND METHODS IN THEIR EFFORTS TO STEM
THE INTIFADAH. ISRAEL'S REPUTATION ABROAD HAS SUFFERED
CONSIDERABLY DURING THE 14 MONTH PALESTINIAN UPRISING THAT
HAS CLAIMED THE LIVES OF AT LEAST 352 PALESTINIANS AND 14
ISRAELIS. NEW METHODS AND TACTICS SUCH AS GREATER FREEDOM TO
SHOOT DEMONSTRATORS AND THE USE OF RUBBER BULLETS WITH STEEL
CORES HAVE INCREASED CONTROVERSY, WITH SEEMINGLY LITTLE OR
NO EFFECT ON THE UPRISING.

01553 BIERMAN, J.; THOMPSON, P.
SCANDAL AND STALEMATE
MACLEAN'S (CANADA'S NEWS MAGAZINE), 102(26) (JUL 89), 17.
THE CONSERVATIVE NEW DEMOCRACY PARTY OFFERED GREEK
VOTERS A CHANCE FOR "KATHARSIS," A THOROUGH CLEANSING OF THE
GOVERNMENT, IF THEY WOULD VOTE THE SCANDAL-RIDDEN
PANHELLENIC SOCIALIST MOVEMENT OUT OF OFFICE. THE VOTERS
COMPLIED BY GIVING NEW DEMOCRACY 44 PERCENT OF THE POLL AND
FORCING PRIME MINISTER ANDREAS PANPANDREOU TO RESIGN.
HOWEVER, THEY LEFT THE CONSERVATIVES SIX SEATS SHORT OF A
MAJORITY IN PARLIAMENT. GREECE IS NOW FACED WITH A CLEAN,
BUT DEADLOCKED GOVERNMENT.

01554 BIERMAN, J.
THE CHALLENGE TO SANCTIONS
MACLEAN'S (CANADA'S NEWS MAGAZINE), 102(11) (MAR 89), 24,
26.
DUE TO SOUTH AFRICAN PROFICIENCY AT "SANCTIONS-BUSTING,"
ATTEMPTS BY THE US AND OTHERS TO APPLY POLITICAL PRESSURE
THROUGH TRADE SANCTIONS HAVE NOT YIELDED SIGNIFICANT RESULTS.
EVEN SOME IN THE ANTI-APARTHEID CAMP ARE BEGINNING TO
QUESTION THE EFFICACY AND THE WORTH OF SANCTIONS. SOME ARGUE
THAT SANCTIONS ACTUALLY HURT THE BLACKS THAT THEY ARE TRYING
TO HELP. ONE OBSERVER SUCCINCTLY STATES "SANCTIONS SIMPLY
STOP ECONOMIC GROWTH WITHOUT CHANGING MINDS."

01555 BIERSCHENK, T.
OIL INTERESTS AND THE FORMATION OF CENTRALIZED GOVERNMENT
IN OMAN, 1920-1970
ORIENT, 30(2) (JUN 89), 205-219.
WHEREAS GEOPOLITICAL FACTORS TEND TO DOMINATE
DISCUSSIONS IN LITERATURE ABOUT THE PERSIANARABIAN GULF,
PUBLICATIONS ON OMAN IN THE FIELDS OF POLITICAL SCIENCE,
SOCIOLOGY, ANTHROPOLOGY AND ISLAMIC STUDIES USUALLY PLACE
LITTLE IMPORTANCE ON THE INFLUENCE OF THE WORLD MARKET. THIS
ARTICLE PURSUES THE OPPOSING POINT OF VIEW, PUTTING FORWARD
THE THESIS THAT LOCAL POLITICAL DEVELOPMENTS, I.E. THE SHIFT
FROM THEOCRACY TO MONARCHY, CAN ONLY BE ADEQUATELY
UNDERSTOOD IN THE CONTEXT OF CHANGES IN WORLD MARKET FORCES.
THE OMANI-SAUDI ARABIAN BORDER CONFLICTS AS WELL AS THE
DISPUTE BETWEEN THE SULTAN OF MUSCAT AND THE IMAM OF OMAN IN
THE 1950S CAN ONLY BE ADEQUATELY INTERPRETATED BY TAKING TWO
EXTERNAL FACTORS OF CENTRAL IMPORTANCE INTO ACCOUNT; THE
SHIFT IN BRITISH INTEREST AWAY FROM PROTECTION OF SEA ROUTES
TO INDIA TO THE SAFEGUARDING OF OIL PRODUCTION IN THE GULF
REGION, AND THE DISSOLUTION OF BRITISH HEGEMONY AS A RESULT
OF BRITISH-AMERICAN RIVAL8 RIES.

01556 BIERSTEKER, T.J.
CRITICAL REFLECTIONS ON POST-POSITIVISM IN INTERNATIONAL
RELATIONS
INTERNATIONAL STUDIES QUARTERLY, 33(3) (SEP 89), 263-267.
YOSEF LAPID CLARIFIES THE NATURE OF RECENT CRITICAL
REFLECTION ON INTERNATIONAL THEORY AND CONTRIBUTES TO
OPENING THE DISCOURSE ON THE SUBJECT. HOWEVER HE UNDERSTATES

THE DIVERSITY, THE HISTORICISM, AND THE CRITICAL NATURE OF POST-POSITIVIST INQUIRY AND EXAGGERATES THE EXTENT TO WHICH PLURALISM, PERSPECTIVISM AND RELATIVISM HAVE TAKEN ROOT IN INTERNATIONAL RELATIONS. HE IS ALSO INSUFFICIENTLY CRITICAL OF POST-POSITIVISM AND DOES NOT SAY ENOUGH ABOUT THE PROBLEM OF CRITERIA FOR EVALUATING ALTERNATIVE EXPLANATIONS. HIS ARTICLE IS ESSENTIALLY A PREFACE TO A LARGER PROJECT, ONE YET TO BE UNDERTAKEN, A PROJECT WHICH WILL NEED MORE CONCRETE, SELF-REFLEXIVE, NUANCED RESEARCH THAT TAKES POST-POSITIVIST CRITICISMS SERIOUSLY AND CONSTRUCTS PLAUSIBLE ALTERNATIVE EXPLANATIONS OF IMPORTANT SUBJECTS.

01557 BIFFEN, J.
UNITED WE FALL?
NATIONAL REVIEW, XLI(12) (JUN 89), 25-26.
THIS ARTICLE DEFINES THE DISPUTE BETWEEN MRS THATCHER AND EUROPEAN COMMISSION PRESIDENT JACQUES DELORS: WHETHER A UNITED EUROPEAN ECONOMY WILL BE SOCIALIST OR FREE. THE SUCCESS ES OF "THATCHERISM" LIE IN THE DISMANTLING OF GOVERNMENT, NOT ITS EXPANSION. THE DELORS VISION OFFERS JUST THE OPPOSITE: EIGHTY PER CENT OF GOVERNMENT FROM BRUSSELS-- AND WITHIN THE DECADE.

01558 BIGGS, T.S.; LEVY, B.
STRATEGIC INTERVENTIONS AND THE POLITICAL ECONOMY OF INDUSTRIAL POLICY IN DEVELOPING COUNTRIES
AVAILABLE FROM NTIS, NO. PB89-202899/GAR. DEC 88, 80.
GIVEN THE DEPENDENCE OF SUCCESSFUL INDUSTRIAL POLICIES ON ECONOMIC AND POLITICAL CONDITIONS, THE PAPER EXPOUNDS THE IMPORTANCE OF ADAPTING INDUSTRIAL STRATEGIES TO LOCAL CAPABILITIES. THE FIRST SECTION FOCUSES ON 'HARD STATES,' I. E., THOSE WITH STRONG GOVERNMENTS, CAPABLE OF DEVISING, IMPLEMENTING, AND SUSTAINING SOCIALLY BENEFICIAL INDUSTRIAL POLICIES. FOLLOWING A TYPOLOGY OF INDUSTRIAL STRATEGIES, THE PAPER ANALYZES THE DISTINCTIVE FEATURES OF INDUSTRIAL EXPANSION IN SOUTH KOREA AND TAIWAN. EXAMPLES OF SUCCESSFUL KOREAN POLICY INTERVENTIONS ARE PRESENTED, AFTER WHICH TAIWAN'S STRATEGY OF 'UNBALANCED GROWTH' AND ITS EFFORTS TO SUSTAIN ENDOGENOUS EXPANSION AND INCREASE THE TECHNICAL CAPABILITIES OF SMALL AND MEDIUM ENTERPRISES ARE EXAMINED. THE SECOND SECTION EXPLORES THE POSSIBLE CONSEQUENCES OF ADOPTING INDUSTRIAL STRATEGIES SUITED FOR HARD STATES IN A 'SOFTER' POLITICAL ENVIRONMENT (SUCH AS THE PHILIPPINES). SUGGESTIONS ARE MADE FOR STRATEGIC INTERVENTIONS MORE SUITED TO SOFT STATES, FOLLOWED BY A DISCUSSION OF INDUSTRIAL POLICIES TO OVERCOME INITIAL PRICE DISTORTIONS.

01559 BIGMAN, L.E.
THE POLITICAL ECONOMY OF THE FOOD QUESTION IN LUSOPHONE WEST AFRICA
DISSERTATION ABSTRACTS INTERNATIONAL, 49(9) (MAR 89), 2777-A.
USING THE THEORY AND METHODOLOGY OF POLITICAL ECONOMY, THE AUTHOR ARGUES THAT THE WAY IN WHICH AFRICAN SOCIETIES WERE INTEGRATED INTO THE WORLD MARKET DIVERTED RESOURCES FROM FOOD PRODUCTION, EXACERBATED EXPLOITATION, CREATED THE CONDITIONS FOR NATIONAL FOOD DEPENDENCY, AND CONTRIBUTED TO THE DEGRADATION OF THE ENVIRONMENT. HE UTILIZES THE CASE STUDIES OF GUINEA-BISSAU AND CAPE VERDE TO SUPPORT HIS HYPOTHESIS.

01560 BILBY, K.
WAR, PEACE, AND MUSIC: THE GUIANAS
HEMISPHERE, 1(3) (SUM 89), 10-12.
THE URBAN AND SEMI-URBAN MAROONS OF FRENCH GUIANA HAVE EVOLVED A MUSICAL SUBCULTURE MUCH LIKE THOSE THAT THRIVE IN MANY PARTS OF CONTEMPORARY AFRICA. THE YOUNG MARRONS OF SAINT LAURENT HAVE ADOPTED A NEW DRUMMING STYLE CALLED "ALEKE" AND FORMED VOLUNTEER ASSOCIATIONS OF DRUMMERS. THEY USE THEIR SONGS AS A VEHICLE FOR SOCIAL COMMENTARY AND POLITICAL PROTEST. WHEN CIVIL WAR BROKE OUT IN SURINAME IN 1986 AND REFUGEES CAME STREAMING INTO SAINT LAURENT, THE ALEKE BANDS WERE QUICK TO WRITE SONGS ABOUT THE TRAUMATIC EVENTS. AS THE CARNAGE CONTINUED IN SURINAME, THE MAROON ENCLAVES OF SAINT LAURENT VIBRATED WITH DEFIANT MUSIC.

01561 BILL, J.A.
POPULIST ISLAM AND U.S. FOREIGN POLICY
SAIS REVIEW, 9(1) (WIN 89), 125-139.
WITH THEIR SOCIETIES CONVULSED BY THE FORCES OF SOCIAL AND POLITICAL CHANGE, MIDDLE EASTERN POLITICAL LEADERS CONSTANTLY SEEK RECIPES AND MODELS THAT WILL BETTER ENABLE THEM TO MEET THE CHALLENGES OF THE DAY. THIS CHALLENGE OF CHANGE CUTS ACROSS THE ENTIRE REGION, WHERE NO SOCIETY IS IMMUNE. THE INTENSITY OF THE CHALLENGE IS MATCHED BY ITS COMPLEXITY, AS CHANGES AFFECT ALL SYSTEMS BY WHICH MIDDLE EASTERN MEN AND WOMEN ORGANIZE THEIR LIVES. THE SIGNS OF CHANGE ARE MOST VIVIDLY SEEN IN THE GAPS, IMBALANCES, AND DIVISIONS THAT DEEPEN DAILY: GAPS BETWEEN RICH AND POOR, URBAN AND RURAL LIFE, MODERN AND TRADITIONAL PRACTICES; IMBALANCES BETWEEN POWER HOLDERS AND POWER SEEKERS; DIVISIONS AMONG ETHNIC GROUPS, RELIGIOUS GROUPS, AND NATION-STATES. IN BRIEF, THE MIDDLE EAST IS TODAY WITNESSING THE COLLAPSE OF TRADITIONAL HUMAN RELATIONSHIPS AND SOCIAL

STRUCTURES; AT THE SAME TIME NEW SYSTEMS REMAIN TO BE BORN. IN THIS CURRENT STATE OF INCOHERENCE MANY MIDDLE EASTERNERS LOOK FORWARD TO A PROMISING IF UNKNOWN FUTURE; OTHERS CHOOSE TO LOOK BACKWARD, TO A MORE FAMILIAR PAST, TO THEIR ROOTS.

01562 BILLE, L.
DENMARK: THE OSCILLATING PARTY SYSTEM
WEST EUROPEAN POLITICS, 12(4) (OCT 89), 42-58.
THE DANISH POLITICAL AND PARTY SYSTEMS, UP TO THE BEGINNING OF THE 1970S, WERE CHARACTERIZED BY A REMARKABLE DEGREE OF STABILITY AND CONSENSUS. THIS VIEW WAS RUDELY SHAKEN BY THE RESULT OF THE 1973 ELECTION. THE AIM OF THIS STUDY IS TO ASSESS WHETHER THE PARTY SYSTEM ON THE PARLIAMENTARY AND GOVERNMENTAL LEVELS CHANGED PERMANENTLY IN 1973, OR WHETHER THE EVENT WAS A SHORT LIVED FLUCTUATION RESULTING FROM AN OUTBURST OF MOMENTARY DISCONTENT, AFTER WHICH THE PARTY SYSTEM GRADUALLY RETURNED TO THE PRE-1973 STATE OF AFFAIRS.

01563 BILSKI, A.
ARMS AND THE STATES
MACLEAN'S (CANADA'S NEWS MAGAZINE), 102(26) (JUL 89), 36-37.
THE ARTICLE COMPARES THE US AND CANADA WITH REGARDS TO FIREARMS. MANY AMERICANS FEEL THE RIGHT TO BEAR ARMS TO BE CONSTITUTIONALLY PROTECTED, BUT ARE INCREASINGLY WORRIED ABOUT THE INCREASE IN VIOLENT CRIME. CANADIANS GENERALLY SUPPORT THEIR NATIONS' MORE STRICT GUN CONTROL LAWS.

01564 BILSKI, A.; RODENBECK, M.; SILVER, E.
DIVIDED TOGETHER
MACLEAN'S (CANADA'S NEWS MAGAZINE), 102(10) (MAR 89), 26.
SOVIET FOREIGN MINISTER EDUARD SHEVARDNADZE MET WITH ISRAELI FOREIGN MINISTER MOSHE ARENS AND PLO LEADER YASSER ARAFAT IN CAIRO. THE SOVIET DIPLOMAT HOPED TO PERSUADE ISRAEL TO ACCEPT HIS PLAN FOR A UNITED NATIONS-SPONSORED INTERNATIONAL PEACE CONFERENCE—ENDORSED BY SYRIA, JORDAN, AND EGYPT— THAT WOULD INCLUDE PLO REPRESENTATIVES. ARENS REJECTED THE OVERTURE OF THE SOVIETS Y CLINGING TO THE LONG-STANDING ISRAELI POLICY OF NOT NEGOTIATING DIRECTLY WITH THE POLO. HOWEVER, THE TWO AGREED TO CONTINUE DIALOGUE IN THE FUTURE, A SIGN WHICH IS LOOKED UPON WITH OPTIMISM BY MANY SUPPORTERS.

01565 BILSKI, A.; KIERNAN, P.; LARSON, J.; LOWTHER, W.; NEMETH, M.
MIAMI'S RACIAL FIRES
MACLEAN'S (CANADA'S NEWS MAGAZINE), 102(5) (JAN 89), 23-25.
THE SHOOTING AND KILLING OF AN UNARMED BLACK MAN BY A MIAMI POLICE OFFICER SPARKED ANOTHER ROUND OF RACIAL RIOTS THAT CAUSED AN ESTIMATED $1 MILLION IN PROPERTY DAMAGE. THE INCIDENT SERVED AS A TRIGGER THAT RELEASED UNDERLYING TENSION AND DISENFRANCHISEMENT ON THE PART OF MIAMI'S BLACKS. POLICE TACTICS, A LONG-STANDING NEGLECT OF THE BLACK COMMUNITY'S PROBLEMS BY MIAMI'S CUBAN DOMINATED POWER STRUCTURE, AND A NEW WAVE OF HISPANIC IMMIGRANTS ALL CONTRIBUTED TO THE UNDERLYING TENSION.

01566 BILSKI, A.; LOWTHER, W.; TEDESCO, T.
NEW BATTLE LINES"
MACLEAN'S (CANADA'S NEWS MAGAZINE), 102(27) (JUL 89), 26-27.
AFTER THE TIANANMEN SQUARE MASSACRE, CHINA'S HARD LINE LEADERS ARE CRACKING DOWN AND SOLIDIFYING THEIR CONTROL. RUMORS OF A MASSIVE PURGE OF ALL PARTY LIBERALS AND OF SECRET EXECUTIONS OF MANY DETAINED DISSENTERS ABOUND. DENG XIAOPING DEFENDED THE ARMY'S CRACKDOWN ON THE PRO-DEMOCRACY MOVEMENT, WHICH HE CALLED A "COUNTERREVOLUTIONARY REBELLION. " ALTHOUGH PEACE HAS APPARENTLY RETURNED TO THE STREETS, THERE REMAINS A CURRENT OF DANGER BENEATH THE CALM.

01567 BILSKI, A.
REVOLT IN A FIEFDOM
MACLEAN'S (CANADA'S NEWS MAGAZINE), 102(7) (FEB 89), 21.
AFTER 35 YEARS OF RULING PARAGUAY AS A VIRTUAL FIEFDOM, PARAGUAY'S PRESIDENT ALFREDO STROESSNER WAS DEPOSED IN A MILITARY COUP THAT LEFT AS MANY AS 300 PEOPLE DEAD. STROESSNER HAD DOMINATED PARAGUAY THROUGH A COMBINATION OF POLITICAL CUNNING AND RUTHLESS REPRESSION. HIS DIVISION OF SPOILS BETWEEN THE PARTY, MILITARY AND BUSINESS COMMUNITY HAD CULTIVATED THEIR SUPPORT AND THE COUP WAS SURPRISING TO MANY PARAGUAYANS.

01568 BIN, F.K.; HUA, W.X.
CHINA'S ECONOMIC REFORMS AND THE GLOBAL ECONOMY
FUTURES, 21(6) (DEC 89), 628-631.
THIS ARTICLE, WRITTEN PRIOR TO THE IMPOSITION OF MARTIAL LAW IN CHINA IN JUNE 1989, CONSIDERS MAJOR TRENDS IN THE GLOBALIZATION PROCESS, DESCRIBES THE NATURE OF CHINA'S DECADE-LONG ECONOMIC REFORM, AND CONCLUDES BY IDENTIFYING THREE MAIN CHARACTERISTICS OF THE FUTURE CHINESE ECONOMY AND ITS ROLE IN THE GLOBAL SYSTEM.

01569 BINDER, L.
    THE CHANGING AMERICAN ROLE IN THE MIDDLE EAST
    CURRENT HISTORY, 88(535) (FEB 89), 65-68, 96-97.
        CHANGING UNITED STATES POLICY BY THE COMMITMENT OF BOTH
    CONTINUE THE PROCESS OF REDUCING TENSION AND EXPANDING
    DISCUSSION FROM THE PRIMARILY MILITARY AND STRATEGIC AREAS
    TO A RANGE OF POLITICAL AND ECONOMIC ISSUES.

01570 BING, A.G.
    PEACE STUDIES AS EXPERIENTIAL EDUCATION
    PHILADELPHIA: ANLS OF AMER ACMY OF POLITICAL AND SOC
    SCIENCE, (504) (JUL 89), 48-60.
        THIS ARTICLE ARGUES THAT PEACE EDUCATION AND GOOD PEACE
    STUDIES AT THE UNIVERSITY LEVEL MUST INCLUDE PEACE ACTION AS
    WELL. DESPITE GENERAL AGREEMENT IN THE PEACE STUDIES FIELD
    THAT SUCH INCLUSION OF PEACE ACTION IS IMPORTANT, FEW
    COLLEGES OR UNIVERSITIES HAVE SUCCESSFULLY INCORPORATED AN
    EXPERIENTIAL COMPONENT INTO THEIR ACADEMIC PROGRAMS. USING
    THE PEACE AND GLOBAL STUDIES PROGRAM AT EARLHAM COLLEGE AS A
    MODEL, THIS ARTICLE ATTEMPTS TO SHOW HOW PEACE ACTION, IN
    THE FORM OF ON-CAMPUS COCURRICULAR EXPERIENCES, OFF-CAMPUS
    INTERNSHIPS, AND FOREIGN STUDY, GIVES NEW MEANING TO THE
    STUDY THAT PRECEDES IT BUT ALSO IS MODIFIED BY FURTHER
    COURSE WORK.

01571 BINGQIAN, W.
    REPORT ON THE IMPLEMENTATION OF THE STATE BUDGET FOR 1988
    AND ON THE DRAFT STATE BUDGET FOR 1989
    BEIJING REVIEW, 32(18) (MAY 89), XI-XVIII.
        THE AUTHOR, WHO IS THE CHINESE MINISTER OF FINANCE,
    REVIEWS THE IMPLEMENTATION OF THE 1988 NATIONAL BUDGET AND
    EXPLAINS THE PROPOSED BUDGET FOR 1989.

01572 BINNS, C.
    RITUAL AND CONFORMITY IN SOVIET SOCIETY: A COMMENT
    JOURNAL OF COMMUNIST STUDIES, 5(2) (JUN 89), 211-219.
        THE ARTICLE IS PRIMARILY A RESPONSE TO THOMAS CUSHMAN'S
    RECENT STRUCTURAL ANALYSIS OF THE SOCIAL FUNCTIONS OF THE
    RITUALS OF THE SOVIET YOUTH ORGANIZATION. THE AUTHOR ARGUES
    THAT CUSHMAN'S METHODOLOGICAL FRAMEWORK IS MISTAKEN AS ARE
    HIS ASSUMPTIONS OF "SOCIAL STABILITY" IN THE USSR. THE
    AUTHOR PROPOSES AN ALTERNATE THEORY THAT, HOPEFULLY, IS
    COMPREHENSIVE AND FLEXIBLE ENOUGH TO DISCERN BROAD
    HISTORICAL DEVELOPMENTS BENEATH A CONFUSION OF CONTRADICTORY
    MANIFESTATIONS.

01573 BINXIAO, W.
    MOSCOW TAKES NEW LOOK AT U.N.
    BEIJING REVIEW, 32(7-8) (FEB 89), 22-24.
        UNDER MIKHAIL GORBACHEV'S NEW POLITICAL THINKING,
    MOSCOW'S COLD ATTITUDE TOWARD THE UNITED NATIONS AND ITS
    POLICY OF CONFRONTATION WITH THE UNITED STATES AT THE U.N.
    HAVE BEEN ALTERED. GORBACHEV HAS EMBRACED THE WORLD BODY AND
    ADVOCATED COOPERATION WITH ITS MEMBER STATES, SAYING THAT
    THE U.N. SHOULD BE A FRONT-LINE FORCE IN RESOLVING THE
    WORLD'S PROBLEMS.

01574 BIRD, R.M.; HORTON, S.
    GOVERNMENT POLICY AND THE POOR IN DEVELOPING COUNTRIES
    UNIVERSITY OF TORONTO PRESS, TORONTO, ONTARIO, CA, 1989,
    240.
        THESE PAPERS DISCUSS BROAD ISSUES OF AGRICULTURAL POLICY,
    STABILIZATION POLICY, AND HOW FISCAL POLICY AFFECTS THE
    POOR. CASE STUDIES EXAMINE SPECIFIC ISSUES IN TAIWAN, INDIA,
    BRAZIL, JAMAICA, TANZANIA, AND COLOMBIA.

01575 BIRD, R.M.
    TAXATION IN PAPUA NEW GUINEA: BACKWARDS TO THE FUTURE?
    WORLD DEVELOPMENT, 17(8) (AUG 89), 1145-1157.
        THIS PAPER EXPLORES THE EVOLUTION, CURRENT PROBLEMS, AND
    POSSIBLE FUTURE DEVELOPMENTS OF THE TAX SYSTEM OF PAPUA NEW
    GUINEA, LEAVING ASIDE THE IMPORTANT QUESTION OF NATURAL
    RESOURCE TAXATION. THE PAPER CONCLUDES THAT THERE IS AT
    PRESENT A SERIOUS MISMATCH BETWEEN THE NATURE OF PAPUA NEW
    GUINEA'S ECONOMY AND ITS TAXES. IN PARTICULAR, TAXATION MUST
    BE EXTENDED TO REACH THE BULK OF ECONOMIC ACTIVITY IN THE
    COUNTRY. NO MATTER WHAT IS DONE IN THIS RESPECT, HOWEVER,
    PAPUA NEW GUINEA IS MOST UNLIKELY TO BE ABLE TO FINANCE ITS
    CURRENT LEVEL OF GOVERNMENT EXPENDITURE IN THE ABSENCE OF
    ADDITIONAL AID OR NATURAL RESOURCE REVENUE. THE MAJOR PUBLIC
    SECTOR PROBLEM CONFRONTING THE COUNTRY IS THEREFORE NOT TAX
    REFORM, BUT EXPENDITURE REFORM.

01576 BIRSEL, R.
    FEW WINNERS IN BURMA'S TEAK WAR
    CULTURAL SURVIVAL QUARTERLY, 13(4) (1989), 36-37.
        THE WORLD'S LAST GREAT TEAK FORESTS ARE THE LATEST
    CASUALTIES IN BURMA'S CIVIL WAR. TIMBER HAS NOW BECOME AN
    ESSENTIAL SOURCE OF INCOME FOR THE ETHNIC MINORITY ARMIES,
    AS WELL AS FOR THE RULING MILITARY REGIME UNDER NE WIN. THE
    1988 PRO-DEMOCRACY UPRISING IN BURMA CONVINCED THE RULERS
    THAT ECONOMIC REFORMS WERE NECESSARY IF THE REGIME WERE TO
    SURVIVE. THE DISASTROUS BURMESE WAY TO SOCIALISM WAS
    OFFICIALLY ABANDONED, FOREIGN TRADE WAS LEGALIZED, AND

MEASURES HERE INTRODUCED TO ATTRACT FOREIGN INVESTMENT. NOW
APPROXIMATELY 20 THAI LOGGING COMPANIES ARE OPERATING IN
BURMA, PAYING BOTH THE INSURGENTS AND THE GOVERNMENT FOR THE
PRIVILEGE.

01577 BISCHOF, B.
    THE DIFFICULTY CALLED "CONFIDENCE"
    AUSTRIA TODAY, (4) (1988), 6-8.
        THE TIMETABLE FORESAW A PERIOD OF TEN MONTHS: ON JULY 31,
    1987 THE THIRD FOLLOW-UP MEETING OF THE CONFERENCE ON
    SECURITY AND COOPERATION IN EUROPE (CSCE) WAS SUPPOSED TO
    HAVE REACHED ITS GOALS. AFTER 25 MONTHS, IT LOOKS AS IF THE
    PERIOD OF NEGOTIATIONS IS GOING TO BE THREE TIMES AS LONG.
    OPTIMISTS ARE PREDICTING THAT THE RESULTS WILL BE THREE
    TIMES AS GOOD AS MIGHT HAVE BEEN EXPECTED. THIS ARTICLE
    SHOWS WHAT A RANGE OF PROBLEMS OF INTERNATIONAL IMPORTANCE
    HAVE BEEN NEGOTIATED. THE CSCE DIPLOMATS ARE NEVERTHELESS
    MANAGING TO BRING MOST OF THEM INTO FORMS THAT ENSURE COMMON
    ACCEPTANCE.

01578 BISHARA, A.
    ISRAEL FACES THE UPRISING: A PRELIMINARY ASSESSMENT
    MIDDLE EAST REPORT, 19(157) (MAR 89), 6-14.
        THE AUTHOR SURVEYS HOW THE INTIFADA HAS INFLUENCED
    ISRAELI ELECTIONS, THE PLATFORMS OF THE EXTREME RIGHTWING
    PARTIES, THE DEBATE OVER THE STRATEGIC IMPORTANCE OF THE
    OCCUPIED TERRITORIES, AND THE ISRAELI ECONOMY.

01579 BISHOP, M.R.; KAY, J.A.
    PRIVATIZATION IN THE UNITED KINGDOM: LESSONS FROM
    EXPERIENCE
    WORLD DEVELOPMENT, 17(5) (MAY 89), 643-657.
        ALTHOUGH THE REASONS FOR PRIVATIZATION VARY ACROSS
    COUNTRIES, IN THE UNITED KINGDOM AS IN OTHER COUNTRIES IT
    ALSO REFLECTS A RENEWED BELIEF IN MARKET FORCES. THE SEARCH
    FOR POLICY OPTIONS THAT EMERGES FROM THIS RENEWAL, HOWEVER,
    NEEDS TO BE TEMPERED BY AN UNDERSTANDING OF MARKET AS WELL
    AS REGULATORY FAILURES. ALTHOUGH PROBLEMS FACING GOVERNMENT
    ENTERPRISES IN DEVELOPED AND DEVELOPING COUNTRIES MAY DIFFER,
    THE OBJECTIVE OF PRIVATIZATION SHOULD BE TO RECONSTRUCT
    THESE ENTERPRISES SO AS TO CREATE CONDITIONS THAT MAKE
    PRIVATE SECTOR OPERATIONS EFFECTIVE AND EFFICIENT. AT THE
    SAME TIME, ONE SHOULD RECOGNIZE THAT THIS MAY REQUIRE
    CONTINUED PUBLIC SECTOR ACTIVITY IN THE SECTOR.

01580 BISTA, D.
    NEPAL IN 1988: MANY LOSSES, SOME GAINS
    ASIAN SURVEY, XXIX(2) (FEB 89), 223-228.
        VIEWED FROM A LONG-TERM PERSPECTIVE, 1988 WAS NOT
    DIFFERENT THAN EARLIER YEARS IN NEPAL. THE ECONOMIC
    PERFORMANCE OF THE GOVERNMENT WAS MARKEDLY BETTER THAN
    PREVIOUS YEARS, BUT PROGRESS WAS NEGATED BY A SERIES OF
    NATURAL DISASTERS INCLUDING AN EARTHQUAKE, FLOODING, AND A
    HUGE HAILSTORM. THE DECISIVE STEPS TAKEN AGAINST CORRUPT
    GOVERNMENT OFFICIALS HERE PRAISEWORTHY, BUT THESE WERE MORE
    THAN COUNTERBALANCED BY THE ACTIONS OF THE PRIME MINISTER IN
    SUBVERTING THE LONG-TERM EVOLUTIONARY PROCESS OF DEMOCRACY.

01581 BIVIN, J.
    POLICY REFORM IN DEVELOPING COUNTRIES: THE INFLUENCE OF
    BILATERAL DONORS
    AVAILABLE FROM NTIS, NO. PB89-162655/GAR, AUG 5 88, 56.
        IT IS CLEAR THAT THE EMPHASIS ON STRUCTURAL ADJUSTMENT
    AND POLICY REFORM WILL BE A FEATURE OF DEVELOPMENT POLICY
    FOR SOME TIME TO COME. BILATERAL DONORS ARE HEAVILY INVOLVED
    IN DEVELOPMENT ASSISTANCE, AND AS SUCH PLAY A ROLE IN
    ADJUSTMENT AND POLICY REFORM AS WELL. THE ROLE IN ADJUSTMENT
    THAT HAS EVOLVED OVER THE PAST FEW YEARS HAS BEEN A
    SECONDARY ROLE IN SUPPORT OF THE MULTILATERAL AGENCIES.
    WHILE THE MULTILATERAL AGENCIES WORK WITH THE DEVELOPING
    COUNTRIES ON THE MACROECONOMIC LEVEL TO ENCOURAGE POLICIES
    THAT WILL RESULT IN SUSTAINED GROWTH, THE BILATERAL DONORS
    SUPPORT THE PROCESS BY EXTENDING LARGER VOLUMES OF
    NONPROJECT AID TO LESSEN THE NEGATIVE IMPACT OF ADJUSTMENT
    PROGRAMS. THIS ROLE IN PROVIDING AID TO SUPPORT DEVELOPING
    COUNTRIES DURING ADJUSTMENT WILL CONTINUE. CASE STUDIES OF
    DONOR POLICIES AND INSTRUMENTS ARE GIVEN FOR UNITED KINGDOM,
    GERMANY, THE NETHERLANDS, FRANCE, SWEDEN, AND JAPAN.

01582 BIZHONG, Z.
    SOUTH KOREA: A SETBACK TO NEGOTIATIONS
    BEIJING REVIEW, 32(19) (MAY 89), 17.
        ON APRIL 13, 1989, SOUTH KOREAN DISSIDENT MOON IK HWAN
    HAS ARRESTED UPON HIS RETURN TO SEOUL AFTER MAKING AN
    UNAUTHORIZED TRIP TO PYONGYANG. MOON IK HWAN HAS OFTEN
    EXPOUNDED HIS VIEWS ON THE REUNIFICATION OF KOREA AND
    DEMANDED THE WITHDRAWAL OF U.S. TROOPS, THEREBY GAINING THE
    SUPPORT OF THE MASSES AND THE ENMITY OF THE SOUTH KOREAN
    AUTHORITIES. THE UPROAR CAUSED BY MOON'S VISIT TO PYONGYANG
    WILL INFLUENCE THE DIRECTION OF SOUTH KOREA'S POLICY AS WELL
    AS THE RELATIONS BETWEEN THE NORTH AND SOUTH.

01583 BJARNASON, B.
    VIEW FROM REYKJAVIK

NATO'S SIXTEEN NATIONS, 34(6) (OCT 89), 29.
THE AUTHOR DISCUSSES ICELAND'S CHANGEABLE POLITICAL
LANDSCAPE, ITS MILITARY COOPERATION WITH NATO, ITS EFFORTS
TO CONTROL ARMS AT SEA, AND ITS LINKS WITH THE EUROPEAN
COMMUNITY.

01584 BJORCK, A.
THE COUNCIL OF EUROPE IN A "COMMON EUROPEAN HOME"
INTERNATIONAL AFFAIRS (MOSCOW), (10) (OCT 89), 34-46.
THE AUTHOR EXPLAINS WHAT THE COUNCIL OF EUROPE IS, THE
REASONS FOR THE COUNCIL'S CHANGING RELATIONS WITH THE SOVIET
UNION AND THE COUNTRIES OF EASTERN EUROPE, AND THE
OPPORTUNITIES FOR INTERNATIONAL COOPERATION REPRESENTED BY
THE COUNCIL OF EUROPE.

01585 BJORGULFSDOTTIR, M.
THE PARADOX OF A NEUTRAL ALLY: A HISTORICAL OVERVIEW OF
ICELAND'S PARTICIPATION IN NATO
FLETCHER FORUM, 13(1) (WIN 89), 71-94.
NINETEEN EIGHTY-NINE IS THE FORTIETH ANNIVERSARY OF THE
NORTH ATLANTIC TREATY ORGANIZATION (NATO), AND SCHOLARS
WORLDWIDE ARE EXAMINING ITS EVOLUTION AND SUCCESS. MEMBER
STATES ENTERING THE ALLIANCE HAD DIFFERING NATIONAL
INTERESTS, BUT ALL HELD A COMMON GOAL OF COLLECTIVELY
DEFENDING THE WEST. ICELAND IS UNIQUE AMONG NATO'S FOUNDING
MEMBERS. IT HAS NEVER HAD ANY ARMY. WHILE IT SUPPORTED, IN
PRINCIPLE, A DEFENSE OF EUROPE, HISTORICALLY, IT HAS AVOIDED
ALLIANCES. NEUTRALITY, COUPLED WITH MAINTAINING A DELICATE
DOMESTIC POLITICAL BALANCE, HAS PRESENTED CHALLENGES FOR THE
ICELANDIC GOVERNMENT. THIS ARTICLE EXAMINES HOW ICELAND,
DESPITE THESE FACTORS, HAS BECOME NATO'S VITAL TRANS-
ATLANTIC LINK, THUS ACQUIRING THE PARADOXICAL TITLE OF
"NEUTRAL ALLY."

01586 BLACHMAN, M.J.; SHARPE, K.E.
THE WAR ON DRUGS: AMERICAN DEMOCRACY UNDER ASSAULT
WORLD POLICY JOURNAL, 7(1) (WIN 89), 135-163.
THIS IS AN ARTICLE WHICH SUGGESTS THAT THE END DOES NOT
JUSTIFY THE MEANS. IT EXAMINES THE LAW-ENFORCEMENT PROGRAM
IN THE WAR AGAINST DRUGS AND DECLARES THAT THE CURRENT U.S.
DRUG POLICY HAS TROUBLING CONSEQUENCES FOR OUR DEMOCRATIC
WAY OF LIFE, IT NOT ONLY THREATENS BASIC LIBERTIES, BUT ALSO
ENCOURAGES THE ABUSE OF OFFICIAL POWER, THUS UNDERMINING
POLITICAL ACCOUNTABILITY, IT EXAMINES THE THREAT TO BASIC
LIBERTIES AND THE MILITARIZATION OF DRUG ENFORCEMENT. IT
SUGGESTS THAT THE WAR ON DRUGS NEEDS TO CHANGE COURSE.

01587 BLACK, D.
TRAVELING IN 21ST CENTURY EUROPE
EUROPE, (292) (DEC 89), 24-25.
WITH THE OPEN MARKET APPROACHING THE EUROPEAN COMMUNITY
(E.C) IN 1992, GREAT STEPS TO MODERNIZE AND UNIFY ITS
TRANSPORTATION SYSTEMS MUST BE TAKEN. THE VARIOUS
CONTINENTAL STATES HAVE ALWAYS RECOGNIZED THEIR ECONOMIC
INTERDEPENDENCE. ALREADY OUTLINED ARE HOPES FOR A NEW
RAILWAY INFRASTRUCTURE, WITH A FLAGSHIP NETWORK OF HIGH-
SPEED LUXURY TRAINS EVENTUALLY RUNNING THE LENGTH AND
BREADTH OF THE E.C. FREIGHT WILL BENEFIT FROM A PLANNED
COMBINATION OF BOTH ROAD AND RAIL, AND A GREATER RELIANCE ON
CONTAINERS THAT WILL BE INTERCHANGEABLE BETWEEN BOTH MODES
OF TRANSPORTATION. IN AIR TRANSPORT, THE LIBERALIZATION OF
RULES ON AIR FARES, CAPACITY, AND MARKET ACCESS IS BEING
PROMOTED. REACTION TO THESE SWEEPING CHANGES HAS BEEN
CONSIDERABLE. GOVERNMENTS FEAR THE EROSION OF NATINAL
SOVEREIGNTY, AND POPULATIONS ARE DUBIOUS. HOWEVER, THE
POLITICALLY AND ECONOMICALLY AWARE SEE THE NECESSITY OF THE
CHANGE.

01588 BLACKER, C.D.
THE NEW UNITED STATES-SOVIET DETENTE
CURRENT HISTORY, 88(540) (OCT 89), 321-324, 357-359.
AS IT APPROACHES THE 1990'S, THE SOVIET UNION IS
ENTERING A NEW ERA. ECONOMIC REFORM (PERESTROIKA), POPULAR
PARTICIPATION (DEMOCRATIZATION) AND GREATER OPENNESS IN
SOCIETY (GLASNOST) ARE THE HALLMARKS OF CHANGE; THIS
EVOLUTION IS APPARENT IN THE SOVIET APPROACH TO FOREIGN
POLICY AND ITS RELATIONS WITH THE UNITED STATES. THE SOVIET
LEADERSHIP UNDERSTANDS ALL TOO WELL THE NEED FOR AN ADROIT
AND CAREFULLY CONSTRUCTED RESPONSE TO UNITED STATES
INITIATIVES IN ARMS CONTROL AND EAST-WEST RELATIONS IN
EUROPE. GIVEN ITS PREOCCUPATION WITH DOMESTIC ISSUES, THE
SOVIET GOVERNMENT MUST CHOOSE ITS BATTLES CAREFULLY.

01589 BLACKMAN, C.N.
NEW DIRECTIONS FOR CENTRAL BANKING IN THE CARIBBEAN
SOCIAL AND ECONOMIC STUDIES, 38(4) (DEC 89), 219-240.
CENTRAL BANKING IN THE CARICOM CARIBBEAN IS EXAMINED AND
ASSESSED FROM THE STANDPOINT OF A COMPARATIVE MODEL WHICH
IDENTIFIES THREE BASIC TYPES OF CENTRAL BANK - DEFINED IN
RESPECT OF THEIR LOCATION ON A CONTINUUM REGISTERING THE
RELATIONSHIP BETWEEN BANK AND GOVERNMENT. THIS MODEL IS USED
AS A REFERENCE FOR IDENTIFYING THE CARIBBEAN CENTRAL BANK
TYPE, AND AN ASSESSMENT IS MADE OF THE APPROPRIATENESS OF
EXISTING CENTRAL BANKS TO CARIBBEAN POLITICAL, ECONOMIC,

SOCIAL AND CULTURAL CIRCUMSTANCES. FUTURE DIRECTIONS FOR
CARIBBEAN CENTRAL BANKING INCLUDE THE ESTABLISHMENT OF A
CARIBBEAN RESERVE SYSTEM AS THE CENTRE-PIECE OF ANY MOVEMENT
TOWARDS REGIONAL ECONOMIC INTEGRATION.

01590 BLACKWILL, R.; LEGRO, J.
CONSTRAINING THE GROUND FORCE EXERCISES OF NATO AND THE
WARSAW PACT
INTERNATIONAL SECURITY, 14(3) (WIN 89), 68-98.
THE ARTICLE EXAMINES THE IMPLICATIONS FOR WESTERN
SECURITY OF SUCH CONFIDENCE AND SECURITY BUILDING MEASURES
(CSBM) AS CONSTRAINTS ON THE GROUND FORCE EXERCISES OF BOTH
NATO AND THE WARSAW PACT. IT EXAMINES THE PURPOSES AND
NATURE OF MILITARY EXERCISES IN EUROPE; THE GOALS AND
CONTENT OF CONSTRAINT PROPOSALS; AND THE TRADE-OFFS INVOLVED
IN ACCEPTING MUTUAL LIMITATIONS ON TRAINING. IT CONCLUDES
THAT THE MAJORITY OF THE PROPOSALS INCLUDING LIMITATIONS ON
THE SIZE, NUMBER, FREQUENCY, DURATION, LOCATION, AND
ACTIVITIES OF EXERCISES WOULD BE DETRIMENTAL TO WESTERN
SECURITY. THE ARTICLE ADVOCATES LOWERING THE NOTIFICATION
FLOORS AND AN INCREASE IN INSPECTION WHICH WOULD DEVELOP A
CLEARER IDEA OF THE QUANTITY AND NATURE OF EACH SIDE'S
TRAINING.

01591 BLAIR, D.D.
"THE HANDMAID'S TALE" AND "THE BIRTH DEARTH": PROPHECY,
PRESCRIPTION, AND PUBLIC POLICY
JOURNAL OF POLITICAL SCIENCE, 17(1-2) (1989), 99-110.
THE AUTHOR COMPARES MARGARET ATWOOD'S "THE HANDMAID'S
TALE" WITH BEN WATTENBERG'S "THE BIRTH DIRTH." ATWOOD,
WRITING FROM A FEMINIST PERSPECTIVE, POSITS A DYSTOPIA IN
WHICH WOMEN ARE REDUCED TO THE FUNCTION OF BEING BREEDERS.
WRITING FROM A NATIONALISTIC PERSPECTIVE, WATTENBERG
DEPLORES THE CURRENT AMERICAN "BIRTH DEARTH," ATTRIBUTES IT
PRIMARILY TO WORKING WOMEN, AND PROPOSES A VARIETY OF PRO-
NATIONALIST REMEDIES. PRO-NATALISM, JUSTIFIED BY AMERICA'S
RELATIVELY LOW FERTILITY RATE, HAS CLIMBED HIGH ON MANY
CONSERVATIVE AGENDAS. THIS MOVEMENT SERIOUSLY JEOPARDIZES
MANY OF THE GAINS ACHIEVED BY FEMINISTS IN RECENT YEARS.

01592 BLAIS, A.; CRETE, J.
CAN A PARTY PUNISH ITS FAITHFUL SUPPORTERS? THE PARTI
QUEBECOIS AND PUBLIC SECTOR EMPLOYEES
CANADIAN PUBLIC ADMINISTRATION, 32(4) (WIN 89), 623-632.
THE PAPER EXAMINES THE ELECTORAL CONSEQUENCES OF THE
PARTI QUEBECOIS' DECISION IN THE FALL OF 1982 TO REDUCE
EXPENDITURES BY DRASTICALLY CUTTING WAGES IN THE PUBLIC
SECTOR. IN SO DOING, THE PARTI QUEBECOIS WAS ATTACKING PART
OF ITS CORE CLIENTELE. THE EPISODE OFFERS THE POSSIBILITY OF
TESTING THE PROPOSITION THAT A PARTY WHICH IGNORES ITS
FAITHFUL SUPPORTERS IS DOOMED TO PERISH. THE ANALYSIS SHOWS
THAT THE MEASURE COST THE PARTI QUEBECOIS A LOSS OF SEVEN
PERCENTAGE POINTS AMONG PUBLIC SECTOR EMPLOYEE; THAT THE
LATTER REACTED AS A GROUP, THEIR VOTING BEHAVIOR NOT BEING
INFLUENCED BY WHETHER OR NOT THEY WERE PERSONALLY AFFECTED
BY THE MEASURE; AND THAT THE TOTAL NET LOSS TO THE PARTI
QUEBECOIS WAS 1.5 PERCENTAGE POINTS. THE PAPER ARGUES THAT
THE MEASURE WAS LESS COSTLY THAN THE THEORETICAL LITERATURE
MIGHT HAVE SUGGESTED AND THAT THE MOVE COULD HAVE BEEN A
SUCCESSFUL ONE HAD THE WHOLE POLICY BEEN HANDLED MORE
SHREWDLY BY THE GOVERNMENT.

01593 BLAIS, A.; COUSINEAU, J.M.; MCROBERTS., K.
THE DETERMINANTS OF MINIMUM WAGE RATES
PUBLIC CHOICE, 62(1) (JUL 89), 15-24.
THIS PAPER ATTEMPTS TO TEST THE DEGREE OF RESPONSIVENESS
OF CANADIAN PROVINCIAL GOVERNMENTS TO DIFFERENT POLITICAL
GROUPS IN ESTABLISHING THEIR RELATIVE MINIMUM WAGE POLICIES
OVER THE 1975-1982 PERIOD. IT DISCUSSES ALTERNATIVE
EXPLANATIONS OF MINIMUM WAGE POLICIES AND FOCUSES ON THE
POLITICAL MARKET APPROACH, WHERE WOMEN, YOUTH, SMALL
BUSINESS AND UNIONS PLAY A ROLE. AN ECONOMETRIC MODEL IS
SPECIFIED AND ESTIMATED ON POOLED ANNUAL TIME SERIES AND
CROSS-SECTION DATA FOR NINE PROVINCES IN CANADA. THE RESULTS
TEND TO SUPPORT MOST OF THE HYPOTHESES.

01594 BLANK, S.
GORBACHEV'S AGENDA AND THE NEXT ADMINISTRATION
COMPARATIVE STRATEGY, 8(4) (1989), 381-398.
THIS ARTICLE EXAMINES THE ROOTS OF GORBACHEV'S POLICIES,
FOCUSING ON SOME OF THE CAUSES OF HIS TURN TOWARDS A NEW
DETENTE WITH THE UNITED STATES UNDER THE RUBRIC OF NEW
THINKING AND THE FORCES THAT IMPELLED THE CHANGE. IT ALSO
EMPHASIZES SOVIET APPROACHES TO THE RESOLUTION OF REGIONAL
CONFLICTS IN THE THIRD WORLD AS A MAJOR COMPONENT OF THIS
POLICY AS OF THE SECOND HALF OF 1988. IT EXAMINES THE
RESULTS OF SOVIET POLICY FAILURES FROM 1976 TO 1985. IT SEES
IN GORBACHEV'S POLICIES THE EFFORT TO OVERCOME THESE
FAILURES BY MEANS OF NEW POLITICAL STATEGIES AND POLICIES
AND SUGGESTS WHAT GOALS MOSCOW IS PURSUING IN ITS EFFORTS TO
ADDRESS REGIONAL CONFLICTS IN ASIA.

01595 BLANK, S.
SOVIET LOW-INTENSITY CONFLICTS: AN AGENDA FOR RESEARCH

CONFLICT, 9(1) (1989), 1-20.
THIS ARTICLE REPRESENTS A PRELIMINARY EFFORT TO UNCOVER
SOME OF THE REASONS FOR THE SOVIET UNION'S POOR SHOWING BOTH
MILITARILY AND POLITICALLY IN AFGHANISTAN BY LOOKING AT SOME
OF THE OUTSTANDING HISTORICAL CHARACTERISTICS OF SOVIET
STRATEGY AND TACTICS IN LOW-INTENSITY CONFLICTS SINCE 1917.
EARLIER IN ITS HISTORY THE SOVIET UNION CREATED NOVEL AND
VIABLE POLITICAL FORMS TO ACCOMPANY ITS MILITARY STRATEGY;
SINCE 1953 THERE HAS BEEN A VISIBLE RELIANCE EXCLUSIVELY
UPON FORCE. THIS NEGLECT OF POLITICAL FACTORS HAS BEEN THE
CAUSE OF SYSTEMATIC INTELLIGENCE FAILURES AND HAS PLACED
ENORMOUS BURDENS UPON THE MILITARY IN SITUATIONS THAT ARE
LIKELY TO DEVELOP INTO LOW-INTENSITY CONFLICTS. IN
AFGHANISTAN POOR POLITICAL AND INTELLIGENCE OPERATIONS WERE
COMBINED WITH AN INAPPROPRIATE MILITARY STRATEGY AND FORCE
STRUCTURE; THE FULL IMPLICATIONS OF THIS UNSOUND APPROACH
MADE THEMSELVES FELT WITH POTENTIALLY PROFOUND CONSEQUENCES
FOR FUTURE SOVIET POLICY.

01596 BLANKFORT, J.
PROPOSITION W
MIDDLE EAST REPORT, 19(157) (MAR 89), 38-40.
ON NOV. 8, 1988, VOTERS IN SAN FRANCISCO AND BERKELEY
OVER WHELMINGLY REJECTED PRO-PALESTINIAN INITIATIVES ON
THEIR BALLOTS. SAN FRANCISCO'S PROPOSITION W, WHICH CALLED
FOR THE USA TO RECOGNIZE A PALESTINIAN STATE "SIDE-BY-SIDE"
WITH ISRAEL, WAS DEFEATED BY 68 TO 32 PERCENT. IN BERKELEY,
A MEASURE THAT WOULD HAVE ESTABLISHED THE GAZA REFUGEE CAMP
OF JABALYA AS A SISTER CITY WAS ALSO DEFEATED.

01597 BLEAKLEY, G.A.
INTERNATIONAL ARMAMENTS COOPERATION
AVAILABLE FROM NTIS, NO. AD-A202 655/7/GAR, SEP 88, 159.
THE PURPOSE OF THIS RESEARCH WAS TO EXAMINE VARIOUS
ASPECTS OF NATO ARMAMENTS COOPERATION. THE STUDY EXAMINED
THE ONGOING MODULAR STANDOFF WEAPON SYSTEM (MSOW) PROGRAM
WITHIN THE CONTEXT OF BROADER STUDY OF OVERALL NATO
COOPERATION. THE MSOW PROGRAM CURRENTLY INVOLVES FIVE
NATIONS IN AN EFFORT TO BUILD A FAMILY OF LONG RANGE
AIRLAUNCHED GROUND ATTACK MISSILES. THE OBJECTIVE OF THE
STUDY WAS TO DETERMINE THE BENEFITS AND DRAWBACKS OF NATO
ARMAMENTS COOPERATION, AS WELL AS THE MILITARY, ECONOMIC,
AND POLITICAL FACTORS THAT INFLUENCE IT. FURTHER, THE STUDY
ATTEMPTED TO DETERMINE WHETHER MSOW'S BENEFITS, DRAWBACKS,
AND INFLUENTIAL FACTORS PARALLELED THOSE OF OVERALL NATO
COOPERATION AND WHETHER THE MSOW PROGRAM WAS PROJECTED TO
YIELD A WEAPON SYSTEM WORTH THE ADDITIONAL EFFORT REQUIRED
IN A JOINT PROGRAM.

01598 BLECHER, M.
CHINA'S STRUGGLE FOR A NEW HEGEMONY
SOCIALIST REVIEW, 19(2) (APR 89), 5-36.
THE ARTICLE REGARDS THE DIFFERENCES BETWEEN THE
GRAMSCIAN APPROACH TO HEGEMONIC CHANGE IN WESTERN CAPITALISM
AND THE EFFORTS TO EFFECT SUCH A CHANGE IN STATE SOCIALIST
COUNTRIES. IT UTILIZES CHINA AS A CASE STUDY AND EXAMINES
THE FRONTAL ATTACKS LAUNCHED ON PRE-REVOLUTIONARY HEGEMONIES
BY MAO AND OTHERS. THE CHINESE CASE SUGGESTS THAT THE
POSSESSION OF EVEN IMMENSE STATE POWER DOES NOT NECESSARILY
SIGNAL AND END POINT TO THE HEGEMONIC STRUGGLE.

01599 BLECHMAN, B.M.; GUTMANN, E.
A $100 BILLION UNDERSTANDING
SAIS REVIEW, 9(2) (SUM 89), 73-100.
THIS ARTICLE PROPOSES A MUTUAL ARMS REDUCTION AGREEMENT
BETWEEN THE SOVIET UNION AND THE UNITED STATES. THIS IDEA
PRESUPPOSES THAT A STRONG ECONOMIC COUNTRY IS AN INVALUABLE
ASSET RELATIVE TO BOTH ECONOMIC AND MILITARY GLOBAL
ADVERSARIES.

01600 BLISHCHENKO, I.
INTERNATIONAL LAW IN A RULE-OF-LAW STATE
INTERNATIONAL AFFAIRS (MOSCOW), (1) (JAN 89), 85-87.
NOW THAT A RULE-OF-LAW STATE IS BEING BUILT IN THE USSR,
THE QUESTION OF THE APPLICABILITY OF INTERNATIONAL LAW
WITHIN THE SOVIET UNION ARISES. DUE TO THE GROWING
INTERDEPENDENCE AND INTERRELATIONSHIP OF ALL STATES IN THE
WORLD, INTERNATIONAL LAW NATURALLY BECOMES MORE IMPORTANT IN
INTERNATIONAL RELATIONS. AN ANALYSIS OF THE BALANCE BETWEEN
THE APPLICATION OF DOMESTIC AND INTERNATIONAL LAW IN THE
USSR REVEALS THAT THE IMPORTANCE OF INTERNATIONAL LAW HAS
BEEN UNDERESTIMATED. A CONSTITUTIONAL AMENDMENT IS NEEDED TO
ENSURE THAT A TREATY SIGNED BY THE USSR IS APPLIED TO THE
ENTIRE TERRITORY OF THE SOVIET UNION AS NATIONAL LAW AND
THAT, IN CASE OF A CONTRADICTION, TREATY LAW SUPERSEDES
NATIONAL LAW.

01601 BLITS, J.
HOBBESIAN FEAR
POLITICAL THEORY, 17(3) (AUG 89), 417-431.
WHILE THE ROLE OF FEAR IN HOBBES'S POLITICAL PHILOSOPHY
HAS RECEIVED CLOSE SCRUTINY IN RECENT YEARS, THE COMMON AND
UNQUESTIONED ASSUMPTION AMONG VIRTUALLY ALL CONTEMPORARY
SCHOLARS IS THAT HOBBES CONSIDERS THE FEAR OF VIOLENT DEATH

MAN'S PRIMARY FEAR. SCHOLARS ASSUME THAT THE POLITICAL LEVEL
IS THE DEEPEST STRATUM OF HOBBESIAN FEAR. THIS PAPER
COMPARES ROUSSEAU'S NATURAL MAN TO HOBBES'S. ROUSSEAU HAS
CRITIZED HOBBES VIEWS, ACCORDING TO HIM, EVEN THOUGH HOBBES
DENIES THAT MAN IS NATURALLY SOCIAL, HOBBES'S NATURAL MAN IS
CHARACTERIZED BY QUALITIES PRODUCED BY SOCIETY RATHER THAN
BY NATURE. ROUSSEAU IS PERFECTLY CORRECT IN DENYING THE TRUE
SOLITUDE OF THE HOBBESIAN MAN, BUT HE IS FUNDAMENTALLY
MISTAKEN OR MISLEADING IN CLAIMING THAT FEAR OF VIOLENT
DEATH IS PRIMARY IN HOBBES'S VEIW. THIS ARTICLE ARGUES THAT
HOBBESIAN FEAR IS BEST UNDERSTOOD AS A PRIMAL, INDETERMINATE
FEAR OF THE UNKNOWN.

01602 BLOICE, C.
THE NATURE OF CONTEMPORARY SOCIALISM
POLITICAL AFFAIRS, LXVIII(8) (AUG 89), 39-41.
THE ARTICLE ARGUES THAT ALTHOUGH CAPITALIST IDEOLOGICAL
WARRIORS HAVE DECLARED THE COLD WAR TO BE OVER AND SOCIALISM
TO BE THE LOSER, SOCIALISM IS NOT WINDING DOWN, IT IS
RETOOLING. IT CONCLUDES THAT CHANGES IN SOCIALIST REGIMES
SUCH AS THE USSR ARE NOT RETREATS FROM SOCIALISM, BUT ARE
REASSERTIONS OF THE DYNAMISM AND CREATIVE STRENGTH OF
MARXISM-LENINISM. ALTHOUGH THE CHANGES ARE MANY AND THE
OBSTACLES SIGNIFICANT, THE ARTICLE CONCLUDES THAT THE FUTURE
IS BRIGHT FOR THE WORLD COMMUNIST AND WORKING CLASS MOVEMENT.

01603 BLOOMFIELD, L.P.
COPING WITH CONFLICT IN THE LATE TWENTIETH CENTURY
INTERNATIONAL JOURNAL, XLIV(4) (AUG 89), 772-802.
THE AUTHOR DISCUSSES THE CAUSES AND PREVENTION OF WAR,
THE TYPES OF LOCAL AND REGIONAL CONFLICTS, PEACEKEEPING AND
PEACEMAKING, AND CONFLICT PREVENTION, INCLUDING RECOGNIZING
EARLY WARNING SIGNALS OF CONFLICTS.

01604 BLOW, R.
BABY BOOM
CAMPAIGNS AND ELECTIONS, 10(3) (OCT 89), 26-30.
ABORTION HAS BEEN CALLED A POLITICIAN'S NIGHTMARE AND A
POLITICAL CONSULTANT'S DREAM. IN ITS INFANCY NOW, THE
ABORTION ISSUE IS EXPECTED TO GROW UP AND DOMINATE
CAMPAIGNING IN THE 1990'S. IN TIME, CONTROL OF SOME STATE
LEGISLATURES MAY SPLIT NOT AS MUCH ALONG PARTY LINES AS
BETWEEN LINES OF CHOICE, FEW ISSUES ARE AS INESCAPABLE ON
BOTH NATIONAL AND LOCAL LEVELS.

01605 BLUM, A.A.
POLITICAL PATERNALISM VS. DEMOCRACY
FREEDOM AT ISSUE, (109) (JUL 89), 16-17.
PATERNALISM PERMEATES THE POLITICAL, ECONOMIC, AND
SOCIAL SYSTEMS OF SINGAPORE. SINGAPORE'S GOVERNMENT LEADERS
ARE THE PARENTS; MANAGEMENT AND THE ELITE ARE THE NEPHEWS
AND NIECES; THE MIDDLE CLASS, THE COUSINS; WORKERS AND THE
POOR, THE CHILDREN. THEY ARE ALL SUPPOSED TO BE PART OF ONE
BIG FAMILY WORKING TOWARD COMMON GOALS, SUCH AS INCREASED
PRODUCTIVITY, WITH FATHER KNOWING WHAT IS BEST FOR HIS
YOUNGER RELATIVES. HE THEREFORE TRIES TO ENGINEER THE
ENVIRONMENT THROUGH A CONTROLLED PRESS SO THAT ALL WILL WORK
TOWARD THE GOALS HE HAS SET.

01606 BLUMSTEIN, J.
GOVERNMENT'S ROLE IN ORGAN TRANSPLANTATION POLICY
JOURNAL OF HEALTH POLITICS, POLICY AND LAW, 14(1) (SPR 89),
5-40.
THIS PAPER INITIALLY CONSIDERS WAYS OF THINKING ABOUT
ORGAN TRANSPLANTATION: SHOULD IT BE TREATED AS A
CATASTROPHIC DISEASE OR AS AN ORDINARY AND ACCEPTED MEDICAL
PROCEDURE? THE ANALYSIS THEN SHIFTS TO THE ROLE THE
GOVERNMENT HAS PLAYED IN INFLUENCING ORGAN TRANSPLANTATION
POLICY. THE FEDERAL GOVERNMENT'S INVOLVEMENT INITIALLY
STEMMED FROM ITS ROLE AS PAYER FOR END-STAGE RENAL DISEASE
SERVICES. IN RECENT YEARS, THE RATIONALE FOR INTERVENTION
HAS CHANGED, AND THE THE MECHANISM FOR IMPLEMENTING
REGULATORY OVERSIGHT HAS SHIFTED TO A PRIVATE NETWORK RUN
FOR THE GOVERNMENT BY THE UNITED NETWORK FOR ORGAN SHARING
(UNOS). THE GOVERNMENT HAS DELEGATED MUCH POLICYMAKING
AUTHORITY TO UNOS, ALTHOUGH THE AUTHOR DEMONSTRATES THAT
THIS IS NOT REQUIRED BY THE APPLICABLE LEGISLATION. THE
ARTICLE RAISES QUESTIONS ABOUT THE RELATIONSHIP BETWEEN UNOS
AND THE FEDERAL GOVERNMENT, ABOUT POTENTIAL CONFLICTS
BETWEEN UNOS GUIDELINES AND STATE LAWS UNDER THE UNIFORM
ANATOMICAL GIFT ACT, AND ABOUT THE IDEOLOGICAL STANCE
UNDERGIRDING MUCH OF CURRENT FEDERAL POLICY IN THE ORGAN
TRANSPLANTATION ARENA.

01607 BLUNDNIKOW, B.
DENMARK DURING THE FIRST WORLD WAR
JOURNAL OF CONTEMPORARY HISTORY, 24(4) (OCT 89), 683-703.
DURING THE FIRST WORLD WAR, DENMARK WAS NEUTRAL--A
STATUS ACHIEVED WITH SOME DIFFICULTY AND ONE THAT THE
COUNTRY HAD TO WORK HARD TO RETAIN. BUT THIS NEUTRALITY WAS
NOT ENTIRELY UNAMBIGUOUS, SINCE THE FOREIGN MINISTER
DECLARED THAT DENMARK WOULD "SHOW FAVORABLE NEUTRALITY"
TOWARD GERMANY AS FAR AS THIS WAS CONSISTENT WITH THE
CONCEPT OF NEUTRALITY. SPECIAL CONSIDERATION OF GERMANY'S

INTERESTS HAS SO DOMINANT IN DANISH FOREIGN POLICY THAT DENMARK WAS READY TO RISK CONTRAVENING THE CONCEPT OF PURE NEUTRALITY. ON THE OTHER HAND, DENMARK ALSO WANTED TO MAINTAIN GOOD RELATIONS WITH BRITAIN.

01608 BLYTHE, J., M.
FAMILY, GOVERNMENT, AND THE MEDIEVAL ARISTOTELIANS
HISTORY OF POLITICAL THOUGHT, X(1) (SPR 89), 1-16.
THE AUTHOR SHOWS THAT DEMONSTRATING THE SIMILARITIES BETWEEN FAMILIAL AND POLITICAL RELATIONSHIPS HAS AN ACTIVE CONCERN OF THIRTEENTH AND FOURTHEENTH CENTURY POLITICAL COMMENTATORS, AND THAT IN MANY CASES THIS CONCERN WENT FAR BEYOND EXPLAINING PRIMITIVE GOVERNMENT AS THE OUTGROWTH OF THE FAMILY. THOSE SCHOLARS WHO ARGUE THAT THE VARIOUS MODES OF RULE ARE SIMPLY THE SAME CONCEPT IN DIFFERENT SIZES HAVE THEREFORE MISINTERPRETED THE WRITINGS OF ARISTOTLE AND OTHER MEDEEVAL PHILOSPHERS.

01609 BO, G.
PROSPECTS FOR THE MIDDLE EAST
BEIJING REVIEW, 32(23) (JUN 89), 15-17.
A NEW MOMENTUM FOR A POLITICAL SETTLEMENT OF THE MIDDLE EAST SITUATION SEEMS TO BE DEVELOPING. THE PALESTINE LIBERATION ORGANIZATION HAS ANNOUNCED ITS RECOGNITION OF ISRAEL. MEANWHILE, CALLS FOR DIALOGUE WITH THE PLO AND AN INTERNATIONAL PEACE CONFERENCE HAVE INCREASED WITHIN ISRAEL. THE EASING OF TENSIONS BETWEEN THE SOVIET UNION AND THE UNITED STATES HAS CONTRIBUTED TO THE MORE OPTIMISTIC OUTLOOK FOR RESOLUTION OF THE MIDDLE EAST CONFLICT.

01610 BOBB, D.
AGNI: CHARIOT OF FIRE
INDIA TODAY, XIV(11) (JUN 89), 10-13.
THE SUCCESSFUL LAWS OF AGNI, INDIA'S FIRST INTERMEDIATE RANGE BALLISTIC MISSILE, AFTER SEVERAL FALSE STARTS, IS A DEMONSTRATION OF HER TECHNOLOGICAL PROWESS. BUT, AS THIS ARTICLE DESCRIBES, THE LAUNCH IS MORE SIGNIFICANT AS A POWERFUL PROJECTION OF MILITARY POWER. IN STRATEGIC TERMS, IT GIVES INDIA UNPRECEDENTED STRIKE CAPABILITY.

01611 BOBB, D.
BREACHING THE WALL
INDIA TODAY, XIV(I) (JAN 89), 14-21.
THE VISIT OF INDIAN PRIME MINISTER RAJIV GANDHI TO CHINA MARKED A NEW BEGINNING IN BILATERAL RELATIONS. GANDHI MET WITH DENG XIAOPING AND ANNOUNCED THAT THE TWO NATIONS HAD AGREED TO FORM A JOINT TASK FORCE TO FIND A SOLUTION TO THE BORDER ISSUE.

01612 BOBB, D.
CLOSER TO REALITY
INDIA TODAY, 14(16) (AUG 89), 40, 42.
THIS IS A REPORT ON INDO-SRI LANKA TALKS WHICH WERE OFFICIALLY LOGGED AS A FAILURE, BUT THE POSITIVE FALL-OUT OF THE TALKS BETWEEN THE TWO COUNTRIES IS THAT THE COMMUNICATION GAP HAS BEEN BRIDGED. DESPITE DIFFERENCES A SOLUTION IS EMERGING. THE ISSUE OF WITHDRAWAL OF THE 45,000 STRONG INDIAN PEACE KEEPING FORCE (IPKF) WAS THE TOPIC OF THE WEEK-LONG DIALOGUE, TIL NOW, MUCH OF THE HOSTILITY BETWEEN DELHI AND COLUMBO HAS BEEN BECAUSE OF THE SERIOUS COMMUNICATION GAP. WITH BOTH SIDES HAVING AGREED TO MAINTAIN CLOSER CONTACTS FROM NOW ON, AT LEAST ONE VITAL BRIDGE HAS BEEN BUILT.

01613 BOBB, D.; DEVADAS, D.; SINGH, R.
CRISIS AT HAND
INDIA TODAY, XIV(3) (FEB 89), 24-26.
ON JANUARY 22, 1989, THE POLITICAL FORTUNES OF THE CONGRESS (I) PARTY PLUMMETED TO A NEW LOW. THE ELECTORAL DEDACLE IN TAMIL NADU WAS, BY ITSELF, SERIOUS ENOUGH. BUT IT WAS ALSO SYMPTOMATIC OF THE BIGGER CRISIS IN THE PARTY AS EVIDENCED BY THE POLITICAL CONVULSIONS IN MADHYA PRADESH AND BIHAR.

01614 BOBB, D.; JAYARAM, P.
SRI LANKA: DANGEROUS DEADLOCK
INDIA TODAY, 19(13) (JUL 89), 22-29.
THIS ARTICLE REPORTS ON THE DEADLOCK POSITIONS OF PRESIDENT PREMADASA AND PRIME MINISTER RAJIV GANDHI OVER THE WITHDRAWAL OF THE INDIAN PEACE KEEPING FORCE (IPKF). IT DESCRIBES THE PANIC AND RESENTMENT OF THE INDIAN COMMUNITY AND THE SITUATION FOR THE NORTH-EAST TAMILS WHO ARE TRAPPED IN THE MIDDLE. IT PREDICTS TROUBLE IN SRI LANKA AS INEVIATABLE.

01615 BOBBIO, N.
THE UPTURNED UTOPIA
NEW LEFT REVIEW, (177) (SEP 89), 37-40.
RECENT POLITICAL EVENTS IN THE EAST HAVE RAISED QUESTIONS ABOUT THE FUTURE OF SOCIALISM. IN THIS ESSAY, THE AUTHOR EMPHASIZES THE CHALLENGE WHICH, IN HIS VIEW, THE FAILURE OF COMMUNIST UTOPIAS HAS LAID AT THE DOOR OF WESTERN LIBERAL DEMOCRACY.

01616 BOBO, L.; LICARI, F.C.
EDUCATION AND POLITICAL TOLERANCE: TESTING THE EFFECTS OF COGNITIVE SOPHISTICATION AND TARGET GROUP AFFECT
PUBLIC OPINION QUARTERLY, 53(3) (FAL 89), 285-308.
THE AUTHORS EXAMINE THE EFFECTS OF EDUCATION AND COGNITIVE SOPHISTICATION ON THE WILLINGNESS TO EXTEND CIVIL LIBERTIES TO NONCONFORMIST GROUPS. A SECONDARY ANALYSIS OF THE 1984 GENERAL SOCIETY SURVEY DATA SHOWS THAT THERE IS A STRONG TOLERANCE DIMENSION THAT CUTS ACROSS GROUPS AND TYPES OF ACTIONS. STRONG POSITIVE EFFECTS OF EDUCATION ON A MULTIPLE TARGET GROUP TOLERANCE SCALE INCLUDE BOTH LEFT-WING AND RIGHT-WING GROUPS. A SUBSTANTIAL FRACTION OF THE EDUCATIONAL EFFECT ON TOLERANCE IS MEDIATED BY COGNITIVE SOPHISTICATION. THE EFFECTS OF EDUCATION ON TOLERANCE ARE STRONG EVEN WHEN A PERSON HAS NEGATIVE FEELINGS TOWARD THE TARGET GROUP.

01617 BOBROW, D.B.
JAPAN IN THE WORLD: OPINION FROM DEFEAT TO SUCCESS
JOURNAL OF CONFLICT RESOLUTION, 33(4) (DEC 89), 571-604.
JAPANESE PUBLIC OPINION ON FOREIGN AND DEFENSE POLICY WARRANTS LONGITUDINAL ANALYSIS AS AN EXTREME CASE OF CHANGE AND LACK OF INTEREST IN INTERNATIONAL DIPLOMATIC AND MILITARY ACTIVISM. DATA FOR THE POST-OCCUPATION PERIOD THROUGH 1984 ARE EXAMINED FOR THE EFFECTS OF AGE, GENERATION, AND SITUATION: MORE RECENT AGGREGATE POLL DATA ARE USED TO CHECK FOR RECENT CHANGES. LITTLE SUPPORT APPEARS FOR STRONG, ONGOING SHIFTS FROM INTERNATIONAL PASSIVISM TO ACTIVISM, ALIGNMENT TO EQUIDISTANCE, DEPENDENCE TO AUTONOMY, MILITARY MINIMIZATION TO EFFORT, OR LACK OF GUIDING PRINCIPLES. GENERATIONAL EFFECTS ARE VERY MODEST AFTER THE EARLY 1970S; AGE-GROUP DIFFERENCES HAVE MORE CONTINUING IMPORTANCE. MAJORITY OPINION IS SCEPTICAL ABOUT THE MERITS OF DEPARTURES FROM THE STATUS QUO, BUTTRESSED BY COUNTERVAILING MINORITIES THAT SUPPORT OPPOSED DIRECTIONS OF CHANGE.

01618 BODANSKY, Y.
WHO KILLED PRESIDENT ZIA--AND HOW?
FREEDOM AT ISSUE, (107) (MAR 89), 23-27.
ON AUG. 17, 1988, PAKISTANI PRESIDENT ZIA UL-HAQ AND 30 OTHERS WERE KILLED IN THE CRASH OF A PAKISTAN AIR FORCE PLANE. THE BOARD OF INQUIRY THAT INVESTIGATED THE TECHNICAL CAUSE OF THE CRASH DISMISSED THE POSSIBILITY OF AN ACCIDENT AND CONCLUDED THAT THE MOST PROBABLE CAUSE WAS A CRIMINAL ACT OR SABOTAGE. A CLOSE EXAMINATION OF THE AVAILABLE TECHNICAL EVIDENCE STRONGLY SUGGESTS THAT THE ASSASSINATION WAS ENGINEERED NOT BY IMPULSIVE OR ILL-TRAINED LOCAL OPPOSITION GROUPS BUT BY THE KGB AND ITS AGENTS.

01619 BODELSON, P.C.
THE POLITICS OF PERSPECTIVE PAYMENT: A LEGISLATIVE CASE STUDY
DISSERTATION ABSTRACTS INTERNATIONAL, 50(5) (NOV 89), 1430-A.
THE AUTHOR PRESENTS A CASE STUDY OF THE ENACTMENT OF A NEW PAYMENT SYSTEM FOR THE MEDICARE PROGRAM, WHICH WAS SIGNED INTO LAW ON APRIL 20, 1983. SHE FINDS THAT THE NEW LAW WAS ENACTED SWIFTLY BECAUSE THE FEDERAL GOVERNMENT APPEARED TO BE FACING A FISCAL CRISIS AND THE SOCIAL SECURITY SYSTEM WAS ON THE VERGE OF BANKRUPTCY.

01620 BODENHEIMER, T.; GOULD, R.
ECONOMIC DECLINE: FERTILE SOIL FOR RIGHT-WING GROWTH; ROLLBACK: RIGHT-WING POWER IN US FOREIGN POLICY
SOUTH END PRESS, BOSTON, MA, 1989, 143-160.
THE CHAPTER EXAMINES ECONOMIC DECLINE AS A KEY FACTOR IN THE INCREASE IN RIGHT-WING POWER AND THEIR ABILITY TO REJUVENATE THE POLICY OF ROLLBACK. IT ANALYZES BOTH THE WORLD ECONOMIC CRISIS OF THE 1970'S AND THE LOSS OF ECONOMIC HEGEMONY BY THE US AND EXAMINES THEIR EFFECTS ON US FOREIGN POLICY. IT SPECIFICALLY EXAMINES THE EFFECTS OF THE DOLLAR DRAIN, THE INTERNATIONALIZATION OF CAPITAL AND THE "LOOTING OF THE US" CAUSED BY MILITARY SPENDING. IT CONCLUDES THAT, IN SHORT, ROLLBACK WAS AN ATTRACTIVE METHOD OF PUTTING THE US BACK ON TOP AGAIN AND THE RIGHT WAS ABLE TO CAPITALIZE ON ITS APPEAL.

01621 BODENHEIMER, T.; GOULD, R.
HOW TO ROLL BACK THE "EVIL EMPIRE"; ROLLBACK: RIGHT-WING POWER IN US FOREIGN POLICY
SOUTH END PRESS, BOSTON, MA, 1989, 37-52.
THE CHAPTER EXPLORES THE FOUNDATIONS OF THE EXTENDED CONFLICT BETWEEN THE US AND SOVIET RUSSIA. IT OUTLINES THE JUSTIFICATIONS THE RIGHT USES IN THEIR WAR ON THE "EVIL EMPIRE" AND THE STRATEGIES USED TO ACHIEVE THEIR GOALS. THESE STRATEGIES INCLUDE ECONOMIC ISOLATION AND THIRD WORLD INSURGENCY. THE ROLE OF ESCALATION DOMINANCE IN THE CONFLICT IS ALSO EXPLORED.

01622 BODENHEIMER, T.; GOULD, T.
ROLLBACK DOCTRINE: UNDERMINING THE UNITED STATES; ROLLBACK: RIGHT-WING POWER IN US FOREIGN POLICY
SOUTH END PRESS, BOSTON, MA, 1989, 217-238.
THIS CONCLUDING CHAPTER ANALYZES THE OVERALL EFFECT OF

ROLLBACK ON THE UNITED STATES. IT ARGUES THAT ROLLBACK
RELATED MILITARY EXPENDITURES STEALS CAPITAL AWAY FROM
DOMESTIC INDUSTRIES, THE SO-CALLED LOOTING OF THE US.
ROLLBACK ALSO IS COUNTERPRODUCTIVE TO THE VERY AIMS IT
OSTENSIBLY TRIES TO ACHIEVE; IT INCREASES THE POLITICAL
ISOLATION OF THE US AND TENDS TO GLORIFY "ENEMIES" OF THE US
AND INCREASE THEIR IMPORTANCE TO A DISPROPORTIONATE LEVEL.
ADHERENTS OF A ROLLBACK POLICY DO NOT UNDERSTAND THE
CHANGING REALITIES OF THE WORLD, ESPECIALLY THE THIRD WORLD
AND THE SOVIET UNION. THE AUTHORS ADVOCATE AN END TO THE
BIPOLAR WORLDVIEW AND THE MYOPIC VIEW THAT ALL COMMUNISTS
ARE EVIL AND GODLESS.

01623 BODENHEIMER, T.; GOULD, R.
    ROLLBACK DOCTRINE: 1945-1980; ROLLBACK: RIGHT-WING POWER
    IN U.S. FOREIGN POLICY
    SOUTH END PRESS, BOSTON, MA, 1989, 11-37.
    THE CHAPTER OUTLINES THE SHIFT FROM A POLICY OF
ISOLATIONISM TO ONE OF "ROLLBACK" THAT TOOK PLACE OVER THE
PAST FORTY YEARS. IT EXAMINES THE CONFICT BETWEEN THOSE WHO
FAVORED A SIMPLE CONTAINMENT OF ENEMIES OF THE US AND THOSE
WHO ADVOCATED THE OVERTHROW OF THOSE GOVERNMENTS. IT
EXAMINES THIRTEEN MAJOR ROLLBACK OPERATIONS INCLUDING KOREA,
CHINA, IRAN, CUBA, AND CHILE. IT CONCLUDES THAT ALTHOUGH THE
OVERALL US FOREIGN POLICY WAS ONE OF CONTAINMENT, THE US
SELECTIVELY ENGAGED IN ROLLBACK OPERATIONS DESIGNED TO
DESTROY SOCIALISM IN THE USSR.

01624 BODENHEIMER, T.; GOULD, R.
    ROLLBACK: RIGHT-WING POWER IN US FOREIGN POLICY
    SOUTH END PRESS, BOSTON, MA, 1989, 272.
    THE BOOK IS ANALYSIS OF THE RIGHT-WING ADVOCATED POLICY
OF ROLLBACK, AN AGRESSIVE POLICY OF OVERTHROWING FOREIGN
GOVERNMENTS IN AN EFFORT TO EXPAND US GLOBAL POWER AND
CONTROL. IT EXAMINES THE METHODS UTILIZED BY THE RIGHT TO
INFLUENCE FOREIGN POLICY, THE SUCCESSES AND FAILURES OF SUCH
POLICIES, AND THE IMPLICATIONS FOR THE US AND FOR WORLD
PEACE. IT ALSO EXAMINES THE CONFLICT BETWEEN TRADITIONAL
CONSERVATIVES AND THE RIGHT-WING WHICH HAS BEEN AT THE HEART
OF FOREIGN POLICY CONFLICTS SINCE THE END OF WORLD WAR II.
IT CONCLUDES WITH AN ANALYSIS OF THE PROSPECTS FOR FUTURE
RIGHT-WING POWER AND INFLUENCE IN THE ARENA OF US FOREIGN
POLICY.

01625 BODENHEIMER, T.; GOULD, R.
    RULING ELITES MOVE TO THE RIGHT; ROLLBACK: RIGHT WING
    POWER IN US FOREIGN POLICY
    SOUTH END PRESS, BOSTON, MA, 1989, 161-178.
    THE CHAPTER ATTEMPTS TO DEMONSTRATE A GENERAL RIGHT-WING
SHIFT IN FOREIGN POLICY ATTITUDES OF THE RULING ELITES WHICH
IS RELATED TO THE WORLD ECONOMIC CRISIS AND THE US ECONOMIC
DECLINE. IT ARGUES THAT BETWEEN 1975 AND 1980, TWO IMPORTANT
DEVELOPMENTS TOOK PLACE: AN INCREASE IN THE POWER OF RIGHT-
WING BUSINESS, AND A MARKED RIGHTWARD SHIFT IN THE VIEWS OF
CONSERVATIVE BUSINESS. IT CONCLUDES THAT DURING THE 1980'S
THE RANGE OF FOREIGN POLICY OPTIONS MOVED CONSIDERABLY TO
THE RIGHT WHEN COMPARED WITH THE 1970'S DETENTE ERA.

01626 BODENHEIMER, T.; GOULD, R.
    THE BREADTH OF RIGHT-WING INFLUENCE: FROM THINK TANKS TO
    DEMOCRATS; ROLLBACK: RIGHT-WING POWER IN US FOREIGN POLICY
    SOUTH END PRESS, BOSTON, MA, 1989, 179-202.
    THE CHAPTER DISCUSSES RIGHT-WING INFLUENCE ON OTHER
ACTORS IN THE POLICY-MAKING PROCESS. THESE ACTORS INCLUDE
THE NEO-INTELLECTUALS, THINK TANKS AND CONSENSUS COUNCILS,
THE TWO MAJOR POLITICAL PARTIES AND THE FOREIGN POLICY
BUREAUCRACY. IT ANALYZES THE OVERALL RIGHTWARD SHIFT OF US
FOREIGN POLICY VIEWS AS INFLUENCED BY THESE ACTORS.

01627 BODENHEIMER, T.; GOULD, R.
    THE GLOBAL ROLLBACK NETWORK: FROM CHIAN KAI-SHEK TO OLIVER
    NORTH; ROLLBACK: RIGHT-WING POWER IN US FOREIGN POLICY
    SOUTH END PRESS, BOSTON, MA, 1989, 53-80.
    THE CHAPTER EXAMINES THE GLOBAL ROLLBACK NETWORK OR
ROLLNET, THE PEOPLE AND INSTITUTIONS DEDICATED TO MAKING
ROLLBACK A REALITY. IT LISTS AND DESCRIBES BRIEFLY THE
ACTORS INVOLVED. THESE INCLUDE: THE CIA, THE MILITARY-
INDUSTRIAL COMPLEX, RIGHT-WING FOREIGN GOVERNMENTS, THE
WORLD ANTI-COMMUNIST LEAGUE, THE "MOONIES", AND ORGANIZED
CRIME AND DRUG SMUGGLERS. THE CHAPTER ALSO OUTLINES SOME OF
THE ACTIVITIES OF ROLLNET AND EXAMINES THEIR INFLUENCE ON
SUCH DIVERSE AREAS AS CHINA, VIETNAM, CENTRAL AMERICA, AND
AFRICA.

01628 BODENHEIMER, T.; GOULD, R.
    THE NEW DRIVE FOR NUCLEAR SUPREMACY; ROLLBACK: RIGHT-WING
    POWER IN US FOREIGN POLICY
    SOUTH END PRESS, BOSTON, MA, 1989, 117-142.
    THE CHAPTER EXPLORES THE EFFECT OF NUCLEAR WEAPONS ON
INTERNATIONAL, PARTICULARLY US-SOVIET RELATIONS. IT EXAMINES
THE NUCLEAR POLICY OF THE US BEGINING WITH THE BRIEF PERIOD
OF NUCLEAR SUPREMACY TO THE PROLIFERATION OF NUCLEAR
STOCKPILES WORLD-WIDE AND THE ACCOMPANYING DOCTRINE OF
MUTUAL ASSURED DESTRUCTION (MAD). IT OUTLINES THE POSITION

OF THE RIGHTWING WITH REGARDS TO NUCLEAR WEAPONS AND THE
SOPHISTICATED STRATEGIES UTILIZED BY THE RIGHT TO STRIVE FOR
NUCLEAR SUPREMACY. THE INFLENCE OF SDI, C31, AND THE 1987
SUMMIT ARE ALSO EXAMINED.

01629 BODENHEIMER, T.; GOULD, R.
    THE PROSPECTS FOR FUTURE RIGHT-WING POWER; ROLLBACK: RIGHT-
    WING POWER IN US FOREIGN POLICY
    SOUTH END PRESS, BOSTON, MA, 1989, 203-216.
    THE CHAPTER ATTEMPTS A FUTURE PREDICITION OF THE
FORTUNES OF THE FAR RIGHT AND THE EXTENT OF THEIR FUTURE
INFLUENCE ON US FOREIGN POLICY. IT OUTLINES THE IMPLICATIONS
OF CONTRAGATE, THE REAGAN-GORBACHEV SUMMITS, AND THE CENTRAL
AMERICAN PEACE PROCESS FOR THE RIGHT. IT CONCLUDES THAT
ALTHOUGH THE RIGHT SUFFERED MANY SETBACKS IN 1987 AND THE
DIVISION BETWEEN THE FAR RIGHT AND TRADITIONAL CONSERVATIVES
CONTINUES TO WIDEN, THE RIGHT WILL MAINTAIN A SIGNIFICANT
INFLUENCE ON US FOREIGN POLICY AND WILL PROBABLY BE THE
CAUSE OF MANY BITTER FOREIGN POLICY BATTLES IN THE FUTURE.

01630 BODENHEIMER, T.; GOULD, R.
    THE REAGAN DOCTRINE: THIRD WORLD ROLLBACK; ROLLBACK: RIGHT-
    WING POWER IN US FOREIGN POLICY
    SOUTH END PRESS, BOSTON, MA, 1989, 81-116.
    THE CHAPTER ANALYZES THE REAGAN DOCTRINE WHICH CONSISTS
PRIMARILY OF A POLICY OF THIRD WORLD ROLLBACK. IT ARGUES
THAT THE REAGAN DOCTRINE AFFIRMS THAT THIRD WORLD ROLLBACK
IS JUSTIFIED AS THE AMERICAN CONTRIBUTION TO A WORLDWIDE
DEMOCRATIC REVOLUTION.; BUT IN FACT, THE MAJOR GROUPS
SUPPORTED BY THE REAGAN DOCTRINE ARE NOT DEMOCRATIC AS
EXAMPLES OF SOUTH AFRICA, EL SALVADOR, NICARAGUA, PRE-
REVOLUTIONARY IRAN, AND THE PHILIPPINES UNDER MARCOS
DEMONSTRATE. THE CHAPTER ALSO ANALYSES REAGAN'S TACTICS OF
POLITICAL, ECONOMIC, PSYCHOLOGICAL, AND MILITARY WARFARE
CALLED LOW INTENSITY CONFLICT. IT CONCLUDES THAT THE RIGHT-
WING WAS UNABLE TO CONVINCE THE REAGAN ADMINISTRATION TO
PURSUE ROLLBACK ON EVERY POSSIBLE FRONT BECAUSE SUCH A
POLICY WAS NOT REALISTIC.

01631 BOGART, W.; ERICKSON, J.
    ON THE DESIGN OF EQUALIZING GRANTS
    PUBLIUS: THE JOURNAL OF FEDERALISM, 19(2) (SPR 89), 33-46.
    THE ARTICLE CONSIDERS THE DESIGN OF GRANTS TO OFFSET
FISCAL DISPARITIES. IT DEFINES A FISCAL DISPARITY AS A
CONDITION IN WHICH TOWNS MUST LEVY A DIFFERENT TAX RATE IN
ORDER TO PROVIDE THE SAME LEVEL OF PUBLIC SERVICES. THE WAYS
OF MEASURING DISPARITIES, AS WELL AS THE METHODS BY WHICH
GRANTS ARE ALLOCATED TO ALLEVIATE DISPARITIES ARE EXAMINES.
THE ARTICLE FOCUSES ON LUMP-SUM GRANTS FOR UNRESTRICTED USE
FROM A STATE GOVERNMENT TO GENERAL PURPOSE LOCAL GOVERNMENTS
WITHIN THAT STATE. IT CONCLUDES WITH AN EXAMPLE OF A GRANTS
FORMULA FOR THE STATE OF NEW JERSEY WHICH MEETS THE AUTHORS'
SPECIFICATIONS.

01632 BOGDAN, C.
    CROSSING THE EUROPEAN DIVIDE
    FOREIGN POLICY, (75) (SUM 89), 56-75.
    THE ARTICLE ANALYZES THE CHANGING CONDITIONS THAT
INCREASE THE HOPE OF AN ALL-EUROPE UNITY. A KEY CHANGE IS
THE DOMESTIC TRANSFORMATION IN THE USSR FROM A VERY
CONSERVATIVE REGIME TO ONE THAT ENCOURAGES REFORM AND
EXPERIMENTATION. A FRAMEWORK FOR ELIMINATING SPHERES OF
INFLUENCE AND FOR ESTABLISHING AND INCREASING UNITY IS
OUTLINED.

01633 BOGDANOR, V.
    DIRECT ELECTIONS, REPRESENTATIVE DEMOCRACY AND EUROPEAN
    INTEGRATION
    ELECTORAL STUDIES, 8(3) (DEC 89), 205-216.
    SINCE 1984, THE EUROPEAN PARLIAMENT HAS GAINED INCREASED
POWER AND WEIGHT WITHIN THE INSTITUTIONAL SYSTEM OF THE
EUROPEAN COMMUNITY. THUS, DIRECT ELECTIONS COULD BE EXPECTED
TO BE OF GREATER IMPORT IN 1989 THAN THEY WERE IN 1984 OR
1979. IN FACT, HOWEVER, DIRECT ELECTIONS ARE INCAPABLE OF
YIELDING THE VERDICT OF THE ELECTORATE ON THE FUTURE OF THE
COMMUNITY. THIS IS NOT ONLY BECAUSE THEY ARE, ALTHOUGH IN
FORM TRANSNATIONAL, IN REALITY A SUMMATION OF TWELVE
SEPARATE NATIONAL CONTESTS; BUT ALSO BECAUSE OF THE VERY
NATURE OF THE PARTY SYSTEMS IN THE MEMBER STATES AND THE
EUROPEAN PARLIAMENT WHICH SERVE TO OBSCURE RATHER THAN
ARTICULATE THE ISSUES INVOLVED IN EUROPEAN INTEGRATION.

01634 BOGDANOR, V.
    PARLIAMENTARY SCRUTINY OF EUROPEAN LEGISLATION
    CONSTITUTIONAL REFORM QUARTERLY REVIEW, 4(4) (WIN 89), 4.
    THIS ARTICLE EXPLAINS HOW THE SPEED OF ADVANCE IN THE
EUROPEAN COMMUNITY FOLLOWING THE SINGLE EUROPEAN ACT, MAKES
THE RECENTLY PUBLISHED FOURTH REPORT FROM THE SELECT
COMMITTEE ON PROCEDURE PARTICULARLY TIMELY. THE COMMITTEE
OUTLINES 'THE CONSTITUTIONAL, LEGAL AND POLITICAL CONTEXT'
OF EUROPEAN LEGISLATION, EMPHASISING THAT IT IS INITIATED BY
THE COMMISSION, A BODY WITH WHICH PARLIAMENT 'HAS NO FORMAL
RELATIONSHIP AND OVER WHICH IT HAS NO DIRECT CONTROL'.
FURTHER, THE GOVERNMENT IS REQUIRED, BY VIRTUE OF BRITISH

MEMBERSHIP OF THE COMMUNITY, TO ACCEPT THE AUTHORITY OF THE
COUNCIL OF MINISTERS, ONLY ONE OF WHOSE 12 MEMBERS IS
ACCOUNTABLE TO THE HOUSE OF COMMONS.

01635 BOGDANOR, V.
THE JUNE 1989 EUROPEAN ELECTIONS AND THE INSTITUTIONS OF
THE COMMUNITY
GOVERNMENT AND OPPOSITION, 24(2) (SPR 89), 199-214.
THE ELECTIONS TO THE EUROPEAN PARLIAMENT IN JUNE 1989
WILL BE ONLY THE THIRD EVER TO BE HELD SIMULTANEOUSLY IN
INDEPENDENT NATION STATES. THEY WILL BE CONCERNED NOT ONLY
WITH THE CHOICE OF MEP'S BUT ALSO WITH DECIDING THE SHAPE
AND FORM OF THE INTERNAL EUROPEAN MARKET. MOST IMPORTANTLY,
THE PARLIAMENT ELECTED IN 1989 COULD PLAY A VITAL ROLE IN
THE FURTHER TRANSFORMATION OF EUROPEAN INSTITUTIONS,
BECOMING IN THE PROCESS A CONSTITUENT ASSEMBLY FOR THE
EUROPEAN COMMUNITY.

01636 BOGDANOV, R.; KORTUNOV, A.
ON THE BALANCE OF POWER
INTERNATIONAL AFFAIRS (MOSCOW), (8) (AUG 89), 3-13.
IT IS NECESSARY FOR SOVIET LEADERS TO OVERCOME THE BIAS
TOWARDS WESTERN MILITARY STRATEGIC THOUGHT, SEEK COMPROMISES,
RENOUNCE THE TRADITIONAL NOTION OF THE ALLEGEDLY INHERENT
AGGRESSIVENESS OF THE WEST, AND MASTER THE ACHIEVEMENTS OF U.
S. AND WESTERN EUROPEAN MILITARY SCIENCE. BUT IN THRUSTING
DEEP INTO THE AMERICANS' STRATEGIC CULTURE, THE SOVIETS MAY
DRIFT TO MECHANICALLY DUPLICATING SOME OF THEIR STRATEGIC
CONCEPTS AND DOCTRINES WITH ALL THEIR SHORTCOMINGS AND
NEGATIVE IMPLICATIONS.

01637 BOGEN, D.; LYNCH, M.
TAKING ACCOUNT OF THE HOSTILE NATIVE: PLAUSIBLE
DENIABILITY AND THE PRODUCTION OF CONVENTIONAL HISTORY IN
THE IRAN-CONTRA HEARINGS
SOCIAL PROBLEMS, 36(3) (JUN 89), 197-224.
THIS PAPER EXAMINES THE VIDEO RECORD OF A SEGMENT OF
OLIVER NORTH'S TESTIMONY BEFORE JOINT CONGRESSIONAL
COMMITTEES INVESTIGATING THE IRAN-CONTRA AFFAIR DURING THE
SUMMER OF 1987 AND ANALYZES THE CONSTITUTIVE RELATIONSHIP
BETWEEN THE TESTIMONY AND AN EMERGENT "MASTER NARRATIVE"
BEING ASSEMBLED BY COMMITTEE INVESTIGATORS FROM A MASS OF
DOCUMENTS AND PRIOR TESTIMONIES. THE DETAILS OF NORTH'S
TESTIMONY DISPLAY THE WITNESS'S BIOGRAPHICAL RELATIONS TO
EVENTS IN THE PAST AS WELL AS HIS MORAL ENTITLEMENTS TO
SPEAK ABOUT THOSE EVENTS IN THE PRESENT CIRCUMSTANCE. IN
CONTRAST, THE COMMITTEES' CONVENTIONAL HISTORICAL ACCOUNT IS
WRITTEN IN AN ANONYMOUS VOICE AS A CHRONOLOGY OF OBJECTIVE
EVENTS, VALIDATED TESTIMONY, AND CERTIFIED DOCUMENTS. THE
PAPER ARGUES THAT ANALYTIC DIFFERENCES BETWEEN
CONVERSATIONAL STORIES AND CONVENTIONAL HISTORIES ARE USED
SYSTEMATICALLY IN THE GENERATION OF TESTIMONY. THE PAPER
FIRST DESCRIBES SOME OF THE DISCURSIVE METHODS THE
INTERROGATOR USES TO ASSIMILATE THE WITNESS'S STORIES TO A
CONVENTIONAL HISTORICAL ACCOUNT AND THEN GOES ON TO DISCUSS
HOW THE WITNESS IS ABLE TO RESIST THE MOVEMENT FROM
BIOGRAPHY TO HISTORY BY EMBEDDING HIS STORIES WITHIN A SET
OF LOCAL ENTITLEMENTS THAT RESIST TRANSLATION INTO A
GENERALIZED NARRATIVE.

01638 BOGOMOLOV, O.T.
SOCIALIST ECONOMIES AT THE TURNING POINT
INTERNATIONAL SOCIAL SCIENCE JOURNAL, (120) (MAY 89),
177-188.
THE AUTHOR SURVEYS THE ECONOMIES OF THE SOCIALIST
COUNTRIES AND ANALYZES THEIR ROLE IN THE INTERNATIONAL
DIVISION OF LABOR.

01639 BOGUSLAVSKY, M.
FOREIGN ECONOMIC ACTIVITY: SAFEGUARDING STATE INTERESTS
FOREIGN TRADE, 4 (1988), 7-11.
THIS ARTICLE EXAMINES THE FOUNDATION OF THE SOVIET
SYSTEM OF EXTERNAL ECONOMIC RELATIONS, THE STATE MONOPOLY IN
LINE WITH THE OBJECTIVE REGULARITIES GOVERNING THE
DEVELOPMENT AND VESTED ECONOMIC INTERESTS OF SOCIALIST
PRODUCTION. PRESENTLY, DEMANDS FOR A RADICAL RESTRUCTURING
OF THE ECONOMIC MECHANISM CALL FOR AN ELIMINATION OF THE GAP
BETWEEN PRODUCTION AND THE FOREIGN MARKET AND MORE
INDEPENDENCE OF DEPARTMENTS DIRECTLY PARTICIPATING IN THE
INTERNATIONAL DIVISION OF LABOR, DISCUSSED IS THE QUESTION
OF HOW TO PRECLUDE THE POSSIBILITY OF PAROCHIAL TENDENCIES
WHICH COULD MINIMIZE THE EFFECTIVENESS OF THIS ACTIVITY.

01640 BOHLEY, B.; DAVIDON, Y.; LANGE, H.; VOIGT, K.
GERMANY AFTER THE WALL
WORLD POLICY JOURNAL, 7(1) (WIN 89), 189-214.
THIS ARTICLE EXPLORES THE FAR-REACHING IMPLICATIONS OF
THE NEWLY OPENED BERLIN WALL -- THE PROSPECT OF
REUNIFICATION IT EXAMINES THE CONCERN OF BONN'S NEIGHBORS,
AS WELL AS THE UNITED STATES, THAT GERMANY IS DETERMINED TO
TRAVEL ITS OWN PATH, EVEN IF THIS MEANS UPSETTING THE
EUROPEAN BALANCE OF POWERS, THE PROSPECT OF AN UPSURGE OF
RIGHT-WING NATIONALISM IN BOTH GERMAN STATES IS EXAMINED THE
ARTICLE OFFERS INTERVIEWS, CONDUCTED AT THE INTERNATIONAL

EAST-WEST WORKSHOP ON COMMON SECURITY, ABOUT GERMANY AFTER
THE WALL.

01641 BOHNING, D.
A YEAR OF ELECTIONS
HEMISPHERE, 1(2) (WIN 89), 8-10.
ONE OF THE BIGGEST ELECTORAL DEMONSTRATIONS IN RECENT
LATIN AMERICAN HISTORY IS TAKING PLACE IN 1989, AS VOTERS IN
EIGHT COUNTRIES ELECT NEW GOVERNMENTS. THE WAVE OF ELECTIONS
TESTS THE REGION'S DEMOCRATIC TREND AND POSES POTENTIAL NEW
POLICY DILEMMAS FOR THE BUSH ADMINISTRATION. IN ADDITION TO
THE LATIN AMERICAN CONTESTS, THERE COULD BE AS MANY AS SIX
NATIONAL ELECTIONS IN THE COUNTRIES OF THE ENGLISHSPEAKING
CARIBBEAN.

01642 BOIES, J.L.
MONEY, BUSINESS, AND THE STATE: MATERIAL INTERESTS,
FORTUNE 500 CORPORATIONS, AND THE SIZE OF POLITICAL ACTION
COMMITTEES
AMERICAN SOCIOLOGICAL REVIEW, 54(5) (OCT 89), 821-833.
THIS PAPER USES DATA FROM THE FEDERAL ELECTIONS
COMMISSION ON POLITICAL ACTION COMMITTEES SPONSORED BY
FORTUNE 500 INDUSTRIALS IN 1976 AND 1980 TO EXAMINE THE
DETERMINANTS OF BUSINESS PAC SIZE. OF THE FIVE GROUPS OF
VARIABLES SUGGESTED BY THE EXTANT PAC LITERATURE -
AVAILABILITY OF RESOURCES, FREE RIDER PROBLEMS, MATERIAL
INTERESTS, PREVIOUS CAMPAIGN ACTIVITY, AND INDUSTRY
CATEGORIES - JUST THE MEASURES OF MATERIAL INTERESTS HAVE
CONSISTENT AND IMPORTANT EFFECTS ON THE LEVEL OF FIRM
POLITICAL ACTIVITY. FIRMS WITH THE RICHEST HISTORY OF
INTERACTION WITH THE STATE, TOP DEFENSE CONTRACTORS, MAJOR
ACQUIRERS OF OTHER BUSINESSES, AND CORPORATIONS PROSECUTED
FOR CRIMINAL ACTS ARE THE MOST POLITICALLY ACTIVE OF LARGE
FIRMS. THUS, WHILE MATERIAL INTERESTS ARE AN IMPORTANT
DETERMINANT OF POLITICAL ACTION, THIS STUDY SUGGESTS ONLY
INTERESTS TIED TO SPECIAL LONG-TERM RELATIONSHIPS WITH THE
STATE SERVE TO INCREASE THE AMOUNT OF POLITICAL ACTION TAKEN
BY LARGE FIRMS. THESE RESULTS SUGGEST THAT THE PLURALIST-
BASED THEORY OF BUSINESS POLITICAL INVOLVEMENT, SO WIDELY
ACCEPTED AMONG CONTEMPORARY PAC RESEARCHERS, IS OF LITTLE
UTILITY FOR EXPLAINING FIRM DIFFERENCES IN POLITICAL
ACTIVITY.

01643 BOK, C.T.
KOREA: THE MASSES - THE SUBJECT OF THE REVOLUTION
WORLD MARXIST REVIEW, 32(4) (APR 89), 38-39.
A STRONG AND WELL-KNIT PARTY IS THE MOST IMPORTANT
WEAPON OF THE REVOLUTION, A POWERFUL INSTRUMENT IN BUILDING
THE NEW SYSTEM. BUT WHILE TOUGHENING THE CORE OF SOCIETY, WE
ARE ALSO MINDFUL OF THE MASSES, THE BASIS OF SOCIETY. THE
WPK CANNOT EXIST OR ACT AT A REMOVE FROM THE PEOPLE,
OTHERWISE THERE WOULD BE NO PROGRESS IN BUILDING SOCIALISM.
BUT IF THE WORKING PEOPLE ARE TO BECOME THE TRUE SUBJECT OF
THE REVOLUTION AND DETERMINE THEIR OWN FUTURE, THEY MUST BE
IDEOLOGICALLY AND ORGANISATIONALLY RALLIED ROUND THE WPK
CENTRAL COMMITTEE. MOREOVER, THE TASK IS TO FORM A SINGLE
WHOLE, A POLITICAL AND SOCIAL ENTITY, WITH THE PARTY AS ITS
BACKBONE, AND THE LEADER AS ITS BRAIN. THIS KIND OF UNITY IS
EXCEPTIONALLY SOLID.

01644 BOLES, J.K.
A POLICY OF OUR OWN: LOCAL FEMINIST NETWORKS AND SOCIAL
SERVICES FOR WOMEN AND CHILDREN
POLICY STUDIES REVIEW, 8(3) (SPR 89), 638-647.
THIS ARTICLE EXAMINES THE WAYS IN WHICH A FEMINIST
FAMILY POLICY AGENDA HAS LED TO SIGNIFICANT POLITICAL ACTION
AND CHANGE WITHIN AMERICAN CITIES. FEMINIST GROUPS, DURING
THE PAST FIFTEEN YEARS, BECAME A PART OF EMERGING LOCAL
WOMEN'S RIGHTS POLICY NETWORKS THAT EFFECTED CHANGES IN
SEVERAL SERVICES FOR WOMEN AND CHILDREN: LIBRARIES
(PROGRAMMING FOR WOMEN AND NONSEXIST CHILDREN'S LITERATURE
ACQUISITIONS POLICIES); PUBLIC EDUCATION (GENDER EQUIT UNDER
TITLE IX); SOCIAL WELFARE (CHILD CARE AND DISPLACED
HOMEMAKER SERVICES); AND CRIMINAL JUSTICE AND HEALTH (THE
TREATMENT OF THE VICTIMS OF RAPE AND DOMESTIC VIOLENCE).
THIS POLICY SUCCESS STEMS NOT ONLY FROM THE WORKINGS OF
TRADITIONAL INTEREST GROUP POLITICS AND POLICY NETWORKS BUT
ALSO FROM THE ASTUTE USE OF POLITICAL SYMBOLS, BUREAUCRATIC
NORMS, AND THE FEDERAL SYSTEM.

01645 BOLES, J.K.
IMAGES OF FEMALE AND MALE ELECTED OFFICIALS: THE EFFECT OF
GENDER AND OTHER RESPONDENT CHARACTERISTICS
JOURNAL OF POLITICAL SCIENCE, 17(1-2) (1989), 19-31.
THE AUTHOR STUDIES THE PERCEPTIONS OF FEMALE AND MALE
ELECTED OFFICIALS. SHE FINDS THAT WOMEN IN ELECTED OFFICE
ENJOY POSITIVE IMAGES AND ARE PERCEIVED AS BEING MORE HONEST
AND MORE CARING THAN MEN IN POLITICS. ALTHOUGH THIS IMAGE
OFFERS WOMEN INITIAL ADVANTAGES IN GAINING OFFICE, THE
ACCEPTANCE OF FEMALE MORAL SUPERIORITY MAY PROVE TO BE A
BARRIER TO EFFECTIVENESS ONCE IN OFFICE. FOR EXAMPLE, WOMEN
MAY BE RELEGATED TO SPECIALIZING IN HEALTH, EDUCATION, AND
WELFARE.

01646 BOLGER, D.P.
TWO ARMIES
PARAMETERS, XIX(3) (SEP 89), 24-34.
THE AUTHOR CONSIDERS THE QUESTION OF THE MISSION OF THE
U.S. ARMY: IS IT TO FIGHT A WAR OR DETER WAR? HE ARGUES THAT
THE USA HAS TWO ARMIES: ONE FOR SHOW AND ONE FOR REAL
FIGHTING. AMERICA'S PAIR OF GROUND FORCES EXIST IN TANDEM,
THE RESULT OF A SHOTGUN WEDDING BETWEEN WHAT WORKED
YESTERDAY AND WHAT IS NEEDED NOW.

01647 BOLKESTEIN, F.
THE LIBERAL INTERNATIONAL: A LIBERAL COMMITMENT TO
INTERNATIONALISM
WASHINGTON QUARTERLY, 12(3) (SUM 89), 101-114.
THE ARTICLE OUTLINES THE GROWTH OF THE INTERNATIONAL
LIBERAL MOVEMENT. IT BEGINS WITH THE MOVEMENT'S ORIGINS IN
EUROPE AND TRACES ITS GROWTH AND EXPANSION TO SOUTH AMERICA.
THE ORGANIZATIONAL STRUCTURE OF THE MOVEMENT IS ANALYZED AS
WELL AS THE MOVEMENT'S STATED GOALS OF ADVANCING FREEDOM,
INDIVIDUALISM, DECENTRALIZATION, PRIVATE ENTERPRISE, AND THE
GURANTEE OF A MINIMUM LEVEL OF WELFARE FOR ALL. THE ARTICLE
ALSO EXPLORES THE FUTURE CHALLENGES FACING LIBERALISM IN THE
WORLD ESPECIALLY AS SOCIALISM BEGINS ITS DECLINE.

01648 BOLLE, M.J.
PRODUCTIVITY, INCOME, AND LIVING STANDARDS
CRS REVEIW, 10(5) (JUN 89), 3-4.
AFTER DECADES OF ROBUST GROWTH, THE ADVANCE IN THE U.S.
STANDARD OF LIVING HAS SLOWED TO A CRAWL. SO FAR, THE U.S.
HAS AVOIDED THE PAIN OF THIS REALITY BY IMPORTING BARGAIN
FOREIGN GOODS AND REDUCING SAVINGS. CONSUMPTION HAS OUTPACED
INCOME WHILE SAVINGS, THE WHEREWITHAL FOR PRODUCTIVITY-
INCREASING INVESTMENT, HAS FALLEN TO AN ALL-TIME LOW. NOW IT
IS QUESTIONABLE WHETHER THE U.S. CAN REVERSE THE DECREASE IN
PRODUCTIVITY AND LIVING STANDARDS.

01649 BOLLEN, K. A.; JACKMAN, R.W.
DEMOCRACY, STABILITY, AND DICHOTOMIES
AMERICAN SOCIOLOGICAL REVIEW, 54(4) (AUG 89), 612-621.
AN EARLY DEBATE IN THE EMPIRICAL STUDY OF POLITICAL
DEMOCRACY CONCERNED THE MEASUREMENT OF DEMOCRACY. INITIAL
WORK EMPLOYED DICHOTOMOUS INDICATORS AND INCORPORATED
STABILITY INTO POLITICAL DEMOCRACY MEASURES. EVIDENCE
ACCUMULATED SHOWING THAT THIS APPROACH COULD ADVERSELY
AFFECT ANALYSES, PARTICULARLY IN THE STUDY OF INCOME
INEQUALITY. DESPITE THIS, SOME RECENT STUDIES HAVE RENEWED
THE FLAWED PRACTICES. CONFUSION CAN RESULT WHEN DEMOCRACY
AND STABILITY ARE CONFOUNDED. STABILITY IS ANALYTICALLY
DISTINCT FROM POLITICAL DEMOCRACY AND SHOULD BE TREATED AS
SUCH EMPIRICALLY. POLITICAL DEMOCRACY IS CONTINUOUS AND
MEASURES OF IT SHOULD REFLECT THIS. IT IS IMPORTANT THAT THE
MEASUREMENT HISTORY OF THIS CONSTRUCT NOT REPEAT ITSELF.

01650 BOLLINGER, W.
VILLALOBOS ON "POPULAR INSURRECTION"
LATIN AMERICAN PERSPECTIVES, 16(3) (SUM 89), 38-47.
IN HIS ARTICLE (THIS ISSUE) VILLALOBOS ARGUES THAT THE
DEMISE OF THE CENTRIST CHRISTIAN DEMOCRATS MARKS THE
COLLAPSE OF A FACADE BEHIND WHICH THE UNITED STATES HAS
CONDUCTED COUNTERINSURGENCY WAR. IF THE FMLN IS CORRECT IN
ITS SOCIAL EXPLOSION PROGNOSIS, IT MAY BE ABLE TO CONVINCE U.
S. POLICYMAKERS JUST HOW DANGEROUS IT IS TO CONTINUE THIS
WAR. AT THAT POINT, LATIN AMERICAN GOVERNMENTS, BUILDING
UPON THEIR CONTADORA AND ESQUIPULAS DIPLOMACY, CAN PLAY A
KEY ROLE IN GUIDING WASHINGTON TOWARD ENDING A WAR THAT THE
UNITED STATES CANNOT WIN.

01651 BOLTHO, A.
OBSTACLES TO MACROECONOMIC COORDINATION IN EUROPE
INTERNATIONAL SPECTATOR, XXIV(3-4) (JUL 89), 175-185.
THIS PAPER LOOKS AT WHETHER AND WHY EEC GOVERNMENTS MAY
HAVE SHIED AWAY FROM COOPERATING IN THE MACROECONOMIC ARENA.
PARTICULARLY IN THE USE OF DISCRETIONARY FISCAL POLICIES AND
PARTICULARLY IN THE 1980S. FOLLOWING AN OVERVIEW OF PAST
COOPERATION, SOME OF THE THEORETICAL AND EMPIRICAL OBSTACLES
THAT MAY HAVE PREVENTED INTRA-EEC COOPERATION ARE SURVEYED.
A CLOSE EXAMINATION IS THEN MADE OF ONE SPECIFIC PROBLEM
THAT MAY HAVE IMPEDED COORDINATION IN EUROPE IN THE RECENT
PAST: THE EXTRAORDINARILY DIFFERENT POSITIONS TAKEN BY
MEMBER COUNTRIES IN THE 1980S ON THE EFFECTIVENESS OF FISCAL
POLICY. THE PAPER CONCLUDES WITH A SUMMARY OF THE ARGUMENTS
AND SUGGESTIONS FOR THE FUTURE.

01652 BOLTON, D.
HAS PEACE BROKEN OUT?
RUSI JOURNAL, 134(3) (FAL 89), 1-2.
THE ARTICLE ANALYZES THE WIDELY HELD PUBLIC PERCEPTION
OF INCREASING GLOBAL PEACE AND SECURITY. IT CONCLUDES THAT
ALTHOUGH SUCH PERCEPTIONS CERTAINLY HAVE SOME BASIS IN FACT,
IT IS IMPORTANT TO VIEW THE VENTS IN THE WORLD WITH CAUTION
AND PRUDENCE. IT CITES TIANANMEN SQUARE AS AN EXAMPLE OF
WHAT A COMMUNIST REGIME MAY DO WHEN PUSHED TOO FAR. IT ALSO
WARNS AGAINST THE PURSUIT OF ARMS CONTROL AGREEMENTS THAT
ARE POLITICALLY BENEFICIAL, BUT DANGEROUS TO THE BALANCE OF

POWER.

01653 BOLTON, J.R.
THE CONCEPT OF THE 'UNITARY UN'
DEPARTMENT OF STATE BULLETIN (US FOREIGN POLICY), 89(2151)
(OCT 89), 74-75.
THE UNITARY UNITED NATIONS CONCEPT PROVIDES A BASIS FOR
DEALING COHERENTLY WITH THE UN SYSTEM ON BOTH BUDGETARY AND
POLICY GROUNDS. IT ALSO OFFERS A PRINCIPLED RULE OF DECISION
TO PRUNE THE THICKET OF UN GOVERNING BODIES. MOREOVER, IT
PERMITS THE REDEFINITION OF THE PROPER LIMITS OF EACH UN
COMPONENT'S RESPONSIBILITIES AND HELPS PREVENT BOTH EMPIRE-
BUILDING AND TURF-FIGHTING.

01654 BOLUKBASIOGLU, S.
THE UNITED STATES-TURKEY INFLUENCE RELATIONSHIP DURING THE
CYPRUS CRISES
DISSERTATION ABSTRACTS INTERNATIONAL, 49(11) (MAY 89),
3496-A.
THE CYPRUS CRISES OF 1964, 1967, AND 1974 AFFECTED THE
ACTIONS OF BOTH TURKEY AND THE USA AND SHAPED THE AMERICAN-
TURKISH INFLUENCE RELATIONSHIP. AFTER THE 1964 CRISIS,
TURKEY REALIZED THAT ITS NATO MEMBERSHIP DID NOT ASSURE THE
PROTECTION OF ITS INTERESTS IN CYPRUS, THEREFORE, THE
TURKISH GOVERNMENT ADOPTED A FLEXIBLE FOREIGN POLICY
DESIGNED TO LESSEN TURKEY'S DEPENDENCY ON THE USA.

01655 BOMSDORF, F.
THE SOVIET UNION'S NORDIC INITIAVE
AUSSEN POLITIK, 40(1) (JAN 89), 55-65.
THE ARTICLE EXAMINES THE SOVIET UNION'S NORDIC
INITIATIVE THAT WAS REFLECTED IN A SPEECH BY MIKHAIL
GORBACHEV IN MURMANSK. IT ANALYZES WHICH PARTS OF THE
INITIAVE ARE NEW AND WHICH ARE MERELY EXTENSIONS OF OLD
POLICIES. GENERALLY, THE CIVILIAN PARTS OF THE INITIAVE ARE
NEW AND THE SECURITY RELATED PARTS ARE NOT. THE ARTICLE ALSO
EXPLORES MOSCOW'S MOTIVES AND AIMS OF THE NORDIC INITIATIVE
AND POSSIBLE WESTERN REACTIONS TO IT.

01656 BONIME, A.R.
THE POLITICS OF CONSTITUTION-MAKING: SPAIN'S TRANSITION TO
DEMOCRACY
DISSERTATION ABSTRACTS INTERNATIONAL, 48(10) (APR 88),
2715-A.
THE STUDY FOCUSES ON ONE OF THE MOST IMPORTANT POLITICAL
DEVELOPMENTS IN THE TRANSITION FROM AUTHORITARIANISM TO
DEMOCRACY: THE CONSTITUTION-MAKING PROCESS AND OUTCOME. IT
CONCLUDES THAT TWO NECESSARY POLITICAL OCCURRENCES FOR A
"TURNING POINT" TOWARDS DEMOCRATIZATION ARE INTERNAL
AUTHORITARIAN ELITE CHANGE AND SOME FORM OF SOCIO-POLITICAL
PLURALIZATION. THE STUDY USES SPAIN AS A CASE TO SUPPORT ITS
CLAIMS.

01657 BONIN, J.J.; STEVENSON, D.E.
RISK ASSESSMENT IN SETTING NATIONAL PRIORITIES
PLENUM PRESS, NEW YORK, NY, 1989, 680.
THIS BOOK IS VOLUME SIX OF A SERIES ON ADVANCES IN RISK
ANALYSIS, IT IS A LARGE COLLECTION OF ARTICLES BY DIFFERENT
AUTHORS, EDITED BY JAMES J. BONIN AND DONALD E. STEVENSON.
IT ADDRESSES THE NEED FOR A HOLISTIC APPROACH TO RISK
ANALYSIS. IT COVERS AN EXTENSIVE SPECTRUM OF RISK AREAS
INCLUDING: RISK IN DEFENSE POLICY DECISIONS; THS SDI AND
NUCLEAR PROLIFERATION FROM A RISK ANALYSIS PERSPECTIVE;
GLOBAL RISK ASSESSMENT; AND THE ROLE OF RISK ASSESSMENT IN
NEW HAMPSHIRE STATE GOVERNMENT

01658 BONN, J.J.; STEVENSON, D.E.; TILLER, M.H.
GLOBAL RISK ASSESSMENT; RISK ASSESSMENT IN SETTING
NATIONAL PRIORITIES
PLENUM PRESS, NEW YORK, NY, 1989, 297-306.
THIS PAPER DISCUSSES THE NEED FOR GLOBAL RISK ASSESSMENT
AND SUGGESTS A GENERAL PHILOSOPHICAL DESIGN APPROACH FOR
SUCH A MONUMENTAL TASK. ONE KEY TO THE SUCCESS OF SUCH AN
ENDEAVOR LIES IN THE INTEGRATION OF GLOBAL RISK ASSESSMENT
DATA NEEDS INTO THE OVERALL FRAMEWORK OF GLOBAL CHANGE STUDY
RECENTLY INITIATED BY SEVERAL ORGANIZATIONS, INCLUDING THE
INTERNATIONAL COUNCIL OF SCIENTIFIC UNIONS. IT IS
EXPLORATORY IN NATURE AND HOPES TO SERVE AS A POINT OF
DEPARTURE FOR MORE DEFINITIVE DESIGN OF A GLOBAL RISK
ASSESSMENT.

01659 BONN, J.J.; PATE-CORNELL, M.E.; STEVENSON, D.E.
RISK IN DEFENSE POLICY DECISIONS; RISK ASSESSMENT IN
SETTING NATIONAL PRIORITIES
PLENUM PRESS, NEW YORK, NY, 1989, 135-150.
THIS PAPER SHOWS HOW THE USE OF RISK ANALYSIS AND
DECISION THEORY CAN IMPROVE THE STRATEGIC DEBATE AND THE
CHOICE OF SOME DEFENSE POLICIES. THREE DIFFERENT LEVELS OF
ABSTRACTION AND QUANTIFICATION IN THE USE OF THESE METHODS
ARE PRESENTED AND ILLUSTRATED. IN ALL THREE CASES, BAYESIAN
TECHNIQUES PERMIT REASONINGS AND CONCLUSIONS THAT ARE NOT
EASILY ACHIEVABLE, IF AT ALL REACHABLE, BY CLASSICAL METHODS
OF STRATEGIC ANALYSIS.

01660 BONN, J.J.; JACHATZ, A.; LYNCH, S.; SCHWALBE, C.;
STEVENSON, D.E.
ROLE OF RISK ASSESSMENT IN NEW HAMPSHIRE STATE GOVERNMENT;
RISK ASSESSMENT IN SETTING NATIONAL PRIORITIES
PLENUM PRESS NEW YORK AND LONDON, 1989, 529-534.
THIS ARTICLE DETAILS THE WORK OF THE ENVIRONMENT HEALTH
RISK ASSESSMENT UNIT WITHIN THE NEW HAMPSHIRE DIVISION OF
PUBLIC HEALTH SERVICES. THIS UNIT IS DESIGNATED AS THE FOCAL
POINT FOR RISK ASSESSMENT IN THE STATE. IT EXAMINES THE ROLE
OF THE UNIT AND GIVES AN EXAMPLE OF THEIR ROLE IN RISK
ASSESSMENT -- THEIR PROGRAM OF EVALUATING RISKS FROM
CONTAMINATION OF PRIVATE DRINKING WATER SUPPLIES. AN
ANALYSIS OF THIS EVALUATION IS GIVEN.

01661 BONN, J.J.; STARR, C.; STEVENSON, D.E.; WHIPPLE, C.
THE STRATEGIC DEFENSE INITIATIVE AND NUCLEAR PROLIFERATION
FROM A RISK ANALYSIS PERSPECTIVE
PLENUM PRESS, NEW YORK, NY, 1989, 151-158.
THE RISKS FROM NUCLEAR WEAPONS AND THE EFFECT OF THE SDI
ON THESE RISKS ARE EXAMINED FROM PERSPECTIVES COMMONLY USED
IN RISK ANALYSIS. TWO PRIMARY ISSUES ADDRESSED ARE HOW RISKS
AND RESPONSES TO RISKS OF NUCLEAR WAR ARE PERCEIVED
DIFFERENTLY DEPENDING ON WHETHER A SHORT-TERM OR LONG-TERM
VIEWPOINT IS TAKEN, AND ON WHETHER SDI INHANCES OR REPLACES
THE TRADITIONAL NUCLEAR ARMS PHILOSOPHY OF MUTUALLY ASSURED
DESTRUCTION. SPECIAL ATTENTION IS GIVEN TO THE DISTINCTION
BETWEEN DEFENSIVE SYSTEMS WHICH PROTECT NUCLEAR WEAPONS FROM
A FIRST STRIKE, AND THEREBY ASSURE THE CAPACITY FOR A
RETALIATORY RESPONSE, AND DEFENSIVE SYSTEMS MEANT TO PROTECT
PEOPLE AND CITIES.

01662 BONNART, F.
ALLIANCES FOR STABILITY
NATO'S SIXTEEN NATIONS, 34(7) (DEC 89), 9.
IN THE RECENT PAST THE BALANCE OF MILITARY THREAT AND
COUNTER-THREAT IN EUROPE PROVIDED A SOMEWHAT ARID BUT
NEVERTHELESS ASSURED STABILITY. THE PRESENT VANISHING
MILITARY THREAT IS COMBINED WITH A GREAT DEAL OF POLITICAL
INSTABILITY. IT IS CONNECTED, MOREOVER, WITH GRAVE ECONOMIC
PROBLEMS. IN THIS ATMOSPHERE, NATO'S DEFENSE AND POLITICAL
ROLES WILL BECOME EVEN MORE IMPORTANT THAN BEFORE.

01663 BONNART, F.
BEYOND MERE NUMBERS
NATO'S SIXTEEN NATIONS, 34(4) (AUG 89), 9.
PRESIDENT GEORGE BUSH HAS PROPOSED TO INCLUDE AMERICAN
TROOPS IN EUROPE AS WELL AS AIRCRAFT AND HELICOPTERS IN THE
CFE NEGOTIATIONS IN VIENNA AND HAS SET A SIX TO TWELVE MONTH
TIMETABLE. BUT HIS INITIATIVE APPEARS TO HAVE BEEN RUSHED
THROUGH WITHOUT MANY OF THE DEEP CALCULATIONS THAT WOULD
NORMALLY PRECEDE SUCH FAR-REACHING PROPOSALS. THE NATO
COUNTRIES DO NOT SEEM TO HAVE THOUGHT DEEPLY ABOUT HOW TO
IMPLEMENT PROPOSED CUTS AND HOW TO VERIFY THE PROVISIONS OF
THE TREATY ONCE IT IS AGREED UPON. THIS OMISSION MAY COST
THEM DEARLY.

01664 BONNART, F.
ONE GERMANY AND NATO?
NATO'S SIXTEEN NATIONS, 34(6) (OCT 89), 5.
IF NATO HAS ACHIEVED ITS OBJECTIVES AND WON A BLOODLESS
VICTORY IN THE STRUGGLE THAT IT HAS WAGED FOR ALMOST HALF A
CENTURY, WHAT IS ITS PURPOSE AND SHOULD IT CONTINUE TO
EXIST? THE PRESENT SOVIET EXPERIMENT MAY MISCARRY AND
COLLAPSE INTO ECONOMIC CHAOS. IF SO, THE CONSEQUENT DISORDER
COULD PRODUCE A COMPLETE POLITICAL REVERSAL WITH HARSH
REPRESSIVE MEASURES AND THE NEED FOR EXTERNAL ACTION TO
REASSERT THE LEADERS' POWER. THEREFORE, IT WOULD BE FOOLISH
TO THROW AWAY THE SOLIDARITY OF THE ALLIANCE AND THE
MECHANISM TO MAINTAIN THE SECURITY OF ITS MEMBERS. BUT
NATO'S PURPOSE TRANSCENDS DEFENSE TO SOLVING THE PROBLEMS OF
CHANGE. A REUNIFIED GERMANY WOULD BE POWERFUL PARTNER IN
THIS UNDERTAKING DUE TO ITS STRENGTH AND ECONOMIC POWER.

01665 BONNART, F.
TESTING TIMES
NATO'S SIXTEEN NATIONS, 34(3) (JUN 89), 9.
DESPITE RECENT ARMS CONTROL PROPOSALS BY GORBACHEV, THE
REALITY OF SOVIET POWER OVER EUROPE WILL REMAIN UNCHANGED.
NEW, MORE MODERN SOVIET MILITARY COMMANDERS WILL SOON SEE
THE ADVANTAGES OF CONCENTRATING THEIR REDUCED RESOURCES TO
CREATE SMALLER BUT FAR MORE EFFECTIVE CONVENTIONAL FORCES.
THE REALITY THAT WESTERN POLITICIANS SHOULD EMPHASIZE IS
THAT AS LONG AS NO SUPRA-NATIONAL POWER EXISTS TO REGULATE
RELATIONS BETWEEN STATES, NO COUNTRY OR GROUPS OF COUNTRIES
WILL EVER GIVE UP THE ABILITY TO PRESERVE ITS SECURITY. THE
SOVIET UNION MUST, THEREFORE, MAINTAIN AN ADEQUATE MILITARY
CAPACITY. THIS IS THE MOST TELLING ARGUMENT FOR MAINTAINING
THE SOLIDARITY AND MILITARY STRENGTH OF NATO.

01666 BONNART, F.
THE SECURITY POLICY OF FRANCE: INTERVIEW WITH THE MINISTER
OF DEFENCE OF FRANCE
NATO'S SIXTEEN NATIONS, 34(6) (OCT 89), 18-21.
FRENCH SECURITY POLICY IS BASED ON THE DETERRENCE

CONCEPT AS EXPRESSED BY FRANCE'S TRIAD OF CONVENTIONAL, PRE-
STRATEGIC AND STRATEGIC FORCES. THESE WILL BE MAINTAINED IN
THE PLAN 2000 FOR ITS ARMED FORCES WITH VARIATIONS IN
EMPHASIS. FRANCE IS A WHOLEHEARTED MEMBER OF THE NORTH
ATLANTIC ALLIANCE BUT WANTS TO SEE A MORE RAPID DEVELOPMENT
OF THE EUROPEAN PILLAR. ALTHOUGH CO-OPERATION IN ARMAMENTS
PRODUCTION HAS HAD FAILURES AS WELL AS SUCCESSES, IMPROVED
RESULTS ARE EXPECTED FROM A RESTRUCTURED DEFENCE INDUSTRY
AND CLOSER TIES ON A EUROPEAN LEVEL. THE PLAN "ARMEES 2000"
WILL PRODUCE A STRONGER AND MORE COHERENT DEFENSIVE FORCE.

01667 BONNELL, V.E.
MOSCOW: A VIEW FROM BELOW
DISSENT, (SUM 89), 311-317.
DECADES OF PREVARICATION AND HYPERBOLE HAVE LEFT THEIR
MARK ON THE SOVIET PEOPLE. ALTHOUGH NEARLY EVERYONE WELCOMES
GLASNOST TO SOME DEGREE, THE REACTIONS TO IT AND PERESTROIKA
ARE MORE VARIED, COMPLEX, AND PROBLEMATIC THAN A WESTERN
OBSERVER MIGHT EXPECT. WESTERN OPTIMISM ABOUT GORBACHEV'S
RECENT REFORMS IS NOT QUITE SHARED IN MOSCOW. THE PEOPLE
HAVE A WORRIED AND SKEPTICAL ATTITUDE TOWARD PERESTROIKA. IT
IS A SORT OF CIVIC CYNICISM: A PROFOUND MISTRUST OF
POLITICAL AUTHORITY AND OFFICIAL DECLARATIONS.

01668 BONNICKSEN, A.L.
HUMAN EMBRYO FREEZING AND IN VITRO FERTILIZATION: POLICY
DIRECTIONS
POLICY STUDIES REVIEW, 8(2) (WIN 89), 380-388.
FREEZING RAISES QUESTIONS ABOUT WHAT POLICIES, IF ANY,
OUGHT TO BE ENACTED REGARDING ITS CLINICAL PRACTICE. THIS
PAPER ARGUES THAT POLICY ON EMBRYO FREEZING SHOULD NOT BE
ENACTED UNTIL MORE IS KNOWN ABOUT FREEZING'S SPECIFIC HARMS
AND BENEFITS IN THE CLINICAL SETTING. IN THE MEANTIME,
EFFORTS SHOULD BE MADE TO ENCOURAGE MORE RIGOROUS SELF-
MONITORING WITHIN THE MEDICAL SECTOR AND GREATER
COMMUNICATION BY PATIENTS ABOUT THEIR EXPERIENCES WITH
FREEZING. THE CHALLENGE OF THE 1990S IS TO DEVELOP WAYS OF
ENCOURAGING AGGRESSIVE SELF-MONITORING BY THE MEDICAL SECTOR.
UNTIL THE GOVERNMENT OVERCOMES ITS RELUCTANCE TO ENACT
POLICY REGARDING TECHNIQUES DEALING WITH HUMAN EMBRYOS, THIS
IS A REALISTIC INTERMEDIARY COURSE OF ACTION.

01669 BONVICINI, G.
THE POLITICAL AND INSTITUTIONAL ASPECTS OF EUROPEAN DEFENCE
INTERNATIONAL SPECTATOR, XXIII(2) (APR 88), 108-116.
THE PROBLEM OF EUROPEAN DEFENSE HAS RECENTLY BECOME A
MAJOR POLITICAL PROBLEM DUE TO TWO IMPORTANT EVENTS: THE
CONCLUSION OF THE SOVIET-AMERICAN AGREEMENT ON SHORT-AND
MEDIUM-RANGE MISSILES AND THE INCREASED FRENCH-GERMAN
MILITARY COOPERATION. THESE EVENTS HAVE LED TO INCREASED
SPECULATION ABOUT EUROPEAN UNION AND WHETHER IT IS A
REALISTIC OR A DESIRABLE GOAL.

01670 BONVICINI, G.; MARE, M.; PIACENTINO, D.
1992: INDUSTRIAL POLICY ISSUES FOR MAJOR EC COUNTRIES
INTERNATIONAL SPECTATOR, XXIII(4) (OCT 88), 230-241.
TJHE AUTHORS CONSIDER SOME OF THE INDUSTRIAL POLICY
ISSUES RELATED TO THE ECONOMIC INTEGRATION OF EUROPE,
INCLUDING HARMONIZATION OF FISCAL POLICY AND REGULATORY
STRUCTURES FOR SAFEGUARDING INDUSTRIAL PROPERTY AND FOR
ECHNICAL STANDARDIZATON AND THE ELIMINATION OF MEASURES
LIMITING OR DISTORTING INTERNATIONAL COMPETITION AMONG
BUSINESSES.

01671 BOO, K.
IT'S NOT JUST WASHINGTON
WASHINGTON MONTHLY, 20(12) (JAN 89), 37, 39-40.
FOR POLITICIANS, NON-RESPONSE IN CASES INVOLVING THE
POOR AND THE POWERLESS HAS BECOME THE BEST RESPONSE.
EVERYWHERE, POOR KIDS WHO RELY ON CITY SERVICES FACE THE
DANGERS OF BUREAUCRATIC APATHY AND INCOMPETENCE. THE ONE
THING THAT ISN'T AT RISK IS THE JOB SECURITY OF MUNICIPAL
EMPLOYEES. THEIR PAYCHECKS ARE THE SAFEST THINGS AROUND.

01672 BOOKCHIN, M.
WHICH WAY FOR THE U.S. GREENS?
NEW POLITICS, 11(2) (WIN 89), 71-83.
IF U.S. GREENS ADOPT DEEP ECOLOGY'S BIOCENTRISM, ITS
DENIGRATION OF HUMAN WORTH, ITS MYSTICAL THRUST, AND ITS
SUBORDINATION OF SOCIAL ISSUES TO A NOTION THAT PLACES
"WILDERNESS" BEFORE SOCIETY AS "THE REAL WORLD," HOWEVER,
THEY WILL EVENTUALLY BECOME A CULT RATHER THAN A MOVEMENT.
OF DIRECT IMPORTANCE TO THE FUTURE OF THE U.S. GREENS IS A
CLEAR UNDERSTANDING OF THE ORIGINS OF THE ECOLOGICAL CRISIS
AND THE MEANS NEEDED TO RESOLVE IT. THAT THE IMMEDIATE
SOURCE OF THE CRISIS IS CAPITALISM, A COMPETITIVE SOCIETY
STRUCTURED AROUND THE NEED TO GROW OR DIE, HAS BEEN
SUFFICIENTLY EMPHASIZED. TO THIS WE MUST ADD A
CIVILIZATIONAL PROBLEM THAT IS, HISTORICALLY, AT LEAST, EVEN
MORE BASIC: THE EXISTENCE OF HIERARCHIES AND OF A
HIERARCHICAL MENTALITY OR CULTURE THAT PRECEDED THE
EMERGENCE OF ECONOMIC CLASSES AND EXPLOITATION.

01673 BOONEKAMP, C.
INDUSTRIAL POLICIES OF INDUSTRIAL COUNTRIES
FINANCE AND DEVELOPMENT, 26(1) (MAR 89), 14-17.
THIS ARTICLE DISCUSSES GOVERNMENT ACTIONS TO FOSTER
SPECIFIC INDUSTRIES, EITHER BY SHIFTING RESOURCES TO
ACTIVITIES THAT WILL USE THEM MORE PRODUCTIVELY IN SUPPORT
OF ADJUSTMENT GOALS OR BY MAINTAINING RESOURCES IN EXISTING
ACTIVITIES FOR SECURITY, POLITICAL, OR OTHER REASONS. THE
AUTHOR LOOKS AT THE DOMESTIC EFFECTS OF THESE POLICIES AND
AT HOW THEY AFFECT TRADE FLOWS, PARTICULARLY THOSE OF
DEVELOPING COUNTRIES.

01674 BOONYAWAT, P.
THE ROLE OF THE GOVERNOR AND THE PROVINCIAL COMMITTEE
SYSTEM IN INTER-AGENCY COORDINATION OF RURAL DEVELOPMENT
PROGRAMS IN THAILAND: FORM VERSUS REALITY
DISSERTATION ABSTRACTS INTERNATIONAL, 49(8) (FEB 89),
2384-A.
THIS DISSERTATION IS AN EXPLORATORY STUDY DESIGNED TO
INVESTIGATE BOTH THE STRUCTURES AND PROCESSES OF DEVELOPMENT
ADMINISTRATION IN THAILAND. IT FOCUSES ON THE MECHANISMS
DESIGNED TO INCREASE INTER-AGENCY COORDINATION AT THE
PROVINCIAL LEVEL AND THE IMPEDIMENTS THAT TEND TO BLOCK
COORDINATION.

01675 BOOTH, A.
INDONESIAN AGRICULTURAL DEVELOPMENT IN COMPARATIVE
PERSPECTIVE
WORLD DEVELOPMENT, 17(8) (AUG 89), 1235-1254.
IN BOTH THE LATE COLONIAL AND THE EARLY POST-
INDEPENDENCE PERIODS, MOST OBSERVERS OF THE INDONESIAN
ECONOMY WERE PESSIMISTIC ABOUT THE PROSPECTS FOR
AGRICULTURAL, AND ESPECIALLY FOODCROP, GROWTH. BUT OVER THE
LAST 15 YEARS, FOOD PRODUCTION GROWTH IN INDONESIA HAS BEEN
AMONG THE FASTEST IN THE WORLD. THIS PAPER EXAMINES THE
REASONS FOR THE ACCELERATED GROWTH AND REVIEWS SOME OF THE
LITERATURE ON ITS DISTRIBUTIVE CONSEQUENCES. COMPARISONS ARE
MADE WITH OTHER EPISODES OF ACCELERATED AGRICULTURAL GROWTH
IN RECENT ASIAN HISTORY, ESPECIALLY THAT OF MEIJI JAPAN. IT
IS SHOWN THAT THERE ARE REMARKABLE SIMILARITIES BETWEEN
AGRICULTURAL DEVELOPMENT INDICATORS IN INDONESIA AND THOSE
IN MEIJI JAPAN. THE CHALLENGE FOR INDONESIAN POLICY MAKERS
IN THE FUTURE WILL BE TO BUILD ON THE AGRICULTURAL SUCCESSES
OF THE PAST TWO DECADES IN ORDER TO CREATE A MORE
DIVERSIFIED ECONOMY AND ENSURE SUSTAINED ECONOMIC
DEVELOPMENT.

01676 BOOTH, W.
GONE FISHING: MAKING SENSE OF MARX'S CONCEPT OF COMMUNISM
POLITICAL THEORY, 17(2) (MAY 89), 205-222.
THE ARTICLE SEEKS TO ANALYZE AND SKETCH CENTRAL ELEMENTS
OF MARX'S CRITIQUE OF CAPITALISM AND TO DERIVE FROM THAT
CRITIQUE THE SENSE OF HIS PORTRAIT OF COMMUNISM. IT FOCUSES
NOT ON THE PHENOMENA OF EXPLOITATION, DOMINATION OF SOCIETY
BY BOURGEOISIE, AND DOMINATION AT THE POINT OF PRODUCTION
WHICH MAKE UP THE TRADITIONAL "PLAIN MARXISM", BUT ON THE
IDEA OF DOMINATION BY AN AUTONOMOUS ECONOMIC PROCESS.

01677 BOOTH, W.J.
EXPLAINING CAPITALISM: THE METHOD OF MARX'S POLITICAL
ECONOMY
POLITICAL STUDIES, XXXVII(4) (DEC 89), 612-625.
THE CENTRAL THESIS OF THIS ARTICLE IS THAT MARX'S
EXPLANATION OF THE SIGNIFICANT PHENOMENA OF THE CAPITALIST
ECONOMY DRAWS UPON A BASIC THEORETICAL SYNTAX OF A
DETERMINIST/LATENT FUNCTIONALIST TYPE. THIS CONCLUSION HAS
THREE CONSEQUENCES. FIRST, IT EXTENDS THE RANGE OF
FUNCTIONALIST EXPLANATION IN MARX BEYOND ITS TRADITIONAL
LOCI, NAMELY THE THEORY OF HISTORY AND THE ANALYSIS OF THE
ROLE OF THE STATE AND OTHER INSTITUTIONS IN STABILIZING
CAPITALISM, INTO THE VERY HEART OF MARX'S PROJECT, HIS
POLITICAL ECONOMY. SECONDLY, IT HAS A POWERFUL, THOUGH
INDIRECT, IMPACT ON OUR UNDERSTANDING OF WHAT MIGHT LOOSELY
BE CALLED THE NORMATIVE COMPONENT OF MARX'S WRITINGS IN AS
MUCH AS IT IDENTIFIES A SPECIFIC SORT OF UNFREEDOM PECULIAR
TO CAPITALIST SOCIETY. THIRDLY, IT SHOWS JUST HOW GREAT A
CHALLENGE IS MOUNTED AGAINST MARX'S PROJECT BY THOSE WHO
SEEK TO RECAST ITS METHOD OF EXPLANATION ALONG
METHODOLOGICAL INDIVIDUALIST LINES. FOR IF THE FIRST TWO
POINTS ARE ACCURATE, RATIONAL-CHOICE MARXISTS ARE DRAWN INTO
A CRITIQUE OF BOTH THE EXPLANATORY AND NORMATIVE CORE OF
MARXISM.

01678 BORBELY, A.F.
FROM PRODUCTION TO CREATION
POLITICAL AFFAIRS, LXVIII(7) (JUL 89), 41-44.
IN ORDER TO ACHIEVE ITS SCIENTIFIC AND SOCIAL GOALS, THE
COMMUNIST PARTY SHOULD ESTABLISH AN INTERDISCIPLINARY
RESEARCH INSTITUTE. IT WOULD BE CHARGED WITH RESEARCHING THE
RELATIONSHIPS BETWEEN THE FOLLOWING KEY MOTIVATION-RELATED
SCIENCES: MARXISM (MOTIVATIONS ON THE COLLECTIVE LEVEL),
PSYCHOANALYSIS (MOTIVATIONS ON THE INDIVIDUAL LEVEL) AND
ARTIFICIAL INTELLIGENCE (MOTIVATIONS ON THE LEVEL OF THE
PERSON/MACHINE INTERFACE). WITH THIS THE CP WOULD INCLUDE

WITHIN ITS ASPIRATIONS A LEADING ROLE IN THE INTERPRETATION
OF, AND ACTIVE PARTICIPATION, IN THE SCIENTIFIC-
TECHNOLOGICAL REVOLUTION. SUCH A LEADERSHIP ROLE WILL BE
NECESSARY TO MAINTAIN PERSPECTIVE WITHIN OUR VERY FAST
CHANGING WORLD AND WOULD COMPLEMENT THE WELL ESTABLISHED
ROLES OF POLITICAL AND MORAL LEADERSHIP.

01679 BORG, P.W.
TELECOMMUNICATIONS AND ECONOMIC DEVELOPMENT IN THE
CARIBBEAN
DEPARTMENT OF STATE BULLETIN (US FOREIGN POLICY), 89(2144)
(MAR 89), 17-20.
ONE OF THE MOST IMPORTANT GOALS OF THE US INTERNATIONAL
COMMUNICATIONS AND INFORMATION POLICY IS TO EXPAND THE
ECONOMIC AND SOCIAL BENEFITS OF THE INFORMATION AGE TO THE
DEVELOPING NATIONS. THERE ARE FEW REGIONS WHERE THE IMPACT
OF RECENT TELECOMMUNICATIONS TECHNOLOGY IS SO EVIDENT OR
WHERE THE POTENTIAL FOR FUTURE GROWTH IS AS GREAT AS IN THE
CARIBBEAN BASIN.

01680 BORGER, J.
THE POVERTY OF RICHES
NEW AFRICAN, (266) (NOV 89), 33.
THIS ARTICLE REPORTS ON A DIAMOND BOOM IN SIERRA LEONE
THAT IS IMPOVERISHING THE COUNTRY AND ITS PEOPLE, IT REPORTS
ON THE SMUGGLING WHICH CONTINUES DESPITE THE NEW MINING
POLICY THAT REQUIRES EVERY EXPORTER SHOW A TURNOVER OF AT
LEAST $500,000 PER MONTH.

01681 BORIN, V.
USSR COMPENSATION-BASED COOPERATION WITH DEVELOPED
CAPITALIST COUNTRIES.
FOREIGN TRADE, 5 (1988), 30-33.
THIS ARTICLE EXAMINES THE COMPENSATION-BASED COOPERATION
OF SOVIET ORGANIZATIONS WITH CAPITALIST FIRMS WHICH HAVE
BECOME AN IMPORTANT FORM OF THE USSR'S FOREIGN ECONOMIC TIES.
THE ECONOMIC ESSENCE OF COMPENSATION-BASED COOPERATION IS
EXPLORED AS WELL AS THE EXPERIENCE, FORMS AND METHODS, AND
EXPORT GROWTH. THE MAIN PROBLEMS OF COMPENSATION-BASED
COOPERATION ARE LISTED WITH DETAILS ABOUT EACH.

01682 BORINSKI, P.
MITIGATING WEST GERMANY'S STRATEGIC DILEMMAS
ARMED FORCES AND SOCIETY, 15(4) (SUM 89), 531-549.
THIS ARTICLE IDENTIFIES THREE STRICTLY STRATEGIC
DILEMMAS CONCERNING WEST GERMANY'S DEFENSE IN THE LATE
EIGHTIES: THE DEFENSE-PROTECTION DILEMMA, THE ARMS CONTROL-
SECURITY DILEMMA, AND THE STRATEGY-RESOURCE DILEMMA. IT
BRIEFLY EXPLAINS EACH DILEMMA AND CRITICALLY EXAMINES THE
MAJOR APPROACHES TO CHANGE UNDER DEBATE TODAY, FOCUSING ON
THE CONTRIBUTION MADE BY THE "ALTERNATIVE DEFENSE" SCHOOL.
CONCLUDING THAT NONE OF THESE APPROACHES CAN SUBSTANTIALLY
ALLEVIATE WEST GERMANY'S STRATEGIC DILEMMAS, THE DISCUSSION
TURNS TO THE IDEA OF "STRUCTURAL INCAPABILITY OF ATTACK," OR
"NONPROVOCATIVE DEFENSE," AS A POSSIBLE BASIS FOR A
SOLTUTION. HAVING CRITIZED THIS IDEA IN ITS CURRENT FORM,
THE ARTICLE ENDS BY SUGGESTING A STRATEGICALLY FEASIBLE WAY
FOR BOTH BLOCS TO MOVE TOWARD FORCE POSTURES STRUCTURALLY
INCAPABLE OF ATTACK AT THE CONVENTIONAL THEATER LEVEL IN
EUROPE.

01683 BORISOV, A.
SOVIET-DUTCH ECONOMIC COOPERATION
FOREIGN TRADE, 9 (1988), 16-18.
THIS ARTICLE REPORTS ON PROGRESS MADE IN SOVIET-DUTCH
RELATIONS SINCE THE SIGNING OF LONG TERM DEVELOPMENT
PROGRAMMES BETWEEN THE USSR AND THE NETHERLANDS SPECIFYING
THEIR ECONOMIC, INDUSTRIAL, TECHNOLOGICAL AND AGRARIAN-
INDUSTRIAL COOPERATION. IT EXAMINES TRADE, IMPORTS,
PROTOCOLS, AND AGREEMENTS BETWEEN THE TWO COUNTRIES.
DISCUSSED ALSO IS COOPERATION IN ENVIRONMENTAL PROTECTION
AND JOINT MANUFACTURING.

01684 BORISOV, Y.
DIPLOMACY OF THE FRENCH REVOLUTION
INTERNATIONAL AFFAIRS (MOSCOW), (8) (AUG 89), 27-38.
THE AUTHOR DISCUSSES THE IMPACT OF THE FRENCH REVOLUTION
ON WORLD HISTORY AND CONSIDERS THE DIPLOMACY OF THE
REVOLUTION.

01685 BORJAS, G.J.
ECONOMIC THEORY AND INTERNATIONAL MIGRATION
INTERNATIONAL MIGRATION REVIEW, 23(3) (FAL 89), 457-485.
THE MODERN LITERATURE ON THE ECONOMICS OF IMMIGRATION
FOCUSES ON THREE RELATED ISSUES: 1) WHAT DETERMINES THE SIZE
AND SKILL COMPOSITION OF IMMIGRANT FLOWS TO ANY PARTICULAR
HOST COUNTRY; 2) HOW DO THE IMMIGRANTS ADAPT TO THE HOST
COUNTRY'S ECONOMY; AND 3) WHAT IS THE IMPACT OF IMMIGRANTS
ON THE HOST COUNTRY'S ECONOMY? THIS ARTICLE REVIEWS THE
THEORETICAL FRAMEWORK AND EMPIRICAL EVIDENCE PROVIDED BY THE
ECONOMICS LITERATURE ON THESE QUESTIONS. IT DEMONSTRATES
THAT THE ECONOMIC APPROACH, USING THE ASSUMPTIONS THAT
INDIVIDUAL MIGRATION BEHAVIOR IS GUIDED BY THE SEARCH FOR
BETTER ECONOMIC OPPORTUNITIES AND THAT THE EXCHANGES AMONG

THE VARIOUS PLAYERS ARE REGULATED BY AN IMMIGRATION MARKET, LEADS TO SUBSTANTIVE INSIGHTS INTO THESE ISSUES.

01686 BORK, R.H.
THE CASE AGAINST POLITICAL JUDGING
NATIONAL REVIEW, 61(23) (DEC 89), 23-28.
THIS ARTICLE IS ADAPTED FROM JUDGE ROBERT BORK'S BOOK, THE TEMPTING OF AMERICA. BORK DEFENDS JUDICIAL RESTRAINT AND REFLECTS UPON THE EXCESSES OF HIS LIBERAL OPPONENTS. HE DESCRIBES HOW IT IS POSSIBLE, AND NECESSARY, FOR A JUDGE TO BASE HIS DECISIONS ON NEUTRAL PRINCIPLES RATHER THAN HIS OWN PREFERENCES AND EXPLAINS THE MINDSET OF HIS OPPONENTS "WHO UNDERSTAND ONLY NAKED POWER," IN LAW AND POLITICS ALIKE.

01687 BORK, R.H.
THE LIMITS OF "INTERNATIONAL LAW"
NATIONAL INTEREST, (18) (WIN 89), 3-10.
USING THE U.S. INVASION OF GRENADA AS AN EXAMPLE, THE BITTER DIVISION BETWEEN HIGH PUBLIC OFFICIALS AND AN UNDEFINED GROUP OF "EXPERTS IN INTERNATIONAL LAW" OVER THE LEGALITY OF WHAT THE UNITED STATES HAD DONE IS EXAMINED IN THIS ISSUE, IT ATTEMPTS TO DEFINE WHAT, EXACTLY, IS INTERNATIONAL LAW? IS IT LAW AT ALL? WHAT PURPOSES DOES IT SERVE? THE EPISODE OF NICARAGUA V. UNITED STATES ILLUSTRATES THE INVERSION OF MANY ESTABLISHED RULES ABOUT THE USE OF FORCE. IT CONCLUDES THAT THERE CAN BE NO AUTHENTIC RULE OF LAW AMONG NATIONS UNTIL NATIONS HAVE A COMMON POLITICAL MORALITY OR ARE UNDER A COMMON SOVEREIGNTY.

01688 BOROSAGE, B.
STILL BUILDING A COALITION OF HOPE
SOJOURNERS, 18(2) (FEB 89), 16-18.
MICHAEL DUKAKIS' 1988 PRESIDENTIAL CAMPAIGN WAS LOST NOT ON TACTICS BUT ON STRATEGY. HIS FAILURE WAS NOT IN THE PACKAGING BUT IN THE MESSAGE.

01689 BOROSAGE, R.
BUSHED AND BEWILDERED
TIKKUN, 4(6) (NOV 89), 46-48.
THIS ARTICLE STATES THAT GEORGE BUSH IS NOT A PROGRESSIVE, BUT REALITY IS FORCING HIM TO ADDRESS WHAT IS ESSENTIALLY A PROGRESSIVE AGENDA. THE COLD WAR IS WANTING; THE JAPANESE AND GERMANS APPEAR TO HAVE WON. NEW TRADE BLOCS ARE FORMING AS THE COMMUNIST BLOC DISSOLVES. THE ADMINISTRATION MUST FACE AN NEW ERA OR GLOBAL COMPETITION WITH AN ECONOMY WEAKENED BY DISSIPATION. ENVIRONMENTAL DEGRADATION IS NO LONGER A NUISANCE, BUT A MAJOR THEAT TO OUR SECURITY. GROWING INEQUALITY AT HOME NOT OFFENDS OUR SENSE OF DECENCY BUT UNDERMINES OUR ECONOMIC FUTURE. THE EVENTS OF 1989 GIVE MANY INDICATIONS THAT THE PEOPLE MAY BE READY FOR A NEW ERA OF PROGRESSIVE MOVEMENT.

01690 BOSSANO, J.
DEFENDING ITS RIGHTS-GIBRALTAR'S POLITICAL AND ECONOMIC FUTURE
PARLIAMENTARIAN, 70(1) (JAN 89), 12-14.
THE AUTHOR PROJECTS ON THE FUTURE OF GIBRALTAR, BY EXPLAINING THE BASIC PHILOSOPHY UNDERLYING GIBRALTAR'S POLICIES FOR THE RESTRUCTURING AND DEVELOPMENT OF THE ECONOMY. BACKGROUND TO ECONOMIC STATUS SHOWS GIBRALTAR'S DEVELOPMENT TO HAVE BEEN IN RESPONSE TO ITS LONGSTANDING ROLE AS A STRATEGIC BRITISH NAVAL AND MILITARY BASE. THE AMALGAM OF RACES, RELIGIONS AND CULTURES IS TRACED. ECONOMIC PLANS WHICH ARE SUMMARIZED INCLUDE THE DIVERSIFICATION OF THE ECONOMIC BASE, WITH AN EMPHASIS ON TOURISM AND SUPPORTING SERVICES, BANKING LAW REFORM, LARGE-SCALE LAND RECLAMATION, AND INCREASING INDEPENDENCE FROM SPAIN. THE AUTHOR SUGGESTS BREAKINS THE BRUSSELS AGREEMENT OF 1984 WHICH WAS SIGNED BY SPAIN AND GREAT BRITAIN.

01691 BOSTON, R.
ADJUSTING THE BREAKS
CHURCH AND STATE, 42(4) (APR 89), 4 (76)-6 (78).
THE SUPREME COURT HAS STRUCK DOWN A TEXAS STATE LAW THAT GRANTED SALES TAX EXEMPTIONS TO RELIGIOUS BOOKS AND MAGAZINES. THE COURT RULED THAT SUCH EXEMPTIONS EXTEND A STATE PREFERENCE TO RELIGIOUS PUBLICATIONS AND RELIGION IN GENERAL, VIOLATING THE FIRST AMENDMENT'S ESTABLISHMENT CLAUSE, WHICH PROHIBITS GOVERNMENT SPONSORSHIP OF RELIGION.

01692 BOSTON, R.
DECADE OF DECISION
CHURCH AND STATE, 42(10) (NOV 89), 4 (220)-10 (226).
U.S. REP. DON EDWARDS SERVES AS CHAIRMAN OF THE HOUSE SUBCOMMITTEE ON CIVIL AND CONSTITUTIONAL RIGHTS, WHICH HAS BEEN CALLED "THE BERMUDA TRIANGLE FOR CONSTITUTIONAL AMENDMENTS." EDWARDS IS AN ARDENT CIVIL LIBERTARIAN WHO CHAMPIONS THE CAUSE OF CHURCH-STATE SEPARATION. HIS LATEST TARGET IS THE COMMUNITY LIFE AMENDMENT, WHICH WOULD AUTHORIZE PRAYER AND BIBLE READING IN THE PUBLIC SCHOOLS.

01693 BOSTON, R.
DIFFERENT DOCTRINE
CHURCH AND STATE, 42(8) (SEP 89), 7 (175)-8 (176).

THE SUPREME COURT'S RULING IN WEBSTER V. REPRODUCTIVE HEALTH SERVICES GIVES STATES NEW POWERS TO REGULATE ABORTION. ALTHOUGH THE JUSTICES STOPPED SHORT OF OVERTURNING ROE V. WADE, THEY INDICATED A WILLINGNESS TO RETURN THE ISSUE TO THE STATES, CREATING THE POTENTIAL FOR ABORTION BATTLES IN ALL STATE LEGISLATURES. IN DISSENTING FROM THE COURT'S DECISION, JUSTICE JOHN PAUL STEVENS DREW EXTENSIVELY ON CHURCH-STATE ARGUMENTS.

01694 BOSTON, R.
FULL COURT PRESS
CHURCH AND STATE, 42(7) (JUL 89), 10 (154).
CONGRESSMAN WILLIAM DANNEMEYER HAS INTRODUCED A CONSTITUTIONAL AMENDMENT TO ALLOW VOLUNTARY PRAYER AND THE TEACHING OF THE JUDEO-CHRISTIAN ETHIC, INCLUDING THE TEN COMMANDMENTS AND CREATIONISM, IN THE PUBLIC SCHOOLS. DANNEMEYER INSISTS THAT THE AMENDMENT'S PURPOSE IS TO RETURN DECISIONS ABOUT PRAYER AND OTHER RELIGION-IN-SCHOOLS ISSUES TO STATE AND LOCAL GOVERNMENTS.

01695 BOSTON, R.
INDEPENDENT'S DAY
CHURCH AND STATE, 42(5) (MAY 89), 7 (103)-8 (104).
A SUPREME COURT DECISION HAS UNANIMOUSLY UPHELD AN EMPLOYEE'S RIGHT TO REFUSE SUNDAY WORK ON RELIGIOUS GROUNDS WITHOUT BEING DENIED STATE UNEMPLOYMENT BENEFITS. THE PLAINTIFF WAS A FUNDAMENTALIST CHRISTIAN WHO SAID THAT HIS PERSONAL INTERPRETATION OF THE BIBLE FORBIDS SUNDAY LABOR, EVEN THOUGH IT IS NOT A STIPULATION OF HIS RELIGIOUS DENOMINATION'S DOGMA. GOVERNMENT OFFICIALS ARGUED THAT THIS BELIEF DID NOT QUALIFY FOR FIRST AMENDMENT PROTECTION BECAUSE IT WAS MERELY A PERSONAL BELIEF AND NOT TIED TO A RECOGNIZED RELIGIOUS GROUP. THE SUPREME COURT DECISION STRONGLY CONFIRMED THE FREE EXERCISE OF RELIGION AND AFFIRMED THE NOTION THAT RELIGIOUS FREEDOM BELONGS TO ALL AMERICANS, NOT JUST THOSE AFFILIATED WITH ORGANIZED RELIGIOUS GROUPS.

01696 BOSTON, R.
MANDATORY MEMBERSHIP?
CHURCH AND STATE, 42(1) (JAN 89), 4-7.
AN ILLINOIS FUNDAMENTALIST CHRISTIAN HAS BROUGHT LITIGATION BECAUSE HE WAS DENIED UNEMPLOYMENT COMPENSATION. HE CLAIMS HE WAS DENIED HIS RELIGIOUS FREEDOM BECAUSE HE REFUSED TO WORK ON SUNDAYS AND THEREFORE WAS DISQUALIFIED BY THE PROSPECTIVE EMPLOYER. AFTER HE WAS REFUSED THE JOB, THE STATE OF ILLINOIS DENIED HIM UNEMPLOYMENT BENEFITS, CLAIMING THAT HIS BELIEF WAS PERSONALLY-HELD AND NOT A TENET OF HIS CHURCH. WHEN THE SUPREME COURT DECISION IS HANDED DOWN ON THE CASE, IT IS EXPECTED TO BREAK NEW GROUND, EITHER REINFORCING BROAD PROTECTIONS OF THE CONSTITUTIONAL RIGHT OF FREE EXERCISE OF RELIGION OR NARROWING THEM TO APPLY ONLY TO MEMBERS OF ORGANIZED RELIGIOUS GROUPS.

01697 BOSTON, R.
PRESCRIPTION FOR CONTROVERSY
CHURCH AND STATE, 42(3) (MAR 89), 8 (56)-12 (60).
WHILE IT IS GENERALLY ACCEPTED THAT ADULTS HAVE THE RIGHT TO REFUSE MEDICAL TREATMENT, THIS PRINCIPLE IS NOT USUALLY EXTENDED TO MINORS. WHEN ADULTS DECIDE TO SHUN MEDICAL CARE FOR CHILDREN IN FAVOR OF SPIRITUAL HEALING AND THE PATIENT DIES, THE RESULT IS AN EMOTIONAL CLASH BETWEEN CHURCH AND STATE. IT IS AN ISSUE THAT IS RAPIDLY COMING TO A HEAD IN THE COURTS.

01698 BOSTON, R.
STATES OF CONFUSION
CHURCH AND STATE, 42(9) (OCT 89), 8 (200)-10 (202).
THE AUTHOR PRESENTS A STATE-BY-STATE SUMMARY OF THE CHURCH-STATE SEPARATION ISSUES CURRENTLY UNDER CONTENTION. THE LIST REVEALS THAT CHURCH-STATE PROBLEMS COME IN A VARIETY OF TYPES, BUT PUBLIC SCHOOL ISSUES AND DISPUTES OVER PAROCHIAL SCHOOL AID TOP THE LIST OF THE MOST FREQUENT.

01699 BOSTON, R.
THE IRS AND THE E-METER SHUFFLE
CHURCH AND STATE, 42(2) (FEB 89), 6 (30)-10 (34).
THE IRS GENERALLY ALLOWS DEDUCTIONS FOR DONATIONS TO RELIGIOUS GROUPS BUT SINCE THE 1970'S HAS REFUSED TO ALLOW SCIENTOLOGISTS TO TAKE DEDUCTIONS FOR AUDITING AND TRAINING. A CASE BROUGHT BY A SCIENTOLOGIST, HERNANDEZ V. COMMISSIONER OF INTERNAL REVENUE, WILL BE HEARD BY THE SUPREME COURT. THE DECISION WILL HAVE IMPORTANT RAMIFICATIONS AFFECTING MANY AMERICAN TAXPAYERS, NOT JUST SCIENTOLOGISTS.

01700 BOSTON, R.
WHEN SYMBOLS CLASH
CHURCH AND STATE, 42(8) (SEP 89), 9 (177)-12 (180).
IN JULY 1989, A SHARPLY-DIVIDED SUPREME COURT RULED THAT GOVERNMENTAL BODIES MAY DISPLAY RELIGIOUS HOLIDAY SYMBOLS, BUT ONLY IF THE SACRED IS MIXED WITH THE SECULAR. FOR EXAMPLE, A CHRISTMAS CRECHE STANDING BY ITSELF GIVES THE IMPRESSION OF STATE ENDORSEMENT OF A RELIGIOUS BELIEF BUT A MIXTURE OF SACRED AND SECULAR CHRISTMAS SYMBOLS WOULD NOT

CONSTITUTE SUCH AN ENDORSEMENT.

01701 BOSWELL, T.
COLONIAL EMPIRES AND THE CAPITALIST WORLD-ECONOMY: A TIME
SERIES ANALYSIS OF COLONIZATION, 1640-1960
AMERICAN SOCIOLOGICAL REVIEW, 54(2) (APR 89), 180-196.
FOR MOST OF THE HISTORY OF THE CAPITALIST WORLD-ECONOMY,
IMPERIAL CONQUEST HAS THE PRINCIPAL FACTOR IN CREATING A
PERIPHERY TO THE EUROPEAN IMPERIAL CORE. THIS STUDY FOCUSES
ON HOW THE DYNAMICS OF THE CAPITALIST WORLD-ECONOMY AFFECTED
THE PATTERN OF COLONIZATION IN THE PERIPHERY. COLONIZATION
IS CONSIDERED A HIERARCHIAL ALTERNATIVE TO MARKET RELATIONS,
INCREASED WHEN MARKET RELATIONS PERFORM POORLY AND SLOWED
WHEN THE MARKET EXPANDS. A TIME SERIES REGRESSION ANALYSIS,
COVERING THE "LONGUE DUREE" OF THE WHOLE SYSTEM, PROVIDES
INITIAL COMPREHENSIVE QUANTITATIVE SUPPORT FOR TWO CENTRAL
PROPOSITIONS IN WORLD-SYSTEM THEORY. THE FINDINGS INDICATE
THAT LONG WAVES OF ECONOMIC EXPANSION AND PERIODS OF
UNICENTRIC HEGEMONY NEGATIVELY AFFECTED THE RATE OF
COLONIZATION. MAJOR WARS AMONG CORE STATES HAD NO IMMEDIATE
IMPACT BUT HAD LONG-TERM POSITIVE EFFECTS. A SHIFT IN THE
INTERNATIONAL REGIME BROUGHT ABOUT BY THE RISE OF SOCIALIST
STATES ALSO CONTRIBUTED TO THE DECLINE OF FORMAL
COLONIZATION. THE FINDINGS POINT TO THE UTILITY OF LONG
WAVES, HEGEMONY, AND INTERNATIONAL REGIMES IN LONG-TERM
HISTORICAL STUDIES OF THE TRADE-OFF BETWEEN MARKET AND
HIERARCHICAL RELATIONS.

01702 BOSWORTH, B.P.; LAWRENCE, R.Z.
AMERICA IN THE WORLD ECONOMY
BROOKINGS REVIEW, 7(1) (WIN 89), 39-52.
IT IS A MISTAKE TO BLAME THE REST OF THE WORLD FOR THE
UNITED STATES' ECONOMIC PROBLEMS. IN THE 1980'S, THE USA HAS
BEEN ON A CONSUMPTION BINGE, SELLING ASSETS AND BORROWING
HEAVILY, BOTH DOMESTICALLY AND ABROAD. THE GROWTH OF
CONSUMPTION HAS FAR OUTSTRIPPED THAT OF PRODUCTION. THE COST
FOR THIS SPENDING SPREE HAS BEEN A SHARP DECLINE IN NATIONAL
SAVING.

01703 BOT, M.
BLACK EDUCATION AND THE ROLE OF THE PRIVATE SECTOR
SOUTH AFRICA FOUNDATION REVIEW, 15(5) (MAY 89), 4-5.
AN OVERVIEW OF THE INFORMATION AVAILABLE ON PRIVATE
SECTOR INVOLVEMENT IN BLACK EDUCATION SHOWS THAT THE RANGE
OF PROGRAMMES PRESENTLY SUPPORTED COVERS VIRTUALLY THE WHOLE
FIELD OF BLACK EDUCATION. WHILE IT INCLUDES MORE TRADITIONAL
AREAS OF SPENDING WITHOUT ANY STRINGS ATTACHED (SUCH AS THE
PROVISION OF FUNDS TO TERTIARY INSTITUTIONS, THE ERECTION OF
BUILDINGS, ETC), IT IS NOTICEABLE THAT NEARLY ALL COMPANIES
MENTION SUPPORT FOR NON-FORMAL EDUCATION PROGRAMMES, A TREND
THAT IS REFLECTED IN THE INCREASED PROPORTION OF SPENDING BY
FIRMS ON ANCILLARY AND SUPPORTIVE PROGRAMMES (SOMETIMES
REFERRED TO AS NONFORMAL EDUCATION) - FROM SEVEN PERCENT IN
1980 TO 26 PERCENT IN 1985, A PERCENTAGE THAT WILL
UNDOUBTEDLY HAVE INCREASED FURTHER. SOME NOTICEABLE TRENDS
ARE CONTINUING, NAMELY INCREASED SUPPORT FOR BURSARIES, IN-
SERVICE TRAINING AND UPGRADING OF TEACHERS, CURRICULUM
ENRICHMENT ESPECIALLY IN ENGLISH, MATHEMATICS AND SCIENCE,
NON-RACIAL SCHOOLING, VARIOUS TYPES OF BRIDGING AND ACADEMIC
SUPPORT PROGRAMMES, CAREER GUIDANCE AND INCREASED SUPPORT
FOR RURAL EDUCATION.

01704 BOUCHARD, J.F.
USE OF NAVAL FORCE IN CRISES: A THEORY OF STRATIFIED
CRISIS INTERACTION (VOLUMES I-III)
DISSERTATION ABSTRACTS INTERNATIONAL, 50(4) (OCT 89),
1081-A.
THE AUTHOR DEVELOPS A THEORY OF STRATIFIED INTERACTION
IN CRISES THAT OCCURS AT THREE LEVELS: POLITICAL, STRATEGIC,
AND TACTICAL. INTERACTIONS AT EACH LEVEL EVOLVE SEPARATELY
AND CAN INDEPENDENTLY INFLUENCE WHETHER OR NOT A CRISIS
ESCALATES TO WAR. HE UTILIZES HIS THEORY IN STUDYING EIGHT
CASES INVOLVING U.S. NAVAL OPERATIONS: THE 1958 TAIWAN
STRAITS CRISIS, THE 1962 CUBAN MISSILE CRISIS, THE 1967 ARAB-
ISRAELI WAR, THE 1973 ARAB-ISRAELI WAR, THE 1964 TONKIN GULF
INCIDENTS, THE 1967 ISRAELI ATTACK ON THE USS LIBERTY, THE
1968 SEIZURE OF THE USS PUEBLO, AND THE 1987 IRAQI ATTACK ON
THE USS STARK.

01705 BOULLATA, K.
PALESTINIAN EXPRESSION INSIDE A CULTURAL GHETTO
MIDDLE EAST REPORT, 19(4) (JUL 89), 24-28.
AN EXAMINATION OF LOCAL CRAFTS AND CULTURAL PRODUCTS IN
PALESTINE INDICATES THAT TRADITIONAL AESTLETIC VALUES HAVE
FOR SOME TIME BEEN RAPIDLY ERODING. THIS ARTICLE EXPLORES
THE PROCESS THAT BRINGS INTO BEING PRODUCTS WHICH STIR A
SENSE OF PRIDE AMONG PALESTINIANS LIVING UNDER OCCUPATION,
AND EXAMINES THE COMPONENTS THAT ENDOW THESE CULTURAL
PRODUCTS WITH THEIR UNIQUELY PALESTINIAN CHARACTER.

01706 BOUMAHDI, B.
A POLITICAL HISTORY OF THE WESTERN SAHARA DISPUTE
DISSERTATION ABSTRACTS INTERNATIONAL, 49(12) (JUN 89),
3861-A.

THE AUTHOR TRACES THE POLITICAL HISTORY OF WESTERN
SAHARA FROM THE FIFTEENTH CENTURY UNTIL THE PRESENT,
EXAMINING THE SITUATION IN LOCAL, REGIONAL, AND
INTERNATIONAL CONTEXTS. AT THE LOCAL LEVEL, THE ROLES OF
MOROCCO AND ALGERIA ARE STRESSED, WHILE AT THE REGIONAL
LEVEL THE EFFECTS OF THE WESTERN SAHARA DISPUTE ON RELATIONS
BETWEEN NORTH AFRICAN STATES AND THE OAU ARE HIGHLIGHTED. AT
THE INTERNATIONAL LEVEL, THE ROLES OF FRANCE, SPAIN, THE
ARAB STATES, THE SUPERPOWERS, AND THE UNITED NATIONS ARE
SCRUTINIZED.

01707 BOURGAULT, J.; DION, S.
BRIAN MULRONEY A-T-IL POLITISE LES SOUS-MINISTRES?
CANADIAN PUBLIC ADMINISTRATION, 32(1) (SPR 89), 63-83.
THIS STUDY EXAMINES WHETHER IT IS TRUE, AS SOME HAVE
CLAIMED, THAT THE MULRONEY GOVERNMENT DID AN UNPRECEDENTED
REORGANIZATION OF THE DEPUTY MINISTERS' STAFF DURING ITS
FIRST TERM. IT QUESTIONS WHETHER THE REORGANIZATION WAS
EXCEPTIONALLY EXTENSIVE AS COMPARED TO THE PRACTICES PRIOR
TO THE CONSERVATIVES AND WHETHER THE REORGANIZATION
CONSTITUTED GREATER POLITICIZATION OF THE DEPUTY MINISTERS
IN THE SENSE THAT THE CONSERVATIVE GOVERNMENT WOULD HAVE
GIVEN PREFERENCE TO SENIOR OFFICIALS WHO SUPPORTED ITS
IDEOLOGY AND ACTION PROGRAMS. TWO INVESTIGATIVE TECHNIQUES
WERE USED: THE MOBILITY INDEX OF DEPUTY MINISTERS (BASED ON
THE NUMBER OF DEPARTURES, APPOINTMENTS AND TRANSFERS) AND A
SERIES OF SEMI-FOCUSED INTERVIEWS WITH SENIOR OFFICIALS AND
POLITICIANS. THE CONCLUSION IS THAT THE DEPUTY MINISTERS
ESCAPED INCREASED POLITICIZATION OF THEIR ROLE EVEN THOUGH
THEY UNDERWENT AN EXCEPTIONALLY DEEP REORGANIZATION DURING
THE FIRST TWO YEARS OF THE CONSERVATIVE MANDATE.

01708 BOURGAULT, J.; DION, S.
GOVERNMENTS COME AND GO, BUT WHAT OF SENIOR CIVIL
SERVANTS? CANADIAN DEPUTY MINISTERS AND TRANSITIONS IN
POWER (1867-1987)
GOVERNANCE, 2(2) (APR 89), 124-151.
THE PURPOSE OF THE ARTICLE IS TO DISCOVER IF THE ARRIVAL
OF NEW GOVERNMENTS TENDED TO ACCELERATE THE MOBILITY OF
SENIOR OFFICIALS, AS MEASURED BY THE NUMBER OF APPOINTMENTS,
DEPARTURES, AND TRANSFERS. IT EXAMINES THE STRATEGIC
CALCULATIONS THAT PERSUADE--OR DISSUADE--NEW GOVERNMENTS TO
CARRY OUT A PURGE OF HIGH RANKING OFFICERS IN THE CIVIL
SERVICE. IT ALSO EXAMINES THE EMPIRICAL EVIDENCE WHICH
INCLUDES THE LIST OF BUREAUCRATS AT THE HEAD OF DEPARTMENTS
AND CENTRAL AGENCIES SINCE THE BEGINING OF THE CONFEDERATION
IN 1867. IT CONCLUDES THAT CHANGES IN POLITICAL PARTIES HAVE
LITTLE EFFECT ON THE TENURE OF DEPUTY MINISTERS IN THE
CANADIAN FEDERAL GOVERNMENT. DEPUTY MINISTERS HAVE BEEN
SURVIVING THE HAZARDS OF POLITICS SINCE THE BEGINING OF THE
CONFEDERATION.

01709 BOURKE, G.
PLAYING POLITICS
AFRICA REPORT, 34(5) (SEP 89), 41-44.
WITH NIGERIA'S FIRST PARTY-BASED ELECTIONS FOR MORE THAN
SIX YEARS DUE BEFORE THE END OF 1989 AND FULL CIVILIAN RULE
SCHEDULED FOR 1992, THERE IS A GROWING BODY OF OPINION THAT
THE MILITARY'S DISENGAGEMENT FROM GOVERNMENT WILL LEAD TO
THE SAME KIND OF CHAOS AND CORRUPTION THAT DOGGED THE
COUNTRY'S TWO PREVIOUS DEMOCRATIC EXPERIMENTS. THE LIFTING
OF THE BAN ON PARTISAN POLITICS PROMPTED CAMPAIGNS BY A
VARIETY OF GROUPS, BUT IN MID-1989, GEN. IBRAHIM BABANGIDA
DISBANDED 13 PARTIES AND SPONSORED TWO NEW ONES IN THEIR
PLACE TO CONTEST THE UPCOMING ELECTIONS.

01710 BOURNE, C.
SOME FUNDAMENTALS OF MONETARY POLICY IN THE CARIBBEAN
SOCIAL AND ECONOMIC STUDIES, 38(2) (JUN 89), 265-290.
THIS PAPER RE-EXAMINES THE QUESTION OF MONETARY
MANAGEMENT. BEGINNING WITH A DISCUSSION OF POLICY OBJECTIVES,
IT PROCEEDS TO ANALYSE THE INFLUENCE OF MONETARY AND CREDIT
VARIABLES ON THE PRICE LEVEL AND THE BALANCE OF PAYMENTS. BY
SO DOING, THE PAPER ATTEMPTS TO ESTABLISH A FEW
MACROECONOMIC FUNDAMENTALS FOR MONETARY POLICY IN THE
COMMONWEALTH CARIBBEAN. THE EMPIRICAL ANALYSIS DRAWS
EXTENSIVELY ON THE AUTHOR'S OWN PRIMARY RESEARCH, BUT SOME
REFERENCE IS ALSO MADE TO THE FINDINGS OF OTHER SCHOLARS.

01711 BOURQUE, G.
TRADITIONAL SOCIETY, POLITICAL SOCIETY AND QUEBEC
SOCIOLOGY: 1945-1980
CANADIAN REVIEW OF SOCIOLOGY AND ANTHROPOLOGY, 26(3) (MAY
89), 394-425.
THE ARTICLE EXAMINES THE MODERNITY OF SOCIOLOGICAL
PRODUCTION IN QUEBEC FROM 1945 TO 1980 AND THE GENERAL
CONDITIONS OF QUEBEC'S EXPRESSION OF ITSELF AS A SOCIETY
DURING THIS PERIOD. IT REGROUPS THIS SOCIOLOGY INTO FOUR
DISTINCT APPROACHES: THE FIRST, FROM 1945 TO 1960 PRESENTED
ITSELF AS A FORM OF CRITICAL KNOWLEDGE OF ADAPTATION WHICH
ILLUSTRATED THE INADAQUECY OF REFERENCES TO TRADITIONALISM.
THE BEGINING OF THE 1960'S MARKED THE TRANSITION TOWARDS THE
PREDOMINANCE OF A REPRESENTATIONAL FORM WHICH THEREAFTER
PRESENTED QUEBEC AS A POLITICAL SOCIETY. IN THE THIRD

TENDENCY A FUNCTIONALIST SOCIOLOGY TOOK ROOT. THE 1970S SAW
IN CONTRADISTINCTION THE AFFIRMATION OF A SOCIETY OF
EMANCIPATION.

01712 BOVARD, J.
   A HAZARDOUS WASTE
   REASON. 21(G) (NOV 89). 32-35.
      THE REGULATIONS OF THE RESOURCE CONSERVATION AND
   RECOVERY ACT (RCRA) ARE INFLEXIBLE AND OFTEN
   COUNTERPRODUCTIVE. A WIDE RANGE OF CRITICS HAVE STATED THAT
   THE RCRA, ALTHOUGH INTENDED TO PROTECT PUBLIC HEALTH AND
   ENCOURAGE RECYCLING, IS UNFAIR, IRRATIONAL, WASTEFUL, SELF-
   DEFEATING, AND INCONSISTENT WITH OTHER ENVIRONMENTAL
   LEGISLATION. EVEN THE ENVIRONMENTAL PROTECTION AGENCY ADMITS
   THAT MANY OF THE RCRA RULES ARE USELESS.

01713 BOVARD, J.
   THE AGRICULTURAL SWAMP
   NATIONAL REVIEW, XLI(2) (FEB 89), 46-48.
      THE AUTHOR DISCUSSES AMERICAN FARM POLICY AND THE USA-
   EUROPEAN COMMUNITY SQUABBLE OVER AGRICULTURAL TRADE.

01714 BOVIN, A.; CHUBARYAN, A.; DASHICHEV, V.; KONSTANTINOV, F.;
   POZHARSKY, V.; SHEINIS, V.; SHISHKOV, Y.; SINISIN, S.;
   STUPISHIN, V.; TROFIMENKO, G.
   OPENNESS IN POLITICS
   INTERNATIONAL AFFAIRS (MOSCOW), (8) (AUG 89), 118-132.
      IN THIS ROUND-TABLE DISCUSSION, SOVIET EXPERTS DISCUSS
   GORBACHEV'S NEW POLITICAL THINKING, NEW THINKING AS AN
   INTERNATIONAL PHENOMENON, AND THE IMPACT OF THE NEW THINKING.

01715 BOWDEN, G.
   LABOR UNIONS IN THE PUBLIC MIND: THE CANADIAN CASE
   CANADIAN REVIEW OF SOCIOLOGY AND ANTHROPOLOGY, 26(5) (NOV
   89), 723-742.
      S.M. LIPSET'S THEORY OF CANADIAN-AMERICAN DIFFERENCES IS
   APPLIED TO THE EXPLANATION OF DIFFERENCES IN UNION DENSITY.
   HYPOTHESES DERIVED FROM THAT THEORY ARE TESTED AGAINST DATA
   ON CANADIAN ATTITUDES TOWARD UNIONS. THE FINDINGS STRONGLY
   AND CONSISTENTLY CONTRADICT THE THEORY. THE IMPLICATIONS FOR
   LIPSET'S THEORY OF CANADIAN-AMERICAN DIFFERENCES ARE
   EXAMINED.

01716 BOWEN, C.M.
   MUNICIPAL INCORPORATION INEQUITIES SYNDROME IN LOS ANGELES
   COUNTY
   DISSERTATION ABSTRACTS INTERNATIONAL, 50(5) (NOV 89),
   1430-A.
      LOS ANGELES COUNTY MUNICIPAL INCORPORATION AND
   ANNEXATION ARE CREATING DISPROPORTIONATE POLITICAL
   REPRESENTATION. RAPID GROWTH HAS GENERATED CONFLICTS AND
   COMPETITION FOR DESIRABLE POPULATIONS AND TERRITORIES, WHILE
   DISADVANTAGED AREAS HAVE BEEN REJECTED. AFTER SURVEYING THE
   SITUATION AND THE CAUSES, THIS DISSERTATION OUTLINES ELEVEN
   RECOMMENDATIONS FOR IMPROVING THE PROBLEM.

01717 BOWEN, J.
   NARRATIVE FORM AND POLITICAL INCORPORATION: CHANGING USES
   OF OF HISTORY IN ACEH, INDONESIA
   COMPARATIVE STUDIES IN SOCIETY AND HISTORY, 31(4) (OCT 89),
   671-693.
      THE ARTICLE EXAMINES THE ROLE OF THE NARRATIVE IN
   DEPICTING THE HISTORY OF RULING AUTHORITY. IT ATTEMPTS TO
   STUDY THE CHANGING HISTORICAL REPRESENTATIONS FOUND IN
   HISTORIES OF GAYO SOCIETY (ACEH PROVINCE, INDONESIA) FORM A
   COMPARATIVE PERSPECTIVE. IT EXAMINES PRE-COLONIAL HISTORIES,
   HISTORIES GREATLY INFLUENCED BY THE DUTCH COLONIAL
   ADMINISTRATION, AND MORE RECENT HISTORIES WHICH SHOW A
   MARKED ISLAMIC INFLUENCE. VIEWS ON AUTHORITY HAVE CHANGED
   OVER THE SAME PERIODS FROM AMBIVALENCE TO INCREASING SUPPORT
   OF THE LEGITIMACY OF RULERS.

01718 BOWER, B.K.
   WAITING FOR MICHELS: AN OPERATIONALIZATION OF THE IRON LAW
   OF OLIGARCHY
   DISSERTATION ABSTRACTS INTERNATIONAL, 50(6) (DEC 89),
   1785-A.
      MICHELS' IRON LAW OF OLIGARCHY ASSUMES THAT GROWING
   ORGANIZATIONS REQUIRE AN INCREASING NUMBER OF INCREASINGLY
   COMPLEX TASKS. IN ORDER TO RESPOND EFFICIENTLY TO THESE
   DEMANDS, CENTRALIZED DECISION-MAKING IS UTILIZED. THIS
   DISSERTATION PROVIDES A COMPREHENSIVE REVIEW OF THE IRON LAW,
   CONSTRUCTS MODELS, ANALYZES THE FINDINGS, AND PRESENTS
   CONCLUSIONS.

01719 BOWERS, D.A. JR.
   EDUCATION REFORM IN THE 1980'S: THE MEDIA, PUBLIC OPINION,
   AND ELITE POLICY-MAKING
   DISSERTATION ABSTRACTS INTERNATIONAL, 50(2) (AUG 89),
   533-A.
      THE AUTHOR EVALUATES THE INFLUENCE THAT THE GENERAL
   PUBLIC, INTEREST GROUPS, AND ELITES HAD ON EDUCATIONAL
   REFORM DURING THE 1980'S. HE SURVEYS EDUCATIONAL REFORM
   ACROSS THE UNITED STATES TO DISCOVER WHICH STATES ARE MORE

LIKELY TO ADOPT REFORMS AND WHICH FACTORS STRONGLY INFLUENCE
THESE STATES. HE FINDS THAT EDUCATIONAL NEED, REGION,
UNIONIZATION OF THE STATE'S POPULATION, VOTER TURNOUT,
STRENGTH OF INTEREST GROUPS, AND INTER-PARTY COMPETITION ALL
AFFECT EDUCATIONAL REFORM. HE USES TEXAS AS A CASE STUDY TO
MORE CLOSELY EXAMINE SOME OF THE FACTORS INVOLVED IN
EDUCATIONAL REFORM.

01720 BOWERS, J.R.
   AGENCY RESPONSIVENESS TO THE LEGISLATIVE OVERSIGHT OF
   ADMINISTRATIVE RULEMAKING: A CASE STUDY OF RULES REVIEW IN
   THE ILLINOIS GENERAL ASSEMBLY
   AMERICAN REVIEW OF PUBLIC ADMINISTRATION, 19(3) (SEP 89),
   217-232.
      STUDENTS OF PUBLIC ADMINISTRATION HAVE LONG MAINTAINED
   THAT FOR BUREAUCRATIC POWER TO BE IN BALANCE WITH
   CONSTITUTIONAL DEMOCRACY, IT MUST BE EXERCISED BY A
   RESPONSIBLE BUREAUCRACY. LEGISLATIVE OVERSIGHT IS ONE MEANS
   BY WHICH TO SECURE THE RESPONSIBLE EXERCISE OF THIS POWER.
   HOWEVER, LITTLE IS KNOWN REGARDING WHY AGENCIES ARE
   RESPONSIVE TO OVERSIGHT. IN THIS ARTICLE THIS QUESTION IS
   EXPLORED BY PRESENTING A CASE STUDY OF BUREAUCRATIC
   RESPONSIVENESS TO A HIGHLY SPECIALIZED AND ROUTINE APPROACH
   TO OVERSIGHT FOUND IN STATE LEGISLATURES-THE LEGISLATIVE
   REVIEW OF ADMINISTRATIVE RULE-MAKING OR "RULES REVIEW." FIVE
   FACTORS THAT APPEAR TO EXPLAIN AGENCY RESPONSIVENESS ARE
   PRESENTED AS ANALYTICAL GENERALIZATIONS THAT MAY FIND
   APPLICATION ELSEWHERE.

01721 BOWERS, J.R.
   REGULATING THE REGULATORS: THE LEGISLATIVE REVIEW OF
   ADMINISTRATIVE RULEMAKING IN ILLINOIS
   DISSERTATION ABSTRACTS INTERNATIONAL, 49(10) (APR 89),
   3150-A.
      THE AUTHOR ANALYZES RULES REVIEW AS A SYSTEMATIC
   RESPONSE BY STATE LEGISLATURES TO THE GROWING ROLE THAT
   STATE AGENCIES PLAY IN LAW-MAKING. HE SUGGESTS THAT RULES
   REVIEW CAN ENABLE STATE LEGISLATURES TO REASSERT THEIR OWN
   LAW-MAKING AUTHORITY AND CAN PROVIDE REGULATORY RELIEF TO
   THE AFFECTED PUBLICS.

01722 BOWERS, S.R.
   PERESTROIKA IN EASTERN EUROPE
   JOURNAL OF SOCIAL, POLITICAL AND ECONOMIC STUDIES, 14(2)
   (SUM 89), 149-187.
      TWO BASIC PATTERNS MAY BE DISCERNED FROM AN EXAMINATION
   OF THE OFFICIAL EAST EUROPEAN REACTION TO PRESSURES FOR
   REFORM. THE MOST CLEARLY RESPONSIVE MODEL IS THAT OF THE
   HUNGARIAN SOCIALIST WORKERS PARTY UNDER THE LEADERSHIP OF
   KAROLY GROSZ. THE MODEL FOR RESISTANCE IS THE GERMAN
   DEMOCRATIC REPUBLIC'S SOCIALIST UNITY PARTY UNDER THE
   LEADERSHIP OF ERICH HONECKER. THE REST OF THE REGION IS
   INCREASINGLY DIVIDED INTO TWO CAMPS. THE PRO-REFORMIST CAMP
   CONSISTS OF POLAND AND, TO A VERY LIMITED EXTENT, BULGARIA.
   CZECHOSLOVAKIA AND ROMANIA ARE FIRMLY ANTI-REFORMIST AND
   THEIR LEADERS ARE IN THE PROCESS OF CONSOLIDATING THEIR
   POSITIONS IN ORDER TO RESIST GROWING PRESSURE FOR BOTH
   ECONOMIC AND POLITICAL REFORMS.

01723 BOWERS, S.R.
   PINOCHET'S PLEBISCITE AND THE CATHOLICS: THE DUAL ROLE OF
   THE CHILEAN CHURCH
   WORLD AFFAIRS, 151(2) (FAL 88), 51-58.
      AS THE PROCESS OF CHILE'S DEMOCRATIZATION HAS PROCEEDED,
   THE RELATIONSHIP BETWEEN THE JUNTA AND THE CHURCH HAS BECOME
   PARTICULARLY SIGNIFICANT AS AN INDICATION OF THE ABILITY OF
   THE REGIME TO WORK WITH NON-GOVERNMENTAL POWER CENTERS IN
   GUIDING NATIONAL DEVELOPMENT ALONG A DEMOCRATIC PATH. THE
   INCREASINGLY VIOLENT CONTEXT OF CHILEAN POLITICS IN 1987 AND
   1988 HAS SERVED AS A REMINDER OF THE DIFFICULTIES OF
   RESOLVING THE JUNTA'S TROUBLED RELATIONSHIP WITH THE SOCIETY
   THAT IT MUST GOVERN BOTH TODAY AND, SHOULD IT WIN THE
   PLEBISCITE, IN THE FUTURE. IT IS THE PURPOSE OF THIS ARTICLE
   TO EXAMINE THE NATURE OF THE RELATIONSHIP BETWEEN THE REGIME
   AND THE CHURCH DURING THIS CRITICAL PERIOD AND TO EVALUATE
   HOW EACH INSTITUTION HAS DEALT WITH THE STRAINS THAT HAVE
   BECOME TYPICAL OF CHILEAN POLITICS. THAT EVALUATION MAY BE
   USEFUL IN MAKING PROJECTIONS ABOUT THE FUTURE OF CHILEAN
   SOCIETY IN THE ERA AFTER THE PLEBISCITE.

01724 BOWKER, M.; WILLIAMS, P.
   SUPERPOWER DETENTE: A REAPPRAISAL
   SAGE PUBLICATIONS, BEVERLY HILLS, CA, 1988, 278.
      THE AUTHORS EXAMINE THE SUPERPOWERS' INTERPRETATIONS OF
   DETENTE AND THE HISTORY OF THEIR INTERESTS IN DETENTE. THEY
   CONSIDER THE IMPACT OF EVENTS IN THE MIDEAST, ANGOLA, AND
   THE HORN OF AFRICA. THEY CONCLUDE THAT IT WAS NOT
   COMPETITION BUT SOVIET SUCCESS IN THE COMPETITION THAT
   HELPED TO SOUR DETENTE. THEY ALSO ARGUE THAT THE MAJOR SHIFT
   IN ATTITUDE OCCURRED IN WASHINGTON RATHER THAN MOSCOW.

01725 BOWLER, S.
   COMPARATIVE ECONOMIC ASSESSMENTS AND THE ENDOGENEITY OF
   LEFT/RIGHT SELF-PLACEMENT: A RESEARCH NOTE

EUROPEAN JOURNAL OF POLITICAL RESEARCH, 17(1) (JAN 89), 35-49.
MUCH OF THE LITERATURE ON POLITICAL ECONOMICS RESTRICTS ITS FOCUS TO THE SHORT-RUN IMPACTS OF ECONOMIC EVENTS IN STUDYING SUCH TOPICS AS VOTE CHOICE OR EXECUTIVE POPULARITY. IN THIS PAPER, THE AUTHOR EXAMINES THE IMPACT OF ECONOMIC EVENTS UPON LONGER-TERM ASPECTS OF VOTER ATTITUDES AND, IN PARTICULAR, UPON VOTER IDEOLOGIES. HE ALSO CONSIDERS THE SCOPE FOR THE INTERPRETABILITY OF ECONOMIC INFORMATION AT AN INDIVIDUAL LEVEL AND PRESENTS STATISTICAL EVIDENCE FROM FOUR EUROPEAN STATES.

01726 BOWLER, S.
VOTER PERCEPTIONS AND PARTY STRATEGIES: AN EMPIRICAL APPROACH
DISSERTATION ABSTRACTS INTERNATIONAL, 50(1) (JUL 89), 245-A.
THE AUTHOR EXAMINES BOTH THE FORMAL AND THE NON-FORMAL LITERATURE ON PARTY COMPETITION CONCERNING THE ABILITY OF POLITICAL PARTIES TO CHANGE THEIR POLICY POSITIONS, IN ORDER TO INFLUENCE VOTER BEHAVIOR.

01727 BOWMAN, J.S.
THE MPA CAPSTONE EXPERIENCE: THE ESSENCE OF ANALYSIS IS SURPRISE
POLICY STUDIES REVIEW, 8(4) (SUM 89), 920-928.
A FINAL COURSE, OR PROJECT, IS A STANDARD REQUIREMENT IN MASTER OF PUBLIC ADMINISTRATION (MPA) PROGRAMS. THIS REQUIREMENT IS INTENDED TO PERMIT THE STUDENT TO DEMONSTRATE ADVANCED ABILITY IN THE DISCIPLINE. THIS ARTICLE EXAMINES ONE SUCH COURSE AT FLORIDA STATE UNIVERSITY. THE COURSE INCLUDED READINGS, EXERCISES, ORAL PRESENTATIONS, AND A WRITTEN REPORT. THIS AUTHOR ASSESSES THE MERITS AND DRAWBACKS OF THE COURSE AS WELL AS NOTES THE UNINTENDED CONSEQUENCES THAT RESULTED. IN CONCLUDING THE ARTICLE, THE AUTHOR MAKES SEVERAL RECOMMENDATIONS FOR FUTURE COURSES BASED ON THE EXPERIENCES GAINED IN THE FLORIDA STATE MODEL.

01728 BOWMAN, R.S.
JEVON'S ECONOMIC THEORY IN RELATION TO SOCIAL CHANGE AND PUBLIC POLICY
JOURNAL OF ECONOMIC ISSUES, 23(4) (DEC 89), 1123-1149.
THIS ARTICLE ATTEMPTS TO EXPLORE THE AREA OF THE INTERSECTION OF THE THEORIST WITH THE SOCIAL SCENE WITH REGARD TO JEVONS. THE HISTORICO-GENETIC METHOD OF ANALYSIS IS FOLLOWED, WHICH PROCEEDS GENERALLY IN INQUIRING ABOUT THE CHANGING HISTORICAL CONTEXT WITHIN WHICH ECONOMIC ANALYSIS SERVES AND THE ADAPTION OF THE RECEIVED BODY OF THEORY TO THE PROBLEM AT HAND. JEVON'S SOCIAL PHILOSOPHY, PROGRAM OF SOCIAL REFORM AND THEORETICAL PERSPECTIVE ARE EXAMINED.

01729 BOWMAN, S.R.
CONVENTIONAL FORCE MODERNIZATION
CRS REVEIW, 10(4) (APR 89), 9-10.
IN THE WAKE OF THE INF TREATY, INTEREST IN THE STATE OF NATO'S CONVENTIONAL FORCES BURGEONED. THE IMPENDING REMOVAL OF A MAJOR PORTION OF NATO'S EUROPEAN-BASED NUCLEAR FORCES LED MANY TO BELIEVE THAT CONVENTIONAL FORCES WOULD HAVE TO SHOULDER A GREATER SHARE OF THE DETERRENT BURDEN. WHILE MOST GENERALLY AGREE THAT NATO MUST MAINTAIN MODERN AND ROBUST CONVENTIONAL FORCES, THE CURRENT INTERNATIONAL POLITICAL AND ECONOMIC ENVIRONMENT PRESENT A NUMBER OF CHALLENGES TO NATO PLANNERS. AMONG THESE CHALLENGES ARE CHANGES IN THE PERCEPTION OF THE WARSAW PACT THREAT TO EUROPE, THE ADVENT OF NEW NEGOTIATIONS TO REDUCE CONVENTIONAL FORCES IN EUROPE, A HEIGHTENED U.S. CONCERN OVER BURDEN-SHARING WITHIN THE NATO ALLIANCE, AND INCREASINGLY CONSTRAINED DEFENSE SPENDING IN VIRTUALLY ALL NATO COUNTRIES.

01730 BOWMAN, S.R.
CORPORATE POWER, IDEOLOGY, AND THE LAW: AN ESSAY ON THE POLITICAL THEORY OF THE CORPORATION IN AMERICA
DISSERTATION ABSTRACTS INTERNATIONAL, 50(4) (OCT 89), 1074-A.
THE STUDY OF THE INTERRELATED ASPECTS OF CORPORATE POWER, IDEOLOGY, AND THE LAW DEMONSTRATES THAT AN ALTERNATIVE TO PREVAILING CONCEPTIONS MAY BE FOUND IN A POLITICAL THEORY OF THE CORPORATION WHICH INCORPORATES AN HISTORICAL ANALYSIS OF THE ROLE OF LAW IN STRUCTURING, MEDIATING, AND JUSTIFYING RELATIONSHIPS OF CONTROL. A CLASS-ANALYTIC POWER APPROACH WHICH IS CONSTRAINED NEITHER BY AN ARTIFICIAL DIVISION OF SOCIAL REALITY NOR BY THE IMPERATIVES OF ECONOMIC DETERMINISM PROVIDES THE ANALYTICAL FRAMEWORK FOR EXAMINING THE EMPIRICAL DIMENSIONS OF CORPORATE POWER CONCEIVED AS RELATIONSHIPS OF CONTROL ROOTED IN THE LAW. THIS APPROACH, WHICH CAN ACCOUNT FOR THE HISTORICAL DEVELOPMENT, ORGANIZATION, AND STRUCTURE OF CORPORATE POWER IN THE UNITED STATES, ALSO PROVIDES THE CONCEPTUAL TOOLS FOR ANALYZING THE IDEOLOGY OF CORPORATE INTERNATIONALISM-THE LIBERAL JUSTIFICATION OF THE ASCENDANT REGIME OF TRANSNATIONAL CORPORATE POWER.

01731 BOWRING, P.; LAU, E.
CASH ON DELIVERY

FAR EASTERN ECONOMIC REVIEW, 142(51) (DEC 89), 13-14.
THE HONG KONG GOVERNMENT BEGAN ITS FORCED REPATRIATION OF VIETNAMESE BOAT PEOPLE IN A PRE-DAWN ACTION THAT SENT NO MORE THAN 50 PEOPLE BACK TO HANOI. EVEN THIS MOVE WAS WIDELY CRITICIZED IN INTERNATIONAL CIRCLES AS BEING HYPOCRITICAL AND SELFISH. BOTH THE HONG KONG AND BRITISH GOVERNMENTS HAVE COME UNDER FIRE FOR THEIR DECISION TO SEND SOME 36,000 UNSCREENED VIETNAMESE BACK TO THEIR HOMELAND. THE INTERNATIONAL OUTCRY PROMPTED THE LOCAL GOVERNMENT TO STATE THAT NO FURTHER FORCED REPATRIATIONS WOULD TAKE PLACE BEFORE THE BRITISH PARLIAMENT DEBATED THE ISSUE.

01732 BOXER, B.
CHINA'S ENVIRONMENTAL PROSPECTS
ASIAN SURVEY, 29(7) (JUL 89), 669-686.
THIS ARTICLE REVIEWS CHINA'S MAJOR ENVIRONMENTAL PROBLEMS IN RELATION TO ECONOMIC ACTIVITIES. IT THEN TRACES THE DEVELOPMENT OF INSTITUTIONS, LAWS, AND OTHER MEASURES TO DEAL WITH PROBLEMS. FINALLY, ENVIRONMENTAL CONSTRAINTS ON CHINA'S MODERNIZATION ARE ASSESSED AS THEY AFFECT CHINA AND THE REGION.

01733 BOYD, R.W.
THE EFFECTS OF PRIMARIES AND STATEWIDE RACES ON VOTER TURNOUT
THE JOURNAL OF POLITICS, 51(3) (AUG 89), 730-742.
THE DECISION TO VOTE IS AFFECTED BY TWO ELEMENTS OF THE ELECTION CONTEXT. ONE IS THE FREQUENCY OF ELECTIONS. PRESIDENTIAL AND STATE PRIMARIES DIVERT RESOURCES AWAY FROM THE GENERAL ELECTION AND REDUCE TURNOUT AMONG THE PERIPHERAL ELECTORATE WHO ARE MOST DEPENDENT ON A MOBILIZATION EFFORT. TAKEN TOGETHER, SPRING AND FALL PRIMARIES LOWERED GENERAL ELECTION BY FIVE PERCENTAGE POINTS NATIONWIDE IN THE 1976, 1980, AND 1984 ELECTIONS. A SECOND ELEMENT OF CONTEXT IS THE ATTRACTIVENESS OF STATEWIDE OFFICES ON THE PRESIDENTIAL YEAR BALLOT. GUBERNATORIAL RACES INCREASE THE PROBABILITY OF VOTING BY 6% IN THOSE STATES THAT STILL ELECT GOVERNORS IN PRESIDENTIAL YEARS. THUS, THE POSTWAR SHIFT OF GUBERNATORIAL RACES TO THE CONGRESSIONAL ELECTION YEAR IS ONE EXPLANATION FOR DECLINING TURNOUT. SENATORIAL RACES DO NOT ATTRACT ADDITIONAL VOTERS TO THE NOVEMBER ELECTION. THESE HYPOTHESES ARE TESTED ON A POOLED SAMPLE OF THE 1976, 1980, AND 1984 CPS ELECTION STUDIES.

01734 BOYER, M.A.
BURDEN-SHARING AND COMPARATIVE ADVANTAGE IN THE WESTERN ALLIANCE SYSTEM: TOWARD A NEW ECONOMIC THEORY OF INTERNATIONAL COOPERATION
DISSERTATION ABSTRACTS INTERNATIONAL, 49(7) (JAN 89), 1948-A.
THE AUTHOR SEEKS TO BROADEN THE SCOPE OF ANALYSES OF SECURITY BURDEN-SHARING WITHIN THE WESTERN ALLIANCE SYSTEM BEYOND THE NARROW APPROACH TAKEN BY PAST WORK IN THE ECONOMIC THEORY OF ALLIANCES. HE CONSIDERS THE NATURE OF BURDEN-SHARING, THE OPTIMALITY OF ALLIANCE SECURITY PROVISION, AND THE FUTURE OF COOPERATION IN THE WESTERN ALLIANCE SYSTEM IN THE FACE OF DECLINING AMERICAN HEGEMONY.

01735 BOYER, M.A.
TRADING PUBLIC GOODS IN THE WESTERN ALLIANCE SYSTEM
JOURNAL OF CONFLICT RESOLUTION, 33(4) (DEC 89), 700-727.
THIS ARTICLE SEEKS TO BROADEN THE SCOPE OF ANALYSES OF SECURITY BURDEN SHARING WITHIN THE WESTERN ALLIANCE SYSTEM BEYOND THE NARROW MILITARY APPROACH TAKEN BY PAST WORK IN THE ECONOMIC THEORY OF ALLIANCES. IN CONTRAST TO THAT WORK, WHICH HAS SHOWN THAT THE WESTERN ALLIES HAVE BEEN PERSISTENTLY FREE RIDING ON THE MILITARY EFFORTS OF THE UNITED STATES, AN ILLUSTRATIVE MODEL IS PRESENTED THAT POSITS THE EXISTENCE OF BURDEN SHARING ACROSS ISSUE AREAS AMONG THE WESTERN ALLIES. THE MODEL YIELDS SIGNIFICANTLY DIFFERENT CONCLUSIONS REGARDING (1) THE NATURE OF ALLIANCE BURDEN SHARING,(2) THE OPTIMALITY OF ALLIANCE SECURITY PROVISION, AND (3) THE FUTURE OF COOPERATION IN THE WESTERN ALLIANCE SYSTEM IN THE FACE OF DECLINING AMERICAN HEGEMONY. ON A THEORETICAL LEVEL, THIS ARTICLE BEGINS TO FORMULATE A NEW ECONOMIC THEORY OF ALLIANCES THAT FOCUSES ON "TRADE" IN PUBLIC GOODS AND ADHERES CLOSELY TO THE RICARDIAN THEORY OF COMPARATIVE ADVANTAGE.

01736 BOYER, P.
ROBUST DEMOCRACY-THE CANADIAN GENERAL ELECTION OF 1988
PARLIAMENTARIAN, 70(2) (APR 89), 72-76.
THE AUTHOR PROVIDES AN OVERVIEW OF THE CANADIAN GENERAL ELECTION OF 1988, WHICH RETURNED 168 PROGRESSIVE CONSERVATIVES TO THE 295-SEAT HOUSE OF COMMONS, AND VOTED PRIME MINISTER MULRONEY INTO A SECOND MAJORITY GOVERNMENT IN SUCCESSION. ON A POLICY LEVEL, THE DISCUSSION COVERS SUCH ISSUES AS CANADA-UNITED STATES RELATIONS IN TERMS OF THE NEW TRADE TREATY. ON A DOMESTIC POLITICAL LEVEL, THE ASCENDENCY OF THE PROGRESSIVE CONSERVATICES AS A GOVERNING PARTY IS DISCUSSED IN THE CONTEXT OF BITTER PARTISANSHIP AND A DESPARATE GRASP FOR POWER BY THE LIBERAL AND NEW DEMOCRATIC PARTIES. THE EFFECTS OF OPINION POLLS IN THESE ELECTIONS ARE DEBATED.

01737 BOYLE, F.
CITIZEN INITIATIVES UNDER INTERNATIONAL LAW: THE
CRIMINALITY OF NUCLEAR WEAPONS
SCANDINAVIAN JOURNAL OF DEVELOPMENT ALTERNATIVES, VIII(2)
(JUN 89), 37-44.
THE ARTICLE ATTEMPTS TO DEFINE IN LEGAL TERMS THE STARK
DILEMMA OF NUCLEAR EXTINCTION THAT CONFRONTS THE HUMAN RACE.
IT ANALYZES THE INHERENT CRIMINALITY OF THE EXISTENCE OF
NUCLEAR WEAPONS AND THE THREAT OF THEIR USE. IT SEEKS TO
ESTABLISH AN AGENDA FOR LAWYERS AROUND THE WORLD TO PURSUE
TO APPLY THEIR TRAINING AND SKILLS TOWARD THE COMPLETE
ELIMINATION OF NUCLEAR WEAPONS.

01738 BOYNE, G.
THE MEASUREMENT OF LOCAL AUTHORITY STAFFING LEVELS
PUBLIC ADMINISTRATION, 67(2) (SUM 89), 228-230.
THE AUTHOR RESPONDS TO A CRITIQUE OF HIS TWO-STAGE
PROCEDURE FOR EVALUATING STAFF CUTS IN LOCAL AUTHORITIES. HE
ARGUES THAT THE SO-CALLED "OPERATIONAL DEFECTS" DO NOT EXIST
AND THAT HIS ORIGINAL STUDY IS VALID AND ACCURATE. (SEE
PUBLIC ADMINISTRATION 1986, V64 PP69-82 AND PUBLIC
ADMINISTRATION 1988, V66 PP457-461)

01739 BOYNTON, G.R.
THE SENATE AGRICULTURE COMMITTEE PRODUCES A HOMEOSTAT
POLICY SCIENCES, 22(1) (MAR 89), 51-80.
THIS PAPER LOOKS BACK TO THE 1960-1973 PERIOD TO
UNDERSTAND AGRICULTURAL POLICY AND POLICY MAKING. THE
ARGUMENT OF THE PAPER IS THAT POLICY AND POLICY MAKING
INTERACT, REACHING WHAT CAN BE UNDERSTOOD AS AN EQUILIBRIUM
IN THE 1970S THAT HAS BEEN REPRODUCED EVER SINCE. THE PAPER
FOCUSES ON THE SENATE AGRICULTURE COMMITTEE. THE POLICY
MAKING OF THE COMMITTEE IS CHARACTERIZED AS A CONSTRAINED
SEARCH THROUGH A POLICY SPACE WITHOUT HAVING AHEAD OF TIME A
CLEAR UNDERSTANDING OF WHAT THE LAW WOULD BECOME AS A RESULT
OF THE SEARCH. THIS CHARACTERIZATION IS CONSISTENT WITH
HERBERT SIMON'S CONCEPTION OF PROCEDURAL RATIONALITY AND IS
CONSISTENT WITH THE INFORMATION AVAILABLE ABOUT THE
COMMITTEE.

01740 BOYTE, H.C.
COMMONWEALTH: THE LANGUAGE OF POPULISM AND THE PRACTICE OF
DEMOCRACY
DISSERTATION ABSTRACTS INTERNATIONAL, 50(4) (OCT 89),
1074-A.
THE TRADITION AND LANGUAGE OF COMMONWEALTH
SIMULTANEOUSLY RESOLVE THE PUZZLE OF POPULISM AND POINT
BEYOND POPULISM TOWARD NEW APPROACHES TO DEMOCRATIC CHANGE
IN TECHNOLOGICAL SOCIETY. AGAINST THE RECENT POLITICAL
ASSAULT ON THE VERY IDEA OF COMMUNAL AND PUBLIC GOODS, THE
EFFORT TO REASSERT THE IMPORTANCE OF COMMONWEALTH FURNISHES
A POWERFUL LANGUAGE FOR TALKING ABOUT THOSE THINGS IN WHICH
MOST CITIZENS FEEL SOME STAKE AND INTEREST. THE POPULIST
SENSE OF VOLUNTARY, CIVIC AGENCY AND POPULAR RESPONSIBILITY
FOR THE COMMONWEALTH COUNTERS BOTH THE STATE-CENTERED
LANGUAGE OF TECHNOCRATIC LIBERALISM AND THE PRIVATIZING
THRUST OF NEO-CONSERVATIVE POLITICS.

01741 BOYTE, H.C.
FACILITATING CITIZENSHIP: AN INTERVIEW WITH PEG MICHELS
NATIONAL CIVIC REVIEW, 78(4) (JUL 89), 259-264.
THIS INTERVIEW WITH AN EXPERIENCED CAMPAIGN FIELD
ORGANIZER AND MANAGER SUGGESTS THAT ATTITUDES TOWARD THE
CURRENT PRACTICE OF ELECTORAL POLITICS OVERLOOK THE
CONNECTION BETWEEN CITIZENSHIP AND EMPOWERMENT. SELF
GOVERNMENT CANNOT BE PASSIVE, AND ACTIVE CITIZENSHIP
REQUIRES BOTH KNOWLEDGE OF ISSUES AND PERSONAL POLITICAL
INVOLVEMENT.

01742 BOYTE, H.C.
OVERVIEW: RETHINKING POLITICS
NATIONAL CIVIC REVIEW, 78(4) (JUL 89), 249-254.
REFLECTION ON THE TRADITIONAL ROLE OF THE TOWN COMMONS
AS A FOCAL POINT OF PUBLIC INVOLVEMENT FOR CITIZENS
UNDERSCORES THE CRISIS OUR DEMOCRATIC INSTITUTIONS FACE: A
TOO RESTRICTIVE DEFINITION OF CITIZENSHIP HAS REDUCED PUBLIC
INVOLVEMENT TO THE MERE CASTING OF BALLOTS AND THE ROLE OF
THE CITIZEN TO MERE CONSUMPTION OF CAMPAIGN RHETORIC. HE
MUST RESTORE INSTITUTIONS OF PUBLIC INVOLVEMENT AND
STRENGTHEN THE CONNECTIONS BETWEEN INDIVIDUAL CITIZENS AND
THE BROADER COMMUNITY.

01743 BOZOKI, A.
A RAINBOW SPECTRUM--POLITICAL TRENDS IN HUNGARY
EAST EUROPEAN REPORTER, 4(1) (WIN 90), 28-30.
ALTHOUGH IDEOLOGY DOES NOT PLAY AN EXCLUSIVE ROLE IN THE
PROCESS OF POLITICAL DIFFERENTIATION IN HUNGARY, THE
COUNTRY'S EXPERIENCES SUGGEST THAT PROCESSES OF POLITICAL
AND IDEOLOGICAL PLURALIZATION OFTEN OVERLAP EACH OTHER. THE
ARTICLE EXAMINES THE SEVEN MAIN POLITICAL TRENDS IN HUNGARY.
THEY INCLUDE: THE BOLSHEVIK CONSERVATIVE FORCES, THE
PRAGMATIC TECHNOCRATS, THE REFORM COMMUNISTS AND DEMOCRATIC
SOCIALISTS, THE CURRENTLY SCHIZOPHRENIC SOCIAL DEMOCRACY

MOVEMENT, THE RADICAL AND LIBERAL DEMOCRATS, THE DEMOCRATIC
POPULISTS, AND THE POPULIST AND RELIGIOUS CONSERVATIVES.

01744 BRACE, P.; COHEN, Y.; GRAY, V.; LOWERY, D.
HOW MUCH DO INTEREST GROUPS INFLUENCE STATE ECONOMIC
GROWTH?
AMERICAN POLITICAL SCIENCE REVIEW, 83(4) (DEC 89),
1297-1308.
IN "THE RISE AND DECLINE OF NATIONS," MANCUR OLSON
DEVELOPED A THEORY THAT HE CLAIMED COULD EXPLAIN DIFFERENCES
IN THE GROWTH RATES OF STATES. SUBSEQUENTLY, VIRGINIA GRAY
AND DAVID LOWERY PRESENTED A RE-SPECIFICATION OF OLSON'S
MODEL AND TESTED THEIR REVISED MODEL WITH DATA FROM U.S.
STATES. IN THIS ARTICLE, PAUL BRACE AND YOUSSEF COHEN ARGUE
THAT THE GRAY-LOWERY MODEL MISSPECIFIES THE DETERMINANTS OF
STATE ECONOMIC GROWTH BY OVERSTATING THE ROLE OF INTEREST
GROUP SIZE AND FAILING TO INCORPORATE CRUCIAL EXOGENOUS
VARIABLES. THEN GRAY AND LOWERY RESPOND TO THE BRACE-COHEN
CRITIQUE.

01745 BRACE, P.
ISOLATING THE ECONOMIES OF STATES
AMERICAN POLITICS QUARTERLY, 17(3) (JUL 89), 256-276.
DESPITE IMPRESSIVE EFFORTS, WE LACK AN EMPIRICALLY
SUPPORTED EXPLANATION OF THE ROLE OF STATE-LEVEL POLITICAL
PROCESSES IN SHAPING STATE ECONOMIC PERFORMANCE. THIS STUDY
INDICATES WHY A CONCRETE UNDERSTANDING OF THE INTERPLAY OF
STATE-LEVEL POLITICAL AND ECONOMIC FORCES HAS BEEN ELUSIVE.
STATE ECONOMIES ARE SENSITIVE TO EXTERNAL INFLUENCES. THIS
SENSITIVITY VARIES SYSTEMATICALLY AND SIGNIFICANTLY OVER
TIME AND BETWEEN STATES. THE MAGNITUDE OF THESE EXTERNAL
INFLUENCES SHOWS THAT BEFORE WE MAY UNRAVEL HOW STATES
INFLUENCE THEIR ECONOMIES, CONSIDERATION MUST BE GIVEN TO
THE EXTRASTATE INFLUENCES THAT CONDITION THE ECONOMIC
ENVIRONMENT OF STATES. POOLED MODELS OF STATE ECONOMIES ARE
ESTIMATED FOR THREE PERIODS: 1968-1973, 1974-1979, AND 1980-
1985. IN GENERAL, STATE ECONOMIES WERE HEAVILY INFLUENCED BY
NATIONAL ECONOMIC TRENDS, BUT OVER TIME THEY HAVE BECOME
MORE ECONOMICALLY INDEPENDENT. STATES ARE ALSO EVALUATED
INDIVIDUALLY. FAST GROWING STATES IN THE 1968-1985 PERIOD
TENDED TO BE THE MOST SENSITIVE TO NATIONAL ECONOMIC
CONDITIONS WHILE SLOWER GROWING STATES WERE MORE AUTONOMOUS.

01746 BRADEMAS, J.; BROWN, H.; HAIG, A.; LAIRD, M.; MUSKIE, E.;
PERCY, C.; SCHLESINGER, J.; SCOWCROFT, B.; VANCE, C.
BUILDING A NEW CONSENSUS: CONGRESS AND FOREIGN POLICY
SAIS REVIEW, 9(2) (SUM 89), 61-71.
THIS ARTICLE OFFERS VARIOUS PROPOSALS ON HOW TO
RECAPTURE THE INITIAL PAST-WORLD WAR II CONSENSUS, WHICH
GUIDED U.S. COLD WAR STRATEGY. OF SPECIAL SIGNIFICANCE IS
THE SECTION ON RESTRUCTURING THE RELATIONSHIP BETWEEN
CONGRESS AND THE INTELLIGENCE GATHERING COMMUNITY. THE
CONSENSUS REPORT PROPOSES A SIGNIFICANT RESTRUCTURING OF A
RELATIONSHIP THAT ALLOWED THE IRAN-CONTRA AFFAIR TO FALL
BETWEEN THE CRACKS OF CHECKS AND BALANCES.

01747 BRADLEY, G.V.
DEVELOPMENTS IN CHURCH-STATE LAW: ANALYSIS AND OPINION
ILLINOIS BAR JOURNAL, 77(15) (NOV 89), 806-813.
THIS ARTICLE EXPLORES ONE FACET OF THE SEEMINGLY EVER-
CHANGING, CONTRADICTORY WORLD OF CHURCH-STATE CONSTITUTIONAL
LAW, WHERE SOME THINGS DO STAY THE SAME. IT CONTENDS THAT
DISPITE SOME APPEARANCES TO THE CONTRARY, COURTS HAVE WED
ESTABLISHMENT AND FREE EXERCISE CLAUSE DOCTRINE IN PURSUIT
OF POLITICAL INCLUSIVENESS AND CIVIL TRANQUILITY, BUT NOT
RELIGIOUS FREEDOM. IT EXPLORES THE ESTABLISHMENT CLAUSE, THE
RISE OF "ENDORSEMENT" ANALYSIS, AND THE CONDUCT EXEMPTION.

01748 BRADSHAW, Y.W.; FRASER, E.
CITY SIZE, ECONOMIC DEVELOPMENT, AND QUALITY OF LIFE IN
CHINA: NEW EMPIRICAL EVIDENCE
AMERICAN SOCIOLOGICAL REVIEW, 54(6) (DEC 89), 986-1003.
THE DEARTH OF CASE STUDIES ON THIRD WORLD URBANIZATION
AND CITY SIZE IS UNFORTUNATE BECAUSE, IN CONTRAST TO CROSS-
NATIONAL RESEARCH, THESE STUDIES CAN EXPLAIN SPECIAL
PATTERNS OF DEVELOPMENT. THIS STUDY UTILIZES THE RECENTLY
PUBLISHED POPULATION ATLAS OF CHINA TO ANALYZE THE
RELATIONSHIP AMONG CITY SIZE, ECONOMIC DEVELOPMENT, AND
PHYSICAL QUALITY OF LIFE. THE DATA ANALYSIS PRODUCES THREE
MAJOR RESULTS. FIRST, ALL-SIZED CITIES ENJOY HIGHER LEVELS
OF ECONOMIC DEVELOPMENT AND PHYSICAL QUALITY OF LIFE
RELATIVE TO NONURBAN AREAS. SECOND, EXTERNALLY ORIENTED
COASTAL CITIES POSSESS HIGHER LEVELS OF ECONOMIC DEVELOPMENT
BUT NOT A BETTER QUALITY OF LIFE. THIRD, EDUCATION AND
INDUSTRIAL EMPLOYMENT CONTRIBUTE TO BOTH ECONOMIC
DEVELOPMENT AND PHYSICAL QUALITY OF LIFE. OVERALL, THESE
FINDINGS SUPPORT MODERNIZATION THEORIES AND SOME ASPECTS OF
THE DEPENDENCY/WORLD-SYSTEMS PERSPECTIVE.

01749 BRADY, D.; BRODY, R.; EPSTEIN, D.
HETEROGENEOUS PARTIES AND POLITICAL ORGANIZATION: THE U.S.
SENATE, 1880-1920
LEGISLATIVE STUDIES QUARTERLY, 15(2) (MAY 89), 205-224.
THE TURN OF THE CENTURY HAS BEEN IDENTIFIED BY SCHOLARS

AS A TIME WHEN BOTH THE HOUSE AND SENATE HAD STRONG LEADERS WHO WERE ABLE TO IMPLEMENT THE REPUBLICAN'S LEGISLATIVE PROGRAM. THIS ARTICLE SHOWS THAT A NECESSARY CONDITION FOR THE STRONG LEADERSHIP EXHIBITED BY THE ALDRICH OLIGARCHY WAS THE EXISTENCE OF A PARTY MEMBERSHIP THAT WAS HOMOGENEOUS IN ITS POLICY PREFERENCES.

01750 BRADY, H.E.; ANSOLABEHERE, S.
THE NATURE OF UTILITY FUNCTIONS IN MASS PUBLICS
AMERICAN POLITICAL SCIENCE REVIEW, 83(1) (MAR 89), 143-164.
(1) VOTERS' PREFERENCES ARE ORDERLY BUT VOTERS DO NOT ALWAYS HAVE PREFERENCES. WHEN THE PERCEIVED DIFFERENCE BETWEEN TWO CANDIDATES IS BELOW SOME THRESHOLD, VOTERS ARE INDIFFERENT BETWEEN THEM. (2) MOST VOTERS CHOOSE CANDIDATES WHOSE ISSUE POSITIONS ARE CONGRUENT WITH THEIR OWN. (3) LACK OF KNOWLEDGE ABOUT CANDIDATES AFFECTS CHOICE AND UTILITY THROUGH TWO ROUTES-INDIFFERENCE AND RISK AVERSION. MOST VOTERS HAVE HIGHLY STRUCTURED UTILITY FUNCTIONS, BUT THE THRESHOLDS AND RISK AVERSION IN THESE FUNCTIONS PLACE RELATIVELY UNKNOWN CANDIDATES AT A DISADVANTAGE IN PRESIDENTIAL PRIMARIES AND OTHER ELECTORAL SITUATIONS. MOREOVER, THE IMPORTANCE OF KNOWLEDGE IN THESE FUNCTIONS SUGGESTS THAT SOCIAL CHOICE THEORISTS MUST TAKE SERIOUSLY THE CLASSIC CONCERNS OF PUBLIC OPINION RESEARCH-THE OPERATION OF THE MEDIA AND THE DYNAMICS OF INFORMATION IN ELECTIONS.

01751 BRADY, N.F.
DEALING WITH THE INTERNATIONAL DEBT CRISIS
DEPARTMENT OF STATE BULLETIN (US FOREIGN POLICY), 89(2146) (MAY 89), 53-56.
THE INTERNATIONAL DEBT CRISIS IS A COMPLEX ACCUMULATION OF A MYRIAD OF INTERWOVEN PROBLEMS AND CONTAINS ECONOMIC, POLITICAL, AND SOCIAL ELEMENTS. RESOLUTION DEPENDS ON A GREAT COOPERATIVE EFFORT BY THE INTERNATIONAL COMMUNITY. IT REQUIRES THE MOBILIZATION OF THE WORLD'S RESOURCES AND THE DEDICATION OF ITS GOODWILL.

01752 BRADY, N.F.
REQUEST FOR U.S. CONTRIBUTIONS TO MULTILATERAL DEVELOPMENT BANKS
DEPARTMENT OF STATE BULLETIN (US FOREIGN POLICY), 89(2147) (JUN 89), 21-30.
THE AUTHOR, WHO IS SECRETARY OF THE TREASURY, SUMMARIZES THE BUSH ADMINISTRATION'S BUDGET PROPOSALS FOR THE MULTILATERAL DEVELOPMENT BANKS AND THE INTERNATIONAL MONETARY FUND'S ENHANCED STRUCTURAL ADJUSTMENT FACILITY. HE ALSO LOOKS AT THE ADMINISTRATION'S PROPOSED DEBT STRATEGY AND AT THE ROLE THE MULTILATERAL DEVELOPMENT BANKS PLAY IN THE INTERNATIONAL DEBT SITUATION.

01753 BRANA-SHUTE, G.
POLITICS AND MILITARISM IN SURINAME
HEMISPHERE, 1(2) (WIN 89), 32-35.
THE AUTHOR SURVEYS SURINAME'S RECENT POLITICAL HISTORY, WHICH HAS BEEN CHARACTERIZED BY CORRUPTION, VIOLENCE, AND FRAGMENTATION OF POWER.

01754 BRAND, J.
FACTION AS ITS OWN REWARD: GROUPS IN THE BRITISH PARLIAMENT 1945-1986
PARLIAMENTARY AFFAIRS, 42(2) (APR 89), 148-164.
THE ARTICLE STUDIES THE GROWTH IN THE NUMBER OF BRITISH FACTIONS SINCE 1945 WITH EMPHASIS ON FACTIONS WITHIN PARLIAMENTARY PARTIES. IT EXAMINES THEIR IDEOLOGY AND GOALS AND ATTEMPTS TO DISCERN THEIR ORIGINS. IT CONCLUDES THAT ALTHOUGH THE NATURE OF THE PARTY IN SOME WAY ENCOURAGES THE GROWTH OF FACTIONS, THE MORE IMPORTANT FACTOR IS THE CHANGES IN SOCIETY THAT THE FACTIONS ARE A REFLECTION OF.

01755 BRAND, J.
KAVANAGH AND MCKENZIE ON POWER
WEST EUROPEAN POLITICS, 12(2) (APR 89), 112-122.
THIS ARTICLE RESPONDS TO AN EARLIER ANALYSIS BY KAVANAGH WHICH CRITICISED THE BASIC THESIS OF MCKENZIE'S BRITISH POLITICAL PARTIES. THE AUTHOR OF THE PRESENT ARTICLE BELIEVES THAT KAVANAGH MADE SOME IMPORTANT CRITICISMS OF MCKENZIE, BUT IT IS STILL TRUE THAT POWER IN THE LABOUR PARTY IS SIMILARLY DISTRIBUTED TO POWER IN THE CONSERVATIVE PARTY - BROADLY THE PARLIAMENTARY PARTY IS AUTONOMOUS, AND THE LEADER, ESPECIALLY IN GOVERNMENT, IS IN CONTROL OF THE PARTY. EVENTS SINCE 1983 HAVE SERVED TO UNDERLINE THIS FACT.

01756 BRANDL, J.E.
DEAR CONSTITUTENT: HERE'S WHERE I STAND
COMMONWEAL, VXVI(21) (DEC 89), 661-662.
THE AUTHOR, WHO IS A MINNESOTA STATE SENATOR, SUGGESTS THAT BOTH PRO-CHOICE AND ANTI-ABORTION POSITIONS ARE TOO EXTREME AND A MODERATE POSITION SHOULD PREVAIL ON THE QUESTION OF ABORTION. HE REJECTS BOTH THE VIEW THAT A FERTILIZED OVUM IS A HUMAN PERSON FROM THE MOMENT OF CONCEPTION AND THE ARGUMENT THAT A WOMAN'S RIGHT TO CHOOSE ABORTION SHOULD BE ABSOLUTE AND INVIOLABLE.

01757 BRANDON, W.P.
CUT OFF AT THE IMPASSE WITHOUT REAL CATASTROPHIC HEALTH INSURANCE: THREE APPROACHES TO FINANCING LONG-TERM CARE
POLICY STUDIES REVIEW, 8(2) (WIN 89), 441-454.
THIS ESSAY QUESTIONS WHETHER THE U.S. GOVERNMENT SHOULD CONTINUE TO FILL THE GAPS IN THE SECURITY OF ELDERLY AMERICANS OR WHETHER THE NEEDS OF OTHER POPULATION SUB-GROUPS OUGHT TO RECEIVE MORE ATTENTION. IT RECOGNIZES THAT INCREMENTALIST POLITICS, DEMOGRAPHY, AND THE CURRENT INTELLECTUAL CLIMATE PROBABLY MAKE LONG-TERM HEALTH CARE THE INEVITABLE FOCUS OF THE NEXT INNOVATION IN SOCIAL AND HEALTH POLICY. THREE BROAD STRATEGIES BY WHICH POLITICAL AND SOCIAL INSTITUTIONS CAN PROVIDE THE NECESSARY RESOURCES FOR LONG-TERM CARE ARE EXAMINED: IMPROVEMENTS IN MEDICAID, SOCIAL INSURANCE, AND PRIVATE LONG-TERM CARE INSURANCE.

01758 BRANDOW, D.
LEAVING KOREA
FOREIGN POLICY, (77) (WIN 89), 77-93.
THIS ARTICLE EXPLORES THE RELATIONSHIP BETWEEN AMERICA AND THE REPUBLIC OF KOREA (ROK). IT SUGGESTS THAT ALTHOUGH THE ROK HAS ADJUSTED SURPRISING WELL TO THE NOVELTIES OF POLITICAL FREEDOM AND DIVIDED GOVERNMENTS, SEOUL'S RELATIONS WITH THE UNITED STATES HAVE DETERIORATED AND ARE LIKELY TO GROW INCREASINGLY STRAINED. IT PROPOSES THAT THE U.S. SHOULD BEGIN WITHDRAWING ITS TROOPS FROM THE KOREAN PENINSULA, AND EVALUATES THE BENEFITS AND RISKS OF AMERICAN DISENGAGEMENT.

01759 BRANDS, H.W.
THE LIMITS OF MANIPULATION: HOW THE UNITED STATES DIDN'T TOPPLE SUKARNO
JOURNAL OF AMERICAN HISTORY, 76(3) (DEC 89), 785-808.
SUKARNO'S OVERTHROW RESULTED FROM DEVELOPMENTS OF ESSENTIALLY INDONESIAN ORIGIN, AND HAD LITTLE TO DO WITH AMERICAN MACHINATIONS, EVEN THOUGH AMERICAN OFFICIALS HAD PRODDED THE INDONESIAN ARMY TO MOVE AGAINST SUKARNO FOR MANY MONTHS. BY THE SUMMER OF 1965 THE JOHNSON ADMINISTRATION, AT A LOSS AS TO WHAT ELSE IT MIGHT DO TO MOTIVATE THE ARMY, HAD BASICALLY GIVEN UP. THE AMERICAN PRESENCE IN INDONESIA DECLINED DRASTICALLY, AND WHILE THOSE AMERICANS WHO REMAINED NO DOUBT CONTINUED TO ENCOURAGE ACTION TO PREVENT THE COUNTRY FROM FALLING COMPLETELY UNDER THE SPELL OF THE LEFT, INDONESIAN AND AMERICAN POLITICS PRECLUDED ANYTHING MORE THAN A HOLDING ACTION. WHEN THE COUP BEGAN IN SEPTEMBER 1965, IT CAUGHT THE US GOVERNMENT, INCLUDING THE CIA, BY SURPRISE.

01760 BRANNEN, M.D.
NATURE OF THE DRUG WAR
AVAILABLE FROM NTIS, NO. AD-A208 729/4/GAR, MAR 31 89, 33.
DURING THE 1988 PRESIDENTIAL CAMPAIGN, BOTH CANDIDATES VIGOROUSLY ADDRESSED THE DRUG PROBLEM. BOTH CANDIDATES REALIZED THAT THE AMERICAN PUBLIC IS BECOMING INCREASINGLY IMPATIENT WITH THE INCREDIBLE DRUG TRAFFIC INTO THE UNITED STATES AND WITHIN OUR BORDERS. THEY AGREED THAT COMPULSIVE DRUG ABUSE THREATENS THE SOCIAL STABILITY OF THE UNITED STATES. INDEED, DRUG USE POSES A CLEAR THREAT TO UNITED STATES NATIONAL SECURITY. SO INEVITABLY ONE OF MANY PROPOSED SOLUTIONS TO THIS PROBLEM HAS BEEN THE USE OF OUR MILITARY RESOURCES TO WIN THE WAR ON DRUGS. THE DEPARTMENT OF DEFENSE HAS BEEN CHARGED WITH THE TASK OF FORMULATING A DETAILED PLAN FOR USE OF UNITED STATES MILITARY RESOURCES IN DRUG WAR. IN STRATEGIC TERMS, THIS WAR MAY BEST BE VIEWED AS A LOW-INTENSITY CONFLICT. AND FROM THE PERSPECTIVE OF STRATEGIC PLANNING, WE MUST NOW CONSIDER THE WAYS, MEANS, AND ENDS OF SUCCESSFULLY RESOLVING THE CONFLICT. LIKEWISE, WE MUST AS WELL VIEW THE CONFLICT COMPREHENSIVELY: HOW CAN WE ELIMINATE THE SUPPLY OF DRUGS. BUT SO LONG AS THE SUPPLY IS AVAILABLE, HOW CAN WE STOP THE FLOW OF DRUGS FROM THEIR SOURCE TO THEIR USERS. MOST IMPORTANTLY, HOW CAN WE REDUCE THE DEMAND FOR DRUGS. THIS STUDY OFFERS AN ANALYSIS OF THE DRUG PROBLEM. IT SPECIFICALLY FOCUSES ON HOW OUR MILITARY RESOURCES CAN BEST BE EMPLOYED TO RESOLVE THE PROBLEM WITHOUT DETRACTING SIGNIFICANTLY FROM OTHER, MORE CONVENTIONAL STRATEGIC MISSIONS OF OUR ARMED FORCES. KEYWORDS: MILITARY OPERATIONS; DRUG TRAFFICKING; LAW ENFORCEMENT. (KT)

01761 BRASHER, C.N.
AN EVALUATION OF THE ABILITY OF MANDATORY WORK PROGRAMS TO REDUCE WELFARE CASELOADS
DISSERTATION ABSTRACTS INTERNATIONAL, 49(11) (MAY 89), 3487-A.
THE AUTHOR STUDIES THE RELATIONSHIP BETWEEN MANDATORY WORK PROGRAMS AND WELFARE CASELOADS TO DETERMINE IF WORKFARE IS EFFECTIVE AND, IF SO, IN WHAT ENVIRONMENTS IT IS MOST EFFECTIVE. HE FOCUSES ON THE COMMUNITY WORK EXPERIENCE PROGRAM (CWEP) AND THE AID FOR FAMILIES WITH DEPENDENT CHILDREN (AFDC) POPULATION. AN INTERSTATE MODEL COMPARES CWEP STATES WITH NON-CWEP STATES WHILE AN INTRASTATE MODEL COMPARES CWEP COUNTIES WITH NON-CWEP COUNTIES IN OHIO. FINDINGS INDICATE THAT CWEP HAS BEEN ASSOCIATED WITH A REDUCTION IN AFDC CASELOADS, ESPECIALLY IN CONSERVATIVE REPUBLICAN JURISDICTIONS.

01762 BRASS, T.
TROTSKYISM, HUGO BLANCO, AND THE IDEOLOGY OF A PERUVIAN
PEASANT MOVEMENT
JOURNAL OF PEASANT STUDIES, 16(2) (JAN 89), 173-197.
DURING 1958-62 THE PROVINCE OF LA CONVENCION IN THE
EASTERN LOWLANDS OF PERU WAS THE SITE OF ONE OF THE MOST
IMPORTANT PEASANT MOVEMENTS IN LATIN AMERICA. A CENTRAL
PARADOX IS THAT ALTHOUGH THE MOVEMENT WAS LED BY AND
REFLECTED THE ECONOMIC INTERESTS OF AN EMERGING STRATUM OF
CAPITALIST PEASANTS, ITS PRINCIPAL MOBILISING IDEOLOGY IN
THE STRUGGLE AGAINST THE LANDLORD CLASS OVER THIS PERIOD WAS
TROTSKYISM. FOR THIS REASON, THE POLITICO-IDEOLOGICAL
UTTERANCES OF HUGO BLANCO, A TROTSKYIST WHO PLAYED A LEADING
ROLE IN THE PEASANT MOVEMENT, TOGETHER WITH HIS VIEWS ON THE
NATURE OF THE CLASS STRUCTURE, THE CLASS STRUGGLE, CLASS
ALLIANCES, ETC., ARE EXAMINED IN ORDER TO ESTABLISH THEIR
CLASS-SPECIFIC ACCEPTABILITY.

01763 BRATTON, M.
THE POLITICS OF GOVERNMENT-NGO RELATIONS IN AFRICA
WORLD DEVELOPMENT, 17(4) (APR 89), 569-587.
SUMMARY. - NON-GOVERNMENTAL ORGANIZATIONS (NGOS),
DESERVEDLY OR NOT, HAVE GAINED A REPUTATION AS THE LEADING
PRACTITIONERS OF RURAL DEVELOPMENT IN AFRICA. AFRICAN
GOVERNMENTS HAVE RESPONDED AMBIGUOUSLY TO THE PRESENCE OF
THESE NEW AGENCIES, VALUING THE ECONOMIC RESOURCES NGOS CAN
RAISE, BUT RESISTING THE POLITICAL PLURALIZATION IMPLIED BY
POPULAR DEVELOPMENT ACTION. THIS ARTICLE DESCRIBES THE
GROWTH OF NGOS IN AFRICA AND PROPOSES A FRAMEWORK FOR
ANALYZING THE DYNAMICS OF GOVERNMENT-NGO RELATIONS. BY MEANS
OF EXAMPLES DRAWN FROM KENYA AND ZIMBABWE, AMONG OTHER
AFRICAN COUNTRIES, THE ARTICLE ILLUSTRATES THE STRATEGIES
USED BY GOVERNMENTS TO EXERCISE CONTROL AND BY NGOS TO
ASSERT AUTONOMY. AN ARGUMENT IS MADE THAT POLITICS, RATHER
THAN ECONOMICS, BEST EXPLAIN THE CONTRIBUTION OF NGOS TO
DEVELOPMENT, AS WELL AS THE ATTITUDE OF GOVERNMENTS TOWARD
THE BURGEONING VOLUNTARY SECTOR.

01764 BRAUER, C.
STAFFING A NEW PRESIDENT: LOST IN TRANSITION
CURRENT, (310) (FEB 89), 28-35.
THE TRANSITION CAN BE A FATEFUL TIME NOT ONLY FOR A NEW
PRESIDENT BUT FOR THE COUNTRY. DURING THIS PERIOD, THE
PRESIDENT MUST MAKE KEY PERSONNEL DECISIONS. SERIOUS ERROR
IS ALL BUT INEVITABLE, GIVEN THE RANGE AND SHEER NUMBER OF
THE APPOINTMENTS AND THE RELATIVELY SHORT TIME A PRESIDENT-
ELECT HAS TO MAKE THEM.

01765 BRAUTIGAM, C.R.
A TENDENCY ANALYSIS OF THE SOVIET RESPONSES TO THE 1980-
1981 POLISH CRISIS
DISSERTATION ABSTRACTS INTERNATIONAL, 50(1) (JUL 89),
250-A.
THE AUTHOR UTILIZES A TENDENCY ANALYTICAL APPROACH TO
STUDY THE SOVIET RESPONSES TO THE 1980-81 POLISH CRISIS IN
ORDER TO: (1) DESCRIBE THE VARIOUS TENDENCIES OF SOVIET
OPINION ON POLAND, (2) TO DETERMINE THE RELATIONSHIP BETWEEN
TENDENCY AND POLICY, AND (3) TO INVESTIGATE THE FACTORS THAT
CONTRIBUTED TO SOVIET POLICY-MAKERS ALIGNING THEMSELVES WITH
PARTICULAR TENDENCIES.

01766 BRAVEBOY-WAGNER, J.A.
THE REGIONAL FOREIGN POLICY OF TRINIDAD AND TOBAGO:
HISTORIAL AND CONTEMPORARY ASPECTS
JOURNAL OF INTERAMERICAN STUDIES AND WORLD AFFAIRS, 31(3)
(FAL 89), 37-62.
THIS ARTICLE EXAMINES THE FOREIGN POLICY OF TRINIDAD AND
TOBAGO TOWARD ITS IMMEDIATE NEIGHBORS IN THE ENGLISH
SPEAKING CARRIBEAN CONSIDERING (A) THE NATURE OF THE
RELATIONSHIP BETWEEN THE THIN-ISLAND COUNTRY AND ITS
NEIGHBORS, (B) ITS ACTIVITIES ON BEHALF OF ITS NEIGHBORS,
AND (C) FACTORS WHICH HAVE INFLUENCED TRINIDAD AND TOBAGO'S
COMMITTMENT AND ACTIVITY ON THE NATIONAL LEVEL.

01767 BRAVERMAN, H.
THE DEGRADATION OF WORK IN THE TWENTIETH CENTURY
MONTHLY REVIEW, 41(5) (OCT 89), 35-47.
THIS ARTICLE, FIRST PUBLISHED IN THE MAY 1982 ISSUE IS A
SLIGHTLY EDITED VERSION OF A TALK THE AUTHOR GAVE IN 1975.
IT DEFINES CAPITALISM AND THE LABOR EXTRACTED UNDER THAT
SYSTEM. IT ANALYSES THE ALIENATION, DEFINED AS TRANSFER OF
OWNERSHIP, WHICH OCCURS, AS WELL AS THE CHEAPENING OF LABOR
POWER. THE INEVIATABILITY OF UNEMPLOYMENT IS EXAMINED. THE
CONCLUSION IS THAT THE ACCUMULATION OF HEALTH AT ONE POLE OF
SOCIETY IS MATCHED AT THE OTHER POLE BY AN ACCUMULATION OF
MISERY.

01768 BRAY, D.
INDIAN INSTITUTES IN ARGENTINA: FROM PATERNALISM TO
AUTONOMY
CULTURAL SURVIVAL QUARTERLY, 13(3) (1989), 68-70.
BEGINNING IN THE 1950S, ARGENTINA DECENTRALIZED STATE
AUTHORITY OVER INDIGENOUS PEOPLES, PASSING IT ON TO THE
PROVINCIAL LEVEL. THIS SET THE STAGE FOR A SIGNIFICANT NEW

PROCESS IN THE EVOLUTION OF ARGENTINE STATE INDIGENOUS
POLICY IN THE DEMOCRATIC PERIOD OF THE 1980S: THE STATE
ESTABLISHED A SERIES OF INDIAN INSTITUTES AT THE PROVINCIAL
LEVEL. THESE INSTITUTES OFTEN HAD BOARDS OF DIRECTORS
LARGELY OR EXCLUSIVELY COMPOSED OF INDIANS AND
DEMOCRATICALLY ELECTED BY THE INDIGENOUS PEOPLES OF THE
PROVINCE, AND LEGISLATIVE MANDATES ADDRESSING A BROAD RANGE
OF THE ECONOMIC AND SOCIAL ISSUES AFFECTING INDIANS. LED BY
NORTHEASTERN FORMOSA PROVINCE IN 1983, INDIAN INSTITUTES
HAVE SINCE BECOME LAW OR HAVE BEEN INTRODUCED AS BILLS IN
PROVINCIAL LEGISLATURES IN CHACO, RIO NEGRO, NEQUEN, SALTA,
AND MISIONES. THESE INSTITUTES USUALLY REPLACE MORE
TRADITIONAL INDIAN AGENCIES WHOSE PRIMARY PURPOSE WAS TO
INTEGRATE INDIANS INTO THE ECONOMY AND MAINTAIN DEPENDENCY.

01769 BRAY, J.
PAKISTAN IN 1989: BENAZIR'S BALANCING ACT
ROUND TABLE, (310) (APR 89), 192-200.
BENAZIR BHUTTO'S COMING TO POWER IN PAKISTAN HAS BROUGHT
A MARKED CHANGE OF MOOD, A SENSE OF HOPE THAT AFTER YEARS OF
MILITARY RULE THE COUNTRY HAS AT LAST ACHIEVED A DEMOCRATIC
BREAKTHROUGH. HOWEVER, THE ARMY HAS ONLY STEPPED BACK, NOT
WITHDRAWN FROM POLITICAL INVOLVEMENT ALTOGETHER. THE ARTICLE
ANALYZES BHUTTO'S IDEOLOGY, THE CIRCUMSTANCES IN WHICH SHE
CAME TO POWER AND THE TIGHT CONSTRAINTS WITHIN WHICH SHE
MUST OPERATE IF DEMOCRACY IS TO SURVIVE IN PAKISTAN.

01770 BRAY, J.
SRI LANKA: THINGS FALL APART?
WORLD TODAY, 45(8-9) (AUG 89), 156-160.
SRI LANKA HAS ACQUIRED A DISMAL REPUTATION AS AN AREA OF
CONFLICT BETWEEN AND WITHIN ITS SINHALESE AND TAMIL
COMMUNITIES. PRESIDENT RANASINGHE PREMADASA HAS PROMISED A
NEW ERA OF NATIONAL RECONCILIATION, BUT HE HAS HAD LITTLE
SUCCESS. HE NOW FACES DEEPENING UNREST IN COLOMBO, THE NORTH,
AND THE EAST AND HAS BEEN FORCED TO RE-IMPOSE A NATIONAL
STATE OF EMERGENCY. AT THE SAME TIME, HE IS LOCKED IN A
BITTER AND SEEMINGLY INTRACTABLE DIPLOMATIC CONFRONTATION
WITH INDIA.

01771 BRAYTON, A.
US MOBILIZATION POLICIES UNDER REAGAN
RUSI JOURNAL, 134(3) (FAL 89), 45-52.
THE ARTICLE EXAMINES THE CHANGES IN MILITARY POLICY
UNDER REAGAN THAT WERE CONNECTED WITH THE INCREASED SPENDING
OF NATIONAL DEFENSE. IT ANALYZES VARIOUS AREAS INCLUDING:
THE ROLE OF RESERVES: NEW EQUIPMENT DISTRIBUTION; NAVAL
FORCES; THE AIR FORCE; MANPOWER POLICIES; MEDICAL READINESS;
EQUIPMENT; AND MOBILIZATION EXERCISES. IT CONCLUDES THAT THE
MOBILIZATION PROGRAMS HAVE GROWN IN IMPORTANCE IN THE REAGAN
YEARS AND RESERVE FORCES HAVE NEVER BEFORE ATTAINED SUCH
HIGH LEVELS OF READINESS.

01772 BREAKWELL, G. M.; DEVEREUX, J.; FIFE-SCHAW, C.
POLITICAL ACTIVITY AND POLITICAL ATTITUDES IN TEENAGERS:
IS THERE ANY CORRESPONDENCE? A RESEARCH NOTE
POLITICAL PSYCHOLOGY, 10(4) (DEC 89), 745-757.
ALTHOUGH CONSIDERABLE ATTENTION HAS BEEN PAID TO
IDENTIFYING THE PROCESSES INVOLVED IN THE POLITICAL
SOCIALIZATION OF YOUNG PEOPLE, VERY LITTLE WORK HAS
ADDRESSED THE RELATIONSHIP BETWEEN YOUNG PEOPLES' POLITICAL
ACTIVITIES AND THEIR POLITICAL ATTITUDES. THIS PAPER REPORTS
A STUDY OF 210 BRITISH 16-18-YEAR-OLDS AND ASSESSES THE
LEVELS OF POLITICAL ACTIVITY IN THIS GROUP AND RELATES THESE
TO POLITICAL ATTITUDES. THE RESULTS SUGGEST THAT GREATER
LEVELS OF ACTIVITY ARE ASSOCIATED WITH INDIVIDUALS HOLDING
LEFT-OF-CENTER POLITICAL VIEWS. SUCH INDIVIDUALS REPORTED
PAYING GREATER ATTENTION TO TV AND NEWSPAPERS WITH A HIGH
POLITICAL CONTENT AND HAVING MORE POLITICAL DISCUSSIONS WITH
TEACHERS AND PARENTS. WHILE THE MORE ACTIVE WERE MORE LIKELY
TO HAVE POLITICAL DISCUSSIONS, POLITICS WAS STILL NOT FOUND
TO BE AN IMPORTANT TOPIC OF DISCUSSION AMONG PEERS.

01773 BRECKENRIDGE, C.A.
THE AESTHETICS AND POLITICS OF COLONIAL COLLECTING: INDIA
AT WORLD FAIRS
COMPARATIVE STUDIES IN SOCIETY AND HISTORY, 31(2) (APR 89),
195-216.
IN THE SECOND HALF OF THE NINETEENTH CENTURY, OBJECTS
FROM INDIA WERE REPEATEDLY ASSEMBLED FOR DISPLAY AT
INTERNATIONAL EXHIBITIONS, KNOWN THEN AND NOW AS WORLD FAIRS.
THEIR TRANSIENCE AND EPHEMERALITY SET WORLD FAIRS APART AS
EXTRAORDINARY PHENOMENA IN THE WORLD OF COLLECTING. THIS
ARTICLE DESCRIBES NINETEENTH-CENTURY WORLD FAIRS AS PART OF
A UNITARY, THOUGH NOT UNIFORM, LANDSCAPE OF DISCOURSE AND
PRACTICE, THAT SITUATED METROPOLE AND COLONY WITHIN A SINGLE
ANALYTIC FIELD, THROUGH PRECISELY SUCH CULTURAL TECHNOLOGIES
AS THE INTERNATIONAL EXHIBITION. SUCH TECHNOLOGIES CREATED
AN IMAGINED ECUMEME: THE VICTORIAN ECUMENE. BY
CONTEXTUALIZING WORLD FAIRS IN THE COLONIAL TOPOS TO WHICH
THEY BELONGED, THIS ESSAY EXAMINES A SMALL PIECE OF THE
PROCESS BY WHICH THIS VICTORIAN ECUMENE WAS CREATED.

01774 BREINER,P.
DEMOCRATIC AUTONOMY, POLITICAL ETHICS, AND MORAL LUCK
POLITICAL THEORY, 17(4) (NOV 89), 550-574.
THIS ARTICLE ATTEMPTS TO VINDICATE RADICAL DEMOCRACY
FROM ITS INSTRUMENTALIST CRITICS. IT DOES SO BY ENLISTING
THE INSTRUMENTALIST'S EMPHASIS ON IRONIC OUTCOMES IN
POLITICAL ACTION TO THE CAUSE OF RADICAL DEMOCRACY. MAX
WEBER'S ARGUMENT FOR A POLITICAL ETHIC OF RESPONSIBILITY AND
JEAN-JACQUES ROUSSEAU'S ARGUMENT FOR POPULAR SOVEREIGNTY ARE
BOTH DISCUSSED. THE INTENT IS TO SHOW PRECISELY HOW A
ROUSSEAUEAN ARGUMENT FOR COLLECTIVE AUTONOMY IN SPITE OF
ITSELF REQUIRES A WEBERIAN ARGUMENT FOR A POLITICAL ETHIC OF
CONSEQUENCES. THIS ETHIC TAKES ACCOUNT OF THE INSEPARABILITY
OF POLITICS FROM MORAL LUCK. MORAL LUCK IS DEFINED AND
DISCUSSED IN DETAIL.

01775 BREMER, L.P. III
COUNTERING TERRORISM IN THE 1980'S AND 1990'S
DEPARTMENT OF STATE BULLETIN (US FOREIGN POLICY), 89(2143)
(FEB 89), 61-64.
AMERICAN COUNTER-TERRORISM POLICY STANDS ON THREE
PILLARS: THE USA WILL NOT ACCEDE TO TERRORIST DEMANDS; THE
USA HAS TAKEN THE LEAD IN PRESSURING STATES THAT SUPPORT
TERRORIST GROUPS AND USE TERRORISM AS PART OF THEIR FOREIGN
POLICY; AND THE USA WILL CONTINUE TO IMPOSE THE RULE OF LAW
ON TERRORISTS AND PUNISH CRIMINAL ACTIONS.

01776 BREMER, L.P. III
COUNTERING TERRORISM: U.S. POLICY IN THE 1980S AND THE
1990S
TERRORISM, 11(6) (1988), 531-537.
THIS IS A TALK GIVEN BY THE AMBASSADOR AT LARGE FOR
COUNTERTERRORISM OF THE U.S. DEPARTMENT OF STATE. HE TALKS
ABOUT U.S. COUNTERTERRORISM POLICY IN THE 1980S AND THE
PRIORITIES FOR THE 1990S, HE DISCUSSES THE THREAT
ENVIRONMENT AND PRIORITIES FOR THE NEW ADMINISTRATION. HE
CONCLUDES THAT SUPPRESSING TERRORISM WILL NOT BE EASY BUT
THAT IT IS POSSIBLE.

01777 BREMER, L.P. III
TERRORISM: ITS EVOLVING NATURE
DEPARTMENT OF STATE BULLETIN (US FOREIGN POLICY), 89(2146)
(MAY 89), 74-78.
THE AUTHOR SURVEYS THE INTERNATIONAL TERRORIST THREAT TO
AMERICAN INTERESTS AND GIVES AN OVERVIEW OF THE US
GOVERNMENT'S COUNTER-TERRORISM POLICY.

01778 BRENDLINGER, N.B.
THE MUTUAL AND BALANCED FORCE REDUCTION NEGOTIATIONS: THE
SOVIET PERSPECTIVE ON VERIFICATION, 1973-1987
DISSERTATION ABSTRACTS INTERNATIONAL, 50(4) (OCT 89),
1081-A.
SINCE 1973, NATO AND THE WARSAW PACT HAVE BEEN
CONDUCTING TALKS TO REDUCE THE NUMBER OF TROOPS IN CENTRAL
EUROPE WITHIN THE FRAMEWORK OF THE MUTUAL AND BALANCED FORCE
REDUCTION (MBFR) NEGOTIATIONS. VERIFICATION HAS
TRADITIONALLY NOT BEEN ACKNOWLEDGED AS IMPORTANT BY THE
SOVIETS, WHO HAVE OBJECTED TO INTRUSIVE ON-SITE MEASURES.
BUT RECENTLY THE SOVIET POSITION ON VERIFICATION HAS BEEN
EVOLVING AWAY FROM THEIR TRADITIONAL SECURITY PARANOIA AND
TOWARD MORE FLEXIBILITY.

01779 BRENNAN, K.; BRODY, R.; HEISSBRODT, D.
THE 40TH SESSION OF THE UN SUB-COMMISSION ON PREVENTION OF
DISCRIMINATION AND PROTECTION OF MINORITIES
HUMAN RIGHTS QUARTERLY, 11(2) (MAY 89), 295-324.
THE ARTICLE REPORTS ON THE ACCOMPLISHMENTS OF THE 40TH
SESSION OF THE SUB-COMMISSION ON PREVENTION OF
DISCRIMINATION AND PROTECTION OF MINORITIES. IT DESCRIBES
THE SIGNIFICANT WORK OF THE SUB-COMMISSION DURING ITS 1988
SESSION INCLUDING: PROTECTING THE HUMAN RIGHTS OF ONE OF ITS
FORMER MEMBERS; RESOLUTIONS REGARD GROSS VIOLATIONS OF HUMAN
RIGHTS IN SPECIFIC COUNTRIES; PROPOSED REFORM OF THE
PROCEDURE OF COUNTRY VIOLATIONS; STUDIES AND REPORTS ON
SPECIFIC HUMAN RIGHTS ISSUES; AND NEW INITIATIVES. THE
ARTICLE ALSO EXAMINES SOME OF THE CENTRAL QUESTIONS POSED BY
OBSERVERS AND MEMBERS OF THE SUB-COMMISSION INCLUDING; DOES
THE SUB-COMMISSION MAKE A UNIQUE CONTRIBUTION TO UN HUMAN
RIGHTS WORK? DO THE MEMBERS OF THE SUB-COMMITTEE TRULY ENJOY
INDEPENDENCE FROM THE GOVERNMENTS WHO NOMINATE THEM?

01780 BRENNER, S.; KROL, J.F.
STRATEGIES IN CERTIORARI VOTING ON THE UNITED STATES
SUPREME COURT
THE JOURNAL OF POLITICS, 51(4) (NOV 89), 828-840.
DO JUSTICES ON THE UNITED STATES SUPREME COURT PURSUE
STRATEGIES IN THEIR CERTIORARI VOTING? THIS ARTICLE INSPECTS
7 TERMS AND DISCOVERS THAT THE JUSTICES USE ERROR CORRECTION,
PREDICTION, AND MAJORITY STRATEGIES, PARTICULARLY WHEN THE
STRATEGIES ARE CONSISTENT WITH EACH OTHER. ALSO INVESTIGATED
ARE THE ERROR CORRECTING AND PREDICTION STRATEGIES THROUGH
THE FOCUS OF LIBERAL AND CONSERVATIVE JUSTICES IN LIBERAL
AND CONSERVATIVE COURTS, THESE TWO STRATEGIES WORK BEST FOR
CONSERVATIVE JUSTICES IN CONSERVATIVE COURTS.

01781 BRENNER, S.; HAGLE, T.; SPAETH, H. J.
THE DEFECTION OF THE MARGINAL JUSTICE ON THE WARREN COURT
WESTERN POLITICAL QUARTERLY, 42(3) (SEP 89), 409-426.
BRENNER AND SPAETH (1988) EXAMINED THE DOCKET BOOKS OF
JUSTICES OF THE UNITED STATES SUPREME COURT AND FOUND THAT
IN 86 PERCENT OF THE WARREN COURT'S MINIMUMWINNING ORIGINAL-
DECISION COALITIONS THAT BROKE UP, THE MARGINAL JUSTICE (I.E.
, THE JUSTICE IDEOLOGICALLY CLOSET TO THE DISSENTERS)
DEFECTED. USE OF A DIFFERENCE OF MEANS TEST AND THE MAXIMUM
LIKELIHOOD ESTIMATION TECHNIQUE PROBIT INDICATE IDEOLOGICAL
CLOSENESS AND THE LACK OF ABILITY OF THE MARGINAL JUSTICE TO
BE THE MOST IMPORTANT FACTORS CONTRIBUTING TO THE DEFECTION
OF THE MARGINAL JUSTICE. ANALYSIS OF THE BEHAVIOR OF THE
FIVE JUSTICES WHO MOST OFTEN WERE MARGINAL SHOWS EACH OF
THEM ALSO RESPONDED IDIOSYNCRATICALLY TO ONE OR MORE
IDENTIFIED CASE CHARACTERISTIC VARIABLES.

01782 BRENTS, B.G.
THE CLASS POLITICS OF AGE POLITICS: THE DEVELOPMENT OF THE
1935 SOCIAL SECURITY ACT
DISSERTATION ABSTRACTS INTERNATIONAL, 49(7) (JAN 89),
1954-A.
THE AUTHOR OFFERS AN HISTORICAL CASE STUDY OF THE
FORMATION OF THE SOCIAL SECURITY ACT OF 1935. SHE FINDS THAT
CLASS STRUGGLE WAS CENTRAL IN THE FORMULATION AS WELL AS THE
ACTUAL MAKING OF SOCIAL SECURITY POLICY.

01783 BRESLAUER, G.
LINKING GORBACHEV'S DOMESTIC AND FOREIGN POLICIES
JOURNAL OF INTERNATIONAL AFFAIRS, 42(2) (SPR 89), 267-282.
THE ARTICLE SPECIFIES THE MAIN COMPONENTS OF MIKHAIL
GORBACHEV'S DOMESTIC AND FOREIGN POLICY AGENDAS, AND THEN TO
ANALYZE THE WAYS IN WHICH GORBACHEV DEFINES THE RELATIONSHIP
BETWEEN THE TWO AGENDAS, BOTH IN HIS LONG-TERM VISION AND IN
HIS SHORT-TERM POLITICAL STRATEGY. WHAT IS DISTINCTIVE ABOUT
THE CURRENT SITUATION IS THE LEADERSHIP'S SENSE OF URGENCY
ABOUT THE NEED TO CREATE ACTIVELY AN INTERNATIONAL
ENVIRONMENT CONDUCTIVE TO THE REALIZATION OF LEADING
DOMESTIC POLICY PRIORITIES WITHOUT SACRIFICING SOVIET HARD-
WON POSITIONS AS A MILITARY AND DIPLOMATIC SUPERPOWER. THE
ARTICLE EXAMINES THE FACTORS LIKELY TO FACILITATE AND
FRUSTRATE GORBACHEV'S EFFORTS AND INQUIRE INTO WHETHER IT IS
IN THE US INTEREST THAT GORBACHEV SUCCEED.

01784 BRESSAND, A.
EUROPEAN INTEGRATION: FROM THE SYSTEM PARADIGM TO NETWORK
ANALYSIS
INTERNATIONAL SPECTATOR, XXIV(1) (JAN 89), 21-29.
THE APPLICATION OF SYSTEM ANALYSIS TO EUROPEAN
INTEGRATION RESTS ON TWO MAJOR WORKING ASSUMPTIONS: (1) THE
BORDERS OF A EUROPEAN SYSTEM AND OF A SET OF WELL DEFINED
SUB-SYSTEMS CAN BE CLEARLY IDENTIFIED. (2) THE MOST
EFFICIENT WAY TO UNDERSTAND THE OVERALL WORKING OF THE
EUROPEAN SYSTEM IS FROM THE OUTSIDE TOWARD THE INSIDE,
STARTING WITH THE INTERACTIONS BETWEEN THE SYSTEM AND ITS
ENVIRONMENT AND WORKING ONE'S WAY INTO SUCCESSIVE LAYERS OF
ORGANIZATION.

01785 BREUER. S.
FOUCAULT AND BEYOND: TOWARDS A THEORY OF THE DISCIPLINARY
SOCIETY
INTERNATIONAL SOCIAL SCIENCE JOURNAL, (120) (MAY 89),
235-248.
MICHEL FOUCAULT DEVELOPED A THERORY OF DISCIPLINARY
SOCIETY THAT HAS BECOME ONE OF THE MOST DISCUSSED MODELS IN
CONTEMPORARY SOCIAL THEORY. THIS ESSAY SUMMARIZES THE MOST
IMPORTANT ARGUMENTS OF FOUCAULT'S CRITICS AND ASSESSES THE
CONTEMPORARY VIABILITY OF HIS THEORY.

01786 BREWIN, C.; MCALLISTER, R.
ANNUAL REVIEW OF THE ACTIVITIES OF THE EUROPEAN
COMMUNITIES IN 1988
JOURNAL OF COMMON MARKET STUDIES, XXVII(4) (JUN 89),
323-358.
THE AUTHORS SUMMARIZE THE ACTIONS TAKEN BY THE EUROPEAN
COMMUNITY BODIES DURING 1988.

01787 BREZEZINSKI, Z.
ENDING THE COLD WAR
WASHINGTON QUARTERLY, 12(4) (FAL 89), 29-34.
THIS ARTICLE SUGGESTS THAT EVEN THE DEBATE OVER THE COLD
WAR'S ALLEGED DEMISE BECOMES PART OF THE WAGING OF THAT WAR,
AND THAT DECISION MAKERS MUST DERIVE POLICY FROM ANALYSIS OF
WHAT HAS BEEN HAPPENING LATELY IN EAST-WEST RELATIONS,
LOOKING AT THE SITUATION FROM ALL ANGLES. IT DETAILS THE
PRESENT SITUATION IN THE USSR. THE NEED FOR A DEFINITION AND
ARTICULATION OF THE TERMINATION OF THE COLD WAR IS EXPLORED.
IT CONCLUDES THAT THE LARGEST ISSUE IS WESTERN RESPONSE TO
THE GENERAL CRISIS OF COMMUNISM.

01788 BRIGGS, W.D.
JOHN F. KENNEDY AND THE FORMATION OF LIMITED WAR POLICY,
19521961: "OUTSIDERS" AS A FACTOR IN DECISIONMAKING

DISSERTATION ABSTRACTS INTERNATIONAL, 50(6) (DEC 89),
1786-A.
    BASED ON THE PUBLIC STATEMENTS OF JOHN F. KENNEDY AND AN
ANALYSIS OF HIS PRIVATE PAPERS AND THOSE OF HIS LEGISLATIVE
ASSISTANTS, THIS STUDY OUTLINES THE ELEMENTS OF THE LIMITED
WAR POLICY ADVOCATED BY KENNEDY. IN ADDITION, THE ROLE OF
"OUTSIDERS" AS AN INFLUENCE ON KENNEDY'S POLICY-MAKING IS
STUDIED.

01789 BRIGOULEIX, B.
    VIEW FROM PARIS
    NATO'S SIXTEEN NATIONS, 34(3) (JUN 89), 13.
    THE APPROACH OF THE EUROPEAN ELECTIONS HAS REVEALED A
SITUATION THAT FRANCE'S POLITICAL LEADERS SEEM TO HAVE
OVERLOOKED: THE OVERWHELMING DESIRE OF THE VOTERS FOR A
CHANGE IN FRENCH POLITICS. ALTHOUGH THIS IS PARTICULARLY
EVIDENT WITHIN THE RIGHT-WING PARTIES, THE PHENOMENON ALSO
EXISTS TO A CERTAIN EXTENT ON THE LEFT. AMONG BOTH LEFT AND
RIGHT PARTIES, THOSE ANXIOUS FOR CHANGE ARE YOUNGER LEADERS,
CREATING A SORT OF "GENERATION GAP" IN FRENCH POLITICS. THE
SPLIT BETWEEN GENERATIONS IS PARTICULARLY EVIDENT IN THE
SOCIALIST PARTY, AS YOUNGER MEMBERS POSITION THEMSELVES FOR
THE TIME WHEN AGEING PRESIDENT FRANCOIS MITTERRAND MUST
LEAVE POLITICS.

01790 BRINTNALL, M.
    FUTURE DIRECTIONS FOR FEDERAL URBAN POLICY
    JOURNAL OF URBAN AFFAIRS, 11(1) (1989), 1-19.
    THIS ARTICLE REVIEWS RECENT NATIONAL URBAN POLICY AND
CONSIDERS THE IMPACT OF THE REAGAN YEARS. SIGNIFICANT
CHANGES HAVE OCCURRED IN U.S. URBAN POLICY SINCE 1980.
FEDERAL PROGRAMS ARE SMALLER, AND THEY OPERATE WITH NEW
RULES; NEW PROBLEMS HAVE MOVED TO THE FOREFRONT OF THE URBAN
AGENDA; AND RESOURCES AVAILABLE AT ALL LEVELS OF GOVERNMENT
HAVE CHANGED. TO ASSESS THE SIGNIFICANCE OF THESE
DEVELOPMENTS, THIS ARTICLE EXAMINES RECENT CHANGES IN THE
IDEAS BEHIND URBAN POLICY, IN THE SHAPE OF FEDERAL PROGRAMS,
IN LEVELS AND DISTRIBUTION OF FEDERAL URBAN SPENDING, AND IN
THE CAPACITY OF STATE AND LOCAL GOVERNMENT TO PERFORM.

01791 BRISKIN, L.
    SOCIALIST FEMINISM: FROM THE STANDPOINT OF PRACTICE
    STUDIES IN POLITICAL ECONOMY: A SOCIALIST REVIEW, (30)
    (FAL 89), 87-114.
    THIS ARTICLE ATTEMPTS TO DEFINE THE POLITICS OF SOCIAL
FEMINISM. THE FIRST PART EXAMINES THE CATEGORIES THROUGH
WHICH THE VARIETY OF FEMINISMS HAVE TRADITIONALLY BEEN
EXPLORED. THE SECOND PART INTRODUCES A MODEL OF FEMINIST
PRACTICE SITUATED WITHIN THE ACTIVIST MAP OF THE WOMEN'S
MOVEMENTS. THE FINAL SECTION USES THE MODEL OF FEMININE
PRACTICE TO HIGHLIGHT THE ORGANIZATIONAL DILEMMAS THAT FACE
FEMINISTS IN THE CANADIAN CONTEXT.

01792 BRISTOW, W.D.; PEYTON, D.E.
    BRAZIL: U.S. STRATEGY FOR THE YEAR 2000
    AVAILABLE FROM NTIS, NO. AD-A209 808/5/GAR, MAR 89, 54.
    BRAZIL IS A STRUGGLING NATION, BOTH POLITICALLY AND
ECONOMICALLY. HER GLOBAL DIPLOMATIC STRATEGY IS ECONOMICALLY
ORIENTED AS SHE COURTS BOTH COMMUNIST AND NONCOMMUNIST
COUNTRIES FOR TECHNOLOGY TRANSFERS AND MARKETS FOR HER
PRODUCTS WHICH INCLUDE A LONG LINE OF MILITARY HARDWARE.
BRAZIL'S DEMOCRATIC FUTURE DEPENDS UPON HER CURRENT
POLITICAL LEADERSHIP'S ABILITY TO STABILIZE AND CORRECT
THESE PROBLEMS BEFORE THE MILITARY ASSUMES CONTROL. FUTURE
UNITED STATES' STRATEGY WITH BRAZIL SHOULD BE IMPROVED
INTERNATIONAL MILITARY EDUCATION AND TRAINING ASSISTANCE,
INFLUENCING THE INTERNATIONAL MONEY MARKETS TO RESTRUCTURE
THIRD WORLD DEBT IN THE INTEREST OF ALL, AND THE OPENING OF
TRADE RESTRICTIONS. POLITICAL SCIENCE, ECONOMICS.

01793 BRITO, C.
    A NEW RESPONSE TO THE CHALLENGE OF THE TIMES
    WORLD MARXIST REVIEW, 32(4) (APR 89), 49-53.
    THE 12TH CONGRESS OF THE PORTUGUESE COMMUNIST PARTY,
HELD IN PORTO IN DECEMBER 1988, WAS A MAJOR LANDMARK IN THE
WORK OF THE NATION'S COMMUNISTS. THE CONGRESS DISCUSSED AND
APPROVED THREE DOCUMENTS OF GREAT SIGNIFICANCE--A NEW PARTY
PROGRAMME, A POLITICAL RESOLUTION AND AMENDMENTS TO THE
STATUTES. PROCEEDING FROM PORTUGUESE REALITIES AND THE
PROTUGUESE REVOLUTIONARY EXPERIENCE, AND DRAWING ON THE
WORLD'S REVOLUTIONARY RECORD, THE NEW PROGRAMME DEFINES THE
SALIENT FEATURES OF THE SOCIALIST SOCIETY THE PCP WANTS TO
BUILD IN PORTUGAL. IN THE COURSE OF ITS SPECIFIC REALISATION,
THIS PROCESS WILL DISPLAY ASPECTS DISTINCTIVE TO PORTUGAL.

01794 BRITTAIN, V.
    AFRICA: WHICH WAY TO GO?
    WORLD MARXIST REVIEW, 32(11) (NOV 89), 75-78.
    THIS ARTICLE DESCRIBES HOW AFRICA'S FUNDAMENTAL ECONOMIC
DIFFICULTIES OVER RECENT YEARS HAVE REFLECTED BOTH THAT
CONTINENTS DECLINING INFLUENCE IN THE INTERNATIONAL FORUMS,
DOMINATED BY THE WEST, AND THE FAILURE OF ANY SOCIALIST
ALTERNATIVE MODEL TO THE NEOCOLONIAL ONE OF MONO-CULTURE
AGRICULTURE ORIENTATED TOWARDS EXPORT. IN ADDITION, THE MOST

PREVALENT TREND WITHIN ALL AFRICAN COUNTRIES, NO MATTER WHAT
POLITICAL SYSTEM THEY HAVE AIMED OR CLAIMED TO BE FOLLOWING,
HAS BEEN THE STIFLING OF DEMOCRACY. THE EFFECT OF THIS
POLITICAL TREND HAS BEEN DRAMATIC IN THE DWARFING OF THE
PRODUCTIVE CAPACITY THROUGHOUT THE CONTINENT, AS THE
ECONOMIC COMMISSION FOR AFRICA RECOGNISED IN ITS MAJOR
REPORT OF MID-1989, ENDORSED BY THE ORGANISATION OF AFRICAN
UNITY.

01795 BRITTON, G.W.; WRONA, N.C.
    AIR QUALITY CONCERNS LOOM LARGE IN YEARS AHEAD
    AMERICAN CITY AND COUNTY, 104(9) (SEP 89), 34, 36.
    IN MANY WAYS, THE NATIONAL CLEAN AIR EFFORT HAS BEEN
SUCCESSFUL, AND AIR QUALITY HAS IMPROVED IN MANY PARTS OF
THE COUNTRY. IN THE FUTURE, GOVERNMENTAL REGULATORY ACTIVITY
WILL INCREASINGLY FOCUS ON FOUR AREAS: ACID RAIN, OZONE AND
CARBON MONOXIDE NON-ATTAINMENTS, AIR TOXICS, AND AIRBORNE
PARTICULATES. EACH POLLUTANT AND THE STRATEGIES FOR
ADDRESSING IT WILL HAVE SIGNIFICANT IMPLICATIONS FOR LOCAL
GOVERNMENTS.

01796 BROADBENT, J.
    STRATEGIES AND STRUCTURAL CONTRADICTIONS: GROWTH COALITION
    POLITICS IN JAPAN
    AMERICAN SOCIOLOGICAL REVIEW, 54(5) (OCT 89), 707-721.
    THE ELITE COALITION THAT PUSHES LOCAL INDUSTRIAL GROWTH
IS COMPOSED OF SIX ACTORS: LOCAL STATE, BUSINESS, AND PARTY
AND NATIONAL STATE, BUSINESS, AND PARTY. THE QUESTION OF
WHICH DOMINATES THE COALITION REFLECTS CURRENT DEBATES ABOUT
THE STRUCTURE OF POWER IN CAPITALIST SOCIETY. THIS PAPER
ADDRESSES THESE DEBATES THROUGH THE DETAILED STUDY OF A
GROWTH COALITION IN A RURAL INDUSTRIALIZATION PROJECT IN
SOUTHERN JAPAN. IT TRACES THE STRATEGIES AND MODES OF
INFLUENCE OF THE SIX ACTORS, THEIR STRUCTURE AND PROCESS,
THROUGH THE 25-YEAR HISTORY OF THE PROJECT. CONTRARY TO THE
"STRONG STATE" IMAGE OF JAPAN, NATIONAL BIG BUSINESS
DOMINATED THE GROWTH COALITION. THE REST OF THE SOCIETY,
INCLUDING THE STATE, ADJUSTED AROUND ITS MOTION. THIS
RESULTED IN POLICIES WHICH FAVORED ECONOMIC GROWTH OVER
SOCIAL NEEDS, GIVING SOME OF THE OTHER ACTORS LEGITIMATION
PROBLEMS. YET, SUCCESS AT RAPID GROWTH PREVENTED THESE FROM
ASSUMING CRISIS PROPORTIONS. THE FINDINGS RUN COUNTER TO
STATE AUTONOMY ARGUMENTS AND SUGGEST CLOSER ATTENTION BE
PAID TO MULTIPLE LEVELS OF STRUCTURE AND PROCESS.

01797 BROCK, D.
    THE THEORY AND PRACTICE OF JAPAN-BASHING
    NATIONAL INTEREST, (17) (FAL 89), 29-40.
    THIS ARTICLE EXAMINES UNITED STATE - JAPAN RELATIONS. IT
EXPLORES THIS ROUND OF U.S. - JAPAN CONFRONTATION AS
CONGRESS PASSED THE 1988 OMNIBUS TRADE ACT AND THE SUPER 301
PROVISION REQUIRING THE PRESIDENT TO CITE "TRADE
LIBERALIZATION PRIORITY" COUNTRIES AND THEN ENTER INTO
NEGOTIATIONS WITH THEM TO DISMANTLE THE TARIFFS, OR OTHER
OBSTACLES DEEMED TO BE EITHER BLOCKING U.S. IMPORTS OR
LIMITING THE EXPANSION OF SERVICES. IT OFFERS OBSERVATIONS
OF THE CHANGING WAY IN WHICH AMERICANS ARE SEEING JAPAN AND
DESCRIBES THE JAPAN-BASHER'S AGENDA. IT CONCLUDES THAT IF
THESE PEOPLE WIN THE POLICY DEBATE, A CRUCIAL POLITICAL AND
MILITARY ALLIANCE - AND THE WORLD ECONOMY - MAY NOT SURVIVE.

01798 BROCK, D.
    THE WORLD OF NARCOTERRORISM
    AMERICAN SPECTATOR, 22(6) (JUN 89), 24-28.
    THE ARTICLE EXAMINES THE HUGE DRUG PROBLEM OF THE US
FROM THE SUPPLY SIDE. IT ANALYZES THE DRUG TRAFFICKING
EFFORTS OF NATIONS AND GROUPS SUCH AS CUBA, NICARAGUA,
PANAMA, AND THE MEDELLIN CARTEL IN COLUMBIA. THE MONEY MADE
FROM DRUG SALES OFTEN GO DIRECTLY TO MARXIST GOVERNMENTS AND
MOVEMENTS IN LATIN AMERICA. THE AUTHOR CAUTIONS AGAINST
UNDUE OPTIMISM OVER STATEMENTS FROM CUBA AND NICARAGUA ABOUT
COOPERATION IN FIGHTING AGAINST THE NARCOTERRORISTS.

01799 BROCKWAY, G.
    HOW WE CAN CONTROL THE INTEREST RATE
    NEW LEADER, LXXII(5) (MAR 89), 13-14.
    THE ARTICLE ARGUES THAT THE BEST WAY TO CONTROL INTEREST
RATES IS TO ENCOURAGE THAT MONEY IS WITHDRAWN FROM
SPECULATION AND MADE AVAILABLE FOR PRODUCTIVE ENTERPRISE.
SUCH A POLICY WOULD BE POLITICALLY DIFFICULT DUE TO THE FACT
THAT A GREAT DEAL OF THE SPECULATION THAT IS CURRENTLY GOING
ON IS FUNDED BY "INSTITUTIONS" AND NOT INDIVIDUALS. HOWEVER,
SUCH A POLICY COUPLED WITH MEASURES TO DECREASE CAPITAL
FLIGHT WOULD HAVE THE ADDITIONAL BENEFIT OF REDUCING
INFLATION.

01800 BROCKWAY, G.
    SOMETHING SEEMS UNBALANCED
    NEW LEADER, LXXII(14) (SEP 89), 14-15.
    THE FACT THAT MICHAEL R. MILKEN MADE $550 MILLION IN
1987 "RAISES QUESTIONS AS TO WHETHER THERE ISN'T SOMETHING
UNBALANCED IN THE WAY OUR FINANCIAL SYSTEM IS WORKING." THE
ARTICLE ASSESSES THIS UNBALANCE AND BLAMES IT ON THE
"CONSERVATIVE FINANCIAL REVOLUTION" WHICH HAS CONSIDERABLY

INCREASED INCOME INEQUALITY IN THE US. IT CONCLUDES THAT
CONSERVATIVES HAVE SIGNIFICANTLY REDUCED THE QUALITY OF LIFE
FOR A LARGE SEGMENT OF THE US POPULATION.

01801 BROCKWAY, G.P.
THE RESERVE'S SILLY NEW EQUATION
NEW LEADER, LXXII(10) (JUN 89), 15-16.
THE AUTHOR HERE ATTEMPTS TO DEBUNK THE MYTH THAT
MATHEMATICAL EQUATIONS SOLVE OR EXPLAIN ECONOMIC PROBLEMS.
FOCUS IS ON CHAIRMAN ALAN GREENSPAN'S TEAM OF THREE
ECONOMISTS AND THEIR FORMULA MV = PQ WHERE M IS MONEY SUPPLY,
V IS VELOCITY OF CHARGE IN MONEY SUPPLY, Q IS THE TOTAL OF
GOODS AND SERVICES PRODUCED AND P EQUALS PRICE LEVEL.

01802 BROCKWAY, G.P.
THE TRUTH ABOUT INFLATION
NEW LEADER, LXXII(3) (FEB 89), 13-14.
THE AUTHOR EVALUATES THE TRADITIONAL PRESCRIPTION FOR
CURING INFLATION ON A MICRO-ECONOMIC LEVEL.

01803 BROCKWAY, G.P.
WHAT HAPPENED TO JIMMY CARTER?
NEW LEADER, 72(18) (NOV 89), 11-13.
THIS IS A FOOTNOTE TO JAMES MACGREGOR BURN'S "THE
CROSSWINDS OF FREEDOM," THIRD AND FINAL VOLUME OF HIS
HISTORY OF "THE AMERICAN EXPERIMENT." BURN'S ANALYSIS OF
CARTER IS THAT HE WAS (AND IS) A DECENT GUY WHO APPARENTLY
THOUGHT DECENCY WAS ENOUGH, WHO HAD A TALENT FOR OFFBEAT
PUBLIC RELATIONS, AND WHO HAD A PROPENSITY FOR SHOOTING
HIMSELF IN THE FOOT. THE FOOTNOTE IS ON HOW THE ECONOMIC
SITUATION AFFECTED CARTER. THE CONSUMER PRICE INDEX,
CONSUMER CREDIT, INFLATION, AND INTEREST RATES ARE EXAMINED.
THE WRITER FEARS THAT WE ARE UNLIKELY TO FIND LEADERS
CAPABLE OF UNDERSTANDING AND LEADING US OUT OF THE SLOUGH OF
CONVENTIONAL ECONOMICS.

01804 BRODER, S.M.
POLITICS OF THE FAMILY: POLITICAL CULTURE, MORAL REFORM,
AND FAMILY RELATIONS IN GILDED AGE PHILADELPHIA
DISSERTATION ABSTRACTS INTERNATIONAL, 49(8) (FEB 89),
2364-A.
THE AUTHOR EXPLORES THE RELATIONSHIP BETWEEN REFORMERS
OF DIVERSE POLITICAL PERSPECTIVES AND PHILADELPHIA'S WORKING
CLASS AND ESTABLISHES THE CENTRALITY OF GENDER AND FAMILY
ISSUES TO CLASS POLITICS IN THE GILDED AGE. SHE PROBES
CONTEMPORARY SOURCES OF REFORM THOUGHT AND THE LABOR PRESS
TO SEE HOW EACH GROUP CONSTRUCTED, SHARED, AND CONTESTED
POLITICAL IMAGES AND THEIR MEANING.

01805 BRODINE, V.
IDEOLOGY AND GLOBAL ECOLOGY
POLITICAL AFFAIRS, LXVIII(9-10) (SEP 89), 15-20.
IN ITS ANALYSIS OF THE CURRENT ENVIRONMENTAL CONDITION,
THE ARTICLE ARGUES THAT BY USING NATURE FOR PROFIT,
CAPITALISM IMPOVERISHES THE WORLD AND THREATENS IT WITH
IRREVERSIBLE DAMAGE. IT OUTLINES SOME OF THE SIGNIFICANT
RISKS ASSOCIATED WITH RESOURCE DEPLETION AND POLLUTION. IT
CONCLUDES WITH SUGGESTIONS FOR REFORM IN BOTH THE SHORT AND
LONG TERM. STOP-GAP PROCEDURES SUCH AS RECYCLING WILL REDUCE
SHORT-TERM POLLUTION AND SAVE RESOURCES, BUT NOTHING SHORT
OF A FULL-SCALE MOBILIZATION OF THE WORKING CLASS WILL SOLVE
MANY OF THE LONG-TERM PROBLEMS.

01806 BRODINE, V. W.
THE ENVIRONMENT: A NATURAL TERRAIN FOR COMMUNISTS
POLITICAL AFFAIRS, LXVIII(1) (JAN 89), 28-33.
COMMUNISTS HAVE A DUTY TO ANALYZE THE RELATIONSHIP OF
ECONOMIC AND POLITICAL SYSTEMS TO THE ENVIRONMENT AND TO
FIND WAYS IN WHICH THE CLASS AND ENVIRONMENTAL STRUGGLES CAN
REINFORCE EACH OTHER.

01807 BRODY, R.; WEISSBRODT, D.
MAJOR DEVELOPMENTS AT THE 1989 SESSION OF THE UN
COMMISSION ON HUMAN RIGHTS
HUMAN RIGHTS QUARTERLY, 11(4) (NOV 89), 586-611.
THE 45TH SESSION OF THE UN COMMISSION ON HUMAN RIGHTS
TOOK A NUMBER OF INCREMENTAL STEPS TOWARDS IMPROVING THE
PROTECTION OF HUMAN RIGHTS THROUGHOUT THE WORLD. THE SESSION
WAS MARKED BY A RELATIVELY SLOW BEGINNING AS A LARGER NUMBER
OF DELEGATES THAN USUAL -- PARTICULARLY IN THE INFLUENTIAL
WESTERN EUROPEAN GROUP -- WERE ATTENDING THEIR FIRST
COMMISSION. THE DELAYS AT THE BEGINNING RESULTED IN MANY
LATE-NIGHT MEETINGS AT THE END OF THE SIXWEEK SESSION.
NEVERTHELESS, BY THE END THE COMMISSION WAS ABLE TO MAKE
MOST OF ITS DECISIONS BY CONSENSUS. A NEW FACTOR IN THE
EXAMINATION OF COUNTRY SITUATIONS WAS THE DECISION OF
BULGARIA, THE GERMAN DEMOCRATIC REPUBLIC, THE UKRAINIAN SSR,
AND THE USSR NOT TO PARTICIPATE IN VOTING ON RESOLUTIONS
CONCERNING ALBANIA, IRAQ, IRAN, AND ROMANIA -- GIVING THOSE
RESOLUTIONS A GREATER CHANCE OF PASSAGE. EXCEPT FOR THE
ISSUE OF CUBA, THE COMMISSION WAS MARKED BY A SLIGHT
DECREASE IN IDEOLOGICAL POLARIZATION AS COMPARED WITH
PREVIOUS SESSIONS. EVEN RESOLUTIONS ON ALBANIA, BURMA, AND
ROMANIA WERE NOT GENERALLY PERCEIVED IN IDEOLOGICAL TERMS.

THIS DECREASE IN IDEOLOGICAL POLARIZATION DID NOT, HOWEVER,
RESULT IN A MUCH NEEDED RESOLUTION ON THE GRAVE HUMAN RIGHTS
ABUSES IN IRAQ. AS TO CUBA, THE UNITED STATES CAUSED THE
COMMISSION TO DEVOTE A CONSIDERABLE AMOUNT OF ITS TIME AND
RESOURCES TO THE HUMAN RIGHTS SITUATION IN THAT COUNTRY.

01808 BROMLEY, D.
INSTITUTIONAL CHANGE AND ECONOMIC EFFICIENCY
JOURNAL OF ECONOMIC ISSUES, XXIII(3) (SEP 89), 735-760.
THE AUTHOR ARGUES AGAINST THE TRADITIONAL VIEW OF
INSTITUTIONAL CHANGE THAT IT IS EITHER IN THE INTEREST OF
ECONOMIC EFFICIENCY, OR IT MERELY REDISTRIBUTES INCOME. HE
PROPOSES A MORE ARTICULATED MODEL FOR UNDERSTANDING AND
EXPLAINING INSTITUTIONAL CHANGE. THE MODEL PROVIDES FOR THE
CONCEPTUAL BASIS FOR AUGMENTING THE TRADITIONAL
EFFICIENCY/EQUITY EXPLANATION OF INSTITUTIONAL CHANGE WITH
TWO OTHER CATEGORIES--THAT OF REALLOCATING ECONOMIC
OPPORTUNITY, AND OF REDISTRIBUTING ECONOMIC ADVANTAGE. THE
AUTHOR ARGUES THAT THIS MORE ELABORATE MODEL WILL ENHANCE
THE ABILITY TO MAKE INSTITUTIONAL CHANGE MORE AMENDABLE TO
RIGOROUS ECONOMIC ANALYSIS.

01809 BROMLEY, D.W.
PROPERTY RELATIONS AND ECONOMIC DEVELOPMENT: THE OTHER
LAND REFORM
WORLD DEVELOPMENT, 17(6) (JUN 89), 867-877.
CONTINUED CONCERN FOR DEVELOPMENT HAS LED TO THE
SUGGESTION THAT PRIVATE PROPERTY RIGHTS SHOULD BE CREATED TO
STIMULATE ECONOMIC DEVELOPMENT. THIS SUGGESTION DERIVES FROM
AN INCOMPLETE UNDERSTANDING OF THE PROPERTY RELATIONS ON THE
PUBLIC DOMAIN LANDS IN THE ARID TROPICS AND FROM A CONFUSION
OF CAUSE AND EFFECT BETWEEN PROPERTY AND ECONOMIC
PRODUCTIVITY. A MODEL OF THE PRIVATE-PUBLIC BOUNDARY IN LAND
IS DEVELOPED THAT CHALLENGES THE VIEW THAT WEALTH WOULD
INCREASE IF LAND AT THE EXTENSIVE MARGIN WERE PRIVATIZED.
THE VARIOUS TYPES OF PROPERTY REGIMES IN LAND ARE DEFINED
AND EXPLAINED.

01810 BROOKS, F.H.
ANARCHISM, REVOLUTION AND LABOR IN THE THOUGHT OF DYER D.
LUM: "EVENTS ARE THE TRUE SCHOOLMASTERS"
DISSERTATION ABSTRACTS INTERNATIONAL, 49(10) (APR 89),
3139-A.
THIS DISSERTATION EXAMINES THE LIFE AND WRITINGS OF DYER
DANIEL LUM (1839-1893), AN AMERICAN LABOR ACTIVIST AND
ANARCHIST. LUM HAS BEEN KNOWN PRIMARILY AS A COMRADE OF THE
COLLECTIVISTIC HAYMARKET ANARCHISTS AND AN ADVOCATE OF
REVOLUTIONARY VIOLENCE. HE WAS ALSO A FOLLOWER OF BENJAMIN
TUCKER'S INDIVIDUALISTIC ECONOMIC VIEWS AND AN APOLOGIST FOR
TRADE UNIONS. THIS ECLECTIC AND SEEMINGLY CONTRADICTORY SET
OF VIEWS IS EXPLAINED PARTLY BY A CLOSE TEXTUAL ANALYSIS OF
LUM'S BOOKS, ARTICLES, AND LETTERS BETWEEN 1885 AND 1893.

01811 BROTHERSON, F. JR.
THE FOREIGN POLICY OF GUYANA, 1970-1985: FORBES BURNHAM'S
SEARCH FOR LEGITIMACY
JOURNAL OF INTERAMERICAN STUDIES AND WORLD AFFAIRS, 31(3)
(FAL 89), 9-35.
THIS ARTICLE EXPLORES GUYANA POLITICS DURING BURNHAM'S
LEADERSHIP, 1970-1985, SOME OF HIS IDEAS AND ACTIONS WERE
MOTIVATED BY ATTEMPTS AT NATION-BUILDING AND FOUNDING A
VIABLE NEW STATE BUT THESE CONCERNS BECAME INVOLVED WITH THE
ESTABLISHMENT AND MAINTENANCE OF BURNHAM'S SUPREME POLITICAL
AUTHORITY. THIS EXPLAINS, TO SOME EXTENT HIS PRE-OCCUPATION
WITH LEGITIMACY. THIS ARTICLE ASSESSES THE DEVELOPMENT AND
IMPLEMENTATION OF HIS POLICIES FOR MOTIVE, CONSEQUENCES, AND
EFFECTIVENESS IN ACHIEVING THEIR GOAL. BACKGROUND ON THE
AUTHORITARIAN POLITICS OF GUYANA ARE GIVEN.

01812 BROUN, J.A.
CHURCH AND PARTY IN HUNGARY
FREEDOM AT ISSUE. (107) (MAR 89), 28-31.
SINCE KAROLY GROSZ ASSUMED POWER IN HUNGARY, THERE HAVE
BEEN CHANGES IN THE COMPOSITION OF THE COMMUNIST PARTY AND
THE INCLUSION OF MORE REFORMISTS. CONSTITUTIONAL CHANGES ARE
IN THE WORKS. ECONOMICALLY, THE GOVERNMENT IS FACED WITH THE
NECESSITY OF RAISING PRICES AND ALLOWING REDUNDANCIES IN
ORDER TO TACKLE MAJOR PROBLEMS. AS IT STANDS NOW, MANY
HUNGARIANS HAVE TO FIND SECOND JOBS TO SUPPORT EVEN SMALL
FAMILIES AND A QUARTER OF THE POPULATION IS BELOW THE
SUBSISTENCE LEVEL. LIFE IS CERTAIN TO BECOME EVEN HARDER
BEFORE IT GETS BETTER. THUS, THE GOVERNMENT MUST SEEK
SUPPORT FROM GROUPS AND INSTITUTIONS OUTSIDE THE PARTY. THE
MOST IMPORTANT OF THESE IS THE CHURCH.

01813 BROWN, A.
NATIONALIST AND ETHNIC UNREST IN THE SOVIET UNION
WORLD POLICY JOURNAL, VI(3) (SUM 89), 469-502.
MIKHAIL GORBACHEV CAME TO POWER IN RUSSIA IN 1985. SINCE
HE HAS EMBARKED ON AN ABITIOUS PROGRAM OF REFORM. IT
UNLEASHED FORCES OF A MAGNITUDE HE COULD NOT HAVE
ANTICIPATED. AS THE NEW SOVIET LEADERSHIP CHARTED A NEW AND
UNPREDICTABLE COURSE IN ITS EFFORT TO ADDRESS DEEPENING
ECONOMIC AND SOCIAL PROBLEMS, THE ACCUMULATED DISCONTENT AND

FRUSTRATION FROM BELOW BEGAN TO BURST FORTH THROUGH FISSURES
IN THE STATE STRUCTURE. UNEXPECTEDLY, MUCH OF THIS PRESSURE
TOOK THE FORM OF NATIONALIST OR ETHNIC UNREST.

01814 BROWN, A.
POLITICAL CHANGE IN THE SOVIET UNION
WORLD POLICY JOURNAL, VI(3) (SUM 89), 469-502.
IN THE SOVIET UNION DRAMATIC AND FUNDAMENTALLY IMPORTANT
CHANGE IS TAKING PLACE. POLITICAL REFORM IS PROCEEDING MUCH
FASTER AND MORE SUCESSFULLY THAN ECONOMIC REFORM. THERE ARE
THREE NEW CONCEPTS THAT HELP TO OPEN UP SPACE FOR NEW
POLITICAL ACTIVITY AND PROVIDE THEORETICAL UNDERPINNING FOR
SOME OF THE CONCRETE REFORMS THAT ARE BEING IMPLEMENTED. THE
FIRST OF THESE CONCEPTS IS THAT OF "SOCIALIST PLURALISM".
THE SECOND CONCEPT ADOPTED IS OF GREAT IMPORTANCE TO THE
ADVANCEMENT OF THE CAUSE OF POLITICAL AND LEGAL REFORM IS
THAT OF PRAVOVOE GOSUDARSTVO, OR THE STATE BASED ON THE RULE
OF LAW. THE AIM OF THIS CONCEPT IS A SYSTEM IN WHICH ALL
INSTITUTIONS AND INDIVIDUALS ARE SUBORDINATE TO THE LAW,
WHICH IS ADMINISTERED BY IMPARTIAL AND INDEPENDENT COURTS.
THE THIRD CONCEPT IS THAT OF "CHECKS AND BALANCES". THIS IS
QUITE NEW IN THE SOVIET CONTEXT. ITS ADOPTION IS A
REMARKABLE DEPARTURE FROM PREVIOUS PATERNS OF SOVIET
THINKING. THE MOST IMPORTANT POINT ABOUT REFORM IN THE
SOVIET POLITICAL SYSTEMS THAT IT IS NOT AN EVENT BUT A
PROCESS AND, IN ALL PROBABILITY, A LONG-TERM PROCESS.

01815 BROWN, C.G.; WINSLOW, T.C.
HEALTH CARE COSTS: RISING HEALTH BILLS COMPEL ACTION
JOURNAL OF STATE GOVERNMENT, 62(3) (MAY 89), 124-126.
THE CONTINUED RISING COST OF HEALTH CARE COMPELS ACTION.
STATE AND FEDERAL COST CONTROL EFFORTS MUST BE EXPANDED AND
NEW INITIATIVES TAKEN. IN CONTROLLING COSTS, HOWEVER, STATE
GOVERNMENTS MUST TAKE CARE TO PROTECT CONSUMERS FROM OVERLY
BURDENSOME PROCEDURES AND INEQUITABLE COST-SHARING.

01816 BROWN, C.H., JR.
THUCYDIDES, HOBBES AND THE LINEAR CAUSAL PERSPECTIVE
HISTORY OF POLITICAL THOUGHT, X(2) (SUM 89), 215-256.
THE PARALLES IN CONCEPTUALIZATION AND PRESENTATION SET
FORTH SUGGEST A STRONGER INFLUENCE OF THUCYDIDES ON HOBBES
THAN HITHERTO RECOGNIZED. HOBBES'S INTENSE STUDY OF
THUCYDIDES (WHICH THE EXERCISE OF MAKING A TRANSLATION MUST
HAVE REQUIRED--ESPECIALLY A TRANSLATION SUCH AS THIS ONE)
WOULD HAVE SIGNIFICANTLY INCREASED HIS RECEPTIVITY TO THE
GALILEAN ARGUMENTS ABOUT MOTION, SEQUENCE, TIME AND CAUSE.
THUCYDIDES WAS NEVER IN ANY WAY REPUDIATED BY HOBBES AFTER
HIS DISCOVERY OF 'SCIENTIFIC' METHODS. ON THE CONTRARY, IN
HOBBES'S OLD AGE HE REAFFIRMED HIS ADMIRATION FOR THE
HISTORIAN, WHOM HE CONSIDERED THE BEST OF THE ANCIENTS, KEPT
HIS TRANSLATION IN PRINT THROUGHTOUT HIS LIFETIME (THREE
PRINTINGS SUBSEQUENT TO THE FIRST EDITION), AND PROBABLY
MEANT IT TO BE INCLUDED AS AN INTEGRAL PART OF HIS OFFERINGS
TO THE PUBLIC ON THE NATURE OF MAN AND SOCIETY.

01817 BROWN, D.
EHTNIC REVIVAL: PERSPECTIVES ON STATE AND SOCIETY
THIRD WORLD QUARTERLY, 11(4) (OCT 89), 1 - 17.
THIS ARTICLE EXPLORES THE IMPLICATION THAT THE STUDY OF
ETHNICITY BECOMES OF CENTRAL CONCERN AS THE STUDY OF
POLITICAL CHANGE SHIFTS TOWARD A FOCUS ON THE ROLE OF
CULTURE AND ON THE CHARACTER OF THE STATE. EXPLORED IN
RELATION TO THE ABOVE IMPLICATION ARE: STATE ELITE, NATIONAL
INDENTITY, STATE INSTITUTIONAL FRAMEWORK; ETHNIC, CLASS,
PATRIMONIAL AND BUREAUCRATIC ELITES. THE IDEOLOGIES OF MONO-
ETHNIC, ETHNICALLY NEUTRAL AND CONSOCIATIONAL NATIONALISM
ARE DETAILED.

01818 BROWN, D.
ETHNIC REVIVAL: PERSPECTIVES ON STATE AND SOCIETY
THIRD WORLD QUARTERLY, 11(4) (OCT 89), 1-17.
THERE HAS BEEN AN ETHNIC REVIVAL SINCE THE 1960'S IN
TERMS OF AN INCREASED INCIDENCE OF ETHNIC CONFLICT AND AN
INCREASED AWARENESS OF THE PHENOMENON BY SOCIAL SCIENTISTS.
BUT THERE HAS BEEN NO CORRESPONDING AWARENESS OF THE
CENTRALITY OF ETHNICITY TO THE STUDY OF DEVELOPMENT. IT IS
ALMOST SHOCKING TO REALIZE JUST HOW LITTLE ATTENTION IS
STILL PAID TO ETHNICITY IN MOST OF THE THEORETICAL WORK THAT
HAS BEEN DONE ON POLITICAL CHANGE. POLITICAL SCIENCE, FROM
THE LATE 1950'S TO THE EARLY 1970'S, HAS DOMINATED BY THE
MODERNISATION PARADIGM IN WHICH ETHNICITY WAS DEPICTED AS A
REMNANT OF TRADITION INEVITABLY DECLINING IN SIGNIFICANCE AS
CULTURAL RATIONALITY AND NATIONAL INTEGRATION DEVELOPED.
ETHNICITY SEEMED TO BE BOTH A MARGINAL AND A TEMPORARY
FEATURE OF POLITICS.

01819 BROWN, F.
COLORADO CITIZENS REWRITE LEGISLATIVE RULES
STATE LEGISLATURES, 15(7) (AUG 89), 14-20.
IN 1988, THE COLORADO VOTERS PASSED A CONSTITUTIONAL
AMENDMENT CALLED "GAVEL," (GIVE A VOTE TO EVERY LEGISLATOR).
ESSENTIALLY, IT OUTLAWED BINDING CAUCUSES AND INSURED THAT
ALL BILLS ARE HEARD. BUT THE NEW RULES HAVEN'T HAD AS MUCH
EFFECT AS PREDICTED BY EITHER PROPONENTS OR OPPONENTS.

01820 BROWN, H.
THE UNITED STATES AND JAPAN: HIGH TECH IS FOREIGN POLICY
SAIS REVIEW, 9(2) (SUM 89), 1-18.
THIS ARTICLE EXAMINES THE ISSUES OF TECHNOLOGY TRANSFER,
CONTROL OF DEFENSE - RELATED TECHNOLOGIES, JAPANESE DEFENSE
SPENDING AND FOREIGN AID, AND WHAT THE POTENTIAL SALE OF
JAPANESE HIGH-TECH EQUIPMENT TO THE SOVIET UNION AND ITS
ALLIES COULD MEAN TO THE INCREASINGLY STRAINED RELATIONSHIP
BETWEEN WASHINGTON AND TOKYO. THE GROWING INFLUENCE OF JAPAN
LOANS ON THE HORIZON OF AMERICA'S FOREIGN AND DOMESTIC
ECONOMIC AND MELITARY POLICY.

01821 BROWN, J.
NO GLASTNOST YET FOR RELIGION IN BULGARIA
THE CHRISTIAN CENTURY, 106(36) (NOV 89), 1124-1125.
THIS ARTICLE DISCUSSES ISSUES OF RELIGIOUS FREEDOM YET
TO BE CONFRONTED IN BULGARIA WHICH IS NOW EXPERIENCING SOME
OF THE OF THE POLITICAL CHANGE THAT HAS COME TO OTHER
EASTERN EUROPEAN COUNTRIES. THE MASS EXODUS OF TURKISH
MUSLIMS IS EXPLORED, AS WELL AS THE EFFECT OF GLASTNOST IN
BULGARIA.

01822 BROWN, J.
THE MILITARY AND SOCIETY: THE TURKISH CASE
MIDDLE EASTERN STUDIES, 25(3) (JUL 89), 387-404.
THE ARTICLE EXAMINES THE RECRUITING METHODS OF THE
TURKISH MILITARY AND THE SOCIO-POLITICAL ATTITUDES OF
INFLUENTIAL MILITARY ELITE. IT ANALYZES THE HISTORICAL
LEGACY OF THE MILITARY IN TURKEY WITH EMPHASIS ON THE
SEPTEMBER 1980 INTERVENTION. IT CONCLUDES THAT MANY OF THE
TURKISH MILITARY ARE RECRUITED FROM "SONS OF MILITARY" AND
CIVIL SERVANTS. FURTHERMORE, THE TURKISH ARMED FORCES HAVE
VENTURED INTO THE POLITICAL ARENA WITH RELUCTANCE. HOWEVER,
THEIR INTERVENTION HAS BEEN REPRESENTATIVE OF TURKISH
SOCIETY AND IS SINCERELY COMMITTED TO THE DEMOCRATIC PROCESS.

01823 BROWN, J. A.
SOCIAL CLASS AND POLITICS: WITH SPECIAL REFERENCE TO NON-
MANUAL WORKERS
DISSERTATION ABSTRACTS INTERNATIONAL, 49(7) (JAN 89),
1944-A.
THE AUTHOR EXPLORES THE RELATIONSHIP BETWEEN SOCIAL
CLASS, POLITICAL BEHAVIOR, POLITICAL ORGANIZATION, AND
SOCIAL CHANGE, WITH PARTICULAR REFERENCE TO NON-MANUAL
WORKERS. PART ONE FOCUSES UPON THE RELATIONSHIP OF SOCIAL
CLASS TO SOCIAL STRUCTURE. PART TWO DISCUSSES THE WAY IN
WHICH AN INDIVIDUAL'S SOCIAL CLASS IDENTITY CAN INFLUENCE
HIS POLITICAL BEHAVIOR, WITH EMPHASIS ON TRADE UNIONS AND
POLITICAL PARTIES.

01824 BROWN, J.C.
PUBLIC REFORM FOR PRIVATE GAIN? THE CASE OF INVESTMENTS IN
SANITARY INFRASTRUCTURE: GERMANY, 1880-1887
URBAN STUDIES, 26(1) (FEB 89), 2-12.
THIS EXAMINATION OF THE ISSUE OF COMPARATIVE PROGRESS IN
SANITARY REFORM FOCUSES ON THE POTENTIAL IMPORTANCE IN
GERMAN TOWNS OF AN UNEQUAL DISTRIBUTION OF WEALTH AND
POLITICAL POWER FOR PUSHING AHEAD PROGRAMS FOR REFORM.

01825 BROWN, J.L.
WHEN VIOLENCE HAS A BENEVOLENT FACE: THE PARADOX OF HUNGER
IN THE WORLD'S HEALTHIEST DEMOCRACY
INTERNATIONAL JOURNAL OF HEALTH SERVICES, 19(2) (1989),
257-278.
DURING THE LAST TWO DECADES, AMERICANS INITIALLY
DISCOVERED THAT MILLIONS OF FELLOW-CITIZENS WERE GOING
HUNGRY, THEN ACTED TO VIRTUALLY ELIMINATE THE PROBLEM, AND,
IN THE 1980S, LEARNED THAT HUNGER HAS REAPPEARED IN EPIDEMIC
PROPORTIONS. HUNGER, PARTICULARLY IN A WEALTHY DEMOCRACY, IS
MOST APPROPRIATELY SEEN AS A FORM OF INSTITUTIONALIZED
VIOLENCE, THE PRODUCT OF IDEOLOGIES THAT FAIL TO DISTRIBUTE
NATIONAL ABUNDANCE IN A MANNER THAT ACHIEVES THE POSSIBLE
GOAL OF PREVENTING HUNGER. THE RETURN OF HUNGER TO THE
UNITED STATES IS ASSOCIATED WITH ECONOMIC AND TAX POLICIES
THAT HAVE REALLOCATED INCOME DISTRIBUTION FROM POOR AND
MIDDLE-INCOME GROUPS TO THE WEALTHY, AND WITH A CONCOMITANT
RELUCTANCE TO UTILIZE THE FEDERAL GOVERNMENT TO PROTECT
NEEDY CITIZENS FROM UNDERNUTRITION ASSOCIATED WITH GROWING
ECONOMIC DEPRIVATION.

01826 BROWN, K.
"TRANSFER" AND THE DISCOURSE OF RACISM
MIDDLE EAST REPORT, 19(157) (MAR 89), 21-22, 47.
REHAVAM ZE'EVI IS THE LEADER OF A NEW ISRAELI POLITICAL
PARTY CALLED "MOLEDET." IT CALLS FOR EXPELLING THE
PALESTINIANS FROM GREATER ISRAEL, NOT BY FORCE BUT BY
AGREEMENT WITH THE NEIGHBORING ARAB STATES.

01827 BROWN, K.L.; FARRAND, R.W.
HUMAN RIGHTS ISSUES IN AFRICA
DEPARTMENT OF STATE BULLETIN (US FOREIGN POLICY), 89(2146)
(MAY 89), 27-32.
THE AUTHORS REVIEW RECENT HUMAN RIGHTS DEVELOPMENTS IN

AFRICAN COUNTRIES, INCLUDING BURUNDI, ETHIOPIA, MOZAMBIQUE, SOMALIA, AND SUDAN.

01828 BROWN, K.V.
CANADIAN SSNS AND THEIR EMPLOYMENT
AVAILABLE FROM NTIS, NO. AD-A201 162/5/GAR, SEP 88, 64.
THROUGH THE PUBLIC FORUM OF THE 1987 WHITE PAPER, THE GOVERNMENT OF CANADA ANNOUNCED ITS INTENTIONS TO MAKE MAJOR CHANGES TO CANADA'S MILITARY AND TO HER DEFENSE POSTURE. AMONG OTHER THINGS, THE WHITE PAPER PUBLICIZED THE PLANNED ACQUISITION OF TEN TO TWELVE NUCLEAR POWERED SUBMARINES. THE GOVERNMENT HOPES THAT THESE SUBMARINES WILL HELP ASSERT CANADA'S CLAIM OF SOVEREIGNTY IN THE WATERS OF THE CANADIAN ARCHIPELAGO INCLUDING THE NORTHWEST PASSAGE. THE UNITED STATES CONSIDERS THE NORTHWEST PASSAGE TO BE A STRAIT USED FOR INTERNATIONAL NAVIGATION AND SUBJECT TO THE RIGHT OF TRANSIT PASSAGE. THE SSNS WILL ALSO HAVE A CLEARLY MARTIAL ROLE IN PROTECTING CANADA'S ECONOMIC INTERESTS AND HER NATIONAL SECURITY RESPONSIBILITIES IN THE ATLANTIC, THE PACIFIC AND THE ARCTIC OCEANS. THIS THESIS EXAMINES THESE REASONS BEHIND CANADA'S DECISION TO ACQUIRE AN SSN FLEET AND THEIR POTENTIAL EMPLOYMENT. THESES.

01829 BROWN, M.E.
UNDERSTANDING CHANGE IN THE SOCIALIST COUNTRIES
SOCIALISM AND DEMOCRACY, (FAL 89), 11-26.
MICHAEL BROWN ARGUES FOR A SELF-CONSCIOUSLY CRITICAL ATTITUDE TOWARDS WHAT HE REGARDS AS THE AMBIGUOUS NATURE OF THE REFORMS INITIATED BY MIKHAIL GORBACHEV AND HIS FOLLOWERS. HE OFFERS INFORMATION AND SOME LIMITS OF ANALYSIS; EXPLORES "PARADIGMATIC" SOCIALISM; EXPLORES SOCIALISM AND DEMOCRACY-THE RIGHTIST INTERPRETATION; AND LOOKS TOWARD A RECONSTRUCTION. HIS CONCLUSIONS ARE PROVISIONAL AND PRESUME IN FAVOR OF THE HISTORY OF SOCIALISM, THOUGH NOT IN FAVOR OF THE IDEALISM THAT HAS RIGHTLY BEEN SUBJECT TO SO MUCH CRITICAL REVIEW.

01830 BROWN, M.L.
DECISION MAKING IN DEVELOPING COUNTRIES REGARDING PARTICIPATION IN REGIONAL ECONOMIC ORGANIZATIONS: COMPARISON OF AN ANDEAN PACT, ECOWAS, AND ASEAN CASE
DISSERTATION ABSTRACTS INTERNATIONAL, 49(10) (APR 89), 3146-A.
DECISIONS MADE BY THE INDIVIDUAL NATION-STATES DETERMINE THE VIABILITY OF COLLECTIVE ORGANIZATIONS. CHILE'S DECISION TO WITHDRAW FROM THE ANDEAN PACT, NIGERIA'S DECISION TO DEPORT ALIEN WORKERS, AND THE PHILIPPINE'S DECISION REGARDING TERRITORIAL CLAIMS OVER THE SABAH REGION HAD LONG-TERM IMPLICATIONS FOR THE WELL-BEING OF THE REGIONAL ORGANIZATIONS TO WHICH THEY BELONGED. TWO OF THESE DECISIONS PRODUCED RESULTS THAT WERE AT ODDS WITH THE INTERESTS OF THE REGIONAL ECONOMIC ORGANIZATION.

01831 BROWN, R.M.
TIMES OF LOYAL OPPOSITION
SOJOURNERS, 18(2) (FEB 89), 20-21.
GEORGE BUSH'S CAMPAIGN VISION WAS A TARNISHED ONE. IT WAS BUILT ON PEOPLE'S FEARS, CHEAP SHOTS, OBFUSCATION OF THE REAL ISSUES, AND THE CONSISTENT TRASHING OF A NOBLE PART OF THE AMERICAN TRADITION (LIBERALISM).

01832 BROWN, S.
CSBM: THE OTHER NEGOTIATIONS
NATO'S SIXTEEN NATIONS, 34(4) (AUG 89), 59-61.
THE DRAMATIC NEW PROPOSALS FOR REDUCING CONVENTIONAL FORCES ANNOUNCED BY PRESIDENT BUSH AT THE NATO SUMMIT IN MAY 1989 WILL ONCE AGAIN OVERSHADOW THE NEGOTIATIONS ON SECURITY AND CONFIDENCEBUILDING MEASURES WHICH RUN IN PARALLEL IN VIENNA. NEVERTHELESS, AS SECURITY ULTIMATELY DEPENDS NOT ONLY ON NUMBERS, TYPES AND LOCATIONS OF FORCES BUT ON THEIR ACTUAL POTENTIAL AND PERMANENT VISIBILITY, IT CAN ONLY BE ACHIEVED BY CREATING A PERMANENT SYSTEM OF OPENNESS AND TRANSPARENCY.

01833 BROWN, W.A.
INDOCHINESE REFUGEES AND RELATIONS WITH THAILAND
DEPARTMENT OF STATE BULLETIN (US FOREIGN POLICY), 88(2134) (MAY 88), 37-41.
THE PARTNERSHIP BETWEEN THE INTERNATIONAL COMMUNITY AND THAILAND IN PROVIDING ASYLUM AND SUBSEQUENT RESETTLEMENT TO INDOCHINESE REFUGEES HAS BEEN ONE OF THE GREAT HUMANITARIAN SUCCESS STORIES OF THE PAST DECADE. YET THAILAND STILL FINDS ITSELF PROVIDING REFUGE TO OVER 400,000 REFUGEES AND THE NUMBERS CONTINUE TO POUR INTO THE COUNTRY. SOME THAIS ARE BEGINING TO QUESTION THE KINGDOM'S GENEROUS FIRST ASYLUM POLICY. THE ARTICLE ADDRESSES THE PROBLEM AND SUGGESTS POSSIBLE SOLUTIONS AS WELL AS OUTLINING CURRENT INTERNATIONAL EFFORTS TO SOLVE THE PROBLEM.

01834 BROWNLEE, W.E.
TAXATION: THE AMERICAN WAY
CURRENT, (315) (SEP 89), 11-17.
MORE THAN MOST NATIONS, AMERICANS GENERALLY HAVE CHOSEN TO RELY ON THE MOST PAINFUL FORMS OF TAXATION (DIRECT LEVIES ON PROPERTY AND INCOME), KEEPING TAXES AT THE FOREFRONT OF PUBLIC ATTENTION. NOT ONLY HAVE AMERICANS BEEN DEEPLY UNFRIENDLY TO THE TAXMAN, BUT THE NATIONAL DEBATES OVER TAXATION HAVE OFTEN BEEN VEHICLES FOR DEFINING LARGER CONFLICTS BETWEEN REGIONS AND CLASSES AND OVER THE MEANING OF "EQUALITY," "FAIRNESS," AND "JUSTICE."

01835 BROWNLEE, W.E.
THE AMERICAN WAY
WILSON QUARTERLY, XIII(2) (SPR 89), 86-98.
THE AUTHOR REVIEWS THE HIGHLIGHTS OF U.S. TAX HISTORY AND RECENT TAX REFORM EFFORTS. SINCE EARLY IN THIS CENTURY, AMERICANS HAVE OPTED FOR MILD "SOAK THE RICH" LEVIES TO REDISTRIBUTE WEALTH. TODAY, AS CONGRESS PONDERS WAYS TO CLOSE THE BUDGET GAP, FURTHER LEVELING OF INCOMES THROUGH TAXATION IS OUT WHILE PRAGMATIC REVENUE INITIATIVES ARE IN. THAT SHIFT MAY BE THE CHIEF POLITICAL LEGACY OF THE EARLY 1980'S.

01836 BRUBAKER, W.R.
THE FRENCH REVOLUTION AND THE INVENTION OF CITIZENSHIP
FRENCH POLITICS AND SOCIETY, 7(3) (SUM 89), 30-49.
THE INSTITUTION AND THE IDEOLOGY OF NATIONAL CITIZENSHIP WERE FIRST WORKED OUT DURING THE FRENCH REVOLUTION. THE REVOLUTION BROUGHT TOGETHER ON A NATIONAL LEVEL FOR THE FIRST TIME THE FORMAL DELIMITATION OF THE CITIZENRY; THE ESTABLISHMENT OF CIVIL EQUALITY, ENTAILING SHARED RIGHTS AND SHARED OBLIGATIONS; THE INSTITUTIONALIZATION OF POLITICAL RIGHTS; THE LEGAL RATIONALIZATION AND IDEOLOGICAL ACCENTUATION OF THE DISTINCTION BETWEEN CITIZENS AND FOREIGNERS. IN SHORT, THE REVOLUTION INVENTED NOT ONLY THE NATION-STATE BUT MODERN CITIZENSHIP.

01837 BRUECKNER, J.K.; O'BRIEN, K.M.
MODELING GOVERNMENT BEHAVIOR IN COLLECTIVE BARGAINING: A TEST FOR SELF-INTERESTED BUREAUCRATS
PUBLIC CHOICE, 63 (1989), 15-42.
THIS PAPER TESTS FOR SELF-INTERESTED BEHAVIOR BY LOCAL-GOVERNMENT BUREAUCRATS ENGAGED IN COLLECTIVE BARGAINING WITH PUBLIC EMPLOYEE UNIONS. A THEORETICAL MODEL IS DEVELOPED THAT SHOWS THE EFFECT OF NISKANEN-STYLE BUREAUCRATIC SELF-INTEREST IN THE TWO STANDARD BARGAINING MODELS: THE DEMAND-CONSTRAINED MODEL AND THE EFFICIENT-BARGAIN MODEL. THESE PREDICTIONS ARE THEN TESTED USING NATIONAL CROSS-SECTION DATA ON UNIONIZED POLICE, FIRE, AND SANITATION WORKERS.

01838 BRUMBAUGH, R.D. JR.; LITAN, R.E.
THE S&L CRISIS: HOW TO GET OUT AND STAY OUT
BROOKINGS REVIEW, 7(2) (SPR 89), 3-13.
THE AUTHORS ESTIMATE THE DIMENSIONS OF THE CURRENT CRISIS AMONG THE UNITED STATES' DEPOSITORY INSTITUTIONS. THEY THEN EXPLAIN THE ORIGINS OF THESE CRISES AND CONCLUDE BY OFFERING SUGGESTIONS FOR RESOLVING THE IMMEDIATE PROBLEMS AND ENSURING THAT THEY DO NOT RECUR.

01839 BRUMBERG, A.
POLAND: STATE AND/OR SOCIETY
DISSENT, (WIN 89), 47-55.
THE AUTHOR DISCUSSES RECENT REFORM EFFORTS IN POLAND AND THE SEE-SAW RELATIONSHIP BETWEEN THE GOVERNMENT AND SOLIDARITY.

01840 BRUMMEL, L.
CAPITALISM AND TECHNOLOGY IN GLOBAL RESPECTIVE: A DISPUTE
THE CHRISTIAN CENTURY, 106(22) (JUL 89), 690-693.
THE AUTHOR FINDS MAX L. STACKHOUSE'S ARTICLE ON GLOBALIZATION "DISTINCTLY PROVINICIAL" IN ITS TREATMENT OF CAPITALISM AND TECHNOLOGY. STACKHOUSE OFFERS A REPLY.

01841 BRUNEAU, T.C.
CONSTITUTIONS AND DEMOCRATIC CONSOLIDATION: BRAZIL IN COMPARATIVE PERSPECTIVE
AVAILABLE FROM NTIS, NO. AD-A208 224/6/GAR, MAR 89, 46.
THE REPORT ANALYZES THE BRAZILIAN EXPERIENCE IN FORMULATING A NEW CONSTITUTION IN 1987-1988 IN COMPARATIVE PERSPECTIVE WITH PORTUGAL AND SPAIN. IT IS DEMONSTRATED HOW THE POLITICAL ACTORS IN BRAZIL PARTICIPATED IN THE CONSTITUTENT ASSEMBLY IN ORDER TO ENSURE THEIR INTERESTS IN THE BASIC DOCUMENT. DUE TO THE POLITICAL DYNAMICS OF THE PERIOD AND THE SEVERE ECONOMIC CRISIS, THE ASSEMBLY WAS EXTREMELY OPEN, OR POROUS, AND THE RESULTING DOCUMENT IS LONG (315 ARTICLES), DETAILED, AND EXTREMELY AMBITIOUS. THERE IS SOME QUESTION, HOWEVER, WHETHER THE POLITICAL STRUCTURES AND ECONOMIC RESOURCES WILL ALLOW FOR A SUBSTANTIAL IMPLEMENTATION OF THE CONSTITUTION.

01842 BRUNEAU, T.C.; HEWITT, W.E.
PATTERNS OF CHURCH INFLUENCE IN BRAZIL'S POLITICAL TRANSITION
COMPARATIVE POLITICS, 22(1) (OCT 89), 39-62.
USING SURVEY DATA COLLECTED IN 1982 AND 1984, THE AUTHORS STUDY THE EXTENT OF CHURCH INFLUENCE IN PRESENT-DAY BRAZIL AND OFFER SOME PRELIMINARY OBSERVATIONS AND PREDICTIONS REGARDING ITS ONGOING INVOLVEMENT IN THIS-

WORLDLY MATTERS.

01843 BRUNING, F.
WHY DID RANDALL ADAMS ALMOST DIE?
MACLEAN'S (CANADA'S NEWS MAGAZINE), 102(13) (MAR 89), .
CAPITAL PUNISHMENT BECOMES A THORNY ISSUE WHEN THE
POSSIBILITY OF EXECUTING INNOCENTS IS THROWN IN. THE CASE OF
RANDALL ADAMS, BROUGHT TO NATIONAL ATTENTION BY THE
DOCUMENTARY "THE THIN BLUE LINE," IS A CAUTION TO THOSE WHO
CLAMOR FOR MORE AND SWIFTER EXECUTIONS IN THE US. ADAMS, WHO
CAME WITHIN THREE DAYS OF BEING EXECUTED, TURNED OUT TO BE
THE INNOCENT VICTIM OF OVERZEALOUS PROSECUTION OF DOUBTFUL
ETHICAL NATURE.

01844 BRUSCO, S.; RIGHI, E.
LOCAL GOVERNMENT, INDUSTRIAL POLICY, AND SOCIAL CONSENSUS:
THE CASE OF MODENA (ITALY)
ECONOMY AND SOCIETY, 18(4) (NOV 89), 405-424.
THE 'EMILIAN MODEL' HAS BECOME WELL KNOWN AS A CASE OF
RAPID ECONOMIC GROWTH BASED ON SMALL FIRMS CONCENTRATED IN
'INDUSTRIAL DISTRICTS'. THIS PAPER GIVES A DETAILED ACCOUNT
OF THREE LOCAL INDUSTRIAL POLICY INITIATIVES ADOPTED IN
MODENA, ONE OF THE PROVINCES OF EMILIA-ROMAGNA IN WHICH THE
FEATURES OF THE MODEL APPEAR CLEAREST. THE POLICY OF
INDUSTRIAL PARKS HAS INTENDED TO MAKE LAND AVAILABLE TO
FIRMS FOR THEIR ORDERLY DEVELOPMENT; THE LOAN GUARANTEE
CONSORTIUM AIMED TO SECURE SPECIAL FINANCING FOR SMALL FIRMS;
AND THE CREATION OF 'REAL SERVICE CENTRES' WAS DIRECTED
TOWARDS SUPPLYING INFORMATION ON TECHNOLOGY AND MARKETS TO
INDUSTRIAL DISTRICTS SPECIALIZING IN PARTICULAR SECTORS. IN
ADDITION TO DESCRIBING THESE INTERVENTIONS, THE PAPER ALSO
SEEKS TO DEMONSTRATE THAT A CLIMATE OF SOCIAL CONSENSUS AND
STRONG CREDIBILITY ON THE PART OF LOCAL GOVERNMENT ARE
NECESSARY PREREQUISITES FOR THE SUCCESS OF LOCAL INDUSTRIAL
POLICIES.

01845 BRUSTEIN, W.
THE SOCIAL ORIGINS OF POLITICAL REGIONALISM, FRANCE, 1849-
1981
UNIVERSITY OF CALIFORNIA PRESS, BERKELEY, CA, 1988, .
THE AUTHOR EXPLORES THE DETERMINANTS OF REGIONAL
POLITICAL LOYALTIES IN WESTERN AND MEDITERRANEAN FRANCE. HE
ARGUES THAT DIFFERENT MODES OF AGRICULTURAL PRODUCTION SHAPE
REGIONAL POLITICS.

01846 BRUZZO, E.A.
ITALY AND SOUTH AFRICA
SOUTH AFRICA INTERNATIONAL, 20(1) (JUL 89), 8-13.
BECAUSE MANY SOUTH AFRICANS ARE LARGELY UNAWARE OF THE
SIGNIFICANCE OF ITALY TO THEIR COUNTRY, BOTH POLITICALLY AND
ECONOMICALLY, AN ITALIAN JOURNALIST PROVIDES AN OUTLINE OF
ITALIAN-SA RELATIONS AND THE PROSPECTS FOR ITALIAN SANCTIONS
IN SOUTH AFRICA. ITALIAN ANTI-APARTHEID ORGANIZATIONS, SA-
ITALIAN COMMERCIAL EXCHANGE, TRADE ANALYSIS, PROSANCTION
MOVEMENTS AND CREDIT ARE EXAMINED. HE CONCLUDES THAT
EXISTING TIES WILL EVENTUALLY SLOWLY, BUT SURELY, CONTINUING
DEVELOPING.

01847 BRYDEN, P. L.
AIDS AND THE POLITICS OF FEAR
POLICY OPTIONS, 10(3) (APR 89), 26-28.
IN PROTECTING THE HUMAN RIGHTS OF AIDS VICTIMS,
GOVERNMENTS MUST STRIKE AN APPROPRIATE BALANCE BETWEEN THE
RIGHTS OF SUFFERERS AND THE ACTION REQUIRED BY THE
LEGITIMATE IMPERATIVES OF PUBLIC HEALTH.

01848 BRYNEN, R.
PLO POLICY IN LEBANON: LEGACIES AND LESSONS
JOURNAL OF PALESTINE STUDIES, XVIII(2) (WIN 89), 48-70.
THE ARTICLE ASSESSES THE PRESENCE OF THE PLO IN LEBANON
DURING THE PERIOD 1967-82. IT ANALYZES THE ALLIANCES THAT
THE PALESTINIANS MADE WITH LOCAL FACTIONS AND THE PLO'S
INDULGENCE IN"TAJAWUZAT", MILITIA LAWLESSNESS, CORRUPTION,
EXTORTION, INTERNECINE FIGHTING, AND VIOLATIONS OF THE CAIRO
AGREEMENT. IT ALSO EXAMINES THE DISUNITY THAT HAMPERED THE
PLO'S EFFORTS IN LEBANON. IT CONCLUDES THAT DIFFICULTIES IN
LEBANON ARE LIKELY TO CONTINUE, AND THE PLO FACES GREAT
DIFFICULTY IN OVERCOMING DISUNITY AND PUBLIC REJECTION IN
LEBANON.

01849 BRYNER, G.
OMB'S REGULATORY REVIEW
BUREAUCRAT, 18(3) (FAL 89), 45-50.
THE AUTHOR EXAMINES THE OBJECTIVES OF THE OMB REGULATORY
REVIEW PROCESS AND THE EXTENT TO WHICH THOSE GOALS HAVE BEEN
ACHIEVED. HE THEN CONSIDERS HOW RELEVANT THOSE GOALS ARE FOR
THE CHALLENGES OF GOVERNMENT REGULATION AND HOW THE OMB
REVIEW PROCESS MIGHT BE RESTRUCTURED.

01850 BRYSON, J. M.; ROERING, W. D.
INITIATION OF STRATEGIC PLANNING BY GOVERNMENTS.
PUBLIC ADMINISTRATION REVIEW, 48(6) (NOV 88), 995-1004.
STRATEGIC PLANNING MAY BE DEFINED AS A DISCIPLINED
EFFORT TO PRODUCE FUNDAMENTAL DECISIONS AND ACTIONS THAT

DEFINE WHAT AN ORGANIZATION (OR OTHER ENTITY) IS, WHAT IT
DOES, AND WHY IT DOES IT. THE STUDY REPORTED HERE TRACKED
THE INITIATION OF STRATEGIC PLANNING BY EIGHT GOVERNMENTAL
UNITS. ALL ARE LOCATED IN THE TWIN CITIES METROPOLITAN AREA
OF MINNESOTA. THE STUDY FOLLOWED THE UNITS UNTIL THEY EITHER
DISCONTINUED THEIR STRATEGIC PLANNING EFFORTS OR COMPLETED A
STRATEGIC PLAN. WHILE AT LEAST SOME PLAN IMPLEMENTATION
EFFORTS WERE UNDERWAY DURING THE STUDY PERIOD, PLAN
IMPLEMENTATION WAS NOT THE PRIMARY FOCUS OF THIS STUDY. THE
OVERALL EFFECTIVENESS OF THE STRATEGIC PLANNING PROCESS
MODEL, THEREFORE, WAS NOT ASSESSED. INSTEAD, THE STUDY TRIED:
(1) TO DOCUMENT WHAT HAPPENS WHEN UNITS OF GOVERNMENT WORK
THROUGH A STRATEGIC PLANNING PROCESS (WHEN THAT PROCESS
REPRESENTS AN INNOVATION FOR THE UNITS) AND (2) TO UNCOVER
THE CONDITIONS NECESSARY FOR SUCCESSFUL INITIATION OF A
STRATEGIC PLANNING PROCESS BY GOVERNMENTAL UNITS. THE REST
OF THIS ARTICLE IS ORGANIZED INTO THREE MAJOR SECTIONS.
FIRST, THE SAMPLE AND RESEARCH METHODS ARE DESCRIBED. SECOND,
THE EFFORTS OF THE EIGHT UNITS ARE REVIEWED AND ANALYZED.
FINALLY, CONCLUSIONS ARE PRESENTED ABOUT THE INITIATION OF
STRATEGIC PLANNING BY GOVERNMENTS.

01851 BRZEZINSKI, Z.
IS THE COLD WAR OVER?
INTERNATIONAL AFFAIRS (MOSCOW), (11) (NOV 89), 32-37.
THE QUESTION OF WHETHER THE COLD WAR HAS ENDED IS NOT
EASY TO ANSWER. PARADOXICALLY, THE DEBATE OVER THE COLD WAR
HAS ITSELF BECOME PART OF THE COLD WAR. THE LOUDER SOME IN
THE WEST AFFIRM THE CONTINUED EXISTENCE OF THE COLD WAR, THE
EASIER IT IS FOR GORBACHEV TO AFFIRM HIS DESIRE TO END THE
CONFLICT AND TO STIGMATIZE THOSE WHO DISPUTE HIS VIEW.
COMPLICATING MATTERS EVEN FURTHER IS THE REALITY THAT ANY
ANSWER NOT ONLY RISKS OVERSIMPLIFYING A COMPLEX HISTORICAL
PROCESS BUT ALSO MAY SERVE AS A SCREEN FOR HIDDEN
IDEOLOGICAL PREFERENCES.

01852 BRZEZINSKI, Z.
POST-COMMUNIST NATIONALISM
FOREIGN AFFAIRS, 68(5) (WIN 90), 1-25.
THE TIME HAS COME FOR THE WEST TO CONFRONT AN ISSUE THAT
FOR YEARS MOST WESTERN SCHOLARS HAVE IGNORED AND THAT
WESTERN POLICYMAKERS STILL CONSIDER TO BE TABOO: THE RISING
TIDE OF NATIONALISM IN EASTERN EUROPE AND THE SOVIET UNION.
THIS LONG-DORMANT ISSUE IS NOW BECOMING, IN A DYNAMIC AND
CONFLICTUAL FASHION, THE CENTRAL REALITY OF THE ONCE
SEEMINGLY HOMOGENEOUS SOVIET WORLD. AS THE COMMUNIST VENEER
FADES AND NATIONALISM SURFACES MORE ASSERTIVELY, THE USA
MUST DEFINE ITS INTERESTS AND FORMULATE A POLICY TO REACT TO
THE CHANGING REALITY.

01853 BRZEZINSKI, Z.
TOWARD A COMMON EUROPEAN HOME
PROBLEMS OF COMMUNISM, XXXVIII(6) (NOV 89), 1-10.
IN A SPEECH TO THE DIPLOMATIC ACADEMY OF THE USSR
MINISTRY OF FOREIGN AFFAIRS, ZBIGNIEW BRZEZINSKI NOTED THE
OBSTACLES ON THE PATH TO A COMMON EUROPEAN HOME, INCLUDING
THE ECONOMIC DIFFICULTIES, AND DISCUSSED THE NEED TO
ARTICULATE COMMON PRINCIPLES AND CONSTRUCT A COOPERATIVE
INSTITUTIONAL FRAMEWORK.

01854 BRZOSKA, M.
THE IMPACT OF ARMS PRODUCTION IN THE THIRD WORLD
ARMED FORCES AND SOCIETY, 15(4) (SUM 89), 507-530.
IN THE LAST 20 YEARS OR SO, THE PRODUCTION OF
CONVENTIONAL ARMAMENTS IN COUNTRIES OF THE THIRD WORLD HAS
INCREASED MARKEDLY. THE MAIN CONSIDERATIONS ARE POLITICAL;
ECONOMICALLY, THERE IS ONLY LIMITED SUPPORT FOR SUCH
INVESTMENTS. OVER TIME, THOUGH, ECONOMIC INTERESTS TEND TO
BECOME ENTRENCHED AND TO SUSTAIN DOMESTIC PRODUCTION. THE
PREDOMINANT QUESTION OF INDEPENDENCE FROM FOREIGN SUPPLIERS
OF WEAPONRY HAS TWO ASPECTS: FIRST, SHORT-RUN INDEPENDENCE
IN AMMUNITIONS, IN WHICH THIRD WORLD ARMS PRODUCTION HAS
BEEN RATHER SUCCESSFUL; AND, SECOND, LONG-RUN INDEPENDENCE
FROM INFLOWS OF TECHNOLOGY AND KNOW-HOW, IN WHICH ONLY A FEW
PRODUCERS HAVE MADE ADVANCES. WHILE DOMESTIC ARMS PRODUCTION
REDUCES A BARRIER FOR ARMS CONTROL IN THE THIRD WORLD, SO
FAR THE IMPACT ON INTERNATIONAL SECURITY HAS NOT BEEN
POSITIVE.

01855 BUCHANAN, G.S.
GOVERNMENTAL AID TO RELIGIOUS ENTITIES: THE TOTAL SUBSIDY
POSITION PREVAILS
FORDHAM LAW REVIEW, 58(1) (OCT 89), 53-86.
PART I OF THIS ARTICLE WILL ENGAGE IN A CRITICAL
ANALYSIS OF THE TOTAL SUBSIDY POSITION AS MANIFESTED IN THE
MUELLER AND KENDRICK DECISIONS AND WILL EXPLORE THE
CONCEPTUAL AND POLICY IMPLICATIONS OF THAT POSITION. PART II
WILL BRIEFLY REVIEW THREE OPTIONS THAT THE COURT COULD
UTILIZE IN ITS ESTABLISHMENT CLAUSE ANALYSIS. WHILE
ACCEPTING THE EMERGENCE OF THE TOTAL SUBSIDY POSITION AS A
FAIT ACCOMPLI THAT CANNOT BE PRACTICALLY REVERSED, PART III
WILL CONCLUDE BY REJECTING THAT POSITION AS APPLIED IN THE
MAJORITY OPINIONS OF MUELLER AND KENDRICK. INSTEAD, IN THE
SPIRIT OF THE MUELLER AND KENDRICK DISSENTS, PART IV OF THIS

ARTICLE URGES THAT THE NO RELIGIOUS USE AND EQUAL ACCESS
RESTRICTIONS OF THE TOTAL SUBSIDY POSITION BE APPLIED MORE
STERNLY IN DETERMINING THE CONSTITUTIONAL VALIDITY OF
GOVERNMENTAL AID TO RELIGIOUS ENTITIES(5) AND THAT ONLY A
NARROW APPLICATION OF THE TOTAL SUBSIDY APPROACH CAN ENSURE
THAT THE ENDURING VALUES EMBODIED IN THE ESTABLISHMENT
CLAUSE ARE ADEQUATELY PROTECTED.

01856 BUCHANAN, J.; VANBERG, V.
    A THEORY OF LEADERSHIP AND DEFERENCE IN CONSTITUTIONAL
    CONSTRUCTION
    PUBLIC CHOICE, 61(1) (APR 89), 15-28.
        IN AN EFFORT TO OFFER AN EXPLANATION FOR THE BEHAVIOR OF
    JAMES MADISON AND OF THOSE WHO DEFERRED TO HIM IN
    CONSTITUTIONAL CONSTRUCTION, THE AUTHORS DEVELOP OF THEORY
    OF "RATIONAL DEFERENCE". THIS THEORY ATTEMPTS TO ANSWER THE
    QUESTION: CAN MODELS OF RATIONAL CHOICE BE EXTENDED TO COVER
    THE BEHAVIOR OF PERSONES WHO ARE OBSERVED TO INVEST SCARCE
    RESOURCES, PARTICULARLY TIME AND INTELLECTUAL ENERGY, IN
    BECOMING MORE FULLY INFORMED ABOUT CONSTITUTIONAL
    ALTERNATIVES? AND SECONDLY, THE QUESTION: CAN SUCH MODELS OF
    RATIONAL CHOICE BE EXTENDED FURTHER TO APPLY TO THE BEHAVIOR
    OF PERSONES WHO ARE OBSERVED TO DEFER TO THE OPINIONS OF
    THOSE WHO DO CHOOSE TO BECOME MORE FULLY INFORMED?

01857 BUCHANAN, J.H. JR.
    CIVITAS: CIVIC EDUCATION TO INFORM AND INVOLVE
    NATIONAL CIVIC REVIEW, 78(4) (JUL 89), 279-284.
        A FORMER MEMBER OF CONGRESS AND CURRENT PRESIDENT OF THE
    COUNCIL FOR THE ADVANCEMENT OF CITIZENSHIP DESCRIBES THE
    CIVITAS FRAMEWORK OF CIVIC EDUCATION, INTENDED TO PROMOTE
    CIVIC RENEWAL BY INSTRUCTING K-12 STUDENTS IN BOTH THE
    PRIVILEGES AND RESPONSIBILITIES OF CITIZENSHIP IN A
    DEMOCRACY.

01858 BUCHANAN, J.M.
    CAMELOT WILL NOT RETURN
    REASON, 20(8) (JAN 89), 36-37.
        THE TURN TO PRIVATIZATION THROUGHOUT THE WORLD STEMS
    PRIMARILY FROM EMPIRICALLY OBSERVED FAILURES IN THE WORKING
    OF POLITICIZED ECONOMIES. PUBLIC CHOICE THEORY HAS PROVIDED
    AN INTELLECTUAL FOUNDATION ENABLING PEOPLE TO UNDERSTAND
    WHAT THEY HAVE OBSERVED. THE IDEAS OF PUBLIC CHOICE THEORY
    MUST BE EXTENDED TO THE EXAMINATION OF ALTERNATIVE SETS OF
    CONSTRAINTS THAT MAY CHANNEL THE PRIVATE UTILITY-MAXIMIZING
    BEHAVIOR OF POLITICAL FUNCTIONARIES IN THE DIRECTION OF THE
    GENERAL INTEREST.

01859 BUCHANAN, P.G.; LOONEY, R.
    RELATIVE MILITARIZATION AND ITS IMPACT ON PUBLIC POLICY
    BUDGETARY SHIFTS IN ARGENTINA, 1963-1982
    AVAILABLE FROM NTIS, NO. AD-A199 953/1/GAR, JUL 88, 77.
        IN SPITE OF A GROWING LITERATURE ON THE SUBJECT,
    ANALYSES OF THE POLICY IMPACT OF MILITARY REGIMES IN LATIN
    AMERICAN REMAIN INCONCLUSIVE. EMPIRICAL ANALYSES HAVE
    NEITHER CONFIRMED OR DENIED THE PROPOSITION THAT MILITARY
    REGIMES HAVE A DECIDED, AND OFTEN NEGATIVE IMPACT ON PUBLIC
    POLICY. IN LIGHT OF THAT, THIS ESSAY ATTEMPTS TO TEST THE
    RELATIVELY SIMPLE ASSUMPTION THAT IT IS THE DEGREE OF
    MILITARY CONTROL OVER THE STATE APPARATUS (I.E. THE RELATIVE
    'DEPTH' OF MILITARIZATION), RATHER THAN THE ADVENT OF A
    MILITARY BUREAUCRATIC REGIME PER SE, THAT HAS THE MOST
    INFLUENCE ON PUBLIC POLICY OUTPUTS, HERE MEASURED IN
    BUDGETARY ALLOCATIONS AT BOTH THE MACROECONOMIC AND
    MICROECONOMIC LEVELS.

01860 BUCK, E.H.; LEE, M.R.
    POLLUTION THREATS TO THE OCEANS
    CRS REVEIW, 10(7) (AUG 89), 13-14.
        INCREASING OCEAN POLLUTION POSES MOUNTING THREATS TO
    MARINE LIFE AND THE QUALITY OF HUMAN LIFE WORLDWIDE.
    INTERNATIONAL EFFORTS TO CONTROL POLLUTION OF THE SEAS HAVE
    BEGUN, BUT MANY UNSOLVED PROBLEMS AND CHALLENGES REMAIN.

01861 BUCKLEY, R.; CROSS, M.; ROBERTS, J.
    JAPAN
    SOUTH, (106) (AUG 89), 81-86.
        OVERSEAS DEVELOPMENT AID IS NOW FIRMLY ESTABLISHED AS
    ONE OF THE BASIC TENETS OF JAPANESE GLOBAL DIPLOMACY, BUT
    THE AVERAGE JAPANESE CITIZEN PAYS LITTLE ATTENTION TO THE
    FOREIGN AID ISSUE. MOST JAPANESE ARE TOO ABSORBED IN
    DOMESTIC POLITICAL INTRIGUE TO SCRUTINIZE THE GOVERNMENT'S
    US$9.1 BILLION OVERSEAS AID PROGRAM.

01862 BUCKLEY, W.F. JR.
    ABORTION: THE DEBATE: WHERE WE STAND
    NATIONAL REVIEW, 61(24) (DEC 89), 25-26.
        THIS INTRODUCTION TO THE COVER STORY AND CONTENDS THAT
    THE BASIC QUESTION IN REGARDS TO ABORTION IS: IS IT POSSIBLE
    TO PRESCIND A DEEPLY FELT MORAL COMMITMENT FROM AN
    INSTITUTIONAL POLITICAL VEHICLE, AND REMAIN LOYAL TO THAT
    POLITICAL VEHICLE? IT EXAMINES THE VIEW POINTS OF ESSAYISTS
    MCGURN AND VAN DEN HAAG, AND POINTS OUT THAT NEITHER ONE OF
    THEM CLARIFIES THE QUESTION OF WHAT THE CORRECT ROAD FOR THE

REPUBLICAN PARTY SHOULD BE. HE CONCLUDES THAT COMITY, EXCEPT
IN OUTRAGEOUS EXTREMES, IS NECESSARY TO THE COMMONHEAL.

01863 BUCKLEY, W.F. JR.
    HOW TO END THE COLD WAR
    NATIONAL REVIEW, 110(21) (NOV 89), 44.
        WM.F. BUCKLEY JR. MAKES A PROPOSAL TO END THE ARMS RACE.
    HE EXAMINES THE COLD WAR IDEOLOGY IN TERMS OF PRESENT USSR
    ECONOMICS AND CONCLUDES THAT ONLY ONE THING WILL SAVE THE
    SOVIET UNION ECONOMICALLY, AND THAT IS HARD CURRENCY. HE
    ALSO EXAMINES SOVIET MILITARY POWER WHICH IS GREATER THAN IT
    HAS EVER BEEN. HE PROPOSES THE PURCHASE BY THE UNITED STATES
    OF SOVIET MILITARY EQUIPMENT, NUCLEAR AND NON-NUCLEAR FOR
    $100 BILLION PER YEAR FOR THE NEXT THREE YEARS AND GIVES HIS
    REASONS FOR THE PROPOSAL.

01864 BUDD, A.P.; CHRISTODOULAKIS, N.; HOLLY, S.; LEVINE, P.
    STABILISATION POLICY IN BRITAIN
    AVAILABLE FROM NTIS, NO. PB89-192827/GAR, NOV 87, 69.
        SINCE THE CONFERENCE MARKS THE 10TH ANNIVERSARY OF THE
    PREVIOUS DEMAND MANAGEMENT CONFERENCE THE AUTHORS HAVE TAKEN
    THE OPPORTUNITY TO RE-EXAMINE THE CONDITION OF THE ECONOMY
    AND THE ROLE OF MACROECONOMIC MODELS IN ANALYZING IT TEN
    YEARS AGO. PART 1 OF THE PAPER DISCUSSES THE LONDON BUSINESS
    SCHOOL (LBS) CONTRIBUTION TO THE 1977 CONFERENCE AND EVENTS
    OF 1978 TO 1981. PART 2 DESCRIBES BRIEFLY THE SUBSEQUENT
    DEVELOPMENTS AND THE CURRENT STATE OF THE LBS MODEL. PART 3
    DISCUSSES THE BALL REPORT AND RECENT DEVELOPMENTS IN OPTIMAL
    CONTROL. IN PART 4 THE AUTHORS APPLY OPTIMAL CONTROL TO THE
    LBS MODEL. THEY DEVISE OPTIMAL POLICIES FOR THE PERIOD 1987
    TO 1995 UNDER ALTERNATIVE WELFARE LOSS FUNCTIONS AND EXAMINE
    IN PARTICULAR THE PROBLEM OF TIME INCONSISTENCY AND THE
    DERIVATION OF ROBUST BUT SIMPLE CONTROL RULES.

01865 BUDICH, W.F.W.
    THE POLITICAL LIFE OF THE NATIONAL INSTITUTE OF MENTAL
    HEALTH: A STUDY OF THE BUREAU WITHIN THE SUB-GOVERNMENT OF
    POLICY MAKING FOR PSYCHIC WELL-BEING
    DISSERTATION ABSTRACTS INTERNATIONAL, 49(10) (APR 89),
    3150-A.
        THE AUTHOR REVIEWS SOME GENERALIZATIONS ABOUT POLICY-
    MAKING SUBSYSTEMS OR TRIANGLES. SAMPLE TRIANGLES ARE
    DESCRIBED TO ILLUSTRATE THEIR PATTERN. THEN THE NATIONAL
    INSTITUTE OF MENTAL HEALTH (NIMH), WHICH LIES WITHIN THE
    TRIANGLE OF POLICY MAKING FOR PSYCHIC WELL-BEING, IS
    COMPARED TO THE ESTABLISHED PATTERN. THE THREE MAJOR NIMH
    ENVIRONMENT COMPONENTS ARE DISCUSSED ONE-BY-ONE: HIGHER
    POLITICAL AUTHORITY, CONGRESS, AND THE ORGANIZED
    CONSTITUENCY.

01866 BUDNER, D.
    FACING THE WALL: THE POLITICS OF WOMEN AND PRAYER
    NEW OUTLOOK, 32(6-7 (292-293)) (JUN 89), 25-26.
        SINCE DECEMBER 1988 A GROUP OF ISRAELI WOMEN FROM
    VARIOUS RELIGIOUS BACKGROUNDS HAS PRAYED TOGETHER AT THE
    WESTERN WALL IN JERUSALEM. THE RESISTANCE AND CRITICISM THE
    GROUP HAS ENCOUNTERED SHED LIGHT ON CERTAIN FUNDAMENTAL
    ISSUES DIVIDING ISRAELI SOCIETY: FREEDOM OF RELIGIOUS
    EXPRESSION, EXTREMIST VIOLENCE, WOMAN'S ROLE IN JEWISH LAW
    AND TRADITION, JURISDICTION OVER HOLY SITES, AND THE
    RELATIONSHIP BETWEEN JEWISH RELIGIOUS LAW AND THE CIVIL LAW.

01867 BUDNER, M.
    THE EMPOWERMENT OF WOMEN: ISRAEL WOMEN'S NETWORK
    NEW OUTLOOK, 32(6-7 (292-293)) (JUN 89), 40-41.
        THE CREATION OF A JUST SOCIETY IN ISRAEL, IN WHICH MEN
    AND WOMEN ARE EQUALLY INVOLVED AT ALL LEVELS OF POWER, WAS
    THE IMPETUS THAT LED A GROUP OF PROFESSIONAL WOMEN,
    REPRESENTING A WIDE RANGE OF THE ISRAELI POLITICAL SPECTRUM,
    TO FOUND THE ISRAEL WOMEN'S NETWORK IN 1984. THE
    ORGANIZATION'S GOAL IS TO REMIND THE PUBLIC OF THE IDEA OF
    EQUALITY FOR ALL CITIZENS EMBODIED IN ISRAEL'S DECLARATION
    OF INDEPENDENCE AND TO PUT IT INTO ACTION.

01868 BUEHRING, G.
    NEW NEGOTIATIONS ON CONVENTIONAL FORCES AND CONFIDENCE-
    AND SECURITY-BUILDING MEASURES IN EUROPE
    DISARMAMENT, XII(2) (SUM 89), 11-17.
        EFFORTS TO CUT CONVENTIONAL FORCES AND ARMAMENTS IN THE
    AREA FROM THE ATLANTIC TO THE URALS HAVE BECOME A CENTRAL
    THEME IN EUROPEAN POLITICS. EUROPE IS BRISTLING WITH ARMED
    FORCES AND CONVENTIONAL WEAPONS OF A MAGNITUDE UNPRECEDENTED
    IN ANY PREVIOUS PEACE-TIME ERA. THIS IMPOSES ENORMOUS
    ECONOMIC BURDENS ON NATO AND THE WARSAW PACT. IN ADDITION TO
    THE OBVIOUS NEED TO REDUCE THESE ECONOMIC BURDENS,
    CONVENTIONAL DISARMAMENT IS NEEDED TO PREVENT REDUCTIONS IN
    NUCLEAR ARMS FROM BEING OFFSET BY GREATER ARSENALS OF
    CONVENTIONAL WEAPONS AND TO GUARD AGAINST A HIGHER RISK OF
    CONVENTIONAL WAR IN EUROPE FOUGHT WITH INTELLIGENT WEAPONS
    ON A COMPUTERIZED BATTLEFIELD.

01869 BUGAJSKI, J.
    NICARAGUA'S SANDINISTA PROJECT: IDEOLOGY, POWER BUILDING,
    AND SOCIAL MANIPULATION

POLITICAL COMMUNICATION AND PERSUASION, 5(4) (1988), 249-264.
THIS PAPER EXAMINES THE IDEOLOGY OF THE NICARAGUAN SANDINISTA NATIONAL LIBERATION FRONT (FSLN) THROUGH AN EVALUATION OF OFFICIAL DECLARATIONS, PUBLISHED OBJECTIVES AND ANALYSES, STATED OBJECTIVES, AND PROGRAMS PURSUED. SINCE ITS SEIZURE OF POWER IN 1979, THE FSLN'S EFFORTS TO "LENINIZE" THE COUNTRY HAVE OCCURRED GRADUALLY AND OFTEN HAVE BEEN CAMOUFLAGED. THE PAPER DESCRIBES THE SANDINISTAS' USE OF "MAGNET" AND "SALAMI" TACTICS TO ATTRACT USEFUL COLLABORATORS AND RESTRICT THE INFLUENCE OF RIVAL POLITICAL ORGANIZATIONS. WHILE THE FSLN OSTENSIBLY HAS TOLERATED OTHER PARTIES' PARTICIPATION IN THE NATIONAL ASSEMBLY, THE SANDINISTAS IN REALITY HAVE REQUIRED SUPPORT FOR FSLN PROGRAMS AND HAVE INCREASED THEIR OWN NUMBERS IN THE ASSEMBLY AND GAINED CONTROL OF THE TOP POSITIONS IN ALL STATE INSTITUTIONS, MINISTRIES, AND THE EXECUTIVE AND LEGISLATIVE BRANCHES OF GOVERNMENT. ORGANIZATIONAL CHANGES HAVE BEEN GEARED TOWARD CENTRALIZATION AND HIERARCHIZATION. AS A RESULT, THE NICARAGUAN STATE HAS BEEN FULLY SUBORDINATED TO THE FSLN. ALTHOUGH THE SANDINISTAS OFFICIALLY ESPOUSE A "MIXED" ECONOMY WITH SOME ROOM FOR A PRIVATE AGRICULTURAL SECTOR AS WELL AS TOKEN POLITICAL OPPOSITION, THE AUTHOR CONCLUDES THAT THEY ARE LIKELY TO CONTINUE ON THEIR COURSE OF INCREASING CENTRALIZED CONTROL OF VIRTUALLY ALL ASPECTS OF PUBLIC LIFE.

01870 BUITER, W.; KLETZER, K.; SRINIVASAN, T.N.
SOME THOUGHTS ON THE BRADY PLAN: PUTTING A FOURTH LEG ON THE DONKEY?
WORLD DEVELOPMENT, 17(10) (OCT 89), 1661-1664.
THE FAILURE OF THE BAKER PLAN TO PRODUCE ANY SIGNIFICANT IMPROVEMENT IN THE CIRCUMSTANCES OF THE HIGHLY INDEBTED MIDDLE-INCOME COUNTRIES HAS NOT SURPRISING. THE PLAN COULD BE READILY DESCRIBED AS A THREE-LEGGED DONKEY. SINCE ONE LEG HAS TOO SHORT, IT IS HARDLY SUPRISING THAT IT DID NOT GO VERY FAR. THE BRADY PLAN COULD BE VIEWED AS AN ATTEMPT TO CORRECT THE FACILITIES OF THE UNSUCCESSFUL BAKER PLAN.

01871 BUKOVSKY, V.
WHO RESISTS GORBACHEV ?
WASHINGTON QUARTERLY, 12(1) (WIN 89), 5-19.
CONTRARY TO POPULAR BELIEF, NO ONE THREATENS GORBACHEV'S POSITION WITHIN THE KREMLIN. SINCE COMING TO POWER IN MARCH 1985, HE REPLACED ALL BUT 5 OF THE 14 POLITBURO MEMBERS, ALL BUT 2 OF THE 6 ALTERNATE MEMBERS, ALL BUT 3 OF THE 12 SECRETARIES OF THE CENTRAL COMMITTEE, AND AT LEAST HALF OF THE CENTRAL COMMITTEE MEMBERS. SPEAKING RECENTLY TO SOVIET NEWS EDITORS, GORBACHEV MENTIONED THAT HE HAS CHANGED 66 PERCENT FO ALL MINISTERS, 61 PERCENT OF ALL REGIONAL PARTY BOSSES AND CHAIRMEN OF THE REGIONAL SOVIETS, AND 63 PERCENT OF ALL DISTRICT PARTY SECRETARIES. AFTER A YOUNG GERMAN PILOT LANDED IN RED SQUARE IN 1987, HE REPLACED MOST OF THE TOP BRASS. IN SHORT, GORBACHEV MUST HAVE AN OVERWHELMING MAJORITY IN EVERY DECISION-MAKING BODY IN THE COUNTRY.

01872 BULARH, G.
THE SELF-SUPPORTING PRINCIPLE IN A FOREIGN TRADE ASSOCIATION
FOREIGN TRADE, 3 (1988), 30-33.
THIS ARTICLE ANALYSES THE NEED FOR PLACING FOREIGN TRADE ORGANIZATIONS ON A FULL SELF-SUPPORTING BASIS FOR RAISING THE EFFECTIVENESS OF USSR'S EXTERNAL ECONOMIC TIES. IT TRACES ECONOMIC DEVELOPMENT FROM THE TIME OF LENIN, THROUGH THE LATE SEVENTIES WHEN FOREIGN TRADE ASSOCIATIONS FIRST CHANGED OVER TO A SELF-SUPPORTING BASIS TO THE PRESENT. IT EXAMINES THE CURRENT FIVE YEAR STRATEGY FOR ECONOMIC AND SOCIAL DEVELOPMENT AND LISTS GUIDELINES FOR DEVELOPING FOREIGN ASSOCIATIONS.

01873 BULL, M.
PERESTROIKA IS CATCHING: THE ITALIAN COMMUNIST PARTY ELECTS A NEW LEADER
JOURNAL OF COMMUNIST STUDIES, 5(1) (MAR 89), 79-82.
THE ARTICLE EXAMINES THE EVENTS THAT SURROUNDED THE RESIGNATION OF ITALIAN COMMUNIST PARTY (PCI) LEADER, ALESSANDRO NATTA. ALTHOUGH MANY REASONS COMBINED TO INFLUENCE NATTA'S DECISION, THE DECLINE OF THE PARTY'S ELECTORAL SUCCES AND POPULAR SUPPORT ARE KEY ELEMENTS. THE ARTICLE ALSO OUTLINES THE CHALLENGES THAT NATTA'S SUCCESSOR, ACHILLE OCHETTO, WILL FACE.

01874 BULLERT, G.
THE CATHOLIC BISHOPS' POLICY ON STRATEGIC DEFENSE: A CASE OF MORAL DISARMAMENT
JOURNAL OF SOCIAL, POLITICAL AND ECONOMIC STUDIES, 14(3) (FAL 89), 283-298.
ON JUNE 25, 1988, THE UNITED STATES CATHOLIC BISHOPS APPROVED A POLICY STATEMENT ON NUCLEAR STRATEGY ENTITLED "BUILDING PEACE: A PASTORAL REFLECTION ON THE RESPONSE TO 'THE CHALLENGE OF PEACE.'" IN THIS ESSAY, THE AUTHOR EXAMINES THE BISHOPS' CURRENT STANCE ON DISARMAMENT AND SECURITY ISSUES, INCLUDING THE STRATEGIC DEFENSE INITIATIVE.

01875 BULLOCK, C.S. III
CONTEMPORARY POLITICS IN THE AMERICAN SOUTH
JOURNAL OF AMERICAN AND CANADIAN STUDIES, (3) (SPR 89), 89-118.
THIS PAPER DETAILS THE CHANGES IN THE AMERICAN SOUTH THAT HAVE OCCURRED SINCE 1949 AND WILL OFFER EXPLANATIONS FOR THOSE CHANGES. THE PRESENTATION INCLUDES BOTH REGIONAL DATA AS WELL AS STATISTICS ON INDIVIDUAL STATES THAT COMPRISE THE ELEVEN-STATE REGION. THIS PAPER TRACES THE SHIFT IN THE ROLE PLAYED BY THE BLACKS FROM PARIAH TO KINGMAKER AND THE TRANSFORMATION OF THE GOP FROM INSIGNIFICANCE TO FULL-FLEDGED COMPETITOR.

01876 BULLOCK, C.S. III
SYMBOLICS OR SUBSTANCE: A CRITIQUE OF THE AT-LARGE ELECTION CONTROVERSY
STATE AND LOCAL GOVERNMENT REVIEW, 21(3) (FAL 89), 91-99.
THIS ARTICLE REVIEWS THE EFFORTS TO ELIMINATE AT-LARGE OR MULTIMEMBER ELECTION DISTRICTS AND REPLACE THEM WITH SINGLE-MEMBER DISTRICTS. THE FIXATION ON DEMANDING SINGLE-MEMBER DISTRICTS RESTS ON TWO ASSUMPTIONS: FIRST, THAT WHITE ELECTED OFFICIALS CANNOT OR WILL NOT REPRESENT BLACK INTERESTS AND, SECOND, THAT WHITES WILL NOT VOTE FOR BLACK CANDIDATES. THE REASONABLENESS OF THESE ASSUMPTIONS IS EXPLORED HERE. THE ARTICLE ALSO EXAMINES WHAT HAS HAPPENED IN SOME HEAVILY BLACK SINGLE-MEMBER DISTRICTS AND SPECULATES ON THE DEGREE TO WHICH BLACK POLICY CONCERNS WILL BE RECEIVED BY COLLEGIAL BODIES WHOSE SINGLE BLACK MEMBER HAS A CONSTITUENCY THAT INCLUDES AN OVERWHELMING SHARE OF THE BLACKS IN THE JURISDICTION. IN ADDITION, RECENT CHANGES IN THE DEMANDS OF CRITICS OF AT-LARGE ELECTIONS WHICH RESULT FROM AN INABILITY TO CREATE PREDOMINANTLY MINORITY SINGLE-MEMBER SEATS ARE REVIEWED.

01877 BULMER-THOMAS, V.
BRITAIN AND LATIN AMERICA: CLOSER IN THE 1990'S?
WORLD TODAY, 45(11) (NOV 89), 198-201.
IF THEY ARE TO BE IMPROVED, BRITISH RELATIONS WITH LATIN AMERICA CAN REST NEITHER ON A SENTIMENTAL APPEAL TO THE PAST NOR EXCLUSIVELY ON HUMANITARIAN GROUNDS. THE RELATIONSHIP WILL HAVE TO REST ON COMMERCIAL FOUNDATIONS, ALTHOUGH THERE IS PLENTY OF SCOPE FOR IMPROVEMENT IN CULTURAL AND POLITICAL RELATIONS AS WELL.

01878 BULMER, S.; PATERSON, W.
WEST GERMANY'S ROLE IN EUROPE: "MAN-MOUNTAIN" OR SEMIGULLIVER"?
JOURNAL OF COMMON MARKET STUDIES, XXVIII(2) (DEC 89), 95-118.
FOLLOWING WORLD WAR II, THE ALLIED POWERS IMPOSED A SET OF DUTIES DESIGNED TO RESTRICT AND PREVENT ANY ABUSE OF AUTONOMOUS WEST GERMAN POWER. TODAY, THE SAME ALLIES ARE BEGINNING, PARADOXICALLY, TO SEEK A GREATER WEST GERMAN ROLE IN A RANGE OF ECONOMIC AND MILITARY ORGANIZATIONS. BUT THOSE CALLING FOR WEST GERMAN LEADERSHIP, WHETHER IN THE EUROPEAN COMMUNITY OR IN THE INTERNATIONAL ECONOMY, ARE REGARDED AS INSENSITIVE IN BONN. THIS ARTICLE EXAMINES HOW THIS SITUATION, WHICH STRIKES AT THE HEART OF WEST GERMANY'S BROAD EUROPEAN POLICY, HAS COME ABOUT. IN DOING SO, IT USES SOME OF THE IMAGERY OF JONATHAN SWIFT'S "GULLIVER'S TRAVELS."

01879 BUNCE, V.
EASTERN EUROPE: IS THE PARTY OVER?
PS: POLITICAL SCIENCE AND POLITICS, XXII(2) (JUN 89), 233-241.
THE AUTHOR DISCUSSES PRESSURES FOR AND AGAINST REFORM IN EASTERN EUROPE, GORBACHEV'S GOALS FOR EASTERN EUROPE, AND THE LIKELY IMPACT OF GLASNOST AND PERESTROIKA IN THE REGION.

01880 BUNCH, B.S.
VARIATIONS IN STATE GOVERNMENT CAPITAL SPENDING AND DEBT PRACTICES: AN EMPIRICAL ANALYSIS
DISSERTATION ABSTRACTS INTERNATIONAL, 50(4) (OCT 89), 1085-A.
THIS DISSERTATION CONSISTS OF THREE RELATED ESSAYS THAT ANALYZE FACTORS THAT MAY INFLUENCE VARIATIONS IN STATE GOVERNMENT CAPITAL SPENDING AND DEBT PRACTICES. THIS RESEARCH FOCUSES ON ANALYZING TO WHAT EXTENT, IF ANY, INSTITUTIONAL FACTORS IMPACT THE LEVEL OF CAPITAL SPENDING AND THE AMOUNT OF DEBT ISSUED BY STATE GOVERNMENTS.

01881 BUNDY, J.
JOHN C. CALHOUN'S REFLECTIONS ON "FEDERALIST" NO. TEN: THE CONCURRENT MAJORITY AS A FOUNDATION FOR AMERICAN PLURALIST THEORY
DISSERTATION ABSTRACTS INTERNATIONAL, 48(10) (APR 88), 2715-A.
THE DISSERTATION ADDRESSES THE QUESTION OF JOHN C. CALHOUN'S ROLE IN FORMULATING A SCHEME DESCRIBING MODERN AMERICAN POLITICS. THE THESIS IS THAT CALHOUN FOUND THE CONCEPT OF THE EXTENDED REPUBLIC AS A SOLUTION TO MAJORITY TYRANNY TO BE INADAQUETE AT LEAST AND DANGEROUS TO LIBERTY AT WORST.

01882 BUNKER, D.
TOPSY-TURVY
INDIA TODAY, XIV(5) (MAR 89), 35.
ONE WAY TO RESOLVE THE PUBLIC DILEMMA REGARDING THE
CHOICE BETWEEN THE CONGRESS (I) AND THE JANATA DAL IN
UPCOMING ELECTIONS IS TO HAVE A TELEVISED DEBATE. THIS
SATIRIC ESSAY DESCRIBES HOW SUCH A DEBATE MIGHT TURN OUT.

01883 BUNKER, S.
THE ETERNAL CONQUEST
NACLA REPORT ON THE AMERICAS, XXIII(1) (MAY 89), 27-35.
BRAZIL'S DEVELOPMENT STRATEGY TREATS THE AMAZON AS A
PANACEA FOR DEBT AND DEFICIT, AS A REGION WHOSE RICHES
SHOULD BE EXPLOITED QUICKLY AND CARELESSLY. MINING FOR
EXPORT, PARTICULARLY OF THE WORLD'S LARGEST IRON DEPOSITS AT
CARAJAS, IS AT THE CORE OF THAT STRATEGY, WHICH PROMISES TO
LEAVE THE REGION EVER POORER BOTH ECOLOGICALLY AND SOCIALLY.

01884 BUNLE, V.
DECLINE OF A REGIONAL HEGEMON: THE GORBACHEV REGIME AND
REFORM IN EASTERN EUROPE
EASTERN EUROPEAN POLITICS AND SOCIETIES, 3(2) (SPR 89),
235-267.
THE ARTICLE ATTEMPTS TO ANALYZE MIKHAIL GORBACHEV'S
IMPACT ON EASTERN EUROPE. IT OUTLINES GORBACHEV'S DIAGNOSIS
OF EAST EUROPEAN PROBLEMS AND HIS POLICIES DESIGNED TO
REMEDY THEM. IT ALSO ASSESSES THE LIKELIHOOD THAT GORBACHEV
WILL SUCCEED IN CREATING A BLOC COMPOSED OF STABLE AND
ECONOMICALLY PRODUCTIVE STATES. IT CONCLUDES THAT ALTHOUGH
GORBACHEV'S RESTRAINTS ARE SIZABLE, HIS ASSETS ARE ALSO
CONSIDERABLE; THEREFORE, THE CASE FOR REFORM STRONGER THAN
WOULD BE OTHERWISE BE THOUGHT.

01885 BUNZEL, J. H.
AFFIRMATIVE-ACTION ADMISSIONS: HOW IT "WORKS" AT UC
BERKELEY
PUBLIC INTEREST, 93 (FAL 88), 111-129.
THIS ARTICLE EXAMINES THE PERFORMANCE OF THE AFFIRMATIVE-
ACTION ETHNIC GROUPS BERKELEY HAS RECRUITED, AND THEN
ANALYSES SOME OF THE RESULTS AND REACTIONS TO BERKELEY'S
POLICIES. THE GOAL WAS TO ENROLL AND ACHIEVE A BALANCE AMONG
UNIVERSITY STUDENTS AND GRADUATES COMPARABLE TO THE ETHNIC,
GENDER, AND INCOME DISTRIBUTION OF CALIFORNIA'S HIGH SCHOOL
GRADUATES.

01886 BUO, S. K.
STRENGTHENING AFRICA'S VOICE
AFRICA REPORT, 34(3) (MAY 89), 51-54.
CREATED TO MAXIMIZE THE CONTINENT'S INFLUENCE IN THE
INTERNATIONAL ARENA, THE OAU HAS SEEN ITS AUTHORITY ERODED
BY THE GROWING INVOLVEMENT OF FOREIGN POWERS IN AFRICA'S
POLITICAL AND ECONOMIC CRISES. REVITALIZING THE ORGANIZATION
AND MAXIMIZING AFRICA'S VOICE ON THE WORLD SCENE SHOULD BE
PARAMOUNT IN CHOOSING A NEW SECRETARY-GENERAL.

01887 BURAWOY, M.
MARXISM WITHOUT MICRO-FOUNDATIONS
SOCIALIST REVIEW, 19(2) (APR 89), 53-86.
THE AUTHOR EXAMINES THE "ANALYTICAL MARXISM" OF ADAM
PRZEWORSKI AND FINDS IT WANTING. ANALYTICAL MARXISTS SEIZE
ON THE LOGICAL FLAWS AND UNSUBSTANTIATED ASSERTIONS OF
ORTHODOX MARXISM TO JUSTIFY ITS WHOLESALE RENOVATION.
HOWEVER, WITHOUT MICRO-FOUNDATIONS, PRZEWORSKI BEGINS BY
CRITICIZING CLASSICAL MARXISM, BUT ENDS UP REPRODUCING
PRECISELY THOSE ASPECTS OF ORTHODOXY WHICH ANALYTICAL
MARXISM CLAIMS TO ABANDON.

01888 BURAWOY, M.
REFLECTIONS ON THE CLASS CONSCIOUSNESS OF HUNGARIAN
STEELWORKERS
POLITICS AND SOCIETY, 17(1) (MAR 89), 1-34.
THE AUTHOR ARGUES THAT THE PRODUCTION REGIMES OF STATE
SOCIALISM ENGENDER DISSENT. LIKE THE CONSENT ORGANIZED UNDER
CAPITALISM, DISSENT TOWARD STATE SOCIALISM IS NOT SIMPLY A
MENTAL ORIENTATION; IT IS EMBEDDED IN DISTINCTIVE AND
COMPULSORY RITUALS OF EVERYDAY LIFE. MOREOVER, UNDER CERTAIN
CONDITIONS, DISSENT LEADS WORKERS TO STRUGGLE FOR THE
TRANSFORMATION OF STATE SOCIALISM TOWARD DEMOCRATIC
SOCIALISM. THIS NEGATIVE CLASS CONSCIOUSNESS PRODUCED BY THE
STATE SOCIALIST REGIME OF PRODUCTION PROVIDES THE RAW
MATERIAL FOR A POSITIVE CLASS CONSCIOUSNESS, A VISION OF AN
ALTERNATIVE ORDER THAT CAN BE FORGED ONLY IN CLASS
MOBILIZATION.

01889 BURAWOY, M.
SHOULD WE GIVE UP ON SOCIALISM?
SOCIALIST REVIEW, 19(1) (JAN 89), 57-74.
THIS ARTICLE OFFERS A CRITIQUE OF SAM BOWLES AND HERB
GINTIS' MILESTONE WORK, DEMOCRACY AND CAPITALISM. THE AUTHOR
CLAIMS THAT PRODUCTION POLITICS IS BOTH RELATIVELY
AUTONOMOUS AND OF VITAL IMPORTANCE, HOWEVER, RECENT MARXIST
THEORY DISSOLVES EITHER THE AUTONOMY OR IMPORTANCE OF WORK-
PLACE CONTESTATIONS. BOWLES AND GINTIS, HE CLAIMS, SACRIFICE
AN ANALYSIS OF THE UNIQUE AND HISTORICAL CHARACTER OF WHAT

THE AUTHOR CALLS "PRODUCTION REGIMES." THE RESULT IS A
REDUCTION OF WORKPLACE POLITICS TO A STRUGGLE FOR
DEMOCRATIZATION, AND A LACK OF APPRECIATION FOR THE
SOCIALIST CHARACTER OF THE STRUGGLES FOR DEMOCRACY OCCURING
IN STATE SOCIALIST SOCIETIES.

01890 BURAWOY, M.
THE FUTURE OF SOCIALISM IN EASTERN EUROPE
SOCIALISM AND DEMOCRACY, (FAL 89), 43-48.
THIS ARTICLE EXPLORES THE FUTURE IN EASTERN EUROPE BY
ANALYZING THE WORKING CLASS CREATED BY SOCIALISM WHICH NOW
WILL TOLERATE SO MUCH INSECURITY. IT DETAILS THE TEMPORARY
RAISE IN THE STANDARD OF LIVING PROVIDED THROUGH SOCIALISM
AND THE RAPID DETERIORATION OF LIVING CONDITIONS AS
SOCIALISM WAS UNABLE TO LIVE UP TO ITS PROMISES, HOWEVER, IT
CONCLUDES THAT NEITHER FREE DEMOCRATS NOR SOCIAL DEMOCRATS,
NEITHER POLISH SOCIOLOGISTS NOR AMERICAN POLITICAL
SCIENTISTS CAN BURY SOCIALISM. IN THE FINAL ANALYSIS ONLY
WORKERS CAN DO THAT AND THEY MAY NOT WANT TO.

01891 BURDEKIN, R.C.K.
PREOBRAZHENSKY'S THEORY OF PRIMITIVE SOCIALIST ACCUMULATION
JOURNAL OF CONTEMPORARY ASIA, 19(3) (1989), 297-307.
IN THIS PAPER, THE POTENTIAL VIABILITY OF
PREOBRAZHENSKY'S LAW OF PRIMITIVE SOCIALIST. ACCUMULATION IS
REASSESSED BY FOCUSING ON THE INTERRELATIONSHIPS BETWEEN
SAVING AND CONSUMPTION ACROSS THE INDUSTRIAL AND AGRARIAN
SECTORS, ALTERNATIVES TO THE PRIMITIVE SOCIALIST
ACCUMULATION PROCESS ARE ALSO CONSIDERED, UTILIZING THE TWO
SECTOR FRAMEWORK DEVELOPED BY KALECKI (1979). ONE OF THE KEY
ISSUES IS THE TRANSFORMATION OF THE RELATIONS OF PRODUCTION
WITHIN THE AGRARIAN SECTOR AND THE INTERPLAY WITH CAPITALIST
MODES OF PRODUCTION DURING THE PROCESS OF ECONOMIC
DEVELOPMENT.

01892 BURG, S.L.; BERBAUM, M.L.
COMMUNITY, INTEGRATION, AND STABILITY IN MULTINATIONAL
YUGOSLAVIA
AMERICAN POLITICAL SCIENCE REVIEW, 83(2) (JUN 89), 535-556.
IN 1981, IN RESPONSE TO THE CENSUS QUESTION ON
NATIONALITY, MORE CITIZENS OF YUGOSLAVIA CHOSE "YUGOSLAV" IN
PLACE OF AN ETHNIC IDENTITY THAN EVER BEFORE. THE AUTHORS
ARGUE THAT THIS IS EVIDENCE OF SHARED POLITICAL IDENTITY AND
ANALYZE THE AGGREGATE DATA ON THE LEVEL OF SOCIAL AND
MATERIAL DEVELOPMENT, POLITICAL SOCIALIZATION, AND INTER-
ETHNIC CONTACT.

01893 BURG, S.L.
THE SOVIET UNION'S NATIONALITIES QUESTION
CURRENT HISTORY, 88(540) (OCT 89), 341-344, 359-362.
GORBACHEV'S ECONOMIC REFORMS HAVE SIGNIFICANTLY
INCREASED SOCIAL AND ECONOMIC HARDSHIPS WITHOUT PRODUCING
MANY MATERIAL BENEFITS. THIS HAS INCREASED THE LEVEL OF
DISSATISFACTION AMONG THE SOVIET PEOPLE. AT THE SAME TIME,
GORBACHEV'S POLITICAL REFORMS HAVE CREATED IDEAL CONDITIONS
FOR THE MOBILIZATION OF ETHNIC IDENTITY BY ACTIVISTS INTENT
ON REDRESSING LONG-HELD GRIEVANCES.

01894 BURGELMAN, J.
POLITICAL PARTIES AND THEIR IMPACT ON PUBLIC SERVICE
BROADCASTING IN BELGIUM: ELEMENTS FROM A POLITICAL-
SOCIOLOGICAL APPROACH
MEDIA, CULTURE, AND SOCIETY, 11(2) (APR 89), 167-193.
SINCE THE 1960'S, THE RELATIONSHIP OF THE POLITICAL
PARTIES IN BELGIUM TO PUBLIC SERVICE BROADCASTING, AND THE
IMPACT OF THE FORMER ON THE LATTER, HAS FREQUENTLY BEEN
DISCUSSED IN THE PRESS AND IN PUBLIC DEBATES. THE BASIC
CONCLUSION OF THE RESEARCH ON THE SUBJECT SEEMS TO BE AS
FOLLOWS: POLITICS CERTAINLY DO INFLUENCE BROADCASTING; FROM
TIME TO TIME, PROBLEMS DO OCCUR BETWEEN THESE TWO
ANTAGONISTIC WORLDS; BUT ON THE WHOLE ONE SHOULD NOT BOTHER
VERY MUCH ABOUT IT. THE TENSIONS THAT OCCUR BETWEEN THE TWO
ARE PART OF THE GAME, WHATEVER THAT GAME MAY BE. THIS ESSAY
CHALLENGES THE APPARENT CONSENSUS IN THE STATE OF RESEARCH
ON THE TOPIC.

01895 BURGIN, E.K.
REPRESENTATIVES' INVOLVEMENT IN FOREIGN POLICYMAKING: THE
INFLUENCE OF SUPPORTIVE CONSTITUENTS
DISSERTATION ABSTRACTS INTERNATIONAL, 50(2) (AUG 89),
533-A.
THE AUTHOR ANALYZES KEY COMPONENTS OF CONGRESSIONAL
POLICYMAKING, FOCUSING ON THE INVOLVEMENT OF LEGISLATORS AND
THE INFLUENCES AFFECTING THAT INVOLVEMENT. SHE ARGUES THAT A
REPRESENTATIVE'S PERCEPTIONS OF THE OPINIONS, DESIRES, AND
POTENTIAL REACTIONS OF SUPPORTIVE CONSTITUENTS SUPPLY THE
PRINCIPAL INFLUENCES ON FOREIGN POLICY PARTICIPATION. SHE
UTILIZES DATA CONCERNING THE ISSUES: CONTRA AID, THE
INTERNATIONAL MONETARY ISSUES: CONTRA AID, THE INTERNATIONAL
MONETARY FUND QUOTA INCREASE, MX MISSILE FUNDING, AND U.S.
MARINES IN LEBANON.

01896 BURK, J.
DEBATING THE DRAFT IN AMERICA

ARMED FORCES AND SOCIETY, 15(3) (SPR 89), 431-448.
MILITARY CONSCRIPTION HAS ALWAYS BEEN A HOT ISSUE IN
AMERICAN POLITICS. DEBATES ABOUT CONSCRIPTION, HOWEVER, DO
NOT ALWAYS REVOLVE AROUND THE SAME ISSUES. IN THIS PA PER,
ARGUMENTS FOR AND AGAINST THE DRAFT OFFERED IN WORLD WAR II
ARE COMPARED WITH AGRUMENTS OFFERED DURING THE VIETNAM WAR.
AN IMPORTANT DIFFERENCE BETWEEN THESE ARGUMENTS IS
DOCUMENTED: WHILE ARGUMENT PRO AND CON DURING THE SECOND
WORLD WAR WAS BASED ON ASSESSMENTS OF THE DRAFT'S IMPACT ON
INDIVIDUAL CITIZENS. THIS SHIFT IN FOCUS IS EXPLAINED AS THE
RESPONSE OF BROAD SECTORS OF PUBLIC OPINION TO LONG-TERM
TRENDS IN PATTERNS OF SOCIAL INTEGRATION THAT ARE NOT
DIRECTLY RELATED TO THE IMMEDIATE PROBLEMS (OR REQUIREMENTS)
OF RAISING AN ARMY FOR WAR.

01897 BURKE, F.; BENSON, G.
WRITTEN RULES: STATE ETHICS CODES, COMMISSIONS, AND
CONFLICTS
JOURNAL OF STATE GOVERNMENT, 62(5) (SEP 89), 195-198.
IN A STRONG EFFORT TO COMBAT THE PUBLIC MISPERCEPTION OF
CONTINUOUS AND PERVASIVE FRAUD, WASTE, AND ABUSE, STATE
GOVERNMENTS HAVE STRENGTHENED THEIR STATUTES ON CONFLICT OF
INTEREST, FINANCIAL DISCLOSURE, AND "REVOLVING DOOR"
PROVISIONS. MANY STATES ARE SEEKING TO MAINTAIN THE HIGHEST
STANDARDS OF ETHICAL CONDUCT THROUGH THE INSTITUTION OF A
MODEL CODE OF ETHICS.

01898 BURKE, J.P.; GREENSTEIN, F.I.
PRESIDENTIAL PERSONALITY AND NATIONAL SECURITY LEADERSHIP:
A COMPARATIVE ANALYSIS OF VIETNAM DECISION-MAKING
INTERNATIONAL POLITICAL SCIENCE REVIEW, 10(1) (JAN 89),
73-92.
THIS ESSAY PRESENTS A FRAMEWORK FOR ANALYZING THE EFFECT
OF PRESIDENTIAL PERSONALITY ON POLICY MAKING, WHILE AVOIDING
THE FALLACY OF SIMPLY "REDUCING" THE EXPLANATION OF
PRESIDENTIAL PERFORMANCE TO THE PRESIDENT'S INDIVIDUAL
CHARACTERISTICS. USING AN APPROACH THAT SIMULTANEOUSLY TAKES
ACCOUNT OF THE LARGER POLITICAL ENVIRONMENT, AND THE
PRESIDENT'S CONSTELLATION OF IMMEDIATE ASSOCIATES (THE
"INSTITUTIONALIZED PRESIDENCY"), AS WELL AS THE PRESIDENT'S
INDIVIDUAL CHARACTERISTICS, THE AUTHORS PRESENT DATA
COMPARING PRESIDENTIAL DECISION-MAKING WITH RESPECT TO
VIETNAM IN 1954 AND 1965. ALL THREE LEVELS OF EVIDENCE MUST
BE EXAMINED TO ESTABLISH WHY THE UNITED STATES DID NOT
INJECT MILITARY FORCE IN 1954 AT THE TIME OF THE FALL OF
DIENBIENPHU AND DID IN 1965, IN THE FACE OF THE INCIPIENT
COLLAPSE OF SOUTH VIETNAM.

01899 BURKE, W.
BEYOND CHARITY AND POLITICS: A JEWISH RESPONSE TO WORLD
HUNGER
PRESENT TENSE, 16(3) (MAR 89), 35-41.
THE ARTICLE EXAMINES THE EFFORTS OF THE AMERICAN JEWISH
WORLD SERVICE, AN ORGANIZATION DESIGNED TO GIVE PEOPLE
TRAPPED BY FAMINE OR POVERTY THE MEANS TO WORK FOR
THEMSELVES. IT FOCUSES ON THE EFFORTS OF THE ORGANIZATION IN
THE PHILLIPINES, MOZAMBIQUE, AND OTHER AREAS.

01900 BURLATSKII, F.
KHRUSHCHEV: STROKES ON A POLITICAL PORTRAIT
SOVIET REVIEW, 30(3) (MAY 89), 52-66.
THE AUTHOR, WHO WAS ONCE A CLOSE ADVISER TO NIKITA
KHRUSHCHEV, RECALLS THE LATE LEADER'S OWN REFORM CAMPAIGN.
DRAWING LESSONS FROM KHRUSHCHEV'S EXPERIENCE THAT MIGHT BE
HELPFUL TO MIKHAIL GORBACHEV, BURLATSKII WARNS AGAINST A
NUMBER OF STRATEGIC ERRORS. HE SAYS THAT GORBACHEV MUST
ESPECIALLY BEWARE OF THE FOLLY OF RELYING ON PARTY AND STATE
CADRES AND ADMINISTRATIVE METHODS TO IMPLEMENT A
RESTRUCTURING OF THE SOVIET SYSTEM.

01901 BURLATSKY, F.
BREZHNEV'S WORDS
ENCOUNTER, LXXII(1) (JAN 89), 66-70.
THE AUTHOR COMPARES THE RISE TO POWER AND THE LEADERSHIP
STYLES OF LEONID BREZHNEV AND NIKITA KHRUSCHEV.

01902 BURLEY, A.
THE ONCE AND FUTURE GERMAN QUESTION
FOREIGN AFFAIRS, 68(5) (WIN 90), 65-83.
THREE DIFFERENT CONCEPTIONS OF WHAT THE GERMAN QUESTION
IS REALLY ALL ABOUT HAVE EMERGED: (1) THE TRADITIONALIST
CONCEPTION, WHICH REVOLVES AROUND THE TASK OF FREEING EAST
GERMANY FROM THE SHACKLES OF COMMUNISM, PAVING THE WAY FOR
THE FORMATION OF A GERMAN NATION-STATE; (2) THE EUROPEANIST
CONCEPTION, WHICH SEEKS TO REUNITE EUROPE SO AS TO SHIFT THE
TWO GERMAN STATES FROM THE PERIMETER OF THE EAST AND WEST
BLOCS TO THE CENTER OF A REVIVED AND INCREASINGLY IMPORTANT
ECONOMIC AND POLITICAL ENTITY; AND (3) THE UNIVERSALIST
CONCEPTION, WHICH VIEWS THE GERMAN QUESTION AS ONE THAT
TRANSCENDS ANY PARTICULAR CONFIGURATION OF THE TWO GERMAN
STATES.

01903 BURMAN, S.G.; JAYAL, N.D.
ENVIRONMENT PROTECTION AND RENEWABLE ENERGY SOURCES

SOUTH ASIA JOURNAL, 3(1/2) (JUL 89), 53-62.
THIS ARTICLE EXAMINES THE EXTENT TO WHICH HISTORY HAS
BEEN SHAPED BY HUMAN CHOICES OF ENERGY TECHNOLOGIES, AND THE
DAMAGE CAUSED BY USING NON RENEWABLE ENERGY SOURCES. IT
GIVES EXAMPLES AND PREDICTED LINKS BETWEEN THE ENERGY
CONSUMPTION PATTERN, NEW TECHNOLOGIES, AND ECOLOGICAL
PROBLEMS, IT PREDICTS THAT RENEWABLE ENERGY SOURCES WILL
PLAY A MORE DOMINATING ROLE IN MEETING THE ENERGY
REQUIREMENTS OF THE WORLD AND WILL BE USEFUL IN KEEPING THE
ECOLOGICAL BALANCES. CONCLUDED IS THE NECESSITY OF NATIONS
OF FORMING LONG-TERM POLICY FOR ALL ENERGY-RELATED
ACTIVITIES AFFECTING SUSTAINABLE DEVELOPMENT IN INFLUENCING
THE CLIMATE ON EARTH.

01904 BURNELL, B.S.; BURNELL, J.D.
COMMUNITY INTERACTION AND SUBURBAN ZONING POLICIES
URBAN AFFAIRS QUARTERLY, 24(3) (MAR 89), 470-482.
FOCUSING ON MULTIFAMILY LAND USE, THIS NOTE DISCUSSES
THE HYPOTHESIS THAT ZONING POLICIES IN A COMMUNITY ARE
RELATED TO THE ZONING POLICIES OF SURROUNDING COMMUNITIES. A
COMMUNITY MAY RESTRICT CERTAIN TYPES OF LAND USE TO PRESERVE
ITS NEIGHBORHOOD QUALITY. AS A RESULT SURROUNDING
COMMUNITIES MAY ADOPT SIMILAR POLICIES TO PREVENT AN INFLUX
THAT WOULD REDUCE NEIGHBORHOOD QUALITY. EMPIRICALLY, A MODEL
IS FORMULATED TO TEST WHETHER THE AMOUNT OF MULTIFAMILY
DEVELOPMENT IN A COMMUNITY IS RELATED TO THE AMOUNT OF
MULTIFAMILY LAND USE IN SURROUNDING COMMUNITIES. OTHER
VARIABLES CONTROL FOR THE EFFECTS OF MARKET FORCES, FISCAL
FACTORS, AND OTHER EFFECTS. THE EMPIRICAL RESULTS ARE
CONSISTENT WITH THE HYPOTHESIS.

01905 BURNS, E.
SQUATTERS' POWER IN SAN MIGUEL TEOTONGO
NACLA REPORT ON THE AMERICAS, XXIII(4) (NOV 89), 29-35.
THE ARTICLE EXAMINES THE PRIMARILY WOMEN-LED SQUATTERS'
MOVEMENT IN THE MEXICO CITY NEIGHBORHOOD OF SAN MIGUEL
TEOTONGO. IT CONCLUDES THAT DESPITE OPPOSITION FROM THE
GOVERNMENT, THE DEMOCRATIC EXERCISE OF POWER FROM THE
NEIGHBORHOOD AND THE WORKPLACE HAS THRUST THE GRASS-ROOTS
MOVEMENT ONTO THE NATIONAL POLITICAL STAGE. THE POLITICAL
POTENTIAL OF THE MOVEMENT GREATLY EXCEEDS ITS CURRENT IMPACT.
HOWEVER, THE PEOPLE OF SAN MIGUEL TEOTONGO AND THEIR
COMPANIONS IN COMMUNITY ORGANIZATIONS ACROSS MEXICO NOT ONLY
MUST PROVIDE LEADERSHIP IN THE RESOLUTION OF THE URBAN
CRISIS, THEY ALSO FACE THE MUCH MORE DAUNTING TASK OF
BUILDING A POLITICAL ALTERNATIVE FOR THE SOCIETY AS A WHOLE.

01906 BURNS, J.
CHINESE CIVIL SERVICE REFORM: THE 13TH PARTY CONGRESS
PROPOSALS
CHINA QUARTERLY, (120) (DEC 89), 739-770.
THE REFORM PROPOSALS OF THE 13TH PARTY CONGRESS PLACE
NEW RESTRICTIONS ON THE SCOPE OF THE PARTY'S JURISDICTION
OVER CADRE MANAGEMENT AND DECLARE THAT SEPARATE METHODS
SHOULD BE USED TO MANAGE CADRE STAFFING ORGANIZATIONS IN THE
COUNTRY'S DIFFERENT EMPLOYMENT SECTORS (ADMINISTRATIVE UNITS,
SERVICE UNITS, AND ECONOMIC ENTERPRISES). THE PROPOSALS
CONCENTRATE ON REFORM OF THE SYSTEM FOR MANAGING THE CADRES
WHO STAFF CHINA'S GOVERNMENTAL BODIES. UNDER THE REFORM,
CADRES WORKING IN GOVERNMENT WILL BE DIVIDED INTO TWO CIVIL
SERVICE STREAMS: POLITICAL CIVIL SERVANTS AND CAREER CIVIL
SERVANTS.

01907 BURNS, J.P.
CHINA'S GOVERNANCE: POLITICAL REFORM IN A TURBULENT
ENVIRONMENT
CHINA QUARTERLY, (119) (SEP 89), 481-518.
DESPITE THE OBJECTION OF MORE CONSERVATIVE ELEMENTS
WITHIN THE CHINESE COMMUNIST PARTY, THE REFORMERS ADOPTED
AND BEGAN TO IMPLEMENT POLITICAL CHANGES DESIGNED TO ALTER
STATE-SOCIETY RELATIONS BY REALIGNING THE ROLE OF THE STATE
IN SOCIETY, WIDENING THE ROLE OF INTELLECTUALS IN THE
STATE'S POLICY PROCESS, RELYING ON ECONOMIC INCENTIVES TO
IMPLEMENT POLICY, AND RENEWING AN EARLIER EMPHASIS ON
INSTITUTION BUILDING TO CONTAIN AND CHANNEL POPULAR
PARTICIPATION. IN EARLY 1989, DENG XIAOPING WITHDREW HIS
SUPPORT FOR THE POLITICAL REFORMERS BECAUSE HE BELIEVED THEY
WERE SUBVERTING THE PARTY'S MONOPOLY ON POWER. THE CCP
LEADERSHIP, BOTH REFORMERS AND CONSERVATIVES, HAD FAILED TO
GRASP THE EXTENT OF THE DECAY IN CHINA'S POLITICAL
INSTITUTIONS, WITH THE RESULT THAT THE POLITICAL REFORM WAS
TOO LITTLE, TOO LATE.

01908 BURNS, W.
ARMS CONTROL IN TRANSITION: THE REAGAN ADMINISTRATION'S
LEGACY
PRESIDENTIAL STUDIES QUARTERLY, XIX(1) (WIN 89), 31-39.
THE ARTICLE EXAMINES THE CHANGES IN THE ARMS CONTROL
POLICY OF THE REAGAN ADMINSTRATION AND THE CHANGES IN THE
INTERNATIONAL ARMS CONTROL CLIMATE OVER THE PAST FEW YEARS.
IT DISCUSSES THE VARIOUS SUMMIT MEETINGS THAT ATTEMPTED TO
BRING ABOUT ARMS REDUCTIONS AND THEIR RELATIVE SUCCESS OR
FAILURE WITH REGARDS TO THE OVERALL PROCESS. IT CONCLUDES
WITH AN ANALYSIS OF THE CURRENT TRENDS AND THEIR FUTURE

IMPLICATIONS.

01909 BURNS, W. J.
"THE CARROT AND THE STICK": ECONOMIC AID AND AMERICAN
POLICY TOWARD EGYPT, 1955-1967
DISSERTATION ABSTRACTS INTERNATIONAL, 49(8) (FEB 89),
2381-A.
THIS STUDY ATTEMPTS TO TRACE THE USE OF ECONOMIC AID AS
AN INSTRUMENT OF AMERICAN POLICY TOWARD EGYPT IN THE NASSER
ERA. CHAPTERS ONE THROUGH SIX PROVIDE DETAILED ACCOUNTS OF
THE U.S.-EGYPTIAN MILITARY AID TALKS THAT PRECEDED THE CZECH
ARMS DEAL IN 1955, OF THE EISENHOWER ADMINISTRATION'S
ATTEMPTS TO BARTER AID FOR THE ASWAN HIGH DAM FOR EGYPTIAN
POLITICAL CONCESSIONS, AND OF THE KENNEDY AND JOHNSON
ADMINISTRATIONS' EFFORTS TO MODERATE EGYPTIAN BEHAVIOR
THROUGH MANIPULATION OF MASSIVE FOOD AID SHIPMENTS. CHAPTER
SEVEN REVIEWS THE OBJECTIVES, TACTICS, AND EFFECTIVENESS OF
AMERICAN AID POLICY IN THE NASSER ERA.

01910 BURNS, W.F.
AN OVERVIEW OF U.S. ARMS CONTROL OBJECTIVES
DEPARTMENT OF STATE BULLETIN (US FOREIGN POLICY), 89(2142)
(JAN 89), 41-44.
THE AUTHOR SURVEYS AMERICAN ARMS CONTROL OBJECTIVES
REGARDING NUCLEAR TESTING, CHEMICAL WEAPONS, NUCLEAR
NONPROLIFERATION, OUTER SPACE, CONVENTIONAL ARMS, STRATEGIC
ARMS, AND VERIFICATION.

01911 BURRIDGE, J.M.
PRESSURE DEFLECTED: JAPAN AND THE 1973 ARAB OIL EMBARGO
DISSERTATION ABSTRACTS INTERNATIONAL, 49(7) (JAN 89),
1948-A.
THE AUTHOR ASSESSES THE EXTENT TO WHICH THE 1973 SUPPLY
REDUCTION BY THE ORGANIZATION OF ARAB PETROLEUM EXPORTING
COUNTRIES SUCCEEDED IN FORCING JAPAN TO ADOPT A MORE PRO-
ARAB FOREIGN POLICY. HE CONCLUDES THAT IT DID NOT RESULT IN
SIGNIFICANTLY GREATER JAPANESE POLITICAL SUPPORT OR ECONOMIC
ASSISTANCE IN THE 1974-78 PERIOD.

01912 BURRIS, B.
TECHNOCRATIC ORGANIZATION AND CONTROL
ORGANIZATION STUDIES, 10(1) (1989), 1-22.
TECHNOCRACY, A NEW TYPE OF ORGANIZATIONAL CONTROL
STRUCTURE, IS DEFINED AND ANALYZED. THE CULMINATION OF A
DIALECTICAL PROCESS OF ORGANIZATIONAL RATIONALIZATION,
TECHNOCRACY TRANSCENDS AND INTEGRATES EARLIER FORMS OF
ORGANIZATIONAL CONTROL, PARTICULARLY TECHNICAL CONTROL,
BUREAUCRATIC CONTROL, AND PROFESSIONAL CONTROL. TECHNOCRATIC
ORGANIZATIONS ARE CHARACTERIZED BY A FLATTENING OF
BUREAUCRATIC HIERARCHIES, A POLARIZATION INTO 'EXPERT' AND
'NON-EXPERT' SECTORS, A SUBSTITUTION OF EXPERTISE FOR RANK
POSITION AS THE PRIMARY BASIS OF AUTHORITY, A DE-EMPHASIS ON
INTERNAL JOB LADDERS IN FAVOUR OF EXTERNAL CREDENTIALING AND
CREDENTIAL BARRIERS, FLEXIBLE CONFIGURATIONS OF
CENTRALIZATION/DECENTRALIZATION, AND OTHER RELATED
ORGANIZATIONAL CHANGES. TECHNOCRACY IS ANALYZED WITH REGARD
TO ITS THEORETICAL BACKGROUND, HISTORICAL DEVELOPMENT,
CONTEMPORARY MANIFESTATIONS, AND SOCIO-POLITICAL
IMPLICATIONS.

01913 BURROWES, R.D.
OIL STRIKE AND LEADERSHIP STRUGGLE IN SOUTH YEMEN: 1986
AND BEYOND
MIDDLE EAST JOURNAL, 43(3) (SUM 89), 437-454.
TWO EVENTS IN SOUTH YEMEN (PDRY) HAVE IMPORTANT AND
POSSIBLY CONFLICTING IMPLICATIONS FOR THE STABILITY,
DEVELOPMENT, AND PROSPERITY OF THE PDRY IN THE COMING YEARS:
THE DISCOVERY OF OIL AND THE VIOLENT INTRAPARTY LEADERSHIP
STRUGGLE. THIS ARTICLE PRESENTS THE CONTEXT IN WHICH WITHIN
SEVERAL MONTHS THESE TWO EVENTS OCCURRED. IT CONCLUDES THAT
IN ALL LIKLIHOOD. THE PDRY WILL FINALLY RESOLVE ITS
INTRAPARTY PROBLEM THROUGH SOME FORM OF RECONCILIATION, AND
THIS WILL PROBABLY ALLOW FOR A GROWTH IN "BROTHERLY"
RELATIONS BETWEEN THE TWO YEMENS. SIMILARLY, THE DISCOVERY
OF OIL BY BOTH YEMENS BODES WELL FOR INCREASING POLITICAL
COOPERATION BETWEEN IF NOT UNIFICATION, OF THE YEMENS AND
FOR JOINT EFFORTS AT SOCIOECONOMIC DEVELOPMENT. THERE ARE
MANY FRIENDS OF "BOTH PARTS OF THE YEMENI HOMELAND" WHO HOPE
FOR SUCH OUTCOMES.

01914 BURSTEIN, C.
TOP QUALITY MANAGEMENT IN FEDERAL AGENCIES
NATIONAL CIVIC REVIEW, 78(2) (MAR 89), 103-113.
LONG RECOGNIZED BY THE PRIVATE SECTOR AS THE MOST
EFFECTIVE WAY TO IMPROVE CUSTOMER SERVICE, FEDERAL AGENCIES
ARE IMPLEMENTING THE "TOTAL QUALITY MANAGEMENT" APPROACH TO
PROVIDE HIGH QUALITY AND TIMELY PRODUCTS AND SERVICES TO THE
FEDERAL TAX-PAYING PUBLIC. BASED ON THE OFFICE OF MANAGEMENT
AND BUDGET'S FY 1990 MANAGEMENT OF THE UNITED STATES
GOVERNMENT REPORT, THIS ARTICLE DESCRIBES SOME FEDERAL
INITIATIVES THAT COULD HOLD LESSONS FOR LOCAL GOVERNMENTS.

01915 BURT, M.R.; COHEN, B.E.
WHO IS HELPING THE HOMELESS? LOCAL, STATE, AND FEDERAL
RESPONSES
PUBLIUS: THE JOURNAL OF FEDERALISM, 19(3) (SUM 89),
111-128.
THIS ARTICLE EXAMINES THE SOURCES OF SUPPORT FOR
SERVICES FOR THE HOMELESS. IT DELINEATES THE EXTENSIVE ROLE
OF THE PRIVATE SECTOR IN BOTH FUNDING AND ACTUALLY
DELIVERING SHELTER, MEAL, AND OTHER SERVICES FOR THE
HOMELESS. IT ALSO INDICATES THE EXTENT TO WHICH CERTAIN
STATES ARE PROVIDING FINANCIAL SUPPORT FOR HOMELESS SERVICES,
AND THE RELATION OF NEW FEDERAL EFFORTS THROUGH PROGRAMS
FUNDED BY THE STEWART B. MCKINNEY HOMELESS ASSISTANCE ACT TO
STATE AND PRIVATE ACTIVITIES.

01916 BURT, R.R.
STATUS OF THE STRATEGIC ARMS REDUCTION TALKS
DEPARTMENT OF STATE BULLETIN (US FOREIGN POLICY), 89(2151)
(OCT 89), 17-19.
THE UNITED STATES APPROACHED ROUND 11 OF THE STRATEGIC
ARMS REDUCTION TALKS (START) AS A RECONNAISSANCE EXERCISE
AND SOUGHT TO CLARIFY THE POLICY POSITIONS OF BOTH PARTIES
AND TO REAFFIRM THE CENTRAL STRUCTURE OF THE JOINT DRAFT
TREATY.

01917 BURTON, C.
THE ROLE OF THE NIC'S IN SOUTHEAST ASIA'S POLITICAL AND
ECONOMIC DEVELOPMENT
INTERNATIONAL JOURNAL, XLIV(3) (SUM 89), 660-675.
TO PROVIDE AN ANALYTICAL CONTEXT FOR INTERPRETING THE
NATURE OF THE RAPIDLY DEVELOPING MUTUAL DEPENDENCE BETWEEN
THE ASIAN NIC'S AND THE SOUTHEAST ASIAN NATIONS, THIS PAPER
FIRST OUTLINES THE CIRCUMSTANCES THAT HAVE SHAPED THE
CONTEMPORARY ECONOMIC STRATEGIES OF THE SOUTHEAST ASIAN
COUNTRIES. NEXT, IT EXAMINES THE IMPACT OF RECENT CHANGES IN
THE POLICIES OF THE SOVIET UNION AND CHINA ON THE SOCIALIST
NATIONS OF INDOCHINA. THE THIRD SECTION ADDRESSES THE
ECONOMIC AND POLITICAL IMPLICATIONS OF THAILAND'S DRAMATIC
SURGE IN ECONOMIC GROWTH. THE CONCLUSION CONSIDERS THE
POTENTIAL GLOBAL SIGNIFICANCE OF CONSOLIDATION AND POLITICAL
INSTITUTIONALIZATION OF THE DEEPENING ECONOMIC TIES BETWEEN
THE MEMBERS OF ASEAN, THE SOCIALIST REGIMES OF INDOCHINA,
AND THE NIC'S.

01918 BURTON, D. W.
POLITICS, PROPAGANDA, AND PUBLIC OPINION IN THE REIGNS OF
HENRY III AND EDWARD I
DISSERTATION ABSTRACTS INTERNATIONAL, 49(8) (FEB 89),
2358-A.
THIS THESIS TRACES THE WAY IN WHICH THE GROWING
POLITICAL CONSCIOUSNESS OF THE ENGLISH NATION IN THE
THIRTEENTH CENTURY LED THE KING TO PAY MORE ATTENTION TO
PUBLIC OPINION AND CONSIDERS THE ARGUMENTS HE USED TO
JUSTIFY HIS POLICIES, IN PARTICULAR HIS MILITARY
UNDERTAKINGS, BEFORE A WIDER PUBLIC AUDIENCE.

01919 BUSBY, M.D.
COOPERATION IN COUNTERING TERRORISM
DEPARTMENT OF STATE BULLETIN (US FOREIGN POLICY), 89(2153)
(DEC 89), 47-49.
THE AUTHOR, WHO IS THE U.S. COORDINATOR FOR COUNTER-
TERRORISM, DISCUSSES INTERNATIONAL COOPERATION IN COMBATTING
TERRORISM, INTERAGENCY ORGANIZATION AGAINST TERRORISM, AND
EXECUTIVE BRANCH MANAGEMENT OF U.S. COUNTER-TERRORISM
EFFORTS. HE STATES THAT THE VERY NATURE OF TERRORISM
REQUIRES A DEFENSE INTERNATIONAL IN SCOPE. THEREFORE,
IMPROVING INTERNATIONAL COOPERATION, BOTH WITH TRADITIONAL
AMERICAN ALLIES AND WITH OTHER NATIONS, MUST BE ONE OF THE
PRIMARY ELEMENTS IN ANY STRATEGY FOR CONTAINING AND
DETERRING TERRORIST ATTACKS.

01920 BUSH, G.
CHANGE IN THE SOIET UNION
DEPARTMENT OF STATE BULLETIN (US FOREIGN POLICY), 89(2148)
(JUL 89), 16-17.
THE AMERICAN POLICY OF CONTAINMENT WORKED FOR 40 YEARS,
BUT NOW IT IS TIME TO MOVE BEYOND CONTAINMENT TO A FOREIGN
POLICY THAT RECOGNIZES THE FULL SCOPE OF THE CHANGES
OCCURING AROUND THE WORLD AND IN THE SOVIET UNION. THE
UNITED STATES NOW SEEKS THE INTEGRATION OF THE SOVIET UNION
INTO THE COMMUNITY OF NATIONS.

01921 BUSH, G.
COMMITMENT TO DEMOCRACY AND ECONOMIC PROGRESS IN LATIN
AMERICA
DEPARTMENT OF STATE BULLETIN (US FOREIGN POLICY), 89(2147)
(JUN 89), 1-3.
IN THIS SPEECH BEFORE THE COUNCIL OF THE AMERICAS
CONFERENCE ON MAY 2, 1989, THE PRESIDENT REVIEWED UNITED
STATES FOREIGN POLICY IN LATIN AMERICA. HE ALSO REAFFIRMED
HIS ADMINISTRATION'S COMMITMENT TO BRINGING DEMOCRACY TO
NICARAGUA.

01922 BUSH, G.
ENCOURAGING POLITICAL AND ECONOMIC REFORMS IN POLAND
DEPARTMENT OF STATE BULLETIN (US FOREIGN POLICY), 89(2147)

(JUN 89), 3-5.
THE US GOVERNMENT IS COMMITTED TO ENCOURAGING POLITICAL
AND ECONOMIC REFORMS THROUGHOUT EASTERN EUROPEAN, INCLUDING
POLAND. THE AMERICAN PEOPLE WANT TO SEE EAST AND CENTRAL
EUROPE FREE, PROSPEROUS, AND PEACEFUL.

01923 BUSH, G.
SECURITY STRATEGY FOR THE 1990'S
DEPARTMENT OF STATE BULLETIN (US FOREIGN POLICY), 89(2148)
(JUL 89), 19-21.
THE UNITED STATES' SECURITY GOALS ARE CONSTANT, BUT THE
STRATEGY USED TO REACH THEM CAN, AND MUST, CHANGE AS THE
WORLD CHANGES. COPING WITH A CHANGING SOVIET UNION IS A
CHALLENGE OF THE HIGHEST ORDER, BUT SECURITY CHALLENGES DO
NOT COME FROM THE EAST ALONE. THE EMERGENCE OF REGIONAL
POWERS ALSO RAPIDLY CHANGING THE STRATEGIC LANDSCAPE.

01924 BUSH, G.
THE FUTURE OF EUROPE
DEPARTMENT OF STATE BULLETIN (US FOREIGN POLICY), 89(2148)
(JUL 89), 18-19.
THE CHANGES THAT ARE OCCURING IN WESTERN EUROPE ARE LESS
DRAMATIC THAN THOSE TAKING PLACE IN THE EAST, BUT THEY ARE
NO LESS FUNDAMENTAL. THE CREATION OF A SINGLE EUROPEAN
MARKET IN 1992 AND NEW FORMS OF COOPERATION WITHIN NATO ARE
TWO CHANGES THAT WILL HELP SHAPE THE FUTURE OF WESTERN
EUROPE. THE CHANGES WILL AFFECT AMERCIAN RELATIONS WITH
WESTERN EUROPE BUT SHOULD NOT ALTER THE BASIC DIMENSIONS OF
THAT RELATIONSHIP.

01925 BUSH, G.
UPCOMING ELECTIONS IN NICARAGUA
DEPARTMENT OF STATE BULLETIN (US FOREIGN POLICY), 89(2150)
(SEP 89), 92.
THE SANDINISTA GOVERNMENT CONTINUES TO SHOW THAT IT
FEARS FREE POLITICAL COMPETITION. THE SANDINISTA ELECTORAL
REFORM LAW IS STACKED IN THE SANDINISTAS' FAVOR AND
PENALIZES PARTIES THAT DID NOT PARTICIPATE IN THE LAST
ELECTION. THE NEW MEDIA LAW ALSO FAILS TO MEET DEMOCRATIC
STANDARDS, AS IT CONTAINS VAGUE PROVISIONS THAT PERMIT
PROSECUTION FOR DEFAMING THE GOVERNMENT. PERMEATING ALL OF
THESE SANDINISTA MEASURES IS GOVERNMENT PROPAGANDA THAT
EQUATES OPPOSITION WITH DISLOYALTY AND CRITICISM WITH
ALLEGIANCE TO A FOREIGN POWER.

01926 BUSH, J.
HOW TO KEEP PRESSURE ON THE SANDINISTAS
AMERICAN SPECTATOR, 22(7) (JUL 89), 16-17.
THE BUSH ADMINISTRATION SHOULD PERSEVERE IN ITS
DETERMINATION TO SUPPORT THE CAUSE OF FREEDOM IN NICARAGUA
AS THE BEST WAY TO SECURING A LASTING PEACE IN CENTRAL
AMERICA. STRONG SUPPORT FOR LEGITIMATE ELECTIONS IN
NICARAGUA IS ESSENTIAL IF THIS GOAL IS TO BE ATTAINED. IF
THE SANDINISTAS ALLOW FREE ELECTIONS, IT IS LIKELY THEY WILL
BE DEFEATED. IF THEY FAIL TO HOLD FREE ELECTIONS, THE
EFFORT FOR FREEDOM IN NICARAGUA WILL CONTINUE BY OTHER MEANS
AND A RENEWAL OF MILITARY ASSISTANCE TO THE RESISTANCE BY
CONGRESS WILL BE IN ORDER.

01927 BUSH, P.O.
THE CONCEPT OF "PROGRESSIVE" INSTITUTIONAL CHANGE AND ITS
IMPLICATIONS FOR ECONOMIC POLICY FORMATION
JOURNAL OF ECONOMIC ISSUES, XXIII(2) (JUN 89), 455-464.
THE PURPOSE OF THIS ARTICLE IS TO EXPLORE THE MANNER IN
WHICH THE IDEA OF "PROGRESSIVE" INSTITUTIONAL CHANGE
PROVIDES A CONCEPTUAL BRIDGE BETWEEN THE THEORY OF
INSTITUTIONAL CHANGE AND THE THEORY OF SOCIAL POLICY
FORMATION IN THE INSTITUTIONALIST LITERATURE. THIS IS
CLEARLY A MATTER OF SOME METHODOLOGICAL SIGNFICANCE; FOR IF
THE CONCEPT DOES PROVIDE SUCH A CONCEPTUAL BRIDGE, THEN THIS
WOULD CONSTITUTE FURTHER EVIDENCE THAT INSTITUTIONAL
ECONOMICS IS A COHERENT BODY OF THOUGHT IN WHICH THEORETICAL
AND APPLIED CONSIDERATIONS CAN BE TIGHLY INTEGRATED. THE
DISCUSSION IS BASED UPON A CONSIDERATION OF THE NON-
CEREMONIAL CONSTRAINTS THAT BOUND THE PROCESS OF
"PROGRESSIVE" INSTITUTIONAL CHANGE.

01928 BUSHEE, G.R.
RISK, PRECEPTIONS, AND INTERNATIONAL CONFLICT: 1816-1965,
AN EXPECTED UTILITY PERSPECTIVE
DISSERTATION ABSTRACTS INTERNATIONAL, 49(7) (JAN 89),
1949-A.
THIS STUDY DEVELOPS AN EXPECTED UTILITY PERSPECTIVE TO
TEST THE PERCEPTUAL ASSUMPTIONS AND HYPOTHESES INCORPORATED
IN MACRO AND MICROLEVEL APPROACHES TO CONFLICT ANALYSIS. THE
STUDY FIRST DELIMIT FOUR SEPARATE PERCEPTUAL APPROACHES BY
EXAMINING THE LEVELS-OFANALYSIS AND PERCEPTUAL VARIABLES
REPRESENTED IN THE LITERATURE.

01929 BUSKY, D.F.
DEFINING DEMOCRATIC SOCIALISM: A CASE STUDY OF THE
FORMATION OF THE BRITISH LABOR PARTY
DISSERTATION ABSTRACTS INTERNATIONAL, 49(11) (MAY 89),
3488-A.

IN ORDER TO DEFINE DEMOCRATIC SOCIALISM, THE AUTHOR
EXAMINES A REPRESENTATIVE DEMOCRATIC SOCIALIST PARTY, THE
BRITISH LABOUR PARTY. HE ANALYZES THE PROGRAMS OF THE THREE
PRINCIPAL ANTECEDENTS OF THE PRESENT LABOUR PARTY: THE
SOCIAL DEMOCRATIC FEDERATION, THE FABIAN SOCIETY, AND THE
INDEPENDENT LABOUR PARTY.

01930 BUSSIERE, E.
SOCIAL WELFARE AND THE COURTS: THE DILEMMAS OF LIBERALISM
DISSERTATION ABSTRACTS INTERNATIONAL, 50(3) (SEP 89),
783-A.
THE AUTHOR EXAMINES THE DILEMMAS THE WELFARE RIGHTS
MOVEMENT POSED FOR THE FEDERAL COURTS, THE NATURE OF THE
COURTS' RESPONSE TO THE POOR PEOPLE'S MOVEMENT, AND THE
IMPLICATIONS FOR THE AMERICAN WELFARE STATE. SHE ANALYZES
THE WARREN COURT'S UNDERSTANDING OF EQUALITY; THE ALLIANCE
BETWEEN THE NATIONAL WELFARE RIGHTS ORGANIZATION AND THE
CENTER ON SOCIAL WELFARE POLICY AND LAW; AND THE VICTORIES
AND SETBACKS THAT LEGAL SERVICES PROGRAM ATTORNEYS
EXPERIENCED IN THE COURTROOM.

01931 BUSZYNSKI, L.
NEW ASPIRATIONS AND OLD CONSTRAINTS IN THAILAND'S FOREIGN
POLICY
ASIAN SURVEY, 29(11) (NOV 89), 1057-1072.
THIS ARTICLE EXAMINES THE CHANGE IN ATTITUDE TOWARD
FOREIGN POLICY IN THAILAND SINCE THE ELECTIONS OF 1988
USHERED IN THE FIRST ELECTED GOVERNMENT SINCE 1976. ELECTED
GOVERNMENTS HAVE DEMONSTRATED AN ABILITY TO INTRODUCE MAJOR
CHANGES AS A REFLECTION OF THE PENT-UP SOCIAL FORCES THEY
REPRESENT, EXTERNAL AND INTERNAL CONSTRAINTS AND NEW
INITIATIVES IN FOREIGN POLICY ARE DETAILED. THAT THE TENSION
BETWEEN ASPIRATIONS AND EXTERNAL CONSTRAINTS WILL
CHARACTERIZE THAILAND'S FOREIGN POLICY IN THE FUTURE AND IS
UNLIKELY TO BE SATISFACTORILY RESOLVED, IS THE CONCLUSION

01932 BUTENKO, A.
ANTAGONISMS UNDER SOCIALISM?
WORLD MARXIST REVIEW, 32(5) (MAY 89), 21-24.
MARXISM HAS ABSOLUTELY NO ROOM FOR THE DOGMATIC AND THE
DOCTRINAIRE, BOTH OF WHICH HINDER A PROPER ANALYSIS OF
REALITY. ANYONE FAMILIAR WITH SOVIET MARXIST STUDIES KNOWS
THAT MANY AUTHORS HAVE BEGUN TO PAY MUCH MORE ATTENTION TO
CONTRADICTIONS UNDER SOCIALISM. THEY DO NOT CONFINE
THEMSELVES TO RECOGNISING THAT ANTAGONISTIC AND NON-
ANTAGONISTIC CONTRADICTIONS ARE OPPOSITES BUT PROCEED, IN
THE SPIRIT OF LENIN'S CALL TO GRASP "THE TRANSITION FROM THE
ONE TO THE OTHER", TO ANALYSE THE CONDITIONS UNDER WHICH NON-
ANTAGONISTIC CONTRADICTIONS CAN BECOME ANTAGONISTIC ONES. A
BETTER UNDERSTANDING OF THE CONTRADICTIONS UNDERLYING SOCIAL
CONFLICTS IS IMPORTANT IN TRYING TO PREVENT THEM
INTENSIFYING. SUCH AN UNDERSTANDING ALONE MAKES IT POSSIBLE
TO DETERMINE PRACTICAL WAYS OF SETTLING CONTRADICTIONS.
GENERALLY SPEAKING, SOCIALISM CAN PREVENT A BREAK BETWEEN
OPPOSITES BECAUSE SOCIETY IS ABLE TO IDENTIFY ITS INTRINSIC
CONTRADICTIONS, TAKE THEM INTO ACCOUNT AND SET IN MOTION
PROCESSES TO SETTLE THEM.

01933 BUTLER, D.
GENERAL ELECTIONS SINCE 1945
CONTEMPORARY RECORD, 3(1) (FAL 89), 18-19.
ELECTION CAMPAIGNS HAVE CHANGED BEYOND ALL RECOGNITION
SINCE 1945. THIS ARTICLE DISCUSSES THE IMPACT OF ELECTIONS
SINCE 1945 ON DEVELOPMENTS IN CAMPAIGN MANAGEMENT. IT
EXPLORES CHANGES IN CAMPAIGNS; THE IMPACT OF THE CAMPAIGN;
THE ROLE OF THE PARTY LEADER AND CONCLUDES THAT ALL
EVOLUTION IS GRADUAL AND THAT ELECTION CAMPAIGNS ENCAPSULATE
WHAT POLITICIANS CAN SELL AND WHAT VOTERS WILL BUY.

01934 BUTLER, G.S.
IN SEARCH OF THE AMERICAN SPIRIT: THE POLITICAL THOUGHT OF
ORESTES BROWNSON
DISSERTATION ABSTRACTS INTERNATIONAL, 50(6) (DEC 89),
1786-A.
ORESTES BROWNSON'S LIFE-LONG SEARCH FOR TRUTH IN MATTERS
RELIGIOUS AND POLITICAL MAY BE ROUGHLY DIVIDED INTO TWO
PHASES: THAT WHICH HE CONDUCTED DURING HIS LIBERAL
PROTESTANT AND AGNOSTIC PERIOD AND THAT WHICH WAS CONDUCTED
DURING HIS ROMAN CATHOLIC PERIOD. THROUGH HIS OWN
EXPERIENCES, BROWNSON ILLUMINATED TWO DISTINCT ASPECTS OF
THE AMERICAN TRADITION. IN DOING SO, HE PROVIDED A VALUABLE
CONTRIBUTION TO THE ONGOING PROCESS OF ARTICULATING AND
DEFINING THE TRUE NATURE OF AMERICAN POLITICAL SYMBOLS.

01935 BUTLER, L.
ETHIOPIA: INSIDE LIBERATED TIGRE
NEW AFRICAN, (262) (JUL 89), 60-62.
THIS ARTICLE EXAMINES CONDITIONS IN TIGRE AFTER THE
ETHIOPIAN "GOVERNMENT" RETREATED. THIS TIME THERE ARE SIGNS
THAT THEY HAVE MADE A PERMANENT RETREAT. THE TPLF (TYGRE
PEOPLE'S LIBERATION FRONT IS TRYING TO REBUILD THEIR
SHATTERED ECONOMY AND RESTORE ESSENTIAL SERVICES.

01936 BUTLER, S.
FREEING HEALTH CARE
NATIONAL REVIEW, 61(24) (DEC 89), 34-36.
THIS ARTICLE EXAMINES THE LIBERAL CLAIM OF DEVOTION TO
THE DREAM OF HIGH-QUALITY HEALTH CARE FOR ALL, WHILE
PURSUING POLICIES THAT MAKE DECENT HEALTH CARE INCREASINGLY
UNAFFORDABLE AND UNAVAILABLE. THE CONSERVATIVE SOLUTION IS
EXPLORED, WHICH MUST BEGIN BY PRESENTING VOTERS WITH A CLEAR
PICTURE OF THE POLICY CHOICES FACING THE COUNTRY, IT
SUGGESTS THAT ONLY BY CHANGING DIRECTION COMPLETELY,
INTRODUCING A REAL MARKET IN HEALTH CARE RATHER TRYING TO
SUPPRESS ALL VESTIGES OF PRICING AND COMPETITION.

01937 BUTLER, S.
RAZING THE LIBERAL PLANTATION: A CONSERVATIVE WAR ON
POVERTY
NATIONAL REVIEW, 110(21) (NOV 89), 27-30.
THIS ARTICLE EXAMINES THE LIBERAL WELFARE ESTABLISHMENT
WHICH IT CLAIMS WHILE PURPORTING TO HELP THE POOR, HAS TAKEN
THEM OVER, AND IS USING THEM AS A MEANS TO POWER. IT
ADVOCATES TWO STRATEGIES - ONE GENERAL, AND THE SECOND
FOCUSED ON EDUCATION - FOR BREAKING THAT POWER, FREEING THE
POOR, AND, NOT INCIDENTALLY, GAINING THE BENEFIT OF THEIR
CONTRIBUTIONS TO SOCIETY. IT SUGGESTS REACHING AN
ACCOMMODATION ON CIVIL RIGHTS, ADOPT A STRATEGY OF
EMPOWERMENT, ATTACK THE POVERTY INDUSTRY AND ALLOWING THE
STATES TO BE INNOVATORS OF ANTI-POVERTY POLICY.

01938 BUTLER, S.M.
PRIVATIZATION AND THE MANAGEMENT OF PUBLIC POLICY
NATIONAL CIVIC REVIEW, 78(2) (MAR 89), 114-126.
WHILE ITS COST-CUTTING POTENTIALITIES ARE MOST OFTEN
USED AS A RATIONALE FOR PRIVATIZATION, THE CONTRACTING
OPTION ALSO MAY PLAY AN IMPORTANT ROLE IN GUIDING POLICY
DECISIONS REGARDING THE GENERAL LEVEL OF PUBLIC SPENDING,
THE SIZE OF THE PUBLIC SECTOR, AND PROMOTION OF THE PUBLIC
GOOD.

01939 BUTLER, W.
INTERNATIONAL LAW, FOREIGN POLICY AND THE GORBACHEV STYLE
JOURNAL OF INTERNATIONAL AFFAIRS, 42(2) (SPR 89), 363-376.
THE ARTICLE EXAMINES THE FOREIGN POLICY OF THE USSR WITH
EMPHASIS ON THE POSITION OF THE SOVIETS ON INTERNATIONAL LAW.
THE ADVENT OF MIKHAIL GORBACHEV AND HIS FAR-REACHING
REFORMS ARE BEGINNING TO AFFECT SOVIET FOREIGN POLICY AS
WELL AS DOMESTIC POLICY? THE SOVIETS ARE BEGINNING TO
ACKNOWLEDGE THE PRIMACY OF INTERNATIONAL LAW, A MOVE THAT
AMOUNTS TO A DRAMATIC REVERSAL OF PREVIOUS FOREIGN POLICY.
THE ARTICLE ATTEMPTS TO EXAMINE THE IMPLICATION OF THE
CURRENT CHANGES.

01940 BUTTERFIELD, J.M.
SOVIET LOCAL AGRICULTURE AND THE RAPO REFORM
DISSERTATION ABSTRACTS INTERNATIONAL, 49(9) (MAR 89),
2793-A.
EVIDENCE INDICATES THAT THE RAION AGROINDUSTRIAL
ASSOCIATION (RAPO) HAS FAILED TO REFORM SOVIET AGRICULTURE.
THREE MAJOR FACTORS ARE CITED FOR THIS FAILURE. THE FIRST IS
INADEQUATE EDUCATION AND TRAINING AMONG LOCAL AGRICULTURAL
MANAGEMENT OFFICIALS. THE SECOND IS DISTRIBUTION OF
AUTHORITY; OFFICIALS IN THE AGRICULTURAL MANAGEMENT
HIERARCHY HAVE BEEN UNWILLING TO GIVE AUTHORITY TO LOCAL
OFFICIALS, WHO HAVE ALSO SHOWN A RELUCTANCE TO TAKE IT.
FINALLY, INTRA-ORGANIZATIONAL FACTORS HAVE COMBINED TO
COMPLICATE LOCAL MANAGEMENT AND UNDERMINE RAPO AUTHORITY.

01941 BUVINIC, M.
INVESTING IN POOR WOMEN: THE PSYCHOLOGY OF DONOR SUPPORT
WORLD DEVELOPMENT, 17(7) (JUL 89), 1045-1057.
DONOR ORGANIZATIONS HAVE SUPPORTED PROJECTS AIMED AT
EXPANDING INCOME-EARNING OPPORTUNITIES FOR POOR WOMEN IN THE
THIRD WORLD SINCE 1975. ALTHOUGH DIFFERING OBJECTIVES HAVE
INFLUENCED DONORS' CHOICE OF INTERVENTIONS, THEY HAVE
GENERALLY FAVORED INCOME-ENHANCING PROJECTS IN THE INFORMAL
ECONOMY CARRIED OUT BY NONGOVERNMENTAL ORGANIZATIONS. MORE
RECENTLY, DONORS ARE SHIFTING TOWARD STRATEGIES THAT
INFLUENCE POLICY OR EMPHASIZE SECTORAL ACTION. DONORS'
EFFORTS HAVE HELPED TO MAINSTREAM WOMEN'S ISSUES IN
EMPLOYMENT AND MICROENTERPRISE DEVELOPMENT POLICY AND
STRENGTHEN ORGANIZATIONS THAT OPEN POOR WOMEN'S ACCESS TO
CAPITAL AND OTHER ASSETS. MAJOR CHALLENGES REMAIN: SUPPORT
FOR MEASURES THAT EXPAND THE DEMAND FOR WOMEN'S LABOR;
RESEARCH THAT INCORPORATES THE OPPORTUNITY COSTS OF WOMEN'S
TIME; AND INTEGRATING THE CONCERNS OF POOR WOMEN INTO THE
ANTIPOVERTY AGENDAS OF MAJOR DONORS.

01942 BUVOLLEN, H.
COMMUNAL LAND AND ARMED CONFLICT IN THE ATLANTIC REGIONS
OF NICARAGUA
SCANDINAVIAN JOURNAL OF DEVELOPMENT ALTERNATIVES, VIII(2)
(JUN 89), 45-58.
THE ARTICLE EXAMINES THE LAND QUESTION OF NICARAGUA'S
ATLANTIC REGIONS WITH REGARDS TO THE CLAIMS OF THE
INDIGENOUS MISKITU, SUMU AND RAMA PEOPLES. IT EXAMINES HOW

THE SANDINISTA LAND REFORM DEALT WITH THE INDIGENOUS CONCEPT
OF LAND USE, HOW THE LAND QUESTION GENERATED CONFLICT WITH
THE AUTHORITIES AND HOW THE AUTONOMY POLICY WILL AFFECT THE
LAND UTILIZATION AND POSSIBILITIES FOR LOCALLY BASED
ECONOMIC DEVELOPMENT.

01943 BUVOLLEN, H.P.
REGIONAL AUTONOMY IN NICARAGUA. A NEW APPROACH TO THE
INDIGENOUS QUESTION IN LATIN AMERICA
ALTERNATIVES, XIV(1) (JAN 89), 123-132.
THE RELATIONSHIP BETWEEN THE SANDINISTA REVOLUTION AND
THE (MISKITU) INDIANS HAS TO A GREAT EXTENT BEEN EXPRESSED
AS AN ARMED CONFLICT SINCE 1981. HOWEVER SEPTEMBER 1987 THE
NICARAGUAN NATIONAL ASSEMBLY RATIFIED A LAW ON AUTONOMY FOR
THE ATLANTIC REGIONS IN EASTERN NICARAGUA DEFINING THEREBY
THE FIRST FORMAL MULTIETHNIC NATION IN LATIN AMERICA. THE
RADICAL CHANGE IN THE SANDINISTA POLICY TOWARDS THE INDIAN
POPULATION HAS NOT ONLY LED TO ADMIRATION BUT ALSO
SKEPTICISM IN THE REGIONS THEMSELVES AND AMONG THE CONCERNED
ABROAD. THIS PAPER FOCUSSES ON THE NICARAGUAN EXPERIENCE IN
THE LIGHT OF THE DISCUSSION ABOUT CLASS AND ETHNICITY,
NATIONAL REVOLUTION AND ETHNODEVELOPMENT.

01944 BUXTON, W.; REHDRICK, D.
THE SOCIOLOGY OF KNOWLEDGE: TOWARD REDEMPTION OF A FAILED
PROMISE
INTERNATIONAL JOURNAL OF POLITICS, CULTURE AND SOCIETY,
2(1) (FAL 88), 66-80.
IN THIS PAPER, THE AUTHORS ARGUE THAT THE SOCIOLOGY OF
KNOWLEDGE, AS GIVEN FORM AND DIRECTION BY MANNHEIM, WAS
NEVER INTENDED TO BE ANOTHER SUBSTANTIVE FIELD OR SEPARATE
DISCIPLINE; IT HAS REPRESENTED A WAY FOR INTELLECTUALS TO
CONFRONT PROBLEMS AT THE FOUNDATIONS OF THEIR DISCIPLINES,
AND A WAY TO BE ENGAGED IN THE PUBLIC SPHERE. MANNHEIM
SOUGHT A WAY FOR INTELLECTUALS TO PARTICIPATE MORE
EFFECTIVELY IN CURBING THE MOVE TOWARD DISORDER AND CHAOS IN
WEIMAR GERMANY. IT WAS THIS PRACTICAL CONCERN THAT LINKED
THE SOCIOLOGY OF KNOWLEDGE WITH "POLITICAL SOCIOLOGY",
PROVIDING THE LATTER WITH THE BASIS FOR PRACTICAL WISDOM.
WHILE COMMENTATORS HAVE ALLUDED TO THE PRACTICAL SIDE OF
MANNHEIM'S THOUGHT, THEY HAVE FAILED TO INDICATE THE
IMPLICATIONS OF THIS ORIENTATION FOR OUR UNDERSTANDING OF
HIS INTENTIONS AND WORK AS A WHOLE.

01945 BUZO, A.
THE CONFUCIAN WAY OF VIOLENCE IN SOUTH KOREA
FAR EASTERN ECONOMIC REVIEW, 141(32) (AUG 88), 42.
AS THE CONTROL OF SOUTH KOREA'S AUTHORITARIAN STATE
WEAKENS, POLITICALLY TINGED VIOLENCE AND BRUTALITY SEEM TO
BE RISING. RIOTING STUDENTS FORM ONLY ONE FACET OF THE
INCREASING VIOLENCE; LABOR UNREST, RELIGIOUS CONFLICT, AND
EVEN ATHLETIC EVENTS HAVE SPURRED THE GROWING PROBLEM.
STUDIES OF POLITICAL VIOLENCE FAIL TO FIND A PATTERN BEYOND
THE CONFLICT BETWEEN FRUSTRATION AND AGGRESSION. KOREANS AS A
PEOPLE SEEM TO EASILY RESORT TO VIOLENCE IN THE PUBLIC ARENA.
A REVERED NATIONALIST ONCE STATED: "THE PEOPLE THINK THAT
TO ATTEND A MEETING IS TO HAVE A FIGHT."

01946 BYERLEE, D.
BREAD AND BUTTER ISSUES IN ECUADORIAN FOOD POLICY: A
COMPARATIVE ADVANTAGE APPROACH
WORLD DEVELOPMENT, 17(10) (OCT 89), 1585-1596.
THE EFFECTS OF POLICY INTERVENTIONS ON PRICE INCENTIVES
AND RESOURCE USE IN WHEAT AND DAIRYING ARE ANALYZED FOR THE
ECUADORIAN SIERRA FROM 1970 TO 1983, A PERIOD OF RAPID
ECONOMIC GROWTH INDUCED BY A BOOM IN PETROLEUM REVENUES.
EXCHANGE RATE AND TRADE POLICIES COMBINED WITH SUBSIDIZED
TRANSPORT SERVICES AND FARM CREDIT TO SUBSTANTIALLY TAX
WHEAT PRODUCERS WHILE MILK PRODUCERS RECEIVED SIGNIFICANT
SUBSIDIES. CONSEQUENTLY SELF-SUFFICIENCY IN WHEAT PRODUCTION
FELL FROM ABOUT 50% IN 1970 TO NEAR ZERO IN 1983, WHILE
IMPORTS OF DAIRY PRODUCTS REMAINED VERY LOW THROUGHOUT THIS
PERIOD OF RAPIDLY EXPANDING DEMAND FOR BOTH BREAD AND
LIVESTOCK PRODUCTS. MEASURES OF COMPARATIVE ADVANTAGE ARE
CONSTRUCTED TO SHOW THAT THESE PRICE DISTORTIONS HAVE LED TO
SUBSTANTIAL INEFFICIENCY IN RESOURCE USE DUE TO THE WIDENING
GAP BETWEEN PRIVATE AND SOCIAL PROFITABILITY FOR WHEAT AND
FOR DAIRYING.

01947 BYERS, R.B.
COMPETING IMAGES OF THE STRATEGIC ENVIRONMENT:
IMPLICATIONS FOR EAST-WEST RELATIONS
INTERNATIONAL SPECTATOR, XXIV(1) (JAN 89), 51-59.
THE PURPOSE OF THE PAPER IS FOURFOLD: (1) TO OUTLINE THE
MAJOR FEATURES OF THE CURRENT EAST-WEST STRATEGIC
ENVIRONMENT; (2) TO INDICATE THOSE DEVELOPMENTS WHICH
SUGGEST THAT THE EXISTING STRATEGIC ENVIRONMENT IS IN
TRANSITION; (3) TO OUTLINE FOUR COMPETING IMAGES OF THE
FUTURE STRATEGIC ENVIRONMENT; AND (4) TO INDICATE SOME OF
THE IMPLICATIONS FOR EAST-WEST RELATIONS FLOWING FROM EACH
OF THE COMPETING IMAGES.

01948 BYRNES, T.A.
MIXING RELIGION AND POLITICS: CATHOLIC BISHOPS IN

CONTEMPORARY AMERICAN POLITICS
DISSERTATION ABSTRACTS INTERNATIONAL, 49(12) (JUN 89), 3855-A.
IN RECENT YEARS, AMERICA'S ROMAN CATHOLIC BISHOPS HAVE TAKEN STRONG POSITIONS ON SEVERAL PUBLIC POLICY ISSUES AND HAVE ACTIVELY PARTICIPATED, BOTH COLLECTIVELY AND INDIVIDUALLY, IN SEVERAL NATIONAL ELECTION CAMPAIGNS. THESE ACTIVITIES COMPRISE A NEW POLITICAL ROLE FOR THE CATHOLIC HIERARCHY IN THAT THEY ARE MUCH LESS PAROCHIAL IN SCOPE AND FAR MORE NATIONAL IN FOCUS THAN PAST POLITICAL ACTIVITIES.

01949 CABAN, P. A.
INDUSTIAL TRANSFORMATION AND LABOR RELATIONS IN PUERTO RICO: FROM "OPERATION BOOTSTRAP" TO THE 1970'S
JOURNAL OF LATIN AMERICAN STUDIES, 21(3) (OCT 89), 559-591.
THIS ESSAY TRACES THE HISTORY OF PUERTO RICAN ECONOMIC CHANGE AND THE RELATIONSHIP BETWEEN INDUSTRIAL TRANSFORMATION AND THE STATE'S CAPACITY TO MANAGE THE OPERATION OF THE ECONOMY, PARTICULARLY INDUSTRIAL RELATIONS UP TO THE LATE 1970S. FOUR FEATURES OF THIS PROCESS ARE EXAMINED: (1) LABOUR RELATIONS DURING THE EARLY PHASE OF INDUSTRIALISATION; (2) THE CHARGES IN THE ECONOMY RESULTING FROM THE EXPANSION OF CAPITAL-INTENSIVE INDUSTRIAL SECTORS; (3) THE IMPACT OF THESE CHANGES ON THE STATE'S CAPACITY TO MANAGE THE POLITICAL ECONOMY, PARTICULARLY ITS FISCAL POLICY; AND (4) HOW THESE CHANGES ALTERED THE NATURE OF STATE-LABOUR RELATIONS.

01950 CABESTAN, J.
THE REFORM OF THE CIVIL SERVICE
CHINA NEWS ANALYSIS, (1383) (APR 89), 1-10.
ONE OF THE KEY POINTS IN ZHAO ZIYANG'S REPORT TO THE THIRTEENTH PARTY CONGRESS WAS THE NEED FOR ESTABLISHMENT OF A PUBLIC SERVICE SYSTEM. SO FAR, EXPERIMENTS HAVE BEEN CARRIED OUT, BUT THE TRADITIONAL STATE CADRE MANAGEMENT SYSTEM HAS NOT YET BEEN ABANDONED.

01951 CAHILL, A.
IRELAND LOOKS TOWARD 1992 (BUT REMEMBERS 1948, 1916, 1798, 1782, AND 1688)
GOVERNANCE, 2(2) (APR 89), 213-220.
THE ARTICLE EXAMINES THE ATTITUDE OF IRELAND IS IT JOINS IN THE MOVEMENT TOWARDS THE TRADE-FRONTIER-FREE EUROPE. IRISH LEADERS HOPE FOR A MILD PUSH TO THEIR ECONOMY AFTER 1992, BUT A MUCH DEEPER ISSUE IS THE POLITICAL ONE OF IRISH INDEPENDENCE AND NATIONALISM. AS EUROPE IS SLOWLY MOVING TOWARDS WHAT MANY VIEW AS A PAN-EUROPEAN POLITICAL CULTURE, IRELAND WHO STUBBORNLY CLINGS TO ITS PAST FILLED WITH BRITISH INJUSTICES COULD FIND ITSELF AN ISOLATIONIST LONER.

01952 CAHILL, A.G.
APPLICATION OF A COGNITIVE RESEARCH STRATEGY TO JOB TRAINING POLICY DECISIONS
DISSERTATION ABSTRACTS INTERNATIONAL, 50(4) (OCT 89), 1085-A.
THE AUTHOR CONTRIBUTES TO POLICY-ANALYTIC THEORY BY EMPLOYING A RESEARCH STRATEGY THAT CAPTURES AND REPRESENTS MULTIPLE REPRESENTATIONS OF PROBLEMS STRUCTURED IN THE MINDS OF POLICY STAKEHOLDERS AND TARGET GROUPS. HE USES AN OCCUPATIONAL GRID TO EXAMINE THE UNDERLYING CRITERIA USED BY A GROUP OF CHRONICALLY UNEMPLOYED INDIVIDUALS IN THE CITY OF PITTSBURGH JOB TRAINING PARTNERSHIP PROGRAM TO EVALUATE THE OCCUPATIONAL CHOICES AVAILABLE TO THEM. THEN HE CONTRASTS THE RESULTS OF THIS STRATEGY WITH THOSE OBTAINED THROUGH STANDARDIZED TESTING PROCEDURES CURRENTLY USED BY THE JTPA STAFF.

01953 CAIDEN, G.E.
THE VALUE OF COMPARATIVE ANALYSIS
INTERNATIONAL JOURNAL OF PUBLIC ADMINISTRATION, 12(3) (1989), 459-475.
CRITICAL QUESTIONS IN BOTH THEORY AND PRACTICE CAN ONLY BE BE ANSWERED THROUGH COMPARATIVE ANALYSIS WHOSE VALUE INCREASES WITH THE GROWING INTERNATIONALIZATION OF PUBLIC ADMINISTRATION. THEORETICALLY, IT HAS LONG BEEN ASSUMED THAT PUBLIC ADMINISTRATION HAS TO BE A DISCIPLINE REACHING BEYOND ONE COUNTRY AND ANY SPECIFIC CULTURE, BUT THE PRACTICAL BENEFITS DERIVED FROM COMPARATIVE ANALYSIS, SUCH AS MORE EFFECTIVE POLICY MAKING, BETTER ADMINISTRATIVE ARRANGEMENTS AND ENHANCED DEVELOPMENT PROSPECTS NEED ALSO TO BE STRESSED. COMPARATIVE BUREAUCRATIC CORRUPTION ILLUSTRATES BOTH THE BENEFITS AND THE DIFFICULT METHODOLOGICAL PROBLEMS ENCOUNTERED, IN THIS CASE REVEALING WHY RICH AND STABLE POLITIES CAN DEPEND ON LEGAL-RATIONAL NORMS WHILE POOR AND UNSTABLE POLITIES ARE MORE SUSCEPTIBLE TO SYSTEMIC DEVIANT CONDUCT BY PUBLIC OFFICIALS.

01954 CAIHONG, H.
CHINESE WARSHIP VISITS HAWAII
BEIJING REVIEW, 32(18) (MAY 89), 36.
ON MARCH 31, 1989, THE CHINESE NAVIGATION TRAINING WARSHIP "ZHENG HE" LEFT QINDAO TO VISIT HAWAII. IT WAS A RETURN VISIT BY THE CHINESE NAVY IN RESPONSE TO THE AMERICAN PACIFIC FLEET'S VISIT TO CHINA IN 1986 AND ALSO THE CHINESE NAVY'S FIRST FRIENDLY VISIT TO A WESTERN COUNTRY. THE CAPTAIN SAID THE VISIT WOULD OPEN A NEW COURSE IN FRIENDLY COMMUNICATIONS BETWEEN THE CHINESE AND AMERICAN NAVIES.

01955 CAIN, B.; LEWIS, I. A.; RIVERS, D.
STRATEGY AND CHOICE IN THE 1988 PRESIDENTIAL PRIMARIES
ELECTORAL STUDIES, 8(1) (APR 89), 23-48.
THE PAPER USES DATA FROM A SERIES OF 12 EXIT POLLS CONDUCTED BY THE LOS ANGELES TIMES TO EXPLAIN THE COURSE OF THE 1988 DEMOCRATIC AND REPUBLICAN PRESIDENTIAL PRIMARY CAMPAIGNS. IT INDICATES THAT THE SO-CALLED "MOMENTUM THEORY" WILL HAVE TO BE REVISED. MOMENTUM IN BOTH RACES WAS SLOWED BY REGIONALISM, AND IN THE DEMOCRATIC CONTEST SPECIFICALLY, BY THE NON-STRATEGIC SUPPORT THAT BLACKS AND AFFLUENT LIBERAL WHITES GAVE JESSE JACKSON. BOTH BUSH AND DUKAKIS STAKED OUT POSITIONS FOR THEMSELVES NEAR THE CENTER OF THE IDEOLOGICAL SPECTRUM IN THEIR RESPECTIVE PARTIES AND THE DISTRIBUTION OF VOTER PREFERENCES SERVED TO MAKE THE MIDDLE AN ADVANTAGEOUS SPOT FOR THE VICTORIOUS CANDIDATES.

01956 CAIN, M.; AL-BADRI, K.S.
AN ASSESSMENT OF THE TRADE AND RESTRUCTURING EFFECTS OF THE GULF COOPERATION COUNCIL
INTERNATIONAL JOURNAL OF MIDDLE EAST STUDIES, 21(1) (FEB 89), 57-69.
THE PECULIAR CHARACTERISTICS OF THE GULF ECONOMIES (INCLUDING EXCESSIVE DEPENDENCE ON A SINGLE PRIMARY SECTOR, THE ACUTE LACK OF SECTORAL LINKAGES, LABOR SHORTAGES, THE WEAK AGRICULTURAL SECTORS, AND THE STRUCTURAL SIMILARITIES RESULTING FROM IMPORT SUBSTITUTION POLICIES) HAVE WORKED AGAINST SECURING A REASONABLE DEGREE OF SUCCESS FOR PAST INTEGRATIVE EFFORTS WITHIN THE GULF REGION AND THE WHOLE ARAB WORLD. BUT THE GULF COOPERATION COUNCIL CONSTITUTES AN UNPRECEDENTED EXPERIENCE FOR THE GULF COUNTRIES, WITH THE BEST CHANCE SO FAR OF PROVIDING THE PREREQUISITES FOR LARGE ECONOMIC GAINS IN THE REGION. ALL PAST INTEGRATION SCHEMES WERE EITHER PARTIAL IN THEIR COVERAGE OR INVOLVED INSTITUTIONS WITH SO MUCH IMPLICIT POLITICAL AND ECONOMIC CONTRADICTION THAT THE PARTICIPATION OF MEMBER COUNTRIES WAS ONLY NOMINAL.

01957 CAIN, S.
AMERICAN JEWS AND THE PALESTINIAN UPRISING
MIDSTREAM, XXXV(4) (MAY 89), 38-41.
AMERICAN JEWS ARE CASTIGATED FOR SPEAKING THEIR MIND ON THE PALESTINIAN UPRISING IN THE WEST BANK AND THE GAZA STRIP BECAUSE THE CRITICS DON'T LIKE WHAT THEY SAY OR BECAUSE THEY DON'T MEET THE CRITICS' STANDARDS OF JEWISH AUTHENTICITY OR LOVE OF ISRAEL. BUT THEY ARE ALSO DECRIED IF THEY DO NOT VENTURE AN OPINION ON THIS TRAUMATIC, HIGHLY PUBLICIZED EVENT. ON ONE HAND, AMERICAN JEWS ARE ENCOURAGED TO SPEAK OUT, PROVIDED THEY HAVE A RECORD OF IDENTIFICATION WITH ISRAEL AND ISRAELIS; INDEED, THEY ARE MORALLY COMPELLED TO DO SO. ON THE OTHER, THEY ARE DISCOURAGED FROM BLAMING THE ISRAELI GOVERNMENT FOR THE ACTS THAT COMPEL A MORAL RESPONSE.

01958 CAISSE, A.
THE QUESTION OF ROLLING BACK THE STATE IN FRANCE
GOVERNANCE, 2(2) (APR 89), 152-171.
THE SIZE AND POWERS OF THE STATE HAVE BEEN AND REMAIN A MAJOR SOURCE OF DEBATE AND DISPUTE IN FRENCH DOMESTIC POLITICS THE ARTICLE EXAMINES THE EFFORTS OF FRANCOIS MITTERAND AND OTHERS TO "ROLL BACK THE STATE" AND THE RESULTS OF SUCH POLICIES. ALTHOUGH THE SOCIALISTS HAVE EXPERIENCED SOME SETBACKS, THEY HAVE ALSO MADE SOME GAINS THAT APPEAR TO BE RELATIVELY IRREVERSIBLE. THESE INCLUDE THE DECENTRALIZATION AND DOWNWARD TRANSFER OF RESPONSIBILITIES AND BUDGETING, COEXISTENCE BETWEEN THAT STATE-OWNED AND PRIVATE ECONOMIC SECTORS, AND THE REHABILITATION OF PRIVATE, AND SEMI-PRIVATE ENTERPRISE. HOWEVER, THE DEBATE IS FAR FROM OVER.

01959 CALABRESE, J.
RAFSANJANI'S FOREIGN POLICY
MIDDLE EAST INTERNATIONAL, (359) (SEP 89), 19-20.
THE WIDELY HELD VIEW THAT NEWLY-ELECTED PRESIDENT RAFSANJANI WILL SIGNIFICANTLY ALTER THE RADICAL POLICES OF HIS SUCCESSOR, THE AYATOLLAH KHOMEINI, IS DUE TO SOME SIGNIFICANT MISCONCEPTIONS. THE FIRST IS THAT RAFSANJANI IS A "PRAGMATIC" OR A "MODERATE." THESE TERMS CARRY QUITE DIFFERENT CONNOTATIONS IN THE ISLAMIC POLITICAL MILIEU. THE SECOND MISCONCEPTION STEMS FROM THE FACT THAT MANY ANALYSTS IGNORE THE SUBTLE CHANGES IN IRANIAN FOREIGN POLICY THAT TOOK PLACE UNDER KHOMEIN'S REIGN. ECONOMIC TIES WITH WEST GERMANY AND ITALY WERE ON THE INCREASE BEFORE THE DEATH OF THE AYATOLLAH; A CLOSE ANALYSIS OF HIS RHETORIC ALSO REVEALS A SHIFT FROM A POLICY OF BALANCED HOSTILITY TO ONE OF BALANCED NEUTRALITY TOWARDS THE SUPERPOWERS.

01960 CALDER, K.E.
ELITES IN AN EQUALIZING ROLE: EX-BUREAUCRATS AS COORDINATORS AND INTERMEDIARIES IN THE JAPANESE GOVERNMENT-BUSINESS RELATIONSHIP
COMPARATIVE POLITICS, 21(4) (JUL 89), 379-404.

JAPAN IS A NATION IN WHICH GOVERNMENT POWER AND
ADMINISTRATIVE ACTIVITIES ARE DEEPLY INTERTWINED WITH THOSE
OF THE PRIVATE SECTOR, MAKING IT DIFFICULT TO DISCUSS PUBLIC
POLICY ABSTRACTED FROM PRIVATE INTEREST. IN THIS ESSAY, THE
AUTHOR EXAMINES ONE ASPECT OF THE JAPANESE GOVERNMENT-
BUSINESS RELATIONSHIP: EX-BUREAUCRATS AS COORDINATORS AND
INTERMEDIARIES.

01961 CALDER, K.E.
THE NORTH PACIFIC TRIANGLE: SOURCES OF ECONOMIC AND
POLITICAL TRANSFORMATION
JOURNAL OF NORTHEAST ASIAN STUDIES, 8(2) (SUM 89), 3-17.
THIS ARTICLE EXPLORES THE CHANGING ECONOMIC AND SECURITY
RELATIONSHIPS AMONG THE UNITED STATES, JAPAN, AND SOUTH
KOREA, WITH PARTICULAR ATTENTION TO THE IMPLICATIONS OF POST-
1985 EXCHANGE-RATE SHIFTS FOR POLITICAL AND ECONOMIC
STABILITY IN THESE THREE NATIONS. THE AUTHOR ARGUES THAT THE
STABILITY AND COHESION OF THIS STRATEGICALLY IMPORTANT NORTH
PACIFIC TRIANGLE, THE ONLY POINT OUTSIDE EUROPE WHERE THE
ECONOMIC AND MILITARY SUPERPOWERS ALL ADJOIN ONE ANOTHER, IS
SIGNIFICANTLY THREATENED BY THE ONGOING SHIFT FROM THE
AMERICAN TO THE JAPANESE MARKET AS THE LOCUS OF REGIONAL
GROWTH, DUE TO DISPROPORTIONATE AND DESTABILIZING ADJUSTMENT
COSTS BEING IMPOSED ON SOUTH KOREA. EXPANDED AMERICAN, AND
ESPECIALLY JAPANESE SUPPORT INITIATIVES ARE THE PRINCIPAL
ALTERNATIVES TO INTENSIFIED KOREAN RELIANCE ON CONTINENTAL
ASIA, THE ARTICLE MAINTAINS.

01962 CALDERON, R.A.
PERESTROIKA AND CENTRAL AMERICA
HEMISPHERE, 1(3) (SUM 89), 33-34.
PERESTROIKA HAS BROUGHT INCREASED CONTACT BETWEEN THE
USSR AND LATIN AMERICA, INCLUDING AN UNPRECEDENTED NUMBER OF
COMMERCIAL, TECHNOLOGICAL, AND CULTURAL ACCORDS.
SIMULTANEOUSLY, THE SOVIETS HAVE ENCOURAGED DEMOCRATIZATION,
CONTADORA NEGOTIATIONS, AND INDEPENDENT FOREIGN POLICIES,
ESPECIALLY FOR MEXICO AND ARGENTINA. BUT, IN GENERAL,
DETENTE HAS NOT REACHED CENTRAL AMERICA AND THE CARIBBEAN.
THE POLITICAL ACTORS OF CENTRAL AMERICA AND THE CARIBBEAN
CONTINUE TO BE IMMERSED IN THE DIALECTICS OF THE COLD WAR,
AND THE AREA'S MARXIST GOVERNMENTS ARE NOT YET EMPLOYING THE
LANGUAGE OF PERESTROIKA.

01963 CALDWELL, C. F.
GOVERNMENT BY CAUCUS: INFORMAL LEGISLATIVE GROUPS IN A ERA
OF CONGRESSIONAL REFORM
JOURNAL OF LAW & POLITICS, V(3) (SPR 89), 625-655.
THE GOAL OF PREVENTING PRIVATE INTERESTS FROM ACHIEVING
THE CONTROVERSIAL "FAVORED POSITION" WITHIN THE LEGISLATIVE
PROCESS IS FEASIBLE. MEETING SUCH A GOAL WOULD NOT SOLVE THE
PROBLEMS OF MONEY AND INFLUENCE WITHIN THE CONGRESS, A
PROBLEM TIED MORE DIRECTLY TO CAMPAIGN FINANCE LAW. THE
LEGISLATIVE SERVICE ORGANIZATIONS (LSO'S) AND INSTITUTES
WILL CONTINUE TO HAVE THEIR INFLUENCE, BUT FURTHER REFORM
COULD CONSTRAIN THE UNAVOIDABLE LINKAGES BETWEEN PRIVATE
INFLUENCE AND THE INTERNAL PROCESSES OF THE HOUSE.

01964 CALDWELL, D.
THE CUBAN MISSILE AFFAIR AND THE AMERICAN STYLE OF CRISIS
MANAGEMENT
PARAMETERS, XIX(1) (MAR 89), 49-60.
MORE THAN ANY OTHER SINGLE EPISODE IN THE HISTORY OF
POST-WORLD WAR II AMERICAN FOREIGN POLICY, THE CUBAN MISSILE
CRISIS CONTRIBUTED TO THE DEVELOPMENT OF AN AMERICAN STYLE
OF CRISIS MANAGEMENT. IN THIS PAPER, THE AUTHOR DESCRIBES
SEVEN ELEMENTS OF THE AMERICAN STYLE OF CRISIS MANAGEMENT
AND THEN EVALUATES THE PRINCIPAL ELEMENTS.

01965 CALDWELL, L.
A CONSTITUTIONAL LAW FOR THE ENVIRONMENT: 20 YEARS WITH
THE NEPA INDICATES THE NEED.
ENVIRONMENT, 31(10) (DEC 89), 6-11, 25-28.
THE US' BASIC DECLARATION OF ENVIRONMENTAL POLICY, THE
NATIONAL ENVIRONMENTAL POLICY ACT (NEPA), WAS THE FIRST
COMPREHENSIVE COMMITMENT IN MODERN TIMES TOWARD RESPONSIBLE
CUSTODY OF THE ENVIRONMENT. THE AUTHOR OF THE ORIGINAL DRAFT
OF THE ACT EXAMINES TWO DECADES OF ITS PERFORMANCE. AFTER AN
ANALYSIS OF WHERE NEPA HAS SUCCEEDED, AND HOW, AND WHERE IT
HAS FAILED, AND WHY, THE ARTICLE EXAMINES THE FEASIBILITY
AND DESIRABILITY OF AN AMENDMENT TO THE CONSTITUTION WHICH
WOULD GUARANTEE ENVIRONMENTAL PROTECTION. IT CONCLUDES THAT
A STATUTE LACKING AN EXPLICIT CONSTITUTIONAL REFERENT IS
MORE EASILY NEGLECTED THAN ONE WITH A SPECIFICALLY
IDENTIFIABLE CONSTITUTIONAL BASIS.

01966 CALHOUN, G
REVOLUTION AND REPRESSION IN TIANANMEN SQUARE
SOCIETY, 26(6) (SEP 89), 21-38.
DRAWING PARTIALLY FROM HIS OWN EXPERIENCES IN BEIJING,
THE AUTHOR RECOUNTS THE EVENTS SURROUNDING THE STUDENT
PROTESTS AT TIANANMEN SQUARE AND THE ENSUING MASSACRE. IT
OUTLINES THE EVENTS FROM THE INITIAL PROTESTS IN LATE APRIL
TO THE FINAL DAYS OF THE MOVEMENT IN EARLY JUNE. IT ALSO
ANALYSES SOME OF THE UNDERLYING CONCEPTS AND CONFLICTS THAT

SHAPED THE MOVEMENT AND THE GOVERNMENT'S RESPONSE.

01967 CALLAMAN, S.
A MORAL OBLIGATION
SOJOURNERS, 18(10) (NOV 89), 18.
THE ARTICLE OUTLINES THE "FEMINIST PRO-CHOICE" POSITION
ON ABORTION. IT HOLDS THAT ALL MEMBERS OF THE HUMAN RACE
HOLD AN INALIENABLE RIGHT TO LIFE AND ARGUES THAT A FETUS
SHOULD NOT BE EXCEPTED FROM PROTECTION. THE ARTICLE OUTLINES
A STRATEGY DESIGNED TO ENSURE THE RIGHT TO LIFE FOR ALL
PEOPLE; IT INCLUDES BANNING LATE ABORTIONS, COUNSELING TO
THOSE CONSIDERING AN ABORTION, AND FAMILY LIFE EDUCATION
BEGINNING IN KINDERGARTEN.

01968 CALLCOTT, M.
THE MUNICIPAL ADMINISTRATION OF NEWCASTLE UPON TYNE, 1835-
1900
DISSERTATION ABSTRACTS INTERNATIONAL, 50(1) (JUL 89),
254-A.
THIS STUDY EXAMINES THE GROWTH AND DEVELOPMENT OF ONE OF
THE MAJOR MUNICIPAL CORPORATIONS OF VICTORIAN ENGLAND FROM
THE PASSAGE OF THE MUNICIPAL CORPORATIONS ACT UNTIL THE END
OF THE NINETEENTH CENTURY. IT IS ARGUED THAT ALTHOUGH THE
ACT OF 1835 INITIALLY IMPOSED VERY LIMITED FUNCTIONS UPON
THE REFORMED CORPORATIONS IT NEVERTHELESS PROVIDED A
FRAMEWORK WITHIN WHICH THOSE CORPORATIONS COULD AND DID
EXPAND IN ROLE. FUNCTION AND RESOURCES IN THE FOLLOWING
SIXTY-FIVE YEARS, ACCEPTING WIDE RESPONSIBILITIES WHICH
NECESSITATED THE CREATION OF A SUBSTANTIAL PROFESSIONAL
BUREAUCRACY.

01969 CALLEO, D.P.
THE AMERICAN ROLE IN NATO
JOURNAL OF INTERNATIONAL AFFAIRS, 43(1) (SUM 89), 19-28.
THIS ARTICLE EXAMINES THE STATUS QUO OF AMERICAN
INVOLVEMENT IN NATO. IT CONTENDS THAT THIS POSITION IS NO
LONGER VIABLE BUT THAT THE SUGGESTED SOLUTIONS OF BURDEN
SHARING AND DISENGAGEMENT ARE INADEQUATE OR INAPPROPRIATE
POLICIES. IT EXAMINES THE AMERICAN STAKE IN EUROPE AND
CONCLUDES THAT THE ALLIANCE SHOULD BE CONTINUED BUT THAT
REFORM IS NECESSARY.

01970 CALMAN, L.J.
WOMEN AND MOVEMENT POLITICS IN INDIA
ASIAN SURVEY, 29(10) (OCT 89), 940-958.
THE INDIAN WOMEN'S MOVEMENT IS DECENTRALIZED INTO VERY
LOOSELY ALLIED ORGANIZATIONS, SOME OF WHICH ARE ASSOCIATED
WITH POLITICAL PARTIES BUT MANY OTHERS ARE "AUTONOMOUS" AND
HAVE EXPLICITLY REJECTED ANY SUCH AFFILIATION. THIS ARTICLE
WILL DESCRIBE THE OVERALL STRUCTURE OF THE WOMEN'S MOVEMENT,
ANALYZING THE IDEOLOGICAL ORIGINS OF THAT STRUCTURE AND
PAYING PARTICULAR ATTENTION TO THE MOVEMENT'S RELATIONSHIP
TO OTHER CONTEMPORARY NONPARTY-AFFILIATED INDIAN MOVEMENTS.
IT WILL SUGGEST SOME POTENTIAL STRENGTHS OF THE RETICULAR
STRUCTURE, NOTING THAT POLITICAL MOVEMENTS MAY SERVE
DIFFERENT FUNCTIONS THAN PARTY AND ELECTORAL POLITICS,
PARTICULARLY THE CREATION OF NEW CHANNELS FOR POLITICAL
PARTICIPATION AND THE DEVELOPMENT OF PERSONAL AND COMMUNITY
EMPOWERMENT. IN THE LONG RUN, THESE MAY ALSO HAVE AN IMPACT
ON GOVERNMENTAL POLICIES AND ACTIONS. I WILL SHOW THAT IN
THE PURSUIT OF THESE GOALS, THE WOMEN'S MOVEMENT HAS BECOME
AN INTEGRAL PART OF THAT BROADER NONPARTY MOVEMENT SECTOR
THAT EMERGED IN INDIA IN THE EARLY 1970S AND BLOSSOMED IN
THE WAKE OF INDIRA GANDHI'S DECLARATION OF AN EMERGENCY IN
1975.

01971 CALVERT, P.
ARGENTINA: THE PRIMACY OF GEOPOLITICS
WORLD TODAY, 45(2) (FEB 89), 33-36.
FROM A GLOBAL PERSPECTIVE, ARGENTINA'S RADICAL
GOVERNMENT SHARES THE CONCERN OF OTHER POWERS WITH THE
NUCLEAR ISSUE AND WELCOMES THE SIGNS OF RAPPROCHEMENT
BETWEEN THE SUPERPOWERS. FROM A REGIONAL PERSPECTIVE, FOUR
SPECIFIC ISSUES STAND OUT IN THE RADICAL FOREIGN POLICY: THE
DEBT CRISIS, RELATIONS WITH CHILE, RELATIONS WITH CENTRAL
AMERICA, AND THE FALKLANDS/MALVINAS QUESTION.

01972 CALVERT, R.L.; MC CUBBINS, M.D.; WEINGAST, B.R.
A THEORY OF POLITICAL CONTROL AND AGENCY DISCRETION
AMERICAN JOURNAL OF POLITICAL SCIENCE, 33(3) (AUG 89),
588-611.
A MAJOR ISSUE IN THE STUDY OF AMERICAN POLITICS IS THE
EXTENT TO WHICH ELECTORAL DISCIPLINE ALSO CONSTRAINS
BUREAUCRATS. IN PRACTICE, EXECUTIVE AGENCIES OPERATE WITH
CONSIDERABLE INDEPENDENCE FROM ELECTED OFFICIALS. HOWEVER,
THE ENTIRE PROCESS OF POLICY EXECUTION IS A GAME AMONG
LEGISLATORS, THE CHIEF EXECUTIVE. AND BUREAUCRATIC AGENTS.
IT INCLUDES THE INITIAL DELEGATION OF AUTHORITY, THE CHOICE
OF POLICY ALTERNATIVES, AND OPPORTUNITIES FOR OVERSIGHT AND
CONTROL. A SIMPLE MODEL OF THIS PROCESS DEMONSTRATES AN
IMPORTANT DISTINCTION BETWEEN BUREAUCRATIC AUTHORITY AND
BUREAUCRATIC DISCRETION. INDEED, IN ITS SIMPLEST FORM, THE
MODEL PREDICTS A WORLD IN WHICH BUREAUCRATS ARE THE SOLE
ACTIVE PARTICIPANTS IN POLICYMAKING, BUT IN WHICH THE CHOICE

OF POLICY IS TRACEABLE ENTIRELY TO THE PREFERENCES OF
ELECTED OFFICIALS. MORE REALISTICALLY, THE MODEL LEADS TO A
PRECISE DEFINITION OF AGENCY DISCRETION. THESE CONCLUSION
HAVE PRACTICAL APPLICATIONS FOR BOTH STUDENTS AND REFORMERS
OF POLICYMAKING.

01973 CALZON, F.
    IN CONVERSATION WITH JEANE J. KIRKPATRICK
    FREEDOM AT ISSUE, (107) (MAR 89), 11-19.
        IN THIS INTERVIEW, THE FORMER U.S. REPRESENTATIVE TO THE
    UNITED NATIONS DISCUSSES THE IMPACT OF MIKHAIL GORBACHEV'S
    POLICIES ON SOVIET-AMERICAN RELATIONS, THE NATURE OF THE
    BUSH ADMINISTRATION, THE FUTURE OF NEO-CONSERVATISM, THE
    REAGAN DOCTRINE, UNITED STATES' POLICY TOWARD CENTRAL
    AMERICA, AND THE DISTINCTION BETWEEN AUTHORITARIAN AND
    TOTALITARIAN REGIMES.

01974 CAMACHO, D.E.
    RAZA POLITICAL DEVELOPMENT AND BEHAVIOR: A CASE OF
    ASSIMILATION
    DISSERTATION ABSTRACTS INTERNATIONAL, 49(11) (MAY 89),
    3488-A.
        BY ANALYZING PLURALIST, ELITIST, AND MARXIST CONCEPTIONS
    OF POWER, THE AUTHOR ENDEAVORS TO EXPLAIN SUCCESSFUL AND
    UNSUCCESSFUL EFFORTS AT COLLECTIVE ACTION BY CHICANOS. HE RE-
    EVALUATES EXISTING THEORIES OF COLLECTIVE ACTION AND STUDIES
    RAZA POLITICAL DEVELOPMENT AND BEHAVIOR.

01975 CAME, B.; ERASMUS, C.
    A NATION IN THE MAKING
    MACLEAN'S (CANADA'S NEWS MAGAZINE), 102(13) (MAR 89), 25,
    27.
        AFTER 75 YEARS OF SOUTH AFRICAN DOMINANCE, NAMIBIA,
    AFRICA'S LAST COLONY, SEEMS READY FOR INDEPENDENCE. A UN
    PEACEKEEPING FORCE HAS BEGUN TO ARRIVE, AND IF ALL GOES AS
    SCHEDULED, THE NATION WILL ACHIEVE INDEPENDENCE BY APRIL,
    1990. PROBLEMS SUCH AS A FEARED EXODUS OF WHITE PROFESSIONAL
    AND MANAGERIAL GROUPS AS WELL AS ECONOMIC WORRIES CLOUD THE
    HORIZON, BUT CANNOT DIM THE HOPE THAT ALL INVOLVED FEEL
    ABOUT THE RECENT DEVELOPMENTS.

01976 CAME, B.
    BLACK-AND-WHITE ISSUES
    MACLEAN'S (CANADA'S NEWS MAGAZINE), 102(4) (JAN 89), 13.
        RACIAL TENSIONS IN TORONTO INCREASED AS SEVERAL POLICE
    OFFICERS WERE CHARGED WITH MANSLAUGHTER FOR THE DEATHS OF
    SEVERAL BLACK CITIZENS OF TORONTO. THE BLACK ACTION DEFENSE
    COMMITTEE AND OTHER ORGANIZATIONS CLAIM THAT MANSLAUGHTER IS
    TOO LENIENT OF A CHARGE AND DEMAND A CHARGE OF MURDER IN
    ORDER TO MAKE HIGHLY VISIBLE THE RACIST NATURE OF THE
    KILLINGS. POLICE GROUPS ARGUE THAT ANY CHARGE IS POLITICALLY
    MOTIVATED AND INTERFERES WITH LAW ENFORCEMENT. THE END
    RESULT IS HIGHER TENSION BETWEEN THE POLICE AND THE TORONTO
    AREA'S VISIBLE MINORITIES.

01977 CAME, B.; MACKENZIE, H.: TEDESCO, T.
    EXECUTION IN CHINA
    MACLEAN'S (CANADA'S NEWS MAGAZINE), 102(26) (JUL 89),
    14-15.
        THE HARD LINE CHINESE GOVERNMENT SHOWED NO SIGNS OF
    EASING UP ON THE "COUNTERREVOLUTIONARIES" THAT DEMONSTRATED
    IN TIANANMEN SQUARE. LESS THAN A MONTH AFTER THE MASSACRE,
    THE GOVERNMENT IS METHODICALLY HUNTING DOWN AND EXECUTING
    "BAD ELEMENTS" AND "RIOTERS." DESPITE WORLDWIDE PROTEST AND
    CONDEMNATION, THE GOVERNMENT HAS ALREADY EXECUTED SOME 30
    CHINESE CITIZENS AND PLANS ON MORE IN THE FUTURE.

01978 CAME, B.; SILVER, E.
    THE WIDENING GULF
    MACLEAN'S (CANADA'S NEWS MAGAZINE), 102(28) (JUL 89), 21.
        IN ISRAEL AND PALESTINE THE INTIFADAH CONTINUED AS A
    PALESTINIAN ISLAMIC FUNDAMENTALIST CAUSED A BUS ACCIDENT
    WHICH KILLED 14 AND INJURED 27. THE INCIDENT DREW ATTENTION
    AWAY FROM THE PEACE NEGOTIATION PROCESS AND GAVE HARD LINE
    ISRAELI FACTIONS, WHO DECLARE THAT NO COMPROMISE WITH
    PALESTINIANS IS POSSIBLE, AMMUNITION TO CONTINUE THEIR
    ATTACKS ON ANY GOVERNMENT SIGN OF DEVIATION FROM THE HARD
    LINE STANCE.

01979 CAMERON, C.M.
    CALCULATION AND CHOICE IN THE JOB OF THE CONGRESSMAN: AN
    INTRODUCTION TO THE THEORY OF SERVICE STRATEGY
    DISSERTATION ABSTRACTS INTERNATIONAL, 49(7) (JAN 89),
    1955-A.
        THE AUTHOR DEVELOPS A FORMAL THEORY OF SERVICE STRATEGY
    FOR RATIONAL, VOTE-SEEKING POLITICIANS, ESPECIALLY MEMBERS
    OF THE US CONGRESS. CONSTRUCTING THE STRATEGY INVOLVES THE
    POLITICIAN IN ANSWERING THREE QUESTIONS: (1) HOW MUCH POLICY-
    MAKING, CONSTITUENCY SERVICE, AND CAMPAIGNING ACTIVITY SHALL
    I UNDERTAKE? (2) ON WHICH VOTING BLOCKS, INTEREST GROUPS, OR
    CONTRIBUTORS SHALL I TARGET MY EFFORTS? (3) HOW SHALL I
    ALLOCATE MY RESOURCES AND MY OWN TIME?

01980 CAMERON, S.
    THE SMOKE TAX MUDDLE
    CONTEMPORARY REVIEW, 255(1485) (OCT 89), 178-180.
        THIS ARTICLE EXAMINES THE BELIEF THAT INCREASING TAXESON
    CIGARETTES WILL CUT SMOKING AND THAT SMOKING IS CONNECTED
    WITH INCOME IN THAT HIGHER INCOME PEOPLE WILL SMOKE MORE. IT
    CONCLUDES THAT THIS IS NOT THE CASE, THAT WITHIN ANY SOCIAL
    CLASS THERE IS NO IMPACT OF PRICE AND INCOME ON SMOKING.

01981 CAMILLER, P.
    BEYOND 1992: THE LEFT AND EUROPE
    NEW LEFT REVIEW, (175) (MAY 89), 5-18.
        PATRICK CAMILLER ARGUES THAT THE RENEWAL OF EUROPE'S
    HITHERTO FRAGMENTED LEFT MUST CENTRALLY ADDRESS THE
    CONTINENT-WIDE POLITICS WHICH HAVE COME ONTO THE AGENDA WITH
    THE REFORM PROCESS IN THE SOVIET UNION AND WHICH ARE
    BECOMING EVER MORE NECESSARY IN AN AGE OF ECONOMIC
    DISLOCATION, ECOLOGICAL DESTRUCTION AND MILITARY INSECURITY.
    SOCIAL-DEMOCRATIC NATIONAL KEYNESIANISM, A CREATURE OF THE
    POST-WAR BOOM, HAS UNIVERSALLY FAILED TO TACKLE THE
    PROLONGED CRISIS OF THE PAST FIFTEEN YEARS. NOR DO THE
    NARROW, HALF-EUROPEAN HORIZONS OF 1992 OFFER ANY SOLID
    PROSPECT OF RECOVERY OF THE PRODUCTIVE ECONOMY, IMBUED AS
    THEY ARE WITH THE ANARCHIC SPIRIT OF CAPITAL UNBOUND. AS THE
    WEST EUROPEAN GOVERNMENTS PREPARE TO GIVE UP MANY OF THEIR
    NATIONAL REGULATORY LEVERS, AN ALLIANCE BETWEEN THE WESTERN
    LEFT AND SOCIALIST REFORM FORCES IN THE EAST COULD THROW
    BACK THE NEO-LIBERAL OFFENSIVE OF THE PAST DECADE AND PLACE
    PLANNED SOCIAL ADVANCE ONCE AGAIN AT THE HEART OF DEBATE ON
    THE CONTINENT.

01982 CAMILLERI, J.
    RETHINKING THE POLITICS OF CHANGE
    ARENA, (87) (WIN 89), 108-126.
        THIS ARTICLE OFFERS A SURVEY OF POSSIBLE AVENUES FOR
    POLITICAL CHANGE WHICH IS NEITHER DETAILED NOR COMPREHENSIVE.
    THE AIM IS TO UNDERLINE THE INADEQUACY OF EXISTING
    INSTITUTIONAL ARRANGEMENTS AND THE WAY THEY REFLECT AND
    REINFORCE THE DOMINANT IDEOLOGY. IT DESCRIBES SOME ALTERNATE
    INSTITUTIONS AND PROCESSES CONSISTENT WITH THE IDEA OF AN
    EGALITARIAN, COMPASSIONATE, TOLERENT AND COSMOPOLITAN
    SOCIETY. IT CONCLUDES THAT RETHINKING THE AUSTRALIAN
    CONSTITUTION IS A TOOL FOR RETHINKING THE MEANING AND ROLE
    OF CITIZENSHIP AND FOR CREATING A NEW SENSE OF IDENTITY AND
    COMMUNITY.

01983 CAMMACK, P.
    REVIEW ARTICLE: BRINGING THE STATE BACK IN?
    BRITISH JOURNAL OF POLITICAL SCIENCE, 19(2) (APR 89),
    261-290.
        RECENT DISCUSSIONS OF THEORIES OF POLITICAL DEVELOPMENT
    OR COMPARATIVE POLITICS HAVE IDENTIFIED A PROCESS OF
    CONVERGENCE BETWEEN HITHERTO MUTUALLY HOSTILE NON-MARXIST
    AND MARXIST OR NEO-MARXIST APPROACHES. IN THIS EASSY, THE
    AUTHOR PROVIDES A DETAILED EXAMINATION OF THE DOUBLE PROCESS
    OF ASSIMILATION AND DISTORTION THAT THE PROCLAMATION OF
    CONVERGENCE INVOLVES BY REFERENCE TO "BRINGING THE STATE
    BACK IN" BY PETER EVANS, DIETRICH RUESCHEMEYER, AND THEDA
    SKOCPOL. HE SEEKS TO REVEAL THE MECHANISMS AT WORK IN THE
    LATEST ATTEMPT BY REPRESENTATIVES OF AMERICAN SOCIAL SCIENCE
    TO EXORCISE THE THREAT POSED BY MARXIST AND NEO-MARXIST
    PERSPECTIVES.

01984 CAMPACCI, N.
    BRAZIL AIMS HIGH
    SOUTH, (109) (NOV 89), 85.
        BRAZILIAN SPACE RESEARCH, A FAVOURED SECTOR OF THE
    MILITARY, IS ADVANCING RAPIDLY. IN 1988, PRESIDENT JOSE
    SARNEY SIGNED AN AGREEMENT WITH CHINA TO JOINTLY BUILD TWO
    REMOTE-SENSING SATELLITES FOR MONITORING NATURAL RESOURCES.
    THE SATELLITE WILL PROVIDE INFORMATION ON NATURAL RESOURCES
    TO BRAZIL, CHINA, AND OTHER THIRD WORLD COUNTRIES, AT A COST
    THEY CAN AFFORD.

01985 CAMPBELL, B.
    PARADIGMS LOST: CLASSICAL ATHENIAN POLITICS IN MODERN MYTH
    HISTORY OF POLITICAL THOUGHT, X(2) (SUM 89), 189-213.
        THIS ARTICLE EXAMINES THE MYTH OF THE CLASSICAL POLIS AS
    AN EXTENDED DEBATING SOCIETY, COMPRISING A BODY OF CITIZENS
    IN A POLITICAL ARENA OR 'PUBLIC SPACE' EVER ENGAGED AT
    DEVELOPING SOME ESSENTIAL PART OF THEMSELVES BY THEIR
    POLITICAL DISCUSSIONS AND CHOICES. THE MYTH HAS HAD A
    STULTIFYING EFFECT ON THE STUDY OF GREEK NOTIONS OF
    POLITICAL PARTICIPATION. THE STULTIFICATION IS MAINLY
    ATTRIBUTABLE TO INADEQUACIES OF THIS CONCEPTION OF THE BIOS
    POLITIKOS AS A RESEARCH MODEL. THE AUTHOR POINTS OUT SOME OF
    THE MORE IMPORTANT OF THESE INADEQUACIES ON TWO FRONTS: ITS
    RENDITION OF THE POLIS AS 'PUBLIC SPACE', AND ITS
    PARTICIPATORY IDEAL, ADVANCED AS A CENTRAL FEATURE OF GREEK
    POLITICAL EXPERIENCE.

01986 CAMPBELL, D.
    BERT CORONA: LABOR RADICAL
    SOCIALIST REVIEW, 19(1) (JAN 89), 41-55.

IN THIS INTERVIEW, HUMBERTO "BERT" CORONA--LABOR ORGANIZER SINCE THE 1930S, CHAMPION OF IMMIGRANT RIGHTS, EARLY LEADER OF CHICANO POLITICS, TEACHER, AND ORAL HISTORIAN-REMINDS US THAT THE US IS ONE OF ONLY TWO INDUSTRIALIZED CAPITALIST STATES IN THE WORLD WHICH BORDERS A THIRD WORLD NATION (SOUTH AFRICA IS THE OTHER). AS SUCH, IMMIGRANT WORKERS ARE AN INSEPARABLE PART OF THE US WORKFORCE; THEY ARE NOT "TEMPORARY" WORKERS, AS SOME WOULD LIKE TO THINK. MEXICAN NATIONALS AND MEXICAN AMERICANS HAVE LONG WORKED IN THE SHIPBUILDING, SHOEMAKING, FOOD PROCESSING, GARMENT AND OTHER INDUSTRIES, AS WELL AS IN AGRICULTURE, AND HAVE LED MANY OF THE STRUGGLES FOR UNIONIZATION IN THOSE INDUSTRIES. CORONA ALSO REMINDS US THAT, JUST AS EUROPEAN IMMIGRANTS IN THE LABOR MOVEMENT WERE SINGLED OUT FOR REPRESSION DURING THE PALMER RAIDS OF THE 1920S, SO WERE MEXICAN AND OTHER LATINO WORKERS SUBJECT TO REPRESSION DURING THE MCCARTHY ERA. IN OUR PRESENT CLIMATE OF HOSTILITY TOWARD UNDOCUMENTED WORKERS, THIS REPRESSION CONTINUES.

01987 CAMPBELL, H.
NAMIBIA: WHAT KIND OF INDEPENDENCE
MONTHLY REVIEW, 41(4) (SEP 89), 9-23.
THIS PAPER GIVES THE BACKGROUND OF THE POLITICAL STRUGGLES THAT AWAIT NAMIBIA AND THE PEOPLE OF SOUTHERN AFRICA AS THE ANTI-APARTHEID STRUGGLE ENTERS A NEW PHASE. THE 1988 AGREEMENT, THE UN RESOLUTION 435, NEGOTIATIONS AND CONCESSIONS AND THE CONTINUING STRUGGLE ARE EACH ADDRESSED. THE CHOICES POSED BY INDEPENDENCE ARE DEFINED.

01988 CAMPBELL, H.
THE MILITARY DEFEAT OF THE SOUTH AFRICANS IN ANGOLA
MONTHLY REVIEW, 40(11) (APR 89), 1-15.
THE HISTORIC AGREEMENT OF FORCES INVOLVED IN THE CONFLICT IN ANGOLA THAT CALLS FOR A SOUTH AFRICAN WITHDRAWAL FROM NAMIBIA AND MOVES TOWARD SELF-DETERMINATION FOR THE PEOPLE'S OF SOUTHER AFRICA WAS NOT SO MUCH THE RESULT OF TENACIOUS NEGOTIATION ON THE PART OF THE US AS IT WAS THE RESULT OF THE DECISIVE MILITARY DEFEAT OF SOUTH AFRICAN FORCES IN ANGOLA. THE ARTICLE OUTLINES THE EVENTS AND CONDITIONS THAT RESULTED IN THE MILITARIZATION OF AFRICA AND THE CONFLICT IN ANGOLA. IT RECOUNTS THE VARIOUS CONFLICTS AND BATTLES THAT TOOK PLACE DURING THE NEARLY 15-YEAR STRUGGLE, AND THE NEGOTIATION PROCESS THAT CULMINATED IN THE RECENT PEACE AGREEMENT.

01989 CAMPBELL, J.; BARNES, I.; PEPPER, C.
1992: THE ILLUSION OF CHANGE
PUBLIC ADMINISTRATION, 67(3) (FAL 89), 319 - 328.
DESPITE ALL THE RECENT PUBILCITY SURROUNDING THE BENEFITS OF A 'EUROPE WITHOUT FRONTIERS' IT WOULD BE WRONG TO ASSUME THAT THE ATTAINMENT OF THIS GOAL IS A FOREGONE CONCLUSION. THE 1992 DEADLINE IS A POLITICAL EXPEDIENT DESIGNED TO CREATE THE IMPRESSION THAT EUROPEAN ECONOMIC INTEGRATION IS AN IRREVERSIBLE PROCESS. HOWEVER, THE REALITY IS THAT THERE IS STILL A LONG WAY TO GO BEFORE EUROPE IS TRULY 'OPEN FOR BUSINESS'. BARRIERS TO TRADE WILL REMAIN DESPITE THE ENTHUSIASM OF THE COMMISSION FOR RADICAL CHANGE, BECAUSE IT IS THE MEMBER STATES WHO FINALLY DECIDE ON THE SHAPE OF NEW INITIATIVES. IN ORDER TO ACHIEVE AGREEMENT COMPROMISES HAVE TO BE MADE, AND THIS REDUCES THE IMPACT OF REFORMS. THE MEASURES TAKEN TO COMPLETE THAT INTERNAL MARKET OF THE EC CAN BECOME EXERCISES IN HARMONIZATION RATHER THAN SIGNIFICANT REFORMS WHICH OFFER DIRECT BENEFITS TO BUSINESS. THIS ARTICLE IS CONCERNED WITH ONE SUCH EXERCISE IN HARMONIZATION, THE INTRODUCTION OF THE SINGLE ADMINISTRATIVE DOCUMENT (SAD).

01990 CAMPBELL, J.C.; BASKIN, M.A.; BAUMGARTNER, F.R.; HALPERN, N.P.
AFTERWARD ON POLICY COMMUNITIES: A FRAMWORK FOR COMPARATIVE RESEARCH
GOVERNANCE, 2(1) (JAN 89), 86-94.
IN THIS ARTICLE, THE GOAL HAS BEEN TO CONVINCE SCHOLARS OF COMPARATIVE PUBLIC POLICY MAKING THAT THE POLICY-COMMUNITIES APPROACH IS BOTH INTERESTING AND ILLUMINATING. THE AUTHORS ARE PERSUADED OF THE LEARNING VALUE OF EXAMINING POLICY COMMUNITIES IN QUITE DISPARATE CONTEXTS - EVEN ACROSS DEMOCRATIC AND AUTHORITARIAN SYSTEMS - AND HOW WELL THIS APPROACH INTEGRATES THE SEPARATE CONCERNS OF HOW INTEREST GROUPS, PARTY SYSTEMS, BUREAUCRATIC ORGANIZATION AND LEADERSHIP STYLES AFFECT POLICY MAKING. IT IS BECAUSE SO MUCH DECISION MAKING IN MODERN GOVERNMENT TAKES PLACE IN AND AROUND POLICY COMMUNITIES THAT UNDERSTANDING THEIR CHARACTERISTICS AND DYNAMICS IS IMPERATIVE IN THE FIELD OF COMPARATIVE PUBLIC POLICY MAKING.

01991 CAMPBELL, J.C.
BUREAUCRATIC PRIMACY: JAPANESE POLICY COMMUNITIES IN AN AMERICAN PERSPECTIVE
GOVERNANCE, 2(1) (JAN 89), 5-22.
JAPAN IS A GOOD TEST CASE FOR SEEING HOW POLICY COMMUNITIES WORK OUTSIDE THE UNITED STATES, WHERE THEY WERE DISCOVERED. ON THE ONE HAND, JAPAN, LIKE THE US, HAS A RELATIVELY FRAGMENTED GOVERNMENTAL SYSTEM, SO THAT A LARGE PORTION OF DECISION-MAKING IS HANDLED AT THE SPECIALIZED LEVEL WITHOUT MUCH CENTRAL INTERVENTION. ON THE OTHER, JAPAN'S STATE STRUCTURE AND POLITICAL CULTURE DIFFER SUBSTANTIALLY FROM THE U.S., ALLOWING US TO GAIN A SENSE OF WHAT CAUSES VARIATIONS IN HOW SPECIALISTS RELATE TO EACH OTHER, AND HOW POLICY COMMUNITIES RELATE TO THE BROADER GOVERNMENTAL SYSTEM. THIS ARTICLE IS AN OVERVIEW OF WHAT CAN BE CALLED THE "BUREAUCRATIC PRIMACY" TYPE OF POLICY COMMUNITY, AS SEEN IN JAPAN IN CONTRAST TO THE UNITED STATES.

01992 CAMPBELL, J.L.
CORPORATIONS, COLLECTIVE ORGANIZATION, AND THE STATE: INDUSTRY RESPONSE TO THE ACCIDENT AT THREE MILE ISLAND
SOCIAL SCIENCE QUARTERLY, 70(3) (SEP 89), 650-666.
TO THE EXTENT THAT THE STATE ENCOURAGES THE FORMATION OF BUSINESS ASSOCIATIONS AND OTHER COLLECTIVE FORMS OF CORPORATE ACTIVITY, THEORISTS OF CORPORATISM AND ORGANIZATIONS HAVE ARGUED THAT IT DOES SO THROUGH THE THREAT OF REGULATORY INTERVENTION. IN CONTRAST, THIS PAPER ARGUES THAT CORPORATE LEADERS ALSO ESTABLISH SUCH ORGANIZATIONS DURING PERIODS OF INDUSTRYWIDE CRISIS WHEN THEY BELIEVE, REGARDLESS OF THE THREAT OF INTERVENTION, THAT THE STATE IS UNABLE TO RESOLVE THE CRISIS FOR THEM. THIS DISTINCTION BETWEEN THE PROBABILITY OF STATE INTERVENTION PER SE AND THE STATE'S CAPACITY FOR ACTUALLY SOLVING INDUSTRY PROBLEMS IS CRUCIAL FOR UNDERSTANDING THE COMMERCIAL NUCLEAR ENERGY SECTOR'S COLLECTIVE ORGANIZATIONAL RESPONSE TO THE ACCIDENT AT THE THREE MILE ISLAND NUCLEAR POWER PLANT. THE IMPLICATIONS FOR CORPORATIST AND ORGANIZATION THEORY ARE EXPLORED.

01993 CAMPBELL, K.
THE SOLDIERS' SUMMIT
FOREIGN POLICY, (75) (SUM 89), 76-91.
THE QUIET DEVELOPMENT OF MILITARY DETENTE OVER THE LAST 2 YEARS HAS OPENED A LASTING NEW ASPECT OF US-SOVIET RELATIONS. THE ARTICLE EXAMINES THE PAST SUPERPOWER MILITARY CONTACTS AND ANALYZES THE DIRECTION AND IMPLICATIONS OF THE CURRENT ONGOING TALKS. IT ALSO OUTLINES SOME OF THE AGENDAS OF THE MEETINGS; SOME OF THE TOPICS OF DISCUSSION INCLUDE: MILITARY STRATEGY, NEW MEANS OF VERIFICATION, EXCHANGES, AND MILITARY PROCUREMENT SCHEDULES.

01994 CAMPBELL, K.J.
THE CRUCIAL CONSTRAINT: CONTAINMENT AND THE AMERICAN MILITARY'S POST-VIETNAM RELUCTANCE TO USE FORCE
DISSERTATION ABSTRACTS INTERNATIONAL, 50(6) (DEC 89), 1793-A.
THE AMERICAN MILITARY SUFFERED ENORMOUS INSTITUTIONAL DAMAGE AND CAME DANGEROUSLY CLOSE TO TOTAL DISINTEGRATION DUE TO THE VIETNAM DEBACLE. FROM VIETNAM, THE MILITARY LEARNED THE VALUE OF DOMESTIC POLITICAL SUPPORT FOR THE SUCCESSFUL USE OF FORCE AND FOR THE HEALTH OF THE MILITARY AS A VIABLE INSTITUTION. CONSEQUENTLY, TODAY'S AMERICAN MILITARY LEADERS ARE CAUTIOUS AND RELUCTANT TO USE FORCE IN A SUSTAINED COMBAT SITUATION UNLESS THEY ARE ASSURED OF DOMESTIC POLITICAL SUPPORT. THIS NEW PRUDENCE UNDERCUTS THE LONGSTANDING POLICY OF CONTAINMENT. THE FAILURE TO RECOGNIZE THE DILEMMA OF CONTAINMENT AND PROVIDE AN ACCEPTABLE ALTERNATIVE BREEDS AMBIGUITY IN AMERICAN FOREIGN POLICY.

01995 CAMPBELL, T.
ARE RIGHTS MEANINGFUL UNDER SOCIALISM?
CRITICAL REVIEW, 3(3) (SUM 89), 554-567.
THIS ARTICLE'S ATTEMPT TO CONSTRUCT A SOCIALIST VERSION OF RIGHTS AND THE RULE OF LAW FAILS BECAUSE IT DOES NOT DRAW ON INDIVIDUALISM POSITIVE RIGHTS ARE INEFFECTIVE BARRIERS TO BOTH THE SCHEMES OF UTOPIAN VISIONARIES WHO COMMAND POLITICAL AUTHORITY AND MORE MUNDANE SOURCES OF THE ABUSE OF POWER. IT LEAVES UNANSWERED THE QUESTION OF WHO WILL DETERMINE THE EXTENT OF THE "NEEDS" THAT WOULD CONSTITUTE SOCIALIST RIGHTS, IN THE ABSENCE OF UNLIMITED RESOURCES TO FULFILL THEM. AND THE REJECTION OF INDIVIDUALISM LEAVES HIM NO MEANS OF ADJUDICATING AMONG CONFLICTING POSITIVE CLAIM-RIGHTS.

01996 CAMPBELL, W.H.
SOVIET THREAT: IS IT DECLINING
AVAILABLE FROM NTIS, NO. AD-A208 559/5/GAR, MAR 89, 62.
SOVIET GENERAL SECRETARY AND PRESIDENT MIKHAIL S. GORBACHEV HAS CAPTIVATED WORLD ATTENTION WITH PROPOSALS FOR WORLD PEACE AND FOR SWEEPING SYSTEMIC CHANGES WITHIN THE SOVIET UNION. IT IS THE PURPOSE OF THIS PAPER TO FIRST EXAMINE WHAT IS OCCURRING WITHIN THE SOVIET UNION TODAY IN THE CONTEXT OF PAST SOVIET BEHAVIOR. THIS ANALYSIS SHOWS THE STRIKING SIMILARITIES BETWEEN THE PROBLEMS AND PROPOSED SOLUTIONS EXISTING TODAY AND THOSE FOUND IN PREVIOUS PERIODS OF SOVIET HISTORY. THE SOVIETS HAVE A CONTINUING PATTERN OF PEACEFUL COEXISTENCE, FRIENDSHIP, AND DETENTE-LIKE POLICIES WHICH RELAX THE TENSIONS IN INTERSTATE RELATIONS AND ALLOW THE SOVIET UNION TO REGAIN THE INITIATIVE AND EMERGE FROM THESE PERIODS WITH RENEWED STRENGTH AND AGGRESSIVENESS. THE SECOND PART OF THIS PAPER EXAMINES SEVERAL AREAS WHERE THE UNITED STATES AND ITS EUROPEAN ALLIES MUST REMAIN ALERT AS

TO THE TRUE INTENTIONS OF THE SOVIET UNION. THIS PAPER CONCLUDES THAT IT IS FAR TOO EARLY TO BELIEVE THE SOVIET UNION HAS MADE A BREAK WITH ITS PAST AND, THEREFORE, TOO EARLY FOR THE WEST TO BEGIN TO BACK DOWN FROM ITS VIGILANCE AND DETERMINATION TO MEET THE SOVIET CHALLENGE FROM A POSITION OF MILITARY STRENGTH.

01997 CANDING, S.C.
INSURGENCY: A FORMIDABLE THREAT TO PHILIPPINE SECURITY
AVAILABLE FROM NTIS, NO. AD-A202 750/6/GAR, APR 88, 85.
A CRITICAL ANALYSIS OF PAST EVENTS, ATTEMPTED SOLUTIONS, AND THE UNDERLYING ASSUMPTIONS IN THE PAST STUDIES OF THE PROBLEM OF INSURGENCY IN THE PHILIPPINES IS PROVIDED BY THE RESEARCH PAPER. IT ADDRESSES THE CHARACTERISTIC AND DYNAMICS OF INSURGENCY PROBLEM FOR CREATING THE SITUATIONS WHICH BROUGHT ABOUT INSURGENCY. FROM THE ROOT CAUSE, THE AUTHOR TRACED THE EVENTS WHICH COMPLICATED THE ISSUES INVOLVED. THE IMPACT OF THE COLONIAL POWERS WHICH DOMINATED THE COUNTRY FOR MORE THAN 400 YEARS WERE SHOWN TO HAVE PLAYED THE GREATER PART. AS THE PAPER CONCLUDED THAT INSURGENCY IS THE MOST FORMIDABLE THREAT TO THE PHILIPPINE NATIONAL SECURITY, IT RECOMMENDS HOLISTIC SOLUTION INVOLVING EFFORTS BY THE WHOLE MACHINERY OF THE PHILIPPINE GOVERNMENT AS NECESSARY TO STOP THE THREAT.

01998 CANFIELD, R.L.
AFGANISTAN: THE TRAJECTORY OF INTERNAL ALIGNMENTS
MIDDLE EAST JOURNAL, 43(4) (FAL 89), 635-648.
AFGANISTAN, AND THE WAY ITS DISPARATE PEOPLES HAVE COME TO FUNCTION AS A NATION, IS THE FOCUS OF ANTHROPOLOGIST, ROBERT CANFIELD'S ARTICLE. HIS STUDY OF THAT SOCIETY'S BASIC "SCAFFOLDING" SUGGESTS WAYS IN WHICH ITS NEAR FUTURE MAY PLAY OUT. CANFIELD DOES NOT TRY TO PREDICT; HE LIMITS HIS FOCUS TO THE COUNTRY'S INTERNAL DYNAMICS. HE DESCRIBES THE BASE FROM WHICH A NEW AFGANISTAN MUST RISE.

01999 CANNON, M.W.
RAISING THE STAKES: THE TAYLOR-ROSTOW MISSION
JOURNAL OF STRATEGIC STUDIES, 12(2) (JUN 89), 125-165.
THE TAYLOR-ROSTOW MISSION TO VIETNAM IN OCTOBER 1961 HAS BEEN LONG RECOGNIZED AS THE KEY EVENT IN A MAJOR TURNING POINT IN THE WAR, BUT IT HAS BEEN LITTLE EXAMINED AND LESS UNDERSTOOD. THIS ESSAY STUDIES THE MISSION IN DETAIL AND CONSIDERS THE QUESTION OF WHETHER IT ACTUALLY MARKED A CHANGE IN AMERICAN POLICY IN VIETNAM, OR MERELY A CONTINUATION.

02000 CANON, D.T.
THE INSTITUTIONALIZATION OF LEADERSHIP IN THE U.S. CONGRESS
LEGISLATIVE STUDIES QUARTERLY, 14(3) (AUG 89), 415-444.
THE THEORY OF INSTITUTIONALIZATION (POLSBY 1968) PROVIDES A FRAMEWORK FOR CREATING HOW CONGRESS HAS CHANGED. THIS PAPER APPLIES THIS THEORY TO LEADERSHIP INSTITUTIONS IN THE HOUSE AND SENATE, FOCUSING ON THE DURABILITY, BOUNDEDNESS, INTERNAL COMPLEXITY, AND UNIVERSAL NORMS AND RULES OF THE LEADERSHIP. EXISTING THEORY DOES NOT FARE AS WELL IN EXPLAINING WHY INSTITUTIONS CHANGE. GRADUAL HISTORICAL FORCES, SUCH AS INCREASED SOCIETAL COMPLEXITY, CANNOT EXPLAIN THE EVOLUTION OF INSTITUTIONS, NOR DO THEY RECOGNIZE THE TENSIONS BETWEEN DIFFERENT ASPECTS OF CHANGE. IT OFFERS A THEORY OF CHANGE, BASED ON PARTISAN STABILITY, EXTERNAL CONDITIONS, MEMBER GOALS, AND THE UTILIZATION OF LEADERSHIP INSTITUTIONS.

02001 CAPELL, E.A.
A FRESHMAN SUCCEEDS IN THE CALIFORNIA LEGISLATURE: PATRICK JOHNSON AND THE CREATION OF THE EMPLOYMENT TRAINING PANEL
DISSERTATION ABSTRACTS INTERNATIONAL, 49(11) (MAY 89), 3488-A.
USING A FRESHMAN LEGISLATOR AS A CASE STUDY, THE AUTHOR SURVEYS HOW THE CALIFORNIA LEGISLATURE OPERATES AND HOW FIRST-TERM LEGISLATORS SUCCEED. SHE FOCUSES ON THE LEGISLATION AUTHORED BY ASSEMBLYMAN PATRICK JOHNSTON, THAT CREATED THE EMPLOYMENT TRAINING PANEL. SHE EXAMINES THE PARTY SYSTEM IN THE LEGISLATURE, THE LEADERSHIP STRUCTURE, THE AUTHOR SYSTEM OF INITIATING LEGISLATION, AND FLOOR ACTIVITIES.

02002 CAPELL, E.A.
A FRESHMAN SUCCEEDS IN THE CALIFORNIA LEGISLATURE: PATRICK JOHNSTON AND THE CREATION OF THE EMPLOYMENT TRAINING PANEL
DISSERTATION ABSTRACTS INTERNATIONAL, 49(11) (MAY 89), 3488-A.
THIS CASE STUDY OF A FRESHMAN LEGISLATOR LOOKS AT HOW THE CALIFORNIA LEGISLATURE OPERATES AND HOW FIRST-TERM LEGISLATORS CAN SUCCEED. IT FOCUSES ON LEGISLATION AUTHORED BY ASSEMBLYMAN PATRICK JOHNSTON THAT CREATED THE EMPLOYMENT TRAINING PANEL.

02003 CAPITANCHIK, D.
THE PEOPLE FAIL TO DECIDE: THE ISRAELI GENERAL ELECTION OF 1988
GOVERNMENT AND OPPOSITION, 24(2) (SPR 89), 142-157.
THE 1988 ISRAELI ELECTION PRODUCED THE SAME STATEMATE

THAT LED TO THE FORMATION OF THE GOVERNMENT OF NATIONAL UNITY IN 1984. THE TWO MAJOR PARTIES EMERGED EVEN MORE NARROWLY DIVIDED, BUT THIS TIME THE BALANCE OF POWER LAY NOT WITH THE SMALLER PARTIES WHOSE DEMANDS COULD BE READILY ACCOMMODATED IN THE PROCESS OF COALITION-BUILDING BUT WITH ORTHODOX AND ULTRA-ORTHODOX RELIGIOUS FACTIONS, FAR REMOVED FROM THE MAINSTREAM OF THE COUNTRY'S POLITICAL LIFE AND PRINCIPAL CONCERNS.

02004 CARALEY, D.
ELECTIONS AND DILEMMAS OF AMERICAN DEMOCRATIC GOVERNANCE: REFLECTIONS
POLITICAL SCIENCE QUARTERLY, 104(1) (SPR 89), 19-40.
WHILE AMERICAN CITIZENS HAVE THE OPPORTUNITY TO VOTE FREELY ON WHO THE PRESIDENT AND MEMBERS OF CONGRESS WILL BE, THEY SEEM TO BE LOSING THEIR INFLUENCE ON WHAT THOSE OFFICIALS DO ONCE IN OFFICE. PRESIDENTIAL AND CONGRESSIONAL ELECTION CAMPAIGNS HAVE BECOME LIKE POPULARITY OR BEAUTY CONTESTS, CON GAMES, AND TELEVISION SPECTACLES. VOTERS CANNOT FIX RESPONSIBILITY FOR SUCCESSFUL OR UNSUCCESSFUL GOVERNMENTAL POLICIES BECAUSE OF THE CONSTITUTIONAL SEPARATION OF POWERS BETWEEN THE PRESIDENT AND CONGRESS AND BECAUSE OF THE HIGH FREQUENCY OF DIFFERENT PARTIES CONTROLLING THE TWO BRANCHES. APPOINTIVE SUPREME COURT JUSTICES HAVE THE POWER TO NULLIFY THE POLICY PREFERENCES OF VOTING MAJORITIES WORKING THROUGH THE PRESIDENT AND CONGRESS.

02005 CARBONE, P. A.
THE NEUTRALITY ACT OF 1794: IS IT BEING VIOLATED BY PRIVATE CITIZENS WHO FUND THE CONTRA REBELS IN NICARAGUA?
POLITICAL COMMUNICATION AND PERSUASION, 5(3) (1988), 191-202.
THE ARTICLE OPENS WITH A REVIEW OF RECENT DEVELOPMENTS WHICH HAVE CAUSED THE NEUTRALITY ACT OF 1794 TO REEMERGE AS A LEGAL ISSUE. THE ARTICLE THEN EXAMINES THE ORIGINS AND PURPOSES OF THE ACT, AS WELL AS THE POLITICAL CLIMATE IN THE UNITED STATES AND THE CIRCUMSTANCES THAT LED TO ITS PASSAGE. THE NEUTRALITY ACT WAS PASSED WITH THE SPECIFIC INTENTION OF REMEDYING THE PRACTICE OF "PRIVATEERING." THIS PROBLEM WAS PREVALENT AT THE TIME THE ACT WAS PASSED BUT IS NO LONGER A PROBLEM. THE ARTICLE EXAMINES EARLY CASE LAW INTERPRETING THE ACT, WITH SPECIFIC ATTENTION TO THE DEFINITIONAL PROBLEM OF HOW TO INTERPRET KEY WORDS AND PHRASES USED IN THE ACT. THE EARLY CASE LAW DEMONSTRATES THAT THE ACTIVITIES OF PRIVATE CITIZENS WHO FUND THE CONTRAS DO NOT VIOLATE THE ACT. ANOTHER IMPORTANT ISSUE ADDRESSED IS HOW THE EXECUTIVE BRANCH INTERPRETS THE ACT. THE ARTICLE SUPPORTS THE POSITION OF THE CURRENT ADMINISTRATION, NAMELY, THAT THE NEUTRALITY ACT DOES NOT APPLY TO THE PRESIDENT WHEN HE IS EXERCISING HIS POWER AS SOVEREIGN OVER THIS NATION'S FOREIGN AFFAIRS. BASICALLY, THE ARTICLE ATTEMPTS TO SHOW THAT THOSE WHO ARE ATTEMPTING TO INVOKE THIS LAW TO PROHIBIT PRIVATE CITIZENS FROM ASSISTING THE DEMOCRATIC RESISTANCE IN NICARAGUA ARE MISINTERPRETING THE PURPOSE AND SCOPE OF THE LAW.

02006 CARBONELL, H.V.
COSTA RICA AND CRISIS IN CENTRAL AMERICA
WORLD MARXIST REVIEW, 31(2) (FEB 88), 30-36.
THE SITUATION IN COSTA RICA, EVENTS OF THE PAST FEW YEARS, AND THE POLICY OF THE PEOPLE'S VANGUARD PARTY OF COSTA RICA ARE EXAMINED IN THE CONTEXT OF THE HISTORICAL EVOLUTION OF LATIN AMERICA AND THE REGION.

02007 CARBONELL, H.V.
COSTA RICA: LEFT UNITY IS OPEN TO ALL
WORLD MARXIST REVIEW, 32(4) (APR 89), 46-49.
ONLY THE UNITY OF THE LEFT AND POPULAR PARTIES, OF THE TRADE UNION, PEASANT AND STUDENT MOVEMENTS, AND INDEED OF THE WHOLE PEOPLE CAN END THE POWER OF BIPARTISANISM. THE PEOPLE'S VANGUARD PARTY OF COSTA RICA PASSED A RESOLUTION WELCOMING THE STEPS TAKEN IN THIS DIRECTION, AS WELL AS THE POSITIVE ATTITUDE ON THE PART OF THE PARTY OF THE COSTA RICAN PEOPLE (PPC) AND THE BROAD DEMOCRATIC FRONT AMONGST OTHERS. THE RESOLUTION SAYS THAT "OUR PARTY'S PLEDGE IS TO GO ON REMOVING THE OBSTACLES TO CONSOLIDATION OF LEFT UNITY AND THE UNIFICATION OF THE BROAD MASSES". ANY SECTARIAN, HEGEMONY-SEEKING OR EXCLUSIVIST ATTITUDES ARE INADMISSIBLE IN UNITARY POLICY, THE CONGRESS STRESSED. UNITY MUST BE OPEN TO ALL THE PATRIOTS AND DEMOCRATS, INCLUDING THE CHRISTIANS AND LEFT SOCIAL DEMOCRATS.

02008 CARCACHE, D.
THE MISKITU COMMUNITIES: RECONSTRUCTION OR AUTONOMY?
CENTRAL AMERICA BULLETIN, 8(6) (MAY 89), 4-5, 8.
WITHIN THE PAST YEAR, AT LEAST TEN THOUSAND NICARAGUAN MISKITUS RETURNED TO THEIR HOMES FROM EXILE IN HONDURAS, WHERE THEY HAD FLED WHEN THE MISURASATA ORGANIZATION WAS BANNED AND ITS LEADERS WERE IMPRISONED FOR DEMANDING AUTONOMY FOR ETHNIC MINORITIES. NOW THE MISKITUS FACE THE ENORMOUS TASK OF RECONSTRUCTURING THEIR COMMUNITIES. THEIR LEADERS ARE PROPOSING THE CREATION OF A POLITICAL ORGANIZATION THAT WOULD BE CALLED "UNIDAD DEL PUEBLO MISKITU." THE MAJORITY OF THE LEADERS HAVE GIVEN UP THEIR ARMS AND THE MILITARY STRUGGLE HAS TRANSFORMED INTO A POLITICAL ONE,

WITH NEW FORCES EMERGING IN ADVANCE OF THE 1990 ELECTIONS.

02009 CARIOU, K.
SASKATCHEWAN: AN ARENA OF SOCIAL STRUGGLE PAST, PRESENT
AND FUTURE
COMMUNIST VIEWPOINT, 21(1) (SPR 89), 3-8.
THIS ARTICLE EXAMINES THE EFFECTS OF THE NEO-
CONSERVATISM OUTLOOK WITHIN MONOPOLY IN CANADA. IT ZEROS IN
ON SASKATCHEWAN WHICH HAS "BECOME A VIRTUAL LABORATORY OF
NEO-CONSERVATISM, THE SCENE OF EXPERIMENTS IN ROLLING BACK
THE GAINS OF THE PEOPLE." IT EXAMINES THE SCOPE AND NATURE
OF THE PROGRESSIVE SOCIAL CHANGES INTRODUCED BY SOCIAL
DEMOCRACY IN SASKATCHEWAN AND THE GOALS THAT THE DEVINE
GOVERNMENT HOPES TO ACHIEVE. IT SUGGESTS THAT THE STRUGGLE
IN SASKATCHEWAN HAS REPERCUSSIONS FOR ALL OF CANADA.

02010 CARLIN, D.R. JR.
A TRAGEDY WITHOUT VILLAINS
COMMONWEAL, CXVI(17) (OCT 89), 517-518.
THE POLITICAL BATTLE OVER ABORTION IN THE USA IS A
HEGELIAN TRAGEDY. BOTH SETS OF ANTAGONISTS, PRO-CHOICE AND
PRO-LIFE, ARE DECENT PEOPLE WITH HONEST MOTIVES. EACH SIDE
IS FIGHTING TO DEFEND A GREAT AND GENUINE VALUE: FREEDOM OF
CHOICE OR HUMAN LIFE.

02011 CARLIN, D.R. JR.
AS AMERICAN AS FREEWAYS
COMMONWEAL, CXVI(13) (JUN 89), 392-393.
THE AUTHOR LOOKS AT THE ANALOGY BETWEEN THE SUPREME
COURT REVERSAL OF PLESSY V. FERGUSON AND THE POTENTIAL
REVERSAL OF ROE V. WADE.

02012 CARLIN, D.R. JR.
DON'T DIE YET
COMMONWEAL, CXVI(9) (MAY 89), 265.
A DISTINCTION MUST BE MADE BETWEEN GORBACHEV'S INTENTION
AND THE LIKELY CONSEQUENCES OF THAT INTENTION. WHATEVER THE
ULTIMATE RESULTS OF HIS REFORMS TURN OUT TO BE, GORBACHEV
REALLY MEANS IT WHEN HE SAYS HE WANTS TO SET THE SOVIET
UNION BACK ON THE TRACK IT STRAYED FROM WHEN STALINISM
REPLACED LENINISM.

02013 CARLIN, D.R. JR.
FIT FOR THE CABINET?
COMMONWEAL, CXVI(5) (MAR 89), 136-137.
THE AUTHOR LOOKS AT THE MORAL ALLEGATIONS AGAINST JOHN
TOWER AND COMPARES THEM TO RUMORS ABOUT THE PRIVATE LIVES OF
JOHN KENNEDY AND MARTIN LUTHER KING, JR.

02014 CARLIN, D.R. JR.
THE FAILURE OF SUCCESS
COMMONWEAL, CXVI(1) (JAN 89), 8.
THE AUTHOR RECOUNTS HIS POLITICAL CAREER, WHICH BEGAN AS
A VOLUNTEER FOR EUGENE MCCARTHY AND HAS TAKEN HIM TO THE TOP
POST IN THE RHODE ISLAND SENATE.

02015 CARLIZIO, L.; CLEMENTS, B.; GEETTER, E.
UNITED STATES POLICY TOWARDS SOUTH AFRICA
HUMAN RIGHTS QUARTERLY, 11(2) (MAY 89), 249-294.
IN ANALYZING THE US POLICY TOWARDS SOUTH AFRICA, THE
ARTICLE EXAMINES SPECIFIC POLICIES SUCH AS TRADE SANCTIONS
AND US ASSISTANCE TO BLACK SOUTH AFRICANS. THE GOALS,
IMPLEMENTATION, AND EFFECTIVENESS OF THESE POLICIES ARE
ANALYZED. OVERALL STRATEGY INCLUDING THE POLICY OF
CONSTRUCTIVE ENGAGEMENT, COMPREHENSIVE SANCTIONS AND US
ASSITANCE ARE ALSO EXAMINED AND RECOMMENDATIONS ARE MADE FOR
FUTURE US POLICY.

02016 CARLSON, A.
A PRO-FAMILY INCOME TAX
PUBLIC INTEREST, (94) (WIN 89), 69-76.
SINCE THE TAX REFORM ACT OF 1986 WAS PASSED, THE
DOMESTIC POLICY DEBATE HAS SHIFTED FROM TAXES TO FAMILIES.
THREE BASIC APPROACHES TO FAMILY POLICY HAVE EMERGED.
PROPONENTS OF AN "IN-KIND" APPROACH TOUT THE EFFICIENCY OF
HAVING THE GOVERNMENT DIRECTLY PROVIDE CERTAIN SERVICES,
SUCH AS DAY CARE AND HEALTH CARE. OTHERS STRESS CORPORATE
BENEVOLENCE, WITH BUSINESSES BEING ENCOURAGED OR FORCED TO
PROVIDE DAY CARE AND PARENTAL LEAVE AS EMPLOYEE BENEFITS.
THE THIRD APPROACH TO FAMILY POLICY FOCUSES ON FAMILY
INCOMES, RECOGNIZING THAT THE WELFARE OF CHILDREN IS HEAVILY
DEPENDENT ON THE SPENDING POWER OF THEIR PARENTS. ALTHOUGH
THIS "IN CASH" METHOD COULD TAKE THE FORM OF MINIMUM WAGE
LAWS OR CHILDREN'S ALLOWANCES, ITS APPLICATION TO TAX POLICY
COULD BE SURPRISINGLY EFFECTIVE.

02017 CARLSON, A.
HELPING CHILDREN: INCOME TAX REFORM
CURRENT, (314) (JUL 89), 12-15.
THREE BASIC APPROACHES TO FAMILY POLICY ARE CURRENT IN
THE USA. PROPONENTS OF THE "IN-KIND" APPROACH TOUT THE
EFFICIENCY OF HAVING THE GOVERNMENT DIRECTLY PROVIDE CERTAIN
SERVICES, SUCH AS DAY CARE. OTHERS STRESS CORPORATE
BENEVOLENCE, WITH BUSINESSES BEING ENCOURAGED OR FORCED TO
PROVIDE DAY CARE AND PARENTAL LEAVE. THE THIRD APPROACH
FOCUSES ON FAMILY INCOMES, RECOGNIZING THAT THE WELFARE OF
CHILDREN IS HEAVILY DEPENDENT ON THE SPENDING POWER OF THEIR
PARENTS. ALTHOUGH THIS "IN-CASH" METHOD CAN TAKE THE FORM OF
MINIMUM WAGE LAWS OR CHILDREN'S ALLOWANCES, ITS APPLICATION
TO TAX POLICY COULD BE SURPRISINGLY EFFECTIVE.

02018 CARLSON, J.M.; BURRELL, B.; DOLAN, K.
IDEOLOGY AND CAMPAIGN ACTIVITY AT THREE LEVELS OF
GOVERNMENT
POLITICAL BEHAVIOR, 11(3) (SEP 89), 273-288.
THIS ARTICLE EXAMINES THE RELATIONSHIP BETWEEN SELF-
DESIGNATED POLITICAL IDEOLOGY, OPINIONS ON TWENTY-ONE ISSUES,
AND CAMPAIGN ACTIVITY AT LOCAL, STATE, AND NATIONAL LEVELS.
THE SAMPLES EXAMINED INCLUDE DELEGATES TO THE 1984 PARTY
CONVENTIONS IN ELEVEN STATES. GENERALLY, THE FINDINGS
INDICATE THAT IDEOLOGY AND ISSUE POSITION ARE MOST STRONGLY
ASSOCIATED WITH ACTIVITY IN NATIONAL CAMPAIGNS. AMONG
DEMOCRATS LIBERALISM IS ASSOCIATED WITH NATIONAL ACTIVITY,
WHEREAS AMONG REPUBLICANS THOSE WHO ARE CONSERVATIVE ARE
MOST ACTIVE IN NATIONAL CAMPAIGNS. SOME IMPORTANT INTRAPARTY
DIFFERENCES ARE FOUND BETWEEN LOCAL CAMPAIGN ACTIVISTS AND
NATIONAL ACTIVISTS. FOR EXAMPLE, AMONG DEMOCRATS LOCAL
CAMPAIGN ACTIVISTS ARE MUCH MORE CONSERVATIVE THAN NATIONAL
ACTIVISTS ON SEVERAL ISSUES.

02019 CARLTON, D.
WERE WE WRONG IN 1939?
NATIONAL REVIEW, XLI(18) (SEP 89), 44-47.
THE AUTHOR ARGUES THAT AMERICA SHOULD HAVE NO REGRETS AT
NOT JUMPING TO THE DEFENSE OF POLAND WHEN HITLER INVADED
THAT COUNTRY IN 1939. THAT BRITAIN AND FRANCE ENTERED THE
FRAY OVER AND EAST EUROPEAN ISSUE REFLECTS THE WARRING OF
POLITICAL FUNCTIONS, ESPECIALLY IN BRITAIN, AT A TIME WHEN
GENERAL ELECTIONS WERE BOOMING. FOR BRITAIN'S PRIME MINISTER
NEVILLE CLAMBERLAIN, HITLER'S AGGESSION BECAME THE DOMESTIC
POLITICAL ISSUE FOR DEBATE AT ELECTION TIME.

02020 CARMACK, R.M.
INDIANS IN BUENOS AIRES, COSTA RICA
CULTURAL SURVIVAL QUARTERLY, 13(3) (1989), 30-33.
THE INDIANS OF COSTA RICA CONTINUE TO BE RELATIVELY
UNKNOWN, EVEN WITHIN THEIR OWN COUNTRY, BECAUSE THERE ARE
FEW OF THEM. DESPITE THEIR SMALL NUMBER, THE KIND OF
POLITICAL TREATMENT THEY RECEIVE AS A NATIVE MINORITY IN A
DEMOCRATIC NATION AND THEIR ULTIMATE SOCIAL FATE ARE OF
CONSIDERABLE SYMBOLIC IMPORTANCE IN THE CONTEXT OF THE
STRUGGLE FOR JUSTICE IN CENTRAL AMERICA.

02021 CARMEN, I.H.
CHESS ALGORITHMS OF SUPREME COURT DECISION MAKING: A
BIOCONSTITUTIONAL POLITICS ANALYSIS
POLITICAL BEHAVIOR, 11(2) (JUN 89), 99-121.
THIS PAPER EXAMINES, FROM A BIOPOLITICAL PERSPECTIVE,
THE METHODOLOGIES BY WHICH SUPREME COURT JUSTICES HAVE
INTERPRETED THE CONSTITUTION, ASSESSING THEIR DECISIONAL
ALGORITHMS AGAINST MODELS OWING AN INTELLECTUAL DEBT TO
EVOLUTIONARY THEORY. THE MODELS THEMSELVES ARE DRAWN FROM
THE CHESS LITERATURE, ITSELF THE MOST VIABLE GAME THEORETIC
CONTEXT FOR "LIVING CONSTITUTIONAL" PLAY. A PROPER
APPRECIATION OF CHESS MASTERY YIELDS THE SALIENT CONCLUSION
THAT A FUNCTIONALIST ALGORITHM OF DATA CHARACTERIZATION IS
OPTIMALLY ADAPTIVE FOR THESE PURPOSES, USUALLY PROVING MORE
ROBUST THAN COMPETING STRUCTURALIST AND HEURISTIC ALGORITHMS
IN RESOLVING COMPLEX CONSTITUTIONAL ISSUES.

02022 CARMI, S.; ROSENFELD, H.
THE EMERGENCE OF MILITARISTIC NATIONALISM IN ISRAEL
POLITICS AND SOCIETY, (17 4) (DEC 89), 5-49.
THIS PAPER EXAMINES THE RISE AND ENTRENCHMENT OF
MILITARISTIC NATIONALISM AS A MOST SIGNIFICANT POLITICAL
DEVELOPMENT IN ISRAEL. FOCUS IS ON HOW THE SOCIALIST
POTENTIAL OF EARLY CLASS STRUGGLES, THE YISHUV, AND THE
LABOR MOVEMENT WAS BLOCKED AND TRANSFORMED DURING THE FIRST
DECADES OF THE ISRAELI STATE. THE AUTHORS ALSO EVALUATE THE
THWARTED POTENTIAL FOR THE EMERGENCE OF A JEWISH SOCIALIST
SOCIETY THAT MIGHT HAVE PRODUCED A VERY DIFFERENT SOCIAL AND
NATIONAL PERSPECTIVE FOR ISRAEL AND PALESTINE. WITH THIS
UNFULFILLED POTENTIAL AS A BACKDROP, OUR ANALYSIS ATTEMPTS
TO REACH A CLEAR UNDERSTANDING OF THE CONDITIONS UNDER WHICH
MILITARISM AND NATIONALISM GAINED ASCENDANCY IN ISRAEL.

02023 CARNESALE, A. (ED.); HAASS, R.N. (ED.); SKINNER, K.K.
LINKAGE; SUPERPOWER ARMS CONTROL: SETTING THE RECORD
STRAIGHT
BALLINGER PUBLISHING COMPANY, CAMBRIDGE, MA, 1987, 275-302.
THE CHAPTER FOCUSES ON LINKAGE: THE TIE BETWEEN ARMS
CONTROL AND THE LARGER US-SOVIET RELATIONSHIP. IT EXAMINES
THE VARIOUS FORMS OF LINKAGE AND ASSESSES THE IMPACT THAT
LINKAGE HAS HAD ON BOTH ARMS CONTROL AND US-SOVIET RELATIONS.
IT CONCLUDES THAT THE DIFFICULTIES INVOLVED IN IDENTIFYING
AND IMPLEMENTING LINKAGE HAVE REDUCED ITS IMPACT ON USSOVIET
RELATIONS.

02024 CARNESALE, A. (ED.); HAASS, R.N. (ED.); HAMPSON, F.O.
SALT I: INTERIM AGREEMENT AND ABM TREATY; SUPERPOWER ARMS
CONTROL: SETTING THE RECORD STRAIGHT
BALLINGER PUBLISHING COMPANY, CAMBRIDGE, MA, 1987, 65-104.
THE CHAPTER EXAMINES THE ABM TREATY AND THE INTERIM
AGREEMENT ON OFFENSIVE STRATEGIC ARMS BEGINING WITH THE
BACKGROUND AND MOTIVATIONS THAT LED TO NEGOTIATIONS. IT
ANALYZES THE EXPECTATIONS THAT DIFFERENT PARTIES HAD GOING
INTO NEGOTIATIONS AND THE RESULTS THEY ACHIEVED. IT
CONCLUDES THAT THE EMERGING STRATEGIC PARTY BETWEEN THE US
AND THE SOVIET UNION WAS THE MOST IMPORTANT PRECONDITION FOR
SALT NEGOTIATIONS. IT ALSO CONCLUDES THAT ALTHOUGH POLITICAL
EXPECTATIONS WERE COMPLEX AND VARIED, THE WORST FEARS OF
SOME WERE NOT REALIZED.

02025 CARNESALE, A. (ED.); FLANAGAN, S.J.; HAASS, R.N. (ED.)
SALT II; SUPERPOWER ARMS CONTROL: SETTING THE RECORD
STRAIGHT
BALLINGER PUBLISHING COMPANY, CAMBRIDGE, MA, 1987, 105-138.
THE CHAPTER EXAMINES THE SALT II TREATY WHICH MANY FEEL
MARKED A TURNING POINT IN NEGOTIATED ARMS CONTROL. IT
OUTLINES THE SHIFTS IN INTERNATIONAL AND DOMESTIC US
POLITICAL MILIEU THAT LED TO THE NEGOTIATIONS AND THEIR
EVENTUAL OUTCOME. IT OUTLINES THE STRATEGIC OBJECTIVES THAT
BOTH SIDES HAD GOING TO THE NEGOTIATING TABLE AND THE
LESSONS THAT CAN BE LEARNED FROM SALT II.

02026 CARNESALE, A. (ED.); BENNETT, A.; HAASS, R.N. (ED.)
THE ACCIDENT MEASURES AGREEMENT; SUPERPOWER ARMS CONTROL:
SETTING THE RECORD STRAIGHT
BALLINGER PUBLISHING COMPANY, CAMBRIDGE, MA, 1987, 41-64.
THE ACCIDENT MEASURES AGREEMENT (AMA) IS A POTENTIAL
MODEL FOR "QUIET" ARMS CONTROL. IT WAS CONSIDERED TO BE
DELINKED FROM OTHER ISSUES IN THE SALT I TALKS AND WAS
CONSIDERED TO BE A PERIPHERAL ISSUE. THE CHAPTER EXAMINES
THE NEGOTIATION THAT LED TO THE RATIFICATION OF THE
AGREEMENT AND THE PROVISIONS OF THE AGREEMENT ITSELF. IT
CONCLUDES THAT ALTHOUGH THE FACTORS THAT MADE THE AMA EASY
TO NEGOTIATATE QUIETLY CAN NOT BE UNIVERSALLY APPLIED TO
OTHER TYPES OF ARMS LIMITATION NEGOTIATIONS, SOME LESSONS
CAN BE LEARNED FROM THE PROCESS.

02027 CARNESALE, A. (ED.); HAASS, R.N. (ED.); WERTHEIMER, J.
THE ANTISATELLITE NEGOTIATIONS; SUPERPOWER ARMS CONTROL:
SETTING THE RECORD STRAIGHT
BALLINGER PUBLISHING COMPANY, CAMBRIDGE, MA, 1987, 139-164.
THE CHAPTER EXAMINES THE HISTORY OF NEGOTIATION INTENDED
TO LIMIT ANTISATELLITE WEAPONS (ASAT). IT CONCENTRATES ON
THE EFFORTS OF THE CARTER ADMINISTRATION TO LIMIT ASATS. IT
CONCLUDES THAT FOUR FACTORS CONTRIBUTED TO THE FAILURE OF
ASAT LIMITATION NEGOTIATIONS: LACK OF SHARED OBJECTIVE, LASS
OF ESSENTIAL EQUIVALENCY, INTERNAL OPPOSITION THAT HAS
TOLERATED BY A PASSIVE WHITE HOUSE, AND VERIFICATION
CONCERNS. IT ALSO OUTLINES HOW ASATS FEEL VICTIM TO THE
"BARGAINING CHIP DILEMMA": IN ORDER TO BE A BARGAINING CHIP
IN NEGOTIATIONS, IT MUST BE VALUABLE, BUT IF IT IS TOO
VALUABLE THE NEGOTIATORS MIGHT NOT BE WILLING TO BARGAIN IT
AWAY.

02028 CARNESALE, A. (ED.); HAASS, R.N. (ED.); HARRIS, E.D.
THE BIOLOGICAL AND TOXIN WEAPONS CONVENTION; SUPERPOWER
ARMS CONTROL: SETTING THE RECORD STRAIGHT
BALLINGER PUBLISHING COMPANY, CAMBRIDGE, MA, 1987, 191-222.
THE BIOLOGICAL AND TOXIC WEAPONS CONVENTION STAND UNIQUE
FROM ALL OTHER POSTWAR ARMS CONTROL AGREEMENTS FOR TWO
REASONS: IT IS THE ONLY INTERNATIONAL AGREEMENT SINCE WORLD
WAR II TO PROVIDE FOR THE ACTUAL ELIMINATION OF AN ENTIRE
CLASS OF WEAPONS FROM THE ARSENALS OF NATIONS, AND IT WAS
STIMULATED, IN LARGE MEASURE, BY A ACT OF UNILATERAL
DISARMAMENT. THE CHAPTER ANALYZES THE BWC, ITS HISTORY, AND
THE MOTIVATIONS WHICH STIMULATED THE NEGOTIATIONS. A CHIEF
MOTIVE OF THE US WAS THE BELIEF THAT BIOLOGICAL WEAPONS WERE
OF LIMITED DETTERENT VALUE.

02029 CARNESALE, A. (ED.); DAALDER, I.H.; HAASS, R.N. (ED.)
THE LIMITED TEST BAN TREATY; SUPERPOWER ARMS CONTROL:
SETTING THE RECORD STRAIGHT
BALLINGER PUBLISHING COMPANY, CAMBRIDGE, MA, 1987, 9-40.
THE CHAPTER ANALYZES THE LIMITED TEST BAN TREATY SIGNED
BY THE US, BRITAIN AND THE SOVIETS IN 1963. IT DISCUSSES THE
UNDERLYING MOTIVES OF THE US TO COME TO THE NEGOTIATING
TABLE AND CONCLUDES THAT ALTHOUGH PUBLIC FEAR OF FALLOUT WAS
A FACTOR, OTHER FACTORS INCLUDING A DESIRE TO DEESCALATE
AFTER THE CUBAN MISSILE CRISIS AND A HOPE FOR IMPROVED US-
SOVIET RELATIONS WERE MORE PROMINENT. THE CHAPTER ALSO
DISCUSSES THE POLITICAL AND STRATEGIC RAMIFICATIONS OF THE
TREATY.

02030 CARNESALE, A. (ED.); HAASS, R.N. (ED.); NYE, J.S. JR.
THE SUPERPOWERS AND THE NON-PROLIFERATION TREATY;
SUPERPOWER ARMS CONTROL: SETTING THE RECORD STRAIGHT
BALLINGER PUBLISHING COMPANY, CAMBRIDGE, MA, 1987, 165-190.
THE CHAPTER STUDIES THE NON-PROLIFERATION TREATY SIGNED
IN 1968. IT OUTLINES THE PROVISIONS OF THE TREATY AND ITS
EFFECTS ON THE INTERNATIONAL SITUATION. IT CONCLUDES BY
LISTING SOME OF THE LESSONS THAT CAN BE LEARNED FROM THE
EXPERIENCE OF NEGOTIATING AND IMPLEMENTING THE NPT. THESE
INCLUDE THE EFFECTIVENESS (OR LACK OF EFFECTIVENESS) OF
BARGAINING FROM STRENGTH AND UNILATERAL RESISTANT. ISSUES
SUCH AS UNCERTAINTY, VERIFICATION, AND COMPLIANCE ARE ALSO
DISCUSSED.

02031 CARNESALE, A. (ED.); HAASS, R.N. (ED.)
VERIFICATION AND COMPLIANCE; SUPERPOWER ARMS CONTROL:
SETTING THE RECORD STRAIGHT
BALLINGER PUBLISHING COMPANY, CAMBRIDGE, MA, 1987, 303-328.
ARMS CONTROL WITHOUT COMPLIANCE CONTROVERSIES IS
UNATTAINBALE. INDEED, THE MORE ARMS CONTROL PRODUCES NEW
AGREEMENTS, THE MORE IT WILL BE THREATENED BY ITS OWN
SUCCESS; CONTENDING WITH CONTESTED COMPLIANCE OF EXISTING
AGREEMENTS AND NEGOTIATING VERIFICATION PROVISIONS OF NEW
ONES COULD WELL COME TO DOMINATE THE AMRS CONTROL AGENDA FOR
THE FORESEEABLE FUTURE. THE CHAPTER OUTLINES THE TWIN
CHALLENGES OF NEGOTIATING MUTUALLY ACCEPTABLE VERIFICATION
PROVISIONS FOR FUTURE AGREEMENTS AND MEETING MUTUALLY
ACCEPTABLE STANDARDS OF COMPLIANCE REGARDING EXISITING
AGREEMENTS AND GIVES SUGGESTIONS TO INCREASE THE
EFFECTIVENESS OF US NEGOTIATING POLICY WITH REGARDS TO THESE
PROBLEMS.

02032 CARNEVALE, D.G.
ORGANIZATIONAL TRUST: A TEST OF A MODEL OF ITS DETERMINANTS
DISSERTATION ABSTRACTS INTERNATIONAL, 49(12) (JUN 89),
3865-A.
THE OBJECTIVE OF THIS RESEARCH IS TO DEVELOP AND TEST A
MODEL OF TRUST FORMATION IN ORGANIZATIONS. THE PARAMETERS OF
THE MODEL ARE BASED ON THE THEORY THAT THE EXISTENCE OF
TRUST IS THE RESULT OF KEY ORGANIZATIONAL AND INDIVIDUAL
ATTRIBUTES. RESULTS FROM THIS STUDY CONFIRM THIS. THE
FINDINGS SUGGEST CONNECTIONS BETWEEN TRUST, THE TYPE OF
WORKPLACE GOVERNANCE REPRESENTED BY ITS ANTECEDENTS, AND THE
POLITICAL IDEOLOGY OF PUBLIC EMPLOYEES.

02033 CARNEY, C.P.
INTERNATIONAL PATRON-CLIENT RELATIONSHIPS: A CONCEPTUAL
FRAMEWORK
SOUTHERN CALIFORNIA LAW REVIEW, 24(2) (SUM 89), 42-55.
DEPENDENCY THEORY HAS CAST NEW LIGHT ON THE WORKINGS OF
THE INTERNATIONAL POLITICAL ECONOMY, AND ON THE RELATIONS
BETWEEN MORE AND LESS DEVELOPED COUNTRIES. INSOFAR AS
DEPENDENCY THEORY AIMS AT SPECIFYING GENERAL SYSTEMIC
CONSTRAINTS ON THE BEHAVIOR OF THIRD WORLD STATES, ITS
ABILITY TO EXPLAIN/PREDICT HOW PARTICULAR THIRD WORLD STATES
RESPOND TO THESE CONSTRAINTS IS LIMITED. THE CONCERN IS WITH
THE FOREIGN POLICY RESPONSES OF THE LDCS. THE COMPARATIVE
FOREIGN POLICY APPROACH TO THIS QUESTION HAS ATTEMPTED TO
ACCOUNT FOR CROSS-NATIONAL VARIATION IN FOREIGN POLICY
RESPONSES OF LDCS WITH VARIATION IN THEIR DOMESTIC FEATURES,
I.E., ATTRIBUTES, CAPABILITIES, AND REGIME TYPES. AN
UNDERSTANDING OF THE FOREIGN POLICIES OF THE LDCS CAN BE
ENHANCED BY ADDING AN EXPLICITLY DYADIC PERSPECTIVE TO
DEPENDENCY AND COMPARATIVE FOREIGN POLICY APPROACHES,
CONCEPTUALIZED AS A FORM OF PATRON-CLIENCY.

02034 CARNOVALE, M.; MERLINI, C.
EAST-WEST RELATIONS AND ARMS CONTROL NEGOTIATIONS: THE
CURRENT SITUATION AND PROSPECTS FOR THE FUTURE
INTERNATIONAL SPECTATOR, XXIII(2) (APR 88), 98-107.
AS A RESULT OF REFORMS WITHIN THE SOVIET UNION, NEW
AREAS ARE OPENING UP AND NEW CHALLENGES ARE FORMING FOR THE
FOREIGN POLICY OF WESTERN EUROPEAN NATIONS TOWARDS THE EAST.
WITH MOSCOW'S PREVIOUS RIGIDITY, THE WEST'S RESPONSE WAS
EXEMPLIFIED BY SIMPLIFIED POSITIONS AND INTERNAL COHESION.
MOSCOW'S NEW ACTIVISM CREATES MORE UNCERTAINTY THAN
DIVERSITY OF OPINION IN AND AMONG WESTERN NATIONS. IN THE
SITUATIONS THAT CONTINUALLY EMERGE AS A RESULT OF
GORBACHEV'S DYNAMISM, POLITICIANS AND COMMENTATORS ARE
UNCERTAIN ABOUT THE RESPONSES TO GIVE. THE UNCERTAINTY HAS
MANIFESTED ITSELF IN ALL AREAS OF EAST-WEST RELATIONS,
INCLUDING ARMS CONTROL TALKS.

02035 CARNOVALE, M.
THE METHODOLOGY OF FORCE CORRELATION AND CONVENTIONAL ARMS
CONTROL
INTERNATIONAL SPECTATOR, XXIV(2) (APR 89), 102-110.
THE AUTHOR ASSESSES THE DIFFERENT APPROACHES TO ANALYSIS
OF THE CORRELATION OF CONVENTIONAL FORCES. IN PARTICULAR, HE
FOCUSES ON THE WAY THEY HAVE BEEN USED TO MEASURE THE
MILITARY CONFRONTATION BETWEEN THE WARSAW PACT AND NATO IN
EUROPE. HE EVALUATES THE PARAMETERS, INPUT OR OUTPUT,
COMMONLY CONSIDERED SIGNIFICANT IN THAT CORRELATION. THEN HE
SUGGESTS ELIMINATING INPUT MEASUREMENTS BECAUSE THEY ARE
GENERALLY UNRELAIBLE AND PARTICULARLY SO IN COMPARISONS
BETWEEN THE ARMED FORCES OF THE EAST AND THE WEST.

02036 CARPENTER, R.
WOODROW WILSON AS A SPEECHWRITER FOR GEORGE CREEL:
PRESIDENTIAL STYLE IN DISCOURSE AS AN INDEX OF PERSONALITY

PRESIDENTIAL STUDIES QUARTERLY, XIX(1) (WIN 89), 117-126.
WOODROW WILSON'S REPUTATION AS A RHETORICAL STYLIST IS
SECURE. YET IN JAMES BARBER'S PROMINENT ASSESSMENT OF
WILSON'S PRESIDENTIAL CHARACTER, THAT "STYLE" IN FINAL
DRAFTS OF DISCOURSE IS PROCLAIMED TO CONTAIN CLUES ABOUT HIS
NEGATIVE PERSONALITY. THIS ANALYSIS FOCUSES ON STYLE EVINCED
IN WILSON'S LONGHAND REVISIONS OF SPEECHES AND
CORRESPONDENCE DRAFTED BY GEORGE CREEL AS CHAIRMAN OF THE
COMMITTEE ON PUBLIC INFORMATION DURING WORLD WAR ONE. THOSE
STYLISTIC ADAPTATIONS ARE NOT SO MUCH THE INDICES OF A
NEGATIVE PERSONALITY IDENTIFIED BY BARBER BUT MORE THE
ADDITIONAL EVIDENCE THAT WILSON HAS BUT A JUDICIOUS AND
EFFECTIVE RHETOR.

02037 CARPENTER, R.C.
GREECE ADRIFT
NATIONAL REVIEW, 61(23) (DEC 89), 17-18.
THIS ARTICLE EXAMINES GREEK PRESENT DAY POLITICS AND THE
RECENT ELECTIONS WHERE FOR THE SECOND TIME IN FIVE MONTHS
THE VOTERS GAVE NO POLITICAL PARTY A CLEAR MANDATE TO GOVERN
THE COUNTRY. IT PREDICTS THAT THIS MEANS FRESH ELECTIONS IN
THE NOT TOO DISTANT FUTURE, WITH PROTRACTED ECONOMIC
INSTABILITY AND UNCERTAIN FOREIGN-POLICY. IT ATTRIBUTES THIS
SITUATION TO WEAK LEADERSHIP IN THE GREEK RIGHT AS IT HAS
"FUMBLED A CHANCE TO ROLL BACK SOCIALISM."

02038 CARR, C.L.
KANT'S THEORY OF POLITICAL AUTHORITY
HISTORY OF POLITICAL THOUGHT, X(4) (WIN 89), 719-731.
KANT'S MORALIZED VERSION OF THE LIBERAL ARGUMENT AVOIDS
THE TRADITIONAL LIBERAL TENSION BETWEEN A COMMITMENT TO
INDIVIDUAL FREEDOM ON THE ONE HAND AND POLITICAL AUTHORITY
ON THE OTHER. YET THE RECONCILIATION ACHIEVED BY THE DOUBLE-
NEGATION ARGUMENT DEPENDS UPON THE LEGITIMACY OF THE KANTIAN
NOTION OF MORAL FREEDOM; AND THERE MAY BE REASONS TO
ENTERTAIN PHILOSOPHICAL DOUBTS ABOUT THE COHERENCE AND
PERSUASIVENESS OF THIS NOTION. THE AUTHOR EXPLAINS HOW THIS
CONCEPT ENABLES US TO CONSTRUCT A THEORY OF POLITICAL
AUTHORITY BASED UPON MORAL RATHER THAN PRUDENTIAL
CONSIDERATIONS.

02039 CARR, M.
PALESTINIAN EDUCATION IN CRISIS
MIDDLE EAST INTERNATIONAL, (360) (OCT 89), 18-19.
THE ARTICLE EXAMINES THE EFFECT OF THE INTIFADA AND THE
RESULTING ISRAELI REPRESSION ON THE PALESTINIAN EDUCATIONAL
SYSTEM. ALTOGETHER OVER 15 MONTHS HAVE BEEN LOST FROM THE
PREVIOUS TWO ACADEMIC YEARS AS A RESULT OF BLANKET CLOSURES
ORDERED BY THE MILITARY. THE ECONOMIC CONSEQUENCES OF THE
INTIFADA HAVE FORCED MANY STUDENTS TO DROP OUT OF FULL-TIME
EDUCATION TO HELP SUPPORT THEIR FAMILIES. ALTHOUGH MOST
PALESTINIANS ARE BEGINNING TO ACCEPT THE ISRAELI DISRUPTION
OF THEIR EDUCATIONAL SYSTEM AS AN UNAVOIDABLE FACT OF LIFE,
THIS DELIBERATE DAMAGE IS ONE OF THE MOST PAINFUL BLOWS
INFLICTED BY THE ISRAELIS.

02040 CARROLL, B.W.
ADMINISTRATIVE DEVOLUTION AND ACCOUNTABILITY: THE CASE OF
THE NONPROFIT HOUSING PROGRAM
CANADIAN PUBLIC ADMINISTRATION, 32(3) (FAL 89), 345-366.
THE PROBLEM OF BUREAUCRATIC ACCOUNTABILITY HAS RECEIVED
CONSIDERABLE ATTENTION IN THE LITERATURE OF PUBLIC
ADMINISTRATION, BUT FEW STUDIES HAVE CONSIDERED THE EXTENT
TO WHICH EXTRA-GOVERNMENTAL AGENCIES ARE HELD ACCOUNTABLE TO
GOVERNMENTS OR LEGISLATURES. THIS PAPER EXAMINES
ADMINISTRATIVE DEVOLUTION AND THE PROBLEM OF ACCOUNTABILITY,
USING THE NON-PROFIT HOUSING PROGRAM AS AN EXAMPLE. IT
ARGUES THAT DEVOLUTION OF PROGRAMS, WITHOUT ADJUSTING FOR
THE RESULTING LOSS OF BUREAUCRATIC CONTROL, LEAVES
GOVERNMENTS WITH LITTLE INFORMATION ABOUT, OR CONTROL OVER,
THE PEOPLE WHO MAKE DECISIONS ABOUT LARGE EXPENDITURES OF
PUBLIC FUNDS. IT CONCLUDES THAT IF THE ADVANTAGES OF USING
THE VOLUNTARY SECTOR FOR SOCIAL SERVICE DELIVERY ARE TO
OUTWEIGH THE PROBLEMS OF REDUCED ACCOUNTABILITY, FORMS OF
CONTROL -SUCH AS INCENTIVES FOR COMPLIANCE AND INTERNAL
PROFESSIONAL STANDARDS -- WHICH DO NOT LIMIT THE AUTONOMY OF
THESE GROUPS, BUT WHICH CAN ENHANCE PRE-AUDIT ACCOUNTABILITY,
NEED TO BE DEVELOPED.

02041 CARROLL, S.J.
THE PERSONAL IS POLITICAL: THE INTERSECTION OF PRIVATE
LIVES AND PUBLIC ROLES AMONG WOMEN AND MEN IN ELECTIVE AND
APPOINTIVE OFFICE
WOMEN AND POLITICS, 9(2) (1989), 51-67.
THIS ARTICE INVESTIGATES SIMILARITIES AND DIFFERENCES IN
THE RELATIONSHIP BETWEEN "PUBLIC" AND "PRIVATE" IN THE LIVES
OF WOMEN AND MEN WHO HOLD ELECTIVE AND APPOINTIVE OFFICE. AN
ANALYSIS OF DATA COLLECTED THROUGH SURVEYS OF FEDERAL
APPOINTEES AND STATE LEGISLATORS INDICATES THAT MEN'S
POLITICAL CHOICES MAY BE MORE INFLUENCED BY PRIVATE SPHERE
CONSIDERATIONS THAN COMMONLY BELIEVED, BUT THAT PRIVATE
SPHERE CONCERNS ARE NEVERTHELESS OF GREATER SIGNIFICANCE TO
WOMEN THAN TO MEN. FINDINGS PROVIDE SUPPORT FOR A
CONCEPTUALIZATION OF PUBLIC AND PRIVATE AS AN INTERRELATED

SYSTEM OF SOCIAL RELATIONS RATHER THAN AS TWO LARGELY
SEPARATE SPHERES OF EXISTENCE.

02042 CARROLL, W.K.; RATNER, R.S.
SOCIAL DEMOCRACY, NEO-CONSERVATISM AND HEGEMONIC CRISIS IN
BRITISH COLUMBIA
CRITICAL SOCIOLOGY, 16(1) (SPR 89), 29-54.
THIS PAPER ADOPTS A GRAMSCIAN PERSPECTIVE IN PRESENTING
A CASE STUDY OF HEGEMONIC CRISIS AND POLITICAL-ECONOMIC
RESTRUCTURING. IN BRITISH COLUMBIA, THE PERIOD FROM 1983
THROUGH 1987 MARKED A DECISIVE SHIFT FROM A VARIANT OF
FORDISM TO A NEO-CONSERVATIVE PROJECT WITH STRONG RESONANCES
OF THATCHERISM. FOCUSING ON THE HISTORICAL SPECIFICITY OF
THE PROVINCE IN THE CANADIAN POLITICAL ECONOMY AND THE
POLITICAL CRISES OF 1983 AND 1987, THIS PAPER EXPLORES THE
STRUCTURAL AND STRATEGIC REASONS FOR THIS TRANSFORMATION,
AND EXAMINES THE OBSTACLES CONFRONTING THE LEFT IN ITS
HESITANT ATTEMPTS TO MOUNT A SUCCESSFUL OPPOSITION AROUND A
COUNTER-HEGEMONIC PROJECT.

02043 CARTER, R. G.
SENATE DEFENSE BUDGETING, 1981-1988: THE IMPACTS OF
IDEOLOGY, PARTY, AND CONSTITUENCY BENEFIT ON THE DECISION
TO SUPPORT THE PRESIDENT
AMERICAN POLITICS QUARTERLY, 17(3) (JUL 89), 332-347.
STUDYING SENATE ROLL CALL VOTES DURING THE REAGAN
ADMINISTRATION SHEDS LIGHT ON THE INTERACTION OF PARTY,
IDEOLOGY, AND LOCAL ECONOMIC BENEFIT AS EXPLANATORY FACTORS
IN A SENATOR'S DECISION TO SUPPORT THE PRESIDENT'S POSITION
ON DEFENSE SPENDING ISSUES. PARTY AND IDEOLOGY ARE FOUND TO
BE THE MOST IMPORTANT OF THESE THREE, BUT THEIR EFFECTS
CHANGE WHEN MOVING FROM CONSIDERATION OF MAJOR PROCUREMENT
ISSUES TO THOSE INVOLVING THE USE, TRAINING, AND READINESS
OF THE NATION'S MILITARY. FURTHER, INCORPORATING ISSUE-BASED
DIFFERENCES AND INDIRECT EFFECTS INTO THE ANALYSIS SUGGESTS
THE EFFECTS OF LOCAL ECONOMIC BENEFIT ARE NOT AS
INCONSEQUENTIAL AS SOME RECENT STUDIES HAVE ARGUED. IN
SUMMARY, THESE FINDINGS FOCUS ATTENTION ON THE ROLE PLAYED
BY ELECTIONS AND THE CIRCUMSTANCES IN WHICH PRESIDENTIAL
LEADERSHIP MAY BE MOST EFFECTIVE ON DEFENSE SPENDING ISSUES.

02044 CARTER, S.K.
TWENTIETH CENTURY RUSSIAN NATIONALISM
JOHN SPIERS PUBLISHING, BRIGHTON, SUSSEX, GB, 1989, 256.
DESPITE LENIN'S ASPIRATIONS TOWARDS SOCIALIST
INTERNATIONALISM, RUSSIAN NATIONALISM HAS ALWAYS BEEN A
POWERFUL FORCE IN RUSSIA AND THE USSR. THIS BOOK EXPLAINS
ITS ORIGINS, ITS SURVIVAL THROUGH THE SOVIET PERIOD, AND ITS
RE-EMERGENCE AS A POLITICAL IDEOLOGY TO BE RECKONED WITH.

02045 CARTWRIGHT, J.
CONSERVING NATURE, DECREASING DEBT
THIRD WORLD QUARTERLY, 11(2) (APR 89), 114-127.
TWO CRISES HAUNT THE THIRD WORLD: THE DEBT BURDEN AND
ENVIRONMENTAL DEGRADATION. IN PART BECAUSE OF THEIR DEBT
BURDEN, MANY THIRD WORLD COUNTRIES ARE RAPIDLY DEPLETING
THEIR STOCK OF NATURAL RESOURCES, WITH THE RESULT THAT THEY
SUFFER FREQUENT DROUGHTS, FLOODS, EROSION, LANDSLIDES, AND
OTHER NATURAL DISASTERS. THE INDUSTRIALIZED COUNTRIES ARE
BEGINNING TO REALIZE THAT THIRD WORLD ENVIRONMENTAL
DEGRADATION WILL ADVERSELY AFFECT THEIR OWN LONG-TERM WELL-
BEING AND THAT THEY SHOULD CONTRIBUTE TO THIRD WORLD
ENVIRONMENTAL PROTECTION AND RESTORATION. HEREIN LIES AN
OPPORTUNITY FOR THE THIRD WORLD TO ACHIEVE A MEASURE OF DEBT
RELIEF WHILE PROTECTING KEY NATURAL ECOSYSTEMS. ONE WIDELY-
DISCUSSED APPROACH INVOLVES THE REDUCTION OF DEBTS OWED TO
WESTERN LENDERS IN EXCHANGE FOR THE CONSERVATION OF NATURAL
ECOSYSTEMS IN THE THIRD WORLD.

02046 CASE, J.
THE INTERNATIONAL PAPER STRIKE: A MILESTONE BATTLE AGAINST
CONCESSIONS AND UNIONBUSTING
POLITICAL AFFAIRS, LXVIII(4) (APR 89), 10-17.
THE INTERNATIONAL PAPERWORKERS' UNION STRIKE THAT ENDED
IN OCTOBER 1988 WAS AN EXPLOSION THAT ATTRACTED AND
EXPRESSED IN CONCENTRATED FORM THE ENERGIES THAT ARE GAINING
MOMENTUM IN THE AMERICAN LABOR MOVEMENT. THE STRIKE FOCUSED
ENERGIES THAT BUILT THROUGHOUT THE 1980'S AS THE ACTIONS OF
CORPORATIONS AND THE REAGAN ADMINISTRATION CUT MORE DEEPLY
INTO THE LIVING AND WORKING CONDITIONS OF AMERICAN LABOR,
ESPECIALLY INDUSTRIAL WORKERS.

02047 CASELLA, A.
THE REFUGEES FROM VIETNAM: RETHINKING THE ISSUE
WORLD TODAY, 45(8-9) (AUG 89), 160-164.
THE UNDERSTANDING REACHED AT THE GENEVA MEETING ON
DISPLACED PERSONS FROM INDOCHINA RESTS ON THE FACT THAT THE
COUNTRIES OF SOUTHEAST ASIA, FOR BOTH SOCIAL AND POLITICAL
REASONS, ARE NOT WILLING TO GRANT PERMANENT ASYLUM TO
REFUGEES FROM VIETNAM. THEY ARE WILLING TO PROVIDE
VIETNAMESE BOAT PEOPLE WITH FIRST ASYLUM, BUT ONLY ON
CONDITION THAT THEY WILL ULTIMATELY BE RESETTLED IN THE WEST.
THIS IMPERATIVE HAS GIVEN THE VIETNAMESE REFUGEE PROBLEM A
UNIQUE INTERNATIONAL DIMENSION. TRADITIONALLY, REFUGEE

PROBLEMS HAVE BEEN REGIONAL ISSUES WITH REGIONAL SOLUTIONS. BUT THIS IS NOT THE CASE WITH THE VIETNAMESE. THEIR FLIGHT INVOLVES THE ADDED DIMENSION OF MOVEMENT FROM ONE OF THE POORER, WAR-SCARRED, THIRD-WORLD NATIONS TO THE INDUSTRIALIZED WORLD.

02048 CASELLA, D.
TAXED IN THE USSR
REASON, 20(11) (APR 89), 46.
SOVIET FINANCE MINISTER VIKTOR SEMENOV HAS SAID THAT THE SOVIET SYSTEM OF TAXATION IS HOPELESSLY UNSCIENTIFIC. THIS HAS LED TO SPECULATION THAT ANOTHER WESTERN INFLUENCE-FILING ANNUAL FINANCIAL RETURNS AND PAYING A PROGRESSIVE INCOME TAX-MAY INVADE SOVIET SOCIETY.

02049 CASEY, B.; CREIGH, S.
"MARGINAL" GROUPS IN THE LABOUR FORCE SURVEY
STP (SOCIALISM: THEORY AND PRACTICE), 36(3) (AUG 89), 282-300.
THE PAPER PULLS TOGETHER THE FINDINGS AND LESSONS FROM A NUMBER OF DISCRETE PIECES OF RESEARCH IN WHICH THE LABOUR FORCE SURVEY (LFS) ANALYSIS HAS PLAYED AN IMPORTANT PART. SUBJECTS OF RESEARCH INCLUDE: THE SELF-EMPLOYED, TEMPORARY WORKERS, OLDER WORKERS/EARLY RETIREES, AND THE LONG-TERM UNEMPLOYED. THE PAPER EXAMINES EACH OF THESE GROUPS AS A SEPARATE ENTITY, AND ALSO ANALYSES HOW THE GROUPS RELATE TO EACH OTHER. THE PAPER CONCLUDES THAT THE LFS HAS BEEN ABLE TO PROVIDE A WEALTH OF DETAIL ON EACH INDIVIDUAL GROUP, BUT ALSO ON GROUP INTERELATIONS AND HOW MEMBERS OF ONE "MARGINAL" GROUP ARE OFTEN SIMULTANEOUSLY MEMBERS OF ANOTHER.

02050 CASEY, L.E.
CONFRONTING THE STATE OF "IRON CAGES": THE PROBLEM OF STATE AUTHORITARIANISM MODERN DEMOCRATIC AND SOCIALIST POLITICAL THEORY
DISSERTATION ABSTRACTS INTERNATIONAL, 50(6) (DEC 89), 1786-A.
STATE AUTHORIANISM IS NOT AN ABERRATION BUT THE END PRODUCT OF A NORMALIZATION DYNAMIC LODGED AT THE VERY HEART OF MODERN POWER RELATIONS. IT IS THIS DYNAMIC WHICH, WHEN TAKEN TO ITS MOST EXTREME FORM IN THE ESTABLISHMENT OF SINGULAR NORMS AROUND WHICH THE STATE INDIVIDUALIZES AND HOMOGENIZES ITS SUBJECTS, YIELDS STATE AUTHORITARIANISM. IN THIS NORMALIZATION PROCESS, COMMUNITIES OF SOCIAL AND CULTURAL DIFFERENCE THAT STAND BETWEEN THE STATE AND THE INDIVIDUAL ARE UNDERMINED.

02051 CASH, J.D.
IDEOLOGY AND AFFECT: THE CASE OF NORTHERN IRELAND
POLITICAL PSYCHOLOGY, 10(4) (DEC 89), 703-724.
IDEOLOGIES ARE CENTRAL TO THE ORGANIZATION OF POLITICAL LIFE AND POLITICAL CONFLICT, YET MOST EMPIRICAL STUDIES TEND TO OBSCURE THEIR SIGNIFICANCE. THIS FAILURE TO TAKE IDEOLOGY SERIOUSLY IS NO MERE OVERSIGHT; RATHER IT ARISES FROM AN ABSENCE OF BOTH ADEQUATE CONCEPTUALIZATIONS AND ADEQUATE METHODS FOR THE ANALYSIS OF IDEOLOGY. SUCH ABSENCES ARE PARTICULARLY EVIDENT WITH REGARD TO THE AFFECTIVE COMPONENT OF IDEOLOGIES, A COMPONENT WHICH IS REGARDED, CHARACTERISTICALLY, AS EPIPHENOMENAL. THIS ARTICLE DRAWS UPON BOTH SOCIAL THEORY AND PSYCHOANALYTIC THEORY IN AN ATTEMPT TO OVERCOME SUCH LACUNAE IN THE STUDY OF IDEOLOGY AND POLITICS. IT FOCUSES UPON UNIONIST IDEOLOGY IN NORTHERN IRELAND AND ATTEMPTS TO ESTABLISH THE INTERNAL DIVERSITY OF THIS IDEOLOGY BY SPECIFYING ITS CORE RULES FOR THE CONSTRUCTION OF THREE MAJOR IDEOLOGICAL POSITIONS. THESE POSITIONS ARE UNDERSTOOD AS THREE MAJOR FORMS OF POLITICAL SUBJECTIVITY. KLEINIAN PSYCHOANALYTIC THEORY IS DRAWN UPON AND REWORKED AS A METHOD FOR THE ANALYSIS OF THESE THREE POSITIONS. HAVING ESTABLISHED THE RULES OF AN AFFECT-LADEN IDEOLOGICAL FORMATION, NAMELY, UNIONISM, A BRIEF SKETCH OF UNIONIST POLITICS IS OFFERED. THIS SKETCH HIGHLIGHTS THE CENTRALITY OF IDEOLOGY, ADEQUATELY UNDERSTOOD, TO POLITICAL CONFLICT IN NORTHERN IRELAND.

02052 CASSADY, A.F.
REFORM OF FEDERAL POSITION CLASSIFICATION: THE NIST ALTERNATIVE
DISSERTATION ABSTRACTS INTERNATIONAL, 50(5) (NOV 89), 1431-A.
THE AUTHOR EXPLAINS HOW A PAY-BAND CLASSIFICATION SYSTEM WAS DESIGNED AND IMPLEMENTED AT THE NATIONAL INSTITUTE OF STANDARDS AND TECHNOLOGY TO IMPROVE ON THE FEDERAL GENERAL SCHEDULE SYSTEM. THE PAY-BANDING WAS AUTHORIZED BY A PROVISION OF THE CIVIL SERVICE REFORM ACT OF 1978 THAT ALLOWS AGENCIES, WITH OPM APPROVAL, TO EXPERIMENT WITH NEW CONCEPTS IN PERSONNEL MANAGEMENT THAT WOULD OTHERWISE BE PROHIBITED.

02053 CASSEL, D.
THE UNITED HOLY LAND FUND
MIDDLE EAST INTERNATIONAL, (364) (DEC 89), 9.
THE ARTICLE OUTLINES THE EFFORTS OF THE UNITED HOLY LAND FUND, A NONPROFIT ORGANIZATION DESIGNED TO GIVE HUMANITARIAN AID TO PALESTINIANS IN GAZA AND THE WEST BANK. ALTHOUGH ITS

EFFORTS HAVE RESULTED IN A SIGNIFICANT TRANSFER OF FUNDS AND MEDICAL SUPPLIES, OPPOSITION FORM THE ISRAEL GOVERNMENT HAS OFTEN SLOWED OR COMPLETELY STOPPED THEIR ATTEMPTS.

02054 CASSESE, S.
THE STATE AND STATE-CONTROLLED AGENCIES AND CORPORATIONS IN POST-WAR ITALY
ITALIAN JOURNAL, III(4) (1989), 19-22.
MUCH HAS BEEN WRITTEN ABOUT THE CONTINUITY BETWEEN THE FASCIST AND THE POST-WAR ADMINISTRATIVE BODIES IN ITALY. THE FACT HAS BEEN WIDELY BEMOANED AND CRITICIZED, AND HISTORIANS HAVE OFTEN ANALYZED IT IN THE YEARS SINCE THE WAR. INDEED, THE CONTINUITY WAS NOT ONLY FORMAL, AFFECTING THE STATE AND ITS INSTITUTIONS, BUT ALSO SUBSTANTIAL, MEANING THAT IT REGARDED BOTH THE MEN AND THE ADMINISTRATIVE APPARATUSES INVOLVED.

02055 CASSTEVENS, T.H.
THE CIRCULATION OF ELITES: A REVIEW AND CRITIQUE OF A CLASS OF MODELS
AMERICAN JOURNAL OF POLITICAL SCIENCE, 33(1) (FEB 89), 294-317.
THIS ARTICLE REVIEWS A MATHEMATICAL MODEL OF THE CIRCULATION OF POLITICAL ELITES. POISSON DISTRIBUTIONS OF TURNOVERS AND EXPONENTIAL DISTRIBUTIONS OF LENGTHS OF TENURE ARE THE MATHEMATICS OF THE MODEL. THESE DISTRIBUTIONS ARE EQUIVALENT IN APPLICATIONS, IF TENURE IS THE TIME BETWEEN TURNOVERS. THE MODEL IS BROAD IN SCOPE; IT HAS BEEN APPLIED TO AT LEAST 30 JURISDICTIONS FROM COUNTIES TO COUNTRIES AND AT LEAST SEVEN TYPES OF INSTITUTIONS FROM COUNTY COMMISSIONERS TO REIGNING MONARCHS IN AT LEAST 25 STUDIES. THE CONSEQUENCES OF THE MODEL ARE STRIKING. CONGRESSIONAL SENIORITY, FOR EXAMPLE, IS NEUTRAL WITH RESPECT TO REELECTABILITY. THE MODEL IS USED IN EXPLANATION, PREDICTION, DEVIANT CASE ANALYSIS, AND MEASUREMENT OF REGIME STABILITY; BUT CONCEPTUAL PROBLEMS ARE TROUBLESOME IN FITTING CURVES, TESTING STATISTICAL THEOREMS, AND DEFINING BODIES SUCH AS CARETAKER CABINETS. NEVERTHELESS, THE MODEL IS A THEORY OF THE CIRCULATION OF ELITES AND, USING A LEAST SQUARES ALGORITHM WITHOUT TRANSFORMATIONS, THE CURVE FITTING CAN BE IMPLEMENTED IN BASIC.

02056 CASTLES, F.G.
BIG GOVERNMENT IN WEAK STATES: THE PARADOX OF STATE SIZE IN THE ENGLISH-SPEAKING NATIONS OF ADVANCED CAPITALISM
JOURNAL OF COMMONWEALTH AND COMPARATIVE POLITICS, XXVII(3) (NOV 89), 267-293.
THIS ARTICLE SEEKS TO USE THE METHODS OF QUANTITATIVE, COMPARATIVE POLITICAL ECONOMY TO LOCATE THE REASONS WHY IN 1960 THE SIZE OF THE STATE IN THE ENGLISH-SPEAKING NATIONS OF ADVANCED CAPITALISM MEASURED IN TERMS OF PUBLIC EMPLOYMENT WAS SO MUCH GREATER THAN ITS SIZE MEASURED IN TERMS OF PUBLIC EXPENDITURE AND WHY THAT DISPARITY HAD DISAPPEARED BY THE EARLY 1980S. IT DOES SO BY A GENERAL ANALYSIS OF THE DETERMINANTS OF BOTH PUBLIC EMPLOYMENT AND PUBLIC EXPENDITURE IN BOTH PERIODS.

02057 CASTLES, F.G.
EXPLAINING PUBLIC EDUCATION EXPENDITURE IN OECD NATIONS
EUROPEAN JOURNAL OF POLITICAL RESEARCH, 17(4) (JUL 89), 431-448.
THIS ARTICLE SEEKS TO EXPLAIN CROSS-SECTIONAL VARIATION IN PUBLIC EDUCATION EXPENDITURE LEVELS AND CHANGE SINCE 1960. FIVE POSSIBLE EXPLANATIONS ARE LOCATED: THE INCREMENTAL PUSH OF PROGRAMME INERTIA, DEMOGRAPHIC AND RELATED PRESSURES, ECONOMIC RESOURCE GROWTH, THE IMPACT OF PARTY AND THE CULTURAL IMPACT OF ROMAN CATHOLICISM. A MULTIVARIATE ANALYSIS DEMONSTRATES THAT EDUCATIONAL EXPENDITURE IS AN ARENA IN WHICH MONOCAUSAL EXPLANATIONS ARE WHOLLY INAPROPRIATE. WITH THE EXCEPTION OF PROGRAMME INERTIA, EACH OF THE EXPLANATIONS IS SEEN TO HAVE AN IMPORTANT BEARING ON THIS ASPECT OF THE PEOPLE'S WELFARE.

02058 CASTLES, F.G.; WIDMAIER, U.: HILDENMANN, R.
THE POLITICAL ECONOMY OF THE PEOPLE'S WELFARE: AN INITIAL PRESENTATION
EUROPEAN JOURNAL OF POLITICAL RESEARCH, 17(4) (JUL 89), 361-365.
MUCH OF THE BEST ANALYSIS IN THE FIELDS DESCRIBED AS "COMPARATIVE SOCIAL AND ECONOMIC POLICY" AND "POLITICAL ECONOMY" IS RETURNING ITS EMPHASIS TO EARLIER CONCEPTIONS OF THE DYNAMIC INTERACTION OF ECONOMY, SOCIAL STRUCTURE, AND THE POLITY OF THE KIND ASSOCIATED WITH NAMES LIKE ALFRED WEBER, JOSEPH SCHUMPETER, AND KARL POLANYI. THESE SCHOLARS ARE SEEKING TO OVERCOME THE FALSE DIVIDE BETWEEN KNOWLEDGE OF THE POLITICAL SYSTEM AND THE ECONOMY, AND THEY ARE DOING SO BY ANALYTICAL APPROACH THAT LOCATES BOTH THE SOCIETAL AND POLITICAL DETERMINANTS OF POLICY PERFORMANCE. THEY ARE CONFRONTING SUCH QUESTIONS AS: WHAT IS THE PEOPLE'S WELFARE, WHAT ARE THE INSTITUTIONAL ARRANGEMENTS BEST DESIGNED TO SECURE IT, AND HOW DO PRESENT SOCIO-ECONOMIC TENDENCIES IMPINGE ON ITS REALIZATION?

02059 CASTRO, F.
LONG LIVE INFLEXIBILITY!
HEMISPHERE, 2(1) (FAL 89), 12.
BIZARRE, COMPLEX, AND INCOMPREHENSIBLE EVENTS ARE
HAPPENING IN THE WORLD. THIS IS WHY, REMEMBERING THE WORDS
OF CAMILO CIENFUEGOS, CUBANS MUST ENTRENCH THEMSELVES BEHIND
THEIR MARXIST-LENINIST IDEAS. THEY MUST EMBRACE THE IDEAS OF
SOCIALISM AND COMMUNISM WITH MORE FERVOR THAN EVER BEFORE.

02060 CATER, N.
A STEP BACKWARDS?
AFRICA REPORT, 34(5) (SEP 89), 32-36.
ONE OF THE MAJOR REASONS BEHIND THE MILITARY'S SEIZURE
OF POWER IN SUDAN HAS BELIEVED TO BE THE AL-MAHDI
GOVERNMENT'S INABILITY TO END THE WAR WITH THE SPLA. HOWEVER,
THE AL-BESHIR JUNTA HAS MADE LITTLE PROGRESS IN THIS REGARD,
OMINOUSLY RAISING THE SPECTER OF PARTITION OF THE SOUTH AND
CLAMPING DOWN ON SUSPECTED OPPONENTS.

02061 CATER, N.
BESAIR'S BIG BASH
NEW AFRICAN, (263) (AUG 89), 16.
THIS ARTICLE REPORTS ON EVENTS BEHIND THE COUP IN SUDAN
WHICH OVERTHREW THE DEMOCRATICALLY ELECTED GOVERNMENT OF
SIDIQ EL MAHDI IN JULY. DISPITE ITS TALK OF PEACE WITH THE
REBELS FIGHTING IN THE SOUTH, THE NEW REGIME HAS TAKEN A
HAWKISH STANCE ON MANY ISSUES. IT DESCRIBES THE REACTION OF
MANY PEOPLE IN SUDAN AND THE ATMOSPHERE OF FEAR THAT IS
RETURNING THE NEW REGIMES LACK OF IMMEDIATE DIRECTION IS A
SOURCE OF DISMAY TO SUDAN'S DEEPLY FRAGMENTED SOCIETY AS
WELL AS TO ITS NEIGHBORS AND TO THE WEST.

02062 CATER, N.
SUDAN'S MR TOUGH GUY
NEW AFRICAN, (OCT 89), 11-12.
THIS STORY IS AN EARLY ASSESSMENT OF SUDAN'S NEW REGIME.
IT REPORTS ON LIEUTENANT GENERAL OMER EL BESHIR'S ATTITUDE
TO THE SOUTH AS WELL AS THE REST OF THE COUNTRY. ALSO
REPORTED ARE THE ACTIONS OF THE CABINET WHO IS AS
INEXPERIENCED IN GOVERNMENT AND DIPLOMACY AS SUDAN'S NEW
LEADER WHOSE STANCE HAS BEEN THAT OF A TOUGH GUY.

02063 CATT, H.
TACTICAL VOTING IN BRITAIN
PARLIAMENTARY AFFAIRS, 42(4) (OCT 89), 548-559.
ONE CONSISTANT FEATURE OF BRITISH ELECTION IN THE 1980S
HAS BEEN INTEREST IN THE PHENOMENA OF TACTICAL VOTING. THIS
ARTICLE ASKS THE FOLLOWING QUESTIONS: WHAT IS TACTICAL
VOTING; HOW WIDESPREAD IS IT IN BRITAIN; HOW CAN THE
EXISTENCE OF TACTICAL VOTING BE EVALUATED AND WHAT IS TOLD
ABOUT ELECTORAL ATTITUDES? IT CONCLUDES THAT TACTICAL VOTING
IS A SYMPTOM OF THE FLAWS IN THE ELECTORAL SYSTEM RATHER
THAN THE ROOT OF THE PROBLEM.

02064 CAUDLE, S.L.
"I SPEAK FOR THE TREES . . ."
POLICY STUDIES REVIEW, 8(4) (SUM 89), 884-890.
THIS ARTICLE CONCENTRATES ON THE NEED FOR GREATER
INFORMATION RESOURCES MANAGEMENT (IRM) EDUCATION IN PUBLIC
ADMINISTRATION PROGRAMS. THE AUTHOR ARGUES THAT CURRENT
MANAGEMENT INFORMATION SYSTEMS TRAINING IS MUCH TOO LIMITED
IN ITS APPROACH, CONCENTRATING ONLY ON THE TECHNOLOGY OF
INFORMATION TRANSFERS. A MORE COMPREHENSIVE TECHNIQUE,
EMPHASIZING ALL OF THE ISSUES OF DATA HANDLING FROM
COLLECTION TO DISTRIBUTION, IS PUT FORWARD. BECAUSE POLICY
DECISIONS ARE AFFECTED BY CRITICAL INFORMATION, PUBLIC
ADMINISTRATORS MUST BE KEENLY AWARE OF THEIR INFORMATION
RESOURCES. IN CONCLUDING THE ARTICLE, THE AUTHOR OFFERS A
POSSIBLE IRM CURRICULUM THAT WOULD PREPARE STUDENTS OF THE
DISCIPLINE TO BE LUCID PRACTITIONERS.

02065 CAVANAGH, R.; CALWELL, C.; GOLDSTEIN, D.; WATSON, R.
TOWARD A NATIONAL ENERGY POLICY
WORLD POLICY JOURNAL, VI(2) (SPR 89), 239-264.
THE ARTICLE DISCUSSES THE CONDITIONS AND CHALLENGES THAT
POLICYMAKERS INTENT ON FORMING A NATIONAL ENERGY POLICY WILL
FACE. THE RECENT UPSWING IN INTEREST IN THE AREA OF ENERGY
IS PRIMARILY DUE TO ENVIRONMENTAL CONCERNS SUCH AS ACID RAIN
AND THE GREENHOUSE EFFECT. POLICYMAKERS WILL NEED TO MAKE
FUNDAMENTAL DECISIONS ABOUT WHETHER TO CONCENTRATE ON FUEL
ACQUISTION OR ON CONSERVATION OF EXISTING FUELS. THE AUTHORS
MAINTAIN THAT FAIR COMPETITION BETWEEN IDEAS IN AN OPEN
FORUM IS THE OPTIMAL FIRST STEP TOWARDS A NATIONAL ENERGY
POLICY.

02066 CEBULA, R.; KOCH, J.
WELFARE POLICIES AND MIGRATION OF THE POOR IN THE UNITED
STATES: AN EMPIRICAL NOTE
PUBLIC CHOICE, 61(2) (MAY 89), 171-176.
THE PAPER INVESTIGATES THE IMPACT OF GEOGRAPHIC WELFARE
BENEFIT DIFFERENTIALS UPON MIGRATION IN THE UNITED STATES.
UNLIKE OTHER RELATED STUDIES, WHICH TYPICALLY FOCUS UPON
BLACK MIGRATION (AS A SURROGATE MEASURE OF MIGRATION OF THE
POOR), THE PRESENT STUDY FOCUSES DIRECTLY UPON MIGRATION OF

THE POOR PER SE. THE EVIDENCE STRONGLY SUGGESTS THAT THE NET
IN-MIGRATION OF THE POOR IS POSITIVELY AND SIGNIFICANTLY
INFLUENCED BY HIGHER NOMINAL AFDC LEVELS AND BY HIGHER REAL
AFDC LEVELS. THE FINDINGS SUPPORT THE "WELFARE MAGNET
HYPOTHESIS".

02067 CEFKIN, J.L.
AFRICA: SIGNIFICANT DEVELOPMENTS
FREEDOM AT ISSUE, (106) (JAN 89), 17-19.
THE AUTHOR BRIEFLY SURVEYS THE ROLE AFRICAN POLICY
PLAYED IN THE 1988 U.S. PRESIDENTIAL CAMPAIGN AND POLITICAL
DEVELOPMENTS IN AFRICA IN 1988, FOCUSING ON LONGSTANDING
INSURGENCIES THAT FINALLY SEEM TO BE MOVING TOWARD
SETTLEMENT.

02068 CEFKIN, J.L.
ISRAEL AND SOUTH AFRICA: RECONCILING PRAGMATISM AND
PRINCIPLE
MIDDLE EAST REVIEW, XXI(2) (WIN 89), 29-40.
FROM 1974 TO 1987, ISRAEL PURSUED POLICIES TO STRENGTHEN
ITS DIPLOMATIC TIES, TRADE, AND OTHER RELATIONS WITH SOUTH
AFRICA. IN SEPTEMBER 1987, ISRAEL IMPOSED ECONOMIC SANCTIONS
ON SOUTH AFRICA. THIS ILLUSTRATES HOW THE ISRAELI-SOUTH
AFRICAN CONNECTION IS CHANGING UNDER THE IMPACT OF NEW
CIRCUMSTANCES. FIVE AFRICAN COUNTRIES HAVE NORMALIZED
RELATIONS WITH ISRAEL IN THE LAST FEW YEARS, AND ADDITIONAL
AFRICAN GOVERNMENTS ARE LIKELY TO FOLLOW. THIS REFLECTS AN
EROSION OF ARAB INFLUENCE, PARTICULARLY THE PLO. AT THE SAME
TIME, THERE IS RECOGNITION OF THE EMERGENCE OF ISRAEL AND
SOUTH AFRICA AS REGIONAL POWERS NOT EASILY COERCED BY
INTERNATIONAL PRESSURES.

02069 CEFKIN, J.L.
SOUTH AFRICA: TOWARD A NEW ORDER
FREEDOM AT ISSUE, (111) (NOV 89), 20-22.
ON SEPTEMBER 6, 1989, SOUTH AFRICA HELD AN ELECTION TO
ITS TRICAMERAL PARLIAMENT. AS EXPECTED, THE NATIONAL PARTY
UNDER THE LEADERSHIP OF F.W. DEKLERK RETAINED POWER BUT WITH
A SUBSTANTIALLY REDUCED MAJORITY. THE CONSERVATIVES REMAINED
THE OFFICIAL OPPOSITION PARTY. THE DEMOCRATS, WHO ADVANCED A
PLAN FOR THE RAPID DISMANTLING OF APARTHEID AND FOR A NEW
CONSTITUTION, DID WELL AND CAN BE COUNTED ON TO DEMAND
PROGRESS TOWARD A NEW ORDER. THERE IS LITTLE DOUBT THAT NEW
REFORMS ARE ON THE AGENDA BECAUSE THE NEED FOR A NEW ORDER
HAS BECOME URGENT.

02070 CERNY, P.G.
THE 'LITTLE BIG BANG' IN PARIS: FINANCIAL MARKET
DEREGULATION IN A DIRIGISTE SYSTEM
EUROPEAN JOURNAL OF POLITICAL RESEARCH, 17(2) (MAR 89),
169-192.
FRENCH DIRIGISME SINCE WORLD WAR II HAS BEEN IDENTIFIED
AT FOUR LEVELS; ECONOMIC PLANNING; THE DOMINANCE OF A NEO-
COLBERTISTE CIVIL ELITE; GAULLISM AND THE FIFTH REPUBLIC;
AND A STATE-LED, CREDIT-BASED SYSTEM FOR FINANCING INDUSTRY.
THE LAST OF THESE WAS SEEN BY ZYSMAN (1977, 1983) AS THE
STRATEGIC CORE OF DIRIGISME, AS IN JAPAN, THROUGH STATE
CONTROL OF INDUSTRIAL PURSE STRINGS. PARADOXICALLY, IT WAS
THE SOCIALIST GOVERNMENTS OF 1981-86, IN RESPONSE TO
DEREGULATION ELSEWHERE, WHICH INITIATED EXTENSIVE CAPITAL
MARKET REFORMS INTENDED TO REPLACE THE STATE-LED, CREDIT-
BASED SYSTEM WITH AN 'ARM-LENGHT' FINANCIAL MARKET SYSTEM.
THESE CONTINUED UNDER THE RIGHT-WING CHIRAC GOVERNMENT.
HOWEVER, THE REFORM PROCESS ITSELF HAS BEEN STATE-LED RATHER
THAN MARKET-LED; AND BOTH RIGIDITIES IN THE MARKETS AND
SHORTCOMINGS IN THE REFORMS HAVE BEEN HIGHLIGHTED BY THE
OCTOBER 1987 CRASH. MUCH DIRIGISME OF A TACTICAL KIND
REMAINS, BUT THE STATE'S POTENTIAL FOR STRATEGIC
INTERVENTION HAS BEEN REDUCED.

02071 CESA, M.
DEFINING SECURITY: THE CASE OF SOUTHERN EUROPE AND THE
SUPERPOWERS IN THE MEDITERRANEAN
DISSERTATION ABSTRACTS INTERNATIONAL, 50(1) (JUL 89),
250-A.
INTERNAL SECURITY IS ALMOST ENTIRELY DEPENDENT ON NON-
MILITARY FACTORS. EXTERNAL SECURITY, ON THE OTHER HAND, CAN
BE RELATED TO BOTH MILITARY AND NON-MILITARY ISSUES. IN THIS
DISSERTATION, THIS BROAD CONCEPTION OF SECURITY IS APPLIED
TO SOUTHERN EUROPE. IN THIS REGION, NATIONAL ACTORS ARE
SENSITIVE TO THREE BASIC SECURITY INTERESTS: FREEDOM OF
NAVIGATION, INTERNATIONAL STABILITY (EXTERNAL SECURITY), AND
DOMESTIC STABILITY (INTERNAL SECURITY).

02072 CEYHUN, F.
THE POLITICS OF INDUSTRIALIZATION IN TURKEY
JOURNAL OF CONTEMPORARY ASIA, 18(3) (1988), 333-357.
TURKEY'S ECONOMIC DEVELOPMENT POLICY IS IN A DILEMMA NOW.
IN ADDIITION TO RISING DEBT, TRADE DEFICITS, UNEMPLOYMENT
AND INFLATION, THE LIBERAL ECONOMIC POLICY WHICH HAS BEEN
PUT TO THE TEST SINCE 1980, WITH THE IMF'S BLESSING, HAS
ALSO WORSENED THE INCOME INEQUALITY. HENCE, TURKEY HAS SEEN
THE FAILURE OF ANOTHER VARIANT OF CAPITALIST ECONOMIC
DEVELOPMENT. FOR MORE THAN THREE AND A HALF DECADES TURKEY

HAS BEEN EXPERIMENTING WITH DIFFERENT INDUSTRIALIZATION POLICIES WITHOUT MUCH SUCCESS. THE QUESTION IS FOR HOW MUCH LONGER WILL THE PEOPLE OF TURKEY BE GUINEA PIGS, AND ENDURE THE PAINS OF THE MISGUIDED POLICIES OF THEIR POLITICIANS? THE ANSWER IS UP TO THE PEOPLE.

02073 CHAKRABRTY, B.
THE COMMUNAL AWARD OF 1932 AND ITS IMPLICATIONS IN BENGAL
MODERN ASIAN STUDIES, 23(3) (JUL 89), 493-524.
THE DEBATE OVER THE SEPARATE AND JOINT ELECTORATES AS RIVAL MODES OF ELECTION TO THE VARIOUS REPRESENTATIVE INSTITUTIONS BY THE BRITISH BEGAN WITH THE SIMLA DEPUTATION OF 1906 AND REMAINED CONTROVERSIAL UNTIL 1947. IT ALSO RAISES DEBATES AMONG CONTEMPORARY HISTORIANS AND POLITICAL SCIENTISTS. AT THIS POINT, THE AVAILABLE EVIDENCE REVEALS THAT THE COMMUNAL AWARD AND THE CONSTITUTIONAL RIGHTS GUARANTEED TO INDIANS UNDER THE ACT WERE THE PRICE THE BRITISH PAID FOR THE CONTINUITY OF THE INDIAN EMPIRE. THIS ARTICLE EXAMINES THE SPECIAL CASE OF BENGAL AND DEALS WITH THE COMPLEX QUESTION OF HOW THE AWARD WAS MADE AND THE REACTIONS OF THE BENGALI POLITICIANS, REGARDLESS OF THEIR RELIGION, ONCE THE ELECTORAL ARRANGEMENT OF THE COMMUNAL AWARD WAS A SETTLED FACT.

02074 CHALIDZE, V.
PERESTROIKA, SOCIALISM, AND THE CONSTITUTION
PHILADELPHIA: ANLS OF AMER ACMY OF POLITICAL AND SOC SCIENCE, (506) (NOV 89), 98-108.
THIS ARTICLE TAKES A GENERAL VIEW OF PERESTROIKA AND ANALYZES CERTAIN POSSIBLE CHANGES IN THE SOVIET CONSTITUTION. THE RECENT STRUGGLE IN SOVIET SOCIETY IS VIEWED AS COMPETITION BETWEEN A PREVIOUS TENDENCY TO UNIFY SOCIAL RELATIONS AND RECENT DEMANDS FOR DEMOCRATIC PLURALISM IN SOCIETY. FURTHER, THE AUTHOR DISCUSSES POSSIBLE CHANGES IN THE SOVIET CONSTITUTION THAT COULD BE BROUGHT ABOUT BY PERESTROIKA. THE SOVIET CONSTITUTION MUST PROVIDE A JURIDICAL DEFINITION OF SOCIALISM IF THE SOVIET UNION IS TO CONTINUE DEVELOPMENT OF A SOCIALIST DEMOCRACY. FINALLY, THE AUTHOR FORMULATES A MODEL JURIDICAL DEFINITION OF SOCIALISM, WHICH SETS FORTH A SOCIALISM OF RIGHTS AND NOT A SOCIALISM OF RESTRICTIONS.

02075 CHAN, A.L.L.
THE DYNAMICS OF POLICY-MAKING IN CHINA: THE CASE OF THE GREAT LEAP FORWARD, 1958
DISSERTATION ABSTRACTS INTERNATIONAL, 49(9) (MAR 89), 2793-A.
THE AUTHOR EMPLOYS THE MULTIPLE CASE-STUDY APPROACH TO EXPLORE POLICY FORMULATION AND IMPLEMENTATION IN CHINA DURING THE GREAT LEAP FORWARD. HE FOCUSES ON THE CENTRAL MINISTRIES AND THE PROVINCES AS POLITICAL ACTORS AND THEIR INVOLVEMENT IN TWO POLICY AREAS: (1) INDUSTRIALIZATION AND (2) RURAL AND AGRICULTURAL CHANGES.

02076 CHAN, G.
CHINA-TAIWAN CONFLICT IN INTERNATIONAL ORGANIZATIONS
CHINA NEWS ANALYSIS, (1397) (NOV 89), 1-9.
THE AUTHOR DESCRIBES THE ORIGIN AND DEVELOPMENT OF THE TWO-CHINA CONFLICT WITHIN THE CONTEXT OF CHINESE PARTICIPATION IN INTERNATIONAL ORGANIZATIONS. HE THEN EXAMINES THE "OLYMPIC FORMULA" OF THE INTERNATIONAL OLYMPIC COMMITTEE AND THE "ICSU FORMULA" OF THE INTERNATIONAL COUNCIL OF SCIENTIFIC UNIONS TO SEE HOW THESE ORGANIZATIONS HANDLE THE TWO-CHINA PROBLEM. HE ASSESSES THE APPLICABILITY OF THESE TWO FORMULAS FOR TACKLING SIMILAR PROBLEMS IN OTHER INTERNATIONAL ORGANIZATIONS, ESPECIALLY THE ASIAN DEVELOPMENT BANK. HE CONCLUDES BY ASSESSING THE IMPLICATIONS OF THE FORMULAS FOR CHINA'S EFFORT TO REUNIFY WITH TAIWAN.

02077 CHAN, G.
SINO-VATICAN DIPLOMATIC RELATIONS: PROBLEMS AND PROSPECTS
CHINA QUARTERLY, (120) (DEC 89), 814-836.
TWO MAJOR FACTORS CONTINUE TO IMPAIR DIPLOMATIC RELATIONS BETWEEN THE PEOPLE'S REPUBLIC OF CHINA AND THE VATICAN: THE "TWO-CHINA" PROBLEM AND THE INDEPENDENCE ISSUE. THE FIRST TWO SECTIONS OF THIS ESSAY DISCUSS THE TWO AREAS OF DISPUTE, DRAWING ON SINO-VATICAN RELATIONS BEFORE AND SINCE 1949 TO SET THEM IN CONTEXT. THE THIRD SECTION EXPLORES THE POSSIBILITIES FOR RECONCILIATION, AND THE FOURTH ANALYZES THE FUTURE PROSPECTS FOR SINO-VATICAN RELATIONS.

02078 CHAN, J.M.; LEE, C.
SHIFTING JOURNALISTIC PARADIGMS: EDITORIAL STANCE AND POLITICAL TRANSITION IN HONG KONG
CHINA QUARTERLY, (117) (MAR 89), 97-117.
THE AUTHORS SEEK TO PROVIDE AN ANALYSIS OF HOW THE PRESS HAS ADAPTED ITS JOURNALISTIC PARADIGMS SINCE, AND BECAUSE OF, THE POLITICAL TRANSITION IN HONG KONG. THEY DEVELOP THE CONCEPT OF A JOURNALISTIC PARADIGM, TRACE THE EMERGENCE OF A DUALISTIC POWER STRUCTURE IN HONG KONG, EXAMINE THE POLITICAL IDEOLOGY AND PARTISAN AFFILIATION OF THE PRESS, AND COMPARE THE DIRECTION AND MAGNITUDE OF EDITORIAL PARADIGM SHIFTS IN RELATION TO PRESS IDEOLOGY.

02079 CHAN, M.; MON, M.C.
MON WOMEN SPEAK OUT FOR PEACE
CULTURAL SURVIVAL QUARTERLY, 13(4) (1989), 34-35.
THE MON ETHNIC GROUP LIVES IN BURMA, THAILAND, CAMBODIA, AND VIETNAM. THESE ESSAYS BY MON WOMEN EXPRESS THEIR HOPES FOR PEACE AND EXPLAIN THE EFFECTS OF BURMA'S FRONTIER WAR ON THEIR LIVES. MON REBELS OPERATE IN SOUTHERN BURMA. IN ADDITION TO FIGHTING BURMESE MILITARY DOMINATION, THEY FIGHT BURMESE ASSIMILATION AND VIEW A RENAISSANCE OF MON CIVILIZATION AS THEIR GOAL.

02080 CHAN, P.H.
FROM COLONY TO NEIGHBOR: RELATIONS BETWEEN JAPAN AND SOUTH KOREA, 1945-1985
DISSERTATION ABSTRACTS INTERNATIONAL, 49(7) (JAN 89), 1949-A.
IN THE 1950'S, JAPAN AND SOUTH KOREA EXCHANGED MUTUAL CONTEMPT AND PRACTISED CONFRONTATIONAL DIPLOMACY. IN 1965, RELATIONS WERE NORMALIZED, FOLLOWING YEARS OF TORTOUS NEGOTIATIONS. BY 1985, A STRONG WORKING RELATIONSHIP AND MUTUAL RESPECT HAD BEEN FIRMLY ESTABLISHED.

02081 CHAN, S.
INCOME DISTRIBUTION AND WAR TRAUMA: A CROSS-NATIONAL ANALYSIS
WESTERN POLITICAL QUARTERLY, 42(3) (SEP 89), 263-282.
THIS PAPER INVESTIGATES THE HYPOTHESIS THAT TRAUMATIC CIVIL OR FOREIGN WAR EXPERIENCE ENCOURAGES MORE EQUITABLE INCOME DISTRIBUTION. THIS HYPOTHESIS IS DERIVED FROM OLSON'S THEORY OF DISTRIBUTIONAL COALITIONS. THE RESULTS OF THE REGRESSION ANALYSES SHOW THAT, AFTER CONTROLLING FOR GNP PER CAPITA, COUNTRIES THAT HAVE UNDERGONE MORE SEVERE AND/OR RECENT CIVIL OR FOREIGN WARS FOUGHT ON THEIR SOILS DO INDEED SIGNIFICANTLY OUTPERFORM OTHERS THAT HAVE NOT HAD THIS EXPERIENCE WITH RESPECT TO THERE INCOME EQUITY. THIS EFFECT OF WAR TRAUMA ENDURES WHEN THE PERCENTAGE OF NATIONAL LABOR FORCE ENGAGED IN AGRICULTURAL PURSUITS, THE LITERACY RATE, THE CRUDE BIRTH RATE, OR THE MILITARY PARTICIPATION RATE (AS MEASURED BY THE NUMBER OF ARMED FORCES PERSONNEL PER 1,000 CITIZENS) IS ENTERED INTO THE REGRESSION ANALYSES AS A COMPETING EXPLANATION. THEREFORE, THE STATISTICAL EVIDENCE IS CONSISTENTLY AND STRONGLY SUPPORTIVE OF THE HYPOTHESIS.

02082 CHAN, S.
INCOME INEQUALITY AMONG LDCS: A COMPARATIVE ANALYSIS OF ALTERNATIVE PERSPECTIVES
INTERNATIONAL STUDIES QUARTERLY, 33(1) (MAR 89), 45-66.
THIS PAPER EMPIRICALLY EXAMINES SEVERAL ALTERNATIVE EXPLANATIONS OF INCOME INEQUALITY AMONG SIXTY-THREE LESS DEVELOPED COUNTRIES (LDCS). IT FINDS SUBSTANTIAL EVIDENCE RELATING THE STOCK OF FOREIGN CAPITAL AND THE RATE OF ECONOMIC GROWTH TO INCOME DISTRIBUTION IN THE MANNER PREDICTED BY THE NEWER DEPENDENCY SCHOOL AND THE MODERNIZATION SCHOOL, RESPECTIVELY. ON THE OTHER HAND, IT FAILS TO FIND SUPPORT FOR THE STATIST PERSPECTIVE, THE DEMOCRACY PERSPECTIVE, AND THE PERSPECTIVE ON DISTRIBUTIONAL COALITIONS. INSTEAD, MILITARY PARTICIPATION AND POPULATION DENSITY ARE FOUND TO EXERCISE A MORE ROBUST AND SIGNIFICANT INFLUENCE IN CURTAILING THE INCOME SHARE OF THE WEALTHY AND IN RAISING THE INCOME SHARE OF THE POOR. THE IMPLICATIONS OF THESE RESULTS FOR THE VARIOUS THEORETICAL TRADITIONS ARE EXPLORED.

02083 CHAN, S.
PAKISTAN AND THE COMMONWEALTH: RETURNING TO THE FOLD?
NEW ZEALAND INTERNATIONAL REVIEW, 14(3) (MAY 89), 19-20.
THE AUTHOR DISCUSSES THE PROSPECT OF PAKISTAN'S READMISSION TO THE COMMONWEALTH AT THE FORTHCOMING COMMONWEALTH HEADS OF GOVERNMENT MEETING. A SIGNIFICANT INCREASE IN TERMS OF THE COMMONWEALTH'S POPULATION AND THE ENHANCEMENT OF THE COMMONWEALTH'S CLAIM TO REPRESENT A SIGNIFICANT PROPORTION OF THE WORLD'S POOR IS NOTED, ALONG WITH THE COMPLETION OF AN ENTIRE GEOGRAPHIC BLOC ENCOMPASSING THE INDIAN SUBCONTINENT. THE AUTHOR OUTLINES THE FIVE COMMONWEALTH BLOCS, EXCLUDING GREAT BRITAIN AND THE IMPLICATIONS OF UNITY WITHIN BLOCS.

02084 CHAN, S.
THE COMMONWEALTH AS AN INTERNATIONAL ORGANIZATION: CONSTITUTIONALISM, BRITAIN AND SOUTH AFRICA
ROUND TABLE, (312) (OCT 89), 393-412.
THE WRITER ATTEMPTS TO DESCRIBE THE RECENT HISTORY OF THE COMMONWEALTH AND TO PUT FORWARD A SENSE OF ITS CONSTITUTIONAL GROWTH. HE PRESENTS AN ACCURATE PICTURE OF THE CONTEMPORARY COMMONWEALTH WITH AN EXPLANATION OF HOW IT ACHIEVED ITS CONTEMPORARY CONDITION. FOREIGN POLICY TOWARDS SOUTHERN AFRICA, BRITAIN AND THE WEST, SANCTIONS AND THE VANCOUVER SUMMIT OF 1987 ARE EXAMINED. ALSO EXPLORED IS A TEST CASE: BRITAIN, THE COMMONWEALTH AND RHODESIAN INDEPENDENCE.

02085 CHAN, S.
THE CONSOLIDATION OF REGIONAL POWER IN THE SOUTH PACIFIC

CONTEMPORARY REVIEW, 255(1485) (OCT 89), 169-172.
THIS ARTICLE DEALS WITH THE DIMINUTION OF INDEPENDENT
NEW ZEALAND IN THE SOUTH PACIFIC REGION. IT EXAMINES NEW
ZEALAND'S INCREASING RELIANCE ON AUSTRALIA FOR DEFENCE
INITIATIVES AND EQUIPMENT. IT REVIEWS THE HISTORY OF THE
REGION'S TWO LOCAL POWERS, AUSTRALIA AND NEW ZEALAND AND THE
DEVELOPING ISSUES OF FOREIGN POLICY, IT CONCLUDES WITH AN
EVALUATION OF AUSTRALIA'S PRESENT POSITION OF POWER.

02086 CHAN, S.
TWO STEPS FORWARD, ONE STEP BACK: TOWARDS A "FREE"
LITERATURE
AUSTRALIAN JOURNAL OF CHINESE AFFAIRS, (19-20) (JAN 88),
81-126.
THE AUTHOR EXAMINES THE STATE OF CHINESE LITERATURE FROM
1979 TO 1987. SHE TRACES THE EVOLUTION OF A NEW LITERARY
POLICY UNDER THE POST-MAO LEADERSHIP OF DENG XIAOPING AND
DISCUSSES THE IMPACT OF THIS POLICY ON CREATIVE WRITING. SHE
SHOWS THAT THE NEW POLICY RETAINS SOME ELEMENTS OF MAO'S
REPRESSIVE LITERARY POLICY WHILE REJECTING OTHERS AND THAT,
AS A RESULT OF DISAGREEMENT OVER BASIC DEVELOPMENT
STRATEGIES, THE CCP LEADERSHIP HAS SOMETIMES STRESSED THE
POLICY'S CONTINUITY WITH MAOISM AND SOMETIMES ITS
DISCONTINUITY. NEVERTHELESS, THIS RELATIVELY LIBERAL POLICY
HAS ALREADY REAPED ITS FIRST FRUIT IN AN UNPRECEDENTED
UPTURN IN BOTH THE QUANTITY AND QUALITY OF CREATIVE WRITING.

02087 CHAND, G.
THE WORLD BANK IN FIJI: THE CASE OF THE SUVA-NADI HIGHWAY
RECONSTRUCTION PROJECT
DEVELOPMENT AND CHANGE, 20(2) (APR 89), 235-267.
THIS ARTICLE EXAMINES THE WORLD BANK'S FIRST PROJECT
LENDING TO THE FIJIAN GOVERNMENT. ON THE BASIS OF
INFORMATION, DATA, AND EVIDENCE PERTAINING TO THIS LOAN, IT
IS ARGUED THAT THE WORLD BANK HAS ACTED ON BEHALF OF
INTERNATIONAL CAPITAL. ISSUES THAT HAVE BEEN CLOSELY
EXAMINED TO ARRIVE AT THIS CONCLUSION ARE THE LOAN CONDITION
AND THEIR IMPACT, PRIVATE SECTOR EFFICIENCY AND THE ECONOMIC
RATE OF RETURN, AND THE DISTRIBUTIONAL IMPACT OF THE PROJECT
FINALLY, TO SUPPORT THE ARGUMENTS, THE PROJECT HAS BEEN
PLACED WITHIN THE WIDER CONTEXT OF CAPITALIST DEVELOPMENT OF
FIJI.

02088 CHANDA, N.
BITING THE BULLET
FAR EASTERN ECONOMIC REVIEW, 141(39) (SEP 88), 24-26.
THE ARTICLE ANALYZES THE CHALLENGES AND DEMANDS THAT
RONALD REAGAN'S SUCCESSOR WILL FACE WITH REGARDS TO EAST
ASIA. THEY INCLUDE THE NEED TO PRESSURE JAPAN, SOUTH KOREA
AND TAIWAN TO OPEN FURTHER THEIR MARKETS, TO CUT DOWN
MILITARY OPERATIONS IN ASIA AND ENCOURAGE JAPAN AND SOUTH
KOREA TP ASSUME A GREATER SHARE OF THE DEFENSE BURDEN, AND
TO COPE WITH A MORE ACTIVE AND SOPHISTICATED SOVIET
DIPLOMACY. THE US WILL ALSO HAVE TO FIND WAYS TO CUT THE
HUGE BUDGET AND TRADE DEFICITS. WHATEVER COURSE THAT
WASHINGTON TAKES, THE ARTICLE CONCLUDES THAT EAST ASIA WILL
HAVE TO DEAL WITH A "LEANER AND MEANER US."

02089 CHANDA, N.
CIVIL WAR IN CAMBODIA?
FOREIGN POLICY, (76) (FAL 89), 26-43.
THIS ARTICLE TAKES A CLOSE LOOK AT THE ROOTS OF CONFLICT
AND THE UNREMITTING ENMITY BETWEEN THE KHMER ROUGE AND ITS
OPPONENTS WHICH TEMPER EXPECTATIONS ABOUT PEACE AND HARMONY
FOR CAMBODIA. EXAMINED ARE FACTORS SUCH AS THE FACT THAT PRK
LEADERS HAVE NO DESIRE TO ACCEPT A DIMINUTION IN THEIR POWER
IN ORDER TO ACHIEVE A SETTLEMENT, AND ALSO THE REBEL
FACTIONS. CHINA'S VIEW IS EXPLORED AND THE ROLE OF THE
UNITED STATES IS RECOMMENDED.

02090 CHANDA, N.
FRIENDS DRIFT APART
FAR EASTERN ECONOMIC REVIEW, 141(27) (JUL 88), 30-32.
AS SOVIET TROOPS CONTINUE THEIR WITHDRAWAL FROM
AFGHANISTAN. CLOSE US-PAKISTAN RELATIONS WHICH HAVE BEEN
BASED LARGELY ON THEIR COMMON OPPOSITION TO THE SOVIET
OCCUPATION ARE COMING UNDER STRAIN. THERE IS CONSIDERABLE
DISAGREEMENT OVER AFGHANISTAN'S FUTURE AS THE US FEARS THAT
IT MAY BE DRAGGED INTO A NEW INVOLVEMENT IN AFGHAN CIVIL
STRIFE BY THROWING SUPPORT BEHIND AN ISLAMIC FUNDAMENTAL
GOVERNMENT SUPPORTED BY PAKISTAN. THERE ARE ALSO BILATERAL
PROBLEMS WHICH WERE LONG IGNORED BECAUSE OF A COMMON
OVERRIDING STRATEGIC OBJECTIVE WHICH NOW WILL HAVE TO BE
DEALT WITH.

02091 CHANDA, N.
SECURITY VS COMMERCE
FAR EASTERN ECONOMIC REVIEW, 141(37) (SEP 88), 98.
AN AUSTRALIAN TO PLAN TO BUY AMERICAN-MADE
COMMUNICATIONS SATELLITES TO BE PUT IN ORBIT BY CUT-RATE
CHINESE LAUNCH SERVICE HAS BROUGHT UP THE ISSUE OF NATIONAL
SECURITY VS COMMERCIAL GAIN. THE ISSUE HAS BEEN HOTLY
DEBATED AT TIMES IN WASHINGTON AND THIS CASE SEEMS TO BE NO
EXCEPTION. THE CURRENT DEBATE IS COMPLICATED BY THE FACT

THAT NO TECH TRANSFER IS INVOLVED AND THE SALE IS BENEFICIAL
TO ONE US COMPANY AND TO A CLOSE TREATY ALLY. ON THE OTHER
HAND IT WOULD BOOST CHINA'S FLEDGLING SPACE LAUNCH INDUSTRY,
A POTENTIAL COMPETITOR. AUSTRALIA AND THE US STATE
DEPARTMENT ARE PUSHING FOR AN EARLY DECISION.

02092 CHANDA, N.
SUPPORT FOR SIHANOUK
FAR EASTERN ECONOMIC REVIEW, 141(28) (JUL 88), 13-14.
IN RESPONSE TO THE GROWING MILITARY MUSCLE OF THE KHMER
ROUGE, THE US IS CONSIDERING SENDING MILITARY AID TO PRINCE
NORODOM SIHANOUK'S RESISTANCE MOVEMENT. HOWEVER, THE
POSITION OF VIETNAM ON THIS ISSUE IS AS OF YET UNKNOWN, AND
THE US IS RELUCTANT TO PURSUE THE POLICY WITHOUT VIETNAM'S
APPROVAL.

02093 CHANDA, N.
THE ANXIOUS WATCH
FAR EASTERN ECONOMIC REVIEW, 141(35) (SEP 88), 14.
AS THE VOID LEFT BY THE LATE PRESIDENT ZIA-UL HAQ
BECOMES PAINFULLY OBVIOUS, THE US IS ANXIOUSLY WATCHING THE
DEVELOPMENTS IN PAKISTAN AND IS ATTEMPTING TO QUIETLY STEER
PAKISTAN ON A MODERATE COURSE THAT WILL GURANTEE THE
PROMISED ELECTIONS IN A FEW MONTHS. INDIA IS ALSO CLOSELY
MONITORING THE SITUATION, BUT DOES NOT EXPECT A MAJOR CHANGE
IN INDO-PAKISTANI RELATIONS IN THE NEAR FUTURE. THE
POSSIBILITY OF ANOTHER MILITARY TAKEOVER SEEMS TO BE IN
NEITHER THE US, NOR INDIA'S INTEREST.

02094 CHANDA, N.
THE END OF AN ERA
FAR EASTERN ECONOMIC REVIEW, 141(36) (SEP 88), 24.
IN RECENT YEARS US-SOVIET AS WELL AS SINO-SOVIET TIES
HAVE IMPROVED MARKEDLY WHICH HAS REULTED IN A LOSST IN THE
ATTRACTION OF WASHINGTON'S CHINA QUESTION. NOW, A CHINESE
REFUSAL TO BAN THE SALE OF BALLISTICMISSILES TO THIRD
PARTIES INCREASE THE TENSION BETWEEN THE US AND CHINA AND
SOME OBERSVERS ARE DECLARING AN "END OF AN ERA" IN US-CHINA
RELATIONS.

02095 CHANDLER, J.A.
THE LIBERAL JUSTIFICATION FOR LOCAL GOVERNMENT: VALUES AND
ADMINISTRATIVE EXPEDIENCY
POLITICAL STUDIES, XXXVII(4) (DEC 89), 604-611.
THERE ARE SEVERAL IMPORTANT JUSTIFICATIONS FOR
AUTONOMOUS UNITS OF LOCAL GOVERNMENT, DERIVED FROM THE
WRITINGS OF J.S. MILL AND LATER THEORIES CONCERNING THE
VALUE OF PLURALISM. THESE ARGUMENTS FAIL TO SHOW THAT LOCAL
GOVERNMENT IS A MORALLY NECESSARY, AS OPPOSED TO EXPEDIENT,
ADJUNCT TO LIBERAL-DEMOCRATIC GOVERNMENT. THE PAPER DEVELOPS
FROM J.S. MILL'S IDEAS ON LIBERTY A MORE SUBSTANTIVE
JUSTIFICATION FOR LOCAL GOVERNMENT BASED ON THE PRINCIPLE
THAT LOCAL GOVERNMENT CAN BE A MEANS FOR ENSURING THAT THE
DETERMINATION OF COLLECTIVE DECISIONS ARE MADE SOLELY BY
THOSE PEOPLE AFFECTED BY THE DECISION.

02096 CHANDLER, W.; BAKVIS, H.
FEDERALISM AND THE STRONG-STATE/WEAK-STATE CONUNDRUM:
CANADIAN ECONOMIC POLICYMAKING IN COMPARATIVE PERSPECTIVE
PUBLIUS: THE JOURNAL OF FEDERALISM, 19(1) (WIN 89), 59-78.
THE ARTICLE EXAMINES CANADA WITHIN A COMPARATIVE
FRAMEWORK AND ASSESS THE "FEDERATIONS AS WEAK STATES"
HYPOTHESIS AS WELL AS THE UTILITY OF THE "STRONG-STATE/WEAK-
STATE" MODEL. ALTHOUGH SOME ASPECTS OF THE CANADIAN FEDERAL
SYSTEM INHIBIT THE ADOPTION OF EFFECTIVE ECONOMIC ADJUSTMENT
POLICIES, THESE FEATURES ARE NOT NECESSARILY FOUND IN OTHER
FEDERAL ARRANGEMENTS. COMPARISONS WITH SWITZERLAND, AUSTRIA,
AND WEST GERMANY SUGGEST THAT, UNDER CERTAIN CIRCUMSTANCES,
FEDERAL POWER SHARING MAY BE CONDUCIVE TO BRINGING ABOUT
BROAD AGREEMENT ON BOTH GOALS AND POLICIES AMONG NATIONAL,
REGIONAL, AND LOCAL GOVERNMENTS AND MAJOR ECONOMIC ACTORS.

02097 CHANDRA, P.
INDIA: SAVING THE FORESTS
THIRD WORLD WEEK, 7(12) (FEB 89), 90-91.
PRIME MINISTER RAJIV GANDHI HAS HALTED TIMBER-CUTTING ON
INDIA'S ANDAMAN AND ISLANDS. GANDHI'S ORDER REPRESENTS A
FUNDAMENTAL DECISION IN FAVOR OF CONSERVATION AND AGAINST
THE PATTERN OF EXPLOITATION ON THE ISLANDS. THE GOVERNMENT
HAS ALSO RESTRICTED IMMIGRATION TO THE ISLANDS AND ORDERED
THE REMOVAL OF PEOPLE WHO SETTLED ON FOREST LAND AFTER 1978.

02098 CHANG-KUEI, L.
HIGH-SPEED SOCIAL DYNAMICS
FREE CHINA REVIEW, 39(10) (OCT 89), 4-7.
POLITICAL AND ECONOMIC MODERNIZATION HAVE PRODUCED
TREMENDOUS SOCIAL CHANGE IN TAIWAN. ONE KEY SOCIAL CHANGE IS
THE SHIFT FROM THE TRADITIONAL VERTICAL RELATIONSHIPS
BETWEEN THE GOVERNMENT AND THE PEOPLE, EMPLOYERS AND WORKERS,
AND TEACHERS AND STUDENTS TO A HORIZONTAL MOTIF. IN
RESPONSE TO THIS TREND, THE GOVERNMENT IS STREAMLINING AND
ENHANCING ITS OWN POLICY-MAKING PROCEDURES AND IS
ENCOURAGING MORE PUBLIC PARTICIPATION IN THE PROCESS OF
DECISION-MAKING AND THE EVALUATION OF PROGRAMS.

02099 CHANG, C.
A DECADE OF SINO-JAPANESE RELATIONS, 1978-1988
DISSERTATION ABSTRACTS INTERNATIONAL, 50(3) (SEP 89),
786-A.
THE AUTHOR SURVEYS SINO-JAPANESE RELATIONS FROM 1978 TO
1988 IN AN ATTEMPT TO DESCRIBE AND EXPLAIN THE COURSE OF
DIALECTICAL DEVELOPMENT OF THE BILATERAL RELATIONSHIP IN
THAT PERIOD. HE EXAMINES INFLUENCES ON THE RELATIONSHIP,
INCLUDING THE PRC'S REFORMULATION OF ITS GLOBAL STRATEGY IN
GENERAL AND SOVIET POLICY IN PARTICULAR, THE RESURGENCE OF
JAPANESE NATIONALISM, THE TAIWAN FACTOR, AND THE LEVEL OF
BILATERAL ECONOMIC RELATIONS.

02100 CHANG, C.
ALIENS IN THEIR ADOPTED LAND
FREE CHINA REVIEW, 39(7) (JUL 89), 32-36.
THE AUTHOR REVIEWS THE STATUS OF THE CHINESE MINORITY IN
SOUTH KOREA, WHERE THE VAST MAJORITY OF THE CHINESE HOLD
TAIWANESE PASSPORTS AND REMAIN FOREIGNERS IN THEIR ADOPTED
LAND, EXCLUDED FROM KEY POSITIONS IN BUSINESS AND THE
GOVERNMENT.

02101 CHANG, C.
LEARNING TO SPEAK OUT
FREE CHINA REVIEW, 39(11) (NOV 89), 37-39.
IN THIS ARTICLE, MEMBERS OF TAIWAN'S MIDDLE CLASS
DISCUSS SUCH ISSUES AS THE ROLE OF THE MIDDLE CLASS IN
DEMOCRATIZATION, MIDDLE CLASS PRIORITIES AMONG DOMESTIC
ISSUES, AND THE IMAGE OF THE MIDDLE CLASS AS A "SILENT
MAJORITY."

02102 CHANG, C.
MAKING IT IN JAPAN
FREE CHINA REVIEW, 39(7) (JUL 89), 42-45.
THE AUTHOR DISCUSSES THE STATUS OF THE CHINESE MINORITY
IN JAPAN, WHICH HAS ATTRACTED LARGE NUMBERS OF TAIWANESE IN
THE LAST DECADE DUE TO ITS RAPID ECONOMIC DEVELOPMENT AND
ECONOMIC OPPORTUNITIES.

02103 CHANG, C.; CHIEN-AI, L.
MINISTERS WITH HEAVY WORKLOADS
FREE CHINA REVIEW, 39(1) (JAN 89), 30-39.
THE CONSTITUTION OF TAIWAN AND REGULATIONS GOVERNING THE
OPERATION OF THE EXECUTIVE YUAN CALL FOR THE APPOINTMENT OF
A NUMBER OF MINISTERS WITHOUT PORTFOLIO. THIS ARTICLE
REVIEWS THE BACKGROUNDS OF TAIWAN'S CURRENT SEVEN MINISTERS
WITHOUT PORTFOLIO AND INCLUDES EXCERPTS FROM INTERVIEWS WITH
FIVE OF THEM.

02104 CHANG, L.H.
FLEXIBLE DIPLOMACY
FREE CHINA REVIEW, 39(5) (MAY 89), 4-9.
IN MARCH 1989 TAIWAN'S PRESIDENT LEE TENG-HUI MADE AN
OFFICIAL STATE VISIT TO SINGAPORE, EVEN THOUGH THE TWO
COUNTRIES DO NOT HAVE OFFICIAL DIPLOMATIC RELATIONS. THE
TRIP WAS SEEN AS A STEP TOWARD THE ADOPTION OF A MORE
FLEXIBLE DIPLOMATIC POLICY BY TAIWAN.

02105 CHANG, L.S.L.
IN PURSUIT OF WEALTH AND POWER: EAST ASIAN NEWLY
INDUSTRIALIZING COUNTRIES IN THE INTERNATIONAL POLITICAL
ECONOMY
DISSERTATION ABSTRACTS INTERNATIONAL, 49(12) (JUN 89),
3861-A.
THIS STUDY EXAMINES THE ECONOMIC DEVELOPMENT OF SOUTH
KOREA AND TAIWAN DURING THE POST-WORLD WAR II PERIOD AND
ASSESSES THE APPLICABILITY AND "FIT" TO THESE TWO COUNTRIES
OF THE THREE MAJOR APPROACHES TO INTERNATIONAL POLITICAL
ECONOMY: ECONOMIC LIBERALISM, MARXISM/RADICALISM, AND
NEOMERCANTILISM. IT FOCUSES ON FOUR MAJOR CONTROVERSIAL
ISSUES OF INTERNATIONAL POLITICAL ECONOMY: THE EFFECTS OF
FOREIGN AID MULTINATIONAL INVESTMENT, AND INTERNATIONAL
TRADE, AND THE ROLE OF THE STATE IN THE DEVELOPMENT OF THIRD
WORLD COUNTRIES.

02106 CHANG, M.M.; SHU, R.L.
REJECTING THE MYTH OF "MODEL MINORITY"
FREE CHINA REVIEW, 39(7) (JUL 89), 48-53.
CHINESE-AMERICANS HAVE OFTEN BEEN CONSIDERED A "MODEL
MINORITY," BASED IN LARGE PART UPON THEIR HIGH SOCIOECONOMIC
ACHIEVEMENTS. BUT MODEL MINORITY STATUS CAN BE A DOUBLE-
EDGED SWORD BECAUSE IT CAN MASK SUBTLE INSTANCES OF
DISCRIMINATION. IN THIS ARTICLE, THE AUTHORS ANALYZE AND
DEBUNK THE MODEL MINORITY THESIS, ESPECIALLY AS IT PERTAINS
TO THE CHINESE IN THE UNITED STATES.

02107 CHANG, Y.; PILLARISETTI, J.R.
DEBT AND THE DEVELOPING COUNTRIES: A NOTE ON OPTIMAL
INTERNATIONAL BORROWING
JOURNAL OF DEVELOPMENT STUDIES, 25(4) (JUL 89), 576-579.
THIS NOTE RE-EXAMINES THE ECONOMIC MODEL OF OPTIMAL
INTERNATIONAL BORROWING FOR LDC'S PROPOSED BY GEMMELL (1988).
PURSUING A RIGOROUS METHODOLOGY, THIS NOTE DERIVES

ALTERNATIVE OPTIMAL DEBT FUNCTIONS AND DISCUSSES THE
CONDITIONS UNDER WHICH THE OPTIMAL DEBT LEVEL IS POSITIVE.
INTERESTING IMPLICATIONS OF THE ANALYSIS. IN THIS NOTE,
INTER ALIA, REST IN IDENTIFYING THE APPROPRIATE ROLE OF
SOCIAL INTER-TEMPORAL CONSUMPTION PREFERENCES IN A MORE
REALISTIC SETTING AND IN PERCEIVING, UNAMBIGUOUSLY, THE
TENDENCY OF 'OVERBORROWING' BY LDCS THAT ONLY SERVICE THEIR
DEBTS OVER LONG PERIODS.

02108 CHANGYOU, Z.; TIANSHEN, W.
CHINA'S INVESTMENTS ABROAD
CHINA RECONSTRUCTS, XXXVIII(4) (APR 89), 26-28.
NOT MANY PEOPLE ARE AWARE THAT CHINESE INVESTMENTS
ABROAD HAVE INCREASED DRAMATICALLY IN THE LAST DECADE.
BETWEEN 1979 AND 1988, CHINA INVESTED US$650 MILLION IN
ABOUT 500 PROJECTS IN 80 COUNTRIES. CHINA'S OVERSEAS
INVESTMENTS ARE AN IMPORTANT PART OF ITS NATIONAL STRATEGY
TO ENCOURAGE INTERNATIONAL ECONOMIC AND TECHNOLOGICAL
COOPERATION. THEY ARE A WAY TO HELP REVITALIZE THE NATIONAL
ECONOMY WHILE PROVIDING VALUABLE TRAINING AND EXPERIENCE FOR
TECHNICIANS AND MANAGERS.

02109 CHANTRASMI, S.
COMMUNISM IN SOUTHEAST ASIA
DISSERTATION ABSTRACTS INTERNATIONAL, 49(9) (MAR 89),
2793-A.
THE AUTHOR EXPLORES THE CAUSES AND DYNAMICS OF POLITICAL
REVOLUTIONS IN SOUTHEAST ASIA. HE STUDIES MARXIST EFFORTS IN
SEVEN COUNTRIES, TAKING LOCAL CHARACTERISTICS INTO ACCOUNT.
HE ASSESSES THE VALIDITY OF COMMONLY-ACCEPTED IDEAS, SUCH AS
THE CONNECTION BETWEEN POVERTY AND COMMUNIST VICTORY AND THE
DOMINO THEORY.

02110 CHAO, W.
SOME STRATEGICAL PROBLEMS IN ATTRACTING FOREIGN CAPITAL
INTO THE PEOPLE'S REPUBLIC OF CHINA.
FOREIGN TRADE, 12 (1988), 20-22.
THIS ARTICLE EXAMINES FOUR AREAS AFFECTING THE
INVESTMENT CLIMATE AND ECONOMIC SITUATION OF CHINA. THESE
AREAS ARE: 1. DETERMINE AND MAINTAIN AN OPTIMAL SCALE ON
WHICH TO ATTRACT FOREIGN INVESTMENTS. 2. CORRECTLY DECIDE
THE AREAS IN WHICH TO USE FOREIGN CAPITAL, 3. INCREASE THE
MICROAND MACROE-EFFECTIVENESS OF THE FORGIEN CAPITAL USED, 4.
IMPROVE MANAGEMENT AT THE MACROLEVEL.

02111 CHARIH, M.
LE PLAN FINANCIER DE LA COMMISSION LAMBERT: EVALUATION ET
MISE EN OEUVRE PAR LE GOUVERNEMENT FEDEDERAL
CANADIAN PUBLIC ADMINISTRATION, 32(3) (FAL 89), 367-381.
THE AUTHOR OF THIS ARTICLE ANALYSES — FROM WITHIN THE
FEDERAL GOVERNMENT -THE TECHNICAL, BUREAUCRATIC AND
POLITICAL DIFFICULTIES THE TRUDEAU GOVERNMENT FACED WHEN
IMPLEMENTING THE FIVE-YEAR FINANCIAL PLAN PROPOSED BY THE
ROYAL COMMISSION ON FINANCIAL MANAGEMENT AND ACCOUNTABILITY.
THE AUTHOR CONCLUDES THAT THE AMENDMENTS MADE TO THAT PLAN
DID, UPON IMPLEMENTATION, SERIOUSLY DIMINISH THE
ACCOUNTABILITY ROLE OF THE GOVERNMENT WITH RESPECT TO
PARLIAMENT.

02112 CHARLOT, JEAN
POLITICAL PARTIES: TOWARDS A NEW THEORETICAL SYNTHESIS
POLITICAL STUDIES, 37(3) (SEP 89), 352-361.
THREE CONCEPTIONS OF THE POLITICAL PARTY CAN BE
DISTINGUISHED. THEY ARE SEILER'S SOCIOCULTURAL CLEAVAGE
APPROACH; LAWSON'S NOTION OF THE LINKAGE PARTY, BASED UPON
PARTICIPATORY, POLICY-RESPONSIVE, CLIENTELE REWARD AND
GOVERNMENT DIRECTIVE LINKAGES; AND OFFERLE'S CONCEPTION OF
PARTIES AS POLITICAL ENTERPRISES CONCENTRATING UPON PARTISAN
SUPPLY TO THE POLITICAL MARKET. AFTER SUGGESTING THAT,
WHATEVER THEIR PARTIAL MERITS, NONE OF THESE APPROACHES
PROVIDES THE BASIS FOR A COMPRHENSIVE THEORY OF POLITICAL
PARTIES, A DUAL PARTY APPROACH IS PREPARED. EVERY PARTY
EXISTS IN AND FOR ITSELF AS WELL AS INTERACTING WITH A
CONSTRAINING ENVIRONMENT. A DIALECTICAL MODEL, BASED UPON
RELATIONS BETWEEN INTERNAL DECISION-MAKING AND EXTERNAL
COMPETITION WITHIN THE CONTEXT OF THE RULES OF THE GAME,
OFFERS THE BEST PROSPECT OF FURTHER ADVANCE IN THE STUDY OF
POLITICAL PARTIES.

02113 CHARLTON, M.
THE GREAT GAME REPLAYED
ENCOUNTER, LXXII(4) (APR 89), 13-24.
IT IS NOW MORE THAN A CENTURY SINCE THE SHADOW OF THE
RUSSIAN EAGLE FIRST BEGAN TO STRETCH DARKLY ALONG THE LINE
OF THE INDIAN FRONTIER. THE SOVIET UNION'S SUDDEN INVASION
OF AFGHANISTAN IN 1979 WAS ANOTHER STEP IN THE LONG, SLOW,
CONTINUOUS HISTORICAL THRUST BY THE RUSSIANS INTO CENTRAL
ASIA.

02114 CHARNEY-MESIBOV, E.
THE SECOND COMMANDMENT: THE POLITICAL NATURE OF THE
ICONOCLASTIC LAW
DISSERTATION ABSTRACTS INTERNATIONAL, 49(8) (FEB 89),
2283-A.

THIS STUDY SHOWS THAT THE PRINCIPLE PURPOSE OF THE
SECOND COMMANDMENT WAS TO SEGREGATE ISRAEL FROM THE OTHER
NATIONS AND TO ENHANCE THE POLITICAL POWER OF THE JERUSALEM
PRIESTHOOD. THIS WAS NEEDED IN THE PRIESTHOOD'S PURSUIT OF
THE FORMATION OF A THEOCRACY WHICH WOULD PROVIDE POWER AND
HEALTH FOR THE PRIESTLY CASTE. THE STUDY SHOWS THAT THE
SECOND COMMANDMENT WAS VARIOUSLY INTEPRETED AND RARELY
OBSERVED BY THE HEBREWS, ISRAELITES, AND JEWS.

02115 CHAROENLOET, V.
THE CRISIS OF STATE ENTERPRISES IN THAILAND
JOURNAL OF CONTEMPORARY ASIA, 19(2) (1989), 206-217.
THIS ARTICLE SUGGESTS THAT THE PRESENT ECONOMIC CRISIS
IN THAILAND IS BEING USED AS A PRETEXT BY THE DOMINANT CLASS
FOR THE IMPLEMENTATION OF A CONSERVATIVE ECONOMIC POLICY AND
THAT PRIVATIZATION IS ONE SUCH POLICY ON THE AGENDA. IT
EXPLORES THE EMERGENCE AND CRISIS OF STATE ACCUMULATION OF
CAPITAL. THE LIMITS OF EXTENSIVE DEVELOPMENT, THE
CONTRADICTIONS OF A HIGHLY CENTRALIZED SYSTEM, SOCIAL
SURPLUS, AND THE DEBT BURDEN ARE ANALYZED IN TURN. THE
POLITICS OF NEO-LIBERALISM IN RELATION TO PRIVATIZATION ARE
EXPLORED AS WELL AS REPERCUSSIONS ON THE LABOR MOVEMENT.

02116 CHASE, R.
GREAT BRITIAN-USSR: A NEW STAGE IN TRADE AND ECONOMIC
COOPERATION
FOREIGN TRADE, 7 (1988), 20-22.
THIS ARTICLE EXAMINES THE IMPORTANT PART THAT TRADE HAS
PLAYED IN THE RELATIONS BETWEEN GREAT BRITIAN AND THE USSR.
IT REPORTS ON EFFORTS MADE BY BOTH COUNTRIES TO RESTORE THE
SLIPPAGE OF TRADE IN RECENT YEARS, IT REPORTS ON THE IMPACT
OF THE SEVERAL DOZEN JOINT UK-USSR WORKING GROUPS COVERING
ALL LEVELS OF INDUSTRIES. EXPLORED ARE THE MANY POINTS OF
COMMON INTEREST, PLUS AN INTENSE PROGRAM OF VISITS IN BOTH
DIRECTIONS.

02117 CHASE, W.
VOLUNTARISM, MOBILISATION AND COERCION: SUBBOTNIKI 1919-
1921
SOVIET STUDIES, XLI(1) (JAN 89), 111-128.
FOLLOWING LENIN'S LEAD, SOVIET HISTORIANS HAVE PRESENTED
THE SOBBOTNIK MOVEMENT OF 1919-21, IN WHICH WORKERS
VOLUNTARILY WORKED OVERTIME WITHOUT PAY TO FURTHER THE CAUSE
OF COMMUNISM, IN THE MOST POSITIVE OF TERMS. WESTERN
HISTORIANS HAVE TENDED TO EMPHASIZE THE COERCIVE ASPECTS OF
THE SYSTEM. THE PURPOSE OF THE ESSAY IS TO EXAMINE THE
EVOLUTION AND CHANGING NATURE OF SUBBOTNIKI IN ORDER TO
UNDERSTAND WHEN AND WHY THEY CHANGED FROM LOCALLY INITIATED,
VOLUNTARY ACTIVITIES TO A MASS MOVEMENT DIRECTED BY THE
PARTY, AND HOW THE FOCUS OF SUBBOTNIK ACTIVITIES CHANGED
DURING THE 1919-1921 PERIOD.

02118 CHATFIELD, C.; DEBENEDETTI, C.; VAN DEN DUNGEN, P.
AMERICAN PEACE ACTIVISM, 1945-1985; PEACE MOVEMENTS AND
POLITICAL CULTURES
UNIVERSITY OF TENNESSEE PRESS, KNOXVILLE, TN, 1988,
222-231.
THIS ESSAY REFLECTS A PRESCRIPTIVE INTERPRETATION THAT
DERIVES FROM THE WRITER'S COMPREHENSIVE STUDY AND HIS
INTENSIVE HISTORY OF THE PEACE MOVEMENTS IN THE VIETNAM ERA.
IT EXPLORES THE DISPARITY BETWEEN EFFORTS INVESTED AND
ACHIEVEMENTS EFFECTED BY AMERICAN PEACE ACTIVISM IN THE
FORTY YEARS FOLLOWING WORLD WAR II. IT FOLLOWS THE STORY OF
AMERICAN PEACE EFFORTS AND ANALYZES THE AREAS OF EFFORTS TO
PERSUADE THE AMERICAN PEOPLE AND THEIR GOVERNMENT THAT THE
COUNTRY'S PRINCIPAL ENEMY WAS INTERNATIONAL WAR, IT
CONCLUDES WITH A VISION OF FUTURE AMERICAN PEACE MOVEMENT
STRATEGY.

02119 CHATFIELD, C.; PATTERSON, D.S.; VAN DEN DUNGEN, P.
CITIZEN PEACE INITIATIVES AND AMERICAN POLITICAL CULTURE;
PEACE MOVEMENTS AND POLITICAL CULTURES
UNIVERSITY OF TENNESSEE PRESS, KNOXVILLE, TN, 1988,
187-203.
THIS ESSAY EXPLORES THE RELATIONSHIP BETWEEN BELIEFS AND
VALUES OF AMERICAN PEACE REFORMERS AND THE PREDOMINANT
VICTORIAN CULTURE IN LATE-NINETEENTH-CENTURY AMERICA. IT
EXAMINES AFFINITY BETWEEN THE PEACE WORKERS' AND MIDDLE-
CLASS VICTORIAN REFORM ATTITUDES AND NEW APPROACHES TO THE
INTERNATIONAL SYSTEM IN THE PEACE MOVEMENT. AN UNDERSTANDING
OF THIS RELATIONSHIP HELPS TO EXPLAIN WAY THE PEACE MOVEMENT
BECAME DIVIDED AND PARALYZED AFTER THE OUTBREAK OF THE
EUROPEAN WAR.

02120 CHATFIELD, C.; DULFFER, J.; VAN DEN DUNGEN, P.
CITIZENS AND DIPLOMATS: THE DEBATE ON THE FIRST HAGUE
CONFERENCE (1899) IN GERMANY; PEACE MOVEMENTS AND
POLITICAL CULTURES
UNIVERSITY OF TENNESSEE PRESS, KNOXVILLE. TN, 1988, 23-39.
THE HAGUE PEACE CONFERENCE FORMED A CHALLENGE TO THE
EXISTING INTERNATIONAL SYSTEM, TO GOVERNMENTS AND DIPLOMATS,
AND TO PEACE MOVEMENTS. ALTHOUGH NATIONAL REACTIONS TO THE
HAGUE PROPOSALS VARIED FROM COUNTRY TO COUNTRY, THEY CAN BE
SEEN AS AN EXPRESSION OF DIFFERENT POLITICAL CULTURES. THIS

CHAPTER DISTINGUISHES AMONG FOUR LINES OF GERMAN RESPONSE TO
THE HAGUE PROPOSALS: THOSE OF DIPLOMATIC AND MILITARY
OFFICIALS, POLITICAL LIBERALS, SOCIALISTS, AND THE SMALL
MINORITY OF PACIFISTS. IT RECORDS THE OFFICIAL POSITION,
SOCIALIST ATTITUDES AND THE ATTITUDE OF THE PEACE MOVEMENT.

02121 CHATFIELD, C.; LUBELSKI - BERNARD, N.; VAN DEN DUNGEN, P.
FREEMASONRY AND PEACE IN EUROPE 1867-1914; PEACE MOVEMENTS
AND POLITICAL CULTURES
UNIVERSITY OF TENNESSEE PRESS, KNOXVILLE, TN, 1988, 81-94.
IN EUROPE, ONLY A PART OF FREEMASONRY WAS INVOLVED IN
PEACE QUESTIONS DURING THE PERIOD BETWEEN 1867 AND 1914. TO
UNDERSTAND WHY, THE WRITER DISTINGUISHES AMONG THE THREE
MAIN CURRENTS THEN EXISTING IN FREE MASONRY: ANGLO-SAXON
FREEMASONRY, LATIN FREEMASONRY, AND GERMANIC AND
SCANDINAVIAN MASONRIES. MASONIC ORGANIZATIONAL TERMS ARE
DEFINED. THE INTERNATIONAL MASONIC CONGRESSES AND BUREAU OF
MASONIC RELATIONS ARE EXPLORED. THE ARTICLE CONCLUDES BY
ADDRESSING HOW THE MASONS COULD ACT EFFECTIVELY TO MAINTAIN
PEACE WHILE THEIR PRESENCE WASN'T SEEN.

02122 CHATFIELD, C.; HOLL, K.; VAN DEN DUNGEN, P.
GERMAN PACIFISTS IN EXILE, 1933-1940; PEACE MOVEMENTS AND
POLITICAL CULTURES
UNIVERSITY OF TENNESSEE PRESS, KNOXVILLE, TN, 1988,
165-184.
THIS IS A REPORT OF SOME OF THE CONCLUSIONS OF RECENT
RESEARCH INTO THE SITUATION OF GERMAN PACIFISTS IN EXILE
AFTER 1933. THE SITUATION FACED BY GERMAN PACIFISTS TOWARDS
THE END OF THE WEIMAR REPUBLIC AND THE WAY THEY REACTED TO
EVENTS AFTER HITLER'S SEIZURE OF POWER ON 30 JANUARY 1933 IS
COMMENTED ON. THEN CONSIDERATION IS GIVEN TO THE FORM OF
PERSECUTION THEY ENCOUNTERED, THEIR EXPERIENCES AND LIVING
CONDITIONS IN EXILE, AND THEIR POLITICAL ACTIVITIES ABROAD.

02123 CHATFIELD, C.; VAN DEN DUNGEN, P.
PEACE MOVEMENTS AND POLITICAL CULTURES
UNIVERSITY OF TENNESSEE PRESS, KNOXVILLE, TN, 1988, 294.
FOR OVER A CENTURY, PRIVATE CITIZENS HAVE WORKED IN
VOLUNTARY ASSOCIATIONS TO PROMOTE PEACE IN THE WORLD. IN
THIS COLLECTION OF ESSAYS, LEADING HISTORIANS FROM EUROPE,
NORTH AMERICA, AND AUSTRALIA EXPLORE THE RELATIONSHIPS
BETWEEN PEACE MOVEMENTS AND THE NATIONAL AND INTERNATIONAL
POLITICAL CULTURES THEY SEEK TO CHANGE. THE AUTHORS RAISE
QUESTIONS OF CONTEMPORARY AS WELL AS HISTORICAL SIGNIFICANCE.
A RECURRENT THEME IS THE NOTION THAT PEACE EFFORTS ARE
CONSTRAINED BY CULTURAL MILIEUX. THE MAGNITUDE OF THE
CHALLENGE FACING PEACE ADVOCATES CAN BE APPRECIATED WHEN
THEY ARE UNDERSTOOD AS BOTH DISSENTERS FROM AND PRESERVERS
OF THEIR POLITICAL CULTURES, THE DIVERSITY OF PEACE
MOVEMENTS, AND THE DIVISIONS WITHIN THEM, RAISES IMPORTANT
ISSUES WHEN THEY ARE ANALYZED AS POLITICAL ORGANIZATIONS.

02124 CHATFIELD, C.; INGRAM, N.; VAN DEN DUNGEN, P.
ROMAIN ROLLAND, INTERWAR PACIFISM AND THE PROBLEM OF PEACE;
PEACE MOVEMENTS AND POLITICAL CULTURES
UNIVERSITY OF TENNESSEE PRESS, KNOXVILLE, TN, 1988,
143-164.
THIS ESSAY EXAMINES ROMAIN ROLLAND'S OPPOSITION TO WAR
AND FOLLOWS THE EVOLUTION OF HIS POLITICAL THOUGHT ON THE
PROBLEMS OF PEACE AND PACIFISM; AND OBSERVES HOW IT WAS
TRANSLATED INTO CONCRETE ACTION IN HIS RELATIONS WITH
PACIFIST AND WAR RESISTANCE ORGANIZATIONS DURING THE
INTERWAR YEARS. IT FOLLOWS THE EVOLUTION FROM INDIVIDUALISM
TO COLLECTIVISM. IT DIVIDES THIS PROCESS INTO THREE PERIODS:
THE GREAT WAR TO ABOUT 1924; 1924 TO THE EARLY THIRTIES; AND
FROM 1932 TO 1939.

02125 CHATFIELD, C.; SUMMY, R.; VAN DEN DUNGEN, P.
THE AUSTRALIAN PEACE COUNCIL AND THE ANTICOMMUNIST MILIEU,
1949-1965; PEACE MOVEMENTS AND POLITICAL CULTURES
UNIVERSITY OF TENNESSEE PRESS, KNOXVILLE, TN, 1988,
233-264.
THIS ARTICLE EXPLORES THE DIRECTION AND THE IMPACT OF
THE MAJOR PEACE BODIES IN AUSTRALIA AFTER WORLD WAR II--THE
AUSTRALIAN PEACE COUNCIL (APC) AND THE WORLD PEACE MOVEMENT
(WPC). IT ALSO EXPLORES CRITICISM OF THE PEACE MOVEMENT THAT
IT WAS SERVING THE INTERESTS OF INTERNATIONAL COMMUNISM. IT
EXAMINES THE ORIGINS OF THE APC - ITS DOMESTIC BACKGROUND
AND FOREIGN LINKS AND ALSO THE MARSHALLING OF THE NEW (WPC)
WITHIN THE OLD (APC). IT CONCLUDES THAT THE EXTREME
ANTICOMMUNISM THAT PLAGUED THE PEACE MOVEMENT SAYS MORE
ABOUT THE SPIRIT OF THE TIMES THAN THE STATE OF THE
GOVERNMENT.

02126 CHATFIELD, C.; VAN DEN DUNGEN, P.; WANK, S.
THE AUSTRIAN PEACE MOVEMENT AND THE HABSBURG RULING ELITE,
1906 - 1914; PEACE MOVEMENTS AND POLITICAL CULTURES
UNIVERSITY OF TENNESSEE PRESS, KNOXVILLE, TN, 1988, 23-39.
THIS CHAPTER EXAMINES THE EXPERIENCE OF THE AUSTRIAN
PEACE MOVEMENT, SET AGAINST THE DEEPENING SOCIAL AND
NATIONAL CONFLICTS AFTER 1906, WHICH SUGGESTS THAT THE
POTENTIAL FOR INFLUENCING GOVERNMENTS IS LIMITED BY THE
POLITICAL CONTEXT AND PERCEPTIONS OF PEACE ADVOCATES. THIS

IS STUDIED IN THE HABSBURG CONTEXT. THE PEACE MOVEMENT IN
AUSTRIA IS ANALYZED. THE BOURGEOIS AND THE SOCIALIST PEACE
RECORDS ARE COMPARED. THE CONCLUSION IS DRAWN THAT PEACE
RESEARCH MUST SEEK SOME MIDDLE GROUND.

02127 CHATFIELD, C.; SIMON, H.; VAN DEN DUNGEN, P.
THE INTERNATIONAL PEACE BUREAU 1892-1917: CLERK, MEDIATOR,
OR GUIDE?; PEACE MOVEMENTS AND POLITICAL CULTURES
UNIVERSITY OF TENNESSEE PRESS; KNOXVILLE, TN, 1988, 67-80.
A HUMAN SOCIETY WHICH WAS TOTALLY UNORGANIZED ON THE
INTERNATIONAL PLANE ABOUNDING WITH RIVALRIES: THIS IS WHAT
PACIFISTS ATTEMPTED TO OVERCOME THROUGH THE ESTABLISHMENT OF
A WORLD COMMUNITY TENDING TOWARD THE HARMONIZATION OF
PARTICULAR INTERESTS, THE INTERNATIONAL PEACE BUREAU (IBP)
WAS ORGANIZED IN THE ATTEMPT. THIS ARTICLE EXPLORES WHETHER
AND TO WHAT EXTENT THE MEN RESPONSIBLE FOR RUNNING THE DAILY
AFFAIRS OF THE IPB - ELIE DUCOMMUN, ALBERT GOBAT, AND HENRI
GOLAY - WERE ABLE OR WILLING TO RECONCILE CONFLICTING IDEAS
AMONG THEIR FELLOW PACIFISTS. IN THE FINAL EVENT, THE
CONCEPTIONS OF HODGSON PRATT, EMILE ARNAUD AND ALBERT GOBAT
PREVAILED OVER THOSE REPRESENTED BY ELIE DUCOMMUN.

02128 CHATFIELD, C.; HERMON, E.; VAN DEN DUNGEN, P.
THE INTERNATIONAL PEACE EDUCATION MOVEMENT, 1919 - 1939;
PEACE MOVEMENTS AND POLITICAL CULTURES
UNIVERSITY OF TENNESSEE PRESS, KNOXVILLE, TN, 1988,
127-142.
THIS CHAPTER EXAMINES PEACE EDUCATION AS AN
INTERNATIONAL MOVEMENT FOLLOWING WORLD WAR I WHICH IN THE
PROCESS LEFT ITS PREWAR ORGANIZATIONAL BASE IN PACIFIST
SOCIETIES. IT DISCUSSES PEACE EDUCATION AS A MORAL
DISARMAMENT AND THE ROLE THE LEAGUE OF NATIONS PLAYED. IT
NOTES THE GROWING ASSERTIVENESS OF THE NONGOVERNMENT
ORGANIZATIONS COORDINATING COMMITTEE AND EXPLORES PEACE
EDUCATION IN THE POLITICAL CONTEXT.

02129 CHATFIELD, C.; JOSEPHSON, H.; VAN DEN DUNGEN, P.
THE SEARCH FOR LASTING PEACE: INTERNATIONALISM AND
AMERICAN FOREIGN POLICY, 1920-1950; PEACE MOVEMENTS AND
POLITICAL CULTURES
UNIVERSITY OF TENNESSEE PRESS, KNOXVILLE, TN, 1988,
204-221.
THIS ARTICLE EXAMINES THE RELATIONSHIP BETWEEN
INTERNATIONALISM AND AMERICAN FOREIGN POLICY. IT EXPLORES
THE POSITIVE IMPACT UPON POST-WORLD WAR II GLOBAL POLITICS
AND FOREIGN POLICY CAUSED BY INTERNATIONALISTS. IT DETAILS
THEIR CALL FOR INTERNATIONAL COOPERATION IN THE AREA OF
ECONOMIC AND SOCIAL DEVELOPMENT, THEIR PROMOTION OF
INTERNATIONAL LAW, AND THEIR ADVOCACY OF INTERNATIONAL
ORGANIZATION AS AN ALTERNATIVE TO UNLIMITED NATIONAL
SOVEREIGNTY. IT ALSO EXAMINES THE RESULTS OF THE LIMITED
NATURE OF THEIR GLOBAL VISION.

02130 CHATFIELD, C.; VAN DEN DUNGEN, P.; WITTNER, L.S.
THE TRANSNATIONAL MOVEMENT AGAINST NUCLEAR WEAPONS, 1945-
1986: A PRELIMINARY SURVEY; THE PEACE MOVEMENTS AND
POLITICAL CULTURES
UNIVERSITY OF TENNESSEE PRESS, KNOXVILLE, TN, 1988,
265-294.
THIS ESSAY EXAMINES THE LARGEST, MOST TURBULENT MOVEMENT
OF MODERN TIMES WHICH HAS BEEN THE TRANSNATIONAL CRUSADE
AGAINST NUCLEAR WEAPONS. IT EXPLORES THE STRENGTHS AND
WEAKNESSES OF THE STRUGGLE TO BAN A PARTICULAR KIND OF
WEAPON TO AVERT A PARTICULAR KIND OF WAR. IT PRESENTS A
SURVEY OF THE FORTY-ONE-YEAR HISTORY OF THE WORLD
ANTINUCLEAR MOVEMENT. IT CONCLUDES THAT ANTINUCLEAR WEAPONS
MOVEMENT HAS SLOWED BUT NOT HALTED THE NUCLEAR ARMS RACE,
AND THAT THE REAL LESSON OF HIROSHIMA IS THAT THERE MUST BE
NO MORE WAR.

02131 CHATFIELD, C.; CHICKERING, R.; VAN DEN DUNGEN, P.
WAR, PEACE, AND SOCIAL MOBILIZATION IN IMPERIAL GERMANY:
PATRIOTIC SOCIETIES, THE PEACE MOVEMENT, AND SOCIALIST
LABOR; PEACE MOVEMENTS AND POLITICAL CULTURES
UNIVERSITY OF TENNESSEE PRESS, KNOXVILLE, TN, 1988, 3-22.
ROGER CHICKERING PROPOSES THAT A SOCIAL MOVEMENT MAY BE
UNDERSTOOD AS A COLLECTIVE BEARER OF AN ALTERNATIVE IDENTITY.
IT EXPLORES THE HISTORY OF THE MIDDLE-CLASS PEACE MOVEMENT
IN IMPERIAL GERMANY AND EXAMINES POINTS OF COMPARISON WITH
THE MOBILIZATION OF OPINION IN THE PATRIOTIC SOCIETIES. IT
QUESTIONS WHETHER MOBILIZATION IS THE APPROPRIATE TERM WITH
WHICH TO ANALYZE THE HISTORY OF THE MOVEMENT. IT CONCLUDES
THAT RECENT CONTROVERSIES OVER THE GERMAN EMPIRE TOOK PLACE
WITHIN A CULTURAL FRAMEWORK AND CONCEPTUAL VOCABULARY WHICH
AGENCIES OF THE STATE HAD PROMOTED IN ORDER TO BUTTRESS AN
AUTHORITARIAN ORDER.

02132 CHATFIELD, C.; VAN DEN DUNGEN, P.; VELLACOTT, J.
WOMEN, PEACE, AND INTERNATIONALISM, 1914-1920: "FINDING
NEW WORDS AND CREATING NEW METHODS"; PEACE MOVEMENTS AND
POLITICAL CULTURES
UNIVERSITY OF TENNESSEE PRESS, KNOXVILLE, TN, 1988,
106-124.
THIS ARTICLE EXPLORES PEACE EFFORTS OF WOMEN PRIOR TO

WORLD WAR I, BY EXAMINING FEMINIST PACIFISM AS A POLITICAL
STATEMENT. IT CONCLUDES THAT THE HISTORY OF ALL WOMEN'S
PEACE MOVEMENTS TEND TO SHOW THAT THOSE WHO CHALLENGE
MILITARISM ARE GENERALLY AMONG THE MOST ADVANCED OF
FEMINISTS WITH A GOOD UNDERSTANDING OF THE SCOPE AND NATURE
OF PATRIARCHY, AND OF WHAT MILITARISM MEANS IN TERMS OF
WOMEN'S POSITION. THE ROOTS OF FEMINIST PACIFISM AND HOW IT
DIVIDED THE SUFFRAGE MOVEMENT ARE DETAILED. WOMEN WERE FOUND
TO BE POWERLESS TO PREVENT WAR.

02133 CHATFIELD, C.; SACRACINO, M.A.; VAN DEN DUNGEN, P.
WOMEN, THE UNWILLING VICTIM OF WAR: THE LEGACY OF OLIVE
SCHREINER (1855-1920); PEACE MOVEMENTS AND POLITICAL
CULTURES
UNIVERSITY OF TENNESSEE PRESS, KNOXVILLE, TN, 1988, 97-105.
THIS CHAPTER EXAMINES THE LEGACY OF OLIVE SCHREINER
WHICH IS HER EFFECTIVE USE OF BOTH FICTION AND ESSAY FORMS
TO IDENTIFY WOMEN WITH CLASSES OPPRESSED AND VICTIMIZED BY
WAR. SHE WAS A COMMITTED PACIFIST AND AN ADVOCATE OF HUMAN
RIGHTS, SEVERAL OF HER NARRATIVE FORM WRITINGS ARE EXPLORED
AND QUOTES ARE GIVEN FROM THEM. IT CONCLUDES BY NOTING THE
EMPHASIS THAT SCHREINER PLACED ON EDUCATION AS A KEY WAY TO
COMBAT RACISM AND WAR, WHICH WAS A PATH WHICH SHE OPENED UP
FOR WOMEN IN HER FICTION, ESSAYS, AND PERSONAL LIFE.

02134 CHAUDHRY, K. A.
THE PRICE OF HEALTH: BUSINESS AND STATE IN LABOR
REMITTANCE AND OIL ECONOMIES
INTERNATIONAL ORGANIZATION, 43(1) (WIN 89), 101-146.
THIS ARTICLE CONTRASTS THE EFFECTS OF STATE-CONTROLLED
OIL REVENUES AND PRIVATELY CONTROLLED LABOR REMITTANCES ON
INSTITUTIONAL DEVELOPMENT, STATE CAPACITY, AND
BUSINESSGOVERNMENT RELATIONS IN SAUDI ARABIA AND THE YEMEN
ARAB REPUBLIC. THESE TWO COUNTRIES REPRESENT EXTREME CASES
OF DEPENDENCE ON EXTERNAL CAPITAL IN DEEPLY DIVIDED
SOCIETIES PRESIDED OVER BY FRAGILE, EMERGING BUREAUCRACIES.
BY TRACING TWO CASES THROUGH A PATTERN OF ECONOMIC BOOM
(1973-83) AND RECESSION (1983-87), THE STUDY DEMONSTRATES
THAT THE TYPE, VOLUME, AND CONTROL OF CAPITAL INFLOWS
DECISIVELY INFLUENCE THE RELATIVE DEVELOPMENT OF THE
BUREAUCRACY'S EXTRACTIVE, DISTRIBUTIVE, AND REGULATORY
CAPACITIES AND AFFECT THE ABILITY OF THE STATE TO RESPOND TO
ECONOMIC CRISIS. IN BOTH CASES, EXTERNAL CAPITAL INFLOWS
PRECIPITATED THE DECLINE OF EXTRACTIVE INSTITUTIONS. HOWEVER,
OIL REVENUES AND LABOR REMITTANCES HAD DIVERGENT EFFECTS ON
BUSINESSGOVERNMENT RELATIONS, AND THIS CIRCUMSCRIBED THE
STATE'S ABILITY TO IMPLEMENT AUSTERITY PROGRAMS DURING THE
RECESSION. DURING THE CRISIS, THE SAUDI GOVERNMENT'S EFFORTS
TO CUT SUBSIDIES TO THE PRIVATE SECTOR AND TO IMPLEMENT
EXTRACTIVE POLICIES WERE BLOCKED BY THE STATE-SPONSORED
MERCHANT CLASS. IN CONTRAST, THE YEMENI GOVERNMENT
INSTITUTED A THOROUGHGOING AUSTERITY PACKAGE THAT TARGETED
THE INDEPENDENT MERCHANT CLASS. IN BOTH CASES, EXTERNAL
CAPITAL INFLOWS DID NOT AUGMENT THE EFFICACY OF THOSE THAT
CONTROLLED THEM. THESE PARADOXICAL OUTCOMES ARE EXPLAINED BY
TRACING THE DIFFERENT EFFECTS OF OIL REVENUES AND LABOR
REMITTANCES ON THE DISTRIBUTION OF ECONOMIC OPPORTUNITY IN
THE PUBLIC AND PRIVATE SECTORS AND THE RESULTING EFFECTS ON
THE REGIONAL, TRIBAL, AND SECTARIAN COMPOSITION OF THE
BUREAUCRACY AND THE COMMERCIAL CLASS.

02135 CHAUVEAU, J.; SAMBA, A.
MARKET DEVELOPMENT, GOVERNMENT INTERVENTIONS, AND THE
DYNAMICS OF THE SMALL-SCALE FISHING SECTOR: AN HISTORICAL
PERSPECTIVE OF THE SENEGALESE CASE
DEVELOPMENT AND CHANGE, 20(4) (OCT 89), 599-620.
THE SENEGALESE FISHERIES SECTOR OCCUPIES A PRIVILEGED
PLACE IN THE STATE'S ECONOMIC RECOVERY POLICY BECAUSE
AUTHORITIES CONSIDER IT TO BE A KIND OF ESCAPE VALVE FOR THE
COUNTRY'S ECONOMY. THE ARTISANAL FISHING SECTOR IS EXPECTED
TO MAKE AN ESSENTIAL CONTRIBUTION TO THE DOMESTIC FOOD
SUPPLY AND TO THE EXPANSION OF EXPORTS, EMPLOYMENT, AND
INVESTMENT. SUCH EXPECTATIONS ARE RELATIVELY NEW ELEMENTS IN
THE LONG HISTORY OF EXTERNAL AND STATE INTERVENTION IN THE
SECTOR. ONLY SINCE 1980, WHEN THE FINDINGS OF BIOLOGICAL AND
SOCIOECONOMIC RESEARCH WERE TAKEN INTO CONSIDERATION, HAS
THE STATE BUREAUCRACY RECOGNIZED THAT CANOE FISHERIES ARE
NOT OSTACLES TO THE GROWTH OF THE SECTOR BUT IMPORTANT
GROWTH STIMULI.

02136 CHAWLA, P.
BALLOT OVER BULLET
INDIA TODAY, XIV(1) (JAN 89), 30-32.
THE ELECTION OF RANASINGHE PREMADASA AS SRI LANKA'S
PRESIDENT INDICATED THE PUBLIC'S DESIRE FOR AN END TO THE
VIOLENCE IN THE ISLAND REPUBLIC. IT WAS ALSO A REBUFF TO
SIRIMAVO BANDARANAIKE'S CONFRONTATIONIST APPROACH TOWARDS
INDIA. AT ONE STROKE, THE PEOPLE DELIVERED THE MESSAGE THAT
THEY HAD HAD ENOUGH AND WANTED THE COUNTRY TO FOLLOW THE
PATH OF CONSTRUCTION AND PROGRESS.

02137 CHAWLA, P.
DOORDARSHAN: HIJACKING THE MEDIUM
INDIA TODAY, XIV(13) (JUL 89), 10-17.

THIS ARTICLE EXAMINES EVIDENCE OF MISUSE OF THE MEDIA BY THE GOVERNMENT. THE OFFICIAL MEDIA HAS BEEN REDUCED TO AN ADVERTISEMENT AGENCY OF THE RULING CLASS, PAID FOR BY THE TAXPAYER. THE OPPOSITION CLAIMS THAT DOORDARSHAN AND AIR ARE NOW THE ELECTORAL WEAPONS OF CONGRESS (I). THE GOVERNMENT INSISTS THAT IT HAS BEEN FAIR.

02138 CHAWLA, P.
DUBIOUS DISMISSAL
INDIA TODAY, XIV(8) (MAY 89), 14-23.
THE STYLE AND METHOD USED TO DISMISS THE JANATA DAL GOVERNMENT IN KARNATAKA WAS YET ANOTHER CASE OF A GOVERNOR USURPING THE POWERS OF THE LEGISLATURE. IT ALSO INDICATED THAT THE CONGRESS(I) IS NOT WAITING UNTIL ELECTION TIME TO DEFEAT GOVERNMENTS IN OPPOSITION-LED STATES IF IT CAN FIND A PRETEXT TO REMOVE THEM EARLIER.

02139 CHAWLA, P.; DILEEP, L.
INVOKING LEGACIES
INDIA TODAY, XIV(1) (JAN 89), 24-27.
THE 1989 ELECTIONS FOR THE TAMIL NADU, NAGALAND, AND MIZORAM ASSEMBLIES WILL BE A POINTER TO THE BIGGER ELECTORAL BATTLE DUE LATER IN THE YEAR AND WILL SET THE TONE FOR IT. WITH THE STAKES SO HIGH, THE REGIONAL PARTIES AND CONGRESS(I) ARE CONCENTRATING ON SIMILAR STRATEGIES: INVOKING THE GODS OF THE PAST, SEARCHING FOR HIGH-PROFILE CANDIDATES, AND WHIPPING UP PAROCHIAL FERVOUR.

02140 CHAWLA, P.; MENON, A.K.
KARUNANIDHI: SMASHING RETURN
INDIA TODAY, XIV(3) (FEB 89), 14-21.
THIRTEEN YEARS AFTER HE WAS REMOVED FROM OFFICE, THIRIKOVALAI MUTHUVEL KARUNANIDHI LED THE DRAVIDA MUNNETRA KAZHAGAM (DMK) TO ELECTION VICTORY IN TAMIL NADU. THE DECISIVE WIN SMASHED THE CONGRESS (I) PARTY'S HOPES OF SECURING A FOOTHOLD IN THE SOUTH.

02141 CHAWLA, P.
MOUNTING INERTIA
INDIA TODAY, XIV(8) (APR 89), 18-21.
THE GOVERNMENT OF RAJIV GANDHI HAS BECOME A MONUMENT TO INERTIA. IT HAS BECOME SO BOGGED DOWN IN LIMITING THE DAMAGES FROM SCANDALS AND POLITICAL EMBARRASSMENTS THAT IT HAS NOT BEEN ABLE TO GET DOWN TO THE BUSINESS OF GOVERNING AND IMPLEMENTING CRUCIAL, TIME-BOUND DECISIONS.

02142 CHAWLA, P.
PANCHAYATI RAJ: FROM DOOR TO "DEHAT"
INDIA TODAY, XIV(10) (MAY 89), 18-21.
PRIME MINISTER RAJIV GANDHI IS MAKING THE BIG PITCH FOR HIS LATEST CAMPAIGN - OPERATION PANCHAYATE RAJ - IN ORDER TO WOO THE COUNTRY'S 300 MILLION RURAL VOTERS. RAJIV'S NEW CLEARLY-DEFINED ELECTORAL STRATEGY AND HIS SLOGAN "POWER TO THE PEOPLE" ARE ELECTORAL GAMBITS SURE TO CONFOUND THE OPPOSITION.

02143 CHAWLA, P.; DILEEP, L.
THE BOTTLE BOMB
INDIA TODAY, XIV(6) (MAR 89), 68-72.
THE GOVERNMENT OF CHIEF MINISTER M. KARUNANIDHI HAS INITIATED A TWO-PRONGED PLAN TO TAKE OVER THE LIQUOR INDUSTRY AND, AT THE SAME TIME, DESTROY THE CLOUT THE LIQUOR BARONS ENJOYED DURING THE MGR REGIME. KARUNANIDHI HAS ZEROED IN ON THE LIQUOR TRADE TO EXTRACT ADDITIONAL REVENUE FOR THE STATE AND HAS ACCUSED AIADMK POLITICIANS OF ACCEPTING BRIBES FROM THE LIQUOR COMPANIES.

02144 CHAZAN, N.
PLANNING DEMOCRACY IN AFRICA: A COMPARATIVE PERSPECTIVE ON NIGERIA AND GHANA
POLICY SCIENCES, 22(3-4) (1989), 325-357.
GHANA AND NIGERIA ARE IN THE MIDST OF GOVERNMENT INITIATED DEMOCRATIZATION PROGRAMS. THE PAPER COMPARES THE DIFFERENT SETTINGS, REASONS, STRATEGIES, PROCEDURES, AND IMPLEMENTATION OF DEMOCRATIZATION EFFORTS IN THESE TWO COUNTRIES. WHILE NIGERIA'S COMPREHENSIVE APPROACH OT DEMOCRATIC PLANNING HAS ENABLED ELITE CONTINUITY. IT HAS NEITHER ASSURED REGIME STABILITY NOR ENHANCED STATE CAPACITIES. IN CONTRAST, GHANA'S PLAN FOR DEMOCRATIC TRANSFORMATION. PURSUED IN A PIECEMEAL FASHION, HAS RESULTED IN REGIME STABILITY AND SOME STATE CONSOLIDATION, BUT NOT IN DEMOCRATIZATION. IN BOTH COUNTRIES, THERE IS LITTLE DOUBT THAT THE UNINTENDED CONSEQUENCES OF EACH APPROACH MAY PROVE MORE SIGNIFICANT THAN THE DIRECT RESULTS OF SUCCESSFUL POLICY IMPLEMENTATION. THUS, EVEN IF THE SPECIFIC DESIGN FOR DEMOCRATIC PROJECT IN THESE WEST AFRICAN STATES MAY NEVERTHELESS BE PROGRESSING.

02145 CHEBRIKOV, V.
REVIEWING THE POLICY ON NATIONALITIES
REPRINTS FROM THE SOVIET PRESS, 49(8) (OCT 89), 24-32.
ON AUGUST 17, 1989 THE SOVIET COMMUNIST PARTY PUBLISHED DRAFT GUIDELINES FOR ITS NEW POLICY ON NATIONALITIES, A DOCUMENT WHICH HAS TO BE DISCUSSED BY THE FORTHCOMING PLENUM OF THE CPSU CENTRAL COMMITTEE ON ETHNIC RELATIONS. THIS IS AN INTERVIEW IN WHICH CPSU CENTRAL COMMITTEE SECRETARY, VIKTOR CHEBRIKOV COMMENTS ON SOME OF THE CLAUSES OF THE DOCUMENT WAS DRAFTED; THE MAIN CAUSES REQUIRING A MAJOR OVERHAUL IN THE POLICY ON NATIONALITIES; THE CONTROVERSY OVER THE AUTHORITY OF THE UNION AND THE REPUBLICS; AND EXPLAINS HOW PROPOSALS AND REMARKS WILL BE SUMMED UP.

02146 CHEEK-MILBY, K.
THE CHANGING POLITICAL ROLE OF THE HONG KONG CIVIL SERVANT
PACIFIC AFFAIRS, 62(2) (SUM 89), 219-234.
THIS PAPER EXPLORES THE POLITICAL ROLE OF CIVIL SERVANTS IN A TRANSITIONAL ENVIRONMENT, THE BRITISH CROWN COLONY OF HONG KONG, WHICH WILL BECOME A SPECIAL ADMINISTRATION REGION OF THE PEOPLE'S REPUBLIC OF CHINA IN 1987. HONG KONG, UNLIKE MOST COUNTRIES HAVE NOT WITNESSED A MERGING OF THE ROLES OF BUREAUCRATS AND POLITICIANS, BUT RATHER A CLEARER DISTINCTION BETWEEN THE TWO WHILE CIVIL SERVANTS HAVE TRADITIONALLY BEEN THE ONLY POLITICAL ACTORS IN THE COLONY, RECENT DEVELOPMENTS HAVE WITNESS THE RISE OF THE NON-CIVIL SERVANT POLITICIAN AND THE CONSEQUENT DECLINE IN THE POLITICAL POWER OF THE HONG KONG CIVIL SERVICE. THIS PAPERS TRACES THIS DEVELOPMENT AND, BASED ON RECENT EMPIRICAL RESEARCH, EXPLORES THE ATTITUDES OF HONG KONG CIVIL SERVANTS TOWARDS HIS CHANGE. IN ADDITION, THE RESEARCH HIGHLIGHTS THE IMPERATIVE NEED FOR A CLEAR DELINEATION OF THE NEW ROLE THAT HONG KONG CIVIL SERVANTS MUST PLAY IN THE POLICY PROCRESS TO ENSURE THE SMOOTH TRANSITION OF POLITICAL POWER IN 1997.

02147 CHEEK, T.
THE "GENIUS" MAO: A TREASURE TROVE OF TWENTY-THREE NEWLY AVAILABLE VOLUMES OF POST-1949 MAO ZEDONG TEXTS
AUSTRALIAN JOURNAL OF CHINESE AFFAIRS, (19-20) (JAN 88), 311-344.
IN THE PAST FEW YEARS TWENTY-THREE VOLUMES OF SPEECHES AND WRITINGS BY MAO ZEDONG, WHICH WERE PREVIOUSLY UNAVAILABLE TO WESTERN SCHOLARS, HAVE BEEN COLLECTED IN THE HARVARD-YENCHING LIBRARY. THIS ARTICLE OFFERS A PRELIMINARY CRITIQUE OF THESE VOLUMES AND THEIR TEXTS, INCLUDING EVIDENCE OF THEIR AUTHENTICITY AND A SUMMARY OF THE TOPICS ON WHICH THEY SHED LIGHT.

02148 CHEN, E.
TIENANMEN: SHOCKED REACTIONS
FREE CHINA REVIEW, 39(8) (AUG 89), 20-23.
THE AUTHOR REVIEWS EVENTS IN TIENANMEN SQUARE IN MAY-JUNE 1989 AND SURVEYS THE REACTIONS TO THE SUPPRESSION OF THE POPULAR PROTEST.

02149 CHEN, K.
HISTORY, THEORY, AND CULTURAL POLITICS: TOWARDS A MINOR DISCOURSE OF MASS MEDIA AND POSTMODERNITY
DISSERTATION ABSTRACTS INTERNATIONAL, 49(8) (FEB 89), 2008-A.
THIS DISSERTATION SEEKS TO UNDERSTAND AND INTERPRET POSTMODERNITY. SUBJECTS INCLUDE POST MODERN INTERPRETIVE ANALYTICS OR STRATEGIES OF ASSEMBLAGE; THE HISTORICAL LOGICS OF CONFIGURATIONS; THE WORKING LOGICS OF POSTMODERN CULTURAL POLITICS IN THREE AXIS: POWER, DESIRE, AND THE SYMBOLIC; AND MASS MEDIA'S STRUCTURAL RELATION TO CULTURAL MICROPOLITICS.

02150 CHEN, L.
LABOR UNIONS AND REGIME TRANSITION IN ARGENTINA
DISSERTATION ABSTRACTS INTERNATIONAL, 49(12) (JUN 89), 3855-A.
DURING ARGENTINA'S LAST MILITARY AUTHORITARIAN ERA (1976-1983), THE LABOR MOVEMENT WAS ONE OF THE FEW CIVILIAN GROUPS CAPABLE OF OPPOSING THE REGIME. BY RELYING ON ITS ABILITY TO MOBILIZE SECTORS OF THE POPULATION OVER BREAD AND BUTTER ISSUES, ITS ORGANIZED BUREAUCRACY, AND ITS TRADITION OF POLITICAL ACTIVISM, LABOR WAS ABLE TO RESIST THE REGIME, DESPITE DISSENSION WITHIN ITS OWN RANKS AND THE GOVERNMENT'S ATTEMPTS TO CIRCUMSCRIBE UNION POLITICAL POWER.

02151 CHEN, M.
A SECTORAL APPROACH TO PROMOTING WOMEN'S WORK: LESSONS FROM INDIA
WORLD DEVELOPMENT, 17(7) (JUL 89), 1007-1016.
BECAUSE GOVERNMENT POLICY MAKERS DO NOT VIEW WOMEN AS PRODUCTIVE WORKERS, WOMEN ARE LEFT OUT OF SECTORAL ECONOMIC PLANNING. DONOR AGENCIES COULD HELP BRING WOMEN INTO THE MAINSTREAM OF THE PLANNING PROCESS AND THE ECONOMY BY COMMISSIONING STUDIES OF WOMEN'S WORK BY SECTORS AND BY SUPPORTING SECTOR-BASED PILOT PROJECTS THAT INVOLVE WOMEN. IN INDIA THIS HAS BEEN DONE SUCCESSFULLY IN AT LEAST TWO FIELDS: DAIRYING AND SILK PRODUCTION. NONGOVERNMENTAL AGENCIES WORKING WITH DONOR AGENCIES HAVE EFFECTIVELY INFLUENCED GOVERNMENT POLICY. THIS HAS NOT, HOWEVER, TAKEN PLACE IN AGRICULTURE, WHERE MOST WOMEN WORK.

02152 CHEN, M.
CHINA IN RECENT CANADIAN THOUGHT
BEIJING REVIEW, 32(26) (JUN 89), 26-29.
THE AUTHOR DISCUSSES THE BACKGROUND TO THE 1970 MUTUAL

RECOGNITION TREATY BETWEEN CANADA AND THE PEOPLE'S REPUBLIC
OF CHINA. THEN HE DISCUSSES CANADIAN IMAGES AND PERCEPTIONS
OF CHINA IN THE PERIOD FROM 1970 TO 1986.

02153 CHEN, P.M.
"PLEASE CALL ME MR. CHING-KUO"
FREE CHINA REVIEW, 39(2) (FEB 89), 4-7.
THE AUTHOR REFLECTS UPON THE LIFE AND WORK OF TAIWAN'S
LATE PRESIDENT CHIANG CHING-KUO, WHO DIED IN JANUARY 1988.

02154 CHEN, T.C.
PEKING-TOKYO CONNECTION
ASIAN OUTLOOK, 25(1) (NOV 89), 32-33.
PEKING'S FOREIGN RELATIONS ARE ERRATIC AND UNPREDICTABLE.
IN THE SHANGHAI COMMUNIQUE OF 1972, PEKING FIRMLY OPPOSED
THE REVIVAL AND EXPANSION OF JAPANESE MILITARISM. SHORTLY
THEREAFTER, THE CHINESE ATTITUDE TOWARD JAPAN CHANGED
ABRUPTY AND DIPLOMATIC RELATIONS WERE ESTABLISHED BETWEEN
PEKING AND TOKYO. TODAY THE ISSUE OF JAPANESE MILITARISM HAS
RAISED ITS UGLY HEAD AGAIN IN PEKING, AND JAPANESE
PARTICIPATION IN CHINESE ECONOMIC DEVELOPMENT HAS BEEN
ERODED.

02155 CHEN, T.C.
THE CAMBODIAN SETTLEMENT
ASIAN OUTLOOK, 25(1) (NOV 89), 17-19.
THE CAMBODIAN SITUATION REMAINS A QUAGMIRE. BASICALLY,
THERE ARE TWO TIERS OF PARTICIPANTS. ONE IS THE MAJOR
CONCERNED COUNTRIES -- VIETNAM, THE UNITED STATES,
COMMUNIST CHINA, AND THAILAND. THE OTHER CONSISTS OF THE
CAMBODIAN FACTIONS -- THE PRESENT PHNOM PENH GOVERNMENT AND
THE THREE FACTIONS OF THE CAMBODIAN RESISTANCE. THE MAIN
PROBLEM IS REACHING AGREEMENT ON THE FORMATION OF THE
GOVERNMENT TO RULE AFTER THE WITHDRAWAL OF THE VIETNAMESE
TROOPS.

02156 CHENEY, J.
THE NEO-STOICISM OF RADICAL ENVIRONMENTALISM
ENVIRONMENTAL ETHICS, 11(4) (WIN 89), 293-327.
FEMININE ANALYSIS HAS CONVINCED THE WRITER OF THIS
ARTICLE THAT CERTAIN TENDENCIES WITHIN THAT FORM OF RADICAL
ENVIRONMENTALISM KNOWN AS DEEP ECOLOGY--WITH ITS SUPPOSED
REJECTION OF THE WESTERN ETHICAL TRADITION AND ITS ADOPTION
OF WHAT LOOKS TO BE A FEMINIST ATTITUDE TOWARD THE
ENVIRONMENT AND OUR RELATIONSHIP TO NATURE--CONSTITUTE ONE
MORE CHAPTER IN THE STORY OF WESTERN ALIENATION FROM NATURE.
IN THIS PAPER THE WRITER DEEPENS HIS CRITIQUE OF THESE
TENDENCIES TOWARD ALIENATION WITHIN DEEP ECOLOGY BY
HISTORICIZING HIS CRITIQUE IN THE LIGHT OF A DEVELOPMENT IN
THE ANCIENT WORLD THAT IS DISQUIETINGLY SIMILAR TO THE RISE
OF DEEP ECOLOGY IN RECENT TIMES--NAMELY, THE RISE OF
STOICISM IN THE WAKE OF THE BREAKUP OF THE ANCIENT POLIS.

02157 CHENEY, R.
CHENEY ON THE ISSUES: COMMENTARY BY THE U.S. SECRETARY OF
DEFENSE
NATO'S SIXTEEN NATIONS, 34(6) (OCT 89), 4-5 (SPECIAL
SECTION).
IN THESE COMMENTS, U.S. SECRETARY OF DEFENSE RICHARD
CHENEY DISCUSSES THE BUSH ADMINISTRATION'S POLICIES
REGARDING DEFENSE IN EUROPE, RELAXED TENSIONS WITH THE
SOVIET UNION, THE U.S. MILITARY BUDGET, AND OTHER ASPECTS OF
AMERICAN DEFENSE.

02158 CHENG-SHU, K.
POWER DIMINISHED BY AMBIGUITY
FREE CHINA REVIEW, 39(11) (NOV 89), 4-7.
TAIWAN'S SOCIAL AND POLITICAL HEALTH IN THE COMING YEARS
COULD DEPEND IN LARGE PART UPON THE ATTITUDES AND ACTIONS OF
ITS LARGE MIDDLE CLASS, ESPECIALLY IF ITS MEMBERS BECOME
MORE ORGANIZED AND WORK TOGETHER TOWARD FOCUSED GOALS. THE
WESTERN CONCEPT OF MIDDLE CLASS REQUIRES SOME CULTURAL
MODIFICATIONS WHEN USED IN A CHINESE CONTEXT, BUT GENERALLY
THE TAIWANESE MIDDLE CLASS CAN BE CHARACTERIZED AS HIGHLY
MOBILE, AMBIGUOUS, DIVERSIFIED, AND PRAGMATIC.

02159 CHENG, H.
THE POLITICAL COMMISSAR SYSTEM IN THE MILITARY: A
COMPARISON OF TWO CHINESE ARMIES
DISSERTATION ABSTRACTS INTERNATIONAL, 49(9) (MAR 89),
2793-A.
THE AUTHOR CHALLENGES BOTH THE "PARTY CONTROL" MODEL AND
THE "CIVILIAN CONTROL" PARADIGM BY COMPARING THE POLITICAL
COMMISSAR SYSTEM'S (PCS) ORIGINS, STRUCTURES, AND FUNCTIONS;
ITS INSTITUTIONAL RATIONALES; AND ITS POLITICAL ROLE IN THE
CHINESE ARMIES: THE PEOPLE'S LIBERATION ARMY OF THE PEOPLE'S
REPUBLIC OF CHINA AND THE ARMY OF THE REPUBLIC OF CHINA. HE
ARGUES THAT THE NATURE OF THE PCS CANNOT BE FULLY UNDERSTOOD
UNLESS IT IS DIVIDED INTO THE PARTY WORK SYSTEM AND THE
POLITICAL WORK SYSTEM.

02160 CHENG, J.
WHITHER CHINA'S REFORM
JOURNAL OF COMMUNIST STUDIES, 5(1) (MAR 89), 32-49.

THE REFORM PROGRAMME IN CHINA WHICH THE THIRTEENTH
CONGRESS OF THE CCP IS TAKEN TO HAVE CONFIRMED, HAS
CONSIDERABLE ECONOMIC ACHIEVEMENTS TO ITS CREDIT, BUT IT
SUFFERS FROM A LACK OF THEORETICAL FOUNDATION, AND FROM
DIVERGENCES AMONG THE REFORMERS THEMSELVES. THESE PROBLEMS
HAVE BEEN COMPOUNDED BY WANING ENTHUSIASM ON THE PART OF THE
POPULATION AND BY A CYNICISM BROUGHT ABOUT BY GROWING
CORRUPTION. THE EXISTENCE OF PRIVILEGE, CORRUPTION AND
WIDENING DIFFERENTIALS SUGGESTS THE NEED FOR POLITICAL
REFORM, BUT HERE TOO THERE ARE DIFFICULTIES. THE
LEADERSHIP'S RESPONSE HAS BEEN TO REST ITS LEGITIMACY ON
ECONOMIC ACHIEVEMENTS. THE DIFFICULTIES THAT IT FACES ARE
LIKELY TO BE DEALT WITH IN THREE PHASES. IN THE SHORT TERM
CORRUPTION AND THE PROBLEMS OF PRICE REFORM WILL BE TACKLED
IN ORDER TO BUILD UP CONFIDENCE AMONG THE PEOPLE - A KIND OF
'SOCIAL COMPACT' OF THE EASTERN EUROPEAN KIND. IN THE MID-
TERM THE GAP BETWEEN RICH AND POOR, AND THE ROLE OF THE
STATE IN THE ECONOMY, WILL ACHIEVE PROMINENCE. IN THE LONG
TERM THE RULE OF LAW AND THE DEVELOPMENT OF EDUCATION ARE
LIKELY TO PROVIDE THE FOCUS.

02161 CHENG, J.Y.S.
HONG KONG: THE DECLINE OF POLITICAL EXPECTATIONS AND
CONFIDENCE
AUSTRALIAN JOURNAL OF CHINESE AFFAIRS, (19-20) (JAN 88),
241-267.
THE SHARP DECLINE OF POLITICAL EXPECTATIONS AND
CONFIDENCE IN HONG KONG IS LARGELY THE RESULT OF PRESSURE
FROM THE CHINESE GOVERNMENT AND THE FAILURE OF THE BRITISH
AND HONG KONG ADMINISTRATIONS TO WITHSTAND THIS PRESSURE.
THIS PAPER TRACES THE SEQUENCE OF EVENTS TO SHOW HOW THE
CHINESE AUTHORITIES LOWERED THE LOCAL COMMUNITY'S POLITICAL
EXPECTATIONS AND LIMITED THE DEVELOPMENT OF DEMOCRACY IN THE
TERRITORY. LONDON'S FAILURE TO FULFIL THE EXPECTATIONS
GENERATED BY THE SINO-BRITISH JOINT DECLARATION CONTRIBUTED
TO THE EROSION OF CONFIDENCE IN HONG KONG'S BRITISH
ADMINISTRATION. ITS LACK OF SENSITIVITY AND CONCERN FOR THE
ASPIRATIONS AND FEELINGS OF THE LOCAL COMMUNITY ON A NUMBER
OF ISSUES REDUCED IT TC A "LAME DUCK" GOVERNMENT IN THE EYES
OF THE HONG KONG PUBLIC.

02162 CHENG, J.Y.S.
POLITICAL MODERNIZATION IN HONG KONG
JOURNAL OF COMMONWEALTH AND COMPARATIVE POLITICS, XXVII(3)
(NOV 89), 294-320.
IN THE PROCESS OF MODERNIZATION, SOCIAL FRUSTRATION AND
SOCIAL CONTRADICTIONS OFTEN PROMOTE POLITICAL PARTICIPATION,
WHEREAS ECONOMIC AND SOCIAL MOBILITY OPPORTUNITIES REDUCE
THE DEMAND FOR POLITICAL PARTICIPATION. IN THE CIRCUMSTANCES
OF INADEQUATE POLITICAL INSTITUTIONALISATION, POLITICAL
PARTICIPATION MAY LEAD TO POLITICAL INSTABILITY. IT IS
BELIEVED THAT HUNTINGTON'S HYPOTHESIS CONTRIBUTES TO AN
UNDERSTANDING OF POLITICAL MODERNISATION IN HONG KONG, AS
THE FOLLOWING DISCUSSION DEMONSTRATES. HUNTINGTON'S
HYPOTHESIS MAY BE SUMMARISED AS FOLLOWS: SOCIAL MOBILISATION
INCREASES THE EXPECTATIONS OF THE INDIVIDUAL AND THE
COMMUNITY AS A WHOLE, AND THEREFORE ENHANCES SOCIAL
FRUSTRATION AS WELL AS EXACERBATING THE CONTRADICTIONS IN
THE COMMUNITY; WHILE THE FRUITS OF ECONOMIC DEVELOPMENT
SATISFY THE DEMANDS OF THE INDIVIDUAL AND THE COMMUNITY, AND
THEREFORE REDUCE SOCIAL FRUSTRATION AND SOCIAL
CONTRADICTIONS.

02163 CHENG, J.Y.S.
THE DEMOCRACY MOVEMENT IN HONG KONG
INTERNATIONAL AFFAIRS, 65(3) (SUM 89), 443-462.
THIS ARTICLE EXPLORES THE IMPORTANCE OF DEMOCRACY AND
FREEDOM IN CHINA AND HONG KONG, AND THE FACT THAT HONG KONG
PEOPLE ARE BECOMING INCREASINGLY AWARE THAT THEIR FUTURE
DEPENDS ON DEVELOPMENTS IN CHINA. IT FOLLOWS THE DEVELOPMENT
OF THE DEMOCRACY MOVEMENT FROM 1970 TO 1985, THEN, THE
DEMOCRACY MOVEMENT'S STRATEGY TO 1988. THEN, THE 1988
ELECTIONS ARE ANALYZED. IT CONCLUDES WITH AN ANALYSIS OF NEW
POLITICAL AWARENESS AND PROSPECTS FOR THE DEMOCRACY MOVEMENT.

02164 CHENG, J.Y.S.
THE POST - 1997 GOVERNMENT IN HONG KONG: TOWARD A STRONGER
LEGISLATURE
ASIAN SURVEY, 29(8) (AUG 89), 731-748.
THIS ARTICLE ANALYZES THE TERMS OF THE DRAFT BASIC LAW
UNDER THE SINO-BRITISH JOINT DECLARATION WITH RESPECT TO THE
GOVERNMENTAL SYSTEM IN HONG KONG BEFORE AND AFTER 1997,
EMPHASIZING THE IMPORTANCE OF A SYSTEM OF CHECKS AND
BALANCES. IT EXPLORES THE CONCERNS OF HONG KONG PEOPLE WHO
ARE INCREASINGLY AGREED ON THE NEED TO ACCELERATE THE
DEVELOPMENT OF REPRESENTATIVE GOVERNMENT IN THE TERRITORY
BEFORE 1997. THE CONCENSUS ON BASIC PRINCIPLES OF THE JOINT
DECLARATION IS DETAILED AS WELL AS RELATIONSHIPS AMONG THE
CHIEF EXECUTIVE, THE EXECUTIVE AUTHORITIES, AND THE
LEGISLATURE.

02165 CHENG, N.
MASSACRE IN PEKING
NATIONAL REVIEW, XLI(14) (AUG 89), 28-31.

THE AUTHOR PLACES THE TIANANMEN TRAGEDY IN HISTORICAL
PERSPECTIVE AND CONCLUDES THAT NEITHER DISSENT NOR
REPRESSION WILL END SOON. BUT THE CRACKDOWN ONLY DRIVES THE
PEOPLE'S DISCONTENT TEMPORARILY UNDERGROUND. AT ANY MOMENT,
IT COULD ERUPT AGAIN.

02166 CHENG, H.
PANAMANIAN POLITICAL CRISIS DEEPENS
BEIJING REVIEW, 32(38) (SEP 89), 17.
IT IS BECOMING MORE DIFFICULT TO FIND A SOLUTION TO THE
U.S.-PANAMANIAN CONFLICT. THE UNITED STATES IS NOT EXPECTED
TO SUSPEND ITS ECONOMIC SANCTIONS WHILE THE PROVISIONAL
GOVERNMENT IS IN OFFICE. BUT WHOEVER HOLDS POWER, THE
LEADERSHIP WILL BE ABLE TO CONSOLIDATE ITS POWER AS LONG AS
IT DOES NOT GIVE UP THE DEMAND THAT SOVEREIGNTY OVER THE
CANAL BE RETURNED TO PANAMA.

02167 CHENGAPPA, R.
HERALDING A NEW REVOLUTION
INDIA TODAY, 14(16) (AUG 89), 38 - 39.
THIS ARTICLE IS A REPORT ON IRAN'S RAFSANJANI'S PROMISES
TO END THE COUNTRY IS ISOLATION. HE BEGINS THE MAMMOTH TASK
OF REBUILDING IRAN'S SHATTERED ECONOMY, HIS STAND IS ONE OF
MODERATION AND HE IS KNOWN AS A PRAGMATIC LEADER. IRAN'S
RELATIONS WITH OTHER COUNTRIES: INDIA, THE U.S., AND THE
USSR ARE EXPLORED.

02168 CHENGAPPA, R.
IRAN AFTER KHOMEINI: ALARM AND INSECURITY
INDIA TODAY, XIV(12) (JUN 89), 30-33.
THE FRENZIED GRIEF THAT FOLLOWED THE DEATH OF AYATOLLAH
KHOMEINI REVEALED THAT HIS LEGACY OF ISLAMIC PURITANISM WILL
CONTINUE TO DOMINATE IRANIAN THINKING. THIS ARTICLE
DESCRIBES HOW, WITH INFLATION SPIRALLING AND THE NEW
LEADERSHIP DIVIDED ON HOW THE COUNTRY SHOULD BE RUN, IRAN'S
FUTURE IS DANGEROUSLY UNCERTAIN, DESPITE THE AYATOLLAH'S
LEGACY.

02169 CHENGRUI, L.
ONLY SOCIALISM CAN DEVELOP CHINA
BEIJING REVIEW, 32(40) (OCT 89), 19-28.
CHINESE LEADER DENG XIAOPING RECENTLY POINTED OUT THAT
ONLY SOCIALISM CAN SAVE CHINA AND ONLY SOCIALISM CAN DEVELOP
CHINA. THE CHINESE HAVE ATTAINED NOTABLE ACHIEVEMENTS IN
ECONOMIC DEVELOPMENT AND IMPROVING THEIR STANDARD OF LIVING
OVER THE PAST FOUR DECADES. THESE SUCCESSES WOULD HAVE BEEN
IMPOSSIBLE WITHOUT THE LEADERSHIP OF THE CHINESE COMMUNIST
PARTY, THE SOCIALIST SYSTEM, THE POLITICAL POWER AT THE
SERVICE OF THE PEOPLE, AND THE PUBLIC OWNERSHIP OF THE MEANS
OF PRODUCTION.

02170 CHENOWETH, E.
HOW TO BRING THE COLD WAR TO AN END
FREEDOM AT ISSUE, (111) (NOV 89), 41-43.
IN ALL THE COMMENTARY ON THE CHANGES IN THE COMMUNIST
WORLD. THERE IS VERY LITTLE SERIOUS STRATEGY REPORTED. THERE
SEEMS TO BE LITTLE ENTHUSIASM IN THE WEST FOR TAKING
ADVANTAGE OF THE SPOILS OF THE COLD WAR OR OF ENTERING A NEW,
MORE DEMOCRATIC AGE. THE LACK OF STRATEGY IS MOST EVIDENT
IN THE POLICIES OF THE UNITED STATES AND WESTERN EUROPE
TOWARDS POLAND, WHERE THE MOST REMARKABLE CHANGES IN EASTERN
EUROPE HAVE TAKEN PLACE.

02171 CHEONG, S.
JAPANESE-SOUTH KOREAN RELATIONS UNDER AMERICAN OCCUPATION,
1945-1952: THE POLITICS OF ANTI-JAPANESE SENTIMENT IN
KOREA AND THE FAILURE OF DIPLOMACY
DISSERTATION ABSTRACTS INTERNATIONAL, 49(8) (FEB 89),
2356-A.
THE MAIN REASON FOR THE DIPLOMATIC DEADLOCK BETWEEN
JAPAN AND THE ROK FROM 1945 TO 1952 WAS THE POLITICAL
POSTURING OF PRESIDENT RHEE, WHO MANIPULATED POPULAR ANTI-
JAPANESE SENTIMENT IN ORDER TO STABILIZE HIS REGIME. BY THE
END OF 1952, SUCH ISSUES AS WAR REPARATIONS AND THE PEACE
LINE, WHICH RHEE HIMSELF HAD CREATED, HAD PENETRATED THE
PUBLIC MIND TO SUCH AN EXTENT THAT IT WAS IMPOSSIBLE FOR THE
KOREAN GOVERNMENT TO ABANDON THEM.

02172 CHEPESIUK, R.
FIGHTING ANARCHY IN COLOMBIA
NEW LEADER, LXXII(14) (SEP 89), 5-8.
MANY COLOMBIANS FEEL THAT THEIR NATION HAS BEEN PLUNGED
INTO A DE FACTO CIVIL WAR. PARAMILITARY ORGANIZATIONS FROM
BOTH THE LEFT AND THE RIGHT CONTINUE TO USE ASSASSINATION AS
A TOOL TO ACCOMPLISH THEIR DESIGNS. BEHIND BOTH FACTIONS
LOOM THE POWERFUL DRUG LORDS. PRESIDENT VIRGILIO BARCO
VARGAS HAS VOWED A RENEWED STRUGGLE TO BREAK COLOMBIAN
POLITICAL AND SOCIAL INSTITUTIONS IS TEARING AND THREATENS
TO COMPLETELY DISINTEGRATE. EVEN THE MOST OPTIMISTIC
OBSERVERS CALCULATE THAT THE "WAR ON DRUGS" WILL EXTEND FAR
INTO THE NEXT CENTURY.

02173 CHERNAVIN, V.
THE PACIFIC IN FOCUS: RESTRAINT MUST BE MUTUAL

REPRINTS FROM THE SOVIET PRESS, 48(2) (JAN 89), 33-36.
WHILE CALLING FOR ACTION TO BUILD CONFIDENCE AND EASE
TENSION IN THE ASIA-PACIFIC REGION, THE SOVIET UNION HAS
ALREADY TAKEN UNILATERAL PRACTICAL STEPS TO REDUCE ITS NAVAL
ACTIVITIES. SPECIFICALLY, THE GEOGRAPHICAL AREA OF PACIFIC
FLEET EXERCISES HAS IN RECENT YEARS BEEN LIMITED EXCLUSIVELY
TO THE SEA OF JAPAN AND THE SEA OF OKHOTSK. IN THE PACIFIC,
TRAINING EXERCISES HAVE TAKEN PLACE ON THE APPROACHES TO
KAMCHATKA, IN CLOSE VICINITY TO THE SOVIET COAST OUR SHIPS
AND AIRCRAFT HAVE NOT PRACTICED STRIKES AT TARGETS IN THE
TERRITORY OF OTHER COUNTRIES. THESE EXERCISES ARE ENTIRELY
OF A DEFENSIVE CHARACTHE SOVIET UNION IS NOW WAITING FOR ITS
PARTNERS TO AGREE TO EMBARK TOGETHER ON A ROAD TO A LASTING
AND SAFE PEACE IN THE REGION.

02174 CHERNYSHOV, V.
WASHINGTON AND THE GENEVA TALKS
REPRINTS FROM THE SOVIET PRESS, 49(9) (NOV 89), 23-25.
THIS ARTICLE ANALYSES THE U.S. POSITION ON SDI AND THE
ABM TREATY AND THE NEED TO RESOLVE FUNDAMENTAL PROBLEMS
WHICH ARE HOLDING BACK THE GENEVA TALKS. IT CONTRASTS BUSH'S
AND REAGAN'S PROPOSALS AND DETAILS THE ECONOMICS AND
CONTINUEING DEVELOPMENT OF THE MISSILE DEFENSE SYSTEM.

02175 CHERVOV, N.
STRATEGIC ARMS REDUCTION TALKS AND FUTURE PROSPECTS
DISARMAMENT, XII(2) (SUM 89), 145-154.
THE AUTHOR REVIEWS RECENT PROGRESS IN ARMS CONTROL AND
CONSIDERS THE OUTLOOK FOR THE SOVIET PROPOSAL TO COMPLETELY
ELIMINATE NUCLEAR WEAPONS BY THE YEAR 2000.

02176 CHESTER, E.W.
IS THE "ALL POLITICS IS LOCAL" MYTH TRUE? THE 1982 HOUSE
RACES AS A CASE STUDY
JOURNAL OF SOCIAL, POLITICAL AND ECONOMIC STUDIES, 14(1)
(SPR 89), 99-116.
THE AUTHOR CLOSELY EXAMINES THE CAMPAIGN LITERATURE
PUBLISHED BY CANDIDATES IN 1982 AND CONSIDERS THE VALIDITY
OF THE MYTH THAT ALL POLITICS IS ESSENTIALLY LOCAL IN NATURE.
HE FOCUSES ON THE 1982 CAMPAIGNS FOR THE U.S. HOUSE OF
REPRESENTATIVES.

02177 CHEUNG, T.
SEEKING NEW SCENARIOS
FAR EASTERN ECONOMIC REVIEW, 142(51) (DEC 89), 28-29.
THE NATURE AND EXTENT OF THE SOVIET THREAT IS SUBJECT TO
ONGOING DEBATE BETWEEN JAPAN'S FOREIGN MINISTRY AND RIGHT-
WING MILITARY FACTIONS. THE BUREAUCRATS SHARE THE OPINION OF
THE U.S. THAT THE WORLDWIDE DECLINE IN TENSION BETWEEN THE
SUPERPOWERS MEANS LESS OF OF A SOVIET THREAT IN THE PACIFIC.
GORBACHEV'S PROMISE TO REDUCE TROOPS AND NAVAL FORCES IN
PACIFIC SUPPORT THESE CLAIMS. HOWEVER, THE RIGHT-WING HAWKS
IN THE MILITARY MAINTAIN THAT RAPPROCHMENT WITH CHINA AND
THE U.S. WILL ALLOW THE USSR TO SPEND MORE OF THEIR
RESOURCES AGAINST JAPAN; THEY FEAR AN INVASION OF THE
NORTHERN ISLAND OF HOKKAIDO AND ARE ATTEMPTING TO INCREASE
JAPAN'S MILITARY CAPABILITIES IN RESPONSE TO THE THREAT. THE
SOVIET OCCUPATION OF FOUR ISLANDS CLAIMED BY JAPAN CONTINUES
TO BE AN INSURMOUNTABLE OBSTACLE TO SOVIET-JAPANESE DIALOGUE;
A FACT THAT PROBABLY SIGNIFIES FURTHER ARMS BUILD-UP IN THE
FUTURE.

02178 CHEUNG, T.
SELF-DEFENSE AND BEYOND
FAR EASTERN ECONOMIC REVIEW, 142(51) (DEC 89), 26-28.
AFTER YEARS OF STEADY BUILD-UP, JAPAN'S SO-CALLED SELF
DEFENSE FORCES RANK AMONG THE WORLD'S LARGEST AND BEST
EQUIPPED. JAPANESE MILITARY LEADERS ARE SUBTLY, BUT STEADILY
BREAKING THE LIMITS AND BARRIERS PLACED ON JAPAN'S MILITARY
ARMAMENTS AFTER WORLD WAR II. AT THE SAME TIME, JAPAN'S
MAJOR RATIONALE FOR MILITARY BUILD-UP, THE SOVIET THREAT, IS
RAPIDLY DIMINISHING. JAPAN'S NEIGHBORS ARE BEGINNING TO
WORRY THAT THE CONTINUED EXPANSION OF JAPAN'S MILITARY MIGHT,
INCLUDING THE ASSIGNMENT OF MILITARY UNITS FOR SECURITY
DUTY FAR FROM JAPANESE SOIL, COULD BECOME A SOURCE OF
INSTABILITY IN AND OF ITSELF.

02179 CHEUNG, T.
THE JAW-JAW WAR
FAR EASTERN ECONOMIC REVIEW, 142(51) (DEC 89), 24.
IN TAIWAN, GROWING APATHY AND CRITICISM OF THE
MILITARY'S PRIVILEGED PLACE AND THE INCREASINGLY PUBLIC
ADVOCACY OF TAIWANESE INDEPENDENCE AMONG SOME OPPOSITION
GROUPS HAS INCREASED APPREHENSIONS AMONG TAIWAN'S HARD-LINE
MILITARY CHIEFS. ALTHOUGH NOT A SHOT HAS BEEN FIRED IN ANGER
IN RECENT YEARS, THE POLITICAL WARFARE BRANCH OF THE
KUOMINTANG IS QUICK TO DECLARE THAT THE WAR BETWEEN CHINESE
NATIONALISTS AND COMMUNISTS REMAINS AS CRITICAL AS EVER.
HOWEVER, THE KMT HARD-LINERS MAY BE FORCED TO ADOPT A MORE
RELAXED POSTURE IN THE FACE OF INCREASED TOLERANCE OF
POLITICAL DIVERSITY BY THE GOVERNMENT.

02180 CHEUNG, T.M.
THE DOCTRINE OF MINIMAL DEFENSE UNFOLDS SLOWLY

FAR EASTERN ECONOMIC REVIEW, 141(31) (AUG 88), 28-29.
ALTHOUGH THE PHASED WITHDRAWAL OF TROOPS FROM
AFGHANISTAN, REMOVAL OF SS-20 MISSILES, THE PULLOUT OF AN
ARMY DIVISION FROM MONGOLIA, AND A SIGNIFICANT CUTBACK IN
NAVAL ACTIVITIES BEYOND TERRITORIAL WATERS HAVE HARDLY
DENTED SOVIET MILITARY CAPABILITIES IN ASIA, SOME ANALYSTS
ARE SEEING THAT FUNDAMENTAL REFORMS OF THE SOVIET MILITARY
COLOSSUS ARE FORTHCOMING. MANY SEE A SHIFT TO "REASONABLE
SUFFICIENCY" AND A MINIMALIST DEFENSE DOCTRINE BY THE
SOVIETS. SOME US DEFENSE SPECIALIST DIFFER, POINTING OUT
THAT THE DOCTRINE HAS ONLY BEEN UTILIZED IN A POLITICAL
CONTEXT AND IS NOT CONNECTED WITH MILITARY SPECIFICS. THEY
POINT TO THE INCREASE IN TROOP NUMBERS, NAVAL FORCES, AND
ARMS SALES TO JUSTIFY THEIR CLAIMS.

02181 CHEUNG, T.M.
THE MOUSE THAT ROARED
FAR EASTERN ECONOMIC REVIEW, 141(38) (SEP 88), 28-29.
BRUNEI'S ABILITY TO DEFEND ITSELF AGAINST AGRESSION,
EXTERNAL OR OTHERWISE IS HIGHLY DEPENDENT ON HELP FROM ITS
ALLIES--ESPECIALLY BRITAIN AND SINGAPORE. WITH THE
POSSIBILITY OF REDUCED BRITISH HELP IN THE FUTURE, THE
SULTANATE IS LOOKING TO OTHER ALTERNATIVES INCLUDING THE
POSSIBILITY OF JOINING THE FIVE POWERS DEFENCE AGREEMENT
COMPRISING SINGAPORE, MALAYSIA, BRITAIN, AUSTRALIA, AND NEW
ZEALAND. BUT AS OF YET, THREATS FROM THE OUTSIDE REMAIN
SMALL, AND THE SULTANATE'S STABILITY MINIMIZES THE RISK OF
INTERNAL INSURGENCY.

02182 CHHIBBER, P.K.; PETROCIK, J.R.
THE PUZZLE OF INDIAN POLITICS: SOCIAL CLEAVAGES AND THE
INDIAN PARTY SYSTEM
BRITISH JOURNAL OF POLITICAL SCIENCE, 19(2) (APR 89),
191-210.
THE AUTHOR ANALYZES POPULAR SUPPORT FOR THE CONGRESS
PARTY OF INDIA IN TERMS OF THE EXPECTATIONS OF THE SOCIAL
CLEAVAGE THEORY OF PARTIES. THE ANALYSIS ILLUSTRATES THE
DEGREE TO WHICH INDIAN PARTISANSHIP CONFORMS TO THE
EXPECTATIONS OF THE THEORY. MORE IMPORTANTLY, THIS SOCIAL
CLEAVAGE THEORY ANALYSIS OFFERS SOME NEW PERSPECTIVES ON (1)
THE INABILITY OF THE INDIAN POLITICAL SYSTEM TO DEVELOP
NATIONAL PARTIES OTHER THAN THE CONGRESS AND (2) THE
DISAGGREGATION OF THE CONGRESS PARTY.

02183 CHI, H.
POLITICAL CONSIDERATIONS II
ASIAN AFFAIRS, AN AMERICAN REVIEW, 16(3) (FAL 89), 157-166.
THE ESSAY SUGGESTS THAT A CHANGE OF CONTEXT IN
NEGOTIATIONS BETWEEN MAINLAND CHINA AND TAIWAN CAN BRING
BOTH SIDES INTO OFFICIAL CONTACT MORE QUICKLY. THIS CHANGE
NOT ONLY INVOLVES SEMANTICS (CHANGING "REUNIFICATION" TO
"TENSION REDUCTION"), BUT ALSO A SUBSTANTIVE CHANGE FROM A
"ZERO-SUM" GAME THAT WILL INEVITABLY PRODUCE CLEAR WINNERS
AND LOSERS TO A "VARIABLE-SUM" GAME IN WHICH BOTH SIDES ONLY
NEGOTIATE THOSE ISSUES THAT CAN PRODUCE MUTUAL BENEFITS NOW
OR IN THE NEAR FUTURE. BY RELEGATING REUNIFICATION TO THE
BACK BURNER, BOTH SIDES CAN JOIN FORCES TO SET IN MOTION A
PROCESS OF TENSION REDUCTION AND CONFIDENCE BUILDING FOR THE
PURPOSE OF FOSTERING MUTUAL RESPECT, UNDERSTANDING, AND
ACCEPTANCE THAT IN THE LONG RUN MAY PROVE TO BE A FAR
SUPERIOR BONDING MATERIAL FOR REUNIFICATION.

02184 CHI, K.S.
PRISON OVERCROWDING AND PRIVATIZATION: MODELS AND
OPPORTUNITIES
JOURNAL OF STATE GOVERNMENT, 62(2) (MAR 89), 70-76.
STATE AND LOCAL GOVERNMENTS ARE TURNING TO THE PRIVATE
SECTOR TO EXPAND THEIR PENAL SERVICES AND TO MANAGE THEIR
CORRECTIONAL FACILITIES, IN ORDER TO REDUCE PRISON
OVERCROWDING. ALTHOUGH THE USE OF THE PRIVATE SECTOR FOR
CORRECTIONAL SERVICES IS NOT NEW, SOME NEW TRENDS ARE
EMERGING. FIRST, SOME STATES HAVE EXPANDED THE AUTHORITY OF
CORRECTIONS DEPARTMENTS AND LOCAL JURISDICTIONS TO MAKE
GREATER USE OF PRIVATE ORGANIZATIONS FOR CORRECTIONAL
SERVICES. SECONDLY, THERE ARE NOW MORE THAN TWO DOZEN FOR-
PROFIT COMPANIES PROVIDING VARIOUS TYPES OF CORRECTIONAL
SERVICES, INCLUDING OFFENDER DETENTION. THIRDLY, STATE AND
LOCAL GOVERNMENTS HAVE COMPLETED CONTRACTS FOR LARGER AND
MORE SECURE CORRECTIONAL FACILITIES.

02185 CHI, S.
AN ECONOMY IN TRANSITION
FREE CHINA REVIEW, 39(4) (APR 89), 4-9.
IN THE 1980'S, TAIWAN'S ECONOMY HAS BEEN CHARACTERIZED
BY FOUR MAJOR TRENDS: (1) INCREASINGLY LARGE FOREIGN
EXCHANGE RESERVES HAVE ACCUMULATED DUE TO TRADE SURPLUSES;
(2) BOTH DOMESTIC CONSUMPTION AND INVESTMENT HAVE FALLEN
BEHIND PRODUCTION; (3) THE SHARE OF THE MANUFACTURING SECTOR
IN TOTAL GNP APPEARED TO REACH ITS PEAK BY THE MID-1980'S,
CALLING FOR A STRUCTURAL CHANGE IN THE FORM OF THE PRIVATE
SECTOR; AND (4) THE GOVERNMENT HAS MANIFESTED A DEFINITE
SHIFT TOWARDS MORE LIBERAL ECONOMIC POLICIES.

02186 CHIA-CHUNG, C.
DEVELOPING CLOSE TIES
FREE CHINA REVIEW, 39(3) (MAR 89), 7.
IN JANUARY 1989, TAIWANESE PREMIER YU KUO-HWA VISITED
THE BAHAMAS, THE DOMINICAN REPUBLIC, AND GUATEMALA. THE
OBJECTIVE WAS TO CULTIVATE DEEPER AND CLOSER FRIENDSHIPS IN
THE CARRIBEAN AND CENTRAL AMERICA. IN HIS TALKS WITH
GOVERNMENT LEADERS, THE PREMIER EMPHASIZED THE "TAIWAN
EXPERIENCE" AND THE VIRTUES OF TAIWAN'S FLEXIBLE SMALL AND
MEDIUM ENTERPRISE-BASED ECONOMIC PROGRAM.

02187 CHIA-MING, S.
MANDATED PRECISION
FREE CHINA REVIEW, 39(9) (SEP 89), 18-19.
THE AUTHOR EXPLAINS THE ORGANIZATION AND FUNCTIONS OF
THE EXAMINATION YUAN, WHICH IS THE BRANCH OF TAIWAN'S FIVE-
YUAN NATIONAL GOVERNMENT IN CHARGE OF THE EXAMINATION,
SELECTION, APPOINTMENT, AND MANAGEMENT OF CIVIL SERVANTS.

02188 CHIAROMONTE, G.
PEACE IS THE REVOLUTIONARY OBJECTIVE
INFORMATION BULLETIN, 25/26(1-2) (JAN 88), 8-9.
IN EVALUATING GORBACHEV'S "NEW THINKING" THE AUTHOR, A
MEMBER OF THE STALION COMMUNIST PARTY LEADERSHIP CONCLUDES
THAT GORBACHEV THINKS AND REFLECTS WITH AN EYE TO NEW GLOBAL
AND HUMAN REALITIES AND IS TRYING TO DRAW FROM THIS
PERSPECTIVE CONCLUSIONS OF A GENERAL CHARACTER VALID FOR
HUMAN KIND AS A WHOLE. SO STUKINGLY NEW AND IMPORTANT A
PERSPECTIVE MUST BE MET WITH COOPERATIVE ACTION WORLDWIDE.

02189 CHICOINE, D.; DELLER, S.; WALZER, N.
THE SIZE EFFICIENCY OF RURAL GOVERNMENTS: THE CASE OF LOW-
VOLUME RURAL ROADS
PUBLIUS: THE JOURNAL OF FEDERALISM, 19(1) (WIN 89),
127-138.
THE DETERIORATION OF THE SUPPLY OF PUBLIC INFRASTRUCTURE
THROUGHOUT THE UNITED STATES HAS BEEN FOUND TO BE
ACCELERATING. THE REASON MOST OFTEN CITED FOR THE INCREASING
RATES OF DETERIORATION IS THE LACK OF AVAILABLE FUNDING, OR
FISCAL STRESS, PRESENT IN MANY LOCAL GOVERNMENTS. A POPULAR
SHORT-TERM SOLUTION TO FISCAL STRESS IS TO DEFER
INFRASTRUCTURE REPAIRS AND/OR REPLACEMENT PROGRAMS. THIS IS
PARTICULARLY TRUE IN RURAL AREAS WHERE A DECLINING
AGRICULTURAL BASE AND REDIRECTED FEDERAL POLICY HAVE PLACED
SIGNIFICANT DOWNWARD PRESSURE ON REVENUES. THE SEARCH FOR A
LONGTERM SOLUTION HAS RENEWED THE DEBATE ABOUT THE OPTIMAL
SIZE OF LOCAL GOVERNMENTS. THE RESEARCH REPORTED HERE
EXAMINES THE ISSUE OF SIZE EFFICIENCY IN THE PRODUCTION OF
LOW-VOLUME RURAL ROADS IN THE MIDWEST. AT ISSUE IS THE
ABILITY OF MIDWEST TOWNSHIPS TO REALIZE SIZE ECONOMIES.
OVERALL, SIZE INEFFICIENCIES WERE IDENTIFIED WHICH SUGGESTS
THAT COST SAVINGS MAY BE REALIZED FROM THE REORGANIZATION OF
THE PRODUCTION OF LOW-VOLUME ROAD SERVICES.

02190 CHIEN-AI, L.
HUMANE AND BENEFICIAL ASSIMILATION
FREE CHINA REVIEW, 39(7) (JUL 89), 10-17.
THE AUTHOR LOOKS AT THE STATUS OF THE ETHNIC CHINESE
MINORITY IN THAILAND.

02191 CHIEN-AI, L.
INVESTING IN A BETTER MALAYSIA
FREE CHINA REVIEW, 39(7) (JUL 89), 23-24.
THE TIME IS RIPE FOR GREATER COOPERATION BETWEEN TAIWAN
AND MALAYSIA, ESPECIALLY IN TERMS OF FOREIGN INVESTMENT.
INCREASED ECONOMIC COOPERATION BETWEEN THE TWO COUNTRIES
WOULD HELP BUSINESS AND MIGHT SMOOTH TOUCHY ETHNIC RELATIONS
BETWEEN THE MALAYSIANS AND THE CHINESE MINORITY.

02192 CHIEN-AI, L.
LIFESTYLES REDEFINED
FREE CHINA REVIEW, 39(11) (NOV 89), 30-34.
RAPID SOCIAL, POLITICAL, AND ECONOMIC CHANGES IN TAIWAN
HAVE STIMULATED EXTENSIVE SHIFTS IN INDIVIDUAL AND FAMILY
LIFESTYLES. AS PART OF THIS TRANSFORMATION, THE MIDDLE CLASS
IS RE-EVALUATING PREVIOUSLY HELD PERCEPTIONS OF SELF,
SOCIETY, AND THE NATION. THERE IS A TREND TOWARD RETHINKING
SUCH BASIC ISSUES AS ETHICAL STANDARDS, ATTITUDES TOWARD
WORK, AND THE APPROPRIATE ROLE OF EDUCATED PEOPLE IN THE
POLITICAL ENVIRONMENT.

02193 CHIEN-AI, L.
OPTIMISM MIXED WITH TENSIONS
FREE CHINA REVIEW, 39(7) (JUL 89), 18-22.
RELIGIOUS, ECONOMIC, AND ETHNIC DIFFERENCES BETWEEN THE
MALAYSIANS AND CHINESE IMMIGRANTS PROVOKE SERIOUS TENSIONS
IN MALAYSIA. ALTHOUGH THE CHINESE GENERALLY ENJOY AN
ECONOMICALLY SUPERIOR POSITION, THEY ENDURE COUNTLESS
RESTRICTIONS. IN 1987, PRIME MINISTER MAHATHIR DECLARED A
STATE OF EMERGENCY DURING WHICH 69 MALAYSIAN CHINESE WERE
ARRESTED AND THREE NEWSPAPERS WERE CLOSED.

02194 CHIEN-AI, L.
VOLUNTEER GROUPS ARISE!

FREE CHINA REVIEW, 39(12) (DEC 89), 53-59.
A SOCIAL MOVEMENT PHENOMENON HAS SWEPT TAIWAN SINCE THE
REPEAL OF MARTIAL LAW IN JULY 1987. NOT ALL OF THE CITIZENS'
ORGANIZATIONS ARE NEW, BUT THEY HAVE BECOME FAR MORE ACTIVE
IN THE PAST TWO YEARS. WHETHER THE ISSUE IS HOUSING, LABOR,
OR THE ENVIRONMENT, THE MEMBERSHIP OF THE GROUPS REFUTES ONE
MUCH-DISCUSSED STEREOTYPE, BECAUSE MANY OF THE ACTIVISTS ARE
DRAWN FROM THE SUPPOSEDLY "SILENT MIDDLE CLASS."

02195 CHIGODO, T.
NAMIBIA: THE COMING VOTE
THIRD WORLD WEEK, 8(11) (MAY 89), 81-82.
MOST FOREIGN OBSERVERS BELIEVE THAT THE SOUTHWEST AFRICA
PEOPLE'S ORGANIZATION (SWAPO) WILL WIN THE UPCOMING
ELECTIONS IN NAMIBIA. BUT A VISIT TO THE NORTHERN REGION OF
OVAMBOLAND, THE MOST POPULOUS AREA OF NAMIBIA, INDICATES
THAT THE RESULTS ARE NOT CERTAIN. MANY OVAMBOS APPARENTLY
HAVE NO LOVE FOR SWAPO.

02196 CHIH-PING, L.
PEKING MASSACRE ANGERS WORLD
ASIAN OUTLOOK, 24(4) (JUL 89), 14-19.
THE TIENANMEN SQUARE MASSACRE HAS BUT A PRELUDE TO
SUBSEQUENT EVENTS. IT HAS FOLLOWED BY A LARGE-SCALE MANHUNT
FOR ACTIVE STUDENT AND INTELLECTUAL LEADERS IN THE DEMOCRACY
MOVEMENT AND FOR ORDINARY CITIZENS WHO CRITICIZED THE
AUTHORITIES DURING THE SHORT-LIVED UPRISING. TENS OF
THOUSANDS OF DEMONSTRATORS AND THEIR SYMPATHIZERS WERE
ARRESTED. THE NAKED VIOLENCE AND BRUTALITY OF THE PEKING
REGIME IMMEDIATELY ANGERED CHINESE PEOPLE OUTSIDE THE
MAINLAND AND DREW SEVERE CONDEMNATION FROM ALL NATIONS WITH
RESPECT TO CIVILIZED PRINCIPLES.

02197 CHIH-PING, L.
TIBETAN TINDERBOX
ASIAN OUTLOOK, 24(3) (MAY 89), 26-28.
IN THE AFTERMATH OF THE MOST RECENT WAVES OF VIOLENT
ANTI-COMMUNIST RIOTING IN LHASA, THE CHINA COMMUNISTS HAVE
BEEN FORCED TO ACKNOWLEDGE THE LOSS OF A LARGE NUMBER OF
TIBETAN LIVES IN THAT ALLEGEDLY "SEMI-AUTONOMOUS" REGION.
SINCE THE RIOTS, THE AREA HAS BEEN UNDER STRICT SURVEILLANCE
AND MILITARY CONTROL BY PEKING'S COMMUNIST DICTATORSHIP.

02198 CHIKVAIDZE, A.
MILITARY CONSTRAINTS ON CANADIAN FOREIGN POLICY
INTERNATIONAL AFFAIRS (MOSCOW), (10) (OCT 89), 74-80.
CANADA'S INVOLVEMENT IN THE CONTINENTAL MILITARY PLANS
AND ACTIVITIES OF THE UNITED STATES SERIOUSLY LIMITS ITS
FOREIGN POLICY OPTIONS. THE ABUNDANCE OF U.S.-CANADIAN
AGREEMENTS IS NO INDICATION THAT CANADA IS AN EQUAL PARTNER
IN THE BILATERAL MILITARY-POLITICAL ALLIANCE NOR THAT CANADA
FULLY SHARES IN THE FRAMING OF COMMON MILITARY POLICY.

02199 CHILDS, D.
EAST GERMANY: COPING WITH GORBACHEV
CURRENT HISTORY, 88(541) (NOV 89), 385-388, 400-401.
THE STRATEGY OF EAST GERMANY'S SOCIALIST UNITY PARTY
LEADERSHIP HAS BEEN TO SEEK AN ALTERNATIVE TO SOVIET-STYLE
REFORM, BUT IT HAS NOT WORKED. AS THE PARTY MOVES TOWARD ITS
TWELFTH CONGRESS IN 1990, MANY MEMBERS WILL BE LOOKING FOR A
CHANGE THAT WILL HERALD A MORE MATURE FORM OF SOCIALISM.

02200 CHIN, M.L.
LEGITIMACY CRISIS IN AUTHORITARIAN REGIMES
DISSERTATION ABSTRACTS INTERNATIONAL, 50(4) (OCT 89),
1075-A.
THE AUTHOR EXPLORES THE DYNAMICS SURROUNDING THE
BREAKDOWN OF MILITARY AUTHORITARIAN REGIMES AND THE
RESUSCITATION OF DEMOCRACY, FOCUSING ON WHY MILITARY
AUTHORITARIAN REGIMES FAIL. HE ARGUES THAT THE VULNERABILITY
OF MILITARY AUTHORITARIAN REGIMES BOILS DOWN TO A LEGITIMACY
CRISIS THAT CAN BE UNDERSTOOD IN TERMS OF THE CONFLICT
BETWEEN THE INDIVIDUAL GOOD AND THE COMMON GOOD.

02201 CHINDALAK, V.
THE THAI NATIONAL CIVIL SERVICE TRAINING CENTER
DISSERTATION ABSTRACTS INTERNATIONAL, 49(10) (APR 89),
3152-A.
THE AUTHOR SURVEYS CIVIL SERVICE TRAINING IN THAILAND.
THAI CIVIL SERVICE TRAINING WAS RANDOM AND UNCOORDINATED
UNTIL 1974, WHEN A TRAINING COORDINATION CENTER WAS CREATED
IN THE THAI CIVIL SERVICE COMMISSION. IN 1980, IT WAS
EXPANDED INTO THE THAI NATIONAL CIVIL SERVICE TRAINING
CENTER, WITH ASSISTANCE FROM THE UNITED NATIONS DEVELOPMENT
PROGRAMME.

02202 CHING, F.
RED STAR OVER HONG KONG
WORLD POLICY JOURNAL, 6(4) (FAL 89), 657-665.
THIS ARTICLE EXAMINES THE EVENTS OF MAY AND JUNE IN
CHINA WHICH HAVE CAST NEW DOUBT ON THE FUTURE OF HONG KONG
AFTER 1997, WHEN THE CROWN COLONY IS TO BE HANDED BACK TO
THE PEOPLE'S REPUBLIC AFTER 156 YEARS OF BRITISH RULE. THIS
DOUBT HAS BEEN SPARKED BY TWO RELATED DEVELOPMENTS: THE

PRECIPITOUS DECLINE IN CONFIDENCE ON THE PART OF THE PEOPLE
OF HONG KONG AS A RESULT OF THE BEIJING MASSACRE, AND THE
STEPPING UP OF PRESSURE BY CHINA ON HONG KONG. RECENT EVENTS
ARE ALSO FORCING BRITAIN TO RETHINK ITS HONG KONG POLICY,
THOUGH THERE IS LITTLE OPTIMISM IN THE COLONY THAT BRITAIN
HAS SUFFICIENT LEVERAGE AT THIS POINT TO EXERT MUCH
INFLUENCE OVER HONG KONG'S FUTURE. THE ARTICLE CONCLUDES
THAT IT REMAINS TO BE SEEN WHETHER CHINA, IN THE COMING
MONTHS, WILL SOFTEN ITS POSITION ON HONG KONG. THERE ARE FEW
SIGNS THAT THIS WILL HAPPEN. HOWEVER, MUCH DEPENDS ON THE
SITUATION IN CHINA. IF THE LEADERS IN BEIJING FEEL CONFIDENT
THAT THEY HAVE REGAINED CONTROL, THEY MAY BE WILLING TO
ALLOW HONG KONG GREATER LEEWAY. BUT IF THEY STILL FEEL
THREATENED, THEY ARE LIKELY TO PUT POLITICAL SURVIVAL AHEAD
OF ECONOMIC INTERESTS AND CONTINUE THE CLAMPDOWN ON HONG
KONG.

02203 CHIPOSA, S.
IMF AUSTERITY LOOMS AGAIN
AFRICAN BUSINESS, (NOV 88), 16-17.
THIS ARTICLE EXAMINES THE FAILURE OF THE ZAMBIAN
GOVERNMENT'S ATTEMPT FOR ECONOMIC INDEPENDENCE FROM THE IMF.
THE ZAMBIANS LOOK FORWARD TO A DIFFICULT YEAR AHEAD EVEN
WITH AN ENLARGED CENTRAL COMMITTEE OF THE UNITED NATIONAL
INDEPENDENCE PARTY. IT EXPLORES THE PROBABILITY OF RESUMED
NEGOTIATIONS WITH THE IMF AND THE WORLD BANK SOON AFTER
ELECTIONS.

02204 CHIRAC, J.
SOVIET CHANGE AND WESTERN SECURITY: THE NEED FOR CARE
CURRENT, (315) (SEP 89), 27-32.
A GROWING NUMBER OF PEOPLE IN WESTERN EUROPE BELIEVE
THAT, THANKS TO THE IMPETUS GIVEN BY GORBACHEV TO CHANGE
WITHIN THE SOVIET UNION AND INTERNATIONALLY, EUROPE MAY SOON
BECOME THE COMMON HOUSE OF ALL PEOPLES. SOME ARE EVEN
INCLINED TO QUESTION THE CONTINUED EXISTENCE OF A MILITARY
THREAT THAT WOULD JUSTIFY THE MAINTENANCE OF THE ATLANTIC
ALLIANCE. BUT WHAT IS NEEDED IS A SOBER AND BALANCED
APPROACH TO EAST-WEST RELATIONS—ONE NEITHER OVERLY FEARFUL
OF THE SOVIET UNION NOR OVERLY FASCINATED WITH THE DRAMA OF
ITS INTERNAL CHANGE.

02205 CHIROT, D.
GETTING THE STORY MISSING THE POINT
DEADLINE, IV 5 (NOV 89), 3-4, 15.
MEDIA COVERAGE OF SIGNIFICANT EVENTS IN EASTERN EUROPE
INCLUDING THE VISIT OF GEORGE BUSH IN JULY HAS BEEN
EXTENSIVE. HOWEVER, THE EMPHASIS HAS BEEN ON IMMEDIATE
ISSUES ONLY. UNDERLYING HISTORICAL LEGACIES, AND THE FACT
THAT EAST EUROPE HAS NEVER BEEN HIGH ON US LIST OF
PRIORITIES, HAVE RECEIVED LITTLE ATTENTION. THE RESULT IS
FEW AMERICANS COMPREHEND THE COMPLEXITIES THAT ARE NECESSARY
FOR AN ADEQUATE UNDERSTANDING OF THE SITUATION.

02206 CHIROT, D.
IDEOLOGY, REALITY, AND COMPETING MODELS OF DEVELOPMENT IN
EASTERN EUROPE BETWEEN THE TWO WORLD WARS
EASTERN EUROPEAN POLITICS AND SOCIETIES, 3(3) (FAL 89),
378-411.
THIS ARTICLE EXPLORES DEVELOPMENT OF INTERWAR EASTERN
EUROPE AND TRIES TO JUDGE JUST HOW INADEQUATE THE RATE OF
ECONOMIC DEVELOPMENT ACTUALLY WAS. IT DOES THIS TO EVALUATE
MODELS OF DEVELOPMENT IN GENERAL AND TO CLARIFY THE MEANING
OF WHAT HAS HAPPENED TO EASTERN EUROPE SINCE THEN. IT
EXPLORES THE ECONOMIC RECORD, AND THEN SOURCES OF DISCONTENT.
IT DESCRIBES ALTERNATIVE MODELS OF DEVELOPMENT AND SOCIAL
CRITICISM. IT ALSO DESCRIBES A PATH WHICH MAY HAVE WORKED
BUT WAS MADE IMPOSSIBLE.

02207 CHISHOLM, P.; LEWIS, P.; LOWTHER, W.
CRACKS IN THE G7 FRONT
MACLEAN'S (CANADA'S NEWS MAGAZINE), 102(10) (MAR 89), 30,
32.
AFTER A SHORT-LIVED SHOW OF HARMONY, CRACKS ARE
BEGINNING TO APPEAR BETWEEN THE US AND OTHER MEMBERS OF THE
SO-CALLED GROUP OF SEVEN (G7). MANY FEAR THE CONTINUED
DETRIMENTAL EFFECT OF THE HUGE US DEFICIT AND THE POSSIBLE
INFLATION RESULTING FROM STRONG GROWTH IN OTHER NATIONS. THE
G7 MEMBERS FACE GROWING TENSIONS UNLESS THEY CAN SOLVE THEIR
DOMESTIC PROBLEMS; FAILURE TO DO SO COULD THROW THE WORLD
ECONOMY INTO A PERIOD OF INSTABILITY THAT NONE OF THEM WOULD
WELCOME.

02208 CHITTICK, W. O.; BILLINGSLEY, K. R.
THE STRUCTURE OF ELITE FOREIGN POLICY BELIEFS
WESTERN POLITICAL QUARTERLY, 42(2) (JUN 89), 201-224.
A LACK OF CONSENSUS ON AMERICAN FOREIGN POLICY HAS LEAD
A NUMBER OF SOCIAL SCIENTISTS TO INVESTIGATE THE STRUCTURE
OF ELITE AND MASS BELIEFS ON FOREIGN POLICY. SO FAR, THESE
EFFORTS HAVE FAILED TO DETERMINE AUTHORITATIVELY HOW MANY
DIMENSIONS THERE ARE TO THE ATTITUDES OF THESE ELITES AND
HOW MANY TYPES OF OPINION AND POLICY ELITES CAN BE
IDENTIFIED WITHIN THIS ATTITUDINAL SPACE. THE PRESENT STUDY
EMPLOYS A NEW DATA-SET ON ELITE BELIEFS TO SHOW THAT THE

ATTITUDES OF OPINION AND POLICY ELITES ARE STRUCTURED ALONG A MINIMUM OF THREE DIMENSIONS AND ENCOMPASS AT LEAST NINE TYPES OF INDIVIDUALS. THE AUTHOR CONCLUDES THAT ALTHOUGH ELITE FOREIGN POLICY BELIEFS ARE COMPLEX, THERE ARE AMPLE OPPORTUNITIES FOR DEVELOPING SUPPORT FOR THE NATION'S FOREIGN POLICY.

02209 CHNOUPEK, B.
JOURNALISM AND NEW POLITICAL THINKING
WORLD MARXIST REVIEW, 31(12) (DEC 88), 107-113.
MEDIA COVERAGE OF THE STEPS TAKEN TO ACHIEVE DISARMAMENT, CONSOLIDATE PEACE AND CREATE A SYSTEM OF UNIVERSAL SECURITY CANNOT BE REDUCED TO OFFICIAL POLICY STATEMENTS, SPEECHES OR VIEWS EXPRESSED BY STATESMEN. IT SHOULD FOCUS PRIMARILY ON PUBLICISING INNOVATIVE IDEAS AND ON SHAPING AND BROADLY REFLECTING PUBLIC OPINION BOTH IN THE EAST AND IN THE WEST. IT FOLLOWS THAT JOURNALISTS ARE TO HELP POOL THE PEACEMAKING EFFORTS OF SCHOLARS, INTELLECTUALS, ARTISTS, EXPERTS IN VARIOUS FIELDS, ATHLETES AND REPRESENTATIVES OF CIVIC ORGANISATIONS AND MOVEMENTS. FOR DIPLOMACY TO BECOME TRULY POPULAR AND FOR THE MASSES TO REALLY HAVE THE FINAL SAY ON VITALLY IMPORTANT ISSUES, INTERNATIONAL RELATIONS NEED FULLFLEDGED GLASNOST WHICH, OVERWHELMINGLY, DEPENDS ON JOURNALISTS.

02210 CHO, H.K.
SOUTH KOREA'S RELATIONS WITH JAPAN, 1951 TO 1987: FROM HOSTILITY TO ACCOMMODATION
DISSERTATION ABSTRACTS INTERNATIONAL, 50(3) (SEP 89), 786-A.
SINCE WORLD WAR II, RELATIONS BETWEEN SOUTH KOREA AND JAPAN HAVE CHANGED DRASTICALLY, FROM OPEN HOSTILITY AND BITTERNESS TO ACCOMMODATION AND COOPERATION. THREE MAJOR FACTORS CONTRIBUTED TO ACCOMMODATION BETWEEN SOUTH KOREA AND JAPAN: (1) GENERATIONAL SHIFTS, (2) STRATEGIC INTERESTS, AND (3) ECONOMIC CONCERNS.

02211 CHO, M.H.
THE NEW STUDENT MOVEMENT IN KOREA: EMERGING PATTERNS OF
KOREA OBSERVER, XX(1) (SPR 89), 93-110.
IDEOLOGICAL ORIENTATION IN THE 1980'S THE PURPOSE OF THIS STUDY IS, FIRST, TO EXAMINE THE EMERGING PATTERNS OF IDEOLOGICAL ORIENTATION AMONG KOREAN COLLEGE-UNIVERSITY STUDENTS IN THE 1980'S. SECOND, IT TRIES TO EXPLAIN THE SOCIAL, POLITICAL, ECONOMIC, AND INTERNATIONAL BACKGROUNDS THAT INFLUENCED THE FORMATION OF IDEOLOGIES OF KOREAN STUDENT MOVEMENTS. THIRDLY, AND OF PARTICULAR CONCERN, ARE THE RISING ANTI-AMERICAN SENTIMENTS AMONG KOREAN STUDENTS AND THE RADICALIZATION OF THE STUDENT ACTIVITIES.

02212 CHOI, R.T.
FOREIGN INTERVENTION IN AFRICAN CONFLICTS: A CASE STUDY OF THE ANGOLAN CONFLICT (1961-1985)
DISSERTATION ABSTRACTS INTERNATIONAL, 50(6) (DEC 89), 1793-A.
THE AUTHOR SEEKS TO MAKE A BALANCED, COMPREHENSIVE STUDY OF FOREIGN INTERVENTION IN INTERNAL AFRICAN CONFLICTS BY CONSIDERING BOTH THE INTERNAL AND EXTERNAL CONDITIONS PRODUCING INTERVENTION. HE USES THE ANGOLAN CONFLICT AS A CASE STUDY AND EMPLOYS C.R. MITCHELL'S CONCEPTUAL FRAMEWORK TO IDENTIFY INTERNAL AND EXTERNAL FACTORS THAT PROMPT FOREIGN INTERVENTION.

02213 CHOI, Y.B.
POLITICAL ECONOMY OF HAN FEITZU
HISTORY OF POLITICAL ECONOMY, 21(2) (SUM 89), 367-390.
IN HAN FEITZU, THE ANCIENT CHINESE PRODUCED POLITICAL ECONOMIC THOUGHT THAT HAS A REMARKABLE RESEMBLANCE IN SCOPE AND APPROACH TO MODERN ECONOMICS, ESPECIALLY THE PUBLIC CHOICE VARIETY. HAN FEITZU IS NOT ONLY REMARKABLE IN HIS CONCEPTION OF HUMAN NATURE, WHICH IS REMINISCENT OF THE "ECONOMIC MAN," BUT ALSO IN ITS RATHER CONSISTENT APPLICATION TO A WIDE RANGE OF ISSUES DEBATED AT THE TIME. MOREOVER, WITH HIS INSISTENCE ON THE PRACTICAL RELEVANCE AND EMPIRICAL VALIDITY OF CONCLUSIONS AND ON THE SEPARATION OF MORALITY FROM POSITIVE ANALYSIS, HAN FEITZU WAS A FORERUNNER OF MODERN SOCIAL SCIENTISTS.

02214 CHOI, Y.H.; KIM, D.H.
KOREA-U.S. TRADE FRICTION: CONTENT ANALYSIS OF THE CHOSUN ILBO, KOREA TIMES, WASHINGTON POST, AND NEW YORK TIMES
KOREA OBSERVER, XX(4) (WIN 89), 507-536.
THE U.S.-SOUTH KOREAN TRADE SITUATION IS STRAINING BILATERAL RELATIONS. THE UNITED STATES HAS BEEN PRESSING KOREA TO OPEN ITS MARKET WIDER WHILE ACCUSING KOREA OF UNFAIR TRADE PRACTICES. KOREANS HAVE STAGED ANTI-AMERICAN PROTESTS OF VARIOUS KINDS TO EXPRESS THEIR DISSATISFACTION WITH AMERICAN PRESSURES ON THEM. THIS PAPER USES CONTENT ANALYSIS OF DAILY NEWSPAPER EDITORIALS IN SOUTH KOREAN AND AMERICAN PUBLICATIONS TO STUDY HOW THE TRADE ISSUE IS PERCEIVED IN THE TWO COUNTRIES AND HOW IT IS AFFECTING RELATIONS.

02215 CHOI, Y.H.
KOREA-U.S. TRADE ISSUES AND KOREANS' ATTITUDE TOWARD TRADE FRICTIONS
KOREA OBSERVER, XX(1) (SPR 89), 39-54.
THIS PAPER ATTEMPTS TO DISCUSS THE PRESENT STATUS OF MAJOR KOREA-U.S. TRADE ISSUES AND TO IDENTIFY THE LEVEL OF KOREANS' UNDERSTANDING OF THE CAUSES OF THE KOREA-U.S. TRADE FRICTIONS AND THEIR FRICTION-REDUCING MEASURES. FOR THIS EMPIRICAL RESEARCH PAPER, A QUESTIONNAIRE SURVEY WAS USED. THIS RESEARCH IS IN THE LASSHELLIAN TRADITION WHICH EMPHASIZES ELITE VALUES AND IDEOLOGY.

02216 CHOLA, M.
ZAMBIAN SUGAR: MORE QUEUES, LESS PROFITS
AFRICAN BUSINESS, (JAN 89), 35.
THIS PAPER REVIEWS THE PROBLEMS RELATED TO SUGAR PRODUCTION IN ZAMBIA. IT REPORTS THAT, ALTHOUGH THE OUTPUT VOLUME HAS INCREASED IN RECENT YEARS, THE ZAMBIAN SUGAR COMPANY OPERATES AT A LOSS AND SHORTAGES EXIST FOR THE CUSTOMERS IN ZAMBIA. THE PROBLEMS ARE ATTRIBUTED TO TOO GREAT EXPORTS, INFLATION AND HIGHER COSTS, PRICES THAT ARE TOO LOW, AND SMUGGLING INTO NEIGHBORING COUNTRIES.

02217 CHOLIERE, Y.
EUROPE: MILITARY INTEGRATION OR COOPERATION IN DISARRANGEMENT
WORLD MARXIST REVIEW, 32(11) (NOV 89), 34-36.
THE FRENCH COMMUNIST PARTY (PCF) IS OPPOSED TO THE CREATION OF NATO'S EUROPEAN NUCLEUS AND TO THE INTEGRATION OF THE FRENCH ARMED FORCES INTO ITS STRUCTURE (INCLUDING THE ESTABLISHMENT OF A FRANCO-WEST GERMAN BRIGADE, OF A JOINT DEFENCE COUNCIL, OR OF ANY JOINT COMMAND). THE PARTY IS AGAINST FRANCE'S COVERT OR OPEN RE-ENTRY INTO NATO'S INTEGRATED MILITARY ORGANISATION AND AGAINST ANY KIND OF EUROPEAN EFFORT TO MANUFACTURE THE ARMS THE NATION NEEDS FOR PURPOSES OF DEFENCE THE PCF MAINTAINS THAT FRANCE SHOULD JOIN VIGOROUSLY THE DRIVE TO ELIMINATE ALL TYPES OF NUCLEAR WEAPONS, INCLUDING ITS OWN STRIKE FORCES; DEMAND AN END TO NUCLEAR TESTS AND TERMINATION OF THE PROGRAMMES FOR THE DEVELOPMENT OF NEW ARMAMENTS; AND DEMAND THAT DEFENCE SPENDING BE REDUCED BY 40 BILLION FRANCS. THIS IS WHAT PCF DEPUTIES WILL ADVOCATE IN THE FORTHCOMING PARLIAMENTARY DEBATE ON UPDATING THE MILITARY PROGRAMME LEGISLATION NOW IN FORCE.

02218 CHOMSKY, N.
NECESSARY ILLUSIONS: THOUGHT CONTROL IN DEMOCRATIC SOCIETIES
SOUTH END PRESS, BOSTON, MA, 1989, .
THE AUTHOR ARGUES THAT THE MEDIA OPERATE IN THE SERVICE OF POWERFUL INSTITUTIONS, NOT IN OPPOSITION TO THEM.

02219 CHOMSKY, N.
THE UNITED STATES AND INDOCHINA: FAR FROM AN ABERRATION
BULLETIN OF CONCERNED ASIAN SCHOLARS, 21(2-4) (APR 89), 76-92.
THIS IS AN ARTICLE DETAILING UNITED STATES "SAVAGERY" IN VIETNAM AS WELL AS IN OTHER COUNTRIES IN THE WORLD, EXAMPLES FROM THE PHILLIPINES AND EL SALVADORAN SUBSTANTIATE CHARGES THAT THE UNITED STATES HAS A PATTERN OF AGGRESSION AND SAVAGERY OF WHICH THE WAR IN INDOCHINA IS TYPICAL, AND NOT AT ALL UNUSUAL, SPECIFIC ACCUSATIONS ARE MADE AND THE U.S. REASONING THAT JUSTIFIED U.S. ACTIONS IS EXPLAINED.

02220 CHON, S.
SOUTH KOREA-SOVIET TRADE RELATIONS: INVOLVEMENT IN SIBERIAN DEVELOPMENT
ASIAN SURVEY, XXIX(12) (DEC 89), 1177-1187.
ALTHOUGH THE SOVIET UNION HAS EXPRESSED SIGNIFICANT INTEREST IN THE DEVELOPMENT OF SIBERIA, THE HARSH NATURAL ENVIRONMENT, THE VASTNESS, THE SPARSE POPULATION, AND THE HUGE DISTANCE BETWEEN EASTERN SIBERIA AND THE POPULATED CENTERS WEST OF THE URALS HAVE ALL HAMPERED EFFORTS AIMED AT DEVELOPMENT. EFFORTS TO UTILIZE JAPAN AS AN ECONOMIC BASE HAVE SIMILARLY FAILED. HOWEVER, THE USSR IS NOW LOOKING TO SOUTH KOREA AS A MUCH MORE EAGER AND WILLING DEVELOPMENT PARTNER. THE ARTICLE BRIEFLY LOOKS AT THE BACKGROUND AND CONDITIONS OF DEVELOPMENT IN SIBERIA. IT ALSO DETAILS THE TRADE AND INVESTMENT RELATIONSHIP WITH SOUTH KOREA AS IT HAS PROGRESSED IN THE 1980S.

02221 CHONG, D.
COLLECTIVE ACTION AND THE CIVIL RIGHTS MOVEMENT
DISSERTATION ABSTRACTS INTERNATIONAL, 49(7) (JAN 89), 1944-A.
THE AUTHOR STUDIES THE DYNAMICS OF COLLECTIVE ACTION, FOCUSING ON TWO MAJOR QUESTIONS: (1) HOW DO RATIONAL INDIVIDUALS DECIDE WHETHER OR NOT TO PARTICIPATE IN COLLECTIVE ACTION ? (2) HOW DO THESE INDIVIDUAL DECISIONS TRANSLATE INTO COLLECTIVE OUTCOMES? THE CIVIL RIGHTS MOVEMENT IS USED AS A CASE STUDY.

02222 CHONGWEI, J.
CHINA'S FOREIGN TRADE STRATEGY

BEIJING REVIEW, 32(31) (JUL 89), 29-32.
CHINA CANNOT ADOPT AN OVERALL EXPORT-ORIENTED POLICY AND
PROMOTE AN ECONOMY GEARED TO FOREIGN MARKETS, LIKE A SMALL
COUNTRY OR AN ISLAND STATE CAN. CHINA MUST ADOPT AN OPEN
STRATEGY OF COMBINING THE PRODUCTION OF IMPORT SUBSTITUTES
WITH AN EXPORT-ORIENTED ECONOMY WHILE EXPANDING ECONOMIC
RELATIONS AND COOPERATION WITH OTHER COUNTRIES AND ENHANCING
ITS COMPETITIVENESS ON THE WORLD MARKET. LOCALITIES AND
INDUSTRIAL DEPARTMENTS WITHIN CHINA MUST, IN ACCORDANCE WITH
THEIR OWN CONDITIONS AND CHARACTERISTICS, ADOPT DIFFERENT
DEVELOPMENTAL STRATEGIES APPROPRIATE TO THE SITUATION OF
SUPPLY AND DEMAND ON THE DOMESTIC AND WORLD MARKETS.

02223 CHOONG, K.
THE PAN-PACIFIC CARD
FAR EASTERN ECONOMIC REVIEW, 142(51) (DEC 89), 60-61.
THE EASING OF INTERNATIONAL POLITICAL AND SECURITY
TENSIONS AS WELL AS THE RISE TO ECONOMIC DOMINANCE OF THE
PACIFIC RIM NATIONS ARE IMPORTANT FORERUNNERS TO SIGNIFICANT
WORLDWIDE ECONOMIC CHANGE. THE ARTICLE EXPLORES VARIOUS
POSSIBLE ECONOMIC BLOCS THAT COULD FORM IN THE PACIFIC IN
THE NEAR FUTURE. THESE INCLUDE: THE YEN BLOC (JAPAN, SOUTH
KOREA, THE ASEAN NATIONS, AUSTRALIA AND NEW ZEALAND), THE
PEKING BLOC (CHINA, NORTH AND SOUTH KOREA, TAIWAN, SINGAPORE,
AND HONG KONG), THE WESTERN PACIFIC BLOC (A COMBINATION OF
THE YEN AND PEKING BLOCS), AND THE PAN-PACIFIC COMMUNITY
(ESSENTIALLY THE WESTERN PACIFIC COMMUNITY, BUT INCLUDING
THE U.S., CANADA, AND PERHAPS CENTRAL AND SOUTH AMERICAN
NATIONS). THE ARTICLE CONCLUDES THAT THE PAN-PACIFIC
ALTERNATIVE IS THE MOST LIKELY AND MOST DESIRABLE OF FUTURE
OPTIONS.

02224 CHOPRA, V.D.
TOWARDS A NEW MODEL OF COOPERATION
WORLD MARXIST REVIEW, 32(8) (AUG 89), 36-39.
THREE YEARS AGO IN VLADIVOSTOK, MIKHAIL GORBACHEV SET
FORTH THE SOVIET PROGRAM FOR ATTAINING SECURITY IN THE ASIA-
PACIFIC REGION. HIS SPEECH GAVE IMPETUS TO THE DEVELOPMENT
OF PEACE PROCESS IN THAT PART OF THE WORLD. IT WAS FOLLOWED
BY THE DELHI DECLARATION, SEVERAL NEW SOVIET PROPOSALS AND
INITIATIVES ADVANCED BY INDIA, VIETNAM, MONGOLIA, INDONESIA
AND OTHER COUNTRIES. DR. CHOPRA, A PROMINENT INDIAN SCHOLAR
DISCUSSES HOW THE PROCESS OF STABILIZATION IS FARING IN ASIA
AND WHAT DIFFICULTIES AND CONTRADICTIONS ARE INVOLVED.

02225 CHORNOVIL, V.
WHY IT'S NECESSARY TO FIND ANSWERS TO THE "NATIONALITIES
QUESTION"
GLASNOST, II(3) (MAY 89), 21-23.
THE 27TH CONGRESS OF THE CPSU HAS ERRONEOUSLY CONCLUDED
THAT THE NATIONALITIES QUESTION IN THE SOVIET UNION HAS BEEN
COMPLETELY AND EQUITABLY RESOLVED AND THAT IN THE FUTURE
ONLY MARGINAL IMPROVEMENTS ARE REQUIRED IN THE PARTY'S
POLICIES. IN FACT, UNSOLVED NATIONALITY PROBLEMS ARE
MANIFESTING THEMSELVES IN POWERFUL WAYS. AND THE
NATIONALITIES QUESTION IS THE MOST IMPORTANT PROBLEM FACING
SOVIET SOCIETY.

02226 CHOUDHURY, M.A.
RESOURCE ENDOWMENT AND ALLOCATION IN ISLAMIC COUNTRIES FOR
ECONOMIC CO-OPERATION
ORIENT, 29(4) (1988), 595-605.
THE MAIN OBJECTIVES OF THIS PAPER ARE TO DELINEATE THE
PRINCIPAL ECONOMIC CHARACTERISTICS OF THE ISLAMIC ECONOMIES
IN RECENT TIMES AND STUDY HOW THESE CHARACTERISTICS CAN GIVE
RISE TO FACTS THAT EXPLAIN THE POTENTIAL FOR ECONOMIC CO-
OPERATION. THE PRINCIPAL INDICATORS EXAMINED ARE GROWTH OF
GDP, LABOUR FORCE, STRUCTURE OF PRODUCTION BY SECTORS,
INVESTMENT, SAVING, CONSUMPTION AND EXPORTS. THE RELATED
INDICATORS ARE CURRENT ACCOUNT BALANCES, DEBT OUTSTANDING,
DEBT SERVICE RATIOS AND EXTERNAL FLOW OF RESOURCES. THE
EMPHASIS IS ON THE ISLAMIC COUNTRIES, BUT A COMPARISON WITH
DEVELOPING COUNTRIES IN GENERAL IS ALSO MADE. SELECTED
ISLAMIC COUNTRIES ARE STUDIED AND THEIR CHOICE IS SOLELY
BASED ON DATA AVAILABILITY. THE COVERAGE HERE IS HOWEVER,
FOR THE LOW- AND MIDDLEINCOME COUNTRIES. THE TABLES AND
DIAGRAMS ARE COLLECTED TOGETHER IN THE STATISTICAL APPENDIX
TO THIS PAPER AND ARE REFERRED TO IN THE TEXT. DEVELOPMENT
CO-OPERATION IS A MULTI-FACETED STUDY IN ECONOMIC
DEVELOPMENT, INTERNATIONAL TRADE AND DEVELOPMENT
INSTITUTIONS. THIS PAPER BRINGS OUT THE ISSUES IN THESE
FIELDS AS FOUND IN THE EMPIRICAL FACTS PRESENTED HERE.

02227 CHOW, E.
FOREIGN WORKERS, LOCAL PROBLEMS
FREE CHINA REVIEW, 39(4) (APR 89), 36-39.
THE INFLUX OF WORKERS FROM SOUTHEAST ASIA IS BEGINNING
TO SEND TREMORS THROUGHOUT TAIWAN, EVEN THOUGH THE NUMBERS
OF FOREIGN WORKERS REMAIN RELATIVELY SMALL. THE GOVERNMENT
NOW FINDS ITSELF FACING IRATE UNIONS AND EMPLOYERS AS IT
TRIES TO REACH A SOLUTION TO THIS THORNY PROBLEM. ITS
RESOLUTION WILL HAVE BROAD IMPLICATIONS FOR THE SUCCESS OF
TAIWAN'S CONTINUED INDUSTRIAL DEVELOPMENT.

02228 CHOW, P.C.Y.
A BALANCING ACT WITH THE U.S.
FREE CHINA REVIEW, 39(4) (APR 89), 20-23.
DUE TO THE TRADE IMBALANCE BETWEEN THE USA AND TAIWAN,
FRICTIONS BETWEEN THE TWO HAVE BECOME A CONSTANT WORRY FOR
BOTH SIDES. IN THIS ARTICLE, THE AUTHOR EXAMINES THE MAJOR
TRADE ISSUES FACING THE TWO NATIONS AND SUGGESTS SOME STEPS
TOWARD THEIR RESOLUTION.

02229 CHRISTENSEN, J. G.
REGULATION, DEREGULATION, AND PUBLIC BUREAUCRACY
EUROPEAN JOURNAL OF POLITICAL RESEARCH, 17(2) (MAR 89),
223-239.
IN 1982, A NEW LIBERAL-CONSERVATIVE GOVERMENT LAUNCHED A
GRAND DEREGULATORY CAMPAIGN AS PART OF ITS PROGRAMME FOR
RESTORING THE DANISH ECONOMY. AFTER SOME INITIAL SUCCESS,
THE CAMPAIGN LOST MOMENTUM. THE GOVERNMENT GRADUALLY
REALISED THAT IT WAS DIFFICULT TO MOBILISE BOTH ECONOMIC
INTERESTS AND PUBLIC OPINION FOR THE CAUSE OF DEREGULATION.
BUREAUCRATIC RESISTANCE AND DISINTEREST AMONG ECONOMIC
INTEREST ORGANISATIONS TOGETHER WITH THE EROSION OF
POLITICAL COMMITMENT TO DEREGULATION AFTER A COUPLE OF YEARS
STOPPED THE CAMPAIGN. STILL, SOME RESULTS WERE REACHED WHERE
LEAST EXPECTED.

02230 CHRISTENSEN, R.
GROWING REPUBLICAN RANKS HELP TOPPLE SPEAKER IN NORTH
CAROLINA
STATE LEGISLATURES, 15(4) (APR 89), 16-19.
NORTH CAROLINA ELECTED A RECORD NUMBER OF REPUBLICANS IN
NOVEMBER 1988. ALTHOUGH THE REPUBLICANS REMAINED A DISTINCT
MINORITY IN THE GENERAL ASSEMBLY, THEY JOINED FORCES WITH
SOME UNHAPPY DEMOCRATS IN THE HOUSE TO OUST LONG-TIME
SPEAKER LISTON RAMSEY.

02231 CHRISTIANSEN, R.E.; STACKHOUSE, L.A.
THE PRIVATIZATION OF AGRICULTURAL TRADING IN MALAWI
WORLD DEVELOPMENT, 17(5) (MAY 89), 729-740.
THIS PAPER EXAMINES THE PRIVATIZATION OF SMALLHOLDER
AGRICULTURAL OUTPUT MARKETING IN MALAWI. DESPITE PROBLEMS
WITH IMPLEMENTING THE PRIVATIZATION PROGRAM, INCLUDING
SERIOUS DISRUPTIONS IN THE SUPPLY OF MAIZE (THE STAPLE FOOD),
THE MOVE TOWARD GREATER PRIVATE SECTOR INVOLVEMENT IN
AGRICULTURAL MARKETING HAS BEEN SUCCESSFUL. NONETHELESS,
SEVERAL MEDIUM-TERM DEVELOPMENT ISSUES (E.G., FOOD SECURITY
AND BUYER AND SELLER OF LAST RESORT FUNCTIONS) NEED TO BE
ADDRESSED IN THE CONTEXT OF RELATIONS BETWEEN THE MARKETING
PARASTATAL (ADMARC) AND THE PRIVATE SECTOR BEFORE THE POLICY
CHANGE CAN BE REGARDED AS FULLY SUCCESSFUL.

02232 CHRISTIE, M.
HOW WASHINGTON WORKS
SOUTH AFRICA FOUNDATION REVIEW, 15(3) (MAR 89), 4,8.
THE AUTHOR PREDICTS THAT AMERICAN PRESSURE AGAINST
APARTHEID WILL INCREASE AND THE COURSE OF US-SOUTH AFRICAN
RELATIONS WILL ULTIMATELY BE DETERMINED BY EVENTS IN SOUTH
AFRICA.

02233 CHRISTIE, M.
U.S. ADOPTS "HANDS-OFF" POLICY
SOUTH AFRICA FOUNDATION REVIEW, 15(11) (NOV 89), 1-2.
THE BUSH ADMINISTRATION AND INFLUENTIAL MEMBERS OF THE
SENATE HAVE REACHED A TACIT UNDERSTANDING THAT A "WAIT AND
SEE" APPROACH TO SOUTH AFRICA IS THE DESIRABLE COURSE IN THE
NEAR FUTURE. ENCOURAGED BY SOUTH AFRICA'S PRESIDENT DE
KLERK'S REFORMS AND APPARENT WILLINGNESS TO COMPROMISE AND
NEGOTIATE, THE U.S. HAS DECLARED THE INTENT OF INITIATING A
POLICY OF "CAUTIOUS CO-OPERATION WITH ALL PARTIES." THE
FUTURE NOW DEPENDS ON THE CONTINUED RATE OF CHANGE.

02234 CHRISTIE, M.
USA: A TENSE BREATHER
SOUTH AFRICA FOUNDATION REVIEW, 15(1) (JAN 89), 4-5.
THE AUTHOR LOOKS AT AMERICAN CONGRESSIONAL SUPPORT FOR
ECONOMIC SANCTIONS AGAINST SOUTH AFRICA. HE PREDICTS THAT
LEGISLATION CALLING FOR COMPREHENSIVE SANCTIONS WILL ONCE
AGAIN BE INTRODUCED IN CONGRESS IN 1989 AND IS LIKELY TO
RECEIVE MORE BIPARTISAN SUPPORT.

02235 CHRISTISON, K.
THE AMERICAN EXPERIENCE: PALESTINIANS IN THE US
JOURNAL OF PALESTINE STUDIES, XVIII(4) (SUM 89), 18-36.
THE ARTICLE CONTAINS A STUDY OF PALESTINIAN-AMERICAN
ATTITUDES TOWARD BEING AMERICAN BASED ON INTERVIEWS WITH
SEVENTY-TWO PALESTINIANS. IT INCLUDES SURVEYS OF ATTITUDES
TOWARDS ASSIMILATION, DISCRIMINATION, POLITICS, AND THE
INTIFADA IN PALESTINE. IT CONCLUDES THAT PALESTINIANS STILL
OFTEN FACE ETHNIC PREJUDICE AND POLITICAL STEREOTYPING.
HOWEVER, THE DIFFICULTIES THE U.S. HAS POSED FOR
PALESTINIANS HAVE SERVED TO REINFORCE THEIR SENSE OF BEING
PALESTINIAN.

02236 CHRISTISON, K.
THE ARAB-ISRAELI POLICY OF GEORGE SHULTZ

JOURNAL OF PALESTINE STUDIES, XVIII(2) (WIN 89), 29-47.
THE ARTICLE EXAMINES THE STANCE AND POLICEES OF GEORGE
SHULTZ DURING HIS TENURE AS SECRETARY OF STATE WITH REGARDS
TO THE MIDEAST. IT ANALYZES SHULTZ'S RESPONSES TO THE
ISRAELI INVASION AND OCCUPATION OF LEBANON, TERRORISM, AND
THE INTIFADAH. THE ARTICLE CONCLUDES THAT SHULTZ'S FOREIGN
POLICY WAS THE PRODUCT AS MUCH OF HIS PERSONALITY AND
PERSONAL STYLE AS OF ANY STRATEGIC PLANNING. ALTHOUGH MANY
OF THE CRISES THAT HE FACED WERE NOT CAUSED BY HIS POLICIES,
HIS REACTIONS WERE OFTEN AD HOC AND WORSENED THE SITUATION.
HIS LEGACY IS AN ARAB WORLD FUNDAMENTALLY SKEPTICAL OF
AMERICA'S JUSTICE AND SPIRIT OF FAIR PLAY, AND AN ISRAEL
THAT IS STRONGER BUT NO MORE SECURE THAN IT WAS WHEN HE TOOK
OFFICE.

02237 CHRISTOFIAS, D.
FACING THE NEW TERRAIN
WORLD MARXIST REVIEW, 31(12) (DEC 88), 26-32.
THE 27TH CPSU CONGRESS WAS RIGHT TO DRAW THE CONCLUSION
THAT THE INTERNATIONAL COMMUNIST MOVEMENT IS AT AN HISTORIC
CROSSROADS, SUCCESSFUL NEGOTIATION OF WHICH LARGELY DEPENDS
ON THE ABILITY OF EACH PARTY TO REASSESS THE FAST-CHANGING
NATIONAL AND INTERNATIONAL TERRAIN. HOWEVER, IT APPEARS THAT
ANY CONTRA-DISTINCTION BETWEEN INTERNATIONAL COMMUNIST UNITY
(REGARDLESS OF WHETHER THE TERM 'PROLETARIAN
INTERNATIONALISM' IS USED OR NOT) AND BROADER INTERACTION OF
THE LEFT, DEMOCRATIC AND PROGRESSIVE FORCES, LOCALLY,
REGIONALLY AND INTERNATIONALLY IS UNPRODUCTIVE. THE PARTY
CAN AND MUST STRENGTHEN THE INTERNATIONAL COMMUNIST MOVEMENT,
ENHANCE ITS ROLE IN WORLD DEVELOPMENT AND, AT THE SAME TIME,
PROMOTE RELATIONS WITH THE SOCIAL DEMOCRATS, DEVELOP
CONTACTS BETWEEN ALL THE CONTINGENTS OF THE WORKING-CLASS
MOVEMENT AND OTHER PROGRESSIVE, LEFT AND DEMOCRATIC FORCES,
ABOVE ALL ON ELIMINATING THE THREAT OF WAR AND SOLVING
UNIVERSAL HUMAN PROBLEMS.

02238 CHRISTOPHER, I.
STEP FORWARD MR. MANLEY
CONTEMPORARY REVIEW, 254(1480) (MAY 89), 241-243.
DESPITE THE LANDSLIDE VICTORY OF THE PNP IT IS IMPORTANT
THAT THE NEW PRIME MINISTER, MR MICHAEL MANLEY, EXPANDS UPON
SOME OF THE SMALL SUCCESSES OF THE DEFEATED SEAGA
ADMINISTRATION. THE JLP DID TRY TO SOLVE SOME OF THE GRAVE
ECONOMIC PROBLEMS AND THEY SCRUPULOUSLY DID ENDEAVOUR TO PUT
PRUDENCE AHEAD OF OTHER CONSIDERATIONS IN THEIR ECONOMIC
POLICY DECISIONS. HOPEFULLY, THE PNP CAN CONTINUE WITH THIS
GOOD WORK.

02239 CHRISTOPHIAS, P.
NEW THINKING AND LOCAL CONFLICTS
WORLD MARXIST REVIEW, 32(10) (OCT 89), 9-12.
THIS PAPER, BY DIMITRIOS CHRISTOPHIAS, GENERAL SECRETARY
OF THE PROGRESSIVE PARTY OF THE WORKING PEOPLE OF CYPRUS
(AKEL), ANSWERS THE QUESTIONS OF HOW NEW POLITICAL THINKING
HELPS LESSEN INTERNATIONAL TENSIONS, SETTLE LOCAL CONFLICTS,
AND COOL HOTBEDS. HE EXAMINES INTERNATIONAL RELATIONS AND
THE INTERNATIONAL ENVIRONMENT OF CONFLICT, AS WELL AS
NATIONAL RECONCILATION, HE CALLS FOR THE SETTLEMENT OF THE
CYPRUS PROBLEM.

02240 CHU-YUAN, C.
A TROUBLED ECONOMY
FREE CHINA REVIEW, 39(11) (NOV 89), 48-53.
THE AUTHOR ANALYZES THE ECONOMIC CAUSES AND EFFECTS OF
THE TIENANMEN SQUARE MASSACRE.

02241 CHU, R.
HISTORICAL RELATIONS
ASIAN AFFAIRS, AN AMERICAN REVIEW, 16(3) (FAL 89), 107-118.
THE AUTHOR EXAMINES THE ISSUE OF TAIWAN'S INDEPENDENCE
FROM A POLITICAL, CULTURAL, LEGAL, AND ECONOMIC PERSPECTIVE.
HE CONCLUDES THAT NONE OF THESE JUSTIFY SEPARATISM AND
INDEPENDENCE. THE UNDERLYING MOTIVATIONS OF THE SEPARATIST
MOVEMENT ARE THE REPRESSION OF THE "FEBRUARY 28" REVOLT BY
THE KUOMINTANG, AND THE FEAR OF COMMUNIST RULE. THE AUTHOR
ADVOCATES THAT ALL CHINESE, SEPARATISTS AND NON-SEPARATISTS
ALIKE, SHOULD WORK FOR A UNIFIED, FREE, AND DEMOCRATIC CHINA.

02242 CHU, Y.
AN AUSPICIOUS YEAR OF SINO-SOVIET RELATIONS
BEIJING REVIEW, 32(5) (JAN 89), 7, 9.
THE YEAR 1988 PROVED TO BE AN AUSPICIOUS ONE FOR SINO-
SOVIET RELATIONS. A POLITICAL BREAKTHROUGH WAS MADE IN
RELATIONS PRIMARILY DUE TO CHANGES IN SOVIET POLICY ON
AFGHANISTAN, MONGOLIA, AND KAMPUCHEA.

02243 CHU, Y.
AUTHORITARIAN REGIMES UNDER STRESS: THE POLITICAL ECONOMY
OF ADJUSTMENT IN THE EAST ASIAN NEWLY INDUSTRIALIZING
COUNTRIES
DISSERTATION ABSTRACTS INTERNATIONAL, 48(10) (APR 88),
2716-A.
IN ANALYZING EAST ASIAN STATES AND THEIR RESPONSES TO
THE CHALLENGE OF INDUSTRIAL UPGRADING AND ECONOMIC STABILITY,

MANY TRADITIONAL APPROACHES ARE OF LIMITED UTILITY.
ALTERNATIVELY, A STATE-CENTERED POLICY MODEL IS MORE
APPLICABLE TO THE VARIOUS CIRCUMSTANCES OF THE EAST ASIAN
NIC'S.

02244 CHU, Y.
SINO-SOVIET RELATIONS: REVIEW AND PROSPECT
BEIJING REVIEW, 32(20) (MAY 89), 7.
THE PAST TWO YEARS HAVE SEEN SOME POSITIVE CHANGES IN
SINO-SOVIET DIPLOMACY, WHICH HAVE LED TO A BREAKTHROUGH IN
ELIMINATING THE THREE OBSTACLES TO IMPROVED RELATIONS--
KAMPUCHEA, AFGHANISTAN, AND THE HEAVY DEPLOYMENT OF SOVIET
TROOPS ALONG THE SINO-SOVIET AND SINO-MONGOLIAN BORDERS.
DURING A VISIT BY CHINESE FOREIGN MINISTER QIAN QICHEN TO
MOSCOW IN LATE 1988, THE TWO COUNTRIES NARROWED THEIR
DIFFERENCES ON THE MAJOR OBSTACLE, KAMPUCHEA, AND REACHED AN
AGREEMENT IN PRINCIPLE ON A SINO-SOVIET SUMMIT IN 1989.
TODAY THE CONDITIONS ARE FINALLY RIPE FOR BOTH CHINA AND THE
SOVIET UNION TO BID FAREWELL TO THE PAST. BUT SAYING
"GOODBYE" IS NOT THE SAME AS FOREGETTING. THE HISTORY OF
SINO-SOVIET RELATIONS OFFERS PRECIOUS EXPERIENCE AND LESSONS
THAT MUST NOT BE FORGOTTEN.

02245 CHU, Y.H.
STATE STRUCTURE AND ECONOMIC ADJUSTMENT OF THE EAST ASIAN
NEWLY INDUSTRIALIZING COUNTRIES
INTERNATIONAL ORGANIZATION, 43(4) (FAL 89), 647-672.
TO EXPLAIN THE DIVERGENCE IN ADJUSTMENT STRATEGIES, THE
ARTICLE EXPLORES THE VARIATIONS IN THE NATIONAL POLITICAL
STRUCTURES OF THE FOUR NICS AND FOCUSES PARTICULARLY ON
THREE ASPECTS OF STATE STRUCTURE: THE ORGANIZATION OF THE
ECONOMIC BUREAUCRACY, THE INSTITUTIONAL LINKS BETWEEN THE
STATE AND PRIVATE SECTOR, AND THE LARGER STATE-SOCIETY
RELATIONS. THE ARTICLE DEMONSTRATES THE USEFULNESS OF MOVING
BEYOND THE GENERALIZATIONS OF THE "DEVELOPMENTAL STATE" VIEW
BY CAREFULLY DISAGGREGATING THESE ASPECTS OF STATE STRUCTURE
AND BY EXPLORING THE ORDERING LOGIC THAT GIVES COHERENCE TO
THEM.

02246 CHUAN, J.
THE TRUE FEATURES OF "DEMOCRATIC FIGHTERS"
BEIJING REVIEW, 32(49) (DEC 89), 23-26.
SOME WESTERN NEWS MEDIA HAVE EXTROLLED WUER KAIXI, YAN
JIAQI, FANG LIZHI, AND OTHER DISSIDENTS AS "DEMOCRATIC
FIGHTERS" CONCERNED ABOUT CHINA AND ITS PEOPLE. THIS ARTICLE
PRESENTS THE TRUTH ABOUT THESE DISSIDENTS AND EXPOSES THEIR
REAL MOTIVES AND CHARACTERS.

02247 CHUBARIAN, A.
WAS AN EARLIER ANTI-NAZI COALITION POSSIBLE?
WORLD MARXIST REVIEW, 32(8) (AUG 89), 30-33.
MUCH PUBLIC INTEREST IN THE GENESIS AND PREHISTORY OF
WORLD WAR II HAS BEEN AROUSED IN CONNECTION WITH THE 50TH
ANNIVERSARY OF THE BEGINNING OF THE MOST TRAGIC AND
DESTRUCTIVE CONFLICT IN HUMAN HISTORY. IN THIS ARTICLE, THE
AUTHOR REFLECTS ON WHETHER AN ANTI-NAZI COALITION COULD HAVE
BEEN FORMED IN THE WAKE OF HITLER'S RISE TO POWER AND WHAT
FACTORS PREVENTED ITS ESTABLISHMENT. HE SUGGESTS THAT THE
LESSONS OF THE PAST CAN HELP US AVOID A REPETITION OF THESE
MISTAKES.

02248 CHUBB, J.E.; YOFFIE, D.B.
AMERICAN TRADE POLICY: AN OBSOLETE BARGAIN?; CAN THE
GOVERNMENT GOVERN?
BROOKINGS INSTITUTION, WASHINGTON, D.C., 1988, 100-138.
THIS ESSAY WHICH EXPLORES AMERICAN TRADE POLICY, BEGINS
WITH AN EXAMINATION OF U.S. TRADE POLICY AND TRADE PROBLEMS.
IT EXAMINES THE U.S. HISTORY OF PROTECTIONISM, DEMAND AND
AVAILABILITY. IT ASKS IF AMERICAN TRADE POLICY IS AN
OBSOLETE BARGAIN AND DISCUSSES GROWING RECIDIVISM AS WELL AS
DEMANDS FOR CONTINGENT PROTECTION. IT PROPOSES AN
INTELLECTUAL CHALLENGE: STRATEGIC TRADE POLICY THEORY AND
OFFERS THE IMPLICATIONS FOR AMERICAN TRADE POLICY AND
INSTITUTIONS.

02249 CHUBB, J.E.; PETERSON, P.E.
CAN THE GOVERNMENT GOVERN?
BROOKINGS INSTITUTION, WASHINGTON, D.C., 1988, 329.
THIS BOOK EXPLORES THE AMERICAN GOAL OF SEEKING MORE
EFFECTIVE GOVERNMENT, AND ASKS THE QUESTION: CAN THE
GOVERNMENT GOVERN? IT EMPHASIZES HOW MUCH WE HAVE YET TO
LEARN ABOUT MAKING OUR GOVERNMENTAL INSTITUTIONS MORE
EFFECTIVE. IT IS PRIMARILY A WORK OF ANALYSIS, NOT OF
ADVOCACY. ALTHOUGH THE AUTHORS DISCUSS A VARIETY OF POLICY
AND INSTITUTIONAL REFORMS THEIR PURPOSE IS NOT SO MUCH TO
INSIST ON ANY PARTICULAR REFORM AS TO EXPLICATE THE CAUSES
AND CONSEQUENCES OF INSTITUTIONAL INTRANSIGENCE, AND TO
CONVINCE POLICYMAKERS THAT THE QUESTION OF GOVERNMENTAL
EFFECTIVENESS HAS BECOME TOO CRITICAL TO BE IGNORED. IT
EXPLORES POLICY AND INSTITUTIONS, AND THEN INSTITUTIONS AND
GOVERNANCE.

02250 CHUBB, J.E.; PETERSON, P.E.
CHAPTER 1: AMERICAN POLITICAL INSTITUTIONS AND THE PROBLEM

OF GOVERNANCE; CAN THE GOVERNMENT GOVERN?
BROOKINGS INSTITUTION, WASHINGTON, D.C., 1988, 1-46.
THIS CHAPTER INTRODUCES THE BOOK, "CAN THE GOVERNMENT
GOVERN?" WHICH EXAMINES THE PROBLEM OF GOVERNANCE THAT THE
COLLISION OF NEW ISSUES AND ESTABLISHED INSTITUTIONS MAY BE
CREATING FOR THE UNITED STATES. THE FIRST PART OF THE BOOK
EXAMINES ENERGY, TRADE, AND THE STABILITY OF THE
MACROECONOMY, AND IN THIS INTRODUCTORY ESSAY THE LONG
DEVELOPMENT OF THE CONTEMPORY GOVERNABILITY PROBLEM IS
TRACED. IT ALSO ARGUES, DRAWING ON THE INDIVIDUAL ESSAYS IN
THE BOOK, THAT THE PROBLEM IS INHERENTLY AND SUBSTANTIALLY
INSTITUTIONAL, AND THEN DISCUSSES THE POLITICALLY DIFFICULT
REQUIREMENTS FOR OVERCOMING IT.

02251 CHUBB, J.E.; PETERSON, P.E.; ROM, M.
MACROECONOMIC POLICYMAKING: WHO IS IN CONTROL?; CAN THE
GOVERNMENT GOVERN?
BROOKINGS INSTITUTION, WASHINGTON, D.C., 1988, 139-184.
THIS ESSAY BEGINS BY EMPHASIZING THE STAKE THAT
PRESIDENTS HAVE IN STABILIZING ECONOMIC GROWTH FOR THE FOUR
TO EIGHT YEARS THEY ARE IN OFFICE. IT DESCRIBES THE
INSTITUTIONAL PROBLEM AND DISCUSSES PRESIDENTIAL INCENTIVES,
AND REJECTS ELECTORAL OR PARTISAN REASONS FOR MANIPULATING
THE ECONOMY. IT DISCUSSES THE FEDERAL RESERVE, THE FEDERAL
OPEN MARKET COMMITTEE, THE PRESIDENT'S RELATIONSHIP TO IT,
AS WELL AS CONGRESS AND FISCAL POLICY. IT CONCLUDES WITH AN
ANALYSIS OF THE FUTURE OF ECONOMIC POLICY MAKING.

02252 CHUBB, J.E.; SHEPSLE, K.A.
THE CHANGING TEXTBOOK CONGRESS; CAN THE GOVERNMENT GOVERN?
BROOKINGS INSTITUTION, WASHINGTON, D.C., 1988, 238-266.
THIS CHAPTER EXAMINES CONGRESS SINCE 1940. IT DETAILS
THE PERIODS OF 1940-1960; AND THE 1970S AND 1980S. IT
SPECULATES ON A PRESENT TEXTBOOK CONGRESS INFLUENCED BY
GEOGRAPHY AND PARTY, A TENUOUS BALANCE ESTABLISHED AMONG
LEGISLATORS, A DECENTRALIZED SUBCOMMITTEE SYSTEM, AND A
RECENTRALIZED AND REINVIGORATED SUBCOMMITTEE SYSTEM. IT
SUGGESTS THE PROBABILITY OF SOME MAJOR INSTITUTIONAL
REORGANIZATION AND THE CONTINUANCE OF FULL SERVICE MEMBERS
OF CONGRESS.

02253 CHUBB, J.E.; KERNELL, S.
THE EVOLUTION OF THE WHITE HOUSE STAFF; CAN THE GOVERNMENT
GOVERN?
BROOKINGS INSTITUTION, WASHINGTON, D.C., 1988, 185-237.
THIS IS A STUDY OF THE DEVELOPMENT OF THE MODERN WHITE
HOUSE STAFF. IT GIVES A HISTORY OF WHITE HOUSE ORGANIZATION
AND TRACES THE DEVELOPMENT OF WHITE HOUSE LINE STAFF, AS
WELL AS ATTEMPTS TO EXPLAIN WHITE HOUSE DEVELOPMENT. IT
ADDRESSES GOVERNABILITY AND THE MODERN WHITE HOUSE.

02254 CHUBB, J.E.; MOE, T.M.
THE POLITICS OF BUREAUCRATIC STRUCTURE; CAN THE GOVERNMENT
GOVERN?
BROOKINGS INSTITUTION, WASHINGTON, D.C., 1988, 267-330.
THIS ESSAY IS AN EFFORT TO UNDERSTAND BUREAUCRACY BY
UNDERSTANDING ITS FOUNDATION IN POLITICAL CHOICE AND SELF-
INTEREST. IT ANALYSES THE BUILDING OF THE BUREAUCRACY BY
INTEREST GROUPS, PRESIDENTS, MEMBERS OF CONGRESS, AND
BUREAUCRATS IN THEIR EFFORTS TO EXERCISE POLITICAL POWER. IT
OUTLINES A THEORETICAL PERSPECTIVE ON THE POLITICS OF
STRUCTURAL CHOICE AND PUTS THIS PERSPECTIVE TO USE IN
EXPLORING THE STRUCTURAL POLITICS OF THREE MODERN
BUREAUCRACIES: THE CONSUMER PRODUCT SAFETY COMMISSION, THE
OCCUPATIONAL SAFETY AND HEALTH ADMINISTRATION, AND THE
ENVIRONMENTAL PROTECTION AGENCY.

02255 CHUBB, J.E.
U.S. ENERGY POLICY: A PROBLEM OF DELEGATION; CAN THE
GOVERNMENT GOVERN?
BROOKINGS INSTITUTION, WASHINGTON, D.C., 1988, 47-99.
THIS ESSAY SUGGESTS THAT MUCH OF THE INSTITUTIONAL
STRUCTURE OF CONTEMPORARY U.S. ENERGY POLICY IS ILL DESIGNED
FOR THE PROBLEMS OF ENERGY SECURITY IN THE 1990S AND BEYOND.
IT SHOWS HOW THAT STRUCTURE HAS BECOME INCONSISTENT WITH AN
EFFECTIVE ENERGY POLICY, AT LEAST IF ONE OF THE POLICY'S
PRIMARY GOALS IS THE PREVENTION OF FUTURE ENERGY CRISIS. IT
ALSO EXPLAINS WHY THE INSTITUTIONAL STRUCTURE WAS CREATED
AND PERSISTS. IT CONSIDERS WHY THE CURRENT RATES OF DOMESTIC
ENERGY PRODUCTION AND CONSUMPTION PRESENT A POTENTIALLY
SERIOUS NATIONAL PROBLEM.

02256 CHUBIN, S.
THE LAST PHASE OF THE IRAN-IRAQ WAR: FROM STALEMATE TO
CEASEFIRE
THIRD WORLD QUARTERLY, 11(2) (APR 89), 1-14.
THROUGHOUT THE 1980'S, THE IRAN-IRAQ WAR WAS PART OF THE
POLITICAL AND STRATEGIC LANDSCAPE OF THE MIDDLE EAST,
ESTABLISHING OR ACCELERATING NEW ALIGNMENTS AND NEW
PRIORITIES. BECAUSE OF ITS LENGTH, ITS BOUTS OF INTENSE
CLASHES ALTERNATING WITH SEASONAL LULLS, AND THE
IMPENTRABILITY OF THE IRANIAN ISLAMIC REVOLUTION, IT GAVE
RISE TO A HOST OF ASSUMPTIONS, BONS MOTS, AND CLICHES THAT
SUBSTITUTED FOR INFORMED ANALYSIS. NO PART OF THE WAR CAME

AS A GREATER SURPRISE TO THE SPECTATORS THAN THE WAY THE WAR
ENDED.

02257 CHUN, K.O.
THE POLITICAL THOUGHT OF CRAWFORD BROUGH MACPHERSON
DISSERTATION ABSTRACTS INTERNATIONAL, 49(11) (MAY 89),
3488-A.
THE POLITICAL THEORY OF C.B. MACPHERSON IS FIRMLY
GROUNDED IN WESTERN LIBERALISM, BUT HIS INDIVIDUALISM IS
ENLIGHTENED BY MARXISM. MACPHERSON'S VIEWS ON DEMOCRACY ARE
FUNDAMENTALLY ETHICAL AND ATTEMPT TO PRESERVE THE INTEGRITY
OF THE INDIVIDUAL AS AN AGENT OF SELF-DEVELOPMENT.

02258 CHUN, R.T.
EVANGELICALISM DIVIDED: AN EXAMINATION OF FACTORS
CONTRIBUTING TO EVANGELICAL POLITICAL DIVERSITY
DISSERTATION ABSTRACTS INTERNATIONAL, 50(2) (AUG 89),
533-A.
AMERICAN EVANGELICALISM HAS OFTEN BEEN PERCEIVED AS
UNIFORMLY POLITICALLY CONSERVATIVE, BUT THIS PERCEPTION HAS
BEGUN TO CHANGE IN RECENT YEARS. THIS DISSERTATION ANALYZED
DATA COLLECTED THROUGH A MAIL SURVEY OF 753 LAYMEN IN
FOURTEEN CHURCHES. THE FINDINGS DEMONSTRATE THAT THE LINK
BETWEEN EVANGELICAL POLITICAL BELIEF AND POLITICAL
CONSERVATISM IS BEST VIEWED AS INDIRECT AND AS MEDIATED BY
OTHER THEOLOGICAL VARIABLES.

02259 CHUNG-YING, C.
DEMOCRACY MOVEMENT SUPPRESSED
FREE CHINA REVIEW, 39(8) (AUG 89), 12-14.
CHINESE STUDENTS ASKED FOR VERY LITTLE IN THE NAME OF
DEMOCRACY AND FREEDOM, BUT THE COMMUNIST PARTY LEADERS SAW A
POWERFUL CHALLENGE TO BOTH THEIR AUTHORITY AND THEIR
POSITION IN THE STUDENTS' PEACEFUL AND RATIONAL APPEAL. THIS
FAILURE TO COMMUNICATE LED TO THE TOTAL ALIENATION OF THE
PARTY LEADERS FROM SOCIETY AS A WHOLE AND TO THE TIENANMEN
SQUARE MASSACRE IN JUNE 1989.

02260 CHUNG, C.
LOCAL AUTONOMY IN KOREA: MYTH AND REALITY
DISSERTATION ABSTRACTS INTERNATIONAL, 49(10) (APR 89),
3140-A.
THE PROPONENTS OF RE-ESTABLISHING LOCAL AUTONOMY IN
KOREA ARGUE THAT IT WOULD LEAD TO GREATER DEMOCRACY AT THE
NATIONAL LEVEL AND REDUCE REGIONAL ECONOMIC DISPARITIES. THE
AUTHOR OF THIS DISSERTATION EXAMINES THOSE ARGUMENTS AND
HYPOTHESIZES THAT AN ELECTED CENTRALIZED GOVERNMENT TENDS TO
ECONOMICALLY REWARD THOSE REGIONS THAT POLITICALLY SUPPORT
IT. HE CONCLUDES THAT LOCAL AUTONOMY IS IMPORTANT FOR
DEMOCRACY AT BOTH THE LOCAL AND THE NATIONAL LEVELS, BUT ITS
DEMOCRATIC MERITS ARE DIFFICULT TO REALIZE. THE ROLE OF
LOCAL AUTONOMY IN NARROWING REGIONAL ECONOMIC DISPARITIES IS
PROBABLY MUCH LESS IMPORTANT THAN THE ROLE PLAYED BY THE
CENTRAL GOVERNMENT.

02261 CHUNG, C.K.
PRESIDENTIAL DECISIONMAKING AND BUREAUCRATIC EXPERTISE IN
KOREA
GOVERNANCE, 2(3) (JUL 89), 267-292.
SINCE 1960, KOREA HAS ACHIEVED ONE OF THE MOST
MIRACULOUS ECONOMIC DEVELOPMENT SUCCESSES IN THE WORLD.
STARTING FROM A WAR-TORN ECONOMY WITH SCARCE NATURAL
RESOURCES, VIRTUALLY NO INDUSTRIAL INFRASTRUCTURE, AND FEW
ENTREPRENEURS, KOREA, NEVERTHELESS, EXPANDED ITS GROSS
NATIONAL PRODUCT (GNP) BY MORE THAN 25 TIMES SINCE THEN.
BECAUSE DEVELOPMENT HAS BEEN STRONGLY GUIDED BY THE STATE,
AND THE PRESIDENT HAS HELD DOMINANT POWER IN THE STATE'S
GOVERNING APPARATUS, KOREAN PRESIDENTS HAVE PLAYED A
DOMINATING ROLE IN THIS PROCESS. PRECISELY HOW THEY PLAYED
THAT ROLE, HOWEVER, IS THE EMPIRICAL ISSUE POSED IN THIS
ARTICLE. COMPARING THE PATTERNS OF PRESIDENTIAL DECISION-
MAKING AND THE ROLE OF BUREAUCRATS IN IT, UNDER PRESIDENT
PARK OF THE 1970S AND UNDER PRESIDENT CHUN OF THE 1980S,
THIS ARTICLE FIRST TRIES TO IDENTIFY THOSE FACTORS THAT
DETERMINE THE RELATIVE STRENGTH OF PRESIDENTIAL POWER VIS-
AVIS CAREER BUREAUCRATS. THEN IT SEEKS TO EXPLAIN, WITHIN
THE FRAMEWORK OF THESE FACTORS, THE DYNAMIC RELATIONSHIP
BETWEEN POLITICAL AUTHORITY AND BUREAUCRATIC EXPERTISE.

02262 CHUNG, E.S.
TRANSITION TO DEMOCRACY IN SOUTH KOREA
ASIAN PROFILE, 17(1) (FEB 89), 25-38.
IN SOUTH KOREA, THERE HAVE BEEN AT LEAST THREE RECENT
REGIME TRANSITIONS: 1960-1961, 1979-1981, AND 1987-1988.
THESE TRANSITIONAL PERIODS PRESENTED SIGNIFICANT
OPPORTUNITIES FOR THE COUNTRY TO MOVE TOWARDS DEMOCRACY. THE
FIRST TWO TRANSITIONS MISCARRIED, BUT THE THIRD ONE HAS SO
FAR BEEN SUCCESSFUL.

02263 CHUNG, J.M.
ELITE ORIENTATION CHANGE AND POLICY CHANGE IN THE POST-
STALIN SOVIET UNION: A GENERATIONAL APPROACH
DISSERTATION ABSTRACTS INTERNATIONAL, 50(1) (JUL 89),
245-A.

THE AUTHOR ENDEAVORS TO EXPLAIN THE RECURRENT SOVIET REFORM EFFORTS IN TERMS OF SOVIET ELITE STRUCTURE, PARTICULARLY THE ORIENTATIONAL STRUCTURE OF THE SOVIET POLITICAL ELITE, DEFINED AS FULL MEMBERS OF THE CENTRAL COMMITTEE OF THE CPSU. HE RELIES HEAVILY ON THE CONCEPT OF POLITICAL GENERATION AND THE GENERATIONAL MODEL OF SOVIET POLITICS. HE CONCLUDES THAT THE CHANGE IN SOVIET ELITE ORIENTATION IS CLOSELY RELATED TO THE RECURRENT EFFORTS FOR SYSTEMATIC REFORM DURING THE POST-STALIN PERIOD.

02264 CHUNG, J.S.
ECONOMIC COOPERATION BETWEEN SOUTH AND NORTH KOREA: PROBLEMS AND POSSIBILITIES
KOREA OBSERVER, XX(1) (SPR 89), 1-20.
ECONOMIC CONTACTS ARE A POLITICALLY MORE NEUTRAL FORM OF BENEFICIAL INTER-KOREAN INTERACTION THAN THE REUNION OF SEPARATED FAMILIES, THE EXCHANGE OF MAIL, OR FREE TRAVEL. ECONOMIC CONTACTS CAN EASILY BE THE INITIAL CONCRETE FORM OF SIGNIFICANT COOPERATION BETWEEN THE TWO KOREAS. CLOSER INTER-KOREAN ECONOMIC RELATIONS WOULD PRODUCE OBVIOUS ECONOMIC BENEFITS FOR BOTH COUNTRIES. MOREOVER, SUSTAINED INTER-KOREAN ECONOMIC COOPERATION COULD HELP TO REDUCE TENSIONS ON THE PENINSULA AND CREATE AN ENVIRONMENT FOR CLOSER NON-ECONOMIC TIES.

02265 CHUNG, W.C.
THE ASSESSMENT OF JAPANESE FOREIGN DIRECT INVESTMENT IN KOREA: A RISK PERSPECTIVE IN KOREAN INDUSTRIALIZATION POLICIES
DISSERTATION ABSTRACTS INTERNATIONAL, 50(2) (AUG 89), 540-A.
GENERALLY, JAPANESE FOREIGN INVESTMENT PROJECTS ARE STRUCTURALLY SECURED BY JOINT VENTURE STRATEGY, BY DOMESTIC AND MULTILATERAL INVESTMENT GUARANTEE SCHEMES, AND BY A TRILATERAL COALITION OF POLITICIANS, BUREAUCRATS, AND FINANCING INSTITUTIONS. YET JAPANESE MANAGERIAL AND ORGANIZATIONAL CHARACTERISTICS ARE OFTEN VIEWED AS A RISK FACTOR IN HOST COUNTRIES. KOREA IS REGARDED BY JAPANESE PRIVATE INVESTORS AS A COUNTRY WITH HIGH MARKET ATTRACTIVENESS BUT HIGH POLITICAL RISK.

02266 CHUNYAN, W.; XIMING, W.
DENG XIAOPING ON PEACE AND WAR
BEIJING REVIEW, 32(14) (APR 89), 20-23.
THE AUTHORS ANALYZE DENG XIAOPING'S THOUGHT ON HOW FUTURE WORLD WARS CAN BE AVOIDED. THEY EXPLORE DENG'S ASSERTION THAT WAR CAN BE AVOIDED BY RELYING ON THE THREE FORCES (THE THIRD WORLD, JAPAN AND EUROPE, AND THE PEOPLE OF THE TWO SUPERPOWERS) AND THE THREE WAYS (THE INTERNATIONAL APPLICATION OF THE ONE COUNTRY-TWO SYSTEMS CONCEPT, MUTUAL ADVANCEMENT THROUGH JOINT DEVELOPMENT, AND THIRD WORLD COOPERATION).

02267 CHURCH, C.
THE SWISS WAY OF CHANGE: POLITICS SINCE THE 1987 ELECTION
WORLD TODAY, 45(7) (JUL 89), 117-121.
THE EVIDENCE OF SWISS POLITICS SINCE 1987 SHOWS THAT CHANGE CAN COME IN DIFFERENT WAYS—SOMETIMES DESPITE, RATHER THAN BECAUSE OF, ELECTIONS AND REFERENDA. THUS, WHILE THE ENVIRONMENT HAS CONTINUED TO BE A MAJOR CONCERN, WITH IMPLICATIONS FOR FOREIGN AS WELL AS DOMESTIC POLITICS, THE SWISS APPROACH HAS BEEN REPLETE WITH AMBIGUITIES. AND ISSUES THAT WERE NOT DISCUSSED MUCH IN THE 1987 ELECTION, LIKE EUROPE, OR DREAMED OF, LIKE THE LEBANESE CONNECTION, HAVE DOMINATED EVENTS SINCE. OVERALL, THE SWISS MUST MAKE ADJUSTMENTS TO LONG-STANDING PRACTICES, EVEN IF THE POPULATION DOES NOT ALWAYS HARM TO THE PROSPECT. FOR ALL ITS SATISFACTION WITH ITS POLITICAL SYSTEM, SWITZERLAND WILL HAVE TO ACCEPT SOME DISSENT AND CHANGE IF IT IS TO BE RECONCILED WITH EMERGING CHALLENGES.

02268 CHURCH, C.H.
BEHIND THE CONSOCIATIONAL SCREEN: POLITICS IN CONTEMPORARY SWITZERLAND
WEST EUROPEAN POLITICS, 12(2) (APR 89), 35-54.
EXISTING APPROACHES DO NOT AID UNDERSTANDING OF CURRENT DEVELOPMENTS IN SWITZERLAND BECAUSE OF THEIR ACCEPTANCE OF CONSOCIATIONALISM. THIS IS LESS CONVINCING AND RELEVANT THAN HAS BEEN APPRECIATED. DESPITE BEING REDEFINED AS DECISION-MAKING OR CONSENSUS POLITICS, IT STILL IGNORES THE NATIONALLY MINDED REALITIES OF SWISS POLITICAL CULTURE AND ITS NEW PROBLEMS. INSTEAD OF CONSOCIATIONALISM ELIMINATING POLITICAL DIVISIONS IN SWITZERLAND NEW ENVIRONMENTAL ISSUES AND FORCES EMERGED FROM THE 1970S. THESE NOW CONSTITUTE A NEW ELEMENT IN SWISS POLITICS AT ODDS WITH THE PREVAILING POLITICAL CULTURE. YET THEY ARE ALSO INFLUENCED BY THIS AND FURTHER GROWTH DEPENDS ON ITS ADAPTABILITY.

02269 CHURCH, F.F.
PROCLAIM LIBERTY THROUGHOUT ALL THE LAND
CHURCH AND STATE, 42(10) (NOV 89), 17 (233)-20 (236).
BECAUSE OF THE FIRST AMENDMENT AND VARIOUS OTHER LAWS ESTABLISHING THE SEPARATION OF CHURCH AND STATE, RELIGION PROSPERS IN THE UNITED STATES UNCOMPROMISED BY THE TAINT OF GOVERNMENT COLLUSION. THE FOUNDING FATHERS ARGUED THAT ANY COLLUSION BETWEEN CHURCH AND STATE WOULD CORRODE THE FOUNDATIONS OF BOTH, AND THEY WERE RIGHT.

02270 CHURCHWARD, L.
CONGRESSIONAL POLITICS - SOVIET STYLE
ARENA, (88) (SPR 89), 17-21.
THIS REPORT ASSESSES THE FIRST SESSION OF THE SOVIET UNION'S NEWLY ESTABLISHED CONGRESS OF PEOPLE'S DEPUTIES IN MOSCOW. IT HAS HAILED AS A PRODUCT OF RESTRUCTURING AND A DEMONSTRATION OF SOVIET DEMOCRACY, ALTHOUGH THERE WERE CONTRADICTIONS REVEALED IN THE WORK OF THE CONGRESS IN THE SOCIAL, ECONOMIC AND POLITICAL ARENAS, IT ANALYZES THE ELECTIONS TO THE CONGRESS WHICH WERE THE MOST DEMOCRATIC SINCE 1918, ALTHOUGH IT WAS NOT ENTIRELY SO. MATTERS OF THE ECONOMY, THE PRESS, SEPARATION OF POWERS, AND ROTATION OF OFFICE WERE EACH CONSIDERED. IT CONCLUDES THAT THE LINES OF POLITICAL AUTHORITY ARE BLURRED AND BEYOND THAT STANDS THE UNDERLYING CONTRADICTION BETWEEN THE STATE AND CIVIL SOCIETY.

02271 CHURCHWARD, L.
THE SOVIET ELECTIONS
ARENA, (87) (WIN 89), 44-46.
THIS ARTICLE REPORTS IN GENERAL AND PARTICULAR ON THE RECENT ELECTIONS IN THE SOVIET UNION WHICH HAVE REVIVED INTEREST IN THE ELECTORAL POLITICS OF THAT COUNTRY. IT EXAMINES THE ELECTORAL SYSTEM AND DISCUSSES THE CHANGES TO THE ELECTORAL LAW AND PRACTICE AND THE INDIRECT ELECTIONS FOR THE SOCIAL ORGANIZATIONS. IT OFFERS INTERPRETATION OF ELECTION RESULTS AND CONCLUDES THAT NEW CIRCUMSTANCES MAY ALLOW THE EMERGENCE OF THE PROFESSIONAL POLITICIAN IN SOVIET LIFE.

02272 CIESLAK, W.
THE WORKING CLASS IN THE COMPUTER AGE: CAN THEY DEFEND THEMSELVES
WORLD MARXIST REVIEW, 32(4) (APR 89), 75-77.
TECHNOLOGICAL PROGRESS IS OPENING UP INCREASINGLY IMPORTANT NEW AREAS OF CLASS STRUGGLE. BUT WHILE IT LIGHTENS AND UPLIFTS WORK, IT OBEYS THE CAPITALIST LOGIC OF EASY PROFIT. THE NEW TECHNOLOGIES ARE BEING USED ON A WIDER SCALE TO DOMINATE LABOUR RELATIONS BY REDUCING JOBS, INCREASING EXPLOITATION AND CONTROL, AND BY MANIPULATING WORKER CONSCIOUSNESS. ORGANISED LABOUR MUST COUNTER THE MONOPOLIES' DRIVE WITH ITS OWN POLICY ON NEW TECHNOLOGIES, BECAUSE EVEN UNDER CAPITALISM A PURPOSEFUL STRUGGLE MAY RESTRICT THEIR ABUSE AND GEAR THEM TO PROGRESSIVE ENDS. A NEW DEMOCRATISATION OF THE ECONOMY MUST GIVE WORKERS FULL PARITY WITH MANAGEMENT. A GUARANTEE OF QUALIFIED AND USEFUL WORK, PROFESSIONAL GROWTH AND ADVANCEMENT MUST BE THE YARDSTICK OF WORKER CONTROL AND INFLUENCE ON PERSONNEL AND BUSINESS MATTERS.

02273 CIMA, R.J.
VIETNAM IN 1988: THE BRINK OF RENEWAL
ASIAN SURVEY, XXIX(1) (JAN 89), 64-72.
1988 WAS A YEAR OF POSSIBILITIES AND INERTIA FOR VIETNAM. LIKE ITS NEIGHBORS CHINA AND THE USSR, THE NATION ENGAGED IN REFORMS THAT ATTEMPTED A FUNDAMENTAL RESTRUCTURING OF THE COMMUNIST ETHIC. CONSERVATIVE ELEMENTS IN GOVERNMENT BALKED AT SOME OF THE MORE RADICAL REFORMS AND VIETNAM'S ECONOMY SUFFERED ACCORDINGLY: INFLATION SOARED TO 1000 PERCENT AND UNEMPLOYMENT ROSE ABOVE 20 PERCENT. HOWEVER, ON THE FOREIGN POLICY FRONT, ATTEMPTS AT CHANGE WERE MORE SUCCESSFUL. 1988 MARKED MORE PROGRESS TOWARDS VIETNAM'S DISENGAGEMENT FROM CAMBODIA THAN SEVERAL OF THE PREVIOUS YEARS COMBINED. VIETNAM'S ATTEMPTS TO INCREASE INTERNATIONAL STANDING, ATTRACT FOREIGN INVESTMENT, AND SECURE FOREIGN AID WERE ALSO MODESTLY SUCCESSFUL. RESISTANCE TO REFORM REAMINS STRONGLY ENTRENCHED, BUT THE COURSE OF CHANGE SEEMS IRREVERSIBLE.

02274 CIMA, R.J.
VIETNAM'S ECONOMIC REFORM: APPROACHING THE 1990S
ASIAN SURVEY, 29(8) (AUG 89), 786-799.
THIS ARTICLE ANALYZES THE NEED FOR ECONOMIC REFORM AS VIETNAMESE LEADERS ARE CONSTRAINED BY ECONOMIC CONSIDERATIONS IN THE DETERMINATION OF NATIONAL POLICY. IT EXPLORES THE PRELUDE TO CHANGE WHICH BEGAN IN THE LATE 1978-EARYL 1979 PERIOD; THEN THE FACTORS WHICH ARE RESISTANT TO CHANGE. DESCRIBED ARE DOMESTIC AND FOREIGN POLICY INNOVATIONS AND THEN THE PROSPECTS FOR THE 1990S ARE OFFERED.

02275 CIMBALA, S.J.
NATO STRATEGY AND NUCLEAR ESCALATION
JOHN SPIERS PUBLISHING, BRIGHTON, SUSSEX, GB, 1989, 256.
THE AUTHOR FOCUSES ON THE KEY DOCTRINES, PLANS, AND POLICIES AT THE CENTER OF THE CONTROVERSY ABOUT WESTERN DETERRENCE AND DEFENSE. HE EXAMINES NATO'S BASIC CONCEPTS OF ESCALATION AND ESCALATION CONTROL IN TERMS OF THEIR LOGICAL CONSISTENCY AND THE IMPLICATIONS FOR POLICY AND STRATEGY.

02276 CLAD, J.
ANATOMY OF A RED REVOLUTION
FAR EASTERN ECONOMIC REVIEW, 141(30) (JUL 88), 12-13.

A SERIES OF DICUMENTS SEIZED BY THE PHILIPPINE MILITARY IN A RAID REVEAL SIGNIFICANT INFORMATION REGARDING THE COMMUNIST PARTY OF THE PHILPPINES AND THE NEW PEOPLE'S ARMY THE DOCUMENTS REVEALED AN EXTENSIVE BANKING NETWORK AND A BUDGET THAT DOUBLED IN 1987. IT ALSO OUTLINES PLANS FOR A NATIONWIDE "STRATEGIC COUNTER OFFENSIVE" IN 1989. THE PARTY AND THE NPA ARE EXPANDING THEIR RANGE OF OPERATIONS AND SOON EVEN AREAS NEAR THE CAPITAL MAY BE THREATENED.

02277 CLAD, J.
COMMISSION'S OMISSIONS
FAR EASTERN ECONOMIC REVIEW, 141(31) (AUG 88), 18-19.
PHILLIPPINE PRESIDENT CORAZON AQUINO'S FIRST PRESIDENTIAL DECREE WAS TO CREATE THE PRESIDENTIAL COMMISSION ON GOOD GOVERNMENT. ITS AIM WAS TO RECOVER "ILL-GOTTEN HEALTH" OF FORMER PRESIDENT MARCOS AND HIS "CRONIES." HOWEVER, RECENT DEVELOPMENTS HAVE RESULTED IN AQUINO CHARGING THE COMMISSION WITH "INEPTNESS, INCOMPETENCE, AND CORRUPTION." ALTHOUGH THE COMMISSION HAS FILED 40 CIVIL SUITS AGAINST VARIOUS MARCOS ASSOCIATES, NONE HAVE SINCE BEEN LITIGATED.

02278 CLAD, J.; CHANDA, N.
HOLDING OUT FOR MORE
FAR EASTERN ECONOMIC REVIEW, 141(32) (AUG 88), 28-29.
TALKS ON THE US BASES IN THE PHILIPPINES WERE SUSPENDED AGAIN AS THE PHILIPPINE GOVERNMENT STUCK TO THEIR DEMAND FOR COMPENSATION OF APPROXIMATELY US $1 BILLION A YEAR. THE US OFFER WAS ABOUT HALF OF THAT FIGURE ALONG WITH A SIZABLE INCREASE IN ECONOMIC AND MILITARY-GRANT AID. ALTHOUGH SOME FEEL THAT THE FILLIPINOS DO NOT WANT THE TALKS TO SUCCEED, MOST ANALYSTS AGREE THAT THE TOUGH STANCE HAS POLITICALLY BENEFICIAL TO THE GOVERNMENT AT A TIME WHEN NATIONALISM WAS HIGH. AS OF YET, THE ULTIMATE FUTURE OF THE USPHILIPPINE BASE AGREEMENT WHICH EXPIRES IN 1991 IS UNKNOWN.

02279 CLAD, J.
INTENSIFYING THE STRUGGLE
FAR EASTERN ECONOMIC REVIEW, 141(31) (AUG 88), 18-19.
ALTHOUGH THE COMMUNIST NEW PEOPLE'S ARMY HAS CONTINUED THEIR ATTEMPTS AT INSURGENCY, THEY ARE EXPERIENCING INCREASED RESISTANCE FROM MANY FRONTS. A PHILIPPINE MILITARY CONCEPT CALLED THE "SPECIAL OPERATIONS TEAM" IS SLOWLY BECOMING AN EFFECTIVE COUNTER-INSURGENCY TOOL AS IS A COMBINATION OF PUBLIC WORKS SPENDING AND BETTER FUNCTIONING PEACE-ANDORDER COUNCILS. COMMUNIST PARTY MILITARY DOCUMENTS THAT WERE SEIZED IN A RECENT RAID REVEAL THE PROBLEMS THAT THE NPA FACES WITH THE INCREASED RESISTANCE FROM A "THREELAYERED APPROACH THAT INTEGRATES CIVILIANS, POLICE, AND MILITARY INTO ONE WORKABLE SECURITY PLAN."

02280 CLAD, J.
MANILA'S HARDY PRIVATEERS
FAR EASTERN ECONOMIC REVIEW, 141(27) (JUL 88), 88-91.
ANNOUNCED SOON AFTER HER ELECTION, AN AMBITIOUS PRIVATIZATION PROGRAM HAS BECOME A CENTERPIECE FOR COROZAN AQUINO'S PRESIDENCY. ALTHOUGH SHE HAS SPOKEN REPEATEDLY IN UNCOMPROMISING TERMS ABOUT HER COMMITMENT TO HAVE THE JOB DONE, THE REALITY IN THE PHILIPPINES IS OTHERWISE. THE POTENTIAL BUYERS OF THE NEARLY 300 GOVERNMENT-CONTROLLED CORPORATIONS ARE MANY, BUT A LACK OF POLITICAL WILL TO DO THE JOB HAS RESULTED IN STALLING TACTICS BY THE GOVERNMENT. SOURCES CLOSE TO THE PROCESS CONSIDER THE PROGAM A FOREGONE FAILURE.

02281 CLAD, J.
PATIENCE WEARS THIN
FAR EASTERN ECONOMIC REVIEW, 141(27) (JUL 88), 12-13.
WHILE PHILIPPINE PRESIDENT CORAZON AQUINO REMAINS SILENT ON THE FUTURE OF US BASES IN HER COUNTRY, FOREIGN SECRETARY RAUL MANGLAPUS HAS BEEN QUITE VOCAL ON THE POINT THAT WASHINGTON NEEDS TO "PAY UP OR GET OUT." FILIPINO DEMANDS FOR GREATLY INCREASED AID AND A BILL PROBITING NUCLEAR WEAPONS THAT WAS ENDORSED BY THE PHILIPPINE SENATE HAVE INCREASED THE STRAIN BETWEEN THE US AND THE PHILIPPINES.

02282 CLAD, J.
REDUNDANT RHETORIC
FAR EASTERN ECONOMIC REVIEW, 141(34) (AUG 88), 26.
PHILIPPINE VICE-PRESIDENT SALVADOR LAUREL HAS COMPLETED HIS POLITICAL ESTRANGEMENT FROM PRESIDENT CORAZON AQUINO, A PROCESS THAT BEGAN ALMOST THE DAY THEY TOOK POWER ALMOST TWO AND ONE HALF YEARS PREVIOUSLY. LAUREL FORMALIZED THE BREAK IN A STRONGLY WORDED LETTER THAT CONDEMNED AQUINO FOR DOING NOTHING WHILE THAT NATION HAD GONE FROM BAD TO WORSE. THE MOVE IS REGARDED AS UNLIKELY TO IMPROVE LAUREL'S POLITICAL INFLUENCE, AND IS EXPECTED TO HAVE LITTLE PRACTICAL EFFECT.

02283 CLAD, J.
TARGETING THE LEGAL LEFT
FAR EASTERN ECONOMIC REVIEW, 141(29) (JUL 88), 23.
RECENT KILLINGS OF TRADE UNIONISTS, LAWYERS, AND OTHER PERSONS ASSOCIATED WITH THE PHILIPPINES' LEGAL LEFT HAVE HIGHLIGHTED THAT PRESIDENT CORAZON AQUINO'S GRIP ON THE

COUNTRY IS STILL INCOMPLETE. THE LATEST CRIMES SHOW NEW TENDENCIES: THE SOCIAL ORIGINS OF AN INCREASING NUMBER OF THE VICTIMS SUGGEST THAT KILLERS ARE PREPARED TO TARGET POLITICALLY ACTIVE MEMBERS OF THE MIDDLE CLASS. ALTHOUGH THE BLAME IS LARGELY UNWARRANTED, MANY BLAME THE GOVERNMENT FOR THE CONTINUED VIOLENCE.

02284 CLAD, J.
THE OBSTACLE COURSE
FAR EASTERN ECONOMIC REVIEW, 142(50) (DEC 89), 28.
INDIA'S NEWLY ELECTED PRIME MINISTER V.P. SINGH CONSOLIDATED HIS GRIP ON HIS OWN JANATA DAL PARTY, BUT AT A PRICE THAT BODES IL FOR HIS GOVERNMENT'S FUTURE COHESION. HIS POLICIES OF EXCLUSION COOPTION OF COMPETING PARTY MEMBERS IS INDICATION OF BOTH HIS DETERMINATION TO RULE THE JANATA DAL, AND THE WEAKNESS OF HIS INITIAL HOLD ON THE PARTY. THE FUTURE OF THE MINORITY GOVERNMENT WILL BE LARGELY DETERMINED BY HOW SINGH DEALS WITH ISSUES SUCH AS THE CORRUPTION OF PAST POLITICIANS IN THE GANDHI ADMINISTRATION, REFORM OF INDIA'S GOVERNMENT CONTROLLED TELEVISION AND RADIO NETWORK, ETHNIC TENSIONS, AND RELATIONS WITH NEPAL AND SRI LANKA.

02285 CLAGGETT, W.
PARTISAN ACQUISITION, POLICY RELEVANT PARTIES AND REALIGNMENTS
WESTERN POLITICAL QUARTERLY, 42(2) (JUN 89), 225-244.
THIS STUDY ATTEMPTS TO EXPLAIN THE ENDURING INTERCOHORT DIFFERENCES IN PARTISAN ACQUISITION. THE RESULTS INDICATE THAT THESE ENDURING GENERATIONAL DIFFERENCES ARE A FUNCTION OF COHORTS' DIRECT EXPOSURE TO POLICY RELEVANT POLITICAL PARTIES DURING THEIR YOUNG ADULT YEARS. THIS RELATIONSHIP HOLDS FOR BOTH THOSE WITH AND WITHOUT PARTISAN PARENTS, EXCEPT THAT THE MAGNITUDE OF IMPACT IS PROBABLY REDUCED FOR THOSE WITH PARTISAN PARENTS. THE ENDURING INTERCOHORT DIFFERENCES IN PARTISAN ACQUISITION AMONG THOSE WITH PARTISAN PARENTS IS SEEMINGLY NOT DUE TO AN ENVIRONMENTALLY INDUCED ALTERATION IN THE EFFECTIVENESS OF PARENTAL PARTISAN SOCIALIZATION.

02286 CLAHE, F.; VORHIES, F.
RELIGION, LIBERTY AND ECONOMIC DEVELOPMENT: AN EMPIRICAL INVESTIGATION
PUBLIC CHOICE, 62(3) (SEP 89), 201-216.
THE EMIRICAL EVIDENCE OF THIS PAPER SHOWS POSITIVE INTERRELATIONSHIPS BETWEEN JUDEO-CHRISTIAN VALUES, POLITICAL ECONOMIC LIBERTY AND ECONOMIC DEVELOPMENT. THE EVIDENCE DOES NOT SUPPORT THE NULL HYPOTHESIS THAT RELIGION, LIBERTY AND DEVELOPMENT ARE UNRELATED. SOCIAL VALUES AND POLITICAL LIBERALISM MERIT CONSIDERATION AS INFLUENCING FACTORS FOR ECONOMIC DEVELOPMENT.

02287 CLANCY, T.
VIEW FROM THE FOURTH ESTATE: LOOK WHO'S SINKING OUR NAVY-- AND OUR ARMY
PARAMETERS, XIX(1) (MAR 89), 109-111.
THE U.S. MILITARY WAS MEANT TO BE NEITHER A JOBS PROGRAM NOR ANOTHER FEDERAL BUREAUCRACY, ALTHOUGH IT HAS BECOME SOMETHING OF BOTH. ITS REAL PURPOSE IS NOT TO PROVIDE FULFILLING CAREERS. ITS GOALS ARE THE PRESERVATION, PROTECTION, AND DEFENSE OF AMERICAN FREEDOM THROUGH THE APPLICATION OF STRUCTURED VIOLENCE. PEOPLE, NOT WEAPONS, FIGHT WARS AND THE MILITARY NEEDS TO RESTORE THE WARRIOR ETHIC. THE MILITARY MUST CHANGE ITS PROGRAMS TO IDENTIFY THE WARRIOR-COMMANDERS, TO NURTURE THEM, TO SELECT THE BEST, AND TO GIVE THEM THE SUPPORT AND EXPERIENCE THEY NEED TO FULFILL THEIR WARTIME MISSIONS.

02288 CLAPP, R.A.J.
REPRESENTING RECIPROCITY, REPRODUCING DOMINATION: IDEOLOGY AND THE LABOR PROCESS IN LATIN AMERICAN CONTRACT FARMING
JOURNAL OF PEASANT STUDIES, 16(1) (OCT 88), 5-39.
THIS ARTICLE EXAMINES CONFLICTING REPRESENTATIONS OF CONTRACT FARMING IN LATIN AMERICA. CONTRACT FARMING ADDRESSES MANY OF THE CONTRADICTIONS OF WAGE LABOUR IN AGRICULTURE, BUT GENERATES ITS OWN. FOR THE COMPANY THESE CONTRADICTIONS INCLUDE INDIRECT CONTROL OF THE LABOUR PROCESS AND THE PROBLEM OF UNCERTAIN SUPPLY; FOR THE FARMER THEY INCLUDE DISGUISED PROLETARIANIZATION AND SELFEXPLOITATION. THE INDIRECT NATURE OF CONTROL MAKES THE UNDERSTANDING AND RELIABILITY OF EACH PARTNER CRUCIAL; THE UNDERSTANDING OF THE CONTRACT IS THEREFORE THE SUBJECT OF MUTED BUT PERVASIVE STRUGGLE. A MORAL ECONOMY OF THE CONTRACT OFFERS ONE FRAMEWORK FOR UNDERSTANDING THE POLITICS OF REPRESENTATION IN CONTRACT FARMING.

02289 CLARK, A.
QUIET REVOLUTION
REASON, 21(3) (JUL 89), 16-23.
ALTHOUGH THE PERIOD OF "UNREST" IN SOUTH AFRICA SEEMS TO TO HAVE SUBSIDED, A QUIET REVOLUTION IS GAINING POWER. SOUTH AFRICANS FROM ACROSS THE COUNTRY'S NUMEROUS DIVIDES ARE STRUGGLING TO BUILD AN ECONOMY UNHINDERED BY THE STATE'S ALL-PERVASIVE RESTRICTIONS. THEIR SUCCESS IS MANIFESTED IN THE

CHANGES THAT INCREASING BLACK ECONOMIC POWER HAS FORCED UPON THE SOUTH AFRICAN GOVERNMENT. AS BLACK BUYING POWER INCREASES, CONCUMER BOYCOTTS ARE BECOMING AN INCREASINGLY EFFECTIVE TOOL OF THE BLACK COMMUNITY. SIMPLY PUT, ECONOMIC GROWTH IS UNDERMINING THE FOUNDATIONS OF APARTHEID.

02290 CLARK, C.
TAIWAN'S POLITICAL ECONOMY AND THE EUROPEAN COMMUNITY
ASIAN PROFILE, 17(6) (DEC 89), 481-496.
THIS PAPER DESCRIBES CURRENT TRADE RELATIONS BETWEEN THE EUROPEAN COMMUNITY AND THE REPUBLIC OF CHINA AS A BASEMARK FOR EVALUATING IMPORTANT EVOLVING ECONOMIC RELATIONS. THE FIRST SECTION BRIEFLY SUMMARIZES TAIWAN'S POLITICAL ECONOMY; THE SECOND CHARTS THE EVOLUTION OF TRADE BETWEEN THE E.E.C. COUNTRIES AND TAIWAN; AND THE THIRD PROVIDES MORE DETAILED DATA ON THE COMMODITY COMPOSITION OF EUROPEAN TRADE WITH THE R.O.C. FINALLY, THE CONCLUSION SPECULATES FROM THESE DATA ABOUT THE FUTURE OF TAIWAN'S TIES WITH THE COMMUNITY.

02291 CLARK, D.; ASTUTO, T.
REAGAN'S FINAL REPORT CARD
SOCIETY, 26(4) (MAY 89), 32-39.
THE PURPOSE OF THE ARTICLE IS TO DETERMINE WHETHER THE ACTIONS OF THE REAGAN ADMINISTRATION PRODUCE A SIGNIFICANT ENDURING CHANGE IN FEDERAL EDUCATION POLICY. IT CONCLUDES THAT A MAJOR REDIRECTION OF FEDERAL EDUCATION POLICY HAS OCCURRED AND THAT THE SCOPE OF THE REDIRECTION WILL BE BROADENED AND MANY OF THE CHANGES WILL BECOME INSTITUTION-ALIZED DURING A NEW ERA OF FEDERAL EDUCATION POLICY. SOME OF THE EFFECTS OF THIS REDIRECTION INCLUDE: THE CONTINUED GROWTH AND INDEPENDENCE OF THE STATE GOVERNMENTS IN EDUCATION POLICY DEVELOPMENT, INCREASED PERFORMANCE STANDARDS, AND AN EMPHASIS ON PARENTAL CHOICE, TRADITIONAL VALUES, AND THE BASICS IN EDUCATION.

02292 CLARK, J.; DARCY, R.; HADLEY, C.D.
POLITICAL AMBITION AMONG MEN AND WOMEN STATE PARTY LEADERS
TESTING THE COUNTERSOCIALIZATION PERSPECTIVE
AMERICAN POLITICS QUARTERLY, 17(2) (APR 89), 194-207.
WHILE DIFFERENCES BETWEEN MEN AND WOMEN IN POLITICAL BEHAVIOR HAVE DECLINED, WOMEN REMAIN UNDERREPRESENTED IN PUBLIC OFFICE IN AMERICA. STUDIES INDICATE THAT EVEN WOMEN IN ELITE POSITIONS IN POLITICAL PARTIES HAVE LESS AMBITION FOR ELECTIVE OFFICE THAN THEIR MALE COUNTERPARTS. THIS ARTICLE EXAMINES THE COUNTERSOCIALIZATION THEORY TO SEE WHETHER POLITICALLY AMBITIOUS WOMEN UNDERGO SIGNIFICANTLY DIFFERENT EXPERIENCES FROM NONAMBITIOUS WOMEN AND FROM AMBITIOUS MEN OR WHETHER FACTORS LEADING TO POLITICAL AMBITION ARE THE SAME FOR BOTH MEN AND WOMEN. MEN AND WOMEN STATE CONVENTION DELEGATES IN 1984 WERE ASKED QUESTIONS REGARDING THEIR DESIRE FOR FUTURE ELECTIVE PUBLIC OFFICES AND THEIR PAST POLITICAL EXPERIENCES. THERE WAS A SIGNIFICANT DIFFERENCE IN THE LEVEL OF POLITICAL AMBITION OF MALE AND FEMALE DELEGATES. HOWEVER, THE CAUSES OF POLITICAL AMBITION APPEAR TO BE DIFFUSE, AND FACTORS LEADING TO POLITICAL AMBITION ARE SIMILAR FOR BOTH MEN AND WOMEN.

02293 CLARK, J.; CLARK, C.
WYOMING WOMEN'S ATTITUDES TOWARD THE MX: THE "OLD" V. "NEW" GENDER GAP
JOURNAL OF POLITICAL SCIENCE, 17(1-2) (1989), 127.
THE AUTHORS RELY ON THE GENDER GAP TO EXPLAIN THE FAIRLY STRONG RELATIONSHIP THAT WAS FOUND BETWEEN GENDER AND ATTITUDES ABOUT PRESIDENT REAGAN'S PROPOSAL TO DEPLOY THE MX MISSILE IN A DENSE-PACK SYSTEM IN WYOMING. THEY ARGUE THAT THE GENDER GAP IN WYOMING IS A MIXTURE OF WHAT MAY BE CALLED THE "OLD" AND THE "NEW" GAPS. GENDER DIFFERENCES IN POLITICAL ATTITUDES AMONG WYOMING RESIDENTS STILL FOLLOW THE OLD PATTERN OF BEING LIMITED TO COMPARATIVELY FEW ISSUES CONCERNING INTERNATIONAL PEACE AND PERSONAL/FAMILY MORALITY AND SECURITY.

02294 CLARK, J.A.
JAPANESE FOREIGN POLICY AND THE WAR IN VIETNAM, 1964-1969
DISSERTATION ABSTRACTS INTERNATIONAL, 50(3) (SEP 89), 787-A.
THE AUTHOR EXAMINES THE VALUES AND ENVIRONMENTS THAT INFLUENCED JAPANESE FOREIGN POLICY DECISION-MAKING IN THE VIETNAM WAR FROM 1964 TO 1969. HE ALSO LOOKS AT HOW RELATIONS WITH THE UNITED STATES AFFECTED JAPANESE POLICY REGARDING VIETNAM.

02295 CLARK, M.
A HIGH-LEVEL FETE
MACLEAN'S (CANADA'S NEWS MAGAZINE), 102(28) (JUL 89), 20.
PARIS BRACING ITSELF FOR AN ONSLAUGHT OF TOURISTS AND DIGNITARIES AS IT PREPARES TO MARK THE 200TH ANNIVERSARY OF THE FRENCH REVOLUTION. THE 15TH ANNUAL ECONOMIC SUMMIT OF THE WORLD'S SEVEN MOST POWERFUL INDUSTRIAL NATIONS IS SCHEDULED TO BE HELD SIMULTANEOUSLY. THE AGENDA FOR THE SUMMIT IN PREVIOUS YEARS HAS BEEN DETERMINED BY TRADE AND FINANCIAL DISPUTES AND BY THE EAST WEST CONFLICT. HOWEVER, THERE HAVE BEEN FEWER DISPUTES THIS YEAR AND MANY OBSERVERS EXPECT A LOW LEVEL SUMMIT. OFFICIALS IN PARIS HAVE STATED

THE SUMMIT WILL FOCUS ON ENVIRONMENTAL PROBLEMS. MUCH RHETORIC IS EXPECTED, BUT ANALYSTS ARE UNSURE AS TO THE SUBSTANTIVE RESULTS OF THE SUMMIT.

02296 CLARK, M.
BRAVE NEW WORLD
MACLEAN'S (CANADA'S NEWS MAGAZINE), 102(2) (JAN 89), 12-13.
AFTER 2 1/2 YEARS OF NEGOTIATIONS AND A FURIOUS NATIONAL DEBATE, THE CANADA-U.S. FREE TRADE AGREEMENT WENT INTO EFFECT. NOW, BUSINESSMEN, BUREAUCRATS AND BARGAIN SHOPPERS ALIKE MUST LEARN TO LIVE WITH THE AGREEMENT--AND WITH THE CONFUSION ARISING FROM THE NEW REGULATIONS. THE CONFUSION OVER THE AGREEMENT IS UNLIKELY TO ABATE FOR A CONSIDERABLE LENGTH OF TIME. UNDER THE TERMS OF THE AGREEMENT, OVER THE NEXT SEVERAL YEARS CANADA AND THE UNITED STATES WILL ENTER INTO MORE THAN A DOZEN SEPARATE NEGOTIATIONS AND STUDIES OF TRADE AREAS, RANGING FROM THE FUTURE OF THE AUTOMOTIVE INDUSTRY AND THE DEFINITION OF SUBSIDIES TO THE USE OF FOOD COLORING.

02297 CLARK, M.
PARTY POLITICS
MACLEAN'S (CANADA'S NEWS MAGAZINE), 102(4) (JAN 89), 10-11.
AS NEW DEMOCRATIC PARTY LEADER ED BROADBENT PREPARES TO STEP DOWN, CANADA'S THIRD PARTY FACES A TIME OF SOUL-SEARCHING AND TESTING. ALTHOUGH THE NDP WON A RECORD NUMBER OF PARLIAMENT SEATS IN NOVEMBER, 1988, IT HAS FAILED TO ACHIEVE THE NEEDED BREAKTHROUGH IN POPULAR SUPPORT. CONTENDERS FOR BROADBENT'S POSITION ARE CONSIDERING VARIOUS SHIFTS IN POLICY AND IDEOLOGY IN AN ATTEMPT TO MAKE THE NDP MORE PALATABLE TO CANADA'S VOTERS. KEY ISSUES INCLUDE INTEGRATION OF WELFARE-STATE PHILOSOPHIES AND NEOCONSERVATIVE ECONOMICS, AND WHETHER THE NDP SHOULD CONTINUE TO SEEK POWER OR MERELY BE CONTENT TO SERVE AS THE SELF-APPOINTED CONSCIENCE OF THE NATION.

02298 CLARK, M.
PASSING ON THE FLAME
MACLEAN'S (CANADA'S NEWS MAGAZINE), 102(11) (MAR 89), 10-11.
THE DECISION OF NEW DEMOCRATIC PARTY LEADER EDWARD BROADBENT TO STEP DOWN ENDED MONTHS OF SPECULATION ABOUT HIS POLITICAL FUTURE. HOWEVER, THE FUTURE OF HIS PARTY IS STILL MUCH IN DOUBT. THE NDP FINDS ITSELF IN A POSITION OF INTENSE SOUL SEARCHING: ELECTORAL FAILURES HAVE NECESSITATED A FUNDAMENTAL RETHINKING ON MANY ISSUES. PARTY OFFICIALS OPTIMISTICALLY LABEL THIS PERIOD AS ONE OF "RENEWING," BUT WITHOUT THE HARD-WORKING, CHARISMATIC BROADBENT, THE PARTY HAS IT WORK CUT OUT FOR IT.

02299 CLARK, M.
SUMMIT SURPRISES
MACLEAN'S (CANADA'S NEWS MAGAZINE), 102(29) (JUL 89), 24.
THE 15TH ANNUAL ECONOMIC SUMMIT WAS TO CONTAIN NO SURPRISES, THE AGENDA HAD BEEN SET MONTHS IN ADVANCE. HOWEVER, MANY UNEXPECTED DEVELOPMENTS CHANGED THE ENTIRE OUTLOOK OF THE SUMMIT. JAPAN OFFERED A $52 BILLION AID PACKAGE FOR THE ENVIRONMENT AND THE DEVELOPING WORLD. MIKHAIL GORBACHEV INTERVENED WITH AN UNPRECEDENTED APPEAL FOR EAST-WEST ECONOMIC COOPERATION WHICH INCLUDED A JOINT ATTEMPT TO EASE THIRD WORLD DEBT. HOWEVER, PERHAPS THE BIGGEST SURPRISE CAME FROM UNINVITED GUESTS: LEADERS OF 24 OF THE WORLD'S POOREST NATIONS WERE BROUGHT FACE TO FACE WITH LEADERS OF THE ELITE ECONOMIC SUPERPOWERS BY FRENCH PRESIDENT FRANCOIS MITTERAND. THE RESULT WAS AN INCREASING CLAMOUR FOR "REGULAR CONSULTATIONS BETWEEN DEVELOPED AND DEVELOPING COUNTRIES AT THE SUMMIT LEVEL."

02300 CLARK, M.; ALLEN, G.; VAN DUSEN, L.
THE NINE-PER CENT BATTLE
MACLEAN'S (CANADA'S NEWS MAGAZINE), 102(26) (JUL 89), 8-10.
CANADIAN GOVERNMENT PROPOSALS FOR A NINE PER CENT FEDERAL GOODS AND SERVICES TAX (GST) HAVE BEEN MET WITH WIDE-RANGING CRIES OF OUTRAGE AND PLEAS FOR EXEMPTION. NO FEWER THAN 3,000 APPEALS FOR SPECIAL TREATMENT HAVE BEEN RECEIVED BY THE GOVERNMENT. THE SWEEPING PROPOSALS, DESIGNED TO RECTIFY THE PROBLEMS OF PREVIOUS TAX PROGRAMS, ARE DESTINED TO BE STRIDENTLY OPPOSED; WHATEVER THE FINAL OUTCOME, IT SEEMS AS IF THE CONSERVATIVE GOVERNMENT HAS ALREADY LOST THE BATTLE TO RENDER THE NEW TAX POLITICALLY PALATABLE.

02301 CLARK, M.L.
SEA, SPACE, AND ICE: NEW FRONTIERS IN INTERNATIONAL NEGOTIATION
DISSERTATION ABSTRACTS INTERNATIONAL, 50(1) (JUL 89), 250-A.
THE AUTHOR REVIEWS ELEVEN NEGOTIATION APPROACHES AND THREE CASE STUDIES, WITH THE GOAL OF IDENTIFYING ASPECTS OF THE INTERNATIONAL NEGOTIATION PROCESS THAT WOULD BE ESPECIALLY USEFUL IN A FUTURE WITHOUT GLOBAL REPRESSION. THE NEGOTIATION APPROACHES INCLUDE SEVERAL TYPES OF CONSENSUAL BEHAVIOR, GROUP DYNAMICS, AND BARGAINING TECHNIQUES. THE THREE CASE STUDIES ARE THE LAW OF THE SEA TREATY, THE 1967 OUTER SPACE TREATY, AND THE ANTARCTIC TREATY SYSTEM.

02302 CLARK, M.T.
THE SOVIET CAMPAIGN AGAINST THE U.S. STRATEGIC DEFENSE
INITIATIVE
DISSERTATION ABSTRACTS INTERNATIONAL, 50(5) (NOV 89),
1427-A.
THE THESIS OF THIS DISSERTATION IS THAT THE SOVIET
POLITICAL CAMPAIGN AGAINST THE U.S. STRATEGIC DEFENSE
INITIATIVE (SDI) IS DESIGNED TO PREVENT THE UNITED STATES
FROM DEPLOYING A BALLISTIC MISSILE DEFENSE (BMD) SYSTEM
CAPABLE OF REDUCING THE IMBALANCE IN U.S. SOVIET STRATEGIC
NUCLEAR FORCE (SNF) VULNERABILITIES. THE THESIS IS EXAMINED
IN TWO PARTS: BACKGROUND ON SOVIET CAPABILITIES FOR
POLITICAL OPERATIONS AND THE POLITICAL CAMPAIGN AGAINST SDI.

02303 CLARK, P. C. JR.
DIPLOMATIC RELATIONS BETWEEN THE UNITED STATES AND THE
SOMOZA GARCIA REGIME, 1933-1956
DISSERTATION ABSTRACTS INTERNATIONAL, 49(8) (FEB 89),
2381-A.
THE AUTHOR STUDIES UNITED STATES RELATIONS WITH
NICARAGUA SINCE 1933, CONCENTRATING ON THE PERIOD AFTER
ANASTASIO SOMOZA GARCIA CAME TO POWER. HIS PRIMARY FOCUS IS
WHETHER OR NOT THERE IS A HISTORICAL BASIS FOR THE
CONTENTION THAT SOMOZA GARCIA WAS KEPT IN POWER BY POLICIES
DESIGNED BY THE UNITED STATES GOVERNMENT.

02304 CLARK, S.G.
EMPLOYEE INVOLVEMENT PROGRAMS: WILL "WIN/WIN" WORK?
NATIONAL CIVIC REVIEW, 78(2) (MAR 89), 94-102.
MANAGERS SEE PARTICIPATORY QUALITY CIRCLES AS A
PRODUCTIVITY BOOSTER; UNIONS AND EMPLOYEE ACTIVISTS VIEW
THEM AS A MORALE AND JOB-SATISFACTION ENHANCER. ALTHOUGH
PRODUCTIVITY AND QUALITY IMPROVEMENT ARE THE RESPONSIBILITY
OF MANAGEMENT, EMPLOYEE-INVOLVEMENT APPROACHES - SUCH AS
QUALITY CIRCLES - PLACE MUCH OF THAT BURDEN IN THE LAPS OF
EMPLOYEES. WHAT'S IN IT FOR EMPLOYEES? THE ANSWER TO THAT
QUESTION WILL DETERMINE WHETHER "WIN/WIN" WILL WORK.

02305 CLARK, W. JR.
BURDENSHARING AND JAPAN
DEPARTMENT OF STATE BULLETIN (US FOREIGN POLICY), 88(2141)
(DEC 88), 30-31.
WILLIAM CLARK COMMENTS ON THE DEFENSE BURDENSHARING
PANEL OF THE HOUSE ARMED SERVICES COMMITTEE'S CONCLUSIONS
WITH REGARDS TO JAPAN. HE EXAMINES DEFENSE AND SECURITY-
RELATED AREAS, REGIONAL COOPERATION, HOST-NATION SUPPORT,
DEFENSE MISSIONS, DEVELOPMENT ASSISTANCE, AND "OUT OF AREA"
INTERESTS.

02306 CLARK, W. JR.
EFFORTS TOWARD PEACE AND RECONCILIATION IN ANGOLA
DEPARTMENT OF STATE BULLETIN (US FOREIGN POLICY), 89(2153)
(DEC 89), 31-32.
THE AUTHOR, WHO IS ACTING ASSISTANT SECRETARY OF STATE
FOR AFRICAN AFFAIRS, DISCUSSES THE ANGOLAN PEACE PROCESS. HE
DISCUSSES U.S. RELATIONS WITH ANGOLA, THE STEPS LEADING TO
GBADOLITE, AND THE GBADOLITE SUMMIT.

02307 CLARK, W. JR.
FY 1990 ASSISTANCE REQUEST FOR EAST ASIA AND THE PACIFIC
DEPARTMENT OF STATE BULLETIN (US FOREIGN POLICY), 89(2146)
(MAY 89), 49-53.
HONORING PRESIDENT BUSH'S PLEDGE TO OFFER ADDITIONAL
FOREIGN AID TO EAST ASIA AND THE PACIFIC REGION IS ESSENTIAL.
THE IMPORTANCE OF FOREIGN AID TO AMERICAN INTERESTS IN THE
ASIA PACIFIC AREA GOES FAR BEYOND DOLLARS AND CENTS.
AMERICAN AID PROGRAMS PROVIDE VISIBLE AND HIGHLY WELCOME
SYMBOLS OF THE UNITED STATES' LONG-TERM COMMITMENT TO REMAIN
ENGAGED IN THE REGION'S AFFAIRS.

02308 CLARK, W. JR.
US-JAPAN RELATIONS
DEPARTMENT OF STATE BULLETIN (US FOREIGN POLICY), 88(2141)
(DEC 88), 27-30.
DEPUTY ASSISTANT SECRETARY FOR EAST ASIAN AND PACIFIC
AFFAIRS WILLIAM CLARK DISCUSSES US-JAPAN RELATIONS. HE
ANALYZES THE CURRENT SITUATION AND TRENDS WITH REGARDS TO
ECONOMIC COOPERATION, DEFENSE COOPERATION, FOREIGN AID
COOPERATION, AND POLITICAL COOPERATION. HE COMMENTS ON
OVERALL RELATIONS AND THEIR DIRECTION AND STATES THAT
ALTHOUGH THERE HAVE BEEN BITTER TRADE DISPUTES, GENERALLY
RELATIONS BETWEEN THE US AND JAPAN ARE "EXCELLENT.

02309 CLARKE, H.D.; ACOCK, A.C.
NATIONAL ELECTIONS AND POLITICAL ATTITUDES: THE CASE OF
POLITICAL EFFICACY
BRITISH JOURNAL OF POLITICAL SCIENCE, 19(4) (OCT 89),
551-562.
THE AUTHORS UTILIZE CO-VARIANCE STRUCTURE ANALYSIS TO
INVESTIGATE THE EFFECTS OF VOTING, CAMPAIGN ACTIVITY, AND
THE OUTCOME OF THE 1984 NATIONAL ELECTION ON POLITICAL
EFFICACY IN THE AMERICAN ELECTORATE.

02310 CLARKE, H.D.; ZUK, G.
THE DYNAMICS OF THIRD-PARTY SUPPORT: THE BRITISH LIBERALS,
1951-79
AMERICAN JOURNAL OF POLITICAL SCIENCE, 33(1) (FEB 89),
196-221.
SINCE MOST ANALYSES OF PARTY POPULARITY HAVE FOCUSED
EXCLUSIVELY ON GOVERNING RATHER THAN OPPOSITION PARTIES,
INTERESTING THEORETICAL QUESTIONS ABOUT THE DETERMINANTS OF
PARTY SUPPORT REMAIN UNANSWERED. ONE NEGLECTED TOPIC
CONCERNS SUPPORT FOR MINOR PARTIES IN MULTIPARTY SYSTEMS. A
STUDY OF SUPPORT FOR THE BRITISH LIBERAL PARTY DURING THE
1951-79 PERIOD SHOWS THAT ITS POPULARITY VARIED IN RESPONSE
TO CHANGES IN THE MACROECONOMY AS WELL AS SYSTEMIC AND
UNANTICIPATED POLITICAL EVENTS AND CONDITIONS. MACROECONOMIC
INFLUENCES ON LIBERAL SUPPORT DO NOT CONFORM TO THE
UBIQUITOUS "REWARDPUNISHMENT" MODEL OF PARTY POPULARITY,
THEREBY SUGGESTING THE LIMITED APPLICABILITY OF KEY
THEORETICAL ASSUMPTIONS IN EXISTING STUDIES OF THE POLITICAL
ECONOMY OF PARTY SUPPORT. MORE GENERALLY, ANALYSES INDICATE
THAT THE POLITICAL CHARACTERISTICS OF PARTIES SUCH AS THE
BRITISH LIBERALS WORK TO PERPETUATE THEIR MINOR PARTY STATUS.
SINCE MANY OF THE FORCES THAT CIRCUMSCRIBED LIBERAL SUPPORT
BETWEEN 1951 AND 1979 REMAIN OPERATIVE TODAY, THE PROSPECTS
OF THE LIBERAL-SDP ALLIANCE FOR "BREAKING THE MOULD" OF
BRITISH POLITICS ARE HIGHLY PROBLEMATIC.

02311 CLARKE, L.
CAPITALISM IS RICHER, DEMOCRACY IS SAFER
SOCIETY, 27(1) (NOV 89), 17-18.
THE ARTICLE EXAMINES THE EFFECT THAT CAPITALISM AND/OR
DEMOCRACY HAVE ON GENERAL SAFETY LEVELS. IT CONCLUDES THAT
CAPITALISM CAN NOT BE LABELLED EITHER THE "BIG DISEASE" OR
THE "BIG CURE"; IT TENDS TO PROMOTE SAFETY WHEN PROFIT IS
ATTACHED, BUT IS LESS DEPENDABLE WHEN PROFITS ARE FEW.
DEMOCRACY, ON THE OTHER HAND, IS CONDUCIVE TO INCREASED
LEVELS OF SAFETY, AND CAN GO A LONG WAY IN NEGATING THE
DAMAGE PERPETUATED BY CAPITALISM.

02312 CLARKE, R.A.
CONFERENCE AGAINST CHEMICAL WEAPONS
DEPARTMENT OF STATE BULLETIN (US FOREIGN POLICY), 89(2152)
(NOV 89), 45-47.
AN INTERNATIONAL GOVERNMENT-INDUSTRY CONFERENCE AGAINST
CHEMICAL WEAPONS WAS HELD IN AUSTRALIA IN SEPTEMBER 1989.
THE CONFERENCE BROUGHT TOGETHER IN A FORMAL SETTING, FOR THE
FIRST TIME, GOVERNMENTS THAT COULD MAKE CHEMICAL WEAPONS OR
COULD ELIMINATE THEM AND INDUSTRIES THAT COULD MAKE CHEMICAL
WEAPONS OR COULD HELP ELIMINATE THEM. THE U.S.
REPRESENTATIVE STATED THAT PRESIDENT GEORGE BUSH AND THE U.S.
GOVERNMENT ARE COMMITTED TO A TOTAL BAN ON CHEMICAL WEAPONS.
HE PROPOSED THREE STEPS THAT WOULD AID THE PROCESS OF
BANNING CHEMICAL WEAPONS: AN END TO SECRECY, CONFIDENCE-
BUILDING, AND THE CREATION OF A FORERUNNER OF THE TECHNICAL
SECRETARIAT THAT WILL BE CREATED WHEN A TREATY IS
IMPLEMENTED.

02313 CLAUDE, I. L., JR.
THE BALANCE OF POWER REVISITED
REVIEW OF INTERNATIONAL STUDIES, 15(2) (APR 89), 77-85.
THE WORLD HAS NOT DISCARDED THE BALANCE OF POWER SYSTEM
IN FAVOUR OF SOME OTHER APPROACH TO THE MANAGEMENT OF
INTERNATIONAL RELATIONS. TO SOME DEGREE, THIS RETENTION OF
BALANCE OF POWER HAS BEEN A MATTER OF GRUDGING ACCEPTANCE,
THE ACKNOWLEDGEMENT THAT WE CANNOT TRANSFORM REALITY BUT ARE
DOOMED TO DOING THE BEST WE CAN WITH WHAT WE HAVE. ONE CAN
BE GRATEFUL FOR THE LIMITED ACHIEVEMENTS OF THE SYSTEM BUT
WORRIED ABOUT ITS FUTURE, AND STILL ACQUIESCE IN THE
NECESSITY OF RELYING UPON THE SELFDIRECTED OPERATIONS OF
STATES FOR SUCH STABILITY AND ORDER AS MANKIND IS LIKELY TO
ENJOY.

02314 CLAUSON, K.L.
THE INTELLECTUAL ELITE OF THE CHRISTIAN RIGHT
JOURNAL OF POLITICAL SCIENCE, 16(1-2) (1988), 24-32.
THE AUTHOR EXPLORES THE VIEWS OF THE "RECONSTRUCTIONIST"
MOVEMENT THAT HAS GREATLY INFLUENCED THE THINKING OF
EVANGELISTS LIKE PAT ROBERTSON AND JERRY FALWELL.

02315 CLAWSON, D.; NEUSTADTL, A.
INTERLOCKS, PACS, AND CORPORATE CONSERVATISM
AMERICAN JOURNAL OF SOCIOLOGY, 94(4) (JAN 89), 749-773.
TWO ALTERNATIVE CORPORATE POLITICAL STRATEGIES ARE
IDENTIFIED FOR POLITICAL ACTION COMMITTEE (PAC)
CONTRIBUTIONS TO CANDIDATES IN THE 1980 CONGRESSIONAL
ELECTIONS: (1) A PRAGMATIC EFFORT TO PROMOTE A PARTICULAR
COMPANY'S BEST INTERESTS AND (2) AN IDEOLOGICAL EFFORT TO
PROMOTE CONSERVATISM. WITH THE USE OF MULTIPLE REGRESSION,
THIS ARTICLE EXAMINES THREE THEORETICAL EXPLANATIONS OF
CORPORATE POLITICAL STRATEGIES. THE EXPECTATIONS OF
CORPORATE LIBERAL THEORY ARE NOT CONFIRMED. RATHER, THERE IS
SUPPORT FOR BOTH STATE STRUCTURE AND INTERLOCK THEORIES. IT
IS ARGUED THAT, AT LEAST IN 1980, BUSINESS POLITICAL
BEHAVIOR WAS IDEOLOGICALLY CONSERVATIVE, WHICH BUSINESS
UNDERSTOOD TO REPRESENT CLASSWIDE RATIONAL INTERESTS.

02316 CLAY, J.W.
IRAQ CRUSHES THE KURDS
CULTURAL SURVIVAL QUARTERLY, 13(2) (1989), 1-2.
ON MARCH 29, 1989, THE IRAQI GOVERNMENT ANNOUNCED THAT MORE THAN 100,000 KURDS WOULD BE REMOVED FROM THE TOWN OF QALADIZA. THE RESETTLEMENT EFFORT WAS SEEN AS PART OF AN OVERALL STRATEGY TO DESTROY THE KURDS AS A PEOPLE. IT WAS REPORTED THAT THE FORMER KURDISH TERRITORY WOULD BE OCCUPIED BY EGYPTIAN SUNNI MUSLIMS, WHO COULD BE EXPECTED TO SHOW MORE LOYALTY TO IRAQ'S SUNNI MUSLIM GOVERNMENT THAN THE KURDS. THE PRESENCE OF URANIUM IN THE KURDS' TERRITORY IS ANOTHER REASON THE GOVERNMENT WANTS TO FORCE THEM OUT.

02317 CLAY, J.W.
THE NUCLEUS FOR INDIGENOUS RIGHTS: PROMOTING EQUALITY IN BRAZIL
CULTURAL SURVIVAL QUARTERLY, 13(4) (1989), 79.
THE NUCLEUS FOR INDIGENOUS RIGHTS (NDI) WAS CONCEIVED IN BRAZIL IN OCTOBER 1988 IN THE AFTERMATH OF THE VICTORIOUS BATTLE TO PRESERVE AND STRENGTHEN THE RIGHTS OF INDIANS UNDER THE NEW BRAZILIAN CONSTITUTION. NDI'S GOAL IS TO MONITOR THE LEGISLATIVE, EXECUTIVE, AND JUDICIAL BRANCHES OF BRAZIL'S GOVERNMENT TO ENSURE THAT THE LETTER - AND SPIRIT - OF BRAZIL'S NEW CONSTITUTION ARE UPHELD. MANY OF THE LAWYERS AND LOBBYISTS WHO WERE ACTIVE IN THE CONSTITUTIONAL DEBATE ARE NOW ON THE NDI STAFF. THEY ARE WORKING TO ASSIST IN DRAFTING THE LAWS AS WELL AS IN IMPLEMENTING AND INTERPRETING THEM, ALL OF WHICH WILL CONTRIBUTE TO FURTHERING THE CAUSE OF INDIGENOUS RIGHTS IN BRAZIL.

02318 CLAY, R.
THE POLITICAL VOCABULARY OF THE POLITIQUES
DISSERTATION ABSTRACTS INTERNATIONAL, 50(1) (JUL 89), 245-A.
THE AUTHOR SKETCHES A PICTURE OF THE OLD, UNDIVIDED RELIGIOUS-POLITICAL-MORAL ORDER AS IT EXISTED IN FRANCE. HE STUDIES SEVERAL FRENCH POLITICAL THEORISTS AND FINDS THAT THEIR WORKS ARE FULL OF RELIGIOUS AND MORAL MATTER. THIS RELIGIOUS AND MORAL MATTER IS NOT ADDITIONAL OR EXTRANEOUS TO THEIR POLITICAL THEORY. IN FACT, THE POLITICAL THEORY DISAPPEARS WHEN MORAL AND RELIGIOUS CRITERIA ARE REMOVED FROM IT. HE FOCUSES CLOSELY ON THE POLITIQUES' ARGUMENTS AND STRATAGEMS ON BEHALF OF THEIR OWN VIEWS. HE EXAMINES THE POLITIQUE ACCOUNT OF CONTEMPORARY HISTORY, THE DEBATE OVER TOLERATION, THE DEBATE OVER LEGISLATIVE POWER, AND THE ATTEMPT TO SUPPRESS POLITICAL DIALOGUE.

02319 CLEARY, R.E.
A CODE OF ETHICS
BUREAUCRAT, 18(1) (SPR 89), 17-19.
THE ENACTMENT OF A CODE OF ETHICS BY THE AMERICAN SOCIETY FOR PUBLIC ADMINISTRATION IN 1984 SUPPORTED EXISTING CODES OF ETHICS IN THE FIELD OF PUBLIC ADMINISTRATION AND MANAGEMENT. IT IS ALSO A MAJOR INDICATOR THAT PUBLIC ADMINISTRATION CAN PROPERLY 3E LABELED A PROFESSION.

02320 CLEARY, S.
THE IMPACT OF THE INDEPENDENCE OF NAMIBIA ON SOUTH AFRICA
SOUTH AFRICA INTERNATIONAL, 19(3) (JAN 89), 117-129.
THE ARTICLE ANALYZES THE IMPACT THAT CHANGING CONDITIONS IN SOUTH WEST AFRICA AND THE EVENTUAL INDEPENDENCE OF THE NATION HASHAD ON SOUTH AFRICAN FOREIGN POLICY AND DOMESTIC POLITICS AS WELL. IT DISCUSSES THE MYTH THAT HAS LONG PERPETUATED BY SOUTH AFRICA THAT SOUTH WEST AFRICA WAS PART OF THE TERRITORY LEGITIMATELY ADMINISTERED BY THE SOUTH AFRICAN GOVERNMENT AND THAT THE SOUTH AFRICAN INVOLVEMENT THERE WAS JUSTIFIED BY THE THREAT OF SOCIALIST EXPANSION.

02321 CLEGG, S.
RADICAL REVISIONS: POWER,DISCIPLINE,AND ORGANIZATIONS
ORGANIZATION STUDIES, 10(1) (1989), 97-116.
TYPICALLY, ORGANIZATION THEORISTS HAVE DEFINED 'POWER' AGAINST 'AUTHORITY' AROUND THE AXIS OF 'LEGITIMACY'. POWER, THUS REGARDED, IS A 'CAPACITY' GROUNDED OUTSIDE THE AUTHORITATIVE STRUCTURE OF THE ORGANIZATION. ORGANIZATIONS HAVE TYPICALLY BEEN REGARDED AS COHERENT AND HOMOGENOUS ENTITIES IN WHICH THESE CAPACITIES OCCUR. AGAINST THESE VIEWS, ORGANIZATIONS ARE DEFINED HERE AS COMPRISING LOCALES, CROSS-CUT BY ARENAS, IN WHICH AGENCIES, POWERS, NETWORKS AND INTERESTS ARE CONSTITUTED. POWER IS NOT A THING BUT A PROCESS CONSTITUTED WITHIN STRUGGLES. POWER IS ALWAYS EMBEDDED WITHIN RULES: THESE CANNOT PROVIDE FOR THEIR OWN INTERPRETATION INDEPENDENTLY OF THOSE AGENCIES WHOSE INTERPRETATIONS INSTANTIATE, SIGNIFY OR IMPLY THEM. SPECIFIC DISCIPLINARY PRACTICES WITHIN ORGANIZATION STUDIES PRESCRIBE THESE INTERPRETATIONS, BUT IT IS ARGUED, THEY CAN PROVIDE NO GENERAL THEORY OF THE ORGANIZATION.

02322 CLEMENT, P.A.
STALIN AND THE SEVENTEENTH CONGRESS OF THE COMMUNIST PARTY OF THE SOVIET UNION: THE PARTY IN CONFLICT
DISSERTATION ABSTRACTS INTERNATIONAL, 48(12) (JUN 88), 3180-A.
ALTHOUGH THE SEVENTEENTH PARTY CONGRESS HAS BEEN VIEWED AS THE APOGEE OF THE STALIN PERSONALITY CULT, CLOSER ANALYSIS OF RECORDS, MEDIA COVERAGE, AND THE ELECTION OF PARTY BODIES REVEALS THAT STALIN DID NOT YET ENJOY FULL DICTATORIAL POWERS. FOR STALIN, THE CONGRESS REPRESENTED A PERSONAL DEFEAT AND IT WAS NOT UNTIL THE NEXT PARTY CONGRESS THAT STALIN WAS ABLE TO PREVAIL OVER HIS MODERATE OPPOSITION.

02323 CLEMENTS, K.P.
COMMON SECURITY IN THE ASIA - PACIFIC REGION: PROBLEMS AND PRESPECTS.
ALTERNATIVES, XIV(1) (JAN 89), 49-76.
IN THE MEDIUM TO LONG TERM THE MARKET PRESSURES FORCING CHANGES TO ASIA-PACIFIC SECURITY POLICIES WILL PROBABLY RESULT IN MORE STRUCTURAL VIOLENCE, NATIONAL RESISTANCE TO HEGEMONIC ECONOMIC TENDENCIES AND AN UNRAVELLING OF ALTERNATIVE SECURITY DOCTRINES. THE CHALLENGE CONFRONTING POPULAR MOVEMENTS, THEREFORE, IS TO ENSURE THAT CURRENT ECONOMIC TRENDS TOWARDS INTEGRATION ARE ACCOMPANIED BY THE ENTRENCHMENT OF COMMON SECURITY POLICIES IN THE ASIA-PACIFIC REGION WHILE SIMULTANEOUSLY GENERATING SPACE FOR ENVIRONMENTALLY SUSTAINABLE AND SOCIALLY JUST DEVELOPMENT STRATEGIES IN THE FUTURE. THIS CHALLENGE REQUIRES NEW SORTS OF STRATEGIC AND TACTICAL THINKING ON THE PARTS OF POPULAR MOVEMENTS INTERESTED IN PROMOTING BOTH PEACE AND JUSTICE. THIS PAPER IS PRIMARILY CONCERNED WITH THE QUESTION OF BUILDING ON EXISTING PRESSURES FOR ECONOMIC INTEGRATION IN ORDER TO CREATE SPACE FOR COMMON SECURITY DOCTRINES IN THE ASIA-PACIFIC REGION.

02324 CLEVELAND, H.
INFORMATION, FAIRNESS AND THE STATUS OF WOMEN
FUTURES, 21(1) (FEB 89), 33.
THIS ARTICLE EXAMINES WOMEN'S LEVEL OF ACCESS TO INFORMATION-AS-ARESOURCE AND REVIEWS THE CURRENT STATUS OF WOMEN WITH REGARD TO POLITICAL POWER AND EMPLOYMENT. A PATTERN OF DEVELOPMENT IN WOMEN'S STRUGGLE FOR FAIRNESS IS ELABORATED, WITH THE KEY DEPENDENT SEEN AS WHAT WOMEN THEMSELVES DO. IN THE CURRENT AGE OF PARTICIPATION WOMEN MAY HAVE THE CULTURAL EDGE, SINCE THE KEYS TO SUCCESS IN LEADERSHIP ARE INCREASINGLY SEEN AS SKILLS IN WORKING WITH OTHER PEOPLE, CONSULTING, AND STRIVING FOR CONSENSUS-ALL SKILLS WHICH WOMEN'S SOCIALIZATION HAS EMPHASIZED.

02325 CLEVELAND, H.
THE AGONY OF ATLANTIC SUCCESS
ITALIAN JOURNAL, III(1) (1989), 15-20.
THE AUTHOR, WHO MANAGED THE ECONOMIC SECTION OF THE ALLIED MILITARY GOVERNMENT IN ITALY DURING AND IMMEDIATELY FOLLOWING WORLD WAR II, REVIEWS THE ALLIED EFFORTS TO ASSIST ITALY IN REBUILDING ITS ECONOMY AFTER THE WAR.

02326 CLEVELAND, P.
LOWERING THE DECIBEL LEVEL
NEW ZEALAND INTERNATIONAL REVIEW, 14(4) (JUL 89), 27-28.
THE UNITED STATES AMBASSADOR TO NEW ZEALAND PRESENTS OBSERVATIONS ABOUT THE PROSPECTS FOR IMPROVED RELATIONS BETWEEN THE UNITED STATES AND NEW ZEALAND. THE NUCLEAR SHIP PROHIBITIONS AND THE CORRESPONDING SUSPENSION OF THE UNITED STATES DEFENSE COMMITMENT TO NEW ZEALAND IS THE MAIN FOCUS OF THE ARTICLE. THE REDUCTION WAS LIMITED, BUT RESULTS OF THE CHANGES PLACED NEWLY EMERGING PRIORITIES ON THE CONTINUING NEED FOR COLLECTIVE ARRANGEMENTS AND NUCLEAR DETERRENCE, WITH THE UNITED STATES IN FAVOR OF MAINTAINING BOTH ARRANGEMENT, AND NEW ZEALAND RECOGNIZING THE FIRST, BUT BUT REJECTING THE SECOND.

02327 CLEVELAND, P.M.
U.S. NEW ZEALAND RELATIONS: SOME PARTING OBSERVATIONS
DEPARTMENT OF STATE BULLETIN (US FOREIGN POLICY), 89(2147) (JUN 89), 45-48.
THE AUTHOR, WHO IS THE AMERICAN AMBASSADOR TO NEW ZEALAND, DISCUSSES RELATIONS BETWEEN THE USA AND NEW ZEALAND IN LIGHT OF THE MAJOR CHANGES TAKING PLACE IN WORLD AFFAIRS.

02328 CLIFFE, L.
FORGING A NATION: THE ERITREAN EXPERIENCE
THIRD WORLD QUARTERLY, 11(4) (OCT 89), 131-147.
THIS ARTICLE DISCUSSES THE ERITREAN EXPERIENCE OF THE NATIONAL QUESTION AND ETHNICITY IN THE HORN OF AFRICA. IT EXAMINES THE ETHNIC COMPOSITION OF ERITREA AND ITS 'NATIONALITIES'; POLITICS AND ETHNICITY IN THE DEVELOPMENT OF THE NATIONALIST MOVEMENT, IN THE LIBERATION STRUGGLE; AND APPROACHES OF THE ERITREAN PEOPLE'S AND APPROACHES OF THE ERITREAN PEOPLE'S POLITICAL PARTICIPATION AND BUILDING ETHNIC UNITY; AND THE PAST AND FUTURE OF CLASS AND ETHNICITY IN ERITREA.

02329 CLIFFORD, M.
A SLOW BOAT TO CHINA
FAR EASTERN ECONOMIC REVIEW, 141(37) (SEP 88), 82-83.
TRADE BETWEEN SOUTH KOREA AND CHINA IS MUSHROOMING. THOWAY TRADE IS EXPECTED TO DOUBLE FROM LAST YEARS US$1.8 BILLION TO AROUND US$3 BILLION THIS YEAR. HOWEVER, MANY

OBSERVERS FEEL THAT KOREA'S CONFIDENCE THAT POLITICAL
RELATIONS WILL FOLLOW ECONOMIC ONES IS MERELY WISHFUL
THINKING. THE CHINESE STILL REFUSE TO EVEN OPEN AN OFFICIAL
TRADE OFFICE IN KOREA, OPTING INSTEAD TO WORK THROUGH A HONG
KONG FIRM. ANY FUTURE IMPROVEMENT IN RELATIONS IS DESTINED
TO OCCUR AT A RATHER SLOW RATE.

02330 CLIFFORD, M.
KOREA INC. ON TRIAL
FAR EASTERN ECONOMIC REVIEW, 141(31) (AUG 88), 44-45.
SOUTH KOREA'S FIRST OPPOSITION DOMINATED NATIONAL
ASSEMBLY HAS MOVED QUICKLY TO PUT ITS IMPRINT ON NATIONAL
ECONOMIC POLICYMAKING. IN THE PROCESS OF GATHERING
INFORMATION FROM THE NATION'S THREE SENIOR ECONOMIC
OFFICIALS, THE BIGGEST REVELATION WAS THE BAIL-OUT COSTS FOR
78 BANKRUPT COMPANIES IN 1986 AND 1987. THE BAIL-OUTS
SYMBOLIZED THE GOVERNMENT-BIG BUSINESS ALLIANCE THAT THE
OPPOSITION HAS CRITICIZED. FOREIGN AND DOMESTIC LENDERS ARE
BEING WARNED THAT THEY SHOULD MAKE LOANS ON THE BASIS OF
CREDIT WORTHINESS AND NOT COUNT ON THE GOVERNMENT TO BAIL
OUT INSOLVENT FIRMS; IN SHORT, KOREA INC. ISN'T WHAT IT USED
TO BE.

02331 CLIFFORD, M.
MAKING JUSTICE BLIND
FAR EASTERN ECONOMIC REVIEW, 141(32) (AUG 88), 16-17.
IN THE FIRST COLLECTIVE PROTEST ACTION IN POST-WAR
HISTORY ABOUT OF A THIRD OF KOREA'S JUDGES HAVE SUCCESFULLY
OPPOSED PRESIDENT ROH TAE WOO'S REAPPOINTMENT OF POLITICALLY
TAINTED SUPREME COURT CHIEF JUSTICE KIM YONG CHUL. ROH THEN
TRIED TO PUSH THROUGH ANOTHER TAINTED NOMINEE WHO WAS
PROMPTLY REJECTED BY THE NATIONAL ASSEMBLY. THE SPARRING IN
THE NATIONAL ASSEMBLY COULD LEAD TO THE COURTS EMERGING AS A
POWERFUL CHECK TO THE GOVERNMENT'S EXECUTIVE BRANCH.

02332 CLIFFORD, M.
MAPPING A NEW COURSE
FAR EASTERN ECONOMIC REVIEW, 141(38) (SEP 88), 80-81.
SOUTH KOREA'S PRESIDENTIAL COMMISSION ON ECONOMIC HAS
COME DOWN HARD IN FAVOR OF LESS PROTECTION FOR AGRICULTURE,
MORE LIBERALIZATION OF TRADE AND LESS GOVERNMENTAL
INTERFERENCE IN CREDIT ALLOCATION. ALTHOUGH THE PROPOSALS IN
AND OF THEMSELVES ARE NOT SIGNIFICANT, WHAT IS SIGNIFICANT
IS THE FACT THAT FOR THE FIRST TIME THE GOVERNMENT IS
PLANNING FOR THE FUTURE IN PUBLIC AND IS ALLOWING INPUT FROM
LIBERAL POLICYMAKERS. THERE IS A GENERAL AGREEMENT THAT
CHANGE IS NOT GOING TO COME QUICKLY BUT MANY FEEL THAT THE
COMMISSION HAS A FIRST IMPORTANT STEP.

02333 CLIFFORD, M.
TALKING ABOUT TALKS
FAR EASTERN ECONOMIC REVIEW, 141(31) (AUG 88), 14-15.
THE RELATIONS BETWEEN NORTH AND SOUTH KOREA MAY HAVE
REACHED THEIR WARMEST POINT IN MORE THAN TWO YEARS. A SOUTH
KOREAN PROPOSAL FOR EXCHANGES BETWEEN THE TWO KOREAS AND
PARLIAMENTARY TALKS WERE MET WITH SWIFT AND ENCOURAGING
RESPONSE FROM THE NORTH. ALTHOUGH NOT A FULL FLEDGED
RAPROACHMENT, THE FACT THAT THE TWO NATIONS ARE EDGING
TOWARDS TALKS IS NOTEWORTHY.

02334 CLIFFORD, M.
THE NOOSE TIGHTENS
FAR EASTERN ECONOMIC REVIEW, 141(33) (AUG 88), 26.
FORMER SOUTH KOREAN PRESIDENT CHUN DOO HWAN WILL
PROBABLY BE FORCED TO TESTIFY BEFORE THE SPECIAL PANELS OF
THE NATIONAL ASSEMBLY LOOKING INTO CORRUPTION AND INTO THE
KWANGJU UPRISING. ALTHOUGH OPPOSTION LEADERS DEMAND ONLY AN
APOLOGY AND A RETURN OF ALL OF CHUN'S ILL-GOTTEN GAINS, THE
FORMER PRESIDENT ISN'T LIKELY TO GIVE IN TO THE WISHES OF
HIS ENEMIES.

02335 CLIFFORD, M.
THE RETURN OF KOREA INC.
FAR EASTERN ECONOMIC REVIEW, 142(52) (DEC 89), 41.
UNSETTLED LABOR RELATIONS, FLAT EXPORTS, AND A DECLINING
ECONOMY HAS BOUGHT ABOUT THE RETURN OF A CRISIS MENTALITY IN
SOUTH KOREA'S ECONOMIC POLICY. PROCLAIMING AN ECONOMIC
CRISIS, A DEPUTY PRIME MINISTER FOR ECONOMIC AFFAIRS
JETTISONED THE GOVERNMENT'S TIGHT LIQUIDITY PACKAGE FOR A
REFLATIONARY ONE. GOVERNMENT ECONOMIC PLANNERS ARE STUCK IN
THE DILEMMA OF INFLUENCING WORKERS TO MODERATE THEIR WAGE
DEMANDS WHILE AT THE SAME TIME KEEPING THE STOCK MARKET UP.
THE RETURN TO A CRISIS/SIEGE MENTALITY MAY MEAN SOLUTIONS,
THE RECORD FOR THE PAST QUARTER CENTURY HAS BEEN QUITE GOOD,
BUT SOME OBSERVERS NOTE THAT THE IDEA OF SOUTH KOREA UNDER
SIEGE IS WEARING THIN IN THE MINDS OF MANY KOREANS.

02336 CLIFFORD, N.R
A TALE OF TWO CITIES
COMMONWEAL, CXVI(15) (SEP 89), 453-455.
LIKE DENG XIAOPING AND LI PENG, THE NEW HEAD OF THE
CHINESE COMMUNIST PARTY, JIANG ZEMIN, SEEMS TO EMBODY THE
CONTRADICTORY DESIRES FOR ECONOMIC ADVANCE AND CONTINUING
TIGHT POLITICAL CONTROLS. SHANGHAI HAS BEEN THE VICTIM OF

CHINESE REPRESSION IN THE PAST; HONG KONG COULD BE IN THE
FUTURE.

02337 CLINE, R.S.
COMMENTARY: THE CUBAN MISSILE CRISIS
FOREIGN AFFAIRS, 68(4) (FAL 89), 190-196.
MIKHAIL GORBACHEV'S TEAM OF OFFICIAL INTELLECTUALS IS
ENGAGED IN A PROGRAM OF HISTORICAL REVISIONISM SERVING
MOSCOW'S INTEREST. SOME OF THE FACTS BEING LAID OUT ARE
MISLEADING OR SIMPLY NOT TRUE, AND THE GEOPOLITCAL THRUST OF
THE SOVIET INTERPRETATION OF HISTORY IS FALSE. THE CUBAN
MISSLE CRISIS IS ONE EVENT THAT HAS BECOME DISTORTED IN
RECENT ACCOUNTS OF THE EPISODE.

02338 CLINGERMAYER, J.C.
THE POLITICAL ECONOMY OF MUNICIPAL ZONING: CONSTITUENCY
DIVERSITY AND INSTITUTIONAL DIFFERENCES
DISSERTATION ABSTRACTS INTERNATIONAL, 50(1) (JUL 89),
246-A.
THE EXTENT TO WHICH CITY COUNCIL MEMBERS WILL ATTEMPT TO
SERVE INTERESTS LOCATED WITHIN A PARTICULAR GEOGRAPHIC AREA
WITHIN THEIR ELECTORAL CONSTITUENCY THROUGH ZONING POLICY
WILL DEPEND UPON THE INTERNAL HOMOGENEITY OF THOSE
CONSTITUENCIES. REPRESENTATIVES OF THE MORE HOMOGENEOUS
CONSTITUENCIES ARE MORE LIKELY TO BE ATTENTIVE TO
GEOGRAPHICALLY-DEFINED INTERESTS THAN ARE REPRESENTATIVES OF
DIVERSE CONSTITUENCIES.

02339 CLINTON, R. L.
SUBSTANTIVE DUE PROCESS, SELECTIVE INCORPORATION, AND THE
LATE-NINETEENTH CENTURY OVERTHROW OF JOHN MARSHALL'S
CONSTITUTIONAL JURISPRUDENCE
JOURNAL OF LAW & POLITICS, V(3) (SPR 89), 499-549.
THE AUTHOR'S THESIS IS THAT MARSHALL'S ALLEGED
"NATIONALISM" IS MORE APPARENT THAN REAL, AND THAT IT MAY BE
LARGELY ATTRIBUTED TO AN IDEA OF JUDICIAL FUNCTION, WIDELY
HELD IN MARSHALL'S DAY, WHICH SERVED AS A LIMITATION ON THE
EXERCISE OF JUDICIAL REVIEW WHEN NATIONAL POWER WAS AT ISSUE.
THE JURISPRUDENCE WHICH RESULTED FROM THE MARSHALL COURT'S
CONCEPTION OF JUDICIAL REVIEW WAS OVERTHROWN IN
COMPREHENSIVE FASHION WITH THE ONSET OF MODERN JUDICIAL
ACTIVISM IN THE LATE-NINETEENTH CENTURY, ENJOYED A BRIEF
RESURGENCE IN THE MID-TWENTIETH CENTURY, AND HAS ONCE AGAIN
REPUDIATED. IN ORDER TO COMPREHEND MORE FULLY THESE
DEVELOPMENTS, THE AUTHOR EXAMINES THE MARSHALL COURT'S
APPROACH TO JUDICIAL REVIEW, AN APPROACH BEST ILLUSTRATED IN
MARBURY V. MADISON, WHEREIN THE AMERICAN DOCTRINE OF
JUDICIAL POWER TO OVERTURN NATIONAL LAWS IS GENERALLY THOUGH
TO HAVE BEEN ESTABLISHED.

02340 CLINTON, R.L.
FEDERAL COURT INVOLVEMENT IN THE APPLICATION OF THE
SURFACE MINING CONTROL AND RECLAMATION ACT OF 1977
POLICY STUDIES REVIEW, 9(1) (AUT 89), 88-97.
THIS ARTICLE SURVEYS 122 FEDERAL CASES REPORTED IN THE
"SURFACE MINING LAW SUMMARY" FROM THE EARLIEST LEGISLATION
UNDER SMCRA TO THE END OF 1987. THE ANALYSIS DISTINGUISHES
BETWEEN CASES IN WHICH ALL OSMRE REGULATIONS OR APPLICATIONS
OF SMCRA WERE UPHELD BY THE FEDERAL COURTS AND THOSE IN
WHICH ONE OR MORE REGULATIONS/APPLICATIONS WERE OVERTURNED.
THE ANALYSIS FURTHER CLASSIFIES THE CASES ACCORDING TO
WHETHER THE DECISIONS WERE FAVORABLE TO INDUSTRY, (OR,
CONVERSELY, TO ENVIRONMENTAL/CITIZEN GROUPS), ACCORDING TO
WHETHER THE ISSUES INVOLVED WERE PRIMARILY OF NARROW PRIVATE
RIGHT (OR, CONVERSELY, OF BROAD PUBLIC POLICY), AND
ACCORDING TO STATE-OFORIGIN. FINALLY, SEPARATE EXAMINATION
OF THOSE CASES IN WHICH OSMRE'S DISCRETION IN THE
ENFORCEMENT OF SMCRA WAS RESTRICTED IS PROVIDED. THE AUTHOR
CONCLUDES THAT BOTH THE FEDERAL COURTS AND OSMRE HAVE BEEN
REASONABLY EVEN-HANDED IN THEIR APPLICATION OF SMCRA.

02341 CLIVE, N.
LETTER FROM GREECE, MID-DECEMBER 1988
GOVERNMENT AND OPPOSITION, 24(1) (1989), 74-80.
AFTER 56 DAYS IN ENGLAND FOR MEDICAL TREATMENT, GREEK
PRIME MINISTER ADREAS PAPANDREOU RETURNED TO ATHENS. THE
PASOK MADE EVERY EFFORT TO STAGE A TRIUMPHAL WELCOME FOR HIS
RETURN BUT IT FELL SHORT OF EXPECTATIONS. PAPANDREOU'S LONG
ABSENCE IN ENGLAND REINFORCED THE DISUNITY IN HIS GOVERNMENT
AND PROVED THAT HIS PERSONAL PRESENCE HAD BEEN SOLIDIFYING
THE GOVERNMENT. BUT HIS POOR HEALTH HAS RAISED QUESTIONS
ABOUT WHETHER HE IS FIT TO CONFRONT PRESSING PROBLEMS.

02342 CLOUGHLEY, B.
BRING THE BOYS HOME FROM THE KURILES, TOO
FAR EASTERN ECONOMIC REVIEW, 141(27) (JUL 88), 28-29.
THE SOVIET OCCUPATION OF THE KURLIE ISLANDS SINCE THE
END OF WORLD WAR II HAS BEEN A MAJOR OBSTACLE TO BETTER
RELATIONS BETWEEN JAPAN AND THE USSR. THE ISLANDS ARE OF
IMMENSE STRATEGIC IMPORTANCE TO THE SOVIETS, AND IF
CONTROLLED BY AN UNFRIENDLY POWER COULD RESULT IN THE
BOTTLING UP OF THE SOVIET'S PACIFIC FLEET BASED IN
VLADIVOSTOK. THERE IS SOME HOPE THAT MIKHAIL GORBACHEV'S
OVERTURE TO JAPAN FOR IMPROVED RELATIONS MAY EVENTUALLY

RESULT IN NEGOTIATIONS OVER THE RETURN OF THE ISLANDS TO JAPANESE CONTROL.

02343 CLUBB, O.E.
AMERICA'S CHINA POLICY
CURRENT HISTORY, 88(534) (JAN 89), 35-36, 56-57.
THROUGHOUT THE 1970'S, THE RADICALLY DIFFERENT WORLD OUTLOOK OF THE MAINLAND CHINESE LEADERSHIP FUELED THE SUSPICIONS OF UNITED STATES' POLICY MAKERS, MANY OF WHOM FEARED A MONOLITHIC COMMUNIST EMPIRE IN CHINA. THE DECADE SAW AN EVOLUTION IN AMERICAN RELATIONS WITH BOTH MAINLAND CHINA AND TAIWAN.

02344 CLUKEY, G.P.
UNITED STATES ECONOMIC RELATIONSHIP WITH JAPAN: IMPLICATIONS FOR U.S. SECURITY
AVAILABLE FROM NTIS, NO. AD-A207/336/9/GAR, MAR 89, 44.
THE UNITED STATES PURSUES, AS PART OF ITS NATIONAL SECURITY STRATEGY, ITS OWN ECONOMIC WELL-BEING AS WELL AS THE ECONOMIC WELL-BEING OF ITS DEMOCRATIC ALLIES IN THE ASIA PACIFIC THEATER. JAPAN IS ITS MOST IMPORTANT ECONOMICALLY, AND A KEY PLAYER IN U.S. FORWARD DEFENSE STRATEGY. THIS STUDY FOCUSES ON THE IMPORTANCE OF A HEALTHY ECONOMIC RELATIONSHIP BETWEEN THE UNITED STATES AND JAPAN. IT ADDRESSES: (1) THE CURRENT U.S. AND JAPAN ECONOMIC SITUATION, (2) ACTIONS TAKEN BY BOTH NATIONS TO IMPROVE AND STRENGTHEN THE U.S.-JAPAN ECONOMIC RELATIONSHIP AND (3) SOME OF THE MAJOR ISSUES AND CONCERNS — FROM AN ECONOMIC AND SECURITY STANDPOINT. THE STUDY ALSO PROVIDES SOME INSIGHT AND BACKGROUND ON RECENT U.S. AND JAPANESE INVOLVEMENT IN THE GLOBAL TRADE, FINANCIAL AID, BANKING AND MONETARY SYSTEMS. FURTHERMORE, IT EXAMINES U.S. AND JAPANESE SUPPORT FOR FREE-TRADE AND OPEN MARKETS. IN THE LAST CHAPTER, MAJOR SECURITY ISSUES ARE SUMMARIZED, AND CONCLUSIONS MADE REGARDING U.S. STRATEGY.

02345 CLUTE, R.E.
THE AMERICAN-SOVIET CONFRONTATION IN AFRICA: ITS IMPACT ON THE POLITICS OF AFRICA
JOURNAL OF ASIAN AND AFRICAN STUDIES, XXIV(3-4) (JUL 89), 159-169.
DESPITE ENORMOUS SOVIET ARMS SUPPLIES TO AFRICA, THE U.S. STRESSED ECONOMIC ASSISTANCE THROUGHOUT THE 1970S AND DID NOT INCREASE ARMS SHIPMENTS. HOWEVER, THE FALL OF THE SHAH OF IRAN, THE LEFTIST REGIME IN MOZAMBIQUE, AND THE SOVIET-CUBAN MILITARY BUILD-UP IN ETHIOPIA AND ANGOLA COMPLETELY CHANGED U.S. STRATEGY IN THE 1980S. AMERICAN EMPHASIS SHIFTED TO THE HORN OF AFRICA. INCREASED AID WAS FUNNELED TO KENYA, SOMALIA, AND THE SUDAN. SUPPORT FOR SOUTHERN AFRICA STATES WAS MINIMAL. THE REAGAN ADMINISTRATION VIEWED SOUTH AFRICA AS A BULWARK AGAINST COMMUNISM AND THE NAMIBIAN QUESTION BECAME STALEMATED.

02346 COATS, W.L. JR.
LDC DEBT: THE ROLE OF THE INTERNATIONAL MONETARY FUND
CONTEMPORARY POLICY ISSUES, VII(2) (APR 89), 41-49.
FOR A COMBINATION OF REASONS THAT DIFFER AMONG COUNTRIES, MANY DEVELOPING COUNTRIES' FOREIGN DEBT SERVICE OBLIGATIONS HAVE BECOME DIFFICULT TO MEET. THE SIZE OF THE PROBLEM IN 1982 RAISED CONCERN OVER THE STABILITY OF THE BANKING SYSTEM. THE INTERNATIONAL MONETARY FUND (IMF) PROVIDED THE FORUM THROUGH WHICH THE INTERNATIONAL COMMUNITY'S STRATEGY FOR MEETING THIS CONCERN HAS EVOLVED. THE IMF ALSO PLAYED, AND CONTINUES TO PLAY, AN ACTIVE ROLE IN HELPING TO FINANCE THE STRUCTURAL AND BALANCE-OF-PAYMENTS ADJUSTMENTS NEEDED IN COUNTRIES WITH DEBT SERVICE PROBLEMS. THE IMF'S INVOLVEMENT IS AN INTEGRAL PART OF THE BROADER STRATEGY, WHICH BUILDS ON THE COOPERATION OF DEBTORS AND CREDITORS, ON A CASE-BYCASE BASIS. THE OBJECTIVE IS TO SHARE THE BURDEN IN A BALANCED WAY.

02347 COBHAM, D.
STRATEGIES FOR MONETARY INTEGRATION REVISITED
JOURNAL OF COMMON MARKET STUDIES, XXVII(3) (MAR 89), 203-218.
AT A TIME WHEN MAJOR CHANGES IN THE DEGREE OF EUROPEAN MONETARY INTEGRATION ARE ONCE AGAIN ON THE POLICY AGENDA, IT IS INTERESTING TO GO BACK TO THE DISCUSSION ON THIS TOPIC THAT TOOK PLACE IN THE 1970S. THIS ARTICLE STARTS BY REVIEWING THAT DISCUSSION AND THEN EXAMINES THE EXPERIENCE OF THE EUROPEAN MONETARY SYSTEM (EMS) IN ITS LIGHT, BEFORE PROCEEDING TO AN ASSESSMENT OF THE STRATEGIES CURRENTLY BEING PROPOSED FOR FURTHER MOVEMENT TOWARDS EUROPEAN MONETARY UNION.

02348 COCHRAN, C.E.
THE DYNAMICS OF TENSION: NORMATIVE DIMENSIONS OF RELIGION AND POLITICS
JOURNAL OF POLITICAL SCIENCE, 16(1-2) (1988), 14-23.
IN A TRULY HEALTHY SOCIETY, PRIVATE RELIGIONS AND PUBLIC LIFE HAVE AN ESSENTIAL NEED FOR ONE ANOTHER. RELIGION, WHICH CAN BE BOTH PRIVATE AND PUBLIC, SHOULD NOT DOMINATE PUBLIC LIFE NOR BE DOMINATED BY IT. RATHER, RELIGION AND POLITICS SHOULD CHALLENGE AND TEST ONE ANOTHER. FOR EXAMPLE, THE

MORAL VALUES OF RELIGION SHOULD SERVE AS A TESTING GROUND OR MEASURING ROD OF THE PROPRIETY OF PUBLIC POLICY.

02349 COCHRAN, C.E.
THE THIN THEORY OF COMMUNITY: THE COMMUNITARIANS AND THEIR CRITICS
POLITICAL STUDIES, 37(3) (FAL 89), 422-435.
WHERE COMMUNITARIAN THEORISTS WERE ONCE VOICES CRYING IN THE WILDERNESS OF POLITICAL PHILOSOPHY, NOW THEY CAMP NEAR THE CENTRE OF THE DISCIPLINE. THIS PAPER APPRAISES THE SUCCESS OF THE NEW COMMUNAL STIRRINGS, PARTICULARLY THE WORK OF ALASDAIR MACINTYRE, MICHAEL SANDEL, MICHAEL WALZER AND BENJAMIN BARBER. IT ALSO EVALUATES AND FINDS WANTING THE LIBERAL CRITICS OF THE NEW COMMUNITARIAN TURN, WHO DEFEND THE 'THIN' THEORY OF THE SELF AGAINST THE 'THICKER', EMBEDDED THEORIES OF SELF ADVANCED BY THE COMMUNITARIANS. THE CRITICS' CONTENTION THAT LIBERAL TOLERANCE AND HUMAN RIGHTS DEPEND ON A 'THIN' THEORY OF THE SELF IS NOT PERSUASIVE. YET THE THEORIES OF COMMUNITY SUBMITTED AS REMEDIES FOR 'THIN' THEORIES OF THE SELF ARE THEMSELVES TOO THIN. FIRST, CONSIDERATION OF INDIVIDUAL ELEMENTS OF COMMUNITY IS TOO NARROW. CHARACTER, FOR EXAMPLE, IS MENTIONED BY MANY OF THE COMMUNITARIANS BUT NOT EXPLORED IN DEPTH. SECONDLY, EVEN THOSE THEORISTS WHO EXAMINE SOME ESSENTIALS IN DEPTH NEGLECT THE RANGE OF REQUIREMENTS, PARTICULARLY AUTHORITY, LOYALTY AND COMMITMENT. THE COMMUNITARIAN LINE OF ARGUMENT, HOWEVER, MAY VERY WELL HELP TO MOVE THEORETICAL AND POLITICAL DEBATE BEYOND THE STERILE CONFINES OF REGNANT IDEOLOGIES.

02350 COCKBURN, P.
DATELINE USSR: ETHNIC TREMORS
FOREIGN POLICY, (74) (SPR 89), 168-184.
THE ARTICLE EXPLORES THE COMPLEXITIES AND CHALLENGES PRESENTED BY THE 104 NATIONALITIES THAT EXIST IN THE USSR. MIKHAIL GORBACHEV'S POLICIES OF GLASNOST AND PERESTROIKA HAVE ENCOURAGED A SURPRISING DEGREE OF OUTSPOKEN NATIONALIST SENTIMENT. ALTHOUGH NATIONALISTIC AGENDAS ARE SOMETIMES IN HARMONY WITH THE DESIRES OF THE CENTRAL GOVERNMENT, THEY ALSO POSE A GRAVE THREAT TO GORBACHEV'S REFORMS. HIS DESIRE TO MAKE DEMOCRATIC CENTRALISM MORE DEMOCRATIC AND LESS CENTRALIST WILL MOST CERTAINLY BE SLOWED IF THE CENTRAL GOVERNMENT HAS TO RESORT TO FORCE TO MAINTAIN ORDER.

02351 COCKBURN, P.
USSR AND ITS ETHNICS: THE DESIRE FOR AUTONOMY
CURRENT, (315) (SEP 89), 33.
RESURGENT NATIONALISM IS AN OPPORTUNITY AS WELL AS A THREAT TO REFORM IN THE USSR. IN THE BALTIC REPUBLICS, LOCAL LEADERS ARE DEMANDING THE VERY POLITICAL AND ECONOMIC DECENTRALIZATION THAT THE KREMLIN SAYS IT WANTS. IN THE BALTICS, GORBACHEV'S REVOLUTION FROM ABOVE IS PRODUCING THE MASS POLITICAL PARTICIPATION THAT HE CONSIDERS ESSENTIAL TO THE SUCCESS OF PERESTROIKA. BUT THE DANGER IS THAT THE DEMAND FOR GREATER CIVIL LIBERTY IS COMBINED WITH A NATIONALIST CHALLENGE TO THE VERY INTEGRITY OF THE SOVIET STATE.

02352 COCKSHOTT, P.; COTTRELL, A.
LABOUR VALUE AND SOCIALIST ECONOMIC CALCULATION
ECONOMY AND SOCIETY, 18(1) (FEB 89), 71-99.
THE USE OF LABOUR VALUES AS A BASIS FOR ECONOMIC CALCULATION IN A SOCIALIST ECONOMY IS DEFENDED. A RESOURCE ALLOCATION MECHANISM IS OUTLINED THAT USES A COMBINATION OF LABOUR VALUE CALCULATION WITH MARKET CLEARING PRICES FOR CONSUMER GOODS. CONDITIONS FOR FULL EMPLOYMENT ARE SPECIFIED. A TYPE THEORETIC ANALYSIS OF ECONOMIC CALCULATION IS PRESENTED. INFORMATION THEORY IS USED TO ESTIMATE THE INFORMATION CONTENT OF REAL PRICE VECTORS. IT IS DEMONSTRATED THAT BOTH PRICES CALCULATIONS AND VALUE CALCULATIONS ARE TYPE THEORY EQUIVALENT AND THAT BOTH INVOLVE INFORMATION LOSS. IT IS SHOWN THAT MODERN COMPUTER TECHNOLOGY IS CAPABLE OF COMPUTING UP TO DATE LABOUR VALUES WITH COMPARATIVE EASE.

02353 CODO, L.C.
ISRAEL'S RETURN TO SUB-SAHARAN AFRICA
JERUSALEM JOURNAL OF INTERNATIONAL RELATIONS, 11(1) (MAR 89), 58-73.
RECENT RESUMPTIONS OF DIPLOMATIC RELATIONS BETWEEN ISRAEL AND AFRICAN COUNTRIES ARE MANIFESTATIONS OF A MORE GENERAL PROCESS WHEREBY ISRAEL IS ATTEMPTING TO REBUILD ITS POLITICAL POSITION IN THE AFRICAN CONTINENT. ISRAEL'S MOTIVATIONS INVOLVE ECONOMIC, POLITICAL, AS WELL AS SECURITY CONSIDERATIONS AND ARE AN ASPECT OF ITS CONTINUING COMPETITION AND CONFLICT WITH THE ARAB STATES.

02354 CODRINGTON, H.
COUNTRY SIZE AND TAXATION IN DEVELOPING COUNTRIES
JOURNAL OF DEVELOPMENT STUDIES, 25(4) (JUL 89), 508-520.
THIS ARTICLE ADDRESSES THE ISSUE OF SIZE AND TAXATION IN POOR COUNTRIES. THE AUTHOR USES THREE CRITERIA OF SIZE TO DETERMINE TWO GROUPS OF VERY LARGE AND VERY SMALL COUNTRIES. AN ANALYSIS OF TAX DATA FOR THE TWO GROUPS REVEALS MARKED

DIFFERENCES IN THE CHOICE OF FISCAL INSTRUMENTS AND THE
DISTRIBUTION OF TAX REVENUE AS WELL AS HIGHER TAX RATIOS FOR
THE SMALL STATES. EVIDENCE BOTH FROM THE LITERATURE AND THIS
STUDY SUGGESTS THAT SMALLNESS GIVES RISE TO FEATURES WHICH
BOTH FACILITATE AND NECESSITATE HIGHER TAX COLLECTIONS.

02355 COE, F.D.
    COMPARABLE WORTH IN PUBLIC EMPLOYMENT
    DISSERTATION ABSTRACTS INTERNATIONAL, 49(7) (JAN 89),
    1955-A.
        THE AUTHOR EXAMINES THE COMPARABLE WORTH EMPLOYMENT
    ISSUE, INCLUDING ITS CULTURAL, ECONOMIC, LEGAL, POLITICAL,
    AND SOCIAL ASPECTS. HE SURVEYS ITS HISTORY, ITS RELATION TO
    JOB EVALUATION, ITS LAWFUL MERITS, AND ITS TREATMENT BY
    STATE AND LOCAL PUBLIC EMPLOYERS.

02356 COFFIN, W.
    THE MAIN DIFFICULTIES ARE YET TO COME
    WORLD MARXIST REVIEW, 32(10) (OCT 89), 32-34.
        THIS ARTICLE, BY WILLIAM COFFIN, PRESIDENT OF
    SANE/FREEZE CAMPAIGN FOR GLOBAL SECURITY (USA), ASSESSES THE
    PRESENT INTERNATIONAL SITUATION AND NEW DEVELOPMENTS IN THE
    US MOVEMENT FOR PEACE AND DISARMAMENT. HE REASSESSES THE
    COLD WAR, PERESTROIKA AND ADDRESSES GEOECONOMICS RATHER THAN
    GEOPOLITICS. HE ADVOCATES THREE MAJOR PROGRAMS: TO BRING
    DOWN THE MILITARY BUDGET, KEEP NUCLEAR WEAPONS PRODUCING
    PLANTS SHUT, AND TO BRING ABOUT LEGISLATION ON CONVERSION.

02357 COHAN, A.S.
    THE STATE IN THE BEDROOM: WHAT SOME ADULTS MAY NOT DO
    PRIVATELY AFTER "HARDWICK V. BOWERS"
    JOURNAL OF AMERICAN STUDIES, 23(I) (APR 89), 41-62.
        IN 1986 THE SUPREME COURT RULED THAT A GEORGIA STATE LAW
    FORBIDDING CONSENSUAL ADULT SODOMY WAS CONSTITUTIONAL. IN
    THIS ESSAY, THE AUTHOR ANALYZES THE OPINION, WHICH WAS
    WRITTEN BY JUSTICE WHITE, EXPLORING THE JUSTICE'S APPARENT
    TURNABOUT IN REASONING SINCE THE 1965 CASE OF GRISWOLD V.
    CONNECTICUT AND OFFERING AN EXPLANATION FOR THAT CHANGE.

02358 COHEN, B.
    A GLOBAL CHAPTER 11
    FOREIGN POLICY, (75) (SUM 89), 109-127.
        THE ARTICLE EXAMINES THE ONGOING PROBLEM OF THIRD WORLD
    DEBT. ALTHOUGH THE US HAS UNVEILED A NEW POLICY TO DEAL WITH
    THE "PROCESS THAT HAS BECOME DEBT-WEARY", THE PROGRAM
    REPRESENTS NO MORE THAN A REFINEMENT OF THE PREVAILING
    STRATEGY RATHER THAN A FUNDAMENTAL REFORM. THE ARTICLE
    PROPOSES A REFORM PLAN THAT INCORPORATES THE FIVE CRUCIAL
    SAFEGUARDS OF SELECTIVITY, FLEXIBILITY, CONDITIONALITY,
    MUTUALITY, AND AUTONOMY. IT PROPOSES THE CREATION OF AN
    INTERNATIONAL DEBT RESTRUCTURING AGENCY THAT WOULD PLAY THE
    ROLE IN LDC DEBT NEGOTIATIONS COMPARABLE OF THAT OF THE
    BANKRUPTCY COURT IN THE CHAPTER 11 PROCEDURE.

02359 COHEN, E.S.
    JUSTICE AND POLITICAL ECONOMY IN COMMERCIAL SOCIETY: ADAM
    SMITH'S "SCIENCE OF A LEGISLATOR"
    THE JOURNAL OF POLITICS, 51(1) (FEB 89), 50-72.
        THE PROBLEM OF ADAM SMITH'S ASSESSMENT OF "COMMERCIAL
    SOCIETY" IS INEXTRICABLY LINKED TO THE NATURE OF THE UNITY
    OF HIS MORAL PHILOSOPHY. IN THIS ARTICLE, THE AUTHOR OFFERS
    AN INTERPRETATION OF SMITH'S "SCIENCE OF A LEGISLATOR" THAT
    LOCATES ITS UNITY AND MEANING IN THE APPLICATION OF A
    CERTAIN METHOD OF ANALYSIS IN HIS THEORY OF JUSTICE AND
    POLITICAL ECONOMY. IN SMITH'S SCIENCE, COMMERCIAL SOCIETY IS
    CONSTITUTED BY A SET OF PRINCIPLES, OR MECHANISMS, THE TWO
    MOST IMPORTANT BEING MORAL SENTIMENTS AND COMPETITIVE
    MARKETS. THESE MECHANISMS TRANSFORM THE PURSUIT OF SELF-LOVE
    TOWARD THE PUBLIC GOOD AND ARE BASED UPON THE FACULTY OF
    SYMPATHY. WHEN PROPERLY GUIDED BY THE LEGISLATOR, THEY YIELD
    BOTH JUSTICE AND OPULENCE. THE EFFECTS OF COMMERCE ON THE
    CHARACTER OF THE LABORING CLASSES, HOWEVER, THREATEN TO
    UNDERMINE MORAL SENTIMENTS AND, THUS, THE BASIS OF JUSTICE
    AND SOCIAL COHESION. THE ADVANCEMENT OF JUSTICE IN
    COMMERCIAL SOCIETY, THEN, WILL DEPEND UPON THE LEGISLATOR'S
    ABILITY TO ENSURE THE PROPER FUNCTIONING OF THESE MECHANISMS
    AND TO PROTECT THE MORAL SENTIMENTS FROM THE CORROSIVE
    EFFECTS OF COMMERCE. SMITH'S SCIENCE PROVIDES A LIMITED AND
    SKEPTICAL ENDORSEMENT OF COMMERCIAL SOCIETY AS A MEANS TO
    THE ESTABLISHMENT OF JUSTICE. IT IS OFFERED AS A GUIDE TO
    THOSE "MEN OF PUBLIC SPIRIT" WHO WOULD ENDEAVOR TO ENSURE
    THE PRESERVATION OF JUSTICE AND THE MORAL TIES THAT BIND THE
    COMMUNITY IN A WORLD INCREASINGLY DOMINATED BY COMMERCE.

02360 COHEN, H.J.
    INDEPENDENCE PROCESS IN NAMIBIA
    DEPARTMENT OF STATE BULLETIN (US FOREIGN POLICY), 89(2152)
    (NOV 89), 43-44.
        NEARLY FOUR MONTHS INTO THE IMPLEMENTATION OF UN
    SECURITY COUNCIL RESOLUTION 435, THE TRANSITION TO NAMIBIAN
    INDEPENDENCE IS FIRMLY IN PLACE. DESPITE SOME DELAYS--
    PRIMARILY CAUSED BY SWAPO'S SURPRISE INCURSION ON APRIL 1,
    1989, AND THE RESULTING ADMINISTRATIVE GLITCHES--ALL PARTIES
    REMAIN COMMITTED TO KEEPING THE INDEPENDENCE PROCESS ON

TRACK AND ENSURING THAT ELECTIONS FOR THE CONSTITUENT
ASSEMBLY ARE HELD IN NOVEMBER 1989.

02361 COHEN, H.J.
    SOUTH AFRICA
    DEPARTMENT OF STATE BULLETIN (US FOREIGN POLICY), 89(2153)
    (DEC 89), 29-30.
        THE BUSH ADMINISTRATION WANTS TO BE ABLE TO SEND SOUTH
    AFRICA A CLEAR SIGNAL OF BROAD, BIPARTISAN SUPPORT FOR A
    POLICY PREMISED ON UNEQUIVOCAL ABHORRENCE OF APARTHEID,
    REFLECTED IN A SUSTAINED U.S. COMMITTMENT TO PROMOTING
    NEGOTIATIONS BETWEEN THE GOVERNMENT IN PRETORIA AND
    LEGITIMATE BLACK REPRESENTATIVES. THE AMERICAN PEOPLE'S
    OUTRAGE AT APARTHEID IS SHARED BY THE BUSH ADMINISTRATION
    AND IS THE IMPETUS FOR THE ADMINISTRATION TO ACCORD PRIORITY
    ATTENTION TO POLITICAL CHANGE IN SOUTH AFRICA.

02362 COHEN, M.
    A PROFUSION OF LAND MINES
    COMMONWEAL, CXVI(9) (MAY 89), 275-278.
        THE KEY TO UNDERSTANDING YITZHAK SHAMIR'S DIPLOMACY IS
    HIS TENACITY. THE ISRAELI PRMIER IS A SHREWD POLITICIAN OF
    PATIENCE AND NERVE. HAVING SECURED THE PREMIERSHIP IN THE
    1988 NATIONAL ELECTION, SHAMIR AND HIS RIGHT-WING LIKUD
    PARTY REINFORCED THEIR DOMESTIC STANDING BY ROUTING THE
    LEFTLEANING LABOR PARTY IN LATE WINTER'S MUNICIPAL ELECTIONS.
    SHAMIR HAS OUTMANEUVERED HIS OPPONENTS WITHIN THE LIKUD AND,
    MORE IMPORTANTLY, HE HAS OUTMANEUVERED LABOR. THE LATTER,
    ALTHOUGH OPPOSED TO THE PREMIER'S POLICIES, NOW SITS IN A
    "NATIONAL UNITY" GOVERNMENT DOMINATED BY HIM.

02363 COHEN, M.
    FORGIVEN AND NEGLECTED
    FAR EASTERN ECONOMIC REVIEW, 141(31) (AUG 88), 14-15.
        IN MARCH 1987, THE PHILIPPINE PRESIDENT CORZON AQUINO
    LAUNCHED A PROGRAM TO ENCOURAGE THE COMMUNIST NEW PEOPLE'S
    ARMY TO "LAY DOWN THEIR ARMS AND REJOIN THE MAINSTREAM OF
    SOCIETY IN A PEACEFUL AND PRODUCTIVE LIFE." THE RETURNEES
    WERE PROMISED AMNESTY FOR ACTS OF SUBVERSION AND ASSISTANCE
    FROM THE GOVERNMENT IN THE FORM OF LOANS, LAND, VOCATIONAL
    TRAINING, HIGHER EDUCATION, AND JOB PLACEMENTS. MORE THAN 7,
    000 NPA REGULARS HAD "SURRENDERED BY THE AMNESTY DEADLINE.
    HOWEVER, MANY ARE FINDING THAT THE GOVERNMENT'S PROMISES ARE
    NOT BEING FULFILLED, MANY SEEM TO BE WORSE OFF THAN THEY
    WERE BEFORE.

02364 COHEN, M.
    RESTRUCTURING THE SYSTEM
    SOCIETY, 26(4) (MAY 89), 40-48.
        THE ARTICLE OUTLINES SOME OF THE CHALLENGES FACING THE
    US EDUCATIONAL SYSTEM IN THE FUTURE. THESE CHALLENGES ARE
    FUNDAMENTALLY DIFFERENT FROM THOSE IT HAS CONFRONTED IN THE
    PAST, LARGELY BECAUSE OF SIGNIFICANT CHANGES IN THE ECONOMIC
    AND SOCIAL FABRIC OF THE COUNTRY. RESPONDING TO THESE NEW
    CHALLENGES WILL REQUIRE A FUNDAMENTAL RESTRUCTURING OF
    SCHOOLS, ESPECIALLY OF THE WAY INSTRUCTION IS PROVIDED AND
    STAFF ROLES AND RESPONSIBILITIES ARE DEFINED. HOWEVER,
    NEEDED CHANGES IN SCHOOLS CANNOT OCCUR WITHOUT CORRESPONDING
    CHANGES IN THE WAY LOCAL DISTRICTS AND STATES OPERATE. ONLY
    BY MAKING CONCORDANT CHANGES AT THE SCHOOL, DISTRICT AND
    STATE LEVELS WILL THE EDUCATION SYSTEM BE ABLE TO RESPOND TO
    THE CHALLENGES OF THE COMING DECADE.

02365 COHEN, M.
    THE END OF JEANE KIRKPATRICK'S IDEOLOGY
    DISSENT,   (SPR 89), 143-145.
        NO THEORY WAS MORE CELEBRATED BY THE COLD WAR WARRIORS
    THAN THAT EXPOUNDED IN JEANE KIRKPATRICK'S "DICTATORSHIPS
    AND DOUBLE STANDARDS." THE REAGAN ADMINISTRATION USED IT TO
    JUSTIFY SUPPORT FOR AN ASSORTMENT OF MISCREANTS RUNNING
    RIGHT-WING REGIMES, ITS HYSTERICAL ANTI-COMMUNISM, AND ITS
    BLOATED DEFENSE BUDGET. BUT AT THE 1988 REPUBLICAN NATIONAL
    CONVENTION, KIRKPATRICK HERSELF PRONOUNCED AN EPITAPH FOR
    HER INTELLECTUAL CLAIM TO FAME.

02366 COHEN, M. P.
    U.S. LEGAL INVOLVEMENT IN VIOLATIONS OF PALESTINIAN RIGHTS
    JOURNAL OF PALESTINE STUDIES, XVIII(3) (SPR 89), 76-95.
        THE PALESTINIAN INTIFADAH THAT BEGAN IN DECEMBER 1987
    HAS FOCUSED WORLD ATTENTION ON THE ISRAELI MILITARY
    OCCUPATION OF THE WEST BANK AND THE GAZA STRIP, AND A VARIETY
    OF REPRESSIVE TACTICS USED BY ISRAEL TO SUSTAIN THAT
    OCCUPATION. ALTHOUGH PALESTINIAN OUTRAGE HAS BEEN DIRECTED
    PRIMARILY AGAINST ISRAEL, ANGER ALSO HAS BEEN VENTED AT THE
    UNITED STATES, WHICH MANY PALESTINIANS CONSIDER COMPLICIT IN
    ISRAEL'S MISCONDUCT. THIS ARTICLE EXPLORES THE LEGAL
    QUESTION OF "COMPLICITY" IN INTERNATIONAL LAW, AND ITS
    APPLICATION TO THE U.S.-ISRAEL RELATIONSHIP AND THE ONGOING
    ISRAELI OCCUPATION.

02367 COHEN, R.; RANGER, R.
    ENFORCING CHEMICALS WEAPONS BAN
    INTERNATIONAL PERSPECTIVES, 18(4) (JUL 89), 9-12.
        CHEMICAL WEAPONS ARE INCREASING IN ATTRACTIVENESS AS THE

WORLD FAILS TO SUPPLY PENALTIES FOR THEIR USE. THE TWO
SECURITY THINKERS WHO WROTE THIS ARTICLE OFFER A FORMULA FOR
CONTROL AND SHARE THEIR ANXIETY AND THEIR HOPE. THEY ANALYZE
LESSONS LEARNED FROM IRAQ AND THE CURRENT CW LIMITS.
EXPLORED IS WHY SANCTIONS FAIL AND POSSIBLE CW VIOLATIONS.
PREVENTIVE ACTION IS SUGGESTED.

02368 COHEN, R.; WILSON, P.A.
TOWARD A U.S. NATIONAL SECURITY STRATEGY FOR THE 1990S:
ASSURING 21ST. CENTURY COMPETITIVENESS
COMPARATIVE STRATEGY, 8(1) (1989), 21-53.
CONTRARY TO WHAT 1980S TRENDS APPEAR TO SUGGEST, U.S.
POLICY MAKERS IN THE NEXT DECADE WILL CONFRONT A DAUNTING
NATIONAL SECURITY CHALLENGE, HAVING TO MAKE CRITICAL CHOICES
OVER THE DISTRIBUTION OF NATIONAL RESOURCES AND DEFENSE
SECTOR INVESTMENT POLICIES. IN A PERIOD OF UNUSUAL
CONSTRAINTS ON NATIONAL RESOURCES, THE U.S. WILL HAVE TO
ENGINEER A STRATEGY THAT REVITALIZES ITS ECONOMY WHILE
MANAGING AN UNCERTAIN SOVIET THREAT WITH FEWER RESOURCES
DEVOTED TO DEFENSE. FAILURE TO NAVIGATE THIS COURSE COULD
LEAD TO A WEAKENING OF THE U.S.'S DEFENSE MOBILIZATION BASE
AND A RETREAT FROM GLOBAL SECURITY OBJECTIVES BY THE
BEGINNING OF THE NEXT CENTURY, AN ESPECIALLY ALARMING RESULT
SINCE THE STAKES INVOLVED IN THIS COMING TEST OF AMERICAN
SKILL AND RESOLVE WILL HAVE BEEN RAISED BY A LOOMING
TRANSCENTURY WEAPONS REVOLUTION THAT HEIGHTENS THE POTENTIAL
FOR DESTABILIZING STRATEGIC ASYMMETRIES. HOW WELL THE U.S.
MEETS THIS TEST WILL STRONGLY INFLUENCE ITS COMPETITIVENESS
IN THE TRANSCENTURY SECURITY ENVIRONMENT.

02369 COHEN, S.F.
THE COLD WAR: A PRESIDENTIAL AGENDA
CURRENT, (311) (MAR 89), 32.
THE COLD WAR, WITH THE US-SOVIET ARMS RACE AS ITS MOST
CHARACTERISTIC EXPRESSION, HAS BECOME THE GREATEST THREAT TO
AMERICA'S NATIONAL INTERESTS IN TWO PROFOUND WAYS. ABOVE ALL,
IT THREATENS OUR NATIONAL SURVIVAL. IT ALSO IS SAPPING
AMERICA'S ECONOMIC HEALTH, WHICH IS AS IMPORTANT FOR REAL
NATIONAL SECURITY AS WEAPONS ARE. IF THE PRESIDENT LACKS THE
VISION AND COURAGE TO END THE COLD WAR, HE WILL BE
NEGLECTING THE BEST INTERESTS OF THE USA.

02370 COHEN, W.
SYMBOLS OF POWER: STATUES IN NINETEENTH CENTURY PROVINCIAL
FRANCE
COMPARATIVE STUDIES IN SOCIETY AND HISTORY, 31(3) (JUL 89),
491-513.
STATUES WERE AN IMMEDIATE AND APPARENTLY UNMEDIATED WAY
OF COMMUNICATING POLITICAL VALUES TO A PEOPLE WHO MIGHT BE
WAVERING IN POLITICAL LOYALTIES. IF THE ORIGINAL SENSE OF
COMMUNITY MIGHT WELL BE THE VILLAGE, THE INTRUSION OF
SYMBOLS THAT LINKED LOCALE WITH LARGE AND HISTORICALLY
SIGNIFICANT EVENTS OF FRANCE HELPED TO CREATE AN IMAGINED
COMMUNITY. IN PART, CIVIC SYMBOLISM MADE IT POSSIBLE FOR
PEOPLE TO IMAGINE COMMON MEMBERSHIP IN THIS COMMUNITY.

02371 COHN, C. E.
NUCLEAR DISCOURSE IN A COMMUNITY OF DEFENSE INTELLECTUALS:
THE EFFECTS OF TECHNO-STRATEGIC LANGUAGE AND RATIONALITY
AND THEIR ROLE IN AMERICAN POLITICAL CULTURE
DISSERTATION ABSTRACTS INTERNATIONAL, 49(8) (FEB 89),
2374-A.
THIS PAPER IS AN EXAMINATION OF THE DISCOURSE OF NUCLEAR
DEFENSE INTELLECTUALS, EXPLORING ITS EFFECTS BOTH WITHIN THE
PROFESSIONAL COMMUNITY AND IN THE WIDER POLITICAL CULTURE.
FEMINIST CRITIQUES OF DOMINANT WESTERN CONCEPTS OF REASON,
AS WELL AS POST-STRUCTURALIST WORK IN DISCOURSE ANALYSIS,
PROVIDE THE INTELLECTUAL FRAME.

02372 COLASANTO, D.; DESTEFANO, L.
ABORTION: PRO-CHOICE POSITION STIRS INCREASED ACTIVISM IN
ABORTION BATTLE
GALLUP REPORT, (289) (OCT 89), 16-20.
AMERICANS WHO BELIEVE A WOMAN HAS A RIGHT TO AN ABORTION
HAVE DRAMATICALLY STEPPED UP THEIR ACTIVISM ON THE ISSUE
DURING THE PAST TEN YEARS. IN ADDITION, THE POPULATION AS A
WHOLE FAVORS THE PRO-CHOICE POSITION. A CLEAR MAJORITY (61
PERCENT) OF AMERICANS DO NOT WANT THE SUPREME COURT TO
OVERTURN ROE V. WADE, WHILE ONLY ONE-THIRD ARE IN FAVOR OF A
REVERSAL.

02373 COLASANTO, D.
PUBLIC WANTS CIVIL RIGHTS WIDENED FOR SOME GROUPS, NOT FOR
OTHERS
GALLUP REPORT, (291) (DEC 89), 13-22.
THIS ARTICLE REPORTS PUBLIC OPINION SURVEYS ON CIVIL
RIGHTS PROGRESS IN THE UNITED STATES, GEORGE BUSH'S
PERFORMANCE IN THE AREA OF CIVIL RIGHTS, THE NEED FOR
PREFERENTIAL TREATMENT OF WOMEN AND MINORITIES, AND
RESPONSIBILITY FOR RACIAL PROBLEMS. BY AN OVERWHELMING
MARGIN, THE AMERICAN PUBLIC WANTS TO SEE THE CIVIL RIGHTS OF
THE ELDERLY AND THE DISABLED RECEIVE MOR ATTENTION. BUT
AMERICAN ARE MUCH LESS SUPPORTIVE OF INCREASED EFFORTS ON
BEHALF OF GROUPS THAT HAVE TRADITIONALLY BEEN THE FOCUS OF

CIVIL RIGHTS PROGRAMS AND LEGISLATION.

02374 COLASANTO, D.
SOCIAL ISSUES: BUSH PRESIDENCY TARNISHED BY GROWING PUBLIC
CONCERN ABOUT POVERTY
GALLUP REPORT, (287) (AUG 89), 2-7.
IN A COUNTRY THAT HAS ENJOYED ALMOST SEVEN YEARS OF
UNINTERRUPTED ECONOMIC GROWTH, THERE IS GROWING PUBLIC
CONCERN ABOUT POVERTY. PRESIDENT BUSH'S PROMISE THAT HE WILL
FORGE A "KINDER, GENTLER NATION" STANDS IN SHARP CONTRAST TO
PUBLIC PERCEPTIONS OF INCREASING POVERTY. AS A RESULT, ONLY
A THIRD OF AMERICANS APPROVE OF BUSH'S HANDLING OF THE
PROBLEMS OF POVERTY AND HOMELESSNESS, WHILE A MAJORITY
DISAPPROVE.

02375 COLBORNE, D.
A THAW IN FRANCO-SA RELATIONS?
SOUTH AFRICA FOUNDATION REVIEW, 15(1) (JAN 89), 7.
THE AUTHOR PREDICTS A SLIGHT THAW IN FRANCO-SOUTH
AFRICAN RELATIONS IN 1989.

02376 COLBORNE, D.
EUROPE AND SOUTHERN AFRICA
SOUTH AFRICA FOUNDATION REVIEW, 15(3) (MAR 89), 7-8.
THE AUTHOR SURVEYS HOW SOUTH AFRICA IS VIEWED IN THE
NETHERLANDS, ITALY, FRANCE, MOZAMBIQUE, AND ZIMBABWE

02377 COLBORNE, D.
FRANCE AND SOUTH AFRICA MID YEAR REVIEW
SOUTH AFRICA FOUNDATION REVIEW, 15(7) (JUL 89), 5.
FRENCH ATTITUDES TO SOUTH AFRICA, AND TO AFRICA AT LARGE,
CAN BE SUMMED UP IN TWO OR THREE PHRASES-- "WAIT AND SEE"
WITH REGARDS TO SOUTH AFRICA, AND DISINVESTMENT AND
MARGINALIZATION WITH REGARDS TO AFRICA IN GENERAL. ALTHOUGH
PUBLIC FUNDS AND AID CONTINUE TO FLOW INTO AFRICA, PRIVATE
INVESTMENT BY FRENCH COMPANIES IS SIGNIFICANTLY DIMINISHING.
DISINVESTMENT IS ALSO PRESENT IN SOUTH AFRICA, BUT, ON THE
WHOLE, THE FRENCH ARE WAITING TO SEE IF F.W. DE KLERK HAS
THE ABILITY AND WILLINGNESS TO INSTIGATE SIGNIFICANT REFORMS.

02378 COLBURN, F.
TURNING TO THE VOTERS IN NICARAGUA
NEW LEADER, LXXII(17) (NOV 89), 5-7.
THE NEXT FEW MONTHS ARE CRITICAL FOR NICARAGUA. THE
SANDINISTA GOVERNMENT WILL FACE A NATIONAL REFERENDUM ON
FEBRUARY 25. VOTER OPINION POLLS ARE CONFUSING. SOME SHOW A
CLOSE RACE BETWEEN DANIEL ORTEGA AND VIOLETA CHAMORRO OF THE
UNITED NICARAGUAN OPPOSITION (UNO). OTHERS SHOW ORTEGA WITH
A CLEAR LEAD. THE ONLY POINT OF AGREEMENT IS THAT A
SIGNIFICANT PERCENTAGE OF VOTERS ARE, AS OF YET, UNDECIDED.

02379 COLE, A.M.
FACTIONALISM, THE FRENCH SOCIALIST PARTY, AND THE FIFTH
REPUBLIC: AN EXPLANATION OF INTRA-PARTY DIVISIONS
EUROPEAN JOURNAL OF POLITICAL RESEARCH, 17(1) (JAN 89),
77-94.
THIS ARTICLE TRACES THE EVOLUTION OF FACTIONS WITHIN THE
FRENCH SOCIALIST PARTY (PS) FROM THE EARLY TWENTIETH CENTURY
UNTIL 1981, WITH SPECIAL REFERENCE TO THE POST-1971 PS AS A
PARTY OF OPPOSITION. IT CONCENTRATES ON THE CAUSES AND
STRUCTURES OF FACTIONS, AS WELL AS THEIR LOCATION TO THE
WIDER POLITICAL SYSTEM AND THE DEGREE OF POLITICAL SPACE
THEY WERE ABLE TO OCCUPY WITHIN THE PARTY. IT ARGUES THAT
FACTIONS WERE DIVIDED BY PERSONAL RIVALRIES (ACCENTUATED BY
THE PRESIDENTIALISED FIFTH REPUBLIC), IDEOLOGICAL AND PARTY
POLICY DIFFERENCES, PARTY STRATEGY, POWER RIVALRIES WITHIN
THE ORGANISATION AND DIFFERENT HISTORICAL ORIGINS. FACTIONS
CORRESPONDED MORE OR LESS TO A SERIES OF IDEAL-TYPES. THESE
WERE THE ORGANISATION FACTION, WHOSE POWER STEMMED FROM ITS
POSITION WITHIN THE PARTY ORGANISATION; THE PARALLEL FACTION,
WHOSE SEPARATE FACTIONAL STRUCTURES PARALLEL OFFICIAL PARTY
ONES, AND THE EXTERNAL FACTION, WHICH ATTEMPTED TO TRANSFORM
EXTERNAL POPULARITY INTO INTERNAL PARTY STRENGTH. FOUR
FACTIONS PREVAILED: MITTERRAND, MAUROY, CERES AND ROCARD.
THOSE HEADED BY PRESIDENTIABLES ENJOYED THE MOST SUCCESS,
WHEREAS THE OTHERS GRADUALLY DECLINED. THE PRESIDENTIALISM
OF THE FRENCH REGIME SET THE PS APART FROM ITS EUROPEAN
COUNTERPARTS.

02380 COLE, J.W.; NYDON, J.A.
CLASS, GENDER, AND FERTILITY: CONTRADICTIONS OF SOCIAL
LIFE IN CONTEMPORARY ROMANIA
EAST EUROPEAN QUARTERLY, XXIII(4) (WIN 89), 469-476.
IN THE MID-1960'S THE ROMANIAN GOVERNMENT SWITCHED FROM
RELATIVELY PERMISSIVE POSITIONS ON ABORTION AND
CONTRACEPTION TO VIGOROUS PRO-NATAL POLICIES. BUT THESE NEW
POLICIES DID NOT EFFECT THE HOPED-FOR LONG TERM INCREASE IN
FERTILITY RATES. DESPITE THE FAILURE OF PRO-NATALIST
POLICIES AND THEIR ROLE IN DISADVANTAGING WOMEN, THE
ROMANIAN GOVERNMENT HAS REMAINED DEDICATED TO ITS POSITION.
THIS PAPER EXAMINES WHY ROMANIA BECAME AND CONTINUES TO BE
PRO-NATALIST AND WHY THE POLICY HAS FAILED.

02381 COLE, R.T.
MICHIGAN GOV. BLANCHARD: MANAGING THROUGH MESSAGES
JOURNAL OF STATE GOVERNMENT, 62(4) (JUL 89), 147-152.
MICHIGAN GOVERNOR JAMES J. BLANCHARD HAS BEEN GIVEN
CREDIT FOR SAVING THE STATE FROM BANKRUPTCY AND PUTTING IT
ON SOLID FINANCIAL GROUND. THE KEY TO HIS SUCCESS HAS BEEN
HIS MESSAGE AND THE INNOVATIVE POLICY SUPPORTED BY IT. HE
COMMUNICATED HIS COMEBACK PLAN DIRECTLY TO THE PUBLIC,
DESCRIBING HIS ASPIRATIONS FOR THE STATE'S FUTURE. BUT
BLANCHARD DID NOT ACT ALONE. HE USED HIS CABINET ADROITLY,
PROVIDING CABINET HEADS WITH THE INFORMATION AND INSPIRATION
NECESSARY TO MANAGE THEIR AGENCIES AND DISSEMINATE HIS
MESSAGE ACROSS THE STATE.

02382 COLEMAN, J.
PRODUCTS LIABILITY REFORM
SOCIETY, 27(1) (NOV 89), 57-66.
THE ARTICLE EXAMINES THE INCREASINGLY COMPLEX WORLD OF
PRODUCT LIABILITY. US MANUFACTURER'S CONCERNS ABOUT EXPOSURE
AND UNCERTAINLY ARE HEIGHTENED BY CURRENT US LIABILITY LAW.
THIS UNCERTAINLY HAS HAD A DIRECT EFFECT ON THE PRODUCTIVITY
OF US MANUFACTURERS. THE ARTICLE OUTLINES THE ONGOING
CHANGES IN LIABILITY LAW; THE GENERAL TREND IS TOWARDS
STRICT LIABILITY IN CONJUNCTION WITH DESIGN DEFECT TESTS. IT
CONCLUDES BY OFFERING SOME SUGGESTIONS FOR REFORM OF THE
CURRENT SYSTEM.

02383 COLEMAN, J.
THE WILD CARDS IN THE 1992 PACK
CONTEMPORARY REVIEW, 254(1480) (MAY 89), 235-240.
THE INESCAPABLE CHARACTER OF THE 1992 ADVENTURE AS IT IS
BEING APPROACHED AT THE MOMENT IS THAT IT IS REVOLUTIONARY
RATHER THAN EVOLUTIONARY AND MAY WELL HAVE ALL THE DANGEROUS
QUALITIES OF REVOLUTION INHERENT IN IT. ITS MOST
ENTHUSIASTIC SUPPORTERS ARGUE THAT UNLESS THE EC GOES THE
WHOLE HOG WITH THE PROJECT NOTHING WILL REALLY HAPPEN AND
THE COMMUNITY WILL SIMPLY DIE A SLOW DEATH. BUT IS THAT
REALLY TRUE? THE STEP BY STEP APPROACH MAY NOT HAVE THE
EMOTIONAL APPEAL OF THE GRAND PLAN BUT THE PRAGMATIST WILL
CERTAINLY ARGUE THAT IT IS THE WAY THAT IS MOST LIKELY TO
SUCCEED IN THE LONGER TERM.

02384 COLEMAN, J.A.
WHO ARE THE CATHOLIC "FUNDAMENTALISTS?"
COMMONWEAL, CXVI(2) (JAN 89), 42-47.
THE AUTHOR SERVEYS THE HISTORY FO CATHOLIC
FUNDAMENTALISTS, THEIR POLITICAL PREFERENCES AND THE POWER
THEY WIELD.

02385 COLEMAN, P.
THE BRIEF LIFE OF LIBERAL ANTI-COMMUNISM
NATIONAL REVIEW, XLI(17) (SEP 89), 34-36.
THIS ARTICLE EXAMINES THE FORMATION AND IMPACT OF NON-
COMMUNIST LEFTIST ORGANIZATION SUCH AS THE CONGRESS FOR
CULTURAL FREEDOM. INTELLECTUAL AMERICAN GOVERNMENT CIRCLES
WERE CONVINCED THAT SUPPORT OF THE NON-COMMUNIST LEFT WOULD
BE THE MOST EFFECTIVE RESPONSE TO THE TOTALITARIAN LEFT.

02386 COLEMAN, P.V.
A STUDY OF THE FEASIBILITY OF USING RETIRED PEACE OFFICERS
AS VOLUNTEERS IN LAW ENFORCEMENT
DISSERTATION ABSTRACTS INTERNATIONAL, 50(2) (AUG 89),
540-A.
IN RESPONSE TO THE CONTINUED REDUCTION IN FUNDS AND
PERSONNEL FOR LAW ENFORCEMENT, THIS DISSERTATION PROPOSES
THAT RETIRED PEACE OFFICERS BE SPECIFICALLY TARGETED FOR
RECRUITMENT AS LAW ENFORCEMENT VOLUNTEERS. TWO MAJOR
OBSTACLES CAN BE ANTICIPATED IN THE IMPLEMENTATION OF A
RETIRED PEACE OFFICER VOLUNTEER PROGRAM. VIGOROUS OPPOSITION
CAN BE EXPECTED FROM POLICE LABOR UNIONS, AND A VARIETY OF
LEGAL AND CIVIL LIABILITY ISSUES WILL BE RAISED.

02387 COLEMAN, R. D.
US-MEXICO RELATIONS: WHO'S IN CHARGE?
MEXICO-UNITED STATES REPORT, II(6) (FEB 89), 3.
UNDER THE REAGAN ADMINISTRATION, US POLICY TOWARD MEXICO
HAS BEEN BASED ON AN IDEOLOGICAL APPROACH FOCUSED ON NICARAGUA
AND NOT ON POLITICAL, SOCIAL, OR ECONOMIC REALITIES IN
MEXICO. SINCE BUSH TOOK OFFICE, OBSERVERS HAVE BEEN WATCHING
TO SEE IF SECRETARY OF STATE BAKER WILL MAKE A RADICAL
DEPARTURE FROM PAST PRACTICES AND ASSUME CONTROL.

02388 COLEMAN, V.
LABOR POWER AND SOCIAL EQUALITY: UNION POLITICS IN A
CHANGING ECONOMY
POLITICAL SCIENCE QUARTERLY, 103(4) (WIN 89), 687-706.
FOCUSING ON THE POST-1960 POLITICS OF THE AFL-CIO, THE
AUTHOR ARGUES THAT AMERICAN LABOR IS BEST UNDERSTOOD AS A
SOCIAL MOVEMENT WHOSE POLITICAL POWER IS DETERMINED BY THE
UNION LEADERSHIP'S ABILITY TO SOLIDIFY PERMANENT LINKAGES
WITH UNORGANIZED SEGMENTS OF THE WORK FORCE. LACKING THE
INSTITUTIONALIZED POWER AFFORDED TO UNIONS IN CLASS-ORIENTED
LABOR PARTY SYSTEMS, AMERICAN LABOR'S INFLUENCE IN NATIONAL
GOVERNMENT IS CONTINGENT UPON THE EXTENT TO WHICH THE STATE

RECOGNIZES UNION LEADERS AS REPRESENTATIVE OF THE LARGER
UNORGANIZED WORK FORCE.

02389 COLEMAN, W.D.
SELF-REGULATION IN THE CANADIAN SECURITIES INDUSTRY: A
STUDY OF THE INVESTMENT DEALERS ASSOCIATION OF CANADA
CANADIAN PUBLIC ADMINISTRATION, 32(4) (WIN 89), 503-523.
THIS ARTICLE EXAMINES AN IMPORTANT SECTOR OF THE ECONOMY,
SECURITIES DEALING, AND SHOWS HOW IT HAS COME TO BE
GOVERNED BY A MIX OF STATE SUPERVISION AND PRIVATE INTEREST
GOVERNMENT. AN INTEREST ASSOCIATION HAS ACHIEVED A UNIQUE
"PUBLIC STATUS" AND HAS ASSUMED RESPONSIBILITY FOR
IMPLEMENTING POLICY AND DISCIPLINING MEMBER FIRMS. THE
DEVELOPMENT OF SELF-REGULATORY MODES OF GOVERNANCE THROUGH
PRIVATE INTEREST GOVERNMENTS, THE ARTICLE SUGGESTS, IS MORE
LIKELY IN HIGHLY CONCENTRATED SECTORS THAT OFFER SPECIALIZED,
TECHNICAL SERVICES RATHER THAN THOSE THAT MANUFACTURE GOODS.
THE ARGUMENT IS DEVELOPED THROUGH A CASE STUDY OF THE
INVESTMENT DEALERS ASSOCIATION OF CANADA AND ITS ROLE IN THE
SECURITIES INDUSTRY. USING A TYPOLOGY OF POLICY NETWORKS,
THE ARTICLE TRACES THE HISTORICAL PATH FROM AN INFORMAL,
PRIMITIVE SYSTEM OF SELF-REGULATION, REQUIRING LITTLE
ATTENTION FROM GOVERNMENT, TO A HIGHLY FORMALIZED SYSTEM,
JOINTLY MANAGED BY COMPLEX STATE AND INDUSTRY ORGANIZATIONS.

02390 COLES,R.
SHAPIRO, GENEALOGY, AND ETHICS
POLITICAL THEORY, 17(4) (NOV 89), 375-379.
MICHAEL SHAPIRO' PROVOCATIVE ARTICLE "POLITICIZING
ULYSSES: RATIONALISTIC, CRITICAL, AND GENEALOGICAL
COMMENTARIES," REVEALS THE DEPOLITICIZING AND
DECONTEXTUALIZING EFFECTS OF CERTAIN RATIONALIST APPROACHES
TO TEXTS AND SOCIAL PRACTICES. SHAPIRO'S ESSAY
SIMULTANEOUSLY AVOIDS ADDRESSING THE IMPORTANT QUESTION OF
THE POSSIBILITY AND DESIRABILITY OF FORULATING A
GENEALOGICAL ETHIC. THE AIM OF THIS REPLY IS TO FIRST
EMPHASIZE THE IMPORTANCE OF THE ETHICAL QUESTION FOR
GENEALOGY IF IT IS TO BE ADEQUATE FOR THE DESIRE FOR FREEDOM
THAT ANIMATES IT, AND SECOND, TO ARGUE THAT THE GENEALOGICAL
DISCOURSE OF WHICH SHAPIRO IS A PART IS, IN FACT, CAPABLE OF
DEVELOPING AN ETHICAL STANCE THAT COULD BE A PROFOUND VOICE
IN THE CONTEMPORARY DEBATE OVER WHAT IS POLICALLY AND
SOCIALLY DESIRABLE.

02391 COLLAMORE, T.J.
MAKING MBO WORK IN THE PUBLIC SECTOR
BUREAUCRAT, 18(3) (FAL 89), 37-40.
ON APRIL 11, 1989, PRESIDENT BUSH ANNOUNCED A GOVERNMENT-
WIDE MANAGEMENT BY OBJECTIVES (MBO) INITIATIVE TO TRACK
PROGRESS IN MEETING KEY POLICY PRIORITIES. THIS ARTICLE
LOOKS AT A SUCCESSFUL PUBLIC-SECTOR MBO SYSTEM THAT IS
ALREADY IN USE IN THE COMMERCE DEPARTMENT.

02392 COLLIE, M.
ELECTORAL PATTERNS AND VOTING ALINGMENTS IN THE US HOUSE
1886-1986
LEGISLATIVE STUDIES QUARTERLY, XIV(1) (FEB 89), 107-128.
CONGRESSIONAL SCHOLARS HAVE EXAMINED THE RELATIONSHIP
BETWEEN ELECTORAL AND INSTITUTIONAL POLITICS FROM A VARIETY
OF PERSPECTIVES. IN THIS TRADITION, THE FOCUS OF THE PAPER
OS ON THE IMPORTANCE OF INDIVIDUALISM IN BOTH ARENAS. THE
CENTRAL PROPOSITION CONSIDERED IS THAT INDIVIDUALISM IN
ELECTORAL POLITICS WILL MANIFEST ITSELF IN INSTITUTIONAL
POLITICS. THE ANALYSIS EXAMINES EVIDENCE ON HOUSE ELECTIONS
AND CONGRESSIONAL VOTING ALIGNMENTS FOR 1886-1986. SPECIAL
ATTENTION IS DEVOTED TO A COMPARISON OF PATTERNS FOR THE NEW
DEAL PARTY SYSTEM AND THOSE FOR THE PRECEEDING PARTY SYSTEM.

02393 COLLIER, K.; ORDESHOOK, P.; WILLIAMS, K.
THE RATIONALLY UNIFORMED ELECTORATE: SOME EXPERIMENTAL
EVIDENCE
PUBLIC CHOICE, 60(1) (JAN 89), 3-30.
IN AN ANALYSIS OF VOTER BEHAVIOR THE ARTICLE REPORTS ON
A SERIES OF EXPERIMENTS IN WHICH VOTERS ARE ALLOWED TO
DECIDE BETWEEN VOTING RETROSPECTIVELY AND PURCHASING
CONTEMPORANEOUS INFORMATION ABOUT THE CANDIDATE CHALLENGING
THE INCUMBENT. IN GENERAL, THE RESULTS CONFORM TO REASONABLE
EXPECTATIONS: VOTERS PURCHASE LESS INFORMATION WHEN THE
CANDIDATE'S STRATEGIES ARE STABLE, AND THEIR LIKELIHOOD THAT
THEIR VOTES MATTER, BY THE RELIABILITY OF THE INFORMATION
AVAILABLE FOR PURCHASE, AND BY THE DEGREE OF INSTABILITY AS
MEASURED BY CHANGES IN EACH VOTER'S WELFARE.

02394 COLLIER, K.E.
ELECTIONS AS INSTITUTIONS
DISSERTATION ABSTRACTS INTERNATIONAL, 49(11) (MAY 89),
3488-A.
THE AUTHOR CHARTS RE-ELECTION RATES AND MARGINS OF
VICTORY FOR ELECTIONS TO THE SENATE, THE HOUSE OF
REPRESENTATIVES, AND THE GOVERNOR'S OFFICE. PREVIOUS
RESEARCH ON JUDICIAL, MUNICIPAL, AND STATE LEGISLATIVE RACES
IS ALSO REVIEWED. THEN THE AUTHOR STUDIES HOW THE IMPACT OF
THE SIZE OF THE ELECTED BODY AND THE SIZE OF THE OFFICE'S
CONSTITUENCY AFFECTS THE USE OF INFORMATION BY VOTERS. HE

ALSO DISCUSSES THE IMPACT OF THE TIMING OF ELECTIONS, NONPARTISAN BALLOTS, AND CONSTRAINTS ON CAMPAIGN INFORMATION.

02395 COLLIER, P.; HOROWITZ, D.
SLOUCHING TOWARDS BERKELEY: SOCIALISM IN ONE CITY
PUBLIC INTEREST, (94) (WIN 89), 47-68.
RADICALS HAVE BUILT A FORMIDABLE POLITICAL MACHINE IN BERKELEY, CALIFORNIA, BUT NOT WITHOUT DISILLUSIONING MANY CITIZENS WHO WORRY THAT THE NEW MACHINE HAS NO SOUL. THE OPPONENTS OF THE RADICAL POLITICAL ELITE ARE NOT ONLY MEMBERS OF THE REPUBLICAN OLD GUARD, A LONG-VANQUISHED MINORITY, BUT ALSO MANY WHO ONCE EMBRACED THE EXPERIMENT IN MUNICIPAL LEFTISM.

02396 COLLINS, C.
THE RISE AND FALL OF THE NATIONAL "DECENTRALIZED AGENCIES" IN COLUMBIA
PUBLIC ADMINISTRATION AND DEVELOPMENT, 9(2) (APR 89), 129-146.
THE PUBLIC SECTOR IN LATIN AMERICA HAS BEEN CHARACTERIZED BY THE PROLIFERATION OF NATIONAL SEMI-AUTONOMOUS BODIES KNOWN AS 'DECENTRALIZED AGENCIES'. THIS ARTICLE FOCUSES ON SUCH AGENCIES IN COLOMBIA FROM THE 1960S ONWARDS. ATTENTION WILL BE PAID TO THEIR INSTITUTIONAL PROLIFERATION AND HOW THIS AFFECTED LOCAL GOVERNMENT, PARTICULARLY IN THE FIELDS OF WATER AND SANITATION. SUCH CHANGES IN STATE ORGANIZATION HAVE NOT BEEN PROBLEM FREE. THE GROWTH OF 'DECENTRALIZED AGENCIES' HAS BEEN ASSOCIATED WITH PROBLEMS OF INEFFICIENCY, ADMINISTRATIVE CONFUSION AND PROBLEMS OF SOCIAL AND POLITICAL UNREST. INDEED, SUCH CONTRADICTIONS HAVE RESULTED IN THE ISSUE OF DECENTRALIZATION BEING PLACED ON THE POLITICAL AGENDA AND THE DEVELOPMENT OF INNOVATIVE AND ADMINISTRATIVE REFORMS THAT COULD BREATHE NEW LIFE INTO LOCAL GOVERNMENT.

02397 COLLINS, N.
GREECE
ELECTORAL STUDIES, 8(3) (DEC 89), 281-287.
THIS ARTICLE REPORTS ON THE OUTCOME OF THE 1989 EUROPEAN ELECTION OF THE REPUBLIC OF IRELAND. IT WAS A DECREASE IN THE VOTE FOR THE TWO LARGEST PARTIES, A CLEAR SWING TO THE LEFT AND THE EMERGENCE OF THE GREEN PARTY. THE SUCCESS OF IRISH PARTIES NOW DEPENDS ON THEIR ECONOMIC APPEAL TO THE ELECTORATE IN GENERAL AND THE LOYALTY OF THEIR TRADITIONAL SUPPORTES IT EXAMINES THE CAMPAIGN, THE PROCEDURE, THE NATIONAL AND EUROPEAN ELECTIONS, AND GIVES THE RESULTS.

02398 COLLINS, P.D.
STRATEGIC PLANNING FOR STATE ENTERPRISE PERFORMANCE IN AFRICA: PUBLIC VERSUS PRIVATE OPTIONS
PUBLIC ADMINISTRATION AND DEVELOPMENT, 9(1) (JAN 89), 65-82.
THIS ARTICLE PRESENTS METHODOLOGIES TO ASSIST GOVERNMENT OFFICIALS IN VARIOUS AFRICAN COUNTRIES WHO HAVE TO DEAL WITH ILL-DEFINED POLICY PROBLEMS ARISING OUT OF PERCEIVED PERFORMANCE SHORTCOMINGS ON THE PART OF STATE ENTERPRISES. IT REVIEWS THE HISTORICAL ROLE AND RECORD OF STATE ENTERPRISE IN AFRICAN ECONOMIES, THE ASSUMPTIONS AND MAJOR ARGUMENTS OF THE 'PRIVATIZATION OPTION' AND THE MAJOR FORMS IN WHICH THE LATTER MAY BE CARRIED OUT. IN A SITUATION WHERE DEBATE HAS TENDED AT TIMES TO GENERATE MORE HEAT THAN LIGHT, THE APPROACH IS A PRAGMATIC ONE, INVOLVING CAREFUL REVIEW OF ALL POLICY ALTERNATIVES, INCLUDING PUBLIC ENTERPRISE REHABILITATION AND A STEP APPLICATION OF PRIVATISATION FEASIBILITY ANALYSIS IN CASES WHERE PUBLIC ENTERPRISE REHABILITATION PROVES UNVIABLE.

02399 COLLINS, R.M.
THE ORIGINALITY TRAP: RICHARD HOFSTADTER ON POPULISM
JOURNAL OF AMERICAN HISTORY, 76(1) (JUN 89), 150-167.
RICHARD HOFSTADTER'S "THE AGE OF REFORM: FROM BRYAN TO FDR" TOUCHED OFF A BITTER CONTROVERSY. CRITICS ACCUSED HIM OF IMPUGNING THE NATION'S RADICAL HERITAGE ON THE BASIS OF INADEQUATE RESEARCH AND UNREPRESENTATIVE EVIDENCE. IN THE EYES OF SOME, HOFSTADTER HAD REDUCED THE POPULISTS TO A HORDE OF XENOPHOBIC, ANTI-SEMITIC, DELUSIONAL CRANKS. ALTHOUGH THE PASSIONS AROUSED BY THE BOOK HAVE LONG SINCE COOLED, THE CONTROVERSY IT GENERATED REMAINS OF INTEREST AND SIGNIFICANCE.

02400 COLLUM, D.
A DREAM COME TRUE
SOJOURNERS, 18(10) (NOV 89), 6.
THE RAPID ASCENT TO POWER OF POLAND'S SOLIDARITY UNION IS CONSIDERED A DREAM COME TRUE FOR GENERATIONS OF POLES WHO HAVE STRUGGLED FOR MORE FREEDOM AND INDEPENDENCE. ALTHOUGH THE DANGERS FACED BY POLAND'S NEW LEADERS ARE SIGNIFICANT, THE FACT THAT SOLIDARITY HAS TAKEN POWER AT ALL IS AN INDICATION THAT BLOODLESS CHANGE FROM OPRESSION TO FREEDOM IS INDEED POSSIBLE.

02401 COLLUM, D.
THE IRON CURTAIN OF SECRECY
SOJOURNERS, 18(5) (MAY 89), 5.

THE ARTICLE DISCUSSES THE "IRON CURTAIN" THAT REMAINS BETWEEN THE CITIZENS OF THE US AND THEIR SECRET GOVERNMENT. THIS PHENOMENON WAS BROUGHT OUT IN SHARP FOCUS DURING THE IRAN-CONTRA SCANDAL AND SUBSEQUENT EFFORTS TO BRING OLIVER NORTH TO TRIAL. THE INTELLIGENCE COMMUNITY'S REFUSAL TO DECLASSIFY IMPORTANT INFORMATION HAS CAUSED MANY OF THE CHARGES AGAINST NORTH TO BE DROPPED ENTIRELY. A RECENT REVEALATION ABOUT A PROPOSED INVASION OF CUBA BEFORE THE DISCOVERY OF MISSILES REVEALS THAT COVERT ACTIONS OF QUESTIONABLE VALIDITY AND MORALITY AND SUBSEQUENT GOVERNMENT COVER-UPS ARE NOTHING NEW.

02402 COLLUM, D.D.
AN OPENING FOR POPULISM
SOJOURNERS, 18(2) (FEB 89), 22-23.
THE AMERICAN PEOPLE DIDN'T WANT TO VOTE FOR GEORGE BUSH IN 1988. THEY WERE FORCED INTO HIS ARMS BY THE ELITIST TECHNOCRAT AT THE TOP OF THE DEMOCRATIC TICKET WHO, UNTIL IT WAS TOO LATE, BETRAYED NO UNDERSTANDING OF OR INTEREST IN THE NEEDS AND ASPIRATIONS OF AVERAGE AMERICANS.

02403 COLLUM, D.D.
GROWING TERROR AND LIMITED RIGHTS IN NORTHERN IRELAND
SOJOURNERS, 18(3) (MAR 89), 6.
GREAT BRITAIN'S DRACONIAN CAMPAIGN AGAINST THE IRISH REPUBLICAN ARMY HAS LED TO SERIOUS INFRINGEMENTS OF CIVIL RIGHTS, INCLUDING DUE PROCESS, TRIAL BY JURY, AND FREEDOM OF THE PRESS. IN FACT, THE REPRESSIVE ABUSES OF THE BRITISH ARMY, COURTS, AND PRISONS HAVE KEPT THE IRA POPULAR ENOUGH TO SURVIVE.

02404 COLLUM, D.D.
OLD THINKING AND NEW WEAPONS
SOJOURNERS, 18(8) (AUG 89), 6.
BUSH RECOGNIZES THE NEED TO APPEASE PROGORBACHEV PUBLIC OPINION IN EUROPE AND AMERICA. BUT HE REFUSES TO ENTERTAIN THOUGHTS OF NON-NUCLEAR WORLD AND IS SURROUNDED BY VOICES, SUCH AS THAT OF HIS DEFENSE SECRETARY RICHARD CHENEY, THAT INSIST THAT A RETURN TO THE BAD OLD DAYS IS INEVITABLE. BETWEEN THE TUGGING OF PAST AND FUTURE, THE PRESIDENT SEEMS PARALYZED. WHILE THE ADMINISTRATION REMAINS FROZEN BY ITS ALLEGIANCE TO OLD VERITIES (AND FRIENDLY DEFENSE CONTRACTORS), THE DEMOCRATS ARE, FOR THE MOST PART, SIMILARLY IMMOBILIZED. FOR THE DEMOCRATS, THE MAIN FREEZING AGENT IS THEIR POLITICAL FEAR OF APPEARING "SOFT ON DEFENSE." AT THIS POINT, IT SEEMS THAT ONLY A DOSE OF SHOCK TREATMENT FROM THE VOTING (AND MARCHING) PUBLIC WILL CAUSE AMERICA'S LEADERS TO STIR FROM THEIR STUPOR AND FACE THE NEW WORLD.

02405 COLMENARES, J.S.
DEEPER CONTRADICTIONS BETWEEN LATIN AMERICA AND IMPERIALISM
WORLD MARXIST REVIEW, 31(2) (FEB 88), 122-129.
A SOLUTION TO THE DEBT PROBLEM IS THE PREREQUISITE FOR A RESUMPTION OF ECONOMIC GROWTH IN THE THIRD WORLD COUNTRIES AND, CONSEQUENTLY, FOR AN IMPROVEMENT OF THE STATE OF EMPLOYMENT IN THE LEADING IMPERIALIST STATES. THE CENTRAL ELEMENT IN THIS PROCESS SHOULD BE A DEMOCRATIC RESTRUCTURING OF THE FINANCIAL SYSTEM, ELIMINATION OF THE DOLLARS' POWER AS WORLD MONEY, AND WASHINGTON'S HEGEMONY IN THE WORLD'S FINANCIAL CENTRES. THERE IS ALSO A NEED TO MODIFY THE DEPENDENT INDUSTRY OF THE LDCS, TO REORIENT IT TOWARDS INTERNAL REQUIREMENTS AND RAW MATERIALS, AND TO FIX FAIR PRICES FOR THEIR GOODS. SO LONG AS TNCS CONTINUE TO BE THE FACTOR BEHIND THE ECONOMIC PERTURBATIONS, IT IS HARD TO IMPLEMENT THE CHARTER OF ECONOMIC RIGHTS AND DUTIES OF STATES OR TO SET UP A NEW INTERNATIONAL ECONOMIC ORDER.

02406 COLODNY, R.
THE US POLITICAL CULTURE OF THE 1930'S AND THE AMERICAN RESPONSE TO THE SPANISH CIVIL WAR
SCIENCE AND SOCIETY, 53(1) (SPR 89), 47-61.
THE ARTICLE EXPLORES THE POLITICAL CULTURE OF THE US BEGINING WITH A BREIF OVERVIEW OF THE 1920'S. IT CONCLUDES THAT THERE WAS NOTHING IN THE POLITICAL CULTURE OF THE AMERICAN PEOPLE IN THE 1920'S TO PREPARE THEM TO FACE THE IMMENSE AND TRAGIC PROBLEMS POSED BY THE NEXT DECADE. IT EXAMINES THE EVENTS THAT SHAPED THE POLITICAL CULTURE OF THE 1930'S AND EXPLORES THE CHANGE OF PUBLIC OPINION WITH REGARDS TO THE SPANISH CIVIL WAR FROM PRO-FACISM TO PRO-REPUBLICANISM. THE GOVERNMENT, HOWEVER, REMAINED NEUTRAL AND ANY SUPPORT GIVEN TO EITHER SIDE WAS ON A STRICTLY VOLUNTEER BASIS.

02407 COLSON, C.; VANNESS, D.H.
A CONSERVATIVE PERSPECTIVE: ALTERNATIVES TO INCARCERATION
JOURNAL OF STATE GOVERNMENT, 62(2) (MAR 89), 59-64.
CONSERVATIVES ARE OFTEN TYPECAST AS CHAMPIONS OF "GET TOUGH ON CRIME" AND "LOCK 'EM UP AND THROW AWAY THE KEY." BUT, INCREASINGLY, CONSERVATIVES OF BOTH MAJOR POLITICAL PARTIES ARE ADVOCATING ALTERNATIVES TO INCARCERATION FOR NON-VIOLENT OFFENDERS. IN FACT, CONSERVATIVES MAY BE THE SINGLE MOST POTENT FORCE FOR PRACTICAL, PRUDENT CRIMINAL JUSTICE REFORM TODAY.

02408 COLVER, H.; REINTART, C.
CAPITALIST DREAMS: CHILE'S RESPONSE TO NINETEENTH-CENTURY
WORLD COPPER COMPETITION
COMPARATIVE STUDIES IN SOCIETY AND HISTORY, 31(4) (OCT 89),
694-721.
THE ARTICLE EXAMINES THE IMPACT OF SUCH REGULATIONS AS
MINING CODES AND MINERAL TAXATION ON THE EFFORTS OF CHILEAN
COPPER ENTREPRENEURS TO COMPETE WORLDWIDE IN THE NINETEENTH
CENTURY. ALTHOUGH THE CONTENTION THAT TODAY'S HIGHLY
REGULATED ECONOMIES KEEP LATIN AMERICANS FROM BEING AS
PRODUCTIVE AS THEIR RESOURCES JUSTIFY, EXTENSION OF THIS
VIEW INTO THE PAST IGNORES EARLIER PRODUCTIVE
ACCOMPLISHMENTS, AS WELL AS SIGNIFICANT EFFORTS AT DIFFERENT
TIMES AND PLACES TO CATS OFF LATIN AMERICA'S MERCANTILE
LEGACY.

02409 COMAROFF, J.; COMAROFF, J.L.
THE COLONIZATION OF CONSCIOUSNESS IN SOUTH AFRICA
ECONOMY AND SOCIETY, 18(3) (AUG 89), 267-296.
THIS ESSAY DOCUMENTS AN EARLY PHASE IN THE COLONIZATION
OF CONSCIOUSNESS, AND THE CONSCIOUSNESS OF COLONIZATION,
AMONG A SOUTH AFRICAN PEOPLE. HERE, AS ELSEWHERE, EUROPEAN
DOMINATION WAS AS MUCH AN ATTEMPT TO SEIZE CONTROL OF THE
SIGNS AND PRACTICES OF EVERYDAY LIFE AS AN EXERCIZE IN
MATERIAL COERCION. NINETEENTH-CENTURY EVANGELISTS IN THE
SOUTH AFRICAN INTERIOR RELIED ON TECHNIQUES OF PERSUASION,
SEEKING TO INTRODUCE AN EXISTENTIAL 'STATE OF COLONIALISM'
WHICH ANTICIPATED THE COLONIAL STATE. WHATEVER ELSE IT MIGHT
HAVE BEEN, THE HISTORY MADE ON THIS FRONTIER WAS ONE OF
STRUGGLE OVER POWER AND MEANING. THE AUTHORS TRACE THE
ATTEMPT OF THE CIVILIZING MISSION TO INVADE THREE DOMAINS OF
AFRICAN LIFE: ITS NATURAL RESOURCES, TECHNIQUES OF
PRODUCTION, AND LANGUAGE IN ORDER TO GRASP HOW NEW
HEGEMONIES WERE LAID DOWN AMIDST LOCAL RESISTANCE, IT IS
NECESSARY TO DISTINGUISH TWO LEVELS OF OPERATION IN
COLONIZING CULTURES. FOR WHILE ITS IDEOLOGICAL MESSAGE WAS
WIDELY REJECTED, THE MISSION ENMESHED LOCAL PEOPLES IN THE
UNDERLYING FORMS OF THE EUROPEAN SYSTEM - THE COMMODITY FORM,
LINGUISTIC FORMS, AND SO ON. THUS WAS INITIATED THE PROCESS
THAT INCORPORATED MANY AFRICAN PEOPLES THE POLITICAL ECONOMY
OF EMPIRE.

02410 COMISKEY, C.M.
ELECTORAL COMPETITION AND THE GROWTH OF PUBLIC SPENDING IN
13 INDUSTRIAL DEMOCRACIES, 1950-1983
DISSERTATION ABSTRACTS INTERNATIONAL, 49(7) (JAN 89),
1945-A.
THE AUTHOR TESTS THE CLAIM THAT COMPETITION BETWEEN
POLITICAL PARTIES OR COALITIONS FOR CONTROL OF THE CENTRAL
GOVERNMENT FOSTERED THE GROWTH OF PUBLIC SPENDING IN 13
INDUSTRIAL DEMOCRACIES BETWEEN 1950 AND 1983.

02411 CONABLE, B.
DEVELOPMENT AND THE ENVIRONMENT: A GLOBAL BALANCE
FINANCE AND DEVELOPMENT, 26(4) (DEC 89), 2-4.
THIS ARTICLE EXPLORES THE EMPHASIS THAT THE WORLD BANK
IS PLACING ON ENVIRONMENTAL CHALLENGE. IT EXAMINES THE
POSSIBLE EFFECTS OF GLOBAL WARMING CAUSED BY THE USE OF
ENERGY BYPRODUCTS AND THE ANTICIPATED INCREASE OF GLOBAL
POPULATION RESULTING IN A GREATER DEMAND FOR ENERGY. WAYS
FOR DEVELOPMENT AND ENVIRONMENT TO COOPERATE ARE EXPLORED.
IT DEFINES THE CARE AND HEALTH OF OUR PLANET AS A GLOBAL
RESPONSIBILITY AND CALLS FOR BOTH THE CHALLENGES OF
DEVELOPMENT AND ENVIRONMENT TO BE RECONCILED.

02412 CONAGHAN, C.M.
ECUADOR SWINGS TOWARD SOCIAL DEMOCRACY
CURRENT HISTORY, 88(536) (MAR 89), 137-141, 154.
THE KEY TASKS FACING ECUADOR'S PRESIDENT RODRIGO BORJA
ARE TO REESTABLISH PUBLIC CONFIDENCE IN THE INSTITUTIONAL
STRUCTURES OF GOVERNMENT AND REINJECT SOBRIETY INTO A
POLITICAL CULTURE THAT HAS BEEN SUBJECTED TO ERRATIC DOSES
OF AUTHORITARIANISM AND POPULISM. HIS GOVERNMENT MUST
WRESTLE WITH THE POLITICAL ILL-WILL AND ECONOMIC DISASTER
LEFT BY THE FEBRES CORDERO ADMINISTRAION.

02413 CONAGHAN, C.M.
ECUADOR: THE POLITICS OF LOCOS
HEMISPHERE, 1(2) (WIN 89), 13-15.
SINCE THE ONSET OF THE ECONOMIC CRISIS IN 1982,
ECUADORAN POLITICS HAS DEVOLVED INTO A HIGHLY PERSONALIZED
AND OFTEN TRIVIALIZED ARENA OF INTRA-ELITE STRUGGLE. THE
STRANGE ATMOSPHERE OF ECUADOR'S RECENT POLITICS REFLECTS THE
DEEPER MALAISE AT WORK INSIDE ITS POLITICAL CULTURE, PARTIES,
AND GOVERNMENT INSTITUTIONS. A KEY TASK FACING PRESIDENT
RODRIGO BORJA IS TO RE-INJECT SOBRIETY AND CREDIBILITY INTO
THE ABUSED DEMOCRATIC SYSTEM. THE IRONY OF ECUADOR'S
POLITICAL SLIDE IS THAT IT OCCURRED DURING THE
ADMINISTRATION OF PRESIDENT LEON FEBRES-CORDERO, WHO HAD
PROMISED TO ELIMINATE CORRUPTION AND ENHANCE POLITICAL
EFFICIENCY AND ECONOMIC PRODUCTIVITY.

02414 CONANT, J.K.
STABILITY, CHANGE, AND LEADERSHIP IN STATE ADMINISTRATION:
1970-1986
STATE AND LOCAL GOVERNMENT REVIEW, 21(1) (WIN 89), 3-10.
ARE LARGE ORGANIZATIONS AS IMPERVIOUS TO ALTERATION AS
MUCH OF THE SCHOLARLY LITERATURE ON ORGANIZATIONAL CHANGE
SEEMS TO INDICATE? THE FINDINGS IN THIS EMPIRICALLY-BASED
STUDY SUGGEST THAT TWO CENTRAL PRESUMPTIONS OF THE
CONTEMPORARY LITERATURE ON ORGANIZATIONAL CHANGE ARE
OVERSTATED OR INACCURATE. THE DATA REVEAL NOT ONLY THAT
CHANGE IN PUBLIC ORGANIZATIONS OCCURS WITH CONSIDERABLE
FREQUENCY BUT ALSO THAT ELECTED AND APPOINTED LEADERS PLAY A
MAJOR ROLE IN BRINGING ABOUT CHANGE.

02415 CONDREN, C.
RADICALS, CONSERVATIVES AND MODERATES IN EARLY MODERN
POLITICAL THOUGHT: A CASE OF THE SANDWICH ISLANDS SYNDROME?
HISTORY OF POLITICAL THOUGHT, X(3) (FAL 89), 525-542.
THE ARTICLE EXAMINES ONE OF THE MAJOR PROBLEMS OF
INTERPRETATION MANIFESTED ACROSS CULTURAL SPACE AND THROUGH
TIME: HOW DOES ONE RENDER THE ALIEN INTELLIGIBLE WITHOUT
UNDULY PREJUDICING THE POSSIBILITY OF UNDERSTANDING THROUGH
TRANSLATORY MISREPRESENTATION? THE AUTHOR EXPLORES THE
RELATED SUB-SETS OF THE POLITICAL LEXICON, LEFT, RIGHT AND
CENTER; AND AT GREATER LENGTH, RADICAL, MODERATE, AND
CONSERVATIVE WITHIN THE CONTEXT OF SEMANTIC CREATIVITY.

02416 CONGLETON, R.D.
CAMPAIGN FINANCES AND POLITICAL PLATFORMS: THE ECONOMICS
OF POLITICAL CONTROVERSY
PUBLIC CHOICE, 62(2) (AUG 89), 101-118.
THIS PAPER EXPLORES THE EXTENT TO WHICH CAMPAIGN
CONTRIBUTIONS OF POLITICALLY GROUPS MAY DRAW CANDIDATES AWAY
FROM THE MEDIAN VOTER POSITION AS CANDIDATES SEEK FUNDS TO
RUN ELECTION CAMPAIGNS, IT DEMONSTRATES THAT THE NECESSITY
OF RAISING CAMPAIGN FUNDS, PROVIDES ANOTHER POSSIBLE
EXPLANATION OF THE CONTROVERSY OBSERVED IN MODERN IT
CONCLUDES THAT THE TACTICS OF CAMPAIGN FINANCE REDUCES THE
LIKELIHOOD THAT A STABLE ELECTORAL EQUILIBRIUM EXISTS EVEN
IN CASES WHERE CANDIDATES COMPETE IN A ONE DIMENSIONAL ISSUE
SPACE.

02417 CONGMING, L.
MODERN CAPITALISM REASSESSED
BEIJING REVIEW, 32(2) (JAN 89), 24-27.
SINCE THE 1950'S, CAPITALISM HAS ADVANCED TO A NEW STAGE
THAT MAY BE CALLED "SOCIAL CAPITALISM." MANY OF ITS PRIMARY
FEATURES, SUCH AS SOCIAL WELFARE PROGRAMS AND JOINT STOCK
COMPANIES, HAVE LAID THE FOUNDATION FOR A PEACEFUL
TRANSITION TO SOCIALISM. A CORRECT UNDERSTANDING OF THIS
MODERN CAPITALISM IS ESSENTIAL TO UNDERSTANDING MODERN
SOCIALISM.

02418 CONKLIN, W. E.
IMAGES OF A CONSTITUTION
UNIVERSITY OF TORONTO PRESS, TORONTO, ONTARIO, CA, 1989,
384.
IN THIS CONJUNCTION OF CONSTITUTIONAL THEORY,
JURISPRUDENCE, LITERARY THEORY, CONSTITUTIONAL LAW, AND
POLITICAL THEORY, WILLIAM CONKLIN TELLS US WHAT A
CONSTITUTION IS NOT: IT IS NOT A TEXT, NOR A COMPENDIUM OF
JUDICIAL AND LEGISLATIVE DECISIONS INTERPRETING A TEXT, NOR
A SET OF DOCTRINES, NOR MORAL/POLITICAL VALUES, NOR CUSTOMS,
NOR A PRIORI CONCEPTIONS. A CONSTITUTION, HE ARGUES, IS AN
IMAGE WHICH EXISTS THROUGH THE LEGAL CONSCIOUSNESS OF A
COMMUNITY. USING A WIDE RANGE OF CANADIAN JUDICIAL DECISIONS
AS EXAMPLES, CONKLIN SHOWS THAT THE CLASSIC CASES HAVE BEEN
THOSE WHERE THE BOUNDARIES OF TWO CONFLICTING IMAGES CLASHED.

02419 CONLAN, T.J.
CONFLICTING TRENDS, COMPETING FUTURES
JOURNAL OF STATE GOVERNMENT, 62(1) (JAN 89), 50-55.
THE FUTURE OF FEDERALISM IS IMPOSSIBLE TO PREDICT. WHILE
STATES ARE VIEWED AS STRONGER THAN EVER, THEY ALSO HAVE LOST
VALUABLE POLITICAL, CONSTITUTIONAL AND FISCAL GROUND IN
RECENT YEARS. THE UNCERTAIN FACTORS SHAPING FEDERALISM MEAN
THAT THE FUTURE OF STATES REMAINS CLOUDY.

02420 CONN, J.L.
CHURCH, STATE, AND ABORTION
CHURCH AND STATE, 42(5) (MAY 89), 4 (100)-6 (102).
THE AUTHOR REVIEWS THE HISTORY OF THE MISSOURI LAW THAT
WAS THE IMPETUS FOR WEBSTER V. REPRODUCTIVE HEALTH SERVICES.
HE FOCUSES ON THE RELIGIOUS FREEDOM AND CHURCH-STATE ISSUES
INHERENT IN THE CASE.

02421 CONN, J.L.
DAY CARE DEBACLE
CHURCH AND STATE, 42(8) (SEP 89), 4 (172)-6 (174).
ON JUNE 23, 1989, THE U.S. SENATE ADOPTED A VOUCHER PLAN
FOR SECTARIAN CHILD CARE AND INSTRUCTION, REJECTING A WHITE
HOUSE SCHEME THAT WOULD EMPHASIZE TAX CREDITS FOR PARENTS.
THE BILL PASSED BY THE SENATE WILL ALLOW STATES TO OFFER
PARENTS "CERTIFICATES" THAT CAN BE USED AT CHURCH-RELATED

PRESCHOOLS AND DAY CARE CENTERS EVEN IF THEY TEACH RELIGION. THE HOUSE OF REPRESENTATIVES HAS NOT VOTED ON THE CHILD CARE PACKAGE.

02422 CONN, J.L.
TESTING "EQUAL ACCESS"
CHURCH AND STATE, 42(3) (MAR 89), 4 (52)-7 (55).
IN FEBRUARY 1989, THE U.S. EIGHTH CIRCUIT COURT OF APPEALS RULED THAT THE EQUAL ACCESS ACT IS CONSTITUTIONAL AND THAT ITS PROVISION REQUIRE HIGH SCHOOLS TO ALLOW STUDENT RELIGIOUS CLUBS TO GATHER. THE COURT RULED THAT SCHOOL OFFICIALS CREATE A "LIMITED OPEN FORUM" WHEN THEY ALLOW EXTRACURRICULAR ACTIVITIES AND MUST ALSO PERMIT BIBLE STUDY. MOREOVER, THE UNANIMOUS DECISION DECLARED THAT A PUBLIC SCHOOL BIBLE CLUB COULD MEET UNDER THE TERMS OF THE FIRST AMENDMENT EVEN IF THE EQUAL ACCESS ACT DID NOT EXIST.

02423 CONN, J.L.
THE LOUISIANA PURCHASE
CHURCH AND STATE, 42(9) (OCT 89), 4 (196)-7 (199).
THE AUTHOR EXAMINES THE HISTORY OF PUBLIC AID TO PAROCHIAL SCHOOLS IN LOUISIANA AND HOW THE WALL OF SEPARATION BETWEEN CHURCH AND STATE HAS BECOME BLURRED IN LOUISIANA'S FUNDING OF EDUCATION.

02424 CONN, J.L.
U.S. CONGRESS RESURRECTS SCHOOL PRAYER ISSUE
CHURCH AND STATE, 42(6) (JUN 89), 7 (127)-8 (128).
ON MAY 9, 1989, THE U.S. HOUSE OF REPRESENTATIVES ADOPTED A LEGISLATIVE MEASURE THAT PROMOTES VOLUNTARY PRAYER IN PUBLIC SCHOOLS. THE MEASURE TOOK THE FORM OF A RIDER ATTACHED TO A VOCATIONAL EDUCATION BILL AND FORBIDS THE ALLOCATION OF FEDERAL VOCATIONAL FUNDS TO ANY EDUCATIONAL AGENCY THAT DENIES OR PREVENTS PARTICIPATION IN PRAYER IN PUBLIC SCHOOLS BY INDIVIDUALS ON A VOLUNTARY BASIS. ALTHOUGH THE AMENDMENT PASSED OVERWHELMINGLY IN THE HOUSE, OBSERVERS SAY THE SENATE IS UNLIKELY TO ADOPT THE PRAYER RIDER WHEN IT VOTES ON THE VOCATIONAL EDUCATION BILL.

02425 CONNELLY, M.; TOMPKINS, G.L.
DOES PERFORMANCE MATTER? A STUDY OF STATE BUDGETING
POLICY STUDIES REVIEW, 8(2) (WIN 89), 288-299.
THIS STUDY EXAMINES THE RELATIONSHIP BETWEEN MEASURES OF EXPENDITURES AND PERSONNEL ON EXECUTIVE DECISION MAKING ON THE BUDGET IN MISSOURI, FY 1979-1985. SPECIFICALLY, IT FOCUSES ON THE INTERACTION OF "MACRO" AND "MICRO" VARIABLES IN THE GOVERNOR'S BUDGET RECOMMENDATIONS, AS DEMONSTRATED BY REVEALING THE CONDITIONS UNDER WHICH CORRELATIONS BETWEEN EXPENDITURES AND PERSONNEL RECOMMENDATIONS ARE WEAK AND STRONG. THE RESULTS INDICATE THAT ATTENTION TO DOLLARS IS NOT ENOUGH TO EXPLAIN STATE POLICY DECISIONS AND THAT STRONG CORRELATIONS ARE NOT AUTOMATIC BETWEEN THE MEASURES, WHICH ARE INFLUENCED BY INTERNAL AS WELL AS EXTERNAL CONSTRAINTS.

02426 CONNER, R.L.
ANSWERING THE DEMO-DOOMSAYERS: FIVE MYTHS ABOUT AMERICA'S DEMOGRAPHIC FUTURE
BROOKINGS REVIEW, 7(4) (FAL 89), 35-39.
FOR THE LAST FIVE YEARS, A SMALL BUT INFLUENTIAL BAND OF FUTURISTS HAVE BEEN WRINGING THEIR HANDS ABOUT US POPULATION TRENDS. THEY FORESEE AN IMMINENT AND THREATENING DECLINE IN THE SIZE OF THE US POPULATION THAT PORTENDS LARGER BUDGET DEFICITS, SOCIAL SECURITY SHORTFALLS, AND A FALL IN AMERICA'S GEOPOLITICAL AND CULTURAL INFLUENCE. THIS FEAR OF POPULATION DECLINE IS BEING USED AS A RATIONALE FOR LARGE INCREASES IN LEGAL IMMIGRATION TO THE USA. BUT THE DEMO-DOOM' RHETORIC IS MORE FEAR THAN FACT.

02427 CONNOLLY, F.W.; BERGIN, T.J.
WHAT DO YOU TEACH POLICY STUDIES EDUCATORS ABOUT COMPUTERS?
POLICY STUDIES REVIEW, 8(4) (SUM 89), 859-864.
COMPUTERS ARE NO LONGER AN IDEA OF THE FUTURE. THEY ARE, RATHER, A COMMON AND EVEN EXPECTED TOOL OF THE PUBLIC ADMINISTRATOR. THE AUTHORS ASSERT THAT STUDENTS OF THE DISCIPLINE MUST HAVE A PRACTICAL KNOWLEDGE OF COMPUTER APPLICATIONS. WHILE IT IS NOT NECESSARY THAT ADVANCED COMPUTER ENGINEERING BE STUDIED, STUDENTS SHOULD NEVERTHELESS BE MADE FAMILIAR WITH THE USES OF THE COMPUTER IN ADMINISTRATION. BEYOND LEARNING HOW TO OPERATE A COMPUTER, THE ARTICLE STATES THAT STUDENTS, ESPECIALLY ADULT LEARNERS, FIRST HAVE TO BE MADE NOT TO FEAR THIS INSTRUMENT OF THE AGE OF INFORMATION SO THAT THEY WILL BE COMFORTABLE WHEN LEARNING ITS APPLICATIONS.

02428 CONOVER, P.J.; FELDMAN, S.
CANDIDATE PERCEPTION IN AN AMBIGUOUS WORLD: CAMPAIGNS, CUES, AND INFERENCE PROCESSES
AMERICAN JOURNAL OF POLITICAL SCIENCE, 33(4) (NOV 89), 912-941.
MUCH THEORY AND RESEARCH SHOWS THAT INFORMATION ABOUT CANDIDATES' ISSUE POSITIONS IS OFTEN DIFFICULT FOR MEMBERS OF THE PUBLIC TO OBTAIN: CANDIDATES TYPICALLY DO NOT GO OUT OF THEIR WAY TO MAKE THEIR POSITIONS CLEAR; THE MEDIA DEVOTE LITTLE TIME TO COVERING CANDIDATES' STANDS ON THE ISSUES;

AND MANY VOTERS HAVE LITTLE INTEREST OR MOTIVATION TO SEARCH OUT INFORMATION ABOUT THE CANDIDATES' POSITIONS. DESPITE THIS, BY ELECTION DAY A SUBSTANTIAL NUMBER OF VOTERS ARE WILLING TO IDENTIFY THE ISSUE POSITIONS OF THE CANDIDATES, AND THESE PERCEIVED POSITIONS ARE OFTEN GOOD PREDICTORS OF VOTE CHOICE. IN THIS PAPER WE CONSIDER THE QUESTION OF HOW VOTERS PERCEIVE CANDIDATES' ISSUE POSITIONS GIVEN LIMITED INFORMATION AND HIGH INFORMATION COSTS. THE MODEL POSITS THAT VOTERS USE PREVIOUSLY ACQUIRED INFORMATION TO INFER WHERE CANDIDATES STAND ON THE ISSUES. IN ADDITION, CHARACTERISTICS OF THE CANDIDATES SERVE AS CUES THAT ALLOW VOTERS TO MAKE INFERENCES FROM SPECIFIC CATEGORIES OF PEOPLE AND POLITICIANS. THE ANALYSIS OF PANEL DATA FROM THE 1976 PRESIDENTIAL ELECTION DEMONSTRATES THE INFLUENCE OF THESE CUES IN THE PERCEPTION OF THE CANDIDATES AND THE ROLE OF THE CAMPAIGN IN STRUCTURING THE CUES THAT VOTERS USE.

02429 CONQUEST, R.
BACK TO THE USSR
NATIONAL REVIEW, XLI(15) (AUG 89), 24-27.
THIS ARTICLE OFFERS A FIRST HAND REPORT ON THE CURRENT SITUATION IN SOVIET COMMUNISM. AS THE AUTHOR REPORTS, FOR POLITICAL AND SOCIAL CHANGE THERE IS AN AGENDA. BUT THE SOVIET UNION IS STILL AT THE STAGE WHEN THE AGENDA HAS NOT YET BEEN TURNED INTO SUBSTANTIAL ACTION. IT IS NOT THE CASE THAT "THE OLD WORLD IS DEAD AND THE NEW INCAPABLE OF BEING BORN": BUT THE DIFFICULTIES OF THE TRANSITION REMAIN.
POL/SYSTEM

02430 CONSTABLE, P.; VALENZUELA, A.
CHILE'S RETURN TO DEMOCRACY
FOREIGN AFFAIRS, 68(5) (WIN 90), 169-186.
THE PATH BACK TO CIVILIAN RULE HAS BEEN LONG AND FRUSTRATING FOR CHILE'S DEMOCRATIC FORCES, BUT THE DIRE PREDICTIONS THAT THE 1988 PLEBISCITE WOULD COLLAPSE IN A CYCLE OF PROTEST AND REPRESSION DID NOT COME TRUE. PINOCHET'S AMBITIONS TO HOLD ONTO POWER WERE THWARTED BY TWO ELEMENTS. FIRST, CHILE'S DEEPLY-ROOTED DEMOCRATIC AND LAW-ABIDING POLITICAL CULTURE SURVIVED 16 YEARS OF REPRESSION. SECONDLY, THE ARMED FORCES HAVE REMAINED HIGHLY DISCIPLINED, PROFESSIONAL, AND UNCORRUPTED.

02431 CONTEH, A.
AFRICAN AND INTERNATIONAL LEGAL PROVISIONS IN THE PEACEFUL SETTLEMENT OF DISPUTES
DISARMAMENT, XII(1) (WIN 89), 44-50.
THERE ARE ADEQUATE LEGAL PROVISIONS CONCERNING THE PEACEFUL SETTLEMENT OF DISPUTES AMONG AFRICAN NATIONS AND THE NON-USE OF FORCE, BOTH IN GENERAL INTERNATIONAL AGREEMENTS AND IN SPECIFIC AFRICAN TREATIES, TO PROVIDE A BASIS FOR STRENGTHENING INTERNATIONAL PEACE, SECURITY, AND COOPERATION. WIDER DISSEMINATION OF INFORMATION ABOUT THESE PROVISIONS IS NEEDED FOR POLITICIANS, SOLDIERS, DIPLOMATS, AND THE PUBLIC-AT-LARGE. THE UNITED NATIONS REGIONAL CENTER FOR PEACE AND DISARMAMENT IN AFRICA IS EDUCATING PEOPLE FOR PEACE THROUGH ITS TRAINING PROGRAMS.

02432 CONWAY, M.M.
THE POLITICAL CONTEXT OF POLITICAL BEHAVIOR
THE JOURNAL OF POLITICS, 51(1) (FEB 89), 3-10.
THE ARGUMENT IS MADE THAT RESEARCH SHOULD INCORPORATE MEASURES OF POLITICAL CONTEXT AND IS ILLUSTRATED THROUGH A DISCUSSION OF THE EFFECTS OF POLITICAL CULTURE ON POLITICAL BEHAVIOR IN THE AMERICAN STATES. THE UTILITY OF USING CULTURE TO ACCOUNT FOR POLITICAL MOBILIZATION PROCESSES AS REPORTED IN SEVERAL RECENT STUDIES IS DISCUSSED. MEASURES OF POLITICAL CULTURE CAN HELP EXPLAIN BOTH DIFFERENCES BETWEEN STATES AND VARIATIONS WITHIN A STATE IN POLITICAL MOBILIZATION PROCESSES.

02433 COOK, B.J.; WOOD, D.B.
PRINCIPAL-AGENT MODELS OF POLITICAL CONTROL OF BUREAUCRACY
AMERICAN POLITICAL SCIENCE REVIEW, 83(3) (SEP 89), 965-980.
B. DAN WOOD INVOKED A PRINCIPAL-AGENT PERSPECTIVE TO ESTABLISH THE IMPORTANCE OF DEMOCRATIC HIERARCHIES IN SHAPING THE OUTPUTS OF PUBLIC BUREAUCRACIES. HE TESTED THE MODEL WITH AIR POLLUTION ENFORCEMENTS OF THE ENVIRONMENTAL PROTECTION AGENCY (EPA) BETWEEN 1977 AND 1985. HIS RESULTS SUGGESTED SOME LIMITATIONS ON BUREAUCRACIES RESPONSIVENESS TO ELECTED POLITICAL INSTITUTIONS, CONSISTENT WITH A PRINCIPAL-AGENT PERSPECTIVE WITH EMPHASIS ON THE AGENT. BRIAN J. COOK CHALLENGES FEATURES OF THE DESIGN AND EMPIRICAL TESTING OF WOOD'S HIERARICHAL MODEL. HE QUESTIONS THE ACCURACY OF WOOD'S CHARACTERIZATION OF THE EXTENT OF EPA AUTONOMY AND POWER. COOK ARGUES THAT A PROPER MODEL REQUIRES RECOGNITION OF THE MULTIPLE PRINCIPAL NATURE OF THE U.S. SYSTEM, AND HE ADEVOCATES CONSIDERATION OF THE NORMATIVE FOUNDATIONS OF PRINCIPAL-AGENT THEORY. WOOD RESPONDS TO BOTH THE SUBSTANTIVE AND METHODOLOGICAL ISSUES RAISED AND SUGGESTS AN ELECTIC APPROACH IN FUTURE RESEARCH.

02434 COOK, E.
MEASURING FEMINIST CONSCIOUSNESS
WOMEN AND POLITICS, 9(3) (1989), 71-88.

THE CONCEPT OF GROUP CONSCIOUSNESS HAS PROVEN USEFUL IN THE ANALYSIS OF POLITICAL AND SOCIAL GROUPS, AND HAS CLEAR UTILITY IN THE STUDY OF FEMINISM. ALTHOUGH SOPHISTICATED MEASURES OF FEMINIST CONSCIOUSNESS HAVE BEEN PROPOSED TO ENABLE SCHOLARS TO OPERATIONALIZE THE CONCEPT IN THE AMERICAN NATIONAL ELECTION STUDIES, THESE MEASURES HAVE PROBLEMS WITH CONTINUITY, OR HAVE CONCEPTUAL PROBLEMS. THIS PAPER PROPOSES A MEASURE THAT CAN BE USED IN ALL AMERICAN NATIONAL ELECTION STUDIES SINCE THE RISE OF THE FEMINIST MOVEMENT, AND PROVIDES DATA THAT SUGGEST THE MEASURE HAS EXTERNAL VALIDITY.

02435 COOK, M.; PIGGOT, J.
THE SHARING SOCIETY
CONTEMPORARY REVIEW, 254(1476) (1989), 25-30.
THE ARTICLE EXAMINES PROFIT SHARING PRACTICES IN GREAT BRITAIN. IT SEEKS TO ANALYZE WHETHER PROFIT SHARING POLICIES HAVE WIDENED OR DEEPENED THE SHAREHOLDING BASE BOTH IN THE SHORT TERM AND THE LONG TERM, AND WHETHER THE IMPACT OF THE STOCK EXCHANGE "CRASH" HAS AFFECTED THE DISTRIBUTION. IT CONCLUDES THAT THE CRASH HAD LITTLE EFFECT ON THE SMALL SHAREHOLDERS AND, DESPITE THE INCREASE IN PROFIT SHARING MEASURES, DISTRIBUTION OF WEALTH IS RELATIVELY THE SAME AS IT WAS IN THE 1970S AND IS UNLIKELY TO CHANGE IN THE FUTURE.

02436 COOK, R. J.
PURITANS, PRAGMATISTS, AND PROGRESS: THE REPUBLICAN COALITION IN IOWA, 1854-1878
DISSERTATION ABSTRACTS INTERNATIONAL, 49(8) (FEB 89), 2364-A.
THE AUTHOR PROBES THE UNDERLYING MOTIVATION OF THE FIRST REPUBLICANS USING IOWA AS A CASE STUDY. HE FOCUSES ON THE INTERPLAY BETWEEN CONSTITUENT ELEMENTS OF THE ANTI-SLAVERY-EXTENSION COALITION, THE POINTS OF DIVERGENCE BETWEEN REPUBLICANS AND DEMOCRATS, AND INTRA-PARTY REACTIONS TO LOCAL AND NATIONAL DEVELOPMENTS.

02437 COOKE, A.
THE PARTITION OF IRELAND AND ITS AFTERMATH
CONTEMPORARY REVIEW, 254(1480) (MAY 89), 250-257.
IF IRELAND HAD NOT BEEN PARTITIONED, THERE WOULD HAVE BEEN CIVIL WAR. IN THE MIDDLE OF 1921 LLOYD GEORGE'S GOVERNMENT SUDDENLY LOST THE WILL TO DEFEAT THE VICIOUS TERRORIST CAMPAIGN WHICH THE IRA HAD BEEN CONDUCTING FOR TWO YEARS IN ORDER TO TRY AND FORCE BRITAIN TO SEVER ALL ITS LINKS WITH IRELAND. TWO FACTORS ABOVE ALL ARE CRUCIAL TO UNDERSTANDING PARTITION. FIRST, NO DEFINITIVE, SCIENTIFIC BOUNDARY SATISFACTORY TO ALL PARTIES EXISTS - ANY MORE THAN IT DOES BETWEEN OTHER COUNTRIES TORN BY COMPETING NATIONALISMS (ONE THINKS AT ONCE OF EASTERN EUROPE). SECOND, THE PHYSICAL DIVISION OF IRELAND IS ONLY A REFLECTION OF A MUCH DEEPER PARTITION. THE REAL PARTITION IS NOT ON THE MAP, BUT IN THE MINDS OF MEN. THUS THE BORDER AS A FRONTIER BETWEEN THE UNITED KINGDOM AND THE REPUBLIC OF IRELAND IS A VERY ROUGH AND READY ATTEMPT TO FOLLOW THE REAL DIVISION OF THE POPULATION.

02438 COOPER, A.F.
RETOUR VERS LE FUTUR: LE COMMERCE D'ECHANGE INTERNATIONAL AU COURS DES ANNEES 80.
ETUDES INTERNATIONALES, XX(2) (JUN 89), 263-282.
THE ARTICLE ANALYZES THE ECONOMIC PRACTICE OF BARTERING. ALTHOUGH BARTER HAS BEEN COMMONLY PORTRAYED AS A DANGEROUS ELEMENT IN INTERNATIONAL RELATIONS AND AS A DESTRUCTIVE ECONOMIC PRACTICE, A CLOSE ANALYSIS WILL REVEAL SIGNIFICANT DIFFERENCES BETWEEN THE 1930S AND THE 1980S. THESE DIFFERENCES INDICATE THAT BARTER IN THE 1980S POINTS NOT TOWARDS A DESTRUCTIVE PAST, BUT TO A DYNAMIC AND COMPLEX FUTURE.

02439 COOPER, A.H.
THE WEST GERMAN PEACE MOVEMENT OF THE 1980'S: HISTORICAL AND INSTITUTIONAL INFLUENCES
DISSERTATION ABSTRACTS INTERNATIONAL, 50(2) (AUG 89), 533-A.
THE AUTHOR APPLIES A "NEW INSTITUTIONALIST" APPROACH TO THE WEST GERMAN PEACE MOVEMENT OF THE 1980'S, FOCUSING ON PEACE GROUPS WITHIN INSTITUTIONS, SUCH AS POLITICAL PARTIES AND CHURCHES. SHE ARGUES THAT INSTITUTIONS PROVIDE THE CRUCIAL LINK BETWEEN MERE ATTITUDE AND MOVEMENT PARTICIPATION.

02440 COOPER, H.F.
STATUS OF THE DEFENSE AND SPACE TALKS
DEPARTMENT OF STATE BULLETIN (US FOREIGN POLICY), 89(2151) (OCT 89), 20-22.
THE AUTHOR, WHO IS THE UNITED STATES' CHIEF NEGOTIATOR AT THE DEFENSE AND SPACE TALKS OF THE CONFERENCE ON DISARMAMENT, DISCUSSES AMERICAN OBJECTIVES IN THE TALKS, THE ABM TREATY, THE SOVIET POSITIONS ON RELEVANT ARMS CONTROL ISSUES, AND AMERICAN INITIATIVES IN ARMS CONTROL.

02441 COOPER, J.; YOUNG, C.
BILL INTRODUCTION IN THE NINETEENTH CENTURY: A STUDY OF INSTITUTIONAL CHANGE
LEGISLATIVE STUDIES QUARTERLY, XIV(1) (FEB 89), 67-106.
CURRENT PROCEDURES FOR BILL INTRODUCTION IN THE U.S. HOUSE WERE NEITHER ORIGINALLY INTENDED NOR QUICKLY ATTAINED. THEY REQUIRED ALMOST A CENTURY TO EMERGE AND WERE TIED TO BASIC STRUCTURAL CHANGES IN A NUMBER OF RELATED AREAS. THUS, TO UNDERSTAND THE EVOLUTION OF BILL INTRODUCTION IS TO UNDERSTAND THE EVOLUTION OF MANY OF THE DEFINING INSTITUTIONAL FEATURES OF THE MODERN HOUSE. VIEWED MORE THEORETICALLY, ANALYSIS OF THIS DEVELOPMENT HAS BENEFITS THAT EXTEND BEYOND BETTER UNDERSTANDING OF THE DYNAMICS OF A PARTICULAR LEGISLATURE. IT PROVIDES AN EXCELLENT CASE STUDY FOR CLARIFYING AND EXAMINING BASIC DIFFERENCES IN MICRO AND MACRO APPROACHES TO INSTUTIONAL ANALYSIS.

02442 COOPER, J.
THE MILITARY AND HIGHER EDUCATION IN THE USSR
PHILADELPHIA: ANLS OF AMER ACMY OF POLITICAL AND SOC SCIENCE, (502) (MAR 89), 108-119.
THE MILITARY DIMENSION OF THE SOVIET HIGHER-EDUCATIONAL SYSTEM IS DIFFICULT TO EXPLORE BECAUSE OF THE STRIKING SCARCITY OF PUBLISHED EVIDENCE. THERE IS A MILITARY PRESENCE AT ALL UNIVERSITIES AND HIGHEREDUCATIONAL INSTITUTES. IT TAKES DIVERSE FORMS, INCLUDING SPECIAL MILITARY DEPARTMENTS AND AN ELABORATE SYSTEM FOR THE MILITARY-PATRIOTIC EDUCATION OF STUDENTS. RESEARCH IS UNDERTAKEN FOR DEFENSE-RELATED CLIENTS, ALTHOUGH SUCH RESEARCH REPRESENTS A MODEST SHARE OF THE TOTAL MILITARY RESEARCH AND DEVELOPMENT EFFORT. IN GENERAL, THE RELATIONSHIP WITH THE MILITARY IS HARMONIOUS, BUT THIS TRADITION OF HARMONY, REFLECTING BROADER SOCIAL ATTITUDES TOWARD THE MILITARY IN SOVIET SOCIETY, HAS COME UNDER STRAIN IN RECENT YEARS AS A RESULT OF CHANGES IN CONSCRIPTION POLICY. IN THE NEW CONDITIONS OF GLASNOST, DISCONTENTS HAVE BEEN ABLE TO FIND OPEN EXPRESSION AND THIS MAY REMAIN THE PATTERN FOR THE FUTURE.

02443 COOPER, M.
A PENSION FOR TROUBLE: THE NEXT S&L CRISIS
WASHINGTON MONTHLY, 21(6) (JUL 89), 24-29.
THE SAVINGS AND LOAN CRISIS HAS CAUSED MANY PEOPLE TO ASK IF THERE ARE ANY OTHER FINANCIAL TIME BOMBS WAITING TO GO OFF. THE ANSWER IS A RESOUNDING YES. THE ARTICLE EXPLORES THE PROBLEMS THAT THE OVER $1 TRILLION OF UNFUNDED LIABILITY CONNECTED WITH THE US PUBLIC PENSION SYSTEM. PUBLIC PENSIONS ARE VERY GENEROUS AND EASY TO ACQUIRE. PERHAPS THE BIGGEST PART OF THE PUBLIC PENSION STORY IS THAT IS HAS BEEN KEPT SO QUIET-- IF ACTION IS NOT TAKEN SOON TO ALLEVIATE THE HUGE AMOUNTS OF UNFUNDED LIABILITY, A FINANCIAL CRISIS THAT WILL DWARF THE S&L CRISIS IS POSSIBLE.

02444 COOPER, M.
JUST TAKE THIS MEDICINE
WASHINGTON MONTHLY, 21(4) (MAY 89), 28, 30.
THE MAJOR CAUSE OF DOUBLE-DIGIT INFLATION IN 20TH-CENTURY AMERICA HAS BEEN SPECIFIC SHORTAGES, SUCH AS OIL SHORTAGES CAUSED BY OPEC. OTHER CAUSES OF RISING PRICES INCLUDE THE BUDGET DEFICIT, MEDICAL COSTS, TRADE BARRIERS, LACK OF LEADERSHIP, THE WEAK DOLLAR, AND MONOPOLY PRICING.

02445 COOPER, W.H.
JAPAN-U.S. TRADE: LOOKING AHEAD
CRS REVEIW, 10(6) (JUL 89), 6-7.
TRADE HAS INCREASINGLY BECOME THE FOCAL POINT OF JAPAN-U. S. RELATIONS. U.S. TRADE DEFICITS WITH JAPAN, JAPANESE UNFAIR TRADE PRACTICES, AND COMPETITION FROM JAPANESE PRODUCTS HAVE DRAWN MUCH ATTENTION FROM U.S. POLICYMAKERS. THE BUSH ADMINISTRATION AND THE 101ST CONGRESS WILL LIKELY FACE MORE CHALLENGES ON ISSUES OF JAPAN-U.S. TRADE.

02446 COPE, R.L.
C.W. DE KIEWIET, THE IMPERIAL FACTOR, AND SOUTH AFRICAN NATIVE POLICY
JOURNAL OF SOUTHERN AFRICAN STUDIES, 15(3) (APR 89), 486-505.
THIS ARTICLE CRITICISES DE KIEWIET'S DISCUSSION, AND ALSO PROVIDES A REASSESSMENT, OF BRITISH IDEAS CONCERNING 'NATIVE POLICY' IN THE 1870S, THE PERIOD IN WHICH CARNARVON ATTEMPTED TO ESTABLISH A BRITISH 'CONFEDERATION' IN SOUTH AFRICA. DE KIEWIET, FOLLOWING MACMILLAN, SAW THE IMPERIAL FACTOR AS A COUNTERWEIGHT TO SETTLER RAPACITY, AND HENCE REPRESENTED CARNARVON'S MOTIVES AS PHILANTHROPIC AND HIS DESIRE FOR A 'UNIFORM NATIVE POLICY' AS A WISH TO PROTECT AFRICANS FROM OPPRESSION AND PROLETARIANISATION. AGAINST THIS, IT IS ARGUED THAT THE PRIORITIES OF GLENELG WERE NOT THOSE OF CARNARVON, AND THAT THE CREATION OF AN AFRICAN WORKING CLASS WAS INESCAPABLE IF A 'CIVILISED' AND ECONOMICALLY EXPANDING DOMINION WAS TO BE ESTABLISHED IN SOUTH AFRICA; AND THAT THE EXPERIENCE OF JAMAICA (WITH ITS SIMILARITIES TO NATAL) AND ELSEWHERE FOLLOWING THE EMANCIPATION OF THE SLAVES, AND THE CONSEQUENT GROWTH OF RACISM AND DECLINE IN PHILANTHROPY, TOGETHER WITH THE GROWTH OF THE BLACK POPULATION IN SOUTH AFRICA IN NUMBERS AND POWER, MADE IT MOST UNLIKELY THAT THE PURPOSE OF IMPERIAL POLICY IN THE 1870S WAS AS DE KIEWIET REPRESENTED IT. THE ARTICLE

CONCLUDES THAT THE PURPOSE OF THE PROPOSED 'UNIFORM NATIVE POLICY' WAS ESSENTIALLY TO STRENGTHEN WHITE SUPREMACY AND SECURE AN ADEQUATE SUPPLY OF FREE WAGE LABOUR.

02447 COPELAND, B.R.
OF MICE AND ELEPHANTS: THE CANADA-U.S. FREE TRADE AGREEMENT
CONTEMPORARY POLICY ISSUES, VII(3) (JUL 89), 42-60.
THIS PAPER CRITICALLY ASSESSES THE FREE TRADE AGREEMENT BETWEEN CANADA AND THE UNITED STATES. REVIEWING THE THEORETICAL LITERATURE ON THE GAINS FROM TRADE AND THE EMPIRICAL LITERATURE ON BILATERAL TRADE LIBERALIZATION REVEALS THAT NO PRESUMPTION SHOULD EXIST THAT BILATERAL FREE TRADE WOULD SIGNIFICANTLY IMPROVE CANADA'S WELFARE. MOREOVER, BECAUSE OF UNCERTAINTY OVER FUTURE ABROGATION OR CONTINGENT PROTECTION ACTIONS, MUCH OF THE PREDICTED RATIONALIZATION OF CANADIAN INDUSTRY MAY NOT OCCUR. IF, ON THE OTHER HAND, FIRMS IN CANADA MAKE MAJOR INVESTMENTS TO TAKE ADVANTAGE OF THE AGREEMENT, CANADA'S BARGAINING POSITION WITH THE UNITED STATES ON TRADE AND OTHER ISSUES COULD BE WEAKENED.

02448 COPELAND, D.
STRUCTURAL ADJUSTMENT IN AFRICA
INTERNATIONAL PERSPECTIVES, XVIII(2) (MAR 89), 11-14.
AFRICAN NATIONS HAVE BEEN ENCOURAGED BY THE INDUSTRIALIZED WORLD TO ENGAGE IN "STRUCTURAL ADJUSTMENT" TO SOLVE THEIR ECONOMIC WOES. MOST OF THE STRUCTURING IS BASED ON A NEOCLASSICAL-LAISSEZ-FAIRE FORMULA THAT USUALLY SIGNALS THE DECREASE OF HEALTH AND EDUCATIONAL BENEFITS, AND OTHER WELFARE MEASURES. MANY NATIONS ARE RETHINKING THEIR ECONOMIC POLICIES; THE ARTICLE EXPLORES SOME OF THE DIRECTIONS THAT THE ECONOMIC CHANGES ARE TAKING INCLUDING A REFORMIST RE-EXAMINATION OF THE SITUATION THAT SEEKS TO MODIFY ADJUSTMENT PROGRAMS BY MAKING THEM SENSITIVE TO HUMAN CONSIDERATIONS. OTHER POLICIES REJECT ADJUSTMENT AS INIMICAL TO THE LONG-TERM INTERESTS OF AFRICA AS A WHOLE.

02449 COPELAND, G.W.
CHOOSING TO RUN: WHY HOUSE MEMBERS SEEK ELECTION TO THE SENATE
LEGISLATIVE STUDIES QUARTERLY, 14(4) (NOV 89), 549-566.
THIS PAPER CONSIDERS THE FACTORS THAT INFLUENCE WHETHER A MEMBER OF THE UNITED STATES HOUSE OF REPRESENTATIVES RUNS FOR THE SENATE, INCLUDING PERSONAL CIRCUMSTANCES, THE OPPORTUNITY STRUCTURE, AND POLITICAL FACTORS. IT CONCLUDES THAT MANY SPECIFIC CONDITIONS DO HAVE AN INFLUENCE ON THE DESIRE OF A HOUSE MEMBER TO EXERCISE PROGRESSIVE AMBITION, BUT THAT THE PROCESS OF DECISION MAKING IS FLUID AND INDIVIDUALISTIC. POTENTIAL CANDIDATES NOT ONLY ARE INFLUENCED BY CONDITIONS, BUT HAVE THE ABILITY TO ACT SO AS TO PROMOTE OPPORTUNITY FOR THEMSELVES.

02450 COPPER, J.F.
TAIWAN: A NATION IN TRANSITION
CURRENT HISTORY, 88(537) (APR 89), 173-176, 198-199.
THE AUTHOR SURVEYS THE RECENT CHANGES IN TAIWAN'S ECONOMY, POLITICS, AND FOREIGN POLICY, ESPECIALLY REGARDING MAINLAND CHINA.

02451 COPSON, R.W.
AFRICA'S WARS AND THEIR CONSEQUENCES
CRS REVEIW, 10(10) (NOV 89), 23-24.
SEVEN AFRICAN COUNTRIES AND TWO NON-INDEPENDENT TERRITORIES WERE AFFLICTED BY PROLONGED WARS DURING THE 1980'S. THESE WARS EXACTED GRAVE COSTS, INCLUDING A DEATH TOLL OF APPROXIMATELY TWO MILLION. THEY INVOLVED ISSUES IMPORTANT TO THE U.S. CONGRESS, SUCH AS ECONOMIC DEVELOPMENT AND HUMAN RIGHTS. DIPLOMATIC INITIATIVES RAISED HOPES FOR PEACE AT THE END OF THE DECADE, BUT PROGRESS WAS FRAGILE.

02452 COPULOS, M.R.
THE ENVIRONMENT: A NORTH-SOUTH CONFLICT
CURRENT, (317) (NOV 89), 35-39.
TO THE SOURCES OF FRICTION BETWEEN THE DEVELOPED AND THE DEVELOPING NATIONS MAY BE ADDED THE ENVIRONMENT. INCREASINGLY, CONFLICTS BETWEEN ECONOMIC DEVELOPMENT AND ENVIRONMENTAL PROTECTION ARE PROVING A SOURCE OF TENSION BETWEEN THE HAVES AND HAVE-NOTS, AND THE SITUATION IS LIKELY TO WORSEN OVER TIME.

02453 COQUERY-VIDROVITCH, C.
ENDURANCE AND CHANGE SOUTH OF THE SAHARA
UNIVERSITY OF CALIFORNIA PRESS, BERKELEY, CA, 1989, 448.
THE AUTHOR EXPLAINS THE PROCESS THAT HAS MADE AFRICA A LAND TORN BY INCESSANT CONFLICT AMONG ITS IMPOVERISHED PEOPLES. SHE FOCUSES ON FOUR MAJOR THEMES: POPULATION, POLITICAL POWER, THE PEASANTRY, AND THE NEW WORLD OF THE CITIES.

02454 CORAK, M.
POLICY IN AN ERA OF FREE TRADE: SOME COMMENTS ON THE DE GRANDPRE REPORT
CANADIAN PUBLIC POLICY--ANALYSE DE POLITIQUES, 15(3) (SEP 89), 335-338.
THIS ARTICLE EXAMINES A RECENT CANADIAN GOVERNMENT-

SPONSORED REPORT, ADJUSTING TO WIN, OR THE SO-CALLED DE GRANDPRE' REPORT. IT EXPLORES THE THREE MAIN SECTIONS: MATTERS OF LABOR SUPPLY, 'PEOPLE ISSUES'; CORPORATE ISSUES; AND SPECIFIC SECTORAL ISSUES. IT PUTS FORWARD SPECIFIC RECOMMENDATIONS WITH THE ATTENTION ON THE CONSTRAINTS AND INSTITUTIONS THAT CONDITION BEHAVIOR. IT CONCLUDES THAT THE REPORT IS AT ITS BEST WHEN SPECIFIC SECTORAL AND CORPORATE ISSUES ARE ADDRESSED, BUT THAT ALL ASPECTS OF IT WILL HAVE AN INFLUENCE UPON THE DEBATE CONCERNING POLICY IN AN ERA OF FREE TRADE.

02455 CORBETT, R.
TESTING THE NEW PROCEDURES: THE EUROPEAN PARLIAMENT'S FIRST EXPERIENCES WITH ITS NEW "SINGLE ACT" POWERS
JOURNAL OF COMMON MARKET STUDIES, XXVII(4) (JUN 89), 359-372.
THE AUTHOR EXAMINES HOW THE EUROPEAN PARLIAMENT HAS UTILIZED THE TWO NEW PROCEDURES INTRODUCED BY THE SINGLE EUROPEAN ACT FOR INVOLVING IT IN THE ADOPTION OF COMMUNITY LEGISLATION: THE ASSENT PROCEDURE AND THE COOPERATION PROCEDURE. SINCE THESE TWO PROCEDURES HAVE BEEN IN FORCE FOR NEARLY TWO YEARS, IT IS POSSIBLE TO MAKE A FIRST ASSESSMENT OF HOW THE PARLIAMENT IS ADAPTING TO AND MAKING USE OF THEM. THE AUTHOR ALSO LOOKS AT SOME OTHER DEVELOPMENTS IN PARLIAMENTARY PROCEDURE ARISING FROM THE ACT.

02456 CORBIN, G.R.
AGENDA-SETTING AND ACID RAIN
DISSERTATION ABSTRACTS INTERNATIONAL, 50(4) (OCT 89), 1075-A.
ATTEMPTS TO ESTABLISH U.S. FEDERAL POLICY TO ABATE ACID RAIN HAVE RESULTED IN POLITICAL STALEMATE. THIS STUDY EMPLOYS AGENDA-SETTING THEORY TO EXPLAIN WHY THAT STALEMATE PERSISTS, FOCUSING ON HOW THE ISSUE IS FRAMED FOR DEBATE, EXPLORING THE UNDERLYING ROOTS OF THE CONFLICT AND THE MOTIVES AND STRATEGIES OF PARTICIPANTS. EXPERTS AND PARTICIPANTS IN THE DEBATE WERE INTERVIEWED AND COMPLETED INTENSIVE QUESTIONNAIRES TO PROVIDE DATA FOR THE STUDY.

02457 CORCORAN-NANTES, Y.
WOMEN IN GRASS-ROOTS PROTEST POLITICS IN SAO PAULO, BRAZIL
DISSERTATION ABSTRACTS INTERNATIONAL, 49(7) (JAN 89), 1994-A.
THE AUTHOR INVESTIGATES THE NATURE OF FEMALE PARTICIPATION IN GRASS-ROOTS PROTEST POLITICS IN DEVELOPING COUNTRIES, FOCUSING ON URBAN SOCIAL MOVEMENTS IN SAO PAULO, BRAZIL.

02458 CORDELL, A. J.
THE EMERGING INFORMATION SOCIETY
POLICY OPTIONS, 10(2) (MAR 89), 14-17.
INFORMATION HAS BECOME PERHAPS THE MOST IMPORTANT INDUSTRY IN THE WESTERN WORLD, DR. CORDELL NOTES. JUST AS THE AUTOMOBILE AGE BROUGHT, ALONG WITH JOBS IN THE AUTO INDUSTRY, WHOLE NEW INDUSTRIES IN ITS WAKE, SO THE COMPUTER IS CREATING NEW INDUSTRIES NOT JUST IN MAKING COMPUTERS, BUT, FAR MORE IMPORTANT, IN CREATING THE CONTENT OF INFORMATION TECHNOLOGY. IDEAS, EXPERIENCES, CONCEPTS AND RAW DATA ARE BEING TURNED INTO COMMODITIES AND SOLD. INFORMATION IS A NEW CAPITAL RESOURCE IN OUR RAPIDLY CHANGING SOCIETY. CANADA, UNFORTUNATELY, IS VERY POORLY POSITIONED FOR THIS NEW WORLD, BECAUSE OF THE SMALLNESS OF POPULATION BASE AND THE OVERWHELMING IMPACT OF THE EMERGING AMERICAN SOFTWARE INDUSTRIES. CANADA MUST COME TO TERMS WITH THE RADICAL SHIFTS BROUGHT ABOUT BY AN INFORMATION ECONOMY, AND SOON.

02459 CORDELL, K.
THE ORIGINS AND DEVELOPMENT OF "DEUTSCHLANDPOLITIK," 1969-1974
DISSERTATION ABSTRACTS INTERNATIONAL, 49(10) (APR 89), 3140-A.
"DEUTSCHLANDPOLITIK" WAS THE PROCESS THAT FORMALLY BEGAN IN 1969 AND CULMINATED IN THE ESTABLISHMENT OF FORMAL DIPLOMATIC LINKS BETWEEN THE TWO GERMAN STATES IN 1974. THIS DISSERTATION TRACES THE EVOLUTION OF "DUETSCHLANDPOLITIK" FROM ITS GENESIS TO IMPLEMENTATION, IN ORDER TO ASSESS WHERE THE POLICY SUCCEEDED AND WHERE IT FAILED.

02460 CORDESMAN, A.H.
NET ASSESSMENT AND DEFENSE RESOURCES: CHALLENGES FOR THE NEXT ADMINISTRATION
WASHINGTON QUARTERLY, 12(2) (SPR 89), 129-149.
NET ASSESSMENT IS THE PROCESS OF ANALYZING ALL THE KEY VARIABLES AFFECTING THE MILITARY BALANCE AND RELATIVE MILITARY POWER AND DETERMINING THEIR IMPACT ON A GIVEN ISSUE. IN TERMS OF DEFENSE RESOURCE MANAGEMENT, IT MEANS ALLOCATING RESOURCES IN A WAY THAT REFLECTS A FULL UNDERSTANDING OF HOW RESOURSES AFFECT THE CURRENT AND FUTURE MILITARY BALANCE AND OF HOW THEY AFFECT THE ABILITY OF U.S. MILITARY FORCES TO EXECUTE NATIONAL STRATEGY AND THEIR ASSIGNED ROLES AND MISSIONS. THE ROLE OF NET ASSESMENT NEEDS TO BE EXPANDED WITNIN DOD. IT SHOULD BE EXPANDED IN THE FULL BUDGET CYCLE WHICH EMBRACES CONGRESSIONAL REVIEW AND PUBLIC PERCEPTION OF DEFENSE. IT MUST PLAY A KEY ROLE LINKING

STRATEGY, FORCE PLANNING, PROGRAMMING, AND BUDGETING.

02461 CORELLI, R.; GILLIES, L.; LAVER, R.; LOWTHER, W.; MANSOUR, V.
AN INFLAMED DEBATE
MACLEAN'S (CANADA'S NEWS MAGAZINE), 102(28) (JUL 89), 36-37.
ABORTION WAS THE FOCUS OF TROUBLING, RANCOROUS DEBATE BOTH IN CANADA AND THE US AS A SERIES OF NARROWLY SPLIT COURT DECISIONS INTENSIFIED THE CONFLICT OVER THE ISSUE. THE DECISION OF THE US SUPREME COURT WHICH UPHOLDS THE CONSTITUTIONALITY OF A MISSOURI STATUTE THAT SEVERELY RESTRICTS ACCESS TO ABORTIONS AND CONTRADICTORY RULINGS IN TWO-ABORTION RELATED CASES IN TORONTO AND WINNIPEG HAVE BROUGHT ABORTION INTO THE FOREFRONT OF PUBLIC CONSCIOUSNESS AND PUBLIC DEBATE. REACTION ON BOTH SIDES WAS IMMEDIATE AND SWIFT AS BOTH PRO CHOICE AND PRO LIFE GROUPS TOOK SIDES ON THE COURT DECISIONS. MANY FEEL THE ISSUE TO BE BEYOND SOLUTION AND MOST AGREE THAT AN EASY SOLUTION DOES NOT EXIST AND THAT ABORTION IS LIKELY TO BE A SIGNIFICANT AND VISIBLE PUBLIC ISSUE FOR YEARS TO COME.

02462 CORMICK, G.
STRATEGIC ISSUES IN STRUCTURING MULTI-PARTY PUBLIC POLICY NEGOTIATIONS
NEGOTIATION JOURNAL, 5(2) (APR 89), 125-132.
MANY OF THE DILEMMAS AND PROBLEMS THAT ARISE IN THE PROCESS OF RESOLVING COMPLEX PUBLIC POLICY DISPUTES CAN BE AVOIDED BY THE ORDERLY AND THOUGHTFUL APPLICATION OF THE MEDIATION PROCESS. THE ARTICLE ATTEMPTS TO OUTLINE A FRAMEWORK OF "PROTOCOLS" FOR THE NEGOTIATION PROCESS THAT WILL FACILITATE SWIFT AND PRODUCTIVE SOLUTIONS TO PROBLEMS. SOME OF THE SUGGESTED FRAMEWORKS INCLUDE THE PURPOSE OF THE NEGOTIATIONS, THE STRUCTURE OF THE NEGOTIATIONS, OPEN MEETINGS, CONFIDENTIALITY, AND THE MEDIA, AND THE USE OF TECHNICAL AND SUBTANTIVE INFORMATION.

02463 CORNING, G.
US-JAPAN SECURITY COOPERATION IN THE 1990'S: THE PROMISE OF HIGH TECH DEFENSE
ASIAN SURVEY, XXIX(3) (MAR 89), 268-286.
A NEW EFFORT TO DEAL CONSTRUCTIVELY WITH THE TRADE AND SECURITY DIMENSIONS OF US-JAPAN RELATIONS SHOULD BE HIGH ON THE FOREIGN POLICY AGENDA OF THE BUSH ADMINISTRATION. THE ARTICLE EXAMINES US OPTIONS TOWARDS JAPAN IN THESE AREAS. IT OUTLINES JAPAN'S VIEWS ON SECURITY AND DEFENSE BURDEN SHARING, AND THE OPTIONS AND PROBLEMS INVOLVED IN HIGH TECHNOLOGY COLLABORATION. IT LISTS SOME POLICY RECOMMENDATIONS FOR FUTURE CONSIDERATION.

02464 CORPUZ, A. G.
DE-MAOIZATION AND NATIONALIST TRENDS IN THE CPP
JOURNAL OF CONTEMPORARY ASIA, 18(4) (1988), 412-429.
THIS ARTICLE OFFERS ONE EXPLANATION FOR THE DE-MAOIZATION AND NATIONALIST TRENDS BY CONSIDERING OVERALL PARTY OBJECTIVES, RHETORIC, AND SPECIFIC INDICATORS OF SUCH TRENDS. THE FOCUS IS ON THE PERIOD FROM THE REESTABLISHMENT OF THE CPP TO THE EARLY 1980S; ALTHOUGH THE AQUINO GOVERNMENT INSTALLED A MORE LIBERAL POLITICAL LATITUDE WHICH AFFECTED THE CPPS STRATEGIES AND TACTICS, THE DE-MAOIZATION AND NATIONALIST TRENDS WERE NOTED WELL BEFORE THE OUSTER OF MARCOS AND THESE REQUIRE AN ASSESSMENT INDEPENDENT OF THE 1986 "SNAP REVOLUTION."

02465 CORRADINI, A.
VERIFICATION AND COMPLIANCE
DISARMAMENT, XII(2) (SUM 89), 155-169.
VERIFICATION IS AN INTEGRAL PART OF ARMS LIMITATION AND DISARMAMENT AGREEMENTS BECAUSE COMPLIANCE WITH SUCH AGREEMENTS MUST BE PROVED. THE UNITED NATIONS HAS DEALT WITH PROBLEMS OF VERIFICATION SINCE ITS INCEPTION, AT BOTH THE DELIBERATIVE AND THE NEGOTIATING STAGES. SEVERAL ARMS LIMITATION AND DISARMAMENT AGREEMENTS CURRENTLY IN FORCE PROVIDE A ROLE FOR THE UNITED NATIONS IN ENSURING COMPLIANCE WITH AGREEMENTS.

02466 CORRADINO, E.A.
THE FOURTH AMENDMENT OVERSEAS: IS EXTRATERRITORIAL PROTECTION OF FOREIGN NATIONALS GOING TOO FAR?
FORDHAM LAW REVIEW, LVII(4) (MAR 89), 617-635.
THIS ARTICLE ARGUES THAT THE FOURTH AMENDMENT WHICH PROTECTS THE INDIVIDUAL'S RIGHT TO BE FREE FROM UNREASONABLE SEARCH AND SEIZURE IS DESIGNED TO PRESERVE THE INDIVIDUAL RIGHTS OF UNITED STATES CITIZENS AND INDIVIDUALS ON UNITED STATES SOIL FROM ARBITRARY AND UNREASONABLE GOVERNMENT ACTIVITY. THIS INTENT IS THWARTED WHEN THE GUARANTEES ARE APPLIED TO FOREIGN NATIONALS ABOARD. WHEN GOVERNMENT ACTION TAKES PLACE ON FOREIGN SOIL NOT SUBJECT TO UNITED STATES SOVEREIGNTY, THE FOURTH AMENDMENT SHOULD NOT BE USED TO GRANT PROTECTION TO ALIENS CLAIMING NO TIES TO THE UNITED STATES.

02467 COSER, L.A.
THE DEATH THROES OF WESTERN COMMUNISM
DISSENT, (SPR 89), 186-191.
COMMUNISM IN WESTERN EUROPE, RATHER THAN BEING AN INSPIRING MESSIANIC MOVEMENT, HAS BECOME A GROTESQUE RELIC. THE SOVIET MORTGAGE ON THE POLITICAL LIFE OF WESTERN EUROPE HAS BEEN LIFTED. THE NEAR DEMISE OF COMMUNISM IN ALL OF WESTERN EUROPE IS A HISTORIC FACT THAT CURRENT COMMENTATORS HAVE NOT YET FULLY APPRECIATED. IT IS AS SIGNIFICANT A FEATURE OF CONTEMPORARY HISTORY AS THE RISE AND FALL OF NAZISM OR THE IMPACT OF THE RUSSIAN REVOLUTION IN THE WEST AFTER 1917.

02468 COSTEA, P.
EASTERN EUROPE'S RELATIONS WITH THE MARXIST-LENINIST REGIMES OF THE THIRD WORLD TO 1988
DISSERTATION ABSTRACTS INTERNATIONAL, 50(6) (DEC 89), 1793-A.
THE AUTHOR ANALYZES THE RELATIONS BETWEEN THE EUROPEAN COMMUNIST COUNTRIES AND THE HANDFUL OF THIRD WORLD STATES THAT CLAIM TO BE BUILDING THE FOUNDATIONS OF SCIENTIFIC SOCIALISM. THE TOTALITARIANIZATION OF SELECTED DEVELOPING COUNTRIES IS THE SOCIALIST WORLD'S MAJOR DEVICE FOR PROMOTING SOCIALISM IN THE THIRD WORLD THE FUNDAMENTAL OBJECTIVES OF SOCIALISM IN THE THIRD WORLD ARE TO DETACH THE "NEO-COLONIAL" WORLD FROM THE PREVAILING INTERNATIONAL ORDER, TO INTEGRATE THE DETACHED COUNTRIES INTO THE SOCIALIST WORLD ORDER, TO SECURE SOCIALIST ECONOMIC OBJECTIVES, AND TO COUNTER THE POLITICAL AND IDEOLOGICAL INFLUENCE OF THE SOCIALIST INTERNATIONAL AND THE PEOPLE'S REPUBLIC OF CHINA.

02469 COTHACH, N.
A VIEW FROM HANOI
INTERNATIONAL AFFAIRS (MOSCOW), (9) (SEP 89), 72-79.
THE SIXTH CONGRESS OF THE COMMUNIST PARTY OF VIETNAM IN LATE 1986 USHERED IN A NEW STAGE IN THE HISTORY OF THE VIETNAMESE REVOLUTION. SINCE THE CONGRESS, VIETNAM HAS EXPERIENCED A PERIOD OF STABLE RENOVATION IN ALL SPHERES OF PARTY AND STATE ACTIVITIES. WITHIN THE GENERAL PROCESS OF RENEWAL, EFFORTS ARE BEING MADE TO INTRODUCE CONSTRUCTIVE CHANGES IN VIETNAMESE FOREIGN POLICY.

02470 COTTAM, M.L.
COGNITIVE PSYCHOLOGY AND BARGAINING BEHAVIOR: PERU VERSUS THE MNCS
POLITICAL PSYCHOLOGY, 10(3) (SEP 89), 445-476.
THIS PAPER EXPLORES THE IMPACT OF COGNITIVE IMAGES ON BARGAINING BETWEEN STATE POLICY MAKERS AND PRIVATE MULTINATIONAL CORPORATIONS (MNCS). THE PAPER BEGINS WITH A DISCUSSION OF THE COGNITIVE IMAGES AND PRESENTS THREE IDEAL-TYPICAL IMAGES OF MULTINATIONAL FIRMS AS PERCEIVED BY THIRD WORLD HOSTS. IT IS THEN ARGUED THAT THE INTERACTION OF IMAGES OF MNCS AND THE SELF PRODUCES DISTINCT BARGAINING PATTERNS WITH MNCS CLASSIFIED IN EACH IMAGE. THE PAPER THEN PRESENTS EXAMPLES OF THESE BARGAINING PATTERNS IN PERUVIAN BARGAINING WITH MNCS DURING THE VELASCO GOVERNMENT.

02471 COTTAM, R.
INSIDE REVOLUTIONARY IRAN
MIDDLE EAST JOURNAL, 43(2) (SPR 89), 168-185.
THE REVOLUTION OF IRAN WAS ONE OF THE GREATEST POPULISTO EXPLOSIONS IN HUMAN HISTORY. HOWEVER, POPULAR SUPPORT FOR THE REGIME BEGAN TO DECLINE SOON AFTER AYATOLIAH KHOMEINI TOOK POWER. THE ARTICLE PRESENTS A DESCRIPTION AND EXPLANATION OF THE FAILURES AND SUCCESSES, BOTH WITH DRAMATIC DIMENSIONS, OF THE REGIME'S FIRST DECADE. IT EXAMINES THE REVOLUTIONARY LEADERSHIP AND THE POLARIZATION THAT RAPIDLY TOOK PLACE. IT ALSO OUTLINES THE ACTIONS OF THE "ACCOMODATING MAJORITY" WHO ADAPTED TO THE REGIME BUT GAVE IT LITTLE OR NO SUPPORT.

02472 COTTON, J.
FROM AUTHORITARIANISM TO DEMOCRACY IN SOUTH KOREA
POLITICAL STUDIES, XXXVII(2) (JUN 89), 244-259.
THE SOUTH KOREA CASE SUPPORTS THE CONTENTION THAT POPULAR DEMANDS FOR POLITICAL PARTICIPATION AND THE WILLINGNESS OF ELITES TO RECOGNIZE THEM ARE THE LIKELY CONSEQUENCES OF MODERNIZATION. THE CONTINUING TRANSFORMATION OF THE POLITICAL SYSTEM SUGGESTS THAT NEITHER THE CORPORATIST NOR THE BUREAUCRATIC AUTHORITARIAN MODELS ARE APPLICABLE TO KOREA. ITS NON-DEMOCRATIC PAST IS BEST SEEN AS A RESPONSE TO SPECIFIC FACTORS, INCLUDING KOREA'S POSITION IN THE PREVAILING WORLD SYSTEM, THE ABSENCE OF COUNTERVAILING ELITES AS A RESULT OF WAR AND RAPID SOCIAL TRANSFORMATION AND THE DEVELOPMENT OF A STRONG AND RELATIVELY INDEPENDENT STATE. THE RECENT DOMESTIC AND INTERNATIONAL IMPACT OF MODERNIZATION HAS BEEN TO REVERSE THE INFLUENCE OF THESE FACTORS, THOUGH ELEMENTS OF THE POLITICAL CULTURE AND THE CONTENTIOUS LEGACY OF THE PAST POSE DIFFICULTIES FOR THE NEW DEMOCRACY. ROH TAE-WOO WILL NEED TO BE SEEN TO BE MAKING A NEW BEGINNING IF THE PERENNIAL LEGITIMACY CRISIS OF THE KOREAN REPUBLIC IS TO BE OVERCOME.

02473 COTTON, J.
NORTH-SOUTH KOREAN RELATIONS: ANOTHER FALSE START?

WORLD TODAY, 45(6) (JUN 89), 104-108.
THE AUTHOR TRACES THE RECENT EVOLUTION OF THE POSITIONS
OF BOTH KOREAN STATES ON INTER-KOREAN RELATIONS. HE ARGUES
THAT THE NEW INITIATIVES TAKEN BY SOUTH KOREA HAVE NOT FOUND
A POSITIVE RESPONSE. NORTH KOREA REMAINS IMPLACABLY OPPOSED
TO ANY STEPS THAT MIGHT LEAD TO THE INSTITUTIONALIZATION OF
THE DIVISION OF KOREA. FOR ITS PART, SOUTH KOREA CAN SEE NO
BASIS FOR PROCEEDING WITH UNIFICATION WITHOUT PRIOR STEPS TO
EASE TENSIONS AND BUILD MUTUAL TRUST. CIRCUMSTANCES HAVE LED
BOTH STATES TO ADDRESS THE PROBLEM ANEW, EVEN THOUGH THEIR
FUNDAMENTAL APPROACHES REMAIN INCOMPATIBLE.

02474 COTTON, J.
OPENING THE GAP: THE DECLINE IN BLACK ECONOMIC INDICATORS
IN THE 1980S
SOCIAL SCIENCE QUARTERLY, 70(4) (DEC 89), 803-819.
THE CLAIMS THAT BLACKS HAVE MADE SUBSTANTIAL ECONOMIC
PROGRESS IN RECENT YEARS ARE CHALLENGED BY TIME SERIES DATA
ON INCOME, OCCUPATION, UNEMPLOYMENT, AND POVERTY RATES, THIS
ARTICLE EXAMINES THE EVIDENCE THAT REVEALS THAT NOT ONLY HAS
THERE BEEN LITTLE IN THE WAY OF REAL ADVANCEMENT, BUT WHAT
FEW GAINS HAVE BEEN MADE ARE IN DANGER OF BEING ERODED IN
THE 1980'S.

02475 COTTON, J.
REDEFINING TAIWAN: 'ONE COUNTRY, TWO GOVERNMENTS'
WORLD TODAY, 45(12) (DEC 89), 213-216.
TAIWAN'S OLD ENMITY TOWARD THE CHINESE MAINLAND IS
FADING WITH THE RELAXATION OF TAIPEI'S "THREE NOES" POLICY.
THE FORMULA NOW FAVORED FOR TAIWAN'S CHANGING RELATIONSHIP
WITH THE MAINLAND IS "ONE COUNTRY, TWO GOVERNMENTS" THOUGH
THIS HAS YET TO BE ADOPTED OFFICIALLY. BECAUSE TAIWAN HAS
FOR SO LONG DEFINED ITSELF AS THE ONLY LEGITIMATE GOVERNMENT
OF CHINA, IT IS CLEAR THAT THIS NEW FLEXIBILITY IS THE
RESULT OF MUCH DELIBERATION. IT IS THE TAIPEI GOVERNMENT'S
CONTENTION THAT INNOVATIONS ARE NECESSARY TO BREAK THE
COUNTRY'S POLITICAL ISOLATION AND ENABLE TAIWAN TO PLAY A
GREATER ROLE IN THE WORLD ECONOMY. DEVELOPMENTS ON THE
MAINLAND HAVE ALSO BEEN A FACTOR IN THE CHANGING POLICY.

02476 COUGHLIN, P.J.
ECONOMIC POLICY ADVICE AND POLITICAL PREFERENCES
PUBLIC CHOICE, 61(3) (JUN 89), 201-216.
THIS ESSAY ARGUES THAT PUBLIC CHOICE OFFERS AN
APPROPRIATE APPROACH FOR THINKING ABOUT ECONOMIC POLICY
ADVICE. FIRST THE AUTHOR DISCUSSES THE NATURE THE POLICY
ADVICE THAT IS PROFFERED BY ECONOMISTS, THEN SPECIFICALLY
SUGGESTS THAT ONE OF THE MOST COMMON MODELING FEATURES IN
THE PUBLIC CHOICE LITERATURE (VIZ., THE ASSUMPTION THAT
INDIVIDUALS HAVE POLITICAL PREFERENCES) MAY BE USEFUL IN
HELPING US UNDERSTAND THE NATURE OF THIS ADVICE. FINALLY,
THE AUTHOR ALSO CARRIES OUT A TENTATIVE EXPLORATION OF THE
IMPLICATIONS OF ACCEPTING THE PERSPECTIVE THAT IS PROVIDED
WHEN THE SUGGESTED MODELING FEATURE IS USED IN THIS CONTEXT.

02477 COUNTEE, S.F.
PUBLIC MANAGERS IN A PRIVATE MANAGER ORIENTED SOCIETY
DISSERTATION ABSTRACTS INTERNATIONAL, 49(12) (JUN 89),
3865-A.
THIS FIELD-BASED RESEARCH DEALT WITH DIFFERENCES BETWEEN
MIDDLE MANAGERS IN PUBLIC AND 'PRIVATE SECTOR ORGANIZATION'S
BY (1) EXAMINING AND ASSESSING HERZBERG'S MOTIVATION-HYGIENE
THEROY AS A CONCEPTUAL MODEL; (2) COMPARING MANAGERS AS TO
JOB SATISFACTION, ORGANIZATIONAL CLIMATE AND MANAGEMENT
TASKS. THE SAMPLE WAS DICHOTOMIZED AMONG PUBLIC AGENCIES OF
STATE AND LOCAL GOVERNMENTS AND PAIRED WITH LIKE PRIVATE NON-
PROFIT ORGANIZATIONS IN NEW YORK STATE.

02478 COUPER, K.
IMMIGRATION, NATIONALITY AND CITIZENSHIP IN THE UK
NEW POLITICAL SCIENCE, 16 (FAL 89), 91-100.
THE AUTHOR FOCUSES IN THE UNITED KINGDOM, SKETCHING THE
BACKGROUND TO THE PRESENT SITUATION REGARDING PATTERNS OF
IMMIGRANT SETTLEMENT IN WESTERN EUROPE AS A WHOLE, AND
DOCUMENTED CONFLICTS OVER CIVIL AND POLITICAL RIGHTS OF THIS
POPULATION. 1981, 1985, AND 1987 ARE YEARS CITED IN WHICH
PREDOMINANTLY YOUNG PEOPLE, BOTH BLACK AND WHITE, CONFRONTED
THE POLICE IN THE INNER CITY AREAS OF MAJOR TOWNS IN THE U.K.
IN CIVIL DISOBEDIENCE ACTS SPRINGING FROM MULTIRACIAL AND
MULTICULTURAL INJUSTICE. THE TERMS IMMIGRANT, INTEGRATION,
ETHNIC MINORITIES, AND EQUALY OPPORTUNITIES ARE EXAMINED.
BRITISH NATIONALITY IS DISCUSSED IN TERMS OF COLONIAL
HISTORY. AN INTERPRETATION OF THE 1981 BRITISH NATIONALITY
ACT IS PROVIDED.

02479 COUTO, R.A.
ECONOMICS, EXPERTS, AND RISK: LESSONS FROM THE CATASTROPHE
AT ABERFAN
POLITICAL PSYCHOLOGY, 10(2) (JUN 89), 309-324.
IN 1966, A COALWASTE PILE COLLAPSED, BURYING AND KILLING
144 CHILDREN AND OTHER RESIDENTS OF ABERFAN, A COALMINING
COMMUNITY IN SOUTH WALES. THIS WAS A CATASTROPHE IN THE
PRECISE SENSE IN WHICH CHARLES PERROW USES THIS TERM AND
RESEMBLED OTHER CATASTROPHES WITH WHICH HE ARE BECOMING ALL
TOO FAMILIAR. THE RECORDS OF THE INVESTIGATING TRIBUNAL AND
INTERVIEWS WITH COMMUNITY LEADERS CONDUCTED IN 1984
RECONSTRUCT THE CATASTROPHE AND ITS CAUSES AND SUGGEST ITS
ENDURING IMPACT ON THE COMMUNITY. FUNDAMENTAL TO THE
CATASTROPHE IS ECONOMIC NEED WHICH PROMOTES TOLERANCE FOR A
HIGH-RISK INDUSTRY. FUNDAMENTAL TO THE AFTERMATH OF THE
CATASTROPHE ARE THE ASSERTION OF COMMUNITY VALUES AND
ABILITIES AND THE DISTRUST OF EXPERTS MAKING DECISIONS FOR
COMMUNITY RESIDENTS.

02480 COVELLO, V., (ED.); MCCALLUM, D., (ED.); PAVLOVA, M., (ED.)
EFFECTIVE RISK COMMUNICATION: THE ROLE AND RESPONSIBILITY
OF GOVERNMENT AND NONGOVERNMENT ORGANIZATIONS
(1989), 370.
THE BOOK IS A COLLECTION OF PAPERS ON THE PROCESS OF
RISK COMMUNICATION. IT EXAMINES THE EFFORTS OF VARIOUS
LEVELS OF GOVERNMENT AS WELL AS NONGOVERNMENTAL
ORGANIZATIONS IN COMMUNICATING SIGNIFICANT HEALTH RISKS TO
SOCIETY. IT EXPLORES THE VARIOUS METHODS IN WHICH RISK CAN
BE COMMUNICATED AND THE CHALLENGES THAT POLICYMAKERS FACE IN
ATTEMPTING TO DO SO. IT ALSO EXAMINES SEVERAL CASE STUDIES
OF AGENCIES AND ORGANIZATIONS IN ACTION.

02481 COVELLO, V., (ED.); MCCALLUM, D., (ED.); PAVLOVA, M.,
(ED.); WILSON, T.
INTERACTIONS BETWEEN COMMUNITY/LOCAL GOVERNMENT AND
FEDERAL PROGRAMS; EFFECTIVE RISK COMMUNICATION: THE ROLE
AND RESPONSIBILITY OF GOVERNMENT AND NONGOVERNMENT
ORGANIZATIONS
PLENUM PRESS, NEW YORK, NY, 1989, 77-82.
THE PURPOSE OF THE CHAPTER IS TO ILLUSTRATE BOTH THE
RISK ASSESSMENT NEEDS OF LOCAL OFFICIALS AND THE WAYS IN
WHICH LOCAL OFFICIALS CAN HELP OTHER LEVELS OF GOVERNMENT
WITH THE RISK COMMUNICATION PROCESS. IT EXPLORES THE
CHALLENGES THAT FACE LOCAL GOVERNMENTS BY FOCUSING ON THE
EXPERIENCE OF ELKHART COUNTY, INDIANA.

02482 COVELLO, V., (ED.); GALBRAITH, P.; MCCALLUM, D., (ED.);
PAVLOVA, M., (ED.)
INTERACTIONS BETWEEN STATE AND FEDERAL PROGRAMS; EFFECTIVE
RISK COMMUNICATION; THE ROLE AND RESPONSIBILITY OF
GOVERNMENT AND NONGOVERNMENT ORGANIZATIONS
PLENUM PRESS, NEW YORK, NY, 1989, 73-77.
THE ARTICLE REVIEWS THE HISTORY OF FEDERAL AND STATE
GOVERNMENTAL COOPERATION IN THE AREA OF RISK COMMUNICATION.
IT CONCLUDES THAT ALTHOUGH GREAT PROGRESS HAS BEEN MADE
TOWARDS HARMONIZATION OF POLICY, MUCH REMAINS TO BE DONE.
THE ARTICLE ALSO ARGUES THAT A COMMITMENT TO JOINT FEDERAL/
STATE PRESS RELEASES USING LANGUAGE APPROPRIATE TO SENSITIVE
ISSUES WOULD IMPROVE RISK COMMUNICATION SIGNIFICANTLY.

02483 COVELLO, V., (ED.); MASON, J.; MCCALLUM, D., (ED.);
PAVLOVA, M., (ED.)
THE FEDERAL ROLE IN RISK COMMUNICATION AND PUBLIC
EDUCATION; EFFECTIVE RISK COMMUNICATION: THE ROLE OF
GOVERNMENT AND NONGOVERNMENT ORGANIZATIONS
PLENUM PRESS, NEW YORK, NY", 1989, 19-27.
THE AUTHOR DISCUSSES THE THREE SETS OF RISKS THAT THE
FEDERAL GOVERNMENT IN THE FORM OF THE CENTERS FOR DISEASE
CONTROL DEALS WITH. THEY ARE: THE RISK OF INFECTIOUS DISEASE,
THE RISKS ASSOCIATED WITH PERSONAL HEALTH-RELATED BEHAVIORS,
AND THE RISKS ASSOCIATED WITH ENVIRONMENTAL HAZARDS BOTH IN
THE WORKPLACE AND THE COMMUNITY. HE ALSO OUTLINES PRINCIPLES
THAT ARE CRITICAL TO CARRYING OUT THE GOVERNMENT'S ROLE IN
RISK COMMUNICATION. THESE INCLUDE CREDIBILITY OF THE SOURCE,
QUALITY OF THE MESSAGE, USE OF INTERMEDIARIES, AND
INVOLVEMENT OF THE CONCERNED PUBLIC.

02484 COVELLO, V., (ED.); ALLEN, F.; MCCALLUM, D., (ED.);
PAVLOVA, M., (ED.)
THE GOVERNMENT AS LIGHTHOUSE: A SUMMARY OF FEDERAL RISK
COMMUNICATION PROGRAMS; EFFECTIVE RISK COMMUNICATION: THE
ROLE AND RESPONSIBILITY OF GOVERNMENT AND NONGOVERNMENT
ORGANIZATIONS
PLENUM PRESS, NEW YORK, NY, 1989, 53-61.
THE ARTICLE GIVES A BRIEF OVERVIEW OF THE 14 FEDERAL
AGENCIES THAT ARE INVOLVED IN RISK COMMUNICATION. IT
EXAMINES THE DIVERSE MISSIONS, MANDATES, AND METHODS OF THE
ORGANIZATIONS AND CONCLUDES THAT SINCE RISK COMMUNICATION IS
POTENTIALLY ONE OF THE MOST POWERFUL DOMESTIC FUNCTIONS OF
GOVERNMENT, IT DESERVES MORE ATTENTION.

02485 COVINGTON, S.R.
NATO AND SOVIET MILITARY DOCTRINE
WASHINGTON QUARTERLY, 12(4) (FAL 89), 73-82.
THIS ESSAY EXAMINES THE SOVIET MILITARY'S VIEW OF
DEFENSIVE DOCTRINE, THE RATIONALE BEHIND ITS WAR PREVENTION
EMPHASIS, AND ITS IMPLICATIONS FOR CONVENTIONAL AND NUCLEAR
FORCE REDUCTIONS, IT ANALYZES THE MAY 1987 WP PROCLAMATION;
STRATEGIC REALITIES; STRATEGY AND WAR PREVENTION; SOVIET
INITIATIVES AND NATO. IT CONCLUDES THAT GRANTING CONCESSIONS
FOR WHAT ARE MISTAKENLY VIEWED AS SOVIET RETREATS COULD
ERODE THE CREDIBILITY OF NUCLEAR DETERRENCE, FLEXIBLE
RESPONSE, AND FORWARD DEFENSE.

02486 COWARD, L.
ATTITUDES TO NUCLEAR DEFENCE: AN INVESTIGATION OF
PROCESSES OF CHANGE IN ELITE AND NON-ELITE BELIEF SYSTEMS
DISSERTATION ABSTRACTS INTERNATIONAL, 49(7) (JAN 89),
1949-A.
THE AUTHOR SEEKS TO DETERMINE HOW MUCH INFORMATION
EXISTS ABOUT ATTITUDES TOWARDS NUCLEAR DETERRENCE AND THE
PROCESSES OF ATTITUDE CHANGE. SHE USES INTERVIEWS WITH A
SAMPLE OF US ELITES WHO HAVE UNDERGONE VARYING DEGREES OF
ATTITUDE CHANGE TOWARDS NUCLEAR DEFENSE AS THE EMPIRICAL
BASIS FOR A MODEL OF ATTITUDE CHANGE.

02487 COWDEN, A.C.
A PUBLIC SECTOR LEXICON: CALIFORNIA STYLE
STATE AND LOCAL GOVERNMENT REVIEW, 21(3) (FAL 89), 116-122.
SINCE THE PASSAGE OF PROPOSITION 13 IN CALIFORNIA,
CITIES HAVE CHANGED MANY OF THEIR APPROACHES TO RAISING
REVENUES AND DELIVERING SERVICES TO THEIR CITIZENS. THIS
PAPER PRESENTS A LEXICON OF APPROACHES WHICH HAVE EVOLVED TO
MEET THE CHALLENGES OF THIS ERA OF FISCAL PRESSURES.
NUMEROUS IDEAS IN GOOD CURRENCY ARE DEFINED AND ILLUSTRATED
WITH PRACTICES ACTUALLY USED IN VARIOUS CALIFORNIA CITIES.

02488 COWLING, M.
THE SOURCES OF THE NEW RIGHT
ENCOUNTER, LXXIII(4) (NOV 89), 3-15.
DURING THE PAST 25 YEARS, THE NEW RIGHT HAS HAD FIVE
FACES, ALL OF WHICH HAVE MANIFESTED PASSION AND CONVICTION,
EVEN WHEN THERE HAS ALSO BEEN MISTRUST OF PASSION AND
CONVICTION, AND ALL OF WHICH HAVE ENDEAVORED TO WRENCH THE
PUBLIC MIND FROM THE GROOVE IT HAD BEEN RUNNING IN SINCE
1940. THESE ARE THE MOVEMENT OF ECONOMIC OPINION AGAINST
KEYNESIANISM, CORPORATISM, AND COLLECTIVISM AND IN FAVOR OF
CAPITALISM, MONETARISM, AND THE FREE MARKET; THE EDUCATIONAL
MOVEMENT THAT DERIVES FROM THE BLACK PAPERS; THE
PARLIAMENTARY, PARTY, AND PUBLIC MOVEMENTS KNOWN AS
POWELLISM AND THATCHERISM; THE MOVEMENT OF ACADEMIC OPINION
KNOWN VARIOUSLY AS THE PETERHOUSE RIGHT, THE LONDON SCHOOL
OF ECONOMICS RIGHT, AND PROFESSOR SCRUTON'S RIGHT; AND A
MOVEMENT AMONG CONSERVATIVE JOURNALISTS.

02489 COX, R.W.
MIDDLEPOWERMANSHIP, JAPAN, AND FUTURE WORLD ORDER
INTERNATIONAL JOURNAL, XLIV(4) (AUG 89), 823-862.
"MIDDLE POWER" AND "FUNCTIONALISM" WERE KEY TERMS IN THE
WORK OF JOHN HOLMES, WHO PROBABLY OFFERED THE MOST
ARTICULATE EXPRESSION OF THE THOUGHT BEHIND CANADIAN
DIPLOMACY IN THE RECONSTRUCTION OF INTERNATIONAL
ORGANIZATION AFTER WORLD WAR II. CANADA HAD AN OVERRIDING
INTEREST IN THE DEVELOPMENT OF INSTITUTIONS AND PRACTICES
CONDUCIVE TO PEACE, TRANQUILITY, AND ORDERLY ADJUSTMENT IN
WORLD POLITICS. MIDDLE POWERS, LIKE CANADA, COULD BE AN
IMPORTANT INFLUENCE TO THIS END BECAUSE, UNLIKE GREAT POWERS,
THEY WERE NOT SUSPECTED OF HARBORING INTENTIONS OF
DOMINATION AND BECAUSE THEY HAD RESOURCES SUFFICIENT TO
ENABLE THEM TO BE FUNCTIONALLY EFFECTIVE. IN THIS ESSAY, THE
AUTHOR DISSOCIATES MIDDLEPOWERSHIP FROM CANADIAN FOREIGN
POLICY IN ORDER TO EXAMINE ITS VALIDITY MORE BROADLY IN
RELATION TO WORLD ORDER AND TO APPLY IT TO THE CASE OF JAPAN.

02490 COX, W.
U.S. PRODUCTIVITY GROWTH AND LIVING STANDARDS
CRS REVEIW, 10(5) (JUN 89), 1-2.
U.S. PRODUCTIVITY GROWTH SLOWED DRAMATICALLY AROUND 1973
AND HAS RECOVERED TO ONLY ABOUT HALF OF ITS EARLIER PACE.
OTHER ADVANCED COUNTRIES, WHILE ALSO EXPERIENCING
PRODUCTIVITY SLOWDOWNS, CONTINUE TO ADVANCE TOWARD THE
AMERICAN INCOME STANDARD AND COULD EQUAL OR EXCEED IT WITHIN
A FEW YEARS. MEANWHILE THE U.S. GOVERNMENT HAS DEVISED NO
EFFECTIVE METHOD TO ACCELERATE THE GROWTH OF U.S.
PRODUCTIVITY AND LIVING STANDARDS.

02491 COY, P.G.
QADDAFI'S REVOLUTION
COMMONWEAL, CXVI(18) (OCT 89), 552-553.
THE QADDAFI REVOLUTION DOES NOT FIT EASILY INTO
TRADITIONAL CATEGORIES. ALTHOUGH IT IS BASICALLY SOCIALIST,
THE MOST IMPORTANT DIMENSIONS OF THE NATIONAL ECONOMY--THE
OIL SECTOR AND PUBLICWORKS PROJECTS--REMAIN AS STATE-
CAPITALISM. THE REVOLUTION ALSO INCLUDES A SIGNIFICANT, IF
LITTLE KNOWN EXPERIMENT IN DIRECT DEMOCRACY, WITH 723 BASIC
PEOPLE'S CONGRESSES AT THE CORE. THESE CONGRESSES COULD BE
LIKENED TO NEW ENGLAND TOWN MEETINGS, DEALING WITH LOCAL AND
DOMESTIC POLICY ISSUES. BUT WHEN BLENDED WTH THE NEAR
AUTOCRACY QADDAFI ENJOYS ON INTERNATIONAL ISSUES, WHERE HIS
NONALIGNMENT AND PAN-ARABISM GENERALLY CARRY THE DAY, THE
MIX RESULTS IN A UNIQUE BREED OF POLITICAL ANIMAL.

02492 COYLE, A.
THE LIMITS OF CHANGE: LOCAL GOVERNMENT AND EQUAL
OPPORTUNITIES FOR WOMEN
PUBLIC ADMINISTRATION, 67(1) (SPR 89), 39-50.
WOMEN MAKE UP THE MAJORITY OF LOCAL GOVERNMENT EMPLOYEES
IN GREAT BRITAIN BUT ARE NOT, HOWEVER, EVENLY REPRESENTED
THROUGHOUT THE EMPLOYMENT STRUCTURE. FROM 1982-7 OVER 200
LOCAL AUTHORITIES ADOPTED EQUAL OPPORTUNITY (EO) POLICIES,
BOTH FOR EMPLOYMENT PRACTICE AND SERVICE DELIVERY, THE AIMS
OF WHICH INCLUDED REDRESSING THIS INEQUITABLE SITUATION FOR
WOMEN. THE ACHIEVEMENTS OF THESE EO POLICIES HAVE PROVED TO
BE VERY LIMITED. MOST HAVE BEEN INTRODUCED WITH FEW
RESOURCES AND LITTLE MANAGERIAL OR POLITICAL SUPPORT AND
WITHOUT MECHANISMS FOR IMPLEMENTATION OR MANAGEMENT
ACCOUNTABILITY. EO REFORMS HAVE BEEN CONTAINED WITHIN THE
EXISTING RELATIONSHIPS AND STRUCTURES OF LOCAL AUTHORITIES
WHEN BY DEFINITION, SUCCESSFUL EO POLICIES WILL UPSET THE
STATUS QUO. NEVERTHELESS IMPORTANT LESSONS HAVE BEEN LEARNED
FROM THIS FIRST PIONEERING PHASE OF EO POLICY DEVELOPMENT.

02493 CRABB, C.V. JR.; MULCAHY, K.V.
THE NATIONAL SECURITY COUNCIL AND THE SHAPING OF U.S.
FOREIGN POLICY
INTERNATIONAL JOURNAL OF INTELLIGENCE AND
COUNTER-INTELLIGENCE, 3(2) (SUM 89), 153-168.
THE AUTHORS FOCUS ON THE PECULIAR NATURE OF THE NATIONAL
SECURITY COUNCIL AS A DECISION-MAKING BODY, EXAMINE THE
UNIQUE POSITION OF THE PRESIDENT IN THE MANAGEMENT OF
NATIONAL SECURITY, AND ANALYZE IN DETAIL THE ROLES THAT
ASSISTANTS FOR NATIONAL SECURITY AFFAIRS HAVE COME TO PLAY
IN THE POLICY-MAKING PROCESS.

02494 CRAIN, R.A.
MAJOR LEGISLATIVE ACCOMPLISHMENTS OF MISSOURI STATE
TEACHERS ASSOCIATION
DISSERTATION ABSTRACTS INTERNATIONAL, 49(7) (JAN 89),
1955-A.
THE AUTHOR SURVEYS FIVE MAJOR AREAS OF LEGISLATION THAT
HAVE BEEN INFLUENCED BY THE MISSOURI STATE TEACHERS
ASSOCIATION.

02495 CRANE, R.
US-INDIA RELATIONS: THE EARLY PHASE, 1941-1945
ASIAN AFFAIRS, AN AMERICAN REVIEW, 15(4) (WIN 89), 189-193.
ROBERT CRANE DISCUSSES THE RELATIONS BETWEEN INDIA AND
THE US FROM THE PERSONAL EXPERIENCE OF BEING A DESK OFFICER
ON SOUTH ASIA IN THE DIVISION OF CULTURAL RELATIONS, US
DEPARTMENT OF STATE. HE OUTLINES THE PRO-BRITISH FACTIONS
AND THE GROWING SUPPORT FOR THE INDIAN INDEPENDENCE MOVEMENT
THAT TOOK PLACE IN THE PERIOD 1941-45. HOWEVER, ON THE WHOLE,
US CONCERN WITH INDIA WAS MINIMAL DURING WARTIME; THE US
GOVERNMENT MRERELY EXPECTED HOSPITALITY FOR THE US MILITARY
IN THE WAR WITH JAPAN. ISSUES SUCH AS INDEPENDENCE WERE
VIEWED AS SOMETHING TO BE TAKEN CARE OF AFTER THE WAR.

02496 CRANE, S.
PUBLIC WORKS FINANCING ENDANGERED
JOURNAL OF STATE GOVERNMENT, 62(1) (JAN 89), 34-35.
FEDERAL ACTION INTERFERING WITH THE ABILITY OF STATES TO
FINANCE PUBLIC WORKS' PROJECTS HAS PROMPTED STATE TREASURERS
TO SEEK A CONSTITUTIONAL AMENDMENT PROTECTING TAX EXEMPTIONS
FOR STATE AND LOCAL FINANCE. RESTRICTIONS ON STATE AND LOCAL
GOVERNMENT FINANCING IMPOSED BY THE 1986 TAX ACT HAVE
CREATED AN ACUTE PROBLEM BECAUSE OF REAGAN'S FEDERALIST
AGENDA. REAGAN ATTEMPTED TO DECENTRALIZE GOVERNMENT BY
PLACING MORE RESPONSIBILITY AT THE STATE AND LOCAL LEVEL. IN
THEORY, THIS POLICY HAS MERIT IN THAT THE GOVERNMENT CLOSEST
TO THE PEOPLE IS MOST LIKELY TO BEST MEET THEIR NEEDS. BUT
THE TAX-EXEMPT BONDS USED TO FINANCE PUBLIC SERVICES ARE NO
LONGER EASILY AVAILABLE BECAUSE STRICT LIMITATIONS HAVE BEEN
PLACED ON HOW THEY MUST BE USED, CREATING FINANCIAL PROBLEMS
FOR STATE AND LOCAL GOVERNMENTS.

02497 CRANOR, J.D.; CRAWLEY, G.L.; SCHEELE, R.H.
THE ANATOMY OF A GERRYMANDER
AMERICAN JOURNAL OF POLITICAL SCIENCE, 33(1) (FEB 89),
222-239.
THE U.S. SUPREME COURT RECENTLY HELD THAT INDIANA'S 1981-
82 STATE LEGISLATIVE REDISTRICTING PLAN WAS CONSTITUTIONAL
DESPITE "DISCRIMINATORY INTENT" TO GERRYMANDER. THE COURT
FOUND THAT THE PLAINTIFFS FAILED TO DEMONSTRATE
"DISCRIMINATORY EFFECT" BECAUSE, AMONG OTHER REASONS, THEY
RELIED ON THE USE OF AGGREGATE STATEWIDE DATA FROM A SINGLE
ELECTION. THIS PAPER ANALYZES REDISTRICTING IN INDIANA
UTILIZING PRECINCT-BY-PRECINCT ELECTION RETURNS AND EXAMINES
SHIFTS IN THE PARTY COMPOSITION OF DISTRICTS. FINDINGS
INDICATE THAT GERRYMANDERING DID TAKE PLACE IN INDIANA AND
THAT BLOCKS OF VOTERS WERE SYSTEMATICALLY SHIFTED TO AND
FROM DISTRICTS AS PART OF AN OVERALL STRATEGY AIMED AT
BENEFITING THE MAJORITY REPUBLICAN PARTY. DISTRICTS
CONTROLLED BY THE REPUBLICANS WERE ALTERED LITTLE, WHILE
DEMOCRATIC DISTRICTS WERE CHANGED SIGNIFICANTLY BY
INTRODUCING LARGE BLOCKS OF "NEW" VOTERS. IN DISTRICTS WHERE
A SEAT HAD CHANGED PARTY HANDS IN THE PAST, A LARGE CORE OF
REPUBLICAN VOTERS WAS CARRIED FORWARD TO THE NEW DISTRICT
WHICH WAS BUTTRESSED BY AN ADVANTAGEOUS SPLIT OF NEW
REPUBLICAN TO DEMOCRATIC VOTERS.

02498 CRANSTON, M.
CAN GOVERNMENT OUTLAW DRUGS?
NATIONAL REVIEW, XLI(19) (OCT 89), 43-45.
IN THIS ARTICLE, THE AUTHOR ACTS AS A "MEDIUM" TO ALLOW
HERBERT SPENCER, THE NINETEENTH CENTURY'S PRE-EMINENT
LIBERTARIAN SOCIOLOGIST, AND SIR JAMES FITZJAMES STEPHEN,
ONE OF THE GREATEST CONSERVATIVE JURISTS OF THE NINETEENTH
CENTURY, TO "DEBATE" PRESIDENT BUSH'S WAR ON DRUGS STRATEGY.
WHAT RESULTS IS A DEMONSTRATION OF THE OPPOSITE POLES OF
GOVERNMENT REGULATION AND LAISSEZ - FAIRE.

02499 CRANSTON, M.
SHOULD WE CELEBRATE THE FRENCH REVOLUTION?
AMERICAN SPECTATOR, 22(6) (JUN 89), 15-17.
THE ARTICLE ANALYZES THE FRENCH REVOLUTION AND CONCLUDES
THAT THERE IS LITTLE IN COMMON WITH THE FRENCH AND AMERICAN
REVOLUTIONS. THERE IS MUCH ABOUT THE FRENCH REVOLUTION THAT
WHEN EXAMINED CLOSELY HARDLY SEEMS LAUDABLE. MANY LATER
REVOLUTIONS SUCH AS THE ONES IN RUSSIA, CUBA, AND CHINA HAVE
CONSCIOUSLY ATTEMPTED TO BE THE HEIRS OF THE FRENCH
REVOLUTION.

02500 CREAMPNEY, L.
PUBLIC GOODS AND POLICY TYPES
PUBLIC ADMINISTRATION REVIEW, 48(6) (NOV 88), 988-994.
DURING 1954-1955, PAUL SAMUELSON DISTINGUISHED PUBLIC
GOODS, COLLECTIVELY CONSUMED BY LARGE GROUPS OF PEOPLE, FROM
PRIVATE GOODS, INDIVIDUALLY EXCHANGED IN THE MARKETPLACE.
THIS PAPER EMPLOYS THE DISTINCTION BETWEEN PUBLIC AND
PRIVATE GOODS TO IDENTIFY THREE DIMENSIONS OF GOVERNMENTAL
ACTIVITY THAT FORM THE BASIS OF AN EIGHTFOLD TYPOLOGY OF
PUBLIC POLICY, AND IT OFFERS SELECTED EXAMPLES OF SPECIFIC
POLICIES THAT FIT THE TYPOLOGY. THE CATEGORIZATION SCHEME
EXPOSES SEVERAL LIMITATIONS IN THE POLICY TYPOLOGIES
PREVIOUSLY OFFERED.

02501 CREMASCO, M.
NATO'S SOUTHERN FLANK AND ITALY'S ROLE IN IT
INTERNATIONAL SPECTATOR, XXIII(2) (APR 88), 79-89.
ON NATO'S SOUTHERN FLANK, THE WORST WORRIES ABOUT
POSSIBLE REPERCUSSIONS FOR EUROPEAN SECURITY COME FROM
EITHER THOSE MEDITERRANEAN CRISES THAT ARE INSIDE THE
ALLIANCE OR THOSE WHICH, APART FROM THEIR NEGATIVE IMPACT ON
SPECIFIC EUROPEAN INTERESTS, COULD LEAD TO A MILITARY
CONFRONTATION BETWEEN THE SUPERPOWERS AND THROUGH ESCALATION,
TO A CONFLICT BETWEEN THE TWO BLOCS IN EUROPE.

02502 CRERAR, A. D.
THE SUSTAINABLE CITY
POLICY OPTIONS, 10(2) (MAR 89), 3-5.
THE CONCEPT OF THE SUSTAINABLE CITY, ARGUES ALISTAIR
CRERAR, OFFERS US AN APPROACH TO THE DEVELOPMENT OF CITIES
IN SUCH A WAY THAT THEIR IMPACT ON THE ENVIRONMENT WILL BE
MINIMIZED. HE BEGINS WITH AN ARGUMENT ABOUT OUR APPROACH TO
CITY DEVELOPMENT, SUGGESTING THAT, FOR HISTORICAL AND
SENTIMENTAL REASONS, POLICY IS TILTED AWAY FROM SENSIBLE
POLICIES TOWARDS OUR URBAN AREAS. THE AUTHOR MOVES FROM THIS
TO A DISCUSSION OF HUMAN RESOURCES AND, USING AN EXAMPLE IN
PAKISTAN, SHOWS HOW AN AREA HEAVILY POPULATED BY REFUGEES
FROM BANGLADESH WAS, IN LARGE MEASURE, REVITALIZED AND
REFURBISHED BY BEING ORGANIZED ON THE BASIS OF SMALL, FACE
TO-FACE UNITS. HE CONCLUDES THAT IT IS POSSIBLE TO BUILD
SUSTAINABLE CITIES, IF WE HAVE THE WILL TO DO SO.

02503 CRICK, B.
LABOUR AND CONSTITUTIONAL CHANGE
CONSTITUTIONAL REFORM QUARTERLY REVIEW, 4(2) (SUM 89), 5.
THE BRITISH LABOUR PARTY HAS ONLY RECENTLY SHOWED ANY
INTEREST IN CONSTITUTIONAL REFORM. HOWEVER, A RECENT POLICY
REVIEW DOCUMENT DOES HINT AT THE POSSIBILITY OF
CONSTITUTIONAL CHANGE DOCUMENT DOES HINT AT THE POSSIBILITY
OF CONSTITUTIONAL CHANGE. WHILE STILL REJECTING THE NOTION
OF A BRITISH BILL OF RIGHTS, THE DOCUMENT DOES STRESS THE
NEED FOR REFORM OF THE HOUSE OF LORDS IN CONJUNCTION WITH
THE CREATION OF TEN ELECTED REGIONAL ASSEMBLIES IN ENGLAND
AND DEVELOPED PARLIAMENTS IN SCOTLAND AND WALES.

02504 CRISTI, F.R.
HEGEL'S CONSERVATIVE LIBERALISM
CANADIAN JOURNAL OF POLITICAL SCIENCE, 22(4) (DEC 89),
717-738.
HEGELIAN SCHOLARSHIP IS RENT BETWEEN CONSERVATIVE AND
LIBERAL INTERPRETATIONS OF HEGEL'S POLITICAL PHILOSOPHY.
THESE ONE-SIDED INTERPRETATIONS MISS HIS ATTEMPTS TO
RECONCILE FREEDOM AND AUTHORITY. THIS ARTICLE SUBMITS THAT
CONSERVATIVE LIBERALISM RIGHTLY DESCRIBES HIS POSTURE. A
DIALECTICAL PROCEDURE ALLOWS HEGEL TO DERIVE RATIONALLY A
CONSERVATIVE STATE FROM THE LIBERAL PRINCIPLES EMBODIED IN
MARKET SOCIETY. THE KEY TO THIS DIALECTICAL DERIVATION LIES
IN THE SPONTANEOUS ORDER THAT SPRINGS NATURALLY FROM THE
SELF-SEEKING BEHAVIOUR OF INDIVIDUALS. HEGEL'S REALIZATION
OF THE NEGATIVE ETHICAL VALUE GENERATED BY THAT SPONTANEOUS
ORDER, AND THE FAILURE OF CORPORATIONS TO DISCIPLINE THE
BUSINESS CLASSES, PROMPTS THE POWERFUL ROLE HE CONFIDES TO

THE STATE AND ITS MONARCH.

02505 CRITCHLEY, W., H.
THE INTERNATIONAL IMPORTANCE OF ECONOMIC DEVELOPMENT IN
THE ARCTIC REGION
ETUDES INTERNATIONALES, XX(1) (MAR 89), 7-26.
THE ECONOMIC DEVELOPMENT OF THE NORTHERN REGIONS OF THE
USSR, UNITED STATES, CANADA, NORWAY AND DENMARK (GREENLAND)
IS EXAMINED WITH REFERENCE TO THE POSSIBLE SOURCES AND
TIMING OF DEVELOPMENT IN EACH STATE. THE CONCLUSION IS THAT
ECONOMIC DEVELOPMENT FOR THESE ARCTIC LITTORAL STATES IS
EXTRAORDINARILY DEPENDENT UPON THE DEVELOPMENT OF NON-
RENEWABLE NATURAL RESOURCES - ESPECIALLY PETROLEUM
HYDROCARBONS - AND, TO A LESSER EXTENT, CERTAIN RENEWABLE
RESOURCES. IN ADDITION, CURRENT WORLD PRICES FOR THE
RELEVANT RESOURCES ARE SUFFICIENTLY LOW THAT DEVELOPMENT
ACTIVITY IN EACH STATE RANGES FROM MODERATE TO MODEST: AS
LONG AS PRICES REMAIN AT THESE LEVELS, THE CURRENT TIMING
AND PACE OF DEVELOPMENT IS NOT LIKELY TO INCREASE. NOTE:
ARTICLE IS PRINTED IN FRENCH

02506 CRITCHLEY, W.H.
CIVILIANIZATION AND THE CANADIAN MILITARY
ARMED FORCES AND SOCIETY, 16(1) (FAL 89), 117-136.
CANADA IS BOTH UNIQUE AND RADICAL IN ITS ORGANIZATION OF
ITS ARMED FORCES BECAUSE IT HAS INTEGRATED AND UNIFIED ITS
ARMED FORCES INTO A SINGLE ENTITY, INSTEAD OF HAVING THREE
DISTINCT BRANCHES OF THE SERVICES AS MOST COUNTRIES DO. THIS
ESSAY FOCUSES ON THE PROBLEMS ASSOCIATED WITH THE
CIVILIANIZATION OF DEFENSE THAT HAS RESULTED FROM THE
IMPLEMENTATION OF THE UNIFICATION POLICY OVER THE PAST TWO
DECADES. SPECIFICALLY, THE AUTHOR CONSIDERS THE PERCEPTION
THAT CIVIL SERVANTS ARE INCREASINGLY PERFORMING "STRICTLY
MILITARY JOBS" AND MAKING "STRICTLY MILITARY DECISIONS" AND
THAT THIS PROBLEM IS A DIRECT RESULT OF THE UNIFICATION
POLICY.

02507 CRITTENDEN, R.; LEA, D.A.M.
WHOSE WANTS IN 'NEEDS-BASED PLANNING'? SOME EXAMPLES OF
UNWRITTEN AGENDAS FROM THE PROVINCIAL INTEGRATED RURAL
DEVELOPMENT PROGRAMMES OF PAPUA NEW GUINEA
PUBLIC ADMINISTRATION AND DEVELOPMENT, 9(5) (NOV 89),
471-486.
THE RHETORIC OF 'NEEDS'-BASED PLANNING REQUIRES LITTLE
REFINING. WHAT MUST BE QUESTIONED AND RECOGNIZED ARE THE
VALUES OF DECISION MAKERS AND THE UNWRITTEN AGENDAS OF THOSE
INVOLVED IN THE PLANNING PROCESS. TAKING THE EXAMPLE OF SOME
OF THE INTEGRATED RURAL DEVELOPMENT PROGRAMMES (IRDPS) IN
PAPUA NEW GUINEA, THIS PAPER LOOKS AT THE WAY PLANNERS AND
OTHERS CAST DEVELOPMENT AND INFORMATION 'NETS'. THESE NETS
ABROGATE INDIGENOUS DEVELOPMENT PROCESSES. THE 'NETS' MAKE
IT EASY FOR DEVELOPMENT PROFESSIONALS AND OTHERS INVOLVED IN
PLANNING TO FOLLOW UNWRITTEN AGENDAS AND DIFFICULT FOR
TARGET GROUPS TO ARTICULATE THEIR 'NEEDS' AND TO UNDERSTAND
WHAT IS GOING ON. IT IS SUGGESTED THAT THESE PROBLEMS ARE
NOT UNIQUE TO PNG AND MAY WELL BE RELEVANT TO 'NEEDS BASED
PLANNING' IN OTHER SITUATIONS.

02508 CROAN, M.
LANDS IN BETWEEN: THE POLITICS OF CULTURAL IDENTITY IN
CONTEMPORARY EASTERN EUROPE
EASTERN EUROPEAN POLITICS AND SOCIETIES, 3(2) (SPR 89),
176-197.
THE ARTICLE ANALYZES THE POLITICS OF CULTURAL IDENTITY
IN PRESENT-DAY EASTERN EUROPE, WITH SPECIAL EMPHASIS ON THE
IDEA OF CENTRAL EUROPE WHICH HAS RECENTLY COME TO BE MUCH
TOUTED IN THE WEST AS A "NEW POLITICAL IDENTITY." CHIEF
CHARACTERISTICS OF THE NEW CENTRAL EUROPE AS CURRENTLY
CONCEIVED INCLUDE A CONTINUED DISTANCING FROM THE SOVIET
UNION, AND AN EMPHASIS ON ELITISM, PESSIMISM, AND
METAPOLITICS. WHETHER OR NOT THE IDEA OF CENTRAL EUROPE HAS
ANY REAL FUTURE, ITS CONTEMPORARY EXPONENTS HAVE ALREADY
BEQUEATHED A RICH, INTELLECTUAL, AND CONTROVERSIAL LEGACY.

02509 CROCKER, C.A.
SOUTHERN AFRICA: EIGHT YEARS LATER
FOREIGN AFFAIRS, 68(4) (FAL 89), 144-164.
THE AUTHOR, WHO WAS US ASSISTANT SECRETARY OF STATE FOR
AFRICAN AFFAIRS FROM 1981 TO 1989, DISCUSSES THE CONCEPT OF
"CONSTRUCTIVE ENGAGEMENT IN THE REGION AS A WHOLE" AS THE
BASIS FOR AMERICAN INVOLVEMENT IN SOUTHERN AFRICA, INCLUDING
THE REPUBLIC OF SOUTH AFRICA.

02510 CROCKER, R.
CONGRESS AND THE POLLS: VOX POPULI
CRS REVEIW, 10(10) (NOV 89), 25-26.
HOW DO MEMBERS OF REPRESENTATIVE BODIES SUCH AS THE U.S.
CONGRESS COME TO KNOW THE VIEWS OF THEIR CONSTITUENTS? THE
ANSWERS TO THIS QUESTION ARE ALMOST AS VARIED AS ARE THE
PERSONALITIES OF THE MEMBERS. EACH REPRESENTATIVE CHOOSES
THE METHOD OR METHODS WITH WHICH HE OR SHE IS THE MOST
COMFORTABLE. THERE ARE SEVERAL TECHNIQUES FOR GAINING
INSIGHT INTO THE VIEWS OF CONSTITUENTS-MAIL, TOWN MEETINGS,
DIRECT DISCUSSIONS WITH CONSTITUENTSNONE OF WHICH IS PERFECT

OR THOROUGH. A NEWER POTENTIAL SOURCE OF INFORMATION ABOUT
CONSTITUENT VIEWS IS POLL RESULTS. LIKE THE ALTERNATIVES,
POLLS AS A SOURCE OF INFORMATION ABOUT THE VIEWS OF THE
REPRESENTED HAVE POSITIVE AND NEGATIVE ASPECTS, BUT MAY
PROVIDE A BROADER PICTURE OF PUBLIC ATTITUDES THAN ANY OF
THE OTHER SOURCES.

02511 CROCKER, T.E.
CHALLENGES AND OPPORTUNITIES IN BASE NEGOTIATIONS
WASHINGTON QUARTERLY, 12(2) (SPR 89), 55-67.
AS THE UNITED STATES ENTERS THE 1990S IT NO DOUBT WILL
FACE GREATER PRESURES TO CONSTRICT FURTHER THE NUMBER OF ITS
OVERSEAS BASES. IT ALSO WILL FACE GREATER DEMANDS BY
EUROPEAN HOST COUNTRIES TO CONTROL NON-NATO USES OF BASES.
AT A MINIMUM, THE UNITED STATES PROBABLY WILL BE REQUIRED TO
PAY MORE FOR CONTINUED ACCESS TO THE BASES IT DOES HAVE.
THESE FINANCIAL PRESSURES WILL COME AT A TIME OF DECLINING
EXPENDITURES FOR DEFENSE AND STATIC SECURITY ASSISTANCE.
THIS ARTICLE TAKES A CRITICAL LOOK AT THE INTERESTS AT STAKE
IN THE U.S. BASES ABROAD AND AT THE WAY IN WHICH U.S.
NEGOTIATORS, PRIMARILY THE DEPARTMENTS OF STATE AND DEFENSE,
SHOULD APPROACH TALKS WITH U.S. ALLIES.

02512 CROFT,S.
MILITARY TECHNOLOGICAL INNOVATION AND STABILITY
FUTURES, 21(5) (OCT 89), 466-479.
A KEY NOTION IN THE MILITARY RELATIONSHIP BETWEEN THE
SUPERPOWERS IS STABILITY. YET IMPROVEMENTS IN NATIONAL
MILITARY CAPABILITIES BROUGHT ABOUT BY TECHNOLOGICAL
INNOVATION MAY DAMAGE STABILITY AND ONE OF THE MOST
IMPORTANT MEANS OF ACHIEVING STABILITY: ARMS CONTROL. THE
INTERACTION OF THE SUPERPOWERS' EFFORTS TO GAIN UNILATERAL
ADVANTAGE MAY PRODUCE A STABLE RELATIONSHIP BETWEEN THEM,
BUT WITHOUT COOPERATION SUCH AN OUTCOME WOULD BE ENTIRELY
FORTUITOUS. THIS ARTICLE ARGUES THAT ONE OF THE MOST
SIGNIFICANT PROBLEMS FACING INTERNATIONAL SECURITY IS NOT
THE EMERGENCE OF NEW MILITARY TECHNOLOGY, BUT RATHER THE
UNMANAGED NATURE OF TECHNOLOGICAL CHANGE. THE ARTICLE CALLS
FOR THE MANAGEMENT OF TECHNOLOGICAL CHANGE IN THE MILITARY
SPHERE IN ORDER TO MAINTAIN STABILITY, AND SUGGESTS THAT
SOME TECHNOLOGICAL DEVELOPMENTS WOULD BE BETTER CONSTRAINED
THAN DEVELOPED.

02513 CROMARTIE, J.; STEWART, J.
FTC ACTIVITY AND PRESIDENTIAL EFFECTS REVISITED
PRESIDENTIAL STUDIES QUARTERLY, XIX(2) (SPR 89), 355-362.
ECONOMIST AND FORMER FTC EXECUTIVE DIRECTOR BRUCE YANDLE
USES RESEARCH BY STEWART AND CROMARTIE PUBLISHED PREVIOUSLY
IN PRESIDENTIAL STUDIES QUARTERLY AS A SPRINGBOARD FOR
FURTHER ANALYSIS OF THE POLITICAL ECONOMY OF THE FTC. HE
PROVIDES NEW DATA AND SUGGESTS THAT PERHAPS THE "PARTY IN
POWER" MODEL'S ATTEMPT TO EXPLAIN REGULATORY POLITICS SHOULD
YIELD TO CONGRESSIONAL AND SPECIAL INTEREST MODELS.
RECONSIDERATIONS OF BOTH STUDIES CLARIFY THE MEANINGS OF THE
FINDINGS AND SUGGEST PATHS FOR FUTURE RESEARCH ON THIS TOPIC
TOPIC. IT IS ALSO SUGGESTED THAT IT IS PROBABLY PREMATURE TO
DISPOSE OF PRESIDENTIAL PARTISANSHIP AS A VARIABLE FOR
ANALYSIS IN FUTURE STUDIES.

02514 CROMER, G.
SAD TALES AND HAPPY TALES: THE POLITICIZATION OF
DELINQUENT LIFE HISTORIES
POLITICAL COMMUNICATION AND PERSUASION, 5(3) (1988),
179-190.
PREVIOUS RESEARCH HAS INDICATED THAT JUVENILE
DELINQUENTS TEND TO HIGHLIGHT THEIR DISMAL PASTS AND PORTRAY
THEMSELVES AS THE VICTIMS OF CIRCUMSTANCES IN ORDER TO
ELICIT FAVORABLE RESPONSES FROM THE VARIOUS AGENTS OF SOCIAL
CONTROL. HOWEVER, THE PRESENT STUDY, BASED ON THE LIFE-
HISTORIES OF TWO GROUPS OF ISRAELI DELINQUENTS, SUGGESTS
THAT THEY SOMETIMES ENGAGE IN THIS PARTICULAR KIND OF
RETROSPECTIVE INTERPRETATION IN ORDER TO BRING ABOUT CHANGES
OF A MUCH MORE FAR-REACHING NATURE. NOT ONLY IS IT AIMED AT
INFLUENCING THE DECISION AS TO THE APPROPRIATE AGENTS OF
SOCIAL CONTACT; IT ALSO CONSTITUTES PART OF A WIDER STRUGGLE
FOR POLITICAL AND CULTURAL LEGITIMACY.

02515 CRONA, E.
MANY MEN SUPPORT ICELAND'S WOMEN'S SLATE
SCANDINAVIAN REVIEW, 77(4) (WIN 89), 26-29.
ICELAND'S WOMEN'S SLATE, WHICH IS THE WORLD'S ONLY
WOMEN'S POLITICAL PARTY, WAS FORMED IN 1983. IN THE 1987
PARLIAMENTARY ELECTIONS, IT RECEIVED MORE THAN TEN PERCENT
OF THE VOTE. THE WOMEN'S SLATE POLICIES CONSTITUTE A BREAK
WITH THE RECENT PAST IN FEMINIST POLITICS. THE PARTY FOCUSES
ON THE GENTLE, NATIVE, NATIONAL, AND SPECIFICALLY FEMALE
PERSPECTIVE, INCLUDING ISSUES CONCERNING CHILDREN AND THE
ELDERLY

02516 CRONIN, A.K.
EAST-WEST NEGOTIATIONS OVER AUSTRIA IN 1949: TURNING POINT
IN THE COLD WAR
JOURNAL OF CONTEMPORARY HISTORY, 24(1) (JAN 89), 125-145.
THE AUTHOR EXAMINES THE CRITICAL FIVE-MONTH PERIOD

BETWEEN JUNE AND NOVEMBER 1949, FOCUSING UPON THE POLICIES
OF THE FOUR GREAT POWERS AND EVALUATING THE EXTENT TO WHICH
THE SOVIET INITIATIVE MAY HAVE BEEN A LOST OPPORTUNITY FOR
THE WESTERN POWERS AND FOR AUSTRIA. THREE QUESTIONS ARE
ADDRESSED: WHAT WAS THE NATURE OF THE SOVIET POLICY SHIFT IN
JUNE 1949? WHY DID THE WESTERN POWERS FAIL TO RESPOND
IMMEDIATELY TO THE SOVIET INITIATIVE? WAS IT A GENUINE
OPPORTUNITY FOR AGREEMENT AND WOULD IT, IN ANY CASE, HAVE
BEEN DESIRABLE TO SIGN AN AUSTRIAN STATE TREATY IN 1949? THE
EPISODE REVEALS A GREAT DEAL ABOUT THE MOTIVATIONS OF THE
USSR AND THE RELATIONS BETWEEN THE WESTERN POWERS IN THE
NEGOTIATIONS OVER AUSTRIA, AS WELL AS IN THE BROADER CONTEXT
OF THE EARLY COLD WAR.

02517 CRONIN, P.M.
SUPERPOWER SUMMITRY: SOVIET-AMERICAN DIPLOMACY AT THE
HIGHEST LEVEL, 1954-1988
JOHN SPIERS PUBLISHING, BRIGHTON, SUSSEX, GB, 1989, 256.
THE AUTHOR STUDIES SUPERPOWER SUMMITRY FROM AN
INTERNATIONAL RELATIONS PERSPECTIVE, EMPHASIZING THE HISTORY
OF SOVIET-AMERICAN SUMMIT MEETINGS FROM THE THREE WARTIME
CONFERENCES THROUGH THE REAGAN-GORBACHEV ENCOUNTER IN MOSCOW
IN 1988. THE APPROACH IS BOTH THEMATIC AND CHRONOLOGICAL,
BREAKING DOWN THE SUMMITS INTO FOUR DISTINCT PHASES.

02518 CRONIN, R.P.
AFGHANISTAN IN 1988: YEAR OF DECISION
ASIAN SURVEY, XXIX(2) (FEB 89), 207-215.
1988 WITNESSED THE BEGINNING OF THE SOVIET TROOP
WITHDRAWAL FROM AFGHANSTAN. HOWEVER, THE FIGHTING CONTINUES
AS REBEL MUJAHIDIN CLASHED WITH GOVERNMENT FORCES. THE
ARTICLE EXAMINES THE BACKGROUND TO THE GENEVA CONVENTION AND
THE WAY IN WHICH IT IS BEING IMPLEMENTED. IT ALSO ASSESSES
THE OPTIONS LEFT TO THE SOVIETS, THE AFGHAN GOVERNMENT, AND
THE RESISTANCE FORCES.

02519 CRONIN, R.P.
JAPAN'S EXPANDING ECONOMIC ROLE AND INFLUENCE IN ASIA
CRS REVEIW, 10(6) (JUL 89), 17-18.
TO ITS ASIAN NEIGHBORS JAPAN HAS EMERGED AS THE
PRINCIPAL AID DONOR, INVESTOR, AND TRADING PARTNER. IT
REMAINS TO BE SEEN WHETHER JAPAN'S INCREASING ROLE WILL
REINFORCE GROWTH IN THE GLOBAL ECONOMIC SYSTEM, TO THE
BENEFIT OF ALL PARTICIPANTS, OR WILL ULTIMATELY HARM U.S.
ECONOMIC AND POLITICAL INTERESTS.

02520 CROSBIE, J.
INTERNATIONAL TRADE: THE CANADIAN PERSPECTIVE
NEW ZEALAND INTERNATIONAL REVIEW, 14(3) (MAY 89), 15-18.
CANADA'S MINISTER FOR INTERNATIONAL TRADE DESCRIBES THE
CANADIAN APPROACH TO THE GATT NEGOTIATIONS AND TRADING LINKS
IN THE ASIA/PACIFIC REGION. HE REPORTS ON PLANS CONCERNING
AGRICULTURAL TRADE WHICH EMERGED FROM MEETINGS WITH THE
CAIRNS GROUP IN NEW ZEALAND, SO THAT THIS MARKET'S PROBLEMS
WILL BE CLEARED UP IN THE GATT URUGUAY ROUNDS. AN IMPASSE ON
AGRICULTURE WHICH DEVELOPED AT THE MONTREAL MINISTERIAL
MEETING IN DECEMBER 1988 IS DISCUSSED. CANADA'S TRADE
FIGURES WITH THE ASIA/PACIFIC REGION ARE REPORTED. OTHER
TOPICS INCLUDE THE RISE IN JAPANESE INVESTMENT IN THE REGION
AS WELL AS NOTABLE ADVANCES IN THE REGION THROUGH THE WORK
OF THE PACIFIC ECONOMIC COOPERATION CONFERENCE

02521 CROTHALL, G.
CHINA REARS A TIGER
SOUTH, (102) (APR 89), 37, 39.
GUANGDONG, CHINA'S RICHEST PROVINCE, IS EMERGING AS A
NEW ASIAN TIGER. IT HAS BEEN AT THE FOREFRONT OF CHINA'S
ECONOMIC REFORM PROGRAM, WHICH HAS BEEN LARGELY ENGINEERED
BY ZHAO ZIYANG. ITS ECONOMY HAS MORE IN COMMON WITH THE FREE-
WHEELING CAPITALISM OF SOUTHEAST ASIA THAN IT DOES WITH THE
STATE PLANNERS IN BEIJING.

02522 CROVITZ, L. G.
THE LEAST RESPONSIVE BRANCH
COMMENTARY, 87(3) (MAR 89), 38-41.
THE CONSTITUTION ESTABLISHED TWO-YEAR TERMS IN THE HOUSE
OF REPRESENTATIVES TO MAKE IT THE BRANCH MOST ACCOUNTABLE TO
VOTERS. BUT THE 99% RE-ELECTION SUCCESS OF INCUMBENTS HAS
TRANSFORMED IT FROM THE MOST RESPONSIVE TO THE LEAST
RESPONSIVE POLITICAL BODY.

02523 CROWDER, G.
THE IDEA OF FREEDOM IN NINETEENTH-CENTURY ANARCHISM
DISSERTATION ABSTRACTS INTERNATIONAL, 49(8) (FEB 89),
2374-A.
THE AUTHOR TRACES THE CENTRAL TRADITION OF NINETEENTH-
CENTURY ANACHISM IN THE WORK OF GODWIN, PROUDHON, BAKUNIN,
AND KROPOTKIN. HIS PRIMARY FOCUS IS ON THEIR SHARED
COMMITMENT TO INDIVIDUAL FREEDOM AS A PRE-EMINENT VALUE.

02524 CROWTHER, A.R.
COMPARABLE WORTH POLICY IN THE STATES
DISSERTATION ABSTRACTS INTERNATIONAL, 50(2) (AUG 89),
540-A.

THE AUTHOR ENDEAVORS TO IDENTIFY THE CURRENT STATUS OF
COMPARABLE WORTH ACTIVITY AT THE STATE LEVEL AND TO ANALYZE
POSSIBLE EXPLANATIONS FOR CURRENT DIFFERENCES IN THE LAWS
AND POLICIES OF THE STATES. SHE BEGINS BY PLACING EACH STATE
INTO ONE OF FOUR CATEGORIES: NO COMPARABLE WORTH ACTIVITY,
PRELIMINARY COMPARABLE WORTH ACTIVITY, SUBSTANTIVE
COMPARABLE WORTH ACTIVITY, AND PAY ADJUSTMENTS. DISCRIMINANT
ANALYSIS REVEALED THAT IDEOLOGICALLY LIBERAL STATES ARE MORE
LIKELY TO HAVE MADE ADJUSTMENTS IN THE SALARIES OF PERSONS
EMPLOYED IN FEMALE-DOMINATED JOBS. THIS CORRELATION BETWEEN
IDEOLOGY AND COMPARABLE WORTH ACTIVITY WAS BY FAR THE MOST
SUBSTANTIAL OF THE FACTORS, WHICH INCLUDED MEASURES OF THE
SOCIOECONOMIC ENVIRONMENT, THE POLICY CONTEXT, AND ATTITUDES
REGARDING WOMEN.

02525 CROWTHER, W.
"CEAUSESCUISM" AND CIVIL-MILITARY RELATIONS IN ROMANIA
ARMED FORCES AND SOCIETY, 15(2) (WIN 89), 207-225.
THIS ARTICLE DISCUSSES THE RELATIONSHIP BETWEEN THE
ROMANIAN ARMED FORCES AND THE LEADERSHIP OF THE ROMANIAN
COMMUNIST PARTY. IT SUGGESTS THAT THIS RELATIONSHIP HAS BEEN
COMPLICATED, AND MADE MORE DIFFICULT, BY ROMANIA'S PURSUIT
OF FOREIGN POLICY AUTONOMY FROM THE SOVIET UNION. CEAUSESCU
HAS RELIED MORE ON DIRECT POLITICAL INTERVENTION AND LESS ON
POSITIVE INDUCEMENTS TO RETAIN CONTROL OF THE ARMED FORCES
THAN HAVE HIS COUNTERPARTS ELSEWHERE IN EASTERN EUROPE.
ROMANIA'S DEFENSE ESTABLISHMENT, LIKE OTHER INSTITUTIONS IN
THAT COUNTRY, HAS BEEN REDUCED TO A STATE OF STAGNATION AND
CANNOT UNDER PRESENT CIRCUMSTANCES BE EXPECTED TO PROVIDE
THE BASIS FOR LEADERSHIP ALTERNATIVE TO THAT OF THE CURRENT
COMMUNIST PARTY ELITE.

02526 CROZIER, B.
CHINA: THE PARTY WINS
NATIONAL REVIEW, XLI(12) (JUN 89), 39-40.
IN THE GRAND CRISIS OF COMMUNISM, NOW UPON US, GORBACHEV
AND DENG HAS BEEN MAKING ANTITHETICAL ERRORS. GORBACHEV HAS
TOLERATED AN UNPRECEDENTED FREEDOM ON INFORMATION AND
CRITICISM, BUT FAILED TO MOVE THE ECONOMY, EVEN MARGINALLY.
THE INTELLECTUALS HAVE BEEN WALLOWING IN THE FREEDOM, WHILE
THE MASSES STAND IN LINE ON THE WAY TO EMPTY SHELVES. DENG
MADE THE OPPOSITE ERROR. HE FREED AGRICULTURE AND CREATED
SPECIAL ECONOMIC ZONES, ENCOURAGING BOTH FOREIGN INVESTMENT
AND (WITHIN LIMITS) LOCAL CAPITALISM. BUT THE LENINIST IN
HIM COULDN'T BEAR THE CHALLENGE OF FREE DEBATE. HE CLAMPED
DOWN ON THE STUDENTS WHO HAD PLASTERED THEIR VIEWS ON
"DEMOCRACY WALL," NOW DEFUNCT. HE FELLED HU YAOBANG AND IS
CLAMPING DOWN ON THE STUDENTS, YET AGAIN. NEITHER OF THESE
MAJOR VARIANTS OF THE LENINIST STATE CAN AFFORD THE LUXURY
OF CONCEDING THAT ECONOMIC AND POLITICAL FREEDOM GO TOGETHER.
MARXISM CONSTRAINS THEIR THOUGHT PATTERNS. "CAPITALISM,"
MARX'S DESIGNATED TARGET FOR DESTRUCTION, IS MERELY THE
ECONOMIC EXPRESSION OF ELECTIVE DEMOCRACY; AND VICE VERSA.

02527 CROZIER, B.
EIN VOLK, EIN REICH, EIN FUROR
NATIONAL REVIEW, 61(20) (OCT 89), 26-27.
THIS ARTICLE APPRAISES THE POSSIBILITY OF A REUNIFIED
GERMANY. IT ASSESS THE LEADERSHIP IN BONN AND THE SOCIAL
DEMOCRATIC OPPOSITION (SPO). THE IMPLICATIONS OF A COMMON
EUROPEAN HOME FOR NATO ARE CONSIDERED.

02528 CROZIER, B.
IN ANDREOTTE'S TENT
NATIONAL REVIEW, XLI(15) (AUG 89), 20.
THIS ARTICLE LOOKS AT THE WESTERN ARAB NATIONS AND THE
NEW ITALIAN PRIME MINISTER WHO HOPES TO APPEASE THEM. PRIME
MINISTERS ANDREOTTE HAS MADE FREQUENT VISITS, SOMETIMES
UNPUBLICIZED TO THE MAGHREB COUNTRIES, ESPECIALLY TO LIBYA
AND ALGERIA. HE IS WORKING ON A PLAN TO ABSORB THE POVERTY
OF ARAB NORTH AFRICA THROUGH SHARED EC PROSPERITY.

02529 CRUZ, R.C.
NEW DIRECTIONS IN SOVIET POLICY TOWARDS LATIN AMERICA
JOURNAL OF LATIN AMERICAN STUDIES, 21(1) (FEB 89), 1-22.
THIS STUDY EXPLORES SOME OF THE CHANGES CURRENTLY TAKING
PLACE IN THE USSR AND THE POSSIBLE IMPACT OF CHANGING SOVIET
FOREIGN POLICY ON LATIN AMERICA. THE ARTICLE BEGINS WITH AN
ANALYSIS OF THE POSSIBLE EFFECTS OF THE ATTEMPTS TO SEPARATE
PARTY AND STATE ON FOREIGN POLICY AND ON THE INTERPRETATION
AND OBSERVANCE OF THE SO-CALLED INTERNATIONALIST OBLIGATIONS
OF THE SOVIET UNION TOWARDS LATIN AMERICA. IT GOES ON TO
INVESTIGATE THE POSSIBLE IMPACT OF PERESTROIKA ON THE
INTERNAL RELATIONS OF COMECON COUNTRIES AND ANY WEAKENING IN
THE COMMITMENT OF ITS MEMBERS TO POLITICAL AND SOCIAL
CHANGES IN THE LATIN AMERICAN REPUBLICS. THESE CHANGES ARE
LOOKED AT PARTICULARLY WITH REFERENCE TO CUBA AND NICARAGUA.
SOME PREDICTIONS ARE ALSO MADE AS TO THE POSSIBLE FUTURE
MOVES THE USSR MIGHT MAKE TO STRENGTHEN AND IMPROVE ITS
RELATIONS WITH THE LARGEST COUNTRIES IN THE REGION, SUCH AS
BRAZIL AND ARGENTINA.

02530 CRYSTAL, J.
COALITIONS IN OIL MONARCHIES: KUWAIT AND QATAR
COMPARATIVE POLITICS, 22(4) (JUL 89), 427-444.
IN RECENT DECADES, KUWAIT AND QATAR HAVE EXPERIENCED
CONTINUITY AT THE VERY TOP OF THEIR POLITICAL SYSTEMS
ACCOMPANIED BY THE WITHDRAWAL OF THE MERCHANT CLASS FROM
FORMAL POLITICAL LIFE. OIL HAS INTRODUCED VERY IMPORTANT
CHANGES IN THE RULING COALITION EVEN AS IT HAS PRESERVED
CONTINUITY AT THE APEX OF THE POLITICAL SYSTEM. THE
BREAKDOWN IN THE OLD RULING COALITION BINDING THE TRADING
FAMILIES AND THE AMIR AND ITS REPLACEMENT BY A NEW SET OF
ELITE ARRANGEMENTS FORM A PATTERNED RESPONSE TO OIL THAT HAS
OCCURRED REPEATEDLY IN THE ARAB STATES.

02531 CUADRA, P.A.
THE SANDINISTAS AND THE U.S. PRESS
HEMISPHERE, 1(2) (WIN 89), 18-19.
FOR CENTRAL AMERICANS, THE PRESS AND FREEDOM OF
EXPRESSION REPRESENT MORE THAN THE FREE PLAY OF OPINION.
THEY ALSO REPRESENT THAT INVISIBLE WALL OF CONTAINMENT AND
DEFENSE AGAINST THE VENERABLE TRADITION OF THE "STRONG MAN"
TYPE OF LEADERSHIP. IN CENTRAL AMERICA THE MOST ELEMENTAL
STRUGGLE FOR FREEDOM OF SPEECH IS PERMANENT AND DRAMATIC, IN
A WAY THAT NORTH AMERICAN JOURNALISTS HAVE NEVER EXPERIENCED.
THUS, U.S. REPORTING ON THE STRUGGLES IN CENTRAL AMERICAN
IS SOMETIMES NAIVE AND DISPLAYS AN OBJECTIVITY THAT CENTRAL
AMERICANS DO NOT UNDERSTAND. THESE SHORTCOMINGS WERE
APPARENT IN U.S. PRESS COVERAGE OF TOMAS BORGE, WHO WAS A
FOUNDER OF THE SANDINISTA FRONT.

02532 CUBANO, A.
TRADE AND POLITICS IN NINETEENTH-CENTURY PUERTO RICO
DISSERTATION ABSTRACTS INTERNATIONAL, 49(7) (JAN 89),
1934-A.
THE AUTHOR STUDIES THE POLITICAL BEHAVIOR OF MERCHANTS
AND LANDOWNERS WHO CHOSE ADAPTATION RATHER THAN
CONFRONTATION WITH SPAIN IN NINETEENTH CENTURY PUERTO RICO.

02533 CUBBIT, D.; CORKILL, D.
ECUADOR: FRAGILE DEMOCRACY
MONTHLY REVIEW PRESS, NEW YORK, NY, 1988, 140.
IN 1979, ECUADOR WAS THE FIRST LATIN AMERICAN COUNTRY IN
WHICH THE MILITARY YIELDED TO CIVILIAN RULE. YET CORRUPTION
AND REPRESSION INCREASED UNDER PRESIDENT LEON FEBRES CORDERO,
AND RECOVERY FROM THE DISASTROUS 1986 EARTHQUAKE HAS BEEN
SLOW. MANY OF ECUADOR'S NATURAL RESOURCES REMAIN
UNDERUTILIZED WHILE OVERDEPENDENCE ON OIL IN A PERIOD OF
DECLINING WORLD OIL PRICES HAS BROUGHT WIDESPREAD HARDSHIP.
AND WHILE THE NEW ADMINISTRATION OFFERS PROGRESSIVES SOME
HOPE, THE LEGACY OF STRONG TIES TO THE U.S. REMAINS, AND
SPLITS WITHIN AND BETWEEN THE MILITARY AND THE RULING CLASS
THREATEN THE COUNTRY'S LONG-TERM STABILITY.

02534 CULBERSON, W.C.
VIGILANTISM IN AMERICA: A POLITICAL ANALYSIS OF PRIVATE
VIOLENCE
DISSERTATION ABSTRACTS INTERNATIONAL, 49(11) (MAY 89),
3489-A.
FOCUSING ON VIGILANTISM, THE AUTHOR ANALYZES CYCLICAL
ASPECTS OF SOCIAL VALUES AND NORMS IN AMERICAN POLITICS.
VIOLENT MEANS HAVE BEEN EMPLOYED FOR A VARIETY OF SOCIAL
ENDS BY INDIVIDUALS AND GROUPS AGAINST INDIVIDUALS, GROUPS,
AND GOVERNMENTAL BODIES THROUGHOUT AMERICAN HISTORY. PRIVATE
VIOLENCE HAS ENCOMPASSED ALL ASPECTS OF AMERICAN POLITICAL
BEHAVIOR.

02535 CULLEN, P.; YANNOPOULOS, G.N.
THE REDISTRIBUTION OF REGULATORY POWERS BETWEEN
GOVERNMENTS AND INTERNATIONAL ORGANISATIONS: THE CASE OF
EUROPEAN AIRLINE DEREGULATION
EUROPEAN JOURNAL OF POLITICAL RESEARCH, 17(2) (MAR 89),
155-168.
THIS PAPER LOOKS AT THE ISSUES RAISED WHEN DEREGULATION
IS ALSO ACCOMPANIED WITH REDISTRIBUTION OF THE RESIDUAL
REGULATORY POWERS BETWEEN GOVERNMENTS AND INTERNATIONAL
ORGANISATIONS BY FOCUSING ON THE EXPERIENCE OF DEREGULATION
OF THE AIRLINE INDUSTRY IN THE EUROPEAN COMMUNITY. THE PAPER
STARTS BY APPLYING A MODEL OF THE POLITICAL MARKET FOR
PROTECTION TO THE SPECIFIC CIRCUMSTANCES OF THE EUROPEAN
AIRLINE INDUSTRY IN AN AN EFFORT TO CLARIFY THE DIFFICULTIES
RAISED WHEN REDISTRIBUTION OF REGULATORY POWERS BETWEEN
DIFFERENT LEVELS OF GOVERNMENT TAKES PLACE. THE FINDINGS OF
THIS ANALYSIS ARE THEN USED TO ELUCIDATE THE EUROPEAN
EXPERIENCE AND IN PARTICULAR TO EXPLAIN THE GAP BETWEEN THE
ORIGINAL PROPOSALS OF THE COMMISSION AND THE FINAL
COMPROMISES WORKED OUT IN THE COUNCIL OF MINISTERS.

02536 CULLEN, R.
SOVIET JEWISH EMIGRATION: TIME FOR A NEW AMERICAN POLICY?
TIKKUN, 4(1) (JAN 89), 34-36.
THE AUTHOR CONSIDERS THE RESPONSE OF THE USA AND OF
AMERICAN JEWRY TO THE SOVIET UNION'S RECENT LIBERALIZATION
OF EMIGRATION.

02537 CULLEN, R.W.
FEDERALISM IN ACTION: THE CANADIAN AND AUSTRALIAN OFFSHORE

DISPUTES COMPARED
DISSERTATION ABSTRACTS INTERNATIONAL, 48(10) (APR 88),
2714-A.
THE INTERGOVERNMENTAL CONFLICT RESULTING FROM DISPUTE
OVER OFFSHORE OIL JURISDICTION IN AUSTRALIA AND CANADA FROM
THE DECADE FOLLOWING WORLD WAR II TO MID-1986 IS THE SUBJECT
OF THIS THESIS. THE CONFLICT RESULTED IN DIFFERENT
RESOLUTIONS IN EACH COUNTRY AND THE MEANS OF ARRIVING AT
THESE RESOLUTIONS DIFFERED ALSO. THE CONDUCT AND OUTCOMES OF
THESE DISPUTES TELL MUCH OF THE RELATIVE STATE OF THE TWO
VARIANTS OF FEDERALISM.

02538 CUMINGS, B.
THE ABORTIVE ABERTURA: SOUTH KOREA IN THE LIGHT OF LATIN
AMERICAN EXPERIENCE
NEW LEFT REVIEW, (173) (JAN 89), 5-32.
IN THIS ESSAY, BRUCE CUMINGS COMPARES AND CONTRASTS THE
DEMOCRATIZATION PROCESS IN LATIN AMERICA WITH THE
INTRODUCTION OF ELECTIVE PROCEDURES INTO THE RULING ORDER OF
SOUTH KOREA. WHILE SALUTING THE SOCIAL COURAGE OF THOSE
STUDENTS AND WORKERS WHO HELPED PUSH BACK SEOUL'S
DICTATORIAL SYSTEM IN 1987-88, CUMINGS ALSO CONSIDERS
STRUCTURAL FACTORS PERMITTING THIS OUTCOME. HE SITUATES
RECENT ATTEMPTS TO UNDERSTAND THIRD WORLD DEMOCRATIZATION ON
THE THEORETICAL TERRAIN OF MARXIST AND NON-MARXIST ACCOUNTS
OF THE REVOLUTIONARY ORIGINS OF CAPITALIST DEMOCRACY IN
EUROPE AND NORTH AMERICA. HE SHOWS HOW THE CLASH OF
REVOLUTION AND COUNTER-REVOLUTION IN KOREA IN 1945-53
EFFECTIVELY ELIMINATED THE PRE-CAPITALIST LANDLORD CLASS IN
THE SOUTH AS WELL AS THE NORTH. HE ALSO EXPLORES THE WAY IN
WHICH THE ROK'S FORMIDABLE CONFIGURATION OF MILITARY AND
ECONOMIC POWER REMAINS SUBORDINATE TO US HEGEMONY AND
COMPLEMENTARY TO JAPAN'S REGIONAL POSTURE. FOR CUMINGS, THE
IMPETUS TO DEMOCRATIZATION REMAINS HOBBLED BY SYSTEMIC
CONSTRAINTS AND HAS STRENGTH ONLY TO THE EXTENT THAT A
DEMOCRATIC OPENING IS BETTER ADAPTED THAN DICTATORSHIP TO
HANDLING THE AWAKENED SOCIAL FORCES OF A CRISIS PERIOD IN A
MORE DEVELOPED CAPITALIST SOCIAL FORMATION.

02539 CUNDY, D.T.
TELEVISED POLITICAL EDITORIALS AND THE LOW-INVOLVEMENT
VIEWER
SOCIAL SCIENCE QUARTERLY, 70(4) (DEC 89), 911-922.
A MAJORITY OF THE COMMERCIAL TELEVISION STATIONS IN THE
UNITED STATES EDITORIALIZE, A TENDENCY THAT INCREASES WITH
MARKET SIZE. A SIGNIFICANT PORTION OF THE EDITORIAL CONTENT
RELATES TO STATE AND LOCAL POLITICS. THE RESULTS OF THIS
STUDY SUGGEST THAT UNDER CONDITIONS OF LOW VIEWER
INFORMATION AND INVOLVEMENT, EDITORIALS CAN HAVE A
SIGNIFICANT INFLUENCE ON IMAGES OF A POLITICIAN. THE
FINDINGS ALSO INDICATE THAT DESPITE THE OPENLY BIASED NATURE
OF AN EDITORIAL, A MESSAGE FROM THAT SOURCE CAN HAVE AS MUCH
OR MORE IMPACT AS THE SAME INFORMATION PRESENTED AS PART OF
THE NEWS.

02540 CUNHAL, A.
PORTUGAL: FOR ADVANCED DEMOCRACY AT THE TURN OF THE CENTURY
INFORMATION BULLETIN, 27 (MAR 89), 13-16.
IN THIS SPEECH, THE GENERAL SECRETARY OF THE PORTUGUESE
COMMUNIST PARTY DISCUSSES THE INTERNATIONAL SITUATION,
PERESTROIKA, PORTUGAL'S INTEGRATION WITH THE EEC, AND THE
APRIL REVOLUTION.

02541 CUNNIGEN, D.
MEN AND WOMEN OF GOODWILL: MISSISSIPPI'S WHITE LIBERALS
DISSERTATION ABSTRACTS INTERNATIONAL, 49(8) (FEB 89),
2404-A.
THE CONTEMPORARY SOUTH'S PROGRESS IN RACE RELATIONS HAS
RESULTED FROM THE COMBINED EFFORTS OF BLACKS, WHITE NORTHERN
LIBERALS, AND WHITE SOUTHERN LIBERALS. THIS DISSERTATION
DEVELOPS A GROUP DEFINITION AND DESCRIPTION OF THE WHITE
SOUTHERN LIBERAL COMMUNITY AND SUMMARIZES THE WHITE SOUTHERN
LIBERAL ATTITUDE ABOUT CONTEMPORARY RACE RELATIONS BY
EXPLORING LIBERAL ACTIVITIES.

02542 CUOMO, M.M.
NEW YORK'S ETHICS REFORM: RESTORING TRUST IN GOVERNMENT
JOURNAL OF STATE GOVERNMENT, 62(5) (SEP 89), 176-179.
WHILE THE ETHICS DEBATE IS NOT RESTRICTED TO GOVERNMENT,
IT HAS A PARTICULARLY CRITICAL ROLE IN ASSURING THE
INTEGRITY AND ACCOUNTABILITY OF GOVERNMENTAL INSTITUTIONS
WHICH, IN TURN, ARE A MEASURE OF THE STRENGTH OF A DEMOCRACY.
WITHOUT AN EFFECTIVE CODE OF CONDUCT THAT APPLIES TO THOSE
WHO GOVERN, GOVERNMENT WILL NOT HAVE THE TRUST AND
CONFIDENCE OF THE PEOPLE. NEW YORK STATE IS PROMOTING
GOVERNMENTAL ACCOUNTABILITY AND ETHICS REFORM THROUGH NEW
LAWS THAT REGULATE THE PRIVATE INTERESTS OF PUBLIC OFFICIALS.

02543 CURRIE, D.; LEWIS, S.W.
COMPARISON OF ALTERNATIVE REGIMES FOR INTERNATIONAL
MACROPOLICY COORDINATION
AVAILABLE FROM NTIS, NO. PB89-192884/GAR, JUL 88, 37.
THE EXPERIENCE OF THE PAST DECADE AND A HALF OF FLOATING
EXCHANGE RATES WITH UNCOORDINATED MACROECONOMIC POLICIES HAS

LED TO RENEWED INTEREST IN SCHEMES OR BLUEPRINTS FOR THE
COORDINATION OF MONETARY, FISCAL AND EXCHANGE RATE POLICIES
BETWEEN COUNTRIES. SUCH BLUEPRINTS OR RULES MAY SERVE TO
AVOID THE COORDINATION FAILURE THAT MIGHT OTHERWISE ARISE
BETWEEN THE MACROECONOMIC POLICY STANCES OF THE MAJOR G7
COUNTRIES. BY FORMULATING POLICY IN TERMS OF EXPLICIT RULES
OR GUIDELINES, SUCH BLUEPRINTS MAY ALSO SERVE TO TAP THE
BENEFITS OF REPUTATION AND CREDIBILITY IN INTERNATIONAL
MACROPOLICY MAKING.

02544 CURRIE, R.F.; SEGALL, A.; TEFFT, B.; TRUTE, B.
MAYBE ON MY STREET: THE POLITICS OF COMMUNITY PLACEMENT OF
THE MENTALLY DISABLED
URBAN AFFAIRS QUARTERLY, 25(2) (DEC 89), 298-321.
THE INCREASING DEINSTITUTIONALIZATION OF THE MENTALLY
DISABLED HAS INSTIGATED RESEARCH ON NEIGHBORHOOD RECEPTIVITY
TO THIS GROUP. USING A RANDOM HOUSEHOLD SAMPLE FROM A
MIDWESTERN CANADIAN CITY, THE AUTHORS INVESTIGATE THE
USEFULNESS OF NEIGHBORHOOD TYPE AND INDIVIDUAL
CHARACTERISTICS IN PREDICTING THE LIKELIHOOD OF SUPPORTIVE
OR OPPOSING POLITICAL RESPONSES FROM RESIDENTS. OVERALL,
THICE AS MANY RESPONDENTS CONSIDER THE PLACEMENT OF
COMMUNITY MENTAL HEALTH FACILITIES IN THEIR NEIGHBORHOOD TO
BE DESIRABLE, COMPARED TO THOSE WHO CONSIDER SUCH FACILITIES
UNDESIRABLE. NEIGHBORHOOD TYPES ARE NOT PARTICULARLY GOOD
PREDICTORS OF ATTITUDES OR INTENDED POLITICAL ACTIONS.

02545 CURRY, M.
U.S. BLACK CHURCHES COORDINATE OPPOSITION TO APARTHEID
SOJOURNERS, 18(3) (MAR 89), 12.
THE BLACK CHURCH SUMMIT ON SOUTHERN AFRICA, HELD IN
JANUARY 1989, MARKED THE FIRST TIME BLACK CHURCHES HAVE
SOUGHT TO COORDINATE THEIR OPPOSITION TO APARTHEID. THE
CHURCH LEADERS CALLED FOR COMPREHENSIVE ECONOMIC SANCTIONS
AGAINST SOUTH AFRICA, REAFFIRMED THE ESSENTIAL CONNECTIONS
BETWEEN BLACKS IN SOUTH AFRICA AND AMERICA, AND ENDORSED THE
WORLD COUNCIL OF CHURCHES' STAND FOR TRUTH: FREE SOUTH
AFRICA CAMPAIGN.

02546 CURRY, R.L. JR.
BASIC NEEDS STRATEGY, THE CONGRESSIONAL MANDATE, AND U.S.
FOREIGN AID POLICY
JOURNAL OF ECONOMIC ISSUES, 23(4) (DEC 89), 1085-1096.
THE GRAVITY OF THE SITUATION IN POORER COUNTRIES,
COUPLED WITH THE ALMOST EXCLUSIVELY MACROECONOMIC ADJUSTMENT
FOCUS TO FUND-SUPPORTED PROGRAMS SUGGESTS A NEED TO SEARCH
FOR AN EFFECTIVE MICROECONOMIC AND SOCIAL FOCUS TO
ASSISTANCE AND DEVELOPMENT STRATEGIES, IT IS THE CONTENTION
OF THIS ARTICLE THAT A SEARCH OUGHT TO INCLUDE A RE-
EVALUATION OF THREE NOW-DEFUNCT POLICY AND INSTITUTIONAL
FEATURES OF THE DEBATE OVER FOREIGN ASSISTANCE THAT TOOK
PLACE DURING THE CARTER PRESIDENCY; THE BASIC HUMAN NEEDS
DEVELOPMENT STRATEGY; THE CONGRESSIONAL MANDATE; AND THE
PROVISIONS OF THE HUMPHERY BILL.

02547 CURTICE, J.
THE 1989 EUROPEAN ELECTION: PROTEST OR GREEN TIDE?
ELECTORAL STUDIES, 8(3) (DEC 89), 217-230.
THE FIRST TWO ROUNDS OF DIRECT ELECTIONS TO THE EUROPEAN
PARLIAMENT HAVE BEEN CHARACTERIZED AS A SET OF SEPARATE
NATIONAL SECOND ORDER ELECTIONS IN WHICH TURNOUT IS LOW,
SMALL PARTIES DO WELL, AND THE ELECTORATE CAST JUDGEMENT ON
THEIR GOVERNMENTS RATHER THAN ON EUROPEAN ISSUES. MANY OF
THOSE FEATURES ARE APPARENT IN THE 1989 ELECTIONS. BUT THERE
WAS A COMMUNITY-WIDE MOVEMENT TOWARDS THE GREENS WHICH WAS
NOT SIMPLY PART OF THE GENERAL SUCCESS FOR SMALL PARTIES,
BUT THE GREENS' GAINS WERE NOT FULLY REFLECTED IN THE
DISTRIBUTION OF STRASBOURG SEATS. THESE ELECTIONS MAY WELL
GIVE A SIGNIFICANT BOOST TO THE SUCCESS OF GREEN PARTIES IN
FUTURE NATIONAL ELECTIONS.

02548 CURTIN, R. T.
CAUTIOUS OPTIMISIM AMONG CONSUMERS
ECONOMIC OUTLOOK USA, 15(1) (SUM 88), 17-19.
THIS ARTICLE EXAMINES CONSUMER CONFIDENCE WHICH HAS
RESULTED IN A LONG EXPANSION OF PERSISTANT STRENGTH. IT
EXPLORES THE INCREASING CONCERN WITH RISING INTEREST RATES
AND RISING INFLATION, BUT ALSO THE OFFSETTING OF THESE
CONCERNS AS CONSUMERS CONTINUE TO FAVORABLY VIEW INCOME AND
EMPLOYMENT PROSPECTS.

02549 CURTIS, M.
THE UPRISING'S IMPACT ON THE OPTIONS FOR PEACE
MIDDLE EAST REVIEW, XXI(2) (WIN 89), 3-12.
THE UPRISING IN THE WEST BANK AND GAZA HAS LASTED AN
UNEXPECTEDLY LONG TIME AND HAS DRAMATICALLY AFFECTED THE
CONSTELLATION OF FORCES IN THE MIDDLE EAST. WHETHER THE
DISORDERS RESULTED FROM A SPONTANEOUS COMBUSTION OF PENT-UP
FORCES OR WERE DELIBERATELY PROVOKED BY ISLAMIC
FUNDAMENTALIST GROUPS IS LESS SIGNIFICANT THAN THE EXTENT OF
THE CONTINUING ACTIVITY AND ITS CONSEQUENCES.

02550 CURTIS, R.
REPRESENTATION AND STATE FORMATION IN THE CANADAS, 1790-

1850
STUDIES IN POLITICAL ECONOMY: A SOCIALIST REVIEW, (28)
(SPR 89), 59-88.
THIS ARTICLE FOCUSES ON EDUCATIONAL ADMINISTRATION AT
THE LOCAL LEVEL IN CANADA WEST. THE AUTHOR DRAWS EXTENSIVELY
UPON LITERATURE CONCERNED WITH THE 19TH CENTURY REVOLUTION
IN GOVERNMENT IN GREAT BRITAIN. IT CONCLUDES THAT THE
EXCERCISE OF STATE POWER IN THIS PERIOD CAN ONLY BE
UNDERSTOOD BY A STUDY OF THE DIFFICULTIES OF CONSTRUCTING
LOCAL INSTITUTIONS WHICH WOULD INCULATE HABITS AND BELIEFS
CONGENIAL TO BOURGEOIS HEGEMONY.

02551 CURWEN, P.
THE KAWTHOOLEI WOMEN'S ORGANIZATION
CULTURAL SURVIVAL QUARTERLY, 13(4) (1989), 32-33.
THE KAWTHOOLEI WOMEN'S ORGANIZATION IS INSEPARABLE FROM
THE KAREN NATIONAL LIBERATION STRUGGLE. THE ESTABLISHMENT OF
THE KAREN WOMEN'S GROUP HAS BEEN DESCRIBED AS "A VICTORY
AGAINST THE BSPP MILITARY REGIME, AGAINST BURMESE CHAUVINISM,
AND AGAINST MALE CHAUVINISM." THE GROUP'S AIMS ARE TO FREE
KAREN WOMEN FROM OPPRESSION AND RAISE THEIR LIVING STANDARDS,
TO RAISE THEIR POLITICAL AND REVOLUTIONARY CONSCIOUSNESS,
TO BE ACTIVE IN THE KAREN REVOLUTIONARY MOVEMENT, AND TO
GAIN EQUAL RIGHTS WITH MEN AND PROTECT THOSE RIGHTS.

02552 CUSACK, T.R.; NOTERMANS, T.; REIN, M.
POLITICAL-ECONOMIC ASPECTS OF PUBLIC EMPLOYMENT
EUROPEAN JOURNAL OF POLITICAL RESEARCH, 17(4) (JUL 89),
471-500.
AN EXAMINATION OF PUBLIC EMPLOYMENT AND EXPENDITURE DATA
FOR 17 OECD COUNTRIES FOR THE PERIOD 1963-1983 REVEALS
DECELERATING GROW H IN THE PUBLIC EMPLOYMENT AFTER 1970,
WHEREAS EXPENDITURE GROWTH RATES HAVE BEEN ACCELERARTING.
TWO CONTRARY TENDENCIES IN PUBLIC SECTOR EMPLOYMENT SINCE
THE EARLY 1970S ARE APPARENT: A GENERAL DECLINE IN GOODS AND
MARKET SERVICES, AND A SIGNIFICANT INCREASE IN COMMUNAL AND
SOCIAL SERVICES. COMPARATIVE EMPIRICAL ANALYSIS, USING A
POOLED CROSS SECTION-TIME SERIES TECHNIQUE, CONFIRMS THE
IMPORTANT CONTRIBUTION OF INCREASING WEALTH TO PUBLIC
EMPLOYMENT GROWTH. SIMILARLY, A STRONG SOCIETAL POSITION FOR
ORGSANIZED LABOR AND INCREASING UNEMPLOYMENT RATES
CONTRIBUTE TO PUBLIC EMPLOYMENT GROWTH, THEREBY SUGGESTING
THE PRESENCE OF A DISCRETIONARY STABILIZATION POLICY.
CONTRAR EXPECTATIONS, HOWEVER, INCREASED TRADE DEPENDENCE
EXERTS A NEGATIVE IMPACT. WITH REGARD TO THE RELATIONSHIP
BETWEEN EXPENDITURE AND EMPLOYEMENT, A GENERAL INCREASE IN
THE EMPLOYMENT CRATION EFFICIENCY OF SPENDING CAN BE
DISCERNED. EMPIRICAL ESTIMATES AGAIN SUGGEST THAT THE
IMPORTANCE OF LABOR IN POLICTAL-ECONOMIC DECISION-MAKING HAS
INTENSIFIED THE EMPLOYMENT CREATION EFFECT OF PUBLIC
SPENDING.

02553 CUSACK, T.R.; ZIMMER, U.
REALPOLITIK AND THE BASES OF MULTISTATE SYSTEM ENDURANCE
THE JOURNAL OF POLITICS, 51(2) (MAY 89), 247-285.
THIS PAPER FOCUSES ON POLICY AND STRUCTURAL FACTORS THAT
PRESERVE OR UNDERMINE THE PLURALISM OF INTERSTATE SYSTEM.
USING A LARGE SCALE COMPUTER SIMULATION MODEL THAT
INCORPORATES MANY OF THE ESSENTIAL ELEMENTS OF THE
"AUTOMATIC STABILIZATION" VERSION OF THE BALANCE OF POWER
THEORY, THE AUTHORS CONDUCT A SYSTEMATIC EXPLORATION OF
ALTERNATIVE REALPOLITIK THESES THAT PURPORT TO DEFINE THE
CONDITIONS AND POLICIES REQUIRED TO PREVENT THE EMERGENCE OF
A HEGEMONIC SYSTEM. THE EXPLORATION RELIES ON NINETY-SIX
EXPERIMENTAL RUNS OF THE MODEL WHEREIN FIVE FACTORS ARE
VARIED. ANALYSIS REVEALS THAT OVEROPTIMISM IN EXPECTATIONS
ABOUT WAR'S OUTCOME PLAYS THE PARADOXICAL ROLE OF MAXIMIZING
THE LENGTH OF SYSTEM ENDURANCE. THE DISTRIBUTION OF POWER
WITHIN THE SYSTEM, ERROR IN DECISION PROCESSES AND
PUNITIVENESS ON THE PART OF VICTORS IN WAR ARE ALSO FOUND TO
HAVE A CONDITIONING ROLE IN THE ENDURANCE OF THE SYSTEM
WHILE NO DISCERNIBLE EFFECT IS APPARENT IN THE CASE OF THE
COSTLINESS OF WAR. ANALYSES FOCUSING ON THE PROCESSES
UNDERLYING THE EVOLUTION OF THE SYSTEM ALSO POINT OUT THE
IMPORTANCE OF CONTEXT-SPECIFIC CONDITIONS IN GENERATING THE
DETERRENCE SITUATIONS REALISTS ARGUE TO BE IMPORTANT WITHIN
THE WORKINGS OF A BALANCE OF POWER SYSTEM.

02554 CUTHBERTSON, K.; TAYLOR, M. P.
MONETARY ANTICIPATIONS AND THE DEMAND FOR MONEY IN THE U.S.
: FURTHER RESULTS
SOUTHERN ECONOMIC JOURNAL, 55(2) (OCT 88), 326-335.
THIS ARTICLE PRESENTS EVIDENCE ON THE SHOCK ABSORBER
HYPOTHESIS FOR THE U.S. WITH THE COVARIANCE MATRIX ESTIMATED,
CONSISTENTLY USING THREE SEPARATE ANTICIPATIONS GENERATING
EQUATIONS. THE RATIONAL EXPECTATIONS-SHOCK ABSORBER
HYPOTHESIS IS TESTED. THE FINDINGS POINT TO THE BELIEF THAT
THE JOINT HYPOTHESIS OF RATIONALITY AND NEUTRALITY IS
DECISIVELY REJECTED.

02555 CVEJANOVICH, G.J. JR.
DEPENDENCE AND DEVELOPMENT IN ARUBA: HOST STATE-FOREIGN
CAPITAL BARGAINING
DISSERTATION ABSTRACTS INTERNATIONAL, 50(2) (AUG 89),

534-A.
THE AUTHOR ANALYZES THE ROLE AND CONSEQUENCES OF
TRANSNATIONAL CORPORATION INVOLVEMENT IN THE DEVELOPMENT
PROCESS, FOCUSING ON THE POLITICAL AND ECONOMIC DEVELOPMENT
OF ARUBA.

02556 CVIJETIC, B.
A HISTORICAL TURNING POINT (II)
REVIEW OF INTERNATIONAL AFFAIRS, (JAN 88), 10-13.
THE AUTHOR ARGUES THAT THE FACT THAT AN AGREEMENT ON THE
DOUBLE-ZERO OPTION HAS BEEN SIGNED IN WASHINGTON; THAT SOME
NEW, HIGHLY SENSITIVE ELEMENTS OF AN AGREEMENT ON DESTROYING
HALF THE NUMBER OF STRATEGIC MISSILES WITHIN THE FAMOUS
"TRAID" HAVE BEEN AGREED UPON; THAT THE NEXT SUMMIT IN
MOSCOW HAS BEEN FIXED WITH THE SPECIFIED AIM OF HAVING START
SIGNED ON THAT OCCASION; THAT DIVERSE FORMS OF BILATERIAL
COOPERATION HAVE BEEN ARRANGED - AND THAT THERE HAS NOT BEEN
ANY BREAKTHROUGH, AT LEAST NOT A PUBLIC ONE, OVER REGIONAL
ISSUES OR HUMAN RIGHTS - INDICATE THAT THE UNITED STATES AND
MOCOW ARE TAKING A MORE FLEXIBLE ATTITUDE WITHOUT DIRECTLY
LINKING AN AGREEMENT IN ONE AREA TO A SIMULTANEOUS AGREEMENT
IN ALL OTHER AREAS.

02557 CYGIELMAN, V.
THE IMPACT OF TWO YEARS OF THE INTIFADA
NEW OUTLOOK, 32(11-12 (297-298)) (NOV 89), 5.
PERHAPS THE MOST CONSPICUOUS RESULT OF THE INTIFADA HAS
BEEN THE RESTORATION OF ISRAEL'S PRE-1967 BORDER. TODAY THE
WEST BANK AND GAZA STRIP ARE SEEN AS FOREIGN TERRITORIES
INHABITED BY A HOSTILE POPULATION WITH STONE-THROWING
YOUNGSTERS READY TO DIE IN THEIR QUEST FOR FREEDOM. MOST
ISRAELIS HAVE COME TO REALIZE THAT PALESTINIAN NATIONAL
DEMANDS CANNOT BE IGNORED OR TALKED AWAY. MANY ALSO
UNDERSTAND THAT THERE IS NO MILITARY SOLUTION TO THE
INTIFADA. ONLY THOSE ISRAELI LEADERS WITH THEIR EYES
HERMETICALLY CLOSED DO NOT SEE THAT THE IDEA OF "GREATER
ISRAEL" HAS EXPIRED DURING THE INTIFADA. BUT THE INTIFADA
HAS BROUGHT FRUSTRATION ALONG WITH HOPE FOR THE PALESTINIANS.
PLO INFLUENCE AMONG THE IMPATIENT PALESTINIAN YOUTH, WHO
FEEL THEIR SACRIFICES ARE NOT BRINGING ENOUGH POLITICAL
PROGRESS, IS BEING ERODED BY THE MORE RADICAL HAMAS AND THE
EXTREME PALESTINIAN LEFT.

02558 CYPHER, J. M.
THE DEBT CRISIS AS "OPPORTUNITY" STRATEGIES TO REVIVE U.S.
HEGEMONY
LATIN AMERICAN PERSPECTIVES, 16(1) (WIN 89), 52-78.
WHILE THE LATIN AMERICAN NATIONS HAVE DONE LITTLE TO
MITIGATE AND MUCH TO FURTHER THE DISARTICULATION OF THEIR
PRODUCTIVE APPARATUSES, THE UNITED STATES HAS PURSUED A
STRATEGY THROUGHOUT THE CRISIS DESIGNED TO REGAIN LOST POWER
OVER THE THIRD WORLD IN GENERAL AND LATIN AMERICA IN
PARTICULAR. IT IS THE PURPOSE OF THIS ARTICLE TO DISCUSS THE
NATURE AND MAGNITUDE OF THE U.S. ECONOMIC OFFENSIVE AGAINST
LATIN AMERICA WHILE FULLY REALIZING THAT THE FINAL OUTCOME
OF THE PRESENT HEIGHTENED RIVALRY COULD BE VERY FAR FROM
THAT SOUGHT BY U.S. POLICYMAKERS. A CRISIS IS BOTH A PERIOD
OF SEEMING (AND REAL) CHAOS AND DANGER AND POTENTIALLY A
PERIOD OF OPPORTUNITY. THE AUTHOR DEMONSTRATES THE SEVERAL
WAYS THAT U.S. POLICYMAKERS HAVE SOUGHT TO USE THE CURRENT
CRISIS TO PARTIALLY REVIVE U.S. HEGEMONY AND REVERSE THIRD
WORLD CHALLENGES TO THAT HEGEMONY THAT BECAME INCREASINGLY
OBVIOUS IN THE DECADE OF THE 1970S.

02559 CZAPUTOWICZ, J.; SCHARF, C.L.
ON THE FUTURE OF POLISH PLURALISM
FREEDOM AT ISSUE, (109) (JUL 89), 28-31.
IN THIS INTERVIEW, ONE OF THE FOUNDERS OF POLAND'S
FREEDOM AND PEACE MOVEMENT DISCUSSES RECENT POLITICAL
CHANGES IN POLAND AND REPORTS THAT YOUNGER POLISH ACTIVISTS
DO NOT SUPPORT LECH WALESA'S PROPOSALS FOR REFORM.

02560 CZUBINSKI, A.
POLITICAL AND MILITARY BALANCE-SHEET OF WORLD WAR II
CONTEMPORARY POLAND, XXII(6) (1989), 21-25.
CZUBINSKI, WHO IS A PROFESSOR AT ADAM MICKIEWICZ
UNIVERSITY, DISCUSSES POLAND'S ROLE IN WORLD WAR II AND
POLISH FOREIGN POLICY UNDER MINISTER OF FOREIGN AFFAIRS
JOZEF BECK.

02561 CZYREK, J.
POLAND: SECURITY IN A CHANGING WORLD
WORLD MARXIST REVIEW, 32(4) (APR 89), 9-12.
GREATER UNIVERSAL SECURITY IMPLIES THAT ALL PARTIES SHOW
THEIR READINESS FOR IT AND NO ONE ACT TO PROMOTE MISTRUST OR
SUSPICION. POLAND FIRMLY BELIEVES IN THE VALIDITY OF THIS
DOCTRINE AND, FOR ITS PART, SEEKS TO CONTRIBUTE TO ITS
PRACTICAL REALISATION. THE DEFENSE COMMITTEE OF THE POLISH
PEOPLE'S REPUBLIC HAS DECIDED TO CUT THE STRENGTH OF THE
NATIONAL ARMY, AND TO REDUCE THE MILITARY BUDGET BY ALMOST
5%. PRIOR TO, AND INDEPENDENTLY OF THAT DECISION, THE WELL-
KNOWN JARUZELSKI PLAN HAS ADVANCED, CONTAINING A NUMBER OF
IDEAS ON DISARMAMENT IN CENTRAL EUROPE FULLY CONSONANT WITH
THE SPIRIT OF THE DOCTRINE IN QUESTION. THE PLAN ALSO

FEATURED A PROPOSAL ON DISCUSSING THE MILITARY DOCTRINES OF
BOTH BLOCS SO AS TO ACT JOINTLY TO MAKE THEM STRICTLY
DEFENSIVE.

02562 CZYREK, J.; STELMACHOWSKI, A.
VIEWPOINT: BEFORE THE ROUND TABLE
POLISH PERSPECTIVES, XXXII(2) (1989), 49-56.
IN THESE INTERVIEWS, TWO POLISH LEADERS DISCUSS THE
RECENT POLITICAL CHANGES IN POLAND AND THE OUTLOOK FOR
CONTINUING POLITICAL REFORM.

02563 D'AMATO, J.V.
CONSTRUCTIVE ENGAGEMENT: THE RISE AND FALL OF AN AMERICAN
FOREIGN POLICY
DISSERTATION ABSTRACTS INTERNATIONAL, 49(10) (APR 89),
3146-A.
THE MAJOR GOAL OF CONSTRUCTIVE ENGAGEMENT WAS TO SUPPORT
AN ASSUMED PROCESS OF EVOLUTIONARY CHANGE WITHIN SOUTH
AFRICA THAT WOULD LEAD TO A NON-RACIAL, PRO-WESTERN, AND
CAPITALIST STATE. THE POLICY WAS PROCESS-ORIENTED AND
ASSUMED A LONG-TERM EFFORT ON BEHALF OF BOTH THE SOUTH
AFRICAN GOVERNMENT AND THE UNITED STATES. THIS DISSERTATION
TRACES THE DEVELOPMENT OF CONSTRUCTIVE ENGAGEMENT FROM ITS
THEORETICAL FOUNDATION AS A REACTION TO THE CONFRONTATIONAL
SOUTH AFRICAN POLICY OF THE CARTER ADMINISTRATION TO ITS
DEMISE IN THE SECOND REAGAN TERM.

02564 D'ANTOINE, H.
BITTER YEARS AHEAD
PACIFIC DEFENCE REPORTER, 16(1) (JUL 89), 13-15.
THE CRISIS CHINA NOW FACES IS OF DENG'S MAKING, HIS
RELUCTANCE TO RETREAT FROM THE POLITICAL STAGE, HIS
INABILITY TO REMOVE THE OLD GUARD FROM ANY INVOLVMENT IN
POLITICS, HIS UNWILLINGNESS OR INABILITY TO INTRODUCE A
PROGRAM OF POLITICAL REFORM, AND HIS RUTHLESS DECISION TO
ORDER THE ARMY TO OPEN FIRE ON THE UNARMED DEMONSTRATORS. IN
THE SHORT TERM, THE PROSPECTS ARE BLEAK. BUT FOR THE LONGER
TERM IN ONE VITALLY IMPORTANT AREA, THERE HAS BEEN A
DRAMATIC, QUALITATIVE CHANGE IN THE ATTITUDES AND RESPONSES
OF AN EXTRAORDINARILY WIDE CROSS-SECTION OF THE CHINESE
POPULATION TOWARDS THE GOVERNMENT AND ITS POLICIES.

02565 D'ANTOINE, H.
THE GREAT LEAP BACKWARDS
PACIFIC DEFENCE REPORTER, 16(6) (DEC 89), 36-41.
THIS ARTICLE DESCRIBES THE ORIGINS OF THE DRAMATIC
EVENTS WHICH SHOOK CHINA DURING THE MAY/JUNE RIOTS OF 1989.
ECONOMIC DIFFICULTIES, SUCH AS MOUNTING INFLATION, GROWING
UNEMPLOYMENT, LOW PRICES FOR AGRICULTURAL PRODUCTS, ALMOST
RAMPANT CORRUPTION, INCOME DISPARITIES AND STEEP INCREASES
IN THE INCIDENCE OF CRIME ENGENDERED A SLOWLY BREWING
DISSATISFACTION WITH THE GOVERNMENT AND ITS POLICIES. THIS
DISSATISFACTION OBSCURED WHAT HAD BEEN A VERY REAL
IMPROVEMENT IN LIVING STANDARDS OVER THE PAST DECADE. THE
RIOTOUS OUTCOME OF THE EVENTS OF JUNE ALSO EXTRACTED A HIGH
PRICE FROM CHINA IN TERMS OF ITS FOREIGN RELATIONS. THE
TRAGEDY OF THIS FOR CHINA IS THAT THE FOREIGN POLICY
SUCCESSES ANTICIPATED FOR 1989 WERE TO FREE CHINA FROM SOME
OF THE IDEOLOGICAL AND TERRITORIAL DISPUTES WHICH HAD
WEIGHED HEAVILY, ALBATROSS-LIKE, INHIBITING IT FOR TWO
DECADES FROM MAKING A WIDER IMPACT ON THE INTERNATIONAL
SCENE.

02566 D'ANTOINE, M.
SUMMIT NO LONGER A PLUME IN GORBACHEV'S HAT
PACIFIC DEFENCE REPORTER, 16(1) (JUL 89), 23-24.
WHILE THE SOVIET UNION HAS REMAINED DISCREETLY QUITE
ABOUT THE EVENTS IN TIAN AN MEN SQUARE, THE DIRECTION THAT
CHINESE FOREIGN POLICY MAY TAKE HAS NOT BEEN MORE OBSCURE
SINCE THE DARK DAYS OF THE CULTURAL REVOLUTION. GORBACHEV'S
PLAN TO ESTABLISH FULL RELATIONS WITH A REFORMIST STATE HAVE
BEEN DASHED AND SOME RUSSIANS ARE NOW ASKING THE QUESTION
WHETHER WHAT HAS HAPPENED IN CHINA MAY NOT ALSO HAPPEN IN
THE SOVIET UNION.

02567 D'AQUINO, N.
EUROPE JOINS THE SPACE RACE
EUROPE, (292) (DEC 89), 26-28.
THE EUROPEANS, THIRD IN THE SPACE RACE AFTER THE UNITED
STATES AND THE SOVIET UNION, ARE JUSTIFIABLY PROUD OF
THEIR RECENT ACHIEVEMENTS IN SPACE. THOUGH EUROPE IS HOLDING
ITS OWN WITH THE U.S. AND THE SOVIET UNION, THE EUROPEAN
SPACE AGENCY (ESA) HAS STRESSED THAT ITS POSITION MUST BE
DEFENDED BY FORMING ALLIANCES ANS COLLABORATING WITH THE
OTHER POWERS. THIS HAS ALREADY TAKEN PLACE WITH SEVERAL
JOINT U.S.-EUROPEAN PROJECTS. ESA'S LONG-TERM STRATEGY HAS
BEEN AGREED UPON AT THE POLITICAL LEVEL BY ITS 13 MEMBER
COUNTRIES. ESA IS PROVING TO BE A PROFITABLE UNDERTAKING.
RECENT CONTRACTS IN THIS SECTOR CONFIRM THAT THE EUROPEAN
SPACE BUSINESS IS BECOMING ECONOMICALLY AS WELL AS
TECHNOLOGICALLY INTERESTING.

02568 D'AQUINO, N.
MEMBER STATE REPORT: ITALY

EUROPE, (285) (APR 89), 36-38, 40.
ITALY'S ECONOMIC GROWTH HAS EXCEEDED THE NORM IN THE
INDUSTRIALIZED WORLD FOR FIVE YEARS RUNNING, AND ENJOYED A
SURPRISING 3.5 PERCENT GROWTH RATE IN 1988. THE UN HAS TAKEN
NOTICE OF ITALY'S NEW FOUND PROSPERITY AND HAS INCREASED THE
DEMANDS ON ITALY FOR CONTRIBUTIONS TO THE BUDGET. HOWEVER,
ALL IS NOT ROSY ON THE DOMESTIC SIDE: LARGE GAPS STILL EXIST
BETWEEN THE RICH NORTH AND THE POOR SOUTH AND POLITICAL AND
LABOR UNREST CONTINUES.

02569 D'ESTAING, V.G.; KISSINGER, H.A,; NAKASONE, Y.
EAST-WEST RELATIONS
FOREIGN AFFAIRS, 68(3) (SUM 89), 1-21.
THE UNITED STATES, JAPAN, AND FRANCE HAVE A RARE
OPPORTUNITY TO CHANGE THE NATURE OF EAST-WEST RELATIONS IN
WAYS BENEFICIAL TO THE WEST, PROVIDED THEY DEVELOP A CLEAR
AGENDA AND STRATEGY. ON THE OTHER HAND, PASSIVITY OR DELAYED
AND UNCOORDINATED REACTION TO SOVIET INITIATIVES WOULD
ENABLE THE KREMLIN TO DEFINE THE EAST-WEST AGENDA AND SERVE
PRIMARILY SOVIET INTERESTS.

02570 D'ESTAING, V.G.
THE TWO EUROPES, EAST AND WEST
INTERNATIONAL AFFAIRS, 65(4) (FAL 89), 653-658.
THIS ARTICLE EXPLORES THE FUTURE OF THE RELATIONS
BETWEEN EAST AND WEST EUROPE. IT SUGGESTS THAT THE FUTURE OF
EUROPE IS FOR EUROPEANS TO DECIDE AND THAT THE TERM THE
'COMMON EUROPEAN HOME' IS THE WRONG METAPHOR. A NEW ECONOMIC
RELATIONSHIP WITH EASTERN EUROPE, AND A COMMUNITY-LEVEL
APPROACH ARE EACH EXPLORED AND THEN THE SOVIET FACTOR IS
ADDRESSED.

02571 D'SOUZA, D.
WHAT EVER HAPPENED TO NEOLIBERALISM?
NATIONAL REVIEW, XLI(10) (JUN 89), 34-36.
THE DEFEAT OF MICHAEL DUKAKIS SIGNALED THE COLLAPSE OF
THE PHILOSOPHY HE REPRESENTED, THE SO-CALLED "NEO-LIBERAL"
APPROACH.

02572 DA CUNHA, M.
NATIVE REALPOLITIK
NACLA REPORT ON THE AMERICAS, XXIII(1) (MAY 89), 19-22.
CONSIDERED AN OBSTACLE BY SOME AND A THREAT BY OTHERS,
THE INDIANS OF THE BRAZILIAN AMAZON HAVE FACED PROSPECTORS,
SOLDIERS, POLICE, AND THE HIRED GUNS OF RANCHERS, LOGGERS
AND MINING COMPANIES. USING SPEARS, ARROWS, AND POLITICAL
SAVVY, THEY ARE FIGHTING BACK WITH SOME SUCCESS.

02573 DAADLDER, H.
THE MOULD OF DUTCH POLITICS: THEMES FOR COMPARATIVE INQUIRY
WEST EUROPEAN POLITICS, 12(1) (JAN 89), 1-20.
THE DUTCH POLITICAL SYSTEM OFFERS MANY FEATURES WORTHY
OF ATTENTION FROM THOSE WHO WISH TO ANALYSE POLITICAL
DEVELOPMENTS IN THIS COUNTRY FROM A COMPARATIVE PERSPECTIVE.
NINE OF THESE ARE INDICATED IN THIS INTRODUCTORY ESSAY: 1.
THE PECULIAR NATURE OF THE STATE WHICH DEVELOPED FROM A
LOOSE CONFEDERACY INTO A UNITARY STATE; 2. REPUBLICAN
TRADITIONS COEXISTING WITH AN OLD DYNASTY BUT A LATE
MONARCHY; 3. THE LASTING EFFECTS OF THE EARLY PRESENCE OF A
PATRICIAN BOURGEOISIE; 4. SPECIAL FEATURES OF PARLIAMENTARY
GOVERNMENT; 5. A RATHER DISTINCTIVE AND PLURALIST
BUREAUCRACY; 6. THE STRONG LEGACY OF DIFFERENT RELIGIOUS AND
IDEOLOGICAL TRADITIONS AND THEIR EFFECT ON THE
CONSOCIATIONAL MODEL WHICH WAS DEVELOPED LARGELY POST HOC; 7.
FRAGMENTATION AND MERGERS IN AN EXTREME MULTIPARTY SYSTEM;
8. THE CORPORATE REALITY OF POLITICS; 9. THE ASSESSMENT OF
AN INCREASE IN DIRECT CONTESTATION.

02574 DACKIH, O.A.
DEFENSE POLICY AND PUBLIC OPINION: THE BRITISH CAMPAIGN
FOR NUCLEAR DISARMAMENT, 1945-1985
DISSERTATION ABSTRACTS INTERNATIONAL, 49(12) (JUN 89),
3861-A.
THE AUTHOR RECOUNTS THE RISE AND FALL OF ANTI-NUCLEAR
ACTIVISM IN GREAT BRITAIN. THE DISSERTATION FOCUSES ON ONE
CENTRAL HYPOTHESIS: THAT CYCLES OF BRITISH NUCLEAR ACTIVISM
ARE CATALYZED BY THE DEVELOPMENT OF FOREIGN SYSTEMS THAT
EVOKE SPECIAL FEELINGS OF SUBORDINATION IN A HEGEMONIC U.S.-
ANGLO RELATIONSHIP AND DEEP-SEATED SYMBOLIC FEARS OF THE
APOCALYPSE.

02575 DADRIAN, E.
DANGER IN DARFUR
NEW AFRICAN, (JAN 88), 22-23.
THIS ARTICLE REPORTS ON THE GRIM SITUATION IN SUDAN'S
WESTERN DARFUR PROVIDENCE. IT DESCRIBES THE KILLINGS BY
BANDITS BACKED BY WEALTHY MERCHANTS AND POLITICANS CONNECTED
WITH THE GOVERNMENT IN KHARTOUM. IT REPORTS ON THE FUR TRIBE
REACTON AND THEIR ENVOLVEMENT IN A SELF PRESERVATION PLAN.

02576 DAHONG, L.
MAINLAND-TAIWAN ECONOMIC RELATIONS ON THE RISE
BEIJING REVIEW, 32(14) (APR 89), 24-27.
ECONOMIC AND TRADE RELATIONS BETWEEN COMMUNIST CHINA AND

TAIWAN HAVE ENTERED A NEW STAGE. SINCE 1988, MAINLAND VESSELS HAVE CALLED AT TAIWANESE PORTS, AND THE VARIETY AND QUANTITY OF PRODUCTS SHIPPED TO TAIWAN ARE EXPECTED TO INCREASE. MEANWHILE, SEVERAL HUNDRED ENTERPRISES BASED IN TAIWAN HAVE BYPASSED OBSTACLES AND INVESTED IN MAINLAND BUSINESSES. MANY LARGE TAIWANESE ENTERPRISES HAVE SENT DELEGATIONS TO THE MAINLAND ON INSPECTION TOURS.

02577 DALE, C.V.
GOVERNMENTALLY MANDATED DRUG TESTING OF PUBLIC EMPLOYEES
CRS REVEIW, 10(8) (SEP 89), 4-5.
MANDATORY PUBLIC EMPLOYEE DRUG TESTING HAS BEEN THE FOCUS OF RECENT GOVERNMENTAL EFFORTS TO COMBAT DRUG ABUSE IN THE WORKPLACE. MOVING ON PARALLEL TRACKS, THE EXECUTIVE BRANCH AND CONGRESS HAVE EACH SOUGHT TO IMPLEMENT PROGRAMS THAT TARGET EMPLOYEES IN CERTAIN SENSITIVE FEDERAL JOBS OR WITHIN FEDERALLY REGULATED INDUSTRIES FOR ROUTINE DRUG TESTING. TOGETHER WITH SIMILAR PROGRAMS ADOPTED BY STATE AND LOCAL GOVERNMENTS, THESE EFFORTS HAVE SPAWNED LAWSUITS CHALLENGING THE AUTHORITY OF GOVERNMENT TO IMPOSE DRUG TESTING WITHOUT REASONABLE SUSPICION OF WORKPLACE DRUG ABUSE. THE SUPREME COURT HAS UPHELD POST-ACCIDENT TESTING OF RAILWAY EMPLOYEES AND TESTING OF CERTAIN CUSTOMS SERVICE EMPLOYEES. BUT IT HAS NOT YET DECIDED THE LEGALITY OF RANDOM TESTING.

02578 DALE, C.V.
MINORITY BUSINESS SET-ASIDES AND THE CONSTITUTION
CRS REVEIW, 10(8) (SEP 89), 6-7.
THE SUPREME COURT, IN STRIKING DOWN A MUNICIPAL MINORITY BUSINESS SET-ASIDE PROGRAM, PROVIDED ADDITIONAL GUIDANCE ON THE CONSTITUTIONAL STANDARDS GOVERNING AFFIRMATIVE ACTION. HOWEVER, AN IMPERFECT JUDICIAL CONSENSUS STILL EXISTS AND IMPORTANT QUESTIONS REMAIN INVOLVING THE ABILITY OF STATES, LOCALITIES, AND CONGRESS TO ENACT AFFIRMATIVE ACTION PROGRAMS.

02579 DALEY, R.A.
LABOR AND INDUSTRIAL CHANGE: THE POLITICS OF STEEL IN FRANCE
DISSERTATION ABSTRACTS INTERNATIONAL, 50(4) (OCT 89), 1075-A.
THE AUTHOR OFFERS A POLITICAL ECONOMY EXPLANATION OF HOW A "WEAK" LABOR MOVEMENT IN FRANCE HAS BEEN ABLE TO AVOID LAYOFFS AND OBTAIN GENEROUS SOCIAL BENEFITS IN AN INDUSTRY THAT HAS VERGED ON BANKRUPTCY FOR THE LAST TWENTY YEARS. HE LOOKS AT HOW STATE INTERVENTION HAS RESPONDED TO THE RADICAL-TRANSFORMATIVE RHETORIC OF FRENCH LABOR, THE INSTABILITY OF INDUSTRIAL RELATIONS, AND THE BACKWARDNESS OF FRENCH BUSINESS.

02580 DALEY, T.
AFGHANISTAN AND GORBACHEV'S GLOBAL FOREIGN POLICY
ASIAN SURVEY, 29(5) (MAY 89), 496-513.
THIS ARTICLE USES THE RECENT WITHDRAWAL OF THE USSR FROM AFGHANISTAN AS A CASE STUDY FOR GORBACHEV'S GLOBAL FOREIGN POLICY. IT ANALYSES THE COSTS-AND CONCLUDES THAT THE COSTS OF STAYING IN AFGHANISTAN DID NOT COME TO EXCEED THE COSTS OF OCCUPATION. WHAT CHANGED INSTEAD WAS THE NEW SOVIET LEADERSHIP PERCEPTION OF THE NATURE OF THOSE COSTS THEMSELVES.

02581 DALLAS, M.D.
INTERMEDIATE RANGE NUCLEAR FORCES TREATY: HISTORY OF ILLUSION
AVAILABLE FROM NTIS, NO. AD-A207 373/2/GAR, MAR 89, 32.
THE PURPOSE OF THIS PAPER IS TO EXAMINE THE INTERMEDIATE-RANGE NUCLEAR FORCE (INF) TREATY IN HISTORICAL PERSPECTIVE. THE THESIS OF THE PAPER IS THAT THE TREATY IS AN ILLUSION. IT IS AN ILLUSION THAT PROMOTES THE IDEA THAT SECURITY CAN BE ACHIEVED EXCLUSIVELY THROUGH ARMS CONTROL, AT THE EXPENSE OF BALANCED AND DIVERSE FORCES ACROSS THE ENTIRE SPECTRUM OF DETERRENCE. ALTHOUGH THE TREATY HAS BEEN FULLY RATIFIED, AND U.S. AND SOVIET OFFICIALS HAVE BEGUN THE PROCESS OF DESTROYING LAUNCHERS, DEBATE STILL RAGES IN NATO CAPITALS OVER THE TREAT'S IMPACT ON ALLIANCE SECURITY AND COHESION. THIS PAPER BEGINS WITH A DISCUSSION OF THE EVOLUTION OF NATO'S DETERRENT STRATEGY. IT CONTINUES WITH A CHRONOLOGY OF EVENTS LEADING TO THE SIGNING OF THE TREATY BY PRESIDENT REAGAN AND GENERAL SECRETARY GORBACHEV ON DECEMBER 8, 1987. THE PAPER ASSESSES THE MILITARY AND POLITICAL IMPACT OF THE TREATY AND ENDS WITH POSSIBLE IMPLICATIONS FOR NATO'S FUTURE AND RECOMMENDATIONS FOR FURTHER ARMS CONTROL NEGOTIATIONS. THE PAPER CONCLUDES THAT THE TREATY HAS NOT ACHIEVED WHAT ITS SUPPORTERS CLAIM. IN FACT THE TREATY IS AN ARMS CONTROL AGREEMENT THAT: (1) IS NOT REMOTELY RELATED TO ITS ORIGINAL PURPOSE; (2) HAS REINFORCED NATO MILITARY INFERIORITY; AND (3) MAY HAVE LAID THE GROUNDWORK FOR THE UNRAVELING OF THE ATLANTIC ALLIANCE.

02582 DALLAS, R.
THE LATIN AMERICAN DEBT CRISIS: IS THERE A WAY OUT?
WORLD TODAY, 45(6) (JUN 89), 99-103.
PARTLY BECAUSE OF THEIR FOREIGN DEBTS BUT MAINLY BECAUSE OF THEIR ECONOMIC MISMANAGEMENT, LATIN AMERICA'S NEW DEMOCRACIES ARE BEING ERODED. THE HOPES OF LATIN AMERICA'S ONCE-OPTIMISTIC VOTERS FOR SOCIAL JUSTICE IN THE FORM OF HIGHER WAGES, BETTER EDUCATION AND HEALTH CARE, AND EQUALITY OF OPPORTUNITY REMAIN UNFULFILLED. IT IS ONLY A MATTER OF TIME BEFORE THE VOTERS' DISILLUSION TURNS TO ANGER. ALTHOUGH ELECTED GOVERNMENTS DO NOT FACE IMMINENT COLLAPSE, THEY ARE LIKELY TO BE REPLACED IN FUTURE ELECTIONS BY LEADERS FARTHER TO THE LEFT OR TO THE RIGHT. AND IF THE REPLACEMENTS FAIL TOO, EXTREMISTS OR GENERALS WILL TAKE OVER. AGAINST THIS BACKGROUND, LATIN AMERICAN ECONOMIC POLICY ASSUMES A NEW URGENCY.

02583 DALLY, P.
HONG KONG: FEARS IN LONDON AND PEKING
ASIAN OUTLOOK, 24(1) (JAN 89), 13-16.
THE AUTHOR DISCUSSES THE FEARS THAT ARE PREVALENT IN LONDON AND PEKING AS THE COLONY OF HONG KONG PREPARES TO BE HANDED OVER TO THE CHINESE COMMUNISTS IN 1997.

02584 DALOS, G.
WHAT IS PAMYAT?
ACROSS FRONTIERS, 5(2) (SUM 89), 7-8, 46-47.
THIS ARTICLE, TRANSLATED FROM HUNGARIAN, IS AN APPRAISAL OF THE PROTEST GROUP, PAMYAT (REMEMBRANCE). IT HAS BEEN CHARACTERIZED "AS THE SPIRITUAL COUNTERPART OF THE WESTERN ULTRA-RIGHT." THE PURPOSE OF THE GROUP IS TO PRESERVE RUSSIAN TRADITIONS, OLD TOWNS, NAMES, RIVERS, ICONS, CHURCHE, THE PAST IN GENERAL ETC. IT EXAMINES WHAT LITTLE IS KNOWN ABOUT THIS OBSCURE GROUP, ITS CHALLENGES, PHILOSOPHY, ACTIVITIES, MEMBERSHIP AND GOALS.

02585 DALPE, R.
LES POLITIQUES D'ACHAT EN TANT QU'INSTRUMENT DE DEVELOPPEMENT INDUSTRIEL
CANADIAN PUBLIC ADMINISTRATION, 32(4) (WIN 89), 564-584.
ALONG WITH MOST INDUSTRIALIZED COUNTRIES, CANADIAN GOVERNMENTS HAVE ADOPTED PROCUREMENT POLICIES WITH VARIOUS INDUSTRIAL DEVELOPMENT OBJECTIVES, SUCH AS GROWTH OF SMALL AND MEDIUM SIZE INDUSTRIES, INNOVATION, AND REGIONAL DEVELOPMENT. THE AUTHOR STUDIES USES WHICH GOVERNMENTS HAVE MADE OF THIS INSTRUMENT AND PROBLEMS WITH WHICH THEY HAVE BEEN CONFRONTED. INTEREST GROUPS AND ENTREPRENEURIAL STRATEGIES PLAY AN IMPORTANT ROLE. DUE TO THE WIDE DIVERSITY OF ACTORS, APPLYING PROCUREMENT POLICIES CONSTITUTES A MAJOR COORDINATION CHALLENGE. HOWEVER, SEVERAL PUBLIC BODIES WITH LARGE BUYING POWERS DO NOT HAVE ESTABLISHED PROCUREMENT POLICIES. FINALLY, A MORE WIDE OPEN ECONOMY FORCES BOTH INDUSTRIES AND GOVERNMENTS TO ADOPT NEW PERSPECTIVES.

02586 DALY, J.
CAUTION LIGHTS
MACLEAN'S (CANADA'S NEWS MAGAZINE), 102(2) (JAN 89), 27.
WHEN CONFRONTED WITH THE ECONOMIC FUTURE OF NORTH AMERICA, MOST ECONOMIC FORECASTERS PREDICT SLOW GROWTH AT BEST IN THE COMING YEARS. THE SPECTER OF HIGH INTEREST RATES AND SLOWER GROWTH IN AMERICA HAS LED MOST ECONOMISTS TO PREDICT THAT CANADA'S SO-CALLED REAL GROSS DOMESTIC PRODUCT WILL GROW ABOUT 2.3 PER CENT IN 1989. AT THE SAME TIME, GOVERNMENT ATTEMPTS TO CONTROL INFLATION WILL LIKELY INCREASE INTEREST RATES. MOST FORECASTERS PREDICT THAT IF A RECESSION OCCURS IN 1990, ONTARIO'S MANUFACTURING AND RESOURCE BASED ECONOMY WILL BE THE HARDEST HIT.

02587 DALY, J.; JENISH, D.
ON THE DENFENSIVE
MACLEAN'S (CANADA'S NEWS MAGAZINE), 102(27) (JUL 89), 36.
CANADIAN FINANCE MINISTER MICHAEL WILSON'S DECISION TO CANCEL A PLAN TO BUY AS MANY AS 12 NUCLEAR SUBMARINES AND TO SLASH $2.74 BILLION FROM PLANNED MILITARY SPENDING OVER THE NEXT FIVE YEARS HAS LEFT CANADA'S DEFENSIVE INDUSTRY IN TURMOIL. FEARS OF LARGE AND LONG-LASTING DAMAGE TO THE PRIVATE SECTOR INDUSTRIES ARE INCREASING. SOME PREDICT THAT CANADA'S DEFENSIVE INDUSTRY MIGHT BE TIPPED DOWN A MUCH SLOWER--AND ULTIMATELY MORE PAINFUL--ROAD TO OBLIVION.

02588 DAMGAARD, E.; SVENSSON, P.
WHO GOVERNS? PARTIES AND POLICIES IN DENMARK
EUROPEAN JOURNAL OF POLITICAL RESEARCH, 17(6) (NOV 89), 731-745.
THE LITERATURE ON PARTY GOVERNMENT, COALITION FORMATION, AND LINKS BETWEEN PARTY AND POLICY TENDS TO ASSUME THAT PARTIES IN GOVERNMENT COMMAND LEGISLATIVE MAJORITIES THAT CAN BE USED TO ENACT DESIRED POLICIES. THIS ASSUMPTION, HOWEVER, DOES NOT APPLY IN GENERAL. IN SCANDINAVIA, AND ESPECIALLY IN DENMARK, THE MINORITY TYPE OF GOVERNMENT IS PREDOMINANT. MINORITY GOVERNMENTS CANNOT GOVERN BY MEANS OF THEIR OWN VOTES. TWO QUESTIONS FOR RESEARCH ARE THEREFORE OBVIOUS. WHY DO SCANDINAVIAN COUNTRIES DEVIATE FROM THE NORMAL PATTERN OF GOVERNMENT FORMATION? AND WHAT ARE THE CONSEQUENCES OF MINORITY GOVERNMENT FOR POLICY MAKING? WHILE THE FIRST QUESTION HAS BEEN TREATED IN RECENT RESEARCH, THIS PAPER CARRIES THE ANALYSIS A STEP FURTHER BY EXPLORING THE POLICY CONSEQUENCES OF MINORITY GOVERNMENT IN DENMARK DURING

THE 1980S. IT IS SHOWN THAT THE GOVERNMENT MAY IN FACT NOT ALWAYS GOVERN, THAT THE GOVERNMENT MAY ACTUALLY BE THE OPPOSITION, AND, CONSEQUENTLY, THAT THE PARTY-POLICY LINK CAN INDEED BE EXTREMELY COMPLEX.

02589 DAMODARAN, N.
INFLUENCE OF PROXY ATTRIBUTES ON MULTI-ATTRIBUTE DECISION ANALYSIS: AN EMPIRICAL INVESTIGATION IN THE CONTEXT OF AIR POLLUTION CONTROL
DISSERTATION ABSTRACTS INTERNATIONAL, 50(6) (DEC 89), 1799-A.
THREE SEPARATE STUDIES IN DECISION ANALYSIS WERE CONDUCTED IN THE CONTEXT OF AIR POLLUTION CONTROL WHEREIN THE PREFERENCES OF INFORMED SUBJECTS WERE INDIVIDUALLY ASSESSED. THE FIRST STUDY DEVELOPED A DECISION MODEL FOR THE CONTROL OF SULFUR DIOXIDE EMISSIONS BY INCORPORATING MULTI-MEDIA EFFECTS OF POLLUTION CONTROL USING BOTH FUNDAMENTAL AND PROXY ATTRIBUTES. THE SECOND STUDY COMPARED FUNDAMENTAL AND PROXY ATTRIBUTES AND TESTED THE HYPOTHESIS THAT PROXY ATTRIBUTES LEAD TO BIASED DECISIONS. THE THIRD STUDY VALIDATED THE RESULTS OF THE PREVIOUS ONE AND WAS EXTENDED TO EXAMINE THE HYPOTHESIS THAT PROXY BIAS COULD BE REDUCED BY APPROPRIATE ELICITATION TECHNIQUES.

02590 DAMUSIS, G.
VIKTORAS PETKUS: LITHUANIAN PATRIOT AND UKRAINIAN HELSINKI MONITORING GROUP MEMBER
UKRANIAN QUARTERLY, XLV(1) (SPR 89), 62-65.
VIKTORAS PETKUS REPRESENTS THE MAIN CURRENT OF LITHUANIAN DISSENT AGAINST THE SOVIET GOVERNMENT. HE WAS FIRST IMPRISONED IN THE POST-WORLD WAR II PERIOD AND WAS ONE OF THE FOUNDING MEMBERS OF THE LITHUANIAN HELSINKI GROUP. PETKUS HAS BEEN ESPECIALLY EAGER TO FOSTER FRIENDSHIP AND COOPERATION AMONG THE BALTS. THE LITHUANIAN HELSINKI GROUP HAS PUBLISHED A NUMBER OF DOCUMENTS ABOUT VIOLATIONS OF HUMAN RIGHTS IN ESTONIA AND LATVIA, AND PETKUS HAS TRIED TO CREATE MORE FORMAL TIES AMONG THE BALTS.

02591 DANDURAND, R. B.; KEMPENEERS, M.; LE BOURDAIS, C.
WHAT FAMILY SUPPORT?
POLICY OPTIONS, 10(2) (MAR 89), 26-29.
A CAREFUL EXAMINATION OF THE DETAILS OF THE 1988-89 BUDGET, UNDERTAKEN BY THREE AUTHORS REPRESENTING LE GROUPE DE REFLEXION ET D'INTERVENTION SUR LES POLITIQUES SOCIALES (GRIPS) SHOWS THAT THERE IS VERY MUCH LESS TO THE BUDGET THAN MEETS THE EYE. IN FACT, MOST OF THE NEW STEPS MERELY RESTORE TO FAMILIES WHAT HAS BEEN TAKEN AWAY IN PREVIOUS BUDGETS. FOR EXAMPLE, THE NEW FAMILY ALLOWANCES MERELY RESTORE THE SITUATION TO THAT OF 1986. A BUDGET BASED ON THE SHORT VIEW AND AIMED AT VOTES RATHER THAN PRINCIPLES IS NOT GOOD ENOUGH. ONLY A POLICY AIMED AT THE MODERN FAMILY, AND ORIENTED TOWARDS THE QUALITY OF LIFE OF ALL SORTS OF FAMILIES, IS WORTHHHHILE, AND THAT APPROACH IS YET TO COME.

02592 DANESHKHU, S.
A PORTRAIT OF RAFSANJANI
MIDDLE EAST INTERNATIONAL, (357) (AUG 89), 16-18.
THE ARTICLE BRIEFLY EXAMINES THE EVENTS THAT SHAPED THE LIFE AND VIEHS OF IRAN'S NEW PRESIDENT, ALI AKBAR HASHEMI RAFSANJANI. IT CONCLUDES THAT THE PRESIDENT PRESENTS A RATHER UNIQUE COMBINATION OF RELIGIOUS AND SECULAR MATTERS, OF EXTREMISM AND PRAGMATISM, AND OF AUTHORITARIANISM AND TEAMWORK. HE IS DESTINED TO BE ONE OF IRAN'S MOST POWERFUL LEADERS, AND WILL LIKELY MOVE IRAN ON THE PATH TOWARDS (RELATIVE) POLITICAL AND ECONOMIC MODERATION.

02593 DANESHKHU, S.
IRAN AFTER KHOMEINI: THE POLITICAL AND ECONOMIC DIMENSIONS
MIDDLE EAST INTERNATIONAL, 353 (JUN 89), 15-16.
THE POST-KHOMEINI ERA, LONG PREDICTED TO BE A PERIOD OF FACTIONAL INFIGHTING, EVEN CIVIL WAR, IN FACT SEEMS TO BE MOVING ALONG WITH INCREDIBLE FLUIDITY. BUT THE LAST TEN YEARS HAVE SHOWN HOW UNPREDICTABLE IRANIAN POLITICS CAN BE, MAKING ANY INSTANT CONCLUSIONS BOTH RISKY AND PREMATURE. WHILE THE PRAGMATISTS, IN THE SHAPE OF THE NEW LEADER AND PRESIDENT, ALI KHAMENEI AND THE SPEAKER OF THE MAJLIS, HOJATOLESLAM ALI AKBAR HASHEMI RAFSANJANI, APPEAR TO HAVE SEHN THINGS UP BETWEEN THEM, THEY FACE A NUMBER OF FORMIDABLE HURDLES IN THE MONTHS TO COME.

02594 DANESHKHU, S.
IRAN'S TEN YEARS OF REVOLUTION: ACHIEVEMENTS AND FAILURES
MIDDLE EAST INTERNATIONAL, (343) (FEB 89), 15-16.
THE MAIN ACHIEVEMENT OF THE ISLAMIC GOVERNMENT HAS BEEN TO SECURE TWO MAJOR OBJECTIVES OF THE REVOLUTION: THE REMOVAL OF THE SHAH AND AN END TO WESTERN INFLUENCE. OTHER AREAS OF PROGRESS INCLUDE BUILDING NEW ROADS, COPING WITH THE HUGE INFLUX OF AFGHAN AND IRAQI REFUGEES, AND EXPANDING THE DEFENSE INDUSTRIES. AGRICULTURE AND ECONOMIC POLICY ARE TWO AREAS OF MAJOR PROBLEMS FOR IRAN'S LEADERS.

02595 DANESHKHU, S.
RAFSANJANI'S CABINET
MIDDLE EAST INTERNATIONAL, (357) (AUG 89), 12-13.

IRAN'S NEWLY ELECTED PRESIDENT, ALI AKBAR HASHEMI RAFSANJANI, MOVED QUICKLY TO PUT IRAN ON THE PATH TO POLITICAL AND ECONOMIC INDEPENDENCE. ONE OF HIS FIRST ACTS WAS A PROPOSAL FOR A SIGNIFICANT CABINET RESHUFFLE. IF RAFSANJANI'S CABINET IS APPROVED, IT WILL BE CONCRETE PROOF OF HIS DESIRE TO RULE IRAN FROM A POSITION OF COMPETENCE RATHER THAN IDEOLOGY. HOWEVER, HARD-LINERS IN IRAN STILL WIELD SIGNIFICANT POWER AND PLAN TO OPPOSE SOME OF RAFSANJANI'S NOMINATIONS. IN ORDER TO SUCCEED, THE PRESIDENT WILL HAVE TO WALK A VERY THIN LINE BETWEEN TRADITIONAL EXTREMISM AND PRAGMATIC MODERATION.

02596 DANFAKA, M.
ON THE ROAD TO MARXIST UNITY
WORLD MARXIST REVIEW, 32(9) (SEP 89), 49-51.
THIS IS AN ARTICLE GIVING COVERAGE TO COMMUNIST PARTY SPLITS. IT LOOKS AT THE REASONS AND REMEDIES FOR NATIONAL COMMUNIST DISUNITY. IT EXAMINES THE ORIGNS OF THE DISUNITY WHICH STEMS FROM THE DIFFICULTIES EXPERIENCED DURING THE 1960S. IT EXAMINES THE SITUATION IN SENGEL AND INVISIONS THE KIND OF FUTURE HOPED FOR. IT CALLS FOR A UNIFICATION OF ALL DEMOCRATIC FORCES ON A NATIONAL AND WORLD SCALE, INCLUDING THOSE OUTSIDE THE MARXIST TENDENCY.

02597 DANIELS, A.
CURTAIN STILL DOWN
NATIONAL REVIEW, 61(24) (DEC 89), 21-23.
ANTHONY DANIELS PONDERS THE SCARS NICOLAE CEAUSESCU CONTINUES TO SEAR INTO THE RUMANIAN PSYCHE. HE CONCLUDES THAT THE CAUSE OF FEAR THERE IS DEEP IN MARXIST-LENINIST IDEOLOGY, WHICH DISTORTS AND DEFORMS HUMAN LIFE WHEREVER IT IS IMPOSED, THANKS TO ITS UNPRECEDENTED ASSAULT ON HUMAN LANGUAGE AND THOUGHT ITSELF. HE CONTRASTS THE STATE IMPOSED TRIBUTES TO CEAUSESCU WITH THE PRESENTED BY OBSERVING DAILY LIFE IN RUMANIA THAT ALL IS NOT WELL THERE HE ALSO EXAMINES THE CONTRADICTIONS IN RUMANIAN SOCIETY.

02598 DANIELS, A.
PEOPLE'S DEMOCRATIC REVUE
NATIONAL REVIEW, XLI(16) (SEP 89), 19-20.
THE AUTHOR REPORTS ON COMMUNISM'S CRUELEST YOKE-THE DEMOCRATIC PEOPLE'S REPUBLIC OF KIM IL-SUNGIA, ON NORTH KOREA. NORTH KOREA IS A FASCIST STATE IN ALMOST PURE FORM AND LEADER KIM SL-SUNG'S TYRANNY ENSURES THAT HUNGER AND POVERTY COULD VERY WELL LAST FOREVER.

02599 DANIELS, P.
THE ITALIAN COMMUNIST PARTY AND THE EUROPEAN PARLIAMENT ELECTIONS OF JUNE 1989
JOURNAL OF COMMUNIST STUDIES, 5(4) (DEC 89), 195-199.
THE 1989 ELECTIONS TO THE EUROPEAN PARLIAMENT (EP) PROVIDED THE ITALIAN COMMUNIST PARTY (PCI) WITH ITS FIRST MAJOR ELECTORAL TEST SINCE ACHILLE OCCHETTO BECAME PARTY SECRETARY IN JUNE 1988. THIS ARTICLE DETAILS THE ELECTION CAMPAIGN AND ITS RESULTS. IT CONCLUDES THAT IT IS STILL TOO EARLY TO SAY WHETHER THE PCL'S ENCOURAGING RESULT IN THE EP ELECTION SIGNALS A LONGER TERM RECOVERY IN ITS ELECTORAL POSITION, BUT THAT THE RESULT DOES REPRESENT A SIGNIFICANT BOOST TO PARTY CONFIDENCE AND STRENGTHENS OCCHETTO IN HIS EFFORTS TO REFORM AND REVITALIZE THE PARTY.

02600 DANILENKO, G.M.
INTERNATIONAL LAW-MAKING FOR OUTER SPACE
SPACE POLICY, 5(4) (NOV 89), 321-329.
WHILE THE NEED FOR ADEQUATE SPACE LAW MAY BE AS URGENT AS EVER, THE INTERNATIONAL COMMUNITY HAS DISCOVERED THAT TODAY IT IS INCREASINGLY DIFFICULT TO REACH CONCENSUS ON STATUES TO GOVERN NEW SPACE ACTIVITIES IN VIEW OF THE NOTICEABLE SLOWDOWN IN THE LAW MAKING PROCESS. SERIOUS DISCUSSIONS ABOUT THE MOST SUITABLE AND EFFECTIVE TECHNIQUES OF SPACE LEGISLATION ARE REQUIRED. THE AUTHOR DISCUSSES THE POLITICAL AND LEGAL PROBLEMS OF MAKING LAWS TO DEAL WITH SPACE AND SPACE ACTIVITIES. A NUMBER OF SUGGESTIONS AIMED AT IMPROVING THE PRESENT LEGISLATIVE PROCESS ARE FORMULATED.

02601 DANOPOULOS, C.P.
DEMOCRATIC UNDERCURRENTS IN PRAETORIAN REGIMES: THE GREEK MILITARY AND THE 1973 PLEBISCITE
JOURNAL OF STRATEGIC STUDIES, 12(3) (SEP 89), 349-368.
THE AUTHOR IDENTIFIES AND DISCUSSES THE REASONS THAT PROMPTED THE AUTHORITARIAN JUNTA, AS THE GREEK MILITARY GOVERNMENT BECAME KNOWN, TO ABOLISH THE MONARCHY AND HAVE ITS DECISION CONFIRMED BY A PLEBISCITE IN 1973. HE ALSO ANALYZES HOW AN ALLEGED 78.4 PERCENT APPROVAL OF THE REGIME'S POSITION LED TO DESTABILIZATION AND CONTRIBUTED TO ITS DEMISE IN JULY 1974. IN ORDER TO BETTER UNDERSTAND THE EVENTS SURROUNDING THE PLEBISCITE AND THE LATTER'S DESTRUCTIVE ROLE, HE BRIEFLY EXAMINES CIVIL-MILITARY RELATIONS IN GREECE.

02602 DAODING, J.
LDP'S DOMINATION ENDS WITH POLL LOSSES
BEIJING REVIEW, 32(33) (AUG 89), 16-17.
IN JULY 1989, JAPAN'S LIBERAL DEMOCRATIC PARTY LOST ITS

MAJORITY IN THE UPPER HOUSE OF THE DIET FOR THE FIRST TIME
SINCE IT WAS FOUNDED IN 1955. THE CRUSHING DEFEAT WAS
ATTRIBUTED TO ITS CORRUPT MONEY POLITICS AND THE RESULTANT
LOSS OF THE PEOPLE'S CONFIDENCE.

02603 DARAWSHE, A.W.
INTERVIEW: ABDEL WAHAB DARAWSHE
AMERICAN-ARAB AFFAIRS, (30) (FAL 89), 36-39.
THIS IS AN INTERVIEW WITH KNESSET MEMBER DARAWSHE,
FOUNDER OF THE DEMOCRATIC ARAB PARTY, AND SPOKESMAN IN THE
ISRAELI PARLIMENT FOR THE PALESTINIAN ARABS UNDER ISRAELI
OCCUPATION AS WELL AS THE PALESTINIANS INSIDE ISRAEL WHO ARE
STRUGGLING FOR EQUALITY. HE GIVES HIS ASSESSMENT OF PRESENT
PALESTINIAN-ISRAELI RELATIONS IN LIGHT OF THE POLITICAL
MOVEMENT IN THE AREA, AND HIS POSITION TOWARD THE SO-CALLED
SHAMIR PEACE PLAN. HE EXPLAINS THE MAIN PROBLEMS FACING THE
PALESTINIAN PEOPLE INSIDE ISRAEL AND EXPLAINS HIS ROLE IN
THE PEACE PROCESS.

02604 DARCY, R.; SCHNEIDER, A.
CONFUSING BALLOTS, ROLL-OFF, AND THE BLACK VOTE
WESTERN POLITICAL QUARTERLY, 42(3) (SEP 89), 347-364.
AN ANALYSIS OF THE VARIOUS BALLOTS USED IN THE 1986
OKLAHOMA GENERAL ELECTION SHOWS THAT SOME BALLOT FORMATS ARE
MORE CONFUSING THAN OTHERS. THE CONFUSING BALLOTS CAUSE
INCREASED VOTER ROLL-OFF EVEN IN HIGHLY SALIENT CONTESTS,
SUCH AS FOR THE UNITED STATES SENATE. FURTHERMORE, THERE IS
AN INTERACTION BETWEEN CONFUSING BALLOTS AND THE VOTER'S
RACE. PRECINCTS WITH GREATER PROPORTIONS OF BLACK CITIZENS
ARE ESPECIALLY IMPACTED BY CONFUSING BALLOT ARRANGEMENTS, AS
ARE PRECINCTS WITH A LARGER PROPORTION OF OLDER CITIZENS. IT
IS PARTICULARLY TROUBLESOME THAT COMMONLY USED BALLOT
FORMATS APPEAR TO DIMINISH THE CONSTITUTIONALLY PROTECTED
VOTE OF BLACK PERSONS.

02605 DARNELL, L.J.
EAST ASIA: A STRATEGIC APPRAISAL OF THE REGION, SOVIET
STRATEGY AND THE U.S. POSTURE
AVAILABLE FROM NTIS, NO. AD-A208 009/1/GAR, APR 89, 60.
DURING THE PAST 20 YEARS, EAST ASIA HAS BECOME A POWER
IN WORLD AFFAIRS PROPORTIONATE TO ITS VAST SIZE AND
POPULATION. AS THE UNITED STATES AND THE SOVIET UNION
CONTINUE THEIR GLOBAL COMPETITION, AMERICAN LEADERS MUST
APPRECIATE THE REGION'S IMPORTANCE AND UNDERSTAND GENERAL
SECRETARY AND PRESIDENT MIKHAIL GORBACHEV'S STRATEGY. GIVEN
THE VITAL IMPORTANCE OF ASIA, THERE IS A NEED FOR THE UNITED
STATES TO REASSESS ITS APPROACH TO THE ASIAN-PACIFIC REGION.
THE PURPOSE OF THIS STUDY IS TO BEGIN THAT EXTRAORDINARILY
IMPORTANT PROCESS. THE STUDY EXAMINES HOW THE EAST ASIAN
NATIONS INFLUENCE THE REST OF THE WORLD. IT EXPLORES HOW THE
SOVIETS HAVE BEEN SUCCESSFULLY IMPLEMENTING THEIR STRATEGY
IN TERMS OF MILITARY, SOCIO-PSYCHOLOGICAL, POLITICAL, AND
ECONOMIC POWER. THE STUDY IDENTIFIES UNITED STATES' VITAL
INTERESTS IN THE REGION AND US POSTURE RELATIVE TO THOSE
INTERESTS. FINALLY, THE CURRENT US STRATEGIC OBJECTIVES ARE
IDENTIFIED AND RECOMMENDED INITIATIVES ARE PRESENTED.

02606 DARNELL, T.
KEEP AMERICA MOVING: CATCH-22 ON WHEELS
AMERICAN CITY AND COUNTY, 104(2) (FEB 89), 30-39.
IF THE FEDERAL COMMITMENT TO SURFACE TRANSPORTATION
CONTINUES TO DIMINISH, AMERICAN CITIES AND COUNTIES WILL
HAVE TO DEVELOP NEW AND EFFECTIVE WAYS TO BUILD
TRANSPORTATION SYSTEMS AND MAINTAIN THE ONES ALREADY IN
PLACE. SURFACE TRAVEL IS EXPECTED TO DOUBLE BY THE YEAR 2020.
FEDERAL, STATE, AND LOCAL GOVERNMENTS MUST INVEST AT LEAST
$95 BILLION ANNUALLY TO MAINTAIN HIGHWAYS, LOCAL ROADS, AND
PUBLIC TRANSIT SERVICES.

02607 DARNELL, T.
KEEPING FAITH, WORKING HARD
AMERICAN CITY AND COUNTY, 104(11) (NOV 89), 54-56, 58, 60,
62.
THE AUTHOR PRESENTS A PROFILE OF ANDREW YOUNG AND
REVIEWS SOME OF YOUNG'S ACHIEVEMENTS AS MAYOR OF ATLANTA,
GEORGIA.

02608 DARNELL, T.
LOCAL GOVERNMENTS STANDING ON THEIR OWN
AMERICAN CITY AND COUNTY, 104(5) (MAY 89), PF2-PF4.
A SURVEY OF LOCAL GOVERNMENT OFFICIALS FOUND THAT ABOUT
SIXTY-THREE PERCENT OF LOCAL GOVERNMENTS ARE EITHER LESS
DEPENDENT OR NO MORE DEPENDENT ON STATE AID NOW THAN THEY
WERE BEFORE THE RECENT FEDERAL CUTBACKS. MOST SURVEY
RESPONDENTS ALSO INDICATED THAT THEY ANTICIPATE NO DRASTIC
CHANGE IN FEDERAL RESPONSIVENESS TO LOCAL FISCAL CONCERNS
UNDER GEORGE BUSH. THE SURVEY COVERED A VARIETY OF ISSUES
CONCERNING THE FEDERAL DEFICIT, TAXATION, AND PUBLIC FINANCE.

02609 DARSHINI, P.
INDIA: "EVE-TEASING"
THIRD WORLD WEEK, 8(3) (MAR 89), 11-12.
THE INDIAN GOVERNMENT IS CRACKING DOWN ON THE GROWING
MENACE OF SEXUAL HARASSMENT, WHICH IS CALLED "EVE-TEASING."

THE GOVERNMENT HAS ACTED AGAINST EVE-TEASING IN THE PAST BUT
THIS TIME, IN ORDER TO SHOW THAT IT MEANS BUSINESS, IT HAS
INTRODUCED A PUNITIVE BILL IN PARLIAMENT.

02610 DASH - YONDON, B.
KEEPING ALIVE THE SPIRIT OF INNOVATION
WORLD MARXIST REVIEW, 31(10) (OCT 88), 54-58.
THE MONGOLIAN PEOPLE'S REVOLUTIONARY PARTY'S MAIN TASK
IN SOLVING THE PRESENT PROBLEMS IS TO IDENTIFY THE CAUSES OF
THE STAGNATION, TO EXTIRPATE THEM BOLDLY AND MASTER THE NEW
THINKING. IT IS IMPERATIVE THAT THE PARTY RENOUNCE THE
MENTALITY OF PASSIVENESS AND INDIFFERENCE PRODUCED BY THE
ADMINISTRATIVE-COMMAND METHODS, THE GREAT DEPENDENCE ON THE
VAGARIES OF THE CLIMATE AND AGE-OLD RELIGIOUS CANONS.

02611 DASH, J.N.
UDAYACHAL MOVEMENT IN ASSAM: A CASE OF SOCIOPOLITICAL
IDENTITY FOR THE BOROS
INDIAN JOURNAL OF POLITICAL SCIENCE, L(3) (JUL 89),
335-342.
THE BODOS IN ASSAM ARE AGITATING FOR THEIR SEPARATE
IDENTITY AND DISTINCT POSITION IN THE NATIONAL LIFE OF INDIA.
STARTING AS A SOCIO-CULTURAL AND ECONOMIC MOVEMENT WITHIN
THE BODO-KACHARI TRIBE IN THE NORTHERN PARTS OF THREE
DISTRICTS WITHIN ASSAM, THE MOVEMENT ORIGINALLY HAD THE
AVOWED GOAL OF IMPROVING THE CULTURAL, ECONOMIC, AND
POLITICAL STATUS OF THE BODO PEOPLE. NOW IT HAS DEVELOPED
INTO A SOCIO-POLITICAL MOVEMENT DEMANDING A SEPARATE STATE
TO BE KNOWN AS "UDAYACHAL."

02612 DASILVA, M.
UNRULY SCHOOLBOYS
FAR EASTERN ECONOMIC REVIEW, 141(27) (JUL 88), 32-33.
THE ANTI-GOVERNMENT RESISTANCE IN SRI LANKA TOOK A NEW
TURN AS THE REBELS ARE ACCUSED OF USING SCHOOL CHILDREN TO
HARASS POLICE AND GOVERNMENT OFFICIALS AND TO ACHIEVE
POLITICAL RESULTS. THE GOVERNMENT HAS ALREADY CLOSED THE
UNIVERSITIES DUE TO THE ACTIONS OF ACTIVIST STUDENTS, BUT
CURRENTLY SEEM TO BE AT A LOSS OF HOW TO HANDLE THE YOUNGER
GROUPS. PRESSURE TO REOPEN THE UNIVERSITIES AND RELEASE
IMPRISONED ACTIVIST STUDENTS HAVE AS OF YET NOT BORNE FRUIT.

02613 DASSU, M.
GORBACHEV AND THE PACIFIC REGION
INTERNATIONAL SPECTATOR, XXIII(3) (JUL 88), 160-173.
UNLIKE THE PAST, THE SOVIET UNION'S SPHERE OF INTEREST
TODAY SEEMS TO ENCOMPASS THE ENTIRE ASIAN PACIFIC REGION.
THE PURPOSE OF THIS ESSAY IS TO DESCRIBE THE CHARACTERISTICS
OF THIS NEW PHASE IN THE SOVIETS' ASIAN POLICY AND TO
CLARIFY THE EXTENT TO WHICH THE CURRENT POLICY MARKS A
DEPARTURE FROM THE PAST.

02614 DATTA, P.K.
POLITICAL SCIENCE IN INDIA: AN ENQUIRY INTO THE PRESENT
STATE OF THE DISCIPLINE
INDIAN JOURNAL OF POLITICAL SCIENCE, L(2) (APR 89),
272-280.
THE AUTHOR TAKES STOCK OF THE STATE OF POLITICAL SCIENCE
KNOWLEDGE IN POST-INDEPENDENCE INDIA AND EXAMINES ITS
RELEVANCE TO THE UNDERSTANDING OF CONTEMPORARY REALITY.

02615 DAVALOS, R.M.
ORGANIZATIONAL CHANGE IN A PUBLIC BUREAUCRACY
DISSERTATION ABSTRACTS INTERNATIONAL, 49(7) (JAN 89),
1955-A.
THE REQUIREMENT THAT ALL DECISIONS MUST ULTIMATELY
ACCOUNT TO SOME POLITICAL PHILOSOPHY IS UNIQUE TO THE PUBLIC
BUREAUCRACY. THE INTENSITY OF THIS POLITICAL INFLUENCE
DETERMINES, TO A GREAT EXTENT, THE STRATEGY AND RATE OF
CHANGE. THIS STUDY EXPLORES HOW THE DESIRES AND EXPECTATIONS
OF ELECTED OFFICIALS EFFECTIVELY LIMIT THE ALTERNATIVES OF
THOSE CHARGED WITH IMPLEMENTING ORGANIZATIONAL CHANGE.

02616 DAVE, R.B.
FROM ECOCRISIS TO ECODEVELOPMENT: MICRO-LEVEL
ENVIRONMENTAL MOVEMENTS IN INDIA
DISSERTATION ABSTRACTS INTERNATIONAL, 50(3) (SEP 89),
783-A.
THE MODERNIZATION APPROACH TO DEVELOPMENT BASED ON A
CONSTANTLY INCREASING USE OF ENERGY, INDUSTRIAL TECHNOLOGIES,
HIGHLY-MECHANIZED AGRICULTURE, AND UNCHECKED GROWTH HAS
CREATED BOTH SOCIAL AND ECOLOGICAL PATHOLOGIES. IN RESPONSE
TO THIS ENVIRONMENTAL-DEVELOPMENTAL CRISIS, THREE
ECODEVELOPMENT APPROACHES HAVE ARISEN: THE ECOPOLITICAL
ECONOMY, THE ECODEVELOPMENT APPROACH TO DEVELOPMENT, AND THE
GANDHIAN APPROACH TO DEVELOPMENT. THIS DISSERTATION EXAMINES
AND COMPARES THE ORIGINS, THEORETICAL FOUNDATIONS, AND ECO-
ALTERNATIVES OF THESE APPROACHES. IT ALSO ANALYZES THREE
CASE STUDIES FROM INDIA.

02617 DAVENPORT, M.
THE CASE FOR A RADICAL SOLUTION
SOUTH, (101) (MAR 89), 16-17.
THE MONTREAL TRADE SUMMIT MAY HAVE FAILED IN BROAD TERMS,

BUT THE EUROPEAN COMMUNITY, THE USA, AND JAPAN DID REACH AN AGREEMENT TO REDUCE BARRIERS ON US$25 BILLION OF TROPICAL AGRICULTURAL PRODUCTS FROM THE THIRD WORLD. EXACTLY HOW THE AGREEMENT WILL BE IMPLEMENTED, AND WHEN, IS UNCLEAR. THE USA AND THE EC HAVE INDICATED THAT THEY WILL WAIT UNTIL MORE PROGRESS IS MADE IN THE WIDER TRADE TALKS OF THE URUGUAY ROUND. BUT THE JAPANESE SAY THEY WILL GO AHEAD.

02618 DAVID ET ERIC GHYSELS, J.-F.
ARE BIASES PREDICTABLE AT THE TIME BUDGET PROJECTIONS ARE ANNOUNCED?
CANADIAN PUBLIC POLICY--ANALYSE DE POLITIQUES, 15(3) (SEP 89), 313-321.
EVERY YEAR THE CANADIAN GOVERNMENT MAKES UP A BUDGET FOR THE FORTHCOMING FISCAL YEAR. DURING THE BUDGET PROCESS, PROJECTIONS ARE MADE OF EXPENDITURES AND RECEIPTS CONTINGENT UPON PREDICTIONS OF KEY MACROECONOMIC VARIABLES. NATURALLY, ONE EXPECTS THAT THE BUDGET DEFICIT OR SURPLUS ACTUALLY REALIZED WILL DIFFER FROM WHAT WAS INITIALLY ANNOUNCED. NEITHER OF THE TWO MAJOR PROTAGONISTS IN THE BUDGET DECISION-MAKING PROCESS, NAMELY THE LEGISLATIVE AND EXECUTIVE BRANCHES OF GOVERNMENT, MAY HAVE AN INTEREST IN USING TRUTHFUL PROJECTIONS, HOWEVER. THE THE PURPOSE OF THE PAPER IS TO FIND EMPIRICAL REGULARITIES. IT IS FOUND THAT 1/ THE DIFFERENCE BETWEEN PROJECTED AND REALIZED BUDGETS IS SUBSTANTIAL; AND 2/ THAT THE DIFFERENCES ARE SYSTEMATICALLY RELATED TO PUBLICLY AVAILABLE INFORMATION AT THE TIME OF THE BUDGET ANNOUNCEMENT. THE PUBLICLY AVAILABLE INFORMATION CONTAINS KEY MACROECONOMIC VARIABLES RELATED TO THE ELECTORAL AND LEGISLATIVE PROCESS. IT IS SHOWN THAT THE BIASES ARE FAIRLY PREDICTABLE AT THE TIME BUDGET PROJECTIONS ARE ANNOUNCED.

02619 DAVID, C.D.
THE THEORY OF THE CULT OF THE OFFENSIVE AND THE CONCEPTUALIZATION OF STRATEGIC CHOICES
ETUDES INTERNATIONALES, 20(3) (SEP 89), 601-624.
THE THEORY OF THE CULT OF THE OFFENSIVE CLEARLY STANDS OUT AMONG THE MOST RECENT WORKS BEING CONDUCTED IN STRATEGIC STUDIES. THE AIM OF THIS ARTICLE IS TO BETTER UNDERSTAND THIS NEW THEORETICAL CONTRIBUTION BY LOOKING AT ITS STRENGTHS AND WEAKNESSES, AND BY APPLYING IT TO THE CASE OF THE EVOLVING AMERICAN NAVAL STRATEGY. THE CENTRAL ELEMENTS OF THIS APPROACH WILL BE ANALYSED IN ORDER TO EXPLAIN THE SIGNIFICANT GROWTH THAT THE AMERICAN NAVY HAS EXPERIENCED SINCE THE START OF THE 1980S. IN THIS MANNER, IT WILL BE POSSIBLE TO PERCEIVE AS MUCH THE APPLICABILITY OF THIS THEORY AS THE RELEVANCE OF THE CASE STUDY, TO SHOW THE VALUE OF STRATEGIC STUDIES AS A FIELD WHICH SEEKS A GREATER UNDERSTANDING OF STRATEGIC CHOICES.

02620 DAVID, C.P.
THE CRISIS IN STRATEGIC STUDIES
ETUDES INTERNATIONALES, 20(3) (SEP 89), 503-515.
THE YOUNG FIELD OF STRATEGIC STUDIES HAS DIFFICULTIES ESTABLISHING A SOLID CONSENSUS ON ITS PURPOSE, BASIC PHILOSOPHY AND MAIN CONCEPTS, BECAUSE THE DEFINITIONS AND MEANINGS GIVEN TO THE NATURE OF RESEARCH IN THAT FIELD ARE LARGELY CONTROVERSIAL. STRATEGISTS HAVE SERIOUS PROBLEMS IN ADDRESSING THE CRITICISMS THAT ARE MADE OF THE FUNDAMENTAL ASSUMPTIONS AND THEORIES THAT UNDERLINE STRATEGIC STUDIES. THIS PAPER EXPLORES THE CAUSES AND IMPLICATIONS OF A CRISIS WHICH NOW PERMEATES HEAVILY THE DEVELOPMENT OF THE FIELD.

02621 DAVID, S. R.
WHY THE THIRD WORLD MATTERS
INTERNATIONAL SECURITY, 14(1) (SUM 89), 50-85.
THIS ARTICLE CONTENDS THAT THE THIRD WORLD IS CENTRAL TO U.S. INTERESTS, AND MAKES THE CASE FOR CONTINUING U.S. INVOLVEMENT THERE. THE AUTHOR RECOGNIZES THAT DEFENDING WESTERN EUROPE AND JAPAN IS A KEY U.S. STRATEGIC OBJECTIVE, BUT HE ARGUES THAT THE PROBABILITY OF COMBAT AND THE POTENTIAL THREATS TO U.S. INTERESTS ARE ALSO GREAT—PERHAPS GREATER-IN THE THIRD WORLD. MANY THIRD WORLD REGIMES ARE UNSTABLE AND MOST POST-1945 CONFLICTS HAVE TAKEN PLACE IN THE THIRD WORLD. U.S. ECONOMIC STAKES IN THE THIRD WORLD ARE NOT LIMITED TO THE PERSIAN GULF; STRATEGIC MINERALS ARE FOUND IN MANY OTHER REGIONS AND U.S. ECONOMIC TIES WITH THE THIRD WORLD CONTINUE TO GROW. AMERICAN PUBLIC CONCERNS ABOUT TERRORISM AND NUCLEAR PROLIFERATION REQUIRE AN ACTIVE U.S. POLICY TOWARD THE THIRD WORLD. THE UNITED STATES, DAVID CONCLUDES, SHOULD AVOID PROTRACTED VIETNAM-LIKE WARS, BUT MUST MAINTAIN THE CAPABILITY TO LAUNCH A MAJOR INTERVENTION THAT CAN ACCOMPLISH ITS GOALS QUICKLY.

02622 DAVIDI, A.
THE ELECTIONS, THE PEACE CAMP, AND THE LEFT
MIDDLE EAST REPORT, 19(157) (MAR 89), 20-21.
THE STEADY DECLINE OF BOTH THE LIKUD AND ALIGNMENT (LABOR) PARTIES IS THE PREDOMINANT TREND IN ISRAELI POLITICS. IN 1988, MORE PEOPLE THAN EVER BEFORE VOTED "NO CONFIDENCE" IN THE MAJOR PARTIES. MANY SUPPORTED FORCES PROPOSING PEACE WITH THE PALESTINIANS OR THOSE ADVOCATING MORE SEVERE REPRESSION.

02623 DAVIDSON, R.H.
MULTIPLE REFERRAL OF LEGISLATION IN THE U.S. SENATE
LEGISLATIVE STUDIES QUARTERLY, 14(3) (AUG 89), 375-392.
A SMALL BUT SIGNIFICANT PORTION OF BILLS AND RESOLUTIONS IN THE U.S. SENATE ARE HANDLED NOT BY THE SINGLE COMMITTEE BUT BY TWO OR MORE COMMITTEES. THE PRACTICE IS OF LONGER STANDING IN THE SENATE THAN IN THE HOUSE OF REPRESENTATIVES, WHICH INSTITUTED MULTIPLE REFERRALS ONLY IN 1975. YET SINCE THE SENATE'S MULTIPLE-REFERRAL RULES WERE BROADENED IN 1977, THE PROPORTION OF MULTIPLY-REFERRED BILLS HAS NOT SOARED, AS IT HAS IN THE HOUSE. NOR HAVE SENATE LEADERS USED THE DEVICE EXTENSIVELY (AS HOUSE LEADERS HAVE) AS A WAY OF ORCHESTRATING AND SCHEDULING COMMITTEE PROCESSING OF HIGH-PRIORITY MEASURES. THIS PAPER DESCRIBES THE SENATE'S USE OF MULTIPLE REFERRALS, USING FIGURES ON OVERALL FREQUENCY OF USE, COMMITTEE VARIATIONS, AND TYPICAL COMMITTEE "PAIRS" IN HANDLING MULTIPLY-REFERRED BILLS. IT EXAMINES THE POLITICS OF INTERCOMMITTEE DELIBERATIONS FROM THE VANTAGE POINT OF THE COMMITTEES AND THE LEADERSHIP. FINALLY, IT SPECULATES ON THE REASONS FOR THE TWO CHAMBERS' CONTRASTING EXPERIENCE WITH MULTIPLE REFERRALS.

02624 DAVIDSON, T.
A TIME OF OPPORTUNITY IN THE MIDDLE EAST
CONTEMPORARY REVIEW, 254(1479) (APR 89), 174-176.
THE OUTLOOK OF PEACE IN THE MIDDLE EAST WILL BE MORE FAVOURABLE OVER THE NEXT TWELVE MONTHS THAN IT HAS EVER BEEN SINCE THE SECOND WORLD WAR. THREE SETS OF CIRCUMSTANCES ARE CONVERGING TO PERMIT A GLIMPSE OF HOPE IN WHAT HAS BEEN A SCENE OF UNRELENTING TRAGEDY FOR MOST OF OUR LIFETIMES. THE FIRST OF THESE FAVOURABLE DEVELOPMENTS IS THE ARRIVAL IN THE WHITE HOUSE OF GEORGE BUSH, WHO WILL EXERCISE MORE PROFESSIONAL LEADERSHIP THAN WE HAVE SEEN FROM WASHINGTON FOR A LONG TIME. THE SECOND NEW FACTOR IS THE ENDING OF THE GULF WAR IN WHICH FOR EIGHT YEARS IRAQ PITTED ITS TECHNICAL SUPERIORITY AGAINST THE VAST HUMAN RESOURCES OF IRAN. THIRDLY, AND THIS IS THE MOST DRAMATIC DEVELOPMENT OF ALL, THE PALESTINE LIBERATION ORGANIZATION (PLO) HAS AT LAST ACKNOWLEDGED THE EXISTENCE OF ISRAEL. PUBLIC OPINION THERE SEEMS TO BE READY TO RECIPROCATE IN SOME MEASURE, ALTHOUGH THE ISRAELI GOVERNMENT IS FAR FROM SHARING THAT VIEW.

02625 DAVIES, B.
BANGKOK ROCKS THE GRAVY BOAT
SOUTH, (108) (OCT 89), 23.
IN THE CONSENSUS-STYLE POLITICS THAT HAVE LONG GOVERNED THAILAND, THERE ARE FEW ISSUES MORE SENSITIVE THAN CHANGE, ESPECIALLY WHEN IT AFFECTS THE PROTECTED BANKING SYSTEM. NOT SURPRISINGLY, THERE WAS A STORM OF PROTEST WHEN FINANCE MINISTER PRAMUAL SABHAVASU OF PROTEST WHEN FINANCE MINISTER PRAMUAL SABHAVASU ANNOUNCED A PACKAGE OF REFORMS THAT INCLUDES THE FREEING OF INTEREST RATES ON FIXED DEPOSITS OF MORE THAN A YEAR AND THE INTRODUCTION OF TAX INCENTIVES ON SAVINGS

02626 DAVIES, B.
FIRST AMONG EQUALS
SOUTH, (107) (SEP 89), 33-35.
ESTABLISHED NEWLY-INDUSTRIALIZING ECONOMIES LIKE SINGAPORE, HONG KONG, AND TAIWAN HAVE BECOME VICTIMS OF THEIR OWN SUCCESS. APPRECIATING CURRENCIES, LABOR SHORTAGES, AND THE NEED TO RECYCLE CURRENT SURPLUSES HAVE SENT COMPANIES QUEUING FOR ALTERNATIVE OFFSHORE PRODUCTION LOCATIONS. THAILAND, MALAYSIA, THE PHILIPPINES, AND INDONESIA ARE ENDEAVORING TO FILL THE VOID AND BECOME THE NEW ASIAN ECONOMIC TIGERS. THE FOUR ARE PURSUING AGGRESSIVE ECONOMIC POLICIES BUT EACH FACES SIGNIFICANT PROBLEMS.

02627 DAVIES, C.
SOLVING THE RUMANIAN PROBLEM
NATIONAL REVIEW, 61(25) (DEC 89), 37.
THIS ARTICLE SUGGESTS THAT THERE ARE MANY REASONS WHY IT MAY BECOME BOTH RIGHT AND EXPEDIENT FOR A DEMOCRATIC COUNTRY TO VIOLATE THE SOVEREIGNTY OF ANOTHER COUNTRY, AND ALL OF THEM APPLY IN THE CASE OF RUMANIA. IT SUGGESTS THAT THE MAIN SOVIET AND WESTERN ANXIETY MUST RELATE TO THE STATE OF TENSION BETWEEN HUNGARY AND RUMANIA CAUSED BY THE RUMANIAN GOVERNMENT'S PERSECUTION OF THE TRANSYLVANIAN MAGYARS IT ADVOCATES AN AGREEMENT AMONG THE AMERICAN, SOVIET, AND EUROPEAN GOVERNMENTS TO REMOVE THE RULERS OF RUMANIA, AND TURN THE COUNTRY INTO A NEUTRAL, DISARMED COUNTRY SPECIALIZING IN BILATERAL TRADE WITH THE SOVIETS.

02628 DAVIES, D.
GADAFFI'S GIRATIONS
NEW AFRICAN, (262) (JUL 89), 16.
THIS ARTICLE EXPLORES GADAFFI'S POLICY OF DESTABILIZATION OF AFRICAN COUNTRIES WHICH CONTINUES DESPITE THE LACK OF ANY COHERENT POLICY, OR OBVIOUS BENEFIT TO LIBYA ITSELF. MANY WEST AFRICAN COUNTRIES, INCLUDING GAMBIA, CHAD, NIGER AND GHANA, ARE SUBJECTED TO GADAFFI'S DESIRE TO OVERTURN NON-REVOLUTIONARY REGIMES.

02629 DAVIES, I.
THE RETURN OF VIRTUE: ORWELL AND THE POLITICAL DILEMMAS OF
CENTRAL EUROPEAN INTELLECTUALS
POLITICS AND SOCIETY, 17(4) (DEC 89), 107-129.
THIS ARTICLE DESCRIBES HOW THE CENTRAL EUROPEAN
INTELLECTUALS, CONSCIOUS THAT "THE LIBERAL TRADITION" MAY
NOT BE STRONG ENOUGH, HAVE TAKEN ON THEMSELVES THE TASK OF
RETHINKING POLITICAL THEORY, IN A WORLD WHERE THE OUTLOOK
FOR A VIRTUOUS POLITICS IS VERY DARK. IF THERE IS A
TRADITION IN WESTERN EUROPE AND NORTH AMERICA THAT IS
CAPABLE OF RESPONDING, IT IS PROBABLY ONE THAT HAS ALWAYS
BEEN CONSCIOUS OF THE ENTIRE SYSTEM OF POST-ENLIGHTENMENT
SOCIETY BEING AMORAL WITHOUT DESPARATELY SEARCHING FOR
ANOTHER EXISTING SYSTEM TO LATCH ONTO, A TRADITION WHICH CAN
BE SEEN IN WILLIAM COBBETT, WILLIAM MORRIS, THOMAS HARDY,
GEORGE ORWELL AND, LATTERLY E.P. THOMPSON.

02630 DAVIES, J. L.
ALLEVIATING POLITICAL VIOLENCE THROUGH ENHANCING COHERENCE
IN COLLECTIVE CONSCIOUSNESS: IMPACT ASSESSMENT ANALYSES OF
THE LEBANON WAR
DISSERTATION ABSTRACTS INTERNATIONAL, 49(8) (FEB 89),
2381-A.
THE AUTHOR RECOUNTS TESTING OF A NEW APPROACH TO PEACE
AND ALLEVIATION OF POLITICAL VIOLENCE BY ENHANCING COHERENCE,
AND THEREBY REDUCING STRESS, IN AN UNDERLYING FIELD OF
COLLECTIVE CONSCIOUSNESS. THE COLLECTIVE PRACTICE OF THE
MAHARISHI TECHNOLOGY OF THE UNIFIED FIELD (INCLUDING
TRANSCENDENTAL MEDITATION AND TM-SIDHI TECHNIQUES) WAS USED
IN AN ATTEMPT TO ENHANCE COHERENCE IN COLLECTIVE
CONSCIOUSNESS AND BEHAVIOR IN LEBANON.

02631 DAVIES, S.
THE ANZAC SHIPS: A MISGUIDED CHOICE
NEW ZEALAND INTERNATIONAL REVIEW, 14(2) (MAR 89), 16-19.
THE AUTHOR, A MEMBER OF PARLIAMENT FOR PENCARROW, NEW
ZEALAND, ARGUES AGAINST THE NEED FOR A FRIGATE-BASED NAVY
(THE ANZAC SHIPS). THE THREE MAINSTAYS OF NEW ZEALAND'S
FOREIGN POLICY ARE SUMMARIZED: TRADE, AID AND DEFENSE; THE
AUTHOR POINTS TO DIMINISHED AID WHICH HAS IMPACTED ON
DEFENCE DECISIONS. SHE ATTACKS STATEMENTS BY THE 1987
DEFENSE REVIEW THAT MAINTAINING THE CAPABILITIES TO OPERATE
OVER SUCH A VAST AREA IS A MAJOR COMMITMENT FOR A SMALL
COUNTRY, WHICH HAS BEEN USED BY THOSE WHO WANT THE ANZAC
SHIPS AND CALLS THIS FASCINATION WITH "BIG SHIPS" THE
REPLACEMENT SYNDROME. A TABLE IS INCLUDED WHICH SUPPORTS HER
BASIC POSITION THAT NAVAL FORCES ARE OVERLAPPING IN CERTAIN
AREAS OF THE REGION.

02632 DAVIES, S.
THE CAPITALISM/SOCIALISM DEBATE IN EAST ASIA
SOCIETY, 26(3) (MAR 89), 29-37.
THE AUTHOR ARGUES THAT THE CAPITALISM/SOCIALISM DEBATE
IS NOT IN EVIDENCE IN EAST ASIA. HE PROPOSES THAT THE
QUESTION THAT SOCIAL SCIENTISTS SHOULD ASK IS "IS THE
CAPITALISM/SOCIALISM DEBATE RELEVANT AS A DEBATE ABOUT THE
THEORETICAL TOOLS NECESARY FOR UNDERSTANDING THE DYNAMICS OF
SOCIAL AND ECONOMIC DEVELOPMENT IN EAST ASIAN SOCIETY?" HE
ANSWERS WITH AN EQUIVOCAL "NOT YET, AND MAYBE NEVER." IN
SHORT, TRYING TO USE THE WESTERN CONCEPTS OF CAPITALISM AND
SOCIALISM WILL NOT EXPLAIN EVENTS AND DEVELOPMENTS THAT ARE
UNIQUE TO EAST ASIA.

02633 DAVIS, C.E.; DAVIS, S.K.; PEACOCK, D.
STATE IMPLEMENTATION OF THE SURFACE MINING CONTROL AND
RECLAMATION ACT OF 1977
POLICY STUDIES REVIEW, 9(1) (AUT 89), 109-119.
THE IMPLEMENTATION OF THE SURFACE MINING CONTROL AND
RECLAMATION ACT (SMCRA) OF 1977 IN COAL PRODUCING STATES IS
GUIDED BY A PARTIAL PREEMPTION POLICY APPROACH THAT
ESTABLISHES A BALANCE BETWEEN FEDERAL AND STATE DECISION-
MAKING AUTHORITY. THE USEFULNESS OF THIS APPROACH IS
ASSESSED BY ANALYZING STATE ENFORCEMENT ACTIONS IN RELATION
THE INSTITUTIONAL CAPACITY OF STATES TO SHOULDER REGULATORY
RESPONSIBILITIES AND THE PROPENSITY OF THE FEDERAL OFFICE OF
SURFACE MINING (OSM) TO OVERSEE STATE ENFORCEMENT ACTIONS
AND, IF NECESSARY, TO UNDERTAKE CORRECTIVE ACTION. RESULTS
INDICATED THAT STATE ADMINISTRATION OF SMCRA WAS CONSTRAINED
BY THE LACK OF EFFECTIVE FEDERAL OVERSIGHT BUT WAS LARGELY
UNAFFECTED BY INTERSTATE DIFFERENCES IN POLITICAL, ECONOMIC,
OR ADMINISTRATIVE CHARACTERISTICS.

02634 DAVIS, D.
CHINESE SOCIAL WELFARE: POLICIES AND OUTCOMES
CHINA QUARTERLY, (119) (SEP 89), 577-597.
IN THE REALM OF SOCIAL WELFARE, THE 1980'S MARKED A
DRAMATIC DEPARTURE FROM THE RECENT PAST IN CHINA. THE
EGALITARIAN IDEALS AND COLLECTIVE SOLUTIONS OF THE MAOIST
ERA DISAPPEARED, TO BE REPLACED BY AN IDEOLOGY THAT
VALIDATES INDIVIDUAL RATHER THAN GROUP GOALS AND PRIVATE
RATHER THAN PUBLIC SOLUTIONS. BUT, WHILE DECOLLECTIVIZATION
AND PRIVATIZATION OF THE WORKPLACE APPEAR TO HAVE NARROWED
INCOME DIFFERENTIALS BETWEEN RURAL AND URBAN RESIDENTS, THE
IDEOLOGICAL AND ADMINISTRATIVE SHIFTS IN THE SOCIAL WELFARE

POLICIES HAVE HAD AN OPPOSITE IMPACT. IN THE AREAS OF
EDUCATION, PENSIONS, AND INCOME MAINTENANCE, THE REFORMS
HAVE WIDENED THE DIFFERENCES BETWEEN THE QUALITY AND
QUANTITY OF SOCIAL SERVICES AVAILABLE TO URBAN AND RURAL
RESIDENTS. AND IN MEDICINE, THE RESULTS HAVE BEEN GAINS FOR
THE WEALTHIEST AND LOSSES FOR THE POOREST RURAL INHABITANTS.

02635 DAVIS, D.B.
AMERICAN EQUALITY AND FOREIGN REVOLUTIONS
JOURNAL OF AMERICAN HISTORY, 76(3) (DEC 89), 729-752.
IF HISTORIANS ARE TO MOVE BEYOND MESSIANIC TYPOLOGIES,
THEY MUST GIVE MORE ATTENTION TO THE WAY REVOLUTIONS HAVE
BEEN COMPARED, DIFFERENTIATED, ACCLAIMED, DENOUNCED, AND
UNDERSTOOD BY DIFFERENT FACTIONS AND CLASSES. THEY MUST KNOW
HOW UNEXPECTED ERUPTIONS OF VIOLENCE AND SEEMING CHAOS WERE
MADE INTELLIGIBLE, HOW THEY WERE INTERPRETED AS MEANINGFUL
EVENTS IN SOME BROAD HISTORICAL PROCESS OR EPIC CONTEST
BETWEEN GOOD AND EVIL. FROM THIS STANDPOINT, THE AMERICAN
ENTHUSIASM FOR THE FRENCH REVOLUTION, WHICH PERSISTED WELL
AFTER THE REIGN OF TERROR, CASTS DOUBT ON THE ALLEGED
CONSERVATISM OF THE AMERICAN REVOLUTION AND PROVIDES INSIGHT
INTO CHANGING PARADIGMS OF EQUALITY AND CHANGING
INTERPRETATIONS OF THE SOURCES OF EVIL.

02636 DAVIS, D.E.
DIVIDED OVER DEMOCRACY: THE EMBEDDEDNESS OF STATE AND
CLASS CONFLICTS IN CONTEMPORARY MEXICO
POLITICS AND SOCIETY, 17(3) (SEP 89), 247-280.
TO ANSWER SOME OF THE CRITICAL QUESTIONS ABOUT THE
MEXICAN STATE AND STATE CONFLICTS OVER DEMOCRATIC REFORM,
THE AUTHOR EXAMINES A HIGHLY CONTENTIOUS AND DIVISIVE DEBATE
OVER A PROPOSED POLITICAL REFORM DISCUSSED BY THE RULING
PARTIDO REVOLUCIONARIO INSTITUCIONAL BETWEEN 1982 AND 1987,
UNDER THE ADMINISTRATION OF PRESIDENT MIGUEL DE LA MADRID.
THE REFORM WAS DESIGNED TO ESTABLISH A LOCALLY-ELECTED
LEGISLATIVE BODY TO REPRESENT MEXICO CITY RESIDENTS AND
BRING DIRECT POPULAR ELECTION OF MEXICO CITY'S MAYOR, TWO
RIGHTS GRANTED TO ALL URBAN RESIDENTS EXCEPT THOSE IN MEXICO
CITY.

02637 DAVIS, D.S.
THE AMERICAN CONSTITUTION AND CATHOLIC CANON LAW
JOURNAL OF CHURCH & STATE, 31(2) (SPR 89), 207-218.
THE AUTHOR CONSIDERS THE IMPLICATIONS OF RECENT
DEVELOPMENTS IN THE ROMAN CATHOLIC CHURCH AS THEY PERTAIN TO
CHURCH-STATE RELATIONS IN THE UNITED STATES, SPECIFICALLY AS
THEY INVOLVE STATE AID TO RELIGIOUSLY-AFFILIATED COLLEGES
AND UNIVERSITIES.

02638 DAVIS, E.
THE FEDERAL BUDGET PROCESS: PROCEDURAL REMEDY FOR CHANGE?
CRS REVEIW, 10(1) (JAN 89), 8-9.
ALTHOUGH THE CONSTITUTION CHARGES THE CONGRESS WITH THE
POWER OF THE PURSE, IT DOES NOT PRESCRIBE A BUDGET SYSTEM.
INSTEAD, THE CONGRESS HAS DEVELOPED A BUDGET SYSTEM ROOTED
IN LONG-STANDING LEGISLATIVE TRADITIONS, ITS OWN RULES AND
PRACTICES, AND VARIOUS BUDGETARY STATUTES. HISTORICALLY THE
CONGRESS HAS ACCOMMODATED CHANGING DEMANDS ON THE BUDGET BY
CHANGING FEDERAL BUDGET PROCEDURES. CONTINUING
DISSATISFACTION WITH THE BUDGET PROCESS, DESPITE RECENT
MAJOR CHANGES, IMPLIES THAT CURRENT DEMANDS ON THE BUDGET
HAVE NOT YET BEEN RESOLVED.

02639 DAVIS, F. L.
PAC CONTRIBUTIONS: THE EFFECTS OF ISSUE SALIENCE AND
CONFLICT
DISSERTATION ABSTRACTS INTERNATIONAL, 49(8) (FEB 89),
2374-A.
PAC CONTRIBUTION TACTICS ARE INFLUENCED BY DISTRICT
CONSTITUENCY OPINION. IN DISTRICTS WHERE ISSUES OF CONCERN
TO AN INTEREST GROUP ARE SALIENT AND CONSTITUENCY OPINION IS
CONSENSUAL, INTEREST GROUPS CONTRIBUTE MORE HEAVILY TO
CANDIDATES HOLDING PIVOTAL LEGISLATIVE POSITIONS, SUCH AS
KEY COMMITTEE MEMBERSHIP. IN DISTRICTS WHERE ISSUES OF
CONCERN TO AN INTEREST GROUP ARE SALIENT AND CONSTITUENCY
OPINION IS DIVIDED, INTEREST GROUPS CONTRIBUTE MORE HEAVILY
ON BEHALF OF POLICY LOYAL CANDIDATES.

02640 DAVIS, J.B.
SMITH'S INVISIBLE HAND AND HEGEL'S CUNNING OF REASON
INTERNATIONAL JOURNAL OF SOCIAL ECONOMICS, 16(6) (1989),
50-66.
THE AFFINITIES OF SMITH'S INVISIBLE HAND NOTION AND
HEGEL'S CUNNING OF REASON ARE EXAMINED THROUGH A STUDY OF
THE KEY LOCATIONS IN WHICH THE INVISIBLE HAND AND CUNNING OF
REASON ARE INTRODUCED. DESPITE THEIR DIFFERENCES IN
ORIENTATION AND PHILOSOPHY, BOTH WRITERS REACH SIMILAR
CONCLUSIONS REGARDING THE PLAY OF SELF-INTEREST AND THE
EMERGENCE OF THE SOCIAL GOOD. SPECIFICALLY, EACH REQUIRES A
DEUS EX MACHINA -- PROVIDENCE OR GEIST -- TO GENERATE THE
NECESSARY TELOS THAT SUPPLEMENTS THEIR RESPECTIVE LOGICAL
ARGUMENTS CONCERNING THE CONCRETE PLAY OF INTEREST. AT THE
SAME TIME, EACH VIEW PROVIDES LITTLE TO EXPLAIN HOW
INDIVIDUALISM CREATES THE GREATER SOCIAL GOOD, SO THAT

RECOURSE IN EACH ARGUMENT TO AN EXTRA-SOCIAL ENTITY OBSCURES THE ACTUAL FUNCTIONING OF THE SOCIAL ORDER. THE COMMON APPROACHES OF THE TWO VERY DIFFERENT THINKERS THUS REFLECTS ON THE GENERAL REQUIREMENTS AND DILEMMAS OF ARGUMENTS CONCERNING THE SOCIAL GOOD AND INDIVIDUAL INTEREST.

02641 DAVIS, J.M.
VIETNAM: WHAT IT WAS REALLY LIKE
MILITARY REVIEW, LXIX(1) (JAN 89), 34-44.
QUESTIONS ABOUT VIETNAM - ABOUT THE EXPERIENCE OF COMBAT AND THE INTEGRITY OF THE SOLDIERS - HAVE RESURFACED OVER THE YEARS. IN THIS MEMOIR, THE AUTHOR ATTEMPTS TO FILL IN THE DETAILS ABOUT WHAT IT WAS LIKE IN VIETNAM, ALLEGED AMERICAN ATROCITIES, AND THE MORALE AND PERSONAL DRAMA OF THE SOLDIERS WHO SERVED.

02642 DAVIS, M.L.; PORTER, P.K.
A TEST FOR PURE OR APPARENT IDEOLOGY IN CONGRESSIONAL VOTING
PUBLIC CHOICE, 60(2) (1989), 101-112.
THE ARTICLE EXAMINES THE QUESTION OF WHETHER POLITICIANS ARE FAITHFUL AGENTS TO THEIR CONSTITUENTS OR WHETHER THEY SOMETIMES IGNORE THE DESIRES OF THEIR PRINCIPALS AND ALLOW THEIR OWN PREFERENCES TO DICTATE THEIR ACTIONS. IT USES THE UNIQUE PROPERTY RIGHTS AFFORDED TO HOLDERS OF POLITICAL OFFICE IS USED AS A COMPARATIVE-STATISTICS TEST FOR THE PRESENCE OF IDEOLOGICAL CONSUMPTION. IT CONCLUDES THAT IDEOLOGICAL CONSUMPTION TENDS TO INCREASE WITH AGE.

02643 DAVIS, T.J.
EMANCIPATION RHETORIC, NATURAL RIGHTS, AND REVOLUTIONARY NEW ENGLAND: A NOTE ON FOUR BLACK PETITIONS IN MASSACHUSETTS, 1773-1777
NEW ENGLAND QUARTERLY, LXII(2) (JUN 89), 248-263.
THIS ARTICLE DESCRIBES THE EFFORTS OF MASSACHUSETTS BLACKS TO MAKE PUBLIC ISSUE OF THE INCONSISTENCY THEY SAW BETWEEN SLAVERY AND THE PROFESSED PRINCIPLES OF THE UNFOLDING REVOLUTION. THE EFFORTS ARE ILLUSTRATED IN FOUR PETITIONS ISSUED BETWEEN JANUARY 1773 AND JANUARY 1777. THE PETITIONS ARE ANALYZED IN CONNECTION WITH BLACKS' SELF-VIEW AND THEIR INCREASING USE OF NATURAL RIGHTS IDEOLOGY AS A RHETORIC OF EMANCIPATION.

02644 DAWSON, E.
THE SATANIC VERSES AND POWER PLAYS IN TEHRAN
PACIFIC DEFENCE REPORTER, 15(10) (APR 89), 36,48.
THE IRAN-IRAQ WAR UNITED THE IRANIAN PEOPLE, PERHAPS AS NEVER BEFORE. RATHER THAN SEEING THEMSELVES IN REGIONAL OR ETHNIC TERMS, THERE IS NOW A REAL SENSE OF IRANIAN NATIONALISM. NOW THAT THE WAR IS OVER, THE REGIME'S VARIOUS FACTIONS ARE BEGINNING TO RE-EMERGE AND TO MANOEUVRE ONCE AGAIN FOR POWER AND INFLUENCE. AS THIS ARTICLE DESCRIBES, 1989 WILL PRESENT A NUMBER OF OPPORTUNITIES FOR WIDESPREAD LEADERSHIP CHANGES - THE ELECTION OF A NEW PRESIDENT, THE SELECTION OF A NEW PRIME MINISTER, PERHAPS THE COMBINING OF THE POSITIONS OF PRIME MINISTER AND PRESIDENT AND, THE DEATH OF AYATOLLAH KHOMEINI.

02645 DAWSON, P.F.
CANADIAN MILITARY MOBILIZATION
ARMED FORCES AND SOCIETY, 16(1) (FAL 89), 37-57.
THE NATURE OF CANADIAN SOCIETY DOES NOT PERMIT A LARGE STANDING FORCE IN THE ABSENCE OF A DIRECT THREAT TO ITS SECURITY. CONTINGENCY PLANNING MUST, THEREFORE, INCLUDE PLANS FOR MOBILIZATION OF THE ARMED FORCES AND SOCIETY AS A WHOLE IN WARTIME. THIS PAPER ANALYZES THE DEVELOPMENT OF MILITARY MOBILIZATION IN CANADA FROM 1867 TO THE PRESENT. THE FACTORS THAT INFLUENCE SECURITY NEEDS AND SOCIETY'S ABILITY TO MOBILIZE TO PROVIDE THOSE NEEDS ARE EXAMINED.

02646 DAWSON, R.; STEVENS, P.S.
DEFENSE EFFECIENCY IN THE 1990'S
WASHINGTON QUARTERLY, 12(2) (SPR 89), 115-128.
THIS ARTICLE REVIEWS THE AGENDA OF REFORMS ESTABLISHED IN 1986 FOR EACH OF FOUR MAJOR ASPECTS OF DEFENSE MANAGEMENT: NATIONAL SECURITY PLANNING AND BUDGETING, MILITARY ORGANIZATION AND COMMAND, ACQUISITION ORGANIZATION AND PROCEDURES, AND CONDUCT AND ACCOUNTABILITY. PROGRESS IN REALIZING SUCH REFORMS HAS VARIED IN THE INTERVENING YEARS. WITH SPECIFIC ACTIONS THIS PROGRESS CAN BE CONTINUED.

02647 DAY, C.L.
OLDER AMERICANS, INTEREST GROUPS, AND AGING POLICY
DISSERTATION ABSTRACTS INTERNATIONAL, 49(11) (MAY 89), 3489-A.
THE ELDERLY EMERGED AS AN IMPORTANT POLITICAL GROUP EARLY IN THE TWENTIETH CENTURY, AS SUPPORT GREW FOR GOVERNMENT OLD-AGE PENSIONS. SINCE SOCIAL SECURITY PASSED IN 1935, OLD-AGE POLITICS HAS EVOLVED FROM A DIFFUSE SOCIAL MOVEMENT TO A STABLE, INFLUENTIAL SET OF ORGANIZATIONS. POLITICAL ORGANIZATIONS FOR THE ELDERLY ARE POWERFUL AND BROADLY REPRESENTATIVE BUT, LIKE INTEREST GROUPS IN GENERAL, THEY STILL LACK THE BROAD COALITION-BUILDING AND ECONOMIC AGENDA-SETTING POWERS OF POLITICAL PARTIES.

02648 DE CUELLAR, J.P.
UNITED NATIONS: THE DYNAMICS OF PEACEMAKING
WORLD MARXIST REVIEW, 32(4) (APR 89), 3-4.
THE LATEST SESSION OF THE GENERAL ASSEMBLY STRENGTHENED POSITIVE TENDENCIES IN INTERNATIONAL RELATIONS. DISCUSSIONS WERE A REFLECTION OF THE GENERAL INTEREST AMONG ALL DELEGATES IN DIALOGUE AND UNDERSTANDING, AND THEIR DECISIONS GAVE A FRESH IMPETUS TO EFFORTS FOR PEACE AND THE SEARCH FOR A BETTER ECONOMIC BALANCE. THE SESSION UNANIMOUSLY APPROVED MANY RESOLUTIONS, PARTICULARLY ON DISARMAMENT. THERE WAS A FURTHER CONVERGENCE OF POSITIONS ON SOCIAL AND HUMANITARIAN PROBLEMS, WITH THE RESULTANT DIALOGUE ON LEGAL ISSUES. THE DECLARATION ON STRENGTHENING THE FUNCTIONS OF THE THE UN WITH REGARD TO THE SETTLEMENT AND PREVENTION OF CONFLICTS WAS APPROVED BY CONSENSUS, AND A DECISION ON OUR BUDGET WAS WORKED OUT.

02649 DE JASAY, A.
IS LIMITED GOVERNMENT POSSIBLE?
CRITICAL REVIEW, 3(2) (SPR 89), 283-309.
THIS ARTICLE IS A PHILOSOPHICAL EXPLORATION OF THE POSSIBILITY OF ACTUALLY LIMITING GOVERNMENT. IT ADDRESSES-- NOT WHETHER GOVERNMENT, BUT HOW MUCH? -- AND THEN EXPLORES THE DIFFICULTIES THAT "HOW MUCH" PRESENTS. IT EXPLORES ISSUES SUCH AS WHO CHOSES FOR WHOM?; THE "OLD SOCIAL CONTRACT"; THE QUEST FOR UNANIMITY; THE QUESTION, CAN IMPARTIAL RULES BE "COMPLETE?"; SPLIT LEVEL CONTRACTARIANISM, HAYAK'S ANALYSIS; AND THE CONSTITUTIONAL LIMITATION OF SOCIAL CHOICE. IT CONCLUDES THAT LIMITED GOVERNMENT WITH POPULAR SOVEREIGNTY IS PRECARIOUS, HISTORICALLY IN RETREAT AND SELF CONTRADICTORY.

02650 DE KERCKHOVE, D.
CONTROL OF THE COLLECTIVE MIND
CANADIAN FORUM, 68(782) (OCT 89), 15-19.
THIS ARTICLE EXAMINES FREE TRADE AND CANADA'S CULTURAL INDUSTRIES. IT FINDS THAT WITH THE FREE TRADE AGREEMENT, CANADA ACCEPTS THE AMERICAN DEFINITION OF CULTURE AS BUSINESS AND THAT THE COMBINATION OF MODERN TECHNOLOGY AND GOVERNMENT INDIFFERENCE CREATS A NEW CHALLENGE TO CANADIAN CULTURE. IT SUGGESTS THAT AS WE ENTER THE COMPETITIVE AND UNFORGIVING WORLD OF GLOBALIZATION, MUCH LARGER RESOURCES WILL HAVE TO BE ALLOCATED TO CULTURE IN ORDER FOR CANADA TO SURVIVE AS AN INDEPENDENT REALITY.

02651 DE ROSA, D.
ASIAN PREFERENCES AND THE GAINS FROM MFN TARIFF REDUCTIONS.
WORLD ECONOMY, 11(3) (SEP 88), 377-396.
THE ARTICLE EXPLORES THE TWO PRINCIPAL COOPERATIVE APPROACHES TO TRADE LIBERALIZATION FACING THE DEVELOPING COUNTRIES OF ASIA: GATT-TYPE RECIPROCAL TRADE AGREEMENTS, WHEREBY REDUCTIONS OF IMPORT BARRIERS ARE IMPLEMENTED ACCORDING TO THE MOST-FAVOURED-NATION (MFN) PRINCIPLE, AND UNCTAD-TYPE TRADE AGREEMENTS, WHEREBY MUTUAL REDUCTIONS OF TRADE BARRIERS ARE ACCOMPLISHED ON A PREFERENTIAL BASIS EXCLUSIVELY AMONG DEVELOPING COUNTRIES. BASED ON DETAILED INFORMATION ABOUT TARIFFS AND OTHER FORMS OF PROTECTION IN THE ASIAN DEVELOPING REGION, AND USING AN ELEMENTARY MODEL OF REGIONAL TRADE FLOWS, AN EXAMINATION IS MADE OF THE IMPLICATIONS FOR NATIONAL ECONOMIC WELFARE OF THESE TWO APPROACHES TO TRADE LIBERALIZATION AS APPLIED TO THE TRADE IN MANUFACTURES OF SEVERAL MAJOR ASIAN DEVELOPING COUNTRIES.

02652 DE SILVA, K.M.
DECENTRALIZATION AND REGIONALISM IN THE MANAGEMENT OF SRI LANKA'S ETHNIC CONFLICT
INTERNATIONAL JOURNAL OF GROUP TENSIONS, 19(4) (WIN 89), 317-338.
THIS ARTICLE EXAMINES HOW ATTEMPTS AT MANAGING SRI LANKA'S ETHNIC RIVALRIES AND TENSIONS THROUGH DISTRICT LEVEL OR PROVINCIAL LEVEL COUNCILS ARE ALWAYS CAUGHT UP IN THE JOSTLING AMONG THE MINORITIES THEMSELVES AS THEY JOCKEY FOR POSITIONS OF ADVANTAGE IN THE RACE FOR POLITICAL AND ECONOMIC GAINS.

02653 DEAK, I.
PACESETTERS OF INTEGRATION :JEWISH OFFICERS IN THE HAPSBURG MONARCHY
EASTERN EUROPEAN POLITICS AND SOCIETIES, 3(1) (WIN 89), 22-50.
THIS IS THE STORY OF THE UNIQUE RELATIONSHIP BETWEEN A CONFESSIONALLY AND ETHNICALLY TOLERANT MONARCHY AND THE JEWS WHO WERE AMONG ITS MOST LOYAL CITIZENS. THE HABSBURG GOVERNMENT HAD OPENED THE WAY TO EMANCIPATION OF ITS JEWISH SUBJECTS WITH VARIOUS TOLERATION PATENTS IN THE LATE 1780S, AND AUSTRIA-HUNGARY FORMALLY EMANCIPATED THE JEWS IN 1867. THE MONARCHY OUTDID THE OTHER EUROPEAN POWERS IN ADMITTING JEWS INTO ITS MOST PRESTIGIOUS INSTITUTION, THE MILITARY OFFICER CORPS, AND ESPECIALLY INTO ITS RESERVE OFFICER BRANCH. BY GRANTING THE OFFICERS' GOLDEN SWORD-KNOT (PORTE-EPEE) TO THOUSANDS UPON THOUSANDS OF JEWISH CIVILIANS, THE EMPEROR SET AN EXAMPLE FOR SOCIETY AS A WHOLE. WITHOUT WITHOUT IT, THE PROCESS OF JEWISH INTEGRATION INTO BUSINESS,

INDUSTRY EDUCATION, THE ARTS, AND THE ADMINISTRATION WOULD HAVE BEEN MUCH MORE DIFFICULT. THIS ESSAY ANALYZES THE CAUSES AND CONSEQUENCES OF THIS EXTRAORDINARY DEVELOPMENT.

02654 DEAKIN, S.
LIBERAL VALUES AND NEW COMMONWEALTH IMMIGRATION: 1961-1981
DISSERTATION ABSTRACTS INTERNATIONAL, 50(4) (OCT 89), 1075-A.
THE AUTHOR EXAMINES THE VALUES AND ATTITUDES OF BRITISH LIBERALS AND SUGGESTS THAT SEVERAL THEMES HAVE BEEN PREDOMINANT IN THE LIBERAL RESPONSE TO RACE POLITICS AND IMMIGRATION. HE FOCUSES ON FIVE THEMES: A SOCIAL DETERMINIST VIEW OF HUMAN BEHAVIOR, A DESIRE FOR RATIONALITY, A DESIRE FOR EQUALITY, A DESIRE FOR PLURALISM, AND A DESIRE FOR COMMUNITY.

02655 DEALTERIIS, M.H.
LOCAL GOVERNMENTS AS IMPLEMENTORS OF PUBLIC POLICY: EXPLAINING VARIANCE IN THE DELIVERY OF WELFARE SERVICES
DISSERTATION ABSTRACTS INTERNATIONAL, 49(10) (APR 89), 3150-A.
THE AUTHOR PROBES HOW POLITICAL VARIABLES AFFECT THE TRANSLATION OF POVERTY INTO WELFARE BENEFITS AT THE COUNTY LEVEL IN NEW YORK. CONTROLLING FOR POVERTY AND PER CAPITA INCOME, HE FINDS THAT PARTISANSHIP AND CONTROL HAVE A MEASURABLE EFFECT ON WELFARE PROGRAMS ADMINISTERED BY THE COUNTIES OF NEW YORK, WHILE COMPETITION DOES NOT. A MODEL OF THE WELFARE PROCESS REVEALS THAT DEMOCRATS HAVE STRUCTURAL REASONS FOR MORE GENEROUS WELFARE POLICIES THAN THE REPUBLICANS.

02656 DEAN, J.
CAN NATO AGREE ON ARMS CONTROL?
TECHNOLOGY REVIEW, 92(7) (OCT 89), 58-68.
THIS ARTICLE EXPLORES THE WARSAW PACT WHICH IS POISED TO END THE COSTLY MILITARY STANDOFF IN EUROPE AND, ALSO, THE SPLITS WITHIN THE WESTERN ALLIANCE WHICH COULD LIMIT PROGRESS. IT SUGGESTS THAT NATO DISAGREEMENT OVER WHETHER TO RESTRICT ON-SITE INSPECTION WILL COMPLICATE THE VERIFICATION DEBATE WITH THE WARSAH PACT AND THAT NATO PROPOSED ARMS-CONTROL SUBREGIONS IN EUROPE ARE GERRYMANDERED AND HARD TO JUSTIFY. THE NEED FOR CONSTANT 50% FORCE CUTS, AND THE NECESSITY OF SOME U.S. NUCLEAR WEAPONS RETAINED IN EUROPE ARE EACH ADDRESSED.

02657 DEAN, J.
CUTTING BACK THE NATO-WARSAW TREATY CONFRONTATION
DISARMAMENT, XII(2) (SUM 89), 18-25.
FOLLOWING THE RATIFICATION OF THE TREATY ON THE ELIMINATION OF INTERMEDIATE-RANGE AND SHORTER-RANGE MISSILES AND THE ANNOUNCEMENT BY GORBACHEV OF SIGNIFICANT UNILATERAL REDUCTIONS IN SOVIET ARMED FORCES, LONG-TERM PROSPECTS FOR A CONTINUING REDUCTION OF THE NATO-WARSAW TREATY MILITARY CONFRONTATION IN EUROPE ARE GENERALLY GOOD, ALTHOUGH THERE ARE MANY COMPLICATIONS THAT COULD IMPEDE THE PROCESS. THE OUTLOOK FOR THE NEW TALKS ON CONVENTIONAL ARMED FORCES IN EUROPE IS MIXED, BUT POSITIVE FACTORS OUTWEIGH THE NEGATIVE ONES AND THERE COULD BE SOME SPECIFIC RESULTS WITHIN THE NEXT FIVE YEARS. BUT ACHIEVING DEEP CUTS IN THE EUROPEAN CONFRONTATION WOULD REQUIRE REVISION OF THE CURRENT WESTERN POSITION.

02658 DEAN, J.W.
MYTHS ABOUT SOUTH AFRICAN SANCTION
INTERNATIONAL PERSPECTIVES, 18(4) (JUL 89), 23-26.
THIS ARTICLE EXPLORES THE CANADIAN VIEW OF THE SITUATION IN SOUTH AFRICA. THE WRITER WANTS TO DESTROY APARTHEID, NOT BY SANCTIONS AND BOYCOTTS, BUT BY GREATER DIRECT AID TO NON-WHITES AND THEIR EDUCATION. IT EXPLORES TWO MYTHS ABOUT SOUTH AFRICA SANCTIONS. MYTH #1: APARTHEID IS SOUTH AFRICA'S BASIC PROBLEM. MYTH #2: SANCTIONS HAVE SERIOUSLY DISRUPTED THE ECONOMY AND WILL SPEED UP THE END OF APARTHEID.

02659 DEAN, K.E.
AN EXAMINATION OF UNANIMOUS DECISION-MAKING ON THE BURGER COURT
DISSERTATION ABSTRACTS INTERNATIONAL, 50(3) (SEP 89), 783-A.
THE AUTHOR ANALYZES THE EXTENT AND NATURE OF UNANIMOUS DECISION-MAKING ON THE BURGER COURT, UTILIZING ALL CIVIL RIGHTS/LIBERTIES AND ECONOMICS DECISIONS ISSUED IN 1969-1985. SHE FINDS THAT THE BURGER COURT'S UNANIMOUS DECISIONS WERE MORE LIKELY TO BE LIBERAL THAN WERE NON-UNANIMOUS ONES. IN CIVIL RIGHTS DECISIONS, THE COURT BECAME MORE CONSERVATIVE OVER TIME, BUT THIS TREND WAS NOT APPARENT IN ECONOMIC MATTERS. IDEOLOGY CLEARLY AFFECTED UNANIMOUS CIVIL RIGHTS DECISIONS, BUT THE EFFECT OF IDEOLOGY WAS NOT APPARENT IN UNANIMOUS ECONOMIC DECISIONS.

02660 DEAN, R.
WHY GORBACHEV MUST CUT DEFENCE SPENDING
WORLD TODAY, 45(8-9) (AUG 89), 128-129.
ONE OF GORBACHEV'S ORIGINAL OBJECTIVES IN CUTTING MILITARY COSTS WAS TO RELEASE RESOURCES TO BOOST INVESTMENT IN THE CIVIL ECONOMY. BUT THE FOCUS HAS CHANGED. IT IS CLEAR FROM RECENT STATEMENTS THAT CUTTING DEFENSE SPENDING IS ALSO EXPECTED TO MAKE A TIMELY CONTRIBUTION TO TWO PRESSING, AND RELATED, PROBLEMS. THE FIRST IS THE BUDGET DEFICIT. THE SECOND IS THE NEED TO IMPROVE LIVING STANDARDS, BOTH TO STRENGTHEN INCENTIVES FOR WORKERS AND TO TRY TO WIN WHOLEHEARTED SUPPORT FOR PERESTROIKA. RESOURCES FORMERLY DEVOTED TO DEFENSE WILL BE USED FOR THE PRODUCTION OF CONSUMER GOODS.

02661 DEANE, H.
MAO'S RURAL POLICIES REVISITED
MONTHLY REVIEW, 40(10) (MAR 89), 1-9.
MAO'S RURAL POLICIES HAD SUCCESSES, AMONG THEM THE CONSTRUCTION OF AN INFRASTRUCTURE OF ROADS, DAMS, CANALS, AND ELECTRIFICATION THAT CONTINUES TO SERVE CHINESE AGRICULTURE; WIDESPREAD HEALTH CARE AND EDUCATION; AND INCREASE IN LAND PRODUCTIVITY; AND THE EMERGENCE, DESPITE MANY DIFFICULTIES, OF A MINORITY OF GENUINE COLLECTIVES, MOST AT THE BRIGADE LEVEL. A SCATTERING OF THEM STILL EXIST AND THRIVE. MORE WOULD HAVE IF THE REFORM WIND STIRRED UP HAD NOT FORCED THE ADOPTION OF THE CONTRACT RESPONSIBILITY SYSTEM. BUT THE RURAL SUCCESSES ACHIEVED BY MAO'S SUSTAINED EFFORTS TO CREATE A NONBUREAUCRATIC SOCIALISM WERE OUTNUMBERED AND OUTWEIGHED BY THE FAILURES, AMONG WHICH WERE CATASTROPHES.

02662 DEARLOVE, J.
BRINGING THE CONSTITUTION BACK IN: POLITICAL SCIENCE AND THE STATE
POLITICAL STUDIES, XXXVII(4) (DEC 89), 521-539.
AT ONE TIME THE STUDY OF POLITICS CENTRED ON THE STATE BUT FOR MUCH OF THIS CENTURY THE EMPHASIS HAS BEEN ON POLITICAL BEHAVIOR AND POLICY-MAKING WITH GOVERNMENTAL DECISIONS EXPLAINED AS A RESPONSE TO SOCIETAL FORCES. IN THE LAST DECADE OR SO, STATECENTRIC THEORISTS HAVE SOUGHT TO BRING THE STATE BACK, ARGUING THAT IT IS MORE AUTONOMOUS THAN SOCIETY-CENTRED THEORISTS HAVE SUGGESTED THE AUTHOR RECORDS THE RETREAT OF THE STATE IN THE ANGLO-AMERICAN STUDY OF POLITICS AND THE RELATED RISE OF A PARTICULAR KIND OF POLITICAL SCIENCE, GOING ON TO OUTLINE THE MORE RECENT GROWTH OF A 'NEW INSTITUTIONALISM' WHICH PLACES THE STATE AT THE VERY CENTRE OF POLITICAL SCIENCE. BRINGING THE STATE BACK IN TO THE STUDY OF BRITISH POLITICS MUST NECESSARILY INVOLVE BRINGING THE CONSTITUTION BACK IN BUT IN WAYS THAT AVOID THE LIMITATIONS OF THE CONSTITUTIONAL APPROACH AND A NARROW LEGALISM.

02663 DEBECKI, R.
DIPLOMATIC RELATIONS RESUMED BETWEEN POLAND AND THE HOLY SEE
CONTEMPORARY POLAND, XXII(9) (1989), 11-13.
AFTER A FIFTY-YEAR HIATUS, POLISH DIPLOMATIC RELATIONS WITH THE HOLY SEE WERE RESUMED ON JULY 17, 1989. IN THIS ARTICLE, THE AUTHOR REVIEWS THE HISTORY OF VATICAN-POLISH DIPLOMACY.

02664 DEBENDETTI, C.
EUROPE 1992 IS A NECESSITY FOR ITALY--AND EUROPE
EUROPE, (285) (APR 89), 39.
THE ARTICLE OUTLINES SOME OF THE OPPORTUNITIES AND CHALLENGES THAT THE EUROPEAN ECONOMIC INTEGRATION OF 1992 WILL PRESENT TO ITALY. IT OUTLINES SOME MEASURES THAT THE GOVERNMENT NEED ADOPT TO TAKE FULL ADVANTAGE OF THE COMING CHANGES. THESE INCLUDE REFORM OF NON-FUNCTIONING PUBLIC SERVICES AND A REDUCTION OF THE HUGE NATIONAL DEBT.

02665 DEBNAM, G.
ADVERSARY POLITICS IN BRITAIN 1964-1979: CHANGE OF GOVERNMENT AND THE CLIMATE OF STRESS
PARLIAMENTARY AFFAIRS, 42(2) (APR 89), 213-229.
THE CENTRAL THEME OF THE ADVERSARY POLITICS THESIS IS THAT FREQUENT CHANGES OF GOVERNMENT IN BRITAIN IN THE 1960'S AND THE 1970'S LED TO POLICY REVERSALS ON A SCALE THAT WAS DAMAGING TO THE ECONOMY AND SOCIETY. THE AUTHOR ANALYZES THE THEORY WITH REGARDS TO THE BRITISH GOVERNMENTS OF 19641979 AND CONCLUDES THAT ADVERSARY POLITICAL THEORISTS WERE GENERALLY CORRECT IN THEIR STATEMENTS ABOUT THE PERIOD. HOWEVER, THEY WERE INCORRECT IN IDENTIFYING THE MECHANISMS BY WHICH THE POLITICAL PHENOMENON OCCURRED.

02666 DEBOE, S.
RELIGION IN THE PEOPLE'S REPUBLIC OF CHINA
FREEDOM AT ISSUE, (109) (JUL 89), 32-33.
ONE AREA OF HUMAN RIGHTS THAT HAS RECEIVED LITTLE ATTENTION IN CHINA IS RELIGIOUS LIBERTY. LIKE MOST COMMUNIST NATIONS, CHINA PROFESSES RELIGIOUS FREEDOM FOR ITS CITIZENS, BUT THE DEED FALLS SHORT OF THE DECLARATION. ALTHOUGH THE BUDDHISTS IN TIBET HAVE RECEIVED MEDIA ATTENTION IN RECENT MONTHS, THERE HAS BEEN VIRTUAL SILENCE ABOUT THE CHRISTIAN COMMUNITIES OF CHINA. PROTESTANTS AND CATHOLICS FORM A VERY SMALL MINORITY OF THE POPULATION, BUT THEY EXPERIENCE A GREAT DEAL OF SEVERE REPRESSION AND HARASSMENT AT THE HANDS OF GOVERNMENT OFFICIALS.

02667 DEBONY, E.
    GATT TALKS ARE BACK ON TRACK
    EUROPE, (286) (MAY 89), 14-15.
        IN APRIL 1988, THE SUCCESSFUL COMPLETION OF THE MID-TERM
    REVIEW OF THE URUGUAY ROUND PUT INTERNATIONAL TRADE BACK ON
    TRACK TOWARD A MAJOR LIBERALIZATION OF TRADE IN GOODS AND
    AGRICULTURE, AS WELL AS EXTENDING THE GATT AUTHORITY TO NEW
    AREAS, SUCH AS TRADE IN SERVICES AND TRADE-RELATED
    INTELLECTUAL PROPERTY RIGHTS.

02668 DEBONY, E.
    THE E.C. PRIES OPEN ITS TELECOM MARKETS
    EUROPE, (285) (APR 89), 18-19, 47.
        PIECE BY PIECE, THE EUROPEAN COMMUNITY COMMISSION HAS
    MOUNTED A MULTI-PRONGED STRATEGY AIMED AT CREATING A SINGLE
    TELECOMMUNICATIONS MARKET IN EUROPE. A CENTRAL GOAL OF THE
    APPROACH IS THE REDUCTION OF THE POWER OF THE NATIONAL
    TELECOMMUNICATIONS MONOPOLIES, THEPOSTAL, TELEPHONE, AND
    TELEGRAPH ADMINISTRATIONS. NOT ONLY DO THE MOVES OF THE
    COMMUNITY REFLECT TECHNOLOGICAL DEVELOPMENTS THAT ARE
    RAPIDLY EATING AWAY AT THESE MONOPOLIES AND ACKNOWLEDGE THAT
    A HARMONIZED APPROACH IS BETTER THAN FREE MARKET CHAOS, THEY
    ARE PROBABLY THE ONLY OPTIONS THAT WOULD BE ACCEPTABLE TO
    THE 12 MEMBER STATES.

02669 DEBOUZY, O.
    THE BALANCE OF AIR FORCES IN EUROPE: THE DEVIL IS IN THE
    DETAILS
    NATO'S SIXTEEN NATIONS, 34(3) (JUN 89), 49-50, 52, 55.
        IN SPITE OF AGREEMENT ON A MANDATE FOR CFE NEGOTIATIONS,
    THE WARSAW PACT HAS BEEN EXERTING PRESSURE TO INCLUDE
    AIRCRAFT AND CLAIMING THAT NATO HAS A CONSIDERABLE NUMERICAL
    SUPERIORITY. BUT A CLOSER LOOK DISPROVES THE STATEMENT: IT
    WOULD BE VALID ONLY IF CERTAIN TYPES OF AIRCRAFT WERE TO BE
    EXCLUDED A PRIORI. ALL AIRCRAFT CAN BE USED FOR VARIOUS
    PURPOSES AND THE DIFFERENCE BETWEEN OFFENSIVE" AND
    "DEFENSIVE" IS HIGHLY ARTIFICIAL. MOREOVER, AT TODAY'S
    FLYING SPEEDS, THEY CAN BE MOVED RAPIDLY AND EASILY IN AND
    OUT OF STRICTLY DEFINED AREAS.

02670 DEBRESSON, C.
    BREEDING INNOVATION CLUSTERS: A SOURCE OF DYNAMIC
    DEVELOPMENT
    WORLD DEVELOPMENT, 17(1) (JAN 89), 1-16.
        INNOVATION, EVEN IN LESS DEVELOPED COUNTRIES, IS THE
    SOURCE OF DYNAMIC GROWTH AND STRUCTURAL TRANSFORMATION. AN
    IMPORTANT FEATURE OF INNOVATION IS THAT IT CLUSTERS. PERHAPS
    THE CLUSTERS OF INNOVATION, MORE THAN THE INDIVIDUAL
    INNOVATIONS, ARE THE SOURCE OF DYNAMIC GROWTH. THE REASONS
    WHY INNOVATIONS CLUSTER ARE REVIEWED: SOME ARE TECHNICAL AND
    EXOGENOUS TO THE ECONOMY; OTHERS ARE ENDOGENOUS TO THE
    ECONOMIC SYSTEM. ALL THESE FORCES COMBINE TO CLUSTER
    INNOVATIVE ACTIVITY. BREEDING INNOVATION CLUSTERS MAY BE THE
    MOST REALISTIC POLICY GOAL FOR A COUNTRY IN ORDER TO PRIME
    THE PUMP OF TECHNOLOGICAL ACCUMULATION AND BRIDGE THE
    TECHNOLOGICAL GAP WITH ADVANCED INDUSTRIAL COUNTRIES.

02671 DECTER, M.
    THE RUSHDIAD
    COMMENTARY, 87(6) (JUN 89), 18-23.
        THE ARTICLE EXAMINES THE REACTIONS OF AUTHORS TO THE
    ISLAMIC UPROAR OVER THE PUBLICATION OF SALMAN RUSHDIE'S THE
    SATANIC VERSES. IT DESCRIBES A MEETING OF FAMOUS AUTHORS AND
    THEIR STATEMENTS ON THE CONTROVERSY.

02672 DEEB, M.
    INTER-MAGHRIBI RELATIONS SINCE 1969: A STUDY OF THE
    MODALITIES OF UNIONS AND MERGERS
    MIDDLE EAST JOURNAL, 43(1) (WIN 89), 20-33.
        THIS ARTICLE EXAMINES THE RATIONALE FOR UNIONS AND
    MERGERS AMONG THE STATES IN NORTH AFRICA. THE PREVAILING
    ASSUMPTION HAS BEEN THAT THE PRIME MOVING FORCE BEHIND THE
    FORMATION OF SUCH UNIONS WAS PAN-ARABISM OR MAGHRIBI UNITY
    AND THAT UNIONS BROKE DOWN OVER MATTERS CONCERNING THE
    IMPLEMENTATION OF SUCH IDEOLOGICAL CONCEPTS. AS THIS ARTICLE
    SHOWS, HOWEVER, THIS FAILS TO EXPLAIN HOW TWO STATES SUCH AS
    MOROCCO AND LIBYA COULD AGREE TO A UNION, ONE WHICH LASTED
    TWO YEARS, WHEN THEY HAVE SUCH DIFFERENT IDEOLOGIES; WHY
    ALGERIA AND LIBYA ARE NOT MORE PERMANENTLY ALLIED SINCE THEY
    HOLD COMPATIBLE VIEWS; OR WHY TUNISIA AND MOROCCO, WHO ALSO
    HOLD SIMILAR VIEWS ON MAGHRIBI AND ARAB AFFAIRS, HAVE NEVER
    BEEN UNITED. ALTERNATIVE EXPLANATIONS ARE EXPLORED HERE.

02673 DEFOIARD, P.A.
    MILITARY SERVICE: FRANCE'S SEA SERPENT
    NATO'S SIXTEEN NATIONS, 34(6) (OCT 89), 36-39.
        LIKE THE PROVERBIAL SEA SERPENT, THE QUESTION OF
    NATIONAL MILITARY SERVICE IN FRANCE DISAPPEARS ONLY TO
    REEMERGE LATER. ITS OPPONENTS CITE TECHNOLOGICAL
    SOPHISTICATION, PROFESSIONAL EFFICIENCY AND ARMS CONTROL,
    WHILE ITS DEFENDERS POINT TO MANPOWER POOL, RESERVE
    AVAILABILITY AND COMPARATIVE COST. THE MOST POWERFUL
    ARGUMENT IS OFTEN IGNORED - ITS SIGNIFICANCE IN INTEGRATING

YOUNG CITIZENS INTO THE COMMUNITY. BEYOND MERE NATIONAL
BOUNDARIES, IT IS A WAY OF SHAPING THE EUROPE OF THE FUTURE.

02674 DEGNAN, D.A.
    WHEN (IF) "ROE" FALLS
    COMMONWEAL, CXVI(9) (MAY 89), 267-269.
        A SUPREME COURT DECISION OVERTURNING ROE V. WADE WILL
    NOT SETTLE THE ISSUE OF LEGAL PROTECTION FOR THE FETUS. MORE
    PROBABLY, IT WILL ONLY DEFINE THE PARAMETERS OF FUTURE
    LEGISLATIVE STRUGGLES IN ALL 50 STATES, BECAUSE UNDER THE
    CONSTITUTION THE INDIVIDUAL STATES HAVE INHERENT POWER TO
    PROTECT LIFE AS PART OF THEIR POWER TO PROVIDE FOR THE
    GENERAL WELFARE.

02675 DEGUTTRY, A.
    THE TRANSNATIONAL CIRCULATION OF INFORMATION ON TERRORISM
    AMONG INVESTIGATING BODIES
    INTERNATIONAL SPECTATOR, XXIII(4) (OCT 88), 270-279.
        THE AUTHOR EXAMINES THE FORMS OF INTERNATIONAL
    COOPERATION USED IN EXCHANGING INFORMATION ON TERRORIST
    ACTIVITIES THAT HELP OFFICIALS ACQUIRE MORE KNOWLEDGE ABOUT
    TERRORISM AND EFFECTIVELY COMBAT THIS TYPE OF CRIMINAL
    ACTIVITY. THE STUDY FIRST EXPLAINS THE WAY IN WHICH THE
    EXCHANGE OF INFORMATION IS REGULATED AND THEN LOOKS AT THE
    ESTABLISHMENT OF INTERNATIONAL DATA BANKS.

02676 DEHAVEN, M.J.
    THE PENETRATION OF OPEN POLITICAL SYSTEMS: A STUDY OF THE
    EFFECTS OF SOVIET BEHAVIOR ON PUBLIC OPINION FOLLOWING THE
    NATO DUAL-TRACK MISSILE DECISION
    DISSERTATION ABSTRACTS INTERNATIONAL, 50(4) (OCT 89),
    1081-A.
        USING A FRAMEWORK SUITABLE FOR ANALYZING COMPARATIVE
    FOREIGN POLICY FORMULATION, THE AUTHOR STUDIES THE YEARS
    IMMEDIATELY FOLLOWING THE 1979 NATO DUAL-TRACK MISSILE
    DECISION. HE HYPOTHESIZES THAT THE SOVIET UNION IS CAPABLE
    OF PENETRATING AND INFLUENCING THE FOREIGN POLICY-MAKING
    PROCESS IN WEST GERMANY AND GREAT BRITAIN BY AFFECTING
    PUBLIC ATTITUDES IN BOTH COUNTRIES. HE CONCLUDES THAT SOME
    WESTERN NATIONS ARE SUSCEPTIBLE TO THE EFFECTS OF SOVIET
    BEHAVIOR AND SOME ARE NOT. SPECIFIC CONTEXTUAL CONDITIONS
    MUST BE EXPLORED IN ORDER TO DETERMINE WHEN IT IS POSSIBLE
    FOR THE PROCESS OF POLITICAL PENETRATION TO BE OPERATIVE.
    GEOPOLITICAL ENVIRONMENT APPEARS TO BE A PRIMARY DETERMINANT
    OF SOVIET BEHAVIOR IN GREAT BRITAIN AND WEST GERMANY.

02677 DEHOUSSE, RENAUD
    FEDELISME, ASYMETRIE ET INTERDENDANCE: AUX ORIGINES DE
    LACTION INTERNATIONAL DES COMPOSANTES DE LETAT FEDERAL.
    ETUDES INTERNATIONALES, XX(2) (JUN 89), 283-310.
        THE ARTICLE EXAMINES THE REASONS THAT IMPEL THE MEMBER
    STATES OF SOME FEDERATIONS TO DEVELOP FOREIGN AFFAIRS POLICY
    INDEPENDENTLY OF EACH OTHER. THE GROWING INTERDEPENDENCE OF
    INDUSTRIALIZED COUNTRIES LEADS TO BOTH AN INCREASE AND A
    DIVERSIFICATION OF INTERNATIONAL CONTACTS BETWEEN PUBLIC
    AUTHORITIES WHICH UNDERMINES THE TRADITIONAL MONOPOLY HELD
    BY EXTERNAL AFFAIRS DEPARTMENTS. IT EMPHASIZES THE FACTORS
    THAT LED TO THE ACTIVISM SHOWN BY BELGIUM'S LINGUISTIC
    COMMUNITIES AND SOME CANADIAN PROVINCES.

02678 DEIBEL, T.
    GRAND STRATEGY LESSONS FOR THE BUSH ADMINISTRATION
    WASHINGTON QUARTERLY, 12(3) (SUM 89), 127-138.
        THE ARTICLE ANALYZES THE FOREIGN POLICY OF NIXON, CARTER,
    AND REAGAN TO DRAW LESSONS FOR THE BUSH ADMINISTRATION AS
    IT PLOTS ITS FUTURE COURSE. IT CONCLUDES THAT BUSH SHOULD
    NOT RELY ON ANY ONE POLICY OF HIS PREDECESSORS, BUT RATHER A
    COMBINATION OF THE BEST POLICIES OF EACH. THE ARTICLE
    EXPLORES THE CHANGES IN US PUBLIC OPINION WITH REGARDS TO
    FOREIGN POLICY AS IT WAS AFFECTED BY VIETNAM AND LATER IRAN
    AND AFGHANISTAN. ALTHOUGH GENERAL US INTERESTS DO NOT
    SIGNIFICANTLY CHANGE BETWEEN ADMINISTRATIONS, BUSH IS FORCED
    TO OPERATE UNDER SOME CONSIDERABLE RESTRAINTS SUCH AS THE
    HUGE BUDGET DEFICIT, A DEMOCRATIC CONGRESS, AND A COMPLACENT
    PUBLIC.

02679 DEIBEL, T.
    REAGAN'S MIXED LEGACY
    FOREIGN POLICY, (75) (SUM 89), 34-55.
        IN ANALYZING THE REAGAN LEGACY WITH REGARDS TO FOREIGN
    POLICY, THE ARTICLE EXAMINES THE GRADUAL SHIFT FROM IDEOLOGY
    TO PRAGMATISM. THIS SHIFT WAS CAUSED IN PART BY CHANGES IN
    THE DOMESTIC AND INTERNATIONAL SCENE INCLUDING GEORGE SHULTZ
    TAKING OVER AS SECRETARY OF STATE, A NOTABLE REACHING OUT TO
    THE SOVIET UNION, THE GENEVA, REYKJAVIK, WASHINGTON, AND
    MOSCOW SUMMIT MEETINGS, AND THE IRAN-CONTRA AFFAIR.

02680 DEIBEL, T.L.
    REAGAN FOREIGN POLICY: A MIXED LEGACY
    CURRENT, (317) (NOV 89), 16-24.
        THE QUESTION OF RONALD REAGAN'S LEGACY IN FOREIGN POLICY
    IS RATHER CONFUSING, BECAUSE THE REAGAN YEARS ENDED SUFFUSED
    WITH IRONY. THE PORTRAYER OF THE "EVIL EMPIRE" WHO SCARED
    MILLIONS WITH CASUAL TALK OF NUCLEAR DEMONSTRATION SHOTS AND

BOMBING THE USSR IN FIVE MINUTES ENDED UP PRESIDING OVER A PROFOUND REDUCTION IN TENSIONS BETWEEN THE USA AND THE SOVIET UNION AND EMERGED AS THE SIGNER OF THE FIRST ARMS TREATY IN HISTORY TO ACTUALLY DESTROY AN ENTIRE CLASS OF PRE-EXISTING WEAPONS.

02681 DEJANVRY, A.; SADOULET, E.
A STUDY IN RESISTANCE TO INSTITUTIONAL CHANGE: THE LOST GAME OF LATIN AMERICAN LAND REFORM
WORLD DEVELOPMENT, 17(9) (SEP 89), 1397-1407.
THIS PAPER SEEKS AN EXPLANATION OF THE LIMITED SUCCESS OF LAND REFORMS IN REDISTRIBUTING LAND IN LATIN AMERICA DURING THE 1960S AND 1970S, IN SPITE OF THEIR WIDESPREAD IMPLEMENTATION. A RATIONAL CHOICE MODEL OF FARMER BEHAVIOR INCORPORATING TRANSACTION COSTS ON LABOR AND CREDIT AND A GAME-THEORETICAL APPROACH BETWEEN LANDLORDS AND THE STATE ARE USED FOR THAT PURPOSE. LAND REFORM FAILED TO BE REDISTRIBUTIVE BECAUSE IT SOUGHT TO FIRST MODERNIZE LARGE FARMS, WHICH ALLOWED LANDLORDS TO REINFORCE THEIR POWER OVER THE STATE. THIS, IN TURN, ENABLED THEM EITHER TO OBTAIN CREDIBLE COMMITMENTS OF NONEXPROPRIATION IF THEY WOULD MODERNIZE, OR TO SUCCESSFULLY USE RENT SEEKING TO EXTERNALIZE THE COST OF MODERNIZATION AND MAKE EXPROPRIATION WITH COMPENSATION NO LONGER FEASIBLE.

02682 DEJANVRY, A.; SADOULET, E.
INVESTMENT STRATEGIES TO COMBAT RURAL POVERTY: A PROPOSAL FOR LATIN AMERICA
WORLD DEVELOPMENT, 17(8) (AUG 89), 1203-1221.
THE ECONOMIC CRISIS THAT STARTED IN 1980 HAS FORCED THE LATIN AMERICAN COUNTRIES TO IMPLEMENT DRASTIC STABILIZATION POLICIES AND STRUCTURAL ADJUSTMENT PROGRAMS. THE CONSEQUENT APPRECIATION OF THE REAL EXCHANGE RATE HAS TRANSFORMED AGRICULTURE INTO THE MOST DYNAMIC SECTOR OF THE ECONOMY. THIS CREATES THE POSSIBILITY OF DEFINING A FORWARD-LOOKING RURAL DEVELOPMENT STRATEGY THAT IS CONSISTENT WITH THIS NEW ROLE FOR AGRICULTURE AND THAT HAS THE POTENTIAL OF SIGNIFCANTLY LESSENING RURAL POVERTY. STARTING FROM A SOCIAL POVERTY MAP FOR THE RURAL AREAS, THE AUTHORS IDENTIFY A FIVE-PRONGED APPROACH THAT INCLUDES (1) FARM-ORIENTED RURAL DEVELOPMENT PROJECTS FOR THE UPPER SUBFAMILY AND FAMILY FARMS; (2) HOUSEHOLD-ORIENTED RURAL DEVELOPMENT PROJECTS FOR THE LOWER SUBFAMILY FARMS; (3) ACCESS TO ADDITIONAL ASSETS FOR THE LANDLESS AND SUBFAMILY FARMERS THROUGH LAND REFORM AND COLONIZATION; (4) EMPLOYMENT CREATION AND LABOR MARKET RATIONALIZATION; AND (5) THE PROMOTION OF BACKWARD, FORWARD, AND FINAL-DEMAND LINKAGES WITH AGRICULTURE LOCATED IN THE RURAL AREAS.

02683 DEJANVRY, A.; SADOULET, E.; YOUNG, L.W.
LAND AND LABOUR IN LATIN AMERICAN AGRICULTURE FROM THE 1950'S TO THE 1980'S
JOURNAL OF PEASANT STUDIES, 16(3) (APR 89), 396-424.
A CONSIDERABLE AMOUNT OF STATISTICAL INFORMATION ON THE EVOLUTION OF THE LATIN AMERICAN PEASANTRY DURING THE LAST 35 YEARS IS USED TO SHOW THAT IT HAS BECOME A LARGE REFUGE SECTOR THAT SYMPTOMISES THE DEVELOPMENTAL FAILURES OF THE REST OF THE ECONOMY. WHILE ECONOMIC GROWTH HAS BEEN RAPID UNTIL THE DEBT CRISIS OF THE EARLY 1980S, NEITHER ACCESS TO LAND NOR EMPLOYMENT CREATION HAS BEEN SUFFICIENT TO REDUCE RURAL POVERTY. AS A RESULT, THE BULK OF THE PEASANTRY NEITHER COMPETES WITH COMMERCIAL FARMING NOR BECOMES DISPOSSESSED OF ACCESS TO A PLOT OF LAND. THROUGH MIGRATION, POVERTY GRADUALLY BECOMES DISPLACED TO THE URBAN SECTOR.

02684 DEJENE, D.
THE ORIGIN OF POLITICAL INSTABILITY IN NIGERIA: THE CASE OF THE FIRST AND SECOND REPUBLIC
DISSERTATION ABSTRACTS INTERNATIONAL, 49(9) (MAR 89), 2798-A.
IN BOTH THE FIRST AND SECOND REPUBLICS, ELITE POLITICAL CULTURE WAS A MAJOR SOURCE OF POLITICAL CONFLICT AND INSTABILITY. BUT, DURING THE FIRST REPUBLIC, ETHNICITY WAS THE MOST DIVISIVE ELEMENT BECAUSE IT WAS THE PRIMARY VEHICLE FOR MOBILIZING POLITICAL SUPPORT REGIONALLY. DURING THE SECOND REPUBLIC, THE ENORMOUS PREMIUM ON POLITICAL POWER LED TO ELECTORAL FRAUD, CORRUPTION, INTOLERANCE, AND LACK OF COMPROMISE, WHICH DESTABILIZED AND ERODED THE LEGITIMACY OF THE RULING GOVERNMENT.

02685 DEJONG, N.
THE FIRST AMENDMENT: A COMPARISON OF NINETEENTH AND TWENTIETH CENTURY SUPREME COURT INTERPRETATIONS
JOURNAL OF POLITICAL SCIENCE, 16(1-2) (1988), 59-69.
THE AUTHOR COMPARES NINETEENTH AND TWENTIETH CENTURY SUPREME COURT INTERPRETATIONS OF THE RELIGIOUS CAUSES OF THE FIRST AMENDMENT. HE EXPLAINS THE VERY DIFFERENT NATURE OF THE TWO INTERPRETATIONS AND THE IMPACT EACH HAS HAD ON AMERICAN SOCIETY.

02686 DEKKER, P.; ESTER, P.
ELITE PERCEPTIONS OF MASS PREFERENCES IN THE NETHERLANDS; BIASES IN COGNITIVE RESPONSIVENESS
EUROPEAN JOURNAL OF POLITICAL RESEARCH, 17(5) (SEP 89),
623-369.
SEVERAL STUDIES HAVE SHOWN DISSIMILARITIES BETWEEN LEADERS AND VOTERS IN TERMS OF POLITICAL ATTITUDES AND POLICY PREFERENCES. THOUGH MANY EXPLANATIONS HAVE BEEN OFFERED FOR THIS PHENOMENON, THE KNOWLEDGE FACTOR HAS BEEN OVERLOOKED. THE BASIC QUESTION OF THIS PAPER IS HOW KNOWLEDGEABLE POLITICIANS ARE OF THE POLITICAL OPINIONS OF THEIR VOTERS AS WELL AS OF THE GENERAL PUBLIC. FORTY-SIX NATIONAL DUTCH POLITICIANS WERE ASKED TO ESTIMATE THE PERCENTAGE OF THE PUBLIC AT LARGE AND OF THEIR OWN VOTERS WHO AGREE WITH SPECIFIC POLITICAL STATEMENTS. THESE ESTIMATES WERE THEN COMPARED WITH THE ACTUAL DISTRIBUTION OF OPINIONS.

02687 DELANEY, K.J.
CONTROL DURING CORPORATE CRISIS: ASBESTOS AND MANVILLE BANKRUPTCY
CRITICAL SOCIOLOGY, 16(2-3) (SUM 89), 51-74.
CHAPTER 11 BANKRUPTCY PROVIDES AN OPPORTUNITY FOR ADDRESSING ISSUES OF POWER AND CONTROL DURING CORPORATE CRISIS. A BROAD NOTION OF POWER IS ESSENTIAL IN UNDERSTANDING THE COMPLEX EVENTS THAT LED TO THE CHAPTER 11 FILING OF THE MANVILLE CORPORATION, FORMERLY THE NATION'S LEADING ASBESTOS MANUFACTURER. THE THEORY OF FINANCE HEGEMONY PLACES THIS CASE IN AN ENTIRELY NEW LIGHT BY TAKING INTO ACCOUNT THE POWER OF THE FINANCIAL COMMUNITY. THE MANVILLE BANKRUPTCY ILLUMINATES SEVERAL MECHANISMS BY WHICH THIS HEGEMONY OPERATES. FROM THIS PERSPECTIVE, CHAPTER 11 BANKRUPTCY IS VIEWED AS A CHOICE MADE FROM A SET OF OPTIONS SEVERELY CONSTRAINED BY OTHER POWERFUL INSTITUTIONS, RATHER THAN A RESULT OF MANAGERIAL INCOMPETENCE OR MARKET FAILURE.

02688 DELAUER, R.D.
THE GOOD OF IT AND ITS PROBLEMS
PHILADELPHIA: ANLS OF AMER ACMY OF POLITICAL AND SOC SCIENCE, (502) (MAR 89), 130-140.
THE EVOLUTION OF THE PRESENT RELATIONSHIPS BETWEEN THE MILITARY ESTABLISHMENT AND THE NATION'S UNIVERSITIES IN THE PERFORMANCE OF DEFENSERELATED RESEARCH AND DEVELOPMENT IS SUMMARIZED. THE PRESENT RELATIONSHIPS AND ORGANIZATIONAL CONCEPTS HAVE THEIR ROOTS IN THE YEARS IMMEDIATELY PRIOR TO WORLD WAR II. THE 25 YEARS FROM THE END OF THE WAR TO 1970 WERE PARTICULARLY SIGNIFICANT IN SHAPING TODAY'S MILITARY-UNIVERSITY COLLABORATION AND COOPERATION. THE VIETNAM ERA AND THE HIGH-INFLATION PERIOD OF THE 1970S CREATED MANY PROBLEMS FOR THE ESTABLISHED RELATIONSHIPS; PARTICULARLY TROUBLESOME WERE THE ANTIWAR SENTIMENT ON MANY CAMPUSES AND THE DECISION BY CERTAIN UNIVERSITIES TO REJECT CLASSIFIED MILITARY RESEARCH EFFORTS. RENEWED SUPPORT OF SCIENCE AND TECHNOLOGY ENDEAVORS IN THE LATE 1970S BROUGHT ABOUT CERTAIN IMPROVEMENTS IN THE MILITARY-ACADEMIC ENVIRONMENT; INNOVATIVE INITIATIVES IN RESEARCH AND DEVELOPMENT ADMINISTRATION IN THE 1980S HAVE FURTHER IMPROVED THESE RELATIONSHIPS. REPRESENTATIVE PROBLEMS AND SOLUTIONS AND POSSIBLE FUTURE DIRECTIONS OF THESE VERY IMPORTANT RELATIONSHIPS ARE REVIEWED AND EXPLORED.

02689 DELEON, R.E.; POWELL, S.S.
GROWTH CONTROL AND ELECTORAL POLITICS: THE TRIUMPH OF URBAN POPULISM IN SAN FRANCISCO
WESTERN POLITICAL QUARTERLY, 42(2) (JUN 89), 307-332.
ON NOVEMBER 4, 1986, SAN FRANCISCO VOTERS PASSED INTO LAW THE MOST AMBITIOUS GROWTH CONTROL MEASURE EVER ENACTED IN THE UNITED STATES. PLACED IN THE CONTEXT OF THREE COMPETING THEORETICAL PERSPECTIVES ON THE POLITICS OF URBAN GROWTH, THIS STUDY ANALYZES THE POLITICAL AND ECONOMIC CONDITIONS THAT MADE THE PROPOSITION M VICTORY POSSIBLE. DRAWING UPON ELECTION STATISTICS, CENSUS TRACT DATA, JOURNALISTIC REPORTAGE, AND PERSONAL INTERVIEWS WITH KEY PARTICIPANTS, THE AUTHORS FOUND THAT SLOW-GROWTH COALITIONS OF PROGRESSIVES, ENVIRONMENTALISTS, WORKING-CLASS HOMEOWNERS, AND RACIAL MINORITIES CAN BE MOBILIZED TO CHALLENGE THE "PREEMPTIVE POWER" OF GROWTH-MACHINE ELITES IN LARGE AMERICAN CITIES.

02690 DELFS, R.; AWANOMARA, S.
ANGLING FOR INFLUENCE
FAR EASTERN ECONOMIC REVIEW, 142(51) (DEC 89), 10-11.
THE U.S. GOVERNMENT'S DECISION TO SEND A HIGH-RANKING ENVOY TO CHINA APPEARS TO HAVE REVERSED THE DOWNWARD MOMENTUM THAT CHARACTERIZED SINO-U.S. RELATIONS SINCE CHINA'S REPRESSION OF PRO-DEMOCRACY DEMONSTRATIONS IN JUNE. MAY CRITICS CHARGE THAT THE VISIT OF NATIONAL SECURITY ADVISER BRENT SCOWCROFT TO BEIJING IS A VIOLATION OF THE BAN ON HIGH-LEVEL CONTACTS—PART OF A SERIES OF SANCTIONS PROTESTING TIANANEMENT SQUARE—AND WILL SEND CHINESE LEADERS THE WRONG MESSAGE. HOWEVER, BUSH;S DECISION TO MAKE A UNILATERAL CONCESSION WILL ULTIMATELY BE JUDGED IN TERMS OF ITS PERCEIVED IMPACT ON THE CURRENT POLITICAL STRUGGLE WITHIN THE CHINESE LEADERSHIP OVER THE LONGER TERM. WORSENING ECONOMIC CONDITIONS IN CHINA AND REFORM IN EASTERN EUROPE HAS LENT NEW HOPE TO CHINA'S EMBATTLED LIBERAL INTELLECTUALS.

02691 DELFS, R.
FANG'S PLEA TO COMRADES: WHAT ABOUT THE THINKERS
FAR EASTERN ECONOMIC REVIEW, 141(27) (JUL 88), 71-73.
ASTROPHYSICIST FANG LIZHI, CHINA'S MOST PROMINENT
DISSIDENT HAS BEEN CALLED "CHINA'S SAKHAROV". MANY
CHARACTERIZE HIM AS A STRONG ADVOCATE OF DEMOCRACY. ALTHOUGH
HE HAS BEEN OUTSPOKEN IN HIS CRITICISM OF THE CHINESE
GOVERNMENT, A CLOSE ANALYSIS OF HIS VIEWS WILL REVEAL THAT
THEY ARE PROFOUNDLY ELITIST, EMPHASIZING THE PUTTING OF
INTELLECTUALS FIRST. REGARDLESS OF HIS POLITICAL PHILOSOPHY,
HE REMAINS A DYNAMIC AND CONTROVERSIAL FIGURE IN CHINA.

02692 DELFS, R.
HARD LINE ON TIBET
FAR EASTERN ECONOMIC REVIEW, 141(27) (JUL 88), 14-15.
ALTHOUGH MANY OBSERVERS FEEL THAT RECONCILIATION BETWEEN
CHINA AND THE DALAI LAMA IS ONLY A MATTER OF TIME, THE GULF
BETWEEN THE TWO STILL APPEARS TO BE QUITE WIDE. CHINA
SUMMARILY REJECTED THE DALAI LAMA'S PROPOSAL THAT TIBET
BECOME A SELF-GOVERNING ENTITY "IN ASSOCIATION" WITH CHINA.
ALTHOUGH THE DALAI LAMA'S POSITION COMPROMISED THE
SOVEREIGNTY OF TIBET IN SOME PEOPLE'S EYES, CHINA SEEMS AS
OF YET UNWILLING TO GRANT ANY AUTONOMY TO THE PROVINCE.

02693 DELFS, R.
POWER TO THE PARTY
FAR EASTERN ECONOMIC REVIEW, 142(49) (DEC 89), 23-25.
A SECRET CHINESE COMMUNIST PARTY DOCUMENT SHOWS THAT THE
PARTY IS ORDERING CHINA BACK TO CENTRAL PLANNING. IT LISTS
DECISIONS ON ECONOMIC POLICY TAKEN BY THE PARTY CENTRAL
COMMITTEE AT ITS RECENT FIFTH PLENUM, CALLING FOR VASTLY
INCREASED SCOPE FOR STATE PLANNING ORGANS AND NEW
RESTRICTIONS ON PRIVATE SECTOR BUSINESSES AND COLLECTIVE
RURAL INDUSTRIES. ALTHOUGH THE DOCUMENT DOES NOT SPEAK OF
DIRECTLY ABOLISHING REFORMS OR ELIMINATING MARKET FORCES,
ITS CALL FOR CORRECTION AND PERFECTION OF REFORMS AND THE
PRESERVATION OF THEIR "SOCIALIST ORIENTATION" SHARPLY
CONTRADICTS THE THRUST OF ECONOMIC REFORMS CARRIED OUT OVER
THE PAST FIVE YEARS UNDER THE LEADERSHIP OF FORMER PREMIER
AND GENERAL SECRETARY ZHAO ZIYANG.

02694 DELGADO, L.
CBO'S AND THE PUBLIC POLICY INITIATIVE: FUNDING A
COLLABORATIVE MODEL
NATIONAL CIVIC REVIEW, 78 3 (MAY 89), 197-201.
THERE IS SURPRISINGLY LITTLE SCHOLARLY RESEARCH
AVAILABLE ON THE EXPERIENCES OF PRIVATE FOUNDATIONS IN
FUNDING COMMUNITY-BASED ORGANIZATIONS (COBS) AND PUBLIC
POLICY EFFORTS. TO AID GRANT MAKERS IN TARGETING THEIR
SUPPORT, SUCCESSFUL AND EFFECTIVE APPROACHES TO COMMUNITY RE
VITALIZATION AND POLICY DEVELOPMENT MUST BE DOCUMENTED.

02695 DELIANG, Q.
AFGHANISTAN: PEACE UNREALIZED
BEIJING REVIEW, 32(3) (JAN 89), 18-19.
IN THE PAST YEAR, THE POLITICAL SETTLEMENT OF THE AFGHAN
ISSUE HAS MADE MAJOR PROGRESS, DUE TO THE EFFORTS OF THE
UNITED NATIONS AND THE CONCERNED PARTIES. THE SIGNING OF THE
GENEVA ACCORDS SIGNIFIED A BLOODLESS VICTORY FOR THE AFGHAN
PEOPLE IN THEIR ARMED FIGHT AGAINST THE SOVIET INVASION AND
ALSO WAS A MAJOR STEP AWAY FROM THE SOVIET UNION'S OLD
FOREIGN POLICY. BUT MILITARY CONFRONTATIONS ON THE
BATTLEFIELDS OF AFGHANISTAN HAVE RECENTLY SHARPENED AND CAST
A SHADOW OVER THE PROSPECTS FOR AN EARLY CEASEFIRE.

02696 DELL, E.
BUCKING THE MARKET: THE ROLE OF POLITICAL INSTITUTIONS --
THE EXAMPLE OF EUROPE
PUBLIC ADMINISTRATION, 67(2) (SUM 89), 211-222.
THE AUTHOR ATTEMPTS TO REFLECT IN A WIDE-RANGING WAY ON
CURRENT THINKING ABOUT THE ROLE OF GOVERNMENT IN RELATION TO
OTHER ECONOMIC ACTORS IN THE ECONOMY. HE SPECIFICALLY
CONCERNS HIMSELF WITH DEDUCTIONS AND CONCLUSIONS ABOUT
EUROPE 1992 AND THE NATURE AND MOTIVATIONS OF THE EUROPEAN
COMMUNITY. HE ALSO EXAMINES THE IMPLICATIONS OF EUROPE 1992
FOR GREAT BRITAIN.

02697 DELLACASA, N.
PRISONER OF THE MNR
NEW AFRICAN, (260) (MAY 89), 16-18.
THE AUTHOR, WHO IS A BRITISH TELEVISION JOURNALIST,
WRITES ABOUT HIS EXPERIENCES WHILE MAKING A FILM ABOUT THE
MOZAMBIQUE NATIONAL RESISTANCE GUERRILLAS IN MOZAMBIQUE. FOR
A YEAR AND A HALF, HE WAS HELD PRISONER IN THE WAR-TORN
COUNTRY WHERE THE MNR HAS GROWN FROM 800 MEN IN 1980 TO A
FORCE THAT HAS PARALYZED THE ECONOMY AND MADE THE COUNTRY
UNGOVERNABLE.

02698 DELORS, J.
EUROPE ON THE WAY TO 1992
INTERNATIONAL AFFAIRS (MOSCOW), (11) (NOV 89), 14-21.
THE PROCESS OF EUROPEAN ECONOMIC INTEGRATION HAS BEEN
FAR FROM SIMPLE. IT HAS BEEN SLOWED BY THE UNFAVOURABLE
ECONOMIC SITUATION, BUT TODAY THE IDEA OF ESTABLISHING A

UNIFIED ECONOMIC AREA BY 1992 IS AGAIN STIRRING THE EUROPEAN
COMMUNITY TO ACTION. THE RENEWED DYNAMISM HAS ATTRACTED THE
ATTENTION OF THOSE WHO DOUBTED THAT THE EUROPEAN COMMUNITY
HAS CAPABLE OF UNITING PEOPLE AND DISPLAYING INITIATIVE. THE
KEEN INTEREST THE SOVIET UNION AND OTHER EASTERN EUROPEAN
COUNTRIES ARE SHOWING IN THE EUROPEAN COMMUNITY IS CLEAR
EVIDENCE OF ITS VIABILITY.

02699 DELVOIE, L.
THE COMMONWEALTH IN CANADIAN FOREIGN POLICY
ROUND TABLE, (310) (APR 89), 137-143.
DURING THE PAST TWO YEARS CANADA HAS PLAYED A
PARTICULARLY ACTIVE AND PROMINENT ROLE IN COMMONWEALTH
AFFAIRS. THE ARTICLE EXAMINES THE "OTHER SIDE OF THE COIN"
BY EXAMINING THE PLACE OR ROLE OF THE COMMONWEALTH IN
CANADIAN FOREIGN POLICY. IT CONCLUDES THAT THE COMMONWEALTH
DOES NOT AND CANNOT OCCUPY A CENTRAL PLACE IN CANADIAN
FOREIGN POLICY. IT CAN, HOWEVER, BE A USEFUL ADJUNCT IN THE
PURSIUT OF CANADIAN INTERESTS IN A FEW COUNTRIES AND SERVES
AS A VEHICLE FOR CANADA TO DEVELOP AND MAINTAIN POLITICAL
AND HUMAN CONTACTS WITH A SIGNIFICANT NUMBER OF DEVELOPING
COUNTRIES.

02700 DEMAS, W.G.
ALISTER MCINTYRE AND CARIBBEAN POLITICAL ECONOMY
SOCIAL AND ECONOMIC STUDIES, 38(2) (JUN 89), 25-35.
FOR MORE THAN A QUARTER-CENTURY, ALISTER MCINTYRE HAS
BEEN INVOLVED IN ANALYZING ISSUES OF POLITICAL ECONOMY
AFFECTING THE CARIBBEAN, THE THIRD WORLD, AND NORTH-SOUTH
RELATIONS. IN THIS ESSAY, THE AUTHOR SURVEYS MCINTYRE'S
CONTRIBUTION TO THE STUDY OF POLITICAL ECONOMY IN THE
CARIBBEAN. HE FOCUSES ON THREE PIONEERING ARTICLES WRITTEN
BY MCINTYRE: "TOWARDS A FIRST APPRAISAL OF WEST INDIAN
MONETARY MANAGEMENT," "THE POLITICAL ECONOMY OF FEDERATION,"
AND "DECOLONIZATION AND TRADE POLICY IN THE WEST INDIES."

02701 DEMEKE, G.
THE RELIABILITY AND ACCURACY OF STATISTICAL SAMPLE SURVEYS
IN THIRD WORLD RURAL SETTINGS
DISSERTATION ABSTRACTS INTERNATIONAL, 49(11) (MAY 89),
3489-A.
THIS STUDY EXAMINES THE EFFICACY OF UTILIZING SAMPLE
SURVEY METHOD AS AN INSTRUMENT OF DATA COLLECTION IN THIRD
WORLD RURAL DEVELOPMENT PROGRAMS. THROUGH A VARIETY OF
RELIABILITY AND VALIDITY TESTS AND COMPARISON WITH KNOWN
POPULATION PARAMETERS OF SAMPLE SURVEY GENERATED DATA, IT
ASSESSES THE ABILITY OF THIS METHODOLOGY TO FURNISH ACCURATE
AND VALID INFORMATION. IN ADDITION, IT REVIEWS VARIOUS DATA
COLLECTION SYSTEMS AT THE DISPOSAL OF RURAL DEVELOPMENT
RESEARCHERS.

02702 DEMELO, J.; STANTON, J.; TARR, D.
REVENUE-RAISING TAXES: GENERAL EQUILIBRIUM EVALUATION OF
ALTERNATIVE TAXATION IN U.S. PETROLEUM INDUSTRIES
JOURNAL OF POLICY MODELING, 11(3) (FAL 89), 425-449.
THIS PAPER ASSESSES RECENT PROPOSALS TO INCREASE TAXES
AND TARIFFS IN THE ENERGY SECTOR TO REDUCE THE U.S. FEDERAL
DEFICIT. THE PAPER ESTIMATES THE WELFARE, FISCAL AND
EMPLOYMENT EFFECTS OF THE MOST COMMON PROPOSALS. THE
ESTIMATES ARE DERIVED FROM A TWELVE-SECTOR GENERAL
EQUILIBRIUM MODEL OF THE U.S. ECONOMY CALIBRATED TO 1984. A
PROPOSED 25 PERCENT IMPORT TARIFF ON CRUDE OIL WOULD RAISE
$7.3 BILLION IN GOVERNMENT REVENUE, WHILE A 15 PERCENT
EXCISE TAX ON PETROLEUM PRODUCTS WOULD RAISE $35 BILLION.
EACH DOLLAR OF GOVERNMENT REVENUE WOULD COME AT A LOSS OF 25
CENTS IN WELFARE IN THE FIRST CASE, BUT AT ONLY A ONE CENT
LOSS IN WELFARE IN THE SECOND. THE PAPER ALSO ESTIMATES THE
LEAST COSTLY (IN TERMS OF WELFARE) COMBINATION OF EXCISE
TAXES AND IMPORT TARIFFS ON THE TWO SECTORS TO RAISE $20
BILLION IN GOVERNMENT REVENUE. THE OPTIMAL TAX STRUCTURE IS
NONUNIFORM, INVOLVING BOTH TAXES AND IMPORT TARIFFS ON OIL,
AND A TARIFF AND SMALL SUBSIDY ON PETROLEUM PRODUCTS TO
COUNTERACT THE DISTORTION INDUCED BY THE TAXATION OF OIL.

02703 DEMETRIUS, F.J.
BRAZIL'S NATIONAL ALCOHOL PROGRAM: TECHNOLOGY AND
DEVELOPMENT IN AN AUTHORITARIAN REGIME
DISSERTATION ABSTRACTS INTERNATIONAL, 50(4) (OCT 89),
1075-A.
THE BRAZILIAN NATIONAL ALCOHOL PROGRAM (PROALCOOL) IS
THE WORLD'S LARGEST AND MOST SOPHISTICATED BIOMASS-TO-ENERGY
PROGRAM. THIS STUDY PROBES THE SOCIAL AND ECONOMIC
CONSEQUENCES OF PROALCOOL DURING ITS FIRST DECADE OF
OPERATION. THEN IT CONSIDERS TWO EXPLANATIONS FOR
PROALCOOL'S TECHNOLOGICAL CHOICES AND THEIR SOCIAL AND
ECONOMIC RESULTS. THE FIRST EXPLANATION FOCUSES ON MARKET
FORCES, WHILE THE SECOND IS A POLITICAL EXPLANATION. THE
STUDY CONCLUDES THAT PROALCOOL CAN BEST BE UNDERSTOOD AS
BOTH AN AGENT AND A PRODUCT OF AN AUTHORITARIAN POLITICAL
REGIME.

02704 DEMONT, J.
A NEW PLAN FOR DEBT
MACLEAN'S (CANADA'S NEWS MAGAZINE), 102(13) (MAR 89),

32-33.
THE PLAN RELEASED BY US SECRETARY OF TREASURY, NICHOLAS BRADY, SIGNALS A FUNDAMENTAL SHIFT IN US POLICY WITH REGARDS TO THIRD WORLD DEBT. SPURRED ON BY UNREST IN VENEZUELA AND OTHER AREAS, THE US IS MOVING TO EASE THE CRIPPLING LATIN AMERICAN DEBT BURDEN. HOWEVER, CANADIAN BANKS ARE UNLIKELY TO FOLLOW THE LEAD OF THE US. THEY HAVE PUBLICLY DEMONSTRATED THEIR OPPOSITION TO FORGIVING FOREIGN DEBT; HOWEVER, INTERNATIONAL ECONOMIC CONDITIONS MAY NECESSITATE MOVING BACK FROM SUCH A HARD-LINE STANCE.

02705 DEMONTGAILHARD, J.D.
CONVENTIONAL DISARMAMENT AND EUROPE
DISARMAMENT, XII(2) (SUM 89), 51-59.
GOVERNMENTS IN THE EAST AND THE WEST CHARACTERIZE THE NEGOTIATIONS OVER CONVENTIONAL ARMS REDUCTION IN EUROPE AS ONE OF THE TESTS OF THE TRANSITION TO A NEW ERA, IN WHICH THE RELAXATION OF MILITARY POSTURES COULD RESULT IN MORE FLUID POLITICAL, ECONOMIC, AND CULTURAL RELATIONS IN EUROPE. SEEN IN THIS LIGHT, THE RECENT INCONCLUSIVE END OF THE MBFR TALKS AFTER 15 YEARS OF NEGOTIATIONS SHOULD SYMBOLIZE THE PASSING TO A RADICALLY NEW APPROACH. BUT THE GOALS AND ULTERIOR MOTIVES OF THE NEGOTIATING PARTIES ARE NOT NECESSARILY THE SAME. THE STAKES AT FUTURE NEGOTIATIONS WILL MAKE THE POLITICAL APPROACH AS IMPORTANT AS A PURELY MILITARY ONE.

02706 DEMOTT, B.
RESURRECTING LIBERALISM: FINDING STANDARDS OF DEBATE
CURRENT, (309) (JAN 89), 14-22.
NEOCONSERVATISM, WHICH IS ESSENTIALLY AN OVERSIMPLIFICATION AND DISTORTION OF THE MID-TWENTIETH CENTURY CRITIQUE OF LIBERALISM, NEEDS NO EXEGESIS. BUT THE IDEAS NEOCONSERVATISM DISTORTED WARRANT CAREFUL RE-EXAMINATION. ACQUAINTANCE WITH THIS ORIGINAL BODY OF THOUGHT, AS IT FIRST EXISTED, COULD BE USEFUL TO ANY WOULD-BE ARCHITECT OF FUTURE POLITICAL RENEWAL.

02707 DENEAULT, G.V.
A STUDY OF (CONGRESSIONAL) APPROPRIATED FUNDING FOR MORALE, WELFARE, AND RECREATION IN THE UNITED STATES AIR FORCE
DISSERTATION ABSTRACTS INTERNATIONAL, 49(7) (JAN 89), 1956-A.
THERE IS A STRONG NEED FOR CONGRESS AND THE DEPARTMENT OF DEFENSE TO DEVELOP A POSITIVE RELATIONSHIP REGARDING MORALE, WELFARE, AND RECREATION PROGRAMS FOR THE MILITARY, IN ORDER TO RECEIVE THE MOST BENEFIT FROM APPROPRIATED FUNDS.

02708 DENICH, B.
PARADOXES OF GENDER AND POLICY IN EASTERN EUROPE: A DISCUSSANT'S COMMENTS
EAST EUROPEAN QUARTERLY, XXIII(4) (WIN 89), 499-506.
EAST EUROPEAN GOVERNMENTS, USING MARXIST FEMINIST PREMISES AS AN IDEOLOGICAL CORNERSTONE OF SOCIAL POLICY, HAVE PROMOTED EMPLOYMENT AS THE ECONOMIC MEANS FOR WOMEN TO GAIN EQUALITY. NOW THAT THE EAST EUROPEAN EXPERIENCE SPANS FOUR DECADES, IT IS TIMELY TO EXAMINE THE INTERPLAY OF THEORY AND REALITY IN WOMEN'S EQUALITY. IT IS IN EVERYDAY LIFE THAT GENDER RELATIONS TAKE FORMS AND THE EFFECTS OF POLICIES CAN BE OBSERVED.

02709 DENITCH, B.
YUGOSLAVIA: THE LIMITS OF REFORM
DISSENT, (WIN 89), 78-85.
ECONOMIC REFORMS REQUIRE SACRIFICES, AND THE RULING COMMUNIST PARTY NO LONGER HAS THE ABILITY TO MOBILIZE OR BULLY SUFFICIENT PUBLIC SUPPORT FOR THESE SACRIFICES UNLESS IT ENTERS INTO A PARTNERSHIP WITH OTHER SOCIAL AND POLITICAL FORCES. "WHICH FORCES?" IS THE QUESTION. THERE ARE THREE POSSIBLE CHOICES: PARTNERSHIP WITH THE TECHNICAL AND MANAGERIAL INTELLIGENTSIA; POPULIST NATIONALISM; ALLIANCE WITH THE MORE SKILLED AND ACTIVE WORKERS AND TECHNICIANS AND THE DEMOCRATIC INTELLIGENTSIA. EACH OF THESE OPTIONS CARRIES ITS OWN POSSIBILITIES AND COSTS. IN YUGOSLAVIA, ALL THREE OPTIONS ARE CURRENTLY BEING TRIED IN DIFFERENT REPUBLICS.

02710 DENMAN, R.
REFLECTIONS ON LEAVING WASHINGTON
EUROPE, 288 (JUL 89), 16.
IN THIS ARTICLE, THE AUTHOR, HEAD OF THE EUROPEAN COMMUNITY COMMISSION'S DELEGATION IN WASHINGTON FROM 1982-1989, REFLECTS ON HIS SEVEN YEAR IN THAT POST. HE FOCUSES ON THE IMPROVEMENTS MADE IN AMERICAN ATTITUDES TOWARD THE EUROPEAN COMMUNITY SINCE THE PLANS FOR A SINGLE EUROPEAN MARKET HAVE SOLIDIFIED AND IMPLEMENTATION IS IMMINENT.

02711 DENNIS, R.
LIBERTARIAN IS AN L-WORD, TOO
REASON, 20(10) (MAR 89), 28-30.
THE POINTS OF AGREEMENT BETWEEN LIBERTARIANS AND LIBERAL DEMOCRATS ARE GREATER THAN MOST PEOPLE THINK. BOTH HAVE A COMMON INTEREST IN FIGHTING A RECURRING AMERICAN POLITICAL PHENOMENON: POPULISM.

02712 DENNISON, B.
WHERE STANDS THE TRADE UNION MOVEMENT?
POLITICAL AFFAIRS, LXVIII(7) (JUL 89), 32-37.
THE U.S. TRADE UNION MOVEMENT IS GOING THROUGH AN ERA OF RAPID AND REMARKABLE CHANGES. NEW GENERATIONS OF UNION LEADERS ARE EMERGING WHO REFLECT, MORE AND MORE, THE MOSAIC OF OUR WORKING CLASS. THEY ARE BLACK, WHITE, LATINO, ASIAN AND NATIVE AMERICAN; THEY ARE WOMEN AND MEN. THIS ARTICLE EXAMINES THE GAINS MADE OF THE LABOR MOVEMENT DURING THE 1980'S. THE DECADE BEGAN WITH THE ELECTION OF THE MOST ANTI-LABOR AND ANTI-UNION U.S. PRESIDENT IN MODERN HISTORY. LABOR HAS SPENT THE DECADE IN PITCHED BATTLE AGAINST A CORPORATE OFFENSIVE THAT HAD THE FULL WEIGHT OF THE EXECUTIVE BRANCH OF GOVERNMENT IN ITS CORNER. THESE NEARLY 10 YEARS OF UNPRECEDENTED STRUGGLE, HAVE HAD A DEEP AND LASTING IMPACT ON THE LABOR MOVEMENT.

02713 DENNISON, B.
YONKERS BATTLES TO END SEGREGATED HOUSING
POLITICAL AFFAIRS, LXVIII(2) (FEB 89), 19-26.
DURING THE SUMMER OF 1988, THE CITY OF YONKERS, NEW YORK, FACED POTENTIALLY BANKRUPTING FINES FOR REFUSING TO BUILD 1,000 UNITS OF AFFORDABLE HOUSING AS PART OF A COURT-ORDERED HOUSING DESEGREGATION PLAN. THE YONKERS CASE ILLUSTRATES THE NATION'S GROWING HOUSING CRISIS AND HOW RACISM HAS ADDED TO THE PROBLEM, MAKING HOUSING MORE EXPENSIVE AND HARDER TO FIND.

02714 DENOON, D.B.H.
JAPAN AND THE U.S.: THE SECURITY AGENDA
CURRENT HISTORY, 88(534) (JAN 89), 37-38, 57.
ALTHOUGH THERE HAS BEEN NO SINGLE, DRAMATIC TURNING POINT, THERE HAS BEEN A MAJOR CHANGE IN U.S.-JAPANESE INTERACTION SINCE 1978. DURING THE CARTER ADMINISTRATION, DISCUSSIONS WITH JAPAN FOCUSED PRIMARILY ON TRADE QUESTIONS AND NEITHER SIDE SHOWED ANY PARTICULAR DESIRE FOR A CHANGE. BUT BY 1983, THE SITUATION WAS FUNDAMENTALLY DIFFERENT. THE COMBINATION OF PERCEIVED AMERICAN WEAKNESS AND THE ELECTION OF RONALD REAGAN, A PRESIDENT COMMITTED TO THE RAPID MODERNIZATION AND EXPANSION OF AMERICAN MILITARY STRENGTH, LAID THE FOUNDATION FOR A TRANSFORMATION OF THE U.S.-JAPANESE SECURITY RELATIONSHIP.

02715 DENZAU, A.
TRADE PROTECTION COMES TO SILICON VALLEY
SOCIETY, 26(3) (MAR 89), 38-42.
THE ARTICLE ATTEMPTS TO ANSWER TWO PRIMARY QUESTIONS ABOUT THE IMPACT OF TRADE PROTECTION ON SILICON VALLEY 1) WHAT ARE THE HIGH-TECH EMPLOYMENT EFFECTS OF INCREASED MEMORY CHIP PRICES? 2) WHAT ARE THE MARKET EFFECTS ON INTEGRATED CIRCUIT (IC) PRODUCERS AND USERS? THE ARTICLE CONCLUDES THAT ROUGHLY ONE JOB IS LOST IN THE ELECTRONICS INDUSTRY FOR EACH JOB SAVED IN THE SEMICONDUCTOR INDUSTRY. FURTHERMORE, AMERICAN TRADE PROTECTION WOULD HAVE THE ADDITIONAL ADVERSE EFFECT OF PUSHING JAPANESE FIRMS INTO NEW IC MARKETS THAT ARE CURRENTLY DOMINATED BY THE US.

02716 DEONIS, J.
BRAZIL ON THE TIGHTROPE TOWARD DEMOCRACY
FOREIGN AFFAIRS, 68(4) (FAL 89), 127-143.
A GROUNDSWELL OF PUBLIC DISILLUSIONMENT WITH BRAZIL'S POLITICAL LEADERSHIP AND AN EXPLOSIVE MOOD OF SOCIAL DISCONTENT HAVE REPLACED THE HIGH HOPES OF 1985 WHEN BRAZIL CELEBRATED THE RESTORATION OF DEMOCRACY. THE MAIN TARGET OF THIS DISILLUIONMENT IS PRESIDENT JOSE SARNEY, WHO HAS BECOME A SYMBOL OF BRAZIL'S FAILURES. THE MAIN BENEFICIARY IS FERNANDO COLOR DE MELLO, WHO IS LEADING AN ANTI-SARNEY CAMPAIGN BASED PRIMARILY ON THE THEME OF PUNISHMENT FOR CORRUPTION IN HIGH PLACES. THE PUBLIC MOOD AND THE LACK OF CLEAR-CUT, TESTED POLITICAL ALTERNATIVES MAKE BRAZIL'S FUTURE HIGHLY UNCERTAIN.

02717 DEPARLE, J.
BEYOND THE LEGAL RIGHT
WASHINGTON MONTHLY, 21(3) (APR 89), 28-29, 32-40, 42-44.
THE ARTICLE EXAMINES LIBERAL AND FEMINIST ATTITUDES TOWARDS THE DIFFICULT ISSUE OF ABORTION. IT CONCLUDES THAT MANY OF THE PROCHOICE CAMP SEEK TO PORTRAY THE ISSUE IN OVERSIMPLISTIC TERMS THAT IGNORE MANY IMPORTANT AND PRESSING ISSUES. THE ARTICLE ATTEMPTS TO ANALYZE SOME OF THESE OFTEN CONTRADICTORY ISSUES AND THEIR IMPLICATIONS FOR THE MORALITY OF ABORTION. IT CONCLUDES THAT ALTHOUGH THERE ARE NO EASY ANSWERS, THE UNDERLYING, OFTEN THORNY, ISSUES THAT SURROUND ABORTION MUST BE DEALT WITH BEFORE A CONCRETE DECISION CAN BE MADE.

02718 DEPARLE, J.
THE JUICE AIN'T NO USE
WASHINGTON MONTHLY, 21(4) (MAY 89), 32-33.
THE AUTHOR ARGUES THAT USING THE DEATH PENALTY MORE OFTEN MAY MAKE SOME PEOPLE FEEL BETTER, BUT IT'S NOT LIKELY TO DETER CRIME.

02719 DEPARLE, J.
THE WORST CITY GOVERNMENT IN AMERICA
WASHINGTON MONTHLY, 20(12) (JAN 89), 33-45.
IN WASHINGTON, D.C., GOVERNMENT MISMANAGEMENT IS SO
COMPLETE THAT THE PASSIVE SINS OF ITS INEPT BUREAUCRACY
RIVAL ANY ACTIVE EXPLOITATION OF THE POOR. AS IN MOST BIG
CITIES, THE CASE AGAINST WASHINGTON'S GOVERNMENT FOCUSES ON
OLD-STYLE SIN AND CORRUPTION. BUT PLAIN CORRUPTION IS
ACTUALLY ONLY A FOOTNOTE COMPARED TO THE QUIET CRUELTY OF
THE DISTRICT'S EVERYDAY BUREAUCRATIC INCOMPETENCE.

02720 DEPARLE, J.
WHAT THE SMARTEST MAN IN WASHINGTON DOESN'T UNDERSTAND.
AND WHY IT WILL HURT YOU.
WASHINGTON MONTHLY, 21(10) (NOV 89), 24-37.
THIS ARTICLE EXAMINES THE FAILURE OF OMB TO RECOGNIZE
AND QUICKLY DEAL WITH CORRUPTION ON THE GOVERNMENT LEVEL,
USING THE HUD AND THE SAVINGS AND LOAN CRISIS AS EXAMPLES,
IT SUGGESTS THAT THE AGENCY NEEDS TO DELVE DEEPER THAN THE
NUMBERS AND GO ON TO PROGRAM ANALYSIS. IT FOLLOWS THE
HISTORY OF THE AGENCY OF GOING FROM BAD TO WORSE.

02721 DEPINIES, J.
DEBT SUSTAINABILITY AND OVERADJUSTMENT
WORLD DEVELOPMENT, 17(1) (JAN 89), 29-43.
A SIMPLE DEBT ACCUMULATION MODEL BASED ON BALANCE-OF-
PAYMENTS IDENTITIES IS ANALYZED AND USED TO PROJECT DEBT-TO-
EXPORT RATIOS IN LATIN AMERICA AND AFRICA UP TO 1990. THE
FUNDAMENTALS OF DEBT DYNAMICS ARE SHOWN TO BE DETERMINED BY
FOUR RATIOS: INTEREST RATE TO EXPORT GROWTH, IMPORT GROWTH
TO EXPORT GROWTH AND THE INITIAL DEBT-TO-EXPORT AND IMPORT-
TO-EXPORT RATIOS. THE RELEVANCE OF THE INITIAL CONDITIONS
AND THE IMPORTANCE OF IMPORT GROWTH ON DEBT DYNAMICS ARE
DISCUSSED. SUSTAINABILITY OF THE DEBT IN TERMS OF KEEPING
DEBT-TO-EXPORT RATIOS ON A DECLINING TREND IS DEFINED AND
USED TO QUANTIFY THE ASSOCIATED AMOUNT OF EXCESS IMPORT
RESTRAINT IN DEBTOR COUNTRIES. TWO TESTS ARE CONSTRUCTED
THAT MEASURE EXCESS RESTRAINT (I.E., OVERADJUSTMENT) BASED
ON THE FUNDAMENTALS OF DEBT DYNAMICS.

02722 DEROSA, M.L.
AN ANALYSIS OF THE CONFEDERATE STATES OF AMERICA
CONSTITUTION IN CONTRADISTINCTION TO THE UNITED STATES
CONSTITUTION AS EXPLICATED BY PUBLIUS
DISSERTATION ABSTRACTS INTERNATIONAL, 48(10) (APR 88),
2716-A.
THE DISSERTATION ANALYZES THE DIFFERENCES AND
DISTINGUISHING CHARACTERISTICS OF THE CONFEDERATE STATES OF
AMERICA CONSTITUTION AND THE US CONSTITUTION. THREE MAJOR
DISTINGUISHING CHARACTERISTICS ARE THE STATUS OF SOVEREGNTY
WITHIN THE CONTEXT OF FEDERALISM, THE APPLICATION OF A
NATIONAL BILL OF RIGHTS, AND THE INSTITUTIONAL CHECKS AND
BALANCES USED BY THE CONFEDERATE CONSTITUTION.

02723 DERRICK, J.; ISLAM, S.
FRISSON IN THE FRANC ZONE
SOUTH, (107) (SEP 89), 28-30.
PROPOSALS AIMED AT FULL ECONOMIC AND MONETARY
INTEGRATION OF THE EUROPEAN COMMUNITY ARE AROUSING CONCERN
ABOUT THE LONGSTANDING MONETARY UNION BETWEEN FRANCE AND 14
AFRICAN COUNTRIES. CENTRAL BANK GOVERNORS FEAR THAT THE
EMERGENCE OF A NEW SINGLE CURRENCY BLOC IN EUROPE WILL
JEOPARDIZE THE PRESENT ARRANGEMENT. PRESIDENT OMAR BONGO OF
GABON HAS SUGGESTED THAT THE FRANC ZONE BE REPLACED BY A
MONETARY SYSTEM LINKING THE EC WITH ALL THE AFRICAN,
CARIBBEAN, AND PACIFIC COUNTRIES THAT PARTICIPATE IN THE
LOME TRADE ARRANGEMENT.

02724 DERTHICK, M.
THE ENDURING FEATURES OF AMERICAN FEDERALISM
BROOKINGS REVIEW, 7(3) (SUM 89), 34-38.
THE AMERICAN STATES MAY BE ENJOYING A RENAISSANCE, BUT
THEY MUST BE WARY OF BEING VICTIMIZED BY THE FEDERAL
GOVERNMENT. CERTAIN REGULATORY EXCESSES OF THE FEDERAL
GOVERNMENT VIS-A-VIS THE STATES HAVE BEEN MODIFIED IN THE
PAST SEVERAL YEARS. YET NOT EVEN UNDER RONALD REAGAN DID THE
FEDERAL GOVERNMENT STEP BACK FROM THE NEW CONSTITUTIONAL
FRONTIERS MAPPED OUT IN THE LAST DECADE OR TWO. THE
PRESIDENT'S EXECUTIVE ORDER OF OCTOBER 1987 ON FEDERALISM
MAY BE INTERPRETED AS AN ATTEMPT TO DRAW BACK, WITH ITS
RHETORICAL STATEMENT OF FEDERALISM AND ITS INSTRUCTIONS TO
EXECUTIVE AGENCIES TO REFRAIN FROM USING THEIR DISCRETION TO
PREEMPT STATE ACTION. BUT TO READ IT IS TO BE REMINDED OF
HOW LITTLE UNILATERAL POWER THE PRESIDENT HAS.

02725 DESAI, U.
ASSESSING THE IMPACTS OF THE SURFACE MINING CONTROL AND
RECLAMATION ACT
POLICY STUDIES REVIEW, 9(1) (AUT 89), 98-108.
THIS PAPER ATTEMPTS TO ASSESS THE IMPACTS OF SMCRA IN
SIX MAJOR SURFACE COAL PRODUCING STATES. ALTHOUGH IT IS NOT
POSSIBLE TO MAKE AN UNQUALIFIED OVERALL NATIONAL ASSESSMENT,
THE EVIDENCE PRESENTED IN THE PAPER INDICATES THAT IN MANY
(BUT BY NO MEANS ALL) CASES, SURFACE COAL MINING IS NOW

CARRIED OUT IN ENVIRONMENTALLY LESS DESTRUCTIVE WAYS THAN
BEFORE THE ACT. HOWEVER, THE ACCOMPLISHMENTS HAVE FALLEN FAR
SHORT OF EXPECTATIONS. THE SITUATION IN SOME STATES HAS
GOTTEN WORSE THAN BEFORE THE ACT. OVERALL, THE IMPACT OF THE
ACT ON THE GROUND HAS BEEN MIXED AND HAS DEPENDED ON THE
RIGOR WITH WHICH THE ACT HAS BEEN IMPLEMENTED IN INDIVIDUAL
COAL STATES.

02726 DESAI, U.
PUBLIC PARTICIPATION IN ENVIRONMENTAL POLICY
IMPLEMENTATION: CASE OF THE SURFACE MINING CONTROL AND
RECLAMATION ACT
AMERICAN REVIEW OF PUBLIC ADMINISTRATION, 19(1) (MAR 89),
49-65.
ENVIRONMENTAL LEGISLATION ENACTED IN THE LAST TWO
DECADES CONTAINS MANY PROVISIONS AND MECHANISMS FOR PUBLIC
PARTICIPATION. HOWEVER, LITTLE SYSTEMATIC INFORMATION IS
AVAILABLE ON ACTUAL USE OF DIFFERENT MECHANISMS OF
PARTICIPATION IN DIFFERENT STAGES OF POLICY IMPLEMENTATION.
THIS STUDY DESCRIBES THE USE OF VARIOUS MECHANISMS BY
PARTICIPANTS IN ONE MAJOR ENVIRONMENTAL POLICY, THE SURFACE
MINING CONTROL AND RECLAMATION ACT (SMCRA). DATA INDICATE
THAT THE ENFORCEMENT STAGE OF POLICY IMPLEMENTATION
GENERATES MOST INDIVIDUAL CITIZEN INVOLVEMENT, AND CITIZEN
COMPLAINTS ARE THE MOST WIDELY USED MECHANISM FOR CITIZEN
PARTICIPATION. HOWEVER, AGGREGATE DATA INDICATE THAT OVERALL
CITIZEN PARTICIPATION IN THE IMPLEMENTATION OF SMCRA HAS
BEEN MODEST. THE PAPER CONCLUDES WITH THOUGHTS ON WHY
EXTENSIVE LEGISLATIVE PROVISIONS FOR CITIZEN PARTICIPATION
ARE NEVERTHELESS JUSTIFIED.

02727 DESCH, M. C.
THE KEYS THAT LOCK UP THE WORLD: IDENTIFYING AMERICAN
INTERESTS IN THE PERIPHERY
INTERNATIONAL SECURITY, 14(1) (SUM 89), 86-121.
THIS ARTICLE ARGUES THAT MANY REGIONS THAT LACK
INTRINSIC IMPORTANCE BECAUSE THEY HAVE NO KEY RESOURCES OR
ARE ECONOMICALLY UNDERDEVELOPED ARE NONETHELESS IMPORTANT TO
THE DEFENSE OF VITAL AREAS, AND THEREFORE HAVE EXTRINSIC
IMPORTANCE TO THE UNITED STATES. DESCH SURVEYS CASES OF
GREAT POWER GRAND STRATEGY FROM THE PELOPONNESIAN WAR TO THE
BRITISH EMPIRE AND FINDS THAT STATES THAT FAILED TO
RECOGNIZE THIS CRUCIAL INTERDEPENDENCE OF INTRINSICALLY AND
EXTRINSICALLY IMPORTANT AREAS TENDED TO COMMIT STRATEGIC
BLUNDERS THAT LED TO THEIR DOWNFALL.

02728 DESCHOUWER, K.
PATTERNS OF PARTICIPATION AND COMPETITION IN BELGIUM
WEST EUROPEAN POLITICS, 12(4) (OCT 89), 28-41.
THIS ARTICLE DEFINES THE PARTY SYSTEM IN A PURELY
SARTORIAN WAY, WHICH SHOWS EXPLICITLY HOW CHANGES IN
CLEAVAGE STRUCTURES OR ELECTORAL BEHAVIOR AFFECT THE PARTY
SYSTEM. THIS STUDY SEEKS CHANGES IN THE PARTY SYSTEM THAT
CAN BE TRACED BACK TO CHANGES IN THE ENVIRONMENT OF THE
PARTY SYSTEM. IT DEMONSTRATES THE LOGIC OF THIS REASONING.
THE SOCIETAL CHANGES AND THE CHANGES OF PARTY-POLITICAL
PARTICIPATION IN BELGIUM ARE DESCRIBED IN SOME DETAIL
BECAUSE THEY ARE IMPORTANT TO UNDERSTAND WHAT IS HAPPENING
IN THE PARTY SYSTEM.

02729 DESILVA, M.
ELECTION MOVES
INDIA TODAY, XIV(2) (JAN 89), 72.
ON FEB. 15, 1989, SRI LANKANS WILL GO TO THE POLL TO
ELECT A PARLIAMENT. FOR NEWLY-ELECTED PRESIDENT RANASINGHE
PREMADASA A SLIGHT SWING IN THE VOTE COULD MEAN A HOSTILE
PARLIAMENT. ALTHOUGH THE JVP AND THE LIBERATION TIGERS OF
TAMIL EELAM ARE UNLIKELY TO PARTICIPATE IN THE ELECTIONS,
OTHER TAMIL MINORITY ORGANIZATIONS HAVE A GOOD CHANCE OF
WINNING SEATS, DUE TO A RECENT CHANGE IN THE RULES GOVERNING
REPRESENTATION IN PARLIAMENT.

02730 DESILVA, M.; TEKWANI, S.
SRI LANKA: BALLOTS VS. BULLETS
INDIA TODAY, XIV(5) (MAR 89), 66-69.
SRI LANKA PRESIDENT PREMADASA'S MAIN CONCERN NOW IS THE
BLOODY CIVIL STRIFE THAT HAS CONVULSED THE COUNTRY FOR FIVE
YEARS. PREMADASA'S ONLY HOPE TO SUCCESSFULLY NEGOTIATE WITH
THE LIBERATION TIGERS OF TARMIL EELAM AND OTHER OUTLAW
GROUPS IS TO CONVINCE THEM OF THE NEED AND HIS DESIRE TO
REMOVE THE INDIAN PEACE-KEEPING FORCES FROM SRI LANKA BY
ELIMINATING THE STRIFE THAT ORIGINALLY NECESSITATED THE
FORCE'S PRESENCE.

02731 DESILVA, M.
TACTICAL TURNABOUT
INDIA TODAY, XIV(8) (MAY 89), 88-89.
IN A DRAMATIC TURNAROUND, THE LIBERATION TIGERS OF TAMIL
EELAM (LTTE) ISSUED A STATEMENT DECLARING ITS WILLINGNESS TO
DISCUSS PEACE WITH REPRESENTATIVES OF THE SRI LANKAN
GOVERNMENT. THE TIMING SUGGESTS AN ADROIT TACTICAL MANOEUVRE
TO TAKE ADVANTAGE OF THE WIDENING GAP BETWEEN COLOMBO AND
INDIA ON THE DEVOLUTION OF POWER TO THE NORTH-EAST COUNCIL.

02732 DESILVA, M.
THE ELUSIVE PEACE
FAR EASTERN ECONOMIC REVIEW, 141(32) (AUG 88), 33.
DESPITE THE EFFORTS OF THE 50,000 STRONG INDIAN
PEACEKEEPING FORCE IN THE NORTH AND SRI LANKAN TROOPS IN THE
SOUTH, PEACE STILL ELUDES THE NATION. THE HARRASSMENT AND
AMBUSHES BY EXTREMIST GROUPS CONTINUE IN DEFIANCE OF THE
INDO-SRI LANKAN PEACE ACCORD. ALTHOUGH SOME EXTREMISTS SEEM
WILLING TO NEGOTIATE, SEVERAL KEY LEADERS CONTINUE TO RESIST
AND HAVE ATTEMPTED TO CONTINUE THE VIOLENCE AND BLOODSHED
THAT HAS ROCKED SRI LANKA FOR YEARS.

02733 DESILVA, M.
THE MOOD OF THE MASSES
FAR EASTERN ECONOMIC REVIEW, 141(30) (JUL 88), 16-17.
THE RESULTS OF BY-ELECTIONS AND PROVINCIAL COUNCIL
ELECTIONS IN SRI LANKA ARE BEING CLOSELY STUDIES BY THE
RULING UNITED NATIONAL PARTY. THEY ARE TRYING TO DETERMINE
THE OPPORTUNE TIME TO DECLARE THE NEXT GENERAL ELECTION
WHICH MUST BE HELD BY AUGUST 1989. ALTHOUGH THE OPPOSITION
SRI LANKA FREEDOM PARTY GAINED GROUND IN THE BY-ELECTIONS,
THE UNITED SOCIALIST ALLIANCE DID NOT PARTICIPATE AND REMAIN
AN UNKNOWN, UNSETTLING FACTOR IN THE UPCOMING ELECTION.

02734 DESILVA, M.
WAKING UP TO REALITY
FAR EASTERN ECONOMIC REVIEW, 141(36) (SEP 88), 26-27.
THE OPPOSITION SRI LANKA FREEDOM PARTY (SLFP) IS
SOFTENING ITS ANTI-INDIA RHETORIC IN HOPES OF WINNING THE
UPCOMING PARLIAMENTARY AND PRESIDENTIAL ELECTIONS. SLEP
LEADERS ARE NOW ACKNOWLEDGING THE "GEOPOLITICAL REALITY" OF
INDIA AS A HUGE NEIGHBOR OF SRI LANKA. HOWEVER, IF THE PARTY
DOES FORM THE NEXT GOVERNMENT OF SRI LANKA, THEY PLEDGE TO
INCREASE PRESSURE FOR THE WITHDRAWAL OF THE 50,000-STRONG
INDIAN PEACEKEEPING FORCE.

02735 DESJARDINS, M.
THE POLITICS OF PENSIONS IN CANADA, 1960-1987
DISSERTATION ABSTRACTS INTERNATIONAL, 49(12) (JUN 89),
3865-A.
THIS THESIS EXAMINES THE EVOLUTION OF CANADIAN PENSION
POLITICS OVER THE LAST TWENTY-FIVE YEARS IN ORDER TO
UNDERSTAND WHY, AFTER CREATING A PUBLIC CONTRIBUTORY PLAN IN
1965, THE STATE REFUSED TO EXTEND ITS REACH FURTHER IN THE
1980S AND RATHER OPTED TO REGULATE EMPLOYER-SPONSORED
PENSIONS. USING AN ANALYTICAL FRAMEWORK WHICH DIFFERS FROM
PREVIOUS STUDIES, IT POSTULATES THAT PENSION POLITICS CAN BE
BEST UNDERSTOOD THROUGH THE ANALYSIS OF CONFLICT WITHIN AND
BETWEEN THE NON-GOVERNMENTAL, INTERGOVERNMENTAL AND
INTRAGOVERNMENTAL ARENAS.

02736 DESMET, A.
GOALS OF THE PEACE FORCES
WORLD MARXIST REVIEW, 32(11) (NOV 89), 40-42.
THE PREVENTION OF WAR IS NOT THE ONLY GOAL OF THE PEACE
MOVEMENT: IT IS IMPORTANT TO KNOW WHAT PEACE WILL BE LIKE,
WHAT ITS CONTENT WILL BE. THE TASKS OF SOCIOECONOMIC
DEVELOPMENT AND OF IMPROVING GENERAL LIVING STANDARDS ARE
CLOSELY LINKED TO THE PROSPECTS FOR STRONGER PEACE. THE
LESSENING OF CONFRONTATION BETWEEN STATES, BROADER FRUITFUL
INTERNATIONAL COOPERATION AND THE RELEASE OF THE HUGE
RESOURCES CURRENTLY SPENT FOR MILITARY PURPOSES AND THEIR
CONVERSION TO PEACEFUL USES COULD SUBSTANTIALLY INFLUENCE
THE PACE AND DIRECTION OF SOCIAL PROGRESS. AS THE WAR DANGER
LESSENS AND THE INTERNATIONAL CLIMATE IMPROVES, THE PEACE
MOVEMENT IS SHIFTING ITS PRIORITIES TO SOCIAL GOALS. THIS IS
ONE OF ITS HALLMARKS TODAY.

02737 DESOTO, H.
THE INFORMALS POSE AN ANSWER TO MARX
SOUTH AFRICA FOUNDATION REVIEW, 15(2) (FEB 89), 4-6.
DEVELOPING ECONOMIES DO NOT WORK FOR TWO REASONS. FIRST,
THE STRUCTURE OF GOVERNANCE AND ECONOMIC ACTIVITY IN MOST
THIRD WORLD COUNTRIES EFFECTIVELY SQUEEZES OUT THE
ENTREPRENEURIAL ELEMENT OF ECONOMIC ACTIVITY. SECONDLY, THE
THIRD WORLD HAS FAILED TO GRASP FULLY THE FUNDAMENTAL LINK
BETWEEN ECONOMIC PARTICIPATION AND POLITICAL PARTICIPATION
AND TO UNDERSTAND THAT PROSPERITY WITHOUT DEMOCRACY IS
IMPOSSIBLE IN A MODERN ECONOMY. PERU'S EXPERIENCES
ILLUSTRATE THESE PRINCIPLES.

02738 DESOTO, H.
WHAT'S WRONG WITH LATIN AMERICAN ECONOMIES?
REASON, 21(5) (OCT 89), 38-42.
THE ARTICLE EXTENSIVELY REPORTS THE RESULTS OF A STUDY
IN PERU THAT ANALYZES THE PREUVIAN ECONOMIC SYSTEM. IT
CONCLUDES THAT DEMOCRACY AND ENTERPRENEURSHIP HAVEN'T FAILED
IN LATIN AMERICA, THEY HAVE NEVER BEEN TRIED. ELECTIONS
WITHOUT DEMOCRACY, REGULATIONS WITHOUT LAW, AND A PRIVATE
SECTOR WITHOUT CAPITALISM ALL COMBINE TO RETARD PROGRESS IN
LATIN AMERICA. HOWEVER, A GROWING "INFORMAL" SECTOR PROMISES
TO GRADUALLY BRING ABOUT CHANGES IN THE SYSTEM.

02739 DESPRETZ, G.
WHO ARE THEY GOING TO FOLLOW?
WORLD MARXIST REVIEW, 31(2) (FEB 88), 50-56.
REAL OPPORTUNITIES EXIST FOR IMPROVING RELATIONS BETWEEN
THE FRENCH COMMUNIST PARTY AND THE YOUNG PEOPLE. FOR YEARS
ON END POLITICIANS OF EVERY HUE HAVE BEEN TRYING TO PERSUADE
THE YOUNG PEOPLE THAT 'IN THE NAME OF FREEDOM AND PROGRESS'
THEY HAVE TO RESIGN THEMSELVES TO PRECARIOUS JOBS,
'FLEXIBLE' EMPLOYMENT, ELITISM AND 'GO-GETTER' IDEOLOGY.
NEVERTHELESS IN GROWING NUMBERS THE YOUNG PEOPLE BECOME
AWARE OF GLARING DIFFERENCES BETWEEN THE OBJECTIVES
PROCLAIMED BY THE AUTHORITIES AND THEIR ACTIONS.

02740 DESSLER, D.
THE USE AND ABUSE OF SOCIAL SCIENCE FOR POLICY
SAIS REVIEW, 9(2) (SUM 89), 203-223.
THIS ARTICLE DISCUSSES THE ETERNAL DISAGREEMENT BETWEEN
THE OLD AND NEW SCHOOL OF INTERNATIONAL RELATIONS THEORY AND
ITS APPLICATIONS. THE ARTICLE HIGHLIGHTS THE DANGERS OF
MANIPULATING THE QUANTITATIVE AND QUALITATIVE ELEMENTS OF
INTERNATIONAL RELATIONS TO SERVE THE PURPOSE OF A
POLICYMAKER.

02741 DESVEAUX, J.A.
STRATEGY, STRUCTURE, AND GOVERNMENT INTERVENTION: AN
ORGANIZATIONAL ANALYSIS OF CANADA'S NATIONAL ENERGY PROGRAM
DISSERTATION ABSTRACTS INTERNATIONAL, 49(8) (FEB 89),
2385-A.
THE AUTHOR EXPLAINS THE RELATIONSHIP BETWEEN STRUCTURES
AND STRATEGIES OF PUBLIC ORGANIZATIONS THAT ATTEMPT MARKET
INTERVENTIONS. THE FOCUS IS ON THOSE ORGANIZATIONS THAT
UNDERTAKE COMPREHENSIVE AND HIGH-RISK STRATEGIES WHEN THE
CONSEQUENCES OF POLICY FAILURE ARE POTENTIALLY HIGH FOR THE
GOVERNMENT AGENCY AND FOR THE ACTORS IN ITS DOMAIN. THE
DEPARTMENT OF ENERGY, MINES, AND RESOURCES OF THE FEDERAL
GOVERNMENT OF CANADA IS USED AS A CASE STUDY.

02742 DETLEFSEN, R.R.
TRIUMPH OF THE RACE-CONSCIOUS STATE: THE POLITICS OF CIVIL
RIGHTS, 1980-86
DISSERTATION ABSTRACTS INTERNATIONAL, 49(11) (MAY 89),
3489-A.
THE AUTHOR ENDEAVORS TO EXPLAIN THE FACTORS THAT IMPEDED
THE REAGAN ADMINISTRATION'S EFFORTS TO RE-ORIENT NATIONAL
CIVIL RIGHTS POLICY TOWARD A COLOR-BLIND, GENDER-NEUTRAL
STANDARD. HE EXAMINES ATTEMPTS BY THE REAGAN ADMINISTRATION,
ACTING PRINCIPALLY THROUGH THE CIVIL RIGHTS DIVISION OF THE
DEPARTMENT OF JUSTICE, TO REFORMULATE CIVIL RIGHTS POLICY
WITH RESPECT TO SPECIFIC ISSUES, SUCH AS AFFIRMATIVE ACTION
AND SCHOOL DESEGREGATION.

02743 DEUDNEY, D.H.
GLOBAL GEOPOLITICS: A RECONSTRUCTION, INTERPRETATION, AND
EVALUATION OF MATERIALIST WORLD ORDER THEORIES OF THE LATE
NINETEENTH AND EARLY TWENTIETH CENTURIES (VOLUMES I AND II)
DISSERTATION ABSTRACTS INTERNATIONAL, 50(6) (DEC 89),
1793-A.
THE AUTHOR MODELS A MATERIALIST WORLD ORDER THEORY IN
WHICH THE LARGEST PHYSICAL FEATURES OF THE EARTH INTERACT
WITH THE NEW INDUSTRIAL CAPABILITIES OF COMMUNICATION,
TRANSPORTATION, AND DESTRUCTION TO DETERMINE MAJOR FEATURES
OF THE WORLD ORDER. HE ALSO SURVEYS THE TRADITION OF
NATURALISM FROM ARISTOTLE THROUGH MONTESQUIEU; CONSIDERS
MAHAN'S ARGUMENT THAT SEA POWER SHAPED EUROPEAN INTERACTION
WITH THE WORLD, THE EUROPEAN STATE SYSTEM, AND THE BRITISH
SYSTEM; AND DISCUSSES EFFORTS BY BURNHAM, HERZ, AND GRAY TO
EXPLAIN THE NUCLEAR ERA.

02744 DEUTSCH, K.A.
MARSHALL PLAN AND UNITED STATES POST WORLD WAR II
INTERESTS IN EUROPE
AVAILABLE FROM NTIS, NO. AD-A209 503/2/GAR, MAR 17 89, 54.
THE MARSHALL PLAN HAS BEEN HERALDED AS ONE OF THE MOST
IMPORTANT AND SUCCESSFUL FOREIGN POLICIES OF THIS CENTURY.
HISTORIANS GENERALLY AGREE THAT IT WAS PRECISELY THE RIGHT
MEDICINE NEEDED TO HEAL WOUNDS AND RESTORE CONFIDENCE ON
BOTH SIDES OF THE ATLANTIC FOLLOWING THE DESTRUCTIVE SECOND
WORLD WAR. IT HAS BEEN CREDITED WITH HELPING CONTAIN THE
SPREAD OF COMMUNISM AND PROVIDING THE FOUNDATION FOR AN
ENDURING ALLIANCE THAT HAS PRODUCED 40 YEARS OF PEACE IN
EUROPE. HOWEVER, THE MARSHALL PLAN HAS ALSO BEEN CRITICIZED
AS A SELFISH U.S. ENDEAVOR AND A PROGRAM THAT DIVIDED EUROPE.
THIS ESSAY INVESTIGATES THE ROLE OF THIS WIDELY ACCLAIMED
PLAN IN U.S. POST-WAR INTERESTS IN EUROPE. IT INCLUDES
ANALYSES OF THE PLAN'S ORIGINS, GOALS, MECHANICS, AND
OVERALL EFFECTIVENESS. IT ALSO EXAMINES BOTH THE SHORT AND
LONG-TERM ECONOMIC, POLITICAL AND MILITARY SIGNIFICANCE OF
THE MARSHALL PLAN, INCLUDING ITS RELATIONSHIP TO THE TRUMAN
DOCTRINE AND CONTAINMENT POLICY. FINALLY, IT FOCUSES ON HOW
THE PLAN HELPED FURTHER U.S. INTERESTS BY FORGING A
COLLECTIVE SECURITY MECHANISM AND A STRONG ECONOMIC
POLITICAL AND MILITARY ALLIANCE NETWORK THAT HAS SHAPED
WESTERN EUROPE AS IT IS KNOWN TODAY.

02745 DEUTSCHER, I.
TIME OF TROUBLE: THE TWENTY-THIRD CONGRESS
MONTHLY REVIEW, 41(4) (SEP 89), 33-45.
THIS ARTICLE OUTLINES IN BROAD TERMS THE BACKGROUND TO
THE SOVIET TWENTY-THIRD CONGRESS. AN ATTEMPT IS MADE TO
DISTINGUISH THE BALANCE BETWEEN THE PROGRESSIVE, SOCIALIST
FORCES IN SOVIET SOCIETY AND THE REACTIONARY ONES. THE
DIFFICULTY OF GAUGING THE STRENGTH OF TRENDS BECAUSE OF THE
LACK OF OPEN DEBATE IS POINTED OUT. THE CONTRIBUTION OF THE
CONGRESS TO THE POLITICAL DEVELOPMENT OF THE USSR IS
ANALYSED.

02746 DEVADAS, D.; SINGH, H.
CHAMBER OF CHAOS
INDIA TODAY, 14(16) (AUG 89), 34-37.
THIS ARTICLE IS A REPORT ON THE EIGHTH LOK SABHA. IT
NOTES THAT IF ANY THING HAS MARKED IT, IT HAS BEEN ANARCHY.
REPORTED IS THAT WITH EACH PASSING YEAR, THE CIVILITY, AND
EUPHORIA OF THE HOUSE OF 1985 HAS PLUMMETED TO DEPRESSINS
DEPTHS OF FUNCTIONAL ANARCHY. ALSO DETAILED IS LEGISLATION
WHICH HAS BEEN SCRAPPY AND REPRESSIVE, AND ALSO THE CONDUCT
OF MEMBERS WHICH HAS BEEN DISMAL.

02747 DEVADAS, D.; MUDGAL, V.
END OF THE ROAD
INDIA TODAY, XIV(2) (JAN 89), 37-38.
SATHANT SINGH AND KEHAR SINGH, CONVICTED OF THE
ASSASSINATION OF PRIME MINISTER INDIRA GANDHI, WERE HANGED
IN DELHI IN JANUARY 1989. IT WAS THE CULMINATION OF THE MOST
SENSATIONAL MURDER CASE EVER IN INDIA. THE CASE HAD RETURNED
TO THE SUPREME COURT A HALF-DOZEN TIMES FOR DISCUSSION OF
CONSTITUTIONAL ISSUES.

02748 DEVATY, S.; HAJEK, M.; JANAT, B.
WILL 28 OCTOBER BRING NATIONWIDE RECONCILIATION?
EAST EUROPEAN REPORTER, 3(4) (SPR 89), 51.
THE ARTICLE IS A STATEMENT BY CHARTER 77 SPOKESPERSONS.
THEY CLAIM THAT THE COMMUNIST GOVERNMENT OF CZECHOSLOVAKIA
HAS SUPPRESSED AND DISTORTED NATIONAL TRADITIONS AND HAS
DESTROYED THE ENVIRONMENT SO AS TO SERIOUSLY THREATEN THE
HEALTH OF FUTURE GENERATIONS. THEY ALSO DEFEND THE RIGHT OF
CZECHS AND SLOVAKS TO DEMONSTRATE ON OCTOBER 28, THE 70TH
ANNIVERSARY OF THE FOUNDATION OF CZECHOSLOVAKIA. SUCH AN ACT
"COULD SEE THE BEGINNING OF NATIONWIDE RECONCILIATION."

02749 DEVAUS, D.; MCALLISTER, I.
THE CHANGING POLITICS OF WOMEN: GENDER AND POLITICAL
ALIGNMENT IN 11 NATINS
EUROPEAN JOURNAL OF POLITICAL RESEARCH, 17(3) (MAY 89),
241-262.
ALTHOUGH THERE HAD BEEN CONSIDERABLE RESEARCH ON THE
CHANGING POLITICS OF WOMEN IN ADVANCED INDUSTRIAL SOCIETIES,
THERE HAD BEEN LITTLE CONSISTENT, CROSS-NATIONAL RESEARCH OF
IDENTITY THE SOURCES OF THESE CHANGES. THE PAPER USES
CLOSELY COMPARABL DATA COLLECTED IN 11 COUNTRIES IN THE
EARLY 1980S TO EXAMINE GENDER DIFFERENCES IN POLITICAL
ALIGNMENTS. THE RESULTS SHOW THAT IN 10 OF THE 11 COUNTRIES,
WOMEN ARE MORE CONSERVATIVE THAN MEN, BY DEFFERING DEGREES.
THE EXCEPTION IS AUSTRALIA, WHERE WOMEN ARE MORE LEFTWING
THAN MEN. THE SOURCES OF THESE GENDER DIFFERENCES ARE SHOWN
TO BE DIFFERENTIAL LEVELS OF WORKFORCE PARTICIPATION AND
RELIGIOSITY BETWEEN MEN AND WOMEN. ONCE THESE AND OTHER
FACTORS ARE TAKEN INTO ACCOUNT THROUGH MULTIVARIATE ANALYSIS,
WOMEN FOLLOW THE AUSTRALIAN PATTERN AND EMERGE AS MORE
LEFTWING THAN MEN IN SIX OF THE 10 COUNTRIES. IN THE
REMAINING FOUR COUNTRIES, GREATER FEMALE CONSERVATISM IS
SUBSTANTIALLY REDUCED ONCE THESE FACTORS ARE TAKEN INTO
ACCOUNT. VARIOUS EXPLANATIONS TO ACCOUNT FOR THESE PATTERNS
ARE DISCUSSED.

02750 DEVEREUX, D.R.
BRITAIN, THE COMMONWEALTH, AND THE DEFENCE OF THE MIDDLE
EAST, 1948-56
JOURNAL OF CONTEMPORARY HISTORY, 24(2) (APR 89), 327-345.
THE MIDDLE EAST WAS ONE OF THE MOST IMPORTANT GLOBAL
REGIONS FOR BRITAIN AFTER 1945. BOTH THE LABOUR AND
CONSERVATIVE GOVERNMENTS BELIEVED IT TO BE VITAL FOR
BRITAIN'S POST-WAR RECOVERY AND HER CONTINUING POSITION AS A
WORLD POWER. EVEN THOUGH WESTERN EUROPE BECAME BRITAIN'S
FIRST PRIORITY FOR DEFENCE AFTER 1950, THE MIDDLE EAST
REMAINED A THEATRE OF GREAT IMPORTANCE AND CONCERN UNTIL
WELL AFTER SUEZ IN 1956. IN MANY RESPECTS, THE MIDDLE EAST
REPLACED INDIA AS THE BASIS FOR BRITAIN'S IMPERIAL OVERSEAS
ROLE, AND ALL THE ARGUMENTS FOR 'PROTECTING THE ROUTES' TO
INDIA WERE USED FOR THE MIDDLE EAST AFTER 1947.

02751 DEVEREUX, M.; WILSON, T.A.
INTERNATIONAL COORDINATION OF MACROECONOMIC POLICIES : A
REVIEW
CANADIAN PUBLIC POLICY--ANALYSE DE POLITIQUES, XV (FEB 89),
20-34.
THIS PAPER REVIEWS THE ISSUES INVOLVED IN INTERNATIONAL
MACROECONOMIC POLICY COORDINATION. WHILE CO-OPERATION
BETWEEN GOVERNMENTS TAKES PLACE AT MANY LEVELS, SUCH AS IN

THE INTERNATIONAL MONETARY FUND (IMF), GENERAL AGREEMENT ON
TARIFFS AND TRADE (GATT) AND THE EUROPEAN COMMUNITY (EC) ETC.
, THERE HAS BEEN MUCH LESS EXPERIENCE WITH DIRECT
INTERNATIONAL AGREEMENTS ON DISCRETIONARY MONETARY AND
FISCAL POLICIES. THE AUTHORS BEGIN WITH A GENERAL SURVEY OF
POSTWAR EXPERIENCE WHICH HAS A BEARING ON POLICY CO-
ORDINATION. DIRECT POLICY AGREEMENTS AT THE SUPRA-NATIONAL
LEVEL HAVE BEEN RARE. NEVERTHELESS, THE INSTITUTIONS OF
INTERNATIONAL TRADE AND FINANCE HAVE CONSTRAINED THE CHOICES
OF NATIONAL ECONOMIC POLICIES TO SOME EXTENT, THEREBY
ACHIEVING CO-ORDINATION OF A KIND. THE PAPER PRESENTS THE
THEORETICAL ARGUMENTS FOR MACROECONOMIC POLICY CO-ORDINATION.

02752 DEVINE, D.
A FREE MARKET IN GOVERNMENT
NATIONAL REVIEW, 61(20) (OCT 89), 40-41.
THIS ARTICLE EXPLORES GOVERNMENT IN AMERICA ON THE LOCAL
LEVEL. IT COMPARES TURN OF THE CENTURY POWER, RESPONSIBILITY,
AND SPENDING TO THE SITUATION TODAY. IT EXAMINES THE
PROGRAM OF PROGRESSIVE REFORMS WHICH REVERSED POWER IN
AMERICA BEING EXERCISED ON A LOCAL LEVEL. IDVOCATES A RETURN
TO MORE LOCAL GOVERNMENTS.

02753 DEVLIN, J. D.
THE ARMY, POLITICS, AND PUBLIC ORDER IN DIRECTORIAL
PROVENCE
DISSERTATION ABSTRACTS INTERNATIONAL, 49(8) (FEB 89),
2385-A.
THE AUTHOR STUDIES THE ROLE PLAYED BY THE ARMY IN
MAINTAINING LAW AND ORDER IN PROVENCE UNDER THE FRENCH
EXECUTIVE DIRECTORY. WHEN THE THERMIDOREANS BREATHED NEW
LIFE INTO THE INSTITUTIONS OF LOCAL GOVERNMENT, THEY
UNLEASHED DISSIDENCE, PARTICULARISM, AND VIOLENCE BORN OF
REVOLUTIONARY EXPERIENCE IN AN AREA TRADITIONALLY ASSOCIATED
WITH EXTREMISM. SINCE THE CIVILIAN LAW ENFORCEMENT AGENCIES
WERE INEFFECTIVE AND POLITICALLY BIASED, THE ARMY WAS CALLED
IN TO ENFORCE THE MANDATES OF GOVERNMENT. SOME OFFICERS
BECAME INVOLVED IN DISSIDENT POLITICS BUT MOST CARRIED OUT
THEIR TASKS AS BEST THEY COULD.

02754 DEVRIES,W.
AMERICAN CAMPAIGN CONSULTING: TRENDS AND CONCERNS
PS: POLITICAL SCIENCE AND POLITICS, XXII(1) (MAR 89),
21-25.
THE AUTHOR SURVEYS TRENDS IN POLITICAL CONSULTING,
INCLUDING ITS TREMENDOUS GROWTH DURING THE PAST 20 YEARS,
THE ENORMOUS INCREASE IN THE AMOUNT OF MONEY SPENT ON
CAMPAIGNS, AND THE SHIFT FROM GENERALIST TO SPECIALIST
CONSULTANTS.

02755 DEWEI, H.
UNLEASHING CHINA'S ECONOMY
NEW ZEALAND INTERNATIONAL REVIEW, 14(4) (JUL 89), 1-7.
THE AUTHOR EXPLAINS THE PROBLEMS CONFRONTING THE CHINESE
ECONOMY. HE SUMMARIZES INDUSTRIAL ADVANCES SINCE THE
ESTABLISHMENT OF THE PEOPLE'S REPUBLIC OF CHINA IN 1949 AND
COMPARES CHINESE CONDITIONS WITH THOSE OF THE NEIGHBORING
SOVIET UNION IN A HISTORICAL SOCIO-POLITICAL CONTEXT. HEAVY
INDUSTRY IS TOO OVEREMPHASIZED, WITH AGRICULTURE AND LIGHT
INDUSTRY BEING WEAK AND REFLECTIVE OF THE OVERLY CENTRALIZED
RIGID SYSTEM OF ECONOMIC MANAGEMENT. REFORMS WHICH HAVE BEEN
INSTATED IN THE LAST DECADE ARE SUMMARIZED, AND INCLUDE
DECISION MAKING POWERS FOR MANAGEMENT, TECHNICAL DEVELOPMENT
AND INCREASED ACCOUNTABLE FOR ECONOMIC EFFICIENCY IN THE
HEAVY INDUSTRIES.

02756 DEWINTER, L.
PARTIES AND POLICY IN BELGIUM
EUROPEAN JOURNAL OF POLITICAL RESEARCH, 17(6) (NOV 89),
707-730.
IN BELGIUM, POLICY STUDIES REPRESENT ONE OF THE
UNDERDEVELOPED BRANCHES OF POLITICAL SCIENCE ACTIVITY.
ESPECIALLY WITH REGARD TO THE RELATIONSHIP BETWEEN PARTY AND
POLICY, BELGIAN POLITICAL SCIENTISTS HAVE REMAINED
REMARKABLY ABSENT FROM THE SCENE. FORTUNATELY, SOME
ECONOMISTS HAVE INVESTIGATED THE MATTER FROM DIFFERENT
PERSPECTIVES. IN THE FIRST PART OF THIS ARTICLE, AN OVERVIEW
OF THEIR RESEARCH RESULTS IS PRESENTED. IN THE SECOND PART,
THE ECONOMISTS' MAJOR RESEARCH FINDING (THE ABSENCE OF A
CLEAR LINK BETWEEN PARTY AND POLICY) IS RELATED TO THE
METHODOLOGY THAT HAS BEEN EMPLOYED, I.E. THE LACK OF
DISAGGREGATION OF THE PARTY VARIABLE. IN THE LAST PART, SOME
SPECIFIC ASPECTS OF THE PARTY-POLICY NEXUS - THE MODES OF
INTERACTION BETWEEN MINISTERS, DEPARTMENTAL ADMINISTRATIONS,
PARLIAMENTARY PARTIES AND PARTY EXECUTIVES - ARE CONSIDERED
WITHIN THE FRAMEWORK OF THE RELATION BETWEEN PARTIES AND
POLICIES.

02757 DEYO, F.C.
LABOR AND DEVELOPMENT POLICY IN EAST ASIA
PHILADELPHIA: ANLS OF AMER ACMY OF POLITICAL AND SOC
SCIENCE, (505) (SEP 89), 152-161.
THE RAPID INDUSTRIAL TRANSFORMATION OF SOUTH KOREA,
TAIWAN, SINGAPORE, AND HONG KONG HAS IN PART BEEN SUSTAINED

BY STATE DEVELOPMENT STRATEGIES ORIENTED EXCLUSIVELY TOWARD
THE NEEDS OF CAPITAL. LESS OFTEN HAVE CRITERIA RELATING TO
THE WELFARE OF WORKERS ENTERED DIRECTLY INTO STATE POLICY
EXCEPT INSOFAR AS SUCH CRITERIA ARE SUPPORTIVE OF GROWTH.
UNDERLYING THIS PATTERN OF STRATEGIC PRIORITIES IS THE
INSULATION OF DEVELOPMENT PLANNERS AND CORPORATE EXECUTIVES
FROM THE POLITICAL DEMANDS AND OPPOSITION OF WORKERS. WHILE
POLITICAL CONTROLS GO SOME DISTANCE IN EXPLAINING THE
POLITICAL WEAKNESS OF EAST ASIAN WORKERS, THE MORE
FUNDAMENTAL CAUSES ARE TO BE FOUND, FIRST, IN THE NATURE OF
EMPLOYMENT RELATIONS IN THESE COUNTRIES AND, SECOND, IN THE
SEQUENCING OF POLITICAL AND ECONOMIC CHANGES DURING THE
COURSE OF INDUSTRIALIZATION.

02758 DEYOUNG, T.J.; PERLMAN, B.J.
TEACHING METHODS IN PUBLIC ADMINISTRATION REVISITED
POLICY STUDIES REVIEW, 8(4) (SUM 89), 852-858.
METHODOLOGY COURSES IN MPA PROGRAMS TEND TO BE UNPOPULAR
WITH STUDENTS AND PROFESSORS ALIKE. THESE SAME COURSES,
HOWEVER, PROVE TO BE AMONG THE MOST VALUABLE WHEN THE
STUDENT IS COMPLETING THE DEGREE PROGRAM OR WHEN THE STUDENT
BECOMES A PRACTITIONER OF PUBLIC ADMINISTRATION. IN THIS
ARTICLE, MANY OF THE MOST WIDELY USED LEARNING MODELS FOR
METHODOLOGY ARE CRITIQUED. IN ADDITION, THE AUTHORS MAKE A
CASE FOR THE USE OF INQUIRY TRAINING TECHNIQUES, ARGUING
THAT THEY ARE MOST APPROPRAITE FOR BOTH STUDENTS AND
PROFESSOR BECAUSE OF THEIR ENVIRONMENTAL SENSITIVITY.

02759 DIAMOND, L.
BEYOND AUTHORITARIARISM AND TOTALITARIANISM: STRATEGIES
FOR DEMOCRATIZATION
WASHINGTON QUARTERLY, 12(1) (WIN 89), 141-163.
THE GLOBAL MOVEMENT FOR DEMOCRACY TODAY HAS MOMENTUM,
BUT HISTORICALLY SUCH MOMENTS OF PROMISE WERE CYCLICAL
SWINGS AND DID NOT LAST. THE CHALLENGE FOR COMMITTED
DEMOCRATIC ACTORS-INDIVIDUALS, INSTITUTIONS, AND NATIONS-IS
TO FASHION STRATEGIES FOR ENGAGING AUTHORITARIAN AND
TOTALITARIAN REGIMES THAT WILL BE CONSISTENT OVER THE LONG
RUN AND COHERENT AND CUMULATIVE IN THEIR EFFECTS. THE LIMITS
TO INTERNATIONAL PRESSURE FOR DEMOCRATIZATION ARE NOT ONLY
INTRINSIC BUT ALSO SELF-IMPOSED BY DEMOCRATIC ACTORS WITH
SHORT ATTENTION SPANS, INFLATED NOTIONS OF THEIR INDIVIDUAL
IMPORTANCE, DIVERGENT POLICIES AND PRIORITIES, AND
SCHIZOPHRENIC, ZIGZAGGING STRATEGIES OF INFLUENCE.
ESTABLISHED DEMOCRATIC INSTITUTIONS AND NATIONS CAN ADVANCE
THE CAUSE OF DEMOCRACY IN OTHER COUNTRIES, BUT FIRST THEY
MUST GET THEIR OWN ACT TOGETHER.

02760 DIAMOND, S.
SPIRITUAL WARFARE: THE POLITICS OF THE CHRISTIAN RIGHT
SOUTH END PRESS, BOSTON, MA, 1989, .
CHAPTERS EXAMINE RELIGIOUS BROADCASTING, AUTHORITARIAN
CHURCHES, CHARISMATIC PRACTICES, CHRISTIAN RIGHT ACTIVISM IN
THE REPUBLICAN PARTY, THE MOBILIZATION OF ANTI-FEMINIST
WOMEN, EFFORTS TO DISCREDIT PROGRESSIVE CHRISTIANITY, AND
LOW-INTENSITY CONFLICT PROJECTS IN CENTRAL AMERICA, SOUTHERN
AFRICA, AND THE PHILIPPINES.

02761 DIAZ-RUIZ, A.
A QUESTION OF PRIORITIES
WORLD MARXIST REVIEW, 32(9) (SEP 89), 68-70.
THIS ARTICLE ASKS IF THERE IS ANY CONTRADICTION BETWEEN
NATIONAL LIBERATION AND UNIVERSAL PEACE. IT SUGGESTS THAT
THE GLOBAL PROBLEMS OF THE MODERN WORLD ARE INDIVISIBLE AND
THAT IT IS WRONG TO ASSUME THAT ANY OF THE MAJOR PROBLEMS
HAS ANY KIND OF PRIORITY. IT FOCUSES ON THE DUTY OF THE
INTERNATIONAL COMMUNIST AND WORKING CLASS MOVEMENT TO
MILITATE FOR PEACE AND SOCIAL PROGRESS. THE LATIN AMERICAN
AND CARIBBEAN SITUATION IS DETAILED AND THE NEED FOR A NEW
INTERNATIONAL ECONOMIC ORDER IS CALLED FOR.

02762 DICKEY, S. A.
GOING TO THE PICTURES IN MADURAI: SOCIAL, PSYCHOLOGICAL,
AND POLITICAL ASPECTS OF CINEMA IN URBAN WORKING CLASS
SOUTH INDIA
DISSERTATION ABSTRACTS INTERNATIONAL, 49(9) (MAR 89),
2706-A.
WORKING CLASS RESIDENTS OF MADURAI, SOUTH INDIA, SPEND A
GREAT DEAL OF TIME AT THE CINEMA AND PURSUING RELATED
ACTIVITIES. THIS DISSERTATION PROBES THE EFFECT OF FILMS ON
THE MADURAI VIEWERS' LIVES, INCLUDING INVOLVING THEM IN
POLITICS. POLITICAL ACTIVISM OFFERS THE VIEWERS AN AVENUE OF
PROTEST AGAINST THEIR OPPRESSIVE SOCIAL SITUATION, AND FAN
CLUBS SOMETIMES PROVIDE OPPORTUNITIES FOR DIRECT POLITICAL
PARTICIPATION WHEN MOVIE STARS RUN FOR PUBLIC OFFICE.

02763 DICKINSON, H.T.
THE IMPACT OF THE FRENCH REVOLUTION ON BRITAIN
CONTEMPORARY REVIEW, 255(1482) (JUL 89), 20-26.
THE ARTICLE STUDIES THE LONG-LASTING IMPACT OF THE
FRENCH REVOLUTION ON NEIGHBORING GREAT BRITAIN. THE CONFLICT
THAT AROSE OUT OF THE REVOLUTION COST BRITAIN MUCH IN BLOOD
AND TREASURE: IT CAUSED SEVERE ECONOMIC DISLOCATION AND
CHANGES IN THE MILITARY STRUCTURE. HOWEVER, MORE SIGNIFICANT

WERE THE CHANGES IN THE POLITICAL AND INTELLECTUAL CLIMATE.
THE ARTICLE CONCLUDES THAT THE FRENCH REVOLUTION HAS A MAJOR
STIMULUS TO RADICAL POLITICAL ACTIVITY THROUGH BRITAIN AND
THE RESULTING LOYALIST COUNTER-REVOLUTION.

02764 DICKS, A.
THE CHINESE LEGAL SYSTEM: REFORMS IN THE BALANCE
CHINA QUARTERLY, (119) (SEP 89), 540-576.
THE INCREASE IN THE SCOPE, COMPLEXITY, AND
SOPHISTICATION OF THE CHINESE LEGAL ENVIRONMENT AND IN THE
VOLUME OF LEGAL ACTIVITY IS NOT THE FORTUITOUS RESULT OF
UNDIRECTED EVOLUTION BUT THE PRODUCT OF A DELIBERATE POLICY
ESPOUSED BY THE LEADERSHIP IN THE LAST DECADE. THE OBJECT OF
THIS ESSAY IS TO PROVIDE A FRAMEWORK WITHIN WHICH THE
RESULTS OF THIS POLICY CAN BE ASSESSED IN THE CONTEXT OF
EVENTS IN CHINA OVER THE PAST FORTY YEARS.

02765 DIEGMUELLER, K.
MIDDLE AMERICA: PRICED OUT OF HOUSE AND HOME
CURRENT, (314) (JUL 89), 16-21.
HOMELESSNESS, PARTICULARLY AMONG FAMILIES, IS LINKED TO
TWO OTHER GROUPS WHO ARE FINDING IT DIFFICULT TO LOCATE AND
ACQUIRE DECENT, AFFORDABLE HOUSING: LOW-INCOME FAMILIES AND
FIRST-TIME HOME BUYERS. THE BUSH ADMINISTRATION IS EXPECTED
TO BUILD A NATIONAL HOUSING AGENDA AROUND THESE THREE GROUPS:
THE HOMELESS, THE LOW-INCOME POPULATION, AND FIRST-TIME
BUYERS.

02766 DIEHL, P.F.
AVOIDING ANOTHER BEIRUT DISASTER: STRATEGIES FOR THE
DEPLOYMENT OF U.S. TROOPS IN PEACEKEEPING ROLES
CONFLICT, 8(4) (1988), 261-270.
THE UNITED STATES CAN HOPEFULLY GAIN INSIGHTS INTO
PEACEKEEPING STRATEGIES FROM THE MNF'S BEIRUT EXPERIENCE AND
THOSE OF OTHER PEACEKEEPING OPERATIONS. THIS ESSAY OFFERS
SOME GUIDELINES ON HOW THE UNITED STATES CAN AVOID ANOTHER
DISASTER AND STILL CONTRIBUTE TO LIMITING GLOBAL CONFLICT
WITHOUT RESORTING TO MILITARY FORCE.

02767 DIENSTBIER, J.
GORBACHEV AND THE STRUGGLE FOR DEMOCRACY IN CZECHOSLOVAKIA
NEW POLITICS, 11(3) (SUM 89), 137-151.
TWENTY YEARS OF "NORMALIZATION" HAS GIVEN CZECHOSLOVAK
SOCIETY AN EXPERIENCE WHICH HAS RADICALLY CHANGED ITS
ATTITUDES AND ASPIRATIONS. PEOPLE'S VIEWS ARE NOW TOTALLY
DIFFERENT FROM WHAT THEY WERE IN 1968. ALTHOUGH IT IS
POSSIBLE TO COMPARE SOME BASIC FEATURES OF SOVIET
RESTRUCTURING WITH THE PRAGUE SPRING, THERE IS NO COMPARISON
BETWEEN THE CURRENT ASPIRATIONS OF SOVIET SOCIETY AND THE
CURRENT ASPIRATIONS OF CZECHOSLOVAK SOCIETY. IN SHORT, THE
CZECHOSLOVAKS ARE YET AGAIN ONE STEP AHEAD IN EXPERIENCE OF
THE PEOPLE OF THE SOVIET UNION.

02768 DIERS, J.
THE STRUGGLE FOR NAMIBIAN INDEPENDENCE
SOJOURNERS, 18(3) (MAR 89), 8-10.
THE AUTHOR LOOKS AT THE "TIMETABLE" FOR NAMIBIAN
INDEPENDENCE AND THE DIFFICULT TASKS THAT WILL CONFRONT THE
NEW STATE.

02769 DIESCHO, J.
FREEDOM AROUND THE CORNER?
AFRICA REPORT, 34(1) (JAN 89), 25-27.
FOR DECADES, NAMIBIANS HAVE WAITED IN THE WINGS AS THEIR
FUTURE HAS BEEN DEBATED AND NEGOTIATED OVER BY THE
DIPLOMATIC WORLD. FROM NORTHERN NAMIBIA, THE LATEST ROUND OF
PEACE TALKS IS BEING REGARDED WITH A WARY EYE, FOR DESPITE
SOUTH AFRICA'S STATED READINESS TO GRANT THE TERRITORY
INDEPENDENCE ON-THE-GROUND REALITIES IN THE WAR-ZONE TELL
ANOTHER STORY.

02770 DIETZ, H.
POLITICAL PARTICIPATION IN THE BARRIADAS A RESEARCH UPDATE
COMPARATIVE POLITICAL STUDIES, 22(1) (APR 89), 122-130.
THIS RESEARCH NOTE UPDATES EARLIER WORK THAT FOCUSED ON
ELECTORAL BEHAVIOR AMONG THE URBAN POOR IN LIMA, PERU. THE
PREVIOUS RESEARCH STOPPED WITH THE 1983 MUNICIPAL ELECTIONS.
THE DATA USED HERE EXTEND THE ANALYSIS THROUGH THE 1985
PRESIDENTIAL ELECTION AND THE 1986 MUNICIPAL ELECTION. THE
RESULTS LARGELY REINFORCE THE HYPOTHESES ORIGINALLY PROPOSED
FOR EXPLAINING THE OBSERVED VACILLATING SUPPORT FOR THE LEFT
BY LOW-INCOME URBAN VOTERS.

02771 DIETZ, J. L.
THE DEBT CYCLE AND RESTRUCTURING IN LATIN AMERICA
LATIN AMERICAN PERSPECTIVES, 16(1) (WIN 89), 13-30.
WHILE THE FINAL IMPACT OF THE ECONOMIC RESTRUCTURING OF
THE POSTDEBT ACCUMULATION STAGE OF THE 1980S CRISIS CANNOT
BE CONFIDENTLY PREDICTED, THERE IS NO DOUBT THAT THE CRISIS
STAGE HAS BEEN CATACLYSMIC FOR THE GREAT MAJORITY IN LATIN
AMERICA WHO HAVE SUFFERED GRIEVOUS REDUCTIONS IN THEIR
PURCHASING POWER. IT IS THE ARGUMENT OF THIS ARTICLE THAT,
FOR A DYNAMIC SEGMENT OF THE RULING ELITES IN LATIN AMERICA,
THE DEBT CYCLE, INCLUDING THE CRISIS PHASE, AUGMENTED THEIR

RELATIVE POSITIONS WITHIN THEIR OWN ECONOMIES, A STATUS,
HOWEVER, WHICH IS NOT NECESSARILY IRREVERSIBLE. THE DEBT
CYCLE HAS CREATED TENSIONS, NEW POWER BASES HAVE
MATERIALIZED, AND CONTRADICTORY PRESSURES HAVE BEEN SET IN
MOTION THAT THREATEN TO TRANSFORM THE EXISTING CONFIGURATION
OF CLASS RELATIONS, NOT THE LEAST OF THESE BEING THE DEEPER
TRANSNATIONALIZATION OF THE ECONOMIES DEMANDED BY THE
INTERNATIONAL FINANCIAL COMMUNITY AS A MEANS OF RESOLVING
THE CRISIS, A "SOLUTION" THAT JEOPARDIZES THE GREATER
NATIONAL ECONOMIC SOVEREIGNTY THAT THE ACCUMULATION STAGE OF
THE DEBT CYCLE INITIATED.

02772 DIGAETANO, A.
CHOICE, RACE, AND PUBLIC SCHOOLS: THE ADOPTION AND
IMPLEMENTION OF A MAGNET PROGRAM
JOURNAL OF URBAN AFFAIRS, 11(3) (1989), 261-282.
ATTENTION TO THE ROLE OF CHOICE IN AMERICAN SCHOOLS HAS
SHIFTED FROM ITS EFFECT ON THE RACIAL COMPOSITION OF THE
STUDENT BODY TO ITS POTENTIAL EFFECT ON THE QUALITY OF
EDUCATION PROVIDED TO STUDENTS. THIS ARTICLE FOCUSES ON THE
ADOPTION AND IMPLEMENTATION OF A SERIES OF ELEMENTARY LEVEL
MAGNET SCHOOLS IN MONTGOMERY COUNTY, MARYLAND, AS A MEANS
FOR IDENTIFYING SOME OF THE POLITICAL AND ORGANIZATIONAL
DYNAMICS LIKELY TO ACCOMPANY AN EXPANDED RELIANCE ON
PROCHOICE MECHANISMS. IMPLEMENTATION OF CHOICE OPTIONS IN
PUBLIC SCHOOL SYSTEMS, IT IS CONCLUDED, WILL ENTAIL MORE
DIFFICULT TRADE OFFS, HIGHER LEVELS OF CONFLICT, AND A MORE
AFFIRMATIVE ROLE FOR THE PUBLIC SECTOR THAN IS COMMONLY
PRESUMED.

02773 DIGAETANO, A.
URBAN POLITICAL REGIME FORMATION: A STUDY IN CONTRAST
JOURNAL OF URBAN AFFAIRS, 11(3) (1989), 261-281.
URBAN POLITICAL ECONOMISTS IN THE 1980S HAVE FOCUSED
MUCH OF THEIR ATTENTION ON URBAN DEVELOPMENT AND THE
POLITICS OF GROWTH. URBAN POLITICAL REGIME ANALYSIS HAS MADE
A SIGNIFICANT CONTRIBUTION TO OUR UNDERSTANDING OF THE
POLITICAL ECONOMY OF URBAN DEVELOPMENT. THIS STUDY APPLIES
REGIME ANALYSIS TO TWO CITIES—BOSTON AND DETROIT—WITH
STARKLY DIFFERENT ECONOMIC CONTEXTS TO DETERMINE THE
RELATIONSHIP BETWEEN UNEVEN DEVELOPMENT AND THE FORM AND
POLICY FOCUS OF URBAN POLITICAL REGIMES.

02774 DIGESER, P.
THE CONVERSATIONAL AND THE CONFRONTATIONAL IN DEMOCRATIC
THEORY
DISSERTATION ABSTRACTS INTERNATIONAL, 49(9) (MAR 89),
2794-A.
BY MODIFYING THOMAS NAGEL'S DISTINCTION BETWEEN AGENT-
NEUTRAL AND AGENT-RELATIVE REASONS, THE AUTHOR ARGUES THAT A
DISTINCTION BETWEEN CONVERSATIONAL AND CONFRONTATIONAL
PREFERENCES CAN BE ESTABLISHED. IF CONVERSATIONAL AND
CONFRONTATIONAL PREFERENCES BOTH PLAY IMPORTANT ROLES IN
LIBERAL DEMOCRACY, THEN BOTH CRITICS AND SUPPORTERS HAVE
UNDER ESTIMATED THIS FORM OF GOVERNMENT. MOREOVER,
PHILOSOPHICAL PSYCHOLOGY CAN PLAY A ROLE IN UNDERSTANDING
LIBERAL DEMOCRACY.

02775 DIIULIO, J. J.
WHAT'S WRONG WITH PRIVATE PRISONS
PUBLIC INTEREST, 92 (SUM 88), 66-83.
THIS ARTICLE RESPONDS TO THE QUESTION IN THE DEBATE OVER
PRIVATIZATION OF CORRECTIONS OF WHETHER THE PRIVATIZATION
MOVEMENT CAN LAST. IT ADDRESSES THREE MAIN CONDITIONS:
SOARING INMATE POPULATIONS; ESCALATING COSTS; AND THE
EFFECTIVENESS OF THE STATUS QUO. THE ISSUES RAISED BY
PRIVATIZATION OF CORRECTIONS ARE EXPLORED.

02776 DIIULIO, J.J.JR.
PUNISHING SMARTER: PENAL REFORMS FOR THE 1990'S
BROOKINGS REVIEW, 7(3) (SUM 89), 3-12.
A STEADY INCREASE IN BOTH THE NUMBER OF CITIZENS BEHIND
BARS AND IN THE NUMBER UNDER COMMUNITY-BASED SUPERVISION IS
INEVITABLE. BUT THERE ARE CORRECTIONAL STRATEGIES THAT, IF
ADOPTED WISELY AND WIDELY, WILL PROTECT THE PUBLIC AND ITS
PURSE MORE EFFECTIVELY THAN CONVENTIONAL APPROACHES. THE
1990'S COULD BE THE DECADE WHEN "PUNISHING HARDER" GIVES WAY
TO "PUNISHING SMARTER." BUT, FOR THAT TO HAPPEN, THE FEDERAL
GOVERNMENT MUST BEGIN TO TREAT CORRECTIONS AS THE MAJOR
NATIONAL DOMESTIC POLICY ISSUE THAT IT HAS BECOME.

02777 DILEO, D.L.
RETHINKING CONTAINMENT: THE ORIGINS AND MEANING OF GEORGE
BALL'S VIETNAM DISSENT
DISSERTATION ABSTRACTS INTERNATIONAL, 49(8) (FEB 89),
2365-A.
THIS STUDY IDENTIFIES FORMER UNDERSECRETARY OF STATE
GEORGE W. BALL AS A CRITIC OF AMERICAN MILITARY INTERVENTION
IN SOUTHEAST ASIA AND ANALYZES HIS DISSENT IN THE CONTEXT OF
THE REALIST SCHOOL OF INTERNATIONAL RELATIONS. THE AUTHOR
EXAMINES THE CULTURAL AND INTELLECTUAL ANTECEDENTS OF BALL'S
VIETNAM DISSENT AND EVALUATES HIS IMPACT ON THE KENNEDY AND
JOHNSON ADMINISTRATIONS.

02778 DILORENZO, T.
ANTITRUST POLICY AND COMPETITION
SOCIETY, 27(1) (NOV 89), 67-71.
THE ARTICLE ANALYZES RECENT CHANGES IN US ANTITRUST
POLICY AND EXAMINES THE EFFECT THAT THEY HAVE ON INDUSTRIAL
PRODUCTIVITY. IT CONCLUDES THAT DESPITE MANY IMPROVEMENTS IN
ANTITRUST POLICY THERE IS MUCH WORK TO BE DONE. ANTITRUST
POLICY STILL STIFLES PRODUCTIVITY, WHILE IGNORING SOME
GLARING INSTANCES OF MONOPOLIZATION. THE ARTICLE SUGGESTS
SOME ANTITRUST REFORM DESIGNED TO IMPROVE AMERICAN
MANUFACTURING COMPETITIVENESS.

02779 DIMA, N.
NICOLAE CEAUSESCU OF COMMUNIST ROMANIA: A PORTRAIT OF POWER
JOURNAL OF SOCIAL, POLITICAL AND ECONOMIC STUDIES, 13(4)
(WIN 88), 429-454.
NICOLAE CEAUSESCU ASSUMED LEADERSHIP OF THE ROMANIAN
COMMUNIST PARTY IN 1965. DURING THE NEXT TEN YEARS, HE
WORKED TO CONSOLIDATE HIS POWER AND TO CONSTRUCT A PERSONAL
DICTATORSHIP. AFTER ANOTHER TEN YEARS, ROMANIA COULD NO
LONGER FUNCTION AS A VIABLE ECONOMIC AND SOCIAL UNIT AND
FELL INTO VIRTUAL BANKRUPTCY. YET, THROUGH THE SETTLED
PROVISIONS OF THE EASTERN EUROPEAN BLOC POLITICAL SYSTEM AND
MORE DIRECTLY THROUGH THE EFFORTS OF CEAUSESCU'S SECRET
POLICE, HIS REGIME REMAINED FIRMLY IN POWER.

02780 DIMAH, A.
THE TRIUMPH OF PRAGMATISM: NIGERIA'S ROLE IN THE
ORGANIZATION OF THE PETROLEUM EXPORTING COUNTRIES
DISSERTATION ABSTRACTS INTERNATIONAL, 50(4) (OCT 89),
1082-A.
THIS STUDY EXAMINES OPEC FROM THE VANTAGE POINTS OF
REGIME THEORY, OLIGOPOLY MODELS, AND CARTEL THEORY. THE
OBJECTIVE IS TO DETERMINE WHICH THEORY, OR ASPECTS OF THE
THEORIES, BEST DESCRIBES OPEC'S ACTIVITIES AND NIGERIA'S
ACTIONS AS A MEMBER OF THE ORGANIZATION.

02781 DIMITRAS, P.E.
GREECE
ELECTORAL STUDIES, 8(3) (DEC 89), 270-280.
THIS ARTICLE EXAMINES THE ELECTIONS IN GREECE IN JUNE
1989. IT DESCRIBES THE EROSION OF POWER OF THE PANHELLIC
SOCIALIST MOVEMENT (PASOK); THE RESULTS OF THE PAPANDREOU
SCANDAL; AND THE NEW ELECTORAL LAW. THE CAMPAIGN IS DETAILED
AND THE RESULTS ANALYZED. THE POST-ELECTORAL GOVERNMENT
FORMATION IS EXPLORED.

02782 DIMITRIJEVIC, V.
HUMAN RIGHTS ARE THE COMMON HERITAGE OF MANKIND
REVIEW OF INTERNATIONAL AFFAIRS, (JAN 88), 28-30.
ALL SOCIETIES ARE CHANGING IN THEIR DESIRE TO CREATE
SOUND FOUNDATIONS FOR ECONOMIC AND OTHER KINDS OF PROGRESS.
INDIVIDUALIST AND LIBERAL STANDS MUST BE MODIFIED BY
RECOGNITION OF SPECIFIC RIGHTS OF SOLIDARITY AND BY
EXPANDING THE NUMBER OF BEARERS OF HUMAN RIGHTS TO INCLUDE
GROUPS OF INDIVIDUALS, WHILE ON THE OTHER HAND THE
TRADITIONALLY COLLECTIVIST SOCIETIES MUST GRADUALLY FREE THE
INDIVIDUAL FROM THE SHACKLES AND LIMITATIONS WHICH PREVENT
HIM FROM ACTING INDEPENDENTLY IN HIS OWN INTEREST AND IN THE
INTEREST OF THE BROADER COMMUNITY. THESE CONDITIONS ARE
RENEWAL IN LIGHT OF CHANGES IN AFRICAN AND ARAB SOCIETIES
OVER THE LAST DECADE.

02783 DING, Y.
OPPOSING INTERFERENCE IN OTHER COUNTRIES' INTERNAL AFFAIRS
THROUGH HUMAN RIGHTS
BEIJING REVIEW, 32(45) (NOV 89), 14-16.
ONE OF THE EXCUSES SOME WESTERNERS USE TO INTERFERE WITH
CHINA'S INTERNAL AFFAIRS IS THAT HUMAN RIGHTS HAVE NO
NATIONAL BOUNDARIES. THIS ARTICLE REFUTES THAT IDEA FROM
THEORETICAL, LEGAL AND PRACTICAL PERSPECTIVES.

02784 DINITZ, S.
REFLECTIONS OF A ZIONIST
MIDSTREAM, XXXV(5) (JUN 89), 3-5.
ZIONISM IS UNDERGOING A SEVERE REAPPRAISAL AND
EVALUATION. SOME OBSERVERS CLAIM THAT, SINCE THE
ESTABLISHMENT OF THE STATE OF ISRAEL, ZIONISM HAS BECOME
OBSOLETE. THEY CLAIM THAT ZIONISM MIGHT HAVE BEEN NECESSARY
AS AN ORGANIZING PRINCIPLE TO OBTAIN THE STATE OF ISRAEL,
BUT ZIONISM AS AN IDEOLOGY, A MOVEMENT OF POLITICAL ACTION,
AND AN ETHICAL SYSTEM DEFINING HUMANITARIAN GOALS FOR THE
JEWISH PEOPLE IS NO LONGER OF VALUE. HOWEVER, THOSE WHO
UNDERSTAND ZIONISM AS THE DYNAMO FOR THE BUILDING UP OF
ISRAEL AND AS THE PRINCIPLE UNITING JEWS AND MAKING ISRAEL
CENTRAL IN THEIR LIVES PERCEIVE THAT THE WORK IS ONLY
BEGINNING. ZIONISM REMAINS RELEVANT UNTIL ISRAELIS CAN
ESTABLISH A SOCIETY OF QUALITY THAT ATTRACTS JEWS FROM ALL
OVER THE WORLD TO SHARE IN THE DEVELOPMENT OF THE JEWISH
STATE.

02785 DINKLAGE, R.I.; ZILLER, R.C.
EXPLICATING COGNITIVE CONFLICT THROUGH PHOTO-COMMUNICATION:
THE MEANING OF WAR AND PEACE IN GERMANY AND THE UNITED

STATES
JOURNAL OF CONFLICT RESOLUTION, 33(2) (JUN 89), 309-317.
SEPARATION OF GROUPS IS ASSOCIATED WITH DIFFERENTIAL
MEANING OF CRUCIAL CONCEPTS, NEGATIVE ATTRIBUTIONS OF THE
SEPARATED PARTIES ARISING FROM COGNITIVE DIFFERENCES, AND AN
ACCOMPANYING INCREASE IN THE PROBABILITY OF CONFLICT. HERE,
THE CRUCIAL CONCEPTS EXAMINED ARE "WAR" AND "PEACE". EIGHTY
CHILDREN FROM GERMANY AND THE UNITED STATES WERE ASKED TO
TAKE ON PHOTOGRAPH THAT REPRESENTS WAR AND ANOTHER THAT
REPRESENTS PEACE. A CONTENT ANALYSIS OF THE PHOTOGRAPHS IN
CONJUNCTION WITH PHOTO-FOCUSED INTERVIEWS SHOWED GERMANY
CHILDREN IN COMPARISON WITH AMERICAN CHILDREN DEPICTED MORE
DESTRUCTION AND NEGATIVE CONSEQUENCES ASSOCIATED WITH WAR
AND MORE PERSON-RELATED PHOTOGRAPHS ASSOCIATED WITH PEACE.
THESE DIFFERENCES IN ORIENTATION MAY BE IRRECONCILABLE
BECAUSE THEY ARE BELOW THE LEVEL OF AWARENESS OF THE GROUP
MEMBERS.

02786 DIPRETE, T.A.
CHAPTER FIVE: PROGRESSIVISM AND PUBLIC PERSONNEL
ADMINISTRATION
PLENUM PRESS, NEW YORK, NY, 1989, 93-118.
CHAPTER FIVE OF THE BOOK, THE BUREAUCRATIC LABOR MARKET
CONTINUES THE STUDY OF THE SHAPING OF RECRUITMENT AND
PROMOTION POLICIES FOR WHITE-COLLAR JOBS. IT DETAILS
PROGRESSIVISM AND PUBLIC PERSONNEL ADMINISTRATION, GIVES THE
CASE FOR THE LONG CAREER LINE AND STUDIES THE TRANSITION
YEARS.

02787 DIPRETE, T.A.
CHAPTER THREE: THE CLERICAL-ADMINISTRATIVE BOUNDARY
PLENUM PRESS, NEW YORK, NY, 1989, 47-72.
IN THIS STUDY OF WHITE-COLLAR JOB LADDERS THE CLERICAL-
ADMINISTRATIVE BOUNDRY IS EXAMINED. CLERICAL HIERCHIES IN
THE FEDERAL GOVERNMENT BEFORE 1850 IS DETAILED, AS WELL AS
THE STANDARD OF LIVING IN GOVERNMENT CLERKS. THE BEGINNING
TRANSFORMATION OF HIGHER CLERICAL WORK, AND THE EMERGENCE OF
ADMINISTRATION ARE STUDIED. HOW TO CHARACTERIZE THE BOUNDRY
IS SUGGESTED.

02788 DIPRETE, T.A.
CHAPTER 1: STRUCTURAL EXPLANATIONS FOR INEQUILITY AND
MOBILITY IN BUREAUCRATIZED ORGANIZATIONS; THE BUREAUCRATIC
LABOR MARKET
PLENUM PRESS, NEW YORK, NY, 1989, 1-30.
THIS CHAPTER GIVES THE INSTITUTIONAL VERSES TECHNICAL
THEORIES OF ORGANIZATIONAL LABOR MARKETS AS WELL AS
ANALYZING THE PUBLIC VERSUS PRIVATE SECTOR ORGANIZATIONS. IT
ALSO GIVES AN OVERVIEW OF THE CHANGING STRUCTURE OF WHITE-
COLLAR WORK IN THE FEDERAL GOVERNMENT.

02789 DIPRETE, T.A.
CHAPTER 10: CONCLUSION: STRUCTURES AND OUTCOMES IN
BUREAUCRATIC LABOR MARKETS; THE BUREAUCRATIC LABOR MARKET
PLENUM PRESS, NEW YORK, NY, 1989, 259-276.
CHAPTER 10 IS THE CONCLUSION OF THE BUREAUCRATIC LABOR
MARKET AND GENERALIZES FROM A CASE STUDY, AS WELL AS, WRAPS
UP ON JOB LADDERS AND JOB MOBILITY; THE EMPIRICAL IMPACT OF
BUREAUCRATIC LABOR MARKETS; AND THE PROFESSIONAL CHARACTER
OF UPPER TIER WORK. IMPLICATIONS FOR POLICY ARE GIVEN.

02790 DIPRETE, T.A.
CHAPTER 2: THE HIERCY OF WHITE-COLLAR WORK
PLENUM PRES, NEW YORK, NY, 1989, 31-46.
THIS CHAPTER EXAMINES THE STRUCTURE OF WHITE-COLLAR JOB
LADDERS, STUDIED ARE THE CHANGES IN THE COMPOSITION OF THE
LABOR FORCE AND THE FORMAL IMPLICATIONS OF THE CHANGE FOR
PROMOTIONS. IT CONCLUDES THAT CHANGES IN THE RECRUITMENT
PATTERNS HAVE OFFSET THE INCREASED PROMOTION CHANCES.

02791 DIPRETE, T.A.
CHAPTER 4: EARLY PERSONNEL MANAGEMENT IN THE FEDERAL CIVIL
SERVICE
PLENUM PRESS, NEW YORK, NY, 1989, 73-92.
CHAPTER FOUR EXAMINES THE SHAPING OF RECRUITMENT AND
PROMOTION POLICIES FOR WHITE COLLAR JOBS. AS IT STUDIES THE
EARLY PERSONNEL MANAGEMENT IN THE FEDERAL CIVIL SERVICE IT
DETAILS THE ONSET OF REFORM. IT ADDRESSES MERIT, THE MERIT
SYSTEM, AND THE QUALIFICATIONS FOR OFFICE. RECRUITMENT
VERSUS PROMOTION IN THE FILLING OF VACANCIES IS ADDRESSED

02792 DIPRETE, T.A.
CHAPTER 6: THE DEVELOPMENT OF A TIERED PERSONNEL SYSTEM IN
THE FEDERAL GOVERNMENT; THE BUREAUCRATIC LABOR MARKET
PLENUM PRESS, NEW YORK, NY, 1989, 119-160.
THIS CHAPTER EXPLORES THE DEVELOPMENT OF A TIERED
PERSONNEL SYSTEM IN THE FEDERAL GOVERNMENT. DETAILED ARE:
HOW VACANCIES WERE TRADITIONALLY FILLED IN THE FEDERAL
GOVERNMENT; THE NEW DEAL AND THE PUSH FOR AN ADMINISTRATIVE
CLASS; THE MATURING BUREAUCRATIC LABOR MARKET; POSTWAR
PROMOTION AND TRAINING POLICIES; THE MATURE LABOR MARKET;
AND, GENDER AND RACIAL INEQUALITY AND THE STRUCTURE OF JOB
LADDERS.

02793 DIPRETE, T.A.
CHAPTER 8: EQUAL EMPLOYMENT OPPORTUNITY AND THE BRIDGING
OF JOB LADDERS; THE BUREAUCRATIC LABOR MARKET
PLENUM PRESS, NEW YORK, NY, 1989, 197-230.
CHAPTER 8 STUDIES EQUAL EMPLOYMENT OPPORTUNITY AND THE
BRIDGING OF JOB LADDERS. IT EXAMINES THE FOLLOWING: EQUAL
EMPLOYMENT OPPORTUNITY AND ITS IMPLICATIONS FOR MOBILITY;
THE EXTENT OF MOBILITY FROM THE LOWER TO THE HIGHER TIER;
SEX AND RACE COMPOSITION OF NEW HIRES AND PROMOTEES; MORE
EVIDENCE ON THE EFFECTIVENESS OF THE BRIDGING STRATEGY IT
ALSO EXPLORES IN DEPTH - MISSING DATA AND THE STATUS OF
WORKERS IN MIXED JOB LADDERS.

02794 DIPRETE, T.A.
THE BUREAUCRATIC LABOR MARKET THE CASE OF THE FEDERAL
CIVIL SERVICE
PLENUM PRESS, NEW YORK, NY, 1989, 341.
THIS BOOK DESCRIBES THE SYSTEM OF ABSTRACTIONS FROM THE
FLOW OF WORK OF THE FEDERAL CIVIL SERVICE AS AN INSTITUTIONA
SET OF VALUED SOCIAL PRACTICES CREATED IN A LONG AND COMPLEX
HISTORICAL PROCESS, IT STUDIES THE HISTORICAL ORIGINS OF
THIS SYSTEM OF ABSTRACTIONS, ESPECIALLY THE CAREER
ABSTRACTIONS. IT ALSO STUDIES THE RELATION OF CAREER
ABSTRACTIONS BUILT INTO THE INSTITUTION TO THE ACTUAL
DEMOGRAPHY OF MOVEMENTS OF EMPLOYEES INTO, THROUGH, AND OUT
OF THE SYSTEM. THE STRUCTURE OF WHITE-COLLAR JOB LADDERS, AS
WELL AS THE SHAPING OF RECRUITMET AND PROMOTION POLICIES FOR
THOSE JOBS A

02795 DIRLIK, A.
POSTSOCIALISM? REFLECTIONS ON "SOCIALISM WITH CHINESE
CHARACTERISTICS."
BULLETIN OF CONCERNED ASIAN SCHOLARS, 21(1) (JAN 89),
33-45.
THE AUTHOR CONSIDERS THE INTERPRETIVE POSSIBILITIES OF A
CONCEPTUALIZATION OF CHINESE SOCIALISM THAT IS PRIMARILY
DECONSTRUCTIVE IN INTENTION. HE ATTEMPTS TO FIND A WAY OUT
OF THE CONCEPTUAL PRISON INTO WHICH CHINESE SOCIALISM IS
FORCED BY IDEOLOGICAL EFFORTS TO CONSTRICT IT BETWEEN
RECEIVED NOTIONS OF CAPITALISM AND SOCIALISM. TO DO SO, HE
DEVELOPS THE CONCEPT OF "POSTSOCIALISM" AND MAINTAINS THAT
IT IS THE MOST ACCURATE DESCRIPTOR OF THE CHINESE SYSTEM.

02796 DIRLIK, A.
THE PATH NOT TAKEN: THE ANARCHIST ALTERNATIVE IN CHINESE
SOCIALISM, 1921-1927
INTERNATIONAL REVIEW OF SOCIAL HISTORY, 39(1) (1989), 1-41.
UNTIL THE LATE 1920S, ANARCHISM WAS STILL A SIGNIFICANT
PRESENCE IN CHINESE RADICAL THINKING AND ACTIVITY, AND TILL
THE MIDDLE OF THE DECADE, GAVE SERIOUS COMPETITION TO THE
COMMUNISTS. THE ESSAY DISCUSSES THE NATURE OF THE ANARCHIST
MOVEMENT IN CHINA, ANARCHIST CRIITICISM OF BOLSHEVIK MARXISM,
AND ANARCHIST REVOLUTIONARY STRATEGY AND ACTIVITY DURING
1921-1927. IT ARGUES THAT WHILE ANARCHISTS WERE QUITE
INNOVATIVE WITH REGARD TO REVOLUTIONARY STRATEGY, THEIR
REPUDIATION OF ORGANIZED POWER DEPRIVED THEM OF THE ABILITY
TO COORDINATE REVOLUTIONARY ACTIVITY ON A NATIONAL SCALE,
AND WHAT SUCCESS THEY ACHIEVED REMAINED LOCAL AND SHORT-
LIVED. INDEED, THE COMMUNISTS WERE ABLE TO MAKE BETTER USE
OF ANARCHIST TACTICS THAN WERE THE ANARCHISTS THEMSELVES.
ANARCHIST CRITIQUE OF POWER RESTED ON A DENIAL OF A CENTER
TO SOCIETY (AND HISTORY). WHILE THIS UNDERCUT THE
ANARCHISTS' ABILITY TO ORGANIZE THE REVLUTIONARY MOVEMENT,
IT IS ALSO REVEALING OF A BASIC PROBLEM OF SOCIALIST
REVOLUTION: THE PROBLEM OF DEMOCRACY. IN IGNORING THE
ANARCHIST CRITIQUE OF POWER, THE SUCCESSFUL REVOLUTIONARIES
DEPRIVED THEMSELVES OF A CRITICAL PERSPECTIVE ON THE PROBLEM
OF SOCIALIST REVOLUTION, AND WERE LEFT AT THE MERCY OF THE
NEW STRUCTURES OF POWER THAT THEY BROUGHT INTO EXISTENCE.
HENCE THE IMPORTANCE OF RECALLING ANARCHISM.

02797 DIRLIK, A.
THE REVOLUTION THAT NEVER WAS: ANARCHISM IN THE GUOMINDANG
MODERN CHINA, 15(4) (OCT 89), 419-462.
IN 1927, ANARCHISTS MADE AN ATTEMPT TO ACQUIRE A VOICE
IN THE GUOMINDANG, PERHAPS EVEN TO SHAPE ITS FUTURE. THEIR
GOAL HAS NOT TO TAKE OVER THE GUOMINDANG POLITICALLY BECAUSE
THEY REJECTED POLITICS, BUT RATHER TO USE THE POSSIBILITIES
THE PARTY OFFERED TO CHANNEL THE CHINESE REVOLUTION IN A
DIRECTION CONSISTENT WITH ANARCHIST GOALS. IN HINDSIGHT, THE
ATTEMPT WAS FUTILE; A LAST DESPERATE, AND SOMEWHAT
OPPORTUNISTIC, ACT IN THE ANARCHISTS' EFFORTS TO RECAPTURE
THE REVOLUTIONARY GROUND THEY HAD LOST OVER THE PREVIOUS
THREE YEARS TO SUCCESSFUL COMMUNIST INROADS AMONG THE MASSES.
FOLLOWING THIS ATTEMPT, ANARCHISM FOR ALL PRACTICAL
PURPOSES WOULD DISAPPEAR AS A SIGNIFICANT FORCE IN CHINESE
RADICALISM. IN THE ATTEMPT, NO LESS THAN IN THE SUPPRESSION
THAT IT INVITED, WAS INSCRIBED THE COMPLEX LEGACY OF THE
HISTORY OF ANARCHISM IN CHINA.

02798 DIRNINGER, C.
SCHMOLLER'S APPROACH TO ECONOMIC POLICY, ESPECIALLY
INDUSTRIAL AND COMMERCIAL POLICY
INTERNATIONAL JOURNAL OF SOCIAL ECONOMICS, 16(9-11) (1989),

117.
OF INTEREST TO THE ECONOMIC HISTORIAN IS THE QUESTION OF
THE RELATION OF THEORETICAL ECONOMIC-POLITICAL CONCEPTS TO
ECONOMIC, SOCIAL AND POLITICAL DEVELOPMENTS WITHIN SOCIETY.
SCHMOLLER'S THEORIES IN THIS REGARD ARE OF INTEREST, BEING
BASED ON THE ACTUAL ECONOMIC DEVELOPMENTS IN HIS OWN TIME.
THE MAIN POINT IS THE PROBLEMS ARISING IN A CAPITALISTIC-
LIBERAL SYSTEM UNDERGOING INDUSTRIALISATION. THE BASIC
ELEMENTS OF SCHMOLLER'S THEORY OF ECONOMIC POLICY ARE
DISCUSSED, THE CENTREPIECE OF WHICH IS THE JUST DIVISION OF
INCOME AND PROPERTY.

02799 DISALVO, C.R.
WHAT'S WRONG WITH OPERATION RESCUE?
COMMONWEAL, CXVI(21) (DEC 89), 664-667.
WHEN WORDS FAIL TO RESOLVE NO-COMPROMISE ISSUES, AN OPEN
SOCIETY HAS TWO CHOICES: POLITICAL VIOLENCE OR CIVIL
DISOBEDIENCE. CIVIL DISOBEDIENCE, PROPERLY PRACTICED, BRINGS
THE OPPOSITION INTO AREAS THAT MAKE PRODUCTIVE DISCUSSION
POSSIBLE. BECAUSE ABORTION REMAINS A CONSTITUTIONALLY
PROTECTED RIGHT, AT THE MOMENT ONLY ONE SIDE CAN EMPLOY
CIVIL DISOBEDIENCE. THE ANT-ABORTION MOVEMENT, LARGELY
THROUGH OPERATION RESUCE, HAS TAKEN ADVANTAGE OF THIS
OPPORTUNITY.

02800 DISCH, L.J.
BREAKING THE SILENCE OF WOMEN IN THE CONVERSATION OF
"MANKIND": THE POLITICAL THEORY OF HANNAH ARENDT
DISSERTATION ABSTRACTS INTERNATIONAL, 50(4) (OCT 89),
1076-A.
HANNAH ARENDT'S STUDIES OF TOTALITARIANISM AND THE HUMAN
CONDITION SUPPORT THE HYPOTHESIS THAT WOMAN'S POLITICAL
VOCABULARY IS DIFFERENT FROM THAT WHICH DOMINATES THE
TRADITION. SHE ILLUSTRATES THE PROBLEM OF ENTRANCE WITH HER
WRITING ON JUDGMENT. IN ADDITION TO ILLUSTRATING THE
PHENOMENON OF ENTRANCE, ARENDT'S WRITING ON JUDGMENT CREATES
THE FOUNDATIONS FOR A NEW UNDERSTANDING OF IT WITH HER
CONCEPT STORYTELLING. SHE INITIATES A VITAL DIALOGUE BETWEEN
CONTEMPORARY FEMINIST AND DEMOCRATIC THEORY.

02801 DISKIN, A.
NOTES ON RECENT ELECTIONS: THE ISRAELI GENERAL ELECTION OF
1988
ELECTORAL STUDIES, 8(1) (APR 89), 75-86.
THE PURPOSE OF THE ARTICLE IS TO DESCRIBE THE BASIC
CHARACTERISTICS OF THE 1988 ELECTIONS OF THE ISRAELI
PARLIAMENT, THE KNESSET. IT OUTLINES THE PARTIES INVOLVED,
THE RESULTS, AND THE EFFECT THAT VARIOUS GROUPS OF VOTERS
HAD ON THE RESULTS INCLUDING THE ARAB VOTE, AND THE JEWISH
ETHNIC VOTE.

02802 DISKIN, L.
THINKING ABOUT A SOCIALIST USA
POLITICAL AFFAIRS, LXVIII(9-10) (SEP 89), 3-5.
THE AUTHOR ARGUES THAT THE INTERNAL KNOT OF ECONOMIC,
SOCIAL AND POLITICAL CONTRADICTIONS THAT CAPITALISM
CONSTANTLY BREEDS GIVES RISE TO THE INEVITABILITY ASPECT OF
SOCIALIST REVOLUTION. HE OUTLINES THE BENEFITS OF A FUTURE
SOCIALIST USA MODELED AFTER A "BILL-OF-RIGHTS SOCIALISM"
ADVOCATE BY GUS HALL AND OTHERS. HE OUTLINES A DEMOCRATIC,
ANTI-MONOPOLY STRATEGY THAT WILL MOBILIZE THE MAJORITY OF
AMERICANS TO ADVANCE SOCIALISM WITHIN THE FRAMEWORK OF THE
CONSTITUTION.

02803 DITTMER, L.
CHINA IN 1988: THE CONTINUING DILEMMA OF SOCIALIST REFORM
ASIAN SURVEY, XXIX(1) (JAN 89), 12-28.
THE ARTICLE BRIEFLY OUTLINES THE ATTEMPTS OF ZHAO ZIYANG
AND OTHER CHINESE REFORMERS TO ENCOURAGE ECONOMIC REFORM. IT
ANALYZES 1988, THE YEAR OF THE "ECONOMIC ROLLER COASTER",
WHICH PITTED THE REFORMERS AGAINST A MOBILIZED ANTIREFORM
JUGGERNAUT. IT ALSO ASSESSES THE FOREIGN POLICY SUCCESSES
AND FAILURES OF THE PEOPLE'S REPUBLIC. IT CONCLUDES THAT
ALTHOUGH THE RESULTS OF CHINA'S REFORMS ARE MIXED, RANGING
FROM AN UNPRECEDENTED LEVEL OF INFLATION, TO A GRADUAL
ACCOMMODATION OF SOME OF THE LESS EXTREME FREE-MARKET
POLICIES, CHINA'S PRAGMATIC, GRADUAL MOVE TOWARDS A NEW
ECONOMIC SYSTEM SEEMS TO BE SUCCEEDING.

02804 DITTMER, L.
SOCIALIST REFORM AND THE PROSPECT OF SINO-SOVIET
CONVERGENCE
STUDIES IN COMPARATIVE COMMUNISM, 22(2/3) (SUM 89),
125-138.
THIS ESSAY EXAMINES PARALLELS THAT HAVE MARKED THE
COURSE OF ECONOMIC REFORM IN CHINA AND THE USSR. IT ARGUES
THAT SOVIET REFORMERS HAVE INCREASINGLY COME TO ADMIRE AND
EMULATE THE CHINESE MODEL. NOTED IS A STRIKING TREND TOWARD
SYSTEMIC CONVERGENCE ALONG SEVERAL DEMENTIONS OF REFORM. IT
ARGUES THAT NEITHER COUNTRY WILL BE SAFE FOR DEMOCRACY AT
ANY TIME IN THE FORSEEABLE FUTURE.

02805 DITTMER, L.
THE TIANANMEN MASSACRE

PROBLEMS OF COMMUNISM, XXXVIII(5) (SEP 89), 2-15.
THE TIANANMEN MASSACRE HAS A WATERSHED EVENT IN THE
HISTORY OF THE PEOPLE'S REPUBLIC OF CHINA WHICH CAN BE
RENDERED SOMEWHAT MORE COMPREHENSIBLE IF IT IS SEEN IN THE
CONTEXT OF A NUMBER OF RECENT DEVELOPMENTS. THE UPHEAVAL
MIGHT BE SAID TO MARK THE CONVERGENCE OF THREE UNRESOLVED,
FESTERING QUESTIONS: THE ROLE OF THE MASSES, THE FUTURE OF
REFORM, AND THE BASIS OF POLITICAL LEGITIMACY.

02806 DIUK, N. M.
M.P. DRAHOMANOV AND THE EVOLUTION OF UKRAINIAN CULTURAL
AND POLITICAL THEORY
DISSERTATION ABSTRACTS INTERNATIONAL, 49(8) (FEB 89),
2358-A.
THE AUTHOR EXAMINES DRAHOMANOV'S POLITICAL IDEAS ON SUCH
SUBJECTS AS POLITICAL FREEDOM IN THE RUSSIAN EMPIRE, THE
NATIONAL QUESTION IN SOCIALISM, THE DEFINITION OF THE
UKRAINIAN NATION, AND THE STRUCTURE AND TACTICS OF THE
RUSSIAN REVOLUTIONARY MOVEMENT.

02807 DIX, R.H.
CLEAVAGE STRUCTURES AND PARTY SYSTEMS IN LATIN AMERICA
COMPARATIVE POLITICS, 22(1) (OCT 89), 23-38.
THE AUTHOR SURVEYS LATIN AMERICA'S EXPERIENCE WITH THE
CONSTRUCTION OF SYSTEMS OF COMPETITIVE PARTY POLITICS.

02808 DIXON, H.J.; MOON, B.E.
DOMESTIC POLITICAL CONFLICT AND BASIC NEEDS OUTCOMES AN
EMPIRICAL ASSESSMENT
COMPARATIVE POLITICAL STUDIES, 22(2) (JUL 89), 178-198.
THIS STUDY UNDERTAKES AN EMPIRICAL INVESTIGATION OF THE
NEAR UNIVERSAL ASSUMPTION THAT DOMESTIC POLITICAL CONFLICT
IS INVARIABLY HARMFUL TO THE SOCIETIES IN WHICH IT OCCURS.
IN PARTICULAR, THE AUTLHRS EXAMINE THE IMPLICATIONS OF
DOMESTIC CONFLICT FOR THE PROVISION OF BASIC HUMAN NEEDS
ONCE THE KNOWN EFFECTS OF AGGREGATE NATIONAL WEALTH ARE
REMOVED. USING A VARIATION OF THE PANEL REGRESSION MODEL,
THE AUTHORS REGRESS AN INDEX OF BASIC NEEDS SATISFACTION ON
MEASURES OF DOMESTIC CONFLICT SCOPE AND INTENSITY, ALONG
WITH SUITABLE CONTROLS, FOR A SAMPLE OF 85 CONTEMPORARY
NATIONS. THE FINDINGS INDICATE THAT THE INTENSITY MEASURE IS
ASSOCIATED WITH LONG-TERM IMPROVEMENTS IN BASIC NEEDS WHILE
THE SCOPE OF CONFLICT CARRIES A NEGATIVE IMPACT FOR BASIC
NEEDS OUTCOMES.

02809 DIZDAREVIC, R.
DOMESTIC SITUATION AND INTERNATIONAL POSITION OF YUGOSLAVIA
YUGOSLAV SURVEY, XXX(2) (1989), 3-20.
IN ACCORDANCE WITH THE CONSTITUTIONAL PROVISION THAT THE
PRESIDENCY OF THE SFRY SHOULD KEEP THE YUGOSLAV ASSEMBLY
INFORMED ABOUT THE SITUATION IN THE COUNTRY AND ITS FOREIGN
POLICY, THE PRESIDENT OF THE PRESIDENCY OF THE SFRY, RAIF
DIZDAREVIC, ADDRESSED BOTH CHAMBERS OF THE ASSEMBLY ON APRIL
20, 1989. DIZDAREVIC REVIEWED YUGOSLAVIA'S DOMESTIC
SITUATION AND ITS INTERNATIONAL POSITION.

02810 DIZEREGA, G.
DEMOCRACY AS A SPONTANEOUS ORDER
CRITICAL REVIEW, 3(2) (SPR 89), 206-240.
THIS ARTICLE DESCRIBES DEMOCRACY AS A SPONTANEOUS ORDER.
IT QUOTES F.A. HAYEK FREQUENTLY IN ITS PRESENTATION. IT
ACKNOWLEDGES THAT HAYEK DID NOT INCLUDE DEMOCRACY IN HIS
ANALYSIS OF SPONTANEOUS ORDER AND ADDRESSES THE FOLLOWING
QUESTIONS: HOW IS IT POSSIBLE TO SAY THAT CONSENT IS THE
FUNDAMENTAL PRINCIPLE UNDERLYING DEMOCRACY EXCEPT IN THE
TRIVIAL SENSE IN WHICH IT UNDERLIES MOST GOVERNMENTS? AND,
HOW CAN A PLETHORA OF SPECIAL INTEREST LEGISLATION BE
CONSIDERED PART OF A SPONTANEOUS ORDER? IN THIS EXAMINATION,
IT ALSO DEMONSTRATES IN WHAT WAYS EGALITARIAN AND
MAJORITARIAN POLITICAL MODELS ARE THEORETICALLY INADEQUATE
AND EVEN MISLEADING TOOLS FOR HELPING TO UNDERSTAND BOTH
DEMOCRACY'S STRENGTHS AND WEAKNESSES.

02811 DLABOHA, I.
UKRAINIAN STUDENTS IN THE UNITED STATES: DOING THEIR BIT
FOR UKRAINE'S INDEPENDENCE
UKRANIAN QUARTERLY, XLV(3) (FAL 89), 273-288.
UKRAINIAN STUDENTS IN THE UNITED STATES HAVE ALWAYS
DISPLAYED AN UNCANNY NATIONAL CONSCIOUSNESS AND
RESPONSIBILITY. EVEN THOUGH THEY LIVED IN THE NEW WORLD,
UKRAINIAN YOUTHS WERE CONSTANTLY REMINED THAT THEIR
SPIRITUAL HOMELAND LAY IN THE UKRAINE. FROM THE VERY
BEGINNINGS OF THE UKRAINIAN COMMUNITY IN THE USA, THE
FOREIGN OCCUPATION OF THE NATIVE LAND AND THE QUEST FOR
UKRAINIAN INDEPENDENCE WERE UPPERMOST IN THE MINDS AND
HEARTS OF THE UKRAINIAN PIONEERS. YOUNG UKRAINIANS WERE
SCHOOLED BY THEIR PARENTS TO REMEMBER THEIR HERITAGE: TO
ATTEND A SATURDAY SCHOOL OF UKRAINIAN STUDIES, TO BELONG TO
A UKRAINIAN YOUTH ORGANIZATION, AND TO READ, WRITE, AND
SPEAK UKRAINIAN.

02812 DLUGIN, L.
DEVELOPMENTS IN THE SOCIALIST WORLD
POLITICAL AFFAIRS, LXVIII(9-10) (SEP 89), 26-30.

THE ARTICLE EXAMINES THE CHANGES TAKING PLACE IN THE
SOVIET SYSTEM OF SOCIALISM. IT ARGUES THAT THE WIDELY HELD
BELIEF THAT SOCIALISM IS DEAD AND THAT THE USSR IS MOVING
TOWARDS A CONVERGENCE WITH CAPITALISM IS FALSE. INSTEAD, THE
USSR IS IMPLEMENTED CHANGES THAT ARE CONSISTENT WITH
SOCIALIST IDEOLOGY AND THAT MOVE IN THE DIRECTION OF GOING
BACK TO LENIN'S CONCEPT OF ALL POWER TO THE SOVIETS. THE
RETOOLING AND STREAMLINING OF SOCIALISM THAT IS CURRENTLY
TAKING PLACE WILL SERVE TO STRENGTHEN SOCIALISM WORLDWIDE.

02813 DLUGIN, L.
THE ULTRA - RIGHT WILL NOT STOP THIS PROCESS
WORLD MARXIST REVIEW, 31(2) (FEB 88), 11-13.
ONE OF THE THINGS THAT CHARACTERIZE THE UNITED STATES
TODAY IS A VERY SHARP DECLINE OF ANTI-COMMUNISM. EVERYTHING
THAT HAS TO DO WITH THE SOVIET UNION AND OTHER SOCIALIST
COUNTRIES IS GREETED WITH GROWING INTEREST IN THE U.S. THE
SUMMIT HAS MADE A TREMENDOUS IMPACT. THE FEW DAYS OF THE
SUMMIT PROVED MORE USEFUL TO OUR PEOPLE THAN WHAT IT
SOMETIMES TOOK YEARS TO ACCOMPLISH: PEOPLE COULD LEARN THE
TRUTH ABOUT SOCIALISM. AMERICANS SAW THE SOVIET LEADER WITH
THEIR OWN EYES, AND IT IS NOW VERY DIFFICULT TO GO BACK TO
THE COLD WAR RHETORIC. IT IS POSSIBLE TO CONSIDER SERIOUSLY
THE FURTHER ISOLATION AND BREAKING-UP OF THE INFLUENCE AND
PROPAGANDA OF THE ULTRA-RIGHT.

02814 DOBELL, A.R.
THE PUBLIC ADMINISTRATOR: GOD OR ENTREPRENEUR? OR, ARE
THEY THE SAME IN THE PUBLIC SERVICE?
AMERICAN REVIEW OF PUBLIC ADMINISTRATION, 19(1) (MAR 89),
1-11.
THIS PAPER DISTINGUISHES ENTREPRENEURIAL BEHAVIOUR IN
THE PUBLIC SERVICE (INNOVATIVE ACTIVITY WHERE THE RISKS AND
BENEFITS ARE ESSENTIALLY PERSONAL OR INFORMED CONSENT CAN
REASONABLY BE PRESUMED) FROM DECISIONS INVOLVING RISKS TO
OTHERS, USUALLY ANONYMOUS AND BEYOND CONSULTATION. IT ARGUES
THAT DECISIONS BY PUBLIC OFFICIALS ARE MORE OFTEN OF THE
LATTER TYPE, IMPOSING RISKS ON OTHERS. THIS LEADS TO A
REQUIREMENT FOR GUIDELINES BASED FIRST ON RIGHTS AND
FUNDAMENTAL PRINCIPLES, THEN ON A CALCULATED RISK-BENEFIT
ANALYSIS, AND FINALLY ON A LIVELY SENSE OF PERSONAL
RESPONSIBILITY. IN THE END, ONLY LEADERSHIP CAN INSTILL A
SHARED SENSE OF ORGANIZATIONAL AND PERSONAL VALUES THAT
ASSURES THE RESPONSIBLE EXERCISE OF ADMINISTRATIVE
DISCRETION IN MAKING RISKY COLLECTIVE DECISIONS.

02815 DOBELL, P. C.
THE NEW SENATE
POLICY OPTIONS, 10(3) (APR 89), 29-32.
SIGNIFICANT, BUT LARGELY UNNOTICED, CHANGES HAVE TAKEN
PLACE IN CANADA'S BODY OF "SOBER SECOND THOUGHT." IN PART,
THESE CHANGES CAME ABOUT BECAUSE OF THE UNUSUAL EXISTENCE OF
A MAJORITY IN THE SENATE OPPOSED TO THE RULING GOVERNMENT.
THE MEECH LAKE ACCORD, WITH ITS NEW METHOD OF APPOINTING
SENATORS, WILL LEND THEM GREATER INDEPENDENCE IN THE FUTURE.

02816 DOBRIANSKY, P.
U.S. HUMAN RIGHTS POLICY: AN OVERVIEW
DEPARTMENT OF STATE BULLETIN (US FOREIGN POLICY), 88(2139)
(OCT 88), 54-57.
THE ARTICLE EXPLORES THE BASIS FOR THE "REALISTIC YET
IDEALISTIC" HUMAN RIGHTS POLICY OF THE US. IT EXAMINES THE
AMRICAN TRADITION THAT FORMS A FOUNDATION FOR US POLICY AND
THE MULTILATERAL AND BILATERAL CHANNELS THROUGH WHICH THE
US ATTEMPTS TO INFLUENCE OTHER NATIONS' HUMAN RIGHTS
POLICIES. IT SEEKS TO DISPEL SEVERAL MYTHS THAT SURROUND
HUMAN RIGHTS SUCH AS THE IDEA THAT EOCNOMIC AND SOCIAL
RIGHTS CONSTITUTE HUMAN RIGHTS OR THAT ECONOMIC DEPRIVATION
IS A VALID RATIONALE FOR DENIAL OF CIVIL/ POLITICAL RIGHTS.

02817 DOBRIANSKY, P.J.
HUMAN RIGHTS AND POLICY: THE AMERICAN TRADITION
CURRENT, (314) (JUL 89), 28-37.
ALTHOUGH HUMAN RIGHTS HAVE BEEN A MUCH DISCUSSED
COMPONENT OF US FOREIGN POLICY SINCE THE EARLY 1970'S,
AMERICAN INTEREST IN THE SUBJECT IS NOT NEW. INDEED,
AMERICAN POLITICAL TRADITION CLEARLY REVEALS A LONGSTANDING
CONCERN WITH PROTECTING THE RIGHTS OF INDIVIDUALS AND
NATIONAL GROUPS. AT THE SAME TIME, IT ALSO MANIFESTS AN EVER-
PRESENT TENDENCY TO FLIRT WITH ISOLATIONISM AND DIRECT
NATIONAL ATTENTION INWARD. THIS SOMEWHAT CONTRADICTORY
COMBINATION OF AMERICAN MORALISM, THE TENDENCY TO
UNIVERSALIZE THE PECULIARLY AMERICAN EXPERIENCE, AND THE
DEEPLY ENTRENCHED ABHORRENCE OF POWER POLITICS ACCOUNT FOR A
CERTAIN TENSION AND INCONSISTENCY IN THE AMERICAN HUMAN
RIGHTS TRADITION.

02818 DOBRIANSKY, P.J.
HUMAN RIGHTS AND U.S. FOREIGN POLICY
WASHINGTON QUARTERLY, 12(2) (SPR 89), 153-169.
PERHAPS THE SINGLE MOST IMPORTANT DILEMMA FOR U.S
DECISION MAKERS IS HOW TO PROMOTE HUMAN RIGHTS IMPROVEMENTS
IN NEWLY CREATED DEMOCRACIES. WHILE TAKING INTO ACCOUNT
CULTURAL AND HISTORICAL FEATURES OF VARIOUS COUNTRIES, THE

UNITED STATES CAN PROPERLY SEEK TO DEVELOP COMMON
INTERNATIONAL HUMAN RIGHTS NORMS AND SECURE THEIR ACCEPTANCE
BY ALL MEMBERS OF THE INTERNATIONAL COMMUNITY. A GOVERNMENT
THAT OPERATES WITHIN THE CONTEXT OF A TRADITIONAL POLITICAL
CULTURE, RESPECTS THE CORPORATE GROUP RIGHTS OF ITS SUBJECTS,
AND PROVIDES OPPORTUNITIES FOR DEMOCRATIC ELECTIONS
DESERVES U.S. SUPPORT AND ENCOURAGEMENT, EVEN IF IT DOES NOT
SUBSCRIBE TO ALL OF THE TENETS OF U.S. DEMOCRATIC TRADITION.

02819 DOBRIANSKY, P.J.
THE BALTIC STATES IN AN ERA OF SOVIET REFORM
DEPARTMENT OF STATE BULLETIN (US FOREIGN POLICY), 89(2147)
(JUN 89), 35-39.
REFUSING TO RECOGNIZE THE LEGITIMACY OF THE FORCED
INCORPORATION OF ESTONIA, LATVIA, AND LITHUANIA INTO THE
SOVIET EMPIRE HAS BEEN A LONGSTANDING, FUNDAMENTAL TENET OF
AMERICAN POLICY TOWARD THE SOVIET UNION. BUT REFORMS
INITIATED BY MIKHAIL GORBACHEV HAVE BEEN FELT THROUGHOUT THE
SOVIET UNION AND ESPECIALLY IN THE BALTIC STATES. THESE
DEVELOPMENTS HAVE SPAWNED A NUMBER OF NEW CHALLENGES AND
OPPORTUNITIES FOR AMERICAN FOREIGN POLICY IN THE AREA.

02820 DOBROCZYNSKI, M.
EUROPEAN RAPPROCHEMENT
POLISH PERSPECTIVES, XXXII(2) (1989), 19-26.
THERE IS NO QUESTIONING THE EXISTENCE OF A RECOGNIZABLE
EUROPEAN IDENTITY, EVEN THOUGH THE TWENTIETH CENTURY HAS
BROUGHT MAJOR CHANGES AND REAPPRAISALS THAT HAVE
SIGNIFICANTLY ALTERED THE SHAPE OF EUROPE AND ITS POSITION
IN THE WORLD. THE SEEMINGLY PARADOXICAL, BUT IN FACT LOGICAL,
CONSEQUENCE OF THE DIVISION OF EUROPE INTO WEST AND EAST
HAS BEEN A WISH TO REBUILD THE CONTINENT'S SPECIFIC UNITY.
BOTH IN THE WESTERN HALF AND IN THE MAJORITY OF THE EAST
EUROPEAN STATES, FORCES WITH AN AUTHENTIC INTEREST IN
BRIDGING THE GULF ARE MAKING THEMSELVES HEARD.

02821 DOBROCZYNSKI, M.
RAPPROCHEMENT OF THE PEOPLES OF EUROPE: DIFFICULTIES AND
PROSPECTS
INTERNATIONAL AFFAIRS (MOSCOW), (2) (FEB 89), 34-41.
SWEEPING CHANGES ARE GRADUALLY ALTERING THE PICTURE OF
THE WORLD TO WHICH WE HAVE BECOME ACCUSTOMED, INCLUDING THE
ESTABLISHED IDEA OF EUROPE AND ITS POSITION IN WORLD AFFAIRS.
DIFFERENCES IN IDEOLOGY AND IN POLITICAL AND ECONOMIC
SYSTEMS HAVE GIVEN RISE TO PSYCHOLOGICAL AND SOCIAL
DISTINCTIONS BETWEEN THE TWO EUROPEAN BLOCS. THE PRESENT
DESIRE TO RESTORE MANY OF THE LOST FEATURES OF EUROPE'S
FORMER COMMON IMAGE IS A PARADOXICAL BUT LOGICAL RESULT OF
THE DIVISION OF EUROPE. THE PUBLIC SEES NO SENSE IN THE
ISOLATION OF THE TWO PARTS OF EUROPE, WHILE POLITICIANS SEEK
OPTIMUM CONDITIONS FOR SECURITY AND ECONOMIC COOPERATION.
THE PROFOUND, INTENSIVE REFORMS UNDERWAY IN INDIVIDUAL
COUNTRIES ARE ENCOURAGING THE RESTORATION OF EUROPEAN UNITY,
WHICH MAY FACILITATE NEW INTIATIVES ON PROMOTING BETTER
INTERNATIONAL RELATIONS.

02822 DOBSON, A.P.
ECONOMIC DIPLOMACY AT THE ATLANTIC CONFERENCE II: A REPLY
TO PRESSNELL AND HOPKINS
REVIEW OF INTERNATIONAL STUDIES, 15(4) (OCT 89), 359-366.
THIS ARTICLE IS A REPLY BY ALAN P. DOBSON CONCERNING HIS
ARTICLE "ECONOMIC DIPLOMACY AT THE ATLANTIC CONFERENCE," HE
ANALYSES THE FOUR ISSUES THAT WERE CHALLENGED AND ANSWERS
THEM. TELEGRAM ABBEY 35; CHURCHILL AND HIS CABINET;
ROOSEVELT AND THE STATE DEPARTMENT; AND DOBSON'S STANDARD OF
CARE AS A HISTORIAN ARE ADDRESSED.

02823 DOBUZINSKIS, L.
THE COMPLEXITIES OF SPONTANEOUS ORDER
CRITICAL REVIEW, 3(2) (SPR 89), 241-266.
THE PURPOSE OF THIS PAPER IS TO SHOW THAT HAYEK
PREMATURELY SYSTEMATIZES SOME OF HIS INNOVATIVE IDEAS INTO
SOMETHING THAT LOOKS SUSPICIOUSLY LIKE AN IDEOLOGY OF
"MARKETISM." THE AUTHOR'S STATED GOAL IS TO MAKE A CLEARER
DISTINCTION BETWEEN HAYEK'S PREMISES AND THE MORE DEBATABLE
CONCLUSIONS THAT HE REACHES. PARALLEL APPROACHES IN THE
NATURAL SCIENCES ARE CONSIDERED BRIEFLY AND THEN IT IS
ARGUED THAT SPONTANEOUS ORDER IS ONLY ONE ASPECT OF THE
COMPLEXITY INHERENT IN HUMAN ACTIONS AND SOCIAL INTERACTIONS.
THE PARALLELS HELP TO BRING TO LIGHT THE DIALECTICAL LINK
BETWEEN ORDER AND CHAOS IN NATURAL AND SOCIETAL PROCESSES.

02824 DOCKRILL, S.
THE EVOLUTION OF BRITAIN'S POLICY TOWARDS A EUROPEAN ARMY,
1950-54
JOURNAL OF STRATEGIC STUDIES, 12(1) (MAR 89), 38-62.
THE AUTHOR ENDEAVORS TO EXPLAIN WHY THE INITIAL
ASSUMPTIONS OF FRANCE AND BRITAIN ABOUT THE LATTER'S
PARTICIPATION IN THE PLEVEN PLAN TURNED OUT TO BE WRONG.
ALTHOUGH BRITAIN DISLIKED THE MAIN FEATURE OF THE FRENCH
PROJECT--SUPRANATIONALITY--IT EVENTUALLY DECIDED TO BECOME
AN ACTIVE SUPPORTER OF THE PLAN AND EXTENDED ITS SECURITY
GUARANTEES TO THE EUROPEAN DEFENSE COMMUNITY (EDC). THE LAST
PHASE OF THE EDC NEGOTIATIONS REVEALED THE EXACT NATURE OF

THE ANGLO-FRENCH DISAGREEMENT ABOUT WEST GERMANY'S MILITARY
INTEGRATION INTO THE WEST.

02825 DODDS, D.
MISKITO AND SUMO REFUGEES: CAUGHT IN CONFLICT IN HONDURAS
CULTURAL SURVIVAL QUARTERLY, 13(3) (1989), 3-6.
SINCE 1981, THE CONFLICTS BETWEEN THE SANDINISTA
GOVERNMENT AND THE INDIGENOUS PEOPLES OF NICARAGUA'S
ATLANTIC COAST HAVE DEMANDED INTERNATIONAL ATTENTION. THE
INDIGENOUS PEOPLES OF NICARAGUA, ESPECIALLY THOSE WHO HAVE
FLED AS REFUGEES INTO HONDURAS, ARE CAUGHT IN THE MIDDLE OF
COMPLEX NATIONAL AND INTERNATIONAL POWER STRUGGLES WITHIN
WHICH THEY STRIVE FOR THEIR OWN CULTURAL SURVIVAL.

02826 DODGE, W.R.
THE EMERGENCE OF INTERCOMMUNITY PARTNERSHIPS IN THE 1980'S
NATIONAL CIVIC REVIEW, 78(1) (JAN 89), 5-14.
CONTRACTION OF FEDERAL FUNDING HAS BEEN ACCOMPANIED BY
REDUCED FEDERAL GUIDANCE. LOCAL GOVERNMENTS BEAR THE DUAL
BURDEN OF BOTH DESIGNING AND FUNDING PROJECTS. THE
INTERJURISDICTIONAL PARTNERSHIP OF THE 1980S ARE
CHARACTERIZED BY TWO THINGS: AN ENCOURAGING CREATIVITY IN
ADDRESSING REGIONAL ISSUES AND A BURGEONING INVOLVEMENT OF
COUNTY GOVERNMENT AS A MAJOR CONVENING AND ADMINISTRATIVE
FORCE.

02827 DOERN, G.B.; PRINCE, M.J.
THE POLITICAL ADMINISTRATION OF SCHOOL CLOSURES:
ADMINISTRATORS, TRUSTEES AND COMMUNITY GROUPS
CANADIAN REVIEW OF SOCIOLOGY AND ANTHROPOLOGY, 15(4) (DEC
89), 450-469.
THIS ARTICLE EXAMINES RECENT EFFORTS BY THE OTTAWA BOARD
OF EDUCATION (OBE) TO CLOSE SEVERAL HIGH SCHOOLS. AFTER
REVIEWING THE EDUCATION LITERATURE ON SCHOOL CLOSURES, THE
AUTHORS DERIVE FIVE PROPOSITIONS WHICH ARE THEN APPLIED TO
THE OBE SITUATION. THE ARTICLE FOCUSES ON THE BASIC ROLES
AND RELATIONSHIPS AMONG OBE ADMINISTRATORS, TRUSTEES AND
COMMUNITY GROUPS. THE OBE CLOSURE PROCESS GENERATED A
DISTINCTIVE KIND OF COMMUNITY AND ADMINISTRATIVE POLITICS,
CHARACTERIZED BY ADVOCACY, LIMITED FLEXIBILITY AND THE
MANIPULATION OF PARTICIPATORY PROCEDURES. THE AUTHORS
CONCLUDE THAT THE OBE PROCESS DID NOT ENHANCE COMMUNITY
TRUST IN LOCAL EDUCATION DECISION-MAKING.

02828 DOGAN, M.; PAHRE, R.
FRAGMENTATION AND RECOMBINATION OF THE SOCIAL SCIENCES
STUDIES IN COMPARATIVE INTERNATIONAL DEVELOPMENT, 24(2)
(SUM 89), 56-73.
AFTER A BRIEF HISTORY OF SCIENCE, THIS ARTICLE ADDRESSES
THE SOCIAL SCIENCES, A LATECOMER TO ACADEMIA. IT EXPLORES
THE NEW HYBRID SUBFIELDS AND PROMOTES THE NEED FOR
OVERLAPPING SPECIALTIES. IT ARGUES THAT HYBRID SPECIALTIES
ARE OF THE MOST IMPORTANCE. IT EXPLORES THE STATE OF THE
DICIPLINES; SPECIALIZATION AND HYBRIDIZATION IN ACADEMIC
JOURNALS; AND TRACES THE PATTERNS OF HYBRIDIZATION.

02829 DOHERTY, H.C.
DEBT IN LATIN AMERICA: TOWARD DEMOCRACY OR DICTATORSHIPS?
FREEDOM AT ISSUE, (110) (SEP 89), 31-35.
THE AUTHOR CONSIDERS SOME ASPECTS OF THE LATIN AMERICAN
DEBT CRISIS, INCLUDING THE UNITED STATES' POLICY SHIFT FROM
THE BAKER PLAN TO THE BRADY PLAN. HE ARGUES THAT COMMON
SENSE DICTATES THAT LATIN AMERICAN DEBT SERVICE MUST BE
SUBSTANTIALLY REDUCED, BOTH AS A PERCENTAGE OF GDP AND AS A
PERCENTAGE OF ANNUAL EXPORTS. THE FIRST STEP IN REDUCING THE
DEBT BURDEN IS TO STOP INCREASING IT.

02830 DOLAN, D.A.
COUNTY GOVERNMENT: PROFESSIONALISM AND STRUCTURE; WHAT
ROLE DO THEY PLAY IN FISCAL HEALTH?
DISSERTATION ABSTRACTS INTERNATIONAL, 50(3) (SEP 89),
789-A.
USING ORDINARY LEAST SQUARES REGRESSION, THE AUTHOR
ANALYZES WHETHER COUNTY GOVERNMENT REFORMS HAVE A
SIGNIFICANT IMPACT ON THE FISCAL HEALTH OF THE COUNTY. A
SERIES OF SOCIOECONOMIC CONSIDERATIONS ARE REPRESENTED BY
FACTOR VARIABLES AND USED AS CONTROL MEASUREMENTS FOR A
CROSS-SECTIONAL ANALYSIS OF COUNTY GOVERNMENTS SERVING
POPULATIONS OF MORE THAN 25,000 PERSONS IN THE STATES OF
FLORIDA, ILLINOIS, AND IOWA.

02831 DOLAN, E.
LETTING GO THE TIGER'S TAIL
REASON, 21(3) (JUL 89), 29-33.
THE ARTICLE ANALYZES THE ECONOMIC REFORMS ENTAILED IN
GORBACHEV'S PERESTROIKA AND THE CHALLENGES THAT SOVIET
ECONOMIC REFORMERS WILL FACE IN THE FUTURE. ECONOMIC
OBSTACLES INCLUDE: THE CAPITAL STRUCTURE, THE ORGANIZATIONAL
STRUCTURE, LEGAL AND CULTURAL FOUNDATIONS, AND MACROECONOMIC
PROBLEMS. ALTHOUGH THE CHALLENGES ARE FORMIDABLE, SUCCESS IS
POSSIBLE WITH THE RIGHT MIX OF PATIENCE AND PRAGMATISM.

02832 DOLINSKI, A.L.; CAPUTO, R.K.; O'KANE, P.
COMPETING EFFECTS OF CULTURE AND SITUATION ON WELFARE

RECEIPT
SOCIAL SERVICE REVIEW, 63(3) (SEP 89), 359-372.
THE DEBATE ABOUT THE RELATIVE INFLUENCE OF CULTURAL AND
SITUATIONAL FACTORS ON WELFARE RECEIPT IS LONG STANDING.
THIS STUDY EXAMINES THE COMPETING EFFECTS OF THESE FACTORS.
RESULTS INDICATE THAT BOTH CULTURE AND SITUATION INFLUENCE
WELFARE RECEIPT. EDUCATION AND WORK EXPERIENCE HERE ABOUT
THREE TIMES AS IMPORTANT AS ATTITUDES IN EXPLAINING THE
VARIANCE IN THE NUMBER OF YEARS WELFARE HAS RECEIVED.

02833 DOLLAR, D.
SOUTH KOREA-CHINA TRADE RELATIONS
ASIAN SURVEY, XXIX(12) (DEC 89), 1167-1176.
THE ARTICLE EXAMINES THE BURGEONING TRADE BETWEEN THE
REPUBLIC OF KOREA AND THE PEOPLE'S REPUBLIC OF CHINA. IT
DESCRIBES THE CURRENT NATURE OF SOUTH KOREA'S TRADE WITH
CHINA AND EXPLORES THE ECONOMIC POTENTIAL FOR EXPANDING THIS
TRADE. IT ALSO CONSIDERS THE POLITICAL AND ECONOMIC FACTORS
WITHIN CHINA THAT WILL INFLUENCE THE DEVELOPMENT OF TRADE
WITH THE ROK AS WELL AS POLITICAL FACTORS WITHIN SOUTH KOREA.
IT CONCLUDES BY ARGUING THAT DIRECT INVESTMENT BY SOUTH
KOREA INTO CHINA CAN ALLEVIATE MANY OF THE PROBLEMS STANDING
IN THE WAY OF GREATER TRADE.

02834 DOLLERY, B.E.
THE TRIUMPH OF MARXIST APPROACHES IN SOUTH AFRICAN SOCIAL
AND LABOUR HISTORY: A COMMENT
JOURNAL OF ASIAN AND AFRICAN STUDIES, XXIV(3-4) (JUL 89),
259-262.
MARTIN MURRAY PROVIDES A SYNOPTIC SURVEY OF RECENT
TRENDS IN SOUTH AFRICAN HISTORIOGRAPHY IN WHICH HE CLAIMS
THAT THE TWIN-PERSPECTIVE MARXIST APPROACH HAS REPLACED THE
LIBERAL ORTHODOXY AS THE DOMINANT PARADIGM. IT IS ARGUED
THAT MURRAY'S SURVEY IS DEFICIENT IN AT LEAST THREE WAYS.
FIRSTLY, THE IMPLICATIONS OF THE DIVISIONS BETWEEN "SOCIAL
HISTORIANS" AND "STRUCTURALISTS" ARE NOT SUFFICIENTLY
EXPLORED. SECONDLY, THE CONTENTIOUS PERIODISATION ISSUE IS
IGNORED. AND THIRDLY, THE IMPACT OF MERLE LIPTON'S
MONUMENTAL STUDY AND THE CONSEQUENT POSSIBILITY OF A
SYNTHESIS EMERGING ARE NEGLECTED.

02835 DOLPHIN, R.
CHILDREN OF CRIME
MACLEAN'S (CANADA'S NEWS MAGAZINE), 102(5) (JAN 89), 43-44.
THE IMMINENT RELEASE OF A BOY WHO HAS CONVICTED OF
MURDERING HIS PARENTS AND SISTER HAS VISIBLY PORTRAYED SOME
OF THE PROBLEMS INHERENT IN CANADA'S YOUNG OFFENDERS ACT.
THE ACT, WHICH REPLACED THE 1908 JUVENILE DELINQUENTS ACT
FIVE YEARS AGO, SETS A THREE YEARS MAXIMUM FOR ANY CRIMINAL
BETWEEN THE AGES OF 12 AND 17. CANADIAN COURTS ARE FACED
WITH THE DILEMMA OF DEALING WITH THE SPECIAL CIRCUMSTANCES
THAT YOUNG OFFENDERS FACE, WHILE AT THE SAME TIME RESPONDING
TO INCREASING CRITICISM AND OUTCRY FROM LAW ENFORCEMENT
OFFICIALS, CRIME VICTIMS, AND THE GENERAL PUBLIC.

02836 DOLPHIN, R.
FUROR OVER FIREARMS
MACLEAN'S (CANADA'S NEWS MAGAZINE), 102(2) (JAN 89), 38.
CANADIAN POLICE FORCES ARE FOLLOWING THEIR UNITED STATES
COUNTERPARTS IN A MOVE TOWARDS USING MORE POWERFUL WEAPONS.
THE SHIFT, PRIMARILY FROM THE STANDARD .38 CALIBER REVOLVER
TO THE MORE POWERFUL .357 MAGUM, HAS BEEN CRITICIZED IN
CANADA. CRITICS ARGUE THAT CANADA IS MUCH MORE PEACEFUL THAN
THE U.S. AND DOES NOT HAVE TO CONTEND WITH THE HEAVILY ARMED
DRUG RUNNERS THAT ARE IN THE U.S. HOWEVER, DESPITE SUCH
PHILOSOPHICAL QUESTIONING, THE MAJORITY OF CANADIAN POLICE
SUPPORT TO CHANGE IN WEAPONRY.

02837 DOMES, J.
THE THIRTEENTH PARTY CONGRESS OF THE KUOMINTANG: TOWARDS
POLITICAL COMPETITION?
CHINA QUARTERLY, (118) (JUN 89), 345-359.
THE AUTHOR EXAMINES HOW THE REFORMS INITIATED BY CHIANG
CHING-KUO FARED AT THE THIRTEENTH PARTY CONGRESS OF THE
KUOMINTANG. HE REVIEWS BOTH THE PREPARATIONS FOR AND THE
DELIBERATIONS OF THE CONGRESS. THEN HE ANALYZES THE RESULTS
OF THE CONGRESS' ACTIONS.

02838 DOMINGUEZ, J.I.
THE CUBAN ARMED FORCES, THE PARTY AND SOCIETY IN WARTIME
AND DURING RECTIFICATION (1986-88)
JOURNAL OF COMMUNIST STUDIES, 5(4) (DEC 89), 45-62.
IN 1986-88 THE CUBAN GOVERNMENT ADOPTED A POLICY OF
'RECTIFICATION' AT HOME, IN PART TO FOSTER NON-MATERIAL
INCENTIVES; ABROAD, IN 1987-88, APPEALING TO PATRIOTISM AND
INTERNATIONALISM, IT SENT 15,000 TROOPS TO ANGOLA TO
REINFORCE 35,000 ALREADY THERE TO CONFRONT SOUTH AFRICA'S
MILITARY. GIVEN CUBA'S POST1950S TRADITION OF 'LEARNING FROM
THE MILITARY', AND THESE TWO APPEALS TO NON-MATERIAL FACTORS,
WERE MILITARY INSTITUTIONS IN NON-COMBAT SITUATIONS MORE
EFFECTIVE THAN CIVILIAN INSTITUTIONS AT PRODUCTIVE,
SOCIALIING, MANAGERIAL AND SYMBOLIC TASKS? AND WHAT OF THE
COMMUNIST PARTY'S WORK-STYLES UNDER THESE CONDITIONS? THE
EVIDENCE INDICATES THAT THE ARMED FORCES PERFORM NO BETTER

THAN CIVILIAN AGENCIES, AND THAT THE COMMUNIST PARTY HAS
BEEN INEFFECTIVE AT THESE TASKS.

02839 DONAHUE, J.; ISAAC, K.
SENATORS AND SOUTH AFRICA
MULTINATIONAL MONITOR, 10(7-8) (JUL 89), 10-11.
AN EXAMINATION OF SENATE FINANCIAL DISCLOSURE REPORTS
FOR 1988 REVEALS THAT MANY SENATORS WHO SUPPORT ECONOMIC
SANCTIONS AGAINST SOUTH AFRICA CONTINUE TO INVEST THEIR OWN
MONEY IN COMPANIES PROFITING FROM APARTHEID. SENATOR JOHN
DANFORTH, WHO SUPPORTED SANCTIONS IN 1986, LEADS THE LIST OF
SENATORS WITH INVESTMENTS IN COMPANIES DOING BUSINESS IN OR
WITH SOUTH AFRICA.

02840 DONINI, P.G.
ITALY AND THE ARAB WORLD
INTERNATIONAL SPECTATOR, XXIII(3) (JUL 88), 174-180.
THE POLICY OF THE ITALIAN STATE TOWARDS THE ARAB WORLD
HAS, SINCE ITS INCEPTION, FOCUSED ON TWO PARTIALLY
INCOMPATIBLE AIMS: (1) TAKING ADVANTAGE OF ITALY'S UNIQUE
GEOGRAPHICAL POSITION IN ORDER TO DEVELOP A SPECIAL
RELATIONSHIP WITH THE WHOLE MEDITERRANEAN BASIN AND (2)
ACTING IN ACCORDANCE WITH A PATTERN SET BY OTHER EUROPEAN
POWERS. THE CYCLICAL WAVERING BETWEEN THE LODESTARS OF
INTEGRATION WITH EUROPE, ON ONE HAND, AND FOSTERING A MORE
INDEPENDENT MEDITERRANEAN POLICY, ON THE OTHER, HAS MARKED
ITALIAN FOREIGN POLICY SINCE 1861.

02841 DONNELLY, W.H.
JAPAN AS A FUTURE NUCLEAR EXPORTER: WHAT IT COULD MEAN TO
THE UNITED STATES
CRS REVEIW, 10(8) (SEP 89), 31-32.
JAPAN'S NUCLEAR INDUSTRY STANDS READY TO COMPETE ON THE
WORLD MARKET IF THE DEMAND FOR NUCLEAR POWER REVIVES. THIS
COULD WEAKEN THE U.S. TRADE BALANCE, A NUCLEAR EXPORT
REVIVAL, AND U.S. INFLUENCE OVER NONPROLIFERATION POLICIES
OF OTHER COUNTRIES.

02842 DONOVAN, M.
PARTY STRATEGY AND CENTER DOMINATIONS IN ITALY
WEST EUROPEAN POLITICS, 12(4) (OCT 89), 114-128.
THIS ANALYSIS OF CHANGE IN THE ITALIAN PARTY SYSTEM
EXAMINES THE ABILITY OF THE THREE MAIN PARTIES TO OFFER
ALTERNATIVE, SYSTEMICALLY DEFINED, POLITICAL/ELECTORAL
STRATEGIES. IT DETAILS THE STRUCTURE OF THE ITALIAN PARTY
SYSTEM; THE CRISIS OF TRANSFORMISM; CENTER-BASED BIPOLARITY -
THE SOCIALIST STRATEGY DOMINANT; AND OFFERS THE OUTLINES OF
A NEW PARTY SYSTEM. IT CONCLUDES THAT THE MAJOR CHANGE IN
THE ITALIAN PARTY SYSTEM IS THE FACT THAT IT IS DIFFICULT TO
INVISAGE THE ITALY OF THE 1990S AS A 'DIFFICULT' DEMOCRACY
WHERE ALTERATION IS RULED OUT.

02843 DOOLEY, B.
ANYONE FOR PRESIDENT?
ENCOUNTER, LXXIII(3) (SEP 89), 45-48.
THE U.S. PRESIDENT'S ROLE IS NO LONGER ALL IT IS CRACKED
UP TO BE. INSTEAD OF CONTROLLING WORLD HISTORY,
INTERNATIONAL EVENTS CONTROL THE PRESIDENT AND CAN BRING HIM
DOWN. AN AMERICAN PRESIDENT SIMPLY CANNOT COMPETE ANY MORE
WITH HIS EUROPEAN COUNTERPARTS WHO ARE NOT ONLY LIKELY TO
HAVE MORE EXPERIENCE IN WORLD AFFAIRS BUT ARE ALSO MORE
LIKELY TO HAVE THE POWER TO NEGOTIATE WITH FOREIGN POWERS,
SAFE IN THE KNOWLEDGE THAT ANY DEALS THEY MAKE WILL BE
ACCEPTED BY THEIR PARLIAMENT AT HOME. A U.S. PRESIDENT MUST
CONSTANTLY WORRY ABOUT MAJORITY SUPPORT IN CONGRESS, WHICH
WEAKENS HIS BARGAINING POWER ABROAD BECAUSE FELLOW
NEGOTIATORS ARE AWARE OF THIS PREDICAMENT.

02844 DORAN, C.F.
SYSTEMIC DISEQUILIBRIUM, FOREIGN PLOICY ROLE, AND THE
POWER CYCLE: CHALLENGES FOR RESEARCH DESIGN
JOURNAL OF CONFLICT RESOLUTION, 33(3) (SEP 89), 371-401.
CONFRONTING WIDESPREAD AMBIGUITIES OF THEORY AND
RESEARCH DESIGN, THIS ARTICLE ESTABLISHES CONDITIONS
UNDERLYING INTERNATIONAL POLITICAL STABILITY FOR STATE AND
SYSTEM. IN TURN, IT (1) DISSECTS THE CYCLE OF RELATIVE POWER
AND ROLE TO ELUCIDATE THE CONCEPT OF GENERAL EQUILIBRIUM,
DEPICTING GRAPHICALLY THE TRAUMA OF ROLE ADJUSTMENT THAT
ACCOMPANIES CRITICAL CHANGES IN RELATIVE POWER; (2) COMPARES
THE EMPIRICAL RESULTS FOR TRANSITIONS AND CRITICAL POINTS
USING THE SAME SET OF DATA; (3) SHOWS MATHEMATICALLY THAT
INVERSIONS IN THE TREND OF SLOPE CAN APPROXIMATE CRITICAL
INTERVALS; AND (4) DEMONSTRATES VIA DIAGRAMS OF EACH STATE'S
CRITICAL CHANGE WHY THE DISEQUILIBRATED SYSTEM 1885-1914
SUCCUMBED TO MASSIVE WORLD WAR. EMPIRICAL RESEARCH ON
SYSTEMS TRANSFORMATION AND MAJOR WAR MUST INCORPORATE BOTH
STRATEGIC POWER BALANCING AND POWER-ROLE EQUILIBRATION FOR
STATES IN THE CENTRAL SYSTEM IN A BROADER CONCEPT LIKE
GENERAL EQUILIBRIUM.

02845 DORAN, C.F.
SYSTEMIC DISEQUILIBRIAM, FOREIGN POLICY ROLE, AND THE POWER
CYCLE.
JOURNAL OF CONFLICT RESOLUTION, 33(1) (SEP 89), 371-401.

CONFRONTING WIDESPREAD AMBIGUITIES OF THEORY AND
RESEARCH DESIGN, THIS ARTICLE ESTABLISHES CONDITIONS
UNDERLYING INTERNATIONAL POLITICAL STABILITY FOR STATE AND
SYSTEM. IN TURN, IT (1) DISSECTS THE CYCLE OF RELATIVE POWER
AND ROLE TO ELUCIDATE THE CONCEPT OF GENERAL EQUILIBRIUM,
DEPICTING GRAPHICALLY THE TRAUMA OF ROLE ADJUSTMENT THAT
ACCOMPANIES CRITICAL CHANGES IN RELATIVE POWER; (2) COMPARES
THE EMPIRICAL RESULTS FOR TRANSITIONS AND CRITICAL POINTS
USING THE SAME SET OF DATA; (3) SHOWS MATHEMATICALLY THAT
INVERSIONS IN THE TREND OF SLOPE CAN APPROXIMATE CRITICAL
INTERVALS; AND (4) DEMONSTRATES VIA DIAGRAMS OF EACH STATE'S
CRITICAL CHANGE WHY THE DISEQUILIBRATED SYSTEM 1885-1914
SUCCUMBED TO MASSIVE WORLD WAR. EMPIRICAL RESEARCH ON
SYSTEMS TRANSFORMATION AND MAJOR WAR MUST INCORPORATE BOTH
STRATEGIC POWER BALANCING AND POWER-ROLE EQUILIBRATION FOR
STATES IN THE CENTRAL SYSTEM IN A BROADER CONCEPT LIKE
GENERAL EQUILIBRIUM.

02846 DORAN, C.F.
TRADE POLICY FOR THE NEW ADMINISTRATION
SAIS REVIEW, 9(1) (WIN 89), 141-155.
THE PERCEPTION OF SOME THAT THE UNITED STATES' ECONOMIC
PROBLEMS ARE EXTERNAL AND THAT AN IMPROVED U.S. TRADE POLICY
CAN SOLVE THE LARGER AND MORE PERSISTENT U.S. ECONOMIC
PROBLEMS IS INCORRECT. THE UNITED STATES' ECONOMIC ILLS ARE,
TO THE CONTRARY, ESSENTIALLY INTERNAL AND SELFINFLICTED, AND
A BAD TRADE POLICY CAN MAKE THEM WORSE. AN IMPROVED TRADE
POLICY ALONE CANNOT GO FAR TOWARD CORRECTING THE ILLS, BUT A
STRONG U.S. ECONOMY ASSISTED BY TIGHT FISCAL POLICY,
REASONABLE MONETARY POLICY, AND STRUCTURAL REFORM CAN GO A
LONG WAY TOWARD LEADING THE WORLD IN THE DIRECTION OF MORE
PRODUCTIVE GLOBAL TRADE RELATIONS.

02847 DORJI, R.
PROTECTION OF ENVIRONMENT IN SOUTH ASIA
SOUTH ASIA JOURNAL, 3(1/2) (JUL 89), 35-42.
THIS ARTICLE ADDRESSES THE MOST EFFECTIVE WAY TO TACKLE
THE PROBLEM OF ENVIRONMENT IS TO ATTACK IT SIMULTANEOUSLY ON
TWO FRONTS -- THE MATERIAL-PHYSICAL AND THE PSYCHOLOGICAL-
SPIRITUAL. LIKE THE MIND AND BODY, EACH HAS ITS INEVITABLE
REPERCUSSIONS ON THE OTHER, AND THE WRITER FEARS THAT ANY
SOLUTION WHICH DOES NOT TAKE COGNIZANCE OF THIS FACT IS, IN
THE LONG RUN, DOOMED TO FAILURE. REGIONAL ACTIVITIES ARE
RECOMMENDED AND THE NEED FOR A WARLESS WORLD IS PROJECTED.

02848 DORMAN, W.
THE CHEMICAL WEAPONS CRISIS: A DEBATE DENIED
DEADLINE, IV(2) (MAR 89), 1-2, 10-12.
US CONFLICT WITH LIBYA, OSTENSIBLY OVER THE ISSUE OF
"ILLEGAL" CHEMICAL WEAPONS BUILD-UP, CULMINATED IN A
DOGFIGHT BETWEEN US AND LIBYAN AIRCRAFT. IT WAS ONLY AFTER
THE INCIDENT THAT THE PRESS BEGAN TO EXAMINE BOTH SIDES OF
THE ISSUE AND WASHINGTON'S SKILLFUL CONTROL OF THE SITUATION
BECAME APPARENT. SIMPLY PUT, "THE ADMINISTRATION'S
POLICYMAKERS CLAIMED THE MORAL HIGH GROUND--AND THE PRESS
CONCEDED IT TO THEM."

02849 DORNBUSCH, R.
THE US ECONOMY AND THE DOLLAR
CANADIAN PUBLIC POLICY--ANALYSE DE POLITIQUES, XV (FEB 89),
10-19.
RENEWED DISCUSSION OF TARGET RANGES FOR EXCHANGE RATES
AND THE CONTINUING LARGE US EXTERNAL DEFICIT RAISES THE
QUESTION WHETHER EXCHANGE RATES ARE SUSTAINABLE AT NEAR
CURRENT LEVELS. THIS ISSUE IS EXPLORED HERE IN THE CONTEXT
OF US MACROECONOMIC ADJUSTMENTS. THE POSITION OF THE DOLLAR
OFFERS A STARTING POINT FOR DISCUSSING WHETHER THE DOLLAR
NEEDS TO DEPRECIATE FURTHER. THE AUTHOR CONCLUDES THAT THIS
IS, INDEED, THE CASE. THE ARGUMENT IS BASICALLY THAT TWO
THIRDS OF THE PRESENT DEFICIT WILL PERSIST EVEN AT THE
CURRENT LEVEL OF THE DOLLAR.

02850 DORNEY, D.C.
A COMPARATIVE ANALYSIS OF THE INFLUENCES OF STATES'
CHARACTERISTICS ON MENTAL HEALTH ALLOCATION STRATEGIES
DISSERTATION ABSTRACTS INTERNATIONAL, 49(8) (FEB 89),
2385-A.
A STATISTICAL PROFILE OF THE 50 STATES WAS GATHERED IN
ORDER TO IDENTIFY THOSE SOCIAL, POLITICAL, ECONOMIC,
GOVERNMENTAL, AND MENTAL HEALTH FUNDING CHARACTERISTICS THAT
INFLUENCED THE USE AND NON-USE OF FORMULAS IN ALLOCATING
MENTAL HEALTH FUNDS. FINDING INDICATE THAT THE DISTRIBUTION
OF RESOURCES IS STRONGLY INFLUENCED BY THE ECONOMIC,
POLITICAL, ORGANIZATIONAL, AND CULTURAL CONTEXT IN EACH
STATE. NEW BUDGETARY PROCEDURES REFLECT A CONSERVATIVE
POLITICAL CLIMATE DEMANDING MORE ACCOUNTABILITY FOR
RESOURCES.

02851 DORON, G.; PEDATZUR, R.
ISRAELI INTELLIGENCE: UTILITY AND COST-EFFECTIVENESS IN
POLICY FORMATION
INTERNATIONAL JOURNAL OF INTELLIGENCE AND
COUNTER-INTELLIGENCE, 3(3) (1989), 347-362.
THE FORMATION OF ISRAELI SECURITY POLICY IS AFFECTED BY

THE JUXTAPOSITION OF AT LEAST FOUR FACTORS: (1) THE
STRUCTURE OF THE INTELLIGENCE COMMUNITY AND THE WAY IT
TRANSMITS RELEVANT INFORMATION TO THE POLICYMAKERS; (2) THE
PERSONAL PREFERENCES OF THE MAJOR POLICYMAKERS, THE MILITARY
CHIEF OF STAFF AND THE HEAD OF AMAN (MILITARY INTELLIGENCE)
AND THEIR PROPENSITIES TOWARD RISK; (3) THE DISCREPANCY
BETWEEN THE CIVILIAN AND MILITARY CONCEPTUALIZATIONS OF THE
SECURITY SITUATION; AND (4) THE RELEVANCE OF THE
INTELLIGENCE DATA GATHERED FOR POLICY FORMATION. THE
COMBINED EFFECT OF THESE FACTORS CREATES A TENDENCY AMONG
ISRAELI POLICYMAKERS TO UNDERSCORE THE INFORMATION PROVIDED
BY THE INTELLIGENCE SYSTEM. THUS ISRAEL EMPLOYS SOMEWHAT
LARGER THAN NECESSARY ARMED FORCES TO ASSURE ITS SECURITY.

02852 DOROSARIO, L.
CHINA'S BROKEN ENGINE
FAR EASTERN ECONOMIC REVIEW, 141(36) (SEP 88), 128-131.
AFTER ALMOST A DECADE OF SLOW, PIECEMEAL REFORM, CHINA'S
STATE INDUSTRIES ARE IN URGENT NEED OF SYSTEMATIC,
FUNDAMENTAL RESTRUCTURING TO ARREST THEIR DECLINE. CURRENTLY
MANY CANNOT SURVIVE WITHOUT SUBSIDIES, EASY LOANS, CHEAP RAW
MATERIALS, AND OTHER FORMS OF GOVERNMENT SUPPORT. THE
ATTEMPTS AT REFORM HAVE FAILED LARGELY DUE TO SELFINTEREST
ON THE PART OF PARTY CADRES, MINISTRY OFFICIALS, AND WORKERS.

02853 DORRANCE, J.C.
THE PACIFIC ISLANDS AND U.S. SECURITY INTERESTS: A NEW ERA
POSES NEW CHALLENGES
ASIAN SURVEY, 29(7) (JUL 89), 698-715.
DEVELOPMENTS WITHIN AND WITHOUT THE PACIFIC ISLAND
REGION NO LONGER PERMIT THE ASSUMPTION THAT IT IS A TRANQUIL
BACKWATER, REQUIRING NEITHER ATTENTION NOR RESOURCES AGAINST
A BACKDROP OF OTHER PRIORITIES. THIS ARTICLE EXAMINES THE
POSITIVE AND UNIQUE CHARACTERISTICS OF THE ISLANDS. THE
AUSTRALIA/NEW ZEALAND, SOVIET, AND U.S. DIMENTIONS ARE
REVIEWED, AS WELL AS U.S. INTERESTS AND OBJECTIVES; ISLAND
STATE SECURITY CONCERNS; AND POSSIBLE U.S. RESPONSES.

02854 DORYAN-GARRON, E.
EXPLAINING DEVELOPMENT STRATEGY CHOICE BY STATE ELITES:
THE COSTA RICAN CASE
DISSERTATION ABSTRACTS INTERNATIONAL, 49(10) (APR 89),
3150-A.
THE AUTHOR IDENTIFIES A SET OF PATTERNS THAT EXPLAIN THE
PROCESS BY WHICH STATE ELITES MAKE DECISIONS AFFECTING
DEVELOPMENT. THESE PATTERNS ARE OUTLINED BY EXAMINING FOUR
INTERVENING VARIABLES: (1) OPPORTUNITIES AND CONSTRAINTS
EMANATING FROM THE INTERNATIONAL POLITICAL ECONOMY, (2) THE
STRENGTH AND NATURE OF THE DEMANDS MADE BY DOMESTIC SOCIAL
ACTORS AND PRESSURE GROUPS, (3) THE POLICY INSTRUMENTS
AVAILABLE TO THE STATE AND THE ELITE, AND (4) THE HISTORICAL
IDEOLOGY OF THE POLICY-MAKING ELITE. THE CASE OF COSTA RICA
IS USED TO ILLUSTRATE THE FINDINGS.

02855 DOUGLAS, S. U.
THE TEXTILE INDUSTRY IN MALAYSIA: COPING WITH PRCTECTIONISM
ASIAN SURVEY, XXIX(4) (APR 89), 416-438.
THE TREND TOWARD PROTECTIONISM IN THE UNITED STATES, ONE
OF THE FIVE COUNTRIES WITH WHICH MALAYSIA HAS BILATERAL
TEXTILE TRADE AGREEMENTS, HAS BEEN ESPECIALLY WORRISOME
BECAUSE NEARLY HALF OF MALAYSIA'S TEXTILE EXPORTS GO THERE.
THIS ARTICLE, BASED ON DATA COLLECTED IN MALAYSIA IN 1986
AND 1987, DESCRIBES THE PROCESSES OF ECONOMIC ADJUSTMENT
MADE BY THE MALAYSIAN TEXTILE AND APPAREL INDUSTRIES IN
RESPONSE TO WORLD MARKETPLACE PRESSURES AND DISTURBANCES.

02856 DOUGLASS, S.
FROM CONTESTED GROUND TO COMMON GROUND
SOJOURNERS, 18(10) (NOV 89), 17.
THE AUTHOR ARGUES THAT ABORTION IS ONE IN A GROUP OF
MANY ISSUES THAT ARE BASED ON DOMINATION AND POWER. THE
ONGOING BATTLE OVER THE RIGHT TO CHOOSE IGNORES THE DEEPER
ISSUE SURROUNDING THE CHOICE ITSELF. SHE CONCLUDES BY
CALLING FOR A RETURN TO MERCY, COMPASSION, AND JUSTICE WITH
AN EMPHASIS ON GENTLE AND LOVING RESPONSES TO UNWANTED
PREGNANCIES.

02857 DOUMANI, B.
ABU FARID'S HOUSE: FAMILY AND POLITICS IN SALFIT
MIDDLE EAST REPORT, 19(157) (MAR 89), 28-33.
THE INTIFADA'S CYCLE OF RESISTANCE AND REPRESSION HAS
INFUSED FAMILIES IN SALFIT AND OTHER PALESTINIAN TOWNS WITH
ONE MIND AND ONE SPIRIT. THE INTIFADA HAS ENGENDERED A
FEELING OF EMPOWERMENT AND SALFIT HAS BEEN REJUVENATED BY
THE STRUGGLE FCR NATIONAL LIBERATION.

02858 DOW, T.
REMEDY THE MARXIAN "QUALITATIVE LEAP" WITH CONFUCIAN-
TAOIST YIN-YANG DIALECTICS
ASIAN PROFILE, 17(2) (APR 89), 113-124.
A MODIFICATION OF THE MUCH DISPUTED MARXIAN "QUALITATIVE
LEAP" BY THE CONFUCIAN-TAOIST YIN-YANG DIALECTICAL MONISTIC
VIEW IS POSSIBLE SO THAT THE UTOPIAN BENT OF THE MARXIAN
"WITHERING AWAY OF THE STATE" IN A CLASSLESS CONDITION COULD

BE CORRECTED WITHOUT ANY BASIC ALTERATION OF EITHER
PHILOSPHICAL SYSTEM.

02859 DOWDING, K.M.
COLLECTIVE ACTION, GROUP ORGANIZATION, AND PLURALIST
DEMOCRACY
DISSERTATION ABSTRACTS INTERNATIONAL, 49(8) (FEB 89),
2422-A.
THE AUTHOR ARGUES THAT GROUPS OF RATIONAL SELF-
INTERESTED MAXIMIZERS CAN OVERCOME THEIR COLLECTIVE ACTION
PROBLEMS, CONTRARY TO THE ACCEPTED RATIONAL CHOICE WISDOM.
ORGANIZATIONS CAN AND DO FORM IN ORDER TO PROVIDE PUBLIC
GOODS. COORDINATORS ARE OFTEN NECESSARY, BUT SELF-INTERESTED
INDIVIDUALS MAY TAKE ON THIS ROLE MERELY TO PROVIDE PUBLIC
GOODS THEY VALUE AND NOT FOR PERSONAL PRIVATE PROFIT.

02860 DOWDY, W.L.
THE CANADIAN NAVY: TORPEDOED AGAIN
ARMED FORCES AND SOCIETY, 16(1) (FAL 89), 99-115.
IN JUNE 1987, A CANADIAN DEFENSE WHITE PAPER ANNOUNCED
THAT THE GOVERNMENT HAD DECIDED TO ACQUIRE A FLEET OF
NUCLEAR-POWERED SUBMARINES. IN APRIL 1989, THE GOVERNMENT
STATED THAT IT HAD DECIDED NOT TO PROCEED WITH THE
ACQUISITION OF THOSE SUBMARINES. THE TWO PRONOUNCEMENTS
ILLUSTRATE A RECURRENT THEME IN CANADIAN NAVAL POLICY. ONCE
AGAIN, THE CANADIAN GOVERNMENT HAS REVERSED A MAJOR
COMMITMENT TO REJUVENATE ITS NAVY. ONCE AGAIN, POLITICAL
EXPEDIENCY HAS PREVAILED. ONCE AGAIN, CANADA HAS CONCEDED
ITS DEPENDENCE ON A STRONGER ALLY FOR THE SECURITY OF ITS
OCEAN ENVIRONMENT. SCARCE GOVERNMENT RESOURCES AND A LOW-
THREAT ENVIRONMENT LARGELY ACCOUNT FOR THE OSCILLATING
FORTUNES OF THE CANADIAN NAVY DURING THE PAST 80 YEARS.

02861 DOWNING, L.; THIGPEN, R.
A DEFENSE OF NEUTRALITY IN LIBERAL POLITICAL THEORY
POLITY, XXI(3) (SPR 89), 512-516.
RECENT ATTACKS ON LIBERAL POLITICAL THEORY HAVE FOCUSED
ON THE CONCEPT OF NEUTRALITY, THE IDEA THAT GOVERNMENT MUST
BE NEUTRAL TOWARD THE HUMAN GOOD. THE DEBATE BETWEEN
LIBERALS AND THEIR CRITICS MIGHT, HOWEVER, PROCEED MORE
SATISFACTORILY IF THE MEANING AND POSSIBILITY OF NEUTRALITY
WERE CLARIFIED. THE AUTHORS OF THIS ARTICLE ATTEMPT THAT,
AND ARGUE THAT WHILE A BLANKET NOTION OF NEUTRALITY IS
INDEFENSIBLE, A CONSTRAINED CONCEPT IS POSSIBLE AND IS
ESSENTIAL TO A FUNDAMENTAL PRINCIPLE OF LIBERAL THEORY,
EQUAL FREEDOM.

02862 DOWTY, A.
THE ASSAULT ON FREEDOM OF EMIGRATION
WORLD AFFAIRS, 151(2) (FAL 88), 85-92.
A SIGNIFICANT PROPORTION OF THE WORLD'S REFUGEES ARE
OUTSIDE THEIR COUNTRIES AT LEAST PARTLY BECAUSE THEIR
GOVERNMENT WANTS THEM THERE, OR IS CONTENT TO SEE THEM THERE,
OR PUTS OTHER PRIORITIES AHEAD OF MAKING THEIR RETURN
POSSIBLE. THIS ATTITUDE OFTEN CORRESPONDS TO A RESTRICTIVE
ATTITUDE ON THE RIGHT OF EMIGRATION, DESPITE THE APPARENT
CONTRAST. THE CLOSE ASSOCIATION WITH MARXIST-LENINIST
REGIMES RAISES THE QUESTION OF HOW DEPENDENT THESE REGIMES
ARE ON SUCH CONTROL. THE EXAMPLES OF BENIN, CONGO, CHINA,
YUGOSLAVIA, HUNGARY, AND (DURING CERTAIN PERIODS) CUBA ALL
SUGGEST THAT THE RELATIONSHIP IS NOT A SIMPLE ONE, AND THAT
UNDER SOME CONDITIONS CONTROL CAN BE LOOSENED WITHOUT
ADVERSE RESULTS, FROM THE REGIME'S PERSPECTIVE.

02863 DOWTY, A.
THE SATANIC VENDETTA: IRAN'S UNHOLY WAR ON THE BAHA'IS
CHURCH AND STATE, 42(4) (APR 89), 7(79)-8(80),10(82).
MUCH ATTENTION HAS BEEN FOCUSED ON THE AYATOLLAH
KHOMEINI'S DEATH THREAT AGAINST AUTHOR SALMAN RUSHDIE. FAR
LESS ATTENTION HAS BEEN PAID TO THE IRANIAN GOVERNMENT'S
EFFORTS TO DESTROY AN ENTIRE RELIGIOUS COMMUNITY. ALTHOUGH
THE BAHA'I FAITH IS ROOTED IN ISLAM AND ORIGINATED IN IRAN,
IRANIAN BAHA'IS MAY BE THE MOST CRUELLY PERSECUTED RELIGIOUS
MINORITY IN THE WORLD TODAY. SINCE CIVIL RIGHTS IN THE NEW
IRAN ARE EXTENDED ONLY TO FOLLOWERS OF RECOGNIZED RELIGIONS
AND THE BAHA'I RELIGION HAS BEEN DENIED LEGAL STATUS,
BAHA'IS HAVE BECOME NON-PERSONS.

02864 DOXEY, M.
CONSRUCTIVE INTERNATIONALISM: A CONTINUING THEME IN
CANADIAN FOREIGN POLICY
ROUND TABLE, (311) (JUL 89), 288-304.
RESPECT FOR INTERNATIONAL INSTITUTIONS AND ENTHUSIASM
FOR ROLE PLAYING WITHIN THEM HAVE BEEN CONSISTENT THEMES IN
CANADIAN FOREIGN POLICY SINCE WORLD WAR II. THIS ESSAY
FOCUSES ON CANADA'S PARTICIPATION IN MULTILATERAL
INSTITUTIONS AND SPECIFICALLY ON THE RECORD OF THE
PROGRESSIVE CONSERVATIVE GOVERNMENT OF BRIAN MULRONEY IN
THIS REGARD. THERE ARE SEVERAL INSTITUTIONS THAT ARE FOCUSED
ON: THE UN, THE COMMONWEALTH, LA FRANCOPHONIE AND NATO.

02865 DOYLE, M.
BLOOD BROTHERS
AFRICA REPORT, 34(4) (JUL 89), 13-16.

RELATIONS BETWEEN SENEGAL AND MAURITANIA REMAIN STRAINED
IN THE WAKE OF THE APRIL 1989 VIOLENCE THAT LEFT MANY DEAD
AND COUNTLESS MORE UPROOTED. DESPITE THE CRUCIAL ROLE PLAYED
BY EACH NATION IN THE ECONOMY OF THE OTHER, THE EXPLOSION OF
LONG-SIMMERING RACIAL TENSIONS MAY HAVE CAUSED IRREPARABLE
DAMAGE AT BOTH THE INTERSTATE AND DOMESTIC LEVELS.

02866 DOYLE, M.
MARGINAL GROUNDS FOR DEBATE
SOUTH, (108) (OCT 89), 33.
THE WEST AFRICAN STATES OF SENEGAL AND GUINEA-BISSAU
HAVE REVIVED A LONGSTANDING SQUABBLE OVER OWNERSHIP OF A
STRETCH OF ATLANTIC SEABED THAT CONTAINS OIL. THE ROW FLARED
UP IN AUGUST 1989 AFTER AN INTERNATIONAL COURT OF
ARBITRATION RULED IN SENEGAL'S FAVOR AND GUINEA-BISSAU
REJECTED THE RULING AS BIASED.

02867 DOYLE, M.
NOUAKCHOTT'S NEW NATIONALISM
AFRICA REPORT, 34(5) (SEP 89), 37-40.
THE RECENT VIOLENCE IN MAURITANIA AND SENEGAL HAS
BROUGHT TO A HEAD LONG-STANDING ETHNIC TENSIONS IN
MAURITANIAN SOCIETY. THE CONFLICT HAS PROVIDED NOUAKCHOTT
WITH AN EXCUSE TO DEPORT SOME 30,000 OF ITS BLACK CITIZENS,
AGAINST WHOM THE AUTHORITIES HAVE LONG HARBORED MISTRUST,
AND TO RE-EMPHASIZE THE ARAB/MOORISH NATIONALISM OF A SECTOR
OF THE POPULATION.

02868 DOYLE, M.
SHUTTERS DOWN ON THE BORDER
SOUTH, (105) (JUL 89), 22-23.
ETHNIC VIOLENCE BETWEEN BLACKS IN SENEGAL AND
MAURITANIAN MOORS COULD HAVE LONG-TERM CONSEQUENCES FOR BOTH
COUNTRIES. MORE THAN 100,000 INDIVIDUALS FLED IN BOTH
DIRECTIONS ACROSS THE BORDER AFTER SENEGALESE TARGETED
MOORISH SHOPS IN SENEGAL, WHICH LED TO REVENGE ATTACKS IN
MAURITANIA AGAINST SENEGALESE WORKERS. THE VIOLENCE WAS
SPARKED BY A BORDER INCIDENT OVER GRAZING RIGHTS.

02869 DRAGADZE, T.
THE ARMENIAN-AZERBAIJANI CONFLICT: STRUCTURE AND SENTIMENT
THIRD WORLD QUARTERLY, 11(1) (JAN 89), 55-71.
ONE CAN ONLY REFER TO THE RECENT ARMENIAN-AZERBAIJANI
CONFLICT IN THE SOVIET UNION AS A TERRIBLE TRAGEDY. THIS IS
NOT ONLY BECAUSE OF THE LOSS OF LIFE AND THE ASSOCIATED
DISRUPTIONS. IT IS ALSO A TRAGEDY BECAUSE THE EVENTS REVEAL
HOW FRAIL ANY PEACE CAN BE, HOW FUTILE UNSUBSTANTIATED
EXPRESSIONS OF INTER-ETHNIC HARMONY VOICED BY GOVERNMENT
AUTHORITIES CAN BE, AND HOW ENDURING THE YOKE OF EMPIRE CAN
BE. FOR THESE REASONS, THE WIDER CONNOTATIONS OF THE
CONFLICT ARE OF CONCERN NOT ONLY FOR THOSE CONNECTED WITH
SOVIET AFFAIRS BUT ALSO FOR ALL FELLOW HUMAN BEINGS. IN
PARTICULAR, THOSE CONCERNED WITH THE THIRD WORLD WILL FIND
SEVERAL PARALLELS WITH OTHER HISTORIES AND OTHER DESTINIES.

02870 DRAGNICH, A.N.
THE RISE AND FALL OF YUGOSLAVIA: THE OMEN OF THE UPSURGE
OF SERBIAN NATIONALISM
EAST EUROPEAN QUARTERLY, XXIII(2) (JUN 89), 183-193.
THE DEMONSTRATIONS THAT ROCKED YUGOSLAVIA IN THE FALL OF
1988 CAN ONLY BE UNDERSTOOD IN THEIR HISTORICAL CONTEXT.
FIRST OF ALL, IT IS IMPORTANT TO KNOW THAT THE
DEMONSTRATIONS INVOLVED THE SERBS, THE LARGEST ETHNIC GROUP
IN YUGOSLAVIA. SECONDLY, HISTORICALLY THE SERBS HAVE BEEN
THE STRONGEST SUPPORTERS OF THE COMMON STATE BUT THAT
SUPPORT SEEMS TO BE EBBING RAPIDLY, WITH POSSIBLE DIRE
CONSEQUENCES FOR THE INTEGRITY OF YUGOSLAVIA AS A STATE.
THIRDLY, THE DEMONSTRATIONS WERE THE CULMINATION OF PROTESTS
THAT HAD BEEN BUILDING DURING THE PAST SIX OR SEVEN YEARS.

02871 DREIER, P.
LOCAL SUCCESS STORIES
COMMONWEAL, CXVI(7) (APR 89), 201-202.
SINCE 1981, FEDERAL HOUSING FUNDS HAVE BEEN SLASHED FROM
MORE THAN $30 BILLION TO LESS THAN $8 BILLION. NEW FUNDING
FOR PUBLIC HOUSING RUN BY LOCAL GOVERNMENT AGENCIES HAS BEEN
VIRTUALLY ELIMINATED. MOST PRIVATE DEVELOPERS HAVE STOPPED
BUILDING LOW-INCOME HOUSING, WHILE NONPROFIT BUILDERS HAVE
TRIED TO FILL THE VACUUM.

02872 DREIFELDS, J.
LATVIAN NATIONAL REBIRTH
PROBLEMS OF COMMUNISM, XXXVIII(4) (JUL 89), 77-95.
LATVIANS ARE CURRENTLY UNDERGOING A REAWAKENING THAT HAS
BECOME PARTICULARLY INTENSE BECAUSE OF FEARS FOR NATIONAL
SURVIVAL. NUMEROUS INDEPENDENT SOCIETIES, MOVEMENTS, AND
GROUPS HAVE SPRUNG UP AND BEEN UNITED IN THE LATVIAN
PEOPLE'S FRONT. RECENTLY, THE FRONT HAS BEGUN TO TALK OF AN
INDEPENDENT LATVIA BASED ON THE RULE OF LAW AND EQUAL RIGHTS
FOR ALL NATIONAL, SOCIAL, AND RELIGIOUS GROUPS. GENERALLY,
LATVIANS HAVE BEEN LESS DARING THAN THEIR BALTIC NEIGHBORS
IN ADVOCATING SOVEREIGNTY, PARTLY FOR DEMOGRAPHIC REASONS,
AND PARTLY TO AVOID ENDANGERING RECENT GAINS.

02873 DREW, S.
EXPECTING THE APPROACH OF DANGER: THE MISSLE GAP AS A
STUDY OF EXECUTIVE - CONGRESSIONAL COMPETITION IN BUILDING
CONSENSUS ON NATIONAL SECURITY ISSUES
PRESIDENTIAL STUDIES QUARTERLY, XIX(2) (SPR 89), 317-336.
THE FULL POWER OF THE AMERICAN PEOPLE WILL BE EVOKED
ONLY WHEN THE AMERICAN PEOPLE AND THE AMERICAN GOVERNMENT
ARRIVE AT A CONSENSUS. IN THE ABSENCE OF SUCH A CONSENSUS IT
IS DIFFICULT TO MOVE A DEMOCRATIC SOCIETY TO ACT EFFECTIVELY
IN FOREIGN AND DEFENSE POLICY. THE MISSLE GAP IS STUDIED AS
AN EXAMPLE OF EXECUTIVE-CONGRESSIONAL COMPETITION IN
BUILDING SUCH A CONSENSUS. THE WEAPONS USED BY LEADERSHIP IN
THE ADMINISTRATION AND THE CONGRESS WHEN IT JOINS IN SUCH A
BATTLE ARE MOST FREQUENTLY PUBLIC STATEMENTS AND DEBATES
DESIGNED TO FORGE A CONSENSUS WHICH WILL ALLOW THE
GOVERNMENT TO ACT. THE SYSTEM ALSO FUNCTIONS WHEN AMERICAN'S
"TRUE INTEREST" LIES NOT IN ACTION, BUT IN RESTRAINT.

02874 DREYER, J.T.
THE PEOPLE'S LIBERATION ARMY AND THE POWER STRUGGLE OF 1989
PROBLEMS OF COMMUNISM, XXXVIII(5) (SEP 89), 41-48.
THE AUTHOR EXPLORES HOW DIFFERENT UNDERSTANDINGS OF THE
CONCEPT OF PROFESSIONALISM SHAPED THE PLA'S RESPONSE TO LI
PENG'S DECLARATION OF MARTIAL LAW IN MAY AND JUNE 1989. SHE
ALSO EXAMINES THE EFFECTS OF THE TIANANMEM MASSACRE ON THE
PUBLIC'S PERCEPTION OF THE PLA AND THE REGIME'S USE OF
PUBLIC RELATIONS EFFORTS TO REPAIR THE DAMAGE. FINALLY,
BECAUSE THE RELIANCE ON THE MILITARY TO RESTORE ORDER IN
BEIJING PORTENDED A POSSIBLE CHANGE IN THE BALANCE OF POWER
BETWEEN THE MILITARY AND CIVILIAN LEADERSHIP, SHE ANALYZES
THE IMPLICATIONS OF THE INCIDENT FOR POLITICAL-MILITARY
RELATIONS.

02875 DREYER, J.T.
THE ROLE OF THE MILITARY
WORLD POLICY JOURNAL, 6(4) (FAL 89), 647-655.
IN THE PEOPLE'S REPUBLIC OF CHINA, ALTHOUGH ONE OF
DENG'S PROFESSED GOALS HAS BEEN TO SEPARATE THE FUNCTIONS OF
THE MILITARY FROM THOSE OF THE PARTY AND GOVERNMENT, THE
PLA'S CONDUCT REVEALED THAT IT CONTINUES TO PLAY A CRITICAL,
AND PERHAPS DECISIVE, ROLE IN CHINESE POLITICS. THIS ARTICLE
EXAMINES A NUMBER OF QUESTIONS. HOW DOES ONE EXPLAIN THE
MILITARY'S APPARENT LACK OF UNITY AND ITS HESITATION IN
IMPLEMENTING THE CRACKDOWN? WHAT ACCOUNTS FOR THE MORE
DECISIVE ACTION OF THE 27TH ARMY? WHAT DOES THE PLA'S ROLE
IN PUTTING DOWN THE DEMONSTRATIONS REVEAL ABOUT CIVIL-
MILITARY RELATIONS IN CHINA TODAY? AND, PERHAPS MOST
IMPORTANT OF ALL, WHAT DO THESE EVENTS PORTEND FOR THE
FUTURE OF POLITICAL AND ECONOMIC REFORM IN THAT COUNTRY?

02876 DREYER, J.T.
UNREST IN TIBET
CURRENT HISTORY, 88(539) (SEP 89), 281-284, 288-289.
THE 1989 RIOTS IN TIBET SHATTERED THE FACADE OF HARMONY
AND PROGRESS FOSTERED BY MORE LIBERAL POLICIES INSTITUTED BY
THE CHINESE. THE BASIC PROBLEM REMAINS: HOW TO RECONCILE
CHINA'S SECURITY NEEDS WITH THE RIGHT OF THE TIBETANS TO
MAKE THEIR OWN DECISIONS.

02877 DRINKWATER, M.
TECHNICAL DEVELOPMENT AND PEASANT IMPROVERISHMENT: LAND
USE POLICY IN ZIMBABWE'S MIDLANDS PROVINCE
JOURNAL OF SOUTHERN AFRICAN STUDIES, 15(2) (JAN 89),
287-305.
THE PAPER PRESENTS AN OUTLINE OF INTERNAL LAND USE
POLICY IN ZIMBABWE AND HOW IT CAME INTO BEING. IT NOTES THE
SIMILARITIES IN LAND USE POLICIES OF BEFORE AND AFTER
INDEPENDENCE AND NOTES THAT THE ATTITUDES AND CONCEPTS OF
RATIONALITY INHERENT IN THE WAY LAND USE POLICIES HAVE BEEN
CONCEIVED AND JUSTIFIED OBSTRUCT UNDERSTANDING BY OFFICIALS
OF THE REASONS WHY THE SCHEMES ARE OPPOSED BY THOSE UPON
WHOM THEY ARE FOISTED.

02878 DROBOT, N.J.
ARMS CONTROL: THE COMMON DENOMINATOR IN SUPERPOWER
RELATIONS
AVAILABLE FROM NTIS, NO. AD-A202 641/7/GAR, APR 88, 48.
THE PURPOSE OF THIS PAPER IS TO HIGHLIGHT ARMS CONTROL
AS A MUTUALLY SHARED INTEREST IN SUPERPOWER RELATIONS.
CHAPTER I ADDRESSES US FOREIGN POLICY VIS-A-VIS THE USSR AND
VICE VERSA, AND FOCUSES ON CURRENT SUPERPOWER NATIONAL
INTERESTS. TODAY, THE USSR IS PREOCCUPIED WITH ECONOMIC
DEVELOPMENT AND IS PROVIDING THE US WITH UNIQUE
OPPORTUNITIES IN ARMS CONTROL CONCESSIONS. THE US IS
CONCERNED WITH STIMULATING ITS ECONOMY AS WELL AND IN
REDUCING FEDERAL BUDGET DEFICITS. CHAPTER II FOCUSES ON THE
SPECIFICS OF THE INTERMEDIATERANGE NUCLEAR FORCE (INF)
TREATY. A REVIEW OF THE BACKGROUND SINCE 1977 LEADING UP TO
THE TREATY IS PRESENTED FOLLOWED BY SPECIFIC TERMS OF THE
TREATY TO INCLUDE THE TYPES OF MISSILE SYSTEMS, TIMETABLES
AND METHODS OF ELIMINATION, AND THE MUTUAL VERIFICATION
SCENARIO. PERSONNEL REQUIREMENTS TO IMPLEMENT THE TREATY ARE
ALSO PRESENTED. CHAPTER III ADDRESSES THE IMPACT OF THE INF
TREATY ON NATO DOCTRINE AND FORCE EMPLOYMENT. CURRENT

CRITICISMS OF THE TREATY THAT RELATE TO THE RESULTING
MILITARY BALANCE IN EUROPE AND US COMMITMENT TO NATO ARE
PRESENTED. US/NATO AND SOVIET/WARSAW PACT THINKING ON SUCH
AREAS AS DEFENSE SUFFICIENCY, MODERNIZATION, AND FUTURE ARMS
CONTROL AGREEMENTS IS ALSO COVERED.

02879 DROWER, G.
    A RETHINK ON BRITAIN'S DEPENDENT TERRITORIES?
    ROUND TABLE, 309 (JAN 89), 12-15.
        THE OFFICIAL BRITISH FOREIGN POLICY OUTLOOK HAS CHANGED,
    HOWEVER, SINCE THE COLONIAL GIVE-AWAY YEARS OF THE 1970S AND
    EARLY 1980S. THERE IS NOW A MORE SELFCONFIDENT EDGE TO
    BRITAIN'S FOREIGN AFFAIRS. WITH THE DEVELOPMENT OF THE 5TH
    AIRBORNE BRIGADE FOR OUT-OF-NATO-AREA OPERATIONS AN
    EFFECTIVE MILITARY MEANS HAS BEEN DEVELOPED BY MEANS OF
    WHICH THE TERRITORIES CAN BE DEFENDED AGAINST EXTERNAL
    ATTACK. THE PRESENT GOVERNMENT IS UNRUFFLED BY HOSTILE
    INTERNATIONAL OPINION AND LARGELY UNCONCERNED AT BRITAIN'S
    LEVEL OF POPULARITY AT THE UNITED NATIONS. FURTHERMORE, THE
    PREVAILING INTELLECTUAL WIND AGAINST RESIDUAL COLONIES HAS
    WANED TO A ZEPHYR. THE UN HAS COME TO REALIZE THE
    DIFFICULTIES POSED BY THE SMALL STATES. ALTHOUGH BRITAIN'S
    REMAINING POSSESSIONS CERTAINLY PREDOMINATE IN THE UN'S LIST
    OF 18 COLONIAL TERRITORIES THE RHETORIC OF ANTIIMPERIALISM
    HAS BECOME RATHER PASSE.

02880 DROZDOV, N.
    USSR-GREAT BRITAIN: SEARCH FOR NEW WAYS TO DEVELOP TRADE
    AND ECONOMIC TIES.
    FOREIGN TRADE, 3 (1988), 22-23.
        THIS ARTICLE REPORTS ON THE 14TH REGULAR SESSION OF THE
    SOVIET-BRITISH PERMANENT INTERGOVERNMENTAL COMMISSION FOR
    COOPERATION IN THE FIELDS OF APPLIED SCIENCE AND TECHNOLOGY,
    TRADE AND ECONOMIC RELATIONS WHICH WAS HELD IN MOSCOW
    OCTOBER 198. THIS SESSION PAID GREATEST ATTENTION TO
    DETERMINING WAYS OF EXPANDING TRADE BETWEEN THE TWO
    COUNTRIES. THIS ARTICLE EXAMINES THE VARIETY OF WAYS THE
    COUNTRIES PLAN TO ACCOMPLISH THIS.

02881 DROZDOVSKY, Y.
    USSR-HUNGARY: A QUALITATIVELY NEW STAGE OF COOPERATION
    FOREIGN TRADE, 6 (1988), 9.
        THIS ARTICLE EXPLORES SOVIET-HUNGARIAN COOPERATION WHICH
    IS CHARACTERIZED BY NEW EVER-GROWING FORMS OF ECONOMIC
    INTERACTION FIRST BY THE ESTABLISHMENT OF DIRECT TIES AND
    SETTING UP OF JOINT VENTURES AND ORGANIZATIONS. IT REPORTS
    ON THE FOCUS OF THE TRADITIONAL PRESS CONFERENCE, HELD AT
    HUNGARY'S TRADE REPRESENTATION IN MOSCOW, WAS ON RESULTS OF
    TRADE RELATIONS, TASKS FOR 1988 AND THE DEVELOPMENT OF
    COOPERATION, TRADE PROTOCOL FOR 1988 IS DISCUSSED.

02882 DRUMMOND, S.
    MALAYSIA AND SINGAPORE: STRAINS AND STRESSES AT BOTH ENDS
    OF THE CAUSEWAY
    WORLD TODAY, 45(4) (APR 89), 69-72.
        WITHIN TEN DAYS, TWO DECISIVE ELECTIONS WERE HELD IN
    MALAYSIA AND SINGAPORE. ON AUGUST 25, 1988, DATUK SHARIR WON
    A BY-ELECTION IN JOHORE BARU. HIS VICTORY WAS SEEN AS A
    DIRECT CHALLENGE TO PRIME MINISTER MOHAMED MAHATHIR. THE
    SINGAPORE ELECTIONS ON SEPTEMBER 3, 1988, USHERED IN THE
    SECOND GENERATION OF THE PEOPLE'S ACTION PARTY. AT THE SAME
    TIME, THEY WERE VIEWED AS A PLEBISCITE ON PROPOSALS TO AMEND
    THE CONSTITUTION.

02883 DRYZEK, J. S; CLARK, M.L.; MCKENZIE, G.
    SUBJECT AND SYSTEM IN INTERNATIONAL INTERACTION
    INTERNATIONAL ORGANIZATION, 43(5) (SUM 89), 475-504.
        RECENT INTEREST IN COGNITIVE APPROACHES TO INTERNATIONAL
    INTERACTION IN GENERAL AND INTERNATIONAL REGIMES IN
    PARTICULAR HAS NOT BEEN MATCHED BY DEVELOPMENT IN THEORY AND
    METHODOLOGY. THIS ARTICLE DETAILS A SYSTEMATIC "SUBJECTIVE"
    APPROACH THAT SEEKS TO MEET THIS NEED. ITS CLAIMS ARE
    DEVELOPED THROUGH ITS COMPARISON WITH THE ACCOMPLISHMENTS
    AND SHORTCOMINGS OF MORE ESTABLISHED APPROACHES TO THE STUDY
    OF INTERNATIONAL INTERACTION AND, IN PARTICULAR,
    MICROECONOMIC FORMAL THEORY. THE SUBJECTIVE ALTERNATIVE CAN
    MODEL BOTH INDIVIDUAL SUBJECTS AND THE SYSTEMS IN WHICH THEY
    ARE PARTICIPATING. AS SUCH, IT OFFERS MUCH MORE IN TERMS OF
    CONTINUITIES AND CONNECTIONS BETWEEN AGENTS AND SYSTEM
    STRUCTURE THAN DO TRADITIONAL PSYCHOLOGICAL ANALYSES IN
    INTERNATIONAL RELATIONS. THE THEORETICAL ARGUMENTS PROCEED
    IN THE CONTEXT OF A STUDY OF COOPERATION AND CONFLICT OVER
    ANTARCTICA AND ITS EVOLVING REGIMES.

02884 DRYZEK, J.S.
    POLICY SCIENCES OF DEMOCRACY
    POLITY, 22(1) (FAL 89), 97-118.
        YEARS AGO, HAROLD LASSWELL PROMISED A POLICY SCIENCE OF
    DEMOCRACY, BUT TO DATE, THE AUTHOR OF THIS ARTICLE CONTENDS,
    MOST EFFORTS AT POLICY ANALYSIS HAVE PROVEN SUBTLY
    ANTIDEMOCRATIC AND OF DUBIOUS RATIONALITY. THE PROBLEM, HE
    ARGUES, IS THAT THE SPORADIC ATTEMPTS TO TAILOR POLICY
    ANALYSIS TO LIBERAL DEMOCRACY TEND TO REINFORCE LIBERAL
    POLITICS AT THE EXPENSE OF EFFECTIVE PROBLEM SOLVING. A

POLICY SCIENCE OF STRONG PARTICIPATORY DEMOCRACY, HE
CONCLUDES, IS CONCEPTUALLY BETTER ABLE TO COMBINE DEMOCRATIC
POLITICS AND RATIONAL POLICY MAKING. ILLUSTRATIONS FROM
PUBLIC POLICY IN AND ABOUT ALASKA SHOW HOW THIS CAN BE
ACHIEVED IN PRACTICE.

02885 DUANZHI, S.
    HUMAN RIGHTS ABUSE OR PREJUDICE?
    BEIJING REVIEW, 32(15) (APR 89), 18-19.
        IN MARCH 1989, BOTH THE U.S. SENATE AND THE EUROPEAN
    PARLIAMENT PASSED RESOLUTIONS ON THE TIBET QUESTION,
    CONDEMNING THE USE OF FORCE BY CHINA IN TIBET AND THE
    ALLEGED HUMAN RIGHTS VIOLATIONS THERE. THE RESOLUTIONS WERE
    IN RESPONSE TO THE IMPOSITION OF MARTIAL LAW IN LHASA AND
    THE SUPPRESSION OF A SEPARATIST RIOT. IN THE WEST, COMMUNIST
    CHINA IS OFTEN CONSIDERED SYNONYMOUS WITH THE SUPPRESSION OF
    FREEDOM AND HUMAN RIGHTS, BUT THIS ATTITUDE IS FOUNDED ON
    IGNORANCE AND PREJUDICE TOWARD THE PEOPLE'S REPUBLIC OF
    CHINA.

02886 DUANZHI, S.
    MONGOLIA RIDES THE TIDE OF REFORM
    BEIJING REVIEW, 32(2) (JAN 89), 21.
        ON DECEMBER 21, 1988, JAMBYN BATMONH, GENERAL SECRETARY
    OF THE MONGOLIAN PEOPLE'S REVOLUTIONARY PARTY AND CHAIRMAN
    OF THE PRESIDIUM OF THE PEOPLE'S GREAT HURAL, CRITICIZED
    PAST MONGOLIAN LEADERSHIP AND PLEDGED TO REFORM THE PARTY. A
    RESOLUTION PASSED AT THE FIFTH PLENARY SESSION OF THE
    NINETEENTH CONGRESS STATED THAT ALL PARTY ORGANIZATIONS AND
    MEMBERS SHOULD VIGOROUSLY CULTIVATE THE PRINCIPLE OF
    COLLECTIVE LEADERSHIP AND THAT MEASURES SHOULD BE TAKEN TO
    REFORM THE CENTRAL COMMITTEE. THERE WILL ALSO BE CHANGES IN
    THE LEGAL SYSTEM, IN ORDER TO SAFEGUARD REFORMS, DEMOCRACY,
    AND OPENNESS.

02887 DUANZHI, S.
    PLUM AND CHERRY JOINTLY BLOSSOM
    BEIJING REVIEW, 32(15) (APR 89), 7.
        A POLITICAL AND DIPLOMATIC SPRING IS WARMING UP SINO-
    JAPANESE RELATIONS. POLITICAL DIALOGUE AND DIPLOMATIC
    CONSULTATIONS HAVE BEEN ESTABLISHED ON A REGULAR BASIS,
    INVOLVING HIGH-LEVEL OFFICIAL AND UNOFFICIAL CONTACTS AND
    EXCHANGES. DESPITE SOME DIFFERENCES, THE BASIC PRINCIPLES
    BEHIND THE DEVELOPMENT OF RELATIONS HAVE BEEN ESTABLISHED AS
    PEACE, FRIENDSHIP, EQUALITY, MUTUAL BENEFIT, TRUST, AND THE
    GOAL OF BUILDING A LONG-TERM, STABLE RELATIONSHIP.

02888 DUANZHI, S.
    RIVAL VISITS HIGHLIGHT EAST-WEST CONTENTION
    BEIJING REVIEW, 32(31) (JUL 89), 15-18.
        IN THE SUMMER OF 1989, U.S. PRESIDENT GEORGE BUSH AND
    SOVIET LEADER MIKHAIL GORBACHEV VISITED EACH OTHER'S ALLIES
    AND THEN SHUTTLED BACK TO THEIR OWN ALLIES IN A DIPLOMATIC
    CONTEST TO WIN INTERNATIONAL SUPPORT AND EXPAND THE
    INFLUENCE OF THEIR RESPECTIVE COUNTRIES. ALTHOUGH BOTH BUSH
    AND GORBACHEV DENIED THAT THEIR VISITS WERE INTENDED TO
    ERODE THE OTHER'S ALLIED SUPPORT, THE COINCIDENCE OF THEIR
    VISITS SUGGESTS THAT A NEW ROUND OF DIPLOMATIC WARFARE IS
    UNDERWAY BETWEEN THE SUPERPOWERS, WITH THE BATTLEGROUND
    PRIMARILY IN EUROPE.

02889 DUANZHI, S.
    SOVIET DIPLOMATIC HARVEST IN 1988
    BEIJING REVIEW, 32(5) (JAN 89), 15-19.
        THE YEAR 1988 SAW UNPRECEDENTED ACTIVITY IN SOVIET
    DIPLOMACY, WHICH MADE BREAKTHROUGHS ON SOME KEY
    INTERNATIONAL QUESTIONS. MAJOR ACHIEVEMENTS INCLUDED THE
    GENEVA ACCORDS ON AFGHANISTAN, RATIFICATION OF THE TREATY ON
    ELIMINATION OF US AND SOVIET INTERMEDIATE-RANGE NUCLEAR
    WEAPONS, AND A UNILATERAL CUT IN SOVIET TROOPS AND
    CONVENTIONAL WEAPONS.

02890 DUANZHI, S.
    VIET NAM'S DOUBTFUL PROMISE
    BEIJING REVIEW, 32(17) (APR 89), 7.
        THE VIETNAMESE GOVERNMENT HAS PLEDGED TO REMOVE ALL ITS
    TROOPS FROM KAMPUCHEA BEFORE THE END OF SEPTEMBER 1989, BUT
    IT IS QUESTIONABLE WHETHER THIS REPRESENTS A MAJOR
    VIETNAMESE POLICY CHANGE. HANOI STILL REFUSES TO ADMIT THAT
    IT LAUNCHED AN AGRESSIVE WAR, PREFERRING TO CONSIDER IT "JUST
    ACTION" AND "SELFLESS ASSISTANCE." MOREOVER, VIETNAM INSISTS
    ON CHOOSING THE COUNTRIES TO SUPERVISE ITS TROOP PULLOUT,
    RATHER THAN PLACING IT UNDER UNITED NATIONS' SUPERVISION.
    VIETNAM HAS ALSO LEFT ITSELF LEEWAY FOR THE RETURN OF ITS
    TROOPS UNDER ANY PRETEXT.

02891 DUBIN, M.F.
    1199: THE BREAD AND ROSES UNION
    DISSERTATION ABSTRACTS INTERNATIONAL, 49(10) (APR 89),
    3140-A.
        THE 1199 IS DISTINCTIVE AMONG U.S. LABOR UNIONS BECAUSE
    IT HAS LONG BEEN AN EXPONENT OF "SOCIAL UNIONISM," AS
    OPPOSED TO "BUSINESS UNIONISM." IT IS A MILITANT UNION,
    ADVERSARIAL TO MANAGEMENT, AND PROMULGATES CLASS

CONSCIOUSNESS. POLITICALLY, IT IS RELATIVELY INDEPENDENT AND OFTEN OPPOSES GOVERNMENT POLICY. IT HAS A UNIQUE STATUS WITHIN THE AFL-CIO AS A "CIVIL RIGHTS" UNION BECAUSE IT IS CLOSELY ALLIED WITH THE BLACK COMMUNITY.

02892 DUBININ, Y.
REPRESENTING PERESTROIKA IN THE USA
INTERNATIONAL AFFAIRS (MOSCOW), (11) (NOV 89), 64-73.
SOVIET DIPLOMATS IN THE UNITED STATES VIEW THEIR WORK AS CO-DEVELOPERS OF THE FOREIGN POLICY OF THE NEW POLITICAL THINKING AND OF INNOVATIVE DIPLOMATIC THOUGHT AS ONE OF THEIR MOST IMPORTANT TASKS. THIS MEANS ENCOURAGING AN IN-DEPTH PERCEPTION OF THE IDEOLOGICAL ASSETS OF PERESTROIKA AND APPRAISING INTERNATIONAL REALITIES IN THE CONTEXT OF PERESTROIKA. IN OTHER WORDS, THE DIPLOMATIC STAFF, AS A WHOLE AND AS INDIVIDUALS, MUST EVOLVE NEW PROFESSIONAL THINKING AND NEW WORKING METHODS. THE TASK OF REORGANIZING THE SOVIET EMBASSY IN WASHINGTON AND OTHER SOVIET MISSIONS IN THE UNITED STATES MUST GO HAND-IN-HAND WITH THE GROWING CAPACITY FOR INDEPENDENT ACTION ON THE PART OF ALL DIPLOMATS.

02893 DUBOIS, W., E., B.
NEGROES AND THE CRISIS OF CAPITALISM IN THE UNITED STATES
MONTHLY REVIEW, 41(1) (MAY 89), 27-35.
IN A REPRINT OF HIS 1953 ARTICLE, W. E. B. DUBOIS DISCUSSES THE CONTINUED EXPLOITATION OF BLACKS IN THE US ESPECIALLY IN THE SOUTH. HE CONCLUDES THAT WHEN BLACKS OBSERVE THE DISCRIMINATION AND EXPLOITATION THAT THEY SUFFER IN THE US AND COMPARE IT TO "COLOR BLIND" NATIONS SUCH AS THE USSR, CHANCES ARE THAT THEY WILL JOIN IN THE SOCIALIST REVOLUTION AND COULD BE A KEY FACTOR IN THE TOPPLING OF US CAPITALISM

02894 DUCAT, C.R.; DUPLEY, R.L.
FEDERAL DISTRICT JUDGES AND PRESIDENTIAL POWER DURING THE POSTWAR ERA
THE JOURNAL OF POLITICS, 51(1) (FEB 89), 98-118.
ANALYSIS OF NEARLY TWO HUNDRED FEDERAL DISTRICT COURT DECISIONS IN CASES INVOLVING THE EXERCISE OF PRESIDENTIAL POWER DURING THE POSTWAR ERA REVEALS TWO VERY DIFFERENT MODELS OF JUDICIAL DECISION MAKING. IN CASES CONCERNING PRESIDENTIAL CONTROL OF FOREIGN AND MILITARY POLICY, JUDICIAL DECISION MAKING APPEARS TO BE DOMINATED BY THE RECOGNITION OF FIXED RULES. SO CLEAR ARE THESE RULES OF DEFERENCE TO THE EXECUTIVE THAT IDENTIFICATION OF THE POLICY-MAKING AREA ALONE CONSTITUTES AN EXCELLENT PREDICTOR OF CASE OUTCOMES. BY CONTRAST, THE STATISTICAL IMPORTANCE OF SUCH PREDICTOR VARIABLES AS PRESIDENTIAL PRESTIGE AND WHETHER THE JUDGE WAS APPOINTED BY THE SAME PRESIDENT AS THAT WHOSE POWERS ARE AT ISSUE IN THE CASE SUGGESTS MUCH GREATER RELATIVISM IN THE JUDICIAL RESPONSE WHEN THE PRESIDENT IS CHALLENGED AS A DOMESTIC POLICYMAKER. AS FAR AS THE FEDERAL DISTRICT COURTS ARE CONCERNED, PRESIDENTIAL POWER OVER FOREIGN AND MILITARY AFFAIRS MAY APTLY BE CALLED "THE POWER TO COMMAND," WHILE THE EXECUTIVE'S POWER IN DOMESTIC AFFAIRS IS BETTER THOUGHT OF AS "THE POWER TO PERSUADE." IN THESE RESPECTIVE MODELS, THE AUTHORS FIND CONFIRMATION OF A DISTINCTION, DEVELOPED HALF A CENTURY AGO BY THE SUPREME COURT IN UNITED STATES V. CURTISS-WRIGHT EXPORT CORP. (200 U. S. 304, 1936), THAT APPROXIMATES THE "TWO PRESIDENCIES" CONCEPT.

02895 DUCHENE, F.
FIRST STATESMAN OF INTERDEPENDENCE?
ENCOUNTER, LXXIII(1) (JUN 89), 32-41.
JEAN MONNET WAS AT THE CENTER OF FOURTH REPUBLIC INNOVATIONS THAT LAID THE FOUNDATIONS FOR FRENCH MODERNIZATION AND EUROPEAN INTEGRATION. IN FACT, IT IS NOT AN EXAGGERATION TO SAY THAT MONNET WAS THE MAJOR STRATEGIST AND STATEMAN OF THE FOURTH REPUBLIC, EVEN THOUGH HE WAS NEITHER A POLITICIAN NOR A CIVIL SERVANT.

02896 DUERST-LAHTI, G.
THE GOVERNMENT'S ROLE IN BUILDING THE WOMEN'S MOVEMENT
POLITICAL SCIENCE QUARTERLY, 104(2) (SUM 89), 249-268.
THE AUTHOR ENDEAVORS TO DEMONSTRATE THAT GOVERNMENTAL ENTITIES CONCERNED WITH WOMEN WERE CRITICAL TO THE NATIONAL MOBILIZATION OF WOMEN IN THE UNITED STATES IN WAYS THAT HAVE NOT BEEN RECOGNIZED. HER ANALYSIS TRACES HOW GOVERNMENT OFFICIALS CONSCIOUSLY AND ACTIVELY USED PUBLIC RESOURCES TO ESTABLISH A LEGITIMATE AGENDA FOR ACTION AND THEN MOBILIZED NATIONWIDE SUPPORT BY CREATING A COMMUNICATION INFRASTRUCTURE TO DISSEMINATE THAT AGENDA—MOST IMPORTANTLY, THROUGH STATE COMMISSIONS ON THE STATUS OF WOMEN.

02897 DUFFIELD, J.S.
THE EVOLUTION OF NATO'S CONVENTIONAL FORCE POSTURE
DISSERTATION ABSTRACTS INTERNATIONAL, 50(5) (NOV 89), 1427-A.
THIS DISSERTATION HAS THREE STATED OBJECTIVES: (1) TO DESCRIBE THE EVOLUTION OF NATO'S CONVENTIONAL FORCE POSTURE IN GREATER DETAIL THAN HAS PREVIOUSLY BEEN POSSIBLE BY USING RECENTLY DECLASSIFIED GOVERNMENT DOCUMENTS; (2) TO EXPLAIN SIGNIFICANT EPISODES IN NATO'S HISTORY THAT AFFECTED

CONVENTIONAL FORCE POLICY; AND (3) TO ASSESS THE PROSPECTS FOR FUTURE CHANGE IN NATO'S CONVENTIONAL FORCES.

02898 DUFFY, G.
A NOTE ON "LABOUR VALUE AND SOCIALIST ECONOMIC CALCULATION"
ECONOMY AND SOCIETY, 18(1) (FEB 89), 100-109.
THE AUTHOR COMMENTS ON "LABOUR VALUE AND SOCIALIST ECONOMIC CALCULATION" BY COCKSHOTT AND COTTRELL. HE EMPHASIZES THE NEED FOR A REASSESSMENT OF THE SUBJECT AND DISCUSSES SOME POSSIBILITIES. HE SEPARATES THE ISSUE OF THE IMPACT OF INCREASING COMPUTING POWER ON THE FEASIBILITY AND DESIRABILITY OF COMPUTING A CENTRAL PLAN FROM THE ISSUE OF USING MARXIAN LABOUR VALUES AS A METHOD OF CALCULATION.

02899 DUFFY, J.M.
CROSS-SECTOR EFFECTS IN THE KEYNESIAN-FIORINAN POLITICAL ECONOMIC MODEL, 1949-1984
DISSERTATION ABSTRACTS INTERNATIONAL, 49(9) (MAR 89), 2734-A.
THE AUTHOR DEVELOPS A POLITICAL ECONOMIC MODEL WITH POLICY, POLITICAL, AND ECONOMIC SECTORS. THE INTERACTIONS OF THE ENDOGENOUS POLITICAL AND ECONOMIC VARIABLES PRODUCE CROSS-SECTOR EFFECTS. THE AUTHOR TESTS THE GENERAL HYPOTHESIS THAT THE ADDITION OF THE CROSS-SECTOR VARIABLES EXPLAINS THE SIGNIFICANTLY GREATER VARIANCE OF THE DEPENDENT VARIABLES.

02900 DUGAN, M.A.
PEACE STUDIES AT THE GRADUATE LEVEL
PHILADELPHIA: ANLS OF AMER ACMY OF POLITICAL AND SOC SCIENCE, (504) (JUL 89), 72-79.
THIS ARTICLE TRACES THE DEVELOPMENT OF PEACE STUDIES ON THE GRADUATE LEVEL, BRIEFLY EXPANDING ON THREE TYPES OF PROGRAMS THAT HAVE EMERGED: CONFLICT-RESOLUTION PROGRAMS, PROGRAMS IN SCHOOLS OF EDUCATION TO TRAIN TEACHERS, AND TRADITIONAL SCHOLARLY ACADEMIC PROGRAMS. INFORMATION ON STRUCTURAL SUPPORTS FOR GRADUATE PEACE STUDIES PROGRAMS IS PROVIDED. THE AUTHOR CONCLUDES BY PRESENTING TWO RECOMMENDATIONS ON THE FUTURE DEVELOPMENT OF GRADUATE PEACE STUDIES: GREATER EMPHASIS ON PEACE ITSELF AND THE FULLER INCORPORATION OF AN ACTION COMPONENT INTO PROGRAMS.

02901 DUGAN, W.E.
THE CHILEAN AND PERUVIAN SYSTEMS OF INTEREST REPRESENTATION: A CASE FOR CORPORATISM?
DISSERTATION ABSTRACTS INTERNATIONAL, 50(2) (AUG 89), 534-A.
EMPLOYING A DISAGGREGATED APPROACH TO THE CONCEPT OF CORPORATISM, THIS ANALYSIS FOCUSES ON THE PATTERNS OF RELATIONS BETWEEN THE STATE AND MULTIPLE INTEREST SECTORS IN CHILE AND PERU FROM THE 1920'S TO THE 1980'S. IT PROVIDES A HISTORICAL ACCOUNT OF THE PATTERNS OF INTEREST REPRESENTATION ACROSS MULTIPLE SECTORS OF SOCIETY, DISTINGUISHING BETWEEN INDUCEMENTS OFFERED BY THE STATE TO INTEREST GROUPS AND CONSTRAINTS THROUGH WHICH THE STATE PRODUCES GROUP COMPLIANCE.

02902 DUHS, A.; ALVEY, J.
SCHUMACHER'S POLITICAL ECONOMY
INTERNATIONAL JOURNAL OF SOCIAL ECONOMICS, 16(6) (1989), 67.
THE WORK OF E.F. SCHUMACHER IS ADDRESSED IN THE BROAD CONTEXT OF ECONOMIC PHILOSOPHY. HIS ECONOMICS PRESENT A FRONTAL ATTACK ON NEO-CLASSICAL ECONOMICS. HE LIKEWISE REJECTS A MARXIST ANALYSIS OF SOCIETY. AND WHILE HE SHARES SOME OF THE CONCERNS OF THE INSTIUTIONALISTS, HE NONETHELESS STANDS APART FROM THEM IN HIS QUESTIONING OF THE MORAL AND PHILOSOPHICAL FOUNDATIONS OF THE DISCIPLINE. SCHUMACHER CAN BE CONSIDERED A MEMBER OF A FOURTH SCHOOL — PHILOSOPHER/ECONOMISTS.

02903 DUIKER, W.J.
UNDERSTANDING THE SINO-VIETNAMESE WAR
PROBLEMS OF COMMUNISM, XXXVIII(6) (NOV 89), 84-88.
THE ORIGINS OF THE SINO-VIETNAMESE CONFLICT, ONCE GENERALLY THOUGHT TO LIE IN BORDER DISPUTES AND THE TREATMENT OF CHINESE NATIONALS IN VIETNAM, HAVE BECOME A HEAVILY DEBATED ISSUE. RECENT STUDIES HAVE FOCUSED ON THE HISTORIC RIVALRY BETWEEN THE COUNTRIES AND THE SUPERPOWER COMPETITION THAT HAS DOMINATED THE POSTWAR PERIOD. ALL OBSERVERS AGREE THAT IT WILL BE SOME TIME BEFORE THESE UNEASY NEIGHBORS REACH AN AMICABLE AND LASTING SOLUTION TO THEIR DIFFERENCES.

02904 DUIKER, W.J.
VIETNAM: THE CHALLENGE OF REFORM
CURRENT HISTORY, 88(537) (APR 89), 177-180, 193-196.
THE AUTHOR REVIEWS VIETNAM'S POLITICAL AND ECONOMIC REFORM EFFORTS. HE ALSO LOOKS AT VIETNAM'S RELATIONSHIPS WITH LAOS, CAMBODIA, AND THE USSR.

02905 DUJMOVIC, N.
MATCHING U.S. SECURITY INTERESTS AND CAPABILITIES IN THE 1990S: THE CHALLENGES FOR PRESIDENT BUSH

FLETCHER FORUM, 13(1) (WIN 89), 31-42.
CAUGHT BETWEEN THE ECONOMIC COSTS OF OVERSTRETCH AND THE POLITICAL PERILS OF UNDERSTRETCH, THE BUSH ADMINISTRATION WILL ATTEMPT TO MANAGE THE CONTEST MUCH LIKE ITS PREDECESSORS. THERE IS ONE SEEMINGLY EASY WAY OUT OF THIS DILEMMA WHICH MAY PROVE SEDUCTIVE TO AN ADMINISTRATION DESPERATE TO RECONCILE US INTERESTS AND CAPABILITIES - BOTH FOR THE SAKE OF THOSE INTERESTS AND TO INCREASE CHANCES FOR REELECTION IN 1992. THIS PATH, UNFORTUNATELY, IS AS POTENTIALLY DISASTROUS AS IT IS TEMPTING. THE REAL CHALLENGE TO THE BUSH ADMINISTRATION FOR THE NEXT FOUR YEARS IS TO AVOID DECLARING THAT THE MAJOR THREAT TO US INTERESTS SINCE WORLD WAR II, THE SOVIET UNION, HAS BECOME BENIGN IN ITS LONG-TERM FOREIGN POLICY OBJECTIVES AND THAT THE UNITED STATES NO LONGER NEED BEAR THE BRUNT OF DEFENDING THE FREE WORLD BECAUSE THE SOVIET UNION IS INEXORABLY MOVING TOWARDS DEMOCRACY VIA PERESTROIKA AND GLASNOST.

02906 DUKES, P.
THE LAST GREAT GAME: USA VERSUS USSR
JOHN SPIERS PUBLISHING, BRIGHTON, SUSSEX, GB, 1989, 300.
THE AUTHOR ARGUES THAT THE RIVALRY OF THE USA AND THE USSR CAN ONLY BE UNDERSTOOD BY ANALYZING THEIR RELATIONSHIP OVER CENTURIES. HE UTILIZES THE CONCEPTS OF EVENT, CONJUNCTURE, AND STRUCTURE TO UNCOVER THE CONTINUITIES AND FOUNDATIONS OF SOVIET-AMERICAN RELATIONS.

02907 DUMONT, G.
UNESCO'S PRACTICAL ACTION ON HUMAN RIGHTS
INTERNATIONAL SOCIAL SCIENCE JOURNAL, (122) (NOV 89), 585-594.
UNESCO'S SUPPORT OF HUMAN RIGHTS IS IN LINE WITH ONE OF ITS ESSENTIAL PURPOSES AS LAID DOWN IN ITS CONSTITUTION: "TO FURTHER UNIVERSAL RESPECT FOR JUSTICE, FOR THE RULE OF LAW, AND FOR THE HUMAN RIGHTS AND FUNDAMENTAL FREEDOMS . . ." IT WAS, THEREFORE, LOGICAL FOR THE UNITED NATIONS COMMISSION ON HUMAN RIGHTS TO ASK UNESCO TO ASSUME RESPONSIBILITY FOR THE TEACHING OF HUMAN RIGHTS, STARTING WITH THE ELABORATION OF A GENUINE SCIENCE CONCERNING THEM. UNESCO TOOK ON THIS TASK IMMEDIATELY AND CONTINUES TO BE RESPONSIBLE FOR IT THROUGH A LARGE NUMBER OF PUBLICATIONS AND THE WORK OF EXPERTS.

02908 DUNCAN, C.
BANK RELIEF, NOT DEBT RELIEF: MEXICO'S ENCOUNTER WITH THE BRADY PLAN
MULTINATIONAL MONITOR, 11(11) (NOV 89), 22-24.
AS MEXICO AND ITS CREDITOR BANKS APPROACH COMPLETION OF NEGOTIATIONS FOR REFINANCING THE COUNTRY'S FOREIGN DEBT, THE PACKAGE IS PROVING TO BE A DISAPPOINTMENT. IF THE ECONOMIC GROWTH THAT MEXICO DESPERATELY NEEDS AFTER SEVEN YEARS OF NEARLY UNBROKEN RECESSION IS DEPENDENT UPON SHARPLY REDUCING FOREIGN DEBT PAYMENTS, THEN THIS AGREEMENT WILL NOT PROVIDE THE SOLUTION. WHATEVER MINIMAL DEBT RELIEF RESULTS FROM MEXICO'S BANK AGREEMENT, ONE THING IS CERTAIN: THE AVERAGE MEXICAN WILL NOT BENEFIT FROM IT.

02909 DUNCAN, I.
PARTY POLITICS AND THE NORTH INDIAN PEASANTRY: THE RISE OF THE BHARATIYA KRANTI DAL IN UTTAR PRADESH
JOURNAL OF PEASANT STUDIES, 16(1) (OCT 88), 40-76.
IN THE LAST 20 YEARS POLITICS IN THE RURAL AREAS OF NORTH INDIA HAS BEEN TRANSFORMED BY THE EMERGENCE OF NON-CONGRESS PARTIES WITH STRONG SUPPORT AMONG THE PROSPEROUS STRATA OF THE PEASANTRY. STUDIES OF THESE DEVELOPMENTS HAVE PLACED DIFFERENT EMPHASES ON THE IMPORTANCE OF CLASS AND CASTE FACTORS, AS WELL AS DRAWING ATTENTION TO THE EXISTENCE OF BLOCS OF POTENTIAL SUPPORT PREVIOUSLY ALIENATED FROM THE CONGRESS. IN UTTAR PRADESH (UP) THE DEFECTION FROM THE CONGRESS OF PEASANT LEADER CHARAN SINGH AND THE FORMATION OF THE BHARATIYA KRANTI DAL (BKD) IN THE LATE 1960S, HAS BEEN SEEN AS ONE OF THE MOST IMPORTANT EXAMPLES OF THESE CHANGES IN RURAL POLITICS. THE PURPOSE OF THIS ARTICLE IS TO EXAMINE THE FORMATION AND INITIAL ELECTORAL FORTUNES OF THE BKD IN ONE LOCALITY AND, AT THE SAME TIME, TO ASSESS THE APPLICABILITY, TO A LOCAL SETTING, OF GENERAL EXPLANATIONS OF THE EMERGENCE AND SUCCESS OF THE PARTY.

02910 DUNCAN, W.
IDEOLOGY AND NATIONALISM IN ATTRACTING THIRD WORLD LEADERS TO COMMUNISM: TRENDS AND ISSUES IN THE LATE TWENTIETH CENTURY
WORLD AFFAIRS, 151(3) (WIN 89), 105-116.
THE ARTICLE EXPLORES THE RELATIONSHIP BETWEEN IDEOLOGY AND NATIONALISM AND HOW THE TWO FUSE TO SHAPE COMMUNISM IN THE THIRD WORLD. IT OUTLINES COMPREHENSIVE DEFINITIONS OF IDEOLOGY, USED THESE CONCEPTS TO AMALGAMATE AND KEEP POLITICAL POWER. IT THEN EXPLORES CONTEMPORARY TRENDS THAT SIGNAL THE NEED FOR CHANGES IN LONG-STANDING THIRD WORLD COMMUNIST TO STIMULATE ECNOMIC GROWTH; THE RISING APPEAL OF CAPITALISM IN THE THIRD WORLD; SOVIET RECOGINIZATION OF STRAINS BETWEEN THE USSR AND NATIONAL COMMUNIST SYSTEMS AS CUBA, NICARAGUA, AND VIETNAM.

02911 DUNDE, C.
LOOKING BACK AT NIXON'S FIRST CHINA TRIP
BEIJING REVIEW, 32(1) (JAN 89), 35-39.
THE AUTHOR RECOUNTS HENRY KISSINGER'S FIRST TRIP TO CHINA IN JULY 1971, WHEN HE MET WITH ZHOU ENLAI, AND THE DIPLOMACY THAT CULMINATED IN PRESIDENT RICHARD NIXON'S FIRST CHINA TRIP.

02912 DUNLEAVY, P.
THE ARCHITECTURE OF THE BRITISH CENTRAL STATE, PART I: FRAMEWORK FOR ANALYSIS
PUBLIC ADMINISTRATION, 67(3) (FAL 89), 249-276.
IN THE BUREAU-SHAPING MODEL OF BUREAUCRACY RATIONALLY SELF-INTERESTED OFFICIALS ARE PRIMARILY CONCERNED TO MAXIMIZE THEIR AGENCIES' CORE BUDGETS, EQUIVALENT TO THEIR RUNNING COSTS. THEY ARE MUCH LESS INTERESTED IN THOSE PARTS OF THEIR OVERALL BUDGET WHICH ARE ALLOCATED AS TRANSFER PAYMENTS TO THE PRIVATE SECTOR OR PASSED ON TO THEIR OTHER PUBLIC SECTOR BODIES. THE VARYING IMPORTANCE OF CORE BUDGETS AND OTHER SPENDING YIELDS A TYPOLOGY OF PUBLIC SECTOR ORGANIZATIONS INTO DELIVERY, TRANSFER, CONTRACTS, REGULATORY AND CONTROL AGENCIES. IN ADDITION, THE BUREAU-SHAPING MODEL IS DEVELOPED IN THIS ARTICLE TO PROVIDE AN EXHUSTIVE CLASSIFICATION OF GOVERNMENT AGENCIES, AND TO REFINE THE ANALYSIS OF SPENDING OVER AND ABOVE CORE BUDGETS. THE METHODOLOGICAL ISSUES INVOLVED IN APPLYING THIS TYPOLOGY EMPIRICALLY TO THE CENTRAL STATE APPARATUS IN BRITAIN ARE EXPLORED. PREVIOUS ATTEMPTS AT 'BUREAUMETRICS' HAVE FAILED TO MESH WITH 'ORDINARY KNOWLEDGE' VIEWS OF WHITEHALL. BY CONTRAST, THE BUREAU-SHAPING MODEL PROVIDES A FRAMEWORK WHICH IS THEORETICALLY SOPHISTICATED, EASILY OPERATIONALIZABLE, AND INTUITIVELY UNDERSTANDABLE. THE SCALE OF PROSPECTIVE HIVINGG OFF FROM THE UK CIVIL SERVICE ORGANIZATION OVER THE NEXT DECADE INDICATES THE VALUE OF ADOPTING A FRAMEWORK WHICH CAN RESPOND METHODOLOGICALLY TO SUCH CHANGES, AND OFFERS A POWERFUL THEORETICAL ACCOUNT OF THEIR DYNAMIC. PART II OF THE PAPER (NEXT ISSUE) PRESENTS THE EMPIRICAL DATA DEMONSTRATING THAT THE BUREAU-SHAPING MODEL IS HIGHLY EFFECTIVE IN SYSTEMIZING AND EXTENDING OUR KNOWLEDGE OF HOW WHITEHALL AND ITS ATTACHED AGENCIES ARE STRUCTURED.

02913 DUNLEAVY, P.
THE ARCHITECTURE OF THE BRITISH CENTRAL STATE, PART II: EMPIRICAL FINDINGS
PUBLIC ADMINISTRATION, 67(4) (WIN 89), 391-417.
PART I OF THIS PAPER EXPLAINED THE NEED TO IMPROVE EXISTING RESEARCH INTO THE BRITISH CENTRAL STATE, OUTLINED THE BUREAU-SHAPING MODEL, AND TACKLED A NUMBER OF METHODOLOGICAL ISSUES INVOLVED IN APPLYING THIS FRAMEWORK. PART II DEMONSTRATES THAT THE BUREAU-SHAPING MODEL IS HIGHLY EFFECTIVE IN SYSTEMATIZING AND EXTENDING OUR KNOWLEDGE OF HOW WHITEHALL AND DIRECTLY ATTACHED AGENCIES ARE STRUCTURED. THE MAIN TYPES OF ORGANIZATIONS IDENTIFIED SHARE MANY SIMILARITIES, SO THAT THE MODEL'S CATEGORIES HAVE A CLEAR INTUITIVE MEANING. AS A RESULT THE BUREAU-SHAPING MODEL CAN EFFECTIVELY COPE WITH ANALYTIC PROBLEMS THAT HAVE CONSTRAINED PREVIOUS 'BUREAUMETRIC' RESEARCH, SUCH AS THE EXTREME VARIATIONS IN THE SIZE OF CENTRAL STATE AGENCIES. THE MODEL ALSO ILLUMINATES BOTH THE DISTRIBUTION OF BUREAU-TYPES ACROSS POLICY SECTORS, AND THE EFFECTS OF DIFFERENT PATTERNS OF ADMINISTRATION ON PUBLIC EXPENDITURE TRENDS UNDER THE THATCHER GOVERNMENT.

02914 DUNLOP, J.B.
GORBACHEV AND RUSSIAN ORTHODOXY
PROBLEMS OF COMMUNISM, XXXVIII(4) (JUL 89), 96-116.
UNDER GORBACHEV, THE SOVIET LEADERSHIP HAS REPLACED THE AGGRESSIVELY ANTI-RELIGIOUS POLICIES OF THE PAST WITH A MORE SUBTLE APPROACH DESIGNED TO MOBILIZE BELIEVERS IN SUPPORT OF PERESTROYKA. EFFORTS HAVE BEEN MADE TO END THE MOST BLATANT FORMS OF DISCRIMINATION AGAINST BELIEVERS. THE RUSSIAN ORTHODOX CHURCH HAS BEEN PRAISED BY STATE LEADERS FOR ITS PATRIOTIC EFFORTS ON BEHALF OF WORLD PEACE, AND THE CHURCH'S POTENTIAL FOR ENGAGING IN CHARITABLE WORK IS BEING EXPLORED. WHILE THE SUBMISSIVE ORTHODOX HIERACHY HAS WELCOMED THESE CHANGES, LAYMEN AND THE LOWER CLERGY CONTINUE TO OBJECT TO THE STATE'S MEDDLING WITH WHAT THEY CONSIDER THE INTERNAL AFFAIRS OF THE CHURCH.

02915 DUNLOP, J.B.
MRS. AQUINO AND THE JOE KAPP SYNDROME
NATIONAL INTEREST, (18) (WIN 89), 77-84.
THIS ARTICLE DESCRIBES WHAT IT CALLS THE JOE KAPP SYNDROME AND SUGGESTS THAT PROMINENT FILIPINO POLITICIANS ARE ON THE BRINK OF FALLIN VICTIM TO THE SYNDROME IN RELATION TO U.S. NEED FOR MILITARY FACILITIES AT ITS AIR AND NAVAL BASES IN THE PHILIPPINES, IT DESCRIBES THE U.S. FACILITIES THERE AND THE IMPACT OF THESE BASES ON THE PHILIPPINE ECONOMY. WAYS TO COUNTERACT FILIPINO OPPOSITION ARE SUGGESTED AS WELL AS THE NEED FOR THE U.S. TO GRADUALLY WITHDRAW FROM THE PHILIPPINES IS EXAMINED.

02916 DUNLOP, J.B.
WILL THE SOVIET UNION SURVIVE UNTIL THE YEAR 2000?
NATIONAL INTEREST, (18) (WIN 89), 65-75.
THIS ARTICLE EXPLORES ANDREI AMALRIK'S PREDICTION OF WAR
BETWEEN THE USSR AND CHINA AND FOCUSES ON THE PERCEPTIVENESS
OF HIS INSIGHTS INTO POSSIBLE FUTURE POLITICAL DEVELOPMENTS
IN THE USSR, THE THINKING OF THE RADICAL REFORMERS IS
DETAILED AND THE ROLES THAT BORIS YELTSIN AND YURI AFANASYEV
PLAY IN THE POLITICAL LEFT ARE EXAMINED. IT OUTLINES FOUR
POSSIBLE FUTURES FOR THE SOVIET UNION AS IT ENTERS THE LAST
DECADE OF THE TWENTIETH CENTURY AND CONSIDERS WHAT EACH OF
THEM WOULD MEAN FOR THE WEST.

02917 DUPLESSIS, L.
THE POLITICISATION OF THE SOVIET SOLDIER BEFORE AND DURING
MILITARY SERVICE
DISSERTATION ABSTRACTS INTERNATIONAL, 49(11) (MAY 89),
3489-A.
THE AUTHOR EXPLORES HOW THE MATURING SOVIET BOY IS
EDUCATED IN HIS PARENTS' HOME, AT SCHOOL, WITHIN YOUTH
MOVEMENTS, AND THROUGH THE MASS MEDIA, ACCORDING TO
COMMUNISTIC, COLLECTIVISTIC, AND MILITARISTIC NORMS. STRONG
EMPHASIS IS PLACED ON PATRIOTISM AND COURAGE IN BATTLE. BUT
THE BUREAUCRATIC PROCEDURES OF ENDOCTRINATION OFTEN LEAD TO
INEFFECTIVE DOGMATIC COMMUNICATION.

02918 DUPRE, L.; O'NEILL, H.
SOCIAL STUCTURES AND SOCIAL ETHICS
REVIEW OF POLITICS, 51(3) (SUM 89), 327-344.
MODERN PRINCIPLES OF MORALITY ARE INADEQUATE FOR SOLVING
THE STRUCTUAL PROBLEMS FACED BY CONTEMPORARY SOCIETIES.
EARLY IN THE MODERN EPOCH THE NORMATIVE, SOCIAL CONCEPT OF
NATURE THAT HAD SUPPORTED GREEK, ROMAN, AND MEDIEVAL ETHICAL
THEORIES, BECAME TRANSFORMED INTO A PURELY EMPIRICAL,
PRIVATE ONE. THUS FOR HOBBES, LOCKE, AND MOST EIGHTEENTH-
CENTURY POLITICAL THEORISTS, THE "STATE OF NATURE" REFFERED
TO THE OPPOSITE OF A SOCIAL STATE, RULED BY LAWFUL CUSTOM,
IT HAD MEANT BEFORE. THE IDEA OF "NATURAL RIGHT" WHICH
GRADUALLY EMERGED AS A SUBSTITUTE PRINCIPLE WAS DEFINED IN
INDIVIDUALIST TERMS. WITH THE NOTION OF "GENERAL WILL"
ROUSSEAU ATTEMPTED TO ESTABLISH A MORE GENUINELY SOCIAL
BASIS FOR THE STATE. YET BY RESTRICTING THE SOCIAL TO THE
POLITICAL HE DEPRIVED ALL ASSOCIATIONS INTERMEDIATE BETWEEN
STATE AND INDIVIDUAL OF ANY INTRINSIC, SOCIAL NORM CAPABLE
OF GUIDING THEIR OWN OPERATIONS FROM WITHIN. BY THE END OF
THE EIGHTEENTH CENTURY ECONOMIC EXCHANGE HAD BEGUN TO WIELD
A POWER SUPERIOR TO THAT POLITICAL LIFE TO WHICH IT HAS
ALLEGED TO BE SOCIALLY SUBORDINATE. IT ENDED UP IMPOSING ITS
PRIVATE OBJECTIVES UPON THE POLITICAL STRUCTURES.
INTERNATIONAL RELATIONS, DEPRIVED OF NORMATIVE AUTHORITY,
REMAINED VOID OF ANY EFFECTIVE, SUPRANATIONAL ARBITRATION.

02919 DUPREEZ, M.
1989: A SCENARIO
SOUTH AFRICA FOUNDATION REVIEW, 15(2) (FEB 89), 7.
IN SOUTH AFRICA, 1981 WILL PROBABLY BE DOMINATED BY FIVE
ISSUES: THE NAMIBIAN INDEPENDENCE PROCESS, THE RELEASE (OR
CONTINUED INCARCERATION) OF NELSON MANDELA, THE
DETERIORATING ECONOMY AND RISING INFLATION RATE, THE GROWING
CONFRONTATION BETWEEN THE NATIONAL PARTY AND THE RIGHT WING,
AND THE GOVERNMENT'S CONTINUED STRATEGY OF REFORM, CO-OPTION,
AND COERCION.

02920 DUQUETTE, D.A.
MARX'S IDEALIST CRITIQUE OF HEGEL'S THEORY OF SOCIETY AND
POLITICS
REVIEW OF POLITICS, 51(2) (SPR 89), 218-240.
THE ARTICLE IS A COMPARATIVE STUDY OF HEGEL AND MARX ON
THE NATURE AND FUNCTION OF THE POLITICAL STATE AND IT ARGUES
THAT MARX'S CRITIQUE OF HEGEL ON THIS TOPIC IS AIMED NOT AT
THE "IDEALISM" OF THE STATE, WHICH CONCERNS THE PRINCIPLE OF
UNIVERSAL FREEDOM, BUT RATHER AT THE "MATERIAL"
PRESUPPOSITIONS OF THE STATE. INDEED, MARX'S CRITIQUE OF
POLITICAL INSTITUTIONS IS PREMISED UPON THE WAY IN WHICH
THEY ARE INFECTED WITH THE EGOISM AND SELF-SEEKING OF CIVIL
(BURGERLICHE) SOCIETY. THE RELATIONSHIP BETWEEN THE VIEWS OF
HEGEL AND MARX ON THESE POINTS IS EXPLORED BY (1) GIVING AN
EXEGESIS OF HEGEL'S CONCEPTION OF CIVIL SOCIETY AS A
FOUNDATION FOR FREEDOM, (2) EXAMINING MARX'S CRITIQUE OF
HEGEL'S THEORY OF THE STATE, (3) DISTINGUISHING THE HEGELIAN
AND MARXIAN PHILOSOPHICAL CONCEPTIONS OF FREEDOM, THE
INDIVIDUAL, AND COMMUNITY, AND (4) EVALUATING THE FAIRNESS
AND COGENCY OF MARX'S CRITIQUE OF HEGEL.

02921 DURAND, B.A.
IMPLEMENTATION OF THE SMALL BUSINESS INNOVATION RESEARCH
PROGRAM AT THE DEFENSE ADVANCED RESEARCH PROJECTS AGENCY
DISSERTATION ABSTRACTS INTERNATIONAL, 49(8) (FEB 89),
2386-A.
THE SMALL BUSINESS INNOVATION RESEARCH PROGRAM HAS
ESTABLISHED IN 1982 TO ENHANCE THE PARTICIPATION OF SMALL
BUSINESS IN FEDERALLY FUNDED RESEARCH AND DEVELOPMENT. THIS
DISSERTATION EXAMINES THE REQUIREMENT FOR THE DEFENSE
ADVANCED RESEARCH PROJECTS AGENCY TO SPEND 1.25% OF ITS

EXTRAMURAL BUDGET ON THIS PROGRAM.

02922 DURASOV, V.A.
PLAN FOR 1990
REPRINTS FROM THE SOVIET PRESS, 49(11/12) (DEC 89), 24-27.
THIS IS A REPORT ON THE SOCIAL AND ECONOMIC PLAN FOR
1990 WHICH HAS BEEN DRAFTED. THE USSR GOVERNMENT HAS
SCRUTINIZED THE DRAFT WITH THE PARTICIPATION OF UNION
REPUBLICS, MINISTRIES AND SCIENTISTS. THE DRAFT PLAN IS NOW
IN THE USSR SUPREME SOVIET. IT DEFINES THE TASKS OF THE
PLANNERS AS: TO REVERSE THE NEGATIVE ECONOMIC TREND AND
PROJECT A STEADY RECOVERY; TO ALLAY SOCIAL TENSION: TO MAKE
AVAILABLE RESOURCES AND TECHNOLOGY FOR THE NEXT FIVE YEAR
PLAN.

02923 DURHAM, M.
THE THATCHER GOVERNMENT AND "THE MORAL RIGHT."
PARLIAMENTARY AFFAIRS, 42(1) (JAN 89), 58-71.
THE RASH OF CONSERVATIVE LEGISLATION APPARENTLY AIMED AT
STIMULAT A "SEXUAL COUNTER-REVOLUTION" IN GREAT BRITAIN.
THIS IS OFTEN ATTRIBUTED TO THATCHERISM WHICH HAS NOT ACTED
PREVIOUSLY DUE TO POLITICAL CAUTION, BUT HAS ALWAYS HELD A
"MORAL COUNTER-REVOLUTION CLOSE TO THE HEART." THE ARTICLE
EXAMINES THE ATTEMPTS OF VARIOUS RIGHT WING GROUPS TO ENACT
CONSERVATIVE LEGISLATION AND CONCLUDES THAT THEIR INFLUENCE
HAS BEEN OVERRATED AND THAT THE GOVERNMENT HAS BE RETICENT
OR EVEN ANTAGONISTIC TO THEIR DESIRES.

02924 DURLAND, W.
ANOTHER REALM
SOJOURNERS, 18(10) (NOV 89), 17.
THE AUTHOR ARGUES THAT SECULAR LAW IS NOT EQUIPPED TO
RESOLVE THE MORALITIES OF ABORTION. HE CALLS FOR A DIVERSION
OF THE ENERGY CURRENTLY SPENT PETITIONING THE COURTS AND
LEGISLATORS TO VIABLE ALTERNATIVES TO ABORTION AND
SUBSTANTIVE SUPPORT AND LONG-RANGE CARE FOR VICTIMIZED WOMEN.

02925 DURNING, A.B.
PEOPLE POWER AND DEVELOPMENT
FOREIGN POLICY, (76) (FAL 89), 66-82.
THIS ARTICLE REPORTS ON GRASS ROOTS EFFORTS OF THIRD
WORLD SELF-HELP ORGANIZATIONS IN THE INTERNATIONAL BATTLE
AGAINST POVERTY AND ENVIRONMENTAL DECLINE. THE IMPACT ON
BOTH THE INTERNATIONAL DEVELOPMENT EFFORT AND ON THE FOREIGN
POLICY OF DONOR GOVERNMENTS IS STUDIED. THE ROLE OF WOMEN IN
COMMUNITY MOVEMENTS IS EMPHASISED. THE NEED FOR AID POLICY
REFORMS IS DOCUMENTED. IT IS PREDICTED THAT COMMUNITY GROUPS
WILL FUNDAMENTALLY ALTER THE WORLD'S POLITICAL LANDSCAPE.

02926 DURR, F.R.
A GRAMM-RUDMAN REPAIR KIT: VIPS
BUREAUCRAT, 18(2) (SUM 89), 53-56.
IF PRESIDENT BUSH AND CONGRESS CANNOT AGREE ON SPENDING
CUTS, GRAMM-RUDMAN WILL KICK IN. BUT THIS COULD WREAK HAVOC
ON BUSH'S DEFENSE BUDGET, WHICH THE PRESIDENT IN COMMITTED
TO PRESERVING. THE RESULT COULD BE CUTS IN WELFARE PROGRAMS
WHERE THERE IS LIKELY TO BE LITTLE OR NO POLITICAL IMPACT OR
OPPOSITION. ONE WAY TO ALLEVIATE THE EFFECTS OF SUCH BUDGET
REDUCTIONS WOULD BE THE EFFECTIVE USE OF VOLUNTEERS IN CARRYING
OUT SOCIAL SERVICE PROGRAMS.

02927 DURSTHOFF, C.
SIGNIFICANT FEATURES OF FISCAL FEDERALISM, 1989
AVAILABLE FROM NTIS, NO. PB89-185490/GAR, JAN 89, 150.
THE VOLUME PROVIDES A SINGLE, CONVENIENT SOURCE OF
COMPARATIVE GOVERNMENT FINANCE INFORMATION FOR POLICYMAKERS,
EDUCATORS, FISCAL ANALYSIS AND OTHER PUBLIC FINANCE
PRACTITIONERS, AS WELL AS THE GENERAL PUBLIC. IT CONTAINS
COMPLETELY REVISED AND UP-TO-DATE INFORMATION ON AGGREGATE
NATIONAL AND STATE ECONOMIC AND FISCAL TRENDS AND ON TAX
RATES.

02928 DUSZA, K.
MAX WELER'S CONCEPTION OF THE STATE
POLITICS AND SOCIETY, 17(4) (DEC 89), 71-105.
THIS ARTICLE HAS TWO GOALS: TO CLARIFY THE CONCEPT OF
THE STATE AS A SPECIFIC ORGANIZATION OF POLITICAL RULE AND
THUS TO HIGHLIGHT THE BACKGROUND THAT IMPARTS MODERN
POLITICS ITS CHARACTERISTIC FEATURES. THIS AUTHOR AGREES
WITH THE "BEHAVIORISTS" THAT COLLECTIVE TERMS LIKE THE STATE
ARE EMPTY WORDS UNLESS ONE CAN DETERMINE WHAT CORRESPONDS TO
THEM IN THE EMPIRICAL WORLD. BUT HE REJECTS THEIR THESIS
THAT THERE IS NO SUCH THING AS A "STATE" IN THE SENSIBLE
WORLD OF HUMAN AFFAIRS BECAUSE THERE ARE ONLY BEHAVIOR
PATTERNS THERE.

02929 DUTTA, D.
POVERTY, PLANNING AND POLITICS: THE PAST DECADE OF INDIA
SCANDINAVIAN JOURNAL OF DEVELOPMENT ALTERNATIVES, VIII(1)
(MAR 89), 117-132.
SINCE THE COLONIAL PERIOD, THE QUESTION OF INDIA'S
POVERTY HAS BEEN IDENTIFIED BY RULING AUTHORITIES AND SOME
SOCIAL SCIENTISTS AS PREDOMINANTLY A SOCIAL AND DEMOGRAPHIC
PHENOMENON AND THEREFORE ITS CAUSES LIE OUTSIDE THE ECONOMIC

AND POLITICAL ARENA. THE PAPER ANALYZES THE ATTEMPTS OF THE GOVERNMENT OF INDIA TO IMPLEMENT "ANTI-POVERTY" MEASURES AND THE RESULTS OF THOSE MEASURES. IT CONCLUDES THAT THE GENERAL FAILURE OF GOVERNMENT ANTI-POVERTY EFFORTS IS DUE TO THE ECONOMIC AND POLITICAL STRUCTURE OF THE COUNTRY, WHERE THE MODERN SEGMENT IS DISPROPORTIONALLY DOMINANT OVER THE TRADITIONAL ONE. POPULATION GROWTH AND SOCIAL BACKWARDNESS MAY HAVE SOME INFLUENCE, BUT THE POLITICAL AND ECONOMIC CAUSES OF POVERTY SHOULD NOT BE IGNORED.

02930 DWIVEDI, O.P.; DUA, B.D.; JAIN, R.B.
IMPERIAL LEGACY, BUREAUCRACY, AND ADMINISTRATIVE CHANGES: INDIA 1947-1987
PUBLIC ADMINISTRATION AND DEVELOPMENT, 9(5) (JUN 89), 253-270.
THE ARTICLE EXAMINES BUREAUCRATIC AND ADMINISTRATIVE CHANGE IN INDIA, BEGINNING WITH INDEPENDENCE IN 1947 TO THE PRESENT. IT ANALYZES THE ENDURING BRITISH LEGACY AND ITS EFFECT ON INDIA'S ATTEMPTS TO FORM ITS OWN DEMOCRATIC GOVERNMENT. IT OUTLINES THE VARIOUS CHANGES THAT HAVE TAKEN PLACE OVER THE PAST FOUR DECADES INCLUDING THE EXPANSION OF PLANNED ECONOMY AND ADMINISTRATIVE GOVERNMENT. IT CONCLUDES THAT THE FACT THAT DEMOCRACY HAS SURVIVED AT ALL IN INDIA IS LAUDABLE. HOWEVER, INDIA IS FACING AND WILL CONTINUE TO FACE SERIOUS PROBLEMS PRESENTED BY COMPLEX ETHNIC DIVERSITY, CLASS STRATIFICATION, AND A DECLINE IN BUREAUCRATIC MORALITY.

02931 DYE, D.R.
AN AUSTERE SALES PITCH FOR VOTES
SOUTH, (104) (JUN 89), 30-31.
AS COSTA RICA GEARS UP FOR ITS ELECTIONS IN FEBRUARY 1990, THE ISSUE THAT PRESIDENTIAL HOPEFULS MUST TACKLE MOST URGENTLY IS THE POLITICAL APPROACH TO MANAGING THE ECONOMIC ADJUSTMENT PROGRAM. ADJUSTMENT IN COSTA RICA HAS BEEN MORE FAR-REACHING AND SUCCESSFUL THAN IN MOST LATIN AMERICAN COUNTRIES. BUT IT HAS LED TO RISING SOCIAL AND ECONOMIC TENSION THAT THREATENS TO BOIL OVER INTO THE POLITICAL ARENA.

02932 DYKSTRA, A.M.
REGION, ECONOMY, AND PARTY: THE ROOTS OF POLICY FORMATION IN PENNSYLVANIA, 1820-1860
DISSERTATION ABSTRACTS INTERNATIONAL, 49(7) (JAN 89), 1938-A.
THIS STUDY RELATES LEGISLATIVE DECISION-MAKING DIRECTLY TO THE PATTERNS OF ECONOMIC GROWTH IN PENNSYLVANIA'S LEGISLATIVE DISTRICTS IN THE NINETEENTH CENTURY. PENNSYLVANIA LEGISLATORS HAD WELL-ESTABLISHED IDEAS ABOUT THE RELATIONSHIP BETWEEN GOVERNMENT AND THE ECONOMY THAT WERE REFLECTED IN CONSISTENT VOTING PATTERNS.

02933 DYOMIN, A.
SERFS IN THE AGE OF PERESTROIKA
GLASNOST, (16-18) (JAN 89), 61-62.
IN THE EARLY 1970'S, RUSSIAN JEWS IN THE VILLAGE OF ILINKA BEGAN TO EMIGRATE TO ISRAEL. REPRESSION BY THE LOCAL AUTHORITIES FOLLOWED IMMEDIATELY. RESIDENTS WERE DENIED PERMISSION TO LEAVE THE KOLKHOZ, THEREBY TURNING THE ILINKA JEWS INTO SERFS. SINCE 1979, NOT ONE FAMILY HAS BEEN GRANTED PERMISSION TO LEAVE. VISITS BY OUTSIDE JEWISH ACTIVISTS HAVE ALSO BEEN PROHIBITED BY LOCAL AUTHORITIES.

02934 DYSON, K.; HUMPHREYS, P.
DEREGULATING BROADCASTING: THE WEST EUROPEAN EXPERIENCE
EUROPEAN JOURNAL OF POLITICAL RESEARCH, 17(2) (MAR 89), 137-154.
THIS ARTICLE IS CONCERNED WITH THE RELATIONSHIP BETWEEN SYSTEMIC AND IDEOLOGICAL CHANGES AFFECTING WEST EUROPEAN BROADCASTING AND THE NATURE OF THE REGULATORY RESPONSES. IN THEORETICAL TERMS THE RESEARCH INTEREST LIES IN THE QUESTION OF THE EXTENT TO WHICH CHANGES IN THE NATURE OF WEST EUROPEAN BROADCASTING REGULATION ARE DETERMINED BY TECHNOLOGICAL FACTORS AND FORCES IN THE INTERNATIONAL POLITICAL ECONOMY. PARTICULAR ATTENTION IS GIVEN TO THE FACTORS IMPEDING OR CONSTRAINING DEREGULATION AND TO THE ARGUMENT THAT NATIONAL INSTITUTIONAL STRUCTURES AND TRADITIONS ARE MEDIATING THE IMPACTS OF TECHNOLOGY, MARKETS AND IDEOLOGY. WHILTS THE ULTIMATE EFFECTS ON FUTURE BROADCASTING REGULATION REMAIN CONTROVERSIAL, CERTAIN BROAD TRENDS CAN BE IDENTIFIED.

02935 E MY, H.V.
FROM A POSITIVE TO A CULTURAL SCIENCE: TOWARDS A NEW RATIONALE FOR POLITICAL STUDIES
POLITICAL STUDIES, XXXVII(2) (JUN 89), 188-204.
THIS ARTICLE SURVEYS DEVELOPMENTS IN RECENT SOCIAL THEORY IN THE COURSE OF OUTLINING A NEW RATIONALE FOR POLITICS FOLLOWING THE SUBJECT'S OWN EXPANSION AND IN THE LIGHT OF DEVELOPMENTS IN POST-EMPIRICIST THOUGHT. IT SUGGESTS REASONS FOR THINKING OF POLITICS AS A CULTURAL RATHER THAN A POSITIVE SCIENCE. IT OUTLINES A NUMBER OF CORE OR PRIMARY POLITICAL PROBLEMS WHICH COMPRISE THE INTELLECTUAL FOUNDATIONS OF THE DISCIPLINE. IT SUGGESTS, OVERALL, THAT POLITICS IS ESPECIALLY CONCERNED WITH MAINTAINING AND IMPROVING THE VIABILITY OF HUMAN

ASSOCIATION(S) IN THE LIGHT OF CONDITIONS CREATED BY THE RISE AND EXPANSION OF COMPLEX SOCIETIES.

02936 EADIE, D.C.
STRATEGIC MANAGEMENT BY DESIGN
NATIONAL CIVIC REVIEW, 78(1) (JAN 89), 37-46.
WHEN APPLIED PROPERLY, STRATEGIC MANAGEMENT TECHNIQUES CNA ASSIST PUBLIC ORGANIZATIONS IN ADAPTING TO CHANGING PRESSURES. ORGANIZATIONS MUST BE AWARE OF HOW THEIR MISSION AND GOALS CAN BE MODIFIED IN RESPONSE TO A DYNAMIC ENVIRONMENT OR CONSTITUENCY. TO MAXIMIZE EFFECTIVENESS IN THE LONG TERM, ORGANIZATIONS MUST IDENTIFY THE ISSUES THEY FACE AND DESIGN OPERATIONAL AND STRATEGIC MANAGEMENT PROCEDURES TO ADDRESS THEM.

02937 EAGLEBURGER, L.S.
THE CHALLENGE OF THE EUROPEAN LANDSCAPE IN THE 1990'S
DEPARTMENT OF STATE BULLETIN (US FOREIGN POLICY), 89(2151) (OCT 89), 37-40.
THE NEXT DECADE IN THE UNITED STATES' RELATIONSHIP WITH EUROPE WILL BE A TRANSITIONAL PERIOD IN WHICH THE PATTERNS OF THE POSTWAR ERA UNDERGO SIGNIFICANT ADJUSTMENT IN THE FACE OF CHANGE IN THE EAST AND THE POLITICAL AND ECONOMIC GROWTH OF WESTERN EUROPE ITSELF. AMERICAN RELATIONS WITH EUROPE WILL BECOME MORE COMPLICATED AS EUROPEANS FORMULATE THEIR OWN RESPONSES TO SOVIET INITIATIVES, SEEK A MORE COHERENT POLITICAL AND ECONOMIC IDENTITY, AND ADOPT MORE ASSERTIVE POSTURES IN DEALING WITH THE USA.

02938 EAGLEBURGER, L.S.
THE OAS AND THE PANAMA CRISIS
DEPARTMENT OF STATE BULLETIN (US FOREIGN POLICY), 89(2152) (NOV 89), 67-75.
THE AUTHOR REVIEWS EVENTS IN THE PANAMA CRISIS IN THE SUMMER OF 1989, FOCUSING ON THE ROLE OF THE ORGANIZATION OF AMERICAN STATES AND ITS ATTEMPTS TO NEGOTIATE THE DEPARTURE OF NORIEGA AND THE FORMATION OF A TRANSITIONAL GOVERNMENT.

02939 EAGLES, C.W.
CONGRESSIONAL VOTING IN THE 1920'S: A TEST OF URBAN-RURAL CONFLICT
JOURNAL OF AMERICAN HISTORY, 76(2) (SEP 89), 528-534.
THE AUTHOR TESTS THE HYPOTHESIS THAT MANY PHENOMENA OF THE 1920'S WERE THE RESULTS OF CONFLICT BETWEEN URBAN AND RURAL AREAS BY ANALYZING ROLL-CALL VOTING IN THE HOUSE OF REPRESENTATIVES.

02940 EAGLES, D.M.
AN ECOLOGICAL PERSPECTIVE ON WORKING CLASS POLITICS: NEIGHBOURHOODS AND CLASS FORMATION IN SHEFFIELD, ENGLAND
DISSERTATION ABSTRACTS INTERNATIONAL, 49(11) (MAY 89), 3490-A.
RECENT STUDIES OF BRITISH ELECTORAL BEHAVIOR BASED ON OPINION SURVEYS HAVE DOCUMENTED A DECLINE IN CLASS VOTING BUT, PARADOXICALLY, AGGREGATE ANALYSES HAVE FAILED TO UNCOVER THIS TREND. THIS DISSERTATION DEVELOPS AND TESTS AN ECOLOGICAL PERSPECTIVE ON THE WORKING CLASS FORMATION PROCESS THAT COULD EXPLAIN THE FINDINGS OF THE AGGREGATE DATA. THE HALLMARK OF THIS PERSPECTIVE IS THE HYPOTHESIS THAT CLASS SENTIMENTS AND POLITICAL BEHAVIOR ARE MOST AFFECTED BY INFLUENCES BASED ON THE RESIDENTIAL NEIGHBORHOOD.

02941 EAGLES, J.; JAMES, C.
BARRIERS FALL DOWN UNDER
FAR EASTERN ECONOMIC REVIEW, 141(27) (JUL 88), 76-77.
AUSTRALIA AND NEW ZEALAND ARE POISED TO SIGN AN AGREEMENT PROVIDING FOR FULL FREE TRADE IN GOODS AND WHAT MINISTERS CLAIM WILL BE THE MOST COMPREHENSIVE AGREEMENT IN THE WORLD SO FAR IN FREE TRADE IN SERVICES. THE AGREEMENT IS THE RESULT OF NEARLY SIX MONTHS OF WORK BY OFFICIALS REVIEWING THE EXISTING CLOSER ECONOMIC TRADE AGREEMENT. ACCELERATION OF THE MOVE TO FREE TRADE REFLECTS THE REALITY THAT A GROWING COMMITMENT EXISTS IN BOTH COUNTRIES TO UNILATERALLY LOWER TRADE BARRIERS.

02942 EAST, C.
A YEAR OF CRISIS
PACIFIC DEFENCE REPORTER, 16(6) (DEC 89), 20-24.
FOR THE PACIFIC RATION OF PAPUA NEW GUINEA, 1989 HAS PRODUCED PROBLEMS OF A NATURE AND MAGNITUDE DEMANDING FROM ITS LEADER RABBIE NAMALIU THE VERY HIGHEST QUALITIES OF LEADERSHIP. THIS ARTICLE DESCRIBES THE SERIOUS DETERIORATION OF LAW AND ORDER, DISPUTES BY LANDOWNERS OVER MINERAL AND LAND RIGHTS, AND AN INCREASING LOSS OF REVENUE CURRENTLY PLAGUING PAPUA. FOCUS IS ON HOW THE LEGACY OF COLONIALISM, WHICH FORMED THE POLITICAL SYSTEM IN PAPUA, MAY BE THE ONE STABILIZING FACTORS OVER THE NEXT FEW YEARS.

02943 EAST, C.
STEADY AS SHE GOES
PACIFIC DEFENCE REPORTER, 16(6) (DEC 89), 26-28.
SIGNS OF LIBERALIZATION IN INDONESIA DURING THE PAST TWO YEARS DO NOT SIGNIFY ANY WEAKENING OF THE PRESENT LEADERSHIP. THIS ARTICLE EXPLAINS HOW LIBERALIZATION WILL BE NUTURED

OVER SUCCESSIVE YEARS SO AS TO AVOID ANY DAMAGE TO NATURAL
DEVELOPMENT AND THE STABILITY OF THE GOVERNMENT.

02944 EASTLAND, T.
CIVIL RIGHTS: A PRESIDENTIAL AGENDA
CURRENT, (310) (FEB 89), 36-38.
CIVIL RIGHTS WAS AMONG THE MANY MATTERS CANDIDATES
FAILED TO ADDRESS IN THE DREARY 1988 PRESIDENTIAL CAMPAIGN.
THIS IS UNFORTUNATE BECAUSE HISTORY PROVES THAT CIVIL RIGHTS
REQUIRES FEDERAL ATTENTION AND THAT PRESIDENTIAL LEADERSHIP
CAN MAKE A CRITICAL DIFFERENCE IN THIS AREA. TWO KEY ISSUES
THAT DEMAND ATTENTION ARE THE PROBLEM OF RACIAL PREFERENCES
AND THE ISSUE OF EQUAL OPPORTUNITY.

02945 EASTLAND, T.
IMPEACHMENT BY OTHER MEANS
COMMENTARY, 88(2) (AUG 89), 40-44.
THE INDEPENDENT-COUNSEL SATUTE CREATES AND BREEDS
POLITICAL IRRESPONSIBILITY. IT ABSOLVES THE PRESIDENT
HIMSELF OF RESPONSIBILITY FOR LAW ENFORCEMENT, AS NEITHER HE
NOR HIS AIDES ANY LONGER MAKE THE MOST IMPORTANT DECISION-
WHETHER TO PROSECUTE. WORSE, THE STATUTE CREATES INCENTIVES
FOR THE PRESIDENT TO BE IRRESPONSIBLE. INSTEAD OF TAKING IT
UPON HIMSELF TO INQUIRE INTO ALLEGED MISCONDUCT OF AIDES AND
DEAL WITH IT ACCORDINGLYWHICH MIGHT INCLUDE STANDING BEHIND
AN AIDE, NOT JUST PROSECUTING OR REMOVING HIM-THE PRESIDENT
CAN SLOUCH OFF HIS OBLIGATION ONTO THE ALL-TOOWILLING
SHOULDERS OF AN INDEPENDENT COUNSEL. THE EXPERIENCE OF THE
PAST ELEVEN YEARS, WHICH HAVE WITNESSED THE OPPOINTMENT OF
MORE THAN NINE INDEPENDENT COUNSELS AND SOME WELL-PUBLICIZED
INVESTIGATIONS, INCLUDING THE NORTH PROBE, ARGUES IN FAVOR
OF MAJOR REFORM OF THE STATUTE, IF NOT ITS REPEAL.

02946 EASTLAND, T.
RACIAL PREFERENCE IN COURT (AGAIN)
COMMENTARY, 87(1) (JAN 89), 32-38.
THE AUTHOR DISCUSSES RECENT SUPREME COURT CASES
INVOLVING RACIAL QUOTAS, INCLUDING CITY OF RICHMOND V. J.A.
CROSON COMPANY AND WYGANT V. JACKSON BOARD OF EDUCATION.

02947 EASTLAND, T.
TOWARD A REAL RESTORATION OF CIVIL RIGHTS
COMMENTARY, 88(5) (NOV 89), 25-29.
THIS ARTICLE ANALYSES THREE 1989 SUPREME COURT RULINGS
INVOLVING RACIAL DISCRIMINATION AND CIVIL RIGHTS--RICHMOND V.
CROSON, WARDS COVE PACKING CO. V. ANTONIO, AND MARTIN V.
WILKS. IT DETAILS EACH CASE AND CONCLUDES THAT IN ALL THREE
CASES ONE IS EITHER FOR OR AGAINST CIVIL RIGHTS OR
AFFIRMATIVE ACTION, BUT INSISTS THAT ONE NEEDS, RATHER, TO
FOCUS ON SPECIFICS. THESE THREE DECISIONS DESCRIBE A COURT
THAT DOES NOT LIKE ILL-CONSIDERED QUOTAS (CROSON) OR UNFAIR
PRESSURE TO ADOPT QUOTAS (ANTONIO) OR UNFAIR PROTECTIONS FOR
QUOTAS (WILKES). THEY ALSO DESCRIBE A COURT WILLING TO TREAT
MATTERS INVOLVING CIVIL RIGHTS EQUALLY.

02948 EASTLAND, T.
WHILE JUSTICE SLEEPS
NATIONAL REVIEW, XLI(7) (APR 89), 24-26.
THE ARTICLE EXAMINES THE AGING US SUPREME COURT AND THE
PROBLEMS IT PRESENTS. AGE AND ITS ACCOMPANYING DISEASE,
SENILITY AND A SIMPLE SLOWING OF THE MENTAL PROCESSES
THREATENS TO THWART THE JUSTICE PROCESS. THE NUMBER OF EVER-
PRESENT AND INCREASINGLY INVOLVED CLERKS IS ALSO ON THE RISE.
THE ARTICLE ADVOCATES MANDATORY RETIREMENT AT 75 AND A
REDUCTION IN THE NUMBER OF CLERKS.

02949 EASTON, S.T.
FREE TRADE, NATIONALISM, AND THE COMMON MAN: THE FREE
TRADE AGREEMENT BETWEEN CANADA AND THE UNITED STATES
CONTEMPORARY POLICY ISSUES, VII(3) (JUL 89), 61-77.
THIS PAPER DISCUSSES THE FORCES THAT HAVE BEEN AT PLAY
IN THE DEBATE OVER THE RECENTLY CONCLUDED CANADA-U.S. FREE
TRADE AGREEMENT. MOST ECONOMISTS AGREE THAT FREE TRADE IS
DESIRABLE AND THAT BOTH PARTIES LIKELY WILL GAIN FROM
SPECIALIZATION AND EXCHANGE. BUT MANY OBJECTIONS TO THIS
AGREEMENT HAVE BEEN RAISED, SOME OF WHICH ARE VERY DIFFERENT
FROM THOSE THAT ECONOMISTS USUALLY CONSIDER. A REVIEW OF THE
AGREEMENT AND MANY OF THE ARGUMENTS RAISED AGAINST IT
REINFORCES THE BASIC CREDO THAT FREER EXCHANGE BETWEEN
CONSENTING PARTIES LEADS TO IMPROVED ECONOMIC WELL-BEING.

02950 EATON, J.
BUREAUCRATIC, CAPITALIST AND POPULIST PRIVATIZATION
STRATEGIES
INTERNATIONAL REVIEW OF ADMINISTRATIVE SCIENCES, 55(3)
(SEP 89), 467-492.
THERE IS MUCH ATTENTION FOCUSED ON THE DIFFERENCES IN
MANAGEMENT BETWEEN THE SOLIALIST AND THE CAPITALIST MARKET
ECONOMIES. WHAT IS USUALLY IGNORED IS THEIR OVERLAP. THERE
ARE EXTENSIVE "SOCIALIST" COMPARTMENTS IN WESTERN ECONOMIES.
PRIVATE ENTERPRISE EXISTS IN ALL ECONOMIC SYSTEMS. SOCIALIST
AND CAPITALIST NATIONS DO NOT DIFFER IN ABSOLUTE TERMS, BUT
TO THE DEGREE TO WHICH THEIR ECONOMY OPERATES WITH PUBLIC
CAPITAL AND THE COMPREHENSIVENESS OF CENTRAL MANAGEMENT

CONTROL. THIS ARTICLE REVIEWS THE MANAGEMENT METHODS OF
BUREACRATIC, CAPITALIST AND POPULIST SYSTEMS. PRIVATIZATION
WITH AND WITHOUT THE SALE OF ASSETS IS DICUSSED, ALONG WITH
POLITICAL AND SIZE CONSTRAINTS.

02951 ECHAVAPPIA, V.
BALAGUER'S BID TO STOP THE DOLLAR DELUGE
SOUTH, (100) (FEB 89), 36-37.
IN AN ATTEMPT TO CURB THE SLIDE OF THE PESO, PRESIDENT
JOAQUIN BALAGUER IS RESISTING THE FLOW OF DOLLARS FROM THE
USA. HE TOOK A POLITICAL GAMBLE WHEN HE CLAMPED DOWN ON
DOMINICAN-OWNED MONEY TRANSFER HOUSES THAT COMPETE FOR
BUSINESS IN NEW YORK CITY. BY CUTTING THE FLOW OF DOLLARS
REMITTED BY EXPATRIATES IN THE USA, HE HAS TAKEN ON NOT ONLY
THE POWERFUL NARCOTICS MAFIA BUT ALSO ORDINARY DOMINICANS
WHO RELY ON THE CASH SENT BY GENEROUS RELATIVES.

02952 ECKERSLEY, R.
GREEN POLITICS AND THE NEW CLASS: SELFISHNESS OR VIRTUE?
POLITICAL STUDIES, XXXVII(2) (JUN 89), 205-223.
THE PREDOMINANTLY NEW MIDDLE-CLASS SOCIAL COMPOSITION OF
THE GREEN MOVEMENT HAS BECOME A MATTER OF INCREASING
INTEREST IN THE WAKE OF THE SUCCESS OF GREEN PARTIES AND THE
GROWTH OF AN INTERNATIONAL GREEN MOVEMENT. THIS PAPER
CONSIDERS THE CONCEPT OF THE 'NEW CLASS' IN RELATION TO TWO
EXPLANATIONS FOR THE SOCIAL COMPOSITION OF THE GREEN
MOVEMENT. THE CLASS-INTEREST ARGUMENT SEEKS TO SHOW THAT
GREEN POLITICS IS A MEANS OF FURTHERING EITHER MIDDLE-CLASS
OR NEW-CLASS INTERESTS WHILE THE 'NEW CHILDHOOD' ARGUMENT
CLAIMS THAT THE DEVELOPMENT OF THE GREEN MOVEMENT IS THE
RESULT OF THE SPREAD OF POSTMATERIAL VALUES, THE MAIN
BEARERS OF WHICH ARE THE NEW CLASS. AGAINST THESE ARGUMENTS
A MORE COMPREHENSIVE EXPLANATION IS PRESENTED, WHICH FOCUSES
ON THE EDUCATION OF THE NEW CLASS AND ITS RELATIVE
STRUCTURAL AUTONOMY FROM THE PRODUCTION PROCESS.

02953 ECKSTEIN, S.
FOREIGN AID CUBAN-STYLE
MULTINATIONAL MONITOR, 10(4) (APR 89), 14-16.
SINCE THE EARLY 1970S CUBA HAS COMMITTED A SMALL BUT
SIGNIFICANT SHARE OF ITS ECONOMIC RESOURCES TO THE THIRD
WORLD. IT IS ONE OF THE FEW THIRD WORLD COUNTRIES TO HAVE A
FOREIGN ASSISTANCE PROGRAM. DESPITE BOTH A SEVERE DEBT
CRISIS THAT HAS BESIEGED ITS ECONOMY AND HEAVY DEPENDENCE ON
SOVIET ASSISTANCE, THE CUBAN AID PROGRAM HAS SURVIVED AND
FLOURISHED. TO WASHINGTON, HOWEVER, CUBAN FOREIGN ASSISTANCE
IS HIGHLY SUSPECT: IT IS AID THAT FLOWS AT THE BEHEST OF THE
SOVIET UNION. BUT THE CUBAN COMMUNIST PARTY INSISTS IT IS A
COMMITMENT OF SCARCE RESOURCES TO "SOCIALIST SOLIDARITY."
NEITHER INTERPRETATION ADEQUATELY REVEALS A DRIVING FORCE
BEHIND THE CIVIL ASSISTANCE PROGRAM SINCE THE LATE 1970S.
THE PROGRAM WAS DESIGNED TO ADDRESS CUBA'S ECONOMIC
RELATIONS WITH WESTERN COUNTRIES. THE CUBAN GOVERNMENT IS
INCREASINGLY TRYING TO CHARGE--IN HARD CURRENCY--FOR ITS
ASSISTANCE, TO MITIGATE ITS SKYROCKETING WESTERN DEBT.

02954 ECKSTEIN, S. (ED.)
POWER AND POPULAR PROTEST: LATIN AMERICAN SOCIAL MOVEMENTS
UNIVERSITY OF CALIFORNIA PRESS, BERKELEY, CA, 1989, 390.
THIS BOOK OF ESSAYS INVESTIGATES THE CAUSES AND
CONSEQUENCES OF PROTEST MOVEMENTS IN LATIN AMERICA.

02955 ECUHARDT, W.
CONDITIONS OF PEACE SUGGESTED BY SOME QUANTITATIVE STUDIES
OF PRIMITIVE WAR
PEACE RESEARCH, 21(3) (AUG 89), 37-39.
ANTHROPOLOGICAL STUDIES INDICATE TEST DEVELOPMENT
CONTRIBUTED TO ALL MEASURES OF PRIMITIVE WARFARE, INTERNAL
AS WELL AS EXTERNAL, AND DEFENSIVE AS WELL AS OFFENSIVE. IT
CONTRIBUTED MOST OF ALL TO OFFENSIVE EXTERNAL WARFARE WHICH,
IN TURN, CONTRIBUTED TO TERRITORIAL EXPANSION AND,
CONSEQUENTLY, TO THE CULTURAL SURVIVAL OF THE MILITARILY
FITTEST. IT SEEMS CLEAR THAT SOMETHING ABOUT PRIMITIVE
CONDITIONS WERE MORE CONDUCIVE TO PEACE THAN MORE DEVELOPED
CONDITIONS, AND ESPECIALLY CIVILIZED CONDITIONS. DEVELOPMENT
HAS ALMOST ALWAYS BEEN ASSOCIATED WITH AUTHORITARIANISM,
THAT IS, WITH LESS FREEDOM AND LESS EQUALITY FOR ALL, WHILE
MORE PRIMITIVE CONDITIONS HAVE ALMOST ALWAYS BEEN ASSOCIATED
WITH MORE FREEDOM AND EQUALITY FOR ALL. IN GENERAL, THEN,
THESE ANTHROPOLOGICAL STUDIES WOULD SUGGEST THAT IF WE
REALLY WANT MORE PEACE IN THE WORLD, WE NEED TO ESTABLISH
MORE FREE AND EQUAL RELATIONS AMONG HUMAN BEINGS AND GROUPS,
INCLUDING NATIONAL GROUPS, RACIAL GROUPS, RELIGIOUS GROUPS,
SEXUAL GROUPS, ETC.

02956 EDELSHTEIN, G.
HOW TO PLUNDER A CHURCH
GLASNOST, II(2) (MAR 89), 16-19, 25.
ACCORDING TO THE OFFICIAL SOVIET LINE, THE CHURCH AND
THE STATE HAVE COMMON HUMANISTIC GOALS, COMMON TASKS, COMMON
PROPAGANDA METHODS, AND COMMON LEADERSHIP. BUT NOT ONE PENNY
TRAVELS FROM THE STATE TO THE CHURCH. THE FLOW OF FUNDS IS
EXCLUSIVELY FROM THE BELIEVERS TO THE GOVERNMENT. BECAUSE
THE CHURCH CONTRIBUTES TO THE STATE COFFERS, THE STATE

ALLOWS THE CHURCH TO COEXIST. UNDER THIS ARRANGEMENT, THE CHURCH IS AN IMPORTANT SOURCE OF UNEARNED INCOME TO THE STATE. NATURALLY, NO ONE CARES IF THIS SYSTEMATIC PLUNDER OF THE RELIGIOUS COMMUNITY VIOLATES STATE LEGISLATION.

02957 EDELSON, B.I.; TOWNSEND, A.
U.S.-SOVIET COOPERATION: OPPORTUNITIES IN SPACE
SAIS REVIEW, 9(1) (WIN 89), 183-197.
THIS ARTICLE ARGUES THAT THE UNITED STATES SHOULD TAKE IMMEDIATE STEPS TOWARD INCREASING ITS LEVEL OF PARTICIPATION IN SPACE ACTIVITIES WITH THE SOVIET UNION. COOPERATIVE ACTIVITIES ARE JUSTIFIED FOR SCIENTIFIC AND SYMBOLIC REASONS AND FOR THE FOCUS THAT THEY COULD PROVIDE FOR THE U.S. PROGRAM. THE UNITED STATES SHOULD NOT SURRENDER THE AUTONOMY OF ITS NATIONAL PROGRAM. RATHER IT SHOULD COORDINATE SOME PARTS OF ITS POLICY WITH OTHER COUNTRIES, INCLUDING THE SOVIET UNION, SO THAT CERTAIN HIGH-PRIORITY MISSIONS CAN BE UNDERTAKEN MORE EFFECTIVELY AND EFFICIENTLY. EMBARKING ON THE MARS ROVER-SAMPLE RETURN AND THE MISSION TO PLANET EARTH ARE GOOD WAYS TO START. THE DIRECTION FOR THESE EFFORTS, HOWEVER, MUST COME FROM THE TOP: THE NEW PRESIDENT MUST ESTABLISH CLEAR AND REALISTIC GOALS FOR THE CIVILIAN SPACE PROGRAM AND COORDINATE THE VARIOUS AGENCIES INVOLVED SO THAT U.S. SPACE ACTIVITIES ARE SUPPORTED BY A UNIFIED POLICY AND BUREAUCRACY.

02958 EDELSTEIN, S.
THE LEGAL RIGHTS OF WOMEN IN ISRAEL
NEW OUTLOOK, 32(6-7 (292-293)) (JUN 89), 16-18.
ACKNOWLEDGING THE POTENTIAL FOR CONTRADICTIONS IN THE LAW IS ESSENTIAL TO UNDERSTANDING THE LEGAL RIGHTS AFFORDED WOMEN IN ISRAEL. AND SOCIAL REALITY IS OF NO LESS IMPORTANCE. LEGISLATION, EVEN THE MOST CAREFULLY WORDED, IS INEFFECTIVE IF IT FALLS ON DEAF EARS. LOW SOCIAL AWARENESS, COMBINED WITH A LEGAL SYSTEM THAT LACKS THE NECESSARY TOOLS TO ENSURE THE RIGHTS OF WOMEN, CREATES AN OFTEN-INEFFECTIVE ARENA FOR PROMOTING GENDER EQUALITY IN ISRAEL.

02959 EDGERTON, D.; HUGHES, K.
THE POVERTY OF SCIENCE: A CRITICAL ANALYSIS OF SCIENTIFIC AND INDUSTRIAL POLICY UNDER MRS. THATCHER
PUBLIC ADMINISTRATION, 67(4) (WIN 89), 419-433.
THE PRESENT GOVERNMENT'S POLICY FOR PUBLICLY FUNDED SCIENCE, WHICH CENTRES ON SELECTIVITY AND CENTRALIZATION, COULD DAMAGE BRITAIN'S CAPACITY TO INNOVATE. THE POLICY FOLLOWS FROM A DESIRE BY GOVERNMENT TO CONTROL THE SCIENTIFIC COMMUNITY AND FROM THE ADVICE OF SOME SCIENTISTS AND SCIENCE POLICY EXPERTS. THIS PAPER DETAILS THE CONTRADICTIONS IN THE GOVERNMENT'S THINKING ON INDUSTRIAL AND SCIENTIFIC QUESTIONS, AND CHALLENGES THE CENTRAL, AND USUALLY UNEXAMINED, ASSUMPTIONS WHICH ARE USED TO JUSTIFY EXISTING POLICY FOR SCIENCE.

02960 EDIE, C.J.
FROM MANLEY TO SEAGA: THE PERSISTENCE OF CLIENTELIST POLITICS IN JAMAICA
SOCIAL AND ECONOMIC STUDIES, 38(1) (MAR 89), 1-35.
PATRON-CLIENT TIES ARE AMONG THE MOST CONSPICUOUS FEATURES OF POLITICAL BEHAVIOUR IN JAMAICA. HUNDREDS OF DEMANDS ARE MADE DAILY ON PUBLIC AND POLITICAL FIGURES IN THE URBAN AREAS OF KINGSTON AND THE RURAL PARISHES. THESE DEMANDS ARE MET LARGELY THROUGH THE INTERVENTION OF THE ELECTED OFFICIALS IN THE AFFAIRS OF THE MUNICIPAL BUREAUCRACY, WHEREBY BUREAUCRATIC ELITES ARE INSTRUCTED TO DISPENSE RESOURCES TO REWARD LOYAL PARTY SUPPORTERS. THIS STUDY SUGGESTS THAT DEMOCRATIC POLITICS IN JAMAICA IS MAINTAINED BY STATE-CONTROLLING PARTY ELITES WHO GRANT PATRONAGE RESOURCES IN EXCHANGE FOR PARTY SUPPORT. INTERNAL POLITICAL ORDER HINGES ON THE POLITICAL DIRECTORATE'S ABILITY TO OBTAIN INTERNATIONAL CAPITAL TRANSFERS.

02961 EDLUND, C.J.
A NEW COMPENSATION STANDARD: EQUAL PAY FOR EQUAL WORTH IN WASHINGTON STATE
DISSERTATION ABSTRACTS INTERNATIONAL, 50(5) (NOV 89), 1431-A.
WASHINGTON COINED THE TERM "COMPARABLE WORTH," LED THE NATION IN CONDUCTING PAY EQUITY STUDIES OF ITS WORK FORCE, AND IS THE ONLY STATE TO IMPLEMENT A NEGOTIATED AGREEMENT. SIX DRIVING FORCES EXPLAIN THE ACTIONS AND ACTIVITIES THAT MOVED THE IDEA FROM CONCEPT TO PRACTICE IN WASHINGTON: AWARENESS OF INEQUITY, ACTION BY KEY POLITICAL ACTORS, ECONOMIC PRESSURES, LITIGATION, TIME CONSTRAINTS, AND PERSONNEL CAPABILITIES.

02962 EDMONDSON. H.
POLITICAL EDUCATION FOR PUBLIC SERVANTS
POLICY STUDIES REVIEW, 8(4) (SUM 89), 834-839.
INCORPORATING DEMOCRATIC VALUES INTO PUBLIC ADMINISTRATION EDUCATION IS NOT AN EASY TASK. TO IGNORE DEMOCRATIC VALUES COMPLETELY, HOWEVER, WOULD BE TO TACITLY CONDONE THE VIOLATION OF THESE PRINCIPLES BY AN ADMINISTRATOR THUS MAKING DEMOCRACY TRAINING ALL THE MORE ESSENTIAL. IN THIS ARTICLE, THE IDEAS OF THE AMERICAN FOUNDERS AND THE IDEAS OF JOHN DEWEY REGARDING DEMOCRACY IN EDUCATION ARE COMPARED. IT IS THE OPINION OF THE AUTHOR THAT THE FOUNDERS AND DEWEY HAD SUCH DIVERGENT VIEW OF TEACHING DEMOCRACY PRECISELY BECAUSE THEY HAD VERY DIFFERENT DEFINITIONS OF DEMOCRACY.

02963 EDSALL, T.B.
CRIME, DRUGS, AND ABORTION WILL SHAPE THE 1990 CAMPAIGNS
STATE LEGISLATURES, 15(7) (AUG 89), 43-44.
IN PUBLIC OPINION POLLS, THE ISSUE OF DRUGS AND CRIME HAS SKYROCKETED TO THE TOP OF VOTERS' PRIORITIES. THE SUPREME COURT'S RECONSIDERATION OF ITS 1973 ABORTION DECISION HAS ALSO COME TO THE FOREFRONT OF POLITICS. BOTH DEMOCRATIC AND REPUBLICAN STRATEGISTS ARE STRUGGLING TO ANTICIPATE HOW THESE TWO ISSUES WILL CHANGE THE POLITICAL LANDSCAPE.

02964 EDWARDS, L.
CONGRESS AND THE ORIGINS OF THE COLD WAR: THE TRUMAN DOCTRINE
WORLD AFFAIRS, 151(3) (WIN 89), 131-142.
THE ARTICLE EXPLORES THE EVENTS THAT LED TO THE ADOPTION OF THE "TRUMAN DOCTRINE." IT OUTLINES THE CONGRESSIONAL BATTLES OVER THE DEGREE OF US SUPPORT FOR GREECE AND TURKEY AGAINST COMMUNIST AGGRESSION AND HOW THE TRUMAN ADMINISTRATION ATTEMPTED TO WIN OVER CONGRESS AND THE NATION. THE RESULT WAS A POLICY THAT CALLED FOR SHIFT AND IMMEDIATE RESPONSES TO COMMUNIST AGGRESSION, FIRST ON AN ECONOMIC LEVEL, THEN ON OTHER FRONTS AS THE SITUATION NECESSITATED. THIS DOCTRINE SIGNALED THE BEGINNING OF THE COLD WAR.

02965 EDWARDS, L.
CONGRESS ON THE ORGINS OF THE COLD WAR: THE TRUMAN DOCTRINE
WORLD AFFAIRS, 151(3) (WIN 88), 131-142.
THIS ARTICLE EXAMINES WHAT PRESIDENT TRUMAN SAID AND DID NOT SAY TO THE JOINT SESSION OF CONGRESS SOME FORTY YEARS AGO. IT EXPLORES THE HEART OF THE TRUMAN DOCTRINE WHICH WAS THAT INTERNATIONAL PEACE AND U.S. SECURITY WERE LINKED, IN RELATION TO THE PROPOSAL OF U.S. HELP TO GREECE AND TURKEY, IT SUGGESTS THAT TO SOME ISOLATIONISTS, THE REAL MENACE WAS NOT THE COMMUNISTS IN GREECE OR TURKEY BUT THOSE INSIDE THE UNITED STATES AND CONCLUDES THAT IN A SENSE, THE PRIMARY ISSUE OF THE SENATE HEARINGS WAS THE DEGREE TO WHICH THE U.S. SHOULD GET "TOUGH" WITH THE SOVIET UNION. IT CONCLUDES WITH THE REASONS FOR WHICH TRUMANS LANGUAGE IN A STATEMENT ISSUED AFTER SIGNING THE BILL IS SIGNIFICANT.

02966 EDWARDS, S.
DEBT CRISIS, TRADE LIBERALIZATION, STRUCTURAL ADJUSTMENT, AND GROWTH: SOME POLICY CONSIDERATIONS
CONTEMPORARY POLICY ISSUES, VII(3) (JUL 89), 30-41.
THIS PAPER ANALYZES SOME DYNAMIC ASPECTS OF TRADE LIBERALIZATION REFORMS WITHIN THE CONTEXT OF THE DEBT CRISIS. IN PARTICULAR, THE PAPER DISCUSSES ISSUES CONCERNING INTENSITY OF LIBERALIZATION, SPEED OF TRADE REFORM, AND THE INTERACTION BETWEEN LIBERALIZATION AND STABILIZATION. IT DEALS WITH ANALYTICAL ISSUES AND DRAWS FROM THE EMPIRICAL EXPERIENCES OF SOME HIGHLY INDEBTED LATIN AMERICAN COUNTRIES.

02967 EDWARDS, S.
EXCHANGE RATE MISALIGNMENT IN DEVELOPING COUNTRIES
AVAILABLE FROM NTIS, NO. PB89-162853/GAR, 1988, 107.
THE BOOK ANALYZES SEVERAL ISSUES RELATED TO THE MISALIGNMENT OF REAL EXCHANGE RATES IN THE DEVELOPING COUNTRIES. CHAPTER 1 DEALS WITH THE THEORY OF EQUILIBRIUM REAL EXCHANGE RATES. THE CHAPTER ALSO ANALYZES THE INTERACTION BETWEEN MACROECONOMIC POLICIES AND REAL EXCHANGE RATES FOR THREE ALTERNATIVE NOMINAL EXCHANGE RATE REGIMES: PREDETERMINED, FREELY FLUCTUATING, AND NONUNIFIED REGIMES. CHAPTER 2 DEALS WITH THE REALIGNMENT OF REAL EXCHANGE RATES, PARTICULARLY PREDETERMINED NOMINAL RATES--THE MOST COMMON EXCHANGE RATE REGIME IN THE DEVELOPING NATIONS. CHAPTER 3 CONTAINS A SUMMARY AND THE MAIN CONCLUSIONS OF THE STUDY. (COPYRIGHT (C) 1988 THE INTERNATIONAL BANK FOR RECONSTRUCTION AND DEVELOPMENT/THE WORLD BANK.)

02968 EELE. G.
THE ORGANIZATION AND MANAGEMENT OF STATISTICAL SERVICES IN AFRICA: WHY DO THEY FAIL?
WORLD DEVELOPMENT, 17(3) (MAR 89), 431-438.
THIS PAPER ARGUES THAT IMPROVING STATISTICAL INFORMATION FOR FOOD SECURITY PLANNING REQUIRES AN ANALYSIS OF THE WAY THAT GOVERNMENT STATISTICAL SERVICES ARE MANAGED AND ORGANIZED. IT IS SUGGESTED THAT THESE SERVICES HAVE FAILED BECAUSE OF A FAILURE OF BOTH SUPPLY AND DEMAND. FURTHER INVESTMENT IN EXISTING ORGANIZATIONS MAY WELL BE INEFFECTIVE WITHOUT A REAPPRAISAL OF THE ROLE THAT INFORMATION PLAYS IN THE DECISION MAKING PROCESS. IT IS SUGGESTED THAT THE DISTINCTION BETWEEN DATA COLLECTION AND DECISION MAKING IS ARTIFICIAL AND THAT CONTINUED SEPARATION OF DATA COLLECTION ACTIVITIES FROM POLICY ANALYSIS HAS RESULTED IN THE DEVELOPMENT OF STATISTICAL ORGANIZATIONS THAT DO NOT MEET THE REAL NEEDS OF GOVERNMENTS.

02969 EFINGER, M.
THE VERIFICATION POLICY OF THE SOVIET UNION
AUSSEN POLITIK, 40(4) (1989), 332 - 348.
THIS ARTICLE FOCUSES ON THE CHANGES IN SOVIET
VERIFICATION POLICY DURING THE PAST FOUR YEARS - 1985 - 1989.
A BRIEF INTRODUCTORY ELUCIDATION OF THE ROLE OF THE
VERIFICATION ISSUE IN ARMS CONTROL IS GIVEN. FOLLOWING, IS A
PRESENTATION OF SOVIET VERIFICATION POLICY SINCE THE SECOND
WORLD WAR. CHANGES IN SOVIET POLICY SINCE 1985 ARE EXAMINED;
AND ALSO THE EXTENT TO WHICH THE CHANGES IMPROVE
RATIFICATION OF PREVIOUS AGREEMENTS.

02970 EGAN, E.
CHILDREN IN CAMBAT
COMMONWEAL, CXVI(4) (FEB 89), 104-105.
THE UN HUMAN RIGHTS COMMISSION NEGOTIATIONS HAVE FAILED
TO ARRIVE AT AN INTERNATIONAL STANDARD FOR DETERMINING WHEN
YOUNGSTERS ARE TOO YOUNG FOR COMBAT. BUT NEGOTIATIONS AR
CONTINUING.

02971 EGEOLU, I.I.
THE ROLE OF THE NIGERIAN PARTY PRESS IN POLITICAL CONFLICT:
AN ANALYSIS OF PARTY PRESS VIEWPOINTS ON THREE MAJOR
ISSUES OF THE NATIONAL PARTY OF NIGERIA AND THE NIGERIA
PEOPLE'S PARTY ACCORD
DISSERTATION ABSTRACTS INTERNATIONAL, 49(9) (MAR 89),
2794-A.
THIS STUDY INVESTIGATES THE ROLE OF THE NIGERIAN PARTY
PRESS DURING THE NPN-NPP POLITICAL CONFLICT THROUGH THE
ANALYSIS OF THEIR VIEWPOINTS ON THREE MAJOR ISSUES: THE
APPOINTMENT OF PRESIDENTIAL LIAISON OFFICERS, THE SECOND
REPUBLIC REVENUE ALLOCATION FORMULA, AND THE KADUNA
IMPEACHMENT.

02972 EGGER, H.
POLAND IS NOT YET LOST
AUSTRIA TODAY, (4) (1989), 4.
AUSTRIA BELIEVES THAT IT IS CAPABLE OF MAKING A SPECIAL
CONTRIBUTION TO THE COMMON EUROPEAN TASK OF PROVIDING
ECONOMIC ASSISTANCE TO BUILD A SOLID FOUNDATION FOR
DEMOCRATIZATION IN EASTERN EUROPE. AUSTRIA HAS ALREADY
LOANED A LARGE SUM TO POLAND. BUT THERE IS NO DOUBT THAT
POLAND NEEDS ADDITIONAL FINANCIAL HELP IN THE FORM OF
"FRESH" CAPITAL. UNFORTUNATELY, MONEY INJECTIONS ALONE WILL
NOT SUFFICE. LIKE ALL THE EASTERN EUROPEAN COUNTRIES, POLAND
NEEDS NEW POLITICAL AND ECONOMIC STRUCTURES.

02973 EGGESBO, B.
ARMAMENT COOPERATION AND LINKS: THE UNITED STATES AND
NORWAY
NATO'S SIXTEEN NATIONS, 34(6) (OCT 89), 61-63 (SPECIAL
SECTION).
ALTHOUGH NORWAY IS NOT A MEMBER OF THE EEC OR THE WEU,
IT PARTICIPATES ACTIVELY IN BOTH EUROPEAN AND TRANS-ATLANTIC
COOPERATIVE ARMAMENTS PRODUCTION. BILATERAL COOPERATION WITH
THE USA HAS BEEN PARTICULARLY STRONG. NORWAY'S GOAL IS TO
STRENGTHEN ITS TIES WITH THE USA AND MAINTAIN NATO'S
STRENGTH ON THE NORTHERN FLANK.

02974 EGRI, C.P.; STANBURY, W.T.
HOW PAY EQUITY LEGISLATION CAME TO ONTARIO
CANADIAN PUBLIC ADMINISTRATION, 32(2) (SUM 89), 274-303.
THIS PAPER PRESENTS A DETAILED CASE ANALYSIS OF THE
EMERGENCE OF FARREACHING PAY EQUITY LEGISLATION (BILL 154)
IN ONTARIO IN 1987 IN ORDER TO TEST A GENERAL ANALYTICAL
FRAMEWORK DESIGNED TO EXPLAIN MAJOR CHANGES IN PUBLIC POLICY.
THREE FACTORS ARE POSTULATED TO BE INSTRUMENTAL IN THE
ATTAINMENT OF NEW LEGISLATIVE INITIATIVES: CHANGES IN
ENVIRONMENTAL VARIABLES (E.G., ECONOMIC AND DEMOGRAPHIC
VARIABLES, HISTORICAL TRENDS AND PRECEDENTS); SHIFTS IN
POLITICAL POWER (E.G., ELECTORAL CHANGES RESULTING IN A
MINORITY GOVERNMENT OR A NEW GOVERNING PARTY, THE PERCEPTION
OF VOTER MANDATED CHANGE); AND CHANGES IN PRESSURE GROUP
BEHAVIOR (E.G., A SHIFT IN THE "BALANCE OF POWER" AMONGST
PRESSURE GROUPS DUE TO CHANGES IN RESOURCES, LEADERSHIP,
POLITICAL INFLUENCE STRATEGIES OR TACTICS, OR THE CREATION
OF NEW PRESSURE GROUPS). THE AUTHORS CONCLUDE THAT ALL THREE
FACTORS WERE IMPORTANT IN EXPLAINING THIS SIGNIFICANT CHANGE
IN PUBLIC POLICY, WITH THE GREATEST WEIGHT BEING ATTRIBUTED
TO SHIFTS IN POLITICAL POWER. THIS FRAMEWORK APPEARS TO BE A
USEFUL STEP IN DEVELOPING A GENERAL THEORY OF MAJOR CHANGES
IN PUBLIC POLICY.

02975 EHLERS, J.A.
IZQUIERDA DEMOCRATICA OR DEMOCRATIC LEFT: A CASE STUDY OF
THE ORIGINS, PHILOSOPHY, ORGANIZATION, AND QUEST FOR POWER
OF A POLITICAL PARTY IN ECUADOR
DISSERTATION ABSTRACTS INTERNATIONAL, 49(8) (FEB 89),
2418-A.
THE AUTHOR TRACES THE DEVELOPMENT OF THE DEMOCRATIC LEFT
POLITICAL PARTY IN ECUADOR FROM 1968 TO 1984. HE STUDIES
PARTY FORMATION, THE PARTY'S ROLE IN THE POLITICAL PROCESS,
AND THEORETICAL CONCEPTS OF DEMOCRATIC SOCIALISM.

02976 EIDINOW, J.
AFTER THE EUROELECTIONS
WORLD TODAY, 45(8-9) (AUG 89), 129-130.
THERE IS EVERY JUSTIFICATION FOR SEEING THE VOTES CAST
IN THE EUROPEAN PARLIAMENT ELECTIONS IN JUNE 1989 AS
EMERGING FROM A SERIES OF NATIONAL ELECTIONS ON A EUROPEAN
SCALE. WITH PERHAPS ONE EXCEPTION AMONG THE MEMBER STATES,
THERE HAS SIMPLY TOO MUCH CROSS-PARTY AGREEMENT ON THE BASIC
COMMUNITY AIMS AND VALUES TO PROVIDE THE CONTRASTS THAT
ALLOW DEBATE.

02977 EIDLIN, F.
THE BREAKDOWN OF NEWSPEAK
POLITICAL COMMUNICATION AND PERSUASION, 5(4) (1988),
225-236.
MANY ATTEMPTS HAVE BEEN MADE TO CREATE NEWSPEAKS. BUT IN
LIGHT OF WHAT IS NOW KNOWN ABOUT SUCH ATTEMPTS, IT IS CLEAR
THAT NOT EVEN THE MOST SUCCESSFUL OF THEM HAS COME ANYWHERE
NEAR TO REALIZATION OF ORWELL'S PROJECTION. RATHER THAN
THESE NEWSPEAKS BECOMING INCREASINGLY FINE-TUNED,
COMPREHENSIVE INSTRUMENTS OF TOTALITARIAN CONTROL, AS
SUGGESTED IN "1984", QUITE AN OPPOSITE DEVELOPMENT HAS TAKEN
PLACE. THE PEOPLES UPON WHOM NEWSPEAKS HAVE BEEN IMPOSED
HAVE LEARNED TO LIVE WITH AND MANIPULATE THESE ARTIFICIAL
LANGUAGES, AND THEIR EFFECTIVENESS HAS DECLINED RATHER THAN
INCREASED OVER TIME. THE PRESENT PAPER EXPLORES THIS
DEGENERATION OF NEWSPEAK, EXAMINING SOME OF THE ASSUMPTIONS
ABOUT LANGUAGE, MAN, AND SOCIETY UNDERLYING ORWELL'S PICTURE
OF THE FUTURE. IT MAKES EXPLICIT THE THEORY OF TOTALITARIAN
CONTROL BASED ON LANGUAGE THAT IS IMPLICIT IN "1984" AND
THEN SHOWS THAT SEVERAL FUNDAMENTAL ASSUMPTIONS OF THIS
THEORY ARE PATENTLY UTOPIAN WHILE OTHERS ARE HIGHLY
IMPLAUSIBLE. APART FROM ITS RICH INSIGHTS INTO THE DYNAMICS
OF TOTALITARIANISM, EVEN THE UTOPIAN ELEMENTS OF "1984" HELP
US TO UNDERSTAND BETTER THE LIMITATIONS OF AS WELL AS THE
POSSIBILITIES FOR TOTALITARIAN CONTROL IN CONTEMPORARY
SOCIETY BY PLACING IN RELIEF THE CONDITIONS THAT WOULD HAVE
TO BE MET FOR SUCH CONTROL ACTUALLY TO BE REALIZED. SETTING
FORTH THESE CONDITIONS MAKES CLEAR WHY THESE CONDITIONS
COULD NEVER BE MET IN REALITY.

02978 EILAM, U.
UNITED STATES-ISRAELI COOPERATION IN DEFENCE: AN ISRAELI
VIEW
NATO'S SIXTEEN NATIONS, 34(6) (OCT 89), 49-51 (SPECIAL
SECTION).
THE GROWING COMPLEXITY AND COST OF MODERN WEAPONS
SYSTEMS HAS DRIVEN ISRAEL TO INCREASE ITS ARMAMENTS
COOPERATION WITH ITS ALLIES. ITS PRINCIPAL PARTNER IS THE
UNITED STATES AND THERE ARE MUTUAL ADVANTAGES. ISRAEL
BENEFITS FROM THE SIZE AND TECHNOLOGICAL EXPERTISE OF THE
USA. IN RETURN, ISRAEL OFFERS COMBAT EXPERIENCE, PRACTICAL
ABILITY, AND HIGHLY TRAINED SPECIALISTS. SINCE ISRAEL'S
DEFENCE INDUSTRY IS TINY COMPARED TO THAT OF WESTERN EUROPE,
IT EXPECTS ITS RELATIONS WITH THE EUROPEAN COMMUNITY AFTER
1992 TO BE STRICTLY COMMERCIAL, BUT IT WILL CONTINUE TO BE
READY TO COOPERATE WITH THE FREE WORLD WHEN COMMON GOALS ARE
SHARED.

02979 EINSTEIN, A.
WHY SOCIALISM
MONTHLY REVIEW, 40(8) (JAN 89), 14-21.
IN THIS ESSAY EINSTEIN DESCRIBES WHAT HE CONSIDERS TO BE
THE EVILS OF CAPITALISM, INCLUDING PRODUCTION FOR PROFIT,
NOT FOR USE, WHICH, IN CONJUNCTION WITH COMPETITION IS
RESPONSIBLE FOR AN INSTABILITY IN THE ACCUMULATION AND
UTILIZATION OF CAPITAL AND EMPLOYMENT. EINSTEIN CONSIDERS
THE WORST EVIL OF CAPITALISM TO BE THE CRIPPLING OF
INDIVIDUALS THROUGHOUT THE EDUCATIONAL SYSTEM THOUGH
INCULCATION OF AN EXAGGERATED COMPETETIVE ATTITUDE WHICH
TRAINS CHILDREN TO WORSHIP ACQUISITIVE SUCCESS.

02980 EISENBERG, C.
THE COMPARATIVE VIEW IN LABOUR HISTORY. OLD AND NEW
INTERPRETATIONS OF THE ENGLISH AND GERMAN LABOUR MOVEMENTS
BEFORE 1914
INTERNATIONAL REVIEW OF SOCIAL HISTORY, 34(3) (1989),
403-432.
COMPARISONS BETWEEN THE ENGLISH AND GERMAN LABOUR
MOVEMENTS HAVE A LONG TRADITION IN HISTORIOGRAPH. IN GERMANY
THEY WERE PRIMARILY DISCUSSED IN THE CONTEXT OF THE "GERMAN
SONDERWEG", A DEBATE WHICH WAS OPENED IN THE 1920S AND
CONTINUES IN THE 1980S. THE ARTICLE PRESENTED HERE ANALYZES
THE METHODOLOGICAL PROBLEMS OF SONDERWEG COMPARISONS OF
LABOUR HISTORY AND CONFRONTS THE MAJOR ARGUMENTS WITH THE
RESULTS OF EMPIRICAL RESEARCH. IT CONCLUDES THAT MANY OLD
SONDERWEG ARGUMENTS CAN NOT WITHSTAND THIS CONFRONTATION.
NEVERTHELESS, THE ARTICLE PROPOSES THAT THE DEBATE SHOULD BE
CONTINUED, SINCE EMPIRICAL RESEARCH FOCUSES ON NEW ASPECTS
AND SUPPORTS THE DIAGNOSIS OF TWO DIFFERENT PATHS OF LABOUR
HISTORY.

02981 EISENSTADT, S.N.; RONIGER, L.; SELIGMAN, A.
CENTRE FORMATION AND POLITICAL PARTICIPATION IN SPAIN AND

ITALY: AN INTERPRETATION OF SOUTHERN EUROPEAN POLITICS;
CENTRE FORMATION, PROTEST MOVEMENTS, AND CLASS STRUCTURE
IN EUROPE AND THE UNITED STATES
FRANCES PINTER PUBLISHERS, LONDON, GB, 1987, 56-75.
RECENTLY, POLITICAL SCIENTISTS INCREASINGLY EMPHASIZE
THAT THE PARALLEL AND SIMILAR DEVELOPMENTS IN MANY ASPECTS
OF THE MEDITERRANEAN POLITICAL SYSTEMS AS WELL AS IN THEIR
PATTERNS OF SOCIAL AND ECONOMIC DEVELOPMENT, WARRANT
SYSTEMATIC STUDY. THE PURPOSE OF THIS ARTICLE IS TO ANALYZE
FROM A COMPARATIVE PERSPECTIVE MAJOR PROCESSES OF CENTRE
FORMATION AND POLITICAL PARTICIPATION IN SOUTHERN EUROPEAN
POLITIES. FOR THIS PURPOSE, TWO HIGHLY DISSIMILAR CASES:
SPAIN, A NATION-STATE WITH A PRONOUNCED RELIANCE ON ITS
IMPERIAL PAST AND ITALY, A NATION-STATE COMPRISED OF
MULTIPLE REGIONAL CENTRES WHICH CRYSTALIZED IN THE
MIDNINETEENTH CENTURY ARE ANALYZED.

02982 EISENSTADT, S.N.; RONIGER, L.; SELIGMAN, A.
CENTRE FORMATION AND PROTEST MOVEMENTS IN EUROPE AND THE
UNITED STATES: A COMPARATIVE PERSPECTIVE; CENTRE FORMATION,
PROTEST MOVEMENTS, AND CLASS STRUCTURE IN EUROPE AND THE
UNITED STATES
FRANCES PINTER PUBLISHERS, LONDON, GB, 1987, 7-23.
THE CHAPTER SPELLS OUT IN GREAT DETAIL THE BASIC
ASSUMPTIONS OF THE SOCIOLOGICAL APPROACH TO COMPARATIVE
CIVILISATIONS AND THEN APPLY IT TO THE EUROPEAN AND AMERICAN
SCENE. IT UTILIZES THE COMPARATIVE APPORACH PARTICULARLY
WITH REFERENCE TO THE SO-CALLED AXIAL AGE CIVILIZATIONS:
CIVILIZATIONS WHICH DEVELOPED IN THE FIRST MILLENIUM BEFORE
THE CHRISTIAN ERA.

02983 EISENSTADT, S.N.; RONIGER, L.; SELIGMAN, A.
SOCIAL STRATIFICATION IN SOUTHERN EUROPE; CENTRE FORMATION,
PROTEST MOVEMENTS, AND CLASS STRUCTURE IN EUROPE AND THE
UNITED STATES
FRANCES PINTER PUBLISHERS, LONDON, GB, 1987, 135-160.
THE CHAPTER IDENTIFIES THE EXISTENCE OF A BASIC
INDETERMINANCY IN THE STRUCTURING OF SOUTHERN EUROPEAN,
SPECIFICALLY SPANISH AND ITALIAN, MODERN SYSTEMS OF
STRATIFICATION. THIS INDETERMINANCY, WHICH PARTAKES OF THE
HISTORICAL EXPERIENCE OF WESTERN EUROPEAN SETTINGS, IMPLIES
THAT THE FORMATION OF HIGHLY DIFFERENTIATED SOCIAL
HIERARCHIES AND A SHARP CONSCIOUSNESS OF STRATA
DIFFERENTIALS HAVE NOT BEEN OBLITERATED IN THE AREA.

02984 EISENSTADT, S.N.; LEVINTHAL, S.; RONIGER, L.; SELIGMAN, A.
SOME PROGRAMMATIC NOTES TOWARDS A COMPARATIVE STUDY OF
STUDENT PROTEST: THE ENGLISH AND ITALIAN CASES; CENTRE
FORMATION, PROTEST MOVEMENTS, AND CLASS STRUCTURE IN
EUROPE AND THE UNITED STATES
FRANCES PINTER PUBLISHER, LONDON, GB, 1987, 76-89.
ALTHOUGH STUDENT PROTESTS ARE AND HAVE BEEN AN INTEGRAL
PART OF THE HISTORY OF MODERN SOCIETY, THE PROTESTS OF THE
1960'S WERE SIGNIFICANTLY DIFFERENT FROM THOSE OF THE PAST.
THE PAPER POINTS OUT THE SPECIFIC CHARACTERISTICS OF STUDENT
PROTEST IN ENGLAND AND ITALY DURING THIS PERIOD. IT MAKES
PARTICULAR REFERENCE TO THE TENDENCY OF THE STUDENT PROTEST
IN ENGLAND TO BE LESS INTENSE, LESS WIDESPREAD AND MORE
INSTITUTIONALIZED THAN THE STUDENT PROTESTS IN OTHER WESTERN
EUROPEAN NATIONS DURING THIS PERIOD.

02985 EISENSTADT, S.N.; RONIGER, L.; SELIGMAN, A.
THE AMERICAN SYSTEM OF STRATIFICATION: SOME NOTES TOWARDS
UNDERSTANDING ITS SYMBOLIC AND INSTITUTIONAL CONCOMITANTS;
CENTRE FORMATION, PROTEST MOVEMENTS, AND CLASS STRUCTURE
IN EUROPE AND THE UNITED STATES
FRANCES PINTER PUBLISHERS, LONDON, GB, 1987, 161-180.
THE CHAPTER ATTEMPTS TO RELATE ONE OF THE MOST SALIENT
FEATURES OF THE AMERICAN STRATIFICATION SYSTEM, NAMELY ITS
LACK OF ANY RIGID STATUS DEMARCATION LINES, WITH THE BASIC
PATTERNING OF CULTURAL ORIENTATIONS, SYMBOLIC AND
INSTITUTIONAL ORDERS OF THE CENTRE AND THE STRUCTURING OF
THE MAJOR ELITE GROUPS IN SOCIETY.

02986 EISENSTADT, S.N.; RONIGER, L.; SELIGMAN, A.
THE FAILURE OF SOCIALISM IN THE UNITED STATES: A
RECONSIDERATION; CENTRE FORMATION, PROTEST MOVEMENTS, AND
CLASS STRUCTURE IN EUROPE AND THE UNITED STATES
FRANCES PINTER PUBLISHERS, LONDON, GB, 1987, 90-118.
FOR MANY, THE MOST BLATANT LACUNA IN AMERICAN SOCI-
POLITICAL LIFE IS THE ABSCENCE OF AN ORGANIZATIONALLY STRONG,
IDEOLOGICALLY COHERENT AND POLTICALLY AUTONOMOUS SOCIALIST
MOVEMENT AND PARTY IN THE US. THE EXISTING SOCIALISM IN THE
US IS DISTINCTLY NON-RADICAL AND SUFFERS EXTENSIVELY FROM
INTERNAL SCHISMS. THE ARTICLE EXAMINES THE DIFFERENT
ANALYSES THAT ATTEMPT TO EXPLAIN THE LACK OF A STRONG
SOCIALIST MOVEMENT IN THE US, EXAMINES SOME OF THEIR
PROBLEMATIC ASPECTS AND PRESENT AN ALTERNATIVE PERSPECTIVE.

02987 EISENSTADT, S.N.; RONIGER, L.; SELIGMAN, A.
THE FRENCH NATION-STATE: CONTINUITIES, TRANSFORMATIONS AND
CENTRE FORMATION; CENTRE FORMATION, PROTEST MOVEMENTS, AND
CLASS STRUCTURE IN EUROPE AND THE UNITED STATES
FRANCES PINTER PUBLISHERS, LONDON, GB, 1987, 24-55.

THE PURPOSE OF THE STUDY IS TO TRACE THE DEVELOPMENT OF
THE FRENCH-NATION STATE ALONG A PARTICULAR LINE OF INQUIRY,
FROM ITS EMERGENCE FROM THE FEUDAL STRUCTURE TO ITS
CRYSTALLIZATION DURING THE PERIOD OF THE THIRD REPUBLIC.
THROUGH THE STUDY OF BASIC CULTURAL ORIENTATIONS AND THE
MODES OF THEIR ARTICULATION BY DIFFERENT GROUP, THE STUDY
ATTEMPTS TO UNDERSTAND HOW THE INTERACTIONS BETWEEN VARIOUS
VALUE ORIENTATIONS, CULTURAL FRAMEWORKS AND INSTITUTIONAL
STRUCTURES, CONTRIBUTED TO THE CRYSTALIZATION OF THE SOCIAL
AND POLITICAL CENTER IN POST-REVOLUTIONARY FRANCE.

02988 EISENSTADT, S.N.; RONIGER, L.; SELIGMAN, A.
THE STRUCTURING OF SOCIAL HIERARCHIES IN COMPARATIVE
PERSPECTIVE; CENTRE FORMATION, PROTEST MOVEMENTS, AND
CLASS STRUCTURE IN EUROPE AND THE UNITED STATES
FRANCES PINTER PUBLISHERS, LONDON, GB, 1987, 121-134.
THE ARTICLE ATTEMPTS TO THROW SOME NEW LIGHT ON THE
STRUCTURING OF SOCIAL HIERARCHIES AND PAYS SPECIAL ATTENTION
TO THE ROLE OF IDEAS IN THIS PROCESS. IT MAKES A CRITICAL
EVALUATION OF THE BASIC ASSUMPTIONS OF SOCIOLOGICAL STUDIES
IN THIS FIELD, WHICH ASSUMPTIONS ARE SHARED TO SOME DEGREE
BY BOTH THE MARXISTS AND THE LIBERAL APPROACHES TO THE
PROBLEM OF CLASS FORMATION.

02989 EJIKE, S.U.
DIRECT INVESTMENT DISPUTES AND U.S. CORPORATE
MULTINATIONALISM IN POST-COLONIAL AFRICA, 1959-1979
DISSERTATION ABSTRACTS INTERNATIONAL, 50(4) (OCT 89),
1082-A.
THE DISSERTATION EXAMINES THE BUSINESS COMPONENT IN U.S.-
AFRICA RELATIONS AND THE HISTORICAL MATRIX OF THIS
RELATIONSHIP, WITH A VIEW TO LOCATING THE STRUCTURE AND THE
IDEOLOGICAL BASIS OF U.S. POLICY CHOICES AND PREFERENCES.
THE FOCUS IS ON THE MULTINATIONAL CORPORATION (MNC) BECAUSE
IT COMPRISED THE BASIC MEDIUM FOR THE CONDUCT OF BUSINESS
RELATIONS BETWEEN AFRICA AND THE U.S. IN THE LAST TWO
DECADES.

02990 EKANDEM, U.O.
THE PROBLEM WITH MAJORITY RULE IN THE GENERAL ASSEMBLY OF
THE UNITED NATIONS: ALTERNATIVE APPROACHES TO CONFLICT
THEORY
DISSERTATION ABSTRACTS INTERNATIONAL, 50(6) (DEC 89),
1794-A.
THE AUTHOR EXAMINES THE CIRCUMSTANCES SURROUNDING THE
FAILURE OF THE GENERAL ASSEMBLY TO IMPLEMENT MOST OF ITS
RESOLUTIONS AND OFFERS A REMEDY. HE IDENTIFIES THREE MAJOR
CAUSES OF THE FAILURE: MAJORITY RULE, THE PRINCIPLE OF
NATIONAL SOVEREIGNTY, AND THE INEQUALITY OF NATIONAL STATUS.
HE CONSIDERS TWO ALTERNATIVES TO MAJORITY RULE: CONSENSUS
BASED ON COMPROMISE AND WEIGHTED VOTING THAT ASSIGNS
PROPORTIONAL VOTING UNITS TO UN MEMBERS.

02991 EL TAYEB, A.A.
THE DEMOCRATIC PROCESS IN SUDAN
WORLD MARXIST REVIEW, 32(8) (AUG 89), 84-87.
THIS ARTICLE DESCRIBES THE LATEST EVENTS IN THE SUDAN
AND THE DEVELOPING COMPLEX SITUATION THERE, IT FINDS THAT
ENDING THE MILITARY DICTATORSHIP HAS NOT BROUGHT ABOUT THE
DESIRED CHANGES IN THAT COUNTRY. WAYS TO COUNTER THE RIGHT-
WING POLICY OF THE GOVERNMENT ARE SUGGESTED. FOUR MAJOR
TASKS OF THE CABINET ARE DETAILED.

02992 EL TAYEB, A.A.
THE IMPERATIVE: A DEMOCRATIC SOLUTION
WORLD MARXIST REVIEW, 32(12) (DEC 89), 75-77.
THE RECORD HAS DEMONSTRATED THAT MILITARY DICTATORSHIP
HAS NOT ONLY BEEN UNABLE TO RESOLVE THE NATION'S MAJOR
PROBLEMS, BUT THAT IT HAS ALSO INVARIABLY PLUNGED THE SUDAN
INTO SEVERE CRISES. CONVERSELY, NATIONAL DEMOCRATIC RULE, IN
SPITE OF ITS SHORTCOMINGS, OFFERS AMPLE OPPORTUNITY AND THE
MOST FAVOURABLE CONDITIONS FOR DEBATE, DIALOGUE AND A SEARCH
FOR THE BEST POSSIBLE WAY OUT OF THE CRISIS.

02993 EL-EID, G. E.
THE IMPACT OF ARAB-ISRAELI WARS ON ARAB STATES' BEHAVIOR
TOWARD THE UNITED STATES AND THE SOVIET UNION: 1965-1975
DISSERTATION ABSTRACTS INTERNATIONAL, 49(8) (FEB 89),
2382-A.
THE AUTHOR ANALYZES THE EFFECTS OF THE 1967 AND 1973
ARAB-ISRAELI WARS ON ARAB BEHAVIOR AND FOREIGN POLICY TOWARD
THE USA AND USSR. HE HYPOTHESIZES THAT THE WARS SHOULD
PRODUCE A MORE CONFLICTUAL ARAB BEHAVIOR TOWARD THE USA AND
A MORE COOPERATIVE BEHAVIOR TOWARD THE USSR. TO A LARGE
EXTENT, THIS STUDY CONFIRMS THE HYPOTHESIS ALTHOUGH ARAB
RESPONSE HAS NOT UNIFORM.

02994 ELADAILEH, A.M.
LEADERSHIP STYLE: THE CASE OF COMMISSIONER ROBERT DEMPSEY,
FLORIDA DEPARTMENT OF LAW ENFORCEMENT
DISSERTATION ABSTRACTS INTERNATIONAL, 50(5) (NOV 89),
1431-A.
ROBERT DEMPSEY WAS EXECUTIVE DIRECTOR OF THE FLORIDA
DEPARTMENT OF LAW ENFORCEMENT FROM 1982 TO 1988. THIS

DISSERTATION STUDIES THE THEORIES AND BEHAVIORS DEMPSEY UTILIZED IN HIS DECISION-MAKING PROCEDURES; HIS LEADERSHIP METHODS, QUALITIES, AND POWER; AND HIS RELATIONSHIPS WITH THE EXTERNAL ENVIRONMENT. IT CONCLUDES THAT DEMPSEY CONSCIOUSLY SOUGHT TO CREATE A NEW LEADERSHIP CLIMATE IN HIS DEPARTMENT AND WORKED WITHIN THE TERMS OF HIS PHILOSOPHY THAT HUMAN RESOURCES ARE THE KEY TO THE AGENCY'S SUCCESS.

02995 ELAIGWU, J.
NIGERIAN FEDERALISM UNDER CIVILIAN AND MILITARY REGIMES
PUBLIUS: THE JOURNAL OF FEDERALISM, 18(1) (WIN 88), 173-188.
NIGERIAN EXPERIENCES WITH MILITARY AND CIVILIAN RULE SUGGESTS THAT MILITARY RULE IS NOT ENTIRELY INCOMPATIBLE WITH FEDERALISM. THE HETEROGENEOUS AND CENTRIFUGAL FORCES THAT OPERATE IN A MULTINATIONAL POLICY LIKE NIGERIA MAKE THE USE OF FEDERAL PRINCIPLES A REASONABLE OPTION FOR MILITARY RULERS. TO SOME EXTENT, FEDERAL PRINCIPLES HAVE BECOME ENTRENCHED IN NIGERIA. TOO GREAT A VIOLATION OF THOSE PRINCIPLES BY A MILITARY REGIME CAN SPARK COMMUNAL CONFLICT AND DESTABLIZE THE REGIME. THE MAJOR DIFFERENCES IN THE OPERATION OF CIVILIAN AND MILITARY FEDERALISM ARE TO BE FOUND IN THE STYLE AND STRUCTURES OF ADMINISTRATION.

02996 ELAM, Y.
ISRAEL'S SOUTH AFRICAN SYNDROME
NEW OUTLOOK, 32(1 (287)) (JAN 89), 33-34.
ISRAEL IS A FACT OF LIFE THAT HAS WON UNIVERSAL RECOGNITION NOT ONLY BECAUSE OF THE STRENGTH IT HAS DEMONSTRATED BUT DUE TO THE INTERNATIONAL LEGITIMACY AFFORDED TO THE ZIONIST MOVEMENT FROM ITS INCEPTION. IT IS ON THIS BASIS THAT ONE MUST EXAMINE AND JUDGE ISRAEL'S BEHAVIOR TOWARD ITS ARAB CITIZENS AND TOWARD THE PALESTINIAN POPULATION IN THE OCCUPIED TERRITORIES. THIS IS WHERE THE COMPARISON BETWEEN ISRAEL AND SOUTH AFRICA, BETWEEN ISRAELI POLICY IN THE OCCUPIED TERRITORIES AND SOUTH AFRICAN APARTHEID, ARISES.

02997 ELANDER, I.; SCHEELE, A.
EVALUATING HOUSING RENEWAL POLICY IN SWEDEN: AN INTEREST-ORIENTED APPROACH
JOURNAL OF URBAN AFFAIRS, 11(4) (1989), 397-410.
DURING THE 1980S A NUMBER OF URBAN RENEWAL PROGRAMS HAVE BEEN INITIATED IN SWEDEN. IN THIS ARTICLE AN INTEREST-ORIENTED APPROACH FOR SYTEMATIC EVALUATION OF HOUSING RENEWAL IS PROPOSED. TAKING A CONTEXTUAL ANALYSIS AS A LOGICAL POINT OF DEPARTURE, TWO FURTHER LEVELS OF EVALUATION ARE IDENTIFIED. THE SECOND ONE IS THEORETICALLY CRUCIAL, I.E. , THE IDENTIFICATION OF INTERESTS AND ACTORS. ON THE THIRD LEVEL, IS THE TASK OF MAPPING THE IMPLEMENTATION STRUCTURE. HERE THE FOCUS IS ON THE WAYS THE DIFFERENT INTERESTS AND ACTORS CONFLICT AND HARMONIZE AS REGARDS THE FORMULATION AND WEIGHING OF NEEDS AND GOALS, THE MOBILIZATION OF RESOURCES, AND THE EXECUTION, REFLECTION, AND FEEDBACK OF POLICY. IT IS ARGUED THAT THESE THREE LEVELS TOGETHER FORM A CONCEPTUAL FRAMEWORK FAVORING COMPARATIVE ANALYSIS OF DIFFERENT CASES AND FACILITATING COMMUNICATION BETWEEN THEORISTS AND PRACTITIONERS. THE METHODOLOGICAL APPROACH IS ILUSTRATED BY REFERENCE TO CURRENT HOUSING RENEWAL PROGRAMS IN SWEDEN.

02998 ELAZAR, D.J.
COURT, CONGRESS, AND CENTRALIZATION
JOURNAL OF STATE GOVERNMENT, 62(1) (JAN 89), 46-49.
THE U.S. SUPREME COURT HAS STOOD THE CONSTITUTION ON ITS HEAD TO GIVE THE CONGRESS THE LAST WORD IN FEDERAL-STATE RELATIONS AT THE SAME TIME THAT CONGRESS HAS STEPPED UP ITS MANDATES ON STATES. DESPITE THIS, STATES ARE TAKING THE LEAD IN POLICY-MAKING, ENCOURAGED BY REAGAN'S NEW FEDERALISM. IN THIS WORST AND BEST OF TIMES, PROTECTING THE RIGHTS OF STATES UNDER THE CONSTITUTION IS IMPORTANT TO THE PRESERVATION OF ALL LIBERTIES.

02999 ELDERSVELD, S.J.; SIEMIENSKA, R.
ELITE CONFLICT ORIENTATIONS IN POLISH AND US CITIES
INTERNATIONAL POLITICAL SCIENCE REVIEW, 10(4) (OCT 89), 309-330.
THIS PAPER ANALYZES THE VALUES OF LOCAL LEADERS IN POLAND AND THE UNITED STATES. A MATCHED SUBSET OF CITIES IS USED. INTERVIEW DATA WERE COLLECTED IN THE 1983-84 PERIOD. THE FOCUS IS ON ELITE VIEWS ABOUT POLITICAL CONFLICT. STRIKING DIFFERENCES WERE FOUND IN THE TYPES OF PROBLEMS SEEN AS SERIOUS IN THEIR COMMUNITIES. YET, SIMILAR PROPORTIONS PERCEIVED AND TOLERATED CONFLICTS TODAY AS IN 1966. INDIVIDUAL LEVEL DATA ON LEADERSHIP POSITION, PARTY AFFILIATION OR STATUS, LENGTH OF TENURE AND AGE REVEALED DIFFERENCES. AND IN BOTH COUNTRIES COMMUNITY DIFFERENCES WERE CONSIDERABLE.

03000 ELDRIDGE, J.
THE CONTRAS AS POLITICAL GYPSIES
HEMISPHERE, 1(2) (WIN 89), 20-21.
DESPITE PRESIDENT GEORGE BUSH'S FEEBLE DECLARATIONS OF COMMITMENT TO THE NICARAGUAN CONTRAS, BOTH DEMOCRATIC AND REPUBLICAN MEMBERS OF CONGRESS HAVE DECLARED THAT THE CONTRA

PROJECT IS DEAD. WITHOUT INCREASED MILITARY AID, THE WAR WILL CONTINUE TO WIND DOWN, LEAVING THOUSANDS OF CONTRAS AND THEIR FAMILIES STRANDED IN HONDURAS. WASHINGTON'S SCENARIOS FOR THE FUTURE IN CENTRAL AMERICA FUNDAMENTALLY NEGLECT THE GENUINE HUMANITARIAN NEEDS OF THE CONTRAS AND THE POLITICAL NEEDS OF HONDURAS.

03001 ELGORAISH, G.A.
NUCLEARIZATION AND STABILITY IN THE MIDDLE EAST
DISSERTATION ABSTRACTS INTERNATIONAL, 49(7) (JAN 89), 1949-A.
THE NUCLEARIZATION OF THE ARAB-ISRAELI CONFLICT AREA HAS ENTAILED SEVERAL RISKS OF NUCLEAR WAR. THIS STUDY ENDEAVORS TO ASCERTAIN AND ASSESS THE LIKELIHOOD OF THE RISKS PRODUCING NUCLEAR WAR, BASED ON PAST EXPERIENCE AND A SURVEY OF EXPERT OPINION. IT ALSO TRACES THE DEVELOPMENT OF THE INTERNATIONAL NUCLEAR INDUSTRY SINCE THE 1950'S, USING THE PRODUCT LIFE CYCLE THEORY.

03002 ELHUSSEIN, A.M.
THE REVIVAL OF 'NATIVE ADMINISTRATION' IN THE SUDAN: A PRAGMATIC VIEW
PUBLIC CHOICE, 9(4) (SEP 89), 437-446.
THE BASIC THEME OF THIS PAPER IS TO TRACE THE PRAGMATIC ATTEMPTS OF DIFFERENT GOVERNMENTS IN THE SUDAN TO REVIVE THE SYSTEM OF NATIVE ADMINISTRATION. THE NEED FOR THIS REVIVAL BECAME CLEAR SHORTLY BEFORE THE OVERTHROW OF NIMEIRY'S GOVERNMENT IN APRIL 1985. THE APPROACHES TO THIS REVIVAL FOLLOWED TWO MAIN LINES. THE FIRST APPROACH ADOPTED PIECEMEAL REFORMS INITIATED BY INDIVIDUAL REGIONAL GOVERNMENTS BEFORE 1986. IN THE SECOND APPROACH THE CENTRAL GOVERNMENT ADOPTED A COMPREHENSIVE STRATEGY TO REVIVE NATIVE ADMINISTRATION. THE IMPLICATIONS OF THESE ATTEMPTS AND THEIR EXPECTED INFLUENCE ON THE NEW MULTI-PARTY SYSTEM IN THE SUDAN ARE BRIEFLY ANALYSED IN THIS PAPER.

03003 ELIA, L.
THE MARSHALL PLAN AND THE EVOLUTION OF DEMOCRACY IN ITALY
ITALIAN JOURNAL, III(1) (1989), 11-14.
THE AUTHOR ANALYZES THE IMPACT OF THE MARSHALL PLAN ON THE HISTORY AND ECONOMY OF ITALY AS IT RE-EMERGED AS A DEMOCRATIC NATION AFTER WORLD WAR II UNDER THE LEADERSHIP OF ALCIDE DE GASPERI.

03004 ELIA, L.
THE REPUBLICAN CONSTITUTION AND THE DEVELOPMENT OF DEMOCRACY IN ITALY
ITALIAN JOURNAL, III(4) (1989), 8-12.
THE AUTHOR REVIEWS MAJOR PROVISIONS OF THE ITALIAN CONSTITUTION RATIFIED IN 1947 AND SURVEYS THE BACKGROUND TO THE CONSTITUTION.

03005 ELIASON, L.C.
THE POLITICS OF EXPERTISE: LEGITIMATING EDUCATIONAL REFORM IN SWEDEN AND THE FEDERAL REPUBLIC OF GERMANY
DISSERTATION ABSTRACTS INTERNATIONAL, 49(12) (JUN 89), 3856-A.
EXPERTS NOT ONLY PROVIDE A BASIS FOR RATIONAL DECISION-MAKING BUT ALSO CONTRIBUTE TO THE LEGITIMATION OF STATE ACTIVITY. THE EDUCATIONAL REFORMS ASSOCIATED WITH THE INTRODUCTION OF COMPREHENSIVE SECONDARY SCHOOLS IN SWEDEN AND WEST GERMANY PROVIDE TWO CASES FOR EXAMINING THE ROLE OF EXPERTISE IN POLICY-MAKING.

03006 ELIOU, C.
VIEW FROM ATHENS
NATO'S SIXTEEN NATIONS, 34(4) (AUG 89), 14.
AS A RESULT OF AN AGREEMENT BETWEEN THE COMMUNISTS AND THE CONSERVATIVE NEW ECONOMY PARTY, GREECE HAS ACQUIRED A NEW GOVERNMENT THAT WILL HOLD OFFICE UNTIL OCTOBER 1989. ITS RESTRICTED MANDATE CENTERS AROUND ENSURING FAIR ELECTIONS IN THE AUTUMN AND CLEANING UP THE RASH OF SCANDALS THAT CONTRIBUTED TO THE DEFEAT OF THE SOCIALIST GOVERNMENT OF ANDREAS PAPANDREOU.

03007 ELKILANI, M. A.
AN EVALUATION OF AGRICULTURAL WATER PROBLEMS IN LIBYA AS AFFECTED BY GOVERNMENT POLICIES
DISSERTATION ABSTRACTS INTERNATIONAL, 49(8) (FEB 89), 2322-A.
THE AUTHOR PROBES THE IMPACT OF WATER INSTITUTIONS AND GOVERNMENT POLICY ON AGRICULTURAL WATER PROBLEMS IN LIBYA FROM 1962 TO 1982. HE FINDS THAT THE PROBLEMS WERE CAUSED BY THE STRUCTURES OF INSTITUTIONS AND GOVERNMENTAL POLICIES.

03008 ELKIN, S.L.
A CHINA WITNESS
PS: POLITICAL SCIENCE AND POLITICS, XXII(3) (SEP 89), 579-580.
IN SEVEN WEEKS FROM LATE APRIL TO EARLY JUNE 1989, CHINA DISPLAYED TO THE WORLD POLITICS AT ITS BEST AND WORST. IT IS IN THE COMPARISON OF THE TWO THAT THE TRUE HORROR OF WHAT OCCURRED CAN BE SEEN.

03009 ELKINS, D.J.
FACING OUR DESTINY: RIGHTS AND CANADIAN DISTINCTIVENESS
CANADIAN JOURNAL OF POLITICAL SCIENCE, 22(4) (DEC 89),
699-716.
THIS ARTICLE ADDRESSES THE SUBJECT OF CANADIAN POLITICAL
CULTURE AND TRADITIONS, AND IN PARTICULAR EMPHASIZED THAT
SOME DISTINCTIVE FEATURES OF CANADIANNESS ARE REVEALED IN
THE CONCEPTION OF RIGHTS WHICH IS ENTRENCHED IN THE CHARTER
OF FREEDOM AND RIGHTS. THE CANADIAN CONSTITUTION CONTAINS
SEVERAL DISTINCTIVE RIGHTS NOT FOUND IN THE UNITED STATES
CONSTITUTION. INDEED, THE COLLECTIVE AND COMMUNITY-BASED
RIGHTS CANADIANS TAKE FOR GRANTED ARE INIMICAL TO AMERICAN
LIBERAL TRADITIONS. NEGATIVE RIGHTS OR INTERPRETIVE
PROVISIONS, SUCH AS THE NON OBSTANTE CLAUSE, ARE UNIQUE TO
CANADA AMONG WESTERN DEMOCRACIES. THE AUTHOR ARGUES THAT
THESE RIGHTS DERIVE FROM THE COUNTRY'S HISTORICAL CONCERNS
WITH RELIGIOUS AND LINGUISTIC COMMUNITIES--ESPECIALLY IN
QUEBEC--AND THAT THEY IN TURN CONDITION HOW POLITICS MUST BE
CONDUCTED IN CANADA.

03010 ELLES, J.
ELECTION 1989
EUROPE, 287 (JUN 89), 24-25.
AS EUROPEAN VOTERS GO TO THE POLLS THIS MONTH TO ELECT
THEIR MEMBERS OF THE EUROPEAN PARLIAMENT (MEP) FOR THE THIRD
TIME IN HISTORY, NOW IS THE TIME TO LOOK AT THE PARLIAMENT'S
RECORD OVER THE PAST FIVE YEARS, ITS LIKELY PRIORITIES FOR
THE NEXT FIVE, AND THE IMPORTANCE OF THIS ELECTORAL PROCESS
TO THE UNITED STATES. AS TO THE LAST, A CONTINUING AND OPEN
DIALOGUE BETWEEN AMERICAN AND EUROPEAN ELECTED DECISION-
MAKERS, WITH AN INPUT FROM THE TRANS-ATLANTIC BUSINESS
COMMUNITY, WILL BE VITAL TO KEEP THE NUMBER OF
MISUNDERSTANDINGS TO A MINIMUM, WHILE SIMULTANEOUSLY
INJECTING IDEAS ON HOW TO SOLVE PROBLEMS BEFORE THEY REACH
BOILING POINTS. THE AIM MUST BE TO BROADEN THE POLITICAL
DIALOGUE, OVER THE YEARS AHEAD, PERHAPS BY A "DECLARATION OF
INTENT" BETWEEN THE TWO SIDES TO DEEPEN THEIR COOPERATION.

03011 ELLIOT, J.
ADMINISTRATIVE REFORM: ANOTHER JAPANESE SUCCESS?
PUBLIC ADMINISTRATION, 67(3) (FAL 89), 339-344.
THIS ARTICLE, DEALING WITH ADMINISTRATIVE REFORM IN
JAPAN, TALKS ABOUT THE PROBLEMS IN THE PUBLIC SECTOR AS WELL
AS THE MACHINERY AND PROCESS OF THE ATTEMPT TO MAKE CHANGE.
IT ANALYSES FIVE REPORTS ISSUED BETWEEN 1981 AND 1983 AIMS
TO RESTORE FISCAL BALANCE WITHOUT INCREASED TAXATION. THE
IMPLEMENTATION OF THE REFORM MEASURES IS DETAILED.

03012 ELLIOT, K. A.
TOO MANY VOICES OF AMERICA
FOREIGN POLICY, (77) (WIN 89), 113-131.
THIS ARTICLE EXAMINES THE KEY ROLE THAT THE UNITED
STATES HAS PLAYED IN THE WORD OF INTERNATIONAL BROADCASTING
SINCE WORLD WAR II, AND THE SUBSEQUENT DEBATE ABOUT THE
GOALS AND STRATEGIES OF AMERICA'S INTERNATIONAL BROADCASTING.
IT EXAMINES THE BROADCASTING STRUCTURE, THE BIAS IN
BROADCASTING, AND THE GLOBAL RANGE POSSIBILITIES, IT SUGGEST
A RESTRUCTURING OF AMERICA'S INTERNATIONAL BROADCASTING
EFFORTS IN ORDER FOR AMERICA TO RETAIN ITS PLACE IN
INTERNATIONAL BROADCASTING.

03013 ELLIOTT, J.E.
GORBACHEV'S PERESTROIKA
CONTEMPORARY POLICY ISSUES, VII(1) (JAN 89), 35-52.
THIS ARTICLE EXAMINES PERESTROIKA, OR THE "STRUCTURAL
TRANSFORMATION OF THE ECONOMY." IT EXPLICATES THE BASES FOR
PERESTROIKA, THE REFORMS' SALIENT ELEMENTS AND THEIR
DIFFERENCES FROM BOTH STALINIST AND POST-STALINIST
EXPERIENCE, THE REFORMS' RELATIONS TO DEMOCRATIZATION AND TO
PRE-STALINIST BOLSHEVIK IDEOLOGY, AND MAJOR ALTERNATIVE
SCENARIOS FOR THE FUTURE.

03014 ELLIOTT, J.E.; CLARK, B.S.
RICHARD HENRY TAWNEY ON THE DEMOCRATIC ECONOMY
INTERNATIONAL JOURNAL OF SOCIAL ECONOMICS, 16(3) (1989),
44-58.
THE RELATIONSHIP BETWEEN CAPITALISM AND DEMOCRACY HAS
BEEN QUESTIONED RECENTLY BY ECONOMISTS AND POLITICAL
SCIENTISTS. IN VIEW OF THIS DEBATE, A REAPPRAISAL IS MADE OF
THE WRITINGS OF RICHARD HENRY TAWNEY, THE ENGLISH ECONOMIST
AND SOCIAL PHILOSOPHER. CENTRAL TO HIS PERSONAL,
INTELLECTUAL AND SOCIO-POLITICAL PROJECT WAS THE IDEAL OF
THE CREATION OF A GENUINELY DEMOCRATIC COMMUNITY. CAPITALISM,
THE PRINCIPLES OF A DEMOCRATIC ECONOMY, INSTITUTIONS AND
PROCESSES, AND THE ALTERNATIVE PERSPECTIVES ON POLITICAL
ECONOMY ARE DISCUSSED.

03015 ELLIS, A.K.
MANIPULATION AND MICRO-MANAGEMENT: THE CONGRESSIONAL
DEFENSE BUDGET PROCESS
DISSERTATION ABSTRACTS INTERNATIONAL, 49(12) (JUN 89),
3862-A.
THE LEGISLATIVE BRANCH MANIPULATES AND MICRO-MANAGES THE
DEFENSE BUDGET AS A MEANS OF OBSTRUCTING, PURSUING, OR

IMPLEMENTING POLICIES THAT OFTEN DIFFER FROM THE EXECUTIVE
BRANCH'S. SINCE THE VIETNAM AND WATERGATE TUMULT, THE BUDGET
PROCESS HAS BECOME THE PRIMARY INSTRUMENT OF LEGISLATIVE
BRANCH CONTROL VIS-A-VIS THE EXECUTIVE BRANCH. NOWHERE HAS
CONGRESSIONAL WILLINGNESS TO USE THE BUDGET TO CHALLENGE
EXECUTIVE BRANCH INITIATIVES BEEN MORE EVIDENT THAN IN
DEFENSE MATTERS.

03016 ELLIS, G.B.; HANNA, K.E.
EVALUATING BIOMEDICAL TECHNOLOGY FOR THE U.S. CONGRESS:
ANIMAL EXPERIMENTATION AND PUBLIC POLICY
POLICY STUDIES REVIEW, 8(2) (WIN 89), 357-367.
THE OFFICE OF TECHNOLOGY ASSESSMENT IS A NONPARTISAN
SUPPORT AGENCY THAT SERVES THE U.S. CONGRESS. IT IS THE
PRIMARY AGENCY OF CONGRESS CHARGED WITH ANALYZING THE
INFLUENCE OF SCIENCE AND TECHNOLOGY ON SOCIETY AND THE
IMPLICATIONS FOR FEDERAL POLICY. IN THIS ESSAY, THE AUTHORS
LOOK AT THE OTA AND AT BIOMEDICAL TECHNOLOGY AS IT APPLIES
TO ANIMAL EXPERIMENTATION AND PUBLIC POLICY.

03017 ELLIS, H.A.
MONTESQUIEU'S MODERN POLITICS: THE SPIRIT OF THE LAWS AND
THE PROBLEM OF MODERN MONARCHY IN OLD REGIME FRANCE
HISTORY OF POLITICAL THOUGHT, X(4) (WIN 89), 665-700.
THE AUTHOR ARGUES THAT MONTESQUIEU'S THE SPIRIT OF THE
LAWS REVEALS ITS AUTHOR TO BE AN AMLIGIOUS MODERNIST,
ANXIOUS ABOUT THE PRESENT THAT HE APPLAUDED AND NOSTALGIC
FOR PASTS THAT HE NEVER CEASED TO ADMIRE.

03018 ELLIS, K.
STORIES WITHOUT ENDINGS: DECONSTRUCTIVE THEORY AND
POLITICAL PRACTICE
SOCIALIST REVIEW, 19(2) (APR 89), 37-52.
THE AUTHOR DISCUSSES THE EFFECT OF DECONSTRUCTION THEORY
ON THE FEMINIST MOVEMENT AND ON WOMEN'S PERCEPTIONS OF
THEMSELVES. DECONSTRUCTION MAKIES THE ASSERTION THAT THE
"AUTHENTIC FEMALE SUBJECT", THE ONE WHICH DEPENDED UPON THE
"TRUTH" OF HER EXPERIENCE WAS AS CONSTRUCTED AS THE OLD
DISCRIMINITORY PERCEPTIONS OF MALE-DOMINATED SOCIETY.

03019 ELLIS, M.H.
THE TASK BEFORE US: CONTEMPORARY JEWISH THOUGHT AND THE
CHALLENGE OF SOLIDARITY
AMERICAN-ARAB AFFAIRS, (30) (FAL 89), 52-71.
TO BEGIN TO ANALYZE JEWISH LIFE IN THE PRESENT AND THE
THEMES WHICH ARE IMPORTANT TO JEWS AND JEWISH COMMUNITIES
AROUND THE WORLD, IT IS IMPORTANT TO ARTICULATE THE
THEOLOGICAL UNDERPINNINGS OF SUCH UNDERSTANDING. THIS
ARTICLE EXPLORES HOLOCAUST THELGY WHICH SPEAKS IN A
PROFOUND WAY TO THE JEWISH PEOPLE, ONE WHICH HAS BECOME
NORMATIVE IN JEWISH CONVERSATION AND ACTIVITY. IT ALSO
EXPLORES JEWISH RESPONSE TO THE PALESTINIAN UPRISING, AND
THE NEED FOR SOLIDARITY AND CRITICAL THOUGHT. IT CONCLUDES
THAT JEWISH RELIGIOUS THOUGHT HAS REACHED AN IMPASSE THAT
CAN BE BROKEN BY THE EMBRACE OF FORMER ENEMIES, WESTERN
CHRISTIANS, AND NEW ENEMIES, THE PALESTINIAN PEOPLE.

03020 ELLISON, C.G.; GAY, D.G.
BLACK POLITICAL PARTICIPATION REVISITED: A TEST OF
COMPENSATORY, ETHNIC COMMUNITY, AND PUBLIC ARENA MODELS
SOCIAL SCIENCE QUARTERLY, 70(1) (MAR 89), 101-119.
NUMEROUS STUDIES HAVE DEMONSTRATED THAT BLACKS TEND TO
PARTICIPATE IN POLITICAL ACTIVITIES AT HIGHER LEVELS THAN
WHITES. IN THIS STUDY DATA FROM THE 1968 AND 1980 AMERICAN
NATIONAL ELECTION SURVEYS ARE USED TO ASSESS THE ETHNIC
COMMUNITY AND COMPENSATORY EXPLANATIONS OF THIS PATTERN, AND
A STRUCTURAL PUBLIC ARENA MODEL IS ADVANCED. THE RESULTS
SUGGEST THE FRUITFULNESS OF FURTHER RESEARCH ON THE
INFLUENCE OF INTERPERSONAL CONTACTS AND SOCIAL NETWORKS ON
BLACK POLITICAL PARTICIPATION.

03021 ELLMAN, M.
THE USSR IN THE 1990'S: STRUGGLING OUT OF STAGNATION
THE ECONOMIST INTELLIGENCE UNIT, LONDON, GB, 1989, .
THE AUTHOR ANALYZES GORBACHEV'S REFORMS, IDENTIFYING
THOSE THAT ARE LIKELY TO WORK NOW, THOSE THAT MAY WORK IN
THE LONG TERM, AND THOSE THAT ARE ONLY PIOUS HOPES. HE ALSO
PRESENTS FIVE SCENARIOS FOR ECONOMIC REFORM IN THE 1990S AND
DISCUSSES THE CAUSES UNDERLYING THE NEW SOVIET THINKING ON
DEFENSE.

03022 ELLNER, S.
ORGANIZED LABOR'S POLITICAL INFLUENCE AND PARTY TIES IN
VENEZUELA: ACCION DEMOCRATICA AND ITS LABOR LEADERSHIP
JOURNAL OF INTERAMERICAN STUDIES AND WORLD AFFAIRS, 31(4)
(WIN 89), 91-129.
THIS ARTICLE EXAMINES THE INTERACTION BETWEEN ACCION
DEMOCRATICA'S (AD) LABOR BUREAU AND THE AD ORGANIZATION
SINCE 1958 IN ORDER TO DETERMINE WHETHER THE APPEARANCE OF
TRANQUIL RELATIONS BETWEEN LABOR AND THE PARTY OVER A PERIOD
OF TIME IS BORNE OUT BY THE FACTS, IT PUTS TO THE TEST THOSE
ANALYSES WHICH VIEW AD'S RELATIONS WITH ITS LABOR SEGMENT AS
LARGELY FREE OF CONFLICT. THE LONG RANGE GOALS OF AD-LABOR,
ITS RELATIONS WITH DIFFERENT FACTIONS WITHIN THE PARTY AND

ITS SUCCESS AS A POLITICAL BARGAINER ARE ANALYSED.

03023 ELLNER, S.
VENEZUELA: NO EXCEPTION
NACLA REPORT ON THE AMERICAS, XXIII(1) (MAY 89), 8-10.
AFTER DECADES OF PROSPERITY CAME TO AN END IN THE EARLY
1980S, ONLY THE MILITANT RHETORIC OF LIBERAL SOCIAL DEMOCRAT
CARLOS ANDRES PEREZ KEPT ALIVE POPULAR FAITH IN VENEZUELA'S
VAUNTED DEMOCRACY. TOUGH TALK RETURNED HIM TO THE PRESIDENCY
AFTER A TEN-YEAR HIATUS, BUT, AS NATIONWIDE RIOTS IN MARCH
SHOWED, PEREZ HAS YET TO TRANSLATE RHETORIC INTO REALITY.

03024 ELLSWORTH, R.
MAINTAINING US SECURITY IN AN ERA OF FISCAL PRESSURE
INTERNATIONAL SECURITY, 13(4) (SPR 89), 16-24.
THE ARTICLE ANALYZES SEVERAL OF THE FISCAL, BUDGETARY,
AND CONTRAVENING SECURITY AND DEFENSE PRESSURES THAT THE
BUSH ADMINISTRATION IS FACING. THESE INCLUDE: LIMITING
DEFENSE SPENDING TO HELP BALANCE THE BUDGET DEFICIT WHILE AT
THE SAME TIME MODERNIZING CERTAIN CONVENTIONAL AND NUCLEAR
WEAPONS SYSTEMS; DEPLOYING ADAQUETE FORCES TO PROTECT US
INTERESTS THROUGHOUT THE WORLD WITHOUT SPREADING US
RESOURCES TOO THIN: AND FOLLOWING THE SOVIET LEAD IN NUCLEAR
ARMS AND CONVENTIONAL ARMS REDUCTION WITHOUT COMPROMISING US
SECURITY OR THE SECURITY OF US ALLIES. THERE IS ALSO AN
ADDITIONAL, DEEPER DILEMMA OF HOW TO GUARD AGAINST A NEW
SOVIET MILITARY THREAT AFTER A FEW YEARS' BREATHING SPELL
WHILE TAKING ADVANTAGE IN THE MEANTIME OF THE SOVIET'S
ATTEMPTS TO SCALE DOWN WORLD TENSIONS AND HOSTILITIES.

03025 ELLWAND, G.
INSIDER TRADING: JAPAN'S GOVERNMENT IS ROCKED BY SCANDAL
MACLEAN'S (CANADA'S NEWS MAGAZINE), 102(2) (JAN 89), 22-23.
A GROWING STOCK SCANDAL--AS WELL AS THE PASSAGE OF AN
UNPOPULAR THREE-PER CENT SALES TAX--HAS UNDERMINED THE
POPULARITY OF THE JAPANESE GOVERNMENT. AS THE JAPANESE MEDIA
EXPOSED AN EVER-INCREASING NUMBER OF INFLUENTIAL POLITICIANS,
INCLUDING KEY MEMBERS OF PARLIAMENT, WHO HAVE BEEN INVOLVED
IN INSIDE TRADING WITH THE RECRUIT COMPANY, PRIME MINISTER
NOBORU TAKESHITA IS RESHUFFLING HIS CABINET IN AN EFFORT TO
DISTANCE HIMSELF FROM THE SCANDAL. HOWEVER, THE SUDDEN
RESIGNATION OF NEWLY APPOINTED JUSTICE MINISTER TAKASHI
HASEGAWA HAS DEALT YET ANOTHER EMBARRASSING BLOW TO THE
GOVERNMENT.

03026 ELLYNE, M.J.
ECONOMIC RELATIONS AND ALLIANCE COHESION IN EASTERN EUROPE:
A HISTORICAL QUANTITATIVE STUDY, 1950-1983
DISSERTATION ABSTRACTS INTERNATIONAL, 49(7) (JAN 89),
1950-A.
THE PURPOSE OF THIS ANALYSIS IS TO INVESTIGATE FIVE
COMMONLY DEBATED HYPOTHESES CONCERNING MACRORELATIONSHIPS
AMONG EAST BLOC MEMBERS' DOMESTIC, INTRABLOC, AND INTERBLOC
ECONOMIC CONDITIONS AND THEIR ALLIANCE COHESION. THE
HYPOTHESES ARE EXPLORED WITHIN A CONCEPTUAL FRAMEWORK OF
EXCHANGE BETWEEN ECONOMIC AND POLITICAL GOODS, FIRST BY
HISTORICAL REVIEW OF EAST EUROPEAN POLICIES AND EVENTS AND
THEN BY QUANTITATIVE ANALYSIS. THIS STUDY UTILIZES ECONOMIC
AND EVENTS DATA (COPDAB) AND ADVANCED QUANTITATIVE METHODS,
INCLUDING THE LISREL PROGRAM.

03027 ELSOM, J.
THE MUDDLED MIND OF MR. HURD
CONTEMPORARY REVIEW, 254(1478) (MAR 89), 132-138.
THE AUTHOR DISCUSSES THE BRITISH "WHITE PAPER ON
BROADCASTING" AND ITS IMPLICATIONS FOR BRITISH TELEVISION.
THE PROPOSED LEGISLATION ATTEMPTS TO ENSURE QUALITY
PROGRAMMING, BUT GIVES THE GOVERNMENT A LICENCE TO CENSOR
ALMOST AT WILL. THE AUTHOR DISCUSSES SEVERAL FLAWS IN THE
PAPER'S REASONING AND SUGGESTS POSSIBLE WAYS OF SOLVING THE
DILEMMAS IT PRESENTS.

03028 ELVIK, H.
VIEW FROM OSLO
NATO'S SIXTEEN NATIONS, 34(7) (DEC 89), 14.
NORWEGIAN PRIME MINISTER JAN P. SYSE OF THE CONSERVATIVE
PARTY HEADS A COALITION COMPOSED OF HIS PARTY, THE CENTRE
PARTY, AND THE CHRISTIAN PEOPLE'S PARTY. IN ORDER TO MUSTER
A MAJORITY IN PARLIAMENT, SYSE'S GOVERNMENT MUST ALSO HAVE
THE VOTES OF THE PROGRESS PARTY. THIS RARE CONSTRUCTION OF A
COALITION GOVERNMENT WITHOUT AN INSTITUTIONALIZED MAJORITY
IN PARLIAMENT IS IN FOR A BUMPY POLITICAL ROAD AHEAD, BUT
ITS DOWNFALL DOES NOT APPEAR IMMINENT. THE MOST SERIOUS
THREAT TO SYSE COMES FROM WITHIN THE COALITIONS. ON THE
QUESTION OF NORWAY'S FUTURE RELATIONS WITH EUROPE AND THE
EEC, TWO OF THE COALITION PARTIES SUPPORT OPPOSITE POSITIONS.

03029 ELY, E.S.
ARMS TRANSFERS AND THE THIRD WORLD: TRENDS AND DEVELOPMENTS
AVAILABLE FROM NTIS, NO. AD-A207 890/5/GAR, JUL 88, 23.
THE ROLE OF ARMS SALES IN WORLD POLITICS HAS GROWN
TREMENDOUSLY SINCE THE END OF WORLD WAR II, PARTICULARLY IN
THE LAST DECADE. THE IMPORTANCE OF ARMS SALES IN
INCREASINGLY EVIDENT IN THE FOREIGN POLICIES OF SUPPLIER AND
RECIPIENT NATIONS, IN REGIONAL POLITICS AND BALANCES, AND IN
EAST-WEST COMPETITION AS IN NORTH-SOUTH RELATIONS. ARMS
SALES HAVE BECOME IN RECENT YEARS A CRUCIAL DIMENSION OF
INTERNATIONAL AFFAIRS. THIS PAPER EXAMINES SEVERAL POSTWAR
TRENDS IN ARMS TRANSFERS AND LOOKS AT WHAT THEIR IMPACT WILL
BE ON THE CONDUCT OF CONFLICT IN THE FUTURE. ONE OF THE
CHALLENGES ENCOUNTERED WHILE RESEARCHING THIS TOPIC WAS THE
SHEER COMPLEXITY OF THE GLOBAL POLITICS OF ARMS SALES. WHAT
WE ARE TALKING ABOUT HERE ARE THE POLITICAL MOTIVES,
ECONOMIC INCENTIVES, AND THE SECURITY PERSPECTIVES OF THE
WORLD. ARMS SALES HAVE ALMOST BECOME A DAILY, ROUTINE
OCCURRENCE. THE INTENT OF THIS PAPER IS TO INCREASE THE
READER'S KNOWLEDGE OF AN EXTREMELY COMPLEX AND NOT
WELLUNDERSTOOD PHENOMENON.

03030 EMMERT, C.F.
JUDICIAL REVIEW IN STATE SUPREME COURTS: 1981-1985
DISSERTATION ABSTRACTS INTERNATIONAL, 50(5) (NOV 89),
1421-A.
THE PRIMARY GOAL OF THIS STUDY IS TO ASSESS THE
POLICYMAKING ROLE WHICH STATE SUPREME COURTS PLAY IN STATE
POLITICAL SYSTEMS. CASES INVOLVING JUDICIAL REVIEW OF STATE
LAWS DECIDED IN THE SUPREME COURTS OF ALL FIFTY STATES ARE
EXAMINED. LEVELS OF JUDICIAL REVIEW OPPORTUNITY AND ACTIVISM
ARE COMPARED ACROSS STATE SUPREME COURTS. STATE-LEVEL
FACTORS ASSOCIATED WITH JUDICIAL REVIEW OPPORTUNITY AND
ACTIVISM ARE ANALYZED.

03031 EMMERT, M.A.
IMPROVING BUSINESS-GOVERNMENT RELATIONS: WHAT IS THE ROLE
AND RESPONSIBILITY OF SCHOOLS OF PUBLIC AFFAIRS
AMERICAN REVIEW OF PUBLIC ADMINISTRATION, 19(2) (JUN 89),
163-173.
THE AUTHOR PROBES THE ROLE OF SCHOOLS OF PUBLIC AFFAIRS
IN PROMOTING AND FACILITATING BUSINESSGOVERNMENT COOPERATION.
A SURVEY OF NATIONAL ASSOCIATION OF SCHOOLS OF PUBLIC
AFFAIRS AND ADMINISTRATION (NASPAA) MEMBERS WAS CONDUCTED TO
DETERMINE IF PUBLIC ADMINISTRATION SCHOOLS ARE CONCERNED
ABOUT THIS ISSUE AND IF THEY ARE INVOLVED IN ACTIVITIES
INTENDED TO FOSTER PUBLIC-PRIVATE RELATIONS AND CROSS-SECTOR
UNDERSTANDING. RESULTS OF THE SURVEY INDICATE THAT SCHOOLS
HAVE A MODEST BUT INCREASING CONCERN ABOUT BUSINESS-
GOVERNMENT RELATIONS AND THAT THIS CONCERN IS TRANSLATED
INTO SOME ACTIONS ON THEIR PART. SCHOOLS OF PUBLIC AFFAIRS
TAKE THEIR PUBLIC SERVICE MISSIONS SERIOUSLY AND ARE ENGAGED
IN A WIDE RANGE OF ACTIVITIES AIMED AT SUPPORTING THE PUBLIC
SECTOR PRACTITIONER. MUCH LESS ENERGY IS DIRECTED TOWARD
PRIVATE SECTOR CONSTITUTENCIES OR TOWARD PROMOTING CROSS
SECTOR COOPERATION OR UNDERSTANDING. A LISTING OF ACTIVITIES
AIMED AT PROMOTING BUSINESS-GOVERNMENT RELATIONS IS COMPILED
AND ACTIVITIES RESPONDENTS THOUGHT TO BE EFFECTIVE ARE
IDENTIFIED.

03032 EMUDONG, C.P.
THE EFFECTS OF WAR-TIME CONTROLS IN THE GOLD-COAST, 1935-
45: A CASE OF THE VULNERABILITY OF AFRICAN SOCIAL CLASSES
IN A DEFENDENT COLONIAL ECONOMY
SCANDINAVIAN JOURNAL OF DEVELOPMENT ALTERNATIVES, 8(4)
(DEC 89), 195-208.
THIS ARTICLE IS PRIMARILY CONCERNED WITH ANALYSING THE
REASONS FOR AND THE EFFECTS OF THE BRITISH SECOND WORLD WAR-
TIME CONTROLS IN THE GOLD COAST, WITH A VIEW TO EXPOSING THE
IMPACT OF THE BRITISH COLONIAL AND IMPERIAL OBJECTIVES AND
PERFORMANCE ON THE EMERGENT SOCIAL CLASSES OF THIS COLONY,
AT THE OUTSET, THE PAPER SPELT OUT WHAT THE CONTROLS STOOD
FOR: FAR FROM BEING MERELY A SET OF EXPEDIENTS TO GRAPPLE
WITH THE PROBLEMS OF THE WAR SITUATION, THE CONTROLS WERE
PART AND PARCEL OF A NEW, INTERVENTIONIST AND CENTRALIST
BRITISH COLONIAL POLITICOECONOMIC POLICY WHICH HAD BEEN
INITIATED EVEN BEFORE THE OUTBREAK OF THE WAR IN RESPONSE TO
THE DICTATES OF THE GREAT DEPRESSION OF THE LATE 1920S TO
THE MID1930S. IN A NUTSHELL, THE CONTROLS NOT ONLY STIFLED
THE DEVELOPMENT OF THE INDIGENOUS RURAL AND URBAN PETTY
BOURGEOISIE INTO A FULLY-PLEDGED BOURGEOISIE, BUT ALSO
UNDERMINED THE SENSE OF CO-OPERATION WHICH HAD EXISTED
BETWEEN THESE EMERGENT CLASSES IN THE 1930S. AND BY
EXTENSION, THE ARTICLE AS A WHOLE GOES A LONG WAY TO TESTIFY
THE VALIDITY OF I.G. SHIVJI'S CONTENTION THAT THE MAIN
REASON WHY "THE SO-CALLED 'NATIONAL BOURGEOISIES' IN AFRICA..
.LACK BOTH THE HISTORICAL MATURITY OF THEIR METROPOLITAN
COUNTERPART AND THE LATTER'S OBJECTIVE ECONOMIC BASE' IS
THAT 'THE NATURAL PROCESS OF THE DEVELOPMENT OF THE
AUTHENTIC NATIONAL BOURGEOISIES AND THE NATIONAL CAPITALISMS
IN AFRICA WAS IRREVERSIBLY ARRESTED BY THESE COUNTRIES
COMING INTO CONTACT WITH ADVANCED CAPITALISMS" HENCE
'AFRICAN STRUCTURES AND CLASSES DEVELOPED IN THE SHADOW OF
FORMAL OR INFORMAL COLONIALISM'.50

03033 ENDICOTT, J.
ASIA FACES THE NEXT CENTURY
NATO'S SIXTEEN NATIONS, 34(2) (APR 89), 17, 19.
THE AUTHOR SURVEYS SOME OF THE SECURITY ISSUES FACING
THE ASIAN POWERS OF JAPAN, CHINA, AND KOREA AS THEY MAKE THE
TRANSITION INTO THE 21ST CENTURY.

03034 ENELOW, J., M.; HINICH, M., J.
  A GENERAL PROBABILISTIC SPATIAL THEORY OF ELECTIONS
  PUBLIC CHOICE, 61(2) (MAY 89), 101-114.
    THE PURPOSE OF THE PAPER IS TO CONSTRUCT A MORE GENERAL
  PROBABILISTIC THEORY OF ELECTIONS TO SHOW WHAT CAUSES
  EQUILIBRIUM AND DISEQUILIBRIUM IN TWO-CANDIDATE ELECTIONS.
  PROSPECTIVE UNCERTAINTY AMONG VOTERS, REDUCED POLICY
  SALIENCE, RISK AVERSE VOTERS, AND RESTRICTIONS ON THE SIZE
  OF THE FEASIBLE SET OF POLICY LOCATIONS ARE ALL STABILIZING
  FACTORS IN TWO-CANDIDATE ELECTIONS.

03035 ENGELSTEIN, D.
  WHAT DOES NEW THINKING MEAN FOR US
  POLITICAL AFFAIRS, LXVIII(7) (JUL 89), 37-40.
    IT SHOULD GO WITHOUT SAYING THAT FOR THE CPUSA, LIKE FOR
  THE CPSU AND OTHER PARTIES, THE NEW THINKING DOES NOT MEAN
  DOWNPLAYNG OR NEGATING OUR MANY IMPORTANT ACHIEVEMENTS. NOW,
  HOWEVER, THE PARTY NEEDS TO EXAMINE THE RELATIONSHIP OF
  OBJECTIVE AND SUBJECTIVE FACTORS INFLUENCING THE GROWTH AND
  DECLINE OF WORKING CLASS CONCIOUSNESS AT DIFFERENT TIMES AND
  IN VARIOUS STRATA OF THE CLASS. PARTY MEMBERS SHOULD ENTER
  INTO CRITICAL, FRUITFUL AND FRATERNAL DISCUSSION WITH THE
  "HISTORICAL SOCIOLOGICAL ANALYSIS" OF THE NEW SCHOOL OF
  LABOR HISTORIANS IN THE USA, AND CONSIDER WHAT WEIGHT TO
  GIVE INFINITELY MORE COMPLEX SOCIAL REALITY IN WHICH HUMAN
  BEINGS ARE TORN IN DIFFERENT AND OFTEN CONFLICTING
  DIRECTIONS BY LOYALTIES ROOTED IN UNION, CLASS, ETHNIC,
  GENDER, IDEOLOGICAL, REGIONAL AND GENERAL IDENTIFICATIONS.

03036 ENGLAND, R.S.
  COMING TO TERMS WITH CONGRESSIONAL REFORM.
  AMERICAN SPECTATOR, (NOV 89), 22-2.
    THIS ARTICLE ASSESSES THE PRESENT SITUATION THAT EXISTS
  IN REFERENCE TO FUNDING POLITICAL COMPAIGNS. IT TARGETS THE
  GROWING SPENDING GAP BETWEEN INCUMBENTS AND CHALLENGERS
  WHICH CONTINUES TO RISE, THE WINNERS OFTEN SPENT TEN TIMES
  THE AMOUNT SPENT BY THE LOSER, THIS DIFFERENCE THREATENS THE
  VIABILITY OF THE ELECTORAL SYSTEM. IT SUGGESTS THAT SPENDING
  BE "FREED UP" SO THA INDIVIDUAL DONORS CAN COMPETE WITH PACS
  - AND GIVE CHALLENGERS A CHANCE TO COMPETE WITH INCUMBENTS.

03037 ENGSTROM, R. L.; COLE, R. L.; TAEBEL, D. A.
  CUMULATIVE VOTING AS A REMEDY FOR MINOUTY VOTE DILUTION:
  THE CASE OF ALAMAGORDO, NEW MEXICO
  JOURNAL OF LAW & POLITICS, V(3) (SPR 89), 469-497.
    DESPITE BEING EQUALLY SUSCEPTIBLE TO DILUTION BY
  SUBMERGENCE AS MORE CONCENTRATED MINORITIES, DISPERSED
  MINORITIES MAY NOT SHARE EQUALLY IN PROTECTION AGAINST THAT
  TYPE OF ELECTORAL DISCRIMINATION. THE INABILITY TO REMEDY
  THE SUBMERGENCE THROUGH A SINGLE-MEMBER DISTRICT ARRANGEMENT
  MAY NOW, AS A CONSEQUENCE OF A RECENT RULING BY THE SUPREME
  COURT IN THORNBURG V. GINGLES, PLACE PROTECTION BEYOND THEIR
  REACH. THIS JUDICIALLY GRANTED EXEMPTION FROM THE STATUTORY
  PROHIBITION AGAINST DILUTIVE SYSTEMS IS BOTH UNFORTUNATE AND
  UNNECCESSARY.

03038 ENTEEN, G.M.
  PROBLEMS OF CPSU HISTORIOGRAPHY
  PROBLEMS OF COMMUNISM, XXXVIII(5) (SEP 89), 76-80.
    UNDER THE INFLUENCE OF GLASNOST', SOME HISTORIANS OF THE
  COMMUNIST PARTY OF THE SOVIET UNION HAVE BEGUN TO QUESTION
  THE TRADITIONAL ASSUMPTIONS OF THEIR APPROACH AND ADVOCATE
  CHANGES IN THE METHODOLOGY OF PARTY HISTORIOGRAPHY. PARTY
  HISTORIANS HAVE SOUGHT EXPANDED ACCESS TO PARTY DOCUMENTS,
  ATTEMPTED TO RECONCILE THE QUEST FOR OBJECTIVITY WITH THE
  CONCEPT OF PARTY-MINDEDNESS, AND DEVISED NEW APPROACHES TO
  THE PERIODIZATION OF PARTY HISTORY. HOWEVER, RECENT EXAMPLES
  OF PARTY HISTORY SHOW THAT DESPITE HISTORIANS' EFFORTS TO
  PROBE MORE DEEPLY INTO THE PARTY'S PAST AND TO MARSHAL NEW
  KINDS OF EVIDENCE, THE STALINIST PARADIGM OF PARTY HISTORY--
  IMPOSED IN THE EARLY 1930'S--REMAINS ESSENTIALLY INTACT.

03039 ENTESSAR, N.
  EGYPT AND THE PERSIAN GULF
  CONFLICT, 9(2) (1989), 111-126.
    THE PURPOSE OF THIS ARTICLE IS TO ANALYZE EGYPT'S
  CHANGING SECURITY ROLE IN THE PERSIAN GULF REGION. FROM 1952
  UNTIL THE LATE 1960S, EGYPT PLAYED A PRIMARILY DESTABILIZING
  ROLE IN THE GULF BY SUPPORTING ANTI-WESTERN RADICAL REGIMES
  AND ATTEMPTING TO UNDERMINE THE LEGITIMACY AND SECURITY OF
  THE PROWESTERN STATES OF THE REGION, ESPECIALLY MONARCHICAL
  IRAN. FOLLOWING EGYPT'S MILITARY DEFEAT IN THE 1967 ARAB-
  ISRAELI WAR, CAIRO GRADUALLY BEGAN TO MODERATE ITS FOREIGN
  POLICY GOALS IN THE GULF. SADAT'S ACCESSION TO POWER IN 1970
  BROUGHT ABOUT A FUNDAMENTAL SHIFT IN THE ORIENTATION OF
  EGYPT'S FOREIGN POLICY AWAY FROM THE SOVIET UNION AND TOWARD
  THE WEST. ALTHOUGH EGYPT'S INFLUENCE DWINDLED AFTER THE
  COUNTRY'S PEACE TREATY WITH ISRAEL, CAIRO IS ONCE AGAIN
  EMERGING AS AN ACTOR IN GULF POLITICS. THE END OF THE IRAN-
  IRAQ WAR AND THE REENTRY OF EGYPT INTO THE ARAB FOLD HAS
  PROVIDED EGYPT A UNIQUE OPPORTUNITY TO CONTRIBUTE TO THE
  STABILITY OF THE GULF AND SERVE AS A BRIDGE BETWEEN WESTERN
  SECURITY INTERESTS AND THOSE OF THE MODERATE STATES OF THE
  PERSIAN GULF.

03040 ENTESSAR, N.
  THE KURDISH MOSAIC OF DISCORD
  THIRD WORLD QUARTERLY, 11(4) (OCT 89), 83-100.
    THE KURDS ARE AN ETHNIC MINORITY NUMBERING SOME 19
  MILLION PEOPLE, PRIMARILY IN TURKEY, IRAN, AND IRAQ WITH
  SMALLER COMMUNITIES IN SYRIA AND THE SOVIET UNION. THIS
  ARTICLE ANALYZES KURDISH COLLECTIVE MOVEMENTS AND STUDIES
  THE IMPACT OF KURDISH ETHNO-NATIONALISM ON CONTEMPORARY
  POLITICS IN TURKEY, IRAN, AND IRAQ.

03041 ENTMAN, R.M.
  HOW THE MEDIA AFFECT WHAT PEOPLE THINK: AN INFORMATION
  PROCESSING APPROACH
  THE JOURNAL OF POLITICS, 51(2) (MAY 89), 347-370.
    THE POLITICAL MESSAGES OF NEWSPAPERS ARE SIGNIFICANTLY
  ASSOCIATED WITH THE SUBSTANTIVE POLITICAL ATTITUDES OF A
  NATIONAL SAMPLE OF THEIR READERS. DIVERSITY OF NEWS
  PERSPECTIVES AND EDITORIAL LIBERALISM SHOW SIGNIFICANT
  RELATIONSHIPS TO READERS' SUPPORT OF INTEREST GROUPS, PUBLIC
  POLICIES, AND POLITICIANS. THE RELATIONSHIPS VARY AMONG SELF-
  IDENTIFIED LIBERALS, CONSERVATIVES, AND MODERATES IN
  ACCORDANCE WITH THE PREDICTIONS OF INFORMATION-PROCESSING
  THEORY. THE STANDARD ASSERTION IN MOST RECENT EMPIRICAL
  STUDIES IS THAT "MEDIA AFFECT WHAT PEOPLE THINK ABOUT, NOT
  WHAT THEY THINK." THE FINDINGS HERE INDICATE THE MEDIA MAKE
  A SIGNIFICANT CONTRIBUTION TO WHAT PEOPLE THINK-TO THEIR
  POLITICAL PERFERENCES AND EVALUATIONS-PRECISELY BY AFFECTING
  WHAT THEY THINK ABOUT.

03042 EPPELMANN, R.
  INTERVIEW WITH PASTOR RAINER EPPLEMANN
  EAST EUROPEAN REPORTER, 4(1) (WIN 89), 23.
    PASTOR RAINER EPPELMANN, CO-FOUNDER OF THE EAST GERMAN
  REFORM GROUP DEMOCRATIC AWAKENING, SPEAKS OF THE AIMS AND
  GOALS OF THE ORGANIZATION AND OF EAST GERMAN REFORM GROUPS
  IN GENERAL. HE OUTLINES HIS REFORM SOCIALIST POSITION WITH
  ITS EMPHASIS ON ECOLOGY, SOCIALISM, AND NON-VIOLENCE. HE
  ALSO COMPARES THE REFORMS GROUPS OF THE EARLY 1980S WITH
  THOSE OF TODAY.

03043 EPSTEIN, B.
  THE REAGAN DOCTRINE AND RIGHT - WING DEMOCRACY
  SOCIALIST REVIEW, 19(1) (JAN 89), 9-38.
    BY ASSOCIATING ITS POLICIES WITH ASPIRATIONS TOWARD
  DEMOCRACY (EVEN THOUGH IN A WAY THAT ULTIMATELY UNDERCUTS
  THE POSSIBILITY OF ITS DEVELOPMENT) THE REAGAN
  ADMINISTRATION HAS CLEARED SPACE FOR INVOLVEMENT IN THE
  THIRD WORLD, AND FOR A MORE SYMPATHETIC HEARING FROM THE
  AMERICAN PUBLIC. IN THIS ARTICLE, THE AUTHOR SHOWS THAT THE
  POLICY OF RIGHT-WING DEMOCRACY RESTS ON A DEFINITION OF
  DEMOCRACY THAT CONTRADICTS THE VALUES COMMONLY ASSOCIATED
  WITH THAT TERM. CRITICS OF THE US ROLE IN THE THIRD WORLD
  NEED TO CHALLENGE THE CLAIM OF THE NEOCONSERVATIVES TO THE
  MANTLE OF DEMOCRACY, AND POINT OUT THAT A PROGRESSIVE
  DEFINITION WOULD PRODUCE A VERY DIFFERENT FOREIGN POLICY.

03044 EPSTEIN, E.J.
  ADMINISTRATIVE LITIGATION LAW: CITIZENS CAN SUE THE STATE
  BUT NOT THE PARTY
  CHINA NEWS ANALYSIS, (1386) (JUN 89), 1-9.
    CHINA'S NEW ADMINISTRATIVE LITIGATION LAW GIVES CITIZENS
  AGGRIEVED BY THE DECISION OF AN ORGAN OF THE STATE
  ADMINISTRATION THE RIGHT TO APPEAL TO THE COURTS. BUT
  APPEALABLE DECISIONS DO NOT INCLUDE THOSE MADE BY THE COURTS,
  THE PROCURACIES, THE LEGISLATURES, OR THE COMMUNIST PARTY,
  WHICH IS A SUPRA-LEGAL ENTITY CONTROLLED ONLY BY THE
  POLITICAL PROCESS. THE NEW LAW IS CLEARLY DESIGNED TO EASE
  POPULAR DISCONTENT WITH BAD ADMINISTRATION WHILE CONTINUING
  TO IMMUNIZE THE PARTY'S POLITICAL POSITION FROM THE
  CUSTOMARILY SHORT, WEAK ARM OF CHINESE LAW.

03045 EPSTEIN, L.; DIXON, W.J.; WALKER, T.G.
  THE SUPREME COURT AND CRIMINAL JUSTICE DISPUTES: A NEO-
  INSTITUTIONAL PERSPECTIVE
  AMERICAN JOURNAL OF POLITICAL SCIENCE, 33(4) (NOV 89),
  825-841.
    THIS STUDY CONCEPTUALIZES THE U.S. SUPREME COURT AS A
  POLITICAL INSTITUTION WHOSE DECISIONMAKING BEHAVIOR OVER
  TIME CAN BE EFFECTIVELY EXPLAINED AND PREDICTED. A FOUR-
  VARIABLE MODEL IS CONSTRUCTED AS A MEANS OF BETTER
  UNDERSTANDING THE COURT'S POLICY OUTPUTS IN CRIMINAL JUSTICE
  DISPUTES. THIS MODEL REPRESENTS COURT DECISIONS AS A
  FUNCTION OF THE INSTITUTION'S POLITICAL COMPOSITION, THE
  GENERALLY STABLE ATTITUDES OF ITS MEMBERS, ITS POLICYMAKING
  PRIORITIES, AND THE POLITICAL ENVIRONMENT. THE RESULTS
  INDICATE THAT THE MODEL HAS SUBSTANTIAL EXPLANATORY AND
  PREDICTIVE CAPACITY WHEN APPLIED TO SUPREME COURT CRIMINAL
  RIGHTS CASES FROM 1946 TO 1986.

03046 ERASMUS, C.
  A GLIMMER OF PEACE
  MACLEAN'S (CANADA'S NEWS MAGAZINE), 102(29) (JUL 89), 26.

THE SOUTH AFRICAN GOVERNMENT, IN AN UNPRECEDENTED MOVE, ALLOWED NEWSPAPERS TO PUBLISH A STATEMENT BY NELSON MANDELA, A BLACK ACTIVIST THAT HAS BEEN IMPRISONED FOR 28 YEARS. THE STATEMENT FOLLOWED A SECRET MEETING BETWEEN MANDELA AND SOUTH AFRICAN PRESIDENT PIETER BOTHA. THE TWO MAN REPORTEDLY DISCUSSED THEIR "MUTUAL COMMITMENT TO PEACEFUL DEVELOPMENT IN SOUTH AFRICA." THESE MOVES BY THE GOVERNMENT HAVE CAUSED BLACK POLITICAL LEADERS TO HOPE THAT THE GOVERNMENT WILL SOON BE WILLING TO TALK WITH THE OUTLAWED ANC AND START ON THE LONG ROAD TOWARD PEACE AND RECONCILIATION IN SOUTH AFRICA.

03047 ERB, R.
THE ROLE OF CENTRAL BANKS
FINANCE AND DEVELOPMENT, 26(4) (DEC 89), 11-13.
THIS ARTICLE SKETCHES OUT SEVERAL FEATURES THAT CHARACTERIZE A STRONG AND EFFECTIVE CENTRAL BANK. IT EXAMINES FOR BANKS: A CLEAR SENSE OF ITS PRIMARY ROLE AND RESPONSIBILITY, GIVES IDEAS FOR A SOLID PROFESSIONAL BASE AND SUGGESTIONS FOR INCREASED PUBLIC UNDERSTANDING. FINALLY, THE ISSUE OF CENTRAL BANK INDEPENDENCE IS BRIEFLY ADDRESSED.

03048 ERFLE, S.; GROFMAN, B.; MCMILLAN, H.
TESTING THE REGULATORY THREAT HYPOTHESIS MEDIA COVERAGE OF THE ENERGY CRISIS AND PETROLEUM PRICING IN THE LATE 1970S
AMERICAN POLITICS QUARTERLY, 17(2) (APR 89), 132-152.
THE AUTHORS ARGUE THAT DURING THE 1979 OIL CRISIS MAJOR DOMESTIC OIL COMPANIES HELD DOWN PRICE INCREASES OF POLITICALLY SENSITIVE OIL PRODUCTS RELATIVE TO THEIR FOREIGN COUNTERPARTS TO REDUCE THE PROBABILITY OF ADVERSE GOVERNMENT ACTION. TO TEST THIS "REGULATORY THREAT" HYPOTHESIS, THE AUTHORS COMPARE THE REACTION OF UNREGULATED FUEL OIL PRICES TO POLITICAL PRESSURE. THEY MEASURE POLITICAL PRESSURE WITH THE LEVEL OF U.S. TELEVISION COVERAGE OF ENERGY ISSUES, AND THEY FIND THAT MEDIA COVERAGE INFLUENCED U.S. HOME HEATING OIL PRICES CHARGED BY DOMESTIC OIL COMPANIES, BUT NOT FOREIGN OIL COMPANIES. IN CONTRAST, FOR THE LESS POLITICALLY SENSITIVE RESIDUAL FUEL OIL, MEDIA COVERAGE DID NOT INFLUENCE PRICES OF EITHER DOMESTIC OR FOREIGN OIL COMPANIES.

03049 ERICKSON, J.
ARMS NEGOTIATIONS IN EUROPE
CURRENT HISTORY, 88(541) (NOV 89), 369-372, 398-399.
TRANSFORMATION OF THE EUROPEAN SECURITY SCENE HAS YET TO MATERIALIZE, ALTHOUGH THE CONVENTIONAL FORCES IN EUROPE NEGOTIATIONS HAVE MARKED SUBSTANTIAL PROGRESS. BUT WESTERN EUROPE IS NOT ON THE ROAD TO TOTAL DENUCLEARIZATION. NATO'S FLEXIBLE RESPONSE HAS NOT BEEN HOPELESSLY IMPAIRED, AND THE WARSAW PACT SEEMS SERIOUSLY COMMITTED TO NEGOTIATIONS.

03050 ERICSON, R.
SOVIET ECONOMIC REFORMS: THE MOTIVATION AND CONTENT OF PERESTROIKA
JOURNAL OF INTERNATIONAL AFFAIRS, 42(2) (SPR 89), 317-332.
THE ARTICLE OUTLINES THE ECONOMIC OBJECTIVES OF PERESTROIKA AND SEEKS TO EXPLORE THE LINKAGE BETWEEN SOVIET FOREIGN POLICY AND DOMESTIC REFORM. THE SHORT-TERM ECONOMIC GOALS REQUIRE A RELAXATION OF INTERNATIONAL TENSION AND AN OPENING TO GREATER INTERNATIONAL INTERACTION. IN THIS MANNER, FOREIGN POLICY CAN BE SEEN AS AN INSTRUMENT FOR FURTHERING ECONOMIC REFORM AND MODERNIZATION.

03051 ERIE, S. P.
RAINBOW'S END: IRISH-AMERICANS AND THE DILEMANS OF URBAN MACHINE POLITICS, 1840-1985
UNIVERSITY OF CALIFORNIA PRESS, BERKELEY, CA, 1988, 374.
THE AUTHOR TRACES THE EMERGENCE, GROWTH, AND DECLINE OF CLASSIC IRISH-AMERICAN POLITICAL MACHINES IN NEW YORK, JERSEY CITY, CHICAGO, SAN FRANCISCO, PITTSBURGH, AND ALBANY. HE STUDIES A RANGE OF ISSUES, INCLUDING THE RELATIONSHIP BETWEEN CITY AND STATE POLITICS, THE MANNER IN WHICH MACHINES SHAPED ETHNIC AND WORKING-CLASS POLITICS, AND THE REASONS CENTRALIZED PARTY ORGANIZATIONS FAILED TO EMERGE IN BOSTON AND PHILADELPHIA DESPITE THEIR LARGE IRISH POPULATIONS.

03052 ERIKSON, R.S.
ECONOMIC CONDITIONS AND THE PRESIDENTIAL VOTE
AMERICAN POLITICAL SCIENCE REVIEW, 83(2) (JUN 89), 567-576.
THIS ANALYSIS DEMONSTRATES THAT THE RELATIVE GROWTH OF PER CAPITA INCOME CHANGE IS AN IMPORTANT DETERMINANT OF POST-WORLD WAR II PRESIDENTIAL ELECTION OUTCOMES. PER CAPITA INCOME CHANGE IS EVEN A BETTER PREDICTOR OF PRESIDENTIAL ELECTION OUTCOMES THAN THE ELECTORATE'S RELATIVE ATTRACTION TO THE DEMOCRATIC AND REPUBLICAN CANDIDATES AS CALIBRATED IN NATIONAL ELECTION STUDY SURVEYS. THE SIGNIFICANCE OF THIS FINDING IS DISCUSSED.

03053 ERIKSON, R.S.; LANCASTER, T.D.; ROMERO, D.W.
GROUP COMPONENTS OF THE PRESIDENTIAL VOTE, 1952-1984
THE JOURNAL OF POLITICS, 51(2) (MAY 89), 337-346.
EXCEPT FOR BIVARIATE ANALYSES, PREVIOUS RESEARCH ON THE GROUP BASIS OF PARTISAN STRENGTH IN THE UNITED STATES HAS FOCUSED ON PARTY IDENTIFICATION AS THE DEPENDENT VARIABLE.

THIS ESSAY EXAMINES THE GROUP BASIS OF THE PRESIDENTIAL VOTE, 1952-1984, USING A MULTIVARIATE LOGIT APPROACH. THE AUTHORS, MULTIVARIATE ANALYSIS SHOWS THE PERSISTENCE OF GROUP-BASED DIVISIONS BETWEEN REPUBLICAN AND DEMOCRATIC VOTERS. AMONG OTHER PATTERNS, CLASS-BASED DIVISIONS HAVE NOTICEABLY INCREASED.

03054 ERIKSON, R.S.; MCIVER, J.P.; WRIGHT, G.C. JR.
POLITICAL PARTIES, PUBLIC OPINION, AND STATE POLICY IN THE UNITED STATES
AMERICAN POLITICAL SCIENCE REVIEW, 83(3) (SEP 89), 729-750.
WHEN COMPARING STATES IN THE UNITED STATES, ONE FINDS LITTLE CORRELATION BETWEEN STATE OPINION AND PARTY CONTROL OF THE STATE LEGISLATURE OR BETWEEN PARTY CONTROL AND STATE POLICY. ALTHOUGH THESE LOW CORRELATIONS SEEMING TO INDICATE THAT PARTISAN POLITICS IS IRRELEVANT TO THE REPRESENTATION PROCESS, THE OPPOSITE IS TRUE. STATE OPINION INFLUENCES THE IDEOLOGICAL POSITIONS OF STATE PARTIES, AND PARTIES' RESPONSIVENESS TO STATE OPINION HELPS TO DETERMINE THEIR ELECTORAL SUCCESS. MOREOVER, PARTIES MOVE TOWARD THE CENTER ONCE IN OFFICE. FOR THESE REASONS, STATE ELECTORAL POLITICS IS LARGELY RESPONSIBLE FOR THE CORRELATION BETWEEN STATE OPINION AND STATE POLICY.

03055 ERIKSON, R.S.
WHY THE DEMOCRATS LOSE PRESIDENTIAL ELECTIONS: TOWARD A THEORY OF OPTIMAL LOSS
PS: POLITICAL SCIENCE AND POLITICS, XXII(1) (MAR 89), 30-35.
WHY DOES A PARTY AS POWERFUL AS THE DEMOCRATIC PARTY CHOOSE TO RUN PRESIDENTIAL CAMPAIGNS THAT ARE SO AMATEURISH AND DISORGANIZED THAT THEY ARE ALMOST GUARANTEED TO FAIL? FROM A RATIONAL CHOICE PERSPECTIVE, ONLY ONE EXPLANATION IS POSSIBLE: IT MUST BE IN THE DEMOCRATS' ELECTORAL INTEREST TO LOSE PRESIDENTIAL ELECTIONS.

03056 ERISMAN, H.M.
THE CARICOM STATES AND US FOREIGN POLICY: THE DANGER OF CENTRALAMERICANIZATION
JOURNAL OF INTERAMERICAN STUDIES AND WORLD AFFAIRS, 31(3) (FAL 89), 141-182.
THIS PAPER EXAMINES THE EXTENT TO WHICH THE CARICOM COUNTRIES EXHIBIT SOCIO-ECONOMIC-POLITICAL CHARACTERISTS CONDUCIVE TO THE EMERGENCE OF AUTHORITARIAN AND/OR VIOLENCE PRONE POLICIES, IT ALSO STUDIES THE IMPACT CREATED BY EXTERNAL VARIABLES- SPECIFICALLY, THE POLICIES AND ACTIVITIES OF THE U.S, IN PARTICULAR THE AID PROGRAMS. THE CENTRAL QUESTION IS HAS US POLICY MADE MAJOR CONTRIBUTIONS TOWARD THE CENTRAL AMERICANIZATION OF THE ANGLOPHONE CARRIBEAN?

03057 ERLICK, J.C.
QUESTIONS FOR THE EAST GERMAN CHURCH
THE CHRISTIAN CENTURY, 106(25) (AUG 89), 791-795.
THIS IS A REPORT ON A "FACE THE PEOPLE" SESSION DURING A FOUR-DAY ECUMENICAL CONFERENCE ON "JUSTICE, PEACE AND INTEGRITY OF CREATION" HELD IN DRESDEN SPRING OF 1989. IT DETAILS THE TYPES OF QUESTIONS ASKED AND FOUND IT RATHER REMARKABLE THAT THE QUESTIONS AND COMMENTS FLOWED STEADILY IN THESE ESSENTIALLY HIERARCHICAL CHURCHES (METHODIST, LUTHERAN, AND LUTHERAN-EVANGELICAL), AND IN A SOCIETY WITH NO TRADITION OF DEMOCRACY. IT EXPLORES THE DILEMMA THE EAST GERMAN CHURCHES FACE IN THE CONTEXT OF CHANGING SOCIALIST SOCIETIES, IT REPORTS THAT THE OFFICIAL CHURCH POSITION BOTH BEFORE AND AFTER THE DRESDEN CONFERENCE IS THAT SOCIAL CHANGE SHOULD BE MADE FROM WITHIN.

03058 ERMACORA, F.
SOUTH TYROL: RESOLVING AND REOPENING A CONFLICT
AUSTRIA TODAY, (4) (1988), 26-31.
IN 1919 THE TREATY OF ST. GERMAIN DECREED THE ITALIAN ANNEXATION OF THE AUSTRIAN CROWN LAND OF TYROL. FOR 70 YEARS, THE POPULATION OF THIS REGION OF THE TYROL HAS BEEN STRUGGLING FOR THE SURVIVAL OF ITS GERMAN-AUSTRIAN CULTURE. THIS ARTICLE REVIEWS THE HISTORY OF THIS REGION SINCE 1915 AND THE CONFLICT OVER ITS DESTINY.

03059 ERNST, U.F.
TRADE, AID, AND DEVELOPMENT: THE EEC EXPERIENCE
AVAILABLE FROM NTIS, NO. PB89-159339/GAR, SEP 87, 111.
THE PAPER REVIEWS THE ARGUMENTS AND EMPIRICAL EVIDENCE OFFERED IN THE LITERATURE RELATED TO THE QUESTION OF TRADE AND DEVELOPMENT, AND ASSESSES THE POLICIES OF THE EUROPEAN ECONOMIC COMMUNITY (EEC) AS A WHOLE AND ITS MEMBER COUNTRIES IN THE AREA OF TRADE AND AID RELATIONSHIPS WITH DEVELOPING COUNTRIES, WHICH INCORPORATE MANY OF THE PRESCRIPTIONS PROFFERED IN THE FRAMEWORK OF THE NEW INTERNATIONAL ECONOMIC ORDER (NIEO), ESPECIALLY WITH RESPECT TO CONCESSIONARY TRADE POLICIES. THE ANALYSIS IN THE PAPER DRAWS PRIMARILY ON EXISTING LITERATURE; WHILE IT PRESENTS SOME EMPIRICAL DATA, IT MAKES NO CLAIM TO ANY ORIGINAL RESEARCH. FOCUSING ON THE DEVELOPING COUNTRIES IN THE AGENCY FOR INTERNATIONAL DEVELOPMENT'S (AID'S) ASIA AND THE NEAR EAST (ANE) REGION, THE REVIEW IS DESIGNED TO CONTRIBUTE TO AID'S POLICY

DIALOGUE WITH HOST GOVERNMENTS BY PROVIDING A BETTER UNDERSTANDING OF THE CONTEXT FOR TRADE POLICIES IN DEVELOPING COUNTRIES, AND BY HIGHLIGHTING THE EXPERIENCE OF A MAJOR DONOR BLOC, THE EEC, WITH THE INTEGRATION OF TRADE AND AID POLICIES.

03060 ESCHBACH, C.L.
DILEMMAS OF SOVEREIGNTY: MEXICAN POLICY TOWARD CENTRAL AMERICA UNDER PRESIDENTS LOPEZ PORTILLO AND DE LA MADRID DISSERTATION ABSTRACTS INTERNATIONAL, 50(6) (DEC 89), 1794-A.
THE AUTHOR DESCRIBES THE PATTERNS OF MEXICAN DIPLOMACY TOWARD CENTRAL AMERICA UNDER PRESIDENTS JOSE LOPEZ PORTILLO AND MIGUEL DE LA MADRID HURTADO. SHE ALSO EXPLAINS WHY MEXICO SOMETIMES CHOOSE TO EXERCISE ITS AUTONOMY THROUGH DIPLOMATIC INITIATIVES THAT CHALLENGE U.S. STRATEGIC INTERESTS AND WHY IT SOMETIMES ACQUIESCES IN THOSE INTERESTS WHILE PURSUING AUTONOMY IN OTHER AREAS.

03061 ESCHET-SCHWARZ, A.
POLITICAL PARTICIPATION IN SWISS REFERENDA AT FEDERAL AND CANTONAL LEVELS: 1879-1981
POLITICAL BEHAVIOR, 11(3) (SEP 89), 255-272.
POLITICAL PARTICIPATION IN THE PROCESS OF SEMIDIRECT DEMOCRACY DIFFERS IN SEVERAL IMPORTANT RESPECTS FROM POLITICAL PARTICIPATION IN ELECTIONS IN REPRESENTATIVE DEMOCRACIES. THIS STUDY DISCUSSES PATTERNS OF PARTICIPATION IN 300 REFERENDA AT THE CANTONAL AND FEDERAL LEVEL IN SWITZERLAND DURING THE 1879-1981 PERIOD. THE PURPOSE OF THIS SURVEY IS TO ACCOUNT FOR CROSS-TEMPORAL AND CROSS-CANTONAL VARIATIONS IN TERMS OF: (A) REFERENDA TYPE, (B) COMPETITION INTENSITY, AND (C) THE INFLUENCE OF A MULTIPLE POLITICAL CULTURE. THE FINDINGS SUGGEST THAT DISTINCTIVE POLITICAL CULTURES AND LIFE STYLES, AND OTHER COLLECTIVE FACTORS ACCOUNT FOR TURN-OUT PERCENTAGES AND COMPETITION INTENSITY. VOTERS TEND TO MOBILIZE ESSENTIALLY TO REJECT CONSTITUTIONAL REVISIONS AND LAWS RATHER THAN ACCEPT THEM. THE SIGNIFICANCE OF CROSS-TEMPORAL DIFFERENCES HAS FOUND TO DIMINISH DURING THE 1952-1981 PERIOD. THIS TENDENCY TOWARD INCREASING STANDARDIZATION OF SWISS POLITICAL PARTICIPATION DOES NOT, HOWEVER, COMPLETELY BLUR THE SPECIFICITY OF PARTICIPATION WITHIN CANTONS, SUGGESTING THAT THE MULTICULTURAL NATURE OF SWISS SOCIETY IS STILL PREVALENT.

03062 ESCHET-SCHWARZ, A.
THE ROLE OF SEMI-DIRECT DEMOCRACY IN SHAPING SWISS FEDERALISM: THE BEHAVIOR OF CANTONS REGARDING REVISION OF THE CONSTITUTION, 1866-1981
PUBLIUS: THE JOURNAL OF FEDERALISM, 19(1) (WIN 89), 79-106.
SWISS FEDERALISM OPERATES AS A SEMI-DIRECT DEMOCRACY INVOLVING REITERATED CONSTITUTIONAL CHOICE BY THE PEOPLE AND THE TERRITORIAL UNITS. IN THIS RESPECT, THE SWISS FEDERAL PROCESS IS UNIQUE IN COMPARISON TO OTHER FEDERAL SYSTEMS. AN ANALYSIS OF CONSTITUTIONAL REFERENDA AND CONSTITUTIONAL INITIATIVES CONDUCTED FROM 1866 TO 1981 HAS UNDERTAKEN IN ORDER TO CHARACTERIZE THE POLITICAL BEHAVIOR OF SWISS CANTONS CONCERNING THE REFERENDA THAT HAVE ALTERED THE ORIGINAL CONSTITUTION OF 1848. THE BEHAVIOR OF THE CANTONS MAY BE EXPLAINED BY THEIR SOCIOPOLITICAL FEATURES. THE SWISS FEDERAL PROCESS IS FOUND TO STRENGTHEN NATION-BUILDING BY MEANS OF THE CONTINUAL ADAPTATION, ALONG WITH SOME INNOVATION, OF THE ORIGINAL CONSTITUTIONAL DESIGN ON THE PART OF THE PEOPLE AS A WHOLE AND THE CANTONS.

03063 ESPING-ANDERSEN, G.
THE THREE POLITICAL ECONOMIES OF THE WELFARE STATE
CANADIAN REVIEW OF SOCIOLOGY AND ANTHROPOLOGY, 26(1) (FEB 89), 10-36.
THE PROTRACTED DEBATE ON THE WELFARE STATE HAS FAILED TO PRODUCE CONCLUSIVE ANSWERS AS TO EITHER THE NATURE OR CAUSES OF WELFARE STATE DEVELOPMENT. THIS ARTICLE HAS THREE AIMS: 1/ TO REINTEGRATE THE DEBATE INTO THE INTELLECTUAL TRADITION OF POLITICAL ECONOMY. THIS SERVES TO PUT INTO SHARPER FOCUS THE PRINCIPAL THEORETICAL QUESTIONS INVOLVED; 2/ TO SPECIFY WHAT ARE THE SALIENT CHARACTERISTICS OF WELFARE STATES. THE CONVENTIONAL WAYS OF MEASURING WELFARE STATES IN TERMS OF THEIR EXPENDITURES WILL NO LONGER DO; 3/ TO 'SOCIOLOGIZE' THE STUDY OF WELFARE STATES. MOST STUDIES HAVE ASSUMED A WORLD OF LINEARITY: MORE OR LESS POWER, INDUSTRIALIZATION OR SPENDING. THIS ARTICLE INSISTS THAT ONE UNDERSTAND WELFARE STATES AS CLUSTERS OF REGIME-TYPES, AND THAT THEIR DEVELOPMENT MUST BE EXPLAINED INTERACTIVELY.

03064 ESPINOSA, A.
PERU: ON A TIGHTROPE
THIRD WORLD WEEK, 7(9) (JAN 89), 66-67.
PERU IS SUFFERING FROM ITS WORST ECONOMIC CRISIS SINCE INDEPENDENCE. MOREOVER, THE TERROR SPREAD BY THE MAOIST SHINING PATH GUERRILLAS IN THE ANDES SEEMS TO BE MORE AND MORE LIKE AN OUTRIGHT WAR, WITH THE SHINING PATH WINNING. THESE PROBLEMS AND OTHERS HAVE LED TO GROWING TENSION BETWEEN PRESIDENT ALAN GARCIA PEREZ AND THE ARMED FORCES HIGH COMMAND AND GENERATED RUMORS OF A FORTHCOMING MILITARY COUP D'ETAT.

03065 ESPOSITO, D.
WOODROW WILSON AND THE ORIGINS OF THE AEF
PRESIDENTIAL STUDIES QUARTERLY, XIX(1) (WIN 89), 127-140.
THE AUTHOR OUTLINES THE EVENTS THAT LED UP TO THE SENDING OF THE US AMERICAN EXPEDITIONARY FORCE (AEF) TO EUROPE BY PRESIDENT WOODROW WILSON. ONCE AMERICA OFFICIALLY ENTERED THE WAR, THE ISSUE OF THE US TROOPS IN EUROPE WAS HOTLY CONTESTED BOTH AT HOME AND AMONG AMERICA'S ALLIES ABROAD. WILSON STOOD AGAINST MUCH OF THE POPULAR OPINION OF THE DAY BY DEMANDING A LARGE AEF TO ACHIEVE HIS VISION OF "PEACE WITHOUT VICTORY." WILSON HAS NOT DISPOSED TO HOARD AMERICAN RESOURCES WHEN THE LIFE OF THE WORLD SEEMED TO BE AT STAKE. WILSON'S POWER TO SUCCEED IN PEACE WOULD BE PROPORTIONAL TO THE EFFORTS THAT THE US WOULD MAKE IN THE WAR, AND THE DIRECTION INDICATED BY WILSON'S DECISIONS IN 1917 TO SEND THE AEF TO FRANCE SHOULD BE UNDERSTOOD AS A CONSCIOUS CHOICE BY THE PRESIDENT TO ACCEPT WHAT COULD AMOUNT TO VIRTUALLY UNLIMITED SACRIFICES TO ACHIEVE HIS ENS.

03066 ESTENSSORO, M.E.
ARGENTINA: TERROR AGAIN
THIRD WORLD WEEK, 7(13) (FEB 89), 100-101.
A CLIMATE OF TENSE UNCERTAINTY PREVAILS IN ARGENTINA, PROVOKED BY THE RECENT REAPPEARANCE OF LEFT-WING TERRORISM. LIKE GHOSTS FROM THE PAST, LEFTIST GUERRILLAS ATTACKED LA TABLADA ARMY BASE, RAISING QUESTIONS ABOUT THE OFFICIAL RESPONSE. IS ARGENTINA PREPARED TO FIGHT TERRORISM WITHIN A DEMOCRATIC AND LEGAL FRAMEWORK? OR WILL IT GIVE EXCESSIVE POWER TO ITS ARMED FORCES, MILITARIZE SOCIETY, AND FIGHT LEFT-WING TERRORISM WITH STATE TERRORISM?

03067 ESTENSSORO, M.E.
PARAGUAY: JOY WITH ANXIETY
THIRD WORLD WEEK, 7(11) (FEB 89), 85-86.
FOLLOWING THE OUSTER OF PRESIDENT ALFREDO STROESSNER, MOST PARAGUAYANS ARE FULL OF BOTH HIGH EXPECTATIONS AND NAGGING ANXIETIES. THEY ARE UNCERTAIN WHETHER THEIR COUNTRY IS MOVING TOWARD DEMOCRACY OR WHETHER THEY WILL SIMPLY HAVE MORE POLITICAL REPRESSION UNDER A DIFFERENT DICTATOR.

03068 ESTLUND, D.; FELD, S.; GROFMAN, B.; WALDRON, J.
DEMOCRATIC THEORY AND THE PUBLIC INTEREST: CONDORCET AND ROUSSEAU REVISITED
AMERICAN POLITICAL SCIENCE REVIEW, 83(4) (DEC 89), 1317-1340.
BERNARD GROFMAN AND SCOTT FELD HAVE ARGUED THAT JEAN-JACQUES ROUSSEAU'S CONTRIBUTIONS TO DEMOCRATIC THEORY CAN BE ILLUMINATED BY INVOKING THE THEORIZING OF THE MARQUIS DE CONDORCET ABOUT INDIVIDUAL AND COLLECTIVE PREFERENCES OR JUDGMENTS. IN THIS ARTICLE, DAVID M. ESTLUND AND JEREMY WALDRON RAISE A NUMBER OF ISSUES ABOUT THE WORK GROFMAN AND FELD.

03069 ETZIONI-HALEVY, E.
ELITE POWER, MANIPULATION, AND CORRUPTION: A DEMO-ELITE PERSPECTIVE
GOVERNMENT AND OPPOSITION, 24(2) (SPR 89), 215-231.
THE AUTHOR CONTRIBUTES TO THE CONTINUING DEBATE ON THE MANNER IN WHICH POWER IS EXERCISED IN WESTERN-STYLE DEMOCRACIES FROM A DEMOCRATIC-ELITE PERSPECTIVE. SHE OFFERS A THEORETICAL EXPOSITION PLACING THIS PERSPECTIVE IN THE SPECTRUM OF THE MAIN THEORIES ON THE SAME TOPIC, WITH SPECIAL REFERENCE TO THE CLASSICAL DEMOCRATIC-ELITE THEORIES OF MAX WEBER, GAETANO MOSCA, JOSEPH SCHUMPETER, AND RAYMOND ARON AND THE CONTEMPORARY PLURALIST-ELITIST THEORIES OF ROBERT DAHL AND GIOVANNI SARTORI.

03070 ETZIONI, A.
STATES OF THE UNION: RECESSION IS NOT A SOLUTION
NEW LEADER, LXXII(6) (MAR 89), 15-16.
THE FEDERAL RESERVE UNDER CHAIRMAN ALAN GREENSPAN IS WELL ON ITS WAY TO INDUCING YET ANOTHER RECESSION, FOR NO GOOD REASON. GREENSPAN HAS PUT THE BRAKES ON THE ECONOMY BY RAISING INTEREST RATES AGAIN.

03071 ETZIONI, A.
WELFARE FOR THE RICH
NEW LEADER, LXXII(8) (MAY 89), 13-14.
WELFARE FOR THE RICH IS THRIVING IN THESE DAYS OF GIANT DEFICITS, SHIFTS TO USERS' FEES AND WORKFARE. THE FEDERAL GOVERNMENT KEEPS USERS' FEES LOW FOR PRIVATE JETS AND HIGH FOR THE GENERAL PUBLIC. YACHTS ENJOY A LARGELY FREE TOWING SERVICE COURTESY OF THE U.S. COAST GUARD. AND THE CURRENT ADMINISTRATION HAS MADE CLEAR ITS WILLINGNESS TO DIG DEEP INTO TAXPAYER POCKETS TO TRANSFER WEALTH TO MANY OWNERS OF SAVINGS AND LOAN (S&L) BANKS. ALSO, THE BUSH ADMINISTRATION IS ADVOCATING THAT CONGRESS APPROVE THE LARGEST TRANSFER PAYMENT YET FROM THE GENERAL TAXPAYERS TO THE WEALTHY FEW: A TAX CUT FOR UNEARNED INCOME (CAPITAL GAINS). ALTHOUGH STOCK AND BOND OWNERSHIP IS NOT CONFINED TO THE SUPERRICH, ABOUT HALF OF THE COUNTRY'S TAXPAYERS OWN NONE OF EITHER. MOST IMPORTANT, THE REAL BENEFITS WOULD FALL WHERE THE OWNERSHIP IS CONCENTRATED: YES, AMONG THE SUPERRICH.

03072 EVANGELISTA, M.
    ISSUE-AREA AND FOREIGN POLICY REVISITED
    INTERNATIONAL ORGANIZATION, 43(1) (WIN 89), 147-172.
    IN THE STUDY OF COMPARATIVE FOREIGN POLICY, TWO SCHOOLS
OF THOUGHT DISAGREE OVER WHAT ACCOUNTS FOR VARIATIONS IN
PROCESSES AND OUTCOMES OF FOREIGN POLICIES WITHIN AND
BETWEEN STATES. ONE HOLDS THAT DIFFERENCES IN THE
CHARACTERISTICS OF THE COUNTRIES IN QUESTION LEAD TO
DIFFERENCES IN THEIR FOREIGN POLICIES. THE OTHER ARGUES THAT
THE IMPORTANT DIFFERENCES ARE NOT BETWEEN COUNTRIES BUT
BETWEEN ISSUE-AREAS. A COMPARISON OF THE SOVIET UNION AND
THE UNITED STATES IN THE ISSUE-AREA OF MILITARY POLICY (IN
PARTICULAR, THE PROCESS OF WEAPONS INNOVATION) SUGGESTS THAT
THE POLICY PROCESSES DIFFER SUBSTANTIALLY, CONTRARY TO WHAT
AN ISSUE-AREA APPROACH WOULD PREDICT. ON THE OTHER HAND, THE
DISTINCTIONS MADE BY SOME STUDENTS OF POLITICAL ECONOMY WHO
FOCUS ON DOMESTIC STRUCTURES APPEAR TO ACCOUNT WELL FOR
DIFFERENCES BETWEEN THE U.S. AND SOVIET PROCESSES OF
INNOVATION. THE DOMESTIC STRUCTURAL APPROACH SHOULD BE
APPLIED TO THE STUDY OF COMPARATIVE MILITARY POLICY AS WELL
AS FOREIGN ECONOMIC POLICY.

03073 EVANIER, D.; SIEFF, M.
    WILL THE SOVIET UNION SURVIVE UNTIL 1994?
    NATIONAL REVIEW, XLI(6) (APR 89), 24, 26-28, 30.
    THIS ARTICLE INCLUDES AN INTERVIEW WITH BORIS SHRAGIN ON
THE FUTURE OF GORBACHEV AND PERESTROIKA. IT ALSO OUTLINES
FOUR GREAT PROBLEMS FACING GORBACHEV: THE ECONOMIC CRISIS,
THE NATIONALITIES CRISIS, THE ECOLOGY CRISIS, AND THE
IDEOLOGY CRISIS.

03074 EVANS-PRITCHARD, A.
    ARGENTINA DRIFTS TOWARD DISASTER
    AMERICAN SPECTATOR, 22(9) (SEP 89), 19-21.
    THE AUTHOR HERE REPORTS ON THE WAGES OF PERONISM'S
ECONOMIC SINS AND CONCLUDES THAT LITTLE REPENTANCE CAN BE
EXPECTED FROM ARGENTINA'S NEW PRESIDENT CARLOS MENEM,
DESPITE HIS CHARM AND GOOD INTENTIONS.

03075 EVANS-PRITCHARD, A.
    VOODOO DEFICITS
    AMERICAN SPECTATOR, 22(2) (FEB 89), 14-15.
    FOR THE EDIFICATION OF GEORGE BUSH RONALD REAGAN'S AND
MARGARET THATCHER'S SUPPLY-SIDE SUCCESSES HAVE ALREADY
PROVED THAT THE KEYNESIAN ORTHODOXIES ON BUDGET DEFICITS AR
BUNK. IF GEORGE BUSH CAN NAVIGATE THROUGH THE REEF OVER THE
NEXT FEW MONTHS, HE COULD FIND HIMSELF SAILING OUT ONTO A
BEAUTIFUL CALM SEA. THE DISMAL EXPECTATIONS FOR HIS
PRESIDENCY ARE ESSENTIALLY FOUNDED ON THE DOOMSDAY DOGMA
THAT THE COUNTRY IS CRIPPLED BY DEBT. WHEN THE "GREAT
DEPRESSION OF THE 1990'S" FAILS TO ARRIVE, PRESIDENT BUSH
WILL LOOK LIKE A MAGICIAN.

03076 EVANS, A.
    EDUCATION FOR A PRODUCTIVE LABOR FORCE
    CRS REVEIW, 10(5) (JUN 89), 8-10.
    THE AUTHOR CONSIDERS ASPECTS OF THE PROBLEM OF EDUCATING
AMERICAN WORKERS, INCLUDING WHAT IS LACKING IN WORKERS'
EDUCATION THAT BUSINESS FINDS MOST TROUBLING, HOW DO
BUSINESSES AND SCHOOLS GO ABOUT CORRECTING THE DEFICIENCIES,
AND WHAT ROLE SHOULD THE FEDERAL GOVERNMENT PLAY IN SOLVING
THIS PROBLEM.

03077 EVANS, C.; TRIPLETT, L.D.
    MEASURING THE IMMEASURABLE?
    STATE LEGISLATURES, 15(3) (MAR 89), 19-21.
    WITHIN THE LAST THREE YEARS, A GROWING NUMBER OF STATE
LEGISLATURES HAVE TRIED TO EVALUATE ENTIRE ECONOMIC
DEVELOPMENT AGENCIES AS WELL AS SPECIFIC PROGRAMS. GIVEN THE
TENS OF MILLIONS OF DOLLARS THAT STATES HAVE POURED INTO
ECONOMIC DEVELOPMENT INITIATIVES IN THE 1980S, PROBLEMS
SURROUNDING THESE ATTEMPTS HAVE RAISED SEVERAL CRITICAL
QUESTIONS, INCLUDING: ARE WE TRYING TO MEASURE THE
IMMEASURABLE? HOW DO WE HOLD ECONOMIC DEVELOPMENT AGENCIES
AND PROGRAMS ACCOUNTABLE?

03078 EVANS, D.G.
    CANADA FACES SENTENCING REFORM
    JOURNAL OF STATE GOVERNMENT, 62(2) (MAR 89), 92-94.
    CANADA, LIKE THE USA, MUST GRAPPLE WITH THE PROBLEMS OF
IMPRISONING AND SUPERVISING GROWING NUMBERS OF OFFENDERS. IN
BOTH COUNTRIES, OVERCROWDING IS AGGRAVATED BY THE PASSAGE OF
EVER MORE PUNITIVE SANCTIONS BY LAWMAKERS ATTEMPTING TO DEAL
WITH PUBLIC SAFETY CONCERNS. THE CANADIAN PARLIAMENT IS
CONSIDERING VARIOUS PROPOSALS TO REFORM SENTENCING AND
EMPHASIZE COMMUNITY SANCTIONS.

03079 EVANS, H.
    NATIONAL DEVELOPMENT AND RURAL-URBAN POLICY: PAST
    EXPERIENCE AND NEW DIRECTIONS IN KENYA
    URBAN STUDIES, 26(2) (APR 89), 253-266.
    THE PAPER COMPARES EARLIER AND CURRENT APPROACHES TO
RURAL-URBAN DEVELOPMENT IN KENYA SINCE ITS ORIGINS IN THE
DEVELOPMENT PLAN OF 1970-74. WHEREAS, EARLIER, RURAL-URBAN
DEVELOPMENT WAS TREATED AS A SELF-CONTAINED POLICY AREA, IT
IS NOW REGARDED AS AN INTEGRAL COMPONENT OF NATIONAL
DEVELOPMENT POLICY. PRIMARY ATTENTION IS GIVEN NOT SO MUCH
TO THE FORM OF THE URBAN SYSTEM, BUT TO THE FUNCTIONING OF
IT. WHILE THE ALLOCATION OF INVESTMENTS IN PHYSICAL
INFRASTRUCTURE REMAINS A KEY INSTRUMENT OF POLICY, OTHERS
INCLUDE THE PROMOTION OF SMALL TOWNS SERVING RURAL AREAS --
KNOWN AS 'RURAL TRADE AND PRODUCTION CENTRES', THE
IMPROVEMENT OF DELIVERY SYSTEMS FOR PUBLIC SERVICES, AND
INCENTIVES FOR BUSINESS, PARTICULARLY SMALL SCALE
ENTERPRISES AND INFORMAL SECTOR ACTIVITIES.

03080 EVANS, M.
    JOHN STUART MILL AND KARL MARX: SOME PROBLEMS AND
    PERSPECTIVES
    HISTORY OF POLITICAL ECONOMY, 21(2) (SUM 89), 273-298.
    THE AUTHOR ASSESSES THE KNOWLEDGE MARX AND MILL HAD OF
EACH OTHER AND LOOKS AT MARX'S REFERENCES TO MILL IN
"CAPITAL." HE NOTES SOME INSTANCES WHEN MARX MISQUOTED MILL
AND CONSIDERS CHARGES OF PLAGIARISM. THEN HE SURVEYS THE
ARGUMENTS OF MARX'S LECTURE ON "VALUE, PRICE, AND PROFIT"
AND SUGGESTS THAT ONE NEGLECTED, THOUGH VERY FLAWED, SOURCE
FOR MARX'S REACTION TO MILL MAY BE FOUND IN A SERIES WRITTEN
BY J.G. ECCARIUS IN "THE COMMONWEALTH."

03081 EVANS, P.B.
    DECLINING HEGEMONY AND ASSERTIVE INDUSTRIALIZATION: U.S.-
    BRAZIL CONFLICTS IN THE COMPUTER INDUSTRY
    INTERNATIONAL ORGANIZATION, 43(2) (SPR 89), 207-238.
    ALTERNATIVE EXPLANATIONS FOR THE FORMATION OF U.S.
FOREIGN ECONOMIC POLICY ARE EXPLORED USING THE ACRIMONIOUS
BUT INCONCLUSIVE CONFLICT BETWEEN THE UNITED STATES AND ITS
LARGEST SOUTH AMERICAN ALLY OVER BRAZIL'S RESTRICTIVE
POLICIES TOWARD THE COMPUTER INDUSTRY. AFTER COMPARING A
POST-DEPENDENCY/ BARGAINING PERSPECTIVE, THE THEORY OF
HEGEMONIC STABILITY, AND STEPHEN KRASNER'S STRUCTURAL
CONFLICT MODEL, THE ARTICLE ARGUES THAT SYSTEMIC
PERSPECTIVES ON FOREIGN ECONOMIC POLICY MUST BE COMPLEMENTED
BY AN ACCOUNT OF THE INTERACTION BETWEEN THE EFFECTS OF
INTERNATIONAL POSITION AND THE DYNAMIC OF DOMESTIC POLITICS.
THE RESULTING POLITICIZED STATE-CENTRIC APPROACH, WHICH
INTEGRATES INTEREST-BASED POLITICS AND IDEOLOGICALLY DEFINED
STATE AIMS, IS PROPOSED AS A MEANS OF MORE FULLY
UNDERSTANDING THE DILEMMAS OF A DECLINING HEGEMON.

03082 EVENSKY, J.
    THE EVOLUTION OF ADAM SMITH'S VIEWS ON POLITICAL ECONOMY
    HISTORY OF POLITICAL ECONOMY, 21(1) (SPR 89), 123-145.
    THE AUTHOR UTILIZES J.G.A. POCOCK'S "STATE OF THE ART"
METHOD TO GAIN A NEW PERSPECTIVE ON THE WORK OF ADAM SMITH.
IN ORDER TO IDENTIFY SMITH'S INTENTIONS AND TO UNDERSTAND
WHY AND HOW THEY CHANGED, THE AUTHOR STUDIES THE LANGUAGE
SMITH HAD AT HIS DISPOSAL AND HOW AND WHY HIS USE OF
LANGUAGE CHANGED. HE FOCUSES ON SMITH'S USE OF THE LANGUAGES
OF POLITICAL DISCOURSE: CIVIL JURISPRUDENCE AND CIVIC
HUMANISM.

03083 EVENSON, J.A.
    THE TRANSITION TIMETABLE
    AFRICA REPORT, 34(2) (MAR 89), 26-30.
    UN SECURITY COUNCIL RESOLUTION 435 CONTAINS MANY
LOOPHOLES WHICH COULD ENABLE SOUTH AFRICA TO UNDERMINE THE
FREE AND FAIR ELECTION PROCESS IN NAMIBIA. THE INTERNATIONAL
COMMUNITY MUST ENSURE THAT THE AIMS OF THE INDEPENDENCE PLAN
ARE NOT SUBVERTED AND THAT THE UN TRANSITION TEAM FULFILLS
ITS MANDATE UNIMPEDED.

03084 EVERSON, J.C.
    FOREIGN DEVELOPMENT ASSISTANCE STRATEGY FOR LATIN AMERICA
    AVAILABLE FROM NTIS, NO. AD-A207 397/1/GAR, MAR 89, 40.
    FOR THE PAST FORTY YEARS, THE UNITED STATES HAS USED
FOREIGN ASSISTANCE AS A POWERFUL INSTRUMENT TO LEAD THE FREE
WORLD IN THE EFFORT TO CONTAIN THE SPREAD OF COMMUNISM AND
TO UNDERWRITE THE GROWTH OF DEMOCRACY. OUR FOREIGN
ASSISTANCE STRATEGY HAS CHANGED MANY TIMES THROUGH THE YEARS
TO REFLECT CHANGED U.S. SECURITY INTERESTS AND PRIORITIES;
AND AS WE PREPARE TO ENTER THE NEXT CENTURY, WE NEED TO
REASSESS OUR NATIONAL GOALS AND PRIORITIES IN LIGHT OF
EMERGING SHORT-AND LONGTERM THREATS. THE INCREASINGLY
SERIOUS PROBLEMS IN LATIN AMERICA THREATEN TO DESTABILIZE
THE SECURITY OF THIS HEMISPHERE IF NOT CHECKED. POPULATION
EXPLOSION AND FAILING ECONOMIES EVENTUALLY WILL BRING SOCIAL
AND POLITICAL TURMOIL ON A UNIMAGINABLE SCALE. POWERFUL DRUG
CARTELS DISTORT THE DEMOCRATIC PROCESS AND GROWTH OF A
NUMBER OF LATIN AMERICAN COUNTRIES TODAY. MORE SIGNIFICANTLY,
THEY SUPPLY THE NARCOTICS THAT POISON OUR OWN SOCIETY. NOT
SINCE THE ALLIANCE FOR PROGRESS, HAS THE UNITED STATES
AFFIRMED THAT ITS LONG-TERM INTERESTS HERE CLOSELY LINKED TO
THE STABILITY AND GROWTH OF THAT REGION. THIS PAPER SUGGESTS
THAT WE MUST RENEW OUR EFFORTS TO SUPPORT NATIONAL
DEVELOPMENT IN LATIN AMERICA AND PROPOSES ADOPTING A
REVITALIZED FOREIGN DEVELOPMENT ASSISTANCE STRATEGY THAT
INCLUDES AN EXPANDED ROLE FOR THE U.S. MILITARY IN THAT

EFFORT. IT EXAMINES THE PROCESS OF NATIONAL DEVELOPMENT, ARGUES THE SIGNIFICANT NEED FOR INCREASED U.S. MILITARY EFFORTS IN THE REGION. FINALLY, IT RECOMMENDS SOME KEY ELEMENTS TO CONSIDER WHEN FORMULATING A NATIONAL FOREIGN DEVELOPMENT ASSISTANCE STRATEGY.

03085 EVRON, B.
RABIN: THE COUNSEL OF DESPERATION
NEW OUTLOOK, 32(2 (288)) (FEB 89), 8.
CAUGHT BETWEEN THE FAILURE OF HARSH MEASURES TO SUPPRESS THE INTIFADA, THE MOUNTING PRESSURES OF A NEARLY-UNITED INTERNATIONAL COMMUNITY TO GRANT THE PALESTINIANS THEIR RIGHTS, AND THE WIDELY-FELT HORROR AT THE INCREASING BRUTALITY, ISRAELI DEFENSE MINISTER YITZHAK RABIN HAS REACTED IN CONTRADICTORY WAYS. ON THE ONE HAND, THE MILITARY BRUTALITY HAS BEEN INTENSIFIED. ON THE OTHER, RABIN HAS OFFERED A PLAN FOR A POLITICAL SOLUTION IN THE OCCUPIED TERRITORIES. HIS PLAN INCLUDES A CEASE-FIRE FOR A PERIOD OF THREE TO SIX MONTHS, TO BE FOLLOWED BY FREE ELECTIONS IN WHICH THE PALESTINIANS WOULD ELECT REPRESENTATIVES TO NEGOTIATE WITH ISRAEL. THE FINAL RESULT WOULD BE A PALESTINIAN FEDERATION OR CONFEDERATION WITH ISRAEL OR JORDAN.

03086 EWA, E.L.
DETERMINANTS OF SOCIAL INTERACTION AMONG NIGERIANS: A RATIONAL CHOICE PERSPECTIVE AND IMPLICATIONS FOR PUBLIC POLICY
DISSERTATION ABSTRACTS INTERNATIONAL, 49(9) (MAR 89), 2795-A.
THE AUTHOR SEEKS TO EXTEND PRIOR THEORETICAL UNDERSTANDING OF SOCIAL ACTION THROUGH A METHODOLOGY THAT LINKS AN INDIVIDUAL'S INTERESTS AND BEHAVIOR TO PERCEIVED SOCIAL OUTCOMES. FIRST, HE EXAMINES CULTURAL CHARACTERISTICS OF INDIVIDUALS FROM THE MAJOR ETHNIC GROUPS OF NIGERIA TO IDENTIFY RELATIONSHIPS BETWEEN PERCEIVED CULTURAL DIFFERENCES AND ATTITUDES TOWARD SOCIAL INTERACTION. HE CONCLUDES THAT, IN ORDER TO PROMOTE SOCIAL INTERACTION ACROSS CULTURES, PLURAL SOCIETIES MUST DEVELOP A NATIONAL IDEOLOGY OR A POLITICAL CULTURE BASED ON AN INTEGRATION OF VALUES THAT REFLECT VARYING SOCIAL INTERESTS.

03087 EWELL, J.
DEBT AND POLITICS IN VENEZUELA
CURRENT HISTORY, 88(536) (MAR 89), 121-124, 147-149.
ECONOMIC PROBLEMS HAVE PLACED STRAINS ON VENEZUELA'S DEMOCRATIC SYSTEM AND ON THE QUALITY OF LIFE. PRESIDENT CARLOS ANDRES PEREZ WILL NEED ALL HIS ENERGY AND CHARISMA TO REACTIVATE VENEZUELA'S DEMOCRACY AND ITS ECONOMY.

03088 EYAL, J.
EASTERN EUROPE: WHAT ABOUT THE MINORITIES?
WORLD TODAY, 45(12) (DEC 89), 205-208.
THE NATIONS OF EASTERN EUROPE ARE CURRENTLY REDEFINING THEIR AIMS AND ASPIRATIONS, THEIR ENEMIES AND THEIR ALLIES. IF THE REGION IS NOT TO RETURN TO A PERIOD OF ENDEMIC INSTABILITY, THE ASPIRATIONS AND FEARS OF ITS PEOPLES MUST BE ACCOMMODATED. THIS WILL REQUIRE CLOSE WEST EUROPEAN INVOLVEMENT IN THE RECONSTRUCTION OF THE REGION'S ECONOMIES AND SOCIAL FABRIC. IT WILL ALSO MEAN GRAPPLING WITH EASTERN EUROPE'S ETHNIC PROBLEMS.

03089 EYAL, J.
INFORMING ON HELSINKI
WORLD TODAY, 45(7) (JUL 89), 109-110.
THE HELSINKI CONFERENCE ON SECURITY AND COOPERATION IN EUROPE (CSCE) PROCESS RELIES ON A MYRIAD OF TREATIES AND DECLARATIONS, SOME LEGALLY BINDING AND SOME WITH ONLY MORAL FORCE, SOME VERY PRECISE AND SOME DELIBERATELY VAGUE. AS LONG AS THE USSR AND ITS ALLIES HAS LITTLE INTEREST IN SEEING THE PROCESS AS AN INTEGRAL WHOLE, SORTING OUT THIS CONFUSING MIX MATTERED LITTLE. BUT, ONCE GORBACHEV BEGAN TAKING THE PROCESS SERIOUSLY, THE SEPARATION OF ITS DIFFERENT ASPECTS BECAME CRUCIAL. IN ORDER TO DO THIS, IT BECAME NECESSARY TO TEMPORARILY SEPARATE THE CSCE INTO DIFFERENT BASKETS. THE LONDON INFORMATION FORUM IN APRIL AND MAY 1989 CONCENTRATED ON THE MASS MEDIA'S ROLE IN THE CSCE PROCESS. DELEGATES ALSO DISCUSSED INTERNATIONAL MEDIA ISSUES, SUCH AS VISA PROBLEMS AND A UNIVERSAL SYSTEM OF ACCREDITATION FOR JOURNALISTS.

03090 EYAL, J.
ROMANIA: A HERMIT UNDER PRESSURE
WORLD TODAY, 45(5) (MAY 89), 85-90.
ROMANIA'S PRESIDENT CEAUSESCU APPEARS INCREASINGLY BELEAGUERED. ISOLATED FROM BOTH THE EAST AND THE WEST, HE SEEMS DETERMINED TO CONTINUE PURSUING POLICIES THAT HAVE RUINED ROMANIA'S ECONOMY AND INTERNATIONAL REPUTATION. LATELY, THERE ARE INDICATIONS THAT CEAUSESCU'S POLICIES ARE EVEN MEETING OPPOSITION FROM WITHIN THE ROMANIAN COMMUNIST PARTY.

03091 FABELLA, R.V.
MONOPOLY DEREGULATION IN THE PRESENCE OF TULLOCK ACTIVITIES
PUBLIC CHOICE, 62(3) (SEP 89), 287-294.
THIS PAPER GIVES THE CONDITION FOR A WELFARE IMPROVING MONOPOLY DEREGULATION WHEN THE DECISION MAKING PROCESS CANNOT BE INSULATED FROM TULLOCK ACTIVITIES AND PLAYERS ARE RISK NEUTRAL. IT CONSIDERS A MODEL WHERE THE DEREGULATION OF A MONOPOLY IS A CONTESTED ISSUE. IT ASSUMES THAT THE DECISION MAKING PROCESS CANNOT BE INSULATED FROM LOBBYING ACTIVITIES, AND DESCRIBES THE FRAMEWORK THAT ALLOWS FOR ONLY ONE WINNER.

03092 FABRICIUS, M.
THE WACKY WAYS WE'RE TAXING FOOD
STATE LEGISLATURES, 15(5) (MAY 89), 20-22.
OF THE 45 STATES THAT IMPOSE A SALES TAX, 26 EXEMPT FOOD. ACCORDING TO ESTIMATES IN STATE TAX EXPENDITURE REPORTS, STATES LOSE ANYWHERE FROM $31 MILLION TO $1.5 BILLION FROM THE SALES TAX EXEMPTION ON FOOD.

03093 FADIA, B.L.; BHATI, P.S.
SARKARIA REPORT AND PROPOSAL FOR INTER-GOVERNMENTAL COUNCIL
INDIAN JOURNAL OF POLITICAL SCIENCE, L(1) (JAN 89), 110-117.
THE SARKARIA COMMISSION WAS APPOINTED IN RESPONSE TO DEMANDS FOR A RE-EXAMINATION OF INDIAN CENTRE-STATE RELATIONS. THIS AROSE DUE TO CRITICISM THAT THE LIMITED FEDERALISM ENVISAGED BY THE INDIAN CONSTITUTION HAS BEEN ERODED, WHETHER BY NATURAL PROCESSES OR WILFULLY, AS A RESULT OF INCREASING CENTRALIZATION AND PERSONALIZATION OF POWER. THE COMMISSION REPORT DOES NOT PROPOSE DRASTIC CONSTITUTIONAL AMENDMENTS BUT ADVOCATES THE REVIVAL OR ESTABLISHMENT OF CERTAIN CONVENTIONS RELATING TO CENTRE-STATE CONSULTATION AND THE REACTIVATION OF DORMANT CONSTITUTIONAL PROVISIONS.

03094 FAINSTEIN, S.S.; FAINSTEIN, N.
THE AMBIVALENT STATE: ECONOMIC DEVELOPMENT POLICY IN THE U.S. FEDERAL SYSTEM UNDER THE REAGAN ADMINISTRATION
URBAN AFFAIRS QUARTERLY, 25(1) (SEP 89), 41-62.
THE REAGAN ADMINISTRATION REDUCED FEDERAL SPENDING ON URBAN AND REGIONAL DEVELOPMENT JUST WHEN THE AMERICAN ECONOMY EXPERIENCED MASSIVE RESTRUCTURING. FEDERAL WITHDRAWALS, HOWEVER, RATHER THAN SIMPLY REDUCING GOVERNMENTAL INTERVENTION IN MARKETS, PRODUCED A SHIFT OF ACTION TO THE STATE AND MUNICIPAL LEVEL. THE IMPACT OF RESTRUCTURING CAUSED STATE AND LOCAL GOVERNMENTS, OFTEN UNDER PRESSURE FROM BUSINESS, TO CREATE A DE FACTO NATIONAL ECONOMIC DEVELOPMENT POLICY. GOVERNMENTS FIERCELY COMPETED WITH ONE ANOTHER IN A SYSTEM OF SUBNATIONAL MERCANTILISM. THE NET EFFECT OF WHICH PROBABLY WAS TO REDUCE TAXATION ON BUSINESS. WHETHER THE U.S. ECONOMY WAS STRENGTHENED AS A WHOLE REMAINS UNCLEAR.

03095 FAINSTEIN, S.S.; FAINSTEIN, N.I.
THE RACIAL DIMENSION IN URBAN POLITICAL ECONOMY
URBAN AFFAIRS QUARTERLY, 25(2) (DEC 89), 187-199.
RACE CONTINUES TO PLAY A CRITICAL INDEPENDENT ROLE IN DETERMINING URBAN OUTCOMES FOR BLACK AMERICANS. BLACKS REMAIN SEGREGATED AND ECONOMICALLY DISAVDANTAGED. THEIR ECONOMIC CONDITION HAS DETERIORATED, WITH DIFFERENCES BETWEEN RACES FAR MORE IMPORTANT THAN STRATIFICATION AMONG BLACKS. BUT THE SPATIAL AND POLITICAL CONTAINMENT OF BLACKS DURING THE LAST DECADE HAS REDUCED THE EFFECT OF BLACK POPULATIONS ON THE ECONOMIC FORTUNES OF CITIES. AS A RESULT, POLITICAL STRATEGIES FOR BLACK ADVANCEMENT FACE SERVERE OBSTACLES AT THE PRESENT TIME.

03096 FAIR, J.D.
THE PEACEMAKING EXPLOITS OF HAROLD TEMPERLEY IN THE BALKANS, 1918-1921
SLAVONIC AND EAST EUROPEAN REVIEW, 67(1) (JAN 89), 68-93.
THE AUTHOR SEEKS TO CONTRIBUTE TO THE DEBATE OVER THE IMPORTANCE OF EXPERT ADVICE IN THE PEACEMAKING PROCESS BY FOCUSING ON AN INDIVIDUAL AND AN ASPECT OF THE PROCESS THAT HAS HITHERTO BEEN OVERLOOKED. THE PAPERS OF HAROLD TEMPERLEY REVEAL MUCH NOT ONLY ABOUT PREVAILING CONDITIONS IN THE BALKANS BUT ALSO ABOUT THE EFFORTS OF ONE MAN, A SCHOLAR AND A SLAVOPHILE, TO INFLUENCE THE COURSE OF EVENTS IN PARIS AND ELSEWHERE. ALONG WITH OTHER EVIDENCE, THEY SHOW THE CONSIDERABLE EXTENT TO WHICH BRITISH POLICY WAS INFLUENCED BY TEMPERLEY'S AUTHORITATIVE ADVICE.

03097 FAIRBANKS, C.H., JR.
GORBACHEV'S CULTURAL RELVOLUTION
COMMENTARY, 88(2) (AUG 89), 23-27.
WITH THE SOVIET ELECTIONS, THE DEMONSTRATIONS IN BEIJING, AND AN ATTEMPTED COUP IN ETHIOPIA, THE GATHERING SENSE OF THE FAILURE OF COMMUNIST REGIMES SUDDENLY SEEMS TO HAVE JELLED. HOWEVER, THE DECLINE OF SUCH SYSTEMS TAKES A LONG TIME. ALSO, THEIR TERMINAL CRISES ARE COMPLEX AND EVENTFUL. EPISODES OF CONSERVATIVE RESTORATION ALTERNATE WITH PERIODS OF EVER MORE RAPID CHANGE AND GROWING OUTSIDE INFLUENCE, AS THE DEEPLY SPLIT SOCIETY TRIES IN VAIN TO FIND A SOLUTION. FINALLY, SUCH TERMINAL CRISES ARE DANGEROUS. THE BRUTAL END IN TIANANMEN SQUARE IS ONLY THE MOST RECENT EXAMPLE.

03098 FAJNZYLBER, F.
GROWTH AND EQUITY VIA AUSTERITY AND COMPETITIVENESS
PHILADELPHIA: ANLS OF AMER ACMY OF POLITICAL AND SOC
SCIENCE, (505) (SEP 89), 80-91.
IN THE FIRST SECTION OF THIS ARTICLE, A COMPARATIVE
ANALYSIS IS UNDERTAKEN OF LATIN AMERICA AND SEMI-
INDUSTRIALIZED COUNTRIES IN OTHER AREAS OF THE WORLD.
ATTENTION IS DRAWN TO THE SPECIFIC FEATURES OF LATIN AMERICA
AS REGARDS ITS LACK OF A STRONG PREDISPOSITION TOWARD THE
INCORPORATION OF TECHNOLOGICAL PROGRESS AND ITS DUBIOUS
ACHIEVEMENTS IN RELATION TO GROWTH, EQUITY, AND
COMPETITIVENESS. IN THE SECOND SECTION, A SIMILAR TYPE OF
COMPARATIVE ANALYSIS IS APPLIED TO THE LEADING COUNTRIES.
FINALLY, SOME REFLECTIONS ARE PRESENTED WITH REGARD TO
DIRECTIONS AND ACTIONS IN LATIN AMERICA AND IN THE NORTH
THAT COULD CONTRIBUTE TO CONFRONTING THE CHALLENGE OF LATIN
AMERICA-THAT IS, TO APPROACHING THE UNTIL NOW EMPTY BOX
WHEREIN GROWTH CONVERGES WITH EQUITY.

03099 FALAH, G.
ISRAELI 'JUDAIZATION' POLICY IN GALILEE AND ITS IMPACT ON
LOCAL ARAB URBANIZATION
POLITICAL GEOGRAPHY QUARTERLY, 8(3) (JUL 89), 229-254.
IN THIS CASE STUDY, THE GALILEE REGION IS EXAMINED
WITHIN THE CONTEXT OF TERRITORIAL CONTROL. SINCE THE REGION
IS CHARACTERIZED BY A LARGE CONCENTRATION OF A NUMERICALLY
DOMINANT ARAB POPULATION, STATE PLANNING POLICYWHICH IS
MOTIVATED BY ZIONIST IDEOLOGY-HAS AIMED AT PREVENTING THE
FORMATION OF AN ARAB 'CORE AREA' THERE. THE POLICY OF
JUDAIZATION, IMPLEMENTED IN VARIOUS STAGES TO CREATE A NEW
AND ALTERNATIVE 'JEWISH CORE' IN MOUNTAINOUS GALILEE, HAS
SIGNIFICANTLY SHAPED THE UNIQUE PATTERN OF URBANIZATION IN
THE LOCAL ARAB SETTLEMENTS. THE FAILURE OF THIS STATE
STRATEGY TO ACHIEVE A POSITIVE JEWISH DEMOGRAPHIC BALANCE
AND TO BREAK UP THE TERRITORIAL CONTINUITY OF ARAB LANDS AND
SETTLEMENTS HAS SERVED TO STRENGTHEN THE ROOTEDNESS OF THE
POPULATION IN THEIR VILLAGES AND HAS ACTED AS A RETARDING
INFLUENCE ON RURAL-URBAN MIGRATION.

03100 FALAH, G.
ISRAELI STATE POLICY TOWARDS BEDOUIN SEDENTARIZATION IN
THE NEGEV
JOURNAL OF PALESTINE STUDIES, XVIII(2) (WIN 89), 71-91.
THE ARTICLE EXAMINES THE POLICY OF THE STATE OF ISRAEL
TOWRDS THE BEDOUIN POPULATION OF THE NEGEV DESERT. THE AIM
OF THE ARTICLE IS, FIRST TO SHOW HOW SEDENTARIZATION AS A
SETTLEMENT POLICY IS USED AS AN OFFICIAL TOOL TO TRANSFORM
BEDOUIN LAND INTO STATE LAND. SECOND, IT DESCRIBES AND
ANALYZES THE VARIOUS MEANS USED TO EVICT AND RELOCATE
BEDOUIN GROUPS FROM THEIR LAND SO AS TO MAKE THE
TRANSFORMATION POSSIBLE. FINALLY, THE ARTICLE EVALUATES AND
ASSESSES THE VIABILITY OF THE EXISTING "PLANNED BEDOUIN
TOWNSHIPS" IN THE NEGEV.

03101 FALCOFF, M.
LEARNING TO LOVE THE MISSILE CRISIS
NATIONAL INTEREST, 16 (SUM 89), 63-73.
THE MISSILE CRISIS HAS TAUGHT THE U.S. POLICY COMMUNITY
THAT CONFRONTATIONS WITH THE SOVIET UNION AT THE NUCLEAR
LEVEL ARE TO BE AVOIDED AT ALL COSTS. IF THIS WAS SO IN 1962,
WHEN THE UNITED STATES POSSESSED OVERWHELMING STRATEGIC AND
NUCLEAR SUPERIORITY (NOT TO MENTION A DECIDEDLY STRONGER
POLITICAL POSITION IN WESTERN EUROPE AND LATIN AMERICA, AND
MUCH BROADER PUBLIC SUPPORT AT HOME THAN ADMINISTRATIONS
WOULD HAVE TODAY), IT SEEMS DISINGENUOUS TO CLAIM THAT WE
COULD RESPOND NOW AS FORCEFULLY AND CREDIBLY TO THE
EMPLACEMENT OF SOVIET STRATEGIC WEAPONRY IN NICARAGUA AS
PRESIDENT KENNEDY DID IN CUBA MORE THAN A QUARTERCENTURY AGO.

03102 FALCOFF, M.
THE ONLY HOPE FOR LATIN AMERICA
COMMENTARY, 87(4) (APR 89), 34-38.
NO VAST INTERNATIONAL TRANSFERS OF WEALTH ARE LIKELY TO
OCCUR IN THE 1990'S. THE ONLY HOPE FOR THE SURVIVAL OF
DEMOCRACY IN LATIN AMERICA IS THE DIFFUSION OF PROPERTY AND
THE ENFRANCHISEMENT OF THOSE WHO ACTUALLY WORK AND CREATE
WEALTH. THE CURRENT ECONOMIC CRISIS IS UNDERMINING THE
STABILITY OF THE REGION AND RAISES THE VERY REAL SPECTER OF
A PLUNGE INTO FULL-DRESS COLLECTIVISM. THE ANSWER TO THIS IS
MORE ECONOMIC FREEDOM, NOT LESS.

03103 FALK, R.
THE FUTURE OF INTERNATIONAL STUDIES: THE QUEST FOR WORLD
ORDER
SCANDINAVIAN JOURNAL OF DEVELOPMENT ALTERNATIVES, 8(3)
(SEP 89), 5-18.
THE FOCUS OF INQUIRY IN INTERNATIONAL STUDIES HAS BEEN
ON POWER POLITICS AND THE STATE SYSTEM. SUCH AN INQUIRY IS
NOT ADEQUATE, FACED WITH GLOBAL PROBLEMS SUCH AS ECOLOGICAL
DECAY FROM ACID RAIN, OZONE DEPLETION, HUMAN HUNGER AND
NUCLEAR WINTER. A SHIFT AWAY FROM NATIONALISTIC VERSIONS OF
TRUTH TO THE GLOBAL INTEREST AND GLOBAL COMMUNITY IS
NECESSARY FOR DEVISING CURES FOR HUMAN SUFFERING. AS THE

IMPORTANCE OF JAPAN AND THE PACIFIC REGION IS INCREASINGLY
RECOGNIZED, IT IS SIGNIFICANT TO ESTABLISH INTERNATIONAL
STUDIES TO EDUCATE YOUTH TO HELP CREATE A BETTER WORLD.

03104 FALLENBUCHL, Z.M.
ECONOMIC NATIONALISM IN THE EASTERN BLOC COUNTRIES
CANADIAN REVIEW OF STUDIES IN NATIONALISM, XVI(1-2) (1989),
153-168.
THE AUTHOR ANALYZES HOW EASTERN EUROPEAN GOVERNMENTS
HAVE USED ECONOMIC NATIONALISM TO SUPPORT THEIR POLICIES;
HOW THEIR SYSTEMS, POLICIES, AND PERFORMANCES DIFFER; HOW
ECONOMIC CONFLICTS AND COMMON INTERESTS INFLUENCE ECONOMIC
NATIONALISM; AND HOW THE LATTER HAS INFLUENCED THE PROCESS
OF ECONOMIC INTEGRATION WITHIN THE COUNCIL FOR MUTUAL
ECONOMIC ASSISTANCE.

03105 FALLESEN, L.
DENMARK'S E.C. RECORD
EUROPE, (291) (NOV 89), 36.
POLICY DIFFERENCES BETWEEN DENMARK AND THE EUROPEAN
COMMUNITY INCLUDE CONFLICTS OVER TAX HARMONIZATION AND
DISCRIMINATORY BIDDING PRACTICES. DESPITE THESE DIFFERENCES,
DENMARK HAS IMPLEMENTED 51 E.C. DIRECTIVES, MORE THAN ANY
OTHER MEMBER EXCEPT FRANCE, WHICH HAS IMPLEMENTED 54.
DESPITE CONTINUED DIFFERENCES, DENMARK STANDS TO PROFIT MUCH
FROM THE SINGLE MARKET.

03106 FALLESEN, L.
MEMBER STATE REPORT: DENMARK
EUROPE, (291) (NOV 89), 34-36,47.
ALTHOUGH THE DANISH ECONOMY HAS PERFORMED AT FAR BELOW
THE EUROPEAN COMMUNITY AVERAGE, DANISH POLITICIANS AND
ECONOMISTS ARE PREDICTING SIGNIFICANT GROWTH IN THE FUTURE.
HOWEVER, THE SUCCESS OF THESE PREDICTIONS DEPEND ON
CONTINUED GLOBAL ECONOMIC GROWTH AND ON CONTINUED BENEFITS
FROM WAGE NEGOTIATIONS. DENMARK ALSO MUST REDUCE ITS HUGE
PUBLIC SECTOR AND HIGH TAX RATES IF IT IS TO FULLY TAKE
ADVANTAGE OF THE COMMON EUROPEAN MARKET.

03107 FARAH, T.E.
POLITICAL CULTURE AND DEVELOPMENT IN A RENTIER STATE: THE
CASE IF KUWAIT
JOURNAL OF ASIAN AND AFRICAN STUDIES, XXIV(1-2) (1989),
106-113.
THIS ARTICLE USES POLITICAL CULTURE TO EXPLAIN KUWAIT'S
SOCIO-ECONOMIC AND POLITICAL DEVELOPMENT. IT ATTRIBUTES
KUWAIT'S POLITICAL STABILITY, ITS SMOOTH TRANSITION FROM A
SUBSISTANCE ECONOMY TO PETROLEUM-INDUCED PROSPERITY AND ITS
ABILITY TO HANDLE HIGH RATES OF SOCIO-ECONOMIC CHANGES TO
THE MANAGEMENT SKILLS OF THE KUWAITI RULING FAMILY AND THE
COMMITMENT OF THE BUREAUCRACY TO THE STATE. THESE TWO
ELEMENTS OF POLITICAL CULTURE EXPLAIN HOW THE KUWAITI REGIME
HAS BEEN ABLE SUCCESSFULLY TO MEET THE CHALLENGES OF
DEVELOPMENT WHICH WOULD OTHERWISE HAVE MADE IT A PRIME
CANDIDATE FOR INSTABILITY. THE ARTICLE CONCLUDES THAT BOND
BETWEEN KUWAITI CITIZENS AND THEIR RULER, WITH THE
BUREAUCRACY PROMOTING AND STRENGTHENING ALLEGIANCE TO THE
STATE AND ITS DEVELOPMENT POLICIES.

03108 FARAI, I.
THE US RESUMES ITS AID - BUT IS THE DIPLOMATIC FENCE
REALLY MENDED?
AFRICAN BUSINESS, (NOV 88), 47-48.
THIS ARTICLE EXPLORES THE HISTORY OF THE RIFT BETWEEN
THE U.S. AND ZIMBABWE WHICH RESULTED IN THE U.S. SUSPENDING
ECONOMIC AID TO ZIMBABWE. IT EXAMINES THE REASONS FOR THE
RESUMPTION OF AID INCLUDING FEAR OF SOVIET INFLUENCE FILLING
THE VOID. IT EXAMINES THE CONTINUING HOSTILITY EXHIBITED BY
ZIMBABWEAN LEADERS TO THE U.S.

03109 FARAZMAND, A.
BUREAUCRACY, DEVELOPMENT, AND REGIME-POLITICS: THE CASE OF
IRAN
INTERNATIONAL JOURNAL OF PUBLIC ADMINISTRATION, 12(1)
(1989), 79-111.
THIS PAPER DEALS WITH THE ROLE OF BUREAUCRACY AND STATE
IN SOCIETY. IT EXAMINES THE POLITICAL REGIME-ENHANCEMENT
ROLE AND ECONOMIC DEVELOPMENT ROLE OF THE MINISTRY OF
AGRICULTURE AND RURAL DEVELOPMENT (MARD) IN IRAN BEFORE AND
AFTER THE REVOLUTION OF 1978-79. WHILE THE MARD TRANSFORMED
RURAL FEUDALISM INTO CAPITALISM AND ENHANCED THE PAHLAVI
REGIME, IT FAILED TO PROMOTE AGRICULTURAL DEVELOPMENT. AN
AGRICULTURALY SELF-SUFFICIENT IRAN BECAME ALMOST TOTALLY
DEPENDENT, AND A MASSIVE RURAL EXODUS OF MORE THAN NINE
MILLION BECAME A MAJOR FORCE FOR THE REVOLUTION OF 1978-79.
TWO MAJOR TRENDS IN POST-REVOLUTIONARY IRAN ARE IDENTIFIED
AND EXPLAINED: INITIAL DEBUREAUCRATIZATION OF SOCIETY ALONG
WITH AN EGALITARIAN AGRICULTURAL AND RURAL POLICY AND THE
REBUREAUCRATIZATION OF SOCIETY AND A POLICY IN FAVOR OF
LARGE PRIVATE LANDHOLDING SINCE 1983. THE AUTHOR ANALYZES
THE NATURE OF GROWING PUBLIC DISSATISFACTION WITH THE
BUREAUCRACY, AND OUTLINES ALTERNATIVES TO REDUCE THIS
DISSATISFACTION AND TO PROMOTE AGRICULTURAL AND RURAL
DEVELOPMENT.

03110 FARER, D.
   REINFORCING DEMOCRACY IN LATIN AMERICA: NOTES TOWARD AN
   APPROPRIATE LEGAL FRAMEWORK
   HUMAN RIGHTS QUARTERLY, 11(3) (AUG 89), 434-451.
      THE AUTHOR EXAMINES VARIOUS ASPECTS OF THE U.S. LEGAL
   SYSTEM IN AN ATTEMPT TO FIND USEFUL PRECEDENTS FOR LATIN
   AMERICAN DEMOCRACIES TO FOLLOW. THESE CONCEPTS INCLUDE: THE
   JUDICIARY AS CONSTITUTIONAL WATCHDOG, RECONSTITUTING OF
   POLITICAL ISSUES AS LEGAL ONES, GUARDING THE RIGHTS OF THE
   WEAK, AND EMPOWERING THE POOR THROUGH THE LEGAL PROCESS. THE
   AUTHOR EXAMINES THE MERITS OF SUBSTANTIVE CONSTITUTIONAL
   REVIEW AS OPPOSED TO INCREMENTAL CHANGE IN LATIN AMERICA.
   THE AUTHOR CONCLUDES THAT THE DIFFERING LOCI OF THE
   PRINCIPAL THREAT TO DEMOCRATIC ORDER (EXECUTIVE POWER IN THE
   U.S. AND THE MILITARY IN LATIN AMERICA) WILL LIMIT THE
   INFLUENCE OF NORTH AMERICAN INSTITUTIONAL DESIGNS ON THE
   ARCHITECTS OF DEMOCRATIC REGIMES IN LATIN AMERICA.

03111 FARER, T.
   ELECTIONS, DEMOCRACY, AND HUMAN RIGHTS: TOWARD UNION
   HUMAN RIGHTS QUARTERLY, 11(4) (NOV 89), 504-521.
      THIS ARTICLE EXPLORES THE REJECTION BY THE REAGAN
   ADMINISTRATION OF ITS PREDECESSOR'S INSISTENCE THAT PROGRESS
   BE SOUGHT WITH RESPECT TO HUMAN RIGHTS IN THE AREAS OF
   PERSONAL SECURITY, POLITICAL RIGHTS, AND ECONOMIC AND SOCIAL
   RIGHTS. THE REAGAN ADMINISTRATION DECLARED THAT THERE WERE
   NO RIGHTS TO PURSUE IN ECONOMICS AND SOCIAL RIGHTS. IT
   EXPLORES THE VIEW THAT THE INTERNATIONAL HUMAN RIGHTS
   MOVEMENT IS GENERALLY INSENSITIVE TO THE LEGITIMATE
   NECESSITIES OF GOVERNMENTS ATTEMPTING TO MAINTAIN PUBLIC
   ORDER. NATIONAL EMERGENCIES AND INTERNATIONAL LAW, ELECTED
   GOVERNMENTS AND THE DEFENSE OF HUMAN RIGHTS, ON AVOIDING
   DIRTY WARS, AND THE MARGIN OF OPPORTUNITY IN SOUTH AMERICA,
   ARE EACH, IN TURN, ANALYZED

03112 FARER, T.J.
   THE UNITED STATES AS GUARANTOR OF DEMOCRACY IN THE
   CARIBBEAN BASIN: IS THERE A LEGAL WAY?
   JERUSALEM JOURNAL OF INTERNATIONAL RELATIONS, 11(3) (SEP
   89), 40-63.
      AN EXPLORATION OF SOME OF THE POSSIBLE WAYS THE UNITED
   STATES COULD INTERVENE TO ENSURE DEMOCRACY IN THE CARIBBEAN
   BASIN WITHOUT RESORTING TO MILITARY MEANS OR ACTIONS THAT
   MIGHT BE CONTROVERSIAL FROM THE STANDPOINT OF INTERNATIONAL
   LAW. THIS ARTICLE EXAMINES THE MILITARY OPTION AND ECONOMIC
   MEASURES AS MEANS, IT QUESTIONS WHETHER DEMOCRACY IS A
   REALITY OR AN ILLUSION AND OFFERS A GUARDEDLY SKEPTICAL
   CONCLUSION.

03113 FARJOUN, E.
   THE GREAT DIVIDE: CONSTRUCTING AN EFFECTIVE ISRAELI
   OPPOSITION
   MIDDLE EAST REPORT, 19(157) (MAR 89), 15-19, 46.
      CONTEMPORARY ISRAELI POLITICS HAVE ONE UNDENIABLE
   CHARACTERISTIC: EXTREME POLARIZATION OF PUBLIC OPINION AND
   POLITICAL NORMS BETWEEN LEFT AND RIGHT, OR BETWEEN LIBERAL
   ZIONISM AND THE MOVEMENT'S CHAUVINIST/RELIGIOUS WING.
   RELIGIOUS FUNDAMENTALISM HAS ACCUMULATED ENORMOUS POLITICAL
   POWER. NON-RELIGIOUS ISRAELIS ARE FRIGHTENED BY THE EVIDENCE
   THAT THIS SIDE IS RAPIDLY BECOMING THE MAJORITY WITHIN THE
   JEWISH ISRAELI POPULATION.

03114 FAROUK-SLUGLETT, M.
   IRAQ AFTER THE WAR (1): THE DEBTS PILE UP
   MIDDLE EAST INTERNATIONAL, (343) (FEB 89), 18-19.
      THE GULF WAR HAS PROFOUNDLY DAMAGED THE ECONOMY OF IRAQ,
   WHICH HAS AMASSED FOREIGN DEBTS ESTIMATED AT $60-80 BILLION.
   IRAQ'S GREATEST DEBTS ARE TO SAUDI ARABIA AND KUWAIT, BUT IT
   WILL PROBABLY NOT REPAY THESE DEBTS SINCE SADDAM HUSSEIN
   CLAIMS THAT IRAQ WAGED THE WAR ON BEHALF OF THE ARABS AS A
   WHOLE. THE WAR HAS STRENGTHENED SADDAM'S POSITION AS THE
   POTENTIAL LEADER OF THE ARAB WORLD. IN THE LONG RUN, THIS
   COULD LEAD TO THE FORGING OF NEW ALLIANCES AMONG THE ARAB
   STATES.

03115 FAROUK-SLUGLETT, M.
   IRAQ AFTER THE WAR (2): THE ROLE OF THE PRIVATE SECTOR
   MIDDLE EAST INTERNATIONAL, (346) (MAR 89), 17-18.
      THE BA'TH PARTY'S DESCRIPTION OF ITSELF AS SOCIALIST AND
   THE STATE'S DOMINANT ROLE IN THE ECONOMY HAS LED TO THE
   MISLEADING ASSUMPTION THAT ITS ECONOMIC POLICIES ARE SOMEHOW
   DIRECTED AGAINST THE ACCUMULATION OF PRIVATE CAPITAL AND
   PRIVATE PROFIT. IN FACT THE REALITY, ALTHOUGH EXTREMELY
   COMPLEX, IS QUITE THE REVERSE AND CLOSELY LINKED TO THE
   CRUCIAL FUNCTION OF THE STATE IN THIRD WORLD COUNTRIES AS
   THE PRINCIPAL GENERATOR OF DEVELOPMENT AND MODERNISATION, AS
   WELL AS OF OPPORTUNITIES FOR PRIVATE CAPITAL ACCUMULATION;
   BUT THE DOMINANCE OF SUCH A "WEALTHY" STATE MAKES FOR A VERY
   CENTRALISED AND BUREAUCRATIC ECONOMIC SYSTEM.

03116 FARQUHARSON, M.
   SALINAS BETS HIS SHIRT
   SOUTH, (110) (DEC 89), 25-26.

WITH AN EXTERNAL DEBT OF US$100 BILLION AND 60 PERCENT
OF THE FEDERAL BUDGET GOING TO SERVICE LOANS, MEXICAN
PRESIDENT SALINAS DE GORTARI SEES NO ALTERNATIVE BUT TO OPEN
UP TO US INVESTMENT, DESPITE THE RISK OF A NATIONALIST
BACKLASH. IF SALINAS FAILS TO PULL OFF AN ECONOMIC MIRACLE,
HIS PRESIDENCY AND PARTY COULD BE IN JEOPARDY AND DOORS
BETWEEN THE TWO NEIGHBORING COUNTRIES COULD CLOSE.

03117 FARQUHARSON, M.
   SALINAS CRACKS THE WHIP
   SOUTH, (108) (OCT 89), 44.
      IN RETURN FOR ONE OF THE WORLD'S MOST PROTECTIVE LABOR
   LAWS, MEXICO'S INSTITUTIONAL REVOLUTIONARY PARTY HAS BEEN
   ABLE TO RELY ON THE SUPPORT OF ORGANIZED LABOR SINCE ITS
   FORMATION. BUT UNDER PRESIDENT SALINAS DE GORTARI, MEXICO IS
   OPENING UP TO FOREIGN INVESTMENT AND CUTTING BACK ON PUBLIC
   SPENDING. AS THE GOVERNMENT'S LARGESSE FOR THE UNIONS DRIES
   UP, THE PARTY IS LOSING SOME OF ITS TRADITIONAL SUPPORT FROM
   LABOR.

03118 FARR, M.
   FEDERAL REPUBLIC OF GERMANY
   EUROPE, (292) (DEC 89), 30, 32, 47.
      THE PEACEFUL REVOLUTION THAT SWEPT EAST GERMANY CAME AS
   WEST GERMANY EXPERIENCED ITS BIGGEST ECONOMIC BOOM IN MORE
   THAN A DECADE. WEST GERMANY, AT THE END OF 1989 HAD THE
   FASTEST GROWING ECONOMY AMONG THE LEADING WESTERN
   INDUSTRIALIZED NATIONS AFTER JAPAN. FOREIGN DEMAND AND
   ORDERS FOR CAPITAL GOODS WERE THE BASIC CAUSES FOR GROWTH,
   ALO WITH RISING CAPITAL INVESTMENTS. DESPITE FEARS AMONG
   MANY WEST GERMAN WORKERS, THE INFLUX OF WELL OVER 600,000
   GERMAN IMIGRANTSETHNIC GERMANS FROM POLAND AND THE SOVIET
   UNION, AND THE INFLUX OF EAST GERMANS-DID NOT HAVE AN
   ADVERSE EFFECT ON UNEMPLOYMENT. MOREOVER, THE AILING EAST
   GERMAN ECONOMY OFFERED ENORMOUS POTENTIAL TO THE WEST. THEIR
   FIRMS WERE OBVIOUS CONTENDERS TO MODERNIZE ITS OUTDATED
   INFRASTRUCTURE AND REVITALIZE ITS ECONOMIC POTENTIAL.

03119 FARZAN, A.
   IRAN: A FEW MONTHS AFTER THE WAR
   WORLD MARXIST REVIEW, 32(4) (APR 89), 73-75.
      WHILE PEACE HAS YET TO BE FIRMLY ESTABLISHED AFTER THE
   DEVASTATIONS OF THE EIGHT-YEAR IRAN-IRAQ CONFLICT, THE END
   TO THE FIGHTING HAS OPENED UP NEW POLITICAL PROSPECTS FOR
   OUR SOCIETY UNDER A CHANGING BALANCE OF SOCIAL FORCES. THE
   MOUNTING POPULAR DISCONTENT OVER THE ECONOMIC HARDSHIPS, AND
   THE FLARE-UPS OF SPONTANEOUS STRUGGLE ON THE HOME FRONT
   REVERBERATED ALL THE WAY TO THE FRONTLINES AND EVENTUALLY
   BECAME ONE OF THE CRUCIAL FACTORS BEHIND THE REGIME'S
   RETREAT AND ITS DECISION TO ACCEPT A CEASE-FIRE.

03120 FATIMA, K.
   THE OTHER SIDE OF U.S. GENEROSITY
   WORLD MARXIST REVIEW, 31(11) (NOV 88), 112-114.
      THROUGH THE EXPORT OF THEIR CAPITAL TO DEVELOPING
   COUNTRIES, THE IMPERIALIST STATES TRANSFER TO THEM A LARGE
   PROPORTION OF THEIR OWN ECONOMIC AND FINANCIAL DIFFICULTIES,
   AND ENSURE THAT THEY REMAIN IN THE ORBIT OF THE WORLD
   CAPITALIST SYSTEM. THIRD WORLD COUNTRIES, ESPECIALLY OIL
   IMPORTERS (INCLUDING PAKISTAN), ARE HARD HIT BY THE SHARP
   CYCLICAL FLUCTUATIONS IN THE WORLD CAPITALIST ECONOMY AND
   MONETARY SYSTEM. THE CRISIS IN THE WORLD MONETARY SYSTEM,
   WHICH HAS LED TO A DETERIORATION IN THE TERMS OF TRADE, THE
   SUDDEN INCREASE IN THE RATE OF INTEREST ON FOREIGN LOANS AND
   THE DECREASE IN THE ACTUAL LOANS AND CREDITS DISBURSED AND
   USED, HAS DEALTH A HEAVY BLOW TO PAKISTAN'S FINANCIAL
   RELATIONS.

03121 FATTON, R. JR.
   THE STATE OF AFRICAN STUDIES AND STUDIES OF THE AFRICAN
   STATE: THE THEORETICAL SOFTNESS OF THE "SOFT STATE"
   JOURNAL OF ASIAN AND AFRICAN STUDIES, XXIV(3-4) (JUL 89),
   170-187.
      IN SPITE OF PROFOUND IDEOLOGICAL AND METHODOLOGICAL
   DIFFERENCES, AFRICAN POLITICAL STUDIES HAVE TENDED TO
   SUBSCRIBE TO THE CONCEPT OF THE "SOFT STATE". THE CONCEPT IS
   GROUNDED IN THE PERCEPTION THAT THE TYPICAL AFRICAN STATE
   CONSTITUTES A WEAK AND CORRUPT BUREAUCRATIC APPARATUS
   BECAUSE IT CONSISTENTLY FAILS TO PROMOTE THE GENERAL
   INTEREST. THIS PERCEPTION IS FLAWED BECAUSE IT IMPLIES THE
   THEORETICAL EXPULSION OF CLASS INTERESTS FROM THE CONCEPT OF
   THE STATE. THE REALITY IS THAT STATES ARE NEVER DIVORCED
   FROM THE MATERIAL, POLITICAL, AND IDEOLOGICAL INTERESTS OF
   THE RULING CLASS. THE STATE IS THEREFORE NEVER "SOFT" IT IS
   ALWAYS AN ORGAN OF DOMINANCE-ALL THE MORE SO IN AFRICAN
   SOCIETIES WHICH ARE TRAVERSED BY PROCESSES OF RULING CLASS
   CONSOLIDATION REQUIRING THE BRUTAL ACCUMULATION AND CLOSURE
   OF WEALTH, PRIVILEGE, AND STATUS.

03122 FAVORSKAIA, A.
   PROOF IN FAVOR OF DEMOCRACY
   SOVIET REVIEW, 30(2) (MAR 89), 54-58.
      IN THIS INTERVIEW, MATHEMATICIAN-CYBERNETICIST IVAR
   PETERSEN DISCUSSES A MATHEMATICAL MODEL OF DEMOCRATIC

DEVELOPMENT PREPARED AT THE INSTITUTE OF CYBERNETICS OF THE EASTONIAN ACADEMY OF SCIENCES. THE MODEL IS CONSIDERED TO BE "SCIENTIFIC PROOF" THAT THE DEMOCRATIC MODEL OF DECISION-MAKING IS THE MOST RATIONAL AND BENEFICIAL FOR SOCIETY, WHILE THE AUTHORITARIAN METHOD OF DECISION-MAKING LEADS TO GREAT LOSSES FOR SOCIETY AS A WHOLE AND IS A CRITICAL BRAKE ON SOCIAL DEVELOPMENT.

03123 FEARNSIDE, P.M.
DEFORESTATION IN AMAZONIA
ENVIRONMENT, 31(4) (MAY 89), 16.
DEFORESTATION MUST BE SLOWED DRASTICALLY AND QUICKLY IF SUSTAINABLE USES OF THE RAIN FOREST ARE TO BE RETAINED. CHEAP AND EFFECTIVE MEASURES INCLUDE TAXING LAND SPECULATION; DISALLOWING PASTURE AS AN "IMPROVEMENT" FOR ESTABLISHING LAND TENURE; HALTING FISCAL INCENTIVES AND OTHER SUBSIDIES FOR DEVELOPMENTS INVOLVING DEFORESTATION; REDUCING AND STRICTLY CONTROLLING ROAD BUILDING; AND STRENGTHENING RIMA PROCEDURES FOR MAJOR DEVELOPMENT PROJECTS. UNLESS THE BRAZILIAN GOVERNMENT SOON ENACTS AND ENFORCES THESE MEASURES, THE FORESTS OF AMAZONIA WILL NOT BE SAVED.

03124 FEHER, F.; HITCHENS, C.; JUDT, T.; LUCZYWO, H.; SKELLY, J.; WESCHLER, L.
ALL CHAOS ON THE EASTER FRONT
DEADLINE, IV(5) (NOV 89), 5-8, 15.
THE ARTICLE CONTAINS EXCERPTS FROM A ROUNDTABLE INTERVIEW OF ACADEMICIANS AND JOURNALISTS DISCUSSING THE ISSUE OF AMERICAN PRESS COVERAGE OF THE EVENTS IN EASTERN EUROPE. THE GENERAL CONSENSUS OF THOSE INTERVIEWED IS THAT ALTHOUGH US PRESS COVERAGE IS, ON BALANCE, OF AN ADEQUATE NATURE, IT OFTEN TENDS TO PORTRAY EVENTS ONLY IN CONTEXT OF THE "CAPITALISM VS SOCIALIASM" BATTLE. THIS CONTEXT OVERSIMPLIFIES MANY OF THE PROBLEMS AND CONDITIONS OF EASTERN EUROPE. US PRESS ALSO IGNORES MANY OF THE FACTIONS AND DIVISIONS WITHIN RESISTANCE AND REFORM GROUPS IN EASTERN EUROPE.

03125 FEHER, F.
ON MAKING CENTRAL EUROPE
EASTERN EUROPEAN POLITICS AND SOCIETIES, 3(3) (FAL 89), 412-447.
THIS ARTICLE DEFINES THE PROBLEM, THE CONCEPTS, AND THE THEORIES INVOLVED WITH THE MAKING OF CENTRAL EUROPE. IT LAYS THE GROUNDWORK BY DESCRIBING THE EXTENSION OF THE CONCEPT "CENTRAL EUROPE,' THE FACT THAT WWII NEVER ENDED LEGALLY, AND THE "GORBACHEV PHENOMENON OR INTERLUDE." IT THEN OFFERS THREE TYPES OF ARGUMENTS WHICH ASSUME OR DENY THE EXISTENCE OF THE "OBJECTIVE FOUNDATIONS" OF CENTRAL EUROPE - GEOGRAPHICAL, CULTURAL - SUBSTANTIVE, AND SUBSTANTIVE AND HISTORICAL. IT THEN ASKS "DOES EUROPE HAVE A CENTER?" AND OFFERS SCENARIOS FOR MAKING CENTRAL EUROPE.

03126 FEHER, F.
THE LEGITIMACY OF THE FRENCH REVOLUTION
FRENCH POLITICS AND SOCIETY, 7(3) (SUM 89), 120-136.
THE AUTHOR ANALYZES THE WEBERIAN TRIPARTITE DIVISION OF LEGITIMATE RULE OR AUTHORITY INTO TRADITIONAL, CHARISMATIC, AND LEGAL (RATIONAL), PARTICULARLY AS IT PERTAINS TO THE FRENCH REVOLUTION.

03127 FEI-LUNG, L.
BALLOT POWER
FREE CHINA REVIEW, 39(12) (DEC 89), 9-15.
THE AUTHOR REVIEWS BASIC FACTS ABOUT TAIWAN'S ELECTORAL SYSTEM AND THE HISTORY OF ELECTIONS IN TAIWAN.

03128 FEI, J.
POLITICAL-ECONOMIC FOUNDATIONS
ASIAN AFFAIRS, AN AMERICAN REVIEW, 16(3) (FAL 89), 119-134.
THE AUTHOR ANALYZES THE POSSIBILITY OF THE REUNIFICATION OF TAIWAN AND MAINLAND CHINA AND CONCLUDES THAT REUNIFICATION IS A HISTORICAL INEVITABILITY. FURTHERMORE, THE FOUNDATION OF THIS UNIFICATION IS BASED ON THE IDENTIFICATION OF CULTURAL VALUES THAT MUST NOT ONLY SERVE THE PURPOSE OF MODERNIZATION BUT MUST ALSO NOT BE DIVORCED FORM THE TRADITIONAL CULTURAL HERITAGE. AFTER AN ANALYSIS OF CHINA'S CONFUCIAN POLITICAL AND ECONOMIC HERITAGE, THE AUTHOR CONCLUDES THAT AN MARKET-ORIENTED ECONOMY AND A DEMOCRATIC GOVERNMENT ARE IMPORTANT PRECONDITIONS TO REUNIFICATION.

03129 FEI, S.
NEW DEVELOPMENTS IN SOUTHERN AFRICA
BEIJING REVIEW, 32(38) (SEP 89), 16-17.
THE AUTHOR REVIEWS THE PROGRESS OF RECENT NEGOTIATIONS IN SOUTHERN AFRICA, HIGHLIGHTING THE LIVINGSTONE TALKS BETWEEN ZAMBIAN PRESIDENT KENNETH KAUNDA AND ACTING SOUTH AFRICAN PRESIDENT F.W. DEKLERK.

03130 FEI, Y.
CHINESE PRESIDENT'S VISIT TO FOUR ARAB NATIONS
BEIJING REVIEW, 32(52) (DEC 89), 7, 9.
IN DECEMBER 1989, CHINESE PRESIDENT YANG SHANGKUN PAID AN OFFICIAL VISIT TO EGYPT, THE UNITED ARAB EMIRATES, KUWAIT, AND OMAN. AS THE FIRST TRIP ABROAD BY THE CHINESE PRESIDENT SINCE THE COUNTER-REVOLUTIONARY REBELLION IN BEIJING, THE VISIT INDICATED THAT CHINA'S DOMESTIC SITUATION WAS STABLE, THAT ITS POLICY OF OPENING TO THE OUTSIDE WORLD REMAINED UNCHANGED, AND THAT ITS INDEPENDENT FOREIGN POLICY HAD NOT CHANGED. THE VISIT ALSO DEEPENED MUTUAL UNDERSTANDING AND TRUST AND PROMOTED THE COMPREHENSIVE DEVELOPMENT OF FRIENDLY RELATIONS BETWEEN CHINA AND THE FOUR COUNTRIES.

03131 FEI, Z.
NEW TRENDS IN TAIWAN
BEIJING REVIEW, 32(2) (JAN 89), 7,9.
FOR SOME TIME THE TAIWAN AUTHORITIES HAVE LOUDLY ADVOCATED AND PURSUED A POLICY OF 'ELASTIC DIPLOMACY,' CLAIMING THEY WISH TO DEVELOP 'OFFICIAL' RELATIONS WITH COUNTRIES HAVING DIPLOMATIC TIES WITH THE PEOPLE'S REPUBLIC OF CHINA. A CURSORY ANALYSIS OF THIS NEW TREND MAKES IT CLEAR THAT THE AIM OF THE TAIWAN AUTHORITIES IS TO CREATE TWO POLITICAL ENTITIES, IN EFFECT TO FABRICATE "TWO CHINAS" OR "ONE CHINA, ONE TAIWAN," AND BY DOING SO INFINITELY DELAY THE REUNIFICATION OF THE MAINLAND AND TAIWAN.

03132 FEIGENBAUM, E.A.
RESTRICTING THE BARBARIAN: CHINA'S FOREIGN TRADE AND THE POLITICS OF EXCLUSION
MICHIGAN JOURNAL OF POLITICAL SCIENCE, (11) (WIN 89), 1-19.
THIS ESSAY IS AN ASSESSMENT OF CHINA'S ATTEMPTS AT RECONCILIATION OF TWO CONSTRUCTS - THE REALITIES OF NATION-STATISM AND A TRADITIONAL GLOBAL CONCEPTION OF UNIVERSAL SCOPE. IT DERIVES ITS IMPETUS FROM THE PRINCIPLE THAT WHILST CHINA MAY HAVE ACCEPTED THE NEED TO ADAPT THESE MODERN REALITIES TO ITS TRADITIONAL WORLD VIEW, THE ABILITY TO DO SO REMAINS HINDERED BY A FAILURE TO DISPOSE OF MANY OF THESE DATED CONCEPTS, IT TRACES THE ROOTS OF THE PROBLEM BY DRAWING HISTORICAL PARALLELS, AND REVIEWING CHINA'S TRADITIONAL GLOBAL ORDER.

03133 FEINBERG, R.E.
DEFUNDING LATIN AMERICA: REVERSE TRANSFERS BY THE MULTILATERAL LENDING AGENCIES
THIRD WORLD QUARTERLY, 11(3) (JUL 89), 71-84.
THE INTERNATIONAL FINANCIAL INSTITUTIONS (IFIS) MUST ADDRESS TWO KEY ISSUES AS THEY CONFRONT THE DEBT AND DEVELOPMENT PROBLEMS OF LATIN AMERICA. BOTH ISSUES CENTRE ON THE URGENT NEED TO REDUCE THE TRANSFER OF RESOURCES FROM LATIN AMERICA TO THE INTERNATIONAL FINANCIAL SYSTEM: FIRST, WHETHER THE IFIS CAN REVERSE THE DISTURBING TREND OF JOINING THE COMMERCIAL BANKS AS NET FINANCIAL DRAINS ON THE CAPITAL-SHORT REGION; AND SECOND, WHAT ROLE THEY SHOULD PLAY IN REDUCING THE PERSISTENT TRANSFER OF FINANCIAL RESOURCES FROM LATIN AMERICA TO PRIVATE LENDERS. BOTH THESE ISSUES ARE CENTRAL TO THE BASIC AGENDA OF THE INTERNATIONAL MONETARY FUND (IMF), THE WORLD BANK, AND THE INTER-AMERICAN DEVELOPMENT BANK (IDB). THESE INSTITUTIONS WERE ESTABLISHED IN PART TO TRANSFER CAPITAL FROM NORTH TO SOUTH AND TO CATALYSE THE MOVEMENT OF PRIVATE CAPITAL TO PROFITABLE INVESTMENTS IN DEVELOPING NATIONS. THE CHALLENGE FACING THE IFIS IN THE 1990S IS TO FULFIL THESE AIMS IN THE FACE OF NEW AND DIFFICULT CIRCUMSTANCES.

03134 FEINERMAN, J.V.
HUMAN RIGHTS IN CHINA
CURRENT HISTORY, 88(539) (SEP 89), 273-276, 293-295.
THE UNIVERSAL SHOCK AND OUTRAGE AT THE CHINESE GOVERNMENT'S ACTIONS IN JUNE 1989 HIGHLIGHTED THE RECENT EVOLUTION OF CHINA'S REPUTATION IN HUMAN RIGHTS. OVER THE PAST DECADE, A "NEW CHINA" SEEMED TO PROMISE GREATER FREEDOM AND POLITICAL REFORMS THAT WOULD REMOVE THE HEAVY HAND OF COMMUNISM FROM DAILY LIFE. A REMARKABLE DEGREE OF TOLERANCE FOR PUBLIC DISAGREEMENT WITH AUTHORITY SEEMED TO BE DEVELOPING.

03135 FELBINGER, C.L.
EFFECTIVE LOCAL GOVERNMENT MANAGEMENT: ROLE EMPHASES OF PUBLIC WORKS DIRECTORS
AMERICAN REVIEW OF PUBLIC ADMINISTRATION, 19(2) (JUN 89), 119-132.
THE AUTHOR EXPLORES WHETHER THE ROLE ORIENTATIONS OF LOCAL PUBLIC WORKS DIRECTORS MIRROR THE ORIENTATIONS AMONG CITY MANAGERS DISCOVERED BY WRIGHT AND RE-EXAMINED AMONG MANAGERS, ASSISTANT MANAGERS, MAYORS, AND MAYORAL ASSISTANTS BY NEWELL AND AMMONDS. HER FINDINGS SHOW THAT ROLE ORIENTATIONS ARE STABLE OVER TIME WITH THE EMPHASIS ON MANAGEMENT. OPERATING IN A POLITICAL ENVIRONMENT (MAYORAL FORM OF GOVERNMENT) DOES NOT AFFECT THIS RELATIONSHIP, AS NEWELL AND AMMONDS FOUND. BUT THERE IS SOME SUPPORT FOR THEIR FINDING THAT POLITICAL AND POLICY ORIENTATIONS INCREASE WITH CITY SIZE. AGE OR TENURE IN THE PROFESSION IS POSITIVELY LINKED WITH A POLICY ORIENTATION. THERE IS NO MASSIVE SHIFT TO POLITICAL AND POLICY ACTIVITIES AMONG ACTORS AT THIS LEVEL OF THE LOCAL HIERARCHY, AT LEAST AMONG LOCAL PUBLIC WORKS DIRECTORS.

03136 FELDMAN, A.
FORMATIONS OF VIOLENCE: THE BODY, NARRATIVITY AND
POLITICAL TERROR IN NORTHERN IRELAND
DISSERTATION ABSTRACTS INTERNATIONAL, 49(9) (MAR 89),
2706-A.
THE CENTRAL HYPOTHESES OF THIS STUDY ARE: (1) ACTS OF
POLITICAL VIOLENCE ARE ANALYZABLE AS INSTRUMENTAL-SYMBOLIC
INFRASTRUCTURES INFORMED BY RELATIONS OF INTERTEXTUALITY AND
TRANSPOSITION; (2) IN NORTHERN IRELAND, THE SYMBOLIC
ORGANIZATION OF VIOLENCE CONSTITUTES A A UNIFORM AND SHARED
MEDIUM OF MATERIAL SIGNIFICATION IRRESPECTIVE OF THE
ANTAGONISTIC IDEOLOGICAL ASCRIPTIONS OF DIFFERENT
PARAMILITARY GROUPS AND THE STATE.

03137 FELDMAN, O.; KAWAKAMI, K.
LEADERS AND LEADERSHIP IN JAPANESE POLITICS: IMAGES DURING
A CAMPAIGN PERIOD
COMPARATIVE POLITICAL STUDIES, 22(3) (OCT 89), 265-290.
THIS ARTICLE ATTEMPTS TO OBSERVE JAPANESE STUDENTS'
PERCEPTIONS OF POLITICAL FIGURES DURING AN ELECTION TIME,
AND TO EXAMINE THE FACTORS THAT MOST DOMINANTLY CONTRIBUTE
TO SUCH IMAGES. EMPLOYING A SAMPLE COLLECTED FROM MORE THAN
1,100 STUDENTS AT FOUR UNIVERSITIES IN JAPAN, THE DISCUSSION
FOCUSES ON MEASURING THE EXTENT TO WHICH THE RESPONDENTS
EVALUATED EACH OF THE POLITICAL FIGURES WHO WERE CANDIDATES
FOR THE PREMIERSHIP, THE WAY THEY STRUCTURED THEIR
EVALUATIONS, AND THE EFFECTS OF VARIABLES SUCH AS POLITICAL
INVOLVEMENT AND MEDIA EXPOSURE ON THIS PROCESS. THE FINDINGS
SHOW THAT, ALTHOUGH THERE WERE NO SIGNIFICANT DIFFERENCES IN
THE LEADERSHIP STYLE OF THE POLITICAL FIGURES, NEGATIVE
EVALUATIONS AS A WHOLE WERE EXPRESSED TOWARD THE CANDIDATE
WITH THE MOST POTENTIAL ABILITY TO BECOME THE PREMIER.
MOREOVER, THE RESPONDENTS CLUSTERED THEIR PERCEPTIONS
ACCORDING TO FIVE CLEAR DIMENSIONS, MOST NOTABLY IN REGARD
TO THE LEADERS' PERFORMANCE AND CONTACT WITH OTHERS. IN
ADDITION, IT WAS FOUND THAT--MORE THAN ANY OTHER FACTOR--THE
MASS MEDIA PLAYED A CRUCIAL ROLE IN DETERMINING THE WAY THE
LEADERS WERE EVALUATED.

03138 FELDMAN, R.
THE NEW PRIVATIZATION
AMERICAN CITY AND COUNTY, 104(9) (SEP 89), 14.
PROPONENTS OF PUBLIC-PRIVATE PARTNERSHIPS, OR THE NEW
PRIVATIZATION, BELIEVE THAT MUCH CAN BE ACHIEVED IN DEALING
WITH THE UNITED STATES' INFRASTRUCTURE CRISIS. THE FIVE KEY
ELEMENTS OF THIS NEW PRIVATIZATION ARE INNOVATIVE USER
CHARGE ARRANGEMENTS, FLEXIBLE MUNICIPAL PROCUREMENT
STRUCTURES, MAXIMIZATION OF MUNICIPAL BALANCE SHEET
POTENTIAL, AGGRESSIVE RISK ALLOCATION TO STIMULATE PRIVATE
INVESTMENT, AND INNOVATIVE FINANCING STRUCTURES.

03139 FELDMAN, R.A.
IMPLEMENTING STRUCTURAL REFORMS IN INDUSTRIAL COUNTRIES
FINANCE AND DEVELOPMENT, 26(3) (SEP 89), 24-26.
THIS ARTICLE OFFERS EXAMPLES FROM FOUR MAIN AREAS OF
REFORM IN THE INDUSTRIAL COUNTRIES WHICH HAS BEEN A VITAL
ASPECT OF POLICYMAKING IN THE 1980S, IT BRIEFLY REVIEWS
EXPERIENCES WITH REFORM AND ILLUSTRATES THEIR EFFECTS ON
AGGREGATE SUPPLY AND DEMAND WITH EXAMPLES FROM SELECTED
ECONOMIES. INCLUDED ARE: GOODS AND SERVICES MARKETS, LABOR
MARKET REFORM, FINANCIAL MARKET REFORM, AND TAX REFORM. THE
FOLLOWS SUBAREAS ARE DETAILED: TELECOMMUNICATIONS, STEEL,
TRANSPORTATION, PRIVATIZATION, AGRICULTURE, TRADE
LIBERALIZATION, WAGES, CONTRACTS, BARGAINING, TRAINING AND
BENEFITS, INTEREST RATES, CAPITAL CONTROLS, PERSONAL INCOME
TAXES, CORPORATE INCOME TAXES AND INDIRECT TAXES.

03140 FELDMAN, S.
SO NEAR BUT YET SO CLOSE: AMERICAN TELEVISION POLITICS IN
THE CANADIAN ELECTION
CANADIAN FORUM, LXVIII(780) (APR 89), 11-12.
THE ARTICLE OUTLINES THE CAMPAIGN STRATEGIES OF CANADA'S
POLITICAL PARTIES WITH EMPHASIS ON THEIR USE OF US
TELEVISION POLITICAL TACTICS. ALL PARTIES ATTEMPTED TO USE
NETWORK NEWS TO THEIR ADVANTAGE BEFORE THE CALL FOR
ELECTIONS WAS ISSUED AND THE IMPACT OF TELEVISION WAS FELT
WITH REAGRDS TO THE DEBATES. ALL IN ALL, THE CONSERVATIVE
AND THE LIBERAL PARTIES DESCENDED TO A STANDARD THAT WOULD
HAVE BEEN UNTENABLE HAD THE AMERICANS NOT PROVIDED A
COMPARABLE MODEL.

03141 FELDMAYER, C.F.
FORCE STRUCTURE IMPLICATIONS OF START
AVAILABLE FROM NTIS, NO. ADA209 674/1/GAR, MAR 89, 39.
THE EMERGING STRATEGIC ARMS REDUCTION TALKS TREATY
(START) WILL REDUCE STRATEGIC NUCLEAR WEAPONS FROM 30-50
PERCENT. THE TREATY WILL MODIFY SOVIET AND AMERICAN
CAPABILITIES, BUT IT WILL NOT ELIMINATE THE NUCLEAR
POTENTIAL FOR EITHER OF THE SUPERPOWERS. START AND ARMS
CONTROL IN GENERAL IS NOT A PANACEA TO REMEDY EASTWEST
RELATIONS; RATHER, ARMS CONTROL IS ONE ELEMENT SUPPORTING A
NATION'S STRATEGY AND HELPS TO DEFINE ITS STRATEGIC POSITION.
THE PRIMARY PURPOSE OF ARMS CONTROL IS TO REDUCE RISKS AND
TO MAINTAIN STRATEGIC STABILITY. STRATEGY AND ARMS CONTROL

MUST BE COORDINATED AND WE OFTEN LINK ARMS CONTROL PROPOSALS
TO FORCE MODERNIZATION PLANS. STRATEGIC WEAPONS, DISARMAMENT.

03142 FELKER, L.S.
LATIN AMERICAN MUNICIPAL GOVERNMENT: THE RISE OF
METAGOVERNMENT
INTERNATIONAL JOURNAL OF PUBLIC ADMINISTRATION, 12(2)
(1989), 331-348.
METAGOVERNMENT, THE EXTRA-LEGAL AND INFORMAL GOVERNMENT
THAT HAS DEVELOPED IN THE SQUATTER SETTLEMENTS AND INFORMAL
ECONOMIC SECTORS OF LATIN AMERICAN NATIONS, IS RAPIDLY
BECOMING THE MOST RELEVENT FORM OF GOVERNMENT FOR MANY LATIN
AMERICANS. THE ROOTS OF THIS PHENOMENON CAN BE FOUND IN THE
EARLY HISTORY OF LATIN AMERICAN MUNICIPAL GOVERNMENTS AND
THE PERSISTENCE OF AN EXCLUSIONIST AND ELITIST SET OF
INSTITUTIONS AND VALUES FROM COLONIAL TIMES TO THE PRESENT.
THE SOCIAL AND ECONOMIC FORCES CONTRIBUTING TO THE RISE OF
METAGOVERNMENT EMANATE FROM THE RURAL REGIONS AND THE HIGH
LEVELS OF POPULATION GROWTH IN THE REGIONS TOGETHER WITH THE
UNBALANCED PATTERNS OF REGIONAL DEVELOPMENT IN THE REGION.
METAGOVERNMENT IS A RESPONSE TO THE EXCLUSIONIST AND ELITIST
POLITICAL CULTURE, AND THE PRODUCT OF NEW SOCIAL FORCES AND
GROUPS ARISING IN URBAN LATIN AMERICA.

03143 FELOCK, R.C.
SUPPORT FOR BUSINESS IN THE FEDERAL DISTRICT COURTS: THE
IMPACT OF STATE POLITICAL ENVIRONMENT
AMERICAN POLITICS QUARTERLY, 17(1) (JAN 89), 96-104.
DESPITE EXTENSIVE LITERATURE RELATING LOCAL
SOCIOECONOMIC AND POLITICAL ENVIRONMENTS TO ECONOMIC OUTPUTS
OF STATE LEGISLATURES AND ADMINISTRATIVE AGENCIES, THERE HAS
BEEN NO COMPARABLE STUDY OF THE IMPACT OF LOCAL
ENVIRONMENTAL FACTORS ON ECONOMIC POLICY OUTCOMES OF EITHER
STATE OR FEDERAL TRIAL COURTS. THIS ARTICLE BEGINS TO FILL
THIS RESEARCH LACUNA BY EXAMINING THE COMBINED AND RELATIVE
EFFECTS OF STATE ECONOMIC DEVELOPMENT POLICIES AND JUDICIAL
BACKGROUND ON FEDERAL DISTRICT COURTS' ECONOMIC POLICYMAKING.
PROBUSINESS STATE DEVELOPMENT POLICIES ARE FOUND TO BE
POSITIVELY RELATED TO SUPPORT FOR BUSINESS IN FEDERAL
DISTRICT DECISIONS. CONCLUSIONS REGARDING THE IMPACT OF
ENVIRONMENTAL FACTORS ON DISTRICT COURT POLICY OUTCOMES ARE
OFFERED ALONG WITH A COMPARISON OF THIS RESEARCH WITH THE
LARGER AND MORE DEVELOPED BODY OF STATE AND LOCAL POLICY
RESEARCH.

03144 FELTS, A.A.
PRACTITIONERS IN THE CLASSROOM: THE VIEW FROM ONE SIDE
POLICY STUDIES REVIEW, 8(4) (SUM 89), 913-919.
PUTTING PRACTITIONERS INTO THE CLASSROOM TO TEACH
GRADUATE PUBLIC ADMINISTRATION COURSES IS A PRACTICE ABOUT
WHICH SURPRISINGLY LITTLE HAS BEEN WRITTEN. THE ISSUES
RAISED IN THIS ARTICLE ARE THE PRACTITIONERS ROLE IN
TEACHING MPA COURSES. THE AUTHOR EXAMINES THREE IMPORTANT
CONSIDERATIONS WHEN PRACTITIONERS BECOME TEACHERS. FIRST,
THE METHOD OF TEACHING IS EXPLORED WITH SPECIAL ATTENTION
BEING GIVEN TO CASE-STUDY TYPE APPROACHES. NEXT, THE
AUTHORITY WORLDS OF ACADEMICS AND PRACTITIONERS ARE COMPARED
WITH SEVERAL DIFFERENCES BEING HIGHLIGHTED. FINALLY, THE
IMAGE WORLD OF PRACTITIONERS IS EXAMINED WITH A KEEN EYE
BEING PLACED ON CRITICAL ANALYSIS.

03145 FENG, N.
EXTERNAL FACTORS PUSH PRIVATIZATION IN AFRICA
BEIJING REVIEW, 32(6) (FEB 89), 15-17.
IN THE 1980'S, A TIDE OF PRIVATIZATION SWEPT ACROSS THE
AFRICAN CONTINENT, BRINGING A MAJOR TURN IN AFRICA'S
STRATEGY OF ECONOMIC DEVELOPMENT. THIS TREND TOWARD AFRICAN
PRIVATIZATION HAS BECOME AN IMPORTANT ISSUE IN THE ECONOMIC
DEVELOPMENT OF THE THIRD WORLD. INTERNAL FACTORS HAVE BEEN
THE MOST IMPORTANT IMPULSES LEADING TO AFRICAN STRUCTURAL
ADJUSTMENTS ON THE BASIS OF PRIVATIZATION, BUT EXTERNAL
FACTORS HAVE ALSO PLAYED A VITAL ROLE.

03146 FENG, T.
THE PROBLEMS AND PROSPECTS OF THE TAIWAN ISSUE
DISSERTATION ABSTRACTS INTERNATIONAL, 50(6) (DEC 89),
1786-A.
THE AUTHOR STUDIES THE NATURE AND THE HISTORICAL ORIGINS
OF THE TAIWAN ISSUE. HE ASSESSES THE INTENTIONS, PERCEPTIONS,
AND BASIC PROPOSITIONS OF BOTH THE REPUBLIC OF CHINA AND
THE PEOPLE'S REPUBLIC OF CHINA. HE ENUMERATES THE POSSIBLE
PEACEFUL FORMULAS FOR SETTLING THE TAIWAN ISSUE AND
EVALUATES THE CONSEQUENCES OF EACH ALTERNATIVE

03147 FENGQI, R.
THE FIGHT AGAINST CORRUPTION GAINS MOMENTUM
CHINA RECONSTRUCTS, XXXVIII(11) (NOV 89), 24-26.
DURING THE STUDENT PROTESTS IN THE SPRING OF 1989, A
MAJOR COMPLAINT INVOLVED OFFICIAL CORRUPTION. ALTHOUGH IT IS
A GROSS DISTORTION TO SAY THAT MOST GOVERNMENT AND PARTY
OFFICIALS ARE CORRUPT, OFFICIAL MALPRACTICE HAS CERTAINLY
INCREASED AND BECOME MORE SERIOUS OVER THE LAST DECADE.
ATTEMPTS HAVE BEEN MADE TO STOP IT, BUT THE PROBLEM IS FAR
FROM SOLVED. THE DEMONSTRATIONS EMPHASIZED THE URGENT NATURE

OF THE PROBLEM, AND GOVERNMENTAL EFFORTS TO ERADICATE
CORRUPT PRACTICES HAVE BEEN REDOUBLED. IN RECENT MONTHS.

03148 FENNO, R.F. JR.
THE SENATE THROUGH THE LOOKING GLASS: THE DEBATE OVER
TELEVISION
LEGISLATIVE STUDIES QUARTERLY, 14(3) (AUG 89), 313-348.
OCCASIONALLY AN INSTITUTION'S MEMBERS TAKE PUBLIC STOCK
OF THEIR STRENGTHS AND WEAKNESSES, THEIR PROBLEMS, AND THEIR
POTENTIAL, WHERE THEY HAVE BEEN AND WHERE THEY OUGHT TO GO.
THESE MOMENTS OF SELF-SCRUTINY AND REFLECTION ARE·USEFUL TO
SCHOLARS. THIS ARTICLE PUTS THE SENATE DEBATE OVER
TELEVISING ITS PROCEEDINGS TO THAT USE. IT PLACES THE DEBATE
IN THE CONTEXT OF A CHANGING SENATE. IT USES THE LANGUAGE OF
THE DEBATE TO EXAMINE CONFLICTING IDEAS ABOUT WHAT THE
SENATE IS, AND OUGHT TO BE, LIKE. IT USES THE ACTUAL
DECISION PROCESS TO ILLUSTRATE THE DISTINCTIVE DELIBERATIVE
FEATURES OF THE INSTITUTION.

03149 FERGUSON, A.
A SEA OF STARS
NATIONAL REVIEW, 110(21) (NOV 89), .
THIS ARTICLE EXPLORES THE POLITICAL USE OF HOLLYWOOD
STARS BY THE LEFT FOR DEMONSTRATIONS ON BEHALF OF THE
HOMELESS, THE FMLN, THE OZONE LAYER, ABORTION RIGHTS ETC. IT
RECOUNTS HOW IN THE EARLY EIGHTIES THAT THE CELEBRITY
NETWORK WAS VAST BUT WITH THE NORMALIZING OF AMERICA,
RESPONSE FROM THE COMMUNITY HAS FALLEN OFF. IT EXAMINES THE
FACT THAT NOW, INCREASINGLY FEWER OF WELL KNOWN STARS ARE
PRESENT AT THESE FUNCTIONS.

03150 FERGUSON, A.
MAD ABOUT MAPPLETHORPE
NATIONAL REVIEW, XLI(14) (AUG 89), 20-21.
THIS ARTICLE CONSIDERS THE FIRST AMENDMENT RIGHTS OF
ROBERT MAPPLETHORPE, WHOSE ARTISTIC "EROTICISM" WAS FUNDED
BY A GRANT FROM THE NATIONAL ENDOWMENT FOR THE ARTS - MUCH
TO THE CHAGRIN OF SEVERAL LESS-THAN-IMPRESSED CONGRESSMEN
AND THEIR CONSTITUENTS.

03151 FERGUSON, T.
BY INVITATION ONLY: PARTY COMPETITION AND INDUSTRIAL
STRUCTURE IN THE 1988 ELECTION
SOCIALIST REVIEW, 19(4) (OCT 89), 73-104.
IN HIS ANALYSIS OF THE 1988 ELECTIONS, THE AUTHOR ARGUES
THAT THE DEMOCRATS LOST PRIMARILY DUE TO THEIR FORFEITURE OF
THEIR ANCESTRAL IDENTIFICATION AS THE PARTY OF PROSPERITY.
WITH THEIR CONSTANT FLIRTATION WITH AUSTERITY AND RAISING
TAXES, THE PARTY HAS LITTLE TO SAY TO ORDINARY AMERICANS ON
MANY ISSUES THAT MATTER MOST TO THEM. IN ADDITION, THE
AUTHOR RELIES ON THE "INVESTMENT APPROACH" TO PARTY POLITICS
AND USES DATA FROM THE FEDERAL ELECTION COMMISSION AND OTHER
SOURCES TO ATTEMPT TO APPLY THE "GOLDEN RULE" TO THE LAST
PRESIDENTIAL ELECTION: TO SEE WHO RULES, FOLLOW THE GOLD.
THE CHANGING ECONOMY AND THE CONSISTENT SUPPORT OF
REPUBLICANS BY BIG BUSINESS VIRTUALLY GUARANTEED A
REPUBLICAN VICTORY.

03152 FERIA, M.
PHILIPPINES
SOUTH, (108) (OCT 89), 59-80.
PRESIDENT CORAZON AQUINO HAS PROVED ADEPT AT POLITICAL
HOUSEKEEPING, HAS PUT COUP RUMORS BEHIND HER, AND HAS
INCREASED ECONOMIC EFFICIENCY. REPORTS INDICATE THAT THE
REBEL MOVEMENT IS WEAKENING, AND MANILA'S POLITICAL PROCESS
SEEMS TO BE SETTLING DOWN. THE RESOURCE-RICH PHILIPPINES IS
PROVING TO BE AN ATTRACTIVE LOCATION FOR COMPANIES LOOKING
FOR A CHEAP PRODUCTION BASE IN SOUTHEAST ASIA, BUT THE
ECONOMY IS BEING HEAVILY TAXED BY DEBT SERVICING.

03153 FERIA, M.; NIEVA, A.M.
THE PHILIPPINES
SOUTH, (100) (FEB 89), 43-54.
ALTHOUGH CORAZON AQUINO HAS NOW WEATHERED THREE STORMY
YEARS IN THE PRESIDENCY, HER PROBLEMS ARE FAR FROM OVER.
INJECTIONS OF FOREIGN CAPITAL AND NEW JOBS ARE REQUIRED TO
CHECK THE COMMUNIST INSURGENCY. BUT INVESTORS WILL REMAIN
CAUTIOUS AS LONG AS POLITICAL STABILITY ELUDES HER. LAST
YEAR'S DOUBLING IN INVESTMENT AND THE 6.4 PER CENT RISE IN
GNP INDICATED A BRIGHTENING BUSINESS CLIMATE. BUT ANALYSTS
ARE WARY OF READING TOO MUCH INTO THESE FIGURES.

03154 FERMAN, B.
SLOUCHING TOWARD ANARCHY: THE POLICY-MAKING/IMPLEMENTATION
GAP REVISITED
GOVERNANCE, 2(2) (APR 89), 198-212.
FOR MORE THAN TWO DECADES POLITICAL SCIENTISTS HAVE
AGONIZED OVER THE LARGE GAP BETWEEN POLICY-MAKING AND
IMPLEMENTATION. SINCE THE POLICYMAKING/IMPLEMENTATION
PROCESS IS USUALLY A TOP-DOWN ONE, MOST ATTEMPTS AT REFORM
ARE ALSO TOP-DOWN AND FALL VICTIM TO THE SAME PROBLEMS. EVEN
SUCCESSFUL ATTEMPTS AT REFORM ARE GENERALLY IDIOSYNCRATIC IN
NATURE AND DIFFICULT TO REPLICATE; HIGH COSTS ALSO LIMIT THE
EFFECTIVENESS OF MANY REFORMS. THE ARTICLE ARGUES THE

REGARDLESS OF THE DIRECTION OF ATTEMPTED REFORMS, THE
STRUCTURE OF AMERICAN POLITICS PUSHES THE
POLICY/IMPLEMENTATION SYSTEM TOWARDS ANARCHY. ELIMINATING
THE GAP BETWEEN POLICYMAKING AND IMPLEMENTATION REQUIRES A
MAJOR RESTRUCTURING OF AMERICAN GOVERNMENT.

03155 FERMON, N.
THE POLITICAL EDUCATION OF SENTIMENT: ROUSSEAU'S TEACHING
ON THE FAMILY AND THE STATE
DISSERTATION ABSTRACTS INTERNATIONAL, 49(10) (APR 89),
3141-A.
ROUSSEAU SHOULD BE SEEN PRIMARILY AS A POLITICAL
REFORMER. HIS NOVELS, "THE NOUVELLE HELOISE" AND "EMILE OR
ON EDUCATION," WERE DIRECT ATTEMPTS TO CHANGE THE MORALS OF
THE FRENCH ARISTOCRACY AND THEY WERE NOT WITHOUT EFFECT.
ROUSSEAU'S POLITICAL THOUGHT VALORIZES THE ROLE OF SENTIMENT
RATHER THAN INTEREST IN CIVIC LIFE AND THE STATE RATHER THAN
THE MARKET AS THE APPROPRIATE REALM IN ORGANIZING SOCIAL
LIFE. IN THE COURSE OF ADDRESSING SPECIFIC PROBLEMS OF
CONTEMPORARY POLITICS, ROUSSEAU RE-DEFINED KEY TERMS OF
POLITICAL DISCOURSE AND ESTABLISHED A NEW SYNTHESIS BETWEEN
AN UNDERSTANDING OF POLITICS AS VIRTUE AND AN UNDERSTANDING
OF POLITICS AS RIGHTS.

03156 FERNANDEZ, D.J.
CUBA: INFLEXIBILIDAD TOTAL?
HEMISPHERE, 2(1) (FAL 89), 10-11.
NEITHER CASTRO'S RHETORIC NOR THE DRAMATIC EVENTS IN THE
SOVIET BLOC ARE APPROPRIATE LENSES THROUGH WHICH TO LOOK AT
CONTEMPORARY CUBAN POLITICS. TO HARP ON CASTRO'S IDEOLOGICAL
RIGIDITY OR TO USE EASTERN EUROPE AS A MODEL FOR WHAT AWAITS
CUBA IS TO MISS TWO FUNDAMENTAL POINTS. CHANGES HAVE BEEN
OCCURRING INSIDE CUBA NOT AS MERE REPERCUSIONS FROM EXTERNAL
EVENTS BUT AS A RESULT OF INTERNAL DYNAMICS. CUBAN HISTORY,
AND SPECIFICALLY THE CUBAN REVOLUTION, HAVE ALWAYS BEEN
ATYPICAL AND SHOULD NOT BE CAST IN THE MOLDS THAT FIT OTHER
SOCIETIES.

03157 FERNANDO, K.
CHRISTIAN PERCEPTION AND ETHNIC CRISIS IN SRI LANKA
SCANDINAVIAN JOURNAL OF DEVELOPMENT ALTERNATIVES, VIII(2)
(JUN 89), 29-36.
THE ARTICLE GIVES BACKGROUND TO THE CURRENT ETHNIC
TENSIONS IN SRI LANKA. IT OUTLINES THE SOURCES AND
IMPLICATIONS OF THE ONGOING CONFLICT BETWEEN THE MAJORITY
SIHNALESE AND THE MINORITY TAMIL COMMUNITIES. IT ALSO
EXPLORES THE ROLE THAT RELIGION AND CHURCHES, WITH EMPHASIS
ON CHRISTIANITY CAN PLAY IN DEFUSING TENSIONS AND CONFLICTS
AND AIDING IN THE FORMATION AND ACHIEVEMENT OF LONG-TERM
SOLUTIONS TO THE PROBLEM.

03158 FERNANDO, T.
INTERNATIONALISM OF ETHNO - POLITICAL ISSUES OF SRI LANKA
AND ITS IMPACT ON FOREIGN RELATIONS
SCANDINAVIAN JOURNAL OF DEVELOPMENT ALTERNATIVES, 8(3)
(SEP 89), 91-94.
THIS ARTICLE BY THE DEPUTY MINISTER OF FOREIGN AFFAIRS
FOR THE GOVERNMENT OF SRI/LANKA BEGINS BY DESCRIBING THE
SOCIETY OF SRI LANKA AND SOME OF THE PROBLEMS A PLURAL
SOCIETY IS VULNERABLE TO, ESPECIALLY WHEN IT HAS ONLY
RECENTLY EMERGED FROM COLONIAL RULE. IT DESCRIBES PRESENT
GOVERNMENT EFFORTS TO MEET TAMIL GREVIENCES ALTHOUGH THE
MORE RADICAL ELEMENTS STILL CALLED FOR SEPARATISM. THE
INTERNATIONALIZATION OF THE ETHNIC CONFLICT IS DETAILED, AND
THE ROLE THAT THE INDIAN GOVERNMENT PLAYED IN SEARCHING FOR
SOLUTIONS.

03159 FEUER, L.
THE INVENTOR OF "PLURALISM"
NEW LEADER, LXXII(13) (SEP 89), 12-13.
THE ARTICLE EXAMINES THE FATHER OF THE CONCEPT OF
POLITICAL PLURALISM, HAROLD J. LASKI. LASKI, A LIBERAL WITH
SOCIALIST LEANINGS, INTRODUCED THE TERM IN 1915. ALTHOUGH
HIS STEADY MOVEMENT FURTHER AND FURTHER LEFT ALIENATED MAY
OF HIS FOLLOWERS, THE WIDESPREAD PURSUIT OF DIFFUSION OF
POWER AMONG A PLURALITY OF INDEPENDENT ASSOCIATIONS STILL
HOLDS CONSIDERABLE APPEAL WORLDWIDE. THE PLURALIST
VOCABULARY IS BECOMING INCREASING UBIQUITOUS AND IS EVEN
ENTERING SOVIET CIRCLES.

03160 FIELD, M.
FRENCH FEDERALISM
FAR EASTERN ECONOMIC REVIEW, 141(28) (JUL 88), 34.
KANAK (INDIGENOUS MELANESIAN) AND FRENCH SETTLER LEADERS
CAME TO AN AGREEMENT ON NEW CALEDONIA'S FUTURE WITH
SURPRISING SPEED. PARTITION OF THE SOUTH PACIFIC TERRITORY-
WHICH MANY VIEWED AS THE ONLY SOLUTION TO THE COMMUNAL
VIOLENCE--WAS REJECTED AS AN OPTION. INSTEAD A FORM OF
FEDERALISM UNDER SCRUTINY OF THE FRENCH STATE WITH A VOTE ON
SELF-DETERMINATION IN 10 YEARS WAS ADVOCATED AND ADOPTED.
MANY VIEW THE AGREEMENT AS A SIGNIFICANT PART OF THE
DECOLONIZATION PROCESS.

03161 FIELDS, A.
GULF COOPERATION COUNCIL: ITS FUTURE IMPACT ON MIDDLE EAST
STABILITY
AVAILABLE FROM NTIS, NO. AD-A207 315/3/GAR, MAR 89, 41.
IN MAY OF THIS YEAR, THE GULF COOPERATION COUNCIL (GCC)
WILL CELEBRATE ITS EIGHTH ANNIVERSARY. PRINCIPALLY FORMED TO
CONSOLIDATE THE ECONOMIC INTERESTS OF SIX PERSIAN GULF
STATES--BAHRAIN, KUWAIT, OMAN, QATAR, SAUDI ARABIA AND THE
UNITED ARAB EMIRATES (UAE)--THE GCC HAS EVOLVED INTO AN
ASTUTE POLITICAL INSTRUMENT WITH EVER INCREASING MILITARY
POWER. FEARFUL THAT THE IRAN-IRAQ WAR WOULD SPREAD TO THE
WESTERN GULF, THE LEVEL OF COOPERATION BETWEEN THE GCC
STATES TRANSCENDED AGE-OLD RIVALRIES AND UNSETTLED DISPUTES.
NOW THAT THE GULF WAR HAS SUBSIDED, THESE OLD RIVALRIES AND
DISPUTES MAY SURFACE, AND SUPERPOWER INITIATIVES MAY CAUSE
MAJOR REGIONAL POLICY CHANGES. THIS PAPER SEEKS TO BROADLY
ANALYZE THE PAST, PRESENT AND FUTURE ROLE OF THE GCC IN THE
GEOPOLITICS OF THE PERSIAN GULF REGION. IT FIRST ADDRESSES
THE SOCIAL THREATS ENDEMIC TO EACH GCC STATE AND THE THREATS
TO STABILITY THEY POSE. NEXT, THE PAPER PROVIDES A BROAD
HISTORICAL PERSPECTIVE OF U.S.-PERSIAN GULF REGIONAL POLICY
INCLUDING HOW IT EVOLVED AND HOW THE IRANIAN REVOLUTION
CAUSED IT TO BE REEVALUATED. FINALLY, THE PAPER SUGGESTS
THAT THE VOID LEFT BY THE DEMISE OF THE TWIN PILLARS POLICY
HAS NOT BEEN FILLED AND THAT ALLOWING THE GCC TO BECOME A DE
FACTO U.S. SURROGATE IS NOT IN THE BEST INTEREST OF REGIONAL
STABILITY.

03162 FIELDS, K.J.
TRADING COMPANIES IN SOUTH KOREA AND TAIWAN
ASIAN SURVEY, 29(11) (NOV 89), 1073-1089.
THIS ARTICLE EXAMINES THE EFFORTS OF GOVERNMENT-INSPIRED
INDUSTRIAL - COMMERCIAL POLICY IN THE POLITICAL ECONOMIES OF
SOUTH KOREA AND JAPAN. IT CHRONICLES THE LARGELY SUCCESSFUL
EFFORT OF THE SOUTH KOREAN STATE TO FOSTER THE DEVELOPMENT
OF LARGE SCALE TRADING COMPANIES AND TAIWAN'S FAILURE TO
ACHIEVE THE SAME OBJECTIVE. THE ANALYSIS OF THE TWO
COMPARABLE CASES NOT ONLY ILLUMINATES THE SPECIFIC
INCENTIVES AND OBSTACLES IN THE TWO ENVIRONMENTS, BUT ALSO
SHEDS LIGHT ON THE FACTORS INFLUENCING THE FATE OF STATE-
IMPLEMENTED INDUSTRIAL POLICIES IN GENERAL.

03163 FIESLER, B.
THE MAKING OF RUSSIAN FEMALE SOCIAL DEMOCRATS, 1890-1917
INTERNATIONAL REVIEW OF SOCIAL HISTORY, 34(2) (1989),
193-226.
THE SOCIAL COMPOSITION OF FEMALE RSDRP MEMBERS (WHO
CONSTITUTED BETWEEN 11% AND 15% OF THE TOTAL PARTY
MEMBERSHIP) PRIOR TO 1917 IS ANALYZED USING PROSOPOGRAPHIC
METHODS. THE ANALYSIS REVEALS THAT WOMEN SOCIAL DEMOCRATS
TENDED TO COME FROM HIGHER SOCIAL CLASSES, AND TO HAVE A
HIGH EDUCATIONAL ATTAINMENT, AND PROFESSIONAL OCCUPATIONS.
THUS, IT IS MISLEADING TO CHARACTERIZE THE RSDRP AS A
"WORKERS' PARTY", FOR ONLY ITS MALE CONTINGENT WAS COMPOSED
MOSTLY OF WORKERS. THE ANALYSIS OF THE PROCESS OF
RADICALIZATION REVEALS THE CULTURAL BARRIERS WHICH THESE
WOMEN HAD TO OVERCOME BEFORE THEY WOULD JOIN THE PARTY.
BREAKING FREE FROM THEIR ROLE IN SOCIETY MEANT, FOR THEM,
LEADING FULLER LIVES AS WOMEN AND AN OPPORTUNITY TO DEDICATE
THEMSELVES TO THE PEOPLE.

03164 FILTZER, D.
THE SOVIET WAGE REFORM OF 1956-1962
SOVIET STUDIES, XLI(1) (JAN 89), 88-110.
THE ARTICLE EXAMINES THE WAGE REFORM IMPLEMENTED UNDER
KHRUSCHEV BEGINING IN 1956. IN ORDER TO UNDERSTAND THE
IMPLICATIONS OF THE WAGE REFORM, THE ARTICLE BEGINS WITH AN
ANALYSIS OF THE MAJOR FEATURES OF THE WAGES SYSTEM UNDER
STALIN, THE REFORM, AND ITS GENERAL RESULTS. THE ARTICLE
ALSO TAKES A DETAILED LOOK AT THE DIFFERENT PROBLEMS THE
REFORM ENCOUNTERED IN INDIVIDUAL INDUSTRIES.

03165 FINCHER, J.
ZHAO'S FALL, CHINA'S LOSS
FOREIGN POLICY, (76) (FAL 89), 3-25.
THIS ARTICLE ANALYSES THE POLITICAL CONSEQUENCES OF THE
ECLIPSE OF ZHAO'S BRILLIANT CAREER CULMINATING IN THE TRAUMA
OF TIANANMEN SQUARE IN JUNE, 1989. IT ADVOCATES MODERATION
WHICH IS UNLIKELY FROM DENG BUT LOOKS FOR ANOTHER ZHAO TO
EMERGE. IT DISCUSSES THE ALTERNATIVES THAT OUTSIDE POWERS
HAVE IN THEIR DEALINGS WITH CHINA.

03166 FINE-DAVIS, M.
ATTITUDES TOWARD THE ROLE OF WOMEN AS PART OF A LARGER
BELIEF SYSTEM
POLITICAL PSYCHOLOGY, 10(2) (JUN 89), 287-308.
THE ROLE OF WOMEN IN IRELAND HAS BEEN A RELATIVELY
TRADITIONAL ONE DUE TO THE STRONG CATHOLIC RELIGIOUS ETHOS
AND OTHER FACTORS. HOWEVER, SINCE THE EARLY 1970'S IRELAND
HAS EXPERIENCED A PERIOD OF RAPID SOCIAL CHANGE RESULTING IN
A NUMBER OF SIGNIFICANT LEGISLATIVE AND ADMINISTRATIVE
REFORMS CONCERNING WOMEN, AS WELL AS A MARKED INCREASE IN
MARRIED WOMEN'S LABOR FORCE PARTICIPATION. HOWEVER, THIS
PARTICIPATION IS STILL QUITE LOW BY U.S. AND EUROPEAN

STANDARDS. THIS PAPER FOCUSSES ON THE ROLE OF ATTITUDES IN
PERPETUATING INEQUALITY AND RIGID SEX-ROLE BEHAVIOR.
ATTITUDINAL DATA FROM A REPRESENTATIVE NATIONWIDE SAMPLE ARE
PRESENTED CONCERNING THE ROLE AND STATUS OF WOMEN. WITH
PARTICULAR REFERENCE TO THE EMPLOYMENT STATUS OF MARRIED
WOMEN. IN ADDITION TO EXPLORING THE DEMOGRAPHIC DETERMINANTS
OF THESE ATTITUDES, A DETAILED EXAMINATION IS MADE OF THEIR
RELATIONSHIP TO OTHER SOCIAL ATTITUDES AND BELIEFS, OF WHICH
A KEY ELEMENT WAS FOUND TO BE RELIGIOSITY. A CASE IS MADE
THAT THESE CONSTITUTE A BELIEF SYSTEM WITH MANY COMPONENTS
REMINISCENT OF THE AUTHORITARIAN PERSONALITY. THE
IMPLICATIONS OF THESE ATTITUDES FOR MARRIED WOMEN'S FUTURE
LABOR FORCE PARTICIPATION AND WELL-BEING ARE DISCUSSED.

03167 FINE, B.
IS THERE SUCH A THING AS "PEOPLE'S CAPITALISM"?
WORLD MARXIST REVIEW, 31(2) (FEB 88), 129-135.
IMPORTANT FOR THE LABOUR MOVEMENT IS THAT IT SHOULD NOT
BE SEDUCED INTO ACCEPTING THE IDEOLOGY OF 'PEOPLE'S
CAPITALISM' AND THAT IT SHOULD RETAIN THE PERSPECTIVE OF
SOCIAL OWNERSHIP AND CLASS CONFLICT AS THE MEANS OF
ACHIEVING THIS STRATEGIC GOAL. THERE ARE SIGNS THAT THE
RIGHT WING OF THE BRITISH LABOUR PARTY COULD ATTEMPT TO
APPROPRIATE THE POLICIES OF 'PEOPLE'S CAPITALISM' IN PLACE
OF SOCIALIST POLICIES. THEY HAVE ALREADY ACCEPTED THE IDEA
OF OWNER-OCCUPATION IN HOUSING AT THE EXPENSE OF PUBLIC
OWNERSHIP. THIS WING MAY WELL PREFER A WORKERS' SHARE SCHEME
OVER NATIONALISATION IN ORDER TO EXERT INFLUENCE ON THE
EMPLOYERS' DECISIONMAKING.

03168 FINGER, H.B.
IS THERE ANOTHER ENERGY CRISIS IN OUR FUTURE?
STATE LEGISLATURES, 15(8) (SEP 89), 30.
THE NATIONAL CONFERENCE OF STATE LEGISLATURES AND THE
NATIONAL GOVERNORS' ASSOCIATION HAVE OVERWHELMINGLY PASSED
RESOLUTIONS ACKNOWLEDGING AMERICA'S NEED FOR NUCLEAR ENERGY.
RECENT DEVELOPMENTS HAVE ALSO SHOWN CONGRESSIONAL SUPPORT
FOR ADDITIONAL NUCLEAR CAPACITY. THIS POLITICAL SUPPORT
REFLECTS THE VIEWS OF THE AMERICAN PUBLIC.

03169 FINGER, J.M.; MESSERLIN, P.A.
EFFECTS OF INDUSTRIAL COUNTRIES' POLICIES ON DEVELOPING
COUNTRIES
AVAILABLE FROM NTIS, NO. PB89-220305/GAR, 1989, 37.
THE REPORT EXAMINES THE CROSS-COUNTRY EFFECTS OF
INDUSTRIAL COUNTRIES' POLICIES ON DEVELOPING COUNTRY TRADE
AND OUTPUT. TOPICS DISCUSSED ARE: INDUSTRIAL POLICIES,
DOMESTIC SUBSIDIES, TARIFFS: PATTERNS AND EFFECTS, NONTARIFF
BARRIERS, EVOLVING FORMS OF PROTECTION, THE CONCENTRATION OF
EXPORTS, EFFECTS ON DEVELOPING COUNTRIES, MAJOR FINDINGS AND
IMPLICATIONS.

03170 FINGER, S.M.; MANELI, M.
ON FLEXIBLE CONTAINMENT
POLITICAL COMMUNICATION AND PERSUASION, 5(4) (1988),
287-290.
THE EMERGENCE OF GORBACHEV AS A DYNAMIC LEADER, FLEXIBLE
IN HIS RELATIONS WITH NONCOMMUNIST COUNTRIES, MAKES THE
RIGID CONTAINMENT PRACTICES OF THE POSTWAR DECADES DECIDEDLY
OUTDATED AND COUNTERPRODUCTIVE. THE INTERNATIONAL CHESSBOARD
HAS BECOME A GAME OF MOVEMENT, SENSITIVITY, AND SUBTLETY.
CONSEQUENTLY, THE UNITED STATES SHOULD USE IN ITS
INTERNATIONAL RELATIONS THE CONCEPT OF PLURALISM THAT WE
HAVE USED TO SUCCESSFULLY AT HOME. THIS MEANS
DIFFERENTIATION AMONG THE VARIOUS MARXIST REGIMES,
CALIBRATING OUR POLICY WITH FLEXIBILITY TOWARD EACH
COUNTRY'S POLICY AND OUR NATIONAL INTERESTS.

03171 FINIFTER, A.W.; FINIFTER, B.M.
PARTY IDENTIFICATION AND POLITICAL ADAPTATION OF AMERICAN
MIGRANTS IN AUSTRALIA
THE JOURNAL OF POLITICS, 51(3) (AUG 89), 599-630.
THE STUDY OF INTERNATIONAL MIGRANTS REVEALS PROCESSES OF
POLITICAL RESOCIALIZATION THAT INCLUDE TRANSLATION,
EXPANSION, AND REPLACEMENT OF PRIOR POLITICAL LEARNING. THIS
PAPER DEMONSTRATES THAT AMERICAN PARTY IDENTIFICATION
INFLUENCES THE POLITICAL ADAPTATION OF AMERICAN MIGRANTS IN
AUSTRALIA BY AFFECTING BOTH WHETHER OR NOT THEY ADOPT AN
AUSTRALIAN PARTY IDENTIFICATION AND THE PARTICULAR PARTIES
THEY SELECT. HOWEVER, POLITICAL IDEOLOGY IS AN EVEN MORE
IMPORTANT FACTOR IN SELECTING A NEW PARTY IDENTIFICATION AND,
IN PARTICULAR, LEADS SOME AMERICAN DEMOCRATS TO CHOOSE A
MORE CONSERVATIVE PARTY, AND SOME AMERICAN REPUBLICANS A
MORE LIBERAL ONE, IN AUSTRALIA. PEOPLE WHO WERE WEAK
PARTISANS IN THE UNITED STATES ARE MORE LIKELY THAN OTHERS
TO RELINQUISH THEIR AMERICAN PARTISANSHIP ONCE IN AUSTRALIA.
OVER AND ABOVE THESE INDIVIDUAL-LEVEL VARIABLES, THE
POLITICAL ENVIRONMENTS IS ALSO INFLUENTIAL: MIGRANTS TEND
FAVOR PARTIES THAT HAVE BEEN ELECTORALLY MORE SUCCESSFUL IN
THE AUSTRALIAN STATE IN WHICH THEY LIVE. THESE AND OTHER
FINDINGS SUGGEST THAT BOTH AMERICAN PARTISANSHIP AND OVERALL
POLITICAL IDEOLOGY PLAY KEY ROLES IN HELPING MIGRANTS TO
ADAPT POLITICALLY TO THEIR NEW ENVIRONMENTS, AND THAT NEW
POLITICAL LEARNING IS GENERALLY DEPENDENT UPON PREVIOUSLY

ESTABLISHED POLITICAL ATTITUDES. NEVERTHELESS, MIGRANTS'
POLITICAL ADAPTATION IS ALSO AFFECTED BY THE POLITICAL
CONTEXT OF THE NEW RESIDENCE.

03172 FINKEL, A.
THE SOCIAL CREDIT PHENOMENON
UNIVERSITY OF TORONTO PRESS, TORONTO, ONTARIO, CA, 1989,
336.
FEW PARTIES IN POLITICAL HISTORY HAVE HAD SUCH A SHIFT
METAMORPHOSIS FROM ONE END OF THE POLITICAL SPECTRUM TO THE
OTHER AS DID THE SOCIAL CREDIT PARTY OF ALBERTA. BETWEEN ITS
ESTABLISHMENT IN THE 1930S AND THE DEFEAT OF THE SOCIAL
CREDIT GOVERNMENT IN 1971, THE PARTY CHANGED FROM A MOVEMENT-
BASED REFORMIST ORGANIZATION TO A CLIQUISH, RELIGIOUS-
ORIENTED OUTFIT WHOSE MAIN PURPOSE WAS TO HOLD THE LEVERS OF
POWER. IN THIS ACCOUNT OF THE SOCIAL CREDIT TRANSFORMATION,
ALVIN FINKEL CHALLENGES EARLIER WORKS WHICH FOCUS PURELY ON
SOCIAL CREDIT MONETARY FIXATIONS AND RELIGIOSITY; HE ARGUES
THAT THE EARLY PARTY IS BEST SEEN AS A COALITION OF
REFORMERS.

03173 FINKEL, S.E.; MULLER, E.N.; SELIGSON, M.A.
ECONOMIC CRISIS, INCUMBENT PERFORMANCE, AND REGIME SUPPORT:
A COMPARISON OF LONGITUDIANAL DATA FROM WEST GERMANY AND
COSTA RICA
BRITISH JOURNAL OF POLITICAL SCIENCE, 19(3) (JUL 89),
329-351.
WHILE MUCH IS KNOWN ABOUT THE EFFECTS OF THE ECONOMY ON
THE POPULARITY AND ELECTORAL FORTUNES OF POLITICAL LEADERS,
POLITICAL SCIENTISTS KNOW VERY LITTLE ABOUT HOW ECONOMIC
DECLINE AND POLITICAL PERFORMANCE INFLUENCE SUPPORT FOR THE
POLITICAL REGIME AND THE STABILITY OF DEMOCRATIC SYSTEMS.
THE AUTHORS USE THREE CROSS-NATIONAL LONMGITUDINAL SURVEYS
TO ADDRESS THIS ISSUE: TWO COLLECTED IN COSTA RICA IN THE
MIDST OF A SEVERE ECONOMIC CRISIS IN THE LATE 1970S AND
EARLY 1980S; AND ONE IN WEST GERMANY DURING THE RECESSION OF
THE MID-1970S. IN BOTH COUNTRIES, OVERALL SUPPORT FOR THE
POLITICAL REGIME REMAINED EXTREMELY HIGH DURING THE ECONOMIC
DECLINE, WHILE SATISFACTION WITH INCUMBENT PERFORMANCE
FLUCTUATED MUCH MORE SHARPLY. MOREOVER, AT THE INDIVIDUAL
LEVEL, CHANGES IN SATISFACTION WITH INCUMBENT PERFORMANCE
WERE ONLY WEAKLY RELATED TO CHANGES IN REGIME SUPPORT. THESE
RESULTS PROVIDE STRONG EVIDENCE SUGGESTING THAT IF
DEMOCRACIES ENTER ECONOMIC DOWNTURNS WITH INITIALLY HIGH
LEVELS OF REGIME SUPPORT THEY WILL BE ABLE TO WITHSTAND EVEN
SEVERE, PROLONGED CRISES OF ECONOMIC PERFORMANCE.

03174 FINKEL, S.E.
EFFECTS OF THE 1980 AND 1984 CAMPAIGNS ON MASS IDEOLOGICAL
ORIENTATIONS: TESTING THE SALIENCE HYPOTHESIS
WESTERN POLITICAL QUARTERLY, 42(3) (SEP 89), 325-346.
RECENT RESEARCH HAS ARGUED AGAINST THE "SALIENCE
HYPOTHESIS," WHICH LINKS CHANGES IN IDEOLOGICAL ORIENTATIONS
IN THE MASS PUBLIC TO CHANGES IN THE IDEOLOGICAL INTENSITY
OF THE POLITICAL ENVIRONMENT. THIS PAPER TESTS THE SALIENCE
HYPOTHESIS IN THREE WAYS: BY EXAMINING CHANGES IN
IDEOLOGICAL ORIENTATIONS WITHIN, AS OPPOSED TO ACROSS,
CAMPAIGNS; BY EXAMINING INDIVIDUAL-LEVEL CHANGE WITH PANEL
DATA FROM THE 1980 ELECTION; AND BY BROADENING THE VARIABLES
TESTED TO INCLUDE MEASURES OF IDEOLOGICAL RECOGNITION AND
AWARENESS. THE RESULTS SHOW THAT AT THE AGGREGATE LEVEL, THE
PUBLIC CHANGED VERY LITTLE IN ITS IDEOLOGICAL EVALUATIONS
DURING THESE ELECTIONS. AT THE INDIVIDUAL LEVEL, THOUGH,
CHANGES WERE CORRELATED TO SOME EXTENT WITH INTEREST IN THE
CAMPAIGN AND WITH EDUCATIONAL ATTAINMENT. THE POLITICAL
ENVIRONMENT APPEARS TO HAVE A DISCERNIBLE, THOUGH LIMITED,
ROLE IN STRUCTURING MASS IDEOLOGICAL EVALUATIONS OVER TIME.

03175 FINKEL, S.E.; MULLER, E.N.; OPP, K.
PERSONAL INFLUENCE, COLLECTIVE RATIONALITY, AND MASS
POLITICAL ACTION
AMERICAN POLITICAL SCIENCE REVIEW, 83(3) (SEP 89), 885-904.
THE AUTHORS PROPOSE TWO MODELS TO EXPLAIN WHY
INDIVIDUALS PARTICIPATE IN COLLECTIVE POLITICAL ACTION--A
PERSONAL INFLUENCE MODEL AND A COLLECTIVE RATIONALITY MODEL.
EACH MODEL OVERCOMES THE FREE-RIDER PROBLEM POSED BY
CONVENTIONAL RATIONAL CHOICE THEORY AND LEFT UNRESOLVED IN
PREVIOUS RESEARCH. THE MODELS ARE TESTED FOR LEGAL AND
ILLEGAL PROTEST BEHAVIORS, USING DATA FROM A NATIONAL SAMPLE
AND TWO SAMPLES OF PROTEST-PRONE COMMUNITIES IN THE FEDERAL
REPUBLIC OF GERMANY. THE PERSONAL INFLUENCE MODEL IS
SUPPORTED FOR BOTH FORMS OF PARTICIPATION, WHILE THE
COLLECTIVE RATIONALITY MODEL IS SUPPORTED FOR LEGAL PROTEST.
THEY DISCUSS IMPLICATIONS OF THE RESULTS FOR GRIEVANCE AND
RATIONAL CHOICE THEORIES OF COLLECTIVE POLITICAL ACTION.

03176 FINKELSTEIN, L.S.
WHAT WAR IN EUROPE? THE IMPLICATIONS OF LEGITIMATE
STABILITY
POLITICAL SCIENCE QUARTERLY, 104(3) (FAL 89), 443-446.
EAST-WEST RELATIONS IN EUROPE ARE AND HAVE BEEN FOR SOME
TIME UNCOMMONLY STABLE. THAT STABILITY REPRESENTS A PRUDENCE
THAT HAS EXISTED EVEN WITHOUT THE PROMISING NEW LEADERSHIP
OF THE SOVIET UNION UNDER MIKHAIL GORBACHEV AND THE REFORMS

THAT HAVE BEEN LAUNCHED THERE, WELCOME THOUGH THEY ARE. IN
THE CONTEXT OF THAT PRUDENCE, NO ISSUES IN EUROPE HAVE
THREATENED EAST-WEST WAS FOR DECADES AND NONE SEEM LIKELY TO.
THUS, A FEAR OF EUROPEAN WAS UNNECESSARILY THREATENS THE
CONSENSUS THAT SHOULD BE THE PRIMARY AIM OF NATO POLICY.

03177 FINKELSTEIN, N.
ISRAEL AND THE "SCOURGE" OF PALESTINIAN MEDERATION
NEW POLITICS, 11(3) (SUM 89), 75-88.
AN INTERNATIONAL CONSENSUS EXISTS FOR RESOLVING THE
PALESTINIAN-ISRAELI CONFLICT. THE ONLY REAL OBSTACLE TO A
NEGOTIATED SETTLEMENT IS THE STEADFAST REFUSAL OF ISRAEL AND
ITS U.S. ALLY TO RECOGNIZE THE PALESTINIAN PEOPLE'S RIGHT TO
SELF-DETERMINATION. FURTHERMORE, THE FIRST CASUALTY OF THIS
CONFLICT HAS BEEN THE TRUTH.

03178 FINKELSTEIN, N.
THE SCOURGE OF PALESTINIAN MODERATION
MIDDLE EAST REPORT, 19(158) (MAY 89), 25-30.
THE PLO MAINSTREAM IS COMMITTED TO AN ACCOMMODATIONIST
SETTLEMENT OF THE MIDDLE EAST CONFLICT. THE TRUTH IS THAT
THE ISRAELI GOVERNMENT DREADS SUCH PALESTINIAN MODERATION.
HISTORICALLY, ISRAEL HAS RESORTED TO EVERY IMAGINABLE DEVICE
TO ISOLATE THE PALESTINIAN MODERATES BECAUSE THEY PUT ITS
OWN UNRELENTING REJECTIONISM IN SUCH STARK RELIEF.

03179 FINLAYSON, J.
US TRADE POLICY: THE REAGAN LEGACY
INTERNATIONAL PERSPECTIVES, XVIII (MAR 89), 3-6.
THE ARTICLE EXPLORES ONE CRUCIAL ELEMENT OF THE
CONTEMPORARY US ECONOMIC PICTURE--THE UNSUSTAINABLE US
EXTERNAL IMBALANCE CAUSED BY ITS LARGE TRADE AND CURRENT
ACCOUNT DEFICITS. IT ASSESSES THE POSSIBLE CONSEQUENCES OF
THESE DEFICITS FOR FUTURE US TRADE POLICY. THE ARTICLE ALSO
OFFERS A BRIEF APPRAISAL OF THE IMPACT OF THE REAGAN ERA ON
AMERICAN TRADE POLICY.

03180 FINN, C.E. JR.
A NATION STILL AT RISK
COMMENTARY, 87(5) (MAY 89), 17-23.
WHEN GAUGED IN TERMS OF STUDENT LEARNING, THE RESULTS OF
THE EXCELLENCE MOVEMENT IN AMERICAN EDUCATION HAVE BEEN
SCANT DESPITE THE EFFORTS OF STATES TO ENACT REFORM
LEGISLATION TO IMPROVE SCHOOLS.

03181 FINN, C.E. JR.
THE CAMPUS: "AN ISLAND OF REPRESSION IN A SEA OF FREEDOM"
COMMENTARY, 88(3) (SEP 89), 17-23.
THIS ARTICLE EXPLORES THE APPLICATION OF THE FIRST
AMMENDMENT WITHIN THE STRUCTURE OF HIGHER EDUCATION. IT
DISCOVERS A GROWING TREND AMONG UNIVERSITIES TO PROHIBIT
CONDUCT THAT "STIGMATIZES OR VICTIMIZES AN INDIVIDUAL ON THE
BASIS OF RACE, ETHNICITY, RELIGION, SEX, SEXUAL ORIENTATION,
CREED, NATIONAL ORIGIN, ANCESTRY, AGE, MARITAL STATUS,
HANDICAP, OR VIETNAM-ERA VETERAN STATUS." IT EXAMINES
EFFORTS ON THE PART OF STUDENTS TO DEMAND CONTROLS IMPOSED
ON CAMPUS BEHAVIOR; AND THE REACTION OF COLLEGE PROFESSORS
WHO FIND THEMSELVES CHALLENGED.

03182 FINN, C.E. JR.
THE CHOICE BACKLASH
NATIONAL REVIEW, 110(21) (NOV 89), 30-32.
THIS ARTICLE CONSIDERS THE EDUCATION ESTABLISHMENT'S
ASSAULT ON PUBLIC SCHOOL CHOICE. IT EXPLORES UPWARD MOBILITY,
PARENTAL VS. STATE DECISION, AND "MARKET PLACE" NEED OF
SCHOOLS. IT ALSO EXAMINES THE ARGUEMENTS AGAINST CHOICE,
PRIVATIZATION, PROTECTIVE PATERNALISM FOR THE POOR. CHAOS
AND IMPOVERISHMENT AND THE IMPOSSIBILITY OF ONE THING BEING
A CURE-ALL. IT INSISTS THAT IT IS FOR THE STUDENT'S BENEFIT
THAT WE MUST SHAPE POLICIES BY WHICH THE SYSTEM OPERATES.

03183 FINN, E.
SO, YE WANT TO GET ELECTED
CANADIAN FORUM, 68(783) (NOV 89), 18-21.
THIS ARTICLE, WRITTEN BY ED FLINN, THIS FIRST LEADER OF
THE NEWFOUNDLAND NDP TAKES THE READER INSIDE ISLAND POLITICS.
HE DESCRIBES HIS EXPERIENCE OF RUNNING AGAINST JOEY
SMALLWOOD, AS WELL AS TRACES THE HISTORY OF THE NEWFOUNDLAND
DEMOCRATIC PARTY. HE DETAILS THE CHALLENGES THE NDP FACES
AND EXPLORES POSSIBILITIES FOR THE FUTURE OF THIS
PROGRESSIVE NEW PARTY.

03184 FINN, J.
FRYING SNOWBALLS IN POLAND
FREEDOM AT ISSUE, (110) (SEP 89), 5-7.
THE AUTHOR DISCUSSES THE JUNE 1989 ELECTIONS IN POLAND
AND THE LINKS BETWEEN THE DECEMBER 1981 CRACKDOWN ON
SOLIDARITY AND ITS RE-EMERGENCE AS A LEGAL, MAJORITY
POLITICAL PARTY EIGHT YEARS LATER.

03185 FINN, J.
THE UNSETTLING SUMMER OF 1989
FREEDOM AT ISSUE, (109) (JUL 89), 3-4.
LATIN AMERICA, EASTERN EUROPE, THE SOVIET UNION, CHINA,

AFGHANISTAN, THE MIDDLE EAST, AND JAPAN HAVE ALL BEEN
UNDERGOING UNPRECEDENTED CHANGE. ALTHOUGH MUCH OF THIS
CHANGE WILL REMAIN INDEPENDENT OF OUTSIDE INFLUENCE, THE
UNITED STATES AND ITS ALLIES MUST GRAPPLE WITH THESE NEW,
STILL SHIFTING CONFIGURATIONS OF POWER AS THEY SHAPE THEIR
OWN FOREIGN POLICIES FOR THE COMING DECADE.

03186 FIORINA, M.; SHEPSLE, K.
IS NEGATIVE VOTING AN ARTIFACT?
AMERICAN JOURNAL OF POLITICAL SCIENCE, 33(2) (MAY 89),
423-439.
NEGATIVE VOTING OCCURS WHEN VOTERS RESPOND MORE STRONGLY
TO POLITICAL ACTIONS OR OUTCOMES THAT THEY OPPOSE THAN TO
COMPARABLE ACTIONS OR OUTCOMES THEY FAVOR. THE PAPER
DISCUSSES THE POSSIBILITY THAT NEGATIVE VOTING IS AN
ARTIFACT. THE MODEL DEVELOPED HAS TOW IMPLICATIONS THAT WILL
HELP TO DETERMINE WHETHER EMPIRICAL FINDINGS ABOUT NEGATIVE
VOTING ARE REAL OR ARTIFACTUAL. FIRST, NEGATIVE VOTING
SHOULD CHARACTERIZE THE BEHAVIOR OF A POLITICIAN'S PREVIOUS
SUPPORTERS. SECOND, NEGATIVE VOTING SHOULD BE STRONGER THE
HIGHER THE PREVIOUS LEVEL OF SUPPORT FOR A POLITICIAN. AN
ANALYSIS OF VOTING IN 1982 AND 1986 HOUSE RACES PRODUCES
EVIDENCE CONSISTENT WITH THESE PROPOSITIONS.

03187 FIORINO, D.J.
TECHNICAL AND DEMOCRATIC VALUES IN RISK ANALYSIS
RISK ANALYSIS, 9(3) (SEP 89), 293-300.
TWO MODELS FOR MAKING DECISIONS ABOUT ENVIRONMENTAL RISK
ARE DISCUSSED IN THIS PAPER -- A TECHNICAL AND A DEMOCRATIC
MODEL. THE PAPER CONSIDERS THE BASIS FOR THE DEMOCRATIC
MODEL AND ARGUES THE VALIDITY OF LAY JUDGMENTS ABOUT RISKS.
IT THEN COMPARES THE DILEMMA IN RISK ANALYSIS WITH ISSUES IN
DEMOCRATIC THEORY AND SUGGESTS SOME PARALLELS, IT THEN
DISCUSSES PRELIMINARY STEPS TOWARD RECONCILING TECHNICAL
WITH DEMOCRATIC VALUES IN RISK ANALYSIS

03188 FIRSOV, F.
WHAT THE COMINTERN'S ARCHIVES WILL REVEAL
WORLD MARXIST REVIEW, 32(1) (JAN 89), 52-57.
THE AUTHOR DISCUSSES THE HISTORY OF THE COMINTERN AND
CONCLUDES THAT OPENING THE COMINTERN'S ARCHIVES TO
HISTORIANS WILL CONTRIBUTE TO THE GOALS OF DISCREDITING
STALINISM AND FURTHERING LENIN'S CONCEPT OF THE COMMUNIST
MOVEMENT.

03189 FISCHER, C.
TURNING THE TIDE? THE KPD AND RIGHT RADICALISM IN GERMAN
INDUSTRIAL RELATIONS, 1925-28
JOURNAL OF CONTEMPORARY HISTORY, 24(4) (OCT 89), 575-597.
GERMANY'S DEFEAT IN THE FIRST WORLD WAR DISCREDITED THE
MONARCHY AND CREATED CONDITIONS IN WHICH A PARLIAMENTARY
REPUBLIC WAS ESTABLISHED AND SOME MAJOR ADVANCES ACHIEVED IN
THE REALM OF ECONOMIC AND SOCIAL POLICY. HOWEVER, THE
REPUBLIC'S FAILURE TO REMOVE THE IMPERIAL ELITES IN THE
ADMINISTRATIVE, MILITARY, JUDICIAL AND, NOT LEAST, ECONOMIC
SECTOR LEFT THIS NEW WEIMAR REPUBLIC RESTING ON FRAGILE
FOUNDATIONS. THESE ELITES WERE SOON TO ATTEMPT TO REVERSE
THE CONSTITUTIONAL AND SOCIO-ECONMIC GAINS REPRESENTED BY
THE REPUBLIC; THE CAPTAINS OF HEAVY INDUSTRY BEING AS ACTIVE
IN THIS AS OTHER ESTABLISHMENT GROUPS.

03190 FISCHER, D.
THE STRATEGIC DEFENSE INITIATIVE AS A CAUSE OF CRISIS
INSTABILITY
JOURNAL OF LEGISLATION, 15(2) (1989), 139-150.
THE ARTICLE EXPLORES THE REASONS FOR AND AGAINST SDI AND
CONCLUDES THAT FOR THE MOST PART, THOSE WHO DISCUSS THE
FEASIBILITY, COST, OR LEGALITY OF SDI MISS THE DEEPER ISSUE
OF SDI PROMOTING CRISIS INSTABILITY. THE AUTHOR ARGUES THAT
SDI WILL INCREASE THE LIKELIHOOD OF PREEMPTIVE STRIKES AND
ACCIDENTAL WAR. THE AUTHOR CONCLUDES THAT THE INCREASED RISK
OF WAR MORE THAN OUTWEIGHS THE PROPOSED BENEFITS OF THE
PROGRAM.

03191 FISCHER, D. H.
THE COASTAL ZONE AS AN ADMINISTRATIVE ENTITY FOR GOVERNING
U.S. MARINE MINERALS DEVELOPMENT
INTERNATIONAL JOURNAL OF PUBLIC ADMINISTRATION, 12(5)
(1989), 707-730.
THE COASTAL ZONE IS BEING PROMOTED AS A SPATIAL UNIT TO
COORDINATE AND ADMINISTER OFFSHORE MINERALS DEVELOPMENT WITH
OTHER COASTAL USES. RATHER THAN AIDING THE ADMINISTRATION OF
MINERALS DEVELOPMENT THE COASTAL ZONE IS BEING USED AS THE
REASON TO BLOCK SUCH DEVELOPMENT. THIS PAPER EXPLORES THE
COASTAL ZONE CONCEPT AS AN ENTITY FOR ADMINISTRATION. IT
CONCLUDES THAT JUST BECAUSE MINERALS MAY BE FOUND IN A
COASTAL ZONE DOES NOT MEAN THAT PHYSICAL ENTITY IS THE MOST
APPROPRIATE VEHICLE FOR ADMINISTERING MINERAL DEVELOPMENT.
ARBITRARINESS AT TO WHAT IS INCLUDED OR EXCLUDED FROM A
COASTAL ZONE AS WELL AS MANY MINERALS IMPACTS BEING FOUND
OUTSIDE OF THE COASTAL ZONE MILITATE AGAINST SUCH AN ENTITY
BEING THE SOLE CRITERION FOR DECISIONMAKING. WHILE THE
COASTAL ZONE MAY BE APPROPRIATE FOR SOME MINERAL DECISIONS,
THE CHOICE TO IMPLEMENT IT MUST BE ARRAYED AGAINST

ALTERNATIVE CRITERIA TO ENSURE A HIGH DEGREE OF
EFFECTIVENESS AND EFFICIENCY IN THOSE DECISIONS.

03192 FISCHER, F.; ZINKE, R.C.
PUBLIC ADMINISTRATION AND THE CODE OF ETHICS:
ADMINISTRATIVE REFORM OR PROFESSIONAL IDEOLOGY?
INTERNATIONAL JOURNAL OF PUBLIC ADMINISTRATION, 12(6)
(1989), 841-854.
THE PRIMARY PROFESSIONAL SOCIETY OF AMERICAN PUBLIC
ADMINISTRATION HAS DEVELOPED A CODE OF ETHICS THAT APPEARS
TO BE LARGELY IRRELEVANT TO THE REALITIES OF BUREAUCRATIC
EXPERIENCE. AN EXPLANATION OF THIS PARADOX CAN BE FOUND IN
THE SOCIOLOGICAL LITERATURE ON THE PROFESSIONS AND CODE-
WRITING. PROFESSIONAL CODES ARE DESIGNED TO REGULATE THE
BEHAVIOR OF A PROFESSION'S MEMBERS, BUT THIS IS GENERALLY
SEEN AS A SECONDARY ASPECT OF A MORE FUNDAMENTAL OBJECTIVE:
THE NEED TO ASSURE THE PUBLIC AT LARGE THAT THE PROFESSION'S
POWER IS BEING EXERCISED RESPONSIBLY. FROM THIS PRESPECTIVE,
THE PUBLIC ADMINISTRATION CODE CAN BE INTERPRETED FIRST AS
PART OF AN ATTEMPT TO LEGITIMATE THE PROFESSION IN THE FACE
OF HOSTILE CHALLENGES TO ITS AUTHORITY, AND SECOND AS AN
EFFORT TO ENGENDER ETHICAL BEHAVIOR. SUCH AN INTERPRETATION
HELPS TO EXPLAIN THE PROFESSION'S FAILURE TO CONFRONT THE
ORGANIZATIONAL AND POLITICAL BARRIERS THAT IMPEDE EFFECTIVE
IMPLEMENTATION OF THE CODE. THE PAPER CONCLUDES WITH AN
OBSERVATION ON THE IMPLICATIONS OF THE ARGUMENT FOR THE
FURTHER DEVELOPMENT OF ETHICS IN PUBLIC ADMINISTRATION.

03193 FISCHER, G.
THE TREATY OF 1963: RETROSPECTIVE AND PERSPECTIVE
DISARMAMENT, XII(2) (SUM 89), 96-108.
THE AUTHOR REVIEWS THE EVENTS THAT LED TO THE PARTIAL
TEST-BAN TREATY OF 1963 AND CONSIDERS ITS IMPACT ON THE
NUCLEAR SITUATION.

03194 FISCHER, P.
CHINA'S LEADERS: LOSS OF CREDIBILITY
AUSSEN POLITIK, 40(4) (1989), 309-320.
DR, PER FISCHER DRAWS UPON HIS PERSONAL EXPERIENCE IN
CHINESE AFFAIRS TO EXPLAIN THE STUDENT REVOLT IN CHINA AND
THE JUNE MASSACRE IN BEIJING THAT CRUSHED IT. HE ANALYSES
THE BACKGROUND OF REFORM CALLED UPON THE DENG XIAOPING AND
QUESTIONS THE USE OF FORCE IN THE HOUR OF CRISIS INSTEAD OF
AGREEING TO A DIALOGUE WITH THE PEOPLE WHO PEACEFULLY
DEMANDED THAT THE PROMISES TO THEM BE KEPT. HE EXAMINES WHAT
THE INTERNATIONAL COMMUNITY CAN DO AND CONCLUDES THAT
RESIGNATION IS INAPPROPRIATE.

03195 FISCHER, P.
MEXICO: TRADING UP
THIRD WORLD WEEK, 8(13) (MAY 89), 99-100.
THE SHRINKING OF MEXICO'S U.S. TRADE SURPLUS WORRIES
SOME MEXICAN ECONOMISTS WHO BELIEVE PRESIDENT CARLOS SALINAS
DE GORTARI'S TRADE LIBERALIZATION HAS PROCEEDED TOO FAR, TOO
FAST. BUT GOVERNMENT ECONOMISTS CLAIM THAT THE PROCESS OF
OPENING THE COUNTRY TO FOREIGN GOODS IS BRINGING DOWN PRICES
AND INFLATION. THE CURRENT IMPORT POLICY FORCES LOCAL
MANUFACTURERS TO BECOME MORE COMPETITIVE AND IMPROVES THEIR
ABILITY TO EXPORT.

03196 FISCHMAN, D.
THE JEWISH QUESTION ABOUT MARX
POLITY, 21(4) (SUM 89), 755-776.
KARL MARX'S ESSAY, "ON THE JEWISH QUESTION," IS COMMONLY
READ AS A CRITIQUE OF LIBERALISM AND NOT FOR WHAT MARX HAS
TO SAY ABOUT JEWS AND JUDAISM. THE AUTHOR OF THIS ARTICLE
ARGUES THAT SO NARROW A READING IS UNFORTUNATE, IN PART
BECAUSE MARX'S ANTI-SEMITIC SLURS NEED TO BE CHALLENGED BUT
ALSO BECAUSE MARX'S ANALYSIS OF THE JEWISH QUESTION ITSELF
ADDS TO AN UNDERSTANDING OF HIS NOTION OF FREEDOM.

03197 FISCHMAN, D.K.
POLITICAL DISCOURSE IN EXILE: KARL MARX AND THE JEWISH
QUESTION OF OUR TIMES
DISSERTATION ABSTRACTS INTERNATIONAL, 49(8) (FEB 89),
2374-A.
THE AUTHOR CONSIDERS JUDAISM IN THE WRITING OF KARL MARX
AND MARX'S RELATION TO HIS JEWISHNESS.

03198 FISHER, B.S.
PARTICIPATORY DEMOCRACY IN CRIME PREVENTION: THE EFFECTS
OF PARTICIPATION ON THE INDIVIDUAL
DISSERTATION ABSTRACTS INTERNATIONAL, 49(11) (MAY 89),
3490-A.
THIS DISSERTATION EXAMINES THE ARGUMENTS MADE BY THE
CLASSICAL AND PARTICIPATORY DEMOCRATS CONCERNING THE
DEVELOPMENTAL BENEFITS OF PARTICIPATION IN DECISION-MAKING.
IT ALSO STUDIES THE "COMMUNITY HYPOTHESIS," WHICH POSITS THE
EFFECTS OF PARTICIPATION IN CRIME PREVENTION ACTIVITIES.
CRIME PREVENTION EFFORTS IN EIGHT NEIGHBORHOODS ARE EXPLORED.

03199 FISHER, J.L.
FORMAL MECHANISMS: HELPING THE GOVERNOR TO MANAGE
JOURNAL OF STATE GOVERNMENT, 62(4) (JUL 89), 131-135.

IMPROVING THE MANAGEMENT OF THE EXECUTIVE BRANCH IS CRITICAL TO THE SUCCESS OF STATE GOVERNMENT. THE NEED FOR BETTER MANAGEMENT IS HEIGHTENED BY THE GROWING COMPLEXITY OF STATE GOVERNMENT ADMINISTRATION, THE EXPANDING ROLE OF STATE GOVERNMENT, AND THE INCESSANT CLAMOR FOR MORE EFFICIENCY. IN THIS ARTICLE, THE AUTHOR DESCRIBES AN EFFORT TO IMPROVE STATE GOVERNMENT MANAGEMENT IN VIRGINIA.

03200 FISHER, K.J.
SMOKE FREE OR FREE TO SMOKE?
AMERICAN CITY AND COUNTY, 104(2) (FEB 89), 53-56.
FOR YEARS, SMOKING HAS BEEN REGULATED AS A FIRE PREVENTION MEASURE. NOW LOCAL GOVERNMENTS INCREASINGLY ARE PASSING REGULATIONS FOR NEW REASONS: TO PROTECT NON-SMOKERS FROM INVOLUNTARILY INHALING SMOKE AND TO PROTECT AGAINST COSTLY LAWSUITS. NEARLY 400 SUCH SMOKING ORDINANCES ARE ON THE BOOKS NATIONWIDE, AND ABOUT 62 PERCENT OF THEM WERE PASSED DURING THE PAST THREE YEARS.

03201 FISHER, L.
HOW THE STATES SHAPE CONSTITUTIONAL LAW
STATE LEGISLATURES, 15(7) (AUG 89), 37-39.
WHILE THE US SUPREME COURT ENJOYS THE REPUTATION OF ISSUING THE LAST WORD ON CONSTITUTIONAL LAW, THE REALITY IS QUITE DIFFERENT. INSTEAD OF A HIERARCHICAL SYSTEM, WITH EACH ISSUE PERCOLATING UP TO THE SUPREME COURT FOR AN ULTIMATE DETERMINATION, THE PROCESS IS PLURALISTIC AND DECENTRALIZED. STATES AND STATE COURTS ALSO PERFORM KEY ROLES IN THE JUDICIAL PROCESS.

03202 FISHER, L.
LEGISLATIVE-EXECUTIVE RELATIONS: SEARCH FOR COOPERATION
CRS REVEIW, 10(1) (JAN 89), 10-11.
CONFLICT BETWEEN THE EXECUTIVE AND LEGISLATIVE BRANCHES IS BOTH INEVITABLE AND CONSTRUCTIVE. HEAD-ON COLLISIONS ARE NATURAL EVENTS FOR SEPARATE BRANCHES THAT HAVE DIFFERENT CONSTITUENCIES AND UNIQUE PREROGATIVES. AFTER THESE INITIAL CLASHES, HOWEVER, THE PUBLIC EXPECTS THE CONGRESS AND THE PRESIDENT TO DISCOVER SOLUTIONS THAT WILL BOTH PROTECT INSTITUTIONAL NEEDS AND ADVANCE THE NATIONAL INTEREST. THE DISTURBING TREND OF RECENT DECADES IS THE DIMINISHING ABILITY OF THE TWO BRANCHES TO RESOLVE THEIR DISPUTES IN AN ATMOSPHERE OF MUTUAL TRUST AND ACCOMMODATION.

03203 FISHER, L.M.
SOUTHERN AFRICA DEVELOPMENT COORDINATING CONFERENCE AND ITS SECURITY IMPLICATIONS
AVAILABLE FROM NTIS, NO. AD-A208 042/2/GAR, APR 89, 57.
POLITICAL INDEPENDENCE TO THE NINE BLACK STATES IN SOUTHERN AFRICA CAME IN VARIOUS FORMS. FOR COUNTRIES LIKE BOTSWANA, LESOTHO, SWAZILAND, TANZANIA AND ZAMBIA THE TRANSITION WAS FAIRLY PEACEFUL. IN CONTRAST, FOR ANGOLA, MOZAMBIQUE AND ZIMBABWE, INDEPENDENCE CAME THROUGH FIERCE BITTER WARS OF LIBERATION. HOWEVER, DESPITE THESE DIFFERENT PATHS TO NATIONHOOD, ALL THESE NINE STATES FACE A NEW CHALLENGE—WHICH IS NATION BUILDING. THE CHALLENGE NOW IS ONE OF CONSOLIDATING POLITICAL INDEPENDENCE THROUGH THE PROVISION OF GOODS AND SERVICES FOR THEIR CITIZENS. IN PURSUIT OF THESE GOALS THE NINE STATES GATHERED TOGETHER IN LUSAKA, APRIL 1980, TO FORM THE SOUTHERN AFRICAN DEVELOPMENT COORDINATION CONFERENCE. THE BIGGEST CHALLENGE FOR THIS NEW GROUPING HAS BEEN SOUTH AFRICA AND ITS ECONOMIC TIES TO THE NINE STATES. VARIOUS ACTIONS BY SOUTH AFRICA TOWARDS ITS NEIGHBORS HAVE CLEARLY DEMONSTRATED THE VULNERABILITY OF THESE NATIONS AS A RESULT OF THESE TIES. THE SADCC GROUPING HAS HAD TO SCALE HIGHER WALLS IN THE FACE OF DESTABILIZATION EFFORTS BY THEIR GIANT NEIGHBOR. THE SUCCESS OF THE GROUP'S EFFORTS HOLDS THE KEY TO THE STRENGTHENING OF THEIR POLITICAL INDEPENDENCE, IMPROVED WELFARE FOR CITIZENS AND PEACE WITHIN THE REGION. IT IS FOR THIS PURPOSE THE SADCC MEMBER COUNTRIES HAVE INCREASED THEIR RESOLVE TO ENSURE ACHIEVEMENT OF THEIR OBJECTIVES IN THE FACE OF GREAT ADVERSITY.

03204 FISHER, R.; KLING, J.
COMMUNITY MOBILIZATION: PROSPECTS FOR THE FUTURE
URBAN AFFAIRS QUARTERLY, 25(2) (DEC 89), 200-211.
THE AUTHORS ADD TO THE DISCUSSION ON THE PROSPECTS OF COMMUNITY MOBILIZATION BY OFFERING FOUR MAJOR POINTS. THE IMPACT OF HUMAN AGENCY, NOT ONLY STRUCTURAL CONDITIONS, MUST BE CONSIDERED. CURRENTLY, THERE ARE DISTINCT SIGNS OF GRASS-ROOTS MOBILIZATION AND A RETURNING ACTIVIST CONSCIOUSNESS. THESE TRENDS AND EVENTS MUST BE SEEN, HOWEVER, AGAINST THE BROAD RESTRUCTURING OF CITIES, WHICH HAS DRAMATICALLY ALTERED THE CONTEXT FOR ORGANIZERS AND PRESENTED NEW, FORMIDABLE BARRIERS. LASTLY, THE SHARPENING OF IDEOLOGICAL CLEAVAGE IS FUNDAMENTAL TO MOBILIZE CONSTITUENCIES AND BRIDGE THE COMMUNITY/CLASS DICHOTOMY THAT CONTINUES TO LIMIT MOST EFFORTS.

03205 FISHER, R.J.
PRENEGOTIATION PROBLEM-SOLVING DISCUSSIONS: ENHANCING THE POTENTIAL FOR SUCCESSFUL NEGOTIATION
INTERNATIONAL JOURNAL, XLIV(2) (SPR 89), 442-474.

THIS ARTICLE EXAMINES THE MANNER AND DEGREE TO WHICH PROBLEM-SOLVING DISCUSSIONS FOCUSSING ON THE BASIC RELATIONSHIP MIGHT FACILITATE THE DECISION OF PARTIES TO MOVE INTO PRENEGOTIATION OR FROM PRENEGOTIATION TO NEGOTIATION. IT IS PROPOSED THAT SUCH DISCUSSIONS CAN HAVE A USEFUL INFLUENCE ON PERCEPTIONS, ATTITUDES, AND ORIENTATIONS IN WAYS THAT WILL IMPROVE BOTH THE PROBABILITY OF NEGOTIATION OCCURRING AND THE LIKELIHOOD OF ITS SUCCESS.

03206 FISHER, S.; COLLETT, M.; FINKEL, A.W.; FUAD, K.; GUTKIN, S.
VENEZUELA
SOUTH, (106) (AUG 89), 39-47.
WHEN CARLOS ANDRES PEREZ BECAME PRESIDENT IN FEBRUARY 1989, HE INHERITED A TROUBLED ECONOMY. AFTER SUCCESSIVE PRICE SLUMPS, VENEZUELA HAS LOST ITS CUSHION OF OIL WEALTH AND THE GOVERNMENT'S TOUGH AUSTERITY PACKAGE TRIGGERED RIOTS IN EARLY 1989. BUT SOME ANALYSTS SAY THE SOCIAL UNREST IS A POLITICAL PROBLEM MASQUERADING AS AN ECONOMIC CRISIS. AS CARACAS BIDS TO ATTRACT FOREIGN CAPITAL TO BOLSTER THE COUNTRY'S INDUSTRIAL GROWTH, THE PRESSURE IS ON PEREZ TO RECOGNIZE THE REAL ISSUES AND DEAL WITH THEM.

03207 FISHLOW, A.
LATIN AMERICAN FAILURE AGAINST THE BACKDROP OF ASIAN SUCCESS
PHILADELPHIA: ANLS OF AMER ACMY OF POLITICAL AND SOC SCIENCE, (505) (SEP 89), 117-128.
THIS ARTICLE EXAMINES THE PRINCIPAL REASONS FOR THE POOR LATIN AMERICAN ECONOMIC PERFORMANCE IN CONTRAST TO ASIAN SUCCESS IN THE LAST DECADE. THESE INCLUDE AN ADVERSE INTERNATIONAL ECONOMY THAT DISCRIMINATED AGAINST LARGE DEBTORS, A SET OF DOMESTIC DISTORTIONS INTRODUCED BY EXCESS EXTERNAL DEBT, AND A POLITICAL INCAPACITY TO IMPLEMENT COHERENT AND CONSISTENT ADJUSTMENT POLICIES.

03208 FISHMAN, A.
THE PALESTINIAN WOMAN AND THE INTIFADA
NEW OUTLOOK, 32(6-7 (292-293)) (JUN 89), 9-11.
THE INFRASTRUCTURE FOR THE ACTIVITIES OF PALESTINAN WOMEN IN THE INTIFADA EXISTED FOR MANY YEARS BEFORE THE UPRISING. AT ITS BASE ARE FOUR LARGE AND RELATIVELY LONG-STANDING WOMEN'S ORGANIZATIONS, EACH IDENTIFIED WITH A DIFFERENT FACTION WITHIN THE PLO: THE ASSOCIATION OF LABOR COMMITTEES, THE ASSOCIATION OF THE WORKING PALESTINIAN WOMAN, THE WOMEN'S ASSOCIATION FOR SOCIAL WORKS, AND THE ASSOCIATION OF THE PALESTINIAN WOMAN. IN NOVEMBER 1988, THE PLO LEADERSHIP CALLED UPON THE WOMEN TO UNITE UNDER THE SUPREME WOMEN'S COUNCIL, BUT SO FAR THIS HASN'T HAPPENED. DUE TO ITS DESIRE TO PRESENT A DEMOCRATIC AND PROGRESSIVE FACE TO THE WORLD, THE PLO IS MAKING AN EFFORT TO EMPHASIZE THE CHANGE IN THE STATUS OF WOMEN IN THE INTIFADA. BUT IT IS DIFFICULT TO BREAK TRADITIONS. THERE ARE SIGNS THAT THE REVOLUTION HAS NOT YET PRODUCED FAIR POLITICAL AND SOCIAL REPRESENTATION FOR WOMEN IN THE OCCUPIED TERRITORIES.

03209 FISHMAN, J.
IMPACT OF THE "INDEPENDENT PLUS" IN THE ELECTION OF '88
POLITICAL AFFAIRS, LXVIII(1) (JAN 89), 12-19.
THE AUTHOR SURVEYS THE PERFORMANCE OF CANDIDATES REPRESENTING THE COMMUNIST AND OTHER MINOR PARTIES IN THE 1988 ELECTIONS.

03210 FISS, O. M.
THE AWKWARDNESS OF THE CRIMINAL LAW
HUMAN RIGHTS QUARTERLY, 11(1) (FEB 89), 1-13.
IT IS TODAY TAKEN AS AXIOMATIC BY THOSE ENGAGED IN THE INTERNATIONAL PROTECTION OF HUMAN RIGHTS THAT EACH AND EVERY VIOLATION OF A HUMAN RIGHT SHOULD BE CRIMINALLY PROSECUTED. THE FACT IS, HOWEVER, THAT DURING THE 1960S -- A PERIOD SOMETIMES REFERRED TO AS THE SECOND RECONSTRUCTION -- THE UNITED STATES HAD AN EXPERIENCE THAT DID NOT CONFORM TO THIS EXPECTATION. THE CRIMINAL PROSECUTION WAS RARE AND EXCEPTIONAL, EVEN THOUGH COMMITMENT TOWARDS THE PROTECTION OF HUMAN RIGHTS WAS THEN FIRM AND UNEQUIVOCAL, PERHAPS MORE SO THAN IN ANY OTHER PERIOD OF US HISTORY. IT WAS THE INJUNCTION, NOT THE CRIMINAL LAW, WHICH BECAME THE PRIMARY LEGAL TOOL FOR THE EXTENSION AND VINDICATION OF HUMAN RIGHTS. THE PURPOSE OF THIS PAPER IS BOTH TO EXPLAIN AND TO JUSTIFY THIS PRACTICE, AND THUS TO SUGGEST THAT THE FIT BETWEEN THE CRIMINAL LAW AND THE PROTECTION OF HUMAN RIGHTS IS NOT AS NATURAL AS IT MIGHT FIRST SEEM.

03211 FITOUSSI, J.; LECACHEUX, J.
GROWTH AND MACROECONOMIC POLICIES IN OECD COUNTRIES
INTERNATIONAL SOCIAL SCIENCE JOURNAL, (120) (MAY 89), 127-148.
SINCE THE EARLY 1980S WORLD GROWTH, WHEN COMPARED WITH THAT OF THE THREE PREVIOUS DECADES, HAS BEEN ON AVERAGE EXTREMELY SLUGGISH. THE PREPONDERANCE OF THE OECD COUNTRIES IN WORLD ECONOMIC ACTIVITY IS AMPLE REASON TO CONSIDER WHAT MAY BE THEIR SHARE OF RESPONSIBILITY FOR THIS STASTE OF AFFAIRS. DESIGNED TO DEAL WITH THE FLUCTUATIONS OF THE CURRENT ECONOMIC SITUATION, THE MACROECONOMIC POLICIES OF THE INDUSTRIAL COUNTRIES STRONGLY INFLUENCE TRENDS IN WORLD

GROWTH, AND CONSEQUENTLY THEIR MAIN FEATURES AND THEORETICAL
FOUNDATIONS WARRANT ANALYSIS.

03212 FITUNI, L.L.
A NEW ERA: SOVIET POLICY IN SOUTHERN AFRICA
AFRICA REPORT, 34(4) (JUL 89), 63-65.
UNDER THE LEADERSHIP OF MIKHAIL GORBACHEV, SOVIET
POLICIES REGARDING REGIONAL CONFLICTS HAVE UNDERGONE A
TRANSFORMATION. THIS ARTICLE PROVIDES THE BACKGROUND TO THE
NEW POLITICAL THINKING AND ITS RELEVANCE TO THE CHANGING
POLITICAL SCENARIO IN SOUTHERN AFRICA.

03213 FITZGERALD, F. T.
THE REFORM OF THE CUBAN ECONOMY, 1976-86: ORGANIZATION,
INCENTIVES, AND PATTERNS OF BEHAVIOR
JOURNAL OF LATIN AMERICAN STUDIES, 21(2) (MAY 89), 283-310.
WITHOUT ATTEMPTING TO DISCUSS EVERY ECONOMIC PROBLEM
THAT OCCURRED IN CUBA FROM 1976 TO 1986, THIS ARTICLE
OUTLINES THE ORDER BENEATH THE ECONOMIC 'CHAOS' AND EXPLAINS
IT IN TERMS OF BOTH 'SYSTEMIC' FACTORS THAT ARE ALWAYS FOUND
IN SOCIALIST ECONOMIES AND 'SOCIO-HISTORICAL FACTORS THAT
ARE ONLY SOMETIMES PRESENT. THE ARTICLE CONCLUDES WITH A
BRIEF ANALYSIS OF THE REVOLUTIONARY LEADERSHIP'S ATTEMPT AT
RECTIFICATION SINCE 1986.

03214 FITZGERALD, G.
IRELAND: SECURITY ISSUES AND FUTURE CHOICES
RUSI JOURNAL, 134(4) (WIN 89), 29-32.
THE ARTICLE TRACES THE DEVELOPMENT OF IRELAND'S QUEST
FOR NEUTRALITY. ALTHOUGH IRELAND HAS DECLARED NEUTRALITY
SINCE ITS FORMATION AS A STATE, ITS ACTIONS WERE OFTEN NON-
BELLIGERENT AT BEST. THE ARTICLE EXAMINES SUCH IMPORTANT
EVENTS AS IRELAND'S ROLE IN WORLD WAR II, IRELAND'S
APPLICATION FOR MEMBERSHIP IN THE EUROPEAN ECONOMIC
COMMUNITY, AND IRELAND'S REACTION TO EEC CALLS FOR SANCTIONS
DURING THE CONFLICT BETWEEN BRITAIN AND ARGENTINA. THE
ARTICLE CONCLUDES WITH AN ANALYSIS OF IRISH PUBLIC OPINION.

03215 FITZGERALD, M.A.
REBELLION AND RETALIATION
AFRICA REPORT, 34(4) (JUL 89), 52-54.
A FAILED ATTEMPT TO OVERTHROW COL. MENGISTU HAILE MARIAM
IN MAY 1989 LED TO THE ELIMINATION OF SCORES OF MILITARY
OFFICERS AND OTHER SUSPECTED SYMPATHIZERS. THE CRACKDOWN,
HOWEVER, HAS FAILED TO QUASH DEEP-ROOTED DISCONTENT WITH THE
ETHIOPIAN GOVERNMENT AND ITS INABILITY TO END THE WAR IN
ERITREA AND TIGRAY.

03216 FITZGERALD, M.A.
THE NEWS HOLE: REPORTING AFRICA
AFRICA REPORT, 34(4) (JUL 89), 59-60.
IN NEWS TERMS, AFRICA IS VIEWED AS A VAST BLACK HOLE
FRINGED BY LIBYA AND SOUTH AFRICA. WITH THE EXCEPTION OF
THESE TWO COUNTRIES, IT IS NOT A PLAYER IN THE GREAT GLOBAL
POWER GAME. AND SO, POLITICAL OBSCURITY COMBINES WITH PRESS
INTIMIDATION TO MAKE IT THE FIRST TO BITE THE DUST WHEN
EDITORIAL BUDGETS ARE TIGHTENED. THIS MAY ALSO BE THE REASON
WHY CENSORSHIP, MANIPULATION OF PUBLIC INFORMATION, AND THE
PERSECUTION OF JOURNALISTS RECEIVE INDIGNANT EDITORIAL
ATTENTION WHEN THEY HAPPEN IN SOUTH AFRICA, BUT ARE FOR THE
MOST PART IGNORED WHEN THEY TAKE PLACE IN BLACK AFRICA.

03217 FITZGERALD, M.W.
"TO GIVE OUR VOTES TO THE PARTY": BLACK POLITICAL
AGITATION AND AGRICULTURAL CHANGE IN ALABAMA, 1865-1870
JOURNAL OF AMERICAN HISTORY, 76(2) (SEP 89), 489-505.
AFTER EMANCIPATION, SOUTHERN AGRICULTURE UNDERWENT A
TRANSFORMATION FROM CENTRALIZED PLANTATION MANAGEMENT TO
DECENTRALIZED TENANT FARMING. IN ALABAMA, THE EMERGENCE OF
DECENTRALIZED TENANT FARMING HAD A POLITICAL DIMENSION,
BECAUSE IT WAS CLOSELY CONNECTED WITH THE UPHEAVAL
ACCOMPANYING CONGRESSIONAL RECONSTRUCTION. THE CRISIS IN
PLANTATION AGRICULTURE DID MUCH TO IMPEL THE EXPLOSIVE
POLITICAL MOBILIZATION OF THE FREEDMEN. THIS POLITICIZATION,
IN TURN, COUNTERACTED THE EFFORTS OF THE LANDOWNERS TO
CONTROL THE LABOR FORCE, THEREBY ENCOURAGING SIGNIFICANT
CHANGES IN COTTON CULTIVATION.

03218 FITZMAURICE, J.
BELGIUM
ELECTORAL STUDIES, 8(3) (DEC 89), 231-236.
THIS ARTICLE EXAMINES THE CAMPAIGN IN BELGIUM WHICH WAS
CONDUCTED IN PARALLEL WITH THE ELECTION OF THE FIRST
REGIONAL COUNCIL FOR BRUSSELS THAT TOOK PLACE ON THE SAME
DAY. THE CAMPAIGN WAS FOUND TO BE ABLE TO EMPHASIZE
CONSENSUS RATHER THAN DIFFERENCE AS THERE WAS SEEN LITTLE TO
BE AT STAKE IN NATIONAL POLITICS. THE COMPULSORY VOTING LAW
IS EXAMINED AND IT IS CONCLUDED THAT BELGIUM HAS ENTERED A
PERIOD OF RELATIVE STABILITY.

03219 FLACKS, O.
WHAT HAPPENED TO THE NEW LEFT?
SOCIALIST REVIEW, 19(1) (JAN 89), 91-110.
THE DISINTEGRATION OF THE YOUTH MOVEMENT, THE FADING OF

REVOLUTIONARY IMAGININGS AND RHETORIC AND THE COLLAPSE OF
THE NATIONAL ORGANIZATIONAL FRAMEWORK OF THE NEW LEFT
CERTAINLY MARKED THE END OF AN ERA IN WHICH VISIONS OF TOTAL
SOCIAL AND PERSONAL TRANSFORMATION SEEMED PLAUSIBLE. WHAT
DID NOT DIE, HOWEVER, WAS THE NEW LEFT PROJECT. THAT PROJECT,
AS DEFINED IN THE LANGUAGE OF EARLY SIXTIES MANIFESTOES AND
IN THE PRACTICES AND PERSPECTIVES OF THOUSANDS OF ACTIVISTS
DURING THE DECADE, COULD NOT GO ON WITHIN THE TERMS AND
CONDITIONS SET IN THE SIXTIES. HOWEVER, THE IDEOLOGY HAS
HELPED DEVELOP WHAT CAME TO BE CALLED THE "NEW" SOCIAL
MOVEMENTS--BOTH FEMINISM AND THE ENVIRONMENTAL MOVEMENT HAD
ROOTS IN THE SIXTIES MOVEMENTS, AND WERE EFFORTS TO
TRANSFORM AND EXTEND THE IDEOLOGICAL CONTENT AND PRACTICAL
RELEVANCE OF RADICALISM.

03220 FLAHERTY, P.
PERESTROIKA AND THE SOVIET WORKING CLASS
STUDIES IN POLITICAL ECONOMY: A SOCIALIST REVIEW, 29 (SUM
89), 39-61.
THIS ESSAY DEMONSTRATES THAT THE SOVIET WORKING CLASS IS
NOT THE REGIMENTED AND DISPIRITED MASS DEPICTED IN
TOTALITARIAN THEORY. INSTEAD FACTORY LIFE IS GOVERNED BY THE
OBSCURE BUT UBIQUITOUS SHOPFLOOR MICRO-POLITICS OF A TACIT
SOCIAL CONTRACT EMBEDDED IN AN EGALITARIAN SUB-CULTURE.
CORPORATISM IN LATE CAPITALISM WILL FAVOR THE DISAGGREGATION
AND WEAKENING OF THE CLASS POWER OF THE LABOUR MOVEMENT, BUT
THE OPERATION OF A SIMILAR "TRIANGLE" OF THE PARTY APPARATUS,
MANAGERIAL TECHNOSTRUCTURE, AND TRADE UNION MACHINE MAY BE
PROMOTING A PROCESS OF CLASS FORMATION IN STATIST SOCIETIES.
THIS WOULD THEN BE A NECESSARY STAGE IN THE MATURATION OF
THE SOVIET WORKING CLASS TOWARDS SELFORGANIZATION AND THE
CAPACITY OF COLLECTIVE ACTION.

03221 FLANAGAN, R.
A HISTORY OF THE POLITICS OF THE UNEMPLOYED, 1884-1939
DISSERTATION ABSTRACTS INTERNATIONAL, 49(8) (FEB 89),
2353-A.
THE AUTHOR TRACES THE DEVELOPMENT OF THE POLITICS OF THE
UNEMPLOYED FROM 1884 TO 1895, THE CRITICAL ROLE OF THE
SOCIALISTS IN THIS DEVELOPMENT, THE POLITICS OF UNEMPLOYED
EX-SERVICEMEN AFTER WORLD WAR I, AND THE ACTIVITIES OF THE
NATIONAL UNEMPLOYED WORKERS' MOVEMENT.

03222 FLANAGAN, T.
THE AGRICULTURAL ARGUMENT AND ORIGINAL APPROPRIATION:
INDIAN LANDS AND POLITICAL PHILOSOPHY
CANADIAN JOURNAL OF POLITICAL SCIENCE, 22(3) (SEP 89),
589-602.
THE EUROPEAN APPROPRIATION OF INDIAN LAND IN NORTH
AMERICA HAS OFTEN BEEN JUSTIFIED THROUGH VERSIONS OF THE
"AGRICULTURAL ARGUMENT" TO THE EFFECT THAT THE INDIANS DID
NOT NEED THE LAND AND DID NOT REALLY OWN IT BECAUSE THEY DID
NOT PERMANENTLY ENCLOSE AND FARM IT. THUS THE EUROPEAN
SETTLERS COULD RESORT TO ORIGINAL APPROPRIATION AS DESCRIBED
IN LOCKE'S SECOND TREATISE. THIS ARTICLE EXAMINES THE
AGRICULTURAL ARGUMENT AS EXEMPLIFIED IN THE WRITINGS OF JOHN
WINTHROP, JOHN LOCKE AND EMER DE VATTEL. ANALYSIS SHOWS THAT
THE ARGUMENT IS FORMALLY CONSISTENT WITH THE PREMISES OF
NATURAL RIGHTS PHILOSOPHY BECAUSE IT ASSUMES THE EQUAL RIGHT
OF BOTH INDIANS AND EUROPEANS TO ENGAGE IN ORIGINAL
APPROPRIATION. BUT THE HISTORICAL RECORD SHOWS THAT THE
ARGUMENT ACTUALLY APPLIED TO ONLY A SMALL PORTION OF THE
LAND ACQUIRED BY THE EUROPEANS. SOVEREIGNTY IS THE ISSUE
THAT SHOULD RECEIVE FURTHER INQUIRY.

03223 FLASKAMP, R.H.
THE DECISION TO SELL: PUSH FACTORS IN THE ARMS TRANSFER
POLICIES OF THE MAJOR WESTERN SUPPLIER STATES
DISSERTATION ABSTRACTS INTERNATIONAL, 49(7) (JAN 89),
1950-A.
IN LIGHT OF THE INCREASING IMPORTANCE OF NON-STRATEGIC
FACTORS IN ARMS TRANSFER POLICY, THE AUTHOR EXAMINES FACTORS
CREATING INCENTIVES FOR THE SUPPLIER STATES TO PARTICIPATE
IN THE INTERNATIONAL ARMS MARKET. HE SURVEYS THE ARMS
TRANSFER POLICIES OF THE USA, UNITED KINGDOM, FRANCE, AND
WEST GERMANY FROM 1971 TO 1980.

03224 FLATH, D.
VERTICAL RESTRAINTS IN JAPAN
JAPAN AND THE WORLD ECONOMY, 1(2) (MAR 89), 187-204.
RESALE PRICE MAINTENANCE (R.P.M), EXCLUSIVE DEALING
STIPULATIONS, AND CUSTOMER RESTRICTIONS ARE ALL WIDESPREAD
IN JAPAN, PARTICULARLY FOR CONSUMER PRODUCTS. ANALYSIS OF
SPECIFIC ANTITRUST CASES DEMONSTRATED THAT STANDARD ECONOMIC
ARGUMENTS CAN ACCOUNT FOR RESTRAINTS BY JAPANESE MAKERS. THE
MODELS THAT APPLY INCLUDE THE MAKER CARTEL AND WHOLESALER
CARTEL THEORIES OF R.P.M., THE SUCCESSIVE MONOPOLY THEORY OF
MAKER-IMPOSED MAXIMUM RESALE PRICE, THE PRICE DISCRIMINATION
THEORY OF R.P.M., AND THE PROTECTION OF MAKER INVESTMENT
THEORY OF EXCLUSIVE DEALING. CLAIMS THAT MARKETING PRACTICES
IN JAPAN ARE BASED ON CULTURE AND TRADITION RATHER THAN
ECONOMIC LOGIC SHOULD BE REGARDED WITH SKEPTICISM.

03225 FLEISCHMAN
POLITICAL TRIALS IN CZECHOSLOVAKIA
ACROSS FRONTIERS, 5(2) (SUM 89), 27.
THIS ARTICLE EXAMINES THE CURRENT WAVE OF PROTEST IN
CZECHOSLOVAKIA AND THE GOVERNMENT CRACKDOWN ON INDEPENDENT
ACTIVITY. IT DETAILS SOME OF THE ARRESTS AND TRIALS OF
PROTEST LEADERS AND THE PSYCHOLOGICAL EFFECT THIS HAS HAD IN
INCREASING THE MOMENTUM OF PROTEST.

03226 FLEMING, J.E.
CONSTITUTIONAL CONSTRUCTIVISM
DISSERTATION ABSTRACTS INTERNATIONAL, 49(7) (JAN 89),
1945-A.
THIS DISSERTATION LAYS THE GROUNDWORK FOR A
CONSTITUTIONAL CONSTRUCTIVISM, A COUNTERPART TO JOHN HART
ELY'S RESTRICTED UTILITARIAN THEORY OF REPRESENTATIVE
DEMOCRACY AND DISTRUST THAT DERIVES FROM JOHN RAWLS'S
CONCEPTIONS OF JUSTIFICATION AND JUSTICE. THE ARGUMENT IS
THAT SUCH A RAWLSIAN THEORY BETTER FITS, JUSTIFIES, AND
REINFORCES THE AMERICAN CONSTITUTIONAL DOCUMENT AND
CONSTITUTIONAL ORDER THAN DOES ELY'S THEORY.

03227 FLENTJE, H.E.
CLARIFYING PURPOSE AND ACHIEVING BALANCE IN GUBERNATORIAL
ADMINISTRATION
JOURNAL OF STATE GOVERNMENT, 62(4) (JUL 89), 161-167.
IN RUNNING THEIR ADMINISTRATIONS, GOVERNORS ARE
SUPPORTED BY THEIR STAFF, BUDGET STAFF, CABINET OFFICERS,
AND THE BUREAUCRACY. SUCCESS IS MORE LIKELY TO COME WHEN A
GOVERNOR CLEARLY UNDERSTANDS AND DEFINES THE PURPOSES OF
EACH AND BALANCES RESPONSIBILITIES AMONG THEM.

03228 FLERAS, A.
TOWARD A MULTICULTURAL RECONSTRUCTION OF CANADIAN SOCIETY
AMERICAN REVIEW OF CANADIAN STUDIES, 29(3) (FAL 89),
307-320.
THIS PAPER WILL DEMONSTRATE HOW THE ENTRENCHMENT OF
MULTICULTURALISM HAS ACCELERATED TRENDS IN REDEFINING
GOVERNMENT-ETHNIC RELATIONS, IN THE PROCESS TRANSFORMING AND
RESHAPING THE RECONSTRUCTION OF CANADIAN SOCIETY ALONG
PLURALISTIC LINES. THE IMPACT AND IMPLICATIONS OF
MULTICULTURALISM ARE EXAMINED IN TERMS OF ITS EVOLUTION FROM
GOVERNMENT POLICY TO ITS CONSTITUTIONAL AND STATUTORY
ENSHRINEMENT AS A FUNDAMENTAL COMPONENT OF NATIONAL DECISION-
MAKING. ALSO DISCUSSED IS THE SHIFT IN PRIORITIES UNDERLYING
CANADIAN MULTICULTURALISM. GOVERNMENT INVOLVEMENT IN
MANAGING RACE AND ETHNIC RELATIONS HAS BECOME INCREASINGLY
FOCUSED UPON ISSUES OF 'ECONOMY' AND 'EQUALITY' RATHER THAN
'CULTURE.' THE 'ETHNICIZATION' OF CANADIAN SOCIETY IS THEN
ANALYZED WITH REFERENCES TO MULTICULTURALISM AS A RENEWABLE
RESOURCE OF STRATEGIC VALUE FOR SHAPING POLITICAL AND ETHNIC
INTERESTS. FINALLY, RECENT DEBATES OVER MULTICULTURALISM ARE
SHOWN TO ENCOMPASS COMPETING IMAGES AND ASSESSMENTS, AS WELL
AS SHIFTING OBJECTIVES AND TACTICS, WHICH STRIKE AT THE CORE
OF CANADIAN NATION-BUILDING.

03229 FLETCHER, J.F.
MASS AND ELITE ATTITUDES ABOUT WIRETAPPING IN CANADA:
IMPLICATIONS FOR DEMOCRATIC THEORY AND POLITICS
PUBLIC OPINION QUARTERLY, 53(2) (SUM 89), 225-245.
OVER THE PAST SEVERAL YEARS, THE ISSUE OF WIRETAPPING
HAS BEEN AT THE CENTER OF A DEBATE REGARDING THE ACTIVITIES
OF THE CANADIAN SECURITY INTELLIGENCE SERVICE (CSIS). THIS
PAPER--BASED UPON DATA FROM A NEW NATIONAL STUDY OF CANADIAN
ATTITUDES TOWARD CIVIL LIBERTIES--EXPLORES TWO QUESTIONS
RELEVANT TO THIS DEBATE: THE STATE OF PUBLIC AND ELITE
OPINION ON THE ISSUE OF WIRETAPPING AND THE IMPLICATIONS OF
THESE ATTITUDES FOR AN UNDERSTANDING OF DEMOCRATIC POLITICS.

03230 FLETCHER, S.R.
TROPICAL DEFORESTATION AND LOSS OF BIOLOGICAL DIVERSITY
CRS REVEIW, 10(7) (AUG 89), 15-18.
THE ACCELERATING WORLDWIDE LOSS OF TROPICAL FORESTS AND
THEIR RICH RESOURCES HAS EVOKED STRONG CONCERN IN THE UNITED
STATES. SINCE VERY LITTLE TROPICAL FORESTLAND EXISTS WITHIN
U.S. BORDERS AND CONCERNS CENTER ON THE ACTIVITIES IN OTHER
COUNTRIES, TROPICAL DEFORESTATION IS AN INTERNATIONAL ISSUE
FOR THE UNITED STATES. CONGRESS IS CURRENTLY CONSIDERING
OPTIONS TO PROVIDE INCENTIVES TO DEVELOPING COUNTRIES THAT
PROTECT THEIR TROPICAL FORESTS.

03231 FLEW, A.
THE PHILOSOPHY OF FREEDOM
JOURNAL OF LIBERTARIAN STUDIES, IX(1) (WIN 89), 69-80.
THE AUTHOR BEGINS BY DISTINGUISHING BETWEEN TWO
FUNDAMENTALLY DIFFERENT, YET INTIMATELY CONNECTED, SENSES OF
THE WORDS "FREEDOM" AND "LIBERTY." THEN HE ARGUES THAT IT
MUST INDEED BE VERY DIFFICULT, IF NOT PRACTICALLY IMPOSSIBLE,
TO BECOME AND TO REMAIN COMMITTED TO THE EXTENSION OF
POLITICAL LIBERTIES AND THE DEFENSE OF POLITICAL FREEDOM SO
LONG AS ONE REFUSES TO RECOGNIZE THAT THE FREEDOM OF THE
WILL "IS ROOTED IN THE VERY QUALITY OF BEING HUMAN."

03232 FLIESS, B.
U.S., E.C. COLLIDE AT GATT REVIEW OVER AGRICULTURE
EUROPE, (283) (JAN 89), 14-15.
IN DECEMBER 1988, REPRESENTATIVES FROM GATT NATIONS
EVALUATED THE PROGRESS OF THE URUGUAY ROUND. THIS
MINISTERIAL LEVEL REVIEW WAS DESIGNED TO GIVE BROAD
POLITICAL GUIDANCE TO A COMPLEX UNDERTAKING AIMED AT
LIBERALIZING WORLD TRADE. THE MINISTERS MADE SIGNIFICANT
PROGRESS IN MOST AREAS, BUT AGRICULTURE HAS A NOTABLE
EXCEPTION.

03233 FLIESS, B.
WORKING TOWARD CLOSER TIES
EUROPE, (289) (SEP 89), 22-23, 47.
THE ARTICLE EXAMINES TRADE RELATIONS BETWEEN THE
EUROPEAN COMMUNITY AND JAPAN. IT CONCLUDES THAT ALTHOUGH THE
RELATIONS ARE DEFINITELY IMPROVING, THE COMMUNITY'S TRADE
DEFICIT WITH JAPAN IS EXPECTED TO WIDEN AGAIN IN 1989. BOTH
SIDES ARE ALSO CONCERNED WITH GUARANTEEING ACCESS TO MARKETS
AND WITH PREVENTING DUMPING. BOTH SIDES MUST WALK THE FINE
LINE BETWEEN "FAIR TRADE" AND PROTECTIONISM IF RELATIONS ARE
TO CONTINUE TO IMPROVE.

03234 FLOISTAD, B.
GREENLAND'S INTERNATIONAL FISHERIES RELATIONS: A COASTAL
STATE IN THE "NORTH" WITH PROBLEMS OF THE "SOUTH"
COOPERATION & CONFLICT: NORDIC JOURNAL OF INTERNATIONAL
POLITICS, XXIV(1) (MAR 89), 35-48.
TWO QUESTIONS ADDRESSED IN THIS ARTICLE. ONE IS WHETHER
GREENLAND, A FISHERIES STATE OF THE "NORTH"", CAN BE SAID TO
HAVE MANY OF THE FEATURE CHARACTERIZING COASTAL STATES OF
THE "SOUTH". THE OTHER QUESTION RELATES TO WHETHER ANY SIGN
OF "NORDISM" CAN BE FOUND IN THE RELATIONSHIP BETWEEN
GREENLAND AND HER NORDIC NEIGHBOURS. HAVING FORMALLY LEFT
THE EUROPEAN COMMUNITY, GREENLAND'S NEED FOR FINANCIAL
FUNDING FROM THE EC PUTS HER IN A SITUATION CHARACTERISTIC
OF THAT COASTAL STATES IN THE THIRD WORLD, NAMELY OF HAVING
SELL THE RESOURCES IN THE SEA TODAY IN ORDER TO DEVELOP HER
NATIONAL FISHERY TOMORROW. ANY SIGN OF SPECIAL
CONSIDERATIONS FROM NORDIC NEIGHBOURS -- "NORDISM" -- IS
FOUND ONLY WHEN IT SUPPORTS, OR AT LEAST DOES NOT COME
CONTRARY TO, THESE COUNTRIES' FOREIGN AND SECURITY POLICY
OBJECTIVES.

03235 FLORA, C.B.; BELLO, R.
THE IMPACT OF THE CATHOLIC CHURCH ON NATIONAL LEVEL CHANGE
IN LATIN AMERICA
JOURNAL OF CHURCH & STATE, 31(3) (AUT 89), 527-542.
STUDIES OF CHANGE IN LATIN AMERICA HAVE BEEN GREATLY
INFLUENCED BY DEPENDENCY THEORISTS WHO HAVE ATTEMPTED TO
LOOK AT THE IMPACT OF PENETRATION OF THE WORLD ECONOMIC
SYSTEM INTO DEVELOPING ECONOMIES ON THE LEVEL OF DEVELOPMENT
AND THE QUALITY OF LIFE IN THOSE COUNTRIES. THE CATHOLIC
CHURCH COULD BE VIEWED AS EITHER A TOOL OF THAT PENETRATION
OR A BLOCK TO IT. THIS STUDY EXAMINES THE INTERRELATIONSHIPS
OF THE CATHOLIC CHURCH WITH OVERALL LEVELS OF DEVELOPMENT,
THE DISTRIBUTION OF THE GOODS AND SERVICES THAT RESULTS IN
AN IMPROVEMENT IN THE QUALITY OF LIFE, AND THE DEGREE OF
DEPENDENCY IN THOSE SOCIETIES.

03236 FLORES, H.
THE SELECTIVITY OF THE CAPITALIST STATE: CHICANOS AND
ECONOMIC DEVELOPMENT
WESTERN POLITICAL QUARTERLY, 42(2) (JUN 89), 377-396.
PLURALISM AND POWER STRUCTURE THEORIES HAVE FAILED TO
EXPLAIN THE SEEMINGLY IMPOSSIBLE SOCIOECONOMIC SITUATION IN
WHICH CHICANOS FIND THEMSELVES IN SAN ANTONIO, TEXAS, AND
LOS ANGELES, CALIFORNIA. HOWEVER, A BETTER UNDERSTANDING OF
THE SYSTEMIC BARRIERS PREVENTING CHICANOS FROM ECONOMICALLY
ADVANCING MAY BE DERIVED BY UNCOVERING THE INSTITUTIONALIZED
RELATIONSHIP BETWEEN THE PRIVATE SECTOR AND LOCAL GOVERNMENT
WITHIN LIBERAL DEMOCRACIES.

03237 FLYNN, G.
PROBLEMS IN PARADIGM
FOREIGN POLICY, (74) (SPR 89), 63-85.
THE ARTICLE OUTLINES THE CHANGES THAT ARE OCCURRING IN
EASTERN AND WESTERN EUROPE DUE TO GORBACHEV'S POLICIES OF
GLASNOST AND PERESTROIKA. IT EXAMINES THE CHALLENGE THESE
CHANGES PROVIDE TO THE WEST: NOT SIMPLY TO USE SOVIET NEW
THINKING TO ENHANCE SHORT-TERM STABILITY IN EUROPE THROUGH
ARMS CONTROL, BUT ALSO TO CHANNEL THE FORCES OF CHANGE IN
THE EAST TO CREATE SOUNDER PRECONDITIONS FOR LONG-TERM
STABILITY. IT OUTLINES THE SOVIET STRATEGIC OBJECTIVES FOR
EUROPE AND THE POSSIBLE WESTERN RESPONSES TO THEM. IT
CONCLUDES THAT MILITARY POLICIES ADDRESS ONLY SYMPTONS AND
THAT BOTH MILITARY AND POLITICAL SOLUTIONS ARE NECESSARY TO
ENSURE LONG-TERM STABILITY.

03238 FLYNN, P.
BRAZIL AND INFLATION: A THREAT TO DEMOCRACY
THIRD WORLD QUARTERLY, 11(3) (JUL 89), 50-70.
THE AUTHOR SURVEYS BRESSER PEREIRA'S HOPES FOR 1989,
FOCUSING ON THE PROBLEM OF INFLATION, THE "SOCIAL PACT," THE

NOVEMBER 1989 ELECTIONS, AND THE SO-CALLED "SUMMER PLAN."

03239 FOLEY, M.W.
CHURCH BEHIND THE SCENES
COMMONWEAL, CXVI(18) (OCT 89), 549-550.
THE ANNOUNCEMENT THAT POPE JOHN PAUL 11 PLANS A TRIP TO
MEXICO IN 1990, TOGETHER WITH THE PAPAL NUNCIO'S UNGUARDED
REMARK THAT CHURCH-STATE RELATIONS ARE UNDER DISCUSSION AT
THE HIGHEST LEVELS OF THE MEXICAN GOVERNMENT PROVOKED A
STORM OF CONTROVERSY, SUGGESTING THAT THE ANTI-CLERICAL
TRADITION ENSHRINED IN MEXICO'S CONSTITUTION IS STILL ALIVE
AND WELL IN INTELLECTUAL AND POLITICAL CIRCLES DISPITE
RECENT HINTS OF A THAW.

03240 FOONER, M.
GOVERNANCE OF INTERPOL; INTERPOL
PLENUM PRESS, NEW YORK, LONDON, 1989, 65 - 88.
THIS CHAPTER DEALS WITH THE DOCUMENTARY FOUNDATION OF
INTERPOL. ITS CONSTITUTION, GENERAL REGULATIONS, AND THE
NATIONAL CENTRAL BUREAU POLICY ARE DETAILED. EXPLORED ARE
THE RULESON INTERNATIONAL POLICE COOPERATION AND ON THE
INTERNAL CONTROL OF INTERPOOL ARCHIVES. THE DILIBERATIVE
ENTITIES, THE GENERAL ASSEMBLY, THE EXECUTIVE COMMITTEE AND
ADVISERS ARE EACH EXAMINED.

03241 FOONER, M.
INTERPOL
PLENUM PRESS, NEW YORK, LONDON, 1989, 241.
THIS BOOK ANALYZES THE WORLD ASSOCIATION OF NATIONAL
POLICE FORCES FOR MUTUAL ASSISTANCE IN THE FIGHT AGAINST
INTERNATIONAL CRIMES AND CRIMINAL CONSPIRACIES - INTERPOL.
THE BOOK PROVIDES THE FIRST COMPREHENSIVE EXPLANATION,
ANALYSIS, AND DOCUMENTATION OF THE ORGANIZATION, FOLLOWING
ITS RESTRUCTURING AND MODERNIZATION IN THE 1980S TO MEET THE
NEW CHALLENGES OF TODAY'S TECHNOLOGICALLY ADVANCED, HEAVILY
ARMED, AND RICHLY FINANCED CRIMINAL ORGANIZATIONS IN AMERICA
AND AROUND THE WORLD. IT INTRODUCES THE READER TO A NEW
PERSPECTIVE ON THE CRIMINALITY OF OUR TIMES.

03242 FOONER, M.
INTERPOL IDENTIFIED; INTERPOL
PLENUM PRESS, NEW YORK, LONDON, 1929, 35-64.
THIS CHAPTER IDENTIFIES INTERPOL AND DISCUSSES THE AIMS,
PURPOSES, PRINCIPLES, POLITICS AND LEGAL STATUS OF THE
ORGANIZATION. IT EXAMINES THE ORIGINS AND HISTORY OF
INTERPOL AND THE NAZI INTRUSION. THE INTERNATIONAL AND THE
UNITED STATES LEGAL STATUS IS PROBED, AS WELL AS ITS ORIGINS
OF U.S. PARTICIPATION, AMBIGUITIES, AND TREASURY DEPARTMENT
MANAGEMENT.

03243 FOONER, M.
ORGANIZATION OF INTERPOL; INTERPOL
PLENUM PRESS, NEW YORK, LONDON, 1989, 89-114.
THIS CHAPTER DEALS WITH THE ORGANIZATION OF INTERPOL
PERSPECTIVES ON ORGANIZATION ARE GIVEN, AS WELL AS POWERS
AND CONTROL ARE DETAILED. FRENCH DOMINATION AND THE PROCESS
ON INTERNATIONALIZATION ARE EXAMINED. AS THE BIPARTITE
STRUCTURE IS EXPLORED, THE OFFICES OF THE GENERAL
SECRETARIATE AND THE SECRETARY GENERAL ARE DESCRIBED. IN
CONCLUSION, THE SIZE, ORIGIN, AND FUNCTIONS OF THE PERMANENT
DEPARTMENTS ARE ALSO DESCRIBED.

03244 FORBES, I.
UNEQUAL PARTNERS: THE IMPLEMENTATION OF EQUAL
OPPORTUNITIES POLICIES IN WESTERN EUROPE
PUBLIC ADMINISTRATION, 67(1) (SPR 89), 19-38.
AS A GENERAL PRINCIPLE, EQUALITY OF OPPORTUNITY ATTRACTS
CONSIDERABLE SUPPORT. HOWEVER, SUCH AGREEMENT DOES NOT
EXTEND TO DEFINITIONS OF EQUAL OPPORTUNITY POLICIES OR TO
THE NEED AND MANNER FOR THEIR IMPLEMENTATION. THESE POLICIES
HAVE A VARIETY OF BOTH IDEOLOGICAL AND HISTORICAL ASPECTS,
AND PATTERNS OF IMPLEMENTATION ARE POLITICALLY AND
CULTURALLY CONDITIONED. TO HIGHLIGHT DIFFERENT APPROACHES TO
EQUAL OPPORTUNITY IMPLEMENTATION, THREE COUNTRIES ARE
COMPARED: FRANCE, THE UNITED KINGDOM AND SWEDEN. INDICES OF
PROGRESS FOR WOMEN ARE PRESENTED AND PERFORMANCES ASSESSED,
AS ARE THE INSTRUMENTS AND MECHANISMS OF IMPLEMENTATION
PREFERRED UNDER DIFFERENT REGIMES. SWEDEN EMERGES WITH THE
MOST SUSTAINED AND EFFECTIVE PUBLIC POLICY ON EQUAL
OPPORTUNITIES, FRANCE DEMONSTRATES THE VALUE OF A MINISTRY
OF WOMEN, WHILE THE POTENTIAL INHERENT IN BRITAIN'S EQUAL
OPPORTUNITIES COMMISSION AND LOCAL AUTHORITY ENDEAVOUR IS
THWARTED BY A LACK OF POLITICAL WILL AT CENTRAL GOVERNMENT
LEVEL.

03245 FORD, D.E.D.
TRANSLATING THE PROBLEMS OF THE ELDERLY INTO EFFECTIVE
POLICIES: AN ANALYSIS OF FILIAL ATTITUDES
POLICY STUDIES REVIEW, 8(3) (SPR 89), 704-716.
THIS PAPER EXAMINES THE POLITICAL IMPLICATIONS OF
CURRENT DECISION MAKING EFFORTS THAT UNDERPIN RECENT COST-
CUTTING MEASURES OF FEDERALLY SUPPORTED PROGRAMS SERVING THE
ELDERLY. CURRENT POLICY CHANGES THAT FAVOR THE PRIVATE
SECTOR (E.G., SHIFTS OF THE COST OF CARE TO OTHER LEVELS OF

GOVERNMENT AND TO ELDERLY INDIVIDUALS AND THEIR FAMILIES)
HAVE ALSO GENERATED A RENEWED INTEREST IN THE POLICY OF
MANDATING FAMILY RESPONSIBILITY. THE PAPER ALSO EXAMINES
ATTITUDES CONCERNING FILIAL RESPONSIBILITY, SUCH AS
MULTIGENERATIONAL LIVING. THE INADEQUACY OF CURRENT POLICY
ANALYS THAT HAS ENCOURAGED THE DISESTABLISHMENT OF THE
CURRENT LONG-TERM CARE SYSTEM AND THE SHIFTING OF CARE COSTS
TO THE PRIVATE SECTOR, ESPECIALLY TO THE INDIVIDUAL AND THE
FAMILY, ARE ALSO EXAMINED.

03246 FORD, M.
KOREANS DRUM UP A NEW DEAL
SOUTH, (104) (JUN 89), 37.
ALONG WITH DEMOCRATIZATION IN SOUTH KOREA HAS COME
INCREASING PRESSURE FROM WORKERS FOR A FAIR SHARE OF THE
ECONOMIC CAKE. FOR YEARS, SOUTH KOREAN COMPANIES ADOPTED AN
AUTHORITARIAN MANAGEMENT STYLE THAT MIRRORED THAT OF SOUTH
KOREA'S MILITARY GOVERNMENTS. MANY BOSSES REGARD THE
ESTABLISHMENT OF DEMOCRATIC UNIONS AS A PERSONAL AFFRONT AND
BELIEVE THAT WORKERS DO NOT NEED FURTHER REWARDS FOR THEIR
CONTRIBUTION TO THE COMPANY AND THE ECONOMY.

03247 FORD, M.
SEOUL PLUGS THE TAX GAP
SOUTH, (109) (NOV 89), 20-21.
IN SOUTH KOREA, YEARS OF DEFICITS ON ITS CURRENT ACCOUNT
HAVE TURNED TO A SURPLUS ACCOMPANIED BY A HIGH GROWTH RATE
TO CREATE AN ECONOMIC BOOM. THIS HAS HIGHLIGHTED A SOCIAL
AND POLITICAL PROBLEM COMMON TO THE WHOLE OF NORTHEAST ASIA:
A GROWING GAP IN THE DISTRIBUTION OF WEALTH. THIS WEALTH GAP
HAS BEEN EXACERBATED BY THE ABSENCE OF TAX AND FISCAL
CONTROLS NORMALLY USED IN DEVELOPED COUNTRIES TO
REDISTRIBUTE INCOME.

03248 FORD, M.
SEOUL PREPARES TO LAY OUT THE WELCOME MAT
SOUTH, (106) (AUG 89), 36.
THE ISSUE OF FOREIGN INVESTMENT IS EMERGING AS A KEY
QUESTION IN THE FUTURE OF SOUTH KOREA'S ECONOMIC POLICY. THE
SEOUL GOVERNMENT HAS PLEDGED TO ALLOW FOREIGNERS TO MAKE
DIRECT INVESTMENTS IN THE SOUTH KOREAN STOCK EXCHANGE BY
1992. IT HAS ALSO AGREED, UNDER PRESSURE FROM THE USA, TO
LIFT RESTRICTIONS ON FOREIGN INVESTMENT BY BANKS, SERVICE
INDUSTRIES, AND OTHER SECTORS. BUT SOME ECONOMISTS FEAR THAT
THE COUNTRY IS NOT STRONG ENOUGH TO RESIST BEING SWAMPED BY
OVERSEAS CAPITAL. JAPAN IS FELT TO BE A PARTICULAR THREAT.

03249 FORD, M.D.
ROCKING THE ROE BOAT
COMMONWEAL, CXVI(11) (JUN 89), 326-328.
THE AUTHOR EXAMINES THE ARGUMENTS SURROUNDING ROE V.
WADE, INCLUDING THE CONTENTION THAT THE SUPREME COURT ACTED
MORE LIKE A LEGISLATURE THAN A COURT IN DECIDING ISSUES THAT
SHOULD BE DEBATED BY ELECTED OFFICIALS.

03250 FORD, T.R.
INDIAN OCEAN DEMANDS MORE ATTENTION
PACIFIC DEFENCE REPORTER, 16(5) (NOV 89), 15-18.
AN ANALYSIS OF THE INDIAN STRATEGIC ENVIRONMENT AND HER
DEFENCE INTERESTS SUPPORTS THE DEVELOPMENT OF A SUBSTANTIAL
INDIAN MILITARY CAPABILITY. HER DEFENCE POLICY INCLUDES
PROTECTION OF THE INDIAN MAINLAND, HER ISLAND TERRITORIES
AND ADJACENT SEA LINES OF COMMUNICATION, AND PROMOTION OF
COMMERCIAL INTERESTS IN THE INDIAN OCEAN REGION. IN ADDITION
INDIAN DEFENCE POLICY SUPPORTS PROTECTION OF INDIAN
NATIONALS IN REGIONAL STATES, REDUCTION OF EXTRA-REGIONAL
POWER INFLUENCE IN THE INDIAN OCEAN, AND ENHANCEMENT OF
INDIAN PRESTIGE AND POSITION AS A MAJOR ASIAN POWER. THIS
ARTICLE EXAMINES AUSTRALIA'S RESPONSE TO INDIA'S BUILD-UP OF
FORCES IN DEFENSE OF INDIAN OCEAN TERRITORIES IN LEFT OF
AUSTRALIA'S OWN STRATEGIC INTERESTS THERE.

03251 FOREMAN, P.
A MEDIA OFFENSIVE
SECHABA, 23(9) (SEP 89), 6-9.
THE ARTICLE DISCUSSES THE VITAL ROLE THE MEDIA PLAYS IN
ENCOURAGING DEMOCRATIC CHANGE AND REFORM IN SOUTH AFRICA. IT
OUTLINES STRATEGIES AND GOALS FOR A MEDIA OFFENSIVE BY THE
"PROGRESSIVE" MOVEMENT AND THE UNDERGROUND FORCES OF THE
AFRICAN NATIONAL CONGRESS. GOALS INCLUDE ORGANIZING THE
MASSES FOR THE ARMED SEIZURE OF POWER, THE WINNING OVER OF
SECTIONS OF THE "ENEMY CAMP" TO THE PROGRESSIVE SIDE, AND
THE DEVELOPMENT OF A NATIONAL CONSCIOUSNESS AND CULTURE.
ACKNOWLEDGING THE IMMENSITY OF THE OBSTACLES FACED, THE
ARTICLE CONCLUDES THAT A DEMOCRATIC MEDIA OFFENSIVE IS
NONETHELESS VITAL.

03252 FOREST, J.
RELIGIOUS OPENINGS IN THE U.S.S.R.
THE CHRISTIAN CENTURY, 106(27) (SEP 89), 848-850.
THIS ARTICLE IS A REPORT ON THE REVITALIZATION OF
RELIGION ON MANY FRONTS IN THE U.S.S.R. IT EXAMINES THE
CHANGE IN LITHUANIA WHICH HAS TAKEN GLASTNOST, PERESTROIKA,
AND DEMOCRATIZATION FURTHER THAN ANY SOVIET REPUBLIC. IT

DISCOVERS THAT THE JEWS ARE BENEFITING FROM POLICY CHANGES, BUT THAT GLASTNOST HAS ALSO MADE ANTI-SEMITISM MORE VISIBLE. IT ALSO FINDS THAT BIBLES ARE MUCH MORE READILY AVAILABLE NOW.

03253 FORESTER, J,; SITZEL, D.
BEYOND NEUTRALITY: THE POSSIBILITIES OF ACTIVIST MEDIATION IN PUBLIC SECTOR CONFLICTS
NEGOTIATION JOURNAL, 5(3) (JUL 89), 251-264.
THE ARTICLE EXAMINES THE IDEOLOGICAL CONFLICT BETWEEN THE CONCEPTS OF ACTIVE AND NEUTRAL MEDIATION. IT PRESENTS A SCORABLE THREE-PARTY MEDIATION EXERCISE FOR TEACHING AND RESEARCH WITH REGARDS TO THE POLITICAL AND ETHICAL INFLUENCE MEDIATORS INEVITABLY EXERT AS THEY MANAGE DISPUTE RESOLUTION PROCESSES. IT EXPLORES THE CONTROVERSIAL QUESTIONS REGARDING POWER, REPRESENTATION, AND NEUTRALITY THAT CHALLENGE BOTH THE DESIRABILITY AND VIABILITY OF PLANNER-MEDIATOR ROLES. IT CONCLUDES THAT ACTIVIST MEDIATION IS A VIABLE, PRACTICAL AND ETHICALLY DESIRABLE STRATEGY.

03254 FORESTIER, K.
A CHINESE PUZZLE
SOUTH, (109) (NOV 89), 94.
CHINA'S EDUCATIONAL SYSTEM FACES A CRISIS ON TWO FRONTS. FIRST, ACADEMICS AND STUDENTS ARE FRUSTRATED BY THE SLOW PACE OF POLITICAL REFORM AND THE LIMITED INTELLECTUAL FREEDOM. THEY ARE BEING HIT HARD BY THE MOST RECENT PURGE OF "BOURGEOIS LIBERAL" IDEAS. SECONDLY, SCHOOLS ARE SUFFERING FROM FINANCIAL NEGLECT, PARTICULARLY IN THE RURAL AREAS.

03255 FORGACS, D.
GRAMSCI AND MARXISM IN BRITAIN
NEW LEFT REVIEW, (176) (JUL 89), 70-90.
THE AUTHOR EVALUATES THE IMPACT OF A CENTRAL FIGURE IN WESTERN MARXISM ON THE THINKING OF THE LEFT. HE TRACES THE INFLUENCE OF GRAMSCI IN GREAT BRITAIN, WHERE DIVERGENT INTERPRETATIONS OF HIS WORK HAVE HELPED TO SHAPE STRATEGIC THEORY SINCE 1968.

03256 FORMAN, S.C.
COMMUNITY PROBLEM SOLVING: THERE ARE NO INTERJURISDICTIONAL PANACEAS
NATIONAL CIVIC REVIEW, 78(1) (JAN 89), 15-24.
COMMITMENT TO REGIONAL PROBLEM SOLVING REQUIRES REGIONAL CITIZENSHIP. SUBURBANIZATION AND WIDESPREAD PREFERENCE FOR THE FLEXIBILITY OF LOCAL CONTROL, HOWEVER, TEND TO COUNTER THE NEEDED SPIRIT OF PARTNERSHIP. REGIONALISM SEEMS AN IDEAL APPROACH TO CERTAIN PROBLEMS; THE QUESTION IS, ARE WE READY FOR IT?

03257 FORRESTER, J.P.
PROFESSIONALISM AND URBAN REFORM: AN ORGANIZATIONAL PERSPECTIVE ON MUNICIPAL FINANCE
AMERICAN REVIEW OF PUBLIC ADMINISTRATION, 19(1) (MAR 89), 67-85.
THE UNCERTAINTY OF INTERGOVERNMENTAL GRANTS-IN-AID IN THE 1980S HAS MADE MUNICIPAL PROFESSIONALISM AN ISSUE THAT DESERVES INCREASING ATTENTION. DEFINING PROFESSIONALISM IN TERMS OF CLASSICAL POLITICAL AND STRUCTURAL REFORM AS WELL AS ADMINISTRATIVE REFORM, THIS ANALYSIS FINDS THAT POLITICALLY REFORMED CITIES ARE NOT NECESSARILY ADMINISTRATIVELY REFORMED. A SUBSEQUENT ANALYSIS EXPLORES THE REASONS PROFESSIONALISM INFLUENCES MUNICIPAL DEPENDENCE ON GRANTS-IN-AID. IN SHORT, PROFESSIONAL GOVERNMENTS DEPEND LITTLE ON STATE AID, WHICH IS NOT TRUE REGARDING THEIR DEPENDENCE ON FEDERAL AID. THESE RESULTS EVEN HOLD WHEN CONTROLLING FOR THE EFFECTS OF URBAN NEED, MUNICIPAL FISCAL POLICIES, AND GRANT ALLOCATIONS. THE FINDINGS SUGGEST THAT MUNICIPALITIES MAY BE IN A POSITION TO MANAGE THEIR DEPENDENCE ON STATE AID, BUT THEIR DEPENDENCE ON FEDERAL AID IS MORE A FUNCTION OF FEDERAL AID OBJECTIVES AND ALLOCATION POLICY.

03258 FORTESCUE, W.
THE DEBATE OF THE FRENCH REVOLUTION
CONTEMPORARY REVIEW, 225(1482) (JUL 89), 12-19.
NOTING THE BICENTENNIAL OF THE FRENCH REVOLUTION IN 1989, THE ARTICLE EXAMINES ONE OF THE MANY LEGACIES OF THE REVOLUTION: THE INTENSE AND ONGOING DEBATE ABOUT IT. THE ARTICLE OUTLINES SOME OF THE MAJOR ARGUMENTS AND IMPLICATIONS OF THE REVOLUTION THAT HAVE BEEN DISCUSSED AND DEBATED ON FOR TWO CENTURIES. SOME VIEW THE REVOLUTION AS EVIDENCE OF THE ONGOING CLASS STRUGGLE PREDICTED BY MARX; OTHERS VIEW IT AS THE BEGINNING OF "ENLIGHTENMENT": STILL OTHERS AS MERELY A VIOLENT EXERCISE IN ANARCHY. THE ARTICLE CONCLUDES THAT ALTHOUGH THE INTERPRETATION OF EVENTS VARY, THERE IS AN ALMOST UNIVERSAL AGREEMENT AS TO THE SIGNIFICANCE OF THE PERIOD 1789-1799.

03259 FORTIN, A.J.
AIDS AND THE THIRD WORLD: THE POLITICS OF INTERNATIONAL DISCOURSE
ALTERNATIVES, XIV(2) (APR 89), 195-214.
AIDS HAS BECOME INCORPORATED INTO THE HISTORIC EAST-WEST SCRAMBLE FOR THIRD WORLD ALLEGIANCES. THE NOW FAMOUS AND DISCREDITED ATTEMPT BY THE SOVIET UNION TO USE AIDS AS A PROPAGANDA DEVICE TO ALIENATE AFRICAN COUNTRIES FROM THE UNITED STATES MUST BE SEEN AS A CLASSIC DISINFORMATION CAMPAIGN. WHILE EVENTUALLY UNSUCCESSFUL, THIS EFFORT CAUSED CONSIDERABLE DELAY AND IRRITATION AMONG THOSE WORKING ON INTERNATIONAL COOPERATIVE EFFORTS TO FIGHT THE EPIDEMIC. THE FOCUS HERE IS WITH THE REPRESENTATIONAL STRATEGIES THAT HAVE BEEN USED TO SITUATE AIDS AS A PROBLEM OF WORLD ORDER, OF ECONOMIC PRODUCTION, OF TECHNOLOGY, AND, OF COURSE, OF HEALTH AND SICKNESS.

03260 FOSSETT, M.A.; KIECOLT, K.J.
THE RELATIVE SIZE OF MINORITY POPULATIONS AND WHITE RACIAL ATTITUDES
SOCIAL SCIENCE QUARTERLY, 70(4) (DEC 89), 820-835.
ANALYSIS OF DATA FROM THE GENERAL SOCIAL SURVEYS AND THE NATIONAL ELECTION STUDIES SHOWS THAT PERCENT BLACK SIGNIFICANTLY AFFECTS WHITE SENSE OF STATUS THREAT FROM BLACKS AND WHITE SUPPORT FOR RACIAL INTEGRATION IN BOTH THE SOUTH AND THE NON-SOUTH. THIS CONFIRMS IMPORTANT, LONG-STANDING ASSUMPTIONS THAT FIGURE PROMINENTLY IN MANY COMPARATIVE STUDIES OF RACIAL INEQUALITY. IT IS ALSO FOUND THAT REGIONAL DIFFERENCES IN STRUCTURAL AND INDIVIDUAL CHARACTERISTICS ARE AT LEAST AS IMPORTANT AS A "SOUTHERN SUBCULTURE" IN EXPLAINING REGIONAL DIFFERENCES IN RACIAL ATTITUDES.

03261 FOSTER, G.D., ET AL
GLOBAL DEMOGRAPHIC TRENDS TO THE YEAR 2010: IMPLICATIONS FOR U.S. SECURITY
WASHINGTON QUARTERLY, 12(2) (SPR 89), 5-24.
THIS ARTICLE EXAMINES THE EXTENT TO WHICH DEMOGRAPHIC DEVELOPMENTS ARE LIKELY TO AFFECT THE SIZE OF COMPOSITION OF MILITARY ESTABLISHMENTS AROUND THE WORLD. ON THE WHOLE, DEMOGRAPHIC FACTORS WILL PRODUCE COMPLETELY DIFFERENT CONCERNS IN THE DEVELOPED WORLD THAN IN THE DEVELOPING WORLD. DECLINING FERTILITY RATES WILL MAKE IT INCREASINGLY DIFFICULT FOR THE UNITED STATES AND ITS NORTH ATLANTIC TREATY ORGANIZATION (NATO) ALLIES AND THE SOVIET UNION AND ITS WARSAW PACT ALLIES ALIKE TO MAINTAIN MILITARY FORCES AT CURRENT LEVELS. IN CONTRAST, EXCEPTIONALLY HIGH FERTILITY RATES IN MOST LDCS, IF NOT MATCHED BY A COMMENSURATE GROWTH OF JOBS, COULD LEAD TO EXPANDED MILITARY ESTABLISHMENTS IN AFFECTED COUNTRIES AS A PRODUCTIVE ALTERNATIVE TO UNEMPLOYMENT. IN OTHER WORDS, WHERE LABOR FORCES ARE SIGNIFICANTLY UNDEREMPLOYED, MILITARY ESTABLISHMENTS MAY HAVE A BUILT-IN MOMENTUM TO CAPITALIZE ON UNUSED MANPOWER FOR PURPOSES OF BOTH INTERNAL AND EXTERNAL SECURITY.

03262 FOSTER, J.; WOOLFSON, C.
CORPORATE RECONSTRUCTION AND BUSINESS UNIONISM: THE LESSONS OF CATERPILLAR AND FORD
NEW LEFT REVIEW, (174) (MAR 89), 51-66.
THE AUTHORS CONSIDER THE EXPERIENCES OF TWO RECENT TRADE-UNION STRUGGLES IN SCOTLAND AGAINST THE KIND OF TRANSNATIONAL LOCATION STRATEGIES THAT THE 1992 EUROPEAN COMMUNITY AGENDA IS DESIGNED TO FACILITATE: THE CATERPILLAR OCCUPATION AGAINST PLANT CLOSURE IN 1987 AND THE FORD MANOEUVRES AT DUNDEE IN 1987-88. AS THE INTERNATIONAL RESTRUCTURING OF CAPITAL GATHERS PACE, IT IS BECOMING EVER MORE EVIDENT THAT THE LEFT MUST MEET THE ECONOMIC AND POLITICAL CHALLENGE AT A GLOBAL LEVEL.

03263 FOURIE, D.
THE ANC LEAVES ANGOLA - IMPLICATIONS
SOUTH AFRICA FOUNDATION REVIEW, 15(5) (MAY 89), 6-7.
WHAT SHOULD BE EXPECTED IN 1989 FROM THE MANUAL OF THE AFRICAN NATIONAL CONGRESS (ANC) FROM ANGOLA IN TERMS OF RECENT TREATIES? SHOULD THE REMOVAL OF BASES AND TRAINING ESTABLISHMENTS TO COUNTRIES FURTHER DISTANT FROM SOUTH AFRICA'S BORDERS REALLY MAKE AN IMPACT ON THE LEVEL OF VIOLENCE PERPETRATED WITHIN SOUTH AFRICA BY THE ARMED ANC OPERATORS? VARIOUS HYPOTHESES ARE POSSIBLE. THE SIMPLE ONE IS THAT NOTHING WILL CHANGE, THAT THE ANC WILL CONTINUE TO FIND AVENUES OF ACCESS TO SOUTH AFRICA AND THAT IN THE PLACE OF TERROR ATTACKS THE INSTRUMENT OF MASS INSURGENCY IN THE TOWNSHIPS WILL BE USED AS A SUBSTITUTE. BUT THERE IS ALSO THE POSSIBILITY THAT INSTEAD OF THE CONTINUATION OF VIOLENCE THE ANC MAY BE COMPELLED TO MODIFY THEIR POLICY OF VIOLENCE. CHANGED ATTITUDES, ESPECIALLY ON THE PART OF THE USSR, MAY INDUCE THE ANC TO SEEK TO SECURE A NEGOTIATING BASE ATTRACTIVE TO THE SOUTH AFRICAN GOVERNMENT.

03264 FOWLER, J.
THE WAR WITHIN THE STATES
NATIONAL REVIEW, XLI(14) (AUG 89), 35-36.
THE WEBSTER DECISION, OR EVEN A COMPLETE REVERSAL OF ROE DOWN THE LINE, CAN ONLY CREATE AN OPPORTUNITY FOR STATE REGULATION. STATE COURTS AND MOST OF THE MEDIA TEND TO BACK ABORTION, AND NEITHER IS DIRECTLY RESPONSIBLE TO THE POLITICAL PROCESS-THOUGH EACH CAN BE GRADUALLY PERSUADED. AND ABORTION ADVOCATES TEND TO IGNORE THEIR FOES' STRENGTH OF COMMITMENT, AS SHOWN IN A RECENT LOS ANGELES TIMES POLL:

46 PER CENT OF PRO-LIFE VOTERS VERSUS ONLY 30 PER CENT OF "PRO-CHOICERS" SAID THEY WOULD SWITCH THEIR VOTE BASED ON THAT SINGLE ISSUE. EACH SIDE IS READY FOR A LONG FIGHT. AND A COMPLEX ONE.

03265 FOWLER, R.B.
RELIGION AND THE ESCAPE FROM LIBERAL INDIVIDUALISM
JOURNAL OF POLITICAL SCIENCE, 16(1-2) (1988), 5-13.
RELIGION SERVES AMERICAN CULTURE BY PROVIDING A HAVEN FROM THE EXCESSES OF LIBERAL INDIVIDUALISM. RELIGION SERVES AS AN ESCAPE FROM THE LIMITATIONS OF LIBERAL CULTURE WITH ITS EMPHASIS UPON SKEPTICISM, UNCERTAINTY, AND RELATIVISM. IT IS LIKE AN ANCHOR OF ABSOLUTISM IN A SEA OF DOUBT. COMMUNITY, WHICH IS AN ESSENTIAL PART OF THE RELIGIOUS EXPERIENCE, HELPS INDIVIDUALS TO ADJUST TO SOCIETY AND ITS NORMS. THUS, RELIGION IS A BUFFER BETWEEN THE EXCESSES OF ATOMISTIC LIBERAL INDIVIDUALISM ON ONE HAND AND THE TOTALITY OF GOVERNMENTAL POWER ON THE OTHER.

03266 FOX, C.J.
FREE TO CHOOSE, FREE TO WIN, FREE TO LOSE: THE PHENOMENOLOGY OF ETHICAL SPACE
INTERNATIONAL JOURNAL OF PUBLIC ADMINISTRATION, 12(6) (NOV 89), 913-930.
THIS PAPER ARGUES THAT, CONTRARY TO SOME POINTS OF VIEW, MOST PUBLIC ADMINISTRATORS HAVE SUFFICIENT DISCRETION TO ACT ETHICALLY; THEY HAVE "ETHICAL SPACE" WITHIN FIELD CONSTRAINTS. THIS CONCLUSION IS ARRIVED AT BY WAY OF A THEORETICAL PERSPECTIVE CALLED PHENOMENOLOGY. ALONG THE WAY WE DESCRIBE THIS ORIENTATION AND TRY TO SHOW ITS RELEVANCE TO PRACTITIONERS.

03267 FOX, D.M.; SCHAFFER, D.C.
HEALTH POLICY AND ERISA: INTEREST GROUPS AND SEMIPREEMPTION
JOURNAL OF HEALTH POLITICS, POLICY AND LAW, 14(2) (SUM 89), 239-260.
THIS PAPER IS A HISTORY OF THE HEALTH POLICY RESULTS OF THE EMPLOYEE RETIREMENT AND INCOME SECURITY ACT OF 1974, PARTICULARLY SECTION 514, WHICH PREEMPTS STATE LAWS "WHICH RELATE TO ANY EMPLOYEE BENEFIT PLAN" BUT PERMITS STATES TO CONTINUE TO REGULATE THE BUSINESS OF INSURANCE. THIS HISTORY EXEMPLIFIES HOW HEALTH POLICY IS OFTEN MADE OUTSIDE CONVENTIONAL ARENAS. ON THE BASIS OF PUBLISHED PRIMARY SOURCES AND INTERVIEWS WITH A NUMBER OF KEY PARTICIPANTS, THE PAPER DESCRIBES HOW INTEREST GROUPS WHICH RARELY ACT TOGETHER COALESCED TO CREATE AND SUSTAIN SEMIPREEMPTION AND ITS EFFECTS ON STATE AND FEDERAL HEALTH POLICY. THE PAPER CONCLUDES WITH AN ASSESSMENT OF RECENT STATE LEGISLATIVE EFFORTS TO ADDRESS THE PROBLEMS CREATED BY ERISA SEMIPREEMPTION. THE IRONICAL RESULTS OF SEMIPREEMPTION OCCURRED BECAUSE OF THE ABSENCE OF A COALITION OF INTEREST GROUPS THAT WAS SUFFICIENTLY STRONG TO RESOLVE THE FUNDAMENTAL QUESTIONS RAISED BY OUR COMMITMENT TO LINKING HEALTH INSURANCE TO EMPLOYMENT.

03268 FOX, E. (ED.)
MEDIA AND POLITICS IN LATIN AMERICAN: THE STRUGGLE FOR DEMOCRACY
SAGE PUBLICATIONS, BEVERLY HILLS, CA, 1988, 208.
"MEDIA AND POLITICS IN LATIN AMERICA" EXAMINES THE DIFFERENT FORCES WHICH HAVE AFFECTED THE MODERN MASS MEDIA IN THE REGION. ELIZABETH FOX PRESENTS AN OVERVIEW OF MEDIA POLICIES, INCLUDING EARLY COMMERCIALIZATION AND GOVERNMENT INTERVENTION, THE MOVEMENTS FOR REFORM, THE IMPACT OF THE DICTATORSHIPS AND THE RECOVERY OF DEMOCRACY. THIRTEEN STUDIES THEN TRACE THE MAJOR THEMES THROUGH NINE COUNTRIES.

03269 FOX, G.
PUTTING THE "PERON" BACK IN
NACLA REPORT ON THE AMERICAS, XXIII(4) (NOV 89), 4-7.
ARGENTINA'S PRESIDENT SAUL MENEM'S PARDONING OF MILITARY CRIMINALS, HIS APPOINTMENT OF BUSINESS EXECUTIVES TO CABINET POSTS, AND HIS ECONOMIC POLICIES THAT HAVE REDUCED THE PEOPLE'S PURCHASING POWER TO NEARLY ZERO, SEEM LIKE UNUSUAL STEPS FOR THE LEADER OF PERONISM, THE NATIONALIST AND POPULIST MOVEMENT THAT GAVE RISE TO THE MONTONERO GUERRILLAS. HOWEVER, THE AUTHOR ARGUES THAT MENEM'S IDEOLOGY IS AS ECLECTIC AS ITS CONSTITUENCY IS DIVERSE. MENEM IS SIMPLY "PUTTING THE PERON BACK IN" IN CONVOLUTED, BUT ASTUTE WAYS.

03270 FOX, J.
TOWARDS DEMOCRACY IN MEXICO?
HEMISPHERE, 1(2) (WIN 89), 40-43.
THE SUMMER OF 1988 MARKED A TURNING POINT IN MEXICO'S POLITICAL TRANSITION. DIVISIONS IN THE MEXICAN GOVERNING ELITE CREATED OPPORTUNITIES FOR ORDINARY PEOPLE TO INFLUENCE EVENTS TO AN UNUSUAL DEGREE. HUNDREDS OF THOUSANDS OF CITIZENS, MANY ALREADY DEMOCRATICALLY ORGANIZED AT THE COMMUNITY LEVEL, PARTICIPATED ACTIVELY IN ELECTORAL POLITICS FOR THE FIRST TIME, CATCHING ANALYSTS COMPLETELY BY SURPRISE. MEXICAN POLITICS WILL NEVER BE THE SAME.

03271 FOX, R.
WAR AND PEACE--AND OIL

AUSTRIA TODAY, (1) (1989), 12, 62.
THE OPEC CONFERENCE IN NOVEMBER 1988 WAS ONE OF THE MOST IMPORTANT IN ITS HISTORY. THE OPEC MINISTERS MET TO TRY TO UNRAVEL SOME VERY KNOTTY PROBLEMS, WHICH THEY HAD ALREADY CONSIDERED WITHOUT SUCCESS AT PREVIOUS MEETINGS AND NOW THREATENED TO PUSH OIL PRICES INTO SINGLE FIGURES. THE GREATEST CHALLENGE WAS REACHING AGREEMENT AMONG ALL 13 MEMBERS, INCLUDING IRAN AND IRAQ. IN THE AFTERMATH OF THE GULF CEASEFIRE, THE ISSUE OF IRANIAN AND IRAQI QUOTAS HAD BECOME CRUCIAL TO OPEC'S CREDIBILITY.

03272 FRAGER, R.A.
CLASS AND ETHNIC BARRIERS TO FEMINIST PERSPECTIVES IN TORONTO'S JEWISH LABOR MOVEMENT, 1919-1939
STUDIES IN POLITICAL ECONOMY: A SOCIALIST REVIEW, (30) (FAL 89), 143-166.
THIS ARTICLE EXAMINES THE HISTORY OF TORONTO'S JEWISH LABOR MOVEMENT WHICH PROVIDES A CRITICAL CONTEXT FOR EXAMINING THE RELATIONSHIP BETWEEN FEMINIST AND SOCIALIST CURRENTS IN CANADA'S PAST. IT ALSO EXPLORES THE RELATIONSHIP BETWEEN THESE CURRENTS AND ETHNIC IDENTITY WITHIN A KEY SECTION OF THE WORKING CLASS. IT CONCLUDES THAT WORKING CLASS JEWISH WOMEN SACRIFICED THEIR OWN POTENTIAL FOR FULL EQUALITY TO MALE-DOMINATED, MALE-DEFINED COLLECTIVITIES OF FAMILY, NATIONALITY, AND CLASS.

03273 FRANCIS, A.A.
THE NEW LAW OF THE SEA AND THE SECURITY INTERESTS OF THE CARICOM STATES
JOURNAL OF INTERAMERICAN STUDIES AND WORLD AFFAIRS, 31(3) (FAL 89), 97-116.
IN 1973 THE THIRD U.N. CONFERENCE ON THE LAW OF THE SEA WAS CONVENED AND EVERY ASPECT OF OCEAN USE WAS REVIEWED. THIS CONCLUDED IN AN 1982 COMPREHENSIVE CONVENTION ON THE LAW OF THE SEA WHICH IS AN ADMIXTURE OF TRADITIONAL PRINCIPLES AND PROGRESSIVE DEVELOPMENTS. THIS ARTICLE EMPHASIZES THOSE ASPECTS WHICH HAV IMPLICATIONS FOR THE SECURITY OF THE SMALL STATES OF THE CARICOM SUB-REGION. SECURITY IS NOT TREATED IN NARROW MILITARY AND STRATEGIC TERMS BUT ARE EXTENDED TO ENCOMPASS ECONOMIC AND POLITICAL ISSUES AS WELL.

03274 FRANCIS, S.
IMPERIAL CONSERVATIVES?
NATIONAL REVIEW, XLI(14) (AUG 89), 37-38.
IN THE RUSH TO DEFEND REAGAN POLICIES FROM THE CAVILS OF THE BOLAND AMENDMENTS AND WAR POWERS ACT. SOME RIGHT-WINGERS HAVE FORGOTTEN THAT CONGRESS SHOULD MEDDLE IN FOREIGN POLICY. ALTHOUGH THE ENEMY OF CHOICE HAS BECOME THE IMPERIAL CONGRESS, THE WAY TO RESIST THE LEGISLATURE IS NOT TO PUT MORE POWER IN THE HANDS OF THE SECRETARY OF STATE.

03275 FRANCK, M.J.
STATESMANSHIP AND THE JUDICIARY
REVIEW OF POLITICS, 51(4) (FAL 89), 510-532.
THIS ESSAY QUESTIONS WHETHER IT IS AS APPROPRIATE AS IT IS COMMON TO SPEAK OF THE FEDERAL JUDICIARY AS LEGITIMATELY ENGAGED IN "STATESMANSHIP"--HOWEVER THAT CONCEPT MAY BE DEFINED OR ELUCIDATED. SCHOLARS OF BOTH THE "INTERPRETIVIST" AND "NONINTERPRETIVIST" SCHOOLS IN CONSTITUTIONAL LAW APPEAR TO SUBSCRIBE TO THE EXPECTATION THAT JUDGES SHOULD BE STATESMEN. SOME POINT TO TOCQUEVILLE FOR SUPPORT OF THIS NOTION. THE ARGUMENT HERE IS THAT TOCQUEVILLE IS UNRELIABLE ON THIS POINT, FOR HE PARTS COMPANY NOT ONLY WITH HIS CONTEMPORARY, JOSEPH STORY, BUT WITH THE FRAMERS OF THE CONSTITUTION. THE FEDERALIST IS EXAMINED FOR ITS THOUGHTS ON THE MEANING AND LOCATION OF STATESMANSHIP IN THE CONSTITUTIONAL ORDER, AND IT IS ARGUED THAT THE ESSAYS ON THE JUDICIARY REVEAL A CONSPICUOUS ABSENCE OF AN EXPECTATION THAT THAT BRANCH SHOULD CONTAIN STATESMEN. INDEED, PUBLIUS ADVANCES AN ARGUMENT THAT CONGRESS SHOULD ACT TO RESTRAIN (THROUGH THE THREAT OF IMPEACHMENT) JUDICIAL TEMPTATIONS TO ENGAGE IN ANY ADVENTURES THAT CAN BE CALLED STATESMANSHIP.

03276 FRANK, A.
THE DEVELOPMENT OF UNDERDEVELOPMENT
MONTHLY REVIEW, 41(2) (JUN 89), 37-51.
THE ARTICLE IS A REPRINT THAT WAS ORIGINALLY WRITTEN IN 1966. IT ARGUES THAT CURRENT THEORIES OF ECONOMIC DEVELOPMENT ARE SKEWED TOWARDS THE EXPERIENCES OF THE EUROPEAN AND NORTH AMERICAN ADVANCED CAPITALIST STATES. ATTEMPTS TO APPLY THESE THEORIES TO THE UNDERDEVELOPED WORLD WOULD THEREFORE BE BIASED AND INACCURATE. THE ARTICLE EXPLORES THE DIFFERENCES BETWEEN THE DEVELOPED AND UNDERDEVELOPED WORLDS AND ANALYZES THE EFFECTS OF THE GLOBAL EXTENSION AND UNITY OF THE CAPITALIST SYSTEM.

03277 FRANK, H.A.
MODEL UTILITY ALONG THE FORECAST CONTINUUM: A CASE STUDY IN FLORIDA LOCAL GOVERNMENT REVENUE FORECASTING
DISSERTATION ABSTRACTS INTERNATIONAL, 49(12) (JUN 89), 3865-A.
THE AUTHOR EVALUATES THE APPLICABILITY OF TIME-SERIES MODELS TO REVENUE FORECASTING IN FLORIDA CITIES. DATA FOR

THE FISCAL YEARS 1982 THROUGH 1985 WERE FIT WITH SEVEN TIME-
SERIES MODELS RANGING IN COMPLEXITY FROM THE MOVING AVERAGE
TO BOX-JENKINS, IN ORDER TO OBTAIN FORECASTS FOR FISCAL YEAR
1986. MEAN ABSOLUTE PERCENTAGE ERROR AND MEAN PERCENTAGE
ERROR OF THE TECHNIQUES TESTED WERE COMPARED, USING ONE- AND
TWO-WAY ANALYSIS OF VARIANCE AND NONPARAMETRIC ANALOGS.

03278 FRANK, P.
PERESTROIKA IN CRISIS
WORLD TODAY, 45(11) (NOV 89), 185-188.
IN ITS ESSENTIALS, THE SOVIET UNION HAS SCARELY CHANGED
AT ALL. DESPITE THE ADVENT OF THE NEW CONGRESS OF PEOPLE'S
DEPUTIES, THE PARTY CLINGS TO ITS MONOPOLY OF POLITICAL
POWER. ALSO, NOTHITHSTANDING THE ATTEMPTS TO DEVOLVE
DECISION-MAKING, THE SOVIET ECONOMY REMAINS IN ALL IMPORTANT
RESPECTS CENTRALLY-PLANNED AND CENTRALLY-CONTROLLED. THE
SOVIET UNION IS STILL A UNIFIED STATE, EVEN THOUGH THE
CLAMOUR FOR INDEPENDENCE AND EVEN SECESSION IS INSISTENT.
THE QUESTION NOW IS: HOW LONG CAN THE SOVIET UNION SURVIVE
IN ITS PRESENT FORM BEFORE THE SHARPENING CONTRADICTIONS
PROVOKE EITHER A SAVAGE BACKLASH OR A REAL QUALITATIVE
CHANGE IN THE DISTRIBUTION OF POWER?

03279 FRANK, R.G.
REGULATORY POLICY AND INFORMATION DEFICIENCIES IN THE
MARKET FOR MENTAL HEALTH SERVICES
JOURNAL OF HEALTH POLITICS, POLICY AND LAW, 14(3) (FAL 89),
477-502.
THIS PAPER ADDRESSES ISSUES RELATED TO THE REGULATION OF
THE DELIVERY OF MENTAL HEALTH SERVICES. THE FOCUS IS
PRIMARILY ON REGULATIONS THAT ARE AIMED AT DEALING WITH THE
CONSEQUENCES OF IMPERFECT INFORMATION IN THE MARKETPLACE.
THE PAPER REVIEWS AND ASSESES WHAT IS KNOWN ABOUT THE IMPACT
OF REGULATIONS ON EFFICIENCY AND EQUITY. ONE CONCLUSION IS
THAT WE KNOW A FAIR AMOUNT ABOUT IMPACTS OF REGULATION ON
PRICES FOR MENTAL HEALTH SERVICE AND VERY LITTLE ABOUT
EFFECTS ON QUALITY OF CARE. A RESEARCH AGENDA IS PROPOSED
BASED ON THE KNOWLEDGE AVAILABLE IN 1988.

03280 FRANKEL, N.
JORDANIAN PALESTINIANS: WHAT DO THEY THINK? (PART 2)
POLITICAL COMMUNICATION AND PERSUASION, 6(1) (1989), 49-86.
REPORTING FROM A NONDEMOCRATIC LAND PRESENTS UNIQUE
PROBLEMS FOR JOURNALISTS AND RESEARCHERS. THIS IS
PARTICULARLY TRUE OF A TRADITIONAL MONARCHY, SUCH AS JORDAN,
WHERE ALL IMPORTANT DECISIONS ARE ULTMATELY THE PREROGATIVE
OF THE MONARCH. JOURNALISTS MUST BE CAREFUL TO STAY WITHIN
CERTAIN BOUNDS. IF THEY ASK THE WRONG QUESTION THEY ARE
LIABLE TO FIND THEMSELVES ON THE NEXT FLIGHT BACK TO THEIR
HOME COUNTRY. QUESTIONS CONCERNING THE LEGITIMACY OF THE
MONARCHY OR THE COMPETENCE OF THE RULING MONARCH ARE
CONSIDERED OUT OF BOUNDS. ONE MUST TRY TO DISCERN THE
UNDERLYING POLITICAL REALITY WITHOUT STRAYING INTO FORBIDDEN
ZONES. THIS STUDY OFFERS A VIEW INTO THE COMPLEX FABRIC OF
JORDANIAN POLITICAL REALITY THROUGH INTERVIEWS WITH
GOVERNMENT OFFICIALS, PROMINENT PRIVATE CITIZENS WITH HIGH-
LEVEL CONNECTIONS, AND FORMER OPPOSITION FIGURES. THE
INTERVIEWS FOCUS ON CRUCIAL AREAS OF FOREIGN AND DOMESTIC
POLICY.

03281 FRANKEL, N.
JORDANIAN PALESTINIANS: WHAT DO THEY THINK? PART I
POLITICAL COMMUNICATION AND PERSUASION, 5(4) (1988),
265-285.
REPORTING FROM A NONDEMOCRATIC LAND PRESENTS PROBLEMS
FOR AMERICAN JOURNALISTS AND RESEARCHERS. THIS IS
PARTICULARLY TRUE OF A TRADITIONAL MONARCHY, SUCH AS JORDAN,
WHERE ALL IMPORTANT DECISIONS ARE ULTIMATELY THE PREROGATIVE
OF THE MONARCH. THE UNDERLYING POLITICAL REALITY IS AS
COMPLEX AS IN A DEMOCRATIC SOCIETY. THIS REALITY IS JUST
MORE DIFFICULT TO DISCERN. IN JORDAN GOVERNMENT OFFICIALS
REFLECT THE CURRENT THINKING OF THE MONARCH. THIS STUDY
PROVIDES A VIEW INTO THE COMPLEX FABRIC OF JORDANIAN
POLITICAL REALITY THROUGH INTERVIEWS WITH GOVERNMENT
OFFICIALS, PROMINENT PRIVATE CITIZENS WITH HIGH-LEVEL
CONNECTIONS, AND FORMER OPPOSITION FIGURES. THE INTERVIEWS
FOCUS ON CRUCIAL AREAS OF FOREIGN AND DOMESTIC POLICY,
INCLUDING RELATIONS WITH THE PALESTINIANS AND ISRAELIS.

03282 FRANKIEWICZ, M.
TWO PATHS: OTHER VIEWS OF THE ROUND TABLE
EAST EUROPEAN REPORTER, 3(4) (SPR 89), 34.
THERE IS CURRENTLY TWO CURRENTS IN THE POLISH OPPOSITION.
ONE IS MADE UP OF THOSE WHO WISH TO REFORM THE PRESENT
SYSTEM; THE OTHER DESIRES TOTAL INDEPENDENCE FROM THE SOVIET
UNION AND THE COMPLETE DESTRUCTION OF COMMUNISM. ALTHOUGH
THE AIMS OF THESE TWO FACTIONS SEEM TO BE MUTUALLY EXCLUSIVE,
THE TRUTH IS THAT THE RADICAL DEMANDS FOR COMPLETE
REVOLUTION GIVE LECH WALESA AND HIS FELLOW MODERATES THE
APPEARANCE OF PRAGMATISM AND PRUDENCE. THE END RESULT IS
THAT THERE IS A GREATER CHANCE FOR SIGNIFICANT, AND PEACEFUL,
REFORM.

03283 FRANKLAND, E.G.
PARLIAMENTARY POLITICS AND THE DEVELOPMENT OF THE GREEN
PARTY IN WEST GERMANY
REVIEW OF POLITICS, 51(3) (SUM 89), 386-411.
THIS STUDY DEALS WITH THE EXPERIENCES OF THE GREENS (DIE
GRUNEN) DURING THE 1980'S AS A NEW "NEW" PARTY IN WEST
GERMAN STATE AND FEDERAL PARLIAMENTS AND SPECIFICALLY WITH
THE GREEN PARLIAMENTARY GROUPS' RELATIONSHIPS WITH THE THE
MOVEMENT-PARTY. THE FOUNDERS OF THE GREENS SOUGHT TO
ORGANIZE AS A DECENTRALIZED, PARTICIPATORY DEMOCRACY.
ACCORDINGLY, THEY DEVELOPED RULES TO HINDER THE EMERGENCY OF
A PROFESSIONALIZED LEADERSHIP AND TO RESTRICT THE AUTONOMY
OF PARLIAME PARLIAMENTARY GROUPS. UTILIZING A COMPARATIVE
APPROACH, THE AUTHOR INVESTIGATES THE EXTENT WHICH THE
GREENS HAVE BECOME "PARLIAMENTARIZED" BY THE NORMALIZING
FORCES OF THE ESTABLISHED SYSTEM AT STATE AND FEDERAL LEVELS.
THIS STUDY RELATES THE GREENS' DEVELOPMENTAL EXPERIENCES TO
THE "CLASSIC" OBSERVATIONS OF DUVERGER, MICHELS, AND OTHERS
ABOUT MODERN PARTY DEVELOPMENT. FINALLY, IT REVIEWS THE
RECENT PERSPECTIVE OF VARIOUS INTRAPARTY GROUPS ABOUT THE
FUTURE OF THE GREENS.

03284 FRANKLIN, B.
TELEVISING LEGISLATURES: THE BRITISH AND AMERICAN
EXPERIENCE
PARLIAMENTARY AFFAIRS, 42(4) (OCT 89), 485-502.
THIS ARTICLE EXPLORES THE OBJECTIVES OF SOME MPS TO THE
BROADCASTING ENTERPRISE AND REVIEWS THE PROGRESS OF THE
SELECT COMMITTEE ON TELEVISING THE PROCEEDINGS OF THE HOUSE
IN PREPARING FOR THE PUBLIC EXPERIENCE IN TELEVISION
BROADCASTING. IT THEN ASSESSES THE EXPERIENCE OF TELEVISING
CONGRESSIONAL PROCEEDINGS IN AMERICA TO ESTABLISH WHAT
LESSONS, IF ANY, MIGHT BE LEARNED BY BRITISH
PARLIAMENTARIANS AND BROADCASTERS.

03285 FRANKLIN, C.H.; KOSAKI, L.C.
REPUBLICAN SCHOOLMASTER: THE U.S. SUPREME COURT, PUBLIC
OPINION, AND ABORTION
AMERICAN POLITICAL SCIENCE REVIEW, 83(3) (SEP 89), 751-772.
THE UNITED STATES SUPREME COURT HAS A HISTORICAL ROLE AS
A "REPUBLICAN SCHOOLMASTER," INCULCATING VIRTUES IN THE
CITIZENRY. THE ROLE AS TEACHER TO THE REPUBLIC ALSO SERVES
THE INTERESTS OF THE COURT. AS THE "WEAKEST BRANCH," THE
SUPREME COURT NEEDS PUBLIC SUPPORT IF ITS DECISIONS ARE TO
BE THE AUTHORS INVESTIGATE THE COURT'S ABILITY TO WIN
POPULAR SUPPORT FOR ITS RULINGS, SPECIFICALLY IN THE CASE OF
ROE V. WADE. THE ANALYSIS SHOWS THAT THE COURT'S DECISION
DID AFFECT PUBLIC ATTITUDES BUT NOT AS PREVIOUS WORK WOULD
PREDICT. WHILE SUPPORT FOR ABORTIONS TO PROTECT HEALTH
INCREASED AS A RESULT OF THE COURT'S DECISION, THE PUBLIC
BECAME MORE POLARIZED OVER "DISCRETIONARY" ABORTIONS. THE
PUZZLE IS WHAT PROCESS CAN ACCOUNT FOR THESE DISPARATE
REACTIONS. THEY DEVELOP A THEORY RESTING ON INTERPERSONAL
INFLUENCES TO EXPLAIN THESE RESULTS, ARGUING THAT THE SOCIAL
INTERPRETATION OF EVENTS DRIVES THE DIFFERING OUTCOMES. THIS
THEORY IS THEN TESTED AGAINST A PURELY PSYCHOLOGICAL
ALTERNATIVE. THE CLOSING DISCUSSION CONSIDERS HOW THESE
RESULTS CAN BE EXTENDED TO THE GENERAL PROBLEM OF PUBLIC
DECISIONS AND POPULAR RESPONSES, INCLUDING PRESIDENTIAL
ACTIONS AND THE INFLUENCE OF THE MEDIA.

03286 FRANKLIN, D.
PERESTROIKA ON THE FARMS
WORLD TODAY, 45(5) (MAY 89), 73-74.
GORBACHEV'S AGRICULTURAL POLICIES EMBRACE A WHOLE RANGE
OF PROBLEMS, UPSTREAM AND DOWNSTREAM FROM THE FARMS. BUT THE
HEART, AND THE MOST CONTROVERSIAL PART OF HIS REFORMS, IS A
PROPOSED REORGANIZATION OF THE FARMS THEMSELVES, WHICH WOULD
AMOUNT TO VIRTUAL RE-PRIVATIZATION. GORBACHEV IS CAREFUL TO
AVOID SAYING THAT HE INTENDS TO UNDO STALIN'S
COLLECTIVIZATION, BUT THE THRUST OF HIS POLICY IS TO
RESTRUCTURE THE FARMS SO THOROUGHLY THAT THE COOPERATIVES
MIGHT SIMPLY WITHER AWAY.

03287 FRANSZOON, D.
CRISIS IN THE BACKLANDS
HEMISPHERE, 1(2) (WIN 89), 36-38.
SURINAME'S CURRENT POLITICAL CRISIS IS ROOTED IN THE
DEEP TENSIONS THAT EXIST BETWEEN ITS ETHNIC COMMUNITIES, AS
MANIFESTED IN THE CIVIL WAR BETHEEN THE MAROONS AND THE
NATIONAL ARMY.

03288 FRANZ, M.G.
IDEOLOGY AND PNEUMAPATHOLOGICAL CONSCIOUSNESS: ERIC
VOEGELIN'S ANALYSIS OF THE SPIRITUAL ROOTS OF POLITICAL
DISORDER
DISSERTATION ABSTRACTS INTERNATIONAL, 50(4) (OCT 89),
1076-A.
ERIC VOEGELIN WAS PERHAPS THE FIRST POLITICAL
PHILOSOPHER TO EXPLAIN IDEOLOGICAL THOUGHT AND ACTIVITY
THROUGH AN ANALYSIS CONDUCTED ON THE LEVEL OF CONSCIOUSNESS.
HIS EFFORT YIELDED THE CONCLUSION THAT IDEOLOGICAL
CONSCIOUSNESS IS A FORM OF SPIRITUAL DISORDER THAT IS
ESSENTIALLY EQUIVALENT TO A PERENNIAL PATTERN OF REBELLION

AGAINST THE MOST FUNDAMENTAL CONDITIONS OF HUMAN EXISTENCE.

03289 FRANZOSI, R.
STRIKE DATA IN SEARCH OF A THEORY: THE ITALIAN CASE IN THE
POSTWAR PERIOD
POLITICS AND SOCIETY, 17(4) (DEC 89), 453-487.
IN THIS PAPER THE AUTHOR DISCUSSES SEVERAL THEORIES OF
INDUSTRIAL CONFLICT: BUSINESS CYCLE, INSTITUTIONALIZATION OF
CONFLICT, AND POLITICAL EXCHANGE THEORIES. THE AUTHOR SHOWS
THAT EACH THEORY HAS SOMETHING TO CONTRIBUTE TO OUR
UNDERSTANDING OF ITALIAN STRIKES, ALTHOUGH NONE CAN FULLY
ACCOUNT FOR THE TEMPORAL DYNAMIC OF STRIKES IN POSTWAR ITALY
AND EACH EXPLAINS ONLY A PARTICULAR FACET OF INDUSTRIAL
CONFLICT. THE ARTICLE FINALLY DEMONSTRATES THAT A PARTICULAR
KIND OF MARXIST THEORY OF CONFLICT PROVIDES A MORE
COMPREHENSIVE EXPLANATION FOR THE AVAILABLE DATA.

03290 FRASER, H.
"WALL OF DEATH" FISHING WORRIES ISLAND STATES
PACIFIC DEFENCE REPORTER, 16(3) (SEP 89), 48-49.
DRIFTNET FISHING IS PRACTISED IN THE REGION BY UP TO 190
JAPANESE AND TAIWANESE VESSELS USING FINE MESHED PLASTIC
DRIFTNETS WHICH ARE UP TO 60 KILOMETRES LONG AND 15 METRES
DEEP. THE COMMONLY CALLED "WALL OF DEATH" PRACTICE
INDISCRIMINATELY CAPTURES VIRTUALLY EVERYTHING SWIMMING NEAR
THE SURFACE OF THE WATER, INCLUDING JUVENILE ALBACORE TUNA,
DOLPHINS AND OTHER MAMMALS. DIVING BIRDS ARE ALSO KILLED BY
ENTANGLEMENT IN THE NETS WHICH THEY CAN'T SEE FROM THE AIR.
FISHERIES EXPERTS IN THE SOUTH PACIFIC BELIEVE THE SOUTHERN
ALBACORE TUNA FISHERY WILL BE DEPLETED WITHIN TWO YEARS IF
THE PRACTICE IS NOT STOPPED. THE NUMBER OF VESSELS OPERATING
IN THE REGION HAS GROWN FROM SEVEN TWO YEARS AGO TO THE
ESTIMATED 190 NOW FISHING. THE TARAWA DECLARATION ADOPTED BY
THE SOUTH PACIFIC FORUM DECIDED ON A MANAGEMENT REGIME THAT
WOULD BAN DRIFTNET FISHING FROM THE REGION. THIS BAN WOULD
BE THE FIRST STEP TOWARDS A COMPREHENSIVE BAN ON THE
PRACTICE.

03291 FRASER, H.
NEW PROBLEMS, NEW CONFIDENCE
PACIFIC DEFENCE REPORTER, 16(6) (DEC 89), 17-18.
THIS ARTICLE DESCRIBES THE CONFIDENCE AND COOPERATION
EVIDENT AT THE SOUTH PACIFIC FORUM, WHICH HELD ITS TWENTIETH
MEETING IN JULY 1989 IN TARAWA, KIRILATI. DESPITE AN AGENDA
PACKED WITH DISCUSSIONS OF DAUNTING PROBLEMS SUCH AS
FISHERIES MONITORING, INTERNATIONAL POLICY AND THE VIOLENCE
OF BOUGAINVILLE, THE SOUTH PACIFIC COMMUNITY MANAGED TO
REACH COLLECTIVE DECISIONS WITHOUT INCIDENT.

03292 FRASER, H.
PNG'S BOUGAINVILLE AGONY
PACIFIC DEFENCE REPORTER, 16(9) (MAR 90), 12.
THE MOVE OF THE NEW GUINEA GOVERNMENT TO MEET THE
BOUGAINVILLE SECESSIONIST MOVES WITH MILITARY FORCE INSTEAD
OF PEACE INITIATIVES FOLLOWS ON THE HEELS OF ESCALATED
VIOLENCE ON THE PART OF THE SELF-STYLED BOUGAINVILLE
REPUBLICAN ARMY. ESSENTIAL PROBLEMS FACING NEW GUINEA IN THE
COMING YEAR ARE TO MAINTAIN UNITY WITHIN THE CENTRAL
GOVERNMENT AND TO RETAIN ITS AUTHORITY IN THE FACE OF THIS
CONTINUING STRONG MILITANT ACTIVITY. THE DELICATE ART OF
KEEPING OPEN CHANNELS OF CUMMUNICATION FOR AN EVENTUAL
BOUGAINVILLE DIALOG MUST BE MAINTAINED.

03293 FRATI, R.
POLITICS ON THE SCREEN
WORLD MARXIST REVIEW, 32(9) (SEP 89), 51-53.
THIS ARTICE EXPLORES HOW THE DEVELOPMENT OF TELEVISION
AND AUDIOVISUAL TECHNOLOGY HAS OPENED NEW HORIZONS FOR
PROPAGANDA, MASS POLITICAL AND CULTURAL WORK, AND FOR
INFLUENCING PUBLIC CONSCIOUSNESS. IT EXAMINES HOW IN ORDER
FOR COMMUNISTS IN THE CAPITALIST WORLD TO BE ABLE TO TAKE
ADVANTAGE OF THIS THEY HAVE TO OVERCOME NUMEROUS OBSTACLES
RESULTING FROM THE SWAY HELD OVER THE MASS MEDIA BY THE
MONOPOLIES. DETAILED IS HOW TV AND VIDEO SERVE THE BRAZILIAN
COMMUNISTS.

03294 FREDERICK, M. J.
THE POLITICS OF PROTRACTED DISPLACEMENT: A CASE STUDY OF
THE OF THE OGADEN SOMALI REFUGEES
DISSERTATION ABSTRACTS INTERNATIONAL, 49(9) (MAR 89),
2799-A.
THE AUTHOR EXAMINES THE REFUGEE POLICY-MAKING PROCESS AT
THE HOST COUNTRY LEVEL, USING THE OGADEN SOMALI REFUGEE
SITUATION AS A CASE STUDY. SHE EVALUATES WHY REFUGEE POLICY
IN SOMALIA HAS BEEN INEFFECTIVE IN PROVIDING A LONG-TERM
SOLUTION, IDENTIFIES PROBLEMS INHERENT IN INTERNATIONAL
REFUGEE POLICY FORMULATION THAT HAVE PRECLUDED A DURABLE
SOLUTION, AND EXAMINES THE RELEVANCE OF THE SOMALI CASE TO
OTHER REFUGEE SITUATIONS.

03295 FREDERIKSEN, P.C.; LOONEY, R.E.
ARMS RACES IN THE THIRD WORLD: ARGENTINA AND BRAZIL
ARMED FORCES AND SOCIETY, 15(2) (WIN 89), 263-270.
THIS ARTICLE EXAMINES WHETHER A SIGNIFICANT PART OF

ARGENTINA'S MILITARY BUDGET OVER A 22-YEAR SPAN CAN BE
ATTRIBUTED TO AN ARMS RACE WITH BRAZIL. MULTIPLE REGRESSION
EQUATIONS ARE ESTIMATED FOR THE PERIOD 1961 AND 1982 AND
SEVERAL SUBPERIODS, TAKING INTO ACCOUNT BRAZIL'S MILITARY
SPENDING, CHANGES IN POLITICAL REGIMES IN ARGENTINA, AND
ALSO THE AVAILABILITY OF ECONOMIC RESOURCES ALLOCATED TO THE
GOVERNMENT. THE RESULTS INDICATE THAT THE RIVALRY EXISTED
UNTIL THE MID-1970S. AS A RESULT OF INCREASED ECONOMIC
COOPERATION BETWEEN THE TWO COUNTRIES SINCE THEN, THE ARMS
RACE HAS GRADUALLY DIMINISHED AND OTHER FACTORS HAVE BECOME
MORE IMPORTANT IN DETERMINING DEFENSE SPENDING LEVELS IN
ARGENTINA.

03296 FREEDMAN, A.
DOING BATTLE WITH THE PATRONAGE ARMY: POLITICS, COURTS,
AND PERSONNEL ADMINISTRATION IN CHICAGO
PUBLIC ADMINISTRATION REVIEW, 48(5) (SEP 88), 847-859.
THIS ARTICLE TRACES THE EVENTS SET IN MOTION BY A
CHICAGO LAWYER, MICHAEL SHAKMAN, WHICH ENDED PATRONAGE IN
CHICAGO'S TRADITIONAL POLITICAL-MACHINE PRACTICES, THROUGH
THE COURT SYSTEM. JUDGEMENTS, NOW KNOWN AS SHAKMAN I,
SHAKMAN II, AND SHAKMAN III ARE EXAMINED, AS WELL AS THE
MAJOR CHANGES RESULTING FROM THE ENDING OF CHICAGO'S OLD
PATRONAGE SYSTEM.

03297 FREEDMAN, J.
WOMEN IN IRAQ
AMERICAN-ARAB AFFAIRS, (29) (SUM 89), 42-46.
THIS ARTICLE EXAMINES SOCIAL CHANGES RESULTING FROM THE
IRAN-IRAQ WAR WHICH ARE BECOMING A PERMANENT CONDITION IN
IRAQ, EXPLORED IS THE GOVERNMENT ROLE IN AFFORDING IRAQ'S
FEMALE CITIZENS ACROSS-THE-BOARD LEGAL RIGHTS, AS WELL AS AN
ELEVATED STATUS WHICH IS FAR SUPERIOR TO THAT OF WOMEN IN
OTHER ARAB NATIONS. DETAILED ARE FEDERATION FIGURES SHOWING
THE PERCENTAGE OF WOMEN'S VOTES IN THE 1984 GENERAL ELECTION
AND THE GOVERNMENT'S BELIEF THAT THE EMANCIPATION OF WOMEN
IS AN INTEGRAL PART OF THE GENERAL LIBERATION OF IRAQ
SOCIETY. IT CONCLUDES THAT IRAQ IS LIKELY TO BECOME THE
MODEL OF WOMEN'S PROGRESS IN THE MIDDLE EAST.

03298 FREEDMAN, L.
GENERAL DETERRENCE AND THE BALANCE OF POWER
REVIEW OF INTERNATIONAL STUDIES, 15(2) (APR 89), 199-210.
GENERAL DETERRENCE HAS BEEN DESCRIBED AS AN
INSTITUTIONALIZED PERCEPTION BY A STATE OR GROUP OF STATES
THAT, DESPITE CONTINUING ANTAGONISM, IT SHOULD NOT EXPECT TO
BE ABLE TO RESOLVE ITS DISPUTES WITH ANOTHER STATE OR GROUP
OF STATES BY MILITARY MEANS. THIS WILL REFLECT AN
UNDERSTANDING OF THE VITAL INTERESTS OF THE DETERRER WHICH
THE DETERRED ACCEPTS MUST BE RESPECTED. THE LONGER THIS
CONDITION LASTS THE MORE STABLE IT IS LIKELY TO BECOME, WITH
A GROWING TOLERANCE OF DISPARITIES IN MILITARY CAPABILITIES
AND ALSO OF POLITICAL CHANGE. GENERAL STABILITY CAN THUS BE
DESCRIBED AS A DETERRENCE RELATIONSHIP WHICH TENDS TOWARDS
THE DISSOLUTION OF ANTAGONISM; GENERAL INSTABILITY SUGGESTS
A TENDENCY TOWARDS CRISIS, AND THE CONSEQUENT PRACTICE OF
IMMEDIATE DETERRENCE.

03299 FREEDMAN, R.O.
RELIGION, POLITICS, AND THE ISRAELI ELECTIONS OF 1988
MIDDLE EAST JOURNAL, 43(3) (SUM 89), 406-422.
ONE OF THE MAJOR SURPRISES OF THE 1988 ISRAELI ELECTIONS
WAS THE GROWTH IN STRENGTH OF ISRAEL'S RELIGIOUS PARTIES.
RELIGIOUS ISSUES PLAYED A SIGNIFICANT ROLE BOTH IN THE
ELECTION CAMPAIGN AND IN POSTELECTION COALITION BARGAINING
THIS ARTICLE EXPLORES THE RAMIFICATIONS OF THESE
DEVELOPMENTS. THE SECULARRELIGIOUS BALANCE IS EXAMINED, AS
WELL AS COALITION NEGOTIATIONS AND A NEW NATIONAL UNITY
GOVERNMENT SEVERAL MAJOR CONCLUSIONS ARE DRAWN AFTER LOOKING
AT THE IMPACT OF RELIGION ON POLITICS.

03300 FREELAND, J.
NATIONALIST REVOLUTION AND ETHNIC RIGHTS: THE MISKITU
INDIANS OF NICARAGUA'S ATLANTIC COAST
THIRD WORLD QUARTERLY, 11(4) (OCT 89), 166-190.
THE ATLANTIC COAST OF NICARAGUA IS HOME TO SIX DIFFERENT
ETHNIC GROUPS, SPEAKING FOUR LANGUAGES. THE MISKITU, THE
LARGEST MINORITY, EVOLVED AS A SEPARATE PEOPLE IN THE
SEVENTEENTH CENTURY FROM THE INTERMARRIAGE OF SUMU INDIANS
WITH ENGLISH PIRATES, SETTLERS, AND ESCAPED AFRICAN SLAVES.
BEFORE THE SANDINISTA REVOLUTION OF 1979, LITTLE WAS KNOWN
OF THE ATLANTIC COAST INDIANS AND LITTLE INTERNATIONAL
CONCERN WAS SHOWN FOR THEIR RIGHTS. THEY BECAME AN ISSUE
ONLY WHEN THE POLICIES OF THE SANDINISTA GOVERNMENT OF
NATIONAL RECONSTRUCTION GENERATED A CONFRONTATION WITH THE
MISKITU.

03301 FREELAND, J.
NATIONALIST REVOLUTION AND ETHNIC RIGHTS: THE MISKITU OF
NICARAGUA'S ATLANTIC COAST
THIRD WORLD QUARTERLY, 11(4) (OCT 89), 166-190.
THIS ARTICLE EXPLORES INTERNATIONAL CONCERN SHOWN FOR
THE MISKITU INDIAN (THE LARGEST MINORITY IN NICARAGUA'S
ATLANTIC COAST) RIGHTS. THIS BECAME AN ISSUE AS THE

SANDINISTA GOVERNMENT IMPLEMENTED THEIR POLICIES OF NATIONAL RECONSTRUCTION. AS THE SANDINISTA APPROACH TO ETHNIC RIGHTS WAS LIMITED AND CONTRADICTORY THE ARTICLE SHOWS HOW THESE CONTRADICTIONS EMERGED, AS POLICY BECAME PRACTICE, AND MET HEAD-ON THE IDEOLOGY OF ETHNIC NATIONALISM WHICH HAD DEVELOPED ON THE COAST, ESPECIALLY AMONG THE MISKITU. CONFLICTING APPROACHES: ETHNICITY VERSUS CLASS, AND NEGOTIATIONS OF THE CONFLICT ARE EXAMINED AND THE AUTONOMY LAW IS DETAILED.

03302 FREELAND, K.
POPULAR MOVEMENT SHAKES UP THE UKRAINE
ACROSS FRONTIERS, 5(2) (SUM 89), 9, 50.
THIS ARTICLE EXAMINES A POPULAR MOVEMENT BY PROMINENT WRITERS, DISSIDENTS, AND POLITICAL ACTIVISTS IN THE UKRAINE, THE MOST POPULOUS NON-RUSSIAN REPUBLIC, IT ANALYSES THE EFFECT THAT THIS MOVEMENT CAN HAVE IN THE "CHAIN OF OPPOSITION" AND THE PROBABLE EFFECT OF OFFICIAL REPRESSION OF THE POPULAR MOVEMENT UPON PERESTROIKA. IT EXPLORES SOME OF THE ISSUES THE GROUP IS CONCERNED WITH - ECOLOGY, PRESERVATION OF NATIONAL MONUMENTS, NATIONAL LANGUAGE, DEMOCRATIZATION.

03303 FREEMAN, C.W. JR.
THE ANGOLA/NAMIBIA ACCORDS
FOREIGN AFFAIRS, 68(3) (SUM 89), 126-141.
THE AUTHOR EXAMINES THE NEGOTIATION OF THE ANGOLA/NAMIBIA ACCORDS, INCLUDING THE CENTRAL ROLE THE USA PLAYED IN RESOLVING THE REGIONAL PROBLEMS IN SOUTHWEST AFRICA.

03304 FREEMAN, J.
FEMINIST ACTIVITIES AT THE 1988 REPUBLICAN CONVENTION
PS: POLITICAL SCIENCE AND POLITICS, XXII(1) (MAR 89), 39-47.
AFTER AN EIGHT-YEAR HIBERNATION, A FEMINIST PRESENCE RE-EMERGED AT THE 1988 REPUBLICAN NATIONAL CONVENTION. IT FOCUSED PRIMARILY ON ABORTION, WHICH STILL DIVIDES THE PARTY DESPITE THE FACT THAT THE FAR RIGHT CONTINUES TO WRITE THE PLATFORM ON ALL ISSUES DIRECTLY AFFECTING WOMEN.

03305 FREEMAN, J.R.; LIN, T.; WILLIAMS, J.T.
VECTOR AUTOREGRESSION AND THE STUDY OF POLITICS
AMERICAN JOURNAL OF POLITICAL SCIENCE, 33(4) (NOV 89), 842-877.
IN MANY RESPECTS POLITICAL SCIENTISTS AGREE ABOUT HOW BEST TO MODEL POLITICAL PROCESSES. BUT WE DISAGREE ABOUT HOW TO TRANSLATE OUR THEORIES INTO STRUCTURAL EQUATIONS; EACH OF US SEEMS TO HAVE OUR OWN STRUCTURAL EQUATION MODEL OF THE SAME THEORY. THIS DISAGREEMENT IS A SERIOUS IMPEDIMENT TO THEORY BUILDING. VECTOR AUTOREGRESSION (VAR) IS A MEANS OF CIRCUMVENTING THIS PROBLEM. WE EXPLAIN THE LOGIC OF THIS ALTERNATIVE MODELING STRATEGY AND EXAMINE ITS RELATIVE VIRTUES. IN PARTICULAR, VAR AND THE MORE FAMILIAR STRUCTURAL EQUATION (SEQ) APPROACHES ARE COMPARED IN TERMS OF THEIR EPISTEMOLOGICAL UNDERPINNINGS, EMPIRICAL POWER, AND USEFULNESS IN POLICY ANALYSIS. THIS COMPARISON SHOWS THAT THE TWO MODELING STRATEGIES ARE BASED ON DIFFERENT CONCEPTIONS OF THEORY AND OF THEORY BUILDING AND THAT, FOR THE FOUR-SIX VARIABLE SYSTEMS WE USUALLY STUDY, THE CHOICE BETWEEN VAR AND SEQ MODELS PRESENTS A TRADE-OFF BETWEEN ACCURACY OF CAUSAL INFERENCE AND QUANTITATIVE PRECISION, RESPECTIVELY. IN ADDITION, VAR MODELS HAVE THE DISADVANTAGE OF BEING UNABLE TO INCORPORATE MULTIPLICATIVE AND NONLINEAR RELATIONSHIPS AS EASILY AS SEQ MODELS. BUT VAR MODELS HAVE THE ADVANTAGE OF PROVIDING A MORE COMPLETE TREATMENT OF POLICY ENDOGENEITY THAN SEQ MODELS. THESE AND OTHER CONTRASTS IN THE TWO MODELING STRATEGIES ARE ILLUSTRATED IN A REANALYSIS OF ALT AND CHRYSTAL'S (1983) PERMANENT INCOME MODEL OF GOVERNMENT EXPENDITURE.

03306 FREEMAN, P.K.; FITZGERALD, M.R.; LYONS, W.
LEGISLATIVE REPRESENTATION ON A TECHNICAL POLICY ISSUE: HAZARDOUS WASTE IN TENNESSEE
SOCIAL SCIENCE JOURNAL, 26(4) (1989), 455-464.
HAZARDOUS WASTE DISPOSAL IS AN EXAMPLE OF AN ISSUE THAT GOVERNMENT OFFICIALS INCREASINGLY MUST CONFRONT BUT FIND DIFFICULT TO RESOLVE -- COMPLEX SCIENTIFIC AND TECHNICAL PROBLEMS THAT FRIGHTEN THE PUBLIC. IN DETERMINING POLICY THE LEGISLATORS MUST ESTIMATE THE ATTITUDES OF THE PUBLIC. THIS STUDY COMPARES LEGISLATORS' OPINIONS WITH CONSTITUENCY OPINIONS USING SURVEYS OF THE GENERAL PUBLIC AND OF LEGISLATORS IN TENNESSEE. IT FINDS THAT CITIZENS ARE MORE CONCERNED THAN THE LAWMAKERS, THAT THEY ARE MORE WILLING TO FIND SOLUTIONS THAN THE LEGISLATORS BELIEVE, AND THAT THEY TRUST SCIENTIFIC EXPERTS MORE THAN THEY TRUST PUBLIC OFFICIALS.

03307 FREI, D.; RULOFF, D.
REASSESSING EAST-WEST RELATIONS: A MACROQUANTITATIVE ANALYSIS OF TRENDS, PREMISES, AND CONSEQUENCES OF EAST-WEST COOPERATION AND CONFLICT
INTERNATIONAL INTERACTIONS, 15(1) (1988), 1-23.
SINCE THE GENEVA, REYKJAVIK, AND WASHINGTON SUMMITS, EAST-WEST RELATIONS ARE GENERALLY EXPECTED TO IMPROVE RAPIDLY. SUCH EXPECTATIONS ARE USUALLY BASED ON THEORETICAL ASSUMPTIONS REGARDING CAUSES AND EFFECTS OF DETENTE. EIGHT HYPOTHESES ARE DISCUSSED AND TESTED EMPIRICALLY BY USING TIME-SERIES DATA FOR THE 1960-84 PERIOD. IT APPEARS THAT THE MOVE TOWARD A STRATEGIC BALANCE IS NOT NECESSARILY CONDUCIVE TO IMPROVED EAST-WEST RELATIONS, NOR DO INDEPENDENT EUROPEAN EFFORTS HAVE A DECISIVE IMPACT ON THE SHAPING OF MAJOR-POWER RELATIONS. IN CONTRAST, DETENTE APPEARS TO BE DIVISIBLE: THE EXTRA-EUROPEAN RIVALRY BETWEEN EAST AND WEST IS HARDLY AFFECTED BY THE EVENTS ON THE MAIN ARENA. FURTHERMORE, AN IMPROVEMENT OF RELATIONS IS NOT A MERE QUESTION OF GOOD WILL: COOPERATIVE INITIATIVES BY THE ONE SIDE ARE USUALLY NOT RESPONDED TO RECIPROCALLY BY THE OTHER. TRADE RELATIONS, RATHER THAN BEING INDEPENDENT STIMULI PROMOTING EAST-WEST DETENTE, HAVE DEVELOPED THEIR OWN MOMENTUM. THE INTERNAL PRESSURE ON DISSIDENTS IS SLOWLY DECREASING IN THE EAST, BUT THE EVIDENCES ARE ONLY WEAK THAT THIS IS ATTRIBUTABLE TO EAST-WEST DETENTE. NOTWITHSTANDING DETENTE, THE PROGRESS IN ARMS CONTROL AND DISARMAMENT HAS NOT YET DAMPENED THE EXPANSION OF MILITARY EXPENDITURES. FINALLY, EAST-WEST RELATIONS APPEAR TO BE VOLATILE AND CYCLICAL IN NATURE. HENCE, IT SEEMS APPROPRIATE TO CAUTION AGAINST A NEW CRISIS AND MAYBE DECLINE OF EAST-WEST RELATIONS IN THE NEARER FUTURE.

03308 FREI, M.
OCCUPIED PALESTINE: A SYMPTOM OF THE TIMES
MIDDLE EAST INTERNATIONAL, 355 (JUL 89), 9-10.
THE INCIDENT OF THE PALESTINIAN ATTACK ON AN ISRAELIOCCUPIED BUS AND ITS BACKLASH ILLUSTRATED ABOVE ALL THAT THE POLITICAL SITUATION IS NOW GETTING OUT OF HAND, BECOMING MORE VICIOUS AND LESS PREDICTABLE. THE ISRAELI AUTHORITIES ARE FACED WITH AN INSOLUBLE PROBLEM. HOW SHOULD ONE PREVENT SUCH ATTACKS? ONE SUGGESTION WAS TO PUT A SCREEN BETWEEN THE BUS DRIVER AND THE PASSENGERS. ANOTHER WAS TO PUT A SCREEN BETWEEN THE OCCUPIED TERRITORIES AND ISRAEL. THIS IDEA HAS GAINED INCREASING ACCEPTANCE OVER THE LAST MONTHS AND THE RECENT INTRODUCTION OF SPECIAL IDENTITY PERMITS FOR PALESTINIAN WORKERS FROM THE GAZA STRIP IS A MOVE IN THAT DIRECTION. BUT ATTEMPTS TO CONFINE PALESTINIAN WORKERS TO THE TERRITORIES HAVE MERELY SHOWN HOW ISRAEL RELIES ON CHEAP LABOUR FROM THE WEST BANK AND GAZA STRIP TO DO THE WORK THAT NO UNEMPLOYED ISRAELI IS AS YET PREPARED TO DO. RIGOROUS PHYSICAL SEGREGATION IS STILL NOT ON THE CARDS BUT PSYCHOLOGICAL SEGREGATION HAS BECOME A REALITY.

03309 FREI, M.
OCCUPIED PALESTINE: DELIBERATE PROVOCATION
MIDDLE EAST INTERNATIONAL, 352 (JUN 89), 8-9.
THE SETTLERS AND THEIR HARD-LINE SUPPORTERS IN THE KNESSET REFER TO THE INTIFADA AS YET ANOTHER ARAB-ISRAELI WAR AND IT IS SIGNIFICANT THAT THE RECENT ESCALATION OF SETTLER VIOLENCE OCCURRED AT A TIME WHEN THERE WERE GROWING FEARS - OR HOPES, FOR THAT MATTER - THAT THE UNIFIED COMMAND OF THE UPRISING WAS ASKING PALESTINIANS TO EXCHANGE STONES FOR FIREARMS. BUT IMMEDIATE WITHDRAWAL OF COMMUNIQUE NO. 40, IN WHICH THERE WAS INDEED A CALL TO EXCHANGE A "LIFE FOR A LIFE", AS A WELL AS A NUMBER OF ASSURANCES FROM TUNIS, ARE AN INDICATION THAT THE PLO IS NOT GOING TO DO THE SETTLERS A FAVOUR PALESTINIANS IN EAST JERUSALEM LIKE PROFESSOR HAVE BEEN EQUALLY ANXIOUS TO STRESS THAT THERE HAS BEEN NO CHANGE IN STRATEGY.

03310 FREI, M.
REOPENING THE SCHOOLS
MIDDLE EAST INTERNATIONAL, 355 (JUL 89), 10-11.
ALL INDICATIONS COMING OUT OF THE ISRAELI MILITARY ESTABLISHMENT IS THAT SCHOOLS IN THE WEST BANK WILL REOPEN SOON. BUT PALESTINIANS ARE LESS CONFIDENT THAT THIS LATEST ISRAELI PROMISE WILL MATERIALISE. AT FIRST THE ISRAELIS DID NOT INDICATE A SPECIFIC TIME BUT LATER STATED THAT ELEMENTARY SCHOOLS WOULD OPEN ON 23 JULY WITH THE OPENING OF HIGH SCHOOLS CONDITIONAL ON THE SUCCESS, FROM THE ISRAELI POINT OF VIEW, OF THE OPENING OF THE ELEMENTARY SCHOOLS. BUT PALESTINIANS ARE DOUBTFUL ABOUT HOW LONG THE SCHOOLS WILL STAY OPEN ONCE THEY IN FACT DO. THE ISRAELIS HAVE TRIED VERY HARD TO FIND A PALESTINIAN "PARTNER" WITH WHOM TO NEGOTIATE ON THIS QUESTION. POLITICAL OBSERVERS FEEL THAT IF ISRAEL WERE TO SUCCEED IN FINDING PALESTINIANS WITH WHOM TO NEGOTIATE ON SCHOOLS, THEN THEY WOULD BE ABLE TO USE THE SAME PALESTINIANS FOR POLITICAL NEGOTIATIONS.

03311 FRENCH, J.D.
INDUSTRIAL WORKERS AND THE BIRTH OF THE POPULIST REPUBLIC IN BRAZIL, 1945-1946
LATIN AMERICAN PERSPECTIVES, 16(63) (FAL 89), 5-27.
THIS ARTICLE CONTENDS THAT VARGAS'S 1945 ELECTORAL LEGISLATION WAS DESIGNED TO ALTER BRAZILIAN ELECTORAL LIFE THROUGH MASS ENFRANCHISEMENT IN URBAN AREAS. IT EXAMINES THE NATURE OF GRASS-ROOTS MOBILIZATION IN THE INDUSTRIAL REGION OF SAO PAULO. IT ESTABLISHES THE CONTOURS OF MASS WORKING CLASS CONSCIOUSNESS, ITS CHARACTERISTICS, PSYCHOLOGY, AND DIRECTION OF DEVELOPMENT. IT ALSO EXAMINES THE MEANS THROUGH

WHICH CHANGE HAS WROUGHT, ALL THIS IN ORDER TO BETTER UNDERSTAND THE POPULAR VOTE OF 1945, THE RELATIVE STRENGTHS OF THE COMMUNIST AND LABOR PARTIES AND THE NATURE OF THE POSTWAR TRADE-UNION MOVEMENT.

03312 FRENDO, M.
THE MEDITERRANEAN BETWEEN EUROPE AND AFRICA: THE ROLE OF THE EUROPEAN COMMUNITY
CONTEMPORARY REVIEW, 254(1480) (MAY 89), 231-234.
THE EUROPEAN COMMUNITY HAS A SPECIAL NEED TO FURTHER ITS PRESENCE, POLITICAL AND STRATEGIC, IN THE MEDITERRANEAN WHICH HAS A REGIONAL IMPORTANCE NOT ONLY AS A FRONTIER BETWEEN EUROPE AND AFRICA, BUT ALSO AS A MAJOR OIL ROUTE, A VITAL LINK OF COMMUNICATION BETWEEN THE INDIAN OCEAN, THE ATLANTIC AND THE BLACK SEA. THE EUROPEAN COUNTRIES IN THE MEDITERRANEAN, IN PARTICULAR ITALY, SPAIN, PORTUGAL, GREECE, AND MALTA (THE FIRST FOUR COMMUNITY MEMBERS, MALTA CURRENTLY AN ASSOCIATE WITH A DECLARED INTENTION OF SEEKING MEMBERSHIP), ARE THE BEST SUITED, CULTURALLY, GEOGRAPHICALLY, HISTORICALLY, TO CARRY OUT THIS TASK FOR EUROPE IN AFRICA THROUGH THE MEDITERRANEAN.

03313 FRENDREIS, J.P.
MIGRATION AS A SOURCE OF CHANGING PARTY STRENGTH
SOCIAL SCIENCE QUARTERLY, 70(1) (MAR 89), 211-220.
BECAUSE THEY ARE UNLIKELY TO BE A PERFECT MATCH OF THE EXISTING ELECTORATE, IN-MIGRANTS MAY FORM THE BASIS FOR AN ALTERNATION IN THE LOCAL PARTISAN BALANCE. THIS NOTE DISCUSSES PARTISAN CHANGE AND THE ROLE MIGRATION MAY PLAY WITHIN IT, AND IDENTIFIES THE CONDITIONS UNDER WHICH MIGRATION IS LIKELY TO HAVE ITS GREATEST EFFECT. THIS EFFECT IS ILLUSTRATED BY AN INTENSIVE ANALYSIS OF A SUN BELT COUNTY WHICH HAS WITNESSED BOTH A WAVE OF MIGRATION-BASED POPULATION GROWTH AND A DRAMATIC CHANGE IN THE LOCAL PARTISAN BALANCE.

03314 FRENDREIS, J.P.
MODELING SPATIAL DIFFUSION: REACTION TO WEILHOFER
COMPARATIVE POLITICAL STUDIES, 22(3) (OCT 89), 343-351.
WELLHOFER'S ADAPTION OF KLINGMAN'S SUGGESTION THAT SPATIAL DIFFUSION BE MODELED AS AN AUTOREGRESSIVE SPATIAL SERIES IS QUESTIONED ON TWO COUNTS. FIRST, THIS APPROACH IS INAPPROPRIATE FOR MOST CLASSES OF DIFFUSION MODELS, INCLUDING DENDRITIC DIFFUSION SYSTEMS, SECOND, THE PROCEDURE BY WHICH WELLHOFER HAS ORDERED THE OBSERVATIONS IN HIS ARGENTINE ILLUSTRATION PRODUCES A DATABASE THAT BEARS ALMOST NO RESEMBLANCE TO THE UNDERLYING PATTERN OF CAUSATION HE WISHES TO EXAMINE AND ACTUALLY CREATES AN ADDITIONAL SOURCE OF BIAS IN THE ANALYSIS.

03315 FRENKEL, O.
CONSTRAINTS AND COMPROMISES: TRADE POLICY IN A DEMOCRACY. THE CASE OF THE US-ISRAEL FREE TRADE AREA
DISSERTATION ABSTRACTS INTERNATIONAL, 49(7) (JAN 89), 1950-A.
THIS DISSERTATION TRACES THE US GOVERNMENT DELIBERATIONS THAT LED TO THE US-ISRAELI FREE TRADE AREA AND DISCUSSES THE NEGOTIATION PROCESS, INCLUDING THE ROLE OF CONGRESS AND INDUSTRY PRESSURE GROUPS. IT DEVELOPS A QUANTITATIVE MODEL THAT USES THE LEVEL OF PROTECTION PRIOR TO THE NEGOTIATIONS AS AN INDICATION OF HOW NEGOTIATORS WOULD TREAT INDIVIDUAL PRODUCTS DURING THE COURSE OF THE FTA NEGOTIATIONS.

03316 FRENKEL, S.
THE PUSHERS: HOW THE GREAT POWERS ARM THE MIDDLE EAST
NEW OUTLOOK, 32(9-10 (295-296)) (SEP 89), 38-42.
THE AUTHOR REVEALS HOW THE GREAT POWERS, INCLUDING WEST GERMANY, FUEL THE ARMS RACE IN THE MIDDLE EAST AND HOW THE VARIOUS REGIONAL ELITES COOPERATE, TO THE DETRIMENT OF THEIR OWN POPULATIONS. HE FINDS THAT ISRAEL IS NO EXCEPTION AND THAT THE ARMS TRADE INCLUDES CHEMICAL WEAPONS ALONG WITH MORE TRADITIONAL WEAPONS AND NUCLEAR ARMS. HE CONCLUDES THAT THE BIG MONEY PLAYERS IN THE MIDEAST ARMS EXPLOSION CONTINUE TO BE THE USA AND THE USSR.

03317 FRENTZEL-ZAGORSKA, J.; ZAGORSKI, K.
EAST EUROPEAN INTELLECTUALS ON THE ROAD TO DISSENT: THE OLD PROPHECY OF A NEW CLASS RE-EXAMINED
POLITICS AND SOCIETY, 17(1) (MAR 89), 89-113.
THE AUTHORS EXAMINE THE STRUCTURAL CONFLICT THAT EXISTS BETWEEN INTELLECTUALS AND THE PARTY-STATE APPARATUS IN CENTRAL-EASTERN EUROPE. THEY DISPUTE SOME OF SZELENYI'S OPINIONS ON THE PAST AND CURRENT SITUATIONS IN THIS PART OF THE WORLD. THEY ALSO CONTRIBUTE TO THE DISCUSSION OF SZELENYI'S THREE SCENARIOS OF FUTURE CHANGES IN SOCIAL AND CLASS ALLIANCES IN EASTERN EUROPE. THEY TREAT THEIR DISCUSSION NOT ONLY AS A CRITICISM OF KONRAD'S AND SZELENYI'S WORKS BUT AS A CONTRIBUTION TO A BETTER UNDERSTANDING OF ONGOING SOCIAL PROCESSES IN STATE-SOCIALIST SOCIETIES. LIKE KONRAD AND SZELENYI, THEY FOCUS ON THE POST-STALINIST PERIOD.

03318 FRETZ, L.
RONALD REAGAN'S FOREIGN POLICY: AN OVERVIEW
NEW ZEALAND INTERNATIONAL REVIEW, 14(4) (JUL 89), 18-22.
THE AUTHOR PROVIDES AN OVERVIEW OF UNITED STATES FOREIGN POLICY DURING THE REAGAN PRESIDENCY, WITH SPECIFIC DATES AND INCIDENTS CITED. EARLY CRITICS, CLAIMS THE AUTHOR WERE THWARTED, WHO HAD BEEN WORRIED THAT HIS "SOVIET BASHING" WOULD LEAD TO INCREASED TENSIONS. THE MIDDLE PERIOD, DURING WHICH REAGAN THE POLICIES OF DETENTE AND ARMS CONTROL IS THE MAJOR AREA WHICH THE AUTHOR ADDRESSES. VARIOUS REASONS ARE EXPLORED WHICH LED REAGAN TOWARDS "SUCCESS": 1) CABINETRY, 2)GORBACHEV'S PERESTROIKA REFORMS, 3)LUCK, 4)THE INF TREATY, 5)TIMING WAS IN HIS FAVOR IN SOME DIFFICULTIES AREAS, I.E., LEBANON, NICARAGUA, AND PANAMA. MILITARY ALLOCATIONS DURING HIS TWO TERMS ARE ALSO DISCUSSED.

03319 FRIDERES, J.; REEVES, W.
THE ABILITY TO IMPLEMENT HUMAN RIGHTS LEGISLATION IN CANADA
CANADIAN REVIEW OF SOCIOLOGY AND ANTHROPOLOGY, 26(2) (MAY 89), 311-332.
A RECENT ANALYSIS OF CANADIAN HUMAN RIGHTS COMMISSION FILES SUGGESTS THAT THE ENFORCEMENT OF LEGISLATED PROHIBITIONS ON DISCRIMINATION MAY BE MORE EASILY IMPLEMENTED FOR SOME GROUNDS OF DISCRIMINATION THAN FOR OTHER GROUNDS OF DISCRIMINATION. AN ANALYSIS OF A SAMPLE OF 1982-83 CASE FILES, SHOWS THAT COMPLAINTS INVOLVING SEX OR DISABILITY ARE MUCH MORE LIKELY TO BE SUBSTANTIATED THAN CASES BASED ON RACE, COLOUR, ETHNICITY OR NATIONAL ORIGIN. USING BOTH QUALITATIVE AND QUANTITATIVE ANALYTICAL PROCEDURES, THE RESULTS SHOW THAT FOR SEX AND DISABILITY CASES, A COMPARATIVE INVESTIGATIVE PROCEDURE WAS EMPLOYED TO ASSESS THE VALIDITY OF THE COMPLAINT WHILE A SEQUENTIAL STYLE OF INVESTIGATION WAS USED IN RACE, COLOUR, ETHNIC OR NATIONAL ORIGIN CASES.

03320 FRIED, E.R.; TREZISE, P.H.
THIRD WORLD DEBT: PHASE THREE BEGINS
BROOKINGS REVIEW, 7(4) (FAL 89), 24-31.
THE AUTHORS DISCUSS THE BRADY PLAN FOR DEALING WITH THE THIRD WORLD DEBT CRISIS, INCLUDING THE EVENTS THAT LED TO IT AND THE PROSPECTS FOR ITS SUCCESS.

03321 FRIEDBERG, A.L.
THE STRATEGIC IMPLICATIONS OF RELATIVE ECONOMIC DECLINE
POLITICAL SCIENCE QUARTERLY, 104(3) (FAL 89), 401-432.
AARON L. FRIEDBERG ANALYZES THE STRATEGIC IMPLICATIONS OF RECENT CHANGES IN AMERICA'S POSITION IN THE WORLD ECONOMY. HE CONCLUDES THAT THESE SHIFTS COULD IMPOSE SUBTLE BUT POWERFUL CONSTRAINTS ON U.S. FREEDOM OF DIPLOMATIC AND MILITARY ACTION.

03322 FRIEDERSDORF, M.L.
CHEMICAL WEAPONS DISPOSAL PROGRAM
DEPARTMENT OF STATE BULLETIN (US FOREIGN POLICY), 89(2147) (JUN 89), 19-21.
THE AUTHOR SUMMARIZES THE UNITED STATES' CHEMICAL STOCKPILE DISPOSAL PROGRAM AND REVIEWS THE PROGRESS THAT HAS BEEN MADE SO FAR IN THE DESTRUCTION PROCESS.

03323 FRIEDLAND, J.
SOUTH AFRICA WOOS ASIA
FAR EASTERN ECONOMIC REVIEW, 141(37) (SEP 88), 83.
SOUTH AFRICA IS TURNING INCREASINGLY TO TAIWAN, HONG KONG, AND INDIRECTLY, TO JAPAN, TO REPLACE A SUBSTANTIAL DECLINE IN DIRECT INVESTMENT FROM EUROPE AND THE US. TWO SEPARATE INVESTMENT MISSIONS FROM THE REPUBLIC CLAIMED IN HONG KONG TO HAVE WON POSITIVE RESPONSE FROM ASIAN BUSINESSMEN.

03324 FRIEDLAND, R.; HECHT, R.
THE TWO BANKS OF JERUSALEM
TIKKUN, 4(3) (MAY 89), 35-38.
THE AUTHORS REPORT ON THE ECONOMICS OF THE INTIFADA AND JEWISH BANKS THAT LAUNDER MONEY FOR THE PLO.

03325 FRIEDMAN, E.
MODERNIZATION AND DEMOCRATIZATION IN LENINIST STATES: THE CASE OF CHINA
STUDIES IN COMPARATIVE COMMUNISM, 22(2/3) (SUM 89), 251-264.
THIS ESSAY ATTEMPTS TO PLACE CHINA'S POST-MAO REFORMS IN A GLOBAL POLITICAL PERSPECTIVE. IT POSITS DEMOCRACY AS THE OPTIMAL ANSWER TO CHINA'S LINGERING POST-FEUDAL CRISIS OF MODERNITY. IT ANALYSES THE POSSIBILITY OF DEMOCRATIZATION FOR CHINA AND IS PESSIMISTIC ABOUT ITS EVENTUALITY.

03326 FRIEDMAN, I.S.
TOWARD WORLD PROSPERITY: RESHAPING THE GLOBAL MONEY SYSTEM
LEXINGTON BOOKS, LEXINGTON, MA, 1987, 317.
THE AUTHOR INTERPRETS THE EVENTS THAT LED TO THE WITHDRAWAL OF VOLUNTARY LENDING BY COMMERCIAL BANKS TO DEVELOPING COUNTRIES. TO RESOLVE THE CURRENT THIRD WORLD DEBT CRISIS, HE ADVOCATES NON-INFLATIONARY GROWTH TO BE ACHIEVED BY SOUND ECONOMIC MANAGEMENT AND THE RESTORATION OF CREDIT-WORTHINESS. HIS SUGGESTED "WAYS AND MEANS" INCLUDE WRITE-OFFS, A DISTINCTION BETWEEN OLD AND NEW DEBT, AN

INTERNATIONAL BANKING COUNCIL FOR COMMERCIAL BANKS, NEW
FORMS OF LENDING, AND AN ENLARGED BAKER PLAN.

03327 FRIEDMAN, S.
BOKSBURG AND THE CP
SOUTH AFRICA FOUNDATION REVIEW, 15(1) (JAN 89), 5.
RESEGREGATION MAY BE IN TROUBLE IN BOKSBURG PRIMARILY
BECAUSE BLACK PEOPLE WILL NOT ACCEPT IT AND THEY NOW HAVE
THE CONSUMER MUSCLE TO STOP IT. BOKSBURG MAY BEGIN TO SHOW
THAT, AS WHITE CITIES BECOME MORE DEPENDENT ON BLACK
SPENDING, THE IDEA OF A CITY RUN ON APARTHEID LINES IS
BECOMING UNWORKABLE.

03328 FRIEDMAN, S.
THE OPPRESSION OF FOREIGN LIBERATION
SOUTH AFRICA FOUNDATION REVIEW, 15(11) (NOV 89), 2.
THE RECENT RELEASE OF EIGHT SENIOR BLACK LEADERS IN
SOUTH AFRICA HAD AN INTERESTING EFFECT ON EXTRA-
PARLIAMENTARY GROUPS. MANY OF THE GROUPS DISMISSED THE
RELEASES AS A MEANINGLESS PLOY. ON THE OTHER HAND, THE MASS
DEMOCRATIC MOVEMENT HAILED THE RELEASE AS A VICTORY, NOT FOR
THE BLACK ORGANIZATIONS, BUT FOR FOREIGN PRESSURE. THESE
REACTIONS ILLUSTRATE THE INCREASING DEPENDENCY BLACK
ORGANIZATIONS FEEL TOWARDS INTERNATIONAL SUPPORT GROUPS.
THOSE WHO DISMISSED THE RELEASES AND THOSE WHO HAILED THEN
HAVE A COMMON CONCERN: THEY WANT TO ENSURE THAT FOREIGN
PRESSURE AGAINST APARTHEID IS STEPPED UP. HOWEVER, FOREIGN
PRESSURE IS UNLIKELY TO EVER BRING ABOUT THE ABOLITION OF
APARTHEID; ONLY DETERMINED AND INDEPENDENT PRESSURE FOR
CHANGE FROM WITHIN CAN FACILITATE MEANINGFUL CHANGE.

03329 FRIEDEN, J.A.
THE ECONOMICS OF INTERVENTION: AMERICAN OVERSEAS
INVESTMENTS AND RELATIONS WITH UNDERDEVELOPED AREAS, 1890-
1950
COMPARATIVE STUDIES IN SOCIETY AND HISTORY, 31(1) (JAN 89),
55-80.
ANALYSIS OF THE ECONOMIC MOTIVES IN IMPERIAL EXPANSION
AND CONTRACTION DEMANDS A DIFFERENTIATED APPROACH TO
ECONOMIC AIMS, FOR THE POLITICAL IMPLICATIONS OF ECONOMIC
ACTIVITIES VARY. THIS STUDY EXPLORES THE POLITICAL
RAMIFICATIONS OF DIFFERENT ECONOMIC INTERESTS AND CONCLUDES
THAT SELLERS OF UNCOMPETITIVE MERCHANDISE AND INVESTORS IN
PRIMARY PRODUCTION FOR EXPORT WILL BE MORE PRONE TO SUPPORT
IMPERIAL INTERVENTION AND DIRECT COLONIALISM THAN WILL
COMPETITIVE EXPORTERS, INVESTORS IN PRODUCTION FOR THE LOCAL
MARKET, AND LENDERS TO FOREIGN GOVERNMENTS.

03330 FROHNEN, B.P.
PHILOSOPHY AND VIRTUE: BURKE, TOCQUEVILLE AND THE
CONTEMPORARY CONSERVATIVE DILEMMA
DISSERTATION ABSTRACTS INTERNATIONAL, 49(10) (APR 89),
3141-A.
CONSERVATIVE POLITICAL PHILOSOPHY HAS GENERALLY BEEN
VIEWED AS BEING CONCERNED WITH PRUDENCE AND PRACTICALITY TO
THE EXCLUSION OF MORE ABSTRACT, METAPHYSICAL ISSUES. BY
EXAMINING THE WORK OF EDMUND BURKE AND ALEXIS DE TOCQUEVILLE,
THIS DISSERTATION SUGGESTS THAT CONSERVATIVE POLITICAL
PHILOSOPHY PROVIDES A JUSTIFICATION FOR A PARTICULAR VIEW OF
THE GOOD LIFE: THE LIFE OF ACCEPTING VIRTUE. RESPECT FOR
EXISTING INSTITUTIONS (PARTICULARLY RELIGION, CONVENTION,
AND ACCEPTED MORALITY) IS FOR THE CONSERVATIVE NOT JUST AN
END IN ITSELF, BUT RATHER ONE ELEMENT IN THE LIFE OF VIRTUE.

03331 FROKE, C.J.
GENDER DIFFERENCES IN THE PUBLIC OFFICE ASPIRATIONS OF
PARTY ACTIVISTS: CHANGE AND STABILITY BETWEEN 1972 AND 1985
DISSERTATION ABSTRACTS INTERNATIONAL, 50(2) (AUG 89),
534-A.
THE AUTHOR EXAMINES CHANGE AND STABILITY IN GENDER
DIFFERENCES CHARACTERIZING ASPIRATIONS TO PUBLIC OFFICE IN
THE TIME PERIOD 1972-1985. HE CONCLUDES THAT THE EXTENT TO
WHICH THERE HAS BEEN CHANGE IN THE DIFFERENCES REFLECTS THE
EVOLVING ROLE OF WOMEN IN POLITICS. THE EXTENT TO WHICH
THERE HAS BEEN STABILITY REFLECTS THE TASK THAT LIES AHEAD
FOR SOCIETY IN DEFINING ITS ROLE EXPECTATIONS FOR MEN AND
WOMEN IN GOVERNMENT.

03332 FROST, H.E.
A CONTENT ANALYSIS OF RECENT SOVIET PARTY-MILITARY
RELATIONS
AMERICAN JOURNAL OF POLITICAL SCIENCE, 33(1) (FEB 89),
91-135.
RELATIONS BETWEEN ELITES OF THE COMMUNIST PARTY OF THE
SOVIET UNION AND THE USSR ARMED FORCES HAVE BEEN A SUBJECT
OF SIGNIFICANT CONTROVERSY FOR WESTERN SCHOLARS. ANALYSES OF
THE BREZHNEVKOSYGIN AND POST-BREZHNEV PERIODS HAVE SUGGESTED
THAT DECISION MAKING INVOLVING UPPER ECHELONS OF THE TWO
GROUPS IS CHARACTERIZED MORE BY COOPERATION THAN CONFLICT,
IN CONTRAST WITH DECISION MAKING IN PREVIOUS PERIODS. THIS
STUDY USES CONTENT ANALYSIS TO INVESTIGATE THE VIEWS OF
PARTY AND MILITARY LEADERS ABOUT FIVE RECENT MILITARY POLICY
ISSUES IN ORDER TO ASSESS THE EXTENT OF TENSION BETWEEN THE
TWO GROUPS. IT CONCLUDES THAT THE COOPERATIVE VIEW, WITH FEW

EXCEPTIONS, DOES MORE ACCURATELY REPRESENT CURRENT HIGH-
LEVEL SOVIET PARTY-MILITARY RELATIONS.

03333 FRUCHTMAN, J.
NATURE AND REVOLUTION IN PAINE'S COMMON SENSE
HISTORY OF POLITICAL THOUGHT, X(3) (FAL 89), 421-438.
THE AUTHOR SEEKS TO DIVINE THE REASON WHY THE EARLIEST
OF THOMAS PAINE'S WORKS, COMMON SENSE, IS CONSIDERED TO BE
HIS MOST POWERFUL. HE CONCLUDES THAT THERE IS MORE TO COMMON
SENSE THAN ITS "RADICAL EGALITARIANISM" OR ITS CAREFULLY
CALIBRATED APPEAL TO THE WORKING POOR, THE URBAN CLASSES OF
MECHANICS, ARTISANS AND TRADESMEN. WHAT IS REMARKABLE IS THE
WAY IN WHICH PAINE LOCATED HIS "RADICAL EGALITARIANISM"
WITHIN THE PREVAILING VIEWS OF NATURE AND COMMON SENSE. THE
AUTHOR EXPLORES PAINE'S USES OF THE TERMS "COMMON SENSE,"
"NATURAL MAN," "NATURE," AND "SOCIABILITY" IN AN ATTEMPT TO
DETERMINE THE APPEAL OF COMMON SENSE TO THE MASSES.

03334 FRY, M. G.
ON THE TRACK OF TREACHERY: THE ASSAULT ON NORMAN
INTERNATIONAL PERSPECTIVES, XVIII(1) (JAN 89), 3-8.
THE AUTHOR CONSIDERS THE CAREER OF CANADIAN DIPLOMAT
HERBERT NORMAN, HIS INVOLVEMENT IN ESPIONAGE, AND HIS
RELATIONSHIP WITH LESTER PEARSON.

03335 FUCHS, L. H.
THERE THEY GO AGAIN
TIKKUN, 4(1) (JAN 89), 37.
IT IS NONSENSE TO SAY THAT JEWS VOTING FOR DUKAKIS
SUFFERED FROM COGNITIVE DISSONANCE. THE FACT THAT EVERY
MAJOR NATIONAL SURVEY SHOWS THAT JEWS SUPPORT LIBERAL
POSITIONS AND PREFER LIBERAL CANDIDATES DOES NOT MAKE THEM
IRRATIONAL. JEWISH VALUES TRANSLATE INTO JEWISH INTERESTS,
WHICH IS WHY JEWS ENDORSE CANDIDATES WITH A STRONG
COMMITMENT TO FIRST AMENDMENT AND SOCIAL JUSTICE ISSUES.
MORE THAN ANY OTHER GROUP, JEWS ARE SENSITIVE TO CIVIC
CULTURE ISSUES: FREEDOM OF SPEECH, FREEDOM OF RELIGION, AND
THE SEPARATION OF CHURCH AND STATE.

03336 FUENTES, M.; FRANK, A.G.
TEN THESES ON SOCIAL MOVEMENTS
WORLD DEVELOPMENT, 17(2) (FEB 89), 179-191.
SOCIAL MOVEMENTS (SM) MOBILIZE SOCIAL POWER APPEALING TO
MORALITY, JUSTICE, SURVIVAL AND IDENTITY. MOST "NEW" SM ARE
NOT NEW, BUT HAVE NEW FEATURES, PARTICULARLY MORE WOMEN'S
PARTICIPATION. THEY ARE CYCLICAL AND RELATED TO LONG
POLITICAL ECONOMIC CYCLES. SM ARE MOSTLY MIDDLE CLASS IN THE
WEST, POPULAR/WORKING CLASS IN THE SOUTH, AND BOTH IN THE
EAST. SOME SM COMPETE OR CONFLICT; OTHERS OVERLAP IN
MEMBERSHIP OR PERMIT COALITIONS. MOST SM SEEK MORE AUTONOMY
AND NOT STATE POWER, WHICH TENDS TO NEGATE THEM. MOST SM ARE
MORE DEFENSIVE AND TEMPORARY THAN OFFENSIVE. BUT THEY ARE
IMPORTANT AGENTS OF SOCIAL TRANSFORMATION, BECAUSE THEIR
PRAXIS REINTERPRETS PARTICIPATORY DEMOCRACY IN CIVIL SOCIETY
AND "TRANSITION TO SOCIALISM." SINCE SM CREATE THEIR OWN
SCRIPTS EN ROUTE, STANDARD OUTSIDE PRESCRIPTIONS SEEM
INAPPROPRIATE.

03337 FUKUI, HARUHIRO
JAPAN IN 1988: AT THE END OF ON ERA
ASIAN SURVEY, XXIX(1) (JAN 89), 1-11.
THE ARTICLE GIVES A BRIEF OVERVIEW OF THE EVENTS THAT
SHAPED JAPAN IN 1988. IT OUTLINES THE UNDERLYING CAUSES OF
JAPAN'S ECONOMIC SUCCESS AND ASSESSES THE PERFORMANCE OF
PRIME MINISTER NOBORU TAKESHITA. IT OUTLINES TAKESHITA'S
OVERALL SUCCESS IN BOTH DOMESTIC AND FOREIGN POLICY FRONTS.
HOWEVER, THE IMMINENT DEATH OF EMPEROR HIROHITO AND
ALLEGATIONS OF SCANDAL CAST A GLOOMY PALL OVER THE END OF
1988.

03338 FUKUYAMA, F.
THE END OF HISTORY?
NATIONAL INTEREST, 16 (SUM 89), 3-18.
WHAT WE MAY BE WITNESSING IS NOT JUST THE END OF THE
COLD WAR, OR THE PASSING OF A PARTICULAR PERIOD OF POSTWAR
HISTORY, BUT THE END OF HISTORY AS SUCH: THAT IS, THE END
POINT OF MANDKIND'S IDEOLOGICAL EVOLUTION AND THE
UNIVERSALIZATION OF WESTERN LIBERAL DEMOCRACY AS THE FINAL
FORM OF HUMAN GOVERNMENT. THE STRUGGLE FOR RECOGNITION, THE
WILLINGNESS TO RISK ONE'S LIFE FOR A PURELY ABSTRACT GOAL,
THE WORLDWIDE IDEOLOGICAL STRUGGLE THAT CALLED FORTH DARING,
COURAGE, IMAGINATION, AND IDEALISM, WILL BE REPLACED BY
ECONOMIC CALCULATION, THE ENDLESS SOLVING OF TECHNICAL
PROBLEMS, ENVIRONMENTAL CONCERNS, AND THE SATISFACTION OF
SOPHISTICATED CONSUMER DEMANDS. IN THE POST-HISTORICAL
PERIOD THERE WILL BE NEITHER ART NOR PHILOSOPHY, JUST THE
PERPETUAL CARETAKING OF THE MUSEUM OF HUMAN HISTORY. PERHAPS
THIS VERY PROSPECT OF CENTURIES OF BOREDOM AT THE END OF
HISTORY WILL SERVE TO GET HISTORY STARTED ONCE AGAIN.

03339 FULLER, G.E.
WAR AND REVOLUTION IN IRAN
CURRENT HISTORY, 88(535) (FEB 89), 81-84, 99-100.
THE AUTHOR ENUMERATES THE REASONS IRAN ACCEPTED A CEASE-

FIRE WITH IRAQ AND IRAN'S FUTURE IN THE AFTERMATH OF THE WAR.

03340 FUMENTO, M.
THE ABESTOS RIP-OFF
AMERICAN SPECTATOR, (OCT 89), 21-26.
THIS ARTICLE EXAMINES THE SITUATION THAT CURRENTLY
EXISTS OF "THE ABESTOS PANIC" IN THE USA. IT DETAILS THE
PROBLEM AS A LIFE SAVING INNOVATION THAT COULD KILL YOU,
DESIGNED TO CORRECT A PROBLEM THAT DOESN'T EXIST, BY
REMOVING MATERIALS THAT AREN'T DANGEROUS UNTIL SOMEBODY
TRIES TO REMOVE THEM, AND ALL THIS AT TREMENDOUSLY HIGH COST
TO THE TAXPAYER. IT STUDIES THE RISK OF LOW-LEVEL EXPOSURE
TO ABESTOS AN LISTS ESTIMATES OF RISK FROM VARIOUS CAUSES
WITH SMOKING THE HIGHEST AT 21,900 DEATHS PER 100,000; AND
ABESTOS IN SCHOOL BUILDINGS AT 1 DEATH PER 100,000, IT
ADVOCATES LEAVING THE "SLEEPING DOG" ALONE.

03341 FUND, J.H.
BEWARE THE GERRYMANDER, MY SON
NATIONAL REVIEW, XLI(6) (APR 89), 34-36.
AS AN EXAMPLE OF THE TYPE OF GERRYMANDERING THAT WILL BE
POSSIBLE USING COMPUTERS AND THE 1990 CENSUS DATA, THE
AUTHOR EXAMINES THE REDISTRICTING THAT PRECEDED THE 1982
CONGRESSIONAL ELECTIONS IN CALIFORNIA.

03342 FURET, F.
THE FRENCH REVOLUTION REVISITED
GOVERNMENT AND OPPOSITION, 24(3) (SUM 89), 264-282.
THE FRENCH REVOLUTION WAS NOT A TRANSITION. IT WAS A
BEGINNING AND AN ORIGINAL VISION. THIS IS WHAT IS UNIQUE IN
THE FRENCH REVOLUTION AND THIS UNIQUENESS HAS BECOME
UNIVERSAL: THE FIRST EXPERIENCE OF DEMOCRACY.

03343 GABBANI, A.S.
FROM IDEOLOGY TO REALISM: A STUDY OF SAUDI-SOVIET RELATIONS
DISSERTATION ABSTRACTS INTERNATIONAL, 50(1) (JUL 89),
251-A.
FOR MANY YEARS, THE SAUDI GOVERNMENT HAS BEEN RELUCTANT
TO ESTABLISH RELATIONS WITH THE SOVIET UNION BECAUSE IT
WISHES TO DISTANCE THE COUNTRY FROM THE INFLUENCES OF
COMMUNISM WITH ALL ITS SECULAR CONSEQUENCES. BUT IT WOULD BE
BENEFICIAL TO BOTH SAUDI ARABIA AND THE SOVIET UNION TO
ESTABLISH POLITICAL RELATIONS. IF RELATIONS WERE ESTABLISHED,
SAUDI ARABIA WOULD HAVE MORE OPPORTUNITY TO DIPLOMATICALLY
AND DIRECTLY INFLUENCE SOVIET GEO-POLITICAL BEHAVIOR WITH
RESPECT TO MIDDLE EASTERN POLITICS. BOTH SAUDI ARABIA AND
THE USSR WOULD BENEFIT FROM DIRECT ECONOMIC RELATIONS.

03344 GABEL, P.
DUKAKIS' DEFEAT AND THE TRANSFORMATIVE POSSIBILITIES OF
LEGAL CULTURE
TIKKUN, 4(2) (MAR 89), 13-16.
FOR PROGRESSIVE FORCES TO SUCCEED, THEY MUST MANIFEST
THEMSELVES IN PUBLIC SPACE IN A WAY THAT LIFTS PEOPLE OUT OF
THEIR SENSE OF ISOLATION AND ENABLES THEM TO FEEL PART OF A
COMMUNITY OF MEANING WITHIN WHICH THEIR DESIRE FOR SOCIAL
CONFIRMATION MIGHT BE REALIZED. ALL CONCRETE PROPOSALS FOR
THE EXPANSION OF ECONOMIC BENEFITS, FOR THE IMPLEMENTATION
OF NEW SOCIAL POLICIES, AND FOR THE EXTENSION OF POLITICAL
RIGHTS MUST BE FRAMED WITHIN AN EVOCATIVE MORAL VISION THAT
ENLIVENS THESE PROPOSALS WITH A SENSE OF SOCIAL CONNECTION
AND PURPOSE.

03345 GABRIEL, O.W.
FEDERALISM AND PARTY DEMOCRACY IN WEST GERMANY
PUBLIUS: THE JOURNAL OF FEDERALISM, 19(4) (FAL 89), 65-80.
IN THIS ARTICLE ON POLITICAL PARTIES, THE WRITER BEGINS
WITH THE THESIS THAT TENSION EXISTS BETWEEN FEDERALISM AND A
DISCIPLINED PARTY SYSTEM, BOTH OF WHICH ARE FOUND IN THE
FEDERAL REPUBLIC. ACCORDING TO THIS THESIS, THE CONSENSUAL
DECISIONMAKING TYPICAL OF FEDERAL SYSTEMS IS CONTRADICTED BY
STRONG PARTISAN CONFLICT, HE THEN LOOKS AT A SECOND THESIS
WHICH SUGGESTS THAT POLITICAL PARTIES ARE CENTRALIZING
FORCES IN A FEDERAL SYSTEM. HE INVESTIGATES THE EFFECT OF
THE GERMAN FEDERAL STRUCTURE ON THE ORGANIZATION OF THE
POLITICAL PARTIES.

03346 GABRIEL, S.; KUMAR, V.
ARMS CONTROL: PRESERVING PEACE FROM NUCLEAR THREAT
INDIAN JOURNAL OF POLITICAL SCIENCE, L(2) (APR 89),
251-262.
THE HUMAN RACE IS SITTING ON A GREAT PILE OF NUCLEAR
WEAPONS. ONE WRONG MOVE, ONE WRONG DECISION, ONE BIG
ACCIDENT COULD PUSH MANKIND INTO THE FLAMES OF NUCLEAR WAR.
ARMS CONTROL NEGOTIATIONS HAVE VIRTUALLY FAILED TO REDUCE
THE LIKELIHOOD OF NUCLEAR OR CONVENTIONAL WAR OR TO EASE
TENSIONS BETWEEN THE UNITED STATES AND THE SOVIET UNION. BUT
THE THIRD WORLD COUNTRIES REALIZE THAT A HALT TO THE ARMS
RACE WOULD PROMOTE A SUBSTANTIAL ACCELERATION OF THE SOCIAL
AND ECONOMIC PROGRESS OF DEVELOPING COUNTRIES AND WOULD MAKE
IT POSSIBLE FOR THEM TO CHANNEL THEIR MATERIAL, FINANCIAL,
AND HUMAN RESOURCES FROM MILITARY TO PEACEFUL, CONSTRUCTIVE
USE.

03347 GACEK, E.
ELECTION LAW FOR SEJM AND SENATE: PLURALISTIC MODEL OF
POLISH PARLIAMENT
CONTEMPORARY POLAND, XXII(5) (1989), 30-35.
THE AUTHOR REPORTS ON THE WORK OF THE SEJM EXTRAORDINARY
COMMITTEE TO REFORM POLISH ELECTION LAWS. IN FORMULATING THE
NEW LAWS, THE COMMITTEE UTILIZED ADVICE AND SUGGESTIONS FROM
THE COUNCIL OF STATE, THE SUPREME COURT, THE OFFICE OF THE
PROSPECUTOR, AND THE JUSTICE MINISTRY. THE GOAL WAS TO
PROMULGATE NEW ELECTIONS LAW THAT CAN BE ONE OF THE DRIVING
FORCES FOR ORDERLY DEMOCRATIC CHANGE IN POLAND.

03348 GACEK, S.A.
LABOR FIGHTS BACK
NACLA REPORT ON THE AMERICAS, 22(6) (MAR 89), 4-6.
THE WORKERS PARTY"S ASTOUNDING VICTORIES IN NOVEMBER'S
MUNICIPAL ELECTIONS HIGHLIGHTED THE DRAMATIC CHANGES THAT
HAVE SWEPT THE LABOR MOVEMENT IN THE PAST TEN YEARS. THE
PATERNALISTIC SYSTEM WHICH KEPT LABOR IN CHECK FOR 40 YEARS
HAS BEEN MORTALLY WOUNDED.

03349 GADDIS, J. L.
LOOKING BACK: THE LONG PEACE
WILSON QUARTERLY, XIII(1) (JAN 89), 42-65.
THE POST-WORLD WAR II SYSTEM OF INTERNATIONAL RELATIONS,
WHICH NOBODY DESIGNED OR EVEN THOUGHT COULD LAST VERY LONG,
WAS BASED NOT UPON THE DICTATES OF MORALITY AND JUSTICE BUT
RATHER UPON AN ARBITRARY DIVISION OF THE WORLD INTO SPHERE
OF INFLUENCE AND INCORPORATED SOME OF THE MOST BITTER
ANTAGONISMS SHORT OF WAR IN MODERN HISTORY. BUT IT HAS NOW
SURVIVED TWICE AS LONG AS THE FAR MORE CAREFULLY DESIGNED
WORLD WAR I SETTLEMENT. AFTER FOUR DECADES, IT SHOWS NO
SIGNS OF DISINTEGRATION, EVEN THOUGH "PEACE" IS NOT THE
FIRST TERM THAT COMES TO MIND WHEN ONE RECALLS THE HISTORY
OF THE COLD WAR.

03350 GADDIS, J.L.
HANGING TOUGH PAID OFF
BULLETIN OF THE ATOMIC SCIENTISTS, 45(1) (JAN 89), 11-13.
DESCRIBED AND EVALUATED IN THIS ARTICLE ARE THE POLICIES
AND EVENTS THAT SHAPED THE RELATIONS BETWEEN THE UNITED
STATES AND THE SOVIET UNION DURING THE REAGAN YEARS. THE
ARTICLE CONCLUDES WITH SUGGESTIONS FOR CONTINUING THE
IMPROVEMENT IN RELATIONS BETWEEN THESE TWO COUNTRIES.

03351 GAGGERO, E.
DEVELOPING COUNTRIES AND SPACE
SPACE POLICY, 5(2) (MAY 89), 107-110.
AS SPACE COMMERCIALIZATION IS BECOMING A REALITY, AND
WITH THE TENDENCY FOR SUCH ACTIVITY TO BE TRANSFERRED TO THE
PRIVATE SECTOR, IT IS TIME FOR THE DEVELOPING COUNTRIES TO
ASSUME A ROLE IN SPACE. THE AUTHOR ARGUES THAT SPACE LAW
COULD BE OF HELP IF THE INTERPRETATION OF TERMS SUCH AS
"COMMON HERITAGE" WERE AGREED ON AND SENSIBLE RULES FOR THE
REGULATION OF COMPETITION IN SPACE ELABORATED. HOWEVER, IT
IS UP TO THE DEVELOPING COUNTRIES THEMSELVES TO BECOME AWARE
OF THE SITUATION, EDUCATE THEIR PUBLIC AND TRAIN THEIR
PERSONNEL THROUGH PARTICIPATION IN COOPERATIVE VENTURES WITH
THE DEVELOPED WORLD.

03352 GAGNON, A.
SOCIAL SCIENCES AND PUBLIC POLICIES
INTERNATIONAL SOCIAL SCIENCE JOURNAL, (122) (NOV 89),
555-566.
THIS ARTICLE ATTEMPTS TO ASSESS THE IMPACT SOCIAL
SCIENCE HAS HAD ON THE FORMULATION OF PUBLIC POLICY IN
LIBERAL DEMOCRATIC SOCIETIES. AS SUCH, IT CAN BE PLACED
WITHIN A LARGER CONTEXT, THAT OF THE SOCIAL AND POLITICAL
ROLES OF INTELLECTUALS.

03353 GAIHA, R.
ON ESTIMATES OF RURAL POVERTY IN INDIA: AN ASSESSMENT
ASIAN SURVEY, 29(7) (JUL 89), 687-697.
THE PURPOSE OF THIS ARTICLE IS TO REVIEW SOME RECENT
ESTIMATES OF RURAL POVERTY IN INDIA BASED ON NATIONAL SAMPLE
SURVEY (NSS) CONSUMER EXPENDITURE DISTRIBUTIONS. IT
CONCENTRATES ON A STUDY BY B.S. MINHAS WHICH FOCUSES ON
CHANGES IN RURAL POVERTY USING DIFFERENT CONSUMER PRICE
DEFLATORS, ADJUSTED AND UNADJUSTED NSS CONSUMER EXPENDITURE
ESTIMATES, AND ALTERNATIVE POVERTY CUT-OFF POINTS, IT FIRST
SUMMARIZES THE PROCEDURE USED IN THE MINHAS STUDY FOR
COMPUTING ALTERNATIVE SERIES OF THE INCIDENCE OF RURAL
POVERTY AND THE IMPORTANT FINDINGS. THIS IS FOLLOWED BY AN
EVALUATION. TO PUT THE DISCUSSION IN PERSPECTIVE, RECENT
EVIDENCE ON RURAL POVERTY AND ITS RELATIONSHIP TO
AGRICULTURAL PRODUCTION AND CONSUMER PRICES IS REVIEWED.

03354 GALBRAITH, J.S.
BRITISH POLICY ON RAILWAYS IN PERSIA, 1870-1900
MIDDLE EASTERN STUDIES, 25(4) (OCT 89), 480-505.
IN THE THIRD QUARTER OF THE NINETEENTH CENTURY THE
PERSIAN GOVERNMENT FACED INTERNAL REVOLT AND RUSSIAN
AGGRESSION WITHOUT. PERSIA TURNED TO BRITAIN AS A COUNTER
BALANCE TO THE SPREAD OF RUSSIAN INFLUENCE. VARIOUS BRITISH

STATESMEN SAW IN PERSIA, OPPORTUNITIES FOR COMMERCIAL EXPANSION BY OPENING UP THE INTERIOR OF THE COUNTRY BY STEAMBOATS AND BY RAILWAYS. THIS ARTICLE EXPLORES THE BACKGROUND OF EFFORTS BY BRITISH GOVERNMENTS TO INDUCE ENTREPRENEURS TO SEEK CONCESSIONS FROM THE SHAW TO OPEN PERSIA TO BRITISH TRAFFIC. EARLY ATTEMPTS TO BUILD A RAILROAD ARE RECORDED, THEN THE BUILDING OF A 900 MILE RR LINE BY BARON JULIUS DE REUTER IS DETAILED.

03355 GALILEE, L.
RENDEZVOUS IN BRUSSELS
NEW OUTLOOK, 32(6-7 (292-293)) (JUN 89), 27-29.
IN MAY 1989, FIFTY WOMEN REPRESENTING ISRAEL, THE OCCUPIED TERRITORIES, AND THE PLO MET IN BRUSSELS TO DISCUSS THE ISRAELI-PALESTINIAN CONFLICT. DESPITE THE DISCUSSIONS, THEY WERE UNABLE TO AGREE ON A UNANIMOUS JOINT STATEMENT OF PRINCIPLES. THE CONFERENCE REVEALED THE PSYCHOLOGICAL DIFFICULTIES, WHICH ARE NO LESS PROBLEMATIC THAN THE POLITICAL OBSTACLES. IT ALSO REVEALED THE VALUE OF INTERPERSONAL MEETINGS, WHICH ARE UNPARALLELED IN THEIR ABILITY TO BREAK DOWN BARRIERS AND ENFORCE A MUTUAL OPENNESS, DESPITE THE ABSENCE OF COMPLETE AGREEMENT OVER EXACT POLITICAL FORMULATIONS.

03356 GALLAGHER, D.
THE EVOLUTION OF THE INTERNATIONAL REFUGEE SYSTEM
INTERNATIONAL MIGRATION REVIEW, 23(3) (FAL 89), 579-598.
THIS ARTICLE EXAMINES THE EVOLUTION OF THE CURRENT INTERNATIONAL SYSTEM FOR RESPONDING TO REFUGEE PROBLEMS AND THE CLIMATE WITHIN WHICH THE LEGAL AND INSTITUTIONAL FRAMEWORK HAS DEVELOPED. IT REVIEWS THE BACKGROUND AND HANDLING OF SOME OF THE KEY REFUGEE MOVEMENTS SINCE WORLD WAR II AND TRACES THE LEGAL AND INSTITUTIONAL ADJUSTMENTS THAT HAVE BEEN MADE TO DEAL WITH NEW REFUGEE MOVEMENTS THAT HAVE OCCURRED PREDOMINANTLY, BUT NOT EXCLUSIVELY, IN THE DEVELOPING WORLD. FINALLY, IT ASSESSES THE ADEQUACY OF THE PRESENT SYSTEM TO MEET THE CHALLENGES AHEAD.

03357 GALLAGHER, M.
DO CONGRESSMEN HAVE MOTHERS?
NATIONAL REVIEW, 61(20) (OCT 89), 38-39, 59.
THIS ARTICLE EXAMINES THE ACT FOR BETTER CHILD CARE AND THE TERMS IN WHICH IT IS BEING DISCUSSED. IT CONSIDERS WHETHER DAY CARE IS JUST AS GOOD FOR KIDS AS STAYING HOME WITH THEIR MOTHERS. IT EXPLORES THE RAMIFICATIONS OF THE ACT WHICH COMES DOWN SQUARELY AGAINST MATERNAL CARE OF CHILDREN.

03358 GALLAGHER, T.
PORTUGAL
ELECTORAL STUDIES, 8(3) (DEC 89), 317-321.
THIS ARTICLE EXAMINES THE 1989 EUROPEAN ELECTIONS IN PORTUGAL, WHICH HAS BEEN A MEMBER OF THE EC FOR A SHORT TIME ONLY. IT PROVIDES A CRITIQUE OF PUBLIC REPRESENTATIVES AND THE MEDIA WITH THEIR PREFERENCE TO BOMBARD VOTERS WITH SLOGANS, RATHER THAN ENCOURAGE AN INTELLIGENT DEBATE ABOUT THE IMPLICATIONS OF EC MEMBERSHIP FOR A FRAGILE PROTECTED ECONOMY. THE ARTICLE EXPLORES ELECTORAL ALLIANCES AND LOW TURNOUT.

03359 GALLAROTTI, G.M.
LEGITIMACY AS A CAPITAL ASSET OF THE STATE
PUBLIC CHOICE, 63 (1989), 43-62.
THIS ARTICLE GIVES A MATHEMATICAL ANALYSIS OF HOW THE STATE OPTIMALLY DIVERSIFIES ITS MANAGEMENT OF SOCIETY SO AS TO MAXIMIZE SOME OBJECTIVE FUNCTION DEFINED OVER RISK AND RETURN (I.E., THE STATE AS A RATIONAL INVESTOR)?; SECOND BY WAY OF A DISCUSSION OF HOW INVESTMENTS IN LEGITIMACY ON THE PART OF THE STATE ENHANCE THE SURVIVAL POTENTIAL OF THE STATE AND LOWER THE TRANSACTION COSTS OF MANAGING SOCIETY. THIS ARTICLE IS ORGANIZED AS FOLLOWS, SECTION 2 DISCUSSES THE CONCEPT OF LEGITIMACY AS A CAPITAL ASSET. SECTION 3 PRESENTS A FORMAL MODEL OF PORTFOLIO DIVERSIFICATION BETWEEN TWO GOVERNMENTAL FUNCTIONS. SECTION 4 DISCUSSES THE SPECIFIC BENEFITS WHICH LEGITIMACY CONFERS ON THE STATE IN TERMS OF THE ECONOMICS OF MANAGING SOCIETY. SECTION 5 BRIEFLY DISCUSSES MARGINAL SUBSTITUTION BETWEEN TANGIBLE AND NONTANGIBLE REWARDS AS A MEANS OF MANAGING RENT POOLS. SECTION 6 PRESENTS SOME CONCLUDING REMARKS.

03360 GALLAROTTI, G.M.
THE ANATOMY OF SPONTANEOUS ORDER: THE EMERGENCE OF INTERNATIONAL MONETARY ORDER BEFORE WORLD WAR I
DISSERTATION ABSTRACTS INTERNATIONAL, 49(10) (APR 89), 3146-A.
ORDERLY, STABLE INTERNATIONAL ECONOMIC SYSTEMS HAVE TRADITIONALLY BEEN SEEN AS THE OUTGROWTH OF INTERNATIONAL MANAGEMENT. THE MANAGERIALIST PARADIGM SUGGESTS THAT INTERNATIONAL ECONOMIC RELATIONS ARE ORDERLY AND STABLE WHEN ONE, A FEW, OR MANY NATIONS DECIDE TO REGULATE INTERNATIONAL PROCESSES RELATED TO THE EXCHANGE OF GOODS, CAPITAL, AND SERVICES. INTERACTIONAL PROCESSES LEFT TO THEMSELVES INVARIABLY DEVOLVE INTO CONFLICTS OF SOME KIND. BUT THE HISTORY OF THE INTERNATIONAL POLITICAL ECONOMY OVER THE PAST HUNDRED YEARS HAS NOT CONSISTENTLY VINDICATED THE

MANAGERIALIST VIEW. THE MOST STRIKING ANOMALY HAS BEEN THE CLASSICAL GOLD STANDARD. INTERNATIONAL MONETARY RELATIONS DURING THE PERIOD 1880-1914 EXHIBITED A VERY HIGH LEVEL OF ORDER.

03361 GALLEGUILLOS-PORTALES, N.H.
THE MAKING OF THE CHILEAN AUTHORITARIAN STATE: A CASE STUDY OF A DEFENSIVE COUP D'ETAT
DISSERTATION ABSTRACTS INTERNATIONAL, 48(12) (JUN 88), 3187-A.
IN THE MORE DEVELOPED COUNTRIES OF THE SOUTHERN CONE OF SOUTH AMERICA, A DISTINCTION CAN BE MADE BETWEEN OFFENSIVE AND DEFENSIVE COUPS. THE COUP D'ETAT THAT TOOK PLACE IN CHILE IN 1973 IS AN EXAMPLE OF A DEFENSIVE COUP: THE NEW RULERS DID NOT ATTEMPT TO CREATE A NEW SOCIO-ECONOMIC, POLITICAL AND CULTURAL PROJECT IN THE BEGINING OF THEIR RULE, THEY WERE MERELY REACTING TO A REVOLUTIONARY SITUATION THAT NEEDED TO BE BROUGHT TO AN END.

03362 GALLIS, P.E.
EUROPEAN ROLES AND RESPONSIBILITIES
CRS REVEIW, 10(4) (APR 89), 18-20.
DIVERGENT PERCEPTIONS OF THE SOVIET THREAT, DOUBTS OVER U.S. LEADERSHIP, GROWING EUROPEAN COOPERATION ON SECURITY ISSUES, AND ECONOMIC COMPETITION ARE EMERGING FACTORS THAT MAY CAUSE NEW FRICTIONS WITHIN THE NATO ALLIANCE IN THE COMING YEARS.

03363 GALLISSOT, R.
IS EUROPE COMBINING TWO FORMS OF RACISM?
NEW POLITICAL SCIENCE, 16 (FAL 89), 79-90.
THE AUTHOR EXPLORES THE CONFLICTS EXPRESSED IN TERMS OF ETHNICITY OR RACE IN EUROPE, WHICH HE EXPRESSES IN CONCRETE TERMS AND AS MODES OF REFERENCE AT THREE DIFFERENT LEVELS. THESE ARE: URBAN, NATION-STATE, AND GLOBAL. EACH OF THESE LEVELS IS GENERALLY CHARACTERIZED. SEGREGATION, WHICH IS JUSTIFIED IN CULTURAL TERMS, IS A PHENOMENA EMERGENT AFTER WORLD WAR II IN EUROPE. IT IS SUGGESTED THAT THIS MIGHT BE A COMBINATION OF TWO FORMS OF RACISM, I.E., COLONIAL AND NATIONALIST RACISM. IMMIGRAT ION, ASSIMILATION, AND THE "IMMEGRE" ARE THEN EXAMINED, IN RELATION TO FRENCH SOCIETY IN PARTICULAR.

03364 GALLOWAY, C.
THE DIKKO AFFAIR AND BRITISH-NIGERIAN RELATIONS
ROUND TABLE, (311) (JUL 89), 323-336.
THE ATTEMPTED KIDNAP FROM BRITAIN OF THE NIGERIAN POLITICIAN UMARA DIKKO IN THE SUMMER OF 1984 WAS BY ANY STANDARDS AN EXTRAORDINARY EVENT, MADE THE MORE SO BECAUSE OF THE INVOLVEMENT ON OPPOSING SIDES OF TWO OSTENSIBLY FRIENDLY COMMONWEALTH GOVERNMENTS. TO UNDERSTAND THE REASONS FOR THE KIDNAP, THE DOMESTIC NIGERIAN BACKGROUND MUST BE CONSIDERED, AND TO UNDERSTAND THE CONTROLLED REACTION OF THE TWO GOVERNMENTS TO THE EVENT SOME ANALYSIS OF THE RELATIONSHIP BETWEEN THE TWO COUNTRIES IS DISCUSSED IN THIS ARTICLE.

03365 GALNOOR, I.
THE ISRAELI ELECTIONS: THE FLIGHT FROM FREEDOM AND RESPONSIBILITY
TIKKUN, 4(1) (JAN 89), 38-40.
THE NOVEMBER 1988 ISRAELI ELECTIONS WERE ABOUT THE INTIFADA, DESPITE THE STRONG DENIAL OF THAT FACT BY MOST VOTERS, AND THE OUTCOME HAS A DEVASTATING STALEMATE. THE RIGHT-WING PARTIES, INCLUDING THE LIKUD, TOOK 42 PERCENT OF THE VOTE WHILE LABOR AND THE OTHER LEFT-WING PARTIES OBTAINED 45 PERCENT.

03366 GALSTER, S.R.; HIPPLER, J.
REPORT FROM AFGHANISTAN
MIDDLE EAST REPORT, 19(158) (MAY 89), 38-42.
THE LAST SOVIET SOLDIERS IN AFGHANISTAN HAVE GONE HOME, CLEARING THE STAGE AROUND KABUL AND OTHER CITIES FOR A MAJOR SHOWDOWN BETWEEN SOVIET-SUPPORTED GOVERNMENT FORCES AND THEIR AMERICAN-SUPPORTED GUERRILLA RIVALS, THE MUJAHIDIN. CONVENTIONAL WISDOM HAS IT THAT THE MUJAHIDIN ARE NOW IN POSITION TO FINALLY TOPPLE THE KABUL REGIME. FORMER PRESIDENT RONALD REAGAN BASED HIS POLICY ON THIS PREMISE-- THAT PEACE IN AFGHANISTAN LAY BEYOND A SOVIET WITHDRAWAL AND THE OVERTHROW OF THE NAJIBULLAH GOVERNMENT. PRESIDENT GEORGE BUSH, HOPING TO PUT HIS OWN IMPRINT ON WHAT CONSERVATIVES VIEW AS THE ONE SOLID VICTORY OF THE REAGAN DOCTRINE, HAS DECIDED TO CONTINUE ARMING THE REBELS AS LONG AS THE RULING PEOPLE'S DEMOCRATIC PARTY OF AFGHANISTAN (PDPA) REMAINS IN POWER.

03367 GALSTON, W.A.
COMMUNITY, DEMOCRACY, PHILOSOPHY: THE POLITICAL THOUGHT OF MICHAEL WALZER
POLITICAL THEORY, 17(1) (FEB 89), 119-130.
THE AUTHOR ARGUE THAT THE OVERALL STORY OF THE JEWISH PEOPLE OCCUPIES A POSITION OF COMPARABLE CENTRALITY IN WALZER'S OWN THOUGHT, FOR IT FURNISHES HIS ROOT-CONCEPT OF A COMMUNITY UNITED, NOT IN FULL AGREEMENT ON FIXED BELIEFS,

BUT RATHER IN ITS COMMITMENT TO INTERPRET A SHARED TEXT, TO ACCEPT AS BINDING (AT LEAST TEMPORARILY) THE INTERPRETATIONS ON WHICH IT CONFERS AUTHORITY, AND TO WEAVE A COMMON LIFE OUT OF THE DENSE, OVERLAPPING SUCCESSION OF SUCH INTERPRETATIONS.

03368 GALSTON, W.A.
PUTTING A DEMOCRAT IN THE WHITE HOUSE
BROOKINGS REVIEW, 7(3) (SUM 89), 21-25.
OVER THE PAST TWO DECADES, TOO MANY AMERICANS HAVE COME TO SEE THE DEMOCRATIC PARTY AS INATTENTIVE TO THEIR ECONOMIC INTERESTS, INDIFFERENT IF NOT HOSTILE TO THEIR MORAL SENTIMENTS, AND INEFFECTIVE IN DEFENSE OF THEIR NATIONAL SECURITY. RATHER THAN FACING REALITY, THE DEMOCRATS HAVE EMBRACED THE POLITICS OF EVASION. THE RESULT HAS BEEN REPEATED DEFEAT IN PRESIDENTIAL ELECTIONS. AND IF THE PARTY DOESN'T CHANGE, IT WILL KEEP LOSING THE PRESIDENCY.

03369 GALSTON, W.A.
THE OBLIGATION TO PLAY POLITICAL HARDBALL
REPORT FROM THE INSTITUTE FOR PHILOSOPHY AND PUBLIC POLICY, 9(1) (WIN 89), 6-7.
DO POLITICIANS HAVE AN OBLIGATION TO PLAY HARDBALL? MUST THEY USE QUESTIONABLE, QUALM-PRODUCING MEANS EVEN IF POLITICS IS A REALM WHERE MORALLY QUESTIONABLE MEANS ARE PARTICULARLY PREVALENT AND MORAL QUALMS PARTICULARLY UNAVOIDABLE? THE NOTION OF AN OBLIGATION TO PLAY HARDBALL, FAR FROM BEING OUTLANDISH, IS IMPLICIT IN A SOUND UNDERSTANDING OF POLITICAL PRACTICE. IN MOST CIRCUMSTANCES, A POLITICIAN DOES NOT STAND ALONE BUT ACTS ON BEHALF OF OTHERS OR IN WAYS THAT AFFECT OTHERS, IN PURSUIT OF CERTAIN ENDS THAT OTHERS HAVE REASON TO EXPECT HIM TO PURSUE. TO BECOME A POLITICIAN MEANS ONE TAKES UPON HIMSELF THE RESPONSIBILITY TO ACT EFFECTIVELY, WHICH OFTEN ENTAILS THE DUTY OF USING HARDBALL TACTICS.

03370 GALTANG, J.
ALTERNATIVE SECURITY POLICIES IN EUROPE
ETUDES INTERNATIONALES, 20(3) (SEP 89), 625-646.
THE TIME HAS COME TO DISCUSS MILITARY DOCTRINE. WE HAVE, FOR MUCH TOO LONG NOW, BEEN DISCUSSING SEPARATE WEAPON SYSTEMS, SOMETIMES SINGLY, SOMETIMES COMBINED, AND NOT THE UNDERLYING RATIONAL. THIS ARTICLE SPELLS OUT ALTERNATIVE SECURITY POLICIES IN THE FIELDS OF MILITARY AND FOREIGN POLICIES. THE READER WILL FIND A LAYMAN'S GUIDE TO MILITARY DOCTRINE, BEGINNING WITH A BASIC DISTINCTION MADE BETWEEN OFFENSIVE AND DEFENSIVE POSTURES, A DISTINCTION BASED ON CAPABILITY AND NOT ON INTENTION. THE ARTICLE WILL SHOW THAT THE DIVISION INTO MILITARY AND POLITICAL MOTIVATIONS IS FAR FROM SHARP, AND NEEDS TO BE BETTER UNDERSTOOD IN ORDER TO DISCUSS AND ASSESS THE IMPLICATIONS OF ALTERNATIVE DOCTRINES FOR EUROPE.

03371 GALTUNG, J.
THE COLD WAR AS AN EXERCISE IN AUTISM: THE US GOVERNMENT, THE GOVERNMENTS OF WESTERN EUROPE, AND THE PEOPLE
ALTERNATIVES, XIV(2) (APR 89), 169-193.
WHAT WE ARE WITNESSING IN THE COLD WAR IS NOT ONLY TWO PARALLEL AUTISMS, BUT TWO DIFFERENT TYPES OF AUTISM, ONE DEMOCRATIC, ONE AUTOCRATIC. THERE IS NO REASON TO ASSUME THAT THE DEMOCRATIC ONE IS LESS AUTISTIC THAN THE AUTOCRATIC VERSION. THE DIFFERENCE IS THAT IN A DEMOCRACY MANY, SOMETIMES MOST, OF THE PEOPLE BELIEVE WHAT THEIR LEADERS SAY EVEN WHEN THEY ARE WRONG, IN AN AUTOCRACY THEY DISTRUST WHAT THE LEADERS SAY EVEN WHEN THEY ARE RIGHT. CHANGE THE EAST FROM AN AUTOCRACY TO A DEMOCRACY (THIS MAY NOT BE AS FAR AWAY AS WE TEND TO ASSUME) AND THE AUTISM MAY MERELY GET MORE FIRMLY ROOTED. WHETHER THAT AUTISM IS CHANGEABLE REMAINS TO BE SEEN VESTED INTERESTS IN STATUS QUO ALL OVER.

03372 GALVIN, J.
A STRATEGY OF THE FUTURE
RUSI JOURNAL, 134(3) (FAL 89), 15-18.
GENERAL GALVIN OUTLINES SEVERAL AREAS OF CONCERN THAT HE WOULD LIKE TO DISCUSS WITH HIS WARSAW PACT COUNTERPART. THESE INCLUDE: THE TRUE MEANING OF SOVIET "BUDGET REDUCTIONS"; MODERNIZATION; THE EXTENT OF UNILATERAL REDUCTIONS; AND THE INCLUSION OF FACTORS OF FORCE, SPACE, AND TIME IN CALCULATIONS OF RELATIVE PARITY BETWEEN THE WARSAW PACT AND NATO. HE CONCLUDES THAT FURTHER NEGOTIATION WILL BE BENEFICIAL FOR BOTH SIDES.

03373 GALVIN, J.
MODERNIZATION OF THEATER NUCLEAR FORCES
NATO'S SIXTEEN NATIONS, 34(1) (1989), 25-27.
NATO'S EUROPEAN-BASED NUCLEAR FORCES ARE AGEING AND HAVE BEEN REDUCED IN NUMBERS BY UNILATERAL DECISIONS OF THE COUNCIL. AS THESE WEAPONS ARE ESSENTIAL FOR THE MAINTENANCE OF NATO'S FLEXIBLE RESPONSE STRATEGY, THEY MUST NOW BE MODERNIZED TO ENSURE THEIR RELIABILITY. IF THESE WEAPONS ARE NOT MODERNIZED, NATO'S ADVERSARIES MAY DOUBT ITS DETERMINATION AND ABILITY TO INFLICT UNACCEPTABLE DAMAGE, THEREBY UNDERMINING THE FOUNDATION OF DETERRENCE. BUT ONCE THE MODERNIZATION PROCESS IS COMPLETED, THESE WEAPONS COULD

BE REDUCED IN ORDER TO ACHIEVE AN EFFECTIVE MINIMUM DETERRENCE.

03374 GALVIN, J.R.
THE NATO ALLIANCE: A FRAMEWORK FOR SECURITY
WASHINGTON QUARTERLY, 12(1) (WIN 89), 85-94.
GIVEN THE OVERALL SIZE AND CONTINUING GROWTH OF SOVIET MILITARY CAPABILITIES, THE MEMBERS OF THE ALLIANCE CLEARLY NEED TO MAINTAIN THEIR VIGILANCE AND TO CONTINUE TO PROVIDE FOR THE COMMON DEFENSE. THIS MEANS THAT NATIONS MUST KEEP THE MEANS FOR MODERNIZATION OR FACE OBSOLESCENCE-THE KISS OF DEATH IN MODERN WELFARE. GIVEN THE GROWING CONSTRAINTS ON NATIONAL RESOURCES, HOWEVER, AND THE INCREASING PRICE OF MODERN WEAPON SYSTEMS, IT IS CRITICAL THAT ALL OF THE ALLIES LOOK FOR METHODS TO IMPROVE THEIR SECURITY AT THE LOWEST POSSIBLE COST. THE NUMBER OF WAYS TO ACCOMPLISH THIS TASK, UNFORTUNATELY, ARE LIMITED. NATIONS CAN NEGOTIATE REDUCTIONS OF SOVIET CAPABILITIES RELATIVE TO NATO, STRETCH THE VALUE OF DEFENSE DOLLARS AND STAY STRONG, OR COMBINE THESE TWO APPROACHES IN SOME WAY TO ACHIEVE AN OPTIMAL OUTCOME.

03375 GAMBLE, A.
THE POLITICS OF THATCHERISM
PARLIAMENTARY AFFAIRS, 42(3) (JUL 89), 350-361.
IN ORDER TO HAVE A FULL UNDERSTANDING OF THATCHERISM AND TO FORM A JUDGEMENT AS TO HOW MUCH OF A RADICAL BREAK THE ELECTION OF THE CONSERVATIVE GOVERNMENT IN 1979 REPRESENTS, IT IS NECESSARY TO EXPLORE THE POLITICS OF THATCHERISM AND THE TRADE-OFFS THAT WERE ESTABLISHED BETWEEN DIFFERENT OBJECTIVES. THE POLITICAL CALCULUS OF THATCHERISM HAS BEEN SHAPED PREDOMINANTLY BY THREE KEY FACTORS--THE DOCTRINES OF THE NEW RIGHT; A PARTICULAR SET OF SPECIAL INTERESTS AND DISTRIBUTIONAL COALITIONS; AND THE DETERMINATION OF THE CONSERVATIVE PARTY TO GAIN AND HOLD POWER. THIS ARTICLE STUDIES THE POLITICS OF THATCHERISM AND CONCLUDES THAT THATCHERISM HAS BEEN MORE ABOUT RESTORING STATE AUTHORITY AND THE POLITICAL FORTUNES OF THE CONSERVATIVE PARTY THAN IT HAS BEEN ABOUT CONSTRUCTING A FREE ECONOMY.

03376 GAMINI, G.; CHAUDHARY, V.
COLOMBO OPENS UP A NEW FRONT
SOUTH, (108) (OCT 89), 45.
HARSH AND VIOLENT TIMES HAVE CREATED AN ECONOMIC AND POLITICAL CRISIS FOR THE GOVERNMENT OF PRESIDENT RANASINGHE PREMADASA. THE SRI LANKAN GOVERNMENT IS PINNING ITS HOPES ON INDUSTRIALIZATION TO SOLVE SOME OF ITS PRESSING ECONOMIC PROBLEMS. BUT THERE IS CONSIDERABLE DOMESTIC DISSATISFACTION WITH THE GOVERNMENT'S CURRENT POLICY, WHICH ENCOURAGES OVERSEAS INVESTORS AT THE EXPENSE OF LOCAL COMPANIES.

03377 GAMM, G.; SHEPSLE, K.
EMERGENCE OF LEGISLATIVE INSTITUTIONS: STANDING COMMITTEES IN THE HOUSE AND SENATE 1810-1825
LEGISLATIVE STUDIES QUARTERLY, XIV(1) (FEB 89), 39-66.
BETWEEN 1810 AND 1825 THE TWO HOUSES OF LEGISLATURE UNDERWENT DRAMATIC AND LASTING TRANSFORMATIONS IN THEIR ORGANIZATIONAL ARRANGEMENTS. BY 1825 EACH CHAMBER HAD A FULLY DEVELOPED SYSTEM OF STANDING COMMITTEES WHICH HAVE DOMINATED ITS PROCEDURES TO THE PRESENT TIME. THE PAPER DOCUMENTS THESE DEVELOPMENTS AND SEEKS TO ACCOUNT FOR THEM BY RATIONAL CHOICE AND ORGANIZATION THEORY.

03378 GAMMON, C.
WHOSE CHOICE?
PRESENT TENSE, 16(6) (SEP 89), 14-23.
THIS ARTICLE, AN ANALYSIS OF THE ABORTION ISSUE, CONCLUDES THAT IN THE WAR OVER ABORTION THERE IS NO COMMON GROUND. IT CONSIDERS THE IDEOLOGY OF EACH SIDE, ONE SIDE CLAIMS THAT IF THE RIGHT TO PRIVACY MEANS ANYTHING, IT IS THE RIGHT OF THE INDIVIDUAL TO BE FREE FROM GOVERNMENT INTRUSION INTO MATTERS SO FUNDAMENTALLY AFFECTING A PERSON AS THE DECISION WHETHER TO BEAR OR BEGET A CHILD. THE OTHER SIDE LAUNCHES WELL-PLANNED ACTIONS OUTSIDE ABORTION CLINICS, USING TACTICS OF NONVIOLENT RESISTANCE TO BLOCK ACCESS AND ACTIVE INTERVENTION TO PERSUADE WOMEN ON THEIR WAY TO GETTING ABORTIONS TO RECONSIDER. THE NECESSITY OF COMMUNICATION ABOUT ABORTION IS CALLED FOR.

03379 GAN, H.J.
CHAPTER 6: INDIVIDUALISM AND LIBERAL DEMOCRACY
FREE PRESS, NEW YORK, NY, 1988, 121-156.
THIS CHAPTER SUGGESTS THAT A DIFFERENT APPROACH TO DEMOCRACY IS REQUIRED: ONE THAT MAKES IT POSSIBLE FOR POLITICAL INSTITUTION TO ACCEPT, AND ADAPT TO, POPULAR INDIVIDUALISM. IT GIVES FIVE PROPOSALS FOR ENHANCING REPRESENTATION AND TALKS ABOUT USER-FRIENDLY GOVERNMENT. IT EXAMINES "NONPOLITICAL" REPRESENTATION AND THE FAILURE OF LIBERAL DEMOCRACY. LIBERAL DEMOCRACY AND THE UNDERCLASS, THE ROLE OF LIBERALS AND THE NEED FOR A VISION OF LIBERAL DEMOCRACY ARE EACH EXPLORED.

03380 GANDASEGUI, M.A.; PRIESTLY, G.
POLITICAL CRISIS AND ECONOMIC AGGRESSION
CENTRAL AMERICA BULLETIN, 8(3) (FEB 89), 1-3, 6-8.

THE AUTHORS STUDY THE POLITICAL AND ECONOMIC ORIGINS OF THE CURRENT CRISIS IN PANAMA AND THE EXTENT TO WHICH U.S. ECONOMIC SACTIONS HAVE AGGRAVATED THE SITUATION. THEY CONCLUDE THAT REAGAN ADMINISTRATION DISAGREEMENTS WITH GENERAL NORIEGA HAVE HAD LITTLE TO DO WITH DRUGS AND MUCH TO DO WITH THE OVERALL U.S. STRATEGY IN CENTRAL AMERICA.

03381 GANDASEGUI, M.A.; PRIESTLY, G.
U.S. ECONOMIC SANCTIONS: AGGRESSION AND ITS CONSEQUENCES
CENTRAL AMERICA BULLETIN, 8(4) (MAR 89), 4-7.
THE AUTHORS ANALYZE THE REASONS FOR, AND CONSEQUENCES OF, THE IMPOSITION OF ECONOMIC SANCTIONS ON PANAMA BY THE UNITED STATES. THEY SHOW THAT WHILE U.S. ECONOMIC SANCTIONS HAVE SEVERELY DAMAGED THE PANAMANIAN ECONOMY, THE ROOTS OF THE CRISIS LAY IN PANAMA'S MODEL OF ECONOMIC DEVELOPMENT.

03382 GANG, G.
IMPLEMENTING THE POLICY OF "ONE COUNTRY, TWO SYSTEMS"
BEIJING REVIEW, 32(52) (DEC 89), 16-20.
DESPITE THE RECENT CLAMOR FROM THE BRITISH WHO WANT TO INTERNATIONALIZE THE HONG KONG ISSUE, THE BASIC PREREQUISITE FOR MAINTAINING LONG-TERM STABILITY AND PROSPERITY IN HONG KONG IS TO SEEK THE COMMON GROUND OF "ONE COUNTRY" AND PRESERVE THE DIFFERENCES OF "TWO SYSTEM." THIS IS THE KEY TO THE FORMULA FOR THE SUCCESSFUL REUNIFICATION OF HONG KONG AND COMMUNIST CHINA.

03383 GANG, Y.
WORLD IMPACT OF SINO-SOVIET NORMALIZATION
BEIJING REVIEW, 32(19) (MAY 89), 14-17.
THE UPCOMING SUMMIT BETWEEN CHINA AND THE SOVIET UNION WILL MARK THE BEGINNING OF THE NORMALIZATION OF THEIR RELATIONS, WHICH SHOULD BRING MULTIPLE BENEFITS TO THE TWO COUNTRIES AND THE REST OF THE WORLD. NORMALIZATION WILL PROMOTE THE RELAXATION OF TENSIONS, STABILITY, AND THE ESTABLISHMENT OF A NEW INTERNATIONAL POLITICAL ORDER.

03384 GANGULT, S.
THE SINO-INDIAN BORDER TALKS, 1981-1989: A VIEW FROM NEW DELHI
ASIAN SURVEY, XXIX(12) (DEC 89), 1123-1135.
CONCENTRATING ON THE PAST DECADE, THE ARTICLE ANALYZES THE BORDER TALKS HELD BETWEEN CHINA AND INDIA. IT EXAMINES THE BACKGROUND OF THE UNDERLYING CONFLICT BEGINNING WITH THE WAR IN 1962, AND FOLLOWS THE DEVELOPMENT OF RELATIONS UP TO THE PRESENT. IT CONCLUDES THAT CHINA HAS MADE THE MAJORITY OF THE INITIATIVES AND THAT THERE IS CONSIDERABLE DIVISION WITHIN THE INDIAN EXTERNAL AFFAIRS MINISTRY ABOUT HOW TO SETTLE THE DISPUTE.

03385 GANGULY, S.
OF GREAT EXPECTATIONS AND BITTER DISAPPOINTMENTS: INDO-US RELATIONS UNDER THE JOHNSON ADMINISTRATION
ASIAN AFFAIRS, AN AMERICAN REVIEW, 15(4) (WIN 89), 212-219.
THE PAPER EXAMINES THREE IMPORTANT EVENTS THAT HAD A PROFOUND IMPACT ON THE COURSE OF INDO-US RELATIONS. THESE ARE THE INDO-PAKISTANI WAR OF 1965, THE RUPEE DEVALUATION OF 1966, AND THE "SELF HELP/SHORT TETHER" AGRICULTURAL POLICIES OF THE JOHNSON ADMINISTRATION. THE PAPER ELABORATES ON THE WAY IN WHICH FUNDAMENTAL DIVERGENCE IN ROLE CONCEPTIONS AFFECTED INDO-US RELATIONS. IT ALSO SPELLS OUT THE INFERENCES THAT INDIAN DECISIONMAKERS DREW FROM THESE EPISODES AND ATTEMPTS TO SHOW HOW THEY COLLECTIVELY CONTRIBUTED TO A DECLINE IN INDO-US RELATIONS.

03386 GANS, H.J.
CHAPTER 1: POPULAR INDIVIDUALISM; MIDDLE AMERICAN INDIVIDUALISM
FREE PRESS NEW YORK, NY, 1988, 1-22.
THIS CHAPTER DEFINES POPULAR INDIVIDUALISM AND EXPLORES THE DESIRE FOR PERSONAL CONTROL. IT IDENTIFIES MIDDLE AMERICANS AND EXPLORES EDUCATION, OCCUPATION, INCOME AND SOCIAL CLASS. IT EXPLORES POPULAR INDIVIDUALISM AS HISTORICAL PROCESS WITH EMPHASIS ON THE POST-WORLD WAR ERA. RISING INCOME, POSTWAR SUBURBANIZATION, "SINGLES", LOOSENING OF TIES TO TRADITIONAL INSTITUTIONS, POLITICAL PROCESS AND CHANGE IN THE NUCLEAR FAMILY ARE EACH EXAMINED.

03387 GANS, H.J.
CHAPTER 2: SOME ECONOMIC AND POLITICAL VALUES; MIDDLE AMERICAN INDIVIDUALISM
FREE PRESS NEW YORK, NY, 1988, 23-42.
THIS CHAPTER EXAMINES HOW MIDDLE AMERICANS MANEUVER IN THE ECONOMY AND DEAL WITH THE GOVERNMENT AGENCIES THAT AFFECT THEIR LIVES. THE PARADOX OF THE DESIRE FOR MORE SERVICES AND LOWER TAXES WHICH REFLECTS A BUILT-IN AMBIVALENCE ABOUT GOVERNMENT AND PRIVATE ECONOMY IS EXPLORED. ALSO ADDRESSED ARE: JOBS, WEALTH, TAXES, THE PROS AND CONS OF PUBLIC SERVICES, THE GOVERNMENT AS THE GUARDIAN OF ECONOMIC SECURITY, AND IDEALISM IN MIDDLE AMERICAN INDIVIDUALISM.

03388 GANS, H.J.
CHAPTER 3: ORGANIZATIONAL AVOIDANCE; MIDDLE AMERICAN INDIVIDUALISM
FREE PRESS, NEW YORK, NY, 1988, 43-66.
THIS CHAPTER ADDRESSES THE VALUES WITH WHICH MIDDLE AMERICANS JUDGE GOVERNMENT AND BUSINESS AND WHICH ARE CONNECTED TO THE STRUCTURE OF THEIR LIVES. IT NOTES THAT MIDDLE AMERICANS ARE LIKELY TO FOLLOW A PATTERN OF ORGANIZATIONAL AVOIDANCE. IT STUDIES INFORMAL GROUPS AND FORMAL ORGANIZATIONS; ACCEPTABLE, UNAVOIDABLE AND AVOIDABLE ORGANIZATIONS; THE MORAL THEMES EXPRESSED BY NIGHT TIME SOAPS; AND MIDDLE AMERICA'S DISTANCE FROM THE LARGER SOCIETY. PATRIOTISM AND MICROSOCIETY AND MACROSOCIETY ARE EXAMINED AND EXPLORED.

03389 GANS, H.J.
CHAPTER 4: POLITICAL PARTICIPATION AND REPRESENTATION; MIDDLE AMERICAN INDIVIDUALISM
FREE PRESS, NEW YORK, NY, 1988, 67-97.
THIS CHAPTER DEALS WITH MIDDLE AMERICAN APATHY TOWARDS PARTICIPATION IN THE POLITICAL PROCESS. IT PRESENTS VARIETIES OF PARTICIPATION AND DESCRIBES UNUSUAL MOTIVES AND UNUSUAL PEOPLE IN RELATION TO POLITICAL ACTIVITY. DISCUSSED IS RESPONSIVENESS AND REPRESENTATION AS A SUBSTITUTE FOR PARTICIPATION. THE QUALITY OF REPRESENTATION IS DISCUSSED AS WELL AS SOCIAL DECENTRALIZATION AND ORGANIZATIONAL CENTRALIZATION.

03390 GANS, H.J.
CHAPTER 5: INDIVIDUALISM, COMMUNITY, AND SOCIETY; MIDDLE AMERICAN INDIVIDUALISM
FREE PRESS, NEW YORK, NY, 1988, 98-120.
THIS CHAPTER EXPLORES THE CRITICISMS OF INDIVIDUALISM AND THE NEED FOR COMMUNAL CONCERNS. IT ALSO EXPLORES THE SHARP DISAGREEMENT BY ADVOCATES OF COMMUNAL VALUES ABOUT THE NATURE OF THAT COMMUNITY. IT CRITIQUES FIVE TYPES OF INDIVIDUALISM AND GIVES A DEFENSE OF POPULAR INDIVIDUALISM. IT REVISITS THE COMMUNAL CRITIQUE AND EXAMINES INDIVIDUALISM AND SOCIETY.

03391 GANS, H.J.
MIDDLE AMERICAN INDIVIDUALISM
FREE PRESS NEW YORK, NY, 1988, 156.
THIS BOOK DEALS WITH SOME FUNDAMENTALS OF AMERICAN LIFE ABOUT ONE OF THE COUNTRY'S BASIC VALUES: INDIVIDUALISM, AS PURSUED BY THE BLUE, WHITE, PINK AND NEWCOLLAR WORKERS CALLED MIDDLE AMERICANS, ITS PURPOSE IS TO UNDERSTAND MIDDLE AMERICANS, AND TO DEFEND THEIR INDIVIDUALISM BY SHOWING HOW LITTLE IT HAS IN COMMON WITH THE INDIVIDUALISM OF CORPORATE AND ENTREPRENEURIAL CAPITALISTS, IT DEFENDS MIDDLE AMERICANS AND ALSO IDENTIFIES THE ECONOMIC AND POLITICAL PROBLEMS CAUSED BY THEM. IT ENDS WITH A NUMBER OF SUGGESTIONS FOR IMPROVING AMERICAN DEMOCRACY, AS WELL AS FOR A WELFARE STATE SUFFICIENTLY EGALITARIAN TO OFFER ECONOMIC SECURITY TO ALL AMERICANS.

03392 GARCIA Y. GRIEGO, L.M.
THE BRACERO POLICY EXPERIMENT: US-MEXICAN RESPONSE TO MEXICAN LABOR MIGRATION, 1942-1955
DISSERTATION ABSTRACTS INTERNATIONAL, 49(7) (JAN 89), 1950-A.
THE AUTHOR REVIEWS THE POLICY RESPONSES OF THE US AND MEXICAN GOVERNMENTS TO MEXICAN LABOR MIGRATION DURING THE PERIOD OF EXPERIMENTATION LEADING UP TO 1955. HE STUDIES HOW EACH GOVERNMENT ESTABLISHED AND PURSUED ITS POLICY OBJECTIVES, THE NATURE OF THE DIFFERENCES WITHIN AND BETWEEN THEM, THE NEGOTIATION PROCESS, THE PLANNING AND EXECUTION OF UNILATERAL ACTION, AND THE POLICY OUTCOMES.

03393 GARCIA, A.M.
THE DEVELOPMENT OF CHICANA FEMINIST DISCOURSE, 1970-1980
GENDER AND SOCIETY, 3(2) (JUN 89), 217-238.
THE DECADE FROM 1970 TO 1980 REPRESENTED A FORMATIVE PERIOD IN THE DEVELOPMENT OF CHICANA FEMINIST THOUGHT IN THE UNITED STATES. DURING THIS PERIOD, CHICANA FEMINISTS ADDRESSED THE SPECIFIC ISSUES AFFECTING THEM AS WOMEN OF COLOR. THEY DEVELOPED AN IDEOLOGICAL DISCOURSE THAT ADDRESSED THREE MAJOR ISSUES: THE RELATIONSHIP BETWEEN CHICANA FEMINISM AND THE IDEOLOGY OF CULTURAL NATIONALISM, FEMINIST BAITING WITHIN THE CHICANO MOVEMENT, AND THE RELATIONSHIP BETWEEN THE CHICANA AND THE WHITE FEMINIST MOVEMENTS. THIS ESSAY DESCRIBES THE DEVELOPMENT OF CHICANA FEMINISM AND COMPARES IT WITH ASIAN AMERICAN AND BLACK FEMINISM.

03394 GARDNER, L.B.
THE CHARACTER AND FORCE OF FEDERAL INCENTIVES AND DISINCENTIVES TO PARTICIPATE IN THE BIOMEDICAL TECHNOLOGY INNOVATION PROCESS
DISSERTATION ABSTRACTS INTERNATIONAL, 49(7) (JAN 89), 1956-A.
THE AUTHOR IDENTIFIES AND CHARACTERIZES SOME OF THE INCENTIVES AND DISINCENTIVES THE FEDERAL GOVERNMENT OFFERS TO INDUSTRY TO COMMERCIALIZE RESEARCH EFFORTS IN BIOMEDICAL TECHNOLOGY. SHE DOCUMENTS AND EVALUATES EIGHT ATTEMPTS TO OBTAIN FEDERAL FUNDING FOR BIOMEDICAL TECHNOLOGY INNOVATIONS

THROUGH THE SMALL BUSINESS INNOVATION PROGRAM AT NIH.

03395 GARDNER, R.; GATI, T.T.; ISRAELYAN, V.; KREMENYUK, V.;
LEONARD, J.; LUCK, E.; PLEKHANOV, S.
SUPERPOWER COOPERATION IN THE U.N.: DREAM OR REALITY
FREEDOM AT ISSUE, (111) (NOV 89), 12-20.
THIS IS AN EDITED TRANSCRIPT OF A ROUNDTABLE DISCUSSION
BY EXPERTS ON THE UNITED NATIONS FROM THE U.N. ASSOCIATION
OF THE UNITED STATES OF AMERICA AND THE SOVIET U.N.
ASSOCIATION. THE GROUP MET IN MOSCOW IN 1989 TO DISCUSS THE
FUTURE OF THE U.N. THE AGENDA INCLUDED ISSUES OF PEACE AND
SECURITY, ARMS CONTROL, U.N. REFORM, THE ENVIRONMENT, HUMAN
RIGHTS, AND INTERNATIONAL ECONOMICS.

03396 GARFINKEL, A.
A POSITIVE ANALYSIS OF MACROECONOMIC POLICY AND
INTERNATIONAL CONFLICT
DISSERTATION ABSTRACTS INTERNATIONAL, 49(8) (FEB 89),
2316-A.
MACROECONOMIC POLICY CAN ONLY BE UNDERSTOOD WITHIN A
GENERAL EQUILIBRIUM CONTEXT IN WHICH THERE IS ACTUAL
CONFLICT OR POTENTIAL FOR CONFLICT AMONG NATIONS. THE AUTHOR
BEGINS BY DEVELOPING A POSITIVE, ECONOMIC THEORY OF MILITARY
SPENDING. THEN SHE CONSIDERS THE INTRODUCTION OF A MILITARY
DRAFT INTO THE THEORY OF OPTIMAL FISCAL POLICY. FINALLY, SHE
SHOWS HOW GOVERNMENTS ACTING OPTIMALLY COULD EMPLOY
FINANCIAL WARFARE PRIOR TO ACTUAL WAR IF THE ENEMY
GOVERNMENT HAS FAILED TO IMMUNIZE ITS FINANCIAL INSTITUTIONS
AGAINST SUCH POLICIES.

03397 GARFINKLE, A.
PLUS CA CHANGE - IN THE MIDDLE EAST
WORLD AFFAIRS, 151(1) (SUM 88), 3-16.
IF THE NEW U.S. ADMINISTRATION CAN DISTINGUISH THE REAL
CHANGES FROM THE APPARENT ONES, IT WILL UNDERSTAND THAT THE
ROAD AHEAD IN THE MIDDLE EAST IS ROCKY BUT, ULTIMATELY,
PASSABLE WITH ENOUGH PATIENCE AND TOLERANCE FOR FRUSTRATION.
CERTAINLY, THINGS ARE MORE FLUID NOW THAN A YEAR AGO, AND
FLUIDITY MEANS OPPORTUNITY. IF IT CAN'T DISTINGUISH, IT WILL
MORE LIKELY SPEED OFF THE ROAD AT THE NEXT SHARP CURVE,
AIDED, NO DOUBT, BY AN OIL SLICK LAID DOWN BY THE PLO. IT
WOULDN'T BE THE FIRST TIME; THE CARTER ADMINISTRATION ERRED
SIMILARLY IN 1977 AND EARLY 1978 AND WAS SAVED FROM IGNOMINY
ONLY BY ANWAR SADAT'S UNUSUAL AMALGAM OF DESPERATION AND
COURAGE.

03398 GARFINKLE, A.M.
THE ATTACK ON DETERRENCE: REFLECTIONS ON MORALITY AND
STRATEGIC PRAXIS
JOURNAL OF STRATEGIC STUDIES, 12(2) (JUN 89), 166-199.
THE AUTHOR CONSIDERS CURRENT ATTITUDES TOWARD DETERRENCE
AND ARGUMENTS OVER ITS EFFECTIVENESS.

03399 GARMENT, S.
THE TOWER PRECEDENT
COMMENTARY, 89(5) (MAY 89), 42-48.
THE AUTHOR REVIEWS THE CONTROVERSY OVER GEORGE BUSH'S
NOMINATION OF JOHN TOWER TO BE SECRETARY OF DEFENSE AND
COMPARES IT TO ROBERT BORK'S NOMINATION TO THE SUPREME COURT.

03400 GARNETT, H.; MERRILL, S.; MILLER, J.D.
URBANIZATION IN AFRICAN DEVELOPMENT: ISSUES AND
OPPORTUNITIES
AVAILABLE FROM NTIS, NO. PB89-159073/GAR, MAR 88, 63.
THE PAPER CONTRIBUTES TO THE FORMULATION OF AN A.I.D.
URBAN POLICY FOR AFRICA. A COMMITMENT TO A CONSCIOUS URBAN
POLICY CALLS FOR EXPANDING THE ARRAY OF A.I.D. COUNTERPARTS
WITHIN THE PUBLIC, PRIVATE, AND INFORMAL SECTORS IN CITIES
AND TOWNS WHO PROVIDE CREDIT, LAND, AND INFRASTRUCTURE TO
LOW-INCOME FAMILIES. THE PAPER ADDRESSES THE PHYSICAL AND
SPATIAL ASPECTS OF ECONOMIC AND SOCIAL DEVELOPMENT
ACTIVITIES. IT SUGGESTS POLICIES FOR MANAGING THE GROWTH OF
CITIES AND TOWNS SO THAT THEY CAN SUPPORT AND SUSTAIN THEIR
OWN DEVELOPMENT. IT EXAMINES THE INSTITUTIONS THAT MUST BE
INTEGRAL TO THAT PROCESS. AND, IT CALLS FOR SUPPORT THROUGH
POLICY DIALOGUE, TRAINING IN DECENTRALIZED DECISION-MAKING,
AND IMPROVED MANAGEMENT OF LOCAL GOVERNMENTS.

03401 GARRETT, B. N.; GLASER, B. S.
CHINESE ASSESSMENTS OF GLOBAL TRENDS AND THE EMERGING ERA
IN INTERNATIONAL RELATIONS
ASIAN SURVEY, XXIX(4) (APR 89), 347-362.
AS A CONSEQUENCE OF CHINESE ANALYSTS' ASSESSMENTS OF
EMERGING GLOBAL TRENDS AND THE REQUIREMENTS OF THE NEW ERA,
BEIJING WILL LIKELY SEE A DIMINISHING NEED FOR ANTI-SOVIET
STRATEGIC COOPERATION WITH THE UNITED STATES. THE SOVIET
THREAT TO CHINA AND TO INTERNATIONAL STABILITY IS PERCEIVED
AS LIKELY TO CONTINUE TO DECLINE AS A RESULT OF THE
SUSTAINABILITY OF WASHINGTON'S ADVANTAGE OVER MOSCOW IN THE
U.S.-SOVIET BALANCE OF POWER AND CONTINUED SOVIET
PREOCCUPATION WITH INTERNAL REFORM AND THE EASING OF
EXTERNAL RELATIONS. AT THE SAME TIME, HOWEVER, CHINESE
PREDICTIONS OF INTENSIFYING ECONOMIC AND TECHNOLOGICAL
COMPETITION IN THE NEW ERA AND GROWING CONCERN THAT BEIJING

MAY FAIL TO NARROW THE GAP WITH THE WEST ARE LIKELY TO
INCREASE THE IMPORTANCE OF SINO-AMERICAN RELATIONS TO CHINA
IN THE COMING DECADE.

03402 GARRETT, G.; LANGE, P.
GOVERNMENT PARTISANSHIP AND ECONMIC PERFORMANCE: WHEN AND
HOW DOES "WHO GOVERNS" MATTER?
THE JOURNAL OF POLITICS, 51(3) (AUG 89), .
THIS ARTICLE RESPONDS TO JACKMAN'S CENTRAL THEORETICAL
AND EMPIRICAL CRITICISMS OF THE AUTHOR'S RESEARCH. IT
CONTENDS THAT THE POLICY CONVERGENCE THESIS IS FAR LESS
PERSUASIVE THAN JACKMAN ASSERTS, AND ALSO THAT HIS EMPIRICAL
TESTS ARE NOT VERY CONCLUSIVE. THIS STUDY INCLUDES THE
NORWEGIAN OUTLIER AND HENCE THE DATA IS MORE SUPPORTIVE OF
THE WRITER'S THESIS IT IS SUGGESTED THAT A POOLED TIME
SERIES, CROSS-SECTION DESIGN MAY PROVIDE BETTER TESTS FOR
THEIR ARGUMENT THAN THOSE PRESENTLY IN DEBATE.

03403 GARRETT, W.R.
RELIGION IN CHINA
THE CHRISTIAN CENTURY, 106(24) (AUG 89), 748-749.
THE STATUS OF RELIGION IN CHINA WHICH WILL INEVITABLY BE
AFFECTED BY THE OUTCOME OF THE COUNTRY'S CURRENT POLITICAL
CRISIS IS EXAMINED IN THIS ARTICLE. THE AUTHOR SURVEYS AND
EVALUATS CHINA'S RELIGIOUS SCENE. IT REMAINS TO BE SEEN
WHETHER FALLOUT FROM EFFORTS TO CRUSH THE STUDENT'S CAMPAIGN
FOR DEMOCRACY WILL CAUSE A NEW ROUND OF RELIGIOUS
PERSECUTION.

03404 GARRIS, E.
LIBERTARIANS BELONG IN THE GOP
REASON, 20(10) (MAR 89), 27-28.
THE NEW RIGHT IS LEADING THE FIGHT TO PLACE SOCIAL
INTOLERANCE AND REVIVAL OF THE COLD WAR AT THE TOP OF THE
GOP AGENDA. SUCH A MOVE WOULD NARROW THE PARTY'S APPEAL BY
EXCLUDING THE KEY TO THE NEW REPUBLICAN MAJORITY.
LIBERTARIANS ARE IN A UNIQUE POSITION TO PUSH FORWARD THE
POLITICAL REALIGNMENT THAT BEGAN WITH THE REAGAN ELECTION OF
1980 AND REDIRECT THE PARTY TO ITS HISTORIC ROOTS AS A PARTY
OF INDIVIDUAL RIGHTS.

03405 GARST, H.D.
CAPITALISM AND LIBERAL DEMOCRACY: STATE STRUCTURES IN
BRITAIN AND GERMANY PRIOR TO WORLD WAR I
DISSERTATION ABSTRACTS INTERNATIONAL, 49(9) (MAR 89),
2795-A.
THE AUTHOR EXAMINES THE INTERPLAY BETWEEN CAPITALISM AND
LIBERAL DEMOCRACY IN BRITAIN AND GERMANY IN THE DECADES
IMMEDIATELY PRIOR TO WORLD WAR I. WHILE BRITAIN HAS BEEN
SEEN AS THE POLITICAL MODEL FOLLOWED BY OTHER CAPITALIST
DEMOCRACIES, GERMANY HAS BEEN VIEWED AS A PECULIAR AND
DEVIANT CASE WHERE THE FAILURE OF STRONG LIBERAL DEMOCRATIC
INSTITUTIONS IS ATTRIBUTED TO PRE-INDUSTRIAL FEUDAL
STRUCTURES. THE AUTHOR CHALLENGES THIS INTERPRETATION OF THE
ANGLO-GERMAN COUPLET.

03406 GARTEN, J.E.
JAPAN AND GERMANY: AMERICAN CONCERNS
FOREIGN AFFAIRS, 68(5) (WIN 90), 84-101.
THE RELATIONSHIPS BETWEEN THE USA AND JAPAN AND GERMANY
ARE CHANGING DRAMATICALLY. IN THE 1990'S, ECONOMIC PRESSURES
ARE LIKELY TO BE THE MAJOR FACTOR RESHAPING TIES AMONG THE
THREE NATIONS. TOKYO AND BONN COULD PRESENT WASHINGTON WITH
ALMOST INTRACTABLE PROBLEMS DERIVING FROM THEIR DOMESTIC
DRIVES AND, IN SOME IMPORTANT CASES, THEIR INTERESTS COULD
CONVERGE IN OPPOSITION TO AMERICA'S NEEDS. THIS COMBINED
CHALLENGE SHOULD LEAD AS QUICKLY AS POSSIBLE TO SERIOUS SOUL-
SEARCHING IN THE BUSH ADMINISTRATION AND CONGRESS.

03407 GARTEN, J.E.
TRADING BLOCS AND THE EVOLVING WORLD ECONOMY
CURRENT HISTORY, 88(534) (JAN 89), 15-16, 54-56.
THE AUTHOR DISCUSSES THE GROWING INFLUENCE OF THE MULTI-
NATIONAL TRADING BLOCS, OR "SUPERBLOCS," IN NORTH AMERICA,
WESTERN EUROPE, AND EAST ASIA ON GLOBAL ECONOMICS AND UNITED
STATES FOREIGN POLICY. HE WARNS THAT THE EVOLUTION OF
REGIONAL SUPERBLOCS HAS THE POTENTIAL TO DIVIDE THE WESTERN
ALLIANCE.

03408 GARTHOFF, R.
REFLECTIONS OF AN AMERICAN
INTERNATIONAL AFFAIRS (MOSCOW), (8) (AUG 89), 70-77.
THE AUTHOR, WHO IS A POLITICAL SCIENTIST AND DIPLOMAT,
EVALUATES THE PROSPECTS FOR FUTURE PROGRESS IN U.S.-SOVIET
RELATIONS AND SPECULATES ABOUT HOW A CHANGE IN U.S.
LEADERSHIP COULD AFFECT THEM. HE SEES A CRUCIAL NEED FOR NEW
THINKING IN BOTH COUNTRIES AND FOR EACH SIDE TO RE-EVALUATE
ITS PERCEPTION OF THE THREAT FROM THE OTHER SIDE.

03409 GARVER, J.
THE "NEW TYPE" OF SINO-SOVIET RELATIONS
ASIAN SURVEY, XXIX(12) (DEC 89), 1136-1155.
VISIT OF SOVIET LEADER MIKHAIL GORBACHEV TO CHINA IN MAY
1989 SIGNALED THE END OF TWO DECADES OF SINO-SOVIET

HOSTILITY. THE ARTICLE ANALYZES THE ORIGINS OF THIS
HOSTILITY AND THE CHANGING CONDITIONS THAT HAVE ALLOWED FOR
THE GRADUAL IMPROVEMENT IN RELATIONS. KEY OBSTACLES TO SINO-
SOVIET RAPPROACHMENT INCLUDE DISAGREEMENT OVER CAMBODIA AND
CHINA'S DESIRE TO MAINTAIN ECONOMIC TIES WITH THE US AND
JAPAN. IN ADDITION, THE BRUTAL REPRESSION IF STUDENT
PROTESTS IN TIANANMEN SQUARE HAS INCREASED TENSION BETWEEN
CHINA AND THE SOVIET UNION. THE ARTICLE CONCLUDES THAT
ALTHOUGH RELATIONS ARE LIKELY TO CONTINUE TO IMPROVE, A FULL
SCALE ALLIANCE IS UNLIKELY AT PRESENT.

03410 GARVEY, J.
     GUARDING OLD GLORY
     COMMONWEAL, CXVI(14) (AUG 89), 423-424.
        IF GEORGE BUSH'S MOVE FOR A CONSTITUTIONAL AMENDMENT TO
     PROTECT THE FLAG FROM THOSE VERY FEW PEOPLE WHO WANT TO BURN
     IT PASSES, IT COULD HAVE TERRIBLE CONSTITUTIONAL CONSQUENCES.
     THE EROSION OF THE BILL OF RIGHTS SHOULD NOT BE TAKEN
     LIGHTLY.

03411 GARVEY, J.
     OFFENSIVE DEFENDERS
     COMMONWEAL, CXVI(6) (MAR 89), 166-168.
        THE AUTHOR LOOKS AT THE AYATOLLAH KHOMEINI'S REACTION TO
     SALMAN RUSHDIE'S "THE SATANIC VERSES." HE NOTES THAT
     HOJATOLISLAM HASHEMI RAFSANJANI STATED THAT THE AYATOLLAH'S
     ORDER TO MURDER RUSHDIE SHOULD NOT BE BLAMED ON IRAN'S
     GOVERNMENT, AN APPARENT ATTEMPT TO DISTINGUISH BETWEEN ON
     ACT OF STATE AND RELIGIOUS FANATICISM.

03412 GARVEY, J.
     RULES OF THE GAME: DEMOCRACY AND ITS LIMITS
     COMMONWEAL, CXVI(22) (DEC 89), 697-698.
        THE MOVEMENT AWAY FROM COMMUNISM AND TOWARD DEMOCRACY IN
     EASTERN EUROPE BRINGS BOTH HOPE AND UNCERTAINTY. IT SHOULD
     BE REMEMBERED THAT THE UGLY AS WELL AS THE GOOD HAS BEEN
     SUPPRESSES. NOT ONLY IS DEMOCRACY ON THE RISE NOW; SO ARE
     RENEWED INTI-SEMITISM IN SOME GROUPS, NATIONALISM IN ITS
     NARROWEST FORM, AND OLD ETHNIC AND RELIGIOUS CONFLICTS.

03413 GASARASI, C.P.
     THE EFFECT OF AFRICA'S EXILES/REFUGEES UPON INTER-AFRICAN
     STATE RELATIONS: CONFLICT AND COOPERATION, 1958-1988
     DISSERTATION ABSTRACTS INTERNATIONAL, 50($) (OCT 89),
     1076-A.
        THE TRANS-BORDER MOVEMENTS AND ACTIVITIES OF AFRICA'S
     EXILES/REFUGEES HAVE SIGNIFICANTLY AFFECTED INTER-AFRICAN
     STATE RELATIONS, AS EVIDENCED BY THE PREPONDERANCE OF
     CONCERN WITHIN AFRICAN STATES THAT THEIR NATIONAL SECURITY
     IS THREATENED BY SUBVERSION BY THEIR NATIONALS ENJOYING
     ASYLUM IN OTHER STATES. THE EROSION OF GENEROUS ASYLUM
     POLICIES IS OCCURRING IN THE AFRICAN STATES, BUT A MORE
     DURABLE SOLUTION WOULD BE THE CREATION OF A FEDERATED STATES
     OF AFRICA, WHICH WOULD RENDER THE PRESENT NATIONAL
     BOUNDARIES OBSOLETE ALONG WITH THE EXILE/REFUGEE STATUS THEY
     CONFER.

03414 GASH, N.
     REFLECTIONS ON THE REVOLUTION
     NATIONAL REVIEW, XLI(13) (JUL 89), 35-38.
        IN THIS ARTICLE, THE AUTHOR CONSIDERS THE FRENCH
     REVOLUTION AS A CATALYST OF THE RISE OF EGALITARIANISM AND
     THE INTERVENTIONIST STATE. HE POSITS THAT THAT THE
     REVOLUTION WAS A SUMMATION OF THE PREVIOUS CENTURY OF
     POLITICAL THOUGHT, AND THE PRECURSOR OF THE NEXT TWO
     CENTURIES OF POLITICAL TURMOIL.

03415 GASPERINI, W.
     PARAGUAY: POST-COUP VOTE
     THIRD WORLD WEEK, 8(9) (APR 89), 69-70.
        ON MAY 1, 1989, PARAGUAYANS WILL ELECT A PRESIDENT AND A
     BICAMERAL CONGRESS. THE PROJECTED PRESIDENTIAL WINNER IS
     GENERAL ANDRES RODRIGUEZ. AS LEADER OF THE COUP THAT OUSTED
     ALFREDO STROESSNER, RODRIGUEZ IS ALREADY CHIEF OF STATE AND
     CONTROLS THE ARMED FORCES. HE ALSO ENJOYS SUPPORT FROM
     ELEMENTS OF THE RULING COLORADO PARTY, WHICH HAS LONG
     DOMINATED PARAGUAY'S ELECTORAL MACHINERY

03416 GASTIL, R.D.
     THE COMPARATIVE SURVEY OF FREEDOM: 1989
     FREEDOM AT ISSUE, (106) (JAN 89), 46-59.
        THE AUTHOR SURVEYS THE PROGRESS TOWARD WORLD FREEDOM AND
     DEMOCRACY IN 1988, LOOKING AT THE CHANGES IN INDIVIDUAL
     COUNTRIES.

03417 GAT, A.
     CLAUSEWITZ'S POLITICAL AND ETHICAL WORLD VIEW
     POLITICAL STUDIES, XXXVII(1) (MAR 89), 97-106.
        THERE HAS BEEN A GREAT DEAL OF CONTROVERSY OVER THE
     PHILOSOPHICAL IMPLICATIONS OF PRUSSIAN MILITARY STRATEGIST
     KARL VON CLAUSEWITZ'S STUDIES OF WAR. THE PAPER CHALLENGES
     THE ACCEPTED OPINION THAT CLAUSEWITZ DID NOT DEAL WITH THE
     ETHICAL ASPECTS OF WAR. IT ARGUES THAT HIS WORKS DOCUMENT AN
     AWARENESS OF THE ETHICAL IMPLICATIONS OF WAR AS WELL AS A

COMPREHENSIVE OUTLOOK REGARDING THE NATURE OF BOTH
INTERNATIONAL RELATIONS AND THE STATE. IT ARGUES THAT THIS
OUTLOOK REFLECTED THE EMERGING WORLD VIEW IN THE GERMANY OF
NATIONAL AWAKENING.

03418 GATES, D.
     AMERICAN STRATEGIC BASES IN BRITAIN: THE AGREEMENTS
     GOVERNING THEIR USE
     COMPARATIVE STRATEGY, 8(1) (1989), 99-123.
        OF LATE, THE PRESENCE OF U.S. FORCES IN SEVERAL EUROPEAN
     STATES HAS COME UNDER SCRUTINY; GREECE, TURKEY, AND SPAIN
     HAVE ALL REVISED THE ACCORDS REGARDING AMERICAN USE OF BASES
     ON THEIR TERRITORY, AND, INDEED, SPAIN RECENTLY REQUESTED
     THAT A SUBSTANTIAL ELEMENT OF THE U.S. FORCES ON ITS SOIL BE
     WITHDRAWN. AFTER THE AMERICAN BOMBING OF LIBYA IN 1986, THE
     PRESENCE OF U.S. COMBAT UNITS IN THE U.K. HAS ALSO BECOME
     CONTROVERSIAL. THE CONCENTRATION OF AMERICAN BASES IN
     BRITAIN IS GREATER THAN IN ANY OTHER EUROPEAN STATE AND,
     FOLLOWING THE 1983 MONTEBELLO DECISION BY NATO DEFENSE
     MINISTERS TO MODERNIZE THEIR NUCLEAR FORCES AND THE RECENT
     AGREEMENT BETWEEN THE U.S. AND USSR ON INTERMEDIATE NUCLEAR
     FORCES, IT SEEMS PROBABLE THAT MORE AIR AND NAVAL UNITS
     COULD BE DEPLOYED THERE. YET THE UNDERSTANDINGS GOVERNING
     THE USE OF BRITISH BASES BY AMERICAN STRATEGIC UNITS SEEM
     DATED AND NEBULOUS. THIS PAPER EXAMINES HOW THEY EVOLVED AND
     WHAT THEIR MAIN PROVISIONS ARE AND ASKS IF THEY COULD OR
     SHOULD BE ALTERED AS MANY HAVE SUGGESTED.

03419 GATES, J.B.; COHEN, J.E.
     PRESIDENTIAL POLICY PREFERENCES AND SUPREME COURT
     APPOINTMENT SUCCESS
     POLICY STUDIES REVIEW, 8(4) (SUM 89), 800-811.
        PRESIDENTIAL APPOINTMENTS TO THE U.S. SUPREME COURT ARE
     MAJOR CONSTITUTIONAL EVENTS. FEW STUDIES ASSESS WHETHER THIS
     POLITICAL PROCESS BENEFITS PRESIDENTS WITH APPOINTMENT
     OPPORTUNITIES. THIS ARTICLE ESTIMATES THE POLICY SUCCESS OF
     PRESIDENTS SINCE EISENHOWER IN APPOINTING FAVORABLE JUSTICES
     ON THE RACIAL EQUALITY ISSUES. PREVIOUS RESEARCH USES THE
     PRESIDENT'S PARTY AFFILIATION AS AN INDIRECT MEASURE OF
     PRESIDENTIAL PREFERENCES. THIS RESEARCH EXAMINES THE
     PRESIDENT'S POLICY STANCE MORE DIRECTLY BY USING
     PRESIDENTIAL PUBLIC STATEMENTS ON RACIAL EQUALITY ISSUES. AN
     ISSUE-SPECIFIC MEASURE OF PRESIDENTIAL PREFERENCES SHOWS
     THAT PRESIDENTS HAVE BEEN MORE SUCCESSFUL IN APPOINTING LIKE-
     MINDED JUSTICES THAN RELIANCE ON PRESIDENTIAL PARTY WOULD
     SUGGEST. REGRESSION ESTIMATES OF THE JUSTICES AGGREGATE
     VOTING RECORD ON RACIAL EQUALITY CASES ARE ROBUST EVEN IN
     LIGHT OF OTHER CONTROLS. THE IMPLICATIONS FOR DEMOCRATIC
     THEORY AND FUTURE RESEARCH ARE DISCUSSED.

03420 GATES, R.M.
     AN OPPORTUNITY UNFULFILLED: THE USE AND PERCEPTION OF
     INTELLIGENCE AT THE WHITE HOUSE
     WASHINGTON QUARTERLY, 12(1) (WIN 89), 35-44.
        THE USEFULNESS OF THE CIA TO PRESIDENTS IN THAT AREA FOR
     WHICH THE CIA WAS PRIMARILY ESTABLISHED-COLLECTION,
     REPORTING, ANALYSIS, AND PRODUCTION OF INFORMATION-AT TIMES
     HAS SUFFERED BECAUSE OF SELF-IMPOSED ISOLATION BY CIA AND
     THE FREQUENT LACK OF TIME AND OFTEN OPPORTUNITY ON THE PART
     OF PRESIDENTS AND THEIR NATIONAL SECURITY TEAMS TO PLAY A
     CENTRAL ROLE IN DEVELOPING INTELLIGENCE POLICY AND STRATEGY.
     THE WHITE HOUSE AND THE INTELLIGENCE COMMUNITY NEED TO
     INTENSIFY THEIR EFFORTS TO ENSURE THAT INTELLIGENCE STRATEGY,
     INVESTMENT, AND POLICY ARE DRIVEN BY A GENUINELY NATIONAL
     PERSPECTIVE AND REQUIREMENTS. ONLY THUS CAN THE TWO
     INSTITUTIONS SEIZE THE OPPORTUNITY FURTHER TO IMPROVE
     INTELLIGENCE SUPPORT TO THE PRESIDENT AND, CONCOMITANTLY,
     BETTER SERVE THE POLICY-MAKING PROCESS.

03421 GATES, S.G.
     THE LIMITS OF CONDITIONALITY: AN EXAMINATION OF INDIVIDUAL
     INCENTIVES AND STRUCTURAL CONSTRAINTS
     DISSERTATION ABSTRACTS INTERNATIONAL, 50(6) (DEC 89),
     1787-A.
        THE AUTHOR DEVELOPS A GAME-THEORETIC MODEL TO STUDY THE
     INTERACTIONS BETWEEN A FOREIGN AID DONOR AND THE RECIPIENT
     WHEN AID IS GIVEN CONDITIONALLY. HE ALSO DEVELOPS AND
     APPLIES A FORMAL MODEL OF BUREAUCRATIC MANAGEMENT TO THE
     CASE OF PAKISTANI IRRIGATION POLICY REFORM. FINALLY, HE USES
     GAME THEORY TO STUDY THE FAILURE OF DONORS TO IMPLEMENT
     SANCTIONS AGAINST RECIPIENTS WHO REFUSE TO COMPLY WITH THE
     CONDITIONS SET FOR THE AID. REFORM IN PAKISTANI IRRIGATION
     POLICY AND U.S. NUCLEAR NONPROLIFERATION POLICY WITH RESPECT
     TO PAKISTAN ARE USED AS CASE STUDIES ON THE EFFECT OF USING
     SANCTIONS.

03422 GAUBATZ, K.T.
     CONSENSUS AND DISSENT: PUBLIC ATTITUDES ABOUT CRIMINAL
     JUSTICE
     DISSERTATION ABSTRACTS INTERNATIONAL, 50(6) (DEC 89),
     1787-A.
        THE AUTHOR EMPLOYS INTENSIVE INTERVIEWS WITH RESIDENTS
     OF OAKLAND, CALIFORNIA, TO PROBE PUBLIC ATTITUDES ABOUT
     CRIMINAL JUSTICE. THROUGH THE USE OF A SCREENING

QUESTIONNAIRE, TWO TYPES OF INTERVIEWEES WERE SELECTED: BELIEVERS (WHO WANT TO "GET TOUGH" ON CRIME) AND DISSENTERS (WHO QUESTION THE WISDOM OF A "GET TOUGH" APPROACH). FOUR MAJOR ANALYTICAL AVENUES ARE PURSUED: THE CONTENT OF THE PARTICIPANTS' VIEWS, THE MOTIVATIONS BENEATH THEIR VIEWS, AN EXPLANATION FOR THE DIVERGENT VIEWS, AND THE STRUCTURE OF THE PARTICIPANTS' VIEWS.

03423 GAUBLEAU, J.J.
FORWARD, TOWARDS LENIN
WORLD MARXIST REVIEW, 32(10) (OCT 89), 48-50.
THIS ARTICLE ADDRESSES THE QUESTION OF WHAT FRENCH COMMUNISTS HAVE DONE IN THE PAST FEW YEARS TO HELP THE YOUNGER GENERATION MASTER LENIN'S METHODOLOGY IN THE LIGHT OF THE REALITIES OF THE LATE 20TH CENTURY. IT EXAMINES THE WRITINGS OF HELENE CARRERE D'ENCAUSE, ALAIN BESANCON AND DOMINIQUE COLAS, AND ALSO ANALYSES LENIN'S OWN IDEAS.

03424 GAUHAR, A.
MANLEY RIDES THE NEW WAVE
SOUTH, (105) (JUL 89), 10-11.
AFTER NEARLY A DECADE AS LEADER OF THE OPPOSITION, MICHAEL MANLEY HAS RETURNED TO THE OFFICE OF PRIME MINISTER OF JAMAICA. HIS POLITICAL BELIEFS AND OBJECTIVES ARE UNCHANGED, BUT HE HAS REVISED HIS VIEW OF THE WORLD ECONOMY AND HAS RE-THOUGHT JAMAICA'S ECONOMIC POLICY.

03425 GAUHAR, A.
TIME TO COME CLEAN
SOUTH, (104) (JUN 89), 10.
NORWEGIAN PRIME MINISTER GRO HARLEM BRUNDTLAND HAS DEVOTED HERSELF TO PERSUADING THE INDUSTRIALIZED WORLD THAT THE ENVIRONMENT CANNOT BE PRESERVED UNLESS PROVERTY, HUNGER, AND DISEASE ARE ELIMINATED. BRUNDTLAND'S CONCERNS ARE SHARED BY THIRD WORLD LEADERS WHO UNDERSTAND THAT THE PROBLEMS OF THE ENVIRONMENT CANNOT BE RESOLVED WITHOUT ADDRESSING THE INTERNATIONAL AND NATIONAL FACTORS THAT PERPETUATE LARGE-SCALE POVERTY.

03426 GAUHAR, H.
CORY'S NEXT CHAPTER
SOUTH, (108) (OCT 89), 10-11.
IN THIS INTERVIEW, PHILLIPPINE PRESIDENT CORAZON AQUINO DISCUSSES THE ISSUES FACING HER COUNTRY, INCLUDING THE QUESTION OF THE FUTURE OF THE AMERICAN MILITARY BASES THERE.

03427 GAWTHROP, L.C.
ETHICS AND DEMOCRACY: THE MORAL DIMENSION
JOURNAL OF STATE GOVERNMENT, 62(5) (SEP 89), 180-184.
VIRTUALLY ALL POLITICAL JURISDICTIONS IN THE UNITED STATES ARE CURRENTLY INVOLVED IN DRAFTING, RE-DRAFTING, AND ENFORCING STANDARDS OF CONDUCT DESIGNED TO INFORM PUBLIC OFFICIALS AND STAFFS WHAT THEY MUST DO TO BE ETHICAL. BUT THE NOTION THAT PUBLIC ETHICS SHOULD BE APPLIED WITH AMORAL DETACHMENT WOULD PROBABLY LEAVE ALL OF THE FOUNDING FATHERS AGHAST.

03428 GAY, R.
POLITICAL CLIENTELISM AND URBAN SOCIAL MOVEMENTS IN RIO DE JANEIRO
DISSERTATION ABSTRACTS INTERNATIONAL, 49(8) (FEB 89), 2419-A.
THROUGH AN ANALYSIS OF THE SOCIAL AND POLITICAL ORGANIZATION OF TWO SLUM COMMUNITIES IN RIO DE JANEIRO, THE AUTHOR FINDS THAT SOCIAL MOVEMENTS PLAY AN IMPORTANT ROLE IN THE DEFINITION OF POLITICAL FORCES IN BRAZIL, NOT ONLY IN TERMS OF GENERATING POLITICAL SUPPORT FOR THE MORE SOCIALLY PROGRESSIVE PARTIES BUT IN TRANSFORMING THE NATURE OF THE POLITICAL PROCESS ITSELF.

03429 GAYNOR, M.
THE PRESENCE OF MORAL HAZARD IN BUDGET BREAKING
PUBLIC CHOICE, 61(3) (JUN 89), 261-267.
IT IS POSSIBLE THAT A BUDGET BREAKING INCENTIVE SCHEME MAY NOT SOLVE THE PROBLEM OF MORAL HAZARD IN TEAM PRODUCTION, DUE TO AN INCENTIVE FOR A PRINCIPAL TO CHEAT ON SUCH AN AGREEMENT. THIS IS A PROBLEM COMMON TO INCENTIVE SCHEMES WHICH RESULT IN AN UNBALANCED BUDGET, WHICH INCLUDE AMONG THEM PROCESSES DESIGNED TO REVEAL DEMAND FOR PUBLIC GOODS. THIS PAPER SHOWS THE CONDITIONS UNDER WHICH CHEATING IS POSSIBLE, AND DESIGNS A PAYMENT SCHEME FOR THE PRINCIPAL WHICH IS FREE OF ANY CHEATING INCENTIVE.

03430 GEBETHNER, S.
INTO THE FOURTH REPUBLIC
POLISH PERSPECTIVES, XXXII(3) (1989), 10-13.
IN POLAND, RECOGNITION OF THE POLITICAL OPPOSITION AND THE RIGHT OF CITIZENS TO FORM OR JOIN DIFFERENT TRADE UNIONS AND ASSOCIATIONS AND THE OPENING OF PARLIAMENTARY ELECTIONS TO RIVAL CANDIDATES HAVE RESULTED IN THE EMERGENCE OF A PLURALIST POLITICAL SYSTEM. THE NEW POLISH POLITICAL SYSTEM MAY BE CALLED A "SOCIALIST PARLIAMENTARY DEMOCRACY," SINCE A PARLIAMENTARY DEMOCRACY IS TAKING SHAPE WITHIN A SOCIALIST SOCIOECONOMIC STRUCTURE.

03431 GEDDES, B.; ZALLER, J.
SOURCES OF POPULAR SUPPORT FOR AUTHORITARIAN REGIMES
AMERICAN JOURNAL OF POLITICAL SCIENCE, 33(2) (MAY 89), 319-347.
THE ARTICLE EXAMINES THE ATTEMPTS OF AUTHORITARIAN GOVERNMENTS TO CONTROL THE FLOW OF NEWS AND INFORMATION TO THE PUBLIC. IT ADAPTS THE EXISTING MAINSTREAM MODEL OF OPINION FORMATION TO CONDITIONS IN AUTHORITARIAN COUNTRIES, ATTEMPTS TO VALIDATE THAT MODEL ON OPINION DATA COLLECTED IN BRAZIL DURING ITS AUTHORITARIAN PERIOD, AND USES THE MODEL TO DERIVE EXPECTATIONS ABOUT PATTERNS OF REGIME SUPPORT THAT EXIST IN DIFFERENT KINDS OF AUTHORITARIAN SYSTEMS. IT CONCLUDES THAT PEOPLE IN THE BROAD MIDDLE RANGES OF PUBLIC AWARENESS, THOSE WHO PAY ENOUGH ATTENTION TO GOVERNMENT MEDIA BUT ARE NOT SOPHISTICATED ENOUGH TO RESIST, ARE TYPICALLY MOST SUSCEPTIBLE TO GOVERNMENT INFLUENCE.

03432 GEE, J.
THREAT TO ISRAEL'S ARABS
MIDDLE EAST INTERNATIONAL, (363) (NOV 89), 11.
THE APPLICATION OF AN AMENDMENT TO ISRAEL"S PREVENTION OF TERRORIST ORDINANCE COULD SIGNIFICANTLY REDUCE THE AMOUNT OF CHARITABLE AID RECEIVED BY PALESTINIANS. THE ORDINANCE MAKES IT ILLEGAL FOR ANYONE TO RECEIVE MONEY OR GOODS FORM A "TERRORIST" ORGANIZATION; IT DEFINES "TERRORIST" SO LOOSELY AS TO INCLUDE ALMOST ANY ORGANIZATION THAT AIDS PALESTINIANS. THE ORDINANCE IS RETROACTIVE AND MANY FEAR IT WILL RESULT IN THE WIDESPREAD CONFISCATION OF PALESTINIAN GOODS AND PROPERTY.

03433 GEEKIE, J.; LEVY, R.
DEVOLUTION AND THE TARTANISATION OF THE LABOUR PARTY
PARLIAMENTARY AFFAIRS, 42(3) (JUL 89), 399-411.
IT IS THE PURPOSE OF THIS ARTICLE TO ELUCIDATE THE KEY IDEOLOGICAL AND PROGRAMMATIC ELEMENTS OF LABOUR'S TRANSFORMATION AND TO OUTLINE THE PRACTICAL CONSEQUENCES IF LABOR CONTINUES ALONG ITS PRESENT ROAD. IT SPECULATES ON THE REASONS WHY LABOR IN SCOTLAND HAS TURNED TOWARDS NATIONALISM, IT CONCLUDES: THAT LABOR'S ADVOCACY OF DEVOLUTIONARY NATIONALISM IS ALSO STATIST DOES NOT MAKE IT ANY LESS NATIONALISTIC.

03434 GEGGUS, D.
RACIAL EQUALITY, SLAVERY, AND COLONIAL SECESSION DURING THE CONSTITUENT ASSEMBLY
AMERICAN HISTORICAL REVIEW, 94(5) (DEC 89), 1290-1308.
THE COLONIAL QUESTION IN THE FRENCH REVOLUTION INVOLVED THREE BROAD ISSUES: SELF-GOVERNMENT FOR FRANCE'S OVERSEAS POSSESSIONS, CIVIL RIGHTS FOR THEIR FREE COLORED POPULATIONS, AND THE ABOLITION OF THE SLAVE TRADE AND SLAVERY ITSELF. THIS ESSAY IS PRIMARILY CONCERNED WITH THE PURSUIT OF RACIAL EQUALITY AND SLAVE EMANCIPATION IN FRANCE, BUT IT IS DIFFICULT TO UNDERSTAND THAT EFFORT WITHOUT REFERENCE TO DEVELOPMENTS IN THE COLONIES AND TO THE CONTEMPORARY DEBATE ABOUT THE LIMITS OF METROPOLITAN CONTROL AND THE THREAT OF WHITE SECESSIONISM WITHIN THE EMPIRE.

03435 GEISE, J.P.
KEEPING FREEDOM POLITICAL: A REPLY TO GRAFSTEIN
SOCIAL SCIENCE QUARTERLY, 70(4) (DEC 89), 855-857.
JACK P. GUEISE, IN A REPLY TO GRAFSTEIN, SUGGESTS THAT ALTHOUGH GRAFSTEIN TENDS TO MAKE THE EXISTENCE OF FREEDOM INTO A SEMANTIC RATHER THAN POLITICAL ISSUE, LESS SEPARATES THE TWO WRITERS THAN MEETS THE EYE. GUEISE CONCLUDES, THE VIRTUE OF SEEING FREEDOM FROM THE PERSPECTIVE HE PROPOSES IS THAT IT COMPELS THE VERY SORT OF ATTENTION TO THE CIRCUMSTANCES OF OUR ACTIONS THAT GRAFSTEIN THINKS IS IMPORTANT. HENCE, FREEDOM IS TO BE SEEN NOT AS SOME ISOLATED PHENOMENON ASSOCIATED WITH THE AUTONOMOUS INDIVIDUAL BUT AS A POSSIBLE FEATURE OF INDIVIDUALS ACTING POLITICALLY. IT IS, AS WELL, A FEATURE THAT NEEDS NURTURING.

03436 GEISE, J.P.
THE RHETORIC AND POLITICS OF LIBERTY
SOCIAL SCIENCE QUARTERLY, 70(4) (DEC 89), 836-850.
THE CONCEPTS OF LIBERTY AND FREEDOM ARE THE CORE OF LIBERAL POLITICAL THOUGHT. THEY ARE ALSO A FOCUS FOR CONTEMPORARY POLITICS. THE PAPER EXAMINES THE VARIOUS DEFINITIONS ASSOCIATED WITH THE NOTION OF LIBERTY, AS WELL AS THE WAYS IN WHICH THESE DEFINITIONS REFLECT THE CONCRETE POLITICAL PREFERENCES OF THEIR EXPONENTS. FINALLY, THE PAPER SUGGESTS A POSSIBLE REVISED UNDERSTANDING OF FREEDOM-AN UNDERSTANDING THAT IS BOTH IN HARMONY WITH LIBERALISM PROPER AND PRESCRIPTIVE FOR A LIBERAL POLITICS.

03437 GELB, B.A.
ECONOMIC IMPLICATIONS OF ENVIRONMENTAL THREATS: A CENTRAL POLICY DILEMMA
CRS REVEIW, 10(7) (AUG 89), 24-26.
BECAUSE THE PATTERN, GROWTH RATE, AND TECHNOLOGY OF INDUSTRIAL CIVILIZATION ARE INEXTRICABLY LINKED TO ENVIRONMENTAL CONDITIONS, CHANGE IN THOSE CONDITIONS OR EFFORTS TO PREVENT CHANGE COULD ALTER HOW PEOPLE MEET THEIR

NEEDS AND WHERE AND HOW THEY LIVE. CONSEQUENTLY, MODERN
ECONOMIES FACE LARGE ADJUSTMENTS IN THEIR QUEST TO FIND
ALTERNATIVES TO POLLUTION-CAUSING SUBSTANCES AND PROCESSES.
THE POLICY CHALLENGE IS GREATLY MAGNIFIED WHEN THE
PROBABILITY, PACE, AND EXTENT OF THE THREAT AND THE COSTS OF
MITIGATING IT ARE POORLY UNDERSTOOD.

03438 GELB, B.S.
    THE PROSPECTS FOR U.S.-SOVIET EXCHANGES
    INTERNATIONAL AFFAIRS (MOSCOW), (9) (SEP 89), 96-102.
        THE AUTHOR DISCUSSES THE AMERICAN APPROACHES TO SOVIET-
    AMERICAN EXCHANGES, BRIEFLY REVIEWS THE DEVELOPMENT OF
    SOVIET-AMERICAN CONTACTS, AND ADVANCES SOME THOUGHTS ON THE
    CURRENT DIRECTION, FUTURE PROSPECTS, AND POTENTIAL OBSTACLES
    TO THE GROWTH OF SOVIET-AMERICAN CONTACTS AND EXCHANGES.

03439 GELB, N.
    BRITONS WORRY ABOUT CIVIL RIGHTS
    NEW LEADER, LXII(4) (FEB 89), 5-6.
        IF THE BRITISH GOVERNMENT HAS ITS WAY, SOCCER FANS WILL
    SOON NEED IDENTIFICATION CARDS TO ATTEND MATCHES. CRITICS
    SAY THE MEASURE WON'T WORK AND THE EXPENSE AND BUREAUCRATIC
    COMPLICATIONS WILL DRIVE THE SMALLER SOCCER TEAMS OUT OF
    BUSINESS. A MORE SERIOUS CRITICISM IS THAT THE SCHEME IS
    ANOTHER EXAMPLE OF PRIME MINISTER THATCHER'S CREEPING
    DESTRUCTION OF FUNDAMENTAL LIBERTIES.

03440 GELB, N.
    LONDON LOSES ITS LUSTER
    NEW LEADER, LXXII(14) (SEP 89), 12-13.
        ALTHOUGH LONDON HAS BEEN LONG REGARDED AS THE "CENTER OF
    CIVILIZATION," MANY NOW FEEL THAT THE GREAT CITY IS LOSING
    SOME OF ITS CHARM. TRANSPORTATION. HOUSING, CRIME, AND
    POLITICAL PROBLEMS ARE BECOMING INCREASINGLY WIDESPREAD AND
    URGENT. ALTHOUGH A US VISITOR MAY FIND LONDON TO BE QUITE
    SAFE AND CLEAN WHEN COMPARED TO NEW YORK OR LOS ANGELES, IT
    IS CLEAR THAT THE BRITISH CAPITAL CITY IS AT LAST BEGINNING
    TO SUFFER FROM BIG-CITY DISEASE.

03441 GELB, N.
    THATCHER AT ODDS WITH EUROPE
    NEW LEADER, LXXII(16) (OCT 89), 12-13.
        AS THE MOVE TO DECISIVELY INTERLOCK THE ECONOMIES OF
    EUROPE GAINS IN POWER AND MOMENTUM, BRITISH PRIME MINISTER
    MARGARET THATCHER IS BECOMING INCREASINGLY UNCOMFORTABLE
    WITH THE DIRECTION OF THE CHANGES. SHE PARTICULARLY FINDS
    FAULT WITH A PROPOSAL FOR A BINDING CHARTER ON HUMAN RIGHTS.
    THE DOCUMENT INCLUDES PROVISIONS FOR A COMMUNITY-WIDE
    MINIMUM WAGE AND MAXIMUM WORKING HOURS STRUCTURE; A
    GUARANTEE OF THE RIGHT TO STRIKE; AND "SOCIAL PROTECTION"
    (UNEMPLOYMENT INSURANCE, WELFARE PAYMENTS ETC) FROM THE
    GOVERNMENT OF WHICHEVER EUROPEAN COMMUNITY A CITIZEN HAPPENS
    TO BE LIVING IN. THATCHER ARGUES THAT THE MINIMUM WAGE
    PROPOSAL WOULD HURT THE POORER NATIONS OF EUROPE AND
    STRIDENTLY DENOUNCES THE SOCIALIST PROVISIONS OF THE
    PROPOSAL. HOWEVER, AS THE 1992 DEADLINE NEARS, IT WILL
    BECOME INCREASINGLY DIFFICULT TO DENY THE MOMENTUM OF THE
    INTEGRATION MOVEMENT.

03442 GELB, N.
    THATCHERISM ISN'T WORKING
    NEW LEADER, LXXII(11) (JUL 89), 8-9.
        MARGARET THATCHER AND HER RULING CONSERVATIVE PARTY ARE
    EXPERIENCING POLITICAL TROUBLES THAT WERE UNIMAGINABLE A
    YEAR AGO. THEIR ONCE ACCURATE SLOGAN "THERE IS NO
    ALTERNATIVE" IS UNDER SERIOUS CONSIDERATION AS LABOUR AND
    GREEN PARTY CANDIDATES ARE BECOMING INCREASINGLY VISIBLE AND
    POWERFUL. THATCHER IS ALSO STRUGGLING WITH INCREASED
    INFLATION AND ENVIRONMENTAL WOES. FOR THE FIRST TIME IN HER
    REIGN, EVEN EMINENT TORIES HAVE DARED TO PUBLICLY CRITICIZE
    HER. ALTHOUGH GENERAL ELECTIONS ARE NOT DUE TO TAKE PLACE
    FOR ANOTHER TWO YEARS, THE "IRON LADY" HAS A LONG ROAD AHEAD
    IF SHE WISHES TO RETAIN POWER.

03443 GELB, N.
    THE PRACTICAL PROBLEMS: EUROPE WITHOUT FRONTIERS
    NEW LEADER, LXXII(1) (JAN 89), 7-8.
        THE DRIVE TOWARD AN ECONOMICALLY UNITED EUROPE BY 1992
    CONTINUES UNABATED, TO THE GROWING ALARM OF THE USA, JAPAN,
    AND OTHER COUNTRIES. OFFICIALS OF THE COMMON MARKET CONTEND
    THAT THIS ANXIETY IS MISPLACED. BUT SOME ARE PRIVATELY
    ADMITTING THAT THERE MAY BE A NEED FOR TEMPORARY PROTECTION
    AGAINST EXTERNAL ECONOMIC COMPETITORS SO INTERNAL EUROPEAN
    INDUSTRIES CAN DEVELOP STRONGER FOUNDATIONS.

03444 GELB, N.
    TROUBLE IN THATCHERLAND
    NEW LEADER, LXXII(6) (MAR 89), 6-7.
        A NUMBER OF FINANCIAL AND HEALTH PROBLEMS ARE PROVOKING
    UNEASE IN GREAT BRITAIN. OF GREATEST CONCERN IS THE FUTURE
    OF THE NATIONAL HEALTH SERVICE. THE THATCHER GOVERNMENT'S
    NEW PLAN FOR ITS TOTAL REORGANIZATION HAS AROUSED WIDESPREAD
    SUSPICION THAT ITS BASIC PRINCIPLES ARE ON THE VERGE OF
    BEING ABANDONED.

03445 GELB, N.
    TURKEY'S IDENTITY PROBLEM
    NEW LEADER, LXXII(8) (MAY 89), 9-10.
        THE TURKS REALIZE THAT IF EASTWEST HOSTILITY IS
    GENUINELY ON A DOWNWARD SPIRAL, EXISTING AMERICAN INTEREST
    IN THEM AS A STAUNCH NATO ALLY IS LIKELY TO DIMINISH. WHEN
    THIS IS COUPLED WITH EUROPE'S STANDOFFISH RESPONSE TO
    TURKISH MEMBERSHIP ENTREATIES, THE FATE OF TURKEY'S
    SECULARIZED MOSLEM SOCIETY IN A SECULARIZED CHRISTIAN
    EUROPEAN AND NATO ALLIANCE BECOMES PROBLEMATIC.

03446 GELB, S.; LEWIS, D.; O'MEARA, D.; SAUL, J. S.
    THE PEOPLE SHALL GOVERN: FROM SOWETO TO LIBERATION IN
    SOUTH AFRICA
    MONTHLY REVIEW PRESS, NEW YORK, NY, 1989, 288.
        THESE ESSAYS CONSIDER THE DEVELOPMENTS IN SOUTH AFRICA
    SINCE THE SOWETO UPRISING IN 1976 AND THE IMPLICATIONS FOR
    THE STRUGGLE TO OVERTHROW APARTHEID. THE AUTHORS CONCENTRATE
    ON FOUR CRUCIAL SPHERES: THE ECONOMY, THE STATE AND THE
    ACTIVITIES OF THE DOMINANT CLASSES, THE EMANCIPATORY
    MOVEMENT, AND THE WORKING CLASS AND THE TRADE UNIONS.

03447 GELFAND, D.; ALLBRITTON, T.
    CONFLICT AND CONGRUENCE IN ONE-PERSON, ONE-VOTE AND RACIAL
    VOTE DILUTION LITIGATION: ISSUES RESOLVED AND UNRESOLVED
    BY BOARD OF ESTIMATE V. MORRIS
    JOURNAL OF LAW & POLITICS, VI(1) (FAL 89), 93-124.
        THE ARTICLE PROVIDES A DISCUSSION OF THE UNITED STATES
    SUPREME COURT'S RECENT DECISION IN BOARD OF ESTIMATE V.
    MORRIS AND AN ANALYSIS OF THE IMPLICATIONS OF THAT DECISION
    FOR ELECTORAL AND GOVERNMENTAL STRUCTURES IN NEW YORK CITY
    AND OTHER AMERICAN MUNICIPALITIES. THESE IMPLICATIONS
    INVOLVE NOT JUST ONEPERSON, ONE-VOTE ISSUES, WITH WHICH THE
    CASE IS DIRECTLY CONCERNED, BUT ALSO A NUMBER OF ISSUES
    RELATED TO RACIAL VOTE DILUTION. IT CONCLUDES THAT THE
    COURT'S ENCOURAGEMENT OF LOCAL GOVERNMENT POSITIONS ELECTED
    ON AN AT-LARGE BASIS IS ON A COLLISION COURSE WITH THE
    COURT'S OTHER DECISIONS IN THE RACIAL VOTE DILUTION AREA.

03448 GELLMAN, P.
    LESTER B. PEARSON. COLLECTIVE SECURITY, AND THE WORLD
    ORDER TRADITION OF CANADIAN FOREIGN POLICY
    INTERNATIONAL JOURNAL, XLIV(1) (WIN 89), 68-101.
        CANADA'S FOREIGN POLICY REVEALS A PREOCCUPATION WITH
    INTERNATIONAL ORGANIZATION THAT ARGUABLY EXCEEDS ANYTHING
    OBSERVED IN THE FOREIGN POLICIES OF OTHER MAJOR
    INDUSTRIALIZED DEMOCRACIES. OF THE MANY CANADIAN OFFICIALS
    WHO HAVE MADE A CASE FOR A WORLD ORDER FOREIGN POLICY, NONE
    HAS BEEN MORE PROMINENT THAN LESTER B. PEARSON. THIS ESSAY
    EVALUATES THE STRENGTH OF PEARSON'S COMMITMENT TO A
    PRINCIPAL VERSION OF HIS WORLD ORDER FOREIGN POLICY, THAT OF
    COLLECTIVE SECURITY. AN ANALYSIS OF PEARSON'S THINKING ABOUT
    THE ETHIOPIAN CRISIS WHEN HE WAS A YOUNG DIPLOMAT, AS WELL
    AS HIS RESPONSE TO THE KOREAN WAR WHEN HE SERVED AS
    SECRETARY OF STATE FOR EXTERNAL AFFAIRS, SUGGESTS THAT HIS
    ADHERENCE TO COLLECTIVE SECURITY WAS MORE COMPLICATED AND
    LESS UNQUALIFIED THAN IS COMMONLY SUPPOSED.

03449 GELLMAN, P.
    THE ELUSIVE EXPLANATION: BALANCE OF POWER "THEORY" AND THE
    ORIGINS OF WORLD WAR I
    REVIEW OF INTERNATIONAL STUDIES, 15(2) (APR 89), 155-182.
        BALANCE OF POWER THEORY DOES NOT END WITH THE PREDICTION
    THAT THE STATES-SYSTEM TENDS TO PROMOTE PARITY IN THE
    DISTRIBUTION OF POWER. THE NUMBER OF GREAT POWERS IN THE
    INTERNATIONAL SYSTEM AFFECTS BOTH THE METHODS THROUGH WHICH
    THE BALANCING OPERATES AND THE CAPACITY OF A STATE OR STATES
    TO MANAGE THAT SYSTEM IN AN ORDERLY FASHION. THE DERIVATIVE
    BALANCE OF POWER PROPOSITIONS WHICH SEEK TO EXPLAIN THE
    BEHAVIOUR OF STATES IN MULTIPOLAR AND BIPOLAR SYSTEMS ARE
    QUITE GENERAL. BALANCE OF POWER PROPOSITIONS MAY
    SIMULTANEOUSLY COVER A RANGE OF DIVERSE OUTCOMES, AND THEY
    MAY BE DIFFICULT TO DISTINGUISH FROM SUB-BALANCE FACTORS AS
    THE FORCE MOST INFLUENCING A PARTICULAR EVENT OR SEQUENCE OF
    EVENTS. NEVERTHELESS, THEY ARE SUFFICIENTLY SPECIFIC TO
    PERMIT OF SOME 'TESTING'; AND ANY ANALYSIS ALONG THESE LINES
    ALSO OUGHT TO BE HELPFUL IN JUDGING THE THEORY AS A WHOLE.

03450 GELLNER, W.
    FEDERALISM AND THE CONTROVERSY OVER THE NEW MEDIA IN WEST
    GERMANY
    PUBLIUS: THE JOURNAL OF FEDERALISM, 19(4) (FAL 89),
    133-146.
        THE POSSIBILITIES OF EXPANDING THE TELEVISION NETWORK BY
    MEANS OF CABLE AND SATELLITE SERVICE HAVE PAVED THE WAY FOR
    THE LANDER TO DETERMINE RELEVANT ORGANIZATIONAL STRUCTURES.
    THE NEWLY COMPLETED STATE MEDIA TREATY SEEMS TO REPRESENT A
    DEFINITE BREAKTHROUGH IN REGULATORY POLICY. THE LEGAL
    REGULATION OF THE NEW MEDIA--CABLE AND SATELLITE TELEVISION--
    FACES FURTHER COMPLICATIONS, HOWEVER, INSOFAR AS NINE LAND
    MEDIA LAWS IMPOSE DIFFERENT LEGAL REQUIREMENTS ON THE NEW
    BROADCASTERS. EVEN SO, DIFFERENCES AMONG THE LANDER IN THE
    AREA OF CABLE TV ARE NO LONGER AS GREAT AS THEY WERE IN THE

PAST, AND A SATELLITE AGREEMENT REACHED BY THE LANDER PROVIDES FOR MORE UNIFORM REGULATION. ALSO, THE FEDERAL CONSTITUTIONAL COURT'S 1986 DECISION EMPHASIZING THE IMPORTANCE OF A UNIFORM SYSTEM OF BROADCASTING AND REQUIRING DUAL PRIVATE AND PUBLIC BROADCASTING MAY HAVE SETTLED THE FUNDAMENTAL POLITICAL DISPUTE AMONG THE LANDER OVER THE NEW MEDIA.

03451 GENDZIER, I.
CONTAINMENT, COUNTERREVOLUTION, AND CREDIBILITY
MIDDLE EAST REPORT, 19(5) (SEP 89), 41-43.
THE ARTICLE REVIEWS CONFRONTING THE THIRD WORLD: UNITED STATES FOREIGN POLICY 1945-1980 BY GABRIEL KOLKO. THE WORK'S OBJECTIVE IS TO EXPLORE US POLICY IN THE THIRD WORLD AS A WHOLE AND TO PROBE THE DEEP STRUCTURES OF POLICY, ESPECIALLY THE INTERPLAY OF ECONOMIC FORCES AND THEIR POLITICAL AND MILITARY EXPRESSIONS. KOLKO EMPHASIZES THE "ESSENTIALLY NONMATERIAL AND SYMBOLIC CONSIDERATIONS THAT INCREASINGLY ENTERED INTO THE UNITED STATES DECISION IN THE THIRD WORLD AFTER ITS FAILURE TO WIN THE KOREAN WAR. IT MAPS THE SHIFT FROM POLICIES OF CONTAINMENT TO AN INCREASING EMPHASIS ON COUNTERREVOLUTION. IT ALSO EXPLORES THE LOSS OF CREDIBILITY THAT THE US HAS EXPERIENCED WORLD WIDE DUE TO FAILURES IN THE MIDDLE EAST AND OTHER AREAS.

03452 GENDZIER, I.
THE UNITED STATES, THE USSR AND THE ARAB WORLD IN NSC REPORTS OF THE 1950'S
AMERICAN-ARAB AFFAIRS, (28) (SPR 89), 22-29.
THE ARTICLE UTILIZES THE NSC REPORTS DURING THE PERIOD 1952-1958 TO ASSESS US AND SOVIET INTENTIONS AND POLICIES IN THE MIDEAST. IT TRACES THE DEVELOPMENT OF US THOUGHT FROM THE POSITION THAT THE USSR WAS NOT CONSIDERED A DIRECT THREAT TO US INTERESTS IN THE MIDEAST (ALTHOUGH FEAR OF INDIRECT INFLUENCE WAS PERVASIVE), TO A PERIOD OF OPEN AND DIRECT COMPETITION. NSC REPORTS ALSO REVEAL THAT INDIGENOUS MOVEMENTS AND FORCES WERE VIEWED AND CLASSIFIED EXCLUSIVELY IN A BIPOLAR FASHION; A GROUP'S ADHERENCE TO ONE OR ANOTHER OF THE TWO GREAT POWERS WAS THE DETERMINING CLASSIFIER.

03453 GENGFU, G.
JAPAN TONES UP DEFENCE POLICY
BEIJING REVIEW, 32(9) (FEB 89), 17-19.
AS THE JAPANESE ECONOMY HAS GATHERED STRENGTH AND THE INTERNATIONAL SITUATION HAS CHANGED, JAPAN'S DEFENSE POLICY HAS REPONDED WITH CHANGES OF ITS OWN. THE JAPANESE GOVERNMENT HAS EMBRACED A NEW STRATEGIC CONCEPT: EXPAND THE SCOPE OF DEFENSE, RECRUIT MORE MILITARY FORCES, INCREASE MILITARY SPENDING, SPEED UP SCIENTIFIC AND TECHNOLOGICAL RESEARCH FOR MILITARY PURPOSES, AND REVISE THE CONSTITUTION. ALL THESE MOVES HAVE AROUSED CONCERN IN NEIGHBORING COUNTRIES.

03454 GENGFU, G.
JAPAN TONES UP DEFENCE POLICY (PART II)
BEIJING REVIEW, 32(10) (MAR 89), 16-19.
IN THE NEXT TEN YEARS, IT IS ANTICIPATED THAT JAPAN'S DEFENSE EXPENSES WILL GROW AT SIX PERCENT AND BE HELD TO 1.5 PERCENT OF THE GNP. SINCE 1981, THE NATIONAL SPENDING ON WELFARE, MEDIUM AND SMALL ENTERPRISES, AND AGRICULTURE HAS BEEN CURTAILED WHILE MILITARY EXPENSES HAVE INCREASED FIVE TO SEVEN PERCENT. THE CHANGES IN JAPAN'S DEFENSE POLICY AND MILITARY STRENGTH ARE CONNECTED TO THE UNITED STATES' DEMAND FOR JAPAN TO INCREASE ITS MILITARY EXPENDITURES AND SHOULDER MORE OF THE RESPONSIBILITY FOR ITS OWN SECURITY.

03455 GENOVESE, M.A.
MONEY AND POLITICS
INTERNATIONAL SOCIAL SCIENCE REVIEW, 64(4) (AUG 89), 172-173.
CAMPAIGN FINANCE REFORM EFFORTS HAVE FAILED PARTLY BECAUSE THE SUPREME COURT RULED THAT PUTTING A SPENDING LIMIT ON CANDIDATES WOULD BE A RESTRICTION ON FREE SPEECH. IF THE COURT MAINTAINS THAT MONEY IS A FORM OF POLITICAL SPEECH, LAWS MUST BE CAREFUL NOT TO RESTRICT THE RIGHT OF INDIVIDUAL POLITICAL EXPRESSION. BUT "ONE MAN, ONE VOTE" IS ALSO A CONSTITUTIONALLY PROTECTED RIGHT AND, THEREFORE, CONGRESS COULD PASS A LAW THAT ALLOWS CANDIDATES TO ACCEPT MONEY ONLY FROM INDIVIDUALS AND GROUPS RESIDING IN THE STATE OR DISTRICT THAT THE CANDIDATE SEEKS TO REPRESENT. THIS WOULD EFFECTIVELY LIMIT CONTRIBUTIONS FROM OUTSIDE POLITICAL ACTION COMMITTEES AND SPECIAL INTERESTS.

03456 GEORGE, B.; LISTER, T.
BRITAIN'S LABOUR PARTY AND DEFENSE: PRINCIPLES OR POWER
WASHINGTON QUARTERLY, 12(2) (SPR 89), 41-53.
ALTHOUGH LABOUR REESTABLISHED ITSELF AT THE 1987 ELECTION AS THE ALTERNATIVE PARTY OF GOVERNMENT, BEATING BACK THE CHALLENGE OF THE CENTRIST ALLIANCE, IT COULD DO NO BETTER THAN ERODE THE CONSERVATIVES' MASSIVE PARLIAMENTARY MAJORITY. LABOUR'S GREATEST HOPE IS THAT THE TIDE OF INTERNATIONAL EVENTS WILL MOVE SWIFTLY IN ITS DIRECTION AND THAT THATCHER WILL BE MAROONED AS THE ONLY WORLD LEADER RELUCTANT TO BARGAIN ON ARMS CONTROL. ALTHOUGH THE DEFENSE

OF THE REALM IS UNLIKELY TO HAVE AS GREAT AN INFLUENCE ON THE RESULT AS THE STATE OF THE ECONOMY AND THE FUTURE OF THE WELFARE STATE, IT IS CERTAIN TO FEATURE IN THE CAMPAIGN.

03457 GEORGE, D.E.
LOW-RODGERS EXPEDITION: A STUDY IN THE FOUNDATIONS OF U.S. POLICY IN KOREA
AVAILABLE FROM NTIS, NO. AD-A205 100/1/GAR, JUN 88, 334.
THIS THESIS REVEALS THE ORIGIN AND SIGNIFICANCE OF THE LOW-RODGERS EXPEDITION OF 1871 IN THE EVOLUTION OF A CONSCIOUS FOREIGN POLICY OF THE UNITED STATES IN EAST ASIA. IT DEALS WITH THE LOW-RODGERS EXPEDITION NOT AS AN ISOLATED EVENT, BUT AS BOTH AN OUTCOME AND ANTECEDENT OF OTHER CLOSELY INTERRELATED EVENTS IN AN UNBROKEN TIME CONTINUUM. CONCENTRATING ON THE FUNDAMENTAL REGIONAL ISSUES OF THE TIMES AND THE NATIONAL CHARACTER AND INTERESTS OF THE UNITED STATES AND THE KINGDOM OF KOREA, THIS THESIS: (1) REVEALS, FOR THE FIRST TIME, THE ORIGINAL 1871 DIARY OF U.S. MINISTER TO CHINA, FREDERICK FERDINAND LOW, AND THE WEALTH OF NEW HISTORICAL DATA THEREIN: HIS MISGIVINGS AND MOTIVATIONS; HIS PLANS AND FAILINGS; AND HIS APPRECIATION FOR THE HISTORICAL IMPORTANCE OF THE MISSION WHICH TODAY BEARS HIS NAME; (2) PROVIDES DEEPER ANALYSIS OF THE CONTEMPORARY EVENTS BEARING ON THE LOW-RODGERS EXPEDITION AND GIVES A DEEPER APPRECIATION OF THE OBSTACLES WHICH WORKED AGAINST ITS SUCCESS FROM THE VERY MOMENT OF ITS INCEPTION; (3) SHOWS WHY MISCONCEPTIONS ABOUT THE EXPEDITION AND SOME PERIPHERAL EVENTS HAVE REMAINED UNCHALLENGED FOR OVER A CENTURY; AND (4) EXPLAINS WHY LOW'S EFFORTS TO OPEN KOREA BEFORE THE 1882 SHUFELDT MISSION FAILED, YET STILL PLAYED A MORE IMPORTANT ROLE IN THE DEVELOPMENT OF U.S. POLICY IN KOREA AND THE OPENING OF KOREA TO THE WESTERN WORLD THAN HAS BEEN RECOGNIZED.

03458 GEORGE, J.
INTERNATIONAL RELATIONS AND THE SEARCH FOR THINKING SPACE: ANOTHER VIEW OF THE THIRD DEBATE
INTERNATIONAL STUDIES QUARTERLY, 33(3) (SEP 89), 269-280.
RECENT DEBATES IN INTERNATIONAL RELATIONS HAVE SEEN SOME OF THE CHARACTERISTIC DICHOTOMIES OF THE DISCIPLINE UNDER SEVERE AND SOPHISTICATED CHALLENGE. THE PROPOSITION, FOR EXAMPLE, THAT THE STUDY OF INTERNATIONAL RELATIONS, IS SOMEHOW "INDEPENDENT" OF MAINSTREAM DEBATES ON THEORY AND PRACTICE IN THE SOCIAL SCIENCES IS NOW WIDELY REJECTED. THE DISCIPLINE CHANGE IN ATTITUDE ON THIS ISSUE OWES MUCH, IN THE 1980S, TO THE INFLUENCES OF AN AS YET SMALL GROUP OF SCHOLARS WHO HAVE INFUSED THE "THIRD DEBATE" IN INTERNATIONAL RELATIONS WITH AN APPRECIATION FOR PREVIOUSLY "ALIEN" APPROACHES TO KNOWLEDGE AND SOCIETY, DRAWN FROM INTERDISCIPLINARY SOURCES, WHICH REPUDIATE (META) THEORETICAL DUALISM IN ALL ITS FORMS. UTILIZING THE SPONGE TERM "POSTPOSITIVISM" YOSEF LAPID HAS CONCENTRATED ON AN IMPORTANT ASPECT OF THE "THIRD DEBATE," ONE WHICH HAS SEEN POSITIVIST BASED PERSPECTIVES REPUDIATED IN FAVOR OF CRITICAL PERSPECTIVES DERIVED, PRIMARILY, FROM DEBATES ON THE PHILOSOPHY OF SCIENCE. THIS PAPER TAKES A BROADER VIEW OF THE "THIRD DEBATE" IN FOCUSING ON SOME OF THE BROADER PATTERNS OF DISSENT IN SOCIAL THEORY THAT ARE NOW EVIDENT IN ITS LITERATURE. IT ARGUES THAT FOR ALL THE DIFFERENCES ASSOCIATED WITH THE NEW CRITICAL SOCIAL THEORY APPROACHES, THEIRS IS CRITIQUE WITH COMMON PURPOSE. ITS PURPOSE: TO HELP US UNDERSTAND MORE ABOUT CONTEMPORARY GLOBAL LIFE BY OPENING UP FOR QUESTIONING DIMENSIONS OF INQUIRY WHICH HAVE BEEN PREVIOUSLY CLOSED OFF AND SUPRESSED; BY LISTENING CLOSELY TO VOICES PREVIOUSLY UNHEARD; BY EXAMINING "REALITIES" EXCLUDED FROM CONSIDERATION UNDER A TRADITIONAL (REALIST) REGIME OF UNITY AND SINGULARITY. ITS PURPOSE, REITERATED: THE SEARCH FOR "THINKING SPACE" WITHIN AN INTERNATIONAL RELATIONS DISCIPLINE PRODUCED BY AND ARTICULATED THROUGH WESTERN MODERNIST DISCOURSE.

03459 GEORGE, M.K.; FAWTHROP, T.
A THAI PEACE OFFENSIVE
SOUTH, (109) (NOV 89), 30, 33.
SINCE PRIME MINISTER CHATICHAI CHOONHAVAN CAME TO POWER IN 1988, HE HAS CHANGED THAILAND'S POLICY TOWARDS CAMBODIA AND VIETNAM, DROPPING THE RIGID BOYCOTT OF THE PREVIOUS REGIME IN FAVOR OF CLOSER TRADE AND MILITARY CONTACTS. CHATICHAI HELD TALKS WITH ALL THE KHMER FACTIONS IN SEPTEMBER 1989 IN AN ATTEMPT TO HAMMER OUT A CEASEFIRE, BUT MILITARY ANALYSTS SAY HE IS LIKELY TO ENGINEER AN AGREEMENT.

03460 GEORGE, M.K.; GORDON-BATES, K.
AQUINO BRACED FOR A WAVE OF DISCONTENT
SOUTH, (105) (JUL 89), 39.
PHILIPPINE UNIONS ARE MOBILIZING AGAINST PLANNED PRICE AND TAX INCREASES AND HAVE ALREADY WON A CAMPAIGN TO RAISE THE MINIMUM WAGE. MANILA HAS MOVED TO STIFFEN ITS LABOR LAWS WITH A BILL THAT THE UNIONS CLAIM IS A VIRTUAL ANTI-STRIKE CHARTER. A MORE SINISTER UNION-BUSTER IS THE NATIONAL ALLIANCE FOR DEMOCRACY, WHICH IS BACKED BY BUSINESS, LEADING POLITICAL FIGURES, AND THE MILITARY. THE ALLIANCE IS PROMOTING ITS OWN NATIONAL UNION IN OPPOSITION TO THE RADICAL UNIONS GROUPED UNDER THE UMBRELLA OF KILUSANG MAYO

UNO.

03461 GEORGE, M.K.; ALAGIAH, G.; VIDAL-HALL, J.
ETHNIC ERUPTION IN THE GLOBAL VILLAGE
SOUTH, (99) (JAN 89), 38-39.
ETHNIC NATIONALISM IS ON THE RISE THROUGHOUT THE WORLD.
THE ISSUE OF ETHNIC REVIVAL WILL PROBABLY DOMINATE THE
1990'S, AS THE SOVIETS' IMBROGLIO IN THE NATIONAL QUESTION
COINCIDES WITH A GLOBAL ETHNIC REVIVAL AND AN UPSURGE IN
LOCALIZED CONFLICTS ROOTED IN RACE, RELIGION, AND CREED.

03462 GEORGE, M.K.; SINGH, S.
HAWKE BIDS FOR STARDOM
SOUTH, (109) (NOV 89), 12-16.
AUSTRALIAN PRIME MINISTER BOB HAWKE HAS INVITED THE SIX
MEMBERS OF ASEAN PLUS JAPAN, SOUTH KOREA, THE USA, CANADA,
NEW ZEALAND, AND AUSTRALIA TO LAUNCH A NEW PACIFIC ECONOMIC
PARTNERSHIP. THE KEY PARTICIPANTS, WITHOUT WHOM PACIFIC
ECONOMIC COOPERATION WOULD BE THREADBARE, ARE THE ASEAN
MEMBERS. BUT SUSPICIONS OF AUSTRALIA'S MOTIVES AND A
CONVICTION THAT THE INITIATIVE OUGHT TO HAVE COME FROM ASEAN
HAVE LED TO COMMENTS THAT THE SIX ARE ONLY GOING TO THE
NOVEMBER 1989 ORGANIZATIONAL MEETING TO SAVE HAWKE
EMBARRASSMENT.

03463 GEORGE, M.K.; GORDON-BATES, K.
JOINT MANOEUVRES IN UNCLE SAM'S WAKE
SOUTH, (101) (MAR 89), 33.
THE WORLD'S WEAPONS MANUFACTURERS ARE TARGETING
SOUTHEAST ASIA AS THEIR KEY MARKET AS NEW DEFENSE STRATEGIES
ARE PLANNED IN ANTICIPATION OF A US WITHDRAWAL FROM THE
PHILIPPINES. THEY PREDICT THAT WEAPONS SALES TO SOUTHEAST
ASIA WILL SOAR OVER THE NEXT TEN YEARS.

03464 GEORGE, M.K.
PACIFIC COURTSHIP
SOUTH, (101) (MAR 89), 31-32.
SOVIET PRESIDENT MIKHAIL GORBACHEV SAYS THERE HAS BEEN A
CHANGE IN THE ATTITUDE OF ASIAN AND PACIFIC NATIONS TOWARDS
MOSCOW SINCE HE UNVEILED HIS NEW POLICY TOWARDS THE REGION
IN 1986. MOSCOW IS PURSUING A NEW RELATIONSHIP BASED ON
PEACE AND SECURITY AND, MOST IMPORTANTLY, MUTUALLY
BENEFICIAL COOPERATION IN TRADE. BUT THE BIG BREAKTHROUGH
HAS YET TO BE ACHIEVED BECAUSE THERE ARE DOUBTS IN SOME
QUARTERS ABOUT MOSCOW'S MOTIVES.

03465 GEORGE, M.K.
SEEING THE GREEN LIGHT
SOUTH, (107) (SEP 89), 12-16.
THE GROWING CLAMOR FOR A CLEANER WORLD IS FORCING
CHANGES ON GOVERNMENTS AND INDUSTRIES, PARTICULARLY IN THE
NORTH. IT IS ALSO OPENING A HUGE MARKET FOR ENVIRONMENTALLY
SAFE PRODUCTS, WHICH THE SOUTH COULD EXPLOIT. THE DOWNSIDE
FOR DEVELOPING COUNTRIES WILL BE FALLING CONSUMPTION AND
IMPORT RESTRICTIONS IN NORTHERN MARKETS FOR COMMODITIES
PRODUCED AT THE EXPENSE OF THE ENVIRONMENT. ENVIRONMENTAL
CONCERNS HAVE OPENED A WINDOW ON THE NORTH-SOUTH DEBATE,
HIGHLIGHTING THE NEED FOR A FAIRER DISTRIBUTION OF RESOURCES
AND PRODUCTS.

03466 GEORGE, M.K.; CHI, J.; MOORE, H.
SOUTH KOREA
SOUTH, (107) (SEP 89), 53-61.
PESSIMISTS SEEM TO OUTNUMBER OPTIMISTS IN SOUTH KOREA
DUE TO THE RISING INFLATION, THE HIGH PRICE OF HOUSING,
LABOR UNREST, PRESSURE FROM THE USA AND THE EUROPEAN
COMMUNITY FOR TRADE LIBERALIZATION, AND DEMANDS FOR
POLITICAL AND SOCIAL REFORM. THE PESSIMISTS SEE LEFTIST
RADICALISM SPREADING AMONG STUDENTS AND WORKERS, THE LABOR
SITUATION GETTING OUT OF HAND, THE COUNTRY LOSING ITS
ECONOMIC ADVANTAGE, AND THE ANTI-AMERICAN MOOD UNDERMINING
SECURITY.

03467 GEORGE, M.K.; FAWTHROP, T.
VIETNAM GETS READY TO RIDE THE WAVE
SOUTH, (103) (MAY 89), 41.
HANOI WANTS TO BE THE NEXT ASIAN INDUSTRIAL TIGER AND IS
LOOKING TO SOUTH KOREA AS A MODEL FOR PROGRAMS THAT, ALONG
WITH VIETNAM'S LARGE RESOURCE BASE, WILL HELP PROPEL IT INTO
THE RANKS OF ASIA'S NEWLY INDUSTRIALIZING ECONOMIES. IN A
BID TO ATTRACT TECHNOLOGY AND INVESTMENT IN ITS INDUSTRIAL
FUTURE, HANOI IS DISCARDING CENTRAL PLANNING FOR A WESTERN-
STYLE MARKET APPROACH.

03468 GEORGE, S.
BRITAIN AND THE EUROPEAN COMMUNITY
CONTEMPORARY RECORD, 2(5) (SPR 89), 15-17.
AT THE END OF 1988, BRITAIN COMPLETED SIXTEEN YEARS AS A
MEMBER OF THE EUROPEAN COMMUNITY (EC). THIS ARTICLE OUTLINES
THE BACKGROUND OF BRITISH ENTRY AND OF THE ARGUMENTS ABOUT
THE CONSEQUENCES OF MEMBERSHIP PUT FORWARD BY ITS SUPPORTERS
AND OPPONENTS. IT APPEARS THAT NEITHER THE WORST FEARS OF
THE OPPONENTS OF MEMBERSHIP NOR THE MORE OPTIMISTIC CLAIMS
OF THE PROPONENTS HAVE BEEN FULLY REALISED. BY ENTERING THE

COMMUNITY, BRITAIN HAS ENSURED THAT IT HAS A VOICE IN THE
MAKING OF DECISIONS WHICH VITUALLY AFFECT ITS FUTURE. EVEN
IF BRITAIN WERE NOT A MEMBER, ITS ECONOMIC FORTUNES WOULD BE
INFLUENCED BY EC POLICIES. MOREOVER, BRITAIN HAS FOUND THAT
BY ACTING IN CONJUNCTION WITH OTHER MEMBER STATES OF THE EC
IT CAN EXERCISE AN INFLUENCE IN WORLD AFFAIRS WHICH HAD
SLIPPED AWAY FROM IT PRIOR TO ENTRY. WERE A NEW REFERENDUM
ON BRITISH MEMBERSHIP TO BE CALLED TODAY, THE ARGUMENTS
WHICH WOULD BE ADVANCED WOULD PROBABLY REMAIN VERY MUCH THE
SAME AS THOSE AT THE TIME OF THE 1975 REFERENDUM.

03469 GERACIOTI, D.
WORKERS OF THE WORLD
MULTINATIONAL MONITOR, 10(7-8) (JUL 89), 18-21.
ON MAY 17, 1988 PRESIDENT RONALD REAGAN SIGNED AN
INTENATIONAL LABOR ORGANIZATION (ILO) CONVENTION. REAGAN'S
ACTION WAS SURPRISING IN LIGHT OF HIS ADMINISTRATION'S
DISMAL RECORD ON LABOR ISSUES. IN ITS 70 YEARS OF EXISTENCE,
THE ILO HAS FORMULATED 168 CONVENTIONS ESTABLISHING BASIC
INTERNATIONAL LABOR STANDARDS IN SUCH AREAS AS FREEDOM OF
ASSOCIATION, OCCUPATIONAL HEALTH AND SAFETY, AND SOCIAL
SECUITY. BUT THE UNITED STATES HAS ONLY RATFIED NINE OF
THESE CONVENTIONS. IN FACT, THE UNITED STATES WITHDREW FROM
THE ILO IN 1977 AFTER BITTERLY CRITIZING THE ILO'S AGENDA AS
TOO POLITICIZED, THOUGH IT RETURNED IN 1980. IT IS ODD THAT
THE UNITED STATES, WHICH CONSIDERS ITSELF THE TORCH BEARER
IN THE INTERNATIONAL HUMAN RIGHTS MOVEMENTS, SHOULD HAVE
SUCH A TULMUTUOUS RELATIONSHIP WITH THE ILO.

03470 GERE, S.B.
INTERPRETATIONS: UNDERSTANDING SOVIET ARMS CONTROL
MOTIVATIONS AND VERIFICATION ATTITUDES
AVAILABLE FROM NTIS, NO. DE89005295/GAR, DEC 88, 29.
THE ROOT MOTIVATION AT THE HEART OF PRESENT SOVIET ARMS
CONTROL MOTIVATIONS AND VERTIFICATION ATTITUDES IS GROUNDED
WITHIN THE BROAD HISTORICAL PERSPECTIVE OF THE RUSSIAN AND
SOVIET MOBILIZATION STRUGGLE. IT IS FROM THIS PERSPECTIVE
THAT PRESENT SOVIET BEHAVIOR IS ROOTED. OUR UNDERSTANDING OF
THIS ROOT MOTIVATION IS ESSENTIAL TO IDENTIFYING
OPPORTUNITIES TO ENHANCE US-SOVIET RELATIONS AND IN TURN OUR
NATIONAL SECURITY. 33 REFS.

03471 GEREFFI, G.
DEVELOPMENT STRATEGIES AND THE GLOBAL FACTORY
PHILADELPHIA: ANLS OF AMER ACMY OF POLITICAL AND SOC
SCIENCE, (505) (SEP 89). 92-104.
IT HAS BECOME COMMONPLACE TO CONTRAST THE NEWLY
INDUSTRIALIZING COUNTRIES (NIC'S) IN LATIN AMERICA AND EAST
ASIA AS HAVING FOLLOWED INWARDORIENTED AND OUTWARD-ORIENTED
DEVELOPMENT STRATEGIES, RESPECTIVELY. THESE ARE NOT MUTUALLY
EXCLUSIVE ALTERNATIVES, HOWEVER. THEY ARE MORE APPROPRIATELY
SEEN AS HISTORICALLY INTERACTING APPROACHES, WITH THE NIC'S
IN BOTH REGIONS MOVING TOWARD MIXED STRATEGIES IN THE 1970S
AND 1980S. IN PARTICULAR, THE DEVELOPMENT OF SECOND-STAGE
IMPORT-SUBSTITUTION INDUSTRIES HAS ALLOWED THE LATIN
AMERICAN AND EAST ASIAN NIC'S TO MEET A VARIETY OF DOMESTIC
DEVELOPMENT OBJECTIVES AND ULTIMATELY TO ENHANCE THE
FLEXIBILITY OF THEIR EXPORT STRUCTURES. THE NIC'S TODAY ARE
PIVOTAL ACTORS IN A GLOBAL MANUFACTURING SYSTEM WITH
INCREASINGLY COMPLEX PRODUCT NETWORKS AND AN UNPRECEDENTED
DEGREE OF GEOGRAPHICAL SPECIALIZATION.

03472 GEREMEK, B.
GOODWILL AND BITTERNESS: GOVERNMENT PARLIAMENT
RELATIONSHIPS
EAST EUROPEAN REPORTER, 4(1) (WIN 89), 59-60.
PROFESSOR BRONISLAW GEREMEK, HEAD OF THE CITIZENS'
PARLIAMENTARY CLUB (OKP), DISCUSSES THE ROLE OF "OPPOSITION"
IN POLAND'S NEW PARLIAMENT. THE OKP CONSISTS OF MP'S AND
SENATORS ELECTED FROM THE "SOLIDARITY" LIST IN THE JUNE
ELECTIONS. IT CONSIDERS ITS ROLE TO BE THE GIVER OF
CONSTRUCTIVE CRITICISM TO TADEUSZ MAZOWIECKI'S GOVERNMENT.
IT HOPES TO ENCOURAGE SOCIAL AND POLITICAL CHANGE AND
CONTINUE THE BENEVOLENT TRENDS IN POLAND.

03473 GEREMEK, B.
SOLIDARITY AND THE POLITICS OF YOUTH
ACROSS FRONTIERS, 5(2) (SUM 89), 21, 48.
THIS ARTICLE IS AN INTERVIEW WITH BRONISLAW GEREMEK,
FULL TIME ADVISOR TO LECH WALESA AND SOLIDARITY. HE SPEAKS
PRIMARILY ABOUT THE YOUNGER GENERATION OF SOLIDARITY, THE 22-
28-YEAR-OLD WORKERS WHO ARE AMONG THE MOST ACTIVE AND
RADICAL MEMBERS OF THE TRADE UNION, AND ABOUT THE
HOPELESSNESS AND FRUSTRATION THAT PERVADE YOUNG POLE'S
ATTITUDES TOWARD THE FUTURE. THE INTERVIEW WAS CONDUCTED
FOLLOWING THE WAVE OF STRIKES IN POLAND LAST FALL.

03474 GERJUOY, E.; BARANGER, E.U.
THE PHYSICAL SCIENCES AND MATHEMATICS
PHILADELPHIA: ANLS OF AMER ACMY OF POLITICAL AND SOC
SCIENCE, (502) (MAR 89), 58-81.
UNIVERSITY FACULTY IN THE PHYSICAL SCIENCES AND
MATHEMATICSTHE QUANTITATIVE SCIENCES-MUST GENERATE THEIR OWN
RESEARCH FUNDS, OFTEN INCLUDING FUNDS TO SUPPORT THEIR

GRADUATE STUDENTS. THE MAJOR FUNDING SOURCE IS THE FEDERAL GOVERNMENT, THROUGH ITS VARIOUS FUNDING AGENCIES; THE COMPETITION FOR RESEARCH FUNDS IS INTENSE. AS A RESULT, AN AGENCY'S FUNDING CRITERIA, WHICH DEPEND ON THE AGENCY'S MISSION, CAN GREATLY INFLUENCE RESEARCH DIRECTIONS IN A BROAD FIELD OF QUANTITATIVE SCIENCE. IN PARTICULAR, SUCH INFLUENCES—AMOUNTING TO A SIGNIFICANT SKEWING OF RESEARCH DIRECTIONS AND SUBFIELD GROWTH IN UNIVERSITY QUANTITATIVE SCIENCE, WITH POSSIBLE EFFECTS ON UNIVERSITY RECRUITING AND ADMINISTRATIVE POLICIES AS WELL—HAVE RESULTED FROM THE MISSION ORIENTATION OF THE DEPARTMENT OF DEFENSE (DOD), COUPLED WITH POSSIBLE MEANS OF ALLEVIATING THE PROBLEMS POSED BY DOD FUNDING OF UNIVERSITY QUANTITATIVE SCIENCE.

03475 GERLICH, P.
DEREGULATION IN AUSTRIA
EUROPEAN JOURNAL OF POLITICAL RESEARCH, 17(2) (MAR 89), 209-222.
SINCE THE NEW GRAND COALITION GOVERNMENT TOOK OFFICE IN 1986, DEREGULATION HAS BECOME AN OFFICIAL GOAL OF GOVERNMENT POLICY IN AUSTRIA. THE ARTICLE DESCRIBES DEBATES, MEASURES AND COUNTERVAILING TENDENCIES IN THREE AREAS OF DEREGULATION: DELEGISLATION, PRIVATIZATION AND THE PROMOTION OF COMPETITION. BECAUSE DEREGULATION INITIATIVE HAVE NOT BEEN VERY EFFECTIVE THE CONCLUSION DISCUSSES POLITICAL CONSTRAINTS AND OPPORTUNITIES FOR SUCH POLICIES IN THE FUTURE.

03476 GERNS, W.
THE BORDERLINE
WORLD MARXIST REVIEW, 31(12) (DEC 88), 33-39.
THE SPECIFIC FEATURE OF THE COMMUNISTS' POLICY ON REFORM IS THAT THEY ARE ACTING AS A FORCE ADVANCING DEMOCRATISATION IN EVERY SPHERE OF SOCIAL LIFE, WITHOUT CREATING ANY ILLUSIONS AND CLEARLY EXPLAINING THE LIMITS OF REFORMS UNDER CAPITALISM. IT ARGUES THE NEED FOR GOING ON TO SOCIALISM EVEN WHEN SOCIALIST TRANSFORMATIONS IN THE COUNTRY ARE NOT ON THE CURRENT AGENDA, AS THEY ARE NOT, FOR INSTANCE, AT THE PRESENT TIME. HOWEVER, THE SIGNIFICANCE OF THE STRUGGLE FOR REFORMS IS DETERMINED NOT LEAST BY THE NEED TO SOLVE GLOBAL PROBLEMS, WHICH HAVE BECOME SO ACUTE IN SOME FIELDS THAT THEIR SOLUTION CANNOT BE DEFERRED UNTIL CAPITALISM IS GOT OUT OF THE WAY. THIS APPLIES PRIMARILY TO THE ESTABLISHMENT OF LASTING PEACE, THE PREVENTION OF AN ECOLOGICAL DISASTER, AND A TOTAL ECONOMIC COLLAPSE IN THE LESS DEVELOPED COUNTRIES, MANKIND'S RELIABLE SUPPLY WITH ENERGY, AND SO ON. THE SOLUTIONS TO THESE PROBLEMS WILL HAVE TO BE FOUND EVEN UNDER CAPITALISM, I.E., IN A WORLD DIVIDED INTO OPPOSITE SOCIAL SYSTEMS.

03477 GERSHMAN, C.
DEMOCRACY AS THE WAVE OF THE FUTURE: A WORLD REVOLUTION
CURRENT, (312) (MAY 89), 18-25.
IN THE STREETS OF LISBON IN 1975, THE PORTUGUESE PEOPLE DEFEATED A DETERMINED DRIVE BY THE COMMUNIST PARTY TO IMPOSE A TOTALITARIAN DICTATORSHIP. AT THE TIME, MANY OBSERVERS FELT THAT THE PORTUGUESE EVENTS REPRESENTED A DECISIVE MOMENT IN THE HISTORY OF POSTWAR EUROPE AND IN THE EVOLUTION OF EAST-WEST RELATIONS. WHAT COULD NOT BE FULLY APPRECIATED WAS THE EXTENT TO WHICH THE PORTUGUESE DRAMA ALSO REPRESENTED A TURNING POINT IN THE WORLDWIDE STRUGGLE FOR FREEDOM AND DEMOCRACY.

03478 GERSHMAN, C.
THE UNITED STATES AND THE WORLD DEMOCRATIC REVOLUTION
WASHINGTON QUARTERLY, 12(1) (WIN 89), 127-139.
DETERMINING WHAT WILL PROMOTE DEMOCRACY IN A PARTICULAR COUNTRY OR SITUATION IS NOT ALWAYS A SIMPLE MATTER. THE APPROACH DESCRIBED ABOVE IS NOT FOOLPROOF, BUT IT WILL MINIMIZE ERROR BY ENSURING THAT PROGRAMS ARE TAILORED TO LOCAL NEEDS AND DO NOT EXPOSE PEOPLE TO MORE RISK THAN THEY ARE PREPARED TO ACCEPT. ALTHOUGH THE ESTABLISHED DEMOCRACIES CAN ASSIST AND FACILITATE THE PROCESS OF DEMOCRATIC CHANGE, IT IS THE PEOPLE THEMSELVES IN THE DEVELOPING COUNTRIES WHO WILL DETERMINE WHETHER DEMOCRATIC SYSTEMS WILL BE ESTABLISHED AND SURVIVE.

03479 GERSHOWITZ, H.
MANAGING SOLID WASTE IN FUTURE SOCIETIES
AMERICAN CITY AND COUNTY, 104(9) (SEP 89), 44, 46.
THE AUTHOR DISCUSSES THE FUTURE OF MUNICIPAL SOLID WASTE MANAGEMENT AND HOW TECHNOLOGICAL, SOCIAL, AND REGULATORY DEVELOPMENTS WILL AFFECT THE PROBLEM OF WASTE DISPOSAL. HE PREDICTS THAT THE PRIMARY METHODS OF HANDLING WASTES WILL NOT CHANGE THE NEXT THREE DECADES. BUT PUBLIC CONCERN ABOUT THE ENVIRONMENT WILL PRODUCE MORE STRINGENT REGULATION AND INCREASED RECYCLING.

03480 GERSON, S.
ON THE STATE OF GOVERNMENT: SOME IDEOLOGICAL QUESTIONS
POLITICAL AFFAIRS, LXVIII(11) (NOV 89), 18-20.
THE ARTICLE BRIEFLY DISCUSSES THE NATURE OF THE STATE AND OF GOVERNMENT AND EMPHASIZES THE DIFFERENCE BETWEEN THE TWO CONCEPTS. THE FORM OF GOVERNMENT IN A CAPITALIST STATE

MAY VARY CONSIDERABLY, BUT IN EACH CASE IT IS DOMINATED BY BIG CAPITAL. THE ARTICLE ALSO OUTLINES THE COMMUNIST PARTY STRATEGY OF UNITING A BROAD ANTI-MONOPOLY COALITION WHOSE COMMON GOAL IS TO REFORM THE "RICH MAN'S STATE" THAT THE US GOVERNMENT IS BECOMING.

03481 GERSONY, R.
WHY SOMALIS FLEE: CONFLICT IN NORTHERN SOMALIA
CULTURAL SURVIVAL QUARTERLY, 13(4) (1989), 45-58.
IN MAY 1988, A LONGSTANDING CIVIL CONFLICT BETWEEN THE INSURGENT SOMALI NATIONAL MOVEMENT AND THE GOVERNMENT OF SOMALIA SUDDENLY INTENSIFIED, CAUSING SUBSTANTIAL NUMBERS OF REFUGEES TO FLEE THE TROUBLED LAND. HUNDREDS OF THOUSANDS OF ETHIOPIAN REFUGEES WHO HAD EARLIER FLED TO SANCTUARY IN NORTHERN SOMALIA WERE ALSO THOUGHT TO BE SEVERELY AFFECTED BY THE INTENSE FIGHTING, WHILE MANY SOMALIS WHO DID NOT FLEE WERE INTERNALLY DISPLACED INSIDE THEIR OWN COUNTRY.

03482 GESSE, T.C.
EDUCATION AS A DETERMINANT OF POLITICAL PARTICIPATION OF NURSE-MIDWIVES
DISSERTATION ABSTRACTS INTERNATIONAL, 50(4) (OCT 89), 1076-A.
POLITICAL PARTICIPATION IS VIEWED BY NURSE-MIDWIVES AS A MECHANISM FOR INVOLVEMENT IN DECISION-MAKING RELATIVE TO THEIR PROFESSION AND TO THE HEALTH CARE OF WOMEN AND INFANTS. THIS STUDY INVESTIGATES POLITICAL PARTICIPATION AMONG NURSE-MIDWIVES AND EXAMINES THE RELATIONSHIPS THAT INFLUENCE THEIR ELECTORAL, NON-ELECTORAL, AND UNCONVENTIONAL POLITICAL ACTIVITIES. FIVE MODES OF POLITICAL PARTICIPATION ARE IDENTIFIED: COMMUNITY/CONTACTING ACTIVITIES, PROTEST, VOTING, CAMPAIGNING, AND PETITIONING.

03483 GETTLEMAN, M.E.
AGAINST CARTESIANISM: PRELIMINARY NOTES ON THREE GENERATIONS OF ENGLISH-LANGUAGE POLITICAL DISCOURSE ON VIETNAM
BULLETIN OF CONCERNED ASIAN SCHOLARS, 21(2-4) (APR 89), 136-144.
THIS IS GETTLEMAN'S STORY OF THE OSS AND VIETNAM'S AUGUST 1945 REVOLUTION. IT BEGINS BY IDENTIFYING ONE OF THE MAIN WAR-LINKED IDEOLOGICAL PROBLEMS - CARTESIAN IMPERIALISM. IT DESCRIBES THREE GENERATIONS OF CARTESIANISM. THE FIRST IS CIRCUMSCRIBED POLITICAL DIVERSITY; THE SECOND IS CONTEMPORARY SCHOLARSHIP; AND THE THIRD IS CARTESIASM PARTIALLY VANQUISHED.

03484 GEYELIN, P.L.
MANAGING THE MEDIA
FLETCHER FORUM, 13(1) (WIN 89), 19-23.
DOES THE SPOTLIGHT OF PRESS ATTENTION SINCERELY ILLUMINATE A NEWSMAKER OR SENSATIONALLY CREATE A NEWS EVENT? GEYELIN SUGGESTS THAT GOVERNMENT ACTIONS SET THE FOREIGN POLICY AGENDA. PLACING JOURNALISTS AT THE MERCY OF POLICYMAKERS AND THE EVENTS THEMSELVES. THUS, TO THE EXTENT THAT FIRST IMPRESSIONS MATTER, THE GOVERNMENT CONTROLS THE FIRST IMPRESSION. TO THE EXTENT THAT PACKAGING AND PRESENTATION ARE IMPORTANT, THE GOVERNMENT CONTROLS THEM AS WELL. IT HAS NOT ONLY THE POWER TO CLASSIFY WHAT IS DOES NOT WANT THE PUBLIC TO KNOW BUT TO DECLASSIFY WHATEVER MAY ADVANCE ITS PURPOSES.

03485 GEYER, H.S.
INDUSTRIAL DEVELOPMENT POLICY IN SOUTH AFRICA: THE PAST, PRESENT, AND FUTURE
WORLD DEVELOPMENT, 17(3) (MAR 89), 379-396.
THE GROWTH CENTER CONCEPT HAS FORMED THE CORNERSTONE OF INDUSTRIAL DEVELOPMENT POLICY IN SOUTH AFRICA SINCE APARTHEID WAS INTRODUCED AS A CONSTITUTIONAL MODEL IN 1948. THIS PAPER ATTEMPTS TO RECAPTURE THE EVOLUTIONARY DEVELOPMENT OF INDUSTRIAL POLICY IN SOUTH AFRICA AND TO UNDERLINE PROMINENT DEFICIENCIES IN PRESENT INDUSTRIAL DEVELOPMENT POLICY. SOUTH AFRICAN INDUSTRIAL POLICY CONTINUES THE SEGREGATION PRACTICES OF THE PAST, DESPITE THE GOVERNMENT'S REPEATED STATEMENTS IN RECENT YEARS THAT IT INTENDS TO MOVE AWAY FROM THE CONCEPT OF APARTHEID. GUIDELINES FOR A REVISION IN INDUSTRIAL DEVELOPMENT THINKINGBASED ON SOUND ECONOMIC PRINCIPLES RATHER THAN CONCEALED POLITICAL PRACTICES-ARE SUGGESTED FOR THE COUNTRY.

03486 GHALEB, M.
SOLIDARITY MOVEMENT: GROWING RESPONSIBILITY
WORLD MARXIST REVIEW, 32(4) (APR 89), 23-24.
THE SPIRIT OF ARAB SOLIDARITY HAS DROPPED, AND IN THE PAST FEW YEARS NARROW NATIONAL INTERESTS HAVE PREVAILED, THE LEADERS OF SOME COUNTRIES TENDING INCREASINGLY TO BEND THEIR POLICIES TO THE DIKTAT OF WORLD IMPERIALISM. BUT RECENT POSITIVE DEVELOPMENTS, SUCH AS THE ENDING OF THE IRAN-IRAQ WAR AND STEPS TOWARDS STABILITY IN THE REGION, GIVE REASON TO HOPE FOR CHANGES FOR THE BETTER.

03487 GHASSEMI, A.
U.S.-IRANIAN RELATIONSHIPS, 1953-1978: A CASE STUDY OF PATRON CLIENT STATE RELATIONSHIPS

DISSERTATION ABSTRACTS INTERNATIONAL, 50(5) (NOV 89),
1428-A.
USING THE PATRON-CLIENT STATE RELATIONSHIP MODEL, THE
AUTHOR INVESTIGATES THE U.S.-IRANIAN RELATIONSHIP AS
POLITICAL AND MILITARY ALLIES FROM 1953 TO 1978. AFTER 1953,
IRAN BECAME A U.S. CLIENT, JOINED THE AMERICAN COLD WAR
ALLIANCE SYSTEM, AND ASSOCIATED ITSELF WITH WESTERN SECURITY
INTERESTS. DURING THE PERIOD UNDER STUDY, THE AMERICAN-
IRANIAN RELATIONSHIP TOOK DIFFERENT FORMS, INCLUDING PATRON-
CLIENT, PATRON-PREVALENCE, AND INFLUENCE PARITY. CHANGE
OCCURRED IN THE RELATIONSHIP TYPE DUE TO THREE FACTORS:
AMERICAN GOAL STRUCTURES, THE SHAH'S THREAT ENVIRONMENT, AND
THE INTERNATIONAL SYSTEM.

03488 GHAZANFAR, S.M.; MONROE, J.
THE IMPACT OF WELFARE AID ON SOCIETY: THE U.S. WELFARE ACT
OF 1988
MANKIND QUARTERLY, 29(4) (SUM 89), 391-400.
WELFARE AID HAS FREQUENTLY BEEN CRITICIZED AS REDUCING
THE INCENTIVE TO PRODUCTIVITY AND WEAKENING FAMILY BONDS.
THE AUTHORS OF THIS ARTICLE EXAMINE THE U.S. WELFARE ACT OF
1988 AND ASSESS ITS POTENTIAL FOR AMELIORATING POVERTY
WITHOUT THESE DRAWBACKS. THEY EXAMINE THE ORIGIN AND CURRENT
STATUS OF THE AID TO FAMILIES WITH DEPENDENT CHILDREN (AFDC)
AND EXPLORE WELFARE REFORM. THEY CONCLUDE THAT AFDC HAS BEEN
REDEFINED TO INCORPORATE THE WORK ETHIC AND SELF-RELIANCE.

03489 GHAZANFAR, S.M.
THE POLITICAL ECONOMY OF PAKISTAN, 1947-88: A CRITICAL
APPRAISAL
SCANDINAVIAN JOURNAL OF DEVELOPMENT ALTERNATIVES, VIII(1)
(MAR 89), 207-214.
THE ESSAY PRESENTS A REVIEW AND CRITICAL COMMENTARY OF A
RECENT BOOK, THE POLITICAL ECONOMY OF PAKISTAN 1947-88, BY
OMAR NORMAN. THE BOOK PROVIDES A RATHER COMPREHENSIVE
COVERAGE OF THE COUNTRY'S DEVELOPMENT SINCE INDEPENDENCE IN
1947, ALTHOUGH THE PRIMARY EMPHASIS IS ON THE POST-1971
PERIOD. THE BOOK IS DISTINGUISHED BY THE FACT THAT IT
EXPLORES THE POLITICAL-ECONOMIC LINKAGES OF PAKISTAN'S
HISTORY. THE ESSAY CRITICALLY EXAMINES MANY OF THE AUTHOR'S
PREJUDICES AND APPARENT BIASES.

03490 GHILAN, M.
A WAR MAY BE ON ITS WAY
NEW POLITICS, 11(3) (SUM 89), 89-95.
THE AUTHOR PERSITS THAT, IN SPITE OF AN OVERALL
IMPROVEMENT IN CHANCES FOR PEACE, STEMMING BASICALLY FROM
PALESTINIAN DIPLOMACY AND FROM THE INTIFADA, THE IMMEDIATE
PROBABILITY IS THAT BEFORE PEACE IS REACHED ANOTHER MAJOR
LOCAL WAR WILL BREAK OUT. POSSIBLY BEFORE THE END OF 1989
AND PROBABLY BETWEEN ISRAEL AND SYRIA, WITH IRAQ
PARTICIPATING, AND WITH LEBANON AND JORDAN AS THE MAIN
BATTLEFIELDS, THE MIDDLE EAST WILL ERUPT AGAIN.

03491 GHILES, F.
ALGERIANS FACE POLITICAL AND ECONOMIC CHALLENGES
MIDDLE EAST INTERNATIONAL, 353 (JUN 89), 16-17.
CONDUCTING RADICAL POLITICAL REFORMS AT A TIME OF
ECONOMIC AUSTERITY IS NOT MAKING THE TASK OF ALGERIA'S
RULERS ANY EASIER, BUT HAD IT NOT BEEN FOR THE COLLAPSE IN
THE PRICE OF OIL AND GAS, WHICH ACCOUNT FOR 97 PER CENT OF
THE COUNTRY'S INCOME, THE REFORMERS WOULD NOT HAVE BEEN ABLE
TO ARGUE THE CASE FOR CHANGE BETWEEN 1985 AND '87. THE
RECENT AGREEMENT WITH THE INTERNATIONAL MONETARY FUND, WHICH
IS TO LEND ALGERIA $565M AND THE LARGE BILATERAL LOANS
EXTENDED BY FRANCE, ITALY, SPAIN AND JAPAN HAVE HELPED, AS
HAVE FIRMER PRICES FOR CRUDE OIL AND A STRONGER DOLLAR. THEY
ARE ALLOWING THE MINISTER OF FINANCE, MR SID AHMED GHOZALI,
TO INCREASE IMPORTS WHILST AVOIDING OVERALL RESCHEDULING.

03492 GHILES, F.
THE PROSPECTS FOR TUNISIA'S ECONOMY
MIDDLE EAST INTERNATIONAL, (349) (APR 89), 18.
THE AUTHOR DISCUSSES THE ECONOMIC REFORMS INSTITUTED BY
TUNISIA'S PRESIDENT BEN ALI.

03493 GIARDINA, D,
NO END IN SIGHT
SOJOURNERS, 18(10) (NOV 89), 8-10.
THE UNITED MINE WORKERS STRIKE AGAINST THE PITTSON
COMPANY CONTINUES INTO ITS SIXTH MONTH. DESPITE CONSIDERABLE
INTERVENTION BY STATE AND FEDERAL COURTS AND SEVERAL
ATTEMPTS AT NEGOTIATION, THE SITUATION REMAINS LARGELY THE
SAME. THE MOVEMENT REMAINS LARGELY NONVIOLENT AND SEEMS
DESTINED TO CONTINUE UNTIL SOME CONCESSIONS ARE GRANTED.

03494 GIARRATANI, F.; HOUSTEN, D.B.
STRUCTURAL CHANGE AND ECONOMIC POLICY IN A DECLINING
METROPOLITAN REGION: IMPLICATIONS OF THE PITTSBURGH
EXPERIENCE
URBAN STUDIES, 26(6) (DEC 89), 549-558.
PUBLIC-PRIVATE PARTNERSHIPS CAN PLAY A VALUABLE ROLE IN
REGIONAL ECONOMIC POLICY, BUT THE NATURE AND EFFECTIVENESS
OF SUCH ALLIANCES DEPENDS ON THE TYPE OF PROBLEMS FACED BY A

REGION. IN THE CONTEXT OF DECLINE, PARTNERSHIPS MAY BE
ORIENTED TO ECONOMIC RENEWAL AND THE REGENERATION OF LOST
ECONOMIC RENTS. THESE OBJECTIVES MAY BE SERVED WHILE THE
OPPORTUNITY COSTS OF POLICY ACTIONS ARE IGNORED, AND WHEN
GROWTH PROSPECTS ARE POOR, THE RISK IS EVER PRESENT THAT
UNINTENDED AND COSTLY CHANGES IN THE SPATIAL DISTRIBUTION OF
ACTIVITY WITHIN A REGION MAY OCCUR AS A RESULT OF GOVERNMENT
POLICY ACTIONS. REGIONAL POLICY IN THE CONTEXT OF DECLINE
MUST FOCUS ALSO ON THE PROBLEMS ASSOCIATED WITH ECONOMIC
ADJUSTMENT, AND PARTNERSHIPS SEEN ILL SUITED TO GIVE FULL
CONSIDERATION TO. SUCH OBJECTIVES.

03495 GIBBINS, R.
CANADIAN FEDERALISM: THE ENTANGLEMENT OF MEECH LAKE AND
THE FREE TRADE AGREEMENT
PUBLIUS: THE JOURNAL OF FEDERALISM, 19(3) (SUM 89),
185-198.
IN RETROSPECT, 1988 MAY TURN OUT TO BE A PIVOTAL YEAR IN
THE EVOLUTION OF CANADIAN FEDERALISM THE NOVEMBER GENERAL
ELECTION WAS DOMINATED BY AN INTENSE NATIONAL DEBATE OVER
THE PROPOSED FREE TRADE AGREEMENT WITH THE UNITED STATES.
ALTHOUGH THE FREE TRADE AGREEMENT WAS SEEN TO HAVE IMPORTANT
RAMIFICATIONS FOR CANADIAN FEDERALISM, COHERENT DISCUSION OF
THOSE RAMIFICATIONS BECAME BLURRED IN THE FACE OF A MUCH
BROADER AND EMOTIONALLY PARTISAN DEBATE. CONCERNS ABOUT THE
NATURE OF CANADIAN FEDERALISM WERE INSTEAD ABSORBED BY, AND
IN PART DISPLACED BY, AN EMERGING NATIONAL DEBATE ON THE
MEECH LAKE CONSTITUTIONAL ACCORD. THE ACCORD HAD BEEN
REACHED BY THE ELEVEN FIRST MINISTERS IN 1987, BUT BY THE
END OF 1988 IT HAD YET TO RECEIVE LEGISLATIVE RATIFICATION
IN MANITOBA AND NEW BRUNSWICK. IN THE AFTERMATH OF THE 1988
ELECTION, DEBATES OVER FREE TRADE AND THE ACCORD HAVE BECOME
PROGRESSIVELY ENTANGLED. WHILE THIS ENTANGLEMENT DID NOT
ALTER THE OUTCOME OF THE FREE TRADE DEBATE, IT HAS HAD
IMPORTANT CONSEQUENCES FOR THE MEECH LAKE ACCORD, AND THUS
FOR THE FUTURE OF CANADIAN FEDERALISM.

03496 GIBBONS, J. R.
CONTEMPORARY POLITICAL CULTURE: POLITICS IN A POSTMODERN
AGE
SAGE PUBLICATIONS, NEWBURY PARK, CA, 1989, 256.
MANY DRAMATIC CHANGES HAVE TAKEN PLACE RECENTLY IN
EUROPEAN POLITICS WHICH HAVE NEITHER BEEN PREDICTED NOR
SUCCESSFULLY EXPLAINED. THESE CHANGES INCLUDE THE WIDESPREAD
POPULAR RECEPTION OF 'NEW RIGHT' IDEAS, THE SUCCESS OF
CONSERVATIVE PARTIES, THE DECLINE OF CONSENSUS POLITICS AND
CORPORATIST COOPERATION, AND THE INCREASING POWER OF THE NEW
MEDIA INFORMATION SYSTEMS. "CONTEMPORARY POLITICAL CULTURE"
EXPLORES THESE PHENOMENA AND CONCLUDES THAT FUNDAMENTAL LONG-
TERM CHANGES ON THE CONTOURS OF EUROPEAN POLITICAL CULTURE
EXPLAIN THE RISE OF THE NEW POLITICS AND RECENT POLITICAL
EVENTS.

03497 GIBBS, J.P.
CONCEPTUALIZATION OF TERRORISM
AMERICAN SOCIOLOGICAL REVIEW, 54(3) (JUN 89), 329-340.
MANY ISSUES AND PROBLEMS SURROUND THE CONCEPTUALIZATION
OF TERRORISM. MOST DEFINITIONS OF THE TERM ARE INDEFENSIBLE
IF ONLY BECAUSE THEY DO NOT SPEAK TO THOSE ISSUES AND
PROBLEMS. AN ASSESSMENT OF CONTENDING DEFINITIONS CAN
TRANSCEND PURELY PERSONAL OPINIONS; AND AN ASSESSMENT CAN BE
UNDERTAKEN WITHOUT A THEORY, EVEN THOUGH AN IMPRESSIVE
THEORY IS THE ULTIMATE JUSTIFICATION OF ITS CONSTITUENT
DEFINITIONS. THE PRESENT CONCEPTUALIZATION GOES BEYOND A
DEFINITION OF TERRORISM BY EMPHASIZING THE DEFINITION'S
BEARING ON FIVE MAJOR CONCEPTUAL QUESTIONS, EACH OF WHICH
INTRODUCES A MAJOR ISSUE AND/OR PROBLEM. THEN IT IS ARGUED
THAT THINKING OF TERRORISM AND OTHER SOCIOLOGICAL PHENOMENA
IN TERMS OF CONTROL PROMOTES RECOGNITION OF LOGICAL
CONNECTIONS AND/OR EMPIRICAL ASSOCIATIONS, EACH OF WHICH
COULD BECOME A COMPONENT OF A THEORY.

03498 GIBERT, S.P.
SAFEGUARDING TAIWAN'S SECURITY
COMPARATIVE STRATEGY, 8(4) (1989), 425-446.
THIS ARTICLE DISCUSSES THE SECURITY OF THE REPUBLIC OF
CHINA ON TAIWAN, EMPHASIZING U.S.-TAIWAN RELATIONS SINCE THE
PASSAGE OF THE TAIWAN RELATIONS ACT AND UNITED STATES ARMS
TRANSFERS TO TAIWAN. DIPLOMATIC AND MILITARY RELATIONS
BETWEEN THE PEOPLE'S REPUBLIC OF CHINA AND THE REPUBLIC OF
CHINA ON TAIWAN AND BETWEEN THE UNITED STATES AND THE TWO
CHINAS ARE ANALYZED IN THE CONTEXT OF EAST ASIAN POLITICAL
AND SECURITY DEVELOPMENTS. THE ARTICLE CONCLUDES BY NOTING
THAT TAIWAN'S SECURITY IS NOT NOW IN JEOPARDY BUT THAT THE
FUTURE DIMINISHED ROLE FOR THE UNITED STATES IN EAST ASIA
WILL REQUIRE TAIWAN TO UNDERTAKE MEASURES TO ENSURE ITS
ABILITY TO DECIDE ITS STATUS FREE FROM COERCION BY MAINLAND
CHINA.

03499 GIBNEY, M.
THE OBLIGATIONS OF INDIVIDUALS
CONTEMPORARY REVIEW, 254(1477) (FEB 89), 85-89.
THE THRUST OF THIS ARTICLE IS TO ARGUE THAT INDIVIDUALS
HAVE MORAL RESPONSIBILITIES THAT TRANSCEND NATIONAL BORDERS.

THIS IS NOT TO SUGGEST THAT POLICYMAKERS IN DEVELOPED NATIONS WILL NOT HAVE THE KINDS OF MORAL OBLIGATIONS UNDER DISCUSSION HERE. IN FACT, GIVEN THEIR UNIQUE POSITION, IT MIGHT WELL BE ARGUED THAT THERE IS AN EVEN GREATER RESPONSIBILITY FOR POLICYMAKERS TO ACT. HOWEVER, THE MORE UNSETTLED PROPOSITION IS THAT INDIVIDUAL CITIZENS HAVE DUTIES TO AID OTHERS.

03500 GIBSON, D.
LIP SERVICE TO THE GREAT LEADER
FAR EASTERN ECONOMIC REVIEW, 141(38) (SEP 88), 17.
THE INCREASING RELATIONS OF NORTH KOREA'S TRADITIONAL ALLIES AND SOUTH KOREA COULD PUT PRESSURE ON PYONGYANG AND ITS LEADER KIM IL SUNG TO BECOME MORE FLEXIBLE. SOUTH KOREA IS PURSUING TRADE AND DIPLOMATIC RELATIONS WITH MANY OF NORTH KOREA'S ALLIES INCLUDING CHINA, HUNGARY, AND THE USSR. ALSO, THE FAILURE OF ALL OF NORTH KOREA'S ALLIES TO SUPPORT AN OLYMPIC BOYCOTT (WITH THE EXCEPTION OF CUBA) HAS PUT PRESSURE ON PYONGYANG TO EASE ITS ISOLATIONIST, RENEGADE STANCE.

03501 GIBSON, J.L.; FRENDREIS, J.P.; VERTZ, L.L.
PARTY DYNAMICS IN THE 1980S: CHANGE IN COUNTY PARTY ORGANIZATIONAL STRENGTH, 1980-1984
AMERICAN JOURNAL OF POLITICAL SCIENCE, 33(1) (FEB 89), 67-90.
IN THIS ARTICLE THE AUTHORS INVESTIGATE CHANGE IN THE STRENGTH OF LOCAL PARTY ORGANIZATIONS IN THE UNITED STATES. FOCUSING ON PARTY ORGANIZATIONS AT THE COUNTY LEVEL, THE WORKING HYPOTHESIS IS THAT PARTY ORGANIZATIONAL STRENGTH HAS INCREASED IN RECENT YEARS. CHANGES IN THE POLITICAL ENVIRONMENT HAVE PRESENTED OPPORTUNITIES FOR PARTY ORGANIZATIONAL CHANGE, WHILE RESOURCES AND MOTIVATIONS FOR ORGANIZATIONAL AND TECHNOLOGICAL INNOVATION HAVE COME FROM SEVERAL SOURCES. THESE INCLUDE THE NATIONAL AND STATE PARTY ORGANIZATIONS, STATE PUBLIC POLICY, AND EXTRAPARTY ORGANIZATIONS. MOREOVER, THE ROLE BELIEFS OF PARTY CHAIRS HAVE NOT BEEN INIMICAL TO THE DEVELOPMENT OF STRONG PARTY ORGANIZATIONS. FINALLY, INTERPARTY ORGANIZATIONAL COMPETITION MAY FUEL THE ORDINARY PROCESSES OF THE DIFFUSION OF ORGANIZATIONAL INNOVATIONS. THESE HYPOTHESES ARE TESTED USING PANEL DATA FOR LOCAL PARTY ORGANIZATIONS FROM THE LATE 1970S AND 1984. THE AUTHORS CONCLUDE BY IDENTIFYING SOME OF THE IMPLICATIONS OF STRENGTHENING LOCAL PARTIES FOR CHANGES IN THE LARGER PARTY AND POLITICAL SYSTEMS.

03502 GIBSON, J.L.
THE POLICY CONSEQUENCES OF POLITICAL INTOLERANCE: POLITICAL REPRESSION DURING THE VIETNAM WAR ERA
THE JOURNAL OF POLITICS, 51(1) (FEB 89), 13-35.
IN THIS ARTICLE THE AUTHOR ANALYZES THE RELATIONSHIP BETWEEN MASS AND ELITE POLITICAL INTOLERANCE AND THE ADOPTION OF REPRESSIVE PUBLIC POLICIES BY THE STATES OF THE UNITED STATES. FOCUS IS ON STATUTES ADOPTED BY THE STATES DURING THE VIETNAM WAR ERA THAT WERE DESIGNED TO QUASH DISSENT ON UNIVERSITY CAMPUSES. THE ANALYSIS REVEALS THAT REPRESSIVE PUBLIC POLICY REFLECTED NEITHER THE INTOLERANCE OF THE MASS PUBLIC NOR THE POLITICAL ELITES IN THE STATE. INSTEAD, RESTRICTIONS ON CAMPUS PROTEST SEEMED TO BE A DIRECT RESPONSE TO LEVELS OF DISRUPTION ON THE CAMPUSES. SOMEWHAT PARADOXICALLY, POLITICAL TOLERANCE SEEMS TO HAVE CREATED THE CONDITIONS FOR DISSENT TO OCCUR, BUT IT FAILED TO BLOCK REPRESSIVE REACTIONS WHEN DISSENT BECAME DISRUPTIVE. MORE INTOLERANT STATES DID NOT ACT REPRESSIVELY, IN PART BECAUSE THE CLIMATE OF INTOLERANCE DISCOURAGED DISSENT IN THE FIRST PLACE. THESE FINDINGS ARE CONTRASTED TO EARLIER RESEARCH ON REPRESSION DURING THE MCCARTHY ERA AND ULTIMATELY, ARE USED TO IMPUGN THE ELITIST THEORY OF DEMOCRACY.

03503 GIBSON, J.L.
THE STRUCTURE OF ATTITUDINAL TOLERANCE IN THE UNITED STATES
BRITISH JOURNAL OF POLITICAL SCIENCE, 19(4) (OCT 89), 562-570.
THE AUTHORS TAKE A FRESH LOOK AT PUBLIC TOLERANCE AND INTOLERANCE OF POLITICAL GROUPS IN THE UNITED STATES.

03504 GIBSON, R.
EUROPE'S NEXT MOVE
SPACE POLICY, 5(3) (AUG 89), 186-187.
SOME TIME BEFORE THE END OF THE FIRST QUARTER OF 1991 THE MINISTERIAL COUNCIL OF THE EUROPEAN SPACE AGENCY (ESA) WILL BE TAKING DECISIONS ABOUT THE DEVELOPMENT PHASES OF THE COLUMBUS AND HERMES PROGRAMS. THE PROSPECTS FOR COMPLETING EITHER PROGRAM WITHIN THE ORGINALLY APPROVED COSTS ARE NOT BRIGHT, AND OPERATIONAL COSTS WILL BE THREE TIMES THE AMOUNT THE ESA SPENDS ON ITS SCIENTIFIC PROGRAM. ARE THEY GOOD VALUE FOR MONEY? THE AUTHOR ARGUES THAT EUROPE IS IN DANGER OF YIELDING TO OTHERS THE LEAD IN THE NEXT GENERATION OF SPACE FLIGHT.

03505 GIDENGIL, E.
CLASS AND REGION IN CANADIAN VOTING: A DEPENDENCY INTERPRETATION

CANADIAN JOURNAL OF POLITICAL SCIENCE, 22(3) (SEP 89), 563-588.
THIS STUDY DEVELOPS A DEPENDENCY INTERPRETATION OF THE INTERPLAY BETWEEN CLASS AND REGION IN INFLUENCING CANADIAN VOTING. THE WEAKNESS OF ANY NATIONAL CLASS CLEAVAGE IN VOTING IS LINKED TO THE SOCIALLY DISINTEGRATIVE EFFECTS OF REGIONAL DEPENDENCY. CLASS CLEAVAGES ARE NOT CONSISTENTLY MANIFESTED IN CANADIAN VOTING BECAUSE CONSISTENT CLASS INTERESTS ARE LACKING. LOG-LINEAR ANALYSES CONFIRM THAT CLASS DOES AFFECT VOTING BUT THIS EFFECT DIFFERS IN BOTH FORM AND INTENSITY DEPENDING ON A REGION'S LOCATION IN THE CENTRE-PERIPHERY SYSTEM. THE IMPACT OF UNION MEMBERSHIP AND LANGUAGE ON THE INTERPLAY BETWEEN CLASS AND REGION IS ALSO EXAMINED.

03506 GIDENGIL, E.
DIVEISITY WITHIN UNITY: ON ANALYZING REGIONAL DEPENDENCY
STUDIES IN POLITICAL ECONOMY: A SOCIALIST REVIEW, 29 (SUM 89), 91-122.
SURPRISINGLY LITTLE SYSTEMATIC ATTENTION HAS BEEN GIVEN TO THE DEFINITION AND IDENTIFICATION OF "REGIONS" IN CANADA. THE DIFFERENCES AMONG THE PROVINCES IN TERMS OF BASIC SOCIAL AND ECONOMIC CHARACTERISTICS, AS WELL AS POLITICAL BEHAVIOUR, ARE SO APPARENT THAT IT IS EASY TO OVERLOOK THE FACT THAT THE PROVINCES ARE THEMSELVES HARDLY HOMOGENEOUS IN THESE RESPECTS. THE APPROACH ADOPTED HERE IS TO USE CLUSTER ANALYSIS TO DETERMINE WHETHER CANADA'S REGIONS IN THE EARLY 1970'S FORMED DISTINCT GROUPS IN TERMS OF THE VARIOUS DIMENSIONS THAT MAKE UP THE DEPENDENCY SYNDROME -- EXTERNAL PENETRATION, RESTRICTED CHOICE, VERTICAL INTERACTION, LACK OF INTEGRATION, FUNCTIONAL INCOMPLETENESS, DEVELOPMENTAL DISPARITIES, AND DIFFERENCES IN LEVEL OF LIVING.

03507 GIDEON, J.P.
DEFENDING AMERICA: THE ESTRANGEMENT OF STRATEGIC DEFENSES, 1945-1985
DISSERTATION ABSTRACTS INTERNATIONAL, 49(7) (JAN 89), 1951-A.
THE AUTHOR REVIEWS PAST AND PRESENT US STRATEGIC AIR DEFENSE DOCTRINE AND ITS INTERACTION WITH OVERALL NATIONAL SECURITY POLICY. EMPHASIS IS PLACED ON THE DEVELOPMENT OF THE STRATEGIC DOCTRINE, THE VARYING PERCEPTIONS OF THE THREAT, THE DECLINE OF AMERICAN AIR DEFENSE CAPABILITY, AND THE POLITICS OF AIR DEFENSE AS REFLECTED IN CONGRESSIONAL ATTITUDES.

03508 GIESECKE, J. R.
MAKING DECISIONS UNDER CHAOTIC CONDITIONS
DISSERTATION ABSTRACTS INTERNATIONAL, 49(8) (FEB 89), 2386-A.
THE AUTHOR COMPARES THE UTILITY OF THE GARBAGE CAN MODEL AND THE POLITICAL BARGAINING MODEL FOR UNDERSTANDING AND MANAGING DECISION-MAKING PROCESSES IN COMPLEX ORGANIZATIONS, USING THREE CATEGORIES OF VARIABLES: CHARACTERISTICS OF THE ORGANIZATION, CHARACTERISTICS OF THE DECISION-MAKING PROCESS, AND THE METHOD BY WHICH THE PROCESS SOLVES PROBLEM.

03509 GILAT, Z.
THE INTIFADA AND THE ISRAELI PRESS
NEW OUTLOOK, 32(11-12 (297-298)) (NOV 89), 37-39.
DURING THE INTIFADA, THE ISRAELI PRESS HAS WORKED UNDER INCREASINGLY SEVERE PRESSURES, WITHOUT THE PROPER TOOLS TO CARRY OUT ITS TASK. DESPITE THE UPSWING IN NEWSWORTHY ACTIVITY, THE QUANTITY OF JOURNALISTIC MANPOWER COVERING THE OCCUPIED TERRITORIES HAS BARELY CHANGED DURING THE TWO YEARS OF THE UPRISING. EACH DAY THERE ARE DOZENS OF INCIDENTS AND INDIVIDUALS WORTHY OF PUBLIC INTEREST, BUT THE NUMBER OF REPORTERS IS INSUFFICIENT TO COVER THEM. IT DOESN'T TAKE LONG FOR THEIR REPORTS TO COLLAPSE UNDER THE BURDEN OF TRYING TO COVER TOO MUCH TERRITORY WITH TOO FEW REPORTERS.

03510 GILBAR, G. G.
THE ECONOMY OF NABLUS AND THE HASHEMITES: THE EARLY YEARS, 1949-56
MIDDLE EASTERN STUDIES, 25(1) (JAN 89), 51-63.
THE RELATIONS BETWEEN THE GOVERNMENT AND NABLUS DEVELOPED IN TWO STAGES: THE FIRST (1949-53) HAS CHARACTERIZED BY THE FOUNDERING OF HOPES FOR AN ECONOMIC BREAKTHROUGH UNDER THE HASHEMITE REGIME AND THE ONSET OF SENTIMENTS OF ALIENATION AND HOSTILITY ON THE PART OF THE POPULATION TOWARDS IT; THE SECOND STAGE (1954-56) WAS MARKED BY THE ATTEMPT TO MODERATE THIS RESENTMENT AND HOSTILITY THROUGH PUMPING IN SOME LIMITED FUNDS FOR THE DEVELOPMENT OF THE CITY. THIS ARTICLE EXAMINES HOWS THESE DEVELOPMENTS LEFT THEIR MARK ON THE CITY'S ECONOMY IN THE PERIOD UNDER STUDY AND LATER.

03511 GILBERT, G.
TOWARD THE WELFARE STATE: SOME BRITISH VIEWS ON THE 'RIGHT TO SUBSISTENCE,' 1768-1834.
REVIEW OF SOCIAL ECONOMY, 46(2) (OCT 88), 144-163.
THE PURPOSE OF THE PAPER, BROADLY STATED, IS TO COMPARE THE VIEWS OF SEVERAL BRITISH THINKERS ON THE JUSTIFICATION OF POOR RELIEF DURING A PERIOD WHEN THE INTRODUCTION OF AN

IRISH POOR LAW AND THE ABOLITION OF THE ENGLISH POOR LAW WERE MATTERS OF INTENSE PUBLIC DEBATE, A DEBATE WHICH BROUGHT TO PUBLIC VIEW MORE EXPLICITLY THAN EVER BEFORE THE IDEOLOGICAL FOUNDATIONS OF STATE ACTION TO ASSIST THE POOR. THE BOLDLY ORIGINAL IDEAS OF AN ANGLICAN CLERGYMAN ON THE NEED FOR A POOR LAW IN IRELAND WILL SET THE CONTEXT FOR THE TWO MAIN CONTENTIONS OF THE PAPER. FIRST, CLASSICAL POLITICAL ECONOMY, CHIEFLY IN THE PERSON OF THOMAS MALTHUS, CHALLENGED BOTH THE "JUSTICE" AND "POLICY" OF POOR RELIEF SO EFFECTIVELY IN THE FIRST TWO DECADES OF THE NINETEENTH CENTURY THAT THE VERY SURVIVAL OF THE POOR LAW WAS PUT IN DOUBT. SECOND, POLITICAL ECONOMY ITSELF, IN A STARTLING REVERSAL DURING THE 1820S, CAME TO ACCEPT THE "POLICY" AND — IN THE CASE OF SEVERAL ECONOMISTS — EVEN THE "JUSTICE" OF STATE ASSISTANCE TO THE POOR.

03512 GILBERT, G. R.; HYDE, A. C.
FOLLOWERSHIP AND THE FEDERAL WORKER
PUBLIC ADMINISTRATION REVIEW, 48(6) (NOV 88), 962-968.
THIS ARTICLE DEFINES "FOLLERSHIP" AS A SPECIAL AND INTERDEPENDENT (AS OPPOSED TO DEPENDENT) ROLE IN THE SUPERVISOR-SUBORDINATE TEAM. THE DYNAMICS OF FOLLOWERSHIP IS EXPLORED AS WELL AS THE DIMENSIONS OF FOLLOWERSHIP ARE DEFINED

03513 GILBERT, J.R.
ECONOMIC AND POLICY IMPLICATIONS OF PROPOSED ARMS SALES OR TRANSFERS TO THE PERSIAN GULF
AVAILABLE FROM NTIS, NO. AD-A205 419/5/GAR, DEC 88, 160.
PRESIDENTS CARTER AND REAGAN EACH ESTABLISHED A NEW UNITED STATES POLICY TO GOVERN SALES OR TRANSFERS OF CONVENTIONAL ARMS TO FOREIGN NATIONS. PRESIDENT CARTER CALLED FOR STRICTER CONTROLS AND AN OVERALL REDUCTION IN ARMS TRANSFERS TO FOREIGN NATIONS. PRESIDENT REAGAN BELIEVED THAT ARMS TRANSFERS TO FRIENDS AND ALLIES STRENGTHENED THE UNITED STATES POSITION IN THE WORLD. THIS THESIS ANALYZES THE SUCCESS OF BOTH ARMS TRANSFER POLICIES IN THE PERSIAN GULF BY COMPARING THE DOLLAR AMOUNT AND TYPE OF EQUIPMENT ACTUALLY TRANSFERRED AGAINST THE FORMAL CONGRESSIONAL NOTIFICATIONS (ARMS EXPORT CONTROL ACT SECTION 36B). FURTHER, IT EXAMINES PROPOSED ARMS SALES AND TRANSFER WITH RESPECT TO STRATEGIC ACCESS OF THE PERSIAN GULF. FINALLY, IT EXAMINES EMPLOYMENT AND FINANCIAL IMPACTS OF THE FOREIGN MILITARY SALES PROGRAM ON THE UNITED STATES ECONOMY. THESES. (FR)

03514 GILBERT, R.E.
MORAL LEADERSHIP IN CIVIL RIGHTS: AN EVALUATION OF JOHN F. KENNEDY
POLITICAL COMMUNICATION AND PERSUASION, 6(1) (1989), 1-19.
THIS STUDY EVALUATES JOHN F. KENNEDY'S RECORD AS A MORAL LEADER AND THE NATION'S TEACHER ON THE ISSUE OF CIVIL RIGHTS. IT BEGINS WITH A BRIEF DISCUSSION OF KENNEDY'S CIVIL RIGHTS RECORD AS A MEMBER OF THE U.S. SENATE AND THEN MOVES INTO AN ANALYSIS OF HIS PRESIDENTIAL YEARS. AS A BRIDGE BETWEEN THE SENATORIAL AND PRESIDENTIAL PERIODS, THE 1960 PRESIDENTIAL CAMPAIGN IS EXAMINED, WITH ATTENTION GIVEN TO THE DEMOCRATIC PARTY PLATFORM, KENNEDY'S CIVIL RIGHTS REMARKS, THE MARTIN LUTHER KING "EPISODE," AND BLACK VOTING BEHAVIOR ON ELECTION DAY.

03515 GILBOA, E.
ISRAEL'S IMAGE IN AMERICAN PUBLIC OPINION
MIDDLE EAST REVIEW, XXI(3) (SPR 89), 25-38.
IT HAS BEEN SUGGESTED THAT THE RECENT DISAGREEMENTS AND SCANDALS IN AMERICAN-ISRAELI RELATIONS, THE PALESTINIAN RIOTS AND ISRAEL'S USE OF FORCE TO STOP THEM, AND THE ISRAELI OBJECTIONS TO THE SHULTZ INITIATIVE HAVE CAUSED SUBSTANTIAL EROSION OF ISRAEL'S TRADITIONAL, FAVORABLE STANDING IN AMERICAN PUBLIC OPINION. THIS HYPOTHESIS IS EXAMINED HERE THROUGH EVALUATION OF THE POSSIBLE EFFECTS OF THE PALESTINIAN RIOTS, AND THE EARLIER CONTROVERSIAL EVENTS, ON AMERICAN ATTITUDES TOWARD KEY U.S.-ISRAELI ISSUES. TO ACCOMPLISH THIS TASK, IT HAS NECESSARY TO COLLECT ALL AVAILABLE RECENT OPINION DATA AND TO PLACE IT WITHIN LONG-TERM TRENDS AND THE APPROPRIATE HISTORICAL CONTEXT.

03516 GILBOA, E.
THE PALESTINIAN UPRISING: HAS IT TURNED AMERICAN PUBLIC OPINION?
ORBIS, 33(1) (WIN 89), 21-37.
IN THE TWO DECADES THAT FOLLOWED THE SIX DAY WAR OF 1967, AMERICAN PUBLIC OPINION WAS HIGHLY FAVORABLE TOWARD ISRAEL AND ITS POLICIES IN THE ARAB-ISRAELI CONFLICT. YET WHEN THE PALESTINIAN UPRISING BEGAN IN DECEMBER 1987, AMERICAN MEDIA STRENUOUSLY CRITICIZED ISRAEL'S RESPONSE TO THE VIOLENCE. DID THIS BARRAGE OF CRITICAL COMMENTARY DIMINISH THE SUPPORT THAT AMERICANS TRADITIONALLY GAVE ISRAEL? SURPRISINGLY, IT DID NOT. AND IN THAT SENSE, WE MAY SAY, THE UPRISING FAILED TO ACHIEVE ONE OF ITS MAIN PURPOSES.

03517 GILES, M. W.; LANCASTER, T.D.
POLITICAL TRANSITION SOCIAL DEVELOPMENT, AND LEGAL MOBILIZATION IN SPAIN

AMERICAN POLITICAL SCIENCE REVIEW, 83(3) (SEP 89), 817-834.
THE AUTHORS EXAMINE COURT USAGE IN SPAIN BETWEEN 1960 AND 1980. DURING THIS PERIOD SPAIN EXPERIENCED RAPID ECONOMIC GROWTH WITH ITS ATTENDANT SOCIAL CHANGE AND DRAMATIC POLITICAL TRANSITION FROM AUTHORITARIANISM TO DEMOCRACY. BOTH THE MOVEMENT TOWARD DEMOCRACY AND SOCIAL DEVELOPMENT ARE FOUND TO BE POSITIVELY LINKED TO INCREASES IN LEGAL MOBILIZATION.

03518 GILIOMEE, H.
THE ELUSIVE SEARCH FOR PEACE
SOUTH AFRICA INTERNATIONAL, 19(3) (JAN 89), 140-151.
THE ARTICLE EXPLORES THE SIMILAR "FATAL EMBRACE" OF OPPOSING FACTIONS IN SOUTH AFRICA, NORTHERN IRELAND, AND ISREAL. IT OUTLINES MUCH OF WHAT IS COMMON TO THE THREE SITUATIONS AND EMPHASIZES THE CONDITIONS THAT MAKE REACHING ANY SORT OF COMPROMISE AGREEMENT SUCH A DIFFICULT TASK. IT OUTLINES SOME PRECONDITIONS FOR PEACE IN SOUTH AFRICA. THEY INCLUDE: THE MUTUAL ACCEPTANCE OF THE LIMITS OF POWER; THE ACCEPTANCE OF A DUAL TRADITION IN SOUTH AFRICAN POLITICAL LIFE AND A REALIZATION THAT A SETTLEMENT WHICH EXCLUDES ONE IS UNWORKABLE; AND THE SHELVING (FOR THE TIME BEING) OF THE CONCEPT OF MAJORITY CONSENT.

03519 GILL, A.; LONG, S.
IS THERE AN IMMIGRATION STATUS WAGE DIFFERENTIAL BETWEEN LEGAL AND UNDOCUMENTED WORKERS?: EVIDENCE FROM THE LOS ANGELES GARMENT INDUSTRY
SOCIAL SCIENCE QUARTERLY, 70(1) (MAR 89), 164-173.
THIS PAPER EXAMINES THE QUESTION OF WHETHER THE LOWER WAGES GENERALLY OBSERVED FOR UNDOCUMENTED WORKERS ARE DUE PRIMARILY TO THEIR IMMIGRATION STATUS OR TO DIFFERENCE FROM LEGAL WORKERS IN OTHER WAGE-RELATED CHARACTERISTICS. WHEN ANALYZING THE WAGES OF HISPANIC GARMENT WORKERS WITH A MODEL THAT INCLUDES CONTROLS FOR HUMAN CAPITAL, PERSONAL, AND JOB CHARACTERISTICS, NO EVIDENCE IS FOUND OF A WAGE DIFFERENTIAL BASED ON IMMIGRATION STATUS. HOWEVER, WHEN THE MODEL IS RESPECIFIED TO EXCLUDE JOB CHARACTERISTICS, EVIDENCE IS FOUND THAT AN IMMIGRATION STATUS WAGE DIFFERENTIAL MAY EXIST.

03520 GILL, G.
IDEOLOGY, ORGANIZATION AND THE PATRIMONIAL REGIME
JOURNAL OF COMMUNIST STUDIES, 5(3) (SEP 89), 285-303.
THE VIEW OF THE COMMUNIST PARTY AS A TIGHTLY ORGANIZED, HIGHLY DISCIPLINED, EFFICIENT POLITICAL STRUCTURE IS LARGELY A MYTH. THE COMMUNIST PARTY WHICH ACHIEVED POWER IN THE SOVIET UNION, AND WHICH WAS THE PROTOTYPE FOR THIS MYTH, WAS UNABLE TO GENERATE HIGH LEVELS OF ORGANIZATIONAL AUTONOMY, INTEGRITY AND COHERENCE. INSTEAD IT DEVELOPED AS AN INSTRUMENT OF A DOMINANT LEADER AND, INTERNALLY, WAS STRUCTURED ON THE BASIS OF THE PATRIMONIAL PRINCIPLE. THIS MEANT THAT ORGANIZATIONAL LINKAGES BETWEEN DIFFERENT LEVELS OF THE PARTY WERE WEAK. IN THIS CONTEXT, THE IDEOLOGY AND THE LEADER CULT INTERTWINED SO AS TO SUSTAIN AND REINFORCE THE PATRIMONIAL STRUCTURE OF POWER WITHIN THE PARTY. THIS LINKAGE OF ORGANIZATIONAL STRUCTURE, IDEOLOGY AND CULT HAS CREATED REAL PROBLEMS FOR THOSE LIKE KHRUSHCHEV AND GORBACHEV WHO HAVE SOUGHT TO REPLACE THE PATRIMONIAL STRUCTURE BY ONE BASED MORE ON THE PARTY'S ORGANIZATIONAL NORMS.

03521 GILL, S.R.; LAW, D.
GLOBAL HEGEMONY AND THE STRUCTURAL POWER OF CAPITAL
INTERNATIONAL STUDIES QUARTERLY, 33(4) (DEC 89), 475-500.
THIS ESSAY SEEKS TO CLARIFY, DEVELOP, AND APPLY CONCEPTS OF POWER AND HEGEMONY WHICH ARE OFTEN LATENT WITHIN THE LITERATURE IN THE FIELD OF INTERNATIONAL POLITICAL ECONOMY. CLARIFICATION IS VITAL, BOTH FOR DEBATE BETWEEN RIVAL PERSPECTIVES AND FOR ATTEMPTS TO GO BEYOND THEM. WE SEE POWER AS HAVING RELATED MATERIAL AND NORMATIVE, BEHAVIORAL AND STRUCTURAL DIMENSIONS. THESE DISTINCTIONS ARE ELABORATED TO HELP EXPLAIN ASPECTS OF THE CHANGING NATURE OF PRESENT-DAY CAPITALISM, WITH PARTICULAR REFERENCE TO ASPECTS OF TRANSFORMATION IN THE 1980S AND BEYOND. PARTLY BUILDING UPON ROBERT COX'S ANALYSIS OF SOCIAL FORCES AND WORLD ORDERS, AND ANTONIO GRAMSCI'S THEORY OF HEGEMONY, WE SEEK TO EXPLAIN SOME OF THE CONDITIONS UNDER WHICH A MORE "TRANSNATIONAL" REGIME OF ACCUMULATION AND AN ASSOCIATED HEGEMONY OF TRANSNATIONAL CAPITAL MIGHT DEVELOP. SUCH A HEGEMONY COULD NEVER BE COMPLETE BECAUSE OF COUNTERHEGEMONIC FORCES AND CONTRADICTORY ELEMENTS IN THE INTERNATIONALIZATION OF CAPITAL. SOME REQUIREMENTS FOR AN ALTERNATIVE COUNTER-HEGEMONIC HISTORIC BLOC ARE SKETCHED, WITH SUGGESTIONS FOR A RESEARCH AGENDA.

03522 GILLEN, D.W.; OUM, T.H.; TRETHEWAY, M.W.
PRIVATIZATION OF AIR CANADA: WHY IT IS NECESSARY IN A DEREGULATED ENVIRONMENT
CANADIAN PUBLIC POLICY—ANALYSE DE POLITIQUES, 15(3) (SEP 89), 285-299.
THE OBJECTIVE OF THIS PAPER IS TO ASSESS THE EFFECT OF THE PRIVATIZATION OF AIR CANADA ON THE ECONOMIC EFFICIENCY OF AIR CANADA ITSELF AND ON THE CANADIAN AIRLINE INDUSTRY. THREE QUESTIONS ARE INVESTIGATED: HOW CONTINUED GOVERNMENT

OWNERSHIP OF AIR CANADA WOULD EFFECT ECONOMIC EFFICIENCY, THE NEW PRIMARY GOAL OF AIR TRANSPORT POLICY; WHAT ADDITIONAL COSTS TO THE INDUSTRY MIGHT ARISE FROM MAINTAINING CROWN OWNERSHIP; AND WHETHER AIR CANADA COULD ACHIEVE NON-ECONOMIC GOALS MORE EFFECTIVELY IF IT WERE TO REMAIN A CROWN CORPORATION. IT FINDS FROM THE TWO COMPLEMENTARY METHODOLOGIES, TOTAL FACTOR PRODUCTIVITY (TFP) AND VARIABLE COST FUNCTION ANALYSIS, THAT CROWN OWNERSHIP OF AIR CANADA HAS HISTORICALLY RESULTED IN A LOSS OF PRODUCTIVE EFFICIENCY OF APPROXIMATELY 23 PER CENT OF TOTAL COSTS. THIS RESULT IS DUE PRIMARILY TO AN OVEREXPANSION OF ITS CAPITAL STOCK. IT ALSO ARGUES THAT MAINTAINING CROWN OWNERSHIP CREATES SIGNIFICANT ENTRY AND EXIT BARRIERS TO THE INDUSTRY AND ROUTES, AS WELL AS ADJUSTMENT COSTS FOR AIR CANADA ITSELF. THESE CONSEQUENCES HAVE SPILLOVER EFFECTS FOR THE REST OF THE INDUSTRY, AND COULD REDUCE THE EFFICIENCY GAINS AVAILABLE FROM DEREGULATION. FINALLY, IT SHOWS THAT THERE IS NO CREDENCE TO THE ARGUMENT THAT A CROWN-OWNED AIR CANADA IS BETTER ABLE TO FULFIL THE SOCIAL GOALS OF GOVERNMENT.

03523 GILLESPIE, C.G.
DEMOCRATIC CONSOLIDATION IN THE SOUTHERN CONE AND BRAZIL: BEYOND POLITICAL DISARTICULATION?
THIRD WORLD QUARTERLY, 11(2) (APR 89), 92-113.
THE AUTHOR ENDEAVORS TO ANSWER THE QUESTION OF WHETHER DEMOCRACY IS BEING CONSOLIDATED IN THREE LATIN AMERICAN COUNTRIES THAT APPEARED TO COMPLETE THE TRANSITION TO DEMOCRACY BETWEEN 1983 AND 1985. ALL THREE COUNTRIES ARE, FOR ONE REASON OR ANOTHER, CRUCIAL CASES FOR THE FUTURE OF LATIN AMERICAN DEMOCRACY: ARGENTINA AND BRAZIL BECAUSE OF THEIR SIZE AND URUGUAY BECAUSE OF ITS PREVIOUS CHARACTER AS A DEMOCRATIC ROLE MODEL FOR THE REGION.

03524 GILLESPIE, C.G.
PARTY STRATEGIES AND REDEMOCRATIZATION: THEORETICAL AND COMPARATIVE PERSPECTIVES ON THE URUGUAYAN CASE
DISSERTATION ABSTRACTS INTERNATIONAL, 50(5) (NOV 89), 1421-A.
IN 1973 URUGUAY'S DEMOCRACY BROKE DOWN AND TWELVE YEARS OF REPRESSIVE MILITARY RULE ENSUED, CULMINATING IN A NEGOTIATED TRANSITION TO DEMOCRACY. IN CONTRAST TO PREVIOUS ACCOUNTS OF THE BREAKDOWN, THIS ANALYSIS FOCUSES ON THE ROLE OF POLITICAL PARTIES AND ELITES IN THE POLITICAL CHANGE. THE AUTHOR DISCUSSES THE WAYS IN WHICH THE PARTIES ADAPTED AND SURVIVED DURING THE AUTHORITARIAN MILITARY RULE, DESPITE THEIR ILLEGALITY. HE ALSO TRACES THEIR EVOLUTION FOLLOWING THE 1980 PLEBISCITE AND THE SHIFT IN THE PATTERN OF ALLIANCES THAT LED TO THE LEGALIZATION OF THE LEFT AND THE ELECTIONS OF NOVEMBER 1984.

03525 GILLESPIE, D.G.
HISTORY, POLITICS, AND THE RUSSIAN PEASANT: BORIS MOZHAEV AND THE COLLECTIVIZATION OF AGRICULTURE
SLAVONIC AND EAST EUROPEAN REVIEW, 67(2) (APR 89), 183-210.
BORIS MOZHAEV'S WORK REFUTES ACCEPTED NOTIONS OF SOVIET AGRICULTURE AND OFFERS A FUNDAMENTAL RE-INTERPRETATION OF HISTORICAL EVENTS, GIVING THE LIE TO HITHERTO "OFFICIAL" HISTORIES. MOZHAEV IS A CONTROVERSIAL WRITER WHO HAS RECEIVED RELATIVELY LITTLE CRITICAL ATTENTION IN THE SOVIET UNION, POSSIBLY BECAUSE HE UNEQUIVOCALLY SUPPORTS THE INDIVIDUAL AT THE EXPENSE OF OFFICIALDOM. BUT HIS NOVEL "RURAL FOLK" HAS AROUSED DEBATE IN THE USSR AND PUTS HIM IN THE FRONT RANK OF MODERN SOVIET WRITERS.

03526 GILLIAM, F.D., JR.; WHITBY, K.J.
RACE, CLASS, AND ATTITUDES TOWARD SOCIAL WELFARE SPENDING: AN ETHCLASS INTERPRETATION
SOCIAL SCIENCE QUARTERLY, 70(1) (MAR 89), 88-100.
THEORIES CONCERNING THE IMPACT OF RACE AND CLASS HAVE UNDEREMPHASIZED THE IMPORTANCE OF THE JOINT EFFECTS OF THESE TWO EXPLANATORY VARIABLES. THIS ARTICLE OFFERS AN EXPLICITLY INTERACTIVE MODEL BASED ON THE CONCEPT OF "ETHCLASS." FOCUSING ON THE BLACK MIDDLE CLASS AS A PRIME EXAMPLE OF AN ETHCLASS, THE AUTHORS FIND THAT UPPER STATUS BLACKS ARE SOMEWHAT MORE CONSERVATIVE THAN THEIR LOWER STATUS RACE PEERS (WITH REGARD TO ATTITUDES TOWARD SOCIAL WELFARE SPENDING) BUT ARE SIGNIFICANTLY MORE LIBERAL THAN THEIR WHITE CLASS PEERS.

03527 GILLMAN, H.
THE CONSTITUTION BESEIGED: T.R., TAFT, AND WILSON ON THE VIRTUE AND EFFICACY OF A FACTION-FREE REPUBLIC
PRESIDENTIAL STUDIES QUARTERLY, XIX(1) (WIN 89), 179-202.
RECENTLY, IN SEPARATE WORKS, RALPH KETCHAM AND THEODORE LOWI DISCUSSED HOW DIFFERENT CONCEPTIONS OF THE RELATIONSHIP BETWEEN INTEREST GROUPS AND THE AMERICAN STATE--ONE DOMINANT AT THE TIME OF THE FOUNDING, THE OTHER PREVALENT DURING THE PAST FEW DECADES--INFLUENCED OR ARE PRESENTLY INFLUENCING PRESIDENTIAL POLITICS. THE ESSAY LOOKS AT A PERIOD OF TRANSITION BETWEEN THESE TWO OPPOSING SETS OF TRADITIONS AND PRACTICES. IN ITS ANALYSIS OF POLITICS DURING THE ROSEVELTTAFT-WILSON ERA, THE ESSAY SEEKS TO EXAMINE HOW THE PRESENCE OF A WELL-DEFINED TRADITION OF POLITICAL LEGITIMACY AVERSE TO "FACTIONAL POLITICS", AFFECTED THE DISCOURSE AND

DECISIONMAKING OF PRESIDENTS AT THE BEGINNING OF THE TWENTIETH CENTURY AS THEY CONTEMPLATED THE RESPONSE OF THE AMERICAN STATE TO INDUSTRIALIZATION.

03528 GILPIN, R.
INTERNATIONAL POLITICS IN THE PACIFIC RIM ERA
PHILADELPHIA: ANLS OF AMER ACMY OF POLITICAL AND SOC SCIENCE, (505) (SEP 89), 56-67.
IN THE HISTORY OF INTERNATIONAL RELATIONS, ECONOMIC, TECHNOLOGICAL, AND DEMOGRAPHIC DEVELOPMENTS HAVE, OVER THE CENTURIES, CAUSED THE CENTER OF ECONOMIC AND POLITICAL ACTIVITIES TO SHIFT FROM ON LOCUS TO ANOTHER. THE MODERN WORLD'S HISTORY CAN BEST BE UNDERSTOOD AS A PROCESS OF HISTORICAL CHANGE THAT BEGAN IN THE MEDITERRANEAN AND SUBSEQUENTLY DIFFUSED NORTH TO ATLANTIC SEABOARD STATES AND THEN SPREAD BOTH WESTWARD ACROSS THE ATLANTIC AND EASTWARD ACROSS THE EURASIAN CONTINENT. FORCES OF CHANGE SWEPT ACROSS BOTH THE NORTH AMERICAN CONTINENT AND EASTERN EUROPE AND EUROPEAN RUSSIA. TODAY, HISTORIC MOVEMENTS OF ECONOMIC, POLITICAL, AND TECHNOLOGICAL FORCES ARE CONVERGING ON THE PACIFIC. A MORE PLURALISTIC WORLD IS RAPIDLY EMERGING IN WHICH THE PACIFIC BASIN NATIONS AND ECONOMIC FORCES WILL PLAY AN INCREASINGLY IMPORTANT ROLE.

03529 GILSDORF, R.R.
GOVERNMENT, EQUALITY AND ECONOMIC GROWTH IN WESTERN EUROPE A CROSS-NATIONAL EMPIRICAL STUDY
GOVERNANCE, 2(4) (OCT 89), 425-459.
THIS ARTICLE ATTEMPTS TO CARRY OUT A SYSTEMATIC COMPARATIVE ANALYSIS OF THE GROWTH/EQUALITY PERFORMANCE OF 18 WEST EUROPEAN NATIONS DURING THE PERIOD OF 1960-1980. IT IS PARTLY EXPLORATORY AND IS EXTENSIVE-ENABLING THE READER TO SEE THE EFFECTS OF BROAD FACTORS ON ECONOMIC PERFORMANCE. THE TWO MAIN OBJECTIVES HAVE BEEN TO DISCOVER WHETHER EQUALITY HAS HINDERED ECONOMIC GROWTH, AND TO TEST HOLLINGSWORTH'S ARGUMENT ON THE POLITICAL - INSTITUTIONAL UNDERPINNINGS OF ECONOMIC PERFORMANCE.

03530 GINDIN, S.
BREAKING AWAY: THE FORMATION OF THE CANADIAN AUTO WORKERS
STUDIES IN POLITICAL ECONOMY: A SOCIALIST REVIEW, 29 (SUM 89), 63-89.
THE DECISION OF THE CANADIAN SECTION OF THE UNITED AUTO WORKERS (UAW) TO FORM ITS OWN CANADIAN UNION HAS ROOTED IN THE DIFFERENT RESPONSES OF UNIONISTS IN THE CANADA AND THE UNITED STATES TO AN INCREASING BELLIGERENCE ON THE PART OF THE CORPORATIONS. A SIMPLE EXPLANATION FOR THE CONTRASTING REACTIONS OF UAW MEMBERS IN THE TWO COUNTRIES TO THE CORPORATE ATTACK FOCUSES ON THE DIFFERENCES IN THEIR NATIONAL ENVIRONMENTS, PARTICULARLY THE DIFFERENT ECONOMIC CONDITIONS WHICH THEY FACED. THE SIGNIFICANCE OF THE SPLIT WAS THAT -- AT A TIME WHEN EVEN THE DEFENSIVE CAPACITIES OF THE LABOUR MOVEMENT WERE IN DANGER OF EVISCERATION -- IT REASSERTED CANADIAN UNIONISM'S VITALITY AS AN INSTITUTION FIGHTING ON BEHALF OF WORKING PEOPLE.

03531 GINSBERG, B.
A POST-ELECTORAL ERA?
PS: POLITICAL SCIENCE AND POLITICS, XXII(1) (MAR 89), 18-20.
THE AUTHOR DISCUSSES POLITICAL CONSULTANTS AS AN EFFECT RATHER THAN A CAUSE, CONNECTING THE RISE OF CONSULTANTS WITH THE DECLINE OF POLITICAL PARTIES.

03532 GIORGIO, A.
COMMUNIST "HUMAN RIGHTS RECORDS"
ASIAN OUTLOOK, 24(2) (MAR 89), 20-22.
A TOP U.S. STATE DEPARTMENT OFFICIAL RECENTLY STATED THAT NORTH KOREA AND CUBA ARE THE WORLD'S WORST VIOLATORS OF HUMAN RIGHTS BECAUSE THEY HAVE ESTABLISHED SYSTEMS OF UNMITIGATED RESTRAINT. UNFORTUNATELY, THE LATEST U.S. STATE DEPARTMENT'S ANNUAL REPORT ON HUMAN RIGHTS WAS NOT VERY CRITICAL OF THE MISERABLE HUMAN RIGHTS RECORDS OF PEKING OR MOSCOW.

03533 GIRAND, M.
RACISM AND IMMIGRATION: FRENCH WEST INDIANS IN THE MAINLAND
NEW POLITICAL SCIENCE, 16 (FAL 89), 71-78.
THE AUTHOR EXAMINES THE REALITIES OF RACISM AGAINST FRENCH WEST INDIANS IN FRANCE AND THE IMPACT THAT THESE ATTITUDES HAVE ON IMMIGRATION LAWS THERE. LINKAGES TO FRANCE'S COLONIAL PAST ARE ESTABLISHED AND APPLIED TO ATTITUDES BEING WITNESSED IN FRANCE FROM THE EMERGING NEW RIGHT. IMMIGRATION LEVELS ARE HISTORICALLY TRACED, WITH STATISTICS REPORTED.

03534 GIROUX, G.
MONOPOLY POWER AND MONITORING: A TEST USING THE GONZALEZ AND MEHAY MODEL
PUBLIC CHOICE, 63(1) (OCT 89), 73-78.
GONZALES AND MEHAY (GM) (1985) DEMONSTRATE THAT LOCAL GOVERNMENTS CAN EXERCISE MONOPOLY POWER, RATHER THAN RESPOND COMPETITIVELY TO VOTER PREFERENCES. A KEY ASUMPTION OF THEIR MODEL IS THAT VOTERS CANNOT EFFECTIVELY MONITOR PUBLIC

OFFICIALS THE PURPOSE OF THIS PAPER IS TO TEST THE RELATIVE
EFFECTIVENESS OF THE FINANCIAL AND COMPLIANCE AUDIT AS A
CONTROL DEVICE TO ASSIST THE MONITORING OF BUREAUCRATS IT
EXPLORES EVIDENCE OF STRATEGIC BEHAVIOR, THE DATA, AND MAKES
AN EMPIRICAL ANALYSIS BEFORE DRAWING CONCLUSIONS.

03535 GIRVAN, N.P.
  TECHNOLOGICAL CHANGE AND THE CARIBBEAN: FORMULATING
  STRATEGIC RESPONSES
  SOCIAL AND ECONOMIC STUDIES, 38(2) (JUN 89), 111-135.
    THIS PAPER EXPLORES SOME OF THE ISSUES ARISING OUT OF
  THE NEED FOR THE CARIBBEAN TO FORMULATE STRATEGIC RESPONSES
  TO GLOBAL TECHNOLOGICAL CHANGE. PART I SETS OUT THE
  PROBLEMATIC. PART II DISCUSSES THE APPROPRIATE ANALYTICAL
  FRAMEWORK FOR THE STUDY OF GLOBAL TECHNOLOGICAL CHANGE AND
  ITS IMPLICATIONS FOR THE CARIBBEAN. WITHIN THIS CONTEXT,
  PART III REVIEWS SOME OF THE LESSONS OF THE LITERATURE ON
  THE HISTORICAL PATTERN OF TECHNOLOGICAL CHANGE AND THE
  CONSTELLATION OF NEW TECHNOLOGIES IN THE CONTEMPORARY PERIOD.
    PART IV MAKES SOME OBSERVATIONS ON THE PATTERN OF ADOPTION
  IN THE CARIBBEAN OF THE CORE GROUP OF NEW TECHNOLOGIES -
  MICROELECTRONICS AND THE RELATED INFORMATION TECHNOLOGY. THE
  PAPER ENDS WITH A DISCUSSION OF SOME OF THE BROADER SOCIAL
  IMPLICATIONS ARISING FROM THE NEED FOR LOCAL INITIATIVES AND
  STRATEGIC RESPONSES.

03536 GIRVIN, B.
  THE TRANSFORMATION OF CONTEMPORARY CONSERVATISM
  SAGE PUBLICATIONS, BEVERLY HILLS, CA, 1988, 232.
    THE AUTHOR STUDIES THE HISTORY OF REPRESENTATIVE
  CONSERVATIVE PARTIES IN EUROPE AND THE USA. THESE NATIONAL
  STUDIES REVEAL THE DIFFICULTIES FACING CONSERVATISM UP TO
  THE EARLY 1970S AND THE SUCCESS OF CONSERVATISM SINCE THEN.
  EXPLANATIONS ARE FOUND IN POLITICAL CULTURES, THE
  CHARACTERISTICS OF PARTICULAR PARTIES OR FORMS OF
  CONSERVATISM, AND THE SOCIAL BASES OF CONSERVATISM.

03537 GITLIN, T.
  POSTMODERNISM: ROOTS AND POLITICS
  DISSENT, (WIN 89), 100-108.
    "POSTMODERNISM" USUALLY REFERS TO A CERTAIN
  CONSTELLATION OF STYLES AND TONES IN CULTURAL WORKS. BUT
  WHAT IS AT STAKE IN THE POSTMODERNISM DEBATE GOES BEYOND ART;
  IT EXTENDS TO THE QUESTION OF WHAT SORT OF DISPOSITION
  TOWARD THE CONTEMPORARY WORLD IS GOING TO PREVAIL THROUGHOUT
  WESTERN CULTURE. THE DISCUSSION OF POSTMODERNISM IS, AMONG
  OTHER THINGS, A DEFLECTED AND DISPLACED DISCUSSION OF THE
  CONTOURS OF POLITICAL THOUGHT, IN THE LARGEST SENSE, DURING
  THE SEVENTIES AND EIGHTIES.

03538 GITLIN, T.
  THE POSTMODERN PREDICAMENT
  WILSON QUARTERLY, XIII(3) (SUM 89), 67-76.
    THE AUTHOR ARGUES THAT THE CONCEPT OF POSTMODERNISM
  TOUCHES ON SOMETHING MORE IMPORTANT THAN THE FADS AND
  FASHIONS OF OUR TIME. IT GOES TO THE HEART OF CONTEMPORARY
  ETHICAL COMMITMENTS AND SOCIAL AND POLITICAL BEHAVIOR.
  DURING THE PAST TWO DECADES, PEOPLE IN THE ADVANCED
  INDUSTRIAL WORLD HAVE ENJOYED A PECULIAR LUXURY: THEY HAVE
  BEEN ABLE TO PLAY WITH THE SURFACES OF THEIR CULTURAL
  HERITAGE WHILE PAYING LITTLE SERIOUS ATTENTION TO ITS
  UNDERLYING VALUES.

03539 GITTELL, M.; ROGOWSKY, E.T.
  LOCAL ORGANIZATIONS AND COMMUNITY DEVELOPMENT: ENERGIZING
  THE SYSTEM
  NATIONAL CIVIC REVIEW, 78(3) (MAY 89), 165-167.
    THE AMERICAN POLITICAL PROCESS HAS LONG BEEN MARKED BY
  THE ACTIVE ROLE OF COMMUNITY AND GRASS-ROOTS ORGANIZATIONS.
  IN SPITE OF CONTINUED CONCENTRATION OF POWER AT FORMAL
  LEVELS OF GOVERNMENT, LOCAL AND COMMUNITY INSTITUTIONS
  REMAIN THE FOCUS OF CITIZEN INVOLVEMENT, THE DIRECT
  PROVIDERS OF SERVICES AND THE ADVOCATES OF LOCAL INTERESTS,
  AND FREQUENTLY THE ONLY REPRESENTATIVES OF LOW-INCOME AND
  MINORITY POPULATIONS AND WOMEN. THEIR RECORD MUST BE
  PRESERVED AND THEIR ROLE REINVIGORATED.

03540 GITTLER, J.B.
  IDEAS ON WAR AND PEACE AMONG THE CLASSICAL GREEK
  DRAMATISTS: AESCHYLUS, SOPHOCLES, EURIPIDES AND
  ARISTOPHANES.
  INTERNATIONAL JOURNAL OF GROUP TENSIONS, 19(4) (WIN 89),
  385-398.
    BOTH TRAGEDY AND COMEDY REFLECTED AND JUDGED THE PASSING
  EVENTS AND DAILY LIVES OF THE ATHENIANS. WE FIND IN THE
  PLAYS DISCUSSIONS OF EMANCIPATION FOR WOMEN, THE RELATION OF
  THE PHYSICAL ENVIRONMENT TO HUMAN LIFE, IDEAS ON LAW AND
  JUSTICE, AND IDEAS ON WAR AND PEACE WHICH IS THE SPECIFIC
  INTEREST OF THIS ARTICLE. THE AUTHOR CITES APPLICABLE
  EXCERPTS ON WAR AND PEACE FROM EACH OF THE RELEVANT PLAYS OF
  THE FOUR DRAMATISTS. THE LIVES OF THE AUTHORS AND SYNOPSES
  OF THE PLAYS FROM WHICH EXCERPTS ARE QUOTED, ARE DETAILED IN
  THE APPENDED NOTES.

03541 GITZ, B.R.
  THE RELIABILITY OF EAST EUROPEAN MILITARY FORCES
  DISSERTATION ABSTRACTS INTERNATIONAL, 50(5) (NOV 89),
  1428-A.
    A CONTINUING PROBLEM IN ESTIMATING WARSAW PACT
  CAPABILITY HAS BEEN THE UNCERTAIN BEHAVIOR OF NON-SOVIET
  FORCES UNDER WAR-TIME CONDITIONS. IN ORDER TO FORECAST SUCH
  BEHAVIOR, THIS DISSERTATION USES A THREE-COMPONENT FRAMEWORK
  BASED UPON USABLE MILITARY RESOURCES, SOVIET/PARTY CONTROL
  MECHANISMS, AND THE VALUE SOCIALIZATION PROCESS.

03542 GIVEL, M.S.
  COMMUNITY SERVICES: THE POLITICS OF A BLOCK GRANT
  DISSERTATION ABSTRACTS INTERNATIONAL, 49(9) (MAR 89),
  2795-A.
    THE AUTHOR STUDIES THE STATES' ASSUMPTION OF THE
  DECENTRALIZED COMMUNITY SERVICES BLOCK GRANT PROGRAM. HE
  FINDS THAT THREE IDEOLOGICALLY - DIVERSE STATES INCREASED
  LOCAL COMMUNITY ACTION AGENCY AUTONOMY, INCREASED AND
  DECREASED LOCAL COMPLEXITY IN A CONTRADICTORY FASHION, AND
  DID NOT CHANGE CLIENT BENEFIT LEVELS. MOREOVER, THE STATES
  DID NOT PROVIDE RECOMPENSATION FOR THE FEDERAL CUTS AND THE
  OVERALL POVERTY LEVEL DID NOT SIGNIFICANTLY CHANGE.

03543 GLAD, B.
  PERSONALITY, POLITICAL AND GROUP PROCESS VARIABLES IN
  FOREIGN POLICY DECISION-MAKING: JIMMY CARTER'S HANDLING OF
  THE IRANIAN HOSTAGE CRISIS
  INTERNATIONAL POLITICAL SCIENCE REVIEW, 10(1) (JAN 89),
  35-61.
    MODELS OF THE DECISION-MAKING PROCESS ASSUMING THE
  RATIONALITY OF THE MAJOR ACTORS ARE NOT APT TO EXPLAIN
  ACTUAL DECISION MAKING BETWEEN STATES WHEN MAJOR VALUES ARE
  AT STAKE. SITUATIONAL, DOMESTIC POLITICAL AND BUREAUCRATIC
  CONSTRAINTS, AS SUGGESTED BY THIS CASE STUDY OF THE US
  RESPONSE TO IRAN'S TAKING OF AMERICAN HOSTAGES, CONSTRAIN
  CHOICES. BEYOND THESE FACTORS, THE CHIEF EXECUTIVE'S OWN
  PERSONALITY IS APT TO HAVE AN IMPACT ON POLICY, ESPECIALLY
  WHEN HE HAS CONSIDERABLE AUTHORITY TO ACT INDEPENDENTLY IN
  THE FOREIGN POLICY ARENA. HIS RESPONSES MAY TO SOME EXTENT
  SHOW GOOD REALITY TESTING, AS EVIDENT IN JIMMY CARTER'S
  REJECTIONS OF MILITARY SANCTIONS AND HIS INITIAL SEARCH FOR
  A DIPLOMATIC RESOLUTION OF THE HOSTAGE ISSUE. BUT THREATS TO
  MAJOR VALUES CAN BRING OUT MORE EGO-DEFENSIVE TRAITS, AS
  EVIDENT IN CARTER'S INFLATION OF THE HOSTAGE ISSUE, HIS
  AVOIDANCE OF QUESTIONS ABOUT THE VIABILITY OF THE RESCUE
  OPERATION AND HIS DIFFICULTIES IN CONFRONTING INCOMPATIBLE
  POLICY GOALS. THE RESULT IN THIS INSTANCE WAS A FAILURE TO
  FULLY CONSIDER POLICY OPTIONS, OTHERWISE FEASIBLE, THAT
  MIGHT HAVE ENTAILED FEWER RISKS FOR THE AMERICAN NATIONAL
  INTEREST.

03544 GLAD, B.
  REAGAN'S MIDLIFE CRISIS AND THE TURN TO THE RIGHT
  POLITICAL PSYCHOLOGY, 10(4) (DEC 89), 593-624.
    RONALD REAGAN'S TURN TO THE POLITICAL RIGHT SERVED
  CERTAIN SOCIAL ADJUSTMENT AND EGO DEFENSIVE NEEDS FOR HIM AT
  A TIME WHEN HIS PERSONAL AND PROFESSIONAL LIFE HAD BOTTOMED
  OUT. A MOVIE CAREER WHICH HAD STARTED OUT AUSPICIOUSLY NEVER
  DID TAKE OFF, AND A MARRIAGE PORTRAYED AS IDYLLIC ENDED IN
  DIVORCE. DRAWING UPON PSYCHOLOGICAL ADAPTATIONS THAT HAD
  SERVED HIM SINCE BOYHOOD - THE ENERGETIC ATTACK ON OBSTACLES
  IN HIS PATH AND THE AVOIDANCE OF EMOTIONAL AND INTELLECTUAL
  AMBIGUITIES - HE WAS ABLE TO FIND NEW ROUTES TO PROFESSIONAL
  AND PERSONAL SUCCESS. HIS TURN TO ANTI-COMMUNISM AND MORE
  GRADUAL EMBRACE OF A CONSERVATIVE POLITICAL PHILOSOPHY
  FACILITATED HIS RISE TO THE PRESIDENCY OF THE SCREEN ACTORS
  GUILD AND PROVIDED HIM WITH NEW OPPORTUNITIES FOR WORK AND
  INFLUENCE. THE TARGETING OF THE COMMUNISTS AND THE FEDERAL
  GOVERNMENT IN WASHINGTON AS THE SOURCES OF ALL THAT HAD GONE
  WRONG IN HOLLYWOOD PROVIDED HIM WITH SAFE OUTLETS FOR THE
  ANGER HE FELT AS A RESULT OF HIS BLOCKED CAREER AND AN
  EXPLANATION OF WHAT HAD HAPPENED TO HIM. THE AVOIDANCE OF
  AMBIGUITY KEPT HIM FROM ANY TROUBLING DOUBTS ABOUT EITHER
  THE MOTIVES OF SOME OF THE LEADERS OF THE ANTI-COMMUNIST
  IMPULSE OR ITS EFFECTS ON THE CAREERS OF THOSE WHO RESISTED
  IT. AN INTERACTIONIST LIFE-HISTORY MODEL IS USED IN THE
  ANALYSIS AND HYPOTHESES SUGGESTED FOR FURTHER RESEARCH.
  INDIVIDUAL SHIFTS ON THE POLITICAL SPECTRUM, AS THIS CASE
  HISTORY SUGGESTS, MAY NOT BE ACCOMPANIED BY COGNITIVE AND
  PSYCHOLOGICAL TRANSFORMATIONS. THREATS TO FUNDAMENTAL VALUES
  MAY WELL INTENSIFY COGNITIVE AND EMOTIONAL RIGIDITIES AS A
  WAY OF AVOIDING ANXIETY.

03545 GLADE, W.
  PRIVATIZATION IN RENT-SEEKING SOCIETIES
  WORLD DEVELOPMENT, 17(5) (MAY 89), 673-682.
    FOUR LATIN AMERICAN COUNTRIES HAVE DEVOTED PARTICULAR
  ATTENTION, THOUGH NOT EQUAL ACTION, TO PRIVATIZATION
  POLICIES, THE IMPLEMENTATION OF WHICH HAS SHED CONSIDERABLE
  LIGHT ON THE DYNAMICS OF RENT-SEEKING SOCIETIES. THE FACT
  THAT DEMOCRATIZATION, IN SOME FORM, IS ALSO UNDERWAY IN EACH
  OF THE FOUR HAS INTENSIFIED THE INTERPLAY OF FORCES THAT
  SHAPE THE IMPLEMENTATION OF PRIVATIZATION PROGRAMS. THE

EXPERIENCES OF MEXICO AND CHILE, IN PARTICULAR, DEMONSTRATE HOW IMPORTANT IT MAY BE TO "PRIVATIZE" THE PRIVATE SECTOR BY REFORMING MACROECONOMIC POLICIES AND OPENING THE ECONOMY TO EXTERNAL COMPETITION BEFORE, OR AT LEAST CONCURRENTLY WITH, TACKLING THE PRIVATIZATION OF THE PUBLIC SECTOR. THE OBSTRUCTIVE FORCE OF RENT-SEEKING BEHAVIOR IS SHOWN MOST CLEARLY IN THE ARGENTINE CASE, WHILE THE BRAZILIAN EXPERIENCE IS USEFUL AS A REMINDER THAT RENT-SEEKING DYNAMICS ARE NOT NECESSARILY INCOMPATIBLE WITH STRUCTURAL TRANSFORMATION AND HIGH RATES OF GROWTH.

03546 GLANTZ, D. M.
SOVIET MILITARY DECEPTION IN THE SECOND WORLD WAR
FRANK CASS JOURNALS, LONDON, GB, 1989, 684.
THIS STUDY OF SOVIET MILITARY DECEPTION DEMONSTRATES THE EXTENT OF SOVIET EXPERIENCES WITH MILITARY DECEPTION AND THE DEGREE TO WHICH THE SOVIETS HAVE STUDIED THEM. ABOVE ALL, IT EMPHASIZES THE IMPORTANCE THE SOVIETS ATTACH TO MILITARY DECEPTION IN A CONTEMPORARY AND FUTURE CONTEXT. THE AUTHOR HAS USED SOVIET SOURCES, SUPPLEMENTED BY MEMOIRS. CAMPAIGN AND OPERATIONAL STUDIES, AND UNIT HISTORIES, CONFIRMING THEM FROM GERMAN RECORDS.

03547 GLASBERG, D.S.
BANK HEGEMONY RESEARCH AND ITS IMPLICATIONS FOR POWER STRUCTURE THEORY
CRITICAL SOCIOLOGY, 16(2-3) (SUM 89), 27-49.
THIS PAPER REVIEWS CASE STUDIES OF BANK HEGEMONY RESEARCH, ILLUSTRATING THE CHALLENGES IT POSES FOR POWER STRUCTURE THEORY TO DEVELOP A MORE DYNAMIC MODEL OF POWER AND TO TAKE INTO ACCOUNT MODERN ORGANIZED CAPITAL FLOW RELATIONSHIPS, BOTH LOCALLY AND GLOBALLY.

03548 GLASER, M.
WATER TO THE SWAMP? IRRIGATION AND PATTERNS OF ACCUMULATION AND AGRARIAN CHANGE IN BANGLADESH
DISSERTATION ABSTRACTS INTERNATIONAL, 50(1) (JUL 89), 255-A.
RESEARCH ON EIGHT BANGLADESH VILLAGES REVEALS THAT THE RESTRUCTURING OF AGRARIAN RELATIONS TO EMPHASIZE OUTPUT AND PRODUCTIVITY OBJECTIVES TAKES DIFFERENT FORMS AND HAS DIFFERENT DEVELOPMENT RESULTS, WHICH ARE DEPENDENT ON THE MICRO-LEVEL POLITICAL ECONOMY. WITH MORE SECURE, HIGHER YIELDS THROUGH IRRIGATION AND WITH A CONTINUING DETERIORATION OF PER CAPITA LAND AVAILABILITY, AGRARIAN RELATIONS IN THE LAND, CREDIT, AND LABOR MARKETS ARE BECOMING MORE PRODUCTIVITY-REDUCING EFFECTS OF MARKET INTERLINKAGES. THE APPEARANCE OF CAPITALIST AGRARIAN RELATIONS HAS NOT DISPLACED MARKET INTERLINKAGES AND WIDER PATRON-CLIENT RELATIONS BUT THESE HAVE ADAPTED TO THE NEEDS OF A CAPITALIST PRODUCTION AND APPROPRIATION RATIONALE.

03549 GLASS, A.
BUSH'S POLITICS OF EVASION
NEW LEADER, LXXII(14) (SEP 89), 3-4.
GEORGE BUSH IS CURRENTLY ENGAGED IN A STRATEGY OF EVADING REALITY WITH REGARDS TO THE SITUATION IN POLAND. WHILE THE POLISH ECONOMY IS OBVIOUSLY IN SHAMBLES, AND THE NEW SOLIDARITY-LED GOVERNMENT DESPERATELY NEEDS FOREIGN AID TO STAVE OFF POPULAR REVOLT, BUSH HAS USED THE STAGGERING US DEFICITS AS AN EXCUSE TO OFFER ONLY PALTRY SUMS TO POLAND. THE AUTHOR FINDS THIS IRONIC SEEING THAT THE US SEEMINGLY HAS PLENTY OF MONEY TO GIVE TO ISREAL, EGYPT, PAKISTAN, AND AFGHANISTAN. BUSH'S LACK OF CONCERN FOR POLAND IS POSSIBLY DUE TO HIS MISUNDERSTANDING OF THE TRULY CRITICAL NATURE OF THE ECONOMY OF POLAND, AND INDEED OF ALL OF EASTERN EUROPE.

03550 GLASS, A.J.
BUSH'S BUDGET TEST
NEW LEADER, LXII(4) (FEB 89), 3-4.
BUSH SEEMS COMMITTED TO PRESERVING THE ECONOMIC AND POLITICAL STATUS QUO. THAT GOAL UNDERLIES HIS REVISIONS TO REAGAN'S FINAL BUDGET. BUT IF BUSH WANTS RESULTS, HE HAS TO SHOW A MODICUM OF GOOD FAITH TOWARD THE DEMOCRATS, WHO CONTROL THE LEGISLATIVE BUDGET-MAKING PROCESS.

03551 GLASS, A.J.
GOOD-BYE TO ALL THAT
NEW LEADER, LXXII(2) (JAN 89), 3-4.
ALTHOUGH IT WASN'T EVIDENT AT THE TIME, REAGAN'S FORTUNE WAS SEALED WHEN HE OVERCAME TWO GRAVE CRISES AT THE START OF HIS PRESIDENCY. THE FIRST CRISIS CAME WHEN HE WAS SHOT. THE SECOND WAS HIS FIRING OF STRIKING GOVERNMENT AIR CONTROLLERS.

03552 GLASSFORD, L.A.
RETRENCHMENT-R.B. BENNETT STYLE: THE CONSERVATIVE RECORD BEFORE THE NEW DEAL, 1930-34.
AMERICAN REVIEW OF CANADIAN STUDIES, 19(2) (SUM 89), 141-158.
THIS ARTICLE FOLLOWS THE ACHIEVEMENTS OF TORY PRIME MINISTER, R.B. BENNETT, DISPITE A BAD PRESS, THE TORY RECORD WAS QUITE SUCCESSFUL, A FACT OFTEN OVERLOOKED BY PUBLIC SUPPORT. IT DESCRIBES BENNETT'S CAMPAIGN PROMISES AND THE STEPS THAT WERE TAKEN TO DELIVER THEM. IT CONCLUDES THAT THE

CONSERVATIVE POLICY RECORD IS QUITE POSITIVE GIVEN THE WORLD ECONOMIC CRISIS.

03553 GLAUBITZ, J.
RAPPROCHEMENT BETWEEN CHINA AND THE SOVIET UNION - BACKGROUND AND PROSPECTS
AUSSEN POLITIK, 40(3) (1989), 251-263.
WITH THE VISIT OF MIKHAIL GORBACHEV TO BEIJING IN MAY 1989, THE RAPPROCHEMENT BETWEEN THE SOVIET UNION AND CHINA WAS FINALLY SEALED. AS DR. JOACHIM GLAUBITZ OF THE STIFTUNG WISSENSCHAFT UND POLITIK IN EBENHAUSEN EXPLAINS, THIS IS IN THE INTERESTS OF BOTH COUNTRIES. UNDER GORBACHEV THE SOVIET UNION, IN ITS EAGERNESS TO IMPROVE RELATIONS WITH CHINA, HAD BECOME INCREASINGLY IMPORTUNATE AS THE CHINESE SKILFULLY CONCEALED THEIR OWN INTEREST. ALTHOUGH THEY STOOD TO GAIN CONSIDERABLY MORE ROOM TO MANOEUVRE IN FOREIGN POLICY, A POLITICAL DIMINUTION OF VIETNAM AND EXPANDED ECONOMIC OPPORTUNITIES, THE CHINESE NEVERTHELESS INSISTED THAT "THREE OBSTACLES" BE REMOVED BEFORE THEY GAVE THEIR HAND TO MOSCOW: SOVIET SUPPORT OF VIETNAM IN CAMBODIA, THE INTERVENTION IN AFGHANISTAN AND THE PERCEIVED MILITARY THREAT ALONG THE SINO-MONGOLIAN-SOVIET BORDER. IN THE EYES OF THE CHINESE, BY EARLY 1989 THE SOVIET UNION HAD SUFFICIENTLY MET THESE CONDITIONS, THUS CLEARING THE WAY FOR A FULL RESUMPTION OF RELATIONS -- POLITICAL, ECONOMIC AND PARTY. AS A RESULT, GORBACHEV WAS ABLE TO MARK OUT BROAD AREAS OF FUTURE ECONOMIC AND CULTURAL COOPERATION, REACH AGREEMENT ON BOTH SUBSTANTIAL TROOP CUTS ALONG THE FRONTIER AND STEPPED-UP NEGOTIATIONS ON DISPUTED STRETCHES OF THEIR COMMON BORDER AS WELL AS RE-ESTABLISH RELATIONS BETWEEN THE RESPECTIVE COMMUNIST PARTIES ON THE BASIS OF COMPLETE EQUALITY AND INDEPENDENCE. THE AGREEMENTS CARRY THE UNMISTAKABLE STAMP OF THE CHINESE, HOWEVER: RELATIONS ARE BASED ON THE "FIVE PRINCIPLES OF PEACEFUL COEXISTENCE" AND NOT ON "SOCIALIST SOLIDARITY", AND THE CHINESE ANTI-BEGEMONY CLAUSE WAS INCLUDED IN THE JOINT COMMUNIQUE. THE PARTIES REMAIN DIVIDED ON A SOLUTION TO THE CAMBODIAN PROBLEM. SO WHILE GORBACHEV'S VISIT MAY HAVE OFFICIALLY BURIED THEIR CONFLIC, THE RIVALRY BETWEEN THE TWO COMMUNIST SUPERPOWERS WILL GO ON.

03554 GLAZER, A.; GROFMAN, B.
WHY REPRESENTATIVES ARE IDEOLOGISTS THOUGH VOTERS ARE NOT
PUBLIC CHOICE, 61(1) (APR 89), 29-40.
ABSTRACT. THROUGH FEW VOTERS APPEAR TO HOLD CONSISTENT IDEOLOGICAL VIEWS, THE ROLL CALL VOTES OF CONGRESSMEN AND SENATORS CAN BE WELL PREDICTED BY IDEOLOGICAL TERMS. AN EXPLANATION FOR THIS PUZZLE IS THAT IDEOLOGY ALLOWS CANDIDATES TO SUCCINCTLY EXPLAIN THEIR VIEWS. BECAUSE IT IS DIFFICULT TO EXPLAIN DETAILED POSITIONS TO VOTERS, A CANDIDATE WHO PRESENTS HIS POSITION IN IDEOLOGICAL TERMS MAY BE ABLE TO DEFEAT A CANDIDATE WHO SUPPORTS A SET OF ISSUE POSITIONS THAT WOULD, IN TOTO, BE PREFERRED BY A MAJORITY OF WELL-INFORMED VOTERS WERE THE VOTERS AWARE OF ALL THE VIEWS OF THAT CANDIDATE. THIS EFFECT CAN BE A POWERFUL ONE. MOREOVER, IDEOLOGY MAY BE A SOURCE OF ELECTROAL STABILITY, AND A MEANS OF PROVIDING REGULARITY AND STRUCTURE TO ELITE POLITICAL DEBATE.

03555 GLEICHER, D.
WAGE RATE DIFFERENTIALS IN CAPITALIST ECONOMIES
SCIENCE AND SOCIETY, 53(1) (SPR 89), 29-46.
THE PAPER BUILDS UPON A PREVIOUS WORK OF THE AUTHOR IN WHICH "SPECIALIZED" LABOR IS INCORPORATED INTO A CLASSICAL MARXIST MODEL OF PRICE DETERMINATION. THIS MODEL PROVIDES A THEORETICAL FRAMEWORK WITHIN WHICH TO PURSUE EXPLANATIONS OF RELATIVE WAGE RATES. THE PAPER OUTLINES THE BASIC FEATURES OF THE MODEL, PROPOSES AN APPROACH LINKING THE RELATIVE WAGE RATES BETWEEN OCCUPATIONS TO THE RELATIVE BARGAINING POWER OF WORKERS EMPLOYED IN THEM, AND DISCUSSES SOME OF THE IMPLICATIONS. THESE INCLUDE THE EXISTENCE OF UNEMPLOYMENT AS A NECESSARY CONDITION OF PROFITABILITY IN CAPITALIST SOCIETY; THE RELATION BETWEEN TRAINING COSTS AND RELATIVE WAGE RATES; AND POSSIBLE POLITICAL/CULTURAL DIVISIONS WITHIN THE CLASS OF WAGE LABORERS.

03556 GLEIJESES, P.
JUAN JOSE AREVALO AND THE CARIBBEAN LEGION
JOURNAL OF LATIN AMERICAN STUDIES, 21(1) (FEB 89), 133-145.
IN MARCH 1945 JUAN JOSE AREVALO BECAME PRESIDENT OF GUATEMALA. HIS INAUGURATION MARKED THE BEGINNING OF AN UNPRECEDENTED DEMOCRATIC PARENTHESIS THAT LASTED UNTIL 1954. AREVALO WAS AN ANTI-COMMUNIST WHO BELIEVED THAT INDIVIDUAL COMMUNISTS SHOULD NOT BE PERSECUTED, A NATIONALIST WHO ACCEPTED THAT GUATEMALA WAS IN THE U.S. SPHERE OF INFLUENCE, AND A REFORMER WHO ESCHEWED RADICAL CHANGE. BUT THE UNITED STATES, WHICH HAD GROWN ACCUSTOMED TO THE SERVILITY OF AREVALO'S PREDECESSORS, WAS NOT PLEASED BY HIM.

03557 GLEIJESES, P.
THE AGRARIAN REFORM OF JACOBO ARBENZ
JOURNAL OF LATIN AMERICAN STUDIES, 21(3) (OCT 89), 453-480.
INAUGURATED PRESIDENT OF GUATEMALA IN 1951, JACOBO ARBENZ PRESIDED OVER THE MOST SUCCESSFUL AGRARIAN REFORM IN THE HISTORY OF CENTRAL AMERICA. BUT PRAISE FOR INITIATING

THE REFORM DOES NOT BELONG SOLELY TO ARBENZ. CREDIT SHOULD
ALSO BE GIVEN TO THE COMMUNIST PARTY OF GUATEMALA, WHOSE
LEADERS WERE ARBENZ'S CLOSEST PERSONAL AND POLITICAL FRIENDS.

03558 GLEWWE, P.; DE TRAY, D.
POOR IN LATIN AMERICA DURING ADJUSTMENT: A CASE STUDY OF
PERU
AVAILABLE FROM NTIS, NO. AD-A204 495/6/GAR, 1989, 55.
THE PAPER PROVIDES A GENERAL OVERVIEW OF THE EFFECTS OF
STRUCTURAL ADJUSTMENT PROGRAMS ON THE POOR, USING PERU'S
ECONOMY AS AN EXAMPLE. THE DEPTH OF PERU'S ECONOMIC PROBLEMS
MAKES IT LIKELY THAT THE PERUVIAN ECONOMY WILL HAVE TO
UNDERGO MAJOR ADJUSTMENTS IN THE NEAR FUTURE. AMONG THE
OPTIONS POLICY MAKERS WILL CONSIDER ARE: REALIGNMENT OF THE
VARIOUS EXCHANGE RATES, TRADE LIBERALIZATION, REMOVAL OF
PRICE DISTORTIONS, AND REDUCTION OF GOVERNMENT EXPENDITURES.
THE ANALYSIS PRESENTED SHOWS HOW HOUSEHOLD LEVEL DATA CAN BE
USED TO ASSESS THE EFFECT OF VARIOUS POLICY OPTIONS ON THE
WELFARE OF THE POOR. (COPYRIGHT (C) 1989 THE INTERNATIONAL
BANK FOR RECONSTRUCTION AND DEVELOPMENT/ THE WORLD BANK.)

03559 GLITMAN, M.W.
SECURITY AND DISARMAMENT, II
DISARMAMENT, XII(3) (AUT 89), 45-53.
THE GOALS OF STABILITY AND PEACE IN FREEDOM, WHICH THE
USA SEEKS FROM ITS SECURITY POLICY, MUST FOR THE FORESEEABLE
FUTURE BE FOUNDED ON A CREDIBLE DETERRENT AND DEFENSE. THAT,
IN TURN, REQUIRES THE RIGHT AMOUNT OF THE RIGHT KIND OF ARMS
FITTED INTO A STRATEGIC AND TACTICAL DOCTRINE. ARMS CONTROL
CAN REINFORCE DETERRENCE AND DEFENSE. IT CAN HELP EMPHASIZE
SYSTEMS THAT INCREASE STABILITY OVER DESTABILIZING ONES. IT
CAN HELP REDUCE THE RISK OF CRISIS DEGENERATING INTO WAR.
BUT IT CANNOT BY ITSELF DETER WAR OR CREATE A DEFENSE.

03560 GLYNN, P.
NUCLEAR REVISIONISM
COMMENTARY, 87(3) (MAR 89), 42-47.
ONE IMPORTANT BY-PRODUCT OF THE PASSIONATE ANTINUCLEAR
CONTROVERSY IN THIS DECADE HAS BEEN A WAVE OF NEW AND
INFLUENTIAL REVISIONIST WRITING ON THE ROLE OF NUCLEAR
WEAPONS IN POSTWAR HISTORY. THE CENTRAL THEME OF THE NEW
REVISIONIST MOVEMENT, BROADLY SPEAKING, IS THE ALLEGED
UNIMPORTANCE OF NUCLEAR WEAPONS -- THEIR LIMITED USEFULNESS
NOT ONLY AS MILITARY WEAPONS BUT ESPECIALLY AS DIPLOMATIC
TOOLS. IN PARTICULARLY, THESE NEWER HISTORIANS ATTEMPT TO
MAKE THE CASE THAT AMERICAN NUCLEAR SUPERIORITY, FOR AS LONG
AS IT LASTED, WAS FAR LESS OF A FACTOR IN INTERNATIONAL
POLITICS, AND LESS CRUCIAL TO AMERICAN SECURITY, THAN HAS
PREVIOUSLY BEEN ASSUMED.

03561 GLYNN, P.
THE DANGERS BEYOND CONTAINMENT
COMMENTARY, 88(2) (AUG 89), 15-22.
TODAY THE CONVICTION IS NIGH UNIVERSAL THAT THE WORLD IS
BECOMING A SAFER PLACE. BUT AS IN THE PAST, THIS VERY
CONVICTION IS HELPING TO MAKE THE WORLD MORE DANGEROUS. FOR
WITH A BLITHENESS EQUALING THE FOLLY OF ANY EARLIER
GENERATION, WE ARE PREPARING TO DISASSEMBLE, PIECE BY PIECE,
THE STRUCTURE THAT HAS GUARANTEED PEACE FOR UPWARD OF FORTY
YEARS. AS IT STANDS, THE LOOSENING OF BARRIERS BETWEEN EAST
AND WEST IS UNLIKELY EITHER TO WEAKEN THE HOLD OF THE RULING
ELITE IN THE SOVIET UNION OR TO ENHANCE THE STABILITY OF THE
WORLD SYSTEM. ON THE CONTRARY, THE LESSONS OF THE NOT-SO-
DISTANT PAST WOULD SUGGEST THAT SUCH A CHANGE IS DESTINED TO
HAVE THE OPPOSITE EFFECT. OPTIMISM ABOUT THIS UNCERTAIN
FUTURE COULD BE OUR UNDOING.

03562 GOBEYN, M.J.
THE EFFECTS OF CAPITAL MOBILITY ON FREE TRADE ZONE
DEVELOPMENT: A POLITICAL ECONOMIC ANALYSIS
MICHIGAN JOURNAL OF POLITICAL SCIENCE, (11) (WIN 89),
46-75.
THIS PAPER EXAMINES THE EMERGENCE OF AND DEVELOPMENTAL
TRENDS WITHIN THIRD WORLD FREE TRADE ZONES. IT WILL BE SHOWN
THAT THE INCREASED MOBILITY OF CAPITAL HAS INFLUENCED
GREATLY THE SOCIAL, ECONOMIC, AND GOVERNMENTAL STRUCTURES OF
MANY OF THESE ZONES. SPECIFICALLY, IT SHALL BE ARGUED THAT
FOREIGN CAPITALISTS, AIDED BY THEIR INCREASED ABILITY TO
QUICKLY RELOCATE MANUFACTURING FACILITIES FROM ONE ZONE TO
ANOTHER, HAVE EFFECTIVELY BEEN ABLE TO MANIPULATE THIRD
WORLD GOVERNMENTS IN THEIR EFFORTS TO SEEK OUT THE MOST
FAVORABLE INVESTMENT CLIMATES. ALSO, IT IS ARGUED THAT LABOR-
RELATED FACTORS, PARTICULARLY WAGE STRUCTURES, ARE THE MOST
IMPORTANT DETERMINANTS OF FOREIGN INVESTMENT IN FREE TRADE
ZONES. THUS, THE MOST ECONOMICALLY SUCCESSFUL ZONES TEND TO
BE LOCATED IN COUNTRIES WHERE REPRESSIVE POLITICAL LABOR
REGIMES ARE ABLE TO MAINTAIN WELL-DISCIPLINED, LOW-WAGE
LABOR SUPPLIES. THESE DEVELOPMENTS ARE THEN LINKED WITH THE
NEW DEPENDENCY THEORY OF THEOTONIO DOS SANTOS, WHICH
MAINTAINS THAT IN TODAY'S GLOBAL ECONOMY THIRD WORLD
COUNTRIES ARE SUBJECT TO A TECHNOLOGICAL-INDUSTRIAL
DEPENDENCE THAT IS BASED UPON THE EXPLOITATIVE TENDENCIES OF
MULTINATIONAL CORPORATIONS.

03563 GOBLE, P.
ETHNIC POLITICS IN THE USSR
PROBLEMS OF COMMUNISM, XXXVIII(4) (JUL 89), 1-14.
UNLIKE IN THE PAST WHEN THE NATIONAL QUESTION HAD BEEN
DECLARED SOLVED ONCE AND FOR ALL, GORBACHEV'S POLICIES OF
GLASNOST' AND REDUCTION OF COERCION, HIS PARTICIPATORY
LEADERSHIP STYLE AND HIS CONCERN WITH EFFICIENCY IN
PROMOTING PERESTROYKA HAVE ALLOWED THE DEVELOPMENT OF WHAT
CAN BE TERMED ETHNIC POLITICS IN THE USSR. THE PRINCIPAL
PLAYERS ARE THE CENTRAL APPARATUS IN MOSCOW, THE RUSSIANS,
BOTH IN THE RSFSR AND IN THE NON-RUSSIAN REPUBLICS, AND THE
NON-RUSSIAN NATIONS. EACH OPERATES WITH DIFFERENT RESOURCES
AND UNDER DIFFERENT CONSTRAINTS TO PROMOTE ITS INTERESTS.
THUS, A ONCE STATIC SITUATION HAS BECOME DYNAMIC,
POTENTIALLY EXPLOSIVE, BUT PERHAPS ULTIMATELY MANAGEABLE.

03564 GOBLE, P.A.
CENTRAL ASIAN STUDIES ON NON-SOVIET ISLAM: A BIBLIOGRAPHIC
GUIDE
MIDDLE EAST JOURNAL, 43(4) (FAL 89), 649-654.
THIS ESSAY HOPES TO LEAD TO A BROADER EXPLOITATION OF
SOVIET CENTRAL ASIAN RESEARCH ON ISLAM OUTSIDE THE SOVIET
UNION. IT INCLUDES A BRIEF SURVEY OF THE HISTORY OF ISLAMIC
STUDIES IN THE FIVE CENTRAL ASIAN REPUBLICS, DESCRIBING BOTH
THEIR INSTITUTIONAL EVOLUTION AND CURRENT PREOCCUPATIONS,
AND, SECOND, AN ANNOTATED LIST OF THE MOST IMPORTANT
BIBLIOGRAPHIC GUIDES TO THIS SUBJECT.

03565 GODET, M.
VIEWPOINT: EUROPE 1992: THE DREAM AND THE REALITY
FUTURES, 21(2) (APR 89), 183-187.
THIS ARTICLE EXAMINES THE GOAL OF A SINGLE INTERNAL
EUROPEAN MARKET TO BE ENACTED BY THE 12 EC STATES BY 31
DECEMBER 1992. THE PUTATIVE BENEFITS PUT FORWARD IN DETAIL
BY THE COMMISSION MAY CAUSE SEVERE PROBLEMS FOR EUROPEAN
REGIONS AND ENTERPRISES, YET MAY PROVIDE OPPORTUNITIES FOR
EUROPE'S COMPETITORS WITHOUT SOME ELEMENT OF EUROPEAN
PROTECTIONISM. AND PARADOXICALLY, THE THE DRIVE TOWARDS
LIBERALISM AND INTERNAL FREE TRADE MAY LEAD TO CENTRALISM
AND ABUSE OF MONOPOLY POWER IN BRUSSELS. THE MAJOR BENEFITS
OF THE DRIVE TOWARDS 1992 DERIVE FROM MOBILIZING DEBATE AND
ANALYSIS, YET THIS SHOULD BE FOUNDED ON EUROPEAN REALITIES,
NOT ILLUSIONS.

03566 GODET, M.
WEST GERMANY: A PARADOXICAL POWER
FUTURES, 21(4) (AUG 89), 344-360.
THIS ARTICLE EXAMINES TWO SEEMINGLY CONTRADICTORY VIEWS
OF WEST GERMANY: THAT ITS ECONOMIC AND INDUSTRIAL SUCCESS
WILL CONTINUE, BASED ON THE EXCELLENT PERFORMANCE OF ITS
PRODUCTIVE SYSTEM AND THE QUALITY OF ITS TRAINING SCHEMES;
OR THAT IT IS A POWER IN DECLINE DUE TO AGEING AND
DEMOGRAPHIC FACTORS, WEAKNESS IN THE SERVICE INDUSTRIES, AND
A RIGID SOCIAL SYSTEM. BASED ON AN ANALYSIS OF THE POLITICAL,
ECONOMIC AND SOCIOCULTURAL REASONS FOR WEST GERMAN POST-WAR
SUCCESS, IT IS HYPOTHESIZED THAT MATERIAL AND INDUSTRIAL
SUCCESS WILL CONTINUE. THE MAJOR FACTOR WHICH MAY PRESAGE
DECLINE IS DEMOGRAPHIC IN ORIGIN, BUT WE SHOULD BEWARE ANY
THESIS OF GERMAN 'SCLEROSIS'.

03567 GODLEY, M.R.
THE SOJOURNERS: RETURNED OVERSEAS CHINESE IN THE PEOPLE'S
REPUBLIC OF CHINA
PACIFIC AFFAIRS, 62(3) (FAL 89), 330-352.
OF THE MANY HONG KONG RESIDENTS WHO UNDERSTANDABLY WORRY
ABOUT THEIR FUTURE AFTER 1997, THE ESTIMATED QUARTER OF A
MILLION RETURNED OVERSEAS CHINESE MAKE A PARTICULARLY
INTERESTING CASE STUDY. ONCE MOTIVATED BY PATRIOTISM OR
ALIENATED BY DETERIORATING CONDITIONS IN SOUTHEAST ASIA,
PARTICULARLY IN INDONESIA, THEY VOTED WITH THEIR FEET A
SECOND TIME WHEN, AFTER BECOMING DISENCHANTED WITH LIFE IN
THE PRC, THEY FLED TO THE BRITISH COLONY. ALTHOUGH MANY
OTHERS HAVE CROSSED THE BORDER BECAUSE OF HARDSHIP OR
POLITICAL VICISSITUDE, THE RETURNED OVERSEAS CHINESE WERE
BRUTALLY MISTREATED DURING THE CULTURAL REVOLUTION WHEN
THEIR VERY "CHINESENESS" WAS OFTEN BROUGHT INTO QUESTION.
THIS ARTICLE RELATES THEIR EXPERIENCES WITHIN THE GENERAL
CONTEXT OF CHINA'S MODERN POLITICAL HISTORY.

03568 GODSON, R.
INTELLIGENCE REQUIREMENTS FOR THE 1990'S
WASHINGTON QUARTERLY, 12(1) (WIN 89), 47-65.
INTELLIGENCE, PARTICULARLY FOREIGN INTELLIGENCE,
CONSISTS OF FOUR MAJOR ELEMENTS-ANALYSIS, COLLECTION,
COUNTERINTELLIGENCE, AND COVERT ACTIONSYMBIOTICALLY RELATED
TO EACH OTHER AND TO OVERALL NATIONAL SECURITY POLICY. THIS
ESSAY CONSIDERS MAJOR REQUIREMENTS OF EACH ELEMENT IN TURN,
ALTHOUGH AFFECTING ANY ONE ELEMENT IS LIKELY TO AFFECT THE
OTHERS AND HAVE CONSEQUENCES FOR OVERALL NATIONAL SECURITY
POLICY FORMULATION AND IMPLEMENTATION.

03569 GOEBEL, S.E.
SOVIET POLITICAL OBJECTIVES IN THE FEDERAL REPUBLIC OF
GERMANY: INSTRUMENTS AND ASSESSMENTS

AVAILABLE FROM NTIS, NO. AD-A199 888/9/GAR, JUN 88, 104.
THIS THESIS EXAMINES APPARENT SOVIET ATTEMPTS TO USE ITS
DETENTE POLICY TO EXPLOIT THE FEDERAL REPUBLIC OF GERMANY'S
MEMBERSHIP IN NATO AND THEREBY EXPAND ITS INFLUENCE IN THE
FRG AND EUROPE AS A WHOLE. IT IS HYPOTHESIZED THAT THE
SOVIET UNION CHOOSES TO EXPLOIT THE FRG'S POSITION IN NATO
BY CULTIVATING A SPECIAL RELATIONSHIP WITH IT AND THEREBY
ACCESSING THE U.S. AND NATO AS A WHOLE, RATHER THAN MAKING
OVERT EFFORTS TO FORCE A NEAR-TERM SPLIT BETWEEN WEST
GERMANY AND THE U.S. THE THESIS FOCUSES ON THE INSTRUMENTS
THE SOVIET UNION USES TO MAXIMIZE ITS INFLUENCE IN THE FRG
AND THE REGION. THESE INSTRUMENTS INCLUDE WEST GERMANY'S
CONCERNS REGARDING NUCLEAR WAR IN EUROPE, OSTPOLITIK AND
GERMAN-GERMAN RELATIONS. KEYWORDS: WEST GERMAN
VULNERABILITIES; SOVIET ACCOMPLISHMENTS AND FAILURES.

03570 GOEL, R.K.; RICH, D.P.
ON THE ECONOMIC INCENTIVES FOR TAKING BRIBES
PUBLIC CHOICE, 61(3) (JUN 89), 269-275.
THIS PAPER PRESENTS AN EMPIRICAL ANALYSIS OF THE FACTORS
AFFECTING BRIBE TAKING BY PUBLIC OFFICIALS. FACTORS
INFLUENCING THE ACCEPTANCE OF BRIBES INCLUDE: THE
PROBABILITY OF BEING CONVICTED, SEVERITY OF PUNISHMENT,
GOVERNMENT SALARY RELATIVE TO PRIVATE SECTOR INCOME, THE
DEMONSTRATION EFFECT, AND THE UNEMPLOYMENT RATE. THE RESULTS
INDICATE THAT HIGHER PROBABILITY OF BEING CONVICTED
DISCOURAGES THE ACCEPTANCE OF BRIBES AS DOES MORE SEVERE
PUNISHMENT. LOW RELATIVE EARNINGS, HIGH UNEMPLOYMENT, AND
THE DEMONSTRATION EFFECT OF AGGREGATE ADVERTISING ALL LEAD
TO INCREASED BRIBE TAKING.

03571 GOERING, J.M.; COULIBABLY, M.
INVESTIGATING PUBLIC HOUSING SEGREGATION: CONCEPTUAL AND
METHODOLOGICAL ISSUES
URBAN AFFAIRS QUARTERLY, 25(2) (DEC 89), 265-297.
THE AUTHORS INVESTIGATE THE CONCEPTS AND EVIDENCE NEEDED
TO UNDERSTAND THE EXTENT OF RACIAL SEGREGATION IN THE
FEDERAL PUBLIC HOUSING PROGRAM OPERATING IN METROPOLITAN
AREAS THROUGHOUT THE UNITED STATES. OVER ONE MILLION UNITS
OF PUBLIC HOUSING IN URBAN AREAS CONSTITUTE AN IMPORTANT,
BUT POORLY UNDERSTOOD, COMPONENT OF OVERALL HOUSING MARKET
SEGREGATION. USING DATA FROM THE U.S. DEPARTMENT OF HOUSING
AND URBAN DEVELOPMENT, THEY DESCRIBE THE DEGREE,
DISTRIBUTION, AND SEGREGATION OF MINORITIES IN HUD-ASSISTED
FAMILY AND ELDERLY HOUSING. THEY ATTEMPT TO EXPLAIN THE
LEVEL AND VARIATION OF PUBLIC HOUSING SEGREGATION THROUGH
EXAMINING LEGISLATIVE, PROGRAMMATIC, AND REGIONAL FACTORS,
THOUGH DIFFERENCES APPEAR AT RELATIVELY LOW LEVELS OF
STATISTICAL SIGNIFICANCE.

03572 GOERTZ, G.; DIEHL, P.F.
A TERRITORIAL HISTORY OF THE INTERNATIONAL SYSTEM
INTERNATIONAL INTERACTIONS, 15(1) (1988), 81-93.
THE AUTHORS CHART THE EVOLUTION OF THE INTERNATIONAL
SYSTEM FROM THE POST-NAPOLEONIC WARS TO THE PRESENT, WITH
SPECIAL REFERENCE TO GROWTH IN THE NUMBER AND CONFIGURATION
OF STATES, AS WELL AS CHANGES IN TERRITORIAL SOVEREIGNTY
INVOLVING THOSE STATES. GROWTH AND CHANGE IN THE
INTERNATIONAL SYSTEM WERE FOUND TO HAVE OCCURRED LARGELY IN
THE 20TH CENTURY. DURING THAT TIME, WAR PLAYED A MAJOR ROLE
IN PRECIPITATING THE GROWTH OF THE INTERNATIONAL SYSTEM,
ALTHOUGH WAR WAS LESS SIGNIFICANT IN CHANGES IN TERRITORIAL
SOVEREIGNTY. THE AUTHORS NOTE THAT MAJOR POWERS WERE
INVOLVED IN ONE-HALF OF THE TERRITORIAL CHANGES AND DISCUSS
IMPLICATIONS FOR THE FUTURE OF THE INTERNATIONAL SYSTEM.

03573 GOERTZEL, T.
EXPLAINING STAR WARS
CRITICAL SOCIOLOGY, 16(2-3) (SUM 89), 205-231.
THE STAR WARS PROPOSAL RESULTED FROM THE CONJUNCTURE OF
SEVERAL FACTORS: AN ORGANIZATIONAL AND TECHNOLOGICAL BASE IN
THE WEAPONS LABORATORIES AND AEROSPACE INDUSTRY, EFFECTIVE
ADVOCACY BY POWERFUL INDIVIDUALS AND ORGANIZATIONS, AND THE
NEED OF THE REAGAN ADMINISTRATION FOR A PUBLIC RELATIONS
RESPONSE TO THE NUCLEAR FREEZE. THE BUREAUCRATIC POLITICS,
DECISION PROCESS, AND SOCIAL MOVEMENTS PARADIGMS ARE MOST
USEFUL FOR EXPLAINING THE INITIATION OF THE PROPOSAL.
RATIONAL ANALYSIS, PRESSURE GROUP, ORGANIZATIONAL PROCESS,
AND GARRISON STATE THEORIES HELP US TO EXPLAIN THE POLICY
OUTCOME.

03574 GOETZE, D.; GALDERISI, P.
EXPLAINING COLLECTIVE ACTION WITH RATIONAL MODELS
PUBLIC CHOICE, 62(1) (JUL 89), 25-40.
THE AUTHORS NOTE THE FAILURE OF A RATIONAL EGOIST MODEL
OF HUMAN BEHAVIOR TO GENERATE SUCCESSFUL PREDICTIONS OF
IMPORTANT POLITICAL AND ECONOMIC BEHAVIORS. THEY PRESENT
ALTERNATIVE MODELS THAT COMBINE RATIONAL, UTILITYMAXIMIZING
FEATURES WITH CONCERNS ABOUT COLLECTIVE WELFARE. THE MODEL
IS COMPARED WITH OTHERS AND TESTED IN AN EXPERIMENTALLY-
INDUCED PUBLIC GOODS GAME AND THE RESULTS INDICATE THAT A
MODEL IN WHICH SUBJECTS ARE PRESUMED TO "TRADE OFF" BENEFITS
TO SELF WITH BENEFITS TO OTHERS PROVIDES A BETTER
EXPLANATION OF ACTUAL CONTRIBUTING BEHAVIOR THAN EITHER THE

RATIONAL EGOIST OR COLLECTIVE WELFARE MODELS.

03575 GOLD, D.
ASSESSING THE BUILDUP ALONG ISRAEL'S EASTERN FRONT
IDF JOURNAL, (17) (SUM 89), 34-38.
THIS ARTICLE ASSESSES THE DANGER FACED BY ISRAEL OF ARAB
WAR ON THE EAST NOW THAT THE DANGER OF AGRESSION FROM EGYPT
HAS BEEN REDUCED. IT EXAMINES THE SCALE OF MILITARY BUILDUP
IN SYRIA, IRAQ, SAUDI ARABIA AND JORDAN DURING THE LAST
DECADE AND THE NECESSITY FOR ISRAEL TO MAINTAIN A MILITARY
POSTURE TO DEFEND ITS EASTERN FRONT. IMPLICATIONS FOR PEACE
ARE DISCUSSED.

03576 GOLD, S.
THE COSTS OF PRIVATIZATION: TURKEY IN THE 1980'S
MULTINATIONAL MONITOR, 11(10) (OCT 89), 11-16.
IN 1980, TURKEY REVERSED A LONGSTANDING POLICY OF
EXTENSIVE STATE INTERVENTION IN THE ECONOMY AND LAUNCHED A
CONCERTED EFFORT TO OPEN ITS ECONOMY MORE FULLY TO THE
DICTATES OF THE MARKETPLACE. PRIOR TO 1980, TURKEY'S ECONOMY
HAD BEEN CHARACTERIZED BY A HEAVY RELIANCE ON STATE
INTERVENTION. THE FUNDAMENTAL TRANSFORMATION OF THE TURKISH
ECONOMY HAS MOVED THE COUNTRY FROM AN INWARD-FOCUSED, IMPORT
SUBSTITUTION-BASED DEVELOPMENT MODEL TOWARD EXPORT-LED
GROWTH AND INDUSTRIALIZATION.

03577 GOLD, S.D.
A NEW WAY TO COMPARE STATES' SPENDING
STATE LEGISLATURES, 15(5) (MAY 89), 10-11.
A NEW RESEARCH TOOL, CALLED A "REPRESENTATIVE
EXPENDITURE SYSTEM," MAY HELP LEGISLATORS GET A BETTER
HANDLE ON HOW GOVERNMENT SPENDING IN ONE STATE COMPARES TO
ANOTHER. ALTHOUGH THE RESEARCH IS STILL IN ITS INFANCY, IT
SHOULD PROVIDE SOME HELPFUL GUIDELINES FOR UNDERSTANDING WHY
ONE STATE SPENDS MORE THAN ANOTHER.

03578 GOLD, S.D.
LOTTERIES: STILL SMALL CHANGE
STATE LEGISLATURES, 15(6) (JUL 89), 14-15.
LOTTERY REVENUE IS GROWING FASTER THAN ANY OTHER STATE
REVENUE SOURCE, BUT IT STARTS FROM A MUCH SMALLER BASE.
LOTTERIES RAISE ONLY 2.6 PERCENT AS MUCH AS TAXES AND, IN
THE BIG PICTURE OF STATE FINANCES, THEY ARE SMALL CHANGE.

03579 GOLD, S.D.
NEW WAYS TO FINANCE INFRASTRUCTURE
STATE LEGISLATURES, 15(3) (MAR 89), 22-25.
THE AUTHOR WEIGHS THE PROS AND CONS OF IMPACT FEES
CHARGED BY LOCAL GOVERNMENTS ON NEW DEVELOPMENT.

03580 GOLD, S.D.
REMEDY FOR THE MANDATE MESS
STATE LEGISLATURES, 15(8) (SEP 89), 16-19.
UNFUNDED STATE MANDATES ARE AN IRRITANT IN STATE-LOCAL
RELATIONS. A PROPOSED CONSTITUTIONAL AMENDMENT PASSED BY
FLORIDA'S LEGISLATURE PROVIDES A PROMISING APPROACH TO THE
PROBLEM.

03581 GOLD, S.D.; ERICKSON, B.M.
STATE AID TO LOCAL GOVERNMENTS IN THE 1980'S
STATE AND LOCAL GOVERNMENT REVIEW, 21(1) (WIN 89), 11-22.
THIS ARTICLE DESCRIBES AND ANALYZES STATE AID TO LOCAL
GOVERNMENT, WITH SPECIAL ATTENTION TO STATE REVENUE-SHARING
PROGRAMS. STATE GOVERNMENTS PROVIDED $130 BILLION OF AID TO
LOCAL GOVERNMENTS IN FISCAL YEAR 1986, WITH EDUCATION
RECEIVING ABOUT FIVE OUT OF EVERY EIGHT DOLLARS OF AID. TO
FACILITATE UNDERSTANDING OF DIFFERENCES IN STATE AID
PROGRAMS AND ANALYSIS OF CHANGES OVER TIME, THE STUDY
PROVIDES COMPARATIVE DATA FOR ALL STATES. IT ALSO BRIEFLY
DESCRIBES MAJOR STATE AID INITIATIVES FOLLOWING THE
TERMINATION OF FEDERAL REVENUE SHARING.

03582 GOLD, S.D.
TAX REFORMS FAIL IN THREE STATES: WHY?
STATE LEGISLATURES, 15(7) (AUG 89), 21-23.
COMPLICATED TAX REFORMS HAVE AN EXTREMELY HARD TIME
WINNING THE APPROVAL OF VOTERS. TAX REFORM IS FAR MORE
LIKELY TO BE ACCOMPLISHED THROUGH THE LEGISLATIVE PROCESS
THAN THROUGH THE BALLOT BOX.

03583 GOLD, S.D.
TAX REVENUES SOAR AND TUMBLE
STATE LEGISLATURES, 15(5) (MAY 89), 30-31.
A RECENT NCSL STUDY OF HOW STATE AND LOW TAX LEVELS HAVE
CHANGED SINCE 1970 DISCLOSED THE FOLLOWING: (1) STATE AND
LOCAL TAXES GREW ROUGHLY IN LINE WITH THE ECONOMY; (2) AS A
PROPORTION OF PERSONAL INCOME, STATE TAXES ROSE MUCH FASTER
THAN LOCAL TAXES; (3) TAX POLICY IN THE 1980'S DIFFERED
GREATLY FROM THAT OF THE 1970'S

03584 GOLD, T.B.
URBAN PRIVATE BUSINESS IN CHINA
STUDIES IN COMPARATIVE COMMUNISM, 22(2/3) (SUM 89),
187-202.

THIS ARTICLE ASSESSES THE RISE OF A LEGALIZED URBAN PRIVATE BUSINESS SECTOR. IT PRESENTS A REVIEW OF TRADITIONAL ROLES OF THE SECOND ECONOMY, THEN EXAMINES MEASURES TO LIMIT PRIVATE ECONOMIC ACTIVITY. THE REBIRTH OF THE PRIVATE SECTOR IS THEN CHRONICLED. IT NOTES THE OFFICIAL DISCRIMINATION AGAINST PRIVATE BUSINESS AS AN AMBIVALENCE OF THE PARTY TO THE ETHOS OF FREE ENTERPRISE, AND ANALYSES REASONS FOR THE AMBIVALENCE.

03585 GOLD, V.
EXTREMISTS IS THE MAINSTREAM
AMERICAN SPECTATOR, 22(7) (JUL 89), 34-35.
THIS ARTICLE DESCRIBES THE GATHERING OF POLITICS AND REPORTERS AT THE COMMEMORATIVE CELEBRATION OF THE SILVES ANNIVERSARY OF THE GOLDUATES PRESIDENTIAL CAMPAIGN, THE CHARGE OF THE RIGHT BRIGADE.

03586 GOLDANSKY, V.
SCIENCE, POLITICS, AND GLASNOST
INTERNATIONAL AFFAIRS (MOSCOW), (9) (SEP 89), 131-137.
THE NEW SOVIET POLICY OF GLASNOST HAS RAISED QUESTIONS ABOUT WHAT GLASNOST REALLY IS, HOW MUCH OF IT SHOULD BE ALLOWED, AND WHOM OR WHAT IT SHOULD OR SHOULD NOT CONCERN. GLASNOST IS ALSO RAISING QUESTIONS IN THE AREAS OF SCIENCE AND TECHNOLOGY.

03587 GOLDBERG, A.C.
WESTERN ANALYSTS REAPPRAISE SOVIET STRATEGIC POLICY
WASHINGTON QUARTERLY, 12(2) (SPR 89), 201-213.
AS MOSCOW MOVES TO MEET THE SIMULTANEOUS DEMANDS OF WESTERN MILITARY AND COMMERCIAL TECHNOLOGICAL COMPETITORS, SOME WINDING DOWN IN EXISTING PROCUREMENT LEVELS AND THE REALLOCATION RESOURCES TO RESEARCH AND DEVELOPMENT OUGHT TO BE ANTICIPATED. HOWEVER, THERE IS NO EVIDENCE THAT THE SOVIET MILITARY SHARES THE MORE EXTREME DISARMAMENT VIEWS EVIDENCED IN THE WRITINGS OF SOME SOVIET ACADEMICIANS. SHORT OF A MAJOR DECISION BY THE POLITBURO TO READJUST SOVIET FORCES IN EUROPE DRAMATICALLY-SOMETHING THAT PROBABLY WOULD EMERGE ONLY FROM PROTRACTED EAST-WEST NEGOTIATIONS-IT IS DOUBTFUL THAT ANY MORE THAN COSMETIC CHANGES WILL OCCUR IN SOVIET OPERATIONAL PLANNING.

03588 GOLDBERG, J.
THE SAUDI MILITARY BUILD-UP: STRATEGY AND RISKS
MIDDLE EAST REVIEW, XXI(3) (SPR 89), 3-14.
THE CONVENTIONAL ANSWER TO WHY THE SAUDIS HAVE PURSUED A MASSIVE MILITARY BUILDUP EXPLAINS THE ENTIRE SAUDI STRATEGY IN TERMS OF PROTECTING THE KINGDOM AGAINST THE GROWING IRANIAN THREAT. BUT A CAREFUL ANALYSIS OF THE SAUDI ARMS PURCHASES RAISES SERIOUS DOUBTS ABOUT THE IRANIAN ARGUMENT. THE SCOPE OF THE ARMAMENTS GOES WELL BEYOND WHAT THE SAUDIS NEED TO PROTECT THEIR WEALTH AND THE VITAL SHIPPING LANES IN THE GULF. MOREOVER, IF ONE EXAMINES THE COMPOSITION OF THE SAUDI SHOPPING LIST, IT IS EASY TO CONCLUDE THAT THE NEW EQUIPMENT IS FAR MORE THAN WHAT THE SAUDIS NEED TO DEFEND EVEN SUCH VULNERABLE TARGETS AS THE OIL TERMINALS AND THE REFINERY COMPLEX IN THE EASTERN PROVINCE. ANOTHER EXPLANATION FOR THE BUILDUP FOCUSES ON ISRAEL AS THE THREAT.

03589 GOLDBERG, S.
SO WHAT IF THE DEATH PENALTY DETERS?
NATIONAL REVIEW, XLI(12) (JUN 89), 42-44.
WHILE THE EMPIRICAL QUESTION CAN BE DEBATED, THE STANDARD THEORETICAL ARGUMENTS AGAINST THE DEATH PENALTY ARE SOPHISTRY. WE HAVE AN ENORMOUS AMOUNT OF BOTH INFORMAL AND FORMAL EVIDENCE--FROM EVERYDAY EXPERIENCE OF SOCIALIZING CHILDREN AND LIMITING ADULT BEHAVIOR AND FROM SUCH "EXPERIMENTS" AS INCREASING THE FEES FOR PARKING VIOLATIONS-- THAT, AS A GENERAL RULE, THE GREATER A PUNISHMENT, THE FEWER PEOPLE WILL BEHAVE IN THE PUNISHED WAY. THUS, IT IS PERFECTLY REASONABLE TO EXPECT THAT THE DEATH PENALTY WOULD HAVE A MORE DISSUASIVE EFFECT THAN WOULD LIFE IMPRISONMENT.

03590 GOLDFIELD, M.
WORKER INSURGENCY, RADICAL ORGANIZATION, AND NEW DEAL LABOR LEGISLATION
AMERICAN POLITICAL SCIENCE REVIEW, 83(4) (DEC 89), 1257-1284.
THE AUTHOR EXAMINES THE INFLUENCE OF WORKER INSURGENCY AND RADICAL ORGANIZATION ON THE PASSAGE AND FINAL FORM OF THE NATIONAL LABOR RELATIONS ACT IN 1935. HE ARGUES THAT OTHER ANALYTIC APPROACHES HAVE FAILED TO TAKE INTO ACCOUNT THE IMPORTANCE OF THIS INFLUENCE AND THE DEGREE TO WHICH IT CONSTRAINED AND STRUCTURED THE RESPONSES OF KEY POLITICAL ACTORS. HE CONCLUDES THAT THE APPROACHES THAT DOWNPLAY THE IMPORTANCE OF WORKER INSURGENCY AND RADICAL ORGANIZATION ARE WRONG IN THE PARTICULARS AND SUSPECT AS GENERAL THEORIES. THIS APPLIES ESPECIALLY TO THE PERSPECTIVE THAT EMPHASIZES THE AUTONOMY OF THE STATE FROM SOCIETAL FORCES.

03591 GOLDFISCHER, D.
MUTUAL DEFENSE EMPHASIS: THE HISTORY AND IMPLICATIONS OF AN ALTERNATIVE APPROACH TO STRATEGIC ARMS CONTROL
DISSERTATION ABSTRACTS INTERNATIONAL, 50(4) (OCT 89), 1082-A.
THE AUTHOR EXAMINES THE HISTORICAL ADVOCACY AND POTENTIAL FEASIBILITY OF A MUTUAL DEFENSE EMPHASIS (MDE) APPROACH TO STRATEGIC ARMS CONTROL. HE TRACES THE PROMOTION OF MDE PROPOSALS DURING THREE PERIODS: THE EARLY 1950'S, THE DECADE PRECEDING THE 1972 ABM TREATY, AND THE 1980'S. HE ARGUES THAT MDE REPRESENTED, AND CONTINUES TO REPRESENT, A PLAUSIBLE ALTERNATIVE TO PREVAILING RATIONALES FOR RELYING PRIMARILY ON OFFENSIVE STRATEGIC WEAPONS.

03592 GOLDING, S.R.
THE FORGING OF A POST-LIBERAL DEMOCRACY: GRAMSCI'S ATTEMPT TO GROUND DEMOCRACY ON THE FRACTURED TERRAIN OF HISTORICAL SUBJECTIVITY
DISSERTATION ABSTRACTS INTERNATIONAL, 50(2) (AUG 89), 534-A.
THE AUTHOR ANALYZES ANTONIO GRAMSCI'S REASSESSMENT OF POLITICS AND POLITICAL STRATEGY IN "QUADERNI DEL CARCERE" AND SUGGESTS THAT GRAMSCI'S WORK LENDS ITSELF TO A POST-LIBERAL THEORIZATION OF DEMOCRACY.

03593 GOLDMAN, E.O.
THE WASHINGTON TREATY SYSTEM: ARMS RACING AND ARMS CONTROL IN THE INTER-WAR PERIOD
DISSERTATION ABSTRACTS INTERNATIONAL, 50(6) (DEC 89), 1794-A.
THE AUTHOR EXAMINES THE EVOLUTION OF THE WASHINGTON TREATY SYSTEM TO HELP EXPLAIN WHY AND HOW ARMS CONTROL SYSTEMS EMERGE AND WHY THEY COLLAPSE. SHE ANALYZES THE ECONOMIC, STRATEGIC, TECHNOLOGICAL, GEOGRAPHIC, AND DOMESTIC CONSTRAINTS FACING THE TREATY POWERS. SHE DEMONSTRATES HOW ARM CONTROL INITIALLY FACILITATED BUT EVENTUALLY OBSTRUCTED FOREIGN POLICY OBJECTIVES IN THE FAR EAST AND AROUND THE GLOBE.

03594 GOLDMAN, M.I.
THE FUTURE OF SOVIET ECONOMIC REFORM
CURRENT HISTORY, 88(540) (OCT 89), 329-332, 348-349.
THE AUTHOR REVIEWS GORBACHEV'S ECONOMIC REFORM EFFORTS, ANALYZES WHY THEY HAVE FAILED, AND SPECULATES ABOUT THEIR FUTURE.

03595 GOLDMAN, S. B.
MEDIA USE AND TIME OF DECISION IN THE 1980 PRESIDENTIAL ELECTION
DISSERTATION ABSTRACTS INTERNATIONAL, 49(9) (MAR 89), 2436-A.
THIS STUDY FOLLOWED 209 REGISTERED VOTERS THROUGH THE 1980 PRESIDENTIAL CAMPAIGN AS THEY MADE THEIR DECISION AMONG JIMMY CARTER, RONALD REAGAN, AND JOHN ANDERSON. THE VOTERS WERE CATEGORIZED AS PRE-CAMPAIGN, CAMPAIGN, POST-DEBATE, OR LAST-MINUTE DECIDERS. TELEVISION VIEWING, NEWSPAPER READING, OTHER COMMUNICATION BEHAVIORS, AND DEMOGRAPHICS WERE ANALYZED FOR THESE VOTERS, UTILIZING THE USES-AND-GRATIFICATIONS APPROACH OF AN ACTIVE, SELECTIVE AUDIENCE.

03596 GOLDMANN, K.
THE LINE IN WATER: INTERNATIONAL AND DOMESTIC POLITICS COOPERATION & CONFLICT: NORDIC JOURNAL OF INTERNATIONAL POLITICS, XXIV(3-4) (DEC 89), 103-116.
IT IS COMMON TO CRITICIZE POLITICAL SCIENTISTS FOR SEPARATING THE INSEPARABLE AND MAKING A SHARP DISTINCTION BETWEEN INTERNATIONAL AND DOMESTIC POLITICS. THE PROBLEM PRESUMABLY IS THAT DIFFERENT MODELS OF THE FUNDAMENTALS OF POLITICS ARE USED BY THOSE CONCERNED WITH INTERNATIONAL AND DOMESTIC POLITICS, THAT THIS SEPARATION REDUCES THEIR ABILITY TO UNDERSTAND BOTH, AND THAT THEREFORE THE SEPARATE MODELS OUGHT TO BE MERGED WITH EACH OTHER. THE MERGER CAN TAKE THE FORM OF ESTABLISHING THE LINKAGES THAT MAY OBTAIN BETWEEN POLITICS AT THE INTERNATIONAL AND THE DOMESTIC LEVELS OR OF PRESUMING THAT THE TWO LEVELS ARE ISOMORPHIC AND HENCE THAT INTERNATIONAL AND DOMESTIC POLITICS ARE NOT JUST INTERRELATED BUT THE SAME. IN THE PAPER, VARIOUS MERGED MODELS OF POLITICS ARE SURVEYED, AND EXAMPLES FROM SWEDISH POLITICS ARE USED TO SUGGEST A VARIETY OF NEW TASKS FOR THE COMPARATIVE STUDY OF POLITICS.

03597 GOLDSCHEIDER, C.
THE DEMOGRAPHIC EMBEDDEDNESS OF THE ARAB-JEWISH CONFLICT IN ISRAELI SOCIETY
MIDDLE EAST REVIEW, XXI(3) (SPR 89), 15-24.
IN ORDER TO CLARIFY THE DEMOGRAPHIC EMBEDDEDNESS OF THE ARAB-JEWISH CONFLICT, THE AUTHOR REVIEWS THE CHANGING DEMOGRAPHIC CONTOURS OF THE MAJORITY-MINORITY RELATIONSHIPS. THIS INCLUDES AN INVESTIGATION INTO THE CHANGING SIZE, GROWTH, AND ETHNIC COMPOSITION OF THE JEWISH AND ARAB POPULATIONS, THE DEMOGRAPHIC FORMATION OF THESE COMMUNITES, THE EVOLUTION OF IMMIGRATION PATTERNS, THE FERITILITY OF JEWISH AND ARAB POPULATIONS, AND THE CHANGING POPULATION PROPORTIONS OF EACH. HE LINKS SOCIAL INEQUALITIES TO DEMOGRAPHIC PROCESSES, EXAMINING THE INDIVIDUAL VIEWS OF ARABS ABOUT JEWS AND JEWS ABOUT ARABS.

03598 GOLDSTEIN, A.
THE DOMAIN OF INQUIRY IN POLITICAL SCIENCE: GENERAL
LESSONS FROM THE STUDY OF CHINA
POLITY, XXI(3) (SPR 89), 517-537.
THE STUDY OF CHINESE POLITICS HAS BEEN FAULTED FOR ITS
SHORTCOMINGS AS SOCIAL SCIENCE, BUT FOR THE MOST PART ITS
CRITICS HAVE IGNORED WHAT THIS ARTICLE ARGUES IS THE CRUCIAL
METHODOLOGICAL WEAKNESS: THE ABSENCE OF AN APPROPRIATELY
DEFINED DOMAIN OF INQUIRY. THE AUTHOR FINDS INSTITUTIONAL
DEFINITIONS OF DOMAINS OF INQUIRY INADEQUATE, SHOWS HOW THEY
HAVE HAMPERED STUDIES OF CHINA, AND SUGGESTS AN ALTERNATIVE.

03599 GOLDSTEIN, J.; LENWAY, S.A.
INTERESTS OR INSTITUTIONS: AN INQUIRY INTO CONGRESSIONAL-
ITC RELATIONS
INTERNATIONAL STUDIES QUARTERLY, 33(3) (SEP 89), 303-328.
THIS ESSAY EXAMINES THE RELATIONSHIP BETWEEN CONGRESS
AND THE INTERNATIONAL TRADE COMMISSION (ITC). USING THE
LOGIC OF PRINCIPAL-AGENT THEORY, WE FIND THAT RISING
CONSTITUENT PRESSURES ON CONGRESS TO INCREASE TRADE
PROTECTIONISM HAVE NOT LED TO INCREASED POLITICAL CONTROL
OVER THE TRADE BUREAUCRACY. THE ESSAY SUGGESTS THAT THE
ABSENCE OF THIS EXPECTED RELATIONSHIP BETWEEN CONGRESS AND
THE ITC MAY BE EXPLAINED BY THE HISTORICAL CIRCUMSTANCES
UNDER WHICH CONGRESS ORIGINALLY DELEGATED POWER. THIS PAPER
ARGUES THAT DELEGATION IN THE 1930S ESTABLISHED RULES AND
NORMS WHICH CONTINUE TO INFLUENCE THE RANGE OF REMEDIES TO
WHICH CONGRESS WILL TURN TO AID AILING INDUSTRIES. THESE
RULES AND NORMS FORESTALL DIRECT CONGRESSIONAL INVOLVEMENT
IN PROTECTIONISM, THEREBY INSULATING THE ITC.

03600 GOLDSTEIN, J.
THE IMPACT OF IDEAS ON TRADE POLICY: THE ORIGINS OF U.S.
AGRICULTURAL AND MANUFACTURING POLICIES
INTERNATIONAL ORGANIZATION, 43(1) (WIN 89), 31-72.
SINCE THE CLOSE OF WORLD WAR II, THE UNITED STATES HAS
SUPPORTED CONTRADICTORY TRADE POLICIES. IN MANUFACTURING,
THE UNITED STATES HAS FOSTERED A LIBERAL TRADE REGIME,
SPURNING GOVERNMENT INVOLVEMENT IN MARKET TRANSACTIONS. IN
AGRICULTURE, IT HAS SANCTIONED POLICIES OF IMPORT
RESTRICTIONS, EXPORT SUBSIDIES, AND IMPORT FEES. THIS
VARIATION IS ROOTED IN DECISIONS THAT WERE MADE IN THE 1930S
AND INSTITUTIONALIZED IN THE 1940S. IN THE WAKE OF THE GREAT
DEPRESSION, POLICYMAKERS CONCLUDED THAT STATE INTERVENTION
HELPED AGRICULTURE AND HURT INDUSTRY. THIS ARTICLE ARGUES
THAT THE CHOICE OF GOVERNMENT POLICY AND ITS APPROPRIATENESS
TO THE ECONOMIC PROBLEMS FACED BY EACH SECTOR REFLECT THE
ACCEPTED KNOWLEDGE AT THE TIME. NEITHER LIBERALIZATION NOR
SUBSIDIZATION WAS INEVITABLE; BOTH WERE ECONOMICALLY VIABLE
OPTIONS. HOWEVER, CENTRAL DECISION-MAKERS MADE CHOICES THAT
WERE OFTEN BASED ON INACCURATE BELIEFS ABOUT THE UTILITY OF
DIFFERENT POLICY OPTIONS.

03601 GOLDSTEIN, M. C.; BEALL, C. M.
THE IMPACT OF CHINA'S REFORM POLICY ON THE NOMADS OF
WESTERN TIBET
ASIAN SURVEY, XXIX(6) (JUN 89), 601-619.
THE ARTICLE EXPLORES THE RELATIONS BETWEEN THE CENTRAL
GOVERNMENT OF CHINA AND THE NOMADIC PEOPLES OF THE REMOTE
TIBETAN PROVINCE OF PHALA. IT OUTLINES THE HISTORY OF
RELATIONS BETWEEN THE TWO GROUPS BEGINNING WITH PRE-
REVOLUTION CHINA AND CULMINATING IN THE REFORMS ATTEMPTED BY
THE CENTRAL GOVERNMENT IN THE 1980'S. THE ARTICLE
CONCENTRATES ON THE MORE RECENT POLICIES AND ATTEMPTS AT
REFORM. IT CONCLUDES THAT THE REFORMS, WHICH ALLOW MORE
RELIGIOUS AND ECONOMIC FREEDOM HAVE HAD AN ON-BALANCE
BENEFICIAL EFFECT UPON THE PEOPLE OF PHALA.

03602 GOLDSTEIN, S.M.
DIPLOMACY AMID PROTEST: THE SINO-SOVIET SUMMIT
PROBLEMS OF COMMUNISM, XXXVIII(5) (SEP 89), 49-75.
THE DRAMATIC DEVELOPMENTS IN CHINESE POLITICS IN THE
SPRING OF 1989 PLAYED A PARADOXICAL ROLE WITH RESPECT TO THE
SIXTH SINO-SOVIET SUMMIT. ON THE ONE HAND, BY TAKING WORLD
ATTENTION AWAY FROM SOMEWHAT LACKLUSTER MEETINGS, THESE
DEVELOPMENTS MASKED THE POTENTIAL FOR FURTHER PROGRESS IN
SINO-SOVIET RELATIONS. THE HECTIC NATURE OF THE SUMMIT, THE
DISTRACTION OF MANY OF ITS PARTICIPANTS, AND ITS MEAGER
DIPLOMATIC OUTPUT TENDED TO OBSCURE THE FACT THAT THE BASIC
SCAFFOLDING FOR A BROADLY-BASED AND FULL BILATERAL
RELATIONSHIP THAT HAD BEEN CONSTRUCTED OVER THE PAST DECADE
REMAINS INTACT. ON THE OTHER HAND, THESE SAME DEVELOPMENTS
EMPHASIZED THE SALIENCE OF DOMESTIC POLITICS AND IDEOLOGY
FOR THE FUTURE DIRECTION OF THESE RELATIONS.

03603 GOLDSTEIN, W.
ECONOMIC GROWTH AND MILITARY POWER: EROSION OF THE
SUPERPOWERS
CURRENT, (309) (JAN 89), 23-31.
THE 1987 WHITE HOUSE SUMMIT AND THE RESULTING ARMS
CONTROL PROPOSALS WERE PROMPTED BY THE REALIZATION THAT
NEITHER SUPERPOWER COULD AFFORD TO MAINTAIN ITS CURRENT
OBLIGATIONS. IT IS BECOMING TOO EXPENSIVE TO MAINTAIN (1)
THE FORCES NEEDED TO POLICE THE SUPERPOWERS' WORLDWIDE

SPHERES OF INFLUENCE; (2) THE NUCLEAR ARSENALS TO GUARANTEE
AN EXTENDED AND ASSURED DETERRENCE; AND (3) THE COMMITMENTS
TO PRESERVE HEGEMONY IN KEY AREAS OF THE THIRD WORLD.

03604 GOLEM, D.
DEVELOPMENTS IN INFRASTRUCTURE FINANCING
AMERICAN CITY AND COUNTY, 104(7) (JUL 89), 10.
AWARENESS OF THE NATION'S INFRASTRUCTURE CRISIS HAS
INCREASED OVER THE PAST FEW YEARS. REDUCED FEDERAL FUNDING
AND LIMITED, INSUFFICIENT REVENUE SOURCES HAVE PLACED THE
BURDEN OF FUNDING INFRASTRUCTURE IMPROVEMENTS AT THE STATE
OR LOCAL LEVEL. THE MAIN DIFFICULTY IN FINANCING CAPITAL
INVESTMENT AS WELL AS INFRASTRUCTURE MAINTENANCE IS THAT THE
VARIOUS LEVELS OF GOVERNMENT ASSUME DIFFERENT
RESPONSIBILITIES FOR EACH SECTOR. COORDINATION AND
COOPERATION AMONG LEVELS OF GOVERNMENT WILL BECOME
INCREASINGLY IMPORTANT, PARTICULARLY BETWEEN STATES AND
LOCALITIES AS THEY STRIVE TO FILL THE FEDERAL FUNDING GAP.

03605 GOLIGHER, G.
HELEN LEVINE
CANADIAN FORUM, LXVIII(784) (DEC 89), 3-4.
THE ARTICLE EXAMINES THE LIFE OF HELEN LEVINE, A
CANADIAN FEMINIST, SOCIAL WORKER, AND ACADEMIC. HER YEARS OF
CRUSADING WAS RECOGNIZED WITH THE NATIONAL PERSONS AWARD
FROM CANADA'S PARLIAMENT. ALTHOUGH HER VIEWS ON MEDICINE,
WOMEN'S RIGHTS, AND VOTING MAY BE CONSIDERED EXTERME BY SOME,
SHE WAS UNDENIABLY A STRONG INFLUENCE FOR SOCIAL CHANGE IN
CANADA.

03606 GOLYGIN, Y.
ECONOMIC COOPERATION BETWEEN THE USSR AND FRG.
FOREIGN TRADE, 10 (1988), 25-29.
THIS ARTICLE TRACES THE HISTORY OF ECONOMIC RELATIONS
BETWEEN THE USSR AND THE FRG WHICH COMMENCED IN THE 1950S,
AND WHICH DEVELOPED ALONG A COMPLICATED PATH FROM
TRADITIONAL TRADE TO MODERN FORMS OF COOPERATION. THE
PRESENT STATE OF ECONOMIC RELATIONS BETWEEN THESE TWO
COUNTRIES MAY ON THE WHOLE BE DESCRIBED AS POSITIVE.

03607 GOMA, O.M.
CRISIS AND INDUSTRIAL REORGANIZATION IN CHILE
JOURNAL OF INTERAMERICAN STUDIES AND WORLD AFFAIRS, 31(1,
2) (SPR 89), 169-192.
THIS ARTICLE PRESENTS A BALANCED VIEW OF THE FAILURES
AND SUCCESSES OF PUBLIC POLICY IN CHILE WITH RESPECT TO
INDUSTRY DURING THE 1973-1988 TIME FRAME, IT ARGUES THAT
INDUSTRIAL POLICY CANNOT BE NARROWLY DEFINED, BUT MUST TAKE
INTO CONSIDERATION SUCH ASPECTS AS A FAIR DISTRIBUTION OF
INCOME, LONG-TERM COMPETITIVENESS, AND HARMONIOUS LABOR
RELATIONS WITHIN A DEMOCRATIC POLITICAL FRAME WORK.

03608 GOMEL, G.; SACCOMANNI, F.; VONA, S.
TRIPOLAR ECONOMIC POLICY COORDINATION: PROBLEMS OF A MULTI-
COUNTRY POLE
INTERNATIONAL SPECTATOR, XXIV(3-4) (JUL 89), 214-234.
SINCE 1985, INTERNATIONAL COOPERATION HAS INVOLVED
MONETARY AUTHORITIES, PARTICULARLY CENTRAL BANKS, TO AN
UNPRECEDENTED EXTENT IN COORDINATED ACTION IN THE FIELD OF
MONETARY AND EXCHANGE RATE POLICIES. THIS FACT HAS
INFLUENCED THE AUTHORS' APPROACH TO THE ISSUE OF ECONOMIC
POLICY COORDINATION (EPC). THEY DO NOT OFFER A NEW MODEL OR
PROVIDE A COMPREHENSIVE THEORETICAL EXPLANATION FOR THE
EVENTS OF 1985-88. RATHER, THEY DESCRIBE THE PROBLEMS AND
THE ACHIEVEMENTS OF EPC AS SEEN BY PRACTITIONERS OF EXCHANGE
RATE AND MONETARY POLICY COORDINATION. THE FIRST SECTION OF
THEIR PAPER BRIEFLY SURVEYS THE LITERATURE ON POLICY
COORDINATION. THE SECOND SECTION DISCUSSES A NUMBER OF
ISSUES THAT ARE CRUCIAL TO THE FEASIBILITY OF POLICY
COORDINATION. THE THIRD ASSESSES THE OUTCOME OF THE EPC
EXERCISE IN 1985-88, FOCUSING ON THE REACTIONS OF MONETARY
AND FINANCIAL MARKETS TO THE IMPLEMENTATION OF THE
COORDINATED STRATEGY, BOTH WITHIN THE G-7 AND THE EMS.

03609 GONDWE, D.K.; GRIFFITH, W.H.
TRADE CREATION AND TRADE DIVERSION: A CASE STUDY OF MDC'S
IN CARIFTA, 1968-1974
SOCIAL AND ECONOMIC STUDIES, 38(3) (1989), 149-175.
THIS PAPER INVESTIGATES THE EFFECTS OF TRADE CREATION
AND TRADE DIVERSON AMONG THE FOUR MDCS OF CARIFTA DURING THE
PERIOD 1968-74. IT ATTEMPTS TO SHED SOME LIGHT ON SOME
POSSIBLE COSTS AND BENEFITS OF ECONOMIC INTEGRATION TO THE
INDIVIDUAL COUNTRIES AS WELL AS TO THE AREA AS A WHOLE.
USING BALASSA'S METHOD, THE PAPER ESTIMATES INCOME
ELASTICITIES OF IMPORT DEMAND, BEFORE AND AFTER INTEGRATION.
THE RESULTS SHOW THAT TRADE CREATION FOR CARIFTA AS A WHOLE
DID TAKE PLACE. HOWEVER, THE BENEFITS OF TRADE CREATION WERE
UNEVENLY DISTRIBUTED. THE PAPER THEREFORE CONCLUDES THAT
EFFECTIVE MECHANISMS MUST BE DEVELOPED TO MINIMIZE THE COSTS
TO MEMBER COUNTRIES AND PREVENT ECONOMIC POLARIZATION.

03610 GONG, H.
THE LEGACY OF CONFUCIAN CULTURE IN MAOIST CHINA
SOCIAL SCIENCE JOURNAL, 26(4) (1989), 363-374.

THIS ARTICLE EXPLORES CONFUCIAN BELIEFS WHICH STRONGLY INFLUENCE THE GOVERNMENT AND SOCIETY OF THE PEOPLE'S REPUBLIC OF CHINA. THE TERMS REN AND LI GIVE DIFFERENT SIDES OF THIS CULTURAL TRADITION. ELEMENTS OF REN ARE THE OBLITERATION OF THE INDIVIDUAL, THE SPIRIT OF SACRIFICE, SELF-RESTRAINT, LACK OF PRIVACY AND IDEOLOGICAL CONTROL. ELEMENTS OF LI ARE A SOCIAL ORDER BASED ON THE WORK UNIT, RESIDENCE AND SUBORDINATION TO THE ELITE.

03611 GONG, X.
POLITICAL AND CONSTITUTIONAL CHARGE IN CHINA
ASIAN THOUGHT AND SOCIETY, XIV(40) (JAN 89), 3-14.
CHINESE CONSERVATIVE LEADERS WILL CONTINUE TO BE CONSTRAINED IN THEIR PURSUIT OF OTHER POLITICAL OBJECTIVES BY THE SUCCESS AND POPULARITY OF BOTH THE ECONOMIC AND POLITICAL REFORM PLATFORM. IN 1987, THEY PLAYED A SUCCESSFUL MINORITY ROLE--CHALLENGING, CONSTRAINING, AND CREATING OBSTACLES--BUT THEIR ROLE IS LIKELY TO BE LIMITED AS LONG AS ECONOMIC AND POLITICAL REFORMS SUCCEED. CHINA CAN ONLY PUT ITS CONFIDENCE IN THE FUTURE, IN CHINA'S YOUNGER GENERATIONS WHO ARE MARKED BY THE OUTSTANDING SUCCESS IN BOTH THE ECONOMIC AND POLITICAL SECTORS THAT THEIR REFORMS HAVE BROUGHT AND WILL BRING FORTH. WHAT CHINA NEEDS MOST TODAY IS A CONCERTED EFFORT TO INSTITUTIONALIZE THE DECISION MAKING PROCESS, TO CARRY OUT THE CONGRESS ENDORSEMENT OF CONTINUED ECONOMIC AND POLITICAL REFORM AND RATIFICATION OF THE "PRIMARY STAGE OF SOCIALISM" AS ITS IDEOLOGICAL BASIS. EVENTUALLY CHINA SHOULD HAVE A CONSTITUTIONALISM WITH CHINESE CHARACTERISTICS, INSTITUTED BOTH ON THE MAINLAND AND TAIWAN, WHICH SHOULD BE UNIFIED, AS A FREE AND PROSPEROUS CHINA.

03612 GONGORA, M.F.T.
THE CONTRIBUTION OF CLASSICAL MILITARY THOUGHT TO MODERN STRATEGIC STUDIES
ETUDES INTERNATIONALES, 20(3) (SEP 89), 535-554.
IN THIS ARTICLE, THE AUTHORS TRY TO DEFINE THE GENERAL CONCEPTUAL FRAMEWORK OF CLASSICAL STRATEGIC THOUGHT IN ORDER TO ASSESS ITS RELEVANCE FOR THE DEVELOPMENT OF CONTEMPORARY STRATEGIC STUDIES. THE ARGUMENT BRINGS OUT THE FACT THAT CLASSICAL STRATEGIC SCHOLARS TENDED TO CONCEPTUALIZE STRATEGY AS THE SCIENTIFIC STUDY OF CONFLICTUAL ACTIONS BETWEEN UNITARY ACTORS, OMITTING BY THIS VERY FACT TO STUDY THE SOCIOPOLITICAL DIMENSIONS OF CONFLICTS, THE IMPACT OF MILITARY TECHNOLOGY OR THE INFLUENCE OF ORGANIZATIONAL AND DECISIONAL PROCESSES ON THE CONDUCT OF WAR. NEVERTHELESS, CLASSICAL STRATEGIC THOUGHT STILL OFFERS AN INVALUABLE BODY OF LITERATURE TO UNDERSTAND THE EVOLUTION OF IDEAS ON WAR, AND A POSSIBLE WAY OF ENRICHING STRATEGIC STUDIES THROUGH THE USE OF ITS DISTINCTIVE COMPARATIVE HISTORICAL PERSPECTIVE.

03613 GONZALES, A.P.
RECENT TRENDS IN INTERNATIONAL ECONOMIC RELATIONS OF THE CARICOM STATES
JOURNAL OF INTERAMERICAN STUDIES AND WORLD AFFAIRS, 31(3) (FAL 89), 63-95.
THIS STUDY EXAMINES THE MOTIVES BEHIND THE INITIATIVES OF CARICOM STATES IN INTERNATIONAL ECONOMICS IN THE POST INDEPENDENCE PERIOD. IT DEMOSTRATES THAT THERE ARE SOME FEATURES - SUCH AS THE EMPHASIS ON SMALLNESS, THE PURSUIT OF DIVERSIFICATION OF ECONOMIC LINKS, AND THE BALANCING OF REGIONALISM AND GLOBALISMHHICH ARE CRITICAL TO UNDERSTANDING CARICOM ECONOMIC POLICY IN THAT ERA. IT FOCUSES ON THE ADJUSTMENTS WHICH HAVE TAKEN PLACE IN THE 1980S. A MORE INTENSE LEVEL OF INTEGRATION DEPENDS ON THE RECOVERY OF SOME OF THE KEY ECONOMIES IN THE REGION.

03614 GONZALES, M.J.
CHINESE PLANTATION WORKERS AND SOCIAL CONFLICT IN PERU IN THE LATE NINETEENTH CENTURY
JOURNAL OF LATIN AMERICAN STUDIES, 21(3) (OCT 89), 385-424.
THE AUTHOR EXAMINES THE HISTORY OF CHINESE PLANTATION WORKERS IN PERU DURING THE PERIOD OF ECONOMIC CRISIS IN THE LATE NINETEENTH CENTURY. HE FOCUSES ON LABOUR RECRUITMENT AND CONTROL BY PLANTERS WHO ATTEMPTED TO MAINTAIN PRODUCTION UNDER EXTREMELY DIFFICULT CONDITIONS. BECAUSE PERUVIAN PLANTERS HAD NEITHER THE CAPITAL NOR THE INCLINATION TO REPLACE CHINESE WORKERS WITH LOCAL WAGE LABORERS, THEY SOUGHT TO RECONTRACT CHINESE WORKERS UNDER TERMS SIMILAR TO CONTRACTS OF INDENTURESHIP AND TO LIMIT THEIR MOBILITY THROUGH DEBT PEONAGE AND CORPORAL PUNISHMENT. THIS WORKED FOR SEVERAL YEARS, BUT GRADUALLY A MAJORITY OF CHINESE COMPLETED THEIR CONTRACTS AND BECAME WAGE LABORERS.

03615 GONZALEZ, L.E.
POLITICAL STRUCTURES AND THE PROSPECTS FOR DEMOCRACY IN URUQUAY
DISSERTATION ABSTRACTS INTERNATIONAL, 50(5) (NOV 89), 1421-A.
URUGUAYAN DEMOCRACY WAS BORN IN 1918 AND HAS BEEN INTERRUPTED TWICE BY AUTHORITARIAN REGIMES, FROM 1933 TO 1942 AND FROM 1973 TO THE MID-1980'S. SEVERAL EXPLANATIONS HAVE BEEN SUGGESTED FOR THE TWO COUPS, FOCUSING ON THE

SOCIAL AND ECONOMIC ENVIRONMENT AND ON THE DYNAMICS OF SHORT-TERM POLITICAL CONFLICTS. THIS STUDY CONCENTRATES ON THE POLITICO-STRUCTURAL FACTORS THAT CREATED A STRUCTURAL PREDISPOSITION FOR THE POLITICAL CHANGE. THESE FACTORS INCLUDE THE FRACTIONALIZATION OF THE MAJOR POLITICAL PARTIES, THE QUASI-PRESIDENTIAL URUGUAYAN INSTITUTIONS, FRAGMENTATION, AND A MARKED INCREASE IN THE POLARIZATION OF THE PARTY SYSTEM.

03616 GONZALEZ, R.; FOLSOM, R.; MEHAY, S.
BUREAUCRACY, PUBLICNESS AND LOCAL GOVERNMENT EXPENDITURES REVISTED: COMMENT
PUBLIC CHOICE, 62(1) (JUL 89), 71-78.
THE AUTHORS OFFER A CRITIQUE OF A RECENT ARTICLE BY PAUL WYCKOFF WHICH DERIVED RELATIONSHIPS BETWEEN BUREAU POWER, CITY SIZE, AND LOCAL GOVERNMENT SPENDING. THEY ARGUE THAT IS DIFFICULT TO RECONCILE WYCKOFF'S FINDINGS WITH THE EMPIRICAL LITERATURE ON THE PUBLICNESS OF LOCAL GOVERNMENT SERVICES AND THAT WYCKOFF'S OWN ASSUMPTIONS TEND TO NEGATE HIS CONCLUSIONS.

03617 GONZALEZ, R.
UNDER THE FLAG OF LAW ENFORCEMENT
NACLA REPORT ON THE AMERICAS, XXII(6) (MAR 89), 22-24.
THE ARTICLE EXAMINES THE EFFORTS OF THE US TO STAMP OUT COCAINE TRAFFIC IN BOLIVIA. US ATTEMPTS TO IMPOSE ITS DRUG CONTROL POLICY IN BOLIVIA HAVE PROVOKED BITTER OPPOSITION FROM THE WELL-ORGANIZED COCA FARMERS UNIONS, AS WELL AS FROM LARGE SECTORS OF THE BOLIVIAN PEOPLE. MANY NOW VIEW US ANTI-DRUG MEASURES AS BEING MORE DANGEROUS TO DEMOCRACY THAN COCAINE ITSELF.

03618 GOODISON, P.
RELATIONS BETWEEN THE EUROPEAN ECONOMIC COMMUNITY AND THE SOUTHERN AFRICAN DEVELOPMENT COORDINATION CONFERENCE-AN ASSESSMENT
DISSERTATION ABSTRACTS INTERNATIONAL, 49(12) (JUN 89), 3856-A.
THE AUTHOR CONSIDERS THE RELATIONSHIP BETWEEN THE COMMISSION OF THE EUROPEAN COMMUNITY AND THE SOUTHERN AFRICAN DEVELOPMENT COORDINATION CONFERENCE. HE TRACES THE EVOLUTION OF THE SADCC INITIATIVE FROM ITS EARLY ROOTS AND EUROPEAN SUPPORT FOR WHAT HAS BEEN AN INNOVATIVE SCHEME IN REGIONAL COOPERATION AMONG IDEOLOGICALLY DIVERSE STATES.

03619 GOODLAND, R.; LEDEC, G.
WILDLANDS: BALANCING CONVERSION WITH CONSERVATION IN WORLD BANK PROJECTS
ENVIRONMENT, 31(9) (NOV 89), 6-11; 27-35.
THIS ARTICLE EXPLORES THE UNFORSEEN AND DISTASTROUS SIDE EFFECTS OF CONVERTING WILDLANDS FOR HUMAN USE. IT DETAILS THE BIOLOGICAL DIVERSITY AND ENVIRONMENTAL SERVICES PROVIDED BY THE WILDLANDS AS WELL AS THEIR FUNCTION SERVED IN MODERN INFRASTRUCTURE IN PROVIDING ENERGY, WATER AND TRANSPORT. IT EXAMINES THE ROLE OF THE WORLD BANK WHOSE PROJECTS INCLUDE CONSERVATION COMPONENTS TO PROTECT THE BANK'S INVESTMENTS AS WELL AS THE "NATURAL CAPITAL" REPRESENTED BY THE BIOLOGICAL DIVERSITY AND ENVIRONMENTAL SERVICES OF WILDLANDS.

03620 GOODMAN, D.S.G.
POLITICAL CHANGE IN CHINA: POWER, POLICY, AND PROCESS
BRITISH JOURNAL OF POLITICAL SCIENCE, 19(3) (JUL 89), 425-444.
THE AUTHOR GENERALIZES ABOUT POLITICAL CHANGE IN COMMUNIST CHINA IN THE PAST FEW YEARS AND REVIEWS ITS IMPACT ON THE STUDY OF CHINA'S POLITICS IN THE WEST.

03621 GOODMAN, M.
WHERE THE BOYS ARE
WASHINGTON MONTHLY, 21(3) (APR 89), 18-20.
THE ARTICLE EXAMINES HOW A WELL-INTENTIONED CIVIL RIGHTS LAW AND A DOSE OF CHAUVINISM HAVE SHOVED WOMEN ADMINISTRATORS OUT OF COLLEGE SPORTS. IT ANALYZES THE DECREASING NUMBERS OF WOMEN IN ADMINISTRATIVE POSITIONS WITHIN THE SPORTS PROGRAMS OF COLLEGES AND THE UNDERLYING REASONS FOR THE DECLINE. IT CONCLUDES THAT ALTHOUGH THERE IS A SIGNIFICANT NUMBER OF QUALIFIED WOMEN, TITLE IX OF THE EDUCATIONAL AMENDMENTS OF 1972 WHICH BARRED SEX DISCRIMINATION IN ANY EDUCATIONAL PROGRAM ALLOWED THE MERGING OF MEN'S AND WOMEN'S ATHLETIC PROGRAMS AT THE EXPENSE OF WOMEN ADMINISTRATORS.

03622 GOODRICH, J.A.
BUSINESS DEVELOPMENT STRATEGIES: AN IMPORTANT COMPARATIVE DIMENSION
INTERNATIONAL JOURNAL OF PUBLIC ADMINISTRATION, 12(3) (1989), 513-531.
GOVERNMENT EFFORTS TO WORK MORE CLOSELY WITH BUSINESSES ARE INCREASINGLY SEEN AS IMPORTANT, AS WE HAVE MOVED FROM DISCUSSIONS ABOUT INDUSTRIAL POLICY TO CONCERNS ABOUT INTERNATIONAL COMPETITIVENESS. HOWEVER OUR IDEAS ABOUT THESE SUBJECTS SUFFER FROM A LACK OF A COMPARATIVE PERSPECTIVE OR AN UNDERSTANDING OF HOW DIFFERENT NATIONS GO ABOUT THIS PROCESS. THE COMPARATIVE STUDY OF NATIONAL STRATEGIES TO

STIMULATE BUSINESS OR TO UPGRADE A COUNTRY'S INDUSTRIAL
PORTFOLIO CAN PRODUCE USEFUL RESULTS. WRITERS WITH
EXPERIENCE IN THE COMPARATIVE ADMINISTRATION FIELD CAN MAKE
A CONTRIBUTION HERE, ESPECIALLY THROUGH THEIR EXPLORATION OF
THE RELATIONSHIP BETWEEN BUREAUCRACY AND SOCIETY, WHICH
SIGNIFICANTLY DEFINES AND CONSTRAINS THESE STRATEGIC
POSSIBILITIES. TO DO THIS, COMPARATIVE ADMINISTRATION
RESEARCHERS WILL NEED TO FOCUS MORE SPECIFICALLY ON BUSINESS
ENTERPRISES AS WELL AS PUBLIC AGENCIES INVOLVED IN BUSINESS
DEVELOPMENT.

03623 GOODSELL, C.T.
DOES BUREAUCRACY HURT DEMOCRACY?
BUREAUCRAT, 18(1) (SPR 89), 45-48.
ONE SCHOOL OF PUBLIC ADMINISTRATION THOUGHT TAKES THE
POSITION THAT BUREAUCRACY PROTECTS ESTABLISHED INTERESTS AND
PERPETUATES EXISTING SOCIAL INJUSTICES. PEOPLE WHO HOLD THIS
VIEW OFTEN FAVOR A MORE ACTIVIST ROLE IN PURSUING SOCIAL
EQUITY AND RESPONSIVENESS TO CITIZENS. OTHERS ARGUE THAT
BUREAUCRACY SHOULD BE THE STRONGHOLD FOR RATIONALISM AND ARE
CONCERNED ABOUT "RUNAWAY BUREAUCRACY." A CASE IS MADE FOR A
SYSTEM OF MULTIPLE CONTROLS, BY THE AUTHOR OF THIS ARTICLE.

03624 GOODSTEIN, L.; MACKENZIE, D.L.
LAW, SOCIETY, AND POLICY; THE AMERICAN PRISON
PLENUM PRESS, NEW YORK AND LONDON, 1989, 1-286.
THIS BOOK BRINGS TOGETHER A GROUP OF CRIMINOLOGIST AND
CORRECTIONAL SCHOLARS WHO WROTE CHAPTERS FOR THIS VOLUME.
EACH AUTHOR WAS CHARGED TO 1) PRESENT THE MAJOR ISSUES; 2)
REVIEW THE EMPIRICAL RESEARCH; AND 3) DISCUSS THE
IMPLICATIONS OF THIS WORK FOR PRESENT AND FUTURE
CORRECTIONAL POLICY. THE GOAL WAS TO EXAMINE THE MAJOR
CORRECTIONAL ISSUES FACING PRISON SYSTEMS. THE CHAPTERS
SCRUTINIZE THE ISSUES FROM THE PERSPECTIVE OF THE SYSTEM,
AND THE INDIVIDUAL, FROM THEORY TO PRACTICAL AND DAILY
MANAGEMENT PROBLEMS, FROM LEGAL TO PSYCHOLOGICAL CONCERNS.

03625 GOODWIN-GILL, G.S.
INTERNATIONAL LAW AND HUMAN RIGHTS: TRENDS CONCERNING
INTERNATIONAL MIGRANTS AND REFUGEES
INTERNATIONAL MIGRATION REVIEW, 23(3) (FAL 89), 526-546.
NOTWITHSTANDING HUMAN RIGHTS LINKAGES, MIGRANTS AND
REFUGEES ARE OFTEN ON THE PERIPHERY OF EFFECTIVE
INTERNATIONAL PROTECTION. STATE SOVEREIGNTY AND SELF-
REGARDING NOTIONS OF COMMUNITY ARE USED TO DENY OR DILUTE
SUBSTANTIVE AND PROCEDURAL GUARANTEES. RECENTLY, EVEN
NONDISCRIMINATION AS A FUNDAMENTAL PRINCIPLE HAS BEEN
QUESTIONED, AS HAS THE SYSTEM OF REFUGEE PROTECTION. THIS
ARTICLE LOCATES BOTH MIGRANTS AND REFUGEES SQUARELY WITHIN
THE HUMAN RIGHTS CONTEXT, CONTRASTING INALIENABLE RIGHTS
WITH THE DEMANDS OF SOVEREIGNTY, AND JUXTAPOSING THE TWO IN
A CONTEXT OF EXISTING AND DEVELOPING INTERNATIONAL STANDARDS.
MIGRATION AND REFUGEE FLOWS WILL GO ON, AND THE DEVELOPED
WORLD, IN PARTICULAR, MUST ADDRESS THE CONSEQUENCES -- LEGAL,
HUMANITARIAN, SOCIOECONOMIC AND CULTURAL. RACISM AND
INSTITUTIONALIZED DENIALS OF BASIC RIGHTS DAILY CHALLENGE
THE COMMON INTEREST. THIS ARTICLE SHOWS HOW THE LAW MUST
EVOLVE, RESPONDING COHERENTLY TO CONTEMPORARY PROBLEMS, IF
THE STRUCTURE OF RIGHTS AND FREEDOMS IS TO BE MAINTAINED.

03626 GOODWIN, J.; SKOCPOL, T.
EXPLAINING REVOLUTIONS IN THE CONTEMPORARY THIRD WORLD
POLITICS AND SOCIETY, 17(4) (DEC 89), 489-510.
THE AUTHORS DISCUSS WHAT THEY CONSIDER TO BE THE MOST
PROMISING AVENUES FOR COMPARATIVE ANALYSES OF CONTEMPORARY
THIRD WORLD REVOLUTIONS. THEY OFFER SOME WORKING HYPOTHESES
ABOUT THE DISTINCTIVELY POLITICAL CONDITIONS THAT HAVE
ENCOURAGED REVOLUTIONARY MOVEMENTS AND TRANSFERS OF POWER IN
SOME, BUT NOT ALL, THIRD WORLD COUNTRIES.

03627 GOODWIN, J.; SKOCPOL, T.
EXPLAINING REVOLUTIONS IN THE CONTEMPORARY THIRD WORLD
POLITICS AND SOCIETY, 17(4) (DEC 89), 489-509.
THIS ANALYSIS SUGGESTS THAT REVOLUTIONARIES IN THE
CONTEMPORARY THIRD WORLD ARE MOST LIKELY TO SUCCEED WHEN
CIVIL SOCIETY AS A WHOLE CAN BE POLITICALLY MOBILIZED TO
OPPOSE AN AUTONOMOUS AND NARROWLY BASED DIRECT COLONIAL
REGIME OR A SULTANISTIC NEO-PATRIMONIAL REGIME. THIS HAS
BEEN A CHARACTERISTIC, IN FACT, OF VIRTUALLY ALL THIRD WORLD
STATES THAT HAVE BEEN TOPPLED BY REVOLUTIONS. IN CONTRAST,
WHEN RADICALS CONFRONT A STATE WITH SIGNIFICANT SOCIAL
CONNECTIONS-EVEN IF THE STATE IS AUTHORITARIAN AND ITS TIES
ARE RESTRICTED TO THE MIDDLE AND UPPER CLASSES-THEN
REVOLUTIONARY COALITION BUILDING BECOMES VERY DIFFICULT.

03628 GOPAL, B.
DYNAMICS OF CENTRE-STATE RELATIONS: EXPERIENCE OF ANDHRA
PRADESH SINCE 1983
INDIAN JOURNAL OF POLITICAL SCIENCE, L(3) (JUL 89),
357-375.
THE SUBJECT OF CENTRE-STATE RELATIONS IN INDIA HAS
ASSUMED CONSIDERABLE IMPORTANCE DUE TO THE DRASTIC CHANGES
IN THE POLITICAL COMPLEXION OF THE STATE AND CENTRAL
GOVERNMENTS. THIS ESSAY EXAMINES THE GOVERNMENT OF ANDHRA

PRADESH SINCE 1983, WHEN A REGIONAL PARTY WAS VOTED TO POWER,
AND ANALYZES THE TENSIONS THAT HAVE DEVELOPED BETWEEN THE
CENTRAL ADMINISTRATION AND THE ANDHRA PRADESH STATE
GOVERNMENT.

03629 GOPAL, S.
OF SKYLARKS AND SHIRTING: THE ENGLISH LANGUAGE IN INDIA
ENCOUNTER, LXXIII(2) (JUL 89), 14-20.
THE AUTHOR CONSIDERS THE STATUS OF THE ENGLISH LANGUAGE,
HINDI, AND REGIONAL LANGUAGES IN INDIA. HE DISCUSSES THE
POLITICAL AND ECONOMIC SIGNIFICANCE ATTACHED TO THE ENGLISH
LANGUAGE FOLLOWING INDIAN INDEPENDENCE.

03630 GORBACHEV, M.
BUILDING UP THE INTELLECTUAL POTENTIAL OF PERESTROIKA
REPRINTS FROM THE SOVIET PRESS, 48(4) (FEB 89), 7-34.
THIS ARTICLE IS THE TEXT OF A SPEECH BY GORBACHEV TO
SCIENTIFIC AND CULTURAL WORKERS AT THE CPSU CENTRAL
COMMITTEE ON JANUARY 6, 1989. GORBACHEV POINTS OUT THAT IN
THE STORMY PROCESS OF REFORM AND ELIMINATION OF OUTDATED
FORMS OF SOCIAL LIFE AND STEREOTYPES, IT IS IMPORTANT TO
RETAIN A SOBER, REALISTIC APPRAISAL OF THE CURRENT
DEVELOPMENTS. APPRECIATING AND PARTICIPATING IN PERESTROIKA
REQUIRES A DIALECTICAL APPROACH TO ALL PROCESSES AND
DIFFICULTIES OF THE TRANSITIONAL PERIOD.

03631 GORBACHEV, M.
ETHNIC RELATIONS AND THE LOGIC OF PERESTROIKA
POLITICAL AFFAIRS, 68(12) (DEC 89), 10-16.
THIS IS EXCERPTED FROM GENERAL SECRETARY MIKHAIL
GORBACHEV'S REPORT ON THE NATIONAL POLICY OT THE COMMUNIST
PARTY OF THE SOVIET UNION, AT THE PLENUM OF THE CPSU CENTRAL
COMMITTEE ON SEPTEMBER 19, 1989. HE STATES THAT THE LOGIC OF
PERESTROIKA AND THEIR DAILY EXPERIENCE HAVE LED THEM TO
CONCLUDE THAT THE NEED FOR COMPREHENSIVE PROFOUND CHANGES IN
ETHNIC RELATIONS IS LONG OVERDUE, HE ADDRESSES THE
NATIONALTY ISSUE AS WELL AS THE PARTY'S INTERNATIONALIST
STANCE. HE STATES THAT ATTEMPTS TO IDEALIZE THE PAST ARE
FUTILE, UNACCEPTABLE AND DO NOT SERVE THE INTERESTS OF THE
WORKING PEOPLE, THE CAUSE OF SOCIALISM. HE ADDRESSES
POLITICAL, ECONOMIC AND INTELLECTUAL ISSUES AND CONCLUDES
THAT ETHNIC IDENTITY SHOULD BE PROTECTED AND THAT EACH
ETHNIC GROUP HAS A RIGHT TO ENJOY ALL THE FRUITS OF
SOVEREIGNTY AND TO DECIDE ALL ISSUES OF ITS DEVELOPMENT AS
IT SEES FIT.

03632 GORBACHEV, M.
GORBACHEV'S SPEECH TO THE CHINESE PUBLIC
REPRINTS FROM THE SOVIET PRESS, 49(2) (JUL 89), 12-29.
MIKHAIL GORBACHEV DISCUSSES DIVERSE ISSUES PERTAINING TO
SINO-SOVIET RELATIONS. THESE INCLUDE: AREAS OF COMMON
INTEREST, BENEFITS OF PAST RELATIONS, ARMS REDUCTION,
SECURITY IN ASIA AND THE PACIFIC, THE KAMPUCHEAN CONFLICT,
ACADEMIC AND ECONOMIC TIES, THE IMPLICATIONS OF PERESTROIKA,
AND RICH-POOR INEQUALITIES. GORBACHEV CONCLUDES THAT ACTIVE
COOPERATION BETWEEN THE USSR AND CHINA WILL ENABLE BOTH
COUNTRIES TO WORK TOWARDS SOLUTIONS OF MANY OF THE WORLD'S
PROBLEMS.

03633 GORBACHEV, M.
MIKHAIL GORBACHEV SPEECH IN BERLIN ON THE OCCASION OF THE
40TH ANNIVERSARY OF THE GDR
REPRINTS FROM THE SOVIET PRESS, 49(11 12) (DEC 89), 33-40.
IN THIS SPEECH GORBACHEV REMARKS ON THE EMERGENCE OF A
STATE OF WORKING PEOPLE IN THE EASTERN PART OF GERMANY WHICH
HAD A SUBSTANTIAL IMPACT ON THE ENTIRE POSTWAR HISTORY OF
EUROPE. HE DETAILS THE SOCIO-ECONOMIC TRANSFORMATIONS WHICH
HAVE BEEN CARRIED OUT IN THE GDR UNDER THE LEADERSHIP OF THE
SOCIALIST UNITY PARTY OF GERMANY. HE EMPHASIZES THAT THE
SOCIALIST WORLD AND ALL MODERN CIVILIZATION ARE
CHARACTERIZED BY THE GROWING DIVERSITY OF FORMS OF
ORGANIZING PRODUCTION, SOCIAL STRUCTURES AND POLITICAL
INSTITUTIONS.

03634 GORBACHEV, M.
MIKHAIL GORBACHEV'S ADDRESS ON THE COMPLETION OF THE FIRST
SESSION OF THE SUPREME SOVIET OF THE USSR
REPRINTS FROM THE SOVIET PRESS, 49(7) (OCT 89), 31-42.
THE FIRST SESSION OF THE SUPREME SOVIET OF THE USSR WAS
CONCLUDED BY MIKHAIL GORBACHEV'S ADDRESS WHERE HE ASSESSES
THE RESULTS OF THE TWO-MONTH-LONG SESSION. HE DESCRIBES THE
EFFORTS OF POLITICAL REFORM, WHICH WILL UTILIZE THE CONCEPT
OF PEOPLES DEPUTIES, ACTING OPENLY AND ALSO WILL FOSTER
ACTIVE CITIZENS, HE EXPRESSES THE HOPE THAT IN THE AUTUMN
SESSION FOCUS WILL BE ON BILLS DEALING WITH THE PRESS AND
OTHER MEDIA, CIVIC ORGANIZATIONS, AND THE FREEDOM OF
CONSCIENCE AS WELL AS IMPROVEMENTS IN ECONOMICS. HE INCLUDES
OTHER AREAS WHERE IMPROVEMENT IS NEEDED IN THIS HOPE-INTER-
ETHNIC RELATIONS, PUBLIC HEALTH, MINER'S STRIKES, CRIME,
INTERNATIONAL RELATIONS, AND FORTH COMING ELECTIONS.

03635 GORBACHEV, M.
NEW STAGE IN SINO - SOVIET RELATION.
REPRINTS FROM THE SOVIET PRESS, 49(3) (AUG 89), 8-22.

THIS IS THE TEXT OF A PRESS CONFERENCE GIVEN BY GORBACHEV ON THE OCCASION OF HIS OFFICIAL VISIT TO CHINA. IN HIS SPEECH HE STRESSES THAT A GOOD NEIGHBOR POLICY AND DEMILITARIZATION OF SINO - SOVIET FRONTIERS IS ESSENTIAL FOR OUR RELATIONS. BOTH RUSSIA AND CHINA MUST CONTINUE TO WORK FOR BRINGING THE ARMED FORCE IN THE FRONTIER AREAS DOWN TO THE LOWEST POSSIBLE LEVEL AND TO ESTABLISH A WORKING MECHANISM FOR NEGOTIATIONS ON THAT TOPIC.

03636 GORBACHEV, M.
OUR POLICY IN ASIA IS OPEN AND WITHOUT ULTERIOR MOTIVES
INFORMATION BULLETIN, 26(23-24) (DEC 88), 3-6.
THIS ARTICLE CONSISTS OF EXCERPTS OF GORBACHEV'S SPEECH IN KRASNOYARSK. THE SOVIET LEADER DESCRIBES SOVIET INITIATIVES AND INVOLVEMENT IN THE ASIA PACIFIC AREA, AND DECLARES THAT THE SOVIET UNION DOES NOT LOOK FOR ANY PRIVILEGES, BENEFITS OR ADVANTAGES IN THE REGION AT THE EXPENSE OF NATIVE POPULATIONS AND OTHE INTERNATIONAL INTERESTS.

03637 GORBACHEV, M.
SOLVING URGENT PROBLEMS OF HARMONIZING INTER - ETHNIC RELATIONS BY JOINT EFFORT AND PERESTROIKA
REPRINTS FROM THE SOVIET PRESS, 48(1) (JAN 89), 32-43.
THE SITUATION IN ESTONIA AND OTHER INTER - ETHNIC PROBLEMS POINT OUT THE NEED FOR BEING CONSISTENT IN IMPLEMENTING THE PRINCIPLES OF THE TERRITORIAL DIVISION OF LABOR AND DEEPENING THE PROCESSES OF ECONOMIC INTEGRATION. THE STRIVING FOR ECONOMIC SEPARATION WOULD HAVE MOST NEGATIVE CONSEQUENCES.

03638 GORBACHEV, M.
SOVIET-AMERICAN SUMMIT: INF TREATY SIGNED
INFORMATION BULLETIN, 25/26(1-2) (JAN 88), 3-4.
THIS ARTICLE CONTAINS THE TEXT OF GORBACHEV'S SPEECH TO THE SOVIET AND AMERICAN PEOPLE ON THE OCCASION OF THE SIGNING OF THE INF TREATY. GORBACHEV APPLAUDS THE NEW THINKING AND CREATIVE BOLDNESS WHICH ENABLED LOTS PARTNERS IN THE TREATY TO FIND WAYS TO ENSURE PEACE AND SECURITY.

03639 GORBACHEV, M.
SPEECH BY MCKHAIL GORBACHEV AT THE UN GENERAL ASSEMBLY
REPRINTS FROM THE SOVIET PRESS, 48(1) (JAN 89), 5-25.
IN HIS FIRST ADDRESS AT THE UN GENERAL ASSEMBLY GORBACHEV DESCRIBES HOW THE AIM OF SOVIET EFFORTS IN THE INTERNATIONAL ARENA AND ONE OF THE KEY PROVISIONS OF THE CONCEPT OF NEW THINKING IS THAT EACH NATION MUST TRANSFORM RIVALRY INTO SENSIBLE COMPETITION ON THE BASIS OF RESPECT FOR FREEDOM OF CHOICE AND BALANCE OF INTERESTS. IN THIS CASE, COMPETITION MAY EVEN BE USEFUL AND BENEFICIAL FROM THE POINT OF VIEW OF THE GENERAL DEVELOPMENT OF THE WORLD. OTHERWISE, IF THE ARMS RACE CONTINUES TO BE ITS MAIN ELEMENT, THIS RIVALRY WILL BE SUICIDAL. MORE AND MORE PEOPLE THROUGHOUT THE WORLD, ORDINARY PEOPLE AND LEADERS, ARE COMING TO REALIZE THIS.

03640 GORBACHEV, M.
SPEECH TO THE CUBAN NATIONAL ASSEMBLY, APRIL 5, 1989
REPRINTS FROM THE SOVIET PRESS, 48(11-12) (JUN 89), 5-20.
THIS ARTICLE IS THE TEXT OF GORBACHEV'S SPEECH, WHEREIN HE DESCRIBES THE IN - DEPTH EXCHANGE OF OPINION BETWEEN HIMSELF AND CASTRO ON A WIDE RANGE OF INTERNATIONAL ISSUES. GORBACHEV STRESSES THAT BOTH CUBA AND THE SOVIET UNION ARE ACTIVELY INVOLVED IN INTERNATIONAL DEVELOPMENT AND ARE VITALLY CONCERNED THAT THE INTERNATIONAL SITUATION BE FAVORABLE FOR THEM TO ACCOMPLISH THE DOMESTIC TASKS THEY HAVE SET THEMSELVES.

03641 GORBACHEV, M.
THE PROGRESS OF PERESTROIKA
WORLD TODAY, 45(6) (JUN 89), 94.
IN THIS ADDRESS ON APRIL 7, 1989, MIKHAIL GORBACHEV SPOKE ABOUT THE SOVIET DOMESTIC SCENE. HE STATED THAT THE SOVIETS HAVE CHOSEN PERESTROIKA FOR THE LONG-TERM AND THERE WILL BE NO TURNING BACK. HE ADMITTED THAT HE WAS EXPERIENCING DIFFICULTIES IN IMPLEMENTING HIS NEW POLICIES BUT STATED THAT THE PROBLEMS DO NOT MEAN THAT THE CONCEPT OF PERESTROIKA IS WRONG. RATHER, THE PROBLEMS ACCENTUATE THE WATERSHED CHARACTER OF THE PERIOD THE USSR IS GOING THROUGH, WHEN THE OLD WAYS ARE STILL ALIVE WHILE THE NEW APPROACHES HAVE NOT YET REACHED FULL SPEED.

03642 GORBACHEV, M.
USSR: A TIME OF CRUCIAL DECISIONS AND PRACTICAL ACTIONS
INFORMATION BULLETIN, 27 (JAN 89), 27-29.
IN THIS SPEECH DELIVERED AT OREL ON NOV. 15, 1988, MIKHAIL GORBACHEV DISCUSSED ECONOMIC AND POLITICAL REFORM IN THE SOVIET UNION.

03643 GORBACHEV, M.
USSR: ALL SHOULD BE DONE TO INCREASE THE AUTHORITY OF SOVIETS
INFORMATION BULLETIN, 26(23-24) (DEC 88), 25-26.
IN THIS ADDRESS GORBACHEV STRESSES THAT IT IS EXTREMELY

IMPORTANT FOR THE SOVIETS TO ADOPT AS SOON AS POSSIBLE THE NEW METHODS OF ECONOMIC MANAGEMENT, TO TAKE INTO THEIR OWN HANDS THE QUESTIONS OF SUPPLYING THE POPULATION WITH FOOD AND INDUSTRIAL GOODS, OF HOUSING AND ITS EQUITABLE DISTRIBUTION, OF DEVELOPING THE SERVICE SECTOR, MAINTAINING LAW AND ORDER AND IMPROVING THE ENVIRONMENT. THE PRINCIPLES OF SELF-FINANCING, SELF SUFFICIENCY AND SELF-MANAGEMENT MUST BE INTRODUCED EVERYWHERE. GLASNOST MUST BE ASSERTED AND INITIATIVE BY LOCAL BODIES AND THE PUBLIC ENCOURAGED. THE SOONER THE LAW ON LOCAL SELFGOVERNMENT AND LOCAL ECONOMIC MANAGEMENT IS DRAFTED AND ADOPTED, THE SOONER THINGS WILL START MOVING.

03644 GORDEYEVA, N.
ENKA AND SOVIET-TURKISH TRADE.
FOREIGN TRADE, 9 (1988), 22-23.
THIS ARTICLE REPORTS AN INTERVIEW WITH SARIK TARA, PRESIDENT OF ENKA, A TURKISH INDUSTRIAL AND TRADE COMPANY. IT OUTLINES SOME OF THE SPHERES OF ACTIVITY OF ENKA, LISTS THE MAIN SOVIET FOREIGN ECONOMIC ORGANIZATIONS ENKA DEALS WITH, AND PROJECTS THE LONG TERM TIES WITH SOVIET ORGANIZATIONS INTO THE FUTURE.

03645 GORDON, B.
ECONOMIC SANCTIONS IN UNITED STATES FOREIGN POLICY: A REVISED FRAMEWORK FOR ANALYSIS
DISSERTATION ABSTRACTS INTERNATIONAL, 49(11) (MAY 89), 3496-A.
THE AUTHOR STUDIES FIVE CASES OF POSTWAR ECONOMIC SANCTIONS IN AMERICAN FOREIGN POLICY THAT DEMONSTRATE THAT, IN SOME INSTANCES, NON-PUBLIC POLICY GOALS ARE OPERATIVE AND MAY BE ENTIRELY DIFFERENT OR EVEN CONTRADICTORY TO PUBLIC SANCTIONS GOALS. THIS HIDDEN AGENDA RESULTS FROM THE TENSION BETWEEN THE PERCEPTIONS OF NATIONAL INTERESTS, ESPECIALLY NATIONAL SECURITY INTERESTS, HELD BY NON-EXECUTIVE DOMESTIC POLITICAL ACTORS IN THE USA AND THOSE HELD BY THE PRESIDENT OR BETWEEN THE PRESIDENT'S PERCEPTIONS OF NATIONAL INTERESTS AND THE GENERALLY ACCEPTED VALUES THAT UNDERLIE FOREIGN POLICY GOALS.

03646 GORDON, C.
MUTUAL PERCEPTIONS OF RELIGIOUS AND SECULAR JEWS IN ISRAEL
JOURNAL OF CONFLICT RESOLUTION, 33(4) (DEC 89), 632-651.
THREE HUNDRED AND EIGHTY ISRAELI STUDENTS IN THE ELEVENTH GRADE, EQUALLY DIVIDED BETWEEN CHILDREN ATTENDING RELIGIOUS SCHOOLS AND CHILDREN ATTENDING SECULAR SCHOOLS, COMPLETED QUESTIONNAIRES ON THE CONFLICT BETWEEN RELIGIOUS AND SECULAR JEWS. INCLUDED HERE QUESTIONS ON ETHNIC AND RELIGIOUS IDENTITY; AMOUNT AND EVALUATION OF INTERACTION BETWEEN THE TWO GROUPS; EVALUATION OF THE PAST, PRESENT, AND FUTURE; AND POSSIBLE SCENARIOS REGARDING SOLUTIONS. IN EACH SET OF QUESTIONS THE STUDENTS WERE ASKED ABOUT THEIR OWN VIEWS AND HOW THEY BELIEVE THE OTHER GROUP SEES THESE ISSUES. ANALYSES COMPARING THE TWO GROUPS REVEALED THAT IN EVERY SET OF QUESTIONS, THE SECULAR VIEWED THE RELIGIOUS SIGNIFICANTLY MORE NEGATIVELY THAN THE RELIGIOUS VIEWED THE SECULAR. THE THEORY THAT EQUAL STATUS CONTACT IS A FACTOR IN CONFLICT RESOLUTION WAS TESTED BY CORRELATING AMOUNT OF ACTUAL CONTACT AND CHOICE OF SOLUTION. CORRELATIONS BETWEEN EVALUATION OF THE RELATIONSHIP AND CHOICE OF SOLUTIONS SHOWED THAT THE MORE POSITIVELY THE STUDENTS VIEWED THE RELATIONSHIP, THE LESS THEY ACCEPTED SOLUTIONS WITH GREAT INTOLERANCE AND LITTLE CONTACT. THE MAJOR INFERENCE OF THIS STUDY, SUPPORTED STRONGLY AND CONSISTENTLY BY THE DATA, IS THAT THE SECULAR, BELIEVING THEIR FREEDOM OF CHOICE AND STYLE OF LIFE TO BE THREATENED, THINK, FEEL, AND ACT ACCORDINGLY. THE RELIGIOUS, WHO DO NOT FACE THIS PROBLEM, SEEM TO BE FAR LESS NEGATIVE AND EXTREME IN THEIR VIEWS.

03647 GORDON, G.F.
ACHIEVING EXCELLENCE IN THE PUBLIC SECTOR: TECHNOLOGY MANAGEMENT AS A PRIORITY FOCUS
DISSERTATION ABSTRACTS INTERNATIONAL, 49(7) (JAN 89), 1956-A.
THIS DISSERTATION EXAMINES ORGANIZATIONAL EFFECTIVENESS IN THE PUBLIC SECTOR, WITH EMPHASIS ON THE FIELD OF TECHNOLOGY MANAGEMENT. THE OBJECTIVE IS TO ANALYZE AND CLARIFY ORGANIZATIONAL EFFECTIVENESS ISSUES WITHIN A FRAMEWORK OF ORGANIZATIONAL THEORY; EVALUATE POTENTIAL BARRIERS TO ACHIEVING EXCELLENCE IN THE PUBLIC SECTOR; DEVELOP A PROFILE OF ORGANIZATIONAL AND MANAGEMENT COMPETENCIES; AND RECOMMEND ACTIONS FOR IMPROVED EFFECTIVENESS.

03648 GORDON, J.
THE FALSE HOPES OF 1950: THE WAFD'S LAST HURRAH AND THE DEMISE OF EGYPT'S OLD ORDER
INTERNATIONAL JOURNAL OF MIDDLE EAST STUDIES, 21(2) (MAY 89), 193-214.
BY 1950, THE SITUATION WITHIN THE WAFD PARTY HAD BECOME VERY VOLATILE. EVEN THOUGH THE WAFD WAS A DYING RELIC OF A DYING AGE, THERE WERE FORCES TRYING TO REVIVE IT AND A STRUGGLE FOR ITS SOUL ENSUED. WHILE THE DIVISION OF THE LEFT AND RIGHT WINGS OF THE WAFD BEARS IMPORT FOR THE HISTORY OF

THE PARLIAMENTARY ERA, IN 1950 THE CABINET WAS THE CRUCIAL BATTLEGROUND. THERE, ASPIRANTS TO PARTY LEADERSHIP SPARRED FOR POSITION IN A CONTEST THAT PROVED FATAL TO GOVERNMENT AND PARTY, CRIPPLING POLICY MAKING AND DRAWING THE WAFD TOWARD ABROGATION OF THE 1936 ANGLO-EGYPTIAN TREATY, A POPULAR BUT POLITICALLY DISASTROUS ACT. INTERNECINE FEUDS AND RIVALRIES WITHIN THE CABINET CHECKED THE INFLUENCE OF NEW IDEAS AND NEW PARTY MEMBERS WHEN THIS WAS PRECISELY WHAT THE PARTY AND THE COUNTRY DESPERATELY NEEDED.

03649 GORDON, M.
SOVIET MIDDLE EAST POLICY AND THE ARAB-ISRAEL CONFLICT
MIDSTREAM, XXXV(9) (DEC 89), 3-8.
THE MIDDLE EAST'S PROXIMITY TO THE SOVIET UNION, ITS STRATEGIC LOCATION, AND ITS OIL AND NATURAL GAS CONFER UPON IT A CRUCIAL IMPORTANCE FOR THE SOVIETS. AN OVERRIDING GOAL OF SOVIET DIPLOMACY SINCE WORLD WAR II HAD BEEN TO EXPAND ITS POWER AND INFLUENCE IN THE MIDEAST WHILE UNDERMINING THE WESTERN, PARTICULARLY THE AMERICAN, POSITION. SINCE GORBACHEV ATTAINED POWER, THERE HAS BEEN NOTHING TO SUGGEST THAT THE SOVIETS HAVE VEERED FROM THIS COURSE; WHAT GORBACHEV HAS DONE IS INTRODUCE INNOVATIVE AND MORE FLEXIBLE TACTICS IN PURSUING SOVIET AMBITIONS. THIS NEW APPROACH HAS BEEN DICTATED BY THE NEED TO FOSTER DETENTE WITH THE WEST AND TO PURSUE PERESTROIKA AT HOME. BY USING NEW MEANS TO REALIZE TRADITIONAL ENDS, GORBACHEV IS GETTING GREATER VALUE FOR HIS MONEY IN PROMOTING MOSCOW'S INTERESTS.

03650 GORDON, M.S.
CAMBRIDGE VOTERS CHALLENGE US POLICY
MIDDLE EAST REPORT, 19(157) (MAR 89), 37-38.
ON NOV. 8, 1988, VOTERS IN CAMBRIDGE AND SOMERVILLE, MASSACHUSETTS, ENDORSED QUESTION 5 BY A MARGIN OF 53 TO 47 PERCENT. QUESTION 5 WAS A NON-BINDING PUBLIC POLICY STATEMENT CALLING ON ELECTED OFFICIALS TO WORK TOWARDS A JUST SETTLEMENT OF THE PALESTINIAN-ISRAELI CONFLICT, INCLUDING THE END OF VIOLATIONS OF PALESTINIAN HUMAN RIGHTS AND ISRAELI OCCUPATION OF THE WEST BANK AND GAZA.

03651 GORDON, P.J.
THE POLITICS OF IMPLEMENTING CHINA'S NUCLEAR DOCTRINE, PART II: 1969-PRESENT
JOURNAL OF NORTHEAST ASIAN STUDIES, 8(2) (SUM 89), 18-37.
THE GROWING INDUSTRIAL BASE IN NORTHERN CHINA NECESSITATES CHINA'S OBTAINING THE CAPABILITY TO DEFEND THOSE AREAS FROM SOVIET ATTACK. CONSEQUENTLY, SINCE THE LATE 1960S, THE PRC HAS BEEN ASSIMILATING MODERN TECHNOLOGY INTO THE MAOIST VIEW OF WARFARE. THE POLITICS OF IMPLEMENTING THE RESULTING PEOPLE'S WAR UNDER MODERN CONDITIONS DOCTRINE HAS AT TIMES BEEN SUBJECT TO INTENSE POLITICAL WARFARE WITH ADVERSE CONSEQUENCES FOR CHINA'S NUCLEAR FORCE POSTURE. PRC LEADERSHIP DECISIONS ALSO REFLECTED THE NEED TO IMPROVE CONVENTIONAL AND TACTICAL NUCLEAR FORCES TO INCREASE THE CREDIBILITY OF THE PLA'S DETERRENT.

03652 GORNICKI, G.
POLAND SPEAKS OUT
EAST EUROPEAN REPORTER, 3(4) (SPR 89), 32.
YEARS OF MARTIAL LAW AND ATTEMPTED SUPPRESSION HAS NOT SLOWED THE ACTIVITIES OF SOLIDARITY AND OTHER POLISH OPPOSITION GROUPS. IN THE FIRST SEMI-DEMOCRATIC ELECTION IN THE SOVIET BLOC SINCE THE 1940'S, SOLIDARITY WON A RESOUNDING VICTORY. HOWEVER, THE VICTORY PUTS BOTH THE RULING COMMUNISTS AND SOLIDARITY IN AN UNEASY POSITION: THE COMMUNISTS FEAR A TOTAL LOSS OF POWER, AND SOLIDARITY FEARS THAT THE OPPOSITION MAY NOT HAVE THE POWER AND EXPERIENCE TO PICK UP THE PIECES.

03653 GORTON, P.
BURMA: DEMOCRACY?
THIRD WORLD WEEK, 8(3) (MAR 89), 19-20.
FOR NEARLY THREE DECADES BURMA HAS LOCKED ITSELF OUT OF THE GLOBAL COMMUNITY, BUT A SENSE IS EMERGING THAT THE AUTHORITARIAN REGIME CANNOT HOLD ON INDEFINITELY. ANTI-ISOLATION TRENDS INCLUDE BURGEONING CONSUMERISM, CRITICISM OF THE U NE WIN JUNTA IN THE INTERNATIONAL MEDIA, AND THE SCARCITY OF FOREIGN AID. A HIGH LITERACY RATE AND AN ACTIVE UNDERGROUND PRESS HAVE ALSO FED THE DISCONTENT THAT COULD LEAD TO CHANGE.

03654 GORTON, P.
CAMBODIA: NEW ALLIANCE
THIRD WORLD WEEK, 8(10) (MAY 89), 77-78.
THE PEOPLE'S REPUBLIC OF KAMPUCHEA HAS CHANGED ITS NAME BACK TO CAMBODIA, RESTORED ITS PRE-COMMUNIST FLAG, AND REFORMED ITS CONSTITUTION. THE SWEEPING CHANGES ARE PART OF A PACKAGE OF CONCESSIONS PRIME MINISTER HUN SEN PRESENTED TO PRINCE NORODOM SIHANOUK IN AN EFFORT TO END THE CIVIL WAR AND UNIFY THEIR COUNTRY. THE MEETING BETWEEN HUN SEN AND SIHANOUK HAD THE QUIET BLESSING OF THE USA AND THE USSR AND AT LEAST THE ACQUIESCENCE OF VIETNAM AND CHINA. WHETHER THE MEETING WILL EVENTUALLY PROVIDE A STABLE AGREEMENT DEPENDS ON THE WILLINGNESS OF ALL THE PLAYERS TO ACCEPT HALF A LOAF

03655 GORTON, P.
CAMBODIA: STILL A PAWN
THIRD WORLD WEEK, 8(1) (MAR 89), 3-4.
THE GREAT MAJORITY OF CAMBODIAN REGUGEES DO NOT WANT TO RETURN TO THEIR NATIVE COUNTRY. NEVERTHELESS, ONCE PEACE COMES TO CAMBODIA, THEY WILL PROBABLY HAVE NO CHOICE. IN ITS SIMPLEST FORM, PEACE IN CAMBODIA MEANS AN END TO THE CIVIL WAR BETWEEN THE GOVERNMENT AND A TRIPARTITE RESISTANCE COALITION. BUT THIS BELIES THE CONTINUING COMPLEXITY OF THE SITUATION.

03656 GORTON, P.
VIETNAM: WAR AGAINST TREES
THIRD WORLD WEEK, 7(9) (JAN 89), 65-66.
INTERNATIONAL EXPERTS SAY THAT VIETNAM IS HEADED IN THE DIRECTION OF OTHER THIRD WORLD COUNTRIES, WHERE THE ENVIRONMENT IS BEING DEVASTATED FOR PROFIT. BUT VIETNAM STILL HAS TIME TO RESCUE ITS ENVIRONMENT, AND A GROWING GOVERNMENT EFFORT MAY STAVE OFF DISASTER. THE GOVERNMENT'S PROGRAM TO REVERSE DEFORESTATION INCLUDES THREE ASPECTS: MASSIVE TREE-PLANTING, TECHNIQUES FOR COMBINING REFORESTATION AND AGRICULTURE, AND EDUCATION ON THE FOLLY OF DESTROYING THE FORESTS.

03657 GOTTFRIED, P.
NIXON VISITED AND REVISITED
NATIONAL REVIEW, XLI(13) (JUL 89), 41-42.
THIS ARTICLE DESCRIBES HOW RICHARD NIXON HAS ACHIEVED THE POSITION OF SENIOR STATESMAN DESPITE ALL THE BEST EFFORTS OF THE MEDIA. THE AUTHOR ATTRIBUTES THIS TO NIXON'S FIRM GROUNDING IN POLITICAL HISTORY AND PHILOSPHY, WHICH MADE HIM MORE INTERESTED IN EXPOUNDING POLITICAL THEORY THAN IN BENDING TO FLEETING PUBLIC WILL.

03658 GOTTLIEB, G.
ISRAEL AND THE PALESTINIANS
FOREIGN AFFAIRS, 68(4) (FAL 89), 109-126.
THE PRESENT OUTLOOK IS GRIM ON THE THREE MAIN CONCERNS OF THE ISRAEL-PALESTINIAN CONFLICT: THE PEACE PROCESS ITSELF, THE ISSUE OF PALESTINIAN REPRESENTATION, AND THE NATURE OF THE PERMANENT SOLUTION. BUT LEADING ISRAELI OFFICIALS AND PALESTINIAN LEADERS HAVE IN FACT STARTED TO DRAW TENTATIVE AND VAGUE IMAGES OF WHAT A PERMANENT SOLUTION MIGHT LOOK LIKE. THOUGH LARGELY UNNOTICED AMID THE RUSH OF DRAMATIC INCIDENTS, THESE IMAGES ARE SIGNIFICANT. THEY FORM A NEW PSYCHOLOGICAL CONTEXT FOR EVERY STEP IN THE PEACE PROCESS.

03659 GOTTSCHALK, L. A.; GILBERT, R.; ULIANA, R.
PRESIDENTIAL CANDIDATES AND COGNITIVE IMPAIRMENT MEASURED FROM VERBAL BEHAVIOR IN CAMPAIGN DEBATES
PUBLIC ADMINISTRATION REVIEW, 48(2) (MAR 88), 613-619.
THIS ARTICLE REPORTS FINDINGS FROM A STUDY TO DETERMINE WHETHER THE PRESIDENTIAL DEBATES CONTAINED EVIDENCE OF SOME KIND OF DISORDER OF VERBAL COMMUNICATION IN THE SPOKEN LANGUAGE OF THE CANDIDATES. A BRIEF INTRODUCTION TO THE SCIENTIFIC ASPECTS OF ASSESSING EVIDENCE OF COGNITIVE IMPAIRMENT FROM SOLELY SPOKEN LANGUAGE ITSELF IS GIVEN. THE PROCEDURE AND METHOD OF TESTING IS PRESENTED AND THE STUDY RESULTS ARE GIVEN.

03660 GOTTSCHALK, M.
THE FAILURE OF AMERICAN POLICY
WORLD POLICY JOURNAL, 6(4) (FAL 89), 667-684.
THIS ARTICLE STATES THAT THE TIME FOR A REASSESSMENT OF SINO-AMERICAN RELATIONS IS LONG OVERDUE. IT EXPLORES CHANGES IN CHINA'S DOMESTIC AND INTERNATIONAL CONDITIONS. AS WELL AS THE CHANGES IN THE NATURE OF ECONOMIC AND STRATEGIC RELATIONS IN MUCH OF THE PACIFIC RIM. IT SUGGESTS THAT BY FAILING TO RETHINK THIS APPROACH, THE SO-CALLED REALISTS HAVE PURSUED A SURREAL PATH IN SINO-AMERICAN RELATIONS THAT HAS NOT ONLY HURT THE CAUSE OF POLITICAL REFORM AND HUMAN RIGHTS IN THE PEOPLE'S REPUBLIC, BUT ALSO AMERICA'S LONG-TERM INTERESTS IN THE REGION

03661 GOTTSCHALK, P.A.
BUILDING PEACE IN SOUTH AFRICA
DISSERTATION ABSTRACTS INTERNATIONAL, 50(4) (OCT 89), 1077-A.
UNLESS BOTH SIDES IN SOUTH AFRICA CAN AGREE ON AN AVENUE FOR SATISFYING THEIR NEEDS, THE CONFLICT WILL PERSIST. THIS DISSERTATION PROPOSES A PROFESSIONALLY-DESIGNED, FULLY SUPPORTED MEDIATION PROCESS FOR DEVELOPING EACH SIDE'S NOTIONS OF CONSTRUCTIVE POWER PREDICATED ON WIN-WIN NEEDS FULFILLMENT. THE PROPOSAL OFFERS A MEANS OF PROVIDING NEW PERSPECTIVES ON NEED RELATIONSHIPS AND UNDERSTANDING OF HOW CONSTRUCTIVE POWER CAN BETTER SATISFY THE NEEDS OF BOTH SIDES.

03662 GOTTSTEIN, P.
THE PLO DIMENSION IN ISRAEL'S FOREIGN POLICY TOWARD EGYPT, JORDON AND MOROCCO
AUSSEN POLITIK, 40(3) (1989), 293-306.
THE ISRAELI GOVERNMENT CONTINUES TO REJECT THE INCLUSION OF THE PALESTINIAN LIBERATION ORGANISATION (PLO) IN MIDDLE

EAST PEACE NEGOTIATIONS, WHETHER IT BE IN A MULTILATERAL OR, EVEN WORSE, BILATERAL CONTEXT. IT HAS BEEN PUT UNDER INCREASING PRESSURE SINCE THE US BEGAN TALKS WITH THE PLO IN TUNIS, NOT LEAST OF ALL BY THE PALESTINIAN UPRISING IN THE OCCUPIED TERRITORIES. IN LOOKING BACK ON THE COALITION BETWEEN THE LABOUR PARTY AND LIKUD BLOC THAT RULED ISRAEL FROM 1984 TO 1988, PETER GOTTSTEIN, M.A., OF THE STIFTUNG WISSENSCHAFT UND POLITIK IN EBENHAUSEN. SEES THE DOGMATIC REJECTION OF THE PLO AS A NEGOTIATING PARTNER AS THE ONE THING LABOUR AND LIKUD HAD IN COMMON. DURING THOSE FOUR YEARS LABOUR'S SHIMON PERES AND LIKUD'S YITZHAK SHAMIR ALTERNATED AS PRIME MINISTER AND FOREIGN MINISTER. PERES HAS THE DRIVING FORCE IN BOTH CAPACITIES WHEN IT CAME TO ESTABLISHING CONTACTS OR INITIATING TALKS WITH MODERATE ARAB GOVERNMENTS. HE SUCCEEDED IN ARRANGING A SUMMIT WITH PRESIDENT MUBARAK IN EGYPT, SOUGHT A MEETING WITH KING HUSSEIN OF JORDON AND WAS INVITED TO MOROCCO BY KING HASSAN II. THUS THE DIALOGUE WITH ALL THREE COUNTRIES HAS RESUMED, AND IN SOME AREAS FURTHER COOPERATION HAS EVOLVED. PERES FAILED TO EXPAND BILATERAL RELATIONS TO SUCH A DEGREE AS TO ENABLE THE UNCOUPLING OF THE PLO ISSUE FROM PROGRESS IN THE PEACE PROCESS, HOWEVER. THAT WOULD HAVE REQUIRED A CHANGE OF POSITION BY THOSE ARAB GOVERNMENTS TO WHOM ISRAEL HAD NOTHING TO OFFER IN RETURN. MOREOVER, PERES' INITIATIVES WERE CONTINUALLY HINDERED BY SHAMIR. THE PRESENT SITUATION IN THE OCCUPIED TERRITORIES OFFERS LITTLE HOPE THAT NEW LIFE CAN BE BREATHED INTO THOSE INITIATIVES IN THE NEAR FUTURE.

03663 GOUGEON, L.
EMERSON, CARLYLE, AND THE CIVIL WAR
NEW ENGLAND QUARTERLY. LXII(3) (SEP 89), 403-423.
THE ARTICLE EXAMINES THE ISSUES THAT RESULTED IN CONFLICT IN THE OTHERWISE FRIENDLY RELATIONS BETWEEN RALPH WADLO EMERSON AND THOMAS CARLYLE. ALTHOUGH EMERSON'S IDEALISM AND OPTIMISM ARE AT ODDS AMERICAN CIVIL WAR. THE TENSIONS THAT DEVELOPED BETWEEN THE US AND GREAT BRITAIN IN THE SPRING AND SUMMER OF 1863 MOVED EMERSON TO PUBLICLY DENOUNCE CARLYLE AND THE BRITISH INTELLECTUAL IN GENERAL. DISAGREEMENT OVER SLAVERY, THE EMANCIPATION PROCLAMATION, AND THE AIMS OF THE UNION LED THE TWO REPRESENTATIVES OF THE AMERICAN AND BRITISH INTELLIGENCIA TO INDULGE IN FREQUENT SCATHING DENUNCIATIONS OF THE OTHER.

03664 GOULD, B.
THE STATE OF SAO PAULO
SOUTH, (101) (MAR 89), 35.
BASED ON THE COFFEE WEALTH OF THE LAST CENTURY, SAO PAULO'S ECONOMY HAS GONE FROM STRENGTH TO STRENGTH, AND THE SOLIDITY OF ITS INDUSTRIAL BASE HAS ENABLED IT TO WITHSTAND RECESSION. SO FAR, SAO PAULO HAS FAILED TO TRANSLATE THIS ECONOMIC PROWESS INTO POLITICAL MUSCLE. BUT THE INCREASINGLY INFLUENTIAL WORKERS' PARTY MAY CHANGE THAT.

03665 GOULD, D.J.
BUREAUCRATIC CORRUPTION IN AFRICA: CAUSES, CONSEQUENCES AND REMEDIES
INTERNATIONAL JOURNAL OF PUBLIC ADMINISTRATION, 12(3) (1989), 427-457.
ONE OF THE CRITICAL POLICY ISSUES IN AFRICAN MANAGEMENT TODAY IS BUREAUCRATIC CORRUPTION THIS PROBLEM HAS IN SOME COUNTRIES REACHED SUCH PROPORTIONS AS TO FRUSTRATE GOOD POLICY INTENTIONS AND TO PARALYZE MANAGEMENT OPERATIONS. THE STUDY EXAMINES THE EXTENT OF BUREAUCRATIC CORRUPTION IN SELECTED AFRICAN COUNTRIES, ANALYZES THEIR POTENTIAL CAUSES, CRITICALLY ASSESSES THEIR CONSEQUENCES ON THE PATTERN OF POLITICAL SOCIO-ECONOMIC AND ADMINISTRATIVE DEVELOPMENT, AND REVIEWS THE EFFECTIVENESS OF REMEDIES PROPOSED OR ACTUALLY TRIED.

03666 GOULD, H.
ANTICOMMUNISM AND ANTOCOLONIALISM: THE DOMESTIC DTEREMINANTS OF DEVELOPING US-INDIAN RELATIONS DURING THE TRUMAN ERA
ASIAN AFFAIRS, AN AMERICAN REVIEW, 15(4) (WIN 89), 194-203.
IN ANALYZING THE RELATIONS BETWEEN THE US AND INDIA DURING THE TRUMAN ERA, THE AUTHOR ATTEMPTS TO EXPLAIN HOW TWO NATIONS WHOSE POLITICAL SYSTEMS WERE MUTUALLY COMPATIBLE AND WHOSE PEOPLE GENUINELY LIKED EACH OTHER FROM THE BEGINING SAW THEIR RELATIONS SOUR AND SINK INTO A PATTERN OF MUTUAL FRUSTRATION. A MAJOR FACTOR IN THE RELATIONS BETWEEN THE TWO NATIONS WAS THE DOMESTIC POLICY THAT PREDOMINATED BOTH NATION'S FOREIGN POLICIES. FOR THE US, IT WAS THE GROWING FERVOR OF ANTICOMMUNISM AND FOR INDIA THE ALREADY STRONG FEELINGS OF ANTICOLONIALISM.

03667 GOULD, J.
THE ENRAGED VOICES OF OPPOSITION
ENCOUNTER, LXXIII(5) (DEC 89), 61-66.
SLOWLY THE OPPONENTS OF THATCHERISM HAVE BEGUN TO RE-GROUP, FORMING NOT ONE MOVEMENT BUT SEVERAL BUSTLING, OVERLAPPING COTERIES. THIS NEW OPPOSITION CRYSTALLIZED IN LATE 1988 IN THE MANIFESTO OF CHARTER 88, WHICH CALLED FOR A FAIR ELECTORAL SYSTEM OF PROPORTIONAL REPRESENTATION, AND IN THE EMERGENCE OF THE JOURNAL "SAMIZDAT," WHICH SEEKS TO

OVERCOME PARTY DIFFERENCES AND CREATE A PROGRESSIVE, POST-THATCHER CONSENSUS.

03668 GOULD, L.
THEODORE ROOSEVELT, WOODROW WILSON, AND THE EMERGENCE OF THE MODERN PRESIDENCY: AN INTRODUCTORY ESSAY
PRESIDENTIAL STUDIES QUARTERLY, XIX(1) (WIN 89), 41-50.
FOR TWENTY YEARS THE PERSONALITIES OF THEODORE ROOSEVELT AND WOODRWOH WILSON AS PRESIDENTS AND POLITICAL RIVALS DOMINATED THE NATIONAL HISTORY OF THE US. THE ESSAY EXAMINES THE EFFECTS OF BOTH PRESIDENTS' TENURE IN THE WHITE HOUSE AND THE LEGACY THAT THEY LEFT. IT CONCENTRATES CHIEFLY ON THE EXPANSION OF PRESIDENTIAL POWERS THAT BOTH PRESIDENTS ENCOURAGED AND TOOK ADVANTAGE OF.

03669 GOULET, D.
PARTICIPATION IN DEVELOPMENT: NEW AVENUES
WORLD DEVELOPMENT, 17(2) (FEB 89), 165-178.
POLITICAL REDEMOCRATIZATION NOW OCCURRING IN NUMEROUS COUNTRIES OF ASIA AND LATIN AMERICA CHALLENGES BOTH THE RULE OF DICTATORS AND THEIR ELITIST DEVELOPMENT STRATEGIES. THIS ESSAY ARGUES THAT NEW MODES OF POPULAR PARTICIPATION ARE NEEDED IN THE TRANSITION TO EQUITABLE DEVELOPMENT. THE AUTHOR CLASSIFIES DIVERSE FORMS OF PARTICIPATION, ASSESSES LESSONS OF EXPERIENCE, ILLUSTRATES NEW FORMS OF PARTICIPATION IN SRI LANKA AND BRAZIL, AND SUMMARIZES THE STRATEGIC IMPORTANCE OF NEW APPROACHES.

03670 GOURE, L.
THE KREMLIN SHAKEUP
GLOBAL AFFAIRS, 4(1) (WIN 89), 1-17.
THIS ARTICLE ANALYZES THE MOVEMENTS IN THE SOVIET UNION REFERRED TO AS PERESTROIKA AND GLASNOST. THE AUTHOR EXPLAINS THAT, TO THE EXTENT THAT THESE TERMS ARE INTERPRETED AS MOVES TOWARD DEMOCRATIZATION, THE SOVIET MEANING OF DEMOCRATIZATION IS QUITE DIFFERENT FROM HOW IT IS UNDERSTOOD IN THE UNITED STATES.

03671 GOUREVITCH, P.A.
THE PACIFIC RIM: CURRENT DEBATES
PHILADELPHIA: ANLS OF AMER ACMY OF POLITICAL AND SOC SCIENCE, (505) (SEP 89), 8-23.
THE DRAMATIC EMERGENCE OF THE PACIFIC REGION POSES A DOUBLE CHALLENGE FOR POLICYMAKERS AND SOCIAL SCIENTISTS. BOTH NEED TO UNDERSTAND CHANGE IN THE REGION AS WELL AS TO ADAPT TOOLS OF ANALYSIS AND GUIDES TO POLICY. TWO LARGE ISSUES DOMINATE DEBATE, THOUGH THERE ARE MANY OTHER IMPORTANT ONES AS WELL. THESE TWO ARE PROSPERITY AND PEACE: WHY HAVE PARTS OF THE ASIAN PACIFIC SIDE GROWN SO QUICKLY WHILE OTHER PARTS OF THE PACIFIC, MUCH OF LATIN AMERICA, AFRICA, AND OTHER AREAS NOT; AND HOW HAVE THESE CHANGES ALTERED THE INTERNATIONAL SYSTEM OF SECURITY? TO ANSWER THESE QUESTIONS, THE ISSUE OF LEVEL OF ANALYSIS MUST BE RAISED.

03672 GOUWS, R.
ECONOMIC AND FINANCIAL PROSPECTS FOR 1989
SOUTH AFRICA FOUNDATION REVIEW, 15(2) (FEB 89), 1-2.
THE AUTHOR SURVEYS SOUTH AFRICA'S RECENT ECONOMIC GROWTH, BALANCE OF PAYMENTS, FINANCIAL MARKETS, AND MONETARY POLICY.

03673 GOW, D.
BEYOND THE PROJECT: THE QUEST FOR SUSTAINABILITY IN THE THIRD WORLD
AVAILABLE FROM NTIS, NO. PB89-162705/GAR, JUN 88, 44.
THE PAPER FOCUSES ON THE GAP BETWEEN CURRENT PRACICE AND WHAT IS KNOWN ABOUT EFFECTIVE DEVELOPMENT MANAGEMENT. DEFINITIONS AND DISCUSSIONS ARE GIVEN FOR THE KEY TERMS 'PROJECTS AND PROGRAMS,' 'THE INTEGRATED APPROACH,' AND 'SUSTAINABLE DEVELOPMENT.' THE PRIMARY CONSTRAINTS TO SUSTAINABLE DEVELOPMENT FALL INTO FIVE CATEGORIES; (1) POLITICAL, ECONOMIC AND FINANCIAL, (2) ENVIRONMENTAL AND NATURAL RESOURCES, (3) TECHNOLOGICAL, (4) INSTITUTIONAL, AND (5) ORGANIZATIONAL. A STRATEGY FOR AN INTEGRATED APPROACH TO SUSTAINABLE DEVELOPMENT IS EXPLAINED.

03674 GOW, J.I.
MEMBERS' SURVEY ON THEORY, PRACTICE, AND INNOVATION IN PUBLIC ADMINISTRATION
CANADIAN PUBLIC ADMINISTRATION, 32(3) (FAL 89), 382-406.
THIS PAPER SUMMARIZES THE RESULTS OF A SURVEY OF IPAC MEMBERS CARRIED OUT IN THE WINTER OF 1987-88. MEMBERS' VIEWS WERE SOUGHT ABOUT THE EDUCATION AND TRAINING OF GOOD SENIOR PUBLIC SERVANTS, ADMINISTRATION CHANGE AND REFORM, AND THE SOURCES OF INNOVATION IN PUBLIC ADMINISTRATION. IN SPITE OF GREAT DIVERSITY IN BACKGROUND AND PRESENT CONDITION, THE MEMBERS SHOWED A HIGH DEGREE OF UNITY IN REGARDING PUBLIC ADMINISTRATION AS A PRACTICAL ACTIVITY VERY MUCH UNDER THE CONTROL OF ADMINISTRATORS. IT IS A WORLD OF NUANCES, WHERE CHANGE DOES OCCUR, BUT NEVER QUITE AS PLANNED AND SELDOM ACCORDING TO THEORY.

03675 GOWA, J.
BIPOLARITY, MULTIPOLARITY, AND FREE TRADE

AMERICAN POLITICAL SCIENCE REVIEW, 83(4) (DEC 89),
1245-1256.
RECENT LITERATURE TYPICALLY ATTRIBUTES THE RELATIVE
SCARCITY OF OPEN INTERNATIONAL MARKETS TO THE PRISONER'S
DILEMMA STRUCTURE OF STATE PREFERENCES WITH RESPECT TO TRADE.
IN THIS ESSAY, THE AUTHOR ARGUES THAT THE PRISONER'S
DILEMMA REPRESENTATION DOES NOT REFLECT THE MOST CRITICAL
ASPECT OF FREE TRADE AGREEMENTS IN AN ANARCHIC INTERNATIONAL
SYSTEM: SECURITY EXTERNALITIES. EXPLICIT CONSIDERATION OF
THESE EFFECTS SUGGESTS THAT A BIPOLAR INTERNATIONAL
POLITICAL SYSTEM HAS AN ADVANTAGE RELATIVE TO ITS MULTIPOLAR
COUNTERPART WITH RESPECT TO THE OPENING OF MARKETS AMONG
STATES. LESS CREDIBLE EXIT THREATS AND STRONGER INCENTIVES
TO ENGAGE IN ALTRUISM WITHIN ITS ALLIANCES EXPLAIN THE
ADVANTAGE OF A TWO-POWER SYSTEM.

03676 GRABER, D. A.
FLASHLIGHT COVERAGE: STATE NEWS ON NATIONAL BROADCASTS
AMERICAN POLITICS QUARTERLY, 17(3) (JUL 89), 277-290.
CONTENT ANALYSIS OF THE EARLY EVENING NATIONAL NEWSCASTS
ON ABC, CBS, AND NBC FROM JULY 1985 TO JUNE 1987 REVEALS
THAT THE NEW FEDERALISM HAS FAILED TO FOCUS NATIONAL MEDIA
ATTENTION ON STATE ISSUES. STATE NEWS WAS EXTREMELY SPARSE,
SPOTLIGHTED A SMALL NUMBER OF STATES, AND LACKED POLITICAL
SUBSTANCE. DISASTER, CRIME, AND TRIVIA STORIES PREVAILED. A
PARALLEL CONTENT ANALYSIS OF STATE NEWS COVERED BY THE NEW
YORK TIMES INDICATES THAT NEWSWORTHY POLITICAL STORIES WERE
PLENTIFUL SO THAT MUCH BETTER COVERAGE OF THIS IMPORTANT
ASPECT OF AMERICAN POLITICS WAS POSSIBLE. WHEN POPULATION IS
USED AS A YARDSTICK OF POLITICAL SIGNIFICANCE, THE CONCERNS
OF MIDWESTERNERS RECEIVED THE LEAST ATTENTION WHILE THE
PACIFIC REGION DOMINATED IN TELEVISION AS WELL AS IN PRINT
NEWS. COMPARED TO NEWS BROADCASTS IN THE SEVENTIES, MEDIA
ATTENTION HAS SHIFTED FROM THE NORTHEASTERN AND NEW ENGLAND
REGIONS TO THE WEST AND SOUTHWEST, POSSIBLY CONTRIBUTING TO
THE ECONOMIC DECLINE OF RUST BELT STATES. STATE NEWS
COVERAGE DURING PRESIDENTIAL CAMPAIGNS SUGGESTS WAYS FOR
INCREASING COVERAGE AT OTHER TIMES.

03677 GRABER, M. A.
OUR (IM)PERFECT CONSTITUTION
REVIEW OF POLITICS, 51(1) (WIN 89), 86-106.
THIS ARTICLE EXPLORES AN ATTITUDE, "PERFECT
CONSTITUTIONALISM." PERFECT CONSTITUTIONALISTS BELIEVE THAT,
PROPERLY INTERPRETED, THE CONSTITUTION REQUIRES THAT OUR
SOCIETY CONFORM TO THE BEST PRINCIPLES OF HUMAN GOVERNANCE.
THIS BELIEF THAT THE CONSTITUTION IS NEARLY FLAWLESS NOT
ONLY UNDERLIES THE SO-CALLED FUNDAMENTAL VALUES STRAND OF
CONSTITUTIONAL THOUGHT BUT ALSO THOSE STRANDS OF
CONSTITUTIONAL ARGUMENT BASED ON CONCEPTIONS OF THE
DEMOCRATIC PROCESS OR THE ORIGINAL INTENTIONS OF THE FRAMERS.
UNFORTUNATELY, EMPIRICAL AND THEORETICAL PROBLEMS RESULT
WHEN CONSTITUTIONAL THEORY IS REDUCED TO POLITICAL
PHILOSOPHY. IN ORDER TO OVERCOME THESE PROBLEMS WE NEED TO
ESSAY A DIFFERENT INTERPRETIVE APPROACH, "IMPERFECT
CONSTUTIONALISM". IMPERFECT CONSTUTIONALISM EMPHASIZES THE
VALUE OF CONSTITUTIONS, EVEN ONES THAT MIGHT BE IMPROVED IN
MANY WAYS.

03678 GRADY, D.O.
ECONOMIC DEVELOPMENT AND ADMINISTRATIVE POWER THEORY: A
COMPARATIVE ANALYSIS OF STATE DEVELOPMENT AGENCIES
POLICY STUDIES REVIEW, 8(2) (WIN 89), 322-340.
THE ABILITY OF STATE LEADERS TO INFLUENCE ECONOMIC
GROWTH AND DIVERSITY WITHIN THEIR STATES IS A DISPUTED ISSUE
WITHIN THE LITERATURE ON STATE ECONOMIC DEVELOPMENT POLICY-
MAKING. THIS RESEARCH CONTRIBUTES TO THIS DEBATE BY
DEVELOPING COMPARATIVE MEASURES OF STATE DEVELOPMENT AGENCY
POWER DRAWN FROM THE EMERGING THEORY ON ORGANIZATIONAL POWER.
IF STATE POLICY LEADERS HAVE INDEPENDENT CONTROL OVER THE
ECONOMIC PERFORMANCE OF THEIR STATES AND IF THAT INFLUENCES
IS EXERCISED THROUGH THE ADMINISTRATIVE UNIT RESPONSIBLE FOR
THAT ACTIVITY, STATES WHICH HAVE SUPPLIED THEIR AGENCIES
MORE RESOURCES AND FREEDOM IN USING THOSE RESOURCES SHOULD
OUTPERFORM THOSE STATES WHICH HAVE NOT.

03679 GRAEBNER, N.A.
AN AMERICAN TRADITION IN FOREIGN AFFAIRS
VIRGINIA QUARTERLY REVIEW, 65(4) (FAL 89), 600-618.
THIS ARTICLE EXAMINES AMERICA'S HISTORICAL DISCARD OF
TRADITION IN GENERAL AND IN FOREIGN AFFAIRS IN PARTICULAR.
IT REVIEWS THE HERITAGE OF TRADITION CALLED UPON BY THE
FOUNDING FATHERS, FOCUSING PARTICULARLY UPON ADAMS, HAMILTON
AND WASHINGTON. IT CALLS FOR A USE OF THE TRADITIONAL
RESPONSE NOW IN A COMPLEX AND TROUBLED WORLD.

03680 GRAFSTEIN, R.
THE THEORY OF FREEDOM
SOCIAL SCIENCE QUARTERLY, 70(4) (DEC 89), 851-854.
THIS IS A RESPONSE TO "THE RHETORIC AND POLITICS OF
LIBERTY" BY JACK P. GEISE. MR. GRAFSTEIN IS SKEPTICAL ABOUT
ATTEMPTS TO REDEFINE FREEDOM. HIS CAVEATS SUGGEST THE
ARGUMENT MUST BE CONDUCTED WITHIN THE FRAMEWORK OF THE
BROADER THEORIES IN WHICH CONCEPTS ARE HOUSED. HE CONCLUDES

THAT WHAT IS MISSING IN THE GEISE REDEFINITION IS A FULLER
RECOGNITION OF THE CORRELATIVE RELATIONS AMONG AGENTS WHO
OPERATE IN A WORLD OF SOCIAL CONSTRAINTS, EXTERNALITIES, AND
NONPUBLIC GOODS.

03681 GRAHAM-YOOLL, A.
AMBIGUITIES OF A PERONIST
SOUTH, (103) (MAY 89), 10-11.
CARLOS MENEM, GOVERNOR OF LA RIOJA PROVINCE, EXPECTS TO
WIN THE PRESIDENCY IN ARGENTINA'S MAY 1989 ELECTION. THE
PERONIST CANDIDATE, MENEM TALKS OF USING A CONSENSUS OF BIG
BUSINESS CORPORATIONS, LABOR, AND GOVERNMENT TO ACHIEVE "A
PRODUCTIVE REVOLUTION."

03682 GRAHAM-YOOLL, A.
HOYTE'S RECIPE FOR ECONOMIC RECOVERY
SOUTH, (100) (FEB 89), 41-42.
UNDER A THREE-YEAR PROGRAM, GUYANA'S PRESIDENT DESMOND
HOYTE PLANS TO RESTORE THE BASIC ECONOMIC INFRASTRUCTURE,
REHABILITATE THE MANUFACTURING SECTOR, AND BROADEN THE
ECONOMIC BASE, WHICH RESTS ON SUGAR, BAUXITE, AND RICE. HE
HAS APPEALED TO THE IMF FOR AN AID PACKAGE TO HELP HIM
SUSTAIN THE RECOVERY PLAN.

03683 GRAHAM, C.; PROSSER, T.
THE CONSTITUTION AND THE NEW CONSERVATIVES
PARLIAMENTARY AFFAIRS, 42(3) (JUL 89), 330-349.
IT IS NOW UNDENIABLE THAT, SINCE THE ADVENT OF THE FIRST
OF MRS. THATCHER'S GOVERNMENTS IN 1979, THERE HAVE BEEN
FUNDAMENTAL CHANGES IN THE STRUCTURE AND WORKINGS OF THE
BRITISH STATE. EVER SINCE THEY FIRST CAME TO POWER, THE
CONSERVATIVES PRESENTED A KEY ELEMENT OF THEIR PROGRAMME AS
BEING A REFORMATION OF STATE STRUCTURES AND PROCEDURES--
OFTEN REFERRED TO AS THE "ROLLING BACK OF THE STATE". WHEN
SEEN LIKE THIS, CONSTITUTIONAL CHANGE BECOMES A CENTRAL
ELEMENT OF THE CONSERVATIVE PROGRAMME RATHER THAN AN
OPTIONAL EXTRA. IN ORDER TO SET THESE MATTERS IN CONTEXT,
THIS ARTICLE DISCUSSES THE NATURE OF CONSTITUTIONS IN
GENERAL AND DRAW ATTENTION TO SPECIFIC FEATURES OF THE
BRITISH CONSTITUTION, BEFORE EXAMINING THE RELATIONSHIP
BETWEEN 'THATCHERISM' AND CHANGES IN THE CONSTITUTION.

03684 GRAHAM, C.B., JR.; WHITBY, K.J.
PARTY - BASED VOTING IN A SOUTHERN STATE LEGISLATURE
AMERICAN POLITICS QUARTERLY, 17(2) (APR 89), 181-193.
THIS ARTICLE USES ESTABLISHED MEASURES OF PARTY
DIFFERENCE AND PARTY COHESION TO ANALYZE THE EFFECTS OF
EMERGING TWO-PARTY COMPETITION IN CONTESTED ROLL CALL VOTES
IN THE SOUTH CAROLINA HOUSE OF REPRESENTATIVES, 1977-1987
THE ANALYSIS ALSO TREATS LEGISLATIVE VOTING IN THE STATE
WITH RESPECT TO THE PARTY AFFILIATION OF GOVERNORS. THE
RESULTS REVEAL LITTLE CONVINCING EVIDENCE OF PARTY AS A
MAJOR REFERENCE SOURCE FOR LEGISLATIVE ROLL CALL BEHAVIOR IN
SOUTH CAROLINA. EVEN THOUGH THERE ARE SOME EXAMPLES OF
STRONGER PARTY-BASED VOTING, THEY APPEAR TO OCCUR IN A
RANDOM FASHION RATHER THAN ON THE BASIS OF A MAJOR,
ORGANIZED ATTEMPT BY LEGISLATORS TO VOTE ALONG PARTY LINES.
THE FINDINGS SUGGEST THAT FURTHER RESEARCH IS NEEDED TO
EXPLORE THE CUES FOR LEGISLATIVE PARTY VOTING IN SOUTH
CAROLINA AND TO IDENTIFY INFLUENCES WITH WHICH TO COMPARE
STATE LEGISLATIVE VOTING EXPERIENCES, PARTICULARLY IN THE
OTHER SOUTHERN STATES.

03685 GRAHAM, C.L.
THE LATIN AMERICAN QUAGMIRE: BEYOND DEBT AND DEMOCRACY
BROOKINGS REVIEW, 7(2) (SPR 89), 42-47.
AT LEAST 12 LATIN AMERICAN NATIONS WILL HOLD
PRESIDENTIAL ELECTIONS IN 1989 OR 1990. FOR MANY THIS WILL
BE THE SECOND ROUND OF ELECTIONS SINCE CIVILIANS TOOK
CONTROL FROM MILITARY REGIMES. BUT CONTINUED ECONOMIC
DETERIORATION THREATENS POLITICAL STABILITY IN THE REGION.

03686 GRAHAM, D.
SDI AND THE COMMON DEFENSE
JOURNAL OF LEGISLATION, 15(2) (1989), 115-118.
THE PRIMARY POLITICAL WRESTLING MATCH OF THE LATE 1980'S
AT LEAST IN THE ARENA OF FOREIGN AFFAIRS AND NATIONAL
SECURITY, HAS FOCUSED ON SDI. HOWEVER, IT WOULD APPEAR THAT
THE ANTI-SDI FORCES FACE A HOPELESS TASK. ON THE TECHNICAL
SIDE THEY MUST PROVE THAT "IT CAN'T BE DONE" WHILE
SCIENTISTS AND ENGINEERS PROVE THAT IT CAN. ON THE MORAL
SIDE THEY MUST BE PREPARED TO KILL SOVIET CITIZENS ON THE
PREMISE THAT THAT OPTION IS SUPERIOR TO DEFENDING OUR OWN.
ON THE LEGAL SIDE THEY MUST ARGUE THAT A TREATY THAT HAS
BEEN VIOLATED BY THE SOVIETS TAKES PRECEDENCE OVER THE
CONSTITUTIONAL MANDATE THAT THE FEDERAL GOVERNMENT "PROVIDE
FOR THE COMMON DEFENSE."

03687 GRAHAM, K.
LOWERING THE NUCLEAR SWORD: NEW ZEALAND, MORALITY AND
NUCLEAR DETERRENCE
NEW ZEALAND INTERNATIONAL REVIEW, 14(2) (MAR 89), 20-25.
THE SECRETARY-GENERAL OF PARLIAMENTARIANS GLOBAL ACTION
IN NEW YORK, DISCUSSES THE MORAL BASIS OF NEW ZEALAND'S ANTI-

NUCLEAR STANCE. HE MAKES CONNECTIONS BETWEEN MORALITY, LAW
AND POLITICS AND DEFINES LAW AS BEING CONTAINED WITHIN THE
BROADER NOTIONS OF MORALITY THAT ARE THE HALLMARKS OF A
SOCIETY'S CIVILIZATION AND CULTURE. HE OUTLINES A HISTORY OF
PACIFISM AND PHILOSOPHICAL PARAMETERS OF "JUST WARS." THE
NUCLEAR AGE AND CHALLENGES FACING COUNTRIES WHO TAKE AN ANTI-
NUCLEAR WEAPONS APPROACH ARE HIGHLIGHTED, WITH A FOCUS ON
NEW ZEALAND'S NATIONAL EXPERIENCES. THE UNITED NATIONS AND
NATO'S POSITIONS ARE ALSO DISCUSSED.

03688 GRAHL, J.; TEAGUE, P.
LABOUR MARKET FLEXIBILITY IN WEST GERMANY, BRITAIN AND
FRANCE
WEST EUROPEAN POLITICS, 12(2) (APR 89), 91-112.
TO RESOLVE THE HIGH UNEMPLOYMENT RATES IN MANY WESTERN
EUROPEAN COUNTRIES, THE NOTION OF LABOUR MARKET FLEXIBILITY
HAS BEEN GAINING FAVOUR WITH ACADEMICS AND POLICY-MAKERS.
THIS ARTICLE EXAMINES THE NOTION OF LABOUR MARKET
FLEXIBILITY IN DETAIL AND ASSESSES THE EXTENT TO WHICH IT
HAS BEEN IMPLEMENTED IN WEST GERMANY, BRITAIN AND FRANCE. IT
IS ARGUED THAT THE MOST SIGNIFICANT DEVELOPMENTS TOWARDS
FLEXIBILTY HAVE OCCURRED IN BRITAIN BECAUSE OF THE THATCHER
GOVERNMENT'S COMMITMENT TO NEO-LIBERAL ECONOMIC POLICIES AND
BECAUSE THE 'VOLUNTARIST' BRITISH INDUSTRIAL RELATIONS
SYSTEM DOES NOT REPRESENT A BARRIER TO THE PURSUIT OF SUCH A
POLICY. BY CONTRAST, THERE HAS BEEN ONLY A PARTIAL
INCORPORATION OF FLEXIBILITY INITIATIVES WITHIN GERMANY AND
FRANCE LARGELY BECAUSE NO GOVERNMENT IN EITHER COUNTRY HAS
BEEN COMMITTED TO A FULL NEO-LIBERAL ASSAULT IN THE EXISTING
DENSE ARRAY OF NATIONAL INDUSTRIAL RELATIONS INSTITUTIONS,
NORMS AND LEGISLATION. THE ARTICLE ALSO ASSESSES THE EXTENT
TO WHICH LABOUR MARKET FLEXIBILITY REPRESENTS A COHERENT AND
WORKABLE APPROACH TO THE CHALLENGE OF RESOLVING UNEMPLOYMENT.
IN SEVERAL IMPORTANT RESPECT, WE FIND IT AN INADQUATE
POLICY TO HELP RESTORE EMPLOYMENT GROWTH IN WESTERN EUROPE.

03689 GRAHL, J.; TEAGUE, P.
THE COST OF NEO-LIBERAL EUROPE
NEW LEFT REVIEW, (174) (MAR 89), 33-50.
A MASS OF PUBLICITY IN THE LAST YEAR HAS PAINTED A
UNIFORMLY ROSY PICTURE OF THE BENEFITS THAT THE SINGLE
MARKET WILL BRING TO THE COUNTRIES OF THE EUROPEAN COMMUNITY
AFTER 1992. JOHN GRAHL AND PAUL TEAGUE TAKE A MORE SOBER
VIEW OF THIS PROCESS. DRAWING ON THE ANALYSES OF THE
REGULATION SCHOOL, THEY ARGUE THAT THE 1992 PROGRAMME WILL
NEITHER ACHIEVE THE MUCHHERALDED AIM OF MARKET INTEGRATION
NOR ENSURE A STABLE RECOVERY OF THE EUROPEAN PRODUCTIVE
ECONOMY.

03690 GRAIG, I.C.
THE PHYICISTS AND THE POLITICIANS: THE PURSUIT OF THE
INTERNATIONAL CONTROL OF ATOMIC WEAPONS, 1943-46
DISSERTATION ABSTRACTS INTERNATIONAL, 50(1) (JUL 89),
251-A.
THIS STUDY EXAMINES THE ACTIVITIES OF THOSE INDIVIDUALS
IN THE US WHO ADVOCATED A PARTICULAR APPROACH TO THE
INTERNATIONAL CONTROL OF ATOMIC WEAPONS IN THE FIRST YEARS
OF THE ATOMIC AGE. THESE INDIVIDUALSPRIMARILY, THOUGH NOT
EXCLUSIVELY, MANHATTAN PROJECT SCIENTISTS AND ADMINISTRATORS-
BELIEVED THAT PEACE IN THE ATOMIC AGE COULD BEST BE ENSURED
THROUGH A SYSTEM OF INTERNATIONAL CONTROL BASED ON THE FREE
INTERCHANGE OF SCIENTIFIC INFORMATION. THIS BELIEF IN THE
NEED FOR FREE INTERNATIONAL SCIENTIFIC INTERCHANGE MADE
THEIR APPROACH UNIQUE.

03691 GRANT, J.P.
AVERTING DISASTER
AFRICA REPORT, 34(4) (JUL 89), 48-51.
THE DIRECTOR OF THE UN'S OPERATION LIFELINE SUDAN
DISCUSSES THE BACKGROUND TO THE HISTORIC AGREEMENT BETWEEN
THE GOVERNMENT AND SPLM TO ALLOW SAFE TRANSIT OF FOOD
SUPPLIES TO THE WAR-TORN SOUTH. ALSO LOOKING AT THE RECENT
MILITARY COUP IN SUDAN, JAMES GRANT OUTLINES PROSPECTS FOR
AN END TO THE CONFLICT, AS WELL AS THE ROLE OF THE
INTERNATIONAL COMMUNITY IN RESOLVING THE NATION'S ONGOING
ECONOMIC CRISIS.

03692 GRANT, W.; MARTINELLI, A.; PATERSON, W.
LARGE FIRMS AS POLITICAL ACTORS: A COMPARATIVE ANALYSIS OF
THE CHEMICAL INDUSTRY IN BRITAIN, ITALY AND WEST GERMANY
WEST EUROPEAN POLITICS, 12(2) (APR 89), 72-90.
LARGE FIRMS AS POLITICAL ACTORS ARE COMPARED IN THE
CHEMICAL INDUSTRY IN THREE COUNTRIES. IN WEST GERMANY, CO-
ORDINATED ACTION THROUGH THE INDUSTRY ASSOCIATIONS IS
IMPORTANT, BUT FIRMS ARE DEVELOPING THEIR OWN POLITICAL
CAPABILITIES. IN ITALY LINKS WITH POLITICAL PARTIES ARE
IMPORTANT, BUT THE OPERATING ENVIRONMENT OF FIRMS HAS BECOME
LESS POLITICISED. BRITAIN CONFORMS MORE TO A 'COMPANY STATE'
MODEL WITH THE GOVERNMENT RELATIONS DIVISIONS OF FIRMS
PLAYING A KEY ROLE. THE GREATEST DIVERGENCE BETWEEN THE
THREE COUNTRIES IS IN TERMS OF RELATIONSHIPS WITH POLITICAL
PARTIES. IN GENERAL, THERE IS A TREND TOWARDS GREATER
CONVERGENCE IN GOVERNMENT-BUSINESS RELATIONS IN THE INDUSTRY
IN THE THREE COUNTRIES, INTERNATIONALISATION BEING A KEY

FACTOR.

03693 GRANT, W.
PRESSURE GROUPS
CONTEMPORARY RECORD, 3(2) (NOV 89), 2-5.
THIS ARTICLE EXAMINES THE STEADY RISE IN INFLUENCE THAT
PRESSURE GROUPS HAVE EXPERIENCED OVER THE LAST 30 YEARS IN
GREAT BRITAIN. IT NOTES THAT THEY INCREASINGLY CHALLENGE
POLITICAL PARTIES AS FOCUSES FOR POLITICAL EXPRESSION. IT
DETAILS THE GROWTH OF SOME OF THE LEADING ENVIRONMENTAL
ORGANIZATIONS INCLUDING GROUPS FOR RURAL PRESERVATION,
NATURE CONSERVATION, AND BIRD PROTECTION. EXPLORED IS THE
IMPACT THAT THE THATCHER GOVERNMENT HAS MADE ON PRESSURE
GROUPS, THE GROWTH OF CONTRACT LOBBYISTS, AND THE SPILLOVER
INTO THE EUROPEAN COMMUNITY. THE CONCLUSION IS DRAWN THAT
ALTHOUGH THERE HAVE BEEN A NUMBER OF CHANGES IN THE PATTERN
OF PRESSURE GROUP ACTIVITY, THE CONTINUITIES ARE AT LEAST AS
IMPORTANT AS THE CHANGES.

03694 GRANT, W.
THE EROSION OF INTERMEDIARY INSTITUTIONS
POLITICAL QUARTERLY (THE), 60(1) (JAN 89), 10-21.
THE ELIMINATION AND DOWNGRADING OF INTERMEDIARY
ORGANIZATIONS IN BRITIAN MAY APPEAR TO BE A PRODUCT OF
THATCHERISM, BUT IN FACT IT DRAWS ON AN OLDER AND STRONGER
TRADITION OF INDIVIDUALISM WHICH IS ROOTED IN THE COUNTRY'S
HISTORY. THIS ARTICLE DESCRIBES THE GOVERNMENT'S ROLE IN
UNDERMINING THE IMPACT OF INTERMEDIARY INSTITUTIONS.

03695 GRANTHAM, C.
PARLIAMENT AND POLITICAL CONSULTANTS
PARLIAMENTARY AFFAIRS, 42(4) (OCT 89), 503-518.
UNLIKE THE MAJORITY OF CONSULTANCY FIRMS, THIS ARTICLE
WILL CONCENTRATE SOLELY ON PARLIAMENT. IN SO DOING IT WILL
ATTEMPT TO SHED SOME LIGHT ON THE FOLLOWING QUESTIONS: WHO
ARE POLITICAL CONSULTANTS? (SPECIALISTS EMPLOYED IN
"POLITICAL CONSULTANCY", "PUBLIC AFFAIRS", "GOVERNMENT
RELATIONS", "LOBBYING", AND "POLITICAL DR".) WHAT ARE THEIR
BACKGROUNDS? WHAT EXACTLY DO THEY DO? AND WITH WHAT EFFECT?
WHAT ARE THE IMPLICATIONS OF THEIR WORK FOR PARLIAMENT?
SHOULD PARLIAMENT RESPOND? AND IF SO, HOW?

03696 GRASSO, K.L.
THE EMERGENCE OF THE LIBERAL DOCTRINE OF TOLERATION IN THE
THOUGHT OF JOHN LOCKE
DISSERTATION ABSTRACTS INTERNATIONAL, 50(5) (NOV 89),
1421-A.
LOCKEAN LIBERALISM ORIGINATED IN AN ATTEMPT TO ADDRESS
THE COMPLEX OF POLITICAL AND EPISTEMOLOGICAL PROBLEMS POSED
BY THE RELIGIOUS WARS AND TO FORMULATE A NEW CIVIL THEOLOGY
FOR ENGLISH SOCIETY. AT THE HEART OF LOCKE'S PROGRAM WAS A
NEW CIVIL THEOLOGY OF TOLERATION.

03697 GRAUBARD, A.
FROM COMMENTARY TO TIKKUN: THE PAST AND FUTURE OF
PROGRESSIVE JEWISH LIBERALS
MIDDLE EAST REPORT, 19(158) (MAY 89), 17-23.
THE AUTHOR COMMENTS ON THE NATIONAL CONFERENCE OF
LIBERAL AND PROGRESSIVE JEWISH INTELLECTUALS, HELD IN
DECEMBER 1988 IN NEW YORK CITY.

03698 GRAY, A.; JENKINS, W.I.
PUBLIC ADMINISTRATION AND GOVERNMENT IN 1988-89
PARLIAMENTARY AFFAIRS, 42(4) (OCT 89), 445-462.
THIS ARTICLE EXPLORES CHANGES IN PATTERNS IN BRITISH
GOVERNMENT AND PUBLIC ADMINISTRATION. MANY ARGUE THAT THE
BIGGEST CHANGE HAS BEEN IN THE RHETORIC OF POLITICS. THE
DEVELOPMENTS DESCRIBED IN THIS ARTICLE ARE PRODUCTS OF THIS
RHETORIC'S INFLUENCE AND REPRESENT A NEW DIRECTION IN THE
WAY GOVERNMENT POWER IS USED TO PROMOTE FREEDOM, IT EXAMINES
THREE SETS OF CONSEQUENCES - THE GOVERNMENT IS BEING
FRAGMENTED INTO A WORLD OF MICRO-POLITICS BASED ON
INDIVIDUAL POLICY AREAS; CHANGES IN THE SYSTEMS OF
RESPONSIBILITY AND ACCOUNTABILITY; AND THE DEMOCRATISATION
OF SERVICE DELIVERY. THESE CHANGES ARE REDEFINING THE
RELATIONSHIP BETWEEN GOVERNMENT AND PARLIAMENT.

03699 GRAY, A., JR.; LAFFER, A.B.
DEBT AND TAXES
NATIONAL REVIEW, XLI(16) (SEP 89), 38-39.
THE AUTHOR REPORT THAT CORPORATE DEBT AND TAKEOVERS HAVE
GROWN EXPLOSIVELY, IN PART BECAUSE THE TAX CODE ENCOURAGES
THEM. IF CONGRESS WANTED TO DO THE RIGHT THING, IT WOULD
START TAXING DEBT AND EQUITY PAYMENTS EQUALLY.

03700 GRAY, C.
INTERPRETING THE 1988 PRESIDENTIAL ELECTION CONSIDERATIONS
ON CONGRESS AND THE PRESIDENCY
PRESIDENTIAL STUDIES QUARTERLY, XIX(2) (SPR 89), 253-258.
THE 1988 PRESIDENTIAL ELECTION PRODUCED A MANDATE. BUSH
WON AT LEAST TWO-THIRDS OF ALL THE STATES IN ALL REGIONS,
WITH A COMPARATIVELY LARGE POPULAR VOTE. THERE WERE FOUR
BASIC THEMES THAT RAN THROUGH THE CAMPAIGN: A VOTE OF
CONFIDENCE IN THE NATIONS ECONOMIC PROGRESS SINCE 1980,

DEFENSE AND FOREIGN POLICY, THE RULE OF LAW, AND "A KINDER
GENTLER NATION". TWO PRINCIPLES WERE DISCUSSED; BUSH RAN AS
A CONSERVATIVE AND TRIED TO PAINT DUKAKIS AS A LIBERAL, AND
ALSO MAINTAINING AND STRENTHENING THE POSITION OF THE
PRESIDENCY. BUSH WOULD LIKE TO STRENTHEN OUR ETHICS LAWS AND
APPLY THEM EQUALLY TO CONGRESS.

03701 GRAY, C.S.; BARNETT, R.W.
GEOPOLITICS AND STRATEGY
GLOBAL AFFAIRS, 4(1) (WIN 89), 18-37.
THIS ESSAY DISCUSSES AND EVALUATES THE VARIOUS CONCEPTS
REGARDING HOW INDIVIDUAL NATIONS DO AND SHOULD STRUCTURE
THEIR DEFENSES WAYS IN WHICH THESE CONCEPTS RELATE TO THE
GOAL OF A GLOBAL SECURITY.

03702 GRAY, J.
THE END OF HISTORY - OR OF LIBERALISM?
NATIONAL REVIEW, 61(20) (OCT 89), 33-35.
THIS ARTICLE ASK THE QUESTION, "DOES THE DEATH OF
COMMUNISM MEAN THE END OF HISTORY?" IT EXPLORES THE
VERTIGINOUS PACE AT WHICH THE POLITICAL AND INTELLECTUAL MAP
IS CHANGING IT EXAMINES THE PEOPLES WHO ARE EMERGING FROM
THE SHADOW OF TOTALITARIANISM AND FINDS THEM TO BE
INDIVIDUALS. IT PREDICTS THE END OF LIBERALISM AS IT GOVERNS
U.S. POLICY, AND CONCLUDES THAT HISTORY WILL NOT END WITH
THE PASSING OF COMMUNISM OR LIBERALISM.

03703 GRAY, J.
THE LAST SOCIALIST?
NATIONAL REVIEW, XLI(12) (JUN 89), 27-31.
ALTHOUGH THE POPE'S THOUGHT SUPPORTS NO CLAIM OF MORAL
EQUIVALENCE BETWEEN EAST AND WEST, IT CAN NEVERTHELESS BE
CRITICIZED ON SEVERAL GROUNDS. IT ENDORSES A BASELESS AND
MISLEADING HISTORY OF WESTERN CAPITALISM AND OF THE WEST'S
RELATIONS WITH DEVELOPING NATIONS. IT DOES NOT SUPPORT
MARXIAN NOTIONS OF CLASS STRUGGLE, BUT IT PROPAGATES A
SOCIALIST CARICATURE OF UNFETTERED CAPITALISM, AND IT
ENVISIONS AN ALTERNATIVE TO BOTH CAPITALISM AND SOCIALISM
THAT IS, IN THE END, ONLY A MIRAGE. WHILE THERE ARE ASPECTS
OF WESTERN CAPITALISM THAT CATHOLIC THOUGHT IS BOUND TO
CONDEMN PAPAL TEACHING GOES ASTRAY INSOFAR AS IT PROPOSES
RADICAL ALTERNATIVES TO THE SYSTEM THAT HAS BROUGHT
PROSPERITY AND LIBERTY TO WESTERN EUROPE, NORTH AMERICA, AND,
INCREASINGLY, THE FAR EAST.

03704 GRAYSON, G.W.
MEXICO-BASHING IN WASHINGTON
HEMISPHERE, 1(2) (WIN 89), 45-48.
PRESIDENT CARLOS SALINAS DE GORTARI HAS MOVED TO
STRENGTHEN TIES WITH THE US. BY SO DOING HE MAY PREEMPT US-
LAUNCHED ATTACKS ON MEXICO, WHICH HAVE BECOME SO FREQUENT IN
RECENT YEARS THAT THE NEOLOGISM "MEXICO-BASHING" HAS ENTERED
THE VOCABULARY OF WASHINGTON DECISIONMAKERS. IN ADDITION TO
MEETING WITH PRESIDENT-ELECT GEORGE BUSH, SALINAS HAS
SELECTED GUSTAVO PETRICIOLI AS HIS AMBASSADOR TO THE US. AN
ECONOMIST AND FORMER FINANCE MINISTER WHO HOLDS A MASTER'S
DEGREE FROM YALE, PETRICIOLI POSSESSES THE STATURE TO BRING
COHERENCE, DYNAMISM, AND GREATER EFFECTIVENESS TO MEXICO'S
PREVIOUSLY UNDERSTAFFED, OVERWORKED, AND SOMETIMES
OUTFLANKED EMBASSY.

03705 GRAZ, L.
ARAB HUMAN RIGHTS
MIDDLE EAST INTERNATIONAL, (364) (DEC 89), 18-19.
ALTHOUGH THE CONCEPT OF HUMAN RIGHTS IS NOT WELL
ACCEPTED IN MANY ARAB STATES, THE ARAB ORGANIZATION FOR
HUMAN RIGHTS (AOHR) IS MAKING SOME PROGRESS. TUNISIA BECAME
THE FIRST ARAB NATION TO AGREE TO ALLOW THE AOHR TO ASSEMBLE
IN 1990; PREVIOUS MEETING WERE HELD IN CYPRUS DUE TO THE
FACT THAT NO ARAB CAPTIAL WOULD HAVE THEM. ALTHOUGH THE ROAD
TO ANYTHING RESEMBLING TRUE HUMAN RIGHTS IS DESTINED TO BE
LONG AND TORTUROUS, AOHR LEADERS REMAIN OPTIMISTIC.

03706 GRAZ, L.
IRAN AND IRAQ: THE UNRELEASED PRISONERS
MIDDLE EAST INTERNATIONAL, (359) (SEP 89), 14.
THE ISSUE OF PRISONERS OF THE IRAN-IRAQ WAR HAS YET TO
BE RESOLVED. SIXTY OR SEVENTY THOUSAND IRAQIS REMAIN AS
PRISONERS OF WAR IN IRAN; HALF AS MANY IRANIANS ARE HELD BY
IRAQ. IRAN HAS REJECTED THE INTERNATIONAL RED CROSS
SUGGESTION THAT AN IMMEDIATE EXCHANGE PRISONERS PRECEDE THE
LABORIOUS UN NEGOTIATIONS. EFFORTS TO PERSUADE IRAQ TO BREAK
THE ICE WITH A "GRAND GESTURE" OF UNCONDITIONALLY RELEASING
A FEW THOUSAND PRISONERS HAVE ALSO FAILED.

03707 GRAZ, L.
IRAQ: SIGNS OF RISING CONFIDENCE
MIDDLE EAST INTERNATIONAL, (349) (APR 89), 13-14.
IRAQ IS CHANGING. THE SCEPTICS AGAIN DARE TO TALK, AND
THE BANS ON CONTACTS WITH FOREIGNERS HAVE BEEN RELAXED.
ECONOMIC LIBERALIZATION IS UNDERWAY. IT IS ALMOST
INCONCEIVABLE THAT THE SHOOTING WAR COULD BREAK OUT AGAIN
WITH IRAN, AND THE IRAQIS DO NOT SEEM UNDULY WORRIED ABOUT
SYRIA AT THE MOMENT.

03708 GRAZ, L.
IRAQ'S POST-WAR CHANGES
MIDDLE EAST INTERNATIONAL, (360) (OCT 89), 16-17.
AS THE PROSPECTS OF LASTING PEACE GROW WITH EACH DAY OF
THE CEASE-FIRE, IRAQ NOW FACES SIGNIFICANT CHALLENGES ON
OTHER FRONTS. THE FINAL RESOLUTION OF CONFLICTS WITH IRAN
OVER THE SHATT AL-ARAB WATERWAY AND PRISONERS OF WAR ARE
SIGNIFICANT. BUT SADDAM HUSSEIN ALSO FACES CONSIDERABLE
CHANGE IN THE THREE PILLARS OF HIS POWER: HIS FAMILY, THE
PARTY, AND THE ARMY. AS HIS POWER BASE DIMINISHES, HE IS
CONSIDERING SIGNIFICANT REFORMS SUCH AS THE LEGALIZATION OF
POLITICAL PARTIES, A NEW CONSTITUTION, AND FREEDOM OF THE
PRESS. THESE REFORMS WILL SERVE AS TESTS OF HUSSEIN'S
CONTINUED APPEAL.

03709 GRAZ, L.
RED CROSS KIDNAP VICTIMS
MIDDLE EAST INTERNATIONAL, (364) (DEC 89), 4.
THE COMPLETE SILENCE ON THE WHEREABOUTS AND FATE OF TWO
SWISS RED CROSS WORKERS WHO DISAPPEARED IN LEBANON IS
WORRYING THE INTERNATIONAL COMMITTEE OF THE RED CROSS (ICRC).
THE USUAL LEBANESE TROUBLE-MAKERS HAVE DENIED ANY
CONNECTION WITH THE DISAPPEARANCE; MEMBERS OF THE ICRC WORRY
THAT THE TWO WERE KIDNAPPED BY FREE LANCE KIDNAPPERS WHO
HAVE SINCE FOUND THEM TO BE "TOO HOT TO HANDLE."

03710 GRAZ, L.; LALOR, P.
SILENT DIPLOMACY
MIDDLE EAST INTERNATIONAL, (341) (JAN 89), 9-10.
SWEDEN IS RE-EMERGING AS AN IMPORTANT, SKILLFUL PLAYER
IN THE MIDDLE EAST DIPLOMATIC NEGOTIATIONS. SWEDISH FOREIGN
MINISTER STEN ANDERSSON WAS LARGELY RESPONSIBLE FOR THE
BEHIND-THE-SCENES WORK THAT LED TO THE BEGINNING OF TALKS
BETWEEN THE PLO AND THE AMERICAN ADMINISTRATION.

03711 GRAZ, L.
THE NEW SOVIET DIRECTION IN THE MIDDLE EAST
MIDDLE EAST INTERNATIONAL, (345) (MAR 89), 18-19.
THE AUTHOR REVIEWS THE IMPROVEMENT OF SOVIET-ARAB
RELATIONS, BEGINNING IN 1985, IN EGYPT, OMAN, AND THE UAE.
HE ALSO LOOKS AT THE SOVIET POSITION IN SAUDI ARABIA, SOUTH
YEMEN, SYRIA, AND IRAQ.

03712 GRAZ, L.
THE PLO AND WHO: A VERY HOT POTATO
MIDDLE EAST INTERNATIONAL, (350) (MAY 89), 11-12.
THE WORLD HEALTH ORGANIZATION IS AT THE CENTER OF A
MAJOR DIPLOMATIC BATTLE BETWEEN PALESTINIANS AND AMERICANS,
BECAUSE THE PALESTINIANS HAVE APPLIED FOR WHO MEMBERSHIP.
THE USA HAS THREATENED TO WITHDRAW FROM THE ORGANIZATION AND
WITHHOLD ITS ANNUAL FINANCIAL CONTRIBUTION IF WHO AFFORDS
THE PLO THIS INTERNATIONAL RECOGNITION.

03713 GRAZ, L.
USSR AND IRAN: MOSCOW VOTES FOR RAFSANJANI
MIDDLE EAST INTERNATIONAL, (354) (JUL 89), 4.
THE RECENT VISIT OF ALI AKBAR HASHEMI RAFSANJANI TO
MOSCOW WAS OF VALUE TO IRAN IN GENERAL, BUT MORE TO THE
POLITICAL FUTURE OF RAFSANJANI PERSONALLY. THE RECEPTION
GIVEN, AND PROMISES OF $6 BILLION WORTH OF BILATERAL ACCORDS
WILL HELP RAFSANJANI IN HIS ELECTION CAMPAIGN. IN ORDER TO
KEEP A POST-REVOLUTIONARY IRAN FROM DRIFTING BACK TO THE
WEST, POSSIBLE FUTURE ARMS SALES WERE ALSO HINTED AT BY THE
SOVIETS

03714 GRAZEBROOK, A.W.
DEFENCE REORGANIZATION A BOLD BUT RISKY MOVE
PACIFIC DEFENCE REPORTER, 16(3) (SEP 89), 54-57.
THIS ARTICLE DESCRIBES THE RISKS AND SIGNIFICANT FLAWS
IN THE PROPOSED REORGANIZATION OF THE AUSTRALIAN DEFENSE
FORCES. THE FLAWS INCLUDE INSUFFICIENT PAY STRUCTURES,
"PACKAGES" WHICH ENCOURAGE THE BEST PEOPLE TO LEAVE THE
FORCE, AND CUTS IN SENIOR POSTINGS WHICH MAY BE PERCEIVED AS
REDUCED OPPORTUNITIES FOR POTENTIAL CAREER OFFICERS.

03715 GRAZEBROOK, A.W.
SOME PROGRESS - SOME PROBLEMS
PACIFIC DEFENCE REPORTER, 15(9) (MAR 89), 21-23.
THIS ARTICLE PROVIDES A REVIEW OF AUSTRALIA'S DEFENSE
CAPABILITIES FOCUSING SPECIFICALLY ON NAVAL FORCE STRUCTURE
AND OPERATIONAL MINE COUNTERMEASURES. THE AUTHOR NOTES THAT,
ALTHOUGH STRONG PROGRESS HAS BEEN MADE IN SOME AREAS, THE
ESTABLISHMENT OF THE NAVY'S MINEHUNTING IS BEHIND SCHEDULE
AND THE NAVY FORCES SERIOUS PROBLEMS IN PERSONNEL.

03716 GRAZIANO, L.
UNEMPLOYMENT: THE VOTER'S CONCEPTION OF REALITY
POLITICAL PSYCHOLOGY, 10(1) (MAR 89), 155-168.
THE ARTICLE FOCUSES ON A QUESTION THAT HAS BEEN THE
SUBJECT OF INTENSE POLITICAL DEBATE: SHOULD NATIONAL
ATTENTION FOCUS ON THE "UNEMPLOYMENT RATE" OR THE EMPLOYMENT
RATE" AS AN ACCURATE INDICATOR OF ECONOMIC CONDITIONS IN THE
US? THE ARTICLE FOCUSES NOT ON ECONOMIC OR POLITICAL

PRINCIPLES, BUT ON THE PRINCIPLE OF HUMAN INFORMATION PROCESSING. PUBLIC DEBATE TREATS DATA AND INFORMATION AS BEING THE SAME ELEMENT WHEN FROM AN INFORMATION PROCESSING PERSPECTIVE, THERE IS A SIGNIFICANT DIFFERENCE BETWEEN THE TWO. THE ESSAY ALSO ATTEMPTS TO SHOW HOW THE PRINCIPLES OF HUMAN COGNITION CAN PROVIDE A TOOL FOR EVALUATING ALTERNATIVE UNEMPLOYMENT MEASURES.

03717 GREEN, D.
REASSESSING THE SACRED TRUST: HEALTH IN THE CAMEROONS DURING THE PERIOD OF MANDATE AND TRUSTEESHIP
DISSERTATION ABSTRACTS INTERNATIONAL, 49(10) (APR 89), 3147-A.
THIS STUDY EXAMINES STRUCTURES OF DEPENDENCY, BROADENING THE USUAL ANALYSIS OF ECONOMIC UNDERDEVELOPMENT TO INCLUDE ATTENTION TO THE UNDERDEVELOPMENT OF HEALTH CARE SYSTEMS. A HISTORICAL ANALYSIS OF HEALTH POLICY IN CAMEROON COMPARES THE SYSTEMS CREATED BY THE BRITISH AND FRENCH DURING THE PERIOD OF MANDATE AND TRUSTEESHIP. AS ADMINISTRATING AUTHORITIES THE BRITISH AND FRENCH PROMISED TO ACT AS GUARDIANS OF THE SACRED TRUST, TO FURTHER THE MATERIAL AND MORAL WELL-BEING OF DEPENDENT PEOPLES. REVISIONIST IN APPROACH, THE STUDY RECONSIDERS THE USUAL CLAIMS OF COLONIAL MEDICAL HISTORY AND PLACES ACTIVITIES TAKEN IN THE NAME OF HEALTH IN A MORE DIRECTLY ECONOMIC AND POLITICAL CONTEXT.

03718 GREEN, D.P.
SELF-INTEREST, PUBLIC OPINION, AND MASS POLITICAL BEHAVIOR
DISSERTATION ABSTRACTS INTERNATIONAL, 50(4) (OCT 89), 1077-A.
THE AUTHOR FORMULATES AND TESTS A SERIES OF HYPOTHESES SPECIFYING THE CONDITIONS UNDER WHICH SELF-INTEREST MANIFESTS ITSELF IN POLITICAL CHOICE. HE BEGINS BY REVIEWING THE THEORETICAL ARGUMENTS SURROUNDING THE CLAIM THAT MAN IS BASICALLY AN APPETITIVE EGOIST. THEN HE ELUCIDATES THE TERMS "INTEREST" AND "SELF-INTEREST" IN ORDER TO PROVIDE A CONCEPTUAL BASIS FOR EMPIRICAL RESEARCH. FINALLY, HE USES SURVEY DATA TO ASSESS THE INFLUENCE OF SELF-INTEREST IN MASS OPINION AND BEHAVIOR.

03719 GREEN, J.C.; GUTH, J.L.
THE MISSING LINK: POLITICAL ACTIVISTS AND SUPPORT FOR SCHOOL PRAYER
PUBLIC OPINION QUARTERLY, 53(1) (SPR 89), 41-57.
EXPLANATIONS FOR THE WIDE GAP BETWEEN STRONG PUBLIC SUPPORT FOR SCHOOL PRAYER AND LACK OF SUPPORT IN CONGRESS HAVE FOCUSED ON THE ATTRIBUTES OF THE PUBLIC. HERE ANOTHER IMPORTANT EXPLICAND IS INVESTIGATED: THE CHARACTERISTICS OF POLITICAL ACTIVISTS. ACTIVIST OPINION MORE NEARLY MATCHES CONGRESSIONAL BEHAVIOR ON SCHOOL PRAYER THAN DOES PUBLIC OPINION. WHILE MANY OF THE SAME DEMOGRAPHIC AND RELIGIOUS VARIABLES EXPLAIN SUPPORT FOR SCHOOL PRAYER AMONG ACTIVISTS AND THE PUBLIC, IDEOLOGY APPEARS TO BE MORE IMPORTANT AMONG ACTIVISTS.

03720 GREEN, J.J.; WHITMORE, B.
OUR PAL POL POT?
COMMONWEAL, CXVI(21) (DEC 89), 668-669.
UNTIL RECENTLY, CAMBODIA'S NASTY GUERRILLA WAS APPEARED TO BE INCHING TOWARD AN END. BUT THE FAILURE OF THE CAMBODIAN FACTIONS TO REACH AN AGREEMENT ON WHETHER THE KHMER ROUGE SHOULD PARTICIPATE IN A FUTURE CAMBODIAN GOVERNMENT HAS DERAILED SETTLEMENT EFFORTS. ALTHOUGH THE USA HAD NO DIRECT ROLE IN PRINCE SIHANOUK'S FALL IN 1970, ITS STRONG SUPPORT FOR THE LON NOL REGIME THAT REPLACED HIM SURELY HAD SOMETHING TO DO WITH THE GROWTH OF POL POT'S KHMER ROUGE. AND THE USA DID BOMB CAMBODIA TO BLOCK THE NORTH VIETNAMESE USE OF THE HO CHI MINH TRAIL.

03721 GREEN, L.G.
TERRORISM AND THE COMMUNICATION UTILITIES: A NATIONAL SECURITY CONCERN
AVAILABLE FROM NTIS, NO. AD-A208 668/4/GAR, FEB 23 89, 27.
INCREASING INTERNATIONAL TERRORIST INCIDENTS, WITH AMERICANS AS THE FOCAL POINT, AND THE SEEMINGLY CHANGING IMAGE OF THE SOVIET UNION COULD CREATE AN ATMOSPHERE CONDUCIVE TO DOMESTIC TERRORISM WITHIN THE UNITED STATES. THIS PAPER WILL EXPLORE THE POTENTIAL CAPABILITIES OF TERRORIST GROUPS. THEN IT WILL EXAMINE THREE PAST COMMUNICATION DISASTERS IN AN ATTEMPT TO DETERMINE IF TERRORISM IS A DOMESTIC THREAT, OR SPECIFICALLY IF THE LOSS OF A MAJOR COMMUNICATION FACILITY IS A THREAT TO NATIONAL SECURITY. EACH DISASTER HAPPENED INDEPENDENTLY OF THE OTHERS. THIS STUDY TAKES THE RESULTS OF THESE ACCIDENTS AND POSTULATES THE EFFECTS OF SIMILAR LEVELS OF DAMAGE CAUSED BY A CONCERTED TERRORIST ACTION. ANALYSIS OF PREAND POST RESPONSES PROVIDES A FOUNDATION FOR RECOMMENDATIONS FOR DEALING WITH TERRORIST THREAT. KEYWORDS: COMMUNICATION DISASTERS, TERRORIST CAPABILITIES, CONCERN FOR DOMESTIC TERRORIST THREAT.

03722 GREEN, R.A.; REED, B.J.
OCCUPATIONAL STRESS AMONG PROFESSIONAL LOCAL GOVERNMENT MANAGERS: INTROSPECTIONS AND A PROGNOSIS

INTERNATIONAL JOURNAL OF PUBLIC ADMINISTRATION, 12(2) (1989), 265-303.
THE AREA OF STRESS RESEARCH IS BROAD AND NOT WELL UNDERSTOOD. LITTLE IS KNOWN ABOUT THE WAYS IN WHICH WORKERS COPE WITH JOB RELATED STRESS. THIS ARTICLE EXPLORES THIS ELEMENT OF STRESS RELATED BEHAVIOR FOR LOCAL GOVERNMENT MANAGERS. AMONG THE MOST IMPORTANT FINDINGS ARE THAT LOCAL MANAGERS PERCEIVE THEIR STRESS LEVELS TO BE EQUAL TO OR GREATER THAN MANY OTHER PROFESSIONS OFTEN ASSOCIATED WITH HIGH DEMAND. IT APPEARS THAT LOCAL MANAGERS SEE OTHER PROFESSIONAL MANAGERS AS FACING INCREASED LEVELS OF STRESS OVER THE PAST DECADE. MANAGERS ALSO SEE THEIR STRESS LEVELS AS EQUAL TO OR GREATER THAN THAT OF PREVIOUS OCCUPATIONS OR OCCUPATIONS THEY MIGHT WISH TO HOLD IN THE FUTURE. WHILE AGE AND LENGTH OF EXPERIENCE APPEAR TO HAVE LITTLE ASSOCIATION WITH PERCEIVED LEVELS OF STRESS, INCREASED EDUCATION DOES APPEAR TO REDUCE SUCH PERCEPTIONS.

03723 GREEN, S.
THE MISGUIDED SEARCH FOR CHRISTIAN AMERICAN
CHURCH AND STATE, 42(5) (MAY 89), 9 (105)-12 (108).
OVER THE PAST TWENTY YEARS, A MOVEMENT HAS EMERGED CALLING FOR THE RECOGNITION OF THE USA AS A CHRISTIAN NATION. SPURRED BY THE WRITINGS OF CONSERVATIVE RELIGIOUS ACTIVISTS, THIS MOVEMENT MAINTAINS THAT AMERICA WAS FOUNDED ON CHRISTIANITY AND THAT PUBLIC OFFICIALS SHOULD ACKNOWLEDGE CHRISTIAN PRINCIPLES THROUGH APPROPRIATE LAWS AND PRONOUNCEMENTS. ITS MEMBERS BELIEVE THAT AMERICA CAN NEVER FULFILL ITS SPECIAL CALLING UNTIL THE GOVERNMENT PUBLICLY ADHERES TO THE CHRISTIAN FAITH. A RECENT EXAMPLE OF THIS THINKING CAN BE SEEN IN THE ARIZONA REPUBLICAN PARTY'S ENDORSEMENT OF A RESOLUTION PROCLAIMING THE USA TO BE A CHRISTIAN NATION.

03724 GREEN, W.
PHARMACEUTICAL RISK MANAGEMENT DECISION-MAKING: THE FOOD AND DRUG ADMINISTRATION AND THE CASE OF DEPO-PROVERA
POLICY STUDIES REVIEW, 8(2) (WIN 89), 420-431.
DEPO-PROVERA HAS BEEN A SCIENTIFIC AND POLITICAL BATTLEGROUND FOR MORE THAN 20 YEARS. AT STAKE HAS BEEN THE REPRODUCTIVE HEALTH OF WOMEN, THE MARKETING OF A LONG-ACTING CONTRACEPTIVE BY A MULTINATIONAL CORPORATION, AND INTERNATIONAL FAMILY PLANNING AND POPULATION CONTROL. ALTHOUGH 80 NATIONS HAVE APPROVED ITS USE, THE USFDA HAS NOT BECAUSE THE DRUG IS SUSPECTED TO BE A CARCINOGEN. THIS ARTICLE FOCUSES ON THE SCIENTIFIC AND POLITICAL ASPECTS OF THE DEBATE OVER DEPO-PROVERA; THE SCIENTIFIC BASIS OF THE FDA DECISION; THE AGENCY'S POLICY JUDGMENTS ABOUT THE RISK; AND THE SCIENTIFIC AND POLITICAL SCRUTINY OF THE FDA'S NEW DRUG DECISIONS.

03725 GREENBAUM, F.
EMPIRE AND AUTONOMY: THE AMERICAN AND NETHERLANDISH REVOLUTIONS
INTERNATIONAL SOCIAL SCIENCE REVIEW, 64(1) (WIN 89), 9-19.
IN "EMPIRE AND AUTONOMY: THE AMERICAN AND NETHERLANDISH REVOLUTIONS IN THE WESTERN TRADITION," FRED GREENBAUM CHALLENGES THOSE WHO PORTRAY THE AMERICAN EXPERIENCE AS UNIQUE. HE TRACES THE EVOLUTION OF THE ISSUES AND IDEAS OF THE AMERICAN REVOLUTION BACK INTO THE EARLY MIDDLE AGES: THE LOCUS OF POWER; RESISTANCE TO TYRANNY; THE SOURCE OF GOVERNMENTAL AUTHORITY, LEGITIMATELY DERIVED FROM GOD AND THE "PEOPLE" (A CHANGING TERM), AND BY TRADITION. IN AN EXAMINATION OF THE SIMILARITIES BETWEEN THE AMERICAN AND NETHERLANDISH REVOLUTIONS, THE AUTHOR SHOWS HOW RESISTANCE TO CENTRALIZATION BY LARGELY AUTONOMOUS PROVINCES, JUSTIFIED WITH THESE IDEAS, EVOLVED INTO WARS OF NATIONAL LIBERATION.

03726 GREENBERG, M.; AMER, S.
SELF-INTEREST AND DIRECT LEGISLATION: PUBLIC SUPPORT OF A HAZARDOUS WASTE BOND ISSUE IN NEW JERSEY
POLITICAL GEOGRAPHY QUARTERLY, 8(1) (JAN 89), 67-78.
ABSTRACT. SIXTY-TWO PERCENT OF THE VOTERS SUPPORTED THE $100 MILLION NEW JERSEY HAZARDOUS WASTE BOND ISSUE IN 1981. ANALYSIS SHOWS THAT SUPPORT INCREASED WITH THE PRESENCE OF MINORITY POPULATIONS, SOCIO-ECONOMIC STATUS, URBANIZATION, YOUNG FAMILIES, AND A HISTORY OF SUPPORT FOR THE DEMOCRATIC PARTYVARIABLES THAT PREVIOUSLY HAVE BEEN IDENTIFIED AS ASSOCIATED WITH SUPPORT FOR ENVIRONMENTAL PROGRAMS. IN ADDITION, COMMUNITIES CLOSER TO HAZARDOUS WASTE SITES STRONGLY SUPPORTED THE BOND ISSUE. NEARLY ALL OF THESE COMMUNITIES ALSO STOOD TO BENEFIT FROM A COMPANION WATER SUPPLY BOND ISSUE. OPPOSITION TO THE BOND ISSUE WAS CENTERED IN SOUTHWEST AND NORTHWEST NEW JERSEY--THAT IS, IN RURAL, RELATIVELY POOR, AND WHITE COMMUNITIES FAR FROM HAZARDOUS WASTE SITES, AND FEARFUL OF LOSING ABUNDANT LOCAL WATER SUPPLIES BECAUSE OF THE WATER BOND ISSUE. THUS, WHILE THE STRONG GENERAL STATEWIDE SUPPORT SUGGESTS THE VOTE WAS A SYMBOL FOR A CLEANER ENVIRONMENT, INTRA-STATE VARIATIONS SUGGEST THAT MOST VOTERS CONSIDERED THEIR PERSONAL BENEFITS AND COSTS BEFORE CASTING BALLOTS.

03727 GREENBERG, M.R.
BLACK MALE CANCER AND AMERICAN URBAN HEALTH POLICY

JOURNAL OF URBAN AFFAIRS, 11(2) (1989), 113-130.
BEFORE RESIGNING AS SECRETARY OF HEALTH AND HUMAN
SERVICES, MARGARET HECKLER TOUCHED OFF A POLITICAL
CONTROVERSY BY RELEASING A REPORT DOCUMENTING THE POOR
QUALITY OF MINORITY HEALTH IN THE UNITED STATES. SECRETARY
HECKLER STATED THAT PUBLIC HEALTH MEASURES WOULD EVENTUALLY
CLOSE THE MINORITY/WHITE HEALTH GAP. BUT CRITICS CONTEND
THAT THE REAGAN ADMINISTRATION'S NEGLECT OF POVERTY, HOUSING,
AND HEALTH SERVICES PROGRAMS HAVE MADE SUCH IMPROVEMENTS
IMPOSSIBLE IN THE FORESEEABLE FUTURE. USING BLACK MALE
CANCER AS A CASE STUDY, THIS ARTICLE EXPLORES THE FACTORS
THAT CONTRIBUTE TO MINORITY DISEASE AND DISCUSSES THE PUBLIC
POLICY RESPONSE.

03728 GREENBLATT, M.
UNION OFFICIALS AND THE LABOR BILL OF RIGHTS
FORDHAM LAW REVIEW, LVII(4) (MAR 89), 601-616.
THIS ARTICLE ATTEMPTS TO CLARIFY THE ANALYSIS FOR
DETERMINING WHETHER THE LABOR-MANAGEMENT RECORDING AND
DISCLOSURE ACT OF 1959 (THE LMRDA) PROTECTS A UNION OFFICIAL.
THE AUTHOR DISCUSSES THE LEGISLATIVE HISTORY OF THE LMRDA,
SHOWING CONGRESSIONAL INTENT TO PROMOTE UNION DEMOCRACY
WHILE MINIMIZING THE LEGISLATION'S IMPACT UPON THE UNION'S
INTERNAL GOVERNANCE. THE AUTHOR CONCLUDES THAT TO FURTHER
THE GOALS OF THE LMRDA, COURTS SHOULD CAREFULLY EXAMINE THE
FACTS OF THE PARTICULAR CASE, AND GRANT RELIEF TO THOSE
UNION OFFICIALS, EITHER APPOINTED OR ELECTED, WHO WERE
REMOVED FROM OFFICE AS PART OF A DELIBERATE ATTEMPT TO
SUPPRESS DISSENTS

03729 GREENE, D.D.
A ZONE OF PEACE OR A BALANCE OF POWER IN THE INDIAN OCEAN?
(VOLUMES I AND II)
DISSERTATION ABSTRACTS INTERNATIONAL, 50(4) (OCT 89),
1082-A.
THE AUTHOR EXAMINES THE PROPOSED INDIAN OCEAN ZONE OF
PEACE FROM THREE PERSPECTIVES: INTERNATIONAL ORGANIZATION,
INTERNATIONAL LAW, AND REGIONAL STRATEGIC ISSUES. THE
CENTRAL ISSUE IS WHETHER A ZONE-OF-PEACE REGIME OR A BALANCE
OF POWER IS THE MOST APPROPRIATE AND MOST LIKELY VEHICLE FOR
PEACE IN THE INDIAN OCEAN REGION.

03730 GREENE, F.
THE UNITED STATES AND AISA IN 1988: A CHANGING ENVIRONMENT
ASIAN SURVEY, XXIX(1) (JAN 89), 89-100.
IN MAKING HIS LAST "GRAND TOUR" OF EAST ASIA IN 1988, US
SECRETARY OF STATE GEORGE SHUTLZ PROCLAIMED THE YEAR TO BE A
VERY ENCOURAGING ONE. THE SOVIET WITHDRAWAL FROM AFGHANISTAN,
THE VIETNAMESE WITHDRAWAL FROM CAMBODIA, THE SOLDIFICATION
OF DEMOCRACY IN SOUTH KOREA AND THE PHILIPPINES, AND THE
GENERAL ECONOMIC GROWTH OF THE REGION WERE ALL GOOD SIGNS.
SHULTZ EMPHASIZED THE PIVOTAL ROLE THAT THE US HAS PLAYED IN
THESE DEVELOPMENTS. HOWEVER, SOME DISCONCERTING DEVELOPMENT
LOOM ON THE HORIZON. REALTIONS WITH KOREA WERE SIGNIFICANTLY
STRAINED, RELATIONS WITH PAKISTAN REMAIN UNCERTAIN, AND THE
ENTIRE REGION IS ADOPTING THE ATTITUDE THAT THE US IS A
NATION IN DECLINE AND ACTING ACCORDINGLY.

03731 GREENE, J.
THE DEBT PROBLEM OF SUB-SAHARAN AFRICA
FINANCE AND DEVELOPMENT, 26(2) (JUN 89), 9-12.
THE ARTICLE REVIEWS THE DEBT SITUATION AND ECONOMIC
PERFORMANCE OF SUB-SAHARAN AFRICAN COUNTRIES AND ANALYZES A
NUMBER OF PROPOSALS FOR REDUCING THEIR DEBT-SERVICE
OBLIGATIONS. IT CONCENTRATES ON DEBT TO GOVERNMENTS AND
INSTITUTIONS AND DOES NOT DISCUSS DEVELOPMENTS AND PROPOSALS
AFFECTING THE COMMERCIAL BANK DEBT OF THE NATIONS.

03732 GREENE, J.
THEODORE ROOSEVELT AND THE BARNES LIBEL CASE: A REAPPRAISAL
PRESIDENTIAL STUDIES QUARTERLY, XIX(1) (WIN 89), 95-106.
AN IMPORTANT EVENT IN THE POLITICAL LIFE OF THEODORE
ROOSEVELT WAS THE 1915 BARNES-ROOSEVELT LIBEL TRIAL IN WHICH
ROOSEVELT WAS ACQUITTED OF THE CHARGES OF LIBEL RESULTING
FROM HIS STATEMENT THAT BARNES WAS A POLITICAL BOSS IN NEW
YORK. THE PURPOSE OF THE ESSAY IS TO REEVALUATE THE EVENTS
LEADING UP TO THE TRIAL, THE REASONS FOR THE CHIEF
COMBATANTS ENTERING INTO THIS PARTICULAR FIGHT, AND SOME OF
THE MORE PERTINENT EVIDENCE PRESENTED IN COURT, SO AS TO
DRAW SEVERAL CONCLUSIONS REGARDING THE CAREER OF BOTH THESE
INFLUENTIAL REPUBLICAN LEADERS. THE TRIAL WAS A WATERSHED
WHICH MARKED THE END OF BARNES'S INFLUENCE IN POLITICS AND A
REJUVENATION OF ROOSEVELT'S INFLUENCE.

03733 GREENE, P.
RACE AFTER WASHINGTON
COMMONWEAL, CXVI(7) (APR 89), 199-200.
THOUGH SOME ANALYSIS DATE THE DECLINE OF BLACK POLITICAL
POWER IN CHICAGO TO ACTING MAYOR EUGENE SAWYER'S DEFEAT BY
STATE'S ATTORNEY RICHARD M. DALEY IN THE MAYORAL PRIMARY, IT
ACTUALLY BEGAN THE VERY NIGHT SAWYER WAS CATAPULTED INTO THE
MAYOR'S SEAT, DECEMBER 1-2, 1987. ON THAT LONG NIGHT, THE
CHICAGO CITY COUNCIL ASSEMBLED FOR NEARLY TWELVE HOURS IN
THE MOST EXTRAORDINARY SESSION IN ITS HISTORY TO CHOOSE A

SUCCESSOR TO THE LATE HAROLD WASHINGTON, LAID TO REST BARELY
TWENTY-FOUR HOURS EARLIER.

03734 GREENE, R.L.
VARIATIONS ON A THEME: POLICY MAKING IN THE UNITED STATES
AND THE SOVIET UNION
DISSERTATION ABSTRACTS INTERNATIONAL, 48(12) (JUN 88),
3187-A.
USING THE AREA OF ENVIRONMENTAL POLLUTION AS A CASE
STUDY, THE DISSERTATION COMPARES THE SOVIET UNION'S DECISION
TO LIMIT INDUSTRIAL DEVELOPMENT ON LAKE BAIKAL WITH OTHER
SOVIET CASE STUDIES, WITH ACCEPTED APPROACHES USED TO
DESCRIBE THE SOVIET POLICY PROCESS, AND WITH US CASE STUDIES
INCLUDING THE PROJECT TO CLEAN UP LAKE FIRE. GENERALIZATIONS
ABOUT THE POLICY PROCESS ARE SUGGESTED AND SIMILARITIES
BETWEEN THE US AND SOVIET SYSTEMS ARE NOTED.

03735 GREENE,F.
"EUROSTYLE" IS IN!
EUROPE, (292) (DEC 89), 36-37.
AMERICANS HAVE HAD A FASCINATION WITH EUROPEAN,
"EUROSTYLE", DESIGNS FOR MOST OF THE EIGHTIES. SOME OF THIS
SUCESS HAS BEEN ATTRIBUTED TO THE FACT THAT EUROPEAN
MANUFACTURERS UNDERSTAND THE IMPORTANCE OF DESIGN AS PART OF
TOTAL PRODUCT DEVELOPMENT, AND GIVE DESIGNERS GREATER
LATITUDE TO BE CREATIVE AND ARTISTIC. EUROSTYLE'S CONTINUING
SUCESS HAS ALSO BEEN ATRIBUTED TO THE GROWING QUALITY
CONSCIOUSNESS ON THE PART OF THE AMERICAN CONSUMER. YOUNG
AMERICANS IN PARTICULAR HAVE DEVELOPED MORE CONFIDENCE IN
THEIR OWN TASTE AS THEY BECOME BETTER EDUCATED AND MORE
TRAVELED.

03736 GREENFIELD, R.
ANOTHER SENIOR SOMALI DIPLOMAT DEFECTS
NEW AFRICAN, (260) (MAY 89), 13.
ONLY A FEW SHORT WEEKS AFTER THE DEFECTION OF THE
COUNSELLOR AND DEPUTY HEAD OF THE MISSION OF THE SOMALI
DEMOCRATIC REPUBLIC OF THE UNITED NATIONS IN GENEVA, HIS
SUCCESSOR AS COUNSELLOR AND CHARGE D'AFFAIRES ALSO SOUGHT
POLITICAL ASYLUM IN THE WEST. THE NEW COUNSELLOR CITED THE
SOMALIAN GOVERNMENT'S DEPLORABLE RECORD ON HUMAN RIGHTS AS
HIS MOTIVATION FOR RESIGNING.

03737 GREENFIELD, R.
BARRE'S UNHOLY ALLIANCE
AFRICA REPORT, 34(2) (MAR 89), 65-68.
THE SOMALIAN GOVERNMENT, INCREASINGLY ISOLATED FROM ITS
TRADITIONAL ALLIES AND UNDER THREAT FROM GUERRILLAS OF THE
SOMALI NATIONAL MOVEMENT, HAS UNLEASHED HARSH REPRESSION
AGAINST THOSE SUSPECTED OF DISLOYALTY. IT IS ALSO TURNING TO
SOME UNLIKELY SOURCES FOR WEAPONS AND SUPPORT.

03738 GREENFIELD, R.
SOMALI PROTEST IN LONDON
NEW AFRICAN, (JAN 88), 23.
THIS ARTICLE REPORTS ON A SOMALI DEMONSTRATION IN LONDON,
CALLING FOR THE RESTORATION OF DEMOCRACY, JUSTICE, AND
CONSENSUS POLITICS IN SOMALIA. THE TURMOIL TAKING PLACE IN
SOMALIA IS DESCRIBED.

03739 GREENFIELD, R.
SOMALIA SLIDES INTO CHAOS
NEW AFRICAN, (266) (NOV 89), 10-11.
THIS ARTICLE EXAMINES THE PRESENT SITUATION IN SOMALIA
AS SOMALI EMBASSIES OVERSEAS HAVE RUN OUT OF MONEY TO PAY
THEIR STAFF OR OUTSTANDING BILLS; THE GOVERNMENT HAS NO
FUNDS TO MAKE ARMS PURCHASES; RIOTS ARE IN MOGADISHU, CLANS
ARE REVOLTING AND THOUSANDS ARE DYING. IT CONCLUDES THAT
SOMALIA IS SLIDING TOWARDS CHAOS.

03740 GREENLAND, H.
THE GREENS AND THEIR POLITICAL PROBLEMS
ARENA, (89) (SUM 89), 23-25.
ATTEMPTS TO FORM GREEN PARTIES IN AUSTRALIA IS MEETING
CONSIDERABLE RESISTANCE FROM AN UNLIKELY SOURCE: THE LEADERS
OF MAINSTREAM ENVIRONMENTAL GROUPS. THE MAINSTREAM-DOMINATED
GREEN ELECTORAL NETWORK (GEN) HAS REPEATEDLY CRITICIZED THE
GREEN ALLIANCE. THE RESPONSE OF THE GREEN ALLIANCE HAS, AS
OF YET, BEEN PASSIVE; ALLIANCE LEADERS HAVE CONTINUALLY
INVITED THE GEN TO JOIN THE ALLIANCE IN COMMON CAUSES AND
ACTIVITIES.

03741 GREENMAN, R.
REFLECTIONS ON 1968 AND BEYOND
NEW POLITICS, 11(2) (WIN 89), 26-32.
THE REAL SHORTCOMING OF THE MOVEMENTS OF THE '60S WAS
NOT THAT THEY FAILED TO ANNIHILATE A VASTLY SUPERIOR
ANTAGONIST, BUT THAT THEY FAILED TO UNDERSTAND, CONSOLIDATE,
AND BUILD ON SOME REAL AND IMPRESSIVE VICTORIES. FOR THE
TRAGEDY HAS THAT FAR FROM BUILDING ON WHAT CAN BE SEEN
HISTORICALLY AS A VICTORY FOR SPONTANEOUS DIRECT ACTION--
THWARTING THE PLANS OF THE NIXON--KISSINGER ADMINISTRATION
TO EXPAND THE WAR IN SOUTHEAST ASIA AND ERADICATE THE
MILITANT BLACK LEADERSHIP--THE MOVEMENT RETREATED INTO

QUIETISM AND DESPAIR. UNACCUSTOMED TO MEASURING TACTICAL VICTORIES IN TERMS OF A LONG RANGE REVOLUTIONARY STRATEGY, THEY MISTOOK PARTIAL GAINS FOR DEFEAT.

03742 GREER, S.
URBANISM AND URBANITY: CITIES IN AN URBAN-DOMINATED SOCIETY
URBAN AFFAIRS QUARTERLY, 24(3) (MAR 89), 341-352.
THE AUTHOR REVIEWS THE FUNCTIONS OF CITIES IN SOCIETIES, INCLUDING SPECIALIZED FUNCTIONS AND THE INTEGRATION OF FUNCTIONS. CITIES ARE SEEN AS MARKETPLACES OF IDEAS, ATTITUDES, ARTIFACTS, AND INNOVATION. THEY ARE THE DRIVING WHEELS OF GREAT CULTURES. THE MODERN CITY HAS EMERGED AS A VAST COLLECTION OF SMALL SUBURBAN TOWNS AROUND A SMALL URBAN CENTER THAT IS LARGELY DESERTED BY NIGHT. WHAT WILL BE THE CONSEQUENCE OF THE LOSS OF THE CITY AS IT ONCE WAS? SOME OBSERVERS FORESEE AN ISOLATION OF FUNCTIONS AND ELITES, A GROWING SOCIAL DISTANCE AMONG THEM, AND A SITUATION CONDUCIVE TO THE FRAGMENTATION OF CULTURE.

03743 GREGOIRE, C.; KANEM, N.
THE CARIBS OF DOMINICA: LAND RIGHTS AND ETHNIC CONSCIOUSNESS
CULTURAL SURVIVAL QUARTERLY, 13(3) (1989), 52-55.
THE 1980'S HAVE WITNESSED A NEW POLITICAL PHENOMENON, CALLED "CARIBISM," IN THE CARIB TERRITORY OF DOMINICA. IT POSITS THAT THE POLARIZATION OF THE CARIB PEOPLE ALONG PARTY LINES IS THE ANTITHESIS OF CARIB UNITY AND THAT WHAT IS NEEDED IS A CARIB PEOPLES' POLITICAL ORGANIZATION THAT WOULD ENLIST THE SUPPORT OF ALL OF THEM IN SECURING A SEAT IN PARLIAMENT. THEN THE CARIB ORGANIZATION COULD BARGAIN WITH THE PARTY THAT WINS A MAJORITY IN PARLIAMENT. CARIBISM ALSO CALLS FOR GREATER AUTONOMY IN THE ADMINISTRATION OF CARIB TERRITORY AFFAIRS, CULTURAL RE-EDUCATION IN THE SCHOOLS, ESTABLISHING INTERNATIONAL LINKAGES TO ASSIST IN THE DEVELOPMENT OF THE TERRITORY, AGRICULTURAL DIVERSIFICATION, REVITALIZATION OF THE CARIB HERITAGE, AND RESOLUTION OF LONGSTANDING BOUNDARY DISPUTES.

03744 GREGOR, J.A.
IN THE SHADOW OF GIANTS: THE MAJOR POWERS AND THE SECURITY OF SOUTHEAST ASIA
HOOVER INSTITUTION PRESS, STANFORD, CA, 1989, 210.
THIS VOLUME SURVEYS THE ECONOMIC, POLITICAL, AND SECURITY SITUATION IN SOUTHEAST ASIA AND HOW THE CIRCUMSTANCES THERE BEAR ON THE INTERESTS OF THE USA, THE USSR, AND THE PEOPLE'S REPUBLIC OF CHINA. THE AUTHOR ADDRESSES THE DANGERS OF INSTABILITY IN THE PHILIPPINES AND OF AN INCREASED SOVIET MILITARY PRESENCE IN THE REGION.

03745 GREGORY, P.R.
SOVIET BUREAUCRATIC BEHAVIOUR: KHOZYAISTUENNIKI AND APPARATCHIKI
SOVIET STUDIES, 61(4) (OCT 89), 511-525.
GORBACHEV'S PERESTROIKA PROGRAM CALLS FOR DRAMATIC CHANGES IN THE SOVIET ECONOMIC BUREAUCRACY. ITS SIZE IS TO BE CUT; IT IS TO INTRUDE LESS IN ENTERPRISE AFFAIRS; AND BUREAUCRATIC ACTIONS ARE TO BE JUDGED MORE ON THE BASIS OF FINAL RESULTS AS ECONOMIC BUREAUCRATS INTERVENE LESS IN ENTERPRISE AFFAIRS, NORMS AND RULES OF CONDUCT SET BY THE BUREAUCRACY ARE TO PLAY A MORE IMPORTANT ROLE. THE CONVENTIONAL WISDOM SUGGESTS THAT OPPOSITION FROM THE ECONOMIC BUREAUCRACY REPRESENTS THE MAJOR THREAT TO THE SUCCESS OF PERESTROIKA. THE EVIDENCE PRESENTED IN THIS PAPER SUGGESTS THAT THE BUREAUCRATIC ATTITUDE TOWARDS REFORM IS NOT UNIFORM, BUT VARIES ACCORDING TO BUREAUCRATIC TYPE.

03746 GREIDER,W.
POLITICS, CENTRAL BANKING, AND ECONOMIC ORDER
CRITICAL REVIEW, 3(3) (SUM 89), 488-504.
THIS ARTICLE PURSUES THE THEME THAT THE FEDERAL RESERVE SYSTEM PROMOTES THE INTERESTS OF WALL STREET--BANKS AND BONDHOLDERS -- OVER THOSE OF MAIN STREET-THE REST OF SOCIETY. THE WEALTH OF FASCINATING OBSERVATIONS ARE, UNFORTUNATELY, ORGANIZED BY A 1950S-STYLE KEYNESIANISM AND A FAITH IN UNLIMITED, MAJORITARIAN DEMOCRACY. NEITHER OF THESE BELIEFS ARE AT ALL ADEQUATE FOR REMEDYING THE DEFICIENCIES OF POLITICAL CONTROL OF THE MONEY SUPPLY, WHICH IS THE REAL PROBLEM.

03747 GREILSAMMER, L.
EUROPEAN POLITICAL COOPERATION: A EUROPEAN FOREIGN POLICY?
JERUSALEM JOURNAL OF INTERNATIONAL RELATIONS, 11(4) (DEC 89), 52-78.
SINCE THE BEGINNING OF THE 1970S, THE MEMBER STATES OF THE EUROPEAN COMMUNITY HAVE SOUGHT TO FORMULATE A COMMON FOREIGN POLICY -- A PROCESS KNOWN AS EUROPEAN POLITICAL COOPERATION. THIS ARTICLE ASSESSES THE RECORD SO FAR, AND FINDS THAT EPC HAS BEEN HAMPERED BY A LACK OF CLARITY REGARDING ITS BASIC PURPOSE. IT EXPLORES THE EPC AS A NEW PHENONENON; THE INSTITUTIONS OF COOPERATION IN FOREIGN POLICY; AND ANALYZES THE PROCESS. IT OFFERS A BALANCE SHEET OF 20 YEARS OF EUROPEAN COOPERATION IN FOREIGN POLICY. IT CONCLUDES WITH A CONSIDERATION OF MAJOR ISSUES OF AN EC FOREIGN POLICY.

03748 GREIPOSA, S.
UNION IN-FIGHTING
NEW AFRICAN, (FEB 88), 26.
THIS ARTICLE REPORTS ON THE INCREASING GOVERNMENT PRESSURE ON ZAMBIA'S TRADE UNIONS. THE LOSS OF FREDERICK CHILUBA AS THE NUBEGW LEADER IS EXAMINED IN RELATION TO REASONS WHY HE LOST HIS POSTION AND WHAT FUTURE THE UNIONS HAVE IN ZAMBIA. THE INTRIGUE IS EXAMINED.

03749 GRENIER, R.
HAVE TYPEWRITER, WILL RUN
NATIONAL REVIEW, XLI(5) (MAR 89), 33-34.
HER ECONOMY RUINED BY SOCIALISM AND FEUDALISM, PERU HAS A WHITE KNIGHT ON THE HORIZON: AUTHOR AND PRESIDENTIAL CANDIDATE MARIO VARGAS LLOSA. THE ULTIMATE CHOICE FOR PERU IS STRAIGHTFORWARD, SAYS THE NEW-BORN POLITICIAN IN A NO-NONSENSE MOOD: DEMOCRACY OR COMMUNISM. BUT HE MUST FIRST WIN AN ELECTION IN THE ROUGH AND TUMBLE OF DAILY POLITICS, AFTER WHICH THE HARD PART WILL BEGIN. VARGAS LLOSA IS UNDER NO ILLUSIONS. WITH PERU IN A STATE OF ECONOMIC, POLITICAL, AND MILITARY CHAOS, HE WILL HAVE HIS WORK CUT OUT FOR HIM. BUT HE HAS A MISSION. "THE TRULY ORIGINAL, REVOLUTIONARY THING FOR LATIN AMERICA," HE SAYS WITH CONVICTION, "IS THE DEMOCRATIC OPTION."

03750 GRENIER, R.
THE ALBANIA OF THE CARIBBEAN
NATIONAL REVIEW, XLI(8) (MAY 89), 41-43.
CASTRO'S VERSION OF COMMUNISM HAS MADE CUBA A BEGGAR NATION, DESTITUTE AND DEPENDENT ON MOSCOW FOR AID THAT BARELY KEEPS THE ECONOMY AFLOAT. SINCE THE USSR HAS EMBRACED GLASNOST AND PERESTROIKA, CUBA'S IDEOLOGICAL LINK WITH MOSCOW IS WEAKER, BECAUSE CASTRO IS FIGHTING BOTH GREATER FREEDOM AND SOVIET-STYLE ECONOMIC REFORMS, CLINGING FERVENTLY TO COMMUNIST MORAL INCENTIVES AND PURITY OF DOCTRINES.

03751 GRENIER, R.
WINTER IN MOSCOW: GORBACHEV'S LONG JOURNEY
NATIONAL REVIEW, 61(25) (DEC 89), 27-29.
THIS ARTICLE EXAMINES SOVIET REFORM. IS ASKS: IS SOVIET REFORM MOVING TOO FAST OR NOT FAST ENOUGH? BOTH, SAY THOSE WHO, TOO THEIR SORROW, KNOW THE SITUATION BEST, IT SUGGEST THAT THE FAILURE OF PERESTROIKA HAS LAID THE STICKS OF POLITICAL DYNAMITE; AND THAT THE EFFICIENCY OF GLASTNOST MAY LIGHT THE FUSE. IT REPORTS ON A COUNTRY NEARING ECONOMIC COLLAPSE, WITH LEVELERS, REFORMERS, DEMOCRATS, AUTHORITARIANS ETC, ALL POISED TO BATTLE AMONG THE RUINS.

03752 GRENZKE, J.
CANDIDATE ATTRIBUTES AND PAC CONTRIBUTIONS
WESTERN POLITICAL QUARTERLY, 42(2) (JUN 89), 245-264.
THIS ARTICLE MAKES THREE CONTRIBUTIONS TO THE DEBATE ABOUT HOW PACS DECIDE TO ALLOCATE THEIR MONEY. FIRST, IT SUGGESTS THAT SOME OF THE CONTROVERSY ABOUT THE IMPORTANCE OF MEMBER POWER TO PAC CONTRIBUTIONS MAY RESULT FROM WEAK MEASURES OF POWER. THE CONCEPT OF POWER USED HERE IS BASED UPON INFORMATION COLLECTED FROM EXTENSIVE INTERVIEWS WITH PAC OFFICIALS, AND THE INDEX THAT HAS BEEN DEVELOPED IS A CLOSER APPROXIMATION OF EACH PAC'S EVALUATION OF WHO HAS POWER. SECOND, INTERVIEWS AND STATISTICAL DATA ESTABLISH THAT MEMBER POWER IS IMPORTANT TO ALMOST ALL OF THE ORGANIZATIONS INVESTIGATED, ALONG WITH CANDIDATE ISSUE POSITIONS, ELECTORAL MARGINALITY, PERSONAL FRIENDSHIPS BETWEEN PAC OFFICIALS AND INCUMBENTS, AND INCUMBENT AGGRESSIVENESS IN PURSUING PAC CONTRIBUTIONS. THIRD, THE DECISIONS OF 120 PACS AFFILIATED WITH 10 ORGANIZATIONS FROM 1975 TO 1982 ARE EXAMINED.

03753 GRENZKE, J.M.
PACS AND THE CONGRESSIONAL SUPERMARKET: THE CURRENCY IS COMPLEX
AMERICAN JOURNAL OF POLITICAL SCIENCE, 33(1) (FEB 89), 1-24.
ALTHOUGH PACS ATTEMPT TO INFLUENCE THE LEGISLATIVE PROCESS WITH CONTRIBUTIONS, THIS RESEARCH FINDS LITTLE EVIDENCE THAT THE CONTRIBUTIONS OF 120 PACS AFFILIATED WITH 10 ORGANIZATIONS AFFECTED THE VOTING PATTERNS OF THE HOUSE MEMBERS WHO SERVED CONTINUOUSLY FROM 1975 TO 1982. IN THE FEW CASES IN WHICH A RELATIONSHIP BETWEEN CONTRIBUTIONS AND A MEMBER'S VOTES IS ESTABLISHED, THE ANALYSIS INDICATES THAT CONTRIBUTIONS ARE A SURROGATE MEASURE OF A MORE IMPORTANT AND LARGER PACKAGE OF SUPPORT FOR THE MEMBER FROM THE INTEREST GROUPS. TWO-STAGE LEAST SQUARES REGRESSION MODELS ARE USED TO TEST THE RELATIONSHIP BETWEEN PAC CONTRIBUTIONS AND A MEMBER'S VOTES, CONTROLLING FOR THE INCUMBENT'S IDEOLOGY AND PARTY, AND THE POLITICAL LEANING OF THE DISTRICT. INTERVIEWS WITH PAC OFFICIALS SUPPLEMENT THE STATISTICAL ANALYSIS.

03754 GRESH, A.
PALESTINIAN COMMUNISTS AND THE INTIFADAH
MIDDLE EAST REPORT, 19(157) (MAR 89), 34-36.

THE AUTHOR DISCUSSES THE HISTORY OF THE PALESTINIAN
COMMUNIST PARTY AND ITS ROLE IN THE INTIFADA.

03755 GRESH, A.
THE FREE OFFICERS AND THE COMRADES: THE SUDANESE COMMUNIST
PARTY AND NIMEIRI FACE-TO-FACE, 1969-1971
INTERNATIONAL JOURNAL OF MIDDLE EAST STUDIES, 21(3) (AUG
89), 393-409.
BY LAYING CLAIM TO A LEADING ROLE FOR THE COMMUNIST
PARTY AND THE WORKING CLASS IN THE 1960'S, THE SUDANESE
COMMUNISTS RAISED THE QUESTION OF POLITICAL LEADERSHIP FOR
THE FIRST TIME. THE SELF-ASSURANCE OF THE COMMUNIST PARTY
AND ITS MOST PRESTIGIOUS LEADER, ABD AL-KHALIQ MAHJUB, GAVE
RISE TO MANY MISUNDERSTANDINGS WITHIN THE PARTY ITSELF AND
WITHIN THE INTERNATIONAL COMMUNIST MOVEMENT, ESPECIALLY IN
THE SOVIET UNION. THE 26 MONTHS OF SUDAN'S POLITICAL HISTORY
ENDING WITH AN ABORTIVE COUP ATTEMPT BY THE EXTREME LEFT IN
JULY 1971 PROVIDE AN INSIGHT INTO THE ESSENTIAL ELEMENTS OF
COMMUNIST STRATEGY IN THE MIDDLE EAST, INCLUDING THAT OF THE
SOVIET UNION.

03756 GRESS, D.
DEMYSTIFYING THE FRENCH REVOLUTION
COMMENTARY, 88(1) (JUL 89), 42-49.
THE LAST TWENTY YEARS HAVE WITNESSED A RADICAL REVISION
OF THE FORMERLY DOMINANT NEWS OF THE FRENCH REVOLUTION. THIS
ARTICLE SHOWS THAT WHAT HAS HAPPENED IN FRENCH POLITICS IN
THE 1970'S AND 1980'S IS THAT THE VERY POLARIZATION
ENGENDERED BY THE REVOLUTION HAS ITSELF VANISHED. THE 1980'S
HAVE SEEN THE EMERGENCE OF AN UNPRECEDENTED CONSENSUS
SPANNING SOCIALISTS, LIBERALS, AND NEO-GAULLISTS. THESE
CIRCUMSTANCES HAVE CONTRIBUTED TO THE DRAMATIC REAPPRAISAL
OF EARLIER ORTHODOXY ABOUT THE REVOLUTION.

03757 GRETTON, M.P.
THE AMERICAN MARITIME STRATEGY: EUROPEAN PERSPECTIVES AND
IMPLICATIONS
RUSI JOURNAL, 134(1) (SPR 89), 19-26.
DURING THE REAGAN ADMINISTRATION, THE UNITED STATES
DEVELOPED A MARITIME STRATEGY IN THE CONTEXT OF NATIONAL AND
NATO SECURITY POLICIES. IT HAS THREE MAIN ELEMENTS:
PEACETIME PRESENCE, CRISIS RESPONSE, AND WAR FIGHTING. IT IS
DIVIDED INTO THREE PHASES: DETERRENCE, SEIZING THE
INITIATIVE, AND CARRYING THE FIGHT TO THE ENEMY.

03758 GREWLICH, K.W.
ITU - TELECOMMUNICATIONS
AUSSEN POLITIK, 40(4) (1989), 349-359.
THE AIM OF THIS ARTICLE IS TO DISCUSS SEVERAL ISSUES
CENTRAL TO INTERNATIONAL TELECOMMUNICATIONS POLICY; TO
DESCRIBE THE SOLUTIONS PROPOSED BY THE ITU; AND TO EVALUATE
THE EFFECTIVENESS OF THESE SOLUTIONS. THE ARTICLE FOCUSES ON
POLITICAL AND ECONOMIC ISSUES OF CENTRAL IMPORTANCE TO THE
TRANSNATIONAL DIMENSION OF THE DEVELOPING INFORMATION
ECONOMY, RATHER THAN ON TECHNICAL MATTERS.

03759 GREWLICH, K.W.
THE STRUGGLE FOR GLOBAL "TELEPRESENCE"
AUSSEN POLITIK, 40(2) (1989), 160-172.
A TREMENDOUS STRUGGLE FOR TELEVISION NORMS AND MARKETS
NOW UNDER WAY WILL MARK THE LAST DECADE OF THIS CENTURY.
HDTV IS THE INTERNATIONAL ACRONYM FOR HIGH DEFINITION
TELEVISION, WHICH IS TO PROVIDE SO-CALLED TELEPRESENCE. AT
STAKE ARE TECHNOLOGY, CONTENT AND COMMERCE WITH AN ESTIMATED
MARKET VOLUME OF 500 MILLIARD DEUTSCHE MARKS, INCLUDING THE
REPLACEMENT OF APPROXIMATELY 600 MILLION TELEVISION SETS IN
THE COMING DECADE. CURRENT DISCUSSIONS AND NEGOTIATIONS HAVE
DRAWN ATTENTION TO A EUROPEAN AUDIOVISUAL DIMENSION AND THE
POSSIBILITIES AFFORDED BY THE EUROPEAN INTERNAL MARKET IN
1992. THE COMMUNITY INTENDS TO LEAVE ITSELF OPEN, BUT NOT TO
LET ITSELF BE FLOODED FROM THE OUTSIDE; THE EUROPEANS WANT
TO BE COMPETITIVE ON THE WORLD MEDIA SCENE. RELEVANT
STRATEGIC CONSIDERATIONS AND INITIATIVES ARE ALREADY UNDER
WAY. THEY SHOULD BE RAPIDLY DEVELOPED FURTHER.

03760 GRIER, K.
ON THE EXISTENCE OF A POLITICAL MONETARY CYCLE
AMERICAN JOURNAL OF POLITICAL SCIENCE, 33(2) (MAY 89),
376-389.
THE PAPER EXAMINES ELECTORAL INFLUENCE ON MONETARY
POLICY AS MEASURED BY M1 MONEY GROWTH. THE AUTHOR FINDS A
SIGNIFICANT FOUR-YEAR ELECTORAL CYCLE IN MONEY GROWTH EVEN
WHEN CONTROLLING FOR THE INFLUENCE OF INTEREST RATES, INCOME,
AND BUDGET DEFICITS. HE ALSO FINDS THE RESIDUAL ELECTORAL
CYCLE PRODUCES THE INCOME AND INFLATION MOVEMENTS ASSOCIATED
WITH THE POLITICAL BUSINESS CYCLE WHEN IT USED IN
SIMULATIONS OF SIMPLE REDUCED FORM MACRO MODELS. THE PAPER
CONCLUDES BY DISCUSSING THE DIFFICULTIES IN RATIONALIZING
CYCLICAL MONETARY POLICY WITH RATIONAL EXPECTATIONS.

03761 GRIER, K.B.
CAMPAIGN SPENDING AND SENATE ELECTIONS, 1978-84
PUBLIC CHOICE, 63(3) (DEC 89), 201-220.
THIS PAPER REPORTS RESULTS SHOWING THAT INCUMBENT

EXPENDITURES HAVE A POSITIVE AND SIGNIFICANT EFFECT ON VOTES
IN THE RE-ELECTION CAMPAIGNS OF INCUMBENT SENATORS. IT
ARGUES THAT THE SIMULTANEITY PROBLEM DESCRIBED BY SCHOLARS
IS NOT THEORETICALLY INEVITABLE, AND PRESENTS A STATISTICAL
SPECIFICATION TEST THAT DOES NOT REJECT THE VALIDITY OF
ORDINARY LEAST SQUARES IN THIS DATASET. IT REVIEWS THE
EXISTING EMPIRICAL LITERATURE AND EXPLAINS AND SUMMARIZES
THE DATA USED IN THE PAPER. IT THEN REPORTS AND INTERPRETS
THE ECONOMETRIC RESULTS AND EXAMINES THE BIGGEST CAMPAIGN
SPENDERS. IT DEMONSTRATES WHY JACOBSON'S SENATE RESULTS
DIFFER FROM THE AUTHORS. IT ADDRESSES THE SIMULTANEITY ISSUE
AND DISCUSSES SOME DIFFERENCE BETWEEN HOUSE AND SENATE
ELECTIONS FOUND IN RECENT RESEARCH.

03762 GRIESEMER, J.R.
TAKING CHARGE: AN ASSESSMENT OF ACTIONS TAKEN BY NEW CITY
MANAGERS TO EFFECTIVELY MANAGE MUNICIPAL ORGANIZATIONS
DISSERTATION ABSTRACTS INTERNATIONAL, 50(1) (JUL 89),
255-A.
THE PURPOSE OF THIS DISERTATION IS TO STUDY THE ACTIONS
TAKEN BY CITY MANAGERS DURING THEIR FIRST TWO YEARS IN
OFFICE TO DETERMINE WHAT TYPE OF ACTIONS, IF ANY, CITY
MANAGERS TAKE TO INITIALLY ESTABLISH THEIR ABILITY TO MANAGE
EFFECTIVELY.

03763 GRIFFIN, L. J.; MCCAMMON, H. J.; O'CONNELL, P. J.
NATIONAL VARIATION IN THE CONTEXT OF STRUGGLE: POSTWAR
CLASS CONFLICT AND MARKET DISTRIBUTION IN THE CAPITALIST
DEMOCRACIES
CANADIAN REVIEW OF SOCIOLOGY AND ANTHROPOLOGY, 26(1) (FEB
89), 37-68.
USING 'GENERAL' MARXIST UNDERSTANDINGS OF THE
DETERMINATION OF UNIONIZATION AND WAGE GROWTH, THE AUTHORS
ESTIMATE A SERIES OF TIME-SERIES MODELS FOR 18 ADVANCED,
STABLE CAPITALIST DEMOCRACIES, FINDING THAT EXPECTATIONS ARE
CONSISTENT WITH THE 1959-80 HISTORIES OF SOME OF THESE
NATIONS AND NOT OF OTHERS. THEY THEN POSIT THAT THESE WITHIN-
NATION HISTORICAL RELATIONSHIPS ARE THEMSELVES A FUNCTION OF
OTHER TEMPORALLY INVARIANT, CROSS-NATIONAL DIFFERENCES
DISTINGUISHING ONE CAPITALIST COUNTRY FROM ANOTHER.
DIFFERENCES IN SOCIAL DEMOCRATIC CONTROL OF GOVERNMENT
ACROSS THE CAPITALIST DEMOCRACIES, IN PARTICULAR, APPEAR
PARTIALLY RESPONSIBLE FOR SOME IMPORTANT COUNTRY-TO-COUNTRY
DIFFERENCES IN THE HISTORICAL RELATIONSHIPS AMONG
PROLETARIANIZATION, UNIONIZATION, STRIKE ACTIVITY, AND WAGE
GROWTH. LABOR MOVEMENTS IN NATIONS WITH SUSTAINED OR
CUMULATIVE SOCIAL DEMOCRATIC REPRESENTATION APPEAR MORE
SUCCESSFUL IN CONVERTING DEPENDENT WORKERS INTO TRADE
UNIONISTS THAN DO OTHER COUNTRIES, BUT ARE LESS SUCCESSFUL
IN USING STRIKES TO EXTRACT WAGE GAINS. THE AUTHORS DISCUSS
FOUR THEORETICAL AND METHODOLOGICAL IMPLICATIONS OF THIS
RESEARCH, INCLUDING THE CONTRADICTORY EFFECTS OF SOCIAL
DEMOCRACY ON CLASS DYNAMICS.

03764 GRIFFIN, S. M.
POLITICS AND THE SUPREME COURT: THE CASE OF THE BORK
NOMINATION
JOURNAL OF LAW & POLITICS, V(3) (SPR 89), 551-604.
THIS ARTICLE IS PRIMARILY CONCERNED WITH THE POLITICAL
MEANING OF THE BORK NOMINATION. JUDGE BORK'S NOMINATION AND
DEFEAT PROVIDED INSIGHT INTO HOW POLITICIANS THINK ABOUT THE
SUPREME COURT AND INTO THE COURT'S ROLE IN OUR SYSTEM OF
GOVERNMENT. THE NOMINATION FORCED SENATORS, FOR EXAMPLE, TO
ARTICULATE THEIR VIEWS ABOUT THE CONSTITUTION AND THE
SUPREME COURT IN A SYSTEMATIC WAY RARELY EQUALLED BY OTHER
DEBATES IN RECENT DECADES. THE NOMINATION REVEALED WITH
GREAT CLARITY THAT THE COURT IS ENMESHED IN A COMPLEX WEB OF
POLITICAL RELATIONSHIPS. DESCRIBING AND ACCOUNTING FOR THIS
INTRICATE SYSTEM REQUIRES A MULTILAYERED APPROACH.

03765 GRIFFITHS, F.
THE SOVIET EXPERIENCE OF ARMS CONTROL
INTERNATIONAL JOURNAL, XLIV(2) (SPR 89), 304-364.
THIS PAPER CONSIDERS FOUR CASES OF SOVIET ARMS
BARGAINING BEHAVIOR SINCE 1917. EACH HAS A TURNING POINT IN
THE READINESS OF THE REGIME TO COME TO TERMS WITH A WORLD IT
HAS SHORN TO TRANSFORM. IN EACH NUCLEAR ARMS BARGAINING
EXERCISE, THE USSR ENGAGED IN PROTRACTED ON-AGAIN, OFF-AGAIN
NEGOTIATIONS WITH THE USA. THIS ESSAY FOCUSES ON THE
PRENEGOTIATION PROCESS IN EACH CASE.

03766 GRIGORIAN, L.
WHAT IS HAPPENIN IN ARMENIA?
ACROSS FRONTIERS, 5(2) (SUM 89), 2-4, 39-43.
THIS ARTICLE EXPLORES RECENT EVENTS IN ARMENIA WHICH
INCLUDE THE EARTHQUAKE, PERESTROIKA, AND ANTI-PERESTROIKA
ACTIVITIES. IT EXPLORES THE DESIRE OF THE ARMENIAN PEOPLE
FOR A DEMOCRATIC MOVEMENT IN ORDER TO NOT BUILD THEIR HOMES
AND LIVES ON THE BASIS OF OLD ATITUDES AND ORDERS. IT
EXPLORES THE REASONS THAT ARMENIA WAS CHOSEN BY THE COMPLEX
OF POWERFUL ANTI-PERESTROLKA FORCES AND CONCLUDES THAT THE
DRAMA IN ARMENIA IS FAR FROM OVER. IT IS THE DRAMA OF
PERESTROIKA.

03767 GRIGORYANTS, S.
CAMPS WITH GUARDS IN WHITE GOWNS
GLASNOST, (16-18) (JAN 89), 34-35.
IN THE SOVIET UNION, IT IS FAR EASIER TO SEND SOMEONE TO
A PSYCHIATRIC HOSPITAL THAN TO A PRISON. IT CAN BE DONE BY
ANY POLICEMAN, NURSE, DEPUTY PROSECUTOR GENERAL, OR ANYONE
WHO HAS EVEN A MODICUM OF SOCIAL STATUS OR PERSONAL TIES TO
A PSYCHIATRIST. OFFICIAL DATA SHOW THAT ABOUT FIVE MILLION
PEOPLE ARE CURRENTLY UNDER PSYCHIATRIC OBSERVATION IN THE
SOVIET UNION. THERE IS REASON TO BELIEVE THAT TORTURE OCCURS
IN SOVIET PSYCHIATRIC HOSPITALS, AS WELL AS CRIMINAL
EXPERIMENTATION ON HEALTHY PERSONS WHO HAVE BEEN FORCIBLY
HOSPITALIZED.

03768 GRIGORYANTS, S.
GRIGORYANTS VISITS THE WEST: EDITOR WARNS THAT REACTIONS
SPEAK LOUDER THAN WORDS
GLASNOST, II(4) (SEP 89), 32-34.
MIKHAIL GORBACHEV'S REACTIONS TO CRITICISM IN THE
CONGRESS OF PEOPLE'S DEPUTIES AND TO THE DEMANDS FOR
INDEPENDENCE BY VARIOUS NATIONALITIES SPEAK LOUDER THAN SUCH
WORDS AS "GLASNOST" AND "PERESTROIKA." THE WEST MUST NOT
PREMATURELY OR NAIVELY EMBRACE GORBACHEV AND HIS REFORM
AGENDA.

03769 GRIGORYANTS, S.
HOW ESTONIA PULLED ITSELF TOGETHER
GLASNOST, II(4) (SEP 89), 22-27.
THE AUTHOR RECOUNTS INTERVIEWS WITH DISSIDENT ESTONIAN
LEADERS, INCLUDING MEMBERS OF THE ESTONIAN NATIONAL
INDEPENDENCE PARTY AND THE ESTONIAN CHRISTIAN ALLIANCE. THE
ESTONIANS DISCUSS THEIR QUEST FOR INDEPENDENCE AND UNITY AS
A PEOPLE.

03770 GRIGORYANTS, S.
MIKHAIL GORBACHEV: WHICH POISON WILL HE CHOOSE?
GLASNOST, II(2) (MAR 89), 51.
GORBACHEV'S REFUSAL TO SOLVE THE NAGORNO-KARABAKH
PROBLEM BY RESTORING THIS ANCIENT PROVINCE TO ARMENIA SHOWS
THAT HE IS UNWILLING TO RIGHT A POLITICAL WRONG REGARDED BY
ARMENIANS AS ONE OF STALIN'S CRIMES. THUS, GORBACHEV HAS
IRREVOCABLY LOST HIS IMAGE AS A STATESMAN STRIVING FOR
JUSTICE AND AS A LEADER DETERMINED TO RIGHT THE WRONGS OF
HIS PREDECESSORS. TENS OF MILLIONS OF SOVIET CITIZENS NOW
VIEW HIM AS NOTHING MORE THAN A POLITICIAN EAGER TO
DISREGARD THE TRAGIC CONDITION OF AN ENTIRE PEOPLE FOR THE
SAKE OF SHORT-TERM ADVANTAGE. IF GORBACHEV CAN MAKE THE
RESOLUTION STICK, THEN HE WILL HAVE DEALT A SEVERE BLOW NOT
ONLY TO ARMENIANS BUT TO ALL OTHER SOVIET NATIONALITIES,
INCLUDING THE RUSSIANS.

03771 GRIGORYANTS, S.
TRAGEDY IN THE TRANSCAUCASUS: IS THE SOVIET GOVERNMENT
UNWILLING OR MERELY INCOMPETENT?
GLASNOST, (16-18) (JAN 89), 6.
ALL CHANGES IN THE USSR AND ALL ATTEMPTS TO PRESERVE THE
STATUS QUO RESULT IN BLOODBATHS. THE SAVAGERY OF SOVIET
SOCIETY AND ITS GOVERNMENT CONTINUES UNCHANGED. THOSE WHO
PERISHED IN THE SUMGAIT MASSACRE WERE THE FIRST VICTIMS OF
PERESTROIKA. GORBACHEV CREATED THE ILLUSION AMONG ARMENIANS
THAT A GREAT MANY THINGS HAD CHANGED FOR THE BETTER. BUT HE
HAS NOW SHOWN HIMSELF TO BE UNWILLING OR INCAPABLE OF
SUBSTANTIATING AND IMPLEMENTING HIS PROMISES.

03772 GRIGORYEV, V.
SOVIET-FINNISH TRADE AND ECONOMIC RELATIONS: TRADITIONS
AND CHANGES
FOREIGN TRADE, 5 (1988), 23-29.
THE CALL FOR AN INTENSIVE DEVELOPMENT OF SOVIET-FINNISH
TRADE DUE TO THE PRESENT RESTRUCTURING OF THE SOVIET UNION'S
ECONOMY AND EXTERNAL ECONOMIC TIES AND THE PROGRESSIVE
CHANGES IN FINNISH INDUSTRY IS EXAMINED IN THIS ARTICLE.
DISCUSSED ARE: PRINCIPLES OF COOPERATION, RESERVES FOR
EXPANDING COOPERATION, AND METHODS TO INTENSIFY COOPERATION.

03773 GRILLI, E.
MACRO-ECONOMIC DETERMINANTS OF TRADE PROTECTIONISM
WORLD ECONOMY, 11(3) (SEP 88), 313-326.
THIS ARTICLE EXPLORES THE USE BY INDUSTRIAL COUNTRIES OF
VARIOUS KINDS OF NON-TARIFF MEASURES TO REGULATE TRADE WHICH
STARTED AGAIN IN THE 1970S. THE ORIGINS OF THE NEW
PROTECTIONISM ARE EXAMINED.

03774 GRIMMETT, R.F.
POLITICAL DIMENSIONS OF THE U.S. MILITARY PRESENCE IN NATO
COUNTRIES
CRS REVEIW, 10(4) (APR 89), 16-17.
ONE CONSEQUENCE OF THE RECENT EASING OF TENSIONS BETWEEN
THE SOVIET BLOC AND THE WEST HAS BEEN TO FOCUS GREATER
ATTENTION ON U.S. MILITARY BASES AND FORCES LOCATED IN NATO
NATIONS. ALTHOUGH AMERICAN BASES WERE ONCE PERCEIVED ALMOST
UNIVERSALLY AS INDISPENSABLE TO THE NATIONAL SECURITY
INTERESTS OF THE VARIOUS HOST NATIONS, THEY ARE NOW VIEWED
IN SOME CASES AS A MIXED BLESSING, AT BEST. THEIR CONTINUED

PRESENCE HAS MADE THEM AN EASY AND POPULAR TARGET OF
CONTROVERSY FOR DOMESTIC POLITICAL ELEMENTS, ESPECIALLY
LEFTIST POLITICAL PARTIES AND LEFTIST FACTIONS WITHIN
PARTIES.

03775 GRIMSSON, O.R.
BACK AT THE TOP OF THE AGENDA: A NUCLEAR TEST BAN
DISARMAMENT, XII(2) (SUM 89), 117-126.
ON THE TWENTY-FIFTH ANNIVERSARY OF THE SIGNING OF THE
PARTIAL TEST-BAN TREATY, A GROUP OF NON-NUCLEAR STATES
FORMALLY ACTIVATED THE TREATY'S AMENDMENT PROCEDURE. THE
PROPOSED AMENDMENT WOULD EXTEND THE PROHIBITION ON NUCLEAR
TESTING IN THE ATMOSPHERE, IN OUTER SPACE, AND UNDER WATER
TO UNDERGROUND TESTS. IF ONE-HALF OR MORE OF THE PARTY
STATES AGREE, THE AMENDMENT COULD ENTER INTO FORCE FOR ALL
PARTIES, EXCEPT FOR THE THREE ORIGINAL NUCLEAR PARTIES (THE
USSR, UK, AND USA), WHICH MUST AGREE TO THE AMENDMENT BEFORE
IT CAN TAKE EFFECT.

03776 GRINDLE, M.S.; THOMAS, J.W.
POLICY MAKERS, POLICY CHOICES, AND POLICY OUTCOMES: THE
POLITICAL ECONOMY OF REFORM IN DEVELOPING COUNTRIES
POLICY SCIENCES, 22(3-4) (1989), 213-248.
THIS ARTICLE PRESENTS AN ANALYTIC MODEL FOR
UNDERSTANDING THE ROLE OF DECISION MAKERS IN BRINGING ABOUT
SIGNIFICANT POLICY AND INSTITUTIONAL CHANGE AND IN
UNDERSTANDING HOW PROCESSES OF AGENDA SETTING, DECISION
MAKING, AND IMPLEMENTATION SHAPE THE CONTENT, TIMING, AND
SUSTAINABILITY OF REFORM INITIATIVES. CENTRAL TO THE MODEL
IS THE ASSERTION THAT POLICY ELITES AND THE POLICY MAKING
PROCESS ARE IMPORTANT DETERMINANTS OF REFORM. THE FRAMEWORK
INDICATES THAT CIRCUMSTANCES SURROUNDING ISSUE FORMATION,
THE CRITERIA THAT DECISION MAKERS USE TO SELECT AMONG
OPTIONS, AND THE CHARACTERISTICS OF SPECIFIC POLICIES ARE
ANALYTIC CATEGORIES THAT EXPLAIN A CONSIDERABLE AMOUNT ABOUT
REFORM OUTCOMES. THE MODEL IS BASED ON CASES DEVELOPED BY
PARTICIPANTS IN TWELVE INITIATIVES TO BRING ABOUT POLICY AND
INSTITUTIONAL CHANGE IN A VARIETY OF DEVELOPING COUNTRIES.

03777 GRINGAUZ, K.
LOSS OF SPACE VELOCITY
SPACE POLICY, 5(3) (AUG 89), 179-182.
PUBLIC DEBTS SURROUNDING THE COSTS AND EFFECTIVENESS OF
THE SPACE RESEARCH PROGRAM ARE GROWING IN THE USSR, DESPITE
(OR PERHAPS BECAUSE OF) A LACK OF HARD INFORMATION. THE
AUTHOR OF THIS ARTICLE ARGUES THAT THE VAST SUMS COMMITTED
TO THE ENERGLYA-BURAN SYSTEM ARE A MONUMENT TO THE SPACE
INDUSTRY'S OVERWEENING AMBITIONS; MEANWHILE USEFUL UNMANNED
PROJECTS ARE BEING HAMPERED BY BUREAUCRATIC MISMANAGEMENT
INHERITED FROM THE BREZHNEV ERA. THE SPACE BUDGET SHOULD BE
BROUGHT UNDER THE CONTROL OF THE NEW SOVIET PARLIAMENT.

03778 GRIPP, R.C.
POLITICAL REFORM IN THREE ASIAN POLITIES
ASIAN PROFILE, 17(2) (APR 89), 189-198.
IN THE 1980'S, REFORM MOVEMENTS TOWARD GREATER DEMOCRACY
HAVE BEEN APPARENT IN THE PHILIPPINES, SOUTH KOREA, AND
TAIWAN. IN THIS ESSAY, THE AUTHOR SURVEYS DEVELOPMENTS IN
THESE COUNTRIES TO DETERMINE THE EXTENT OF DEMOCRATIC
DEVELOPMENT THERE.

03779 GROBAR, L.M.; PORTER, R.C.
BENOIT REVISITED: DEFENSE SPENDING AND ECONOMIC GROWTH IN
LDC'S
JOURNAL OF CONFLICT RESOLUTION, 33(2) (JUN 89), 318-345.
IN THE EARLY 1970S, EMILE BENOIT SHOCKED DEVELOPMENT
ECONOMISTS BY PRESENTING POSITIVE CROSS-COUNTRY CORRELATIONS
BETWEEN MILITARY EXPENDITURE RATES AND ECONOMIC GROWTH RATES
IN LESS DEVELOPED COUNTRIES (LDCS). THIS ARTICLE REVIEWS THE
LONG DEBATE THAT HAS FOLLOWED. WHILE SOME STUDIES UNCOVER
EVIDENCE OF POSITIVE EFFECTS OF MILITARY SPENDING THROUGH
HUMAN CAPITAL FORMATION AND TECHNOLOGICAL "SPIN-OFF" EFFECTS,
MODELS THAT ALLOW MILITARY SPENDING TO AFFECT GROWTH
THROUGH MULTIPLE CHANNELS FIND THAT. WHILE MILITARY SPENDING
MAY STIMULATE GROWTH THROUGH SOME CHANNELS, IT RETARDS IT
THROUGH OTHERS, AND THE NET EFFECT IS NEGATIVE. THE MOST
IMPORTANT NEGATIVE EFFECT IS THAT HIGHER MILITARY SPENDING
REDUCES NATIONAL SAVING RATES, THEREBY REDUCING RATES OF
CAPITAL ACCUMULATION. THE EXISTENCE OF POSITIVE EFFECTS OF
MILITARY SPENDING ON ECONOMIC GROWTH, AS CONJECTURED BY
BENOIT, STILL CANNOT BE RULED OUT. HOWEVER, THE RECENT
ECONOMETRIC EVIDENCE POINTS TO THE CONCLUSION THAT THESE
POSITIVE EFFECTS, IF THEY EXIST, ARE SMALL RELATIVE TO THE
NEGATIVE EFFECTS AND THAT, OVERALL, MILITARY SPENDING HAS A
WEAK BUT ADVERSE IMPACT ON ECONOMIC GROWTH IN DEVELOPING
COUNTRIES.

03780 GROENEWEGEN, J.; BELJE, P.
THE FRENCH COMMUNICATION INDUSTRY DEFINED AND ANALYZED
JOURNAL OF ECONOMIC ISSUES, 23(4) (DEC 89), 1059-1074.
THE PURPOSE OF THIS ARTICLE IS TO EVALUATE PUBLIC POLICY
IN THE FRENCH TELECOMMUNICATION SECTOR, TO ANSWER QUESTIONS
CONCERNING THE KIND OF POLICY DEVELOPED. THE ARTICLE
DESCRIBES THE STRATEGIES OF ENTERPRISES, GOVERNMENT AGENCIES,

AND RESEARCH INSTITUTIONS AND TRIES TO ANALYZE THE FORCES
BEHIND THE DYNAMICS OF THE SUBSYSTEM OF THE INDUSTRY. IT
DISCUSSES THE NETWORK APPROACH WHICH SHOWS REMARKABLE
SIMILARITIES WITH THE SOCIAL FABRIC MATRIX. THEN, THE
CONCEPTS OF THE NETWORK APPROACH ARE APPLIED TO A
DESCRIPTION, ANALYSIS, AND EVALUATION OF PUBLIC POLICY IN
THE FRENCH TELECOMMUNICATION SECTOR. A FINAL EVALUATION
CONCLUDES THE PAPER.

03781 GROFMAN, B.; HANDLEY, L.
   BLACK REPRESENTATION: MAKING SENSE OF ELECTORAL GEOGRAPHY
   AT DIFFERENT LEVELS OF GOVERNMENT
   LEGISLATIVE STUDIES QUARTERLY, 15(2) (MAY 89), 265-280.
   THE NUMBER OF MINORITIES SERVING IN LEGISLATURES,
COUNCILS, AND GOVERNING BOARDS VARIES GREATLY ACROSS REGIONS
OF THE COUNTRY AND ACROSS LEVELS OF GOVERNMENT. FOR EXAMPLE,
ON THE NATIONAL LEVEL, THERE ARE MORE BLACK MEMBERS OF
CONGRESS IN THE NORTH THAN IN THE SOUTH, WHILE AT THE LOCAL
LEVEL MORE BLACKS SERVE IN THE SOUTH THAN IN THE NORTH. THIS
PAPER ACCOUNTS FOR THE VARIATION IN BLACK REPRESENTATION
PRIMARILY AS AN INTERACTION OF THE CONCENTRATION OF BLACKS
(IN BOTH RAW POPULATION NUMBERS AND IN POPULATION
PERCENTAGES) AND THE SIZE OF THE CONSTITUENCY UNIT.

03782 GROFMAN, B.; HANDLEY, L.
   MINORITY POPULATION PROPORTION AND BLACK AND HISPANIC
   CONGRESSIONAL SUCCESS IN THE 1970S AND 1980S
   AMERICAN POLITICS QUARTERLY, 17(4) (OCT 89), 436-445.
   THIS ARTICLE LOOKS AT THE RELATIONSHIP BETWEEN A
CONGRESSIONAL DISTRICT'S BLACK AND HISPANIC POPULATION
PROPORTION AND THE LIKELIHOOD OF ELECTION OF EITHER. IT
SHOWS THAT BLACK AND HISPANIC GAINS APPEAR TO BE DUE TO AN
INCREASE IN THE NUMBER OF DISTRICTS WITH SUBSTANTIAL
MINORITY POPULATION RATHER IN THE WILLINGNESS OF NONMINORITY
VOTERS TO SUPPORT MINORITY CANDIDATES. IT FOCUSES ON THE
IMPORTANCE OF THE COMBINED MINORITY POPULATION AS A
DETERMINATE OF MINORITY ELECTORAL SUCCESS.

03783 GROFMAN, B.
   RICHARD NIXON AS PINOCCHIO, RICHARD II, AND SANTA CLAUS:
   THE USE OF ALLUSION IN POLITICAL SATIRE
   THE JOURNAL OF POLITICS, 51(1) (FEB 89), 163-173.
   THE APPROACH TO THE USES OF METAPHOR AND ALLUSION IN
POLITICAL SATIRE IS ROOTED IN THE INTERACTION VIEW OF
METAPHOR OFFERED BY THE PHILOSOPHER MAX BLACK. THIS ARTICLE
FOCUSES ON ONE CENTRAL ILLUSTRATION, THE ASSERTION THAT
"RICHARD NIXON IS PINOCCHIO"-CONTAINED IN A 1970S MONOLOGUE
BY THE POLITICAL SATRIST DAVID FRYE. THE AUTHOR ARGUES THAT
THE MEANING ATTACHED TO THIS ASSERTION REQUIRES US TO KNOW
ABOUT BOTH RICHARD NIXON AND PINOCCHIO. THE MORE HE KNOW OF
EACH, THE MORE SOPHISTICATED WILL BE OUR UNDERSTANDING OF
WHAT MAKES THIS ALLUSION BOTH SATIRICAL AND APT. ALSO, FOR
AN ALLUSION TO WORK, IT MUST NOT CONTAIN ELEMENTS THAT
APPEAR TO CONTRADICT THE SATIRIST'S CENTRAL THRUST, AND THAT
CENTRAL THRUST MUST BE COMPREHENSIBLE TO THE AUDIENCE EVEN
IF SOME OF THE FINE POINTS MAY BE MISSED. MOREOVER, SOME
ALLUSIONS ARE "RICHER" AND MORE SUCCESSFUL THAN OTHERS, SUCH
AS THAT OF NIXON AS PINOCCHIO. TO DEMONSTRATE THESE POINTS,
THE AUTHOR CONTRASTS TWO OTHER ALLUSIONS INVOLVING NIXON,
ONE PORTRAYING HIM AS RICHARD II, THE OTHER AS SANTA CLAUS.

03784 GROFMAN, B.
   THE COMPARATIVE ANALYSIS OF COALITION FORMATION AND
   DURATION: DISTINGUISHING BETWEEN-COUNTRY AND WITHIN-
   COUNTRY EFFECTS
   BRITISH JOURNAL OF POLITICAL SCIENCE, 19(2) (APR 89),
   291-302.
   MOST AUTHORS TREATING CABINET-COALITION FORMATION HAVE
ATTEMPTED TO MODEL FEATURES OF CABINET FORMATION, SUCH AS
CABINET DURATION OR CABINET TYPE, LARGELY OR ENTIRELY USING
DATA POOLED FROM ALL CABINETS IN A NUMBER OF DIFFERENT
COUNTRIES OVER SOME CONSIDERABLE TIME PERIOD. BUT, IF THE
ANALYST IS NOT VERY CAREFUL, RESULTS OF POOLED CROSS-
NATIONAL DATA MAY LEAD TO MISTAKES ABOUT CAUSAL STRUCTURE
AND A CONFUSION OF WITHIN-COUNTRY AND BETWEEN-COUNTRY
EFFECTS.

03785 GROGAN, S.E.
   THE GUERRILLA AS MIDWIFE: THE END OF UNION (IRELAND) AND
   THE THE MANDATE (PALESTINE)
   DISSERTATION ABSTRACTS INTERNATIONAL, 49(8) (FEB 89),
   2375-A.
   IRELAND AND PALESTINE CLEARLY ILLUSTRATE THE PROBLEMS
THAT RESPONSIBLE PARLIAMENTARY GOVERNMENTS FACE WHEN
CHALLENGED BY GUERRILLA INSURRECTION. SINN FEIN AND ZIONIST
GOALS WERE ACHEIVED BY COMPREHENSIVE GUERRILLA STRATEGIES
THAT SKILLFULLY EXPLOITED BRITISH ECONOMIC WEAKNESS, THE
RELUCTANCE OF BRITISH HOME OPINION TO SANCTION ALL-OUT
COUNTERINSURGENCY MEASURES, AND THE CABINET'S FEAR OF
ALIENATING THE USA. VIOLENCE WAS MERELY ONE ELEMENT OF THE
GRAND STRATEGY.

03786 GROGAN, S.E.
   THE RESULT-ORIENTATION OF WILLIAM O. DOUGLAS: POLITICAL

ACTIVITIES ON AND OFF THE BENCH
DISSERTATION ABSTRACTS INTERNATIONAL, 49(8) (FEB 89),
2375-A.
   RESULT-ORIENTATION, INSTITUTIONORIENTATION, AND
DOCTRINEORIENTATION ARE IMPORTANT IN EXPLAINING THE
POLITICAL BEHAVIOR OF SUPREME COURT JUSTICE IN THIS STUDY,
THE AUTHOR CONSIDERS THE RESULT-ORIENTATION OF ASSOCIATE
JUSTICE WILLIAM O. DOUGLAS. SHE EXAMINES HIS JUDICIAL AND
EXTRA-JUDICIAL BEHAVIOR, STUDYING HOW HE ATTEMPTED TO SHAPE
AMERICAN LAW AND POLITICS

03787 GROLL, S.; ORZECH, Z.B.
   FROM MARX TO THE OKISHIO THEOREM: A GENEALOGY
   HISTORY OF POLITICAL ECONOMY, 21(2) (SUM 89), 253-272.
   THE OKISHIO THEOREM WAS FIRST PRESENTED IN 1961 IN NABUO
OKISHIO'S PAPER "TECHNICAL CHANGES AND THE RATE OF PROFIT"
AND DEALS WITH A CRITICISM OF THE MARXIAN LAW OF THE
TENDENTIAL FALL OF THE RATE OF PROFIT. THE ARGUMENT
CONTAINED IN THE OKISHIO THEOREM GOES BACK IN A STRAIGHT
LINE TO TUGAN-BARANOWSKY AND TO MARX HIMSELF. IN "CAPITAL I"
MARX PROPOSED AN ALTERNATIVE THEORY OF TECHNICAL CHANGE AND
ACCUMULATION THAT, LIKE THE OKISHIO THEOREM, ARRIVES AT A
RISING RATHER THAN FALLING RATE OF PROFIT IN A CAPITALIST
ECONOMY.

03788 GROMYKO, A.
   AFRICA: CONTINENT AT THE THRESHOLD
   INTERNATIONAL AFFAIRS (MOSCOW), (9) (SEP 89), 87-95.
   THE AUTHOR ARGUES THAT IT IS NECESSARY TO DISCARD SOME
FIXED STEREOTYPES IN ORDER TO UNDERSTAND AND BE UNDERSTOOD
IN AFRICA. HE DECLARES THAT THE TIME HAS COME FOR AN
ANALYSIS OF THE REAL WAYS OF ATTAINING SOCIAL AND ECONOMIC
PROGRESS IN THE THIRD WORLD.

03789 GROS, D.
   PARADIGMS FOR THE MONETARY UNION OF EUROPE
   JOURNAL OF COMMON MARKET STUDIES, XXVII(3) (MAR 89),
   219-230.
   THE NOTION OF A EUROPEAN MONETARY UNION CAN BE
INTERPRETED IN DIFFERENT WAYS. TO MOST NON-ECONOMISTS IT
PROBABLY IMPLIES A SINGLE EUROPEAN CURRENCY AND A EUROPEAN
CENTRAL BANK. TO ECONOMISTS, HOWEVER, A MONETARY UNION
IMPLIES ONLY (IN THE WORDS OF THE 1970 WERNER PLAN): 'THE
IRREVOCABLE FIXING OF PARITIES AND THE TOTAL LIBERALIZATION
OF CAPITAL MOVEMENTS'. TO OTHERS STILL, A MONETARY UNION
MIGHT BE REACHED IF THERE IS A WIDELY USED EUROPEAN PARALLEL
CURRENCY. THIS ARTICLE ARGUES THAT THESE PARADIGMS IMPLY
DIFFERENT DEGREES OF MONETARY INTEGRATION AND THAT THE
BENEFITS THAT CAN BE EXPECTED FROM A MONETARY UNION FOR
EUROPE DEPEND ON THE DEGREE OF MONETARY INTEGRATION. WHICH
PARADIGM SHOULD BE CHOSEN, THEREFORE, DEPENDS ON THE REASONS
FOR WHICH A MONETARY UNION FOR EUROPE IS DEEMED DESIRABLE.

03790 GROSS, J.
   SOCIAL CONSEQUENCES OF WAR: PRELIMINARIES TO THE STUDY OF
   IMPOSITION OF COMMUNIST REGIMES IN EAST CENTRAL EUROPE
   EASTERN EUROPEAN POLITICS AND SOCIETIES, 3(2) (SPR 89),
   198-214.
   IN SPITE OF THE ENORMOUS IMPACT THE SECOND WORLD WAR HAD
ON THE FATE OF EAST CENTRAL EUROPEAN SOCIETIES, NO GENERAL
HISTORIES OF WARTIME REGIMES IN THESE COUNTRIES ARE
CURRENTLY AVAILABLE. THE ARTICLE OUTLINES SOME OF THEY KEY
THEMES THAT A SOCIAL HISTORY OF EASTERN EUROPE WOULD TREAT.
IT SEEKS TO INTERPRET EVENTS IN SUCH A WAY AS TO RECONCILE
THE FACT THAT ALTHOUGH EASTERN EUROPEAN NATIONS EXPERIENCED
THE WAR IN VASTLY DIFFERENT WAYS, THEY ALL WERE CONSOLIDATED
INTO COMMUNIST RULE. IT ANALYZES THE SOCIAL, POLITICAL, AND
ECONOMIC CONDITIONS THAT COULD POSSIBLY HAVE INFLUENCED SUCH
AN OUTCOME.

03791 GROSSE, R.
   RESOLVING LATIN AMERICA'S TRANSFER PROBLEM
   WORLD ECONOMY, 11(3) (SEP 88), 417-435.
   THE ARTICLE BEGINS WITH A DISCUSSION OF THE TRANSFER
PROBLEM. THE SECTION AFTER THAT OUTLINES SOME OF THE KEY
CHARACTERISTICS OF THE PREVIOUS THREE TRANSFER PROBLEMS IN
THIS CENTURY. THEN, FOCUSSING ON THE CURRENT LATIN AMERICAN
PROBLEM PROJECTIONS ARE MADE OF THE ABILITIES OF SEVERAL
COUNTRIES TO REPAY THEIR DEBTS OVER THE NEXT FIVE YEARS.
BOTH THE HISTORY AND THE PROJECTIONS LEAD TO A CONCLUSION
THAT SOME OF THE EXISTING FOREIGN DEBT WILL NEVER BE REPAID,
BE IT THROUGH DEFAULT, LOAN DEVALUATION, GOVERNMENT POLICY
INTERVENTION AND/OR INFLATING AWAY SOME OF THE REAL VALUE.
THE BASIC RESULT OF THE ANALYSIS IS A CONCLUSION THAT THE
PROBLEM WILL LINGER INDEFINITELY, BUT THAT SOME PROMISING
STEPS HAVE BEEN TAKEN BY THE PRIVATE SECTOR WHICH COULD WELL
ELIMINATE THE CRISIS NATURE OF THE PROBLEM AND LEAD TO
RENEWED LENDING BY COMMERCIAL BANKS AND FOREIGN DIRECT
INVESTMENT INTO THE REGION.

03792 GROSSMAN, J.
   THE POLITICS OF "STAR WARS"
   JOURNAL OF LEGISLATION, 15(2) (1989), 93-102.
   THE ARTICLE EXAMINES THE UNDERLYING POLITICAL

FOUNDATIONS OF SDI. IT CONCLUDES THAT THE POLITICAL MOTIVES
HAVE SUPERCEDED EVEN NATIONAL SECURITY CONCERNS AND THAT SDI
IS AN ATTEMPT OF THE POLITICAL RIGHT TO TAKE THE INITIAVE
FROM THE INCREASINGLY POPULAR PEACE MOVEMENTS. SDI HAS
APPEALED TO AMERICAN NATIONALISM AND TO THE PREVAILING
AMERICAN "MOOD", BUT SEEMS TO BE LACKING IN CONCRETE
TECHNICAL JUSTIFICATION.

03793 GROSSMAN, P., J.
    FISCAL DECENTRALIZATION AND GOVERNMENT SIZE: AN EXTENSION
    PUBLIC CHOICE, 62(1) (JUL 89), 63-70.
        THIS PAPER ANALYZES ONE METHOD GOVERNMENTS EMPLOY TO
    CIRCUMVENT THE DISCIPLINE OF A COMPETITIVE SYSTEM OF FISCAL
    FEDERALISM - INTERGOVERNMENTAL COLLUSION IN THE FORM OF
    INTERGOVERNMENTAL GRANTS. GRANTS, IT IS ARGUED, SERVE TO
    ENCOURAGE THE EXPANSION OF THE PUBLIC SECTOR BY
    CONCENTRATING TAXING POWERS IN THE HANDS OF THE CENTRAL
    GOVERNMENTS AND BY WEAKENING THE FISCAL DISCIPLINE IMPOSED
    ON GOVERNMENTS FORCED TO SELF-FINANCE THEIR EXPENDITURES.
    THE RESULTS REPORTED SUGGEST THAT INTERGOVERNMENTAL GRANTS
    DO ENCOURAGE GROWTH IN THE PUBLIC SECTOR. THE RESULTS OFFER
    FURTHER SUPPORT FOR THE USE OF MONOPOLY GOVERNMENT
    ASSUMPTIONS IN PUBLIC SECTOR MODELING.

03794 GROTH. A.J.
    TOTALITARIANS AND DEMOCRATS: ASPECTS OF POLITICAL-MILITARY
    RELATIONS 1939-1945
    COMPARATIVE STRATEGY, 8(1) (1989), 73-97.
        FOCUSING ON GERMANY AND THE USSR AS TOTALITARIAN STATES,
    AND BRITAIN, U.S., AND FRANCE AS DEMOCRATIC STATES, AND
    RELYING LARGELY ON BIOGRAPHICAL AND AUTOBIOGRAPHICAL SOURCES,
    SEVERAL DEMOCRATIC-TOTALITARIAN CONTRASTS ARE ADDRESSED;
    DEMOCRATIC STATES ARE CHARACTERIZED BY GENERALLY MORE
    STRUCTURED, LEGAL-RATIONAL RELATIONSHIPS AT THE TOP LEVELS
    OF POLITICAL-MILITARY HIERARCHIES WITH MUCH GREATER RELIANCE
    ON COMMITTEE AND OTHER VOLUNTARY COORDINATING MECHANISMS OF
    THE MILITARY ESTABLISHMENTS; MORE INVOLVEMENT BY MILITARY IN
    STRATEGIC ISSUES; MORE DIFFUSE AND OFTEN POLITICALLY
    SIGNIFICANT STATUS AS WELL AS GREATER PROFESSIONAL AUTONOMY
    FOR THE MILITARY; MUCH LESS DRASTIC MILITARY ACCOUNTABILITY
    FOR FAILURE, BUT ALSO MUCH MORE PUBLIC-LEGAL ACCOUNTABILITY
    BY MILITARY PROFESSIONALS. THE IMPACT OF THESE DIFFERENCES
    ON THE BATTLEFIELD APPEARS TO HAVE BEEN MIXED WITH SOME
    SIGNIFICANT ADVANTAGES ACCURING TO THE TOTALITARIAN STATES.

03795 GROTSCH, E.; LOBMEYER, H.
    ETHNICITY AND INTER-STATE RELATIONS IN THE MIDDLE EAST
    ORIENT, 30(3) (SEP 89), 350-354.
        THE AUTHORS REPORT ON A COLLOQUIUM HELD BY THE FREE
    UNIVERSITY OF BERLIN, "ETHNICITY AND INTERNATIONAL CONFLICT
    IN THE MIDDLE EAST." THREE MAIN PROBLEMS DISCUSSED WERE:
    CROSS-BORDER SOLIDARITY BETWEEN DOMINANT AND MARGINALIZED
    SEGMENTS OF SOCIETY IN DIFFERENT STATES; THE INFLUENCE OF
    INTERNAL FRAGMENTATION ON FOREIGN POLICY; AND DIVIDED
    NATIONS OR THE EXTERNAL "INTERIOR": ARAB UNITY AND THE
    SEVERAL ARAB STATES. SPECIFIC CASE STUDIES DISCUSSED IN
    THESE CONTEXTS INCLUDE: THE IRAQI SHI'A AND THEIR RELATIONS
    WITH IRAN; THE KURDS IN THE IRAN-IRAQ CONFLICT; GREECE'S
    MUSLIM MINORITY; LEBANON; SYRIA; PAN-ARABISM; AND SRI LANKA.

03796 GROVE, E.
    AND THAT WAS THE FUTURE... PREDICTING THE NAVAL FUTURE:
    THE UK EXPERIENCE
    FUTURES, 21(2) (APR 89), 169-182.
        NAVAL HISTORY IS A STRIKING EXAMPLE OF CONSTANT
    ADAPTATION TO TECHNOLOGICAL DEVELOPMENT--STEAM WARSHIPS,
    IRONCLADS, DREADNOUGHTS, SUBMARINES, AIRCRAFT CARRIERS, AND
    NUCLEAR SUBMARINES. AS ERIC GROVE SHOWS IN THIS SURVEY OF
    NAVAL DEVELOPMENTS IN THE UK BEFORE AS WELL AS AFTER
    HIROSHIMA, THE ATOMIC BOMB AND THE END OF EMPIRE HAVE
    COMBINED TO MAKE NAVAL STAFFS RETHINK THEIR STRATEGY AND THE
    DESIGNS OF THEIR WARSHIPS. HIS CONCLUSION IS THAT THE ONLY
    ACCEPTABLE PREDICTIONS ARE THOSE THAT TAKE ACCOUNT OF
    CONTEMPORARY TRENDS--POLITICAL AND ECONOMIC--HOWEVER
    UNWELCOME THEY MAY APPEAR.

03797 GROVE, R.
    SCOTTISH MISSIONARIES, EVANGELICAL DISCOURSES AND THE
    ORIGINS OF CONSERVATION THINKING IN SOUTHERN AFRICA 1820-
    1900
    JOURNAL OF SOUTHERN AFRICAN STUDIES, 15(2) (JAN 89),
    163-187.
        THE PAPER EXAMINES THE CONDITIONS UNDER WHICH COLONIAL
    STATES IN SOUTHERN AFRICA EVOLVED AN INTEREST IN
    CONSERVATION AND PROBES THE RESPECTIVE MOTIVATIONS OF
    SCIENTISTS AND THE STATE IN ADOPTING CONSERVATIONIST IDEAS.
    IT ARGUES THAT CONSERVATIONISM IN THE CAPE AROSE OUT OF A
    COINCIDENCE BETWEEN CHANGING PRECEPTS IN WESTERN SCIENCE AND
    A COLONIAL CRISIS, TRIGGERED INITIALLY BY DROUGHT. THESE
    IDEAS DEVELOPED AGAINST THE BACKGROUND OF A PRE-EXISTING AND
    PRECOCIOUS AWARENESS OF THE SPPED OF ENVIRONMENTAL CHANGE IN
    THE WORKS OF TRAVELLERS AND MISSIONARIES IN THE LATE
    EIGHTEENTH AND EARLY NINETEENTH CENTURIES.

03798 GROVOGUI, S.N.
    CONFLICTING SELVES IN INTERNATIONAL LAW: AN ANALYSIS OF
    COLONIALISM AND DECOLONIZATION IN NAMIBIA
    DISSERTATION ABSTRACTS INTERNATIONAL, 49(11) (MAY 89),
    3497-A.
        BEGINNING WITH THE PONTIFICAL BULL OF POPE ALEXANDER VI,
    THE AUTHOR EXAMINES THE EMERGENCE OF THE EUROPEAN EGO AS THE
    CENTER AROUND WHICH THE DISCOURSE OF INTERNATIONAL POLITICS
    HAS BEEN CONSTRUCTED. HE TRACES THE GENEALOGY OF THE CONCEPT
    OF SOVEREIGNTY AND SELF-DETERMINATION IN INTERNATIONAL LAW
    AND FINDS THAT THEY WERE FORMULATED TO REINFORCE THE DESIRES
    OF EUROPEANS TO DOMINATE NON-EUROPEANS. THE RESISTANCE OF
    NAMIBIANS TO DOMINATION AND THE RESPONSE OF EUROPEAN POWERS
    TO THE NATIONALISTS ARE USED TO DEMONSTRATE THE IDEOLOGICAL
    NATURE OF THE LAW AND THE FALLACY OF THE CLAIMS MADE BY MOST
    INTERNATIONAL LEGAL THEORISTS.

03799 GRUBER, R.
    GERMANY: END OF POSTWAR ERA
    SOUTH AFRICA FOUNDATION REVIEW, 15(3) (MAR 89), 5.
        GERMANY IS UNDERGOING A PERIOD OF TRANSITION. THE THREE
    MAJOR POLITICAL, PARLIAMENTARY PARTIES HAVE SEEN THEIR
    TRADITIONAL ROLE AND SUPPORT BASE WITHER IN RECENT YEARS.
    NEW PARTIES ARE EMERGING ANOTHER SIGN OF CHANGE IS THE
    GERMAN ATTITUDE TOWARDS THE SUPERPOWERS AS WEST GERMANS FEEL
    LESS THREATENED BY THE SOVIET UNION.

03800 GRUBER, R.
    PERESTROIKA AND APARTHEID
    SOUTH AFRICA FOUNDATION REVIEW, 15(11) (NOV 89), 7-8.
        UNTIL THE ADVENT OF PERESTROIKA, THE SOVIET UNION HAD
    NOT REALLY HAD A COHERENT POLICY TOWARDS SOUTH AFRICA.
    HOWEVER, THE NEW EMPHASIS ON RESOLUTION OF REGIONAL
    CONFLICTS HAS LED THE USSR TO PURSUE A POLICY ENCOURAGING
    NEGOTIATION AND SETTLEMENT AMONG SOUTH AFRICANS. ALTHOUGH
    UNWILLING TO ABANDON THEIR LONG-STANDING FRIENDSHIP WITH THE
    ANC, SOVIET OFFICIALS HAVE DECLARED INTEREST IN ESTABLISHING
    TIES WITH OTHER POLITICAL ORGANIZATIONS IN SOUTH AFRICA.

03801 GRUBER, R.
    WEST GERMANY: OVER TO PRETORIA
    SOUTH AFRICA FOUNDATION REVIEW, 15(1) (JAN 89), 6.
        THE AUTHOR REVIEWS DEVELOPMENTS IN WEST GERMAN-SOUTH
    AFRICAN RELATIONS IN 1988.

03802 GRUNES, R.A.
    CREATIONISM, THE COURTS, AND THE FIRST AMENDMENT
    JOURNAL OF CHURCH & STATE, 31(3) (AUT 89), 465-486.
        ALTHOUGH COUCHED IN THE LANGUAGE OF CONSTITUTIONAL LAW,
    THE CREATIONISM-EVOLUTION CONTROVERSY IS ESSENTIALLY A
    POLITICAL DISPUTE INVOLVING GROUPS WITH RADICALLY DIFFERENT
    VALUES AND AGENDAS. SCIENTISTS, EDUCATORS, MAINLINE CLERGY,
    AND CIVIL LIBERTARIANS ARE THE MAJOR OPPONENTS OF "CREATION
    SCIENCE." ON THE OTHER SIDE ARE THE ORGANIZATIONS OF THE NEW
    CHRISTIAN RIGHT THAT SEEK TO RESTORE RELIGION AND A GOD-
    CENTERED ENVIRONMENT TO CLASSROOMS. IN THE CASE OF "EDWARDS
    V. AGUILLARD" THE SUPREME COURT USED ITS ESTABLISHMENT
    CLAUSE TEST TO STRIKE DOWN A DELIBERATE, CALCULATED ATTEMPT
    BY FUNDAMENTALIST GROUPS TO BRING RELIGION INTO THE
    CLASSROOM AND TO PLACE SCIENCE EDUCATION UNDER RELIGIOUS
    CONTROL.

03803 GRUNTORAD, J.
    NEW GROUPS GROW STRONGER DESPITE REPRESSION
    EAST EUROPEAN REPORTER, 3(4) (SPR 89), 67-68.
        THE ARTICLE INCLUDES A BRIEF LIST AND DESCRIPTION OF
    SEVERAL NEW INDEPENDENT GROUPS IN CZECHOSLOVAKIA. THEY
    INCLUDE: THE INITIATIVE FOR SOCIAL DEFENSE (ISO), THE
    MOVEMENT FOR CIVIL LIBERTIES (HOS), THE JOHN LENNON PEACE
    CLUB (MKJL), A DEFENSE COMMITTEE ON BEHALF OF PEACE
    ACTIVISTS, THE CZECHOSLOVAK HELSINKI COMMITTEE (CSHV), CZECH
    CHILDREN, OBRODA (REVIVAL) CLUB FOR SOCIALIST RECONSTRUCTION,
    THE ASSOCIATION FOR THE STUDY OF DEMOCRATIC SOCIALISM
    (SSDS), THE CLUB FOR LEGAL SUPPORT (KPP), AND THE EAST
    EUROPEAN INFORMATION AGENCY (VIA). THE ARTICLE OUTLINES THE
    STRUCTURE, IDEOLOGY, AND GOALS OF EACH GROUP.

03804 GRUSHIN, B.A.
    PUBLIC OPINION IN THE SYSTEM OF MANAGEMENT
    SOVIET REVIEW, 30(6) (NOV 89), 31-39.
        HOWEVER THEORETICIANS MAY INTERPRET PUBLIC OPINION AND
    HOWEVER THEY MAY RESOLVE QUESTIONS ABOUT ITS STRENGTHS AND
    WEAKNESSES, PUBLIC OPINION DOES NOT YET PLAY THE ROLE IT
    DESERVES TO PLAY, AND SHOULD ALREADY HAVE BEEN PLAYING, IN
    THE WHOLE SYSTEM OF SOCIALIST SOCIAL RELATIONS AND
    ESPECIALLY IN THE SYSTEM OF SOCIAL MANAGEMENT. IT IS
    IMPORTANT TO ACCURATELY MEASURE THE RANGE OF PUBLIC OPINION
    AND THEN TAKE IT INTO ACCOUNT IN THE FORMULATION OF SOVIET
    PUBLIC POLICY.

03805 GRUSKY, S.
    THE CHANGING ROLE OF THE US MILITARY IN PUERTO RICO
    SOCIAL AND ECONOMIC STUDIES, 36(3) (SEP 87), 37-76.
        THIS PAPER EXAMINES THE CHANGING ROLE OF THE US MILITARY

IN PUERTO RICO. THE GEOSTRATEGIC ROLE OF THE ISLAND FROM
SPANISH COLONIAL TIMES TO THE LATE 1970S IS SUMMARIZED.
SPECIFIC RECENT CHANGES IN MILITARY INFRSTRUCTURE IS
EXAMINED. ALSO, THE CHANGING ECONOMIC ROLE OF THE US
MILITARY IS DISCUSSED.

03806 GUANG, W.
WORLD PRESSED FOR NEW POLITICAL ORDER
BEIJING REVIEW, 32(1) (JAN 89), 7,9.
THE WORLD LEADERSHIP HAS A MISSION TO SET UP A NEW
INTERNATIONAL POLITICAL ORDER BASED ON THE FIVE PRINCIPLES
OF PEACEFUL COEXISTENCE: MUTUAL RESPECT FOR SOVEREIGNTY AND
TERRITORIAL INTEGRITY, MUTUAL NON-AGGRESSION, NON-
INTERFERENCE IN ANOTHER COUNTRY'S INTERNAL AFFAIRS, EQUALITY
AND MUTUAL BENEFIT, AND PEACEFUL COEXISTENCE. THE
ESTABLISHMENT OF THIS NEW INTERNATIONAL POLITICAL ORDER
REQUIRES THE ELIMINATION OF HEGEMONISM AND POWER POLITICS
FROM INTERNATIONAL RELATIONS.

03807 GUAZZONE, L.
KUWAIT'S NATIONAL SECURITY POLICY AND ITS INFLUENCE ON THE
GULF REGION
INTERNATIONAL SPECTATOR, XXIV(2) (APR 89), 63-71.
THE AUTHOR ANALYZES THE ROOTS AND PATTERNS OF KUWAIT'S
SECURITY POLICY, FIRST THROUGH THE HISTORICAL LESSONS THAT
HAVE SHAPED KUWAITI PERCEPTIONS OF THE EXTERNAL ENVIRONMENT
AND THEN THROUGH THE EVOLUTION OF FOREIGN POLICY PATTERNS
THAT THESE EXPERIENCES HAVEE GENERATED. THEN SHE EXAMINES
KUWAIT'S SECURITY POLICY DURING THE IRAN-IRAQ WAR AND
DESCRIBES THE SECURITY ROLE OF KUWAIT'S DOMESTIC AND
MILITARY POLICIES.

03808 GUCKIAN, N.J.
BRITISH RELATIONS WITH TRANS-JORDAN, #1920-1930
DISSERTATION ABSTRACTS INTERNATIONAL, 49(10) (APR 89),
3147-A.
THE AUTHOR EXAMINES BRITISH POLICY TOWARDS TRANS-JORDAN
FROM 1920 TO 1930, THE FORMATIVE PERIOD DURING WHICH THE
FOUNDATIONS OF THE PRESENT HASHEMITE KINGDOM OF JORDAN WERE
LAID THE HISTORY OF TRANS-JORDAN DURING THIS PERIOD IS THE
STORY OF THE CONSOLIDATION OF BRITAIN'S POSITION IN THE
TERRITORY, THE BUILDING OF AN ARAB GOVERNMENT THAT WAS
INDEPENDENT OF PALESTINE, THE ESTABLISHMENT OF THE
TERRITORIAL FRONTIERS, THE DEVELOPMENT OF AN ARAB ARMY UNDER
BRITISH OFFICERS, THE IMPOSITION OF FINANCIAL DISCIPLINE ON
ABDULLAH'S REGIME, AND THE DEVELOPMENT OF A BRITISH-
CONTROLLED AIR AND LAND ROUTE TO IRAQ AND THE PERSIAN GULF.

03809 GUDAVA, E.
THE TRAGEDY OF GEORGIA
GLASNOST, II(3) (MAY 89), 4-10.
THE AUTHOR RECOUNTS THE EVENTS OF APRIL 9, 1989, IN
TBILISI, SOVIET GEORGIA. HE CLAIMS THAT WHAT BEGAN AS A
PEACEFUL DEMONSTRATION ENDED WITH MASS MURDER BY THE SOVIET
SPECIAL FORCES.

03810 GUDMUNDSON, L.
PEASANT, FARMER, PROLETARIAN: CLASS FORMATION IN A
SAMLLHOLDER COFFEE ECONOMY, 1850-1950
HISPANIC-AMERICAN HISTORICAL REVIEW, 69(2) (MAY 89),
221-258.
COSTA RICAN COFFEE-BASED SOCIETY WITNESSED A "PEASANT TO
FARMER" TRANSITION IN AGRICULTURE, BY WHICH A SUBSISTANCE-
ORIENTED PEASANTRY WAS TRANSFORMED INTO PROPERTIED AND
PROPERTYLESS, EMPLOYER AND LABORER CLASSES. THIS WAS LENGHTY
AND HIGHLY AMBIGUOUS PROCESS BUT ONE IN WHICH A HEALTHY
SMALL HOLDER GROUP, OR RURAL PETTY BOURGEOISIE OF SORTS, WAS
CONSOLIDATED BY THE EARLY TWENTIETH CENTURY. THE PROCESS
INVOLVED BOTH POLITICAL MOBILIZATION AND SOCIAL CHANGE,
PARTICULARLY THE GROWING RESTRICTION OF PARTIBLE INHERITANCE
TO FAVOR SONS OVER DAUGHTERS. OF ALL THE SOCIAL CLASSES
PRESENT IN THE COUNTRYSIDE, THE WELL-TO-DO PRODUCER
(NONPROCESSOR) GROUP AND ITS HISTORY ARE THE PRIMARY FOCUS
OF THIS STUDY.

03811 GUERRIERI, P.; PADOAN, P.C.
TWO-LEVEL GAMES AND STRUCTURAL ADJUSTMENT: THE ITALIAN CASE
INTERNATIONAL SPECTATOR, XXIV(3-4) (JUL 89), 128-140.
THE AUTHORS PRESENT A SIMPLE FRAMEWORK THAT BUILDS ON
THE IDEA OF TWO-LEVEL GAMES. THEY OFFER A DETERMINATION OF
THE WIN SET THAT IS BASED ON THE IDEA OF A GOVERNMENT
MAXIMIZING ITS REPUTATION ABROAD (VIS-A-VIS OTHER
GOVERNMENTS) AND POPULARITY AT HOME (VIS-A-VIS INTEREST
GROUPS AND THE STATE BUREAUCRACY). THE WAY IN WHICH THE
STRUCTURE AND NATURE OF INTERNATIONAL REGIMES INFLUENCE THE
INTERACTION BETWEEN THE TWO LEVELS OF POLITICS IS
DEMONSTRATED. THEN A NEW LEVEL IS INTRODUCED: THE POLICY AND
POLITICS OF STRUCTURAL ADJUSTMENT. ITALY IS USED AS A CASE
STUDY.

03812 GUERTNER, G.L.
CONVENTIONAL DETERRENCE AFTER ARMS CONTROL
PARAMETERS, XIX(4) (DEC 89), 67-79.
CONVENTIONAL ARMS CONTROL AND MODERNIZATION PROGRAMS CAN

SHAPE A STRATEGIC ENVIRONMENT THAT FURTHER DEGRADES SOVIET
CAPACITY FOR MOMENTUM AND QUICK MILITARY VICTORY. THE
INHERENT ADVANTAGE OF THE ATTACKER IN GAINING THE INITIATIVE
OVER THE DEFENDER MUST BE REVERSED BEFORE WESTERN INTERESTS
ARE SECURE. THE GROWING LETHALITY OF NATO'S CONVENTIONAL
FORCES AND GORBACHEV'S NEW MILITARY THINKING IN THE FORM OF
NONOFFENSIVE DEFENSE MAKE THIS POSSIBLE FOR THE FIRST TIME
IN POSTWAR EUROPE.

03813 GUEULLETTE, A.
FINANCING THE ACQUISITION OF WESTERN TECHNOLOGY IN THE
CONTEXT OF THE HUNGARIAN REFORM
SOVIET STUDIES, 61(4) (OCT 89), 592-601.
THE QUESTIONS OF HOW FAR CAN THE REFORMS IN HUNGARY BE
SAID TO HAVE CONTRIBUTED TO ENTERPRISES' AUTONOMY IN
DECISION-MAKING AND TO THE FINANCING OF TECHNOLOGICAL
DEVELOPMENT, AND IF THERE IS A REAL DIVERGENCE FROM THE
CHARACTERISTICS OF THE CENTRALLY PLANNED ECONOMY ARE
ADDRESSED IN THIS ARTICLE. THE MAIN PRINCIPLES OF THE NEW
ECONOMIC MECHANISM ARE EXAMINED IN ORDER TO ANSWER THESE
QUESTIONS STUDIED ARE, ECONOMIC REFORM AND THE CAPITAL
MARKET, TRANSFER OF TECHNOLOGY, INDEBTEDNESS AND ECONOMIC
POLICY.

03814 GUEYE, S.P.
THE CRISIS OF URAT CIVILIZATION?
WORLD MARXIST REVIEW, 32(11) (NOV 89), 59-62.
THIS ARTICLE EXPLORES THE VALUE AND PURPOSE OF THE
CONCEPT OF "PROGRESS" IN VIEW OF SOME OF THE PRESENT
CONTRADICTIONS OF INDUSTRIALIZATION AND CERTAIN "MISLAPS" OF
MODERN TECHNOLOGY. THE AUTHOR CONTENDS THAT THE EUROAMERICAN
MODEL OF DEVELOPMENT, WHICH HAS ACHIEVED FORMIDABLE PROGRESS
IN TERMS OF SCIENTIFIC KNOWLEDGE, HAS PUSHED HUMANITY INTO A
SITUATION WHEREBY THE PRESENT LOGIC OF DEVELOPMENT URGENTLY
REQUIRES CHANGE IN ORDER TO AVOID A UNIVERSAL CATASTROPLE.

03815 GUICHERD, C.
ANOTHER WAY TO PEACE
COMMONWEAL, CXVI(22) (DEC 89), 704-706.
THE AUTHOR DISCUSSES THE OFFICIAL FRENCH CATHOLIC STANCE
ON NUCLEAR DETERRENCE AS EVIDENCED BY THE FRENCH BISHOPS AND
OTHER FRENCH CATHOLIC ATTITUDES TOWARD NUCLEAR ARMS.

03816 GUIDA, R.A.
THE COSTS OF FREE INFORMATION
PUBLIC INTEREST, (97) (FAL 89), 87-95.
THE AUTHOR DISCUSSES THE USES AND ABUSES OF THE FREEDOM
OF INFORMATION ACT, WHICH MAKES THE AMERICAN GOVERNMENT MORE
OPEN AND ACCOUNTABLE BUT ALSO CREATES ADDITIONAL WORK FOR
GOVERNMENT AGENCIES.

03817 GUILLAUMONT, P.; GUILLAUMONT, S.
THE IMPLICATIONS OF EUROPEAN MONETARY UNION FOR AFRICAN
COUNTRIES
JOURNAL OF COMMON MARKET STUDIES, XXVIII(2) (DEC 89),
139-154.
AS 1992 APPROACHES, THE POLITICAL AND ECONOMIC
AUTHORITIES OF THE FRANC ZONE STATES ARE BECOMING
INCREASINGLY CONCERNED ABOUT THE IMPLICATIONS OF EUROPEAN
ECONOMIC INTEGRATION. IN PARTICULAR, THE LIKELIHOOD OF THE
ESTABLISHMENT OF A EUROPEAN MONETARY UNION HAS SPARKED A
WAVE OF CONCERN. BUT THE ESTABLISHMENT OF EMU WOULD NOT
REQUIRE THE RULES OF THE FRANC ZONE TO BE MODIFIED, EVEN IF
IT WOULD IN SOME RESPECTS CHANGE ITS ECONOMIC IMPLICATIONS.
THE EMU WOULD MAKE POSSIBLE, AND DESIRABLE, MONETARY
COOPERATION BETWEEN THE AFRICAN SIGNATORIES OF THE LOME
CONVENTION AND THE EC AS A WHOLE, WHICH WOULD REINFORCE THE
FRANCO-AFRICAN MONETARY COOPERATION NOW IN EXISTENCE.

03818 GUILLEN-R., A.
CRISIS, THE BURDEN OF FOREIGN DEBT, AND STRUCTURAL
DEPENDENCE
LATIN AMERICAN PERSPECTIVES, 16(1) (WIN 89), 31-51.
THIS ARTICLE ATTEMPTS TO ADVANCE THE STUDY OF LATIN
AMERICA'S EXTERNAL DEBT. IT ANALYZES THE HISTORICAL PROCESS
OF INDEBTEDNESS, THE CAUSES AND FACTORS CONDITIONING ITS
ORIGINS AND RAPID GROWTH, THE INTERNAL UTILIZATION OF THE
LOANS OBTAINED, AND THE IMPACT OF DEBT SERVICE ON ECONOMIC
GROWTH AND THE ACCUMULATION OF CAPITAL. ALTHOUGH SEVERAL OF
THE HYPOTHESES SET FORTH IN THIS WORK ARE APPLICABLE TO
LATIN AMERICA AS A WHOLE, THEY ARE MAINLY FOUNDED ON THE
MEXICAN CASE.

03819 GUILLORY, T.
CANADA: THE DECISION TO PROCURE NUCLEAR ATTACK SUBMARINES
AND ITS SIGNIFICANCE FOR NATO
AVAILABLE FROM NTIS, NO. AD-A201 669/9/GAR, SEP 88, 99.
IN JUNE 1987 THE CANADIAN GOVERNMENT ANNOUNCED PLANS TO
PROCURE 10 TO 12 NUCLEAR ATTACK SUBMARINES (SSNS). THE
EVIDENCE SUGGEST THAT, FOR SOME CANADIANS, A PRIMARY PURPOSE
FOR THIS SUBMARINE PROGRAM MAY NOT BE TO ENHANCE THE
SECURITY OF NATO, BUT INSTEAD TO ASSERT CANADA'S SOVEREIGNTY,
PRINCIPALLY AGAINST THE UNITED STATES, IN THE ARCTIC REGION.
THE THESIS DISCUSS THE DECISION AND ITS POSSIBLE

IMPLICATIONS FOR THE SECURITY OF NORTH AMERICA AND NATO. IT
IS ARGUED THAT THE UNITED STATES MUST CONTINUE TO HAVE
UNIMPEDED ACCESS TO THE ARCTIC REGION TO COUNTER THE EVER
INCREASING THREAT POSED BY SOVIET NUCLEAR BALLISTIC MISSILE
SUBMARINES (SSBNS). FINALLY THE THESIS SUGGESTS A POSSIBLE
SOLUTION TO THE CURRENT SOVEREIGNTY DEBATE AND A POTENTIAL
STRATEGY FOR EMPLOYING THESE SNN TO ENHANCE THE SECURITY OF
NORTH AMERICA AND NATO AS A WHOLE. KEYWORDS: NAVAL
PROCUREMENT; NUCLEAR POWERED SUBMARINE THREATS; ARCTIC
REGIONS ACCESS; SOVEREIGNTY; CANADA AS A NAVAL POWER;
DETERRENCE; NATIONAL INTERESTS; THESES.

03820 GUIRGUIS, S.A.
THE IMAGE OF EGYPT IN "THE NEW YORK TIMES," 1956, 1967,
1979
DISSERTATION ABSTRACTS INTERNATIONAL, 49(8) (FEB 89),
2009-A.
THE AUTHOR COMPARES THE IMAGE OF EGYPT PRESENTED BY "THE
NEW YORK TIMES" DURING THREE TIME PERIODS. THE SUEZ CRISIS
OF 1956, THE EGYPTIAN-ISRAELI WAR OF 1967, AND THE PEACE
TREATY OF 1979. HER OBJECTIVE IS TO DETERMINE THE EXTENT TO
WHICH CHANGES IN THE PROJECTED IMAGE OF EGYPT WERE SIMILAR
TO OR DIFFERENT FROM CHANGES IN AMERICAN-EGYPTIAN GOVERNMENT
RELATIONS.

03821 GUITON, M.V.; MARVICK, E.W.
FAMILY EXPERIENCE AND POLITICAL LEADERSHIP: AN EXAMINATION
OF THE ABSENT FATHER HYPOTHESIS
INTERNATIONAL POLITICAL SCIENCE REVIEW, 10(1) (JAN 89),
63-71.
LASSWELL'S EFFORTS IN THE 1930S TO USE THE FINDINGS OF
PSYCHOANALYTIC CASE STUDIES FOR UNDERSTANDING PERSONALITY
PATTERNS IN POLITICAL LEADERSHIP HAVE BEEN FOLLOWED ONLY BY
SLOW PROGRESS. SOME OBSTACLES TO SUCH APPLICATION ARE
IDENTIFIED. CASE MATERIAL FROM THE PSYCHOANALYTIC TREATMENT
OF A SMALL NUMBER OF PATIENTS WHOSE FATHERS WERE ABSENT IN
WARTIME IS USED TO EXEMPLIFY CERTAIN PROMISING STRATEGIES
FOR OVERCOMING SUCH OBSTACLES. THE DISCUSSION SUGGESTS THE
NEED FOR THE PSYCHOPOLITICAL INVESTIGATOR TO EXAMINE CLOSELY
THE DETAILS OF VARIOUS INTRAPSYCHIC RESPONSES TO EARLY
FAMILY EXPERIENCE. FOR THIS, THE STUDY OF CLINICAL
LITERATURE IS THE BEST RESOURCE.

03822 GUNDLE, S.
ITALY
ELECTORAL STUDIES, 8(3) (DEC 89), 288-295.
AS IN MOST MEMBER NATIONS OF THE EC, EUROPEAN ELECTIONS
IN ITALY ARE HEAVILY CONDITIONED BY DOMESTIC POLITICAL
EVENTS. THIS ARTICLE EXPLORES ITALY'S 1989 POLITICAL
CAMPAIGN ISSUES AND PERSONALITIES, IT EXAMINES THE EFFECT OF
WORDS AND IMAGES PROJECTED BY THE MEDIA AND ANALYZES
ELECTION RESULTS.

03823 GUNLICKS, A.
CONSTITUTIONAL LAW AND THE PROTECTION OF SUBNATIONAL
GOVERNMENTS IN THE UNITED STATES AND WEST GERMANY
PUBLIUS: THE JOURNAL OF FEDERALISM, 18(1) (WIN 88),
141-158.
THE ARTICLE EXPLORES THE RELATIONS BETWEEN FEDERAL AND
SUBNATIONAL GOVERNMENTS IN THE US AND WEST GERMANY. IT
EXPLORES THE HISTORY OF FEDERALISM IN BOTH NATIONS AND
CONCLUDES THAT CONSTITUTIONAL PROVISIONS IN WEST GERMANY
GRANT THE STATES A GENERAL PROTECTION COMPARABLE TO THE
TENTH AMMENDMENT. HOWEVER, IN BOTH CASES RECENT ACTION BY
COURTS HAVE LIMITED THE PROTECTION FROM FEDERAL INTRUSION
THAT THE STATES ENJOYED PREVIOUSLY.

03824 GUNN, P.
AN ARTEFACT OF LATE FORDISM? THE SOCIAL SECURITY REVIEW
ARENA, 86 (FAL 89), 44-50.
THE SOCIAL SECURITY REVIEW, SOMETIMES KNOW AS THE 'CASS
REVIEW', WAS ANNOUNCED BY THE MINISTER FOR SOCIAL SECURITY,
BRIAN HOWE, IN DECEMBER 1985. IT WAS PRESENTED AS THE FIRST
'FUNDAMENTAL RE-EXAMINATION OF EXISTING PROGRAMS AND
PRIORITIES' IN THE SOCIAL SECURITY AREA IN AUSTRALIA SINCE
THE CURTIN LABOR GOVERNMENT ESTABLISHED THE BASIS FOR THE
POST-WAR WELFARE STATE IN THE 1940S. WHERE THERE IS
INNOVATION, IT IS MAINLY IN THE FORM OF RETHINKING THE
SOCIAL SECURITY SYSTEM AS AN 'ACTIVE' 'SPRINGBOARD' INTO THE
LABOUR MARKET RATHER THAN A 'PASSIVE' 'SAFETY NET'. THIS IS
ACCOMPANIED BY FAIRLY GENERAL DISCUSSION OF LINKAGES OF
INCOME SUPPORT OF THE VARIOUS CATEGORIES WITH LABOUR MARKET
PROGRAMMES.

03825 GUNTHER, R.
ELECTORAL LAWS, PARTY SYSTEMS, AND ELITES: THE CASE OF
SPAIN
AMERICAN POLITICAL SCIENCE REVIEW, 83(3) (SEP 89), 835-858.
USING AGGREGATE, SURVEY, AND IN-DEPTH ELITE INTERVIEW
DATA FROM SPAIN IN THE 1970S AND 1980S, THE AUTHOR
DEMONSTRATES THAT THE "MECHANICAL" EFFECT OF THE SPANISH
ELECTORAL LAW IS AS STRONG AS THAT OF MANY SINGLE-MEMBER
CONSTITUENCY SYSTEMS. BUT THE "DISTAL" EFFECT OF THE
ELECTORAL LAW ON THE PARTY SYSTEM IS SHOWN TO BE COMPLEX AND

MULTIFACETED, NOT DIRECT AND DETERMINISTIC. THE PERCEPTIONS,
CALCULATIONS, STRATEGIES, AND BEHAVIOR OF PARTY ELITES PLAY
A CRUCIAL INTERVENING THE ELECTORAL LAW AND THE OVERALL
SHAPE OF THE PARTY SYSTEM.

03826 GUOCANG, H.
THE ROOTS OF THE POLITICAL CRISIS
WORLD POLICY JOURNAL, 6(4) (FAL 89), 609-620.
THE CHINESE GOVERNMENT HAS SUCCEEDED IN SUPPRESSING BUT
NOT ERADICATING THE MOVEMENT FOR DEMOCRACY IN THE PEOPLE'S
REPUBLIC OF CHINA. WHILE THE CURRENT REGIME IS A
TRANSITIONAL ONE IT MAY BE ABLE TO CONSOLIDATE ITS POWER
ENOUGH TO STAVE OFF A RAPID DEMISE. THIS ARTICLE EXAMINES
THE BACKGROUND LEADING UP TO THE DEMONSTRATIONS IN TIANANMEN
SQUARE. IT EXPLORES THE POLITICAL AND ECONOMIC SITUATION,
THE BEIJING SPRING AND EFFORTS ON THE PART OF THE GOVERNMENT
TO SUPRESS THE PROTESTS.

03827 GUOGUAN, L.
A SWEET AND SOUR DECADE
BEIJING REVIEW, 32(1) (JAN 89), 22-28.
LIU GUOGUANG, VICE-PRESIDENT OF THE CHINESE ACADEMY OF
SOCIAL SCIENCES, CASTS A CRITICAL EYE OVER THE URBAN AND
RURAL ECONOMIC REFORMS OF THE LAST TEN YEARS. AS HE POINTS
OUT, THE GAINS HAVE BEEN ENORMOUS. BUT IF THEY ARE TO BE
SUSTAINED AND CONTINUED. CARE MUST BE TAKEN IN SELECTING THE
RIGHT POLICIES FROM THE VARIOUS CONTENDING PROPOSALS NOW
BEING PUT FORWARD IN CHINESE ECONOMIC CIRCLES.

03828 GUOJIAN, H.
STRENGTHENING TAXATION'S ROLE AS AN ECONOMIC LEVER
BEIJING REVIEW, 32(32) (AUG 89), 20-23.
CHINA IS ADOPTING A SERIES OF MEASURES TO STRENGTHEN ITS
TAX SYSTEM. THE NEW MEASURES ARE DESIGNED TO CONSOLIDATE
TAXATION AS THE MAIN SOURCE OF STATE REVENUE AND TO DEVELOP
ITS REGULATORY ROLE IN THE BATTLE AGAINST INFLATION AND THE
MAINTENANCE OF A REASONABLE DISTRIBUTION OF WEALTH.

03829 GUOYOU, L.
U.S. ROLE IN ASIAN ECONOMY
BEIJING REVIEW, 32(32) (AUG 89), 32-34.
THE ECONOMIC BOOM IN JAPAN, SOUTH KOREA, SINGAPORE, HONG
KONG, AND TAIWAN MAY BE THE MOST NOTEWORTHY DEVELOPMENT IN
INTERNATIONAL AFFAIRS IN THE LAST THIRTY YEARS BECAUSE IT
MARKS THE RISE OF THE REGION'S POWER IN THE WORLD. IN A VERY
SHORT TIME, ASIA HAS NARROWED THE GAP BETWEEN THE EAST AND
THE WEST AND STARTED A HISTORICAL SHIFT OF ECONOMIC POWER
FROM WEST TO EAST. THE MOST IMPORTANT DYNAMIC TO DRIVE THIS
ECONOMIC THRUST CAME FROM THE UNITED STATES, AS DID MOST OF
THE MANAGERIAL SKILL AND TECHNOLOGY.

03830 GUPPY, N.
PAY EQUITY IN CANADIAN UNIVERSITIES, 1972-73 AND 1985-86
CANADIAN REVIEW OF SOCIOLOGY AND ANTHROPOLOGY, 26(5) (NOV
89), 743-758.
THE GAP IN THE AVERAGE EARNINGS OF WOMEN AND MEN HAS
NARROWED VERY LITTLE OVER TIME. LEGISLATION BASED ON 'EQUAL
PAY FOR EQUAL WORK' HAS PROVED INEFFECTIVE. IT IS HOPED THAT
NEW LEGISLATION BASED ON 'EQUAL PAY FOR WORK OF EQUAL VALUE'
WILL FACILITATE THE ATTAINMENT OF A FAIRER BALANCE IN THE
INCOMES WOMEN AND MEN. THIS PAPER REVIEWS THE EVIDENCE FOR
WAGE DISCRIMINATION ON WHICH THE MORE RECENT LEGISLATION
RESTS. NEW EVIDENCE OF A LONGITUDINAL NATURE DEMONSTRATES A
SLOW DECLINE IN WAGE DISPARITIES BETWEEN 1972 AND 1986 IN
THE CANADIAN UNIVERSITY SYSTEM. ESTIMATES OF CHANGING LEVELS
OF WAGE DISCRIMINATION ARE PROVIDED. THE FINDINGS ALSO SHOWS
THAT EVEN IF PAY EQUITY LEGISLATION IS COMPLETELY SUCCESSFUL,
THE INCOMES OF WOMEN AND MEN WILL STILL DIFFER
SUBSTANTIALLY.

03831 GUPTA, A.
THE POLITICAL ECONOMY OF POST-INDEPENDENCE INDIA - A
REVIEW ARTICLE
JOURNAL OF ASIAN STUDIES, 48(4) (NOV 89), 787-797.
IN ATTEMPTING TO DEVELOP A PERSPECTIVE ON POLITICAL
ECONOMY THROUGH AN ANALYSIS OF A FEW BOOKS, THE AUTHOR HAS
CHOSEN TO CONCENTRATE ON FOUR CRUCIAL THEMES: THEORIES OF
THE STATE: THE ASSOCIATION OF THE STATE, REGIME, AND PARTY;
THE FORMULATION OF STATE POLICIES; AND THE IMPLEMENTATION OF
POLITICS. HE CONCLUDES THE ARTICLE BY IDENTIFYING AREAS THAT
HAVE NOT BEEN ADDRESSED: INDIAN VILLAGES; THE MANNER IN
WHICH REGIMES AND STATES SEEK LEGITIMACY; GENDER; AND
ELITISM.

03832 GUPTA, S.
A FRIENDLY VISITOR
INDIA TODAY, XIV(3) (FEB 89), 77.
AMERICAN CONGRESSMAN STEPHEN J. SOLARZ, WHO HAS BEEN
DESCRIBED AS A "PRO-INDIAN ZIONIST WHOSE CONSTITUENCY IS NOT
BROOKLYN BUT BOMBAY," VISITS THE SOUTH ASIAN SUBCONTINENT
OFTEN. A STAUNCH OPPONENT OF ZIA, HE IS A STOUT SUPPORTER OF
BENAZIR BHUTTO. THE CHANGE IN PAKISTAN'S GOVERNMENT HAS
ALTERED SOLARZ'S POSITION ON CAPITOL HILL AND ALLOWED HIM TO
BE FRIENDLY WITH BOTH INDIA AND PAKISTAN.

03833 GUPTA, S.
AFGHANISTAN: CONDEMNED TO FRATRICIDE
INDIA TODAY, XIV(5) (MAR 89), 50-53.
WITH THE DEPARTURE OF THE LAST SOVIET TROOPS FROM
AFGHANISTAN, THE GOVERNMENT FORCES LED BY PRESIDENT
NAJIBULLAH GOT READY FOR A LAST-DITCH BATTLE WITH THE
FACTION-RIDDEN MUJAHEDIN. AS CONVERGING HORDES OF ABDUL HAG,
THE GUERRILLA LEADER DOMINATING THE KABUL REGION, THREATENED
TO BLAST THE CITY WITH MISSILES, THE RESIDENTS OF KALUL CAME
TO REALIZE THAT FRACTRICIDAL CONFLICT WILL LIKELY BE THEIR
FATE NOW THAT THE SUPERPOWERS HAVE BARTERED AFGHANISTAN'S
FUTURE FOR A TENUOUS PEACE OF THEIR OWN.

03834 GUPTA, S.
AFGHANISTAN: STEPPING UP THE FIRE
INDIA TODAY, XIV(7) (APR 89), 32-35, 37.
AS A MAJOR STEP IN THEIR MOVE TOWARDS KABUL, THE AFGHAN
MUJAHEDIN INTENSIFIED THEIR OFFENSIVE AGAINST THE TOWN OF
JALALABAD WHILE OPENING UP NEW FRONTS ELSWHERE. THEIR
PROGRESS WAS SLOW AND LOSSES HIGH, BUT THEY ARE BEGINNING TO
TAKE THEIR TOLL ON THE GOVERNMENT FORCES. THE FRATRICIDAL
WAR CONTINUES AND THREATENS TO DRAW IN OTHER REGIONAL POWERS.

03835 GUPTA, S.
ARMS FOR THE ASKING
INDIA TODAY, XIV(14) (JUL 89), 42-47.
THE ARTICLE EXAMINES THE ARMS TRADE THAT ORIGINATES IN
THE TOWN OF DARRA ADAM KHEL IN PAKISTAN. LONG A SOLID
SUPLIER OF WEAPONS FOR SIKH EXTREMISTS AND REBELS FROM SRI
LANKA, DARRA'S ARMS MARKET EXPANDED ENORMOUSLY AFTER THE
SOVIET INVASION OF AFGHANISTAN. HOWEVER, THE TOWN HAS
RECENTLY SUFFERED A SIGNIFICANT SLUMP IN TRADE. RIFLES,
MORTARS, ANTI-AIRCRAFT GUNS, ROCKET LAUNCHERS, AND MINES ARE
STILL OPENLY AVAILABLE WITH NO QUESTIONS ASKED.

03836 GUPTA, S.
BUTA SINGH: COURTIER UNDER CROSFIRE
INDIA TODAY, XIV(10) (MAY 89), 10-12.
HOME MINISTER BUTA SINGH, RAJIV GANDHI'S HATCHET MAN, IS
HIMSELF UNDER RELENTLESS ATTACK: FIRST, OVER THE THAKKAR
COMMISSION REPORT, THEN THE DISMISSAL OF THE BOMMAI
GOVERNMENT IN KARNATAKA. THIS ARTICLE DESCRIBES HOW NEW
REVELATIONS ABOUT DUBIOUS BUSINESS DEALS INVOLVING HIS
FAMILY HAVE REKINDLED THE FUREY OF HIS OPPONENTS.

03837 GUPTA, S.
DAY OF THE DRAGON
INDIA TODAY,   (JUL 89), 38-42.
THIS ARTICLE REPORTS ON CHINA FOLLOWING THE TIANANMEN
MASSACRE WHERE AUTHORITIES HAVE UNLEASED A CAMPAIGN OF
PROPAGANDA AND TERROR NOT SEEN SINCE THE CHINESE REVOLUTION.
IT DETAILS THE ALL-OUT MEDIA CAMPAIGN TO SUBDUE THE
POPULATION, UNMINDFUL OF WORLDWIDE REVULSION, AND REPORTS ON
THE EXECUTION OF SEVERAL DEMOCRACY AGITATION LEADERS.

03838 GUPTA, S.
DEFYING THE PAST
INDIA TODAY, XIV(2) (JAN 89), 24-26.
IN DECEMBER 1988, RAJIV GANDHI BECAME THE FIRST INDIAN
PRIME MINISTER TO VISIT PAKISTAN IN NEARLY THREE DECADES.
THE INDIAN LEADER AND BENAZIR BHUTTO SIGNED ACCORDS ON THE
AVOIDANCE OF DOUBLE TAXATION AND ON CULTURAL EXCHANGES AND
AGREED TO SIGN A DOCUMENT FORBIDDING ATTACKS ON ONE
ANOTHER'S NUCLEAR INSTALLATIONS.

03839 GUPTA, S.
STATE OF SIEGE
INDIA TODAY, XIV(6) (MAR 89), 62-65.
FOLLOWING THE SOVIET WITHDRAWAL, AFGHAN TROOPS HAVE
CONTINUED TO HOLD OUT AGAINST THE REBELS. NAJIB HAS
DISPLAYED MUCH GREATER TENACITY AND POLITICAL ACUMEN THAN
WESTERN OBSERVERS HAD CREDITED HIM WITH. BY COLLECTING A
FORMIDABLE ARSENAL AND ASSEMBLING HIS MOST EXPERIENCED
MILITARY COMMANDERS AND PARTY FUNCTIONARIES IN KABUL, NAJIB
HAS SHOWN A WILLINGNESS TO FIGHT RATHER THAN RETREAT INTO
IGNOMINIOUS SAFETY.

03840 GUPTA, S.; ROY, B.
STUNNING MANOEUVRE
INDIA TODAY, 14(15) (AUG 89), 14-20.
THIS ARTICLE REPORTS ON CURRENT HAPPENINGS IN INDIA. THE
CAG REPORT HAS SUDDENLY ALTARED ALL EQUATIONS AND POWER
BALANCES. THE OPPOSITION HAS BEEN REVITALISED AND ITS EN
MASSE RESIGNATION FROM LOK SABHA HAS PUT THE CONGRESS(1) ON
THE DEFENSIVE. THE REPORT QUESTIONS THE PROCESS OF SELECTION
AND PURCHASE OF THE CONTROVERSIAL BEFORS GUN.

03841 GUPTA, S.; LIPSCHITZ, L.; MAYER, T.
THE COMMON AGRICULTURAL POLICY OF THE EC
FINANCE AND DEVELOPMENT, 26(2) (JUN 89), 37-39.
THE EUROPEAN COMMUNITY (EC) AS A GROUP IS THE LEADING
IMPORTER AND THE SECOND LARGEST EXPORTER OF AGRICULTURAL
COMMODITIES IN THE WORLD. THE COMMUNITY'S SHARE OF WORLD

EXPORTS IS NOT ONLY LARGE, BUT HAS GROWN SINCE THE INCEPTION
OF THE COMMON AGRICULTURAL POLICY (CAP) IN THE 1960'S. THE
ARTICLE ASSESSES THE IMPACT OF THE CAP ON TRADE AND
PRODUCTION PATTERNS IN EC MEMBER COUNTRIES AS WELL AS THE
REST OF THE WORLD. IT ALSO DISCUSSES THE REFORMS THAT HAVE
BEEN SPURRED BY THE HEAVY COSTS OF THE CAP ON THE EC AND ITS
ADVERSE EFFECTS ON INTERNATIONAL TRADING RELATIONS.

03842 GUPTA, S.; DEVADAS, D.; NOORANI, A.G.; TRIPATHI, S.
WIDENING THE WEB
INDIA TODAY, XIV(8) (APR 89), 22-27.
MORE THAN FOUR YEARS AFTER THE ASSASSINATION OF INDIRA
GANDHI AND EXACTLY FOUR MONTHS AFTER HER ASSASSINS WERE
HANGED, THE GOVERNMENT CHARGED FOUR MORE PERSONS WITH
PARTICIPATING IN THE CONSPIRACY. IN SO DOING, IT REOPENED
THE CONTROVERSY ABOUT THE CRIME.

03843 GUPTA, U.S.
BIHAR: CLERK POWER - RANCHI COURTS FACE ANARCHY
INDIA TODAY, XIV(5) (MAR 89), 28.
THE STATE OF AFFAIRS IN RANCHI COURTS IS DEPLORABLE: THE
CLERKS INTIMEDATE JUDICIAL MAGISTRATS, EXTORT MONEY FROM
LITIGANTS, AND IN GENERAL, CALL THE SLOTS. A RECENT BOYCOTT
BY LAWYERS AND A SPATE OF VIGILANCE RAIDS HAS HAD ONLY ONE
POSITIVE EFFECT: CLERKS ARE NOW MORE DISCREET ABOUT
DEMANDING MONEY.

03844 GUPTA, V.P.
INDIAN ADMINISTRATIVE DEVELOPMENT IN THE EIGHTIES:
IMPEDIMENTS AND CATALYSTS IN VIEW OF FIVE-YEAR PLAN
INDIAN JOURNAL OF POLITICAL SCIENCE, L(2) (APR 89),
263-271.
THE AUTHOR HIGHLIGHTS SOME ISSUES IN THE AREA OF INDIAN
ADMINISTRATIVE DEVELOPMENT, OFFERING BOTH DIAGNOSIS AND
REMEDIES FOR THE FAILURES EXPERIENCED DURING THE COURSE OF
THIRTY-FIVE YEARS OF DEVELOPMENT PLANNING.

03845 GURDILEK, R.
VIEW FROM ANKARA: EYE OF THE STORM
NATO'S SIXTEEN NATIONS, 34(6) (OCT 89), 8.
THE SENSITIVE ISSUE OF SELECTING A SUCCESSOR TO TURKEY'S
PRESIDENT KENAN EVREN ILLUSTRATES THE UNCERTAINTY AND
COMPLEXITY OF TURKISH POLITICS. MOST POLITICAL OBSERVERS
BELIEVE A DAMAGING POWER STRUGGLE IS INEVITABLE BETWEEN
PRIME MINISTER OZAL'S WESTERN-ORIENTED TECHNOCRAT PROTEGES
AND THE ONCE-POWERFUL ISLAMIC FUNDAMENTALIST FACTION BIDDING
FOR A COMBACK. IF THE FUNDAMENTALISTS REGAIN THEIR INFLUENCE,
MANY MOTHERLAND PARTY DEPUTIES SAY THE RESULT WOULD BE A
TIDAL WAVE OF DEFECTIONS TO THE CONSERVATIVE TRUE PATH PARTY.

03846 GURDON, C.
A CLAMOR RISES AT THE GATES OF KHARTOUM
SOUTH, (104) (JUN 89), 11.
AS SADIQ EL-MAHDI CLINGS TO POWER IN SUDAN'S NEW 23-MAN
CABINET, THE MINISTERS FACE CRUCIAL ECONOMIC DECISIONS
PREPARATORY TO A POSSIBLE CIVIL WAR SETTLEMENT. BILATERAL
CREDITORS ARE LIKELY TO PRESS FOR STRUCTURAL READJUSTMENT,
BUT IT IS QUESTIONABLE WHETHER A FRAGILE PEACE SETTLEMENT
COULD SURVIVE STRINGENT AUSTERITY MEASURES.

03847 GUSFIELD, J.R.
CONSTRUCTING THE OWNERSHIP OF SOCIAL PROBLEMS: FUN AND
PROFIT IN THE WELFARE STATE
SOCIAL PROBLEMS, 36(5) (DEC 89), 431-441.
LINKS BETWEEN THE EMERGENCE OF SOCIAL PROBLEMS AND THE
WELFARE STATE ARE EXAMINED, WITH PARTICULAR ATTENTION TO THE
PLACE OF THE "TROUSLED PERSONS" PROFESSIONS, MASS MEDIA AND
EDUCATIONAL INSTITUTIONS, THE PLACE OF THE LANGUAGE OF
CONFLICT AND CONSENSUS IN SOCIAL PROBLEMS ACTIVITIES,
CONTESTED AND UNCONTESTED DEFINITIONS OF PROBLEM CONDITIONS
HOW MEANINGS AND PROBLEMS ARE TRANSFORMED, AND HOW
MOBILIZATION ACTIVITIES CONTRIBUTE TO THESE TRANSFORMATIONS.
THE PAPER ENDS WITH A PLEA TO MOVE THE STUDY OF SOCIAL
PROBLEMS CLOSER TO THE STUDY OF HOW SOCIAL MOVEMENTS AND
INSTITUTIONS AFFECT AND ARE AFFECTED BY THE INTERPRETATIONS,
THE LANGUAGE, AND THE SYMBOLS THAT CONSTITUTE SEEING A
SITUATION AS A SOCIAL PROBLEM IN HISTORICAL AND
INSTITUTIONAL CONTEXT.

03848 GUSHEE, D.E.; JUSTUS, J.R.
STRATOSPHERIC OZONE DEPLETION
CRS REVEIW, 10(7) (AUG 89), 11-12.
POLITICAL LEADERS HAVE CREATED, THROUGH MULTILATERAL
NEGOTIATIONS UNDER UNITED NATIONS' AUSPICES, AN
INTERNATIONAL TREATY TO STOP GROWTH IN CFC AND HALON USE
AROUND THE WORLD. THE MONTREAL PROTOCOL ON SUBSTANCES THAT
DEPLETE THE OZONE LAYER WENT INTO EFFECT ON JANUARY 1, 1989.
WHEN THE PROTOCOL WAS CONSUMMATED, IT WAS VIEWED AS A
STUNNING ACHIEVEMENT, BRINGING TOGETHER FOUR DOZEN COUNTRIES
THAT ACCEPTED A MANDATE TO RESHAPE A MAJOR INDUSTRIAL SECTOR.
NOW THESE SAME SIGNATORIES APPEAR TO BE WILLING TO GO EVEN
FURTHER IN RESPONSE TO THE MOST RECENT DATA.

03849 GUSTAFSON, M.; ROSENBERG, J.
THE FAITS OF FRANKLIN ROOSEVELT
PRESIDENTIAL STUDIES QUARTERLY, XIX(3) (SUM 89), 559-566.
THIS ARTICLE CITES EVIDENCE TO ILLUSTRATE THE LINKAGE
THAT EPISTED BETWEEN ROOSEVELT'S RELIGIOUS VALUES AND HIS
POLITICAL IDEOLOGY. AN ANALYSIS OF THE RELATIONSHIP GIVES AN
INDICATION OF THE KIND OF SOCIETY ROOSEVELT ENVISIONED FOR
THE FUTURE.

03850 GUSTAITIS, A.
THE POPULAR FRONT IN ESTONIA
GLASNOST, II(2) (MAR 89), 76-77.
INTENSE GRASSROOTS POLITICAL ACTIVITY IN ESTONIA HAS
GIVEN RISE TO A POPULAR, PRO-PERESTROIKA MOVEMENT KNOWN AS
THE NATIONAL FRONT. NUMEROUS INDEPENDENT AND UNOFFICIAL
ORGANIZATIONS HAVE ENDORSED THE FRONT, INCLUDING THE COUNCIL
ON CULTURE, THE SOCIETY FOR AN ENLIGHTENED PEOPLE, THE GREEN
MOVEMENT, AND THE ESTONIAN INDEPENDENT SOCIAL FORUM. THE
MEMBERS SEE PERESTROIKA AS A CHANCE TO GAIN MORE
INDEPENDENCE AND GUARANTEE THE DEVELOPMENT OF THE REPUBLIC
UNDER FEDERAL PRINCIPLES.

03851 GUSTAVSON, M.R.
SOME THOUGHTS ON FRG (FEDERAL REPUBLIC OF GERMANY)
AVAILABLE FROM NTIS, NO. DE89005947/GAR, 1988, 2.
EARLY IN AUGUST M.R. GUSTAVSON HAD AN OPPORTUNITY TO
MEET WITH A NUMBER OF INDIVIDUALS IN THE FEDERAL REPUBLIC OF
GERMANY TO DISCUSS NATIONAL SECURITY ISSUES. HE ALSO TALKED
WITH PAUL ZINNER, WHO HAS SPENT MUCH OF THIS SUMMER THERE
CONDUCTING INTERVIEWS. THE ATTACHMENT SUMMARIZES SOME OF THE
NATIONAL SECURITY VIEWS WHICH WERE ENCOUNTERED. RECOUNTED
HERE ARE ONLY THOSE VIEWS WHICH HAVE A SUBSTANTIAL NUMBER OF
BACKERS AND WHICH MAY BE OF PARTICULAR INTEREST TO OTHERS AT
LLNL AND WITHIN DOE.

03852 GUTMANN, A.
THE CENTRAL ROLE OF RAWLS'S THEORY
DISSENT, (SUM 89), 338-342.
POLITICAL THINKING IN THE ACADEMY HAS CHANGED SINCE THE
EARLY 1960'S IN AT LEAST THREE SIGNIFICANT WAYS. FIRST, MOST
RIGHTS ADVOCATES NOW EMBRACE PART OF THE MARXIST CRITIQUE
AND DEFEND NOT ONLY THE TRADITIONAL LIST OF CIVIL AND
POLITICAL LIBERTIES BUT ALSO MORE EQUAL DISTRIBUTION OF
INCOME, WEALTH, EDUCATION, JOB OPPORTUNITIES, HEALTH CARE,
AND OTHER GOODS ESSENTIAL TO SECURE THE WELFARE AND DIGNITY
OF THE DISADVANTAGED. SECONDLY, MOST PROMINENT POLITICAL
PHILOSOPHERS ARE NOW RIGHTS THEORISTS. THIRDLY, GRAND
POLITICAL THEORY IS ONCE AGAIN ALIVE IN THE ACADEMY. ALL OF
THESE CHANGES ARE ATTRIBUTABLE TO THE INFLUENCE OF "A THEORY
OF JUSTICE" BY JOHN RAWLS.

03853 GUTMANN, A. (ED.)
DEMOCRACY AND THE WELFARE STATE
PRINCETON UNIVERSITY PRESS, LAWRENCEVILLE, NJ, 1988, 352.
THE ESSAYS IN THIS VOLUME EXPLORE THE MORAL FOUNDATIONS
AND THE POLITICAL PROSPECTS OF THE WELFARE STATE IN THE
UNITED STATES. AMONG THE QUESTIONS ADDRESSED ARE THE
FOLLOWING: HAS PUBLIC SUPPORT FOR THE WELFARE STATE FADED?
CAN A DEMOCRATIC STATE PROVIDE WELFARE WITHOUT PRODUCING
DEPENDENCY ON WELFARE? WHY AND IN WHAT WAYS DOES THE WELFARE
STATE DISCRIMINATE AGAINST WOMEN? CAN WE JUSTIFY LIMITING
IMMIGRATION FOR THE SAKE OF SAFEGUARDING THE WELFARE OF
AMERICANS? HOW CAN ELEMENTARY AND SECONDARY EDUCATION BE
DISTRIBUTED CONSISTENTLY WITH DEMOCRATIC VALUES?

03854 GUTTERIDGE, W.
CHANGING SOVIET ATTITUDES TO SOUTH AFRICA: SOME FIRST HAND
IMPRESSIONS
SOUTH AFRICA FOUNDATION REVIEW, 15(6) (JUN 89), 3, 8.
THE AUTHOR PRESENTS HIS IMPRESSIONS ON THE EFFECTS THAT
SOVIET CHANGES SUCH AS PRESTROIKA AND CHANGES IN FOREIGN
POLICY WILL HAVE ON SOUTH AFRICA. HE ARGUES THAT THE SOVIETS
ARE BEGINNING TO SEE PARALLELS BETWEEN THE RACIAL TENSION
SURROUNDING APARTHEID AND THEIR OWN ETHNIC AND RACIAL
TROUBLES IN ARMENIA, THE BALTIC STATES, AND OTHER AREAS.
SOVIET ACKNOWLEDGEMENT OF THE FUTILITY OF ARMED STRUGGLE TO
SOLVE THE PROBLEM AS WELL AS QUIET PRESSURE FOR NEGOTIATIONS
SEEMS TO BE ON THE INCREASE.

03855 GUYOT, E.; CLAD, J.
REGAINING THE INITIATIVE
FAR EASTERN ECONOMIC REVIEW, 141(38) (SEP 88), 40-41.
A RECENT ARMED FORCES OF THE PHILIPPINES (AFP) STUDY
WARNS THAT THE COMMUNIST INSURGENCY IS "SLOWLY GAINING THE
STRATEGIC INITITIAVE." TO COUNTER THE GROWING THREAT, THE
STUDY PROPOSES A CHANGE OF TACTICS FROM THE CURRENT SEARCH
AND DESTROY CAMPAIGNS OF "SHORT DURATION" TO A WAR OF QUICK
DECISION TO BE FOUGHT OVER THE NEXT TWO OR THREE YEARS.
DESPITE THE STUDY'S UNCONVENTIONAL PROPOSALS, THE MILITARY
SEEMS TO HAVE ACCEPTED ITS MAIN THRUST: THE NEED FOR A WAR
OF QUICK DECISION.

03856 GWALA, N.
POLITICAL VIOLENCE AND THE STRUGGLE FOR CONTROL IN

PIETERMARITZBURG
JOURNAL OF SOUTHERN AFRICAN STUDIES, 15(3) (APR 89),
506-524.
THE FOCUS OF THE PAPER IS EDENDALE, THE SECOND LARGEST
TOWNSHIP IN PMB. THIS PAPER LOOKS INTO THE FOLLOWING ASPECTS.
FIRSTLY, A SOCIAL AND ECONOMIC PROFILE OF THE PMB TOWNSHIPS,
WITH PARTICULAR EMPHASIS ON EDENDALE, INCLUDING SOME
ADMINISTRATIVE ASPECTS OF THESE TOWNSHIPS. SECONDLY, AN
ATTEMPT IS MADE TO EXPLAIN THE SOCIAL AND POLITICAL
INTERESTS BATTLING FOR THE CONTROL OF EDENDALE. THIRDLY, THE
BASIS OF INKATHA'S ATTEMPTS AT ESTABLISHING ITS HEGEMONY IN
PMB TOWNSHIPS IS ANALYSED. LASTLY, THE PAPER CONCLUDES BY
DRAWING SOME LESSONS FOR THE STRUGGLE AGAINST INKATHA IN
NATAL.

03857 HA, M.
THE IMPACT OF REAL ESTATE SPECULATION CONTROL POLICY: AN
INTERRUPTED TIME-SERIES EVALUATION FOR THE REPUBLIC OF
KOREA
DISSERTATION ABSTRACTS INTERNATIONAL, 50(6) (DEC 89),
1799-A.
THE AUTHOR OFFERS AN EMPIRICAL ANALYSIS OF THE EFFECT OF
THE COMPREHENSIVE REAL ESTATE SPECULATION CONTROL POLICY IN
SOUTH KOREA AND DERIVES THEORETICAL IMPLICATIONS ABOUT
REGULATORY POLICY MECHANISMS, PROCESS, AND CONTEXT IN A NON-
WESTERN SOCIETY.

03858 HAAS, M.
THE POLITICS OF SINGAPORE IN THE 1980S
JOURNAL OF CONTEMPORARY ASIA, 9(1) (1989), 48-77.
THIS ARTICLE ANALYZES THE 1980S CAMPAIGN IN SINGAPORE TO
SNUFF OUT DEMOCRACY. THE RESULTING SITUATION WAS THAT THERE
WERE FEW POLITICAL INSTITUTIONS BETWEEN THE STATE AND THE
PEOPLE. THE ALIENATION OF THE MASSES FROM THE GOVERNMENT LED
TO THE RISE OF VARIOUS FORMS OF POLITICAL DISSENT. A
REVOLUTION AT THE TOP WAS ESTABLISHING SUB-FACISM, NAMELY,
RIGHTIST TOTAL CONTROL OF SOCIETY WITHOUT ANY APPARENT
LEGITIMATING IDEOLOGY. A DETAILED NARRATIVE ON THESE
DEVELOPMENTS IS OFFERED

03859 HAAS, P.
DO REGIMES MATTER? EPISTEMIC COMMUNITIES AND MEDITERRANEAN
POLLUTION CONTROL
INTERNATIONAL ORGANIZATION, 43(5) (SUM 89), 377-404.
INTERNATIONAL REGIMES HAVE RECEIVED INCREASING ATTENTION
IN THE LITERATURE ON INTERNATIONAL RELATIONS. HOWEVER,
LITTLE ATTENTION HAS BEEN SYSTEMATICALLY PAID TO HOW
COMPLIANCE WITH THEM HAS BEEN ACHIEVED. AN ANALYSIS CF THE
MEDITERRANEAN ACTION PLAN, A COORDINATED EFFORT TO PROTECT
THE MEDITERRANEAN SEA FROM POLLUTION, SHOWS THAT THIS REGIME
ACTUALLY SERVED TO EMPOWER A GROUP OF EXPERTS (MEMBERS OF AN
EPISTEMIC COMMUNITY), WHO WERE THEN ABLE TO REDIRECT THEIR
GOVERNMENTS TOWARD THE PURSUIT OF NEW OBJECTIVES. ACTING IN
AN EFFECTIVE TRANSNATIONAL COALITION, THESE NEW ACTORS
CONTRIBUTED TO THE DEVELOPMENT OF CONVERGENT STATE POLICIES
IN COMPLIANCE WITH THE REGIME AND WERE ALSO EFFECTIVE IN
PROMOTING STRONGER AND BROADER RULES FOR POLLUTION CONTROL.
THIS SUGGESTS THAT IN ADDITION TO PROVIDING A FORM OF ORDER
IN AN ANARCHIC INTERNATIONAL POLITICAL SYSTEM, REGIMES MAY
ALSO CONTRIBUTE TO GOVERNMENTAL LEARNING AND INFLUENCE
PATTERNS OF BEHAVIOR BY EMPOWERING NEW GROUPS WHO ARE ABLE
TO DIRECT THEIR GOVERNMENTS TOWARD NEW ENDS.

03860 HAASS, R.
DEALING WITH FRIENDLY TYRANTS
NATIONAL INTEREST, (15) (SPR 89), 40-48.
THE ARTICLE DEALS WITH AN ISSUE THAT HAS TROUBLED US
POLICYMAKERS FOR DECADES: DEALING WITH FRIENDLY TYRANTS. IT
ANALYZES INSTANCES OF US RELATIONS WITH AUTHORITARIAN
REGIMES IN THE PAST AND PRESENT AND ATTEMPTS TO FORMULATE
SOME BASIC PRINCIPLES AND TACTICS THAT WILL PROVE USEFUL FOR
FUTURE POLICYMAKERS. SOME OF THE FACTORS THAT NEED TO BE
ASSESSED ARE: THE REGIME'S VULNERABILITY, THE NATURE OR
SEVERITY OF THE RULE, THE POSSIBILITY OF ALTERNATIVES, AND
THE INTENSITY OF US INVOLVEMENT. THE ARTICLE CONCLUDES BY
ADVOCATING FLEXIBILITY AND REALISM WHEN DEALING WITH
AUTHORITARIAN REGIMES.

03861 HAASS, R.N.
DEMOCRACY AND TYRANNY: DEALING WITH FRIENDLY TYRANTS
CURRENT, (316) (OCT 89), 34.
IT MAY BE NO EXAGGERATION TO SAY THAT UNITED STATES
POLICY TOWARD PRO-AMERICAN, RIGHT-WING, AUTHORITARIAN RULERS
CONSTITUTES THE MOST CONTROVERSIAL FOREIGN POLICY QUESTION
BEFORE THE US GOVERNMENT. ONE APPROACH WOULD HAVE THE USA
CONTINUE TO SUPPORT A FRIENDLY AUTHORITARIAN REGIME ON THE
GROUNDS THAT IT HAS SERVED AMERICAN POLITICAL, ECONOMIC, AND
MILITARY INTERESTS AND WILL CONTINUE TO DO SO IF IT SURVIVES.
ANOTHER SCHOOL OF THOUGHT ADVOCATES WITHDRAWING AMERICAN
SUPPORT FROM AUTHORITARIAN ELITES ON THE GROUNDS THAT THEY
CONTRADICT AMERICAN VALUES.

03862 HABERMAS, J.
TWENTY YEARS LATER

DISSENT, (SPR 89), 250-256.
IN THIS INTERVIEW, ONE OF WEST GERMANY'S BEST-KNOWN
POLITICAL PHILOSOPHERS CONSIDERS THE POLITICAL MOVEMENT OF
THE LATE 1960'S AND HOW IT BROUGHT CHANGES THAT CONTINUE TO
INFLUENCE POLITICS TODAY.

03863 HABIB, H.
BANGLADESH: PEACE OFFER
THIRD WORLD WEEK, 8(13) (MAY 89), 100-101.
IN AN EFFORT TO END THE GUERRILLA WAR IN THE CHITTAGONG
HILL TRACTS, BANGLADESHI PRESIDENT HUSSAIN MOHAMMED ERSHAD
DECLARED AN AMNESTY FOR TRIBAL INSURGENTS AND URGED THE
FIGHTERS TO RETURN TO NORMAL VILLAGE LIFE. THE MINORITY
TRIBES IN THE TRACTS ARE TRYING TO OUST BENGALI SETTLERS WHO
HAVE COME FROM THE OVERCROWDED PLAINS BELOW. THE
TRIBESPEOPLE, WHO ARE MOSTLY BUDDHISTS OR ANIMISTS, FEAR
THEY WILL LOSE THEIR CULTURAL AND ETHNIC IDENTITY TO THE
MOSLEM BENGALIS. THE HILL PEOPLE ALSO WANT TO REGAIN THE
REGIONAL AUTONOMY THEY ENJOYED UNDER BRITISH COLONIAL RULE.

03864 HABIB, K.
THE GLOBAL CHARACTER OF THIRD WORLD PROBLEMS
WORLD MARXIST REVIEW, 32(8) (AUG 89), 69-72.
THIS ARTICLE IS A CONTINUATION OF WMR'S DISCUSSION ON
HOW TO OVERCOME UNDERDEVELOPMENT IN THE MODERN WORLD. IT
STATES THAT THE INTERNATIONAL COMMUNITY HAS A DUTY TOWARDS
DEVELOPING NATIONS TO ANALYSE THE EXPERIENCE AMASSED,
COLLECT AND STUDY NEW PROPOSALS, AND ADOPT THE BEST
SOLUTIONS. IT SUGGESTS THAT THE ROUTE FOR ELIMINATING THE
CURRENT STATE OF AFFAIRS IS A MAJOR OVERHAUL OF THE ECONOMIC
AND SOCIAL STRUCTURES OF THIS GROUP OF COUNTRIES. IT OFFERS
SPECIFIC STEPS FOR OVERCOMING "UNDERDEVELOPMENT."

03865 HABIB, K.
THE PEACE PROCESS MUST BE ADVANCED
WORLD MARXIST REVIEW, 32(4) (APR 89), 71-73.
IT HAS BECOME PERFECTLY OBVIOUS THAT WAR CANNOT BE A
MEANS OF SETTLING CONFLICTS BETWEEN STATES, THAT IT MERELY
WORSENS THE SITUATION AND COMPOUNDS THE DIFFICULTIES. ONCE
WAR BREAKS OUT, IT IS IMPOSSIBLE TO ANTICIPATE HOW LONG IT
WILL LAST, THE CONSEQUENCES FOR THE COUNTRIES INVOLVED, OR
THE SCALE ON WHICH OTHER STATES WILL BE DRAWN INTO THE
CONFLICT AND UNIVERSAL SECURITY JEOPARDISED. THE ONLY WAY TO
SETTLE INTERNATIONAL AND REGIONAL CONFLICTS TODAY IS BY
NEGOTIATION, WITH RESTRAINT AND DIALOGUE AND WITHOUT THE USE
OF FORCE. THE INTERNATIONAL COMMUNITY IS FACED WITH THE
RESPONSIBLE AND NOBLE TASK OF MAINTAINING THE MOMENTUM OF
THE PEACE PROCESS THROUGH THE GENERAL POSITIVE SHIFTS NOW
UNDER WAY. THESE ARE HAVING AN INFLUENCE ON ALL STATES AND
POLITICAL FORCES, THEREBY HELPING TO IMPROVE RELATIONS
BETWEEN THEM ON THE ONE HAND, AND PROTECTING BASIC HUMAN
RIGHTS AND FREEDOMS ON THE OTHER. THESE CHANGES SHOULD HELP
TO PROTECT THE LONG-SUFFERING IRAQI AND IRANIAN PEOPLES.

03866 HACKER, J.
THE BERLIN POLICY OF THE USSR UNDER GORBACHEV
AUSSEN POLITIK, 40(3) (1989), 232-250.
THE YARDSTICK AND CRUCIAL QUESTION OF THE SOVIET BERLIN
POLICY HAS ALWAYS BEEN AND STILL IS TODAY THE INCORPORATION
OF WEST BERLIN INTO INTERNATIONAL TREATIES OF THE FEDERAL
REPUBLIC OF GERMANY. A SPECIAL TERRITORIAL CLAUSE, THE SO-
CALLED FRANK-FALIN FORMULA, WAS ALREADY ELABORATED IN THIS
CONTEXT IN 1972. IT WAS ALSO APPLIED MUTATIS MUTANDIS IN THE
DECLARATION BETWEEN THE EUROPEAN COMMUNITY AND THE COUNCIL
FOR MUTUAL ECONOMIC ASSISTANCE IN 1988. WHEREVER THE
SPECIFIC INTERESTS OF THE SOVIET UNION IN THE FIELDS OF
TRADE AND ECONOMIC COOPERATION WERE NOT AT STAKE MOSCOW HAS
EVADED THE ISSUE. AGREEMENT COULD ONLY BE REACHED ON THE SO-
CALLED PERSON-RELATED SOLUTION; AS, FOR EXAMPLE, IN THE
AGREEMENT ON SCIENTIFIC AND TECHNICAL COOPERATION IN 1986.
PROF. DR. JENS HACKER FROM THE INSTITUTE OF POLITICAL
SCIENCES AT THE UNIVERSITY OF REGENSBURG EXPLAINS THESE
RECURRENT DIFFICULTIES BY REFERRING TO THE REPEATED ATTEMPT
BY THE SOVIET UNION TO INTERPRET THE PRINCIPLE OF AN
INDEPENDENT POLITICAL ENTITY INTO THE 1971 BERLIN SETTLEMENT
FOR THE CITY'S WESTERN SECTORS. AT THE SAME TIME THE SOVIET
UNION SUPPORTS THE CLAIM BY THE GERMAN DEMOCRATIC REPUBLIC
THAT EAST BERLIN, WHICH ON ACCOUNT OF ITS FOUR-POWER STATUS
BELONGS TO BERLIN AS A WHOLE, IS THE CAPITAL OF THE GDR. ON
THE ONE HAND, THE SOVIET UNION INSISTS ON THE CONTINUATION
OF RIGHTS AND RESPONSIBILITIES FOR GERMANY AS A WHOLE AND
FOR BERLIN, WHICH IS SHARES WITH THE WESTERN VICTOR POWERS.
ON THE OTHER HAND, IT REJECTS THE AFFILIATION OF WEST BERLIN
AS A LAND OF THE FEDERAL REPUBLIC OF GERMANY, A STATUS
CONFIRMED BY THE CLAUSE IN THE BERLIN SETTLEMENT RELATING TO
THE MAINTENANCE AND DEVELOPMENT OF TIES WITH THE FEDERAL
REPUBLIC OF GERMANY. WEST BERLIN IS NOT A SEPARATE ENTITY
UNDER INTERNATIONAL LAW. IT ONLY HAS RELATIONS WITH ONE
STATE -- THE FEDERAL REPUBLIC OF GERMANY -- AND ITS EXTERNAL
INTERESTS ARE REPRESENTED BY THE FEDERAL REPUBLIC OF GERMANY.
THERE IS NO SIGN OF A WILLINGNESS ON THE PART OF THE SOVIET
UNION, EVEN UNDER GORBACHOV, TO MOVE THESE CONTRADICTIONS
AND ACCEPT THE NORMS OF ESTABLISHED LEGAL PRACTICE IN THE
RELATIONS BETWEEN WEST BERLIN AND THE FEDERAL REPUBLIC OF

GERMANY.

03867 HACKETT, D.W.; KABIR, M.
IS ATLANTIC CANADA BECOMING MORE DEPENDENT ON FEDERAL
TRANSFERS?
CANADIAN PUBLIC POLICY--ANALYSE DE POLITIQUES, XV(1) (MAR
89), 43-48.
THIS STUDY UNDERTAKES AN EMPIRICAL ANALYSIS TO EXAMINE
THE PROPOSITION THAT THE ATLANTIC PROVINCES HAVE BECOME
INCREASINGLY DEPENDENT ON FEDERAL TRANSFER PAYMENTS IN
RECENT YEARS. A FRAMEWORK IS DEVELOPED WITHIN WHICH THE
QUESTION OF DEPENENCE OF THE ATLANTIC PROVINCES ON TRANSFER
PAYMENTS FOR THE PERIOD 1962-84 IS ANALYSED. THE ANALYSIS
INDICATES THAT PER CAPITA TOTAL FEDERAL TRANSFERS TO THE
REGION INCREASED AT A FASTER RATE THAN THE NATIONAL AVERAGE.
HOWEVER, PER CAPITA FEDERAL REVENUE RAISED IN THE REGION,
COMPARED TO THE COUNTRY AS A WHOLE, INCREASED AT AN EVEN
FASTER RATE, THE CONCLUSION REACHED IS THAT WHILE ATLANTIC
PROVINCES ARE DEPENDENT ON FEDERAL TRANSFER PAYMENTS, THE
LEVEL OF DEPENDENCE HAS BEEN DECREASING IN COMPARISON TO THE
NATIONAL AVERAGE IN RECENT YEARS.

03868 HADAR, L.T.
PRESS AND GOVERNMENT IN ISRAEL: FROM FRIENDS TO ADVERSARIES
MIDSTREAM, XXXV(9) (DEC 89), 9-12.
LIKE RICHARD NIXON, WHO PERCEIVED THE AMERICAN MEDIA TO
BE CONTROLLED BY THE EASTERN LIBERAL ELITE, ISRAELI'S LIKUD
LEADERSHIP HAS REGARDED THE MAJOR PRINT AND BROADCAST MEDIA
TO BE UNDER THE INFLUENCE OF A SECULAR, LEFT-OF-CENTER
ASHKENAZI MINORITY WHOSE VIEWS OF ISRAEL'S FUTURE AND THE
PALESTINIAN PROBLEM CLASH WITH THAT OF THE LIKUD AND ITS
NATIONALISTIC, TRADITIONAL SEPHARDI SUPPORTERS. THE LIKUD
HAS SUCCEEDED IN IMPOSING "A REIGN OF TERROR" ON THE ISRAELI
BROADCASTING AUTHORITY, BUT THE PRINT MEDIA HAS BEEN MORE OF
A PROBLEM.

03869 HADAR, L.T.
THE "STRATEGIC ASSET" CONCEPT: DECLINE AND FALL?
MIDSTREAM, XXXV(7) (OCT 89), 10-16.
A CERTAIN UNEASINESS EXISTS IN GEORGE BUSH'S WASHINGTON
AMONG FRIENDS AND SUPPORTERS OF ISRAEL IN THE EXECUTIVE
BRANCH, ON CAPITOL HILL, IN THE ORGANIZED JEWISH COMMUNITY,
AND AMONG PRO-ISRAELI LOBBYISTS. THESE PEOPLE HAVE A SENSE
THAT, CONTRARY TO PUBLIC APPEARANCES, NOT ALL IS WELL ON THE
AMERICAN-ISRAELI FRONT, THAT SOMETHING IS HAPPENING BEHIND
THE SCENES IN THE UNDERCURRENTS OF THE AMERICAN-ISRAELI
CONNECTION. THEY ARE WORRIED ABOUT THE FUTURE OF AMERICAN
FOREIGN POLICY ON ISRAEL.

03870 HADARI, S.A.
UNINTENDED CONSEQUENCES IN PERIODS OF TRANSITION:
TOCQUEVILLE'S "RECOLLECTIONS" REVISITED
AMERICAN JOURNAL OF POLITICAL SCIENCE, 33(1) (FEB 89),
136-149.
TOCQUEVILLE'S RECOLLECTIONS ANALYSES THE UNEXPECTED
CHAIN OF EVENTS DURING A PERIOD OF RAPID SOCIAL CHANGE. THE
AUTHOR'S READING OF THIS NEGLECTED TEXT UNCOVERS THREE
FORMAL MODELS OF UNINTENDED CONSEQUENCES IN SUCH PERIODS OF
TRANSITION AND FORCES A REEVALUATION OF TOCQUEVILLE'S
APPROACH AS A POLITICAL THEORIST: NO LONGER A PROPHET, BUT
RATHER A CAUTIOUS STUDENT OF SOCIAL PROCESSES ACUTELY AWARE
OF THEIR UNDERDETERMINATION. THE MODELS ARE CLASSIFIED
INITIALLY BY THE RELATION BETWEEN INTENDED AND ACHIEVED
GOALS--OVERSHOOTING, UNDERSHOOTING, AND BOOMERANG--AND OFFER
A GENERAL EXPLANATION OF THE GENESIS OF EACH EFFECT.

03871 HADDAD, A.E.
A CORRELATIONAL-STRUCTURAL MODEL OF POLITICAL INSTABILITY
IN THE ARAB WORLD
DISSERTATION ABSTRACTS INTERNATIONAL, 49(12) (JUN 89),
3857-A.
THE AUTHOR CONSTRUCTS A MODEL FOR THE SIGNIFICANT
DETERMINANTS OF POLITICAL INSTABILITY AND ITS NATURE IN THE
ARAB WORLD. HE UTILIZES FOUR MODELS THAT ILLUSTRATE THE
TURMOIL COMPONENT OF POLITICAL INSTABILITY, THE ELITE
STRUGGLE COMPONENT, THE FREQUENCY OF EXECUTIVE TURNOVER
COMPONENT, AND A COMBINED MODEL OF THE PRECEDING THREE
COMPONENTS.

03872 HADENIUS, S.
THE SWEDISH PARLIAMENTARY ELECTION OF SEPTEMBER 1988:
RESULTS AND IMPLICATIONS
SCANDINAVIAN REVIEW, 77(1) (SPR 89), 13-22.
THE AUTHOR EXPLAINS THE BACKGROUND TO THE 1988 SWEDISH
PARLIAMENTARY ELECTION AND SURVEYS THE RESULTS.

03873 HADLEY, C.D.; MORASS, M.; NICK, R.
FEDERALISM AND PARTY INTERACTION IN WEST GERMANY,
SWITZERLAND, AND AUSTRIA
PUBLIUS: THE JOURNAL OF FEDERALISM, 19(4) (FAL 89), 81-98.
THE FEDERALISM ESTABLISHED IN THE CONSTITUTIONS OF THE
FEDERAL REPUBLIC OF GERMANY, SWITZERLAND, AND AUSTRIA, IN
ADDITION TO THE COMMON LANGUAGE OF THESE COUNTRIES,
DISTINGUISHES THEM FROM THE OTHER WEST EUROPEAN COUNTRIES,

WHICH LEAN TOWARD CENTRALLY ORGANIZED STATES. AFTER
EXAMINING THE HISTORICAL FOUNDATION AND DEVELOPMENT OF THE
FEDERAL SYSTEMS IN THE THREE COUNTRIES, THE ARTICLE ANALYZES
THE SEGMENTATION, FEDERAL-STATE INTERACTION, AND INTRAPARTY
EFFECTS OF POLITICAL PARTIES IN THEM. WHILE FEDERALISM IS
STRENGTHENED BY THE HETEROGENEITY AND REGIONAL SOLIDARITY OF
THE POLITICAL PARTIES IN SWITZERLAND, FEDERALISM HAS BECOME
A PURE "PARTY FEDERALISM" IN THE FEDERAL REPUBLIC OF GERMANY
AND AUSTRIA.

03874 HADLEY, C.D.; STANLEY, H.H.
SUPER TUESDAY 1988: REGIONAL RESULTS AND NATIONAL
IMPLICATIONS
PUBLIUS: THE JOURNAL OF FEDERALISM, 19(3) (SUM 89), 19-38.
FOURTEEN SOUTHERN AND BORDER STATES ESTABLISHED A SAME-
DAY PRESIDENTIAL PRIMARY ON 8 MARCH 1988. THIS ANALYSIS
SHOWS THAT THIS SUPER TUESDAY, IN SEVERAL SENSES, WAS LESS
THAN SUPER. THE RESULTS TURNED OUT TO BE LESS SATISFYING
THAN ITS DEMOCRATIC FOUNDERS PREFERRED BUT LESS UPSETTING
THAN ITS CRITICS ANTICIPATED. DESPITE SUPER TUESDAY, IOWA
AND NEW HAMPSHIRE REMAINED DOMINANT IN THE 1988 PRESIDENTIAL
PRIMARIES. ALTHOUGH VOTER TURNOUT INCREASED SLIGHTLY OVER
1984 AND THE RESULTS CONTRIBUTED MIGHTILY TOWARD SETTLING
THE NOMINATION IN THE REPUBLICAN PARTY, SUPER TUESDAY
NEITHER SETTLED THE DEMOCRATIC NOMINATION NOR GAVE
MEANINGFUL MOMENTUM TO THE MORE MODERATE DEMOCRATIC
CANDIDATES.

03875 HAENSCM, K.
THE EUROPEAN COMMUNITY AND THE SOVIET UNION.
PLURAL SOCIETIES, 18(2) (MAR 89), 2-22.
THIS ARTICLE DESCRIBES HOW IT WAS THAT SOVIET COMMUNIST
TERRITORIAL ASPIRATIONS IN EUROPE BOOSTED THE UNIFICATION OF
WESTERN EUROPE OVER MANY YEARS, WHILE THE SUCCESS OF THE
COMMUNITY DEMONSTRATED THE FALLACY OF THE SOVIET DOCTRINE
THAT COMPETITIVE ANARCHY BETWEEN NATIONAL ECONOMIES IN THE
ADVANCED STAGE OF CAPITALISM WOULD LEAD TO THEIR MUTUAL
DESTRUCTION.

03876 HAERI, S.
FRANCE AND IRAN: COMMERCIAL LINKS
MIDDLE EAST INTERNATIONAL, (359) (SEP 89), 13-14.
DESPITE A TENSE POLITICAL SITUATION DUE TO THE DEATH
SENTENCE OF SALMAN RUSHDIE AND THE LEBANESE CRISIS,
RELATIONS BETWEEN FRANCE AND IRAN HAVE CONTINUED TO STEADILY
IMPROVE. RENEWED DIALOGUE ON POLITICAL, ECONOMIC AND
REGIONAL DIFFERENCES AND ON EXPANDING FUTURE COOPERATION
HAVE CREATED A "POSITIVE" ATMOSPHERE. ALTHOUGH FRANCE AND
IRAN SUPPORT DIFFERENT SIDES IN THE LEBANESE CONFLICT,
FRANCE HAS AGREED NOT TO INTERVENE MILITARILY, AND ECONOMIC
TIES BETWEEN FRANCE AND IRAN CONTINUE TO INCREASE.

03877 HAERI, S.
IRAN AND SYRIA: WARNING TO TAIF
MIDDLE EAST INTERNATIONAL, (360) (OCT 89), 7-8.
AS LEBANESE PARLIAMENTARIANS WERE MEETING IN TAIF,
SEVERAL INFLUENTIAL PRO-IRANIAN AND PRO-SYRIAN LEBANESE AND
PALESTINIAN LEADERS MET IN TEHRAN. THEIR AIM WAS TO COUNTER
ANY DECISION THAT THE MPS MAY MEET AT TAIF. ALTHOUGH SYRIA
AND IRAN AGREE ON THEIR DESIRE TO SEE LEBANON RULED BY ARABS,
THEY DIFFER SHARPLY ON EXACTLY HOW THIS IS TO BE DONE. THE
RESULT IS A STRANGE COMBINATION OF COOPERATION AND TENSION
BETWEEN THE TWO NATIONS.

03878 HAERI, S.
IRAN AND USSR: A NEW CHAPTER?
MIDDLE EAST INTERNATIONAL, 353 (JUN 89), 11-12.
THE SOVIET UNION IS EXPECTED TO BECOME IRAN'S MAIN
TRADING PARTNER IF ALL THE AGREEMENTS DISCUSSED DURING THE
PAST MONTHS ARE SIGNED. THEY INCLUDE RAILWAY, ROAD, HOUSING,
POWER STATIONS, DAMS, SHIPPING AND OIL PROJECTS, WHICH ARE
TO BE FINANCED THROUGH THE SALE TO THE SOVIET UNION OF THREE
BILLION CUBIC FEET OF NATURAL GAS.

03879 HAERI, S.
IRAN GOES FOR A CLEVER COMPROMISE
MIDDLE EAST INTERNATIONAL, 352 (JUN 89), 3-4.
DESPITE THE FACT THAT IN HIS WILL, PARTS OF WHICH WERE
READ BY PRESIDENT KHAMENEI, AYATOLLAH KHOMEINI STRESSED THE
NECESSITY OF FOLLOWING HIS "NO TO THE EAST, NO TO THE WEST"
POLICY, HE DID NOT GIVE ANY SPECIFIC DIRECTIVE TO HIS
SUCCESSOR. THIS, ACCORDING TO OBSERVERS, WILL GIVE KHAMENEI
A RELATIVELY FREE HAND IN FORMULATING HIS OWN FOREIGN POLICY,
WHICH IS LIKELY TO BE MORE PRAGMATIC THAN THE ONE PURSUED
BY THE OLD REVOLUTIONARY LEADER. NOTWITHSTANDING THAT IN HIS
WILL KHOMEINI STIGMATISED KING FAHD OF SAUDI ARABIA AND
OTHER ARAB LEADERS (SUCH AS HUSSEIN OF JORDAN, HASSAN OF
MOROCCO, MUBARAK OF EGYPT, SADDAM OF IRAQ) AS "REACTIONARY",
DIPLOMATS EXPECT A MARKED IMPROVEMENT IN IRAN'S RELATIONS
WITH ITS NEIGHBOURS AND OTHER NATIONS, INCLUDING THE WEST.

03880 HAERI, S.
IRAN: CHANGE OF DIRECTION
MIDDLE EAST INTERNATIONAL, (346) (MAR 89), 9-10.

IN A MAJOR SHIFT IN THE TRADITIONAL DIRECTION OF ITS
FOREIGN POLICY, IRAN IS PREPARING TO INTEGRATE ITSELF MORE
INTO ASIA WHILE LESSENING TIES WITH THE MIDDLE EAST. THE WAR
AGAINST IRAQ PERSUADED IRAN'S RULERS THAT THE FUTURE OF THE
COUNTRY LIES MORE WITH ITS ASIAN NEIGHBORS TO THE EAST THAN
WITH THE ARAB NEIGHBORS TO THE WEST.

03881 HAERI, S.
IRAN: HARDLINERS REEMERGE
MIDDLE EAST INTERNATIONAL, (342) (JAN 89), 14.
IN THE GUISE OF ERADICATING INTERNATIONAL DRUG
TRAFFICKERS, THE IRANIANS HAVE EXECUTED MORE THAN 300 PEOPLE
WITHIN A FEW WEEKS. BUT THE OPERATIONS ARE REALLY AIMED AT
CRUSHING THE OPPOSITION FROM WITHIN. THE FAILURE OF THE
IRANIAN ECONOMY TO IMPROVE FOLLOWING THE CEASE-FIRE GAVE THE
HARDLINERS AN OPPORTUNITY TO BLAME THE MODERATES AND DEMAND
RETRIBUTION.

03882 HAERI, S.
IRAN: INVITATION TO MURDER
MIDDLE EAST INTERNATIONAL, (350) (MAY 89), 12-13.
HASHEMI RAFSANJANI CAUSED AN INTERNATIONAL OUTCRY IN MAY
1989 WHEN HE URGED PALESTINIANS TO LAUNCH A CAMPAIGN OF
KILLING AND SABOTAGE AGAINST WESTERNERS "TO STOP ISRAEL'S
FOLLIES," THE CALL STUNNED WESTERN OBSERVERS WHO SEE
RAFSANJANI AS A "MODERATE" IRANIAN LEADER. ACCORDING TO SOME
SOURCES, RAFSANJANI WAS FORCED TO MAKE THE DECLARATION TO
PROVE THAT HE IS STILL A COMMITTED ANTI-WESTERN
REVOLUTIONARY.

03883 HAERI, S.
IRAN: NEW HARD-LINE APPOINTMENTS
MIDDLE EAST INTERNATIONAL, (359) (SEP 89), 12-13.
THE NOMINATIONS OF IRAN'S PRESIDENT RAFSANJANI OF
ASSADOLLAH LEJEVARDI, "THE BUTCHER OF EVIN," AND OTHER HARD-
LINERS FOR CABINET POSTS REDUCED HOPES THAT IRAN COULD
FINALLY EMERGE FROM TEN YEARS OF POLITICAL CONVULSIONS AND
ECONOMIC PARALYSIS. ALTHOUGH THE PRESIDENT HAD LITTLE CHOICE
THAN TO BOW TO THE DEMANDS OF HARD-LINE FACTIONS IN IRAN,
THE NOMINATIONS DO NOT BODE WELL FOR THE PROSPECTS OF
ECONOMIC AND POLITICAL REFORM.

03884 HAERI, S.
IRAN: ONE HORSE RACE?
MIDDLE EAST INTERNATIONAL, 353 (JUN 89), 12.
ACCORDING TO INFORMED SOURCES IN TEHRAN, THE DECISION TO
ADVANCE THE ELECTION'S DATE HAD BEEN FORCED ON THE LEADERS
FOR SEVERAL REASONS. FIRST, IF CANDIDATES SUCH AS AHMAD
KHOMEINI WERE ALLOWED TO RUN AND SERIOUSLY CHALLENGE MR
RAFSANJANI, THEY WOULD CREATE A DELICATE SITUATION WHICH
COULD BE EXPLOITED, NOT ONLY BY OPPONENTS OF THE PRESENT
MODERATE LEADERS, BUT ALSO BY PROFESSIONAL TROUBLE-MAKERS.
THIS MIGHT THROW THE WHOLE SYSTEM'S FUTURE INTO JEOPARDY.
SECOND, THE ELECTION OF PRESIDENT KHAMENEI AS AYATOLLAH
KHOMEINI'S SUCCESSOR HAS LEFT A VACUUM AT THE TOP WHICH IT
WOULD BE WISE TO FILL AS SOON AS POSSIBLE. AND THIRD, THERE
IS AN URGENT NEED TO OPEN UP THE SOCIO-ECONOMIC CLIMATE. NOW
KHOMEINI HAS GONE, CRITICISM OF THE REGIME FOR ITS FAILURES
WILL BE FAR LESS RESTRAINED.

03885 HAERI, S.
IRAN: RAFSANJANI JUMPS ON THE BANDWAGON
MIDDLE EAST INTERNATIONAL, (349) (APR 89), 15-16.
IRANIAN LEADER RAFSANJANI HAS CLAIMED THAT A NETWORK OF
SPIES WORKING FOR THE UNITED STATES HAS BEEN DISCOVERED IN
IRAN AND DESTROYED.

03886 HAERI, S.
IRAN: SPATE OF EXECUTIONS
MIDDLE EAST INTERNATIONAL, (341) (JAN 89), 15-16.
THE ISLAMIC REPUBLIC HAS FINALLY CONFIRMED WESTERN MEDIA
REPORTS OF THE EXECUTION OF SEVERAL LEADING CLERGYMEN AS
WELL AS THOUSANDS OF POLITICAL PRISONERS, MOSTLY LEFT-
WINGERS BELONGING TO THE MARXISTISLAMIC ORGANIZATION OF THE
PEOPLE'S MUJAHEDIN. THE ADMISSION STIRRED A WAVE OF NEW
INTERNAL CLASHES AND INTENSE, HEATED DEBATES ABOUT THE ISSUE.

03887 HAERI, S.
IRAN: THE PINCER CLOSES
MIDDLE EAST INTERNATIONAL, (354) (JUL 89), 6.
LESS THAN A MONTH AFTER THE DEATH OF AYATOLIAH KHOMEINI
THE NEW LEADER OF THE ISLAMIC REPUBLIC HOJATOLESLAM ALI
KHAMENEI AND MAJLIS SPEAKER RAFSANJANI ARE ALREADY AT ODDS
WITH EACH OTHER. RAFSJANI HAS COMPLAINED OF KHAMENEI'S
INTRUSION INTO HIS FOREIGN POLICY DOMAIN AND HAS ATTACKED
KHAMENINI'S STRIDENT ANTI-WESTERN POSTURE. RAFSANJANI'S
PROBLEMS ARE COMPOUNDED BY THE PRESENCE OF THE AYATOLLAH'S
SON AHMAD WHO IS RECIVING PRESSURE TO ENTER THE IRANIAN
POLITICAL WORLD.

03888 HAERI, S.
IRAN: THE PURGE BEGINS
MIDDLE EAST INTERNATIONAL, (347) (MAR 89), 12-13.
THE RESIGNATION OF AYATOLLAH HUSSEINALI MONTAZERI AS THE

DESIGNATED SUCCESSOR TO AYATOLLAH KHOMEINI'S SPIRITUAL
LEADERSHIP OF THE IRANIAN REVOLUTION HAS LEFT THE COUNTRY
VIRTUALLY IN THE HANDS OF THE HARD-LINE RADICALS. THEIR NEXT
TARGET WILL UNDOUBTEDLY BE THE SPEAKER OF THE MAJLIS,
HOJATOLESLAM HASHEMI RAFSANJANI.

03889 HAERI, S.
  IRAN: THE SUCCESSORS
  MIDDLE EAST INTERNATIONAL, (344) (FEB 89), 14.
    HOJATOLESLAM HASHEMI RAFSANJANI HAS CONFIRMED THAT THE
  ISLAMIC REPUBLIC'S CONSTITUTION MAY SOON BE CHANGED TO ALLOW
  HIM TO BECOME THE FIRST US-STYLE PRESIDENT OF IRAN. WHILE
  IRAN'S PRESENT PRESIDENTIAL SYSTEM IS SIMILAR TO FRANCE'S,
  THE NEXT IRANIAN PRESIDENT IS EXPECTED TO HAVE EXECUTIVE
  POWERS THAT WILL NECESSITATE A CHANGE IN THE CONSTITUTION.
  RAFSANJANI ALSO CONFIRMED THAT THE AYATOLLAH MONTAZERI WILL
  SUCCEED THE AYATOLLAH KHOMEINI.

03890 HAERI, S.
  IRAN: WARNING TO RAFSANJANI
  MIDDLE EAST INTERNATIONAL, (351) (MAY 89), 13.
    AHMAD KHOMEINI, THE 44-YEAR OLD SON OF THE AYATOLLAH HAS
  WARNED MAJLIS SPEAKER RAFSANJANI AGAINST ANY ATTEMPT AT
  SUCCEEDING HIS FATHER. THE WARNING WAS ISSUED IN RESPONSE TO
  A NEWSPAPER ARTICLE THAT CONSIDERED THE POSSIBILITY OF
  RAFSANJANI AS IRAN'S NEXT LEADER.

03891 HAERI, S.
  PARIS CONFERENCE ON KURDS
  MIDDLE EAST INTERNATIONAL, (361) (OCT 89), 14.
    THE FIRST INTERNATIONAL CONFERENCE ON THE KURDS WAS HELD
  IN PARIS IN OCTOBER. REPRESENTATIVES OF THE KURDISH
  MINORITIES OF IRAN, IRAQ, TURKEY, SYRIA, AND THE USSR MET
  AND DEBATED SUCH DIVERSE ISSUES AS IRAQ'S USE OF CHEMICAL
  WEAPONS ON KURDISH VILLAGES, THE FATE OF SOVIET AND TURKISH
  KURDS, AND THE POSSIBILITY OF A UN OBSERVER SEAT FOR THE
  KURDISH PEOPLE. THE CONFERENCES FRANK PORTRAYAL OF THE LESS
  THAN IDEAL CONDITIONS THAT KURDS FACE IN MANY NATIONS
  BROUGHT SIGNIFICANT PROTEST FROM TURKEY, IRAN, IRAQ, AND
  SYRIA.

03892 HAERI, S.
  RAFSANJANI AND IRAN'S ECONOMY
  MIDDLE EAST INTERNATIONAL, (360) (OCT 89), 13-15.
    IN OPPOSITION TO THE STATEMENTS OF IRAN'S HARD-LINE
  CLERICAL RULERS, PRESIDENT RAFSANJANI DECLARED THAT THE
  PROBABILITY OF RETURNING TO WAR WITH IRAQ IS SMALL. HE
  DECLARED THAT IRAN SHOULD CONCENTRATE INSTEAD ON IRAN'S
  STRUGGLING ECONOMY. HE SINGLED OUT INFLATION AS A PROBLEM
  THAT NEEDS TO BE DEALT WITH AND CALLED FOR INCREASED
  INDUSTRIAL OUTPUT AND THE PRIVATIZATION OF SOME STATE
  INDUSTRIES. THE POSSIBILITY OF TECHNICAL OR FINANCIAL AID
  FROM ABROAD WAS NOT MENTIONED.

03893 HAERI, S.
  RAFSANJANI'S CABINET ENDORSED
  MIDDLE EAST INTERNATIONAL, (358) (SEP 89), 13.
    IRAN'S PRESIDENT ALI AKBAR HASHEMI RAFSANJANI PLEDGED TO
  "CLEAN UP" THE COUNTRY'S INEFFICIENT ADMINISTRATION. TO
  ACCOMPLISH THIS DAUNTING TASK, HE PROPOSED A RADICAL
  RESHUFFLING OF THE CABINET. ALTHOUGH THE CABINET NOMINEES
  INCLUDED MANY THAT WERE OPPOSED BY IRAN'S MANY HARD-LINE
  FUNDAMENTALISTS, THE CABINET WAS OVERWHELMINGLY APPROVED IN
  THE IRANIAN PARLIAMENT.

03894 HAERI, S.
  RAFSANJANI'S ECONOMIC PLAN
  MIDDLE EAST INTERNATIONAL, (361) (OCT 89), 13-14.
    IRAN'S PRESIDENT HASHEMI RAFSANJANI ANNOUNCED A FAR-
  REACHING PROGRAM OF ECONOMIC REFORMS ON THE SAME DAY THAT
  FORMER INTERIOR MINISTER MOHTASHAMI WAS SENT TO SEMI-EXILE
  IN QOM. MANY OBSERVERS SEE A CONNECTION; MOHTASHAMI, THE
  LEADER OF A HARD-LINE GROUP WHO ADVOCATED ECONOMIC SELF-
  RELIANCE, WOULD BE SURE TO DISAGREE WITH RAFSANJANI'S
  PROGRAM OF WIDESPREAD PRIVATIZATION AND RECEIPT OF LARGE
  AMOUNTS OF FOREIGN AID. ALTHOUGH NOT YET OFFICIALLY
  RECOGNIZED IRAN WOULD HAVE TO RECEIVE SOME OF THE NECESSARY
  FUNDS FROM WESTERN SOURCES.

03895 HAERI, S.
  RAFSANJARI'S HERCULEAN TASK
  MIDDLE EAST INTERNATIONAL, 356 (AUG 89), 15.
    AS THE NEW PRESIDENT OF THE ISLAMIC REPUBLIC, RAFSANJANI
  FACES THE AWESOME TASK OF WRESTLING WITH IMMENSE AND
  PRESSING PROBLEMS WITHOUT ENJOYING THE "PROTECTIVE, BLESSING
  HAND" OF THE IMAM. INFLATION RUNS AT MORE THAN 300 PER CENT
  (OFFICIALLY ONLY 50 PER CENT IS ADMITTED); UNEMPLOYMENT IS
  HIGH; PRICES ARE BEYOND THE REACH OF 95 PER CENT OF THE
  POPULATION. OPINIONS HOLDS THAT RAFSANJANI WILL ENJOY THREE
  TO FOUR MONTHS OF GRACE. IF THE PEOPLE, WHO ARE NOT AFRAID
  OF HIM AS THEY WERE OF KHOMEINI, FEEL THAT HE IS TRYING TO
  EASE THEIR BURDEN, THEY WILL COOPERATE WITH HIM; IF NOT, THE
  NEW PRESIDENT CAN EXPECT A VERY ROUGH RIDE.

03896 HAERI, S.
  SUDAN AND IRAN
  MIDDLE EAST INTERNATIONAL, (363) (NOV 89), 13-14.
    A REPORT IN MARDOM, THE OFFICIAL ORGAN OF THE IRANIAN
  TUDEH (PRO-MOSCOW COMMUNIST) PARTY, STATES THAT SUDAN'S
  RULING GENERAL OMAR AL-BASHIR LED A "SECRET" DELEGATION TO
  IRAN. IT ALSO CLAIMS THAT IRAN PROMISED TO SEND SUDAN OIL
  AND MILITARY HARDWARE AS WELL AS REVOLUTIONARY GUARDS
  OFFICERS TO AID BASHIR IN HIS FIGHT AGAINST "COMMUNISM, THE
  WEST, AND THE CHRISTIAN REBELLION OF THE SOUTH."

03897 HAERI, S.
  THE PASSWORD IS REVISION
  MIDDLE EAST INTERNATIONAL, (343) (FEB 89), 13-14.
    PRESIDENT SEYYED ALI KHAMENEI HAS ACCUSED THE WESTERN
  MEDIA OF PLOTTING AGAINST IRAN BY CLAIMING THAT REVISIONISTS
  ARE QUESTIONING THE REVOLUTION. KHAMENEI HAS DECLARED THAT
  THE IRANIANS WILL NEVER DEVIATE FROM THEIR REVOLUTIONARY
  PRINCIPLES. BUT MANY OBSERVERS BELIEVE THE LATEST BATTLE IN
  TEHRAN IS CENTERED AROUND THE QUESTION OF REVISION, AND THE
  PRESIDENT'S DENIAL IS SEEN AS PROOF.

03898 HAERI, S.
  TROUBLE IN IRAN
  MIDDLE EAST INTERNATIONAL, (364) (DEC 89), 12.
    THREE MONTHS AFTER BEING SWORN IN, IRANIAN PRESIDENT
  RAFSANJANI SEEMS TO HAVE FAILED TO WIN THE CONFIDENCE OF THE
  PRIVATE SECTOR, THE TRADE AND BUSINESS COMMUNITIES, AS WELL
  AS THE INTELLECTUAL MIDDLE CLASS. IN LESS THAN THREE WEEKS,
  IRAN SAW RIOTING IN TEHRAN'S BAZAAR, CLASHES BETWEEN
  STUDENTS AND REVOLUTIONARY GUARDS, AND A REBELLION IN A
  SOUTHWESTERN TOWN. THE GOVERNMENT'S HARSH REPRESSION OF
  THESE EVENTS HAS ONLY INCREASED TENSION.

03899 HAERI, S.
  TURKEY GETS A RAP
  MIDDLE EAST INTERNATIONAL, (347) (MAR 89), 15.
    TURKISH - IRANIAN RELATIONS DETERIORATED RAPIDLY IN
  EARLY 1989, WITH ANKARA EXPELLING AN UNDISCLOSED NUMBER OF
  "UNDESIRABLE" IRANIANS, BELIEVED TO BE AGENTS OF THE IRANIAN
  MINISTRY OF INFORMATION.

03900 HAERI, S.
  WARNINGS
  MIDDLE EAST INTERNATIONAL, (348) (APR 89), 9.
    IRAN'S MAJLIS SPEAKER AND ARMED FORCES COMMANDER-IN-
  CHIEF HOJATOLESLAM RAFSANJANI CLEARLY AND EXPLICITY WARNED
  FRANCE THAT A RETURN TO LEBANON WOULD RESULT IN THE SAME
  "HUMILIATION" IT SUFFERED IN SEPTEMBER, 1983 WHEN 53 FRENCH
  PARATROOPERS WERE KILLED WHEN THEIR HEADQUARTERS WAS BLOWN
  UP BY IRANIAN-TRAINED SHI'ITE COMMANDOS. THE IRANIAN
  ANNOUNCEMENT CAME AT THE REQUEST OF SYRIA WHO DOES NOT WISH
  TO DAMAGE ITS OWN INTERNATIONAL STANDING ESPECIALLY VIS A
  VIS THE US. SYRIA ALSO DOES NOT WISH TO JEOPARDIZE A
  POTENTIAL STATE VISIT TO PARIS. IRAN, WHO HAS NO RELATIONS
  WITH THE US TO JEOPARDIZE, WAS MORE THAN WILLING TO ISSUE
  THE WARNING.

03901 HAEUSER, P.N.
  EXPLAINING STATE VARIATIONS IN COMMUNITY COLLEGE POLICIES
  DISSERTATION ABSTRACTS INTERNATIONAL, 49(12) (JUN 89),
  3857-A.
    LIKE TRADITIONAL STUDIES OF STATE AID TO LOCALITIES,
  THIS ANALYSIS IS BASED ON THE ASSUMPTION THAT ATTRIBUTES
  CHARACTERIZING A STATE PROVIDE AN EXPLANATION OF STATE
  POLICY DECISIONS. THE SPECIFIC FOCUS OF THIS STUDY IS STATE
  POLICY AFFECTING COMMUNITY COLLEGE SYSTEMS, INCLUDING STATE
  OVERSIGHT, STATE CENTRALIZATION OF MANAGERIAL PROCEDURES,
  AND THE USE OF EQUALIZATION IN FUNDING PROCEDURES.

03902 HAGAN, J.
  PATTERNS OF ACTIVISM ON STATE SUPREME COURTS
  PUBLIUS: THE JOURNAL OF FEDERALISM, 18(1) (WIN 88), 97-116.
    THE STUDY EXAMINES PATTERNS OF JUDICIAL CONFLICT AND
  POLICY ACTIVISM DURING 1930-1980 ON THE SUPREME COURTS OF
  CALIFORNIA, MICHIGAN, NEW JERSEY, NORTH CAROLINA, VIRGINIA,
  AND WEST VIRGINIA. THE FINDINGS INDICATE THAT DRAMATIC
  SHIFTS FROM PASSIVITY TO ACTIVISM TAKE PLACE OVER VERY SHORT
  PERIODS OF TIME, AND THAT WHEN A SHIFT TO JUDICIAL ACTIVISM
  DOES OCCUR, IT IS DUE MAINLY TO A CHANGE IN COURT
  COMPOSITION INVOLVING THE INTRODUCTION OF "MAVERICK"
  JUSTICES. FURTHERMORE, OF THE FOUR COURTS IN THE STUDY THAT
  UNDERWENT A TRANSITION TO ACTIVISM, NONE HAVE SUBSEQUENTLY
  BECOME NON-ACTIVIST.

03903 HAGAN, J.D.
  DOMESTIC POLITICAL REGIME CHANGES AND FOREIGN POLICY
  RESTRUCTURING IN WESTERN EUROPE: A CONCEPTUAL FRAMEWORK
  AND INITIAL EMPIRICAL ANALYSIS
  COOPERATION & CONFLICT: NORDIC JOURNAL OF INTERNATIONAL
  POLITICS, XXIV(3-4) (DEC 89), 141-162.
    THIS ARTICLE PRESENTS AN INITIAL INVESTIGATION INTO THE
  CASUAL LINKAGE BETWEEN DOMESTIC POLITICAL REGIME CHANGES AND
  FOREIGN POLICY RESTRUCTURING IN WESTERN EUROPE. A

THEORETICAL FRAMEWORK IS DEVELOPED THAT INCORPORATES THREE
ELEMENTS: A TYPOLOGY OF FOUR KINDS OF REGIME CHANGE, A
CONCEPTUALIZATION OF SHIFTING REGIME PROPERTIES (THE
LEADERSHIP'S ORIENTATION TO FOREIGN AFFAIRS AND ITS INTERNAL
POLITICAL FRAGMENTATION) THAT UNDERLAY SIGNIFICANT REGIME
CHANGES, AND THREE DIMENSIONS OF FOREIGN POLICY
RESTRUCTURING LIKELY TO BE AFFECTED BY CHANGES IN DOMESTIC
POLITICAL CONDITIONS. ALSO REPORTED ARE RESULTS FROM A
PRELIMINARY EMPIRICAL ASSESSMENT OF REGIME CHANGE EFFECTS ON
TRENDS IN WESTERN EUROPEAN VOTING IN THE UNITED NATIONS,
TRADE WITH THE SOVIET UNION, AND MILITARY BUDGETS OVER THE
PAST TWO DECADES.

03904 HAGAN, J.D.
DOMESTIC POLITICAL REGIME CHANGES AND THIRD WORLD VOTING
REALIGNMENTS IN THE UNITED NATIONS
INTERNATIONAL ORGANIZATION, 43(5) (SUM 89), 505-541.
THIS ARTICLE PRESENTS A CROSS-NATIONAL ANALYSIS OF THE
RELATIONSHIP BETWEEN DOMESTIC POLITICAL REGIME CHANGES AND
VOTING REALIGNMENTS OF THIRD WORLD NATIONS IN THE UNITED
NATIONS (UN). IT SEEKS TO MOVE BEYOND EXISTING RESEARCH THAT
HAS ASSUMED THAT FOREIGN POLICY IS ROOTED IN POLITICAL AND
ECONOMIC STRUCTURES AND CHANGES ONLY WHEN A POLITICAL
REVOLUTION OCCURS. IT ARGUES THAT A WIDER VARIETY OF REGIME
CHANGES -RANGING FROM THOSE INVOLVING MAINSTREAM POLITICAL
PARTIES TO MILDER ONES SUCH AS FACTIONAL SHIFTS IN SINGLE-
PARTY REGIMES -- CAN ALSO PROVOKE MAJOR REALIGNMENTS. USING
A NEW DATA SET ON THIRD WORLD REGIMES, THE ARTICLE EXAMINES
THE IMPACT OF REGIME CHANGES FOR EIGHTY-SEVEN NATIONS ON
THEIR UN VOTING PATTERNS DURING THE PERIOD FROM 1946 TO 1984.
ALTHOUGH THE FINDINGS INDICATE THAT REVOLUTIONS ARE MOST
LIKELY TO PROVOKE MAJOR VOTING REALIGNMENTS, THEY ALSO SHOW
THAT THE MORE FREQUENT, NONREVOLUTIONARY TYPES OF REGIME
CHANGES ARE ASSOCIATED WITH MANY VOTING REALIGNMENTS. A
MAJOR IMPLICATION OF THESE FINDINGS IS THAT FOREIGN POLICY
CHANGES REFLECT A COMPLEX SET OF DOMESTIC REGIME FACTORS,
INCLUDING LEADERSHIP BELIEF SYSTEMS AND INTERNAL POLITICAL
CONSTRAINTS, AS WELL AS ASPECTS OF POLITICAL STRUCTURE.

03905 HAGE, J.; FINSTERBUSCH, K.
THREE STRATEGIES OF ORGANIZATIONAL CHANGE: ORGANIZATIONAL
DEVELOPMENT, ORGANIZATIONAL THEORY AND ORGANIZATIONAL
DESIGN
INTERNATIONAL REVIEW OF ADMINISTRATIVE SCIENCES, 55(1)
(MAR 89), 29-58.
ALTHOUGH THE THIRD WORLD TRAILS THE WEST IN THE SKILL OF
WORKERS, THE QUANTITY AND QUALITY OF CAPITAL AND
TECHNOLOGIES, AND THE EFFECTIVENESS OF ORGANIZATIONS, IT IS
MAKING TREMENDOUS EFFORTS TO BETTER EDUCATE ITS POPULATION,
INCREASE ITS CAPITAL AND IMPROVE ITS TECHNOLOGIES AND IS
ALSO LOOKING TO THE WEST TO LEARN HOW TO IMPROVE ITS
ORGANIZATIONS. THE ARTICLE SEEKS TO COMBINE THE THREE
LITERATURES OF: 1) THE PSYCHOLOGY OF HUMAN RELATIONS AND/OR
ORGANIZATIONAL DEVELOPMENT; 2) THE SOCIOLOGY OF
ORGANIZATIONS AND/OR ORGANIZATIONAL THEORY AND 3) MANAGEMENT
SCIENCE AND/OR ORGANIZATIONAL DESIGN INTO A WORKABLE
FRAMEWORK AND APPLY IT TO A THIRD WORLD CASE OF
ORGANIZATIONAL IMPROVEMENT.

03906 HAGER, C.J.
TECHNOLOGICAL DEMOCRACY: BUREAUCRACY AND CITIZENRY IN THE
WEST GERMAN ENERGY DEBATE
DISSERTATION ABSTRACTS INTERNATIONAL, 49(12) (JUN 89),
3857-A.
LONG A PART OF GERMAN THEORETICAL DISCOURSE, THE
QUESTION OF DEMOCRATIC PARTICIPATION IN THE MODERN
TECHNOLOGICAL STATE HAS GAINED NEW SALIENCE WITH THE RECENT
RISE OF GRASSROOTS CITIZEN PROTEST IN WEST GERMANY. THIS
DISSERTATION CONSIDERS THE CONFLICT BETWEEN EXPERT
BUREAUCRACY AND CITIZENS IN WEST BERLIN'S ENERGY POLICY.

03907 HAGER, M.M.
READING THE TEA LEAVES OF PROTEST
MONTHLY REVIEW, 41(4) (SEP 89), 24-32.
THIS ARTICLE ATTEMPTS TO CLARIFY THE JOURNALISTIC
APPROACH OF ASSESSING THE WIDER SIGNIFICANCE OF THE RECENT
VIOLENCE IN CHINA. THE PROBABILITY OF CHINA'S DEVELOPING A
DEMOCRATIC SOCIALISM IS CONSIDERED. SYMBOLS USED IN THE
DEMONSTRATIONS ARE ANALYSED. THE PARELLELISM BETWEEN THE
CULTURAL REVOLUTION AND THE 1989 DEMOCRACY MOVEMENT IS
STUDIED.

03908 HAGGARD, S.
THE EAST ASIAN NIC'S IN COMPARATIVE PERSPECTIVE
PHILADELPHIA: ANLS OF AMER ACMY OF POLITICAL AND SOC
SCIENCE, (505) (SEP 89), 129-141.
PURELY ECONOMIC ANALYSES OF THE EAST ASIAN NEWLY
INDUSTRIALIZING COUNTRIES HAVE OVERLOOKED THE POLITICS OF
THEIR GROWTH. WHY WERE THESE COUNTRIES ABLE TO PURSUE
STRATEGIES THAT COMBINED RAPID GROWTH WITH A RELATIVELY
EQUITABLE DISTRIBUTION OF INCOME? THE REASON LIES PARTLY IN
EXTERNAL CONDITIONS, INCLUDING EXPANDING WORLD TRADE, AND,
IN THE CASE OF TAIWAN AND KOREA, PRESSURE FROM THE UNITED
STATES FOR POLICY REFORM. DOMESTIC SOCIAL AND POLITICAL

CONDITIONS WERE ALSO AUSPICIOUS, HOWEVER. EXPORT-LED GROWTH
HAS FACILITATED BY WEAK LABOR MOVEMENTS AND THE ABSENCE OF
LEFTIST OR POPULIST PARTIES. A RELATIVELY BRIEF PERIOD OF
IMPORT-SUBSTITUTION POLICIES PREVENTED THE DEVELOPMENT OF
STRONG PROTECTIONIST BUSINESS INTERESTS. EQUITY WAS ADVANCED
BY LAND REFORMS IN KOREA AND TAIWAN AND BY THE ABSENCE OF A
RURAL SECTOR IN HONG KONG AND SINGAPORE. NO EXPLANATION IS
COMPLETE, HOWEVER, WITHOUT REFERENCE TO THE STRENGTH OF THE
EAST ASIAN STATES, INCLUDING THEIR INSULATION FROM INTEREST-
GROUP PRESSURES AND THEIR COHESIVE, MERITOCRATIC
BUREAUCRACIES.

03909 HAGHIGHAT, D.
INTERPRETING U.S. POLICY TOWARD IRAN DURING THE EARLY COLD
WAR YEARS
DISSERTATION ABSTRACTS INTERNATIONAL, 50(2) (AUG 89),
535-A.
THE AUTHOR STUDIES U.S. POLICY TOWARD IRAN DURING THE
EARLY COLD WAR YEARS, FOCUSING ON THE NATIONALIST REGIME OF
MOHAMMAD MOSSADEGH. HE ARGUES THAT MOST ANALYSES FAIL TO
EXAMINE U.S. POLICY TOWARD IRANIAN NATIONALISM IN THE
CONTEXT OF THE RISING POWER OF THE UNITED STATES AND THE
DECLINING POWER OF GREAT BRITAIN. BOTH THE USA AND THE USSR
WERE DETERMINED TO FILL THE POWER VACUUM CREATED WHEN GREAT
BRITAIN BEGAN TO LOSE ITS STRONG FOOTHOLDS IN IRAN. MOREOVER,
TRADITIONALIST AND REVISIONIST STUDIES DO NOT ANALYZE U.S.
POLICY IN DIRECT RELATION TO THE INTERNAL POLITICAL STRUGGLE
IN IRAN.

03910 HAGLE, T.M.
A COGNITIVE-CYBERNETIC THEORY OF JUDICIAL DECISION MAKING:
A THEORY AND EMPIRICAL ANALYSIS OF UNITED STATES SUPREME
COURT DECISION MAKING
DISSERTATION ABSTRACTS INTERNATIONAL, 50(3) (SEP 89),
784-A.
THE COGNITIVE-CYBERNETIC THEORY OF JUDICIAL DECISION
MAKING IS CHARACTERIZED BY FOUR MAIN PRINCIPLES:
SIMPLIFICATION OF A COMPLEX PROBLEM, A STABLE DECISIONAL
ENVIRONMENT, A FOCUS ON A SMALL NUMBER OF MAJOR FACTORS, AND
A LIMITED CHOICE SET. THIS DISSERTATION USES THE SEARCH AND
SEIZURE DECISIONS OF THE US SUPREME COURT FROM 1961 THROUGH
1987 TO TEST THE THEORY.

03911 HAGOPIAN, E.C.
FROM MARONITE HEGEMONY TO MARANITE MILITANCY: THE CREATION
AND DISINTEGRATION OF LEBANON
THIRD WORLD QUARTERLY, 11(4) (OCT 89), 101 - 117.
THE THESIS OF THIS ARTICLE IS THAT MARONITISM, BECAUSE
OF THE WAY IT DEFINES MARONITE IDENTITY, SHARES WITH ZIONISM
MANY OF THE IDEOLOGICAL MYTHOLOGIES THAT INFORMED THE
CREATION OF THE STATE OF ISRAEL AS A JEWISH STATE. THIS
ARTICLE REVIEWS THE IDEOLOGICAL EVOLUTION OF THE MARONITES
OF LEBANON THAT LED FIRST TO THE ESTABLISHMENT OF MARONITE
IDENTITY AND HEGEMONY IN THE EARLY STAGES OF LEBANON, AND
ALSO TO THE MARONITE MILITANCY OF THE 1970S AND 1980S, THE
CULMINATION OF WHICH WAS THE DISINTEGRATICN OF THE
LEBANONESE STATE.

03912 HAGOPIAN, E.C.
MARONITE HEGEMONY TO MARONITE MILITANCY: THE CREATION AND
DISINTEGRATION OF LEBANON
THIRD WORLD QUARTERLY, 11(4) (OCT 89), 101-117.
MARONITISM, BECAUSE OF THE WAY IT DEFINES MARONITE
IDENTITY, SHARES WITH ZIONISM MANY OF THE IDEOLOGICAL
MYTHOLOGIES THAT INFORMED THE CREATION OF THE STATE OF
ISRAEL AS A JEWISH STATE. THE IDEOLOGICAL COMMONALITY STEMS
FROM THE SHARED COMMITMENT TO THE EXCLUSION OF OTHER GROUPS,
BOTH SOCIALLY AND POLITICALLY. CONTEMPORARY MARONITISM, IN
RESPONSE TO DEMOGRAPHIC AND IDEOLOGICAL CHALLENGES TO ITS
HEGEMONY, SOUGHT TO EMULATE THE JEWISH STATE BY CREATING A
CHRISTIAN MAJORITY AND CHRISTIAN-DOMINATED STATE IN LEBANON
USING THE SAME IDEOLOGICAL STRATEGY AS ZIONISM, BUT IT
FAILED. THE FAILURE CAN BE ATTRIBUTED TO MANY FACTORS, BUT
PRIMARILY TO HISTORICAL TIMING AND CONTEXT AND TO MARONITE
IDEOLOGICAL SELF-DELUSION.

03913 HAHN, B.
WILL THE PLA TAKE OVER?
PACIFIC DEFENCE REPORTER, 16(3) (SEP 89), 13-15.
RECENT DISCUSSIONS BETWEEN A NUMBER OF VERY SENIOR PLA
OFFICERS REFLECT A NERVOUSNESS OR SERIOUS CONCERN OVER THE
ENFORCEMENT OF A TOO CONSERVATIVE POLITICAL LINE AT THE
EXPENSE OF LOSING INTERNATIONAL RESPECT AND SUPPORT FOR
THEIR MODERNIZATION PROGRAMS AND ACQUISITION OF "STATE-OF-
THE-ART" TECHNOLOGY. SHOULD A MAJOR DIVISION OCCUR IN THE
CCP LEADERSHIP OVER SERIOUS INTERNAL ECONOMIC OR POLITICAL
ISSUES AND SITUATIONS, THE PLA WILL, UNDOUBTEDLY, ACT
DECISIVELY TO PROTECT ITS INTERESTS.

03914 HAHN, J.W.
POWER TO THE SOVIETS?
PROBLEMS OF COMMUNISM, XXXVIII(1) (JAN 89), 34-46.
AS PART OF HIS PROGRAM OF PERESTROYKA AND AS A MEANS OF
OUSTING OFFICIALS OPPOSED TO IT, MIKHAIL GORBACHEV TARGETED

THE LOCAL SOVIETS FOR REFORM. UNTIL RECENTLY, THESE LOCAL
COUNCILS HAD BEEN LARGELY POWERLESS BODIES ELECTED FROM A
SINGLE SLATE OF CANDIDATES NOMINATED BY LOCAL PARTY AND
GOVERNMENT OFFICIALS. TO REINVIGORATE THE SOVIETS, GORBACHEV
AND OTHER REFORMERS PROPOSE MULTICANDIDATE ELECTIONS AND THE
INSTITUTIONALIZATION OF CONTROLS BY THE SOVIETS OVER THEIR
EXECUTIVE COMMITTEES AND LOCAL ADMINISTRATIVE DEPARTMENTS.
REFORMERS ALSO SEEK TO REGULATE AND IN SOME WAYS LIMIT PARTY
CONTROL OVER THE SOVIETS AND TO SYSTEMATIZE RELATIONS
BETWEEN THE SOVIETS AND THE ENTERPRISES OPERATING ON THEIR
RESPECTIVE TERRITORIES. THE OUTCOME OF THESE EFFORTS IS NOT
YET KNOWN, BUT THE SUCCESS OF THE REFORM DEPENDS UPON THE
PARTY'S WILLINGNESS TO RESTRICT ITS POWER OVER LOCAL
GOVERNMENT AND, ULTIMATELY, THE EMERGENCE OF A DEMOCRATIC
POLITICAL CULTURE IN THE USSR.

03915 HAI, C.R.
    WHAT THE YOUNG GENERATION LIVES FOR
    WORLD MARXIST REVIEW, 31(10) (OCT 88), 59-63.
       KOREAN YOUTH HAVE A CHERISHED GOAL: TO SECURE PEACE IN
    KOREA AND ATTAIN ITS PEACEFUL REUNIFICATION. YOUNG PEOPLE
    IDENTIFY WITH THE STRUGGLE OF THEIR CONTEMPORARIES IN SOUTH
    KOREA, WHERE THE ANTI-US AND ANTI-FACIST MOVEMENT OF THE
    POPULAR MASSES HAS RECENTLY INTENSIFIED. APART FROM ENDING
    THE NEOCOLONIAL US DOMINANCE, IT IS A MOVEMENT FOR NATIONAL
    DIGNITY, SOVEREIGN RIGHTS, A DEMOCRATISATION OF SOCIETY AND
    THE COUNTRY'S REUNIFICATION.

03916 HAIBAO, Y.; PING, L.
    GROWTH SLOWS IN DEVELOPMENT ZONES
    BEIJING REVIEW, 32(1) (JAN 89), 40-42.
       THE TIDE OF FOREIGN CAPITAL FLOWING INTO CHINA'S 13
    ECONOMIC AND TECHNOLOGICAL DEVELOPMENT ZONES WILL PROBABLY
    SLOW IN 1989 DUE TO THE MEASURES ADOPTED TO STABILIZE THE
    ECONOMY AND CURB INFLATION. THESE INCLUDE A SERIES OF
    MEASURES CANCELLING THE ALLOCATION OF NEW FUNDS, RAISING THE
    BANK RATE, CUTTING BACK ON CONSTRUCTION PROJECTS, AND
    DECREASING THE NUMBER OF NEW LOANS.

03917 HAIBO, L.
    BENAZIR BHUTTO ON PAK-CHINESE TIES
    BEIJING REVIEW, 32(7-8) (FEB 89), 14-15.
       IN THIS INTERVIEW, PAKISTANI PRIME MINISTER BENAZIR
    BHUTTO SAID THAT HER 1989 STATE VISIT TO CHINA WAS AN
    EXPRESSION OF PAKISTANI-CHINESE FRIENDSHIP. SHE ALSO
    DISCUSSED THE SITUATION IN AFGHANISTAN, PAKISTANI-INDIAN
    RELATIONS, AND IMPORTANT DOMESTIC ISSUES.

03918 HAIBO, L.
    BUSH VISITS CHINA AND FRIENDS
    BEIJING REVIEW, 32(10) (MAR 89), 9-10.
       PRESIDENT GEORGE BUSH SERVED AS HEAD OF THE U.S. LIAISON
    OFFICE IN BEIJING IN 1974-75 AND MADE FOUR ADDITIONAL TRIPS
    TO CHINA BEFORE ASSUMING THE PRESIDENCY. UNLIKE HIS
    PREDECESSORS, BUSH HAS MANY ORDINARY CHINESE FRIENDS,
    INCLUDING THOSE WHO ATTENDED THE SAME CHRISTIAN CHURCH WHEN
    HE LIVED IN BEIJING. UNDER BUSH, U.S.-SINO RELATIONS COULD
    ADD MORE DIMENSIONS, FUNCTIONING ON LEADER-TO-PEOPLE AND
    PEOPLE-TO-PEOPLE LEVELS AS WELL AS THE LEADER-TO-LEADER
    PLANE.

03919 HAIBO, L.
    MARTIAL LAW: DECLARED BUT NOT ENFORCED
    BEIJING REVIEW, 32(22) (MAY 89), 9-11.
       ON MAY 19, 1989, PREMIER LI PENG DELIVERED A HEATED
    MIDNIGHT SPEECH TO THE PARTY, GOVERNMENT OFFICIALS, AND ARMY
    CADRES AND DECLARED THAT BEIJING WAS IN A CRITICAL SITUATION.
    HE SAID THAT THE "ANARCHIC STATE" IN BEIJING WAS BECOMING
    WORSE, THAT LAW AND ORDER WERE THREATED, AND THAT A FEW
    PEOPLE WERE USING THE HUNGER STRIKERS AS HOSTAGES TO FORCE
    THE PARTY AND GOVERNMENT TO AGREE TO THEIR POLITICAL
    CONDITIONS. PRESIDENT OF STATE YANG SHANGKUN SAID THAT THE
    CAPITAL'S SOCIAL ORDER AUTHORITIES HAD NO ALTERNATIVE BUT TO
    SEND TROOPS INTO BEIJING.

03920 HAIBO, L.
    SINO-INDIAN RELATIONS USHER A NEW ERA
    BEIJING REVIEW, 32(1) (JAN 89), 9-10.
       INDIAN LEADER RAJIV GANDHI VISTED CHINA ON DECEMBER 19-
    23, 1988 AND BECAME THE FIRST INDIAN PRIME MINISTER TO DO SO
    IN 34 YEARS. HIS VISIT WAS GENERALLY CONSIDERED A GENUINE
    STARTING POINT FOR IMPROVED RELATIONS. BOTH COUNTRIES
    EXPRESSED A READINESS TO SOLVE PROBLEMS THAT HINDER SUCH
    PROGRESS, ESPECIALLY THE BOUNDARY ONE, THROUGH PEACEFUL AND
    FRIENDLY CONSULTATIONS.

03921 HAIBO, L.
    SINO-SOVIET SUMMIT: NORMALIZATION AT LAST
    BEIJING REVIEW, 32(22) (MAY 89), 7, 9.
       WHEN PRESIDENT MIKHAIL GORBACHEV ARRIVED IN BEIJING ON
    MAY 15, 1989, HE BECAME THE FIRST SOVIET LEADER TO VISIT
    CHINA IN 30 YEARS. DURING HIS FOUR-DAY STAY, HIS MEETINGS
    WITH CHINESE LEADERS SIGNALLED A COMPREHENSIVE END TO THE
    STRAINED RELATIONS OF THE LAST DECADES AND OPENED BROAD

PROSPECTS FOR FRIENDSHIP AND CO-OPERATION.

03922 HAIBO, L.
    STALIN'S IMAGE FADES IN CHINA
    BEIJING REVIEW, 32(20) (MAY 89), 11-12.
       THE CHINESE PEOPLE ARE OUTRAGED BY THE REVELATIONS ABOUT
    JOSEPH STALIN AND THE RECENT DISCLOSURE OF HIS MANY CRIMES
    AND ERRORS. THE STALINIST CULT IS COMING UNDER ATTACK IN
    CHINA, ALONG WITH HIS NON-MARXIST AND NON-SOCIALIST THEORIES
    AND PRACTICES.

03923 HAIBO, L.
    TAIWANESE INVITED TO DISCUSS UNITY
    BEIJING REVIEW, 32(2) (JAN 89), 9-11.
       MAINLAND CHINESE OFFICIALS HAVE EXPRESSED THEIR
    WILLINGNESS TO DISCUSS THE COUNTRY'S REUNIFICATION WITH ALL
    PARTIES, ORGANIZATIONS, AND PEOPLES IN TAIWAN. THE CHINESE
    COMMUNIST PARTY CENTRAL COMMITTEE HAS PROPOSED THAT THE
    PARTY AND THE KUOMINTANG SHOULD MAKE CONTACT AND NEGOTIATE
    ON AN EQUAL BASIS AS SOON AS POSSIBLE.

03924 HAILEY, M.E.
    THE POLITICAL AND SOCIAL ATTITUDES OF CHURCH OF CHRIST
    MINISTERS
    DISSERTATION ABSTRACTS INTERNATIONAL, 49(11) (MAY 89),
    3490-A.
       THE AUTHOR STUDIES THE POLITICAL AND SOCIAL ACTIVITIES
    OF CHURCH OF CHRIST MINISTERS AND HOW THEY FIT INTO THE
    FRAMEWORK OF THE NEW RELIGIOUS RIGHT. HE CONCLUDES THAT,
    ALTHOUGH THE CHURCH OF CHRIST MINISTERS BELONG TO THE
    CONSERVATIVE EVANGELICAL CULTURE, THERE IS ONLY A MODEST
    RESIDUUM OF SUPPORT FOR THE NEW RELIGIOUS RIGHT AMONG THE
    MINISTERS, WHO ARE POLITICALLY ACTIVE ONLY TO A LIMITED
    DEGREE.

03925 HAINSWORTH, P.
    NORTHERN IRELAND
    ELECTORAL STUDIES, 8(3) (DEC 89), 313-316.
       THIS ARTICLE EXAMINES THE 1989 EUROPEAN ELECTIONS IN
    NORTHERN IRELAND, NOTING ITS UNIQUE SINGLE TRANSFERABLE VOTE
    (STV) ELECTORAL SYSTEM. IT EXPLORES THE CAMPAIGN, CANDIDATES,
    ISSUES AND RESULTS IT CONCLUDES THAT THE RESULTS WERE QUITE
    PREDICTABLE AND THAT THIS TENDED TO REDUCE INTEREST IN THE
    ELECTION. PERSONALITY AND PRECEDENT PREDOMINATED.

03926 HAJIME. S.
    THE DAY THE MOUNTAINS MOVED
    JAPAN ECHO, XVI(4) (WIN 89), 14-22.
       THE RESULTS OF THE JULY 1989 TOKYO METROPOLITAN ASSEMBLY
    ELECTIONS POINT TO A DRAMATIC SHIFT IN THE JAPANESE
    POLITICAL CLIMATE. THE RULING LIBERAL DEMOCRATIC PARTY LOST
    TWENTY SEATS IN THE ELECTION, WHILE SOCIALIST OR SOCIALIST-
    BACKED CANDIDATES WON 36 SEATS, TRIPLING THEIR PREVIOUS
    REPRESENTATION. ONE-THIRD OF THE WINNING SOCIALIST
    CANDIDATES WERE WOMEN, AN INDICATION OF THE RAPID
    TRANSFORMATION UNDERWAY IN JAPAN'S TRADITIONALLY MALE-
    DOMINATED SOCIETY.

03927 HAJNICZ, A.
    POLAND WITHIN ITS GEOPOLITICAL TRIANGLE
    AUSSEN POLITIK, 40(1) (JAN 89), 30-40.
       THE AUTHOR PRESENTS VIEWS EXPRESSED BY PARTICIPANTS OF A
    CONSERVATORIUM, "POLAND IN EUROPE". THE SUBJECT OF THE
    CONSERVATORIUM OFTEN IS OFTEN ALTERNATE POLITICAL SOLUTIONS
    TO POLISH DILEMMAS THAT DO NOT COINCIDE WITH GOVERNMENT
    POLICY. THE AUTHOR DISCUSSES THE "YALTA STATE": A POLAND
    DEPENDENT ON AND SURROUNDED BY THE USSR. HE DISCUSSES THE
    NEED THE RID POLAND OF THE SYNDROME OF GERMAN DANGER AND THE
    SOVIET PROTECTORATE AND PURSUE RECONCILIATION AND
    NORMALIZATION OF RELATIONS WITH BOTH THE GERMANS AND THE
    RUSSIANS AND ACQUIRE THE STATUS OF A PERFECTLY NORMAL
    EUROPEAN COUNTRY.

03928 HAK, T.A.A.; HAK, B.A.
    THE ARAB WORLD IN FLUX
    NEW OUTLOOK, 32(2 (288)) (FEB 89), 45-46.
       IN 1989 THE WORLD WILL WITNESS THE PALESTINIAN PEACE
    STRATEGY AND ITS TRANSFORMATION INTO A PAN-ARAB PEACE
    STRATEGY. THIS PEACE STRATEGY WILL BE BUILT UPON THE
    FOLLOWING FOUNDATIONS: PALESTINIAN RECOGNITION OF ISRAEL'S
    EXISTENCE; READINESS TO NEGOTIATE WITH ISRAEL IN THE
    FRAMEWORK OF AN INTERNATIONAL CONFERENCE; ACCEPTANCE OF THE
    IDEA OF PEACEFUL COEXISTENCE BETWEEN ISRAEL AND THE
    INDEPENDENT PALESTINIAN STATE; AND ACCEPTANCE OF THE FACT
    THAT THE INDEPENDENT PALESTINIAN STATE WILL BE ESTABLISHED
    WITHIN THE FRAMEWORK OF THE 1967 BORDERS.

03929 HALACHMI, A.
    AD-HOCRACY AND THE FUTURE OF CIVIL SERVICE
    INTERNATIONAL JOURNAL OF PUBLIC ADMINISTRATION, 12(4)
    (1989), 617-650.
       NEGATIVE ATTITUDES OF CITIZENS TOWARD BUREAUCRATS, THE
    GROWING ATTENTION TO CONTRACTING OUT AND PRIVATIZATION, AND
    THE INCREASING SENSE OF PROFESSIONALISM AMONG PUBLIC SECTOR

EMPLOYEES WILL SHAPE THE FUTURE OF THE CIVIL SERVICE. THE NEED TO EMPLOY TECHNOCRATS IN ORDER TO CARRY OUT MISSIONS THAT ARE GROWING IN COMPLEXITY REQUIRES NEW ORGANIZATIONAL ARRANGEMENTS. FOR SOME AGENCIES ALVIN TOFFLER'S IDEA OF AD-HOCRACY MAY BE THE BASIS FOR SUCH NEW ARRANGEMENTS.

03930 HALDON, J.
THE FEUDALISM DEBATE ONCE MORE: THE CASE OF BYZANTIUM
JOURNAL OF PEASANT STUDIES, 17(1) (OCT 89), 5-40.
THIS ARTICLE TAKES UP ONE ASPECT OF THE DEBATE ON FEUDALISM AND NONEUROPEAN SOCIETIES. THROUGH A REVIEW OF ELEMENTS OF THE SOCIAL AND ECONOMIC HISTORY OF THE LATE ROMAN AND BYZANTINE STATES, IT SEEKS TO DEMONSTRATE, FIRST, HOW AND WHY THESE SOCIAL FORMATIONS SHOULD BE CONSIDERED FEUDAL; SECOND, THAT A BROAD APPLICATION OF THE CONCEPT OF THE FEUDAL MODE OF PRODUCTION AS A CONCEPT OF POLITICAL ECONOMY IS BOTH THEORETICALLY MORE VALID AND ANALYTICALLY MORE FRUITFUL THAN ITS RESTRICTION TO THE EXAMINATION OF TYPES OF SOCIETY TRADITIONALLY IDENTIFIED AS FEUDAL ON THE BASIS OF THEIR INSTITUTIONAL AND SUPERSTRUCTURAL APPEARANCE. THE CRUCIAL POINT IN THIS CONTEXT IS THE RIGOROUS SEPARATION OF CONCEPTS BELONGING TO THEORETICAL AND HEURISTIC CATEGORIES SUCH AS MODE OF PRODUCTION FROM THE FORMS WHICH THESE CONCEPTS EXPRESS IN SPECIFIC HISTORICAL SOCIETIES.

03931 HALE, D.
PICKING UP REAGAN'S TAB
FOREIGN POLICY, (74) (SPR 89), 145-167.
THE ARTICLE EXAMINES THE ECONOMIC CHALLENGES THAT THE US AND THE WORLD WILL FACE IN THE NEXT DECADE. MANY ECONOMISTS PREDICT ANOTHER WORLD DEPRESION REMINISCENT OF THE 1930'S, AND ALTHOUGH MANY OF THE CONDITIONS ARE SIMILAR, THE ROLE OF GOVERNMENT AND THE STRUCTURE OF ECONOMIC POLICYMAKING ARE DIFFERENT ENOUGH TO PROBABLY AVERT A DOMINO-LIKE COLLPASE OF THE US'S FINANCIAL INSTITUTIONS. HOWEVER, PROBLEMS SUCH AS THE HUGE BUDGET DEFICIT, BALANCE OF PAYMENTS DEFICIT, AND EXTERNAL DEBT CAN STILL CAUSE MAJOR ECONOMIC DISLOCATIONS AND PROBLEMS. IT EXAMINES TRENDS IN THE CHANGING WORLD ECONOMY, WHICH INCLUDE THE DECLINE OF THE US IN ABSOLUTE TERMS, THE RISE OF JAPAN AND DEMOGRAPHIC CHANGES IN THE US AND EUROPE.

03932 HALE, D.D.
MUST WE BECOME JAPANESE
NATIONAL REVIEW, 61(20) (OCT 89), 30-32; 59.
THIS ARTICLE EXAMINES JAPAN'S INDISPUTABLE ECONOMIC SUCCESS WHICH EVOKES ENVY, AND TEMPTS THE US TOWARD IMITATION. IT EXPLORES THE BUSH ADMINISTRATION'S INCLINATION TOWARDS JAPANESE ECONOMICS AND POINTS OUT THAT THE JAPANESE FORMULA IS ONE PART FAVORABLE INVESTMENT CLIMATE AND ONE PART CAREFUL TINKERING BY A COMPETENT AND PRESTIGIOUS CIVIL SERVICE WHICH, THE AUTHOR CLAIMS, WE WON'T SEE SOON, THE AUTHOR CONTENDS THAT WE NEED TO KNOW MORE ABOUT THE REASONS FOR JAPANESE SUCCESS BEFORE WE TRY TO ADAPT POLICIES TO OUR OWN CIRCUMSTANCES.

03933 HALE, S.
THE STATUS OF WOMEN INDIA
PACIFIC AFFAIRS, 62(3) (FAL 89), 364-381.
CURRENT RESEARCH ON THE CHANGING STATUS OF WOMEN IN INDIA RAISES ISSUES AT THE CORE OF THEORETICAL DEBATES CONCERNING THE INTERRELATIONS BETWEEN GENDER, ETHNIC, RELIGIOUS, AND ECONOMIC HIERARCHIES WITHIN SOCIETY. STEADILY INCREASING NUMBERS OF INDIA WOMEN ARE GAINING ACCESS TO EDUCATION AND TO PAID EMPLOYMENT OUTSIDE THEIR HOMES. THESE WOMEN ACQUIRE INDEPENDENCE AND STATUS IN TERMS OF ECONOMIC SUCCESS THAT POTENTIALLY CONFLICTS WITH THEIR TRADITIONALLY SUBORDINATE AND SEGREGATED STATUS AS WOMEN IN RELATIONS WITH MEN.

03934 HALL, B.W.
PEACE STUDIES AS IF SOVIET STUDIES MATTERED
PHILADELPHIA: ANLS OF AMER ACMY OF POLITICAL AND SOC SCIENCE, (504) (JUL 89), 106-116.
STUDENTS OF PEACE STUDIES AND SOVIET STUDIES SHOULD PROVIDE COMPLEMENTARY TOOLS OR MIRRORS FOR INTERPRETING CONTEMPORARY INTERNATIONAL POLITICS, BUT THEY ARE NOT RESPONDING TO THIS CALL. THE SERIOUSNESS OF THE INTELLECTUAL LACUNAE CREATED BY SOVIET STUDIES AND PEACE STUDIES SCHOLARS WORKING IN ISOLATION FROM EACH OTHER IS ADDRESSED IN THIS ARTICLE IN SEVERAL WAYS. FIRST, CLAIMS ABOUT EXISTING DIFFERENCES IN THE TWO APPROACHES ARE ESTABLISHED. SECOND, THE CONSTRUCTIVE, NONOVERLAPPING CONTRIBUTIONS EACH APPROACH CAN MAKE IN UNDERSTANDING CONTEMPORARY SOVIET POLITICS ARE ILLUSTRATED THROUGH A DUAL ANNOTATION OF A SPEECH BY GORBACHEV. FOLLOWING COMMENTS ON THIS PARTICULAR TEXT MADE FROM A PEACE STUDIES PERSPECTIVE AND A SOVIET STUDIES PERSPECTIVE, THE ARTICLE ADDRESSES PARTICULAR ISSUES THAT MAY BE UNDERSTOOD MORE DEEPLY BY INCORPORATING THE TWO APPROACHES. IN CONCLUSION, AN ASSESSMENT IS MADE OF THE PROMISE OF COLLABORATIVE WORK IN SOVIET STUDIES AND PEACE STUDIES.

03935 HALL, G.
SOME AIMS AND GUIDELINES FOR THE CPUSA IDEOLOGICAL CONFERENCE
POLITICAL AFFAIRS, LXVIII(5) (MAY 89), 3-6.
THE AUTHOR ENUMERATES IDEOLOGICAL QUESTIONS THAT AMERICAN COMMUNISTS SHOULD FOCUS ON: THE CLASS STRUGGLE, RACISM, NATIONALISM, MALE SUPREMACY, GREAT POWER CHAUVINISM, THE DEFENSE OF MARXISM-LENINISM, AND THE THEORY OF THE PARTY.

03936 HALL, G.
THE CARICATURE OF "COMMUNISM"
POLITICAL AFFAIRS, LXVIII(1) (JAN 89), 2-5.
THE MAIN PREMISE OF ANTI-COMMUNISM DOES NOT CONCERN THE PHILOSOPHY, THE THEORIES, OR THE PRACTICES OF THE COMMUNIST PARTY. ANTI-COMMUNISM PROJECTS A CARICATURE OF COMMUNISM BASED UPON VERY SENSITIVE AND EMOTIONALLY-CHARGED ISSUES, INCLUDING PATRIOTISM, DEMOCRACY, AND RELIGION.

03937 HALL, G.
THE WORLD IN TRANSITION
POLITICAL AFFAIRS, LXVIII(3) (MAR 89), 3-16.
THE AUTHOR SPECULATES ON THE COURSE THE BUSH ADMINISTRATION WILL TAKE, ESPECIALLY IN THE AREAS OF INTERNATIONAL RELATIONS AND RACE RELATIONS. HE ALSO CONSIDERS THE STATE OF SOCIALISM AND THE COMMUNIST PARTY IN THE USA.

03938 HALL, G.
USA: OUR GOAL - WORKING CLASS UNITY, LEFT UNITY
INFORMATION BULLETIN, 25/26(1-2) (JAN 88), 9-12.
THIS ARTICLE CONTAINS EXCERPTS FROM THE MAIN REPORT BY GUS HALL TO THE 24TH NATIONAL CONVENTION OF THE CPUSA. FOCUS IS ON AN EVALUATION OF THE IDEOLOGICAL STUMBLING BLOCKS TO LEFT UNITY. ANY SUCCESSFUL LEFT ALLIANCE MUST BE CONSTRUCTIVE, NOT PROVOCATIVE AND MUST LEAVE ANTI-COMMUNISM BEHIND THOSE WHO CONTINUE TO MAKE ANTI-COMMUNISM THE PRIMARY QUESTION FOR LABOR IN PLACE OF THE BATTLES AGAINST THE TRANSNATIONALS WILL SOON BECOME IRRELEVANT.

03939 HALL, G.
USA: THE PEOPLE'S MOOD IS CHANGING
INFORMATION BULLETIN, 26(21-22) (NOV 88), 14-15.
THE CHAIRMAN OF THE COMMUNIST PARTY USA DESCRIBES THE SENSE OF HOPE AND REVIVED EXPECTATION OCCASIONED OF THE END OF REAGANISM IN THE UNITED STATES.

03940 HALL, H.K.; NELSON, D.R.
INSTITUTIONAL STRUCTURE AND TIME HORIZON IN A SIMPLE MODEL OF THE POLITICAL ECONOMY: THE LOWI EFFECT
INTERNATIONAL SPECTATOR, XXIV(3-4) (JUL 89), 153-174.
THIS PAPER PROPOSES AN ENDOGENOUS ECONOMIC POLICY MODELING APPROACH. ENDOGENOUS POLICY MODELS ATTEMPT AN EXPLICIT REPRESENTATION OF THE PROCESSES THAT GENERATE PAY-OFFS TO POLITICAL ACTIVITY IN A GENERAL POLITICAL-ECONOMIC EQUILIBRIUM. THE SIMPLEST FORM OF THIS APPROACH ASSUMES THAT CITIZEN PREFERENCES OVER ECONOMIC POLICY ARE STRICTLY DETERMINED BY THEIR RELATIONSHIP TO THE ECONOMY. THIS PAPER DEVELOPS A FORMAL LINK BETWEEN THE INSTITUTIONALIST AND INDIVIDUALIST THEORIES BY ILLUSTRATING THE EFFECT OF INSTITUTIONAL STRUCTURE ON THE INCENTIVES TO POLITICAL ACTION. THE RESULTS YIELD A TYPOLOGY SIMILAR TO THAT OBSERVED IN LOWI'S CLASSIC WORK LINKING INSTITUTIONALIZED POLICY TYPES TO POLITICAL ACTION.

03941 HALL, M.G.; BRACE, P.
ORDER IN THE COURTS: A NEO-INSTITUTIONAL APPROACH TO JUDICIAL CONSENSUS
WESTERN POLITICAL QUARTERLY, 42(3) (SEP 89), 391-408.
THIS STUDY ATTEMPTS TO BRIDGE THE GAP IN THE STUDY OF JUDICIAL POLITICS BETWEEN TRADITIONAL INSTITUTIONAL ANALYSIS AND ATTITUDINAL THEORY BY APPLYING CONCEPTS DRAWN FROM THE NEO-INSTITUTIONAL PERSPECTIVE TO DISSENT BEHAVIOR IN STATE SUPREME COURTS. NEOINSTITUTIONALISM EMBRACES RATIONAL CHOICE ASSUMPTIONS ABOUT HUMAN BEHAVIOR, WITH PARTICULAR ATTENTION TO HOW INSTITUTIONAL ARRANGEMENTS SHAPE PURPOSIVE BEHAVIOR. FROM THIS PERSPECTIVE, DISSENT IS VIEWED NOT MERELY AS THE COLLECTIVE EXPRESSION OF INDIVIDUAL ATTITUDES OR POLICY PREFERENCES BUT A COMPLEX INTERACTION OF VALUES AND STRUCTURES. MODELS INCORPORATING VARIABLES DERIVED FROM THE NEO-INSTITUTIONAL PERSPECTIVE WERE ESTIMATED USING ORDINARY LEAST SQUARES REGRESSION. ABSENT ANY PERSONAL ATTRIBUTE OR CASE CHARACTERISTICS, THESE MODELS CAN EXPLAIN UP TO 36 PERCENT OF THE VARIANCE IN STATE SUPREME COURT DISSENT RATES FOR 1966 AND 1981. NEO-INSTITUTIONALISM APPEARS TO BE A PROMISING APPROACH FOR THE FIELD OF JUDICIAL BEHAVIOR.

03942 HALL, R.G.
TYRANNY, WORK AND POLITICS: THE 1818 STRIKE WAVE IN THE ENGLISH COTTON DISTRICT
INTERNATIONAL REVIEW OF SOCIAL HISTORY, 34(3) (1989), 433-470.
CRITICS OF E. P. THOMPSON HAVE QUESTIONED HIS EMPHASIS ON THE TIES BETWEEN RADICALISM AND TRADE UNIONISM IN EARLY NINETEENTH-CENTURY ENGLAND; HISTORIANS HAVE LIKEWISE

DESCRIBED THE 1818 STRIKES AS SIMPLE WAGE DISPUTES IN WHICH THE RADICALS PLAYED A NEGLIGIBLE ROLE. THIS ESSAY CHALLENGES THESE ASSUMPTIONS ABOUT THE 1818 STRIKES AND RADICALISM. IN THE SUMMER OF 1818, WHEN A WIDE RANGE OF GRIEVANCES TOUCHED OFF THE STRIKE WAVE, THE RADICALS RALLIED TO THE SIDE OF THE TRADES AND SOMETIMES SERVED AS LEADERS OF THE STRIKES; THAT SUMMER THE RADICALS AND STRIKING TRADES ALSO DREW UPON AND CONTRIBUTED TO A SHARED REPERTOIRE OF OLD AND NEW TACTICS AND FORMS OF ACTION.

03943 HALL,P.
AND THAT WAS THE FUTURE... THE PLANNERS' WORLD
FUTURES, 21(5) (OCT 89), 498-507.
THE MOST SACRED WORD IN ANY MODERN POLITICAL DICTIONARY ARE: POPULATIONS, PROGRAMMES, PLANNING, PEOPLE. THE CONVICTIONS BEHIND THOSE PRESSURE INDICATORS HAVE SHAPED THE FUTURE FOR BILLIONS OF HUMAN BEINGS-FROM THE PLACE OF THE AUSTRALIAN ABORIGINES IN THE OUTBACK TO THE FIRST INHABITANTS OF THE VAST NEW TOWNS THAT BEGAN TO SPREAD ACROSS THE UK COUNTRYSIDE DURING THE 1950S. THE LESSON OF THE VARIOUS UK POST-WAR BUILDING PROGRAMMES, IS THAT THE NATION GETS THE CITIES THE POLITICIANS AND PLANNERS THINK WILL BE GOOD FOR THE PEOPLE. NOT SO LONG AGO, IN THE 1950S, THE GOOD WORDS SPOKE OF CLEARANCES, REDEVELOPMENT, MEGASTRUCTURES, HIGH-LEVEL WALKWAYS. THEN, THE WORLD CHANGED IN THE LATE 1960S AND THE NEW WORDS LOOKED TO REHABILITATION, PRESERVATION, PEDESTRIANIZATION, AND HOUSING WITH A HUMAN SCALE.

03944 HALLAJ, M.
THE PLO'S PEACE OFFENSIVE: FALSE START OR NEW BEGINNING?
MIDDLE EAST INTERNATIONAL, (343) (FEB 89), 19-20.
IT IS TOO EARLY TO ASSESS THE CONSEQUENCES OF THE PLO'S RECENT PEACE OFFENSIVE. NEW GOVERNMENTS HAVE RECENTLY COME INTO POWER IN THE UNITED STATES AND ISRAEL, EACH BURDENED WITH ITS OWN HANDICAPS THAT COULD IMPEDE ITS ABILITY TO MAKE THE NECESSARY FRESH START IN SEARCH OF ARAB-ISRAELI PEACE.

03945 HALLENBECK, R.A.
AFFECTING THE MEASURED APPLICATION OF MILITARY FORCE FOR POLITICAL ENDS: INSIGHTS FROM AMERICA'S INTERVENTION IN LEBANON, 1982-84
DISSERTATION ABSTRACTS INTERNATIONAL, 48(10) (APR 88), 2721-A.
THE DISSERTATION EXAMINES THE US MILITARY AND DIPLOMATIC INTERVENTION IN LEBANON DURING THE PERIOD AUGUST 1982 TO FEBRUARY 1984. IT COMPARES ASPECTS OF THE US INTERVENTION IN LEBANON WITH THE US INVOLVEMENT IN VIETNAM AND KOREA AND SEEKS TO DETERMINE HOW AND WHY US EFFORTS FAILED TO ACHIEVE ITS OBJECTIVES. IT ATTEMPTS TO DETERMINE CAUSE AND EFFECT RELATIONSHIPS THAT ARE GENERALIZABLE TO THESE AND OTHER ATTEMPTS TO APPLY MILITARY FORCE TO ACHIEVE POLITICAL ENDS.

03946 HALLIDAY, F.
THE REVOLUTION'S FIRST DECADE
MIDDLE EAST REPORT, 19(156) (JAN 89), 19-21.
THE AUTHOR SURVEYS THE ACHIEVEMENTS AND PROBLEMS OF THE ISLAMIC REPUBLIC OF IRAN AS IT ENTERS ITS SECOND DECADE.

03947 HALPERN, N.
SOCIAL SCIENTISTS AS POLICY ADVISERS IN POST-MAO CHINA: EXPLAINING THE PATTERN OF ADVICE
AUSTRALIAN JOURNAL OF CHINESE AFFAIRS, (19-20) (JAN 88), 215-240.
THE AUTHOR STUDIES THE STATE'S INFLUENCE ON SOCIAL SCIENCE AND THE INFLUENCE OF SOCIAL SCIENTISTS ON THE STATE IN POST-MAO CHINA. SHE FOCUSES ON THE TWO AREAS WHERE SOCIAL SCIENTISTS HAVE DEVELOPED INSTITUTIONALIZED ADVISORY ROLES: ECONOMICS AND INTERNATIONAL RELATIONS.

03948 HALPERN, N.P.
ECONOMIC REFORM AND DEMOCRATIZATION IN COMMUNIST SYSTEMS: THE CASE OF CHINA
STUDIES IN COMPARATIVE COMMUNISM, 22(2/3) (SUM 89), 139-152.
THIS ESSAY EXAMINES THE RELATIONSHIP BETWEEN ECONOMIC REFORM AND POLITICAL DEVELOPMENT IN POST-MAO CHINA, IT ARGUES THAT WHILE ECONOMIC REFORM IN CHINA HAS BEEN CLOSELY LINKED WITH RATIONALIZATION AND INTELLECTUAL FREEDOM, IT HAS BY NO MEANS DIRECTLY ENGENDERED PLURALISM AND DEMOCRATIZATION. IT CONCLUDES THAT POLITICAL DEVELOPMENTS IN CHINA ARE BETTER EXPLAINED BY BY TRAUMAS OF THE CULTURAL REVOLUTION AND POWER STRUGGLE THAN BY "OPENNESS."

03949 HALPERN, N.P.
POLICY COMMUNITIES IN A LENINIST STATE: THE CASE OF THE CHINESE ECONOMIC POLICY COMMUNITY
GOVERNANCE, 2(1) (JAN 89), 23-41.
THIS ARTICLE DEMONSTRATES THAT AN ECONOMIC POLICY COMMUNITY CAME INTO EXISTENCE IN CHINA OF THE EARLY 1960'S AND THAT IT WAS ABLE TO SERVE AS A MECHANISM FOR EXPERTS' IDEAS TO EXERT SOME INFLUENCE ON POLICY OUTCOMES. IT SHOWS THAT LEADERSHIP PREDISPOSITIONS, AS MUCH AS STATE STRUCTURE, DETERMINE THE ROLE AND IMPACT OF POLICY COMMUNITIES AND THE

INFLUENCE OF EXPERTS.

03950 HALSTEAD, G.H.
A NEW CONCEPT OF SECURITY
INTERNATIONAL PERSPECTIVES, XVIII(3) (MAY 89), 3-6.
NATO'S VERY SUCCESS IS NOW ONE OF ITS PROBLEMS. THE ESSENTIAL ELEMENTS ON WHICH WESTERN SECURITY HAS RESTED SINCE THE SECOND WORLD WAR ARE NOT SELF-GENERATING. THERE ARE THREE: THE ROUGH EAST-WEST BALANCE OF POWER, GLOBAL STABILITY AND TRANSATLANTIC SOLIDARITY -- AND THEY HAVE IN FACT BEEN UNDERGOING IMPORTANT MODIFICATIONS OVER THE YEARS. ON BOTH SIDES THERE HAS BEEN A RELUCTANCE TO ADAPT TO THE NEW REALITIES OF GREATER EQUALITY. THE AMERICANS ACCUSE THE EUROPEANS OF CRITICIZING US POLICIES, AND OF FAILING TO CARRY THEIR FAIR SHARE OF THE DEFENCE BURDEN. THE EUROPEANS CHARGE THE AMERICANS WITH FAILING TO TAKE ADEQUATE ACCOUNT OF EUROPEAN VIEWS, AND OF USING THEIR LEADERSHIP POSITION TO EXACT ECONOMIC CONCESSIONS. IT IS NOT A GOOD BASIS FOR A HEALTHY PARTNERSHIP.

03951 HALSTEAD, J.
THE POLITICAL AND STRATEGIC IMPORTANCE OF THE ARCTIC: A CANADIAN PERSPECTIVE
ETUDES INTERNATIONALES, XX(2) (MAR 89), 27-44.
THE ARCTIC LENDS A SPECIAL DIMENSION TO CANADIAN FOREIGN AND DEFENSE POLICIES BECAUSE IT IS THE MOST HARSH AND THE LEAST POPULATED PART OF CANADA, IT IS WHERE AMERICAN SECURITY INTERESTS IMPINGE MOST INSISTENTLY AND IT IS THE HAM IN THE SUPERPOWER SANDWICH. MOREOVER, THE ARCTIC IS BEING DRAWN INCREASINGLY INTO THE INTERNATIONAL SYSTEM, WITH IMPORTANT POLICY IMPLICATIONS: CANADA CANNOT EXPECT TO DEVELOP EFFECTIVE POLICIES TO DEAL WITH ITS OWN ARCTIC IN ISOLATION FROM OTHER COUNTRIES; AND CANADA'S ABILITY TO CARRY SUCH POLICIES OUT WILL DEPEND ON THE EXTENT TO WHICH IT CAN EXERCISE EFFECTIVE CONTROL OVER ITS VAST TERRITORY. THESE IMPLICATIONS ARE OF PARTICULAR IMPORTANCE TO CANADA'S R RELATIONS WITH THE UNITED STATES. TRADITIONALLY CANADA HAS DEALT BILATERALLY WITH THE UNITED STATES ON SUCH MATTERS BUT THE TIME HAS COME TO SUPPLEMENT THE BILATERAL CHANNELS WITH MULTILATERAL APPROACHES WHEREVER POSSIBLE, IN ORDER TO EMPHASIZE THE POINT THAT THE DEFENCE OF NORTH AMERICA IS AN INTEGRAL PART OF THE DEFENCE OF THE NORTH ATLANTIC TREATY AREA. IN ACCORDANCE WITH THIS CONCEPT, VARIOUS MEASURES SHOULD BE CONSIDERED TO REINFORCE THE STRATEGIC UNITY OF NATO, TO ENSURE THAT DEFENCE MEASURES IN THE ARCTIC ARE CONSISTENT WITH STRATEGIC STABILITY AND WITH ARMS CONTROL POLICIES, AND TO ESTABLISH IN THE ARCTIC A REGIME OF MUTUAL SECURITY, BOLSTERED BY A CONCERTED PROGRAM OF CIRCUMPOLAR COOPERATION. NOTE: ARTICLE PRINTED IN FRENCH

03952 HALSTEAD, J.
VIEW FROM OTTAWA
NATO'S SIXTEEN NATIONS, 34(2) (APR 89), 29-30.
IN A ROUGH-AND-TUMBLE CAMPAIGN, THE PROGRESSIVE CONSERVATIVES UNDER PRIME MINISTER BRIAN MULRONEY GAINED A SECOND TERM IN POWER IN CANADA'S 1988 ELECTION. THE MOST EMOTIONAL CAMPAIGN ISSUE WAS THE CANADA-US FREE TRADE AGREEMENT, BUT THE ISSUE THAT PROBABLY DECIDED THE OUTCOME WAS LEADERSHIP. DOMESTIC POLICY QUESTIONS HERE MUCH LESS PROMINENT, WHILE DEFENSE POLICY NEVER BECAME AN IMPORTANT ISSUE AND OTHER FOREIGN POLICY MATTERS WERE VIRTUALLY IGNORED. THE LACK OF DEBATE ON DEFENSE POLICY SEEMS TO INDICATE A BROAD CONSENSUS AMONG CANADIANS ON CERTAIN BASIC TENETS.

03953 HALTON, M.R.
LEGISLATING ASSIMILATION: THE ENGLISH-ONLY MOVEMENT
THE CHRISTIAN CENTURY, 106(36) (NOV 89), 1119-1120.
THIS ARTICLE EXAMINES THE PITCHED BATTLE WHICH IS UNDERWAY BETWEEN THOSE WHO CONSIDER THAT, FOR THE SAKE OF AMERICA'S COHESION, ENGLISH MUST BE LEGISLATED THE OFFICIAL LANGUAGE THROUGH CONSTITUTIONAL AMENDMENTS, AND THOSE WHO CONSIDER SUCH ATTEMPTS TO BE BIGOTED. IT TAKES THE STANCE THAT LEGISLATION MAKING ENGLISH THE OFFICIAL U.S. LANGUAGE IS UNNECESSARY; THERE ARE GENTLER WAYS TO BRING ABOUT ASSIMILATION.

03954 HAMBLETON, R.
URBAN GOVERNMENT UNDER THATCHER AND REAGAN
URBAN AFFAIRS QUARTERLY, 24(3) (MAR 89), 359-388.
RECENT DEVELOPMENTS AFFECTING URBAN GOVERNMENT IN BRITAIN AND THE UNITED STATES ARE EXAMINED IN THIS ARTICLE. THE SOCIOECONOMIC TRENDS AFFECTING CITIES ARE SIMILAR, AND CENTRAL GOVERNMENT FINANCIAL SUPPORT TO CITY GOVERNMENT HAS BEEN REDUCED IN BOTH COUNTRIES. THE THATCHER GOVERNMENT, HOWEVER, COMBINES ECONOMIC LIBERALISM WITH A SWEEPING COMMITMENT TO POLITICAL CENTRALIZATION, WHICH WOULD BE UNTHINKABLE IN THE UNITED STATES. THE RESULT IS THAT BRITISH URBAN GOVERNMENT, IN CONTRAST TO AMERICAN EXPERIENCE, HAS BECOME HIGHLY POLITICIZED AND CONFLICTUAL.

03955 HAMBURGER, A. C.
PUBLIC SCHOOLS AND PUBLIC HEALTH: EXCLUSION OF CHILDREN WITH AIDS

JOURNAL OF LAW & POLITICS, V(3) (SPR 89), 605-624.
THIS NOTE ADDRESSES THE PROPER ROLE OF DIFFERENT LEVELS OF GOVERNMENT IN EXCLUDING CHILDREN WITH ACQUIRED IMMUNE DEFICIENCY SYNDROME (AIDS) FROM PUBLIC SCHOOLS. IT DOES NOT PROPOSE DETAILED GUIDELINES, BECAUSE THE MEDICAL CRITERIA WILL BE IN FLUX AS KNOWLEDGE AND TREATMENT OF THE DISEASE DEVELOP. INSTEAD, IT SEEKS TO DETERMINE WHICH LEVELS OF GOVERNMENT HAVE THE LEGAL AUTHORITY, INSTITUTIONAL COMPETENCY, AND THE POLITICAL WILLPOWER TO ESTABLISH RULES ABOUT THE EXCLUSION OF CHILDREN WITH AIDS FROM SCHOOL. THE NOTE ARGUES THAT EACH STATE SHOULD DETERMINE ITS OWN RULES REGARDING WHEN CHILDREN WITH AIDS SHOULD BE EXCLUDED FROM SCHOOL.

03956 HAMID, N.; NABI, I.
PRIVATE FINANCE COMPANIES IN LDC'S: LESSONS FROM AN EXPERIMENT
WORLD DEVELOPMENT, 17(8) (AUG 89), 1289-1297.
IN MANY LDCS LIBERALIZING THE FINANCIAL SECTOR WILL INVOLVE CREATING NEW FINANCIAL INSTITUTIONS IN THE PRIVATE SECTOR TO ATTRACT UNTAPPED SAVINGS AND PROVIDE NEW SERVICES. THIS PAPER PROVIDES A DETAILED ACCOUNT OF AN EXPERIMENT WITH PRIVATE FINANCE COMPANIES (PFCS) IN PAKISTAN. THE COMPLEX LEGAL, IDEOLOGICAL AND ECONOMIC FACTORS WHICH EXPLAIN THE INITIAL SUCCESS AND THE ULTIMATE FAILURE OF THAT EXPERIMENT ARE IDENTIFIED. IT IS CONCLUDED THAT PFCS HAVE AN IMPORTANT ROLE IN MOBILIZING RURAL SAVINGS, BUT TO SAFEGUARD DEPOSITORS A LEGAL FRAMEWORK HAS TO BE PROVIDED. CARE SHOULD BE TAKEN THAT NATIONALIZED BANKS, ACTING IN THEIR SELF-INTEREST AS MONOPOLISTS, DO NOT CREATE HURDLES IN THE PROVISION OF SUCH MINIMUM REGULATION.

03957 HAMILTON, C.
RELIGIOUS IMPERATIVE FOR PEACE
MIDDLE EAST INTERNATIONAL, (362) (NOV 89), 19-20.
THE ARTICLE VIEWS THE CURRENT SITUATION IN ISRAEL AND PALESTINE FROM A RELIGIOUS PERSPECTIVE. THE AUTHOR ARGUES THAT NO RELIGION, BE IT MUSLIM, CHRISTIAN, OR JEWISH, JUSTIFIES THE CURRENT REPRESSION AND TERRORISM THAT IS TAKING PLACE IN THE MIDDLE EAST. HE CALLS FOR A RETURN TO THE BELIEF IN RECONCILIATION, SHARED BY ALL RELIGIONS, THAT WOULD AID IN EASING AND EVENTUALLY SOLVING MIDDLE EASTERN CONFLICTS.

03958 HAMILTON, C.
THE IRRELEVANCE OF ECONOMIC LIBERALIZATION IN THE THIRD WORLD
WORLD DEVELOPMENT, 17(10) (OCT 89), 1523-1530.
THIS ESSAY ARGUES THAT POLICIES OF ECONOMIC LIBERALIZATION MAY INHIBIT GROWTH AND DEVELOPMENT IN THIRD WORLD COUNTRIES. THE IDEA THAT GOVERNMENT INTERVENTION STIFLES ENTREPRENEURIAL INITIATIVE AND LEADS TO MISALLOCATION OF RESOURCES IS OFTEN INAPPROPRIATE TO THE INSTITUTIONAL CONDITIONS AND ECONOMIC STRUCTURES OF THIRD WORLD COUNTRIES. IN THESE COUNTRIES, THE ADVERSARIAL RELATIONSHIP BETWEEN PRIVATE BUSINESS AND GOVERNMENT IS FOREIGN. CONSEQUENTLY, THE IMPACT OF INTERVENTIONIST POLICIES—AS WELL AS THEIR FORM—DIFFERS FROM THAT ALLEGED FOR THE WEST.

03959 HAMILTON, D.
THE WALL BEHIND THE WALL
FOREIGN POLICY, (76) (FAL 89), 176-197.
THIS ARTICLE FOCUSES ON THE IDEOLOGICAL POSITION THAT THE GDR IS TRYING TO MAINTAIN IN A CHANGING WORLD. THE BALANCE OF POWER IN EUROPE WHICH EAST GERMANY MAINTAINS IS ANALYSED. THE GDR'S ECONOMIC PROWESS IS EXAMINED AS WELL AS THE THREE-FOLD SQUEEZE THE ECONOMY FACES: 1) SOVIET PERESTROIKA, 2) EXPORTS TOT HE WEST, AND 3) RISING CONSUMER DEMANDS OF ITS OWN POPULATION EAST GERMANY'S RELATIONSHIP WITH THE USSR. AND THE ROLE OF THE CHURCH ARE EXAMINED THE FACT THAT THE GDR IS NOT RIPE FOR REVOLUTION, BUT HAS ENTERED AN IMPORTANT PHASE OF TRANSITION IS EXPLORED AS THIS CAN BE A CRITICAL DETERMINANT IN THE POST-COLD WAR ORDER IN EUROPE.

03960 HAMILTON, L.; BLOOMFIELD, L.; MCNAMARA, R.S.; MROZ, J.; PIADYSHEV, B.
REGIONAL CONFLICTS: ROUND TABLE DISCUSSION
INTERNATIONAL AFFAIRS (MOSCOW), (11) (NOV 89), 84.
IN THIS ROUND TABLE DISCUSSION, AMERICAN AND SOVIET EXPERTS DISCUSS REGIONAL CONFLICTS, THE SUPERPOWER ROLE IN THE THIRD WORLD, AND RELATED TOPICS.

03961 HAMILTON, L. H.
CHALLENGES FOR UNITED STATES POLICY IN THE MIDDLE EAST
MIDDLE EAST JOURNAL, 43(1) (WIN 89), 7-15.
US POLICY IN THE MIDDLE EAST HAS FOCUSED ON THE PEACE PROCESS, ON TRYING TO FACILITATE DIRECT TALKS BETWEEN THE PARTIES, ON SUPPORTING UN RESOLUTION 242, AND ON THE PRINCIPLE OF LAND FOR PEACE. IF THE PEACE PROCESS IS TO GO FORWARD, THE UNITED STATES MUST PROVIDE EFFECTIVE LEADERSHIP. IN 1988, SECRETARY SHULTZ GAVE THE PEACE PROCESS HIGH VISIBILITY AND PRIORITY. BUT BEFORE 1988 -- AND FOR SIX

YEARS -- THE UNITED STATES DID NOT MAKE A FULL-FLEDGED COMMITMENT TO PURSUING THE PEACE PROCESS. THIS WAS, IN PART, BECAUSE THE GAPS AMONG THE PARTIES' POSITIONS APPEARED UNBRIDGEABLE. AMERICAN LEADERSHIP CAN ONLY BE PROVIDED BY THE PRESIDENT AND THE SECRETARY OF STATE AND, TO SUCCEED, THAT LEADERSHIP MUST BE SUSTAINED.

03962 HAMILTON, L.A.
STRUCTURAL CHANGE, PARAPROFESSIONALS, AND URBAN MANAGEMENT: A CASE STUDY OF SUCCESSFUL ORGANIZATIONAL IMPROVEMENT
DISSERTATION ABSTRACTS INTERNATIONAL, 49(7) (JAN 89), 1957-A.
THIS DISSERTATION IS A CASE STUDY OF ORGANIZATIONAL CHANGE IN AN URBAN COUNTY GENERAL ASSISTANCE PROGRAM THAT EMPLOYED PARAPROFESSIONALS. STRATEGIES DIRECTED TOWARD CHANGING EMPLOYEE BEHAVIORS (NORMATIVE) ARE CONTRASTED WITH STRATEGIES DIRECTED AT CHANGING THE STRUCTURE OF THE SYSTEM (STRUCTURAL). FACTORS DETERMINING THE SELECTION OF THE CHANGE STRATEGY ARE ENUMERATED, WITH SPECIAL FOCUS ON THE LEVEL OF ORGANIZATION AS A KEY CRITERION.

03963 HAMILTON, M.
THE PROMISED LAND
MIDDLE EAST INTERNATIONAL, (346) (MAR 89), 19-20.
THE AUTHOR DISCUSSES THE CHRISTIAN DUTY TO SUPPORT THE EXISTENCE AND SECURITY OF THE ISRAELI STATE WHILE WORKING TO PROVIDE THE PALESTINIANS WITH INDEPENDENCE AND SECURITY.

03964 HAMILTON, M.P.
THE RELIGIOUS NEED FOR PEACE IN THE MIDDLE EAST
AMERICAN-ARAB AFFAIRS, (30) (FAL 89), 89-93.
WHILE OTHER SCHOLARS IN THE SYMPOSIUM FOR RELIGIOUS LEADERS IN 1989 SPOKE ON THE POLITICAL AND RELIGIOUS DIMENSIONS OF THE ISRAELI-PALESTINIAN CONFLICT, REV. HAMILTON'S (OF THE WASHINGTON CATHEDRAL) CONTRIBUTION WAS PERSONAL. HE TOLD STORIES, OFFERED OPINIONS AND GROUPED THEM UNDER THEOLOGICAL CATEGORIES. HE ADDRESSED THE CREATION, THE ROLE OF THEOLOGY, AND RECONCILATION. HE CONCLUDES WITH THREE MAXIMS FOR PEACEMAKERS.

03965 HAMILTON, R. H.
AMERICAN ALL-MAIL BALLOTING: A DECADE'S EXPERIENCE
PUBLIC ADMINISTRATION REVIEW, 48(5) (SEP 88), 860-866.
THIS ARTICLE CONCENTRATES ON THE THREE MOST IMPORTANT BENEFITS FROM AN ARRAY OF ADVANTAGES. THESE INCLUDE (1) A DECREASE IN OVERALL COSTS OF HOLDING ELECTIONS; (2) INCREASED VOTER PARTICIPATION/CONVENIENCE; AND (3) AN INCREASE IN THE INTEGRITY OF ELECTIONS AS A RESULT OF MORE TIME FOR VOTERS TO CONSIDER ISSUES BEFORE CASTING THEIR BALLOTS. IT ALSO FACILITATES THE ABILITY OF THE ELDERLY, INFIRM, HANDICAPPED, AND THOSE TEMPORARILY UNABLE TO PARTICIPATE ON A SPECIFIC TIME AND DATE TO VOTE. ALL-MAIL BALLOTING IS, HOWEVER, A BARRIER TO VOTING BY THOSE WITH NO FIXED ADDRESS, BUT IN-PERSON VOTING AT POLLING PLACES RARELY DEALS WITH THAT ISSUE EITHER.

03966 HAMM, M.R.
CHALLENGES TO NATO AFTER THE INF TREATY
CONTEMPORARY REVIEW, 254(1479) (APR 89), 184-189.
INSOFAR AS THE INF-TREATY CAN BE ASSESSED TODAY, ITS MILITARY BENEFITS TO NATO APPEAR QUESTIONABLE, WHILE ITS CONCRETE DRAWBACKS ARE READILY APPARENT. THIS POINT WAS REPEATEDLY MADE BY WITNESSES IN THE RATIFICATION HEARINGS OF THE US SENATE JUST RELEASED IN PRINT. NEVERTHELESS, VIRTUALLY ALL OF THEM CALLED FOR THE RATIFICATION OF THE TREATY FOR POLITICAL REASONS. NEITHER NATO'S POLITICAL NOR MILITARY LEADERS EVER REALLY SCRUTINIZED THE RAMIFICATIONS OF THE 'ZERO-OPTION' BEFORE OR AFTER IT WAS PROPOSED BY THE ALLIANCE IN NOVEMBER OF 1981. ADMITTEDLY SOME HAD SECOND THOUGHTS IN THE INTERIM, BUT REJECTING THE ZERO-SOLUTION WOULD HAVE CALLED INTO QUESTION NATO'S COMMITMENT TO ARMS CONTROL, JEOPARDIZED PUBLIC SUPPORT FOR THE ALLIANCE, AND RISKED THE POTENTIAL POLITICAL GAINS THAT MIGHT BE ACHIEVED IN THE TREATY'S AFTERMATH.

03967 HAMM, M.R.
POLITICAL SPRINGTIME IN EUROPE: CHALLENGES AND OPPORTUNITIES OF SYSTEMIC CHANGE
CONTEMPORARY REVIEW, 255(1484) (SEP 89), 118-123.
THIS ARTICLE EXPLORES THE TERMINAL CRISIS OF COMMUNISM AND THE ONSET OF THE POST-COMMUNIST AGE. IT ADDRESS CONCERNS ABOUT HOW THIS NEW AGE IS TO COME ABOUT; HOW IT IS GOING TO LOOK; WHAT WILL BE ITS IMPACT ON EUROPE'S GEOPOLITICAL LANDSCAPE; AND, SPECIFICALLY, HOW THE DIFFICULT ISSUE OF GERMAN UNITY WILL BE HANDLED? IT COVERS A VISIT TO THE FEDERAL REPUBLIC FROM GORBACHEV AND THE AGREEMENTS AND DECLARATIONS SIGNED DURING THE VISIT. IT SUGGESTS THAT THE WESTERN ALLIES REASSESS ITS ATTITUDE TOWARD EUROPE AND EUROPEAN POLITICAL AND MILITARY INTEGRATION.

03968 HAMMAMI, K.
SYRIA: HOW TO GET OUT OF THE CRISIS
WORLD MARXIST REVIEW, 32(5) (MAY 89), 74-76.
FROM THE NATIONAL PROGRESSIVE FRONT TO THE TRADE UNIONS

TO THE BROAD WORKING MASSES, PROTEST IS MOUNTING AGAINST THE
"SOLUTIONS" BEING IMPOSED BY THE PARASITIC BOURGEOISIE.
PEOPLE UNDERSTAND THAT SYRIA CAN'T GO ON RESISTING
IMPERIALIST AND ZIONIST CONSPIRACIES WITHOUT OVERCOMING THE
CRISIS. THE FIGHT FOR IMPROVEMENT STEMS NOT ONLY FROM THE
MAJORITY'S DAILY NEEDS, BUT ALSO FROM THE REQUIREMENTS OF
SUCH ECONOMIC GROWTH AS WOULD MEET THE POPULAR INTEREST,
FURTHER SOCIAL PROGRESS, AND STRENGTHEN NATIONAL
INDEPENDENCE. AS A CURE FOR THE CRISIS, THE SYRIAN COMMUNIST
PARTY SUGGESTS THAT THE PUBLIC SECTOR SHOULD BE MADE THE
STANDARD-BEARER OF THE ECONOMY. THIS CALLS FOR IMPROVING ITS
MANAGEMENT, RAISING ITS PROFITABILITY, AND EXPANDING THE
SECTOR BY CREATING NEW ENTERPRISES WHICH WOULD RELY MAINLY
ON LOCAL RESOURCES.

03969 HAMMAN, J.A.
THE ALLOCATION OF FEDERAL AID: THE DISTRIBUTION OF FEDERAL
MASS TRANSPORTATION ASSISTANCE FROM 1965-1986
DISSERTATION ABSTRACTS INTERNATIONAL, 50(2) (AUG 89),
535-A.
THE AUTHOR CONSIDERS TWO PROBLEMS FOUND IN THE EXISTING
LITERATURE ON FEDERAL AID ALLOCATION. THE FIRST CONCERNS THE
ALMOST EXCLUSIVE FOCUS GIVEN TO COMMITTEE INFLUENCES. THE
SECOND IS THE IMPLICIT ASSUMPTION THAT INFLUENCES AND
RESULTING FEDERAL AID DISTRIBUTIONS ARE INVARIANT OVER TIME.
HE DEVELOPS A TEMPORAL MODEL OF FEDERAL AID ALLOCATIONS THAT
STRESSES DYNAMICS AND THREE PROBLEMS THAT PROGRAM MANAGERS
COMMONLY FACE: IDENTIFYING A CORE CLIENTELE AND DEVISING
WAYS TO ASSIST THEM, EXPANDING THE CORE AND MEETING ITS
CHANGING NEEDS, AND MAKING ADJUSTMENTS TO OUTSIDE CHALLENGES
TO THE PROGRAM AFTER IT HAS BEEN ESTABLISHED. THE MODEL IS
TESTED BY EXAMINING THE HISTORY OF THE FEDERAL MASS TRANSIT
SECTION 3 DISCRETIONARY PROGRAM FROM FISCAL 1965 TO 1986.

03970 HAMMAR, T.
COMPARING EUROPEAN AND NORTH AMERICAN INTERNATIONAL
MIGRATION
INTERNATIONAL MIGRATION REVIEW, 23(3) (FAL 89), 631-637.
INTERNATIONAL MIGRATION IS A VAST, COMPLEX AND
HETEROGENEOUS FIELD OF STUDY. IT REQUIRES NOT ONLY KNOWLEDGE
ABOUT DYNAMIC PROCESSES IN THE PAST AND AT PRESENT AND IN
VARIOUS REGIONS OF THE WORLD, BUT ALSO INTERDISCIPLINARY
COOPERATION, NOT LEAST IN ORDER TO ACHIEVE A GOOD
THEORETICAL DEVELOPMENT. THIS ARTICLE ADDRESSES WHETHER
IMMIGRATION IS PERMANENT OR TEMPORARY, ADDRESSES THE LEGAL
STATUS OF ALIENS AND GIVES A LONG TERM PRESPECTIVE.

03971 HAMMOND, J.L.
RESETTLEMENT AND RURAL DEVELOPMENT IN NICARAGUA
MONTHLY REVIEW, 41(5) (OCT 89), 22-34.
THIS ARTICLE TRACES THE DEVELOPMENT OF ASENTAMIENTOS,
RESETTLEMENT CAMPS, IN NICARAGUA BOTH BEFORE AND AFTER THE
WAR. AS AN EFFORT TO IMPLEMENT BROADER REVOLUTIONARY GOALS
IN PREVIOUSLY NEGLECTED RURAL AREAS THIS RELOCATION IS MORE
THAN A RESPONSE TO MILITARY NECESSITY. PRODUCTION IS
DESCRIBED, AS WELL THE GENERAL OPERATION OF THE COOPERATIVE.
THE POLITICAL, MATERIAL, AND ADMINISTRATIVE PROBLEMS FACED
BY THE ASENTAMIENTOS ARE ADDRESSED.

03972 HAMMOND, S.J.
CONSCIOUSNESS AND COMMUNITY: A POLITICAL SYMPHONY IN THE
DIMENSIONS OF FREEDOM
DISSERTATION ABSTRACTS INTERNATIONAL, 50(5) (NOV 89),
1422-A.
THE AUTHOR STUDIES THE RELATIONSHIP BETWEEN INDIVIDUAL
AND COMMUNITY, BOTH AS A CONCEPT AND AS CONCRETE REALITY, TO
ESTABLISH THE CONNECTION BETWEEN THE SPIRIT OF HUMAN
CONSCIOUSNESS AT A GIVEN LEVEL AND THE SOCIAL LIFE-WORLD AND
TO ADVANCE THE NOTION OF HUMAN ASSOCIATION AS RADICALLY
RELATIONAL. HE DEVOTES A LARGE PORTION OF THE STUDY TO THE
EXAMINATION OF EPISTEMOLOGICAL CONSTRUCTS AND THEIR
INFLUENCE ON POLITICS AND POLITICAL THEORY.

03973 HAMMOND, S.W.
CONGRESSIONAL STAFF AIDS AS CANDIDATES AND AS U.S.
REPRESENTATIVES
SOCIAL SCIENCE JOURNAL, 26(3) (1989), 277-288.
SINCE THE EARLY 1970S, CONGRESSIONAL STAFF JOBS HAVE
BECOME A MORE FREQUENT ROUTE TO HOUSE ELECTION THAN
PREVIOUSLY, FORMER LEGISLATIVE AIDS, ONCE IN OFFICE, ACHIEVE
LEADERSHIP POSITIONS IN THE HOUSE MORE QUICKLY THAN THEIR
COLLEAGUES. THIS STUDY HAS IMPLICATIONS FOR POLITICAL
RECRUITMENT, PARTIES, AND THE OPERATIONS OF GOVERNMENT. IT
RAISES QUESTIONS ABOUT THIS RECENT DEVELOPMENT IN THE
POLITICAL PROCESS.

03974 HAMMOND, W.M.
THE ARMY AND PUBLIC AFFAIRS: ENDURING PRINCIPLES
PARAMETERS. XIX(2) (JUN 89), 57-74.
THROUGHOUT MUCH OF ITS HISTORY, THE ARMY HAS FOUND IT
DIFFICULT TO RECONCILE THE PUBLIC'S RIGHT TO KNOW WITH ITS
OWN NEED FOR SECRECY DURING WARTIME. IN THE 20TH CENTURY,
THE ARMY INITIATED FORMAL PUBLIC AFFAIRS PROGRAMS TO DEAL
WITH THIS DILEMMA. IN THIS PAPER, THE AUTHOR SURVEYS THE

HISTORY OF THE ARMY'S PUBLIC RELATIONS EFFORTS AND LOOKS FOR
THE LESSONS TO BE LEARNED FROM IT.

03975 HAMPSON, F.
WINNING BY THE RULES: LAW AND WARFARE IN THE 1980'S
THIRD WORLD QUARTERLY, 11(2) (APR 89), 31-62.
THE AUTHOR EXPLORES WHETHER LAW AND HUMAN RIGHTS RULES
ARE APPLICABLE TO THE CONDUCT OF HOSTILITIES. HE PROBES WHAT
CONTEMPORARY CONFLICTS IN THE THIRD WORLD REVEAL ABOUT THE
POSSIBILITY OF REGULATING WAR BY LAW. HE ALSO EXAMINES THE
CLAIM THAT MILITARY EFFICIENCY IS INCOMPATIBLE WITH LEGAL
OBLIGATIONS ATTRIBUTED TO STATES IN WARTIME.

03976 HAMPSON, F.O.
HEADED FOR THE TABLE: UNITED STATES APPROACHES TO ARMS
CONTROL PRENEGOTIATION
INTERNATIONAL JOURNAL, XLIV(2) (SPR 89), 365-409.
THE AUTHOR EXAMINES FOUR CASES OF ARMS CONTROL
NEGOTIATIONS INVOLVING THE UNITED STATES, ADDRESSING THREE
MAJOR QUESTIONS: WHY DO STATES CHOOSE TO BECOME INVOLVED IN
ARMS CONTROL NEGOTIATION? WHY DID THESE FOUR CASES GET TO
THE BARGAINING TABLE? WHAT FACTORS SHAPED THE UNITED STATES
GOVERNMENT'S SUBSTANTIVE POSITION PRIOR TO THE NEGOTIATIONS
THEMSELVES?

03977 HANAK, L.; SHOUKEIR, M.
A YEAR OF HOPE
WORLD MARXIST REVIEW, 31(12) (DEC 88), 20-25.
THE FOURTH SOVIET-AMERICAN SUMMIT IN THE PAST THREE
YEARS GAVE A POWERFUL IMPETUS TO PROGRESS IN THE STRUGGLE
FOR NUCLEAR DISARMAMENT. BUT THE WORLD EXPECTED A MUCH
GREATER CONTRIBUTION -SPECIFICALLY, WITH REGARD TO HALVING
THE STRATEGIC CAPABILITIES. HAD THE US POSITION ON THIS
ISSUE NOT BEEN NEGATIVE, SUCH AN AGREEMENT COULD HAVE BEEN
CONCLUDED STILL, THERE REMAINS AN INCONTROVERTIBLE TRUTH:
WITH EACH PASSING DAY AND WITH EACH PASSING YEAR, THE
MOVEMENT OF PEACE CHAMPIONS IS GROWING, AND NEW
REPRESENTATIVES OF DIFFERENT CLASSES AND SOCIAL GROUPS ARE
JOINING THE STRUGGLE FOR A WORLD WITHOUT WARS, WEAPONS OR
VIOLENCE. THE FUTURE OF THE HUMAN RACE DEPENDS TO A GREAT
EXTENT ON THE WAY THESE FORCES WILL ACT.

03978 HANCHER, L.; MORAN, M.
INTRODUCTION: REGULATION AND DEREGULATION
EUROPEAN JOURNAL OF POLITICAL RESEARCH, 17(2) (MAR 89),
129-136.
'DEREGULATION' IS BEST CONCEIVED AS COVERING TWO
SEPARATE SETS OF PROCESSES: CHANGES TO THE STRUCTURE OF
RULES EMBODIED IN REGULATORY SYSTEMS; AND DISTRUBANCES TO
THE STABILITY OF THOSE SYSTEMS DUE TO THE INABILITY OF
SYSTEM 'GOVERNORS' TO FUNCTION EFFECTIVELY. THE MOST
STRIKING FEATURE OF DEREGULATION IS VARIETY-IN INCIDENCE,
FORM AND EXTENT. THIS VARIETY IS A FUNCTION OF THREE BROAD
SETS OF VARIABLES: PLACE, NOTABLY NATIONAL SETTING; TIME,
NOTABLY THE HISTIRICAL EPOCH AND THE STAGE IN A REGULATORY
CYCLE DEREGULATION HAPPENS; AND ARENA, NOTABLY THE ECONOMIC
ARENA AND POLICY NETWORKS WHERE DEREGULATION TAKES PLACE.

03979 HAND, R.G.
PUBLIC SECTOR ORGANIZATIONAL EFFECTIVENESS
DISSERTATION ABSTRACTS INTERNATIONAL, 49(9) (MAR 89),
2802-A.
INTERVIEW DATA, ANALYZED IN TERMS OF MANAGERS' LEVEL OF
ORGANIZATION (STATE OR COUNTY) AND VALUE ORIENTATION
(PRAGMATIC, MORAL/ETHICAL, OR AFFECTIVE), INDICATE THAT
STATE AND COUNTY MANAGERS HAVE DIFFERENT ORGANIZATIONAL
VALUES. THE MAJORITY OF THE STATE MANAGERS FALL INTO THE
PRAGMATIC ORIENTATION WHILE COUNTY MANAGERS PRIMARILY HAVE A
MORAL/ETHICAL ORIENTATION. PRAGMATIC MANAGERS IN THIS SURVEY
RATED THE ORGANIZATION SIGNIFICANTLY HIGHER THAN THE
MORAL/ETHICAL-ORIENTED OR THE AFFECT-ORIENTED MANAGER.

03980 HANDKE, W.
CHINA IS DIFFERENT: ECONOMIC REFORM-DEMOCRACY OPENING
AUSSEN POLITIK, 40(2) (1989), 129-138.
WHEN THE CHINESE SPEAK OF DEMOCRATIZATION, IT OUGHT NOT
TO BE MEASURED WITH WESTERN NOTIONS OF DEMOCRACY. WHEN THE
CHINESE SPEAK OF OPENING, THE WEST OUGHT NOT TO EXPECT AN
OPENING OF THE SYSTEM. THIS ARTICLE ATTEMPTS TO PUT THE
RELEVANT CONCEPTS IN ORDER SO THAT BOTH THE QUALITY AND THE
POSSIBLE DIMENSIONS OF THE REFORMS UNDER WAY IN CHINA CAN BE
ASSESSED REALISTICALLY. DEMOCRATIZATION DOES NOT MEAN THE
COMMUNIST PARTY IS RELINQUISHING ITS LEADING ROLE. RATHER,
IT MEANS POWER IS BEING DECENTRALISED BY DELEGATING
RESPONSIBILITY. SO THE ANNOUNCED SEPARATION OF PARTY AND
ADMINISTRATION IS NOTHING MORE THAN A SHIFT OF THE PARTY'S
LEADING ROLE TO THE ISSUANCE OF BASIC GUIDELINES AND THE
TASK OF GENERAL SUPERVISION.

03981 HANDLEY, P.
BACK TO BUSINESS
FAR EASTERN ECONOMIC REVIEW, 141(34) (AUG 88), 57-58.
THE CABINET LINE-UP PRIME MINISTER CHATICHAI CHOONHAVAN,
THAILAND'S FIRST ELECTED HEAD OF GOVERMENT IN 12 YEARS

INSPIRES LITTLE CONFIDENCE AMONG BUSINESS LEADERS OR
ECONOMISTS. FEARS OF INEXPERIENCE, CORRUPTION AND HIGH
SPENDING ARE AMONG THE REASONS WHY CHATICHAI'S CHOICES ARE
NOT ENTHUSIASTICALLY HAILED BY THE NATIONS BUSINESSMEN. THE
ADMINISTRATION IS TAKING A PRO-BUSINESS STANCE, BUT MANY
OBSERVERS FEEL THAT THE LACK OF COMPETENCE WILL RESULT IN
POLICIES THAT WILL NOT BE IN THE BEST NATIONAL INTEREST.

03982 HANEY, J. D.
THE MATURITY OF EXPERT POWER: COMPUTER INFORMATION SYSTEMS
WITHIN SMALL GOVERNMENT ORGANIZATIONS
DISSERTATION ABSTRACTS INTERNATIONAL, 49(8) (FEB 89),
2386-A.
WITHIN GOVERNMENT ORGANIZATIONS, THOSE HIGHER IN THE
HIERARCHY WILL HAVE GREATER POWER THAN LOWER-LEVEL EMPLOYEES.
AN EXCEPTION TO THIS RULE IS KNOWN AS "THE POWER OF LOWER
LEVEL PARTICIPANTS." THIS DISSERTATION DEMONSTRATES THIS
PHENOMENON WITH COMPUTER SPECIALISTS WHOSE ABILITY TO SOLVE
COMPUTER-RELATED PROBLEMS CREATES A POWER RELATIONSHIP OVER
THE USER DEPARTMENTS.

03983 HANF, K.
DEREGULATION AS REGULATORY REFORM: THE CASE OF
ENVIRONMENTAL POLICY IN THE NETHERLANDS
EUROPEAN JOURNAL OF POLITICAL RESEARCH, 17(2) (MAR 89),
193-207.
DEREGULATION IN THE NETHERLANDS HAS BEEN ASSOCIATED WITH
THE PERCEIVED CRISIS OF THE WELFARE STATE. BUT IN THE AREA
OF ENVIRONMENTAL POLICY IT HAS NOT MEANT DISMANTLING THOSE
SUBSTANTIVE REGULATIONS DESIGNED TO PROMOTE IMPROVED
ENVIRONMENTAL QUALITY. DEREGULATION IN ENVIRONMENTAL
MANAGEMENT HAS INVOLVED THE RETENTION OF OVERALL REGULATORY
OBJECTIVES WHILE STRIVING TO SIMPLIFY AND STREAMLINE
EXISTING REGULATORY PROCEDURES AND DEVELOPING ALTERNATIVES
TO THE MORE TRADITIONAL INSTRUMENTS OF REGULATION.
DEREGULATION IN THIS AREA IS A PRIME EXAMPLE OF 'RE-
REGULATION'- OF STEPS TAKEN TO MAKE EXISTING REGULATIONS
MORE EFFECTIVE, OR TO REPLACE RULES WITH OTHER INSTRUMENTS
DESIGNED TO ACHIEVE MORE EFFECTIVELY AND EFFICIENTLY THE
SAME BEHAVIOURAL CHANGES SOUGHT WITH THE ORIGINAL REGULATORY
SCHEME.

03984 HANIOGLU, M. S.
NOTES ON THE YOUNG TURKS AND THE FREEMASONS, 1875-1908
MIDDLE EASTERN STUDIES, 25(2) (APR 89), 186-197.
GREAT DIFFERENCES SEPARATED THE FREEMASONS FROM THE
YOUNG TURKS. IN SPITE OF THESE DIFFERENCES, THE FACT
REMAINED THAT THE FREEMASONS SUPPORTED THE YOUNG TURKS AND
WERE MORE THAN SATISFIED WITH THE REINSTATEMENT OF
CONSTITUTION; IT WAS STILL CLEAR TO THEM THAT THE BULK OF
THE POPULACE, NOW FIRED BY THE EMERGENCE OF TURKISH
NATIONALISM, WOULD BE UNMOVED BY ANY IDEA OF REVIVING A
BYZANTINE STATE OR BY THE PROSPECT OF RESOLVING THE TENSIONS
BETWEEN THE DIFFERENT ETHIC GROUPS IN THE EMPIRE. THE
FREEMASONS UNDERSTOOD THAT THEIR ALLIANCE WITH THE YOUNG
TURKS HAD BEEN BASED ON MUTUAL INTEREST AND THAT SIMILAR
ALLIANCES HAD BEEN CONTRACTED WITH ARMENIAN, BULGARIAN AND
ALBANIAN COMMITTEES IN 1907-08. THE INESCAPABLE REALITY WAS
THAT THESE DIFFERENT MOVEMENTS WERE FOLLOWING DIVERGENT
PATHS.

03985 HANKISS, E.
DEMOBILIZATION, SELF-MOBILIZATION, AND QUASI -
MOBILIZATION IN HUNGARY, 1948-1987
EASTERN EUROPEAN POLITICS AND SOCIETIES, 3(1) (WIN 89),
105-151.
THIS PAPER SHOWS THAT THERE ARE GOOD REASONS TO ANALYZE
SOCIOECONOMIC PROCESSES IN POSTWAR HUNGARY AS THE OUTCOMES
OF A MULTIPLE-ACTOR GAME, RATHER THAN ANALYZING THEM IN
TERMS OF A ONEACTOR GAME AS WAS USUAL IN THE 1950S AND 1960S.
IN SPITE OF MASSIVE MOBILIZATIONAL AND DEMOBILIZATIONAL
STRATEGIES ON THE PART OF ELITE, HUNGARIAN SOCIETY HAS NEVER
BEEN COMPLETELY DOMINATED AND PARALYZED, NOT EVEN IN THE
LATE 1940S AND EARLY 1950S. THE MAJORITY OF THE POPULATION
HAVE DEVELOPED A NUMBER OF STRATEGIES OF SELF-MOBILIZATION,
WITH WHICH THEY HAVE BEEN ABLE TO WIDEN THEIR SPHERE OF
ACTION. THEY HAVE BEEN ABLE, TO A CERTAIN EXTENT, TO PROTECT
THEIR INTERESTS, INFLUENCE POLICY IMPLEMENTATIONS, AND OPEN
UP SPHERES OF RELATIVE AUTONOMY.

03986 HANKISS, E.
REFORMS AND THE CONVERSION OF POWER
EAST EUROPEAN REPORTER, 3(4) (SPR 89), 8-9.
THE AUTHOR ARGUES THAT ALTHOUGH REFORMS IN EASTER EUROPE
ARE UNDENIABLY NECESSARY, THEY MAY SERVE CONFLICTING
INTERESTS. HE OUTLINES HOW THE RULING ELITE MAY ATTEMPT TO
UTILIZE POLITICAL AND MARKET REFORMS TO CONVERT THEIR
ILLEGITIMATE BUREAUCRATIC POWER INTO LEGITIMATE POWER AND
THUS MAINTAIN THEIR HEGEMONY OVER THE GENERAL POPULACE. HE
DEMONSTRATES THE IMPORTANCE OF AWARENESS OF THIS POSSIBILITY
AND OF THE PROPER REACTION TO CALLS FOR REFORM.

03987 HANKS, C.A.
THE INTERORGANIZATIONAL IMPLEMENTATION OF STATE HEALTH

POLICY: A NETWORK APPROACH
DISSERTATION ABSTRACTS INTERNATIONAL, 50(4) (OCT 89),
1086-A.
THIS DISSERTATION IS AN IMPLEMENTATION ANALYSIS OF THREE
STATE HEALTH POLICIES ADOPTED TO IMPROVE ACCESS TO MATERNAL
AND CHILD HEALTH SERVICES IN TEXAS FROM 1983-86. THE AUTHOR
UTILIZES THE NETWORK APPROACH TO ANALYZE AND COMPARE THE
STRUCTURE AND DECISION PROCESS OF SIX POLICY SUBSYSTEMS, IN
ORDER TO EXPLAIN PROGRAM PERFORMANCE.

03988 HANNAH, J.P.; INDYCK, M.
BEYOND THE SHULTZ INITIATIVE: THE NEW ADMINISTRATION AND
THE PALESTINIAN PROBLEM
SAIS REVIEW, 9(1) (WIN 89), 87-106.
THIS PAPER ARGUES THAT THE INTENSIFICATION OF THE
CONFLICT BETWEEN ISRAEL AND THE PALESTINIANS HAS RENDERED
PEACEMAKING MORE URGENT, BUT ALSO MORE DIFFICULT. BARRING A
DRAMATIC CHANGE IN THE REGIONAL SITUATION (SUCH AS A
FUNDAMENTAL SHIFT IN THE PLO'S ATTITUDE TOWARD PEACE WITH
ISRAEL), ATTEMPTS TO ACHIEVE A RAPID BREAKTHROUGH ON THE
PEACE PROCESS WILL BE EXTREMELY DIFFICULT, AND MAY EVEN
PROVE COUNTERPRODUCTIVE. TRADITIONAL AMERICAN DIPLOMATIC
ACTIVISM THAT SEEKS TO PRODUCE A CAMP DAVID-STYLE
NEGOTIATION IN SHORT ORDER SHOULD THEREFORE GIVE WAY,
INITIALLY, TO A LESS AMBITIOUS, BUT MORE SUSTAINED APPROACH
THAT FIRST TRIES TO LAY THE GROUNDWORK FOR EVENTUAL
NEGOTIATIONS. SUCH AN APPROACH WILL REQUIRE THE NEW
PRESIDENT TO PROMOTE A RIPENING PROCESS THAT HELPS TO
RESHAPE THE POLITICAL ENVIRONMENT WITHIN WHICH ISRAELIS AND
PALESTINIANS INTERACT, STRENGTHENING THE FORCES OF
MODERATION ON BOTH SIDES SO THAT A NEGOTIATED SETTLEMENT
BECOMES POSSIBLE OVER TIME.

03989 HANNIBALSSON, J.B.
ICELAND ON THE INTERNATIONAL ECONOMIC SCENE
SCANDINAVIAN REVIEW, 77(2) (SUM 89), 19-23.
THE NEAT SEPARATION OF POLICY CONCERNS INTO DOMESTIC
ISSUES, ON THE ONE HAND, AND EXTERNAL OR INTERNATIONAL
ISSUES, ON THE OTHER, IS NOT ONLY AN ABSTRACTION BUT AN
ILLUSORY ONE AT THAT. THE CASE OF ICELAND'S NEW VALUE-ADDED
TAX ILLUSTRATES THIS TRUISM. ICELAND'S VALUE-ADDED TAX HAS
REGARDED, ON THE DOMESTIC SIDE, AS AN EXTREMELY IMPORTANT
STEP TOWARDS STRENGTHENING GOVERNMENT FINANCES. IN THE
INTERNATIONAL CONTEXT, IT WAS NECESSARY TO REPLACE ICELAND'S
SALES TAX WITH A VALUE-ADDED TAX IF ICELAND INTENDS TO
FOLLOW AND ENJOY SOME OF THE BENEFITS OF THE CREATION OF A
UNIFIED EUROPEAN MARKET IN 1992.

03990 HANNUM, H.
INTERNATIONAL LAW AND COMBODIAN GENOCIDE: THE SOUNDS OF
SILENCE
HUMAN RIGHTS QUARTERLY, 11(1) (FEB 89), 82-138.
CAMBODIA HAS BEEN A PARTY TO THE CONVENTION ON THE
PREVENTION AND PUNISHMENT OF THE CRIME OF GENOCIDE3 SINCE
ITS ENTRY INTO FORCE IN 1951 AND ACCEPTED THE COMPULSORY
JURISDICTION OF THE INTERNATIONAL COURT OF JUSTICE IN 1957.
YET THERE HAS BEEN NO EFFORT TO INVOKE THE JURISDICTION OF
THE COURT IN ORDER TO VERIFY AND CONDEMN THE VIOLATIONS OF
INTERNATIONAL LAW COMMITTED BY THE KHMER ROUGE GOVERNMENT OF
DEMOCRATIC KAMPUCHEA. THIS ARTICLE EXAMINES THE FEASIBILITY
OF BRINGING AN APPLICATION TO THE INTERNATIONAL COURT OF
JUSTICE, UNDER THE TERMS OF ARTICLE IX OF THE GENOCIDE
CONVENTION OR ARTICLE 36 OF THE STATUTE OF THE COURT. IT
CONCLUDES THAT SUCH AN APPLICATION WOULD BE LEGALLY FEASIBLE
AND POLITICALLY DESIRABLE AND THAT THE FAILURE OF ANY STATE
THUS FAR TO INSTITUTE PROCEEDINGS BEFORE THE COURT IS AN
INDEFENSIBLE ABDICATION OF INTERNATIONAL RESPONSIBILITY.

03991 HANPING, Z.
THE GANDHI VISIT: LANDMARK IN SINO-INDIAN RELATIONS
CHINA RECONSTRUCTS, XXXVIII(4) (APR 89), 32-33.
WHEN RAJIV GANDHI ARRIVED IN BEIJING IN DECEMBER 1988,
HE BECAME THE FIRST INDIAN PRIME MINISTER TO VISIT CHINA IN
34 YEARS. FOLLOWING DECADES OF ESTRANGEMENT AND OCCASIONAL
BORDER CONFLICT, THE KEYNOTE OF THE GANDHI VISIT WAS THE
NEED FOR COOPERATION, MUTUAL UNDERSTANDING, AND THE
RESTORATION OF HARMONIOUS SINO-INDIAN RELATIONS.

03992 HANRIEDER, W.F.
THE GERMAN-AMERICAN ALLIANCE AT FORTY
AUSSEN POLITIK, 40(2) (1989), 148-159.
AS THE GERMAN-AMERICAN PARTNERSHIP REACHES MATURITY, IT
IS ALSO SUBJECT TO INCREASING STRAINS AS BOTH PARTIES
CONFRONT THE CHALLENGES OF A SHIFTING EAST-WEST MILITARY
BALANCE, THE DIMINISHED CREDIBILITY OF THE AMERICAN NUCLEAR
COMMITMENT TO EUROPE, ECONOMIC AND MONETARY DISAGREEMENTS,
THE EUROPE OF 1992, AND THE QUESTION OF HOW TO APPROACH A
NEW EUROPEAN POLITICAL ORDER IN THE 1990S. THIS ARTICLE
ARGUES THAT THE UNITED STATES CREATED ATLANTIC AND WEST
EUROPEAN ALLIANCES TO CONTAIN NOT ONLY THE SOVIET UNION BUT
ALSO THE FEDERAL REPUBLIC AND THAT NOW, WHEN AMERICA'S
POSTWAR STRATEGY OF DOUBLE CONTAINMENT HAS ERODED, THE
UNITED STATES MUST SUPPLANT IT WITH A DIPLOMACY THAT TREATS
THE FEDERAL REPUBLIC AS AN EQUAL PARTNER, RESTORES

COMPLEMENTARITY TO AMERICA'S GERMANY AND SOVIET POLICY, AND
EASES THE WAY TOWARDS A NEW EUROPEAN POLITICAL ORDER.

03993 HANSBERRY, L.
THE SCARS OF THE GHETTO
MONTHLY REVIEW, 41(3) (JUL 89), 52-55.
THIS IS A REPRINT FROM VOLUME 16, 1965 MONTHLY REVIEW
(MR) OF A TALK GIVEN BY LORRAINE HANSBERRY TO MR IN APRIL OF
THAT YEAR. MS. HANSBERRY DESCRIBES THE DISADVANTAGES OF
GROWING UP IN THE BLACK GHETTO SHE DISCRIBES HER OWN
EXPERIENCE OF NOT BEING TAUGHT ARITHMETIC OR HOW TO SWIM
BECAUSE HER SCHOOL LACKED A POOL. SHE ACCUSES THE RULING
CLASS IN THE U.S. OF REFUSING TO ADMIT THE REAL "SCOPE,
SCALE AND CHARACTER" OF THEIR OPPRESSION OF BLACKS. SHE
CALLS UPON A NER ORDER OF THOUGHT FOR REVOTUTION AGAINST THE
PRESENT ORGANIZATION OF AMERICAN SOCIETY.

03994 HANSEN, D.P.
CONVENANTAL ETHICS AND ECONOMIC POLICY: THE INDUSTRIAL
POLICY DEBATE RECONSIDERED
DISSERTATION ABSTRACTS INTERNATIONAL, 49(7) (JAN 89),
1951-A.
PUBLIC POLICIES REPRESENT MORAL CHOICES ABOUT PREFERRED
FUTURES. IN THIS DISSERTATION, THE AUTHOR MAKES A
COMPARATIVE ANALYSIS OF DIFFERENT TYPES OF INDUSTRIAL POLICY
PROPOSALS AS THEY ARE FRAMED BY MORAL CONCERNS. HE ALSO
SKETCHES A PROPOSAL FOR A COVENANTAL POLICY ETHIC.

03995 HANSEN, K.
ARE COALITIONS REALLY ON THE RISE?
STATE LEGISLATURES, 15(4) (APR 89), 11-12.
DUE TO THE DECLINE IN PARTY DISCIPLINE AND THE
INCREASING INDEPENDENCE OF LEGISLATORS, FORMING COALITIONS
TO TAKE CONTROL OF A LEGISLATIVE CHAMBER IS BECOMING MORE
COMMON. IN THIS ARTICLE, THE PROS AND CONS OF LEGISLATIVE
COALITIONS ARE DISCUSSED.

03996 HANSEN, K.
THE ETHICAL DILEMMA OF HEALTH CARE
STATE LEGISLATURES, 15(9) (OCT 89), 8-13.
HEALTH CARE RATIONING HAS IGNITED A HEATED ETHICAL
DEBATE, ESPECIALLY AMONG THOSE WHO BELIEVE HEALTH CARE IS A
RIGHT, NOT A PRIVILEGE. IN THIS ARTICLE, THE AUTHOR LOOKS AT
OREGON'S NEW PROGRAM TO PROVIDE HEALTH INSURANCE FOR
EVERYONE.

03997 HANSEN, S.
INDUSTRIAL POLICY AND CORPORATISM IN THE AMERICAN STATES
GOVERNANCE, 2(2) (APR 89), 172-197.
WITH REFERENCE TO RECENT TRENDS IN INDUSTRIAL POLICY IN
THE AMERICAN STATES, THE ARTICLE EXPLORES THE QUESTION:
"DOES THE TERM CORPORATISM HAVE ANY VALIDITY IN THE AMERICAN
CONTEXT?" ALTHOUGH ON A NATIONAL LEVEL THE GOVERNMENT HAS
ABJURED MOST SECOR-SPECIFIC INDUSTRIAL POLICIES, MANY STATES
HAVE ADOPTED A MUCH MORE INTERVENTIONIST STANCE. THE ARTICLE
ARGUES THAT THERE HAVE BEEN CONSIDERABLE CHANGES, BOTH IN
THE SUBSTANCE OF STATE ECONOMIC POLICIES AND IN THE PROCESS
THROUGH WHICH THEY ARE DEVELOPED, IMPLEMENTED, AND EVALUATED.
ALTHOUGH THE CHANGES DO NOT FIT THE MODEL OF EUROPEAN
CORPORATION, PRESSURE GROUP MODELS ARE NO LONGER ADEQUATE TO
EXPLAIN THE CHANGES.

03998 HANSEN, S.
TARGETING IN ECONOMIC DEVELOPMENT: COMPARATIVE STATE
PERSPECTIVES
PUBLIUS: THE JOURNAL OF FEDERALISM, 19(2) (SPR 89), 47-62.
THE ARTICLE EXAMINES RECENT EFFORTS TO TARGET STATE
INDUSTRIAL POLICY ALONG THREE DIMENSIONS: SECTORAL AID TO
SPECIFIC BUSINESSES OR ECONOMIC ACTIVITIES, GEOGRAPHIC AID
TO GROWING OR DECLINING REGIONS, AND DIRECT ASSISTANCE TO
THE UNEMPLOYED. WHILE THE STATES HAVE DONE BETTER WITH
SECTORAL TARGETING THAN OPPONENTS OF A FEDERAL INDUSTRIAL
POLICY FEARED, INDUSTRIAL POLICY MUST COMPETE WITH MANY
OTHER STATE PROGRAMS, INCLUDING MORE TRADITIONAL ECONOMIC
DEVELOPMENT EFFORTS BASED ON ADVERTISING AND TAX
EXPENDITURES. ONLY A FEW STATES HAVE MANAGED TO CHANNEL MUCH
STATE AID TO DISPLACED WORKERS OR DISTRESSED COMMUNITIES.
DESPITE SOME EVIDENCE AS TO THE SUCCESS OF INDUSTRIAL POLICY
FOCUSED ON LIMITED AREAS OR ACTIVITIES, DILUTION OF POLICY
FOCUS AND UNDERINVESTMENT OF RESOURCES CHARACTERIZE STATE
INDUSTRIAL POLICY EFFORTS TO DATE.

03999 HANSMANN, H.
THE ECONOMICS AND ETHICS OF MARKETS FOR HUMAN ORGANS
JOURNAL OF HEALTH POLITICS, POLICY AND LAW, 14(1) (SPR 89),
57-86.
IN 1984, FEDERAL LEGISLATION OUTLAWING PAYMENT FOR HUMAN
ORGANS FOR TRANSPLANTATION HAS ADOPTED AFTER ONLY CURSORY
DISCUSSION OF THE UNDERLYING POLICY ISSUES. MORE CONSIDERED
ANALYSIS SUGGESTS THAT THIS PROHIBITION MAY BE OVERLY BROAD.
IT APPEARS POSSIBLE TO DESIGN SUITABLY REGULATED MARKET-TYPE
APPROACHES TO THE ACQUISITION AND ALLOCATION OF CADAVERIC
ORGANS (AND PERHAPS OF ORGANS FROM LIVING DONORS AS WELL)
THAT WILL BE NEITHER UNDULY OFFENSIVE TO ETHICAL

SENSIBILITIES NOR EASILY ABUSED AND THAT MAY YIELD
SIGNIFICANT IMPROVEMENTS OVER THE EXISTING SYSTEM OF ORGAN
PROCUREMENT, WHICH PRESENTS IMPORTANT ETHICAL AND PRACTICAL
PROBLEMS OF ITS OWN. MOREOVER, WHATEVER ULTIMATE JUDGEMENT
WE REACH CONCERNING THE MERITS OF MARKETS FOR TRANSPLANTABLE
ORGANS, ANALYSIS OF THE SOURCE OF THE INITIAL MORAL
RESISTANCE TO THE COMMERCIALIZATION THAT LIES BEHIND
MEASURES SUCH AS THE 1984 LEGISLATION OFFERS INSIGHTS INTO
THE RESPECTIVE ROLES OF MARKET AND NONMARKET INSTITUTIONS IN
GENERAL.

04000 HAO, Y.
CHINA'S 1.2 BILLION POPULATION TARGET FOR THE YEAR 2000:
WITHIN OR BEYOND?
AUSTRALIAN JOURNAL OF CHINESE AFFAIRS, (19-20) (JAN 88),
165-183.
AFTER A BRIEF REVIEW OF THE FERTILITY CHANGES AND FAMILY-
PLANNING PROGRAMS IN CHINA AND DISCUSSIONS ON A NUMBER OF
DEMOGRAPHIC FACTORS RELEVANT TO TARGET FULFILMENT, THIS
PAPER PRESENTS A PROJECTION FOR THE CHINESE POPULATION FOR
THE YEAR 2000. IT THEN COMPARES THE RESULTS WITH SIMILAR
PROJECTIONS FROM OTHER SOURCES. THE MAJOR PURPOSE IS TO
ARGUE THAT THE 1.2 BILLION TARGET WILL EVENTUALLY BE
EXCEEDED. THE DATA USED IN THIS PAPER COME MAINLY FROM
FAMILY-PLANNING SERVICE STATISTICS AND THE 1985 REGIONAL IN-
DEPTH FERTILITY SURVEY, WHICH WAS CONDUCTED BY THE CHINESE
STATE BUREAU OF STATISTICS IN HEBEI, SHAANXI, AND SHANGHAI.
THE PROJECTION IS BASED ON THE 1982 NATIONAL CENSUS DATA.

04001 HAPPY, J.R.
ECONOMIC PERFORMANCE AND RETROSPECTIVE VOTING IN CANADIAN
FEDERAL ELECTIONS
CANADIAN JOURNAL OF POLITICAL SCIENCE, XXII(2) (JUN 89),
377-387.
THIS STUDY EXAMINES THE RETROSPECTIVE ECONOMIC VOTING
MODEL FOR CANADIAN FEDERAL ELECTIONS, 1930 THROUGH 1979. THE
ANALYSIS SHOWS THAT CHANGE IN PERSONAL OR DISPOSABLE INCOME
HAS A SIGNIFICANT, DIRECT IMPACT ON INCUMBENCY VOTING WHILE
INFLATION ENTERS THE VOTING CALCULUS INDIRECTLY, AS A
(PARTIAL) DEFLATOR OF NOMINAL INCOME, AND UNEMPLOYMENT HAS
NO EFFECT. DISPOSABLE INCOME IS A BETTER PREDICTOR OF
INCUMBENCY VOTING THAN IS PERSONAL INCOME, NOMINAL INCOME
VARIABLES PREDICT BETTER THAN REAL VALUES AND VARIABILITY IN
INCOME PERFORMANCE IS NEGATIVELY RELATED TO INCUMBENCY
VOTING. THE STUDY CONCLUDES THAT VOTER ATTRIBUTION OF
RESPONSIBILITY FOR INCOME PERFORMANCE IS FOCUSSED AND
SPECIFIC, INCOME STABILITY AS WELL AS INCOME GROWTH ARE
DEMANDED THROUGH INCUMBENCY VOTING, AND VOTERS ARE AFFECTED
BY MONEY ILLUSION.

04002 HAQ, F.
ISLAMIC REFORMISM AND THE STATE: THE CASE OF THE JAMMATT-
IISLAMI OF PAKISTAN
DISSERTATION ABSTRACTS INTERNATIONAL, 49(10) (APR 89),
3141-A.
THE JAMMATT-I-ISLAMI WAS FOUNDED IN 1941 TO INCULCATE A
REVITALIZED ISLAMIC WORLD-VIEW AMONG MUSLIMS. IT OUTLINED A
PROGRAM FOR ESTABLISHING AN ISLAMIC POLITICAL SYSTEM, AN
ISLAMIC SOCIAL SYSTEM, AND AN ISLAMIC ECONOMIC SYSTEM. IT
ALSO BUILT A WELL DISCIPLINED ORGANIZATION TO ACTIVELY
STRUGGLE FOR THE CREATION OF AN ISLAMIC ORDER. THE
ORGANIZATION HAS HAD A MIXED SUCCESS RECORD. THE JAMMATT HAS
BEEN SUCCESSFUL IN CAPTURING IDEOLOGICAL HEGEMONY IN
PAKISTAN BUT HAS FAILED TO SEIZE POLITICAL POWER AND HAS NOT
MET ITS GOALS IN ELECTIONS.

04003 HAQQANI, H.
CALLING ALL CONSERVATIVES
FAR EASTERN ECONOMIC REVIEW, 141(29) (JUL 88), 30.
WITH PLANS FOR A GENERAL ELECTION ALMOST COMPLETE,
PAKISTAN'S PRESIDENT ZIA-UL HAQ IS BEGINNING QUIET
NEGOTIATIONS WITH PAKISTANI POLITICIANS IN AN ATTEMPT TO
FORM A RIGHT WING COALITION AGAINST BENAZIR BHUTTO'S
PAKISTAN PEOPLE'S PARTY. HE IS ALSO CONSIDERING INTRODUCING
PROPORTIONAL REPRESENTATION WHICH WOULD MAKE IT IMPOSSIBLE
TO SECURE AN ABSOLUTE MAJORITY.

04004 HAQQANI, H.
POWER UP FOR GRABS
FAR EASTERN ECONOMIC REVIEW, 141(35) (SEP 88), 12-13.
PAKISTAN'S PRESIDENT ZIA-UL HAQ'S SUDDEN DEATH IN AN
AIRCRAFT CRASH HAS BROUGHT THE COUNTRY INTO ANOTHER PHASE OF
POLITICAL UNCERTAINTY. ZIA HAD RULED FOR 11 YEARS AND HAD
BECOME A FIXTURE IN PAKISTANI POLITICS. FEARS THAT THE
MILITARY WOULD RUSH IN TO FILL THE VACUUM WHICH ZIA LEFT ARE
AS OF YET UNFOUNDED. ACCORDING THE THE PAKISTANI
CONSTITUTION, POWER WAS TRANSFERRED TO SENATE CHAIRMAN
GHULAM ISHAQ KHAN. NOW ALL OF THE VARIOUS POLITICAL PARTIES
AND FACTIONS ARE WAITING TO SEE WHAT THE MILITARY DOES
BEFORE MAKING ANY BOLD MOVES.

04005 HAQQANI, H.
PUTTING ASIDE DIFFERENCES
FAR EASTERN ECONOMIC REVIEW, 141(30) (JUL 88), 32.

FOR THE MOMENT, PAKISTAN'S MAIN OPPOSTION ALLIANCE, THE MOVEMENT FOR THE RESTORATION OF DEMOCRACY HAS PUT ASIDE THEIR VARIOUS DIFFERENCES IN A DISPLAY OF UNITY TO PRESSURE PRESIDENT ZIA-UL HAQ TO DECLARE EARLY ELECTIONS. THE ALLIANCE IS PLANNING RALLIES IN SEVERAL CITIES TO DEMONSTRATE THE PUBLIC'S SUPPORT FOR ELECTIONS. PAKISTAN PEOPLE'S PARTY LEADER BENAZIR BHUTTO AND OTHERS ARE TRYING TO AVOID ANY FORM OF VIOLENT CONFRONTATION TO NOT ALLOW ZIA AN EXCUSE TO POSTPONE THE ELECTIONS.

04006 HAQQANI, H.
SHIFTING SANDS OF PATRONAGE
FAR EASTERN ECONOMIC REVIEW, 141(38) (SEP 88), 35.
PAKISTAN'S POLITICAL PARTIES ARE CALLING FOR THE DISMISSAL OF CARETAKER STATE GOVERNMENTS APPOINTED BY THE LATE PRESIDENT ZIA-UL HAQ, ARGUING THAT NEUTRAL MINISTERS WERE A PREREQUISITE FOR FAIR ELECTIONS. BUT PRESIDENT GHULAM ISHAQ KHAN -- WHO DOES NOT WISH TO SEND THE WRONG SIGNAL TO THE ARMED FORCES BY SEEMINGLY FAVORING THE OPPOSITION-- APPEARS TO BE WAITING FOR THE OUTCOME OF KEY DECISIONS IN THE SUPREME COURT BEFORE MAKING HIS NEXT MOVE. THE COURTS ARE ATTEMPTING TO DECIDE ISSUES SUCH AS THE CONSTITUTIONALITY OF NON-PARTY ELECTIONS AND OF ZIA'S DECISION TO DISSOLVE PARLIMENT.

04007 HAQQANI, H.
SPLITTING THE DIFFERENCE
FAR EASTERN ECONOMIC REVIEW, 141(27) (JUL 88), 29-30.
IN ORDER TO MAINTAIN THE PERCEPTION OF UNITY, AFGHAN RESISTANCE LEADERS HAVE ACCPETED AN ISLAMIC DOMINATED INTERIM GOVERNMENT THAT WILL MOVE TO AFGHANISTAN AS SOON AS THE REBELS TAKE A MAJOR CITY. ALTHOUGH MANY INDEPENDENT MUJAHIDEEN LEADERS ARE DISSATISFIED WITH THE STRUCTURE OF THE INTERIM GOVERNMENT, THEY ARE WILLING TO SUPPORT IT AT LEAST UNTIL THE COMMUNIST GOVERNMENT IS OVERTHROWN,

04008 HAQQANI, H.
STRIKING AT SYMBOLS
FAR EASTERN ECONOMIC REVIEW, 141(31) (AUG 88), 23.
BY FIXING A DATE FOR THE GENERAL ELECTIONS, PAKISTANI PRESIDENT ZIA-UL HAQ PRE-EMPTED STREET PROTESTS CALLING FOR AN ELECTION SCHEDULE: AND BY DECLARING THAT THE ELECTIONS WOULD BE HELD ON A NON-PARTY BASIS HE INFURIATED AS WELL AS CONFUSED PAKISTAN'S OPPOSITION PARTIES. FOR FEAR OF A CRACKDOWN, THE OPPOSITION IS UNABLE TO REACT VIOLENTLY. THE DENIAL OF THE USE OF PARTY SYMBOLS WILL MEAN THAT THE LARGELY ILLETERATE VOLTERS WILL BE UNABLE TO IDENTIFY THE OPPOSITION CANDIDATES.

04009 HAQQANI, H.
TIGHTENING THE BELT
FAR EASTERN ECONOMIC REVIEW, FEER(28) (JUL 88), 82.
IN RESPONSE TO THE COUNTRY'S CHRONIC BUDGET DEFICIT, PAKISTAN HAS FORMED A NEW BUDGET THAT ENVISAGES A SUBSTANTIAL INCREASE IN GOVERNMENT REVENUE THROUGH NEW TAXES AND PLUGGING OF LOOPHOLES IN TAX COLLECTION. HOWEVER MANY OBSERVERS FEEL THAT THE MEASURES WILL NOT BE ENOUGH TO DEAL WITH THE DEFICIT. ALTHOUGH MORE MEASURES MIGHT BE NECESSARY, THEY ARE UNLIKELY TO COME DUE TO THE GENERAL ELECTION WHICH PRESIDENT ZIA-UL HAQ PLANS TO HOLD LATER IN THE YEAR.

04010 HAQQANI, H.
TOO MANY PARTIES
FAR EASTERN ECONOMIC REVIEW, 141(27) (JUL 88), 30-31.
ALTHOUGH PAKISTAN'S POLITICAL PARTIES SEEM UNANIMOUS IN DEMANDING IMMEDIATE GENERAL ELECTIONS FOLLOWING PRESIDENT ZIA-UL HAQ'S DISSOLUTION OF THE GOVERNMENT, THAT IS THE ONLY THING THAT THEY CAN AGREE ON. A RECENT CONFERENCE OF FIFTEEN OPPOSITION PARTIES DEMONSTRATED THE DISUNITY AND DIVISION WITHIN THE RANKS OF THE ANTI-ZIA MOVEMENT. THE MAIN OPPOSITION GROUP, BENAZIR BHUTTO'S PAKISTAN PEOPLE'S PARTY HOPES TO WIN AN ELECTION ON ITS OWN STRENGTH, BUT WITHOUT THE SUPPORT OF OTHER OPPOSITION GROUPS, THEIR TRIUMPH IS NOT A SURE THING.

04011 HARBOUR, F.
THE ABM TREATY, NEW TECHNOLOGY AND THE STRATEGIC DEFENSE INITIATIVE
JOURNAL OF LEGISLATION, 15(2) (1989), 119-138.
THE ARTICLE EXAMINES THE ONGOING CONFLICT BETWEEN THE PROPONENTS OF SDI WHO FAVOR A BROAD INTERPRETATION OF THE ABM TREATY AND THOSE WHO FAVOR A NARROW INTERPRETATION. IT ANALYZES THE TEXT OF THE ABM TREATY, THE SUBSEQUENT PRACTICE OF THE TWO PARTIES, AND THE UNCLASSIFIED PORTION OF THE NEGOTIATING RECORD AND CONCLUDES THAT BOTH PARTIES TO THE TREATY INTENDED ITS PROHIBITIONS ON TESTING AND DEVELOPMENT TO COVER SPACE-BASED TECHNOLOGY NOT BASED ON FAMILIAR PRINCIPLES AND COMPONENTS. MUCH OF WHAT THE US NEEDS TO KNOW ABOUT MORE ADVANCED SYSTEMS CAN BE DISCOVERED IN THE NEXT DECADE, AND WITHIN THE PARAMETERS OF THE NARROW INTERPRETATION. IN THE MEANTIME, IT WOULD BE BOTH UNNECESSARY AND IMPRUDENT TO RUPTURE THE ABM TREATY IN ORDER TO PURSUE A TECHNOLOGY WHOSE VALUE TO THE US IS AT BEST OPEN TO QUESTION.

04012 HARBOUR, F.V.
CONSCRIPTION AND SOCIALIZATION: FOUR CANADIAN MINISTERS
ARMED FORCES AND SOCIETY, 15(2) (WIN 89), 227-247.
THIS PAPER INVESTIGATES THE ROLE OF ADULT EXPERIENCE IN THE DEVELOPMENT OF ELITE ATTITUDES ABOUT DEFENSE. SPECIFICALLY, THE STUDY TRACES THE EFFECT OF DIFFERING EXPERIENCES IN WORLD WAR I ON THE ATTITUDES TOWARD CONSCRIPTION HELD BY FOUR KEY CANADIAN MINISTERS DURING WORLD WAR II. H. L. MACKENZIE KING AND C. G. POWER OPPOSED COMPULSORY SERVICE BOTH IN WORLD WAR I AND IN NOVEMBER 1944 DURING A CRISIS THAT CAME WITHIN HOURS OF BRINGING DOWN THE ADMINISTRATION OF PRIME MINISTER MACKENZIE KING. J. L. RALSTON AND T. A. CRERAR, ON THE OTHER HAND, SUPPORTED CONSCRIPTION BOTH DURING WORLD WAR I AND IN NOVEMBER 1944. DURING WORLD WAR I, PERSONAL ATTACHMENT TO THE ANTICONSCRIPTIONIST HEAD OF THE FEDERAL LIBERAL PARTY AND TO PARENTS WHO OPPOSED COMPULSORY SERVICE SEEMED TO INFLUENCE THE TWO WHO OPPOSED CONSCRIPTION. FIRSTHAND EXPOSURE TO OPPOSITION AND A PRIOR INCLINATION TO BE SYMPATHETIC TO QUEBEC ALSO APPARENTLY CONTRIBUTED TO NEGATIVE ATTITUDES.

04013 HARDER, J.K.B.
THE ROLE OF THE LOCAL PASTOR IN THE POLITICAL MOBILIZATION OF EVANGELICAL PROTESTANTS
DISSERTATION ABSTRACTS INTERNATIONAL, 49(9) (MAR 89), 2795-A.
THIS DISSERTATION ANALYZES THE POLITICAL ROLE OF THE LOCAL PASTOR BY ANALYZING DATA COLLECTED THROUGH A MAIL QUESTIONNAIRE SENT TO 600 CLERGYMEN IN THE SOUTHERN BAPTIST, INDEPENDENT BAPTIST, AND ASSEMBLIES OF GOD CHURCHES. THE AUTHOR TESTS THE HYPOTHESIS THAT THE MORE CONTACT MINISTERS HAVE WITH THE NATIONAL ORGANIZATIONS OF THE NEW CHRISTIAN RIGHT AND THE MORE THEY REFLECT THE MOVEMENT'S ATTITUDES ON POLITICAL ISSUES, THE MORE LIKELY THEY ARE TO "PREACH POLITICS" FROM THE PULPIT AND TO ENCOURAGE THEIR CONGREGATION TO BE POLITICALLY ACTIVE.

04014 HARDIN, C.M.
A CHALLENGE TO POLITICAL SCIENCE
PS: POLITICAL SCIENCE AND POLITICS, XXII(3) (SEP 89), 595-599.
POLITICAL SCIENTISTS NEED TO GIVE MAJOR ATTENTION TO THE SEPARATION OF POWERS BETWEEN THE PRESIDENT AND THE CONGRESS IN THE CONSTITUTION. THEY ALSO NEED TO CONSIDER THAT THE VIABILITY OF CONSTITUTIONAL DEMOCRACY REQUIRES ANOTHER KIND OF SEPARATION OF POWERS: THAT BETWEEN THE GOVERNMENT AND THE OPPOSITION, EACH WITH ITS LEADER, EACH WITH ITS LEGISLATIVE BASE AND POPULAR SUPPORT.

04015 HARDING, N.
EQUAL OPPORTUNITIES FOR WOMEN IN THE NHS: THE PROSPECTS OF SUCCESS?
PUBLIC ADMINISTRATION, 67(1) (SPR 89), 51-64.
THE POSITION OF WOMEN IN THE NHS SUGGESTS WIDESPREAD LATENT DISCRIMINATION. THE PROSPECTS OF DEVELOPING EQUALITY OF OPPORTUNITY ARE NOT PROMISING, AS NEITHER EXTERNAL AGENCIES NOR INTERNAL MANAGERS ARE CAPABLE OF BRINGING ABOUT THE NECESSARY CHANGES. HOWEVER, CHANGING DEMOGRAPHIC FACTORS MIGHT RESULT IN ENLIGHTENED PERSONNEL POLICIES WHICH WILL ASSIST THE DEVELOPMENT OF EQUAL OPPORTUNITIES.

04016 HARDWICK, K.R.
COUNTY DISTRIBUTION OF MUNICIPALITY-ORIENTED SERVICES
DISSERTATION ABSTRACTS INTERNATIONAL, 49(8) (FEB 89), 2375-A.
MUNICIPALITY-ORIENTED SERVICES ARE PAID FOR BY ALL COUNTY TAXPAYERS BUT TEND TO BENEFIT CERTAIN MUNICIPALITIES MORE THAN OTHERS. IN THIS DISSERTATION, THE AUTHOR USES A CROSS-SECTIONAL MULTIPLE REGRESSION DESIGN TO EXPLAIN THE LEVEL OF BENEFITS THAT ACCRUE TO THE MUNICIPALITIES THAT COMPRISE BROOME COUNTY, NEW YORK.

04017 HAREVEN, S.
FOUR BUS STOPS AWAY
NEW OUTLOOK, 32(1 (287)) (JAN 89), 22-27.
THE AUTHOR LOOKS AT THE ROUTINE, EVERYDAY CHANGES IN LIFE IN THE OCCUPIED TERRITORIES BROUGHT ABOUT BY THE INTIFADA. HE STATES THAT THIS PROFOUND CHANGE, WHICH IS BEING OVERSHADOWED BY THE VIOLENCE, IS PROBABLY THE MOST IMPORTANT THING THAT IS HAPPENING TODAY AMONG THE ARABS OF THE TERRITORIES.

04018 HARHOFF, F.
ARCTIC SECURITY POLICY: A GREENLAND PERSPECTIVE
ETUDES INTERNATIONALES, XX(1) (MAR 89), 45-60.
THE DEVELOPMENT THROUGH THE PAST TWO DECADES HAS SHOWN INCREASING MILITARY AND POLITICAL TENSIONS IN, AND A CORRESPONDING MILITARY STRUCTURALIZATION OF THE ARCTIC, PARTLY BECAUSE OF THE FACT THAT ARCTIC WATERS OF BOTH SUPER-POWERS ARE GEOGRAPHICALLY ADJACENT IN THIS REGION, AND PARTLY BECAUSE NEW WARFARE TECHNOLOGY, NOTABLY WITH NUCLEAR POWERED AND ARMED SUBMARINES, HAS FACILITATED ADVANCED MISSILE LAUNCHING OPPORTUNITIES IN ARCTIC WATERS. THE

ARTICLE OUTLINES THE LEGAL AND POLITICAL STRUCTURE OF THE
GREENLAND HOME RULE AND ARGUES THAT THE HOME RULE SHOULD
HAVE A DECISIVE SAY IN SECURITY POLICY MATTERS, SINCE THIS
MAY DRAW FURTHER ATTENTION TOWARDS THE GLOBAL ENVIRONMENTAL
RISKS AND DISASTER FOLLOWING FROM NUCLEAR OR CHEMICAL
CONTAMINATION AND INCREASE THE PRESSURE FOR A PEACEFUL
FUTURE IN THE ARCTIC.

04019 HARKABI, Y.; FRIEDMAN, R.
      ISRAEL'S FATEFUL HOUR
      WORLD POLICY JOURNAL, VI(2) (SPR 89), 357-370.
         FORMER ISRAELI HEAD OF MILITARY INTELLIGENCE YEHOSHAFAT
      HARKABI DISCUSSES THE SUBJECT OF HIS NEW BOOK ISRAEL'S
      FATEFUL HOUR: THE FUTURE OF THE OCCUPIED TERRITORIES. HE
      EXAMINES THE SIGNIFICANCE OF THE PLO PEACE INITIATIVE AND
      ITS IMPLICATIONS FOR THE FUTURE. HE ANALYZES THE FACTORS
      THAT LED TO THE PLO CHANGE OF STANCE AND THE ISRAELI
      REACTION. HE CONCLUDES THAT ISRAEL WILL EVENTUALLY NEGOTIATE
      WITH THE PLO OUT OF POLITICAL AND MILITARY NECESSITY AND
      SOME SORT OF COMPROMISE WILL BE REACHED.

04020 HARKABI, Y.
      THE ROAD TO PEACE: KEYNOTE SPEECH
      NEW OUTLOOK, 32(3-4 (289-290)) (MAR 89), 11-12.
         THE PLO'S ACCEPTANCE OF THE PRINCIPLE OF A TWO-STATE
      SETTLEMENT IS A HISTORICAL DEVELOPMENT OF MOMENTOUS
      SIGNIFICANCE. HISTORICALLY, THE ISRAELI SIDE UPHELD THE
      PRINCIPLE OF PARTITION, OR A TWO-STATE SOLUTION, WHILE THE
      PALESTINIANS CALLED FOR ONE STATE, NEGATING THE IDEA OF A
      JEWISH NATION. NOW THE ROLES ARE REVERSED. THE OFFICIAL
      ISRAELI LEADERSHIP CALLS FOR A ONE-STATE SOLUTION IN WHICH
      PALESTINIANS WILL HAVE A FORM OF AUTONOMY UNDER ISRAELI
      SOVEREIGNTY. THIS POSITION IS VIEWED UNFAVORABLY BY MANY AND
      THE BALANCE OF SUPPORT WITHIN THE INTERNATIONAL COMMUNITY
      WILL NOW START SHIFTING FROM ISRAEL TO THE PLO.

04021 HARKNESS, J.
      THE ECONOMIC COST OF AIDS IN CANADA
      CANADIAN REVIEW OF SOCIOLOGY AND ANTHROPOLOGY, 15(4) (DEC
      89), 405-413.
         FORMING A RATIONAL ANTI-AIDS POLICY - GUIDED, SAY, BY A
      COST-BENEFIT ANALYSIS - IS DIFFICULT (IF NOT IMPOSSIBLE)
      WITHOUT KNOWING THE COST INVOLVED. PRESUMABLY, AIDS
      CURRENTLY IMPOSES SUBSTANTIAL COST ON CANADIAN SOCIETY. THE
      DIRECT COSTS OF AIDS ARE RELATIVELY SMALL. THE PRINCIPLE
      COST IS INDIRECT, BEING THE LOSS OF HUMAN CAPITAL (OR
      POTENTIAL OUTPUT) AS A RESULT OF THE PREMATURE DEATH OR
      DISABILITY OF AIDS VICTIMS. SUCH HUMAN CAPITAL COSTS SHOULD
      BE AN INPUT INTO ANY AIDS-RELATED POLICY DECISION. THE MAIN
      PURPOSE OF THIS PAPER IS TO ESTIMATE THE REDUCTION IN
      CANADA'S CURRENT HUMAN CAPITAL STOCK AS THE RESULT OF AIDS.
      THIS REDUCTION WAS FOUND TO BE ABOUT A BILLION DOLLARS IN
      1988. SECTION I GIVES A BACKGROUND ON AIDS AND DESCRIBES THE
      CURRENT CANADIAN SITUATION. THE LOSS OF CANADIAN HUMAN
      CAPITAL IS THEN ESTIMATED IN SECTION II. SECTION III THEN
      BRIEFLY TREATS SOME OF THE MAIN DIRECT COSTS OF AIDS.
      FINALLY, CONCLUSIONS ARE FOUND IN SECTION IV.

04022 HARMEL, P.
      A WIDER WORLD: THE HARMEL DOCTRINE UPDATED
      NATO'S SIXTEEN NATIONS, 34(1) (1989), 29-33.
         LOOKING BACK AT THE LAST YEARS OF ICY EAST-WEST
      RELATIONS, THE PRESENT THAW IS ENCOURAGING. IT MAY WELL
      ANNOUNCE THE DAWN OF A NEW RELATIONSHIP OF COOPERATION IN
      EUROPE, WHICH WILL ENABLE BOTH SIDES TO BREATHE MORE FREELY
      AND INCREASE THEIR PROSPERITY. THUS, THIS IS A FAVORABLE
      TIME TO DEVELOP AND ENLARGE THE DIALOGUE BETWEEN COUNTRIES
      OF DIFFERING POLITICAL SYSTEMS IN ORDER TO CONSIDER THE
      CHANGES OCCURRING IN NORTH-SOUTH RELATIONS AND THE
      UNIVERSALIZATION OF THE WORLD. THE THIRD WORLD NEEDS MASSIVE
      HELP THAT CAN ONLY BE PROVIDED THROUGH A VAST COMMON EFFORT
      BY THE MORE INDUSTRIALIZED COUNTRIES OF THE EAST AND WEST.

04023 HARMON, J.
      AID'S BIGNESS COMPLEX
      MULTINATIONAL MONITOR, 10(9) (SEP 89), 7-8.
         IN 1987, CONGRESS PASSED "MICROENTERPRISE LOAN"
      LEGISLATION MANDATING A NEW, EXPERIMENTAL STRUCTURE FOR
      DEDEVELOPMENT AID LOANS. THE NEW PROGRAM INVOLVED TARGETING
      INDIGENT INDIVIDUALS WITH SMALL INFUSIONS OF CASH, AND MANY
      ADVOCATES BELIEVED THAT IT OFFERED A CREATIVE REMEDY FOR
      SOME OF THE POVERTY IN THE THIRD WORLD, BUT NOW, EVALUATIONS
      FROM SEVERAL SOURCES ARE REPORTING THAT THE UNITED STATES
      AGENCY FOR INTERNATIONAL DEVELOPMENT (AID) HAS NOT COMPLIED
      WITH THE SPIRIT OF THE LAW.

04024 HARMSEN, R.A.
      OF GRANDEUR AND COMPRIMISE: THE CONSTITUTION OF THE FRENCH
      FIFTH REPUBLIC
      DISSERTATION ABSTRACTS INTERNATIONAL, 49(11) (MAY 89),
      3491-A.
         THE AMBIGUITY OF THE 1958 FRENCH CONSTITUTION IS A
      PRODUCT OF THE CONTRADICTIONS AND LIMITATIONS OF GAULLIAN
      AND GAULLIST CONSTITUTIONAL THOUGHT AS POLITICALLY

REINFORCED BY THE TREIZE MAI CRISIS. THE COMPROMISING
CIRCUMSTANCES OF TREIZE MAI HOLD THE HISTORICAL KEY TO
UNDERSTANDING THE NATURE OF THE FIFTH REPUBLIC CONSTITUTION,
WHICH IS FUNDAMENTALLY CHARACTERIZED BY AN ANTIMONY
INVOLVING STATIST AND LIBERAL DOCTRINAL PROVISIONS.

04025 HARMSEN, R.A.
      OF GRANDEUR AND COMPROMISE: THE CONSTITUTION OF THE FRENCH
      FIFTH REPUBLIC
      DISSERTATION ABSTRACTS INTERNATIONAL, 49(11) (MAY 89),
      3491-A.
         THE AMBIGUITY OF THE 1958 FRENCH CONSTITUTION IS A
      PRODUCT OF THE CONTRADICTIONS AND LIMITATIONS OF GAULLIAN
      AND GAULLIST CONSTITUTIONAL THOUGHT AS POLITICALLY
      REINFORCED BY THE COMPROMISING CIRCUMSTANCES OF THE "TREIZE
      MAI" CRISIS. GENERAL DEGAULLE'S CONSTITUTIONALISM MUST BE
      VIEWED IN TERMS OF A BROADLY DEFINED AND HISTORICALLY-
      DERIVED DESIRE TO EFFECT A RECONCILIATION BETWEEN THE STATE
      AND THE REPUBLIC. THE CONSTITUTION ITSELF IS FUNDAMENTALLY
      CHARACTERIZED BY AN ANTIMONY INVOLVING STATIST AND LIBERAL
      DOCTRINAL PROVISIONS.

04026 HARON, N.
      THE MALAY REGIMENT, 1933-1955: A POLITICAL AND SOCIAL
      STUDY OF A COLONIAL MILITARY ESTABLISHMENT IN MALAYSIA
      DISSERTATION ABSTRACTS INTERNATIONAL, 49(7) (JAN 89),
      1989-A.
         THE AUTHOR STUDIES THE DOCTRINES APPLICABLE TO FORMING A
      COLONIAL ARMY AND HOW THESE DOCTRINES WERE APPLIED IN THE
      RAISING OF THE MALAY REGIMENT. HE LOOKS AT THE POLITICAL,
      CULTURAL, AND SOCIO-ECONOMIC FACTORS THAT INFLUENCED BRITISH
      POLICY IN THIS CASE.

04027 HARP, G.J.
      REPUBLICAN POSITIVISTS: THE AMERICAN COMTEAN TRADITION,
      1850-1920
      DISSERTATION ABSTRACTS INTERNATIONAL, 48(10) (APR 88),
      2711-A.
         THE STUDY FOCUSES ON SEVERAL REPRESENATIVE LATE
      NINETEENTH AND EARLY TWENTIETH-CENTURY FIGURES IN AN ATTEMPT
      TO CONSTRUCT A COMPOSITE PORTRAIT OF THE AMERICAN COMTEAN
      TRADITION. IT CONCLUDES THAT ALTHOUGH COMTE WAS AN IMPORTANT
      RESOURCE FOR THOSE INVOLVED IN THE RECONSTRUCTION OF
      AMERICAN LIBERALISM, FEW AMERICAN COMTISTS REMAINED LONG IN
      THE ORTHODOX CAMP.

04028 HARRIES, O.
      IS THE COLD WAR REALLY OVER?
      NATIONAL REVIEW, 110(21) (NOV 89), .
         THIS ARTICLE EXPLORES THE PARADIGM THAT HAS SERVED THE
      WORLD WELL FOR THE LAST 40 YEARS TO EXPLAIN THE WORLD AND
      ORDERING PRIORITIES, WHICH IS NOW BREAKING DOWN. WITH THE
      POSSIBILITY OF THE COLD WAR ENDING, IDEAS ABOUT
      MULTIPOLARITY AND INTERDEPENDENCE ARE EXAMINED, AS WELL AS
      THE POSSIBILITY OF WAR BECOMING OBSOLESCENT IF NOT ENTIRELY
      OBSOLETE. IT CALLS FOR THE NECESSITY OF DEFINING THE
      CHARACTER OF THE NEW ERA INTO WHICH WE ARE MOVING, FOR
      WITHOUT A MODEL THAT BEARS A REASONABLY CLOSE RESEMBLANCE TO
      EMERGING REALITIES, THE CHANCES OF FORMULATING SOUND
      POLICIES WILL BE SLIM.

04029 HARRINGTON, M.
      MARKETS AND PLANS: IS THE MARKET NECESSARILY CAPITALIST?
      DISSENT, (WIN 89), 56-70.
         THE ACTUAL FUNCTIONING OF SOME OF THE WORLD'S MOST
      IMPORTANT CONTEMPORARY MARKETS--THE CAPITALIST WORLD MARKET
      THAT INTEGRATES NORTH AND SOUTH, FOR INSTANCE--IS VICIOUSLY
      AND COMPLETELY AT ODDS WITH THE VIRTUES IMPUTED TO THEM. BUT
      IN THE DIMLY FORESEEABLE AND UTTERLY INTERNATIONAL FUTURE OF
      THE NEXT 50 YEARS OR SO, MARKETS CAN BE AN IMPORTANT
      INSTRUMENT OF FREE CHOICE RATHER THAN PERVERSE
      MALDISTRIBUTION, IF THEY ARE REORGANIZED WITHIN A SOCIALIST
      CONTEXT. IN THE ADVANCED WELFARE STATES, SOCIALISTS HAVE
      ALREADY REMOVED SOME CRITICAL AREAS OF LIFE FROM THE MARKET
      ECONOMY.

04030 HARRINGTON, M.
      TOWARD A NEW SOCIALISM
      DISSENT, (SPR 89), 153-163.
         THE AUTHOR CONSIDERS THE THIRD WORLD'S DEBT PROBLEM AND
      WHAT IT COULD MEAN TO THE POLITICAL REGIMES IN COUNTRIES
      THAT ARE SUFFERING ECONOMIC HARDSHIPS DUE TO THE STRAIN OF
      REPAYING THEIR DEBTS.

04031 HARRIS, E.D.
      STEMMING THE SPREAD OF CHEMICAL WEAPONS
      BROOKINGS REVIEW, 8(1) (WIN 90), 39-45.
         A HALT TO THE SPREAD OF CHEMICAL WEAPONS CANNOT COME TOO
      SOON. ALREADY TWELVE COUNTRIES OUTSIDE NATO AND THE WARSAW
      PACT ARE THOUGHT TO POSSESS OR TO BE DEVELOPING CHEMICAL
      WEAPONS. THIS ARTICLE IDENTIFIES THESE COUNTRIES, CONSIDERS
      THE IMPLICATIONS OF THE CONTINUED PROLIFERATION OF CHEMICAL
      WEAPONS, AND DISCUSSES POTENTIAL SOLUTIONS TO THE PROBLEM.

04032 HARRIS, J.B.
THE DOMESTIC POLITICS OF AMERICAN ARMS CONTROL POLICY,
1954-1979
DISSERTATION ABSTRACTS INTERNATIONAL, 49(7) (JAN 89),
1951-A.
THE AUTHOR STUDIES SEVEN CASES OF NUCLEAR ARMS CONTROL
DECISION-MAKING OVER THE COURSE OF SIX PRESIDENTIAL
ADMINISTRATIONS, USING A VARIABLE DOMESTIC STRUCTURES MODEL
OF ARMS CONTROL POLICY-MAKING. THE CASES ARE EISENHOWER AND
THE TEST BAN NEGOTIATIONS; KENNEDY AND THE PARTIAL TEST BAN
TREATY; JOHNSON AND SALT I; NIXON AND THE ABM TREATY; NIXON,
SALT I, AND MIRV; NIXON, FORD, AND SALT II; AND CARTER AND
THE SALT II TREATY.

04033 HARRIS, L.
A DEEPER LOOK AT US AGRICULTURE
POLITICAL AFFAIRS, LXVIII(6) (JUN 89), 16-21.
THE ARTICLE EXAMINES THE DECLINE OF THE US FARMER. IT
EXAMINES THE FACTORS THAT HAVE LED TO THE DECREASED PROFIT
ACCRUED BY FARMERS. THE FUTURE OUTLOOK SEEMS TO BE MORE OF
THE SAME: THE CONTINUED INDUSTRIALIZATION OF AGRICULTURE AND
THE CONTINUED SEPARATION OF THOSE WHO WORK THE LAND FROM
THOSE WHO OWN THE LAND. IT ALSO EXAMINES THE MEASURES THAT
FARMERS ARE TAKING TO SLOW OR STOP THE DECAY OF THEIR
PROFESSION SUCH AS THE HARKIN/GEPHARDT "SAVE THE FAMILY FARM
ACT" AND THE HALTHILL PLAN.

04034 HARRIS, L.
EUROPE AND NORTH AFRICA: A RELATIONSHIP NEEDING ATTENTION
MIDDLE EAST INTERNATIONAL, (348) (APR 89), 18-19.
THE ARTICLE EXAMINES AN OFTEN OVERLOOKED BUT
INCREASINGLY IMPORTANT SECTOR OF EUROPEAN RELATIONS: NORTH
AFRICA. IT OUTLINES THE FACTORS THAT MAKE NORTH AFRICA
IMPORTANT TO EUROPE AND THE INCREASING COMMERCIAL RELATIONS
BETWEEN THE TWO REGIONS. IT ALSO ANALYZES THE PROBLEMS OF
STAGGERING EXTERNAL DEBT AND RAPIDLY INCREASING POPULATION
AS IT ATTEMPTS TO PREDICT THE FUTURE OF EUROPEAN-NORTH
AFRICAN RELATIONS.

04035 HARRIS, L.
SAUDI ARABIA AND CHINA: MUTUAL INTERESTS
MIDDLE EAST INTERNATIONAL, (351) (MAY 89), 14.
SAUDI ARABIA REMAINS THE ONLY ARAB STATE WITHOUT
DIPLOMATIC TIES TO CHINA, BUT THE OPENING OF TRADE OFFICES
MAKES SUCH A MOVE SEEM INCREASINGLY LIKELY. A DESIRE FOR
WEAPONS, CONCERN FOR THE STATUS OF MUSLIMS IN CHINA, AND A
DESIRE TO INFLUENCE SINO-IRANIAN RELATIONS HAVE ALL COMBINED
TO WEAKEN SAUDI ARABIA'S LONGSTANDING POLICY OF RESTRICTING
RELATIONS WITH COMMUNIST REGIMES.

04036 HARRIS, P.
MORAL PROGRESS AND POLITICS: THE THEORY OF T. H. GREEN
POLITY, XXI(3) (SPR 89), 538-562.
T. H. GREEN HAS BECOME SOMETHING OF A NEGLECTED FIGURE
AMONG AMERICAN POLITICAL THEORISTS, PERHAPS BECAUSE HIS
FOCUS ON THE SOCIAL CHARACTER OF MAN IS NOT ALTOGETHER
COMPATIBLE WITH SOME OF THE MORE EXTREME VERSIONS OF LIBERAL
INDIVIDUALISM NOW IN VOGUE. THIS ARTICLE EXAMINES GREEN'S
CONCEPTION OF MORAL PROGRESS AND THE WAYS IN WHICH HE
THOUGHT POLITICAL INSTITUTIONS AND POLITICAL ACTIVITY
CONTRIBUTE TO IT. THE AUTHOR ARGUES THAT GREEN'S THEORY OF
MORAL PROGRESS IS ULTIMATELY UNSATISFACTORY, BUT DOES HELP
TO ILLUMINATE HIS POLITICAL PHILOSOPHY BY UNDERSCORING HIS
GRADUALIST AND CAUTIOUS VIEW OF THE ROLE OF POLITICS IN
PROMOTING THE "MORALISATION" OF INDIVIDUALS.

04037 HARRIS, R.A.
FEDERAL-STATE RELATIONS IN THE IMPLEMENTATION OF THE
SURFACE MINING CONTROL AND RECLAMATION ACT OF 1977
POLICY STUDIES REVIEW, 9(1) (AUT 89), 69-78.
THE FEDERAL SURFACE MINING CONTROL AND RECLAMATION ACT
OF 1977 NOT ONLY ESTABLISHED NATIONAL PERFORMANCE STANDARDS
AND PERMITTING PROCEDURES FOR THE COAL INDUSTRY BUT ALSO
PROVIDED FOR STATE PRIMACY. ULTIMATELY, STATE PRIMACY IS AN
EXPERIMENT IN COOPERATIVE FEDERALISM, A SHARING OF AUTHORITY
AND RESPONSIBILITY BETWEEN THE STATES AND THE FEDERAL
GOVERNMENT TO INSURE BOTH THE GENERAL WELFARE AND
SENSITIVITY TO LOCAL CONDITIONS. THE HISTORY OF SURFACE
MINING REGULATION IS INSTRUCTIVE BECAUSE IT POINTS OUT THE
PITFALLS AND PROMISE OF COOPERATIVE FEDERALISM AS WELL AS
THE CRITICAL ROLE OF THE COURTS IN MAKING STATE PRIMACY WORK.

04038 HARRISON, B.T.
THE WANING OF THE AMERICAN STUDENT PEACE MOVEMENT OF THE
SIXTIES
PEACE RESEARCH, 21(3) (AUG 89), 1-16.
THIS ARTICLE EXAMINES WHY SIXTIES ACTIVISM IN AMERICA
WARED WITH THE DOWN OF THE SEVENTIES. THE AUTHOR OPINES THAT
ACTIVIST MOVEMENTS OF THE SIXTIES WERE LIMIT AROUND A CULT
OF YOUTH AND WERE THEREFORE PRECONDITIONED TO SELF-DESTRUCT.
ALSO, THE VERY SUCCESSES THE MOVEMENT HAD GAINED DRAINED
SOME MOMENTUM OUT OF IT. VIETNAM DID END, CURL RIGHTS LAWS
WERE CREATED AND COLLEGES DID ALLOW STUDENT REPRESENTATION
ON GOVERNING LANDS. AMERICAN INSTITUTIONS ACCOMMODATED AND
ABOLISHED THE DISSENT.

04039 HARRISON, F.
THE POSITION OF WOMEN IN PAKISTAN
CONTEMPORARY REVIEW, 254(1476) (JAN 89), 12-17.
THE ARTICLE EXAMINES SEVERAL EXAMPLES OF PAKISTANI LAWS
THAT DISCRIMINATE AGAINST WOMEN. THESE RANGE FROM LEGAL
CODES THAT STATE THAT THE EVIDENCE OF ONE MAN IS WORTH THAT
OF TWO WOMEN TO LAWS THAT BAN WOMEN FROM ATTENDING SPORTS
EVENTS. THE ARTICLE CONCLUDES THAT TO CHANGE PAKISTAN'S
DISCRIMINATORY LAWS WOULD BE MERELY A SYMBOLIC GESTURE; THE
UNDERLYING DISREGARD FOR WOMEN'S RIGHTS, AND FOR HUMAN
RIGHTS IN GENERAL, WOULD REDUCE THE ACTUAL IMPACT OF LEGAL
CHANGES TO A BARE MINIMUM.

04040 HARRISON, F.
WOMEN'S MOVEMENTS IN PAKISTAN
CONTEMPORARY REVIEW, 254(1481) (JUN 89), 298-303.
ALL THE WOMEN'S GROUP IN PAKISTAN CONSTITUTE A
FRAGMENTED, BUT ESSENTIAL WOMEN'S MOVEMENT IN ITS EARLY
STAGES. THE WORK THE GROUPS DO MUST NOT BE UNDERMINED, BUT
PRIMARILY LACKING IS A CONSCIOUSNESS AMONGST ORDINARY WOMEN
OF THE RIGHTS AND EQUALITY THEY ARE OWED. WITHOUT MASS
FEMALE AWARENESS, THERE IS NO HOPE OF COMBATTING PREJUDICED
SOCIAL ATTITUDES EFFECTIVELY.

04041 HARRISON, T.
SO MUCH SEEMED POSSIBLE
NEW POLITICS, 11(2) (WIN 89), 33-37.
THIS ARTICLE PROVIDES A REVIEW AND COMMENTARY OF TODD
GITLIN'S LOOK THE SIXTIES: YEARS OF HOPE, DAYS OF RAGE. THE
AUTHOR OPINES THAT, ALTHOUGH SOME OF GITLIN'S THREADS GET A
LITTLE TANGLED IN HIS ATTEMPT TO EXPLAIN THE ORIGINS AND
EVOLUTION OF THE SIXTIES LEFT, ON THE WHOLE HIS ANALYSIS IS
SENSIBLE AND THOROUGH.

04042 HARRISS, K.
NEW ALLIANCES: SOCIALIST-FEMINISM IN THE EIGHTIES
FEMINIST REVIEW, (31) (SPR 89), 34-54.
THIS PAPER EXPLORES SOME OF THE ISSUES FACING BRITISH
WOMEN WHO WANT TO PURSUE BOTH FEMINIST AND SOCIALIST AIMS.
IN PARTICULAR, IT LOOKS AT THE FRAGMENTATION OF THE WOMEN'S
LIBERATION MOVEMENT INTO MANY IDENTITY GROUPS, THE WAY IN
WHICH MUNICIPAL SOCIALISM ADDRESSED THESE GROUPS IN THE
1980'S, AND THE ENTRY OF MANY SOCIALIST-FEMINISTS INTO LOCAL
GOVERNMENT. THE AUTHOR ARGUES THAT INVOLVEMENT IN LOCAL
GOVERNMENT IS NOT A SOLUTION TO THE QUESTION OF HOW TO UNITE
SOCIALISM WITH FEMINISM AND THAT, ON THE CONTRARY, LOCAL
GOVERNMENT HAS OFTEN TAKEN UP THE POLITICS OF IDENTITY IN
WAYS THAT REPEAT PROBLEMS OF FRAGMENTATION.

04043 HARSANYI, I.
HURRANTY AT A CROSSROADS
WORLD MARXIST REVIEW, 32(11) (NOV 89), 62-63.
THE TERM "NEW THINKING" MUST NOT BE USED AS A TROJAN
HOUSE DISTRACTING THE WORLD'S OPPRESSED FROM THE STRUGGLE
FOR INDEPENDENCE AND SECURITY. HUMANTY IS AT A CROSSROADS
BECAUSE IT IS CONFRONTED BY NEW PROBLEMS WHICH CANNOT BE
RESOLVED SINGLEHANDEDLY BY ANY ONE SOCIAL FORMATION OR GROUP
OF STATES. SOLUTION CAN ONLY BE PRODUCED TOGETHER AND MUST
BE THE IMPERATIVE UNDERLYING THE AND NEW POLITICAL THINKING.
"

04044 HARSCH, E.
A YEAR AFTER THE COUP, WHERE DOES THE ECONOMY STAND?
AFRICAN BUSINESS, (DEC 88), 30-31.
THIS ARTICLE ASSESES THE MIDPOINT OF BURKINA FASO'S FIVE-
YEAR ECONOMIC DEVELOPMENT PLAN LAUNCHED IN 1986. THE
ACHIEVEMENTS ARE HIGHLIGHTED THOUGH MANY DIFFICULTIES AND
OBSTACLES FACE THE BURKINABE ECONOMY. IT EXAMINES THE BEST
PERFORMING SECTORS WHICH ARE INDUSTRY, HEALTH, EDUCATION,
AGRICULTURE AND WATER.

04045 HARSCH, E.
AFTER ADJUSTMENT
AFRICA REPORT, 34(3) (MAY 89), 46-50.
ARE AFRICAN ECONOMIES REALLY BETTER OFF AFTER HAVING
ADOPTED STRUCTURAL ADJUSTMENT PROGRAMS PROMOTED BY THE WORLD
BANK AND THE IMF? CONTROVERSY HAS BEEN RAGING BETWEEN
PROPONENTS OF REFORM, IN PARTICULAR THE WORLD BANK, AND THE
ECONOMIC COMMISSION FOR AFRICA, WHICH FINDS LITTLE
IMPROVEMENT IN AFRICA'S OVERALL GROWTH AND RATE OF
DEVELOPMENT.

04046 HARSCH, E.
AMOS SAWYER: FIGHTING FOR RIGHTS
AFRICA REPORT, 34(4) (JUL 89), 27-30.
THE OCTOBER 1985 ELECTIONS IN LIBERIA, WHICH WERE MARKED
BY WIDESPREAD IRREGULARITIES, WERE FOLLOWED BY A WAVE OF
SEVERE POLITICAL REPRESSION. AS A RESULT, MANY LIBERIAN
OPPOSITION POLITICAL LEADERS WERE FORCED INTO EXILE. IN 1988,
A NUMBER OF THEM FORMED THE ASSOCIATION FOR CONSTITUTIONAL
DEMOCRACY IN LIBERIA. AMOS SAWYER IS ONE OF THE ACDL'S MOST
PROMINENT SPOKESMEN.

04047 HARSCH, E.
    CECELIA JOHNSON: A WOMAN'S PLACE
    AFRICA REPORT, 34(2) (MAR 89), 61-64.
        GHANA'S WOMEN FACE SPECIAL PROBLEMS CREATED BY THE
    DEVELOPMENT PROCESS. THE 31ST DECEMBER WOMEN'S MOVEMENT HAS
    ORGANIZED TO DRAW GHANAIAN WOMEN INTO THE PROCESS, BOTH
    POLITICALLY AND THROUGH OTHER PRODUCTIVE ACTIVITIES.

04048 HARSCH, E.
    HOW POPULAR IS THE FRONT?
    AFRICA REPORT, 34(1) (JAN 89), 57-61.
        IN OCTOBER 1988, PRESIDENT BLAISE COMPAORE'S POPULAR
    FRONT CELEBRATED THE FIRST ANNIVERSARY OF THE COUP IN WHICH
    CAPT. THOMAS SANKARA WAS KILLED, HOWEVER, PUBLIC SUPPORT FOR
    THE "RECTIFICATION" PROCESS IS FAR FROM SECURE. THE
    GOVERNMENT HAS BEEN WALKING A CAREFUL LINE BETWEEN
    PORTRAYING THE LATE PRESIDENT'S POLICIES AS ERRONEOUS AND
    RETAINING MANY OF HIS INITIATIVES, CREATING CONFUSION AND
    MALAISE AMONG THE BURKINABE PEOPLE.

04049 HARSCH, E.
    LIVING DANGEROUSLY
    AFRICA REPORT, 34(2) (MAR 89), 56-60.
        A WILY POLITICAL SURVIVOR, PRESIDENT SAMUEL DOE IS NOW
    BESET WITH AN UNPRECEDENTED ECONOMIC CRISIS WHICH EVEN
    AMERICAN FINANCIAL EXPERTS COULDN'T RESOLVE. WITH CRACKDOWNS
    CONTINUING ON ANY SIGN OF DISSENT, LIBERIA'S OPPOSITION
    PARTIES ARE NOW LOOKING AT NEW STRATEGIES TO CHALLENGE DOE'S
    RULE.

04050 HARSCH, E.
    ON THE ROAD TO RECOVERY
    AFRICA REPORT, 34(4) (JUL 89), 21-26.
        DESPITE CONSIDERABLE CONTROVERSY ABOUT THE BENEFITS AND
    DRAWBACKS OF STRUCTURAL ADJUSTMENT PROGRAMS IN AFRICA, THERE
    IS GENERAL AGREEMENT THAT GHANA'S ECONOMIC REFORM EFFORTS
    HAVE ACHIEVED POSITIVE RESULTS. THIS ARTICLE ANALYZES WHAT
    HAS MADE THE GHANAIAN PROGRAM A SUCCESS AND WHETHER IT CAN
    BE EMULATED ELSEWHERE ON THE CONTINENT.

04051 HARSCH, E.
    THE RURAL REVOLT
    AFRICA REPORT, 34(6) (NOV 89), 62-66.
        IMPOVERISHED BLACK SOUTH AFRICANS IN THE COUNTRYSIDE ARE
    UP IN ARMS AGAIN IN THE CLASSIC CONFLICT OVER LAND
    DISTRIBUTION. THIS TIME, HOWEVER, THEY ARE MORE POLITICIZED
    AND EVEN TRADITIONAL HOMELAND CHIEFS ARE JOINING THE
    ANTIAPARTHEID OPPOSITION.

04052 HART-LANDSBERG, M.
    SOUTHKOREA: LOOKING AT THE LEFT
    MONTHLY REVIEW, 41(3) (JUL 89), 56-70.
        THIS ARTICLE TRACES THE BACKGROUND AND DYNAMICS OF A
    LEFT-LED MOVEMENT DEMANDING A UNIFIED AND PROGRESSIVE KOREA
    WHICH HAS REEMERGED IN THE SOUTH. IT TRACES JAPANESE AND US
    IMPERIALISM AND THE RISE AND FALL OF THE LEFT; GOVERNMENT
    POLICIES AND LIBERAL RESISTANCE; THE KWANGJU UPRISING AND
    THE RESURGENCE OF THE LEFT, AND HOW THE REVOLUTIONARY
    PROCESS IS GAINING MOMENTUM.

04053 HART, D.B.; MUNGER, M.C.
    DECLINING ELECTORAL COMPETITIVENESS IN THE HOUSE OF
    REPRESENTATIVES: THE DIFFERENTIAL IMPACT OF IMPROVED
    TRANSPORTATION TECHNOLOGY
    PUBLIC CHOICE, 61(3) (JUN 89), 217-228.
        THIS PAPER ADVANCES THE HYPOTHESIS THAT IMPROVEMENTS IN
    THE NATIONAL TRANSPORTATION AND COMMUNICATION INFRASTRUCTURE
    ARE RESPONSIBLE FOR THE 'VANISHING MARGINALS' OR THE
    INCREASED ELECTORAL SECURITY OF U.S. REPRESENTATIVES. THE
    AUTHORS ASSUME THAT MARGIN AND SECURITY ARE DIRECTLY
    AFFECTED BY THE AMOUNT OF TIME A LEGISLATOR, OR A MEMBER OF
    HER STAFF, DEVOTES TO DIRECT CONTACT WITH CONSTITUENTS IN
    THE HOME DISTRICT. FORMALLY, THE AUTHORS DEMONSTRATE THAT A
    DECLINE IN THE TIME OPPORTUNITY COST ASSOCIATED WITH TRAVEL
    TO THE DISTRICT IMPROVES VICTORY MARGINS, WHERE THEY PROXY
    IMPROVEMENT IN TRANSPORTATION TECHNOLOGY BY USING A DISTANCE
    VARIABLE ACROSS THREE DIFFERENT HISTORICAL SAMPLES: 1890,
    1928, AND 1970. THIS PROPOSITION OFFERS A POTENTIALLY MORE
    FUNDAMENTAL EXPLANATION OF DECLINING ELECTORAL COMPETITION
    THAN EXISTING EXPLANATIONS FOCUSING ON PROFESSIONALISM,
    CAREERISM, REDISTRICTING AND BUREAUCRATIC CASEWORK. IN FACT,
    THE TECHNOLOGY/ COMMUNICATION HYPOTHESIS MAY WELL ENCOMPASS
    SUCH EXPLANATIONS.

04054 HART, J.
    URILE AMERICA SLEPT
    NATIONAL REVIEW, XLI(17) (SEP 89), 32-34.
        THE AUTHOR DESCRIBES HOW THE DEADLY HIATUS IN AMERICAS
    LEADERSHIP - FROM THE POINT WHEN ROOSEVELT'S HEALTH AND
    JUDGEMENT BEGAN TO FAIL TO THE POINT WHEN TRUMAN AWOKE TO
    THE REALITY OF SOVIET INTENTIONS - LED TO YALTA AND PATSDOM,
    THE BETRAYAL OF THE POLES, THE IMPOSITION OF COMMUNIST
    GOVERNMENTS IN EASTERN EUROPE, THE ZECHOSLOVAK COUP, AND, ON

THE OTHER SIDE OF THE WORLD, THE LOSS OF CHINA AND THE
INVASION OF SOUTH KOREA.

04055 HART, M.
    ALMOST BUT NOT QUITE: THE 1947-48 BILATERAL CANADA -U.S.
    NEGOTIATIONS
    AMERICAN REVIEW OF CANADIAN STUDIES, XIX(1) (SPR 89),
    25-58.
        BECAUSE THE 1947-48 NEGOTIATIONS WERE CONCEIVED AND
    PURSUED IN SECRET AND WERE QUIETLY ABANDONED WITHOUT ANY
    PUBLIC DEBATE, THEY HAVE ASSUMED QUALITY OF UNREALITY, AS A
    BIZARRE EVENT WITH NO BASIS IN CONTEMPORARY THOUGHT AND
    DEBATE. WHILE THIS VIEW OF THE PAST MAY FIT FOR THOSE WHO
    HAVE BECOME ENAMORED OF A UNIDIMENSIONAL VIEW OF CANADA AS
    THE UNCOMPROMISING CHAMPION OF POSTWAR MULTILATERALISM,
    THERE WAS DEBATE, AND FOR THE ARCHITECTS OF THAT
    MULTILATERALISM, THE CHOICE WAS NOT BETWEEN MULTILATERALISM
    OR BILATERALISM, BUT BETWEEN VARIOUS MEANS TO THE SAME END,
    A PROSPEROUS AND INDEPENDENT CANADA.

04056 HART, N.
    GENDER AND THE RISE AND FALL OF CLASS POLITICS
    NEW LEFT REVIEW, (175) (MAY 89), 19-47.
        LITTLE CONSCIOUS ATTEMPT HAS BEEN MADE TO INVESTIGATE
    THE SIGNIFICANCE OF GENDER DIFFERENTIALS IN HOUSEHOLD
    CONSUMPTION AND LABOR IN GREAT BRITAIN. IN THIS ESSAY, THE
    AUTHOR ASSEMBLES EVIDENCE OF A SYSTEMATIC INEQUALITY BETWEEN
    MALE AND FEMALE PATTERNS OF MATERIAL LIFE, LEADING TO A
    CHARACTERISTIC GENDER GAP IN POLITICS.

04057 HARTLE, D.G.
    PERCEPTIONS OF THE EXPENDITURE BUDGET PROCESS: SURVEY OF
    FEDERAL AND PROVINCIAL LEGISLATORS AND PUBLIC SERVANTS
    CANADIAN PUBLIC ADMINISTRATION, 32(3) (FAL 89), 427-448.
        THIS PAPER PRESENTS THE RESULTS OF A MAILED
    QUESTIONNAIRE SURVEY OF A SAMPLE OF ELECTED AND APPOINTED
    OFFICIALS IN THE FEDERAL AND PROVINCIAL LEVELS OF GOVERNMENT
    IN WHICH THE RESPONDENTS' OPINIONS WERE REQUESTED CONCERNING
    SOME PROCEDURAL, TECHNICAL AND POLITICAL ASPECTS OF THE
    EXPENDITURE BUDGET PROCESS IN THEIR JURISDICTIONS. THE
    RESULTS WERE TABULATED SO AS TO PERMIT COMPARISONS BETWEEN
    THE OPINIONS OF RESPONDENTS WITHIN EACH OF THE TWO LEVELS OF
    GOVERNMENT AND FROM POLITICIANS AND BUREAUCRATS AT EACH
    LEVEL SEPARATELY AND AT BOTH LEVELS COMBINED. THERE WERE
    THREE HYPOTHESES TO BE TESTED: WHETHER POLITICAL RATHER THAN
    TECHNICAL BARRIERS INHIBIT THE EVALUATION OF GOVERNMENT
    EXPENDITURE PROGRAMS; WHETHER POLITICIANS ARE MORE
    "REALISTIC" THAN BUREAUCRATS; AND WHETHER OFFICIALS, BOTH
    ELECTED AND APPOINTED, AT THE PROVINICAL LEVEL OF GOVERNMENT
    ARE MORE "REALISTIC" THAN THOSE AT THE FEDERAL LEVEL.

04058 HARTLEY, A.
    AFTER THE THATCHER DECADE
    FOREIGN AFFAIRS, 68(5) (WIN 90), 102-118.
        "THATCHERISM" HAS NOT BEEN MERELY A SERIES OF POLITICAL
    MEASURE. STARTING WITH THE AIMS OF STIMULATING INDIVIDUAL
    EFFORT AND ENTERPRISE AND WEANING CITIZENS FROM DEPENDENCE
    ON THE STATE, IT HAS CREATED OR TRIGGERED A SOCIAL AND
    ECONOMIC REVOLUTION, THE RESULTS OF WHICH WILL CONTINUE TO
    BE FELT FOR MANY YEARS AND WHICH CANNOT BE REVERSED BY
    SUBSEQUENT GOVERNMENTS. THATCHER HAS CREATED A NEW ELECTORAL
    FOLLOWING MORE IN TUNE WITH AN EGALITARIAN POST-INDUSTRIAL
    SOCIETY THAN WITH HER PARTY'S TRADITIONAL SUPPORTERS. THE
    POLITICAL CONSEQUENCES CAN BE SEEN ON BRITAIN'S ELECTORAL
    MAP.

04059 HARTLEY, A.
    AFTER 1992: MULTIPLE CHOICE
    NATIONAL INTEREST, (15) (SPR 89), 29-39.
        THE ARTICLE CONCERNS ITSELF WITH SEVERAL OF THE
    ALTERNATIVE FUTURES FOR EUROPE AFTER 1992. IT ANALYZES MANY
    OF THE FACTORS THAT WILL DETERMINE THE SHAPE OF THE EUROPEAN
    COMMUNITY AFTER THE LEGISLATION DESIGNED TO STRENGTHEN AND
    CONSOLIDATE THE EUROPEAN COMMUNITY IS PASSED. IT PAYS
    SPECIAL ATTENTION TO THE CHALLENGES POSED BY A REFORMING
    SOVIET UNION AND MIKHAIL GORBACHEV TO EUROPE IN GENERAL AND
    WEST GERMANY IN PARTICULAR.

04060 HARTLEY, A.
    BETWEEN EAST AND WEST
    ENCOUNTER, LXXII(2) (FEB 89), 77-78.
        BRITISH INTELLECTUALS, IN A SPECTRUM RANGING FROM WHAT
    WAS ONCE THE ALLIANCE TO "MARXISM TODAY," HAVE CHOSEN TO
    IDENTIFY THEMSELVES WITH THE EAST EUROPEAN INTELLIGENTSIA'S
    RESISTANCE TO TYRANNY. IT IS A POWERFUL, IF BACKHANDED,
    TRIBUTE TO THE RUSSIAN AND CZECH DISSIDENTS THAT THE VERY
    MENTION OF THEM SHOULD CONJURE UP IDEAS OF FREEDOM AND THE
    RULE OF LAW. IN THE YEARS TO COME, EASTERN EUROPE'S
    INTELLECTUAL OUTPUT WILL AFFECT THE WEST IN MANY WAYS.

04061 HARTLEY, A.
    REVOLUTION AND ROMANTICISM
    ENCOUNTER, LXXII(3) (MAR 89), 76-77.
        IT IS THE NATURE OF GREAT HISTORICAL EVENTS TO BRING

WITH THEM ALTERED CULTURAL CONDITIONS THAT MAY EXPRESS OR
CAUSE, ACCORDING TO ONE'S POINT OF VIEW, THE POLITICAL
UPHEAVALS OF THE TIME. THERE IS AN OBVIOUS SUITABILITY IN
THE ROMANTIC MOVEMENT COMING TO BIRTH DURING THE FRENCH
REVOLUTION. FOR WHAT WAS ROMANTICISM IF NOT AN ACUTE SENSE
OF MUTABILITY, OF THE CHANGES WROUGHT BY TIME UPON HUMAN
BEINGS? WHAT WAS THE FRENCH REVOLUTION IF NOT AN UNDERLINING
OF THE POSSIBILITIES OF SUDDEN TRANSFORMATION INHERENT IN
THE HUMAN CONDITION?

04062 HARTLEY, A.
    SAVING MR. RUSHDIE?
    ENCOUNTER, LXXIII(1) (JUN 89), 73-77.
        BECAUSE THE ISSUES RAISED BY THE SALMAN RUSHDIE AFFAIR
    ARE IMPORTANT AND LIKELY TO APPEAR MORE SIGNIFICANT AS TIME
    PASSES, THE AUTHOR REVIEWS THE EVENTS SURROUNDING
    PUBLICATION OF "THE SATANIC VERSES," INCLUDING THE AYATOLLAH
    KHOMEINI'S CONDEMNATION OF IT.

04063 HARTMANN, R.
    A BREAK IN THE CLOUDS: A RECORD OF RAPPROCHEMENT
    WORLD MARXIST REVIEW, 32(9) (SEP 89), 36.
        THIS REPORT BY FRG AMBASSADOR, RUDIGER HARTMANN, ONE OF
    THE CHIEF NEGOTIATORS IN THE VIENNA TALKS ON CONVENTIONAL
    ARMS IN EUROPE, GIVES HIS IMPRESSION OF THE PROGRESS SO FAR,
    AND THE PROSPECTS AHEAD IN THE TALKS. MR HARTMANN BELIEVES
    THAT THERE ARE A NUMBER OF FACTORS BEHIND THE PRESENT
    RAPPROCHEMENT BETWEEN EAST AND WEST. HE EXPRESSES THESE
    FACTORS AND ALSO THE DIFFERENCES IN THE NEGOTIATIONS. HE
    BELIEVES THAT DEADLINES DO WORK AND THAT BOTH SIDES WANT AN
    EARLY AGREEMENT.

04064 HARTZ, F.; BOHLEY, B.; GUZINSKI, D.; HARTZ, M.; JAGER, K.;
    PELCH, V.; SIEGERT, C.
    EAST GERMANY: SOLIDARITY--BOTH ACKNOWLEDGED AND GIVEN
    EAST EUROPEAN REPORTER, 3(4) (SPR 89), 71-72.
        MEMBERS OF THE PEACE AND HUMAN RIGHTS INITIATIVE, A
    POLISH-CZECHOSLOVAK SOLIDARITY GROUP EXPRESS THEIR EMPATHY
    WITH SIMILAR MOVEMENTS IN EAST GERMANY. RECENT EVENTS IN
    EAST GERMANY, INCLUDING THE REPRESSION OF DEMONSTRATIONS AND
    CENSORSHIP OF PUBLICATIONS, CLEARLY DEMONSTRATE THAT THE
    GERMAN DEMOCRATIC REPUBLIC HAS NOT KEPT ITS PROMISES TO
    GUARANTEE HUMAN RIGHTS.

04065 HARUO, N.
    KOREA'S SAEMAUL MOVEMENT: "CAPACITATION" IN DEVELOPMENT
    JAPAN QUARTERLY, XXXVI(3) (JUL 89), 294-299.
        SOUTH KOREA'S SAEMAUL MOVEMENT OFFERS VALUABLE LESSONS
    FOR DEVELOPMENT PROGRAMS THROUGHOUT THE THIRD WORLD.
    "CAPACITATION," OR IMPROVING CAPABILITIES TO SOLVE
    SOCIOECONOMIC PROBLEMS, IS THE VERY CORE OF THE SAEMAUL-
    MOVEMENT TYPE OF DEVELOPMENT. OTHER THIRD WORLD COUNTRIES
    SHOULD EXAMINE BOTH THE CONCEPT OF CAPACITATION AND SOUTH
    KOREA'S EFFORTS.

04066 HARUO, S.
    HANDLING THE INFLUX OF FOREIGN WORKERS
    JAPAN ECHO, XVI(1) (SPR 89), 23-28.
        ATTRACTED BY JAPANESE ECONOMIC PROSPERITY, UNSKILLED
    WORKERS ARE SLIPPING INTO JAPAN UNINVITED. THE GOVERNMENT
    PROHIBITS THE EMPLOYMENT OF THE ILLEGAL ALIENS, BUT IT HAS
    PROVED POWERLESS TO HALT THE SWIFT RISE IN THEIR NUMBERS.
    THE INFLUX HAS REACHED THE POINT WHERE IT MAY SET OFF A
    CHAIN REACTION OF PROBLEMS RIPPLING THROUGH JAPANESE SOCIETY.
    AND JAPAN'S RESPONSE TO THESE PROBLEMS WILL HAVE
    REPERCUSSIONS IN THE INTERNATIONAL COMMUNITY.

04067 HARVEY, A.D.
    BRITAIN'S WAR AIMS IN THE FIRST WORLD WAR
    CONTEMPORARY REVIEW, 255(1483) (AUG 89), 92-100.
        EUROPE FOUND ITSELF AT WAR SO SUDDENLY IN AUGUST 1914
    THAT IT WAS ONLY AFTER THE FIRST CLASH OF ARMIES THAT THE
    VARIOUS GOVERNMENTS BEGAN TO FACE THE PROBLEM OF EXPLAINING
    TO THEIR PEOPLES NOT ONLY WHY THE WAR HAD STARTED BUT ALSO
    WHAT OBJECTIVES NEEDED TO BE SECURED BEFORE IT COULD BE
    HONORABLY ENDED. AS FAR AS BRITAIN WAS CONCERNED, THERE WERE
    NO TERRITORIAL CLAIMS AGAINST GERMANY AND IT WAS NECESSARY
    TO FIND SOME OTHER WAR AIM. VARIOUS OBJECTIVES WERE OFFERED
    AT TIMES DURING THE WARGERMAN HEGEMONY, PRUSSIAN MILITARISM,
    CONSTITUTIONAL LIBERTY AND POPULAR GOVERNMENT, THE TURKISH
    EMPIRE, NATIONALITY, THE CHAMPIONSHIP OF SMALL NATIONS, AND
    THE CHANGING SITUATION IN PETROGRADWERE ALL USED AS WAR AIMS
    AT ONE TIME OR ANOTHER.

04068 HARVEY, L.
    THE POST-MODERNIST TURN IN FEMINIST PHILOSOPHY OF SCIENCE
    ARENA, (88) (SPR 89), 119-133.
        THIS ARTICLE AIMS TO HIGHLIGHT SOME OF THE THEORETICAL
    AND POLITICAL DANGERS ATTENDING RECENT DEVELOPMENTS IN
    FEMINIST PHILOSOPHY OF SCIENCE WHICH ENTAIL A THOROUGHGOING
    RELATIVISM WITH RESPECT TO OUR UNDERSTANDING OF SCIENCE, IT
    ARGUES FOR A SUSTAINED EFFORT TO OVERCOME THE TENSIONS AND
    CONTRADICTIONS GENERATED BY TWO CONFLICTING PROJECTS-
    FEMINIST 'SUCCESSOR SCIENCE PROJECTS' AND POST-MODERNISM VIA

A CRITIQUE OF SANDRA HARDING'S SOMEWHAT AMBIVALENT POSITION
IN THIS DEBATE.

04069 HASEL KORN, A.
    SELECTIVE TERRORISM
    NATIONAL REVIEW, XLI(16) (SEP 89), 21-22.
        THE AUTHOR REPORTS THAT TERRORISTS' NEWEST TERRORIST
    TACTIC MAY BE THE DEADLIEST OF ALL: IMPROVING THEIR IMAGE.
    THE "SELECTIVE TERRORISM" APPROACH, ADOPTED BY A GROWING
    LIST OF TERRORIST ORGANIZATIONS, INCLUDING THE PLO, AVOIDS
    "NONCUMBATANT TARGETS," THIS TACTIC SEEKS TO EXPLOIT THE
    AMBIGUITY INHERENT IN ANY DEFINITION OF WHAT CONSTITUTES
    "TERRORISM."

04070 HASKINS, R.; BROWN, H.
    THE DAY-CARE REFORM JUGGERNAUT
    NATIONAL REVIEW, XLI(4) (MAR 89), 40-41.
        AS ENSHRINED IN THE DEMOCRATS' ACT FOR BETTER CHILD CARE,
    CHILD CARE BOILS DOWN TO THE FAMILIAR LIBERAL APPROACH TO
    SOCIAL PROBLEMS: INTERVENE DIRECTLY IN THE MARKET, PUT
    RESTRICTIONS ON THE TYPE OF SERVICE AND WHO CAN PROVIDE IT,
    AND THEN DOLE OUT FEDERAL CASH IN SUBSIDIES SO THAT MILLIONS
    OF FAMILIES BECOME DEPENDENT ON THE GOVERNMENT.

04071 HASLAM, J.
    THE UN AND SOVIET UNION: NEW THINKING?
    INTERNATIONAL AFFAIRS, 65(4) (FAL 89), 677-684.
        THIS ARTICE EXPLORES QUESTIONS ABOUT SOVIET COMMITMENT
    TO THE UN AND THE LIMITS TO THE EXTENSION OF THE 'NEW
    THINKING; TO THE INTEGRATION OF USSR INTO THE EXISTING
    INTERNATIONAL ORDER. THE OLD SOVIET ATTITUDE TO THE UN IS
    REVIEWED AS WELL AS TRADITIONAL SOVIET FOREIGN POLICY.
    CHANGES ARE EXAMINED, AS WELL AS SOVIET PROPOSALS AND
    GORBACHEV'S UN SPEECH.

04072 HASSAN, A.
    BIRTH OF A STATE
    NEW OUTLOOK, 32(1 (287)) (JAN 89), 29-30.
        IN THIS INTERVIEW, MAHMOUD DARWISH, A MEMBER OF THE PLO
    EXECUTIVE COMMITTEE AND THE AUTHOR OF THE PALESTINIAN
    DECLARATION OF INDEPENDENCE, ANSWERS QUESTIONS ABOUT THE
    ESTABLISHMENT OF A PALESTINIAN STATE AND THE SIGNIFICANCE OF
    THE DECLARATION.

04073 HASSAN, H. B. A.
    CONFLICT MANAGEMENT IN THE MIDDLE EAST: THE AMERICAN ROLE
    IN THE EGYPTIAN-ISRAELI PEACE TREATY (1973-1979)
    DISSERTATION ABSTRACTS INTERNATIONAL, 49(9) (MAR 89),
    2799-A.
        THE AUTHOR EVALUATES THREE MAJOR HYPOTHESES: (1)
    SUCCESSFUL AMERICAN INTERVENTION IN THE MIDEAST RELIED ON A
    GREAT SHIFT IN STRUCTURAL RELATIONS IN THREE DOMAINS, AND
    KISSINGER'S STRATEGY FACILITATED THE NEXT PHASE OF
    NEGOTIATIONS. (2) THE USA PLAYED A LEADING ROLE IN THE
    BARGAINING PROCESS. (3) THE RESULTS OF THE CONFLICT
    RESOLUTION WERE WEAK BECAUSE THEY ACCOMMODATED ONLY THE
    INVOLVED PARTIES.

04074 HASSAN, H. M.
    SNM REJECTS PEACE PROPOSALS
    NEW AFRICAN, (257) (FEB 89), 37.
        PRESIDENT SIYAD BARRE HAS OFFERED TO NAME SOMEONE OF
    ISAQ ORIGIN AS PRIME MINISTER, BUT THE SNM HAS REJECTED THE
    OFFER. THE SNM IS ALSO OPPOSED TO THE PRESIDENT'S SON OR HIS
    HALF-BROTHER ASSUMING THE PRESIDENCY. THE SNM HAS PROPOSED
    ADAN ABDULLE OSMAN AS A TRANSITIONAL PRESIDENT, BUT THE
    VETERAN POLITICIAN HAS REJECTED THE PROPOSAL.

04075 HASSAN, K.I.
    PRESCRIPTIONS FOR ENSLAVEMENT
    WORLD MARXIST REVIEW, 31(11) (NOV 88), 114-118.
        THE INDEPENDENCE OF MOST DEVELOPING COUNTRIES DOES NOT
    EXTEND BEYOND THE POLITICAL FRAMEWORK, AND THEY REMAIN
    ECONOMICALLY TIED TO THEIR FORMER COLONIAL MASTERS, AND THAT
    IS WHY THE LIVING STANDARDS ARE NOT IMPROVING. IF THEY ARE
    TO LIBERATE THEMSELVES FROM THE CLUTCHES OF IMPERIALISM,
    THEY MUST RESTRUCTURE THE OLD, COLONIAL SYSTEM OF THE
    ECONOMY WHICH THEY HAVE INHERITED, AND THAT DEPENDS ABOVE
    ALL ON TRANSFORMATIONS IN THE SYSTEM OF STATE POWER. BUT THE
    FACT IS THAT IN MOST DEVELOPING COUNTRIES THERE HAS BEEN NO
    ESSENTIAL CHANGE IN ITS CLASS NATURE.

04076 HASSAN, P.
    REGIONAL RESPONSES TO ENVIRONMENTAL DEGRADATION IN SOUTH
    ASIA
    SOUTH ASIA JOURNAL, 3(1/2) (JUL 89), 43-52.
        THIS ARTICLE PROJECTS THE NEEDS OF THE RAPIDLY GROWING
    PAKISTAN POPULATION. IT CONCLUDES THAT THIS GROWTH WILL
    DIRECTLY LEAD TO OVER-EXPLOITATION OF THE COUNTRY'S NATURAL
    RESOURCES, IRRETRIEVABLY IMPAIRING THE QUALITY OF HUMAN LIFE
    FOR FUTURE GENERATIONS. IT EXAMINES THE PAKISTAN
    ENVIRONMENTAL PROTECTION ORDINANCE. THE IMMENSE COMMONALITY
    OF THE COUNTRIES OF SOUTH ASIA IS NOTED AND SOME OF THE
    AREAS FOR REGIONAL COOPERATION ARE OUTLINED.

04077 HASSAN, R.M.; AHMED, S.; FLETCHER, L.B.
UNEQUAL WEALTH ACCUMULATION AND INCOME INEQUALITY IN A
UNIMODAL AGRICULTURE: SUDAN'S RADAD IRRIGATION SCHEME
JOURNAL OF DEVELOPMENT STUDIES, 26(1) (OCT 89), 120-130.
PATTERNS OF INCOME, SAVINGS, AND WEALTH ACCUMULATION OF
TENANT FARMERS IN THE RAHAD IRRIGATION SCHEME OF SUDAN WERE
EXAMINED. ALTHOUGH LAND AND IRRIGATION WATER ARE PUBLICLY
OWNED AND EQUALLY DISTRIBUTED IN THESE SCHEMES, UNEQUAL
ACCESS TO CAPITAL HAS FOUND TO INFLUENCE STRONGLY THE
DISTRIBUTION OF FAMILY INCOME AND THE SAVING AND
ACCUMULATION CAPACITIES OF THE TENANT FARMERS. ANALYSIS
USING LORENZ CURVES AND GINI COEFFICIENTS REVEALED A HIGH
POSITIVE CORRELATION BETWEEN WEALTH AND FAMILY INCOME. THE
AVERAGE WEALTH GAP BETWEEN POOR AND RICH HOUSEHOLDS
INCREASED BY 28 PER CENT OVER THE YEAR OF THE STUDY. TO
REDUCE RELATIVE POVERTY, IMPROVED CREDIT AND MARKETING
SYSTEMS PLUS MORE RESEARCH AND EXTENSION SUPPORT TO ENHANCE
PRODUCTIVITY AND CREATE HIGHER ON-FARM INCOMES FOR THE
POORER TENANTS ARE NEEDED. IN ADDITION, MACRO AND SECTOR
POLICIES THAT SUBSIDISE LABOUR-SAVING TECHNOLOGIES AND LOWER
INCENTIVES FOR EXPORT AND DOMESTIC CROP PRODUCTION NEED TO
BE REFORMED TO PROMOTE GREATER EMPLOYMENT AND HIGHER OFF-
FARM EARNINGS FOR THE POORER HOUSEHOLDS.

04078 HATCH, O.
THE POLITICS OF PICKING JUDGES
JOURNAL OF LAW & POLITICS, VI(1) (FAL 89), 35-54.
SENATOR ORRIN HATCH EXAMINES THE SENATE'S JUDICIAL
SELECTION PROCEDURES, THE CONSTITUTIONAL BACKGROUND OF THE
APPOINTMENT AND CONFIRMATION PROCESS, AND HOW THE CURRENT
PRACTICE OF THE SENATE JUDICIARY COMMITTEE IS A THREAT TO AN
INDEPENDENT JUDICIARY. HE CONCLUDES THAT THE INCREASINGLY
POLITICAL NATURE OF THE DECISIONS THAT FEDERAL JUDGES OFTEN
UNDERTAKE MAKES THE TEMPTATION TO POLITICIZE THE APPOINTMENT
PROCESS NEARLY IRRESISTIBLE. FURTHERMORE, THIS TEMPTATION
WILL ALWAYS EXIST UNTIL THE ONCE-PREVAILING ETHIC OF
JUDICIAL SELF-RESTRAINT CAN BE REINVIGORATED. IF THE CURRENT
ABUSE OF THE ADVICE AND CONTENT POWER CONTINUES, THE
INTEGRITY OF THE JUDICIAL SELECTION MAY BE IRREPARABLY
HARMED.

04079 HATEM,M.
EGYPTIAN UPPER - AND MIDDLE-CLASS WOMEN'S EARLY
NATIONALIST DISCOURSES ON NATIONAL LIBERATION AND PEACE
WOMEN AND POLITICS, 9(3) (1989), 49-70.
MOST EGYPTIAN WOMEN REMAIN TORN BETWEEN THEIR SUPPORT
FOR NATIONAL LIBERATION STRUGGLES THAT UNITE THEM WITH MEN
AND PEACE, WHICH THEY INTUITIVELY FAVOR IN CONFLICT
SITUATIONS. THE FIRST HALF OF THIS ARTICLE EXAMINES THE WAY
THAT EGYPTIAN/COMMITMENT TO NATIONAL WOMEN'S RIGHTS THUS
GIVING THOSE VIOLENT NATIONAL STRUGGLES POSITIVE
CONNOTATIONS. THE SECOND HALF DISCUSSES THE CONTRIBUTION OF
THE EGYPTIAN FEMINIST UNION.

04080 HATRY, H.P.; SKIDMORE, F.
THE PRIVATE SECTOR IN STATE SERVICE DELIVERY: EXAMPLES OF
INNOVATIVE PRACTICES
NATIONAL CIVIC REVIEW, 78(2) (MAR 89), 127-133.
TAX-LIMITATION REFERENDA AND A PRESIDENTIAL
ADMINISTRATION BULLISH ON PRIVATIZATION HAVE RESULTED IN
WIDESPREAD USE OF THE PRIVATE SECTOR TO DELIVER STATE AND
LOCAL SERVICES. FOR YEARS THE STRAGGLERS OF THE
PRIVATIZATION MOVEMENT, STATES HAVE MORE RECENTLY TAKEN
RESPONSIBLE AND INNOVATIVE STEPS TOWARD INVOLVING THE
PRIVATE SECTOR IN THE AREAS OF PARKS AND RECREATION AND
HUMAN SERVICES.

04081 HATTER, D.; BINKLEY, A.; LAKE, D.
CANADA
SOUTH, (106) (AUG 89), 53-60.
OFFICIALS AT THE CANADIAN INTERNATIONAL DEVELOPMENT
AGENCY ARE REASSESSING THEIR OVERSEAS AID STRATEGY IN THE
WAKE OF A DEFICIT-CUTTING NATIONAL BUDGET, IN WHICH FOREIGN
AID AND DEFENSE SPENDING ARE THE TWO MAIN VICTIMS. SINCE
CANADA'S COMMITMENTS TO MULTILATERAL INSTITUTIONS ARE LONG-
TERM, AID CUTBACKS WILL MAINLY AFFECT BILATERAL PROGRAMS.
OFFICIALS SAY CANADA MUST NOW EMPHASIZE THE NON-FISCAL
ELEMENTS OF ITS AID, STRESSING QUALITY RATHER THAN QUANTITY.

04082 HATTERY, M.R.
REVENUE SUPPORT FOR LOCAL PUBLIC SERVICES: A COMPARATIVE
ANALYSIS OF GENERAL PURPOSE AID AND LOCAL OPTIONAL TAXES
DISSERTATION ABSTRACTS INTERNATIONAL, 49(10) (APR 89),
3150-A.
THE AUTHOR COMPARES TWO FISCAL POLICY OPTIONS THAT HAVE
THE POTENTIAL OF PROVIDING THE REVENUE NEEDS OF LOCAL
GOVERNMENTS IN NEW YORK. THE TWO ALTERNATIVES ARE (1) STATE
GENERAL PURPOSE AID AND (2) AN EXPANSION OF LOCAL GOVERNMENT
TAXING OPTIONS.

04083 HAUG, F.
LESSONS FROM THE WOMEN'S MOVEMENT IN EUROPE
FEMINIST REVIEW, (31) (SPR 89), 107-116.
THE AUTHOR DISCUSSES THE PROBLEMS AND FUTURE DIRECTIONS
FOR SOCIALIST-FEMINIST POLITICS IN EUROPE. ONE ISSUE THAT
SHE CONSIDERS IS THE QUESTION OF QUOTAS FOR MINIMUM FEMALE
REPRESENTATION IN POLITICAL SITUATIONS. FOR EXAMPLE,
FEMINISTS IN THE FEDERAL REPUBLIC OF GERMANY AND THE
SCANDINAVIAN COUNTRIES HAVE PERSUADED SOME POLITICAL PARTIES
AND OTHER ORGANIZATIONS TO RESERVE A MINIMUM NUMBER OF SLOTS
FOR WOMEN TO BE SELECTED FOR ELECTORAL LISTS OR ELECTED TO
EXECUTIVE COMMITTEES. IT IS DEBATABLE WHETHER THIS IS AN
ADVANCE FOR FEMINISM OR MERE TOKENISM.

04084 HAUS, L.A.
THE POLITICAL ECONOMY OF EAST-WEST TRADE NEGOTIATIONS:
EAST EUROPEAN COUNTRIES AND THE GATT
DISSERTATION ABSTRACTS INTERNATIONAL, 50(3) (SEP 89),
787-A.
THE AUTHOR IDENTIFIES THE MAJOR POLITICAL-ECONOMIC
ISSUES THAT HAVE INFLUENCED THE OUTCOMES OF NEGOTIATIONS
BETWEEN EAST EUROPEAN COUNTRIES AND THE GATT. SHE ALSO
EXAMINES THE MAJOR FACTORS THAT HAVE INFLUENCED THE POLICIES
OF WESTERN COUNTRIES TOWARD THESE NEGOTIATIONS. THEN SHE
EVALUATES TO WHAT EXTENT, AND UNDER WHAT CONDITIONS, FOREIGN
POLICY IN THE WEST WAS INFLUENCED BY GATT NORMS AND RULES,
GEOPOLITICAL GOALS, AND COMMERCIAL INTERESTS.

04085 HAUSMAN, D.M.
ARE MARKETS MORALLY FREE ZONES?
PHILOSOPHY AND PUBLIC AFFAIRS, 18(4) (FAL 89), 317-333.
THIS ARTICLE EXPLORES DAVID GAUTHIER'S STATEMENT THAT A
PERFECTLY COMPETITIVE MARKET IS "A MORALLY FREE ZONE." IT
FOCUSES ON GAUTHIER'S VIEWS, BUT THE POINTS ARE GENERAL AND
THE ISSUES ARE OF WIDER IMPORTANCE. IT ARGUES THAT REAL
MARKETS ARE NOT PERFECTIVELY COMPETITIVE AND THAT THEIR
IMPERFECTIONS ARE MORALLY SIGNIFICANT. IT DETAILS GAUTHIER'S
VIEW AND EXPLORES THE QUESTION "CAN INITIAL HOLDINGS BEAR
THE MORAL BURDEN?"

04086 HAVEL, V.
CARDS ON THE TABLE
ACROSS FRONTIERS, 5(2) (SUM 89), 28-29, 47.
THIS ARTICLE EXAMINES THE CURRENT POLITICAL FEELING OF
THE PEOPLE OF CZECHOSLOVAKIA AS THEY ARE BEGINNING TO OPENLY
SHOW THAT THEY ARE NO LONGER WILLING TO APATHETICALLY
ACQUIESCE IN THE FORCIBLY IMPOSED STATUS QUO. ALSO, THE
REACTION OF THE GOVERNMENT TO THE CHANGES IS DISCUSSED.
ANALYSED IS THE MANIFESTO OF THE MOVEMENT FOR CIVIL FREEDOM
WHICH PRESENTS NEW IDEAS AS A POINT OF DEPARTURE FOR
POLITICAL WORK.

04087 HAVEL, V.
THERE IS NOTHING TO BE SORRY FOR
EAST EUROPEAN REPORTER, 3(4) (SPR 89), 59.
THE ARTICLE IS THE TEXT OF VACLAV HAVEL'S SPEECH AT HIS
FIRST TRIAL IN THE DISTRICT COURT OF PRAGUE. HE PROCLAIMS
HIS INNOCENCE AND DEFENDS THE ACTIONS OF CHARTER 77 AND
OTHER INDEPENDENT ACTIVIST GROUPS. HE ALSO OUTLINES THE
FUTILITY IN LABELLING ANY REFORM MOVEMENT AS BEING "ANTI-
STATE" OR "ANTI-SOCIALIST."

04088 HAVEMAN, R.H.
TARGETING THE POOR: NEW POLICY FOR THE NEW POVERTY
CURRENT, (310) (FEB 89), 11-19.
AFTER THE REAGAN ADMINISTRATION, THE PROBLEMS OF POVERTY
AND INEQUALITY ARE AGAIN ON THE NATION'S PLATE, IN SOME WAYS
IN MORE VIRULENT FORM THAN IN THE 1960'S. BUT NOW, UNLIKE
THE ERA OF THE GREAT SOCIETY, THERE IS LITTLE ROOM TO
MANEUVER. SLOW ECONOMIC GROWTH AND RECORD DEFICITS HAVE MADE
NEW EFFORTS DIFFICULT TO CONTEMPLATE. IF THE UNITED STATES
WANTS TO REDUCE POVERTY AND PROMOTE EFFICIENCY AND GROWTH, A
NEW WAY OF REDUCING INEQUALITY MUST BE FOUND. THE NEW
STRATEGY MUST RECOGNIZE THE CHANGES IN POVERTY AND
INEQUALITY. IT MUST CORRECT THE INEFFICIENCIES FOSTERED BY
CURRENT POLICIES. IT MUST AIM NOT AT EQUALIZING OUTCOMES,
BUT AT EQUALIZING OPPORTUNITIES.

04089 HAVEMANN, A.
THE VIZIER AND THE RA'IS IN SALJUQ SYRIA: THE STRUGGLE FOR
URBAN SELF-REPRESENTATION
INTERNATIONAL JOURNAL OF MIDDLE EAST STUDIES, 21(2) (MAY
89), 233-242.
BY SALJUQ TIMES, THE VIZIERATE HAD FOR SOME TIME BEEN A
WELL-ESTABLISHED FEATURE OF ISLAMIC GOVERNMENT AND THE
VIZIER EXERCISED GREATER AUTHORITY ON BEHALF OF THE TURKISH
SULTANS THAN AT ANY PREVIOUS TIME. THIS ESSAY EXAMINES THE
RELATIONSHIP BETWEEN THE INSTITUTION OF THE VIZIERATE AND
THAT OF THE HEADSHIP IN SALJUQ DAMASCUS AND ALEPPO.

04090 HAVEMANN, P.
AFTER SOCIAL JUSTICE: DAWKINS IN SASKATCHEWAN
ARENA, 86 (FAL 89), 28-33.
THE INCORPORATION OF THE ACADEMY UNDER THE BANNER OF
ECONOMIC RATIONALISM REQUIRES THE ERADICATION OF THE
'LIBERAL' VISION BY MEANS OF INTELLECTUAL SUPPRESSION, UNDER-
FUNDING, ELIMINATION OF PROGRAMMES WITHOUT ACADEMIC DUE

PROCESS, AND THE CONNIVANCE OF ACADEMICS THEMSELVES. IN THIS ARTICLE, THE ASSAULT ON THE INSTITUTIONAL ARRANGEMENTS OF THE LIBERAL WELFARE STATE AND THE ACADEMY IS VIEWED AGAINST THE BACKGROUND OF NEO-CONSERVATIVE SUCCESSES IN CANADA -- EPITOMIZED BY THE FREE TRADE DEAL. DISMANTLING HAS INVOLVED THE ERADICATION OF 'INEFFICIENCIES' IN THE UNIVERSITY SECTOR AND THE INCORPORATION OF THE ACADEMY INTO A 'COLLABORATIVE' PARTNERSHIP WITH THE CORPORATE SECTOR.

04091 HAWES, G.
AQUINO AND HER ADMINISTRATION: A VIEW FROM THE COUNTRYSIDE
PACIFIC AFFAIRS, 62(1) (SPR 89), 9-28.
THIS ARTICLE EVALUATES THE QUALITY OF DEMOCRACY IN THE PHILIPPINE COUNTRYSIDE. BASED ON INTERVIEWS CONDUCTED DURING 1986 AND 1987 WITH PEASANTS, WORKERS, PARTY OFFICIALS, CANDIDATES, AND UNDERGROUND ACTIVISTS, THE CONCLUSION IS DRAWN THAT DEMOCRACY (AT LEAST IN THE COUNTRYSIDE) IS INCOMPLETE AND SEVERELY FLAWED. THE ARTICLE FURTHER ARGUES THAT THE RESTORATION OF THE PRE-MARTIAL LAW POLITICAL SYSTEM MEANS THAT MOST PARTIES ARE ONCE AGAIN ORGANIZED FROM THE TOP DOWN AND THAT THE POOR ARE STRUCTURALLY EXCLUDED FROM PARTICIPATION IN DECISION MAKING BOTH WITHIN THE POLITICAL PARTIES AND THE POLICY ARENA. THIS LACK OF MEANINGFUL PARTICIPATION FOR THE POOR COUPLED WITH AN INCREASE IN THE LEVEL OF MILITARY VIOLENCE IN THE COUNTRYSIDE HELPS TO EXPLAIN THE CONTINUED MASS SUPPORT FOR THE REVOLUTIONARY MOVEMENT FIGHTING AGAINST THE AQUINO GOVERNMENT.

04092 HAWES, M. K.
MULRONEY AND THE AMERICANS: A NEW ERA?
INTERNATIONAL PERSPECTIVES, XVIII(1) (JAN 89), 9-12.
THE AUTHOR ASSESSES BRIAN MULRONEY'S FIRST-TERM RECORD ON CANADIAN-AMERICAN RELATIONS.

04093 HAWI, G.
A REVOLUTION IN CONSCIOUSNESS AND POLITICS
WORLD MARXIST REVIEW, 32(9) (AUG 89), 8-12.
THE WORLD MARXIST REVIEW COMMISSION ON THE INTERNATIONAL COMMUNIST MOVEMENT AND EXCHANGES OF PARTY EXPERIENCE ASKS THE QUESTION: HOW ARE SISTER PARTIES RESTRUCTURING THEIR ACTIVITY IN FACE OF RAPIDLY CHANGING NATIONAL AND WORLD REALITIES? THE LEADER OF THE LEBANESE COMMUNIST PARTY ANSWERS IN THIS ARTICLE. IT REVIEWS THE GLOBAL CHARACTER OF THE NEW POLITICAL THINKING WHICH REQUIRES A FRESH LOOK AT REVOLUTION, IT CONCLUDES THAT THE ULTIMATE VICTORY OF SOCIALISM REQUIRES PEACE. IT EXAMINES CAPITALISM DEMOCRACY, HUMANISM, ECONOMIC DEVELOPMENT, AND REFORM IN LEBANAN.

04094 HAWI, G.
LEBANON: TASK OF THE NEW STAGE IN THE STRUGGLE
INFORMATION BULLETIN, 25/26(1-2) (JAN 88), 26-28.
IN THIS INTERVIEW, THE GENERAL SECRETARY OF THE LEBANESE COMMUNIST PARTY OFFERS AN ANALYSIS OF THE SITUATION IN HIS COUNTRY AND DISCUSSES THE TASKS AT HAND FOR THE LEBANESE NATIONAL - PATRIOTIC FORCES.

04095 HAWK, B.G.
AFRICANS AND THE 1965 U.S. IMMIGRATION LAW
DISSERTATION ABSTRACTS INTERNATIONAL, 49(11) (MAY 89), 3491-A.
REFUGEE AND IMMIGRATION POLICY ARE THE RESULT OF INTERPLAY BETWEEN THE AGENDAS OF THE EXECUTIVE AND LEGISLATIVE BRANCHES OF GOVERNMENT. IF THE ISSUE WERE SIMPLY THE NUMBER OF IMMIGRANTS, POLICY WOULD BE MERELY A MATTER OF SETTING A LIMIT AND ALLOCATING SLOTS ON A RANDOM BASIS. A STUDY OF AFRICAN IMMIGRATION TO THE USA UNDER THE 1965 LAW REVEALS INTERESTING FACTS ABOUT THE GOALS AND CONSEQUENCES OF THE POLICY, PARTICULARLY THE INTERPLAY OF SKILLS CRITERIA AND ETHNIC DISCRIMINATION.

04096 HAWKINS, K.D.
ASSESSMENT OF BRAZIL'S ECONOMIC AND ENERGY PROBLEMS
AVAILABLE FROM NTIS, NO. AD-A202 090/7/GAR, APR 88, 57.
BRAZIL, A LARGE THIRD WORLD COUNTRY WITH SIGNIFICANT POTENTIAL, WAS WELL ON ITS WAY TOWARD ENTERING DEVELOPED NATION STATUS WHEN THE ORGANIZATION OF PETROLEUM EXPORTING COUNTRIES (OPEC) RAISED THE PRICE OF OIL IN 1973. THIS PRICE RISE HIT BRAZIL PARTICULARLY HARD BECAUSE IMPORTS SUPPLIED APPROXIMATELY 80 PERCENT OF ITS ENERGY NEEDS. BRAZIL'S PROBLEM THEN BECAME ONE OF HOW TO COUNTER THE ECONOMICALLY DEVASTATING IMPACT OF THE COSTLY ENERGY IMPORTS. IF ADEQUATE ALTERNATIVES TO IMPORTED OIL COULD BE DEVELOPED, IT WAS THOUGHT BRAZIL'S ECONOMIC PROBLEMS WOULD APPARENTLY BE OVER. BRAZIL WORKED HARD ON THE PROBLEM AND MADE DRAMATIC PROGRESS OVER A 15-YEAR PERIOD. HOWEVER, DURING THIS 15-YEAR PERIOD BRAZIL AMASSED THE LARGEST FOREIGN DEBT OF ANY THIRD WORLD COUNTRY, MOST OF WHICH HAS INCURRED PAYING FOR IMPORTED ENERGY. THIS HUGE DEBT REPLACED THE ORIGINAL ENERGY DEPENDENCE PROBLEM, AND BRAZIL IS NO BETTER OFF ECONOMICALLY THAN WHEN THE ENERGY CRISIS EFFECTIVELY STOPPED ECONOMIC GROWTH. BRAZIL'S ECONOMIC PROBLEMS CARRY CERTAIN IMPLICATIONS FOR UNITED STATES POLICY PLANNERS, AND THE AUTHOR MAKES RECOMMENDATIONS REGARDING THESE IMPLICATIONS.

04097 HAWKINS, R.B. JR.
LINKING CONSTITUTIONAL REFORM TO LOCAL SELF-GOVERNANCE
JOURNAL OF STATE GOVERNMENT, 62(1) (JAN 89), 31-33.
IN TODAY'S COMPLEX INFORMATION AGE, A HIERARCHICAL STRUCTURE OF POWER BASED ON COMMAND AND CONTROL DOES NOT WORK WELL. YET THE FEDERAL GOVERNMENT IS USURPING STATE AND LOCAL CONTROL, EVEN THOUGH CITIZENS ARE DEMANDING MORE VOICE IN GOVERNING THEIR LOCAL INSTITUTIONS. WHAT IS NEEDED IS A CONSTITUTIONAL AMENDMENT TO RESTORE THE BALANCE OF POWER IN THE U.S. FEDERAL SYSTEM.

04098 HAWXHURST, J.
SOUTH AMERICAN ELECTIONS
SOJOURNERS, 18(10) (NOV 89), 10-12.
ARGENTINA, BOLIVIA, CHILE, BRAZIL, URUGUAY, COLOMBIA, AND PERU HAVE MADE SIGNIFICANT STRIDES TOWARDS DEMOCRACY. CITIZENS OF THESE NATIONS ARE CELEBRATING THE DEMOCRATIC TRANSFER OF POWER THAT WAS TRIGGERED BY THE COLLAPSE OF THE ECONOMICALLY AND POLITICALLY BANKRUPT MILITARY DICTATORSHIPS. POPULIST MOVEMENTS AND CANDIDATES ARE GAINING IN POPULARITY, BUT ANY ELECTED CANDIDATE WILL FACE SIGNIFICANT ECONOMIC CHALLENGES AND POTENTIAL UNREST.

04099 HAY, K.A.J.
ASEAN AND THE SHIFTING TIDES OF ECONOMIC POWER AT THE END OF THE 1980'S
INTERNATIONAL JOURNAL, XLIV(3) (SUM 89), 640-659.
IN THIS ARTICLE THE CURRENT ECONOMIC SITUATIONS OF FIVE ASEAN COUNTRIES ARE BRIEFLY REVIEWED. CONSIDERATION IS THEN GIVEN TO THE IMPORTANCE OF FOREIGN TRADE IN MAINTAINING THE PACE OF ASEAN DEVELOPMENT, PARTICULARLY THE REQUIREMENT FOR MARKET ACCESS TO NORTH AMERICA, EUROPE, AND EAST ASIA. THE DEFICIT AND DEBT PROBLEMS OF THE UNITED STATES ARE SEEN TO CAST A LONG SHADOW OVER CONTINUED ASEAN TRADE EXPANSION AND TO REDUCE THE CASH THAT THE UNITED STATES HAS TRADITIONALLY HAD AVAILABLE FOR FOREIGN AID AND INVESTMENT. ASEAN'S PERCEPTIONS OF EMERGING TRADE BLOCS IN NORTH AMERICA AND EUROPE ALSO OCCASION UNEASINESS AND CAUSE ITS MEMBER-STATES TO DRAW CLOSER TO WESTERN PACIFIC ALTERNATIVES. JAPAN'S ROLE IN ASEAN AS A DISPENSER OF CASH IS GROWING. MOREOVER, JAPAN AND OTHER EAST ASIAN COUNTRIES CAN PROVIDE MUCH OF THE TECHNOLOGY, KNOW-HOW, AND MANAGEMENT TECHNIQUES REQUIRED FOR ACCELERATED INDUSTRIALIZATION. BUT THESE NEIGHBOURS HAVE LESS EXPERIENCE AND FEWER CAPABILITIES TO HELP THE ASEAN STATES WITH PROBLEMS OF BALANCING GROWTH, PROVIDING EQUITY IN INCOME DISTRIBUTION, ALLEVIATING POVERTY, AND PRESERVING THE ENVIRONMENT. HERE, ASEAN MUST CONTINUE TO LOOK TO NORTH AMERICA, EUROPE, AND THE MULTILATERAL AGENCIES.

04100 HAYAT, S.
HOW CHARISMATIC WAS QUAID-I-AZAM JINNAH?
ASIAN PROFILE, 17(6) (DEC 89), 563-572.
QUAID-I-AZAM MOHAMMAD ALI JINNAH WAS THE CREATOR OF PAKISTAN. SOME WRITERS HAVE DESCRIBED HIM AS "CHARISMATIC." OTHERS, USING THE SAME INFORMATION ABOUT HIS POLITICAL CAREER, HAVE FOUND HIM TO LACK CHARISMA. THIS PAPER EXPLORES THIS ISSUE THROUGH A REVIEW OF THE RELEVANT LITERATURE. THE UNDERLYING HYPOTHESIS IS THAT THE DIFFERING ASSESSMENTS OF JINNAH'S CHARISMA HAVE ARISEN MORE FROM A SUPERFICIAL READING OF THE CONCEPT OF CHARISMA THAN FROM DIFFICULTY IN UNDERSTANDING THE NATURE OF HIS POLITICAL LEADERSHIP.

04101 HAYDEN, F.G.
INSTITUTIONALISM FOR WHAT: TO UNDERSTAND INEVITABLE PROGRESS OR FOR POLICY RELEVANCE?
JOURNAL OF ECONOMIC ISSUES, XXIII(2) (JUN 89), 633-645.
IN TWO RECENT PAPERS, ANNE MAYHEW CHALLENGED THE APPROACH AND PURPOSE OF INSTITUTIONALISM (MAYHEW 1987A, 1987B). HER MESSAGE WAS THAT INSTITUTIONALISM SHOULD BE CONCERNED WITH DESCRIBING CULTURES IN ORDER TO UNDERSTAND THE INEVITABLE FLOW OF HUMAN PROGRESS, AND SHOULD NOT BE UNDERTAKING ANALYSIS FOR THE PURPOSE OF SOCIAL EVALUATION AND POLICY. THE PURPOSE OF THIS ARTICLE IS TO DEMONSTRATE THE INSUFFICIENCY OF THE BASE UPON WHICH THAT MESSAGE WAS CONSTRUCTED.

04102 HAYES-RENSHAW, F.; LEQUESNE, C.; LOPEZ, P.M.
THE PERMANENT REPRESENTATIONS OF THE MEMBER STATES TO THE EUROPEAN COMMUNITIES
JOURNAL OF COMMON MARKET STUDIES, XXVIII(2) (DEC 89), 119-138.
THE AUTHOR STUDIES THE PERMANENT MISSIONS OF THE MEMBER STATES TO THE EUROPEAN COMMUNITY BODIES, INCLUDING THE HISTORY OF THEIR CREATION, THEIR INTERNAL ORGANIZATION, AND THE ROLE THEY PLAY IN THE ELABORATION AND NEGOTIATION OF THE NATIONAL POSITION IN THE COUNCIL OF MINISTERS. THREE MEMBER STATES--FRANCE, IRELAND, AND SPAIN--ARE USED AS CASE STUDIES BECAUSE THEY DIFFER IN A NUMBER OF SIGNIFICANT WAYS AND REPRESENT A MICROCOSM OF THE EUROPEAN COMMUNITY.

04103 HAYES, K.
FULLY PRO-LIFE
SOJOURNERS, 18(10) (NOV 89), 22.
THE AUTHOR ARGUES THAT MERELY ARGUING OVER WHEN HUMAN

LIFE BEGINS OR HOW TO SAVE UNBORN CHILDREN IGNORES A VITAL
ELEMENT: THE MOTHER. SHE ADVOCATES, ALONG WITH LEGAL
SOLUTIONS, INCREASED SUPPORT SYSTEMS AND AVAILABILITY OF
ALTERNATIVES FOR WOMEN WITH UNPLANNED PREGNANCIES--
ESPECIALLY POOR WOMEN. WITHOUT THIS TWO-PRONGED APPROACH,
ANY ATTEMPT TO SOLVE THE PROBLEM OF ABORTION WILL FALL SHORT
OF THE MARK.

04104 HAYS, R.
STATE-LOCAL RELATIONS IN POLICY IMPLEMENTATION: THE CASE
OF HIGHWAY TRANSPORTATION IN IOWA
PUBLIUS: THE JOURNAL OF FEDERALISM, 18(1) (WIN 88), 79-96.
THIS ARTICLE EXAMINES RELATIONSHIPS BETWEEN STATE
AGENCIES AND LOCAL COMMUNITIES, USING SURVEY AND INTERVIEW
DATA FROM A CASE STUDY OF THE IOWA DEPARTMENT OF
TRANSPORTATION. IT ARGUES THAT THESE RELATIONSHIPS OFTEN
PARALLEL THE AGENCY-CLIENTELE RELATIONSHIPS OBSERVED BY
PUBLIC ADMINISTRATION SCHOLARS. THE AGENCY DERIVES SIMILAR
BENEFITS FROM LOCAL GOVERNMENT SUPPORT AS FROM PRIVATE
CLIENTELE SUPPORT, NAMELY, AN INDEPENDENT POWER BASE THAT
HELPS TO PRESERVE ITS FLOW OF RESOURCES AND ITS
ADMINISTRATIVE AUTONOMY. IDOT POSSESSES FORMIDABLE POLITICAL
RESOURCES IN THE BREADTH AND INTENSITY OF ITS CLIENTELE, BUT
THE KEY TO IDOT'S SUCCESS IS THE SKILLFUL UTILIZATION OF
THOSE RESOURCES THROUGH AN ADMINISTRATIVE STRATEGY STRESSING
THE DEVELOPMENT OF WIDELY ACCEPTED TECHNICAL DECISION-
CRITERIA AND AN ADMINISTRATIVE STYLE EMPHASIZING
ACCESSIBILITY, RESPONSIVENESS, AND FLEXIBILITY. A SURVEY OF
MAYORS AND LOCAL BUSINESS LEADERS SHOWS THAT THIS STRATEGY
HAS GENERATED WIDESPREAD POSITIVE PERCEPTIONS OF THE
DEPARTMENT AMONG THESE CLIENTELE GROUPS.

04105 HAYWARD, S.
PASSION OVER PRUDENCE
REASON, 21(7) (DEC 89), 43-44.
THIS ARTICLE IS A REVIEW OF THE BOOK "CITIZENS: A
CHRONICLE OF THE FRENCH REVOLUTION" BY SIMON SCHAMA, IT
EXPLORES THE HISTORICAL DEBATE WHICH HAS CONVERVED WITH THE
POLITICAL DEBATE AS TO ITS PLACE IN HISTORY, "CITIZENS"
ADDRESSES ITSELF TO ISSUES AS WELL AS AS THE LIBERAL, MARYIST,
AND BURK'S VIEWS OF THE REVOLUTION. IT IS IN A NARRATIVE
FORM THAT PROVIDES INTERPRETATIONS AS EVENTS UNFOLD BEFORE
THE READER, IT ILLUMINATES MANY OF THE BASIC POLITICAL
QUESTIONS THE REVOLUTION FACED. "CITIZENS" COMES DOWN
SQUARELY AS THE FRENCH REVOLUTION AS A CATASTROPHE
PROCEEDING FROM RATHER UNREMARKABLE POLITICAL CAUSES.

04106 HAZARD, H.A.
RESOLVING DISPUTES IN INTERNATIONAL TRADE
DISSERTATION ABSTRACTS INTERNATIONAL, 50(2) (AUG 89),
536-A.
THE AUTHOR EXAMINES THE DISPUTE-SETTLEMENT MECHANISMS OF
THE GENERAL AGREEMENT ON TARIFFS AND TRADE (GATT) AND
EVALUATES THEIR EFFECTIVENESS IN RESOLVING CONFLICTS IN
INTERNATIONAL TRADE.

04107 HAZELKORN, E.
WHY IS THERE NO SOCIALISM IN IRELAND? THEORETICAL PROBLEMS
OF IRISH MARXISM
SCIENCE AND SOCIETY, 53(2) (SUM 89), 136-164.
THIS ARTICLE ASKS WHETHER THE THEORETICAL FRAME WORK IN
WHICH IRISH SOCIALISM OPERATES HAS CONTRIBUTED TO THE
WEAKNESS OF MARXISM AND LABOR. IT STUDIES SOCIAL AND
POLITICAL CONSERVATISM WHICH HAS BEEN ALMOST INVERSELY
PROPORTIONAL TO THE LONG ORGANIZATIONAL HISTORY OF IRISH
SOCIALISM. IT INVESTIGATES THE LACK OF IRISH WORKING CLASS
UNITY AND ITS IMPACT ON THE THEORETICAL AND POLITICAL
PRACTICE OF IRISH MARXISM AND THE EARLY YEARS OF THE LABOUR
PARTY.

04108 HAZELL, R.
FREEDOM OF INFORMATION IN AUSTRALIA, CANADA, AND NEW
ZEALAND
PUBLIC ADMINISTRATION, 67(2) (SUM 89), 189-210.
IN 1982, AUSTRALIA, CANADA AND NEW ZEALAND INTRODUCED
FREEDOM OF INFORMATION LAWS. THE ARTICLE SUMMARIZES THE MAIN
FEATURES OF THE LEGISLATION AND DISCUSSES THE DIFFERENT
APPEAL MECHANISMS; THE IMPLICATIONS FOR MINISTERIAL
ACCOUNTABILITY; THE LEVEL OF TAKE-UP; ADMINISTRATIVE COSTS
AND BENEFITS ETC. APART FROM THE REQUESTS FOR PERSONAL FILES,
THE LEVEL OF DEMAND HAS BEEN RELATIVELY LOW; MINISTERIAL
ACCOUNTABILITY REMAINS UNCHANGED; THE LEGISLATION HAS
SUCCESSFULLY PROTECTED GOVERNMENT SECRETS; AND THE OVERALL
COSTS HAVE NOT PROVED TO BE TOO GREAT. IT CONCLUDES THAT FOI
HAS NOT REALIZED ITS MORE AMBITIOUS OBJECTIVES, SUCH AS
INCREASING PUBLIC PARTICIPATION IN DECISION-MAKING, BUT AT
THE SAME TIME, IT HAS NOT FUFILED MANY OF ITS OPPONENTS'
WORST FEARS.

04109 HAZLETON, W.A.; HOY-HAZLETON, S.
TERRORISM AND THE MARXIST LEFT: PERU'S STRUGGLE AGAINST
SENDERO LUMINOSO
TERRORISM, 11(6) (1988), 471-470.
THE POLITICAL BALANCE IN PERU SINCE THE RETURN OF

DEMOCRATIC GOVERNMENT IN 1980 HAS SHIFTED TO THE LEFT, AND
THE UNITED LEFT (IZQUIERDA UNIDA OR IU) IS CONSIDERED A
SERIOUS CONTENDER IN THE 1990 ELECTIONS. THIS PAPER
INVESTIGATES IU'S PROSPECTS FOR SUCCESS IN PRESENTING A
CLEAR ALTERNATIVE WITHIN THE COUNTRY'S MARXIST COALITION AND
IN UNDERMINING SUPPORT FOR THE ARMED REVOLUTIONARY GROUP
SENDERO LUMINOSO. THE ORIGINS OF IU ARE TRACED FROM THE 1978
CONSTITUENT ASSEMBLY ELECTIONS, AND ITS ORGANIZATION,
STRUCTURE, AND TACTICS ARE EVALUATED IN TERMS OF ITS
EFFECTIVENESS. IF IT ACHIEVES POWER, IT WILL FACE ITS
GREATEST CHALLENGE FROM SENDERO LUMINOSO, THE MILITANT
MAOIST GROUP THAT HAS BEEN RESPONSIBLE FOR MUCH OF THE
TERRORISM THAT HAS GRIPPED PERU IN THIS DECADE. THE AUTHORS
DESCRIBE SENDERO'S STRATEGY AND TACTICS AND THOSE OF ITS
CHIEF RIVAL, THE MRTA. FINALLY THE PAPER EXPLORES IU'S
ALTERNATIVES FOR DEALING WITH THESE RADICAL LEFTIST GROUPS
AND THE POLITICAL VIOLENCE THEY EXPOUSE.

04110 HAZLETT, T.W.
THE FAIRNESS DOCTRINE AND THE FIRST AMENDMENT
PUBLIC INTEREST, (96) (SUM 89), 103-116.
THE AUTHOR DISCUSSES THE FEDERAL COMMUNICATIONS
COMMISSION'S FAIRNESS DOCTRINE AND HOW VARIOUS PRESIDENTIAL
ADMINISTRATIONS HAVE INTERPRETED IT. HE ALSO CONSIDERS THE
ISSUE OF WHETHER THE FAIRNESS DOCTRINE VIOLATES THE FIRST
AMENDMENT OF THE CONSTITUTION.

04111 HEAD, I.L.
SOUTH-NORTH DANGERS
FOREIGN AFFAIRS, 68(3) (SUM 89), 71-86.
THE NORTH-SOUTH RELATIONSHIP IS A DIVERSE AND CONFUSING
WEB. TO UNDERSTAND, TO RESPOND EFFECTIVELY, AND TO ENSURE A
CONSTRUCTIVE OUTCOME IS AS DEMANDING A TASK AS ANY THAT
FACES HUMANKIND. IT IS DEMANDING NOT ONLY IN TERMS OF
SUBSTANCE, BUT ALSO BECAUSE OF ATTITUDES WELL ENTRENCHED IN
BOTH NORTH AND SOUTH. IT IS THE MOST IMPORTANT TASK, SINCE
IT SUBSUMES, OR INEVITABLY WILL SUBSUME, ALL THE OTHERS. THE
NORTH MAY BE MOST IN PERIL BECAUSE THE MOMENTUM OF EVENTS
IMPACTING UPON IT IS IN EXCESS OF ITS WILLINGNESS TO RESPOND.
IF IT IS NOT WILLING TO BECOME AWARE, TO CHANGE ITS
UNSUSTAINABLE ATTITUDE OF SUPERIORITY, AND TO TAKE ACTION TO
REDUCE DRAMATICALLY IN THE SOUTH THE BROAD INCIDENCE OF
ABSOLUTE POVERTY, THEN NORTH ECONOMIC WELFARE, SOCIAL
TRANQUILITY AND POLITICAL STABILITY WILL NOT SIMPLY BE AT
RISK-INCREASINGLY THEY WILL BE IN JEOPARDY.

04112 HEALEY, E.J.
CANADA AND THE UNITED STATES: PARTNERS IN DEFENSE
NATO'S SIXTEEN NATIONS, 34(6) (OCT 89), 13-14, 17 (SPECIAL
SECTION).
FORMAL US-CANADIAN DEFENSE COOPERATION DATES BACK TO
WORLD WAR II AND THE NEED TO DEFEND THE SAME CONTINENT,
WHICH HAS SPAWNED SEVERAL BILATERAL SECURITY AGREEMENTS.
ARMAMENTS COOPERATION PREDATES THE 1988 FREE TRADE AGREEMENT
IN THE FORM OF NUMEROUS DEFENCE DEVELOPMENT AND DEFENCE
PRODUCTION ARRANGEMENTS. THE DEFENCE PRODUCTION SHARING
PROGRAM GIVES CANADIAN INDUSTRY AN EQUAL OPPORTUNITY TO
COMPETE WITH US INDUSTRY ON A COMMERCIAL BASIS. NOW, AS
EUROPE MOVES TOWARD A SINGLE ECONOMIC MARKET, CANADA IS
SUPPORTING EFFORTS TOWARD GREATER DEFENCE COOPERATION AND
DEVELOPMENT OF A NATO INDUSTRIAL BASE.

04113 HEALEY, N.M.
"COMPLETING THE INTERNAL MARKET" IN EUROPE: THE ROAD TO
1992
CONTEMPORARY REVIEW, 254(1481) (JUN 89), 281-288.
THE OBJECTIVE OF 1992 CREATE A 'SINGLE', OR COMMON,
MARKET IN EUROPE, DEFINED BY THE EUROPEAN COMMUNITY (EC) AS
'AN AREA WITHOUT INTERNAL FRONTIERS IN WHICH THE FREE
MOVEMENT OF GOODS, PERSONS, SERVICES AND CAPITAL IS ENSURED.
" THIS ARTICLE OFFERS AN OVERVIEW OF 1992 AGAINST THE
ECONOMIC AND POLITICAL BACKGROUND OF THE INITIATIVE. IT
ARGUES THAT WHILE THE ULTIMATE GOAL OF A EUROPE SANS
FRONTIERES MAY NEVER BE ACHIEVED, THE ADVANCES MADE IN THE
PRESENT DRIVE FOR GREATER UNITY ARE TO BE WELCOMED.

04114 HEALEY, N.M.
A DECADE OF CONSERVATIVE ANTI-INFLATION POLICY: WHAT HAS
GONE WRONG?
CONTEMPORARY REVIEW, 255(1487) (DEC 89), 297-302.
THIS ARTICLE EXAMINES INFLATION IN BRITAIN IN THE 60'S
AND 70'S AND THE GOVERNMENT'S ATTEMPT TO RIGHT THE EXCESSES
OF THE PAST. SINCE THE INFLATION RATE IS STILL THE SAME,
THIS ARTICLE ASKS WHAT HAS GONE WRONG; WAS GOVERNMENT
STRATEGY FLAWED IN SOME WAY; DID THE GOVERNMENT MISHANDLE
ITS EXECUTION?; THEN ATTEMPTS TO PROVIDE ANSWERS TO THESE
AND RELATED QUESTIONS. IT CONCLUDES THAT IN THE FINAL
ANALYSIS ANTI-INFLATION POLICY CANNOT BE DIVORCED FROM THE
SUPPLY-SIDE.

04115 HEALEY, N.M.
THE US BUDGET DEFICIT AND THE 1988 PRESIDENTIAL CAMPAIGN
CONTEMPORARY REVIEW, 254(1479) (APR 89), 169-173.
THE REASON FOR THE RELUCTANCE OF MESSRS BUSH AND DUKAKIS

TO JOIN IN IDEOLOGICAL COMBAT OVER THE DEFICIT ISSUE WAS
THAT, BY ACCIDENT RATHER THAN DESIGN, THE TWO POLITICAL
PARTIES FOUND THEIR TRADITIONAL ROLES IN WHAT WOULD
OTHERWISE HAVE BEEN A SET-PIECE SKIRMISH DISCONCERTINGLY
REVERSED. THE REPUBLICANS, HISTORICALLY WEDDED TO THE IDEALS
OF 'SOUND MONEY' AND BALANCED BUDGETS, HAVE PRESIDED OVER
THE LARGEST BUDGET DEFICITS IN AMERICAN HISTORY DURING MR
REAGAN'S EIGHT YEARS IN THE WHITE HOUSE CONVERSELY, THE
DEMOCRATIC PARTY, WHICH PIONEERED DEFICIT FINANCING DURING
THE KENNEDY-JOHNSON ERA, HAS BEEN A LONG-STANDING ADVOCATE
OF BUDGET DEFICITS TO COUNTER UNEMPLOYMENT. BOTH PARTIES
THUS LACKED THE IDEOLOGICAL BAGGAGE AND THE POLITICAL
COMMITMENT TO SWITCH SIDES EFFECTIVELY IN THE PRE-ELECTION
BUDGET DEBATE.

04116 HEARD, A.
RECOGNIZING THE VARIETY AMONG CONSTITUTIONAL CONVENTIONS
CANADIAN JOURNAL OF POLITICAL SCIENCE, XXII(1) (MAR 89),
63-82.
ABSTRACT. THIS ARTICLE ARGUES THAT THE TRADITIONAL VIEWS
OF CONSTITUTIONAL CONVENTIONS HAVE FAILED TO ILLUMINATE THE
VARIETY AMONG THIS IMPORTANT GROUP OF CONSTITUTIONAL RULES.
A FRESH EXAMINATION OF CONVENTIONAL RULES EXPLAINS HOW THEY
MAY VARY IN PRECISION, ACCEPTANCE AND IMPORTANCE TO BASIC
CONSTITUTIONAL PRINCIPLES AND PROCESSES. A HIERARCHIAL
ORDERING OF FIVE TYPES OF CONSTITUTIONAL RULES IS PROPOSED
AS A REPLACEMENT FOR THE SIMPLE DICHOTOMY BETWEEN USAGE AND
CONVENTION THAT IS CURRENTLY ACCEPTED. THE IMPLICATIONS OF
SUCH AN ORDERING, WHICH REACH BEYOND MERE ANALYTIC
CLASSIFICATION, ARE THEN DISCUSSED.

04117 HEARL, D.
LUXEMBOURG
ELECTORAL STUDIES, 8(3) (DEC 89), 296-304.
THIS ARTICLE EXPLORES ELECTIONS IN LUXEMBOURG AS ONE EC
MEMBER STATE IN WHICH, IN TERMS OF OUTCOME AND CAMPAIGNING,
EUROPEAN ELECTIONS MATTER THE LEAST. THE TECHNICAL FEATURES
& THE COUNTRY'S SMALL SIZE AND CONSEQUENT HIGH RATIO OF
CANDIDATES TO VOTERS, COMBINE TO MAKE 'PERSONALIZED' VOTING
MUCH MORE IMPORTANT IN LUXEMBOURG THAN IN ANY OTHER EC
MEMBER STATE. THE POLITICAL PARTIES, THE CAMPAIGN ISSUES,
AND THE EUROPEAN CAMPAIGN ARE EACH EXAMINED AND THE RESULTS
ARE DETAILED.

04118 HEATH, J.M.
THE INSTITUTIONALISED REVOLUTION
ENCOUNTER, LXXII(3) (MAR 89), 3-7.
THE AUTHOR BRIEFLY REVIEWS THE REVOLUTIONARY PERIOD IN
MEXICO THAT BEGAN UNDER FRANCISCO MADERO IN 1910 AND ENDED
IN 1940, WHEN GENERAL MANUEL CARDENAS DECIDED NOT TO RUN FOR
A SECOND TERM AS PRESIDENT AND THE PRINCIPLE OF "NO RE-
ELECTION" WAS FINALLY ESTABLISHED.

04119 HEATHERLY, C., (ED.); EISENACH, J.; PINES, B., (ED.)
A WHITE HOUSE STRATEGY FOR DEREGULATION; MANDATE FOR
LEADERSHIP III: POLICY STRATEGIES FOR THE 1990S
THE HERITAGE FOUNDATION, WASHINGTON, DC, 1989, 87-103.
THE ARTICLE EXAMINES THE RECORD OF THE REAGAN
ADMINISTRATION WITH REGARDS TO GOVERNMENTAL REGULATION. IT
CONCLUDES THAT ALTHOUGH THEIR STATED GOAL WAS DEREGULATION
AND REDUCTION OF THE SIZE OF GOVERNMENT, THEIR LEGACY WAS
ONE OF MERELY SLOWING GOVERNMENT GROWTH. THE NEW PRESIDENT
WILL ALSO FACE SIGNIFICANT CHALLENGES TO ANY ATTEMPTS AT
DEREGULATION, BUT INCREMENTAL IMPROVEMENTS ARE POSSIBLE. THE
ARTICLE OUTLINES A STRATEGY TO CLEARLY IDENTIFY OBJECTIVES
OF REGULATORY POLICY, RETAKE CONTROL FROM CONGRESS, AND TO
IMPLEMENT A REGULATORY BUDGET.

04120 HEATHERLY, C., (ED.); MOFFIT, R.; PINES, B., (ED.); TESKE,
R.
CONGRESSIONAL RELATIONS AND PUBLIC AFFAIRS; MANDATE FOR
LEADERSHIP III: POLICY STRATEGIES FOR THE 1990S
THE HERITAGE FOUNDATION, WASHINGTON, DC, 1989, 817-836.
IN ITS ANALYSIS OF CONGRESSIONAL RELATIONS AND PUBLIC
AFFAIRS THE ARTICLE BEGINS WITH BACKGROUND INFORMATION
INCLUDING THE INSTITUTIONAL SETTING, THE AGENCY SETTING, AND
THE PEOPLE AND PROCESSES INVOLVED. THE ARTICLE ALSO OUTLINES
STRATEGIC PRINCIPLES NECESSARY TO GUARANTEE SUCCESS
INCLUDING KNOWING WHEN TO COMPROMISE, SEIZING THE INITIATIVE,
AND MOBILIZING SUPPORT. THE ARTICLE ALSO EXAMINES THE
IMPORTANCE OF PUBLIC AFFAIRS AND INTEREST GROUPS AND
ILLUSTRATES THE PRINCIPLES IN ACTION IN A CASE STUDY
INVOLVING THE ADOPTION OF MEDICARE PROSPECTIVE PAYMENT IN
1983.

04121 HEATHERLY, C., (ED.); HOLMES, K.; PINES, B., (ED.); RIVKIN,
D.
EXECUTIVE-LEGISLATIVE RELATIONS AND US NATIONAL SECURITY;
MANDATE FOR LEADERSHIP: POLICY STRATEGIES FOR THE 1990S
THE HERITAGE FOUNDATION, WASHINGTON, DC, 1989, 477-486.
THE ARTICLE EXPLORES THE RELATIONSHIP BETWEEN THE
EXECUTIVE BRANCH AND THE LEGISLATURE IN THE AREA OF FOREIGN
POLICY AND NATIONAL SECURITY. SPECIAL EMPHASIS IS PLACED ON
THE INCREASING ENCROACHMENTS OF AN "IMPERIAL" CONGRESS ON

TRADITIONAL EXECUTIVE POWERS. THE ACTIONS OF THE REAGAN
ADMINISTRATION AND ITS ATTEMPTS TO DECREASE THIS
ENCROACHMENT ARE ALSO DISCUSSED. THE ARTICLE CONCLUDES WITH
RECOMMENDATIONS FOR THE FUTURE PRESIDENT DESIGNED TO "DRAW
THE LINE" ON CONGRESSIONAL MICROMANAGEMENT OF FOREIGN POLICY
AND ESTABLISH A "PRINCIPLED APPROACH" TO EXECUTIVE-
LEGISLATIVE RELATIONS.

04122 HEATHERLY, C., (ED.); BUTLER, H.; PINES, B., (ED.);
RUSSELL, W.; YANDLE, B.
INDEPENDENT REGULATORY AGENCIES; MANDATE FOR LEADERSHIP
III: POLICY STRATEGIES FOR THE 1990S
THE HERITAGE FOUNDATION, WASHINGTON, DC, 1989, 399-418.
MUCH OF THE RESPONSIBILTY FOR ADMINISTERING AND
ENFORCING FEDERAL REGULATORY LAWS FALLS TO AGENCIES OUTSIDE
THE ORTHODOX CABINET DEPARTMENTS. KNOWN GENERICALLY AS
"INDEPENDENT REGULATORY AGENCIES", THEY ARE NOT UNDER DIRECT
CONTROL OF THE PRESIDENT. THE CHAPTER OUTLINES AND EXAMINES
THE FUNCTIONS OF SOME OF THESE AGENCIES INCLUDING THE
FEDERAL COMMUNICATIONS COMMISSION, THE FEDERAL TRADE
COMMISSION, AND THE SECURITIES AND EXCHANGE COMMISSION. IT
EXAMINES THE ACTIVITIES OF THESE AGENCIES UNDER THE REAGAN
ADMINISTRATION AND OFFERS SUGGESTIONS FOR FUTURE POLICYMAKERS

04123 HEATHERLY, C., (ED.); MOORE, S.; PINES, B., (ED.)
MANAGING THE FEDERAL BUDGET; MANDATE FOR LEADERSHIP III:
POLICY STRATEGIES FOR THE 1990S
THE HERITAGE FOUNDATION, WASHINGTON, DC, 1989, 63-86.
THE ARTICLE DISCUSSES WHAT IS "PERHAPS THE MOST CRITICAL
DOMESTIC POLICY CHALLENGE CONFRONTING THE NEW ADMINISTRATION:
THE ENORMOUS BUDGET DEFICIT. THE AUTHOR ARGUES THAT A
BALANCED BUDGET BY 1993 WITHOUT NEW TAX INCREASES OR PAINFUL
CUTS IN SPENDING IS POSSIBLE. HE OUTLINES A SERIES OF
STRATEGIES DESIGNED TO MAINTAIN STEADY ECONOMIC GROWTH, HOLD
THE GROWTH RATE OF TOTAL SPENDING TO BETWEEN THREE AND FOUR
PERCENT ANNUALLY, AND BLOCK THE PASSAGE OF NEW SPENDING
INITIAVES THAT WOULD INCREASE THE DEFICIT. HE OUTLINES A NEW
BUDGET ACT AND A FOUR YEAR DEFICIT REDUCTION STRATEGY THAT
WOULD BALANCE THE BUDGET BY THE NEXT PRESIDENTIAL ELECTION.

04124 HEATHERLY, C., (ED.); PINES, B., (ED.)
MANDATE FOR LEADERSHIP III; POLICY STRATEGIES FOR THE 1990S
THE HERITAGE FOUNDATION, WASHINGTON, DC, 1989, 927.
THE BOOK IS A COLLECTION OF POLICY RECOMMENDATIONS FOR
THE CONSIDERATION OF THE NEXT PRESIDENT. IT ANALYZES THE
WHITE HOUSE AND POLICY LEADERSHIP, DOMESTIC POLICY, FOREIGN
POLICY AND NATIONAL DEFENSE, AND AGENCY MANAGEMENT OF POLICY
INITIATIVES AND GIVES SUGGESTIONS REGARDING A PLETHORA OF
SPECIFIC AGENCIES AND POLICIES. BASIC GOALS ADVOACTED
INCLUDE STRENGTHENING THE IDEALS OF INDIVIDUAL LIBERTY,
LIMITED GOVERNMENT, FREE ENTERPIRSE, AND A STRONG NATIONAL
DEFENSE.

04125 HEATHERLY, C., (ED.); PINES, B., (ED.); UHLMANN, M.
ORGANIZING FOR POLICY LEADERSHIP: A MEMO TO THE PRESIDENT;
MANDATE FOR LEADERSHIP III: POLICY STRATEGIES FOR THE 1990S
THE HERITAGE FOUNDATION, WASHINGTON, DC, 1989, 23-38.
THE AUTHOR LOOKS AHEAD TO THE NEW PRESIDENT AND THE JOB
OF ORGANIZING THE EXECUTIVE BRANCH. HE GIVES SUGGESTIONS
REGARDING THE FORMATION AND STRUCTURE OF THE WHITE HOUSE
STAFF, THE CABINET, THE OFFICE OF MANAGEMENT AND BUDGET, THE
DOMESTIC POLICY STAFF, AND THE NATIONAL SECURITY COUNCIL. HE
ARGUES THAT THE OPTIMAL ORGANIZATION WILL BE OPEN AND
FLEXIBLE AND WILL EMPHASIZE THE AUTHORITY AND THE
ACCOUNTABILITY OF THE PRESIDENT.

04126 HEATHERLY, C., (ED.); MORRIS, J.; PINES, B., (ED.)
POLICY-MAKING BY REGULATION AND GOVERNMENT-BY-LAWSUIT;
MANDATE FOR LEADERSHIP III: POLICY STRATEGIES FOR THE 1990S
THE HERITAGE FOUNDATION, WASHINGTON, DC, 1989, 867-882.
RECENT STATISTICS DISCLOSE THAT A HIGHLY DECENTRALIZED
AND FRAGMENTED FEDERAL GOVERNMENT IS DOING A GREAT DEAL OF
REGULATING AND AN EXTRAORDINARY AMOUNT OF LITIGATING. THE
CHAPTER OFFERS SOME INSIGHTS INTO HOW THE CHALLENGES AND
PROBLEMS PRESENTED BY THIS LITIGATION MAZE CAN BE VIEWED AS
OPPORTUNITIES FOR ADVANCING THE ADMINISTRATION'S POLICY
AGENDA. IT EXAMINES THE POLICYMAKER AS REGULATOR AND AS
LITIGATOR AND STUDIES THE REGULATORY PROCESS IN ORDER TO
GIVE THE NEXT PRESIDENT RECOMMENDATIONS ON HOW TO ACHIEVE
DESIRED GOALS AND AGENDAS.

04127 HEATHERLY, C., (ED.); IKLE, F.; PINES, B., (ED.)
PUBLIC DIPLOMACY; MANDATE FOR LEADERSHIP III: POLICY
STRATEGIES FOR THE 1990S
THE HERITAGE FOUNDATION, WASHINGTON, DC, 1989, 635-644.
IN CONTRAST TO TRADITIONAL DIPLOMACY, WHICH DEALS WITH
GOVERNMENT OFFICIALS, PUBLIC DIPLOMACY SEEKS TO ADVANCE
FOREIGN POLICY OBJECTIVES BY INFLUENCING THE GENERAL
PUBLIC'S ATTITUDES TOWARD AND PERCEPTIONS OF CURRENT WORLD
AFFAIRS. THE CHAPTER ANALYZES THE EFFORTS OF THE REAGAN
ADMINISTRATION TO REVERSE THE DOWNWARD TREND OF THE WORLD
IMAGE OF THE US. IT ALSO OFFERS POLICY RECOMMENDATIONS
DESIGNED TO INCREASE FAVORABLE PUBLIC PERCEPTION OF THE US.
BASIC GOALS OF THESE POLICIES INCLUDE: TELL THE TRUTH TO THE

WORLD ABOUT THE US AND ITS FOREIGN POLICY, CONVEY THE
ADVANTAGES OF THE AMERICAN POLITICAL AND ECONOMIC SYSTEM AND
DEMOCRATIC CAPITALISM IN GENERAL, AND ENCOURAGE NATIONS TO
ATTAIN AND GUARD INDIVIDUAL LIBERTIES, HUMAN RIGHTS,
DEMOCRATIC POLITICAL INSTITUTIONS, AND PRIVATE FREE-MARKET
ECONOMIC ENTERPRISE.

04128 HEATHERLY, C., (ED.); PINES, B., (ED.); VALIS, W.
PUBLIC LIASON AND COALITION BUILDING; MANDATE FOR
LEADERSHIP III: POLICY STRATEGIES FOR THE 1990S
THE HERITAGE FOUNDATION, WASHINGTON, DC, 1989, 51-62.
IN ITS ANALYSIS OF RELATIONS BETWEEN THE PRESIDENT AND
THE GENERAL POPULACE OF THE US THE ARTICLE FOCUSES ON THE
OFFICE OF PUBLIC LIASON (OPL) AND ITS PRECURSORS. IT
OUTLINES A BRIEF HISTORY OF THE OPL BEGINING WITH THE
EISENHOWER ADMINISTRATION AND EXAMINES THE ROLE AND
STRUCTURE OF THE OPL. SOME OF THE STRATEGIC AND OPERATIONAL
FUNCTIONS OF THE OPL INCLUDE: CONSTITUENCY BUILDING, POLICY
ADVOCACY, AND POLICY FACILITATION. THE ARTICLE CONCLUDES
WITH A BRIEF ANALYSIS OF WHAT MAKES A SUCCESSFUL OPL.

04129 HEATHERLY, C., (ED.); GRIZZLE, C.; PINES, B., (ED.)
THE DEPARTMENT OF AGRICULTURE; MANDATE FOR LEADERSHIP III:
POLICY STRATEGIES FOR THE 1990S
(1989), 137-154.
THE ARTICLE EXAMINES THE DEPARTMENT OF AGRICULTURE, ITS
FUNCTIONS, AND SOME OF THE INSTITUTIONAL CONSTRAINTS THAT
LIMIT ITS INFLUENCE AND EFFECTIVENESS. IT OUTLINES THE
RECORD OF THE REAGAN ADMINISTRATION WITH REGARDS TO
AGRICULTURE. IT CONCLUDES WITH A SERIES OF POLICY
RECOMMENDATIONS REGARDING AGRICULTURE REFORM. THESE INCLUDE:
REFORMING FARM SUBSIDY PROGRAMS, EXPANDING TRADE IN
AGRICULTURAL PRODUCTS, REDUCING FARMER DEPENDENCY ON FEDERAL
CREDIT, IMPROVING THE INCENTIVES FOR LAND CONSERVATION, AND
TARGETING ASSISTANCE PROGRAMS TO THE NEEDY.

04130 HEATHERLY, C., (ED.); LACY, J.; PINES, B., (ED.)
THE DEPARTMENT OF COMMERCE AND THE US TRADE REPRESENTATIVE;
MANDATE FOR LEADERSHIP III: POLICY STRATEGIES FOR THE
1990S
THE HERITAGE FOUNDATION, WASHINGTON, DC, 1989, 155-174.
THE ARTICLE ANALYZES THE DEPARTMENT OF COMMERCE AND ITS
FUNCTIONS AND THE RECORD OF THE REAGAN ADMINISTRATION WITH
REGARDS TO TRADE. IT OUTLINES THE GOALS OF INCREASED US
COMPETITIVENESS AS EMBODIED IN INCREASED NATIONAL STANDARDS
OF LIVING AND ECONOMIC GROWTH, INCREASED CONSUMER CHOICE,
AND EXPANDED OPPORTUNITIES FOR PRODUCTIVE EMPLOYMENT. IT
OUTLINES POLICY RECOMMENDATIONS DESIGNED TO FURTHER THESE
GOALS. THESE INCLUDES ESTABLISHING FREE TRADE AREAS,
REMOVING IMPORT RESTRICTIONS, REMOVING EXPORT RESTRICTIONS,
PROTECTING PROPERTY RIGHTS, ENCOURAGING COMMERCIAL USE OF
SPACE, REORGANIZING THE INTERNATIONAL TRADE ADMINISTRATION,
AND ELIMINATING UNNECESSARY OFFICES. THE ARTICLE CONCLUDES
WITH SPECIFIC INITIAVES SUGGESTED FOR IMMEDIATE
IMPLEMENTATION.

04131 HEATHERLY, C., (ED.); HOLMES, K.; KOSMINSKY, J.; PINES, B.,
(ED.); SCHNEIDER, W.; ZAKHEIM, D.
THE DEPARTMENT OF DEFENSE; MANDATE FOR LEADERSHIP III:
POLICY STRATEGIES FOR THE 1990S
THE HERITAGE FOUNDATION, WASINGTON, DC, 1989, 685-798.
THE DEPARTMENT OF DEFENSE IS THE SUBJECT OF EXTENDED
ANALYSIS IN THIS CHAPTER. THE ACTIONS OF THE REAGAN
ADMINISTRATION WITH REGARDS TO DEFENSE ARE ANALYZED AS ARE
THE INSTITUTIONAL CONSTRAINTS THAT THE DEPARTMENT OPERATES
UNDER. SPECIFIC TOPICS OF DISCUSSION INCLUDE: STRATEGIC
OFFENSIVE FORCES, STRATEGIC DEFENSE, ARMS CONTROL, MILITARY
SPACE POLICY, THE MILITARY SERVICES, THE US AND NATO, LOW
INTENSITY CONFLICT, STRATEGIC TRADE, DEFENSE MANAGEMENT AND
ACQUISITIONS, AND DEFENSE INDUSTRIAL PREPAREDNESS.

04132 HEATHERLY, C., (ED.); KIMBERLING, C.; PINES, B., (ED.)
THE DEPARTMENT OF EDUCATION; MANDATE FOR LEADERSHIP III:
POLICY STRATEGIES FOR THE 1990S
THE HERITAGE FOUNDATION, WASHINGTON, DC, 1989, 175-194.
THE ARTICLE ARGUES THAT THE NATION'S TEACHERS, PUPILS,
AND SCHOOLS DO NOT NEED A FEDERAL DEPARTMENT OF EDUCATION,
BUT ACKNOWLEDGES ITS EXISTENCE AND OUTLINES ITS FUNCTIONS.
IT REVIEWS THE RECORD OF THE REAGAN ADMINISTRATION WITH
REGARDS TO EDUCATION AND OFFERS POLICY RECOMMENDATIONS FOR
FUTURE EDUCATIONAL POLICY. THESE INCLUDE POLICIES THAT WOULD
ENCOURAGE EQUITY AND CHOICE, RESTORE EXCELLENCE TO
ELEMENTARY AND SECONDARY EDUCATION, REFORM VOCATIONAL
EDUCATION AND TRAINING, AND IMPROVE FINANCIAL ACCOUNTABILITY
FOR HIGHER EDUCATION.

04133 HEATHERLY, C., (ED.); COPULOS, M.; PINES, B., (ED.)
THE DEPARTMENT OF ENERGY; MANDATE FOR LEADERSHIP III:
POLICY STRATEGIES FOR THE 1990S
THE HERITAGE FOUNDATION, WASHINGTON, DC, 1989. 195-212.
THE ARTICLE OUTLINES THE FUNCTIONS AND ROLES OF THE US
DEPARTMENT OF ENERGY. IT ALSO ANALYZES SOME OF THE
CHALLENGES THAT WILL CONFRONT THE DOE IN THE FUTURE AND
OUTLINES POTENTIAL SOLUTIONS FOR POLICY CONSIDERATION. SOME

OF THE ACTIONS PROPOSED INCLUDE THE UPGRADING OF PRODUCTION
OF NUCLEAR MATERIALS, THE REVIVING OF THE NUCLEAR INDUSTRY,
THE ESTABLISHMENT OF STRONGER INCENTIVES TO IMPROVE DOMESTIC
OIL AND NATURAL GAS PRODUCTION, IMPROVEMENT OF THE
ENVIRONMENT THROUGH THE USE OF NATURAL GAS AND ALCOHOL FUELS,
THE DEREGULATION OF THE ELECTRIC UTILITY INDUSTRY, AND THE
MERGING OF THE DEPARTMENTS OF ENERGY AND INTERIOR. THE
MAJORITY OF THE PROPOSED REFORMS EMPHASIZE THE APPROACH USED
BY THE REAGAN ADMINISTRATION WHICH FOCUSES ON MARKET FORCES
AND DEREGULATION.

04134 HEATHERLY, C., (ED.); BUTLER, S.; DOCKSAI, R.; FERRARA, P.;
PINES, B., (ED.)
THE DEPARTMENT OF HEALTH AND HUMAN SERVICES; MANDATE FOR
LEADERSHIP III: POLICY STRATEGIES FOR THE 1990S
THE HERITAGE FOUNDATION, WASHINGTON, DC, 1989, 229-284.
THE DEPARTMENT OF HEALTH AND HUMAN SERVICES IS THE
LARGEST DOMESTIC CABINET DEPARTMENT. IT HANDLES MATTERS
RANGING FROM THE SOCIAL SECURITY SYSTEM TO HEALTH CARE FOR
THE POOR. THE ARTICLE IS DIVIDED INTO THREE SECTIONS: HEALTH,
WELFARE, AND SOCIAL SECURITY. IT OUTLINES THE FUNCTIONS OF
THE AGENCY, THE INSTITUTIONAL CONSTRAINTS THAT THE AGENCY
OPERATES UNDER AND EXAMINES THE RECORD OF THE REAGAN
ADMINISTRATION WITH REGARDS TO THESE ISSUES. THE ARTICLE
ALSO PROPOSES A PLETHORA OF REFORMS IN EACH AREA RANGING
FROM DECENTRALIZATION OF THE WELFARE SYSTEM TO REFORMING
INDIVIDUAL RETIREMENT ACCOUNTS.

04135 HEATHERLY, C., (ED.); FERRARA, P.; PINES, B., (ED.)
THE DEPARTMENT OF HOUSING AND URBAN DEVELOPMENT; MANDATE
FOR LEADERSHIP III: POLICY STRATEGIES FOR THE 1990S
THE HERITAGE FOUNDATION, WASHINGTON, DC, 1989, 285-304.
THE ARTICLE STATES THAT THE GOAL OF THE DEPARTMENT OF
HOUSING AND URBAN DEVELOPMENT SHOULD BE TO PROVIDE HOUSING
ASSISTANCE DIRECTLY TO THE POOR IN AN EFFICIENT,
COSTEFFECTIVE MANNER THAT HARNESSES FREE-MARKET COMPETITION
AND INCENTIVES. IT OUTLINES A SUMMARY OF THE FUNCTIONS OF
THE HUD AND ANALYZES THE RECORD OF THE REAGAN ADMINISTRATION
WITH REGARDS TO THIS AGENCY. IT PROPOSES THE USE OF HOUSING
VOUCHERS TO EMPOWER THE POOR, THE INCREASE OF RESIDENT
MANAGEMENT AND OWNERSHIP OF PUBLIC HOUSING, SPURRING
COMPETITION IN HOUSING FINANCE, AND THE ELIMINATION OF
WASTEFUL FEDERAL ECONOMIC DEVELOPMENT PROGRAMS. THE ISSUE OF
HOMELESSNESS IS ALSO ADDRESSED.

04136 HEATHERLY, C., (ED.); BREGER, M.; PINES, B., (ED.)
THE DEPARTMENT OF JUSTICE; MANDATE FOR LEADERSHIP III:
POLICY STRATEGIES FOR THE 1990S
THE HERITAGE FOUNDATION, WASHINGTON, DC, 1989, 323-342.
THE ARTICLE DISCUSSES THE WIDE RANGE OF RESPONSIBILITIES
THAT THE DEPARTMENT OF JUSTICE FACES. THESE RANGE FROM
ENFORCING THE NATION'S CIVIL LAWS TO MANAGING FEDERAL PRISON.
IT OUTLINES THE AGENCIES MANY FUNCTIONS AND OFFERS POLICY
PROPOSALS TO MEET THE GOALS OF CREATING A COLOR-BLIND
SOCIETY, WINNING THE WAR ON DRUGS, PROTECTING AMERICANS FROM
CRIME, ENSURING ACCESS TO JUSTICE, AND ASSURING ETHICS IN
GOVERNMENT. PROPOSED RESTRUCTURING OF THE DEPARTMENT AS WELL
AS SPECIFIC POLICIES SUCH AS PRISON REFORM, REFORM IN
IMMIGRATION POLICY, AND TORT LAW REFORM ARE ALSO DISCUSSED.

04137 HEATHERLY, C., (ED.); PETERSON, W.; PINES, B., (ED.)
THE DEPARTMENT OF LABOR AND THE NATIONAL LABOR RELATIONS
BOARD; MANDATE FOR LEADERSHIP III: POLICY STRATEGIES FOR
THE 1990'S
THE HERITAGE FOUNDATION, WASHINGTON, DC, 1989, 343-360.
THE DEPARTMENT OF LABOR ADMINISTERS FEDERAL UNEMPLOYMENT
AND JOB TRAINING PROGRAMS, ENFORCES FEDERAL SAFETY AND WAGE
REGULATIONS, AND IN GENERAL OVERSEES US LABOR POLICY. THE
NATIONAL LABOR RELATIONS BOARD IS AN INDEPENDENT REGULATORY
AGENCY WHICH PROTECTS EMPLOYEE RIGHTS AND DEALS WITH LABOR
MANAGEMENT RELATIONS. THE ARTICLE EXAMINES THE RECORD OF THE
REAGAN ADMINISTRATION WITH REGARDS TO THESE ISSUES AND
OFFERS SUGGESTIONS FOR FUTURE POLICY. SOME OF THE GOALS AND
PROPOSALS INCLUDE: EDUCATING THE PUBLIC ON PRODUCTIVITY AND
FLEXIBILITY, BLOCKING MANDATED BENEFITS LEGISLATION,
EXPANDING EMPLOYEE CHOICE, OUTLAWING LABOR VIOLENCE,
ESTABLISHING MARKEY WAGES, EXPANDING THE RIGHT TO WORK AT
HOME, AND HALTING SUBSTANCE ABUSE IN THE WORKPLACE.

04138 HEATHERLY, C., (ED.); JONES, G.; PINES, B., (ED.)
THE DEPARTMENT OF THE INTERIOR; MANDATE FOR LEADERSHIP III:
POLICY STRATEGIES FOR THE 1990'S
THE HERITAGE FOUNDATION, WASHINGTON, DC, 1989, 305-322.
THE ARTICLE BRIEFLY EXAMINES THE FUNCTIONS OF THE
DEPARTMENT OF THE INTERIOR AND ASSESSES THE SUCCESSES AND
FAILURES OF THE REAGAN ADMINISTRATION. IN PROPOSING FUTURE
POLICY, THE ARTICLE UTILIZES TWO POLITICAL PRINCIPLES: THAT
THE GOVERNMENT SHOULD LEAVE TO THE PRIVATE SECTOR THOSE
ACTIVITIES THAT THE PRIVATE SECTOR CAN PERFORM BETTER, AND
THAT GOVERNMENT ACTIVITIES THAT MEET MAINLY STATE AND LOCAL
NEEDS SHOULD BE ADMINISTERED BY THOSE LEVELS OF GOVERNMENT.
SOME OF THE PROPOSED REFORMS INCLUDE: PUBLIC LAND MANAGEMENT
REFORM, THE DECENTRALIZATION OF PARK AND WILDERNESS AREAS
OWNERSHIP, THE IMPROVEMENT OF ACCESS TO FEDERALLY OWNED

MINERALS, AND THE INTRODUCTION OF MARKETS FOR WATER. REFORMS
REGARDING POLICY TOWARDS AMERICAN INDIANS AND THE US
TERRITORIES ARE ALSO DISCUSSED.

04139 HEATHERLY, C., (ED.); HUMBERT, T.; PINES, B., (ED.)
THE DEPARTMENT OF THE TREASURY; MANDATE FOR LEADERSHIP III:
POLICY STRATEGIES FOR THE 1990S
THE HERITAGE FOUNDATION, WASHINGTON, DC, 1989, 439-462.
THE DEPARTMENT OF THE TREASURY IS PRINCIPALLY
RESPONSIBLE FOR FORMULATING AND RECOMMENDING ECONOMIC,
FINANCIAL, TAX, AND FISCAL POLICIES. THE ARTICLE EXAMINES
THE TREASURY DEPARTMENT AND SUGGESTS FUTURE REFORMS TO SOLVE
CURRENT FISCAL AND BUDGETARY PROBLEMS. THESE REFORMS INCLUDE:
A REORGANIZATION OF THE DEPARTMENT, THE CONSTRUCTION OF A
NEUTRAL, YET PRO-FAMILY TAX SYSTEM, LONG AND SHORT TERM
SOLUTIONS TO THE THRIFT CRISIS, BANKING LAW REFORM, AND
POLICIES DESIGNED TO STABILIZE INTERNATIONAL FINANCE AND
MONETARY POLICY.

04140 HEATHERLY, C., (ED.); PINES, B., (ED.); STANLEY, R.
THE DEPARTMENT OF TRANSPORTATION; MANDATE FOR LEADERSHIP
III: POLICY STRATEGIES FOR THE 1990S
THE HERITAGE FOUNDATION, WASHINGTON, DC, 1989, 419-438.
THE DEPARTMENT OF TRANSPORTATION (DOT) WAS AN IMPORTANT
TOOL FOR THE REAGAN ADMINISTRATION IN THE MOVEMENT TOWARDS
DEREGULATION. AFTER A BRIEF SUMMARY OF THE FUNCTIONS OF THE
VARIOUS AGENCIES THAT MAKE UP THE DOT AND A DISCUSSION OF
THE INSTITUTIONAL CONSTRAINTS THAT THEY OPERATE UNDER, THE
ARTICLE OUTLINES A SERIES OF GOALS AND POLICIES REGARDING
THE FUTURE OF THE DOT. THESE INCLUDE: RESTRUCTURING AND
PRICING AIRPORT AND AIRWAY SERVICES; PROTECTING AIRLINE
COMPUTER RESERVATION SYSTEMS FROM REGULATION; IMPROVING
RAILROAD INDUSTRY EFFICIENCY; COMPLETING TRUCKING
DEREGULATION; ABOLISHING THE INTERSTATE COMMERCE COMMISSION;
ENDING PROTECTION FOR THE MARITIME INDUSTRY; AND
RESTRUCTURING FEDERAL SUPPORT FOR MASS TRANSIT.

04141 HEATHERLY, C., (ED.); CLARK, N.; PINES, B., (ED.)
THE ENVIRONMENTAL PROTECTION AGENCY; MANDATE FOR
LEADERSHIP III: POLICY STRATEGIES FOR THE 1990S
THE HERITAGE FOUNDATION, WASHINGTON, DC, 1989, 213-228.
IN ITS ANALYSIS OF THE EPA. THE AUTHOR ARGUES THAT THE
REAGAN ADMINISTRATION HAD A RARE OPPORTUNITY TO REFORM
AMERICA'S FLAWED ENVIRONMENTAL PROTECTION PROGRAMS, BUT
LARGELY FAILED TO DO SO. THE ARTICLE OUTLINES THE REAGAN
ENVIRONMENTAL RECORD AND EXAMINES THE FUNCTIONS OF THE EPA
AND THE INSTITUTIONAL CONSTRAINTS THAT IT OPERATED UNDER. IN
ORDER TO REVERSE THE TREND OF FEDERAL MISHANDLING OF
ENVIRONMENTAL ISSUES SEVERAL POLICIES ARE PROPOSED INCLUDING:
IMPROVING THE EFFECTIVENESS AND EFFICIENCY OF SUPERFUND,
THE USE OF MARKET MECHANISMS TO CLEAN THE AIR, THE EXPANSION
OF STATE AND LOCAL RESPONSIBILITY FOR SEWAGE WASTEWATER
TREATMENT, AND THE REMOVAL OF DISINCENTIVES TO PRIVATIZED
WASTEWATER TREATMENT.

04142 HEATHERLY, C., (ED.); CLINE, R.; PINES, B., (ED.)
THE INTELLIGENCE COMMUNITY; MANDATE FOR LEADERSHIP III:
POLICY STRATEGIES FOR THE 1990S
THE HERITAGE FOUNDATION, WASHINGTON, DC, 1989, 645-652.
THE CHAPTER ARGUES THAT A STRONG INTELLIGENCE COMMUNITY
IS VITAL TO THE SURVIVAL OF DEMOCRACY IN A WORLD WHERE
CLOSED SOCIETIES CAN TAKE ADVANTAGE OF A DEMOCRACY'S
OPENNESS. IT OUTLINES THE PROBLEMS AND CHALLENGES THAT THE
REAGAN ADMINISTRATION FACED WITH REGARDS TO INTELLIGENCE AND
OUTLINES GOALS FOR THE FUTURE PRESIDENT. THESE INCLUDE:
DIRECTING INTELLIGENCE COLLECTION, IMPROVING LANGUAGE AND
AREA EXPERTISE, STREAMLINING CONGRESSIONAL OVERSIGHT, AND
STRENGTHING COUNTERINTELLIGENCE.

04143 HEATHERLY, C., (ED.); DEVINE, D.; PINES, B., (ED.)
THE OFFICE OF PERSONNEL MANAGEMENT; MANDATE FOR LEADERSHIP
III: POLICY STRATEGIES FOR THE 1990S
THE HERITAGE FOUNDATION, WASHINGTON, DC, 1989, 361-378.
THE CHAPTER EXAMINES THE OFFICE OF PERSONNEL MANAGEMENT
(OPM) AND ITS FUNCTIONS IN THE FEDERAL GOVERNMENT. IT
ANALYZES THE CHALLENGES THAT THE NEW PRESIDENT WILL FACE
WITH REGARDS TO THE OPM. THESE INCLUDE: PROTECTING
PRESIDENTIAL AUTHORITY, INJECTING FLEXIBILITY INTO FEDERAL
PAY AND BENEFITS POLICY, IMPROVING FEDERAL RETIREMENT POLICY,
RECRUITING SKILLED PERSONNEL, INSTITUTING PAY FOR
PERFORMANCE MANAGEMENT, SIMPLIFYING THE DISCIPLINARY AND
APPEALS PROCESS, EXPOSING THE FLAWS OF "COMPARABLE WORTH",
AND OPPOSING CHANGES TO THE 1939 HATCH ACT.

04144 HEATHERLY, C., (ED.); CORDIA, L.; PINES, B., (ED.)
THE PEOPLE FACTOR: MANAGING PRESIDENTIAL PERSONNEL;
MANDATE FOR LEADERSHIP III: POLICY STRATEGIES FOR THE 1990S
THE HERITAGE FOUNDATION, WASHINGTON, DC, 1989, 103-119.
THE ARTICLE EXAMINES THE CRITICAL PROCESS OF SELECTING
AND MANAGING PRESIDENTIAL PERSONNEL. IT PROVIDES AN OVERVIEW
OF PRESIDENTIAL STAFFING PATTERNS FROM THE KENNEDY
ADMINISTRATION TO THE REAGAN ADMINISTRATION. IT CONCLUDES
WITH RECOMMENDATIONS REGARDING POLICY DIRECTION, PERSONNEL
CRITERIA, AND TIMETABLE OF PERSONNEL SELECTION.

04145 HEATHERLY, C., (ED.); PINES, B., (ED.)
THE POLITICS OF PRESIDENTIAL LEADERSHIP; MANDATE FOR
LEADERSHIP III: POLICY STRATEGIES FOR THE 1990S
THE HERITAGE FOUNDATION, WASHINGTON, DC, 1989, 9-23.
THE ARTICLE EXAMINES THE OPPORTUNITIES AND CHALLENGES
THAT WILL FACE THE NEXT PRESIDENT. HE WILL FACE NOT ONLY
PRESSING ISSUES SUCH AS HUGE BUDGET DEFICITS AND AN IMMENSE
DRUG PROBLEM, BUT ALSO A CONGRESS INSISTING ON CONTROLLING
LARGE AREAS OF AUTHORITY THAT WERE TRADITIONALLY THOUGHT TO
BE WITHIN THE PROVINCE OF THE PRESIDENT AND GOVERNMENT THAT
IS MATCHLESS FOR SHEER SIZE. THE ARTICLE OUTLINES A SET OF
PRINCIPLES AND STRATEGIES THAT WILL ENABLE THE NEXT
PRESIDENT TO BUILD ON THE SUCCESSES OF THE REAGAN
ADMINISTRATION AND DECREASE CONGRESSIONAL ENCROACHMENT ON
PRESIDENTIAL POWERS.

04146 HEATHERLY, C., (ED.); GRIBBIN, H.; PINES, B., (ED.)
THE PRESIDENT AND THE CONGRESS: THE OFFICE OF LEGISLATIVE
AFFAIRS; MANDATE FOR LEADERSHIP III: POLICY STRATEGIES FOR
THE 1990S
THE HERITAGE FOUNDATION, WASHINGTON, DC, 1989, 39-50.
IN ITS ANALYSIS OF THE RELATIONSHIP BETWEEN THE
PRESIDENT AND CONGRESS, THE ARTICLE FOCUSES PRIMARILY ON THE
OFFICE OF LEGISLATIVE AFFAIRS (OLA). IT OUTLINES THE BUDGET,
STAFF MEMBERS, AND FUNCTIONS OF THE OLA AND DISCUSSES THE
"NIXONIAN" AND "JOHNSONIAN" MODELS OF RELATIONS BETWEEN
EXECUTIVE AND LEGISLATIVE BRANCHES OF GOVERNMENT. IT
EXAMINES THE ACHIEVEMENTS AND FAILURES OF THE REAGAN YEARS
WITH REGARDS TO THIS RELATIONSHIP AND ISSUES POLICY
RECOMMENDATIONS FOR THE FUTURE PRESIDENT.

04147 HEATHERLY, C., (ED.); KEYES, A.; PINES, B., (ED.)
THE UNITED NATIONS; MANDATE FOR LEADERSHIP III: POLICY
STRATEGIES FOR THE 1990S
THE HERITAGE FOUNDATION, WASHINGTON, DC, 1989, 653-664.
IN ITS ANALYSIS OF THE UN, THE ARTICLE FOCUSES ON THE
INCREASINGLY ANTI-US SENTIMENT THAT HAS AFFECTED UN POLICIES
AND PROCEDURES. IT EXAMINES THE EFFORTS OF THE REAGAN
ADMINISTRATION TO REVERSE THIS TREND, BUT CONCLUDES THAT
MUCH REMAINS TO BE DONE. FUTURE POLICY RECOMMENDATIONS
INCLUDE: A RETHINKING OF US PARTICIPATION IN THE UN, RAISING
THE STATE DEPARTMENT'S STAKE IN THE UN, HALTING UN-BASED
SOVIET ESPIONAGE, AND ACHIEVING UN BUDGET REFORM.

04148 HEATHERLY, C., (ED.); LENARD, T.; PINES, B., (ED.)
THE UNITED STATES POSTAL SERVICE; MANDATE FOR LEADERSHIP
III: POLICY STRATEGIES FOR THE 1990S
HERITAGE FOUNDATION, WASHINGTON, DC, 1989, 379-398.
UNLIKE MANY OTHER FEDERAL AGENCIES, THE UNITED STATES
POSTAL SERVICE IS NOT UNDER DIRECT CONTROL OF THE PRESIDENT
OR CONGRESS. HOWEVER, THE PRESIDENT STILL CAN HAVE AN EFFECT
ON HOW THE USPS IS RUN AND MANAGED. THE CHAPTER OUTLINES THE
FUNCTIONS OF THE USPS AND EXAMINES THE RELATIONSHIP BETWEEN
THE USPS AND THE REAGAN ADMINISTRATION. IT ALSO OUTLINES
FUTURE POLICY RECOMMENDATIONS INCLUDING: RECOGNIZING THE
IMPORTANCE OF POSTAL APPOINTMENTS, RESTRUCTURING THE BOARD
OF GOVERNORS, FORGING A NEW LABOR POLICY, AND ENCOURAGING
COMPETITION IN MAIL DELIVERY.

04149 HEBNER, C.J.
SECURITY ASSISTANCE IN THE MODERNIZATION OF THE PEOPLE'S
FEDERATION ARMY
AVAILABLE FROM NTIS, NO. AD-A202 691/2/GAR, SEP 88, 87.
THIS STUDY CONCLUDES THAT INCREASED INTERACTIONS BETWEEN
THE UNITED STATES (US) AND THE PEOPLE'S REPUBLIC OF CHINA
(PRC) WILL BE BENEFICIAL FOR BOTH COUNTRIES AND FOR GLOBAL
POLITICAL STABILITY. AN EXAMINATION OF CURRENT SECURITY
ASSISTANCE PROGRAMS BETWEEN THE COUNTRIES WILL ENABLE US TO
ENHANCE THE SUCCESS OF FUTURE PROJECTS. THIS THESIS REVIEWS
BRIEFLY THE HISTORICAL BACKGROUND OF RELATIONS BETWEEN THE
PRC AND THE WORLD IN GENERAL AND SPECIFICALLY BETWEEN THE
PRC AND THE US. AFTER SUMMARIZING THE BASIC GOALS OF GENERAL
SECURITY ASSISTANCE PROGRAMS THIS THESIS EXAMINES THE
ARGUMENTS FOR AND AGAINST THESE PROGRAMS. IT PROVIDES A
SUMMARY OF THE PEOPLE'S LIBERATION ARMY (PLA) MODERNIZATION
PROGRAM WITH A FOCUS ON THE CAPABILITIES OF THE PRC
AEROSPACE INDUSTRIAL BASE. FINALLY, THIS WORK PROVIDES A
TECHNICAL ANALYSIS OF THE PEACE PEARL FOREIGN MILITARY SALES
PROGRAM WITH A POLITICAL ANALYSIS OF THE POTENTIAL FOR
FUTURE PROGRAMS BETWEEN THE US AND THE PRC.

04150 HECHT, J.L.; OLIVER, J.K.
SAVINGS, CAPITAL FORMATION, AND NATIONAL SECURITY
SAIS REVIEW, 9(2) (SUM 89), 111-128.
THE AUTHORS HERE LINK THE IDEA OF HIGHER SAVINGS AND
RETHINKING THE APPLICATION OF U.S. CAPITAL FORMATION TO
NATIONAL SECURITY, PROPOSING A GOVERNMENTAL SYSTEM THAT
WOULD GIVE EQUAL WEIGHT TO ECONOMIC, POLITICAL AND MILITARY
STABILITY.

04151 HECHT, S.
CHICO MENDES: CHRONICLE OF A DEATH FORETOLD
NEW LEFT REVIEW, (173) (JAN 89), 47-56.

THE AUTHOR DRAWS ON HER KNOWLEDGE OF THE BRAZILIAN
AMAZON TO EXPLAIN THE NATURE OF THE IMPENDING DISASTER THERE
AND TO SHOW HOW A GOVERNMENT-BACKED FEVER OF LAND-GRABBING
AND SPECULATION HAS STRIPPED VAST AREAS OF SOIL FOR NO
RATIONAL LONG-TERM BENEFIT. THE OLD SYSTEM OF DEBT PEONAGE
HAS FINALLY LOST ITS GRIP. BUT THE ANCESTRAL CLASS SAVAGERY
OF BRAZILIAN LANDOWNERS MANIFESTED ITSELF IN THE MURDER OF
THE ACRE RUBBER-TAPPERS' LEADER, CHICO MENDES. THE LIFE AND
DEATH OF MENDES CLEARLY DEMONSTRATE THAT ECOLOGICAL ISSUES
CAN AND MUST BE FUSED WITH THE STRUGGLES OF THE SOCIAL AND
POLITICAL FORCES IN THE REGION.

04152 HECKART, B.
     THE CITIES OF AVIGNON AND WORMS AS EXPRESSIONS OF THE
     EUROPEAN COMMUNITY
     COMPARATIVE STUDIES IN SOCIETY AND HISTORY, 31(3) (JUL 89),
     462-490.
        AS EUROPEANS REBUILT AND DEVELOPED THEIR CITIES IN THE
     PERIOD AFTER WORLD WAR II, THEY ALSO CHARTED THE COURSE OF
     THEIR UNIFICATION. FRANCE AND WEST GERMANY PLAYED KEY ROLES
     IN THIS UNIFYING PROCESS; A COMPARISON OF THEIR URBAN
     PLANNING EXPERIENCES PROVIDES INSIGHT INTO THE DYNAMICS OF
     THE COMMUNITY'S FORMATION AND GROWTH. THIS STUDY EXPLORES
     THE RELATIONSHIP BETWEEN THE EUROPEAN COMMUNITY AND ITS
     URBAN FORMS BY INVESTIGATING HOW TWO TOWNS--AVIGNON, FRANCE
     AND WORMS, WEST GERMANY--TREATED THEIR INNER CITIES DURING
     THE THREE DECADES FOLLOWING WORLD WAR II.

04153 HEDLUND, R.D.
     ENTERING THE COMMITTEE SYSTEM: STATE COMMITTEE ASSIGNMENTS
     WESTERN POLITICAL QUARTERLY, 42(4) (DEC 89), 597-626.
        ALTHOUGH MUCH IS KNOWN ABOUT THE SELECTION OF COMMITTEES
     IN THE U.S. CONGRESS, MUCH LESS IS KNOWN ABOUT THE PROCESSES
     AND OUTCOMES OF COMMITTEE ASSIGNMENTS IN THE STATES. USING
     CROSS-TIME MEMBER REQUEST DATA FROM BOTH POLITICAL PARTIES
     IN WISCONSIN, THIS STUDY EXAMINES THE APPROPRIATENESS OF THE
     ACCOMMODATION PORTION OF SHEPSLE'S INTEREST-ADVOCACY-
     ACCOMMODATION SYNDROME FROM HIS U.S. HOUSE STUDY. THESE DATA
     INDICATE THAT, IN SPITE OF A DISPROPORTIONATE NUMBER OF
     MEMBER REQUESTS FOR PERCEIVED IMPORTANT COMMITTEES, BOTH
     MAJORITY AND MINORITY PARTY LEADERS HAVE ACHIEVED HIGH
     LEVELS OF SUCCESS IN SATISFYING MEMBER REQUESTS FOR
     COMMITTEE MEMBERSHIPS AND LEADERSHIP POSTS. SUCH FINDINGS
     HAVE IMPORTANT IMPLICATIONS FOR COALITION BUILDING AND PARTY
     SUPPORT IN LEGISLATIVE CHAMBERS.

04154 HEGARTY, D.
     SOUTH PACIFIC SECURITY ISSUES: AN AUSTRALIAN PERSPECTIVE
     CONFLICT, 8(4) (1988), 311-326.
        THE INTERNATIONAL PROFILE OF THE SOUTH PACIFIC REGION
     HAS RISEN SUBSTANTIALLY IN RECENT YEARS THROUGH A
     COMBINATION OF INCREASED EXTERNAL POWER INTEREST,
     PARTICULARLY THAT BY THE SOVIET UNION AND LIBYA, AND BY
     EVENTS INTERNAL TO THE REGION, THE MOST DRAMATIC OF WHICH
     HAVE BEEN THE COUP IN FIJI AND THE THE CRISIS IN NEW
     CALEDONIA. IN VARYING DEGREES THE ANZUS DISPUTE, DIFFERENCES
     BETWEEN THE REGIONAL STATES OVER FOREIGN POLICY AND SECURITY
     ISSUES, AND THE CONTINUING POTENTIAL FOR STRIFE IN THE
     REGION'S TWO LOCAL CONFLICT SITUATIONS (NEW CALEDONIA AND
     THE PAPAU NEW GUINEA/INDONESIA BORDER AREA), HAVE TENDED TO
     UNSETTLE WHAT HAS ONCE A CALM AND TRANQUIL "LAKE." THIS
     PAPER DISCUSSES SOME OF THE KEY SECURITY ISSUES IN THE SOUTH
     PACIFIC AND THEIR IMPACT ON AUSTRALIA'S REGIONAL SECURITY
     ENVIRONMENT. IN PARTICULAR, THE PAPER EXAMINES THE PAPUA NEW
     GUINEA/INDONESIA BORDER ISSUE, THE POTENTIAL FOR CONFLICT
     THERE, AND THE APPROACHES BY THE TWO GOVERNMENTS FOR
     MANAGING THE PROBLEM.

04155 HEGARTY, DAVID
     PAPUA NEW GUINEA IN 1988: POLITICAL CROSSROADS?
     ASIAN SURVEY, XXIX(2) (FEB 89), 181-188.
        1988 WAS SIMILAR TO PRECEDING YEARS IN PAPUA NEW GUINEA
     IN THAT THE ESTABLISHED MANNER OF PARLIAMENTARY POLITICS--
     FREQUENT FLOOR CROSSING, SHIFTING FACTIONAL ELEMENTS, AND
     UNSTABLE COALITIONS--WAS PREVALENT. IN JULY AMID ACCUSATIONS
     OF CORRUPTION THE RULING COALITION WAS TOPPLED, BUT THE
     REPLACEMENT COALITION WAS EQUALLY UNSTABLE. ANALYSTS ARE
     RAISING SERIOUS QUESTIONS AS TO THE OVERALL STABILITY OF
     PAPUA NEW GUINEA'S POLITICAL SYSTEM AND DEMOCRATIC
     INSTITUTIONS. WARMING OF RELATIONS WITH PACIFIC NEIGHBORS
     CHARACTERIZED THE NATION'S FOREIGN POLICY WITH THE
     SIGNIFICANT EXCEPTION OF CONTINUED CLASHES WITH INDONESIA.
     ECONOMIC GROWTH WAS MODEST, BUT POLITICAL UNREST AND DOUBTS
     AS TO THE BENEFITS OF RELYING HEAVILY ON A MINING ECONOMY
     LOOM ON THE ECONOMIC HORIZON.

04156 HEGEDUS, I.
     THE STRUGGLE FOR POLITICAL PLURALISM: THE FIRST CONGRESS
     OF THE ASSOCIATION OF YOUNG DEMOCRATS (FIDESZ)
     EAST EUROPEAN REPORTER, 3(4) (SPR 89), 17-20.
        THE ARTICLE OUTLINES THE AIMS AND RECENT ACTIVITIES OF
     THE ASSOCIATION OF YOUNG DEMOCRATS (FIDESZ). IT RECOUNTS THE
     DECISIONS MADE AT ASSOCIATION CONGRESSES AND THE EFFORTS OF
     THE GOVERNMENT TO DISCOURAGE AND REPRESS FIDESZ ACTIVITIES.

THE ARTICLE CONCLUDES WITH A STATEMENT OF THE POLITICAL
GOALS AND AGENDA OF FIDESZ. AMONG THE MOST EMPHASIZED GOALS
IS THE REMOVAL OF THE DICTATORIAL CHARACTER OF THE PRESENT
POLITICAL SYSTEM, AND THE GUARANTEE OF POLITICAL FREEDOM AND
INDEPENDENCE.

04157 HEHIR, J.B
     ZERO-PLUS GAME
     COMMONWEAL, CXVI(2) (JAN 89), 39-40.
        THE ISRAELI-PALESTINIAN CONFLICT READILY LEADS TO ZERO-
     SUM CONCEPTIONS (I.E., "IF I WIN, YOU LOSE"). BUT THE ONLY
     POSSIBILITY FOR GRASPING THE POTENTIAL OF THE NEW MOVEMENT
     IN THE MIDEAST IS TO SHIFT FROM A ZERO-SUM TO A PLUS-SUM
     CONCEPTION (I.E., THERE ARE SOME OUTCOMES THAT BENEFIT BOTH
     PARTIES).

04158 HEHIR, J.B.
     DECADE OF DECISION
     COMMONWEAL, CXVI(12) (JUN 89), 362-363.
        WHILE THERE WILL BE CONTINUITY ON THE TOPIC OF ARMS
     CONTROL IN THE 1990'S THERE WILL ALSO BE THREE CHANGES IN
     THE WAY THE SUPERPOWERS ADDRESS THAT TOPIC. THE NEXT DECADE
     WILL SEE A PRIMACY OF THE POLITICAL OVER THE STRATEGIC, A
     NEAR EQUALITY OF IMPORTANCE BETWEEN CONVENTIONAL AND NUCLEAR
     NEGOTIATIONS, AND A NEED TO ADDRESS THE SYSTEMIC AS WELL AS
     THE SUPERPOWER DIMENSION OF ARMS CONTROL. SUPERPOWER

04159 HEHIR, J.B.
     EAST-WEST, NORTH-SOUTH
     COMMONWEAL, CXVI(20) (NOV 89), 614-615.
        POPE JOHN PAUL II BELIEVES THAT THE CATHOLIC CHURCH IS
     PREPARED BY ITS HISTORY AND CALLED BY ITS VOCATION TO HELP
     SHAPE THE FUTURE DIRECTION OF THE WORLD. HE CLEARLY
     MANIFESTS A CONSCIOUSNESS THAT HIS PERSONAL HISTORY AS WELL
     AS THE CATHOLIC CHURCH'S PERVASIVE PRESENCE IN AREAS OF
     MAJOR POLITICAL AND SOCIAL CHANGE (EASTERN EUROPE, LATIN
     AMERICA, AND THE PHILIPINNES) PROVIDE HIM WITH A PULPIT AND
     A PERSPECTIVE THAT COMMAND AN ATTENTIVE AUDIENCE IN THE
     INTERNATIONAL COMMUNITY. HE HAS CALLED FOR THE LINKAGE OF
     THE EAST-WEST DIMENSION OF WORLD POLITICS WITH THE NORTH-
     SOUTH ISSUES.

04160 HEIDAR, K.
     NORWAY: LEVELS OF PARTY COMPETITION AND SYSTEM CHANGE
     WEST EUROPEAN POLITICS. 12(4) (OCT 89), 143-156.
        THIS IS A REPORT ON CHANGES IN THE NORWEGIAN PARTY
     SYSTEM OVER THE LAST TWO DECADES. IT EXAMINES GOVERNMENT,
     PARLIAMENT, ELECTION AND ORGANIZATION. THIS APPROACH IS USED
     BECAUSE OF THE QUESTION OF THE APPROPRIATE LEVEL OF
     THEORETICAL GUIDANCE APPLIED TO A PARTICULAR SUBJECT. IT
     EXPLORES, ALSO, THE VARIOUS ATTEMPTS MADE AT LABLELLING THE
     NORWEGIAN PARTY SYSTEM AND IDENTIFIES ITS CHANGES IN THE
     POST-WAR ERA.

04161 HEIDEMANN, M.A.
     REGIONAL ECOLOGY AND REGULATORY FEDERALISM: WISCONSIN'S
     QUANDARY OVER TOXIC CONTAMINATION OF GREEN BAY
     DISSERTATION ABSTRACTS INTERNATIONAL, 50(6) (DEC 89),
     1799-A.
        THE AUTHOR CONSIDERS HOW RECENT TRENDS IN AMERICAN
     FEDERALISM AFFECT THE NEED FOR ENVIRONMENTAL REGULATIONS
     TAILORED TO SPECIFIC ECOLOGICAL REGIONS. USING A CASE STUDY
     APPROACH, SHE EXAMINES EFFORTS BY WISCONSIN TO CONTROL WATER
     POLLUTION IN GREEN BAY. SHE HYPOTHESIZES THAT POLLUTION
     CONTROL EFFORTS IN WISCONSIN, PARTICULARLY FOR TOXINS, ARE
     HAMPERED BY OVER-DEPENDENCE ON FEDERAL REGULATIONS.

04162 HEIDEMANN, S.
     RESULTS OF EGYPTIAN POLICY FOR ENCOURAGEMENT OF FOREIGN
     DIRECT INVESTMENTS: THE PARTICIPATION OF GERMAN FIRMS
     DURING THE 1980'S
     ORIENT, 30(2) (JUN 89), 221-249.
        ON THE ONE HAND, THE BASIC LEGAL REQUIREMENTS FOR
     FOREIGN INVESTMENTS IMPROVED DURING THE 80S; ON THE OTHER
     HAND, JOINT VENTURES WITH STATE-OWNED COMPANIES WERE
     ABANDONED, THUS CLOSING COOPERATION POTENTIALS FOR LARGE-
     SCALE INDUSTRIAL PROJECTS. IN THE CASE OF GERMANY, A
     SYSTEMATIC EXAMINATION OF THE INVESTMENT BUREAUS'S DATA
     SHOWS THE NUMBER OF PROJECTS TO BE ONE FOURTH LOWER (AT MOST
     32 PROJECTS) AND THE AMOUNT OF CAPITAL PARTICIPATION TO BE
     ONE THIRD LOWER (APPROXIMATELY 15 MILLION US-$). ONLY EIGHT
     OF THE 32 FIRMS ARE PARTIALLY OR WHOLLY DIRECTED BY GERMAN
     MANAGEMENT; THEY MAKE UP THREE FOURTHS OF THE GERMAN CAPITAL
     PARTICIPATION. THE INITIATIVE FOR ESTABLISHING, AMONG OTHERS,
     LARGER-SCALE JOINT VENTURES WITH MULTINATIONAL ENTERPRISES
     MAINLY CAME FROM THE EGYPTIAN SIDE. THEIR FOREMOST INTEREST
     WAS GEARED TOWARD GERMAN TECHNOLOGY AND MANAGEMENT. THE MAIN
     PROBLEM THESE FIRMS HAVE IS SECURING A HIGH QUALITY AND
     PRODUCTIVITY LEVEL.

04163 HEIDENHEIMER, A.J.
     PROFESSIONAL KNOWLEDGE AND STATE POLICY IN COMPARATIVE
     HISTORICAL PERSPECTIVE: LAW AND MEDICINE IN BRITAIN,
     GERMANY, AND THE UNITED STATES

INTERNATIONAL SOCIAL SCIENCE JOURNAL, (122) (NOV 89), 529-553.
PROFESSION AND POLICY ARE TERMS THAT HAVE ACQUIRED DISTINCT, ALBEIT POORLY BOUNDED, MEANINGS IN ENGLISH BUT LACK EQUIVALENTS IN OTHER LANGUAGES. PARTICULAR PROFESSIONS LIKE THOSE OF LAW AND MEDICINE, ON THE OTHER HAND, HAVE MAINTAINED RATHER SIMILAR MEANINGS AND IDENTITIES IN VARIOUS WESTERN NATIONAL SETTINGS. BUT WITHIN THESE NATIONAL SETTINGS SUBCOMPONENTS OF THE LEGAL AND MEDICAL PROFESSIONS HAVE, OVERTIME, CHANGED THEIR RELATIONSHIPS TO EACH OTHER, AS WELL AS TO THE STATE AND TO THEIR CLIENTS. HENCE A HISTORICAL ANALYSIS MAY FOCUS ON HOW, THROUGH THEIR INTERACTIONS WITH STATE STRUCTURES, PROFESSIONS HAVE CONTRIBUTED TO SHAPING DIFFERENCES IN NATIONAL POLICY PROFILES.

04164 HEILEMANN, J.
CONGRESS'S WATCH DOG: MOSTLY IT STILL GOES FOR THE CAPILLARIES
WASHINGTON MONTHLY, 21(10) (NOV 89), 38-44.
THIS ARTICLE ANALYSES THE JOB DESCRIPTION OF THE GENERAL ACCOUNTING OFFICE (GAO) AND HOW WELL IT IS DOING ITS JOB. IT EXPLORES THE GAO'S PAST PREOCCUPATION WITH MINUTIAE AND SUBMITS THAT IT CONTINUES TO MISS THE GOVERNMENT'S MAIN PROBLEMS. THE HUD SCAN IS EXPLORED IN THIS LIGHT.

04165 HEILMAN, J.G.; JOHNSON, G.W.
SYSTEM AND PROCESS IN CAPITAL-INTENSIVE PRIVATIZATION: A COMPARATIVE CASE STUDY OF MUNICIPAL WASTEWATER TREATMENT WORKS
POLICY STUDIES REVIEW, 8(3) (SPR 89), 549-572.
CAPITAL-INTENSIVE PRIVATIZATION (CIP) IS AN OPTION FOR INFRASTRUCTURE PROJECT DEVELOPMENT. ADVOCATES CLAIM THAT CIP GENERATES COST SAVINGS THROUGH EFFICIENCIES INHERENT IN THE COORDINATED DESIGN, CONSTRUCTION, AND OPERATION OF FACILITIES. THE PRESENT PAPER ASSESSES THESE CLAIMS IN THE FIELD OF MUNICIPAL WASTEWATER TREATMENT FACILITIES (WWHS). IT PRESENTS CASE-STUDY RESULTS AND AGGREGATE DATA ON SEVEN OF THE FIRST PRIVATIZED WWHS AND ON SEVEN COMPARABLE GRANT-FUNDED FACILITIES. THE ANALYSIS RELIES ON THE CONCEPTS OF SYSTEM AND PROCESS. IT CONCLUDES THAT CIP CHANGES THE SYSTEM OF PLAYERS AND THE PROCESSES THROUGH WHICH THEY INTERACT. IN DOING SO, CIP GENERATES EFFICIENCIES OF TIME AND COST IN PROJECT DESIGN AND CONSTRUCTION. IT ALSO MAY CHANGE ACCOUNTABILITY MECHANISMS, TRADE EFFICIENCY OFF AGAINST ACCOUNTABILITY, AND RAISE ISSUES OF COMPATIBILITY WITH THE NATURE OF THE STATE. THESE MATTERS BEAR DIRECTLY ON THE CURRENT DEBATES OVER TAX AND BUDGET POLICY GENERATED BY INCREASED DEMANDS FOR SERVICES, LIMITED RESOURCES, AND DEFICIT REDUCTION MANDATES.

04166 HEIM, D.
A COMPASSIONATE MIDDLE GROUND
SOJOURNERS, 18(10) (NOV 89), 19-20.
ALTHOUGH ABORTION HAS APPARENTLY SPLIT THE NATION INTO TWO EXTREME CAMPS, IN REALITY A CONSIDERABLE MAJORITY OF AMERICANS ARE SOMEWHERE IN THE MIDDLE BETWEEN PRO-LIFE AND PRO-CHOICE. DRAWING FROM THE EXPERIENCE OF FRANCE AND OTHER EUROPEAN NATIONS, THE ARTICLE EXPLORES POSSIBLE AVENUES OF LEGISLATION THAT WOULD SATISFY THE DESIRES OF THOSE WHO STAND IN THE "COMPASSIONATE MIDDLE GROUND."

04167 HEIMAN, B.J.
THE CONDUCT OF INTERNATIONAL ECONOMIC RELATIONS IN THE BUSH ADMINISTRATION
FLETCHER FORUM, 13(1) (WIN 89), 9-17.
THE UNITED STATES ADOPTED THE "OPEN DOOR" POLICY ONE HUNDRED YEARS AGO. TODAY, THE APPOINTMENT OF JAMES BAKER AS SECRETARY OF STATE HIGHLIGHTS THIS THEME OF DIPLOMATIC EMPHASIS ON TRADE NEGOTIATIONS. HEIMAN TELLS US WHAT WE MIGHT EXPECT IN THE REALM OF INTERNATIONAL ECONOMIC RELATIONS UNDER THE NEW ADMINISTRATION, AND WHY. BAKER'S SUBSTANTIVE KNOWLEDGE OF WORLD TRADE MARKETS AND INTERNATIONAL MONETARY SYSTEMS PRESAGE AN EVOLUTION IN AMERICAN TRADE NEGOTIATIONS. GLOBAL ECONOMIC CONDITIONS, ESPECIALLY THE "THIN DEFICITS" OF THE UNITED STATES, FAVOR THE USAGE OF SEQUENTIAL BILATERAL AGREEMENTS AND AGGREGATE TRADE ACCORDS. FURTHER, THE PRESIDENTIAL FAVOR BAKER ENJOYS AS SECRETARY OF STATE ENCOURAGES AN INCREASED EMPHASIS ON THE LINKAGE BETWEEN ECONOMIC RELATIONS AND DIPLOMACY.

04168 HEIN, GORDON R
INDONESIA IN 1988: ANOTHER FIVE YEARS FOR SOEHARTO
ASIAN SURVEY, XXIX(2) (FEB 89), 119-128.
THE ARTICLE EXAMINES INDONESIA IN 1988 WITH EMPHASIS ON POLITICAL, ECONOMIC, AND FOREIGN POLICY ISSUES. INDONESIA'S POLITICS REMAINED ESSENTIALLY UNCHANGED AS THE RULING GOLKAR PARTY CONTINUED ITS DOMINANCE AND REELECTED PRESIDENT SOEHARTO TO A FIFTH FIVE-YEAR TERM. ON THE ECONOMIC FRONT, DECLINING OIL PRICES, INCREASING UNEMPLOYMENT, AND INCREASING DEBT THREATENED TO STAGNATE THE NATION'S GROWTH. HOWEVER, ENERGETIC ATTEMPTS TO INCREASE NON-OIL EXPORTS RESULTED IN MODEST GROWTH IN 1988. THE CHIEF FOREIGN POLICY EVENTS OF 1988 WERE INDONESIA'S HOSTING OF THE JAKARTA

INFORMAL MEETING (JIM) DESIGNED TO RESOLVED THE KAMPUCHEAN CONFLICT, INDONESIA'S CAMPAIGN FOR CHAIRMANSHIP OF THE NONALLIGNED MOVEMENT.

04169 HEINE, J.
COUNTDOWN FOR PINOCHET: A CHILEAN DIARY
PS: POLITICAL SCIENCE AND POLITICS, XXII(2) (JUN 89), 242-246.
THE AUTHOR GIVES AN EYEWITNESS ACCOUNT OF THE OCT. 5, 1988, PLEBISCITE IN BRAZIL.

04170 HEINZ, D.
CHRUCH, SECT, AND GOVERNMENTAL CONTROL: SEVENTH-DAY ADVENTISTS IN THE HASBURG MONARCHY
EAST EUROPEAN QUARTERLY, XXIII(1) (MAR 89), 109-115.
HISTORICALLY, CATHOLICISM HAS EXERTED IMMENSE POWER AND INFLUENCE IN AUSTRIAN POLITICAL, CULTURAL, AND EDUCATIONAL LIFE. SINCE THE MID-19TH CENTURY WHEN SMALLER RELIGIOUS SECTS, SUCH AS THE SEVENTH-DAY ADVENTISTS, BEGAN TO APPEAR IN AUSTRIA-HUNGARY AS A REACTION TO THEOLOGICAL RATIONALISM, THEY HAVE HAD TO FACE OPPOSITION FROM TWO SIDES: CHURCH AND STATE. THIS CONFLICT HAS BEEN A DOMINANT THEME IN THE HISTORY OF ANGLO-AMERICAN MISSION OUTREACH IN HABSBURG AUSTRIA.

04171 HEINZIG, D.
CHINA BETWEEN THE SUPERPOWERS
ASIAN THOUGHT AND SOCIETY, XIV(40) (JAN 89), 47-52.
THE DEVELOPMENT OF CHINA'S RELATIONS WITH THE SUPERPOWERS HAS BEEN DETERMINED BY RADICAL CHANGES THAT TOOK PLACE IN BOTH DIRECTIONS AND AT INTERVALS OF AROUND TEN YEARS. THE FIRST DECADE, THE 1950'S, WAS CHARACTERIZED BY THE ALLIANCE WITH MOSCOW AND CONCURRENT CONFLICT WITH WASHINGTON; THE SECOND, THE 1960'S, BY A DUAL CONFRONTATION WITH BOTH SUPERPOWERS; THE THIRD, THE 1970'S, BY DETENTE WITH THE USA WHILE RELATIONS WITH THE USSR REMAINED TENSE; AND FINALLY, THE FOURTH, THE 1980'S, BY A GRADUAL RAPPROACHMENT WITH MOSCOW WHILE RELATIONS WITH WASHINGTON HAVE REMAINED RELAXED. RECENTLY, THE SELF-ASSURED POST-MAO LEADERSHIP IN PEKING HAS SKILLFULLY APPLIED ITS NEW FLEXIBILITY TO GAIN ADVANTAGES WITHOUT ALLOWING ITSELF TO LAPSE INTO TOO GREAT OF A DEPENDENCY ON EITHER OF THE SUPERPOWERS.

04172 HEISBOURG, F.
ECONOMY AND SECURITY: CONSTRAINTS AND OPPORTUNITIES
INTERNATIONAL SPECTATOR, XXIII(2) (APR 88), 74-78.
THERE IS NO DIRECT OR LINEAR CORRELATION BETWEEN ECONOMY AND SECURITY, BUT THERE IS A COMPLEX LINK BETWEEN ECONOMIC PERFORMANCE AND POLITICO-MILITARY POWER. THE LACK OF CLARITY IN THIS REGARD IS BORNE OUT BY THE DIFFICULTY OF ESTABLISHING AN IRREVOCABLE LINK BETWEEN THE LEVEL OF DEFENSE EXPENDITURE AND ECONOMIC GROWTH. SOME OF THE FASTEST-GROWING ECONOMIES IN THE WORLD ARE ALSO AMONG THOSE WHOSE DEFENSE SPENDING REPRESENTS A PROPORTION HIGHER THAN THE AVERAGE IN WESTERN EUROPE. YET IT WOULD BE A MISTAKE TO ASSUME THAT THERE ARE NO LINKS. IT IS AT LEAST ARGUABLE THAT HIGH LEVELS OF DEFENSE SPENDING ON TOP OF A RIGID ECONOMY AND AN AGEING SOCIETY WILL ACCELERATE ECONOMIC DECLINE, WHEREAS HIGH DEFENSE EXPENDITURES IN QUICKLY GROWING ECONOMIES WILL NOT HINDER GROWTH SO LONG AS THE SHARE OF GNP DEVOTED TO DEFENSE DECLINES OVER TIME. SIMILARLY, A THRESHOLD PROBABLY EXISTS IN THE OTHER DIRECTION.

04173 HEJKA-EKINS, A.
TEACHING ETHICS IN PUBLIC ADMINISTRATION
PUBLIC ADMINISTRATION REVIEW, 48(5) (SEP 88), 885-891.
THIS ARTICLE DESCRIBES THE CURRENT STATUS OF ETHICS EDUCATION IN GRADUATE PROGRAMS OF PUBLIC ADMINISTRATION AND POLICY. FIRST, THREE PRIMARY ISSUES OF DEBATE IN THE LITERATURE REGARDING ETHICS EDUCATION ARE IDENTIFIED. SECOND, DEVELOPMENT OF A QUESTIONNAIRE USED TO SURVEY ETHICS INSTRUCTORS IS DISCUSSED. THIRD, A REPORT ON THE FINDINGS OF THIS SURVEY, CONDUCTED IN NOVEMBER 1986, IS PRESENTED. FINALLY, QUESTIONS REGARDING THE STATUS OF ETHICS EDUCATION AND THE IMPLICATIONS FOR FUTURE RESEARCH ARE EXPLORED.

04174 HELLER, A.; FEHER, F.
DOES SOCIALISM HAVE A FUTURE?
DISSENT, (SUM 89), 371-375.
DOES SOCIALISM HAVE A FUTURE? THIS QUESTION HAS BEEN ASKED FOR ALMOST TWO HUNDRED YEARS, WHENEVER SOCIALISM AS THEORY AND MOVEMENT REACHED A CRITICAL PERIOD. THERE CAN BE LITTLE DOUBT THAT SOCIALISM, BOTH AS A MOVEMENT AND A THEORY, IS NOW LIVING THROUGH ONE OF ITS GREATEST TRIALS. THE INCREASINGLY BLUNT ADMISSIONS BY THE RULING BUREAUCRACIES OF SOVIET-TYPE SOCIETIES THAT THEIR LONG AND, AS FAR AS HUMAN LIVES ARE CONCERNED, EXPENSIVE EXPERIMENTS HAVE FAILED POLITICALLY AND ECONOMICALLY THREATENS THE SOCIALIST IDEA, HOWEVER DEFINED, WITH EXTINCTION.

04175 HELLIWELL, J. F.
FROM NOW TILL THEN: GLOBALIZATION AND ECONOMIC CO-OPERATION
CANADIAN PUBLIC POLICY--ANALYSE DE POLITIQUES, XV (FEB 89),

71-77.
THIS PAPER DEALS WITH THE CURRENT STATE OF GROWTH AND
IMBALANCES AMONG THE MAJOR INDUSTRIAL COUNTRIES, WITH
SPECIAL REFERENCE TO JAPAN AND THE UNITED STATES, AND TO THE
LIKELY PROSPECTS FOR, AND EFFECTS OF, FUTURE MACROECONOMIC
POLICY CHANGES. THE AUTHOR TAKES A LONGER-TERM FOCUS ON THE
WORLD ECONOMY, AND DEALS WITH SOME OF THE IMPLICATIONS OF
GLOBALIZATION FOR INTERNATIONAL POLICY CO-ORDINATION.

04176 HELLMANN-RAJANAYAGAM, D.
THE TAMIL MILITANTS--BEFORE THE ACCORD AND AFTER
PACIFIC AFFAIRS, 61(4) (WIN 89), 603-619.
THE ARTICLE DISCUSSES THE IDEOLOGY AND PROGRAMME OF SOME
OF TH MAJOR MILITANT TAMIL GROUPS BEFORE AND AFTER THE
INTERVENTION OF THE INDIAN PEACE KEEPING FORCE (IPKF) IN
NORTHERN SRI LANKA. BESIDES THE LTTE, THE SO-CALLED
"TRISTAR" (EPRLF,PLOT, AND TELO) AND EROS, WHO TRY TO STEER
A MIDDLE COURSE BETWEEN LTTE AND IPKF, ARE DISCUSSED. WHILE
LTTE ALWAYS HAD DOUBTS ABOUT AN ACTIVE INDIAN INTERVENTION
IN SRI LANKA AND PURSUED PRIMARILY NATIONALIST OBJECTIVES,
THE OTHER GROUPS WELCOMED THE INDIAN INTERVENTION TO A
GREATER OR LESSER DEGREE AND ARE NOW WILLING AND READY TO
COOPERATE WITH THE IPKF. AFTER A SHORT "HONEYMOON," THE LTTE
HAVE NOW TURNED COMPLETELY AGAINST THE IPKF AND ARE ACTIVELY
RESISTING IT. THE ARTICLE CONCLUDES THAT WHAT THE LTTE WANT
IS TOTAL POLITICAL CONTROL OF A COMBINED NORTHERN AND
EASTERN PROVINCE IN ORDER TO CONSOLIDATE THEIR POWER BASE.

04177 HELMS, L.B.; HENKIN, A.B.; SINGLETON, C.A.
THE LEGAL STRUCTURE OF POLICY IMPLEMENTATION;
RESPONSIBILITIES OF AGENCIES AND PRACTITIONERS
SOCIAL SERVICE REVIEW, 63(2) (JUN 89), 180-198.
AGENCIES AND PRACTITIONERS RESPONSIBLE FOR THE
IMPLEMENTATION OF SOCIAL POLICY ARE BOUND BY COMPLEX LEGAL
REQUIREMENTS AND RESTRAINTS. TO FACILITATE FIT BETWEEN THE
INTENT OF STATUTES AND THE OPERATION OF PROGRAMS,
PRACTITIONERS SHOULD ACQUIRE A BASIC UNDERSTANDING OF THE
LEGAL PRINCIPLES THAT GUIDE ADMINISTRATIVE PROCESSES IN
PUBLIC POLICY IMPLEMENTATION, ESPECIALLY THOSE RELATED TO
HUMAN SERVICES ORGANIZATIONS. IN THE PRESENT ARTICLE, THE
AUTHORS ORGANIZE AND EXPLAIN ASPECTS OF ADMINISTRATIVE LAW
IMPORTANT TO PROFESSIONALS IN DIRECT SERVICE AGENCIES.

04178 HEMMER, H.; MANNEL, C.
ON THE ECONOMIC ANALYSIS OF THE URBAN INFORMAL SECTOR
WORLD DEVELOPMENT, 17(10) (OCT 89), 1543-1552.
THIS PAPER EXAMINES THE LINKS AND INTERACTIONS BETWEEN
THE FORMAL AND THE INFORMAL SECTOR IN DEVELOPING COUNTRIES.
IT IS ARGUED THAT BOTH THE FACTOR AND THE PRODUCT MARKETS
SHOW THESE LINKS. BASED ON THE ASSUMPTION THAT FOR MOST
PRODUCTS DEMAND CONSISTS OF A SPECIFIC AND A NONSPECIFIC
DEMAND, THE PAPER PRESENTS AN ANALYSIS OF THE PRODUCT AND
LABOR MARKETS AND DISCUSSES THE EFFECTS OF SHIFTS IN DEMAND
ON DEVELOPMENT STRATEGIES. IT CONCLUDES THAT SUCCESSFUL
MEASURES HAVE TO INCLUDE THE INFORMAL AS WELL AS THE FORMAL
SECTOR.

04179 HENDERSON, D.R.
ARE WE ALL SUPPLY-SIDERS NOW?
CONTEMPORARY POLICY ISSUES, VII(4) (OCT 89), 116-128.
THE TERM "SUPPLY-SIDER" HAS COME TO MEAN SOMEONE WHO
BELIEVES THAT AN X PERCENT CUT IN TAX RATES WILL--THROUGH
ITS EFFECT ON THE INCENTIVE TO WORK, TO SAVE AND INVEST, AND
TO AVOID AND EVADE TAXES--LEAD TO MUCH LESS THAN AN X
PERCENT CUT, AND PERHAPS EVEN TO AN INCREASE, IN TAX
REVENUES. NOT ALL ECONOMISTS ARE SUPPLY-SIDERS IN THIS SENSE,
BUT MANY MORE ARE NOW THAN WERE DURING THE 1970S. THE
REASON FOR THE SWITCH IS THE EVIDENCE THAT HAS ACCUMULATED
ON THE INCENTIVE EFFECTS OF TAXES. MANY STUDIES HAVE SHOWN
THAT CUTS IN TAX RATES FOR THE HIGHEST-INCOME TAXPAYERS
ACTUALLY HAVE INCREASED THE GOVERNMENT'S REVENUE. A KEY
REASON FOR THIS EFFECT IS NOT A LARGE ELASTICITY OF LABOR
SUPPLY BUT RATHER A LARGE ELASTICITY OF TAX AVOIDANCE WITH
RESPECT TO TAX RATES. THE MOST IMPORTANT POLICY IMPLICATION
OF THIS EVIDENCE IS THAT THE GOVERNMENT CANNOT INCREASE ITS
REVENUE SUBSTANTIALLY WITHOUT TAXING THE NON-RICH.

04180 HENDERSON, G.
THE US AND LIBYA: EYEBALL TO EYEBALL FOR THE LAST TIME
MIDDLE EAST INTERNATIONAL, (342) (JAN 89), 8-9.
THE AUTHOR EXAMINES RONALD REAGAN'S ACCUSATIONS
REGARDING LIBYA'S ALLEGED CHEMICAL WEAPONS PLANT AT RABTA.

04181 HENDERSON, G.; NEFF, D.
THE USSR AND LIBYA: BOMBERS FOR THE COLONEL; CAREFUL TIMING
MIDDLE EAST INTERNATIONAL, (348) (APR 89), 6-7.
WHILE MIKHAIL GORBACHEV WAS MEETING FIDEL CASTRO IN CUBA,
AND ISRAEL'S YITZHAK SHAMIR WAS IN WASHINGTON, THE US
ARRANGED FOR THE LEAK OF INFORMATION REGARDING THE SOVIET
SALE OF ADVANCED FIGHTER-BOMBERS TO LIBYA. THE TIMING WAS
IMPECCABLE: IT REINFORCED THE IDEA THAT ISRAEL WAS STILL
THREATENED BY ITS ARAB NEIGHBORS AND NEEDED ADDITIONAL US
AID TO DEFEND ITSELF, AND IT ALSO SERVED TO EMBARASS
GORBACHEV ESPECIALLY AS HE MOVEDON TO GREAT BRITAIN. IT

DISTRACTED ATTENTION FROM GORBACHEV'S REFORMS AND NEW
THINKING. ALL IN ALL, IT AMOUNTED TO A CONSIDERABLE
POLITICAL VICTORY FOR THE LINGERING COLD WARRIORS ON CAPITAL
HILL.

04182 HENDERSON, H.; WILMS, H.
THE BUSH ADMINISTRATION: AFTER THE HONEYMOON
BUREAUCRAT, 18(2) (SUM 89), 13-14.
GEORGE BUSH DID NOT CAMPAIGN TO UNDO THE PROGRAMS OF THE
PRECEDING PRESIDENT NOR DOES HIS ADVENT MARK A CHANGE IN THE
GOVERNING PARTY, ALTHOUGH HIS APPEARS TO BE A LESS
DOCTRINAIRE ADMINISTRATION THAN REAGAN'S. THE BUSH
ADMINISTRATION HAS BEEN MARKED BY AN EARLY WILLINGNESS TO
WORK MORE CLOSELY WITH CONGRESS AND THE CAREER BUREAUCRACY
THAN THE REAGAN ADMINISTRATION. THIS PRAGMATIC AND
COOPERATIVE STRAIN, HOWEVER, HAS NOT YET BEEN MARKED BY A
CLEARLY-DEFINED SET OF PRIORITIES ARTICULATED IN READILY
UNDERSTOOD TERMS.

04183 HENDERSON, L.J.
NEIGHBORHOOD POWER IN THE CAPITOL: ADVISORY NEIGHBORHOOD
COMMISSIONS IN WASHINGTON, D.C.
NATIONAL CIVIC REVIEW, 78(3) (MAY 89), 209-215.
INITIATED IN 1975 UNDER THE PROVISIONS OF D.C. LAW 1-21,
ADVISORY NEIGHBORHOOD COMMISSIONS (ANCS) HAVE FACED
CHALLENGES HEADY ENOUGH TO TEST ANY CITIZEN INSTITUTION IN
URBAN AMERICA. WHAT HAS BEEN THE ROLE OF ANCS IN THE
DISTRICT'S QUEST FOR FULL AUTONOMY AND POWER IN THE
INTERGOVERNMENTAL SYSTEM OF THE NATION?

04184 HENDERSON, R.D.
SOUTH AFRICA SANCTIONS AT WORK
INTERNATIONAL PERSPECTIVES, XVIII(3) (MAY 89), 17-19.
ECONOMIC SANCTIONS AGAINST SOUTH AFRICA SHOULD NOT BE
PUNITIVE, BUT RATHER SHOULD BE DESIGNED TO MAKE THE
RETENTION OF ITS APARTHEID SYSTEM PROHIBITEDLY COSTLY AND
THUS HASTEN ITS ABOLITION. TOWARD THIS GOAL, FURTHER
SANCTIONS SHOULD BE TARGETED A THAT COUNTRY'S VULNERABLE
FINANCIAL SECTOR, INCLUDING COMMERCIAL ENTERPRISES BASED
OUTSIDE THE COUNTRY BUT CONTROLLED BY SOUTH AFRICAN CONCERNS.

04185 HENDRICK, R.
TOP-DOWN BUDGETING, FISCAL STRESS, AND BUDGETING THEORY
AMERICAN REVIEW OF PUBLIC ADMINISTRATION, 19(1) (MAR 89),
29-48.
RECENT BUDGETING LITERATURE ARGUES THAT MANY GOVERNMENTS
BUDGET IN A TOP-DOWN MANNER, ESPECIALLY UNDER FISCAL STRESS,
AND THAT INCREMENTAL BUDGETING THEORY IS ACCURATE ONLY FOR
BOTTOMUP BUDGETING PROCEDURES WHEN RESOURCES ARE PLENTIFUL.
HOWEVER, FEW STUDIES SYSTEMATICALLY COMPARE CHANGES UNDER
DIFFERENT CONDITIONS TO ASSESS THEIR CLAIMS. THIS STUDY
ADDRESSES THIS PROBLEM BY TESTING A MODEL THAT CONTAINS BOTH
MANAGERIAL AND INCREMENTAL INDICATORS OF BEHAVIOR. THE MODEL
IS ESTIMATED USING POOLED, CROSSSECTIONAL, TIME-SERIES
ANALYSIS UNDER FOUR DIFFERENT ENVIRONMENTAL CONDITIONS:
FISCAL AUSTERITY/TOP-DOWN BUDGETING, FISCAL
AUSTERITY/BOTTOMUP BUDGETING, FISCAL PROSPERITY/TOP-DOWN
BUDGETING AND FISCAL PROSPERITY/BOTTOM-UP BUDGETING.

04186 HENDRICKS, F.
LOOSE PLANNING AND RAPID RESETTLEMENT: THE POLITICS OF
CONSERVATION AND CONTROL IN TRANSKEI, SOUTH AFRICA, 1950-
1970
JOURNAL OF SOUTHERN AFRICAN STUDIES, 15(2) (JAN 89),
306-325.
ATTEMPTS BY VARIOUS GOVERNMENT AGENCIES TO IMPLEMENT
PROGRAMS OF CONSERVATION IN SOUTH AFRICA WERE GENERALLY
FAILURES. THE PAPER LOOKS AT THE ATTEMPTS TO REINVIGORATE
TRIBALISM IN THE RESERVES AND ATTEMPTS TO GIVE AS MANY
AFRICANS AS POSSIBLE THE IMPRESSION OF A STAKE IN THE LAND
OF THE RESERVES OFTEN COMPETED WITH AND SUPERCEDED ATTEMPTS
TO IMPLEMENT CONSERVATION PROGRAMS. THE INTRODUCTION OF THE
BANTU AUTHORITIES IN THE 1950'S WAS THE FIRST STEP IN THE
PROCESS THAT ULTIMATELY DERAILED ALL ATTEMPTS AT
CONSERVATION.

04187 HENDRIXSON, K.L.
SEEKING THE ECONOMIC KINGDOM: THE IMPACT OF STATE MAJORITY
OWNERSHIP OF THE GHANA BAUXITE COMPANY ON COMPANY
PERFORMANCE
DISSERTATION ABSTRACTS INTERNATIONAL, 50(6) (DEC 89),
1795-A.
WITH THE ONSET OF STATE MAJORITY OWNERSHIP, THE GHANA
BAUXITE COMPANY BEGAN A TEN-YEAR DECLINE IN COMMERCIAL
PERFORMANCE. IN THIS DISSERTATION, THE AUTHOR EXAMINES THE
LINKAGE BETWEEN STATE OWNERSHIP AND POOR PERFORMANCE. SHE
HYPOTHESIZES THAT THE FIRM'S PERFORMANCE WAS AFFECTED BY A
CONFLICT IN GOALS BETWEEN THE GOVERNMENT AND THE COMPANY.
SHE ALSO HYPOTHESIZES THAT THE DEGREE OF AUTONOMY HELD BY
MANAGEMENT IS LINKED TO THE EFFICIENCY OF THE FIRM'S
OPERATIONS.

04188 HENDY, J.
THE TORIES' LEGISLATIVE STICK

WORLD MARXIST REVIEW, 32(6) (JUN 89), 64-66.
THIS ARTICLE EXAMINES THE IMPACT THAT THE CONSERVATIVE
GOVERNMENT HAS HAD UPON LABOR REFORM. IT CLAIMS THAT
LEGISLATIVE CHANGES SERVE TWO FUNCTIONS: FIRST IS TO INHIBIT
TRADE UNION ACTIVITY BY THE IMPOSITION OF LEGAL PENALTIES;
THE SECOND IS TO DO SO BY INFLUENCING THE ATTITUDES AND
THINKING OF WORKING PEOPLE AND TRADE UNIONISTS. IT EXPLORES
THE JUXTAPOSING OF THE INDIVIDUAL AND THE COLLECTIVE; AND
INDIVIDUALIZING LABOR RELATIONS IN ORDER TO BREAK
TRADITIONAL COLLECTIVISM AND SOLIDARITY IT SUGGESTS THAT IT
IS CRUCIAL TO FORM A POLICY FOR THE FUTURE.

04189 HENIG, J.R.
CHOICE, RACE, AND PUBLIC SCHOOLS: THE ADOPTION AND
IMPLEMENTATION OF A MAGNET PROGRAM
JOURNAL OF URBAN AFFAIRS, 11(3) (1989), 243-259.
ATTENTION TO THE ROLE OF CHOICE IN AMERICAN SCHOOLS HAS
SHIFTED FROM ITS EFFECT ON THE RACIAL COMPOSITION OF THE
STUDENT BODY TO ITS POTENTIAL EFFECT ON THE QUALITY OF
EDUCATION PROVIDED TO STUDENTS. THIS ARTICLE FOCUSES ON THE
ADOPTION AND IMPLEMENTATION OF A SERIES OF ELEMENTARY LEVEL
MAGNET SCHOOLS IN MONTGOMERY COUNTRY, MARYLAND, AS A MEANS
FOR IDENTIFYING SOME OF THE POLITICAL AND ORGANIZATIONAL
DYNAMICS LIKELY TO ACCOMPANY AN EXPANDED RELIANCE ON
PROCHOICE MECHANISMS. IMPLEMENTATION OF CHOICE OPTIONS IN
PUBLIC SCHOOL SYSTEMS, IT IS CONCLUDED, WILL ENTAIL MORE
DIFFICULT TRADE OFFS, HIGHER LEVELS OF CONFLICT, AND A MORE
AFFIRMATIVE ROLE FOR THE PUBLIC SECTOR THAN IS COMMONLY
PRESUMED.

04190 HENKELS, M.
THE ROLE OF BUREAUCRATIC EXPERTISE IN NUCLEAR WASTE POLICY:
AGENCY POWER AND POLICY DEVELOPMENT
DISSERTATION ABSTRACTS INTERNATIONAL, 50(1) (JUL 89),
256-A.
THIS DISSERTATION EXPLORES THE ROLE OF AGENCY EXPERTISE
IN THE NUCLEAR WASTE POLICY PROCESS DURING THREE PERIODS:
(1) 1957-1959 WHEN NUCLEAR WASTES ENTERED THE PUBLIC AGENDA,
(2) 1970-1972 WHEN THE ATOMIC ENERGY COMMISSION ATTEMPTED TO
ESTABLISH A WASTE REPOSITORY IN KANSAS, AND (3) 1984-1986
DURING THE DEPARTMENT OF ENERGY'S IMPLEMENTATION OF THE
NUCLEAR WASTE POLICY ACT OF 1982. THE STUDY EVALUATE WHETHER
THE PRECONDITIONS FOR DEPENDENCE ON OR DEFERENCE TO AGENCY
EXPERTISE HAVE BECOME LESS FAVORABLE, WEAKENING AGENCY
CONTROL OF THE POLICY PROCESS.

04191 HENKIN, L.
INFLUENCE, MARGINALITY, AND CENTRALITY IN THE
INTERNATIONAL LEGAL SYSTEM
JERUSALEM JOURNAL OF INTERNATIONAL RELATIONS, 11(2) (JUN
89), 49-67.
ALTHOUGH A BASIC INTERNATIONAL LEGAL ORDER, REFLECTING
ESTABLISHED CUSTOMARY LAW, IS NOW IN PLACE, THE RULES AND
POLITICS OF LAWMAKING CONTINUE, ON THE WHOLE, TO FAVOR STATE
AUTONOMY. THERE IS AN URGENT NEED FOR NEW LAW THAT WOULD
ADDRESS THE STILL-UNMET NEEDS OF MANY NATIONS, BUT THIS
WOULD REQUIRE FAR GREATER POLITICAL WILL AND COOPERATION
AMONG THE ACTORS.

04192 HENKIN, L.
THE UNIVERSITY OF THE CONCEPT OF HUMAN RIGHTS
PHILADELPHIA: ANLS OF AMER ACMY OF POLITICAL AND SOC
SCIENCE, (506) (NOV 89), 10-16.
THE IDEA OF HUMAN RIGHTS IS RELATED BUT NOT EQUIVALENT
TO JUSTICE, THE GOOD, DEMOCRACY. STRICTLY, THE CONCEPTION IS
THAT EVERY INDIVIDUAL HAS LEGITIMATE CLAIMS UPON HIS OR HER
SOCIETY FOR DEFINED FREEDOMS AND BENEFITS. AN AUTHORITATIVE
CATALOG OF RIGHTS IS SET FORTH IN THE UNIVERSAL DECLARATION
OF HUMAN RIGHTS. THE RIGHTS OF THE UNIVERSAL DECLARATION ARE
POLITICALLY AND LEGALLY UNIVERSAL, HAVING BEEN ACCEPTED BY
VIRTUALLY ALL STATES, INCORPORATED INTO THEIR OWN LAWS, AND
TRANSLATED INTO INTERNATIONAL LEGAL OBLIGATIONS. ASSURING
RESPECT FOR RIGHTS IN FACT, HOWEVER, WILL REQUIRE THE
CONTINUED DEVELOPMENT OF STABLE POLITICAL SOCIETIES AND OF
THE COMMITMENT TO CONSTITUTIONALISM. VIRTUALLY ALL SOCIETIES
ARE ALSO CULTURALLY RECEPTIVE TO THOSE BASIC RIGHTS AND
HUMAN NEEDS INCLUDED IN THE UNIVERSAL DECLARATION THAT
REFLECT COMMON CONTEMPORARY MORAL INTUITIONS. OTHER RIGHTS,
HOWEVER NOTABLY, FREEDOM OF EXPRESSION, RELIGIOUS AND ETHNIC
EQUALITY, AND THE EQUALITY OF WOMEN - CONTINUE TO MEET DEEP
RESISTANCE.

04193 HENNAYAKE, S. K.
THE PEACE ACCORD AND THE TAMILS IN SRI LANKA
ASIAN SURVEY, XXIX(4) (APR 89), 401-415.
THE INTERNATIONAL MEDIA HAS NOT ADEQUATELY REPORTED THE
EVENTS IN SRI LANKA SINCE JULY 1987 WHEN INDIA AND SRI LANKA
SIGNED THE PEACE ACCORD DESIGNED TO END THE GUERRILLA WAR
WAGED BY THE TAMIL SEPARATISTS AND EFFECT A PERMANENT
SOLUTION TO THE TAMIL PROBLEM IN THE COUNTRY. THIS ARTICLE
VERY BRIEFLY ANALYZES RECENT POLITICAL DEVELOPMENTS IN SRI
LANKA, ESPECIALLY IN THE TAMIL-DOMINATED NORTH. IN ADDITION
TO PUBLISHED MATERIAL, THE AUTHOR HAS USED INFORMATION FROM
INFORMAL INTERVIEWS CONDUCTED IN SIR LANKA DURING THE FIRST

HALF OF 1988.

04194 HENNESSY, A.
THE CUBAN REVOLUTION: A WIDER VIEW
JOURNAL OF COMMUNIST STUDIES, 5(4) (DEC 89), 3-16.
THE CUBAN REVOLUTION HAS BEEN MARKED BY AN INDEPENDENCE
OF FOREIGN MODELS, GREATER PROXIMITY TO THE THIRD WORLD THAN
TO ORTHODOX MARXISM, AND REMARKABLE STABILITY AND LEADERSHIP
CONTINUITY. ITS MOST SALIENT CHARACTERISTIC HAS BEEN ITS
VOLUNTARISM. THE REVOLUTION HAS 'LATIN-AMERICANIZED' CUBA,
WHICH BEFORE 1959 LOOKED MORE TO THE USA AND SPAIN THAN TO
THE CARIBBEAN OR LATIN AMERICA.

04195 HENNINGHAM, S.
A DIALOGUE OF THE DEAF: ATTITUDES AND ISSUES IN NEW
CALEDONIAN POLITICS
PACIFIC AFFAIRS, 61(4) (WIN 89), 633-652.
THE NEW FRENCH GOVERNMENT IS ENGAGED IN THE HARD TASK OF
RECONCILING THE PRO-INDEPENDENCE (INDIGENOUS MELANESIAN)
KANAKS OF NEW CALEDONIA WITH THEIR "LOYALIST" PRO-FRANCE
SETTLER OPPONENTS. THE TERRITORY IS SMALL, BUT THE CONFLICT
HAS IMPLICATIONS FOR THE SECURITY AND STABILITY OF THE
SOUTHWEST PACIFIC. TO HELP EXPLAIN THE CONFLICT, AND HOW IT
MIGHT BE RESOLVED, THE PAPER REVIEWS THE REFORMIST POPULISM
OF THE UNION CALEDONIENNE PARTY IN THE 1950S AND 1960S AND
EXAMINES THE DIFFERENCES IN ATTITUDES WHICH EMERGED BETWEEN,
BUT ALSO WITHIN, THE RIVAL NATIONALIST AND LOYALIST BLOCS IN
THE 1970S AND 1980S. A REVIVAL OF THE TOLERANCE OF THE UNION
CALEDONIENNE IN ITS EARLY YEARS WOULD IMPROVE PROSPECTS FOR
A LASTING COMPROMISE. THE GOVERNMENT APPARENTLY HOPES TO
ESTABLISH FEDERAL INDEPENDENCE WITH CLOSE LINKS WITH FRANCE,
BUT PARTITION IS POSSIBLE SHOULD CONCILIATION FAIL.

04196 HENNINGHAM, S.
PLURALISM AND PARTY POLITICS IN A SOUTH PACIFIC STATE:
VANUATU'S RULING VANUA'AKU PATI AND ITS RIVALS
CONFLICT, 9(2) (1989), 171-196.
TO HELP PUT INTO CONTEXT THE POLITICAL UPHEAVALS DURING
1988 IN THE SMALL SOUTH PACIFIC ISLAND COUNTRY OF VANUATU,
THIS ARTICLE REVIEWS THE HISTORY AND CHARACTER OF THE RULING
VANUA'AKU PATI (VP), AND ITS VARIOUS RIVALS, BOTH BEFORE AND
SINCE INDEPENDENCE IN 1980. THE ARTICLES ARGUES THAT
ALTHOUGH THE CRISIS AROSE FROM A LEADERSHIP CONTEST BETWEEN
PRIME MINISTER LINI AND VP SECRETARY-GENERAL SOPE, IT ALSO
REFLECTED VANUATU'S UNDERLYING REGIONAL AND ETHNIC DIVISIONS.
THE ARTICLE CONCLUDES THAT TENSIONS AND DISRUPTIONS ARE
LIKELY TO CONTINUE, THREATENING DEMOCRACY.

04197 HENNINGSEN, M.
DEMOCRACY: THE FUTURE OF A WESTERN POLITICAL FORMATION
ALTERNATIVES, 64(3) (JUL 89), 327-342.
DEMOCRACY EVOKES CONTRADICTORY RESPONSES AROUND THE
WORLD. WHILE GLOBAL NEWS CREATES THE IMPRESSION AS IF
DEMOCRACY HERE THE FOCAL POINT OF GLOBAL ATTENTION
EVERYWHERE, A CLOSER LOOK REVEALS A RATHER MELANCHOLY
POLITIC CLIMATE WHICH SEEMS TO PREVAIL IN THE POSTINDUSTRIAL
SOCIETIES OF THE WEST. THIS PAPER IS AN ATTEMPT AT
INTERPRETING THIS PARADOX IN THE CONTEXT OF THE HISTORY OF
DEMOCRACY AS A WESTERN POLITICAL FORMATION. THE PAPER WILL
REVISIT SOME OF THE MAJOR WESTERN CONFIGURATIONS DURING THE
PAST 200 YEARS IN ORDER TO UNDERSTAND BETTER THE CONTRAST
BETWEEN GLOBAL HOPE AND WESTERN MELANCHOLY. THE HISTORICAL
REEXAMINATION MAY ALSO SHED SOME LIGHT ON THE TENSIONS
VISIBLE IN THOSE SOCIETIES WHICH ARE NOW UNDERGOING MAJOR
PROCESSES OF SOCIAL RESTRUCTURING. HOWEVER, THE ROOTS OF
WESTERN MELANCHOLY LIE NOT ONLY IN THE PAST. A NEW SOCIAL
AGENDA ADDS URGENCY TO THE PROBLEMS ALL WESTERN DEMOCRATIC
SOCIETIES WILL HAVE TO COPE WITH IN THE FUTURE.

04198 HENRY, B.
JAMAICA: TURNABOUT
THIRD WORLD WEEK, 7(9) (JAN 89), 77-78.
IN 1980, MANY JAMAICANS THOUGHT THEY WERE SAVING THEIR
COUNTRY FROM COMMUNISM WHEN THEY ELECTED RIGHT-WINGER EDWARD
P.G. SEAGA AND TURNED PRIME MINISTER MICHAEL N. MANLEY OUT
OFFICE. NOW IT APPEARS LIKELY THAT THE VOTERS WILL TURN
THEIR BACKS ON SEAGA AND RETURN MANLEY TO OFFICE IN THE
FEBRUARY 1989 ELECTION.

04199 HENRY, C.
JESSE JACKSON AND THE DECLINE OF LIBERALISM IN
PRESIDENTIAL POLITICS
BLACK SCHOLAR, 20(1) (JAN 89), 2-11.
THE ARTICLE ANALYZES THE APPARENT DECLINE OF LIBERALISM
AND ASKS THE QUESTION OF WHY DID THE PARTY OF FRANKLIN D
ROOSEVELT DENY ITS HERITAGE. IT EXAMINES THE LIBERAL
TRADITION AND THE RISE OF CONSERVATISM. AS GENERAL TRENDS.
IT ALSO SEEKS TO ISOLATE SPECIFIC FACTORS IN THE 1988
PRESIDENTIAL ELECTION THAT RESULTED IN A REPUBLICAN VICOTRY.
IT ALSO ATTEMPTS A BRIEF PROGNOSIS OF THE FUTURE OF THE
LIBERAL MOVEMENT.

04200 HENRY, D. JR.
LIBERTY AND SOPHISTICATION

JOURNAL OF STATE GOVERNMENT, 62(1) (JAN 89), 28-30.
WHEN THE U.S. CONSTITUTION WAS WRITTEN, THE 10TH
AMENDMENT WAS INSISTED UPON AS A SAFEGUARD AGAINST EXCESS BY
THE CENTRAL GOVERNMENT. TODAY ANOTHER CONSTITUTIONAL
AMENDMENT IS NEEDED TO RESTORE THE 10TH AMENDMENT'S
PROTECTION OF LIBERTY AND PROPERTY FROM AN UNRESTRAINED
FEDERAL GOVERNMENT.

04201 HENRY, R.M.
INEQUALITY IN PLURAL SOCIETIES: AN EXPLORATION
SOCIAL AND ECONOMIC STUDIES, 38(2) (JUN 89), 69-110.
THE PAPER FOCUSES ON INEQUALITY IN PLURAL SOCIETIES AND
QUESTIONS WHETHER THE INVERTED 'U' HYPOTHESIS ON THE
RELATIONSHIP BETWEEN INEQUALITY AND PER CAPITA INCOME IS AS
EASILY ESTABLISHED AS COMPARED TO MORE HOMOGENEOUS SOCIETIES.
SINCE THERE ARE INTERVENING STRUCTURAL FACTORS THAT WOULD
DISTURB THE NEATNESS OF THAT ASSUMED RELATIONSHIP,
ECONOMISTS NEED TO APPLY ALTERNATIVE HYPOTHESES IN EMPIRICAL
WORK ON DISTRIBUTION IN SUCH SOCIETIES.

04202 HENSCHEN, B.M.; SIDLOW, E.I.
THE SUPREME COURT AND THE CONGRESSIONAL AGENDA - SETTING
PROCESS
JOURNAL OF LAW & POLITICS, 5(4) (SUM 89), 685-724.
AS AN IMPORTANT FIRST STEP IN THE POLICYMAKING PROCESS,
THE SETTING OF THE AGENDA IS CRITICAL IN DETERMINING THE
PROBLEMS GOVERNMENT ADDRESSES AND THE POLICIES IT PRODUCES.
THE PURPOSE OF THIS STUDY IS TO EXPLORE THE ROLE THE COURT
MAY PLAY IN AGENDA-SETTING BY LOOKING AT CASES THAT PROMPTED
CONGRESSIONAL ACTION AND THE FORCES THAT MAY HAVE INTERVENED
IN THE PROCESS BY WHICH THE COURT "PUT" JUDICIAL POLCIES ON
THE CONGRESSIONAL AGENDA. SPECIFICALLY, IT EXAMINES SUPREME
COURT CASES IN TWO STATUTORY POLICY AREAS, LABOR AND
ANTITRUST, THAT PROVOKED CONGRESSIONAL RESPONSE IN THE FORM
OF LEGISLATION DESIGNED TO ENACT INTO LAW THE DECISION OF
THE COURT, SUPPLEMENT OR CLARIFY THE COURT'S INTERPRETATION,
MODIFY THE COURT'S DECISION, OR REVERSE A SUPREME COURT
RULING.

04203 HENZE, P.B.
CONTRASTS IN AFRICAN DEVELOPMENT: THE ECONOMIES OF KENYA
AND ETHIOPIA, 1975-1984
AVAILABLE FROM NTIS, NO. AD-A208 309/5/GAR, APR 89, 35.
THIS DOCUMENT COMPARES KENYAN AND ETHIOPIAN ECONOMIC
DEVELOPMENT DURING THE CRUCIAL DECADE 19751984. BOTH
COUNTRIES EXPERIENCED BASIC CHANGES IN LEADERSHIP DURING THE
PERIOD ETHIOPIA IN 1974 AND KENYA IN 1978. THE MILITARY
JUNTA (DERG) THAT SEIZED POWER IN ETHIOPIA ABANDONED PRO-
WESTERN POLICIES WITH THE AIM OF BUILDING A MARXIST-LENINIST
ECONOMY AND POLITICAL STRUCTURE; THE NEW KENYAN LEADERSHIP
REMAINED PRO WESTERN. ALTHOUGH BOTH SUFFERED BECAUSE OF
PETROLEUM PRICE INCREASES, DROUGHT, FOOD SHORTAGES, AND
MILITARY THREATS, KENYA EMERGED FROM THE DECADE WITH GOOD
PROSPECTS FOR ECONOMIC GROWTH TO ACCOMMODATE ITS INCREASING
POPULATION. ETHIOPIA, ON THE OTHER HAND, MADE NO SIGNIFICANT
ECONOMIC PROGRESS. THE SITUATION CLEARLY DEMONSTRATED THE
SUPERIORITY OF KENYA'S MIXED ECONOMY, WHICH EMPHASIZED
PRIVATE INITIATIVE AND PEASANT AGRICULTURE, OVER ETHIOPIA'S
MARXIST-LENINIST SYSTEM.

04204 HENZE, P.B.
IS THERE HOPE FOR THE HORN OF AFRICA: REFLECTIONS ON THE
POLITICAL AND ECONOMIC IMPASSES
AVAILABLE FROM NTIS, NO. AD-A200 260/8/GAR, JUN 88, 33.
THIS NOTE IS THE EXTENDED AND UPDATED VERSION OF A PAPER
THAT WAS PRESENTED AT A CONFERENCE ON CRISIS IN THE HORN OF
AFRICA: CAUSES AND PROSPECTS, AT THE WOODROW WILSON
INTERNATIONAL CENTER FOR SCHOLARS, SMITHSONIAN INSTITUTION,
WASHINGTON, D.C., JUNE 1987. THE STUDY, WHICH DRAWS ON THE
AUTHOR'S VISIT TO ETHIOPIA IN MARCH 1987, REVIEWS THE
DESTABILIZING EFFECTS ON THE HORN OF AFRICA OF INCREASING
SOVIET ACTIVISM; FAMINE IN ETHIOPIA AND SUDAN, AND ERITREA;
AND SOMALIAN IRREDENTISM. THE AUTHOR BELIEVES THAT TO
ALLEVIATE THE ECONOMIC AND POLITICAL DETERIORATION OF THE
REGION, WESTERN GOVERNMENTS MUST JOIN IN SETTING UP AN
INTERNATIONAL PEACE AND MEDIATION COMMISSION THAT WOULD WORK
TOWARD (1) THE ACCEPTANCE BY THE COUNTRIES INVOLVED OF DE
FACTO BORDERS AND ARBITRATION OF DISPUTES; (2) THE
PERSUASION OF FOREIGN POWERS TO CEASE SUPPORT OF SEPARATISM
AND DISSIDENCE; (3) A MORATORIUM ON ARMS SHIPMENTS TO THE
REGION; (4) THE CREATION OF AN INTERNATIONAL GROUP TO
MONITOR COMPLIANCE WITH THE PEACE PROCESS AND HUMAN RIGHTS
STANDARDS; (5) ADHERENCE BY ALL DONORS TO COMMON CRITERIA
FOR THE PROVISION OF EMERGENCY RELIEF AND DEVELOPMENT AID;
AND (6) INCREASED REGIONAL ECONOMIC DEVELOPMENT AID.

04205 HEPBURN, D.L.
COOPERATION AND CONFIDENCE-BUILDING MEASURES IN LATIN
AMERICA AND THE CARIBBEAN
DISARMAMENT, XII(3) (AUT 89), 77-82.
THE LATIN AMERICAN AND CARIBBEAN REGION HAS MISSED SOME
OPPORTUNITIES TO COOPERATE IN THE PAST, BUT RECENT
INITIATIVES HAVE BEEN ENCOURAGING AND GOVERNMENTS SEEM TO BE
LOOKING FOR AVENUES OF COOPERATION AND MEANS OF CONFIDENCE-

BUILDING.

04206 HEPER, M.
MOTHERLAND PARTY GOVERNMENTS AND BUREAUCRACY IN TURKEY,
1938-1988
GOVERNANCE, 2(4) (OCT 89), 460-471.
THE TURISH POLITICAL SYSTEM WITH ITS OTTOMAN LEGACY
STANDS OUT AS A UNIQUE EXAMPLE OF A MODERNIZING POLITY WITH
A DISTINCT STATE TRADITION. THIS ARTICLE EXPLORES THE SHARP
CENTER-PERIPHERY CONFLICT IN TURKEY WHICH PLACED ITS
INDELIBLE STAMP ON LATER PERIODS AND PLACES RECENT
DEVELOPMENTS WITH RESPECT TO PUBLIC BUREAUCRACY IN
PERSPECTIVE AS THIS PARTICULAR EVOLUTION IS KEPT IN MIND.
EXPLORED ARE FOUR POLICIES TO REDUCE THE SCOPE OF CIVIL
BUREAUCRACY IN TURKISH POLITICS: PRIVATIZATION,
SIMPLIFICATION, DECENTRALIZATION AT THE LOCALITIES AND
REDUCED BUREAUCRACY AT THE CENTER.

04207 HEPPENHEIMER, T.A.
MR. NOSE CONE AND THE WEAPON OF OPENNESS
REASON, 20(11) (APR 89), 37-39.
THE AUTHOR PROFILES PHYSICIST ARTHUR KANTROWITZ, WHO HAS
ADVOCATED THE ESTABLISHMENT OF A SCIENCE COURT TO DEBATE AND
ADVISE THE NATION'S LAWMAKERS ON TECHNOLOGICAL ISSUES. HE
HAS STATED THAT A SCIENCE COURT WOULD HAVE THE VIRTUE OF
OPENNESS, WHICH HE VIEWS AS THE KEY TO AMERICA'S STRENGTH.

04208 HERB, G.H.
PERSUASIVE CARTOGRAPHY IN GEOPOLITIK AND NATIONAL SOLIALISM
POLITICAL GEOGRAPHY QUARTERLY, 8(3) (JUL 89), 271-288.
THE ARTICLE EXAMINES THE USE OF PERSUASIVE CARTOGRAPHY
BY BOTH THE GERMAN SCHOOL OF "GEOPOLITIK" AND BY THE
NATIONAL SOCIALISTS. ALTHOUGH THE TWO MOVEMENTS SHARED MANY
CAUSES, THE ARTICLE CONCLUDES THAT THE PERSUASIVE MAPS
DIFFERED NOT ONLY IN THEIR GRAPHIC FORM BUT ALSO IN THEIR
POLITICAL CONTENT.

04209 HERBST, J.
PROSPECTS FOR REVOLUTION IN SOUTH AFRICA
POLITICAL SCIENCE QUARTERLY, 103(4) (WIN 89), 665-686.
SOME SCHOLARS AND MANY INSIDE THE AFRICAN NATIONAL
CONGRESS NOW ARGUE THAT A QUANTITATIVE INCREASE IN THE
CURRENT FORM OF POPULAR PROTEST MAY LEAD TO A SUCCESSFUL
REBELLION IN SOUTH AFRICA. THEREFORE, AN EXAMINATION OF THE
REVOLUTIONARY OPPORTUNITIES AND CONSTRAINTS CREATED BY THE
MOST RECENT OUTBREAK OF PROTEST IS NECESSARY IF THE FUTURE
EVOLUTION OF SOUTH AFRICA IS TO BE UNDERSTOOD. AFTER ARGUING
THAT THE PRESENT PROTEST ACTIVITIES DO NOT POSE A THREAT TO
THE CONTINUED EXISTENCE OF THE WHITE REGIME, THIS ESSAY
SUGGESTS WHAT DEVELOPMENTS WOULD INDICATE THAT A TRULY
REVOLUTIONARY SITUATION IS DEVELOPING IN SOUTH AFRICA.

04210 HERBST, J.
THE CREATION AND MAINTENANCE OF NATIONAL BOUNDARIES IN
AFRICA
INTERNATIONAL ORGANIZATION, 43(4) (FAL 89), 673-692.
A PARADOX IS CENTRAL TO THE NATURE OF POLITICAL
BOUNDARIES IN AFRICA: THERE IS WIDESPREAD AGREEMENT THAT THE
BOUNDARIES ARE ARBITRARY, YET THE VAST MAJORITY OF THEM HAVE
REMAINED VIRTUALLY UNTOUCHED SINCE THE LATE 1800S, WHEN THEY
WERE FIRST DEMARCATED. THIS ARTICLE ARGUES THAT, CONTRARY TO
CURRENT THEORIES, THE PRESENT BOUNDARY SYSTEM REPRESENTS A
RATIONAL RESPONSE BY BOTH THE COLONIALISTS AND THE PRESENT-
DAY AFRICAN LEADERS TO THE CONSTRAINTS IMPOSED BY THE
DEMOGRAPHIC AND ETHNOGRAPHIC STRUCTURE OF THE CONTINENT.
USING THIS FRAMEWORK OF ANALYSIS, THE ARTICLE EXAMINES THE
INSTITUTIONS THAT FORMULATED THE DECISION-MAKING RULES FOR
THE CREATION AND MAINTENANCE OF BOUNDARIES IN AFRICA,
DISCUSSES THE CONDITIONS UNDER WHICH COOPERATION AMONG
STATES HAS OCCURRED, AND EXPLORES THE PROSPECTS FOR FUTURE
CHANGES IN THE BORDERS OF AFRICAN STATES.

04211 HERF, J.
A POLITICAL CULTURE IN CRISIS THE CASE FOR KOHL
NATIONAL INTEREST, (17) (FAL 89), 55-62.
THIS ARTICLE OFFERS A REVIEW OF THE ESSENTIALS OF WEST
GERMANY'S DEMOCRATIC POLITICAL CULTURE WHICH PLACES
DEVELOPMENTS SINCE 1960 IN FOCUS. IT EXPLORES THE IMPACT ON
WEST GERMAN POLITICAL CULTURE OF HELMUT KOHL, AS HE
CONTINUED TO SPEAK A LANGUAGE OF FREEDOM VERSUS
TOTALITARIANISM AND DEMOCRACY VERSUS DICTATORSHIP. IT
CONCLUDES THAT THE WEST GERMAN POLITICAL SCENE TODAY
CONSISTS OF A POPULAR FRONT OF THE LEFT, A MILITANTLY
DEMOCRATIC CENTER AND RIGHT, AND A REVIVAL OF THE OLD, ANTI-
DEMOCRATIC RIGHT, AND THAT THE SPLIT BETWEEN THE DEMOCRATIC
RIGHT AND THE UNDEMOCRATIC RIGHT REMAINS A CHASM FOR HELMUT
KOHL.

04212 HERLIHY, P.H.
PANAMA'S QUIET REVOLUTION: COMARCA HOMELANDS AND INDIAN
RIGHTS
CULTURAL SURVIVAL QUARTERLY, 13(3) (1989), 17-24.
PANAMA HAS SEEN THE EMERGENCE OF A REVOLUTIONARY CONCEPT:
THE COMARCA, OR INDIAN HOMELAND. THE COMARCA HAS BECOME THE

FUNDAMENTAL OBJECTIVE OF THE PANAMANIAN INDIANS' MODERN
POLITICAL CONDUCT. BECAUSE THE KUNA AND CHOCO INDIANS HAVE
ALREADY GAINED COMARCA STATUS FOR PARTS OF THEIR TERRITORY,
THEIR POLITICS FOCUS MORE SPECIFICALLY ON THE ADMINISTRATIVE
PROBLEMS CREATED BY PRESSURES FROM OUTSIDE SOURCES. BUT THE
GUAYMI AND TERIBE ARE STILL LOBBYING FOR HOMELANDS, WHILE
THE BRIBRI HAVE REMAINED LARGELY APART FROM THE POLITICAL
PROCESS.

04213 HERMAN, L.G.
  PRIMAL POLITICS: A PHILOSOPHICAL STORY OF GOOD AND EVIL
  DISSERTATION ABSTRACTS INTERNATIONAL, 49(10) (APR 89),
  3141-A.
    THE AUTHOR ARGUES THAT THE PROFUSION OF CRITICAL GLOBAL
  PROBLEMS FACING THE WORLD TODAY IS SYMPTOMATIC OF A
  POTENTIALLY CATASTROPHIC TURNING POINT IN INDUSTRIAL
  CIVILIZATION. USING THE DECONSTRUCTION OF WESTERN
  CIVILIZATION BY THE FRANKFURT SCHOOL PHILOSOPHERS AS A
  STARTING POINT, HE SUGGEST THAT WHAT IS AT STAKE IS THE
  MEANING AND VIABILITY OF CIVILIZATION IN ITS ENTIRETY.

04214 HERMANN, M.C.; HERMANN, C.E.
  WHO MAKES FOREIGN POLICY DECISIONS AND HOW: AN EMPIRICAL
  INQUIRY
  INTERNATIONAL STUDIES QUARTERLY, 33(4) (DEC 89), 361-388.
    AT THE APEX OF FOREIGN POLICY MAKING IN ALL GOVERNMENTS
  OR RULING PARTIES ARE ACTORS WITH THE ABILITY TO COMMIT THE
  RESOURCES OF THE GOVERNMENT AND THE POWER TO PREVENT OTHER
  ENTITIES WITHIN THE GOVERNMENT FROM REVERSING THEIR POSITION
  - THE ULTIMATE DECISION UNIT. ALTHOUGH THIS DECISION UNIT
  MAY CHANGE WITH THE NATURE OF THE POLICY PROBLEM AND WITH
  TIME, ITS STRUCTURE WILL SHAPE A GOVERNMENT'S FOREIGN POLICY.
  IN THIS PAPER HE PROPOSE THREE TYPES OF DECISION UNITS:
  PREDOMINANT LEADERS, SINGLE GROUPS, AND MULTIPLE AUTONOMOUS
  ACTORS. EACH OF THESE EXISTS IN ONE OF SEVERAL CONDITIONS
  THAT HELP TO DETERMINE WHETHER THE DECISION UNIT AFFECTS
  FOREIGN POLICY LARGELY THROUGH THE PRE-EXISTING KNOWLEDGE,
  BELIEFS, AND STYLE OF THOSE PARTICIPATING IN THE UNIT (A
  SELF-CONTAINED UNIT) OR WHETHER FACTORS OUTSIDE THE DECISION
  UNIT MUST BE TAKEN INTO CONSIDERATION IN UNDERSTANDING THE
  RESULTS OF THE DECISION-MAKING PROCESS (AN EXTERNALLY
  INFLUENCEABLE UNIT). THE HYPOTHESES THAT SELF-CONTAINED
  UNITS WILL ENGAGE IN MORE EXTREME FOREIGN POLICY BEHAVIOR
  THAN EXTERNALLY INFLUENCEABLE UNITS AND THAT SINGLE GROUP
  DECISION UNITS WILL SHOW MORE EXTREME FOREIGN POLICY
  BEHAVIOR THAN THOSE COMPRISED OF MULTIPLE AUTONOMOUS ACTORS
  ARE EXAMINED USING DATA FROM TWENTY-FIVE NATIONS DURING THE
  DECADE FROM 1959 OR 1968.

04215 HERMASSI, E.
  THE FRENCH REVOLUTION AND THE ARAB WORLD
  INTERNATIONAL SOCIAL SCIENCE JOURNAL, (119) (FEB 89),
  33-44.
    AS A GLOBAL HISTORICAL PHENOMENON, THE FRENCH REVOLUTION
  SET ITS SEAL ON A NEW TYPE OF SOCIETY AND GAVE RISE TO A
  VAST EXPANIONIST MOVEMENT. ITS IMPACT, THOUGH INDIRECT, HAS
  HIGHLY SIGNIFICANT IN THE ARAB WORLD.

04216 HERNANDEZ, CAROLINA, G.
  THE PHILIPPINES IN 1988: REACHING OUT TO PEACE AND
  ECONOMIC RECOVERY
  ASIAN SURVEY, XXIX(2) (FEB 89), 154-164.
    AFTER AN ANALYSIS OF DEVELOPMENTS IN THE PHILIPPINES IN
  THE AREAS OF POLITICS, ECONOMICS, AND FOREIGN RELATIONS IN
  1988, THE ARTICLE CONCLUDES THAT, ON BALANCE, 1988 HAS A
  YEAR WHEN THE PHILIPPINES SHOWED MORE HOPEFUL SIGNS OF
  ECONOMIC RECOVERY AND PERHAPS PEACE. ECONOMIC GROWTH WAS
  ABOVE THE GOVERNMENT TARGETED RATE. DESPITE CONTINUED
  CONFLICT BETWEEN THE GOVERNMENT AND THE COMMUNIST PARTY OF
  THE PHILIPPINES' NEW PEOPLE'S ARMY AND ACCUSATIONS OF
  WIDESPREAD POLITICAL CORRUPTION THE ABSENCE OF ANY COUP
  ATTEMPTS HAS A HEARTENING SIGN.

04217 HERNANDEZ, L.; CARLSEN, L.
  GRASSROOTS CHALLENGES
  HEMISPHERE, 1(2) (WIN 89), 52-54.
    MEXICO'S 1988 PRESIDENTIAL ELECTION GAVE A VOICE TO A
  WIDESPREAD PHENOMENON THAT HAS BEEN QUIETLY GROWING FOR
  YEARS. GRASSROOTS MOVEMENTS PREPARED THE GROUND FOR THE
  MASSIVE ANTI-INSTITUTIONAL REVOLUTIONARY PARTY EXPRESSION ON
  ELECTION DAY. THESE MOVEMENTS HAVE EVOLVED FROM THE
  AFTERMATH OF THE GOVERNMENT'S ANTI-STUDENT REPRESSION, WHICH
  HAS SPAWNED A GENERATION OF SOCIAL ACTIVISTS. THE MOVEMENTS
  HAVE GAINED FORCE AS SURVIVAL MECHANISMS IN A SETTING OF
  AUTHORITARIAN GOVERNMENT AND ECONOMIC CRISIS. GRASSROOTS
  MOVEMENTS PROVIDE THE KEY TO UNDERSTANDING THE CHANGING
  POLITICAL CLIMATE OF MEXICO.

04218 HERNANDEZ, L.; CARLSEN, L.
  RURAL STRUGGLE
  HEMISPHERE, 1(2) (WIN 89), 55.
    FOR DECADES, XOXOCOTLA, MEXICO, HAS LED A DUAL POLITICAL
  LIFE. ON THE ONE HAND, ITS RESIDENTS HAVE MANAGED TO
  CONSERVE THE PRINCIPAL FEATURES OF THEIR POLITICAL

TRADITIONS. A LOCAL ASSEMBLY CONTINUES TO ELECT THE TOWN'S
GOVERNING LEADERSHIP AND THE ELDERLY STILL PLAY A VITAL ROLE
IN COMMUNITY AFFAIRS. ON THE OTHER HAND, LOCAL CONCERNS HAVE
BEEN INCREASINGLY SUBORDINATED TO THE POLICIES AND WHIMS OF
FEDERAL AND STATE AUTHORITIES.

04219 HERO, R.E.
  MULTIRACIAL COALITIONS IN CITY ELECTIONS INVOLVING
  MINORITY CANDIDATES: SOME EVIDENCE FROM DENVER
  URBAN AFFAIRS QUARTERLY, 25(2) (DEC 89), 342-351.
    THIS RESEARCH EXAMINES THE ELECTORAL COALITIONS OF
  MINORITY CANDIDATES ELECTED CITYWIDE. THE FOCUS IS ON THE
  ELECTION OF A HISPANIC AS MAYOR AND A BLACK AS CITY AUDITOR
  OF DENVER. ALTHOUGH THE COALITIONS THAT ELECTED THE TWO
  MINORITY CANDIDATES ARE SIMILAR IN MANY RESPECTS, THERE ARE
  SOME NOTABLE DIFFERENCES. PERHAPS MOST INTERESTING ARE THE
  LEVELS OF BLACK SUPPORT FOR THE HISPANIC CANDIDATE AS
  COMPARED TO THE HISPANIC SUPPORT FOR THE BLACK CANDIDATE.
  AND THE LEVEL OF NONMINORITY SUPPORT FOR THE BLACK AUDITOR
  CANDIDATE IS SOEMWHAT HIGHER THAN THAT FOR THE HISPANIC
  MAYORAL CANDIDATE. THESE FINDINGS ARE INTEGRALLY IMPORTANT
  BUT THERE ARE ALSO BROADER IMPLICATIONS.

04220 HERO, R.E.; BEATTY, K.M.
  THE ELECTIONS OF FEDERICO PENA AS MAYOR OF DENVER:
  ANALYSIS AND IMPLICATIONS
  SOCIAL SCIENCE QUARTERLY, 70(2) (JUN 89), 300-310.
    THIS ANALYSIS ILLUMINATES THE IMPACT OF ETHNICITY, PARTY
  AFFILIATION, AND INCREASED TURNOUT IN THE ELECTIONS OF
  FEDERICO PENA AS MAYOR OF DENVER IN 1983 AND 1987.
  SUBSTANTIAL EVIDENCE OF "RACIAL VOTING" IS FOUND. PARTY
  AFFILIATION HAD A CLEAR IMPACT, ESPECIALLY IN 1987. A
  STRATEGY OF SELECTIVELY INCREASING TURNOUT APPEARS TO HAVE
  BEEN EFFECTIVE AND MAY HAVE BEEN A DECIDING FACTOR. THE
  BROADER IMPLICATIONS OF THESE FINDINGS, FOR BOTH ELECTIONS
  AND GOVERNANCE, ARE BRIEFLY DISCUSSED.

04221 HERO, R.E.
  THE U.S. CONGRESS AND AMERICAN FEDERALISM: ARE
  'SUBNATIONAL' GOVERNMENTS PROTECTED?
  WESTERN POLITICAL QUARTERLY, 42(1) (MAR 89), 93-106.
    A MAJOR ASSUMPTION OF AMERICAN FEDERALISM IS THAT STATE
  AND LOCAL GOVERNMENTS ARE "PROTECTED" FROM NATIONAL
  GOVERNMENT INTRUSIONS BY STRUCTURAL FEATURES INHERENT IN THE
  NATIONAL GOVERNMENT, PRINCIPALLY THE REPRESENTATION OF .
  STATES AND THEIR SUBUNITS IN THE SENATE AND HOUSE,
  RESPECTIVELY. THE PURPOSE OF THIS PAPER IS TO CONSIDER THIS
  ASSUMPTION AND TO PROVIDE SEVERAL SOURCES OF EVIDENCE WHICH
  ARE PERTINENT TO THESE ISSUES. FIRST, SEVERAL POINTS WHICH
  HAVE BEEN RAISED IN OBJECTION TO THE ASSUMPTION ARE
  PRESENTED AND CRITIQUED. SOME GENERAL DEVELOPMENTS WHICH ARE
  RELEVANT TO THE ASSUMPTION ARE NEXT DISCUSSED. EMPIRICAL
  EVIDENCE, CONGRESSIONAL VOTES ON "FEDERALISM ISSUES"
  AGGREGATED BY STATE CONGRESSIONAL DELEGATION, IS THEN
  EXAMINED TO ASSESS THE ASSUMPTION. THERE IS MODEST EVIDENCE
  OF SUPPORT FOR FEDERALISM BUT IT IS DIFFICULT TO ASCERTAIN
  HOW STATE DELEGATIONS CONSTRUCT THAT SUPPORT. IT SEEMS THAT
  FEDERALISM'S SIGNIFICANCE, AS MANIFESTED IN CONGRESSIONAL
  ROLL-CALL VOTES, IS INTERSTITIAL AND/OR MEDIATIVE.

04222 HERRING, C.
  ACQUIESCENCE OR ACTIVISM? POLITICAL BEHAVIOR AMONG THE
  POLITICALLY ALIENATED
  POLITICAL PSYCHOLOGY, 10(1) (MAR 89), 135-154.
    THIS PAPER FOCUSES ON FACTORS ASSOCIATED WITH MASS
  SOCIETY AND RELATIVE DEPRIVATION THEORIES AS DETERMINANTS OF
  POLITICAL BEHAVIOR AMONG THE POLITICALLY ALIENATED. RESULTS
  FROM CONTINGENCY TABLE AND LOGIT ANALYSIS SUGGEST THAT NOT
  ONLY DO THE ALIENATED DIFFER FROM THEIR NONALIENATED
  COUNTERPARTS, BUT ALSO THERE ARE SUBSTANTIAL VARIATIONS
  AMONG THE ALIENATED: (1) THOSE WITH ORGANIZATIONAL
  AFFILIATIONS AND TRUST IN OTHERS ARE LESS LIKELY TO BE
  "POLITICAL DROPOUTS"; (2) THOSE WHO FEEL WORSE OFF OR
  UNDEREMPLOYED ARE LESS LIKELY TO BE "POLITICAL RITUALISTS";
  (3) THOSE WITH ORGANIZATIONAL AFFILIATIONS ARE MORE LIKELY
  TO ENGAGE SIMULTANEOUSLY IN CONVENTIONAL AND UNCONVENTIONAL
  MODES OF PARTICIPATION; AND (4) THOSE WHO ARE UNTRUSTING AND
  THOSE WHO FEEL UNDEREMPLOYED ARE SIGNIFICANTLY MORE LIKELY
  TO BE INVOLVED AS PROTESTORS. MASS SOCIETY AND RELATIVE
  DEPRIVATION THEORIES HELP DISTINGUISH AMONG THE POLITICALLY
  ALIENATED, BUT THEIR PREDICTIONS ABOUT THE RELATIVE
  FREQUENCIES OF DIFFERENT REACTIONS TO ALIENATION ARE NOT
  BORNE OUT.

04223 HERRING, R.J.
  DILEMMAS OF AGRARIAN COMMUNISM: PEASANT DIFFERENTIATION,
  SECTORAL AND VILLAGE POLITICS
  THIRD WORLD QUARTERLY, 11(1) (JAN 89), 89-115.
    LAND REFORM PRESENTS THE AGRARIAN LEFT WITH A DOUBLE-
  EDGED SWORD: AN ISSUE THAT MOBILIZES THE POOR BUT
  SIMULTANEOUSLY THREATENS TO DESTROY THE VERY SOCIAL-
  STRUCTURAL NICHE WHICH EFFECTUATES THAT MOBILIZATION
  POTENTIAL. AGRARIAN COMMUNISM IN INDIA HAS DIVERGED ALONG
  THESE LINES. KERALA'S COMMUNISTS RECOGNIZED THE THREAT OF

EMBOURGEOISEMENT BUT PRESSED TO ABOLISH THE LANDLORD-TENANT
NEXUS WITH A LAND-TO-THE-TILLER REFORM. ELECTORAL COMMUNISM
IN WEST BENGAL AVERTED THE THREAT OF EMBOURGEOISEMENT.
REJECTING LAND-TO-THE-TILLER, BENGAL'S COMMUNIST PARTY
SETTLED FOR THE LAND POLICY OF CONSERVATIVE REGIMES: TENANCY
REFORM. THE CRUCIAL POLITICAL DIFFERENCE IS THAT TENANTS
REMAIN DEPENDENT ON POLITICAL-ADMINISTRATIVE MEANS TO RETAIN
PROPRIETARY CLAIMS.

04224 HERRNSON, P.S.
NATIONAL PARTY DECISION MAKING, STRATEGIES, AND RESOURCE
DISTRIBUTION IN CONGRESSIONAL ELECTIONS
WESTERN POLITICAL QUARTERLY, 42(3) (SEP 89), 301-325.
NATIONAL PARTY ORGANIZATIONS HAVE RECENTLY BECOME ACTIVE
CONGRESSIONAL CAMPAIGNERS. THIS STUDY EXAMINES THE NATIONAL
PARTIES' DECISION-MAKING PROCESSES, STRATEGIES, AND THE
DISTRIBUTION OF PARTY RESOURCES TO CANDIDATES IN THE 1984
CONGRESSIONAL ELECTIONS. THE RESULTS SHOW THAT THE
REPUBLICAN NATIONAL AND CONGRESSIONAL CAMPAIGN COMMITTEES
PROVIDED MORE CAMPAIGN ASSISTANCE TO CONGRESSIONAL
CANDIDATES THAN DID THEIR DEMOCRATIC COUNTERPARTS. COMPARED
TO THE DEMOCRATS, THE REPUBLICANS MORE CLEARLY TARGETED
COORDINATED EXPENDITURES AND CAMPAIGN SERVICES TO
COMPETITIVE CANDIDATES, SOUTHERNERS, NONINCUMBENTS, AND
CANDIDATES POSSESSING HIGH QUALITY CAMPAIGN ORGANIZATIONS.
THE DEMOCRATS, HOWEVER, MORE CLEARLY TARGETED CAMPAIGN
CONTRIBUTIONS TO NONINCUMBENTS. THE NATIONAL PARTIES'
RESOURCES, ORGANIZATIONAL CHARACTERISTICS, AND DECISION-
MAKING PROCESSES HAD A MAJOR IMPACT ON THE DISTRIBUTION OF
PARTY CAMPAIGN ASSISTANCE.

04225 HERRON, D.R.
THE IDEA OF FEDERALISM IN WESTERN EUROPE AFTER WORLD WAR
II: AN ANALYSIS OF THE GOALS AND TACTICS OF THE EUROPEAN
UNION OF FEDERALISTS (UEF)
DISSERTATION ABSTRACTS INTERNATIONAL, 48(10) (APR 88),
2721-A.
THE NOT WELL UNDERSTOOD CONCEPT OF "FEDERALISM" WITH
REGARDS TO THE EFFORTS TO CREATE A EUROPEAN FEDERATION AFTER
WORLD WAR II IS THE SUBJECT OF THE DISSERTATION. THE WRITING
AND ACTIONS OF THE LEADERS OF THE EUROPEAN UNION OF
FEDERALISTS ARE EXAMINED TO REVEAL THE TWO DIFFERENT
MEANINGS OF THE TERM "FEDERALISM" THAT WERE IN USE IN THE
LATE 1940'S. ONE WAS BASED ON THE ANGLO-AMERICAN TRADITION
OF FEDERALISM AND CAME TO BE KNOWN AS INTERNATIONAL
FEDERALISM. THE OTHER WAS BASED ON FRENCH TRADTIONS AND
BECAME KNOWN AS INTEGRAL FEDERALISM.

04226 HERZ, B.
BRINGING WOMEN INTO THE ECONOMIC MAINSTREAM
FINANCE AND DEVELOPMENT, 26(4) (DEC 89), 22-25.
THIS ARTICLE EXPLORES CONCERN FOR DEVELOPING NATIONS
WOMEN FOR ECONOMIC REASONS AS WELL AS EQUITY AND POLITICAL
GROUNDS. IT DETAILS HOW WOMEN CONTRIBUTE SUBSTANTIALLY TO
ECONOMIC GROWTH, HELPING MAKE HEADWAY IN REDUCING POVERTY
IMPROVING FAMILY WELFARE, SLOWING DOWN POPULATION GROWTH AND
SAVING THE ENVIRONMENT. IT EXAMINES EVIDENCE WHICH SUGGESTS
THAT EFFORTS TO IMPROVE OPPORTUNITIES FOR WOMEN CAN BE COST
EFFECTIVE, BUT THAT IT WILL BE IMPORTANT TO REFINE AND TEST
INNOVATIVE APPROACHES, AS IT EXPANDS INTO MORE COUNTRIES AND
A GREATER NUMBER OF FIELDS.

04227 HERZFELD, C.
TECHNOLOGY AND NATIONAL SECURITY: RESTORING THE US EDGE
WASHINGTON QUARTERLY, 12(3) (SUM 89), 171-184.
THE ARTICLE EXAMINES THE LEVEL OF TECHNOLOGY IN THE US
WHERE DECADES OF NEGLECT HAVE SERIOUSLY UNDERMINED THE US
STRATEGY FOR AFFORDABLE DETERRENCE BASED ON QUALITATIVE
SUPERIORITY. IT OUTLINES THE EXTENT OF THE PROBLEM BY A
DETAILED COMPARISON WITH SOVIET MILITARY TECHNOLOGY AND
SEEKS TO OUTLINE TO BASIC CAUSES OF THE PROBLEM WHICH
INCLUDES A DECREASING AMOUNT OF RESOURCES DEVOTED TO DEFENSE
RELATED TECHNOLOGY, A MANAGEMENT PROCESS THAT HAS THE EFFECT
OF IMPEDING TECHNOLOGICAL INNOVATION, AND THE HIGHLY
EMOTIONAL AND CONFRONTATIONAL ATMOSPHERE BETWEEN THE
GOVERNMENT AND THE DEFENSE INDUSTRY. THE ARTICLE CONCLUDES
WITH PROPOSALS FOR SIGNIFICANT AND FUNDAMENTAL REFORM THAT
WOULD HELP THE US REGAIN ITS TECHNOLOGICAL EDGE.

04228 HERZOG, D.
UP TOWARD LIBERALISM
DISSENT, (SUM 89), 355-359.
THE AUTHOR DISCUSSES THE RENAISSANCE OF LIBERALISM,
FOCUSING ON THREE RECENT PUBLICATIONS: "LIBERAL EQUALITY" BY
AMY GUTMANN, "BENJAMIN CONSTANT AND THE MAKING OF MODERN
LIBERALISM" BY STEPHEN HOLMES, AND "ANOTHER LIBERALISM:
ROMANTICISM AND THE RECONSTRUCTION OF LIBERAL THOUGHT" BY
NANCY ROSENBLUM.

04229 HESS, S.
MAKING IT HAPPEN: THOUGHTS FOR A NEW PRESIDENT ON PROCESS,
PEOPLE, AND THE PRESS
BROOKINGS REVIEW, 7(1) (WIN 89), 69-78.
THERE IS NO SHORTAGE OF POLICY AND PROGRAM PROPOSALS

FROM WHICH A NEW PRESIDENT CAN CHOOSE. BUT A PROPOSAL'S
MERITS ALONE WILL NOT MAKE IT "HAPPEN." MAKING IT HAPPEN
DEPENDS ON THE SKILL OF THE ASSISTANTS AND ADVISERS THE
PRESIDENT CHOOSES. THE PATHS HE PICKS, AND THE WAY HE
RELATES TO THE PRESS--AMONG OTHER FACTORS.

04230 HETTINGER, E.C.
JUSTIFYING INTELLECTUAL PROPERTY
PHILOSOPHY AND PUBLIC AFFAIRS, 18(1) (WIN 89), 31-52.
NATURAL RIGHTS TO THE FRUITS OF ONE'S LABOR ARE NOT BY
THEMSELVES SUFFICIENT TO JUSTIFY COPYRIGHTS, PATENTS, AND
TRADE SECRETS, THOUGH THEY ARE RELEVANT TO THE SOCIAL
DECISION TO CREATE AND SUSTAIN INTELLECTUAL PROPERTY
INSTITUTIONS. THIS ANALYSIS SUGGESTS THAT THE ISSUE TURNS ON
CONSIDERATIONS OF SOCIAL UTILITY. WE MUST DETERMINE WHETHER
OUR CURRENT COPYRIGHT, PATENT, AND TRADE SECRET STATUTES
PROVIDE THE BEST POSSIBLE MECHANISMS FOR ENSURING THE
AVAILABILITY AND WIDESPREAD DISSEMINATION OF INTELLECTUAL
WORKS AND THEIR RESULTING PRODUCTS.

04231 HEWINGS, G.J.D.; FONSECA, M.; GUILHOTO, J.; SONIS, M.
KEY SECTORS AND STRUCTURAL CHANGE IN THE BRAZILIAN ECONOMY:
A COMPARISON OF ALTERNATIVE APPROACHES AND THEIR POLICY
IMPLICATIONS
JOURNAL OF POLICY MODELING, 11(1) (SPR 89), 67-90.
ATTEMPTS TO IDENTIFY KEY SECTORS IN AN ECONOMY WITH
INPUT-OUTPUT MODELS HAVE BEEN A SOURCE OF CONSIDERABLE
DEBATE. IN THIS PAPER, SEVERAL OLD AND NEW APPROACHES TO THE
PROBLEM ARE EVALUATED WITH REFERENCE TO THE BRAZILIAN
ECONOMY USING THE INPUT-OUTPUT MODELS FOR 1959, 1970 AND
1975. TWO ALTERNATIVE APPROACHES ARE SUGGESTED IN THIS PAPER.
THE FIRST OF THESE FOCUSES ON KEY COEFFICIENTS THROUGH THE
IDENTIFICATION OF FIELDS OF INFLUENCE ASSOCIATED WITH
CHANGES IN THESE COEFFICIENTS, INCLUDING THE EFFECTS OF
SIMULTANEOUS CHANGES IN MORE THAN ONE COEFFICIENT. THE
SECOND APPROACH DECOMPOSES THE INTERINDUSTRY TRANSACTIONS
INTO A SET (HIERARCHY) OF FLOWS. IT IS CLAIMED THAT THE
FLOWS ASSOCIATED WITH THE HIGHER LEVELS OF THE HIERARCHY CAN
BE CONSIDERED AS THE KEY FLOWS OR MOST IMPORTANT
TRANSACTIONS. THESE NEW APPROACHES ARE COMPARED TO EARLIER
TECHNIQUES TO EXAMINE THE DEGREE TO WHICH IMPORTANT CHANGES
IN THE ECONOMY COULD BE DETECTED.

04232 HEWISON, G.
THE HARD BUT NECESSARY TASK OF RENEWAL
WORLD MARXIST REVIEW, 32(9) (SEP 89), 3-6.
THIS ARTICLE REVIEWS THE STRUGGLE OF SOCIALISM VERSUS
IMPERIALISM AND CAPITALISM, EMPHASISING THE ERRORS AND
MISCALCULATIONS MADE DURING THE LAST 20 YEARS WHEN
COMMUNISTS WERE LULLED INTO ACTING AS THOUGH NOTHING THAT
IMPERIALISM DID OR COULD DO COULD CHECK THE "TRIUMPHAL"
MARCH OF THE REVOLUTIONARY FORCES. IT CALLS FOR A
REALIZATION THAT SOCIALISM HAS NOT ULTIMATELY FAILED AND FOR
"NEW POLITICAL THINKING" AS THE STRUGGLES ON THE
INTERNATIONAL SCENC CONTINUE. IT EXPLORES THE NEED IN CANADA
TO CONTINUE THE REVOLUTION AND TO REALIZE THE DIFFERENCE IN
SOCIALISM IN A COUNTRY SUCH AS CANADA COMPARED TO SOCIALISM
IN A THIRD WORLD ECONOMY IS SUBSTANTIAL.

04233 HEXIN, W.
LATIN AMERICA EXPLORES NEW ECONOMIC PATHS
BEIJING REVIEW, 32(32) (AUG 89), 15-18.
DURING THE LAST DECADE, LATIN AMERICAN ECONOMIES HAVE
GENERALLY WORSENED. APART FROM THE INFLUENCE OF THE
INTERNATIONAL ECONOMIC ENVIRONMENT, THE DEFICIENCIES IN THE
ECONOMIC STRUCTURE OF LATIN AMERICA AS WELL AS ERRORS IN
DEVELOPMENT STRATEGIES AND POLICIES HAVE BEEN THE MAIN
FACTORS IN THE SHARP UPS AND DOWNS IN LATIN AMERICAN
ECONOMIC DEVELOPMENT.

04234 HEYDEN, F.G.
PUBLIC PENSION POWER FOR SOCIOECONOMIC INVESTMENTS
JOURNAL OF ECONOMIC ISSUES, 23(4) (DEC 89), 1027-1046.
THIS ARTICLE IS A FIRST STEP TOWARD THE DEVELOPMENT OF
SOCIAL FABRIC MATRIX (HEYDEN 1982) DATA BASE FOR STATE AND
LOCAL PUBLIC PENSION FUNDS. THE ARTICULATION OF THE PRIMARY
CRITERIA THAT FLOW FROM THE BASIC SOCIAL BELIEFS IS THE MAIN
PURPOSE OF THE ARTICLE. IT PROPOSES THAT A RIGOROUS APPROACH
TO POLICY MAKING CANNOT BE DEVELOPED UNLESS THE EXPLICIT
PRIMARY CRITERIA IS FORMULATED WHICH CAN GUIDE ANALYSIS,
INVESTMENT, AND ADMINISTRATION.

04235 HEYWOOD, P.
SPAIN
ELECTORAL STUDIES, 8(3) (DEC 89), 322-330.
THIS ARTICLE EXAMINES THE 1989 EUROPEAN ELECTIONS IN
SPAIN WHICH WHICH WERE OF CRITICAL IMPORTANCE FOR DOMESTIC
POLITICS, AN ANALYSIS OF CURRENT PROBLEMS IS PROVIDED, AND
THE IMPLICATIONS OF THE BASQUE AND CATALONIAN PREFERENCE IS
EXPLORED. THE CAMPAIGN AND ELECTION RESULTS ARE DETAILED.

04236 HICKEY, D.
AMERICAN TECHNOLOGICAL ASSISTANCE, TECHNOLOGY TRANSFERS
AND TAIWAN'S DRIVE FOR DEFENSE SELF-SUFFICIENCY

JOURNAL OF NORTHEAST ASIAN STUDIES, VIII(3) (FAL 89),
44-61.
AMERICAN TECHNOLOGICAL ASSISTANCE AND A PLENTIFUL SUPPLY
OF HARD CURRENCY HAVE ENABLED TAIWAN TO MAKE IMPRESSIVE
STRIDES IN ITS CAMPAIGN FOR DEFENSE SELF-SUFFICIENCY. THIS
STUDY EXAMINES AMERICA'S SUPPORT FOR TAIWAN'S DRIVE FOR
DEFENSE SELF-SUFFICIENCY. IT OUTLINES PRESENT AMERICAN
POLICY ON TAIWAN'S ARMS DEVELOPMENT, EXPLORES RECENT
PROGRESS IN ITS WEAPONS RESEARCH AND DEVELOPMENT PROGRAM,
AND DISCUSSES POTENTIAL BENEFITS AND LIABILITIES THAT SUCH A
PROGRAM MAY POSE FOR THE UNITED STATES. IN CONCLUSION, IT
EXPLAINS WHY CONTINUING THE PRESENT POLICY IS IN THE BEST
INTERESTS OF THE UNITED STATES.

04237 HICKS, A.; PATTERSON, W.D.
ON THE ROBUSTNESS OF THE LEFT CORPORATIST MODEL OF
ECONOMIC GROWTH
THE JOURNAL OF POLITICS, 51(3) (AUG 89), 662-675.
CONTRARY TO CLAIMS BY JACKMAN, HICKS'S REVISION OF THE
LANGE-GARRETT MODEL OF 1974-1980 ECONOMIC GROWTH RATES
RECEIVES ROBUST EMPIRICAL SUPPORT FROM REGRESSION ANALYSES
OF LANGE AND GARRETT'S ORIGINAL FIFTEEN CASES. JACKMAN'S
CRITICISMS OF HICKS'S (1988) "EXPANDED" MODEL FOUNDER ONCE
STATISTICALLY APPROPRIATE PROCEDURES ARE USED TO GAUGE THE
STABILITY OF HICKS'S ESTIMATES AND STATISTICAL TESTS.
JACKMAN'S CRITICISMS OF HICKS'S "ELEMENTARY" MODEL COME
UNDONE ONCE THE EXPOSITORY FUNCTION OF THE "ELEMENTARY"
MODEL IS CLARIFIED AND THE THEORETICAL AND EMPIRICAL MERITS
OF HICKS'S "CATCH-UP" SPECIFICATION RELATIVE TO THOSE OF
JACKMAN'S "INERTIAL" SPECIFICATION ARE ELABORATED. AS FOR
JACKMAN'S TWO PRINCIPAL THEORETICAL CRITICISMS, THAT BASED
ON A MAJORITARIAN/ CONSENSUS CONCEPTION OF GOVERNMENT STANDS
UP POORLY TO AN EXAMINATION OF THE SEMINAL TEXT UNDERLYING
THAT CONCEPTION, WHILE THAT CRITICISM ROOTED IN THE DOWNSIAN
THEORETICAL TRADITION APPEARS, AT BEST, PRECARIOUSLY
SUPPORTED BY THAT INTELLECTUAL LINEAGE.

04238 HICKS, A.; AMBUHL, M.; SWANK, D.H.
WELFARE EXPANSION REVISITED: POLICY ROUTINES AND THEIR
MEDIATION BY PARTY, CLASS, AND CRISIS, 1957-1982
EUROPEAN JOURNAL OF POLITICAL RESEARCH, 17(4) (JUL 89),
401-430.
POST-WAR WELFARE EFFORT (I.E., WELFARE SPENDING AS A
SHARE OF NATIONAL INCOME) IN ADVANCED CAPITALIST POLITICAL
DEMONCRACIES IS PROPOSED TO RESULT FROM POLICY ROUTINES
EMPHASIZED IN THE TRADITIONAL ACADEMIC LITERATURES
COMPLEMENTED AND MEDIATED BY CLASS-LINKED FACTORS STRESSED
IN THE 'NEW POLITICAL ECONOMY' LITERATURE. BOTH SETS OF
FACTORS ARE INTEGRATED INTO A SINGLE CONCEPTION OF STATE
POLICY-MAKING. IN THIS, SELF-INTERESTED ELITE AND
ADMINISTRATIVE STATE PERSONNEL RESPOND TO THEIR ENVRONMENTS
BY MEANS OF RELATIVELY DISCRETIONARY AND RELATIVELY
AUTOMATIC POLICY ROUTINES, RESPECTIVELY. LEFT AND NON-LEFT
GOVERNMENTS MEDIATE THESE ROUTINES AND DO SO DIFFERENTLY IN
DIFFERENT LONG-TERM INSTITUTIONAL (STRONG-UNION VERSUS WEAK-
UNION) AND MACROECONOMIC (EXPANSIONARY VERSUS CRISIS)
CONTEXTS. WELFARE EXPANSION IS FOUND TO BE AMPLY EXPLAINED
BY THE PROPOSED CONTEXTS MARKED BY 'LEFT CORPORATISM' (OR
STRONG UNIONS) AND/OR BY RELATIVELY 'EXPANSIONARY ECONOMIC
CLIMATES'. IRONICALLY, LEFT-PARTY GOVERNMENTS IN LEFT
CORPORATIST CONTEXTS ARE FOUND TO BE PARTICULARLY SENSITIVE
OF INFLATION WHERE TRANSFER SPENDING IS CONCERNED. WHERE
UNIONS ARE STRONG, POLICY MAKING IS GENERALLY LESS
INCREMENTAL AND MORE FLEXIBLE. AFTER 1973, POLICY
SENSITIVITY TO REAL ECONOMIC GROWTH OR DECLINE LOOMS LARGE,
AND WORKING-CLASS-LINKED POLITICS ARE MUTED WHERE UNIONS ARE
WEAK, MOST ESPECIALLY WHERE THEY ARE DECENTRALIZED.

04239 HICKSON, D.J.; BUTLER, R.J.; CRAY, D.; MALLORY, G.R.;
WILSON, D.C.
DECISION AND ORGANIZATION - PROCESSES OF STRATEGIC
DECISION MAKING AND THEIR EXPLANATION
PUBLIC ADMINISTRATION, 67(4) (WIN 89), 373-390.
STRATEGIC DECISIONS SHAPE THE COURSE TAKEN BY AN
ORGANIZATION, WHETHER IT BE IN THE PUBLIC SECTOR OR THE
PRIVATE SECTOR. AN ANALYSIS IS REPORTED OF 150 CASES OF THE
MAKING OF SUCH DECISIONS IN BOTH PUBLICLY AND PRIVATELY
OWNED ORGANIZATIONS. THREE TYPES OF DECISIONMAKING PROCESS
ARE IDENTIFIED, SPORADIC, FLUID, AND CONSTRICTED.
DIFFERENCES DUE TO THE NATURE OF THE SUBJECT MATTER UNDER
DECISION, AND TO THE NATURE OF THE ORGANIZATION, ARE
EXAMINED. DIFFERENCES IN THE PROPENSITY TO SPORADIC DECISION-
MAKING PROCESSES IN THE ADMINISTRATION OF PUBLICLY OWNED
ORGANIZATIONS ARE DESCRIBED.

04240 HIDENORI, I.
SLIGHTING TAIWAN IS BEHIND THE TIMES
JAPAN QUARTERLY, XXXVI(1) (JAN 89), 69-74.
IN TAIWAN, GRADUAL LIBERALIZATION HAS BEEN GOING ON
SINCE 1986. IN THE FINAL YEARS OF HIS RULE, CHIANG CHING-KUO
INITIATED A SERIES OF POLITICAL REFORMS THAT INCLUDED
LIFTING MARTIAL LAW AND PERMITTING THE FORMATION OF
OPPOSITION PARTIES. IN JULY 1988, THE PARTY CONGRESS OF THE
RULING KUOMINTANG ENDED THE MONOPOLY RULE OF THE CHIANG

FAMILY. THE GROWING VOICE AMONG THE TAIWANESE CALLING FOR
POLITICAL FREEDOM AND DEMOCRATIZATION HERALDS A SHIFT FROM
THE OLD AUTHORITARIAN REGIME TO A NEW DEMOCRATIC SYSTEM. BUT
SOME OBSERVERS ARGUE THAT IT WILL TAKE FIVE YEARS TO LEARN
IF REPRESENTATIVE DEMOCRACY HAS REALLY TAKEN ROOT IN TAIWAN.

04241 HIEBERT, M.
KHMER ROUGE RUSE?
FAR EASTERN ECONOMIC REVIEW, 141(35) (SEP 88), 32.
IN AN ATTEMPT TO COUNTER THE GROWING FEARS THAT THE
KHMER ROUGE MAY TRY TO BATTLE BACK INTO POWER AFTER THE
WITHDRAWAL OF VIETNAMESE TROOPS FROM CAMBODIA, THEY HAVE
PROPOSED A PEACE PLAN THAT WOULD REDUCE THE SIZE OF THE
KHMER ROUGE. FORCES TO THE SAME LEVEL AS OTHER REISTANCE
FACTIONS. THE PLAN ALSO CALLED FOR AN INTERIM GOVERNMENT
HEADED BY PRINCE SIHANOUK. SOME SEE THE PROPOSAL AS A RESULT
OF CHINESE PRESSURE TO BLOCK ANY KHMER ROUGE ATTEMPT TO
SEIZE POWER.

04242 HIEBERT, M.
SOCIALIST STAGNATION
FAR EASTERN ECONOMIC REVIEW, 141(30) (JUL 88), 20-21.
19 MONTHS AFTER THE VIETNAMESE COMMUNIST PARTY ELECTED
NGUYEN VAN LINH TO SPEARHEAD ITS EFFORTS TO RESCUE THE
COUNTRY FROM NEAR ECONOMIC RUIN AND GROWING POLITICAL
MALAISE, VIETNAM'S TROUBLES SEEM TO BE DEEPENING AS IS THE
POLITICAL UNREST. THE GOVERNMENT IS RECEIVING CRITICISM FROM
HANOI'S SOVIET BLOC ALLIES AND EVEN FROM WITHIN PARTY RANKS.
RUNAWAY INFLATION AND FAMINE IN THENORTHERN PROVINCES HAVE
ERODED THE GOVERNMENT'S CREDIBILITY, AND THE FIRST CONTESTED
ELECTION FOR THE PREMIERSHIP IN SOCIALIST VIETNAM REVEALED
THE INCRESING PARTY DISUNITY.

04243 HIEBERT, M.
STILL SEEING RED
FAR EASTERN ECONOMIC REVIEW, 142(49) (DEC 89), 25.
POLITICAL CHANGE IN THE SOVIET UNION AND EASTERN EUROPE
HAS HAD TWO DIRECT RESULTS IN THEIR POLICY TOWARDS CAMBODIA.
IN AN IMPORTANT SHIFT IN FOREIGN POLICY, EASTERN EUROPEAN
NATIONS HAVE BEGUN TO ENCOURAGE THE LEADERS OF CAMBODIA AND
VIETNAM TO ACCOMODATE THE KHMER ROUGE. LED BY HUNGARY, THE
COMMUNIST BLOC HAS BEEN INCREASINGLY VOCAL IN ITS ADVOCATING
OF A COALITION GOVERNMENT THAT INCLUDES KHMER ROUGE ELEMENTS.
IN ADDITION, ECONOMIC REFORMS IN SOVIET BLOC COUNTRIES IS
LIKELY TO RESULT IN SIGNIFICANT CUTS IN FINANCIAL AID TO
PHNOM PENH.

04244 HIEBERT, M.
THE COMPROMISE CANDIDATE
FAR EASTERN ECONOMIC REVIEW, 141(27) (JUL 88), 34.
DO MUOI WAS ELECTED VIETNAM'S PREMIER IN THE NATIONAL
ASSEMBLY'S FIRST TWO-CANDIDATE POLL AND WILL NOW HAVE TO
GRAPPLE WITH AN ECONOMIC CRISIS AND DECLINING PUBLIC
CONFIDENCE IN THE COMMUNIST PARTY. LITTLE IS KNOWN ABOUT THE
VIEWS OF THE NEW PREMIER, BUT RECENT SPEECHES SUGGEST THAT
HE SUPPORTS ECONOMIC REFORM WHICH MANY DEEM NECESSARY TO
AVERT FUTURE FOOD SHORTAGES AND TAME THE INFLATION THAT IS
CURRENTLY AVERAGING 60% PER MONTH.

04245 HIEBERT, M.
WITHDRAWAL SYMPTOMS
FAR EASTERN ECONOMIC REVIEW, 141(28) (JUL 88), 14.
VIETNAM WITHDREW ITS MILITARY HIGH COMMAND FROM CAMBODIA,
MARKING THE FIRST MAJOR STEP IN HANOI'S EFFORT TO TURN THE
DEFENCE OF CAMBODIA OVER TO THE GOVERNMENT THAT VIETNAM
INSTALLED NEARLY A DECADE AGO. SPURRED ON BY PRESSURE FROM
THE USSR AND BY THE SEEMINGLY ENDLESS CAUSLTIES THAT RESULED
FROM THE OCCUPATION, VIETNAM HAS PLEDGED TO REMOVE 50,000 OF
ITS TROOPS AND PLACE THE REMAINING 50-70,000 SOLDIERS UNDER
CAMBODIAN COMMAND. MANY CAMBODIAN GOVERNMENT OFFICIALS FEAR
THAT CHAOS AND BLOODSHED WILL FOLLOW THE WITHDRAWAL.

04246 HIETT, P.
"NEW" PARTY IN ALGERIA
MIDDLE EAST INTERNATIONAL, (364) (DEC 89), 12-13.
THE SOCIALIST FORCES FRONT HAS THE POTENTIAL TO BECOME
THE STRONGEST OPPOSITION PARTY FACING ALGERIA'S RULING FLN.
THE MAIN REASON IS HOCINE AIT AHMED, A REVERED NAME IN
ALGERIAN REVOLUTIONARY HISTORY, WHO HAS ASSUMED LEADERSHIP
OF THE SOCIALIST FORCES FRONT. AIT AHMED ARRIVES ON A
TREMULOUS SCENE MARKED BY WIDESPREAD RIOTING AND SIGNIFICANT
RESISTANCE TO PRESIDENT CHADLI'S PROPOSED REFORMS. SOME
OBSERVERS FEEL THAT HE HAS A SIGNIFICANT CHANCE FOR SUCCESS
IF HE CAN CASH IN ON HIS REPUTATION AND TAKE ADVANTAGE OF
CURRENT POLITICAL CONDITIONS.

04247 HIETT, P.
ALGERIA'S FLN CONGRESS
MIDDLE EAST INTERNATIONAL, (365) (DEC 89), 11-12.
AN EXTRAORDINARY CONGRESS OF ALGERIA'S RULING FLN WAS
HELD IN HOPES OF FURTHERING THE POLITICAL AND ECONOMIC
REFORMS INTRODUCED BY PRESIDENT CHADLI BENJEDID. HOWEVER,
THE MOOD OF THE CONGRESS SHIFTED, AND REFORMERS NOT ONLY
FOUND THEIR PROPOSALS REJECTED, THEY ALSO HAD TO FIGHT HARD

TO RETAIN THE REFORMS THEY INSTITUTED PREVIOUSLY. THE SUDDEN
TURNABOUT WAS THE RESULT OF CHADLI'S DESIRE TO MIMIC THE
GLASNOST OF MIKHAIL GORBACHEV BY ALLOWING THE OLD GUARD IN
CONGRESS TO SPEAK. MOST OBSERVERS FEEL THAT THE PACE OF
REFORM IN ALGERIA WILL BE SIGNIFICANTLY SLOWED IN THE NEXT
FEW YEARS.

04248 HIETT, P.
    BEN ALI AND THE FUNDAMENTALISTS
    MIDDLE EAST INTERNATIONAL, (363) (NOV 89), 12-13.
        HOPES OF ADDITIONAL DEMOCRATIC REFORMS WERE DASHED BY
    TUNISIA'S PRESIDENT BEN ALI. HE DECLARED IN AN ANNIVERSARY
    SPEECH THAT THE POSSIBILITY OF A TUNISIAN RELIGIOUS PARTY IS
    NONEXISTENT; FURTHERMORE, HE REFUSED TO HELP THE LEGALIZED
    OPPOSITION PARTIES. TUNISIA'S WIDELY ACCLAIMED REFORM
    MOVEMENT SEEMS TO BE GRINDING DOWN TO A HALT.

04249 HIETT, P.
    HASSAN MANEUVERS
    MIDDLE EAST INTERNATIONAL, (364) (DEC 89), 13.
        KING HASSAN OF MOROCCO CALLED ON THE UN TO DRAW UP A
    REFERENDUM ON THE ISSUE OF SELF-DETERMINATION IN THE WESTERN
    SAHARA. HE DECLARED THAT IF THE UN IS UNABLE TO ORGANIZE A
    REFERENDUM IN TWO YEARS, THAT HE WOULD "DRAW THE NECESSARY
    CONCLUSIONS" AND CONDUCT ONE OF HIS OWN. THIS ANNOUNCEMENT
    HAS BEEN ALTERNATELY INTERPRETED AS A MOVE TO DEFLECT
    INTERNATIONAL CRITICISM; AN ATTEMPT TO DELAY ANY REAL PEACE
    SETTLEMENT; OR A GENUINE EFFORT TO END THE 14 YEARS OF
    FIGHTING IN THE WESTERN SAHARA.

04250 HIETT, P.
    LIBYA'S ARMED FUNDAMENTALISTS; QADHAFI'S DAY OF MOURNING
    MIDDLE EAST INTERNATIONAL, (362) (NOV 89), 13-14.
        LIBYA'S MUMMAR QADHAFI MADE A RARE ADMISSION TO THE
    EXISTENCE OF FUNDAMENTALIST ISLAMIC GROUPS WHO OPPOSE HIM.
    HE DECLARED IN A NATIONALLY TELEVISED SPEECH THAT HE WOULD
    CRUSH ANY ISLAMIC MOVEMENT WHICH OPPOSED HIM. OUTSIDE
    SOURCES BELIEVE THAT PUBLIC ADMISSION OF THE PROBLEM'S
    EXISTENCE DEMONSTRATES THAT OPPOSITION TO QUADHAFI HAS GROWN
    CONSIDERABLY. QADHAFI ALSO EXPERIENCED OPPOSITION OF ANOTHER
    KIND WHEN A LARGE PORTION OF LIBYA'S POPULATION IGNORED HIS
    "DAY OF MOURNING" FOR THE VICTIMS OF ITALIAN COLONIALISM.
    HIS ATTEMPT TO CAMPAIGN FOR "WAR DAMAGES" FELL ON DEAF EARS
    IN ITALY.

04251 HIETT, P.
    THIRD POLISARIO OFFENSIVE
    MIDDLE EAST INTERNATIONAL, (363) (NOV 89), 14.
        THE WESTERN SAHARA GROUP POLISARIO LAUNCHED WHAT MIGHT
    BE ITS BIGGEST ATTACK AGAINST THE MOROCCAN DEFENSIVE WALL
    SINCE ENDING ITS UNILATERAL TRUCE AT THE BEGINNING OF
    OCTOBER. ALTHOUGH CLAIMS OF LOSSES VARIED BY THE SOURCE,
    BOTH SIDES AGREED THAT IT WAS PERHAPS THE LARGEST CONFLICT
    THUS FAR. SOME MOROCCAN OPPOSITION GROUPS ADVOCATE THE
    INTERNATIONALIZATION OF THE CONFLICT BY CALLING FOR AN
    EXTRAORDINARY SUMMIT OF THE ARAB MAGHREB UNION, BUT KING
    HASSAN SEEMS TO BE WILLING TO WAIT A FEW MONTHS FOR THE
    ORDINARY SUMMIT TO TAKE PLACE.

04252 HIETT, P.
    TUNISIA'S FUNDAMENTALISTS
    MIDDLE EAST INTERNATIONAL, (361) (OCT 89), 12.
        THE TENSION IN TUNISIA BETWEEN THE GOVERNMENT AND THE
    ISLAMIC FUNDAMENTALIST "AL-NAHDA" MOVEMENT BECAME APPARENT
    IN CRITICISM OF RECENT EDUCATIONAL REFORMS. CHANGES IN
    TEXTBOOK POLICY AND AN ATTEMPT TO ENFORCE THE BAN ON
    HEADSCARVES BROUGHT SIGNIFICANT AND OUTSPOKEN OBJECTION FROM
    MANY ISLAMIC FUNDAMENTALISTS. AL-NAHDA LEADERS CLAIM TO HAVE
    BEEN SUBJECT TO POLICE HARASSMENT DUE TO THEIR DEMAND FOR
    THE MINISTER OF EDUCATION'S RESIGNATION. IN A TIME OF
    INCREASING DEMOCRATIZATION OF TUNISIA, IT REMAINS CLEAR THAT
    THE AL-NAHDA, THE GOVERNMENT'S MOST FORMIDABLE ENEMY, IS NOT
    YET CONSULTED WHEN THE GOVERNMENT SEEKS THE WILL OF THE
    PEOPLE.

04253 HIETT, P.
    TUNISIA"S NEW PRIME MINISTER
    MIDDLE EAST INTERNATIONAL, (360) (OCT 89), 10-11.
        THE PACE OF POLITICAL CHANGE IN THE MAGHREB HAS BEEN
    FAST AND FURIOUS. TUNISIA JOINED THE RANKS OF NATIONS
    CHANGING LEADERS WITH THE DISMISSAL OF PRIME MINISTER
    BACCOUCHE. ALTHOUGH HIS REPLACEMENT, DR. HAMID QARHI, HAS
    LITTLE GOVERNMENT EXPERIENCE, HE IS AN OLD PARTY HAND AND IS
    MORE LIKELY TO FOLLOW THE PACE OF PRESIDENT'S BEN ALI'S
    PROPOSED REFORMS.

04254 HIETT, P.
    WESTERN SAHARA FLARE-UP
    MIDDLE EAST INTERNATIONAL, (361) (OCT 89), 12-13.
        AFTER A YEAR OF RELATIVE CALM, THE POLISARIO LAUNCHED
    TWO LARGE ATTACKS AGAINST THE FORCES OF MOROCCO'S KING
    HASSAN. POLISARIO CLAIMS THAT HASSAN'S FAILURE TO MOVE
    TOWARDS ANY SETTLEMENT IN THEIR ONGOING TALKS PROVOKED THE
    ATTACKS. HASSAN COUNTERS THAT THA ALTHOUGH SUCH TALKS NEVER

OCCURED, THERE CERTAINLY WOULD BE NO PROSPECT OF FUTURE
NEGOTIATIONS. THE RENEWAL OF HOSTILITIES HAS SIGNIFICANT
REGIONAL IMPLICATIONS. RELATIONS BETWEEN MOROCCO, ALGERIA,
AND MAURITANIA ALL ARE FEELING INCREASED STRAIN DUE TO THE
FIGHTING.

04255 HIGGS, R.
    BEWARE THE PORK-HAWK
    REASON, 21(2) (JUN 89), 28-34.
        THE CONGRESSIONAL "PORK-HAWK" THRIVES ON MICROMANAGING
    THE DEFENSE PROGRAM, STIPULATING NOT ONLY HOW MUCH WILL BE
    SPENT FOR BROAD DEFENSE PURPOSES BUT HOW MUCH WILL BE SPENT
    FOR EACH OF THE SEVERAL THOUSAND LINE ITEMS IN THE ANNUAL
    DEFENSE BUDGET AND EXACTLY HOW THE PENTAGON MUST MANAGE THAT
    SPENDING.

04256 HIGGS, R.
    DO LEGISLATORS' VOTES REFLECT CONSTITUENCY PREFERENCE? A
    SIMPLE WAY TO EVALUATE THE SENATE
    PUBLIC CHOICE, 63(2) (NOV 89), 175-182.
        THIS ARTICLE GIVES A METHOD WHICH CAN BE APPLIED TO ANY
    DATA ON SENATORIAL VOTING. ITS APPLICATION SHOWS THAT QUITE
    OFTEN MANY SENATORS DEPART FROM CONSTITUENCY PREFERENCE.
    THIS FINDING REFUTES THE HYPOTHESIS THAT "OURS IS A PERFECT
    POLITICAL MARKET."

04257 HIGLEY, J.; BURTON, M.G.
    THE ELITE VARIABLE IN DEMOCRATIC TRANSITIONS AND BREAKDOWNS
    AMERICAN SOCIOLOGICAL REVIEW, 54(1) (FEB 89), 17-32.
        STABLE DEMOCRATIC REGIMES DEPEND HEAVILY ON THE
    "CONSENSUAL UNITY" OF NATIONAL ELITES. SO LONG AS ELITES
    REMAIN DISUNIFED, POLITICAL REGIMES ARE UNSTABLE, A
    CONDITION WHICH MAKES DEMOCRATIC TRANSITIONS AND DEMOCRATIC
    BREAKDOWNS MERELY TEMPORARY OSCILLATIONS IN THE FORMS
    UNSTABLE REGIMES TAKE. DISUNITY APPEARS TO BE THE GENERIC
    CONDITION OF NATIONAL ELITES, AND DISUNITY STRONGLY TENDS TO
    PERSIST REGARDLESS OF SOCIOECONOMIC DEVELOPMENT AND OTHER
    CHANGES IN MASS POPULATIONS. THE CONSENSUALLY UNIFIED ELITES
    THAT ARE NECESSARY TO STABLE DEMOCRACIES ARE CREATED IN ONLY
    A FEW WAYS, TWO OF THE MOST IMPORTANT OF WHICH INVOLVE
    DISTINCTIVE ELITE TRANSFORMATIONS. AFTER ELABORATING THIS
    ARGUMENT, THE AUTHORS EXAMINE THE RELATIONSHIP BETWEEN
    ELITES AND REGIMES IN WESTERN NATION-STATES SINCE THEY BEGAN
    TO CONSOLIDATE AFTER 1500. THIS APPROACH MAKES SENSE OF THE
    WESTERN POLITICAL RECORD, DOES MUCH TO CLARIFY PROSPECTS FOR
    STABLE DEMOCRACIES IN DEVELOPING SOCIETIES TODAY, AND MAKES
    THE INCREASINGLY ELITE-CENTERED ANALYSIS OF DEMOCRATIC
    TRANSITIONS AND BREAKDOWNS MORE SYSTEMATIC.

04258 HIGONNET, P.
    SOCIABILITY, SOCIAL STRUCTURE, AND THE FRENCH REVOLUTION
    SOCIAL RESEARCH, 56(1) (SPR 89), 99-126.
        THE FRENCH REVOLUTION HAS NOT A SOCIAL REVOLUTION. ITS
    FIRST CAUSE WAS NEITHER SOCIAL NOR ECONOMIC. ITS MOTOR WAS
    THE CULTURAL TRANSFORMATION OF THE COUNTRY'S POSSESSING,
    ADMINISTRATIVE, AND EDUCATED ELITES IN THE PRECEDING CENTURY.
    THE POLITICS OF 1789-99 ORIGINATED IN THE PRE-REVOLUTIONARY
    RESTRUCTURING OF THE ANCIENT ASSUMPTIONS ON THE NATURE OF
    THE PUBLIC AND THE PRIVATE. THUS, THE FIRST CAUSE OF THE
    REVOLUTION LAY IN THE ELITES' RENEWED DEFINITIONS OF BOTH
    THE EMPOWERED SELF AND THE EMPOWERED NATION.

04259 HIJAB, N.
    ARAB NGO'S MEET IN CAIRO
    MIDDLE EAST INTERNATIONAL, (363) (NOV 89), 14.
        MANY ARAB INTELLECTUALS WONDER IF DEMOCRACY IN THEIR
    REGION MIGHT FOLLOW THE SWEEPING CHANGES IN EASTERN EUROPE
    AND THE SOVIET UNION. HOWEVER, MOST ACKNOWLEDGE THE FUTILITY
    OF COUPS AND THE LACK OF MOMENTUM OF POPULAR MOVEMENTS IN
    ARAB NATIONS. THEY LOOK INSTEAD TO NON-GOVERNMENTAL
    ORGANIZATIONS (NGO) AS A POSSIBLE "BACK DOOR TO DEMOCRACY."
    THE FIRST ARAB NGO CONFERENCE WAS HELD IN CAIRO PROVIDES
    MODEST HOPE THAT THESE ORGANIZATIONS COULD BE AN IMPETUS FOR
    BENEFICIAL REFORM.

04260 HIJAB, N.
    THE STRATEGY OF THE POWERLESS
    MIDDLE EAST INTERNATIONAL, (350) (MAY 89), 17-18.
        THE PALESTINIAN STRATEGY TO EMPOWER THE POWERLESS HAS
    THREE MAIN ELEMENTS. THE FIRST IS TO MOBILIZE AND POLITICIZE
    THE PALESTINIAN PEOPLE BEHIND AN ORGANIZATION REPRESENTING
    THEIR INTERESTS, THE PLO. SECONDLY, THE STRATEGY HAS BEEN TO
    MAINTAIN THE UNITY OF THE PALESTINIAN MOVEMENT BY HAVING THE
    WIDEST POSSIBLE REPRESENTATION OF PALESTINIAN SOCIETY IN THE
    PLO. AN ACHIEVABLE POLITICAL PROGRAM HAS BEEN THE THIRD
    MAJOR ELEMENT.

04261 HILAIRE, M.
    THE USE OF FORCE IN BLOC SITUATION AND THE DEVELOPMENT OF
    DOCTRINAL RULES OF THE GAME IN THE WESTERN HEMISPHERE
    DISSERTATION ABSTRACTS INTERNATIONAL, 49(11) (MAY 89),
    3497-A.
        THE AUTHOR STUDIES HOW LAW AND POLITICS INTERACT IN BLOC
    SITUATIONS AND THE IMPACT OF THAT INTERACTION ON THE

INTERNATIONAL LEGAL ORDER. HE FOCUSES ON THE INFLUENCE OF
THE UNITED STATES' RULES OF THE GAME IN THE WESTERN
HEMPISHERE AND HOW THEY REGULATE RELATIONS BETWEEN THE USA
AND THE SOVIET UNION AND THEIR SUBORDINATES. HE EXAMINES
FOUR CASES OF US INTERVENTION IN THE WESTERN HEMISPHERE TO
ILLUSTRATE THE PRACTICAL APPLICATION OF THE RULES OF THE
GAME IN CRISIS SITUATIONS.

04262 HILL, C.
    1939: THE ORIGINS OF LIBERAL REALISM
    REVIEW OF INTERNATIONAL STUDIES, 15(4) (OCT 89), 319-328.
        1939 WAS NEITHER ONE THING NOR THE OTHER. IT WAS THE
    LAST GOLDEN YEAR OF PEACE AT THE END OF A PERIOD OF
    EXPANSION AND CONFIDENCE, AS 1914 HAD SEEMED TO BE, AND IT
    WAS NOT THE START OF A DRAMATIC NEW ERA, AS WAR HAD BEEN IN
    1775 AND REVOLUTION IN 1917. RATHER, 1939 WAS THE ANTE-
    CHAMBER THROUGH WHICH THE NATIONS OF EUROPE WERE SLOWLY
    USHERED INTO WAR, AND ITS ASSOCIATION WITH REACTIVE AND
    HESISTANT POLICY-MAKING HAS COMPOUNDED THE SENSE OF
    DETERMINISM. THIS ARTICLE CHALLENGE SUCH A PERSPECTIVE IN
    TWO WAYS: FIRST IT WILL SUGGEST THAT THE EVENTS OF 1939 ARE
    IN THEMSELVES RATHER MORE SIGNIFICANT THAN IS SOMETIMES
    ASSUMED, AND SECOND IT WILL SEE 1939 AND THE WAR WHICH THEN
    UNSTOPPABLY UNROLLED, AS HAVING INITIATED CHANGES WHICH ARE
    STILL BEING WORKED OUT IN THE NATURE AND QUALITY OF
    INTERNATIONAL RELATIONSHIPS, AS WELL AS MAJOR PARTICULAR
    DEVELOPMENTS LIKE THE RISE OF AMERICAN POWER AND THE
    DIVISION OF GERMANY.

04263 HILL, C.T.
    AGENCY RESPONSIBILITY FOR CIVILIAN TECHNOLOGY
    CRS REVEIW, 10(5) (JUN 89), 17-18.
        UNTIL RECENTLY, NO FEDERAL AGENCY HAD ASSUMED A LEAD
    ROLE IN FINANCING CIVILIAN TECHNOLOGY. NOW, HOWEVER, BOTH
    THE NEW FEDERAL TECHNOLOGY ADMINISTRATION (FTA) IN THE
    DEPARTMENT OF COMMERCE AND THE DEFENSE ADVANCED RESEARCH
    PROJECTS AGENCY (DARPA) IN THE DEPARTMENT OF DEFENSE HAVE
    SUCH RESPONSIBILITIES. DECIDING THE PROPER ROLE OF EACH
    AGENCY HAS BECOME A KEY POLICY ISSUE.

04264 HILL, C.T.
    SCIENCE AND THE BUDGET: AN UPDATE
    CRS REVEIW, 10(2) (FEB 89), 28-30.
        THE FEDERAL GOVERNMENT SPENDS MORE THAN $60 BILLION EACH
    YEAR ON RESEARCH AND DEVELOPMENT TO SERVE MANY PUBLIC GOALS.
    IN THIS ERA OF TIGHT BUDGET CONSTRAINTS, THE CONGRESS AND
    THE EXECUTIVE BRANCH ARE SEEKING BETTER WAYS TO SET
    PRIORITIES FOR FUNDING AMONG DIVERSE SCIENTIFIC AND
    TECHNOLOGICAL OPPORTUNITIES. THIS ARTICLE SUMMARIZES RECENT
    IMPORTANT DEVELOPMENTS CONCERNING THIS ISSUE.

04265 HILL, K.
    THE POLITICAL BEHAVIOR OF AFRICAN METHODIST EPISCOPAL
    CHURCH MEMBERS IN DETROIT: THE INFLUENCE OF CONTEXT,
    COGNITION, AND SOCIO-PHYSCHOLOGICAL CHARACTERISTICS
    DISSERTATION ABSTRACTS INTERNATIONAL, 49(12) (JUN 89),
    3857-A.
        HOW PEOPLE THINK, LEARN, AND COGNITIVELY ORGANIZE
    INFORMATION ABOUT POLITICS INFLUENCES THEIR POLITICAL
    BEHAVIOR. THIS RESEARCH INVESTIGATES THESE COGNITIVE
    FUNCTIONS BY EXAMINING THE INFLUENCE OF CHURCH CONTEXT, THE
    PERCEPTIONS OF THAT CONTEXT, AND THE GENERAL ORIENTATIONS
    EMBEDDED IN MEMORY ON THE POLITICAL BEHAVIOR OF BLACK CHURCH
    MEMBERS IN DETROIT.

04266 HILL, K.; HURLEY, P.
    UNIFORM STATE LAW ADOPTIONS IN THE AMERICAN STATES: AN
    EXPLANATORY ANALYSIS
    PUBLIUS: THE JOURNAL OF FEDERALISM, 18(1) (WIN 88),
    117-126.
        THE ARTICLE EXAMINES THE UNIFORM LAW MOVEMENT WHICH
    BEGAN IN 1892. IT EXPLORES THE POPULARITY OF UNIFORM STATE
    LAWS AND THE VARIOUS FACTORS THAT ACCOUNT FOR STATE
    RESPONSIVENESS TO UNIFORM LAWS. IT CONCLUDES THAT MOST
    UNIFORM LAW PROPOSALS ARE MET WITH ONLY MODEST SUPPORT.
    POLITICAL CULTURE WAS FOUND TO BE THE ONLY SIGNIFICANT
    EXPLANATORY FACTOR: MORALISTIC STATES HAVE, ON AVERAGE, THE
    HIGHEST ADOPTION RATE, TRADITIONALISTIC STATES HAVE THE
    LOWEST.

04267 HILL, L.E.
    CULTURAL DETERMINISM OR EMERGENT EVOLUTION: AN ANALYSIS OF
    THE CONTROVERSY BETWEEN CLARENCE AYRES AND DAVID MILLER
    JOURNAL OF ECONOMIC ISSUES, XXIII(2) (JUN 89), 465-471.
        THE PURPOSE OF THIS ESSAY IS TO SPECIFY AND TO ANALYZE
    THE THE ISSUES INVOLVED IN THE AYRES-MILLES CONTROVERSY IN
    ORDER TO ELUCIDATE INSTITUTIONALIST-INSTRUMENTALIST THEORY
    OF ECONOMIC CAUSATION.

04268 HILL, R.
    GORBACHEV MARCHES ON
    JOURNAL OF COMMUNIST STUDIES, 5(1) (MAR 89), 74-78.
        THREE-AND-A-HALF YEARS INTO HIS TENURE OF THE POSITION
    OF CPSU CENTRAL COMMITTEE GEENERAL SECRETARY, MIKHAIL

GORBACHEV SHOW NO SIGNS OF RELENTING IN HIS BID TO
"RESTRUCTURE" THE SOVIET POLITICAL SYSTEM. HE CONTINUES TO
REORGANIZE THE PARTY AND THE GOVERNMENT; THOSE WHO HAVE BEEN
RELUCTANT TO SUPPORT HIS REFORMS ARE MORE AND MORE OFTEN
FINDING THEMSELVES OUT IN THE COLD. HOWEVER, GORBACHEV'
APPEARS TO BE UNSURE OF THE POLITICAL SYSTEM TOWARDS WHICH
HE IS ATTEMPTING TO IMPEL THE SOVIET UNION. ONLY ONE THING
REMAINS CERTAIN: DESPITE ALL OF THE DEMOCRATIC REFORMS, THE
COMMUNIST PARTY IS TO REMAIN THE RULING PARTY.

04269 HILL, R.B.
    ECONOMIC FORCES, STRUCTURAL DISCRIMINATION, AND BLACK
    FAMILY INSTABILITY
    REVIEW OF BLACK POLITICAL ECONOMY, 17(3) (WIN 89), 5-23.
        THE SOCIAL AND ECONOMIC GAINS ACHIEVED BY BLACK FAMILIES
    DURING THE 1960S WERE SEVERELY ERODED DURING THE SEVENTIES
    AND EIGHTIES. ACCORDING TO THE THESIS OF THE DECLINING
    SIGNIFICANCE OF RACE, THIS CRISIS IS MAINLY CONCENTRATED
    AMONG THE BLACK "UNDERCLASS" AND IT IS BROAD SOCIETAL TRENDS,
    NOT RACISM, THAT IS MAINLY RESPONSIBLE FOR THEIR INCREASED
    DEPRIVATION. THIS THESIS FAILS TO ASSESS THE ROLE OF
    INSTITUTIONALIZED RACISM AS IT IS MANIFESTED IN "UNINTENDED"
    OR "STRUCTURAL" DISCRIMINATION, I.E., THE DISPROPORTIONATE
    ADVERSE EFFECTS OF ECONOMIC TRENDS AND POLICIES ON THE
    FUNCTIONING OF LOW-INCOME AND MIDDLE-INCOME BLACK FAMILIES.
    MOREOVER, SOCIAL FORCES OR POLICIES THAT HAVE RACIALLY
    DISPARATE ADVERSE EFFECTS ARE "DISCRIMINATORY" BY RESULT,
    WHETHER INTENDED OR NOT. THE MAJOR ECONOMIC TRENDS THAT
    AFFECTED BLACK FAMILIES ADVERSELY DURING THE SEVENTIES AND
    EIGHTIES WERE: BACKTO-BACK RECESSIONS, DOUBLE-DIGIT
    INFLATION, AND INDUSTRIAL AND POPULA TION SHIFTS. THE KEY
    ECONOMIC POLICIES THAT UNDERMINED BLACK FAMILY STABILITY
    HAVE BEEN: ANTI-INFLATION FISCAL AND MONETARY POLICIES,
    TRADE POLICIES, PLANT CLOSINGS, SOCIAL WELFARE, BLOCK GRANTS,
    AND FEDERAL PER CAPITA FORMULAS FOR ALLOCATING FUNDS TO
    STATES AND LOCAL AREAS THAT HAVE NOT BEEN CORRECTED FOR THE
    CENSUS UNDERCOUNT.

04270 HILL, R.J.; IIVONEN, J.
    GORBACHEV AT THE TOP
    JOURNAL OF COMMUNIST STUDIES, 5(3) (SEP 89), 329-339.
        THIS ARTICLE EXAMINES THE ABILITY OF MIKHAIL GORBACHEV
    TO PULL OFF ASTOUNDING POLITICAL COUPS, WHILE CONSISTENTLY
    AND PUNCTILIOUSLY OBSERVING ALL THE FORMALITIES OF PARTY AND
    STATE PROTOCOL. IT ALSO DETAILS HIS EFFORTS AT ADJUSTING THE
    PARTY MEMBERSHIP. REFORM OF THE STATE ELECTION SYSTEM AND
    THE POLITICAL CULTURE OF REPRESENTATIVES ARE EACH EXPLORED.
    IT CONCLUDES THAT THIS IS A POSITIVE EXPERIMENT IN BUILDING
    DEMOCRACY.

04271 HILLHOUSE, R. J.
    A REEVALUATION OF SOVIET POLICY IN CENTRAL EUROPE: THE
    SOVIET UNION AND THE OCCUPATION OF AUSTRIA
    EASTERN EUROPEAN POLITICS AND SOCIETIES, 3(1) (WIN 89),
    83-104.
        WHILE RESEARCH HAS FOCUSED PRIMARILY UPON FACTORS
    EXTERNAL TO AUSTRIA TO ACCOUNT FOR THE REVERSAL IN SOVIET
    POLICY, CONDITIONS WITHIN AUSTRIA THAT COULD HAVE INFLUENCED
    THE TURNABOUT HAVE BEEN LARGELY NEGLECTED. CAREFUL
    EXAMINATION OF THE RELATIONSHIP BETWEEN THE ORIGINAL
    INCENTIVES FOR THE USSR TO OCCUPY EASTERN AUSTRIA AND THE
    STATE OF THESE FACTORS AT THE TIME OF THE CONCLUSION OF THE
    STATE TREATY CONTRIBUTES TO A MORE COMPLETE UNDERSTANDING OF
    SOVIET MOTIVES IN CENTRAL EUROPE. THAT THE ECONOMIC
    INTERESTS OF THE USSR WERE CLOSELY INTERRELATED WITH THE
    SOVIET APPROVAL OF THE AUSTRIAN STATE TREATY HAS LONG BEEN
    IGNORED. IN ORDER TO EXPLORE THE DEVELOPMENT OF SOVIET
    INTERESTS IN AUSTRIA, THE AUTHOR FIRST BRIEFLY REVIEWS THE
    ALLIED PLANNING ON THE OCCUPATION OF AUSTRIA AND THE
    INTERNAL POLITICAL SITUATION IN AUSTRIA. THROUGH A DETAILED
    ANALYSIS OF SOVIET ECONOMIC POLICY AND A REASSESSMENT OF
    SOVIET PROFITS FROM AUSTRIA, THE AUTHOR EXAMINES SOVIET
    POLICY'S SHIFT FROM POLITICAL TO ECONOMIC PRIORITIES.
    FINALLY, WITH A REEVALUATION OF SOVIET ECONOMIC STRATEGY, HE
    CONCLUDES THAT ECONOMIC FACTORS PLAYED A MAJOR ROLE IN THE
    SUDDEN SOVIET AGREEMENT TO THE AUSTRIAN STATE TREATY.

04272 HILLIER, B.
    TIME INCONSISTENCY AND THE THEORY OF SECOND BEST
    SCOTTISH JOURNAL OF POLITICAL ECONOMY, 36(3) (AUG 89),
    253-265.
        THE PAPER DRAWS TOGETHER THE WORK OF HILLIER AND
    MACLCOMSON (1984) ON THE MICROECONOMIC FOUNDATIONS OF THE
    TIME INCONSISTENCY PROBLEM, WITH SOME RECENT WORK BY ROGERS
    (1987) ON THE IMPLICATIONS OF TIME INCONSISTENCY FOR SOME
    TRADITIONAL WELFARE THEORETIC RESULTS. THE ANALYSIS OF THE
    INTERACTIONS BETWEEN A GOVERNMENT MACROECONOIC POLICY MAKER
    AND A PRIVATE SECTOR POPULATED WITH RATIONAL MAXIMIZING
    AGENTS INTERPRETS THE WHOLE PROBLEM AS A DYNAMIC CASE IF
    LIPSEY AND LANCASTER'S THEORY OF SECOND BEST (1956). THE
    AUTHORS EMPHASIZES THE SIMPLICITY OF THE MODEL FROM WHICH
    THE RESULTS ARE DERIVED, AS WELL AS THE ROLE OF CONFLICT.

04273 HILLS. C.A.
    URUGUAY ROUND AND U.S. TRADE POLICY: A FOUNDATION FOR THE
    FUTURE
    DEPARTMENT OF STATE BULLETIN (US FOREIGN POLICY), 89(2152)
    (NOV 89), 53-54.
        THE BUSH ADMINISTRATION'S TRADE POLICY EMPHASIZES
    OPENING MARKETS. NOT CLOSING THEM, AND CREATING AN EVER-
    EXPANDING GLOBAL TRADING SYSTEM BASED UPON CLEAR AND
    ENFORCEABLE RULES. TO ACHIEVE THIS, THE ADMINISTRATION HAS
    DESIGNED A THREE-PRONGED STRATEGY. FIRST, THE UNITED STATES
    IS COMMITTED TO THE SUCCESSFUL CONCLUSION OF THE URUGUAY
    ROUND OF MULTILATERAL TRADE TALKS BY THE DECEMBER 1990
    DEADLINE. SECONDLY, IN A MANNER THAT IS CONSISTENT WITH U.S.
    AIMS IN THE URUGUAY ROUND, THE BUSH ADMINISTRATION WILL
    PURSUE BILATERAL AND REGIONAL MARKET-OPENING INITIATIVES.
    THIRDLY, THE USA WILL USE THE STRENGTH OF ITS DOMESTIC
    MARKET TO FURTHER ITS OBJECTIVES IN THE URUGUAY ROUND. THE
    OVERRIDING OBJECTIVE IN ALL U.S. TRADE POLICY IS TO GET
    GOVERNMENT OUT OF BUSINESS.

04274 HILLS, J.
    NEO-CONSERVATIVE REGIMES AND CONVERGENCE IN
    TELECOMMUNICATIONS POLICY
    EUROPEAN JOURNAL OF POLITICAL RESEARCH, 17(1) (JAN 89),
    95-113.
        STARTING FROM THE PROPOSITION THAT NEO-CONSERVATIVE
    GOVERNMENTS WOULD WISH TO INCREASE COMPETITION IN THE
    TELECOMMUNICATIONS MARKET AND THAT SOCIALIST GOVERNMENTS
    WOULD WISH TO RETAIN A NETWORK MONOPOLY WHICH PROTECTS SMALL
    CONSUMERS, THIS PAPER EXPLORES TELECOMMUNICATIONS POLICY IN
    A NUMBER OF INDUSTRIALISED COUNTRIES. IT ARGUES THAT THERE
    IS LITTLE CONVERGENCE BETWEEN POLICIES ADOPTED BY NEO-
    CONSERVATIVE REGIMES AND THAT SOCIALIST GOVERNMENTS ARE AS
    LIKELY TO LIBERALISE OR PRIVATISE THE TELECOMMUNICATIONS
    MONOPOLY. A NUMBER OF EXPLANATORY VARIABLES ARE EXPLORED,
    INCLUDING FEDERALISM, TRADE UNION STRENGTH AND INDUSTRIAL
    POLICY GOALS. THE ARTICLE CONCLUDES THAT THE CONJUNCTURE OF
    POLITICAL AND ECONOMIC INTERESTS IN ANY ONE COUNTRY IS
    LIKELY TO BE DIFFERENT FROM THAT IN ANY OTHER. THESE
    CONJUNCTURES DETERMINE OUTCOMES IN POLICY TERMS AND NO
    COUNTRY IS LIKELY TO FOLLOW CLOSELY AMERICAN EXPERIENCE IN
    LIBERALISATION.

04275 HILLYARD, P.; PERCY-SMITH, J.
    THE COERCIVE STATE REVISITED
    PARLIAMENTARY AFFAIRS, 42(4) (OCT 89), 533-547.
        THE BOOK "THE COERCIVE STATE: THE DECLINE OF DEMOCRACY
    IN BRITAIN "ANALYZED JUST HOW MUCH FREEDOM HAD BEEN LOST IN
    RECENT YEARS AND HOW THE STATE HAD ASSUMED EVEN GREATER
    POWERS. THE AIM OF THIS ARTICLE IS NOT TO DESCRIBE IN DETAIL
    THE CONTENTS OF THE BOOK BUT TO SHOW HOW THERE HAS BEEN NO
    REVERSAL IN THE TRENDS NOW HAPPENING IN BRITAIN. IT SUGGESTS
    THAT RECENT DEVELOPMENTS HAVE LED TO FURTHER DECLINE OF
    DEMOCRACY AND MORE COERCION. IT EXAMINES THE POLITICAL
    SYSTEM, CENSORSHIP, USE OF PROPAGANDA, THE AMOUNT OF PUBLIC
    INFORMATION, TRADE UNIONS, AND THE POLICE.

04276 HILTERMANN, J.
    HUMAN RIGHTS AND THE PALESTINIAN STRUGGLE FOR LIBERATION
    JOURNAL OF PALESTINE STUDIES, XVIII(2) (WIN 89), 109-118.
        THE ARTICLE EXAMINES THE INTIFADAH AND ITS IMPLICATIONS
    FOR THE PEOPLE OF PALESTINE. IT ANALYZES THE INFRASTRUCTURE
    OF THE RESISTANCE AND THE ACTIONS TAKEN BY ISRAEL TO REPRESS
    IT. THE ARTICLE CONCLUDE THAT DESPITE THE INCREASE IN
    ISRAELI REPRESSION, THE MOVEMENT IS INCREASING IN STRENGTH
    AND IS BEGINING TO PAY OFF.

04277 HILTERMANN, J.
    OCCUPATIONAL HAZARDS
    MIDDLE EAST INTERNATIONAL, (360) (OCT 89), 14.
        THE ARTICLE EXAMINES THE ISRAELI PRATICE OF SENDING
    PALESTINIAN UNDESIRABLES TO "ADMINISTRATIVE DETENTION" IN
    KETZIOT, A REMOTE DESERT TOWN. ACCORDING TO AMNESTY
    INTERNATIONAL THOUSANDS OF PALESTINIAN STUDENTS, JOURNALISTS,
    DOCTORS, LAWYERS, AND LABORERS HAVE BEEN DETAINED IN
    KETZIOT.

04278 HILTERMANN, J.R.
    HUMAN RIGHTS AND THE MASS MOVEMENT: THE FIRST YEAR OF THE
    INTIFADAH
    JOURNAL OF PALESTINE STUDIES, XVIII(3) (SPR 89), 126-133.
        IN THE OCCUPIED TERRITORIES THE PERIOD UNDER REVIEW, THE
    FIRST YEAR OF THE INTIFADAH, HAS BEEN CHARACTERIZED BY AN
    ESCALATION OF REPRESSION AND VIOLENCE AS THE PALESTINIAN
    NATIONAL MOVEMENT ACHIEVED A NUMBER OF SIGNIFICANT POLITICAL
    VICTORIES, NOT LEAST OF WHICH WAS THE DECLARATION OF AN
    INDEPENDENT STATE ON 15 NOVEMBER 1988. THE ISRAELI RESPONSE
    TO THE PLO'S SUCCESS WAS A FURTHER RELAXATION OF STATED
    CONSTRAINTS WITH REGARD TO THE ARMY'S METHODS OF PUTTING AN
    END TO THE POPULAR UPRISING TEMPERED, IN EARLY 1989, BY
    ATTEMPTS TO APPEASE THE POPULATION BY SUMMONING AND
    CONSULTING WITH ITS PERCEIVED LOCAL REPRESENTATIVES. THE
    MAIN TYPES OF MEASURES USED BY THE ISRAELI AUTHORITIES HAVE
    BEEN: ARMED EFFORTS TO END STREET DEMONSTRATIONS; COLLECTIVE

AND ARBITRARY PUNISHMENTS INTENDED TO SERVE BOTH AS
DETERRENTS AND REPRISALS; ASSAULTS ON THE INSTITUTIONAL AND
ORGANIZATIONAL INFRASTRUCTURE OF PALESTINIAN SOCIETY AND
RESISTANCE; AND ATTEMPTS TO REDUCE MEDIA COVERAGE OF THE
UPRISING.

04279 HILTON, I.; FERIA, M.; FORD, M.; JIANG, Y.; JIANGSHAN, X.;
    QIDE, C.; QINGHAU, Z.; ROBERTI, M.; SHU, B.; SPARKS, S.
    CHINA
    SOUTH, (108) (OCT 89), 81-108.
        AT THE FIRST TRADE FAIR IN BEIJING FOLLOWING THE JUNE
    1989 UPRISING, WESTERN AND JAPANESE COMPANIES WERE
    CONSPICUOUS BY THEIR ABSENCE. BY CONTRAST, COUNTRIES SUCH AS
    SOUTH KOREA, CZECHOSLOVAKIA, AND INDIA WERE WELL REPRESENTED.
    THE DETENTE WITH INDIA, BEGINNING WITH THE DECEMBER 1988
    SUMMIT BETWEEN RAJIV GANDHI AND DENG XIAOPING, HAS MAJOR
    POLITICAL IMPLICATIONS FOR THE ASIAN SUPERPOWERS AND THEIR
    ZONES OF INFLUENCE, AS DID THE SUBSEQUENT SUMMIT BETWEEN
    DENG AND GORBACHEV. THESE RAPPROCHEMENTS ARE NOT PLEASING TO
    THE STRIDENT REALPOLITIK PRACTITIONERS OF THE USA, WHO WANT
    CHINA TO BALANCE THE USSR AND ARGUE THAT IT DOES NO GOOD TO
    ISOLATE OR PUNISH THE CHINESE.

04280 HIMMELFARB, G.
    VICTORIAN VALUES/JEWISH VALUES
    COMMENTARY, 87(2) (FEB 89), 23-31.
        THE AUTHOR CONSIDERS PRIME MINISTER THATCHER'S ADVOCACY
    OF A RETURN TO VICTORIAN VALUES AND BEATRICE POTTER WEBB'S
    ESSAY ON THE JEWISH COMMUNITY IN EAST LONDON IN THE 1880'S.

04281 HIMMELFARB, M.
    AMERICAN JEW: DIEHARD CONSERVATIVES
    COMMENTARY, 87(4) (APR 89), 44-49.
        THE 1988 PRESIDENTIAL VOTING SHOWED THAT AMERICAN JEWS
    ARE DIEHARD CONSERVATIVES IN THE SENSE THAT THEY REFUSE TO
    CHANGE. TIMES HAVE CHANGED AND AMERICA HAS CHANGED. MOST
    WHITES ONCE VOTED FOR DEMOCRATIC PRESIDENTIAL CANDIDATES BUT
    HAVE SWITCHED TO VOTING FOR REPUBLICANS. PRACTICALLY ALONE
    AMONG WHITE VOTERS, AMERICAN JEWS HAVE HARDLY CHANGED.

04282 HINCHMAN, L.P.; HINCHMAN, S.K.
    "DEEP ECOLOGY" AND THE REVIVAL OF NATURAL RIGHT
    WESTERN POLITICAL QUARTERLY, 42(3) (SEP 89), 201-228.
        THE WRITINGS OF DEEP ECOLOGISTS-THE ENVIRONMENTAL
    MOVEMENT'S MOST RADICAL AND CONSISTENT THINKERS-REVEAL THE
    OUTLINES OF A POLITICAL THEORY AT ODDS WITH THE MAIN
    CURRENTS OF CONTEMPORARY THOUGHT. THIS THEORY REVIVES, IN A
    NOVEL FORM, AN ESSENTIAL ELEMENT OF ARISTOTELIAN NATURAL
    RIGHT: THAT WHAT IS "RIGHT BY NATURE" INVOLVES THE FULL
    UNFOLDING OF AN ENTITY WITHIN ITS PROPER CONTEXT. BUT THIS
    CONTEXT PROVES TO BE UNDAMAGED NATURE AS A WHOLE (NOT JUST
    THE POLIS), AND THE FULL UNFOLDING OF HUMAN BEINGS
    PRESUPPOSES THAT OF OTHER BEINGS AS WELL. CONFUSIONS ARISE,
    HOWEVER, WHEN DEEP ECOLOGISTS TRY TO INFER FROM NATURAL
    PARADIGMS, SUCH AS UNDISTURBED ECOSYSTEMS, THE PROPER ORDER
    FOR HUMAN SOCIETY. SLIGHTING THE GENUINELY ARISTOTELIAN
    FACTOR OF RATIONAL SPEECH AND POLITICAL PARTICIPATION, DEEP
    ECOLOGISTS OFTEN SLIP INTO A FACILE "NATURALISM" WHICH SEEKS
    TO ASSIMILATE POLITICS TO QUASI-AUTOMATIC, UNREFLECTIVE
    ORGANIC PROCESSES.

04283 HINCHMAN, L.P.
    VIRTUE OF AUTONOMY: ALASDAIR MACINTYRE'S CRITIQUE OF
    LIBERAL INDIVIDUALISM
    POLITY, 21(4) (SUM 89), 635-654.
        THIS ARTICLE PROBES THE WRITINGS OF ALISDAIR MACINTYRE,
    PARTICULARLY "AFTER VIRTUE", FOR THE CONCEPT OF SOCIETY AND
    POLITICS THAT UNDERLIE HIS ETHICS. THE AUTHOR ARGUES THAT
    MACINTYRE TREATS THE DISORDER OF MORAL LANGUAGE AS A SYMPTOM
    OF DEEPER SOCIAL, POLITICAL, AND HUMAN DISINTEGRATION
    EVIDENT IN THE EMERGENCE OF THE MODERN AUTONOMOUS INDIVIDUAL.
    HE CONCLUDES BY MAKING THREE CLAIMS AGAINST MACINTYRE (1)
    ENLIGHTENMENT INDIVIDUALISM WAS NOT JUST A CONTINGENT
    MISTAKE; (2) MACINTYRE'S OWN ARGUMENTS ARE PARTLY COMPATIBLE
    WITH THE ENLIGHTENMENT VIEWS HE CRITICIZES; AND (3)
    MACINTYRE TACITLY ACCEPTS FAR MORE OF THE ENLIGHTENMENT
    POSITION THAN HIS THEORIES WOULD SEEM TO JUSTIFY.

04284 HINE, R.C.
    CUSTOMS UNION ENLARGEMENT AND ADJUSTMENT: SPAIN'S
    ACCESSION TO THE EUROPEAN COMMUNITY
    JOURNAL OF COMMON MARKET STUDIES, XXVIII(1) (SEP 89), 1-28.
        IN THE SHORT TERM, SPAIN AND ITS EUROPEAN COMMUNITY
    PARTNERS MUST COME TO GRIPS WITH THE ADJUSTMENT PROBLEMS
    CREATED BY SPAIN'S MEMBERSHIP IN THE EC CUSTOMS UNION. THESE
    PROBLEMS ARE PARTICULARLY SEVERE BECAUSE SPAIN IS A LARGE,
    HEAVILY PROTECTED COUNTRY AND A RELATIVELY POOR ONE. THE
    REQUIRED TARIFF CHANGES ARE MARKEDLY ASYMMETRIC BECAUSE MOST
    OF SPAIN'S EXPORTS TO THE EC ALREADY HAD RELATIVELY LIBERAL
    ACCESS BEFORE 1986, WHILE SPAIN'S IMPORTS FROM ALL SOURCES
    WERE HEAVILY RESTRICTED. OVER THE LONGER TERM, THE NATURE OF
    THE SPECIALIZATION PROCESS IN THE EUROPEAN ECONOMY WILL HAVE
    IMPORTANT IMPLICATIONS FOR ADJUSTMENT.

04285 HINNEBUSCH, R.A.
BUREAUCRACY AND DEVELOPMENT IN SYRIA: THE CASE OF
AGRICULTURE
JOURNAL OF ASIAN AND AFRICAN STUDIES, XXIV(1-2) (1989),
79-93.
THIS ARTICLE EXAMINES THE SYRIAN BUREAUCRACY THROUGH A
CASE STUDY OF ITS ROLE IN AGRICULTURAL DEVELOPMENT. IT
ANALYSES THE DEGREE OF TECHNOCRATIC RATIONALITY IMPARTED TO
AGRARIAN POLICY, THE EFFECTIVENESS OF THE BUREAUCRACY IN
CARRYING OUT AGRICULTURAL POLICY, THE BENEFICIAL ROLE OF THE
BUREAUCRACY FOR THE AGRARIAN ECONOMY AND THE PEASANTRY, AND
THE POLITICAL CONSEQUENCES OF THE SYRIAN BUREAUCRACY'S ROLE
IN AGRICULTURE. IT ALSO INDICATES THAT WHILE SENIOR PUBLIC
OFFICIALS PLAY A ROLE IN SHAPING AGRARIAN POLICY, THIS ROLE
IS IN TURN SHAPED BY BA'THIST IDEOLOGY AND A POLITICAL
STRUCTURE THAT VESTS CONTROL OVER HIGH POLICY IN THE
PRESIDENCY AND THE RULING PARTY AND NOT IN THE MINISTERIAL
BUREAUCRACY. THIS ARRANGEMENT INFLUENCES AGRICULTURAL
PLANNING, ADMINISTRATIVE LEADERSHIP, AND PATRONAGE POLITICS.
THIS PAPER CONCLUDES THAT DESPITE THE FLAWS THAT AFFLICT THE
AGRARIAN APPARATUS, THE SYRIAN BUREAUCRACY HAS PUT IN PLACE
DEVELOPMENT PROGRAMS OF GREAT BENEFIT TO AGRICULTURE.

04286 HINSLEY, H.
THE EUROPEAN COMMUNITY: A BODY-POLITIC OR AN ASSOCIATION
OF STATES?
WORLD TODAY, 45(1) (JAN 89), 1-3.
THE EUROPEAN COMMUNITY IS AN ASSOCIATION OF STATES. IT
IS A SINGULAR FEATURE OF THE COMMUNITY THAT ITS INAUGURATION
AND EARLY DEVELOPMENT WERE HEAVILY INFLUENCED BY THE
CONVICTION THAT IT WOULD EVENTUALLY CULMINATE IN THE
CREATION OF A UNITED STATES OF WESTERN EUROPE. AFTER NEARLY
40 YEARS OF EVOLUTION, FACTS CAST DOUBT ON THE VALIDITY OF
THAT BELIEF. IT IS UNLIKELY THAT THE EUROPEAN COMMUNITY WILL
EVOLVE INTO A BODY-POLITIC IN THE FORESEEABLE FUTURE.

04287 HIPPLER, J.
KURDISH REFUGEES STILL IN CAMPS
MIDDLE EAST REPORT, 19(5) (SEP 89), 12.
THE 50,000 KURDISH REFUGEES THAT FLED FROM ATTACKS BY
THE IRAQI ARMY ARE NOW VIRTUAL PRISONERS IN TWO REFUGEE
CAMPS IN TURKEY. SOME ARGUE THAT THE TURKISH GOVERNMENT
FEARS CONTACT BETWEEN THE POLITICIZED IRAQI KURDS AND
TURKEY'S OWN REPRESSED KURDISH MINORITY. THE RESULT IS THAT
THE REFUGEES ARE KEPT IN SQUALID CONDITIONS AND ARE
"GUARDED" BY TURKISH SOLDIERS.

04288 HIRD, J.A.
THE USE AND QUALITY OF COST-BENEFIT ANALYSIS IN THE
FEDERAL GOVERNMENT
DISSERTATION ABSTRACTS INTERNATIONAL, 50(4) (OCT 89),
1086-A.
THIS STUDY EXAMINES THE QUALITY AND USE OF COST-BENEFIT
ANALYSIS IN TWO FEDERAL AGENCIES, USING A QUANTITATIVE
REVEALED PREFERENCE ANALYSIS OF CBA AT THE ARMY CORPS OF
ENGINEERS AND A QUALITATIVE CASE-STUDY ANALYSIS FOR THE
NATIONAL HIGHWAY TRAFFIC SAFETY ADMINISTRATION.

04289 HIRSCH, P.; LOHMANN, L.
CONTEMPORARY POLITICS OF ENVIRONMENT IN THAILAND
ASIAN SURVEY, XXIX(4) (APR 89), 439-451.
CONTEMPORARY POLITICS OF ENVIRONMENT IN THAILAND REFLECT
BOTH CONTINUITIES AND NEW DEVELOPMENTS. AS DURING THE 1970'S,
ENVIRONMENTAL POLITICS CONTINUE TO PROVIDE AN OUTLET FOR
DEEPER POLITICAL ISSUES CONCERNING LEGAL AND ILLEGAL ACCESS
TO RESOURCES BY DIFFERENT GROUPS IN SOCIETY. WITHIN THIS
POLITICAL CULTURE, HOWEVER, HAS EMERGED A SIGNIFICANT
INCREASE IN PARTICIPATION BY RURAL POPULATIONS. THE EMERGING
ALLIANCES IN THAI ENVIRONMENTAL POLITICS CANNOT AFFORD TO
NEGLECT INVOLVING THOSE MOST DIRECTLY AFFECTED BY
DEGRADATION OF THE COUNTRY'S NATURAL RESOURCE BASE.

04290 HIRSCH, P.
THE STATE IN THE VILLAGE: INTERPRETING RURAL DEVELOPMENT IN
DEVELOPMENT AND CHANGE, 20(1) (JAN 89), 35-56.
THAILAND MOST STUDIES OF VILLAGE AND STATE ARE LOCKED
INTO ONE OF TWO ALTERNATIVE PARADIGMS. THE FIRST DEALS WITH
THE ENTRY OF VILLAGE INTO STATE AND IS ILLUSTRATED BY THE
MODERNIZATION MOULD OF DEVELOPMENT, WHEREBY INCREASING
SPATIAL INTEGRATION OF NATIONAL POLITY AND ECONOMY RESULTS
IN A RATIONALIZATION OF BACKWARD INSTITUTIONS AND PEASANT
PARTICIPATION IN THE WIDER SOCIETY. THE SECOND PARADIGM IS
CONCERNED WITH EXTENSION OF STATE POWER AND HEGEMONY INTO
THE VILLAGE AND THE LOCKING OF THIRD WORLD PEASANTRIES INTO
EXPLOITATIVE RELATIONS OF PRODUCTION AS A RESULT OF THEIR
INTEGRATION INTO THE WIDER SPATIAL POLITICAL ECONOMY. THE
PARADIGMATIC GULF BETWEEN THESE TWO MAY HAVE OBSCURED A
REFLEXIVE RELATIONSHIP BETWEEN TWO SETS OF PROCESSES, A
RELATIONSHIP THAT CAN BE DETECTED IN THE PRAXIS AND
DISCOURSE OF STATE-LED RURAL DEVELOPMENT. THIS PAPER
EXAMINES RURAL DEVELOPMENT AS IT AFFECTS THE CHANGING
RELATIONSHIP BETWEEN A THAI VILLAGE AND THE THAI STATE.

04291 HIRSCHMANN, N.J.
FREEDOM, RECOGNITION, AND OBLIGATION: A FEMINIST APPROACH
TO POLITICAL THEORY
AMERICAN POLITICAL SCIENCE REVIEW, 83(4) (DEC 89),
1227-1244.
THE AUTHOR ARGUES THAT A FEMINIST METHODOLOGY CAN HELP
LIBERAL POLITICAL THEORY MOVE BEYOND THE PROBLEMS THAT IT
HAS BEEN RECYCLING SINCE THE SEVENTEENTH CENTURY. TAKING
POLITICAL OBLIGATION AS THE FOCUS FOR HER ANALYSIS, THE
AUTHOR SHOWS HOW FEMINIST PSYCHOANALYTIC AND PSYCHOLOGICAL
THEORY CAN HELP UNCOVER THE STRUCTURAL SEXISM OF LIBERAL
THEORY AND EPISTEMOLOGY AND POINT THE WAY TOWARD MORE
CONSISTENT, AND LESS BIASED, THEORETICAL FORMULATIONS.
REJECTING THE ESSENTIALIST VIEW OF GENDER DIFFERENCE THAT
HAS BEEN ATTRIBUTED TO THIS LITERATURE, SHE ARGUES THAT IT
IS MORE APPROPRIATE TO READ IT AS A SYMBOLIC LANGUAGE OF
POWER AND AS A HEURISTIC DEVICE FOR UNCOVERING THE GENDERED
DIMENSIONS OF SUPPOSEDLY "NEUTRAL" CONCEPTS LIKE OBLIGATION.

04292 HIRSHLEIFER, J.
CONFLICT AND RENT-SEEKING SUCCESS FUNCTIONS: RATIO VS.
DIFFERENCE MODELS OF RELATIVE SUCCESS.
PUBLIC CHOICE, 63(2) (NOV 89), 101-112.
THE RENT-SEEKING COMPETITIONS STUDIED BY ECONOMISTS FALL
WITHIN A MUCH BROADER CATEGORY OF CONFLICT INTERACTIONS THAT
ALSO INCLUDES MILITARY COMBATS, ELECTION CAMPAIGNS,
INDUSTRIAL DISPUTES, LAWSUITS, AND SIBLING RIVALRIES. IN THE
RENT-SEEKING LITERATURE, EACH PARTY'S SUCCESS PI (WHICH CAN
BE INTERPRETED EITHER AS THE PROBABILITY OF VICTORY OR AS
THE PROPORATION OF THE PRIZE WON) HAS USUALLY BEEN TAKEN TO
BE A FUNCTION OF THE RATIO OF THE RESPECTIVE RESOURCE
COMMITMENTS. ALTERNATIVELY, HOWEVER, PI MAY INSTEAD BE A
FUNCTION OF THE DIFFERENCE BETWEEN THE PARTIES' COMMITMENTS
TO THE CONTEST. THE CONTEST SUCCESS FUNCTION (CSF) FOR THE
DIFFERENCE FORM IS A LOGISTIC CURVE IN WHICH, AS IS
CONSISTENT WITH MILITARY EXPERIENCE, INCREASING RETURNS
APPLY UP TO AN INFLECTION POINT AT EQUAL RESOURCE
COMMITMENTS. A CRUCIAL FLAW OF THE TRADITIONAL RATIO MODEL
IS THAT NEITHER ONESIDED SUBMISSION NOR TWO-SIDED PEACE
BETWEEN THE PARTIES CAN EVER OCCUR AS A COURNOT EQUILIBRIUM.
IN CONTRAST, BOTH OF THESE OUTCOMES ARE ENTIRELY CONSISTENT
WITH A MODEL IN WHICH SUCCESS IS A FUNCTION OF THE
DIFFERENCE BETWEEN THE PARTIES' RESOURCE COMMITMENTS.

04293 HISAE, S.
THE POLITICAL AWAKENING OF WOMEN
JAPAN QUARTERLY, XXXVI(4) (OCT 89), 381-385.
THE RECENTLY INTENSIFIED POLITICAL CONSCIOUSNESS OF
JAPANESE WOMEN WAS CLEARLY EVIDENT IN THE RESULTS OF THE
JULY 23, 1989, ELECTION IN THE HOUSE OF COUNCILORS. THE
JAPAN SOCIALIST PARTY, LED BY A WOMAN, INCREASED ITS
REPRESENTATION BY 24 SEATS, 11 OF WHICH WENT TO WOMEN. IN
ALL, 22 WOMEN WERE ELECTED TO THE UPPER HOUSE FROM
OPPOSITION PARTIES.

04294 HITCHCOCK, D.I. JR.
THE UNITED STATES IN A CHANGING PACIFIC RIM: ASIAN
PERCEPTIONS AND THE U.S. RESPONSE
WASHINGTON QUARTERLY, 12(4) (FAL 89), 123-138.
A VIEW WIDELY HELD THROUGHOUT MUCH OF NORTH AND
SOUTHEAST ASIA TODAY IS THAT SINCE THE UNITED STATES HAS WON
THE COLD WAR, NOW IS THE TIME TO MOVE IN (TO ASIA) AND TO
CAPITALIZE ON IT IN EVERY WAY. THIS ARTICLE SUGGESTS THE
NEED FOR GRADUAL CHANGE IN THE U.S. APPROACH TO THE REGION.
THE EAST ASIAN SUCCESS STORY HAS PROVIDED ASIA WITH A NEW
SENSE OF SELF-CONFIDENCE AND THE U.S. MUST TAKE NOTICE OF
THIS AND ANTICIPATE ITS IMPLICATIONS EXAMINED ARE: THE
SOVIET PRESENCE; THE CHANGING U.S. ROLE; THE IMPORTANCE OF
ECONOMIC FACTORS; AND THE POTENTIAL FOR REGIONAL SECURITY
COOPERATION.

04295 HLUBEK, G.J.
U.S. SECURITY ASSISTANCE TO THIRD WORLD NATIONS: WHAT
DRIVES CONGRESSIONAL SUPPORT
AVAILABLE FROM NTIS, NO. AD-A202 033/7/GAR, SEP 88, 105.
SINCE THE VIETNAM WAR, CONGRESS HAS INCREASINGLY
ASSERTED ITSELF IN U.S. FOREIGN POLICY, INCLUDING SECURITY
ASSISTANCE RELATIONSHIPS WITH THIRD WORLD NATIONS. THIS HAS
LED TO SIGNIFICANT CONFLICT BETWEEN THE EXECUTIVE AND
LEGISLATIVE BRANCHES, AND THE NEED TO EXPLAIN CONGRESSIONAL
VOTING BEHAVIOR ON SECURITY ASSISTANCE. USING 15 CASES
INCLUDING AID TO THE CONTRAS AND EL SALVADOR DURING THE
REAGAN PRESIDENCY, THIS THESIS INVESTIGATES THE RELATIVE
IMPACT OF VARIOUS FACTORS ON CONGRESSIONAL SUPPORT FOR
SECURITY ASSISTANCE, INCLUDING PUBLIC OPINION AND THE LEVEL
OF SOVIET BLOC ASSISTANCE. THE RESEARCH CONCLUDES THAT THE
MOST POWERFUL DETERMINANT IS THE THIRD WORLD GOVERNMENT
WHOSE BEHAVIOR CONGRESS IS TRYING TO CHANGE.

04296 HO, K.L.
INDIGENIZING THE STATE: THE NEW ECONOMIC POLICY AND THE
BUMIPUTERA STATE IN PENINSULAR MALAYSIA
DISSERTATION ABSTRACTS INTERNATIONAL, 50(1) (JUL 89),
246-A.

THE AUTHOR ASSESSES THE POLITICAL IMPACT OF THE NEW
ECONOMIC POLICY (NEP) IN PENINSULAR MALAYSIA FROM 1971 TO
THE PRESENT. HE EXPLORES THE CAUSE-AND-EFFECT RELATIONSHIPS
AMONG THE POWERFUL ECONOMIC, POLITICAL, AND SOCIAL CURRENTS
GENERATED BY THE NEP AND THE MALAYSIAN STATE. HE ARGUES THAT
THIS PROVIDES THE MOST FRUITFUL POINT OF DEPARTURE FOR
UNDERSTANDING THE STRUCTURE OF THE MALAYSIAN STATE, ITS
POLITICS, AND STATE-SOCIETY RELATIONS IN THE POST-1970
PERIOD.

04297 HO, L.H.
NATIONAL SECURITY FOR THE REPUBLIC OF KOREA AND THE MAJOR
POWERS
AVAILABLE FROM NTIS, NO. AD-A202 215/0/GAR, APR 88, 54.
THE KOREAN PENINSULA WAS DIVIDED AT THE 38TH PARALLEL BY
THE GREAT POWERS IN 1945, AND KOREA HAS BECOME A KEY AREA OF
MAJOR POWERS (UNITED STATES, USSR, JAPAN, AND CHINA)
INTERACTION. ALL THE MAJOR POWERS IN THE CONTEMPORARY
INTERNATIONAL SYSTEM HAVE VITAL INTERESTS IN THE KOREAN
PENINSULA. THIS PENINSULA IS THE ONLY AREA IN THE WHERE
THESE POWERS INTERACT FACE-TO-FACE. THIS REPORT REVIEWS THE
INTERACTIONS OF THE MAJOR POWERS ON THE KOREAN PENINSULA AND
THE MILITARY POSTURE OF BOTH KOREAS AND ATTEMPTS TO CLARIFY
KOREA'S POSITION IN THE POWER RELATIONSHIP BETWEEN THOSE
FOUR BIG POWERS WITH FOCUS ON KOREA'S TASKS IN THE FUTURE.

04298 HOADLEY, S.
TAIWAN AND NEW ZEALAND
NEW ZEALAND INTERNATIONAL REVIEW, 14(4) (JUL 89), 8-12.
THE AUTHOR DISCUSSES TAIWAN'S STATUS IN THE SOUTH
PACIFIC REGION. AREAS OF ACTIVITY WHICH ARE ASSESSED, WITH A
FOCUS ON RELATIONS TO NEW ZEALAND, INCLUDE DIPLOMATIC TIES,
PROFITABLE TRADE, AND CULTURAL AND INTELLECTUAL EXCHANGES
WITH NEW ZEALAND. TOURISM RATES OF TAIWANESE (BASED ON VISA
FIGURES) ARE REPORTED AS HIGH, AND TAIWAN-NEW ZEALAND
STUDENT EXCHANGES HAVE GROWN. TAIWAN IS INCLUDED AS ONE OF
THE "FOUR TIGERS" ALONG WITH SOUTH KOREA, HONG KONG, AND
SINGAPORE. . PERCAPITA FIGURES ON TAIWAN ARE INCLUDED.

04299 HOBBS, H.H.
AMERICAN CITIES IN INTERNATIONAL PERSPECTIVE: LOCAL
GOVERNMENTS IN FOREIGN AFFAIRS
DISSERTATION ABSTRACTS INTERNATIONAL, 49(12) (JUN 89),
3862-A.
LOCAL GOVERNMENTS ARE MOVING BEYOND TRADITIONAL URBAN
CONCERNS TO FORGE A NEW SPHERE OF INFLUENCE IN INTERNATIONAL
ISSUES. TO EXAMINE THIS PHENOMENON, THE AUTHOR IDENTIFIES
FOUR POLITICAL ISSUES THAT HAVE ATTRACTED CITY INTEREST: THE
COMPREHENSIVE TEST BAN MOVEMENT, NUCLEAR FREE ZONE
DECLARATIONS, ANTI-APARTHEID/DIVESTMENT CAMPAIGNS, AND
SANCTUARY FOR CENTRAL AMERICAN REFUGEES.

04300 HOBSBAWM, E.
FAREWELL TO THE CLASSIC LABOUR MOVEMENT?
NEW LEFT REVIEW, (173) (JAN 89), 69-74.
THIS IS THE TEXT OF A LECTURE DELIVERED AT A MEETING TO
COMMEMORATE 125 YEARS OF THE SPD IN BONN IN 1988. THE AUTHOR
SURVEYS THE HISTORY OF THE SOCIALIST AND COMMUNIST PARTIES,
SUGGESTING A DECLINE OF THE CLASS CONSCIOUSNESS ON WHICH
THEY WERE TRADITIONALLY BASED AND NOTING THE CONTINUING
STRENGTH OF THEIR PRESENCE WITHIN THE POLITICAL ARENAS OF
THE WEST.

04301 HOBSBAWM, E.J.
THE MAKING OF A "BOURGEOIS REVOLUTION"
SOCIAL RESEARCH, 56(1) (SPR 89), 5-32.
WHAT USUALLY HAPPENS TO REVOLUTIONS SUFFICIENTLY DISTANT
FROM THE PRESENT IS THAT THEY ARE EITHER TRANSFORMED INTO
NON-REVOLUTIONS (THAT IS, INTEGRATED INTO HISTORICAL
CONTINUITY OR EXCLUDED FROM IT AS INSIGNIFICANT TEMPORARY
INTERRUPTIONS) OR THEY ARE CELEBRATED BY PUBLIC RITES OF
PASSAGE SUITABLE TO THE OCCASIONS THAT MARK THE BIRTH OF
NATIONS AND/OR REGIMES. THEY REMAIN CONTROVERSIAL ONLY AMONG
HISTORIANS. ATTEMPTS TO APPLY THESE TWO TECHNIQUES OF
ELIMINATING THE CONTROVERSIAL ASPECTS OF THE FRENCH
REVOLUTION HAVE BEEN MADE BY REPUBLICANS AND BY THE
POLITICAL RIGHT. BUT THESE ATTEMPTS HAVE FAILED.

04302 HOCHSCHILD, J.L.
EQUAL OPPORTUNITY AND THE ESTRANGED POOR
PHILADELPHIA: ANLS OF AMER ACMY OF POLITICAL AND SOC
SCIENCE, (501) (JAN 89), 143-155.
THIS ARTICLE IS CONCERNED WITH PEOPLE WHO SO LACK
MARKETABLE SKILLS AND MATERIAL RESOURCES THAT THEY ARE
EXCLUDED FROM MAINSTREAM SOCIETY AND WHO LACK FAITH THAT
THEY CAN SUCCEED THROUGH CONVENTIONAL MEANS. THEY ARE
USUALLY POOR, BUT THEY ARE A SMALL SUBSET OF THE POOR AND
ARE NOT NECESSARILY POOR THROUGHOUT THEIR LIVES. MOST ARE
EXCLUDED BECAUSE THE AMERICAN RHETORIC OF EQUAL OPPORTUNITY
FOR ALL IS BELIED BY POLITICAL CHOICES THAT DENY TO SOME ANY
CHANCE OF SUCCESS. PROGRAMS TO ENABLE THE ESTRANGED POOR TO
ENTER MAINSTREAM SOCIETY MUST PROVIDE SKILLS, A STARTING
PLACE, AND FAITH IN THE POSSIBILITY OF ACHIEVEMENT. SUCH
PROGRAMS ARE LONG-LASTING, INTENSIVE, AND COMPREHENSIVE-THUS

COSTLY. TO ENSURE THAT ESTRANGEMENT IS NOT REPRODUCED IN THE
NEXT GENERATION, PROGRAMS TO AID THE POOR MUST, FURTHERMORE,
ELIMINATE GENDER BIASES IN THEIR PRESCRIPTIONS AND MUST
CHANGE THE STRUCTURAL CONDITIONS THAT CREATE THE GAP BETWEEN
THE PROMISE AND PRACTICE OF EQUAL OPPORTUNITY. THESE
PROGRAMS SHOULD NOT NECESSARILY BE TARGETED ON MINORITIES OR
THE POOR, BUT SHOULD BUILD ON AMERICANS' SUPPORT FOR SOCIAL
POLICIES THAT GIVE EVERYONE A CHANCE FOR AT LEAST SOME
SUCCESS.

04303 HOCKETT, J.D.
JUSTICE ROBERT H. JACKSON AND THE ROLE OF THE SUPREME
COURT IN AMERICAN POLITICS
DISSERTATION ABSTRACTS INTERNATIONAL, 49(11) (MAY 89),
3491-A.
THE AUTHOR ANALYZES THE JUDICIAL FUNCTION FROM THE
PERSPECTIVE OF JUSTICE ROBERT H. JACKSON, WHOSE WORK AFFORDS
A COMPELLING INTERPRETATION OF THE SUPREME COURT'S PROPER
ROLE IN A REPUBLICAN FORM OF GOVERNMENT. JACKSON'S
PHILOSOPHY IS CHARACTERIZED BY CERTAIN CONSIDERATIONS THAT
LIMIT THE PURVIEW OF JUDICIAL JUDGMENT AND DISTINGUISH HIS
THEORY FROM NONINTERPRETATIVE APPROACHES TO CONSTITUTIONAL
ADJUDICATION.

04304 HODGES, S.
WAR GAMES IN THE PACIFIC
SOJOURNERS, 18(10) (NOV 89), 10.
THE PACIFIC NAVAL EXERCISE (PACEX) OF THE US MILITARY
FORCES THREATENS TO DAMAGE THE ONGOING PEACE PROCESS BETWEEN
THE US, USSR, AND NORTH KOREA. PACEX, WHICH COMBINES THE
FORCES OF THE US WITH JAPANESE, SOUTH KOREAN, PHILIPPINE,
THAI, INDONESIAN, AUSTRALIAN, AND CANADIAN FORCES, IS THE
LARGEST JOINT MILITARY EXERCISE EVER HELD IN THE ASIA-
PACIFIC REGION. MANY OBSERVERS FEAR THE DETRIMENTAL EFFECT
THAT PACEX MAY HAVE ON THE WARMING GLOBAL POLITICAL CLIMATE.

04305 HOEFLER, J.M.
THE LOCAL IMPLEMENTATION OF PUBLIC MANPOWER PROGRAMS:
PUTTING PUBLIC CHOICE TO THE EMPIRICAL TEST IN A PROCESS
EVALUATION OF MUNICIPAL SERVICE DELIVERY
DISSERTATION ABSTRACTS INTERNATIONAL, 49(12) (JUN 89),
3866-A.
PUBLIC CHOICE PREDICTS THAT JUDICIOUS USE OF INDIVIDUAL
INCENTIVES, COMPETITIVE FRAGMENTATION, AND INCREASED
DEVOLUTION OF PROGRAMMATIC AUTHORITY ARE THE KEYS TO
UNDERSTANDING AND IMPROVING THE PERFORMANCE OF LOCAL SERVICE
DELIVERY AGENCIES. IN THIS DISSERTATION, THESE PUBLIC CHOICE
HYPOTHESES ARE TESTED EMPIRICALLY USING PUBLIC FUNDED,
LOCALLY IMPLEMENTED EMPLOYMENT AND TRAINING PROGRAMS AS THE
RESEARCH FOCUS. FINDINGS INDICATE THAT (1) PERSONAL
INCENTIVES CAN HAVE SUBSTANTIAL, AND USUALLY POSITIVE,
IMPACTS ON PROGRAM EFFECTIVENESS, (2) DEVOLUTION TO THE
STATE WAS FOUND TO HAVE A MILDLY NEGATIVE IMPACT, WHILE
DEVOLUTION TO THE LOCAL LEVEL APPEARS MORE PROMISING, AND
(3) THE QUALITY AND QUANTITY OF SERVICES WERE FOUND
GENERALLY TO BE DILUTED BY INTRA-LOCAL FRAGMENTATION.

04306 HOEKMAN, B.M.
DETERMINING THE NEED FOR ISSUE LINKAGES IN MULTILATERAL
TRADE NEGOTIATIONS
INTERNATIONAL ORGANIZATION, 43(4) (FAL 89), 693-714.
IN MULTILATERAL TRADE NEGOTIATIONS, TRADE-OFFS USUALLY
ARE MADE WITHIN THE ISSUE-AREAS THAT ARE ON THE AGENDA. IN
THE ABSENCE OF CROSS-ISSUE TRADE-OFFS (LINKAGES), AGREEMENT
MAY NOT BE POSSIBLE. TO MAXIMIZE BOTH THE POTENTIAL GAINS
FROM TRADE AND THE SCOPE FOR AGREEMENT, NEGOTIATORS NEED TO
BE WILLING AND ABLE TO CONSIDER THE FEASIBILITY OF ISSUE
LINKAGES. THIS RAISES THE PRACTICAL PROBLEM OF DETERMINING
WHEN SUCH TRADE-OFFS ARE LIKELY TO BE NECESSARY. ALTHOUGH
QUANTITATIVE METHODS OF POLICY ANALYSIS HAVE BEEN DEVELOPED,
THEY HAVE NOT BEEN WIDELY USED BY POLICYMAKERS, IN PART
OWING TO THE FACT THAT NEGOTIATIONS FOCUS LARGELY ON
NONTARIFF MEASURES. THIS ARTICLE PROPOSES A QUALITATIVE
APPROACH TO THE PROBLEM AND APPLIES IT TO THE TOKOYO AND
URUGUAY ROUND NEGOTIATIONS ON SAFEGUARDS TO PROTECT DOMESTIC
INDUSTRIES FROM PROBLEMS RELATED TO INCREASES IN IMPORTS.

04307 HOEKSTRA, D.
NEUSTADT, BARBER AND PRESIDENTIAL STATESHIP: THE PROBLEM
OF LINCOLN
PRESIDENTIAL STUDIES QUARTERLY, XIX(2) (SPR 89), 285-300.
ABRAHAM LINCOLN HAS BEEN CONSISTENTLY CHOSEN BY SCHOLARS
AS THE GREATEST AMERICAN PRESIDENT, ONE WAY OF TESTING THE
EXPLANATORY POWER OF CURRENT MODELS OF THE PRESIDENCY-SUCH
AS THOSE OF RICHARD NEUSTADT AND JAMES DAVID BARBER - IS TO
EXAMINE HOW USEFUL THEY ARE IN HELPING US TO UNDERSTAND THE
NATURE OF LINCOLN'S STATESMANSHIP; THIS ANALYSIS REQUIRES
BOTH A PROBING OF HOW PRESIDENTIAL INTENTION IS ANALYZED BY
NEUSTADT AND BARBER AND, AS A CORRECTIVE TO THEIR MODELS, A
RECONSTRUCTION OF LINCOLN'S GUIDING INTENTIONS, AS THEY
CULMINATED IN THE EMANCIPATION PROCLAMATION.

04308 HOFF, J.; ANDERSEN, J.
THE DANISH CLASS STRUCTURE

ACTA SOCIOLOGICA, 32(1) (MAR 89), 23-52.
THE ARTICLE ANALYZES THE DANISH CLASS STRUCTURE AND
COMPARES IT WITH OTHER NATIONS. SEEN IN AN INTERNATIONAL
PERSPECTIVE, THE DANISH CLASS STRUCTURE IS VERY SIMILAR TO
THE SWEDISH, AND WHEN COMPARED TO THE USA, IT IS
CHARACTERIZED BY A SMALL PETTY BOURGEOISIE AND A LARGE
NUMBER OF SEMI-AUTONOMOUS EMPLOYEES. THE ARTICLE ALSO SHOWS
THAT IT IS IMPORTANT TO ACCOUNT FOR THE CLASS COMPOSITION OF
THE POPULATION OUTSIDE THE LABOR FORCE.

04309 HOFF, S.B.
PRESIDENTIAL SUPPORT IN THE VETO PROCESS, 1889-1985
DISSERTATION ABSTRACTS INTERNATIONAL, 50(6) (DEC 89),
1787-A.
THE AUTHOR TRACES THE HISTORY OF THE VETO, BOTH PRIOR TO
AND THROUGHOUT AMERICAN CONSTUTUTIONAL HISTORY. THE
RELATIONSHIP BETWEEN SEVEN INDICATORS OF SUPPORT FOR THE
PRESIDENT AND THE ANNUAL VETO FREQUENCY FROM 1889 TO 1985 IS
EXAMINED, USING MULTIPLE REGRESSION. FIVE SUPPORT INDICATORS
ARE FOUND TO SIGNIFICANTLY AFFECT VETO USE: THE YEAR WITHIN
THE PRESIDENTIAL TERM, THE TERM BEING SERVED BY THE
PRESIDENT, THE LEVEL OF UNEMPLOYMENT, THE NUMBER OF PUBLIC
BILLS PASSED BY CONGRESS, AND WHETHER THE PRESIDENT WAS
ELECTED OR SUCCEEDED TO OFFICE.

04310 HOFFMAN-LANGE, U.
POSITIONAL POWER AND POLITICAL INFLUENCE IN THE FEDERAL
EUROPEAN JOURNAL OF POLITICAL RESEARCH, 17(1) (JAN 89),
51-76.
FEDERAL REPUBLIC OF GERMANY METHODS OF ELITE
IDENTIFICATION MEASURE DIFFERENT ASPECTS OF POWER IN
SOCIETIES. THE RELATIONSHIP BETWEEN THE POSITIONAL AND THE
DECISIONAL METHODS WAS STUDIED EMPIRICALLY, USING DATA FROM
A 1981 WEST GERMAN ELITE SURVEY. IN THIS SURVEY, RESPONDENTS
DETERMINED THROUGH THE POSITIONAL METHOD WERE ASKED TO NAME
THEIR INTERACTION PARTNERS FOR (POLITICAL) ISSUED IN WHICH
THEY WERE ACTIVELY INVOLVED. THE RESULTS SHOW THAT
INCUMBENCY OF AN ELITE POSITION IS A CRUCIAL PRECONDITION
FOR BECOMING POLITICALLY INFLUENTIAL. ONLY A SMALL NUMBER OF
LEGISLATORS, JOURNALISTS, AND ACADEMICS WHO DID NOT HOLD AN
ELITE POSITION WERE MENTIONED AS KEY INFLUENTIALS. THE SAME
DATA WERE ALSO USED TO DETERMINE THE DENSER PART OF THE WEST
GERMAN ELITE NETWORK WHICH WAS MADE UP OF 559 CORE DECISION-
MAKERS. THE SECTOR COMPOSITION OF THIS ELITE CIRCLE
UNDERLINES THE INTERMEDIATING ROLE OF POLITICAL LEADERS AND
SENIOR CIVIL SERVANTS.

04311 HOFFMAN, S.
THE EUROPEAN COMMUNITY AND 1992
FOREIGN AFFAIRS, 68(4) (FAL 89), 27-47.
THE AUTHOR REVIEWS THE PROGRESS THAT THE EUROPEAN
COMMUNITY HAS MADE IN ITS EFFORTS TO ESTABLISH A SINGLE
MARKET BY 1992 AND DISCUSSES THE SIGNIFICANCE OF THAT
DEVELOPMENT.

04312 HOFFMEYER, U.
POLITICAL ECONOMY OF REPUTATION: CREDIBILITY,
MACROECONOMIC POLICY MAKING AND SHIFTING EXPECTATIONS IN A
TWO-PARTY DEMOCRACY
AVAILABLE FROM NTIS, NO. PB89-192751/GAR, NOV 88, 45.
THE PAPER ADDRESSES THE PROBLEM OF MACROECONOMIC POLICY
DESIGN IN A DEMOCRACY WHERE TWO PARTIES COMPETE FOR THE ROLE
OF GOVERNMENT RESPONSIBLE FOR POLICY MAKING. SUCH POLICY
MAKING IS ASSUMED TO BE CONTINGENT ON PRIVATE AGENT'S
EXPECTATIONS WHICH IN TURN ARE INFLUENCED BY PAST GOVERNMENT
BEHAVIOR. THE PAPER PROCEEDS BY DESCRIBING THE ECONOMY, THE
POLICY OPTIONS AVAILABLE FOR THE (POTENTIAL) DECISION MAKER
AND THE UNDERLYING ELECTION MECHANISM OF THE POLITICAL
SYSTEM BEFORE COMBINING ALL THREE ASPECTS.

04313 HOFHANSEL, C.
EXPLAINING STATE AUTONOMY AND STATE CAPACITY: A COMPARISON
OF US AND WEST GERMAN POLICIES ON ARMS AND NUCLEAR EXPORTS
AND EAST-WEST TRADE
DISSERTATION ABSTRACTS INTERNATIONAL, 50(3) (SEP 89),
784-A.
THIS DISSERTATION ANALYZES TWO CENTRAL THEORETICAL
CONCERNS OF STATIST LITERATURE (STATE AUTONOMY AND STATE
CAPACITY) IN THE CONTEXT OF POLICY-MAKING IN TWO STATES IN
THREE DIFFERENT ISSUE AREAS. THE EMPIRICAL CORE CONSISTS OF
SIX CASE STUDIES INVOLVING A WEST GERMAN REACTOR EXPORT TO
ARGENTINA, AN AMERICAN REACTOR EXPORT TO THE PHILIPPINES,
AMERICAN AND WEST GERMAN ARMS SALES TO SAUDI ARABIA, WEST
GERMAN PARTICIPATION IN THE SIBERIAN GAS PIPELINE DEAL, AND
THE REAGAN ADMINISTRATION'S ATTEMPT TO BLOCK THIS DEAL.

04314 HOFSTETTER, C.R.; SCHULTZE, W.A.
SOME OBSERVATIONS ABOUT PARTICIPATION AND ATTITUDES AMONG
SINGLE PARENT WOMEN: INFERENCES CONCERNING POLITICAL
TRANSLATION
WOMEN AND POLITICS, 9(1) (1989), 83-105.
HYPOTHESES CONCERNING POLITICAL TRANSLATION AND
PARTICIPATION ARE TESTED USING AN EXTREMELY LARGE DATA SET
DRAWN FROM 33 FIELD POLL SURVEYS REPRESENTING CALIFORNIA

ADULTS, 1978-1986. STATISTICAL CONTROLS FOR NUMEROUS SOCIAL
AND ATTITUDINAL VARIABLES ARE EXECUTED BY REGRESSION
ANALYSIS. SINGLE PARENT FEMALES ARE FOUND TO BE CONSIDERABLY
MORE NEGATIVE IN EVALUATIONS OF REAGAN AND REAGANOMICS THAN
OTHERS. RESULTS ARE VIEWED AS A CONSEQUENCE OF ADAPTATION TO
PROBLEMS SINGLE PARENT FEMALES FACE AND RESPONSE TO
POLITICAL LEADERSHIP RATHER THAN FITTING MORE TRADITIONAL
STRUCTURAL MODELS OF TRANSLATION. KEY FINDINGS REMAIN ROBUST
EVEN AFTER CONTROL FOR SOCIAL AND POLITICAL VARIABLES.

04315 HOFTE, R.; OOSTINDIE, G.
UPSIDE-DOWN DECOLONIZATION
MACLEAN'S (CANADA'S NEWS MAGAZINE), 102(4) (WIN 89), 28-31.
THE PROSPECTS FOR THE INDEPENDENCE OF HOLLAND'S
CARIBBEAN POSSESSIONS ARE CLOUDED BY QUESTIONS OF ECONOMIC
VIABILITY AND POLITICAL FRAGMENTATION, AS WELL AS DOMESTIC
POLITICS IN THE NETHERLANDS. THE ANTILLEANS UNDERSTANDABLY
HOLD THAT THESE PROBLEMS NEED TO BE SOLVED BEFORE CHANGES IN
THE RELATIONSHIP WITH THE NETHERLANDS CAN BE ADDRESSED.

04316 HOGAN, H.
THE DRUG PROBLEM: OVERVIEW
CRS REVEIW, 10(10) (NOV 89), 1-3.
THE FEDERAL GOVERNMENT, LONG ASSUMING A LEAD IN DRUG
CONTROL, HAS VASTLY EXPANDED ITS ROLE IN RECENT YEARS.
BESIDES MORE TRADITIONAL CONCERNSIMPORT CONTROL,
INTERNATIONAL CONTROL EFFORTS, REGULATION OF THE
PHARMACEUTICAL INDUSTRY AND THE MEDICAL USE OF CONTROLLED
DRUGS, AND RESEARCH AND INNOVATION-THE FEDERAL GOVERNMENT
TODAY MAKES GRANTS TO STATES AND LOCALITIES FOR A VARIETY OF
DRUG ABUSE PREVENTION AND CONTROL PURPOSES, PROVIDES AID TO
INDIVIDUAL FOREIGN COUNTRIES FOR DRUG CONTROL, AND MAKES THE
RESOURCES OF THE ARMED SERVICES AVAILABLE FOR DRUG LAW
ENFORCEMENT UNDER CERTAIN CIRCUMSTANCES. SPENDING FOR DRUG
CONTROL HAS RISEN FROM $82 MILLION IN FY69 TO AN ESTIMATED
$5.7 BILLION IN FY89.

04317 HOGAN, H.; DOYLE, C.
THE FEDERAL RESPONSE: A GROWING ROLE
CRS REVEIW, 10(10) (NOV 89), 11-13.
THE FEDERAL ROLE IN THE PREVENTION OF DRUG ABUSE WAS
ORIGINALLY LIMITED TO IMPORT CONTROL, BUT IT HAS BEEN
BROADENED TO INCLUDE A DOMESTIC REGULATORY SCHEME, RESEARCH,
AND ASSISTANCE TO NON-FEDERAL ENTITIES FOR TREATMENT AND
PREVENTION. IN THIS ARTICLE, THE AUTHORS OFFER A HISTORICAL
OVERVIEW OF HOW FEDERAL POLICY TOWARDS DRUG ABUSE HAS
CHANGED SINCE 1887, WHEN THE FIRST FEDERAL LAW TO DISCOURAGE
THE NON-MEDICAL USE OF A DEPENDENCY-PRODUCING DRUG WAS
PASSED.

04318 HOGAN, J.
THEODORE ROOSEVELT AND THE HEROES OF PANAMA
PRESIDENTIAL STUDIES QUARTERLY, XIX(1) (WIN 89), 79-94.
THIS ESSAY EXAMINES THE STORY OF THE PANAMA CANAL MADE
LEGENDARY BY THEODORE ROOSEVELT AND OTHER POPULAR
STORYTELLERS DURING CONSTRUCTION OF THE CANAL. RESPONDING TO
EARLY CRITICISM OF THE PROJECT, ROOSEVELT ATTACKED THE
"SENSATION MONGERS" AND CAMPAIGNED TO TRANSFORM THE STORY OF
THE CANAL INTO AN INSPIRATIONAL TALE OF AMERICAN POWER,
INGENUITY, AND PERSEVERANCE. DOZENS OF POPULAR AUTHORS,
ESSAYISTS, AND LECTURERS JOINED ROOSEVELT IN CELEBRATING THE
PROJECT, AND TOGETHER THEY CREATED A NEW SYMBOL OF AMERICA'S
RISE TO WORLD LEADERSHIP AND A NEW GENERATION OF UNIQUELY
AMERICAN HEROES.

04319 HOGAN, J. Q.
LOCALISM, THE UNEXAMINED FAITH: INFORMAL GOVERNANCE IN
CONTEMPORARY SMALL COMMUNITIES
DISSERTATION ABSTRACTS INTERNATIONAL, 49(8) (FEB 89),
2376-A.
THE AUTHOR STUDIES THE STRUCTURE AND PROCESSES OF LOCAL
SELF-GOVERNMENT IN UNINCORPORATED SMALL PLACES. SHE USES
FIELDWORK IN FIVE RURAL CALIFORNIA COMMUNITIES (1) TO
DESCRIBE HOW COMMUNITIES WITHOUT GOVERNMENTS PURSUE THEIR
NEED FOR SELF-GOVERNANCE AND REPRESENTATION AND (2) TO
GENERALIZE ABOUT LOCAL GOVERNANCE UNDER CONDITIONS OF
SMALLNESS AND UNINCORPORATED STATUS.

04320 HOGAN, J.V.
POLITICS AND PARTY MANAGEMENT IN THE HOUSE OF LORDS, 1846
TO 1865
DISSERTATION ABSTRACTS INTERNATIONAL, 49(8) (FEB 89),
2387-A.
THE AUTHOR STUDIES THE POLITICS AND TECHNIQUES OF PARTY
MANAGEMENT IN THE HOUSE OF LORDS DURING THE MID-19TH CENTURY,
FOCUSING ON THE EFFORTS OF PARTY LEADERS AND WHIPS AS THEY
WORKED TO WIN MAJORITIES DURING A PERIOD OF CONFUSED PARTY
ALIGNMENTS.

04321 HOGAN, M.J.
THE MARSHALL PLAN: AMERICA, BRITAIN, AND THE
RECONSTRUCTION OF WESTERN EUROPE, 1947-1952
CAMBRIDGE UNIVERSITY PRESS, CAMBRIDGE, GB, 1987, 445.
THIS ACCOUNT OF THE MARSHALL PLAN ILLUMINATES BOTH THE

VISION AND THE SHORT-SIGHTEDNESS OF POLICY LEADERS IN THE
RECONSTRUCTION OF WESTERN EUROPE FOLLOWING WORLD WAR II. IT
CLARIFIES THE CONTRIBUTIONS OF MAJOR AGENCIES AND THE
TRANSNATIONAL ORGANIZATION CREATED TO ADMINISTER THE PLAN.
THE ANALYSIS FOCUSES ON THE PRINCIPAL ACTORS AS REVEALED
THROUGH THEIR MEMORANDA, LETTERS, AND OTHER DOCUMENTS.

04322 HOHMANN, H.
SOVIET PERSTROIKA, ECONOMIC REFORM AND INTEGRATION
PROBLEMS IN EASTERN EUROPE
JOURNAL OF COMMUNIST STUDIES, 5(1) (MAR 89), 18-31.
THE ARTICLE EXAMINES THE SOVIET INTEREST IN OTHER
SOCIALIST COUNTRIES AND THEIR ATTEMPTS AT ECONOMIC REFORMS.
IT IS NOT ONLY AN INTEREST IN LEARNING, BUT AN INTEREST IN
CONTROLLING, AND AN INTEREST IN COOPERATION. THESE FORMS OF
INTEREST ARE ANALYZED IN A PATTERN WHICH SEEKS TO AID THE
INCREASE OF UNDERSTANDING OF SOVIET BEHAVIOR. THE ARTICLE
ALSO DISCUSSES THE PROBLEM OF "TRANSFERABILITY" WHICH MAKES
IT DIFFICULT FOR THE SOVIETS TO COPY OTHER NATIONS' REFORMS.
IT CONCLUDES WITH AN ANALYSIS OF THE EFFECTS OF EASTERN
EUROPEAN REFORMS ON GORBACHEV'S BROAD ATTEMPT WITHIN THE
USSR.

04323 HOJMAN, D.E.
NEOLIBERAL ECONOMIC POLICIES AND INFANT AND CHILD
MORTALITY: SIMULATION ANALYSIS OF A CHILEAN PARADOX
WORLD DEVELOPMENT, 17(1) (JAN 89), 93-108.
THE PARADOX OF DETERIORATING LIVING STANDARDS FOR THE
POOREST COEXISTING WITH DECLINING INFANT AND CHILD MORTALITY
RATES DURING THE 1970S IS EXPLAINED BY A SIMULTANEOUS MODEL
WHERE THESE RATES AND THE BIRTH RATE ARE ENDOGENOUS. PARTIAL-
AND GENERAL-EQUILIBRIUM RESULTS CONFLICT; SOME APPARENTLY
SATISFACTORY POLICY TOOLS HAVE COUNTERPRODUCTIVE IMPACTS;
ACTION ON SMALL GROUPS OF SELECTED POLICY VARIABLES IS MORE
EFFECTIVE THAN OVERALL ECONOMIC AND SOCIAL WELFARE EXPANSION;
AND POLICY EFFECTS DIFFER ACCORDING TO SOCIAL CLASS. THE
ROLE OF MIDWIFE VISITS, AVERAGE REAL EARNINGS, AND CHEAP
ENERGY FOR POOR URBAN HOUSEHOLDS ARE EMPHASIZED. PERVERSELY,
HIGH UNEMPLOYMENT ALSO CONTRIBUTED TO THE ACTUAL MORTALITY
DECLINE DURING THE PERIOD.

04324 HOLBROOK-PROVOW, T.M.
ECONOMIC CONDITIONS AND AMERICAN NATIONAL ELECTION
OUTCOMES: EVIDENCE FROM SPACE AND TIME
DISSERTATION ABSTRACTS INTERNATIONAL, 49(8) (FEB 89),
2376-A.
STATE AND NATIONAL ECONOMIC CONDITIONS ARE MUCH MORE
IMPORTANT DETERMINANTS OF PRESIDENTIAL ELECTION OUTCOMES
THAN CONGRESSIONAL ELECTION OUTCOMES. CONGRESSIONAL
ELECTIONS ARE DOMINATED BY TWO STATE-LEVEL POLITICAL
VARIABLES-PARTISANSHIP AND INCUMBENCY, ALTHOUGH THE NATIONAL
ECONOMY DOES HAVE A SLIGHT IMPACT.

04325 HOLCOMBE, R.
THE MEDIAN VOTER IN PUBLIC CHOICE THEORY
PUBLIC CHOICE, 61(2) (MAY 89), 115-126.
THE MEDIAN VOTER MODEL HAS FALLEN FROM BEING ONE OF THE
MOST SOLIDLY ESTABLISHED MODELS IN PUBLIC CHOICE TO A STATE
OF ALMOST VIRTUAL ABANDONMENT. THE ARTICLE REVIEWS THE ROLE
OF THE MEDIAN VOTER MODEL IN PUBLIC CHOICE THEORY, PAYING
SPECIAL ATTENTION TO RESEARCH THAT INDICATES THAT THE MODEL
IS VALID ONLY IS VERY SPECIAL CONDITIONS THAT SELDOM EXIST
IN REALITY. IT CONCLUDES THAT THE MEDIAN VOTER MODEL IN THE
PUBLIC SECTOR HAS SERVED MUCH THE SAME ROLE AS THE MODEL OF
PURE COMPETITION IN THE PRIVATE SECTOR. BOTH PROVIDE A
FOUNDATION UPON WHICH VARIOUS COMPLICATIONS THAT REFLECT
REALITY CAN BE ADDED. JUST BECAUSE THE MEDIAN VOTER MODEL IS
NOT DESCRIPTIVE OF EVERY POLITICAL MARKET DOES NOT MEAN THAT
IT CAN NOT PROVIDE A SOLID FOUNDATION FOR THE ANALYSIS OF
PUBLIC SECTOR DEMAND.

04326 HOLCOMBE, R.G.
A NOTE ON SENIORITY AND POLITICAL COMPETITION
PUBLIC CHOICE, 61(3) (JUN 89), 285-288.
THERE IS A TENDENCY TO VIEW POLITICAL COMPETITION AS
BETWEEN PARTIES SINCE ON ELECTION DAY A MEMBER OF ONE PARTY
WILL BE OPPOSED BY A MEMBER OF ANOTHER PARTY, BUT THIS
OBSCURES THE ACTUAL NATURE OF THE COMPETITION. AS REVEALED
BY THEIR ACTIONS, INCUMBENTS ARE MORE CLOSELY ALLIED WITH
OTHER INCUMBENTS IN A DIFFERENT PARTY THAN WITH THEIR OWN
PARTY MEMBERS WHO ARE CHALLENGING THOSE OTHER INCUMBENTS.
WERE THIS NOT SO, MEMBERS OF THE MINORITY PARTY WOULD FAVOR
A WEAKENING OF THE SENIORITY SYSTEM IN ORDER TO ENHANCE THE
PARTY'S OPPORTUNITY TO REPLACE INCUMBENTS AND BECOME THE
MAJORITY PARTY. THUS, UNDERSTANDING WHY THE SENIORITY SYSTEM
IS A STABLE POLITICAL INSTITUTION ALSO LENDS INSIGHT INTO
THE NATURE OF POLITICAL COMPETITION.

04327 HOLDGATE, M.W.
PLANNING FOR OUR COMMON FUTURE: OPTIONS FOR ACTION
ENVIRONMENT, 31(8) (OCT 89), 15-17; 38-41.
THIS ARTICLE EXPLORES THE CRITICAL IMPLICATIONS FOR
PUBLIC POLICY AT THE NATIONAL AND INTERNATIONAL LEVELS
CAUSED BY RECENT PREDICTIONS OF CLIMATE CHANGE. IT ALSO
EXPLORES WHAT MUST BE DONE TO PREVENT TURMOIL AS A
CONSEQUENCE OF GLOBAL CHANGE AND DISCOVERS THAT THERE IS
LESS EVIDENCE OF EFFECTIVE NATIONAL ANALYSIS AND PLANNING
AND THAT WHAT THERE IS LIES MOSTLY IN THE DEVELOPED WORLD.
THE DIRECTOR GENERAL OF THE WORLD CONSERVATION UNION
PROPOSES POLICY STRATEGIES BY WHICH NATIONS CAN AVOID AND
LIMIT SUCH CHANGE WHERE POSSIBLE AND ADAPT TO WHEN NECESSARY.

04328 HOLIK, J.
CONVENTIONAL STABILITY
DISARMAMENT, XII(2) (SUM 89), 26-33.
THE SIMULTANEOUS OPENING OF NEGOTIATIONS ON THE
REDUCTION OF CONVENTIONAL ARMED FORCES IN EUROPE AND ON
CONFIDENCE- AND SECURITY-BUILDING MEASURES MARKS THE
BEGINNING OF A NEW PHASE IN THE EFFORT TOWARDS GREATER
SECURITY IN EUROPE. THE CORE PROBLEM OF EUROPEAN SECURITY,
THE DESTABILIZING IMBALANCE IN CONVENTIONAL FORCES, CAN AT
LAST BE TACKLED. THE GOAL MUST BE TO ELIMINATE ASYMMETRIES.
IN VIEW OF THE PRESENT SUPERIORITY OF THE WARSAW PACT
COUNTRIES IN THE CONVENTIONAL SPHERE, THIS CAN BE ACHIEVED
ONLY THROUGH ASYMMETRICAL REDUCTIONS.

04329 HOLLAND, R.G.
THE NEW DOMINION
NATIONAL REVIEW, XLI(18) (SEP 89), 25-26.
THIS ARTICLE EXAMINES THIS ISSUES AND CANDIDATES IN THE
1989 VIRGINIA GUBERNATORIAL RACE. THE ELECTION OF EITES
CANDIDATE, DEMOCRAT LAURENCE DOUGLAS WILDER OR REPUBLICAN
JOHN MARSHALL COLEMAN, WILL SIGNIFY A NEW CHAPTER IN THE
DEVELOPMENT OF THE NEW SOUTH.

04330 HOLLANDER, P.
IDEOLOGICAL NOISE
ENCOUNTER, LXXIII(5) (DEC 89), 67-70.
FROM THE EARLIEST DAYS OF THE SOVIET SYSTEM, PROPAGANDA
HAS BEEN A MASSIVE, OBTRUSIVE, AND UBIQUITOUS PRESENCE: A
RELENTLESS EFFORT ON THE PART OF SOVIET AUTHORITIES WHO HAVE
INVESTED VAST RESOURCES AND MANPOWER IN IT. PROPAGANDA IS
APPLIED IDEOLOGY, WHICH MAY EXPLAIN THE RELATIVELY MINOR
AMOUNT OF STUDY IT HAS INSPIRED IN THE WEST, BECAUSE
BELITTLING THE IMPORTANCE OF IDEOLOGY IN SOVIET POLITICS HAS
BEEN CONGENIAL TO BOTH A CRITICAL AND A SYMPATHETIC VIEW OF
THE SOVIET SYSTEM.

04331 HOLLINGTON, J.
INVESTING IN EUROPEAN PROPERTY
EUROPE, (292) (DEC 89), 38-40, 47.
THE PROSPECT OF A UNITED EUROPE PRESENTS SUBSTANTIAL
OPPORTUNITIES FOR THE PROPERTY MARKET. TO CAPITALIZE UPON
THEM, HOWEVER, THE BUSINESS COMMUNITY MUST BE AWARE OF THE
VARIETY OF RESTRICTIONS, LEGISLATIONS, AND SEPARATE
ECONOMIES THAT EXIST IN EACH MEMBER STATE. THE DEMAND FOR
PRIME PROPERTY WILL GROW AS THE PACE OF BUSINESS ACCELERATES
IN THE SINGLE MARKET. MANY NON-EUROPEAN COMPANIES ARE
ALREADY POSITIONING THEMSELVES TO TAKE ADVANTAGE OF THE
SINGLE MARKET BY ESTABLISHING OPERATION IN THE EUROPEAN
COMMUNITY. ONCE ESTABLISHED IN THE E.C., COMPANIES MUST
DEVELOP THROUGH ACQUISTIONS, MERGERS AND ORGANIC GROWTH.
BUSINESSES WILL NEED SUITABLE PROPERTIES IN THE RIGHT
LOCATION AND AT THE RIGHT PRICE IN ORDER TO EXPAND.
UNFORTUNATELY, IT IS NOT THAT STRAIGHTFORWARD. THE UPROOTING
OF TRADITIONS, THE MERGING OF SEPARATE ECONOMIES, AND
LEGISLATION WILL NOT CHANGE OVERNIGHT.

04332 HOLLINGWORTH, C.
PROSPEROUS FACADE HIDES DEEP ANXIETY
PACIFIC DEFENCE REPORTER, 16(6) (DEC 89), 43-44.
THE SITUATION IN HONG KONG, WHICH IS DUE TO RETURN TO
CHINESE SOVEREIGNTY IN 1997, HAS GROWN MORE CRITICAL
THROUGHOUT THE YEAR AS A RESULT OF DEVELOPMENTS OUTSIDE THE
COLONY. THESE INCLUDE THE ARRIVAL OF THOUSANDS OF BOAT
PEOPLE FROM VIETNAM, WHERE THE ECONOMIC CONDITION HAS
REACHED ROCK BOTTOM; AND THE TRAGIC EVENTS IN PEKING'S TIAN
AN MEN SQUARE IN JUNE WHICH HAVE CAUSED HONG KONG RESIDENTS
TO DEVELOP DEEP FEARS OF THE PEOPLE'S LIBERATION ARMY (PLA)
WHICH, WITHOUT DOUBT, WILL BE DEPLOYED IN THE TERRITORY WHEN
THE CHINESE TAKE OVER. THIS ARTICLE DESCRIBES HOW, BEHIND A
HIGHLY SUCCESSFUL FACADE, THE INHABITANTS OF HONG KONG ARE
GENERALY UNHAPPY AND DEEPLY CONCERNED ABOUT THEIR FUTURE.

04333 HOLLINGWORTH, C.
YANG'S POLITICAL COMMISSARS BACK IN AUTHORITY
PACIFIC DEFENCE REPORTER, 16(1) (JUL 89), 16-17.
YANG IS RESPONSIBLE FOR HAVING REACTIVATED THE POLITICAL
COMMISSARS IN THE PLA SHORTLY AFTER THE MASSIVE STUDENT
DEMONSTRATIONS BEGAN IN APRIL FOLLOWING THE DEATH OF THE
FORMER REFORMIST SECRETARY GENERAL OF THE COMMUNIST PARTY --
HU YAOBANG WHO WAS DISMISSED IN 1985. THE COMMISSARS WERE
RELIEVED TO REOPEN THEIR STUDY GROUPS -- FOR POLITICAL
INDOCTRINATION -- BECAUSE THEY HAD FEARED THEY MIGHT BE
DISMISSED IN THE NEXT ROUND OF CUTS ENVISAGED IN THE PLA.
ALTHOUGH ALL SEVEN REGIONAL MILITARY COMMANDERS WERE
APPOINTED BY DENG, MAJOR CHANGES ARE EXPECTED.

04334 HOLLIS, R.
FROM FORCE TO FINANCE, BRITAIN'S ADAPTATION TO DECLINE: #
TRANSFORMING RELATIONS WITH SELECTED ARAB GULF STATES, #
1965-1985
DISSERTATION ABSTRACTS INTERNATIONAL, 49(11) (MAY 89),
3497-A.
THE AUTHOR ASSESSES THE ABILITY OF BRITAIN TO MAXIMIZE
THE BENEFITS AND MINIMIZE THE COSTS OF RETREAT FROM EMPIRE.
AS A CASE STUDY, SHE USES THE CHANGE IN BRITAIN'S
RELATIONSHIPS WITH THE ARAB STATES OF THE LOWER GULF (KUWAIT,
BAHRAIN, QATAR, THE UNITED ARAB EMIRATES, AND OMAN) BETWEEN
1965 AND 1985.

04335 HOLLIS, R.
TACTICAL DYNAMICS OF THE INTIFADA AND ISRAEL"S RESPONSE
RUSI JOURNAL, 134(4) (WIN 89), 23-28.
THE ARTICLE EXAMINES THE INTIFADA IN TERMS OF GENERAL
PRINCIPLES WHICH HAVE CHARACTERIZED INSURGENCIES AND
COUNTERINSURGENCIES IN THE PAST. IT FOCUSES ON SPECIFIC
TACTICS WHICH HAVE CONSEQUENCES FOR THE QUEST FOR A
RESOLUTION OF THE CONFLICT. THE AUTHOR OFFERS SOME THOUGHTS,
BASED ON PERSONAL OBSERVATIONS AND CONVERSATIONS AND
INTERVIEWS WITH PARTIES ON BOTH SIDES, ABOUT THE
DISTINGUISHING CHARACTERISTICS OF THE STRUGGLE.

04336 HOLLOWAY, D.
STATE SOCIETY AND THE MILITARY UNDER GORBACHEV
INTERNATIONAL SECURITY, 14(3) (WIN 89), 5-24.
THE ARTICLE COMPARES CIVIL-MILITARY RELATIONS IN THE
USSR DURING THE BREZHNEV ERA WITH THE RAPIDLY CHANGING
RELATIONS INITIATED BY MIKHAIL GORBACHEV. IT ARGUES THAT THE
EMERGENCE OF AN INDEPENDENT PUBLIC OPINION HAS ALREADY HAD
AN IMPORTANT EFFECT ON SOVIET CIVIL-MILITARY RELATIONS,
HELPING TO SET IN MOTION A PROCESS OF DEMILITARIZATION. HOW
PUBLIC ATTITUDES HAVE AFFECTED THE FOUR ISSUES OF
"DEDOVSHCHINA" (THE BULLYING OF NEW CONSCRIPTS), STUDENT
DEFERMENTS, MILITARY REFORM, AND RELATIONS WITH THE BALTIC
REPUBLICS ARE DISCUSSED. THE ARTICLE CONCLUDES THAT
DEMOCRATIZATION AND DEMILITARIZATION HAVE GONE HAND IN HAND,
BUT THE FUTURE DEVELOPMENT OF THESE PROCESSES REMAINS
UNCERTAIN.

04337 HOLLOWAY, N.
FAIR WEATHER FRIENDS
FAR EASTERN ECONOMIC REVIEW, 141(36) (SEP 88), 117.
A RESULT OF PRIME MINISTER NOBORU TAKESHITA'S VISIT TO
CHINA IS THAT JAPAN MAY SOON BE THE NUMBER ONE INVESTOR IN
THE PEOPLE'S REPUBLIC OF CHINA. A NEW AGREEMENT WHICH GIVES
A LEGAL BASIS TO PROTECT JAPAN'S CHINESE INVESTMENTS AND
GIVE THOSE INVESTMENTS "NATIONAL TREATMENT" WILL LIKELY
RESULT IN AN INCREASE IN CHINA. THE SIGNING OF AN AGREEMENT
WILL LIKELY GIVE IMPETUS TO OTHER NATIONS' ATTEMPTS TO REACH
SIMILAR AGREEMENTS WITH CHINA.

04338 HOLLOWAY, N.
THE RISING WORLD STAR
FAR EASTERN ECONOMIC REVIEW, 141(34) (AUG 88), 20-22.
JAPAN'S EMERGENCE AS AN IMPORTANT PLAYER ON THE WORLD
STAGE HAS MIRRORED THE RISE OF THE YEN AGAINST MAJOR
INTERNATIONAL CURRENCIES. MANY FEEL THAT THE ZENITH WAS
REACHED WHEN PRIME MINISTER NOBORU TAKESHITA PROPOSED A $50
BILLION INCREASE IN FOREIGN AID AND PROPOSED METHODS TO DEAL
WITH THIRD WORLD DEBT AT THE TORONTO SUMMIT AND "STOLE THE
SHOW" FROM RONALD REAGAN AND MARGARET THATCHER. IT APPEARS
THAT JAPAN IS ACTING AS STANDARD BEARER FOR EAST ASIA AND IS
DEMANDING TO BE ACCEPTED BY THE US AND EUROPE ON MORE EQUAL
TERMS THAN IN THE PAST.

04339 HOLLOWAY, N.
THE YEN AS DIPLOMAT
FAR EASTERN ECONOMIC REVIEW, 141(34) (AUG 88), 22-23.
JAPANESE ATTITUDES TO FOREIGN POLICY ISSUES HAVE CHANGED
GREATLY OVER THE PAST TWO YEARS. THE RISE IN THE YEN SINCE
1985 HAS BEEN THE MAIN CAUSE. THE FACT THAT BUSINESS HAS
EMERGED STRONGER AS A RESULT OF THE YEN'S ASCENT, DESPITE
DIRE PREDICTIONS, HAS ENORMOUSLY BOOSTED JAPAN'S
SELFCONFIDENCE. THE YEN HAS ALSO BECOME A VITAL TOOL OF
DIPLOMACY. THE US CANNOT MAKE A BIG DECISION ON MONETARY
POLICY WITHOUT CONSULTING ITS MAIN CREDITOR, JAPAN.

04340 HOLLOWAY, S.
REAGAN'S EFFECT ON STUDENTS: A SURVEY
INTERNATIONAL PERSPECTIVES, XVIII(2) (MAR 89), 7-10.
THE PAPER PRESENTS THE RESULTS OF A SURVEY OF THE
FOREIGN POLICY ATTITUDES OF FIRST-YEAR COLLEGE STUDENTS IN
SOME CANADIAN AND AMERICAN UNIVERSITIES. THE PURPOSE OF THE
SURVEY WAS TO DETERMINE THE EFFECT OF REAGAN'S FOREIGN
POLICY ON THE GENERAL POPULACE AND TO DETERMINE WHETHER
REGAN'S LEGACY REVERSED THE EARLIER ATTITUDES CAUSED BY
VIETNAM. THE CONCLUSIONS WERE INDICATIVE OF THE AMBIVALANCE
OF BOTH AMERICANS AND CANADIANS TOWARDS REAGAN. IN SHORT,
THEY SAID "YES" TO THE MAN AND "NO" TO HIS POLICIES.

04341 HOLLYDAY, J.
A TARGET OF CHEMICAL WARFARE
SOJOURNERS, 18(8) (AUG 89), 14-16.
THIS ARTICLE DESCRIBES THE CHEMICAL POISONING OF SOUTH
AFRICAN CHURCH LEADER FRANK CHIKANE. THE INCIDENT WAS THE
CULMINATION OF A LONG SERIES OF DETENTIONS AND TORTURES AT
THE HANDS OF THE SOUTH AFRICAN STATE. HOWEVER, THE THREATS
AND VIOLENCE HAVE DONE NOTHING TO TURN CHIKANE AROUND: HE IS
DETERMINED TO SEE AN END TO APARTHEID IN SOUTH AFRICA.

04342 HOLLYDAY, J.
COURTING DISCRIMINATION
SOJOURNERS, 18(9) (OCT 89), 4.
THIS EDITORIAL EXAMINES THE HYPOCRISY OF THE INDIGNANT
RESPONSE TO THE SUPREME COURT'S RULING ON FLAG BURNING WHILE
IN THE SAME SUMMER THE COURT RULED AGAINST MINORITY WORKERS
IN ALASKA, FOR WHITE FIRE FIGHTERS IN ALABAMA, AGAINST WOMEN
EMPLOYEES OF AT&T, AND AGAINST A BLACK WOMEN CLAIMING
HARASSMENT IN NORTH CAROLINA. IT SUGGESTS THAT IF THE FLAG
IS OUR ACCLAIMED STANDARD OF DECENCY, THEN LET US MAKE THIS
A DECENT NATION FOR ALL OF US.

04343 HOLLYDAY, J.
NO EASY ANSWERS
SOJOURNERS, 18(10) (NOV 89), 14-16.
THE ARTICLE GIVES AN OVERVIEW TO THE CURRENT ABORTION
SITUATION IN THE US. FEW ISSUES HAVE BEEN SO DIVISIVE AND SO
DIFFICULT TO FIND SOLUTIONS. RECENT SUPREME COURT DECISIONS
GUARANTEE THAT THE BATTLE AHEAD WILL CONTINUE TO BE LONG AND
MESSY.

04344 HOLLYDAY, J.
WAITING FOR A DAY IN THE SUN
SOJOURNERS, 18(2) (FEB 89), 14-15.
AFTER THE 1988 REPUBLICAN CONVENTION, THE MAN WHO WANTED
"A KINDER, GENTLER AMERICA" LAUNCHED A NASTY OFFENSIVE
AGAINST HIS DEMOCRATIC RIVAL. GEORGE BUSH GOT AWAY WITH HIS
LIES AND DISTORTIONS. TOO MANY PEOPLE READ HIS LIPS INSTEAD
OF HIS RECORD. DUKAKIS EVENTUALLY JOINED THE NEGATIVITY FRAY.
AND HE SPENT MUCH OF HIS TIME TRYING TO DODGE AND DISTANCE
HIMSELF FROM MOST ANYTHING SOUNDING VAGUELY LIBERAL, WAITING
FAR TOO LONG TO ATTEMPT TO ARTICULATE ANY ALTERNATIVE VISION
FOR THE COUNTRY. BY THEN, THE MOMENTUM AND HOPE OF THE
DEMOCRATIC CONVENTION WERE GONE.

04345 HOLM, H.
A DEMOCRATIC REVOLT? STABILITY AND CHANGE IN DANISH
SECURITY POLICY 1979-1989
COOPERATION & CONFLICT: NORDIC JOURNAL OF INTERNATIONAL
POLITICS, XXIV(3-4) (DEC 89), 179-197.
THE EVENT IN MANY EUROPEAN COUNTRIES FOLLOWING THE
INTENSE SECURITY DEBATES SINCE 1979 HAVE REVITALIZED
ARGUMENTS ABOUT THE RELATIONSHIP BETWEEN DEMOCRACY AND
SECURITY POLICY CHANGE. FROM TOCQUEVILLE ONWARDS, MANY HAVE
ARGUED THAT SECURITY POLICY SHOULD BE SHIELDED FROM THE
DEMOCRATIC PROCESS. AN ANALYSIS OF DANISH SECURITY POLICY
CONTENT AND THE DECISION-MAKING PROCESS IN THE YEARS 1979-
1989 IS USED HERE TO PROVIDE AN ANSWER TO THIS DEBATE.
REPRESENTATION, PARTICIPATION AND INFORMATION ARE USED AS
INDICES FOR THE DEMOCRATIZATION OF DANISH SECURITY POLICY,
AND IT IS CONCLUDED THAT DESPITE A CLEAR TREND TOWARDS
INCREASED PARTICIPATION AND INFORMATION, BOTH THE CONTENT OF
DANISH SECURITY POLICY AND THE DECISION-MAKING PROCESS HAVE
REMAINED STABLE.

04346 HOLM, H.
SDI SUCCESSES AND SDI FAILURES: A EUROPEAN PERSPECTIVE
JOURNAL OF LEGISLATION, 15(2) (1989), 171-178.
THE ARTICLE CONCENTRATES ON HOW SDI IS VIEWED IN WESTERN
EUROPE. IT EXPLORES THE MANY FACES OF SDI SUCH AS SDI AS A
DEFENSIVE PANACEA, A RESEARCH PROGRAM, A METHOD OF ENHANCING
DETERRENCE, AS AN OVERALL WESTERN DEFENSE, AND AS A
BARGAINING CHIP. IT EXPLORES THE POLITICAL SUCCESS OF SDI IN
WESTERN EUROPE AS NATIONS WHO WERE ONCE IN OPPOSITION ARE
NOW BEGINING TO SUPPORT THE PROGRAM. HOWEVER, THE PROGRAM'S
DIVISIVENESS, UNCERTAINTIES, AND COST ALMOST GUARNTEE THAT
IT WILL NOT DEVELOP BEYOND THE STAGE OF A WEAPONS
MODERNIZATION AND RESEARCH PROGRAM.

04347 HOLM, H.
WATER EXPORTS: SPECULATIONS OF A PUBLIC LOBBYIST
CANADIAN FORUM, LXVIII(780) (APR 89), 7-10.
THE ARTICLE EXAMINES THE ATTITUDES OF CANADIANS TOWARDS
ONE OF CANDA'S MOST PRIZED RESOURCES: ITS WATER. IT ALSO
ANALYZES THE EFFECT THAT THE CANADAD-UP FREE TRADE AGREEMENT
WILL HAVE ON FUTURE CANADIAN EXPORTS OF WATER TO THE US. IT
CONCLUDES THAT CANADA HAS PROBABLY LOST CONTROL OF ITS WATER
RESERVES AND IS FINANCING ITS OWN DEMISE.

04348 HOLME, J.
NOTES ON COMMUNIST POLITICAL ACTION
POLITICAL AFFAIRS, LXVIII(7) (JUL 89), 40-41.
THE QUESTION FOR COMMUNISTS NOW, AS IN THE PAST, IS NOT
WHETHER TO WORK WITH DEMOCRATS, BUT WHICH DEMOCRATS TO WORK

WITH AND HOW. DEMOCRATS, LIKE OTHERS, SHOULD BE JUDGED NOT
BY PARTY LABELS, BUT BY THE STANDS THEY TAKE ON ISSUES OF
CONCERN TO THE WORKING CLASS AND ITS ALLIES. RULING
CLASS/CORPORATE FORCES WITHIN THE DEMOCRATIC PARTY CONTROL
THE LION'S SHARE OF THE MONEY AND TALENT REQUIRED TO WAGE
SUCCESSFUL ELECTION CAMPAIGNS. THESE CORPORATE FORCES ARE
ALWAYS READY TO OPPOSE PROGRESSIVE CANDIDATES (E.G. JESSE
JACKSON), AND, IF NECESSARY, THEY WILL ABANDON PARTY UNITY
BY BOYCOTTING PROGRESSIVE CANDIDATES WHO MANAGE TO SECURE
THE DEMOCRATIC PARTY NOMINATION.

04349 HOLME, R.
    ARE RIGHTS UNDER THREAT IN BRITAIN?
    CONTEMPORARY RECORD, 3(1) (FAL 89), 26-27.
        THIS ARTICLE TRACES THE HISTORY OF A BILL OF RIGHTS IN
    BRITISH GOVERNMENT STARTING WITH 1688. IT CLAIMS THAT
    'CONSTITUTIONAL RIGHTS' OF THE INDIVIDUAL IS A CONTRADICTION
    IN TERMS, FOR ALL CONSTITUTIONAL RIGHTS REST IN THE
    SOVEREIGN STATE. IT CONCLUDES THAT THE SYSTEM, AS A WHOLE,
    NEEDS FUNDAMENTAL REFORM.

04350 HOLMER, A.F.; BELLO, J.H.
    THE 1988 TRADE BILL
    DEPARTMENT OF STATE BULLETIN (US FOREIGN POLICY), 89(2144)
    (MAR 89), 11-14.
        THE FINAL 1988 TRADE BILL SIGNED BY THE PRESIDENT
    CLEARLY CONTINUES RATHER THAN CONTORTS TRADITIONAL US TRADE
    POLICY AND RENEWS THE US COMMITMENT TO THE MULTILATERAL
    TRADING SYSTEM. IT DOES NOT LEGISLATE BARRIERS TO CLOSE THE
    AMERICAN MARKET AND CREATE "FORTRESS AMERICA" RATHER, IT
    PROVIDES BETTER TRADE REMEDY TOOLS TO USE JUDICIOUSLY TO
    OPEN FOREIGN MARKETS

04351 HOLMES, H.A.
    BIOLOGICAL WEAPONS PROLIFERATION
    DEPARTMENT OF STATE BULLETIN (US FOREIGN POLICY), 89(2148)
    (JUL 89), 43-45.
        THE AUTHOR, WHO IS ASSISTANT SECRETARY FOR POLITICO-
    MILITARY AFFAIRS, DISCUSSES THE FOREIGN POLICY IMPLICATIONS
    OF BIOLOGICAL WEAPONS PROLIFERATION. HE INCLUDES BACKGROUND
    ON THE DEVELOPMENT OF UNITED STATES POLICY ON BIOLOGICAL
    WEAPONS AND ON THE PRESENT STATE OF PLAY IN THIS AREA.

04352 HOLMES, H.A.
    FOREIGN POLICY IMPLICATIONS OF BIOLOGICAL WEAPONS
    DEPARTMENT OF STATE BULLETIN (US FOREIGN POLICY), 89(2151)
    (OCT 89), 22-24.
        THE AUTHOR DISCUSSES THE PROLIFERATION OF BIOLOGICAL
    WEAPONS, THE BIOLOGICAL AND TOXIC WEAPONS CONVENTION, AND
    THE US BIOLOGICAL DEFENSE RESEARCH PROGRAM.

04353 HOLMES, H.A.
    FY 1990 SECURITY ASSISTANCE REQUEST
    DEPARTMENT OF STATE BULLETIN (US FOREIGN POLICY), 89(2147)
    (JUN 89), 52-54.
        THE AUTHOR DISCUSSES THE BASIC PURPOSES OF SECURITY
    ASSISTANCE AS AN INSTRUMENT OF AMERICAN FOREIGN AND NATIONAL
    SECURITY POLICY, RECENT FUNDING REDUCTIONS, AND THE BUSH
    ADMINISTRATION'S FUNDING REQUESTS AND LEGISLATIVE PROPOSALS
    FOR FY 1990.

04354 HOLMES, J.E.; ELDER, R.E., JR.
    OUR BEST AND WORST PRESIDENTS: SOME POSSIBLE REASONS FOR
    PERCEIVED PERFORMANCE
    PRESIDENTIAL STUDIES QUARTERLY, XIX(3) (SUM 89), 529-557.
        THE TWELVE BEST AND TWELVE WORST AMERICAN PRESIDENTS ARE
    COMPARED IN TERMS OF THIRTY-EIGHT INDICATORS. ABOUT HALF OF
    THESE INDICATORS REVEAL DEFINITE OR POSSIBLE STATISTICALLY
    SIGNIFICANT DIFFERENCES BETWEEN THE TWO GROUPS. THIRTY-SIX
    AMERICAN PRESIDENTS ARE RANK ORDERED USING THE 1983 MURRAY
    AND BLESSING SURVEY OF HISTORIANS. A COMPARISON OF
    INDICATORS FOR THE TOP AND BOTTOM THIRDS IS EMPHASIZED,
    ALTHOUGH DATA FOR ALL PRESIDENTS IS INCLUDED. INDICATORS
    MEASURED FOR EACH PRESIDENT ARE DIVIDED INTO GROUPS
    INCLUDING BACKGROUND, HIGH-LEVEL GOVERNMENTAL EXPERIENCE,
    POLITICAL CONSENSUS, FOREIGN POLICY ASSERTIVENESS,
    PROSPERITY, MOTIVES EXPRESSED IN FIRST INAUGURAL ADDRESSES,
    AND BARBER TYPES. HIGH-LEVEL GOVERNMENTAL EXPERIENCE
    GENERALLY IS THE LEAST SIGNIFICANT SERIES OF INDICATORS.
    MOST OFTEN BACKGROUND DOES NOT TEST AS SIGNIFICANT, BUT
    THERE ARE POSSIBLE EXCEPTIONS. TOP PRESIDENTS GENERALLY
    DIFFER FROM BOTTOM PRESIDENTS BY PUBLISHING MORE BOOKS
    BEFORE ASSUMING OFFICE, ENJOYING MORE POLITICAL CONSENSUS
    AND PROSPERITY DURING THEIR TERMS, BEING MORE POSITIVE AND
    POSSIBLY MORE ACTIVE, BEING MORE ASSERTIVE ON FOREIGN POLICY
    ISSUES, AND POSSIBLY HAVING POWER ORIENTATIONS WHICH ARE
    GREATER THAN THEIR AFFILIATION AND ACHIEVEMENT ORIENTATIONS.
    THE CONCLUSION PLACES INDICATORS IN AN OVERALL CONTEXT.

04355 HOLST, J.J.
    CONVENTIONAL STABILITY IN EUROPE
    SCANDINAVIAN REVIEW, 77(2) (SUM 89), 7-18.
        EAST-WEST RELATIONS HAVE COME TO AN IMPORTANT CROSSROADS.
    THE LONG-TERM AIM SHOULD BE TO TRANSFORM THE POST-WAR

DIVISION OF EUROPE, WITH ITS HEAVILY ARMED MILITARY
ALLIANCES, INTO A SECURITY ORDER BASED ON THE PRINCIPLES OF
ARMS REDUCTION AND COMMON SECURITY. SUCH A FRAMEWORK OF
SECURITY SHOULD PROVIDE BOTH POLITICAL AND MILITARY
STABILITY, THUS REDUCING UNCERTAINTY, FEAR, AND TENSION.

04356 HOLSTI, K.J.
    MIRROR, MIRROR ON THE WALL, WHICH ARE THE FAIREST THEORIES
    OF ALL?
    INTERNATIONAL STUDIES QUARTERLY, 33(3) (SEP 89), 255-262.
        OVER THE LAST CENTURY OUR FIELD HAS BORROWED EXTENSIVELY
    FROM THE EPISTEMELOGICAL FOUNDATIONS OF HISTORIANS, NATURAL
    SCIENTISTS, AND VARIOUS FORMS OF POSITIVISM. POST-MODERNISM
    AS APPLIED TO INTERNATIONAL RELATIONS IS A REACTION TO THE
    EXCESSIVE CLAIMS AND ASPIRATIONS OF THE "BEHAVIORAL
    REVOLUTION." LAPID'S ESSAY CONCISELY ENUMERATES AND
    EVALUATES ITS COUNTER-CLAIMS. WHERE POST-MODERNISM WILL LEAD
    REMAINS PROBLEMATIC. ITS STANCE OF METHODOLOGICAL AND
    THEORETICAL RELATIVISM AND ITS CALL FOR THE DECONSTRUCTION
    OF CLASSICAL AND MORE RECENT INTERNATIONAL RELATIONS
    THEORIES COULD LEAD TO THE ABANDONMENT OF RIGOROUS BASES FOR
    EVALUATING ADDITIONS TO KNOWLEDGE, TO AN INDIFFERENCE TO THE
    REALITIES OF INTERNATIONAL LIFE, AND TO THE PROMOTION OF
    FADS. THE ESSAY DISCUSSES THE SOURCES AND VIRTUES OF
    THEORETICAL PLURALISM AND ARGUES THAT IN LIGHT OF THE
    INCREASING COMPLEXITY OF INTERNATIONAL RELATIONS, OUR FIELD
    WILL NECESSARILY BE CHARACTERIZED BY A MULTIPLICITY OF
    THEORIES. THE SEARCH FOR A SINGLE, AUTHORITATIVE THEORETICAL
    OR EPISTEMELOGICAL STANCE IS LIKELY TO BE HARMFUL FOR THE
    GENERATION OF RELIABLE KNOWLEDGE IN THE FIELD.

04357 HOLSTI, O.R.
    THE POLITICAL PSYCHOLOGY OF INTERNATIONAL POLITICS: MORE
    THAN A LUXURY
    POLITICAL PSYCHOLOGY, 10(3) (SEP 89), 495-500.
        THIS PAPER ELABORATES OF THE OBSERVATIONS OF ROBERT
    JARVIS CONCERNING THE LIMITS OF STRUCTURAL EXPLANATIONS, THE
    NEGLECT OF NATIONALISM, AND THE COLLABORATIONS OF HISTORIANS.
    IT PROVIDES A REALISTIC DIAGNOSIS OF THE CHALLENGES AND
    OPPORTUNITIES FOR POLITICAL PSYCHOLOGY.

04358 HOLZER, M.
    PUBLIC SERVICE: PRESENT PROBLEMS, FUTURE PROSPECTS
    INTERNATIONAL JOURNAL OF PUBLIC ADMINISTRATION, 12(4)
    (1989), 585-594.
        THE CONCEPT OF PUBLIC SERVICE, WHICH IS TOO OFTEN
    APPROACHED SIMPLISTICALLY, IS WORTHY OF BOTH SUPPORT AND
    SERIOUS REEXAMINATION. CONTRIBUTORS TO THIS SYMPOSIUM
    PROVIDE FOUR DISTINCT PERSPECTIVES WHICH, TAKEN AS A WHOLE,
    PROVIDE AN OPTIMISTIC VIEW OF POSSIBILITIES FOR SOLVING
    PROBLEMS ASSOCIATED WITH THIS NECESSARY AND PRODUCTIVE LINK
    IN OUR SOCIAL FABRIC.

04359 HOLZER, R.
    WHAT NEXT WITH COMMUNISM?
    EAST EUROPEAN REPORTER, 4(1) (WIN 89), 78-79.
        THE ARTICLE EXAMINES THE CONSIDERABLE AMOUNT OF
    DISAGREEMENT OVER THE "DEMISE" OF COMMUNISM IN POLAND. IT
    CONCLUDES THAT THE CURRENT POLISH SITUATION NO LONGER LENDS
    ITSELF TO A DESCRIPTION AND ANALYSIS IN TERMS OF THE
    TRADITION CONFLICT BETWEEN THE COMMUNIST AUTHORITIES AND A
    DEMOCRACY-HUNGRY SOCIETY. INSTEAD, BOTH THE COMMUNISTS AND
    SOLIDARITY ARE EXPERIENCING INCREASED DIVERGENCE INTO
    FACTIONS WHO PURSUE RADICALLY DIFFERENT POLICIES. THE END
    RESULT IS "COMMUNISM IS GONE, THE COMMUNISTS HAVE REMAINED."

04360 HOLZGREFE, J. L.
    THE ORIGINS OF MODERN INTERNATIONAL RELATIONS THEORY
    REVIEW OF INTERNATIONAL STUDIES, 15(1) (JAN 89), 11-26.
        IT IS CLEAR THAT NO SINGLE AUTHOR CAN BE ACCORDED THE
    TITLE OF 'FOUNDER' OF MODERN INTERNATIONAL RELATIONS THEORY.
    EACH OF THE PRINCIPAL ASPECTS OF MODERN INTERNATIONAL
    RELATIONS THEORY WERE FIRST FORMULATED BY DIFFERENT WRITERS
    AND IT WAS NOT UNTIL THE LATE SEVENTEENTH OR EARLY
    EIGHTEENTH CENTURIES THAT THEY WERE WELDED BY WRITERS SUCH
    AS PUFENDORF AND VATTEL INTO MODERN THEORIES OF
    INTERNATIONAL RELATIONS. THAT THIS WAS SO IS NEITHER VERY
    SURPRISING NOR PARTICULARLY INTERESTING. WHAT IS OF GREATER
    IMPORTANCE ARE THE HISTORICAL CAUSES OF THIS DEVELOPMENT. IT
    IS A COMMON CONCEIT AMONG INTELLECTUALS THAT THEORY AND
    PRACTICE STAND IN A RECIPROCAL RELATIONSHIP; THEORY INFORMS
    PRACTICE AND PRACTICE INFORMS THEORY. IN THE PRESENT CASE,
    HOWEVER, THERE APPEARS TO BE A MARKED DISJUNCTION BETWEEN
    THE TWO. IN ALMOST EVERY INSTANCE PRACTICAL CHANGES WERE IN
    ADVANCE OF THEORETICAL DEVELOPMENTS BY FIFTY TO ONE HUNDRED
    YEARS. INDEED, THE GAP WAS SO GREAT THAT CHANGES IN
    INTERNATIONAL RELATIONS THEORY WERE SELDOM MORE THAN POST
    FACTO RATIONALIZATIONS OF ACTUAL HISTORICAL DEVELOPMENTS.

04361 HOLZMAN, F.D.
    POLITICS AND GUESSWORK: CIA AND DIA ESTIMATES OF SOVIET
    MILITARY SPENDING
    INTERNATIONAL SECURITY, 14(2) (FAL 89), 101-131.
        THE PRIMARY PURPOSE OF THIS ARTICLE IS TO EVALUATE THE

CIA'S ESTIMATES OF ME/GNP. IT RAISES QUESTIONS REGARDING THE METHODOLOGIES EMPLOYED IN AGGREGATING THE DATA COLLECTED BY THE U.S. GOVERNMENT. IT INTRODUCES THE METHODOLOGIES USED AND OFFERS A HISTORY OF THE CHANGES IN ESTIMATES BETWEEN 1965 AND 1984, AND THE IMPACT OF THE 1982 PRICE REFORM ON THE ESTIMATES, IT ATTEMPTS TO EXPLAIN HOW THE INCONSISTENCIES AND PUZZLES COULD HAVE DEVELOPED. IT CONCLUDES THAT THE ESTIMATES AFTER 1975 TENDED TO BE SIGNIFICANTLY BIASED UPWARD AND THAT THEY MIGHT HAVE CONTRIBUTED TO U.S. FOREIGN POLICY DECISIONS THAT WERE NOT IN THE BEST INTERESTS OF THE U.S.

04362 HOMER-DIXON, T.F.; KARAPIN, R.S.
GRAPHICAL ARGUMENT ANALYSIS: A NEW APPROACH TO UNDERSTANDING ARGUMENTS, APPLIED TO A DEBATE ABOUT THE WINDOW OF VULNERABILITY
INTERNATIONAL STUDIES QUARTERLY, 33(4) (DEC 89), 389-410.
ARGUMENTS AND DEBATES ABOUT POLITICS ARE ACTIVITIES CENTRAL TO A DEMOCRACY. UNDERSTANDING ARGUMENTS ACCORDING TO COMMON FRAMES OF REFERENCE IS NOT A STRAIGHTFORWARD TASK BUT DEMANDS MUCH CRITICAL INTELLIGENCE AND SKILL. TO AID IN EVALUATING AND CRITICIZING ARGUMENTS, WE PRESENT IN THIS PAPER A QUASIFORMAL ANALYTICAL METHODOLOGY THAT USES A GRAPHICAL SCHEME SYNTHESIZED FROM THE WORK OF TOULMIN AND OTHERS. ARGUMENTS ARE ANALYZED INTO SETS OF PROPOSITIONS STRUCTURALLY LINKED BY SUPPORT, ATTACK, AND "WARRANTING" RELATIONS. THIS METHOD HAD ADVANTAGES OVER OTHERS, SINCE IT IS WELL-ADAPTED TO INFORMAL REASONING AND SINCE IT HELPS IDENTIFY IMPLICIT PRINCIPLES OF ARGUMENTATION (WARRANTS), UNSUPPORTED CLAIMS, CIRCULARITIES IN REASONING, LINES OF POSSIBLE ATTACK, AND STRUCTURAL RELATIONS BETWEEN SUB-ARGUMENTS. ANYONE CAN USE THE GRAPHICAL TEMPLATE OF ARGUMENT ELEMENTS AND RELATIONS AS A GUIDE IN ANALYZING POLITICAL (OR OTHER) ARGUMENTS FOR A VARIETY OF CRITICAL PURPOSES. THIS PAPER HAS CHOSEN TO APPLY THE METHOD TO A DEBATE ABOUT THE STRATEGIC WINDOW OF VULNERABILITY, A DEBATE CHOSEN FOR ITS CONTINUING POLITICAL RELEVANCE AND THE RICHNESS OF ITS ARGUMENT STRUCTURE. IT PRESENTS GRAPHS AND THEIR VERBAL INTERPRETATIONS, AND HOPES TO ENCOURAGE OTHERS TO USE THIS METHOD IN THEIR OWN CRITICAL RESEARCH.

04363 HONECKER, E.
IN SUPPORT OF NUCLEAR - FREE ZONES
INFORMATION BULLETIN, 26(19-20) (OCT 88), 11-13.
HONECKER DESCULES HOW THE FREEING OF CENTRAL EUROPE FROM NUCLEAR WEAPONS MEETS THE GENIUNE SECURITY INTERESTS OF ALL THE EUROPEANS. A NUCLEAR-FREE CORRIDOR COULD DO MUCH TO LOWER THE LEVEL OF THE ARMED CONFRONTATION ON OUR CONTINENT. THE PROCESS OF CONFIDENCE-BUILDING WOULD BE DEEPENED. THERE WOULD BE FURTHER OPPORTUNITIES FOR CONTINUED DISARMAMENT. THE WARNING TIME WOULD BE INCREASED. THE DANGER OF SURPRISE ATTACK WOULD BE REDUCED. CONSEQUENTLY, IT MAKES SENSE FOR ALL THE STATES, BIG AND SMALL, TO GIVE SERIOUS THOUGH TO THESE POTENTIALITIES AND PROSPECTS. ALL THE PEOPLES AND STATES WOULD STAND TO GAIN IN TERMS OF SECURITY.

04364 HONECKER, E.
UNITY AND DIVERSITY
WORLD MARXIST REVIEW, 32(2) (FEB 89), 3-7.
ALL-ROUND COOPERATION BETWEEN THE SOCIALIST COUNTRIES UNDER THE LEADERSHIP OF THE FRATERNAL PARTIES ON THE BASIS OF THE PRINCIPLES OF EQUALITY, INDEPENDENCE, AND RESPONSIBILITY TO ONE'S OWN PEOPLE AND MUTUAL BENEFIT IS AMONG THE GAINS OF SOCIALISM. THE POINT OF DEPARTURE IS THE CONCEPTION OF SCIENTIFIC SOCIALISM WORKED OUT BY MARX AND ENGELS, ACCORDING TO WHICH THE NEW SOCIETY IS BUILT WITH AN EYE TO THE CONDITIONS OF EACH COUNTRY. THERE IS NOTHING NEW IN THE IDEA, FOR INSTANCE, THAT THERE IS NO SINGLE MODEL THAT HOLDS GOOD FOR ALL THE SOCIALIST COUNTRIES, AS THAT WOULD RUN COUNTER TO THE EXISTING REALITIES AND THE AVAILABLE EXPERIENCE.

04365 HONG, L.
HOUSING CONSTRUCTION AND REFORM
CHINA RECONSTRUCTS, XXXVIII(8) (AUG 89), 8-11, 59.
THE AUTHOR REVIEWS THE HOUSING SHORTAGE IN CHINA AND THE GOVERNMENT'S EFFORTS TO ALLEVIATE IT. IN MARCH 1988, THE LEADING GROUP ON HOUSING SYSTEM REFORM OF THE STATE COUNCIL DECLARED THAT IN THREE TO FIVE YEARS CHINA WOULD BEGIN A REFORM PROGRAM IN ALL URBAN AREAS, DESIGNED TO PROVIDE ADEQUATE SHELTER AT AN AFFORDABLE COST.

04366 HONG, S.
AVIATION POLICY-MAKING IN SOUTH KOREA
DISSERTATION ABSTRACTS INTERNATIONAL, 49(7) (JAN 89), 1957-A.
THE RELATIONSHIP BETWEEN THE GOVERNMENT AND THE AIRLINES IN SOUTH KOREA CAN BE CHARACTERIZED AS CORPORATISM. AVIATION POLICY-MAKING CAN BE CLASSIFIED INTO TWO TYPES, DEPENDING ON WHO PLAYS THE MAJOR ROLE AND WHO HAS THE PRIMARY INTEREST IN THE POLICY ISSUE UNDER DISCUSSION: (1) INDUSTRIAL ACTORS OR INTEREST GROUPS AND (2) STATE AGENCIES OR GOVERNMENT AUTHORITIES.

04367 HONG, Z.
POLITICAL REFORM AND CIVIL SERVICE SYSTEM
BEIJING REVIEW, 32(29) (JUL 89), 32-34.
THE AUTHOR DISCUSSES THE ANCIENT CHINESE CIVIL SERVICE SYSTEM AND THE CHINESE GOVERNMENT'S CURRENT EFFORTS TO REFORM THE POLITICAL APPARATUS.

04368 HONGQI, W.
TIRANA STARTS TO OPEN ITS DOOR
BEIJING REVIEW, 32(17) (APR 89), 17-18.
SINCE RAMIZ ALIA TOOK OFFICE, SUBTLE YET POSITIVE CHANGES HAVE BEEN OCCURRING IN ALBANIA. ALBANIA HAS THROWN OUT SOME RIGID, OUTDATED DOGMAS AND STARTED ON A NEW INNOVATIVE ROAD. THE ALBANIAN PARTY OF LABOR HAS CHANGED ITS WORKING EMPHASIS AND ADOPTED SOME NEW THEORETICAL CONCEPTS. REFORM AND INNOVATIONS ARE NOW UNDERTAKEN WITHOUT THE LEAST HESITATION, ESPECIALLY IN THE AREA OF MANAGEMENT.

04369 HONGZHI, X.
GDR: STABLE AND PERMANENT ECONOMIC GROWTH
BEIJING REVIEW, 32(31) (JUL 89), 18-19.
THE GERMAN DEMOCRATIC REPUBLIC IS ONE OF SEVERAL SOCIALIST COUNTRIES WITH A LONG, STABLE TRACK RECORD OF ECONOMIC DEVELOPMENT. THE SOCIALIST UNITY PARTY OF GERMANY AND THE GOVERNMENT FORMULATED POLICIES SUITED TO THE CONDITION OF THE COUNTRY AND HAVE OVERSEEN THE INNOVATION AND CONTINUANCE OF THESE POLICIES. THE GOVERNMENT HAS PLACED SPECIAL EMPHASIS UPON EDUCATION AND THE DEVELOPMENT OF TECHNOLOGY.

04370 HONIG, E.
THE POLITICS OF PREJUDICE
MODERN CHINA, 15(3) (JUL 89), 242-274.
THE AUTHOR SURVEYS THE ECONOMIC STATUS OF THE SUBEI PEOPLE AND ANALYZES THE PROCESS THROUGH WHICH SUBEI PEOPLE WERE TRACKED INTO A PARTICULAR SECTOR OF THE SHANGHAI LABOR MARKET. THE ARTICLE THEN SUGGESTS THAT ECONOMIC STATUS IS NOT ENOUGH TO ACCOUNT FOR THE PREJUDICE AGAINST SUBEI NATIVES AND THAT POLITICAL FACTORS MUST BE CONSIDERED AS WELL. MORE PRECISELY, THE INTERSECTION OF ECONOMIC RELATIONS AND POLITICAL CULTURE MUST BE EXAMINED.

04371 HOOD, S.
POETRY AND POLITICS: A CONVERSATION WITH ERICH FRIED
NEW LEFT REVIEW, (173) (JAN 89), 57-68.
THE AUTHOR INTERVIEWS ERICH FRIED, ONE OF THE LAST MAJOR LINKS WITH THE INTER-WAR GENERATION OF LEFT-WING SOCIALISTS IN GERMANY AND AUSTRIA. ALTHOUGH FRIED LIVED MOST OF HIS ADULT LIFE IN LONDON, HIS REPUTATION AND INFLUENCE AS AN OUTSTANDING POET, NOVELIST, AND ESSAYIST HAS REMAINED HIGHEST IN GERMANY AND HAS BEEN STEADILY GROWING IN THE DECADE SINCE THE FORMATION OF THE GREENS.

04372 HOOGLUND, E.
THE ISLAMIC REPUBLIC AT WAR AND PEACE
MIDDLE EAST REPORT, 19(156) (JAN 89), 4-12.
THE AUTHOR SURVEYS MAJOR EVENTS IN RECENT IRANIAN HISTORY, INCLUDING THE TOLL EXACTED BY THE IRAN-IRAQ WAR, THE CEASEFIRE, AND THE RECONSTRUCTION EFFORT.

04373 HOOK, S.
CIVILIZATION AND ITS MALCONTENTS
NATIONAL REVIEW, XLI(19) (OCT 89), 30-33.
THE ACADEMIC LEFT ARGUES THAT COURSES IN WESTERN CULTURE ARE INCERENTLY BIASED AGAINST WOMEN, PERSONS OF COLOR, AND MINORITIES. THE AUTHOR HERE REBUTS THIS ARGUMENT, STATING THAT TO POLITICIZE THE CURRICULUM FOR HUMANITIES BY DECREEING VALUES LOOKS ARE SUITABLE AND REPRESENTATIVE OF THE "EXPLOITED, OPPRESSED AND HITHERTO UNRECOGNIZED" IS TO CLERY THAT, IN THE COURSE OF HISTORY, CERTAIN LOOKS HAD MORE INFLUENCE OVER HISTORICAL AND PHILOSOPHICAL DEVELOPMENT THAN OTHERS. WHETHER OR NOT THESE LOOKS ARE "POLITICALLY CORRECT" SHOULD BE IRRELEVANT.

04374 HOOLE, F.W.; HUANG, C.
THE GLOBAL CONFLICT PROCESS
JOURNAL OF CONFLICT RESOLUTION, 33(1) (MAR 89), 142-163.
THE RELATIONSHIP BETWEEN DOMESTIC AND INTERNATIONAL CONFLICT IS THE PRIMARY FOCUS OF THIS ARTICLE. THE AUTHORS USE THE INTERNATIONAL SYSTEM AS THE UNIT OF ANALYSIS AND EMPLOY A DYNAMIC TIME SERIES RESEARCH ORIENTATION. THEY PRESENT EMPIRICAL EVIDENCE SUPPORTING THE IDEA THAT THE CHANGE IN MAGNITUDE OF DOMESTIC CONFLICT AND THE CHANGE IN MAGNITUDE OF INTERNATIONAL CONFLICT ARE INTIMATELY RELATED IN A BEHAVIOR PATTERN, WHICH THEY CALL "THE GLOBAL CONFLICT PROCESS."

04375 HOON, S.J.
JUST A LITTLE CLOSER
FAR EASTERN ECONOMIC REVIEW, 141(37) (SEP 88), 28.
DESPITE STRIDENT RHETORIC ABOUT CHINA, TAIWAN'S MAINLAND POLICY HAS BECOME MORE FLEXIBLE SINCE A RECENT NATIONAL CONGRESS OF THE RULING KUOMINTANG. THE "THREE NO'S" POLICY OF NO NEGOTIATIONS, NO CONTACT, AND NO COMPROMISE WITH

PEKING IS QUIETLY AND OF INGENIOUSLY BEING IGNORED. THERE IS A DISTINCT POSSIBILITY THAT NEARLY ALL TAIWAN RESIDENTS IN THE FUTURE WILL BE ALLOWED TO VISIT CHINA, THE VOLUME OF TRADE WITH CHINA IS ALSO ON THE INCREASE AND HIGH LEVEL ACADEMICIANS ARE VISITING THE MAINLAND IN INCREASING NUMBERS.

04376 HOON, S.J.
LEE'S JUGGLING ACT
FAR EASTERN ECONOMIC REVIEW, 141(29) (JUL 88), 20-21.
THE ELECTION OF PRESIDENT LEE TENG-HUI AS CHAIRMAN OF TAIWAN'S RULING KUOMINTANG HAS PUT HIM IN THE POSITION TO BE ABLE TO CONSOLIDATE HIS GRIP ON THE PARTY. ALTHOUGH HE IS IN FAVOR OF SIGNIFICANT POLITICAL REFORM, THE PACE OF LIBERALIZATION IS LIKELY TO BE SLOW DUE TO THE STRONG BLOC OF ENTRENCHED CONSERVATIVES.

04377 HOON, S.J.
MANDATE WITH A STING
FAR EASTERN ECONOMIC REVIEW, 141(30) (JUL 88), 18-19.
THE RULING KUOMINTANG STRONGLY ENDORSED PRESIDENT LEE TENGHUI'S PROGRAM OF POLITICAL AND SOCIAL REFORMS BY ELECTING MOST OF HIS NOMINEES FOR THE NEWLY EXPANDED 180-MEMBER CENTRAL COMMITTEE. IN THE FIRST FREE ELECTION FOR THE COMMITTEE IN THE KMT'S 94 YEAR HISTORY, SOME 1,200 DELAGATES DEALT A PUNISHING BLOW TO THE POLITICAL PRESTIGE OF PRIME MINISTER YO KOU-HWA AND OTHER HARD-LINE CONSERVATIVES.

04378 HOON, S.J.
MESSENGER SPURNED
FAR EASTERN ECONOMIC REVIEW, 141(35) (SEP 88), 26.
AN AMERICAN-CHINESE PROFESSOR RETURNED FROM PERKING WITH WHAT APPEARED TO BE DRAMATIC INITIAVES THAT SHOWED CHINA TO BE IN A COMPROMISING MOOD WITH REGARDS TO REUNIFICATION WITH TAIWAN. A FEW DOZEN ACADEMICS OFTEN SHUTTLE ACROSS THE TAIWAN STRAIT TO EXCHANGE IDEAS AND ODS THAT CANNOT BE OFFICIALLY EXCHANGED. HOWEVER, TAIWAN DOES NOT GIVE MUCH CREDENCE TO THE "DRAMATIC BREAKTHROUGHS" THAT THEY HEAR ABOUT THROUGH THE ACADEMIC GRAPEVINE. THE MOST RECENT MESSAGE WAS REJECTED AS BEING "ALL PHONY" AND TAIWAN'S POLICY OF THE "THREE NO'S" WAS REITERATED.

04379 HOON, S.J.
PARTING OF THE WAYS
FAR EASTERN ECONOMIC REVIEW, 141(33) (AUG 88), 27.
SOUTH KOREA AND TAIWAN HAVE BEEN STAUNCH ALLIES FOR NEARLY 40 YEARS, BUT RECENT DEVELOPMENTS ARE CHILLING THE RELATIONS BETWEEN THE TWO NATIONS. THE MAIN CAUSE IS THE INCREASING ATTENTION THAT SEOUL IS PAYING TO MOSCOW AND PEKING, ONCE THE DECALRED ENEMIES OF BOTH STATES. INDIRECT TRADE BETWEEN SOUTH KOREA AND CHINA AMOUNTS TO US$1.5 BILLION A YEAR AND SEEMS TO BE ON THE RISE. DESPITE THE PROTESTATIONS OF NORTH KOREA, A STRONG ALLY OF THE PEOPLE'S REPUBLIC, SOME ARE PREDICTING FULL DIPLOMATIC RELATIONS BETWEEN SEOUL AND PEKING WITHIN TWO YEARS. TAIWAN IS NOW BECOMING INCREASINGLY ISOLATED AS THE WORLD SHIFTS TO INCREASING TIES TO PEKING.

04380 HOON, S.J.; MALIK, M.
THE CORRUPTION OF MATESHIP
FAR EASTERN ECONOMIC REVIEW, 141(30) (JUL 88), 26-27.
ALTHOUGH CORRUPTION IN AUSTRALIA HAS EXISTED SINCE THE FIRST WHITE SETTLEMENT 200 YEARS AGO, A RECENT STRING OF SCANDALS HAS BROUGHT CORRUPTION TO THE FOREFRONT AND HAS RAISED QUESTIONS ABOUT ITS EXTENT AND ITS FUTURE. A FORMER STATE ATTORNEY-GENERAL AND MINISTER FOR PLANNING AND DEVELOPMENT IS BEING INVESTIGATED POSTHUMOUSLY FOR ALLEGEDLY ACCEPTING BRIBES INVOLVING REZONING; A FORMER CHIEF MAGISTRATE HAS JAILED FOR INFLUENCING ANOTHER MAGISTRATE IN A TRAIL OF A FRIEND: APOLICE OFFICER IS BEING TRIED FOR PERVERTING THE COURSE OF JUSTICE IN INVESTIGATIONS INTO A HEROIN DEAL. THE QUESTION OF "MATESHIP": "WHERE DOES DOING A FRIEND A FAVOR AND BEING REPAID WHEN IT IS POSSIBLE END AND CORRUPTION BEGIN" IS BEING ASKED BY MANY IN AUSTRALIA.

04381 HOON, S.J.
TWO LEES TOGETHER
FAR EASTERN ECONOMIC REVIEW, 141(31) (AUG 88), 30.
IN HIS FIRST CONCRETE MOVE SINCE BEING APPOINTED PARTY CHAIRMAN, LEE TENG-HUI SHUFFLED THE CABINET AND SUBMITTED A CLEAR CUT AGENDA FOR THE NEXT SESSION OF THE LAWMAKING LEGISLATIVE YUAN. MANY SEE LEE'S FIRM ACTION AS PROOF OF HIS FIRM GRIP ON THE RULING KUOMINTANG AND A RECEEDING IN POWER OF THE OLD GUARD FACTION WHO FLED MAINLAND CHINA IN 1947. ALONG WITH LEE, LEE HUAN HAS RISEN TO BECOME THE SECOND MOST POWERFUL FIGURE IN TAIWAN SHIFTING THE CORE OF POWER TO WHAT IS NOW CALLED A LEE-LEE AXIS.

04382 HOOPER, J.
KING HASSAN IN MADRID
MIDDLE EAST INTERNATIONAL, (360) (OCT 89), 11.
THE VISIT OF MOROCCO'S KING HASSAN TO SPAIN CONFIRMED SOME OF HIS WORST FEARS. HE WAS MERCILESSLY CRITICIZED BY THE SPANISH MEDIA ON HIS HUMAN RIGHTS RECORD, HIS DREAM FOR A BRIDGE ACROSS GIBRALTAR, AND HIS UNPUNTUALITY. HOWEVER,

THE DIPLOMATIC RESULTS OF THE THREE-DAY VISIT HERE IMPRESSIVE. THE TWO COUNTRIES AGREED TO AN ANNUAL SUMMIT OF HEADS OF GOVERNMENT; THEY ALSO SIGNED A MILITARY COOPERATION PACT WHICH FACILITATES JOINT TRAINING EXERCISES AND THE SALE OF ARMS FROM SPAIN TO MOROCCO.

04383 HOOPER, J.
THE SPANISH BRIDGE TO THE MIDDLE EAST
MIDDLE EAST INTERNATIONAL, (354) (JUL 89), 15.
THE ARTICLE OUTLINES THE ROLE OF SPAIN IN THE MIDDLE EAST PEACE PROCESS. SPAIN HAS HAD A LONG AND VARIED HISTORY WITH REGARDS TO BOTH MUSLIMS AND TO JEWS. RECENTLY, SPAIN HAS INCREASED ITS RELATIONS WITH ISRAEL AND ALREADY RECOGNIZES THE PLO. SPAIN HAS HIGHLIGHTED ITS ROLE AS PRESIDENT OF THE EEC IN FORMULATING EUROPEAN POLICY TOWARDS THE MIDEAST AND IN ENCOURAGING ALL PARTIES INVOLVED, INCLUDING THE US AND THE SOVIET UNION, TO COME NEARER TO THE NEGOTIATING TABLE.

04384 HOOPER, R.
MIKHAIL GORBACHEV'S ECONOMIC RECONSTRUCTION AND SOVIET DEFENSE POLICY
RUSI JOURNAL, 134(2) (SUM 89), 15-22.
THERE IS A WIDE KNOWLEDGE THAT THE SOVIET ECONOMY HAS STAGNATED AND REACHED A CRISIS SITUATION. SOVIET PRESIDENT, MIKHAIL GORBACHEV HAS PROMOTED WIDE-RANGING REFORMS. ONE OF THE REFORMS, RESTRUCTING, WILL TAKE A GREAT DEAL OF TIME, MONEY AND EFFORT FROM THE CITIZENS. INVESTMENT IN SOCIAL PROGRAMS AND THE REFORMS OF INDUSTRY AND MANAGEMENT WILL BE NEEDED. AS FAR AS DEFENSE, SOVIET FOREIGN MINISTER EDUARD SHEVARDNADZE IS QUOTED, "WE MUST INHANCE THE PROFITABILITY OF OUR FOREIGN POLICY AND ENSURE THAT RELATIONS WITH OTHER STATES BURDEN OUR ECONOMY TO THE LEAST POSSIBLE EXTENT." FOR RESTRUCTURING, THE WHOLE OF THE SOVIET SOCIETY MUST BECOME MORE EFFICIENT AND LESS BUREAUCRATIC. IN FOREIGN POLICY, SOVIET COMMITMENTS NEED TO CUT BACK, ALLOWING DOMESTIC REFORMS TO FLOURISH IN A STABLE AND PEACEFUL INTERNATIONAL ENVIRONMENT.

04385 HOORN, E.
COMECON STATES COMPETE AGAINST EACH OTHER FOR FOREIGN INVESTMENT
AUSTRIA TODAY, (1) (1989), 18.
SOMETHING THAT WOULD HAVE BEEN UNTHINKABLE JUST A FEW YEARS AGO IS REALITY TODAY, AND TOMORROW MAY WELL BE OUTDATED: THE MEMBER STATES OF THE COMECON ECONOMIC COMMUNITY IN EASTERN EUROPE ARE COMPETING HARD AGAINST EACH OTHER FOR THE FAVOURS OF FOREIGN INVESTORS. THE SITUATION IS ACTUALLY GROTESQUE, BUT IT IS BITTER REALITY FOR THOSE CONCERNED: THE DISGRACEFULLY LOW WAGES IN THE COMMUNIST FACTORIES ARE PRESENTED AS BAIT TO ENTICE CAPITALISTS FROM THE WEST TO COME AND SET UP JOINT VENTURES. FOREIGN MAJORITY HOLDINGS AND FOREIGN MANAGEMENT ARE PART OF THE PRICE THAT GOVERNMENTS ARE PREPARED TO PAY FOR THE ECONOMIC STIMULUS. IN THE BACKGROUND LURKS THE HOPE THAT THE LETHARGY OF THE WORKERS WILL BE BROKEN BY THE OUTSIDE INFLUENCES. BUT FEW PEOPLE IN EASTERN EUROPE WILL SEE ANYTHING OF THE PRODUCTS.

04386 HOORN, E.
HOPE FOR PERESTROIKA
AUSTRIA TODAY, (4) (1988), 23-24.
THE CONTINUING CRITICAL ECONOMIC SITUATION IN THE COMECON REGION HAS HAD PARADOXICAL EFFECTS. IT IS PRECISELY THOSE COUNTRIES LIKE EAST GERMANY AND CZECHOSLOVAKIA THAT ARE DRAGGING THEIR FEET OVER REFORMS THAT HAVE BEEN "PROTECTED" FROM THE PARTLY CHAOTIC AND TOTALLY FRUSTRATING TRANSITIONAL EFFECTS AND, FROM THE POINT OF VIEW OF THEIR WESTERN PARTNERS, REMAIN FOR THE MOMENT PREDICTABLE IN THEIR STAGNATING STABILITY. THE BOOM ANTICIPATED IN 1989 IN THE WEST IS EXPECTED TO IMPROVE THE COMECON GROUP'S EXPORT CHANCES AND WITH IT THE EAST'S FOREIGN EXCHANGE SITUATION AND CREDITWORTHINESS.

04387 HOORN, E.
WHY GORBACHEV IS FINDING THINGS SO DIFFICULT
AUSTRIA TODAY, (3) (1989), 20.
SOVIET CITIZENS ARE ENJOYING FAR MORE FREEDOM THAN HITHERTO, AS A RESULT OF GLASNOST. PERESTROIKA, HOWEVER, IS CONSTANTLY GENERATING NEW PROBLEMS AND THE SUPPLY OF GOODS IS STEADILY DETERIORATING. THE OLD PONDEROUS ECONOMIC SYSTEM IS STILL DOMINANT, BUT IT HAS LOST ITS POWER AND AUTHORITY. THE PLANNED ECONOMY IS NO LONGER FUNCTIONING; YET THE NEW, MORE MARKET-ORIENTED SYSTEM IS STILL A THING OF THE FUTURE. THE HUGE BUDGET DEFICIT IS ONE OF THE MAJOR CAUSES OF THE COUNTRY'S CURRENT ECONOMIC WOES.

04388 HOOVER, J.
THE FOUNDATION OF THE COMMUNITARIAN STATE IN THE THOUGHT OF FRIEDRICH SCHLEIERMACHER
HISTORY OF POLITICAL THOUGHT, X(2) (SUM 89), 295-312.
IN ORDER TO EXPLICATE SCHLEIERMACHER'S UNIQUE DEFENCE OF THE STATE THE AUTHOR CONSIDERS FIRST OF ALL HIS OBJECTIONS TO TWO NORMATIVE APPROACHES TO POLITICAL AUTHORITY, ONE BELONGING TO THE MODERN NATURAL LAW VIEW AND THE OTHER

ASSOCIATED WITH ROMANTICISM. THE AUTHOR THEN TAKE UP
SCHLEIERMACHER'S CRITICISMS OF THE TWO ACCOUNTS OF THE
ORIGIN OF THE STATE WHICH CORRESPOND TO THESE TWO TRADITIONS.
THE FINAL SECTIONS OF THIS DISCUSSION TURN TO
SCHLEIERMACHER'S POSITIVE ACCOUNT OF THE STATE, CONSIDERING
IN ORDER ITS NATURAL BASES, ITS DEVELOPMENT, AND ITS MATURE
FORM.

04389 HOPKINS, M.
    CHINA'S FORBIDDEN SUBJECT
    NEW LEADER, LXII(4) (FEB 89), 7-9.
        CHINA HAS A NATIONAL NETWORK OF LABOR CAMPS THAT HOLD
    SOME POLITICAL DETAINEES ALONG WITH CRIMINALS. BUT
    STATISTICS ARE SCARCE AND SUSPECT. THE MOST DILIGENT
    INVESTIGATORS FIND IT IMPOSSIBLE TO GIVE AN ACCURATE
    PORTRAIT OF HUMAN RIGHTS VIOLATIONS UNDER DENG XIAOPING.

04390 HOPKINS, M.
    HOW CHINA MANAGES THE PRESS
    NEW LEADER, LXXII(8) (MAY 89), 3-4.
        CHINESE AUTHORITIES DEAL WITH THE EDITORS OF ABOUT 1,000
    MAJOR NEWSPAPERS, 5,000 MAGAZINES AND MORE THAN 1,000
    TELEVISION AND RADIO CENTERS. AMONG THE EDITORIAL STAFFS AND
    LOCAL PARTY COMMITTEES THERE ARE CONSERVATIVES AND
    REFORMISTS, THE CAUTIOUS RURAL OFFICIALS AND THE OUTWARD
    LOOKING URBAN CADRES. PRESS CENSORSHIP CONSEQUENTLY IS
    APPLIED UNEVENLY. ITS ERRATIC NATURE IS ONE REASON WHY MANY
    CHINESE JOURNALISTS HAVE BEEN CHAMPIONING A LAW TO DEFINE
    THE "FREE PRESS" GUARANTEED IN CHINA'S CONSTITUTION. A
    COMMISSION HAS BEEN DEBATING A DRAFT LAW FOR YEARS, AND A
    FINAL PROPOSAL MAY BE COMPLETED BY THIS FALL.

04391 HOPKINS, M.
    LAST DAYS OF CHINA'S OLD GUARD
    NEW LEADER, 72(18) (NOV 89), 7-8.
        THIS ARTICLE EXAMINES CHINA SIX MONTHS AFTER THE
    MASSACRE IN TIANANMEN SQUARE. IT EXPLORES RECENT ECONOMIC
    GAINS THAT HAVE NOW BEEN REVERSED BY GOVERNMENT POLICY,
    HOWEVER THE GOVERNMENT HAS STOPPED SHORT OF IMPOSING SOME OF
    THE SEVEREST MEASURES EXPECTED, PERHAPS DUE TO INTERNAL
    RESISTANCE. IT DETAILS THE ISOLATION OF CHINESE LEADERSHIP
    DIPLOMATICALLY WITH MOST OF THE WORLD. IT CONCLUDES THAT
    WITH EACH MONTH THAT WITNESSES THE DISINTEGRATION OF
    COMMUNIST TOTALITARIAN RULE ELSEWHERE, THE IDEOLOGICAL
    OBSOLESCENT OF THE CHINESE OLD GUARD BECOMES MORE
    DESPERATELY APPARANT - ESPECIALLY TO THE CHINESE.

04392 HOPKINS, M.
    THE NEW TRUTH IN CHINA
    NEW LEADER, LXXII(11) (JUL 89), 5-7.
        THE STREETS OF BEIJING ARE RELATIVELY QUIET AND PEACEFUL.
    HOWEVER, THE HARD-LINE GOVERNMENT IS STILL STRUGGLING TO
    DEAL WITH THE SUPPRESSION OF THE TIANANMEN SQUARE
    DEMONSTRATIONS. THOUSANDS OF CITIZENS HAVE BEEN DETAINED FOR
    QUESTIONING AS POLICE SEARCH FOR THE "RUFFIANS" RESPONSIBLE
    FOR THE UPRISING. THE MEDIA IS ENGAGED IN A STRATEGY OF
    ORWELLIAN DISINFORMATION IN WHICH THE THOUSANDS OF BANNER-
    HAVING STUDENTS AND WORKERS OF MAY ARE DISMISSED AS A
    HANDFUL OF "COUNTERREVOLUTIONARY HOOLIGANS." MEANWHILE, THE
    GOVERNMENT IS FACING INCREASINGLY SEVERE ECONOMIC PROBLEMS
    AND AN IMPENDING STRUGGLE TO SUCCEED AN AGING DENG XIAOPING.

04393 HORAN, M.J.
    THE CAREER PLATEAU AMONG PROFESSIONAL/TECHNICAL
    SPECIALISTS IN THE FEDERAL GOVERNMENT
    DISSERTATION ABSTRACTS INTERNATIONAL, 50(3) (SEP 89),
    789-A.
        THE AUTHOR EXAMINES THE PHENOMENON OF CAREER PLATEAUING
    FROM THE VIEWPOINT OF THE PROFESSIONAL/TECHNICAL SPECIALISTS
    EMPLOYED BY THE FEDERAL GOVERNMENT. SHE ASKS THE FOLLOWING
    QUESTIONS: WHAT EFFECT, IF ANY, DOES PLATEAUING HAVE ON
    THOSE EXPERIENCING IT? DOES PLATEAUING GROW IN IMPORTANCE
    AND EFFECT OVER TIME? WHAT CAN BE DONE TO ALLEVIATE THE
    ADVERSE EFFECTS OF PLATEAUING?

04394 HORIGUCHI, R.
    ELECTION PROTECTS DEFENCE TREATY
    PACIFIC DEFENCE REPORTER, 16(10) (APR 90), 33.
        THIS ARTICLE DESCRIBES HOW THE RECENT JAPANESE ELECTIONS
    REFLECT A MOVE TOWARD STABILITY OVER CHANGE. THE RETURN TO
    POWER OF THE CONSERVATIVE LIBERAL DEMOCRATIC PARTY, WHICH
    WON A COMFORTABLE 257 SEATS IN THE 512 SEAT HOUSE OF
    REPRESENTATIVES, MARKS AN ENDORSEMENT OF THE PARTY WHICH LED
    JAPAN TO UNPRECEDENTED ECONOMIC SUCCESS. THE VICTORY ALSO
    ASSURES THE CONTINUITY OF THE JAPAN-US SECURITY SYSTEM WHICH
    WOULD HAVE BEEN JEOPARDIZED HAD AN OPPOSITION COALITION
    GAINED POWER.

04395 HORIGUCHI, R.
    STRAINS IN US DEFENCE RELATIONS
    PACIFIC DEFENCE REPORTER, 15(9) (MAR 89), 39-40.
        JAPAN'S EMERGENCE AS A FINANCIAL AND ECONOMIC SUPERPOWER
    THAT HAS ENHANCED ITS INTERNATIONAL POLITICAL STATURE, HAS
    GIVEN RISE TO FRICTION BETWEEN TOKYO AND WASHINGTON THAT,

FREQUENTLY HAS LED TO EMOTIONAL OUTBURSTS WITH STRONG
NATIONALISTIC OVERTONES ON BOTH SIDES. THIS ARTICLE
DESCRIBES HOW THESE OUTBURSTS HAVE CAST A SHADOW ON THE
DEFENSE RELATIONS BETWEEN THE TWO COUNTRIES. THE AUTHOR
DESCRIBES THE TWO PRINCIPLE SOURCES FOR THIS SITUATION AS 1)
THE CONDUCT OF US FORCES STATIONED IN JAPAN, AND 2) THE
CONTINUED LAGGLING OVER THE JOINT DEVELOPMENT OF JAPAN'S
NEXT TOP OF THE LINE DUAL-PURPOSE MILITARY JET, CODE-NAMED
FSX.

04396 HORIGUCHI, R.Y.
    CONTROVERSIAL BLUEPRINT FOR DEFENCE
    PACIFIC DEFENCE REPORTER, 15(10) (APR 89), 35.
        IF THE NUCLEAR DETERRENT CONTINUES TO RETAIN ITS
    EFFECTIVENESS, CONDITIONS HAVE EVOLVED TO CAST DOUBTS ON
    AMERICA'S ABILITY TO PROVIDE A SUFFICIENT CONVENTIONAL
    MILITARY POWER TO COME TO JAPAN'S ASSISTANCE IN THE EVENT OF
    A MULTI-THEATRE WORLD CONFLICT. THIS ARTICLE EXAMINES THE
    OUTCOME OF A JOINT US-JAPAN STUDY LAUNCHED IN 1989 WHICH
    EVALUATES HOW TO COPE WITH SUCH AN EVENTUALITY. IT CONTAINS
    THE SEEDS OF A HEATED CONTROVERSY IN JAPAN, WHERE SOME SEE
    IN THIS UNDERTAKING THE RISK OF TRAPPING THE COUNTRY IN THE
    GLOBAL MILITARY STRATEGY OF THE UNITED STATES.

04397 HORIGUCHI, R.Y.
    DEFENCE AGENCY SEES SOVIET THREAT
    PACIFIC DEFENCE REPORTER, 16(5) (NOV 89), 53.
        THE JAPANESE GOVERNMENT IN AN OFFICIAL DOCUMENT HAS
    DESCRIBED IN UNPRECEDENTED DETAIL THE DESTRUCTION AND
    DEPLOYMENT OF SOVIET FAR EASTERN FORCES IN AREAS ADJOINING
    JAPAN. THE JAPANESE DEFENSE AGENCY CONSIDERS SOVIET MILITARY
    DEPLOYMENTS TO BE A THREAT TO JAPANESE SECURITY, AND THE
    AGENCY HAS UNDERTAKEN STEPS TO COUNTERACT THAT THREAT. AS
    THIS ARTICLE DESCRIBES, THE JAPANESE HAVE ENGAGED IN VARIOUS
    AIR, GROUND, AND WATER EXERCISES WITH U.S. FORCES ENGAGED IN
    PACEX-89.

04398 HORIGUCHI, R.Y.
    HINTS OF US WITHDRAWAL
    PACIFIC DEFENCE REPORTER, 16(6) (DEC 89), 49-50.
        A HINTED AT REDUCTION IN THE UNITED STATES TROOP LEVEL
    IN SOUTH KOREA HAS INJECTED A NEW FACTOR IN THE POLITICALLY
    CHANGED ATMOSPHERE IN THE SOUTHERN HALF OF THE DIVIDED
    PENINSULA. MILITARY AND CIVILIAN OFFICIALS IN BOTH THE
    UNITED STATES AND KOREA WORRY THAT THE BURDEN ON SOUTH KOREA
    TO STAND ALONE AGAINST NORTH KOREA WOULD EXACERLATE SOUTH
    KOREA'S CURRENT ECONOMIC SYMPTOMS, WHICH POINT TO DECLINING
    GROWTH, RISING UNEMPLOYMENT, AND INFLATION.

04399 HORMATS, R.D.
    REDEFINING EUROPE AND THE ATLANTIC LINK
    FOREIGN AFFAIRS, 68(4) (FAL 89), 71-91.
        THE FUTURE SHAPE OF EUROPE WILL DEPEND HEAVILY ON
    WHETHER THE EUROPEAN COMMUNITY CAN ACHIEVE SUFFICIENT
    COHESION AND PROSPERITY TO ACCOMPLISH TWO TASKS: (1) TO
    GENERATE FORCES IN EASTERN EUROPE STRONG ENOUGH TO DRAW
    REFORM-MINDED NATIONS THERE MORE CLOSELY INTO THE WEST'S
    ECONOMIC AND POLITICAL ORBIT WITHOUT THREATENING MOSCOW TO
    THE POINT THAT IT INTERVENES AND (2) TO CREATE FORCES IN
    WESTERN EUROPE STRONG ENOUGH THAT THE WEST GERMANS WILL SEE
    ANY FUTURE ASSOCIATION BETWEEN THEIR COUNTRY AND EAST
    GERMANY WITHIN A COMMUNITY CONTEXT. THROUGHOUT THIS PROCESS,
    US-EUROPEAN RELATIONS WILL BE ALTERED AS THE WEST EUROPEANS
    SEEK TO REDUCE THEIR POLITICAL DEPENDENCE ON WASHINGTON, AS
    TENSIONS WITH THE SOVIETS EASE, AND AS PROGRESS IS MADE IN
    ROLLING BACK THE DIVISION OF EUROPE.

04400 HORN, G.
    REDUCTION OF CONVENTIONAL ARMED FORCES AND ARMAMENTS IN
    EUROPE
    DISARMAMENT, XII(2) (SUM 89), 34-40.
        IN VIEW OF THE UNPRECEDENTED QUANTITIES OF WEAPONS,
    TROOPS, AND MILITARY EQUIPMENT INVOLVED, THE NEGOTIATIONS ON
    CONVENTIONAL ARMED FORCES IN EUROPE MAY BE THE MOST COMPLEX
    DISARMAMENT TALKS EVER UNDERTAKEN. THE COMPLICATED PROBLEMS
    MUST BE ADDRESSED WITH FLEXIBILITY AND CLEAR OBJECTIVES.
    APPROACHES THAT FAIL TO TAKE ACCOUNT OF BROAD
    INTERRELATIONSHIPS ARE BOUND TO FAIL SOONER OR LATER. THE
    ULTIMATE GOAL MUST BE TO ORGANIZE EUROPEAN ARMIES THAT ARE
    INTENDED SOLELY TO GUARANTEE THE SECURITY OF THE INDIVIDUAL
    COUNTRIES AND ARE SUITABLE ONLY FOR THE RELIABLE DEFENSE OF
    SOVEREIGNTY AND TERRITORIAL INTEGRITY. THIS MEANS THAT THEY
    MUST BE INCAPABLE OF ATTACK, WHETHER STRATEGIC OR
    OPERATIONAL, AGAINST THE TERRITORY OF ANOTHER COUNTRY.

04401 HORN, M.J.
    THE POLITICAL ECONOMY OF PUBLIC ADMINISTRATION:
    ORGANIZATION, CONTROL, AND PERFORMANCE OF THE PUBLIC SECTOR
    DISSERTATION ABSTRACTS INTERNATIONAL, 50(2) (AUG 89),
    540-A.
        THE AUTHOR USES A TRANSACTIONS COST APPROACH TO EXPLAIN
    THE ORGANIZATION OF PUBLIC ADMINISTRATION. HE APPLIES THIS
    APPROACH TO THREE PUBLIC SECTOR FUNCTIONS: THE PUBLIC
    PROVISION OF GOODS FOR SALE, REGULATION, AND TAX-FINANCED

BUREAUCRATIC PRODUCTION. THE APPROACH EXPLAINS A NUMBER OF
THE CHARACTERISTIC FEATURES OF PUBLIC SECTOR ORGANIZATION
AND WHY THEY VARY.

04402 HORNE, D.A.
PUBLIC POLICY MAKING AND PRIVATE MEDICAL CARE IN THE
UNITED KINGDOM SINCE 1948
DISSERTATION ABSTRACTS INTERNATIONAL, 49(8) (FEB 89),
2387-A.
THE THESIS EXAMINES PUBLIC POLICIES TOWARDS THE
PROVISION OF PRIVATE MEDICAL CARE IN GREAT BRITAIN FOLLOWING
THE INCEPTION OF NHS IN 1948. IT APPLIES THE CONCEPT OF THE
'ASSUMPTIVE WORLD' TO THE PROCESSES OF POLICY FORMULATION
AND IMPLEMENTATION IN THE ARENA OF PRIVATE MEDICINE IN ORDER
TO ASSESS THE CONCEPTS' STRENGTHS AND WEAKNESSES AND ITS
RELEVANCE TO POLICY AS AN INTELLECTUAL DISCIPLINE.

04403 HORNER, C.
SECURING COMPETENCE AND CHARACTER IN PUBLIC SERVICE
GOVERNANCE, 2(2) (APR 89), 115-123.
THE ARTICLE EXAMINES THE CONTROVERSY OVER CIVIL SERVICE
HIRING. THE WAY THAT PEOPLE HAVE BEEN BROUGHT INTO THE CIVIL
SERVICE HAS ALWAYS BEEN CONSIDERABLY MORE THAN A PRACTICAL
OR TECHNICAL MATTER--IT IS AN IMPORTANT MORAL AND POLITICAL
ISSUE, AS WELL. THE ARTICLE EXAMINES THE EFFORTS TO
RECONCILE THE CONCEPT OF ADVANCEMENT ON THE BASIS OF MERIT
AND THE BELIEF THAT ADVANCEMENT TO ALL. IT OUTLINES THE NEW
POLICIES OF THE OFFICE OF PERSONNEL MANAGEMENT (OPM)-THE
CHIEF PERSONNEL AGENCY FOR THE FEDERAL GOVERNMENT--IN THEIR
ATTEMPTS TO PROVIDE QUALIFIED AND FAIR EMPLOYMENT. THE
POLICIES INCLUDE A WIDE VARIETY OF ALTERNATIVES SUCH AS
DIRECT RECRUITING AND HIRING ON THE BASIS OF GRADE POINT
AVERAGE, AND A BATTERY OF JOB SPECIFIC COGNITIVE EXAMS,
WHICH ARE DESIGNED TO INCLUDE MEASURES OF EXPERIENCE AND
PERSONAL VALUES.

04404 HOROWITZ, D.L.
CAUSE AND COMSEQUENCE IN PUBLIC THEORY: ETHNIC POLICY AND
SYSTEM TRANSFORMATION IN MALAYSIA
POLICY SCIENCES, 22(3-4) (1989), 249-287.
THIS ARTICLE UNDERTAKES A SYSTEMATIC ASSESSMENT OF THE
SOURCES AND SYSTEMIC CONSEQUENCES OF POLICY. IT BEGINS WITH
A STATEMENT OF CONTRASTING THEORIES OF THE SOURCES OF POLICY.
ONE STRAND OF COMPARATIVE THEORY EMPHASIZES NATIONAL
CULTURES AND ELITE BELIEFS AS THE MAIN SOURCES OF POLICY;
ANOTHER STRESSES THE CROSS-NATIONAL IMPERATIVES OF
PARTICULAR POLICY PROGRAMS OF INTERNATIONAL DIFFUSION, AND
OF COMMON POLICY PROCESSES. DRAWING ON LONGITUDINAL DATA ON
AN ARRAY OF ETHNIC POLICIES IN MALYSIA, THE STUDY HIGHLIGHTS
THE LIMITS OF CULTURAL-DETERMINIST THEORIES OF POLICY. IT
SHOWS THAT ELITE BELIEFS CHANGE OVER TIME, OFTEN CREATING
LAYERS OF POLICY BASED ON VARYING PREMISES; THAT ONE SET OF
BELIEFS CAN OVERCOME ANOTHER, INCONSISTENT SET; THAT
CRITICAL EVENTS CAN ALTER THE BALANCE OF AUTHORITATIVE
BELIEFS; AND THAT, WHERE BELIEFS ARE IN CONFLICT, ORGANIZED
INTERESTS HAVE ROOM FOR MANEUVER, MOREOVER, THE INTERACTION
OF A MIX OF OPERATIVE BELIEFS CAN PRODUCE OUTCOMES VERY MUCH
AT VARIANCE WITH WHAT POLICYMAKERS WISH OR ANTICIPATE.
FINALLY, ON THE SYSTEMIC EFFECTS OF POLICY, THE STUDY SHOWS
THAT INTERESTS CREATED BY EARLIER POLICY CAN BE DECISIVE
ACTORS IN THE SHAPING OF LATER POLICY. POLICY ITSELF CAN
CHANGE THE ENTIRE STRUCTURE OF THE POLITICAL SYSTEM - AN
OUTCOME CLEARLY DEMONSTRTED IN THE CASE OF MALAYSIA.

04405 HOROWITZ, D.L.
INCENTIVES AND BEHAVIOUR IN THE ENTHNIC POLITICS OF SRI
LANKA AND MALAYSIA
THIRD WORLD QUARTERLY, 11(4) (OCT 89), 18 - 37.
THIS ARTICLE EXPLORES THE ISSUES RAISED BY THE
DEVELOPMENT OF CONFLICT AND CONFLICT-REDUCING MECHANISMS
PATTERNS OF BEHAVIOUR OF TWO COUNTRIES, SRI LANKA AND
MALAYSIA, ARE EXAMINED AND THE ARTICLE ARGUES THAT THERE ARE
SYSTEMATIC DIFFERENCES INDERPINNING THE TWO PATTERNS. IT
ADDRESSES THE RAW CONDITIONS OF CONFLICT AND THE
INSTITUTIONS THAT ARISE TO REDUCE THE CONFLICT. IT CONCLUDES
THAT SEVERE CONFLICT CAN BE REDUCED BY DELIBERATE ACTION,
WHILE MODERATE CONFLICT, IF LEFT UNATTENDED, CAN GROW INTO
SERIOUS ETHNIC PROBLEMS.

04406 HOROWITZ, D.L.
INCENTIVES AND BEHAVIOUR IN THE ETHNIC POLITICS OF SRI
LANKA AND MALAYSIA
THIRD WORLD QUARTERLY, 11(4) (OCT 89), 18-35.
RECENT DEVELOPMENTS IN SRI LANKAN AND MALAYSIAN ETHNIC
CONFLICT RAISE IMPORTANT ISSUES ABOUT THE DEVELOPMENT OF
CONFLICT AND CONFLICT-REDUCING MECHANISMS. FOR TWENTY-FIVE
YEARS, SRI LANKA EDGED CLOSER AND CLOSER TO OUTRIGHT WARFARE
BETWEEN TAMILS AND SINHALESE, UNTIL THE TAMIL TIGER
INSURGENCY EMBROILED THE ISLAND IN FIGHTING SO SEVERE THAT
THE SRI LANKANS CALLED UPON INDIAN ASSISTANCE TO CONTAIN THE
GUERRILLAS. MALAYSIA, BY CONTRAST, HAS MOVED SEVERAL TIMES
TO THE PRECIPICE, ONLY TO DRAW BACK. THE ARGUMENT OF THIS
ARTICLE IS THAT THERE ARE SYSTEMATIC DIFFERENCES
UNDERPINNING THE TWO PATTERNS. THOSE DIFFERENCE PERTAIN BOTH

TO THE RAW CONDITIONS OF CONFLICT AND TO THE INSTITUTIONS
THAT ARISE OR ARE DEVISED TO REDUCE THE CONFLICT. ALTHOUGH
CONFLICT CONDITIONS AND INSTITUTIONAL SETTING RELATE TO EACH
OTHER IN SUBTLE WAYS, THEY ALSO HAVE A DEGREE OF INDEPENDENT
VARIATION. SEVERE CONFLICT CAN BE REDUCED BY DELIBERATE
ACTION, WHILE RELATIVELY MODERATE CONFLICT, IF LEFT
UNATTENDED OR, WORSE, NURTURED UNDER UNFAVOURABLE POLITICAL
INSTITUTIONS, CAN GROW INTO QUITE SERIOUS ETHNIC PROBLEMS.

04407 HOROWITZ, D.L.
IS THERE A THIRD-WORLD POLICY PROCESS?
POLICY SCIENCES, 22(3-4) (1989), 197-212.
IN FIELD AFTER FIELD, SOME POLITICAL SCIENTISTS HAVE
ARGUED FOR DISTINGUISHING WESTERN POLITIES FROM DEVELOPING
POLITIES, WHILE OTHERS HAVE ARGUED FOR INCLUSIVE TREATMENT.
THIS ESSAY ASSESSES THESE DIVERGENT PERSPECTIVES AS THEY
RELATE TO PULBIC POLICY MAKING. ON THE ONE HAND, IT IS CLEAR
THE SYSTEMIC FRAMEWORKS OF POLICY (THE INSTITUTIONS,
PARTICIPANTS, RESOURCES, THE WEIGHT OF THE STATE RELATIVE TO
THE SOCIETY, AND THE CAPACITY OF THE STATE TO WORK ITS WILL)
ALL VARY BETWEEN DEVELOPING AND WESTERN COUNTRIES. THE SAME
IS TRUE FOR THE SCOPE OF POLICY ACTIVITY, THE CONFIGURATION
OF ISSUES, AND TE ACTUAL CONTENT OF POLICY. ONE THE OTHER
HAND, THE POLICY PROCESS APPEARS TO DISPLAY REGULARITIES
THAT TRANSCEND THE CATEGORIES OF WESTERN OR THIRD WORLD
STATE. THE ESSAY GOES ON TO EXPLAIN THE DIVERGENCES OF
POLICY IN TERMS OF DISPARATE ACCESS TO RESOURECES, LEVELS OF
ECONOMIC DEVELOPMENT, AND SOCIAL PATTERNS. THE CONVERGENCE
OF PROCESS IS EXPLAINED IN TERMS OF THE DEEPER EXIGENCIES OF
HUMAN PROBLEM SOLVING IN HIGHLY STRUCTURED CONTEXTS.

04408 HOROWITZ, I.
THE PUBLIC COSTS OF PRIVATE BLESSINGS: FUNDAMENTALS OF THE
ECONOMIC ROLE OF GOVERNMENT
STUDIES IN COMPARATIVE INTERNATIONAL DEVELOPMENT, 24(1)
(SPR 89), 39-46.
THE MAIN THRUST OF THIS OVERVIEW IS TO DEMONSTRATE HOW
THE SHIFT OF GOVERNMENT AUTHORITY OVER TIME-FROM A DEFENSE
OF THE REALM AGAINST FOREIGN INTRUDERS TO AN ADJUDICATION OF
CONFLICTING CITIZEN CLAIMS-HAS CREATED A NEW SET OF PROBLEMS
AND CHALLENGES FOR THE MODERN STATE IN SEARCH OF DEVELOPMENT
IT IS ARGUED THAT THE POWER OF THE STATE EXPANDS AS
TRADITIONAL FORMS OF ECONOMIC RIVALRIES AND CLASS CLAIMS
WEAKEN, AND AS RECOURSE TO LEGAL DECISION-MAKING BECOMES
WIDELY ACCEPTED BY ALL SOCIAL AND ECONOMIC SECTORS.
GOVERNMENT HAS PROVEN BETTER ABLE TO SATISFY EXISTING CLAIMS
THAN AT INITIATING NEW FORMS OF SOCIAL RELATIONS.
EXPERIENCES IN A VARIETY OF ECONOMIC STRUCTURES THUS ARGUE
FOR A CONTINUED INTERPLAY OF PUBLIC AND PRIVATE, FEDERAL AND
PERSONAL CLAIMS.

04409 HOROWITZ, I.L.
SOCIOLOGY AND SUBJECTIVISM
SOCIETY, 26(5) (JUL 89), 49-54.
THE COMMON DENOMINATOR OF SUBJECTIVISM IN SOCIAL SCIENCE,
AND SOCIOLOGY IN PARTICULAR, RESIDES IN THE TENDENCY TO
DENY THAT HUMAN BEHAVIOR IS NORMALLY DRIVEN BY A REASONED
RESPONSE TO A KNOWABLE REALITY. THE AUTHOR DOES NOT DISPUTE
THE ROLE OF SUBJECTIV FACTORS IN DECISION MAKING, OR EVEN
THE PLACE OF HUMAN WILL IN DIRECTING THE COURSE OF EVENTS;
IN THIS ARTICLE HE DENIES THAT THE SUBJECTIVE ELEMENT
OBLITERATES ALL OBJECTIVE ELEMENTS. TO SAY THAT THE WORLD
HAS NO RULES IN THE NAME OF IDEOLOGY IS NO BETTER THAN TO
OFFER A DIET OF STRICT DETERMINISM.

04410 HOROWITZ, I.L.
TRIUMPHALISM IN THE CRUCIBLE OF TRAGIC POLITICS
ENCOUNTER, LXXII(5) (MAY 89), 34-36.
BERTRAND DE JOUVENEL IS A SADLY NEGLECTED, BADLY
MALIGNED FIGURE WHOSE WORK RANGED FROM NEWSPAPER REPORTING
TO POLITICAL THEORY. DE JOUVENEL OFFERS INTRIGUING CROSS-
OVER POINTS BETWEEN LIBERAL AND CONSERVATIVE THROUGHT,
NATIONALIST AND COSMOPOLITAN SENTIMENT, AND RIGHTIST AND
LEFTIST POLITICAL ACTION. HE REFLECTS THE MAIN TENDENCIES OF
FRENCH LIFE AND THOUGHT BETWEEN THE TWO WORLD WARS AND THE
MAJOR MOVEMENTS IN FRENCH THOUGHT AFTER WORLD WAR II.

04411 HORTON, S.; MCLAREN, J.
SUPPLY CONSTRAINTS IN THE TANZANIAN ECONOMY: SIMULATION
RESULTS FROM A MACROECONOMETRIC MODEL
JOURNAL OF POLICY MODELING, 11(2) (SUM 89), 297-313.
ECONOMIC EVENTS OF THE 1970S AND EARLY 1980S (WORLD
RECESSION AND DISRUPTION OF INTERNATIONAL TRADE AND FINANCE)
HIT SUB-SAHARAN AFRICA PARTICULARLY BADLY. THERE HAS BEEN
HEATED DEBATE AS TO THE ROLE OF ADDITIONAL EXTERNAL
RESOURCES AND DOMESTIC ADJUSTMENT MEASURES IN ECONOMIC
RECOVERY. THIS PAPER USES A SUPPLY CONSTRAINED
MACROECONOMETRIC MODEL OF THE TANZANIAN ECONOMY TO SIMULATE
THE EFFECTS OF SEVERAL ALTERNATIVE STRATEGIES. THE RESULTS
HIGHLIGHT THE PROBLEMS OF EITHER A STRATEGY OF DEVALUATION
OR OF MORE EXTERNAL AID ALONE. ONE INEXPENSIVE POLICY
ADVOCATED IS THAT OF FREEING PROJECT AID FOR GENERAL BALANCE
OF PAYMENTS SUPPORT.

04412 HOSLE, V.
MORALITY AND POLITICS: REFLECTIONS ON MACHIAVELI'S PRINCE
POLITICS AND SOCIETY, 17(4) (DEC 89), 51-69.
THE COUNTERENLIGHTENMENT TENDENCIES OF THE LAST CENTURY
HAVE LED TO A PROFOUND DEMORALIZATION OF POLITICS,
ESPECIALLY IN THE TOTALITARIAN STATE, WHICH IS UNIQUE IN
WORLD HISTORY. AS A RESULT, MANY PEOPLE, PARTICULARLY AMONG
THE YOUNG, SEEM TO THINK THAT DRAWING ANY DISTINCTION
BETWEEN INDIVIDUAL ETHICS AND POLITICS NECESSARILY LEADS TO
POWER POSITIVISM, I.E., TO THE DOCTRINE THAT THERE ARE NO
VALIDITY CLAIMS BEYOND THE FACTUAL DISTRIBUTION OF POWER. IN
THIS CONTEXT THE AUTHOR ADDRESSES THE PHILOSOPHICAL
QUESTIONS: HOW IS IT POSSIBLE TO JUSTIFY THE DEVIATION OF
POLITICAL ACTION FROM ACKNOWLEDGED FUNDAMENTAL MORAL NORMS
WITHOUT FALLING INTO A RELATIVISTIC POWER POSITIVISM? MAY OR
MUST THE ACTIONS OF THE STATEMAN DIFFER, FOR REASONS OF
STATE, FROM THOSE OF A PRIVATE PERSON?

04413 HOSMER, C.; JAMALI, M.
COULD A RECHARTERED UNITED NATIONS HELP PREVENT A NUCLEAR
WAR?
INTERNATIONAL JOURNAL ON WORLD PEACE, VI(1) (JAN 89),
31-40.
THE ARTICLE EXAMINES FOUR SIGNIFICANT WEAKNESSES OF THE
UNITED NATIONS AND PROPOSES SOLUTIONS THAT ARE DESIGNED TO
REDUCE THE RISK OF NUCLEAR WAR. THE FOUR WEAKNESSES ARE LACK
OF MUSCLE, THE UNFAIR WEIGHT OF SMALL NATIONS, THE EXCLUSIVE
AND UNLIMITED UN VETO, AND THE POWERLESS INTERNATIONAL COURT
OF JUSTICE. THE AUTHOR PROPOSED THE DELEGATION TO THE UN
SOLE CONTROL OF THE WORLD'S NUCLEAR WEAPONS, A GRADED VOTING
SYSTEM BASED ON POPULATION AND MONETARY CONTRIBUTIONS,
MECHANISMS FOR VETO OVERIDE, AND AN INCREASE IN AUTHORITY OF
THE INTERNATIONAL COURT OF JUSTICE. ALTHOUGH THESE CHANGES
ARE SOMEWHAT IMPRACTICAL, THE INEFFECTIVENESS OF ALL OTHER
METHODS WILL FORCE THE INEVITABLE REALIZATION OF THE
NECESSITY AND EFFICACY OF THE PROPOSAL.

04414 HOTSON, J. H.
THE PLUTO EXPERIMENT
POLICY OPTIONS, 10(3) (APR 89), 13-14.
CONVENTIONAL ECONOMICS CANNOT EXPLAIN WHY CANADA HAS
APPARENTLY LOST THE ABILITY TO CONTROL ITS MONETARY SYSTEM
AND WHY IT IS SUFFERING FROM STAGFLATION. THE AUTHOR ARGUES
THAT INFLATION IS BUILT INTO ANY SYSTEM THAT ALLOWS INTEREST
RATES TO GET OUT OF HAND AND THAT A DEBT MONEY ECONOMY CAN
AVOID COLLAPSE ONLY IF INTEREST RATES ARE MATCHED BY
PRODUCTIVITY INCREASES.

04415 HOUGH, J.F.
GORBACHEV'S POLITICS
FOREIGN AFFAIRS, 68(4) (WIN 90), 26-41.
VARIOUS ANALYSES HAVE BEEN OFFERED TO EXPLAIN MIKHAIL
GORBACHEV'S POLITICS. THE EXPLANATION THAT MAY BE CLOSEST TO
THE TRUTH SUGGESTS THAT GORBACHEV IS A VERY SKILLED
POLITICIAN WHO KNOWS WHAT HE IS DOING, THAT HE IS OPERATING
A POLITICAL SYSTEM USING TRADITIONAL LEVERS OF POWER, AND
THAT HE IS RESPONDING TO AND MANIPULATING SOCIAL FORCES OF A
TYPE THAT WERE ANTICIPATED IN AMERICAN THEORIES OF
TOTALITARIANISM AND MODERNIZATION OF THE 1950'S. IN ORDER TO
UNDERSTAND WHAT IS HAPPENING IN THE SOVIET UNION, IT IS
NECESSARY TO ASK SOME FUNDAMENTAL QUESTIONS: WHAT ARE THE
MAJOR FORCES OF CONTEMPORARY SOVIET HISTORY? HOW IS
GORBACHEV TRYING TO DIRECT THEM AND USE THEM?

04416 HOUGH, R.L.
SOLIDARISMO--THREAT TO FREE TRADE UNIONS
FREEDOM AT ISSUE, (108) (MAY 89), 17-21.
THE FREE TRADE UNION MOVEMENTS IN CENTRAL AMERICA FACE A
VERY COMPLEX THREAT. TRADE UNION LEADERS SEE SOLIDARITY AS
ENDANGERING THEIR SURVIVAL SINCE BOTH COMPETE FOR THE
ALLEGIANCE OF THE SAME CONSTITUENCY. BUT THERE ARE
ADDITIONAL, MORE SUBSTANTIAL REASONS FOR TRADE UNION FEAR OF
SOLIDARITY.

04417 HOUHOULAS, P.
DEFENCE COOPERATION BETWEEN GREECE AND THE UNITED STATES
NATO'S SIXTEEN NATIONS, 34(6) (OCT 89), 38-39 (SPECIAL
SECTION).
GREEK DEFENCE EXPENDITURE EQUALS ONE OF THE HIGHEST
PERCENTAGES OF GDP IN WESTERN EUROPE. GREECE CONTRIBUTES
ACTIVELY TO COOPERATIVE ARAMENTS PROJECTS WITHIN NATO,
PURSUING THE AIMS OF IMPLEMENTING COMMON NATO GOALS AND
DEVELOPING ITS DOMESTIC DEFENCE INDUSTRY. IN THE FRAMEWORK
OF THE TRADITIONALLY FRIENDLY RELATIONS BETWEEN GREECE AND
THE USA, GREECE HAS ALSO ESTABLISHED DEFENCE COOPERATION
WITH THE UNITED STATES. IN THE FUTURE, GREECE INTENDS TO
IMPROVE ITS DEFENCE EXCHANGE BALANCE AND BECOME MORE
COMPETITIVE IN THE INTERNATIONAL ARMAMENTS MARKET.

04418 HOUSE, R.
HIDDEN BOOM IN BRAZIL
SOUTH, (108) (OCT 89), 40-41.
BRAZIL'S BUSINESS LOBBY IS PUSHING THE GOVERNMENT TO
ENFORCE LEGISLATION AGAINST THE COUNTRY'S BOOMING INFORMAL

ECONOMIC SECTOR, WHICH IS ESTIMATED TO COST THE GOVERNMENT
ABOUT US$20 BILLION ANNUALLY IN LOST TAX REVENUE AND TAKES
BUSINESS AWAY FROM MERCHANTS WHO OPERATE LEGALLY. THE
INFORMAL SECTOR IS NOW RESPONSIBLE FOR FORTY PERCENT OF
BRAZIL'S US$352 BILLION GDP AND REPRESENTS A TURNOVER OF
MORE THAN US$100 BILLION. IT HAS REDUCED UNEMPLOYMENT AND
BOOSTED ECONOMIC GROWTH BY AN ESTIMATED THREE PERCENT IN
1988.

04419 HOUSE, R.
SARNEY'S BATTLE ZONES
SOUTH, (100) (FEB 89), 35-36.
BRAZILIAN PRESIDENT JOSE SARNEY'S PLAN TO REVITALIZE THE
POVERTY-STRICKEN NORTHEAST BY ESTABLISHING AT LEAST SEVEN
EXPORT-PROCESSING ZONES IN THE REGION IS IN DANGER OF BEING
STILLBORN. BIG BUSINESS SAYS IT IS A CASE OF TOO LITTLE TOO
LATE AND THAT THE PROPOSED ZONES WOULD SIMPLY BECOME CENTERS
FOR INSTITUTIONALIZED CONTRABAND.

04420 HOUSE, R.
THE STRUGGLE FOR AMAZON SURVIVAL
SOUTH, (103) (MAY 89), 77.
PRESIDENT JOSE SARNEY IS PAINTING HIMSELF INTO A CORNER
BY DENOUNCING OUTSIDE ATTEMPTS TO HELP CURB THE EXPLOITATION
OF THE AMAZON. BY PANDERING TO THE STRONG BRAZILIAN
NATIONALIST SENTIMENTS THAT THE INTERNATIONAL ONSLAUGHT ON
BRAZIL'S ENVIRONMENTAL STANCE HAVE AROUSED, SARNEY IS MAKING
IT DIFFICULT TO ACCEPT THE FOREIGN HELP HE NEEDS TO PROMOTE
DEVELOPMENT WITHOUT DESTROYING THE FORESTS.

04421 HOUSHOLDER, T.
AND THE BEAT GOES ON
CAMPAIGNS AND ELECTIONS, 10(2) (AUG 89), 9-10.
IN THE SPRING OF 1989, THERE WERE THREE SPECIAL
CONGRESSIONAL ELECTIONS WITHIN A FOUR-WEEK PERIOD. THEY WERE
BILLED AS FACE-OFFS BETWEEN THE TWO NATIONAL PARTIES, WHO
RESPONDED WITH ENORMOUS AMOUNTS OF MONEY AND ATTENTION. IN
THE END, NEITHER PARTY RECEIVED A LOT IN RETURN FOR THEIR
INVESTMENT, ALTHOUGH THE DEMOCRATS WON IN INDIANA AND
ALABAMA. THE REPUBLICANS WON ONLY IN WYOMING, WHERE THE
PARTY HAS A DECISIVE EDGE IN THE NUMBER OF REGISTERED VOTERS.
CANDIDATES IN BOTH PARTIES STUCK WITH THE ISSUES THAT HAD
TAKEN GEORGE BUSH TO VICTORY, AND NEGATIVE ADVERTISING WAS
OMNIPRESENT.

04422 HOUSMAN, D.; FRELK, J. J.
A DETERRENT THAT DETERS
NATIONAL REVIEW, XLI(8) (MAY 89), 33-35.
CONGRESS WANTS TO BUY THE MIDGETMAN MISSILE AND THAT MAY
BE A GOOD IDEA. BUT NO SERIOUS PLAN FOR STRATEGIC
MODERNIZATION CAN IGNORE THE STRATEGIC DEFENSE INITIATIVE.

04423 HOVELSEN, L.
COMMUNISM, RELIGION, FREEDOM
FREEDOM AT ISSUE, (108) (MAY 89), 6.
IN THIS INTERVIEW, MILOVAN DJILAS ANSWERS QUESTIONS
ABOUT WHY COMMUNISM DOESN'T WORK AND WHY FREEDOM OF RELIGION
IS ESSENTIAL. HE ALSO WARNS THAT RELIGION BECOMES DANGEROUS
WHEN IT IS LINKED TO AN IDEOLOGY AND THAT ORTHODOX ANTI-
COMMUNISM IS A THREAT WHEN IT BECOMES AN IDEOLOGY.

04424 HOVI, J.
THE EVOLUTION OF COOPERATION: SOME NOTES ON THE IMPORTANCE
OF IMPORTANCE OF DISCRIMINATION
COOPERATION & CONFLICT: NORDIC JOURNAL OF INTERNATIONAL
POLITICS, XXIV(2) (JUN 89), 55-68.
THIS PAPER COMPARES PROSPECTS FOR COOPERATION IN
COMPOUND PRISONER'S DILEMMA SUPERGAMES UNDER TWO DIFFERENT
REGIMES -- ONE WHERE DISCRIMINATING BEHAVIOR IS ALLOWED, AND
ONE WHERE IT IS EFFECTIVELY BANNED. THREE "STAGES" IN THE
EVOLUTIONARY PROCESS ARE BEING DISCUSSED. FIRST, THE AUTHOR
CONSIDERS THE CONDITIONS UNDER WHICH A PROCESS TOWARDS
COOPERATION CAN BE INITIATED. IT IS FOUND THAT THESE
CONDITIONS TEND TO BE MORE STRICT WHEN DISCRIMINATION IS
BANNED THAN WHEN IT IS ALLOWED,. SECOND, THE PROSPECTS FOR
EXPANSION OF COOPERATIVE STRATEGIES, ONCE ESTABLISHED, ARE
INVESTIGATED. IT IS CONCLUDED THAT WHEN DISCRIMINATION IS
EFFECTIVELY BANNED, A GROUP OF COOPERATORS CANNOT EXPECT
OTHERS TO JOIN IN ON A VOLUNTARY BAIS. THIS IS A VERY
DIFFERENT SITUATION FROM THE ONE EXISTING UNDER A REGIME
WHERE DISCRIMINATION IS ALLOWED. FINALLY, THE PAPER
CONSIDERS THE POSSIBLE STABILITY PROPERTIES UNDER EACH
REGIME, OF A SITUATION CHARACTERIZED BY UNIVERSAL COOPERATION.
IT IS INDICATED THAT ALTHOUGH A BAN OR DISCRIMINATION DOES
NOT INHIBIT STABILITY, IT MIGHT AT LEAST MAKE IT MORE
FRAGILE.

04425 HOWARD, A.E.D.
FEDERALISM AT THE BICENTENNIAL
JOURNAL OF STATE GOVERNMENT, 62(1) (JAN 89), 12-19.
THE AUTHOR ARGUES THAT AMERICAN FEDERALISM IS NOT EASY
TO DEFINE, UNDERSTAND, OR EXPLAIN BECAUSE IT IS AS MUCH THE
PRODUCT OF HISTORICAL CIRCUMSTANCES AS OF PHILOSOPHICAL
DESIGN. HE REVIEWS SOME OF THE MILESTONES IN THE DEVELOPMENT

OF AMERICAN FEDERALISM.

04426 HOWARD, M.
IDEOLOGY AND INTERNATIONAL RELATIONS
REVIEW OF INTERNATIONAL STUDIES, 15(1) (JAN 89), 1-10.
THE FIRST DUTY BOTH OF THE THEORIST AND OF THE
PRACTITIONER OF INTERNATIONAL RELATIONS IS EMPATHY: THE
CAPACITY TO ENTER INTO OTHER MINDS AND UNDERSTAND IDEOLOGIES
WHICH HAVE BEEN FORMED BY ENVIRONMENT, HISTORY AND EDUCATION
IN A VERY DIFFERENT MOULD FROM OUR OWN. THE MOST DIRECT WAY
OF DOING THIS IS OF COURSE TO STUDY THE LANGUAGES WHICH BOTH
EXPRESS AND CREATE THESE DIFFERENCES BETWEEN NATIONS.
ENGLISH IS NOT THE NATIVE LANGUAGE OF THOSE WITH WHOM WE ARE
DEALING, AND IS NOT A NATURAL OR EFFECTIVE VEHICLE FOR THEIR
IDEAS. IT ENABLES THEM TO UNDERSTAND US A LITTLE BETTER THAN
WE CAN UNDERSTAND THEM, BUT IT CAN GIVE AN ILLUSION OF
MUTUAL UNDERSTANDING WHERE NONE IN FACT EXISTS. WHETHER OR
NOT WE POSSESS THE KEY WHICH LANGUAGES PROVIDE TO THE
UNDERSTANDING OF OTHER PEOPLES AND THEIR IDEOLOGIES, THERE
IS ANOTHER WHICH LIES WITHIN THE GRASP OF ALL OF US: THE
STUDY OF THEIR HISTORY. IF WITHOUT LANGUAGES WE ARE COLOUR-
BLIND, WITHOUT HISTORY WE ARE GROPING IN TOTAL DARKNESS.
HISTORY ENABLES US TO UNDERSTAND OURSELVES AS WELL AS OTHER
CULTURES. IT TEACHES US WHAT WE MAY AND MAY NOT EXPECT IN
OUR MUTUAL RELATIONS. IT TEACHES US OUR OWN LIMITATIONS, AND
THUS A CERTAIN HUMILITY. IN DEALING WITH A MULTICULTURAL,
MULTI-IDEOLOGICAL WORLD, THAT IN ITSELF IS NOT A BAD
BEGINNING.

04427 HOWARD, M.
PUBLIC SECTOR FINANCING IN JAMAICA, BARBADOS, AND TRINIDAD
AND TOBAGO
SOCIAL AND ECONOMIC STUDIES, 38(3) (1989), 119-148.
THIS PAPER EXAMINES THE MODE OF PUBLIC SECTOR FINANCING
IN THE CARIBBEAN COUNTRIES OF JAMAICA, BARBADOS AND TRINIDAD
AND TOBAGO DURING THE RECESSIONARY PERIOD 1974-1984. THE
ANALYSIS DEALS ONLY WITH CENTRAL GOVERNMENT FINANCES. THE
PAPER EXAMINES TAX STRUCTURE CHANGES AS WELL AS DEFICIT
FINANCING IN THE THREE COUNTRIES. THE PAPER CONCLUDES THAT
THERE HAS BEEN A FUNDAMENTAL SHIFT TO INDIRECT TAXATION AS A
METHOD OF FINANCING IN JAMAICA AND BARBADOS. FURTHER, MONEY
CREATION WAS EMPLOYED AS THE PRIMARY METHOD OF FINANCING THE
FISCAL DEFICIT IN JAMAICA DURING RECESSION, AND THIS HAD
IMPLICATIONS FOR THE BALANCE OF PAYMENTS. THE DEPENDENCE ON
OIL SECTOR REVENUES IN TRINIDAD AND TOBAGO IS ALSO
HIGHLIGHTED.

04428 HOWARD, M.
1989: A FAREWELL TO ARMS?
INTERNATIONAL AFFAIRS, 65(3) (SUM 89), 407-414.
THIS ARTICLE PUTS THE SUBJECTS OF NATO ARMS REDUCTION
AND OF CHANGES IN STRATEGIC DOCTRINE IN AN HISTORICAL
CONTEXT. IT PLACES PRESIDENT GORBACHEV'S WORDS AND ACTIONS
AS PART OF A TRANSFORMATION NO LESS FUNDAMENTAL AND FAR
REACHING THAN THOSE WHICH OCCURRED IN FRANCE IN 1789; A
GENUINE REVOLUTION IN WHICH A NEW, LITERATE, EDUCATED MIDDLE
CLASS IS BREAKING THE SHACKLES OF AN INCOMPETENT AND
OBSCURANTIST ANCIEN REGIME.' IT SUGGESTS THAT WE ARE
WITNESSING THE ESTABLISHMENT OF A NEW ORDER BASED ON
INTELLIGENT ANALYSIS, REASONED DISCUSSION, AND COOPERATION
WITH ITS NEIGHBORS, AND THAT WHILE GIVING DUE WEIGHT TO THE
CONTINUATION OF EXISTING INSTITUTIONS AND ATTITUDES,
FUNDAMENTAL AND IRREVERSIBLE CHANGES ARE TAKING PLACE.

04429 HOWE, D.W.
WHY THE SCOTTISH ENLIGHTMENT WAS USEFUL TO THE FRAMERS OF
THE AMERICAN CONSTITUTION
COMPARATIVE STUDIES IN SOCIETY AND HISTORY, 31(3) (JUL 89),
572-587.
A COMPARATIVE LOOK AT THE SOCIETIES OF SCOTLAND AND
AMERICA IN THE EIGHTEENTH CENTURY PROVIDES MANY PARALLELS.
BOTH THE SCOTTISH ENLIGHTENMENT AND THE CONSTITUTION OF THE
UNITED STATES ARE EXAMINED HERE AS CREATIONS OF PARTICULAR
SOCIAL GROUPS LOCATED IN PARTICULAR HISTORICAL CONTEXTS AND
IMPLEMENTING PARTICULAR AGENDAS. THE FRAMERS OF THE AMERICAN
CONSTITUTION WERE A FLEXIBLE, INNOVATIVE, AND ABOVE ALL,
PRACTICAL LOT. IF THEY FOUND THE SCOTTISH ENLIGHTENMENT
SUPREMELY RELEVANT AND HELPFUL, THIS SHOULD REVEAL SOMETHING
OF WHAT THE AMERICAN FOUNDERS INTENDED, AND WHAT THEIR PLANS
FOR THE PROPOSED CONSTITUTION WERE. IN THE LAST ANALYSIS,
THE FRAMERS OF THE AMERICAN CONSTITUTION FOUND THE THINKERS
OF THE SCOTTISH ENLIGHTENMENT SUITED THEIR PURPOSES BECAUSE
THE SOCIAL SITUATION AND GOALS OF THE TWO GROUPS WERE
REMARKABLY SIMILAR.

04430 HOWE, G.
EUROPE'S ROLE IN NATO'S FIFTH DECADE
RUSI JOURNAL, 134(2) (SUM 89), 1-6.
1989 SAW THE 40TH ANNIVERSARY OF THE SIGNING OF THE
NORTH ATLANTIC TREATY (NATO). IT HAS NOT ALWAYS BEEN
SELFEVIDENT THAT THERE WAS A SPECIFIC ROLE FOR EUROE WITHIN
THE ALLIANCE. IN RECENT YEARS, HOWEVER, AS THE AMERICANS
HAVE DEVOTED MORE ATTENTION TO OTHER AREAS OF THE WORLDTHE
PACIFIC, SOUTHWEST ASIA, CENTRAL AMERICA-THE NOTION THAT

EUROPE MUST INTEREST ITSELF IN ITS OWN DEFENCE HAS BECOME
WIDELY ACCEPTED.

04431 HOWE, G.
SOVIET FOREIGN POLICY UNDER GORBACHEV
WORLD TODAY, 45(3) (MAR 89), 40-45.
SOVIET POLICIES ARE CHANGING. A POWERFUL INTERNAL FORCE
IS AT WORK, BUT REFORM HAS SO FAR CREATED MORE PROBLEMS THAN
IT HAS SOLVED. YET THERE ARE NOW UNPRECEDENTED OPPORTUNITIES
FOR THE WEST TO WORK WITH THE SOVIET UNION TO BUILD A BETTER
PEACE THAN THE ONE FOLLOWING THE SECOND WORLD WAR. THE WEST
MUST STAY UNITED AND FREE OF ILLUSIONS; THE SOVIET SYSTEM
WILL REMAIN VERY DIFFERENT FROM THE WEST'S. IT IS EASY TO
DOUBT SOVIET INTENTIONS, BUT IT ALSO EASIER THAN EVER BEFORE
TO PUT THEM TO THE TEST.

04432 HOWE, G.I
HONG KONG--FAITH IN THE FUTURE
PARLIAMENTARIAN, 70(3) (JUL 89), 123-126.
THE OUTGOING BRITISH FOREIGN SECRETARY TO CHINA
DISCUSSES THE FUTURE FOR HONG KONG, IN LIGHT OF THE JOINT
DECLARATION SIGNED IN 1984 BETWEEN CHINA AND GREAT BRITAIN.
PROVISIONS OF THE JOINT DECLARATION ARE SUMMARIZED, WITH
EMPHASIS GIVEN TO THE EFFECTS WHICH ARE INDICATED FOR HONG
KONG'S AUTONOMY (POLITICALLY AND ECONOMICALLY), FOREIGN AND
DEFENSE AFFAIRS IN HONG KONG, AND LIMITS ON TRADE CONTROLS
BY CHINA. THE JOINT DECLARATION IS BEING DEBATED; THE AUTHOR
MAINTAINS THAT IT REMAINS THE CENTRAL ELEMENT IN THE
SAFEGUARDING OF HONG KONG'S FUTURE. CONSIDERATION IS GIVEN
TO THE HISTORICAL EVENTS OF TIANANMEN SQUARE IN CHINA. THE
VIETNAMESE BOAT PEOPLE AND THEIR PLIGHT IS ALSO DISCUSSED.

04433 HOWE, I.
CHINA!
DISSENT, (SUM 89), 291-292.
THE MOST STRIKING ASPECT OF THE POLITICAL MOVEMENT IN
CHINA IN MAY 1989 IS THE SUDDEN UPSURGE OF ENERGY AND THE
FLOWERING OF INGENUITY AMONG PEOPLE WITHOUT ANY PREVIOUS
EXPERIENCE IN POLITICS, PEOPLE WHO HAVE BEEN HELD DOWN FOR
DECADES BY A REPRESSIVE DICTATORSHIP. THE VERY MASSES WHOM
SO MANY REALPOLITIK ANALYSTS HAD CONFIDENTLY RELEGATED TO
THE ROLE OF PASSIVITY AND DOCILITY, EITHER BECAUSE OF ABSURD
NOTIONS ABOUT THE CHINESE NATIONAL CHARACTER OR THEORIES
ABOUT MODERN SOCIETY, HAVE SUDDENLY DISPLAYED THE SPIRIT OF
GOOD-NATURED MILITANCY THAT OFTEN OCCURS AT THE OUTSET OF
POPULAR REVOLUTIONS.

04434 HOWE, I.; CHAPIN, J.; HARRINGTON, M.; JUDIS, J.; SCHEUER,
J.; SIEGEL, F.
INTO THE BUSH YEARS
DISSENT, (WIN 89), 5-10.
THE AUTHORS DISCUSS THE 1988 PRESIDENTIAL ELECTION
CAMPAIGN AND THE PROSPECTS FOR THE BUSH ADMINISTRATION. THEY
CONSIDER THE IMPORTANCE OF ADVERTISING IN THE CAMPAIGN, THE
FAILURE OF NEOLIBERALISM, AND WHO DESERVES RESPONSIBILITY
FOR THE OF THE DEMOCRATIC PARTY.

04435 HOWLAND, N.D.
THE UNITED STATES AND ANGOLA, 1974-88: A CHRONOLOGY
DEPARTMENT OF STATE BULLETIN (US FOREIGN POLICY), (89
2143) (FEB 89), 16-24.
THE AUTHOR TRACES EVENTS IN ANGOLA BEGINNING WITH THE
1974 MILITARY COUP IN PORTUGAL THAT BROUGHT TO POWER A NEW
GOVERNMENT DEDICATED TO GRANTING INDEPENDENCE TO PORTUGUESE
COLONIES. THE CHRONOLOGY INCLUDES A SUMMARY OF US POLICY
TOWARD ANGOLA THROUGHOUT THE TURMOIL OF THE 1970'S AND
1980'S.

04436 HOWLETT, M.
THE 1987 NATIONAL FOREST SECTOR STRATEGY AND THE SEARCH
FOR A FEDERAL ROLE IN CANADIAN FOREST POLICY
CANADIAN PUBLIC ADMINISTRATION, 32(4) (WIN 89), 545-563.
AFTER OBTAINING OFFICE IN 1984, THE FEDERAL CONSERVATIVE
GOVERNMENT BEGAN A LENGTHY PROCESS OF CONSULTATIONS AND
CONFERENCES INTENDED TO DEFINE A NEW, EXPANDED, FEDERAL ROLE
IN CANADIAN FOREST POLICY. DESPITE THEIR BEST EFFORTS,
HOWEVER, THE 1987 NATIONAL FOREST SECTOR STRATEGY WHICH
EMERGED FROM THIS PROCESS ENVISIONED ONLY A VERY RESTRICTED
FEDERAL ROLE IN THE SECTOR. ON THE BASIS OF A SURVEY OF
FEDERAL GOVERNMENT ACTIVITY IN THE FOREST SECTOR SINCE 1867,
IT IS ARGUED THAT THE MOST RECENT FEDERAL INITIATIVE (LIKE
SIMILAR ATTEMPTS MADE IN 1949, 1966, AND 1978) FOUNDERED ON
THE OBSTACLES PRESENTED TO ANY EXPANDED FEDERAL ROLE BY THE
FACT THAT RESOURCE OWNERSHIP AND CONSTITUTIONAL AUTHORITY
OVER THE FOREST RESOURCE ARE VESTED IN THE PROVINCIAL
GOVERNMENTS.

04437 HOWLETT, M.P.
FOREST POLICIES IN CANADA: RESOURCE CONSTRAINTS AND
POLITICAL CONFLICTS IN THE CANADIAN FOREST SECTOR
DISSERTATION ABSTRACTS INTERNATIONAL, 49(9) (MAR 89),
2802-A.
THE AUTHOR ESTABLISHES A FRAMEWORK OF POLICY ANALYSIS IN
THE NATURAL RESOURCE SECTOR, BASED ON THE EVALUATION OF

FACTORS PERTAINING TO THE RESOURCE PRODUCTION PROCESS AND
ASSOCIATED POLITICAL CONFLICTS. THEN HE APPLIES THIS
FRAMEWORK TO THE HISTORY OF FOREST POLICY DEVELOPMENT IN
CANADIAN FEDERAL, PROVINCIAL, AND TERRITORIAL GOVERNMENTS.

04438 HOWSE, J.; VAN DUSEN, L.
UPSET IN THE WEST
MACLEAN'S (CANADA'S NEWS MAGAZINE), 102(13) (MAR 89),
12-13.
A VICTORY BY CANADA'S 16-MONTH OLD REFORM PARTY
SURPRISED PRIME MINISTER BRIAN MULRONEY AND THE RULING
CONSERVATIVES. THE TORIES EXPECTED THE OUTCOME OF THE
ALBERTA BY-ELECTION TO BE PREDETERMINED BY THEIR VICTORY IN
THE FEDERAL ELECTION. THE REFORM PARTY MP, DEBORAH GREY,
CAMPAIGNED ON SUCH WESTERN IRRITANTS AS OFFICIAL
BILLINGUALISM, THE SLOW PROGRESS OF SENATE REFORM, AND THE
LACK OF INFLUENCE EXERTED BY WESTERN MPS IN THE HOUSE OF
COMMONS, ALTHOUGH GREY IS CURRENTLY THE ONLY REFORM MP IN
PARLIAMENT, PARTY LEADERS CLAIM SHE IS JUST THE TIP OF THE
ICEBERG.

04439 HOXIE, R.G.
THE PRESIDENCY, THE CONGRESS, AND THE COURT AS VIEWED FROM
THE FEDERALIST
PRESIDENTIAL STUDIES QUARTERLY, XIX(3) (SUM 89), 465-470.
IN THIS ARTICLE THE AUTHOR SEEKS TO GIVE PERSPECTIVE ON
ALL THREE BRANCHES OF THE AMERICAN GOVERNMENTS OF 1789 AND
OF 1989 BY FOCUSING ON THE INSIGHTS OF THE FEDERALIST ESSAYS.

04440 HOYER, S.H.
THE UNITED STATES AND EASTERN EUROPE IN THE NEXT FOUR YEARS
WASHINGTON QUARTERLY, 12(2) (SPR 89), 171-181.
EVEN IF REFORM CONTINUES IN THE SOVIET UNION AND EASTERN
EUROPE, AMERICANS SHOULD NOT EXPECT A STEADY ASCENT TOWARD
LIBERALIZATION. PROGRESS WILL PROBABLY BE PUNCTUATED BY
BACKSLIDING AND INCIDENTS OF REPRESSION, WHICH WILL ELICIT
DOMESTIC PRESSURE FOR REPRISALS. IN DETERMINING THE
APPROPRIATE RESPONSE, CONGRESS CAN PLAY AN IMPORTANT ROLE.
ALTHOUGH BITTER PARTISANSHIP HAS OFTEN CHARACTERIZE U.S
POLICY TOWARD OTHER AREAS OF THE WORLD, SUCH AS CENTRAL
AMERICA, CONSENSUS OVER EASTERN EUROPE HAS TRADITIONALLY
BEEN EASIER TO REACH. WITH EASTERN EUROPE LIKELY TO BECOME
INCREASINGLY VISIBLE AND NEWSWORTHY IN THE COMING YEARS,
HOWEVER, IT IS VITAL THAT CONGRESS MAKE EVERY EFFORT TO
MAINTAIN A RATIONAL, BIPARTISAN APPROACH.

04441 HRADILEK, T.; NEMCOVA, D.; VONDRA, S.
CHINA: COMMON STRUGGLE FOR COMMON AIMS
EAST EUROPEAN REPORTER, 3(4) (SPR 89), 71.
THE ARTICLE IS A CHARTER 77 DOCUMENT THAT EXPRESSES
SOLIDARITY BETWEEN PRO-DEMOCRACY MOVEMENTS IN EASTERN EUROPE
AND THE PEOPLE'S REPUBLIC OF CHINA. THE AUTHORS PRAISE THE
EFFORTS OF STUDENTS IN PEKING AND SHARPLY CRITICIZE THE
GOVERNMENT CRACKDOWN; THEY ARGUE THAT THE CHINESE
GOVERNMENT'S "CONSENT TO BARBARITY IS BARBARITY ITSELF."

04442 HRADILEK, T.
TALKS, NOT TRUNCHEONS!
EAST EUROPEAN REPORTER, 3(4) (SPR 89), 53-54.
THIS CHARTER 77 DOCUMENT RESPONDS TO CLAIMS OF THE
CZECHOSLOVAKIAN GOVERNMENT THAT CHARTER 77 AND OTHER
INDEPENDENT GROUPS WERE PLANNING MASS VIOLENCE, DRIVING
YOUNG PEOPLE TO SUICIDE, AND PLANTING BOMBS IN PUBLIC PLACES.
THE AUTHORS RESPOND THAT ALL OF THE PLANNED DEMONSTRATIONS
WERE PEACEFUL, DESPITE BRUTAL POLICE REPRESSION. THEY ALSO
ARGUE THAT THE GOVERNMENT'S RESORT TO VIOLENCE ROBS THEM OF
ANY LEGITIMACY THEY ONCE ENJOYED.

04443 HRBEK, R.
GERMANY
ELECTORAL STUDIES, 8(3) (DEC 89), 254-261.
THIS ARTICLE IS AN ANALYSIS OF ELECTION RESULTS IN WEST
GERMANY. A MAJOR FEATURE IS THE DECREASING ATTRACTIVENESS OF
THE TWO BIG CATCH-ALL-PARTIES. ALSO RECOGNIZED IS: NO PARTY
WON AN ABSOLUTE MAJORITY IN ANY ONE LAND; A REGIONALIZATION
OF VOTING BEHAVIOR BECAME OBVIOUS; A TREND TOWARDS THE
FRAGMENTATION OF THE PARTY SYSTEM BECAME OBVIOUS. IT
CONCLUDES THAT AS A RESULT OF THE ELECTION THE GERMAN
COMPONENT IN THE EUROPEAN PARLIAMENT BECAME WEAKER IN THE
SOCIALIST PARTY GROUP AND IN THE GROUP OF THE EUROPEAN
PEOPLE'S PARTY.

04444 HSIA, T.
THE SUPREME COURT IN OTHER COUNTRIES
CRS REVEIW, 10(8) (SEP 89), 26-27.
MOST OF THE NATIONS OF THE WORLD HAVE AN INSTITUTION
COMPARABLE IN SOME RESPECTS TO THE U.S. SUPREME COURT. BUT
THE ATTRIBUTES OF THESE COURTS VARY ENORMOUSLY. THIS ARTICLE
SUMMARIZES THE DISTINCTIVE FEATURES OF SEVERAL HIGH COURTS,
INCLUDING THOSE OF GREAT BRITAIN, CANADA, AND INDIA.

04445 HSIUNG, J.
FROM THE VANTAGE OF THE BEIJING HOTEL: PEERING INTO THE
1989 STUDENT UNREST IN CHINA

ASIAN AFFAIRS, AN AMERICAN REVIEW, 16(2) (SUM 89), 55-62.
MUCH OF THIS ARTICLE IS BASED ON THE AUTHOR'S ON-THE-
SPOT OBSERVATIONS IN THE PEOPLE'S REPUBLIC OF CHINA FROM
JUNE 11 APRIL THROUGH 10 JUNE 1989. HE HAS IN BEIJING AND
SAW THE PROLONGED STUDENT PROTEST AT CLOSE RANGE. AFTER
BRIEFLY OUTLINING THE EVENTS OF THE REVOLUTION, THE AUTHOR
DISCUSSES THE LESSONS PEOPLE CAN DRAW FROM THE TRAGIC
EPISODE. HE OFFERS A CRITIQUE OF THE MISTAKES THAT RESULTED
IN THE TRAGEDY AND SUGGESTS WHAT CHINA SHOULD DO IN ITS
AFTERMATH.

04446 HSIUNG, J.
POLITICAL CONSIDERATIONS I
ASIAN AFFAIRS, AN AMERICAN REVIEW, 16(3) (FAL 89), 145-156.
THE ARTICLE CONTAINS AN ANALYSIS OF SEVERAL IMPORTANT
POLITICAL CONSIDERATIONS SURROUNDING THE ISSUE OF CHINESE
REUNIFICATION. IT EXPLORES THE ORIGINS OF THE "TAIWAN
IMPASSE," THE CURRENT POSITIONS OF BOTH SIDES, RECENT
DEVELOPMENTS IN TAIWAN, AND POSSIBLE U.S. ROLES IN
RESOLUTION OF CURRENT PROBLEMS. THE ARTICLE CONCLUDES THAT
WHILE FULL-SCALE REUNIFICATION IS NOT LIKELY UNTIL MAINLAND
CHINA "CATCHES UP" WITH TAIWAN VIA ECONOMIC LIBERALIZATION
AND MODERNIZATION, SIGNIFICANT NEGOTIATIONS ARE CURRENTLY
POSSIBLE AND DESIRABLE.

04447 HSU, L.
SERIOUS IMAGE PROBLEMS
FREE CHINA REVIEW, 39(10) (OCT 89), 47-49.
IN A FEW SHORT HOURS IN TIENANMEN SQUARE, THE CHINESE
LEADERSHIP DEMOLISHED AN INTERNATIONAL IMAGE THEY HAD BEEN
CULTIVATING FOR A DECADE. IN THIS INTERVIEW, JAW-LING JOANNE
CHANG ANALYZES THE IMPACT OF CHINA'S CURRENT DOMESTIC
SITUATION ON ITS INTERNATIONAL RELATIONS.

04448 HSU, R.C.
CHANGING CONCEPTIONS OF THE SOCIALIST ENTERPRISE IN CHINA,
1979-1988
MODERN CHINA, 15(4) (OCT 89), 499-524.
THIS ARTICLE EXAMINES HOW CHINESE ECONOMISTS'
CONCEPTIONS OF SOCIALIST ENTERPRISE IN THE POST-MAO PERIOD
HAVE EVOLVED IN RESPONSE TO THE CHANGING PROBLEMS OF BOTH
THE ENTERPRISE AND THE POLITICAL ECONOMY. THE ARTICLE IS
DIVIDED INTO THREE SECTIONS. IN THE FIRST, THE TRADITIONAL
RELATIONSHIP BETWEEN THE STATE AND THE ENTERPRISE AND THE
JUSTIFICATION FOR SUCH A RELATIONSHIP ARE OUTLINED. SECTION
TWO EXPLAINS HOW ECONOMISTS IN 1979-1985 COME TO QUESTION
THAT JUSTIFICATION AND PROPOSED VARIOUS WAYS TO CHANGE THAT
RELATIONSHIP. SECTION THREE DISCUSSES HOW NEW CONCEPTS OF
THE "RATIONAL" SOCIALIST ENTERPRISE EMERGED IN 1985-1988.
BEFORE DISCUSSING THESE TOPICS, HOWEVER, IT IS USEFUL TO
HIGHLIGHT THE ROLE OF THE ENTERPRISE IN CHINA'S
MICROECONOMICS IN ORDER TO PROVIDE THE SETTING.

04449 HU, W.
THE STRATEGIC SIGNIFICANCE OF THE REPUBLIC OF CHINA ON
TAIWAN
DISSERTATION ABSTRACTS INTERNATIONAL, 50(5) (NOV 89),
1428-A.
THE AUTHOR DEVELOPS A CONTEMPORARY APPROACH TO THE
CONCEPT OF STRATEGIC SIGNIFICANCE AND APPLIES IT TO AN
ANALYSIS OF THE STRATEGIC SIGNIFICANCE OF THE REPUBLIC OF
CHINA ON TAIWAN. THE APPROACH IS BASED ON THREE FUNDAMENTAL
CRITERIA: A COUNTRY'S NATIONAL CAPABILITY, ITS EGO-
PERCEPTION OF ITS SIGNIFICANCE IN A GLOBAL AND REGIONAL
CONTEXT, AND OTHER COUNTRIES' PERCEPTIONS OF THE STATE'S
STRATEGIC SIGNIFICANCE TO THEIR INTERESTS.

04450 HU, X.
SITUATION DETERIORATING IN PANAMA
BEIJING REVIEW, 32(23) (JUN 89), 18.
ON MAY 11, 1989, U.S. PRESIDENT GEORGE BUSH ORDERED
ADDITIONAL TROOPS TO THE PANAMA CANAL ZONE TO REINFORCE
FORCES ALREADY THERE. BUSH SAID THAT THE TROOPS WERE NEEDED
TO PROTECT THE SECURITY OF U.S. PERSONNEL AND INTERESTS. THE
ACTION WAS TAKEN AFTER PANAMA'S ELECTORAL TRIBUNAL NULLIFIED
THE PRESIDENTIAL ELECTIONS HELD ON MAY 7.

04451 HUA, Z.
SUPERPOWER RELATIONS ENTER NEW STAGE
BEIJING REVIEW, 32(51) (DEC 89), 13-14.
AS THE TWO-DAY INFORMAL SUMMIT BETWEEN U.S. PRESIDENT
GEORGE BUSH AND SOVIET LEADER MIKHAIL GORBACHEV CONCLUDED ON
DECEMBER 3, 1989, BOTH LEADERS DECLARED THAT A NEW STAGE HAS
BEGINNING IN U.S.-SOVIET RELATIONS. THEY STATED THAT THEY
HAD AGREED TO RESOLVE ALL ACUTE ISSUES INVOLVING THE TWO
SUPERPOWERS BY POLITICAL MEANS, AVOID MILITARY INTERFERENCE
IN EASTERN EUROPE, WORK TOGETHER TO CONCLUDE ARMS CONTROL
AGREEMENTS, AND PROVIDE SUPPORT FOR THE SOVIET REFORM EFFORT.

04452 HUANG, C.
THE STATE AND FOREIGN INVESTMENT THE CASES OF TAIWAN AND
SINGAPORE
COMPARATIVE POLITICAL STUDIES, 22(1) (APR 89), 93-121.
THE INFLUENCE OF A HOST STATE ON DIRECT FOREIGN

INVESTMENT ATTRACTS THE ATTENTION OF SCHOLARS MUCH LESS THAN DO THE CONSTRAINTS OF THE LATTER ON THE FORMER. THIS STUDY ADDRESSES THE IMPACT OF STATE REGULATORY POLICIES ON THE ROLES OF INWARD FOREIGN INVESTMENT IN TAIWAN AND SINGAPORE'S MANUFACTURING SECTOR. THE SIMILARITIES BETWEEN THE TWO SMALL ASIAN OPEN ECONOMIES ARE FIRST DISCUSSED. THE DIFFERENT ROLES PLAYED BY THE FOREIGN INVESTORS IN THEIR ECONOMIES ARE THEN COMPARED. A REVIEW OF THE LITERATURE IN ORTHODOX THEORIES AND RADICAL POINTS OF VIEW REVEALS SEVERAL POSSIBLE EXPLANATORY VARIABLES FOR SUCH DIFFERENCES. THROUGH THE LOGIC OF THE "MOST SIMILAR SYSTEMS" DESIGN, OR METHOD OF DIFFERENCE, SOME SEEMINGLY PLAUSIBLE FACTORS ARE RULED OUT, DUE TO THEIR SIMILARITIES IN THE TWO CHOSEN ENTITIES. IT IS FOUND THAT SOME PULL FACTORS (SUCH AS GEOGRAPHIC LOCATION, COLONIAL LEGACY, EXTERNAL POLITICAL ENVIRONMENT, AND INDIGENOUS INDUSTRIAL CAPACITY) AND CONVERSION FACTORS (SUCH AS STATE POLICIES TOWARD FOREIGN INVESTMENT) MAY BE RESPONSIBLE FOR THE DIFFERENCES BETWEEN THE TWO ISLANDS. A MORE DETAILED ANALYSIS IS THEN GIVEN TO THE CONVERSION FACTORS IN GENERAL AND THE STATE REGULATORY POLICIES TOWARD FOREIGN CAPITAL IN PARTICULAR. FINALLY, SOME GENERAL HYPOTHESES ABOUT THE CONVERSION FACTORS IN THE HOST STATE-FOREIGN CAPITAL RELATIONSHIP APPLICABLE TO MOST INDUSTRIALIZING COUNTRIES ARE SUGGESTED FOR FURTHER TESTING IN FUTURE STUDIES.

04453 HUAT, T.C.
CONFUCIANISM AND NATION BUILDING' IN SINGAPORE
INTERNATIONAL JOURNAL OF SOCIAL ECONOMICS, 16(8) (1989),
5-16.
THE OUTSTANDING ECONOMIC GROWTH OF SEVERAL EAST ASIAN COUNTRIES HAS ATTRACTED WORLD ATTENTION. MANY OBSERVERS HAVE ATTRIBUTED THE SUCCESS OF THESE CONFUCIAN COUNTRIES TO THEIR COMMON CULTURAL VALUES, SUCH AS RESPECT FOR AUTHORITY, LOYALTY TO GOOD LEADERS, PREFERENCE FOR ORDER, HARD WORK, THRIFT AND EMPHASIS ON EDUCATION. THE ABOVE FACTORS SEEM TO HAVE WORKED IN SINGAPORE, ALTHOUGH SOME RESEARCHERS HAVE OBSERVED THAT ECONOMIC SUCCESS AND RAPID CHANGES HAVE ERODED THESE TRADITIONAL VALUES. IN SINGAPORE, THE POLITICAL LEADERS HAVE NOW CAUTIONED SINGAPOREANS AGAINST ASSIMILATING ALIEN VALUES AND BECOMING A PSEUDO-WESTERN SOCIETY. THEY HAVE CALLED FOR A SET OF NATIONAL PRINCIPLES BASED ON ASIAN VALUES TO GUIDE SINGAPOREANS INTO THE NEXT CENTURY.

04454 HUBER, J.D.
VALUES AND PARTISANSHIP IN LEFT-RIGHT ORIENTATIONS:
MEASURING IDEOLOGY
EUROPEAN JOURNAL OF POLITICAL RESEARCH, 17(5) (SEP 89),
599-621.
THIS PAPER ANALYZES WHETHER LEFT-RIGHT SCALES PROVIDE AN INTERVAL MEASURE OF CITIZEN ISSUE ATTITUDES THAT IS COMPARABLE ACROSS EIGHT WESTERN EUROPEAN COUNTRIES. TWO COMMONLY HELD VIEWS OF LEFT-RIGHT SELF-PLACEMENT ARE JUXTAPOSE: (1) THE THEORY THAT ISSUE ATTITUDES ARE PRIMARY COMPONENT OF LEFT-RIGHT SELF-PLACEMENT, AND (2) THE THEORY THAT PARTISANSHIP IS THE PRIMARY COMPONENT OF LEFT-RIGHT SELF-PLACEMENT, WHICH ENTAILS THAT LEFT-RIGHT SCALES WILL TAKE ON DIFFERENT SUBSTANTIVE MEANINGS IN COUNTRIES WITH DIFFERENT TYPES OF PARTY SYSTEM. DISTANCE MEASURES AND LEAST SQUARES REGRESSION SHOW THAT LEFT-RIGHT SCALES ARE GENERALLY AN APPROPRIATE INSTRUMENT FOR CROSS-NATIONAL TESTS OF THEORIES THAT HAVE AS AN EXPLANATORY VARIABLE THE IDEOLOGICAL ORIENTATIONS OF VOTERS.

04455 HUBERMAN, L.
WHY SOCIALISM IS NECESSARY
MONTHLY REVIEW, 41(6) (NOV 89), 22-36.
THIS IS THE TEXT OF A TALK BY LEO HUBERMAN AT A CONFERENCE ON LATIN AMERICA HELD AT THE UNIVERSITY OF NIJMEGEN, HOLLAND, ON NOVEMBER 6, 1968. IT ORIGINALLY APPEARED IN THE JANUARY 1969 ISSUE OF MONTHLY REVIEW. IT ANALYZES THE STATUS OF LATIN AMERICAN COUNTRIES WHICH ARE POVERTY STRICKEN EVEN THOUGH THEY HAVE AMPLE NATURAL RESOURCES. IT EXAMINES THE U.S. ALLIANCE FOR PROGRESS AID PROGRAM AND CONCLUDES THAT THE PLAN CAN NOT WORK. IT DEMONSTRATES WHY SOCIALISM WOULD MAKE POSSIBLE BOTH POLITICAL AND ECONOMIC INDEPENDENCE, USING CUBA AS AN EXAMPLE OF ACHIVEMENT THROUGH SOCIALISM.

04456 HUBERT, P.J.
PARTY PRESS AND PROPAGANDA IN PARTIES OF THE LEFT IN
BRITAIN (VOLUMES I AND II)
DISSERTATION ABSTRACTS INTERNATIONAL, 49(11) (MAY 89),
3491-A.
THE AUTHOR EXAMINES SIX BRITISH LEFT-WING PARTY NEWSPAPERS FOR 1978-1982: THE MORNING STAR, LABOUR WEEKLY, TRIBUNE, MILITANT, SOCIALIST CHALLENGE, AND SOCIALIST WORKER. THE COVERAGE GIVEN TO THE FALKLANDS WAR IS USED TO ILLUSTRATE THEIR DIFFERENCES IN FORM AND CONTENT. THE LENINIST MODEL IS RE-EXAMINED TO DISCERN HOW IT IS REFLECTED IN THE NEWSPAPERS AND ITS CONTINUED RELEVANCE AS A GUIDE TO SOCIALIST PAPERS.

04457 HUDSON, V.M.; HYER, E.
HOMER LEA'S GEOPOLITICAL THEORY: VALOR OR IGNORANCE?
JOURNAL OF STRATEGIC STUDIES, 12(3) (SEP 89), 324-348.
THE AUTHORS STUDY HOMER LEA'S GEOPOLITICAL THEORY AND HIS CONCEPT OF THE "GREAT GAME." AN AMERICAN, LEA WAS A CLOSE ADVISER TO CHINESE REFORMERS K'ANG YU-WEI AND LIANG CH'I-CH'AO, AN AIDE TO SUN YAT-SEN, A PROPHETIC MILITARY STRATEGIST, AND THE AUTHOR OF SEVERAL BOOKS ON WORLD AFFAIRS.

04458 HUDSON, V.M.; HERMANN, C.F.; SINGER, E.
THE SITUATIONAL IMPERATIVE: A PREDICTIVE MODEL OF FOREIGN
POLICY BEHAVIOR
COOPERATION & CONFLICT: NORDIC JOURNAL OF INTERNATIONAL
POLITICS, XXIV(3-4) (DEC 89), 117-139.
FOREIGN POLICY BEHAVIORS, DEFINED IN TERMS OF THE INTENSITY OF AFFECT AND COMMITMENT AN ACTOR CONVEYS TO EXTERNAL RECIPIENTS USING VARIOUS INSTRUMENTS OF STATECRAFT, ARE EXPLAINED IN TERMS OF A SITUATIONAL MODEL. THE MODEL REPRESENTS AN EXTERNALLY-DEFINED PREDISPOSITION THAT WILL INFLUENCE ANY GROUP OF POLICY-MAKERS TO ACT IN A CERTAIN WAY ONCE THEY RECOGNIZE A SPECIFIC FOREIGN PROBLEM. IN ADDITION TO DIFFERENT TYPES OF SITUATIONS, THE MODEL INCLUDES AS ITS VARIABLES THE CONFIGURATION OF ROLES ASSUMED IN A SITUATION BY OTHER INTERNATIONAL ENTITIES. IT ALSO INCLUDES A SET OF RELATIONSHIPS, EACH CAPABLE OF ASSUMING DIFFERENT VALUES, THAT EXIST BETWEEN THE ACTOR AND OTHER ROLE OCCUPANTS. FOR EACH TYPE OF SITUATION A DECISION LOGIC IS DEVELOPED AND EXPRESSED IN A DECISION TREE. EACH BRANCH OF THE DECISION TREE CONSTITUTES A HYPOTHESIS ABOUT THE CONFIGURATION OF BEHAVIOR PROPERTIES THAT WILL LIKELY RESULT. THE MODEL IS ILLUSTRATED BY REFERENCE TO TWO CASES OF FOREIGN POLICY DECISION-MAKING--THE ZAMBIAN GOVERNMENT'S RESPONSE TO THE UNILATERAL DECLARATION OF INDEPENDENCE BY THE WHITE REGIME IN RHODESIA IN 1965 AND THE RESPONSE OF THE UNITED STATES GOVERNMENT TO THE IMPENDING WAR BETWEEN BRITAIN AND ARGENTINA OVER THE FALKLANDS IN 1982.

04459 HUEGLIN, T.
THE POLITICS OF LIMITED PLURALISM: WEST GERMANY AS A
PARADIGMATIC CASE
STUDIES IN POLITICAL ECONOMY: A SOCIALIST REVIEW, (28)
(SPR 89), 111-136.
THIS ARTICLE ARGUES THAT THE WEST GERMAN CONCENSUS OF LABOR/BUSINESS/GOVERNMENT, EVEN AT ITS APOGEE IN THE LATE 1960S WAS MORE APPARENT THAN REAL. IT ADDRESSES THE RERESSION OF MARGINALS AND THE NUMBER OF PERMANENTLY UNEMPLOYED WHICH HAS GIVEN RISE TO THE GREEN PARTY, THE SUCCESS OR FAILURE OF WHICH HAS MASSIVE IMPLICATIONS FOR THE FUTURE OF WEST GERMAN DEMOCRACY.

04460 HUFBAUER, G.
BEYOND GATT
FOREIGN POLICY, (77) (WIN 89), 64-76.
THIS ARTICLE EXAMINES THE CROSS ROADS IN TRADE POLICY THAT THE U.S. IS NOW CONFRONTED WITH, IT PROPOSES A TRADE GOAL THAT BEST CAPTURES THE OUTWARD-LOOKING, LEVEL-PLAYING-FIELD THEMES OF U.S. POLICY WHICH IS A BROAD FREE ZONE OF FREE COMMERCE WITH LIKEMINDED COUNTRIES - A FREE TRADE AND INVESTMENT AREA (FTIA) OF THE ORGANIZATION FOR ECONOMIC COOPERATION AND DEVELOPMENT (OECD). IT ADDRESSES THE TRADE DEFICIT AND EXPLORES THE POLITICS OF FREE TRADE. IT CONCLUDES WITH TEN POSSIBLE TENATS OF AN OECD FTIA.

04461 HUFTON, O.
WOMEN IN REVOLUTION
FRENCH POLITICS AND SOCIETY, 7(3) (SUM 89), 65-81.
THROUGHOUT THE FRENCH REVOLUTION, WOMEN OFTEN INTERVENED DRAMATICALLY IN ACTIONS THAT HAD, OR WERE INTENDED TO HAVE, IMMENSE POLITICAL CONSEQUENCES. IN THIS ESSAY, THE AUTHOR ENDEAVORS TO DRAW PORTRAITS OF THREE DIFFERENT TYPES OF WOMEN, EACH OF WHOM HAS PASSED INTO REVOLUTIONARY MYTHOLOGY, HAD AN IMPACT ON THE REVOLUTION, OR HAS HAD A LASTING INFLUENCE ON THE HISTORY OF FRENCH FEMINISM.

04462 HUGHES, J.
THE IRKUTSK AFFAIR
SOVIET STUDIES, XLI(2) (APR 89), 228-253.
THE PAPER EXAMINES THE POLITICAL CRISIS, KNOWN AS THE "IRKUTSK AFFAIR", WHICH ENVELOPED THE SIBERIAN PARTY ORGANIZATION DURING THE GRAIN CRISIS OF 1927-28. IT SEEKS TO ILLUMINATE THE MANNER IN WHICH POWER RELATIONSHIPS, WHETHER INTER-REGIONAL, CENTER-PERIPHERY OR BETWEEN STALIN AND HIS CLIENTS IN THE PARTY OPERATED IN THE SOVIET STATE AT THIS TIME. IT FOCUSES PARTICULARLY ON THE WAY SIBERIAN REGIONAL FACTORS INFLUENCED THESE POWER RELATIONSHIPS AND DISTORTED THE PRACTICAL IMPLEMENTATION OF POLICY DIRECTIVES FROM THE CENTRAL AUTHORITIES.

04463 HUGHES, T.P.
U.S. SUPPORT FOR SOVIET TECHNOLOGY: A LESSON FROM HISTORY
CURRENT, (315) (SEP 89), 18-26.
ONE OF THE MOMENTOUS AND ALMOST FORGOTTEN CHAPTERS OF MODERN HISTORY CONCERNS THE BOLSHEVIKS' FIERCE DETERMINATION BETWEEN THE WARS TO ADOPT THE INDUSTRIAL LEGACY AND METHODS

OF THE UNITED STATES. FOR THE BOLSHEVIKS OF THE 1920'S, AMERICAN INDUSTRIALISM HAS CRUCIAL TO THE SUCCESS OF THE COMMUNIST STATE. MIKHAIL GORBACHEV MAY KNOW ABOUT THIS CHAPTER OF SOVIET-AMERICAN RELATIONS BECAUSE PERESTROIKA WITHOUT AMERICAN TECHNICAL AND MANAGERIAL INPUT MUST BE NO MORE CONCEIVABLE TO HIM THAN WAS A SOCIALIST FUTURE WITHOUT AMERICAN-STYLE INDUSTRY TO LENIN.

04464 HUGICK, L.
ABORTION: MAJORITY CRITICAL OF ABORTION DECISION, BUT MOST AMERICANS FAVOR SOME NEW RESTRICTIONS
GALLUP REPORT, (286) (JUL 89), 5-12.
AMERICANS REMAIN DEEPLY DIVIDED IN THEIR ATTITUDES TOWARD THE ABORTION ISSUE. NEITHER SIDE OF THE DEBATE CAN CLAIM TO HAVE A MAJORITY OF THE PUBLIC FIRMLY IN ITS CAMP. WHILE MOST AMERICANS OPPOSE A COMPLETE REVERSAL OF ROE V. WADE, MOST WOULD FAVOR SOME NEW ABORTION RESTRICTIONS AT THE STATE LEVEL.

04465 HUGICK, L.
AMERICANS, CANADIANS, EUROPEANS SAY NATO IS STILL NEEDED
GALLUP REPORT, (289) (OCT 89), 2-3.
THE RELAXATION OF TENSIONS BETWEEN THE WEST AND THE SOVIET UNION UNDER GORBACHEV HAS YET TO CONVINCE WESTERN PUBLIC OPINION THAT NATO HAS OUTLIVED ITS USEFULNESS. A POLL IN 12 NATO MEMBER COUNTRIES FOUND HIGH LEVELS OF SUPPORT FOR MAINTAINING NATO THROUGHOUT THE AMERICAS AND WESTERN EUROPE. ONLY IN SPAIN WAS THERE SIGNIFICANT SENTIMENT FOR DISBANDING NATO.

04466 HUGICK, L.
PUBLIC EMBRACES CHANGES IN EASTERN EUROPE WITH FEW EXCEPTIONS
GALLUP REPORT, (291) (DEC 89), 2-9.
THE POLITICAL AND SOCIAL CHANGES IN EASTERN EUROPE ARE BEING EMBRACED BY AMERICANS, WITH FEW RESERVATIONS. AS SOVIET DOMINANCE OF HER FORMER SATELLITES WANES, AMERICANS PREDICT A BETTER LIFE FOR THE PEOPLE OF EASTERN EUROPE AND A MORE PEACEFUL WORLD. BUT THE AMERICAN PUBLIC IS EVENLY DIVIDED OVER WHETHER EVENTS IN EASTERN EUROPE SIGNAL THE BEGINNING OF THE END OF COMMUNISM IN THE WORLD. OVERWHELMINGLY AMERICANS FEEL THAT MORE IS LIKELY TO BE GAINED THROUGH A REDUCTION IN INTERNATIONAL TENSIONS THAN MIGHT BE LOST AS A RESULT OF WEAKENING THE MILITARY ALLIANCES THAT ARE OFTEN GIVEN CREDIT FOR KEEPING PEACE SINCE WORLD WAR II. RELATIVELY FEW AMERICANS ARE VERY CONCERNED ABOUT THE PROSPECT OF A REUNIFIED GERMANY, WHILE MORE THAN THREE-FOURTHS OF AMERICANS HAVE A FAVORABLE OPINION OF MIKHAIL GORBACHEV.

04467 HUGICK, L.
PUBLIC SEES NORTH SENTENCE AS FAIR
GALLUP REPORT, (286) (JUL 89), 21-22.
A PLURALITY OF AMERICANS FEEL THAT OLIVER NORTH WAS TREATED FAIRLY BY THE JUDGE WHO SENTENCED HIM FOR HIS CONVICTION IN THE IRAN-CONTRA CASE. AS EXPECTED, REACTIONS TO THE SENTENCING DIFFER ALONG POLITICAL LINES. REPUBLICANS (55 PERCENT) ARE MORE LIKELY THAN DEMOCRATS OR INDEPENDENTS TO FEEL THE SENTENCE WAS FAIR.

04468 HUGICK, L.
SOVIETS AND AMERICANS GENERALLY OPTIMISTIC ABOUT PEACE IN THE NEW YEAR
GALLUP REPORT, (291) (DEC 89), 10-12.
THIS ARTICLE REPORTS THE RESULTS OF A GALLUP INTERNATIONAL SURVEY TAKEN IN THIRTY-SIX COUNTRIES. GENERALLY, THE SURVEY FOUND AMERICANS AND SOVIETS TO BE OPTIMISTIC ABOUT THE PROSPECTS FOR INTERNATIONAL PEACE IN 1990 WHILE EUROPEANS ARE DIVIDED ABOUT THE PROSPECTS FOR PEACE. MOMENTUM TOWARD GERMAN REUNIFICATION MAY BE RESPONSIBLE FOR THE GUARDED ATTITUDE TOWARD PEACE EXPRESSED BY SOME WEST EUROPEANS.

04469 HUGICK, L.
THE ADMINISTRATION: BUSH RATES HIGH ON EASTERN EUROPE, "NICE GUY" IMAGE; LOWER ON ECONOMY AND OTHER DOMESTIC ISSUES
GALLUP REPORT, (290) (NOV 89), 4-10.
THIS ARTICLE REPORTS PUBLIC OPINION SURVEYS ON THE PERFORMANCE OF PRESIDENT GEORGE BUSH AND VICE PRESIDENT DAN QUAYLE. THE POLLS IDENTIFY THE REDUCTION OF EAST-WEST TENSIONS AS ONE OF THE KEYS TO BUSH'S SEVENTY-PERCENT APPROVAL RATING WITH THE AMERICAN PUBLIC. DESPITE THE HIGH APPROVAL RATING, THE SURVEYS REVEAL SOME TROUBLING SIGNS FOR THE PRESIDENT BECAUSE THE RATINGS FOR HIS HANDLING OF SPECIFIC DOMESTIC ISSUES ARE SIGNIFICANTLY LESS POSITIVE THAN THOSE HE RECEIVES FOR HIS HANDLING OF INTERNATIONAL RELATIONS. THERE IS GROWING DISAPPROVAL OF HIS HANDLING OF THE ECONOMY, THE FEDERAL BUDGET DEFICIT, THE DRUG PROBLEM, THE ABORTION ISSUE, AND THE PROBLEMS OF POVERTY AND HOMELESSNESS.

04470 HUIJUN, C.
MOSCOW OPENS ITS ECONOMIC DOORS
BEIJING REVIEW, 32(20) (MAY 89), 15-18.
SINCE THE 27TH CONGRESS OF THE SOVIET COMMUNIST PARTY, THE SOVIET UNION HAS BEEN PURSUING A STRATEGY OF ACCELERATED SOCIO-ECONOMIC DEVELOPMENT AND EXTENSIVE REFORM IN THE ECONOMIC AND POLITICAL SECTORS. THE STRATEGY HAS INCLUDED THE ADOPTION OF A SERIES OF POLICIES TO OPEN ITS ECONOMY TO THE OUTSIDE WORLD. SOME RESULTS HAVE BEEN ACHIEVED, BUT DIFFICULTIES AND PROBLEMS STILL PERSIST.

04471 HULME, D.L. JR.
THE VIABILITY OF INTERNATIONAL SPORT AS A POLITICAL WEAPON: THE 1980 US OLYMPIC BOYCOTT
DISSERTATION ABSTRACTS INTERNATIONAL, 49(7) (JAN 89), 1951-A.
THE AUTHOR ADDRESSES THE GENERAL QUESTION OF THE DEGREE TO WHICH POLITICAL LEADERS CAN HOPE TO UTILIZE SPORT IN A PUNITIVE FASHION IN THE INTERNATIONAL ARENA. HE STUDIES THE 1980 US OLYMPIC BOYCOTT OF THE MOSCOW GAMES IN DETAIL.

04472 HULNICK, A.S.
DETERMINING U.S. INTELLIGENCE POLICY
INTERNATIONAL JOURNAL OF INTELLIGENCE AND COUNTER-INTELLIGENCE, 3(2) (SUM 89), 211-224.
A STUDY OF THE RECENT PAST REVEALS THAT THE MAKING OF U. S. INTELLIGENCE POLICY HAS HAPPENED MORE BY ACCIDENT THAN BY DESIGN, SOMETIMES DRIVEN AS MUCH BY EVENTS ABROAD AS BY THE UNDERSTANDING OF INTELLIGENCE NEEDS AT HOME. NEITHER THE STRUCTURE OF THE INTELLIGENCE SYSTEM NOR ITS VARIOUS MISSIONS AND FUNCTIONS WERE DEVELOPED BY POLICYMAKERS SITTING WITHIN THE NATIONAL SECURITY COUNCIL DELIBERATING THE ISSUES. RATHER, THE SYSTEM WAS BORN AND NURTURED ALMOST AS AN ADJUNCT TO OTHER POLITICAL ACTIVITY. IN THIS ESSAY, THE AUTHOR DISCUSSES HOW INTELLIGENCE POLICY SHOULD BE CREATED, WHO SHOULD BE MAKING IT, AND HOW IT SHOULD BE IMPLEMENTED AND CONTROLLED.

04473 HUMES, B.D.
ESSAYS ON INSTITUTIONAL CHANGE: THE CHOICE AND EFFECTS OF LEGISLATIVE RULES
DISSERTATION ABSTRACTS INTERNATIONAL, 49(9) (MAR 89), 2796-A.
THE AUTHOR ANALYZES THE EFFECTS OF COMMITTEE JURISDICTIONS AND GERMANENESS RULES UNDER VARIOUS COMBINATIONS OF DECISION-MAKING PROCESSES, AGENDAS, AND VOTERS' EXPECTATIONS. HE DETERMINES THAT DIFFERENT POLICY OUTCOMES RESULT WHEN THE SEQUENTIAL DECISION-MAKING PROCESS DOES, OR DOES NOT, INCLUDE CONFERENCE COMMITTEES. HE ALSO SHOWS THAT THE CHOICE OF GERMANENESS RULES IN AN INSTITUTIONAL SETTING IS GENERICALLY UNSTABLE.

04474 HUMMEL, R.
I'D LIKE TO BE ETHICAL, BUT THEY WON'T LET ME
INTERNATIONAL JOURNAL OF PUBLIC ADMINISTRATION, 12(6) (NOV 89), 855-866.
TO BE ETHICAL, THE MEMBER OF A MODERN ORGANIZATION MUST KNOW WHAT THE WORK REQUIRES OF HIM (OR HER), WHAT THE ORGANIZATION REQUIRES OF HIM, AND WHAT OTHERS REQUIRE OF HIM. BUT MODERN ORGANIZATIONS PUT DOING ONE'S JOB BEFORE DOING ONE'S WORK AND BEFORE ONE'S DUTY TO ONE'S FELLOW MAN. BECAUSE THEY DO SO STRUCTURALLY, THE INDIVIDUAL USUALLY CANNOT KNOW WHAT THE EFFECT OF DOING ONE'S DUTY IS ON DOING A GOOD PIECE OF WORK OR ON OTHER HUMAN BEINGS. THIS ARTICLE ATTEMPTS TO MAKE A BEGINNING TO SHOW HOW FAR REMOVED THE STRUCTURE OF KNOWLEDGE IN MODERN ORGANIZATION IS FROM CONSTITUTING THE BASIS FOR ETHICAL BEHAVIOR. THE MEANS CHOSEN IS A PHENOMENOLOGICAL RECONSTRUCTION OF THE ETHICAL FIELD THAT LINKS THE INDIVIDUAL TO OBJECTS, OTHERS, AND SELF.

04475 HUMMEL, R.P.
TOWARD A NEW ADMINISTRATIVE DOCTRINE: GOVERNANCE AND MANAGEMENT FOR THE 1990'S
AMERICAN REVIEW OF PUBLIC ADMINISTRATION, 19(3) (SEP 89), 175-196.
THREE SUCCESSIVE TERMS OF MARKET-ORIENTED PRESIDENTS RAISE DIFFICULTIES FOR FEDERAL BUREAUCRATS IN LEGITIMATING PAST ADMINISTRATIVE DOCTRINE AND PRACTICES, WHICH WERE GOVERNMENT-CENTERED. THE PRESENT ARTICLE RESPONDS TO CHARLES LEVINE'S CALL FOR A NEW ADMINISTRATIVE DOCTRINE THAT IS MORE FULLY DESCRIPTIVE OF THE NEEDS AND ROUTINES OF TODAY'S FEDERAL CIVIL SERVANTS THAN A DOCTRINE BASED ON EITHER A LIBERAL OR NEO-CONSERVATIVE IDEOLOGY. THE AUTHOR INTRODUCES THE CONCEPT OF DOCTRINE INTO PUBLIC ADMINISTRATION DISCOURSE IN ORDER TO CLARIFY THE DIFFERENCES IN IDEOLOGY, DOCTRINE, AND PRACTICES BETWEEN AN ERA OF TOP-DOWN LIBERAL PROGRESSIVISM AND THE ERA OF BOTTOM-UP NEO-CONSERVATIVE PROGRESSIVISM THAT DAWNED WITH THE FIRST REAGAN ADMINISTRATION. THE PURPOSE IS TO TAKE A FIRST STEP IN DESCRIBING EMERGING ADMINISTRATIVE REALITIES THAT BOTH TRADITIONAL BUREAUCRATS AND FREE-MARKETEERS MUST RECOGNIZE.

04476 HUMPHREYS, C.; JAEGER, H.
AFRICA'S ADJUSTMENT AND GROWTH
FINANCE AND DEVELOPMENT, 26(2) (JUN 89), 6-8.
ALTHOUGH SUB-SAHARAN AFRICA IS OFTEN VIEWED WITH DESPAIR

AS A CONTINENT IN UNRELENTING DECLINE, CLOSER EXAMINATION
REVEALS A MORE COMPLEX, LESS DISMAL PICTURE. THE ARTICLE
EXAMINES THE ECONOMIC SITUATION IN SUB-SAHARAN AFRICA AND
CONCLUDE THAT COUNTRIES THAT ARE IMPLEMENTING PROGRAMS OF
ECONOMIC REFORM AND ADJUSTMENT SHOW SIGNS OF ECONOMIC
RECOVERY. IT EXAMINES MANY OF THE POLICY REFORMS INCLUDING
REFORMS IN EXCHANGE RATES, AGRICULTURAL POLICY, GOVERNMENT
PRICING AND MARKETING POLICIES, PUBLIC FINANCE, AND PUBLIC
ENTERPRISE.

04477 HUMPHRIES, R.
    THE CONSERVATIVE PARTY
    SOUTH AFRICA FOUNDATION REVIEW, 15(6) (JUN 89), 6,8.
        THE ARTICLE EXPLORES THE STATUS AND POTENTIAL FORTUNES
    OF THE CONSERVATIVE PARTY AS ANOTHER GENERAL ELECTION
    APPROACHES MOST OBSERVERS SEE THE COMING ELECTION AS A
    CRITICAL "MAKE OR BREAK" ELECTION FOR THE CP. RECENT
    SQUABBLES WITHIN THE RULING NATIONAL PARTY INCREASE THE CP'S
    CHANCES FOR SUCCESS, BUT THE CP WILL HAVE TO MAKE GREAT
    STRIDES TO OVERCOME ITS NEGATIVE IMAGE AND THE ADVANTAGES OF
    THE INCUMBENT NATIONAL PARTY.

04478 HUNDERT, E., J.; NELLES, P.
    LIBERTY AND THEATRICAL SPACE IN MONTESQUIEU'S POLITICAL
        THEORY: THE POLITICS OF PUBLIC LIFE IN THE PERSIAN LETTERS
    POLITICAL THEORY, 17(2) (MAY 89), 223-246.
        THE PAPER EXAMINES THE CONCEPT FIRST DISSECTED BY
    MONTESQUIEU IN THE PERSIAN LETTERS THAT A THEATRICALLY
    AMBIGUOUS SOCIAL UNIVERSE OF PERFORMERS IS AT THE HEART OF
    THE CONCEPT THAT LIBERTY IS UNDERSTOOD AS THAT CONDITION IN
    WHICH THE INNER PERSON. IS SHIELDED FROM PUBLIC SCRUTINY BY
    A PERSON'S FREEDOM TO ACT, AND BY THE NECESSITY OF A
    PERSON'S ACTING, ON THE PUBLIC STAGE. IT ALSO FOCUSES ON THE
    CONCEPT THAT AN UNTHEATRICAL POLITICS, FREE OF AMBIGUITY,
    VIOLATES NATURAL LAW AND IS A CONDITION OF DEPOTISM, AND
    THAT A THEATRICALIZED POLITICS IS A PREREQUISITE OF LIBERTY.

04479 HUNITIE, M.F.
    THE CAPITAL BUDGET IN THE JORDANIAN PUBLIC SERVICE:
        OBJECTIVES, PROCESSES, DECISION-MAKING, ISSUES, AND
        INSTITUTIONS
    DISSERTATION ABSTRACTS INTERNATIONAL, 49(12) (JUN 89),
    3866-A.
        THE AUTHOR COMPARES CAPITAL BUDGETING IN JORDAN TO
    CAPITAL BUDGETING IN DEVELOPING COUNTRIES IN GENERAL. HE
    FINDS BOTH SIMILARITIES AND DIFFERENCES. SIMILARITIES
    INCLUDE THE LACK OF ADEQUATE BUDGETARY CHARACTERISTICS, ILL-
    DEFINED AND INAPPROPRIATE APPLICATION OF REFORMS, INADEQUATE
    PLANNING, AND INEQUITABLE DISTRIBUTION OF FUNDS AMONG
    REGIONS. BUT JORDAN ENJOYS A HIGH DEGREE OF INTERNATIONAL
    CREDIBILITY BECAUSE REPAYMENT OF LOANS AND FINANCIAL
    OBLIGATIONS IS A PRIORITY OF ITS CAPITAL BUDGET. MOREOVER,
    JORDAN APPLIES RATIONAL INCREMENTAL AND REPETITIVE-
    ALLOCATIVE DECISION-MAKING TECHNIQUES IN ALLOCATING ITS
    GENERAL BUDGET.

04480 HUNTER, J.
    COCAINE AND CUTOUTS: ISRAEL'S UNSEEN DIPLOMACY
    LINK, 22(1) (JAN 89), 1-3.
        THE ARTICLE EXPLORES THE ALLEGATIONS THAT THE CIA, IN
    COOPERATION WITH ISRAEL HAS ENGAGED IN A "GUNS FOR DRUGS"
    CAMPAIGN INTENDED TO AID THE CONTRAS IN NICARAGUA. IT
    EXAMINES THE TESTIMONY OF SOME KEY WITNESSES THAT CLAIM THAT
    THE "HARARI NETWORK" COOPERATED WITH PANAMA'S GENERAL
    NORIEGA AND THE MEDELLIN CARTEL IN COLUMBIA AND DELIVERED
    COCAINE TO THE US IN RETURN FOR ARMS TO THE CONTRAS.

04481 HUNTER, J.
    ISRAEL AND ETHIOPIA
    MIDDLE EAST INTERNATIONAL, (364) (DEC 89), 15.
        ETHIOPIA ANNOUNCED THE RESUMPTION OF DIPLOMATIC
    RELATIONS WITH ISRAEL. A LONG TRADITION OF CLOSE RELATIONS
    AND MILITARY AID WAS BROKEN WHEN ETHIOPIA JOINED THE
    ORGANIZATION OF AFRICAN UNITY IN 1973. HOWEVER, THE TWO
    NATIONS HAVE RECENTLY BEEN COOPERATING IN AREAS SUCH AS
    AGRICULTURE AND THE IMMIGRATION OF ETHIOPIAN JEWS TO ISREAL.
    THE RESUMPTION OF RELATIONS WILL ALLOW AS MANY AS 16,000
    JEWS TO IMMIGRATE TO AN ALREADY STRAINED ISRAEL.

04482 HUNTER, J.; KIDRON, P.
    ISRAEL-SOUTH AFRICAN MILITARY DEALS
    MIDDLE EAST INTERNATIONAL, (362) (NOV 89), 11-12.
        A SERIES OF REPORTS AIRED BY THE NBC TELEVISION NETWORK
    PROVIDES MANY PREVIOUSLY UNKNOWN DETAILS ABOUT ISRAEL
    NUCLEAR WEAPON AND MISSILE PROGRAMS AND ABOUT ITS TRANSFER
    OF THESE TECHNOLOGIES TO SOUTH AFRICA. ISRAEL REPORTEDLY HAS
    EXCHANGED MISSILE TECHNOLOGY IN RETURN FOR TEST SITES AND A
    SUPPLY OF URANIUM. NBC ALSO CLAIMS THAT ISRAEL PROVIDED MUCH
    OF THE TECHNOLOGY FOR THE DEVELOPMENT OF NEW SOUTH AFRICAN
    AIRCRAFT. WHILE ANY ATTEMPT BY ISRAELI PRESS TO PRINT
    INFORMATION ABOUT ISRAELI NUCLEAR MISSILE PROGRAMS IS
    STRICTLY CENSORED, SOME NEWSPAPERS HAVE CIRCUMVENTED THE
    CENSORSHIP BY SIMPLY REPRINTING FOREIGN REPORTS.

04483 HUNTER, J.
    ISRAEL'S MAN IN PANAMA
    LINK, 22(1) (JAN 89), 3-4.
        THE ARTICLE EXAMINES THE ACTIVITIES OF MIKE HAHARI, A
    MOSSAD OFFICER WHO BECAME A SUPPORTER OF PANAMA'S GENERAL
    MANUEL ANTONIO NORIEGA. HARARI WAS SAID TO HAVE REBUILT THE
    PANAMANIAN ARMED FORCES AND AIDED NORIEGA'S DRUG TRAFFICKING.

04484 HUNTER, J.
    ISRAEL'S MEN
    LINK, 22(1) (JAN 89), 7-10.
        THE ARTICLE ANALYZES, IN ADDITION TO MIKE HARARI IN
    PANAMA, ISRAEL'S "CUTOUTS" IN OTHER AREAS OF THE WORLD
    INCLUDING GUATEMALA, HONDURAS, SIERRA LEONE, BELIZE, CHINA,
    AND AFRICA. MOST OF "ISRAEL'S MEN" HAVE BEEN INVOLVED WITH
    ARMS SALES OF BOTH THE OVERT AND COVERT VARIETY.

04485 HUNTER, J.
    ISRAEL'S SUPPORT FOR NORIEGA
    MIDDLE EAST INTERNATIONAL, (362) (NOV 89), 12-13.
        DESPITE INCREASING US PRESSURE, ISRAEL CONTINUES TO
    MAINTAIN CLOSE TIES WITH PANAMA. ISRAEL HAS REFUSED TO
    RECALL MIKE HARARI, PANAMA'S HONORARY CONSUL IN ISRAEL. HE
    HAS TRAINED MEDELLIN DRUG CARTEL FORCES, SMUGGLED ARMS FOR
    THE US, SMUGGLED DRUGS INTO THE US, AND FUNCTIONS AS MANUEL
    NORIEGA'S CHIEF SECURITY OFFICER. WASHINGTON CAN ONLY APPLY
    MILD PRESSURE TO ISRAEL BECAUSE OF US INVOLVEMENT IN SOME OF
    HARARI'S EARLIER ILLICIT INVOLVEMENT IN THE "SECRET WAR"
    AGAINST NICARAGUA.

04486 HUNTER, J.
    SOUTH AFRICA: ISRAEL'S FRIEND IN NEED?
    MIDDLE EAST INTERNATIONAL, (348) (APR 89), 16-18.
        AS US PUBLIC OPINION BEGINS TO TURN AGAINST ISRAEL, THE
    POSSIBILITY EXISTS THAT ISRAEL WILL PURSUE CLOSER RELATIONS
    WITH THE REPUBLIC OF SOUTH AFRICA. THERE ALREADY IS A GREAT
    DEAL OF CLANDESTINE MILITARY COOPERATION BETWEEN THE TWO
    NATIONS; ISRAEL IS ALSO SUSPECTED OF AIDING SOUTH AFRICA TO
    CIRCUMVENT THE TRADE EMBARGOES PLACED ON SOUTH AFRICA BY THE
    US AND EUROPE. THE ONLY FACTOR THAT MIGHT LIMIT INCREASED
    ISRAELI-SOUTH AFRICAN COOPERATION IS THE INTERNATIONAL
    STIGMA THAT WOULD RESULT FROM OPENLY BEFRIENDING THE
    APARTHEID REGIME.

04487 HUNTER, J.
    SOVIET JEWS: REDIRECTING TO ISRAEL
    MIDDLE EAST INTERNATIONAL, (354) (JUL 89), 10.
        JEWISH GROUPS IN THE US HAVE SHIFTED POLICY AND ARE NOW
    ADVOCATING THE RESETTLEMENT OF SOVIET JEWS IN ISRAEL. THE
    THOUSANDS OF SOVIET JEWS WHO ARE WAITING FOR VISAS IN ITALY
    AND THE THOUSANDS MORE THAT ARE EXPECTED TO LEAVE THE USSR
    ARE STRAINING THE RESOURCES OF JEWISH GROUPS IN THE US AND
    ARE SWAMPING THE STATE DEPARTMENT. ISRAEL WILL ALSO FIND IT
    DIFFICULT TO FIND JOBS AND HOUSING FOR THE IMMIGRANTS.

04488 HUNTER, J.
    THE US AND ISRAEL: REVERBERATIONS FROM THE POLLARD CASE
    MIDDLE EAST INTERNATIONAL, (351) (MAY 89), 13.
        ALTHOUGH JONATHAN JAY POLLARD WAS SENTENCED TO A LIFE
    TERM FOR SPYING FOR ISRAEL SOME THREE YEARS PREVIOUSLY, THE
    US CONTINUES TO PURSUE THE CASE--TO ISRAEL'S GREAT CHAGRIN.
    THE JUSTICE DEPARTMENT HAS ASKED FOR PERMISSION TO
    INTERROGATE A NUMBER OF INDIVIDUALS CONNECTED WITH THE CASE,
    A REQUEST WHICH IS LIKELY TO NOT BE ALLOWED BY THE ISRAELI
    GOVERNMENT WHO FEELS THAT IT HAS TIME TO CLOSE THE CASE THAT
    HAS SOURED RELATIONS BETWEEN THE TWO NATIONS' INTELLIGENCE
    AGENCIES.

04489 HUNTER, J.
    THE US ATTITUDE TO SOVIET JEWS
    MIDDLE EAST INTERNATIONAL, (359) (SEP 89), 14-15.
        A NEWLY DRAFTED US POLICY LIMITS THE NUMBER OF SOVIET
    EMIGRANTS ADMITTED TO THE US AN MAY CHANNEL MANY SOVIET JEWS
    TO ISRAEL. THE REASONS FOR THE 50,000 PERSON CEILING HAVE
    BEEN GIVEN ALTERNATELY AS A REACTION TO GLASNOST AND
    PERESTROIKA, OR A PURELY FINANCIAL MEASURE (IT COSTS ABOUT
    $5,000 TO TRANSPORT AND SETTLE EACH SOVIET JEW). HOWEVER,
    SOME OBSERVERS ARGUE THAT THE MEASURE RESULTED FROM ISRAELI
    PRESSURE; ISRAEL HAS REPEATEDLY ATTEMPTED TO INCREASE THE
    NUMBER OF SOVIET JEWS WHO CHOSE TO GO TO ISRAEL.

04490 HUNTER, J.
    THE US-IRAN ARMS DEAL: WHY ANOTHER CASE WAS DROPPED
    MIDDLE EAST INTERNATIONAL, (342) (JAN 89), 18-20.
        THE AMERICAN GOVERNMENT HAS DROPPED CHARGES AGAINST FOUR
    ISRAELIS AND FIVE INTERNATIONAL BUSINESSMEN ACCUSED OF
    TRYING TO SELL $2.5 BILLION WORTH OF AMERICAN-MADE WEAPONS
    TO IRAN. FEDERAL PROSECUTORS STATED THAT THEY WOULD BE
    UNABLE TO DISPROVE BEYOND REASONABLE DOUBT THE DEFENDANTS'
    CLAIM THAT THEY WERE ACTING UNDER THE SAME AUTHORITY INVOKED
    BY THE REAGAN ADMINISTRATION FOR ITS SECRET ARMS-FOR-
    HOSTAGES DEALINGS WITH IRAN.

04491 HUNTER, J.
    US AND ISRAEL: NO MORE NUCLEAR COOKIES
    MIDDLE EAST INTERNATIONAL, (354) (JUL 89), 9-10.
        AFTER YEARS OF UNOFFICIAL COMPLICITY, THE US IS BEGINNING
    TO REDUCE ITS INVOLVEMENT IN THE ISRAELI DEVELOPMENT OF
    NUCLEAR WEAPONS. RECENT REVEALATIONS MAKE WASHINGTON'S
    STANDARD "SEE NO EVIL" POLICY SEEM RIDICULOUS. ISRAEL IS
    ESTIMATED TO POSSESS SOME 200 NUCLEAR WEAPONS WHICH MAKES IT
    THE WORLD'S SIXTH LARGEST NUCLEAR POWER. ALTHOUGH THE US IS
    DENOUNCING THE SPREAD OF NUCLEAR WEAPONS AND RESTRICTING
    ISRAELI ACCESS TO US WEAPONS LABS AND RESEARCH FACILITIES,
    MANY OBSERVERS STATE THAT THE US'S RENOUNCIATION OF NUCLEAR
    PROLIFERATION IS ONLY HALF-HEARTED.

04492 HUNTER, R.
    WHAT NEXT FOR GERMANY - AND EUROPE?
    EUROPE, (292) (DEC 89), 34-35.
        THIS ARTICLE STATES THAT ONE DAY THE TWO GERMAN STATES
    WILL BE UNIFIED IN A SINGLE SOVEREIGNTY. THAT MUST BE THE
    INESCAPABLE CONSEQUENCE OF EVENTS SUCH AS THE OPENING OF THE
    BERLIN WALL. THE ISSUE, THEREFORE, SHOULD NOT BE ABOUT THE
    WHETHER OF GERMAN UNIFICATION BUT ABOUT THE HOW AND WHEN OF
    IT. DUE TO THE SUDDENESS OF THE EVENTS IN EAST GERMANY, THE
    IDEA OF A UNIFIED NATION HAS COME INTO PLAY WITHOUT ADEQUATE
    PREPARATION OR AN UNDERSTANDING OF WHAT IT WOULD MEAN TO THE
    CITIZENS. THUS, IT IS IMPERATIVE TO ACT IN WAYS THAT WILL
    KEEP THE WEST PREPARED FOR ANY EVENTUALITY. THERE IS ALSO
    THE QUESTION OF A PLACE FOR A UNIFIED GERMANY IN THE
    EUROPEAN COMMUNITY. THE ARTICLE CONCLUDES THAT THE GERMAN
    FUTURE DEPENDS UPON THE EUROPEAN FUTURE THROUGHOUT THE
    CONTINENT.

04493 HUNTER, R.E.
    BERLIN: FORTY YEARS ON
    FOREIGN AFFAIRS, 68(3) (SUM 89), 41-52.
        THE AUTHOR DISCUSSES THE PROSPECTS FOR A REUNIFIED
    GERMANY AND A SINGLE BERLIN AND THE RAMIFICATIONS FOR
    INTERNATIONAL RELATIONS.

04494 HUNTER, R.E.
    BEYOND THE COLD WAR: THE EUROPEAN AGENDA
    WASHINGTON QUARTERLY, 12(4) (FAL 89), 35-52.
        THIS ARTICLE EXPLORES THE U.S. AGENDA FOR CHANGE IN
    EUROPE THAT WILL INCLUDE SHARED EFFORTS WITH OTHER STATES -
    EAST AND WESTTO END THE DIVISION OF EUROPE AND THAT CAN
    INCLUDE SOME REDUCTION OF U.S. FORCES NOW BASED ON THE
    CONTINENT. THE RECASTING OF THE PURPOSE OF NATO FROM AN
    ALLIANCE DESIGNED TO CONTAIN THE PROJECTION OF SOVIET POWER
    AND INFLUENCE TO ONE DESIGNED TO RECONCILE FUNDAMENTAL
    DIFFERENCES SEPARATING EAST FROM WEST IS EXAMINED. THE
    ESSENTIALS FOR EUROPEAN MILITARY SECURITY: EASTERN EUROPE;
    SOVIET POWER AND INFLUENCE; U.S. POWER AND INFLUENCE; AND
    THE GERMAN PROBLEM ARE EACH ANALYZED.

04495 HUNTER, R.E.
    THE REAGAN ADMINISTRATION AND THE MIDDLE EAST
    CURRENT HISTORY, 88(534) (JAN 89), 41, 57-58.
        DURING THE REAGAN ADMINISTRATION, THE UNITED STATES
    ABANDONED ITS ONCE ACTIVE POLICIES IN THE VOLATILE MIDDLE
    EAST. BECAUSE THE 1979 EGYPTIAN-ISRAELI PEACE TREATY REDUCED
    THE RISKS OF MAJOR ARAB-ISRAELI CONFLICT AND U.S.-SOVIET
    CONFRONTATION, IT ALSO SEEMED TO REDUCE THE REAGAN
    ADMINISTRATION'S NEED TO TRY TO NEGOTIATE PEACE. BUT BY
    ABSTAINING FROM ITS EXPECTED ROLE, THE USA NEITHER REMOVED
    ITSELF FROM DANGER NOR INCREASED THE SECURITY OF ITS
    INTERESTS.

04496 HUNTER, S.
    TERRORISM: A BALANCE SHEET
    WASHINGTON QUARTERLY, 12(3) (SUM 89), 17-32.
        THE ARTICLE STUDIES THE EXTENT AND EFFECT OF TERRORISM.
    IT SEEKS TO OVERCOME SOME OF THE DEFINITIONAL PROBLEMS THAT
    THE INTERNATIONAL COMMUNITY HAS GRAPPLED WITH FOR A QUARTER
    CENTURY. IT EXPLORES TERRORISM AS A POLITICAL PHENOMENON AND
    AS AN INSTRUMENT OF POLICY ESPECIALLY WITH REGARDS TO IRAN,
    SYRIA, AND LIBYA. IT OUTLINES THE EFFORTS OF THE
    INTERNATIONAL COMMUNITY TO COMBAT TERRORISM. IT CONCLUDES
    THAT ALTHOUGH TERRORISM HAS BEEN AND STILL REMAINS A
    SIGNIFICANT PROBLEM, THE LAST 10 YEARS OF TERRORISM HAS NOT
    IN ANY SIGNIFICANT WAY AFFECTED REGIONAL OR INTERNATIONAL
    BALANCES OF POWER; IN FACT, THOSE NATIONS THAT HAVE ESPOUSED
    TERRORISM AS A INSTRUMENT OF POLICY HAVE SUFFERED MORE THAN
    THE VICTIMS IN TERMS OF NATIONAL AND HUMAN LOSSES, AS WELL
    AS IN TERMS OF POWER AND PRESTIGE.

04497 HUNTER, S. T. (ED)
    THE POLITICS OF ISLAM REVIVALISM: DIVERSITY AND UNITY
    INDIANA UNIVERSITY PRESS, BLOOMINGTON, IN, 1988, 320.
        THESE ESSAYS ANALYZE THE IMPACT OF ISLAMIC REVIVALIST
    MOVEMENTS IN THE MAJOR MUSLIM COUNTRIES, WITH THE EXCEPTION
    OF TURKEY AND BANGLADESH.

04498 HUNTER, S.T.
    POST-KHOMEINI IRAN

FOREIGN AFFAIRS, 68(5) (WIN 90), 133-149.
    MOST OBSERVERS OF IRANIAN AFFAIRS EXPECTED THAT
KHOMEINI'S DEATH WOULD CREATE A POWER VACUUM IN IRAN, WITH
INTENSE INFIGHTING AMONG ITS ISLAMIC LEADERSHIP. DURING THE
MONTHS IMMEDIATELY PRECEDING KHOMEINI'S DEATH, LEADERS WERE
ENGAGED IN A HEATED DEBATE OVER THE REFORM OF THE ISLAMIC
CONSTITUTION. MANY BELIEVED THAT IF THE CONSTITUTIONAL
PROBLEM WAS NOT RESOLVED DURING THE AYATOLLAH'S LIFETIME,
THERE WOULD BE OPEN CONFLICT AND PERHAPS CIVIL WAR. DESPITE
THESE DIRE PREDICTIONS, THE TRANSITION OF POWER HAS
SURPRISED EVEN THE MOST OPTIMISTIC OF OBSERVERS AS IRAN'S
EMERGING LEADERS HAVE DISPLAYED UNEXPECTED UNITY AND
ALACRITY IN FILLING THE POLITICAL VACUUM.

04499 HUNTER, W., J.; NELSON, M. A.
    INTEREST GROUP DEMAND FOR TAXATION
    PUBLIC CHOICE, 62(1) (JUL 89), 41-62.
        ACKNOWLEDGING THAT RESEARCHERS HAVE TYPICALLY IGNORED
    THE DETERMINANTS OF THE TAX STRUCTURE OF THE PUBLIC SECTOR,
    THE AUTHORS OUTLINE A BEHAVIORAL MODEL OF POLITICAL INTEREST
    GROUPS THAT CAN BE EMPLOYED TO GAIN INSIGHTS INTO THE
    POLITICAL SELECTION OF TAXES. THE THEORY PROVIDES A GENERAL
    COMPLIMENT TO THE WELL-DOCUMENTED ANALYSIS OF SPECIAL
    INTEREST DEMAND FOR PUBLIC EXPENDITURES.

04500 HUNTINGTON, S
    NO EXIT-THE ERRORS OF ENDISM
    NATIONAL INTEREST, (17) (FAL 89), 3-11.
        THIS ARTICLE EXPLORES A MAJOR THEORETICAL AND ACADEMIC
    ISSUE IN 1989 - THE THEORY OF ENDISM. IT EXAMINES THREE
    MANIFESTATIONS OF ENDISM THE END OF THE COLD WAR, WARS AMONG
    NATION STATES, AND OF HISTORY. THE MESSAGE OF ENDISM IS
    "WE'VE WON!" WHICH PROVIDES AN ILLUSION OF WELL BEING, THE
    CONSEQUENCES OF WHICH ARE DANGEROUS AND SUBVERSIVE, TWO
    FALLACIES OF ENDISM ARE DETAILED AND IT CONCLUDES THAT TO
    HOPE FOR THE BENIGN END OF HISTORY IS HUMAN; TO EXPECT IT TO
    HAPPEN IS UNREALISTIC; AND TO PLAN ON IT HAPPENING IS
    DISASTROUS.

04501 HUNTINGTON, S.P.
    VIEW FROM THE FOURTH ESTATE: NO EXIT, THE ERRORS OF ENDISM
    PARAMETERS, XIX(4) (DEC 89), 93-97.
        THE AUTHOR REVIEWS TWO RECENT MANIFESTATIONS OF ENDISM:
    THE END OF THE COLD WAR AND THE END OF WAR BETWEEN
    DEMOCRATIC NATIONS. HE QUESTIONS WHETHER THESE TWO PHENOMENA
    ARE GENUINE AND IRREVERSIBLE AND WHETHER THE OPTIMISM OF
    THOSE WHO BELIEVE IN A PEACEFUL FUTURE IS MISPLACED.

04502 HURD, M.
    THE CHALLENGE OF CHANGE: WATER MANAGEMENT IN THE 1990'S
    AMERICAN CITY AND COUNTY, 104(11) (NOV 89), 38-40, 42, 44.
        THE 1986 AMENDMENTS TO THE SAFE DRINKING WATER ACT
    PROMISE TO MAKE A PROFOUND IMPACT ON THE WAY WATER SYSTEMS
    ARE MANAGED AND OPERATED. SCORES OF NEW FEDERAL REGULATIONS
    FOR PREVIOUSLY UNREGULATED WATER SUPPLY CONTAMINANTS, ALONG
    WITH INCREASES IN MONITORING, REPORTING, AND TESTING
    REQUIREMENTS WILL MAKE LIFE HARDER FOR LOCAL GOVERNMENTS.
    EFFECTIVE LONG-RANGE PLANNING WILL BE THE KEY TO COPING WITH
    THE CHANGES SCHEDULED TO TAKE EFFECT OVER THE NEXT FEW YEARS.

04503 HURLEY, P.A.
    PARTISAN REPRESENTATION AND THE FAILURE OF REALIGNMENT IN
    THE 1980S
    AMERICAN JOURNAL OF POLITICAL SCIENCE, 33(1) (FEB 89),
    240-261.
        THIS PAPER ADVANCES THE CONCEPT OF PARTISAN
    REPRESENTATION AND SUGGESTS THAT SUCH REPRESENTATION PLAYS A
    ROLE IN THE PROCESS OF REALIGNMENT. PARTISAN REPRESENTATION
    FOCUSES ATTENTION ON HOW WELL THE PARTIES IN CONGRESS, AS
    GROUPS, REPRESENT THEIR RANK-ANDFILE IDENTIFIERS, AS GROUPS.
    IMPROVED PARTISAN REPRESENTATION WITHIN THE ADVANTAGED PARTY,
    AS WELL AS INCREASED CONGRUENCE BETWEEN INDEPENDENTS AND
    THE ADVANTAGED PARTY SHOULD BE IMPORTANT FACTORS IN
    TRANSFORMING SHORT-TERM ELECTORAL CHANGE INTO DURABLE NEW
    PATTERNS OF PARTISAN PREFERENCE AND VOTING BEHAVIOR. FAILURE
    TO REPRESENT WELL BOTH EXISTING IDENTIFIERS AND INDEPENDENTS
    SHOULD INHIBIT THE PROCESS OF REALIGNMENT. SINCE THE PUBLIC
    OPINION DATA NECESSARY TO TEST THIS HYPOTHESIS ARE
    UNAVAILABLE FOR ANY PERIOD OF REALIGNMENT, THE HYPOTHESIS IS
    TESTED BY EXAMINING THE FAILED REALIGNMENT OF THE 1980S WITH
    THE EXPECTATION THAT THE RELATIONSHIP OF REPUBLICAN HOUSE
    VOTING PATTERNS TO THE ISSUE PREFERENCES OF REPUBLICANS AND
    INDEPENDENTS IN THE MASS PUBLIC SHOULD NOT IMPROVE BETWEEN
    1980 AND 1984. A COMPARISON OF PUBLIC OPINION WITH HOUSE
    ROLL CALL VOTING IN THE 97TH AND 98TH CONGRESSES SUPPORTS
    THE NULL HYPOTHESIS, AS EXPECTED.

04504 HURLEY, P.A.; WILSON, R. K.
    PARTISAN VOTING PATTERNS IN THE U.S. SENATE, 1887-1986
    LEGISLATIVE STUDIES QUARTERLY, 15(2) (MAY 89), 225-250.
        THIS ARTICLE DESCRIBES PATTERNS OF PARTY VOTING, PARTY
    COHESION AND PARTY STRENGTH IN THE U.S. SENATE FROM 1877
    THROUGH 1986, AND REPLICATE, FOR THE SENATE, EARLIER
    EXPLANATORY MODELS DEVELOPED FOR THE HOUSE OF

REPRESENTATIVES. THE ARTICLE THEN REFINES AND EXTENDS THESE MODELS TO CORRECT FOR AUTOCORRELATION AND MEASURMENT PROBLEMS IN THE REPLICATED ANALYSIS.

04505 HURST, H.
THE CANBERRA SCENE: CHEMICAL WEAPONS: A DECLARATION OF "WAR"
PACIFIC DEFENCE REPORTER, 16(4) (OCT 89), 16-17.
THERE IS AN EXISTING INTERNATIONAL ANTI-CHEMICAL WARFARE TREATY - THE GENEVA PROTOCOL OF 1925 - BUT IT IS BASED ON THE HONOR SYSTEM, WITH NO PROVISION FOR VERIFICATION. ADOPTION OF THE GENEVA PROTOCOL FOLLOWED USE BY GERMANY OF POISONOUS GASES IN WORLD WAR I. THAT CAUSED THOUSANDS OF CASUALTIES ON BOTH SIDES AND MANY AUSTRALIAN SOLDIERS WERE AMONG THE VICTIMS. THIS ARTICLE DESCRIBES AN AUSTRALIA-HOSTED MEETING IN CANBERRA IN SEPTEMBER 1989 AT WHICH GOVERNMENT AND INDUSTRY REPRESENTATIVES FROM MANY NATIONS GATHERED TOGETHER TO DISCUSS ELIMINATION OF CHEMICAL WARFARE FOR GOOD.

04506 HURTADO, M.E.; FARQUHARSON, M.; HOUSE, R.
BUY, BUY THE AMERICAN PIE
SOUTH, (109) (NOV 89), 28-30.
LATIN AMERICAN COUNTRIES HAVE DISCOVERED THAT THE TRADE CORD THAT BINDS THEM TO THE USA IS HARDER TO LOOSEN THAN THEY HAD ANTICIPATED. BRAZIL HAS WORKED HARDER THAN ANY OTHER LATIN AMERICAN COUNTRY TO DIVERSIFY ITS EXPORT MARKETS. ITS POLICY BORE FRUIT IN THE 1970'S, BUT THE ECONOMIC CRISIS OF THE EARLY 1980'S EXPOSED THE FRAGILITY OF THE NEW MARKETS IN DEVELOPING COUNTRIES. NOW BRAZIL, LIKE THE REST OF LATIN AMERICA, HAS BEEN FORCED TO TURN AGAIN TO THE USA. MEANWHILE, ECONOMIC ANALYSTS PREDICT A CONTINUING SLIDE IN BRAZIL'S US TRADE.

04507 HURTADO, M.E.
CALLING UP THE SPECTRES
SOUTH, (99) (JAN 89), 35.
THE USA IS EXPECTED TO TRY TO INFLUENCE THE OUTCOMES OF 1989 ELECTIONS IN GRENADA, PANAMA, AND EL SALVADOR. IF GRENADA HOLDS ELECTIONS IN 1989, THE USA IS EXPECTED TO PRESSURE THE OPPONENTS OF FORMER PRIME MINISTER ERIC GAIRY INTO UNITY IN ORDER TO STOP GAIRY'S BID FOR OFFICE. IN PANAMA, THE USA WILL PROBABLY HAVE TO WATCH WHILE GENERAL NORIEGA WINS AS THE CANDIDATE SUPPORTED BY THE UNITED DEMOCRATIC ALLIANCE COALITION. IN EL SALVADOR, IT SEEMS LIKELY THAT ALFREDO CRISTIANI, THE RIGHT-WING ARENA CANDIDATE, WILL WIN THE PRESIDENTIAL ELECTION.

04508 HURTADO, M.E.
CHILE AT THE THRESHOLD
SOUTH, (106) (AUG 89), 10-11.
IN DECEMBER 1989 CHILEAN VOTERS WILL GO TO THE POLLS TO CHOOSE A NEW PRESIDENT AND PARLIAMENT. THE 17-PARTY CENTRE-LEFT COALITION, THE CONCERTACION, IS EXPECTED TO WIN. ITS LEADERS ARE OPTIMISTIC THAT THEY WILL HAVE A SMOOTH TRANSITION AND WILL NOT HAVE TO FEND OFF THE TYPE OF MILITARY INTERFERENCE THAT HAS PLAGUED THE GOVERNMENTS OF PRESIDENT ALFONSIN IN ARGENTINA AND PRESIDENT GARCIA IN PERU.

04509 HURTADO, M.E.
GOLDEN ROAD TO BLOODSHED
SOUTH, (102) (APR 89), 10-11.
PRESIDENT CARLOS ANDRES PEREZ DID NOT EXPECT THE FURY WITH WHICH VENEZUELAN TEACHERS, STUDENTS, WORKERS, THE UNEMPLOYED, PEASANTS, AND SLUM-DWELLERS REACTED TO HIS IMF-INSPIRED AUSTERITY MEASURES. BUT HUNDREDS WERE KILLED IN SEVERAL DAYS OF RIOTING IN FEBRUARY AND MARCH 1989. WHAT HAPPENED IN VENEZUELA COULD HAVE REPERCUSSIONS BEYOND ITS BORDERS. POLITICAL TRENDS SPREAD QUICKLY IN SOUTH AMERICA AND THERE IS ENOUGH COMMON GROUND TO ARGUE THAT MOST OF ITS NEIGHBORS ARE ALSO READY TO EXPLODE.

04510 HURTADO, M.E.
INTO THE DEEP FREEZE
SOUTH, (103) (MAY 89), 75-76.
IN MAY 1989, A HELSINKI MEETING WILL REVIEW THE VIENNA CONVENTION ON THE OZONE LAYER AND ITS MONTREAL PROTOCOL IN LIGHT OF DISCOVERIES ABOUT THE RATE AT WHICH CHEMICAL EMISSIONS ARE DEPLETING THE WORLD'S PROTECTIVE SHIELD. FOR THE THIRD WORLD, THE KEY ISSUE IS HOW MUCH DEVELOPING COUNTRIES WILL BE EXPECTED TO REDUCE EMISSIONS AND HOW THIS COMPARES WITH STANDARDS FOR THE BIG INDUSTRIAL POLLUTERS OF THE NORTH.

04511 HURTADO, M.E.; HOUSE, R.
NEW RIDERS OF THE POPULIST WAVES
SOUTH, (99) (JAN 89), 34-35.
AS CHILE PREPARES TO JOIN THE WAVE OF NEW LATIN AMERICAN DEMOCRACIES IN 1989, THE TIDE IS ALREADY MOVING ON TOWARD THE LEFT. BEFORE RODRIGO BORJA WON ECUADOR'S PRESIDENCY IN 1988, PRESIDENT GARCIA OF PERU WAS THE LONELY EXPONENT OF WELFARE POLITICS IN SOUTH AMERICA. NOW BORJA AND GARCIA ARE LIKELY TO BE JOINED BY CARLOS MENEM IN ARGENTINA, JAIME PAZ ZAMORA IN BOLIVIA, AND LEONEL BRIZOLA OR LUIS INACIO DA

SILVA IN BRAZIL. THE STRICTURES IMPOSED BY FOREIGN DEBT SEEM TO BE TURNING LATIN AMERICANS AGAINST POLITICIANS OFFERING MORE OF THE SAME AND LEADING TO POPULAR DISILLUSIONMENT WITH TRADITIONAL POLITICIANS.

04512 HURTADO, M.E.
THE SHAME OF NATIONS
SOUTH, (104) (JUN 89), 77-78.
POLITICAL EMBARRASSMENT WILL REMAIN THE STRONGEST INCENTIVE FOR STOPPING TOXIC WASTE DUMPING IN THE THIRD WORLD, EVEN AFTER THE NEW INTERNATIONAL TREATY REGULATING CROSS-BORDER TRADE IN HAZARDOUS WASTE GOES INTO EFFECT IN 1990. LIKE MANY OTHER INTERNATIONAL ACCORDS, THIS ONE HAS NO MEANS OF ENFORCEMENT. MOREOVER, IT FALLS SHORT OF THE BAN FAVORED BY AFRICAN COUNTRIES, IN PARTICULAR.

04513 HURTADO, M.E.
US TRADES ON THE WORK ETHIC
SOUTH, (106) (AUG 89), 29-30.
THE USA HAS CAST ITSELF IN THE UNPOPULAR ROLE OF POLICING WORKERS' RIGHTS, FOLLOWING ITS FAILURE TO SECURE ENOUGH INTERNATIONAL SUPPORT FOR A CAMPAIGN TO PENALIZE COUNTRIES WITH POOR WORKING STANDARDS. AS THE ONLY INDUSTRIAL NATION TO WITHDRAW TRADE PREFERENCES UNILATERALLY FROM COUNTRIES THAT FAIL TO OBSERVE MINIMUM LABOR STANDARDS, IT HAS NOW STEPPED UP PRESSURE TO INCORPORATE A SIMILAR MECHANISM INTO GATT. BUT CRITICS SAY THE UNITED STATES' CONCERN FOR WORKERS' RIGHTS IS MERELY A COVER FOR PROTECTIONISM AND AN ATTEMPT TO PREVENT THE USE OF CHEAP LABOR TO COMPETE WITH AMERICAN GOODS.

04514 HURWITZ, J.; PEFFLEY, M.; RAYMOND, P.
PRESIDENTIAL SUPPORT DURING THE IRAN-CONTRA AFFAIR; AN INDIVIDUAL-LEVEL ANALYSIS OF PRESIDENTIAL REAPPRAISAL
AMERICAN POLITICS QUARTERLY, 17(4) (OCT 89), 359-385.
THIS ARTICLE USES NATIONAL ELECTION STUDIES PANEL DATA TO INVESTIGATE PRESIDENTIAL SUPPORT BOTH BEFORE AND AFTER THE MAJOR REVELATIONS IN THE IRAN-CONTRA AFFAIR TO DETERMINE THE REASONS BEHIND THE EROSION OF PRESIDENT REAGAN'S SUPPORT BASE AND THE CHARACTERISTICS OF INDIVIDUALS WHO DID, AND DID NOT, ADJUST THEIR VIES OF THE PRESIDENT SUBSEQUENT TO THE REVELATIONS. IT FINDS THAT HIS PERFORMANCE WAS MOST SERIOUSLY QUESTIONED BY THOSE DISAPPROVING OF HIS CENTRAL AMERICAN POLICY.

04515 HUSAIN, S., S.
REVIVING GROWTH IN LATIN AMERICA
FINANCE AND DEVELOPMENT, 26(2) (JUN 89), 2-5.
THE ARTICLE EXAMINES THE ECONOMIC QUAGMIRE THAT MANY LATIN AMERICAN NATIONS HAVE FOUND THEMSELVES IN. IT OUTLINES THE ORIGINS OF THE CURRENT PROBLEMS INCLUDING THE ROLE OF GOVERNMENT, INEFFECENT INDUSTRIALIZATION, AND OVER-RELIANCE ON EXTERNAL FINANCE. IT ESTABLISHES AN AGENDA FOR REFORM AND ANALYZES THE ROLE THAT THE WORLD BANK CAN PLAY IN ASSISTING ECONOMIC REFORM AND GROWTH.

04516 HUSATNI, F.
INTERVIEW WITH FAYSAL HUSAYNI
JOURNAL OF PALESTINE STUDIES, XVIII(4) (SUM 89), 3-17.
THE ARTICLE IS AN INTERVIEW OF FAYSAL HUSAYNI, A WELL KNOWN PALESTINIAN IN THE OCCUPIED TERRITORIES. HE SPEAKS OF HIS EXPERIENCE WITH THE PALESTINIAN INDEPENDENCE MOVEMENT. HIS RANGE OF EXPERIENCE INCLUDES ARMED STRUGGLE, SEVERAL PRISON STAYS, AND INVOLVEMENT IN MANY POLITICAL ORGANIZATIONS SUCH AS THE ARAB STUDIES SOCIETY. HE ALSO SPEAKS OF THE INTIFADA, THE ISRAELI CRACKDOWN AND THE POSSIBILITY OF NEGOTIATIONS BETWEEN THE PLO AND ISRAEL.

04517 HUSSAIN, A.
SUSTAINABLE DEVELOPMENT AND REGIONAL COOPERATION
SOUTH ASIA JOURNAL, 3(1/2) (JUL 89), 17-26.
THIS ARTICLE EXPLORES THE NEED FOR A NEW DEVELOPMENT PATH FOR SOUTH ASIA. IT QUESTIONS: CAN WE ACHIEVE IN OUR THINKING AND PRACTICE, A NEW RELATIONSHIP BETWEEN MAN, NATURE AND GROWTH. IN PART I IS EXAMINED THE RESOURCE POTENTIAL OF SOUTH ASIA AND THE EXTENT OF ITS DEGRADATION. IN PART II IS PRESENTED AN OUTLINE OF AN APPROACH TO SUSTAINABLE DEVELOPMENT THROUGH ESTABLISHING A LINK BETWEEN TWO LEVELS OF DEVELOPMENT PRAXIS: GRASS ROOTS ORGANIZATION ON THE ONE HAND, AND REGIONAL COOPERATION FOR HUMAN AND NATURAL RESOURCE DEVELOPMENT, ON THE OTHER.

04518 HUSSAIN, M.
CHINA FILLS A "VACUUM" IN THE MIDDLE EAST
MIDDLE EAST INTERNATIONAL, (351) (MAY 89), 17.
THE ARTICLE DESCRIBES THE EFFORTS OF CHINA TO FILL THE "VACUUM" CREATED IN THE MIDDLE EAST BY DISILLUSIONMENT WITH BOTH SUPERPOWERS. IT OUTLINES CHINA'S OBJECTIVES IN THE AREA AND THE METHODS THAT BEIJING IS USING TO INCREASE ITS INFLUENCE IN THE AREA. THE PRIMARY FOREIGN POLICY TOOL IN THE MIDEAST THUS FAR HAS BEEN THE SALE OF SOPHISTICATED ARMAMENTS TO PAKISTAN, IRAN, AND SAUDI ARABIA.

04519 HUSSAIN, M.
IRAN FORGES NEW LINKS
MIDDLE EAST INTERNATIONAL, (344) (FEB 89), 17-18.
DIPLOMATIC DEVELOPMENTS HAVE CONTRIBUTED TO A CLOSER
CONVERGENCE OF INTERESTS BETWEEN TEHRAN AND ISLAMABAD THAT
MAY EVENTUALLY LEAD TO THE EVOLUTION OF A NEW REGIONAL
COALITION OF THE MUSLIM STATES OF PAKISTAN, IRAN, AND
AFGHANISTAN. THREE RECENT DEVELOPMENTS ARE PARTICULARLY
RELEVANT: THE UPGRADING OF SOVIET-IRANIAN RELATIONS,
TEHRAN'S ACTIVISM ON THE AFGHAN ISSUE, AND THE GROWING
INTIMACY BETWEEN PAKISTAN AND IRAN.

04520 HUSSAIN, M.
IRAN'S FOREIGN POLICY
MIDDLE EAST INTERNATIONAL, (361) (OCT 89), 15-16.
ALTHOUGH OPEN WARFARE BETWEEN IRAN AND IRAQ HAS CEASED,
THE UNDERLYING TENSION BETWEEN THE TWO NATIONS CONTINUES.
IRAN IS VIGOROUSLY PURSUING FOREIGN POLICY AIMS IN LEBANON
AND AFGHANISTAN WHICH PIT IRAN AGAINST IRAQ AND SAUDI ARABIA.
IN COOPERATION WITH SYRIA, IRAN CONTINUES TO PROMOTE A
GRAND ALLIANCE OF VARIOUS ISLAMIC, NATIONALIST, LEFTIST, AND
PALESTINIAN FACTIONS IN LEBANON. TEHRAN IS ALSO ACTIVELY
INVOLVED IN PURSUING POLITICAL SOLUTIONS IN AFGHANISTAN.
THESE ACTIONS REFLECT AN INCREASING PRESENCE IN THE MIDEAST
FOR THE ISLAMIC REPUBLIC.

04521 HUSSAIN, M.
THE MUSLIM QUESTION IN INDIA
JOURNAL OF CONTEMPORARY ASIA, 19(3) (1989), 279-296.
THE ARTICLE EXPLORES THE MUSLIM QUESTION WHICH STILL
LOOMS LARGE IN DIVIDED SECULAR-INDEPENDENT INDIA WITHOUT ANY
SOLUTION AT SIGHT. IT DESCRIBES THE SOCIAL, POLITICAL, AND
DEMOGRAPHIC MILIEU; THE POLITICAL STRUCTURE AND HUMAN RIGHTS;
AND NEW DIMENSIONS IN THE COMMUNAL SITUATION-SECULAR SOCIAL
MOVEMENT AND NONSECULAR EXPRESSIONS (I) AND THE HINDU-SIKH
CONFLICT (II). IT OFFERS THE MUSLIM STRATEGY FOR SURVIVAL
AND THE POLEMICS OF SURVIVAL STRATEGY. IT CONCLUDES THAT A
SUCCESSFUL SOLUTION OF THE MUSLIM QUESTION FUNDAMENTALLY
DEPENDS ON THE SUCCESS OF THE LEFT FORCES IN TRANSFORMING
INDIA TO THE SOCIALIST PATH.

04522 HUSSAIN, Z.
RELIGIOUS ROW
INDIA TODAY, XIV(6) (MAR 89), 66.
PAKISTANI PROTESTS OVER SALMAN RUSHDIE'S "THE SATANIC
VERSES" HAVE BEEN LED BY OPPOSITION AND RELIGIOUS LEADERS.
THE MAIN OBJECTIVE OF THE PROTESTS HAS BEEN TO STIR UP
RELIGIOUS FRENZY AND UNDERMINE THE GOVERNMENT OF BENAZIR
BHUTTO.

04523 HUSSEIN, S.A.
ISLAM AND POLITICS IN MALAYSIA, 1969-1982: THE DYNAMICS OF
COMPETING TRADITIONS
DISSERTATION ABSTRACTS INTERNATIONAL, 50(5) (NOV 89),
1422-A.
THE 1970'S SAW THE RISE OF THE REVIVALIST MOVEMENT IN
MALAYSIA REPRESENTED BY THREE ORGANIZATIONS: ABIM, ARQAM,
AND TABLIGH. BY 1982, THESE GROUPS HAD BEEN LARGELY
NEUTRALIZED POLITICALLY BECAUSE THE MOVEMENT'S BASE WAS
LIMITED MAINLY TO THE SMALL, URBAN MIDDLE CLASS AND THE
SUPERIOR FORCE OF THE DOMINANT ISLAMIC TRADITION
OVERSHADOWED THEM.

04524 HUSSEIN, S.M.
OFFENSE, DEFENSE, AND PREEMPTION (AN EXPECTED UTILITY
APPROACH TO THE THEORY OF INTERNATIONAL CONFLICT)
DISSERTATION ABSTRACTS INTERNATIONAL, 50(1) (JUL 89),
251-A.
IN THIS DISSERTATION, WAR IS MODELED AS A DECISION
PROBLEM UNDER UNCERTAINITY. ACTORS CHOOSE BETWEEN TWO
LOTTERIES; ONE OFFERS THE OPTION AND CONSEQUENCES OF USING
FORCE WHILE THE SECOND LOTTERY OFFERS THE CHOICE AND
CONSEQUENCES OF DOING NOTHING. THE MODEL IS USED TO SPECIFY
THE CONDITIONS UNDER WHICH ACTORS WILL USE FORCE OFFENSIVELY,
DEFENSIVELY, OR PREEMPTIVELY. THE MODEL SUGGESTS THAT TWO
FACTORS THAT WERE NOT EXPLICIT IN PREVIOUS ANALYSES, COST
AND REVISED EXPECTATION, ARE CRUCIAL TO THE DECISION TO GO
TO WAR.

04525 HUSSEINI, F.
A NEW FACE TO THE MIDDLE EAST
NEW OUTLOOK, 32(11-12 (297-298)) (NOV 89), 14-15.
THE PALESTINIAN PEOPLE ARE STRUGGLING IN ORDER TO CREATE
TWO STATES: A PALESTINIAN STATE AND AN ISRAELI STATE, LIVING
SIDE-BY-SIDE. THE PALESTINIANS WANT PEACE AND THAT CAN ONLY
BE ACHIEVED THROUGH DIALOGUE WITH THE ENEMY OR A
REPRESENTATIVE OF THE ENEMY'S GOVERNMENT. THE ISRAELIS MUST
ALSO DECIDE WHO THEIR ENEMY IS AND WHAT THEY WANT FROM THAT
ENEMY. IF THEY WANT TO REACH A SOLUTION TO THE CONFLICT,
THEY MUST SPEAK WITH THAT ENEMY OR THE REPRESENTATIVE OF THE
PALESTINIANS--THE PLO.

04526 HUSTON, J.A.
FIFTEEN GREAT MISTAKES OF THE COLD WAR

WORLD AFFAIRS, 151(1) (SUM 88), 35-45.
AFTER FORTY YEARS OF COLD WAR IN WHICH THE UNITED STATES
HAS HAD TO FACE ONE CRISIS AFTER ANOTHER IN DEALING WITH THE
SOVIET UNION AND THE COMMUNIST WORLD, THE AUTHOR EXAMINES
WHERE THE UNITED STATES MAY HAVE GONE WRONG IN A NUMBER OF
ITS POLICY DECISIONS: THE FIFTEEN GREAT MISTAKES OF THE COLD
WAR. THREE FAULTY ASSUMPTIONS LAY BENEATH MANY OF THESE
MISTAKES. ONE IS THE ASSUMPTION OF A COMMUNIST MONOLITH,
WITH NO DIFFERENCES AMONG RUSSIANS, CHINESE, KOREANS,
VIETNAMESE, OR CUBANS. ANOTHER IS THE ASSUMPTION THAT THE
NUCLEAR BOMB IS JUST ANOTHER WEAPON, AND THAT PARITY IS TO
BE CALCULATED ACCORDING TO NUMBERS IN THE SAME WAY AS OTHER
WEAPONS. THE THIRD IS THAT THERE IS NO LIMIT TO MILITARY
EXPENDITURES, AND THAT IN ANY CASE MILITARY EXPENDITURES
HAVE NO ADVERSE EFFECT ON THE ECONOMY.

04527 HUTCHISON, T.
LEGISLATING VIA VETO
STATE LEGISLATURES, 15(1) (JAN 89), 20-22.
CONCEIVED AS A LEGITIMATE TOOL FOR RESTRAINING STATE
SPENDING, THE ITEM VETO IS NOW REGULARLY USED AS A TOOL OF
GUBERNATORIAL POLICYMAKING AND IS OFTEN USED TO UNDERMINE
THE INTENTIONS OF THE LEGISLATURE.

04528 HUTH, P.K.
THE DILEMMA OF DETERRENCE: CREDIBILITY VS. STABILITY
ESCALATION AND CONFLICT RESOLUTION IN CRISES FROM 1885 TO
1984
DISSERTATION ABSTRACTS INTERNATIONAL, 48(10) (APR 88),
2722-A.
IN ORDER TO DETERMINE UNDER WHAT CONDITIONS EXTENDED
DETERRENCE IS LIKELY TO SUCCEED OR FAIL, HYPOTHESES WERE
FORMULATED REGARDING: THE BALANCE OF MILITARY FORCES, THE
CRISIS BARGAINING STRATEGIES OF THE DEFENDER, THE PAST
BWHAVIOR OF THE DEFENDER, AND THE EXTENT OF ECONOMIC AND
MILITARY TIES BETWEEN DEFENDER AND PROTEGE. THESE HYPOTHESES
WERE TESTED ON THE UNIVERSE OF HISTORICAL CASES OF ATTEMPTED
DETERRENCE FROM 1885 TO 1984 PROBIT ANALYSIS.

04529 HUXLET, M.
READING PLANNING POLITICALLY
ARENA, (89) (SUM 89), 116-132.
THE AUTHOR EXAMINES THE LANGUAGE, ASSUMPTIONS, AGENDAS,
AND METHODS OF PROBLEM IDENTIFICATION IN SHAPING MELBOURNE'S
FUTURE, A VICTORIAN MINISTRY OF PLANNING AND ENVIRONMENT
DOCUMENT. HE SEEKS TO EXAMINES THE WAYS IN WHICH PLANNING
DISCOURSE AFFECTS THE WAY IN WHICH PROBLEMS ARE CONCEIVED
AND SOLUTIONS PROPOSED. HE CONCLUDES THAT, IN THE CASE OF
SHAPING MELBOURNE'S FUTURE, WHAT AT FIRST APPEARS TO BE A
POLICY CONCERNED WITH SOCIAL DEMOCRATIC IDEALS--
REDISTRIBUTION, SOCIAL JUSTICE AND ECONOMIC GROWTH--AT BEST,
CAN BE SHOWN TO BE A RECIPE FOR MORE OF THE SAME, OR AT
WORST, A CONTRIBUTION TO INCREASED INEQUALITY.

04530 HUXLEY, C.
ARAB GOVERNMENT WAKES UP TO AIDS THREAT
MIDDLE EAST REPORT, 19(6) (NOV 89), 24-25.
THIS ARTICLE REPORTS ON THE SPREAD OF AIDS IN THE MIDDLE
EAST WHICH BEGAN LATER THAN IN THE WEST OR IN AFRICA AND
APPEARS TO HAVE DIFFERENT CHARACTERISTICS. IT ESTABLISHES
THAT AS YET THERE IS NO SINGLE MEANS OF TRANSMISSION AND
THAT EDUCATION IS THE MOST EFFECTIVE MEANS OF PREVENTION.

04531 HWEE, D.O.
CONSCRIPT MILITARY FORCE AS A CREDIBLE DEFENSE SYSTEM FOR
A SMALL NATION: THE CASE OF SINGAPORE AND TAIWAN
AVAILABLE FROM NTIS, NO. AD-A199 851/7/GAR, JUN 13 88, 161.
THE CONSCRIPT SYSTEM IS CURRENTLY USED BY A LARGE NUMBER
OF COUNTRIES, INCLUDING THE MAJORITY OF SMALL NATIONS. THIS
STUDY EXAMINES THE APPROPRIATENESS AND EFFECTIVENESS OF A
CONSCRIPT MILITARY FORCES (FOREIGN) AS A CREDIBLE DEFENSE
SYSTEM FOR SMALL COUNTRIES. THIS STUDY ANALYZES THE FACTORS
WHICH CAUSED SINGAPORE AND TAIWAN TO HAVE A CONSCRIPT
SYSTEMS. THE FACTORS INCLUDE GEOGRAPHY, THREAT ASSESSMENT,
DEFENSE POLICY, HISTORICAL CIRCUMSTANCES, POPULATION/SOCIETY,
AND ECONOMIC CONSIDERATIONS. THE ANALYSIS OF THE
EFFECTIVENESS OF THE CONSCRIPT SYSTEM COVERS FOUR MILITARY
CRITERIA AND FOUR NON-MILITARY CRITERIA WHICH RELATE TO THE
OPERATIONAL READINESS OF THE ARMED FORCES AND THE
CONTRIBUTION OF THE MILITARY SYSTEM TO INTERNAL NATIONAL
OBJECTIVES. THE STUDY SHOWS THAT GIVEN THE INHERENT FACTORS
AND CONSTRAINTS, THE CONSCRIPT SYSTEM IS SUITABLE IN
PROVIDING SINGAPORE AND TAIWAN WITH THE TYPE OF MILITARY
FORCE REQUIRED FOR THEIR DEFENSE NEEDS. THE CONSCRIPT SYSTEM
HAS BEEN EFFECTIVE IN CONTRIBUTING TO THE MILITARY
EFFICIENCY OF THE ARMED FORCES AS WELL AS IN SUPPORTING
OTHER NON-MILITARY NATIONAL INTERNAL OBJECTIVES. THE STUDY
PROVIDES INSIGHTS INTO THE RATIONALE FOR A SMALL COUNTRY'S
ADOPTION OF A CONSCRIPT SYSTEM AND THE EFFECTIVENESS OF THE
SYSTEM. IT ALSO PROVIDES A CONCEPTUAL FRAMEWORK THAT WILL
FACILITATE ANALYSIS OF THE CHOICE AND EFFECTIVENESS OF A
CONSCRIPT SYSTEM.

04532 HYDE-PRICE, A.
PERESTROIKA OR UMGESTALTUNG? EAST GERMANY AND THE
GORBACHEV REVOLUTION
JOURNAL OF COMMUNIST STUDIES, 5(2) (JUN 89), 185-210.
THE ARTICLE EXPLORES THE CHANGING NATURE OF GDR-SOVIET
RELATIONS IN THE 1980'S, CONCENTRATING ON THE GORBACHEV
PERIOD. IT ALSO SEEKS TO ASSESS THE STABILITY AND CAPACITY
FOR CHANGE IN THE EAST GERMAN POLITICAL SYSTEM. EAST
GERMANY'S RESPONSE TO THE REFORMS IN THE USSR HAS BEEN
PARADOXICAL: PERESTROIKA AND GLASNOST HAVE BEEN RESISTED,
BUT MUCH OF GORBACHEV'S FOREIGN POLICY AND "NEW THINKING"
HAS BEEN ENDORSED. THE ARTICLE CONCLUDES THAT SIGNIFICANT
STRUCTURAL REFORMS HILL BECOME UNAVOIDABLE IN THE 1990'S,
BUT THEY ARE LIKELY TO FOLLOW A UNIQUELY GERMAN PATTERN,
RATHER THAN A SOVIET-STYLE PERESTROIKA.

04533 HYLAND, W.G.
SETTING GLOBAL PRIORITIES: A NEW U.S. FOREIGN POLICY
CURRENT, (312) (MAY 89), 26-33.
EVEN THOUGH THE UNITED STATES' FOREIGN-POLICY FOUNDATION
IS STURDY AND SHOULD NOT BE TAMPERED WITH AND EVEN THOUGH
THE USA SHOULD MAINTAIN ITS ALLIANCES WITH JAPAN AND WESTERN
EUROPE, THE USE NEEDS A NEW FOREIGN POLICY. THE THREAT TO
AMERICAN NATIONAL SECURITY IS CHANGING AND THE
SUPERSTRUCTURE OF AMERICAN POLICY, WHICH HAS ERECTED IN
RESPONSE TO THAT THREAT, IS COLLAPSING.

04534 HYMAN, J.
TRIAL ADVOCACY AS AN IMPEDIMENT TO WISE NEGOTIATION
NEGOTIATION JOURNAL, 5(3) (JUL 89), 237-250.
THE ARTICLE ANALYSES THE APPARENT CONFLICT BETWEEN THE
SYSTEM OF ADVERSARIAL LITIGATION AND ALTERNATIVE METHODS OF
PROBLEM-SOLVING NEGOTIATION AND MEDIATION. IT CONCENTRATES
ON FOUR KEY AREAS OF CONFLICT BETWEEN THE LITIGATOR AND THE
"WISE" NEGOTIATIOR: THE USE OF FACTS, THE USE OF LEGAL RULES
AND PRINCIPLES, THE EXERCISE OF CONTROL OVER THE DISPUTANTS
AND THE DISPUTE, AND THE STANCE THE PROFESSIONAL TAKES
TOWARDS THE DISPUTING PARTIES' MEANS AND ENDS. IT CONCLUDES
THAT ALTHOUGH THE CONFLICT IS QUITE REAL, IT IS NOT AS DEEP
AS IT MAY AT FIRST APPEAR.

04535 IANNELLO, K.P.
A FEMINIST FRAMEWORK FOR ORGANIZATIONS
DISSERTATION ABSTRACTS INTERNATIONAL, 50(2) (AUG 89),
541-A.
THE AUTHOR INVESTIGATES FEMINIST CLAIMS WITH REGARD TO
ORGANIZATIONS AND FOCUSES ON THE RELATIONSHIP BETWEEN
POLITICAL IDEALS AND HIERARCHY WITHIN ORGANIZATIONS. OF
PARTICULAR INTEREST IS ANARCHIST FEMINIST THEORY THAT HOLDS
THE DEVELOPMENT OF NON-HIERARCHICAL STRUCTURE AS A GOAL. THE
MAJOR RESEARCH QUESTION IS: TO WHAT EXTENT HAVE ANARCHIST
FEMINISTS BEEN ABLE TO CREATE AND MAINTAIN NON-HIERARCHICAL
STRUCTURES WHILE STILL ATTAINING, TO A REASONABLE EXTENT,
ORGANIZATION GOALS?

04536 IBRAHIM, B.
POLICIES AFFECTING WOMEN'S EMPLOYMENT IN THE FORMAL SECTOR:
STRATEGIES FOR CHANGE
WORLD DEVELOPMENT, 17(7) (JUL 89), 1097-1107.
WOMEN'S PARTICIPATION IN THE FORMAL WORKFORCE IS
INCREASING IN MOST DEVELOPING COUNTRIES, BUT WORK CONDITIONS,
WAGES, AND JOB SECURITY ARE DECLINING. AS GOVERNMENTS
RETREAT FROM POLICIES DESIGNED TO PROTECT WORKERS AND
ENHANCE THEIR EMPLOYMENT, THE SPECIAL NEEDS OF WOMEN WORKERS
ARE NEGLECTED. INTERNATIONAL PRESSURES FOR STRUCTURAL
ADJUSTMENT IN DEVELOPING ECONOMIES HAVE RESULTED IN
RELAXATION OF LABOR LAWS, PRIVATIZATION OF INDUSTRY AND
SERVICES, AND THE ENCOURAGEMENT OF INTERNATIONAL INVESTMENT.
JOINT ACTION IS CALLED FOR AMONG GOVERNMENTS, DONORS,
RESEARCHERS, AND LABOR ACTIVISTS. THEY SHOULD EXAMINE THE
JOB CREATION PROCESS FOR POSSIBLE INTERVENTIONS IN
INVESTMENT DECISIONS AND ADDRESS THE NATURE OF LABOR LAWS,
THE EXTENT OF THEIR APPLICATION, AND THE ABILITY OF UNIONS
AND OTHER WORKERS' ORGANIZATIONS TO LOBBY FOR EFFECTIVE
DEFENSE OF WORKERS' RIGHTS.

04537 IBRAHIM, M.
THE CAUSES BEHIND THE EXPLOSION OF RELIGIOUS EXTREMISM
WORLD MARXIST REVIEW, 31(11) (NOV 88), 92-98.
THIS ARTICLE IS AN ATTEMPT TO TACKLE THE SUBJECT OF
RELIGIOUS EXTREMISM IN EGYPT IN THEORETICAL AND PRACTICAL
TERMS AND TO DISCUSS ISSUES THAT NOT ONLY COLOUR ALL
DOMESTIC AFFAIRS BUT HAVE ALSO EMERGED AS A FACTOR OF THE
IDEOLOGICAL STRUGGLE CURRENTLY UNDER WAY WITHIN THE ECP AND
THE LEFT IN GENERAL.

04538 IBRAHIM, O.F.
THE FABRIC OF RULE: A STUDY OF THE POSITION OF TRADITIONAL
RULING FAMILIES IN THE POLITICS OF KANO STATE, NIGERIA,
1960-1983
DISSERTATION ABSTRACTS INTERNATIONAL, 50(4) (OCT 89),
1078-A.
THIS STUDY TESTS THE HYPOTHESES: (A) THAT THE
TRADITIONAL RULING FAMILIES OF KANO STATE HAVE CONTINUED TO
DOMINATE KANO STATE POLITICS SINCE INDEPENDENCE AND (B) THAT
SUCCESSIVE GOVERNMENTS OF KANO STATE HAVE CONTINUED TO MAKE
POLICIES THAT FAVOR TRADITIONAL INSTITUTIONS.

04539 IFTEKHARUZZAMAN
THE CHIMERA OF DISARMAMENT IN SOUTH ASIA
SOUTH ASIA JOURNAL, 2(4) (APR 89), .
THE MAIN ARGUMENT OF THIS PAPER IS THAT IN THE SOUTH
ASIAN CONTEXT, COMPLETE DISARMAMENT IS AN IMPOSSIBLE TARGET
TO ACHIEVE. CONTRARY TO THE BELIEF OF SOME ANALYSTS, THE
REGION IS SPENDING MUCH MORE THAN IT CAN AFFORD ON ARMS AND
DEFENCE. PROBLEMS INHERENT IN THE PROCESS OF NATIONBUILDING,
PARTICULARLY THE DISTORTED PROCESS OF POLITICO-ECONOMIC
DEVELOPMENT ON THE ONE HAND, AND PECULIARITIES IN REGIONAL
CONFIGURATION ON THE OTHER, ACCOUNT FOR THE CONTINUED URGE
FOR A REGIONAL ARMS RACE. THE INVOLVEMENT OF THE EXTERNAL
POWERS IN THE REGION, PARTICULARLY THE US AND THE USSR,
CONTINUE TO ADD THE GLOBAL DIMENSION TO THE SOUTH ASIAN ARMS
RACE. WHILE COMPLETE DISARMAMENT IN THE REGION WOULD REMAIN
IMPOSSIBLE IN ALL LIKELIHOOD, THE TREND OF ARMS BUILDUP CAN
BE HOPEFULLY REVERSED THROUGH PROGRESS IN NATION-BUILDING
EFFORTS IN EACH OF THE SOUTH ASIAN COUNTRIES ALONGWITH
CONCRETE MEASURES FOR REGIONAL CONFIDENCE-BUILDING ON A
SUSTAINED BASIS. THE NEED FOR REGIONAL COOPERATION IS TO BE
SPECIFICALLY UNDERSCORED IN THIS CONTEXT AS A CATALYST.

04540 IGNATIEFF, M.
CITIZENSHIP AND MORAL NARCISSISM
POLITICAL QUARTERLY (THE), 60(1) (JAN 89), 63-74.
WERE LIBERALS, SOCIAL DEMOCRATS AND SOCIALISTS TO WORK
THEMSELVES FREE OF THE SEDUCTIVE PLEASURES OF MORAL
SUPERIORITY ABOUT THE VANALITY OF THE MARKET AND FALSE
NOSTALGIA ABOUT THE VANISHED COMPASSION OF THE OLD CIVIC
CONTRACT, THEY MIGHT BE ABLE TO DEVELOP A ROBUST ALTERNATIVE
VISION TO MARKET CONSERVATISM. AS LONG AS IT IS BELIEVED
THAT SUCH AN ALTERNATIVE DEPENDS ON MOBILIZING THE WELL-
SPRINGS OF CIVIC ALTRUISM, AND THAT SUCH WELL-SPRINGS ARE
BEING STEADILY POISONED BY THATCHERIAN GREED, THERE CAN BE
LITTLE GROUNDS FOR HOPE AT ALL. BUT THE HISTORY OF
CITIZENSHIP SHOULD SHOW THAT THE 20TH CENTURY CITIZENSHIP OF
ENTITLEMENT WAS NOT BUILT ON ALTRUISM SO MUCH AS EMERGING
AWARENESS OF THE INDISSOLUBLE INTERDEPENDENCE OF PRIVATE AND
PUBLIC UTILITIES IN THE MODERN WORLD.

04541 IKENBERRY, G.J.
RETHINKING THE ORIGINS OF AMERICAN HEGEMONY
POLITICAL SCIENCE QUARTERLY, 104(3) (FAL 89), 375-400.
G. JOHN IKENBERRY EXPLORES UNITED STATES POLICIES TOWARD
EUROPEAN POSTWAR RECONSTRUCTION AND INTERNATIONAL ORDER IN
AN EFFORT TO UNDERSTAND THE ORIGINS AND NATURE OF AMERICAN
HEGEMONIC POWER. HE ARGUES THAT DESPITE THE PREPONDERANCE OF
AMERICAN ECONOMIC AND MILITARY CAPABILITIES AFTER WORLD WAR
II, THE UNITED STATES WAS LESS SUCCESSFUL IN CARRYING OUT
ITS POSTWAR POLICIES THAN OFTEN THOUGHT.

04542 IMBERT, C.
THE END OF FRENCH EXCEPTIONALISM
FOREIGN AFFAIRS, 68(4) (FAL 89), 48-60.
THE PARTICULARLY FRENCH PASSION THAT LEADS INTELLECTUALS
AND POLITICIANS TO WANT TO BUILD SOCIETY ACCORDING TO
THEORETICAL CONSTRUCTS IS COMING TO AN END. IT WAS BORN FROM
A REVOLUTIONARY MYTHOLOGY AND IT IS DYING AT A TIME WHEN
THAT MYTHOLOGY IS FADING AWAY. THE CURRENT PHRASE IN FRANCE
IS "THE REVOLUTION IS OVER," WHICH MEANS THAT MODERN
HISTORIANS HAVE BLOWN TO PIECES ITS LEGENDARY DIMENSION AND
THAT, ABOVE ALL, THE LONG IDEOLOGICAL FURROW PLOWED BY THE
COUNTRY'S HISTORY THROUGH THE TWO CENTURIES SINCE THE FRENCH
REVOLUTION IS DRAWING TO AN END.

04543 INAYATULLAH
SOCIAL SCIENCES IN PAKISTAN: AN EVALUATION
INTERNATIONAL SOCIAL SCIENCE JOURNAL, (122) (NOV 89),
617-633.
THE AUTHOR TRACES THE DEVELOPMENT OF SOCIAL SCIENCES IN
PAKISTAN AND EVALUATES THE PRESENT STATE OF SOCIAL SCIENCES
THERE. THE DIFFUSION OF SOCIAL SCIENCES IN THE INDIAN
SUBCONTINENT WAS SLOW, PARTICULARLY IN THOSE AREAS NOW
COMPRISING PAKISTAN. SINCE INDEPENDENCE AND PARTICULARLY
DURING THE 1960'S, SOCIAL SCIENCES PICKED UP MOMENTUM IN
PAKISTAN. BY 1983, THERE WERE ABOUT SIXTY SOCIAL SCIENCE
DEPARTMENTS IN TWELVE UNIVERSITIES. IN ADDITION, THERE WERE
APPROXIMATELY ONE DOZEN INSTITUTES IN THE PUBLIC SECTOR
ENGAGED IN SOCIAL SCIENCE RESEARCH, AND A LARGE NUMBER OF
GOVERNMENT IN-SERVICE TRAINING INSTITUTIONS USING SOCIAL
SCIENCES IN THEIR TRAINING.

04544 INAYATULLAH, N.
LABOR AND DIVISION OF LABOR: CONCEPTUAL AMBIGUITIES IN
POLITICAL ECONOMY
DISSERTATION ABSTRACTS INTERNATIONAL, 49(10) (APR 89),
3142-A.
USING TEXTUAL ANALYSIS, THIS STUDY TRACES THE DIVISION
OF LABOR IN MODERN POLITICAL ECONOMY BACK TO CLASSICAL
POLITICAL ECONOMY, PARTICULARLY SMITH AND MARX. A CRITIQUE

OF THEIR CONCEPTUALIZATION OF THE DIVISION OF LABOR IS USED
TO SHED LIGHT ON MODERN USES OF THE TERM, PARTICULARLY IN
WALLERSTEIN. IT IS DEMONSTRATED THAT MODERN AMBITUITIES
INHERENT IN THE TERM ORIGINATED IN THE INSECURE FOUNDATIONS
OF CLASSICAL THEORIES.

04545 INBAR, E.
THE "NO CHOICE WAR" DEBATE IN ISRAEL
JOURNAL OF STRATEGIC STUDIES, 12(1) (MAR 89), 22-37.
THE ACRIMONIOUS DEBATE IN ISRAEL OVER THE INVASION OF
LEBANON UNQUESTIONABLY REFLECTS A RISE IN WIDESPREAD TENSION
AND DEEP CLEAVAGE IN ISRAELI SOCIETY. THIS ARTICLE FOCUSES
ON ONE ASPECT OF THE CONTROVERSY, THE POSITION OF THE
ISRAELI POLITICAL ELITE ON THE WAR. THE AUTHOR EXAMINES THE
VARIOUS WAYS IN WHICH THE CONCEPT OF A "NO CHOICE WAR" HAS
BEEN UNDERSTOOD AND THE GENERAL TENDENCY TO VIEW WAS AS A
PHENOMENON OVER WHICH ISRAEL HAS LITTLE CONTROL.

04546 INBAR, M.; YUCHTMAN-YAAR, E.
THE PEOPLE'S IMAGE OF CONFLICT RESOLUTION: ISRAELIS AND
PALESTINIANS
JOURNAL OF CONFLICT RESOLUTION, 33(1) (MAR 89), 37-66.
THIS ARTICLE PRESENTS A COMPARISON OF POLITICAL
PREFERENCES FOR SOLUTIONS TO THE ISRAELIARAB CONFLICT OF
THREE SAMPLES OF RESPONDENTS SYNCHRONOUSLY INTERVIEWED:
ISRAELI JEWS, ISRAELI ARABS, AND WEST BANK ARABS. THE
RESULTS INDICATE NO SOLUTION IS SIMULTANEOUSLY ENDORSED AT
THE GRASS ROOTS BY A PLURALITY OF ISRAELI JEWS ON THE ONE
HAND, AND ISRAELI ARABS OR WEST BANK ARABS ON THE OTHER.
NONETHELESS, BOTH JEWS AND ARABS DISTINGUISH BETWEEN IDEAL
(COVETED) SOLUTIONS, AND REALITY-BOUND ONES THEY COULD LIVE
WITH AND WOULD ACCEPT. WITHIN NATIONALITIES, ATTITUDES VARY
TO A LIMITED EXTENT ACCORDING TO SOCIAL CHARACTERISTICS SUCH
AS EDUCATION AND RELIGIOSITY. ADDITIONALLY, AMONG ISRAELI
ARABS ATTITIDES ARE SIGNIFICANTLY AFFECTED BY LOCALITY OF
RESIDENCE, ESPECIALLY AMONG RURAL DWELLERS, WHICH IS A
REMINDER OF THE ENDURING RELEVANCE OF THE TRADITIONAL-MODERN
DIMENSION OF ANALYSIS FOR THIS POPULATION.

04547 INBARI, P.
ELECTIONS IN JORDAN: TEST RUN FOR THE TERRITORIES?
NEW OUTLOOK, 32(11-12 (297-298)) (NOV 89), 43-44.
THE WEST AND EAST BANKS OF THE JORDAN RIVER ARE TIED TO
EACH OTHER. THE INTIFADA AFFECTS NOT ONLY THE PALESTINIANS
IN THE OCCUPIED TERRITORIES, BUT THEIR BROTHERS AND SISTERS
ACROSS THE RIVER AS WELL. IF ANYONE NEEDED PROOF OF THIS,
GOT IT WITH THE VICTORY OF THE RELIGIOUS LISTS IN THE
JORDANIAN GENERAL ELECTIONS (NOVEMBER 8, 1989), WHICH CAN BE
VIEWED AS A KIND OF TEST RUN FOR THOSE PLANNED FOR THE
OCCUPIED TERRITORIES. MOST OF THE SUPPORT FOR THE ISLAMIC
LISTS CAME FROM PALESTINIAN AREAS OF JORDAN, AND IT IS
REASONABLE TO ESTIMATE THAT AT LEAST HALF OF THE EAST BANK
PALESTINIANS VOTED FOR LISTS SIMILAR TO HAMAS OR THE ISLAMIC
JIHAD MOVEMENTS IN THE OCCUPIED TERRITORIES. THE SUCCESS OF
THESE ISLAMIC GROUPS IS THEREFORE LIKELY TO BE EVEN MORE
IMPRESSIVE IN ELECTIONS IN THE WEST BANK AND GAZA.

04548 INBARI, P.
THE REAL MESSAGE
NEW OUTLOOK, 32(1 (287)) (JAN 89), 19-20.
FOR THE MOST PART, ISRAELIS TOOK NOTE ONLY OF THE
EXTERNAL, SUPERFICIAL SIGNALS THAT EMERGED FROM THE
PALESTINE NATIONAL COUNCIL DEBATES IN ALGERIA, THEREBY
MISSING THE PROFOUND HISTORICAL MESSAGES OF THE COUNCIL. IT
IS NECESSARY TO STUDY THE DECLARATION OF THE INDEPENDENT
PALESTINIAN STATE ALONG WITH UN RESOLUTION 181 AND
RESOLUTION 242 TO UNDERSTAND THE TRUE SIGNIFICANCE OF THE
MEETING.

04549 INDRA, A.
CZECHOSLOVAKIA, FEBRUARY 1948: DIALECTICS OF REVOLUTION
WORLD MARXIST REVIEW, 31(2) (FEB 88), 13-22.
THE MAIN RESULT OF THE NATIONAL DEMOCRATIC REVOLUTION
WAS THE REBIRTH OF THE STATE INDEPENDENCE OF THE CZECH AND
SLOVAK PEOPLES. THE COMMUNISTS' DEDICATION AND VALOUR IN THE
STRUGGLE AGAINST FASCISM AND THEIR ROLE IN THE RESISTANCE AT
HOME AND ABROAD WERE FORCEFUL PROOF THAT THE COMMUNIST PARTY
OF CZECHOSLOVAKIA WAS A MOST CONSISTENT DEFENDER OF NATIONAL
INTERESTS AND THAT THE REBORN REPUBLIC COULD NOT BE GOVERNED
WITHOUT IT. AS FOR THE RIGHT POLITICAL PARTIES OF THE BIG
BOURGEOISIE, THEIR 'HURRAY-PATROITISM' CRUMBLED DOWN IN THE
FACE OF NAZISM AND THEY THEMSELVES ULTIMATELY LOST FACE.

04550 INGLE, S.
CHANGE, POLITICS AND THE PARTY SYSTEM
PARLIAMENTARY AFFAIRS, 42(1) (JAN 89), 23-36.
THE ARTICLE ATTACKS THE NOTION OF A LOGICAL, RATIONAL,
AND STABLE TWO-PARTY SYSTEM IN GREAT BRITAIN. IT MAINTAINS
THAT THE HISTORY OF BRITISH POLITICAL PARTIES INDICATES A
DIVERSITY, COMPLEXITY, AND CAPACITY FOR CHANGE WHICH RENDERS
THE "TWO-PARTY" LABEL QUITE MISLEADING. THE FACT THAT
POLITICAL PARTIES HAVE CHANGED PROFOUNDLY IN THE PAST SEEMS
TO INDICATE THE PROPENSITY FOR FUTURE CHANGE AS WELL. THE
AUTHOR CONCLUDES THAT THERE IS NO SOUND, RATIONAL BASIS FOR

THE ASSUMPTION THAT THE CURRENT SYSTEM IS OPTIMAL OR
SUPERIOR TO OTHER SYSTEMS AND CALLS FOR A "CHANGE OF
GOVERNMENT" IN GREAT BRITAIN.

04551 INGRAM, D.
COMMONWEALTH FOR A NEW WORLD
ROUND TABLE, (312) (OCT 89), 383-392.
THIS ARTICLE EXPLORES THE PART THE COMMONWEALTH CAN PLAY
AS THE OLD GROUPINGS THAT WERE MOULDED IN THE 1940S AND
1950S BREAK DOWN. IT SUGGESTS THAT THE COMMONWEALTH, AS A
GROUPING OF MEDIUM AND SMALL POWERS, IS IN A POSITION TO
WATCH AND ACT ON BEHALF OF THE PEOPLES AND COUNTRIES OF
AFRICA. IT ALSO SUGGESTS THAT NEW CIRCUMSTANCES DEMAND NEW
THINKING, AND THAT MULTILATERALISM WILL RETURN TO POPULARITY.
SOUTHERN AFRICA AND HUMAN RIGHTS ARE EXPLORED AS WELL AS
OTHER ISSUES.

04552 INGRAM, D.
ELECTORAL FURORE
NEW AFRICAN, (OCT 89), 18.
THIS ARTICLE REPORTS ON THE UNACCEPTABLE ELECTORAL
SYSTEM FOISTED ON THE NAMBIANS BY THE SOUTH AFRICAN
GOVERNMENT. THE CONCERN THAT THE PROCEDURE IS SO COMPLICATED
THAT IT COULD LEAD TO DELAY, MISCALCULATION, AND
GERRYMANDERING IS ADDRESSED.

04553 INOGUCHI, T.
SHAPING AND SHARING PACIFIC DYNAMISM
PHILADELPHIA: ANLS OF AMER ACMY OF POLITICAL AND SOC
SCIENCE, (505) (SEP 89), 46-55.
THIS ARTICLE ATTEMPTS TO ELUCIDATE THE UNDERLYING
CONSIDERATIONS AND CALCULATIONS OF ONE OF THE MAJOR ACTORS
OF THE PACIFIC REGION, JAPAN, IN SHAPING AND SHARING THE
MUCH VAUNTED PACIFIC DYNAMISM. KEEPING IN MIND THE ENORMOUS
ECONOMIC VIGOR ACCOMPANIED BY A MEASURE OF UNCERTAINTY IN
PACIFIC INTERNATIONAL RELATIONS, THE ARTICLE ATTEMPTS TO
ANALYZE FROM A JAPANESE PERSPECTIVE THE CURRENT
CONFIGURATION OF IDEAS AND PRACTICES UNFOLDING IN THE REGION.
FIRST, THE MAJOR FEATURES OF PACIFIC DYNAMISM ARE
DELINEATED. SECOND, THE SUPERPOWERS' PREOCCUPATION WITH
DOMESTIC DIFFICULTIES ARE TOUCHED ON AS ONE OF THE MAJOR
TRIGGERING MECHANISMS ENCOURAGING MORE REGIONALIST FORCES
THROUGHOUT THE WORLD. THIRD, JAPANESE CALCULATIONS
SURROUNDING PACIFIC DYNAMISM ARE DELINEATED, WITH MAJOR
COUNTERACTIONS TO PACIFIC DYNAMISM BY OTHER MAJOR ACTORS
ALSO TAKEN INTO ACCOUNT.

04554 IONESCU, G.
POLITICAL UNDERCOMPREHENSION OR THE OVERLOAD OF POLITICAL
COGNITION
GOVERNMENT AND OPPOSITION, XVI(4) (AUT 89), 413-426.
THE AUTHOR FOCUSES ON THE FOLLOWING QUESTION: CAN MODERN
POLITICAL JUDGMENT ITSELF, BEFORE IT SETS POLITICAL
ENGINEERING OR POLICY-MAKING IN MOTION, COMPREHEND (IN THE
DOUBLE MEANING OF THE EXPRESSION) THE ISSUES UPON WHICH IT
SHOULD BE EXERTED IN THEIR INDIVIDUAL ESOTERICISM AND IN
THEIR COLLECTIVE ARRAY?

04555 IONESCU, G.
READING NOTES, WINTER 1989
GOVERNMENT AND OPPOSITION, 24(2) (SPR 89), 232-239.
IN THE USA, THE BUDGET PROCESS IS A POLITICAL OPERATION
WHICH IS THE RESULT OF ELECTORAL OPERATIONS AND OF THE
TECHNIQUE OF ADVERSARIAL PROMISSORY POLITICS. THE POLITICAL
ELITE IN CURRENT AMERICAN POLITICS IS TOO WEAK EVEN TO TRY
TO TELL THE VOTERS THAT THEY SHOULD ACCEPT SOME TEMPORARY
SACRIFICES IN THE SUPREME INTEREST OF THEIR COUNTRY. SELDOM
HAS THE SAYING "THEY WANT TO HAVE THEIR CAKE AND EAT IT TOO"
PROVED MORE APT THAN IN THE CASE OF THE PRESENT AMERICAN
ELECTORATE.

04556 IRESON, W.R.; IRESON, C.J.
LAOS: MARXISM IN A SUBSISTENCE RURAL ECONOMY
BULLETIN OF CONCERNED ASIAN SCHOLARS, 21(2-4) (APR 89), 59
- 75.
THIS ARTICLE PROVIDES AN OVERVIEW OF LAOS -- ITS LIFE
AND PEOPLE. IT DESCRIBES THE EARLY LAOS KINGDOMS, LAOS UNDER
THE FRENCH, THE INDEPENDENCE MOVEMENT AND THE BEGINNINGS OF
THE SECOND INDOCHINA WAR. THE THIRD COALITION AND THE PATHET
LAO VICTORY, AND THE CONSOLIDATION OF THE NEW GOVERNMENT ARE
DETAILED. CONTINUING PROBLEMS AND ISSUES OF WAR-RELATED
SITUATIONS, RELATIONS WITH OTHER COUNTRIES, THE ECONOMY,
POLITY, HEALTH, AND EDUCATION ARE EACH CONSIDERED A LOOK AT
CONTEMPORARY LAOS BEYOND THE VILLAGE IS MADE AND ECONOMIC
AND POLITICAL LIBERATION IS DISCUSSED.

04557 IRONSIDE, P.A.
THE DEVELOPMENT OF BERTRAND RUSSELL'S SOCIAL AND POLITICAL
THOUGHT, #1895-1938
DISSERTATION ABSTRACTS INTERNATIONAL, 49(10) (APR 89),
3142-A.
THE AUTHOR STUDIES THE SOCIAL AND POLITICAL THOUGHT OF
BERTRAND RUSSELL IN TERMS OF RESTORING IT TO ITS IMMEDIATE
INTELLECTUAL CONTEXT AND RELOCATING IT WITHIN THE TRADITION

OF LIBERAL CULTURAL CRITICISM. RUSSELL IS DISCUSSED BOTH AS AN EDWARDIAN INTELLECTUAL AND AS A WRITER WHO SUSTAINED THE CLERISY TRADITION OF ENGLISH CULTURAL CRITICISM. THE STUDY IS ORGANIZED AROUND A DETAILED ANALYSIS OF "PRINCIPLES OF SOCIAL RECONSTRUCTION."

04558 IRVINE, L.
CRISES OF THE LEGITIMATE: MATT COHEN AND TIMOTHY FINDLEY
AMERICAN REVIEW OF CANADIAN STUDIES, XIX(1) (SPR 89), 15-23.
THE WAYS THAT NOVELISTS RESPOND TO THE CULTURAL CRISES PROMULGATED BY ESSAYISTS AND CRITICS VARY CONSIDERABLE. THE TWO OF CONCERN HERE, THE CANADIANS MATT COHEN AND TIMOTHY FINDLEY, USE THEIR MANY NOVELS AND SHORT STORIES, THEIR INTERVIEWS, JOURNALISM, ESSAYS AND LITERARY CRITICISM TO ILLUSTRATE OVER AND OVER AGAIN THEIR INTERPRETATIONS OF WHAT IT MEANS TO BE MEMBERS OF A "NEW WORLD" NATION, OF HOW POST-COLONIAL COUNTRIES MAINTAIN THEIR LINKS WITH THE CULTURES AND HISTORIES OF THE PAST, OF THE RELATIONSHIPS THAT CONTINUE TO EXIST BETWEEN NORTH AMERICA AND EUROPE (PERHAPS BECAUSE THEY ARE CANADIAN WRITERS, COHEN AND FINDLEY PAY PARTICULAR ATTENTION TO ENGLAND AND FRANCE), OF THE PECULIAR INTERSECIONS BETWEEN PRIVATE AND PUBLIC EXPERIENCE, OF THE RELATIONSHIPS BETWEEN VARIOUS TECHNOLOGIES AND THE HUMANITIES, BETWEEN SCIENCE AND CULTURE, AND OF THE ETHICAL ROLE OF THE IMAGINATIVE WRITER IN THE LATTER PART OF THE TWENTIETH CENTURY. BOTH OF THEM REPEATEDLY ARTICULATE THE BREAKDOWN OF CULTURAL HOMOGENEITY. THEY ACKNOWLEDGE THAT WESTERN INSTITUTIONS, AS THESE INTERSECT WITH AND INFLUENCED BY HISTORY, PHILOSOPHY, RELIGION AND LITERATURE, ARE NOT STABLE, AND THAT THE NARRATIVES THAT EXPLAIN THEM AND TO WHICH THEY OFTEN GIVE RISE NEED CONSTANT REVISION.

04559 IRWIN, G.; VAN HOLSTEYN, J.
DECLINE OF THE STRUCTURED MODEL OF ELECTORAL COMPETITION
WEST EUROPEAN POLITICS, 12(1) (JAN 89), 21-41.
THE DUTCH POLITICAL PARTY SYSTEM IS TO A GREAT EXTENT THE RESULT OF DEVELOPMENTS DURING THE NINETEENTH CENTURY. SEPARATE POLITICAL PARTIES EMERGED FOR THE MOST IMPORTANT SUB-CULTURAL GROUPS IN THE SOCIETY - CATHOLICS, PROTESTANTS, AND WORKERS - AS WELL AS FOR THE MORE ESTABLISHED LIBERALS. FROM THE TIME OF THE INTRODUCTION OF UNIVERSAL SUFFRAGE UNTIL THE MID-1960S FIVE POLITICAL PARTIES DOMINATED POLITICS, AND ELECTORAL CHOICE WAS HIGHLY STRUCTURED ALONG THE LINES OF SOCIAL GROUPS. IN THE 1960S CHANGES BEGAN TO OCCUR THAT AFFECTED THE RELATIONSHIP BETWEEN THE INDIVIDUAL, THE GROUP, AND THE PARTIES. THIS WAS PARTICULARLY IMPORTANT FOR THE RELIGIOUS PARTIES AS CHURCH ATTENDANCE DECLINED AND THE NUMBER OF PERSONS INDICATING NO RELIGIOUS PREFERENCE INCREASED. ECONOMIC DEVELOPMENTS PRODUCED CHANGES IN THE CLASS STRUCTURE THAT ALSO AFFECTED ELECTORAL RESULTS. ANALYSIS OF VOTER CHOICE OVER THE PAST 20 YEARS SHOWS THAT THE VOTE IS FAR LESS STRUCTURED ALONG CLASS AND RELIGIOUS LINES THAN IT HAD BEEN DURING THE EARLIER PERIOD.

04560 IRWIN, G.; VAN HOLSTEYN, J.
TOWARDS A MORE OPEN MODEL OF COMPETITION
WEST EUROPEAN POLITICS, 12(1) (JAN 89), 112-138.
THE ARTICLE ANALYZES THE MANY CHANGES THAT HAVE OCCURRED IN THE NETHERLANDS DURING THE PAST TWO DECADES. IN TERMS OF ELECTORAL POLITICS, RELIGION AND CLASS NO LONGER PROVIDE A SUFFICIENT EXPLANATION OF VOTER CHOICE. THE TWO IDEOLOGICAL DIMENSIONS--SOCIO-ECONOMIC AND RELIGIOUS-SECULAR--CONTINUE TO DEFINE "HEARTLANDS" IN WHICH PARTIES CAN RELY ON CONSIDERABLE SUPPORT, BUT A "BATTLEFIELD" ALSO EXISTS IN THE IDEOLOGICAL ISSUE SPACE IN WHICH PARTIES COMPETE FOR SUPPORT. THE MODEL OF VOTER CHOICE HAS MOVED FROM HIGHLY STRUCTURED TO A MORE OPEN MODEL OF COMPETITION.

04561 IRWIN, T.H.
SOCRATES AND ATHENIAN DEMOCRACY
PHILOSOPHY AND PUBLIC AFFAIRS, 18(2) (SPR 89), 184-205.
THE MAIN EXPLICIT AIM OF I.F. STONE'S BOOK THE TRIAL OF SOCRATES, IN HISTORICAL--TO DISCOVER THE HISTORICAL TRUTH ABOUT SOCRATES, HIS DOCTRINES, AND THE ATTITUDE OF THE ATHENIAN PUBLIC TO THE MAN AND THE DOCTRINES. THA AUTHOR OF THIS ARTICLE CONTENDS, HOWEVER, THAT STONE'S ERRORS ARE SO FREQUENT AND SO SERIOUS THAT NO READERS SHOULD SUPPOSE THEY HAVE BEEN GIVEN GOOD REASONS FOR BELIEVING WHAT HE SAYS ABOUT SOCRATES. HE FAILS EVEN TO RAISE SOME OF THE FUNDAMENTAL QUESTIONS THAT HAVE BEEN DISCUSSED BY STUDENTS OF SOCRATES. HIS HISTORICAL JUDGMENTS ARE ARBITRARY. AND HIS ACCOUNT OF SOCRATES' PHILOSOPHY IS A CARICATURE BASED ON MISUNDERSTANDING.

04562 IRWIN, Z.
ISRAEL AND THE SOVIET UNION: A SLOW THAW
WORLD TODAY, 45(5) (MAY 89), 74-76.
MIKHAIL GORBACHEV'S ACCESSION TO GENERAL SECRETARY OF THE SOVIET COMMUNIST PARTY IN 1985 WAS FOLLOWED BY THE CESSATION OF VITUPERATIVE SOVIET ANTI-ZIONIST PROPAGANDA AND THE BREAKING OF THE TABOOS OF HIGH-LEVEL DIPLOMATIC CONTACT BETWEEN THE USSR AND ISRAEL. SOVIET-ISRAELI RELATIONS SINCE THEN SUGGEST A PROGRESSIVE, IF AWKWARD, EXERCISE IN PHASES

THAT SEEK TO DEMONSTRATE MUTUAL CREDIBILITY WHILE ASSURING THIRD-PARTY CRITICS OF BOTH GOVERNMENTS THAT RAPPROCHEMENT WILL NOT COME CHEAPLY. THE SOVIETS HAVE REGISTERED NOT ONLY A PREDICTABLE RENEWAL OF INTEREST IN THE ARAB-ISRAELI CONFLICT BUT ALSO A DESIRE TO ADVANCE BILATERAL RELATIONS. THE TWO GOALS MAY NOT BE EASILY RECONCILED.

04563 ISA CONDE, N.
THE TIME OF REVOLUTIONS IS NOT PAST
WORLD MARXIST REVIEW, 32(10) (OCT 89), 3-8.
THIS PAPER WRITTEN BY GENERAL SECRETARY, NARCISO ISA CONDE, OF THE DOMINICAN COMMUNIST PARTY, ADVOCATES THAT REVOLUTIONS RENEW THE WORLD AND THAT EVERY SIGNIFICANT ERA IN HISTORY HAS BEEN BORN IN THE CRUCIBLE OF REVOLUTIONARY STRUGGLE. IT DETAILS THE LESSONS OF HISTORY AND NEW TYPES OF REVOLUTIONS. IT DESCRIBES THE PRICE AND FORMS OF STRUGGLE, REASSESSES THE ROLE OF DEMOCRACY AND ASSESSES THE PROSPECTS FOR THE FUTURE.

04564 ISAAC, J.C.
ON REBELLION AND REVOLUTION
DISSENT, (SUM 89), 376-384.
IN "THE REBEL," ALBERT CAMUS OFFERS A POLITICAL VISION THAT IS NEITHER MARXIST NOR LIBERAL. IT FALLS WITHIN THE RANGE OF DEMOCRATIC SOCIALISM. BUT CAMUS'S DEMOCRATIC SOCIALISM IS NOT SIMPLY A JOINING OF DEMOCRATIC NORMS TO A SOCIALIST VISION. IT IS BASED UPON A MUCH MORE SERIOUS QUESTIONING OF THE OPTIMISM AND HUMANISM OF THE ENLIGHTENMENT. IT IS A DEMOCRATIC SOCIALISM WITHOUT APPEAL, WITH NO RELIANCE UPON ANY KIND OF TRANSCENDENTAL IMPERATIVE AND WITH NO GUARANTEE OF HISTORICAL SUCCESS.

04565 ISAACMAN, A.F.
THE PATH TO PEACE
AFRICA REPORT, 34(6) (NOV 89), 50-54.
PEACE REMAINS THE PRINCIPAL ITEM ON PRESIDENT JOAQUIM CHISSANO'S AGENDA, FOR WITHOUT IT, THE VERY SURVIVAL OF THE MOZAMBICAN NATION IS THREATENED. KEY TO THE PEACE PROCESS ARE DIPLOMATIC EFFORTS BY MOZAMBIQUE AND THE INTERNATIONAL COMMUNITY TO PERSUADE SOUTH AFRICA TO ABANDON RENAMO.

04566 ISARD, W.; DUNCAN, K.
A THOUSAND AND ONE PH.D. DISSERTATION TOPICS: THE SUMMARY OF THE 1988 THIRD WORLD PEACE SCIENCE CONGRESS
CONFLICT MANAGEMENT AND PEACE SCIENCE, 10(2) (SPR 89), 77-98.
THIS ARTICLE EXAMINES THE NUMEROUS PAPERS PRESENTED AT THE WORLD PEACE SCIENCE CONGRESS. THE CENTRAL FOCUS OF THE CONGRESS WAS ON WAR AND PEACE AND THE PAPERS EXPLORED TERRORISM, GUERRILLA WARFARE AS WELL AS HOW TO MITIGATE THE ARMS RACE AND TO LESSEN MILITARY EXPENDITURES

04567 ISASI-DIAS, A.
MUJERISTAS: A NAME OF OUR OWN
THE CHRISTIAN CENTURY, 106(18) (MAY 89), 560-561.
THE AUTHOR EXPLORES THE SEARCH OF HISPANIC FEMINISTS FOR A PROPER NAME FOR THEMSELVES. SHE OPTS FOR "MUJERISTA" (WOMANIST). SHE DISCUSSES THE EMERGENCE OF MUJERISTA THEOLOGY: A COMBINATION OF FEMINISTIC THEOLOGY, LATIN AMERICAN LIBERATION THEOLOGY, AND CULTURAL THEOLOGY.

04568 ISLAM, N.
COLONIAL LEGACY, ADMINISTRATIVE REFORM AND POLITICS: PAKISTAN 1947-1987
PUBLIC ADMINISTRATION AND DEVELOPMENT, 9(3) (JUN 89), 253-270.
THE PAPER PRESENTS AN ANALYSIS OF THE KEY ELEMENTS OF THE BRITISH COLONIAL LEGACY WHICH LAID DOWN THE FOUNDATIONS OF PAKISTAN'S ADMINISTRATIVE SYSTEM. IT REVIEWS THE MAJOR REFORM PROPOSALS, THEIR OUTCOMES AND THEIR POLITICAL CONTEXT DURING THE LAST FOUR DECADES OF PAKISTAN'S EXISTENCE. IT ALSO DISCUSSES THE IMPACT OF REFORM ON THE KEY ADMINISTRATIVE INSTITUTIONS WHICH DOMINATE THE BUREAUCRATIC SYSTEM IN THE COUNTRY. IT CONCLUDES THAT THE PERSISTENT COLONIAL LEGACY, THE FRAGMENTATION OF POLITICAL POWER, AND THE ABSENCE OF EFFECTIVE POLITICAL INSTITUTIONS HAVE PREVENTED THE IMPLEMENTATION OF GLOBAL ADMINISTRATIVE REFORM IN PAKISTAN.

04569 ISLAM, S.
EUROPEAN AID TO PALESTINE
MIDDLE EAST INTERNATIONAL, (365) (DEC 89), 10.
USING STRONGER THAN USUAL LANGUAGE, LEADERS OF THE EUROPEAN COMMUNITY DEPLORED THE "CONTINUOUS DETERIORATION OF THE SITUATION IN THE OCCUPIED TERRITORIES," AND VOICED THEIR CONCERN OVER ISRAEL'S FAILURE TO GUARANTEE BASIC HUMAN RIGHTS IN AREAS SUCH AS EDUCATION AND HEALTH IN PALESTINE. THEY ALSO AGREED TO DOUBLE THE AMOUNT OF DIRECT FINANCIAL AID TO PALESTINIANS IN THE OCCUPIED TERRITORIES AND "SUBSTANTIALLY INCREASE" ALL OTHER FORMS OF INDIRECT ASSISTANCE TO GAZA AND THE WEST BANK.

04570 ISMCHENKO, I.; KMAZANOV, V.
SOVIET TRADE AND ECONOMIC INTERCOURSE WITH LATIN AMERICAN

DEVELOPING COUNTRIES
FOREIGN TRADE, 8 (1988), 26-30.
THIS ARTICLE ANALYSES THE EXISTING STATE OF TRADE BETWEEN THE USSR AND LATIN AMERICAN COUNTRIES. DUE TO THE FACT THAT MUTUAL TRADE REMAINS SMALL IN VOLUME AND LIMITED IN THE RANGE OF GOODS TRADED, VARIOUS METHODS OF INCREASING TRADE ARE EXPLORED. THESE INCLUDE: INTERRELATED EXPORT/IMPORT OPERATIONS, THE CONSTRUCTION OF INTERPRISES ON A COMPENSATION BASIS, THE ESTABLISHMENT OF MIXED FIRMS AND JOINT VENTURES AND THE ESTABLISHMENT OF STABLE LINKS INVOLVING THE PRODUCTION SECTOR OF PARTNERS, THE USSR SEES LATIN AMERICAN COUNTRIES AS PROMISING TRADING PARTNERS.

04571 ISPAHANI, M.
VARIETIES OF MUSLIM EXPERIENCE
WILSON QUARTERLY, XIII(4) (AUT 89), 63-72.
THE AUTHOR SURVEYS THE VARIETY OF CONTEMPORARY MUSLIM CULTURES AND STATES. SHE FINDS THAT THE DIVERSITY ALLOWS MANY LIBERAL AND MODERATE MUSLIMS TO CHALLENGE THE FUNDAMENTALISTS' NOTION OF A SINGLE, ORTHODOX MUSLIM STATE WITHOUT ABANDONING THE VISION OF A UNIFIED COMMUNITY OF BELIEVERS.

04572 ISRAELI, R.
CONSUL DE FRANCE IN MID-NINETEENTH-CENTURY CHINA
MODERN ASIAN STUDIES, 23(4) (OCT 89), 671-704.
THE ARTICLE EXAMINES TWO FRENCH CONSULATES IN MID-NINETEENTH CENTURY CHINA. THE CONSULATE IN CANTON REPRESENTS THE FIRST AND MOST INTENSE INITIAL ARENA OF CONFLICT BETWEEN CHINESE AND FOREIGNERS DURING THE BATTLE FOR OPENING UP CHINA. THE CONSULATE IN HANKOW, AN INLAND CITY OF LESSER IMPORTANCE, OPENED UP AT THE SECOND STAGE OF WESTERN PENETRATION INTO THE HEARTLAND OF CHINA. THE ACCOUNTS OF THE FRENCH CONSULS IN CHINA REVEAL THE EXTENT TO WHICH THEIR TEMPERAMENT, WORLD-VIEW, BACKGROUND, ZEAL, LUST, AND LIFESTYLE, COULD DETERMINE, NO LESS THAN THE DICTATED OR PERCEIVED INTEREST OF THEIR COUNTRY, THE RESULTS OF THEIR MISSION TO CHINA.

04573 ISRAELYAN, V.
ON DIPLOMATIC NEGOTIATIONS
INTERNATIONAL AFFAIRS (MOSCOW), (1) (JAN 89), 75-84.
THE AUTHOR DISCUSSES THE CLASSIC APPROACH TO DIPLOMATIC NEGOTIATIONS AND RECENT U.S.-SOVIET TALKS ON ARMS LIMITATION.

04574 ISSAHI, C.
EMPIRE BUILDERS, CULTURE MAKERS, AND CULTURE IMPRINTERS
JOURNAL OF INTERDISCIPLINARY HISTORY, XX(2) (AUT 89), 177-196.
THE AUTHOR EXPLAINS THE DIFFERENCE BETWEEN EMPIRE BUILDERS, CULTURE MAKERS, AND CULTURE IMPRINTERS. THEN HE STUDIES WHAT ENABLED CERTAIN PEOPLES, AND NOT OTHERS, TO IMPRINT THEIR LANGUAGE AND CULTURE OVER A VAST AREA. FOR EXAMPLE, WHY DID THE ROMANS AND NOT THE GREEKS FOUND A MAJOR CULTURAL AREA? DID THEY ACHIEVE THIS FEAT BECAUSE THEY WERE MORE SUCCESSFUL AS EMPIRE BUILDERS AND POSSESSED GREATER POLITICAL AND MILITARY SKILL? WHAT OTHER FACTORS WERE IMPORTANT?

04575 ISSAHI, C.
REAPPRAISING THE FRENCH REVOLUTION: THERE WERE COSTS AS WELL AS BENEFITS
CURRENT, (317) (NOV 89), 4-9.
THE ACHIEVEMENTS OF THE FRENCH REVOLUTION WERE GREAT AND HAVE RECEIVED THEIR DUE. BUT LIKE ALL HUMAN EVENTS, IT HAD ITS COSTS, WHICH HAVE ATTRACTED FAR LESS ATTENTION. IN THIS ARTICLE, THE AUTHOR ENDEAVORS TO POINT OUT THESE COSTS AND ASSIST THE READER IN JUDGING TO WHAT EXTENT THEY OFFSET THE REVOLUTION'S POSITIVE ASPECTS.

04576 ISSRAELIAN, E.
GORBACHEV'S MURMANSK INITIATIVE AND CONFIDENCE BUILDING MEASURES IN THE ARCTIC
ETUDES INTERNATIONALES, XX(1) (MAR 89), 61-70.
IN HIS SPEECH AT MURMANSK ON OCTOBER 1, 1987, GENERAL SECRETARY GORBACHEV PRESENTED A PROGRAMME TO RADICALLY LOWER THE LEVEL OF MILITARY CONFRONTATION IN THE ARCTIC AND PROPOSED A NUMBER OF CONFIDENCE-BUILDING MEASURES. THE MURMANSK INITIATIVE REPRESENTS A SIGNIFICANT CONTRIBUTION TO THE WHOLE PROCESS OF CONFIDENCE-BUILDING BY PROPOSING, IN PARTICULAR: TO LIMIT THE NUMBER OF LARGE EXERCISES BY NAVAL AND AIR FORCES IN THE NORTHERN SEAS; TO INVITE OBSERVERS TO SUCH EXERCISES; TO INCLUDE BARENTS SEA, ALONG WITH OTHER NORTHERN SEAS, IN A ZONE OF PEACE; TO BAN ANTI-SUBMARINE ACTIVITIES IN AGREED AREAS OF THE NORTHERN AND WESTERN ATLANTIC; TO INCLUDE THE REDUCTION OF MILITARY ACTIVITIES IN THE ARCTIC ON THE AGENDA OF THE SECOND STAGE OF THE CONFERENCE ON CBM AND DISARMAMENT IN EUROPE; TO REDUCE NAVAL ACTIVITIES IN INTERNATIONAL STRAITS; AND TO PURSUE THE ESTABLISHMENT OF A NORDIC NUCLEAR WEAPON-FREE ZONE FOR WHICH THE SOVIET UNION WOULD ACT AS GUARANTOR.

04577 ISUPOV, V.
DIRECT TIES: ECONOMIC CONDITIONS.

FOREIGN TRADE, 9 (1988), 3-6.
THIS ARTICLE ADDRESSES THE QUESTION, "TO WHAT EXTENT DO THE ECONOMIC CONDITIONS OF THE EXISTING MECHANISM OF ECONOMIC MANAGEMENT MEET THE ECONOMIC INTERESTS OF ENTERPRISES AND ASSOCIATIONS?" IT STUDIES FORMAL RIGHTS AND REALITIES, THE DIRECT TIES MATERIAL BACKUP PROBLEMS AND PRICE INFORMATION PROBLEMS IN THE CMEA COUNTRIES.

04578 ITO, K.
AN EMERGING REGIONAL REGIME: ASEAN AS THE MINI-MAX REGIME
DISSERTATION ABSTRACTS INTERNATIONAL, 50(2) (AUG 89), 537-A.
IN ORDER TO UNDERSTAND WHY AND HOW ASEAN WORKS, THE AUTHOR EXAMINES FOUR CASE STUDIES: THE PHILIPPINES' TERRITORIAL CLAIM TO SABAH, INTRA-ASEAN TRADE LIBERALIZATION, ASEAN'S AND THE INDIVIDUAL ASEAN STATES' APPROACH TO JAPAN AS THE DOMINANT ECONOMIC PARTNER, AND ASEAN'S AND THE INDIVIDUAL ASEAN STATES' APPROACH TO THE KAMPUCHEA CONFLICT.

04579 ITOH, M.
JAPANESE PERCEPTIONS OF THE SOVIET UNION: JAPANESE FOREIGN POLICY ELITES' PERCEPTIONS OF THE SOVIET UNION AND JAPANESE FOREIGN POLICY TOWARDS THE SOVIET UNION
DISSERTATION ABSTRACTS INTERNATIONAL, 50(5) (NOV 89), 1428-A.
THE AUTHOR STUDIES JAPANESE FOREIGN POLICY ELITES' PERCEPTIONS OF THE USSR AND HOW THEY INFLUENCE JAPAN'S FOREIGN POLICY DECISION-MAKING TOWARD THE USSR. HIS THEORETICAL FRAMEWORK POSTULATES A CORRELATION AMONG EVENTS (INDEPENDENT VARIABLE), FOREIGN POLICY ELITES' PERCEPTIONS (INTERVENING VARIABLE), AND FOREIGN POLICY OUTPUTS (DEPENDENT VARIABLE).

04580 IVANOV, I.
THE STATE MONOPOLY OF FOREIGN TRADE: TODAY'S FORMS AND PROBLEMS
FOREIGN TRADE, 4 (1988), 4-6.
THIS ARTICLE TRACES STATE MONOPOLY OF FOREIGN TRADE AS IT CONTINUES TO GROW AND STRENGTHEN. THE NEED FOR AN INNOVATED APPROACH TO THE USSR'S EXTERNAL ECONOMIC RELATIONS IS EXAMINED, AS WELL AS THE NEED FOR A RESTRUCTURING OF IT, LENIN'S CRITERIA FOR ASSESSING THE METHODS OF EXTERNAL ECONOMIC RELATIONS MANAGEMENT IS REVIEWED. SOLUTIONS TO PROBLEMS IN THIS AREA, CONSIDERED A TASK FOR STATE AND PARTY, ARE ADVOCATED.

04581 IVANOV, R.
KHRUSHCHEV IN AMERICA
INTERNATIONAL AFFAIRS (MOSCOW), (11) (NOV 89), 107-114.
NIKITA KHRUSHCHEV'S VISIT TO THE UNITED STATES IN 1959 MARKED A BREAKTHROUGH IN RELATIONS BETWEEN THE TWO SUPERPOWERS OF THE COLD WAR ERA. KHRUSCHEV'S VISIT WAS CONSIDERED A SUCCESS, EVEN THOUGH ALL THE HOPES IT INSPIRED DID NOT MATERIALIZE.

04582 IVANOV, Y.
ON CAPITOL HILL
INTERNATIONAL AFFAIRS (MOSCOW), (8) (AUG 89), 91-96.
THE AUTHOR LOOKS AT THE OPERATIONS OF THE U.S. CONGRESS AND WHAT THEY MIGHT TEACH THE SOVIETS AS THEY DEMOCRATIZE THEIR OWN CONGRESS OF PEOPLE'S DEPUTIES.

04583 IVERSON, P.
PRESIDENTIAL ADDRESS: COWBOYS AND INDIANS, STOCKMEN AND ABORIGINES: THE RURAL AMERICAN WEST AND THE NORTHERN TERRITORY OF AUSTRALIA SINCE 1945
SOCIAL SCIENCE JOURNAL, 26(1) (1989), 1-14.
THE ARTICLE EXAMINES THE EXPERIENCE OF THE AMERICAN INDIANS AND THE NATIVE ABORIGINES OF AUSTRALIA AND SEEKS TO DEVELOP SOME COMMON THEMES IN THEIR HISTORY. IT OUTLINES THE COMMON IMPACT OF WORLD WAR II, ECONOMIC DEVELOPMENT, AND URBANIZATION. IT ALSO EXPLORES THE RIGHTS TO THE LAND OF BOTH PEOPLES AND THEIR MODERN IDENTITY.

04584 IYAYI, O.V.
FOREIGN INVESTORS' PERCEPTIONS OF NIGERIAN PUBLIC POLICY ON FOREIGN INVESTMENT
DISSERTATION ABSTRACTS INTERNATIONAL, 49(12) (JUN 89), 3866-A.
BECAUSE NIGERIAN FINANCIAL INSTITUTIONS ARE UNABLE TO ADEQUATELY FINANCE THE NATION'S PRIVATE SECTOR, THE IMPORTATION OF FOREIGN CAPITAL IS NECESSARY TO HELP ACHIEVE PUBLIC POLICY GOALS FOR ECONOMIC DEVELOPMENT. THIS STUDY PROBES FOREIGN INVESTOR PERCEPTIONS OF THE EFFECTS OF NIGERIAN PUBLIC POLICY ON FOREIGN INVESTMENT THERE. FINDINGS INDICATE THAT FOREIGN INVESTORS CONSIDER NIGERIAN PUBLIC POLICY TO BE A DISINCENTIVE. MOREOVER, THEY BELIEVE THAT MOST OF THE GOVERNMENT REGULATIONS HAVE FAILED TO ACHIEVE THEIR INTENDED OBJECTIVES.

04585 IYENGAR, S.
HOW CITIZENS THINK ABOUT NATIONAL ISSUES: A MATTER OF RESPONSIBILITY
AMERICAN JOURNAL OF POLITICAL SCIENCE, 33(4) (NOV 89),

878-900.
A DOMAIN-SPECIFIC MODEL OF PUBLIC OPINION IS PROPOSED IN
WHICH ATTRIBUTION OF ISSUE RESPONSIBILITY IS A SIGNIFICANT
DETERMINANT OF INDIVIDUALS' ISSUE OPINIONS AND ATTITUDES.
TWO DIMENSIONS OF ISSUE RESPONSIBILITY ARE ASSESSED: CAUSAL
RESPONSIBILITY FOCUSES ON THE ORIGINS OF THE ISSUE, WHILE
TREATMENT RESPONSIBILITY FOCUSES ON ALLEVIATION OF THE ISSUE.
THE MODEL IS TESTED WITH A SAMPLE OF FOUR ISSUES: POVERTY,
RACIAL INEQUALITY, CRIME, AND TERRORISM. THE RESULTS
INDICATE THAT FOR ALL FOUR ISSUES ATTRIBUTIONS OF
RESPONSIBILITY SIGNIFICANTLY AFFECT ISSUE OPINIONS
INDEPENDENTLY OF PARTISANSHIP, LIBERALCONSERVATIVE
ORIENTATION, INFORMATION, AND SOCIOECONOMIC STATUS. IN
GENERAL, AGENTS OF CAUSAL RESPONSIBILITY ARE VIEWED
NEGATIVELY WHILE AGENTS OF TREATMENT RESPONSIBILITY ARE
VIEWED POSITIVELY. IN CONCLUSION, THE IMPORTANCE OF DOMAIN-
SPECIFICITY FOR PUBLIC OPINION RESEARCH IS CONSIDERED.

04586 IZYUMOV, A.; KORTUNOV, A.
REDEFINING SOVIET FOREIGN POLICY
HEMISPHERE, 1(3) (SUM 89), 30-32.
THE REALIGNMENT OF THE SUPERPOWERS IS PRESENTING NEW
FOREIGN POLICY OPTIONS AND CONSTRAINTS THAT COULD BE
IMPORTANT IN LATIN AMERICA AS THE REGION PURSUES ECONOMIC
RECOVERY AND DEMOCRATIZATION. SOVIET GLASNOST AND
PERESTROIKA PROMISE TO HAVE A SIGNIFICANT REGIONAL IMPACT IN
THE COMING DECADE.

04587 JABBRA, J.G.
BUREAUCRACY AND DEVELOPMENT IN THE ARAB WORLD
JOURNAL OF ASIAN AND AFRICAN STUDIES, XXIV(1-2) (1989),
1-11.
IN THEIR EFFORTS TO MOVE THEIR COUNTRIES FORWARD SINCE
WORLD WAR II, ARAB LEADERS HAVE SEEN THE BUREAUCRACY AS
CENTRAL TO THEIR DEVELOPMENT ENDEAVORS. BUREAUCRACIES IN THE
ARAB WORLD HAVE BEEN CALLED UPON TO MAINTAIN LAW AND ORDER,
EXECUTE THE DECISIONS OF THE POLITICAL LEADERSHIP, CARRY OUT
THE ROUTINE FUNCTIONS OF STATE, AND PROMOTE SOCIO-ECONOMIC
AND POLITICAL DEVELOPMENT. IT HAS BEEN A COMMONLY-HELD
BELIEF THAT, SHOULD THE BUREAUCRACY NOT PLAY AN EFFECTIVE
ROLE IN DEVELOPMENT, POLITICAL AND SOCIO-ECONOMIC PROBLEMS
OF STAGGERING MAGNITUDE MAY ENSUE AND THREATEN TO DISLOCATE
THE VERY FABRIC OF SOCIETY. UNFORTUNATELY, ARAB COUNTRIES
HAVE LEARNED THAT THEIR BUREAUCRACIES ARE ILL-EQUIPPED TO
CARRY OUT THE DAUNTING TASK OF DEVELOPMENT.

04588 JABER, N.
FALL-OUT FROM THE SAUDI EXECUTIONS
MIDDLE EAST INTERNATIONAL, (360) (OCT 89), 7-8.
RELATIONS BETWEEN SAUDI ARABIA AND KUWAIT ARE SINGULARLY
COOL AFTER THE SAUDI EXECUTION OF 16 SH'ITE KUWAITI
NATIONALS. THE SAUDIS CLAIM THAT IRAN WAS BEHIND THE BOMBING
OF MECCA DURING THE ANNUAL HAJJ PILGRIMAGE, SUPPOSEDLY
CARRIED OUT BY THE KUWAITIS. KUWAIT, WHO IS INTENT IN
NORMALIZING RELATIONS WITH IRAN, HAVE MAINTAINED A STONY
SILENCE TOWARDS SAUDI ARABIA.

04589 JABER, N.
IRAQ AND THE KURDS: PACIFICATION THROUGH DEPORTATION
MIDDLE EAST INTERNATIONAL, (349) (APR 89), 14-15.
ACCORDING TO REPORTS FROM NORTHERN IRAQ AND KURDISH
LEADERS IN EXILE, THE REGIME OF SADDAM HUSSEIN HAS BEGUN
IMPLEMENTING PLANS TO DEPORT THOUSANDS OF KURDISH CIVILIANS
FROM THEIR HOMES. BUT RELIABLE INFORMATION ON THE SCALE OF
THE GOVERNMENT PLAN IS HARD TO COME BY.

04590 JABES, J.; ZUSSMAN, D.
ORGANIZATIONAL CULTURE IN PUBLIC BUREAUCRACIES
INTERNATIONAL REVIEW OF ADMINISTRATIVE SCIENCES, 55(1)
(MAR 89), 95-116.
THE ARTICLE STUDIES ORGANIZATIONAL CULTURE IN PUBLIC
SECTOR ORGANIZATIONS USING THE PRIVATE SECTOR AS A
COMPARISON. THE OBJECTIVE OF THE ARTICLE IS TO LOOK AT
DIFFERENCES AND SIMILARITIES, IF ANY, IN THE WAY SENIOR
MANAGERS DESCRIBE THEIR ORGANIZATION'S ORIENTATION, THEIR
ATTITUDES TOWARDS LOYALTY, THEIR PERCEPTION OF
ORGANIZATIONAL GOALS AND THE DEGREE TO WHICH THEY VIEW THEIR
ORGANIZATIONS AS BEING ORIENTED TO PEOPLE. IT FOLLOWS THE
COMPARISON BY RELATING CULTURAL DIMENSIONS TO OUTCOME
MEASURES OF WORK SATISFACTION IN ORDER TO DETERMINE THE
IMPORTANCE AND ROLE THAT ORGANIZATIONAL CULTURE PLAYS IN
PUBLIC AND PRIVATE SECTOR ORGANIZATIONS.

04591 JABLONSKY, D.
THE NAZI PARTY IN DISSOLUTION: HITLER AND THE VERBOTZEIT,
1923-1925
FRANK CASS JOURNALS, LONDON, GB, 1989, 248.
THE VERBOTZEIT REFERS TO THE PERIOD FROM 1923 TO 1925 IN
WHICH THE NAZI PARTY WAS BANNED IN BAVARIA. THIS BOOK
EXAMINES THE EFFECT THIS SUPPRESSION HAD ON THE LEADERSHIP
STRUCTURE OF THE NAZI PARTY AND ON THE CONSEQUENT POSITION
OF THAT PARTY WITHIN THE VOLKISCH MOVEMENT. MOST IMPORTANTLY,
THE FAILURE OF THE LEADERSHIP STRUCTURE WITHIN THE NAZI
PARTY AS WELL AS IN THE VOLKISCH MOVEMENT EMPHASIZED THE
PIVOTAL ROLE OF THE IMPRISONED ADOLF HITLER, WHO WAS
INCREASINGLY VIEWED BY ALL AS THE ONE PERSON CAPABLE OF
BRINGING ORDER OUT OF THE VOLKISCH CHAOS.

04592 JACKLIN, M.
CONSERVATIVE DEMOCRATS ARE VICTORIOUS IN CONNECTICUT HOUSE
STATE LEGISLATURES, 15(4) (APR 89), 13-15.
IN CONNECTICUT'S 1989 LEGISLATIVE SESSION, DEMOCRATIC
DISSIDENTS CONVINCED HOUSE REPUBLICANS TO HELP THEM OUST THE
LIBERAL SPEAKER FOR A MORE CONSERVATIVE LEADER. BUT THE
CONSERVATIVE DEMOCRATS SAID THAT THE COALITION WITH THE
REPUBLICANS WAS ONLY TEMPORARY.

04593 JACKMAN, R.W.
THE POLITICS OF ECONOMIC GROWTH, ONCE AGAIN
THE JOURNAL OF POLITICS, 51(3) (AUG 89), 646-661.
PAPERS BY LANGE AND GARRETT AND BY JACKMAN HAVE DEBATED
WHETHER THE POLITICAL AND ECONOMIC POWER OF THE LEFT
INFLUENCES ECONOMIC GROWTH IN THE WESTERN INDUSTRIAL
DEMOCRACIES. MOST RECENTLY, HICKS (1988) HAS CONCLUDED THAT
THEY DO, ONCE LANGE AND GARRETT'S MODEL IS MODIFIED, DESPITE
MY CLAIM TO THE CONTRARY. THIS PAPER SHOWS THAT THERE IS NO
EVIDENCE FOR THE CLAIMS ADVANCED BY HICKS. FIRST IT
DEMONSTRATES THAT HICKS'S ELEMENTARY REVISION IS MISGUIDED
AND INSUFFICIENT TO SALVAGE THE LANGE-GARRETT HYPOTHESIS.
SECOND, IT ESTABLISHS THAT THE ESTIMATES FOR HIS EXPANDED
MODEL ARE NOT ROBUST, BUT INSTEAD DEPEND ENTIRELY ON
INFLUENTIAL OBSERVATIONS. THIRD, IT REVIEWS SOME CRUCIAL
THEORETICAL ISSUES THAT ARE MISCONSTRUED BOTH BY LANGE AND
GARRETT AND BY HICKS AND SUGGEST AN ALTERNATIVE APPROACH TO
THE POLITICS OF ECONOMIC GROWTH.

04594 JACKSON, J.
A CALL TO COMMON GROUND
BLACK SCHOLAR, 20(1) (JAN 89), 12-18.
THE ARTICLE IS THE SPEECH DELIVERED BY JESSE JACKSON TO
THE DEMOCRATIC NATIONAL CONVENTION. HE APPEALS TO THE
"RAINBOW COALITION" TO FIND COMMON GROUND AND WORK TOGETHER
IN THE COMING MONTHS AND YEARS. COMMON GROUND IS DEEMED
NECESSARY FOR MUTUAL SURVIVAL AND NECESSARY TO REVERSE MANY
OF THE DAMAGING POLICIES OF THE REAGAN ADMINISTRATION. HE
CONCLUDED BY CHALLENGING YOUTH TO CREATE A NEW VALUE SYSTEM
AND TO "NEVER SURRENDER" TO A HIGH MORAL CHALLENGE, TO DRUGS,
TO MALNUTRITION, ILLITERACY, INEQUALITY, AND AIDS.

04595 JACKSON, J.
INTERMEDIATE STAGES ON THE ROAD TO SOCIALISM
POLITICAL AFFAIRS, LXVIII(8) (AUG 89), 19-24.
THE ARTICLE EXPLORES POLICIES AND PRACTICES DESIGNED TO
PLACE THE COMMUNIST PARTY, USA ON THE CUTTING EDGE OF THE
CLASS STRUGGLE. IT ATTEMPTS TO OUTLINE INTERMEDIATE STAGES
ON THE ROAD TO SOCIALISM AND DIVIDES FUTURE TASKS INTO THREE
AREAS: "ALLHUMANITY TASKS," "WORKING-CLASS TASKS," AND "THE
SPECIAL AND MASS TASKS" OF THE PARTY ITSELF. SPECIFIC AREAS
OF POLITICAL ACTIVITY IS ALSO SUBDIVIDED INTO THREE AREAS OF
EMPHASIS: DISARMAMENT, ANTIDISCRIMINATION, AND DEMOCRACY.
THE AUTHOR CONCLUDES THAT THE ADOPTION OF SUCH A VISION WILL
ENABLE THE PARTY TO SOLVE PROBLEMS THAT CLASS-STRUCTURED
SOCIETY CANNOT DEAL WITH.

04596 JACKSON, J.E.; KING, D.C.
PUBLIC GOODS, PRIVATE INTERESTS, AND REPRESENTATION
AMERICAN POLITICAL SCIENCE REVIEW, 83(4) (DEC 89),
1143-1164.
THE AUTHORS ESTIMATE A MODEL OF HOUSE MEMBERS' ROLL CALL
VOTING DECISIONS EMBODYING SOME HYPOTHESES ABOUT
REPRESENTATION, INCLUDING ESTIMATES OF THE INFLUENCE OF
DISTRICT OPINION ON BROAD COLLECTIVE ISSUES RELATIVE TO
PERSONAL ECONOMIC INTERESTS, OF THE EFFECT OF ELECTORAL
SECURITY ON CONSTITUENCY RESPONSIVENESS, AND OF THE
DIFFERENCE IN CONSTITUENCY AND PARTY VOTING AMONG
REPUBLICANS AND DEMOCRATS. THIS MODEL IS ESTIMATED WITH
VOTES TAKEN DURING DELIBERATIONS ON THE 1978 TAX REFORM ACT,
IMPORTANT BECAUSE IT WAS A SIGNIFICANT CHANGE FROM THE TAX
REFORMS PASSED IN THE LATE 1960S AND 1970S, MARKED THE FIRST
APPEARANCE OF THE KEMP-ROTH PROPOSED TAX CUT, AND
REPRESENTED A CONCERTED EFFORT BY REPUBLICANS TO MAKE TAX
POLICY A BROAD NATIONAL ISSUE. FINDINGS INDICATE THAT
CONSTITUENT PREFERENCES FOR REDISTRIBUTION ARE IMPORTANT
INFLUENCES ON REPRESENTATIVES' DECISIONS AND THAT
REPUBLICANS EXHIBITED A GREATER DEGREE OF PARTY VOTING THAN
THE DEMOCRATS WHILE THE DEMOCRATS BETTER REPRESENTED THEIR
CONSTITUENT'S PREFERENCES.

04597 JACKSON, J.E.
W.E.B. DU BOIS: LIGHT FOR THE PATH
POLITICAL AFFAIRS, LXVIII(7) (JUL 89), 2-6.
DU BOIS PERCEIVED THE EQUALITY, JUSTICE AND DEMOCRACY
CAUSE OF AFRICAN AMERICANS AS BEING A COMPONENT PART OF THE
GLOBAL STRUGGLE BETWEEN THE MAIN DIVISION, THE PRIMARY
CONTRADICTION OF CLASS SOCIETY. HE COUNTED AFRICAN AMERICANS
AS A PARTICULAR PART OF THAT SECTION OF HUMANKIND WHO ARE
THE WORKING PRODUCERS, THE REAL CREATORS OF MATERIAL AND
SPIRITUAL VALUES. FREEDOM COMES FROM STRUGGLE AGAINST THOSE

WHO USURPED AND ARROGATED TO THEMSELVES FOR THEIR OWN
AGGRANDIZEMENT AND POSITIONS OF POWER, THE FRUITS OF THE
LABOR AND THE CREATIVE TOIL OF OTHERS.

04598 JACKSON, J.K.
   JAPANESE INVESTMENT IN THE UNITED STATES
   CRS REVEIW, 10(6) (JUL 89), 11-13.
   JAPANESE INVESTMENT IN THE UNITED STATES INCREASED
SHARPLY DURING THE 1980'S. THE ALLURE OF THESE INVESTMENTS
PLACED STATE AND LOCAL GOVERNMENTS IN BIDDING WARS AND
FUELED THE DEBATE WITHIN CONGRESS OVER THE ADEQUACY OF THE
PRESENT SYSTEM OF COLLECTING DATA ON FOREIGN INVESTMENTS.
ANOTHER FACTOR IN THE DEBATE IS THE APPARENT EASE WITH WHICH
JAPANESE FIRMS CAN BUY AMERICAN ASSETS, CONTRASTED WITH WHAT
SOME AMERICANS VIEW AS A MORE RESTRICTIVE ENVIRONMENT ABROAD.

04599 JACKSON, M.
   PEOPLE'S TARGETS FOR THE 101ST CONGRESS
   POLITICAL AFFAIRS, LXVIII(5) (MAY 89), 13-20.
   PERHAPS MORE NOW THAN AT ANY OTHER TIME, LABOR, THE
GRASS ROOTS MOVEMENTS, AND LARGE COALITIONS ARE WORKING
TOGETHER TO DEMAND THAT CONGRESS BE RESPONSIBLE TO THE
PEOPLE THAT ELECTED THEM. THE 101ST CONGRESS HAS BEFORE IT
MANY BILLS THAT ARE CENTRAL TO THE DEMANDS OF LABOR,
COMMUNITY ORGANIZATIONS, WOMEN, RELIGIOUS GROUPS, AND CIVIL
RIGHTS COALITIONS. LABOR'S AGENDA FOR CONGRESS HAS 40 MAJOR
DEMANDS THAT RANGE FROM "AIRLINE LABOR PROTECTION" TO
"WELFARE REFORM."

04600 JACKSON, W.D.
   NEW SERVICES FOR BANKS?
   CRS REVEIW, 10(9) (OCT 89), 8-10.
   ARE BANKS IN A SPECIAL CATEGORY? OR ARE THEY JUST
ANOTHER KIND OF FIRM, LIKE FINANCE COMPANIES? IF BANKS ARE
TO BE CONSIDERED AS FIRMS, COULD THEY BE TREATED AS
COMPONENTS OF THE MANUFACTURING SECTOR? IN THE AFTERMATH OF
THE RECENT FIRREA LEGISLATION, THESE BASIC QUESTIONS ONCE
AGAIN MAY BE BROUGHT BEFORE THE CONGRESS.

04601 JACOBS, C.W.
   CARROT-AND-STICKING THE BUREAUCRATS: MERIT PAY IN THE
   FEDERAL CIVIL SERVICE
   DISSERTATION ABSTRACTS INTERNATIONAL, 49(9) (MAR 89),
   2803-A.
   A THREE-PART STUDY OF THE 1978 CIVIL SERVICE REFORM ACT,
THIS THESIS EXPLORES THE REASONS THAT PAY-FOR-PERFORMANCE
STRATEGIES FAIL TO REFORM PUBLIC BUREAUCRACIES. PART ONE
TRACES THE POLITICAL AND LEGISLATIVE HISTORY OF CSRA. PART
TWO RECOUNTS THE IMPLEMENTATION PROCESS. PART THREE ANALYZES
TWO MERIT PAY PERFORMANCE MEASUREMENT TOOLS (MBO AND BARS)
AND REVIEWS AN EMPIRICAL STUDY OF THE USE OF THESE SYSTEMS
BY FEDERAL MANAGERS.

04602 JACOBS, D.C.
   POLITICAL BOULWARISM: BARGAINING DURING THE REAGAN YEARS
   NEGOTIATION JOURNAL, 5(4) (OCT 89), 349-356.
   THIS ARTICLE EXAMINES BARGAINING DURING THE REAGAN YEARS.
IT LABELS REAGAN AS A PRACTICAL CONSERVATIVE (ANTI-UNION)
AND SUGGESTS THAT HE COMBINED PRACTICAL CONSERVATISM WITH AN
EFFECTIVE "BOULWARISTIC" APPEAL TO WORKERS WHO MAY BE
OTHERWISE RESISTANT TO THE IDEOLOGICAL PROGRAM OF THE
PRACTICAL RIGHT. BOULWARISM IS DEFINED AND DESCRIBED AND
THEN THE ARTICLE ILLUSTRATES HOW REAGAN USED THIS TECHNIQUE
DURING HIS PRESIDENCY. IT THEN BRIEFLY EXPLORES THE DUKAKIS,
DUNLOP, AND BUSH'S USE OF BARGAINING AN AN IMMENSELY
POWERFUL SOCIAL TOOL.

04603 JACOBSEN, C.
   ON TOP OF THE WORLD: NORDIC EXPERIENCE AND THE NORDIC
   COUNCIL
   SCANDINAVIAN REVIEW, 77(4) (WIN 89), 14-19.
   THE NORDIC COUNCIL IS A UNIT DEVOTED TO COLLABORATION
BETWEEN THE NORDIC PARLIAMENTS AND THE NORDIC GOVERNMENTS.
THE NORDIC COUNCIL OF MINISTERS IS RESPONSIBLE FOR THE
COLLABORATION BETWEEN THE NORDIC GOVERNMENTS AND THE NORDIC
COUNCIL. THE NORDIC COMMUNITY MODEL AND OFFICIAL NORDIC
COOPERATION REPRESENT MAJOR INTERNATIONAL POWER EVEN THOUGH
EACH MEMBER OF THE NORDIC COUNCIL IS BOUND BY DIFFERENT
TREATIES. FOR EXAMPLE, DENMARK IS THE ONLY NORDIC COUNTRY IN
THE EUROPEAN COMMUNITY. DENMARK, ICELAND, AND NORWAY ARE
MEMBERS OF NATO WHILE FINLAND AND SWEDEN PREFER NEUTRALITY.

04604 JACOBSOHN, G. J.
   ALTERNATIVE PLURALISMS: ISRAELI AND AMERICAN
   CONSTITUTIONALISM IN COMPARATIVE PERSPECTIVE
   REVIEW OF POLITICS, 51(2) (SPR 89), 159-189.
   CONSTITUTIONAL TRANSPLANTATION, THE PROCESS BY WHICH THE
CONSTITUTIONAL PRACTICE OF ONE SOCIETY BECOMES AN IMPORTANT
SOURCE FOR THE LEGAL DEVELOPMENT OF ANOTHER, HAS FIGURED
IMPORTANTLY IN THE INSTITUTIONAL EVOLUTION OF NEW POLITIES.
THIS ARTICLE EXAMINES THE CONSTITUTIONAL EXPERIENCE OF
ISRAEL AND THE UNITED STATES, TWO SOCIETIES THAT SHARE A
LANGUAGE OF JURISPRUDENTIAL DISCOURSE WHILE DIFFERING
SIGNIFICANTLY IN A NUMBER OF POLITICALLY RELEVANT WAYS. IN

PARTICULAR, THE FACT THAT BOTH SOCIETIES CAN BE DESCRIBED AS
PLURALISTIC ONLY CONCEALS THE FACT THAT THEY REPRESENT
ALTERNATIVE MODELS OF PLURALISM THAT MAY RENDER PROBLEMATIC
THE TRANSFERABILITY OF CONSTITUTIONAL OUTCOMES FROM ONE
PLACE TO ANOTHER. THUS, THE LITERATURE OF MODERN
CONSTITUTIONALISM, WHICH HAS TENDED TO EMPHASIZE THE RIGHTS-
BASED LIBERAL ETHIC OF INDIVIDUALISM, IS ARGUABLY MORE
COMPATIBLE WITH AN AMERICAN MODEL IN WHICH THE PRINCIPLES OF
THE "PROCEDURAL REPUBLIC" ARE MORE UNPROBLEMATICALLY
EMBRACED.

04605 JACOBSON, C.
   SAME GAME, DIFFERENT PLAYERS: PROBLEMS IN URBAN PUBLIC
   UTILITY REGULATION, 1850-1987
   URBAN STUDIES, 26(1) (FEB 89), 13-31.
   THE AUTHOR EXPLAINS BASIC FACTORS THAT HAVE HISTORICALLY
CONFRONTED EFFORTS TO PROTECT PUBLIC AND GOVERNMENTAL
INTERESTS IN THE PROVISIONS OF GOODS PROVIDED BY PUBLIC
UTILITY INDUSTRIES. A MAJOR FOCUS IS THE IMPLICATIONS OF THE
USE OF FIXED AND NETWORKED DISTRIBUTION SYSTEMS FOR THE
SORTS OF ISSUES THAT MUST BE FACED IN ORDER TO PROTECT
PUBLIC INTERESTS. ANOTHER AREA OF CONCERN IS HOW DIFFERENCES
IN THE NATURE OF THE MARKETS SERVED BY THESE INDUSTRIES HAVE
CONTRIBUTED TO DIFFERENCES IN GOVERNMENT INVOLVEMENT.

04606 JACOBSON, D.
   THEORIZING IRISH INDUSTRIALIZATION: THE CASE OF THE MOTOR
   INDUSTRY
   SCIENCE AND SOCIETY, 53(2) (SUM 89), 165-191.
   JACOBSON TACKLES THE KEY QUESTION FOR THE IRISH LEFT:
THE ECONOMY. THE PROBLEMS OF POOR INFRASTRUCTURE, THE
ABSENCE OF INDIGENOUS INDUSTRY, THE PREVALENCE OF SMALL-
SCALE INEFFICIENT AGRICULTURE, AND HIGH UNEMPLOYMENT HAV
EBEEN HALLMARKS OF THE IRISH ECONOMY FOR DECADES; BOURGEOIS
STRATEGIES HAVE EMBRACED ORTHODOX FISCAL MEASURES, AUTARKY,
AND INTERNATIONALIZATION OF THE ECONOMY. JACOBSON EXAMINES
THE IMPACT OF THESE VARYING STRATEGIES ON IRELAND IN A
REVIEW OF MODELS OF ECONOMIC DEVELOPMENT: DEPENDENT
INDUSTRIALIZATION, SEMI-PERIPHERY/NON-"WHITE SETTLER," NEO-
COLONIAL, AND CAPITALIST COLONIAL UNDERDEVELOPMENT. USING
THE IRISH MOTOR INDUSTRY AS A CASE IN POINT. HE CONSIDERS
THE IMPLICATIONS FOR THE IRISH ECONOMY OF MEMBERSHIP IN THE
EUROPES COMMUNITY. UNLIKE SOME ON THE IRISH LEFT WHO ARGUE
FOR DISENGAGEMENT FROM EUROPE, JACOBSON ARGUES THAT THE
EUROPEAN COMMUNITY OFFERS THE ONLY REALISTIC CHANCE FOR
INDUSTRIALIZATION AND SOCIALISM IN IRELAND.

04607 JACOBSON, G.C.; WOLFINGER, R.E.
   INFORMATION AND VOTING IN CALIFORNIA SENATE ELECTIONS
   LEGISLATIVE STUDIES QUARTERLY, 14(4) (NOV 89), 509-530.
   SENATORS SEEKING REELECTION ARE MUCH MORE VULNERABLE
THAN REPRESENTATIVES, AND SENATORS FROM THE LARGEST STATES
ARE THE MOST VULNERABLE OF ALL. PATTERNS OF INFORMATION AND
VOTING BEHAVIOR IN THE 1980 AND 1986 SENATE ELECTIONS IN
CALIFORNIA PROVIDE SOME POSSIBLE EXPLANATIONS. THE
RELATIVELY LOW SALIENCE OF ALAN CRANSTON, THE INCUMBENT IN
BOTH ELECTIONS, RAISED THE IMPORTANCE OF THE CAMPAIGNS AND
OF OTHER SHORT-TERM FACTORS. ONLY AN ATTRACTIVE, WELL-
FINANCED CHALLENGER COULD DERIVE ANY ADVANTAGE FROM THIS
CIRCUMSTANCE, HOWEVER, AND CRANSTON ESCAPED SUCH A THREAT
UNTIL 1986. WHEN FORCED BY AN ABLE OPPONENT, THE INCUMBENT
WAS ABLE TO COUNTER WITH HIS OWN CAMPAIGN TO FRAME THE
ISSUES AND DEFINE THE CONTEST.

04608 JACOBSON, G.C.
   STRATEGIC POLITICIANS AND THE DYNAMICS OF U.S. HOUSE
   ELECTIONS, 1946-86
   AMERICAN POLITICAL SCIENCE REVIEW, 83(3) (SEP 89), 773-794.
   ANALYSIS OF BOTH DISTRICT-LEVEL AND AGGREGATE TIME-
SERIES DATA FROM POSTWAR HOUSE ELECTIONS SUPPORTS THE THESIS
THAT STRATEGIC POLITICAL ELITES PLAY A PIVOTAL ROLE IN
TRANSLATING NATIONAL CONDITIONS INTO ELECTION RESULTS AND
THEREFORE IN HOLDING MEMBERS OF CONGRESS COLLECTIVELY
ACCOUNTABLE FOR THE GOVERNMENT'S PERFORMANCE. MORE HIGH-
QUALITY CANDIDATES RUN WHEN PROSPECTS APPEAR TO FAVOR THEIR
PARTY; THEY ALSO WIN SIGNIFICANTLY MORE VOTES AND VICTORIES
THAN OTHER CANDIDATES IN EQUIVALENT CIRCUMSTANCES. THUS,
STRATEGIC CAREER DECISIONS BOTH REFLECT AND ENHANCE NATIONAL
PARTISAN TIDES. THE ELECTORAL IMPORTANCE OF STRATEGIC
POLITICIANS HAS GROWN OVER TIME IN TANDEM WITH THE TREND
TOWARD CANDIDATE-CENTERED ELECTORAL POLITICS. THIS HAS
RENDERED THE EFFECTS OF NATIONAL FORCES LESS AUTOMATIC, MORE
CONTINGENT, THUS THREATENING THE CAPACITY OF ELECTIONS TO
ENFORCE SOME DEGREE OF COLLECTIVE RESPONSIBILITY.

04609 JACOBSON, J.
   SINK WITH THE DEMOCRATS OR BUILD AN AMERICAN LEFT
   NEW POLITICS, 11(2) (WIN 89), 5-14.
   THE AUTHOR PROTESTS A POLICY BASED ON LESSER EVILISM, A
POLICY OF WORKING WITHIN THE DEMOCRATIC PARTY AND
CAMPAIGNING FOR ITS CANDIDATES, OF CONCENTRATING THE
ENERGIES OF THE LEFT IN REALIGNING OR REFORMING THE
DEMOCRATIC PARTY AS A SUBSTITUTE STRATEGY FOR TRYING TO
BUILD A MEANINGFUL AMERICAN LEFT. THE REALITY IS THAT IN THE

AFTERMATH OF LEFT PARTICIPATION IN THE DUKAKIS-BENSTEN
CAMPAIGN THE LEFT IS WEAKER AND MORE DEMORALIZED THAN BEFORE.
THE DEMOCRATIC PARTY REMAINS NO LESS SHABBY, SHODDY AND
CONSERVATIVE. HAD DUKAKIS WON, DISILLUSIONMENT AND
DEMORALIZATION WOULD ONLY HAVE BEEN DELAYED SINCE A DUKAKIS-
BENSTEN ADMINISTRATION COULD NOT HAVE MET EVEN THE LEFT'S
MOST MODEST EXPECTATIONS.

04610 JACOBSON, J.
THE CRACKS WIDER
NEW POLITICS, 11(3) (SUM 89), 101-107.
IT IS UNDERSTANDABLE WHY SO MANY CHINESE PROTESTERS HOLD
GORBACHEV IN SUCH HIGH REGARD CONSIDERING THE GAP BETWEEN
THE REFORMS OF GLASNOST IN THE SOVIET UNION AND THE
HARSHNESS OF THE CHINESE COMMUNIST SYSTEM. BUT OBJECTIVELY
VIEWED, THAT ESTEEM IS UNWARRANTED. GORBACHEV HAS NO
INTENTION OF ADVANCING OR INSTITUTIONALIZING THE FREEDOMS
AND SOCIAL JUSTICE IN THE SOVIET UNION THAT THE CHINESE
PEOPLE ARE DEMANDING FOR THEIR COUNTRY. WHAT THEY WANT MAKES
THEM "HOTHEADS" AND IF GORBACHEV HAS HIS WAY, IT WILL HAPPEN
ONLY IN FAIRY TALES, NEVER IN SOVIET LIFE. OF COURSE,
GORBACHEV DID BACK OFF FROM HIS HARSH CHARACTERIZATION WHICH
WAS DAMAGING TO HIS IMAGE AND POLITICALLY INJUDICIOUS. BUT
IT WAS AN INSTINCTIVE AND CANDID REACTION AND SHOULD NOT BE
FORGOTTEN.

04611 JAFFA, H.V.
A RIGHT TO PRIVACY?
NATIONAL REVIEW, XLI(5) (MAR 89), 51-52.
THE RIGHT TO PRIVACY IS NOT A WHIT MORE ABSTRACT,
METAPHYSICAL, OR GENERAL THAN ANY OF THE OTHER RIGHTS THAT
ARE CONSTITUTIONALLY PROTECTED. BOTH THE COURTS AND THE
LEGISLATURES MUST GIVE CONCRETE DEFINITION TO ALL SUCH
RIGHTS BY SAYING WHAT THEY DO PERMIT AND WHAT THEY DO NOT
PERMIT IN ACTUAL CIRCUMSTANCES.

04612 JAGAN, J.
FIGHTING BUREAUCRACY AND BELIEVING IN PEOPLE
WORLD MARXIST REVIEW, 32(8) (AUG 89), 62-64.
THIS ARTICLE REPORTS ON THE REMARKABLE ACHIEVEMENTS MADE
BY THE PEOPLE'S PROGRESSIVE PARTY (PPP) IN GUYANA DUE TO
THEIR ADHERERENCE TO DEMOCRATIC METHODS AND THE TECHNIQUES
THEY USED TO OVERCOME A BUREAUCRACY BUILT IN BY THE BRITISH
TO PREVENT ANY SUBSTANTIAL GAINS BY THE PPP. IT EXAMINES
GAINS MADE IN THE AREAS OF HEALTH SERVICES, AGRICULTURE,
EDUCATION, HOUSING, LAND SETTLEMENT, TRANSPORT SERVICES, AND
PUBLIC UTILITIES. IT CONCLUDES THAT AFTER THEY WERE KICKED
OUT OF OFFICE THAT THE COUNTRY IS BANKRUPT AND THAT
PRODUCTION HAS PLUMMETED.

04613 JAGAN, J.
IN THE NAME OF REVOLUTIONARY CHANGE
WORLD MARXIST REVIEW, 32(1) (JAN 89), 29-32.
THE AUTHOR REPORTS ON THE 23RD CONGRESS OF THE PEOPLE'S
PROGRESSIVE PARTY OF GUYANA.

04614 JAHANPOUR, F.
IRAN AFTER KHOMEINI
WORLD TODAY, 45(8-9) (AUG 89), 150-153.
THE DEATH OF THE AYATOLLAH KHOMEINI MARKED THE END OF AN
ERA, BOTH FOR IRAN AND FOR THE CAUSE OF ISLAMIC
FUNDAMENTALISM AS A WHOLE. KHOMEINI LED A REVOLUTION THAT
CHALLENGED THE DOMINANCE OF WESTERN CIVILIZATION. NOT ONLY
DID HE REVERSE THE COURSE OF MODERNIZATION AND
WESTERNIZATION IN IRAN, HE BREATHED NEW LIFE INTO ISLAMIC
MOVEMENTS THROUGHOUT THE WORLD. UNFORTUNATELY, HE PROPAGATED
A HARSH, FANATICAL, AND INTOLERANT ISLAM, NOT IN KEEPING
WITH THE HIGHEST PEAKS OF ISLAMIC CIVILIZATION. IRAN'S
FUTURE WITHOUT KHOMEINI IS UNCERTAIN. IF THE NEW LEADERS CAN
INSURE ECONOMIC GROWTH, INTERNAL STABILITY, AND THE EASING
OF SOCIAL AND RELIGIOUS PRESSURES, THEY SHOULD HOLD ONTO
THEIR POWER. IF THEY FAIL, THE COUNTRY WILL BE VULNERABLE TO
SOCIAL UNREST AND A POSSIBLE COUP.

04615 JAHSHAN, K.
US MEDIA TREATMENT OF THE PALESTINIANS SINCE THE INTIFADA
AMERICAN-ARAB AFFAIRS, (28) (SPR 89), 81-88.
THE AUTHOR, UTILIZING A PERSONAL SURVEY OF US NEWSPAPER
AND TELEVISION MEDIA, EXAMINES AND CRITIQUES THE US COVERAGE
OF THE INTIFADA. HE CONCLUDES THAT ALTHOUGH QUANTITATIVE
COVERAGE IS IMPRESSIVE, QUALITY IS LACKING FOR SECERAL
REASONS. THESE INCLUDE THE FACT THAT THERE HAS BEEN NO
SERIOUS ATTEMPT TO PORTRAY FROM A HUMAN-INTEREST ANGLE THE
PALESTINIAN SUFFERING, THE FACT THAT US MEDIA COVERAGE HAS
BEEN CONTENT TO FOLLOW THE FOCUS, TREND AND PACE SET BY THE
OFTEN BIASED ISRAELI MEDIA, THE LACK OF CONSISTENCY, AND US
TIMIDITY WITH REGARDS TO ISRAELI RESTRICTION OF MEDIA
COVERAGE IN PALESTINE.

04616 JAIN, H.; HACKETT, R.
MEASURING EFFECTIVENESS OF EMPLOYMENT EQUITY PROGRAMS IN
CANADA: PUBLIC POLICY AND A SURVEY
CANADIAN PUBLIC POLICY--ANALYSE DE POLITIQUES, XV(2) (JUN
89), 189-204.

EMPLOYMENT EQUITY (EE) REFERS TO COMPREHENSIVE PLANNING
PROCESS BY AN EMPLOYER TO IDENTIFY AND REMOVE DISCRIMINATION
IN EMPLOYMENT POLICIES AND PRACTICES. THE ARTICLE SEEKS TO
DETERMINE THE EXTENT TO WHICH KEY COMPONENTS OF AN EE
PROGRAM AS DEFINED BY THE CANADA EMPLOYMENT AND IMMIGRATION
COMMISSION (CEIC) ARE REPRESENTED WITHIN EE PROGRAMS, ASSESS
THE FEASIBLITY OF PUTTING THE CEIC CRITERIA TO OPERATIONAL
USE, AND DEVELOP AN EFFECTIVE SCORING SCHEME THAT RECOGNIZES
THE DIFFERENTIAL IMPORTANCE OF EACH CRITERION TO THE
ACHIEVEMENT OF EE. THE RESULTS HIGHLIGHT THE STRENGTHS AND
WEAKNESSES OF EXISTING PROGRAMS AND DEMONSTRATE THE
USEFULNES OF THE EE INDEX AS A TOOL FOR ASSESSING THE
POTENTIAL EFFECTIVENESS OF EE PROGRAMS.

04617 JAMA, A.A.
HORN OF AFRICA CONFLICT
AVAILABLE FROM NTIS, NO. AD-A207 996/0/GAR, MAR 89, 31.
AMONG THE MOST FAR-REACHING CONSEQUENCES OF COLONIALISM
IN AFRICA HAS BEEN THE PARTITION OF THE CONTINENT INTO
POLITICAL UNITS WHOSE BORDERS WERE DETERMINED ON THE BASIS
OF EUROPEAN INTERESTS. WHERE ETHNIC GROUPS WERE DIVIDED BY
AN ARTIFICIAL BORDER, THERE IS PRESSURE FOR TERRITORIAL
REVISIONS WITH THE OBJECT OF ACHIEVING UNITY WITHIN THE
BORDERS OF ONE STATE. SUCH PRESSURES ARE AT THE ROOT OF THE
POLITICAL PROBLEMS OF THE HORN OF AFRICA. THE ETHIOPIAN
DENIAL OF THE OGADEN SOMALIS' RIGHTS FOR SELF-DETERMINATION
SET THE STAGE FOR AN INEVITABLE CONFLICT, INVOLVING NOT
MERELY THE LOCAL AFRICANS BUT OUTSIDE GOVERNMENTS AND EVEN
THE SUPERPOWERS. THE LOCAL CONFLICT ON THE HORN PERMITTED
THE APPLICATION OF SOVIET POWER AND MILITATED AGAINST A
COMMENSURATE WESTERN RESPONSE; THUS THE RUSSIAN INTERVENTION
REVERSED THE OUTCOME OF THE CONFLICT IN FAVOR OF ETHIOPIA
MILITARILY AT THE PRESENT TIME. THE PURPOSE OF THIS PAPER IS
TO DESCRIBE THE STRUGGLE OF THE SOMALIS FOR THEIR FREEDOM
AND COMPLETE INDEPENDENCE FROM COLONIALISM, IN GENERAL. AND
THE OGADEN SOMALIS, IN PARTICULAR, WHO ARE TRYING TO ACHIEVE
WHAT THEIR BROTHERS ACHIEVED ALREADY AND WITH THEIR HELP.

04618 JAMES, A.
THE REALISM OF REALISM: THE STATE AND THE STUDY OF
INTERNATIONAL RELATIONS
REVIEW OF INTERNATIONAL STUDIES, 15(3) (JUL 89), 215-229.
THIS ARTICLE ATTEMPTS TO TAKE ACCOUNT OF WHAT IS
PROBABLY BEHIND SOME OF THE MORE OUTWARDLY SOPHISTICATED
CRITICISM OF LARGE-R-REALISM. IT HAS TO DO WITH THE INTEREST
OF SOME STUDENTS OF INTERNATIONAL MATTERS IN THE WAY IN
WHICH UNDERSTANDING PROGRESSES, AND OF THEIR HAVING NOTED
THE FACT THAT IN THE AREA OF NATURAL SCIENCE GREAT STRIDES
ARE REPORTED TO HAVE BEEN MADE BY WHAT HAS BEEN CALLED
'PARADIGM SHIFT'--THAT IS TO SAY, A BASIC CHANGE IN THE
WHOLE WAY OF LOOKING AT THINGS. THE ACADEMIC SUBJECT OF
INTERNATIONAL RELATIONS HAS SUFFERED FROM A CERTAIN AMOUNT
OF CRITICISM FROM OUTSIDE AND DOUBT FROM WITHIN, AND MUCH OF
THIS HAS HAD TO DO WITH ITS ABILITY--OR, RATHER, ITS
INABILITY--TO DEAL WITH ITS SUBJECT MATTER IN AN
APPROPRIATELY 'SCIENTIFIC' WAY. MORE SPECIFICALLY, THE
ABSENCE OF GENERAL THEORY OF A SUFFICIENTLY PRECISE KIND HAS
BEEN PARTICULARLY WORRYING IN SOME QUARTERS. ACCORDINGLY,
THE POSSIBILITY THAT THE SUBJECT NEEDS TO BE LOOKED AT IN A
NEW WAY HAS APPEAL. THE OPINION MAY, HOWEVER, BE VENTURED
THAT EFFORTS TO RECREATE INTERNATIONAL RELATIONS WILL
ULTIMATELY PROVE FUTILE. THEY MAY FOR A WHILE POSSESS A
CERTAIN TRENDY ATTRACTION, BUT THE INTELLECTUAL FOUNDATIONS
ON WHICH THEIR IDEAS REST ARE SO INSECURE THAT IN TIME THEIR
EDIFICE MAY BE EXPECTED TO DISINTEGRATE INTO ITS SEVERAL
PARTS.

04619 JAMES, A.
THE UN FORCE IN CYPRUS
INTERNATIONAL AFFAIRS, 65(3) (SUM 89), 481-500.
INTERNATIONAL PEACEKEEPING HAS HAD A SOMEWHAT CHEQUERED
AND STACCATO HISTORY IN TERMS OF BOTH ITS SUCCESS AND OF THE
FREQUENCY WITH WHICH IT HAS APPEARED, IT IS IMPORTANT THAT
THERE SHOULD BE A REALISTIC COMPREHENSION OF BOTH THE
LIMITATIONS AND THE POSSIBILITIES OF PEACEKEEPING. THE
EXPERIENCE OF THE PEACEKEEPING FORCE WITH THE LONGEST
HISTORY - THE UN FORCE IN CYPRUS (UNFLCYP) ILLUSTRATES THIS.
THIS DETAILED ANALYSIS CONSIDERS THE ISSUES OF THE NON-
SETTLEMENT OF THE PROBLEM WHICH BROUGHT ABOUT ITS CREATION
WHICH CAUSES CONDEMNATION OF THIS FORCE BY SOME, WHILE
OTHERS CLAIM THAT MAINTENANCE OF CALM IN CYPRUS IS A
CONSEQUENCE OF ITS PRESENCE. IT CONCLUDES THAT UNIFLCYP HAS
PROVIDED A VIVID DEMONSTRATION OF THE VALUABLE POTENTIAL
WHICH RESIDES IN THE DEVICE OF INTERNATIONAL PEACEKEEPING.

04620 JAMES, C.
MORE OF THE SAME
FAR EASTERN ECONOMIC REVIEW, 141(32) (AUG 88), 65.
DESPITE A RECESSION THAT HAS BEEN DEVELOPING OVER THE
PAST NINE MONTHS, THE FIFTH BUDGET OF NEW ZEALAND FINANCE
MINISTER ROGER DOUGLAS STILL EMPHASIZES THE MEDIUM-TERM. IT
CALLS FOR A NZ$2 BILLION (US$1.3 BILLION) REDUCTION IN
FOREIGN DEBT THROUGH ASSET SALES, TOUGH MEASURES TO CUT
STATE SPENDING AND NO LET UP IN THE ANTI-INFLATIONARY DRIVE.

CUTS IN COMPANY TAXES, GOODS AND SERVICES TAX, AND PERSONAL
TAXES ARE NOT IN THE MAKING EITHER.

04621 JAMES, C.
RECLAIMING THEIR HERITAGE
FAR EASTERN ECONOMIC REVIEW, 141(37) (SEP 88), 36-42.
OVER A CENTURY OF FOREIGN DOMINATION TOOK ITS TOLL ON
NEW ZEALAND'S INDIGINOUS MAORI PEOPLE. THEY LOST THE VAST
MAJORITY OF THEIR LAND TO ENTERPRISING FOREIGNERS AND
DECADES OF LITIGATION FAILED TO REGAIN BUT A FRACTION OF
THEIR PREVIOUS HOLDINGS. HOWEVER, RECENT COURTS HAVE BEEN
MUCH MORE ATTENTIVE TO THE DEMANDS OF THE MAORIS AND THEIR
CLAIMS OF LAND ARE BEGINING TO BE HONORED.

04622 JAMES, D.
IS MEXICO REALLY PRIVATIZING?
MEXICO-UNITED STATES REPORT, II(7) (APR 89), 4-5.
THE MEXICAN GOVERNMENT CLAIMS THAT IT HAS PRIVATIZED
MANY STATE-OWNED ENTERPRISES. BUT A DETAILED ACCOUNT OF THE
NUMBER OF STATE-OWNED COMPANIES THAT HAVE BEEN DISPOSED OF
AND THEIR ECONOMIC IMPORTANCE RAISES QUESTIONS ABOUT
MEXICO'S DRIVE TO PRIVATIZE.

04623 JAMES, D.
1991 ELECTIONS SEEN AS KEY TEST
MEXICO-UNITED STATES REPORT, 111(2) (NOV 89), 1-2.
MEXICO'S MIDTERM ELECTIONS ARE CONSIDERED THE ACID TEST
OF PRESIDENT SALINAS'S EFFORT TO MODERNIZE AND DEMOCRATIZE
THE POLITICAL SYSTEM. SALINAS HAS BEEN SUCCESSFUL IN
COMBATING INFLATION AND SECURING AN AGREEMENT ON MEXICO'S
SIGNIFICANT FOREIGN DEBT. IN ADDITION, BILATERAL RELATIONS
WITH THE UNITED STATES ARE IMPROVING. HOWEVER, MOST
OBSERVERS ARGUE THAT WITHOUT SIGNIFICANT AND VISIBLE
DEMOCRATIC REFORM, SALINAS WILL FACE CONSIDERABLE POLITICAL
CHALLENGE IN THE FUTURE.

04624 JAMES, D.R.
CITY LIMITS ON RACIAL EQUALITY: THE EFFECTS OF CITY-SUBURB
BOUNDARIES ON PUBLIC SCHOOL DESEGREGATION, 1968-1976
AMERICAN SOCIOLOGICAL REVIEW, 54(6) (DEC 89), 963-985.
THE CLASSIC QUESTION PROMPTING THIS STUDY IS: HOW DO
STATE STRUCTURES CREATE SOCIAL INEQUALITIES? CLASS THEORIES
ARGUE THAT LOCAL-STATE FRAGMENTATION SERVES THE INTERESTS OF
DOMINANT CLASSES BY PROTECTING CLASS PRIVILEGES AND BY
MANAGING SOCIAL CONFLICTS AND DEMOBILIZING INSURGENCIES.
INSTITUTIONALISTS ARGUE THAT FRAGMENTATION HINDERS POLICY
IMPLEMENTATION AND TENDS TO MAKE THE METROPOLIS UNGOVERNABLE.
RATIONAL CHOICE OR MARKET MODELS CLAIM THAT LOCAL-STATE
FRAGMENTATION SERVES DEMOCRACY BECAUSE CITIZENS WHO ARE NOT
SATISFIED WITH ONE LOCAL GOVERNMENT MAY CHOOSE ANOTHER. THIS
STUDY EVALUATES THE ADEQUACY OF THESE THEORIES IN EXPLAINING
METROPOLITAN SCHOOL SEGREGATION.

04625 JAMES, H.
IMAGES OF OTHERS: THE ROOTS OF GERMAN IDENTITY
ENCOUNTER, LXXII(1) (JAN 89), 23-33.
THE AUTHOR CONSIDERS THE QUESTION OF WHAT MAKES A NATION,
A NATION. HE DECLARES THAT NATIONALISM DEPENDS ON THE
APPLICATION OF IMAGINATION TO FORMULATE, AND SOMETIMES EVEN
INVENT, COMMON FEATURES--SUCH AS A SHARED HISTORY, COMMON
LANGUAGE, OR SHARED TRADITIONS. THEN HE EXAMINES THE
ESTABLISHMENT OF THE GERMAN STATE IN 1871 AND WHAT GERMAN
IDENTITY MEANT.

04626 JAMES, L.E.
MISSOURI'S DIOXIN CONTAMINATION, 1968-1988: THE POLITICS
AND ADMINISTRATION OF HAZARDOUS WASTE CATASTROPHE
DISSERTATION ABSTRACTS INTERNATIONAL, 49(11) (MAY 89),
3501-A.
BUILDING ON J. KENNETH BENSON'S THEORY OF
INTERORGANIZATIONAL NETWORKS, THE AUTHOR STUDIES THE NETWORK
ASSOCIATED WITH MISSOURI'S DIOXIN CONTAMINATION OVER A 20-
YEAR PERIOD. SHE ALSO ASSESSES THE FACTORS IDENTIFIED IN
"PARTICIPATION IN AMERICAN POLITICS: THE DYNAMICS OF AGENDA
BUILDING" TO DETERMINE THEIR IMPACT ON THE SCOPE OF THE
INTERORGANIZATIONAL NETWORK.

04627 JAMES, P.
STRUCTURE AND CONFLICT IN WORLD POLITICS: A TIME-SERIES
ANALYSIS OF INTERNATIONAL CRISES, 1929-1979.
ETUDES INTERNATIONALES, XX(4) (DEC 89), 791-816.
ONE OF THE MOST INTRACTABLE DEBATES IN THE FIELD OF
WORLD POLITICS CONCERNS THE LINKAGE OF SYSTEMIC STRUCTURE TO
INTERNATIONAL CONFLICT. THE DIALOGUE HAS FOCUSED ON THE
RELATIVE MERITS OF BIPOLAR VERSUS MULTIPOLAR AND, MORE
RECENTLY, POLYCENTRIC STRUCTURES. ADVOCATES OF EACH SYSTEM
HAVE THEIR ADHERENTS AND, FOR SOME TIME NOW, HAVE AGREED TO
DISAGREE. MOST OF THE DEBATE OVER STRUCTURE AND CONFLICT
THUS FAR HAS BEEN CAST IN TERMS THAT DO NOT FACILITATE ITS
RESOLUTION. THE OBJECTIVE OF THIS STUDY IS TO WORK TOWARD A
MORE COMPELLING EMPIRICAL JUDGMENT OF THE COMPETING CLAIMS.
SPECIFICALLY, THAT INVOLVES REVISION OF THE CENTRAL CONCEPTS.
STRUCTURE CANNOT BE ASSESSED ONLY IN TERMS OF DISTRIBUTION
OF POWER; THE CONCEPT ALSO SHOULD INCORPORATE THE NOTION OF

AUTONOMOUS DECISION CENTRES. WITH RESPECT TO CONFLICT, MOST
COMMONLY REFERRED TO AS INSTABILITY, WAR IS HELD TO BE A
LESS COMPREHENSIVE MEASUREMENT THAN INTERNATIONAL CRISIS.
RENEWED TESTING FOCUSES ON THE LINKAGE OF STRUCTURE TO
CONFLICT AS SO DEFINED. DATA FROM THE INTERNATIONAL CRISIS
BEHAVIOUR PROJECT ON 280 CASES FROM 1929 TO 1979 PROVIDE THE
EVIDENCE TO COMPARE THE PHASES OF STRUCTURE. THE DIFFERENCES
THAT EMERGE AMONG MULTIPOLARITY, BIPOLARITY AND POLYCENTRISM
WITH RESPECT TO PATTERNS OF CONFLICT ARE GENERALLY
CONSISTENT WITH THEORETICAL EXPECTATIONS.

04628 JAMES, P.; MICHELIN, R.
THE CANADIAN NATIONAL ENERGY PROGRAM AND ITS AFTERMATH:
PERSPECTIVES ON A ERA OF CONFRONTATION
AMERICAN REVIEW OF CANADIAN STUDIES, XIX(1) (SPR 89),
59-81.
ALTHOUGH THE LITERATURE GENERATED BY THE NEP AND ITS
AFTERMATH IS VAST, CERTAIN ASPECTS OF THIS IMPORTANT PUBLIC
REMAIN UNEXPLORED. SPECIFICALLY, THE PHASE OF CONFRONTATION
FROM OCTOBER 1980 TO THE 1981 CANADA-ALBERTA AGREEMENT MIGHT
BE DEALT WITH IN MORE RIGOROUS TERMS, IN ORDER TO OBTAIN
GREATER UNDERSTANDING OF THE POLICY PROCESS. THUS THE
OVERALL PURPOSE OF THIS STUDY IS TO IDENTIFY THE ESSENTIAL
CHARACTER OF THE INTENSE CONFLICT OVER ENERGY POLICY AT THE
OUTSET OF THE DECADE.

04629 JAMES, P.; HARVEY, F.
THREAT ESCALATION AND CRISIS STABILITY: SUPERPOWER CASES,
1948-1979
CANADIAN JOURNAL OF POLITICAL SCIENCE, 22(3) (SEP 89),
523-546.
USING A MODIFIED VERSION OF CHICKEN, REFERRED TO AS THE
THREAT GAME, BRAMS AND KILGOUR HAVE DEVELOPED A THEORETICAL
MODEL OF THREAT ESCALATION AND STABILITY IN SUPERPOWER
CRISES. MORE SPECIFICALLY, THEY DERIVE EXPLICIT THRESHOLDS
FOR SUFFICIENT PRE-EMPTION TO STABILIZE A CRISIS BEFORE IT
ESCALATES OUT OF CONTROL. AN APPROPRIATE DEGREE OF COERCION
THEREBY IS DESIGNATED FOR THE RESPONSE TO AN ADVERSARY, IN
ORDER TO DETER FURTHER ESCALATION. THE OVERALL OBJECTIVE OF
THIS STUDY IS TO USE DATA ON SUPERPOWER CRISES TO TEST A
MODIFIED VERSION OF THE MODEL DEVELOPED BY BRAMS AND KILGOUR.
MIXED RESULTS EMERGE FROM TESTING THE MOST GENERAL
PROPOSITIONS. THE CHOICE OF RESPONSE LEVEL USUALLY DOES NOT
SURPASS THE MODEL'S RECOMMENDED VALUE. HOWEVER,
STABILIZATION IS FEASIBLE IN VIRTUALLY ALL CRISES AND, WHEN
AN ACTOR DOES MEET THE THRESHOLD, SATISFACTION WITH THE
OUTCOME OCCURS MORE FREQUENTLY THAN OTHERWISE. TWO MORE
SPECIFIC HYPOTHESES ALSO ARE TESTED, WITH PARTIAL SUPPORT
FOR THE MODEL ONCE AGAIN BEING THE RESULT.

04630 JAMES, P. A.
POLITICAL (IN)STABILITY: A MODEL OF PRE AND POST
REVOLUTIONARY NICARAGUA
DISSERTATION ABSTRACTS INTERNATIONAL, 49(8) (FEB 89),
2376-A.
THIS DISSERTATION COMBINES A DYNAMIC ANALYSIS OF REGIME
ENVIRONMENT AND REGIME STABILITY. NICARAGUA FROM 1977 TO
1981 IS USED AS A CASE STUDY.

04631 JAMESON, F.
MARXISM AND POSTMODERNISM
NEW LEFT REVIEW, (176) (JUL 89), 31-46.
IN A PREVIOUS ARTICLE, THE AUTHOR IDENTIFIED
POSTMODERNISM AS THE CULTURAL LOGIC OF LATE CAPITALISM. IN
THIS ESSAY, HE REPLIES TO CRITICS OF HIS POSITION AND
CONTINUES HIS ATTEMPT TO ANALYZE THE SYSTEMIC COHERENCE OF A
SOCIAL AND CULTURAL PHENOMENON THAT SPURNS ANY TOTALIZING
AMBITION.

04632 JAMMEH, S.C.
STATE INTERVENTION IN AGRICULTURAL PRICING AND MARKETING
IN SENEGAL: THE POLITICS OF BUDGETARY REALLOCATION
DISSERTATION ABSTRACTS INTERNATIONAL, 49(7) (JAN 89),
1957-A.
IT IS VIRTUALLY INEVITABLE THAT POLICYMAKERS OPERATING
IN THE CONTEXT OF A POLITICAL MACHINE DEPLOY ECONOMIC POLICY
TO ADVANCE THEIR SOCIAL AGENDA. IN SENEGAL, POLICYMAKERS
FREQUENTLY MANIPULATE AGRICULTURAL PRICES AND SERVICES TO
REALLOCATE BUDGETARY REVENUES TO A SMALL GROUP OF MACHINE
STAFFERS AND AGENTS. THEY DO THIS DESPITE EVIDENCE THAT SUCH
POLICIES DAMAGE AGRICULTURAL GROWTH AND LONG-TERM
DEVELOPMENT.

04633 JANDA, K.
REGIONAL AND RELIGIOUS SUPPORT OF POLITICAL PARTIES AND
EFFECTS ON THEIR ISSUE POSITIONS
INTERNATIONAL POLITICAL SCIENCE REVIEW, 10(4) (OCT 89),
349-370.
POLITICAL SOCIOLOGY ASSUMES THAT SOCIAL CLEAVAGES ARE
MANIFESTED IN POLITICAL ALIGNMENTS. THIS RESEARCH FOCUSES ON
THE CLEAVAGE FACTORS OF REGION AND RELIGION IN GROUP SUPPORT
OF NATIONAL POLITICAL PARTIES. IT DISCUSSES PROBLEMS IN
ANALYZING THESE FACTORS ACROSS CULTURES AND ILLUSTRATES THE
PROBLEMS BY ANALYZING SOCIAL SUPPORT FOR APPROXIMATELY 150

PARTIES IN 53 NATIONS IN ALL CULTURAL-GEOGRAPHIC AREAS OF
THE WORLD. REGIONAL AND RELIGIOUS PATTERNS OF SUPPORT
CLEARLY AFFECT PARTIES' POSITIONS ON ISSUES. REGIONALLY
HOMOGENEOUS PARTIES TEND TO OPPOSE NATIONAL INTEGRATION, AND
RELIGIOUSLY HOMOGENEOUS PARTIES TEND TO OPPOSE THE
SECULARIZATION OF SOCIETY. MOREOVER, PARTIES' POSITIONS ON
SECULARIZATION ALSO DEPEND HEAVILY ON THEIR SPECIFIC
RELIGIOUS COMPOSITION.

04634 JANICAUD, D.
HEIDEGGER'S POLITICS: DETERMINABLE OR NOT?
SOCIAL RESEARCH, 56(4) (WIN 89), 819-848.
THE AUTHOR CONSIDERS THE QUESTION OF A POSSIBLE
"AFFINITY" BETWEEN THE DISCIPLINE OF PHILOSOPHY AND
TOTALITARIAN POWER. SHE EXAMINES THE POSSIBILITY OF A
NEGATIVE LINK, RATHER THAN A DIRECT LINK, BETWEEN
HEIDEGGER'S POLITICS AND PHILOSOPHY. WHILE LOCATING NOTHING
POLITICALLY DETERMINATE IN HEIDEGGER'S A-POLITICS, SHE
NEVERTHELESS HOLDS THAT IT CONTAINS A DANGER IN "THE WILL TO
FOUND A POLITICS ANEW ON THE ONTOLOGICAL DIFFERENCE ALONE."

04635 JANKOVIC, N.
CAPITALISM, SOCIALISM, AND ECONOMIC GROWTH
INTERNATIONAL JOURNAL OF POLITICS, CULTURE AND SOCIETY,
2(4) (SUM 89), 523-536.
IN THIS PAPER CERTAIN BROAD PRINCIPLES REGARDING GROWTH
AND DISTRIBUTION WHICH PREVAIL IN POST-KEYNESIAN THEORY, BUT
BELONGING TO THE CLASSICAL TRADITION, ARE APPLIED TO THE
MODEL OF A SOCIALIST ECONOMY WHICH RESEMBLES THAT OF OTHER
CONTEMPORARY EASTERN EUROPEAN ECONOMIES. THE ULTIMATE CAUSES
OF GROWTH AND THE OVERALL PROBLEMS OF ITS STABILITY UNDER
SOCIALISM ARE CONSIDERD IN THE FIRST SECTION. THE CRUCIAL
PROBLEM OF FUNCTIONAL INCOME DISTRIBUTION IN SOCIALISM, I.E.
THE LEVEL OF GOVERNMENT'S FREEDOM OF VARY THE
CONSUMPTION/INVESTMENT RATIO IN ORDER TO INDUCE FASTER
GROWTH, IS CONSIDERED IN THE SECOND SECTION. IT IS ARGUED IN
CONCLUSION THAT CONTEMPORARY CAPITALISM AND SOCIALISM SHARE
A COMMON FUNDAMENTAL ECONOMIC PROBLEM, PROVIDE DIFFERENT
ANSWERS DEPENDING ON THE ECONOMIC AND POLITICAL PHILOSOPHY
OF THEIR GOVERNMENTS AND, HENCE, BELONG TO THE HIGHER STAGES
OF DEVELOPMENT OF THE SAME INDUSTRIAL MODE OF PRODUCTION.

04636 JANKOWIAK, W.R.
THE LAST HURRAH? POLITICAL PROTEST IN INNER MONGOLIA
AUSTRALIAN JOURNAL OF CHINESE AFFAIRS, (19-20) (JAN 88),
269-288.
THE AUTHOR STUDIES THE STUDENT UNREST AND PROTEST STRIKE
OF 1981-82 AS A MEANS TO IDENTIFY THE HISTORICAL AND
SOCIOLOGICAL FACTORS RESPONSIBLE FOR PERIODICALLY MOBILIZING
MONGOLS AND, IN SOME CASES, RESTRAINING THEM FROM TAKING
THEIR GRIEVANCES TO THE STREET AND DEMANDING JUSTICE FROM
THE STATE. IN ADDITION, AN ANALYSIS OF THE STUDENTS'
GRIEVANCES PROVIDES AN OPPORTUNITY TO ASSESS THE
DIFFICULTIES, INHERENT IN FEDERALISM, OF IMPLEMENTING A
VIABLE AUTONOMOUS REGION POLICY WHILE SIMULTANEOUSLY
STRIVING FOR NATIONAL INTEGRATION.

04637 JANNUZZI, G.
POLITICAL AND ECONOMIC ASPECTS OF EUROPEAN SECURITY
INTERNATIONAL SPECTATOR, XXIII(1) (JAN 88), 3-6.
IN THE EUROPEAN DEBATE ON SECURITY, THREE CONCENTRIC
CIRCLES SHOULD BE CONSIDERED: THE FIRST AND CENTRAL ONE
CONCERNS MILITARY DEFENCE; THE SECOND ONE INCLUDES ARMS
LIMITATION AND CONTROL; THE THIRD CONCERNS THE GENERAL
POLITICAL AND ECONOMIC FRAMEWORK IN WHICH SECURITY IS TO BE
CONSIDERED.

04638 JANSEN, G.
BEIRUT AFTER THE CEASE-FIRE
MIDDLE EAST INTERNATIONAL, (361) (OCT 89), 4-5.
THE ARTICLE ARGUES THAT THE IMAGE OF BEIRUT AS A CITY OF
RUBBLE FILLED WITH THOUSANDS OF CASUALTIES IS SIGNIFICANTLY
EXAGGERATED. ALTHOUGH UNDENIABLY BATTERED, THE CITIZENS OF
LEBANON'S CAPITAL SEEM WILLING TO GET ON WITH LIVING THEIR
LIVES-WITHOUT INTERRUPTIONS. ANY FACTION WHO BREAKS THE SIX
MONTH-OLD CEASE-FIRE IS SURE TO EARN ALMOST UNIVERSAL
CONDEMNATION.

04639 JANSEN, G.
BENAZIR UNDERCUTS THE ISLAMIC MILITANTS
MIDDLE EAST INTERNATIONAL, (343) (FEB 89), 14.
THE SUNNIS OF PAKISTAN HAVE BUCKED THE TREND OF THE
ISLAMIC ORTHODOX IN IRAN. SAUDI ARABIA, AND THE GULF STATES
TO SUBORDINATE WOMEN. SAUDI ARABIA, IRAN, AND THEIR ACOLYTE
MULLAHS IN PAKISTAN OPENLY OPPOSED BENAZIR BHUTTO'S BID TO
BECOME THE RULER OF THE ISLAMIC REPUBLIC OF PAKISTAN. BUT,
HAVING BEATEN THE MUSLIM MALE CHAUVINISTS, BHUTTO
IMMEDIATELY DECLARED THAT SHE WOULD OPPOSE DISCRIMINATION
AGAINST WOMEN.

04640 JANSEN, G.
CATS - PAWS IN THE IRAQ - SYRIA TUSSLE
MIDDLE EAST INTERNATIONAL, 353 (JUN 89), 9-10.
APART FROM THE SAUDIS AND THE LEBANESE MUSLIMS AND

DRUZES, THERE IS AN ARAB AND INTERNATIONAL CONSENSUS THAT
SYRIA SHOULD REMOVE ITSELF FROM LEBANON. BUT THIS CONSENSUS
HAD MADE NO IMPACT ON THE POLICY OF THE THICK-SKINNED
SYRIANS. THE SIMPLEST SOLUTION WOULD BE THE WITHDRAWAL OF
ALL FOREIGN FORCES AND INFLUENCES FROM LEBANON - IRAQI,
SYRIAN AND ISRAELI IN SOUTH LEBANON, THIS LAST A SYRIAN
PREREQUISITE FOR ITS WITHDRAWAL: INDEED THAT IS WHAT THE
ARAB LEAGUE HAS ALREADY CALLED FOR. YET THE CHANCES OF ANY
SUCH THING HAPPENING IN THE NEAR OR THE NOT-SO-NEAR FUTURE
ARE VIRTUALLY NIL.

04641 JANSEN, G.
DEMOCRACY AND FUNDAMENTALISM
MIDDLE EAST INTERNATIONAL, (365) (DEC 89), 9.
THE GENERAL ELECTION IN JORDAN IN NOVEMBER OF 1989 DID
MORE THAN RESTORE A MEASURE OF PARLIAMENTARY DEMOCRACY TO
JORDAN'S POLITICAL LIFE; OF FAR GREATER IMPORT WAS THE FACT
THAT IT ESTABLISHED A CONNECTION BETWEEN DEMOCRATIC PRACTICE
AND THE GROWTH OF THE POLITICAL POWER OF ISLAMIC
FUNDAMENTALISM. THE POLITICAL VICTORY OF A SIGNIFICANT
NUMBER OF FUNDAMENTALISTS HAS CAUSED CONCERN FOR JORDAN'S
LEADERS, AS WELL AS THE LEADERS OF OTHER MIDEAST STATES WHO
HAVE TRIED TO RESTRAIN THEIR INFLUENCE IN THE PAST.

04642 JANSEN, G.
IRAN AND IRAQ: STALEMATE HARDENED
MIDDLE EAST INTERNATIONAL, (341) (JAN 89), 15.
THE STALEMATE IN THE GULF WAR NEGOTIATIONS CONTINUED IN
JANUARY 1989 WHEN IRAN ANNOUNCED THAT IT WOULD NOT RETURN TO
GENEVA TO RESUME TALKS UNTIL THE UN GENERAL SECRETARY FINDS
COMPROMISE SOLUTIONS TO THE MAIN ISSUES. THE DISCUSSION HAD
BOGGED DOWN TWO MONTHS EARLIER DUE TO DIFFERENCES BETWEEN
THE TWO SIDES ON THE PRIORITY TO BE GIVEN TO THE VARIOUS
CLAUSES IN UN RESOLUTION 598.

04643 JANSEN, G.
IRAN AND IRAQ: THE TILT IN IRAN'S FAVOUR
MIDDLE EAST INTERNATIONAL, (344) (FEB 89), 12.
IRAN IS GAINING MORE ADVANTAGE THAN THE IRAQIS FROM THE
CEASE-FIRE BECAUSE THE PEACE TALKS IN GENEVA HAVE BEEN
DEADLOCKED FOR THREE MONTHS. THE TALKS BROKE DOWN BECAUSE OF
DISAGREEMENT OVER PRIORITIES. THIS INACTIVITY IS GOOD FOR
IRAN BECAUSE IT ALLOWS THE COUNTRY TO REBUILD ITS STRENGTH.

04644 JANSEN, G.
IRAQ'S ELECTION: A TASTE OF DEMOCRACY
MIDDLE EAST INTERNATIONAL, (348) (APR 89), 11.
THE GENERAL ELECTION IN IRAQ WAS A REFLECTION OF THE
PEOPLE'S DEMAND FOR CHANGE AND REFORM. WHILE THE WAR WAS
BEING FOUGHT, THE GENERAL CONSENSUS WAS TO ACCEPT THE
CURRENT POLITICAL CONDITIONS, BUT THE CESSATION OF
HOSTILITIES HAVE BROUGHT ON INCREASED PRESSURE FOR A CHANGE
FROM THE ONE-PARTY RULE OF SADDAM HUSSEIN AND HIS BA'TH
PARTY. THE GENERAL ELECTION GAVE THE PEOPLE A CHOICE BETWEEN
PARTY CANDIDATES AND "INDEPENDENT" CANDIDATES AND THREE
FOURTHS OF THE ELECTORATE PARTICIPATED. THE FUTURE OF
DEMOCRACY NOW LIES WITH THE NEWLY ELECTED PARLIAMENTARIANS
AND THEIR ABILITY AND WILLINGNESS TO SUPPORT FURTHER REFORM
AND CHANGE.

04645 JANSEN, G.
IRAQI AND THE KURDS: "FINAL SOLUTION"?
MIDDLE EAST INTERNATIONAL, 352 (JUN 89), 11-12.
THE IRAQI AUTHORITIES MAKE NO GREAT SECRET OF THE FACT
THAT THEY ARE TRYING TO CREATE A "SECURITY ZONE", PERHAPS 30-
40 MILES WIDE. AND EMPTY OF KURDISH INHABITANTS, ALONG THE
FRONTIER WITH IRAN. THUS THE GUERRILLAS WILL NOT BE ABLE TO
RECEIVE SUPPORT FROM ANY KURDISH POPULATION. NEARER TO THE
BORDER THE KURDISH VILLAGES ARE BEING DESTROYED SO THAT THE
AREA IS COMPLETELY DEPOPULATED, BUT FARTHER INTO IRAQ THE
PLAN IS TO REPLACE THE KURDS WITH ARABS, IF ANY CAN BE FOUND
READY TO COOPERATE WITH WHAT COULD BE A HAZARDOUS
UNDERTAKING.

04646 JANSEN, G.
ISLAMIC CONFERENCE ORGANIZATION: SNUB TO IRAN
MIDDLE EAST INTERNATIONAL, (346) (MAR 89), 8-9.
THE SPRING 1989 MEETING OF THE ISLAMIC CONFERENCE
ORGANIZATION (ICO) WAS AN INSTRUCTIVE AND CHASTENING
EXPERIENCE FOR IRAN. THE MEETING EMPHASIZED THE FACT THAT
IRAN, AS THE ONLY SHIITE GOVERNMENT IN THE MUSLIM WORLD, CAN
MAKE A LOT OF NOISE BUT CANNOT IMPOSE ITS WILL ON THE
MAJORITY OF MUSLIMS. THE EPISODE CONFIRMED IRAN'S UNEASY
RELATIONSHIP WITH THE ICO.

04647 JANSEN, G.
NEGOTIATING THE NON-NEGOTIABLE
MIDDLE EAST INTERNATIONAL, (350) (MAY 89), 19.
"EVERYTHING IS NEGOTIABLE". THOSE WORDS USED BY ISRAELI
PRIME MINISTER YITZHAK SHAMIR WERE SUPPOSED TO INDICATE A
NEW FLEXIBILITY, A RELAXATION IN HIS USUALLY RIGID
NEGATIVISM. BUT THAT IS NOT NECESSARILY SO, EVEN THOUGH
SECRETARY OF STATE JAMES BAKER SEIZED ON THEM AS SHOWING A
REAL, HOPEFUL CHANGE, ADDING THAT SHAMIR EVEN INCLUDED

"SOVEREIGNTY OVER THE OCCUPIED TERRITORIES" IN THE
"EVERYTHING", AN INTERPRETATION THAT IS IN FACT QUESTIONABLE.

04648 JANSEN, G.
NINTH NON-ALIGNED SUMMIT
MIDDLE EAST INTERNATIONAL, (358) (SEP 89), 8.
THE NINTH SUMMIT OF THE NON-ALIGNED MOVEMENT WAS MARKED
BY A SIGNIFICANT LACK OF ARAB PARTICIPATION. THE HEADS OF
STATE OF IRAN, SYRIA, MOROCCO, AND IRAQ ALL FAILED TO ATTEND
THE SUMMIT. AS A RESULT, THE ONLY MIDEAST ISSUE THAT WAS
DISCUSSED IN DEPTH WAS PALESTINE. YASSER ARAFAT HAS CHOSEN
AS THE REGIONAL SPOKESMAN FOR ALL OF ASIA AND SPENT MOST OF
HIS TIME DISCUSSING THE PLO PEACE INITIATIVE AND THE
INTIFADA. THE ONLY OTHER ARAB FIGURE WHO CAUGHT ATTENTION
WAS LIBYA'S QADHAFI, WHO ARRIVED IN RAINY BELGRADE WITH
CAMELS AND A BEDUIN TENT.

04649 JANSEN, G.
SYRIA AND IRAN COMING UNSTUCK
MIDDLE EAST INTERNATIONAL, (363) (NOV 89), 6.
SYRIA AND IRAN WERE UNITED BY MUTUAL HATRED OF IRAQ.
HOWEVER, WITH THE END OF THE IRAN-IRAQ WAR, THE TWO NATIONS
ARE FINDING THAT THEY HAVE LESS IN COMMON. DISAGREEMENT OVER
THE TAIF AGREEMENT ON LEBANON HAS BECOME A MAJOR CAUSE OF
CONFLICT BETWEEN IRAN AND SYRIA. SOME OBSERVERS NOTE THAT
SYRIA MAY USE THE ARAB LEAGUE SPONSORED AGREEMENT TO WORK
ITS WAY AWAY FROM IRAN AND BACK INTO THE ARAB FAMILY. IF THE
LEBANON CONFLICT IS RESOLVED, SYRIA STILL FACES A SHAKY
ECONOMY AND A BLEAK FUTURE.

04650 JANSEN, G.
THE HOSTAGE CRISIS
MIDDLE EAST INTERNATIONAL, (357) (AUG 89), 8.
ALTHOUGH THE MARONITE-SYRIAN CONFLICT APPEARS TO HAVE
"FROZEN" THE HOSTAGE ISSUE, THE CRISIS IS BY NO MEANS OVER.
ISRAEL'S KIDNAPPING OF SHAIKH ABD AL-KARIM OBEID HAS
RESULTED IN MANY PROPOSALS FOR THE RELEASE OF THE SHAIKH,
THE WESTERN HOSTAGES, ISRAELI SERVICEMEN HELD IN LEBANON,
AND OTHER ARAB AND PALESTINIAN PRISONERS. SUCH DIVERSE
POWERS AS IRAN AND PAKISTAN HAVE INCREASED THEIR INVOLVEMENT
IN THE DIPLOMATIC WRANGLING. AS OF YET, THE IMPASSE
CONTINUES AS NO PROPOSAL HAS RECEIVED ISRAEL'S APPROVAL.

04651 JANSEN, G.
THE IRANIAN MUJAHEDIN: MARXISTS, MUSLIMS OR BOTH?
MIDDLE EAST INTERNATIONAL, 355 (AUG 89), 19-20.
SINCE 1981 THE MUJAHEDIN HAS UNDERGONE MANY VICISSITUDES.
IN THAT YEAR IT ATTEMPTED AN OPEN, ARMED CHALLENGE TO THE
KHOMEINI REGIME WHICH WAS DEFEATED; THE TOP LEADERSHIP WENT
INTO EXILE AND THE MEMBERSHIP WENT UNDERGROUND AND IS STILL
PERSECUTED. IN EXILE THE MUJAHEDIN CHANGED ITS CHARACTER AND
BECAME A "RELIGIO-POLITICAL SECT." FROM THE START THE GROUP
MADE CLEAR THAT WHILE IT STUDIED AND ACCEPTED MARXIST
ECONOMICS IT AVOIDED MARXIST PHILOSOPHY "IN ORDER TO PROTECT
ITS RELIGIOUS SUSCEPTIBILITIES". A HANDBOOK PUBLISHED ON THE
EVE OF THE ISLAMIC REVOLUTION DECLARED: "WE SAY 'NO' TO
MARXIST PHILOSOPHY, ESPECIALLY TO ATHEISM. WE SAY 'YES' TO
MARXIST SOCIAL THOUGHT, PARTICULARLY ITS ANALYSIS OF
FEUDALISM, CAPITALISM AND IMPERIALISM."

04652 JANSEN, G.
THE NEW CONSTITUTIONAL PROPOSALS
MIDDLE EAST INTERNATIONAL, (362) (NOV 89), 4.
THE ARTICLE OUTLINES THE PROPOSED REFORMS OF THE TAIF
ACCORDS. THEY INCLUDE: PROVISIONS WHICH RADICALLY DIMINISH
THE POWER OF THE PRESIDENT; AN INCREASE OF MEMBERSHIP OF A
HALF CHRISTIAN AND HALF MUSLIM PARLIAMENT; AND INCREASED
POWER AND RESPONSIBILITY TO THE CABINET. THESE CHANGES ARE
THE FIRST MAJOR CONSTITUTIONAL SHIFTS SINCE 1926.

04653 JANSEN, G.
THE POPE SPEAKS OUT
MIDDLE EAST INTERNATIONAL, (358) (SEP 89), 19-20.
A STATEMENT BY THE POPE ACCUSING SYRIA OF BEING SOLELY
RESPONSIBLE FOR "GENOCIDE" AGAINST LEBANESE CHRISTIANS WILL
MOST LIKELY INCREASE TENSIONS BETWEEN MUSLIMS AND CHRISTIANS
THROUGHOUT THE MIDEAST. OBSERVERS NOTE THAT THE POPE'S
INTERVENTION WILL INCREASE LONG-TERM TENSION BY RAISING
QUESTIONS ABOUT THE LOYALTY OF ALL ARAB CHRISTIANS; IN THE
SHORT TERM IT WILL ALSO ENCOURAGE THE HARD-LINE MARONITES
NOT TO COMPROMISE BECAUSE IT FOSTERS THE IMPRESSION THAT,
LIKE THE CRUSADES OF CENTURIES PAST, WESTERN HELP IS ON THE
WAY.

04654 JANSEN, G.
THE POPE TRIES TO MAKE AMMENDS
MIDDLE EAST INTERNATIONAL, (360) (OCT 89), 7.
POPE JOHN PAUL II ATTEMPTED TO REPAIR THE DAMAGE DONE TO
THE CHRISTIAN-MUSLIM NEGOTIATIONS BY HIS ACCUSATION THAT THE
SYRIANS WERE PRACTICING "GENOCIDE" AGAINST THE LEBANESE
"CHRISTIANS." IN A MUCH STRESSED STATEMENT, HE DIRECTLY
ADDRESSED THE MUSLIM PEOPLE IN A CALL FOR UNITY AND
SETTLEMENT.

04655 JANSEN, G.
THE PRESSURES ON KING FAHD
MIDDLE EAST INTERNATIONAL, (347) (MAR 89), 11-12.
THE MARCH 25, 1989, MEETING BETWEEN HUSSEIN, MUBARAK,
AND ARAFAT PRESENTED TWO ULTIMATUMS TO KING FAHD. THE ARAB
LEADERS HAVE CALLED ON SAUDI ARABIA TO SUMMON A SUMMIT
MEETING OF THE ARAB LEAGUE AND TO LIFT THE SUSPENSION OF
EGYPT'S MEMBERSHIP.

04656 JANSEN, G. H.
AYATOLLAH KHOMEINI: AN ASSESSMENT
MIDDLE EAST INTERNATIONAL, 352 (JUN 89), 14-15.
KHOMEINI'S FAME GAINED FROM THE MULTIPLIER EFFECT OF THE
SIMULTANEITY OF HIS POLITICAL REVOLUTION - THE OVERTHROW OF
THE PAHLAVI MONARCHY - AND HIS ISLAMIC INNOVATION - THE
VILAYET E-FAQIH OR ISLAMIC STATE. IN THE FIRST PLACE, AN
ANTI-MONARCHIAL "REVOLUTION" WAS NOTHING NEW IN IRAN: THE
SECULAR NATIONALISTS LED BY MOSSADEGH FORCED THE SHAH INTO A
PANIC-STRICKEN FLIGHT IN 1953 WITHOUT ANY OF THE BLOODSHED
OF THE LATER KHOMEINI VERSION. SECOND, THE SO-CALLED
"ISLAMIC REVOLUTION" HAS TURNED OUT NOT TO BE SO
REVOLUTIONARY; THE CLASS STRUCTURE OF IRAN HAS NOT GREATLY
CHANGED AND THERE ARE STILL EXTREMES OF RICH AND POOR IN THE
CITIES AND IN THE COUNTRYSIDE. DESPITE ALL THEIR LATER
VENERATION OF KHOMEINI, HE WAS NOT ABLE TO INSPIRE HIS
FELLOW CLERICS, EXCEPT A HANDFUL, TO FOLLOW HIS POLITICAL
ANTIMONARCHIST EXAMPLE.

04657 JANSEN, G. H.
THE DEATH SQUADS
MIDDLE EAST INTERNATIONAL, 356 (AUG 89), 10.
WHAT THE ISRAELIS DO NOT WANT THE WORLD TO KNOW IS THAT
BESIDES THE INTIFADA ON THE STREETS, A SECRET WAR BETWEEN
THE INTELLIGENCE SYSTEMS OF BOTH SIDES IS ALSO BEING WAGED.
ISRAELIS MURDER INDIVIDUALS WHOM THEY THINK ARE DANGEROUS,
SOMETIMES QUITE MISTAKENLY, WHILE THE PALESTINIANS KILL
THOSE WHO THEY BELIEVE ARE SPIES AND COLLABORATORS WITH THE
ISRAELI ENEMY. SIXTY COLLABORATORS HAVE BEEN EXECUTED SO FAR
AND THE LATEST COMMUNIQUE FROM THE UNIFIED COMMAND OF THE
INTIFADA CAUTIONED THAT VICTIMS MUST FIRST BE POSITIVELY
IDENTIFIED AS COLLABORATORS BEFORE ACTION IS TAKEN. THE MAIN
MOTIVATION OF THESE PERSONS IS MONEY; THE INTIFADA - THE
FREQUENT STRIKES AND THE LIMITATIONS OF BUSINESS TO JUST
THREE HOURS A DAY - HAS ADDED TO PALESTINIANS' ECONOMIC
HARDSHIPS.

04658 JANSEN, M.
CYPRUS TALKS STALLED
MIDDLE EAST INTERNATIONAL, (358) (SEP 89), 13-14.
SETTLEMENT NEGOTIATIONS BETWEEN GREEK AND TURKISH
CYPRIOT LEADERS STALLED OVER INTERPRETATION OF "IDEAS" PUT
FORTH BY UN SECRETARY-GENERAL PEREZ DE CUELLAR. ALTHOUGH THE
GREEK CYPRIOTS ACCEPTED DE CUELLAR'S PROPOSAL FOR A UNITED
FEDERAL REPUBLIC CONSISTING OF TWO "FEDERATED STATES"
ADMINISTERED BY THE TWO COMMUNITIES, TURKISH REPRESENTATIVES
CONTINUE TO ARGUE OVER THE PROPOSAL. THE TURKISH
REPRESENTATIVES ALSO EXPRESSED THEIR RESENTMENT AT THE
GROWING INTERNATIONAL PRESSURE AIMED AT FORCING CONCESSIONS.

04659 JANSEN, M.
CYPRUS: STILL TALKING
MIDDLE EAST INTERNATIONAL, (344) (FEB 89), 14-15.
THE AUTHOR REVIEWS THE GREEK AND TURKISH PROPOSALS UNDER
CONSIDERATION FOR A POLITICAL SETTLEMENT IN CYPRUS.

04660 JANSEN, M.
HOW THE PLO CHARTER HAS BECOME "CADUC"
MIDDLE EAST INTERNATIONAL, (350) (MAY 89), 4.
PLO CHAIRMAN YASSER ARAFAT WAS ON FIRM GROUND WHEN, ON 2
MAY 1989, HE DECLARED THE PALESTINE NATIONAL CHARTER TO BE
CADUC. OVER THE PAST 20 YEARS THE CHARTER'S ORIGINAL
MAXIMALIST PRINCIPLES HAVE BEEN ERODED, BYPASSED AND FLATLY
CONTRADICTED BY LEGISLATION ADOPTED BY SUCCESSIVE PALESTINE
NATIONAL COUNCILS IN VOTES EXCEEDING THE TWO-THIRDS MAJORITY
REQUIRED TO AMEND OR ABROGATE THE CHARTER.

04661 JANSEN, M.
INFLAMMATORY AND ILL-CONCEIVED
MIDDLE EAST INTERNATIONAL, 356 (AUG 89), 15-16.
NEGOTIATIONS ON A CYPRUS SETTLEMENT MAY, PARADOXICALLY,
HAVE BEEN BOOSTED RATHER THAN SET BACK BY THE MINI-CRISIS
PRECIPITATED ON 19-20 JULY BY AN ILL-CONCEIVED DEMONSTRATION
BY GREEK CYPRIOT WOMEN IN THE UN BUFFER ZONE SEPARATING THE
ISLAND'S TWO COMMUNITIES. THIS OUTBURST OF "HELLENISM" COULD
SPUR EUROPE, THE US AND THE USSR, WHICH ARE PROMOTING A
CYPRUS SETTLEMENT, TO PUT PRESSURE ON THE TWO SIDES TO
ACCEPT A DOCUMENT JUST TABLED BY THE SECRETARY-GENERAL. HIS
PROPOSALS INCLUDE THE WITHDRAWAL OF MOST FOREIGN FORCES FROM
CYPRUS, THE ESTABLISHMENT OF ETHNIC ZONES WITH CEILINGS FOR
SETTLEMENT EACH OF THE ZONES BY MEMBERS OF THE OTHER
COMMUNITY, A REDUCTION FROM 37 TO 26 PER CENT OF THE AREA
HELD BY TURKISH CYPRIOTS AND CONSTITUTIONAL CHECKS AND
BALANCES. SEPTEMBER HAS BEEN FIXED AS THE DEADLINE

04662 JANSEN, M.
    THE ARAB MILITARY DETERRENT
    MIDDLE EAST INTERNATIONAL, (344) (FEB 89), 16.
        POLITICO-MILITARY DEVELOPMENTS GENERATED BY THE IRAN-
    IRAQ WAR HAVE PRODUCED A NEW STABLE EQUILIBRIUM BETWEEN THE
    ARABS AND ISRAEL. FOR THE FIRST TIME SINCE ITS ESTABLISHMENT,
    ISRAEL'S FORCES CANNOT SIMPLY ATTACK AT WILL ANY ARAB STATE
    OR COMBINATION OF STATES. THIS SHIFT IN THE MILITARY
    POSITION DID NOT HAPPEN BECAUSE THE ARABS ACQUIRED A
    QUANTITATIVE OR QUALITATIVE EDGE OVER ISRAEL. THE ARABS
    REMAIN UNABLE TO MATCH ISRAEL'S VAST STATE-OF-THE-ART
    ARSENAL, WHICH MEANS THAT THE ARABS CANNOT LAUNCH AN
    OFFENSIVE. BUT THE ARABS HAVE WEAPONS OF MASS DESTRUCTION
    WHICH COULD CAUSE HEAVY CIVILIAN CASUALTIES IF DEPLOYED
    AGAINST ISRAEL'S CROWDED COASTAL CITIES. THE ARABS NOW HAVE
    EFFECTIVE DETERRENT POWER.

04663 JANSEN, M.
    THE PALESTINIANS' "GUARDIAN ANGELS"
    MIDDLE EAST INTERNATIONAL, 356 (AUG 89), 9.
        THE PALESTINIANS HAVE "GUARDIAN ANGELS", CIVIL AND HUMAN
    RIGHTS GROUPINGS, BOTH PALESTINIAN AND ISRAELI, WHICH
    COLLECT INFORMATION ABOUT ABUSES, REPORT ON THEM AND
    INTERVENE WITH THE OCCUPATION AUTHORITIES ON BEHALF OF
    INDIVIDUALS. THERE IS THE ISRAELI FOUNDED AND FUNDED "HOT
    LINE FOR VICTIMS OF VIOLENCE" WHICH RUNS AN OFFICE IN EAST
    JERUSALEM STAFFED BY VOLUNTEER STUDENTS FROM THE HEBREW
    UNIVERSITY, BOTH ISRAELI AND PALESTINIAN. FIVE TO SEVEN
    PEOPLE COME TO THEM DAILY. IN THEIR FIRST YEAR THEY HAVE
    HANDLED OVER 700 CASES. THE PALESTINIAN HUMAN RIGHTS
    INFORMATION CENTRE COOPERATES "ON A STRICTLY NON-POLITICAL,
    HUMANITARIAN BASIS" WITH THE ISRAELI CITIZENS RIGHTS
    MOVEMENT OF SHULAMIT ALONI, WHICH TAKES UP VIOLATIONS
    DIRECTLY WITH THE AUTHORITIES. AL-HAQ, OR LAW IN THE SERVICE
    OF MAN, AND THE ISRAELI LEAGUE FOR HUMAN AND CIVIL RIGHTS
    ALSO SEND INVESTIGATORS INTO THE FIELD AND MAKE
    REPRESENTATIONS TO A GOVERNMENT WHICH OCCASIONALLY LISTENS.

04664 JANUS, M.
    PRIVATIZING CORRECTIONS: SYMBOLIC AND POLICY ISSUES
    BUREAUCRAT, 18(1) (SPR 89), 32-36.
        INTEREST IN THE PRIVATIZATION OF CORRECTIONS HAS SURGED
    DUE TO THE INCREASING INMATE POPULATIONS, TIGHT GOVERNMENTAL
    BUDGETS, GROWING COURT INTERVENTION IN THE ADMINISTRATION OF
    CORRECTIONS, DISENCHANTMENT WITH THE GOVERNMENT'S ABILITY TO
    PERFORM ANY TASK EFFECTIVELY, AND A FONDNESS FOR PRIVATE
    SECTOR VALUES. IN THIS ARTICLE, THE AUTHOR IDENTIFIES THE
    POTENTIAL SUBSTANTIVE AND SYMBOLIC IMPACTS OF PRIVATE
    CORRECTIONS AND PROVIDES A DETAILED FOCUS ON THE SYMBOLIC
    AND PUBLIC POLICY IMPLICATIONS OF PRISONS FOR PROFIT.

04665 JANWAL, M.
    END USER COMPUTING IN ASIAN COUNTRIES: POLICY LESSONS FOR
    DEVELOPMENT ADMINISTRATION
    PUBLIC ADMINISTRATION AND DEVELOPMENT, 9(5) (NOV 89),
    513-522.
        END USER COMPUTING REQUIRES POLICY INITIATIVES VERY
    DIFFERENT FROM THOSE NEEDED FOR COMPUTERIZATION IN ORDER TO
    DEAL WITH THE SPECIFIC ISSUES OF INITIATION, DEVELOPMENT AND
    INSTITUTIONALIZATION. MICROCOMPUTERS PROVIDE A SERVICE AND
    NOT GOODS OR SAVINGS AND REQUIRE AN EMPHASIS ON THE DYNAMICS
    OF THE SYSTEM, WHERE BOTH STRATEGIC ISSUES AND OPERATIONAL
    PRIORITIES HAVE TO BE SET. THE PROCESS IS ORGANIZATIONAL,
    RATHER THAN A TECHNOLOGICAL OR A PLANNING EXERCISE. IT
    REQUIRES GOVERNMENTS TO GUIDE THE CHANGE THROUGH DELIBERATE
    DECISION MAKING. THE OBJECTIVE HAS TO BE TO OBTAIN THE
    SUPPORT OF USERS AT DIFFERENT LEVELS. IN THIS PAPER ASIAN
    EXPERIENCES ARE COMPARED WITH WESTERN EXPERIENCES TO
    DETERMINE A FRAMEWORK FOR LOOKING AT THE PROCESS. THE
    LIMITED SET OF STRATEGIES FOR SUCCESS HAVE ALSO BEEN
    IDENTIFIED.

04666 JARAUSCH, K.H.; ARMINGER, G.
    THE GERMAN TEACHING PROFESSION AND NAZI PARTY MEMBERSHIP:
    A DEMOGRAPHIC LOGIT MODEL
    JOURNAL OF INTERDISCIPLINARY HISTORY, XX(2) (AUT 89),
    197-225.
        THE AUTHORS STUDY THE GERMAN TEACHING PROFESSION IN THE
    THIRD REICH, WHEN IT WAS HIGHLY STRATIFIED BY EXAMINATIONS
    AND ENTITLEMENTS. THE PROFESSIONAL CLEAVAGES HERE REINFORCED
    BY DEMOGRAPHIC DIVISIONS, WHICH COMBINED WITH OTHER FACTORS
    TO DIVIDE THE VOCATION. GIVEN SUCH CLEAVAGES, IT IS NO
    WONDER THAT GERMAN TEACHERS SELDOM SPOKE WITH A UNITED VOICE.
    THIS MAKES THE UNIFORMITY AND BREATH OF NAZIFICATION OF
    GERMAN EDUCATORS ALL THE MORE SURPRISING.

04667 JARBAWI, A.; HUNTER, R.
    SHAMIR'S ELECTION PLAN
    MIDDLE EAST INTERNATIONAL, (358) (SEP 89), 15-16.
        THE ARTICLE EXAMINES THE FIVE MONTH-OLD PEACE PLAN OF
    ISRAEL'S PRIME MINISTER, YITZHAK SHAMIR. IT ANALYZES BOTH
    THE INTERNAL AND INTERNATIONAL PRESSURES THAT LED TO THE
    INITIAL PROPOSAL FOR ELECTIONS ON THE OCCUPIED TERRITORIES.
    IT TRACES THE DEVELOPMENT OF THE PLAN AS QUALIFYING DEMANDS

WERE PLACED ON IT BY THE PLO AND BY LIKUD RIGHT-WINGERS SUCH
AS ARIEL SHARON. ALTHOUGH THE FACT THAT THE PLAN STILL
EXISTS IN ANY FORM IS SOMEWHAT OF A MIRACLE, LITTLE PROGRESS
TOWARDS SOLVING THE FUNDAMENTAL QUESTION OF SOVEREIGNTY IN
THE OCCUPIED TERRITORIES HAS BEEN MADE. THE ARTICLE
CONCLUDES THAT THE PEACE PLAN IS MERELY A PLOY TO BUT TIME
FOR ISRAEL IN HOPES THAT THE INTIFADA AND INTERNATIONAL
PRESSURE WILL SLOW DOWN.

04668 JARRETT, J.E.
    RECENT SERVICE-DELIVERY IMPROVEMENTS IN STATE AND LOCAL
    GOVERNMENTS
    NATIONAL CIVIC REVIEW, 78(2) (MAR 89), 85-93.
        IN SPITE OF A GENERAL PUBLIC PERCEPTION - ARTICULATED
    MOST EFFECTIVELY BY PROPONENTS OF PRIVATIZATION - THAT
    GOVERNMENT EMPLOYEES ARE NEITHER PRODUCTIVE NOR QUALITY
    ORIENTED, NUMEROUS EXAMPLES OF SERVICE-IMPROVEMENT EFFORTS
    MAY BE CITED. WHETHER INITIATED BY LINE WORKERS OR TOP
    MANAGEMENT, INVOLVING HIGH TECHNOLOGY OR MERELY MORE
    EFFICIENT USE OF CURRENT RESOURCES, SERVICE-DELIVERY AND
    OPERATIONAL IMPROVEMENTS INDICATE A MOVE TOWARD GREATER
    ACCOUNTABILITY IN PUBLIC AGENCIES.

04669 JARUZELSKI, W.
    CHANGING POLAND IN A CHANGING EUROPE
    CONTEMPORARY POLAND, XXII(7) (1989), 28-31.
        THE VECTOR OF CHANGE IN POLAND IS NOT WITHOUT ITS
    IMPORTANCE FOR THE WHOLE EUROPEAN SITUATION. POLAND IS
    LOCATED AT A KEY GEOGRAPHIC JUNCTURE ON THE CONTINENT.
    THROUGH POLAND LIES THE SHORTEST WAY FROM WEST TO EAST, FROM
    NORTH TO SOUTH. FOR CENTURIES, POLAND HAS BEEN AN IMPORTANT
    ELEMENT IN EUROPEAN STRATEGIC SCHEMES, IRRESPECTIVE OF THE
    ALTERING ALIGNMENT OF FORCES. NOW POLAND HAS UNDERTAKEN
    POLITICAL AND ECONOMIC REFORMS THAT REFLECT THE CHANGING
    INTERNATIONAL SITUATION AS WELL AS ITS OWN INTERNAL NEED FOR
    CHANGE.

04670 JARUZELSKI, W.
    POLAND: SOCIALISM CORRECTS ITSELF
    INFORMATION BULLETIN, 26(21-22) (NOV 88), 5-7.
        JARIZELSKI COMMENTS THAT THE POLISH INITIATIVES FOR
    INCREASED DEMOCRACY, ARMS CONTROL AND ECONOMIC REFORM COULD
    APPEAR AND AROUSE REAL INTEREST ONLY THANKS TO THE OPENNESS
    IN EAST-WEST RELATIONS THAT HAS BEEN CREATED BY THE NEW
    THINKING AND THE SOVIET PEACE OFFENSIVE. THE SOVIET-AMERICAN
    DIALOGUE IS OF DECISIVE IMPORTANCE.

04671 JARVIS, A.
    THE AUSTRALIAN CONSTITUTIONAL REFERENDUM: 1988
    ELECTORAL STUDIES, 8(1) (APR 89), 87-90.
        THE ARTICLE OUTLINES THE FOUR CONSTITUTIONAL REFERENDUMS
    THAT TOOK PLACE IN AUSTRALIA IN 1988. IT ANALYZES THE
    REFERENDUM STRUCTURE, THE NATURE OF THE REFERENDUMS
    THEMSELVE THE CAMPIAGN FOR SUPPORT, AND THE END RESULTS.

04672 JASON, P.
    ENGINEERING DEMOCRACY
    NEW AFRICAN, (OCT 89), 39.
        THIS ARTICLE REPORTS ON THE PROGRESS OF THE NIGERIAN
    MILITARY GOVERN MENT IN IT'S EFFORTS TO ESTABLISH THE
    DEMOCRATIC PROCESS THERE. THAT THE INTENSE DESIRE TO SEE
    THAT FAIR PLAY, MODERATION AND CONSENSUS OPERATES AT ALL
    LEVELS IN THE HANDOVER TO CIVILIAN RULE MAY BE INTERFERING
    WITH THE VERY DEMOCRACY THE GOVERNMENT WANTS TO ESTABLISH IS
    EXPLORED. THE MASS OF CONTRADICTIONS IS ANALYSED.

04673 JASON, P.
    FIKA DEPARTURE AND CIVIL SERVICE REFORMS
    AFRICAN BUSINESS, (JUN 88), 19-20.
        THIS ARTICLE REPORTS ON CIVIL SERVICE REFORMS INSTITUTED
    BY NIGERIAN PRESIDENT, BABANGIDA. IT DESCRIBES THE
    RESISTANCE OF THE CIVIL SERVANTS AFFECTED BY THE REFORM AND
    THE ENSUING POWER STRUGGLES. THE EFFECTIVENESS OF THE
    REFORMS IS QUESTIONED BY OTHERS ALSO WHO FEAR THAT TOO MUCH
    POWER IN THE HANDS OF A MINISTER MAY RESULT IN FINANCIAL
    MISMANAGEMENT. THE REPORTING SYSTEM IS DESCRIBED.

04674 JASON, P.
    NIGERIA BASHES THE PRESS
    NEW AFRICAN, (258) (MAR 89), 40.
        ONCE THE BASTION OF PRESS FREEDOM IN AFRICA, NIGERIA IS
    NOW PASSING LEGISLATION THAT WILL BE MORE REPRESSIVE THAN
    SOUTH AFRICA'S. IN THE PAST, NIGERIA'S TOP JOURNALIST HAVE
    LED A MEDIA WAR AGAINST CORRUPTION IN HIGH PLACES. IF SOME
    JOURNALISTS ARE OUTLAWED AND OTHERS ARE INTIMIDATED BY THE
    NEW LAW, THE AUTHORITIES WILL BE ASSURED OF A SYCOPHANTIC
    PRESS THAT PANDERS TO THE WHIMS OF THE RULERS.

04675 JASON, P.
    WILL THE ARMY GO?
    NEW AFRICAN, (260) (MAY 89), 25-26.
        NIGERIA'S MILITARY HANDOVER TO CIVILIANS WILL BEGIN IN
    EARNEST IN 1989 AND CLIMAX WITH LOCAL GOVERNMENT ELECTIONS
    IN 1992. BUT THERE IS GROWING SCEPTICISM ABOUT THE

TRANSITION. NIGERIANS CONCEDE THAT ANY MILITARY GOVERNMENT IS USUALLY MINDFUL OF WHO SUCCEEDS IT, BUT THEY DID NOT EXPECT THE GOVERNMENT TO GO ABOUT SELECTING ITS SUCCESSORS SO OPENLY.

04676 JAUDON, B.
PULLING THE PLUG ON NUCLEAR POWER
SOJOURNERS. 18(3) (MAR 89), 4.
DESPITE TREMENDOUS COST OVERRUNS, GROSS MISMANAGEMENT, CLIMBING INTEREST RATES, AND SLUMPING DEMAND, NUCLEAR POWER IS HANGING ON. IT REMAINS ON A LIFE-SUPPORT SYSTEM FROM THE FEDERAL GOVERNMENT, WHICH HAS REFUSED TO PULL THE PLUG ON THE DYING INDUSTRY. MEANWHILE, THE PUBLIC IS LEFT WITH THE BILL AS THE UTILITIES THAT OWN THE NUCLEAR FACILITIES ATTEMPT TO HIKE THEIR RATES TO RECOUP THEIR LOSSES.

04677 JAUDON, B.
THE BRUTALITY OF EL SALVADOR'S "DEMOCRACY"
SOJOURNERS. 18(7) (JUL 89), 4.
THE ESCALATING REPRESSION AGAINST SALVADORAN CIVILIANS COMES JUST WEEKS AFTER ARENA WON THE PRESIDENTIAL ELECTION. IT DEFEATED THE CHRISTIAN DEMOCRATS, WHO HAD FALLEN FROM GRACE, AND THE DEMOCRATIC CONVERGENCE, WHICH IS STILL IN THE EMBRYONIC STAGE SINCE ITS CANDIDATES RETURNED FROM EXILE LESS THAN TWO YEARS AGO. ARENA'S VICTORY WAS HAILED BY THE BUSH ADMINISTRATION AS ANOTHER VICTORY FOR DEMOCRACY IN EL SALVADOR. BUT DEMOCRACY REQUIRES MORE THAN JUST ELECTIONS. AND U.S. OFFICIALS HAVE SIMPLY LOOKED THE OTHER WAY AS THE SALVADORAN AUTHORITIES HAVE SHOWN JUST WHAT KIND OF BRUTAL DEMOCRACY THEY ARE CAPABLE OF.

04678 JAUDON, B.
TURNING HOUSING INTO A RIGHT
SOJOURNERS, 18(8) (AUG 89), 8-12.
FEDERAL NEGLECT, DISINVESTMENT, AND GENTRIFICATION IN RECENT DECADES HAVE INSTEAD LED TO A HOUSING CRISIS THAT IS UNMATCHED IN U.S. HISTORY, ACCORDING TO ADVOCATES FOR AFFORDABLE HOUSING. IF A CONSENSUS EXISTS AMONG ACTIVISTS ABOUT WHAT IS NEEDED, IT IS THAT THE FEDERAL GOVERNMENT MUST BECOME A PLAYER AGAIN AND REINVEST IN AFFORDABLE HOUSING PROGRAMS. FEW, HOWEVER, BELIEVE THAT KEMP HAS THE ADMINISTRATION SUPPORT PRESIDENT BUSH PROMISED HIM WHEN HE ACCEPTED THE POST AT HUD, A PROBLEM THAT SO FAR HAS PREVENTED ANY SIGNIFICANT FEDERAL HOUSING INITIATIVES.

04679 JAYARAM, P.
SRI LANKA: CHARTING A NEW COURSE
INDIA TODAY, XIV(10) (MAY 89), 50-52.
BY INITIATING PEACE PARLEYS WITH LIBERATION TIGERS OF TAMIL EELAM (LTTE) WITHOUT NEW DELHI'S PRESENCE, THE PREMADASA GOVERNMENT HAS EMPHASIZED THAT IT INTENDS TO WORK OUT ITS OWN SOLUTIONS TO THE CONTINUING ETHNIC STRIFE WITHOUT THE INDIAN PEACEKEEPING FORCE IN SRI TANKA.

04680 JAYASINGHE, E.
THE DECLARATION OF THE INDIAN OCEAN AS A ZONE OF PEACE AND ITS IMPLEMENTATION
DISARMAMENT, XII(3) (AUT 89), 120-129.
ESTABLISHING A ZONE OF PEACE IN THE INDIAN OCEAN WILL BE ARDUOUS AND HIGHLY COMPLEX AND WILL REQUIRE AN ATMOSPHERE OF MUTUAL TRUST AND CONFIDENCE. IT WILL DEMAND GREAT UNDERSTANDING AND THE COOPERATION OF ALL PARTIES INVOLVED. IT WILL REQUIRE RE-EXAMINATION AND ADJUSTMENTS OF NATIONAL AND GROUP INTERESTS. HOW BEST AND HOW SOON AN AGREEMENT ON THE ESTABLISHMENT OF A PEACE ZONE IN THE INDIAN OCEAN CAN BE REACHED WILL DEPEND, TO A GREAT EXTENT, NOT ON THE PREVAILING CONDITIONS IN THE INDIAN OCEAN REGION OR ELSEWHERE BUT ON THE POLITICAL WILL OF MEMBER STATES TO PROMOTE INTERNATIONAL PEACE AND SECURITY.

04681 JAYRAM, P.; CHAWLA, P.
SRI LANKA: A DIPLOMATIC DEADLOCK
INDIA TODAY, XIV(12) (JUN 89), 70-71.
THIS ARTICLE DESCRIBES THE STANDOFF BETWEEN SRI LANKAN PRESIDENT R. PREMSDASA AND INDIAN PRIME MINISTER RAJIV GANDHI OVER THE QUESTION OF THE WITHDRAWAL OF THE INDIAN PEACEKEEPING FORCE (IPKF) FROM THE NORTHEASTERN PROVINCES. IT IS NOT GOING TO ADD TO INDIA'S PRESTIGE OF THE IPKF PULLS OUT AND ANOTHER ROUND OF BLOODY ENCOUNTERS ENSUES. BUT PREMADASA IS DETERMINED TO OUST THE IPKF SOON.

04682 JEAN, C.
ECONOMIC IMPLICATIONS OF THE USE OF NEW TECHNOLOGIES IN DEVELOPMENT OF NATO FORCES
INTERNATIONAL SPECTATOR, XXIII(1) (JAN 88), 43-52.
THE CONCEPT OF EMERGING TECHNOLOGIES IS AN EXPRESSION OF THE WEST'S INTENT TO COMPENSATE FOR THE WARSAW PACT'S QUANTITATIVE SUPERIORITY WITH A HIGHER LEVEL OF TECHNOLOGY. EMERGING TECHNOLOGIES INCLUDE A VAST RANGE OF AVANT-GARDE TECHNICAL DEVELOPMENTS IN DIVERSE SECTORS FROM MICRO-ELECTONICS TO SOPHISTICATED SOFTWARE, FROM NEW MATERIALS TO BIO-ENGINEERING. IT IS DIFFICULT TO ASSESS BOTH THE COST OF ET'S AND THEIR CONCRETE APPLICATIONS. IT IS ALSO DIFFICULT TO EVALUATE WHAT THEIR ACTUAL EFFECT ON THE WEST'S DEFENSE

CAPABILITIES WILL BE AND WHAT CHANGES IN FORCE STRUCTURE AND DOCTRINE THEY MAY ENTAIL.

04683 JEANNOT, T.M.
MORAL LEADERSHIP AND PRACTICAL WISDOM
INTERNATIONAL JOURNAL OF SOCIAL ECONOMICS, 16(6) (1989), 14-38.
BOOK VI OF ARISTOTLE'S NICOMACHEAN ETHICS IS COMMENTED ON, SHOWING ITS RELEVANCE TO SOME THEMES IN CONTEMPORARY MORAL PHILOSOPHY. IT IS ARGUED THAT THE CLASSICAL APPROACH TO MORALITY (ARISTOTLE) AND THE ENLIGHTENED APPROACH (KANT) NEED NOT COMPOSE ANTINOMY. INSTEAD, THE ARISTOTELIAN EMPHASES ON THE DEVELOPMENT OF VIRTUOUS CHARACTER AND THE NATURE OF PRACTICAL WISDOM COALESCE WITH THE KANTIAN EMPHASIS ON AUTONOMY -- WHAT FALK CALLS "RESPONSIBLE SELF-DIRECTION" -- IN THE PERSON OF THE MORAL LEADER. IN PARTICULAR, GREAT MORALISTS HAVE RECOGNISED THAT MORAL WISDOM IS NOT MAINLY A MATTER OF STRICT OBEDIENCE TO RULES. WHILE RULES HAVE THEIR PLACE, THE SUBJECT MATTER OF ETHICS CANNOT BE DETERMINED BY A QUASI-MATHEMATICAL FORMALISM. OVER-EMPHASIS ON THE FORMALISM OF THE CATEGORICAL IMPERATIVE OBSCURES KANT'S MORE FUNDAMENTAL EMPHASIS ON AUTONOMY. THE AUTONOMOUS PERSON, ABLE TO EXERCISE MORAL LEADERSHIP, CULTIVATES THE ARISTOTELIAN VIRTUE OF PHRONESIS.

04684 JEFFE, S.B.
GUN CONTROL: A SHIFT IN ATTITUDES
STATE LEGISLATURES, 15(5) (MAY 89), 12-15.
STATE LEGISLATORS ACROSS THE NATION RESPONDED TO THE STOCKTON, CALIFORNIA, SCHOOLYARD MASSACRE BY INITIATING THE MOST INTENSIVE EXAMINATION OF FIREARMS REGULATION IN 20 YEARS. THERE WAS A SIMILAR FLURRY OF ACTIVITY IN CONGRESS. EVEN LEADERS LIKE PRESIDENT BUSH AND CALIFORNIA'S GOVERNOR DEUKMEJIAN BEGAN TO TAKE A SECOND LOOK AT THE ISSUE.

04685 JEFFERSON, G.H.
POTENTIAL SOURCES OF PRODUCTIVITY GROWTH WITHIN CHINESE INDUSTRY
WORLD DEVELOPMENT, 17(1) (JAN 89), 45-57.
THIS PAPER PRESENTS AN APPROACH FOR MODELING AND ESTIMATING POTENTIAL SOURCES OF PRODUCTIVITY GROWTH WITHIN FOUR MAJOR SECTORS OF CHINESE INDUSTRY - THE STATE AND COLLECTIVE SECTORS AND HEAVY AND LIGHT INDUSTRY. THE FINDINGS, BASED UPON INDUSTRIAL DATA FROM 293 CHINESE COUNTIES, INDICATE THAT SUBSTANTIAL PRODUCTIVITY GAINS CAN BE ACHIEVED BY TRANSFERRING TECHNOLOGY FROM THE STATE TO THE COLLECTIVE SECTOR, EXPLOITING ENTERPRISE AND AGGLOMERATIVE SCALE ECONOMIES, AND REALLOCATING INVESTMENT AND LABOR TO TAKE ADVANTAGE OF LARGE DISPARITIES BETWEEN FACTOR RETURNS AMONG THE SECTORS. THE IMPLICATIONS FOR THE RESULTS OF SEVERAL IDIOSYNCRACIES OF CHINESE INDUSTRIAL PRICES AND DATA ARE EXAMINED.

04686 JEFFERY, R.
THE POLITICS OF HEALTH IN INDIA
UNIVERSITY OF CALIFORNIA PRESS, BERKELEY, CA, 1988, 368.
THE AUTHOR SUMMARIZES THE STATUS OF PUBLIC HEALTH AND HEALTH SERVICES IN INDIA BEFORE INDEPENDENCE. AFTER CONSIDERING THE LEGACY OF BRITISH RULE, HE ASSESSES PATTERNS OF HEALTH EXPENDITURE, THE EDUCATION OF HEALTH PERSONNEL, AND THE OPERATION OF HEALTH INSTITUTIONS SINCE 1947.

04687 JELAVICH, B.
TSARIST RUSSIA AND THE BALKAN SLAVIC CONNECTION
CANADIAN REVIEW OF STUDIES IN NATIONALISM, XVI(1-2) (1989), 209-226.
THE RELATIONSHIP OF TSARIST RUSSIA TO THE EAST EUROPEAN NATIONAL MOVEMENTS IN THE NINETEENTH CENTURY WAS EXCEEDINGLY COMPLEX AND AFFECTED BOTH RUSSIAN DOMESTIC AND FOREIGN POLICY. THIS ESSAY LOOKS AT THE REACTION OF THOSE RESPONSIBLE FOR THE DIRECTION OF RUSSIAN FOREIGN AFFAIRS, EMPHASIZING THE ATTITUDES OF THOSE WHO MADE THE CONCRETE DECISIONS RATHER THAN THE OPINIONS OF THOSE WHO CONSIDERED NATIONALITY PROBLEMS IN GENERAL OR HAD A SPECIFIC INTEREST IN ONE OR MORE OF THE MOVEMENTS.

04688 JENCKS, H.W.
THE MILITARY IN CHINA
CURRENT HISTORY, 88(539) (SEP 89), 265-268, 291-293.
THE MASSACRE OF UNARMED DEMONSTRATORS IN TIANANMEN SQUARE REVERSED A DECADE-LONG TREND OF MILITARY PROFESSIONALIZATION AND DISENGAGEMENT FROM POLITICS BY THE CHINESE PEOPLE'S LIBERATION ARMY.

04689 JENISCH, U.
THE NORTH SEA--INTERNATIONAL LAW OF THE SEA AND ENVIRONMENTAL PROTECTION
AUSSEN POLITIK, 40(1) (JAN 89), 76-93.
THE ARTICLE EXAMINES THE GROWING PROBLEM OF ENVIRONMENTAL POLLUTION IN THE NORTH SEA. IT ALSO EXAMINES THE VARIOUS AGREEMENTS THAT VARIOUS NATIONS IN THE EUROPEAN COMMUNITY HAVE MADE TO ATTEMPT TO ARREST THE SPREAD OF POLLUTION. IT EXPLORES THE VARIOUS CAUSES OF POLLUTION AND CONCLUDE THAT A LARGE PART OF POLLUTION IS CAUSED BY RIVERS

AS OPPOSED TO COASTAL AREAS; THIS FACT NECESSITATES FURTHER
ACTION INLAND.

04690 JENISH, D.
ABORTION ON TRIAL
MACLEAN'S (CANADA'S NEWS MAGAZINE), 102(30) (JUL 89),
14-17.
EIGHTEEN MONTHS AFTER THE SUPREME COURT OF CANADA
DECLARED THE COUNTRY'S ABORTION LAW UNCONSTITUTIONAL,
ABORTION RIGHTS ARE ONCE AGAIN UNDER ATTACK. THE
CONTROVERSIAL CASES OF BARBARA DODD AND CHANTAL DAIGLE HAVE
BROUGHT THE EVER DIVISIVE ISSUE INTO THE PUBLIC EYE ONCE
AGAIN. AS THE COURTS MOVE TO DECIDE ON THESE AND OTHER CASES,
THE BATTLE LINES IN THE SEEMINGLY NEVER ENDING BATTLE OVER
ABORTION RIGHTS ARE ONCE AGAIN DRAWN.

04691 JENISH, D.
LOOKING AHEAD
MACLEAN'S (CANADA'S NEWS MAGAZINE), 102(1) (JAN 89), 10-13.
THE ARTICLE EXAMINES THE RESULTS OF AN ANNUAL POLL AMONG
CANADIANS. THE RESULTS INDICATE THAT THE MAJORITY OF
CANADIANS ARE CONFIDENT THAT THEIR CURRENT PROSPERITY WILL
CONTINUE. HOWEVER, MANY OF THE ARE CONCERNED WITH THE
CHANGING QUALITY OF LIFE, INCLUDING CHANGES AFFECTING
PERSONAL SAFETY, HOUSING, THE ENVIRONMENT, AND MORALS AND
MANNERS.

04692 JENISH, D.; DALT, J.; WALLACE, B.
TAKEOVER FEVER HITS CANADA
MACLEAN'S (CANADA'S NEWS MAGAZINE), 102(5) (JAN 89), 30-33.
CANADIAN BUSINESS MOVES FURTHER ONTO THE WORLD STAGE AS
THREE UNRELATED TRANSACTIONS IN THE CANADIAN BEER, AIRLINE,
AND OIL INDUSTRIES--WITH A TOTAL PRICE TAG OF $6.7 BILLION--
ALLOWED VICTORS TO CLAIM CORPORATIONS EMPLOYING 12,800
WORKERS AND HOLDING ASSETS OF $5.1 BILLION. QUESTIONS ABOUT
THE IMPACT OF THE MERGERS (SUCH AS INCREASED PRICE DUE TO
LACK OF COMPETITION) REMAIN, BUT THE DRAMATIC RESTRUCTURING
SIGNALS THE BEGINNING OF A NEW ECONOMIC ERA IN CANADA.

04693 JENKINS, D.
BILL HAYDEN: A NATIONALIST, A SOCIALIST AND A REPUBLICAN
FAR EASTERN ECONOMIC REVIEW, 141(37) (SEP 88), 26-27.
THE ARTICLE ANALYZES BILL HAYDEN'S FIVE-AND-A-HALF
TENURE AS AUSTRALIA'S FOREIGN MINISTER. IT CONCLUDES THAT
HAYDEN WAS A COMPETENT, DILIGENT, AND HARD WORKING AND HARD
TRAVELLING MINISTER. HOWEVER, THE JOB IS A DIFFICULT ONE AND
HAYDEN MAY HAVE HAD LESS IMPACT THAN HE HAD HOPED FOR.
HAYDEN RECENTLY LEFT HIS POST TO ASSUME THE POST OF
AUSTRALIA'S GOVERNOR-GENERAL.

04694 JENKINS, J.C.; BRENTS, B.G.
SOCIAL PROTEST, HEGEMONIC COMPETITION, AND SOCIAL REFORM:
A POLITICAL STRUGGLE INTERPRETATION OF THE ORIGINS OF THE
AMERICAN WELFARE STATE
AMERICAN SOCIOLOGICAL REVIEW, 54(6) (DEC 89), 891-909.
RECENT NEO-MARXIAN AND STATE-CENTRIC ANALYSES OF THE
ORIGINS OF THE AMERICAN WELFARE STATE HAVE MISSPECIFIED THE
AUTONOMY OF THE STATE, THEREBY CONFLATING POLICY FORMULATION
WITH POLICY-MAKING AND MISSING THE COMPLEX POLITICAL
STRUGGLES THAT SHAPED THE FORMULATION OF THE SOCIAL SECURITY
ACT OF 1935. SYNTHESIZING POULANTZAS'S "CLASS STRUGGLE"
THEORY OF STATE WITH SOCIAL PROTEST THEORY AND DOMHOFF'S
ANALYSIS OF CAPITALIST DOMINANCE, THE AUTHORS ADVANCE A
POLITICAL STRUGGLE THEORY THAT IDENTIFIES TWO MAJOR
PROCESSES LEADING TO SOCIAL REFORMS: (1) SUSTAINED PROTEST
WAVES BY EXCLUDED GROUPS AND THREATENED POLITY MEMBERS THAT
CREATE A SENSE OF POLITICAL CRISIS AMONG ELITES; AND (2)
HEGEMONIC COMPETITION BETWEEN CAPITALIST BLOCS THAT USE
POLICY-PLANNING AND ELECTORAL INVESTMENTS TO PROMOTE
ALTERNATIVE POLITICAL PROGRAMS. THIS MODEL IS THEN APPLIED
TO THE FORMULATION OF THE SOCIAL SECURITY ACT. UNEMPLOYED
PROTESTS, INDUSTRIAL STRIKES, AND MIDDLE-CLASS REFORM
MOVEMENTS, INTERACTING WITH ELECTORAL INSTABILITY, CREATED
AN ELITE SENSE OF POLITICAL CRISIS. SIMULTANEOUSLY, RIVAL
CAPITALIST BLOCS CENTERED IN BANK GROUPS AND INDUSTRIAL
SEGMENTS COMPETED FOR POLITICAL DOMINANCE, CREATING
OPPORTUNITIES FOR PROTEST AND PLACING MAJOR REFORMS ON THE
NATIONAL POLITICAL AGENDA.

04695 JENKINS, J.C.; ECKERT, C.M.
THE CORPORATE ELITE, THE NEW CONSERVATIVE POLICY NETWORK,
AND REAGANOMICS
CRITICAL SOCIOLOGY, 16(2-3) (SUM 89), 121-144.
THIS ARTICLE PROVIDES A POLICY HISTORY OF THE
FORMULATION OF THE REAGANOMICS PROGRAM AND ITS INSERTION
INTO THE NATIONAL POLITICAL AGENDA, SHOWING THAT IT STEMMED
FROM POLICY-PLANNING EFFORTS OF A NEW CONSERVATIVE NETWORK
OF POLICY ORGANIZATIONS. THE AUTHORS ALSO PROVIDE AN ELITE
ANALYSIS OF THE STRUCTURE OF THIS POLICY NETWORK, SHOWING
THAT THE INNER CIRCLE AND UPPER TIER OF THE CAPITALIST CLASS
SUPPORTED THE AUSTERITY CAMP AS WELL AS THE TRADITIONAL
KEYNESIAN MODERATES, WHILE SUNBELT COWBOYS TENDED TO SUPPORT
THE MORE CONSERVATIVE SUPPLY-SIDERS. THE CORPORATE ELITE
REMAINS THE HEGEMONIC GROUP WITHIN THE CAPITALIST CLASS,

WORKING IN COALITION WITH A NEWLY MOBILIZED COWBOY STRATUM.

04696 JENKINS, P.
UNDER TWO FLAGS; PROVOCATION AND DECEPTION IN EUROPEAN
TERRORISM
TERRORISM, 11(4) (1988), 263-274.
THE STUDY OF TERRORISM IS OFTEN COMPLICATED BY THE
TENDENCY OF GROUPS TO ISSUE FALSE OR MISLEADING CLAIMS OF
RESPONSIBILITY, A PRACTICE WHICH DATES BACK AT LEAST TO THE
LATE NINETEENTH CENTURY. THIS PAPER DESCRIBES AND
CATEGORIZES VARIOUS PATTERNS OF FALSE CLAIMS AND
ATTRIBUTIONS IN CONTEMPORARY EUROPEAN TERRORISM. THESE
DECEPTIONS ARE PRACTICED BOTH BY TERRORIST GROUPS THEMSELVES
AND SOMETIMES BY OFFICIAL AGENCIES. THE PAPER ALSO ARGUES
FOR A MORE SUBTLE AND CRITICAL EVALUATION OF CLAIMS OF
RESPONSIBILITY THAN HAS BEEN FOUND IN SOME RECENT ACCOUNTS
OF TERRORIST MOVEMENTS.

04697 JENKINS, T.
NICARAGUA'S LOST DECADE
SOUTH, (107) (SEP 89), 10-11.
NICARAGUA'S ECONOMY IS IN SHREDS. POPULAR SUPPORT FOR
THE REVOLUTION HAS BEEN ERODED. THE CONSENSUS AMONG
INTERNATIONAL OBSERVERS IS THAT THE SANDINISTAS WILL LOSE AT
THE POLLS IN FEBRUARY 1990 IF THE ELECTIONS ARE FREE AND
FAIR.

04698 JENKINS, T.
THE WAR BUSH WANTS TO FORGET
SOUTH, (99) (JAN 89), 31.
THE BUSH TEAM IS PREPARING FOR THE DEMISE OF THE CONTRAS
WITH A NEW POLICY: ACTIVE CONTAINMENT. THIS MEANS THE USA
WILL ATTEMPT TO ISOLATE NICARAGUA AND AT THE SAME TIME
PROVIDE MORE RESOURCES FOR THE OTHER CENTRAL AMERICAN
COUNTRIES, BOTH MILITARY AND ECONOMIC. THE USA WILL ALSO
PRESSURE ITS ALLIES TO STARVE NICARAGUA OF CASH AND RESTRICT
TRADE EVEN MORE THAN AT PRESENT. THE REGIONAL FOCUS WILL
MOVE TO EL SALVADOR.

04699 JENNINGS, B.
ETHICAL POLITICS VS. POLITICAL ETHICS: TOO MUCH OF A GOOD
THING?
JOURNAL OF STATE GOVERNMENT, 62(5) (SEP 89), 173-175.
IN THE NEW ETHICAL CLIMATE OF GOVERNMENT, THERE IS A
DANGER THAT THE QUEST FOR A MORE ETHICAL POLITICS IS BEING
TRANSFORMED INTO A CYNICAL MODE OF POLITICIZED ETHICS.

04700 JENSEN, H.; JANSSEN, B.; MASTERMAN, S.
A COMMON HOME
MACLEAN'S (CANADA'S NEWS MAGAZINE), 102(28) (JUL 89),
18-19.
PROMOTING HIS VISION OF GLASNOST AND PERESTROIKA, SOVIET
LEADER MIKHAIL GORBACHEV VISITED BOTH PARIS AND BUCHAREST.
HIS RECEPTION IN PARIS WAS NOT AS WARM AS THE "GORBYMANIA"
THAT SWEPT BONN, GERMANY THE PREVIOUS MONTH. HOWEVER, HE WAS
ABLE TO SIGN SEVERAL SIGNIFICANT AGREEMENTS WITH FRENCH
PRESIDENT FRANCOIS METTERRAN. IN BUCHAREST, HE PROCLAIMED
THE RIGHT OF EASTERN EUROPEAN NATIONS TO PURSUE THEIR OWN
PATHS WHILE RESPECTING THOSE OF OTHERS.

04701 JENSEN, H.; TUREK, B.
A VOTE FOR JARUZELSKI
MACLEAN'S (CANADA'S NEWS MAGAZINE), 102(30) (JUL 89), 26.
GENERAL WOJCIECH JARUZELSKI WON THE POLISH PRESIDENTIAL
ELECTION BY A MERE ONE VOTE AFTER A MARATHON 6 1/2 HOURS OF
PROCEDURAL WRANGLING AND NINE SEPARATE BALLOTS. ALTHOUGH HE
DECLARES HIS DESIRE TO BE A "PRESIDENT OF CONSENSUS," HIS
FOUNDATION IS EXTREMELY SHAKY. IRONICALLY, IT IS THE
GENERAL'S ERSTWHILE FOES IN THE SOLIDARITY TRADE UNION THAT
WERE RESPONSIBLE FOR HIS VICTORY. HOWEVER, MANY VIEW
JARUZELSKI AS THE ONLY ONE WHO COULD ENSURE STABILITY IN
POLAND IN A TIME OF ECONOMIC DISLOCATION AND RADICAL
POLITICAL CHANGE.

04702 JENSEN, H.; MACKENZIE, H.
DOOMSDAY FLIGHT
MACLEAN'S (CANADA'S NEWS MAGAZINE), 102(30) (JUL 89),
24-25.
THE CRASH OF UNITELD AIRLINES FLIGHT 232 KILLED 110 AND
RAISED SERIOUS QUESTIONS ABOUT DC-10 AIRCRAFT. THE FAA HAS
YET TO CONFIRM THE CAUSE OF THE CRASH, BUT A REEVALUATION OF
THE AGING FLEET OF DC-10S SEEMS WARRANTED.

04703 JENSEN, H.; MASTERMAN, S.; TUREK, B.
WOOING THE EAST
MACLEAN'S (CANADA'S NEWS MAGAZINE), 102(29) (JUL 89), 22-3.
AS THE FIRST US PRESIDENT TO VISIT POLAND IN 12 YEARS
AND THE FIRST EVER TO VISIT HUNGARY, GEORGE BUSH HAS A
"DELICATE MISSION" TO PERFORM. HE SCORED HIGH MARKS FOR
RHETORIC AND DIPLOMACY, BUT LOW ON SUBSTANCE: THE PROMISED
AMOUNT OF FOREIGN AID HAS SIGNIFICANTLY SMALLER THAN
EXPECTED. BUSH DECLARED HIS AIM WAS TO PROMOTE THE
DEMOCRATIZATION OF THE EAST BLOC WITHOUT ANTAGONIZING
MIKHAIL GORBACHEV; HE WAS SOMEWHAT SUCCESSFUL, BUT ECONOMIC

TURMOIL THREATENS TO CAUSE A DEGREE OF INSTABILITY THAT
SPEECHMAKING CANNOT HOPE TO OVERCOME.

04704 JENSEN, R.J.
THE CAUSES AND CURES OF UNEMPLOYMENT IN THE GREAT
DEPRESSION
JOURNAL OF INTERDISCIPLINARY HISTORY, XIX(4) (SPR 89),
553-583.
THE REFRAIN "UNEMPLOYED THROUGH NO FAULT OF THEIR OWN"
REVERBERATED THROUGHOUT THE 1930'S AND ECHOES DOWN TO THE
PRESENT. "NO FAULT" IMPLIES THAT NO CHARACTERISTIC OR
DEFICIENCY OF THE WORKERS CAUSED THEIR UNEMPLOYMENT AND THAT
INDIVIDUAL EFFORT TO REMEDY THE SITUATION COULD NOT HELP. AS
USED IN THE POLITICAL DEBATE REGARDING THE NECESSITY OF
GOVERNMENT INTERVENTION IN THE ECONOMY, IT ASSUMED THAT
MACRO-, NOT MICRO-SOLUTIONS WERE NEEDED, AND THAT POLITICAL
STEPS WERE NECESSARY. RELYING ON NEW DATA, NEW ECONOMIC
MODELS, AND A HALF-CENTURY OF PERSPECTIVE, THIS ESSAY
EXPLORES THE QUESTIONS INVOLVED IN THIS ISSUE: WERE THE
UNEMPLOYED OF THE 1930'S FAULTLESS? WERE THE FLAWS OF
CAPITALISM RESPONSIBLE FOR THEIR PLIGHT? DID THE PROGRAMS OF
HERBERT HOOVER AND FRANKLIN D. ROOSEVELT HELP OR HURT?

04705 JENSON, J.
"DIFFERENT" BUT NOT "EXCEPTIONAL": CANADA'S PERMEABLE
FORDISM
CANADIAN REVIEW OF SOCIOLOGY AND ANTHROPOLOGY, 26(1) (FEB
89), 69-94.
THIS PAPER ARGUES THAT CANADA DID NOT EXPERIENCE A
POSTWAR SETTLEMENT SIMILAR TO THOSE OF OTHER ADVANCED
INDUSTRIAL SOCITIES AFTER 1945. THE CANADIAN WELFARE STATE
AND OTHER KEYNESIAN-STYLE MACROECONOMIC POLICIES WERE NOT
SUSTAINED BY A CLASS-DIVIDED PARTY SYSTEM BUT IMPLICATED,
INSTEAD, THE INSTITUTIONS OF FEDERALISM. THIS DIFFERENCE IN
THE POLITICS OF CANAIAN ECONOMIC POLICY NO LONGER APPEARS
EXCEPTIONAL, AS SO MUCH OF THE NEW CANADIAN POLITICAL
ECONOMY ARGUES, IF WE BRING TO BEAR THE THEORETICAL
PERSPECTIVE OF THE FRENCH REGULATION APPROACH AND ADD TO
THAT APPROACH THE CONCEPT OF A 'PARADIGM' WHICH ORDERS THE
SOCIAL RELATIONS OF FORDISM IN CANADA. IT WAS THIS PARADIGM
WHICH ENTERED INTO CRISIS ALONG WITH PRODUCTION-BASED
RELATIONS IN THE 1970S. THE CRISIS OF FORDISM IN CANADA,
GIVEN THE PARTICULARITIES OF THE FORDIST PARADIGM, IS, THEN,
A CRISIS OF THE POLITICAL ARRANGEMENTS OF FEDERALISM MORE
THAN IT IS ONE OF THE PARTY SYSTEM.

04706 JENSON, J.
FROM "BABA COOL" TO A "VOTE UTILE": THE TRAJECTORY OF THE
FRENCH "VERTS"
FRENCH POLITICS AND SOCIETY, 7(4) (FAL 89), 1-15.
THE FRENCH "VERTS" IS A MOVEMENT WHOSE TIME HAS COME.
DRAMATIC NEW PUBLIC VISIBILITY FLOWS NOT ONLY FROM SERIOUS
EFFORTS ON THE PART OF A SMALL GROUP OF "VERTS" BUT ALSO
FROM THE WORKINGS OF ELECTORAL INSTITUTIONS, RISING POPULAR
CONCERN ABOUT THE ENVIRONMENT, AND THE EXISTENCE OF
POLITICAL OPENINGS CREATED BY THE FOUNDERING PCF AND EXTREME
LEFT AND BY THE SOCIALISTS' CENTRIST STRATEGY. NEVERTHELESS,
IT IS NOT AT ALL CLEAR THAT THE FRENCH "VERTS" HAVE THE
STRENGTH TO BECOME A PERMANENT PART OF THE NATIONAL
POLITICAL SCENE.

04707 JENSON, J.
PARADIGMS AND POLITICAL DISCOURSE: PROTECTIVE LEGISLATION
IN FRANCE AND THE UNITED STATES BEFORE 1914
CANADIAN JOURNAL OF POLITICAL SCIENCE, XXII(2) (JUN 89),
235-258.
THIS ARTICLE EXAMINES THE DIFFERENCES IN PRE-1914 FRANCE
AND THE UNITED STATES IN TWO KINDS OF STATE POLICIES
REGULATING WOMEN'S BEHAVIOUR, THOSE "PROTECTING" THE
CONDITION UNDER WHICH WOMEN PARTICIPATED IN CERTAIN
OCCUPATIONS AND THOSE PROVIDING INFANT AND MATERIAL
PROTECTION. THOSE POLICIES ARE EXAMINED TO ILLUMINATE THE
ARGUMENT THAT POLITICS, INCLUDING STATE POLICIES, MAKES AN
IMPORTANT CONTRIBUTION TO THE MAINTENANCE AND CHANGE OF
ONGOING SYSTEMS OF SOCIAL RELATIONS. CENTRAL TO THIS
ARGUMENT IS THE NOTION THAT MEANING SYSTEMS AROUND WHICH
ACTORS CONSTITUTE COLLECTIVE IDENTITIES ARE A CRUCIAL
ANALYTIC FOCUS FOR UNDERSTANDING STABILITY AND CHANGE. AT
THE END OF THE NINETEENTH CENTURY HEGEMONIC SOCIETAL
PARADIGMS, CONSTRUCTED OUT OF THE PROCESSES
INSTITUTIONALIZING NEW SOCIAL RELATIONS, EMERGED IN FRANCE
AND THE US. THE FRENCH PARADIGM OF "CITIZEN-PRODUCER" AND
THE AMERICAN ONE OF "SPECIALIZED CITIZENSHIP" HAD QUITE
DIFFERENT IMPLICATIONS FOR THE PATTERNS OF GENDER RELATIONS
EMBEDDED WITHIN THEM. THESE IMPLICATIONS ARE VISIBLE IN THE
TREATMENT OF WOMEN'S WORK AND MATERNITY IN THESE YEARS OF
THE EMERGING WELFARE STATE.

04708 JENSHOLD, J.M.
RURAL ROAD DEVELOPMENT IN THE RSFSR, 1971-75: POLITICAL
DIMENSIONS OF SOVIET INFRASTRUCTURE POLICY
DISSERTATION ABSTRACTS INTERNATIONAL, 50(5) (NOV 89),
1422-A.
THE CONDITION OF THE RURAL ROAD NETWORK HAS LONG BEEN

RECOGNIZED AS A MAJOR IMPEDIMENT TO ECONOMIC DEVELOPMENT
PLANS IN THE SOVIET UNION. POLITICAL CONSIDERATIONS OF THE
COMMUNIST PARTY ELITE DO NOT ENCOURAGE THE ADOPTION OF LONG-
TERM POLICIES THAT REQUIRE HEAVY INVESTMENTS AND PRODUCE
DEFERRED RESULTS. THIS CARRIES IMPLICATIONS FOR REFORM
EFFORTS IN THE SOVIET UNION, BECAUSE PERIODS OF REFORM ARE
TIMES OF HIGH POLITICAL VULNERABILITY FOR CENTRAL COMMITTEE
MEMBERS AND REGIONAL OFFICIALS. RISK-AVERSE BEHAVIOR IS
REINFORCED DURING SUCH PERIODS.

04709 JERVIS, R.
DEBATES ON DETERRENCE: SECURITY AND MUTUAL SECURITY
ETUDES INTERNATIONALES, 20(3) (SEP 89), 557-576.
THIS ARTICLE DEALS WITH TWO GENERAL ARGUMENTS ABOUT HOW
NUCLEAR WEAPONS MIGHT PRODUCE OR PREVENT WAR, BOTH BASED ON
THEMES PRESENT IN PRE-NUCLEAR ERAS. THE FIRST DEBATE IS OVER
WHETHER TRADITIONAL MILITARY POLICIES INCREASE OR DECREASE
THE LIKELIHOOD OF WAR, WHETHER A POLICY RELYING ON IMPLICIT
OR EXPLICIT THREATS DETER OR PROVOKE. THE SECOND DEBATE
CENTERS ON HOW NUCLEAR WEAPONS ARE BROUGHT INTO THE
FRAMEWORK OF FORCE AND THREATS, AND HOW DETERRENCE CAN BE
MADE MOST EFFECTIVE, THROUGH A POSTURE OF DETERRENCE BY
DENIAL VERSUS DETERRENCE BY PUNISHMENT. INVOLVED IN THESE
ARGUMENTS ARE DISPUTES OVER INTERNATIONAL POLITICS, THE
NATURE AND INTENTIONS OF THE SOVIET UNION, AND THE CHANGES
BROUGHT ABOUT BY NUCLEAR WEAPONS.

04710 JETLY, N.
INDIA'S SECURITY PERSPECTIVES IN SOUTH ASIA IN THE EIGHTIES
CONFLICT, 8(4) (1988), 295-309.
IT IS INEVITABLE IN THE INEXORABLE LOGIC OF
INTERNATIONAL POLITICS THAT PROBLEMS OF ITS OWN SECURITY AND
THOSE OF REGIONAL PEACE AND STABILITY WOULD CONTINUE TO
REMAIN THE CENTER OF INDIA'S FOREIGN POLICY CONCERNS. THIS
PAPER PROPOSES TO TAKE UP INDIA'S RESPONSE TO THE SECURITY
ENVIRONMENT AT THREE LEVELS: DOMESTIC, REGIONAL, AND
EXTERNAL.

04711 JETLY, N.
INDIA AND THE SRI LANKAN ETHNIC TANGLE
CONFLICT, 9(1) (1989), 77-88.
IN THE SCHEME OF SOUTH ASIAN POLITICS, INDIA FINDS
ITSELF IN AN UNENVIABLE POSITION. INDIA'S CENTRALITY AND
STABILITY PUT IT IN THE THANKLESS ROLE OF REGIONAL MEDIATOR,
THIS SERVING ONLY TO ALIENATE ITS NEIGHBORS. MOST OF INDIA'S
EFFORTS IN THIS REGARD HAVE BEEN ON BEHALF OF SRI LANKAN
NATIONAL UNITY. THIS PAPER ADDRESSES INDIA'S NECESSARY BUT
UNWELCOME ROLE IN UNDOING THE SRI LANKAN ETHNIC TANGLE.

04712 JI, B.
LOCAL RESPONSES TO INTERGOVERNMENTAL AID IN THE UNITED
STATES: 1977-1982
DISSERTATION ABSTRACTS INTERNATIONAL, 50(6) (DEC 89),
1787-A.
THE AUTHOR REVIEWS THE PATTERN OF FEDERAL AID TO LOCAL
GOVERNMENTS AND HOW IT CHANGED DRAMATICALLY DURING THE
REAGAN ADMINISTRATION. IN 1977, WHEN THE CARTER
ADMINISTRATION EMPHASIZED TARGETING AID TO NEEDY COMMUNITIES,
LOW-INCOME LOCALITIES BENEFITED GREATLY FROM FEDERAL
CATEGORICAL AID PROGRAMS. UNDER REAGAN, WEALTHIER
COMMUNITIES WERE MORE LIKELY TO PARTICIPATE IN FEDERAL GRANT
PROGRAMS BECAUSE FEDERAL CATEGORIAL MONIES DID NOT TARGET
EITHER LOW-INCOME SUBURBS OR BLACK SUBURBS.

04713 JI, G.
ADHERING TO THE NORMS IN STATE-TO-STATE RELATIONS
BEIJING REVIEW, 32(41) (OCT 89), 4.
SINCE THE QUELLING OF THE COUNTER-REVOLUTIONARY
REBELLION IN BEIJING IN JUNE 1989, THE INTERNATIONAL
COMMUNITY HAS GRADUALLY OBTAINED A COMPREHENSIVE, OBJECTIVE
UNDERSTANDING OF THE INCIDENT. THE ATTITUDE OF SOME
COUNTRIES TOWARD CHINA IS CHANGING, AND THEY ARE PREPARING
TO RESUME POLITICAL, ECONOMIC, AND SOCIAL TIES. BUT SOME
PEOPLE IN THE WEST HAVE VOICED A DIFFERENT VIEW. THEY ARGUE
THAT THE RESTORATION AND DEVELOPMENT OF RELATIONS WITH CHINA
SHOULD DEPEND ON THE CHINESE GOVERNMENT'S COMMITMENT TO
RESPECT FUNDAMENTAL HUMAN RIGHTS AND TO CARRY OUT GENUINE
REFORM AND OPENING UP TO THE OUTSIDE WORLD.

04714 JI, G.
THE NON-ALIGNED MOVEMENT AT A TURNING POINT
BEIJING REVIEW, 32(39) (SEP 89), 7.
THE NINTH SUMMIT OF NON-ALIGNED COUNTRIES, HELD IN
SEPTEMBER 1989, REFLECTED THE PREVAILING MOOD IN
INTERNATIONAL RELATIONS. BECAUSE ECONOMIC DEVELOPMENT IS THE
MOST URGENT PROBLEM CONFRONTING THE NON-ALIGNED COUNTRIES,
ECONOMIC MATTERS WERE GIVEN TOP PRIORITY. ALTHOUGH THE
GENERAL TREND IN INTERNATIONAL RELATIONS IS TOWARD DETENTE,
THE ECONOMIC DISPARITY BETWEEN NORTH AND SOUTH IS CONTINUING
TO GROW AND THE THIRD WORLD'S DEBT BURDEN IS BECOMING MORE
SERIOUS.

04715 JIABAO, C.
VIETNAM'S "FINAL WITHDRAWAL" A HOAX

BEIJING REVIEW, 32(42) (OCT 89), 16-17.
AT THE INTERNATIONAL CONFERENCE ON KAMPUCHEA IN JULY AND
AUGUST 1989, THE VIETNAMESE REPRESENTATIVES RAISED OBSTACLES
TO ENSURE THAT THE MEETING FAILED. VIETNAM IS CLINGING
OBSTINATELY TO ITS SET POLICY OF PARTIAL SETTLEMENT OF THE
KAMPUCHEAN ISSUE. IN REALITY, THE PARTIAL SETTLEMENT SETTLES
NOTHING BECAUSE HANOI HAS NOT FULLY WITHDRAWN ITS FORCES
FROM KAMPUCHEA. WHILE PUBLICLY DECLARING THAT IT HAS REMOVED
ALL ITS TROOPS, VIETNAM HAS HIDDEN QUITE A FEW THERE.

04716 JIAN, C.
THE KEY TO PREVENTING A DEBT CRISIS
BEIJING REVIEW, 32(14) (APR 89), 27-29.
TEN YEARS AGO, CHINA HAD NEITHER EXTERNAL NOR INTERNAL
DEBTS. BUT THE PURSUIT OF THE POLICIES OF REFORM AND OPENING
TO THE OUTSIDE WORLD HAS REQUIRED FOREIGN LOANS AND
EFFECTIVE USE OF DEBT. AFTER AN INITIAL PERIOD OF CAUTION,
CHINA HAS RAPIDLY STEPPED UP THE SCALE OF ITS BORROWING,
BOTH DOMESTICALLY AND EXTERNALLY. THE BORROWED MONEY HAS
PLAYED A MAJOR ROLE IN INSTILLING NEW VITALITY INTO THE
CHINESE ECONOMY, BUT CHINA MUST BE CAREFUL TO AVOID THE TYPE
OF DEBT CRISIS THAT NOW PLAGUES MANY THIRD WORLD COUNTRIES.
THE KEY TO PREVENTING SUCH A CRISIS LIES IN ADAPTING THE
ECONOMY TO HIGH INTEREST RATES AND ESTABLISHING EFFICIENT
INDUSTRIES AND ENTERPRISES.

04717 JIANG, L.
BUSH'S FOREIGN POLICIES: A REALISTIC OUTLOOK
BEIJING REVIEW, 32(9) (FEB 89), 14-16.
THOUGH THE BUSH ADMINISTRATION JUST ENTERED OFFICE, ITS
FOREIGN POLICY HAS ALREADY DRAWN WORLDWIDE ATTENTION. THE
PREVAILING VIEW IS THAT BUSH WILL FOLLOW REAGAN'S DIPLOMATIC
LINE IN ORDER TO ENSURE A REPUBLICAN POLICY CONTINUITY. BUT
THE BUSH ERA WILL HAVE ITS OWN FEATURES AND CANNOT BE MERELY
A CARBON COPY OF REAGAN'S. JUDGING BY REMARKS MADE BY
PRESIDENT BUSH AND SECRETARY OF STATE BAKER, A DISTINCT MARK
OF BUSH'S FOREIGN POLICY WILL BE AN EMPHASIS ON PRAGMATISM
AND REALISTIC DIPLOMACY.

04718 JIANG, L.
NON-ALIGNED MOVEMENT AIMS AT MODERNIZATION
BEIJING REVIEW, 32(36) (SEP 89), 15-17.
A WIDE RANGE OF ISSUES WILL BE DISCUSSED AT THE NINTH
SUMMIT OF THE HEADS-OF-STATE OF THE NON-ALIGNED MOVEMENT IN
SEPTEMBER 1989. THIS ARTICLE BRIEFLY REVIEWS PAST NAM
SUMMITS AND ILLUSTRATES HOW THE NAM'S MAJOR CONCERNS HAVE
CHANGED SINCE THE FIRST SUMMIT IN 1961.

04719 JIANGUO, Y.
A FEW WORDS ABOUT MARTIAL LAW
BEIJING REVIEW, 32(38) (SEP 89), 7.
ALTHOUGH CHINA'S POLITICAL SITUATION HAS STABILIZED,
MARTIAL LAW WILL CONTINUE FOR A TIME IN PARTS OF BEIJING,
BECAUSE IT ENSURES GOOD SOCIAL ORDER AND NORMAL ACTIVITIES
IN ALL ASPECTS OF LIFE, INCLUDING TOURISM AND FOREIGN TRADE.

04720 JIANGUO, Y.
HOPE OF CHINA'S AGRICULTURE
BEIJING REVIEW, 32(33) (AUG 89), 19-22.
THE ECONOMIC REFORM THAT BEGAN A DECADE AGO IN CHINA
MADE ITS FIRST BREAKTHROUGHS IN RURAL AREAS, BUT SOME
OBSERVERS ARE WORRIED THAT THE MOTIVATING FORCE BEHIND RURAL
REFORM HAS SUBSIDED. THEY FEAR THAT CHINESE AGRICULTURE WILL
BECOME BOGGED DOWN AND LESS PRODUCTIVE. EXPERIMENTS ON THE
HUANGHE-HUAIHE-HAIHE PLAIN, HOWEVER, INDICATE THAT IT IS
POSSIBLE TO RAISE PRODUCTION FURTHER BY TRANSFORMING LOW-
YIELDING LAND AND RAISING PER-UNIT OUTPUT. THE KEY LIES IN
ADHERING TO THE GOVERNMENT'S POLICY OF ENCOURAGING AND
SUPPORTING AGRICULTURAL DEVELOPMENT.

04721 JIANGUO, Y.; YUEQI, S.
THREE GORGES PROJECT (1): DREAM AND REALITY
BEIJING REVIEW, 32(27) (JUL 89), 19-35.
A LARGE NUMBER OF CHINESE AND FOREIGN EXPERTS HAVE SPENT
YEARS INVESTIGATING THE POSSIBILITY OF BUILDING A MAMMOTH
DAM TO PROVIDE FLOOD CONTROL AND ELECTRICITY IN THE THREE
GORGES OF THE CHANGJIANG RIVER. SHARP DIFFERENCES HAVE
ARISEN OVER THE PROJECT AND THE CENTRAL GOVERNMENT HAS
ORDERED A RE-STUDY. THIS IS THE FIRST TIME SINCE THE
FOUNDING OF NEW CHINA THAT THE GOVERNMENT HAS RECONSIDERED
AN APPROVAL WHICH IT HAD ALREADY GIVEN IN PRINCIPLE.

04722 JIANGUO, Y.
TWO VIEWS ON REFORM
BEIJING REVIEW, 32(45) (NOV 89), 7.
THERE ARE TWO DIAMETRICALLY OPPOSED VIEWS ON REFORM AND
OPENING. ONE HOLDS THAT REFORM AND OPENING SHOULD BE BASED
ON THE FOUR CARDINAL PRINCIPLES, AIMED AT EVENTUALLY
BUILDING SOCIALISM WITH CHINESE CHARACTERISTICS; THE SECOND
ADVOCATES "TOTAL WESTERNIZATION" OF CHINA IN AN ATTEMPT TO
TRANSFORM SOCIALIST CHINA INTO A CAPITALIST COUNTRY.
PRACTICE HAS PROVED THAT WITHOUT REFORM AND THE OPEN POLICY
BASED ON THE FOUR CARDINAL PRINCIPLES, THE ACHIEVEMENTS
ALREADY GAINED WOULD HAVE BEEN IMPOSSIBLE. LIKEWISE

CONTINUATION OF ITS ESTABLISHED POLICY IS NECESSARY SO THAT
CHINA CAN REALIZE ITS GOALS FOR THE FUTURE.

04723 JIANGUO, Y.
WILL ECONOMIC CURBS HIT OVERSEAS INVESTMENT?
BEIJING REVIEW, 32(10) (MAR 89), 7.
CURRENTLY CHINA IS STRIVING TO SCALE DOWN ITS OVERHEATED
ECONOMY, IMPROVE ITS ECONOMIC ENVIRONMENT AND RECTIFY ITS
ECONOMIC ORDER. CHINESE LEADERS HAVE REITERATED: THESE
EFFORTS WILL NOT AFFECT CHINA'S OPEN POLICY. WHILE CHINA
CURTAILS ITS ECONOMIC GROWTH, ITS DOORS REMAIN OPEN TO
FOREIGN INVESTMENT. SIMULTANEOUSLY, IT WILL STRICTLY UPHOLD
AND PROTECT CONTRACTS FOR FOREIGN-FUNDED PROJECTS, INCLUDING
THOSE ALREADY IN OPERATION.

04724 JIANJUN, L.
MINISTER HE KANG ON CHINA'S AGRICULTURE
BEIJING REVIEW, 32(18) (MAY 89), 20-24.
DURING THE PAST FOUR YEARS, CHINESE AGRICULTURE HAS MADE
LITTLE PROGRESS. IN THIS INTERVIEW, THE CHINESE MINISTER OF
AGRICULTURE ANSWERS QUESTIONS ABOUT THE PROBLEMS AND THE
MEASURES THE GOVERNMENT PLANS TO TAKE TO IMPROVE THE
SITUATION FOR CHINA'S FARMERS.

04725 JIANMIN, W.
PROSPECTS FOR TAIWAN-U.S. TRADE
BEIJING REVIEW, 32(50) (DEC 89), 31-32.
TAIWAN, WHICH HAS AN ENORMOUS TRADE SURPLUS WITH THE
UNITED STATES, HAS COME UNDER PRESSURE FROM AMERICAN
PROTECTIONISM IN RECENT YEARS. THIS SHARPENING OF TRADE
FRICTION HAS HAD A SERIOUS IMPACT ON TAIWAN'S ECONOMY AND
ITS RELATIONS WITH WASHINGTON.

04726 JIANQUN, P.
ECONOMIC DEVELOPMENT IN MINORITY REGIONS
CHINA RECONSTRUCTS, XXXVIII(12) (DEC 89), 8-13.
CHINA HAS 55 MINORITY NATIONALITIES, WHO ACCOUNT FOR
EIGHT PER CENT OF THE COUNTRY'S POPULATION. IN THE PAST THE
MINORITY PEOPLES, WHO RESIDE MOSTLY IN REMOTE BORDER AREAS,
LIVED IN ECONOMIC AND SOCIAL ISOLATION. DURING THE PAST
DECADE, MAJOR CHANGES HAVE OCCURRED IN MINORITY AREAS. IN
THIS ARTICLE, SIX TOP OFFICIALS OF THE STATE NATIONALITIES
AFFAIRS COMMISSION DISCUSS THE STATUS OF CHINA'S MINORITIES.

04727 JIAOMING, L.
THE ARAB LEAGUE: UNITY STRENGTHENED
BEIJING REVIEW, 32(24-25) (JUN 89), 17-18.
THE 1989 EXTRAORDINARY ARAB SUMMIT FOCUSED ON THE
PALESTINIAN PROBLEM, THE LEBANON ISSUE, AND IRAN-IRAQ
RELATIONS. THE SUMMIT STRENGTHENED ARAB UNITY, AS EGYPT
RETURNED TO THE ARAB LEAGUE AND A SPIRIT OF RECONCILIATION
PREVAILED AFTER YEARS OF DIVISION WITHIN THE ARAB WORLD.

04728 JIAQUAN, L.
MORE ON REUNIFICATION OF TAIWAN WITH THE MAINLAND
BEIJING REVIEW, 32(3) (JAN 89), 26-30.
SINCE THE DEATH OF CHIANG CHING-KUO, A SERIES OF NEW
IDEAS ON THE REUNION OF TAIWAN AND THE CHINESE MAINLAND HAVE
BEEN PROPOSED. IN THIS ARTICLE, THE AUTHOR REVIEWS THESE
PROPOSALS AND GROUPS THEM INTO EIGHT CATEGORIES.

04729 JIAQUAN, L.
TAIWAN'S NEW MAINLAND POLICY RAISES CONCERN
BEIJING REVIEW, 32(21) (MAY 89), 23-25.
SINCE LATE MARCH 1989, TAIWANESE OFFICIALS HAVE BEEN
OPENLY ADVOCATING A POLICY OF "ONE COUNTRY, TWO EQUAL
GOVERNMENTS." THIS POLICY DIFFERS FROM MAINLAND CHINA'S "ONE
COUNTRY, TWO SYSTEMS" FORMULA IN THREE MAJOR WAYS. THE FIRST
DIFFERENCE CONCERNS THE PRINCIPLE OF SOVEREIGNTY AND WHETHER
TAIWAN IS A SOVEREIGN NATION. THE SECOND DIFFERENCE IS THE
QUESTION OF EQUALITY AND WHETHER THE TWO POLITICAL ENTITIES
ARE POLITICAL EQUALS. THE THIRD DIFFERENCE IS HOW THE
TRANSITION PERIOD TO PEACEFUL REUNIFICATION WOULD WORK.

04730 JIARONG, Y.
THE DEVELOPMENT OF COMECON AND ITS PROSPECTS
BEIJING REVIEW, 32(38) (SEP 89), 14-16.
THE AUTHOR REVIEWS THE ACHIEVEMENTS OF COMECON DURING
ITS FORTY-YEAR HISTORY AND ENUMERATES SOME OF THE PROBLEMS
FACING THE MEMBERS OF THE ORGANIZATION.

04731 JIAYAN, Y.
WHAT DOES "THE RIVER DIES YOUNG" ADVOCATE?
BEIJING REVIEW, 32(34) (AUG 89), 14, 19-21.
THE CHINESE TV SERIES "THE RIVER DIES YOUNG" HAS EVOKED
HEATED DEBATES IN IDEOLOGICAL AND THEORETICAL CIRCLES. THE
SERIES' WRITERS HAVE EXPRESSED THEIR CONCERN AND ANXIETIES,
WITH THE GOAL OF CHANGING CHINA'S BACKWARD STATUS. BUT,
OWING TO THEIR LACK OF SUFFICIENT BACKGROUND IN THEORY AND
THEIR INADEQUATE KNOWLEDGE, MANY OF THEIR BASIC THESES AND
JUDGMENTS ARE INCORRECT AND EVEN HARMFUL. FOR EXAMPLE, THE
SERIES TOTALLY NEGATES THE LONG-STANDING CULTURAL TRADITION
OF A GREAT NATION AND EXEMPLIFIES THE ATTITUDE OF NATIONAL
NIHILISM, PESSIMISM, AND HISTORICAL FATALISM.

04732 JIBU, B.
STRENGTHENING SOCIAL WELFARE
BEIJING REVIEW, 32(5) (JAN 89), 31-32.
OVER THE LAST FEW YEARS, CHINESE SOCIAL WELFARE AND
RELIEF INSTITUTIONS HAVE STRIVED TO EXTEND THE RANGE OF
THEIR WELFARE PROVISIONS AND EQUIP THEMSELVES WITH MODERN
MEDICAL FACILITIES. AT THE SAME TIME, PRIVATE WELFARE
INSTITUTIONS HAVE BEGUN TO APPEAR IN SOME OF CHINA'S
PROVINCES AND AUTONOMOUS REGIONS. THE TOTAL NUMBER OF PEOPLE
IN NEED OF SOCIAL WELFARE IS HUGE. FORTY MILLION DISABLED
SERVICEMEN AND FAMILIES OF REVOLUTIONARY MARTYRS RECEIVE
SPECIAL CARE FROM THE STATE, AND ANOTHER 100 MILLION PEOPLE
RECEIVE SOME FORM OF SOCIAL RELIEF.

04733 JIE, T.H.
TECHNOLOGICAL INNOVATION IN KOREA: AN EMPIRICAL
INVESTIGATION INTO THE EFFECT OF GOVERNMENT INNOVATION
INCENTIVE POLICIES, MARKET PRESSURE AND COMPETITION, AND
FIRM'S ORGANISATION STRUCTURE TO THE TECHNOLOGICAL
INNOVATION BEHAVIOR IN KOREAN FIRMS
DISSERTATION ABSTRACTS INTERNATIONAL, 50(2) (AUG 89),
541-A.
THE AUTHOR EXAMINES SOME OF THE MAJOR FACTORS THAT SEEM
TO HAVE AFFECTED TECHNOLOGICAL INNOVATION IN KOREAN FIRMS.
HE STUDIES GOVERNMENT INNOVATION INCENTIVE POLICIES, MARKET
PRESSURE AND COMPETITION, AND THE ORGANIZATIONAL STRUCTURE
OF KOREAN FIRMS IN RELATION TO THEIR EFFECTS ON
TECHNOLOGICAL INNOVATION BEHAVIOR. HE FINDS THAT THE RAPID
INTERNATIONALIZATION AND RELATED CULTURAL CHANGES HAVE BEEN
VERY INFLUENTIAL IN KOREA'S INDUSTRIALIZATION AND
TECHNOLOGICAL PROGRESS.

04734 JILLSON, C.
POLITICAL CULTURE AND THE PATTERN OF CONGRESSIONAL
POLITICS UNDER THE ARTICLES OF CONFEDERATION
PUBLIUS: THE JOURNAL OF FEDERALISM, 18(1) (WIN 88), 1-26.
THE ARTICLE ATTEMPTS TO BRING A BROAD TRADITION OF
SOCIOCULTURAL ANALYSIS TO BEAR IN UNDERSTANDING THE PATTERN
AND CHARACTER OF CONGRESSIONAL POLITICS IN THE FIRST
AMERICAN NATIONAL GOVERNMENT. THE APPROACH CENTERS ON THE
STUDY OF POLITICAL CULTURE AND THE ROLE OF IDEAS IN SHAPING
THE PERFORMANCE OF INSTITUTIONS AND ATTEMPTS TO PLACE VALUES,
OR CONFLICTS BETWEEN ALTERNATIVE VALUE SYSTEMS AT THE HEART
OF DISCUSSIONS OF POLITICAL DEVELOPMENT AND CHANGE IN
REVOLUTIONARY AMERICA. IT UTILIZES THAT THREE POLITICAL
SUBCULTURES--MORALISTIC IN NEW ENGLAND, INDIVIDUALISTIC IN
THE MIDDLE ATLANTIC STATES, AND TRADITIONALISTIC IN THE
SOUTH--TO PROVIDE A BASIS FOR AN EXPLANATION OF FACTIONAL
DIVISIONS WHICH APPEARED IN THE CONGRESS OF THE ARTICLES OF
CONFEDERATION.

04735 JIMENEZ-HUERTA, E.R.
STATE CONTROL AND POLITICAL PARTICIPATION IN LOW-INCOME
SETTLEMENTS IN THE FEDERAL DISTRICT, MEXICO
DISSERTATION ABSTRACTS INTERNATIONAL, 50(2) (AUG 89),
541-A.
THE AUTHOR IS CONCERNED WITH THE RELATIONSHIP BETWEEN
THE MEXICAN STATE AND "COLONOS" IN THE CITY. SHE SHOWS HOW
THE STATE HAS ATTEMPTED TO CONTROL "COLONOS" THROUGH THE
ORGANS OF CITIZEN REPRESENTATION AND EXPLAINS WHY THESE
ATTEMPTS HAVE FAILED. SHE EMPHASIZES THAT CONCEPTIONS OF THE
MEXICAN POLITICAL SYSTEM AS AUTHORITARIAN-CORPORATIST ARE
REDUCTIONIST BECAUSE THEY DEFINE THE POLITICAL SYSTEM AS
ONLY THE STATE AND ITS PARTY, THE PRI. CONTRARY TO THIS VIEW,
SHE ARGUES THAT INDEPENDENTLY ORGANIZED BODIES DO EXIST AND
THAT THEY CONTRIBUTE TO THE SHAPE OF THE POLITICAL SYSTEM.
FURTHERMORE, THE PERCEPTION OF AN UNDIVIDED STATE IS FALSE.
IN FACT, IT IS FRACTIONALIZATION WITHIN THE STATE THAT
PARTLY EXPLAINS THE STATE'S INCREASING FAILURE TO EXERCISE
TIGHT CONTROL OVER "COLONOS."

04736 JIN, S.
CHINA AND HUMAN RIGHTS
CHINA RECONSTRUCTS, XXXVIII(1) (JAN 89), 43-46.
THE AUTHOR SURVEYS SOME BASIC THEORIES OF HUMAN RIGHTS.
THEN HE REVIEWS THE STATUS OF HUMAN RIGHTS IN THE PEOPLE'S
REPUBLIC OF CHINA IN THE CONTEXT OF THE UNIVERSAL
DECLARATION OF HUMAN RIGHTS.

04737 JING, Z.
FORTY YEARS OF SOCIALIST ECONOMIC CONSTRUCTION
CHINA RECONSTRUCTS, XXXVIII(10) (OCT 89), 32-33.
ALTHOUGH CHINA HAS EXPERIENCED MANY DIFFICULTIES SINCE
1949, IT HAS ESTABLISHED A STRONG INDUSTRIAL BASE,
SIGNIFICANT TRADE RELATIONS WITH THE INTERNATIONAL COMMUNITY,
AND VASTLY IMPROVED AGRICULTURAL PRODUCTION. CHINA'S
ECONOMIC GROWTH HAS BEEN EXTREMELY RAPID. BUT, BECAUSE OF
CHINA'S HUGE POPULATION, PER CAPITA PRODUCTION OF MAJOR
AGRICULTURAL AND INDUSTRIAL RAW MATERIALS FALLS FAR SHORT OF
THE LEVEL IN THE DEVELOPED COUNTRIES.

04738 JINGBEN, R.
REFORM AND SOCIETY

WORLD MARXIST REVIEW, 32(1) (JAN 89), 14-16.
BASED ON THEIR OWN EXPERIENCES AND THOSE OF OTHER
SOCIALIST COUNTRIES, THE CHINESE HAVE INSTITUTED A THREE-
FOLD SET OF REFORMS. FIRST, THE ADMINISTRATIVE ALLOCATION OF
MATERIAL RESOURCES, FUNDS, AND LABOR MUST BE REPLACED BY A
COHERENT, DEVELOPED MARKET SYSTEM. SECONDLY, INDUSTRIAL AND
COMMERCIAL ENTERPRISES MUST TURN TO SELF-FINANCING AND SELF-
SUFFICIENCY WHILE KEEPING AN EYE ON THE MARKET. THIRDLY, THE
ADMINISTRATIVE AGENCIES THAT FORMERLY HANDED DOWN ECONOMIC
INDICATORS TO THE ENTERPRISES MUST BE TRANSFORMED AND
CHARGED WITH OVERALL REGULATION AND CONTROL.

04739 JINGHONG, Z.
"CHINA HAS NOT BEEN ISOLATED"
BEIJING REVIEW, 32(47) (NOV 89), 38-40.
AFTER THE STUDENT UNREST AND THE COUNTER-REVOLUTIONARY
REBELLION THAT HIT CHINA'S CAPITAL CITY OF BEIJING IN MAY
AND JUNE, 1989, MANY ORDINARY CITIZENS EXPRESSED THEIR
UNDERSTANDING AND SUPPORT FOR THE CHINESE GOVERNMENT'S
ACTIONS.

04740 JIRO, A.
QUIETING SOCIAL SECURITY NIGHTMARES
JAPAN QUARTERLY, XXXVI(2) (APR 89), 141-145.
THE RAPID PACE AT WHICH THE JAPANESE POPULATION IS AGING
IS UNPARALLELED IN ANY OTHER INDUSTRIALIZED NATION. THE
POTENTIAL IMPACT OF THIS AGING POPULATION ON THE NATIONAL
PENSION AND HEALTH CARE SYSTEMS IS LEADING THE MINISTRY OF
HEALTH AND WELFARE TO RETHINK SOME OF ITS POLICIES. IT HAS
ALREADY PROPOSED TO RAISE THE AGE AT WHICH PRIVATE-SECTOR
RETIREES COULD BEGIN RECEIVING THEIR OLD-AGE PENSIONS.

04741 JISI, W.
IDEALISM, REALISM: THE WEAVE OF US CHINA POLICY
BEIJING REVIEW, 32(3) (JAN 89), 14-18.
CONTRADICTION AND INTERACTION, A DELICATE WEAVING OF
REALISTIC INTEREST AND IDEOLOGICAL CONSIDERATIONS, FROM THE
MAIN FIBRES IN THE CLOAK OF U.S. DIPLOMATIC POLICY.
REALISTIC DIPLOMACY TENDS TO BE CONSERVATIVE. DEFENDING
PEACE IS ITS MAIN THRUST. IDEALISM, HOWEVER, IS MORE BENT
TOWARD PROMOTING TRANSFORMATIONS OF WORLD POLITICS. AMERICAN
IDEALISTS SEE THE WORLD THROUGH STAR-SPANGLED GLASSES. THEY
SEE THEIR NATION AS THE MOST MORAL COUNTRY IN THE WORLD AND
JUDGE THE POLITICAL SYSTEMS OF OTHER COUNTRIES ACCORDING TO
THEIR OWN CRITERIA. THIS STRAND OF AMERICAN DIPLOMACY HAS
BEEN EVIDENT IN UNITED STATES' POLICY TOWARD TAIWAN AND
COMMUNIST CHINA.

04742 JISI, W.
IDEALISM, REALISM: THE WEAVE OF US CHINA POLICY (PART II)
BEIJING REVIEW, 32(4) (JAN 89), 16-18.
THE NEW AMERICAN NATIONALISM THAT APPEARED IN THE EARLY
1980'S WAS CHARACTERIZED BY A RENEWED ANTI-COMMUNISM. THIS
BRAND OF RED-BASHING WAS OPPOSED TO SOVIET EXPANSIONISM AND
AIMED AT CREATING A GLOBAL POLICY THAT WOULD KEEP ANY
COMMUNISTS FROM ASSUMING POWER. THOUGH HE GAVE LIP SERVICE
TO THE PRINCIPLE OF REALISM IN INTERNATIONAL DIPLOMACY,
RONALD REAGAN MADE ALMOST NO MENTION OF THE BALANCE OF POWER
PRINCIPLE IN INTERNATIONAL RELATIONS OR OF THE WORLD'S TREND
TOWARDS MULTIPOLARIZATION. REAGAN DIPLOMACY, ESPECIALLY
DURING HIS FIRST TERM, WAS CLEARLY EARMARKED BY IDEOLOGY,
RATHER THAN REALISM. HIS ATTEMPTS TO APPLY HIS ANTI-
COMMUNIST IDEAS TO CHINA POLICY NEARLY WRECKED SINO-AMERICAN
RELATIONS.

04743 JITSURO, T.
MAKING JAPAN A BETTER PARTNER
JAPAN ECHO, XVI(2) (SUM 89), 69-74.
THE BUSH ADMINISTRATION IS LIKELY TO MARK THE BEGINNING
OF A TRANSITION IN U.S.-JAPANESE RELATIONS. EVEN THOUGH BUSH
IS EXPECTED TO MAINTAIN AN ANTI-PROTECTIONIST STANCE IN
TRADE AFFAIRS, HE WILL COME UNDER MOUNTING PRESSURE FOR
PROTECTION FROM THE CONGRESSIONAL DEMOCRATS, WHO INCREASED
THEIR MAJORITY IN THE 1988 ELECTION. THE 1988 OMNIBUS TRADE
ACT HAS GIVEN THE ADMINISTRATION POWERFUL WEAPONS FOR
RETALIATORY ATTACKS IN SUCH AREAS AS TRADE AND INVESTMENT;
THE QUESTION IS WHETHER BUSH WILL BE PERSUADED TO WIELD THEM.

04744 JIYE, W.
THE STATE, THE MARKET, AND THE ENTERPRISE
BEIJING REVIEW, 32(15) (APR 89), 20-25.
ONE OF THE MAJOR GOALS OF CHINA'S REFORM PROGRAM IS THE
CREATION OF AN ECONOMIC SYSTEM IN WHICH "THE STATE REGULATES
THE MARKET, THE MARKET GUIDES THE ENTERPRISE." IN THIS
ARTICLE, THE AUTHOR EXPLAINS HOW SUCH A SYSTEM WORKS AND
ENUMERATES THE SEVEN MAJOR ISSUES THAT FORM THE BACKDROP FOR
NATIONAL ECONOMIC POLICY. THESE INCLUDE POPULATION GROWTH,
SURPLUS RURAL LABOR, UNEVEN DEVELOPMENT, AND CHANGES IN THE
STRUCTURE OF OWNERSHIP.

04745 JOBERT, B.
THE NORMATIVE FRAMEWORKS OF PUBLIC POLICY
POLITICAL STUDIES, 37(3) (FAL 89), 376-386.
THIS ARTICLE SUGGESTS SOME TOOLS FOR THE ANALYSIS OF

SOCIAL CONCEPTIONS THAT SHAPE THE POLICY-MAKING PROCESS. IT
DEFINES THE THREE DIMENSIONS OF POLICY FRAMEWORKS AND THEIR
LINKS WITH THE RELATED NOTIONS OF PARADIGM AND MYTH. IT
ANALYSES THE INSTITUTIONALIZATION OF POLICY FRAMEWORK
BUILDING AND ITS IMPACT ON POWER RELATIONS WITHIN THE FRENCH
POLICY-MAKING PROCESS.

04746 JOCHNOWITZ, G.
THE WORDS OF MARX, THE METHODS OF LENIN
NATIONAL REVIEW, XLI(14) (AUG 89), 31-32.
THE PROBLEM WITH MAO ZEDONG HAS NOT THAT HE
MISUNDERSTOOD MARXISM BUT THAT HE UNDERSTOOD IT VERY WELL.
MARX LOOKED FORWARD TO AN ERA WITHOUT MERCHANTS AND
THEREFORE WITHOUT SPECIALIZATION, WHEN ONE WOULD "REAR
CATTLE IN THE EVENING (AND) CRITICIZE AFTER DINNER," THIS IS
ENTIRELY CONSISTENT WITH CLOSING THE SCHOOLS AND EXILING
PROFESSIONALS TO THE COUNTRYSIDE; MAO HAS NOT
MISINTERPRETING MARX.

04747 JOCHNOWITZ, G.
TRUE POWER TO THE PEOPLE
NATIONAL REVIEW, XLI(12) (JUN 89), 22-23.
THIS ARTICLE DESCRIBES UNREST AND CRACKDOWN IN CHINA
WHICH EXTEND BEYOND TIANANMEN SQUARE. A MONTH AGO, EVERY
CHINESE THOUGHT HE WAS THE ONLY ONE WHO LONGED FOR FREEDOM
AND DEMOCRACY. NOW EVERYONE KNOWS THAT THE CHINESE PEOPLE
HAVE HELD THE EQUIVALENT OF AN ELECTION AND VOTED DOWN THEIR
LEADERS. THE PEOPLE ARE BEGINNING TO REALIZE HOW MUCH POWER
THEY HAVE.

04748 JOCKEL, J.T.; SOKOLSKY, J.J.
DEFENCE WHITE PAPER LIVES AGAIN
INTERNATIONAL PERSPECTIVES, 18(4) (JUL 89), 5-7.
THIS PAPER EXPLORES SOME BRIGHT SIDES TO THE DEFENCE
WHITE PAPER THAT WAS SO SAVAGED BY THIS YEAR'S COST-CUTTING
BUDGET - WHICH MIGHT NOT BE TOTALLY LOST. IT SUGGESTS
RESTRUCTURING THE CANADIAN ARMED FORCES IN A NORTHWARD AND
MARITIME ORIENTATION, INCLUDING AN INHANCED COMMITMENT TO
NATO'S NORTHERN FLANK, WHICH WOULD BE A RECOMMITMENT TO
COLLECTIVE DEFENCE.

04749 JOFFE, G.
MAURITANIA: RACE RIOTS
MIDDLE EAST INTERNATIONAL, (350) (MAY 89), 13-14.
ON MAY 3, 1989, THE MAURITANIAN GOVERNMENT EXPELLED ALL
SENEGALESE, A DECISION LIKELY TO USHER IN A COMPLETE
EXCHANGE OF POPULATIONS BETWEEN ITSELF AND ITS SOUTHERN
NEIGHBOR. RELATIONS BETWEEN THE TWO WEST AFRICAN NATIONS
HAVE OFTEN BEEN FRAUGHT WITH ETHNIC TENSIONS. THE CURRENT
CRISIS MEANS THAT MAURITANIA'S RELATIONS WITH BLACK AFRICA
ARE LIKELY TO WORSEN AND NOUAKCHOTT WILL HAVE TO LOOK TO THE
ARAB MAGHREB UNION FOR AID AND SUPPORT.

04750 JOFFE, G.
MOROCCO
SOUTH, (107) (SEP 89), 81-89.
OVER THE PAST SIX YEARS, THE MOROCCAN GOVERNMENT HAS
FOLLOWED IMF PRESCRIPTIONS FOR REDUCING PUBLIC SECTOR
EXPENDITURES AND REORIENTING THE ECONOMY TOWARDS EXPORT-LED
GROWTH. IT HAS MADE SUCH SIGNIFICANT PROGRESS WITH ITS
RESTRUCTURING PROGRAM THAT IT HAS BECOME A MODEL OF IMF-
STYLE ECONOMIC REFORM. OFFICIALS ANTICIPATE THAT THE
RESTRUCTURING WILL BE COMPLETE WITHIN FIVE YEARS.

04751 JOFFE, G.
MOROCCO AND POLISARIO: HASSAN SQUARES THE CIRCLE
MIDDLE EAST INTERNATIONAL, (342) (JAN 89), 13-14.
ON JAN. 4, 1989, KING HASSAN FINALLY MET WITH LEADERS OF
HIS MOST INVETERATE OPPONENT, THE POLISARIO FRONT. OTHER
MEETINGS MAY FOLLOW AS BOTH SIDES GET ON WITH THE TASK OF
RECONCILING THEIR POSITION IN ADVANCE OF THE LONG-PROMISED
SELF-DETERMINATION REFERENDUM IN WESTERN SAHARA.

04752 JOFFE, J.
NATO AND THE DILEMMAS OF A NUCLEAR ALLIANCE
JOURNAL OF INTERNATIONAL AFFAIRS, 43(1) (SUM 89), 29-46.
THIS ARTICLE EXAMINES THE BALANCE WHICH ALL ALLIANCIES
MUST STRIKE BETWEEN AUTONOMY AND OBLIGATION. IT FURTHER
ANALYSES TWO NOVEL FACTORS THAT ARE UNPRECEDENTED. ONE IS
THE INTRUSION OF NUCLEAR WEAPONS, THE OTHER IS BIPOLARITY.
IT STUDIES THE REASONS FOR THE ENDURANCE OF NATO AND
EXPLORES ITS FUTURE.

04753 JOFFE, J.
THE REVISIONISTS - MOSCOW, BONN, AND THE EUROPEAN BALANCE
NATIONAL INTEREST, (17) (FAL 89), 41-54.
THIS ARTICLE SUGGESTS THAT THERE ARE ONLY THREE NATIONS
THAT CAN CHANGE THE EUROPEAN STATUS QUO AND THAT GERMANY AND
RUSSIA ARE DOING SO WITH ALL DELIBERATE, THOUGH CAUTIOUS,
SPEED. IT DEFINES GERMANY AND RUSSIA AS IN THE VANGUARD IN
THE SYSTEM CHANGE AND THE UNITED STATES AS ONE OF THE STATUS
QUO POWERS. IT EXPLORES THE QUEST FOR REDUCED DEPENDENCE AND
INCREASED OPTIONS WHICH DRIVES THE DIPLOMACY OF ANY STATE -
AND ALL THE MORE SO WEST GERMANY'S, WHICH COULD ONLY REGAIN

AUTONOMY BY ENCASING IT IN THE WESTERN COALITION, IT
CONCLUDES BY EXPLORING WHERE THE BASIC INTERESTS OF GERMANY
AND RUSSIA MEET WITH THOSE OF THE UNITED STATES WHERE
SKILLFUL STATECRAFT CAN YET REJOIN THE TWO HALVES OF EUROPE.

04754 JOHAL, S.
INDIA'S SEARCH FOR CAPITAL ABROAD
ASIAN SURVEY, 29(10) (OCT 89), 971-982.
THIS ARTICLE CONSIDERS THE ECONOMIC AND POLITICAL
BACKGROUND TO THE ECONOMIC DISAGREEMENTS BETWEEN INDIA AND
THE UNITED STATES, AND EXAMINES THE POLICIES OF BOTH
COUNTRIES TOWARD INDIA'S IMF LOAN, IDA FUNDING, AND INDIA'S
APPLICATION TO BORROW FOR THE FIRST TIME FROM THE ADB. IT
ARGUES THAT INDIA IS LESS LIKELY TO BE INFLUENCED BY U.S.
POLICIES AS THE U.S. REDUCES ITS FUNDING TO THE IDA AND ADF,
AND THAT IN 1989 INDIA IS LESS VULNERABLE TO SHIFTS IN U.S.
POLICY IN THE IMF AND THE MULTILATERAL DEVELOPMENT BANKS
(MDBS) THAN IT WAS IN 1980.

04755 JOHN, K.E.
1980-1988 NEW HAMPSHIRE PRESIDENTIAL PRIMARY POLLS
PUBLIC OPINION QUARTERLY, 53(4) (WIN 89), 590-605.
THE AUTHOR DISCUSSES THE USE OF TRACKING POLLS IN THE
NEW HAMPSHIRE PRIMARIES. THE ARTICLE CONTAINS A COMPILATION
OF NEW HAMPSHIRE PRESIDENTIAL PRIMARY POLLS, INCLUDING DATA
FROM TRACKING POLLS AND OTHER SURVEYS CONDUCTED THROUGHOUT
THE 1980'S. FINAL ELECTION RESULTS ARE ALSO PROVIDED.

04756 JOHNS, M.C.
THE REAGAN ADMINISTRATION'S RESPONSE TO STATE-SPONSORED
TERRORISM
CONFLICT, 8(4) (1988), 241-259.
IN THE 1980S, STATE-SPONSORED TERRORISM HAS BECOME A
MAJOR FOCUS OF ATTENTION AND SUBJECT TO DEBATE AMONG
NATIONAL SECURITY POLICYMAKERS. EXAMINATION OF THE REAGAN
ADMINISTRATION'S EXPERIENCE IN DEALING WITH THIS PHENOMENON
OVER ALMOST A DECADE CAN PROVIDE INSIGHT FOR FUTURE POLICY
DECISIONS. THIS ANALYSIS FIRST DEFINES AND DISTINGUISHES
WHAT CONSTITUTES STATE-SPONSORED TERRORISM; IT THEN TRACES
THE EVOLUTION OF THE AMERICAN GOVERNMENT'S POLICIES DURING
THE REAGAN YEARS AND DISCUSSES BOTH THE SUCCESSES AND
FAILURES THAT RESULTED. THE ARTICLE CONCLUDES WITH
RECOMMENDATIONS AND OBSERVATIONS CONCERNING THE DIRECTION OF
U.S. NATIONAL SECURITY POLICY CONCERNING STATE-SPONSORED
TERRORISM.

04757 JOHNSON-FREESE, J.
A MODEL FOR MULTINATIONAL SPACE COOPERATION
SPACE POLICY, 5(4) (NOV 89), 288-300.
IT IS BECOMING INCREASINGLY CLEAR THAT SPACE ACTIVITIES
CAN BENEFIT FROM INTERNATIONAL COOPERATION, BUT CONCERNS
ABOUT NATIONAL INTERESTS REMAIN. THIS ARTICLE EXAMINES THE
EXPERIENCE OF THE INTER-AGENCY CONSULTATIVE GROUP (IAGG),
WHICH ACHIEVED STRIKING SUCCESS IN COORDINATING THE EFFORTS
OF THE USA, THE USSR, THE EUROPEAN SPACE AGENCY, AND JAPAN
TO STUDY HALLEY'S COMET. SUBSEQUENTLY, THE IAGG HAS
UNDERTAKEN A NEW PROJECT. FOCUSED ON SOLAR-TERRESTRIAL
SCIENCE, AND FURTHER EXPANSION COULD FOLLOW. HOWEVER, THE
GROUP'S SUCCESS HAS DEPENDED ON SCRUPULOUS RESPECT FOR
MEMBER'S NATIONAL AUTONOMY. AND SO IT IS UNLIKELY TO HERALD
THE FORMATION OF A SUPRANATIONAL SPACE AGENCY IN THE NEAR
FUTURE.

04758 JOHNSON, C.
RETHINKING JAPANESE POLITICS: A GODFATHER REPORTS
FREEDOM AT ISSUE, (111) (NOV 89), 5-11.
JAPANESE POLITICS ARE CHANGING A LOT AND THE NATURE,
MEANING, AND SIGNIFICANCE OF THESE CHANGES ARE HIGHLY
CONTROVERSIAL BOTH IN JAPAN AND IN THE UNITED STATES. IN
THIS ARTICLE, THE AUTHOR CONSIDERS WHAT THESE CHANGES MEAN
FOR AMERICAN RELATIONS WITH JAPAN.

04759 JOHNSON, C.
THEIR BEHAVIOR, OUR POLICY
NATIONAL INTEREST, (17) (FAL 89), 17-27.
THIS ARTICLE ARGUES THAT THE STRUCTURE OF WORLD POLITICS,
INCLUDING INTERNATIONAL ECONOMIC RELATIONS IS AT A GENUINE
TURNING POINT. IT DEFINES THE 'STRUCTURE' OF INTERNATIONAL
RELATIONS AND OFFERS SIX MAJOR TRENDS CHANGING THE STRUCTURE
OF GLOBAL AFFAIRS. IT DISCUSSES BRIEFLY THE FIRST FIVE OF
THESE TRENDS IN RELATIONSHIP TO THE SIXTH AND THEN ADDRESSES
THE PROBLEM OF JAPAN ITSELF. EXPLORED ARE: THE END OF
HEGEMONY; COMMUNIST DISCREPITUDE AND THE PACIFIC; THE TRADE-
DEFENSE LINKAGE; EUROPE AND JAPAN, ADVERSARIAL TRADE;
PROBLEMS FOR JAPAN AND SUGGESTIONS FOR WHAT AMERICA SHOULD
DO.

04760 JOHNSON, D.
NEW MEGALOMANIA OR OLD PATRIOTISM?
ENCOUNTER, LXXII(4) (APR 89), 3-7.
FEW WEST OR EAST GERMANS CONSIDER THEMSELVES TO BE A
DANGER TO ANYBODY. THE PASSIVE POLITICAL ROLE THAT DEFEAT
FORCED UPON THE NEW WEST GERMAN STATE IS NOW A THING OF THE
PAST, BUT THE MENTAL HABITS THAT IT INCULCATED HAVE SURVIVED.

TO WEST GERMANS THE IDEA THAT THEIR OWN STATE COULD BE THE UNWITTING CAUSE OF HAVOC IN THE WESTERN CAMP IS ALIEN AND, CONSEQUENTLY, LIABLE TO ENRAGE THEM.

04761 JOHNSON, G.D.
CAPITALISM, PROTESTANTISM, AND THE PRIVATE FAMILY: COMPARISONS AMONG EARLY MODERN ENGLAND, FRANCE, AND THE AMERICAN COLONIES
SOCIOLOGICAL INQUIRY, 59(2) (SPR 89), 144-164.
THE STUDY OF WESTERN FAMILY CHANGE LIES DISINTEGRATED, DIVIDED INTO TWO LARGELY INDEPENDENT INTELLECTUAL COMMUNITIES--FAMILY HISTORY AND THEORETICAL FAMILY SOCIOLOGY. AN INTEGRATION OF THE TWO FIELDS IS PROPOSED. THE RESULTS OF FAMILY HISTORICAL RESEARCH FROM THREE NATIONAL CASES, ENGLAND, FRANCE, AND THE NORTH AMERICAN COLONIES, ARE USED TO EVALUATE CRITICALLY THE FAMILY THEORIES OF PARSONS, SECCOMBE, ZARETSKY, AND HORKHEIMER. THE PATTERN OF FAMILY ORGANIZATION REGARDED AS MODERN, INCLUDING THE DIFFERENTIATION OF THE FAMILY FROM OTHER SOCIAL INSTITUTIONS, THE EMERGENCE OF COMPANIONATE MARRIAGE, AND THE CONSOLIDATION OF AUTHORITY OVER THE FAMILY IN THE ROLE OF THE FATHER, CHARACTERIZE THE FAMILY SYSTEMS OF ENGLAND AND THE COLONIES BETTER THAN THAT OF FRANCE. A THEORY OF MODERN FAMILY ORGANIZATION IS PROPOSED THAT IDENTIFIES THE EMERGENCE OF A CULTURALLY DOMINANT MIDDLE CLASS AND THE INSTITUTIONALIZATION OF PROTESTANTISM AS FACILITATING CONDITIONS FOR THE DEVELOPMENT OF THIS PRIVATE FAMILY SYSTEM.

04762 JOHNSON, J.
SUMMIT CREATES COMMON E.C. FRONT EASTERN EUROPE
EUROPE, (292) (DEC 89), 22, 47.
ON NOVEMBER 18, 1989 THE EUROPEAN COMMUNITIES (E.C.) HEADS OF STATE AND GOVERNMENT MET IN PARIS TO DISCUSS THE BREAK NECK PACE OF REFORM IN EASTERN EUROPE. THE E.C.'S LEADERS EXAMINED THE POSSIBILITIES OF SETTING UP A EUROPEAN DEVELOPMENT BANK, TO PROVIDE AID TO THE REFORMING EAST EUROPEAN ECONOMIES. THE PROPOSED BANK "WILL INVOLVE ALL COUNTRIES THAT SUPPLY CAPITAL AND WILL CHANNEL IT TO ALL THE (EASTERN EUROPEAN) COUNTRIES THAT ENGAGE IN REFORM." IT IS EVIDENT THAT ECONOMIC ASSISTANCE IS CONTITIONAL ON CONTINUED PROGRESS TO DEMOCRACY.

04763 JOHNSON, L.
COVERT ACTION AND ACCOUNTABILITY: DECISION-MAKING FOR AMERICA'S SECRET FOREIGN POLICY
INTERNATIONAL STUDIES QUARTERLY, 33(1) (MAR 89), 81-110.
THE STUDY EXAMINES THE WAY IN WHICH THE US DECIDES UPON AND OVERSEES THE USE OF COVERT ACTION. IT EXPLORES THE DEFINITIONAL NUANCES OF COVERT ACTION AND EXAMINES THE MAGNITUDE OF FUNDING FOR COVERT ACTION FOR THE YEARS 1947-1986. IT ALSO PRESENTS GLOBAL TARGETING PRIORTIES FOR COVERT ACTION AND EXPLORES THE PROCEDURES BY WHICH THE GOVERNMENT APPROVES OF AND REVIEWS COVERT ACTION. DURING THE FORD AND CARTER ADMINISTRATIONS, THIS DECISION PROCESS EVOLVED INTO A COMPLEX MATRIX OF CHECKPOINTS AND OVERSEERS, INCLUDING UNPRECEDENTED LEGISLATIVE INVOLVEMENT. THE REAGAN YEARS HAVE PRODUCED DRAMATIC EVIDENCE THAT THESE EFFORTS AT CLOSER SUPERVISION OF AMERICA'S SECRET FOREIGN POLICY HAVE FALLEN SHORT OF THE GOALS ESPOUSED BY REFORMERS.

04764 JOHNSON, L.K.
STRATEGIC INTELLIGENCE: AN AMERICAN PERSPECTIVE
INTERNATIONAL JOURNAL OF INTELLIGENCE AND COUNTER-INTELLIGENCE, 3(3) (1989), 299-332.
STRATEGIC INTELLIGENCE, WHICH IS VITAL TO THE UNITED STATES AND ALL OTHER DEVELOPED NATIONS, CONSISTS OF TWO THINGS: (1) THE COLLECTION-AND-ANALYSIS OF INFORMATION ABOUT GLOBAL CONDITIONS - ESPECIALLY POTENTIAL THREATS TO A NATION'S SECURITY AND (2) BASED ON THIS INFORMATION, THE USE OF SECRET INTELLIGENCE AGENCIES TO HELP PROTECT THE NATION AGAINST HARM AND ADVANCE ITS INTERESTS ABROAD. INFORMATION AND RESPONSE - THE ESSENCE OF DECISIONMAKING - IS A LINKAGE MADE ALL THE MORE CRITICAL IN THE FACE OF MODERN DOOMSDAY-WEAPONS AND FRAGILE ECONOMIC DEPENDENCIES.

04765 JOHNSON, P.E.
THE BY-PRODUCT HYPOTHESIS AND ITS RAMIFICATIONS
DISSERTATION ABSTRACTS INTERNATIONAL, 49(9) (MAR 89), 2796-A.
THE AUTHOR IDENTIFIES THE ORGANIZATIONAL STRUCTURES BY WHICH INTEREST GROUPS RAISE AND ALLOCATE FUNDS. THEN HE APPLIES HIS FINDINGS TO THE EARLY YEARS OF THE AMERICAN FEDERATION OF LABOR. HE UTILIZES THE BY-PRODUCT THEORY OF INTEREST GROUP POLITICS, WHICH HOLDS THAT GROUP INFLUENCE RESULTS FROM THE DIVERSION OF FUNDS FROM NONPOLITICAL PROGRAMS BY GROUP LEADERS.

04766 JOHNSON, R.A.
AFFIRMATIVE ACTION AS A WOMAN'S ISSUE
JOURNAL OF POLITICAL SCIENCE, 17(1-2) (1989), 114-126.
THE AUTHOR TRACES THE DEVELOPMENT OF FEDERAL AFFIRMATIVE ACTION POLICY FROM THE ISSUING OF EXECUTIVE ORDERS BY PRESIDENTS ROOSEVELT, KENNEDY, AND JOHNSON TO ITS FULL IMPLEMENTATION IN THE DEPARTMENT OF LABOR. THEN SHE SUMMARIZES AND EVALUATES ALL THE AFFIRMATIVE ACTION CASES DECIDED BY THE SUPREME COURT, STARTING WITH THE BAKKE DECISION. FINALLY, SHE CONSIDERS THE WAYS AFFIRMATIVE ACTION INCREASES OPPORTUNITIES FOR WOMEN.

04767 JOHNSON, R.H.
THE PERSIAN GULF IN U.S. STRATEGY
INTERNATIONAL SECURITY, 14(1) (SUM 89), 122-160.
THIS ARTICLE ADDRESSES THE QUESTION OF WHETHER THE GULF DESERVES ITS CURRENT STATUS AND PRIORITY IN U.S. GRAND STRATEGY AND WHETHER A MULTI-DIVISION RAPID DEPLOYMENT FORCE IS LIKELY TO PROVIDE A USEFUL RESPONSE TO THE MOST PROBABLE THREATS. IN THE FOUR MAJOR PARTS OF THE ARGUMENT THE AUTHOR DEMONSTRATES THAT THE U.S. VIEW OF THE THREAT AND THE STAKES HAD ITS SOURCE IN MISUNDERSTANDINGS OF THE EVENTS OF THE 1970S; THAT A SEVERE OIL SUPPLY CRISIS IN THE 1990S—AND PROBABLY BEYOND—IS MUCH LESS LIKELY THAN GENERALLY ASSUMED; THAT THE POTENTIAL THREATS TO U.S. INTERESTS FROM THE SOVIETS, THE GULF OIL PRODUCERS, OR LOCAL CONFLICTS HAVE ALMOST CERTAINLY BEEN OVERSTATED; AND THAT A RAPID DEPLOYMENT FORCE CAPABLE OF LARGE-SCALE INTERVENTION ON THE GROUND IS VERY UNLIKELY TO BE USEFUL IN DEALING WITH EITHER THE MORE PROBABLE OR THE MORE UNLIKELY THREATS. THE AUTHOR CONCLUDES THAT A STRATEGY THAT LIMITS DIRECT U.S. MILITARY INVOLVEMENT MAINLY TO AIR AND SEA POWER MAKES A GREAT DEAL MORE SENSE.

04768 JOHNSON, S.
NAMIBIA: INDEPENDENCE
THIRD WORLD WEEK, 8(4) (MAR 89), 29-30.
ILLEGAL PRE-ELECTION HARASSMENT AND VIOLENCE BY SOUTH AFRICAN-CONTROLLED SECURITY FORCES HAVE BEEN ALLEGED IN NAMIBIA. THE SOUTHWEST AFRICA PEOPLE'S ORGANIZATION (SWAPO), WHICH FOR MANY YEARS HAS LED A POLITICAL AND GUERRILLA-WARFARE CAMPAIGN FOR INDEPENDENCE FROM SOUTH AFRICA, HAS BEEN THE TARGET OF THE ALLEGED ILLEGAL POLITICAL INTERFERENCE.

04769 JOHNSON, T.V.
DEMOCRATIC DEMANDS AND CLASS CONSCIOUS FORCES
POLITICAL AFFAIRS, LXVIII(2) (FEB 89), 14-18.
IT IS GENERALLY UNDERSTOOD ON THE LEFT THAT THE WORKING CLASS WILL COME TO REALIZE THE NECESSITY OF SOCIALISM THROUGH ITS PARTICPATION IN STRUGGLES TO WIN ITS CLASS DEMANDS WITHIN THE CAPITALISM SYSTEM-THAT IS, THROUGH THE DEMOCRATIC STRUGGLE. JUST AS IMPORTANT IS THE REALIZATION THAT DEMOCRATIC STRUGGLES WILL NOT AUTOMATICALLY LEAD THE WORKING CLASS TO THIS REVELATION. IT IS ONLY IF THESE STRUGGLES ARE LED BY THE CLASS-CONSCIOUS FORCES THAT THE WORKING CLASS WILL COME TO THIS REALIZATION. THE AUTHOR CONSIDERS HOW JESSE JACKSON AND THE BLACKS' STRUGGLE ARE RELATED TO THIS CONCEPT.

04770 JOHNSON, T.V.
MARTIN LUTHER KING, JR: A DIFFERENT IMAGE
POLITICAL AFFAIRS, LXVIII(1) (JAN 89), 9-11.
IN "WHERE DO WE GO FROM HERE: CHAOS OR COMMUNITY?" MARTIN LUTHER KING SET FORTH THREE IMPORTANT THEMES: (1) AFRO-AMERICAN TRADE UNION UNITY, (2) THE ROLE OF AFRO-AMERICAN TRADE UNIONISTS, AND (3) THE NECESSITY FOR FUNDAMENTAL CHANGES IN THE ECONOMIC STRUCTURE.

04771 JOHNSTON, G. K.
SOCIALIST THOUGHT AND THE TRANSITION TO SOCIALISM IN ADVANCED SOCIETIES
DISSERTATION ABSTRACTS INTERNATIONAL, 49(8) (FEB 89), 2376-A.
THE AUTHOR EXPLORES THE RELATIONSHIP BETWEEN DISCUSSIONS OF THE TRANSITION TO SOCIALISM AND CONCEPTUALIZATIONS OF THE FORM THAT SOCIALISM MIGHT TAKE. HE CONSIDERS THE WORK OF MARX, MORRIS, LENIN, AND THE THEORETICIANS OF THE SECOND INTERNATIONAL. HE ARGUES THAT ANY SUSTAINED DISCUSSION OF THE FORM THAT SOCIALISM MIGHT TAKE HAS TO THINK THROUGH THE RELATIONSHIP BETWEEN PRINCIPLES, STRUCTURES, AND INSTITUTIONS, BUT SUCH INITIATIVES ARE UNLIKELY, IN THEMSELVES, TO BE DECISIVE IN SECURING SUPPORT FOR THE SOCIALIST PROJECT.

04772 JOHNSTON, R.; PATTIE, C.
A NATION DIVIDING? ECONOMIC WELL-BEING, VOTER RESPONSE AND THE CHANGING ELECTORAL GEOGRAPHY OF GREAT BRITAIN
PARLIAMENTARY AFFAIRS, 42(1) (JAN 89), 37-57.
THE ARTICLE CLOSELY ANALYZES BRITAIN'S ELECTORAL GEOGRAPHY FROM THE PERIOD 1979-1987. IT CONCLUDES THAT SPATIALLY, BRITAIN IS BECOMING INCREASINGLY POLARIZED SO THAT "THE PARTISANSHIP OF INDIVIDUALS IS INFLUENCED MORE BY WHERE THEY LIVE THAN WHAT THEY DO." THE INCREASE IN SPATIAL POLARIZATION RESULTS FROM THE GROWING ECONOMIC AND SOCIAL POLARIZATION OF THE COUNTRY. THE FUTURE WILL DEPEND ON A COMBINATION OF TWO THINGS: THE DEGREE TO WHICH THE SOCIAL AND ECONOMIC CHANGES UNDER THATCHERISM FAVOR ONE PART OF THE COUNTRY OVER THE OTHERS; AND THE DEGREE TO WHICH THE OPPOSITION PARTIES RESTRUCTURE THEIR POLICIES AND STRATEGIES TO FIGHT THATCHERISM ON ITS HOME GROUND.

04773 JOHNSTON, R.J.; JOHNSTON C.J.; PATTIE, C.J.
THE IMPACT OF CONSTITUENCY SPENDING ON THE RESULT OF THE
1987 BRITISH GENERAL ELECTION
ELECTORAL STUDIES, 8(2) (AUG 89), 143-156.
MOST ANALYSTS OF BRITISH GENERAL ELECTIONS BELIEVE THAT
THE CONSTITUENCY CAMPAIGNS HAVE VERY LITTLE IMPACT ON THE
OUTCOME. USING CAMPAIGN EXPENDITURE AS A SURROGATE FOR
CONSTITUENCY CAMPAIGN ACTIVITY, ANALYSES OF THE 1987 GENERAL
ELECTION INDICATE THAT IT WAS SIGNIFICANTLY RELATED TO THE
OUTCOME. WHATEVER THE CAUSAL RELATIONSHIP, LOCAL PARTY
ORGANIZATIONS CLEARLY BELIEVE IT IS NECESSARY TO SPEND MONEY
ON THEIR CAMPAIGNS, AND PRESUMABLY BELIEVE THAT SUCH
SPENDING IS EFFECTIVE. INDEED, RELATIVE TO THE LEGALLY-
IMPOSED LIMITS, THEY INCREASED THEIR REPORTED SPENDING
BETWEEN 1983 AND 1987. SO WAS THEIR EXPENDITURE RELATED TO
THE RESULT IN 1987; DID IT POTENTIALLY INFLUENCE THE PATTERN
OF VOTING? THIS ANALYSES SUGGESTS THAT IT DID.

04774 JOHNSTON, R.J.
VOTING SHIFTS IN NEW ZEALAND BETWEEN 1984 AND 1987.
ANALYSES OF ESTIMATED CONSTITUENCY FLOW-OF-THE-VOTE
MATRICES
POLITICAL SCIENCE, 41(1) (JUL 89), 1-17.
IN SOME RESPECTS, THE NEW ZEALAND GENERAL ELECTION OF
AUGUST 1987 WAS RELATIVELY UNREMARKABLE EVENT. FEW SEATS
CHANGED HANDS AND THE GOVERNMENT HAS RETURNED WITH ITS
MAJORITY ALMOST UNSCATHED. BUT THESE SIMPLE FACTS MASK
CONSIDERABLE UNDERLYING CHANGE, WHICH IS THE SUBJECT OF THIS
ESSAY.

04775 JOHNSTON, W.
HAS THERE BEEN A GROWTH IN THE INTERNATIONAL ORDER?
TEACHING POLITICAL SCIENCE, 16(3) (SPR 89), 107-121.
THE BOOK, "THE EXPANSION OF INTERNATIONAL SOCIETY" MAKES
A MAJOR CONTRIBUTION TO THE ADVANCEMENT OF THE UNDERSTANDING
OF INTERNATIONAL POLITICS. THREE STRENGTHS OF THE BOOK ARE
OUTLINED: IT IS GLOBAL IN ITS SWEEP; THE COMPARATIVE
ANALYSIS OF DIFFERENT HISTORICAL ERAS IN INTERNATIONAL
POLITICS IS CENTRAL; AND, THE CONTROLLING IMPORTANCE OF
RULES IN INTERNATIONAL POLITICS IS EMPHASIZED. THE FOUR
PARTS OF THE BOOK COVER: THE FIRST GLOBAL INTERNATIONAL
SYSTEM, THE ENTRY OF NON-EUROPEAN STATES INTO INTERNATIONAL
SOCIETY, THE CHALLENGE TO WESTERN DOMINANCE, AND THE NEW
INTERNATIONAL SOCIETY. THE BOOK IS OF EXTRAORDINARY VALUE
BECAUSE OF THE MANY PROFOUND PROBLEMS THE READER IS
COMPELLED TO ADDRESS, THIS ARTICLE CONCLUDES.

04776 JOHNSTONE, D.
TURKEY'S OTHER NATO LINK
MIDDLE EAST REPORT, 19(5) (SEP 89), 17-18.
BILATERAL RELATIONS BETWEEN THE US AND TURKEY, BACKED BY
SUBSTANTIAL ARMS MODERNIZATION AID, DOMINATE TURKEY'S
RELATIONS WITH NATO. HOWEVER, THE FEDERAL REPUBLIC OF
GERMANY IS INCREASING MILITARY AID TO TURKEY AND RELATIONS
BETWEEN THE TWO NATIONS ARE APPROACHING THE LEVEL OF THE PRE-
WORLD WAR I IMPERIALIST AGE. GERMAN AID IS ESPECIALLY
ENTICING TO TURKEY BECAUSE IT DOES NOT COME WITH THE
IDEOLOGICAL STRINGS THAT ARE OFTEN ATTACHED TO US AID. THE
DIMINISHING COLD WAR AND CONTINUED US FRIENDLINESS TOWARDS
ISRAEL BOTH SERVE TO INCREASE THE ATTRACTIVENESS OF
BILATERAL RELATIONS BETWEEN TURKEY AND THE FRG.

04777 JOLLY, C.M.; GADBOIS, M.A.
FOREIGN AID AS A PROMOTIONAL STRATEGY
REVIEW OF BLACK POLITICAL ECONOMY, 18(1) (SUM 89), 59-74.
DEVELOPED COUNTRIES ARE MOTIVATED BY SEVERAL FORCES WHEN
ALLOCATING AID TO DEVELOPING COUNTRIES. THE FORCES COULD BE
HUMANITARIAN IN ONE COUNTRY AND COMMERCIAL SELF-INTERESTS IN
ANOTHER. THE PRINCIPAL OBJECTIVE OF THIS STUDY WAS TO
DETERMINE THE EFFECTIVENESS OF AID AS A PROMOTIONAL STRATEGY
FOR TRADE AND TO INVESTIGATE WHETHER MAJOR DONOR COUNTRIES
ARE OPTIMALLY ALLOCATING THEIR AID RESOURCES TO INCREASE
THEIR EXPORT AND TOTAL TRADE.

04778 JONES-HENDRICKSON, S.B.
FINANCIAL STRUCTURE AND ECONOMIC DEVELOPMENT IN THE
ORGANISATION OF EASTERN CARIBBEAN STATES
SOCIAL AND ECONOMIC STUDIES, 38(4) (DEC 89), 71-93.
THIS PAPER EXAMINES THE NEXUS BETWEEN FINANCIAL
STRUCTURE AND ECONOMIC DEVELOPMENT IN SEVEN COUNTRIES OF THE
ORGANISATION OF EASTERN CARIBBEAN STATES. THE ANALYSIS IS AN
EKISTIC ONE: IT IS CONDUCTED WITH THE BASIC NEEDS OF THE
INDIVIDUAL STATE AND THE ENTIRE COMMUNITY AS ITS FRAME OF
REFERENCE. THE METHOD IS ECLECTIC: THOSE FEATURES FROM
VARIOUS SYSTEMS AND DOCTRINES WHICH BUTTRESS THE AGRUMENTS
ARE USED. THE PAPER LOOKS AT THE STRUCTURE, ECONOMIC
DEVELOPMENT, THE INTERACTION OF STRUCTURE AND GROWTH, DIRECT
AND INDIRECT TAXES, SUBSIDIES, REVENUE, AID, LOANS AND
GRANTS.

04779 JONES, A.; MOSKOFF, W.
NEW COOPERATIVES IN THE USSR
PROBLEMS OF COMMUNISM, XXXVIII(6) (NOV 89), 27-39.
AS A MEANS OF SPURRING INDIVIDUAL INITIATIVE, THE NEW
SOVIET COOPERATIVES HAVE BEEN HIGHLY SUCCESSFUL. THEY
PROVIDE A WIDE RANGE OF CONSUMER GOODS AND SERVICES,
ALTHOUGH AT PRICES CONSIDERABLY HIGHER THAN IN THE STATE
SECTOR. AFTER AN EARLY WAVE OF FAVORABLE LEGISLATION AND
PUBLICITY, THE COOPERATIVES ARE ENCOUNTERING STRONG PUBLIC
HOSTILITY, NEW OFFICIAL RESTRICTIONS, AND INCREASINGLY HEAVY
TAXATION.

04780 JONES, C.
GORBACHEV AND THE WARSAW PACT
EASTERN EUROPEAN POLITICS AND SOCIETIES, 2(3) (SPR 89),
215-234.
THE ESSAY IDENTIFIES THREE UNCHANGING MILITARY-POLITICAL
OBJECTIVES OF THE WARSAW PACT AND AN ENDURING SET OF
MECHANISMS DESIGNED TO ACHIEVE THESE OBJECTIVES. IT ARGUES
THAT THE DEPARTURES OF MIKHAIL GORBQACHEV FROM PREVIOUS
SOVIET POSITIONS ON NUCLEAR AND CONVENTIONAL FORCE LEVELS,
DRAMATIC AS THEY ARE, PURSUE IN FACT THE TRADITIONAL
MILITARY-POLITICAL OBJECTIVES DEPENDENT ON THE PRESERVATION
OF THE TRADITIONAL MECHANISMS OF THE WARSAW PACT.

04781 JONES, C.B.
MALTA AFTER 25 YEARS OF INDEPENDENCE
CONTEMPORARY REVIEW, 255(1486) (NOV 89), 262-266.
THIS YEAR MALTA CELEBRATES THE 25TH ANNIVERSARY OF ITS
ACCESSION TO INDEPENDENCE FROM UNDER 180 YEARS OF BRITISH
RULE. THIS ARTICLE EXAMINES THE TWO DISTINCT FORMS OF
GOVERNMENT DURING THE 25 YEARS - THE NATIONALISTS (CHRISTIAN
DEMOCRATIC IDEALS) AND THE LABOURITES (SOCIALISM). IT
FOCUSES IN ON THE PERIOD OF TIME THAT THE COUNTRY HAD TO
DECIDE MATTERS OF LOCAL SELF-GOVERNMENT, AND ALSO TO FORGE A
NEW FOREIGN POLICY TOWARDS THE UNITED NATIONS AND TO DECIDE
WHETHER TO FIT IN WITH THE WEST OR EASTERN BLOC IDEALS, IT
CONCLUDES THAT MALTA IS LOOKED UPON WITH MORE RESPECT ABROAD
THAN BEFORE.

04782 JONES, C.O.
GOVERNING WHEN IT'S OVER: THE LIMITS OF PRESIDENTIAL POWER
BROOKINGS REVIEW, 7(4) (FAL 89), 11-15.
"GOVERNING WHEN IT'S OVER" MEANS FIGURING OUT NOT ONLY
HOW TO GOVERN WHEN THE ELECTION IS OVER BUT ALSO HOW TO
GOVERN IN THE FACE OF SERIOUS CHALLENGES TO THE PRESIDENT'S
RIGHT OR POWER TO DO SO. SUCH CIRCUMSTANCES AS SCANDALS, THE
LACK OF A MANDATE, OR BEING A LAME DUCK RAISE QUESTIONS
ABOUT THE PRESIDENT'S ABILITY TO GOVERN.

04783 JONES, D.L.
THE DYNAMICS OF CONTEMPORARY INTERNATIONAL CONFLICT
DISSERTATION ABSTRACTS INTERNATIONAL, 49(10) (APR 89),
3147-A.
CONTEMPORARY INTERNATIONAL CONFLICTS HAVE BEEN DOMINATED
BY PROTRACTED LOCAL HOSTILITIES AMONG THIRD WORLD
PARTICIPANTS AND BY THE COMPETITIVE INTERVENTIONS OF
EXTERNAL MAJOR POWER ADVERSARIES. BECAUSE VITAL MAJOR POWER
INTERESTS ARE OFTEN AT STAKE, SUCH CONFLICTS RAISE THE
SPECTOR OF THE TRANSFORMATION OF INDIRECT AND LIMITED FORMS
OF MAJOR POWER CONFLICT INTO DIRECT, MORE INTENSE FORMS.
THIS DISSERTATION EXPLICATES THE DYNAMIC PROCESSES THROUGH
WHICH SUCH CONFLICTS ARE ESCALATED OR THROUGHT WHICH THEY
ARE CONSTRAINED. THE 1965 AND 1971 INDO-PAKISTANI WARS ARE
USED AS CASE STUDIES.

04784 JONES, D.S.; IYER, T.K.K.
THE NATURE OF POLITICAL CONVENTIONS IN A WRITTEN
CONSTITUTIONAL ORDER: A COMPARATIVE PERSPECTIVE
GOVERNANCE, 2(4) (OCT 89), 405-424.
POLITICAL AND CONSTITUTIONAL DEVELOPMENTS HAVE OCCURRED
WHICH HAVE CALLED INTO QUESTION THE NATURE OF POLITICAL
CONVENTIONS. TO UNDERSTAND SUCH DEVELOPMENTS, A CLEAR
APPRECIATION OF THE ROLE OF CONVENTIONS AND THEIR IMPORTANCE
IN THE EVOLUTION OF A POLICY IS NECESSARY. BY CONSIDERING
EXAMPLES OF CONVENTIONS IN DIFFERENT SYSTEMS OF GOVERNMENT,
THIS ARTICLE ATTEMPTS TO SHED FURTHER LIGHT ON THEIR NATURE
AND PURPOSE.

04785 JONES, D.T.
ELIMINATING CHEMICAL WEAPONS: LESS THAN MEETS THE EYE
WASHINGTON QUARTERLY, 12(2) (SPR 89), 83-92.
CHEMICAL WEAPONS (CW) ISSUES ARE FERMENTING ANEW. IN
EXAMINING POTENTIAL ARMS-CONTROL AGREEMENTS, SUCH AS START
OR CONVENTIONAL FORCE REDUCTIONS, A CW AGREEMENT IS
BEGINNING TO ASSUME AN AIR OF BEING "DOABLE." SOME
INTERNATIONAL MOMENTUM HAS DEVELOPED IN ITS FAVOR, AND THE
SOVIETS HAVE MADE A NUMBER OF POSITIVE MOVES. IF A U.S.
REVIEW CONCLUDES THAT THE POTENTIAL FOR RESTRICTING FURTHER
CW PROLIFERATION AND ELIMINATING EXISTING CW STOCKS
OUTWEIGHTS THE MILITARY RISKS STEMMING FROM VERIFICATION
LIABILITIES, CW INITIATIVES WILL BECOME HIGHLY VISIBLE.
STILL, THIS WILL ONLY BE THE BEGINNING OF A RENEWED
NEGOTIATING EFFORT, NOT THE END, AS RECENT MULTILATERAL
NEGOTIATIONS SUGGEST AT LEAST TWICE THE AMOUNT OF TIME IS
REQUIRED AS ORIGINALLY ESTIMATED.

04786 JONES, D.W.
FOREIGN TRADE, THE MULTINATIONAL ENTERPRISE, AND REGIONAL
ECONOMIC CHARGE IN THE UNITED STATES
AVAILABLE FROM NTIS, NO. DE88007678/GAR, 1988, 14.
THIS PAPER IDENTIFIES THE SCOPE FOR LOCATIONAL
ANALYSISREGIONAL AND SPATIAL ECONOMICS, OR IN GENERAL,
ECONOMIC GEOGRAPHY - TO CONTRIBUTE TO THE ASSESSMENT OF THE
ROLE OF INTERNATIONAL TRADE AND THE MULTINATIONAL ENTERPRISE
ACTIVITY IN CHANGING THE REGIONAL PATTERN OF ECONOMIC
ACTIVITY IN THE UNITED STATES. RECENT TRENDS IN ACTUAL TRADE
PATTERNS AND IN THE THEORY OF TRADE AND THE MULTINATIONAL
ENTERPRISE ARE REVIEWED.

04787 JONES, E.; MUTUURA, J.
THE SUPPLY RESPONSIVENESS OF SMALL KENYAN COTTON FARMERS
JOURNAL OF DEVELOPING AREAS, 23(4) (JUL 89), 535-544.
THIS ARTICLE STUDIES THE ECONOMIC POLICY OF THE KENYAN
GOVERNMENT TO INCREASE COTTON PRODUCTION TO SELF-SUFFICIENCY
AS PRODUCTION DECLINES, THE COTTON INDUSTRY IN KENYA IS
CONFRONTED WITH INSTABILITY OF SUPPLIES COUPLED WITH LOW
PRODUCTION LEVELS. THESE PROBLEMS ERODE MUCH-NEEDED FOREIGN
EXCHANGE AND CREATE CONSIDERABLE UNCERTAINTY AMONG FARM
PRODUCERS AND POLICYMAKERS AS TO THE FUTURE OUTLOOK FOR
COTTON AS AN ENTERPRISE. ECONOMIC PLANNERS ARE UNCERTAIN
CONCERNING WHETHER ABRUPT CHANGES IN PRODUCTION ARE DUE TO
RELATIVE PRICE CHANGES AMONG COMMODITIES OR TO OTHER
PROBLEMS BEYOND THE FARM GATE. THIS STUDY IS THEREFORE
INTENDED TO (1) IDENTIFY AND EMPIRICALLY ESTIMATE THOSE
FACTORS THAT DETERMINE COTTON PRODUCTION; (2) EXAMINE THE
RELATIVE IMPACTS OF THESE FACTORS; AND (3) OFFER SUGGESTIONS
AND/OR POLICY RECOMMENDATIONS FOR INCREASING COTTON
PRODUCTION.

04788 JONES, G.
LOCAL GOVERNMENT AND 1992
CONSTITUTIONAL REFORM QUARTERLY REVIEW, 4(2) (SUM 89), 4.
BRITISH LOCAL AUTHORITIES HAVE BECOME MORE AWARE OF THE
OPPORTUNITIES AND CHALLENGES OFFERED TO THEM BY THE EUROPEAN
SINGLE INTERNAL MARKET. IN NOVEMBER 1988, LOCAL AUTHORITY
ASSOCIATIONS JOINED FORCES TO SET UP THE LOCAL GOVERNMENT
INTERNATIONAL BUREAU (LGIB), A LIAISON BETWEEN LOCAL
GOVERNMENTS AND THE OVERALL COMMUNITY. A RECENT LGIB
PUBLICATION STRONGLY SUPPORTS ECONOMIC INTEGRATION WITH
EUROPE, WHILE AT THE SAME TIME MAINTAINS THE IMPORTANCE OF
LOCAL AUTONOMY.

04789 JONES, G. S. (ED.); MARINI, J. A. (ED.)
THE IMPERIAL CONGRESS: CRISIS IN THE SEPARATION OF POWERS
HERITAGE FOUNDATION, WASHINGTON, DC, 1989, 384.
"THE IMPERIAL CONGRESS" EXAMINES THE SERIOUS STRUCTURAL
PROBLEMS OF A CONGRESS THAT HAS STEPPED OUTSIDE THE
BOUNDARIES OF ITS POWER AS SET FORTH IN THE CONSTITUTION.
THE BOOK ARGUES THAT CONGRESS HAS USURPED POLICY MAKING
POWER THAT TRADITIONALLY BELONGED TO THE EXECUTIVE BRANCH.
IT IS DIVIDED INTO THREE SECTIONS: "THE CONSTITUTIONAL
FRAMEWORK OF SEPARATED POWERS," "CONGRESS AT WORK AND PLAY,"
AND "RECLAIMING AMERICAN POLITICS."

04790 JONES, G.W.
A REVOLUTION IN WHITEHALL? CHANGES IN BRITISH CENTRAL
GOVERNMENT SINCE 1979
WEST EUROPEAN POLITICS, 12(3) (JUL 89), 238-261.
SINCE THE CONSERVATIVES CAME TO POWER IN 1979 THERE HAVE
BEEN IMPORTANT CHANGES IN BRITISH CENTRAL GOVERNMENT WHICH
HAVE THEIR INTELLECTUAL ORIGINS IN MANAGERIALIST THINKING OF
THE 1960S, BUT OWE THEIR RECENT IMPLEMENTATION TO THE
COMMITMENT OF THE PRIME MINISTER TO REFORM THE CIVIL SERVICE
ALONG LINES ADVOCATED BY 'NEW RIGHT' OR 'PUBLIC CHOICE'
THEORISTS. WHILE MOST INSTITUTIONAL REFORMS OF DEPARTMENTS
WERE FOR POLITICAL REASONS, CHANGES IN THE PROCESSES OF THE
CIVIL SERVICE CAN BE SEEN AS AN EXTENSION OF DEVELOPMENTS
BEGINNING WITH THE RAYNER SCRUTINIES, AND MOVING THROUGH THE
FINANCIAL MANAGEMENT INITIATIVE AND THE EFFICIENCY STRATEGY
TO EXECUTIVE AGENCIES. THE BRITISH UNIFIED CIVIL SERVICE IS
CHALLENGED BY PRESSURES FOR FRAGMENTATION, BUT LIMITS TO THE
CHANGES ARE SET BY THE DOMINANCE OF THE CONCEPTS OF
MINISTERIAL RESPONSIBILITY TO PARLIAMENT, PARLIAMENTARY
AUDIT, AND OF TREASURY CONTROL.

04791 JONES, K. B. (ED.); JONASDOTTIR, A. G. (ED.)
THE POLITICAL INTERESTS OF GENDER: DEVELOPING THEORY AND
RESEARCH WITH A FEMINIST FACE
SAGE PUBLICATIONS, NEWBURY PARK, CA, 1989, 256.
KATHLEEN JONES AND ANNA JONASDOTTIR START FROM THE
PREMISE THAT CONTEMPORARY POLITICAL THEORY IS INADEQUATE
WHEN APPROACHED FROM THE PERSPECTIVE OF GENDER. THIS VOLUME
INDICTS CONTEMPORARY POLITICAL ANALYSIS FOR ITS SILENCE
ABOUT OR IGNORANCE OF WOMEN'S INTERESTS AND CHALLENGES THE
HYPOTHESIS THAT THE CENTRAL CONCEPTS OF POLITICAL THOUGHT,
AND ITS BASIC TECHNIQUES, ARE VALUE NEUTRAL. THE
CONTRIBUTORS GO ON TO CONSIDER HOW POLITICAL THEORY AND
POLITICAL COMMUNITIES WOULD APPEAR IF WOMEN'S INTERESTS WERE
ADDRESSED. IN PARTICULAR, THEIR AIM IS TO RECONSTRUCT THE
METHODOLOGY OF POLITICAL ANALYSIS TO CONCEPTUALIZE POLITICAL

REALITY IN TERMS OF GENDER.

04792 JONES, P.
REVIEW ARTICLE: RE-EXAMINING RIGHTS
BRITISH JOURNAL OF POLITICAL SCIENCE, 19(1) (JAN 89),
69-96.
THE CONFIDENCE AND CONVICTION WITH WHICH RIGHTS ARE
ASSERTED IN THE MARKETPLACE OF POLITICS IS NOT UNDERWRITTEN
BY ANY SUBSTANTIAL PHILOSOPHICAL AGREEMENT ON THE CHARACTER,
CONTENT, OR FOUNDATIONS OF RIGHTS. WHAT RIGHTS ARE, WHAT
THEY ENTAIL, WHAT RIGHTS SHOULD BE ATTRIBUTED TO PEOPLE, AND
WHY ARE ALL SUBJECTS OF PROFOUND DISAGREEMENT. IN THIS
ARTICLE, THE AUTHOR EXAMINES SIX RECENT STUDIES OF RIGHTS
THAT FORM A SUBSTANTIAL CONTRIBUTION TO THE DEBATE.

04793 JONES, R.
DEADLOCKED
STATE LEGISLATURES, 15(6) (JUL 89), 23-27.
ONE PARTY IS SUPPOSED TO CONTROL A LEGISLATIVE CHAMBER,
BUT THAT'S NOT ALWAYS THE WAY IT WORKS. WHEN A CHAMBER IS
SPLIT EVENLY BETWEEN DEMOCRATS AND REPUBLICANS, RESOLVING
THE PARTISAN STALEMATE IS CHALLENGING, OFTEN CALLING FOR
CREATIVE SOLUTIONS. BUT THE WORK OF THE LEGISLATURE CAN
PROCEED, DESPITE THE FREQUENT TIE VOTES.

04794 JONES, R.
PAKISTAN AND THE UNITED STATES: PARTNERS AFTER AFGHANISTAN
WASHINGTON QUARTERLY, 12(3) (SUM 89), 65-90.
THE ARTICLE EXPLORES THE RELATIONS BETWEEN THE US AND
PAKISTAN WITH EMPHASIS ON THE COOPERATION IN THE AFGHANISTAN
CONFLICT. IT TRACES BENAZIR BHUTTO'S RISE TO POWER AND
ANALYZES HOW THE ELECTIONS IN PAKISTAN HAVE CHANGED THE
DOMESTIC SCENE. IT EXAMINES WHERE PAKISTAN IS HEADED OVER
THE NEXT FIVE YEARS AND WHAT CHALLENGES LIE AHEAD FOR US
POLICYMAKERS. IT SUGGESTS THE OUTLINES OF AN AFFIRMATIVE US
APPROACH THAT ACKNOWLEDGES THE IMPORTANCE OF THE
RELATIONSHIP TO US INTERESTS AND SEEKS TO KEEP IT EFFECTIVE
AS A PARTNERSHIP, WHILE TAKING ON THE FORESEEABLE CHALLENGES.

04795 JONES, R.H.
"IN GOD WE TRUST" AND THE ESTABLISHMENT CLAUSE
JOURNAL OF CHURCH & STATE, 31(3) (AUT 89), 381-417.
THE ISSUE OF WHETHER COMMON SYMBOLIC PRONOUNCEMENTS,
SUCH AS "IN GOD WE TRUST," VIOLATE THE FIRST AMENDMENT'S
ESTABLISHMENT PROHIBITION WARRANTS RE-EXAMINATION. THIS
ESSAY ARGUES THAT THE GOD-REFERENCES FAIL THE SUPREME
COURT'S ESTABLISHMENT CLAUSE DOCTRINES BUT DO NOT IN FACT
VIOLATE THE ESTABLISHMENT CLAUSE. THE ESSAY BEGINS BY
REVIEWING THE BACKGROUND ISSUES CONCERNING SYMBOLISM,
RELIGION, AND INTERPRETATIONS OF THE ESTABLISHMENT CLAUSE.
THEN WHY THE GOVERNMENTAL PRONOUNCEMENTS CONTAINING "GOD"
FAIL THE SUPREME COURT'S ESTABLISHMENT CLAUSE DOCTRINES IS
DISCUSSED. FINALLY, A JUSTIFICATION FOR UPHOLDING THESE
PRONOUNCEMENTS AS CONSTITUTIONAL IS ADVANCED.

04796 JONES, S.F.
MARXISM AND PEASANT REVOLT IN THE RUSSIAN EMPIRE: THE CASE
OF THE GURIAN REPUBLIC
SLAVONIC AND EAST EUROPEAN REVIEW, 67(3) (JUL 89), 403-434.
THE AUTHOR STUDIES THE FOLLOWING QUESTIONS: WHAT FACTORS
MADE THE GURIAN MOVEMENT SO SUCCESSFUL? WHAT WAS THE ROLE OF
ETHNIC, DEMOGRAPHIC, GEOGRAPHICAL, AND SOCIO-ECONOMIC
FACTORS? WHAT DID THE GURIAN REPUBLIC LOOK LIKE AND HOW DID
IT FUNCTION? WHAT WAS THE APPEAL OF SOCIAL DEMOCRACY TO THE
GURIAN PEASANTRY AND HOW DID IT PERCEIVE THE AGRARIAN
POLICIES OF GEORGIAN SOCIAL DEMOCRATS? WHICH PEASANTS WERE
INVOLVED, HOW POLITICALLY CONSCIOUS WERE THEY, AND WHAT WERE
THEIR GOALS AND METHODS?

04797 JONES, T.; PLANT, R.
IS LABOUR ABANDONING ITS SOCIALIST ROOTS?
CONTEMPORARY RECORD, 3(2) (NOV 89), 6-8.
THIS IS A DEBATE WHERE TUDOR JONES ARGUES THAT LABOUR IS
ABANDONING ITS ROOTS, AND RAYMOND PLANT PUTS THE CASE FOR
THE DEFENCE. JONES CONTENDS THAT LABOUR HAS VIRTUALLY
ABANDONDED IT'S TRADITIONAL COMMITTMENT TO PUBLIC OWNERSHIP
AND IS ANTIPATHETIC TOWARDS A MARKET ECONOMY. HE DETAILS
EXAMPLES OF PUBLIC OWNERSHIP AND ANALYSES PARTY MEMBER
RESPONSE TO A MARKET ECONOMY. HE EXAMINES THE REVISIONIST
PROJECT AND ITS CLAIM THAT PUBLIC OWNERSHIP IS A MEANS
RATHER THAN AN END. HE CONTENDS THAT THE SOCIAL OWNERSHIP OF
THE DECISIVE PARTS OF THE MEANS OF PRODUCTION IS THE ONLY
PERMENANT BASIS FOR A SOCIALIST, CLASSLESS SOCIETY. RAYMOND
PLANT REVIEWS 3 DOCUMENTS THE LABOUR PARTY HAS PUBLISHED
CONNECTED WITH THE OVERALL REVIEW OF POLICY WHICH IT
UNDERTOOK AFTER THE 1987 ELECTION DEFEAT. HE DETAILS THE
CONTROVERSY THE REVIEW HAS CAUSED AND THE DEGREE TO WHICH
THE PARTY HAD BECOME ON THE IDEOLOGICAL DEFENSIVE, KENESIAN
ECONOMIC MEASURES ARE EXAMINED. HE CONCLUDES THAT TODAYS
WORLD REQUIRES A DIFFERENT APPROACH TO THE PUBLIC SECTOR.

04798 JONES, W.; JONSON, J.A.
AIDS: THE URBAN POLICYMAKING CHALLENGE
JOURNAL OF URBAN AFFAIRS, 11(1) (1989), 85-102.

THE ARTICLE EXAMINES THE IMMENSE CHALLENGE POSED TO URBAN POLICYMAKERS BY THE SPREAD OF AIDS. AIDS IS FORCING POLICYMAKERS TO ENGAGE IN UNUSUAL EFFORTS AT LARGE AND NONINCREMENTAL CHANGE WHILE POSSESSING VERY LITTLE UNDERSTANDING OF THE ULTIMATE NATURE OF THE DISEASE. DEALING WITH ADIS WILL REQUIRE "AMBITIOUS DECISIONMAKING STYLES" IMPLEMENTED ON A LOCAL LEVEL. THE ARTICLE EXAMINES SOME OF THE SPECIFIC CHALLENGES THAT WILL HAVE TO BE CONFRONTED INCLUDING TREATMENT COSTS, LEGAL AND ADMINISTRATIVE RESPONSIBILITIES, AND WORKPLACE CONCERNS.

04799 JORDAN, A.A.; GRANT, R.L.
EXPLOSIVE CHANGE IN CHINA AND THE SOVIET UNION: IMPLICATIONS FOR THE WEST
WASHINGTON QUARTERLY, 12(4) (FAL 89), 97-112.
THE FUNDAMENTAL TRANSFORMATIONS UNDERWAY IN CHINA AND THE SOVIET UNION AMOUNT TO SECOND REVOLUTIONS. TO GAUGE THE DEPTH AND CHARACTER OF THESE TRANSFORMATIONS, AND THEIR MEANING FOR THE WEST, THIS ARTICLE EXAMINES THEIR ORIGINS AND DYNAMICS. THE ROOTS AND CHARACTER OF REFORM, THE PROSPECTS FOR SUCCESS, AND THE IMPLICATIONS FOR THE WEST ARE EXPLORED, IT CONCLUDES THAT WHILE REFORM IS POSSIBLE, AND PROSPECTS FOR MAJOR ECONOMIC SUCCESS ARE DIM, THE IMPLICATIONS FOR SOVIET REFORM ARE POSITIVE FOR THE WEST.

04800 JORDAN, E.
THE EXCLUSION OF WOMEN FROM INDUSTRY IN NINETEENTH-CENTURY BRITAIN
COMPARATIVE STUDIES IN SOCIETY AND HISTORY, 31(2) (APR 89), 273-296.
IT IS ARGUED HERE THAT THE SEXUAL DIVISION OF LABOR IN NINETEENTH CENTURY BRITAIN HAD TWO DIMENSIONS: THE SEX-TYPING OF JOBS WITHIN THOSE INDUSTRIES WHICH EMPLOYED WOMEN, AND THE ALMOST TOTAL EXCLUSION OF WOMEN FROM MANY OF THE NEW AND EXPANDING SECTORS. MOST SCHOLARLY ATTEMPTS TO ACCOUNT FOR THE SEXUAL DIVISION OF LABOR HAVE CONCENTRATED ON THE SEX-TYPING OF JOBS, BUT THE PROPOSED EXPLANATIONS CANNOT BE GENERALIZED TO EXPLAIN THE EXCLUSION OF WOMEN FROM WHOLE INDUSTRIES. THE ANSWER MAY LIE, IN PART AT LEAST, IN AN ANDROCENTRIC BLINDNESS CREATED IN MIDDLE-CLASS EMPLOYERS BY THEIR ACCEPTANCE OF THE DOMESTIC IDEOLOGY, WITH ITS ENDORSEMENT OF SEPARATE SPHERES FOR MEN AND WOMEN.

04801 JORGE, A.; SALAZAR-CARILLO, J.
THE LATIN AMERICAN ECONOMIC DEBT AND PUBLIC POLICY
JOURNAL OF INTERAMERICAN STUDIES AND WORLD AFFAIRS, 31(1, 2) (SPR 89), 233-248.
THIS ARTICLE ARGUES THAT ONLY SUSTAINED GROWTH IN LATIN AMERICA CAN LEAD TO AN ACCEPTABLE SOLUTION OF THE DEBT CRISIS, IT SUGGESTS THAT SUSTAINED SOCIAL AND ECONOMIC DEVELOPMENT MUST REMAIN THE PREMIER PUBLIC POLICY GOAL FOR THE WESTERN HEMISPHERE, IT FUTHERMORE SUGGESTS THAT SUSTAINED ECONOMIC EXPANSION IN THE U.S., EUROPE, AND JAPAN PROVIDES THE BEST HOPE OF PREVENTING A FINANCIAL BREAKDOWN AND ECONOMIC SLOWDOWN IN THE AMERICAS.

04802 JORGENSEN, J.
THE EUROPEAN COMMUNITY: THE CHALLENGE OF 1992
NEW ZEALAND INTERNATIONAL REVIEW, 14(3) (MAY 89), 7-10.
THE HEAD OF THE EUROPEAN COMMUNITY'S DELEGATION TO NEW ZEALAND OUTLINES THE PURPOSES AND IMPLICATIONS OF THE SINGLE EUROPEAN MARKET, FORECAST FOR THE YEAR 1992. HE PUTS FORTH ARGUMENTS WHHICH SUPPORT THE MOVEMENT AS KEY TO CREATING AN ENVIRONMENT FOR BUSINESS AND LABOR, FREE OF RESTRICTIVE BARRIERS AND TO PROVIDING A STRENGTHENING OF EUROPEAN COMMUNITY FOUNDATIONS IN ORDER TO COMPETE IN THE WORLD MARKET. A REPORT BY PAOLO CECCHINI ON THE "COSTS OF NON-EUROPE" IS CITED WHICH IDENTIFIED THE REAL ECONOMIC VALUE OF INTEGRATED MARKETS IN AN ARRAY OF INDUSTRIAL SECTORS AND HIGHLIGHTED THE COSTS OF DIVISION INTO TWELVE SEPARATE MARKETS.

04803 JOSEPH, H.
SOUTH AFRICA: SOME GLASNOST ON THE WOMEN'S QUESTION
INFORMATION BULLETIN, 27(3-4) (FEB 89), 10-11.
THE TIME HAS COME TO CRITICALLY EXAMINE THE VACUUM OF WOMEN'S LEADERSHIP IN THE DEMOCRATIC AND LIBERATION MOVEMENT. FALLACIES AND JUSTIFICATIONS MUST STOP. WE NEED NO SELF-DECEPTION. THE MILITANCY OF WOMEN IN SHOPFLOOR STRUGGLES, IN CIVIC AND COMMUNITYBASED BATTLES OF RENT, BUS, AND CONSUMER BOYCOTTS DO NOT MATCH THE INADEQUATE PRESENCE OF WOMEN ON LEADING BODIES. CATCH PHRASES AND PAPER RESOLUTIONS OF WOMEN'S EQUALITY ARE WORN-OUT. WINDOW DRESSING OF ONE OR TWO WOMEN ON EXECUTIVES CANNOT BE SUFFICIENT. THE FIGHT AHEAD DEMANDS STRONG AND SEASONED WOMEN'S LEADERSHIP, A LEADERSHIP THAT WILL PLAY A CRUCIAL ROLE IN THE TOUGH TIMES AHEAD!

04804 JOSEPH, L.
THE E.C. IN SOUTH ASIA
EUROPE, (290) (OCT 89), 24-25.
THE ARTICLE OUTLINES THE EUROPEAN COMMUNITY'S COMBINATION OF LOW-KEY PRESENCE AND SOMETIMES AGGRESSIVE DIPLOMACY IN SOUTH ASIA. IN CONTRAST TO LARGE SCALE HANDOUTS, THE E.C. HAS CONCENTRATED ON TECHNICAL ASSISTANCE AND

FINANCIAL ASSISTANCE THAT IS "UNLINKED" TO FOREIGN POLICY. DESPITE ITS QUIET NATURE, THE EFFORTS HAVE BEEN REMARKABLY SUCCESSFUL IN IMPROVING THE STANDARD OF LIVING AND INDEPENDENCE OF SOUTH ASIAN NATIONS.

04805 JOSEPH, R.A.
SYMBOLIC POLITICS IN THE HIGH TECHNOLOGY DEBATE IN AUSTRALIA
DISSERTATION ABSTRACTS INTERNATIONAL, 49(12) (JUN 89), 3857-A.
SINCE THE EARLY 1980'S, HIGH TECHNOLOGY HAS BEEN PROMINENT IN POLITICAL DEBATE IN AUSTRALIA. EMPHASIZING THE ROLE OF POLITICAL LANGUAGE IN POLITICAL ACTIVITY, THIS STUDY ANALYZES AUSTRALIA'S HIGH TECHNOLOGY DEBATE AS A SEQUENCE OF EVENTS OR NEWS. THEN THE POLICY-MAKING PROCESS IS PROBED, USING THE SYMBOLIC FORMS OF POLITICAL MYTH AND RITUAL.

04806 JOSEPHSON, M.
ETHICS LEGISLATION: PROBLEMS AND POTENTIAL
STATE LEGISLATURES, 15(6) (JUL 89), 50.
THERE ARE TWO STAGES TO ETHICAL BEHAVIOR: KNOWING WHAT IS RIGHT, AND DOING IT. IN GOVERNMENT, BOTH ARE DIFFICULT. BECAUSE THERE WILL ALWAYS BE TENSION BETWEEN ETHICAL IDEALS AND PRACTICAL POLITICS, THOSE WHO WANT TO IMPROVE THE MORAL QUALITY OF GOVERNMENT NEED TO RECOGNIZE THE INHERENT LIMITATIONS OF LAWS AND ACKNOWLEDGE THE IMPORTANCE OF FINDING OTHER WAYS TO ENHANCE ETHICAL CONSCIOUSNESS AND COMMITTMENT.

04807 JOSEPHSON, M.S.
TRAVERSING THE MINE FIELD OF PUBLIC SERVICE ETHICS
JOURNAL OF STATE GOVERNMENT, 62(5) (SEP 89), 185-188.
IN RECENT YEARS, MANY IN GOVERNMENT HAVE COME TO SEE THEMSELVES AS STANDING ON SHIFTING SANDS OF PROPRIETY. THEY BELIEVE THAT THE STANDARDS OF ETHICS, DETERMINED BY A HOSTILE PRESS AND FICKLE PUBLIC, CHANGE ERRATICALLY WITHOUT NOTICE. THERE IS A WIDESPREAD PERCEPTION THAT CONDUCT WHICH WAS ACCEPTABLE YESTERDAY CAN OVERNIGHT BECOME THE SOURCE OF CRITICISM AND SCORN. CONDUCT ONCE THOUGHT TO BE WITHIN THE MORES OF POLITICAL AND GOVERNMENT ETHICS CAN RESULT IN LOSS OF OFFICE AND EVEN CRIMINAL PROSECUTION. TO REGAIN PUBLIC TRUST IN GOVERNMENT, PUBLIC OFFICIALS NEED TO ADHERE TO HIGHER STANDARDS OF INTEGRITY IN PERFORMING THEIR DUTIES THAN ARE REQUIRED BY LAWS AND REGULATIONS.

04808 JOSHI, B.R.
NATIONAL IDENTITY AND DEVELOPMENT: INDIA'S CONTINUING CONFLICT
CULTURAL SURVIVAL QUARTERLY, 13(2) (1989), 3-7.
IN INDIA, THE LIST OF BLACK LAWS RESTRICTING CIVIL LIBERTIES IS GROWING, AND THE EXAMPLES OF OFFICIALLY SANCTIONED VIOLATIONS OF HUMAN RIGHTS ARE MULTIPLYING. ALL ARE INSTITUTED BY WINNERS OF PROVINCIAL AND NATIONAL CONFRONTATIONS WHO, TRYING TO STABILIZE THEIR POWER, FIND THAT THEY HAVE ENSURED ALIENATION AND CONFLICT THAT WILL FURTHER DESTABILIZE THE ENTIRE SYSTEM. SOCIAL AND ECONOMIC CHANGE IS, IN LARGE PART, RESPONSIBLE FOR THIS DILEMMA. AT THE VERY LEAST, THE LOCAL ENVIRONMENT, THE OCCUPATIONS, THE CULTURE, AND EVEN THE PHYSICAL EXISTENCE OF SOME ETHNIC GROUPS WILL BE SNUFFED OUT. AT WORST, MORE SEGMENTS OF SOCIETY WILL FIND THEMSELVES IN CONFLICT WITH ONE ANOTHER UNDER CONDITIONS THAT WILL DESTROY THE FABRIC OF SOCIETY AND INDIA'S STRAINED ECOSYSTEM.

04809 JOSHI, G.
FOREST POLICY AND TRIBAL DEVELOPMENT
CULTURAL SURVIVAL QUARTERLY, 13(2) (1989), 17-22.
THE AUTHOR ASSESSES THE NATURE AND EXTENT OF FOREST DWELLERS' DEPENDENCE ON INDIA'S FORESTS AND THE EXTENT TO WHICH THE FOREST POLICY IMPLEMENTED BY DIFFERENT STATES AND UNION TERRITORIES ENSURES THAT THEIR BASIC NEEDS ARE MET. HE ALSO CONSIDERS HOW THE GOVERNMENT'S FOREST POLICY SEEKS TO IMPROVE THE SOCIOECONOMIC CONDITIONS OF THE FOREST DWELLERS.

04810 JOVE, S.; ALVARES, S.
THE VIEW FROM SPAIN
WORLD MARXIST REVIEW, 31(12) (DEC 88), 86-93.
THIS ARTICLE CITES HISTORICAL FACTORS AS THE BASIC REASON WHY THE OUTCOME OF WORLD WAR II DID NOT RESULT IN RADICAL SOCIAL CHANGES IN WEST EUROPEAN COUNTRIES. THESE FACTORS WERE ALSO CRUCIAL IN ALLOWING IMPERIALISM TO MAINTAIN THE FRANCO DICTATORSHIP IN SPAIN AND THE SALAZAR-CAETANO DICTATORSHIP IN PORTUGAL UNTIL 1974-1977.

04811 JREISAT, J.E.
BUREAUCRACY AND DEVELOPMENT IN JORDAN
JOURNAL OF ASIAN AND AFRICAN STUDIES, XXIV(1-2) (1989), 94-105.
BUREAUCRACY IS THE MAJOR INSTRUMENT OF SOCIO-ECONOMIC DEVELOPMENT IN JORDAN. IT FUNCTIONS WITHIN AN ENVIRONMENTAL OF SCARCE RESOURCES, OVERPOWERING POLITICAL LEADERSHIP, AND PARTICULARISTIC CULTURAL HABITS. THIS STUDY REVIEWS NOT ONLY THE PROGRESS MADE TOWARDS ACHIEVING THE GOALS OF NATIONAL DEVELOPMENT BUT ALSO THE OBSTACLES THAT RETARD MODERNIZATION

EFFORTS. IT EXAMINES SPECIFIC BUREAUCRATIC PATHOLOGIES IN THE JORDANIAN POLITICAL-ADMINISTRATIVE STRUCTURE: CLERKISM, CENTRALISM, NEPOTISM, INCOMPETENCE, AND THE NEGATIVE EFFECTS OF SUCH FACTORS ON DEVELOPMENT AND ADMINISTRATIVE EFFECTIVENESS. THE EXAMINATION OF OFFICIAL ADMINISTRATIVE REFORM EFFORTS IN JORDAN INDICATES THAT THE SUBSTANTIVE ISSUES OF REFORM HAVE NOT BEEN EFFECTIVELY ARTICULATED OR MANAGED.

04812 JUHNKE, W.E.
PRESIDENT TRUMAN'S COMMITTEE ON CIVIL RIGHTS: THE INTERACTION OF POLITICS, PROTEST, AND PRESIDENTIAL ADVISORY COMMISSION
PRESIDENTIAL STUDIES QUARTERLY, XIX(3) (SUM 89), 593-610.
JUHNKE ANALYZES THE 1946-47 TRUMAN COMMITTEE ON CIVIL RIGHTS. TRUMAN WAS CONCERNED BY MOB VIOLENCE AGAINST BLACKS IN THE SUMMER OF 1946. THIS HAD CAUSED THE NAACP TO CREATE THAT YEAR A NATIONAL EMERGENCY COMMITTEE AGAINST MOB VIOLENCE. THIS, IN TURN, PROMPTED TRUMAN IN 1946 TO APPOINT A 25 MEMBER PRESIDENT'S COMMITTEE ON CIVIL RIGHTS. THE COMMITTEE'S REPORT TO SECURE THESE RIGHTS, WAS OF LANDMARK PROPORTIONS, THE FIRST SUCH PRESIDENTIAL COMMITTEE REPORT CALLING UPON THE FEDERAL GOVERNMENT TO BECOME THE GUARDIAN OF THE NATION'S CIVIL RIGHTS. IT DIRECTLY LED TO THE END OF SEGREGATION AND DISCRIMINATION IN BOTH THE ARMED FORCES AND IN THE FEDERAL CIVIL SERVICE. IT BEGAN THE LONG ROAD TO BE CLIMAXED IN THE EISENHOWER ADMINISTRATION WITH THE END OF SEGREGATION IN PUBLIC SCHOOL.

04813 JULIEN, G.
LES STYLES DE GESTION DES CADRES SUPERIEURS VUS PAR LES PROFESSIONELS DE LA FONCTION PUBLIQUE DU QUEBEC
CANADIAN PUBLIC ADMINISTRATION, 32(3) (FAL 89), 449-461.
THE COMPROMISE TO BE REACHED BETWEEN THE PRODUCTIVITY REQUIREMENTS OF PUBLIC SERVICES AND THE DEMORALIZATION OF PROFESSIONALS POSES A MAJOR CHALLENGE TO SENIOR MANAGERS IN THE QUEBEC CIVIL SERVICE. THIS ARTICLE PRESENTS THE RESULTS OF A STUDY CONDUCTED AMONG PROFESSIONALS IN ORDER TO IDENTIFY THE MANAGEMENT STYLES ADOPTED BY MANAGERS TO STRENGTHEN MORALE AND IMPROVE SERVICE PRODUCTIVITY. THIS STUDY USES A THREE-PRONGED MODEL TO DISTINGUISH A RANGE OF NINE STYLES. USING THIS MODEL, THE STYLES ARE DEFINED NOT ONLY BY THE INTEREST EXPRESSED IN POWER. THE STORY TOLD BY THE PROFESSIONALS IS COMPARED TO THAT OF THE MANAGERS, AMONG WHOM A STUDY WAS CONDUCTED IN 1980.

04814 JULL, P.
THE ARCTIC AND INUIT INTERNATIONALISM
ETUDES INTERNATIONALES, XX(1) (MAR 89), 115-130.
THE DRIVING FORCE BEHIND INUIT INTEREST IN INTERNATIONAL AFFAIRS HAS BEEN THE DETERMINATION TO SOLVE THE PROBLEMS OF UNDER-DEVELOPMENT, ENVIRONMENTAL DAMAGE, SOCIAL INJUSTICE, INADEQUATE LEGAL RECOGNITION AND LIMITED OR NON-EXISTENT SELFGOVERNMENT. TO ASSIST IN THE SOLUTION OF THESE PROBLEMS, THE INUIT CIRCUMPOLAR CONFERENCE (ICC) WAS FOUNDED IN 1977. THE CONFERENCE, WHICH IS PRESENTLY HEADED BY A CANADIAN INUIT (MARY SIMON), HOLDS A GENERAL ASSEMBLY EVERY THREE YEARS AND SERVES AS THE VEHICLE FOR OVERALL INUIT IDENTITY AND INTERESTS IN THE WORLD. THIS IDENTITY HAS BEEN DEVELOPED IN SPITE OF INTERNATIONAL BOUNDARIES AND EASTWEST CONFLICTS. THUS, THE NEXT GENERAL ASSEMBLY, TO BE HELD IN SISIMUIT (GREENLAND) IN 1989, WILL BE THE FIRST WHERE SOVIET INUIT WILL JOIN THEIR KIN FROM ALASKA, CANADA AND GREENLAND. THEY WILL CONTINUE TO ADDRESS SUCH FUNDAMENTAL ISSUES AS: THE DEVELOPMENT OF AN OVERALL ARCTIC POLICY; THE PROTECTION OF THE ENVIRONMENT; SUSTAINABLE DEVELOPMENT; INTERNATIONAL ABORIGINAL RIGHTS; AND THE ONGOING MILITARIZATION OF THE ARCTIC, WHICH IS A CAUSE OF GREAT CONCERN TO ALL INUIT.

04815 JUN, N.
JAPAN'S ECONOMIC CCOPERATION: NEW VISIONS WANTED
JAPAN QUARTERLY, XXXVI(4) (OCT 89), 392-403.
THE AUTHOR CONSIDERS JAPAN'S OFFICIAL DEVELOPMENT ASSISTANCE PROGRAM, WHICH HAS RISEN FROM $1.4 BILLION IN 1977 TO $11 BILLION IN 1989--MAKING JAPAN THE WORLD'S BIGGEST FOREIGN DEVELOPMENT AID DONOR.

04816 JUSTER, F. T.
ECONOMIC POLICY ISSUES AND THE ELECTION: DOES IT MATTER WHO WINS?
ECONOMIC OUTLOOK USA, 15(2) (FAL 88), 14-20.
THIS ARTICLE LOOKS AT SOME BASIC DIFFERENCES BETWEEN REPUBLICANS AND DEMOCRATS IN BOTH VALUES AND ANALYTIC JUDGMENTS THAT HAVE AN INFLUENCE ON THE EVOLUTION OF POLICY, SPECULATES ABOUT THE PROBABLE POLICY DIFFERENCES BETWEEN THE TWO CANDIDATES, AND EXAMINES THE ECONOMIC POLICY ISSUES THAT SEEM MOST IMPORTANT OVER THE NEXT SEVERAL YEARS. IT CONCLUDES WITH SOME JUDGMENTS ABOUT THE WAY A BUSH OR DUKAKIS PRESIDENCY WOULD HANDLE SOME OF THE ISSUES.

04817 JUSTER, F. T.
THE POLITICAL ECONOMY SCOREBOARD: AN UPDATE
ECONOMIC OUTLOOK USA, 15(2) (FAL 88), 8-13.
IN 1986 A SIMILIAR ARTICLE EXAMINED THE RECORD OF ALL

SIX POSTWAR ADMINISTRATIONS IN THE U.S., AND LOOKED AT THE BEHAVIOR OF BOTH REAL AND FINANCIAL VARIABLES TO ASSESS DIFFERENCES IN THE OUTCOMES ACHIEVED BY VARIOUS ADMINISTRATIONS, AS WELL AS TO DETERMINE THE ECONOMIC OUTCOMES THAT SEEMED MOST IMPORTANT TO VOTERS. THIS ARTICLE UPDATES THE INFORMATION BASE, ADDS A FEW NEW MEASURES THAT RELATE TO ECONOMIC OUTCOMES, AND REEXAMINES THE QUESTION OF VOTER PREFERENCES.

04818 JWAIN, G.R.
TITO: THE FORMATION OF A DISLOYAL BOLSHEVIK
INTERNATIONAL REVIEW OF SOCIAL HISTORY, 34(2) (1989), 248-271.
TITO ROSE TO LEAD THE YUGOSLAV COMMUNIST PARTY BY STRESSING HIS LOYALTY TO LENIN. AS A "LEFT" CRITIC OF "RIGHT LIQUIDATIONISM" HIS VIEWS COINCIDED WITH THE LEFT TURN IN THE COMINTERN WHICH CLIMAXED WITH THE MOLOTOV-RIBBENTROP PACT. DURING THE "IMPERIALIST" WAR, TITO, LIKE LENIN, WROTE ONLY OF THE ARMED UPRISING AND THE PROLETARIAN REVOLUTION; FOR HIM THIS BEGAN WITH THE GERMAN INVASION OF APRIL 1941. HOWEVER, TITO'S EXPERIENCES IN MOSCOW DURING THE HEIGHT OF THE PURGES ENABLED HIM TO GET THE MEASURE OF STALIN. TWICE HE EMERGED UNSCATHED FROM ACCUSATIONS OF TROTSKYISM, AND IN HIS WRITINGS BEGAN TO EXPLORE THE DIFFERENCES BETWEEN LENINISM AND STALINISM.

04819 KABRA, K. N.
METHODS OF NATIONALISATION IN INDIA: 1947-80
JOURNAL OF CONTEMPORARY ASIA, 18(3) (1988), 318-332.
THIS ARTICLE PROVIDES A STUDY OF METHODS OF NATIONALISATION WHICH WERE DEPLOYED IN INDIA DURING 1947-80. THE AUTHOR POINTS OUT THE ROLE OF THE CHOICE OF METHODS OF NATIONALISATION IN THE PROCESS OF NATIONALISATION. THIS IS FOLLOWED, BY A DISCUSSION OF THE CONSTITUTIONAL PROVISIONS AND LEGAL FRAMEWORK GOVERNING NATIONALISATIONS IN INDIA. THIRD, THERE IS AN ACCOUNT OF THE EXTENT TO WHICH VARIOUS METHODS OF NATIONALISATION WERE USED. AN ATTEMPT TO ANALYSE THE FACTORS AFFECTING THE CHOICE OF VARIOUS METHODS CONCLUDES THE ARGUMENT. IN DISCUSSION, THE AUTHOR COMPARES AND CONTRASTS THE IMPLICATIONS OF THE ALTERNATIVE METHODS USED FOR NATIONALISATION IN INDIA, TO SHOW HOW THE CHOICE OF THE METHODS OF NATIONALISATIONS AS AN AREA OF SECONDARY DECISION-MAKING ACQUIRED A GREAT DEAL OF SUBSTANTIVE SIGNIFICANCE. IN PARTICULAR ATTENTION IS DRAWN TO REPEATED INSTANCES OF MANAGERIAL TAKE-OVER PRIOR TO NATIONALISATION. AS THE INDIAN DEVELOPMENT STRATEGY AND ITS UNDERLYING POLITICAL AND ECONOMIC BASIS CHANGES, IT MAY WELL BECOME NECESSARY IN FUTURE TO GO IN FOR THE FORMULATION OF AN EXPLICIT POLICY STATEMENT ABOUT NATIONALISATION AND IT SHOULD FORM PART OF EITHER THE DEVELOPMENT STRATEGY OR THE INDUSTRIAL POLICY.

04820 KACI, A.
THE STATE CENTRALIZATION AND CONTROL OF THE BROADCASTING MEDIA IN ALGERIA FROM 1962 TO 1982: APPLICATION AND SHORTCOMINGS
DISSERTATION ABSTRACTS INTERNATIONAL, 49(9) (MAR 89), 2437-A.
ALGERIA'S POST-INDEPENDENCE RADIODIFFUSION TELEVISION ALGERIENNE EVIDENCED FIVE MAIN CHARACTERISTICS: (1) FAILURE OF THE ELITES TO RETHINK BROADCASTING; (2) PRIVILEGED DISSEMINATION OF OFFICIAL POLITICAL DISCOURSE; (3) TOLERANCE OF FINANCIAL, PERSONNEL, AND PRODUCTION MISMANAGEMENT IN EXCHANGE FOR POLITICAL ALLEGIANCE; (4) CONTROL OF THE BROADCASTING PROFESSION; AND (5) A PATERNALISTIC CONCEPTION OF ITS AUDIENCES.

04821 KADES, C.L.
THE AMERICAN ROLE IN REVISING JAPAN'S IMPERIAL CONSTITUTION
POLITICAL SCIENCE QUARTERLY, 104(2) (SUM 89), 215-248.
THE AUTHOR REVIEWS THE EXTRAORDINARY PROCESS BY WHICH THE CURRENT JAPANESE CONSTITUTION CAME INTO BEING AND, IN LIGHT OF THAT PROCESS, EXAMINES WHY IT HAS CONTINUED TO EXIST WITHOUT FORMAL CHANGE.

04822 KAEMPFER, W.H.; WILLETT, T.D.
COMBINING RENT-SEEKING AND PUBLIC CHOICE IN AN ANALYSIS OF TARIFFS VERSUS QUOTAS
PUBLIC CHOICE, 63(1) (OCT 89), 79-86.
THIS IS A RESPONSE TO A RECENT ARTICLE IN THIS JOURNAL, WHERE RICHARD MCKENZIE MAKES TWO MAJOR ARGUMENTS ON THE IMPLICATIONS OF ADOPTING A RENT-SEEKING PERSPECTIVE FOR ANALYZING THE COMPARATIVE EFFICIENCY OF TARIFFS AND QUOTAS. THE AUTHORS DISAGREE WITH A SPECIFIC CONCLUSION THAT IF A GOVERNMENT EMPLOYS TARIFFS, THEN MORE RESTRICTIVE TRADE POLICIES WILL BE ADOPTED THAN IF QUOTAS AND VOLUNTARY REPORT RESTRAINTS ARE USED. IT STUDIES RENT-SEEKING IN A BROADER PUBLIC CHOICE CONTEXT AND CONCLUDES THE EMPIRICAL EVIDENCE IS THAT WHERE QUOTAS ARE USED, PROTECTION IS HIGH.

04823 KAGARLITSKY, B.
A DIFFICULT HEGEMONY
ACROSS FRONTIERS, 5(2) (SUM 89), 11-14, 36-38.
THIS PAPER DETAILS THE DIFFICULTIES ENCOUNTERED IN THE

EFFORT TO CREATE A POPULAR FRONT. THE TASK OF ESTABLISHING A
MASS DEMOCRATIC ORGANIZATION IS DETAILED. EXAMINED ARE THE
EVENTS AND HURDLES ENCOUNTERED BY THE SEVERAL GROUPS VYING
FOR OFFICIAL RECOGNITION AS THE OFFICIAL POPULAR FRONT AS
MOSCOW'S INDEPENDENT LEFT EMERGES AS AN ORGANIZED FORCE.

04824 KAGARLITSKY, B.
    ANOTHER HOT SUMMER
    ACROSS FRONTIERS, 5(3) (FAL 89), 7-8; 29-31.
        THIS ARTICLE DESCRIBES THE ORIGIN AND IMPACT OF THE
    MINER'S STRIKE IN THE SOVIET UNION. SINCE THE GOVERNMENT HAS
    UNABLE TO OFFER A RAPID AND SUBSTANTIVE IMPROVEMENT IN THE
    MINER'S LIVING CONDITIONS, THEIR ONLY HOPE WAS SELF-RELIANCE
    AND INDEPENDENT ACTION. THE LOCAL AUTHORITIES' ATTITUDE
    TOWARD EVENTS IS DESCRIBED AS WELL AS OFFICIAL PRESS
    REACTION. EFFORTS BY THE PARTY APPARATUS TO WARD OFF
    POLITICAL DEMANDS IS DESCRIBED AS INNEFFECTIVE.

04825 KAGARLITSKY, B.
    SOVIET UNION: BIRTH OF THE SOCIALIST PARTY
    EAST EUROPEAN REPORTER, 4(1) (WIN 89), 86-89.
        THE ARTICLE IS AN INTERVIEW WITH BORIS KAGARLITSKY, A
    SOVIET ACTIVIST AND FOUNDER OF THE SOCIALIST PARTY IN THE
    USSR. HIS VIEWS ARE LEFT OF MAINSTREAM PERESTROIKA WHICH HE
    ATTACKS FOR BEING TOO VAGUE AND LADEN WITH BUREAUCRACY. HE
    DISCUSSES THE SOCIAL, GEOGRAPHICAL, AND IDEOLOGICAL
    COMPOSITION OF THE SOCIALIST PARTY AS WELL IS THE
    ORGANIZATION'S FUTURE AIMS. THE ETHNIC AND NATIONALITY
    PROBLEMS THAT TROUBLE THE SOVIET UNION, THE FUTURE OF
    PERESTROIKA, AND THE POSSIBILITY OF A FREE-MARKET ORIENTED,
    PLURALISTIC SOVIET UNION ARE ALSO TOPICS OF DISCUSSION.

04826 KAGARLITSKY, B.
    THE IMPORTANCE OF BEING MARXIST
    NEW LEFT REVIEW, (178) (NOV 89), 29-36.
        THE AUTHOR CONSIDERS THE PLACE OF MARXIST IDEOLOGY AND
    THE POSITION OF THE LIBERAL INTELLIGENTSIA IN GORBACHEV'S
    SOVIET UNION.

04827 KAGIAN, J.
    DECUELLAR'S HOPES
    MIDDLE EAST INTERNATIONAL, (344) (FEB 89), 12-13.
        OFFICIALS FROM IRAN AND IRAQ ARE EXPECTED TO MEET WITH
    UN LEADERS IN NEW YORK IN FEBRUARY 1989 TO PREPARE FOR A NEW
    ROUND OF PEACE TALKS.

04828 KAGIAN, J.
    SECURITY COUNCIL STATEMENT
    MIDDLE EAST INTERNATIONAL, (357) (AUG 89), 6-7.
        THE UNITED NATIONS SECURITY COUNCIL ISSUED A STATEMENT
    CALLING FOR AN END TO ALL FIRING AND SHELLING ON LAND AND ON
    SEA IN LEBANON AND FOR OBSERVANCE OF A TOTAL AND IMMEDIATE
    CEASE-FIRE BY ALL PARTIES. ALTHOUGH THE GOAL OF THE
    STATEMENT IS CERTAINLY LAUDABLE, IT IS CLEAR THAT THE UN IS
    ATTEMPTING TO SHIFT RESPONSIBILITY OF THE CONFLICT'S
    RESOLUTION AWAY FROM THE INTERNATIONAL COMMUNITY AND ONTO
    THE ARAB COMMUNITY.

04829 KAH, M.A.B.
    ECOWAS, SECURITY, AND DEVELOPMENT
    DISARMAMENT, XII(1) (WIN 89), 104-109.
        THE AUTHOR DISCUSSES HOW ECONOMIC COOPERATION, IN
    GENERAL, AND ECOWAS, IN PARTICULAR, CAN SERVE AS AN
    INSTRUMENT OF PEACE AND SECURITY. ALL MEMBER STATES OF
    ECOWAS HAVE AN EQUAL STAKE IN ITS SUCCESS AND CONTINUED
    SURVIVAL, WHICH CAN BE ACHIEVED ONLY IF THE STATES ACCEPT
    ECOWAS AS THE CENTERPIECE IN THE FORMULATION AND CONDUCT OF
    THEIR WEST AFRICAN POLICY.

04830 KAISER, F.M.
    THE WATCHERS' WATCHDOG: THE CIA INSPECTOR GENERAL
    INTERNATIONAL JOURNAL OF INTELLIGENCE AND
    COUNTER-INTELLIGENCE, 3(1) (SPR 89), 55-75.
        THE DIFFERENCE BETWEEN CONGRESS AND THE EXECUTIVE BRANCH
    OVER THE POTENTIAL CREATION OF A STATUTORY INSPECTOR GENERAL
    FOR THE CIA REFLECT MORE THAN DISAGREEMENTS OVER THE
    SPECIFIC AUTHORITY AND DUTIES OF THE POST. AT THE HEART, THE
    DISPUTE REFLECTS A CONFLICT OVER LEGISLATIVE VERSUS
    EXECUTIVE POWERS AND INTERESTS AND OVER CONGRESSIONAL
    ABILITY TO OVERSEE AND CONTROL INTELLIGENCE MATTERS. THIS
    ARTICLE CONSIDERS THE CONFLICT IN LIGHT OF EFFORTS TO
    RESTRUCTURE THE OFFICE, PARTICULARLY AS A STATUTORY OFFICE
    WITH FEATURES SIMILAR TO THOSE UNDER THE AMENDED 1978
    INSPECTOR GENERAL ACT.

04831 KAISER, K.
    A VIEW FROM EUROPE: THE US ROLE IN THE NEXT DECADE
    INTERNATIONAL AFFAIRS, 65(2) (SPR 89), 209-224.
        ALTHOUGH AMERICA'S RELATIVE WEIGHT IS DRCREASING AS A
    NEW MULTIPOLAR STRUCTURE OF WORLD POLITICS EMERGES, ITS
    POWER AND IMPACT WILL REMAIN FORMIDABLE AND DECISIVE IN
    PRACTICALLY EVERY AREA OF WORLD POLITICS. THE ARTICLE
    EXAMINES SOME OF THE VERY DIFFERENT CHALLENGES THAT THE US
    WILL FACE IN THE FUTURE. SUBJECT AREAS COVERED INCLUDE:

MAINTAINING THE GLOBAL ECONOMIC SYSTEM WHICH INCLUDES
DEALING WITH PROBLEMS SUCH AS PROTECTIONISM AND THIRD WORLD
DEBT; MANAGING EAST-WEST RELATIONS: THE DEVELOPMENT OF THE
NATO ALLIANCE; AND GLOBAL TASKS OF WORLD ORDER WHICH INCLUDE
DEALING WITH NUCLEAR PROLIFERATION, THE SPREAD OF ADVANCED
WEAPONS TECHNOLOGY, AND ENVIRONMENTAL DETERIORATION.

04832 KAISER, K.
    WHY NUCLEAR WEAPONS IN TIMES OF DISARMAMENT?
    WORLD TODAY, 45(8-9) (AUG 89), 134-139.
        TODAY'S DEBATES OVER NUCLEAR WEAPONS ARE DOMINATED BY
    CONCEPTS AND ISSUES THAT ARE BASICALLY MARGINAL, LIKE THE
    MODERNIZATION OF TACTICAL NUCLEAR FORCES, BUT WHICH CONCEAL
    MORE FUNDAMENTAL QUESTIONS THAT ARE OFTEN EITHER OVERLOOKED
    OR CONSCIOUSLY NOT ADDRESSED. THE TENOR OF THE NUCLEAR
    DEBATE WITHIN WEST GERMANY AND WITHIN NATO HAS CHANGED
    DRAMATICALLY. THE PRESENT SITUATION IS CHARACTERIZED BY A
    STRIKING CONTRAST BETWEEN A RADICAL QUESTIONING OF THE BASIC
    RULES OF WESTERN SECURITY POLICY OF THE LAST FEW DECADES, ON
    ONE HAND, AND AN OFTEN DESPERATE CLINGING TO TRADITIONAL
    PRINCIPLES, ON THE OTHER.

04833 KAKAR, M.H.
    AFGHANISTAN: IS PEACE POSSIBLE?
    FREEDOM AT ISSUE, (110) (SEP 89), 35-36.
        AFGHAN POLITICS HAS BECOME MORE INTERNATIONAL AND LESS
    NATIONAL IN THE RECENT PAST BECAUSE THE DECISIONS AFFECTING
    AFGHAN NATIONAL LIFE ARE IN REALITY MADE BY OTHER POWERS IN
    THE REGION, DESPITE THE SOVIET UNION'S APPARENT MILITARY
    WITHDRAWAL. UNDER DIFFERENT NAMES AND PRETEXTS, THESE POWERS
    SERVE THE NATIONAL INTERESTS OF THEIR OWN LANDS. UNLESS AND
    UNTIL THE HANDS OF THESE FOREIGN POWERS CEASE TO STRETCH
    INTO AFGHANISTAN, THE PROSPECTS FOR PEACE ARE DIM.

04834 KAKARIA, A.
    BENAZIR'S TOUR DE FORCE
    INDIA TODAY, XIV(12) (JUN 89), 73.
        THIS ARTICLE DESCRIBE BENAZIR BHUTTO'S TRIUMPHANT VISIT
    TO THE UNITED STATES DURING WHICH SHE MANAGED TO MEET EVEN
    TOUGH AMERICAN LEGISLATORS WITH A FEMININE APPEAL THAT WAS
    ACCENTUATED BY HER STATUS AS THE FIRST EVER FEMALE LEADER OF
    A MUSLIM NATION.

04835 KALHLA, P.
    CLEARING THE LOGJAM
    MACLEAN'S (CANADA'S NEWS MAGAZINE), 102(2) (JAN 89), 16.
        SINCE THE 1986 GRANTING OF AMNESTY TO IMMIGRANTS,
    REFUGEES CLAIMANTS HAVE FLOODED TO CANADA FROM TURKEY,
    BRAZIL, PORTUGAL AND ELSEWHERE, OVERWHELMING THE
    GOVERNMENT'S ABILITY TO PROCESS THEM. A NEW POLICY
    ENGINEERED BY IMMIGRATION MINISTER BARBARA MCDOUGALL
    ATTEMPTS TO CLEAR THE ENORMOUS BACKLOG. THE POLICY RECEIVED
    IMMEDIATE CRITICISM FROM MANY OF THE SOME 85,000 PEOPLE WHO
    ARE PROCESSING CLAIMS FOR REFUGEE STATUS. MANY ARGUE THAT
    THE POLICY IS TOO STRICT AND WILL RESULT IN MASS
    DEPORTATIONS WHICH IN TURN WILL DAMAGE CANADA'S ECONOMY. THE
    FUROR IS UNLIKELY TO DIE DOWN SOON, BUT HEARINGS ARE NOT
    SCHEDULED TO BEGIN UNTIL APRIL OF 1990.

04836 KALOGEROPOULOU, E.
    ELECTION PROMISES AND GOVERNMENT PERFORMANCE IN GREECE:
    PASOK'S FULFILMENT OF ITS 1981 ELECTION PLEDGES
    EUROPEAN JOURNAL OF POLITICAL RESEARCH, 17(3) (MAY 89),
    289-311.
        THE 'MANDATE THEORY' OF DEMOCRACY RESTS ON THE IDEA THAT
    ELECTORS CHOOSE POLITICAL PARTIES ON THE BASIS OF THE
    ALTERNATIVE GOVERNMENT PROGRAMMES THEY OFFER DURING AN
    ELECTION CAMPAIGN. THUS, THE QUESTION OF WHETHER OR NOT
    PROGRAMMES ARE FULFILLED IN GOVERNMENT IS CENTRAL IN
    ASSESSING THE EFFECTIVENESS OF DEMOCRATIC PROCESSES. IN ITS
    ELECTION MANIFESTO FOR THE 1981 GENERAL ELECTION IN THEN
    OPPOSITION SOCIALIST PARTY, PASOK, PROPOSED A RADICAL REFORM
    OF GREEK SOCIETY. THE DEGREE TO WHICH ITS PROPOSALS WERE
    ACTUALLY IMPLEMENTED IN ITS FIRST PERIOD OF OFFICE (1981-85)
    POINTS UP THE CONSTRAINTS FACING ANY REFORMIST PARTY TRYING
    TO FULFIL ITS PROMISES. FOLLOWING RECENTLY PUBLISHED
    RESEARCH ON PLEDGE FULFILMENT IN BRITAIN AND CANADA, THIS
    STUDY IDENTIFIES THE DEFINITE PLEDGES MADE BY PASOK IN ITS
    1981 ELECTORAL MANIFESTO AND CHECKS HOW FAR THEY ACTUALLY
    FOUND THEIR WAY INTO GOVERNMENT OUTPUTS UP TO 1985.

04837 KALU, C.N.
    THE PERCEPTIONS OF EX-PARTICIPANTS ON THE EFFECTIVENESS OF
    THE NATIONAL YOUTH SERVICE CORPS (NYSC) IN NIGERIA
    DISSERTATION ABSTRACTS INTERNATIONAL, 49(7) (JAN 89),
    1958-A.
        IN ORDER TO PROVIDE A RESEARCH BASE FOR DETERMINING THE
    OPERATIONAL EFFECTIVENESS OF THE NYSC, THE AUTHOR RATES THE
    PERCEPTIONS OF EX-PARTICIPANTS ON THE EFFECTIVENESS OF THE
    NYSC OF NIGERIA. HE DISCOVERS A STATISTICAL RELATIONSHIP
    BETWEEN ACHIEVEMENT AND ADEQUACY OF ADMINISTRATIVE SERVICES,
    ZONE OF ORIGIN, AND THE IMPACT OF THE PROGRAM ON THE
    RESPONDENTS.

04838 KAMALUDDIN, S.
    POLITICS OF SPLITTING
    FAR EASTERN ECONOMIC REVIEW, 141(33) (AUG 88), 25-26.
    THE PRACTICE OF BREAKING UP POLITICAL PARTIES IN
BANGLADESH IS AS OLD AS THE COUNTRY ITSELF AND RECENT EVENTS
PROVED TO BE NO EXCEPTION TO THE GENERAL RULE. TWO OF THE
MAJOR OPPOSITION PARTIES: THE BANGLADESH NATIONALIST PARTY
AND THE AWAMI LEAGUE ARE BOTH SUFFERING FROM INTERNAL
DISSENT AND STRIFE WHICH IS REDUCING THEIR IMAGE AND
INFLUENCE AND ALMOST ASSURING ANOTHER VICTORY OF THE RULING
JATIYA PARTY.

04839 KAMARA, E.F.
    CONTINUITY OR CHANGE: AMERICAN FOREIGN POLICY OF HUMAN
RIGHTS UNDER THE CARTER AND THE REAGAN ADMINISTRATION WITH
PARTICULAR EMPHASIS ON SOUTHERN AFRICA, 1977-1984
    DISSERTATION ABSTRACTS INTERNATIONAL, 50(2) (AUG 89),
537-A.
    THE AUTHOR ASSESSES THE EXTENT TO WHICH HUMAN RIGHTS
BECAME THE MAJOR FOREIGN POLICY GOAL OF THE CARTER
ADMINISTRATION IN SOUTHERN AFRICA AND THE ROLE IT PLAYED IN
THE REAGAN POLICY IN THE REGION. THE POST-VIETNAM POLITICAL
ENVIRONMENT AND PERSONAL BELIEFS SHAPED CARTER'S FOREIGN
POLICY INTO A PROGRAM OF HUMAN RIGHTS WHILE POWER
CONSIDERATIONS AND FEAR OF COMMUNISM SHAPED REAGAN'S POLICY.

04840 KAMATH, S.J.
    CONCEALED TAKINGS: CAPTURE AND RENT-SEEKING IN THE INDIAN
SUGAR INDUSTRY
    PUBLIC CHOICE, 62(2) (AUG 89), 119-138.
    IN THIS PAPER, TESTS ARE DEVELOPED AND IMPLEMENTED FOR
DISCRIMINATING BETWEEN THE APPLICABILITY OF ALTERNATIVE
THEORIES OF REGULATION WHEN APPLIED TO THE INDIAN SUGAR
INDUSTRY SINCE THE EARLY 1950S. IT DISCUSSES THE NATURE OF
CONTROLS AND THEIR CONSEQUENCES IN THE INDUSTRY. A
DISCUSSION OF THE TWO MAJOR ALTERNATIVE THEORIES OF
REGULATION AND THE 'CAPTURE' THEORY IN PARTICULAR IS
PRESENTED, IT DEVELOPES AND IMPLEMENTS THE TESTS AND
EXAMINES THE RESULTS. CONCLUSIONS ARE THEN PRESENTED.

04841 KAMERMAN, S.B.; KAHN, A.J.
    FAMILY POLICY: HAS THE UNITED STATES LEARNED FROM EUROPE?
    POLICY STUDIES REVIEW, 8(3) (SPR 89), 581-598.
    IN THIS ARTICLE, THE AUTHORS FOCUS ON WHETHER SOCIETAL
LEARNING HAS OCCURRED ACROSS THE ATLANTIC WITH REGARD TO
FAMILY POLICY AND WHAT, IF ANYTHING, THE U.S. HAS LEARNED OR
BORROWED FROM EUROPE. THE AUTHORS CONCLUDE THAT THERE HAS
BEEN SOME BORROWING, ALBEIT MODEST; CURRENTLY, SOME OF THAT
LEARNING IS REFLECTED IN AN EXPANDING CHILD POLICY DEBATE.

04842 KAMINSKI, B.
    THE ANATOMY OF THE DIRECTIVE CAPACITY OF THE SOCIALIST
STATE
    COMPARATIVE POLITICAL STUDIES, 22(1) (APR 89), 66-92.
    THIS ARTICLE DISCUSSES THE PROBLEM OF THE DIRECTIVE
CAPACITY OF THE SOCIALIST STATE, DEFINED AS THE ABILITY TO
IDENTIFY OPPORTUNITIES AVAILABLE WITHIN BOTH THE DOMESTIC
AND INTERNATIONAL POLITICAL ECONOMY AND TO DEVELOP AND
IMPLEMENT POLICIES. THE FOCUS IS NOT ON HOW THE DIRECTIVE
CAPACITY OF THE SOCIALIST STATE IS ACTUALLY USED BY THE
ELITES BUT ON THE IDENTIFICATION OF BASIC MECHANISMS SHAPING
IT. THE FOLLOWING QUESTIONS ARE ADDRESSED: WHAT IS THE
RELATIONSHIP BETWEEN POLITICS AND ECONOMICS IN STATE
SOCIALISM, AND HOW DOES IT DETERMINE DIRECTIVE CAPACITY?
WHAT ARE THE UNDERLYING STRUCTURES THAT SHAPE THE SOCIALIST
STATE/ ECONOMY INTERACTION? WHAT MECHANISMS HAVE DEVELOPED
WITHIN THE FRAMEWORK OF STATE SOCIALISM THAT COMPENSATE FOR
LACK OF PRESSURES TOWARD HIGHER EFFICIENCY? WHAT ARE THE
SYSTEM'S LIMITATIONS AND WHAT STRATEGIES ARE AVAILABLE TO
INCREASE THE DIRECTIVE CAPACITY?

04843 KAMINSKI, B.; SOLTAN, K.
    THE EVOLUTION OF COMMUNISM
    INTERNATIONAL POLITICAL SCIENCE REVIEW, 10(4) (OCT 89),
371-392.
    THE PAPER PRESENTS A FRAMEWORK FOR UNDERSTANDING THE
EVOLUTION OF COMMUNISM. IT SUGGESTS THAT THE POLITICO-
ECONOMIC SYSTEM OF COMMUNIST REGIMES MAY BE USEFULLY SEEN AS
AN INSTITUTIONALLY AND IDEOLOGICALLY CONSTRAINED BARGAINING
GAME. WE DISTINGUISH THREE STAGES OF THE DEVELOPMENT OF THIS
"GAME" -- PURE COMMUNISM, LATE COMMUNISM, AND CONSTITUTIONAL
COMMUNISM. PURE COMMUNISM IS CHARACTERIZED BY AN ASPIRATION
TO THE TOTAL CONTROL OVER SOCIETY, AND A STRONG COMMITMENT
TO IDEOLOGY. CONSTRAINTS ON BARGAINING WEAKEN IN LATE
COMMUNISM, RESULTING IN A SYSTEM WITH DISTINCTIVE ECONOMIC
AND POLITICAL FEATURES, WHICH WE DESCRIBE. CONSTITUTIONAL
COMMUNISM IS AN IDEAL TYPE BASED ON THE CURRENT WAVE OF
REFORM, IN WHICH THE POWER OF COMMUNISTS IS LIMITED WITHOUT
BEING UNDERMINED. ITS CHIEF INGREDIENTS ARE THE RULE OF LAW,
SEPARATION OF POWERS, COMMUNIST CORPORATISM, GLASNOST, AND
THE MARKET.

04844 KAMPELMAN, M.M.
    DIPLOMACY IN AN ELECTION YEAR AND BEYOND
    DEPARTMENT OF STATE BULLETIN (US FOREIGN POLICY), 88(2141)
(DEC 88), 38-40.
    AMBASSADOR MAX KAMPELMAN DISCUSSES THE CHALLENGES THAT
THE US AND ITS DIPLOMATS WILL FACE IN THE COMING ELECTION
YEAR AND IN THE FURTHER FUTURE. THE OVERRIDING CONCERN OF
ALL DIPLOMACY SHOULD BE THE ATTAINMENT OF PEACE BUILT ONLY
ON THE FOUNDATION OF JUSTICE, FREEDOM, AND THE RULE OF LAW.
HE EXAMINES THE "MORAL DIMENSION" OF FOREIGN POLICY AND THE
ROLE THAT THE SOVIET UNION WILL PLAY IN THE WORLDWIDE EFFORT
FOR PEACE IN THE YEARS AHEAD.

04845 KAMPELMAN, M.M.
    THE RULE OF LAW IN THE SOVIET UNION
    FREEDOM AT ISSUE, (111) (NOV 89), 23-26.
    THE FIRST BLUSH OF GLASNOST HAS THROWN NEW LIGHT ON THE
SOVIET LEGAL SYSTEM. CRITICISMS OF THE OLD WAYS NOW COMPETE
FOR SPACE IN SOIVET JOURNALS AND NEWSPAPERS WITH PROPOSALS
FOR REVISIONS. VAST CHANGES AFFECTING THE ADMINISTRATION OF
JUSTICE ARE BEING ADVANCED. PRESIDENT GORBACHEV HAS
RESURRECTED A TERM ONCE CONDEMNED AS HOPELESSLY BOURGEOIS TO
EXPLAIN THE NEW LEGAL GOALS. THAT TERM, AN EMPTY VESSEL YET
TO BE FILLED, IS "THE RULE OF LAW." THE FATE OF THAT CONCEPT
MAY SERVE AS A WEATHER VANE FOR THE FATE OF PERESTROIKA AS A
WHOLE. WHEN WE EVALUATE A COUNTRY, THERE ARE FEW CRITERIA
MORE TELLING THAN ITS PRACTICE OF LAW.

04846 KAMPEN, T.
    THE ZUNYI CONFERENCE AND FURTHER STEPS IN MAO'S RISE TO
POWER
    CHINA QUARTERLY, (117) (MAR 89), 118-134.
    THE AUTHOR RECOUNTS SOME IMPORTANT DETAILS ABOUT THE
ZUNYI CONFERENCE, INTERPRETS THEM, AND EXPLAINS THE
DIFFICULTIES THAT ARISE IN STUDYING THIS PERIOD OF CHINESE
COMMUNIST PARTY HISTORY. HE ALSO CONSIDERS THE IMPORTANCE ON
THE CONFERENCE AS IT RELATES TO THE RISE OF MAO ZEDONG.

04847 KAMRAVA, M.
    INTELLECTUALS AND DEMOCRACY IN THE THIRD WORLD
    JOURNAL OF SOCIAL, POLITICAL AND ECONOMIC STUDIES, 14(2)
(SUM 89), 227-234.
    DICTATORSHIPS HAVE LONG BEEN AN INSEPARABLE FEATURE OF
MANY THIRD WORLD GOVERNMENTS. WHILE BOTH THE WEST AND THE
EASTERN BLOC COUNTRIES HAVE HAD THEIR OWN SHARE OF
DICTATORIAL REGIMES, THE THIRD WORLD HAS BECOME SYNONYMOUS
WITH POWER-HUNGRY DICTATORS AND DESPOTIC POLITICAL SYSTEMS.
THE TASK OF THIS ESSAY IS TWO-FOLD: (1) TO SEE WHETHER THERE
ARE DOMINANT SOCIAL AND CULTURAL CHARACTERISTICS WITHIN
THIRD WORLD SOCIETIES THAT ARE PARTICULARLY CONDUCIVE TO THE
DEVELOPMENT OF DICTATORSHIPS AND (2) TO EXPLORE POSSIBLE
SOLUTIONS FOR PREVENTING THE OCCURRENCE OF CYCLES OF
POLITICAL DESPOTISM IN THOSE SOCIETIES. THE SOLUTION, IT IS
ARGUED, HAS MUCH TO DO WITH THIRD WORLD INTELLECTUALS.

04848 KAN, H.
    THE REAGAN ADMINISTRATION AND THE EXPANSION OF THE
MILITARY-INDUSTRIAL COMPLEX
    JOURNAL OF AMERICAN AND CANADIAN STUDIES, (3) (SPR 89),
43-74.
    REAGAN'S EFFORTS TO RAPIDLY INCREASE U.S. MILITARY
EXPENDITURES LED TO A WIDESPREAD DEBATE. GIVEN THE
IMPLICATIONS OF THE DEBATE, THIS PAPER ATTEMPTS TO ANSWER
SOME OF THE CRUCIAL QUESTIONS ARISING FROM THE EXPANSION OF
THE MILITARYINDUSTRIAL COMPLEX DURING REAGAN'S
ADMINISTRATION. SOME QUESTIONS ADDRESSED ARE: WHAT ARE THE
ORIGINS OF THIS MILITARY BUILD-UP? WHAT IS THE POLITICAL,
MILITARY AND ECONOMIC BACKGROUND OF THIS PHENOMENON? WHAT
ARE THE CONSEQUENCES OF THE HUGE MILITARY EXPENDITURES
ALLOCATED BY THE REAGAN ADMINISTRATION?

04849 KANAUKA, A.V.
    THE CHANGING ROLE OF SCIENTISTS AND TECHNOLOGISTS IN
DEFENSE POLICY CREATION
    DISSERTATION ABSTRACTS INTERNATIONAL, 49(12) (JUN 89),
3867-A.
    THE AUTHOR CONSIDERS THE DIRECT AND INDIRECT ROLE THAT
SCIENTISTS AND TECHNOLOGISTS PLAY IN THE CREATION OF U.S.
DEFENSE POLICY AND HOW THAT ROLE HAS CHANGED SINCE WORLD WAR
I. SOME NORMATIVE ARGUMENTS ON THE FUTURE ROLE OF SCIENTISTS
AND TECHNOLOGISTS ARE ALSO PRESENTED.

04850 KANET, R.E.
    SOVIET FOREIGN POLICY AND THE END OF THE POSTWAR ERA
    PS: POLITICAL SCIENCE AND POLITICS, XXII(2) (JUN 89),
225-232.
    GORBACHEV AND OTHER SOVIET POLITICAL LEADERS HAVE
RELEGATED CLASS WARFARE TO A SECONDARY POSITION AS A
DETERMINANT OF SOVIET FOREIGN POLICY. THEY ARGUE THAT
OVERCOMING THE THREAT TO HUMAN EXISTENCE POSED BY GLOBAL
PROBLEMS IS MORE IMPORTANT.

04851 KANG, J.
    SPORTS, MEDIA, AND CULTURAL DEPENDENCY
    JOURNAL OF CONTEMPORARY ASIA, 18(4) (1988), 430-443.
    CONTRARY TO THE PREVALENT MYTH, SPORTS IS NOT A LANGUAGE

EVERYONE CAN SPEAK. IN SEMIOTIC TERMS, SPORT IS UNIVERSAL ON
THE LEVEL OF THE CODE, THE "PHONEMIC" LEVEL, THE BODY. BUT
IT IS NOT UNIVERSAL ON THE "MORPHEMIC" OR SEMANTIC LEVELS,
THE PARTICULAR POLITICAL ORGANIZATIONS REPRESENTED BY EACH
SPORT. INTERNATIONAL SPORT MERELY REFLECTS THE WORLD
POLITICAL STRUCTURE. AS INTERNATIONAL SPORT NOW CANNOT BE
CONCEIVED AS BEING INDEPENDENT FROM THE MASS MEDIA, IT HAS
BECOME ONE OF THE MOST EFFECTIVE MARKETING INSTRUMENTS IN
THE CAPITALIST WORLD SYSTEM. TELEVISION SPORT COVERAGE ACTS
AS "MASS PROPAGANDA," THEREBY SUSTAINING WESTERN LIFESTYLES
IT DRAMATIZES "OUR SENSE OF ORDER" AND ENFORCES CONSERVATIVE
VALUES, THUS PAVING THE WAY FOR CULTURAL IMPERIALISM.

04852 KANIN, D.B.
  NORTH KOREA: INSTITUTIONAL AND ECONOMIC OBSTACLES TO
  DYNAMIC SUCCESSION
  JOURNAL OF SOCIAL, POLITICAL AND ECONOMIC STUDIES, 14(1)
  (SPR 89), 49-76.
    KIM IL-SONG, ABSOLUTE RULER OF THE PEOPLE'S DEMOCRATIC
  REPUBLIC OF KOREA, IS ATTEMPTING TO PROTECT HIS LEGACY WITH
  THE FERVOR OF AN EGYPTIAN PHAROAH PREPARING FOR THE AFTER-
  LIFE. KIM'S CONCERN IS SIMPLE: HOW CAN HE PREVENT THE
  POSTHUMOUS DENIGRATION OF HIS LIFE AND WORK THAT DEVOURED
  JOSEPH STALIN AND MAO ZEDONG? HIS ANSWER IS EQUALLY SIMPLE:
  CHOOSE A SUCCESSOR WHO IS ABSOLUTELY DEPENDENT ON THE
  PRESERVATION OF KIM'S STATURE AND ASSURE THE TRANSFER OF
  POWER BEFORE KIM'S OWN DEATH.

04853 KANT, S.
  EVOLUTION OF ADMINISTRATIVE AREAS IN MEDIEVAL INDIA, WITH
  SPECIAL REFERENCE TO PUNJAB
  ASIAN PROFILE, 17(1) (FEB 89), 61-74.
    THE MEDIEVAL MUSLIM PERIOD OF INDIAN HISTORY WITNESSED
  THE SUPERIMPOSITION OF ISLAMIC POLITY AND PIETY OVER THE
  POLITICAL AND ADMINISTRATIVE INSTITUTIONS THAT HAD EVOLVED
  ON INDIAN SOIL UNDER THE TRADITIONS AND CUSTOMS OF THE HINDU
  RELIGION. PUNJAB, DUE TO ITS FRONTIER LOCATION IN THE
  NORTHWESTERN REGION, BORE THE RUDE SHOCK OF CHANGE FIRST.
  THE MUSLIM RULERS TESTED THE POLITICAL AND ADMINISTRATIVE
  THEORIES THAT THEY BROUGHT FROM THEIR NATIVE LANDS FIRST ON
  PUNJAB. THEN THESE POLITICAL AND ADMINISTRATIVE METHODS WERE
  EXTENDED TO OTHER PARTS OF INDIA.

04854 KANTE, M.
  THE IMPLEMENTATION OF THE SAHEL REGIONAL FINANCIAL
  MANAGEMENT PROJECT, 1982-86: A CASE STUDY IN STRATEGIC
  MANAGEMENT
  DISSERTATION ABSTRACTS INTERNATIONAL, 49(10) (APR 89),
  3151-A.
    THIS THESIS DEMONSTRATES HOW THEORETICAL MODELS AND
  EMPIRICAL KNOWLEDGE OF ORGANIZATIONS AND THEIR MANAGEMENT
  MAY BE APPLIED TO THE STUDY OF PROGRAM IMPLEMENTATION IN THE
  THIRD WORLD. USING A STRATEGIC MANAGEMENT FRAMEWORK
  DEVELOPED BY SAMUEL PAUL, THIS DISSERTATION EXAMINES THE
  HYPOTHESIS THAT THE ENVIRONMENT OF THE HOST COUNTRY HAS A
  CRITICAL IMPACT ON THE PERFORMANCE OF ORGANIZATIONS THE FIT
  OR LACK OF FIT BETWEEN THE ORGANIZATIONAL POLICIES AND
  STRUCTURES AND THE HOST ENVIRONMENT DIRECTLY CORRELATES WITH
  PROJECT PERFORMANCE. DATA FOR THE STUDY IS DRAWN FROM THE
  SAHEL REGIONAL FINANCIAL PROJECT.

04855 KANWISHER, N.
  COGNITIVE HEURISTICS AND AMERICAN SECURITY POLICY
  JOURNAL OF CONFLICT RESOLUTION, 33(4) (DEC 89), 652-675.
    THE AUTHOR ARGUES THAT CERTAIN POLITICAL MISCONCEPTIONS
  AND FALLACIES RESIST COUNTER-ARGUMENT BECAUSE THEY ARE
  REINFORCED BY PARTICULAR REASONING SHORTCUTS KNOWN AS
  "COGNITIVE HEURISTICS." ALTHOUGH HEURISTICS SAVE TIME AND
  MENTAL WORK, THEY CAN LEAD TO ERROR BECAUSE THEY ARE BASED
  ON VIOLABLE ASSUMPTIONS. SHE DISCUSSES SEVEN COGNITIVE
  HEURISTICS AND THE PARTICULAR SECURITY FALLACIES THEY
  PERPETUATE--FROM THE DOMINO THEORY TO THE IDEA THAT
  DETERRENCE REQUIRES FORCE MATCHING. FINALLY, THE SCOPE AND
  LIMITATIONS OF SUCH PSYCHOLOGICAL EXPLANATIONS ARE DISCUSSED.

04856 KAPCIA, A.
  MARTI, MARXISM AND MORALITY: THE EVOLUTION OF AN IDEOLOGY
  OF REVOLUTION
  JOURNAL OF COMMUNIST STUDIES, 5(4) (DEC 89), 161-183.
    IDEOLOGY, NOW RELATIVELY NEGLECTED, IS CLEARLY A
  DIMENSION BASIC TO THE WHOLE PROCESS OF REVOLUTIONARY CHANGE
  IN CUBA. DEVELOPING FROM TRADITIONS OF RADICAL NATIONALISM
  AND A POLITICAL CULTURE OF DISSIDENCE, CUBANISMO BECAME AN
  IDEOLOGICAL ALTERNATIVE SUFFICIENT TO CONTRIBUTE
  FUNDAMENTALLY TO THE POPULAR SUPPORT FOR BOTH INSURRECTION
  AND RADICALIZATION. WITH INSTITUTIONAL INSTRUMENTS FOR
  POLITICAL SOCIALIZATION LACKING IN THE 1960S, IT WAS ABLE TO
  FUSE WITH NEWER INPUTS TO BECOME ITSELF A POWERFUL MEANS OF
  MASS POLITICIZATION, LEADING TO BOTH THE 'NEW MAN' ETHOS AND,
  LATER, THE CURRENT 'RECTIFICATION' PROCESS.

04857 KAPEPULA, N.
  PRICE DECONTROL SPARKS RIOTS
  NEW AFRICAN, (264) (SEP 89), 28-29.

THIS ARTICLE REPORTS ON RIOTS, A PRICE EXPLOSION AND
RUNAWAY INFLATION IN ZAMBIA AS A RESULT OF DECONTROLLED
PRICES. DETAILED IS HOW PRESIDENT KAUNDA HAS COME FULL
CIRCLE AND HAS DECONTROLLED PRICE IN PRECISELY THE WAY URGED
BY THE IMF IN 1985-87. IT EXPLORES PUBLIC SUPPORT SOLELY BY
LOCAL INDUSTRIALIST, MURRY SANDERSON, AND OPPOSING VIEWS BY
TRADE UNION OFFICIALS. IT ALSO ADDRESSES ABUSE AND MISUSE OF
THE PRICE DEREGULATION BY TRADERS. BLACK MARKET TRADER
AGGRESSION AND SKYROCKETING PRICES OF COMMODOTIES ARE
DETAILED.

04858 KAPLAN, D.H.
  "MAITRES CHEZ NOUS": THE EVOLUTION OF FRENCH-CANADIAN
  SPATIAL IDENTITY
  AMERICAN REVIEW OF CANADIAN STUDIES, 19(4) (WIN 89),
  407-428.
    A KEY QUESTION MUST BE WHY FRENCH CANADIANS HAVE BECOME
  OF LATE MORE ASSERTIVE OF THEIR POLITICAL DESTINY. IT IS THE
  PRIMARY GOAL OF THIS PAPER TO ARGUE THAT THIS RESURGENCE
  RELATES TO A GENERAL SHIFT IN RELEVANT INSTITUTIONS, AND
  SPECIFICALLY TO THE SPATIAL IMPLICATIONS OF THESE
  INSTITUTIONS. FRENCH CANADA HAS ALWAYS PRESERVED A MANIFOLD
  SET OF INSTITUTIONS APART FROM ENGLISH CANADA, AND THREE OF
  THEM HAVE EXERTED A PROFOUND IMPACT ON HER SOCIETY: THE
  IMPLANTATION OF THE EARLY SEIGNEURIAL SYSTEM, THE ROMAN
  CATHOLIC CHURCH, AND THE INSTITUTIONS OF GOVERNMENT WITHIN
  THE PROVINCE OF QUEBEC. THOSE INSTITUTIONS HAVE SOMETIMES
  COLLABORATED BUT, BY AND LARGE, THEY HAVE OFFERED COMPETING
  CONCEPTIONS OF SOCIAL ORGANIZATION (GUINDON, 1960). EACH
  INSTITUTION IS VIEWED IN TERMS OF HOW ITS POSITION CHANGES
  RELATIVE TO THE OTHERS. THESE FLUCTUATIONS HAVE BROUGHT
  ABOUT CONCOMITANT REALIGNMENTS IN SPATIAL ORGANIZATION AND
  PERCEPTION, WHICH IN TURN HAVE AFFECTED THE MANNER IN WHICH
  FRENCH CANADA HAS EXPRESSED ITS IDENTITY.

04859 KAPLAN, H.
  POLICY AND RATIONALITY: THE REGULATION OF CANADIAN TRUCKING
  UNIVERSITY OF TORONTO PRESS, TORONTO, ONTARIO, CA, 1989,
  240.
    VOCAL CRITICISM HAS COME FROM SOME QUARTERS OVER
  GOVERNMENT'S FAILURES IN REGULATING OF CANADIAN
  TRANSPORTATION. HAROLD KAPLAN ASSESSES THAT CRITICISM AND
  CONSIDERS THE FACTORS THAT CREATE THE GAP BETWEEN
  EXPECTATIONS AND REALITY IN GOVERNMENTAL SOLUTIONS. KAPLAN
  DEVELOPS AN APPROACH TO POLICY-MAKING DERIVED FROM SOCIAL
  SYSTEMS THEORY. IN IT, DECISION-MAKING OR SOCIAL ACTION IS
  SEEN TO RESULT FROM THE INTERPLAY OF FOUR SPECIALIZED ACTION
  SUBSYSTEMS OR 'GAMES.'

04860 KAPLAN, R.
  DRUNK ON FRENCH HISTORY
  FREEDOM AT ISSUE, (110) (SEP 89), 23-27.
    QUESTIONS ABOUT STATE SOVEREIGNTY, CULTURAL IMPERIALISM,
  AND NATIONALISM ARE IN THE AIR IN FRANCE, AS WELL AS IN
  GERMANY AND GREAT BRITAIN AND THROUGHOUT EUROPE. IT IS GOOD
  THAT THEY ARE BEING DISCUSSED BUT IT WOULD BE EVEN BETTER IF
  MAINSTREAM FRENCH POLITICIANS TOOK THEM SERIOUSLY. IF THE
  COLD WAR IS OVER, THEN THERE MUST BE A RESURGENCE OF
  NATIONAL AND RELIGIOUS FEELING. IT WOULD BE IRONIC INDEED IF
  THE DEMOCRATIC NATIONS, HAVING WON THE BATTLE FOR DEMOCRACY,
  FORGOT HOW TO WAGE THE BATTLE OF NATIONHOOD. AND, OVER THE
  NEXT SEVERAL YEARS, THAT IS GOING TO BE THE BIG ISSUE IN
  FRANCE AND IN EUROPE.

04861 KAPLAN, R.
  LETTER FROM FRANCE: TOWARD CONSENSUS
  FREEDOM AT ISSUE, (107) (MAR 89), 20-21.
    THE DEPOLITICIZATION OF FRENCH POLITICS SEEMS TO BE WELL
  UNDERWAY. FRENCH PUBLIC OPINION HAS GONE SO FAR TOWARD "LE
  LIBERALISME" THAT SOCIALISM BARELY DARES TO SPEAK ITS NAME,
  EVEN THOUGH FRANCOIS MITTERAND AND MICHEL ROCARD REMAIN
  POPULAR POLITICIANS. WITH THE EXCEPTION OF THE COMMUNISTS
  AND THE NATIONAL FRONT, THERE IS A CONSENSUS ON THE BROAD
  LINES OF FRENCH POLICY. FOR EXAMPLE, ON FOREIGN POLICY,
  THERE IS AGREEMENT THAT THE COUNTRY SHOULD KEEP ITS GUARD UP,
  WATCH OVER ITS INTERESTS, AND TRY TO MAINTAIN THE LEAD,
  POLITICALLY IF NOT ECONOMICALLY, AMONG THE EUROPEAN NATIONS.

04862 KAPS, C.
  DELORS PROPOSES "NEW PARTNERSHIPS" WITH U.S.
  EUROPE, 288 (JUL 89), 14-15.
    INSTEAD OF DENOUNCING HIM AS THE "PROTECTIONIST GATE
  KEEPER OF FORTRESS EUROPE," THE UNITED STATES IS WARMLY
  WELCOMING EUROPEAN COMMUNITY COMMISSION PRESIDENT JACQUES
  DELORS AS THE REPRESENTATIVE OF A EUROPE STRIVING TO BE A
  SERIOUS AND RESPONSIBLE POLITICAL FORCE IN THE WORLD. AT A
  RECENT MEETING WITH PRESIDENT BUSH, DELORS CALLED FOR A NEW
  AND PROFOUND PARTNERSHIP BETWEEN THE EUROPEAN COMMUNITY AND
  THE UNITED STATES, PRUDENTLY AVOIDING THE PETTY AND OFTEN
  TEDIOUS QUARRELS OVER TRADE ISSUES.

04863 KAPSTEIN, E.B.
  LOSING CONTROL
  NATIONAL INTEREST, (18) (WIN 89), 85-90.

THIS ARTICLE IS AN ASSESSMENT OF NATIONAL SECURITY AND
THE GLOBAL ECONOMY. IN TIMES OF WAR AND CRISIS, THE AMERICAN
ECONOMY HAS BEEN ONE OF THE COUNTRY'S GREAT MILITARY ASSETS,
THE WRITER EXPLORES AMERICA'S NOW CRUMBLING DEFENSE
INDUSTRIAL BASE. HE EXAMINES AMERICA'S GROWING DEPENDENCE ON
FOREIGN SUPPLIERS FOR BOTH HIGH-TECH AND LOW TECH SUPPLIES.
HE OFFERS THREE APPROACHES TOWARDS A SOLUTION AND CONCLUDES
THAT THE U.S. MUST ASSEMBLE A BETTER DATA BASE; MUST MAKE IT
EASIER FOR CONTRACTORS TO COMMERCIALIZE "DUAL-USE"
TECHNOLOGY, AND MUST MAINTAIN ACCESS TO ALLIED COUNTRIES.

04864 KAPSTEIN, E.B.
    RESOLVING THE REGULATOR'S DILEMMA: INTERNATIONAL
    COORDINATION OF BANKING REGULATIONS
    INTERNATIONAL ORGANIZATION, 43(2) (SPR 89), 323-347.
        UNDER THE LEADERSHIP OF THE UNITED STATES AND GREAT
    BRITAIN, A MULTILATERAL AGREEMENT ON BANK CAPITAL STANDARDS
    WAS REACHED IN DECEMBER 1987. THIS AGREEMENT SUGGESTS THAT
    THE INTERPLAY OF MARKET FACTORS, CONSENSUAL KNOWLEDGE, AND
    LEADERSHIP BY POWERFUL STATES CAN LEAD TO INTERNATIONAL
    POLICY COORDINATION. THE ARTICLE DESCRIBES THE MULTILATERAL
    NEGOTIATIONS THAT LED TO THIS BANKING ACCORD.

04865 KAPUSTIN, M.
    DIALECTICS BY COMMAND: REVOLUTIONISM IN PHILOSOPHY AND THE
    PHILOSOPHY OF REVOLUTIONISM
    SOVIET REVIEW, 30(6) (NOV 89), 58-81.
        PERESTROIKA BEGAN WITH THE DEVELOPMENT OF A NEW
    POLITICAL THINKING, RESURRECTING THE SPIRIT OF TRUE LENINISM.
    SOVIET SOCIETY MUST NOW DECISIVELY REPUDIATE THE STALINIST
    LEGACY IN ALL AREAS OF SOCIAL CONSCOUSNESS, INCLUDING
    LITERATURE, AESTHETICS, PHILOSOPHY, AND SOCIAL SCIENCE.

04866 KAPUTIKYAN, S.
    AN OPEN LETTER (APRIL 5, 1988): SILVA KAPUTIKYAN ADDRESSES
    ALL HONEST SCIENTISTS, WRITERS, AND ARTISTS
    GLASNOST, (16-18) (JAN 89), 30-33.
        THE AUTHOR BRIEFLY REVIEWS THE HISTORY OF THE ARMENIAN
    PEOPLE, THE ANNEXATION OF KARABAKH AND NAKHICEVAN TO
    AZERBAIJAN UNDER STALIN, AND THE SOURCES OF DISCONTENT IN
    KARABAKH.

04867 KARAGANOV, S.
    THE USA AND COMMON EUROPEAN HOME
    INTERNATIONAL AFFAIRS (MOSCOW), (8) (AUG 89), 17-26.
        CONTRADICTIONS IN THE AMERICAN APPROACH TO EUROPE
    REFLECT THE FACT THAT INTER-ATLANTIC RELATIONS AND U.S.
    FOREIGN POLICY TOWARDS EUROPE HAVE REACHED A BOUNDARY LINE.
    THIS IS THE RESULT OF A FUNDAMENTAL CHANGE IN THE MILITARY
    BALANCE IN EUROPE, THE RESTORATION OF THE TREND TOWARDS
    STRONGER ECONOMIC AND POLITICAL POSITIONS FOR WESTERN EUROPE,
    AND THE DYNAMIC PROCESSES UNDERWAY IN EASTERN EUROPE.

04868 KARAOSMANOGLU, A.L.
    TURKEY AND NATO
    NATO'S SIXTEEN NATIONS, 34(7) (DEC 89), 46-48, 50-51.
        TURKEY'S CONTRIBUTION TO THE ALLIED DEFENCE OF EUROPE'S
    SOUTHERN REGION IS UNQUESTIONED. TURKEY'S NEED FOR SECURITY
    ASSISTANCE FROM ITS PARTNERS IS GRADUALLY LESSENING AS
    ALLIED HELP CONTRIBUTES TO THE DEVELOPMENT OF TURKISH
    DEFENCE-RELATED INDUSTRY. IN THE CHANGING STRATEGIC
    ENVIRONMENT, NATO'S FLEXIBLE RESPONSE STRATEGY MUST BE
    MAINTAINED AND, ALTHOUGH THE EUROPEAN PILLAR SHOULD BE
    STRENGTHENED, TURKEY IS OPPOSED TO A FURTHER REGIONALIZATION
    OF DEFENCE. THE GRECO-TURKISH DISAGREEMENT OVER THE AEGEAN
    HAS CAUSED TENSION BETWEEN THE TWO ALLIES AND WEAKENED THE
    SOUTHERN FLANK. BUT THE DIALOGUE INITIATED BY THE DAVOS
    PROCESS CONTINUES, FACILITATING A SERIOUS EXAMINATION OF THE
    DISPUTE.

04869 KARASAPAN, O.
    GULF WAR REFUGEES IN TURKEY
    MIDDLE EAST REPORT, 19(156) (JAN 89), 33-35.
        A LARGELY IGNORED BY-PRODUCT OF THE IRANIAN REVOLUTION
    AND THE GULF WAR HAS BEEN THE LARGE INFLUX OF REFUGEES INTO
    TURKEY. THE ECONOMIC BENEFITS OF TURKISH NEUTRALITY DURING
    THE GULF WAR LED ANKARA TO DOWNPLAY THE PROBLEM, BUT THE
    RECENT ARRIVAL OF KURDISH REFUGEES HAS STRAINED REGIONAL
    TIES AND CLOUDED TURKISH HOPES FOR LUCRATIVE POST-WAR
    RECONSTRUCTION DEALS. THE LARGE IRANIAN REFUGEE POPULATION
    OF A MILLION OR MORE IS ALSO CAUSING WORRIES, AS STRUGGLES
    AMONG IRANIAN POLITICAL GROUPS SPILL OVER INTO TURKEY.

04870 KARASAPAN, O.
    TURKEY AND US STRATEGY IN THE AGE OF GLASNOST
    MIDDLE EAST REPORT, 19(5) (SEP 89), 4-10,22.
        THE ARTICLE EXAMINES THE MILITARY RELATIONSHIP BETWEEN
    THE US AND TURKEY OVER THE PAST FEW DECADES. THE TWO NATIONS
    DEVELOPED CLOSE MILITARY TIES IN THE FORTIES AND FIFTIES DUE
    TO A COMMON DESIRE TO CONTAIN SOVIET EXPANSION. DESPITE
    COUPS, COUNTERINSURGENCIES, AND CRISES (NOTABLY THE 1964
    CYPRUS CRISIS), THE TWO NATIONS HAVE MAINTAINED A WORKING
    RELATIONSHIP FOR FIVE DECADES. HOWEVER, AS THE THREAT OF
    COMMUNISM DIMINISHES, TURKEY FEARS THAT IT WILL BE LEFT IN

ITS TENUOUS GEOPOLITICAL SITUATION WITHOUT NEEDED WESTERN
AID. ALTHOUGH THE POLITICAL CHAOS OF THE 1970S IS UNLIKELY
TO REOCCUR, THE LEADERS OF TURKEY WILL FACE SIGNIFICANT
POLITICAL, MILITARY, AND ECONOMIC CHALLENGES AND CHOICES IN
THE YEARS TO COME.

04871 KARDAM, N.
    DO ORGANIZATIONS CHANGE? A COMPARATIVE ANALYSIS OF THE
    INCORPORATION OF GENDER ISSUES INTO DEVELOPMENT ACTIVITIES
    OF THE UNITED NATIONS DEVELOPMENT PROGRAMME, THE WORLD
    BANK, AND THE FORD FOUNDATION
    DISSERTATION ABSTRACTS INTERNATIONAL, 50(3) (SEP 89),
    787-A.
        THE AUTHOR STUDIES THE POLICY IMPACT OF THE GLOBAL
    WOMEN'S MOVEMENT ON THREE INTERNATIONAL DEVELOPMENT AGENCIES:
    THE UN DEVELOPMENT PROGRAMME, THE WORLD BANK, AND THE FORD
    FOUNDATION. PROCEDURAL, PROGRAMMATIC, BUDGETING, AND
    STAFFING CHANGES ARE ASSESSED AND EXPLAINED IN TERMS OF
    ORGANIZATIONAL ENVIRONMENTS AND INTERNAL BARGAINING
    PROCESSES.

04872 KAREITHI, P.; BEHN, S.; ONSTAD, E.
    KENYA
    SOUTH, (99) (JAN 89), 43-51.
        A DECADE OF PRESIDENT DANIEL ARAP MOI'S LEADERSHIP HAS
    PRODUCED PROGRESS IN KENYA, BUT IT WOULD BE PREMATURE TO
    CELEBRATE THE COUNTRY'S ECONOMIC ACHIEVEMENTS. IMPORTANT
    POLICIES ARE STILL BEING OVERHAULED AND KEY SECTORS ARE
    BEING RESTRUCTURED IN LINE WITH IMF AND WORLD BANK
    REQUIREMENTS. PRIVATIZATION AND IMPORT LIBERALIZATION ARE
    THE CENTRAL PLANKS OF THE CURRENT REFORM PROGRAM.

04873 KARGALITSKY, B.
    THE RETURN OF STALIN?
    NEW POLITICS, 11(2) (WIN 89), 125-132.
        IN SPITE OF ALL THE EFFORTS OF LIBERAL PUBLICISTS AND
    REPEATED OFFICIAL CONDEMNATION, STALIN'S CULT OF PERSONALITY
    HAS NOT LEFT THE STAGE, AND THE DISCUSSIONS ABOUT THE PAST
    HAVE BECOME EVEN MORE INTENSE. THE PROBLEM OF STALIN HAS NOT
    MOVED FROM THE CENTER OF ATTENTION PRECISELY BECAUSE THE
    SOCIAL AND POLITICAL STRUCTURES ESTABLISHED IN HIS EPOCH
    CONTINUE TO EXIST EVEN IF IN A MODIFIED FORM. STALINISTS
    HAVE NO NEED TO SEARCH FOR NEW SOLUTIONS TO EXISTING
    PROBLEMS. THEY CAN RELY ON AN ACCUMULATED ARSENAL OF
    MEASURES. AT WORST, THEY CAN FALL BACK ON FOREIGN
    EXPERIENCES, INCLUDING THOSE OF LATIN AMERICAN MILITARY
    REGIMES. THEY HAVE POLITICAL AND ORGANIZATIONAL EXPERIENCE,
    RESOLVE AND A TALENT FOR DEMAGOGUERY BY NO MEANS
    CHARACTERISTIC OF THE LIBERALS. BEHIND THE STALINISTS ARE A
    SIGNIFICANT NUMBER OF PEOPLE WHO ARE TIRED OF INSTABILITY
    AND RETAIN FAITH IN THE PATRIARCHAL-AUTHORITARIAN VALUES
    DRUMMED INTO THEIR MINDS FOR DECADES.

04874 KARGER, H.J.; STOESZ, D.
    WELFARE REFORM: MAXIMUM FEASIBLE EXAGGERATION
    TIKKUN, 4(2) (MAR 89), 23-25, 118-122.
        WITH THE FAMILY SUPPORT ACT OF 1988, CONSERVATIVE
    PROPONENTS OF WELFARE REFORM ARE WAXING HYPERBOLIC ABOUT THE
    IDEA THAT WELFARE RECIPIENTS SHOULD WORK. BUT, WITH FEW
    EXCEPTIONS, THE WELFARE REFORM PRODUCED AT THE END OF THE
    REAGAN ADMINISTRATION IS THE MOST PUNITIVE AND INADEQUATE
    ADDITION TO AMERICAN WELFARE SINCE THE WORKHOUSE.

04875 KARIEL, H.S.
    THE DESPERATE POLITICS OF POSTMODERNISM
    UNIVERSITY OF MASSACHUSETTS PRESS, 1989, .
        THE AUTHOR SEEKS TO EXPLOIT THE POSSIBILITIES OFFERED BY
    THE POSTMODERN AGE. HE ATTEMPTS TO BREAK PREVAILING
    CONNECTIONS AND DESIGN NEW ONES. HE SEEKS TO BRING WHAT HE
    TAKES TO BE POSTMODERN PRACTICES INTO A STILL UNACKNOWLEDGED
    CONTEXT-AN ORIENTATION THAT MANDATES A LIGHTNESS OF BEING IN
    THE FACE OF MODERNITY, OF OPPRESSIVE EVENTS THAT MAKE IT
    HARD TO RELATE TO THINGS, TO BRING EXPERIENCE INTO
    RELATIONSHIP.

04876 KARIN, D.B.
    TOWARDS THE EMPIRE STATE: NEW YORK POLITICS AND ECONOMIC
    GROWTH, 1800-1815
    DISSERTATION ABSTRACTS INTERNATIONAL, 48(10) (APR 88),
    2712-A.
        THE STUDY FOCUSES ON NEW YORK'S "PUBLIC LEADERS" AND
    THEIR ACTIONS TO PROMOTE ECONOMIC DEVELOPMENT IN THE STATE
    BETWEEN 1800 AND 1815. MORE SPECIFICALLY, THE DISSERTATION
    ANALYZES THE EFFORTS OF LEADING NEW YORKERS TO EXPEDITE ROAD
    BUILDING, MANUFACTURING, AND BANKING.

04877 KARKLINS, R.
    PERESTORIKA AND ENTHNOPOLITICS IN THE USSR
    PS: POLITICAL SCIENCE AND POLITICS, XXII(2) (JUN 89),
    208-214.
        EVENTS IN THE NON-RUSSIAN REPUBLICS OF THE USSR CAN BE
    PROPERLY ANALYZED ONLY WITHIN THE CONTEXT OF POLITICAL
    CHANGE AT THE CENTER OF POWER IN MOSCOW. (1) GORBACHEV'S
    POLICIES HAVE A DIFFERENT IMPACT IN NONRUSSIAN REGIONS THAN

AT THE CENTER; (2) HIS POLICIES ARE CONTRADICTORY AND THIS
CREATES PROBLEMS IN THE UNION-REPUBLICS; (3) NATIONALITY
POLICY ITSELF HAS BEEN INSENSITIVE TO THE INTERESTS OF THE
NONRUSSIANS.

04878 KARKLINS, R.
THE ORGANIZATION OF POWER IN SOVIET LABOR CAMPS
SOVIET STUDIES, XLI(2) (APR 89), 276-297.
ALTHOUGH THE PRISON SHOULD NOT BE TAKEN UNCRITICALLY AS
A SOCIETY IN MICROCOSM, THE COMPARATIVE ISOLATION OF ITS
SOCIAL PROCESS FROM THE IMPACT OF EXTERNAL VARIABLES
PROVIDES A RARE OPPORTUNITY FOR SYSTEMIC ANALYSIS. THE
PURPOSE OF THE PAPER IS TO PINPOINT THE MAIN POLITICAL
FEATURES IF THE CAMP SYSTEM IN THE USSR. IT EXAMINES THE
ORGANIZATIONAL STRUCTURE OF LABOR CAMPS SINCE STALIN AND
DISCUSSES THE PRIMARY MECHANISMS OF CONTROL. IT ALSO
EXAMINES INMATE PROTESTS AND THE EFFECT THAT THEY HAD ON THE
POWER PROCESS. IT CONCLUDES THAT THE TYPICAL IMAGE OF SOVIET
LABOR CAMPS BEING A PURELY REPRESSIVE INSTITUTION IS A GROSS
OVERSIMPLIFICATION; IN REALITY, RELATIONS BETWEEN CAPTOR AND
CAPTIVE ARE INTERACTIVE AND COMPLEX.

04879 KARLINER,J.
CENTRAL AMERICA'S OTHER WAR
WORLD POLICY JOURNAL, 6(4) (FAL 89), 787-810.
THIS ARTICLE EXAMINES THE ENVIRONMENTAL CRISIS THAT
CENTRAL AMERICA NOW FACES. THERE IS EVIDENCE THAT CENTRAL
AMERICAN GOVERNMENT RECOGNIZE THE IMPORTANCE OF ECOLOGICAL
STABILITY TO ECONOMIC, SOCIAL, AND POLITICAL STABILITY IN
THE REGION. THE CRISIS, UNPARALLELED IN ITS HISTORY, IS
EXPLORED AS WELL AS UNDERDEVELOPMENT, AND THE CONTRADICTIONS
OF AGRO-EXPORT. IT CONCLUDES THAT TO ACHIEVE REAL REGIONAL
SECURITY WILL REQUIRE THE U.S. GOVERNMENT TO BREAK WITH
IDEOLOGICALLY SHORT-SIGHTED PATTERN AND TO ADOPT AN APPROACH
THAT OFFERS CENTRAL AMERICA ALTERNATIVE DEVELOPMENT OPTIONS
BASE ON ENVIRONMENTAL SUSTAINABILITY, DEMOCRATIC
PARTICIPATION, AND SOCIAL EQUITY.

04880 KARLOV, G.
SOVIET PERESTROIKA: A VIEW FROM THE INSIDE
GLASNOST, II(4) (SEP 89), 18-20.
THREE YEARS AFTER THE PROCLAMATION OF PERESTROIKA, THE
SOVIET PEOPLE ARE SKEPTICAL ABOUT IT. THEY ARE NOT
INDIFFERENT TO IMPROVEMENTS IN THE REALM OF FOREIGN AFFAIRS,
AND THEY ARE HAPPY FOR THOSE FAMILIES WHOSE SONS HAVE
RETURNED FROM AFGHANISTAN. YET THE SHELVES IN THE STORES
REMAIN EMPTY, AND HAVING SOMETHING TO EAT MUST PRECEDE
FREEDOM. DISILLUSIONMENT PREDOMINATES BECAUSE REAL
PERESTROIKA HAS YET TO BEGIN. MIKHAIL GORBACHEV HAS DONE
WHAT MOST NEW LEADERS DO: HE HAS CORRECTED THE MOST OBVIOUS
BLUNDERS OF HIS PREDECESSORS. THAT'S ALL. HE HAS TACKLED
ONLY THE EASIER PROBLEMS: THOSE IN THE SPHERE OF FOREIGN
POLICY AND THOSE ON THE SURFACE OF SOVIET DOMESTIC LIFE.

04881 KARMI, G.
WHY ISRAEL DOES NOT SAY "YES" TO ARAFAT
MIDDLE EAST INTERNATIONAL, (349) (APR 89), 17-18.
THE REAL EXPLANATION FOR ISRAEL'S INTRACTABILITY ON
PALESTINE DOES NOT LIE IN THE OFFICIAL ISRAELI LINE ABOUT
SECURITY AND PALESTINIAN TERRORISM. IT HAS MUCH MORE TO DO
WITH GUILT AND LEGITIMACY. THE FEAR ABOUT LEGITIMACY HAS
BEEN EXPRESSED OPENLY BY MANY ISRAELIS. THE GUILT STEMS FROM
THE BRUTAL TRUTH THAT THE JEWISH STATE WAS ESTABLISHED AT
THE EXPENSE OF THE PALESTINIANS.

04882 KARSH, E.
A MARRIAGE OF CONVENIENCE: THE SOVIET UNION AND ASAD'S
SYRIA
JERUSALEM JOURNAL OF INTERNATIONAL RELATIONS, 11(4) (DEC
89), 1-26.
NEITHER THE PARTON-CLIENT-RELATIONSHIP NOR THE TAIL-WAGS-
THEDOG PARADIGM SUFFICES TO DESCRIBE THE SOVIET-SYRIAN
RELATIONSHIP. SYRIA CANNOT BE CONSIDERED A SOVIET CLIENT,
AND NOR CAN THE USSR BE SEEN AS A PASSIVE, REACTIVE ACTOR;
INSTEAD, THE RELATIONSHIP COMES CLOSER TO BEING ONE OF
STRATEGIC INTERDEPENDENCE. THIS ARTICLE SEEKS TO EXAMINE THE
APPLICABILITY OF THESE TWO PARADIGMS TO THE USSR'S RELATIONS
WITH SYRIA. IT FOCUSES ON THE ARAB-ISRAELI CONFLICT, SYRIA'S
INTERVENTION IN THE LEBANESE CIVIL WAR, AND THE
FORMALIZATION OF SOVIET-SYRIAN RELATIONS-AND ANALYZES THE
NATURE AND CHARACTERISTICS OF THE INFLUENCE INTERACTION
BETWEEN THE TWO COUNTRIES.

04883 KARSTEN, S.G.
GORBACHEV'S PERESTROIKA: BEGINNING OF A SOVIET SOCIALIST
MARKET ECONOMY?
INTERNATIONAL JOURNAL OF SOCIAL ECONOMICS, 16(6) (1989),
39-49.
TO WHAT EXTENT MIKHAIL GORBACHEV'S GLASNOST AND
PERESTROIKA ANTICIPATE THE PARADIGM OF A SOCIALIST MARKET
ECONOMY IS INVESTIGATED. GORBACHEV, LIKE CHINA'S DENG
XIAOPING, REALISES THAT SOCIOECONOMIC THEORIES WHICH
ABSTRACT THEMSELVES FROM THE OBSERVATIONS AND NEEDS OF DAILY
LIFE HAVE LITTLE RELEVANCE. THAT IS, A MEANINGFUL PARADIGM

HAS TO PAY ATTENTION TO SOCIETY'S VALUES, ESPECIALLY TO THE
INTERRELATIONSHIP OF PERSONAL INITIATIVE, MORALITY, LAW,
GOVERNMENT AND PUBLIC POLICY. HENCE, GORBACHEV ADVOCATES THE
ESTABLISHMENT OF MORE FAVOURABLE SOCIO-ECONOMIC CONDITIONS
TO LAY THE FOUNDATION FOR A "FUNCTIONAL SOCIALIST SOCIAL
MARKET ECONOMY", HOWEVER DEFINED, IN THE SOVIET UNION.

04884 KARUPPAIYAN, V.
AGRARIAN TENSION IN A THANJAVUR VILLAGE
INDIAN JOURNAL OF POLITICAL SCIENCE, L(1) (JAN 89), 64-73.
ALTHOUGH AGRARIAN SOCIETIES ARE KNOWN FOR THEIR PEACEFUL,
GOLDEN LIFESTYLES, THEY HAVE CONFLICTS AND TENSIONS
INHERENT WITHIN THEM. THIS PAPER ENDEAVORS TO EXPLAIN
AGRARIAN TENSION WITHIN A WEST THANJAVUR VILLAGE CALLED
"KOOTHUR," WITH PARTICULAR REFERENCE TO THE DISTRIBUTION OF
POWER IN INTRA-CASTE AND INTER-CASTE FACTIONS. POLITICAL
POWER, ECONOMIC POWER, SOCIAL POWER, AND PHYSICAL POWER ALL
CONTRIBUTE TO THE TENSIONS WITHIN A SOCIETY.

04885 KARVELIS, L. JR.
THE SEC IS COMING!
AMERICAN CITY AND COUNTY, 104(1) (JAN 89), 10.
THE SECURITIES AND EXCHANGE COMMISSION RECENTLY ISSUED
ITS FINAL REPORT ON THE DEFAULT OF THE WASHINGTON PUBLIC
POWER SUPPLY SYSTEM ON $2.25 BILLION IN NUCLEAR CONSTRUCTION
BONDS. THE MUCH PUBLICIZED DEFAULT, TOGETHER WITH NEW YORK'S
MARKET CLOSURE IN THE MID-1970'S, PROMPTED THE SEC TO
PROPOSE NEW REGULATIONS REGARDING TIMELY AND COMPLETE
MUNICIPAL DISCLOSURE.

04886 KASHLEV, Y.
CONVENTIONAL DISARMAMENT IN EUROPE
DISARMAMENT, XII(2) (SUM 89), 41-50.
THE MEETING OF THE FOREIGN MINISTERS OF THE STATES
PARTICIPATING IN THE CSCE PROCESS IN MARCH 1989 MARKED THE
BEGINNING OF NEGOTIATIONS ON CONVENTIONAL ARMED FORCES IN
EUROPE AND ON FURTHER MEASURES FOR IMPROVING CONFIDENCE AND
SECURITY IN EUROPE. THE SUCCESS OF THE TALKS DEPENDS ON
WHETHER THE PARTICIPANTS WILL BE ABLE TO OVERCOME ROUTINE
AND WHETHER THEY WILL BRING CREATIVE APPROACHES TO THE
DISCUSSION. FRESH OUTLOOKS, NEW PROPOSALS, AND DECISIONS ARE
NEEDED. THE USSR AND THE OTHER MEMBERS OF THE WARSAW TREATY
ORGANIZATION ARE READY TO EXAMINE ANY PROPOSALS DIRECTED
TOWARD THE ENHANCEMENT OF STABILITY ON THE CONTINENT AT
LOWER LEVELS OF MILITARY CONFRONTATION, ON THE BASIS OF
EQUALITY AND NON-INFRINGEMENT OF THE SECURITY OF ANY OF THE
PARTIES INVOLVED AND WITH THE GUARANTEE OF VERIFICATION.

04887 KASPRZYK, L.
SCIENCE AND TECHNOLOGY POLICY AND GLOBAL CHANGE
INTERNATIONAL SOCIAL SCIENCE JOURNAL, (121) (AUG 89),
433-440.
THE AUTHOR SURVEYS THE DIFFERENCES IN SCIENCE AND
TECHNOLOGY POLICY IN CAPITALIST AND SOCIALIST COUNTRIES. HE
COMPARES SCIENCE AND TECHNOLOGY POTENTIAL IN THE EAST AND
WEST, ALONG WITH THEIR CHOICE OF RESEARCH AND DEVELOPMENT
PRIORITIES.

04888 KASS, H.D.; ZINKE, R.C.
ETHICS AND PUBLIC ADMINISTRATION: CRITIQUE AND
RECONSTRUCTION
INTERNATIONAL JOURNAL OF PUBLIC ADMINISTRATION, 12(6)
(1987), 835-840.
THIS ARTICLE SERVES AS AN INTRODUCTION TO THE
PUBLICATION, INTERNATIONAL JOURNAL OF PUBLIC ADMINISTRATION,
NOV. 1989. IT REVIEWS THE COLLECTION OF ARTICLES AND
OBSERVES THE RENEWED INTEREST IN ADMINISTRATIVE ETHICS SINCE
WATERGATE.

04889 KASS, H.D.
EXPLORING AGENCY AS A BASIS FOR ETHICAL THEORY IN AMERICAN
PUBLIC ADMINISTRATION
INTERNATIONAL JOURNAL OF PUBLIC ADMINISTRATION, 12(6) (NOV
89), 949-970.
THIS ARTICLE ARGUES THAT AGENCY, THE NORMATIVE THEORY
ASSOCIATED WITH THE "ACTING FOR" RELATIONSHIP IN SOCIETY,
HAS HAD A PROFOUND, BUT OFTEN UNRECOGNIZED AFFECT ON ETHICS
IN PUBLIC ADMINISTRATION. ACCORDINGLY, IT SEEKS TO PROVIDE A
BRIEF REVIEW OF AGENCY THEORY AS IT APPLIES TO CONTEMPORARY
AMERICAN PUBLIC ADMINISTRATION. THE REVIEW PROVIDES AN
OVERVIEW OF AGENCY THEORY, GIVES AN EXAMPLE OF HOW DEEPLY IT
INFLUENCES AMERICAN PUBLIC ADMINISTRATION, SHOWS HOW IT
FACILITATES ETHICAL ACTION IN ADMINISTRATION AND REVIEWS
SOME OF THE MAJOR OBSTACLES TO EMPLOYING AGENCY THEORY IN
THE MODERN AMERICAN ADMINISTRATIVE STATE.

04890 KASS, I.
GORBACHEV'S STRATEGY: IS OUR PERSPECTIVE IN NEED OF
RESTRUCTURING
COMPARATIVE STRATEGY, 8(2) (1989), 181-190.
THE PURPOSE OF THE ESSAY IS TO ANALYZE THE OBJECTIVE
IMPERATIVES WHICH DRIVE SOVIET STRATEGY AT THE CURRENT STAGE
AND SET A FRAMEWORK FOR ASSESSING THE IMPLICATIONS OF THAT
STRATEGY FOR US NATIONAL SECURITY. IT ANALYZES THE LACK OF A

COHERENT, PROACTIVE US POLICY VIS-A-VIS THE USSR AND THE UNDERLYING CAUSES OF THIS DEFICIENCY IN US FOREIGN POLICY.

04891 KASTELINA, L.
THE VIEW FROM THE EUROPEAN PARLIAMENT
WORLD MARXIST REVIEW, 32(9) (SEP 89), 65-67.
THE AUTHOR CONTENDS THAT THE WAY IN WHICH THE SINGLE EUROPEAN MARKET IS BEING BUILT IS NOT THE BEST ONE. SHE EXPLORES WHAT THE SINGLE MARKET WILL BRING, AND URGES CONTROL OF THE PROCESS OF INTEGRATION RATHER THAN RESISTANCE. SHE ADDRESSES THE QUESTION OF THE NATIONAL SOVEREIGNTY OF THE EEC COUNTRIES AND QUESTIONS HOW THE ESTABLISHMENT OF SUPRANATIONAL STRUCTURES WILL AFFECT IT. IT IS SUGGESTED THAT THE LEFT AND THE LABOUR MOVEMENT SHOULD PAY ATTENTION TO THE WHOLE RANGE OF PROBLEMS THROWN UP BY THE PROCESS OF INTEGRATION.

04892 KATEB, G.
INDIVIDUALISM, COMMUNITARIANISM, AND DOCILITY
SOCIAL RESEARCH, 56(4) (WIN 89), 921-942.
THE AUTHOR PRESENTS THE CASE FOR LIBERAL, RIGHTS-BASED INDIVIDUALISM, WITH ITS INSTITUTIONS OF REPRESENTATIVE DEMOCRACY AND CAPITALISM, AGAINST ITS COMMUNITARIAN CRITICS. HIS DEFENSE IS AIMED AT SHOWING THAT FOUCAULT'S THEORY OF DOCILITY, WHICH PURPORTS TO REVEAL THAT MODERNITY'S LIBERATION OF THE INDIVIDUAL IS ONLY A NEW SERVITUDE, IS ACTUALLY MORE APPROPRIATELY APPLIED TO COMMUNITARIANISM. THE AUTHOR'S ARGUMENTS CONSIDER BOTH PEOPLE'S NEEDS, ACCORDING TO THE COMMUNITARIANS, AND THE COMMUNITARIAN CRITICS' OWN NEEDS. HE FINDS THAT BOTH SETS OF NEEDS ARE RETROGRESSIVE, ENTAILING A DISTRUST OF FREEDOM AND A THREAT TO DIGNITY, THAT THEY ARE INHOSPITABLE TO DIVERSITY AND DISAGREEMENT, AND THAT THEY REQUIRE LEADERSHIP AND A DISPOSITION TO BE LED.

04893 KATEB, G.
HOBBES AND THE IRRATIONALITY OF POLITICS
POLITICAL THEORY, 17(3) (AUG 89), 355-391.
THIS ARTICLE STATES THAT IT IS COMMONLY UNDERSTOOD THAT CONCERN WITH CIVIL WAR DOMINATES THOMAS HOBBES'S POLITICAL THEORY. FOR HOBBES, CIVIL WAR IS ALWAYS SENSELESS. IF HE THINKS THAT MUCH OF POLITICAL ACTIVITY IS IRRATIONAL, HE FINDS CIVIL WAR THE PERFECTION OF SUCH IRRATIONALITY. THE QUESTION ADRESSED HERE, IS WHY HIS CONCERN WITH CIVIL WAR IS AS ALL-ABSORBING AS IT IS. HOBBES MAY BE READ AS PROVIDING THREE DISTINCT ARGUMENTS TO SHOW THE UNWISDOM OF DELIBERATELY CARRYING SOCIAL DISAGREEMENT TO THE POINT OF VIOLENCE. THE FIRST OF THESE IS CALLED THE EXTREME ARGUMENT, DEFINED HERE AS THE AIMS FOR WHICH CIVIL WARS ARE FOUGHT (OR THREATEN TO BE FOUGHT) AND THE MOTIVES THAT INVEST SUCH OBJECTIVES WITH THEIR LETHAL POWER. HOBBES FOUND THESE BOTH DICREDITABLE. THE SECOND OR MODERATE ARGUMENT WORKS WITH THE ASSUMPTION THAT RELIGIOUS AND POLITICAL DOCTRINES ARE, IN HOBBES AGE, THE SOURCE OF THE ENERGY BEHIND TUBULENCE, SEDITION, AND CIVIL WAR. THE UNEXPECTED ARGUMENT IS THE LAST OF THE THREE. HERE, HOBBES DOES NOT SO MUCH ARGUE AS RECURENTLY SUGGEST THAT DISTURBING OR SHATTERING SOCIAL PEACE IS IRRATIONAL BECAUSE IT WEAKENS OR EVEN ELIMINATES A SOCIETY'S ABILITY TO CONDUCT INTERNATIONAL RELATIONS AND TO FIGHT WAR AGAINST FOREIGNERS. THESE THREE ARGUMENTS ARE DISCUSSED IN DEPTH.

04894 KATES, G.
JEWS INTO FRENCHMEN: NATIONALITY AND REPRESENTATION IN REVOLUTIONARY FRANCE
SOCIAL RESEARCH, 56(1) (SPR 89), 213-232.
ON SEPTEMBER 27, 1791, THE FRENCH CONSTITUENT ASSEMBLY PASSED A LAW GRANTING FULL POLITICAL RIGHTS TO ASHKENAZIC JEWS, BUT THIS JEWISH EMANCIPATION WAS NOT ALWAYS WELL RECEIVED AT THE LOCAL GOVERNMENT LEVEL. LEADING JEWS WERE STUBBORNLY DETERMINED TO ACQUIRE THEIR FULL POLITICAL RIGHTS AND EQUALLY DETERMINED TO MAINTAIN THEIR RELIGIOUS IDENTITY. FRENCH REVOLUTIONARY LEADERS INSISTED UPON THE PRINCIPLES OF RELIGIOUS FREEDOM AND EQUALITY BEFORE THE LAW, EVEN AT THE RISK OF OFFENDING LOCAL CONSTITUENCIES. THUS, THE FRENCH BECAME THE FIRST MODERN EUROPEAN NATION-STATE TO OFFER JEWS POLITICAL EQUALITY.

04895 KATES, G.
THE GIRONDINS: CHAMPIONS OF REPRESENTATIVE DEMOCRACY
FRENCH POLITICS AND SOCIETY, 7(3) (SUM 89), 82-89.
THE AUTHOR RE-EXAMINES THE GIRONDINS AND THEIR CONTRIBUTION TO THE FRENCH REVOLUTIONARY PERIOD.

04896 KATHLENE, L.
UNCOVERING THE POLITICAL IMPACTS OF GENDER: AN EXPLORATORY STUDY
WESTERN POLITICAL QUARTERLY, 42(2) (JUN 89), 397.
THIS STUDY ANALYZES GENDER DIFFERENCES AMONG STATE LEGISLATORS. BASED ON PSYCHOLOGICAL RESEARCH OF MORAL REASONING PROCESSES, TWO ATTITUDINAL CONSTRUCTS ARE DEVELOPED TO REPRESENT DIVERGENT ATTITUDE AND VALUE ORIENTATIONS RELEVANT TO THE POLITICAL CONTEXT. THE CONSTRUCTS ARE OPERATIONALIZED THROUGH A VARIANT OF DISCOURSE ANALYSIS USED IN SOCIOLINGUISTICS. THIS

EXPLORATORY STUDY APPLIES THE METHODOLOGY TO INTERVIEW DATA WITH TEN STATE LEGISLATORS, WITH THE RESULT THAT THE ATTITUDINAL CONSTRUCTS ARE ABLE TO DESCRIBE DIFFERING POLICY APPROACHES RELATED TO GENDER. DUE TO THE SMALL, EXPERIMENTAL NATURE OF THE STUDY, NO GENERALIZATIONS CAN BE MADE; BUT THE PRELIMINARY RESULTS SHOW PROMISE FOR STUDYING HOW GENDER DIFFERENCES IMPACT PUBLIC POLICY. A FOLLOW-UP, MORE COMPREHENSIVE STUDY IS BEING CONDUCTED UNDER THE DIRECTION AND FUNDING OF THE CENTER FOR THE AMERICAN WOMAN AND POLITICS, EAGLETON INSTITUTE OF POLITICS AT RUTGERS UNIVERSITY.

04897 KATZ, M.
EVOLVING SOVIET PERCEPTIONS OF US STRATEGY
WASHINGTON QUARTERLY, 12(3) (SUM 89), 157-170.
SOVIET PERCEPTIONS ABOUT US STRATEGY HAVE UNDERGONE AN IMPORTANT EVOLUTION OVER THE PAST 20 YEARS. THE ARTICLE OUTLINES THE CHANGING CONDITIONS AND CHANGING PERCEPTIONS OF THE USSR OVER FOUR PERIODS DURING THE PAST 20 YEARS: THE NIXON YEARS, THE FORD-CARTER YEARS, THE FIRST REAGAN ADMINISTRATION, AND THE SECOND REAGAN ADMINISTRATION. IT CONCLUDES WITH SOME OF THE LESSONS THAT THE SOVIETS HAVE LEARNED SUCH AS THE FACT THAT TAKING ADVANTAGE OF A DECREASE IN PUBLIC SUPPORT FOR DEFENSE BY INCREASING THE SOVIET MILITARY PRESENCE IN THE THIRD WORLD MAY BE COUNTERPRODUCTIVE IN THE LONG RUN, AND OUTLINES SOME POSSIBLE FUTURE TRENDS IN SOVIET PERCEPTIONS.

04898 KATZ, N.H.
CONFLICT RESOLUTION AND PEACE STUDIES
PHILADELPHIA: ANLS OF AMER ACMY OF POLITICAL AND SOC SCIENCE, (504) (JUL 89), 14-21.
THIS ARTICLE EXPLORES SOME OF THE KEY SOURCES OF AND REASONS FOR THE RAPID GROWTH OF CONFLICT-RESOLUTION PROGRAMS IN HIGHER EDUCATION IN THE UNITED STATES. IT HIGHLIGHTS SOME BENEFITS, AS WELL AS DILEMMAS, OF ACADEMIC WORK IN CONFLICT RESOLUTION. IN ADDITION, THE AUTHOR PROMOTES THE VIEWPOINT THAT CONFLICT-RESOLUTION CONTENT AND APPROACH SHOULD BE INFUSED BY PERSPECTIVES AND VALUES FROM PEACE STUDIES, SUCH AS CONCERNS FOR ISSUES OF SOCIAL JUSTICE AND FAIRNESS, AND STRATEGIES FOR NONVIOLENT SOCIAL CHANGE.

04899 KATZEN, L.
AFRICA'S MAN-MADE CRISIS
ENCOUNTER, LXXII(5) (MAY 89), 68-71.
AFRICA'S PROBLEMS ARE NOT PRIMARILY CAUSED BY BAD WEATHER, POOR RESOURCES, OR OTHER EXTERNAL FACTORS BEYOND GOVERNMENTAL CONTROL. ESSENTIALLY, ITS PROBLEMS HAVE BEEN MAN-MADE BY BAD GOVERNMENT IN THE POST-COLONIAL ERA. THE PROBLEMS HAVE BEEN LONG-TERM, MULTI-SECTORAL, AND SELF-REINFORCING OVER SEVERAL DECADES. GOVERNMENTAL POLICY INADEQUACIES HAVE BEEN MANIFEST IN AT LEAST THREE CRITICAL AREAS: A CONSISTENT BIAS AGAINST AGRICULTURE IN MOST SUB-SAHARAN COUNTRIES; TRADE AND EXCHANGE-RATE POLICIES THAT HAVE OVERPROTECTED INEFFICIENT IMPORT-SUBSTITUTING INDUSTRY AND HARMED AGRICULTURE; AND A WIDESPREAD NEGLECT OF MANPOWER CONSTRAINTS.

04900 KATZENSTEIN, L.
CONTROLLING THE POLITICAL ARRIVAL OF BALLISTIC MISSILE DEFENSE
JOURNAL OF LEGISLATION, 15(2) (1989), 103-114.
THE ARTICLE EXPLORES THE BROAD BASE OF SUPPORT FOR SDI AMONG THE SCIENTIFIC COMMUNITY, THE BUREAUCRACY, THE CONSERVATIVE CAMP, AND EVEN AMONG MODERATE DEMOCRATS. IT CONCLUDES THAT SOME FORM OF STRATEGIC DEFENSE IS INEVITABLE AND THE CONTROVERY SHOULD NOT BE OVER WHETHER STRATEGIC DEFENSE SHOULD BE UTILIZED, BUT OVER WHAT KIND OF STRATEGIC DEFENSE SHOULD BE UTILIZED.

04901 KATZENSTEIN, M.F.
ORGANIZING AGAINST VIOLENCE: STRATEGIES OF THE INDIAN WOMEN'S MOVEMENT
PACIFIC AFFAIRS, 62(1) (SPR 89), 53-71.
THE ARTICLE EXAMINES THE KIND OF POWER AND RESOURCES THAT THE INDIAN WOMEN'S MOVEMENT HAS UTILIZED IN THE STRUGGLE TO BRING ATTENTION TO WOMEN'S SUBORDINATION. THE ARGUMENT PRESENTED HERE IS THAT BY FOCUSING ON ISSUES OF VIOLENCE AGAINST WOMEN (RAPE, DOWRY DEATHS, WIFE-BEATING), THE INDIAN WOMEN'S MOVEMENT HAS BEEN ABLE TO PROVOKE MEDIA NOTICE, TO SECURE PUBLIC AND STATE ATTENTION TO WOMEN'S ISSUES AND THUS TO EXERT INFLUENCE FAR IN EXCESS OF ITS NUMERICAL POWER OR ORGANIZATIONAL COHESIVENESS. WHAT GIVES A SOCIAL MOVEMENT STRENGTH IS NOT JUST THE ABILITY TO CREATE ORGANIZATIONAL NETWORKS, STRONG LEADERSHIP, ACCESS TO FUNDS-ATTRIBUTES USUAL LY THOUGHT OF AS MOVEMENT "RESOURCES." AT LEAST AS CRITICAL IS THE CAPACITY OF A MOVEMENT TO PRODUCE NEW MEANINGS AND TO ACT AS SIGNIFYING AGENTS. "NAMING" THE VIOLENCE INFLICTED AGAINST WOMEN, THE INDIAN FEMINIST MOVEMENT HAS BEGUN A PROCESS OF RE-VIEWING THE WAY WOMEN ACROSS A BROAD SPECTRUM OF INDIAN SOCIETY SEE THEMSELVES AS WELL AS THE WAY WOMEN'S EXPERIENCES ARE UNDERSTOOD BY THOSE IN POSITIONS OF PROMINENCE IN SOCIETY AND WITHIN THE STATE.

04902 KAUCK, D.M.
AGRICULTURAL COMMERCIALIZATION AND STATE DEVELOPMENT IN
CENTRAL AMERICA: THE POLITICAL ECONOMY OF THE COFFEE
INDUSTRY FROM 1838 TO 1940
DISSERTATION ABSTRACTS INTERNATIONAL, 49(8) (FEB 89),
2419-A.
THE AUTHOR FOCUSES ON THE HISTORICAL IMPACT OF THE
DEVELOPMENT OF COFFEE CULTIVATION ON AGRARIAN POLITICS AND
THE PROCESS OF STATE FORMATION IN GUATEMALA, EL SALVADOR,
AND COSTA RICA. HE SEEKS TO DETERMINE THE EXTENT TO WHICH
THE DIVERGENT PATTERNS OF MODERN POLITICAL DEVELOPMENT IN
CENTRAL AMERICA WERE RELATED TO STRUCTURAL DIFFERENCES IN
THE LEADING EXPORT SECTOR.

04903 KAUFMAN-OSBORN, T.V.
POLITICS AND THE INVENTION OF REASON
POLITY, 21(4) (SUM 89), 679-710.
THIS ESSAY DRAWS LOOSELY UPON JOHN DEWEY'S PUBLISHED AND
UNPUBLISHED WORKS TO LOCATE THE ORIGIN OF PHILOSOPHY'S
INVERSION OF THE ONTOLOGICAL RELATIONSHIP BETWEEN
PREREFLECTIVE EXPERIENCE AND THE THINKING IT OCCASIONALLY
ELICITS. ARGUING THAT REASON OWES ITS BIRTH TO A FORMALIZED
REIFICATION OF THE KNOW-HOW EMBODIED IN THE SKILLS AND
PRODUCTS OF ANTIQUITY'S CRAFTS, THE AUTHOR SUGGESTS THAT
CONTEMPORARY POLITICAL THEORY IS ILL ADVISED TO TURN TO
CLASSICAL PHILOSOPHY TO DEFEND THE CAUSE OF DEMOCRACIC
POLITICS AS BEING NOT TO REHABILITATE THE CLASSICAL
TRADITION BUT TO OVERCOME IT, AND HE CONCLUDES BY SKETCHING
A POLITICAL REASON THAT MOVES IN THIS DIRECTION.

04904 KAUFMAN, E.
ISRAEL AND CENTRAL AMERICA: ARMS SALES AND THEIR
SIGNIFICANCE
NEW OUTLOOK, 32(2 (288)) (FEB 89), 29-33.
THE MAIN REASONS FOR ISRAEL'S MILITARY EXPORTS ARE
ECONOMIC, STRATEGIC, AND POLITICAL. IN CENTRAL AMERICA,
WHICH IS A MAJOR MARKET FOR ISRAELI ARMS, THE ECONOMIC
FACTOR IS PARAMOUNT. CENTRAL AMERICA HAS PROVIDED ISRAEL
WITH A RARE OPPORTUNITY TO SELL ITS OLDER WEAPONS, WHICH ARE
OBSOLETE DUE TO THE HIGHLY TECHNICAL LEVEL OF THE MIDDLE
EAST ARMS RACE BUT STILL USEFUL TO CENTRAL AMERICAN
COMBATANTS. PARTICULARLY SINCE THE EMERGENCE OF THE
SANDINISTA REGIME IN NICARAGUA, A NEW GEOPOLITICAL SITUATION
HAS DEVELOPED, CHARACTERIZED BY AN INCREASE IN BOTH LOCAL
AND TRANSNATIONAL TENSIONS AND ARMED GUERRILLA GROUPS. SINCE
THE USA HAS IMPOSED RESTRICTIONS ON ITS ARMS TRANSFERS TO
THE REGION, ISRAELI AGENTS HAVE FREQUENTLY WON THE STATUS OF
MAJOR SUPPLIER TO CENTRAL AMERICAN REGIMES.

04905 KAUFMAN, E.; TSUR, N.
WALKING A TIGHTROPE
PRESENT TENSE, 16(6) (SEP 89), 39-44.
THIS ARTICLE EXPLORES THE AMBIGUOUS SITUATION IN WHICH
ISRAEL FINDS ITSELF IN THE ARENA OF MALTREATMENT OF
PRISONERS. THIS QUESTION HAS GAINED ATTENTION IN THE MORE
THAN TWO DECADES THAT HAVE ELAPSED SINCE 1967, RESULTING IN
ISRAEL'S OCCUPATION OF THE WEST BANK AND GAZA. THE
INCREASINGLY CONFRONTAL SITUATION WHICH HAS DEVELOPED
BETWEEN ISRAEL AND THE PALESTINIAN ARABS LIVING UNDER
MILITARY RULE HAS PRODUCED A CORRESPONDING DETERIORATION IN
HUMAN RIGHTS STANDARDS, AS RESISTANCE TO ISRAELI MILITARY
PRESENCE GROWS, SO DOES THE LEVEL OF PUNITIVE MEASURES
DESIGNED TO CHECK AND PUNISH UNREST. EXAMINED IS ISRAELI LAW
AND ITS RAMIFICATIONS.

04906 KAUFMAN, R.
COVERAGE OF THE PENTAGON SCANDAL: LETTING THE JUSTICE
DEPARTMENT OFF THE HOOK... AGAIN
DEADLINE, III(6) (NOV 88), 1-2, 9-10.
PRESS COVERAGE OF THE CURRENT PENTAGON FRAUD AND BRIBERY
INVESTIGATION, CODE NAMED "ILL WIND" HAS BEEN MORE
EXHAUSTIVE THAN COVERAGE OF PREVIOUS SCANDALS. HOWEVER, ONCE
AGAIN THEY SEEM TO BE MISSING THE CRITICAL FACT THAT
ALTHOUGH THE GOVERNMENT IS CURRENTLY ENGAGED IN MUCH
ACCUSING AND FINGER POINTING, THE END RESULT WILL PROBABLY
NOT AMOUNT TO MUCH. PREVIOUS INVESTIGATIONS AND INDICTMENTS
HAVE RESULTED IN LITTLE OR NO CONCRETE PENALTIES FOR LAW-
BREAKING DEFENSE CONTRACTORS.

04907 KAUFMAN, R.G.
THE UNITED STATES AND NAVAL LIMITATION, 1921-1938
DISSERTATION ABSTRACTS INTERNATIONAL, 49(10) (APR 89),
3147-A.
THIS STUDY ANALYSES, SYSTEMATICALLY AND FROM THE
AMERICAN POINT OF VIEW, THE NAVAL ARMS LIMITATION PROCESS OF
THE INTERWAR YEARS WITH GREAT BRITAIN AND JAPAN, WHICH
CULMINATED IN THREE TREATIES: THE WASHINGTON NAVAL TREATY OF
1922, THE LONDON NAVAL TREATY OF 1930, AND THE LONDON NAVAL
TREATY OF 1936. IT FOCUSES MAINLY ON THE NEGOTIATIONS
LEADING UP TO THE TREATIES; THE DOMESTIC POLITICS OF NAVAL
LIMITATION; THE QUEST TO MEASURE PARITY MEANINGFULLY;
AMERICAN DECISIONMAKERS' HOPES AND EXPECTATIONS FOR THE
TREATIES; THE DOCTRINAL PREMISES, THEORIES OF THE ARMS RACE,
AND TECHNOLOGICAL ASSUMPTIONS UNDERPINNING THE TREATIES; THE

POLITICS OF VERIFICATION; THE EFFECTS OF THE NAVAL TREATIES
AND THE PROCESS OF NAVAL LIMITATION ON NAVAL DOCTRINE AND
DEPLOYMENT; THE CONSEQUENCES OF POLITICAL ASYMMETRIES
BETWEEN OPEN AND CLOSED SOCIETIES FOR THE COURSE AND OUTCOME
OF THE NEGOTIATIONS; HOW AND WITH WHAT SUCCESS AMERICAN
DECISIONMAKERS ATTEMPTED TO RECONCILE NAVAL LIMITATION WITH
U.S. FOREIGN POLICY COMMITMENTS AND MILITARY CAPABILITIES.

04908 KAUFMAN, R.R.
THE POLITICS OF ECONOMIC ADJUSTMENT POLICY IN ARGENTINA,
BRAZIL, AND MEXICO: EXPERIENCES IN THE 1980'S AND
CHALLENGES FOR THE FUTURE
POLICY SCIENCES, 22(3-4) (1989), 395-413.
DURING THE DEBT CRISIS OF THE 1980'S NEW DEMOCRATIC
GOVERNMENTS IN ARGENTINA AND BRAZIL EXPERIMENTED WITH
HETERODOX APPROACHES TO ECOMOMIC STABILIZATION. WHEREAS
MEXICO'S DOMINANT PARTY REGIME ADOPTD A FAR MORE ORTHODOX
LONE OF ADJUSTMENT. NONE OF THESE APPROACHES HAD LED TO A
SUSTAINED RECOVERY BY THE END OF THE DECADE. DIFFERENCE IN
POLICY CHOICE ARE ATTRIBUTABLE TO GOALS AND BELIEFS OF TOP
DECISIONMAKING OFFICIALS AND TO THE WAY THE INSTITUTIONAL
FEATURES OF THEIR RESPECTIVE POLITICAL REGIMES TIME HORIZONS
AND VULNERABILITY TO DOMESTIC DISTRIBUTIVE PRESSURES.
CONVERGING ECONOMIC OUTCOMES ARE ATTRIBUTABLE TO UNDERLYING
STUCTURAL PROBLEMS THAT CUT ACROSS THESE DISTINCTIONS:
POLITICAL CONSTRAINTS ON THE MANAGEMENT OF FISCAL DEFICITS,
AND INTERNATIONAL POWER ASYMMETRIES IMPEDING SIGNIFICANT
REDUCTIONS IN THE EXTERNAL DEBT BURDEN.

04909 KAUFMANN, J.W.
CHANGING FACE OF SOVIET STRATEGY
AVAILABLE FROM NTIS, NO. AD-A202 639/1/GAR, MAY 88, 132.
THE SOVIET UNION IS OUR MAIN COMPETITOR FOR POWER AND
INFLUENCE IN THE WORLD. IT HAS THE POWER TO DESTROY OUR
SOCIETY, AS WE KNOW IT, WITHIN HOURS. TO PREVENT THIS FROM
HAPPENING, WE MUST UNDERSTAND THE SOVIET'S POLITICAL AND
MILITARY OBJECTIVES AND STRATEGY RELATING TO GLOBAL CONFLICT.
EVIDENCE EXISTS THAT SUGGESTS THAT THE SOVIETS MAY HAVE
MADE, OR MAY BE IN THE PROCESS OF MAKING, SERIOUS REVISIONS
IN THEIR GLOBAL NUCLEAR AND CONVENTIONAL STRATEGY AND
DOCTRINE. THIS PAPER BRIEFLY TRACES THE HISTORY OF SOVIET
MILITARY STRATEGY AND DOCTRINE SINCE WORLD WAR II AND
PRESENTS EVIDENCE THAT THEY ARE AT A CROSSROAD IN THEIR
STRATEGIC THINKING. THEY ARE CURRENTLY WEIGHING THE ECONOMIC,
POLITICAL, AND MILITARY CONSEQUENCES OF CONTINUING A
CONFRONTATIONAL, OFFENSIVE NUCLEAR WARFIGHTING STRATEGY,
DOCTRINE, AND FORCE POSTURE AND ARE CONSIDERING A CHANGE TO
A LESS THREATENING AND AFFORDABLE POSTURE. A BRIEF LOOK AT
THEIR REACTION TO PRESIDENT REAGAN'S STRATEGIC DEFENSE
INITIATIVE AND GENERAL SECRETARY GORBACHEV'S LATEST ARMS
CONTROL INITIATIVES REINFORCES THE ARGUMENT THAT A SHIFT IN
SOVIET STRATEGY MAY TAKE PLACE IN THE NEAR FUTURE IF AMERICA
LETS IT HAPPEN.

04910 KAUNDA, L.
BLACK AGAINST BLACK
NEW AFRICAN, (MAR 88), 18-19.
THIS ARTICLE REPORTS ON CIVIL WAR, BLACK AGAINST BLACK,
GOING ON IN SOUTH AFRICA. IT DESCRIBES THE ANGUISH THAT
PEOPLE ARE EXPERIENCING BECAUSE OF THE NUMEROUS DEATHS,
SEIZING OF CHILDREN TO FIGHT, AND DISRUPTION OF DAILY LIFE
IN PIETERMARITZBURG.

04911 KAUTZER, K.M.
MOVING AGAINST THE STREAM: AN ORGANIZATIONAL STUDY OF THE
OLDER WOMEN'S LEAGUE
DISSERTATION ABSTRACTS INTERNATIONAL, 49(8) (FEB 89),
2414-A.
UTILIZING SELZNICK'S THEORY OF LEADERSHIP, THE AUTHOR
EXAMINES THE NATURE AND EFFECTIVENESS OF THE LEADERSHIP OF
TISH SOMMERS DURING HER TENURE AS PRESIDENT OF THE OLDER
WOMEN'S LEAGUE FROM 1980 TO 1985. FINDINGS ILLUMINATE BOTH
STRENGTHS AND WEAKNESSES IN SELZNICK'S THEORY AND DOCUMENT A
RANGE OF HIGHLY SUCCESSFUL AND INNOVATIVE STRATEGIES USED BY
OWL LEADERSHIP TO PROMOTE ITS GOALS.

04912 KAVADLO, C.
SITUATED FRATERNIZATION: THE EUDAEMONIC SUBLIMATION OF
RELIGION
INTERNATIONAL JOURNAL OF POLITICS, CULTURE AND SOCIETY,
2(2) (WIN 88), 257-276.
IN THIS STUDY OF THE LEISURE LIFE OF URBAN WORKERS, THE
AUTHOR POINTS TO THE SECULAR EQUIVALENT OF REDEMPTION THEY
FIND IN THEIR ESCAPE INTO THE EFFERVESCENCE OF LOUNGE RIGHT
LIFE. IN THE LOUNGE, ALL IS CONTRIVED TO BOLSTER THE EGO AND
SELF-ESTEEM THOSE WHO OTHERWISE ARE THE UNRECOGNIZED OF THE
WORLD THE SERVICE WORKERS, GARBAGE COLLECTORS, MAINTENANCE
MEN, TRUCK DRIVERS, PLUMBERS, TAXI DRIVERS, ET AL.

04913 KAVAN, J.
NO RATIONALE FOR THE SURVIVAL OF YUGOSLAVIA?
EAST EUROPEAN REPORTER, 3(4) (SPR 89), 46.
THE ARTICLE IS AN INTERVIEW WITH TOMAZ MASTNAK, A
SLOVENIAN PEACE ACTIVIST AND JOURNALIST. MASTNAK DISCUSSES

SUCH SUBJECTS AS THE DECLINE OF SOCIALISM AND THE RISE OF
NATIONALISM IN YUGOSLAVIA. HE OUTLINES SOME OF THE PROBLEMS
THAT RESULT FORM INCREASED NATIONALIST AND ETHNIC TENSIONS.
HE WARNS AGAINST THE DANGERS OF THE GROWING POWER OF SERBIAN
STRONG MAN SLOBODAN MILOSEVIC. HE PAINTS A PICTURE OF A
YUGOSLAVIA THAT IS INCREASINGLY FRAGMENTED AND UNSTABLE.

04914 KAVAN, J.
THE ICE HAS CRACKED, BUT WILL IT MELT
EAST EUROPEAN REPORTER, 3(4) (SPR 89), 49-51.
THE ARTICLE EXAMINES THE RECENT SPATE OF DEMONSTRATIONS
AND THE EFFORTS OF THE HARD-LINE CZECHOSLOVAKIA GOVERNMENT
TO REPRESS THEM AND REMAIN IN POWER. THE CONSERVATIVES IN
GOVERNMENT HOPE THAT THEY WILL BE ABLE TO KEEP THE PRESSURE
FOR REFORMS AT BAY UNTIL THE END OF THEIR LIVES OR UNTIL--AS
THEY EXPECT-- GORBACHEV IS DEPOSED BY THEIR FRIENDS IN THE
KREMLIN. HOWEVER, THE INCREASINGLY COURAGEOUS ACTIVISM OF
THE CITIZENS OF CZECHOSLOVAKIA HAS RAISED TENSION TO MUCH
HIGHER LEVELS.

04915 KAW, M.
PREDICTING SOVIET MILITARY INTERVENTION
JOURNAL OF CONFLICT RESOLUTION, 33(3) (SEP 89), 402-429.
THIS ARTICLE ATTEMPTS TO EXPLAIN AND PREDICT SOVIET
INTERVENTION IN CONFLICTS ABROAD DURING 1950-1987. A
GEOPOLITICS DRIVEN MODEL OF SOVIET CALCULUS FOR INTERVENTION
PREDICT WHICH OF FOUR LEVELS OF INTERVENTION WILL BE UNTAKEN:
VERBAL/DIPLOMATIC OR LESS, ARMS DELIVERY, LIMITED PERSONNEL,
OR LARGE-SCALE PERSONNEL SUPPORT. WHEN TESTED ON 403
DIVERSE CIVIL AND INTERSTATE CONFLICTS ADAPTED FROM THE
CORRELATES OF WAR AND CONFLICT AND PEACE DATA BANK PROJECTS,
THE MODEL PROVED CORRECT IN 88% OF THE CASES. TWO OTHER
PREDICTIVE RULES - THE MODAL AND THE MIRROR IMAGE
ALTERNATIVES--WERE ALSO TESTED AND USED AS BASELINES FOR
COMPARISON. THE RESULTS SHOW MOSCOW RARELY WIELDS THE SWORD
EXCEPT TO RESCUE AN EMBATTLED ALLY OR A POTENTIAL CLIENT.
ALTHOUGH IT INTERVENED MORE FREQUENTLY DURING THE 1970S, AN
INCREASE IN THE NUMBER OF BELEAGUERED CLIENTS SEEMS TO
ACCOUNT FOR THE TRENDLINE. THE FINDINGS OFFER USEFUL
CORRECTIVES TO COLD WAR AND MIRROR IMAGE THEORIES.

04916 KAW, M.
SOVIET SUPPORT OF REVOLUTIONS: NEITHER POWER NOR GLORY
INTERNATIONAL INTERACTIONS, 15(2) (1989), 95-111.
THIS STUDY EXAMINES WHY THE SOVIET UNION SUPPORTS
REVOLUTIONARY MOVEMENTS AND HOW LIKELY ITS SUPPORT WILL TAKE
THE FORM OF DIRECT MILITARY ASSISTANCE. THREE HYPOTHESES
ABOUT ITS PRIMARY MOTIVE FOR BACKING INSURGENTS ARE TESTED
ON 126 CIVIL CONFLICTS DURING 1950-87. THE "EASILY
SATISFIED" HYPOTHESIS, WHICH CONTENDS REBELS ARE SUPPORTED
TO ERADICATE NOT IDEOLOGICALLY REGRESSIVE NOR POLITICALLY
ALOOF REGIMES, BUT ONLY THOSE VIRULENTLY ANTISOVIET, BEST
ACCOUNTS FOR THE VARIATIN IN SOVIET BEHAVIOR. SOVIET LEADERS
ARE NOT ONLY HIGHLY SELECTIVE IN BACKING REVOLUTIONS, THEIR
SUPPORT IS USUALLY CONFINED TO MORAL EXHORTATIONS. A SURVEY
TURNED UP ONLY 3 TO 5 INSTANCES OF DIRECT MILITARY
ASSISTANCE TO GUERILLA MOVEMENTS COMPARED TO 16 INSTANCES OF
TANGIBLE AID FOR EMBATTLED GOVERNMENTS. THESE FINDINGS
INDICATE THE NEED TO REVISE COLD WAR VIEWS OF THE USSR AS AN
ACTIVE PROMOTER OF REVOLUTIONS.

04917 KAWAGUCHI, H.
JAPAN'S EVOLING DEFENCE POLICY
NATO'S SIXTEEN NATIONS, 34(2) (APR 89), 21-24, 27.
JAPAN ENTERED A NEW ERA AFTER THE TRAUMA OF THE SECOND
WORLD WAR. BY VIRTUE OF ITS CONSTITUTION, IT RENOUNCED WAR
AS A SOVERIGN RIGHT OF THE NATION AND ONLY MAINTAINED
MINIMUM ARMED FORCES ADEQUATE FOR IMMEDIATE SELF-DEFENCE.
HOWEVER, AS SOVIET MILITARY POWER GREW IN THE POST-WAR YEARS,
THIS REQUIREMENT HAD TO BE SEEN IN TERMS OF INCREASED
DEFENCES, AT THE SAME TIME, JAPAN'S PRINCIPAL ALLY, THE
UNITED STATES, CALLED FOR GREATER EFFORTS. MORE AND BETTER
DEFENCE RESOURCES ARE NOW BEING MADE AVAILABLE, ALBEIT IN A
HIGHLY CAUTIOUS WAY IN THE PRESENT IMPROVED EAST-WEST
CLIMATE, FORCE IMPROVEMENTS WILL NOT BE SPECTACULAR. THEY
WILL BE SUFFICIENT FOR A ROBUST DEFENCE - AND NOT FOR MORE.

04918 KAWANO, K.
THE FRENCH REVOLUTION AND THE MEIJI ISHIN
INTERNATIONAL SOCIAL SCIENCE JOURNAL, (119) (FEB 89),
45-52.
THE FRENCH REVOLUTION AND THE MEIJI ISHIN DIFFER
SIGNIFICANTLY IN TERMS OF CLASS RELATIONS AND INTERNATIONAL
INFLUENCE. NEVERTHELESS, THEY WERE BOTH TREMENDOUS SOCIAL
UPHEAVALS THAT DIRECTLY LED TO THE CREATION OF MODERN STATES.

04919 KAWELL, J.A.
GOING TO THE SOURCE
NACLA REPORT ON THE AMERICAS, XXII(6) (MAR 89), 13-21.
THE ARTICLE ASSESSES THE EFFECTIVENESS OF US ANTI-DRUG
EFFORTS IN PERU'S COCA-GROWING HUALLAGA VALLEY. US FORCES
ARE OFTEN CAUGHT UP IN A NO-WIN QUANDARY OF DRUG LORDS AND
GUERRILLAS. IT CONCLUDES THAT US POLICY HAS, AS OF YET,
ABYSMALLY FAILED TO STEM THE GROWTH OF THE COCAINE INDUSTRY,

AND THREATENS TO DRAW THE US INTO A VAST AND BITTER WAR.

04920 KAWELL, J.A.
THE ADDICT ECONOMIES
NACLA REPORT ON THE AMERICAS, XXII(6) (MAR 89), 33-38.
THE ARTICLE EXAMINES THE INCREASING COCAINE TRADE AND
ITS EFFECT ON THE ECONOMIES OF COLUMBIA, PERU, AND BOLIVIA.
IT ARGUES THAT VIEWING COCAINE SOLELY AS A MORAL ISSUE OFTEN
CLOUDS THE UNDERLYING ECONOMIC IMPORTANCE OF THE DRUG TRADE
TO TH ECONOMIES OF LATIN AMERICA. HOWERVE, THE ARTICLE
CONCLUDES THAT THERE WILL BE LITTLE LONG-TERM ECONOMIC
BENEFIT TO THE COCAINE TRADE FOR LATIN AMERICA. LIKE SILVER,
TIN, AND RUBBER BEFORE IT, IT WILL BENEFIT A RICH FEW FOR A
BRIEF SPACE OF TIME BEFORE SUCCUMBING TO CHANGING WORLD
TRENDS.

04921 KAHIANI, N.
THE REVOLUTION CAN DEFEND ITSELF
WORLD MARXIST REVIEW, 32(12) (DEC 89), 72-74.
THE APRIL REVOLUTION OF 1978, ACCOMPLISHED UNDER THE
LEADERSHIP OF THE PEOPLE'S DEMOCRATIC PARTY OF AFGHANISTAN,
WAS OBJECTIVELY CONDITIONED BY THE LONG STRUGGLE OF THE
AFGHAN PEOPLE FOR DEMOCRACY AND NATIONAL DEVELOPMENT.
HOWEVER, THE PROVOCATIVE STAND OF THE BIG FEUDAL LORDS,
BUREAUCRATS AND OTHER OPPONENTS OF TRANSFORMATION, AS WELL
AS INTERFERENCE FROM THE PAKISTANI MILITARY AND HEGEMONIC US
CIRCLES EXACERBATED THE REPUBLIC'S DIFFICULTIES. IF THE USA
AND PAKISTAN BEGIN TO HONOUR THEIR COMMITMENTS UNDER THE
GENEVA ACCORDS, THERE WILL APPEAR A REAL OPPORTUNITY FOR
DIALOGUE BETWEEN ALL SIDES, RECONCILIATION AND NATIONAL
CONCORD, AND FOR THE FORMATION OF A COALITION GOVERNMENT
INVOLVING ALL POLITICAL FORCES CONCERNED.

04922 KAYE, L.
CAPITAL FRIGHT
FAR EASTERN ECONOMIC REVIEW, 142(49) (DEC 89), 52-53.
INVESTMENT ABROAD BY TAIWAN'S BUSINESSMEN IS INCREASING
AT AN INCREDIBLE RATE. RAPID SOCIAL CHANGE, GALLOPING
CONSUMERISM, AND THE LIFTING OF MARTIAL LAW HAVE COMBINED TO
INCREASE CRIME RATES, ESPECIALLY AGAINST HIGH-PROFILE
ENTREPRENEURS AND EXECUTIVES. THE CRIME WAVE, ALONG WITH
WAGE INFLATION, SPIRALLING ENVIRONMENTAL CLEAN-UP COSTS, AND
LABOR UNREST HAVE LED TO SIGNIFICANT CAPITAL FLIGHT.
TAIWAN'S GOVERNMENT HAS RESPONDED WITH TOUGHER LAWS AGAINST
CRIME AND LABOR UNREST, BUT OPINION REMAINS SPLIT AS TO
WHETHER THE MEASURES WILL HAVE ANY NOTICEABLE EFFECT.

04923 KAYE, L.
OPPOSITION ONSLAUGHT
FAR EASTERN ECONOMIC REVIEW, 142(50) (DEC 89), 22-23.
TAIWAN'S OPPOSITION DEMOCRATIC PROGRESSIVE PARTY (DPP)
HAD A SURPRISINGLY GOOD SHOWING AT THE POLLS, CAPTURING %38
OF THE POPULAR VOTE IN THE CITY AND COUNTY EXECUTIVE RACES
AND WINNING 21 PARLIAMENTARY SEATS. THE KUOMINTANG'S (KMT)
CAPTURING OF ONLY %53 OF THE POPULAR VOTE IS A REFLECTION OF
GROWING VOTER DISCONTENT WITH THE RULING GOVERNMENT. THE
ELECTION RESULTS REVEAL THAT BOTH THE KMT AND THE DPP STILL
HAS A GOOD DEAL OF POST-ELECTION SOUL-SEARCHING TO DO,
ESPECIALLY ON THE ISSUE OF TAIWAN'S INDEPENDENCE. BOTH
PARTIES MUST ALSO DEAL WITH INTERNECINE FACTIONAL SQUABBLES
THAT HAVE HAMPERED THEIR EFFECTIVENESS IN THE PAST.

04924 KAYSEN, C.
CAN UNIVERSITIES COOPERATE WITH THE DEFENSE ESTABLISHMENT?
PHILADELPHIA: ANLS OF AMER ACMY OF POLITICAL AND SOC
SCIENCE, (502) (MAR 89), 29-39.
DEEPLY INFLUENCED BY THEIR EXPERIENCES IN WORLD WAR II,
THE MILITARY SERVICES AND THE DEPARTMENT OF DEFENCE BECAME
IMPORTANT AND SUPPORTIVE FUNDERS OF ACADEMIC SCIENCE-CHIEFLY
THE PHYSICAL SCIENCES-IN THE POSTWAR PERIOD. THEY MADE AN
IMPLICIT CONTRACT WITH THE ACADEMY, PROVIDING SUPPORT UNDER
THE GOING RULES: THE PURSUIT OF NEW KNOWLEDGE; INVESTIGATOR
INITIATIVE; PUBLICATION OF THE RESULTS; AND SOME FORM OF
PEER REVIEW AS THE ALLOCATIVE INSTRUMENT. IN RETURN, THE
ACADEMY OFFERED NEW SCIENCE AND TRAINED SCIENTISTS. THE
RELATION PERSISTS, BUT CHANGES IN THE POLITICAL CONTEXT, THE
INTERNAL CAPABILITIES OF THE DEFENSE DEPARTMENT, AND THE
GROWTH OF OTHER FORMS OF SUPPORT HAVE CHANGED IT IN A LONG-
LASTING WAY. NONETHELESS, THERE ARE GOOD REASONS ON BOTH
SIDES TO CONTINUE THE RELATION, AND A WILLINGNESS BY BOTH TO
ACCEPT THE TERMS OF THE IMPLICIT CONTRACT WOULD ALLOW IT TO
CONTINUE.

04925 KAZA, J.
FIGHTING FOR "SOCIALIST PLURALISM" IN LATVIA
NEW LEADER, LXXII(2) (JAN 89), 12-14.
THE SUPREME SOVIET HAS APPROVED CHANGES THAT MAINTAIN
THE KREMLIN'S EXTENSIVE POWERS OVER THE UNION REPUBLICS AND
EFFECTIVELY CLOSE THE FAST TRACK TO REFORM THROUGH LOCAL
AUTONOMY, INITIATIVE, AND DIVERSITY. SINCE THE VOTE ON THESE
CONSTITUTIONAL CHANGES, THE NEO-STALINISTS HAVE CONSOLIDATED
THEIR POWER AND STARTED TO SHOW THEIR TEETH AGAINST THE
REBELLIOUS BALTS.

04926 KAZI, M.
ISLAND GLASNOST
NEW AFRICAN, (260) (MAY 89), 20-21.
THE SEYCHELLES PEOPLE'S PROGRESSIVE FRONT HAS RULED THE
ISLANDS SINCE A COUP OVERTHREW PRESIDENT JAMES MANCHAM IN
JUNE 1977. AFTER YEARS OF POLITICAL REPRESSION, THE SPPF HAS
NOW EMBARKED ON A NEW STRATEGY, SHELVING HARD-LINE SOCIALISM
AND GIVING THE PUBLIC A DOSE OF GLASNOST. THE CHURCH IS
BEING RESTORED TO ITS FORMER STATUS, AND THE ECONOMY IS
BEING LIBERALIZED.

04927 KAZUHISA, O.
JOINT FIGHTER DEVELOPMENT: SECURITY SACRIFICED AGAIN
JAPAN ECHO, XVI(3) (AUT 89), 66-69.
FOR THE TIME BEING JAPAN AND THE UNITED STATES HAVE
SMOOTHED OVER THEIR DIFFERENCES REGARDING JOINT DEVELOPMENT
OF THE FSX, THE NEXT-GENERATION SUPPORT FIGHTER FOR JAPAN'S
AIR SELF-DEFENSE FORCE. THE DOMINANT IMPRESSION THAT EMERGES
FROM THE CONTROVERSY, WHICH WAS RESOLVED THROUGH MAJOR
CONCESSIONS BY TOKYO IN RESPONSE TO PRESSURE FROM WASHINGTON,
IS THAT THE DEBATE WAS CONDUCTED AT A LOW LEVEL, WITHOUT
GENUINE DIALOGUE BASED ON THE NORMS OF INTERNATIONAL
RELATIONS AND WITHOUT ANY REFERENCE TO THE LESSONS OF
HISTORY. THE MOST REGRETTABLE ASPECT OF JAPAN'S BEHAVIOR IS
THAT ONCE AGAIN THE COUNTRY SACRIFICED SECURITY IN AN EFFORT
TO ALLEVIATE ECONOMIC FRICTION.

04928 KAZUO, N.
FLAWS IN THE "CONTAINING JAPAN" THESIS
JAPAN ECHO, XVI(4) (WIN 89), 52-57.
THE AUTHOR RESPONDS TO JAMES FALLOWS' ADVOCACY OF THE
NEED FOR "CONTAINING JAPAN." AFTER COMMENTING ON THE TONE OF
FALLOWS' ESSAY AND CRITICIZING THE SHORTCOMINGS IN THE
ECONOMIC THEORIZING OF JAPAN-BASHERS IN GENERAL, THE AUTHOR
REBUTS SOME OF FALLOWS' SPECIFIC CHARGES AND ARGUES THAT
THEY ARE BASED ON A MISUNDERSTANDING OF THE MECHANISMS THAT
GUIDE ECONOMIC ACTIVITY IN JAPAN AND AROUND THE WORLD.

04929 KEALEY, L.; SANGSTER, J.
BEYOND THE VOTE: CANADIAN WOMEN AND POLITICS
UNIVERSITY OF TORONTO PRESS, TORONTO, ONTARIO, CA, 1989,
416.
THESE ESSAYS SURVEY THE ACTIVITIES OF CANADIAN WOMEN WHO
HAVE WORKED WITHIN THE MAINSTREAM POLITICAL PARTIES; THOSE
WHO HAVE WORKED FOR SPECIFIC GOALS, SUCH AS PEACE; AND
OTHERS WHO HAVE WORKED OUTSIDE THE MAINSTREAM IN THE
SOCIALIST AND LABOUR MOVEMENTS.

04930 KEAN, T.H.
STATES MUST TAKE THE LEAD IN PROTECTING WETLANDS
STATE LEGISLATURES, 15(9) (OCT 89), 30.
THE NATIONAL WETLANDS FORUM HAS RECOMMENDED THAT STATES
TAKE THE LEAD IN WETLANDS REGULATION BY PREPARING WETLANDS
CONSERVATION PLANS THAT WOULD ESTABLISH A COMPREHENSIVE
PROGRAM TO INSURE NO OVERALL NET LOSS OF WETLANDS IN THE
SHORT TERM. THEN THE STATES, NOT THE FEDERAL GOVERNMENT,
WOULD BECOME RESPONSIBLE FOR WETLANDS REGULATION.

04931 KEANE, J.
EIRE AND UNIFIL: MORE DEATHS IN LEBANON
MIDDLE EAST INTERNATIONAL, (347) (MAR 89), 15-16.
THE DEATHS OF THREE IRISH SOLDIERS NEAR BRA'SHIT ON
MARCH 21, 1989, BRINGS TO 11 THE NUMBER OF SOLDIERS KILLED
IN ACTION WHILE SERVING WITH THE UNITED NATIONS INTERIM
FORCE IN LEBANON. THE IRISH GOVERNMENT IS INVESTIGATING THE
INCIDENT BEFORE ANNOUNCING A DECISION ON WHETHER OR NOT IT
WILL REPLACE ITS TROOPS THAT ARE DUE FOR ROTATION.

04932 KEANE, J.
THE EEC AND IRAN: FINANCIAL EXPEDIENCY
MIDDLE EAST INTERNATIONAL, (347) (MAR 89), 15.
IRELAND'S DECISION TO TAKE THE LEAD IN RESTORING NORMAL
DIPLOMATIC RELATIONS WITH IRAN, FOLLOWING THE BREAK OVER
DEATH THREATS TO SALMAN RUSHDIE, WAS THE RESULT OF FINANCIAL
EXPEDIENCY RATHER THAN A POLITICAL GESTURE. THE DECISION OF
SUCH EEC COUNTRIES AS ITALY, SPAIN, AND GREECE TO FOLLOW
IRELAND'S LEAD IS OF SMALL CONCERN TO BRITAIN, BUT IT IS
WATCHING ANXIOUSLY FOR ANY SIGN OF WEAKENING RESOLVE ON THE
PART OF FRANCE OR GERMANY.

04933 KEARNEY, R. C.; SINMA, C.
PROFESSIONALISM AND BUREAUCRATIC RESPONSIVENESS: CONFLECT
OR COMPATIBILITY?
PUBLIC ADMINISTRATION REVIEW, 48(1) (JAN 88), 571-579.
THIS PAPER DOES NOT CLAM THAT PROFESSIONALISM IS A
PANACEA FOR ALL THE ILLS OF BUREAUCRACY. BUT IT AGREES WITH
SUCH NOTABLES AS ARISTOTLE, JOHN STUART MILL, WOODROW WILSON,
AND MAX WEBER THAT THE PRESERVATION OF A DEMOCRATIC SYSTEM
DEPENDS UPON THE COMPETENCE OF EXPERTS IN GOVERNMENT TO
PRESERVE MODERN DEMOCRACY.1 FOLLOWING A DISCUSSION OF THE
CHARACTERISTICS AND NATURE OF PROFESSIONALISM, DON K.
PRICE'S (1965) MODEL OF THE FOUR ESTATES IS REVIEWED AND
RECONCEPTUALIZED TO DEMONSTRATE THE INCREASING
INTERPENETRATION OF THE "FOUR ESTATES," PARTICULARLY THE

PROFESSIONS AND ADMINISTRATION. THE RECONCEPTUALIZATION
EMPHASIZES HOW THE EXPANDED ROLE OF THE PROFESSIONAL
ADMINISTRATOR HAS BENEFITTED BUREAUCRATIC RESPONSIVENESS.
AFTER TAKING INTO ACCOUNT THE PRINCIPAL CRITICISMS OF
PROFESSIONALISM, ITS ADVANTAGES ARE DESCRIBED. THE
CONCLUSION IS THAT WHEN CONSIDERED WITHIN THE CONTEXT OF
EXISTING INTERNAL AND EXTERNAL CHECKS ON ADMINISTRATIVE AND
PROFESSIONAL DISCRETION, PROFESSIONALISM DOES NOT PRECLUDE
BUREAUCRATIC RESPONSIVENESS. DUAL STREAMS OF PROFESSIONALISM
CONSTITUTE NOT A THREAT TO BUT A PROMISE OF BUREAUCRATIC
RESPONSIVENESS. INDEED, IT IS SUBMITTED THAT PROFESSIONALISM,
IN CONJUNCTION WITH OTHER INSTITUTIONS, PROCESSES, AND
DEVELOPMENTS IN PUBLIC ADMINISTRATIONS, STRENGTHENS
BUREAUCRATIC RESPONSIVENESS AND HELPS TO INSURE THE SURVIVAL
OF THE DEMOCRATIC SYSTEM.

04934 KEARSLEY, H.J.
COUNTERING INSTITUTIONALIZED RACISM
CONTEMPORARY REVIEW, 254(1477) (FEB 89), 94-97.
FOR A SOCIETY TO BE SUFFERING FROM INSTITUTIONALISED
RACISM, IT MUST BE PROVABLE THAT CERTAIN RACIAL ELEMENTS OF
THAT SOCIETY ARE SYSTEMATICALLY NOT RECEIVING EQUAL
OPPORTUNITIES IN COMPARISON TO THE REMAINDER OF THAT SOCIETY.
THE LACK OF EQUAL TREATMENT BY THE STRUCTURE MUST BE
ACTIVELY COUNTERED THROUGH AFFIRMATIVE ACTION. IT IS UP TO
THOSE WHO HAVE ENJOYED THE FRUITS OF THAT SYSTEM FOR SO LONG
TO ENSURE NOW, AT LAST, THE FRUITS WILL BE EQUALLY
DISTRIBUTED, IRRESPECTIVE OF THE COLOUR OF ONE'S SKIN.

04935 KEATING, M.
THE DISINTEGRATION OF URBAN POLICY: GLASGOW AND THE NEW
BRITAIN
URBAN AFFAIRS QUARTERLY, 24(4) (JUN 89), 513-536.
IN THE PAST, THE CONFLICT BETWEEN THE GROWTH AND
DISTRIBUTIONAL ASPECTS OF URBAN POLICY HAS NOT BEEN A MAJOR
ISSUE IN BRITAIN. IN GLASGOW, THE INSTITUTIONAL REFORMS OF
THE 1970S HERALDED A COMPREHENSIVE, PUBLIC-SECTOR-DIRECTED
PROGRAM FOR URBAN REGENERATION. IN THE 1980S, POLICY HAS
DISINTEGRATED UNDER THE IMPACT OF RECESSION, LOCAL FISCAL
CUTBACK, AND CENTRAL GOVERNMENT AND AGENCY INTERVENTION. A
CONFLICT BETWEEN GROWTH AND DISTRIBUTION IS POSED. GLASGOW
EMERGES AS A DUAL CITY, WITH SUBSIDIZATION OF DOWNTOWN
BUSINESS AND AMENITIES BUT WIDESPREAD DEPRIVATION,
ESPECIALLY ON THE PERIPHERY - REFLECTING CONDITIONS MORE
WIDELY SEEN IN THE "NEW BRITAIN."

04936 KECHICHIAN, J.A.
THE GCC AND THE WEST
AMERICAN-ARAB AFFAIRS, (29) (SUM 89), 20-31.
THIS ARTICLE EXPLORES FOUR CONCLUSIONS REACHED BY THE
GULF COOPERATION COUNCIL (GCC) BY THE END OF THE 1980S
INVOLVING THE AREAS OF ACCESS, THE SOVIET UNION, COMMONALITY,
AND SECURITY. IT EXAMINES THE GCC STATES' PERCEPTION OF
THESE FOUR AREAS AND COMPARES THEM TO WESTERN VIEWS. IT
EXPLORES WHAT THE WEST CAN DO TO PRESERVE ITS LONG TERM
INTERESTS IN THIS VITAL REGION OF THE WORLD, AS WELL AS
WHETHER OR NOT THE GCC STATES CAN ACCOMPLISH SECURITY
OBJECTIVES AND REMAIN INDEPENDENT FROM THE WEST.

04937 KEDEM, P.; BAR-LEV, M.
DOES POLITICAL SOCIALIZATION IN ADOLESCENCE HAVE A LASTING
INFLUENCE? THE ENDURING EFFECT OF ISRAELI YOUTH MOVEMENTS
ON THE POLITICAL IDEOLOGY AND BEHAVIOR OF THEIR GRADUATES
POLITICAL PSYCHOLOGY, 10(3) (SEP 89), 391-416.
THE LONG-TERM EFFECTS OF MEMBERSHIP IN ISRAELI YOUTH
MOVEMENTS ON THE POLITICAL SOCIALIZATION OF THEIR ADOLESCENT
MEMBERS, AND THEIR SUBSEQUENT POLITICAL IDEOLOGY AND
INVOLVEMENT AFTER LEAVING THE MOVEMENTS WERE STUDIED ON A
REPRESENTATIVE SAMPLE (N = 1250) OF ISRAELI UNIVERSITY
STUDENTS. THIS RESEARCH'S MAIN CONTRIBUTION TO POLITICAL
SOCIALIZATION STUDIES IS THAT IT OFFERS A MEANS BY WHICH TO
ANALYZE A SOCIALIZATION EFFECT DIRECTED SOLELY AT THE
ADOLESCENT, TO CONTROL (AT LEAST STATISTICALLY) OTHER
CONFOUNDING CHILDHOOD INFLUENCES, AND TO ENABLE RELATING
THEIR ADULT POLITICAL IDEOLOGY TO THIS INFLUENCE. THE WIDE
AGE RANGE OF ISRAELI STUDENTS (DUE TO THEIR 3-YEAR ARMY
SERVICES AND NEED TO WORK) AND THE SIZE OF THE CONTROL GROUP
(THOSE WHO HAD NEVER JOINED A YOUTH MOVEMENT) HELPED TO
SURMOUNT MANY OF THE DIFFICULTIES THAT OCCUR IN LONGITUDINAL
AND COHORT STUDIES. AS WITH ANY FIELD STUDY, PERFECT PROOF
IS NOT FEASIBLE. IT IS IMPOSSIBLE TO VERIFY IF ALL THE
SOCIALIZATION AGENTS WERE ACCOUNTED FOR, OR WHETHER SOME
SPURIOUS CORRELATIONS HAD OCCURRED BUT, WITHIN THE CONFINES
OF THIS RESEARCH METHOD, THE HYPOTHESES, ON THE WHOLE, WERE
CONFIRMED: (1) ADULT POLITICAL IDEOLOGIES OF FORMER YOUTH
MOVEMENT MEMBERS CORRESPONDED TO THEIR MOVEMENTS' OFFICIAL
IDEOLOGIES, WHILE IDEOLOGIES OF NONMEMBERS WERE MORE ERRATIC;
(2) POLITICAL INVOLVEMENT WAS HIGHER AMONG FORMER YOUTH
MOVEMENT MEMBERS THAN AMONG NONMEMBERS. THE RESULTS ARE
DISCUSSED WITHIN THE LIFESPAN THEORIES OF POLITICAL
SOCIALIZATION.

04938 KEDOURIE, E.
REPORTING ISLAM

ENCOUNTER, LXXII(2) (FEB 89), 74-76.
EVEN THOUGH MEANS OF TRANSPORT HAVE BECOME IMMEASURABLY
SPEEDIER AND MEANS OF COMMUNICATION INSTANTANEOUS IN RECENT
YEARS, INFORMATION ABOUT EVENTS IN MOST OF THE WORLD IS MORE
DIFFICULT TO OBTAIN. THERE ARE MANY REASONS FOR THIS DECLINE
OR REGRESSION IN THE ABILITY OF JOURNALISTS TO KEEP THEIR
READERS INFORMED ABOUT HAPPENINGS IN THE NON-WESTERN WORLD,
INCLUDING THE WORLD OF ISLAM. POLITICAL CONDITIONS IN MANY
COUNTRIES IN ASIA AND AFRICA HAVE SINCE THE ADVENT OF
INDEPENDENCE PUT GREATER OBSTACLES IN THE PATH OF REPORTERS.
INFORMATION ABOUT CURRENT EVENTS HAS BECOME A MATTER OF
STATE, TO BE MANIPULATED OR SUPPRESSED IN THE INTEREST OF
THE RULERS. MOREOVER, NEWSPAPER READERSHIP HAS CHANGED
GREATLY WITH THE ADVENT OF MASS LITERACY. TODAY'S MASS
READERSHIP HAS A MUCH NARROWER, LESS INFORMED INTEREST IN
PUBLIC AFFAIRS THAN THE ELITE READERS OF YESTERDAY.

04939 KEECH, W.R.; PAK, K.
ELECTORAL CYCLES AND BUDGETARY GROWTH IN VETERANS' BENEFIT
PROGRAMS
AMERICAN JOURNAL OF POLITICAL SCIENCE, 33(4) (NOV 89),
901-911.
WHILE MANY STUDIES HAVE GENERATED NEGATIVE FINDINGS
REGARDING THE GENERAL EXISTENCE OF ELECTORAL CYCLES IN
ECONOMIC PHENOMENA, WE HAVE FOUND AN APPARENTLY ROBUST
ELECTORAL CYCLE IN VETERANS' BENEFITS. THIS PATTERN WAS
FOUND BETWEEN 1961 AND 1978, BUT HAS DISAPPEARED SINCE THEN.
THIS ARTICLE USES THIS CASE TO INVESTIGATE THE POSSIBILITY
THAT ELECTORAL CYCLES MIGHT CONTRIBUTE TO THE GROWTH OF
GOVERNMENT SPENDING. USING TWO DIFFERENT METHODS OF
INFERENCE, IT FINDS NO STRONG BASIS TO CONCLUDE THAT SUCH
CYCLES CAUSE INCREASING PUBLIC SECTOR GROWTH.

04940 KEEN, M.
MAKING THE MOST OF AFRICAN AGRICULTURE
AFRICAN BUSINESS, (AUG 88), 14-15.
THIS ARTICLE REPORTS ON THE NINTH AGI-ENERGY ROUND-TABLE
HELD IN GENEVA IN JUNE OF 1988 WHICH WAS ORGANISED TO HELP
DEVELOPING COUNTRIES TO MAKE THE MOST OF THEIR AGRICULTURAL
RESOURCES TWO ISSUES RAISED AT THE CONFERENCE WITH
PARTICULAR RELEVANCE TO AFRICA ARE EXAMINED: 1) THE DEBATE
OVER THE DISBANDMENT OF AGRICULTURAL MARKETING BOARDS, AND
2) HOW AFRICA MIGHT ENCOURAGE MORE FOREIGN INVESTMENTS.

04941 KEENES, E.
PARADIGMS OF INTERNATIONAL RELATIONS: BRINGING POLITICS
BACK IN
INTERNATIONAL JOURNAL, XLIV(1) (WIN 89), 41-67.
THE AUTHOR ENDEAVORS TO GIVE RENEWED DIRECTION TO THE
INTER-PARADIGM DEBATE IN INTERNATIONAL RELATIONS. HE ARGUES
THAT THE DEBATE SHOULD NOT BE ENTIRELY A COMPETITIVE AND
COMPARATIVE SEARCH FOR A GENERAL THEORY OF INTERNATIONAL
RELATIONS THAT ESTABLISHES THE LEGITIMATE PARAMETERS OF THE
FIELD. YET, AT THE SAME TIME, PLURALISM, RELATIVISM, AND
INCOMMENSURABILITY SHOULD NOT PUSH THE VARIOUS PARADIGMS
INTO BEING SIMPLY IDEALIST WORLD-VIEWS OR TEXTS THAT BEAR A
CONTESTED CORRESPONDENCE WITH REALITY. THE AUTHOR'S INTENT
IS TO GIVE RENEWED CLARITY TO THE EXPLICITLY POLITICAL
CONTENT OF THE PARADIGMS, TO SHOW HOW EACH EXPRESSES THE
WORLD AS A MORE OR LESS DISTINCTIVE, YET NOT EXCLUSIVE,
POLITICAL SPACE.

04942 KEGLEY, C.K. JR.
THE BUSH ADMINISTRATION AND THE FUTURE OF AMERICAN FOREIGN
POLICY: PRAGMATISM, OR PROCRASTINATION?
PRESIDENTIAL STUDIES QUARTERLY, 19(4) (FAL 89), 717-732.
THIS ARTICLE PRESENTS A PESSIMISTIC PORTRAYAL OF
AMERICAN FOREIGN POLICY. IT PORTRAYS CONTINUITY IN AMERICAN
FOREIGN POLICY SINCE THE BEGINNINGS OF THE COLD WAR IN 1945
AND SUGGESTS THAT THE BUSH ADMINISTRATION IS NOT PREPARED TO
CHANGE THOSE POLICIES. IT PORTRAYS AN ADMINISTRATION
UNRESPONSIVE TO NEW OPPORTUNITIES AND QUARRELS WITH THE VIEW
THAT DEEDS ARE MORE IMPORTANT THAN WORDS IN JUDGING SOVIET
POLICY.

04943 KEITH, R.C.
WHAT HAPPENED TO CHINESE "DEMOCRACY?"
INTERNATIONAL PERSPECTIVES, 18(4) (JUL 89), 3-4.
CHINA KEEPS THE EDITORS OF "INTERNATIONAL PERSPECTIVES"
TROUBLED BY THEIR INABILITY TO UNDERSTAND WHAT IS EXACTLY
HAPPENING. THEY SUGGEST THAT SOME OF THAT BEWILDERMENT CAN
BE REDUCED BY A KNOWLEDGE OF THE RECENT PAST OF THE CHINESE
COMMUNIST PARTY AND ITS LEADERS. A UNIVERSITY OF CALGARY
SCHOLAR, RONALD KEITH, NARROWS THAT GAP BY EXPLORING THE
ABSENCE OF PRAGMATISM IN THE CHARACTER OF DENG XIAOPING, HIS
ALLEGIENCE TO SOCIALISM, AND HIS REJECTION OF "BALANCE OF
POWER."

04944 KEITH, S.R.
THE FIRST POLITICAL SCIENTIST: HERODOTUS OF HALICARNASSUS
DISSERTATION ABSTRACTS INTERNATIONAL, 50(6) (DEC 89),
1788-A.
THE AUTHOR REVIEWS HERODOTUS' INVESTIGATIONS IN EGYPT,
HIS THEORY OF HUMAN NATURE AND POLITICAL ORGANIZATION AS

REVEALED BY THE PRIMITIVE PEOPLES OF RUSSIA AND AFRICA, HOW
HIS THEORY EXPLAINS HIS RECOUNTING OF POLITICAL EVENTS, AND
HIS "DEBATE ON GOVERNMENT."

04945 KELLAS, J. G.
SCOTTISH AND WELSH PARTIES
CONTEMPORARY RECORD, 2(6) (SUM 89), 8-11.
THE AUTHOR SURVEYS NATIONALIST POLITICAL PARTIES IN
WALES AND SCOTLAND.

04946 KELLAS, J.G.
PROSPECTS FOR A NEW SCOTTISH POLITICAL SYSTEM
PARLIAMENTARY AFFAIRS, 42(4) (OCT 89), 319-532.
THIS ARTICLE EXPLORES A NEW PHASE IN THE POLITICS OF
SCOTLAND, ENTERED INTO IN 1989. IN ORDER TO UNDERSTAND
SCOTTISH POLITICS, IT EXAMINES BOTH THE STRUCTURE OF
POLITICAL INSTITUTIONS IN SCOTLAND AND THE POLITICAL
BEHAVIOR OF THE SCOTTISH PEOPLE. THE DEMAND FOR
CONSTITUTIONAL CHANGE TOWARDS DEVOLUTION AND INDEPENDENCE IS
DETAILED, AS WELL AS THE DESIRE FOR A PEACEFUL TRANSITION TO
DEVOLUTION AND TO SOME KIND OF REPRESENTATION IN THE EC.

04947 KELLEHER, F.A.
GENDER, STATE POLICY, AND PROFESSIONAL POLITICS: PRIMARY
SCHOOL TEACHERS IN FRANCE, 1880-1920
DISSERTATION ABSTRACTS INTERNATIONAL, 49(9) (MAR 89),
2781-A.
BETWEEN 1880 AND 1914, NATIONAL POLICIES BASED ON
POLITICAL AND IDEOLOGICAL CONSIDERATIONS PROVIDED THE
CATALYST FOR THE RAPID ENTRY OF LAY WOMEN INTO PRIMARY
SCHOOL TEACHING IN FRANCE. BECAUSE THE STATE PRESERVED A SEX-
SEGREGATED SYSTEM, TEACHING ASSIGNMENTS AND ROLE
DESCRIPTIONS WERE GENDER-SPECIFIC AND EXPLICITLY POLITICAL.
INCORPORATION INTO THE CIVIL SERVICE SYSTEM VASTLY ENHANCED
FEMALE CAREER PROSPECTS WHILE BLOCKING MOBILITY FOR YOUNGER
MEN. THE RESULT WAS A FRAGMENTATION OF INTERESTS AND THE
DEVELOPMENT OF SEVERAL DISTINCT SELF-DEFINITIONS AMONG
TEACHERS.

04948 KELLER, E.J.
REVOLUTIONARY ETHIOPIA: FROM EMPIRE TO PEOPLE'S REPUBLIC
INDIANA UNIVERSITY PRESS, BLOOMINGTON, IN, 1989, 320.
ALTHOUGH A POLITICALLY ASTUTE STATESMAN, EMPEROR HAILE
SELASSIE WAS UNABLE TO COPE WITH THE ECONOMIC, SOCIAL, AND
POLITICAL CRISES THAT OCCURRED DURING THE MODERNIZATION OF
HIS BUREAUCRATIC STATE AND EVENTUALLY PRECIPITATED THE
REVOLUTION. IN THIS BOOK, THE AUTHOR EXAMINES THE CAUSES OF
THE REVOLUTION AND THE ENSUING SOCIALIST REGIME'S
UNSUCCESSFUL EFFORTS TO RECONSTITUTE ETHIOPIAN SOCIETY ON
THE FOUNDATIONS OF A NEW INSTITUTIONS AND A NEW SOCIAL MYTH.

04949 KELLER, L.F.
CITY MANAGEMENT, PUBLIC ADMINISTRATION AND THE AMERICAN
ENLIGHTENMENT
INTERNATIONAL JOURNAL OF PUBLIC ADMINISTRATION, 12(2)
(1989), 213-249.
HISTORY HAS OFTEN BEEN IGNORED IN EXAMINING
ADMINISTRATION AT THE LOCAL LEVEL. IN THIS ARTICLE THE
CAREERS OF THREE PUBLIC ADMINISTRATORS ARE STUDIES, TWO
ACADEMICS AND A PRACTITIONER. THE PRACTITIONER HELPED SHAPE
CITY MANAGEMENT AND THE IDEALS OF THE TWO ACADEMICS
CHARACTERIZE THE FIELD AT THAT TIME. THE FOUNDATIONS THEY
LAID HAVE IN MANY WAYS PROVED LONG LASTING IN SPITE OF THEIR
BELIEFS IN SOME DUBIOUS ASSUMPTIONS. MOST IMPORTANTLY, THESE
FOUNDATIONS ARE RELEVANT FOR THE FUTURE ADMINISTRATION OF
THE AMERICAN CITY.

04950 KELLEY, A.E.; BOWMAN, L.; HULBARY, W.E.
GENDER, PARTY, AND POLITICAL IDEOLOGY: THE CASE OF MID-
ELITE PARTY ACTIVISTS IN FLORIDA
JOURNAL OF POLITICAL SCIENCE, 17(1-2) (1989), 6-18.
THE AUTHORS DOCUMENT THE IMPORTANCE OF GENDER AS A
VARIABLE IN ACCOUNTING FOR POLITICAL ATTITUDES AMONG PARTY
ACTIVISTS IN FLORIDA. UTILIZING A 1984 SURVEY, THE AUTHORS
DEVELOP A POLITICAL IDEOLOGY SCALE THAT THEY RELATE TO
GENDER, PARTY, AND SOCIAL CHARACTERISTICS. THEY FIND THAT
PARTISANSHIP IS THE MAJOR DISCRIMINATING VARIABLE BUT THAT
GENDER IS OFTEN RELATED TO IDEOLOGICAL DIFFERENCES AMONG
PARTY ACTIVISTS, REGARDLESS OF PARTY AFFILIATION. SOCIAL
CHARACTERISTICS EXPLAIN WHY SOME WOMEN AND MEN ARE MORE
LIBERAL OR CONSERVATIVE THAT WOULD BE EXPECTED ON THE BASIS
OF PARTISANSHIP ALONE.

04951 KELLEY, B.C.
FUTURE OF THE MEXICAN POLITICAL SYSTEM
AVAILABLE FROM NTIS, NO. AD-A208 127/1/GAR, MAR 89, 153.
THIS THESIS IS AN ASSESSMENT OF THE VIABILITY AND
SUSTAINABILITY OF THE MEXICAN CORPORATIST POLITICAL SYSTEM
INSTITUTED IN 1929. WHAT IS THE FUTURE OF MEXICAN POLITICS
OVER THE NEXT 20 YEARS. SINCE 1929, THIS SYSTEM OF
GOVERNMENT HAS BEEN THE MOST STABLE IN LATIN AMERICA. THERE
HAVE BEEN NO PRESIDENTIAL ASSASSINATIONS, NO MILITARY COUPS,
AND NO EARLY DEPARTURES FROM OFFICE: ALL THE ABOVE BEING
ACCOMPLISHED WITH A JUDICIOUS BLEND OF REPRESSION AND CO-

OPTATION. HOWEVER, THERE ARE SIGNS THAT THE FLEXIBILITY OF
THIS SYSTEM IS NO LONGER SUFFICIENT TO MAINTAIN GOVERNMENT
IN ITS CURRENT FORM. THROUGH A LOOK AT THE CAUSES OF THE
1911 REVOLUTION, THE RESULTING POLITICAL STRUCTURE, THE
CURRENT PROBLEMS, AND THE ATTEMPTS AT REFORM, WHAT BECOMES
APPARENT IS THAT SOME TYPE OF CHANGE SEEMS ALMOST
UNAVOIDABLE. JUST WHAT THIS CHANGE MIGHT BE, TO INCLUDE THE
TIMING AND FORM OF SAID CHANGE, IS THE FOCUS OF THIS THESIS.

04952 KELLEY, D.M.
     STATISM, NOT SEPARATIONISM, IS THE PROBLEM
     THE CHRISTIAN CENTURY, 106(2) (JAN 89), 48-52.
     THE AUTHOR DISCUSSES SEPARATION OF CHURCH AND STATE. HE
CONSIDERS THE ELIGIBILITY OF CHURCH-RELATED AGENCIES FOR TAX
FUNDS TO PERFORM PUBLIC SERVICES.

04953 KELLEY, P. C.
     THE POLITICAL STRATEGIES OF TRADE ASSOCIATIONS: A GROUNDED
     THEORY STUDY (VOLUMES I-II)
     DISSERTATION ABSTRACTS INTERNATIONAL, 49(9) (MAR 89),
     2712-A.
     THE AUTHOR SEEKS TO DETERMINE THE PRECONDITIONS FOR
POLITICAL INVOLVEMENT BY TRADE ASSOCIATIONS, TO IDENTIFY THE
POLITICAL BEHAVIORS OF TRADE ASSOCIATIONS, TO INFER THE
FACTORS THAT SHAPE THESE BEHAVIORS, AND TO DETERMINE THE
GENERAL CHARACTERISTICS OF POLITICAL ACTIVITY AMONG TRADE
ASSOCIATIONS.

04954 KELLNER, P.
     ADAPTING TO THE POSTWAR CONSENSUS: LABOR
     CONTEMPORARY RECORD, 3(2) (NOV 89), 13-15.
     THIS SYMPOSIUM FOCUSES ON THE TWO CANADIAN RADICAL
GOVERNMENTS SINCE 1945: THE LABOR GOVERNMENT OF 1945-51
WHICH ESTABLISHED POSTWAR CONCENSUS; AND THE CONSERVATIVE
GOVERNMENT SINCE 1979, WHICH HAS LARGELY DISMANTLED IT. IT
DISCUSSES HOW LABOR HAS CHANGED ITS POLICIES AND IMAGE UNDER
THE STIMULUS OF THE THATCHER GOVERNMENTS, IT DESCRIBES LABOR
FROM 1979 TO 1983, THE KINNOCK REVOLUTION, AND WHY KINNOCK
SUCCEEDED WHERE GAITSKELL FAILED, THE TWO PHASES OF CHANGE
ARE DETAILED.

04955 KELLOGG, P.
     STATE, CAPITAL AND WORLD ECONOMY: BUKHARIN'S MARXISM AND
     THE "DEPENDENCY/CLASS" CONTROVERSY IN CANADIAN POLITICAL
     ECONOMY
     CANADIAN JOURNAL OF POLITICAL SCIENCE, XXII(2) (JUN 89),
     337-362.
     IN THE LATE 1960S AND EARLY 1970S, "LEFT-NATIONALIST"
DEPENDENCY THEORIES DOMINATED CANADIAN POLITICAL ECONOMY.
HOWEVER, CANADA DEFIED THE PREDICTIONS OF DEPENDENCY THEORY
AND DEVELOPED ALL THE CLASS RELATIONS APPROPRIATE TO
ADVANCED CAPITALIST SOCIETIES. THE ORIGINS OF CANADIAN
INDUSTRIAL CAPITALISM HERE NOT SUCH THAT THE COUNTRY WAS
LOCKED INTO A STAPLE-TRAP, NOTWITHSTANDING THE VERY REAL
RELIANCE OF THE ECONOMY ON STAPLE-EXPORT. IN RECENT YEARS, A
NUMBER OF POLITICAL ECONOMISTS HAVE OFFERED AN "ORTHODOX"
MARXIST CRITIQUE OF DEPENDENCY TO ACCOUNT FOR THESE AND
OTHER WEAKNESS IN ITS OVERALL FRAMEWORK. THIS ARTICLE FIRST
SUMMARIZES THE DEPENDENCY ARGUMENTS, THEN THE ARGUMENTS OF
ITS MARXIST CRITICS, AND FINALLY INTRODUCES A SUMMARY LOOK
AT THE IDEAS OF NIKOLAI BUKHARIN, A LITTLE-EXAMINED BUT
NONETHELESS IMPORTANT THEORIST WHOSE INSIGHTS ON THE
RELATIONSHIP BETWEEN THE STATE AS A CAPITALIST AND THE
GROWING INTERNATIONALIZATION OF ECONOMIC LIFE ARE KEY TO A
MARXIST RE-THEORIZATION OF CANADIAN POLITICAL ECONOMY.

04956 KELLOUGH, J.E.
     THE 1978 CIVIL SERVICE REFORM AND FEDERAL EQUAL EMPLOYMENT
     OPPORTUNITY
     AMERICAN REVIEW OF PUBLIC ADMINISTRATION, 19(4) (DEC 89),
     313-324.
     THE ISSUE OF FEDERAL EQUAL EMPLOYMENT OPPORTUNITY (EEO)
IS EXPLORED BY EXAMINING EMPLOYMENT TRENDS FOR BLACKS AND
WOMEN IN MIDDLE- AND HIGHER-LEVEL POSITIONS AND LOOKING FOR
POSSIBLE IMPACTS OF ELEMENTS OF THE 1978 CIVIL SERVICE
REFORM DESIGNED TO ADVANCE EEO. USING AN INTERRUPTED TIME-
SERIES MULTIPLE-REGRESSION MODEL, THE RATE OF INCREASE IN
BLACK EMPLOYMENT WAS FOUND TO DECLINE SLIGHTLY FOLLOWING THE
REFORM. FOR WOMEN, HOWEVER, LONG-TERM EMPLOYMENT TRENDS IN
THE MIDDLE-LEVEL GRADES APPEAR UNCHANGED, WHEREAS THE
EMPLOYMENT RATE IN HIGHER GRADES INCREASED FOLLOWING THE
1978 REFORM.

04957 KELLY, H.; WYCKOFF, A.
     STATISTICS AND POLICY: DISTORTING ECONOMIC ACTIVITY
     CURRENT, (314) (JUL 89), 22-27.
     GOVERNMENT STATISTICS ARE AT THE CENTER OF THE AMERICAN
INFORMATION-BASED ECONOMY. BUT THE FEDERAL GOVERNMENT FACES
A CRISIS IN THE WAY IT COLLECTS, ANALYZES, AND DISSEMINATES
INFORMATION. THE ABILITY TO FORM A REALISTIC PICTURE OF
WHAT'S HAPPENING TO THE ECONOMY AND TO AMERICAN SOCIETY IS
GETTING WORSE RATHER THAN BETTER. AND THIS IS MAKING IT MORE
DIFFICULT TO MAKE GOOD PUBLIC POLICY AND GOOD BUSINESS
DECISIONS.

04958 KELLY, J.; WOOLCOCK, S.
     GATT: A MID-TERM AGREEMENT
     WORLD TODAY, 45(6) (JUN 89), 92-93.
     ON APRIL 8, 1989, SENIOR TRADE OFFICIALLY REACHED
AGREEMENT ON THE GATT URUGUAY ROUND MID-TERM REVIEW AND
AVERTED THE POTENTIAL COLLAPSE OF THE NEGOTIATIONS OVER A
DISPUTE ON AGRICULTURAL POLICY BETWEEN THE USA AND THE
EUROPEAN COMMUNITY. PROGRESS WAS ALSO MADE IN THREE OTHER
PROBLEM AREAS: INTELLECTUAL PROPERTY, TEXTILES, AND
SAFEGUARDS.

04959 KELLY, J.A.
     THE UNITED STATES IN SOUTHEAST ASIA: A POLITICAL-SECURITY
     AGENDA
     WASHINGTON QUARTERLY, 12(4) (FAL 89), 113-122.
     U.S. POLICIES IN SOUTHEAST ASIA NEED A NEW ASSESSMENT-
CIRCUMSTANCES DIFFER GREATLY FROM THOSE THAT SHAPED THE
CURRENT BASIC U.S. APPROACH. THIS ARTICLE MAKES THREE
PRELIMINARY OBSERVATIONS ABOUT THE ENVIRONMENT SHAPING U.S.
POLICY AND LOOKS TOWARD ENDING THE 1980S AND STARTING THE
1990S, IT THEN OFFERS POLICY PRESCRIPTIONS FOR THE UNITED
STATES AND ALERTS THE U.S. TO SOME DANGERS TO BE AVOIDED, IT
CONCLUDES THAT THE BEGINNING OF A NEW ADMINISTRATION IS A
GOOD TIME TO MAKE THE ASSESSMENT.

04960 KELLY, J.H.
     RECENT EVENTS IN THE MIDDLE EAST
     DEPARTMENT OF STATE BULLETIN (US FOREIGN POLICY), 89(2152)
     (NOV 89), 61-63.
     THE AUTHOR, WHO IS ASSISTANT SECRETARY OF STATE FOR NEAR
EASTERN AND SOUTH ASIAN AFFAIRS, DISCUSSES EVENTS OCCURRING
IN THE FALL OF 1989 IN THE MIDDLE EAST, LEBANON, AND IRAN.
HE FOCUSES ON PROGRESS IN THE MIDEAST PEACE PROCESS.

04961 KELLY, J.H.
     U.S. DIPLOMACY IN THE MIDDLE EAST
     DEPARTMENT OF STATE BULLETIN (US FOREIGN POLICY), 89(2151)
     (OCT 89), 44-45.
     THE AUTHOR, WHO IS THE STATE DEPARTMENT'S ASSISTANT
SECRETARY FOR NEAR EASTERN AND SOUTH ASIAN AFFAIRS,
DISCUSSES AMERICAN DIPLOMATIC POLICY IN THE MIDEAST,
INCLUDING THE US DIALOGUE WITH THE PLO AND THE PROSPECTS FOR
IMPROVED RELATIONS WITH IRAN FOLLOWING KHOMEINI'S DEATH.

04962 KELLY, R.M.; BURGESS, J.
     GENDER AND THE MEANING OF POWER AND POLITICS
     WOMEN AND POLITICS, 9(1) (1989), 47-82.
     THIS PAPER EXAMINES THE EXTENT TO WHICH WOMEN AS A GROUP
HAVE A DISTINCTIVE UNDERSTANDING OF POLITICS AND POWER.
USING THE THEORETICAL FRAMEWORK OF THE PERCEPTUAL-
REPRESENTATIONAL SYSTEM AND THE ASSOCIATIVE GROUP ANALYSIS
(AGA) METHODOLOGY, THE STUDY EXAMINES THE SUBJECTIVE
DIFFERENCES IN POLITICAL MEANINGS OF 148 MALE AND FEMALE
DELEGATES ATTENDING THEIR RESPECTIVE DEMOCRATIC AND
REPUBLICAN NATIONAL CONVENTIONS IN 1984. THE DATA DO NOT
INDICATE THAT A UNIQUE MALE OR FEMALE SUBJECTIVE POLITICAL
CULTURE EXISTS. BOTH REPUBLICAN MEN AND DEMOCRATIC WOMEN
COMPREHEND A POLITICS OF CONNECTEDNESS. THEY DIFFER IN TERMS
OF THE NATURE, PURPOSES, AND TYPE OF CONNECTEDNESS.

04963 KELLY, T.J.
     SOVIET AFGHANISTAN EXPERIENCE AS A REFLECTION OF SOVIET
     STRATEGIC CULTURE
     AVAILABLE FROM NTIS, NO. AD-A209 189/0/GAR, MAY 4 89, 80.
     SOVIET STRATEGIC CULTURE IS A HISTORICAL CONCEPT WHICH
DESCRIBES THE CHARACTERISTIC SOVIET APPROACHES TO
INTERNATIONAL AFFAIRS. IN ITS MOST DEVELOPED, UTILITARIAN
FORM, IT PROJECTS PROBABLE SOVIET POLITICAL AND DIPLOMATIC
BEHAVIOR. THE SOVIET INVASION OF AFGHANISTAN AND SUBSEQUENT
OPERATIONS PROVIDE A PERSPECTIVE FROM WHICH TO JUDGE SOVIET
CONSISTENCY WITH THEIR NORMALLY EXPECTED METHODS. THIS PAPER
EXAMINES SOVIET PERFORMANCE IN AFGHANISTAN TO DETERMINE ITS
CONSISTENCY WITH SOVIET STRATEGIC CULTURE. CONCLUSIONS AND
IMPLICATIONS ARE DRAWN WHICH SHOW THE SOVIET WITHDRAWAL FROM
AFGHANISTAN AS A SIGNIFICANT DEPARTURE FROM THE TRADITIONS
OF SOVIET STRATEGIC CULTURE. ONGOING SOVIET ATTEMPTS TO
MASSIVELY RESTRUCTURE THEIR SYSTEM THUS PORTEND A PERIOD OF
GREAT AMBIGUITY. GENERAL SECRETARY GORBACHEV'S NEW THINKING
CONFOUNDS THE USE OF THIS HISTORICAL CONCEPT. HENCE, THE
UTILITY OF SOVIET STRATEGIC CULTURE AS A PREDICTIVE CONCEPT
SEEMS GREATLY REDUCED.

04964 KELMAN, S.
     MAKING PUBLIC POLICY: A HOPEFUL VIEW OF AMERICAN GOVERNMENT
     BASIC BOOKS, NEW YORK, NY, 1987, 332.
     THE AUTHOR ANALYZES THE MAJOR INSTITUTIONS OF AMERICAN
GOVERNMENT: CONGRESS, THE PRESIDENCY, THE BUREAUCRACY, AND
THE SUPREME COURT. THEN THE ASSESSES THE POLICY MAKING
PROCESS IN AMERICAN GOVERNMENT.

04965 KELSEY, T.
     FREEDOM UP FOR THE CHOP
     SOUTH, (110) (DEC 89), 129.

TURKISH PRIME MINISTER TURGUT OZAL MAKES NO SECRET OF HIS HOSTILITY TOWARD THE PRESS. THE GOVERNMENT CURRENTLY IS PURSUING 35 LEGAL ACTIONS, RANGING FROM SLANDER TO THE ILLEGAL PUBLICATION OF A DEATH NOTICE, AND IN MOST OZAL IS INSISTING ON PRISON TERMS. THE PUBLICATION OF AN ARTICLE ABOUT CORRUPTION IN THE HIGHEST ECHELONS OF THE TURKISH GOVERNMENT HAS DRAWN THE MOST ANGER FROM OZAL.

04966 KELSEY, T.
RENAISSANCE BEGINS IN IRAQ'S SHATTERED CITIES
SOUTH, (109) (NOV 89), 40-41.
NOTHING INDICATES MORE CLEARLY IRAQ'S COMMITMENT TO RECONSTRUCTION THAN THE FEVERISH ACTIVITY AT THE SOUTHERN PORTS OF BASRA AND FAW, WHICH WERE HEAVILY DAMAGED DURING THE GULF WAR. THE DRIVE HAS THE AIR OF A CRUSADE, AS THE IRAQIS OFFER IT AS EVIDENCE THAT THE COUNTRY IS COMMITTED TO LASTING PEACE. BUT THE RECONSTRUCTION IS EXACTING A HEAVY PRICE IN AN ECONOMY ON THE BRINK OF COLLAPSE.

04967 KEMP, J.
EARLY PHASED DEPLOYMENT OF SDI AS A NATIONAL INSURANCE POLICY
JOURNAL OF LEGISLATION, 15(2) (1989), 81-88.
THE ESSAY EXAMINES THE POLICY REASONS FOR THE ACCELERATED PHASED DEPLOYMENT OF SDI. IT DISCUSSES SOVIET ARMS CONTROL VIOLATIONS AND SOVIET INITIAVES IN SPACE AND FOCUSES ON THE SOVIET NEGOTIATIONS PUSH AGAINST SDI. IT EXPLAINS THE RATIONALE SUPPORTING A US GO-AHEAD FOR ACCELERATED SDI DEPLOYMENT AND CONSIDERS AN ACCIDENTAL LAUNCH PROTECTION SYSTEM PLAN AS A FIRST STEP. THE ESSAY CONCLUDES WITH AN EVALUATION OF THE FUTURE OF SDI.

04968 KEMP, S.
WOMEN IN THE STRUGGLE FOR PEACE
SECHABA, 23(7) (JUL 89), 13-15.
THOUGH SOME IMPORTANT LAWS HAD BEEN CHANGED AS A START TO ADDRESSING THE PROBLEMS FACED BY WOMEN IN ZIMBABWE, DISCRIMINATION AGAINST WOMEN REMAINS A BARRIER DIFFICULT TO OVERCOME. AT THE "WOMEN IN THE STRUGGLE FOR PEACE" CONFERENCE IN HARARE ZIMBABWEAN WOMEN STRESSED THE IMPORTANCE OF INTEGRATING THE STRUGGLE FOR WOMEN'S EMANCIPATION WITH THE STRUGGLE FOR NATIONAL LIBERATION. ONE OF THE ERRORS MADE AFTER INDEPENDENCE WAS IN NOT ORGANISING THE WOMEN WHO HAD SUPPORTED THE STRUGGLE IN THE RURAL AREAS.

04969 KEMPELMAN, M.
DIPLOMACY IN AN ELECTION YEAR AND BEYOND
WORLD AFFAIRS, 151(3) (WIN 89), 99-103.
MAX KAMPELMAN, COUNSELOR OF THE STATE DEPARTMENT, SPEAKS OF THE GROWING IMPORTANCE OF DIPLOMACY IN THE CHANGING GLOBAL CONDITIONS THAT ARE SURE TO CONTINUE IN THE FUTURE. HE ANALYZES THE MORAL IMPLICATIONS OF DIPLOMACY, WAR, AND PEACE, AND GIVES THESE CONCEPTS SPECIFIC APPLICATION WITH REGARDS TO THE RECENT CHANGES IN THE SOVIET UNION. HE ARGUES THAT THE CHANGES IN THE USSR MUST BE MET WITH PRUDENCE AND FLEXIBILITY. HE CONCLUDES Y DISCUSSING THE IMPORTANCE OF FREEDOM AND ITS RELATIONSHIP TO SOCIETIES OF THE FUTURE.

04970 KEMPER, V.
THE ROAD TO PALESTINE
SOJOURNERS, 18(4) (APR 89), 14-24.
ISRAEL'S OCCUPATION OF THE WEST BANK AND GAZA STRIP IS, IN ITS MOST BASIC FORM, THE MIDDLE EASTERN INCARNATION OF APARTHEID. ONE RACIAL AND ETHNIC GROUP HAS, THROUGH A SUCCESSION OF WARS, LAND SEIZURES, ECONOMIC ARRANGEMENTS, AND UNJUST LAWS AND POLICIES, CREATED A TWO-TIERED, SHARPLY SEGREGATED SOCIETY IN WHICH THE RIGHTS AND PRIVILEGES OF ONE GROUP ARE GAINED AND PRESERVED THROUGH THE DELIBERATE EXPLOITATION AND OPRESSION OF ANOTHER.

04971 KENDE, I.
ROLE AND POSSIBILITIES OF NON-NUCLEAR STATES IN EUROPE
PEACE AND THE SCIENCES, 1 (1989), 54-60.
PRESENT DAY EUROPEAN CONDITIONS OFFER MANY POSSIBILITIES OF DIFFERENT TYPES FOR TAKING STEPS TO INCREASE SECURITY. EVERY EUROPEAN COUNTRY, NO MATTER OF WHAT SOCIAL SYSTEM, OF WHICH MILITARY DOCTRINE OR OF WHICH MILITARY ALLIANCE, HAS THE POSSIBILITY TO INITIATE SUCH STEPS, TO PARTICIPATE IN SUCH ACTIONS OR JOIN THEM. THE NON-NUCLEAR COUNTRIES CAN PLAY ROLES WHICH MAY SIGNIFICANTLY INFLUENCE THE EUROPEAN SITUATION, BY TAKING A COMMON STAND, PARTICULARLY IF THEY AGREE ON JOINT ACTIONS. AGREEMENTS OF THIS TYPE CAN CONTRIBUTE TO THE FURTHER STRENGTHENING OF MUTUAL CONFIDENCE, HELP TO TAKE STEPS TO CONTINUE REDUCING TENSION OR PROCEED IN DISARMAMENT, AND FINALLY, TO CONSOLIDATE COMMON SECURITY IN EUROPE.

04972 KENDRICK, S.; MC CRONE, D.
POLITICS IN A COLD CLIMATE: THE CONSERVATIVE DECLINE IN SCOTLAND
POLITICAL STUDIES, XXXVII(4) (DEC 89), 589-603.
AN IMPORTANT FEATURE OVER THE LAST 30 YEARS HAS BEEN THE INCREASING SHORTFALL IN THE CONSERVATIVE VOTE IN SCOTLAND COMPARED WITH ENGLAND. THE CONSERVATIVE PARTY, DESPITE

SOCIAL STRUCTURAL DISADVANTAGES IN TERMS OF HOUSING TENURE AND SOCIAL CLASS, DID USUALLY WELL UNTIL THE MID-1950S, PARTICULARLY AMONG UNIONISTS AND PROTESTANTS. AFTER CONSIDERING THE HISTORICAL AND RELIGIOUS FACTORS EXPLAINING EARLIER CONSERVATIVE POLITICAL STRENGTH, IT IS ARGUED THAT TWO FACTORS HELP TO EXPLAIN THE CHANGING POLITICS OF THE STATE IN SCOTLAND: THE ESTABLISHMENT OF SCOTLAND AS A SEPARATE UNIT OF ECONOMIC MANAGEMENT IN POPULAR PERCEPTION AND THE GREATER DEPENDENCE ON DIRECT STATE INVOLVEMENT. THE SCOTTISH ECONOMIC DIMENSION HAS MADE SCOTLAND AN IDEOLOGICAL CATEGORY LARGELY INCOMPATIBLE WITH CONSERVATIVE ENGLISH /BRITISH NATIONAL RHETORIC AS EMPLOYED BY MRS THATCHER.

04973 KENNAN, G.F.
AFTER THE COLD WAR
PARAMETERS, XIX(3) (SEP 89), 97-104.
TO PROMOTE THE NORMALIZATION OF EAST-WEST RELATIONS AND TO SHAPE THE FUTURE IN A MANNER COMMENSURATE WITH ITS POSITIVE POSSIBILITIES, AMERICA'S FIRST CONCERN SHOULD BE TO REMOVE, INSOFAR AS IT LIES WITHIN ITS POWER TO DO SO, THOSE FEATURES OF U.S. POLICY AND PRACTICE THAT HAVE THEIR ORIGINS AND RATIONALE IN OUTDATED COLD WAR ASSUMPTIONS AND, THEREFORE, LACK CURRENT JUSTIFICATION. TO SOME EXTENT, THIS HAS ALREADY BEEN DONE. CULTURAL EXCHANGES AND PEOPLE-TO-PEOPLE CONTACTS ARE PROCEEDING BRISKLY, AND THE SAME MAY BE SAID OF SCHOLARLY EXCHANGES. PROGRESS HAS ALSO BEEN MADE IN THE COMMERCIAL FIELD, BUT OBSTACLES REMAIN. THERE IS NO PRESENT JUSTIFICATION FOR THESE OBSTACLES AND REMOVING THEM SHOULD PRESENT NO PROBLEMS.

04974 KENNEDY, B.
REFINANCING THE CPP: THE COST OF ACQUIESCENCE
CANADIAN PUBLIC POLICY--ANALYSE DE POLITIQUES, XV(1) (MAR 89), 34-42.
THIS ARTICLE SCRUTINIZES THE RELATIONSHIP BETWEEN THE CPP AND THE PROVINCES UNDER THE NEW CPP FINANCIAL ARRANGEMENTS. IT BRIEFLY RECALLS THE GENESIS OF THE CPP AND THAT OF ITS CLOSE RELATIVE, THE QUEBEC PENSION PLAN. THE FINANCIAL ARRANGEMENTS IN EFFECT FROM 1966 THROUGH 1986 ARE THEN ALONG WITH SOME OF THE OPTIONS FOR REFORM THAT WERE EXPLORED BY THE DEPARTMENT OF INSURANCE. THESE ARE CONTRASTED WITH THE NEW FINANCIAL ARRANGEMENTS PUT INTO EFFECT IN JANUARY 1987. THE CONCLUSION DRAWN FROM COMPARISON OF THESE ARRANGEMENTS IS THAT THE CPP IS AND WILL CONTINUE TO BE A PROGRAM INTENDED TO SERVE TWO QUITE DISTINCT PURPOSES: PAYING PENSIONS AND RAISING REVENUE FOR PROVINCIAL GOVERNMENTS. SPECIFICALLY, THE EFFECTIVE TRANSFER FROM THE CPP TO THE PROVINCES IS ESTIMATED TO BE ABOUT $1.2 BILLION PER YEAR.

04975 KENNEDY, M.; BIATECKI, I.
POWER AND THE LOGIC OF DISTRIBUTION IN POLAND
EASTERN EUROPEAN POLITICS AND SOCIETIES, 3(2) (SPR 89), 300-328.
ALTHOUGH "EFFECTIVENESS" AND "EGALITARIANISM" ARE SUPPOSED TO BE DETERMINING FACTORS DETERMINING SOCIALISM'S LOGIC OF DISTRIBUTION, POWER IS ALSO AN IMPORTANT FACTOR. THE ARTICLE CONSIDERS THE RELATIONSHIP BETWEEN POWER AND THE LOGIC OF DISTRIBUTION IN POLAND. DRAWING ON RECENT POLISH SOCIAL RESEARCH, THE AUTHORS ARGUE THAT POWER RESOURCES ARE CONSTRAINED THROUGH A SYSTEM OF VASSALAGE AND THEIR TRANSLATION INTO PRIVELEGE IS DISTORTED THROUGH THE OPERATION OF A GENERALIZED MARKET.

04976 KENNEY, M.; FLORIDA, R.
JAPAN'S ROLE IN A POST-FORDIST AGE
FUTURES, 21(2) (APR 89), 136-151.
THE SHIFT AWAY FROM MASS PRODUCTION INDUSTRIES TO NEW INFORMATIONINTENSIVE INDUSTRIES IS LEADING TO SPECULATION ON WHAT WILL SUPERSEDE THE FORDIST MODEL OF INDUSTRIAL ORGANIZATION. THIS ARTICLE OUTLINES ALTERNATIVE MODELS ADVANCED AS POTENTIAL REPLACEMENT FOR FORDISM, AND PRESENTS A NEW POST-FORDIST FUTURE, BASED UPON EXPLORATION OF THE POST-WAR EVOLUTION OF JAPAN. FUJITSUISM IS POSED AS A POTENTIAL POST-FORDIST FORM OF INDUSTRIAL ORGANIZATION, AND IS INVESTIGATED AS A NEW MECHANISM FOR SUSTAINED ECONOMIC GROWTH PARTICULARLY SUITED TO THE INFORMATION AGE.

04977 KENNEY, P.J.; RICE, T.W.
AN EMPIRICAL EXAMINATION OF THE MINIMAX HYPOTHESIS
AMERICAN POLITICS QUARTERLY, 17(2) (APR 89), 153-162.
IN THIS ARTICLE THE AUTHORS EXAMINE EMPIRICALLY THE MINIMAX HYPOTHESIS. THE HYPOTHESIS HOLDS THAT INDIVIDUALS ARE MOTIVATED TO INCUR THE MINIMAL COSTS OF VOTING IN ORDER TO AVOID THE MAXIMUM REGRET: THEIR PREFERRED CANDIDATE LOSING BY A SINGLE VOTE. THE RESULTS OF THIS STUDY SUGGEST THAT A SUBSTANTIAL NUMBER OF PEOPLE APPARENTLY DO EMPLOY A MINIMAX DECISION-MAKING PROCESS. OVER ONE-THIRD OF THE INDIVIDUALS INTERVIEWED REPORTED SOMETIMES WORRYING THAT IF THEY ABSTAIN FROM VOTING THEIR FAVORITE CANDIDATE MIGHT LOSE. IN ADDITION, THESE RESPONDENTS HERE SIGNIFICANTLY MORE LIKELY THAN THOSE WHO EXPRESSED NO WORRY TO CLAIM THEY VOTED IN 1984 AND TO SAY THEY PLANNED TO VOTE IN 1986. AND PERHAPS MOST INTRIGUING, FURTHER ANALYSIS SUGGESTS THAT INDIVIDUALS

MAY BE MORE LIKELY TO EMPLOY MINIMAX DECISION MAKING THAN
EXPECTED UTILITY DECISION MAKING.

04978 KENSUKE, Y.; MITSUHIDE, Y.
DIRECTING JAPAN'S AID EFFORTS
JAPAN ECHO, XVI(1) (SPR 89), 8-12.
IN RECENT YEARS JAPAN HAS INCREASED ITS FOREIGN AID
UNTIL IT HAS BECOME THE WORLD'S LARGEST AID-GIVING NATION.
THE ERA IN WHICH JAPAN COULD FOLLOW THE LEAD OF LARGER
DONORS HAS ENDED. THE GLOBAL COMMUNITY NOW EXPECTS JAPAN TO
EXERCISE LEADERSHIP AND DEVELOP AN AID PHILOSOPHY BEFITTING
ITS STATUS AS THE TOP DONOR.

04979 KENT, T.
FIVE STEPS TO BETTER POLICY
POLICY OPTIONS, 10(1) (JAN 89), 25-26.
PUBLIC POLICY FORMATION DEPENDS ON INSTITUTIONS AS WELL
AS PEOPLE, AND CANADA'S INSTITUTIONS NEED REFORM. CANADA'S
CABINET NEEDS TO BE REDUCED IN SIZE, AND THE ECONOMIC
COUNCIL OF CANADA SHOULD BE REVITALIZED OR DISPLACED. NEW
INSTITUTIONS ARE NEEDED TO DEAL WITH FEDERAL-PROVINCIAL
RELATIONS, AND A NEW APPROACH TO THE APPOINTMENT OF JUDGES
IS REQUIRED. FINALLY, A MEDIA INSTITUTE IS NEEDED TO
ENCOURAGE BETTER JOURNALISM AND RAISE THE QUALITY OF PUBLIC
INFORMATION.

04980 KERESZTES, P.
THE NEW HURGARIAN REVOLUTION
AMERICAN SPECTATOR, 22(7) (JUL 89), 28-29.
DISMANTLING THE FREAKISH APPARATUS INSTITUTIONALIZED
DURING THE IRON CURTAIN'S EXISTENCE WILL REQUIRE CROSSING A
NO MAN'S LAND NO ONE HAS YET SURVIVED. ECONOMIC OVERHAUL, IN
SHORT, WILL PROVE TO BE FAR MORE DIFFICULT TO ACHIEVE THAN
THE EVIDENTLY CONTENTIOUS CHANGES IN THE POLITICAL STRUCTURE.
IT'S ONE THING TO EMBRACE THE PRINCIPLES OF PROPERTY RIGHTS
AND MARKET ECONOMICS IN A BROAD SENSE, AS THE SOVIET, POLISH,
AND HUNGARIAN COMMUNISTS HAVE BEEN DOING FOR SOME TIME NOW.
IT'S FAR TRICKIER, HOWEVER, TO REDISTRIBUTE FARMLAND
COLLECTIVIZED DECADES AGO - AND BUDAPEST HAS YET TO MOVE ON
THIS FUNDAMENTAL REFORM.

04981 KERRIGAN, J.E.; LUKE, J.S.
PUBLIC ADMINISTRATION EDUCATION AND TRAINING IN THE THIRD
WORLD: PROBLEMS AND OPPORTUNITIES
POLICY STUDIES REVIEW, 8(4) (SUM 89), 904-912.
NATIONS OF THE THIRD WORLD ARE NOT DEVELOPING AS QUICKLY
AS THEIR POTENTIAL SUGGESTS THEY SHOULD. THIS ARTICLE POSITS
THAT ONE OF THE MAJOR REASONS FOR THIS LACK OF DEVELOPMENT
IS A SCARCITY OF TRAINED PUBLIC MANAGERS. TEACHING CITIZENS
OF DEVELOPING COUNTRIES PUBLIC ADMINISTIN PRESENTS A
SPECIAL CHALLENGE. THE AUTHORS POINT OUT THAT THE EMPHASIS
IN TRAINING THESE INDIVIDUALS SHOULD BE PLACED ON PRACTICAL
LEARNING. IN ADDITION, CURRICULUM SHOULD NOT BASED SOLELY ON
THE AMERICAN MODEL, BUT SHOULD RECOGNIZE THE CULTURAL AND
ECONOMIC DISSIMILARITIES THAT EXIST. THE AUTHORS CLOSE THE
ARTICLE BY SUGGESTING SOME POSSIBLE TRAINING APPROACHES FOR
DEVELOPING NATIONS.

04982 KERSELL, J.E.
A NEW APPROACH TO NATIVE RIGHTS
POLICY OPTIONS, 10(1) (JAN 89), 7-9.
THE CANADIAN FEDERAL GOVERNMENT RECENTLY SIGNED
AGREEMENTS IN PRINCIPLE ON THE ISSUE OF ABORIGINAL RIGHTS
WITH THE NATIVES OF THE YUKON AND NORTHWEST TERRITORIES. IN
THIS ARTICLE, THE AUTHOR ARGUES THAT NOW IS THE TIME TO LOOK
A STEP FURTHER, AT THE CASE FOR ACCEPTING NATIVE COMMUNITIES
ON THEIR OWN TERMS AS THE POLITICAL BASE FOR FUTURE
DEVELOPMENT.

04983 KERSHAW, I.
THE NAZI STATE: AN EXCEPTIONAL STATE?
NEW LEFT REVIEW, (176) (JUL 89), 47-69.
THE CHARACTER OF THE NAZI STATE AND HITLER'S ROLE IN IT
HAVE ALWAYS POSED A PROBLEM FOR HISTORICAL EXPLANATION.
WHILE STATIC LIBERAL THEORIES OF TOTALITARIANISM HAVE FAILED
TO PROBE BENEATH THE SURFACE OF POLITICAL FORM, OR EVEN TO
ACCOUNT FOR THE STRUCTURAL COMPLEXITY OF THE THIRD REICH,
SIMPLISTIC ECONOMIC DETERMINISM IS UNABLE TO GRASP THE
RELATIVE AUTONOMY OF THE MOVEMENT THAT CULMINATED IN THE
EXTERMINATION CAMPS AND DEMENTIA. DRAWING ON ALTERNATIVE
TRADITIONS OF ANALYSIS, THIS ESSAY ARGUES THAT THE NAZI
PERIOD CAN ONLY BE UNDERSTOOD IN TERMS OF A SHIFTING
RELATIONSHIP BETWEEN BIG CAPITAL, THE STATE AND THE PARTY,
AND HITLER HIMSELF.

04984 KESSIDES, C.; KING, T.; NUTI, M.; SOKIL, C.
FINANCIAL REFORM IN SOCIALIST ECONOMIES
AVAILABLE FROM NTIS, NO. PB89-220271/GAR, 1989, 253.
CONTENTS: FINANCIAL REFORM IN SOCIALIST ECONOMIES:
WORKSHOP OVERVIEW; MONETARY AND FINANCIAL ASPECTS OF
GORBACHEV'S REFORM; MONETARY REFORMS IN BULGARIA; FINANCIAL
ASPECTS OF THE ECONOMIC REFORM IN POLAND; CHINA'S REFORM OF
THE FINANCIAL AND TAX SYSTEMS; THE REORGANIZATION OF THE
BANKING SYSTEM IN HUNGARY; FEASIBLE FINANCIAL INNOVATION

UNDER MARKET SOCIALISM; SHAREHOLDING SCHEMES IN THE YUGOSLAV
ECONOMY; STRUCTURAL REFORM AND FINANCIAL REFORM IN CHINA;
THE BEGINNINGS OF A CAPITAL MARKET IN HUNGARY; SOCIALIST
STOCK COMPANY: THE MISSING LINK IN ECONOMIC REFORM;
FINANCIAL SYSTEM FOR RESTRUCTURING THE YUGOSLAV ECONOMY; THE
ROLE OF SMALL-SCALE INDUSTRY IN YUGOSLAVIA'S ECONOMIC
DEVELOPMENT; ECONOMIC REFORM AND MONETARY COOPERATION IN THE
CMEA; ALTERNATIVE MODES OF FINANCIAL ORGANIZATION; THE BASIS
OF CHINA'S BANKING REFORM; BALANCE OF PAYMENTS ADJUSTMENT
AND FINANCIAL CRISIS IN YUGOSLAVIA.

04985 KETT, I.
THE CRITICAL JEWISH ISSUE
MIDSTREAM, XXXV(2) (FEB 89), 41-45.
THE FOUNDING OF ISRAEL IN 1948 WAS ONLY A PARTIAL
REALIZATION OF THE JEWISH DREAM. BY AND LARGE, WESTERN JEWRY
HAS IGNORED THE IMPLICATIONS OF JEWISH HISTORY, TO ITS OWN
DETRIMENT AND TO THAT OF ISRAEL. THE JEWISH PEOPLE, AND MORE
SPECIFICALLY THE JEWS OF AMERICA, ARE FORFEITING A PRECIOUS
WINDOW IN HISTORY. WHAT THE IMPLICATIONS WILL BE AND WHAT
PRICE WILL BE PAID ARE ONLY PARTIALLY DISCERNIBLE AT THIS
POINT IN TIME. BUT CERTAINLY THE FOUNDERS OF THE ZIONIST
MOVEMENT AND THOSE WHO PROCLAIMED THE JEWISH STATE IN 1948
NEVER ENVISIONED THAT, TO A LARGE DEGREE, WESTERN JEWRY
WOULD ALMOST TOTALLY DISREGARD THE CALL TO RETURN TO ZION.
AS A RESULT, AMERICAN JEWRY IS PROBABLY DESTINED TO REMAIN
FOREVER OUTSIDE THE STRUGGLE FOR JEWISH NATIONAL FULFILLMENT.
THE INCREASING IRRELEVANCE OF DIASPORA JEWRY TO THE
SECURITY AND FUTURE OF ISRAEL BECOMES MORE APPARENT EACH DAY.

04986 KEYES, C.
BUDDHIST POLITICS AND THEIR REVOLUTIONARY ORIGINS IN
THAILAND
INTERNATIONAL POLITICAL SCIENCE REVIEW, 10(2) (APR 89),
121-142.
THE ARTICLE ARGUES THAT THAI POLITICS, WHICH HAVE BEEN
INFLUENCED BY A NUMBER OF BUDDHIST MOVEMENTS IN THE PAST TWO
DECADES, CAN ONLY BE UNDERSTOOD IF IT IS RECOGNIZED THAT THE
THAI POLITICAL ORDER HAS UNDERGONE A MAJOR REVOLUTIONARY
TRANSFORMATION WHICH STEM FROM THE REFORMATIONS OF BUDDHISM
BEGUN IN THE MID NINETEENTH CENTURY. THESE REFORMATIONS LED
TO A FUNDAMENTAL SHIFT IN THE PRACTICAL INTERPRETATION OF
THE BUDDHIST THEORY OF ACTION WHICH, IN TURN HAS TO AN
INCREASING NUMBER OF PEOPLE VIEWING THEMSELVES AS BEING
SUFFICIENTLY FREED FROM THE CONSTRAINTS OF THE PREVIOUS
KARMA TO EFFECT SIGNIFICANT CHANGES IN THEIR LIVES AND THOSE
OF THE WORLD WHICH THEY LIVE.

04987 KEYSSAR, E.
HISTORY AND THE PROBLEM OF UNEMPLOYMENT
SOCIALIST REVIEW, 19(4) (OCT 89), 15-34.
THIS ARTICLE ADDRESSES THE PROBLEM OF UNEMPLOYMENT FROM
THE STANDPOINT OF: OVER THE LAST 100 YEARS UNEMPLOYMENT HAS
STAYED ROUGHLY THE SAME, IT EXAMINES THE HISTORICAL RECORD
OF UNEMPLOYMENT WHICH RAISES SOME SERIOUS QUESTIONS ABOUT
POLITICS, ECONOMICS, AND PUBLIC POLICY IN THE UNITED STATES
SINCE THE GREAT DEPRESSION. IT CONCLUDES THAT THERE EXISTS A
POLITICAL AND CULTURAL ATMOSPHERE THAT DEFLECTS INQUIRY AND
SANCTIONS INACTION, AND OFFERS LESSONS TO BE LEARNED.

04988 KGOPE, T.
ASPECTS OF ARMED STRUGGLE
SECHABA, 23(3) (MAR 89), 22-24.
THE ARTICLE DISCUSSES ARMED STRUGGLE AS A NECESSARY
COMPONENT OF THE OVERALL STRUGGLE FOR LIBERATION IN SOUTH
AFRICA. IT DISCUSSES THE ROLE OF THE REVOLUTIONARY ARMY, ITS
ORGANIZATION, AND ULTIMATE GOALS. IT EXAMINES THE IMPORTANCE
OF MASS ACTION IN ANY STRUGGLE FOR FREEDOM AND INDEPENDENCE.

04989 KHADKA, N.
SOUTH ASIAN CLASICIATION FOR REGIONAL COOPERATION: A
NEPALESE PERSPECTIVE
ROUND TABLE, 309 (JAN 89), 65-87.
THE GROWING INTERNATIONAL DISPARITY IN THE STANDARDS OF
LIVING BETWEEN THE DEVELOPED AND THE DEVELOPING COUNTRIES
AND CONSEQUENTLY THE LOSS OF LEVERAGE FOR NEGOTIATION FOR AN
EQUITABLE SHARING OF ECONOMIC BENEFITS ARISING FROM UNEQUAL
EXCHANGE IN THE INTERNATIONAL DIVISION OF LABOUR BY THE
LATTER PROVIDED AN IMPETUS FOR ATTEMPTS TO FORGE CLOSER
COOPERATION, AMONG SOUTH ASIAN COUNTRIES. EVEN IF IT DOES
NOT GIVE IMMEDIATE ECONOMIC BENEFITS, EFFORTS AT REGIONAL
COOPERATION COULD DEFINITELY HELP NEPAL TO SEAL OFF EXTERNAL
HINDRANCES WHILST HELPING TO PRESERVE ITS NATIONAL IDENTITY
AS AS WELL AS GOING AHEAD WITH DEVELOPMENT EFFORTS. IT HAS
TO BE BORNE IN MIND THEREFORE THAT MOST OF NEPAL'S INTERNAL
PROBLEMS HAVE EXTERNAL DIMENSIONS WHICH MEANS THAT PEACE AT
HOME IS THE MOST IMPORTANT ELEMENT TO SAFEGUARD AGAINST
UNWANTED INTRUSIONS FROM EXTERNAL FRONTS. AND PEACE AT HOME
IS ACHIEVED ONLY THROUGH NATIONAL CONSENSUS ON SOME
FUNDAMENTAL ISSUES SUCH AS POLITICAL PARTICIPATION,
STRATEGIES OF DEVELOPMENT AND THE ACCEPTABLE DIMENSIONS OF
EXTERNAL RELATIONS.

04990 KHAI, P.V.
TRANSFORMATION IN VIETNAM AS EXEMPLIFIED BY ONE CITY
WORLD MARXIST REVIEW, 31(2) (FEB 88), 116-122.
CREATIVE DYNAMISM HAS ALWAYS BEEN A FEATURE OF THE
WORKING PEOPLE OF HO CHI MINH CITY, WITH ITS LONG-STANDING
REVOLUTIONARY TRADITIONS. SOCIALIST EMULATION AND THE SCOPE
OF THE MOVEMENT ARE CLOSELY LINKED WITH THE RIGHTS AND
INTERESTS OF EVERY INDIVIDUAL WORKER, AND OF THE COLLECTIVES
AT THE ENTERPRISES AND ORGANISATIONS. SOCIALIST CONSTRUCTION
IN VIETNAM IS BEING CARRIED ON IN THE LIGHT OF PRESIDENT HO
CHI MINH'S PRECEPT: "THE PARTY MUST WORK OUT A GOOD PLAN TO
DEVELOP THE ECONOMY AND CULTURE SO AS TO KEEP RAISING THE
PEOPLE'S LIVING STANDARDS."

04991 KHALID, A.F.B.H.
ISLAMIC LAW AND LAND IN THE STATE OF SELANGOR, MALAYSIA:
PROBLEMS OF ADMINISTRATION AND ISLAMISATION
DISSERTATION ABSTRACTS INTERNATIONAL, 50(6) (DEC 89),
1800-A.
THIS STUDY BEGINS WITH THE HISTORICAL BACKGROUND OF
SELANGOR AND THE CONTRIBUTION MADE BY THE EARLY IMMIGRANTS
TOWARD THE ECONOMIC DEVELOPMENT OF THE STATE. IT THEN
CONSIDERS THE ARRIVAL OF THE BRITISH IN 1874 AND THE
COMMERCIAL TREATIES SIGNED BETWEEN THEM AND THE RULERS OF
SELANGOR THAT REINFORCED THEIR AUTHORITY OVER THE POLITICAL,
ECONOMIC, AND ADMINISTRATIVE AFFAIRS OF THE STATE. THE
ADMINISTRATION OF "FARAID," "HAKAF," "BAITULMAL," AND
"ZAKAT" ARE EXAMINED FROM 1874 TO THE EARLY 1980'S.

04992 KHALILZAD, Z.
THE UNITED STATES IN SOUTH ASIA
CURRENT HISTORY, 88(542) (DEC 89), 417-420, 451-453.
THE AUTHOR REVIEWS THE RECENT PAST REGARDING UNITED
STATES INTERESTS AND FOREIGN POLICY IN SOUTH ASIA. THEN HE
SPECULATES ABOUT FUTURE AMERICAN POLICY THERE AND WARNS THAT
"DECREASING UNITED STATES ACTIVITY IN SOUTH ASIA WOULD NOT
SERVE AMERICAN INTERESTS."

04993 KHAMBATA, F.; KHAMBATA, D.
EMERGING CAPITAL MARKETS: A CASE STUDY OF EQUITY MARKETS
IN INDIA
JOURNAL OF DEVELOPING AREAS, 23(3) (APR 89), 425-438.
IN ORDER TO STREAMLINE AND IMPROVE THE EFFICIENCY OF
INDIAN EQUITY MARKETS A NUMBER OF ISSUES NEED TO BE RESOLVED.
THIS STUDY REVIEWS THE GROWTH AND DEVELOPMENT OF THE INDIAN
EQUITY MARKETS, BEGINNING WITH THE LEGISLATIVE AND FISCAL
FRAMEWORK AND THE ROLE AND OPERATIONS OF THE KEY
INSTITUTIONAL PLAYERS. THE DEMAND, SUPPLY AND OWNERSHIP
STRUCTURE OF EQUITY IS PRESENTED, AND THE CHARACTERISTICS OF
THE PRIMARY AND SECONDARY MARKET FOR EQUITIES ARE EVALUATED.

04994 KHAN, A.
FORCASTING A LOCAL GOVERNMENT BUDGET WITH TIME SERIES
ANALYSIS
STATE AND LOCAL GOVERNMENT REVIEW, 21(3) (FAL 89), 123-129.
THIS PAPER PRESENTS A SIMPLE APPLICATION OF THE BOX-
JENKINS METHOD TO FORECAST THE GENERAL FUND (GF) REVENUE AND
EXPENDITURE OF A LOCAL GOVERNMENT USING TIME SERIES DATA. IT
USES A UNIVARIATE ARIMA MODEL TO PRODUCE THE NECESSARY
FORECASTS. THE MODEL IS ALSO USED TO UNDERSTAND THE BUDGET
BALANCE IN TERMS OF THE DEFICITS AND SURPLUSES GENERATED BY
THE FORECAST VALUES. THE AVAILABLE BUDGET SERIES IS SOMEWHAT
SHORTER THAN IS CONSIDERED IDEAL FOR MOST ARIMA MODELS; THE
FORCASTS PRESENTED IN THIS PAPER SEEM FAIRLY REASONABLE,
HOWEVER.

04995 KHAN, M.A.
GEOPOLITICAL DYNAMICS OF SOUTHWEST ASIA: THE AFTERMATH OF
AFGHANISTAN AND IRAN - IRAQ WAR
AVAILABLE FROM NTIS, NO. AD-A209 069/4/GAR, MAR 89, 47.
IN THE AFTERMATH OF THE SOVIET'S WITHDRAWAL FROM
AFGHANISTAN AND THE END OF IRAN-IRAQ WAR, THE SOUTHWEST
ASIAN REGION IS PASSING THROUGH A PERIOD OF INTENSE
READJUSTMENTS. HAVING REMAINED THE ARENA OF DECADE LONG
INTRA-REGIONAL RIVALRIES AND THE SUPERPOWERS COMPETITION,
THE REGION IS CONVULSIVE AND UNSTABLE AND WILL TAKE TIME
BEFORE COOLING DOWN TO A STABLE MASS. THE THREE COUNTRIES ON
THE SOVIET UNION'S PERIPHERY, AFGHANISTAN, PAKISTAN AND IRAN,
WERE AFFECTED BY THE SOVIET INTERVENTION IN AFGHANISTAN IN
VARYING DEGREE WHEREAS IRAN WAS ALSO ENGAGED IN A
DEBILITATING WAR OF ATTRITION WITH IRAQ. NOTWITHSTANDING THE
NATURE OF EXPERIENCES AND RELATIONSHIP OF THREE COUNTRIES
WITH THE SUPERPOWERS AND THEIR RESPECTIVE INTERNAL DYNAMICS,
THE GEOPOLITICAL FACTORS POINT TOWARDS A COOPERATIVE REGIME
IN THIS WAR-TORN REGION. THE RESEARCH FOCUSES ON THE
REGIONAL DYNAMICS OF THE FORESTATED COUNTRIES AND THEIR
EFFECTS ON THE SUPERPOWERS, PARTICULARLY ON THE UNITED
STATES' STRATEGY IN THE REGION. THE RESEARCH FURTHER
CONCLUDES THAT IF THE UNITED STATES IS PREPARED AND WILLING
TO CONSOLIDATE ITS POSITION VIS-A-VIS THE SOVIET UNION BY
HELPING STABILIZATION IN THE REGION, IT COULD CONSIDERABLY
DRAW DOWN ITS MILITARY PRESENCE AND IN FACT MAY FALL BACK TO
THE NIXON DOCTRINE.

04996 KHAN, M.M.
RESISTANCE TO ADMINISTRATIVE REFORM IN BANGLADESH, 1972-
1987
PUBLIC ADMINISTRATION AND DEVELOPMENT, 9(3) (JUN 89),
287-30.
THE ARTICLE EXAMINES THE EFFORTS OF BANGLADESH TO
IMPLEMENT ADMINISTRATIVE REFORMS DESIGNED TO REBUILD THE
NATION AFTER ITS BLOODY CIVIL WAR. IT OUTLINES THE POLITICAL
LEGACY LEFT BY PREVIOUS PERIODS OF COLONIALISM AND
DOMINATION BY PAKISTAN AND PAST ATTEMPTS AT REFORM. IT
CONCLUDES THAT PAST ATTEMPTS OF ADMINISTRATIVE REFORM HAVE
NOT BEEN SUCCESSFUL IN MEETING STATED GOALS. LACK OF
CONSENSUS ABOUT THE GOVERNMENT SYSTEM, INCREASING
ENCROACHMENT OF MILITARY PERSONNEL ON THE PUBLIC SERVICE,
AND CONTROVERSY OVER THE STATUS OF GENERALISTS AND
SPECIALISTS WITHIN THE PUBLIC SECTOR WILL BE SIGNIFICANT
PROBLEMS THAT FUTURE ADMINISTRATIVE REFORMERS WILL FACE.

04997 KHAN, S.
PAKISTAN: P.M. AS RIOT TARGET
THIRD WORLD WEEK, 8(1) (MAR 89), 1-2.
IN PAKISTAN, THE MUSLIM CAMPAIGN AGAINST SALMAN RUSHDIE
INCLUDED DENUNCIATIONS OF BENAZIR BHUTTO. THE PRIME
MINISTER'S RIGHT-WING OPPONENTS IN THE RELIGIOUS PARTIES AND
THE CLERGY HAVE CONSTANTLY QUESTIONED HER RELIGIOUS
CREDENTIALS TO RULE THE COUNTRY. IN PROTESTING AGAINST
RUSHDIE'S "THE SATANIC VERSES," THEY SAW AN OPPORTUNITY TO
ATTACK BHUTTO AS WELL AS THE BOOK.

04998 KHAN, S.U.
U.S. WEAPONS ACQUISITION AND EXPORT: EXPLORING THE
DOMESTIC CONNECTION
DISSERTATION ABSTRACTS INTERNATIONAL, 49(11) (MAY 89),
3497-A.
EXTERNAL FACTORS DO NOT FULLY EXPLAIN THE COMPLEXITY OF
RECENT UNITED STATES' ARMS SALE PRACTICES. IN ORDER TO
IDENTIFY ALL THE FACTORS INVOLVED, THIS DISSERTATION
UNDERTAKES A TWO-LEVEL STUDY. AT THE THEORETICAL LEVEL, IT
IDENTIFIES THOSE DOMESTIC FACTORS MOST LIKELY TO INFLUENCE
US ARMS SALES. AT THE EMPIRICAL LEVEL, IT SEEKS TO DETERMINE
WHETHER SUCH FACTORS ACTUALLY HAVE INFLUENCED THE SALES.

04999 KHARBANDA, V.P.
SCOPE FOR SINO-INDIAN AGREEMENT ON SCIENCE AND TECHNOLOGY
CHINA REPORT, 25(2) (APR 89), 171-174.
THIS ARTICLE GIVES A BRIEF AND BROAD OUTLINE OF THE
POSSIBLE AREAS WHERE INDIA AND CHINA COULD COOPERATE
EFFECTIVELY FOR MUTUAL BENEFIT. IT EXPLORES THE AREAS OF
BIOTECHNOLOGY, INFORMATION TECHNOLOGIES, ENERGY AND
AUTOMATION, AS WELL AS TRANSPORT AND COMMUNICATIONS,
ENVIRONMENT PROTECTION, MEASUREMENT AND STANDARDISATION, AND
THE RECYCLING OF WASTE.

05000 KHAVARI, A.
PLAYING AT PEACE
WORLD MARXIST REVIEW, 32(12) (DEC 89), 70-72.
IRAQ AND OTHER ARAB COUNTRIES FEAR THE ISLAMIC
REVOLUTION WITH ITS POLICY OF ISLAMIC FUNDAMENTALISM. FOR
ITS PART, IRAN HAS NOT FORGOTTEN THE BEGINNING OF THE WAR
AND THE SOLIDARITY OF MANY ARAB COUNTRIES WITH IRAQ. TO SUM
UP, THE TERRITORIAL CLAIMS AND THE MUTUAL SUSPICION AND FEAR,
AS WELL AS THE DESPOTIC RULE AND ABSENCE OF DEMOCRATIC
FREEDOMS IN THESE COUNTRIES, MAKE PEACEFUL SETTLEMENT VERY
DIFFICULT.

05001 KHAVARI, A.
THOSE WHO FIND PEACE DEADLIER THAN POISON
WORLD MARXIST REVIEW, 31(10) (OCT 88), 11-16.
IRAN AND IRAQ REACHED A CEASEFIRE AGREEMENT IN AUGUST
1988 AND ENTERED DIRECT PEACE TALKS. IN THIS ARTICLE, THE
FIRST SECRETARY OF THE TUDEH CENTRAL COMMITTEE OF IRAN
ANALYSES BELOW THE CAUSES AND PROGRESS OF THE WAR, EXPLAINS
WHY IT WAS WAGED FOR EIGHT LONG YEARS IN THE TEETH OF COMMON
SENSE, AND PRESENTS HIS PARTY'S POSITION ON THE PRESENT
PHASE OF THE CONFLICT.

05002 KIAMBA, M.
THE INTRODUCTION AND EVOLUTION OF PRIVATE LANDED PROPERTY
IN KENYA
DEVELOPMENT AND CHANGE, 20(1) (JAN 89), 121-147.
THE INTRODUCTION OF CAPITALIST DEVELOPMENT IN KENYA
ORIGINATED DURING THE LAST YEARS OF THE 19TH CENTURY DURING
THE COUNTRY'S INCORPORATION INTO THE BRITISH COLONIAL EMPIRE.
WITH RELATIVELY LIMITED CAPITAL RESOURCES, AN AFRICAN LABOR
FORCE, AND EXTENSIVE POLITICAL INTERVENTION BY THE COLONIAL
STATE, THE EUROPEAN FARMER-SETTLER EMBARKED ON CAPITALIST
AGRICULTURAL DEVELOPMENT, LARGELY FOR EXPORT TO BRITAIN. IN
THIS BROAD CONTEXT, THIS ESSAY EXPLORES THE INTRODUCTION AND
EVOLUTION OF PRIVATE LANDED PROPERTY IN KENYA, AS PART OF
THE LARGER PROCESS OF COLONIZATION. ALONG WITH COLONIZATION
AND CAPITALISM CAME THE DISSOLUTION OF THE OLD, CUSTOMARY
LAND RELATIONS OF THE AFRICANS AND THEIR TRANSFORMATION INTO
A PATTERN COMPATIBLE WITH CAPITALIST DEVELOPMENT.

05003 KIDON-ONYANG, M.
     CHAOS IN KARAMOJA
     NEW AFRICAN, (APR 88), 15-16.
        THIS ARTICLE IS A REPORT ON WHAT IT IS REALLY LIKE IN
     KARAMOJA. IT DESCRIBES THE CORRUPTION IN RELIEF OPERATIONS,
     BANDITRY ON THE ROADS, CATTLE RAIDING, VILLAGES DESTROYED,
     PEOPLE KILLED AS A PART OF EVERYDAY LIFE THERE.

05004 KIDRON, P.
     A CRITICAL CONGRESS FOR SHAMIR
     MIDDLE EAST INTERNATIONAL, 353 (JUN 89), 3-4.
        THE MOST EXPLOSIVE ISSUE IN ISRAELI POLITICS IS THE
     FORTHCOMING MEETING OF THE LIKUD CENTRAL COMMITTEE, WHICH IS
     TO CONSIDER THE PEACE PLAN INITIATED BY THE PARTY'S LEADER,
     PRIME MINISTER YITZHAK SHAMIR. FEW OBSERVERS EXPECT THE
     RIVAL CAMPS TO RISK A FULLSCALE SHOWDOWN. THE VITRIOLIC
     RHETORIC NOTWITHSTANDING, THERE IS TOO MUCH AT STAKE,
     NOTABLY LIKUD'S UNINTERRUPTED 12-YEAR HOLD ON OFFICE. IF THE
     GOVERNMENT HERE BROUGHT DOWN BY DISSENTION WITHIN THE PARTY,
     THERE IS A VERY REAL POSSIBILITY OF ITS LABOUR RIVALS
     SWIFTLY STEPPING IN TO FORGE A COALITION WITH THE RELIGIOUS
     PARTIES AND THE MODERATE LEFT. LIKUD WOULD HAVE TO FIGHT THE
     ENSUING ELECTION FROM A POSITION OF INFERIORITY AS A
     POWERLESS OPPOSITION, WHILE THE PRESTIGE OF OFFICE MIGHT
     RESTORE LABOUR TO THE NEAR-PERMANENT GRASP ON POWER IT LOST
     IN 1977.

05005 KIDRON, P.
     ABIE NATHAN GAOLED; SYRIAN PILOT DEFECTS
     MIDDLE EAST INTERNATIONAL, (361) (OCT 20), 8-10.
        TWO PILOTS HAVE CAUSED NO SMALL STIR IN ISRAEL. ABIE
     NATHAN, WELL-KNOWN IN ISRAEL FOR HIS WORLD WAR II EXPLOITS
     AND HIS DARE-DEVIL SOLO MISSIONS TO EGYPT IN THE 1960'S WAS
     JAILED FOR SIX MONTHS IN ISRAEL FOR MEETING PLO CHAIRMAN
     YASSER ARAFAT. NATHAN'S POPULARITY WAS EVIDENT AS A 1,000-
     VEHICLE MOTORCADE OF SYMPATHIZERS ESCORTED HIM TO PRISON.
     ANOTHER PILOT GAINED NOTORIETY BY FLYING AN ADVANCED MIG 23
     FROM SYRIA TO ISRAEL. HIS DEFECTION AND THE "CAPTURE" OF
     SUCH SOPHISTICATED WEAPONRY IS A WINDFALL FOR ISRAEL.
     HOWEVER, THE FACT THAT HE FLEW THROUGH ISRAELI AIRSPACE FOR
     SEVERAL MINUTES WITHOUT BEING INTERCEPTED CAUSED
     CONSIDERABLE PUBLIC CONCERN OVER THE STATE OF ISRAEL'S
     VAUNTED AIR DEFENSE SYSTEM.

05006 KIDRON, P.
     CONFRONTATION POSTPONED
     MIDDLE EAST INTERNATIONAL, (348) (APR 89), 4-5.
        IN ITS ANALYSIS OF THE IMPLICATIONS FOR ISRAEL OF PRIME
     MINISTER SHAMIR'S VISIT TO THE US, THE ARTICLE CONCLUDES
     THAT THE MOST IMPORTANT RESULT OF THE MEETING WAS THAT THE
     LONG DREADED SHOWDOWN FAILED TO MATERIALIZE. THE
     CONFRONTATION WAS AVOIDED PARTIALLY DUE TO SHAMIR'S
     CONCESSION THAT ELECTIONS IN THE OCCUPIED TERRITORIES NEED
     NOT BE LINKED TO THE END OF THE INTIFADA. ALTHOUGH SHAMIR
     MANAGED TO AVOID CONFRONTATION IN WASHINGTON, HARD-LINERS
     LED BY ARIEL SHARON ARE HEATING UP THE CONFLICT IN ISRAEL
     WITH THEIR DEMANDS FOR A TOTAL SUPRESSION OF THE INTIFADA
     AND CONTINUED COLONIZATION OF THE OCCUPIED TERRITORIES.

05007 KIDRON, P.
     CONSTERNATION IN ISRAEL
     MIDDLE EAST INTERNATIONAL, (359) (SEP 89), 3-5.
        THE ANNOUNCEMENT OF MUBARAK'S "TEN POINTS" HAS THROWN
     TOP ISRAELI POLITICIANS INTO A STATE OF DISARRAY.
     DEMONSTRATING THEIR INITIAL SURPRISE AT THE ANNOUNCEMENT
     BOTH YITZHAK SHAMIR AND MOSHE ARENS EXPRESSED GUARDED
     SUPPORT FOR THE MEASURE. HOWEVER, ONCE ARIEL SHARON AND
     OTHER HARD-LINERS APPLIED PRESSURE, THEY SOON RETREATED TO A
     MORE TRADITIONAL REJECTION OF THE PROPOSAL. THIS ISSUE
     THREATENS TO SPLIT THE UNSTEADY LABOUR-LIKUD COALITION THAT
     IS CURRENTLY RULING ISRAEL.

05008 KIDRON, P.; HUNTER, J.
     ISRAEL AND THE COCAINE BARONS
     MIDDLE EAST INTERNATIONAL, (358) (SEP 89), 3-4.
        A VIDEOTAPED RECORDING OF AN ISRAELI OFFICER TRAINING
     MEDELLIN NARCO-TERRORISTS BROUGHT SIGNIFICANT CRITICISM OF
     THE ONGOING PRACTICE OF ISRAEL'S MILITARY MEN AIDING
     TERRORISTS AND DICTATORS THE WORLD OVER WITH EQUIPMENT AND
     EXPERTISE. WHETHER ACTING UNDER STATE COMMAND, OR SIMPLY
     INDEPENDENT ACTS OF SOLDIERS OF FORTUNE, ISRAELI MILITARY
     MEN HAVE BEEN INVOLVED IN AID AND ASSISTANCE TO COLOMBIAN
     DRUG LORDS AND NICARAGUAN CONTRAS.

05009 KIDRON, P.
     ISRAEL AND THE PALESTINIANS: WHAT RABIN PROPOSES AND WHY
     MIDDLE EAST INTERNATIONAL, (343) (FEB 89), 5-7.
        ISRAELI DEFENCE MINISTER YITZHAK RABIN CONTINUES TO PLAY
     A DUAL ROLE IN THE MIDEAST SITUATION. WHILE HE ORDERS THE
     ARMY AND THE MILITARY LEADERS TO TIGHTEN THE SCREWS ON THE
     PALESTINIANS, HE IS ALSO MAKING POLITICAL OVERTURES TO THE
     LOCAL PALESTINIAN LEADERSHIP. HIS PEACE PLAN IS THE FIRST
     SERIOUS PROPOSAL FOR GIVE-AND-TAKE TO BE OFFERED BY A SENIOR
     ISRAELI LEADER, BUT IT HAS EVOKED MIXED REACTIONS.

05010 KIDRON, P.
     ISRAEL CAUTIONS SYRIA
     MIDDLE EAST INTERNATIONAL, (357) AUG 89), 5-6.
        THE INCREASING CONFLICT IN LEBANON HAS CAUSED ISRAELI
     DEFENSE MINISTER YITZHAK RABIN TO ISSUE STERN WARNINGS TO
     SYRIA THAT ISRAEL'S DECLARED "RED LINES" MUST NOT BE CROSSED.
     ISRAEL'S CONCERN WITH MAINTAINING THE STATUS QUO THAT WAS
     ESTABLISHED BY THE (1974) DISENGAGEMENT-OF-FORCES AGREEMENT
     IS READILY APPARENT; AFTER THE BITTER EXPERIENCES OF THE
     1982-1985 INVASION OF LEBANON, MANY ISRAELIS DO NOT WISH TO
     SEE ADDITIONAL MILITARY INVOLVEMENT. MEANWHILE, ISRAELI
     SPOKESMEN WASTED NO TIME SCORING PROPAGANDA POINTS OF OF THE
     LEBANESE CONFLICT; NOT ONLY DOES IT DRAW ATTENTION AWAY FROM
     THE OCCUPIED TERRITORIES, BUT IT DEMONSTRATES THE QUAGMIRE
     THAT THE ARAB WORLD FINDS ITSELF IN.

05011 KIDRON, P.
     ISRAEL GLOATS TOO SOON
     MIDDLE EAST INTERNATIONAL, 356 (AUG 89), 5-6.
        WHETHER COLONEL WILLIAM HIGGINS WAS INDEED EXECUTED IN
     RETALIATION FOR ISRAEL'S ABDUCTION OF SHAIKH ABD AL-KARIM
     OBEID, OR WHETHER - AS ISRAELI SPOKESMEN CLAIM THE EVENT
     MERELY GAVE HIS CAPTORS A PRETEXT TO REVEAL HIS DEMISE WHICH
     ACTUALLY OCCURRED MONTHS EARLIER, THE REVELATION ENGINEERED
     A SHARP CHANGE OF MOOD IN ISRAEL. THE SMUG GLOATING WHICH
     INITIALLY HAILED THE "SUPERBLY EXECUTED" COMMANDO RAID
     ABRUPTLY SWITCHED TO GRAVE ANXIETY OVER POSSIBLE HARM TO
     RELATIONS WITH THE US, SHOULD WASHINGTON HOLD ISRAEL
     RESPONSIBLE FOR HIGGINS' DEATH. BY OPENLY BOASTING OF THE
     ABDUCTION, ISRAEL HUMILIATED THE SHI'ITES, LEAVING THEM NO
     CHOICE BUT EQUALLY SWIFT AND BRUTAL RETALIATION.

05012 KIDRON, P.
     ISRAEL: "WE CAN'T GO ON LIKE THIS"
     MIDDLE EAST INTERNATIONAL, (350) (MAY 89), 7-9.
        THE SHAMIR PEACE INITIATIVE HAS YET TO BE APPROVED BY
     THE ISRAELI CABINET. IN FACT, THE DETAILS OF THE PLAN ARE
     STILL BEING WORKED OUT BY A FOUR-MAN COMMITTEE THAT INCLUDES
     SHAMIR, DEFENSE MINISTER RABIN, FOREIGN MINISTER ARENS, AND
     FINANCE MINISTER PERES.

05013 KIDRON, P.
     ISRAEL: EUPHORIA OVER
     MIDDLE EAST INTERNATIONAL, (357) (AUG 89), 9.
        THE SELF-CONGRATULATORY MOOD OF ISRAEL'S RULING
     ESTABLISHMENT OVER THE ABDUCTION OF SHAIKH ABD AL-KARIM
     OBEID ABRUPTLY ENDED WITH THE EXECUTION OF US COLONEL
     WILLIAM HIGGINS. THE RESULTING INTERNATIONAL OUTCRY CAUSED A
     QUICK REVERSAL OF ISRAELI RHETORIC. THE INTERROGATION OF THE
     SHAIKH ALSO REVEALED THAT TWO OF THE THREE ISRAELI
     SERVICEMEN WHO WERE BELIEVED TO BE HELD BY LEBANESE MILITIA
     DIED WITHIN HOURS OF THEIR CAPTURE. THIS NEWS LEAKED OUT TO
     THE FAMILIES OF THE SOLDIERS BEFORE OFFICIAL ANNOUNCEMENT
     AND COMPOUNDED THE RAPIDLY GROWING EMBARRASSMENT OF ISRAEL'S
     RULING ESTABLISHMENT.

05014 KIDRON, P.
     ISRAEL: PINNING HOPES ON THE ARABS
     MIDDLE EAST INTERNATIONAL, (349) (APR 89), 4-5.
        FROM THE ONSET OF THE DISTURBANCES IN JORDAN IN APRIL
     1989, ISRAELIS HAVE DRAWN PARALLELS WITH EVENTS IN THE WEST
     BANK AND GAZA. OVERALL, THERE ARE HOPES THAT IF HUSSEIN'S
     EFFORTS TO REGAIN CONTROL INVOLVE HARSH MEASURES, THIS WILL
     VINDICATE ISRAELI FORCE AGAINST THE INTIFADA AND OFFSET
     ISRAEL'S TARNISHED IMAGE. THERE IS ALSO HOPE THAT THE
     JORDANIAN DISTURBANCES WILL SOMEHOW RESOLVE THE THORNY ISSUE
     OF ELECTIONS IN THE OCCUPIED TERRITORIES.

05015 KIDRON, P.
     ISRAEL: PLETHORA OF PLANS
     MIDDLE EAST INTERNATIONAL, (354) (JUL 89), 7-8.
        THE MIDEAST PEACE PROCESS IS CURRENTLY BEING DELUGED BY
     PEACE PLANS FROM VARIOUS SOURCES. SOME OF THE IDEAS ARE
     NOTHING NEW, BUT SOME EXHIBIT ORIGINALITY AND A FRESH A
     APPROACH. ALL SIDES INVOLVED UNDERSTANDABLY DESIRE TO
     PROTECT THEIR OWN INTERESTS WHICH GENERALLY NEGATES THE
     USEFULNESS OF MANY OF THE PROPOSALS, BUT A FEW OF THE MORE
     DARING PLANS, SUCH A PROPOSED ISRAEL-PALESTINE-JORDANIAN
     CONFEDERATION, OR A PLAN THAT ADVOCATES ISRAEL'S RELINQUISH
     THE OCCUPIED TERRITORIES IN RETURN FOR MEMBERSHIP IN THE
     EUROPEAN COMMUNITY AND NATO, MAY HAVE THE APPEAL NECESSARY
     TO SPARK TRUE PROGRESS FOR PEACE IN PALESTINE.

05016 KIDRON, P.
     ISRAEL: SHAMIR'S MYSTERIOUS IDEAS
     MIDDLE EAST INTERNATIONAL, (347) (MAR 89), 6-8.
        THE AUTHOR SPECULATES ABOUT PEACE PLANS LIKELY TO BE
     PROPOSED BY YITZHAK SHAMIR AND SHIMON PERES IN THE NEAR
     FUTURE.

05017 KIDRON, P.
     ISRAEL: SHARON RALLIES HIS TROOPS
     MIDDLE EAST INTERNATIONAL, (345) (MAR 89), 13-14.

ISRAEL'S INDUSTRY AND COMMERCE MINISTER ARIEL SHARON
MISSES NO OPPORTUNITY TO DISSOCIATE HIMSELF FROM PRIME
MINISTER YITZHAK SHAMIR AND FOREIGN MINISTER MOSHE ARENS,
WHOM HE REGARDS AS TOO SOFT. ALTHOUGH HE IS CAREFUL TO AVOID
A DIRECT CONFRONTATION WITH SHAMIR, SHARON CONSTANTLY
COMPLAINS ABOUT THE GOVERNMENT'S INACTION AND LACK OF
LEADERSHIP.

05018 KIDRON, P.
ISRAEL: THE PAY-OFF
MIDDLE EAST INTERNATIONAL, (344) (FEB 89), 10-11.
NEGOTIATIONS BETWEEN ISRAELI FINANCE MINISTER SHIMON
PERES AND HISTADRUT LEADERS PRODUCED AN AGREEMENT THAT A
COST-OF-LIVING INCREASE OF 12% WILL BE COMPENSATED BY A WAGE
RISE OF NO MORE THAN 3%. IN RETURN FOR ITS ACCOMMODATION ON
WORKERS' PAY, THE GOVERNMENT WILL GIVE AID TO BOLSTER SOME
OF THE HISTADRUT'S FAILING VENTURES AND GUARANTEE BANK LOANS
FOR HISTADRUT-OWNED CONCERNS.

05019 KIDRON, P.
ISRAEL"S POLITICAL DISARRAY
MIDDLE EAST INTERNATIONAL, (360) (OCT 89), 3-4.
THE SIMULTANEOUS VISITS OF ISRAELI FINANCE MINISTER
SHIMON PERES AND FOREIGN MINISTER MOSHE ARENS TO THE US
UNDERSCORED THE INCREASING CONFLICT IN ISRAEL'S POLITICAL
CIRCLES. CONFLICT OVER EGYPTIAN PRESIDENT MUBARAK'S PEACE
PLAN AND ISRAELI PRIME MINISTER YITZHAK SHAMIR'S OWN PEACE
PLAN HAVE SPLIT THE POWER-SHARING LABOUR AND LIKUD PARTIES
EVEN FURTHER APART. IN ADDITION, INTRA-PARTY STRIFE IS
RAMPANT. IF THESE CONFRONTATIONS DO NOT ABATE, IT REMAINS
UNLIKELY THAT ANY CONCRETE PROGRESS TOWARDS PEACE WILL BE
ACHIEVED.

05020 KIDRON, P.
LABOUR'S EMPTY BLUSTER
MIDDLE EAST INTERNATIONAL, 355 (JUL 89), 6-7.
ALTHOUGH CLEARLY UNCOMFORTABLE OVER ITS ROLE AS SHAMIR'S
JUNIOR PARTNER, LABOUR SEEMS TO HAVE FEW PRACTICAL
ALTERNATIVES. IT WOULD BE HARD TO CHOOSE A WORSE TIME FOR
PULLING OUT OF THE COALITION. THE PARTY'S LAST REMAINING
POWER-BASE IS THE HISTRADRUT TRADE UNION FEDERATION, WHOSE
ECONOMIC ENTERPRISES, STILL IN GRAVE DIFFICULTIES, ARE IN
URGENT NEED OF MASSIVE GOVERNMENT AID. IF LABOUR OPTED FOR
THE OPPOSITION BENCHES, THAT AID WOULD BE JEOPARDISED; THE
PARTY'S TARNISHED IMAGE WOULD HARDLY BE IMPROVED BY ITS
INDUSTRIAL EMPIRE'S PLUNGE INTO BANKRUPTCY.

05021 KIDRON, P.
LITTLE JOY FOR ISRAEL
MIDDLE EAST INTERNATIONAL, (345) (MAR 89), 5.
THE FRUITLESSNESS OF THE ARENS-SHEVARDNADZE TALKS
HIGHLIGHTS THE ISRAELI DILEMMA REGARDING THE SOVIET UNION.
ISRAEL GENUINELY WANTS TO NORMALIZE RELATIONS WITH MOSCOW,
BUT PRIME MINISTER YITZHAK SHAMIR AND HIS HARDLINE
COLLEAGUES ARE RELUCTANT TO GRANT THE USSR A SIGNIFICANT
ROLE IN MIDEAST DIPLOMACY, DUE TO MOSCOW'S SUPPORT FOR
PALESTINIAN SELF-DETERMINATION AND RUSSIAN INSISTENCE THAT
ISRAEL SURRENDER ITS 1967 CONQUESTS.

05022 KIDRON, P.
PERES FACES ISRAEL'S ECONOMIC ABYSS
MIDDLE EAST INTERNATIONAL, (342) (JAN 89), 17-18.
SHIMON PERES PLAN TO SAVE THE FAILING ISRAELI ECONOMY
GOT OFF TO AN INAUSPICIOUS START. WITH CABINET MEMBERS
REFUSING TO CUT THEIR BUDGETS, PERES WAS FORCED TO SHIFT THE
BURDEN TO ORDINARY CITIZENS, WHO MUST NOW PAY 10-30% MORE
FOR STAPLE FOODSTUFFS AND PUBLIC TRANSPORTATION BECAUSE
GOVERNMENT SUBSIDIES WERE ABRUPTLY WITHDRAWN.

05023 KIDRON, P.
PERES' ECONOMIC PLAN
MIDDLE EAST INTERNATIONAL, (358) (SEP 89), 9.
UNDER HEAVY FIRE FOR THE GROWING UNEMPLOYMENT IN ISRAEL,
FINANCE MINISTER SHIMON PERES UNVEILED A PLAN TO CREATE NEW
JOBS BY MEANS OF 100 SELECTED PROJECTS, TO BE RAMMED THROUGH
BY A MINISTERIAL COMMITTEE EMPOWERED TO BYPASS NORMAL
LICENSING PROCEDURES. THE PLAN WAS CRITICIZED BOTH FOR THE
BYPASSING OF ALL EXISTING PROCEDURES AND FOR THE FACT THAT
PERES' PROJECTS ARE UNLIKELY TO GENERATE MANY NEW JOBS.

05024 KIDRON, P.
PERES' TRIBULATIONS
MIDDLE EAST INTERNATIONAL, 353 (JUN 89), 4-5.
WHEN PERES UNDERTOOK THE FINANCE PORTFOLIO LAST DECEMBER,
HE EVIDENTLY LOOKED FORWARD TO SWIFT AND IMPRESSIVE SUCCESS
IN HEALING THE ECONOMY, THEREBY ALLOWING HIM TO SALVAGE HIS
TATTERED POLITICAL REPUTATION AND LAUNCH HIMSELF ON THE PATH
BACK TO THE PRIME MINISTER'S OFFICE. PERES SET ABOUT HIS
TASK AT A SPANKING PACE, HOLDING NIGHTLONG CONSULTATIONS
WITH LEADING ECONOMISTS AND HEADS OF BUSINESS AND TRADE
UNIONS. WITHIN DAYS, HE HAD INITIATED A HASTY TWO-STAGE
DEVALUATION OF THE OVER-PRICED SHEKEL AND OTHER VIGOROUS
STEPS TO STIMULATE THE FLAGGING ECONOMY AFTER YEARS OF
MISMANAGEMENT BY LIKUD. BUT IN SPITE OF HIS ENERGETIC

APPROACH, THE WHEELS ARE SLOWING DOWN.

05025 KIDRON, P.
SHAMIR LOSES A RELIGIOUS PARTY . . . AND FAILS IN
HISTRADRUT ELECTIONS
MIDDLE EAST INTERNATIONAL, (363) (NOV 89), 8-10.
ISRAELI PRIME MINISTER YITZHAK SHAMIR IS SUFFERING
POLITICAL SETBACKS BOTH IN PARLIAMENT, AND IN THE HISTRADRUT,
A HUGE ISRAELI TRADE CONFEDERATION. WHILE THE DEFECTION OF
THE DIMINUTIVE AGADAT YISRAEL PARTY IS INSIGNIFICANT IN
TERMS OF PARLIAMENTARY ARITHMETIC, IT COULD SIGNAL THAT
ISRAEL'S ULTRA-ORTHODOX RELIGIOUS PARTIES HAVE HAD ENOUGH OF
SHAMIR'S "SHABBY TREATMENT." A FULL-SCALE ABANDONMENT OF
SHAMIR COULD HAVE SIGNIFICANT REPERCUSSIONS. LOSSES IN THE
HISTRADRUT ELECTIONS ALSO SIGNAL THE WANING OF POWER FOR
SHAMIR AND THE LIKUD PARTY.

05026 KIDRON, P.
SHAMIR STANDS FIRM
MIDDLE EAST INTERNATIONAL, (361) (OCT 89), 8-9.
DESPITE A FLURRY OF DIPLOMATIC ACTIVITY, IT SEEMS THAT
LITTLE PROGRESS TOWARDS A RESOLUTION OF THE ISRAELI-
PALESTINIAN CONFLICT WILL BE MADE. A KEY OBSTACLE IS THE
HARD-LINE STANCE TAKEN BY PRIME MINISTER YITZHAK SHAMIR; HE
HAS UNEQUIVOCALLY STATED THAT IF THE PLO IS REPRESENTED IN
THE PALESTINIAN DELEGATION, ISRAEL WILL NOT PARTICIPATE.
SUCH AN UNCOMPROMISING POLICY WILL ALMOST CERTAINLY SCUTTLE
ANY NEGOTIATION ATTEMPTS.

05027 KIDRON, P.
SHAMIR'S RELATIONS WITH WASHINGTON
MIDDLE EAST INTERNATIONAL, (362) (NOV 89), 6-7.
THE FAILURE OF PRESIDENT GEORGE BUSH TO INVITE ISRAELI
PRIME MINISTER YITZHAK SHAMIR TO WASHINGTON IS AN INDICATION
OF THE CURRENT LEVEL OF TENSION BETWEEN ISRAEL AND THE US.
THE CHIEF SORE SPOT IS SHAMIR'S REJECTION OF SECRETARY OF
STATE JAMES BAKER'S PROPOSED "FIVE POINTS." ISRAEL HAS
DEMANDED THE RIGHT TO DOMINATE THE PROPOSED PEACE
NEGOTIATIONS TO AN EXTENT UNPRECEDENTED IN DIPLOMATIC
PROTOCOL. A FAILURE TO RESOLVE THIS CONFLICT WILL
SIGNIFICANTLY SET BACK THE PEACE PROCESS IN THE MIDDLE EAST.

05028 KIDRON, P.
SHARMIR BENDS WITH THE WIND
MIDDLE EAST INTERNATIONAL, 355 (JUL 89), 5-6.
YITZHAK SHAMIR RIDES TO THE TIDE, ENDEAVOURING ONLY TO
REMAIN AFLOAT. WHEN HIS "PEACE INITIATIVE" CAME UNDER FIRE
FROM WITHIN THE RANKS OF HIS OWN LIKUD PARTY, THE PRIME
MINISTER FACED A POTENTIALLY BRUISING SHOWDOWN WITH THE
REBELS WHO HAD RALLIED AROUND ARIEL SHARON AND HIS DEMANDS
FOR TOUGHER TERMS. BUT WHEN THE LIKUD CENTRAL COMMITTEE
CONVENED ON 5 JUNE, SHAMIR SHUNNED A TRIAL OF STRENGTH WITH
HIS PARTY ADVERSARIES, PREFERRING THE WELL TRIED TACTIC OF
"IF YOU CAN'T BEAT 'EM, JOIN 'EM", BY INCORPORATING INTO HIS
OWN SPEECH ALL THE "STIFFENERS" THEY DEMANDED. HOWEVER
UNDIGNIFIED, THIS TWISTING AND TURNING HAS LEFT SHAMIR WITH
A TACTICAL ADVANTAGE OVER HIS IMMEDIATE POLITICAL
COLLOCUTORS: UNLIKE THEM, HE HAS RETAINED A CERTAIN FREEDOM
OF MANOEUVRE. BY BOWING TO ONE AND ALL, HE HAS PLACED
HIMSELF AT THE FOCAL POINT OF ALL THE CONFLICTING PRESSURES,
DUCKING TO ALLOW THEM TO CANCEL ONE ANOTHER OUT. AS THE DUST
CLEARS, THE NEW "PARALLEL OF FORCES" EMERGES WITH STRIKING
CLARITY.

05029 KIDRON, P.
SHARON FOR THE USSR?
MIDDLE EAST INTERNATIONAL, (357) (AUG 89), 9.
A VISIT OF SOVIET GEORGIA'S TRADE DELEGATION NOT ONLY
LED TO DISCUSSION OF JOINT SOVIET-ISRAELI ECONOMIC VENTURES,
BUT ALSO AN INVITATION TO ISRAEL'S MINISTER OF INDUSTRY AND
TRADE, ARIEL SHARON, TO VISIT THE USSR. THE MEDIA HULLABALOO
THAT RESULTED APPARENTLY EMBARRASSED THE SOVIET UNION INTO
DENYING THE INVITATION.

05030 KIDRON, P.
SIGNS OF STRESS: VIGILANTE VIOLENCE
MIDDLE EAST INTERNATIONAL, 352 (JUN 89), 6-8.
IN RECONSTITUTING THE EXITS FROM THE GAZA STRIP AS A DE
FACTO BORDER, WITH THE ID CARDS AS MAKESHIFT VISAS, THE
ISRAELI AUTHORITIES ARE IMPLICITY CONCEDING THAT THE
OCCUPIED TERRITORIES ARE A SEPARATE NATIONAL AND POLITICAL
ENTITY. IT CAN INDEED BE SEEN AS A MARK OF THE SUCCESS OF
THE INTIFADA THAT THE AUTHORITIES OVERCAME AN EVIDENT
RELUCTANCE TO INSTITUTE THE STEP, THE LATTER BEING A FURTHER
INDICATION THAT, AFTER 19 MONTHS OF THE PALESTINIAN UPRISING,
THE ISRAELI ESTABLISHMENT IS IN PROFOUND CONFUSION OVER THE
CORRECT RESPONSE.

05031 KIDRON, P.
STONEWALLING
MIDDLE EAST INTERNATIONAL, (346) (MAR 89), 4-5.
THE WASHINGTON VISIT OF ISRAELI FOREIGN MINISTER MOSHE
ARENS HAD THE AIR OF A NON-EVENT. MOST OF HIS TIME WAS TAKEN
UP WITH MEDIA APPEARANCES BECAUSE THE MAIN PURPOSE OF HIS

MISSION HAS TO GENERATE A SEMBLANCE OF ACTIVITY WHILE, IN
FACT, ENDEAVORING TO DELAY OR BLOCK ANY GENUINE MOVEMENT.

05032 KIDRON, P.
THE COALITION AGAIN, THANKS TO ARAFAT
MIDDLE EAST INTERNATIONAL, (341) (JAN 89), 4-5.
ISRAEL'S NATIONAL UNITY COALITION IS BACK IN BUSINESS
AFTER A BITTER ELECTION CAMPAIGN. WHILE THE PARLIAMENTARY
DEADLOCK BETWEEN LIKUD AND LABOUR HAS DICTATED PARITY IN THE
NUMBER OF MINISTERIAL PROTFOLIOS ALLOTTED TO EACH PARTY, THE
TERMS OF THEIR AGREEMENT MARK A MARGINAL SHIFT IN FAVOUR OF
THE LIKUD. CREDIT FOR THE RENEWAL OF THE ALLIANCE SHOULD GO
TO PRESSURES CREATED BY YASSAR ARAFAT, A FALTERING ECONOMY,
STATESMANLIKE INDUCEMENTS, AND SORDID POLITICAL INTERESTS.

05033 KIDRON, P.
THE INTIFADA'S COST TO ISRAEL
MIDDLE EAST INTERNATIONAL, (365) (DEC 89), 18-19.
THE ARTICLE EXPLORES THE EFFECT THAT THE INTIFADA HAS
HAD ON ISRAEL. IT CONCLUDES THAT THE ECONOMIC EFFECT HAS
BEEN MIXED. SOME SHORT TERM LOSES DUE TO DECLINING TOURISM,
THE LOSS OF CHEAP ARAB LABOR AND THE LOSS OF THE WEST BANK
AS A MARKET, ARE COUNTERED BY THE LONG TERM BENEFITS OF THE
FORCED MODERNIZATION OF ISRAELI INDUSTRY. THE INTIFADA HAS
HAD A SIGNIFICANT EFFECT ON MILITARY MORALE AND DISCIPLINE;
POLARIZATION AMONG NOT ONLY MILITARY PERSONNEL, BUT THE
POPULATION AS A WHOLE IS INCREASING. PERHAPS THE MOST
SIGNIFICANT EFFECT IS THE RAISING OF ISRAELI PUBLIC
CONSCIOUSNESS TO THE INESCAPABLE NECESSITY OF DEALING WITH
THE PROBLEM.

05034 KIDRON, P.
WINKS AND NODS, BUT SHAMIR'S PLAN REMAINS ELUSIVE
MIDDLE EAST INTERNATIONAL, (342) (JAN 89), 3-5.
FOR MONTHS, ISRAELI PRIME MINISTER YIZHAK SHAMIR CLAIMED
TO HAVE A PEACE PLAN BUT FAILED TO RELEASE ANY DETAILS. THEN
THE EXISTENCE OF THE PLAN WAS PLACED IN DOUBT BY SHAMIR
HIMSELF, WHO TOLD EUROPEAN VISITORS THAT "THE LIKUD HAS NO
PEACE PLAN AND NO SUCH PLAN CAN BE EXPECTED IN THE
FORSEEABLE FUTURE." FORESEEABLE FUTURE."

05035 KIDRON, P.
YES, THEY ARE JEWS
MIDDLE EAST INTERNATIONAL, 356 (AUG 89), 11-12.
IN THEIR BITTER REARGUARD BATTLE AGAINST THE
CONSERVATIVE-REFORM TIDE, ISRAEL'S ORTHODOX RABBIS REFUSE TO
RECOGNISE THE VALIDITY OF CONVERSIONS. THIS REFUSAL FOUND
TANGIBLE EXPRESSION WHEN OFFICIALS OF THE INTERIOR MINISTRY -
LONG AN ORTHODOX DOMAIN - REFUSED TO ISSUE SUCH CONVERTS
WITH IDENTITY CARDS DESIGNATING THEIR RELIGION AS JEWISH.
WITHOUT REGISTRATION AS "JEW", THE CONVERT COULD ENCOUNTER
DIFFICULTY IN FINDING EMPLOYMENT OR GAINING A SECURITY
CLEARANCE, AND BE AT A MARKED DISADVANTAGE IN FAMILY
DISPUTES, WHICH COME UNDER THE JURISDICTION OF RELIGIOUS
COURTS; THEIR CHILDREN COULD FACE OBSTACLES WHEN THEY WISH
TO MARRY. THIS BEING A MATTER OF CRUCIAL IMPORTANCE, A
NUMBER OF CONVERTS ACCORDINGLY PETITIONED THE SUPREME COURT,
WHICH FOUND IN THEIR FAVOUR AND INSTRUCTED THE INTERIOR
MINISTRY TO REGISTER THEM AS JEWS.

05036 KIDRON, R.
SHAMIR'S PLAN--AND THE THREATS
MIDDLE EAST INTERNATIONAL, (351) (MAY 89), 3-5.
THE ARTICLE OUTLINES THE PEACE PLAN OF ISRAELI PRIME
MINISTER YITZHAK SHAMIR AND ANALYZES ITS IMPLICATIONS. THE
PEACE INITIATIVE WAS ACCOMPANIED BY THREATS TO ANYONE WHO
ATTEMPTED TO TORPEDO IT, BUT THE GREATEST OPPOSITION TO THE
PLAN IS LIKELY TO COME FROM SHAMIR'S OWN CABINET.

05037 KIECHEL, C.
SOMETHING HAPPENED
NATIONAL REVIEW, XLI(13) (JUL 89), 23-24.
THIS ARTICLE EXAMINES WHY POLAND HAS A BETTER CHANCE TO
REFORM THAN THE SOVIET UNION. POLAND HAS SOME ADVANTAGES ITS
BIG BROTHER TO THE EAST DOESN'T SHARE. FIRST: POLES
THEMSELVES. POLES, TYPICALLY INDIVIDUALISTIC, ARE CLOSET
CAPITALISTS: WELL-EDUCATED POLES COULD BE MODERN ONES.
POLAND'S SECOND GREAT ADVANTAGE IS AGRICULTURE. POLISH LAND
WAS NEVER COLLECTIVIZED, AND TODAY MORE THAN 75 PER CENT OF
IT IS PRIVATELY OWNED. THE VAST MAJORITY OF PRIVATE FARMERS
ARE PEASANTS, NOT AGRICULTURAL SHIFT WORKERS LIKE THOSE WHO
TOIL ON RUSSIA'S COLLECTIVIZED FARMS. POLAND'S THIRD GREAT
ECONOMIC ADVANTAGE IS THE CATHOLIC CHURCH. IF AND WHEN
POLAND IMPLEMENTS REAL FREE-MARKET POLICIES, THERE WILL BE A
NECESSARY STAGE OF PRIMITIVE CAPITALISM, WITH GROWING
DISPARTIES IN INCOME AND WEALTH. THE CATHOLIC CHURCH
PROVIDES A COMMUNITY, A SAFETY VALVE THAT CAN HELP DIFFUSE
THE SOCIAL TENSIONS THAT MAY ARISE.

05038 KIEL, L.D.
PUBLIC ADMINISTRATION IN THE POST-INDUSTRIAL ERA:
ADAPTATION OR DRIFT?
DISSERTATION ABSTRACTS INTERNATIONAL, 50(6) (DEC 89),
1800-A.

THE AUTHOR EXAMINES THE PRESENT STATE OF THE ACADEMIC
FIELD OF PUBLIC ADMINISTRATION WITHIN THE THEORETICAL
FRAMEWORK OF THE POST-INDUSTRIAL SOCIETY. HE FOCUSES ON THE
RELATIVE ADAPTATION OF ACADEMIC PUBLIC ADMINISTRATION TO THE
TECHNOLOGICAL REQUISITES OF MANAGEMENT DECISION-MAKING IN
THE POST-INDUSTRIAL ERA.

05039 KIELMANSEGG, P.G.
WEST GERMANY'S CONSTITUTION: RESPONSE TO THE PAST OR
DESIGN FOR THE FUTURE?
WORLD TODAY, 45(10) (OCT 89), 175-179.
THE AUTHOR EVALUATES THE IMPACT THE BASIC LAW HAS HAS ON
THE DEVELOPMENT OF CONSTITUTIONAL DEMOCRACY IN WEST GERMANY
SINCE 1949. HE IDENTIFIES AND OUTLINES FOUR FUNDAMENTAL
PRINCIPLES THAT SHAPED THE CONSTITUTION AND COMPARES THE
IMPORTANCE OF THE CONSTITUTION TO THAT OF SOCIAL AND
ECONOMIC FACTORS.

05040 KIELMAS, M.
CENTRAL MEDITERRANEAN OIL SEARCH POINTS TO LIBYA
MIDDLE EAST INTERNATIONAL, 352 (JUN 89), 17-18.
AFTER A YEAR OF SUBTLE BRIDGE-BUILDING WITH
INTERNATIONAL INDUSTRY AND A MINIMUM OF FUSS, LIBYA HAS
EMERGED AS AN OVERALL FAVOURITE IN THE CENTRAL
MEDITERRANEAN'S RENEWED OIL SEARCH. WHILE FOR LIBYA THIS
MEANS A RESUMPTION OF SYSTEMATIC OIL EXPLORATION AFTER WHAT,
IN PRATICAL TERMS, HAS BEEN A 20-YEAR HIATUS, THE EFFORTS OF
OTHER MEDITERRANEAN COUNTRIES SUCH AS TUNISIA, ALGERIA AND
MALTA TO ATTRACT THE OIL INDUSTRY'S INTEREST ARE LIKELY TO
BE PUSHED EVEN FURTHER INTO THE SHADE. LIBYA'S OVERWHELMING
ADVANTAGE IS THAT IT IS THE ONLY COUNTRY IN THE
MEDITERRANEAN REGION WHERE IT IS STILL POSSIBLE TO FIND BIG
OIL.

05041 KIELMAS, M.
THE SOVIET-IRANIAN DEAL - MORE WORDS THAN SUBSTANCE
MIDDLE EAST INTERNATIONAL, 355 (JUL 89), 16-17.
WITH OIL AND ENERGY MATTERS FIGURING SO HIGHLY IN THE
RECENT SOVIET-IRANIAN ECONOMIC AGREEMENT, IT IS NO SMALL
TWIST OF HISTORICAL IRONY THAT THE FIRST TREATY SIGNED
BETWEEN THESE TWO NATIONS IN 1723 LEGITIMISED THE RUSSIAN
ANNEXATION OF THE FUTURE OIL PROVINCE OF BAKU. CENTRAL TO
THE DEAL ARE IRANIAN GAS EXPORTS TO THE SOVIET UNION.
IRANIAN GAS SUPPLIES PIPED TO THE SOVIET CAUCASIAN REPUBLICS
OF ARMENIA, GEORGIA AND AZERBAIJAN, WERE CUT IN 1980 WHEN
IRAN QUADRUPLED THE PRICE. THE SUBSEQUENT HARDSHIP SUFFERED
IN THESE REGIONS PERSUADED THE SOVIET AUTHORITIES TO
UNDERTAKE A MAJOR GAS SUPPLY PROJECT FROM THE HUGE WESTERN
SIBERIAN FIELDS TO THE CAUCASUS. WHAT THE DEAL REPRESENTS IS
THAT AFTER 266 YEARS AND THREE INVASIONS (THE OTHER TWO WERE
IN 1813 AND 1941), IRAN AND THE USSR ARE TAKING THE FIRST
TENTATIVE STEPS TO RECONCILE THEIR TORTUOUS HISTORY. HASHEMI
RAFSANJANI'S SENTIMENTS IN MOSCOW SUPPORTING THE AFGHAN
REBELS DEMONSTRATED THAT THE TWO SIDES WILL CONTINUE TO
MANIPULATE THE REGION'S MINORITIES, SOMETHING REMINISCENT OF
PETER THE GREAT WITH THE ARMENIANS AND GEORGIANS AND STALIN
WITH AZERBAIJAN. NEVERTHELESS, THE INTERESTS OF GOOD
NEIGHBOURLINESS PERHAPS REQUIRED AN ELABORATE ECONOMIC
WRAPPING, EVEN THOUGH MUCH OF IT WILL PROVE ILLUSORY.

05042 KIGGUNDU, M.; HOBBS, C.F.
THE DEPLOYMENT OF CANADIAN EXPERTS AND TEACHERS IN
INTERNATIONAL DEVELOPMENT
CANADIAN PUBLIC ADMINISTRATION, 32(1) (SPR 89), 1-22.
THE PURPOSE OF THIS PAPER IS TWOFOLD. FIRST, IT EXAMINES
THE DEPLOYMENT OF CANADIAN EXPERTS AND TEACHERS IN
INTERNATIONAL DEVELOPMENT. SECONDLY, IT ASSESSES THE EXTENT
TO WHICH THE DISTRIBUTION OF CANADIAN EXPERTISE AMONG
DEVELOPING COUNTRIES IS CONSISTENT WITH THE CANADIAN POLICY
OF CONCENTRATING ON THE NEEDS OF THE POOREST OF THE POOR AND
THOSE IN GREATEST NEED. THE RESULTS SHOW THAT OVER ONE-HALF
OF ALL CANADIAN EXPERTS GO TO AFRICA AND THAT ABOUT 20 PER
CENT ARE WOMEN, MOSTLY IN TRADITIONAL FEMALE-DOMINATED
PROFESSIONS. USING MORE OBJECTIVE SOCIAL AND ECONOMIC
DEVELOPMENT INDICATORS, SUCH AS THE PHYSICAL QUALITY OF LIFE
INDEX AND DISPARITY REDUCTION RATES, HOWEVER, THE RESULTS
SHOW THAT THE DEPLOYMENT OF CANADIAN EXPERTISE DOES NOT
REFLECT THE REAL NEEDS OF MANY OF THE DEVELOPING COUNTRIES
RECEIVING AID FROM THE CANADIAN INTERNATIONAL DEVELOPMENT
AGENCY. THESE CONTRADICTIONS AND INCONSISTENCIES ARE
DISCUSSED IN THE LIGHT OF COMPETING AND OFTEN CONFLICTING
FOREIGN POLICY OBJECTIVES WHICH OFTEN OVERRIDE THE
LEGITIMATE DEVELOPMENT NEEDS OF THE MOST NEEDY COUNTRIES.
SPECIFIC SUGGESTIONS ARE MADE TO ALLEVIATE SOME OF THE
INCONSISTENCIES.

05043 KIHL, Y.H
SOUTH KOREA'S RISE TO PROMINIENCE
CURRENT HISTORY, 88(537) (APR 89), 165-168, 192-193.
IN THE LATE 1980'S, SOUTH KOREA IS A SUCCESS STORY IN
TERMS OF ITS IMPRESSIVE GAINS IN ECONOMIC DEVELOPMENT AND
ITS STRIDES TOWARD DEMOCRACY. MOREOVER, DUE TO THE DIFFERENT
RATES OF ECONOMIC GROWTH AND SOCIOPOLITICAL DEVELOPMENT, THE
BALANCE BETWEEN THE TWO KOREAS HAS COME TO FAVOR THE SOUTH

OVER THE NORTH.

05044 KIHL, Y.W.
INTRA-REGIONAL CONFLICT AND THE ASEAN PEACE PROCESS
INTERNATIONAL JOURNAL, XLIV(3) (SUM 89), 598-615.
IN THE MANILA DECLARATION OF 15 DECEMBER 1987, THE HEADS
OF STATE OF THE SIX MEMBERS OF THE ASSOCIATION OF SOUTH-EAST
ASIAN NATIONS (BRUNEI, INDONESIA, MALAYSIA, THE PHILIPPINES,
SINGAPORE, AND THAILAND) REAFFIRMED THEIR COMMON RESOLVE TO
ESTABLISH A ZONE OF PEACE, FREEDOM AND NEUTRALITY (ZOPFAN)
FOR THE REGION. DESPITE THIS DECLARATION OF PEACEFUL INTENT,
THE POSSIBILITY REMAINS THAT OLD DISPUTES BOTH WITHIN
COUNTRIES AND BETWEEN COUNTRIES MAY FLARE ANEW. THIS ESSAY
SEEKS TO IDENTIFY THESE LATENT CONFLICTS AND TO CLARIFY
THEIR SOURCE AND NATURE. FURTHER IT EXAMINES THE FUTURE
OPPORTUNITIES FOR THESE CONFLICTS - AS WELL AS PROBLEMS
ARISING FROM GLOBAL AND REGIONAL CHANGES IN THE EXTERNAL
ENVIRONMENT - TO BE RESOLVED OR AT LEAST CONTAINED THROUGH
THE ASEAN FRAMEWORK AND THE STRENGTHENING OF SECURITY AND
TRADE LINKS AMONG ITS MEMBERS.

05045 KILGOUR, D.; KIRSNER, J.
CALL OFF THE PARTY
POLICY OPTIONS, 10(2) (MAR 89), 36.
THE DOMINANCE OF PARTY DISCIPLINE IN THE CANADIAN HOUSE
OF COMMONS IS SO GREAT, THE AUTHORS ARGUE, THAT PARTY
LEADERS COULD CAST A PROXY VOTE ON BEHALF OF THEIR FOLLOWERS
WITHOUT THEIR NEED TO BE PRESENT IN THE HOUSE OF COMMONS.
THIS INTERFERES WITH THE MP'S ABILITY TO REPRESENT HIS
CONSTITUENCY PROPERLY, SINCE HE WILL HAVE TO VOTE WITH THE
PARTY EVEN IF HIS OWN AREA IS NOT IN AGREEMENT. THEY SUGGEST
A SIGNIFICANT LOOSENING OF THE BONDS OF DISCIPLINE IN LINE
WITH THE CUSTOM OF OTHER DEMOCRACIES, AND ADOPTION OF THE
MCGRATH REPORT ON PARLIAMENTARY REFORM'S PROVISION FOR MANY
MORE FREE VOTES IN THE COMMONS.

05046 KILJUNEN, K.
TOWARD A THEORY OF THE INTERNATIONAL DIVISION OF
INDUSTRIAL LABOR
WORLD DEVELOPMENT, 17(1) (JAN 89), 109-138.
THE OBJECTIVE OF THIS STUDY IS TO CONTRIBUTE TO THE
CURRENT DEVELOPMENT THEORY AND DEVELOPMENT POLICY DEBATE.
THE AIM IS TO ILLUMINATE CONTROVERSIES WITHIN INTERNATIONAL
TRADE THEORY OVER THE EXPLANATION OF STRUCTURAL CHANGES IN
THE INTERNATIONAL DIVISION OF LABOR AND THE ASSUMPTION THAT
SPECIALIZATION IS BENEFICIAL TO ALL PARTICIPANTS. THE
STARTING POINT OF THIS INQUIRY IS THE CONVENTIONAL THEORY OF
COMPARATIVE ADVANTAGE. IN RECENT YEARS, SOME NEW
EXPLANATIONS HAVE EMERGED, AIMED AT QUALIFYING THE
DETERMINATION OF COMPARATIVE ADVANTAGE. FURTHERMORE, THERE
ARE APPROACHES THAT OPPOSE ALTOGETHER SPECIALIZATION BASED
ON COMPARATIVE ADVANTAGE. THESE VARIOUS THEORETICAL ACCOUNTS
ARE PRESENTED IN ORDER TO FIND CONCEPTS AND CATEGORIES TO
DESCRIBE THE CHANGING PATTERN OF THE INTERNATIONAL DIVISION
OF INDUSTRIAL LABOR.

05047 KILLIAN, J.H.
ELEVENTH AMENDMENT JURISPRUDENCE: THE COURT CONFOUNDS
CONGRESSIONAL POWER
CRS REVEIW, 10(8) (SEP 89), 3-5.
AMONG THE DIVISIVE ISSUES COMING BEFORE THE SUPREME
COURT ARE QUESTIONS OF FEDERALISM. A HALLMARK OF ONE GROUP
OF JUSTICES HAS BEEN FEDERAL SUPREMACY; THAT OF ANOTHER
GROUP HAS BEEN STATE IMMUNITY FROM FEDERAL REGULATION. FOR
THE MOMENT, CONGRESSIONAL POWER TO REGULATE STATES UNDER THE
COMMERCE CLAUSE IS PREDOMINANT, BUT IMPLEMENTING REGULATION
THROUGH SUITS IN FEDERAL COURTS BY AFFECTED INDIVIDUALS
AGAINST STATES OR STATE OFFICERS HAS BEEN CURTAILED BY
AGGRESSIVE JUDICIAL ENFORCEMENT OF THE ELEVENTH AMENDMENT.

05048 KIM, B.
BRINGING AND MANAGING SOCIOECONOMIC CHANGE: THE STATE IN
KOREA AND MEXICO
DISSERTATION ABSTRACTS INTERNATIONAL, 49(8) (FEB 89),
2377-A.
THE SALIENT FEATURE AMONG LARGER NEWLY INDUSTRIALIZING
COUNTRIES IS PERVASIVE STATE INTERVENTION. THE EXPANSION AND
GROWTH IN ITS ROLE ARE DISCERNIBLE ACROSS CULTURAL REGIONS
AND REFLECT THE WIDELY-SHARED DIFFICULTIES THAT ARE ENTAILED
IN RESOURCE MOBILIZATION AND STRUCTURAL TRANSFORMATION.
HOWEVER, SIMILAR STATE TASKS ARE PURSUED DIFFERENTLY, AND
POLITICAL OUTCOMES MAY DIVERGE SHARPLY FROM THE ONES THAT
WERE ORIGINALLY INTENDED.

05049 KIM, E.
EXPLAINING SOVIET-JAPANESE RELATIONS, 1972-1985: DOMESTIC
POLITICS VERSUS THE GLOBAL SUPERPOWER RIVALRY
DISSERTATION ABSTRACTS INTERNATIONAL, 50(3) (SEP 89),
787-A.
TWO EXPLANATIONS HAVE BEEN ADVANCED IN THE STUDY OF
MOSCOW-TOKYO RELATIONS BETWEEN 1972 AND 1985. THE DOMESTIC
POLITICS MODEL FOCUSES ON CHANGES IN THE RESPECTIVE DOMESTIC
POLITICS, WHILE THE SUPERPOWER RELATIONS MODEL EMPHASIZES
THE VICISSITUDE OF THE GLOBAL SUPERPOWER RIVALRY. THIS

DISSERTATION CONCLUDES THAT THE SUPERPOWER PERSPECTIVE
PROVIDES A CAUSE-EFFECT EXPLANATION OF SOVIET-JAPANESE TIES,
WHILE THE DOMESTIC PERSPECTIVE HELPS EXPLAIN WHETHER OR NOT
A CERTAIN POLICY WAS ADOPTED IN A PARTICULAR SITUATION.

05050 KIM, G.
WESTERN INTERVENTION IN KOREA, 1950-54
DISSERTATION ABSTRACTS INTERNATIONAL, 50(4) (OCT 89),
1083-A.
THIS DISSERTATION LOOKS AT WHY THE WESTERN POWERS
INTERVENED IN THE KOREAN WAR AND HOW THEY PURSUED THEIR
OBJECTIVES.

05051 KIM, H.
CAMPUS RADICALS FACE THE IDEOLOGICAL GAP
FAR EASTERN ECONOMIC REVIEW, 141(36) (SEP 88), 91-93.
THE ARTICLE EXAMINES THE ONGOING EFFORTS OF SOUTH KOREAN
UNIVERSITY STUDENTS TO CONTINUE DEMONSTRATING FOR
REUNIFICATION WITH NORTH KOREA. IT OUTLINES THE LOOSE, BUT
EFFECTIVE ORGANIZATION THAT EXISTS ON CAMPUSES WHOSE PURPOSE
IS TO INDOCTRINATE YOUNGER STUDENTS TO THE CAUSE. IT ALSO
LOOKS AT THE GROWING GENERATION GAP WHICH SEPARATES AN OLDER
GENERATION WHICH REMEMBERS THE WAR AND VIEWS THE US AS
KOREA'S BENEFACTORS, AND THE RISING YOUTH WHICH NOW MAKE UP
NEARLY THREE-QUARTERS OF THE POPULATION AND IS INCREASINGLY
ANTI-AMERICAN.

05052 KIM, H.
EQUIDISTANCE OR SPLIT-INTEREST: CHINA BETWEEN TWO KOREAS
IN EDUCATIONAL AND CULTURAL RELATIONS, 1945-1988
KOREA OBSERVER, XX(4) (WIN 89), 455-478.
FOUR MAJOR FACTORS SEEM TO INFLUENCE CHINESE FOREIGN
POLICY TOWARD NORTH AND SOUTH KOREA IN TERMS OF THE
PERCEPTION OF THE BALANCE OF POWER: (1) THE UNITED STATES'
INTEREST IN THE KOREAN PENINSULA AS IT RELATES TO AMERICAN
SECURITY NEEDS; (2) JAPAN'S INTEREST IN KOREA AS IT RELATES
TO THE FORMERS SECURITY NEEDS AND ITS TRADE WITH SOUTH KOREA;
(3) THE SOVIET UNION'S SECURITY NEEDS AND ITS ALLIANCE WITH
NORTH KOREA; AND (4) THE POSSIBLE POLITICAL REALITY OF A
UNIFIED KOREA. THESE FOUR FACTORS, WORKING AT TIMES
INDEPENDENTLY AND AT TIMES IN CONCERT, HAVE SHAPED CHINESE
INTERNATIONAL RELATIONS WITH THE TWO KOREAS.

05053 KIM, H. K.
THE POLITICAL ECONOMY OF INDUSTRIAL ADJUSTMENT STRATEGIES
IN SOUTH KOREA: A COMPARATIVE STUDY OF THE TEXTILE, STEEL,
AND SEMICONDUCTOR INDUSTRIES
DISSERTATION ABSTRACTS INTERNATIONAL, 49(8) (FEB 89),
2377-A.
THE AUTHOR USES A SECTORAL APPROACH TO ANALYZE CHANGING
PATTERNS OF STATE INTERVENTION OVER DIFFERENT PHASES OF
INDUSTRIALIZATION IN SOUTH KOREA. THE TEXTILE, STEEL, AND
SEMICONDUCTOR INDUSTRIES ARE EXAMINED IN DETAIL. THE ROLE OF
THE STATE HAS VARIED SYSTEMATICALLY ACROSS SECTORS AND OVER
FOUR DEVELOPMENTAL PHASES: (A) IMPORT SUBSTITUTION
INDUSTRIALIZATION, (B) EXPORT-ORIENTED INDUSTRIALIZATION
(EOI), (C) EOI DEEPENING, AND (D) SECONDARY EOI.

05054 KIM, H.N.
THE 1988 PARLIAMENTARY ELECTION IN SOUTH KOREA
ASIAN SURVEY, 29(5) (MAY 89), 480-495.
THIS ESSAY ANALYSES THE RESULTS OF THE 1988 ELECTION,
EMPHASIZING FACTORS THAT CONTRIBUTED TO BRINGING ABOUT THE
SO-CALLED YADAE YOSO (LARGE OPPOSITION AND SMALL GOVERNMENT
PARTY) PHENOMENON IN THE PARLIAMENTARY ELECTION, IN ADDITION,
IT ATTEMPTS TO EVALUATE THE IMPLICATIONS OF THE ELECTION
RESULTS FOR THE FUTURE OF THE SOUTH KOREAN PARTY SYSTEM.

05055 KIM, I.C.
POLITICAL ALIENATION IN RURAL SOUTH KOREA: A SOCIOECONOMIC
ANALYSIS
DISSERTATION ABSTRACTS INTERNATIONAL, 49(8) (FEB 89),
2387-A.
THE AUTHOR STUDIES CONTEMPORARY POLITICAL ALIENATION IN
RURAL SOUTH KOREA AND ITS IMPACT ON DEVELOPMENT. HE USES A
CONCEPTUAL COLLAPSED AND COMBINED MODEL OF POLITICAL
ALIENATION TO DIFFERENTIATE LEVELS AND DISPOSITIONS OF
POLITICAL ALIENATION AND THEIR CONNECTIONS TO POLICY
NONCOMPLIANCE AND NONTRADITIONAL PARTICIPATION OF THE
ALIENATED POPULACE.

05056 KIM, J.
RECENT ANTI-AMERICANISM IN SOUTH KOREA: THE CAUSES
ASIAN SURVEY, 29(8) (AUG 89), 749-763.
THE INTENT OF THIS ARTICLE IS TO ANALYZE THE CAUSES OF
ANTI-AMERICANISM IN SOUTH KOREA IN BOTH LONG RANGE AND
IMMEDIATE TERMS AND TO UNDERSTAND THE MEANING OF THE
PHENOMENON. THE GENERAL PERSPECTIVE IS EXPLORED AS WELL AS
THE CHANGING PERCEPTIONS OVER THE LAST THREE GENERATIONS.
RECENT ISSUES AND CONFLICTING VIEWS ARE IDENTIFIED. IT
CONCLUDES THAT RATIONAL CRITICISM OF THE UNITED STATES IS
NOT FUNDAMENTALLY HARMFUL TO EITHER COUNTRY.

05057 KIM, J.
TECHNOLOGY DEVELOPMENT STRATEGY AND THE RELATIONSHIP
BETWEEN TECHNOLOGY IMPORT AND DOMESTIC RESEARCH AND
DEVELOPMENT (R&D)
DISSERTATION ABSTRACTS INTERNATIONAL, 50(6) (DEC 89),
1788-A.
THE MAJOR PURPOSE OF THIS STUDY WAS TO DEVELOP A MEANS
TO UNDERSTAND THE RELATIONSHIP BETWEEN TECHNOLOGY IMPORT AND
DOMESTIC RESEARCH AND DEVELOPMENT. ALTHOUGH MUCH OF THE
DISCUSSION FOCUSES ON THE JAPANESE AND KOREAN EXPERIENCE IN
TECHNOLOGY DEVELOPMENT, THE STATISTICAL ANALYSIS OF THE
RELATIONSHIP BETWEEN TECHNOLOGY IMPORT AND DOMESTIC R&D
ENCOMPASS OTHER COUNTRIES. THE STATISTICAL FINDINGS SUGGEST
THAT THE RELATIONSHIP BETWEEN A COUNTRY'S TECHNOLOGY IMPORT
AND ITS DOMESTIC AND INDUSTRIAL R&D IS STRONGLY CORRELATED
WITH ITS TECHNOLOGY DEVELOPMENT STRATEGY.

05058 KIM, P. S.
JAPANESE TRAINING PROGRAMS IN THE PUBLIC SECTOR
ASIAN THOUGHT AND SOCIETY, XIV(40) (JAN 89), 15-30.
CRITICS ARGUE THAT JAPAN'S TRAINING PROGRAM IN THE
PUBLIC SECTOR HAS SERIOUS SHORT COMINGS. FIRST, THEY ASSERT
THAT IT CONCENTRATES TOO MUCH ON LEGAL SUBJECTS AT THE
EXPENSE OF ECONOMICS, POLITICS, AND OTHER SOCIAL SCIENCE
TOPICS WHICH ARE EQUALLY IMPORTANT TO THE TRAINEES. BECAUSE
LECTURE HAS BEEN THE PRIMARY METHOD OF INSTRUCTION, TRAINEES
OFTEN FIND THE CURRICULUM BORING. THE CRITICS RECOMMEND THAT
MORE SEMINARS AND DISCUSSIONS SHOULD BE INCORPORATED INTO
THE TEACHING METHODS. THIRD, THEY ARGUE THAT THE PRESENT
TRAINING PROGRAMS HAVE A ONE-DIMENSIONAL HORIZONTAL ASPECT,
SINCE TRAINEES USUALLY ARE AT THE SAME RANK, AND HAVE
APPROXIMATELY THE SAME AGE, EDUCATIONAL BACKGROUND, AND
LEVEL OF SENIORITY. THE CRITICS CONTEND THAT BECAUSE THE
RELATIONSHIPS WITHIN AN AGENCY ARE MORE VERTICAL, IN
ACCORDANCE WITH OFFICIAL HIERARCHY, THE INSTRUCTORS SHOULD
USE SIMULATION METHODS TO ORIENT THE TRAINEES PROPERLY IN
THE MULTIDIMENSIONAL ASPECTS OF PUBLIC ADMINISTRATION.
FINALLY, THEY SAY THAT THE TRAINING FACILITIES AND EQUIPMENT
ARE POOR IN VIEW OF JAPAN'S CURRENT PROSPERITY, AND THAT
THERE ARE NEITHER ENOUGH QUALIFIED FULL-TIME INSTRUCTORS NOR
ENOUGH UP-TO-DATE TEACHING MATERIALS. CONSEQUENTLY, THE
INSTRUCTION IS UNEVEN IN QUALITY AND OFTEN INEFFECTIVE.

05059 KIM, S.
DEPENDENCY, STATE AND ECONOMIC DEVELOPMENT: #A CROSS-
NATIONAL ANALYSIS
DISSERTATION ABSTRACTS INTERNATIONAL, 49(11) (MAY 89),
3501-A.
THE AUTHOR STUDIES THE EFFECTS OF ECONOMIC DEPENDENCY
AND PRIOR LEVELS OF DEVELOPMENT ON A COUNTRY'S ECONOMIC
GROWTH. HYPOTHESES STEMMING FROM DEPENDENCY, DEPENDENT
DEVELOPMENT, STRUCTURAL BLOCKAGE ANALYSIS, MODERNIZATION,
AND CAPITALISM ARE EXAMINED.

05060 KIM, S.
POLITICAL INSTABILITY: A CRITICAL ANALYSIS OF THE CONCEPT
FROM THE STANDPOINT OF POLITICAL DEVELOPMENT
KOREA OBSERVER, XX(2) (SUM 89), 137-162.
THE AUTHOR ENDEAVORS TO MAKE SENSE OF THE VARIOUS
APPROACHES AND INDICATORS THAT HAVE BEEN USED TO EXPLAIN THE
PROBLEM OF POLITICAL INSTABILITY AND POLITICAL DEVELOPMENT.
HE ATTEMPTS TO CLARIFY THE CONCEPTUAL INADEQUACIES OF
POLITICAL INSTABILITY BY EXAMINING THE MOST COMMONLY
RECURRING DEFINITION IN THE CONTEMPORARY LITERATURE OF
POLITICAL SCIENCE.

05061 KIM, S.
THE POLICY AND POLITICS OF ENVIRONMENTAL PROTECTION IN THE
REPUBLIC OF KOREA
DISSERTATION ABSTRACTS INTERNATIONAL, 50(6) (DEC 89),
1788-A.
THIS STUDY EXAMINES THE EMERGENCE, DEVELOPMENT, AND
INSTITUTIONALIZATION OF ENVIRONMENTAL POLICY IN THE REPUBLIC
OF KOREA. A STUDY OF THE POLICY PROCESS THAT ESTABLISHED THE
OFFICE OF ENVIRONMENT REVEALS THE CHARACTERISTICS OF POLICY-
MAKING IN AN AUTHORITARIAN REGIME: THE WIDE DECISION-MAKING
AUTHORITY OF THE PRESIDENT, THE DOMINANCE OF THE EXECUTIVE
BRANCH, THE PASSIVE ROLE OF THE LEGISLATURE, AND THE NEAR
EXCLUSION OF THE PUBLIC. THE EXPERIENCE OF ENVIRONMENTAL
REGULATION IN KOREA SHOWS BOTH THE POTENTIAL AND THE LIMITS
OF ENVIRONMENTAL PROTECTION IN A RAPIDLY INDUSTRIALIZING
COUNTRY.

05062 KIM, S.H.
THE IMPACT OF POLITICS AND ECONOMICS ON POVERTY IN
ADVANCED CAPITALIST COUNTRIES
DISSERTATION ABSTRACTS INTERNATIONAL, 50(3) (SEP 89),
784-A.
THE AUTHOR ANALYZES THE RELATIVE IMPACTS OF ECONOMIC
GROWTH AND SOCIAL WELFARE SPENDING ON POVERTY IN THE USA AND
13 WESTERN EUROPEAN COUNTRIES IN THE POSTWAR ERA. HE ALSO
EXPLORES HOW GENERAL ECONOMIC AND POLITICAL CONDITIONS HAVE
AFFECTED THE LEVELS OF POVERTY IN THESE COUNTRIES.

05063 KIM, T.K.
INDUSTRIALIZATION AND AUTHORITARIANISM IN THE REPUBLIC OF
KOREA, 1963-1983
DISSERTATION ABSTRACTS INTERNATIONAL, 48(10) (APR 88),
2717-A.
THE STUDY EXAMINES THE POLITICAL CONSEQUENCES OF
INDUSTRIAL DEVELOPMENT IN SOUTH KOREA. IT CONCLUDES THAT
POLITICAL AUTHORITARIANISM IS LIKELY TO ATTEND HIGHER LEVELS
OF INDUSTRIALIZATION IN THE LATER DEVELOPERS, AND ECONOMIC
CRISIS AND POLITICAL CONFLICT NEGATIVELY AFFECT THE DEGREE
OF POLITICAL DEMOCRACY.

05064 KIM, T.T.
NORTH KOREAN TERRORISM: TRENDS, CHARACTERISTICS, AND
DETERRENCE
TERRORISM, 11(4) (1988), 289-308.
THE ARTICLE EXAMINES NORTH KOREAN TERRORISM: ITS HISTORY,
CHARACTERISTICS, AND POSSIBLE MEANS OF DETERRING IT. A
STUDY OF THE TRENDS OVER THE PAST FOUR DECADES REVEALS
INCREASING LETHALITY AND INTERNATIONALIZATION OF TERRORISM
BY HIGHLY MOTIVATED IDEOLOGUES WHO HAVE A HIGH PROPENSITY
TOWARD SELF-DESTRUCTION. ALTHOUGH PATCHWORK POLICIES CAN BE
SUCCESSFUL IN CERTAIN CIRCUMSTANCES, ONLY A BROAD-BASED
INTERNATIONAL COUNTER-TERRORIST POLICY WILL BE OF ANY LONG-
TERM DETERRENCE TO THE TERRORISTS FROM THE NORTH.

05065 KIM, W.
CONFLICT AMONG GREAT POWERS: POWER DISTRIBUTION, ALLIANCE,
AND THE ONSET OF WAR
DISSERTATION ABSTRACTS INTERNATIONAL, 50(1) (JUL 89),
252-A.
ALLIANCES ARE A VITAL FACTOR IN THE DECISION TO ENGAGE
IN MAJOR POWER CONFLICT, AND THEORIES THAT DO NOT TAKE
ALLIANCES INTO ACCOUNT WILL PROVE DEFICIENT IN BOTH
EXPLANATORY AND PREDICTIVE POWER. CATACLYSMIC WARS ARE
MANIPULABLE AND ARE UNDER HUMAN CONTROL. WORLD PEACE CANNOT
BE DISTURBED WHEN THE GROUP OF NATIONS THAT SUPPORTS THE
STATUS QUO FINDS WAYS TO MAINTAIN ITS POWER PREPONDERANCE
OVER THE CHALLENGING GROUP OF NATIONS THAT ARE UNHAPPY WITH
THE EXISTING INTERNATIONAL ORDER.

05066 KIM, W.
POWER, ALLIANCE, AND MAJOR WARS, 1816-1975
JOURNAL OF CONFLICT RESOLUTION, 33(2) (JUN 89), 225-273.
FOR YEARS, STUDENTS OF INTERNATIONAL POLITICS HAVE
ATTEMPTED TO EXPLAIN SEEMINGLY CONTRADICTORY PERSPECTIVES
ABOUT THE RELATIONSHIP BETWEEN POWER DISTRIBUTION AND THE
ONSET OF WAR, AND BETWEEN ALLIANCE FORMATION AND THE
INCIDENCE OF WAR. POWER TRANSITION THEORISTS CLAIM THAT WAR
IS MOST LIKELY WHEN POWER IS EQUALLY DISTRIBUTED AMONG
NATIONS AND THAT ALLIANCES HAVE LITTLE OR NO IMPACT ON THE
LIKELIHOOD OF MAJOR WARS, WHEREAS BALANCE-OF-POWER THEORISTS
SUGGEST THAT WAR IS LESS LIKELY WHEN POWER IS EQUALLY
DISTRIBUTED AND THAT ALLIANCES PLAY A CRITICAL ROLE IN THE
INCIDENCE OF WAR. IN THIS RESEARCH, SEVERAL PROPOSITIONS
SUGGESTED BY THE POWER TRANSITION THEORY ARE TESTED FOR
MAJOR WAR CASES FROM 1816 TO 1975. THE MAIN FINDINGS SHOW
THAT ALLIANCES PLAY A SIGNIFICANT ROLE IN THE INCIDENCE OF
MAJOR WARS AND THAT THE PROBABILITY OF WAR INCREASES WHEN
THE TWO ALLIANCE COALITIONS, NOT THE TWO NATIONS IN A DYAD,
HAVE APPROXIMATELY EQUAL POWER. THESE FINDINGS CONFIRM
NEITHER THE BALANCE-OF-POWER PERSPECTIVE NOR THE VIEW OF THE
POWER TRANSITION MODEL. IN ADDITION, THE POWER TRANSITION
AND THE RATE OF GROWTH HYPOTHESES CLAIMED BY THE POWER
TRANSITION THEORY ARE NOT EMPIRICALLY SUPPORTED.

05067 KIMBALL, C.
THE NEW MOMENT
SOJOURNERS, 18(4) (APR 89), 26-31.
AFTER YEARS OF POLITICAL DEADLOCK, THERE IS NOW
CONSIDERABLE MOVEMENT ON ALL SIDES OF THE ISRAELI-
PALESTINIAN CONFLICT. THE SHARP RHETORIC AND INTRANSIGENT
POSITIONS SO CHARACTERISTIC OS THIS TRAGIC CONFRONTATION
HAVE GIVEN WAY IN SOME QUARTERS TO MORE MODERATE,
ACCOMMODATING POSITIONS THAT CALL FOR NEGOTIATED SETTLEMENT.
THE LARGE MAJORITY OF ISRAELI JEWS DEEPLY DESIRE A DURABLE
PEACE. THEIR FIRST REQUIREMENT, WITH GOOD REASON, WILL BE
VERY FIRM SECURITY GUARANTEES. IN SPITE OF THE CURRENT
MILITARY CONFIGURATION, THE EXPERIENCE OF HISTORY AND
GEOGRAPHICAL AND DEMOGRAPHIC REALITIES POSE REAL DANGERS.
PEOPLE BESET BY INSECURITY FOR MORE THAN THREE MILLENNIA ARE
UNDERSTANDABLY SLOW TO RISK THE MEASURE OF SECURITY THEY
HAVE ACHIEVED.

05068 KIMCHE, J.
ARAFAT'S ROAD TO "PEACE"
MIDSTREAM, XXXV(2) (FEB 89), 3-5.
DESPITE YASIR ARAFAT'S AVOWED COMMITMENT TO PEACE, THE
RESOLUTIONS PUBLISHED AT THE END OF THE PLO EXECUTIVE
MEETING IN DECEMBER 1988 LEFT NO ROOM FOR MISUNDERSTANDING.
THE STATEMENTS INCLUDED NO REFERENCE TO PEACE OR TO A DESIRE
FOR PEACE OR TO A PLO COMMITMENT TO PEACE WITH ISRAEL. THERE
HAS NO MENTION OF ISRAEL OTHER THAN AS THE ENEMY THAT MUST
BE OVERCOME. THERE HAS NO HINT OF A TWO-STATE SOLUTION, NO

REFERENCE TO SECURITY COUNCIL RESOLUTION 242, AND NO MENTION
OF RECOGNIZING AND ACCEPTING ISRAEL'S EXISTENCE.

05069 KIMCHE, J.
TEN YEARS OF EGYPTIAN PEACE AND PALESTINIAN WAR
MIDSTREAM, XXXV(7) (OCT 89), 3-5.
THE AUTHOR REVIEWS THE BACKGROUND TO THE 1978 CAMP DAVID
ACCORDS AND EGYPTIAN PRESIDENT ANWAR SADAT'S MOTIVATIONS FOR
SIGNING THEM.

05070 KIMELDORF, H.
REDS OR RACKETS? THE MAKING OF RADICAL AND CONSERVATIVE
UNIONS ON THE WATERFRONT
UNIVERSITY OF CALIFORNIA PRESS, BERKELEY, CA, 1989, 270.
AMERICAN LABOR UNIONS TRADITIONALLY HAVE NOT BEEN AS
RADICALIZED AS THEIR EUROPEAN COUNTERPARTS. IN THIS BOOK,
THE AUTHOR ANALYZES THE DIVERGENT SOURCES OF RADICALISM AND
CONSERVATISM WITHIN THE AMERICAN LABOR MOVEMENT. HE FOCUSES
ON THE POLITICAL CONTRAST BETWEEN EAST AND WEST COAST
LONGSHOREMEN FROM WORLD WAR 1 THROUGH THE EARLY YEARS OF THE
COLD WAR.

05071 KIMENYI, M.S.; SHUGHART, W.F., II
POLITICAL SUCCESSIONS AND THE GROWTH OF GOVERNMENT
PUBLIC CHOICE, 62(2) (AUG 89), 173-179.
THIS NOTE INVESTIGATES EMPIRICIALLY THE EFFECT OF
POLITICAL SUCCESSION ON THE GROWTH OF GOVERNMENT IN LIMITED
AUTOCRACIES USING KENYA AS AN EXAMPLE. IT ADDRESSES THE
PROBLEM CONFRONTING A LEADER OF AN AUTOCRATIC GOVERNMENT IS
THAT OF MAINTAINING A STABLE SUPPORTING COALITION POLITICAL
TRANSITION IN KENYA IS STUDIED AND IT IS CONCLUDED THAT A
SIGNIFICANT INCREASE IN THE SIZE OF THE KENYAN GOVERNMENT
FOLLOWING SUCCESSION CAN BE EXPECTED.

05072 KINCAID, J.
A PROPOSAL TO STRENGTHEN FEDERALISM
JOURNAL OF STATE GOVERNMENT, 62(1) (JAN 89), 36-45.
THIS ARTICLE CALLS ATTENTION TO THE ROLE OF THE U.S.
SUPREME COURT IN NATIONALIZING THE FEDERAL SYSTEM AND
ADVANCES A PROPOSAL THAT THE U.S. SUPREME COURT BE
CONSTITUTIONALLY REQUIRED TO REACH A THREE-FOURTHS VOTE TO
VOID A STATE LAW OR LOCAL ORDINANCE. THIS RULE WOULD APPLY
TO STATE OR LOCAL ACTS THAT ARE SAID TO VIOLATE THE U.S.
CONSTITUTION OR A FEDERAL STATUTE ENACTED PURSUANT TO
CONGRESSIONAL AND PRESIDENTIAL INTERPRETATIONS OF NATIONAL
POWER UNDER THE U.S. CONSTITUTION.

05073 KING, D.S.
POLITICAL CENTRALIZATION AND STATE INTERESTS IN BRITAIN
THE 1986 ABOLITION OF THE GLC AND MCCS
COMPARATIVE POLITICAL STUDIES, 21(4) (JAN 89), 467-494.
THIS ARTICLE ADDRESSES CONTEMPORARY STATE THEORY BY
EXAMINING THE ROLE OF STATE INTERESTS AND THE CONSTRAINTS
UPON STATE AUTONOMY IN RECENT CENTRAL-METROPOLITAN RELATIONS
IN BRITAIN. THE ABOLITION OF THE GREATER LONDON COUNCIL AND
SIX METROPOLITAN COUNTY COUNCILS IN BRIIAN IN 1986 IS
ANALYZED BY REFERENCE TO LIBERAL, MARXIST, AND STATIST
PROPOSITIONS ABOUT STATE AUTONOMY AND STATE INTERESTS. THREE
VERSIONS OF THE STATIST PERSPECTIVE ARE DELINEATED, AND IT
IS ARGUED THAT AN UNDERSTANDING OF CENTRAL STATE INTERESTS
IS NECESSARY FOR A COMPLETE ACCOUNT OF THE 1986 ABOLITION.

05074 KING, D.S.
US FEDERALISM AND THE REAGAN ADMINISTRATION
CONTEMPORARY RECORD, 3(2) (NOV 89), 35-38.
THIS ARTICLE TRACES THE HISTORY OF THE US POLITICAL
SYSTEM WHICH HAS BEEN FEDERAL SINCE THE DECLARATION OF
INDEPENDENCE. IT TRACES THE WEAKENING OF STATE POWER AND THE
REVERSAL IN THE REAGAN ADMINISTRATION IT EXAMINES PRESIDENT
REAGAN'S RADICAL AGENDA OF REGULATORY REFORM, CUTTING
FEDERAL GRANTS AND CREATING BLOCK GRANTS. URBAN POLICY,
HOUSING, WELFARE, ECONOMIC DEVELOPMENT ARE EXPLORED IN THE
CONTEXT OF EXPANDING STATES ROLES.

05075 KING, G.
EVENT COUNT MODELS FOR INTERNATIONAL RELATIONS:
GENERALIZATIONS AND APPLICATIONS
INTERNATIONAL STUDIES QUARTERLY, 33(2) (JUN 89), 123-147.
THIS ARTICLE DEVELOPS AN APPROACH TO MODELING AND
STATISTICAL ANALYSIS BASED EXPLICITLY ON ESTIMATING
CONTINUOUS PROCESSES FROM OBSERVED EVENT COUNTS. TO
DEMONSTRATE THIS CLASS OF MODELS, THE AUTHOR PRESENTS
SEVERAL NEW STATISTICAL TECHNIQUES DEVELOPED FOR AND APPLIED
TO DIFFERENT AREAS OF INTERNATIONAL RELATIONS. THESE INCLUDE
THE INFLUENCE OF INTERNATIONAL ALLIANCES ON THE OUTBREAK OF
WAR, THE CONTAGIOUS PROCESS OF MULTILATERAL ECONOMIC
SANCTIONS, AND RECIPROCITY IN SUPERPOWER CONFLICT. THE
AUTHOR ALSO SHOWS HOW ONE CAN EXTRACT CONSIDERABLY MORE
INFORMATION FROM EXISTING DATA AND RELATE SUBSTANTIVE THEORY
TO EMPIRICAL ANALYSES MORE EXPLICITLY WITH THIS APPROACH.

05076 KING, G.
REPRESENTATION THROUGH LEGISLATIVE REDISTRICTING: A
STOCHASTIC MODEL

AMERICAN JOURNAL OF POLITICAL SCIENCE, 33(4) (NOV 89),
787-824.
THIS PAPER BUILDS A STOCHASTIC MODEL OF THE PROCESSES
THAT GIVE RISE TO OBSERVED PATTERNS OF REPRESENTATION AND
BIAS IN CONGRESSIONAL AND STATE LEGISLATIVE ELECTIONS. THE
ANALYSIS DEMONSTRATES THAT PARTISAN SWING AND INCUMBENCY
VOTING, CONCEPTS FROM THE CONGRESSIONAL ELECTIONS LITERATURE,
HAVE DETERMINATE EFFECTS ON REPRESENTATION AND BIAS,
CONCEPTS FROM THE REDISTRICTING LITERATURE. THE MODEL SHOWS
PRECISELY HOW INCUMBENCY AND INCREASED VARIABILITY OF
PARTISAN SWING REDUCE THE RESPONSIVENESS OF THE ELECTORAL
SYSTEM AND HOW PARTISAN SWING AFFECTS WHETHER THE SYSTEM IS
BIASED TOWARD ONE PARTY OR THE OTHER. INCUMBENCY, AND OTHER
CAUSES OF UNRESPONSIVE REPRESENTATION, ALSO REDUCE THE
EFFECT OF PARTISAN SWING ON CURRENT LEVELS OF PARTISAN BIAS.
BY RELAXING THE RESTRICTIVE PORTIONS OF THE WIDELY APPLIED
"UNIFORM PARTISAN SWING" ASSUMPTION, THE THEORETICAL
ANALYSIS LEADS DIRECTLY TO AN EMPIRICAL MODEL ENABLING ONE
MORE RELIABLY TO ESTIMATE RESPONSIVENESS AND BIAS FROM A
SINGLE YEAR OF ELECTORAL DATA. APPLYING THIS DATA FROM SEVEN
ELECTIONS IN EACH OF SIX STATES, THE PAPER DEMONSTRATES THAT
REDISTRICTING HAS EFFECTS IN PREDICTED DIRECTIONS IN THE
SHORT RUN: PARTISAN GERRYMANDERING BIASES THE SYSTEM IN
FAVOR OF THE PARTY IN CONTROL AND, BY FREEING UP SEATS HELD
BY OPPOSITION PARTY INCUMBENTS, INCREASES THE SYSTEM'S
RESPONSIVENESS. BIPARTISAN-CONTROLLED REDISTRICTING APPEARS
TO REDUCE BIAS SOMEWHAT AND DRAMATICALLY TO REDUCE
RESPONSIVENESS. NONPARTISAN REDISTRICTING PROCESSES
SUBSTANTIALLY INCREASE RESPONSIVENESS BUT DO NOT HAVE AS
CLEAR AN EFFECT ON BIAS. HOWEVER, AFTER ONLY TWO ELECTIONS,
PRIMA FACIE EVIDENCE FOR REDISTRICTING EFFECTS EVAPORATE IN
MOST STATES. FINALLY, ACROSS EVERY STATE AND TYPE OF
REDISTRICTING PROCESS, RESPONSIVENESS DECLINED SIGNIFICANTLY
OVER THE COURSE OF THE DECADE. THIS IS CLEAR EVIDENCE THAT
THE PHENOMENON OF "VANISHING MARGINALS," RECOGNIZED FIRST IN
THE U.S. CONGRESS LITERATURE, ALSO APPLIES TO THESE
DIFFERENT TYPES OF STATE LEGISLATIVE ASSEMBLIES. IT ALSO
STRONGLY SUGGESTS THAT REDISTRICTING COULD NOT ACCOUNT FOR
THIS PATTERN.

05077 KING, J.D.
INTERPARTY COMPETITION IN THE AMERICAN STATES: AN
EXAMINATION OF INDEX COMPONENTS
WESTERN POLITICAL QUARTERLY, 42(1) (MAR 89), 83-92.
STUDIES OF AMERICAN STATE POLITICAL SYSTEMS COMMONLY
EMPLOY RANNEY'S INDEX OF INTERPARTY COMPETITION. THIS PAPER
EXPLORES THE RANNEY INDEX, CONSIDERING INTERCORRELATIONS
AMONG ITS VARIOUS COMPONENTS AND TREATING EACH AS A
DEPENDENT VARIABLE. THE DISTINCTIVENESS OF COMPETITION IN
GUBERNATORIAL ELECTIONS IS EVIDENT, LEADING TO THE
CONCLUSION THAT THE FOLDED RANNEY INDEX TAPS COMPETITION
WITHIN THE LEGISLATIVE BRANCH RATHER THAN THE OVERALL
COMPETITIVE NATURE OF A STATE'S POLITICAL SYSTEM.

05078 KING, M.B.
MIX TEC POLITICAL IDEOLOGY: HISTORICAL METAPHORS AND THE
POETICS OF POLITICAL SYMBOLISM
DISSERTATION ABSTRACTS INTERNATIONAL, 49(8) (FEB 89),
2285-A.
THE AUTHOR RECONSTRUCTS THE POLITICAL IDEOLOGY OF THE
MIXTEC PEOPLE OF MEXICO ON THE EVE OF THE SPANISH CONQUEST.
HE FOCUSES ON THE STRUCTURE AND ORGANIZATION OF MIXTEC
POLITICAL IDEOLOGY, THE SEMIOTIC STRUCTURE, AND THE
IDEOLOGICAL SUPPORT AND REGULATION OF MIXTEC SEGMENTARY
POLITICAL ORGANIZATION.

05079 KING, P.
JUSTIFYING TOLERANCE
HISTORY OF POLITICAL THOUGHT, X(4) (WIN 89), 733-743.
THIS ARTICLE RAISES THE QUESTION OF WHETHER TOLERANCE
CAN BE SEEN TO FIT MORE INTO ONE TRADITION OF THOUGHT THAN
ANOTHER. THE AUTHOR'S SUMMARY VIEW OF THE MATTER IS THAT ONE
IS WELL-PLACED TO LOCATE TOLERANCE WITHIN ANY TRADITION, AT
LEAST WHERE THERE IS EXPRESS OR IMPLICIT EVIDENCE OF SOME
FORM OF CONTENTION FOR IT. INASMUCH AS TOLERANCE IS NOT A
UNIVERSAL VALUE (IN THE SENSE EARLIER STIPULATED), AND
INASMUCH AS THE POTENTIAL OBJECTS OF TOLERANCE WITHIN
DIFFERENT TRADITIONS NECESSARILY DIFFER, THEN IT WOULD
APPEAR IN PRINCIPLE TO BE PERFECTLY POSSIBLE TO INCORPORATE
SOME (NOT ANY) LEGITIMATE AND COHERENT PLEA FOR TOLERANCE
WITHIN EVERY TRADITION WITHOUT DOING THE LEAST VIOLENCE
EITHER TO THE TRADITION OR TO THE TOLERANCE.

05080 KIRBY, J.
AN ACCENT ON HARMONY
FREE CHINA REVIEW, 39(7) (JUL 89), 4-9.
THAILAND HAS ASSIMILATED ITS ETHNIC CHINESE MINORITY
WITH MORE SUCCESS THAN ANY OTHER NATION IN SOUTHEAST ASIA.
BUT ETHNIC RELATIONS BETWEEN THE THAIS AND ITS CHINESE
IMMIGRANTS HAVE NOT ALWAYS BEEN IDEAL. IN THIS ARTICLE, THE
AUTHOR LOOKS AT HOW INTER-RACIAL HARMONY HAS BEEN
ESTABLISHED IN A REGION PREVIOUSLY TORN APART BY STRIFE
AMONG COMPETING ETHNIC AND POLITICAL GROUPS.

05081 KIRBY, J.
FROM OPIUM TO FRUIT
FREE CHINA REVIEW, 39(2) (FEB 89), 47-53.
FOR MOST OF ITS MODERN HISTORY, MUCH OF THAILAND'S
NORTHERN FRONTIER HAS BEEN ONLY NOMINALLY UNDER THE
POLITICAL CONTROL OF THE THAI GOVERNMENT. BUT A SUSTAINED 20-
YEAR EFFORT BY THE THAI GOVERNMENT, WITH THE ASSISTANCE OF A
HOST OF INTERNATIONAL AGENCIES, HAS NOW TRANSFORMED THE
REGION. SUCCESS IS DUE IN GREAT PART TO THE EFFORTS OF
TAIWAN'S VOCATIONAL ASSISTANCE COMMISSION FOR RETIRED
SERVICEMEN, WHICH HAS INTRODUCED NEW AND PROFITABLE CASH
AGRICULTURAL CROPS TO THE AREA.

05082 KIRBY, J.
OVERSEAS ASSISTANCE: NEW GOLD IN THE TRIANGLE
FREE CHINA REVIEW, 39(8) (AUG 89), 68-71.
ONE OF TAIWAN'S MORE SIGNIFICANT FOREIGN AID PROGRAMS
HAS HELPED UPGRADE THE INFRASTRUCTURE AND AGRICULTURAL
PRODUCTIVITY OF AN IMPOVERISHED AREA OF THAILAND KNOWN AS
THE "GOLDEN TRIANGLE." EFFORTS HAVE FOCUSED ON THE CHINESE
LIVING THERE. CALLED THE "JIIN HAW," THESE CHINESE ARE THE
REMNANTS OF A NATIONALIST CHINESE ARMY THAT RETREATED INTO
THAILAND AFTER THE CHINESE COMMUNISTS TOOK THE MAINLAND.

05083 KIRCHHEIMER, D.W.
PUBLIC ENTERPRENEURSHIP & SUBNATIONAL GOVERNMENT
POLITY, 22(1) (FAL 89), 119-142.
THE ENTREPRENEURIAL SPIRIT IS USUALLY ASSOCIATED WITH
PRIVATE AND NOT PUBLIC INSTITUTIONS. THIS ARTICLE, HOWEVER,
ARGUES THAT GOVERNMENT'S RESPONSE TO THE MUCH EXPANDED
SOCIAL ROLE IT TOOK IN THE 1930S AND 1960S IS BEST
UNDERSTOOD AS A KIND OF EXPERIMENTATION AKIN TO
ENTERPRENEURSHIP. USING NEW YORK AS A CASE STUDY, THE AUTHOR
DEVELOPS THE ELEMENTS OF A THEORY OF PUBLIC ENTREPRENEURSHIP
AS AN INSTITUTIONAL RESOURCE IN INTERGOVERNMENTAL RELATIONS.

05084 KIRK-WESTERMAN, C.; BILLEAUX, D.M.; ENGLAND, R.E.
ENDING SEXUAL HARASSMENT AT CITY HALL: POLICY INITIATIVES
IN LARGE AMERICAN CITIES
STATE AND LOCAL GOVERNMENT REVIEW, 21(3) (FAL 89), 100-105.
SEXUAL HARASSMENT IS AN OLD PROBLEM, BUT A NEW ISSUE.
BASED ON A SURVEY OF PERSONNEL DIRECTORS, THIS STUDY
EXAMINES POLICY INITIATIVES TAKEN BY GOVERNMENTS IN LARGE
AMERICAN CITIES TO END SEXUAL HARASSMENT AT WORK. FINDINGS
SUGGEST THAT MUNICIPAL GOVERNMENT OFFICIALS HAVE IMPLEMENTED
POLICIES, GRIEVANCE PROCEDURES, AND TRAINING PROGRAMS TO
ADDRESS THE PROBLEM OF SEXUAL HARASSMENT AT THE LOCAL LEVEL.

05085 KIRKMAN, K.E.
GRADUATION IN THE GENERALIZED SYSTEM OF PREFERENCES: THE
PROJECTED IMPACT ON REMAINING BENEFICIARIES IN THE UNITED
STATES SCHEME
WORLD DEVELOPMENT, 17(10) (OCT 89), 1597-1600.
THE PAPER EXPLORES THE ISSUE OF "GRADUATION" IN THE
GENERALIZED SYSTEM OF PREFERENCES USING AN EXPORT SIMILARITY
INDEX TO ANALYZE THE EFFECTS OF THE US DECISION TO GRADUATE
HONG KONG, SINGAPORE, SOUTH KOREA, AND TAIWAN FROM ITS GSP
SCHEME IN 1989. THE GRADUATION OF SINGAPORE WILL HAVE A
GREATER IMPACT ON REMAINING GSP BENEFICIARIES THAN WILL THE
GRADUATION OF HONG KONG OR SOUTH KOREA. SOME OF THE
REMAINING BENEFICIARIES WILL BENEFIT MORE THAN OTHERS; THE
ASEAN COUNTRIES ARE THE CLEAREST POTENTIAL GAINERS, BUT THE
ABILITY TO GAIN IS NOT LIMITED TO THE HIGHEST INCOME OR
LARGEST CURRENT BENEFICIARIES AMONG GSP-ELIGIBLE COUNTRIES.

05086 KIRKPATRICK, J.J.
HOW THE PLO WAS LEGITIMIZED
COMMENTARY, 88(1) (JUL 89), 21-28.
THIS ARTICLE CHRONICLES THE RISE OF PLO STATUS AND THE
UNDERMINING OF ISRAEL'S INSIDE THE UN GENERAL ASSEMBLY AND
OTHER INSTITUTIONS OF THE THIRD WORLD INCLUDING THE
ORGANIZATION OF AFRICAN UNITY, THE ISLAMIC CONFERENCE AND
THE NON-ALIGRED MOVEMENT. AS SET FORTH IN THE PALESTINIAN
NATIONAL COVENANT ADOPTED IN JULY 1968, THE GOAL OF THE PLO
IS THE REPLACEMENT OF ISRAEL WITH A PALESTINIAN STATE. THAT
THE UN HAS INCORPORATED MANY OF THE COVENANT'S KEY
PROPOSITIONS IN RESOLUTIONS OF THE GENERAL ASSEMBLY WAS THE
FIRST STEP IN A CONTINUING PROCESS OF LEGITIMAZATION FOR THE
PLO.

05087 KIRKPATRICK, J.J.
MY FALKLAND WAR AND THEIRS
NATIONAL INTEREST, (18) (WIN 89), 11-20.
THIS ARTICLE, BY JEANE KIRKPATRICK, EXPLORES THE BRITISH
AND THE U.S. REACTION TO THE FALKLANDS WAR. FIRST SHE
OBSERVES THAT THE WAR WAS ONE OF THE TRULY UNEXPECTED EVENTS
OF THE POSTWAR PERIOD AND QUOTES THE WRITINGS OF MICHAEL
CHARLTON. THEN SHE DESCRIBES THE BELIEFS OF THE
INTERNATIONAL COMMUNITY ABOUT THE VALIDITY OF BRITISH
INTERVENTION. SHE EXAMINES THE IMPACT OF THE WAR ON U.S. -
LATIN AMERICAN RELATIONS. SHE CONCLUDES THAT BRITAIN EMERGED
FROM THE WAR STRONGER, AND THAT THE U.S. EMERGED, WEAKENED
IN THE HEMISPHERE, AND NO STRONGER IN EUROPE.

05088 KIRKWOOD, R.; JEFFREY, T.P.
THE WRIGHT STUFF
NATIONAL REVIEW, XLI(7) (APR 89), 35-36.
HOUSE SPEAKER JIM WRIGHT IS GOING ON TRAIL BEFORE HIS
PEERS ON CHARGES OF VIOLATING HOUSE RULES. THE CHARGES ARE
SIGNIFICANT: DODGING OUTSIDE-INCOME RESTRICTIONS, FILING
INCOMPLETE FINANCIAL DISCLOSURES AND ACCEPTING ILLEGAL
GRATUITIES. HOWEVER, THE IMMENSELY MORE SIGNIFICANT CHARGE
OF PRECIPITATING THE CURRENT SAVINGS AND LOAN CRISIS GOES
UNSAID. IF WRIGHT FALLS FROM OFFICE, IT WILL BE FOR
INFRACTIONS OF HOUSE ETHICS RULES, RATHER THAN FOR PLAYING
POLITICAL GAMES THAT ENDED UP COSTING BILLIONS TO TAXPAYERS.

05089 KIRMANI, N.
THE URUGUAY ROUND: REVITALIZING THE GLOBAL TRADING SYSTEM
FINANCE AND DEVELOPMENT, 26(1) (MAR 89), 6-8.
THE AUTHOR REVIEWS THE PROGRESS MADE TO DATE IN THE
URUGUAY ROUND OF THE GATT.

05090 KIRP, D. L.
COMPASSION FATIGUE: HONG KONG AND THE BOAT PEOPLE
AMERICAN SPECTATOR, 22(4) (APR 89), 16-19.
ACTING ON ORDERS FROM BRITAIN, HONG KONG'S GOVERNMENT
HAS DECLARED THAT VIETNAMESE ARRIVING AFTER JUNE 15, 1988,
WILL BE TREATED NOT AS "GENUINE REFUGEES" BUT AS ILLEGAL
IMMIGRANTS. THEY WILL BE IMPRISONED. CUT OFF FROM
INTERNATIONAL ORGANIZATIONS, AND DENIED ANY POSSIBILITY OF
RESETTLEMENT IN THE WEST.

05091 KIRSCHBAUM, S.J.
SLOVAK NATIONALISM IN THE FIRST CZECHOSLOVAK REPUBLIC,
1918-1938
CANADIAN REVIEW OF STUDIES IN NATIONALISM, XVI(1-2) (1989),
169-187.
THE AUTHOR ENDEAVORS TO PLACE SLOVAK NATIONALISM IN THE
FIRST CZECHOSLOVAK REPUBLIC IN ITS PROPER PERSPECTIVE.
TRADITIONALLY, SLOVAK NATIONALISM HAS EVOKED EITHER OUTRIGHT
CONDEMNATION OR RIGHTEOUS EXPLANATION. BUT THE INHERENT
CONTRADICTIONS WITHIN EACH PERSPECTIVE, AS WELL AS THE
EMPIRICAL EVIDENCE, SUGGEST THAT NEITHER APPROACH IS
SATISFACTORY IN EXPLAINING THE ROLE AND CONTENT OF SLOVAK
NATIONALISM.

05092 KIRTON, C.D.
DEVELOPMENT PLANNING IN THE GRENADA REVOLUTION: APPLYING
AFROSIBER
SOCIAL AND ECONOMIC STUDIES, 38(3) (SEP 89), 1-52.
THE MNEMONIC TERM AFROSIBER REPRESENTS THE NINE STAGES
OF A PLANNING METHODOLOGY DEVELOPED BY TREVOR FARRELL, A
CARIBBEAN ECONOMIST. THIS ARTICLE EXAMINES AFROSIBER AS AN
'OPERATIONAL FRAMEWORK' WHICH CAN BE UTILIZED BY PLANNING
TECHNICIANS FOR PLAN PREPARATION PURPOSES. IT USES THE
METHODOLOGY TO ASSESS THE PLANNING EXPERIENCE DURING THE
GRENADA REVOLUTION. FURTHER, IT SEEKS TO ESTABLISH THE
EXTENT TO WHICH THE VARIOUS STAGES OF THE METHODOLOGY WERE
RELEVANT, USEFUL, AND ACTUALLY IMPLEMENTED AS PART OF
GRENADA'S DEVELOPMENT PLANNING PROCESS.

05093 KIRTON, C.D.
GRENADA AND THE IMF: THE PRG'S EXTENDED FUND FACILITY
PROGRAM, 1983
LATIN AMERICAN PERSPECTIVES, 16(3) (SUM 89), 121-144.
THIS ARTICLE PROVIDES AN OVERVIEW OF GRENADA'S IMF
PROGRAM WHICH WAS APPROVED IN MID-1983 AND ABORTED A FEW
MONTHS LATER FOLLOWING THE U.S. INVASION OF THE COUNTRY. HE
ARGUES THAT THE APPROACH OF THE PEOPLE'S REVOLUTIONARY
GOVERNMENT (PRG) TO THE IMF WAS BASED UPON THE EXPECTATION
THAT ONCE THE IMF GAVE ITS "SEAL OF APPROVAL" TO GRENADA A
MUCH MORE FAVORABLE "ECONOMIC CLIMATE" WOULD ENSUE, LEADING
TO INCREASED LEVELS OF PARTICIPATION OF BOTH DOMESTIC AND
FOREIGN CAPITAL IN THE COUNTRY'S DEVELOPMENT EFFORTS. KIRTON
CONCLUDES THAT GRENADA'S POSITION WAS MADE LESS
DISADVANTAGEOUS (VIS-A-VIS FUND CONDITIONALITY) SIMPLY
BECAUSE THE ECONOMIC SITUATION HAD NOT DETERIORATED SO BADLY
AS TO WARRANT TOTAL DEPENDENCE ON IMF FUNDING AT ALL COSTS,
AND THAT SOME OF THE MEASURES INTRODUCED AS PART OF THE
PROGRAM MAY HAVE BEEN IMPLEMENTED BY THE PRG (THE "NON-IMF
ALTERNATIVE"), EVEN WITHOUT THE INSISTENCE OF THE IMF.

05094 KIRYANOVA, M.
USSR-CHINA: PROSPECTS FOR DEVELOPING TRADE AND ECONOMIC
RELATIONS.
FOREIGN TRADE, 11 (1988), 2-4.
THIS ARTICLE EXPLORES MUTUAL TRADE GROWTH BETWEEN USSR
AND CHINA, OVER RECENT YEARS THE RANGE OF GOODS HAS
SIGNIFICANTLY EXPANDED AND CHANGES IN THE TRADE PATTERNS
OCCURRED. THE AUTHOR EXAMINES TRADE AND ECONOMIC RELATIONS,
BORDER TRADE, COOPERATION, TRANSPORTATION, AND THE SOVIET-
CHINESE COMISSION FOR ECONOMIC, TRADE, SCIENTIFIC AND
TECHNICAL COOPERATION.

05095 KIS, J.
TURNING POINT IN HUNGARY
DISSENT, (SPR 89), 235-241.

THE PRESENT CRISIS IN HUNGARY WAS PRECEDED BY AN
UNUSUALLY LONG PERIOD OF TRANQUILITY. THE AUTHOR OF THIS
ARTICLE BEGINS BY EXAMINING THE ROOTS OF THIS EXCEPTIONAL
POLITICAL STABILITY LASTING MORE THAN A QUARTER OF A CENTURY.
THEN HE CONSIDERS THE CLIMATE FOR REFORM IN HUNGARY.

05096 KISKER, G.
THE WEST GERMAN FEDERAL CONSTITUTIONAL COURT AS GUARDIAN
OF THE FEDERAL SYSTEM
PUBLIUS: THE JOURNAL OF FEDERALISM, 19(4) (FAL 89), 35-52.
THIS ARTICLE DESCRIBES AND ANALYZES THE ROLE THAT COURTS
HAVE PLAYED IN DEVELOPING AND TRANSFORMING THE WEST GERMAN
FEDERAL SYSTEM. IT FIRST RECALLS SOME BASIC STRUCTURES OF
THAT SYSTEM. THEN THE COURTS, IN PARTICULAR THE FEDERAL
CONSTITUTIONAL COURT, THEIR JURISDICTION, AND THEIR
PROCEDURES WILL BE DISCUSSED AND A SURVEY IS MADE OF THE
MOST OUTSTANDING LEGAL CONTROVERSIES IN GERMAN FEDERALISM.
THE FINAL SECTION ASKS WHETHER THE RULINGS OF THE FEDERAL
CONSTITUTIONAL COURT AMOUNT TO A "JUDICIAL PHILOSOPHY" ON
FEDERALISM.

05097 KISSINGER, H.
U.S.-SOVIET RELATIONS: CONFRONTATION OR COOPERATION
WORLD MARXIST REVIEW, 31(2) (FEB 88), 78-82.
BY THE 21ST CENTURY THERE WILL BE FIVE TO SIX POWER
CENTERS IN THE WORLD, EACH OF THEM ATTEMPTING TO ASSERT A
GREATER ROLE IN THEIR IMMEDIATE AREA. IF THAT HAPPENS, THE
KIND OF GLOBAL COMPETITION THAT THE UNITED STATES AND THE
SOVIET UNION HAVE HAD WILL NOT MAKE ANY SENSE ANY MORE, AND
IF, INDEED, IN THE IMMEDIATE PERIOD AHEAD, THE SOVIET UNION
AND THE UNITED STATES WERE TO SLIDE, BY MISTAKE OR BY DESIGN,
INTO A CONFLICT, THEY WOULD BE EXHAUSTING THEMSELVES OVER
ISSUES THAT THE EVOLUTION OF HISTORY AND OF GEOPOLITICS MAY
MAKE IRRELEVANT. IF PRESENT TRENDS IN THE WORLD CONTINUE, IF
EACH SIDE KEEPS ENCOURAGING EVERY CRISIS EVERYWHERE AND
SETTLES NONE, WE RUN THE HUGE DANGER THAT SOONER OR LATER
SOMETHING HAPPENS LIKE WORLD WAR I, IN WHICH NONE OF THE
LEADERS HAD THE SLIGHTEST INTENTION OF PRODUCING THE
CONSEQUENCES THAT CAME ABOUT.

05098 KISTIAKOWSKY, V.
MILITARY FUNDING OF UNIVERSITY RESEARCH
PHILADELPHIA: ANLS OF AMER ACMY OF POLITICAL AND SOC
SCIENCE, (502) (MAR 89), 141-154.
SINCE THE MISSION OF THE DEPARTMENT OF DEFENSE (DOD) AND
THE PURPOSES OF THE UNIVERSITIES DO NOT COINCIDE, THE
QUESTION WHETHER THIS IS PRAGMATICALLY IMPORTANT IS EXAMINED.
RELEVANT EVENTS IN RECENT HISTORY ARE MENTIONED, AND THE
REASONS GIVEN IN SUPPORT OF DOD FUNDING OF UNIVERSITY
RESEARCH ARE SUMMARIZED. FIVE CONSEQUENCES OF SUCH SUPPORT
ARE THEN DISCUSSED: DISTORTION OF THE BALANCE BETWEEN
RESEARCH FIELDS, CHANGE OF EMPHASIS WITHIN RESEARCH FIELDS,
CLASSIFICATION AND OTHER RESTRICTIONS, CONSEQUENCES FOR
GRADUATE STUDENTS, AND POLITICAL CONSEQUENCES. SOCIAL
RESPONSIBILITY FOR THE END USE OF RESEARCH IS THEN
CONSIDERED, AND IT IS SUGGESTED THAT SOCIAL RESPONSIBILITY
SHOULD BECOME AN IMPORTANT UNIVERSITY CRITERION OF
EXCELLENCE. THE ARTICLE CONCLUDES THAT THE NEGATIVE
CONSEQUENCES OF DOD FUNDING FAR OUTWEIGH ITS PERCEIVED
BENEFITS, AND SUGGESTS THAT THE UNIVERSITIES SHOULD WORK TO
ESTABLISH A STRONG CIVILIAN BASE OF RESEARCH FUNDING INSTEAD
OF LOBBYING FOR DOD SUPPORT

05099 KITAHARA, M.
DOUGLAS MACARTHUR AS A FATHER FIGURE IN OCCUPIED JAPAN
AFTER WORLD WAR II
INTERNATIONAL SOCIAL SCIENCE REVIEW, 64(1) (WIN 89), 20-28.
UNTIL THE END OF WORLD WAR II, THE JAPANESE CONCEIVED OF
THEIR RELATIONSHIP WITH THE EMPEROR IN TERMS OF THE
EXTENSION OF THE PARENT-CHILD RELATIONSHIP. AFTER THE
SURRENDER, DOUGLAS MACARTHUR ADMINISTERED OCCUPIED JAPAN AS
AN AUTHORITARIAN, YET PATERNALISTIC, SUPREME COMMANDER IN
CHIEF, AND THE JAPANESE WERE FORCED TO REALIZE THAT
MACARTHUR EXISTED OVER AND ABOVE THE EMPEROR. FOR THIS
REASON, THE JAPANESE BEGAN TO LOOK AT HIM AS A NEW FATHER
FIGURE. ON HIS PART, MACARTHUR CONCEIVED OF HIMSELF AS THE
GUARDIAN OF THE JAPANESE, WHO, IN HIS OPINION, WERE
INFANTILE AND HAD TO BE EDUCATED. THE PERCEPTION AND
EXPECTATION OF EACH OTHER COINCIDED NEATLY, AND THE JAPANESE
BEGAN TO IDENTIFY WITH HIM AND, LATER, WITH THE AMERICANS AS
A WHOLE.

05100 KITCHEN, R.
ADMINISTRATIVE REFORM IN JAMAICA: A COMPONENT OF
STRUCTURAL ADJUSTMENT
PUBLIC CHOICE, 9(4) (SEP 89), 339-356.
JAMAICA IS CURRENTLY UNDERGOING A MAJOR INNOVATIVE
ADMINISTRATIVE REFORM PROGRAMME (ARP). THE IMPETUS FOR THE
ARP STEMS FROM THE REALIZATION THAT WEAK PUBLIC
ADMINISTRATION (AS PREVAILED IN JAMAICA) IS A MAJOR OBSTACLE
TO THE IMPLEMENTATION OF ECONOMIC REFORMS. THE ARP THUS
BECAME A SIGNIFICANT PLANK OF THE WORLD BANK'S STRUCTURAL
ADJUSTMENT LENDING TO JAMAICA. THE JAMAICAN PROGRAMME IS
PROBABLY THE LEADING AND MOST AMBITIOUS ATTEMPT AT

ADMINISTRATIVE REFORM IN THE THIRD WORLD, AND THE
EXPERIENCES AND LESSONS LEARNT CAN BE APPLIED TO THE MANY
DEVELOPING COUNTRIES WHICH ARE CONTEMPLATING OR IMPLEMENTING
SIMILAR PROGRAMMES. THE JAMAICAN EXPERIENCE INDICATES THAT
THE MOST IMPORTANT INGREDIENTS FOR SUCCESS ARE POLITICAL
COMMITMENT AT THE HIGHEST LEVEL, A DETERMINED EXTERNAL
AGENCY, A CAREFULLY DESIGNED BUT FLEXIBLE PARTICIPATORY
PROGRAMME WHICH LEARNS AS IT PROGRESSES, AND GOOD
COMMUNICATION OF THE REFORM PROPOSALS. ADMINISTRATIVE REFORM
IS A LONG-TERM PROCESS, AND IT WOULD BE DANGEROUS TO PITCH
EXPECTATIONS TOO HIGH.

05101 KITEME, B.C.
THE CULT OF STALIN: NATIONAL POWER AND THE SOVIET PARTY-
STATE
DISSERTATION ABSTRACTS INTERNATIONAL, 50(5) (NOV 89),
1423-A.
THE CULT OF STALIN WAS A LEADERSHIP-ADMINISTRATIVE
SYSTEM THAT ASSISTED IN IMPLEMENTING RAPID AND FAR-REACHING
CHANGE. FROM 1929 TO 1953, ITS FUNCTION WAS TO RESERVE THE
SOLE POLICY-MAKING ROLE TO STALIN, TO MOBILIZE PARTY SUPPORT
FOR HIS POLICIES, AND THEREBY TO TRANSFORM SOCIETY. THIS
MODE OF BUILDING CENTRALIZED POLITICAL AND ECONOMIC POWER IN
THE NAME OF STALIN WAS PROMOTED BY THE ASCENDANT SECOND-
LEVEL LEADERSHIP IN THEIR CONFLICT WITH THE OPPOSITION FOR
POSITION AND POLICY SUPPORT FROM THE PARTY CADRES. THE CULT
DREW ON IMAGES OF AUTHORITY FROM TSARIST RUSSIA, THE
BOLSHEVIK PERIOD, AND VARIOUS NON-RUSSIAN ETHNIC CULTURES TO
IDEALIZE PROGRESS THROUGH MILITARY-POLITICAL ACTION.

05102 KITSCHELT, H.
THE INTERNAL POLITICS OF PARTIES: THE LAW OF CURVILINEAR
DISPARITY REVISITED
POLITICAL STUDIES, 37(3) (SEP 89), 400-421.
ONE OF THE FEW EFFORTS TO LINK SYSTEMIC AND
ORGANIZATIONAL DETERMINANTS OF PARTY STRATEGIES IS PROVIDED
BY WHAT JOHN MAY DUBBED THE 'LAW OF CURVILINEAR DISPARITY'.
ACCORDING TO THIS LAW, VOTERS, PARTY ACTIVISTS AND LEADERS
HAVE NECESSARILY DIVERGENT POLITICAL IDEOLOGIES. THESE
SYSTEMATIC DIFFERENCES ARE ATTRIBUTABLE TO THE ACTIVISTS'
MOTIVATIONS AND THE CONSTRAINTS OF PARTY COMPETITION. THIS
PAPER ARGUES THAT THE LAW IS EMPIRICALLY VALID ONLY UNDER
DISTINCTIVE BEHAVIOURAL, ORGANIZATIONAL AND INSTITUTIONAL
CONDITIONS, WHICH ARE NOT SPECIFIED IN ITS GENERAL
FORMULATION THUS, THE LAW IS ONLY A SPECIAL CASE IN A
BROADER THEORY RECONSTRUCTING THE INTERACTION BETWEEN
CONSTITUENCIES, INTRA-PARTY POLITICS AND PARTY COMPETITION.
THIS ALTERNATIVE THEORY IS PARTIALLY TESTED WITH SURVEY DATA
FROM PARTY ACTIVISTS IN THE BELGIAN ECOLOGY PARTIES AGALEV
AND ECOLO.

05103 KITSENKO, O.
PAKISTAN: GOVERNMENT CHANGED. WHAT NEXT?
REPRINTS FROM THE SOVIET PRESS, 48(5) (MAR 89), 28-30.
A NEW PRIME MINISTER, BENAZIR BHUTTO, AND A NEW
DEMOCRATIC CIVILIAN GOVERNMENT LED BY PAKISTAN PEOPLE'S
PARTY (PPP) SIGNAL SIGNIFICANT CHANGES FOR PAKISTAN. HOWEVER,
BHUTTO AND THE PPP FACE CONSIDERABLE CHALLENGES IN THE FORM
OF WIDESPREAD ETHNIC TENSIONS, LARGE FOREIGN DEBT, AND A
LACK OF AN ABSOLUTE MAJORITY IN THE NATIONAL ASSEMBLY.
FOREIGN RELATIONS WITH INDIA AND THE USSR ARE LIKELY TO
IMPROVE, A TREND WHICH COULD, OVER THE LONG-TERM, RELIEVE
SOME OF THE PRESSURE ON PAKISTAN'S STRAINED BUDGET THROUGH A
DECREASED NEED FOR DEFENSE EXPENDITURES.

05104 KIVA, A.
DEVELOPING COUNTRIES, SOCIALISM, CAPITALISM
INTERNATIONAL AFFAIRS (MOSCOW), (3) (MAR 89), 54-63.
THE AUTHOR DISCUSSES HOW SOVIET THOUGHT AND POLICIES
REGARDING DEVELOPING COUNTRIES HAVE CHANGED SINCE THE 1960'S.

05105 KIVENGERE, H.
IN DEFENCE OF UGANDA'S NRA
NEW AFRICAN, (256) (JAN 89), 14-15.
THE AUTHOR BRIEFLY REVIEWS UGANDA'S RECENT HISTORY AND
DEFENDS THE NATIONAL RESISTANCE ARMY'S RECRUITMENT OF CHILD
SOLDIERS. SHE ARGUES THAT THE CHILDREN, AND OTHER UGANDANS,
ARE FARING BETTER UNDER THE NATIONAL RESISTANCE GOVERNMENT
THAN UNDER AMIN OR OBOTE.

05106 KIYOFUKU, C.
WHOSE BURDEN IS SHARED DEFENSE?
JAPAN QUARTERLY, XXXVI(1) (JAN 89), 18-24.
JAPANESE SECURITY ANALYSTS ARE IN A QUANDARY AS TO WHAT
THE UNITED STATES REALLY WANTS JAPAN TO DO IN TERMS OF
DEFENSE. THE USA SEEMS TO WANT JAPAN TO INCREASE ITS DEFENSE
SPENDING. BUT IF JAPAN SPENDS MORE, IS IT TO USE THE
ADDITIONAL FUNDS TO BUILD A DEFENSE CAPABILITY THAT WOULD
RENDER DEPENDENCE ON THE USA UNNECESSARY AND INVALIDATE THE
TREATY OF MUTUAL COOPERATION AND SECURITY BETWEEN THE TWO
COUNTRIES? OR IS INCREASED SPENDING TO BE USED STRICTLY TO
EASE THE AMERICAN DEFENSE BUDGET? HAS JAPAN ALREADY GONE
BEYOND THE PERMISSIBLE LIMIT IN ITS DEFENSE BUILDUP, CAUSING
ANY FURTHER EXPANSION DUE TO AMERICAN PRESSURE TO BE SEEN

INTERNATIONALLY AS DETRIMENTAL TO WORLD PEACE?

05107 KIYOKO, T.
CONFLICTING CONCEPTS ON THE EMPEROR
JAPAN QUARTERLY, XXXVI(1) (JAN 89), 50-55.
FROM THE TIME OF THE MEIJI RESTORATION UNTIL THE END OF
WORLD WAR II, THE ROLE OF THE EMPEROR WAS INTERPRETED IN TWO
WAYS. ONE IMAGE WAS THAT OF THE EMPEROR AS A LIVING DEITY, A
SUPREME BEING ON EARTH. THE OTHER WAS THAT THE EMPEROR WAS A
MAN ABOVE MEN, A MONARCH LIMITED BY THE RATIONAL AND
DEMOCRATIC INTERPRETATIONS EXPRESSED IN THE CHARTER OATH.
AFTER WORLD WAR II, EMPEROR HIROHITO ISSUED AN IMPERIAL
RESCRIPT RENOUNCING HIS DIVINITY AND REAFFIRMING THE
DEMOCRATIC IDEAS EXPRESSED IN THE CHARTER OATH PROCLAIMED BY
THE EMPEROR MEIJI.

05108 KLATT, H.
FORTY YEARS OF GERMAN FEDERALISM: PAST TRENDS AND NEW
DEVELOPMENTS
PUBLIUS: THE JOURNAL OF FEDERALISM, 19(4) (FAL 89),
185-202.
THIS ARTICLE TRACES THE MAJOR DEVELOPMENTS IN GERMAN
FEDERALISM FROM 1949 TO THE PRESENT. FROM A SYSTEM BASED ON
A CONCEPT OF "DUAL FEDERALISM," WHICH WAS DIFFERENT IN
IMPORTANT WAYS FROM THE AMERICAN SYSTEM, GERMAN FEDERALISM
BECAME SOMEWHAT MORE LIKE THE POSTWAR AMERICAN COOPERATIVE
FEDERALISM. CRITICISM OF THIS SYSTEM IN THE 1970S LED TO
VARIOUS REFORM EFFORTS, WHICH MADE LITTLE HEADWAY UNTIL THE
1980S AND THE FORMATION OF A CDU/CSU-FDP COALITION
GOVERNMENT UNDER CHANCELLOR HELMUT KOHL. THE "TURNABOUT"
PROMISED BY THIS GOVERNMENT AND CARRIED OUT TO SOME EXTENT
INCLUDED PLANS AND POLICIES TO STRENGTHEN THE LANDER BY SOME
SORTING OUT OF FUNCTIONS. THESE EFFORTS WERE SUCCESSFUL AT
FIRST, BUT THE FEDERAL GOVERNMENT HAS ORIENTED ITS POLICIES
MORE TOWARD THE NATIONAL ARENA. FINANCIAL CONSTRAINTS, THE
NATIONALIZATION OF BASIC RIGHTS, TECHNOLOGICAL CONCERNS, AND
PRESSURES BY THE EC HAVE LED TO NEW TENDENCIES TOWARD
INTERGOVERNMENTALIZING AND CENTRALIZING THE RELATIONS
BETWEEN THE FEDERATION AND LAND GOVERNMENTS.

05109 KLEBE, E.
PUBLIC HEALTH RESOURCES: WHO CUTS THE PIE?
CRS REVEIW, 10(3) (MAR 89), 6-8.
FEDERAL "HEALTH DOLLARS" ARE SPENT IN TWO MAIN AREAS:
THE FINANCING AND DELIVERY OF SPECIFIC MEDICAL SERVICES FOR
INDIVIDUALS, WHICH ARE CALLED "PERSONAL HEALTH SERVICES,"
AND PUBLIC HEALTH PROGRAMS, WHICH ARE USUALLY DIRECTED AT
ENTIRE POPULATIONS AND ARE UNDERTAKEN TO PREVENT DISEASE BY
PROMOTING HEALTHFUL ENVIRONMENTS, BEHAVIORS, AND LIFESTYLES.
PUBLIC HEALTH PROGRAMS COMPETE FOR FEDERAL FUNDING WITH SUCH
PERSONAL HEALTH SERVICES AS MEDICARE AND MEDICAID.

05110 KLEBE, E.R.
DEMAND REDUCTION THROUGH TREATMENT AND PREVENTION
CRS REVEIW, 10(10) (NOV 89), 14-16.
INCREASINGLY, POLICYMAKERS IN THE CONGRESS AND THE
ADMINISTRATION HAVE BEGUN TO SUPPORT THE PREMISE THAT THE
PROBLEM OF DRUG ABUSE WILL BE DIMINISHED ONLY WHEN THE
DEMAND FOR DRUGS IS DRAMATICALLY REDUCED. THIS REDUCTION CAN
BE ACCOMPLISHED IN TWO WAYS: BY HELPING TO REHABILITATE
THOSE WHO USE AND ARE ADDICTED TO DRUGS AND BY PREVENTING
THE INITIAL USE AND EVENTUAL ABUSE OF DRUGS. ONE ELEMENT OF
PREVENTION IS DETERRENCE THROUGH LAW ENFORCEMENT MEASURES.

05111 KLEEMAN, R.
GRAY AREAS OF FEDERAL ETHICS LAW
BUREAUCRAT, 18(1) (SPR 89), 7-11.
PUBLIC EMPLOYEES WILL BEHAVE IN AN ETHICAL MANNER ONLY
IF THE STANDARDS AND LEGAL SANCTIONS ARE CLEAR AND
PERSUASIVE. HOWEVER, AT LEAST IN THE FEDERAL SECTOR, THIS
OFTEN IS NOT THE CASE. THIS ARTICLE DESCRIBES SOME OF THE
"GRAY AREAS" IN FEDERAL ETHICS LAWS, NOTING BOTH CONFUSING
PERMISSIBLE ACTION AND TERMS.

05112 KLEEMEIER, L.
POLICY REFORM AND RURAL DEVELOPMENT ASSISTANCE IN TANZANIA
PUBLIC CHOICE, 9(4) (SEP 89), 405-416.
TANZANIA FOR A LONG TIME REFUSED TO REFORM ITS ECONOMIC
POLICIES ALONG THE LINES RECOMMENDED BY THE WORLD BANK AND
IMF. EVENTUALLY THE FOREIGN EXCHANGE CRISIS FORCED THE
GOVERNMENT TO MAKE THE CHANGES ADVOCATED BY ITS OWN
PRAGMATIC ECONOMISTS AND THE WESTERN DONOR COMMUNITY. THE
REFORMS WERE NECESSARY, BUT NOT A PANACEA FOR ALL THE
PROBLEMS WHICH HAD PLAGUED RURAL DEVELOPMENT PROGRAMMES OVER
THE PAST DECADE. THREE BIG PROBLEMS STILL FACE BASIC-NEEDS
PROGRAMMES: THE GOVERNMENT ADMINISTRATION HAS VERY LITTLE
CAPACITY TO MANAGE OR BACK UP PROGRAMMES; NEITHER THE
NATIONAL NOR DISTRICT GOVERNMENTS CAN AFFORD THEM; AND RURAL
RESIDENTS HAVE NOT COMPENSATED FOR EITHER OF THESE
DEFICIENCIES THROUGH THEIR OWN PARTICIPATION AND
CONTRIBUTIONS. THIS ARTICLE LOOKS AT TWO BASIC-NEEDS
PROGRAMMES IN THE RURAL WATER SUPPLY SECTOR TO ILLUSTRATE
HOW THESE LONG-STANDING PROBLEMS CONTINUE TO AFFECT
IMPLEMENTATION. BOTH PROGRAMMES ARE FUNDED AND IMPLEMENTED

BY DONORS. THE CONCLUSION IS THAT DONORS HAVE NOT BEEN
SUFFICIENTLY SELF-CONSCIOUS AND INNOVATIVE IN GRAPPLING WITH
THE MORE INTRACTABLE PROBLEMS FACING RURAL PROGRAMME
ASSISTANCE IN TANZANIA.

05113 KLEER, J.
A VIEW FROM POLAND-EUROPE 1992: FEARS, WISHES, PROSPECTS
CONTEMPORARY POLAND, XXII(8) (1989), 3-8.
THE AUTHOR CONSIDERS THE CHANGES THAT WESTERN EUROPE'S
SINGLE MARKET WILL MAKE AFTER 1992 AND SPECIFICALLY HOW IT
WILL AFFECT THE CMEA.

05114 KLEER, J.
NEW RULES OF THE ECONOMIC GAME
CONTEMPORARY POLAND, XXII(1) (1989), 1-3.
ON DECEMBER 23, 1988, THE SEJM PASSED TWO LAWS OF
FUNDAMENTAL IMPORTANCE FOR THE FUTURE ECONOMIC SHAPE OF
POLAND. THE FIRST CONCERNS BUSINESS ACTIVITY, WHILE THE
SECOND GOVERNS BUSINESS WITH FOREIGN EQUITY PARTICIPATION.
THE CHANGES THAT THEY ENTAIL WILL RESULT IN A TRUE
REVOLUTION IN THE POLISH ECONOMIC MODEL, WITH EQUAL TERMS
FOR THE PRIVATE AND PUBLIC SECTORS.

05115 KLEIN, D.
THE CHANCES OF CAPITALISM WITHOUT GUNS
WORLD MARXIST REVIEW, 31(12) (DEC 88), 13-20.
MILITARISM WITH ITS DEEP ROOTS IN MODERN CAPITALISM IS
CLASHING EVER MORE STRONGLY WITH ENTREPRENEURIAL INTERESTS.
THEREFORE, ONE CANNOT RULE OUT A FAVORABLE REGROUPING OF
DIFFERENT FACTIONS OF THE STATEMONOPOLY, MONOPOLY AND NON-
MONOPOLY BOURGEOISIE AND, AS A CONSEQUENCE, THE POSSIBILITY
THAT ITS REALISTIC SECTION WOULD JOIN US IN THE CONVERSION
EFFORT AND IN THE CREATION, ON THE BASIS OF THE LATEST
TECHNOLOGIES AND OF COOPERATION, OF ENVIRONMENTALLY SAFE
INDUSTRIES. IN TERMS OF ITS DEPTH, SCOPE AND DIVERSITY OF
SOCIAL EFFECTS, THE PRESENT REVOLUTION IN THE PRODUCTIVE
FORCES IS SUPERIOR TO ALL PREVIOUS LEAPS IN MANKIND'S
TECHNOLOGICAL DEVELOPMENT; THEREFORE, IT MAKES NEW SOCIAL
PRACTICE POSSIBLE.

05116 KLEIN, I.J.
SOVIET STRATEGIC CULTURE, 1917-1965
DISSERTATION ABSTRACTS INTERNATIONAL, 49(10) (APR 89),
3148-A.
IMPORTANT SOURCES OF SOVIET STRATEGIC CULTURE ARE THE
THOUGHT OF MARX, ENGELS AND LENIN AND THE EXPERIENCE OF THE
RUSSIAN CIVIL WAR. ITS CHIEF CANONS ARE: (1) ONLY THE
COMPLETE DESTRUCTION OF AN ENEMY CAPITALIST REGIME AND ITS
ARMED FORCES ARE ACCEPTABLE POLITICAL GOALS IN WAR; (2)
THESE GOALS MUST BE CONSUMMATED THROUGH OFFENSIVE
OPERATIONAL MANEUVER; (3) MILITARY POWER IS ONLY AN
EMBODIMENT OF THE INHERENT ECONOMIC, POLITICAL AND MORAL
STRENGTH OF THE STATE; (4) AS HISTORICALLY THE MOST
PROGRESSIVE STATE, THE SOVIET UNION MUST ADOPT THE MOST
MODERN WEAPONS AND OPERATIONAL METHODS.

05117 KLEIN, J.
THE THEORY AND PRACTICE OF ARMS CONTROL: RESULTS AND
PERSPECTIVES
ETUDES INTERNATIONALES, 20(3) (SEP 89), 647-664.
ARMS CONTROL, AS DEVELOPED BY AMERICAN CIVILIAN
STRATEGISTS IN THE LATE 1950S, SOUGHT TO MAINTAIN THE
EQUILIBRIUM UPON WHICH MUTUAL DETERRENCE WAS DEPENDENT, AND
STROVE TO PREVENT DIRECT CONFLICT BETWEEN THE TWO NUCLEAR
PROTAGONISTS. HAS IT EXHAUSTED ITS VIRTUALITY AND WILL THERE
BE A RETURN TO THE TRADITION OF GENERAL AND TOTAL
DISARMAMENT? ONE COMES TO ASK WITHIN THE FRAMEWORK OF THIS
ANALYSIS, WHETHER THE WASHINGTON TREATY OF DECEMBER 1987
INTRODUCES A NEW ELEMENT TO ARMS CONTROL, OR WHETHER IT
CLOSELY FOLLOWS THE METHODS USED IN FORMER AGREEMENTS. IN AN
EFFORT TO BETTER COMPREHEND THIS QUESTION, THE PAST
EXPERIENCES IN ARMS CONTROL WILL BE EXAMINED BEFORE MAKING
ANY CONJECTURES ON ITS ANTICIPATED EVOLUTION, ALL THE WHILE
TAKING INTO CONSIDERATION THE NEW APPROACHES USED IN THE
AMERICAN-SOVIET RELATIONS, THE PROBLEMS CREATED BY
TECHNOLOGICAL INNOVATION, AND THE INTENTIONS OF BOTH THE
SMALL AND MEDIUM STATES.

05118 KLENIEWSKI, N.
URBAN ECONOMIC DEVELOPMENT
DISSENT, (WIN 89), 15-17.
IN THE PAST FIFTEEN YEARS, THE HEALTH OF THE LOCAL
ECONOMY HAS BECOME THE PRESSING URBAN POLICY ISSUE. ALTHOUGH
THE OLDER MANUFACTURING CITIES ARE MOST IN NEED OF AN
ENERGETIC POLICY, THE ISSUE IS A TOP PRIORITY FOR VIRTUALLY
EVERY CITY ADMINISTRATION. A REVIEW OF CITY STRATEGIES
REVEALS A COMMON WISDOM ON ECONOMIC DEVELOPMENT. DEVELOPMENT
POLICY THAT STRESSES MANUFACTURING IS DERIED AS "SMOKESTACK
CHASING" WHILE LOCAL GOVERNMENTS PURSUE TOURISTS, SHOPPERS,
AND CORPORATE OFFICES. FURTHERMORE, MOST CITIES ARE WILLING
TO PROVIDE HEFTY PUBLIC SUBSIDIES TO STIMULATE THAT KIND OF
PRIVATE INVESTMENT IN THEIR DOWNTOWN AREAS.

05119 KLEPAC, H.P.; GEORGE, W.L.
   TRENDS IN NATO CONVENTIONAL STRATEGY
   ETUDES INTERNATIONALES, 20(3) (SEP 89), 577-598.
      THE PURPOSE OF THIS ARTICLE IS TO CONCENTRATE ON THE
   CONVENTIONAL STRATEGY OF EUROPE IN ORDER TO BRING TO LIGHT
   ITS NEW TRENDS, ALL THE WHILE DEMONSTRATING THE PRINCIPAL
   ROLE THAT NEW TECHNOLOGY MAINTAINS WITHIN THIS EVOLUTIONARY
   PROCESS. EMPHASIS WILL BE PLACED UPON THE RECENT CHANGES IN
   WESTERN DOCTRINES, IN ORDER TO DISTINGUISH THE DIFFERENCES
   BETWEEN THE DOCTRINES OF AIR LAND BATTLE AND FOLLOW-ON-
   FORCES ATTACK (FOFA), AND THOSE WHICH PRECEDED THEM. AN
   ATTEMPT WILL THEN BE MADE TO COMPARE THE RECENT DEVELOPMENTS
   IN THE CONCEPTUAL MODELS OF WAR OF ATTRITION AND WAR OF
   MANEUVER, SO AS TO DETERMINE WHETHER THESE NEW DOCTRINES
   CORRESPOND TO EITHER THE FIRST OR SECOND MODEL. THIS
   ANALYSIS SHOULD THUS PERMIT A BETTER UNDERSTANDING OF THE
   DEBATE WHICH ENCOMPASSES THE CONVENTIONAL STRATEGY OF EUROPE.

05120 KLEPAK, H.P.
   VERIFICATION OF A CENTRAL AMERICAN PEACE ACCORD
   AVAILABLE FROM NTIS, NO. PB89-204911/GAR, 1989, 93.
      THE PAPER DISCUSSES THE BACKGROUND TO, POSSIBLE CONTEXTS
   OF, AND LIKELY DIFFICULTIES WITH AN EVENTUAL CENTRAL
   AMERICAN PEACE ACCORD, PARTICULARLY ITS VERIFICATION. IT
   BEGINS WITH A BRIEF ANALYSIS OF THE POLITICAL, MILITARY AND
   DIPLOMATIC BACKGROUND OF THE REGIONAL CRISIS, SETTING THE
   SCENE FOR A LOOK AT THE VERIFICATION ASPECTS OF THE PEACE
   NEGOTIATIONS AND AGREEMENTS TO DATE: CONTADORA, ESQUIPULAS
   II, AND SAPOA. IT THEN ATTEMPTS TO SHOW WHAT KIND OF FURTHER
   AGREEMENT ONE MIGHT SEE IN THE FUTURE, DOING THIS BY
   EXAMINING BOTH 'MINIMUM' AND 'MAXIMUM' CONTENT POSSIBILITIES.
   THIS IS FOLLOWED BY A LENGTHY DISCUSSION OF THE
   VERIFICATION IMPLICATIONS OF SUCH AGREEMENTS AND THE
   POLITICAL, GEOGRAPHICAL, SOCIAL AND TECHNICAL DIFFICULTIES
   THEY MIGHT POSE.

05121 KLICH, I.
   ARAB DOUBTS ABOUT MENEM
   MIDDLE EAST INTERNATIONAL, 355 (JUL 89), 14.
      AN ARGENTINE-ARAB CHAMBER OF COMMERCE DELEGATION, WHICH
   VISITED THE MIDDLE EAST AND NORTH AFRICA TO PROMOTE A TRADE
   EXHIBITION, IS PRESIDENT CARLOS MENEM'S FIRST CONTACT WITH
   THE ARABS SINCE HE WAS VOTED INTO OFFICE. THIS IS PRESUMABLY
   DUE TO THE BAD PRESS HIS ELECTION CAMPAIGN RECEIVED ABROAD,
   AND TO THE FACT THAT EARLY IN THE 1960S MENEM DESCRIBED IN
   AN ARAB LEAGUE PUBLICATION THE CONSERVATIVE ARAB STATES AS
   "ALLIES OF IMPERIALISM AND ACCOMPLICES OF ZIONISM". WHILE
   MENEM NO LONGER SEEMS TO SUBSCRIBE TO THESE AND OTHER VIEWS
   IN TUNE WITH THOSE OF THE EGYPTIAN LEADERSHIP OF THE DAY, HE
   HAS TO BUILD UP THE ARAB MONARCHS' CONFIDENCE. THE SAME IS
   THE CASE WITH THE EGYPTIANS, WHO HAVE LONG SHED NASSER'S
   ANTI-IMPERIALIST RHETORIC.

05122 KLICH, I.
   ARGENTINA: WILL MENEM BE EVEN-HANDED?
   MIDDLE EAST INTERNATIONAL, (351) (MAY 89), 15.
      ARGENTINA'S NEXT PERONIST PRESIDENT, CARLOS MENEM, IS OF
   SYRIAN MUSLIM PARENTAGE, BUT CONVERTED TO CHRISTIANITY; HIS
   WIFE HAS PROUDLY DECLARED HER ATTACHEMENT TO HER ANCESTORS'
   FAITH AND WILL BECOME LATIN AMERICA'S FIRST MUSLIM FIRST
   LADY. MANY SEE THE ADVENT OF MENEM AS AN INDICATION THAT
   ANTI-ARAB PREJUDICE HAS DECREASED SIGNIFICANTLY IN ARGENTINA.
   ALTHOUGH THE MIDDLE EAST HAS NEVER FIGURED PROMINENTLY IN
   ARGENTINE INTERNATIONAL RELATIONS, MENEM'S BACKGROUND HAS
   GIVEN RISE TO QUESTIONS AS TO WHAT ATTITUDE A FUTURE
   GOVERNMENT WILL TAKE TOWARDS THE ARABS AND ISRAELIS.

05123 KLICH, I.
   CHILEAN GRAPES: WHO DID IT?
   MIDDLE EAST INTERNATIONAL, (347) (MAR 89), 16.
      AN ISRAELI ULTRA-NATIONALIST ZIONIST MOVEMENT HAS
   CLAIMED RESPONSIBILITY FOR THE CYANIDE FOUND IN CHILEAN
   GRAPES EXPORTED TO THE USA. THE GROUP SAID THAT THE
   POISONING WAS INTENDED TO PUNISH THE USA FOR TALKING WITH
   THE PLO.

05124 KLICH, I.
   ISRAEL AND CHILE: DOUBTS ON THE KFIR DEAL
   MIDDLE EAST INTERNATIONAL, (344) (FEB 89), 11-12.
      ISRAEL'S ROLE AS THE BROKER OF AN ILL-FATED TRANSFER OF
   CHILEAN F-5 FIGHTERS TO IRAN SEEMS TO HAVE IRKED THE USA,
   WHICH HAS RESPONDED BY PERSUADING CHILE TO POSTPONE, IF NOT
   DROP ALTOGETHER, THE ACQUISITION OF KFIR COMBAT PLANES.

05125 KLICH, I.
   ISRAELI'S IN COLOMBIA
   MIDDLE EAST INTERNATIONAL, (364) (DEC 89), 17-18.
      THE DETENTION OF TWO ISRAELI RESERVE OFFICERS BY THE
   COLOMBIAN GOVERNMENT RAISES THE QUESTION OF ISRAEL'S
   CONNECTION WITH COLOMBIAN DRUG CARTELS. ALTHOUGH DIFFICULT
   TO SUBSTANTIATE, ACCUSATIONS OF DEATH SQUADS BEING TRAINED
   BY ISRAELI MILITARY EXPERTS ARE BEING VOICED.

05126 KLIMENKO, V.
   INDEPENDENT TRADE UNION ORGANIZING IN THE USSR
   ACROSS FRONTIERS, 5(3) (FAL 89), 10-11.
      THIS IS AN INTERVIEW WITH THE COORDINATOR FOR PUBLIC
   RELATIONS, ASSOCIATION OF SOCIALIST TRADE UNIONS, IT
   ADDRESSES THE ORIGINATION OF AN INDEPENDENT TRADE UNION
   FEDERATION; ITS ROLE IN SOCIETY; AND HOW IT WOULD DIFFER
   FROM THE OFFICIAL UNIONS, IT ALSO EXPLORES THE TRADE UNIONS
   POLITICAL GOALS AND THE COORDINATOR'S OUTLOOK FOR THE FUTURE.

05127 KLINTWORTH,G.
   CHINA'S INDOCHINA POLICY
   JOURNAL OF NORTHEAST ASIAN STUDIES, VIII(3) (FAL 89),
   25-43.
      CHINA HAS MADE VIRTUALLY ALL THE GAINS IT CAN EXPECT
   FROM THE WAR IN CAMBODIA. THESE INCLUDE ITS REGIONAL
   INFLUENCE, ITS RELATIONS WITH THAILAND AND THE SUPERPOWERS,
   AND ITS PUNISHMENT OF VIETNAM. CONTINUED SUPPORT FOR THE
   UNIVERSALLY CONDEMNED KHMER ROUGE RISKS UNDERMINING CHINA'S
   REGIONAL STANDING FOR NO CERTAIN GAIN. IT COULD FORESTALL
   NEW POSSIBILITIES FOR CHINA IN PHNOM PENH AND EVEN IN HANOI.
   THUS, CHINA WILL PROBABLY DUMP THE KHMER ROUGE WHEN THE TIME
   IS RIPE. ACCEPTANCE BY CHINA OF THE REALITIES OF HUN SEN'S
   CAMBODIA-PROVIDED IT SURVIVES-MAY BE A NOTTOO-DISTANT
   PROSPECT.

05128 KLOSKO, G.
   POLITICAL OBLIGATION AND GRATITUDE
   PHILOSOPHY AND PUBLIC AFFAIRS, 18(4) (FAL 89), 352-358.
      THIS ARTICLE EXAMINES THE VIEW THAT POLITICAL
   OBLIGATIONS CAN BE EXPLAINED AS OBLIGATIONS OF GRATITUDE
   STEMMING FROM BENEFITS THE INDIVIDUAL RECEIVES FROM THE
   STATE, AS RECENTLY REVIVED BY A.D.M. WALKER. THE AUTHOR
   BELIEVES THAT WALKER'S ATTEMPT TO SKETCH OUT A WORKABLE
   THEORY OF POLITICAL OBLIGATION IS LESS THAN SUCCESSFUL, AND
   EXPLAINS WHY.

05129 KLOTEN, N.
   THE DELORS REPORT: A BLUEPRINT FOR EUROPEAN INTEGRATION?
   WORLD TODAY, 45(11) (NOV 89), 191-194.
      THE AUTHOR EXAMINES THE DELORS REPORT, WHICH WAS
   PREPARED BY A GROUP OF EXPERTS TO SERVE AS A GUIDE TO
   ECONOMIC AND MONETARY UNION IN WESTERN EUROPE.

05130 KLOTEN, N.
   TOWARDS A EUROPEAN CENTRAL BANK SYSTEM
   INTERNATIONAL SPECTATOR, XXIII(4) (OCT 88), 243-251.
      UNTIL A SHORT TIME AGO, THE OPTION OF A EUROPEAN CENTRAL
   BANK WAS SEEN AS THE FINAL STAGE OF A LONG-TERM PROCESS OF
   INTEGRATION. TODAY, IT IS CONSIDERED TO BE VIABLE MONETARY
   POLICY ALTERNATIVE IN THE FORESEEABLE FUTURE. THE INTEREST
   IN AN ECB SOLUTION REFLECTS EUROPEAN POLICY MOTIVES AND, AS
   SUCH, ALSO EXPRESSES IMPATIENCE REGARDING WHAT HAS BEEN
   ACHIEVED SO FAR.

05131 KLUTZNICK, P.M.
   THE ROAD TO PEACE
   NEW OUTLOOK, 32(2 (288)) (FEB 89), 38-39.
      IN RECENT MONTHS, THERE HAS BEEN AN UNUSUAL NUMBER OF
   GESTURES POINTING TO THE PROSPECT FOR AN APPROACH TO PEACE
   BETWEEN ISRAEL AND SOME OF ITS NEIGHBORS. FOR YEARS, ANY
   GESTURE BY ONE SIDE WAS MET WITH SKEPTICISM AND DOUBTS BY
   THE OTHER. THIS HAS BEEN AN ENDEMIC SITUATION AND IS NOT AN
   ATMOSPHERE CONDUCIVE TO PROGRESS TOWARD THE ULTIMATE GOAL.
   WHILE AN ELEMENTARY TRUST HAS NOT YET BEEN ACHIEVED, THERE
   IS NOW AT LEAST A SLIGHT MOVEMENT IN THAT DIRECTION.

05132 KNAPP. K.A.
   CORRECTIONAL POLICIES: BALANCING REFORMS WITH RESOURCES
   JOURNAL OF STATE GOVERNMENT, 62(2) (MAR 89), 79-83.
      CONTEMPORARY SENTENCING REFORMS IN THE UNITED STATES
   TYPICALLY FOLLOW ONE OF TWO PATHS. THE FIRST APPROACH
   EMPHASIZES NON-CUSTODIAL COMMUNITY CORRECTIONS PROGRAMS FOR
   OFFENDERS WHO DO NOT SERIOUSLY THREATEN PUBLIC SAFETY AND
   OTHERWISE WOULD BE SENT TO PRISON. THE SECOND PATH IS
   STRUCTURED SENTENCING. THE DESIRE FOR SENTENCES THAT ARE
   FAIR AND PROPORTIONAL TO THE OFFENSE WAS A DRIVING FORCE IN
   STRUCTURED SENTENCING AS STATES SOUGHT WAYS TO REDUCE
   DISPARITIES IN SENTENCES FOR SIMILAR CRIMES. WHILE THE TWO
   TYPES OF SENTENCING REFORM COEXIST, THEIR PATHS TEND NOT TO
   CROSS. SINCE THIS SEPARATION CAN BE DETRIMENTAL, A COMPUTER
   MODEL HAS BEEN DEVELOPED TO SHOW POLICY-MAKERS THE IMPACT ON
   STATE AND LOCAL CORRECTIONAL RESOURCES OF THE TWO TYPES OF
   SENTENCING REFORMS.

05133 KNEE, S.
   THE DIPLOMACY OF NEUTRALITY: THEODORE ROOSEVELT AND THE
   RUSSIAN POGROMS OF 1903-1906
   PRESIDENTIAL STUDIES QUARTERLY, XIX(1) (WIN 89), 71-78.
      THE ISSUE OF THE EXTENT TO WHICH THE NATION SHOULD BE A
   CHAMPION OF HUMAN RIGHTS INTERNATIONALLY HAS BEEN MUCH WE
   DEBATED OVER THE PAST TWO DECADES. THE PROBLEM IS NOT A NEW
   ONE, AS THE AUTHOR'S SURVEY OF THEODORE ROOSEVELT'S RESPONSE
   TO RUSSIAN POGROMS REVEALS. THE PRESIDENT HAD TO BALANCE THE

LIMITED IMPACT ON THE RUSSIAN AUTOCRACY OF AMERICAN PROTESTS
ABOUT THE TREATMENT OF JEWS IN THAT COUNTRY AGAINST THE
ENTHUSIASM AND FERVOR OF THOSE IN THE US WHO WERE OUTRAGED
AT THE REPRESSIVE POLICIES OF CZAR NICHOLAS II AND HIS
GOVERNMENT. THE HUMAN RIGHTS ASPECT OF THE MATTER ALSO
BECAME ENTANGLED WITH ROOSEVELT'S ASIAN DIPLOMACY THAT
SOUGHT TO RESTRAIN RUSSIAN POWER IN MANCHURIA AND ELS WHERE
IN NORTH CHINA AND KOREA?

05134 KNEEN, P.
SOVIET SCIENCE POLICY UNDER GORBACHEV
SOVIET STUDIES, XLI(1) (JAN 89), 67-87.
THE ARTICLE EXAMINES THE INCREASED EMPHASIS PLACED ON
SCIENCE AS A SOLUTION TO MANY OF THE PROBLEMS IN THE USSR BY
MIKHAIL GORBACHEV. SCIENCE IS CURRENTLY VIEWED AS A MEANS TO
AID THE NATION'S ATTEMPT TO EMERGE INTO THE "RESTRUCTURED"
WORLD OF THE 1990'S THE ARTICLE OUTLINES THE CHANGES THAT
ARE BEING INTRODUCED INTO THE ORGANIZATION OF THE USSR
ACADEMY OF SCIENCES AND IN ITS PERSONNEL POLICY, ALONG WITH
INCREASED MATERIAL SUPPORT. THE IMPACT OF THESE CHANGES ARE
ALSO ASSESSED.

05135 KNEISEL, E.
THE JOB BEGINS AT SCHOOL
POLICY OPTIONS, 10(2) (MAR 89), 24-25.
CANADA CANNOT MEET THE CHALLENGE OF INTERNATIONAL
COMPETITION UNTIL IT IMPROVES ITS EDUCATIONAL APPROACH,
ARGUES MR. KNEISEL. WHILE COMPETITIVENESS DEPENDS ON
PRODUCTIVITY AND PRODUCTIVITY ON TECHNOLOGY, THESE ARE IN
THE HANDS OF THE PRIVATE SECTOR WHILE EDUCATION, THE PROCESS
THAT PREPARES OUR WORKERS AND MANAGERS, IS IN GOVERNMENT
HANDS. THE AUTHOR SUGGESTS A SEVEN-POINT PROGRAM TO BRING
GREATER INVOLVEMENT OF THE PRIVATE SECTOR INTO THE CLASSROOM,
AND TO IMPROVE TEACHING TECHNIQUES.

05136 KNELMAN, F.H.; ALDRIDGE, R.C.
HOW INF IS DISARMING
PEACE RESEARCH, 21(1) (JAN 89), 13-16.
IN THIS ARTICLE THE AUTHORS ATTEMPT TO PROVE THEIR
CONTENTION THAT THE SPLINTERING AND WEAKENING OF THE NEW
RIGHT COALITION IN THE US, THE STRENGTH OF THE EUROPEAN
PEACE MOVEMENT, THE SHADOW OF IRAN-CONTRAGATE, AND
GORBACHEV'S ACCOMMODATION TO US DEMANDS, FORCED REAGAN TO
SAY "YES" TO THE INF TREATY (INFT).

05137 KNIGHT, V.C.
NAMIBIA'S TRANSITION TO INDEPENDENCE
CURRENT HISTORY, 88(538) (MAY 89), 225-228, 239-241.
EVEN AS AN INDEPENDENT COUNTRY, NAMIBIA WILL REMAIN
DEPENDENT ON SOUTH AFRICA FOR TRANSPORT, TRADE, AND CURRENCY
TRANSACTIONS. MOREOVER, TRIBAL SEPARATION FOSTERED BY SOUTH
AFRICA'S LONG OCCUPATION WILL BE SLOW TO DISAPPEAR.

05138 KNIRSCH, P.
PEACE MOVEMENT AND PEACE RESEARCH AS PART OF THE DETENTE
MOVEMENT
PEACE AND THE SCIENCES, 1 (1989), 68-71.
THE CHANGES THAT ARE NOW OCCURRING IN INTERNATIONAL
RELATIONS MAKE IT NECESSARY FOR MANY OF THOSE IN THE PEACE
MOVEMENT TO RETHINK THEIR POSITIONS. ABOVE ALL, THIS
MOVEMENT WILL HAVE TO REFRAIN FROM PARTISANSHIP IN THE
FUTURE - THERE IS NO SOCIALIST OR CAPITALIST PEACE, BUT ONLY
THE MUTUAL PEACEFUL COEXISTENCE OF ALL PEOPLES OR NATIONS.
THE PEACE MOVEMENT MUST PREVENT THESE DIFFERENCES OF OPINION
FROM LEADING TO CONFLICTS OF DOGMATICALLY DEFENDED OPINIONS.
INSTEAD, BY MEANS OF HONEST MUTUAL DISCUSSION IT SHOULD BE
POSSIBLE TO ARRIVE AT A CONSENSUS ACCEPTABLE TO ALL THOSE
AFFECTED BY A PARTICULAR PROBLEM (COUNTRIES, PEOPLES,
SYSTEMS, INTEREST GROUPS).

05139 KNORR, K.
MILITARY TRENDS AND FUTURE WORLD ORDER
JERUSALEM JOURNAL OF INTERNATIONAL RELATIONS, 11(2) (JUN
89), 68-95.
THE AUTHOR IDENTIFIES THE MAJOR MILITARY TRENDS THAT
REVEALED THEMSELVES IN RECENT DECADES AND SEEM TO HOLD SWAY
WITH UNDIMINISHED STRENGTH. IN DISCUSSING THESE TRENDS THE
AUTHOR TURNS FIRST TO THE KEY RELATIONSHIP BETWEEN THE TWO
SUPERPOWERS, AND THEN, SUCCESSIVELY, TO THE FIRST WORLD OF
CAPITALIST-DEMOCRATIC NATIONS, THE SECOND WORLD OF COMMUNIST
STATES, AND THE THIRD WORLD OF MORE OR LESS NONALIGNED
COUNTRIES. IN EACH INSTANCE, THE EFFECTS OF THE MILITARY
TRENDS ARE EXPLORED AS THEY AFFECT RELATIONS WITHIN EACH
WORLD AND AS THEY IMPINGE ON RELATIONS AMONG THE THREE
WORLDS.

05140 KNORR, L.
DISTURBANCE OF THE CONSENSUS IN NATO AND OVERCOMING
"DETERRENCE"
PEACE AND THE SCIENCES, 1 (1989), 39-53.
THE NEW THINKING AND APPROACH CHARACTERIZED BY THE USSR
SECURITY POLICY SINCE THE ACCESSION OF M. GORBACHEV TO
OFFICE DEEPENED THE DISTURBANCE OF THE CONSENSUS WHICH
EXISTED BETWEEN THE MORE REALISTIC AND THE TRADITIONAL

FORCES ORIENTED TOWARDS CONFRONTATION IN NATO. AS THIS
ARTICLE DESCRIBES, THE OPPOSITIONS MARKING THE DISTURBANCE
OF THE CONSENSUS AND THE CONTROVERSIAL DIFFERENTIATION CAN
BE OBSERVED BETWEEN THE USA AND THE STATES IN WESTERN EUROPE
BOTH IN VIEW OF THE DIVERGING INTERESTS, AND BETWEEN
CONSERVATIVE QUARTERS IN THE NATO STATES. (THERE IS AN
ADDITIONAL CONTRADICTION BETWEEN OFFICIAL STATEMENTS AND THE
ACTUAL POSITION: SOMETIMES A RESULT OF THE EXERCISED
POLITICAL PRESSURE BY AGGRESSIVE FORCES, SOMETIMES THE
PRODUCT OF THE ATTEMPTED MISLEADING OF THE PUBLIC.)

05141 KNOSHOO, T.N.
ENVIRONMENTAL PRIORITIES AND SUSTAINABLE DEVELOPMENT
SOUTH ASIA JOURNAL, 3(1,2) (JUL 89), 27-34.
THE ENVIRONMENT IS A HOLISTIC CONCEPT AND ENCOMPASSES
ALL ASPECTS OF DEVELOPMENT, INCLUDING ECONOMICS, THE
ELIMINATION OF POVERTY, AND ENSURING WORLD PEACE. THE
OBJECTIVE OF THIS PAPER IS TO IDENTIFY PRIORITY AREAS WHERE
APPROPRIATE ACTION COULD LEAD TO SUSTAINED DEVELOPMENT.
THESE AREAS HAVE TO BE IDENTIFIED IN RELATION TO THE
PARTICULAR SOCIAL, CULTURAL AND ECONOMIC MILIEU PREVAILING
IN EACH COUNTRY. THE TWELVE AREAS WHERE PRIORITY ACTION IS
NEEDED ARE GIVEN.

05142 KNOX, M.L.
TURNING RIGHT
AFRICA REPORT, 34(2) (MAR 89), 41-42.
THE PRETORIA GOVERNMENT MADE USE OF THE FLAP OVER THE
CONSERVATIVE PARTY'S REINSTITUTION OF "PETTY APARTHEID" IN
BOKSBURG TO ENHANCE ITS REFORMIST IMAGE AND DISCREDIT THE
RIGHT-WING. HOWEVER, THE BOKSBURG TOWN COUNCIL WAS ONLY
UPHOLDING WHAT IS STILL THE LAW THROUGHOUT APARTHEID SOUTH
AFRICA.

05143 KNUTSEN, M. H. O.
SOCIAL CLASS, GENDER, AND SECTOR EMPLOYMENT AS POLITICAL
CLEAVAGES IN SCANDINAVIA
ACTA SOCIOLOGICA, 32(2) (1989), 181-202.
POLITICAL CLEAVAGES IN WESTERN DEMOCRACIES HAVE
TRADITIONALLY BEEN CONNECTED TO POSITIONS IN THE LABOUR
MARKET. DURING THE LAST 10-15 YEARS, RESEARCH HAS
ESTABLISHED THAT THE EXPLANATORY POWER OF HIERARCHICAL
STATUS VARIABLES HAS BEEN MARKEDLY REDUCED. THE PRESENT
STUDY EXAMINES THE RELATIVE IMPORTANCE OF SOCIAL CLASS AND
TWO OTHER STRUCTURAL CLEAVAGES WHICH HAVE BEEN EMPHASIZED IN
RECENT POLITICAL SOCIOLOGY: SECTOR EMPLOYMENT AND GENDER.
THESE VARIABLES ARE STUDIED IN RELATION TO VARIOUS MEASURES
OF POLITICAL VALUE PRIORITIES (INTEREST-BASED LEFT-RIGHT
VALUES, SUPPORT FOR THE WELFARE STATE, AND MATERIALIST/POST-
MATERIALIST VALUES) AND PARTY PREFERENCE IN A COMPARATIVE
SCANDINAVIAN CONTEXT (DENMARK, NORWAY, AND SWEDEN). IT IS
CONCLUDED THAT SOCIAL CLASS STILL HAS CONSIDERABLE IMPACT.
SECTOR EMPLOYMENT HAS, HOWEVER, APPROACHED SOCIAL CLASS AS
AN IMPORTANT CLEAVAGE, WHILE THE IMPACT OF GENDER IS
RELATIVELY SMALL.

05144 KNUTSEN, O.
CLEAVAGE DIMENSIONS IN TEN WEST EUROPEAN COUNTRIES A
COMPARATIVE EMPIRICAL ANALYSIS
COMPARATIVE POLITICAL STUDIES, 21(4) (JAN 89), 495-534.
THE PRESENT ARTICLE DISCUSSES DIFFERENT APPROACHES FOR
IDENTIFYING EMPIRICAL CLEAVAGE DIMENSIONS AND CONCLUDES THAT
A SO-CALLED CLEAVAGE-DEFINED APPROACH IS MOST APPROPRIATE
FOR IDENTIFYING AND INTERPRETING PARTY DIMENSIONS. IT IS
FURTHER ARGUED THAT DISCRIMINANT ANALYSIS IS A POWERFUL
STATISTICAL TOOL FOR ANALYZING CLEAVAGE DIMENSIONS IN
ACCORDANCE WITH A CLEAVAGE-DEFINED APPROACH. USING DIFFERENT
STRUCTURAL VARIABLES THAT ARE INCORPORATED IN THE LIPSET-
ROKKAN MODEL FOR PARTY CLEAVAGES IN WESTERN EUROPE, AND TWO
IDEOLOGICAL DIMENSIONS (CALLED LEFT-RIGHT MATERIALISM AND
MATERIALISM/POSTMATERIALISM) AS "INPUT" FOR THE DIMENSIONAL
ANALYSES, DATA FROM NORWAY AND THE EUROPEAN COMMUNITY
COUNTRIES (BASED ON EURO-BAROMETER 16 FROM 1981) ARE
ANALYZED AND RELATED TO THE COMPARATIVE LITERATURE ON
CLEAVAGE STRUCTURE IN WESTERN EUROPE.

05145 KO, S.
JAPAN'S TRADE WITH CHINA AND SOUTH KOREA
KOREA OBSERVER, XX(2) (SUM 89), 163-176.
THIS STUDY ATTEMPTS TO ANALYZE THE COMMODITY STRUCTURE
OF JAPAN'S TRADE WITH CHINA AND SOUTH KOREA AND TO DRAW
CONCLUSIONS FOR COMPARATIVE ADVANTAGES OF TRADING BETWEEN
JAPAN AND CHINA, BETWEEN JAPAN AND SOUTH KOREA, AND BETWEEN
SOUTH KOREA AND CHINA. IT PRIMARILY FOCUSES ON THE PERIOD
FROM 1982 TO 1986 DURING WHICH TIME THE TRADE RELATIONS
BETWEEN JAPAN AND THE TWO COUNTRIES WERE VIGOROUS. IN
ADDITION, THE PERIOD UNDER STUDY IS RECENT ENOUGH TO SHOW
THE GENERAL TREND OF THEIR TRADE RELATIONS.

05146 KO, S.
NATIONALIZATION POLICY OF THE BRITISH LABOUR PARTY: ITS
DEVELOPMENT, IDEOLOGY, AND RELATION TO THE DYNAMICS OF
INTRA-PARTY POLITICS (VOLUMES I AND II)
DISSERTATION ABSTRACTS INTERNATIONAL, 50(4) (OCT 89),

1078-A.
THE BRITISH LABOUR PARTY'S NATIONALIZATION POLICIES HAVE
BEEN SYSTEMATICALLY DILUTED WHEN THEY HAVE PASSED FROM PARTY
PROGRAMS TO ELECTION MANIFESTOS AND, AGAIN, FROM ELECTION
MANIFESTOS TO POLICY PERFORMANCE IN GOVERNMENT. THE
LIMITATIONS ON POLICY ARTICULATION AND IMPLEMENTATION CAN BE
FOUND IN THE TRADITIONAL DUALISM OF LABOUR SOCIALISM. THE
DOMINANCE OF THE TRADE UNIONS IN THE PARTY'S POLICY-MAKING
STRUCTURE IS ANOTHER MAJOR CONSTRAINT UPON THE DEVELOPMENT
OF NATIONALIZATION.

05147 KOBYLKA, J.F.
LEADERSHIP ON THE SUPREME COURT OF THE UNITED STATES:
CHIEF JUSTICE BURGER AND THE ESTABLISHMENT CLAUSE
WESTERN POLITICAL QUARTERLY, 42(4) (DEC 89), 545-568.
WARREN BURGER'S RESIGNATION BROUGHT THE USUAL
RETROSPECTIVE ANALYSES OF HIS TENURE AS CHIEF JUSTICE. THE
CONSENSUS EMERGED THAT HE FAILED TO ACHIEVE HIS POLICY GOALS
BECAUSE HE WAS AN INEFFECTIVE LEADER. THIS FAILURE HAS
DESCRIBED IN TERMS OF HIS "SOCIAL" AND "TASK" DEFICIENCIES.
BURGER DID NOT ACHIEVE MANY OF HIS JURISPRUDENTIAL GOALS,
BUT AN INDIVIDUAL FOCUS OBSCURES THE CONTEXTUAL FACTORS THAT
CONDITIONED HIS CAPACITY FOR POLICY LEADERSHIP. WHILE
EXAMINATION OF THIS PHENOMENON ON HISTORICAL COURTS HAS
INCLUDED TREATMENT OF CONTEXT, THAT OF CONTEMPORARY COURTS -
LARGELY BECAUSE OF THE INAVAILABILITY OF ARCHIVAL DATA - HAS
FAILED TO DO SO. HOWEVER, SENSITIVE USE OF AVAILABLE
QUALITATIVE INDICATORS, IN CONJUNCTION WITH QUANTITATIVE
SOURCES, ALLOWS ASSESSMENT OF THE IMPORTANCE OF CONTEXT TO
INFLUENCE EFFORTS ON CONTEMPORARY COURTS. THIS PROVIDES FOR
A FULLER CONCEPTUALIZATION AND EXAMINATION OF "MODERN"
JUDICIAL LEADERSHIP. THIS IS DEMONSTRATED THROUGH ANALYSIS
OF BURGER'S ATTEMPTS TO MOLD ESTABLISHMENT CLAUSE DOCTRINE.

05148 KOCS, S.A.
FRANCE, GERMANY, AND THE POLITICS OF MILITARY ALLIANCE,
1955-1987
DISSERTATION ABSTRACTS INTERNATIONAL, 50(2) (AUG 89),
535-A.
SINCE REALISM AND LIBERALISM OFFER CONTRASTING
EXPLANATIONS FOR THE PATTERN OF RELATIONS AMONG LIBERAL
STATES IN THE POST-WAR WORLD, THIS DISSERTATION PROPOSES TWO
TESTS OF THE REALIST AND LIBERAL MODELS. THE FIRST EXAMINES
THE STRATEGIC POLICIES OF CONTEMPORARY LIBERAL STATES TO
DETERMINE WHETHER THEIR UNDERLYING LOGIC IS REVISIONIST (THE
REALIST HYPOTHESIS) OR RISK-AVERSE (THE LIBERAL HYPOTHESIS).
THE SECOND TEST SURVEYS THE ARMS PROCUREMENT POLICIES OF
LIBERAL STATES TO DETERMINE WHETHER THE POLICIES ARE SHAPED
BY THE DESIRE TO MINIMIZE STRATEGIC VULNERABILITIES VIS-A-
VIS ALLIED STATES (THE REALIST HYPOTHESIS) OR ARE
INCREASINGLY GOVERNED BY COST AND PERFORMANCE CRITERIA (THE
LIBERAL HYPOTHESIS).

05149 KODIKARA, S.U.
POLITICAL DIMENSIONS OF SAARC
SOUTH ASIA JOURNAL, 2(4) (APR 89), 349-371.
IN CONSIDERING THE POLITICAL DIMENSIONS OF THE SOUTH
ASIAN ASSOCIATION FOR REGIONAL COOPERATION, ONE HAS TO TAKE
INTO ACCOUNT THE TWO 'PARAMETRIC GIVENS' WHICH DETERMINE THE
NEXUS OF RELATIONS BETWEEN STATES IN THE SOUTH ASIAN REGION.
ONE PERTAINS TO THE COMMONALITY OF INTERESTS; THE OTHER TO
ASYMMETRIES ARISING FROM DIVERGENCES AND DISPARATENESS IN
SIZE, POPULATION, AND ECONOMIC POTENTIAL. THERE IS NO DOUBT
THAT A COMMON CIVILISATIONAL MATRIX, WHICH BINDS THE SOUTH
ASIAN COUNTRIES HAS REINFORCED THIS COMMONALITY OF INTERESTS.
MOREOVER, THE GEOGRAPHICAL BARRIERS OF THE SUBCONTINENT
ITSELF, BOUND AS IT IS BY THE HIMALAYAS IN THE NORTH AND THE
INDIAN OCEAN ON ITS OTHER SIDES, HAS INVESTED THE REGION
WITH A NEW GEOPOLITICAL SIGNIFICANCE. THE CONCEPT OF
REGIONAL SECURITY HAS BECOME AN IMPORTANT PARAMETER OF THE
POLITICAL DIMENSIONS OF SAARC. THIS CONCEPT OF SAARC
SECURITY IS THE FOCUS OF THIS ARTICLE.

05150 KODIKARA, S.U.
THE CONTINUING CRISIS IN SRI LANKA: THE JVP, THE INDIAN
TROOPS, AND TAMIL POLITICS
ASIAN SURVEY, 29(7) (JUL 89), 716-724.
THIS ARTICLE EXAMINES THE THREEFOLD CRISIS THAT SRI
LANKA IS ENGULFED IN, WHICH THREATENS THE UNITY AND
INTEGRITY OF THE NATION. THE JUP-LED ANTI-INDIAN CAMPAIGN
POSES THE MOST IMMEDIATE CRISIS. ALSO EXPLORED IS PRESIDENT
PREMADASA'S CALL FOR THE WITHDRAWAL OF INDIAN TROOPS AND THE
LINKAGE OF THE WITHDRAWAL TO THE GRANTING OF MORE POWERS TO
THE TAMIL AREAS. IT CONCLUDES THAT IT WILL BE THE MUSLIMS OF
THE EASTERN PROVINCE WHO WILL DECIDE ITS FUTURE.

05151 KOEHN, P.; NEGASH, G.
IRANIAN EMIGRES AND NON-RETURNEES: POLITICAL EXILES OR
ECONOMIC MIGRANTS
SCANDINAVIAN JOURNAL OF DEVELOPMENT ALTERNATIVES, VIII(2)
(JUN 89), 79-110.
THE ARTICLE USES EXTENSIVE IN-PERSON INTERVIEWS TO
EXAMINES THE EXPRESSED REASONS FOR LEAVING OR NOT RETURNING
TO ONE'S HOMELAND AMONG A SAMPLE OF IRANIAN EXILES LIVING IN

THE US. THE ANALYSIS DIFFERENTIATES BETWEEN EMIGRES, THOSE
WHO HAVE NO INTENTION OF RETURNING, AND NON-RETURNEES, THOSE
WHO DECIDE TO REMAIN OVERSEES AFTER LEAVING IRAN. HOWEVER,
BOTH GROUPS DEMONSTRATED SIMILAR RESULTS: OVER 80 PERCENT OF
THE NONRETURNEES AND 75 PERCENT OF THE EMIGRES OPTED FOR
PERMANENT EXILE FOR POLITICAL REASONS.

05152 KOEHN, P.
LOCAL GOVERNMENT INVOLVEMENT IN NATIONAL DEVELOPMENT
PLANNING; GUIDELINES FOR PROJECT SELECTION BASED UPON
NIGERIA'S FOURTH PLAN EXPERIENCE
PUBLIC CHOICE, 9(4) (SEP 89), 417-436.
THIS ARTICLE IS CONCERNED WITH EFFECTIVE LOCAL
GOVERNMENT PARTICIPATION AT THE PROJECT SELECTION STAGE IN
THE DEVELOPMENT PLANNING PROCESS. THE CONTEXT FOR ANALYSIS
IS NIGERIA'S FIRST EXPERIENCE WITH LOCAL INVOLVEMENT IN
NATIONAL PLANNING. A NOVEL EVALUATION SCHEME IS ELABORATED
AND APPLIED IN ASSESSING THE PROPOSALS SUBMITTED BY TWO
LOCAL GOVERNMENTS, KADUNA AND BAUCHI, FOR INCLUSION IN THE
FOURTH NATIONAL DEVELOPMENT PLAN. THE FINDINGS REVEAL
SERIOUS DISTORTIONS IN BOTH LOCAL DEVELOPMENT PLANS AND
DEMONSTRATE THE UTILITY OF EMPLOYING AN UNCOMPLICATED
MULTIDIMENSIONAL IMPACT ANALYSI SCHEME IN THE EVALUATION AND
SELECTION OF PROJECT PROPOSALS.

05153 KOELBLE, T.A.
PARTY STRUCTURES AND DEMOCRACY MICHELS, MCKENZIE, AND
DUVERGER REVISITED VIA THE EXAMPLES OF THE WEST GERMAN
GREEN PARTY AND THE BRITISH SOCIAL DEMOCRATIC PARTY
COMPARATIVE POLITICAL STUDIES, 22(2) (JUL 89), 199-216.
IN RECENT YEARS A NUMBER OF NEW POLITICAL PARTIES HAVE
EMERGED IN WESTERN EUROPE WITH NOVEL FORMS OF INTRAPARTY
ORGANIZATIONS. THIS ARTICLE ADDRESSES SOME OF THE QUESTIONS
RAISED BY MICHELS, MCKENZIE, AND DUVERGER ABOUT OLIGARCHIC
TENDENCIES AND UNDEMOCRATIC FEATURES IN PARTY ORGANIZATION
IN LIGHT OF THE EXPERIENCE OF TWO NEW PARTIES. THE DATA
SUGGESTS THAT MICHELS'S "IRON LAW OF OLIGARCHY," WHILE
SUPERFICIALLY TRUE, DOES NOT HOLD EQUALLY WELL ACROSS BOTH
CASES. THE ORGANIZATION OF THE WEST GERMAN GREEN PARTY,
WHILE NOT COMPLETELY SUCCESSFUL IN AVOIDING OLIGARCHIC
TENDENCIES, DOES INHIBIT LEADERSHIP DOMINATION OF THE
MEMBERSHIP AND PARTY ACTIVISTS. THE BRITISH SOCIAL
DEMOCRATIC PARTY (SDP) EXHIBITS STRONG OLIGARCHIC TENDENCIES
BECAUSE THE PARTY WAS FOUNDED BY A GROUP OF PARTY NOTABLES
WHO DESIRED TO AVOID ACTIVIST DOMINATION. IN OTHER WORDS,
THE ORIGINS OF THE PARTY-THE INTENTIONS AND POLICY GOALS OF
ITS FOUNDERS-PLAY AN IMPORTANT ROLE IN SHAPING
ORGANIZATIONAL STRUCTURE. OLIGARCHY IS NOT AN INESCAPABLE
OUTCOME OF ORGANIZATION.

05154 KOFORD, K.
DIFFERENT PREFERENCES, DIFFERENT POLITICS: A DEMAND-AND-
STRUCTURE EXPLANATION
WESTERN POLITICAL QUARTERLY, 42(1) (MAR 89), 9-32.
DIFFERENT TYPES OF LEGISLATIVE POLITICS ARE EXPLAINED BY
THE DISTRIBUTION AND INTENSITY OF LEGISLATORS' DEMANDS.
DEMANDS ARE LEGISLATORS' WILLINGNESS TO PAY FOR VICTORY ON A
BILL. DIFFERENT DEMAND DISTRIBUTIONS REQUIRE DIFFERENT
INSTITUTIONAL STRUCTURES AND "POLITICS" FOR THE LEGISLATORS
TO OBTAIN THE RESULTS THEY WANT. THE TYPES OF POLITICS ARE
SIMILAR TO LOWI'S TYPOLOGY OF INTEREST-GROUP INTERACTION.
THE PAPER DESCRIBES THE DEMAND DISTRIBUTIONS FORMALLY AND
THEN IDENTIFIES THE INSTITUTIONAL STRUCTURES AND "POLITICS"
REQUIRED TO WRITE AND PASS BILLS FOR DISTRIBUTIVE,
REGULATIVE, AND REDISTRIBUTIVE DEMAND DISTRIBUTONS. APPLYING
THE PRINCIPLE TO CASE STUDIES, DIFFERENCES FROM LOWI'S
CLASSIFICATION ARE FOUND; THE ACTUAL POLITICS ARE BETTER
PREDICTED BY THE DEMAND APPROACH.

05155 KOFORD, K.
DIMENSIONS IN CONGRESSIONAL VOTING
AMERICAN POLITICAL SCIENCE REVIEW, 83(3) (SEP 89), 949-964.
WHILE DIMENSIONAL STUDIES OF CONGRESSIONAL VOTING FIND A
SINGLE IDEOLOGICAL DIMENSION, REGRESSION ESTIMATES FIND
SEVERAL CONSTITUENCY AND PARTY DIMENSIONS IN ADDITION TO
IDEOLOGY. IN THIS ESSAY, THE AUTHOR RESCALES SEVERAL
UNIDIMENSIONAL STUDIES TO SHOW THEIR INCREASED
CLASSIFICATION SUCCESS OVER THE NULL HYPOTHESIS THAT VOTES
ARE NOT UNIDIMENSIONAL. SEVERAL NULL HYPOTHESES ARE EXPLORED.

05156 KOH, B.C.
NORTH KOREA IN 1988: THE FORTIETH ANNIVERSARY
ASIAN SURVEY, XXIX(1) (JAN 89), 39-45.
1988 MARKED THE FORTIETH ANNIVERSARY OF THE DEMOCRATIC
PEOPLE'S REPUBLIC OF KOREA AND OF NORTH KOREAN PRESIDENT KIM
IL SUNG'S PRESIDENCY. DESPITE A MASSIVE PROPAGANDA CAMPAIGN
AIMED AT ECONOMIC PROGRESS, WORLD ATTENTION WAS AIMED AT
SOUTH KOREA. NORTH KOREA IS ALSO SUFFERING IN THE
INTERNATIONAL SCENE AS IT CLINGS TO HARD LINE IDEOLOGY WHILE
ITS NEIGHBORS TO THE NORTH, CHINA AND THE SOVIET UNION, ARE
ENGAGING IN FAR-FLUNG REFORMS. ALL IN ALL, IT WAS A
DIFFICULT YEAR FOR NORTH KOREA: IT MADE HERCULEAN EFFORTS TO
SURMOUNT ECONOMIC DIFFICULTIES AT HOME, BUT FOUND ITSELF
INCREASINGLY ISOLATED INTERNATIONALLY.

05157 KOHLER, M.A.
COMMENTS ON THE STATE AND FUNCTION OF THE ARABIZATION
POLICY IN MOROCCO
ORIENT, 30(2) (JUN 89), 269-286.
THE ARTICLE TRIES TO EXPLAIN THE POSITION OF
TRADITIONALISTS AND LEFTISTS IN FAVOUR OF MORE "ARABIZATION"
OF EDUCATION AND ADMINISTRATION-A CULTURAL CHOICE, BUT MUCH
MORE A CALL FOR POLITICAL PARTICIPATION AND EMANCIPATION FOR
THE ARABOPHONE MAJORITY BELONGING TO LOWER STRATAS OF THE
MOROCCAN SOCIETY-AND THE GOVERNMENT WHICH, CAUTIOUSLY
SUPPORTED BY THE MONARCH, IN RETURN OPTS FOR INTENSIFIED
FRENCH LESSONS IN SCHOOLS AND REFUSES FURTHER "ARABIZATION".
ALTHOUGH IN THE DEBATE ONLY PEDAGOGICAL AND DIDACTICAL
ARGUMENTS ARE USED, THERE IS STRONG EVIDENCE FOR THE
SUPPOSITION THAT A POLITICAL AND ECONOMICAL ELITES'
RESISTANCE AGAINST "ARABIZATION" AT LEAST PARTLY HAS
SOMETHING TO DO WITH THE ATTEMPT TO RESERVE KEYPOSTS TO
MEMBERS OF THEIR OWN GROUP -ALL OF THEM EDUCATED IN PRIVATE
MOROCCAN OR FRENCH CULTURAL MISSION SCHOOLS WHICH HAVE NOT
BEEN AFFECTED BY "ARABIZATION".

05158 KOHLI, A.
POLITICS OF ECONOMIC LIBERALIZATION IN INDIA
WORLD DEVELOPMENT, 17(3) (MAR 89), 305-328.
ATTEMPTS AT "LIBERALIZING" INDIA'S IMPORT-SUBSTITUTION
MODEL OF DEVELOPMENT HAVE HAD A MIXED RECORD. SOME SUCCESS
IN CHANGING THE POLICY REGIME HIGHLIGHTS THE ROLE OF A NEW
TECHNOCRATIC LEADERSHIP THAT HAS RECEIVED SUPPORT FROM BOTH
INDIAN BUSINESS GROUPS AND FROM EXTERNAL AID AGENCIES.
CONVERSELY, "POPULAR SECTORS" WITHIN INDIA-INCLUDING THE
RANK AND FILE OF THE RULING PARTY, THE ORGANIZED WORKERS IN
THE PUBLIC SECTOR, AND THE NUMERICALLY SIGNIFICANT MIDDLE
AND LOWER PEASANTRY-HAVE REGISTERED THEIR OPPOSITION. WHILE
THE GOVERNMENT REMAINS COMMITTED TO LIBERALIZING THE ECONOMY,
THE MOMENTUM HAS SLOWED DOWN AND, GIVEN THE PRESSURES OF
ELECTORAL POLITICS, A POPULIST ECONOMIC PROGRAM HAS BEEN
SIMULTANEOUSLY READOPTED. IT APPEARS THAT THE MARRIAGE OF
POLITICAL AND ECONOMIC LIBERALISM MAY NOT BE AN EASY ONE IN
COUNTRIES LIKE INDIA.

05159 KOHN, H.; BADASH, L.
UNIVERSITY EDUCATION FOR THE NUCLEAR AGE
PHILADELPHIA: ANLS OF AMER ACMY OF POLITICAL AND SOC
SCIENCE. (504) (JUL 89), 22-36.
THIS ARTICLE DISCUSSES THE RESPONSE OF THE UNIVERSITY,
AS AN INSTITUTION, TO THE NUCLEAR PREDICAMENT, THAT IS, TO
THE THREAT OF A MAJOR NUCLEAR WAR AND ITS IMPLICATIONS. THE
SUBJECT IS TREATED IN A RATHER BROAD CONTEXT INCLUDING
TEACHING, RESEARCH, CONFERENCES, AND COMMUNITY EDUCATION.
THE MAIN EMPHASIS, HOWEVER, IS ON UNDERGRADUATE EDUCATION.
THE AUTHORS' OWN INSTITUTION, THE UNIVERSITY OF CALIFORNIA,
IS EXAMINED IN THE GREATEST DETAIL. THE AUTHORS CONCLUDE
THAT THE UNIVERSITY'S ROLE IS STILL VERY INADEQUATE, AND
THEY ESTIMATE THE MAGNITUDE OF THE REQUIRED ADDITIONAL
EFFORTS. THE ARTICLE ENDS WITH SOME SUGGESTIONS FOR MAKING
THE UNIVERSITY MORE EFFECTIVE IN RESPONDING TO THE NUCLEAR
PREDICAMENT.

05160 KOHNO, M.
JAPANESE DEFENSE POLICY MAKING: THE FSX SELECTION, 1985-
1987
ASIAN SURVEY, 29(5) (MAY 89), 457.
THIS ARTICLE JAPAN - US MILITARY TIES AND QUESTIONS
AMERICAN MOTIVES AS JAPAN FEELS PRESSURE FROM WASHINGTON. IT
EXAMINES THE RECENT SELECTION OF THE NEXT GENERATION FIGHTER
SUPPORT OF THE ASDF. THE FSX SELECTION PROVIDES A VIHICLE TO
ANALYSE JAPANESE DEFENSE POLICY FORMULATION IN THE BROADER
CONTEXT OF THE CONTEMPORARY US - JAPAN ALLIANCE.

05161 KOHUT, A.; HUGICK, L.
BUSH CHINA POLICY BROADLY SUPPORTED
GALLUP REPORT, (285) (JUN 89), 13-17.
PUBLIC REACTION TO EVENTS IN CHINA IN THE FIRST HALF OF
1989 IS IN LINE WITH OFFICIAL UNITED STATES GOVERNMENT
POLICY. WHILE LARGE MAJORITIES OF AMERICAN FAVOR SUSPENDING
US ARMS SALES AND GIVING POLITICAL ASYLUM TO CHINESE
STUDENTS STUDYING IN THE USA, A SOLID MAJORITY OPPOSES
BREAKING OFF RELATIONS WITH CHINA AND A PLURALITY OPPOSE
RECALLING THE US AMBASSADOR FROM BEIJING.

05162 KOHUT, A.; HUGICK, L.
COLOMBIANS QUESTION WORTH OF DRUG WAR; AMERICANS SKEPTICAL
IT CAN BE WON
GALLUP REPORT, (288) (SEP 89), 2-11.
A POLL CONDUCTED IN THE USA AND COLOMBIA FOUND THE
PEOPLE OF BOTH COUNTRIES DIVIDED OVER THE WAR AGAINST THE
COLOMBIAN DRUG CARTELS. WHILE FEELING PERSONALLY THREATENED
BY DRUGS AND VIOLENCE, MANY COLOMBIANS QUESTIONED WHETHER
THE GOVERNMENT'S CRACKDOWN ON COCAINE DEALERS WOULD BENEFIT
THE COUNTRY IN THE LONG RUN. MOST COLOMBIANS CITED THE
DEMAND FOR ILLEGAL DRUGS IN THE USA AS THE MAJOR SOURCE OF
THE PROBLEM AND RESENTED U.S. PRESSURE ON THEIR GOVERNMENT.
AMERICANS CITED DRUGS AS THE NATION'S TOP PROBLEM BUT WERE

SKEPTICAL ABOUT THE CHANCES THAT PRESIDENT BUSH'S ANTI-DRUG
PROGRAM WOULD MAKE MUCH OF A DENT IN THE DEMAND FOR ILLEGAL
NARCOTICS.

05163 KOHUT, A.; HUGICK, L.
MIDDLE EAST: PUBLIC FAVORS MILITARY ACTION IF DIPLOMATIC
EFFORTS TO FREE HOSTAGES STALL
GALLUP REPORT, (287) (AUG 89), 8-11.
A GALLUP POLL SHOWS THAT ONLY HALF OF AMERICANS ARE
OPTIMISTIC THAT CURRENT EFFORTS TO FREE THE HOSTAGES IN
LEBANON WILL SUCCEED SOON, AND TWO-THIRDS WOULD FAVOR SOME
FORM OF AMERICAN MILITARY ACTION IF DIPLOMACY FAILS TO
PRODUCE RESULTS IN THE SHORT TERM. THE POLL ALSO REVEALS
THAT ISRAEL'S IMAGE IN THE USA HAS SUFFERED SOME DAMAGE AS A
RESULT OF ITS ABDUCTION OF A SHIITE CLERIC IN AN ATTEMPT TO
WIN THE RELEASE OF SOME ISRAELI SOLDIERS BEING HELD IN
LEBANON. BUT, AT THE SAME TIME, AMERICAN SYMPATHIES FOR THE
PALESTINIAN ARAB POSITION HAVE ALSO DECLINED IN THE FACE OF
MIDEAST TERRORISM DIRECTED AT AMERICANS.

05164 KOHUT, A.; HUGICK, L.
POLITICS: REPUBLICAN PARTY'S IMAGE AT A HIGH POINT
GALLUP REPORT, (286) (JUL 89), 2-4.
POSITIVE FEELINGS ABOUT THE STATE OF THE AMERICAN
ECONOMY AND THE INTERNATIONAL SITUATION HAVE HELPED TO
RETURN THE IMAGE OF THE REPUBLICAN PARTY TO THE POSTWAR HIGH
IT ENJOYED UNDER RONALD REAGAN PRIOR TO THE IRAN-CONTRA
SCANDAL. IN MID-1989, AMERICANS SEE THE REPUBLICANS AS MORE
QUALIFIED THAN DEMOCRATS TO KEEP THE COUNTRY PROSPEROUS,
MAINTAIN THE PEACE, AND HANDLE THE NATION'S TOP PROBLEM.

05165 KOHUT, A.; HUGICK, L.
SPACE: TWENTY YEARS AFTER APOLLO 11, AMERICANS QUESTION
SPACE PROGRAM'S WORTH
GALLUP REPORT, 286(13-20) (JUL 89), 13-20.
TWENTY YEARS AFTER AMERICAN FIRST PUT MEN ON THE MOON,
THE PUBLIC SHOWS ONLY A LIMITED COMMITMENT TO THE U.S. SPACE
PROGRAM. AMERICAN'S LUKEWARM ATTITUDE ABOUT FUTURE SPACE
EXPLORATION IS A CONSEQUENCE OF INCREASED CONCERN WITH
DOMESTIC PROBLEMS, COUPLED WITH DECREASED CONCERN FOR THE U.
S.-SOVIET RIVALRY WHICH PROPELLED THE SPACE RACE DURING THE
1960S.

05166 KOHUT, A.; HUGICK, L.
TAXES AND FEDERAL PROGRAMS: PUBLIC SUPPORTS HIGHER TAXES
FOR DOMESTIC PROGRAMS; EDUCATION, DRUG WAR LEAD THE LIST
GALLUP REPORT, (289) (OCT 89), 4-10.
MOST AMERICANS SAY THEY WOULD PAY HIGHER TAXES TO TACKLE
THE SOCIAL PROBLEMS OF THE LATE 1980'S BUT WOULD BALK AT
HIGHER TAXES AS A MEANS OF REDUCING THE DEFICIT. A POLL
INDICATES THE PUBLIC IS MOST WILLING TO PAY FOR IMPROVING
PUBLIC EDUCATION, FIGHTING DRUGS, HELPING THE HOMELESS, AND
PROVIDING LONG-TERM HEALTH CARE FOR THE ELDERLY. DEFENSE
SPENDING AND SPACE EXPLORATION RATE AS AMERICANS' LOWEST
PRIORITIES FOR NEW SPENDING.

05167 KOHUT, A.; SHRIVER, J.
THE ENVIRONMENT: ENVIRONMENT REGAINING A FOOTHOLD ON THE
NATIONAL AGENDA
GALLUP REPORT, (285) (JUN 89), 2-12.
FOR THE FIRST TIME IN MORE THAN A DECADE, A SIGNIFICANT
PROPORTION OF THE PUBLIC CONSIDERS ENVIRONMENTAL ISSUES TO
BE THE MOST IMPORTANT PROBLEM FACING THE NATION. DEPLETION
OF THE OZONE LAYER AND THE GLOBAL WARMING TREND HAVE BECOME
MAJOR CONCERNS OF THE GOVERNMENTS OF INDUSTRIALIZED NATIONS.
THE BUSH ADMINISTRATION HAS ANNOUNCED THAT THE WORLD
ENVIRONMENT WILL BE HIGH ON THE AGENDA AT AN INTERNATIONAL
CONFERENCE IN JUNE 1989 AND AT AN ECONOMIC SUMMIT SCHEDULED
FOR JULY 1989.

05168 KOICHI, M.
PROBLEMS IN THE AID PROGRAM
JAPAN ECHO, XVI(1) (SPR 89), 13-18.
IN THE 1980'S JAPANESE FOREIGN AID HAS GROWN RAPIDLY,
DESPITE THE FIRM CLAMPDOWN ON OTHER GOVERNMENT EXPENDITURES
DESIGNED TO RESTORE HEALTH TO PUBLIC FINANCE. BUT HOW THE
OUTLAYS ARE SPENT IS AS IMPORTANT AS THEIR SIZE. IN THIS
ARTICLE, THE AUTHOR SURVERYS THE AIMS OF THE JAPANESE
FOREIGN AID PROGRAM AND THE EFFECTIVENESS OF ITS PREVIOUS
SPENDING. HE CONCLUDES WITH SOME SUGGESTIONS ON HOW TO
IMPROVE THE AID POLICY.

05169 KOJI, H.
A HALF-HEARTED ANTI-APARTHEID POLICY
JAPAN QUARTERLY, XXXVI(3) (JUL 89), 267-274.
IN DECEMBER 1988, THE UN GENERAL ASSEMBLY DEBATE ON
COMPREHENSIVE, COMPULSORY SANCTIONS AGAINST SOUTH AFRICA
CULMINATED IN A RESOLUTION THAT CRITICIZED JAPAN, BECAUSE
JAPAN HAD BECOME PRETORIA'S BIGGEST TRADING PARTNER IN 1987.
THE RESOLUTION SENT SHOCK WAVES THROUGH THE JAPANESE
GOVERNMENT. THE MINISTRY OF FOREIGN AFFAIRS SOUGHT OUT
AFRICAN NATIONS TO EXPLAIN THAT JAPAN HAS BEEN TRYING TO CUT
BACK ITS TRADE WITH SOUTH AFRICA, WHILE THE MINISTRY OF
INTERNATIONAL TRADE AND INDUSTRY APPEALED TO THE BUSINESS

COMMUNITY TO EXERCISE MORE SELF-RESTRAINT IN ITS DEALINGS
WITH SOUTH AFRICANS.

05170 KOLAKOWSKI, L.
ARE WE TO WAIT FOR A MIRACLE?
EAST EUROPEAN REPORTER, 3(4) (SPR 89), 41-42.
MANY AMONG POLAND'S OPPOSITION GROUPS CRITICIZE LECH
WALESA AND OTHERS FOR NEGOTIATING WITH THE RULING COMMUNIST
PARTY. THEY ARGUE THAT NEGOTIATING WITH THE GOVERNMENT
COMPROMISES THE PRINCIPLES OF THE POLITICAL OPPOSITION. THE
AUTHOR RESPONDS THAT SUCH A VIEWPOINT IS UNREALISTIC: CHANGE
FROM COMPLETELY WITHOUT THE EXISTING SYSTEM IS NEXT TO
IMPOSSIBLE WITH THE EXCEPTION OF WIDESPREAD AND BLOODY
REVOLUTION. HE LAUDS WALESA AND OTHER MODERATES FOR TAKING
THE FIRST, PRAGMATIC STEPS TOWARDS WIDESPREAD REFORM.

05171 KOLGANOV, A.; BUZGALIN, A.
HOW HAS THE "ADMINISTRATIVE SYSTEM" CREATED?
SOVIET REVIEW, 30(6) (NOV 89), 40-57.
THE AUTHORS INVESTIGATE THE RELATIONSHIP BETWEEN THE
PATTERNS OF DEVELOPMENT OF THE ECONOMIC SYSTEM OF SOVIET
SOCIETY IN THE 1920'S AND 1930'S AND THE SOCIAL-CLASS BASE
OF THE ADMINISTRATIVE SYSTEM, OR STALINISM.

05172 KOLLAND, F.
THE PERCEPTION OF CULTURE AND CULTURAL INFLUENCE: THEIR
ROLE IN TECHNOLOGY TRANSFER (FOREIGN MANAGEMENT AND THE
MEXICAN LIFE STYLE: RESULTS OF A SURVEY IN MEXICO)
SCANDINAVIAN JOURNAL OF DEVELOPMENT ALTERNATIVES, VIII(2)
(JUN 89), 59-78.
IN A RESEARCH PROJECT, CONDUCTED IN MEXICO, 100
EXECUTIVES OF TRANSNATIONAL CORPORATIONS WERE CONFRONTED
WITH THE QUESTION ABOUT THE INFLUENCE OF EVERYDAY MEXICAN
LIFE, THE NATIONAL CULTURE ON TECHNOLOGY TRANSFER. IN
ANALYZING THE DATA, USING E.G. THE THEORETICAL CONCEPT OF
MODAL-PERSONALITY, THREE TYPES OF PERCEPTIONS OF THE MEXICAN
CULTURE WERE DERIVED: THE HEDONIST, THE REFUSER AND THE
UNCERTAIN. THE DIFFERENT PERCEPTIONS ARE DETERMINING THE
TRANSFER OF TECHNOLOGY IN A CERTAIN WAY. WHEREAS EXECUTIVES,
VIEWING THE MEXICAN AS A "REFUSER" UNDERTAKE FEWER CHANGES
IN CONNECTION WITH IMPORTED TECHNOLOGY THOSE, WHO SEE THE
MEXICAN PERSONALITY AS POSITIVELY OR IN TRANSITION PLAN MORE
TECHNICAL RENEWALS AS WELL AS EMPLOYEES' TRAINING.

05173 KOLOSOVSKY, A.
RISK ZONES IN THE THIRD WORLD
INTERNATIONAL AFFAIRS (MOSCOW), (8) (AUG 89), 39-49.
THE AUTHOR CONSIDERS THE DIVERSITY OF THE THIRD WORLD,
THE TENDENCY TO ANALYZE THIRD WORLD RELATIONSHIPS IN TERMS
OF EAST-WEST RELATIONS, AND THE RISK ZONES OF THE THIRD
WORLD.

05174 KON, I.
THE PSYCHOLOGY OF SOCIAL INERTIA
SOVIET REVIEW, 30(2) (MAR 89), 59-76.
THE AUTHOR WRITES OF THE NEED FOR A FUNDAMENTAL
REORIENTATION OF THE CONSERVATIVE VALUE SYSTEM THAT PERVADES
CONTEMPORARY SOVIET SOCIETY. AMONG THE TRADITIONAL WAYS OF
THINKING THAT MUST BE CHALLENGED ARE THE EQUATION OF
GOODNESS WITH OBEDIENCE, THE FEAR OF WHATEVER IS NOVEL OR
UNIQUE, AND AN UNHEALTHY REVERENCE FOR AUTHORITY.

05175 KONONOV, V.; ONISMCHUK, Y.
SOVIET UNION-TURKEY: NEW FORMS OF ECONOMIC AND TECHNICAL
COOPERATION
FOREIGN TRADE, 8 (1988), 23-25.
THIS ARTICLE EXAMINES CONDITIONS WHICH HAVE CREATED
FAVOURABLE OPPORTUNITIES FOR TRADE AND ECONOMIC TIES TO
DEVELOP BETWEEN THE USSR AND TURKEY, AGREEMENTS SIGNED OVER
THE LAST 25 YEARS WHICH HAVE CONSOLIDATED RELATIONS AND
SHAPED LEGAL FRAMEWORK ARE DETAILED. TECHNICAL ASSISTANCE,
PROJECTS ON CONTRACT TERMS, TRIPARTITE AGREEMENTS, THE
ESTABLISHMENT OF EXPORT ORIENTED JOINT VENTURES, AND A NEW
FORM OF INVESTMENT KNOWN AS BOT (BUILD, OPERATE, TRANSFER)
ARE EACH EXPLORED.

05176 KONVITZ, M.R.
THE ORIGINAL INTENT OF THE FRAMERS: WHAT THE ESTABLISHMENT
CLAUSE MEANS
MIDSTREAM, XXXV(9) (DEC 89), 13-18.
CHIEF JUSTICE WILLIAM H. REHNQUIST IS ONE OF THE
FOREMOST ADVOCATES OF THE JURISPRUDENCE OF ORIGINAL INTENT
AND JUDICIAL RESTRAINT. IN THIS ARTICLE, THE AUTHOR REVIEWS
A SUPREME COURT CASE IN WHICH REHNQUIST ELABORATED AND
APPLIED HIS PHILOSOPHY OF ORIGINAL INTENT.

05177 KOPER, G.; VERMUNT, R.
THE EFFECTS OF PROCEDURAL ASPECTS AND OUTCOME SALIENCE ON
PROCEDURAL FAIRNESS JUDGMENTS
SOCIAL JUSTICE RESEARCH, 2(4) (DEC 89), 289-302.
THE EFFECTS OF PROCESS CONTROL AND DECISION CONTROL ON
PROCEDURAL FAIRNESS JUDGEMENTS ARE EXAMINED WITH REGARD TO
THE PROCEDURE USED BY COMMERCIAL BANKS IN GRANTING BUSINESS
CREDITS TO ENTREPRENEURS. MALE AND FEMALE ENTREPRENEURS WITH

EXPERIENCE IN REQUESTS FOR BUSINESS CREDITS WERE INTERVIEWED
ABOUT SEVERAL ASPECTS OF THE PROCEDURE FOR GRANTING BUSINESS
CREDIT. RESPONDENTS HAD EITHER A POSITIVE OR A NEGATIVE
EXPERIENCE WITH CREDIT GRANTING (I.E., THE REQUEST WAS OR
WAS NOT REWARDED). THE OUTCOME-ORIENTED AND THE PROCEDURE-
ORIENTED EXPLANATIONS FOR THE EFFECTS OF PROCESS CONTROL ON
PROCEDURAL FAIRNESS JUDGEMENTS ARE DISCUSSED. THE RESULTS
SHOW THAT, CONTRARY TO EXPECTATION, PROCESS CONTROL HAD NO
EFFECT ON THE PROCEDURAL FAIRNESS JUDGMENTS. ON THE CONTRARY,
PERCEIVED SERIOUSNESS OF TREATMENT, AS WELL AS THE
PREDICTED EFFECTS OF DECISION CONTROL, DID INFLUENCE
PROCEDURAL JUSTICE JUDGMENTS. MOREOVER, SOME SUPPORT WAS
FOUND FOR THE CONTENTION THAT SERIOUSNESS OF TREATMENT
FUNCTIONS AS PRECONDITION FOR PROCESS CONTROL EFFECTS (TYLER,
1987). NEITHER THE OUTCOME-ORIENTED, NOR THE PROCEDURE-
ORIENTED EXPLANATION COULD FULLY ACCOUNT FOR THE FINDINGS.
IT IS ASSUMED THAT THE SPECIFIC ASPECTS OF THE SITUATION ARE
RESPONSIBLE FOR THE RESULTS, INDICATING HOW IMPORTANT THE
SITUATIONAL CONTEXT IS IN RESEARCH CONCERNING PROCEDURAL
JUSTICE.

05178 KOPETZKI, C.
THE LIMITS OF IMMUNITY
AUSTRIA TODAY, (4) (1988), 9-12.
THE SOVEREIGNTY OF THE PEOPLE OVER THE INSTITUTIONS OF
STATE IS ONE OF THE MOST FUNDAMENTAL PRINCIPLES OF DEMOCRACY.
THE IMMUNITY OF THE PEOPLE'S REPRESENTATIVES IN PARLIAMENT,
THEIR PROTECTION FROM ARBITRARY ACTION AGAINST THEM IN THE
EXECUTION OF THEIR PARLIAMENTARY FUNCTIONS, IS A LOGICAL
CONSEQUENCE. THIS PRINCIPLE IS RIGOROUSLY DEFENDED IN THE
LEGISLATURES OF ALL DEMOCRATIC STATES; THEY RESERVE TO
THEMSELVES THE DECISION OF WHETHER OR NOT ONE OF THEIR
MEMBERS MAY BE ARRESTED OR HAVE HIS OR HER HOME SEARCHED. IT
MAY AT TIMES APPEAR THAT THE IMMUNITY PRIVILEGE IS
ANACHRONISTIC AND SUPERFLUOUS, OR THAT AT LEAST ITS
BOUNDARIES ARE SET TOO WIDE. IN AUSTRIA, THE SIMULTANEOUS
OCCURRENCE OF SEVERAL "IMMUNITY CASES" HAS LED TO A LIVELY
DEBATE WHICH MAY WELL BE OF INTEREST ELSE WHERE. THE
PRINCIPLE IN QUESTION IS THE LIMIT OF IMMUNITY

05179 KOPPEL, B.; PLUMMER, M.
JAPAN'S ASCENDANCY AS A FOREIGN-AID POWER
ASIAN SURVEY, 29(11) (NOV 89), 1043-1056.
THERE IS A NEED FOR AN ANALYSIS OF JAPAN'S COOPERATION
EFFORTS FROM THE PERSPECTIVE OF DEVELOPING COUNTRIES IN ASIA.
THIS ARTICLE ADDRESSES THIS NEED BY EXAMINING TRADE,
INVESTMENT, AND OFFICIAL DEVELOPMENT ASSISTANCE
RELATIONSHIPS BETWEEN JAPAN AND ASIA AND ASKS WHETHER FROM
THE PERSPECTIVE OF DEVELOPING COUNTRIES IN ASIA, DO THESE
RELATIONSHIPS INDICATE THE EMERGENCE OF A HEGEMONIC
ASSOCIATION WITH JAPAN? THE ANALYSIS OFFERED IS INTENDED AS
SUGGESTIVE RATHER THAN CONCLUSIVE.

05180 KOPVILLEM, P.; STEELE, S.
A KEENER EARTH WATCH
MACLEAN'S (CANADA'S NEWS MAGAZINE), 102(1) (JAN 89), 18-20.
THE FUTURE OF THE EARTH'S ENVIRONMENT CAUSED HEIGHTENED
CONCERN AMONG CANADIANS IN 1988. A NATIONWIDE POLL INDICATES
THAT A STATISTICALLY SIGNIFICANT 1.6 PER CENT OF RESPONDENTS
CITED ENVIRONMENTAL PROBLEMS AS CANADA'S SINGLE MOST
IMPORTANT ISSUE. IN ADDITION, A MAJORITY SAID THAT THEY WERE
WILLING TO SPEND UP TO $1,000 PER HOUSEHOLD EACH YEAR TO BUY
SAFER PRODUCTS. THIS ENVIRONMENTAL CONCERN IS MORE
SIGNIFICANT IN LIGHT OF THE FACT THAT CANADA'S POLITICIANS
FOCUSED ALMOST EXCLUSIVELY ON FREE TRADE IN THE RECENT
FEDERAL ELECTIONS.

05181 KOPVILLEM, P.; ALLEN, G.
A NETWORK OF CLINICS
MACLEAN'S (CANADA'S NEWS MAGAZINE), 102(30) (JUL 89), 19.
DR. HENRY MORGANTALER HAS LONG BEEN IN THE FOREFRONT OF
THE ABORTION BATTLE IN CANADA. AFTER YEARS OF LEGAL BATTLES,
HE WAS FINALLY VINDICATED BY THE CANADA SUPREME COURT'S 1988
DECISION WHICH TO OPEN UP CLINICS AND IS CONTINUING TO FIGHT
LEGAL BATTLES IN PROVINCIAL COURTS AT AND AGE WHEN PEOPLE
ARE CONSIDERING RETIREMENT.

05182 KOPVILLEM, P.; ALLEN, G.; BROSNAHAN, M.; SHARIFF, S.;
WALMSLEY, A.
AN ANGRY RACIAL BACKLASH
MACLEAN'S (CANADA'S NEWS MAGAZINE), 102(28) (JUL 89),
14-16.
IN 1971, THEN-PRIME MINISTER PIERRE TRUDEAU OFFICIALLY
ADOPTED MULTICULTURALISM, THE IDEA THAT PEOPLE OF DIFFERENT
ETHNIC BACKGROUNDS COULD LIVE IN HARMONY WITHOUT LOSING
THEIR CULTURAL DISTINCTIVENESS, AS A TOUCHSTONE FOR CANADIAN
SOCIETY. HOWEVER CANADIAN REALITY HAS FALLEN FAR SHORT OF
THE IDEAL. OPINION POLLS REVEAL THAT A GROWING NUMBER OF
CANADIANS EXPRESS INTOLERANCE NOT ONLY OF MINORITIES, BUT
TOWARD THE IDEA OF ETHNIC DIVERSITY ITSELF. ALTHOUGH MANY
ACKNOWLEDGE AND ACCEPT THE ECONOMIC NECESSITY OF IMMIGRATION
IN A NATION WITH A DECLINING BIRTH RATE, THE FACT THAT
INCREASING NUMBERS ARE COMING TO CANADA FROM THEIR WORLD
NATIONS IS INCREASING TENSION AND UNCERTAINTY.

05183 KORBONSKI, A.
THE POLITICS OF ECONOMIC REFORMS IN EASTERN EUROPE: THE
LAST THIRTY YEARS
SOVIET STUDIES, XLI(1) (JAN 89), 1-19.
IN DISCUSSING ECONOMIC REFORMS IN SELECTED EAST EUROPEAN
COUNTRIES, THE AUTHOR VIEWED THE REFORMS AS BOTH THE CAUSE
AND EFFECT OF SOCIO-POLITICAL AND ECONOMIC CHANGES IN THE
REGION. ONE OF THE PURPOSES OF THIS PAPER IS TO RE-EXAMINE
THIS CONCLUSION REGARDING THE DUAL ROLE OF ECONOMIC REFORMS
AS BOTH AN OUTCOME AND CATALYST OF SOCIO-POLITICAL AND
ECONOMIC DEVELOPMENT IN SELECTED EAST EUROPEAN COUNTRIES,
MOSTLY CZECHOSLOVAKIA, HUNGARY, AND POLAND. THE PAPER GIVES
A BRIEF ANALYSIS OF INTERNAL POLITICAL AND ECON MIC CHANGES
IN THE REGION WHICH HAVE EITHER TRIGGERED, OR BECOME
INFLUENCED BY, THE REFORMS IN THE PAST TWO DECADES.

05184 KORDAN, B.S.
ETHNICITY, THE STATE, AND WAR: CANADA AND THE UKRAINIAN
PROBLEM (1939-1945), A STUDY IN STATECRAFT
DISSERTATION ABSTRACTS INTERNATIONAL, 49(7) (JAN 89),
1945-A.
POLITICAL REALISM HAS FUNDAMENTALLY CONDITIONED THE
NATURE OF MODERN STATECRAFT. BUT WITHIN THE CONTEXT OF
LIBERAL DEMOCRACY, REALISM OFTEN POSES A CONTRADICTION
BETWEEN THE STATE AGENDA (USUALLY DEFINED IN TERMS OF
NATIONAL INTEREST) AND THE UNDERLYING POLITICAL CULTURE. THE
CONTRADICTION APPEARS WHEN DURING THE SECOND WORLD WAR THE
PRINCIPLES WHICH INFORMED WESTERN ALLIED OBJECTIVES AND
CANADIAN WAR AIMS WERE AT ODDS WITH THE PREMIER AGENDUM OF
STATE SECURITY. THE THESIS ARGUES THAT THIS CONTRADICTION
SIGNIFICANTLY MODIFIED THE BEHAVIOUR OF THE CANADIAN STATE
WITH RESPECT TO THE UKRAINIAN NATIONALIST COMMUNITY IN
CANADA.

05185 KORET, H.
HELSINKI IN PARIS
NEW LEADER, LXXII(11) (JUL 89), 12-14.
THE ARTICLE REPORTS ON THE PROCEEDINGS AT THE FIRST
ANNUAL HUMAN DIMENSION CONFERENCE HELD IN PARIS. FOR THE
FIRST TIME IN THE NEARLY 15-YEAR-OLD HELSINKI PROCESS THE
MEETING DID NOT SINGLE OUT THE SOVIET UNION AS THE PRINCIPAL
PERPETRATOR OF HUMAN RIGHTS ABUSES; INSTEAD ROMANIA,
BULGARIA, AND OTHER EASTERN EUROPEAN NATIONS WERE
CONCENTRATED UPON. A MECHANISM DESIGNED IN VIENNA TO HELP
ENFORCE COMPLIANCE WITH THE HUMAN RIGHTS DECISIONS HAS
YIELDED SIGNIFICANT RESULTS. MANY OBSERVERS ARE CONFIDENT
ABOUT CONTINUED PROGRESS IN THE FUTURE.

05186 KOREY, H.
ADVANCING THE HELSINKI PROCESS
NEW LEADER, LXXII(3) (FEB 89), 7-9.
THE HELSINKI ACCORD HAS NOT ACHIEVED ALL OF ITS HUMAN
RIGHTS AIMS, BUT THE STANDARDS ARE NOW MUCH HIGHER AND MORE
SPECIFIC. EMBRYONIC IMPLEMENTATION PROCEDURES HAVE BEEN PUT
IN PLACE AND A CONTINUOUS REVIEW PROCESS HAS BEEN SET IN
MOTION.

05187 KOREY, H.
JACKSON-VANIK AND ITS MYTHS
MIDSTREAM, XXXV(6) (AUG 89), 7-11.
WITH THE ESCALATION OF SOVIET JEWISH EMIGRATION, IT WAS
INEVITABLE THAT THERE WOULD BE DISCUSSION OF THE JACKSON-
VANIK AMENDMENT TO THE U.S. TRADE REFORM ACT. THAT AMENDMENT
LINKS THE GRANTING OF MOST FAVORED NATION (MFN) TARIFF
TREATMENT AND EXPORT-IMPORT BANK CREDITS AND CREDIT
GUARANTEES TO THE REMOVAL OF EMIGRATION BARRIERS. BUT A
WAIVER PERMITS THE GRANTING OF TRADE BENEFITS UNDER
CIRCUMSTANCES THAT ARE LESS THAN UNRESTRICTED FREE
EMIGRATION.

05188 KORIONOV, V.
SEARCHING FOR "COUNTER-ARGUMENTS
REPRINTS FROM THE SOVIET PRESS, 48(2) (JAN 89), 26-28.
THE SOVIET UNION HAS NEVER BARRED ITSELF FROM THE REST
OF THE WORLD. BEGINNING FROM LENIN'S DECREE ON PEACE, OUR
PIONEERING IDEA OF COLLECTIVE SECURITY, OUR PARTICIPATION IN
THE ANTI-HITLER COALITION, AND OUR VIGOROUS INVOLVEMENT IN
UN ACTIVITIES, THE SOVIET UNION HAS ALWAYS BEEN FOR GREATER
INTERNATIONAL COOPERATION. IT IS ANOTHER MATTER THAT UNDER
STALIN AND BREZHNEV WE DID NOT ALWAYS USE ALL THE
OPPORTUNITIES AND POLITICAL INSTRUMENTS FOR GREATER
INTERNATIONAL UNDERSTANDING. HOWEVER, THESE PERIODS HAVE
PASSED.

05189 KORKUT, F.C.
A COMPARATIVE CASE ANALYSIS OF U.S. CRISIS DIPLOMACY:
CYPRUS, 1963-64 AND 1974
DISSERTATION ABSTRACTS INTERNATIONAL, 48(10) (APR 88),
2722-A.
THE DISSERTATION IS A STUDY OF US FOREIGN POLICY AND
CRISIS DIPLOMACY DURING THE 1963-64 AND 1974 CYPRUS CRISES
AND WITHIN THE CONTEXT OF THE EASTERN MEDITERRANEAN AS A
REGIONAL SUBSYSTEM. THE UNDERLYING MOTIVES BEHIND US ACTIONS

ARE ANALYZED TO DETERMINE WHETHER THE "CONTINUITY" OR
REDUCTIONIST COLD WAR MODEL OR THE "STATE DEPARTMENT" OR A
SYSTEMIC ACKNOWLEDGEMENT OF THE LIMITED INFLUENCE OF THE US
IN THE REGION ARE MORE APPLICABLE IN THIS CASE.

05190 KORNILOV, L.
HEAD OF CZECHOSLOVAK GOVERNMENT ADDRESSES PERESTROIKA IN
HIS COUNTRY
REPRINTS FROM THE SOVIET PRESS, 49(9) (NOV 89), 33-40.
THIS ARTICLE IS AN INTERVIEW OF LADISLAV ADAMEC, HEAD OF
THE CZECKOSLOVAK GOVERNMENT ABOUT THE PRESENT STAGE OF
PERESTROIKA THERE. IT ADDRESSES CURRENT PROBLEMS OF ECONOMIC
GROWTH, SOCIAL PATTERNS, GOVERNMENT WORK, PUBLIC
ORGANIZATIONS AND GLASTNOST.

05191 KORNIYENKO, G.
SHORTAGE OF GOODWILL HINDERS GENEVA TALKS
REPRINTS FROM THE SOVIET PRESS, 49(11/12) (DEC 89), 45-50.
ON SEPTEMBER 7, THE WARSAW TREATY ORGANIZATION AND NATO
STARTED ANOTHER ROUND OF TALKS ON EUROPEAN ARMS REDUCTIONS
ON SEPTEMBER 25, THE SOVIET UNION AND THE U.S. RESUMED TALKS
ON NUCLEAR AND SPACE ARMAMENTS, FOLLOWED BY NEGOTIATIONS OF
A NUCLEAR TEST BAN. THE ARTICLE ANALYZES PREVIOUS ROUNDS,
THEIR ACHIEVEMENTS AND FAILURES, AND FUTURE ACTIONS FOR A
RADICAL TURN IN THE DISARMAMENT PROCESS.

05192 KORNYSMEV, V.
SOVIET-ARGENTINE TRADE AND ECONOMIC TIES
FOREIGN TRADE, 5 (1988), 34-35.
THIS ARTICLE DETAILS THE QUALITATIVELY NEW FEATURES DUE
TO A NUMBER OF NEW INTERGOVERNMENTAL TRADE AGREEMENTS
BETWEEN THE USSR AND ARGENTINA. THE GROWTH IN TOTAL MUTUAL
TRADE AS A RESULT OF THESE AGREEMENTS IS OBSERVED. RESULTS
OF THE 10TH MEETING OF THE SOVIET-ARGENTINA JOINT COMMISSION
ON TRADE, ECONOMIC, SCIENTIFIC, AND TECHNICAL COOPERATION
HELD IN BUENOS AIRES IN OCTOBER 1987 ARE EXAMINED AND THE
RECENT DECREASE IN TRADE WILL BE TURNED AROUND DUE TO
STRATEGIES PLANNED AT THE COMMISSION.

05193 KOROSENYI, A.
NEW COALITIONS IN HUNGARIAN POLITICS
EAST EUROPEAN REPORTER, 4(1) (WIN 89), 30-31.
THE ARTICLE EXAMINES THE VARIOUS POLITICAL COALITIONS
THAT ARE BEING FORMED IN ANTICIPATION OF HUNGARY'S
APPROACHING ELECTIONS. THE SEEMINGLY MOST POWERFUL COALITION
CONSISTS OF THE HUNGARIAN DEMOCRATIC FORUM (MDF), THE
SMALLHOLDERS PARTY, THE CHRISTIAN DEMOCRATIC PARTY, AND THE
BAJCSY-ZSILINSZKY PARTY. THIS RIGHT-WING "NATIONAL CENTRE"
HAS A GOOD CHANCE OF DEFEATING THE RULING MSZMP ON ITS OWN
WITHOUT THE HELP OF OTHER OPPOSITION PARTIES. THE LEFT
REMAINS DIVIDED BETWEEN THE SOCIAL DEMOCRATIC PARTY, THE
FEDERATION OF FREE DEMOCRATS (SZDSZ), THE FEDERATION OF
YOUNG DEMOCRATS (FIDESZ), AND THE FACTIONS OF THE MSZP/MSZMP
(RULING COMMUNISTS). THE ARTICLE EXPLORES POTENTIAL
COALITIONS OF THE LEFT AND CONCLUDES THAT NONE OF THE
POSSIBILITIES ARE LIKELY TO CHALLENGE THE GROWING POWER OF
THE RIGHT.

05194 KOROSTELEV, V.A.
THE REBIRTH OF SMALL-SCALE COMMODITY PRODUCTION
SOVIET REVIEW, 30(1) (JAN 89), 64-76.
IN THE PAST, SOVIET LEADERS INCORRECTLY ASSUMED THAT
SOCIALISM IS IMMUNE TO THE NEGATIVE ASPECTS OF CONCENTRATION
OF PRODUCTION. OVER TIME, MANY LARGE SOVIET ENTERPRISES AND
ASSOCIATIONS HAVE BECOME REAL MONOPOLIES WITH ALL THE
ATTENDANT CONSEQUENCES. AS A RESULT OF CONCENTRATION, THE
LARGE ENTERPRISES HAVE CEASED TO PRODUCE ALL THE GOODS
REQUIRED BY CONSTANTLY GROWING AND CONTINUOUSLY CHANGING
HUMAN NEEDS. THE SHORTAGES HAVE BEEN MOST NOTICEABLE IN
CONSUMER PRODUCTS, SUCH AS CLOTHING. THE EXISTING STRUCTURE
OF PRODUCTION AND THE TRADITIONAL BRANCH SYSTEM OF
MANAGEMENT DOES NOT GUARANTEE THE SOVIET CONSUMER ALL THE
LUXURIES HE WANTS. SMALL-SCALE COMMODITY PRODUCTION CAN HELP
FILL THE GAP BETWEEN THE CONSUMER'S DESIRES AND WHAT IS
AVAILABLE.

05195 KORPI, H.
POWER, POLITICS, AND STATE AUTONOMY IN THE DEVELOPMENT OF
SOCIAL CITIZENSHIP: SOCIAL RIGHTS DURING SICKNESS IN
EIGHTEEN OECD COUNTRIES SINCE 1930
AMERICAN SOCIOLOGICAL REVIEW, 54(3) (JUN 89), 309-328.
THE EXTENSION OF SOCIAL CITIZENSHIP VIA MODERN SOCIAL
POLICIES IS A FUNDAMENTAL MACROLEVEL SOCIAL CHANGE OF THE
PAST HUNDRED YEARS. THIS PAPER ATTEMPTS TO REORIENT THE
EMPIRICAL STUDY OF SOCIAL POLICY DEVELOPMENT FROM ITS
PRESENT CONCENTRATION ON AGGREGATED SOCIAL EXPENDITURES TO A
FOCUS ON THE MULTIDIMENSIONAL ASPECTS OF THE DEVELOPMENT OF
WELFARE STATES, SOCIAL RIGHTS, AND SOCIAL CITIZENSHIP. ON
THE BASIS OF A NEW DATA SET DESCRIBING THE DEVELOPMENT OF
CITIZENS' SOCIAL RIGHTS IN THE MAIN SOCIAL INSURANCE
PROGRAMS IN 18 OECD COUNTRIES SINCE 1930, CAUSAL HYPOTHESES
DERIVED FROM PLURALIST INDUSTRIAL, NEO-MARXIST, POPULAR
PROTEST, STATE AUTONOMY, AND POWER RESOURCES APPROACHES ARE
TESTED. ON THE CRUCIAL ISSUE OF THE ROLE OF LEFT GOVERNMENT

PARTICIPATION IN THE EXTENSION OF SOCIAL RIGHTS, THE
HYPOTHESES OF THE POWER RESOURCES APPROACH ARE SUPPORTED.

05196 KORTE, K.
    JAPAN AND THE SINGLE EUROPEAN MARKET
    AUSSEN POLITIK, 40(4) (1989), 397 - 407.
        THIS ARTICLE EXAMINES THE ACCURACY OF THE "FORTRESS
    EUROPE" IMAGE AND JAPAN'S LIKELY STRATEGY FOR 1992. IT
    DETAILS THE SINGLE EUROPEAN MARKET AND THIRD-COUNTRY
    RELATIONS; THE HARMONIZATION OF TRADE BARRIERS; AND TOKYO'S
    NEW STRATEGY TOWARD EUROPE. IT ARGUES THAT JAPANESE EFFORTS
    WILL CENTER ON SIGNIFICANTLY INCREASING DIRECT INVESTMENTS.

05197 KORYAGIN, A.
    WHEN JUSTICE IS BLIND--TO REALITY
    GLASNOST, (16-18) (JAN 89), 39, 42.
        THE NEW "STATUTES ON THE CONDITIONS AND PROCEDURES OF
    RENDERING PSYCHIATRIC ASSISTANCE" SHOULD BE REGARDED AS THE
    RELUCTANT RESPONSE OF THE SOVIET GOVERNMENT TO PUBLIC
    ACTIVISM INSIDE THE USSR AND ABROAD. THIS RESPONSE FOLLOWS
    MANY YEARS OF PROTEST AGAINST THE USE OF PSYCHIATRY AS A
    TOOL OF POLITICAL REPRESSION. THE NEW ATTITUDE TOWARD
    PSYCHIATRY IS REFLECTED IN THE RELEASE OF DISSIDENTS FROM
    PSYCHO-PRISONS AND THE NEW DISCUSSION ABOUT IMPROVING
    PSYCHIATRIC SERVICES IN THE USSR.

05198 KOSAI, Y.
    REBUILDING THE JAPAN-U.S. RELATIONSHIP
    JAPAN AND THE WORLD ECONOMY, 1(3) (JUL 89), 229-242.
        THIS ESSAY DESCRIBES SOME OF THE MAJOR CHANGES THAT ARE
    TAKING PLACE IN JAPANESE TRADE PATTERNS AND ARGUES THAT
    THERE IS HOPE FOR RECTIFYING THE IMBALANCE. THE AUTHOR
    DISCUSSES HOW TO CONTAIN AND ROLL BACK PROTECTIONISM, WHILE
    RECOGNIZING THAT MUCH OF JAPAN-U.S. TRADE IS IN FACT
    REGULATED. FINALLY, HE POINTS OUT THAT, BY VIRTUE OF THEIR
    LEADING POSITIONS WITHIN THE WORLD ECONOMY, JAPAN AND THE
    UNITED STATES CANNOT SIMPLY DEAL WITH THEIR IMMEDIATE
    CONCERNS BUT MUST COOPERATE FOR THE TOTAL DEVELOPMENT OF THE
    LARGER WORLD ECONOMY. FINALLY, THE AUTHOR ARGUES THAT THIS
    GLOBAL PERSPECTIVE IS FAR FROM COMPLICATING, AND THAT THE
    RELATIONSHIP SHOULD ACTUALLY MAKE IT EASIER TO SOLVE THE
    BILATERAL ISSUES.

05199 KOSCHWITZ, H.
    CONTEMPORARY RELATIONS BETWEEN STATES: OPEN AND PUBLIC
    DIPLOMACY
    AUSSEN POLITIK, 40(2) (1989), 139-147.
        WHAT PUBLIC DIPLOMACY HAS ACCOMPLISHED SINCE THE SECOND
    WORLD WAR IN INTENSITY AND EXPANSION MAY OUTSTRIP THE
    OBJECTIVES OF OPEN DIPLOMACY AS PROCLAIMED AND INTRODUCED
    AFTER THE FIRST WORLD WAR. INDEED, IT MAY EVEN CALL THE
    DEMOCRATISATION OF INTERNATIONAL RELATIONS INTO QUESTION.
    THE DEPLOYMENT OF SO MANY AMBASSADORS AND EMISSARIES IN THE
    WEST, ESPECIALLY IN WESTERN EUROPE AND IN THE FEDERAL
    REPUBLIC OF GERMANY, PROVIDES DAILY PROOF OF THE INTENSIVE
    USE OF THE WAYS AND MEANS OF PUBLIC DIPLOMACY. THE TREND
    FROM OPEN TO PUBLIC DIPLOMACY SEEMS IRREVERSIBLE.

05200 KOSHIW, J.V.
    FIRST CONGRESS OF THE POPULAR MOVEMENT FOR THE
    RECONSTRUCTION OF THE UKRAINE (RUKH)
    ACROSS FRONTIERS, 5(3) (FAL 89), 12-13; 32.
        THIS ARTICLE REPORTS ON THE CONGRESS HELD TO DEMAND AN
    INDEPENDENT UKRANIAN STATE, IT EXAMINES THE STATUTE,
    PROGRAMME, RESOLUTIONS & ELECTED LEADERS OF THE MOVEMENT, IT
    ALSO EXPLORES THE THREE MAIN GROUPINGS AT THE CONGRESS:
    DELEGATES FROM WESTERN UKRAINE; FROM THE DONBASS; AND FROM
    KIEV, IT REPORTS ON THE RESULTS FROM A SURVEY CARRIED OUT BY
    CONGRESS OF THE DELEGATES BACKGROUNDS.

05201 KOST, K.
    THE CONCEPTION OF POLITICS IN POLITICAL GEOGRAPHY AND
    GEOPOLITICS IN GERMANY UNTIL 1945
    POLITICAL GEOGRAPHY QUARTERLY, 8(4) (OCT 89), 369-386.
        THE HISTORY OF GERMAN GEOGRAPHY ASCRIBES THE ABERRATIONS
    OF THE DISCIPLINE FROM 1900-1945, ESPECIALLY DURING THE
    NATIONAL SOCIALIST PERIOD, MAINLY TO THE NEGATIVE INFLUENCE
    OF GEOPOLITICS. THE EXAMPLE OF THE POLITICAL CONCEPTS OF
    POLITICAL GEOGRAPHY AND GEOPOLITICS, HOWEVER, SHOWS THAT THE
    LACK OF THEORETICAL FOUNDATIONS AND IDEOLOGICAL ONE-
    SIDEDNESS ARE RESPONSIBLE FOR THIS DEVELOPMENT. ACCORDINGLY,
    GEOPOLITICS WAS NOT AN INNOVATION BUT ONLY REINFORCES
    PATTERNS OF THINKING WHICH HAVE BEEN A COMPONENT OF THE
    GERMAN GEOGRAPHY SINCE THE END OF THE 19TH CENTURY AND ONLY
    MADE POSSIBLE THE RISE OF GEOPOLITICS.

05202 KOSTELANICK, D.
    THE GYPSIES OF CZECHOSLOVAKIA: POLITICAL AND IDEOLOGICAL
    CONSIDERATIONS IN THE DEVELOPMENT OF POLICY
    STUDIES IN COMPARATIVE COMMUNISM, XXII(4) (WIN 89),
    307-322.
        THE ARTICLE EXAMINES THE "GYPSY PROBLEM" IN
    CZECHOSLOVAKIA (WITH SOME COMPARISONS TO HUNGARY AND POLAND).
    THE AUTHOR SEEKS TO DETERMINE HOW A REGIME COMMITTED TO THE

SOCIAL, POLITICAL, AND ECONOMIC EQUALITY OF ALL CAN ALLOW
SUCH DISPARITY BETWEEN THE GYPSIES AND THE GENERAL
POPULATION. HE EXAMINES PUBLIC POLICY, BIRTH RATES, ECONOMIC
FACTORS (SUCH AS EMPLOYMENT), HOUSING, AND EDUCATION, AND
ATTEMPTS TO RECONCILE THE FIGURES WITH THE STIGMA OF RACISM.
HE CONCLUDES THAT GYPSIES HAVE TRADITIONALLY FILLED TABOO OR
LOW PAYING ROLES IN SOCIETY, AND THE POLICIES OF THE
GOVERNMENT DEMONSTRATE THE RULERS' DESIRE TO ENSURE THAT THE
GYPSIES REMAIN IN THEIR LOW SOCIAL AND ECONOMIC STATION.

05203 KOSTERMAN, R.; FESHBACH, S.
    TOWARD A MEASURE OF PATRIOTIC AND NATIONALISTIC ATTITUDES
    POLITICAL PSYCHOLOGY, 10(2) (JUN 89), 257-274.
        THE MULTIDIMENSIONALITY OF PATRIOTIC AND NATIONALISTIC
    ATTITUDES AND THEIR RELATIONSHIP TO NUCLEAR POLICY OPINIONS
    WERE INVESTIGATED. ONE HUNDRED AND NINETY-FOUR COLLEGE
    STUDENTS, 24 HIGH SCHOOL STUDENTS, AND 21 BUILDING
    CONTRACTORS WERE ADMINISTERED THE 120-ITEM
    PATRIOTISM/NATIONALISM QUESTIONNAIRE. ONE HUNDRED AND SIXTY-
    SIX OF THE COLLEGE STUDENTS WERE CONCURRENTLY ADMINISTERED
    THE 18-ITEM NUCLEAR POLICY QUESTIONNAIRE. AN ITERATED
    PRINCIPAL FACTOR ANALYSIS WAS PERFORMED ON THE
    PATRIOTISM/NATIONALISM QUESTIONNAIRE AND SIX FACTORS WERE
    EXTRACTED FOR VARIMAX ROTATION. THE RESULTS INDICATED THAT
    THE FACTORS WERE INTERPRETABLE AND DISTINCT. FURTHER
    ANALYSES INDICATED THE PREDICTIVE VALIDITY OF THE SUBSCALES
    DERIVED FROM THE SIX FACTORS FOR THE NUCLEAR POLICY
    QUESTIONNAIRE, AND EXPLORATORY ANALYSES OF VARIANCE EXAMINED
    THE EFFECTS OF SELECTED DEMOGRAPHIC VARIABLES. THE FINDINGS
    SUPPORT THE CONTENTION THAT PATRIOTIC/NATIONALISTIC
    ATTITUDES ENTAIL MULTIPLE DIMENSIONS, AND THAT THEY ARE
    DIFFERENTIALLY RELATED TO NUCLEAR POLICY OPINIONS. THE
    AUTHORS CONCLUDE THAT RESEARCHERS NEED TO BE MORE ATTENTIVE
    TO THIS MULTIDIMENSIONALITY, ESPECIALLY THE DISTINCTION
    BETWEEN PATRIOTISM AND NATIONALISM.

05204 KOSZEG, F.
    DEMOCRACY WITHIN THE WARSAW PACT
    EAST EUROPEAN REPORTER, 3(4) (SPR 89), 12-14.
        FERNEC KOSZEG, A LEADER OF THE HUNGARIAN ALLIANCE OF
    FREE DEMOCRATS, DISCUSSES THE PACE AND IMPLICATIONS OF THE
    POLITICAL REFORMS SWEEPING HUNGARY. HE ALSO OUTLINES THE
    STRATEGY OF THE FREE DEMOCRATS INCLUDING PLANNED CHANGES IN
    THE LAW, PROPERTY SYSTEM, AND WELFARE SYSTEM. HE ALSO
    OUTLINES THE EFFORTS OF THE OPPOSITION TO GARNER PUBLIC
    SUPPORT WITH EMPHASIS ON THE "COMMON WORKER" RESIDING
    OUTSIDE OF BUDAPEST.

05205 KOTANDZHYAN, A.
    THE SECRETS OF SOVIET GLASNOST
    GLASNOST, (16-18) (JAN 89), 65-66.
        THE HISTORY OF THE POLITICAL RESTRUCTURING OF ARMENIA
    DATES BACK TO THE JANUARY 1975 PLENARY SESSION OF THE
    CENTRAL COMMITTEE OF THE ARMENIAN COMMUNIST PARTY. THAT IS
    WHEN THE LEADERSHIP OF THE REPUBLIC, UNDER THE GUISE OF
    FIGHTING NEGATIVE SOCIAL PHENOMENA, BEGAN TO APPOINT ITS OWN
    TEAM OF PEOPLE TO RUN THE "SHADOW ECONOMY." IT BECAME THE
    NORM TO PROMOTE THE LEADERS' RELATIVES AND CRONIES TO KEY
    POSITIONS AND TO EXTEND PATRONAGE TO SUCH PEOPLE AT EVERY
    LEVEL OF THE PARTY, THE GOVERNMENT, AND THE ECONOMY. THE
    SUSCEPTIBILITY OF CADRES TO MANIPULATION WAS GUARANTEED BY
    INVOLVING THEM IN THE CONSPIRATORIAL CIRCLE OF GRAFT AND
    "SHADOW TAXATION."

05206 KOTHARI, R.
    THE NEW DETENTE: SOME REFLECTIONS FROM THE SOUTH
    ALTERNATIVES, 64(3) (JUL 89), 289-300.
        HUMAN HISTORY IS WITNESS TO MAJOR REVERSALS IN WORLD
    AFFAIRS, ESPECIALLY AFTER THE BALANCE OF FORCES THAT GOVERN
    THE WORLD HAVE GONE SO OFF THE KEEL AND APPEAR CLOSE TO THE
    ABYSS. HOWEVER SOME LEADERS HAVE BEEN MOVING OUT OF THEIR
    SINGLE-CONSTITUENCY FOCI AND HAVE REALIZED THE
    INTERRELATIONSHIP BETWEEN DIMENSIONS IT IS WITH RESPECT TO
    THE INTERRELATIONSHIPS THAT ARE LIKELY TO BE IGNORED OR LEFT
    OUT OF CONSIDERATION, AND THE CONSEQUENCES OF FOCUSING ON
    SINGLE DIMENSIONS OR LIMITED CONCERNS, THAT THIS ARTICLE
    RAISES CERTAIN ISSUES, POSES DOUBTS AND APPREHENSIONS THAT
    ARISE, AND SUGGESTS, BOTH FOR THE MOVEMENTS AND FOR THE
    COMMUNITY OF EXPERTS CONCERNED WITH PUBLIC POLICY, POSSIBLE
    INTERVENTIONS THAT ARE SENSITIVE TO THE INTERRELATIONSHIPS
    AND ARE CAPABLE OF SAFEGUARDING THE INTERESTS OF THOSE THAT
    CONTINUE TO BE MARGINALIZED BY GOVERNMENTS AND RULING ELITES,
    PERHAPS MORE SO AS A RESULT OF CHANGED PERCEPTIONS OF THE
    HUMAN AGENDA THAN HAS THE CASE EARLIER.

05207 KOTKIN, J.
    AMERICA'S RISING SUN
    REASON, 20(8) (JAN 89), 22-27.
        AMERICA HAS BECOME A NATION OBSESSED WITH FOREBODINGS OF
    DECLINE, BUT THE APOSTLES OF DECLINE ARE DISTORTING THE
    OBJECTIVE REALITY OF AMERICA'S ACTUAL SITUATION. AMERICA'S
    RESILIENCY RESTS UPON THREE PILLARS: MASSIVE IMMIGRATION, AN
    ENTREPRENEURIAL OPEN ECONOMY, AND VAST NATURAL RESOURCES.

05208 KOTOWSKI, D.
TOWARDS THE DIPLOMATIC ROAD: POLAND-THE VATICAN CITY
CONTEMPORARY POLAND, XXII(5) (1989), 4-6.
THERE IS EVERY INDICATION THAT POLAND WILL BECOME THE
FIRST SOCIALIST COUNTRY TO ESTABLISH FULL DIPLOMATIC
RELATIONS WITH THE HOLY SEE. IT HAS BEEN REPORTED THAT
RELATIONS WILL BE NORMALIZED IN THE FORM OF A CONVENTION
THAT WILL STIPULATE THE PRINCIPLES OF THE ACTIVITIES
PERMITTED THE ROMAN CATHOLIC CHURCH IN POLAND, THE TYPES OF
TIES BETWEEN THE UNIVERSAL CHURCH AND THE LOCAL CHURCH IN
POLAND, APPOINTMENT OF BISHOPS ORDINARIES, DELIMITATION OF
DIOCESAN BOUNDARIES, RELATIONS BETWEEN THE POLISH GOVERNMENT
AND THE HOLY SEE, AND IMPLEMENTATION OF THE FREEDOMS OF
CONSCIENCE, CREED, AND WORSHIP.

05209 KOTTAB, D.
OUTBURST OF ANGER IN NABLUS
MIDDLE EAST INTERNATIONAL, (359) (SEP 89), 8.
NABLUS, THE LARGEST CITY ON THE WEST BANK ERUPTED IN
ANGER AT RUMORS THAT THE BODIES OF TWO PALESTINIANS SHOT IN
A CONFLICT WITH ISRAELI SOLDIERS WERE BEING USED FOR ORGAN
DONATION IN ISRAEL. THE DEATH OF TWO PALESTINIANS AND THE
RESULTING COVER-UP INCREASED THE TENSION THAT AN ISRAELI
CURFEW HAD ALREADY BEGUN. AUTHORITIES CAUTIOUSLY LIFTED
CURFEW AND REIMPOSED IT ON THE ENTIRE CITY AS A RESULT OF
WIDESPREAD ATTACKS. AUTHORITIES FINALLY BOWED TO PRESSURE,
EXHUMED THE BODIES, AND ALLOWED AN AUTOPSY. HOWEVER, TENSION
IN THE CITY REMAINS HIGH.

05210 KOTTAB, D.
WEST BANK'S MIXED REACTION
MIDDLE EAST INTERNATIONAL, (359) (SEP 89), 7-9.
ALTHOUGH THE GENERAL OUTLOOK IN THE OCCUPIED TERRITORIES
REMAINS BLEAK, SOME PALESTINIANS ARE GUARDEDLY OPTIMISTIC
ABOUT THE POSSIBILITY OF A POLITICAL BREAKTHROUGH AS A
RESULT OF THE EGYPTIAN PROPOSALS. THE FACT THAT THE EGYPTIAN
PROPOSALS HAVE RECEIVED THE APPROVAL OF THE US AND ISRAEL'S
LABOUR PARTY GIVES THE NEGOTIATION PROCESS SOME HOPE.
HOWEVER, MANY SIGNIFICANT OBSTACLES REMAIN. THESE INCLUDE
THE MEMBERSHIP OF THE PALESTINIAN DELEGATION AND THE AGENDA
OF THE TALKS. THESE FUNDAMENTAL OBSTACLES HAVE CAUSED MANY
PALESTINIANS TO ADOPT A "WAIT AND SEE" POLICY WITH REGARDS
TO THE FUTURE.

05211 KOURVETARIS, G.A.
POLITICAL ELITES AND PARTY ORGANIZATION IN GREECE: AN
ENTREPRENEURIAL MODEL
JOURNAL OF SOCIAL, POLITICAL AND ECONOMIC STUDIES, 14(2)
(SUM 89), 189-214.
BECAUSE OF THEIR STRATEGIC LOCATION, ELITE GROUPS
DIRECTLY OR INDIRECTLY INFLUENCE POLICIES AND DECISIONS THAT
HAVE FAR-REACHING CONSEQUENCES FOR POLITICAL AND SOCIAL
CHANGE. THIS IS CLEARLY THE CASE IN GREECE, WHERE THE RULING
PASOK PARTY AND THE MAJOR OPPOSITION PARTY (NEW DEMOCRACY)
ARE ORGANIZED AROUND CHARISMATIC POLITICAL LEADERS, WHEREAS
THE KKE (COMMUNIST PARTY) OPERATES ON A STRICT BASIS OF
MARXIST ORGANIZATIONAL PRINCIPLES.

05212 KOVACS, Z.
BORDER CHANGES AND THEIR EFFECT ON THE STRUCTURE OF
HUNGARIAN SOCIETY
POLITICAL GEOGRAPHY QUARTERLY, 8(1) (JAN 89), 79-86.
ABSTRACT. THE TRIANON PEACE TREATY (1920) RESULTED IN
HUNGARY LOSING 71 PERCENT OF ITS TERRITORY AND 64 PERCENT OF
ITS POPULATION. THE EFFECTS OF THIS BORDER CHANGE ON THE
URBAN PATTERN AND HIERARCHY ARE DESCRIBED BY RECONSTRUCTING
THE PRE-WORLD WAR II URBAN SYSTEM AND DOCUMENTING THE
SUBSEQUENT DEMISE OF MANY OF THE TOWNS. THE PRESENT-DAY
DEVELOPMENT OF TOWNS ALONG THE BORDER IS CONSIDERED AS PART
OF THE NATIONAL SETTLEMENT PATTERN POLICY.

05213 KOVALEV, A.
THE AFRICAN ORGANIZATION IGADD: TASKS AND PROBLEMS
FOREIGN TRADE, 5 (1988), 36.
THIS REPORT DETAILS THE MAIN PURPOSE OF THE INTER-
GOVERNMENTAL AUTHORITY FOR DROUGHT AND DEVELOPMENT (IGAAD)
ESTABLISHED IN 1988 BY SIX EAST AFRICAN COUNTRIES. EXAMINED
ARE THE PROPOSALS IN THE FORM OF COMPREHENSIVE PROJECTS FOR
PRESENTATION TO DONATING COUNTRIES AND INTERNATIONAL
ORGANIZATIONS. THE RESULTS OF THE FIRST OF THE DONAR
CONFERENCES WERE NOT PROMISING, BUT AID FROM THE WORLD
COMMUNITY CONTINUES TO ARRIVE.

05214 KOVALICK, W.W. JR.
IMPROVING FEDERAL INTERAGENCY COORDINATION: A MODEL BASED
ON MICRO-LEVEL INTERACTION
DISSERTATION ABSTRACTS INTERNATIONAL, 49(9) (MAR 89),
2803-A.
THIS DISSERTATION POSITS A MODEL FOR FEDERAL INTERAGENCY
COOPERATION THAT MOVES BEYOND TRADITIONAL
INTERORGANIZATIONAL COORDINATION LITERATURE AND ITS EXCHANGE-
BASED CONCEPTS OF COOPERATION. DRAWING UPON THE PRINCIPLES
OF AUTHENTIC MANAGEMENT FOUNDED IN HUMANISTIC PSYCHOLOGY AND
NEGOTIATION LITERATURE, IT SUGGESTS THAT INTERORGANIZATIONAL

COOPERATION IS DEVELOPED AND NURTURED AT THE MICRO LEVEL.
THE EXPERIENCE OF THE INTERAGENCY REGULATORY LIAISON GROUP
IS APPLIED TO A MICRO-LEVEL MODEL.

05215 KOVEL, J.
TWO SPIRITUAL REVOLUTIONARIES
MONTHLY REVIEW, 40(8) (JAN 89), 22-34.
THIS ARTICLE DESCRIBES THE REVOLUTIONARY WORK OF MIGUEL
MARMOL, ONE OF THE FOUNDING MEMBERS OF THE SALVADORIAN
COMMUNIST PARTY, AND JAMES CARNEY, AND AMERICAN JESUIT
KILLED BY SECURITY FORCES IN HONDURAS FOR REVOLUTIONARY
ACTIVITY AMONG THE PEASANTRY. THE AUTHOR USES THE MEMOIRS OF
THESE MEN AS A SPRINGBOARD FOR AN EVALUATION OF THE
RELATIONSHIP BETWEEN RELIGION AND REVOLUTION.

05216 KOVYLIAKOV, A.
HOW THEY KILLED THE SUMY EXPERIMENT; IT'S NOT EASY BEING
INDEPENDENT; THE RISE AND FALL OF "IDEA"
ACROSS FRONTIERS, 5(2) (SUM 89), 10-11.
THIS LETTER INQUIRES INTO THE CAUSES OF THE DEMISE OF
THE SCIENTIFIC-PHILOSOPHICAL CLUB IN THE CITY OF SUMY AND
CONCLUDES THE PERESTROIKA IS NOT BEING EFFECTIVE AND THAT
THE STALINIST STYLE OF LEADERSHIP REMAINS TENACIOUS. IT
FOLLOWS THE ORIGINS, GOALS, ACTIVITIES AND SUPPRESSION OF
THE CLUB.

05217 KOZAK, M.G.
CUBA: A THREAT TO PEACE AND SECURITY IN OUR HEMISPHERE
DEPARTMENT OF STATE BULLETIN (US FOREIGN POLICY), 89(2152)
(NOV 89), 75-78.
THE UNITED STATES' PRINCIPAL CONCERNS REGARDING CUBA
HAVE BEEN AND REMAIN CUBA'S RELATIONSHIP WITH THE SOVIET
UNION; CUBA'S SUPPORT FOR TERRORISM AND EFFORTS TO
DESTABILIZE DEMOCRATIC GOVERNMENTS, ESPECIALLY IN THE
AMERICAS; AND WIDESPREAD HUMAN RIGHTS ABUSES AND POLITICAL
REPRESSION WITHIN CUBA. MORE RECENTLY, THE USA HAS HAD
SERIOUS DIFFERENCES WITH THE CASTRO REGIME REGARDING
NARCOTICS TRAFFIC.

05218 KOZAK, M.G.
FY 1990 ASSISTANCE REQUEST FOR LATIN AMERICA AND THE
CARIBBEAN
DEPARTMENT OF STATE BULLETIN (US FOREIGN POLICY), 89(2147)
(JUN 89), 59-66.
THE AUTHOR SUMMARIZES THE MAJOR POLITICAL TRENDS IN
LATIN AMERICA AND THE CARIBBEAN, THE FUNDAMENTAL PRINCIPLES
UNDERLYING UNITED STATES FOREIGN AID IN THE REGION, AND THE
BUSH ADMINISTRATION'S FOREIGN AID PROPOSALS FOR LATIN
AMERICA AND THE CARIBBEAN IN FY 1990.

05219 KOZHEMYAKOV, A.
THE MECHANISM OF FRENCH FOREIGN POLICY
INTERNATIONAL AFFAIRS (MOSCOW), (7) (JUL 89), 35-44.
FRENCH DIPLOMACY HAS FOR CENTURIES BEEN VIEWED, WITH
GOOD REASON, AS CLASSICAL AND AS ONE OF THE WORLD'S LEADING
DIPLOMACIES. THE SKILL OF FRENCH POLITICIANS AND DIPLOMATS
HAS REPEATEDLY PROVED THAT A HIGHLY PROFESSIONAL, TACTICALLY
EXPERIENCED, AND FLEXIBLE DIPLOMACY CONTRIBUTES IN LARGE
MEASURE TO A STATE'S LEVERAGE AND PRESTIGE IN WORLD POLITICS.
FRANCE OWES MUCH TO THE STRUCTURE OF ITS CONTEMPORARY
FOREIGN POLICY MECHANISM, ITS LEGAL STANDARDS AND HIERARCHIC
PRINCIPLES, AND THE PLACE AND INFLUENCE OF THE VARIOUS PARTS
OF THIS MECHANISM, PRIMARILY THE FOREIGN MINISTRY.

05220 KOZLOV, N.N.; WEITZ, E.D.
REFLECTIONS ON THE ORIGINS OF THE "THIRD PERIOD": BUKHARIN,
THE COMINTERN, AND THE POLITICAL ECONOMY OF WEIMAR GERMANY
JOURNAL OF CONTEMPORARY HISTORY, 24(3) (JUL 89), 387-410.
THE AUTHORS STUDY THE ORIGINS OF THE THIRD PERIOD AND
ARGUE THAT THE FORMULATION OF POLICY INVOLVED NOT ONLY
IMMEDIATE POLITICAL ISSUES BUT ALSO LONG-STANDING
THEORETICAL DISPUTES CONCERNING THE ORIGINS OF THE BREAKDOWN
OF CAPITALISM. THE COMINTERN DISPUTE OF THE 1920'S TURNED ON
THE VARIED ANALYSES OF THE RELATIVE STABILIZATION OF
CAPITALISM, BUT THE TERMS OF THE DEBATE STRETCH BACK TO
ARGUMENTS AMONG LEADING FIGURES OF THE SECOND INTERNATIONAL.
BUKHARIN'S IDENTIFICATION OF THE THIRD PERIOD DERIVED FROM
HIS CONTRIBUTION TO THIS DEBATE, IN WHICH HE FORMULATED HIS
VIEWS ON STATE CAPITALISM AND ARGUED THAT CAPITALISM'S
BREAKDOWN DERVIED FROM DISPROPORTIONALITY AND NOT FROM A
CHRONIC SHORTCOMING IN EFFECTIVE DEMAND.

05221 KOZLOV, V.A.
THE HISTORIAN AND PERESTROIKA
SOVIET REVIEW, 30(2) (MAR 89), 19-38.
THE AUTHOR LOOKS AT HOW THE ROLE OF HISTORIANS AND
HISTORICAL ACCOUNTS OF THE SOVIET PAST ARE CHANGING DUE TO
PERESTROIKA. HE DISCUSSES THE POPULARITY OF FICTION AND
JOURNALISTIC WRITING AS AN ALTERNATIVE TO DRY, IMPLAUSIBLE,
AND PLATITUDINOUS OFFICIAL HISTORIES AND CALLS ON HISTORIANS
TO SATISFY THE NEED FOR KNOWLEDGE OF THE PAST.

05222 KOZMA, F.
A FORECASTER'S CONTRIBUTION TO POLEMICS

WORLD MARXIST REVIEW, 31(2) (FEB 88), 73-77.
ECONOMIC PATTERNS IN VARIOUS COUNTRIES AND REGIONS ARE
LIKELY TO BE DETERMINED BY TWO MUTUALLY DEPENDENT FACTORS,
NAMELY, THE INTELLECTUAL POTENTIAL AND THE AMOUNT AND
QUALITY OF THE AVAILABLE RESOURCES. ANY SHORTAGE OF EITHER
MAY CAUSE OR FURTHER THE DEPENDENCE OF ECONOMICALLY BACKWARD
COUNTRIES.

05223 KOZREIN, Y.; KUVSREINOV, V.
FOREIGN TRADE ASPECTS OF DIRECT TIES BETWEEN ORGANIZATIONS
OF THE CMEA COUNTRIES
FOREIGN TRADE, 6 (1988), 2-4.
THIS ARTICLE EXAMINES THE IMPORTANCE OF DIRECT TIES
BETWEEN THE ECONOMIC ORGANIZATIONS OF THE CMEA COUNTRIES.
THE TASKS SET BY THE 27TH CONGRESS OF THE CPSU TO DEEPEN
SOCIALIST ECONOMIC INTEGRATION ARE EXPLORED. A COMPREHENSIVE
LISTING OF FOREIGN TRADE THEMES UTILIZED BY THE USSR WITHOUT
INTERMEDIARY-SPECIALIZED FOREIGN TRADE ORGANIZATIONS
PARTICIPATION IS GIVEN, PLANS TO SPEED UP EXCHANGE WITHIN
THE SYSTEM OF DIRECT TIES ARE DETAILED. FUTURE COMPARATIVE
STUDIES TO FURTHER DIRECT TIES ARE NEEDED

05224 KOZYREV, A.; SHUMIKHIN, A.
EAST AND WEST IN THE THIRD WORLD
INTERNATIONAL AFFAIRS (MOSCOW), (3) (MAR 89), 64-74.
CURRENT WORLD CONDITIONS DEMAND THAT THE SOVIET UNION
ACHIEVE A STABLE BALANCE OF INTERESTS WITH OTHER MAJOR
POWERS WITH REGARD TO THE THIRD WORLD. THE BIDDING OF
HISTORY DICTATES THAT THIS DIVERSE, CONTRADICTORY, AND
RAPIDLY CHANGING WORLD SHOULD BE NOT ONLY A BETTER PLACE TO
LIVE BUT SHOULD ALSO STOP GENERATING DANGEROUS INTERNATIONAL
CRISES AND CONFLICTS THAT DIRECTLY OR INDIRECTLY INVOLVE THE
SUPERPOWERS. BOTH THE USSR AND THE USA MUST STRIVE FOR
GREATER COOPERATION IN THE THIRD WORLD.

05225 KOZYREV, A.
EAST AND WEST: FROM CONFRONTATION TO COOPERATION AND CO-
DEVELOPMENT
INTERNATIONAL AFFAIRS (MOSCOW), (10) (OCT 89), 3-13, 57.
PROFOUND CHANGES IN SOVIET DOMESTIC AFFAIRS ARE
INSEPARABLE FROM REVOLUTIONARY REFORMS IN SOVIET FOREIGN
POLICY. THIS MAKES IT POSSIBLE TO LOOK FOR CONSTRUCTIVE
SOLUTIONS TO MAJOR PROBLEMS AND TO PROPOSE PRACTICAL WAYS OF
SHAPING INTERNATIONAL RELATIONS MARKED BY COOPERATION AND CO-
DEVELOPMENT AMONG STATES. THIS CANNOT BE ACCOMPLISHED BY
SIMPLY MAKING A DECISION AND SWEARING FROM THEN ON TO PUT
ONE'S TRUST IN COOPERATION RATHER THAN CONFRONTATION. STATES
ON BOTH SIDES OF THE BARRICADES MUST REGARD ONE ANOTHER AS
REAL PARTNERS. THIS REQUIRES COMPATIBILITY AND, IN MANY
CASES, CONVERGENCE OF FUNDAMENTAL INTERESTS AND VALUES.

05226 KRAFT, M.E.; FREEMAN III, A.M.
INTRODUCTION: ECONOMIC AND POLITICAL ISSUES IN RISK
ANALYSIS
RISK ANALYSIS, 9(3) (SEP 89), 279 - 282.
THE PAPERS COLLECTED IN THIS ISSUE OF "RISK ANALYSIS"
ARE FROM A CONFERENCE HELD IN APRIL 1988 AT THE UNIVERSITY
OF WISCONSIN, MADISON. THE CONFERENCE WAS INTENDED TO
EXPLORE EMERGING ISSUES IN RISK ASSESSMENT AND MANAGEMENT
FROM THE PERSPECTIVE OF THE SOCIAL SCIENCES. THE SIX PAPERS
REFLECT DIVERSE RESEARCH ON ENVIRONMENTAL RISKS. CLIMATE
CHANGE, POLITICAL AND INSTITUTIONAL ISSUES, HOW RISK
ANALYSIS AND POLITICS INTERACT, POLICIES TO REDUCE RISK, AND
THE ROLE OF THE INSURANCE SYSTEM IN MANAGING RISKS
ASSOCIATED WITH HAZARDOUS CHEMICALS ARE EACH ADDRESSED.

05227 KRAHN, H.; TANNER, J.
BRINGING THEM BACK TO SCHOOL
POLICY OPTIONS, 10(2) (MAR 89), 23-24.
A LARGE MINORITY OF ONTARIO ADOLESCENTS WERE SHOWN TO BE
DISSATISFIED WITH THE PROVINCIAL EDUCATION SYSTEM IN THE
REPORT OF THE RADWANSKI COMMISSION. THE PROBLEM APPLIES
NATIONWIDE, BUT PROFS. TANNER AND KRAHN SUGGEST, ON THE
BASIS OF A STUDY UNDERTAKEN IN EDMONTON, THAT THE RADWANSKI
REPORT HAS LEFT OUT AN EQUALLY IMPORTANT ASPECT -- HOW TO
ENTICE THE DROP-OUTS TO RETURN TO SCHOOL. THIS SURVEY SHOWED
THAT MANY OF THOSE WHO LEFT ARE ANXIOUS FOR MORE EDUCATION,
AND, UNDER THE RIGHT CONDITIONS, WOULD GO BACK TO SCHOOL.
THE BIG PROVISO WAS THAT IT NOT BE TO THE KIND OF HIGH
SCHOOL THEY KNEW BEFORE. THIS ARGUES THAT THERE IS A NEED TO
PROVIDE A MORE ADULT AND LESS REGIMENTED SETTING THAN THE
CONVENTIONAL HIGH SCHOOL FOR MANY OF THE DROP-OUTS.

05228 KRAINES, O.
RELIGIOUS SYMBOLS ON PUBLIC PROPERTY: IS IT CONSTITUTIONAL?
MIDSTREAM, XXXV(8) (NOV 89), 42-44.
THE QUESTION OF RELIGIOUS SYMBOLS ON PUBLIC PROPERTY HAS
NOT YET BEEN RESOLVED. ONE MIGHT CONCLUDE THAT THE WALL OF
SEPARATION BETWEEN CHURCH AND STATE SHOULD MEAN THAT NO
RELIGIOUS SYMBOLS MAY BE DISPLAYED ON PUBLIC PROPERTY. ON
THE OTHER HAND, ONE MIGHT CONCLUDE THAT THE GUARANTEE OF
RELIGIOUS FREEDOM SHOULD MEAN THAT SUCH DISPLAYS ARE
PERMITTED AS LONG AS ALL RELIGIONS' SYMBOLS ARE TREATED
EQUALLY. THREE IMPORTANT CASES INVOLVING RELIGIOUS SYMBOLS

ON PUBLIC PROPERTY WERE HEARD BY THE SUPREME COURT IN LAST
FEW YEARS.

05229 KRAKAU, A.; DIEHL, O.
THE UNILATERAL REDUCTION IN CONVENTIONAL ARMS BY THE USSR
AUSSEN POLITIK, 40(2) (1989), 119-128.
WHEN THE SOVIET UNION AND THE OTHER WARSAW PACT
COUNTRIES IMPLEMENT PLANS TO DIMINISH THEIR QUANTITATIVE
SUPERIORITY OVER NATO, THEY WILL HAVE TAKEN A STEP TOWARD
REDUCING THE MOST OFFENSIVE AND THREATENING ELEMENTS OF
THEIR CONVENTIONAL POTENTIAL. THAT IS EXACTLY IN LINE WITH
THE CHARGE THE CONFERENCE ON SECURITY AND COOPERATION IN
EUROPE (CSCE) GAVE TO THE CONVENTIONAL STABILITY TALKS (CST)
THAT HAVE BEGUN IN VIENNA. IN ANNOUNCING HIS DECISION TO
MAKE UNILATERAL CUTS IN ARMED FORCES, GORBACHEV MADE MORE
THAN JUST A NEGOTIATING PROPOSAL. NEVERTHELESS THE
CAPABILITY OF THE WARSAW PACT TO LAUNCH AN INVASION REMAINS
INTACT. THE AUTHORS HERE RULE OUT NATO'S ACKNOWLEDGING
GORBACHEV'S MOVE AS AN ADVANCE CONCESSION AND THEN GIVING
THE SOVIETS A QUICK PRO QUO.

05230 KRAMER, M.
ARABISTIK AND ARABISM: THE PASSIONS OF MARTIN HARTMANN
MIDDLE EASTERN STUDIES, 25(3) (JUL 89), 283-300.
THE INFLUENCE IF EUROPEAN SCHOLARSHIP UPON MIDDLE
EASTERN NATIONALISTS IS SCARCELY ACKNOWLEDGED. HOWEVER, A
CLOSE ANALYSIS OF THE WRITINGS OF NINETEENTH-CENTURY FOREIGN
SCHOLARS WILL REVEAL STRIKING SIMILARITIES WITH THE
TWENTIETH CENTURY OPINIONS OF ARAB NATIONALISTS. THE ARTICLE
FOCUSES ON THE TRAVELS AND WRITINGS OF MARTIN HARTMANN, A
GERMAN SCHOLAR. HARTMANN WAS ONE OF THE FIRST TRULY
DISINTERESTED FRIENDS OF ARAB NATIONALISM. ALTHOUGH HIS
DREAMS OF ARAB UNITY WERE NOT REALIZED, HIS EFFORTS AND
WRITINGS CAN BE VIEWED AS A SIGNIFICANT PRECURSOR TO THE
ARAB NATIONALISM OF THIS CENTURY.

05231 KRAMER, M.
BEYOND THE BREZHNEV DOCTRINE: A NEW ERA IN SOVIET-EAST
EUROPEAN RELATIONS?
INTERNATIONAL SECURITY, 14(3) (WIN 89), 25-67.
THE ADVENT OF MIKHAIL GORBACHEV WITH HIS FAR-REACHING
REFORMS HAS SIGNIFICANTLY AFFECTED THE "BREZHNEV DOCTRINE."
THE ARTICLE EXPLORES THE WAYS THAT SOVIET EAST-EUROPEAN
RELATIONS HAVE CHANGED, AND MAY CONTINUE TO CHANGE, UNDER
GORBACHEV. IT BEGINS BY TRACING THE EVOLUTION OF SOVIET
FOREIGN POLICY IN THE LATTER HALF OF THE 1980S, WITH
EMPHASIS ON THE IMPORTANT SHIFT THAT TOOK PLACE IN 1988.
1988 WAS A WATERSHED YEAR DURING WHICH FAR GREATER LATITUDE
FOR INTERNAL POLITICAL LIBERALIZATION AS WELL AS ECONOMIC
REFORM WAS GIVEN. THE ARTICLE ALSO DISCUSSES THE DANGERS AND
OBSTACLES THAT GORBACHEV HAS ENCOUNTERED OR IS LIKELY TO
ENCOUNTER. IT CONCLUDES WITH GUIDELINES FOR THINKING ABOUT
THE FUTURE OF SOVIET-EAST EUROPEAN RELATIONS, WITH
PARTICULAR EMPHASIS ON THE PROSPECTS FOR A CONTINUED
RELAXATION OF SOVIET POLICY.

05232 KRAMER, M.
SOVIET MILITARY POLICY
CURRENT HISTORY, 88(540) (OCT 89), 337-340, 349-353.
ALTHOUGH SOVIET MILITARY POWER, BOTH NUCLEAR AND NON-
NUCLEAR, HAS CONTINUED TO GROW SINCE 1985, GORBACHEV HAS
BEEN LAYING THE GROUNDWORK TO REDUCE MILITARY PRODUCTION AND
THE SIZE OF THE SOVIET ARMED FORCES OVER THE NEXT DECADE.
THUS, THE PROSPECT OF RADICAL CHANGE IN SOVIET MILITARY
POLICY CAN NO LONGER BE RULED OUT.

05233 KRAMER, M.
THE SPECTER OF COMMUNISM
POLITICAL THEORY, 17(4) (NOV 89), 607-637.
THIS ARTICLE FOCUSES ON A SMALL SET OF WRITINGS GROUPED
TOGETHER BY G.A. COHEN. CHIEF AMONG THESE TEXTS IS KARL
MARX'S THEORY OF HISTORY. FIRST DISCUSSED IS AN OUTLINE OF
COHEN'S PRINCIPAL ARGUMENTS RELATING TO HIS SO-CALLED
PRIMARY THESIS. NEXT IS A FULL-SCALE CURTIQUE, PROBING
CERTAIN POINTS OF CONFLICT BETWEEN COHEN'S MODE OF
EXPRESSION AND HIS PRIME SUBSTANTIVE THEMES. THE BASIC
CONCLUSION IS: IF MARXISM IS PROFOUNDLY UNSATISFYING, THAT
IS BECAUSE IT STAYS UNATTUNED TO ITS OWN APORIAS.

05234 KRAPELS, E.N.
REVITALIZING U.S. OIL SECURITY POLICY
SAIS REVIEW, 9(2) (SUM 89), 185-201.
ALTHOUGH THE UNITED STATES HAS BEEN THROUGH TWO OIL
CRISES IN THE PAST SEVENTEEN YEARS, OLD HABITS ARE HARD TO
BREAK. THIS ARTICLE EVALUATES THE PROSPECT OF U.S. OIL
POLICY REPEATING PAST MISTAKES. THE ISSUE OF ENERGY SECURITY,
IN LIGHT OF EVER-INCREASING DOMESTIC CONSUMPTION AND
FOREIGN IMPORTS, ADDRESSES A PRIMARY FACET OF U.S. FOREIGN
POLICY. AS THIS AUTHOR POINTS OUT, OIL HAS MADE GOBAL
PLAYERS OUT OF SINGLE RESOURCE COUNTRIES THAT WOULD RECEIVE
LITTLE U.S. ATTENTION OTHERWISE.

05235 KRAPIEC, M.A.
TOTALITARIANISM AND WAR

POLISH PERSPECTIVES, XXXII(1) (1989), 22-25.
THE AUTHOR CONSIDERS HOW WORLD WAR II ORIGINATED AND HOW SUCH WARS CAN BE AVOIDED IN THE FUTURE.

05236 KRASNER, S.D.
REALIST PRAXIS: NEO-ISOLATIONISM AND STRUCTURAL CHANGE
JOURNAL OF INTERNATIONAL AFFAIRS, 43(1) (SUM 89), 143-160.
THIS ARTICLE EXAMINES THE PRESENT POLICY OF THE UNITED STATES TOWARDS EUROPE AND ITS OTHER ALLIES AND PREDICTS THAT NEO-ISOLATIONISM WILL CHARACTERIZE THESE RELATIONS IN THE FUTURE. IT DETAILS THE NEED FOR REEVALUATING U.S. POLICY AND THE ADVANTAGES OF DOING SO. IT FOCUSES ON THE IDEA THAT THE FUTURE OF AMERICAN VALUES DEPENDS MORE ON THE AMERICAN ECONOMY THAN ON THE POWER OF ITS MILITARY.

05237 KRASUCKI, L.
ON THE HORIZON: 11TH PUWP CONGRESS
CONTEMPORARY POLAND, XXII(9) (1989), 4-10.
THE AUTHOR REPORTS ON THE 13TH PLENUM OF THE POLISH UNITED WORKERS' PARTY CENTRAL COMMITTEE.

05238 KRATOCHWIL, F.
THE CHALLENGE OF SECURITY IN A CHANGING WORLD
JOURNAL OF INTERNATIONAL AFFAIRS, 43(1) (SUM 89), 97-118.
THIS ARTICLE EXAMINES THE CHALLENGES OF THE POSTWAR AGE. IT ANALYSES THE ORIGINAL THREAT AND THE PRESENT PROMISING PROSPECTS FOR NEGOTIATIONS BETWEEN EAST AND WEST. THE SECOND CHALLENGE OF CREATEING A MORE ENCOMPASSING, STABLE AND VIABLE ORGANIZATION OF POLITICAL LIFE IS TREATED.

05239 KRAUS, J.
ECONOMIC ADJUSTMENT AND REGIME CREATION IN NIGERIA
CURRENT HISTORY, 88(538) (MAY 89), 233-237, 249-250.
SINCE THE MILITARY OVERTHREW NIGERIA'S CIVILIAN GOVERNMENT IN DECEMBER, 1979, SUCCESSOR MILITARY GOVERNMENTS HAVE STRUGGLED TO COPE WITH THE MAJOR CONSEQUENCES OF NIGERIA'S DISASTROUS POLITICAL ECONOMY. THE CRUCIAL CONCERNS HAVE BEEN THREE: MANAGING A TRAUMATIC, DEEP RECESSION AND UNDERTAKING AN IMPORTANT STRUCTURAL ADJUSTMENT IN THE ECONOMY; DEVELOPING AND SUSTAINING POLITICAL LEGITIMACY AMONG AN IMPOVERISHED PUBLIC UNPREPARED BY POLITICAL EXPERIENCE TO ENDURE HARSH AUTHORITARIANISM; AND RECREATING A MORE ACCOUNTABLE AND LESS CORRUPT DEMOCRATIC POLITICAL SYSTEM THAN THE REGIME OF 1979-1983.

05240 KRAUS, J. F.
THE NEW BOSSES: MACHINES AND ELECTORAL SYSTEMS IN URBAN AMERICA
DISSERTATION ABSTRACTS INTERNATIONAL, 49(8) (FEB 89), 2377-A.
THE AUTHOR INVESTIGATES THE ROLE OF TRADITIONAL POLITICAL PARTY ORGANIZATIONS IN ELECTORAL POLITICS IN NEW YORK CITY IN THE MID-1980'S, FOCUSING ON THE COUNTY PARTY ORGANIZATIONS AND THE LOCAL POLITICAL CLUBS.

05241 KRAUS, L.G.
THE DEMOCRACY ISSUE: REFORM THROUGH THE CONSTITUTION
ROVI PUBLISHERS, BELVEDERE, CA, 1987, 275.
THE AUTHOR ARGUES THAT AN ACT OF CONGRESS IS ALL THAT IS NECESSARY TO EFFECTIVELY ELIMINATE THE ELECTORAL COLLEGE AND SIMPLIFY THE ELECTION OF THE PRESIDENT. THIS WOULD ASSURE ONE-PERSON, ONE-VOTE RULE AND SUPERSEDE THE PRESENT SCHEME OF ELECTIONEERING STRATEGY GENERATED BY THE EXISTING SYSTEM.

05242 KRAUS, M.
GORBACHEV'S CHALLENGE, THE USSR, AND EASTERN EUROPE
FREEDOM AT ISSUE, (106) (JAN 89), 23-26.
THE AUTHOR SURVEYS POLITICAL DEVELOPMENTS IN THE SOVIET UNION IN 1988 AND WHAT THEY WILL MEAN IN DOMESTIC AND INTERNATIONAL SITUATIONS, INCLUDING SOVIET RELATIONS WITH EASTERN EUROPE.

05243 KRAUS, R.
EASTERN EUROPE AS AN ALTERNATE WEST FOR CHINA'S MIDDLE CLASS
STUDIES IN COMPARATIVE COMMUNISM, XXII(4) (WIN 89), 323-336.
THE ARTICLE EXAMINES HOW EASTERN EUROPE FUNCTIONS AS A SOCIALIST FILTER FOR BOURGEOIS CULTURE. ALTHOUGH POPULIST REVOLUTION OFTEN DENIED THE CHINESE MIDDLE CLASS ACCESS TO OUTSIDE CULTURE, EASTERN EUROPE HAS REMAINED THE MOST SIGNIFICANT SOURCE OF WESTERN CULTURE. EASTERN EUROPEAN CULTURE HAS HELPED SMOOTH THE ALLIANCE BETWEEN POPULIST, NATIVIST, AND COSMOPOLITAN MODELS TO THE CHINESE URBAN MIDDLE CLASS AS THEY STRIVE FOR SELF-IDENTIFICATION.

05244 KRAUSE, A.
HUNGARY EXEMPLIFIES NEW ERA IN EAST-WEST RELATIONS
EUROPE, (283) (JAN 89), 30-31, 54.
IN JUNE, 1988, COMECON OFFICIALLY RECOGNIZED THE EUROPEAN COMMUNITY, AND A BROAD AGREEMENT TO PROMOTE COOPERATION WAS SIGNED. IN SEPTEMBER, HUNGARY AND THE EC SIGNED A SIMILAR AGREEMENT. THE RESULTS OF THE NEW ACCORDS HAVE BEEN SMALL THUS FAR, BUT HUNGARIANS REMAIN OPTIMISTIC DESPITE MAJOR ECONOMIC OBSTACLES AND POLITICAL UNCERTAINTIES.

05245 KRAUSE, A.
1992'S IMPACT ON AMERICAN BUSINESS ACCELERATES
EUROPE, 287 (JUN 89), 16-17.
NEW SIGNS OF CONFLICT AND TENSION ON BOTH SIDES OF THE ATLANTIC HAVE THROWN COLD WATER ON THE IDEA THAT THE BUSH ADMINISTRATION HAS RECOGNIZED THE NEED FOR AN ALL-ENCOMPASSING APPROACH TO WESTERN EUROPE'S ACCELERATING EFFORT NOT ONLY TO INTEGRATE ECONOMICALLY, BUT ALSO TO BECOME A MORE FORCEFUL, UNITED VOICE. THUS, SAY MANY OBSERVERS, IT IS MORE URGENT THAN EVER THAT THE BUSH ADMINISTRATION--STARTING WITH PRESIDENT BUSH AND SECRETARY OF STATE JAMES BAKER-BEGIN TO FOCUS MORE INTENTLY ON EUROPEAN EFFORTS TO INTEGRATE ECONOMICALLY AND, ACCORDING TO SOME U.S. BUSINESS LEADERS, TO SOUND MORE POSITIVE. NOT EVEN THE MOST ARDENT SUPPORTERS OF EUROPE'S EFFORTS WOULD ARGUE THAT AMERICA SHOULD NOT BE VIGILANT. BUT THAT IS NOT A STRATEGY. AND WE ARE A LONG WAY FROM THE EARLY 1970S AND "THE YEAR OF EUROPE," WHICH MANY AMERICANS HAVE FORGOTTEN.

05246 KRAUSE, L.B.
CHANGES IN THE INTERNATIONAL SYSTEM: THE PACIFIC BASIN
PHILADELPHIA: ANLS OF AMER ACMY OF POLITICAL AND SOC SCIENCE, (505) (SEP 89), 105-116.
THE ECONOMICS OF THE PACIFIC BASIN HAVE BEEN MUCH MORE SUCCESSFUL THAN THOSE IN OTHER AREAS DURING THE 1980S. ECONOMIC GROWTH IN THE PACIFIC HAS BEEN HIGH AND INFLATION HAS BEEN WELL CONTAINED. FIVE FACTORS SEEM TO BE MOST IMPORTANT IN EXPLAINING THIS SUCCESS. FIRST, THESE ECONOMIES HAVE MANAGED TO FORM A CONSENSUS TO PROMOTE GROWTH RATHER THAN OTHER SOCIETAL GOALS. SECOND, THE PEOPLE WORK VERY HARD. THIRD, THEY SAVE AND INVEST AN UNUSUALLY LARGE SHARE OF THEIR CURRENT INCOMES. FOURTH, THEY IMPLEMENT MARKET-CONFORMING ECONOMIC POLICIES THAT ARE PARTICULARLY OUTWARD LOOKING. FINALLY, THESE ECONOMIES BENEFIT FROM A REGIONAL FACTOR THAT COMES FROM BEING SURROUNDED BY OTHER SUCCESSFUL COUNTRIES. LEADERSHIP IN THE PACIFIC BASIN HAS BEEN SUPPLIED BY THE UNITED STATES; HOWEVER, JAPAN HAS TAKEN ON A MORE PROMINENT ROLE IN RECENT YEARS AND MAY BECOME DOMINANT IN THE FUTURE.

05247 KRAUTHAMMER, C.
UNIVERSAL DOMINION: TOWARD A UNIPOLAR WORLD
NATIONAL INTEREST, (18) (WIN 89), 46-49.
THIS ARTICLE IS AN ANSWER TO THE SERIES QUESTION: WHAT SHOULD AMERICA'S PURPOSE BE IN THE CONDITIONS LIKELY TO PREVAIL DURING THE REST OF THIS CENTURY NOW THAT THE COLD WAR IS CHANGING ITS CHARACTER IN RADICAL WAYS. THIS WRITER SUGGESTS THAT THE UNITED STATES GO ALL THE WAY AND STOP AT NOTHING SHORT OF UNIVERSAL DOMINION. HE REVIEWS THE PREDICTABLE STANCES OF PALEOCONSERVATIVES, NEOCONSERVATIVES, AND LIBERALS, AND EXAMINES ISOLATION VERSUS THE DEMOCRATIC CRUSADE.

05248 KRAUZE, E.
ENGLAND, THE UNITED STATES AND THE EXPORT OF DEMOCRACY
WASHINGTON QUARTERLY, 12(2) (SPR 89), 189-197.
AFTER MANY CENTURIES OF LIVING WITH DEMOCRACY AS THE ART OF LIMITING POWER, THE ENGLISH UNDERSTOOD THE NECESSITY OF LIMITING THEIR OWN POWER. IN CONTRAST, U.S. HISTORY RECOGNIZES NEITHER THE NOTION OF LIMITS NOR THE PRIDE OF DISSEMINATING DEMOCRACY BEYOND ITS BORDERS. IN ITS INTELLECTUAL HISTORY, THERE IS NO BURKE OR MACAULAY, AND, IN ITS POLITICAL HISTORY, THERE IS BUT ONE GLADSTONE. TRUE, BY SAVING EUROPE IN WORLD WAR II AND BY IMPLEMENTING THE MARSHALL PLAN, THE UNITED STATES SAVED EUROPEAN DEMOCRACY. THERE IS A SUBTLE DIFFERENCE, HOWEVER, IN FOSTERING THE CAUSE OF DEMOCRACY IN TIMES OF PEACE AND IN TIMES OF WAR. THE UNITED STATES HAS DONE THE BIG JOB BUT FAILED TO DO THE LITTLE JOB-THE ONE THAT NEEDS PATIENCE, WISDOM, AND DECADES OR CENTURIES OF EFFORT.

05249 KREISBERG, P.
CONTAINMENT'S LAST GASP
FOREIGN POLICY, (75) (SUM 89), 146-163.
FOR 40 YEARS THE CENTRAL PILLAR OF US SECURITY POLICY IN ASIA HAS BEEN THE CONTAINMENT OF COMMUNIST STATES. THE ARTICLE TRACES THE DEVELOPMENT OF US CONTAINMENT POLICY AND OUTLINES THE POLITICAL AND SECURITY TIES BETWEEN THE US AND JAPAN, SOUTH KOREA, THE PEOPLE'S REPUBLIC OF CHINA, THE PHILIPPINES, AUSTRALIA, AND OTHERS--ALL OF WHICH WERE BUILT ON ANTICOMMUNIST ALLIANCES. IT EXPLORES THE CURRENT CONDITIONS OF DECREASED SUPERPOWER TENSION AND LESSENED COMMUNIST THREAT AND EXAMINES THE FUTURE US OPTIONS IN AN ARENA WHERE CONTAINMENT ALONE IS NOT A SUFFICIENT TIE TO BIND NATIONS TOGETHER.

05250 KREISBERG, P.
THE UNITED STATES, SOUTH ASIA AND AMERICAN INTERESTS
JOURNAL OF INTERNATIONAL AFFAIRS, 43(1) (SUM 89), 83-96.
THIS ARTICLE EXAMINES THE ROLE SOUTH ASIA MIGHT PLAY IN AMERICA'S VIEW OF THE WORLD. IT EXAMINES THE POSSIBILITIES FOR THE US TO CONTINUE TO BUILD A LONG TERM STRATEGY OF

FRIENDLY RELATIONS. IT EXPLORES THE ROLES THAT BOTH INDIA
AND PAKISTAN WILL PLAY IN THIS AND DISCUSSES THE CHALLENGES
INVOLVED.

05251 KREMER, N.
SAVIMBI STATES HIS TERMS
NEW AFRICAN, (260) (MAY 89), 26.
IN A NEWS CONFERENCE, JONAS SAVIMBI SUMMARIZED HIS
DEMANDS FOR AN ANGOLAN PEACE SETTLEMENT, CALLING FOR DIRECT
NEGOTIATIONS WITH THE MPLA, WHICH WOULD LEAD TO A
TRANSITIONAL GOVERNMENT OF NATIONAL UNITY FOLLOWED BY
NATIONAL ELECTIONS TWO YEARS LATER. HE ALSO PROPOSED RE-
OPENING THE BENGUELA RAILWAY ON CONDITION THAT IT NOT BE
USED FOR LOGISTICAL PURPOSES.

05252 KRENZ, E.
POWER, DEMOCRACY, LAW
WORLD MARXIST REVIEW, 32(10) (OCT 89), 21-24.
THIS ARTICLE DEALS WITH MAJOR ASPECTS OF BUILDING
SOCIALISM IN THE GERMAN DEMOCRATIC REPUBLIC. IT EXAMINES THE
INVOLVEMENT OF THE PEOPLE IN DECISION MAKING AT THE LEVEL OF
STATE AND SOCIETY. IT ALSO EXAMINES THE SOCIALIST UNITY
PARTY OF GERMANY AS THE LEADING POLITICAL PARTY AND DETAILS
ITS GOALS, INTERESTS, CONCERNS AND PROJECTS.

05253 KRENZLER, H.
TOWARD HEALTHY AND OPEN WORLD MARKETS
EUROPE, (292) (DEC 89), 16-17.
THE UNITED STATES AND THE EUROPEAN COMMUNITY (E.C.) BOTH
HAVE OPEN TRADING SYSTEMS. BOTH THE U.S. AND THE E.C. HAVE
FREEDOM OF ESTABLISHMENT, THE PRINCIPLES OF CONSUMER CHOICE,
AND OF AN INDEPENDENT, UNNCORRUPTED LEGAL SYSTEM. BECAUSE OF
THESE OPEN MARKETS, THE U.S. AND E.C. ACCOUNT FOR MORE THAN
A THIRD OF WORLD TRADE. THE HEALTH OF THE WORLD ECONOMY
DEPENDS ON THESE TWO MARKETS REMAINING OPEN. IT IS
FUNDAMENTAL TO THE SURVIVAL OF THE SYSTEM THAT BOTH
COUNTRIES OBSERVE COMMON COMMITMENTS, SUCH AS THE GENERAL
AGREEMENT ON TARIFFS AND TRADE.

05254 KREOTSIALOV, I.
USSR-INDIA: NEW TRENDS IN TRADE AND ECONOMIC RELATIONS
FOREIGN TRADE, 3 (1988), 12-17.
THIS ARTICLE EXPLORES SOVIET-INDIAN RELATIONS AS AN
EXAMPLE OF COOPERATION BETWEEN TWO GREAT FORCES OF OUR TIMES
-- THE WORLD OF SOCIALISM AND THE WORLD BORN OF THE NATIONAL
LIBERATION STRUGGLE. THE ARTICLE EXAMINES TRADE AGREEMENTS,
THE CREATION OF JOINT VENTURES, NEW PROJECTS, AND OTHER
ASPECTS OF THE POSITIVE, GROWING TRADE ECONOMIC RELATIONS
BETWEEN THE TWO COUNTRIES.

05255 KREPON, M.
SPYING FROM SPACE
FOREIGN POLICY, (75) (SUM 89), 92-108.
THE ARTICLE EXAMINES THE ONGOING EFFORTS OF MANY NATIONS
TO DEVELOP OR INCREASE THEIR SPACE PROGRAMS. IT DISCUSSES
THE MILITARY IMPLICATIONS OF SPACE TECHNOLOGY WITH
PARTICULAR EMPHASIS ON "SPYING SATELLITES" SUCH AS LANDSAT
AND THE FRENCH SPOT SATELLITE. IT OUTLINES SOME POTENTIAL
BENEFICIAL USES OF SPACE TECHNOLOGY SUCH AS REFEREEING
SUPERPOWER COMPLIANCE DISPUTES, BUILDING CONFIDENCE IN
MULTILATERAL ARMS CONTROL AGREEMENTS, AND DETERRING SURPRISE
ATTACKS. IT CONCLUDES THAT ALTHOUGH THE FUTURE OF SPACE
TECHNOLOGY IS UNCERTAIN, THE ADVANCE OF SATELLITE TECHNOLOGY
SEEMS DESTINED TO INCREASE THE EROSION OF GOVERNMENTAL
CONTROL AND COULD HAVE DAMAGING SECURITY IMPLICATIONS. THE
ARTICLE PROPOSES THE USE OF SAFEGUARDS AGAINST THE NEGATIVE
APPLICATIONS OF SATELLITE TECHNOLOGY.

05256 KRIESI, H.
NEW SOCIAL MOVEMENTS AND THE NEW CLASS IN THE NETHERLANDS
AMERICAN JOURNAL OF SOCIOLOGY, 94(5) (MAR 89), 1078-1116.
THE CLASS BASE OF THE SO-CALLED NEW SOCIAL MOVEMENTS IS
ANALYZED USING DATA FROM THE DUTCH NATIONAL ELECTION SURVEY
OF 1986. THIS ANALYSIS IS LINKED TO THE THEORY ON THE "NEW
CLASS," RECONCEPTUALIZED AS THOSE IN THE NEW MIDDLE CLASS
WHO TRY TO DEFEND THEIR RELATIVE AUTONOMY AGAINST THE
ENCROACHMENT OF THE "TECHNOCRATS." THE ANALYSIS SHOWS THAT,
ALTHOUGH THE DUTCH NEW SOCIAL MOVEMENTS ARE SUPPORTED BY
BROAD SEGMENTS OF THE POPULATION, THEIR INNER CIRCLES ARE
PREDOMINANTLY CONSTITUTED BY SEGMENTS OF THE
RECONCEPTUALIZED NEW CLASS: THE YOUNG SPECIALISTS IN SOCIAL
AND CULTURAL SERVICES AND SOME OF THE YOUNG ADMINISTRATIVE
SPECIALISTS IN PUBLIC SERVICE. IN ADDITION, THE ANALYSIS
DOCUMENTS THE LIBERALIZING EFFECT OF EDUCATION FOR THE
YOUNGER COHORTS AND SUGGESTS A PROFOUND CHANGE OF VALUES IN
THE POSTWAR PERIOD.

05257 KRIESI, H.
THE POLITICAL OPPORTUNITY STRUCTURE OF THE DUTCH PEACE
MOVEMENT
WEST EUROPEAN POLITICS, 12(3) (JUL 89), 295-312.
THIS ARTICLE ANALYSES THE POLITICAL OPPORTUNITY
STRUCTURE OF THE DUTCH POLITICAL SYSTEM WITH RESPECT TO NEW
SOCIAL MOVEMENTS IN GENERAL, AND THE DUTCH PEACE MOVEMENT IN

PARTICULAR. IT IS SHOWN THAT THE PREVAILING STRATEGY OF THE
DUTCH POLITICAL SYSTEM IS ONE OF INTEGRATION, AND THAT THE
DOMINANT PARTY ON THE LEFT (THE SOCIAL DEMOCRATIC PARTY)
WENT THROUGH A PROCESS OF TRANSFORMATION WHICH OPENED IT UP
TO THE NEW CHALLENGERS AT PRECISELY THE MOMENT WHEN THE
CYCLE OF PROTEST OF THE NEW SOCIAL MOVEMENTS TOOK OFF. THE
CONSEQUENCES OF THE HIGH DEGREE OF OPENNESS OF THE DUTCH
SYSTEM ARE THEN DOCUMENTED ON THE BASIS OF A DETAILED
ANALYSIS OF THE ALLIANCE STRUCTURE OF THE DUTCH PEACE
MOVEMENT.

05258 KRINSKY, I.; ROTENBERG, W.
THE TRANSITION TO COMPETITIVE PRICING ON THE TORONTO STOCK
EXCHANGE
CANADIAN PUBLIC POLICY--ANALYSE DE POLITIQUES, XV(2) (JUN
89), 135-144.
ON APRIL 1, 1983 COMMISSION RATES ON TRANSACTIONS OF ALL
SIZES BECAME NEGOTIABLE ON THE TORONTO STOCK EXCHANGE (TSE).
UNDER THE NEW COMPETITIVE PRICING ARRANGEMENT, BROKERAGE
FIRMS ESTABLISH THEIR OWN RATE STRUCTURES AND COMPETE IN THE
MARKETPLACE ON THE BASIS OF PRICE, CONTENT AND QUALITY OF
SERVICE. THIS STUDY EXAMINES THE FIRST TWO YEARS OF
TRANSITION TO NEGOTIATED RATES. THE SPEED AND MAGNITUDE OF
RATE REDUCTIONS, AND THEIR DISTRIBUTION ACROSS INVESTOR
CATEGORIES, INDICATE THE NATURE AND POWER OF THE BROKERAGE
CARTEL THAT IS CURRENTLY BEING DISMANTLED IN CANADA.

05259 KRIPS, M.
POLITICS WITH A DIFFERENCE--AND ONTOLOGICAL RELATIVITY
ARENA, (89) (SUM 89), 55-69.
THE AUTHOR CONSIDERS THE WORKS OF DERRIDA AND QUINE IN A
RESPONSE TO THE CLAIMS THAT THERE IS A COMPLICITY BETWEEN
POST-STRUCTURALISM AS AN INTELLECTUAL MOVEMENT AND THE
ABSTRACTED, "POST-MODERN" FORM OF SUBJECTIVITY REQUIRED BY
THE INTERSECTION OF THE COMMODITY FORM WITH MODERN MASS
MEDIA. HE HOPES TO ILLUSTRATE A "LESS TENDENTIOUS APPROACH"
TO SOME POST-STRUCTURALIST THESES. HE CONCLUDES THAT
DECONSTRUCTION MAY BE INEVITABLE, BUT THE QUESTION REMAINS
OF WHETHER IT SHOULD BE MORE ACTIVELY PURSUED IN PARTICULAR
LOCATIONS.

05260 KRISHAN, G.
TRENDS IN REGIONAL DISPARITIES IN INDIA
ASIAN PROFILE, 17(3) (JUN 89), 243-262.
THE AUTHOR EXPLORES THE EMERGING REGIONAL DIMENSION OF
THE INDIAN DEVELOPMENT EXPERIENCE SINCE INDEPENDENCE. THE
STUDY IS BASED ON A SURVEY OF THE RELEVANT RESEARCH MATERIAL
PREVIOUSLY PUBLISHED ON THE SUBJECT AND ON AN ANALYSIS OF
DATA PERTAINING TO SELECT INDICATORS OF DEVELOPMENT. THE
AUTHOR ENDEAVORS TO EXPLAIN THE PERSISTENT POVERTY IN INDIA,
WHY VARIOUS REGIONS WITHIN INDIA DIFFER IN TERMS OF THEIR
RELATIVE DEVELOPMENT LEVELS, AND WHAT UNDERLYING FACTORS
ACCOUNT FOR THE PATTERN OF REGIONAL DISPARITIES.

05261 KROEF, J.
THE UNITED STATES AND VIETNAM: THE IMPERATIVES OF
RECONCILIATION
CURRENT RESEARCH ON PEACE AND VIOLENCE, XII(1) (1989),
1-14.
THOUGH IT HAS BEEN OVER A DECADE SINCE OFFICIAL WAR
BETWEEN THE UNITED STATES AND VIETNAM, RELATIONSHIPS BETWEEN
THE TWO NATIONS HAVE NEVER BEEN FRIENDLY. THE U.S. AND ITS
FRIENDS IN ASEAN (THE ASSOCIATION OF SOUTHEAST ASIAN
NATIONS), LED MOST OF THE WORLD COMMUNITY IN ISOLATING THE
NOW UNIFIED SOCIALIST REPUBLIC OF VIETNAM FROM INTERNATIONAL
TRADE, FINANCIAL ASSISTANCE AND DEVELOPING NORMAL DIPLOMATIC
RELATIONS. WHEN THE VIETNAM GOVERNMENT INVADED CAMBODIA, IT
SERVED AS A DECISIVE FACTOR IN AMERICAN POLICY
CONSIDERATIONS. THIS ARTICLE STATES THAT A STEADY
INCREMENTAL NORMALIZATION OF US DIPLOMATIC RELATIONS,
BEGGINNING WITH A RENEWED EXPLORATION OF THE OPENING OF
DIPLOMATIC INTEREST SECTIONS, AND CORRELATED WITH A
VIETNAMESE WITHDRAWAL FROM CAMBODIA THAT DOES NOT LEAD TO A
DANGEROUS POWER VACUUM THERE SEEM TO BE THE NECESSARY NEW
POLICY CHOICES. THE US NEEDS TO BE FAR MORE AND DIRECTLY
INVOLVED IN DEVELOPING STRATEGIES THAT WILL LEAD TO AN
INTERNATIONAL PEACEKEEPING FORCE.

05262 KRUCHEM, T.
THE CONFLICT BETWEEN MORAL ATTITUDES AND POLITICAL
RESPONSIBILITY: THE FOREIGN POLICY OF THE FEDERAL REPUBLIC
OF GERMANY TOWARDS SOUTH AFRICA
SOUTH AFRICA INTERNATIONAL, 19(4) (APR 89), 188-203.
WITH REGARD TO ITS CONTRIBUTION TO BREAKING DOWN
APARTHEID, THE FOREIGN POLICY OF THE FEDERAL REPUBLIC OF
GERMANY IS EXAMINED AS THAT OF A WESTERN COUNTRY WITH VERY
CLOSE ECONOMIC, CULTURAL, RELIGIOUS AND TRADE UNION LINKS
WITH SOUTH AFRICA. IN THIS CONNECTION THE ASPECTS RELATING
TO NAMIBIA ARE LARGELY IGNORED. THE QUESTIONS POSED ARE: WHO
ARE THE RELEVANT PROTAGONISTS INVOLVED IN GERMAN FOREIGN
POLICY VIS-A-VIS SOUTH AFRICA? WHAT ARE THEIR INTERESTS? THE
AUTHOR IDENTIFIES AND EXAMINES THE SOCIAL
SECTORS/ORGANIZATIONS THAT HAVE INTERESTS RELATED TO SOUTH
AFRICA AND ACCORDINGLY ACT AS FOREIGN POLICY PROTAGONISTS.

THESE INCLUDE: THE BUSINESS COMMUNITY; TRADE UNIONS: CHURCHES; POLITICAL PARTIES; SUPPORTERS OF THE REFORMIST POLICY OF THE SOUTH AFRICAN GOVERNMENT; AND, FUNDAMENTALIST APARTHEID OPPONENTS.

05263 KRUKS, S. (ED.); RAPP, R. (ED.); YOUNG, M.B. (ED.)
PROMISSORY NOTES: WOMEN AND THE TRANSITION TO SOCIALISM
MONTHLY REVIEW PRESS, NEW YORK, NY, 1989, 416.
THESE ESSAYS DEBATE THE PROSPECTS FOR A TRUE MARRIAGE OF FEMINISM AND SOCIALISM BY EXAMINING THE POSITION OF WOMEN IN SOCIALIST THOUGHT AND PRACTICE FROM MARX TO THE PRESENT. CASE STUDIES EXAMINE THE STATUS OF WOMEN IN CUBA, NICARAGUA, MOZAMBIQUE, YEMEN, VIETNAM, WEST BENGAL, POST—MAO CHINA, HUNGARY, THE GERMAN DEMOCRATIC REPUBLIC, AND THE USSR.

05264 KRUPNICK, M.
EDWARD SAID: DISCOURSE AND PALESTINIAN RAGE
TIKKUN, 4(6) (NOV 89), 21-24.
THE ARTICLE DISCUSSES THE EFFORTS OF PALESTINIAN WRITER EDWARD SAID TO CREATE A NATIONAL IDENTITY FOR PALESTINIANS. SAID ARGUES THAT THE TRADITIONAL STORY OF THE EXODUS GIVES THE JEWS IN ISRAEL A FRAME OF REFERENCE WITH WHICH TO DISCUSS THE CURRENT SITUATION. THIS FRAME OF REFERENCE LIMITS FUTURE DISCUSSION AND DEBATE ON THE PALESTINIAN QUESTION BY COMPLETELY OVERSHADOWING ANY ARAB CLAIM TO THE LAND. SAID HAS DILIGENTLY SOUGHT FOR A FOUNDATION FOR A PALESTINIAN NATIONAL NARRATIVE AND HAS ALSO WORKED TO DEMYSTIFY THE ORIGINAL EXODUS STORY. THE AUTHOR CONCLUDES THAT SAID'S WORK IS A REFLECTION OF PAIN--THE PAIN OF A DISPERSED, STORYLESS PEOPLE FIGHTING FOR IDENTITY.

05265 KRUPNIK, M.
EDWARD SAID: DISCOURSE AND PLESTINIAN RAGE
TIKKUN, 4(6) (NOV 89), 21-24.
THIS ARTICLE ADDRESSES THE PROBLEM OF PALESTINIAN IDENTITY AS SEEN BY EDWARD SAID. IT ANALYSES THE WALZER-SAID DEBATE BECAUSE IT AFFORDS A VIEW OF ISRAELI-PALESTINIAN CONFLICT, AND DISCUSSES SAID'S PROPOSAL TO DELEGITIMISE A CONONICAL TEXT, BACKED BY THE REASONING: HOW BETTER TO AVENGE THE INJURY OF POLITICAL EXCLUSION THAN TO DISCREDIT THE STORIES BY WHICH YOUR ENEMY MAKES SENE OF ITSELF A PEOPLE?

05266 KRYGIER, M.
POLAND: LIFE IN AN ABNORMAL COUNTRY
NATIONAL INTEREST, (18) (WIN 89), 55-64.
THIS ARTICLE DESCRIBES LIFE IN POLAND. IT DETAILS THE SHAMBLES OF THE POLISH ECONOMY AND CALLS EVERYDAY LIFE "HARD, DRAB AND EXAUSTING." IT ALSO EXPLORES THE INDUSTRIAL SOCIETY WHICH HAS PRODUCED A NATION OF RENAISSANCE MEN, AND ESPECIALLY WOMEN. THE DEPTH OF THE CRISIS IS DETAILED AND SOLIDARITY'S ROLE IS EXAMINED. POLAND'S INABILITY TO DECIDE WHAT THE RUSSIANS AND THE UNITED STATES WILL DO NEXT IS EXPLORED, AS WELL AS THEIR NEED FOR HELP IN ORDER TO SUCCEED.

05267 KUBALKOVA, V.; CRUICKSHANK, A. A.
A RAMBO COME TO JUDGEMENT: FRED HALLIDAY, MARRISM AND INTERNATIONAL RELATIONS
REVIEW OF INTERNATIONAL STUDIES, 15(1) (JAN 89), 37-47.
THIS ARTICLE POINTS OUT WEAKNESSES CHARACTERISTIC OF HALLIDAY'S REPLY ARTICLE THROUGHOUT WHETHER IN THOSE PARTS (1) THAT PERTAIN TO HALLIDAY'S REPLY TO THE AUTHORS' ARTICLE ON THE NEW COLD WAR, (2) IN THOSE THAT COME PROPERLY UNDER THE HEADING OF REVIEW-ARTICLE IN REFERENCE TO THE WHOLE OF OUR WORK, (3) IN HIS REJECTION OF THE ADJECTIVE 'CRITICAL' AND (4) IN HIS REJECTION OF THE ADJECTIVE 'REVISIONIST' THAT THE AUTHORS USED TO DESCRIBE THEORIES OF NEW COLD WAR. THE AUTHORS EXAMINE HIS ARGUMENT IN THIS ORDER AND CONCLUDE (5) WITH SOME COMMENTS ON HALLIDAY'S POSITIVISM VIS-A-VIS HIS NOTION OF 'VIGILANTISM'.

05268 KUBRICHT, A.P.
UNITED STATES—CZECHOSLOVAK RELATIONS DURING THE KENNEDY ADMINISTRATION
EAST EUROPEAN QUARTERLY, XXIII(3) (SEP 89), 355-364.
JOHN F. KENNEDY WON EXTENSIVE SUPPORT FROM AMERICAN LIBERALS BECAUSE OF HIS APPARENTLY LESS CONFRONTATIONAL AND CALMER RHETORICAL APPROACH TO EASTERN EUROPE AND THE COMMUNIST THREAT. ON THE OTHER HAND, HE WAS CAPABLE OF SURPRISING HIS LIBERAL SUPPORTERS BY APPEARING TO ACCEPT TRADITIONAL FEARS OF SOVIET EXPANSION. KENNEDY'S WILLINGNESS TO CREATE INTERNAL PRESSURES IN THE SOVIET SATELLITES WAS EVIDENT. HE INTRODUCED POLICIES AND TACTICS THAT MAY HAVE SEEMED LESS THREATENING THAN MILITARY CONFRONTATION BUT WERE STILL DIRECTED AT ELIMINATING SOVIET INFLUENCE IN EASTERN EUROPE.

05269 KUEH, Y.Y.
THE MAOIST LEGACY AND CHINA'S NEW INDUSTRIALIZATION STRATEGY
CHINA QUARTERLY, (119) (SEP 89), 420-447.
THIS ARTICLE IS DIVIDED INTO TWO PARTS. THE FIRST CONSIDERS CHINA'S INDUSTRIAL PERFORMANCE IN TERMS OF THE PACE AND PATTERN OF INDUSTRIALIZATION, REGIONAL INDUSTRIAL DISTRIBUTION, AND TECHNOLOGICAL CHANGE. THIS ANALYSIS IS SET IN THE CONTEXT OF THE POLICY BACKGROUND AGAINST WHICH INDUSTRIAL CHANGES HAVE OCCURRED. THE SECOND SECTION OF THE ARTICLE EXAMINES THE NATURE AND SCOPE OF THE MODIFICATIONS TO THE MAOIST STRATEGY OF INDUSTRIALIZATION AFTER THE LATE 1970'S, ESPECIALLY THE POSSIBLE LONG—TERM IMPACT ON EXISTING SECTORAL, REGIONAL, AND TECHNOLOGICAL IMBALANCES. THIS INCLUDES DISCUSSION OF HOW THE NEW DEVELOPMENT STRATEGY IS LIKELY TO AFFECT CHINA'S EFFORTS TO DISMANTLE THE SOVIET-STYLE SYSTEM OF CENTRAL PLANNING AND ITS ECONOMIC RELATIONS WITH THE WEST.

05270 KUENNE, R.E.
CONFLICT MANAGEMENT IN MATURE RIVALRY
JOURNAL OF CONFLICT RESOLUTION, 33(3) (SEP 89), 554-566.
RIVALRY IS A FORM OF CONFLICT IN WHICH RELATIVELY FEW OPPONENTS MUST MAKE DECISIONS IN FULL KNOWLEDGE THAT RIVALS WILL PERCEIVE THOSE DECISIONS AS INTERFERING TO A GREATER OR LESSER EXTENT WITH THEIR WELFARES. ACTORS' AUTONOMOUS ACTIONS MUST BE UNDERTAKEN ONLY AFTER OPPONENTS' POTENTIAL REACTIONS HAVE DISCOUNTED THE FAVORABLE EFFECTS ON THE INITIATING AGENT'S WELFARE IN THE ABSENCE OF SUCH REACTIONS. THIS PAPER DEFINES AN ENVIRONMENT OF MATURE RIVALRY IN WHICH THIS PROSPECTIVE INTERACTION OF DECISIONS TAKES PLACE IN A MANNER THAT RESTRAINS CONFLICT THROUGH THE FOSTERING OF MIND-SETS, INSTITUTIONS, AND CONDITIONS THAT ENHANCE COOPERATION. THE ROLE OF UNCERTAINTY IS FEATURED AS A FACILITATOR OF THESE STABILIZING TENDENCIES. A FORMAL FRAMEWORK FOR ANALYZING THE SOLUTION PROCESS IN CONTEXTS OF MATURE RIVALRY IS PRESENTED USING THE THEORY OF RIVALROUS CONSONANCE.

05271 KUGELMASS, S.P.
COMPUTER INTEGRATION IN NEW YORK CITY MUNICIPAL GOVERNMENT AS OF FISCAL YEAR 1986
DISSERTATION ABSTRACTS INTERNATIONAL, 50(4) (OCT 89), 1086-A.
MUNICIPAL COMPUTER INFORMATION SYSTEMS (CIS) REPRESENT A GROWING PROPORTION OF MUNICIPAL GOVERNMENT RESOURCES. THIS DISSERTATION DESCRIBES AND ANALYZES THE ALLOCATION OF MUNICIPAL RESOURCES FOR CIS, THE GOVERNMENTAL AND ORGANIZATIONAL PURPOSES SERVED BY THE SYSTEMS, AND THE EXTENT TO WHICH THEY ARE USED. NEARLY 800 OPERATIONAL CIS WERE STUDIED IN 50 NEW YORK CITY MUNICIPAL AGENCIES.

05272 KUGLER, J.,; ORGANSKI, A.F.K.
THE END OF HEGEMONY?
INTERNATIONAL INTERACTIONS, 15(2) (1989), 113-128.
THIS STUDY CHALLENGES THE NOTION THAT THE UNITED STATES IS A DECLINING HEGEMON, OR THAT THE WESTERN REGIME IS IN PERIL. COMPARISONS OF ECONOMIC OUTPUT, TRADE, AND POWER STATISTICS INDICATE THAT THE UNITED STATES CONTINUES TO HOLD A MORE FAVORABLE POSITION THAN PREVIOUS HEGEMONS DID AT COMPARABLE PERIODS IN THE TRAJECTORY OF THEIR RULE IN RELATION TO BOTH ITS ALLIES AND OPPONENTS. MOST IMPORTANT, INDICATORS OF POWER (UNLIKE ECONOMIC INDICATORS) SUGGEST THE POWER DISTRIBUTION IN THE WORLD ORDER HAS VARIED LITTLE SINCE WORLD WAR II AND CONTINUES TO INSURE AMERICAN DOMINANCE. THE PRECEPTION OF A WITHERING AMERICAN HEGEMONY IS A TRENDY BUT INACCURATE ASSESSMENT OF OUR TIME.

05273 KULIK, S.
FELLING TREES WITH A SHOVEL
REPRINTS FROM THE SOVIET PRESS, 49(11/12) (DEC 89), 15-18.
THE SOVIET AND AMERICAN POSITIONS ON CHEMICAL WEAPONS HAVE NOTICABLY GROWN CLOSER AS A RESULT OF THE MEETINGS BETWEEN THE TWO COUNTRIES' FOREIGN MINISTERS IN WYOMING, THEREBY INCREASING CHANCES THAT CHEMICAL WEAPONS MAY BE FINALLY PROHIBITED AND ELIMINATED. DESPITE THE OBVIOUS PROGRESS IN THIS SPHERE, THE WESTERN MASS MEDIA FROM TIME TO TIME COME UP WITH INCREDIBLE STORIES ABOUT THE CHEMICAL WEAPONS OF THE FUTURE. SOME ARTICLES QUOTE INTELLIGENCE SOURCES WHICH CLAIM THAT THE SOVIET UNION HAS DEVELOPED A NEW TYPE OF CHEMICAL WEAPONS - GENETIC. THIS ARTICLE IS AN EXCLUSIVE INTERVIEW DURING WHICH A POLITICAL COMMENTATOR DISCUSSES THE PROBLEM WITH THE CHIEF OF THE CHEMICAL TROOPS OF THE SOVIET DEFENCE MINISTRY, AND ALSO A LEADING EXPERT ON CHEMICAL WEAPONS.

05274 KULKARNI, V.G.
STRAINING AT THE SEAMS
FAR EASTERN ECONOMIC REVIEW, 141(27) (JUL 88), 16-18, 20-21.
TO A VISITOR, SURFACE APPEARANCES IN BURMA HAVE REMAINED THE SAME SINCE THE COUNTRY LAPSED INTO-IMPOSED SOLITARY CONFINEMENT. HOWEVER, RESIDENT DIPLOMATS HAVE BEGUN TO SENSE A SLOW UNDERCURRENT OF CHANGE. THE ECONOMIC SYSTEM HAS STEADILY DETERIORATED AND THE STATE'S COFFERS ARE ALMOST EMPTY. ANY WORSENING OF THE ECONOMIC SITUATION MAY RESULT IN INCREASED DISCONTENT AMONG THE NORMALLY STOIC POPULACE AND EVENTUALLY FORCE POLITICAL CHANGE AWAY FROM THE ONE-PARTY RULE OF THE MILITARY.

05275 KUM, J.M.
LEADERSHIP PERCEPTION AND INTERSTATE CONFLICT IN AFRICA

(1960-1985)
DISSERTATION ABSTRACTS INTERNATIONAL, 49(10) (APR 89),
3148-A.
THE IMAGES LEADERS HOLD OF ONE ANOTHER MAY OR MAY NOT
FOSTER AN ENVIRONMENT CONDUCIVE TO CONFLICT. IN THIS
DISSERTATION, THE AUTHOR EXAMINES THE DYNAMIC BETWEEN THE
SUBJECTIVE IMAGES THAT AFRICAN LEADERS HOLD OF ONE ANOTHER,
THEIR PERCEPTION OF EVENTS, AND OTHER FACTORS THAT
CONTRIBUTE TO INTERSTATE CONFLICT.

05276 KUMAR, D.K.
U.S. POLICY TOWARD JAMAICA, 1962-1982
DISSERTATION ABSTRACTS INTERNATIONAL, 49(10) (APR 89),
3148-A.
THE AUTHOR TESTS A MODIFIED VERSION OF A THEORETICAL
APPROACH PROPOSED BY VLOYANTES TO ANALYZE UNITED STATES
POLICY TOWARD THE CARIBBEAN. THE BASIC THESIS OF THE MODEL
IS THAT GEOGRAPHIC REGIONS ADJACENT TO THE SUPERPOWERS ARE
REGARDED BY THESE POWERS AS WITHIN THEIR SPHERES OF
INFLUENCE. THE MODEL IS APPLIED TO A STUDY OF U.S. RELATIONS
WITH JAMAICA FROM 1962 TO 1982.

05277 KUMAR, R.
CONTEMPORARY INDIAN FEMINISM
FEMINIST REVIEW, (33) (AUT 89), 20-29.
THE AUTHOR FOCUSES ON THE MAIN CURRENTS OF THE WOMEN'S
LIBERATION MOVEMENT IN CONTEMPORARY INDIA AND THE COURSE
THEY HAVE FOLLOWED OVER THE LAST TEN YEARS, WITH OCCASIONAL
DIGRESSIONS TO LOOK AT THE MOVEMENT'S EARLIER HISTORY.

05278 KUMAR, R.
THE FEMINIST MOVEMENT IN INDIA
NEW POLITICS, 11(2) (WIN 89), 148-155.
THIS ARTICLE DESCRIBES THE MAIN CURRENTS IN INDIAN
FEMINISM, AND EXAMINES THE COURSE THEY HAVE TAKEN OVER THE
LAST TEN YEARS. WOMEN'S ISSUES HAD BECOME SO WIDELY
RECOGNIZED THAT THE CENTER AND RIGHT PARTIES FORMED WOMEN'S
FRONTS, AND SPECIAL ATTENTION BEGAN TO BE PAID TO WOMEN IN
MOST GENERAL MOVEMENTS OF THE '80S, ALTHOUGH IT WAS MORE
NOTICEABLE IN PEASANT THAN IN WORKERS' MOVEMENTS. PERHAPS IN
REACTION, MOVEMENTS AGAINST FEMINIST OR WOMEN'S RIGHTS IDEAS
WERE STARTED BY SECTIONS OF TRADITIONALIST SOCIETY, AND
SINCE THE MID-'80S, FEMINISTS HAVE SUFFERED MORE SERIOUS
DEFEATS THAN EVER BEFORE.

05279 KUNCE, F.
NO DISPOSABLES
SOJOURNERS, 18(10) (NOV 89), 21.
TWO SEPARATE DECISIONS OF THE US SUPREME COURT SEEM TO
INDICATE THAT SOME ELEMENTS OF SOCIETY ARE CONSIDERED TO BE
"DISPOSABLE." ONE DECISION CONCLUDED THAT THE DEATH PENALTY
IS APPROPRIATE FOR THE MENTALLY RETARDED AND FOR THOSE AS
YOUNG AS 16 YEARS OLD WHEN THEY COMMITTED THEIR CRIME. THE
OTHER UPHELD AN EARLIER DECISION TO ALLOW ABORTION.

05280 KUNDE, J.E.; SHANAHAN, M.; WOLFE, M.P.
TRAINING FOR ELECTED LEADERSHIP: HEADING INTO THE 1990'S
NATIONAL CIVIC REVIEW, 78(6) (NOV 89), 428-438.
MANY OF THE LEADERSHIP QUALITIES AND SKILLS DEMONSTRATED
BY ELECTED OFFICIALS PRIOR TO THEIR PUBLIC ROLES ARE NOT
TRANSFERABLE TO THE PUBLIC SECTOR. MEANWHILE, THE CHALLENGES
TO LOCAL GOVERNMENTS--LEGAL, FISCAL, RISK AND CONFLICT
MANAGEMENT, ENVIRONMENTAL--HAVE REACHED HERETOFORE UNKNOWN
LEVELS OF URGENCY AND COMPLEXITY. ELECTED OFFICIALS NEED
ACCESS TO TRAINING FOR EFFECTIVE, COLLABORATIVE GROUP
DECISION MAKING.

05281 KUNIHIRO, M.
THE EXTERNAL IMPLICATIONS OF 1992, I: A JAPANESE VIEW
WORLD TODAY, 45(2) (FEB 89), 29-31.
THE AUTHOR, WHO IS JAPAN'S DEPUTY MINISTER OF FOREIGN
AFFAIRS, DISCUSSES JAPANESE HOPES AND FEARS RELATING TO THE
ESTABLISHMENT OF A SINGLE EUROPEAN MARKET IN 1992.

05282 KUNTJORO-JAKTI, H.U.
EXTERNAL AND DOMESTIC COALITIONS OF THE BUREAUCRATIC
AUTHORITARIAN STATE IN INDONESIA
DISSERTATION ABSTRACTS INTERNATIONAL, 50(1) (JUL 89),
246-A.
THE AUTHOR TRACES THE EVOLUTION OF DOMESTIC POLITICAL-
ECONOMIC COALITIONS IN THE INDONESIAN STATE SINCE THE
INCEPTION OF THE NEW ORDER REGIME IN 1966 AND EVALUATES THE
INFLUENCE OF THESE COALITIONS ON ECONOMIC POLICY. HE ALSO
LOOKS AT THE RELATIONSHIP BETWEEN THESE COALITIONS AND THEIR
COUNTERPARTS IN THE LIBERAL DEMOCRATIC PARTY OF JAPAN,
INDONESIA'S MAJOR TRADING PARTNER AND A DOMINATING FORCE IN
INDONESIAN ECONOMIC GROWTH.

05283 KUNZLE, D.
REVOLUTIONARY RESURRECTION: THE CHURCH OF SANTA MARIA DE
LOS ANGELES AND THE SCHOOL OF PUBLIC MINUMENTAL ART IN
MANAGUA, NICARAGUA
LATIN AMERICAN PERSPECTIVES, 16(2) (SPR 89), 47-60.
THE ARTICLE DISCUSSES THE DEVELOPMENT OF A SERIES OF

MURALS IN A CHURCH IN NICARAGUA. THE FACT THAT THE ART IS
ENCOURAGED BY THE SANDINISTA GOVERNMENT AND THE FACT THAT
THE CHURCH EXISTS AT ALL IS EVIDENCE THAT THE IMAGE OF
RELIGIOUS INTOLERANCE THAT THE SANDINISTA GOVERNMENT HAS IN
THE US, IS INACCURATE.

05284 KUO-SHU, L.
ADJUST, REVISE, AND REFORM
FREE CHINA REVIEW, 39(1) (JAN 89), 8-11.
SWEEPING REFORMS ARE NEEDED IN TAIWAN'S FINANCIAL SYSTEM
TO BRING GREATER INTERNATIONAL AND DOMESTIC STRENGTH TO
TAIWAIN, IN LINE WITH ITS INCREASED PROSPERITY AND ECONOMIC
ROLE IN THE WORLD COMMUNITY. WHILE THE GOVERNMENT HAS
ALREADY TAKEN SOME STEPS TO MODERNIZE THE SYSTEM, MUCH
REMAINS TO BE DONE.

05285 KUO-SHU, L.
RESTRUCTURING THE ECONOMY
FREE CHINA REVIEW, 39(10) (OCT 89), 32-35.
IN THE LATE 1980'S, TAIWAN FINDS ITSELF GRAPPLING WITH A
HUGE TRADE IMBALANCE WITH THE USA AND A RAPID APPRECIATION
OF THE NEW TAIWAN DOLLAR. BECAUSE IT IS DEPENDENT ON THE
AMERICAN MARKET AND LACKS RETALIATORY LEVERAGE, TAIWAN IS A
LIKELY TARGET OF UNITED STATES' PROTECTIONIST MEASURES. IN
ADDITION, DUE TO RISING PUBLIC AWARENESS FROM ACCELERATED
POLITICAL DEMOCRATIZATION, THE GOVERNMENT CAN NO LONGER
IGNORE THE PROBLEMS OF POLLUTION, PUBLIC SERVICES, AND
WELFARE. IT MUST RESTRUCTURE ITS POLICY TO GIVE GREATER
PRIORITY TO THE ENVIRONMENT, CONSUMER PROTECTION, AND SOCIAL
WELFARE.

05286 KUO-TAI, H.
THE STRUGGLE BETWEEN THE KUOMINTANG AND THE CHINESE
COMMUNIST PARTY ON CAMPUS DURING THE WAR OF RESISTANCE,
1937-1945
CHINA QUARTERLY, (118) (JUN 89), 300-323.
FROM 1937 TO 1945 HIGHER EDUCATION WAS ONE OF THE MAIN
ARENAS OF THE STRUGGLE BETWEEN THE KUOMINTANG AND THE
CHINESE COMMUNIST PARTY. IN THIS PAPER, THE AUTHOR REVIEWS
HOW THE CCP ESTABLISHED ITS UNDERGROUND ORGANIZATIONS IN
UNIVERSITIES AND DEVELOPED ITS STRONGHOLD IN HIGHER
EDUCATION. THEN HE DISCUSSES THE KMT'S COUNTERMEASURES,
INCLUDING THE CREATION OF KMT PARTY BRANCHES, THE THREE
PEOPLE'S PRINCIPLES YOUTH CORPS ON CAMPUS, AND YOUTH LABOUR
CAMPS ALONG THE BORDER REGIONS.

05287 KUO, J.
FAILURE AT CHUNGKING: POLITICAL NEGOTIATIONS IN POST-WAR
CHINA
DISSERTATION ABSTRACTS INTERNATIONAL, 50(4) (OCT 89),
1083-A.
WHEN THE SINO-JAPANESE WAS ENDED IN AUGUST 1945, THE TWO
MAJOR PARTIES IN CHINA WERE IN A STATE OF CIVIL CONFLICT. IN
SEPTEMBER AND OCTOBER, THEY HELD NEGOTIATIONS, WITH FOUR
ISSUES PREDOMINATING: THE POLITICAL CONSULTATIVE CONFERENCE,
THE NATIONAL ASSEMBLY, MILITARY REORGANIZATION, AND THE
LIBERATED AREAS. OF THE FOUR, THE LAST TWO WERE MATTERS OF
ESSENCE FOR THE COMMUNISTS AND NON-NEGOTIABLE PRINCIPLES FOR
THE NATIONAL GOVERNMENT. AT THE END OF THE NEGOTIATIONS,
THEY AGREED TO HOLD A POLITICAL CONSULTATIVE CONFERENCE AND
ISSUED AN OPTIMISTIC JOINT COMMUNIQUE, BUT, IN FACT, NOT A
SINGLE PROBLEM HAD BEEN SOLVED.

05288 KUO, W.H.
ECONOMIC REFORMS AND URBAN DEVELOPMENT IN CHINA
PACIFIC AFFAIRS, 62(2) (SUM 89), 188-203.
CHINA'S URBAN POLICY-MAKERS HAVE RECENTLY EXPERIENCED
MOUNTING SOCIAL PRESSURES TO IMPPROVE THEIR URBAN CONDITIONS.
THIS PAPER ARGUES THAT SOME OF THE URBAN DEVELOPMENT
PROBLEMS CONFRONTED BY ECONOMIC REFORMERS ORIGINATED IN THE
STALINIST MODEL OF ECONOMIC DEVELOPMENT INSTITUTED IN
PREREFORM YEARS. OVERSTRESS ON THE DEVOLOPMENT OF HEAVY
INDUSTRY AND A CENTRALIZED ECONOMIC PLANNING SYSTEM DEPRIVED
THE CITIES OF ORGANIZATION STRUCTURES WHICH WOULD HAVE
ENABLED THEM TO ACHIEVE SOUND URBAN DEVELOPMENT. THE
ECONOMIC REFORMS OF RECENT YEARS HAVE INITIATED SOME URBAN-
ORGANIZATION AND POLICY CHANGES. HOWEVER, THE PACE AND
MAGNITUDE OF CHANGE AMONG CITIES VARIES, AS DOES THEIR
ABILITY TO RESOLVE THEIR EXISTING URBAN UNDERDEVELOPMENT
PROBLEMS. ANALYSIS REVEALS CHINESE URBAN POLICY-MAKERS ARE
STILL REACTING MAINLY TO SOCIAL PRESSURES RESULTING FROM
ECONOMIC GROWTH. THE SERVICE NEEDS OF THE CITIES DO NOT SEEM
TO HAVE PLAYED A SIGNIFICANT ROLE IN THE DATA INSOFAR AS THE
ALLOCATION OF URBAN CAPITAL INVESTMENT FUNDS AND THE
IMPROVEMENT OR URBAN SERVICE ARE CONCERNED.

05289 KUPCHAN, C.A.
AMERICAN GLOBALISM IN THE MIDDLE EAST: THE ROOTS OF
REGIONAL SECURITY POLICY
POLITICAL SCIENCE QUARTERLY, 103(4) (WIN 89), 4.
STUDENTS OF AMERICAN INVOLVEMENT IN THIRD WORLD REGIONS
OFTEN SHARE A COMMON CRITICISM OF US SECURITY POLICY: THE
USA TENDS TO MISUNDERSTAND INDIGENOUS POLITICAL CHANGE AND
MISTAKES NATIONALISM AND NEUTRALISM FOR SOVIET IDEOLOGY AND

INFLUENCE. THIS ESSAY EVALUATES THIS ARGUMENT AND EXAMINES THE ROOTS OF US REGIONAL SECURITY POLICY IN THE MIDDLE EAST. TWO QUESTIONS ARE ADDRESSED: HAS THE USA TENDED TO REACT INAPPROPRIATELY TO POLITICAL CHANGE IN THE MIDDLE EAST BY FOCUSING ON THE SOVIET THREAT MORE THAN REGIONAL CONCERN? IF THERE IS SUCH A BIAS, WHAT IS ITS SOURCE?

05290 KURAN, T.
ON THE NOTION OF ECONOMIC JUSTICE IN CONTEMPORARY ISLAMIC THOUGHT
INTERNATIONAL JOURNAL OF MIDDLE EAST STUDIES, 21(2) (MAY 89), 171-191.
THE AUTHOR DESCRIBES AND EVALUATES THE NOTION OF ECONOMIC JUSTICE THAT APPEARS IN ISLAMIC ECONOMICS. HE BEGINS BY DEFINING THE MAIN PRINCIPLES OF JUSTICE SUBSCRIBED TO BY ISLAMIC ECONOMISTS. THEN HE PRESENTS A SYNOPSIS OF THE INJUNCTIONS THEY PROPOSE TO ENSURE THAT SOCIETY ADHERES TO THESE PRINCIPLES. BY AND LARGE, THESE INJUNCTIONS REST ON A FAULTY MODEL OF HUMAN CIVILIZATION AND LEAVE FAR MORE ROOM FOR INTERPRETATION THAN THE ISLAMIC ECONOMISTS ACKNOWLEDGE. IN MANY CONTEXTS, THEY BRING THE PRINCIPLES OF JUSTICE INTO CONFLICT, BOTH WITH ONE ANOTHER AND WITH OTHER ISLAMIC PRINCIPLES. THUS, AN ISLAMIC SOCIETY BASED ON THESE PRINCIPLES MUST INEVITABLY CONTAIN SEEDS OF DISHARMONY.

05291 KURAN, T.
SPARKS AND PRARIE FIRES: A THEORY OF UNANTICIPATED POLITICAL REVOLUTION
PUBLIC CHOICE, 61(1) (APR 89), 41-74.
A FEATURE SHARED BY CERTAIN MAJOR REVOLUTIONS IS THAT THEY WERE NOT ANTICIPATED, THE ARTICLE ATTEMPTS TO EXPLAIN THIS PHENOMENON; THE EXPLANATION HINGES ON THE OBSERVATION THAT PEOPLE WHO COME TO DISLIKE THEIR GOVERNMENT ARE APT TO HIDE THEIR DESIRE FOR CHANGE AS LONG AS THE OPPOSITION SEEMS WEAK. THE ARTICLE STUDIES CERTAIN POLITICAL REVOLUTIONS INCLUDING THE FRENCH REVOLUTION OF 1789, THE RUSSIAN REVOLUTION OF 1917, AND THE IRANIAN REVOLUTION OF 1978-79 AND CONCLUDES THAT A GOVERNMENT THAT APPEARS UNSHAKABLE MIGHT SEEMITS SUPPORT CRUMBLE FOLLOWING A SLIGHT SURGE IN THE OPPOSITION'S APPARENT SIZE, CAUSED BY EVENTS INSIGNIFICANT IN AN OF THEMSELVES.

05292 KURER, O.
JOHN STUART MILL ON GOVERNMENT INTERVENTION
HISTORY OF POLITICAL THOUGHT, X(3) (FAL 89), 457-480.
TRADITIONAL THOUGHT INDICATES THAT JOHN STUART MILL'S POSITION ON GOVERNMENT INTERVENTION WAS INCONSISTENT, A A COMBINATION OF LIBERTARIANISM AND AUTHORITARIANISM. THE AUTHOR DIFFERS. HE ESTABLISHES A SET OF ETHICAL PRINCIPLES THAT UNDERLIE AND JUSTIFY THE RULES OF GOVERNMENT INTERVENTION AND ULTIMATELY PROVIDE A THEORY OF WHEN AND HOW THE GOVERNMENT SHOULD INTERVENE. HE THEN SHOWS HOW MILL APPLIES THIS THEORY TO PRACTICAL POLITICS. MILL EMERGES AS HAVING HELD A COHERENT AND SOPHISTICATED VIEW OF GOVERNMENT INTERVENTION, AND AS HAVING CONSISTENTLY PROPOSED POLICIES DERIVED FROM THIS ETHICAL STANCE.

05293 KURODA, Y.
JAPAN, THE ARAB WORLD AND ISRAEL
AMERICAN-ARAB AFFAIRS, (28) (SPR 89), 9-21.
THE PAPER ATTEMPTS TO CHARACTERIZE THE NATURE AND SCOPE OF JAPANESE VIEWS ON THE ARAB-ISRAELI CONFLICT AND ON THE ARAB WORLD IN GENERAL. IT EXAMINES THE HISTORICAL PERSPECTIVE, JAPANESE PUBLIC OPINION ON NORTH AFRICA AND "WEST" ASIA, AND RECENT JAPANESE DIPLOMATIC AND TRADE RELATIONS WITH THE REGION. IT ALSO EXAMINES ARAB PERCEPTIONS OF JAPANESE CULTURE. THE PAPER CONCLUDES THAT, OUTSIDE OF CONCERN FOR MIDEASTERN OIL, THE JAPANESE ARE INDIFFERENT TO THE CONFLICTS IN THE REGION. UNLIKE THE WEST, JAPAN DOES NOT SHARE COMMON RELIGIOUS AND CULTURAL TIES WITH THE REGION AND MAINTAIN ONLY AN ECONOMIC INTEREST IN THE MIDEAST.

05294 KURON, J.
THE ROUND TABLE: INSTEAD OF REVOLUTION
EAST EUROPEAN REPORTER, 3(4) (SPR 89), 32-34.
THE ARTICLE ANALYZES THE NEGOTIATIONS THAT ARE TAKING PLACE IN POLAND BETWEEN THE RULING COMMUNIST PARTY AND OPPOSITION GROUPS. THE AUTHOR ACCEPTS THE NECESSITY OF NEGOTIATION, BUT CAUTIONS AGAINST OVERCONFIDENCE. HE ALSO OUTLINES IMPORTANT ITEMS THAT SHOULD BE ON THE NEGOTIATIONS OPPOSITION'S AGENDA. THESE INCLUDE: A CONCRETE RIGHT TO SELF-ORGANIZATION, MORE ACCESS TO THE MEDIA, AND, ULTIMATELY, COMPLETELY FREE ELECTIONS. THE AUTHOR CONCLUDES BY DEMONSTRATING THE IMPORTANCE OF THESE TALKS, NOT ONLY FOR POLAND, BUT FOR THE ENTIRE SOVIET BLOC.

05295 KURTH, J.R.
THE PACIFIC BASIN VERSUS THE ATLANTIC ALLIANCE: TWO PARADIGMS OF INTERNATIONAL RELATIONS
PHILADELPHIA: ANLS OF AMER ACMY OF POLITICAL AND SOC SCIENCE, (505) (SEP 89), 34-45.
FOR MANY YEARS, THE STUDY OF INTERNATIONAL ECONOMY AND INTERNATIONAL SECURITY, TWO FIELDS OF INTERNATIONAL RELATIONS, HAS BEEN BASED RESPECTIVELY UPON THE TWO CONCEPTS

OF INTERNATIONAL LIBERALISM AND EXTENDED DETERRENCE. BOTH CONCEPTS DEVELOPED OUT OF THE CONDITIONS OF THE ATLANTIC/EUROPEAN ARENA AFTER WORLD WAR II; TOGETHER THEY FORM THE ATLANTIC ALLIANCE PARADIGM. THIS PARADIGM POORLY FITS THE PACIFIC/ASIAN WORLD. IN REGARD TO THE INTERNATIONAL ECONOMY, THE EAST ASIAN STATES ARE ADHERENTS NOT OF INTERNATIONAL LIBERALISM BUT OF INTERNATIONAL MERCANTILISM. IN REGARD TO INTERNATIONAL SECURITY, THEY ARE CASES NOT OF EXTENDED DETERRENCE BUT OF FINITE DETERRENCE. TOGETHER, THESE CONCEPTS FORM THE PACIFIC BASIN PARADIGM. THE 1990S WILL BE A PERIOD OF CONFLICT BETWEEN THESE TWO INTERNATIONAL RELATIONS PARADIGMS, THE DECLINING ONE OF THE UNITED STATES AND THE AMERICAN HALF CENTURY AND THE RISING ONE OF THE EAST ASIAN POWERS AND THE FUTURE.

05296 KURTI, L.
"RED CSEPEL:" WORKING YOUTH IN A SOCIALIST FIRM
EAST EUROPEAN QUARTERLY, XXIII(4) (WIN 89), 445-468.
THE AUTHOR EXPLORES THE COMPLEX AND OFTEN MISUNDERSTOOD ISSUE OF THE INTERRELATIONSHIP OF AGE, GENDER, AND INEQUALITY. HE USES A SPECIFIC CASE STUDY BASED ON HIS OWN FIELD WORK EXPERIENCES AMONG WORKING YOUTH IN HUNGARY.

05297 KURTZ, K.T.
NO CHANGE-FOR A CHANGE
STATE LEGISLATURES, 15(1) (JAN 89), 28-30.
FOR DECADES, STATE LEGISLATURES HAD EXTRAORDINARILY HIGH RATES OF TURNOVER. BUT THE 1988 ELECTIONS PRODUCED REMARKABLY LITTLE CHANGE, AND STABILITY OF STATE LEGISLATIVE MEMBERSHIP IS NOW AT AN ALL-TIME HIGH. THAT'S GOOD FOR THE PARTY IN CONTROL, AND IT'S PRODUCING A DIFFERENT TYPE OF LEGISLATURE.

05298 KURZ, R.J.
BUSH'S FIRST STAND
HEMISPHERE, 2(1) (FAL 89), 4-5.
THE WINDS OF CHANGE HAVE BEEN BLOWING THROUGH CENTRAL AMERICA, SHAKING AND EVEN BLOWING AWAY THE OLD STRUCTURES OF REGIONAL INTERNATIONAL RELATIONS. THE PRESSURES GIVING RISE TO THESE POWERFUL WINDS EMANATE MORE FROM THE POLITICAL CURRENTS OF MOSCOW AND WASHINGTON THAN FROM THOSE OF CENTRAL AMERICA, BUT IT IS THE CENTRAL AMERICANS WHO MUST FACE THE CONSEQUENCES. IN MOSCOW, THE DEMISE OF THE BREZHNEV DOCTRINE AND THE BREAKUP OF THE SOVIET BLOC IN EASTERN EUROPE SENT AN IMPORTANT POLITICAL MESSAGE TO CUBA AND NICARAGUA. IN WASHINGTON, THE REAGAN DOCTRINE SEEMED TO YIELD TO THE BUSH ADMINISTRATION'S PRAGMATISM, ALTHOUGH THE TRADITION OF CENTRAL AMERICAN INSTABILITY AND U.S. INTERVENTION CONTINUES IN PANAMA.

05299 KURZWEILL, J.
MASS STRUGGLE, POLITICS, AND COALITION
POLITICAL AFFAIRS, LXVIII(6) (JUN 89), 33-36.
THE ARTICLE DISCUSSES ELECTORAL POLITICS FROM THE VIEWPOINT OF THE COMMUNIST PARTY, USA AND ITS PROGRAM THAT CHARACTERIZES THE ANTI-MONOPOLY STRUGGLE. IT OUTLINES THE FORCES OF ELITISM, RACISM, SEXISM, AND OPPORTUNISM THAT THE ANTI-MONOPLOY FORCES MUST CONTEND WITH. IT ESTABLISHES PARTY STRATEGY AND GOALS AND PURSUES POSSIBLE COALITIONS WITH THE PEACE MOVEMENT WOMENT'S MOVEMENT, AND OTHER RIGHTS MOVEMENTS. IT CONCLUDES THAT THE COMMUNIST PARTY IS CENTRAL TO THE STRUGGLE FOR EQUALITY AND THE EVENTUAL RESULT OF A SOCIALIST USA.

05300 KUTSENKO, G.
THE PRIDE OF OUR PROFANED COUNTRY
GLASNOST, II(2) (MAR 89), 59.
THE ISSUE OF POLITICAL PRISONERS IN THE SOVIET UNION IS STILL A BURNING ONE. IN FEBRUARY 1987, THE SUPREME SOVIET PASSED THE DECREE ON PARDONS FOR POLITICAL PRISONERS. UNFORTUNATELY, NUMEROUS POLITICAL PRISONERS REMAIN INCARCERATED BECAUSE THEY REFUSE TO SIGN AN OATH THAT THEY WILL NOT BREAK THE LAW. REALIZING THAT THE GOVERNMENT IS ATTEMPTING TO DECEIVE SOVIET SOCIETY AS WELL AS THE OUTSIDE WORLD, MANY PRISONERS REFUSE TO SUBMIT ANY STATEMENTS RATHER THAN TO PARTICIPATE IN THE CHARADE.

05301 KUTTAB, D.
A CONCESSION OF SORTS
MIDDLE EAST INTERNATIONAL, (346) (MAR 89), 11.
THE DECISION BY THE ISRAELI GOVERNMENT TO REPLACE REGULAR ARMY TROOPS WITH UNITS OF THE BORDER POLICE MARKED THE START OF A NEW POLICY AIMED AT AVOIDING FATAL CONFRONTATIONS WITH PALESTINIAN PROTESTORS. BUT THE NEW POLICY DID NOT IMMEDIATELY PRODUCE RESULTS AND PALESTINIANS DOUBTED THAT THE BORDER POLICE WOULD BE ANY SOFTER THAN THE REGULAR ARMY.

05302 KUTTAB, D.
A DELAYING GIMMICK
MIDDLE EAST INTERNATIONAL, (348) (APR 89), 5-6.
ALTHOUGH THEY DO NOT WANT TO APPEAR "REJECTIONIST", MOST PALESTINIANS FEEL THAT ISRAELI PRIME MINISTER SHAMIR'S CALL FOR ELECTION IS MERELY A TACTIC TO END THE INTIFADA AND

DELAY THE EVENTUALITY OF REAL SUBSTANTIVE TALKS WITH THE PLO.
PALESTINIAN LEADERS HAVE A DIFFICULT DECISION TO MAKE WITH
REGARDS TO SHAMIR'S ELECTION PLAN: A BOYCOTT WOULD LET
ISRAEL OF THE HOOK AND JUSTIFY CONTINUED REPRESSION OF THE
INTIFADA, BUT AN AGREEMENT TO PARTICIPATE WOULD ACHIEVE
LIMITED POLITICAL GAINS AT BEST.

05303 KUTTAB, D.
       A WAY OF BY-PASSING ELECTIONS
       MIDDLE EAST INTERNATIONAL, 355 (JUL 89), 8-9.
       IT IS UNCLEAR WHETHER PALESTINIANS WOULD WANT TO DO
ANYTHING TO SAVE SHAMIR. IT IS POSSIBLE THAT BY HELPING HIM
SURVIVE PALESTINIANS CAN MAKE CERTAIN SHORT-TERM GAINS. ON
THE OTHER HAND, BY DENYING HIM SUCH MEETINGS PALESTINIANS
WOULD CONTRIBUTE TO THE FALL OF THE COALITION GOVERNMENT.
THIS WOULD MEAN ELECTIONS SOMEWHERE DOWN THE LINE AND THE
POSSIBILITY OF AN ALLLIKUD GOVERNMENT. BUT IF THE COALITION
GOVERNMENT FELL, PALESTINIANS WOULD HAVE TO WAIT EVEN LONGER
BEFORE THE POSSIBILITY OF A GENUINE PEACE PROCESS COULD BEGIN.
THUS IF SHAMIR DECIDED TO INVITE PALESTINIANS TO MEET HIM,
IT WOULD NOT BE EASY FOR THEM TO SAY NO.

05304 KUTTAB, D.
       BEIT SAHUR DEFIES ISRAEL
       MIDDLE EAST INTERNATIONAL, (360) (OCT 89), 9-10.
       THE BATTLE OF WILLS BETWEEN ISRAEL AND THE RESIDENTS OF
THE PALESTINE TOWN OF BEIT SAHUR HAS GONE SINCE THE FIRST
CALL BY THE INTIFADA LEADERSHIP TO STOP PAYING TAXES.
UNLIKE OTHER TOWNS WHO WERE FORCED INTO SUBMISSION, BEIT
SAHUR HAS MAINTAINED A UNITED REFUSAL TO PAY VALUE-ADDED-
TAXES IMPOSED BY THE ISRAELIS. ISRAELI ATTEMPTS TO SUBDUE
THE TOWN THROUGH THE USE OF CURFEWS, HARASSMENT, AND
WIDESPREAD CONFISCATION OF PERSONAL GOODS HAVE LARGELY
FAILED.

05305 KUTTAB, D.
       BEIT SAHUR HOLDS OUT
       MIDDLE EAST INTERNATIONAL, (361) (OCT 89), 10-11.
       THE TAX REVOLT AT BEIT SAHUR CONTINUES. AS INTERNATIONAL
ATTENTION INCREASES, SO DO THE ISRAELI ATTEMPTS TO BREAK THE
TOWN'S RESOLVE BY ARRESTS, NIGHT CURFEWS, AND THE CONTINUED
CONFISCATION OF HOUSEHOLD GOODS AND MACHINERY. ATTEMPTED
DIPLOMATIC SOLUTIONS TO THE STALEMATE HAVE YIELDED NO FRUIT.

05306 KUTTAB, D.
       CURFEWS AND KILLINGS MARK THE ANNIVERSARY
       MIDDLE EAST INTERNATIONAL, (365) (DEC 89), 3-4.
       ISRAEL SOUGHT TO STOP LARGE PUBLIC DEMONSTRATIONS ON THE
SECOND ANNIVERSARY OF THE INTIFADA BY ENFORCING PROLONGED
CURFEWS. HOWEVER, SOME AREAS WERE NOT PUT UNDER CURFEW, AND
CLASHES BETWEEN DEMONSTRATORS AND ISRAELI'S RESULTED IN TEN
PALESTINIAN DEATHS OVER FOUR DAYS. AS NEWS OF THE KILLINGS
SPREAD, FURTHER DEMONSTRATIONS TOOK PLACE, RESULTING IN
FURTHER VIOLENCE AND DEATH.

05307 KUTTAB, D.
       HUSSEINI DEBATES IN PRISON
       MIDDLE EAST INTERNATIONAL, (343) (FEB 89), 7-8.
       ISRAELI DEFENCE MINISTER YITZHAK RABIN UNVEILED HIS
PROPOSAL FOR ENDING THE INTIFADA AFTER HE RECEIVED CABINET
APPROVAL FOR HARDENING HIS IRON-FIST POLICY. PALESTINIAN
LEADER FAISAL HUSSEINI WAS PRESENTED WITH A BLUEPRINT OF
RABIN'S PLAN BEFORE IT WAS PUBLICLY ANNOUNCED. HUSSEINI
EXPRESSED OPPOSITION TO MANY SPECIFIC POINTS BUT ADMITTED
THAT IT CONTAINED SOME POSITIVE ELEMENTS.

05308 KUTTAB, D.
       ID CARDS AND "TOURISTS"
       MIDDLE EAST INTERNATIONAL, (357) (AUG 89), 10-11.
       THE HOSTAGE CRISIS AND THE ESCALATION OF THE LEBANESE
CIVIL WAR HAS PROVIDED COVER FOR INCREASED ISRAELI
REPRESSION IN THE OCCUPIED TERRITORIES IN HOPES OF CRUSHING
THE INTIFADA. ECONOMIC PRESSURES, MOVEMENT CONTROLS, AND
FREQUENT CLASHES WITH PALESTINIANS HAVE ALL BEEN UTILIZED IN
HOPES OF INSTILLING THE FEAR THAT PALESTINIANS ONCE HAD. TWO
KEY POINTS OF CONFLICT ARE THE US OF MAGNETIC IDENTIFICATION
CARDS FOR WORKERS IN THE GAZA STRIP AND ALLEGATIONS THAT
ISRAELI UNDERCOVER TEAMS, DISGUISED AS TOURISTS, ARE
ASSASSINATING PALESTINIAN ACTIVISTS.

05309 KUTTAB, D.
       OCCUPIED PALESTINE: ANGER AND FRUSTRATION
       MIDDLE EAST INTERNATIONAL, (347) (MAR 89), 9-10.
       PALESTINIANS BELIEVE THAT THE USA AND ISRAEL ARE
DRAGGING THEIR FEET IN FINDING A POLITICAL SOLUTION TO THEIR
PROBLEMS. MOREOVER, THE PALESTINIANS HAVE NOT EXPERIENCED
ANY RELAXATION OF ISRAEL'S "IRON FIST" POLICIES. THIS IS
LEADING TO UNEASE IN THE OCCUPIED TERRITORIES, WHERE THE
INTIFADA IS BECOMING MORE VIOLENT AND THERE ARE CALLS FOR
ARMED STRUGGLE.

05310 KUTTAB, D.
       OCCUPIED PALESTINE: BEIT SAHUR BATTLES ON; BLACK PANTHERS
       IN NABLUS; UNRWA UNDER ATTACK

MIDDLE EAST INTERNATIONAL, (362) (NOV 89), 10-11.
       THE ARTICLE BRIEFLY OUTLINES THREE EVENTS IN THE
OCCUPIED TERRITORIES. THE TAX REVOLT IN BEIT SAHUR CONTINUES
DESPITE INCREASED ISRAELI PROPAGANDA AND HARASSMENT. ISRAEL
IS RECEIVING INCREASED CRITICISM FROM CHRISTIAN CHURCHES FOR
ITS REPRESSION OF THE REVOLT. IN NABLUS, PALESTINIAN
AUTHORITIES ARE ATTEMPTING TO STOP THE "BLACK PANTHERS," A
GROUP WHICH SPECIALIZES IN KILLING COLLABORATORS. NINETEEN
PALESTINIANS HAVE BEEN KILLED BY THE GROUP THUS FAR. ISRAEL
IS CONTINUING TO HAMPER THE EFFORTS OF THE UNRWA, A
PALESTINIAN RELIEF ORGANIZATION. UNRWA ATTEMPTS TO PROVIDE
FOR BOTH SHORT AND LONG-TERM NEEDS OF THE PALESTINIAN
COMMUNITY HAVE BEEN SLOWED BY RECENT ISRAELI RAIDS.

05311 KUTTAB, D.
       OCCUPIED PALESTINE: BLOODY END TO RAMADAN
       MIDDLE EAST INTERNATIONAL, (350) (MAY 89), 5-6.
       THE MONTH OF RAMADAN 1989 SAW AN INTENSIVE LEVEL OF
CONFRONTATIONS BETWEEN THE ISRAELI ARMY AND PALESTINIAN
DEMONSTRATORS, WITH A RECORD NUMBER OF PALESTINIANS KILLED
AND THE PROSPECTS FOR A POLITICAL BREAKTHROUGH GROWING
INCREASINGLY DIM. PALESTINIAN LEADERS ISSUED A STATEMENT
REJECTING THE IDEA OF ELECTIONS BEFORE AN ISRAELI TROOP
WITHDRAWAL AND REAFFIRMING UNQUALIFIED SUPPORT FOR THE PLO.

05312 KUTTAB, D.
       OCCUPIED PALESTINE: DEPORTATIONS AND TRICKS
       MIDDLE EAST INTERNATIONAL, (354) (JUL 89), 11.
       THE ISRAELI USE OF DEPORTATIONS TO DEAL WITH THE
PALESTINIAN INTIFIDA (UPRISING) CAME AS A SURPRISE TO SOME,
ESPECIALLY AFTER DEFENCE MINISTER RABIN HAD DECLARED THAT
DEPORTATIONS WERE INNEFECTIVE. ISRAELI COLLABORATORS, IN AN
ATTEMPT TO FOSTER THE ILLUSION OF INTERNAL CONFLICT AMONG
PALESTINIANS HAVE SET SEVERAL CARS OF PALESTINIAN
NATIONALIST LEADERS ABLAZE.

05313 KUTTAB, D.
       OCCUPIED PALESTINE: ESCALATING CASUALTIES
       MIDDLE EAST INTERNATIONAL, (342) (JAN 89), 11-12.
       THE INTIFADA INTENSIFIED IN EARLY 1989, AS DID ISRAELI
DETERMINATION TO CRUSH IT BY FORCE. AT THE SAME TIME, MORE
AND MORE PALESTINIAN LEADERS CAME OUT PUBLICLY IN SUPPORT OF
WEST BANK MUNICIPAL ELECTIONS.

05314 KUTTAB, D.
       OCCUPIED PALESTINE: ESCALATION
       MIDDLE EAST INTERNATIONAL, (349) (APR 89), 6-8.
       IN APRIL 1989, THERE WAS A MARKED ESCALATION IN THE
INTIFADA AS THE PALESTINIANS RETALIATED AGAINST THE LATEST
ROUND OF ISRAELI REPRESSION AND KILLINGS.

05315 KUTTAB, D.
       OCCUPIED PALESTINE: ISRAELISS CAUGHT NAPPING
       MIDDLE EAST INTERNATIONAL, (348) (APR 89), 10.
       THE ARTICLE OUTLINES A RECENT UPRISING AT THE AL-AQSA
MOSQUE WHERE THOUSANDS OF DEMONSTRATORS ATTACED ISRAELI
SOLDIERS AND POLICE AND HURLED STONES AT THE WAILING WALL.
ELEVEN ISRAELIS AND PALESTINIANS WERE HURT AND A
ULTRANATIONALIST ISRAELI GROUP CLAIMED RESPONSIBILITY FOR A
RETALITORY ATTACK IN WHICH ONE ARAB WAS KILLED AND THREE
OTHERS WERE WOUNDED.

05316 KUTTAB, D.
       OCCUPIED PALESTINE: THE MUNICIPAL ELECTION ISSUE
       MIDDLE EAST INTERNATIONAL, (341) (JAN 89), 6-7.
       ISRAELI LEADERS HAVE SUGGESTED THE POSSIBILITY OF
ELECTIONS IN THE OCCUPIED TERRITORIES, BUT THE PROPOSAL HAS
EVOKED ANGRY REACTION FROM THE PALESTINIANS, WHO DO NOT WANT
TO PROVIDE AN ALTERNATIVE LEADERSHIP AND WEAKEN PRESSURE ON
ISRAEL TO TALK DIRECTLY TO THE PLO.

05317 KUTTAB, D.
       OCCUPIED PALESTINE: WIELDING A HEAVIER STICK
       MIDDLE EAST INTERNATIONAL, (351) (MAY 89), 8.
       EVEN AS THE ISRAELI GOVERNMENT WAS DRAFTING A PEACE
PROPOSAL, THE VIOLENCE AND REPRESSION IN THE OCCUPIED
TERRITORIES INCREASED. APPARENTLY THE ISRAELIS WERE ENGAGING
IN A CLASSIC CARROT AND STICK OPERATION BY WIELDING A
HEAVIER STICK WHILE DANGLING THE CARROT OF ELECTIONS.

05318 KUTTAB, D.
       PALESTINIANS RESTRAINED
       MIDDLE EAST INTERNATIONAL, (364) (DEC 89), 8-10.
       THE 15TH OF NOVEMBER MARKED THE FIRST ANNIVERSARY OF THE
DECLARATION OF PALESTINIAN INDEPENDENCE. PALESTINIANS
CELEBRATED THIS EVENT IN A GENERALLY NON-VIOLENT MANNER.
HOWEVER, UNDERLYING THE JOYFUL CELEBRATION WAS THE GROWING
SUSPICION THAT NON-VIOLENCE AND NEGOTIATION WERE NOT
CHANGING CONDITIONS. SOME PALESTINIAN SPLINTER GROUPS ARE
RESORTING TO VIOLENCE DESPITE THEIR LEADERS CALLS FOR PEACE.
THE TENSION IS INCREASED BY THE FACT THAT THOUSANDS OF
PALESTINIANS ARE LANGUISHING IN OVERCROWDED ISRAELI JAILS.

05319 KUTTAB, D.
SHAMIR'S "SECRET" TALKS
MIDDLE EAST INTERNATIONAL, 356 (AUG 89), 8.
SHAMIR HAS ABLE TO USE THE NEWS OF THE MEETINGS WITH
PALESTINIANS TO IMPROVE THE PROSPECTS OF HIS OWN PEACE PLAN,
IN SERIOUS TROUBLE AT HOME AND ABROAD DUE TO THE CONSTRAINTS
PLACED ON IT BY THE LIKUD CENTRAL COMMITTEE. BY NOT
REVEALING WHICH PALESTINIANS HE HAD MET, SHAMIR HAS ABLE TO
DEFUSE NEGATIVE REACTION FROM LIKUD, WHICH WOULD BE ANGERED
IF IT WAS KNOWN THAT HE MET PRO-PLO PALESTINIANS.
PALESTINIANS WANTED THE MEETINGS TO BE PUBLICISED FOR
EXACTLY THE SAME REASON THAT THE ISRAELIS WANTED THEM KEPT
SECRET. THEY WANTED TO DISPROVE THE ALLEGATIONS OF
PALESTINIAN INTIMIDATION. THEY WANTED TO SHOW THAT THE PLO
KNOWS ABOUT THE MEETINGS AND THEY WANTED TO CONFIRM THE
CLAIMS THAT ISRAEL WAS CONDUCTING INDIRECT NEGOTIATIONS WITH
THE PLO.

05320 KUTTAB, D.
SPEAKING PLAINLY
MIDDLE EAST INTERNATIONAL, (351) (MAY 89), 6.
THE MEETING OF PALESTINIANS FROM THE OCCUPIED
TERRITORIES AND US REPRESENTATIVES HAS UNSATISFACTORY TO
BOTH SIDES. THE AMERICANS MADE LITTLE PROGRESS IN PUSHING
THE ACCEPTANCE OF SHAMIR'S PEACE PLAN, AND THE PALESTINIANS
INSISTED ON DIRECT NEGOTIATIONS WITH PLO REPRESENATIVES IN
TUNIS. ALTHOUGH BOTH SIDES SPOKE QUITE FRANKLY, LITTLE
PROGRESS WAS MADE.

05321 KUTTAB, D.
THE INTIFADA
MIDDLE EAST INTERNATIONAL, (358) (SEP 89), 5-6.
AS PALESTINIANS CONSIDERED THEIR OPTIONS WITH REGARDS TO
CONTINUING THE INTIFADA, ISRAEL MADE THE DECISION EASIER BY
GIVING THE MOVEMENT ADDITIONAL IMPETUS THROUGH ITS REDOUBLED
EFFORTS TO REPRESS THE MOVEMENT. ATTEMPTS TO ISSUE MAGNETIC
SECURITY CARDS TO WORKERS IN GAZA RESULTED IN HUGE
DEMONSTRATIONS. REPRESSION AND BRUTALITY CONTINUED
THROUGHOUT THE OCCUPIED TERRITORIES AS THE DEATH COUNT
CLIMBED TO 655.

05322 KUTTAB, D.
THE INTIFADA'S SECOND YEAR
MIDDLE EAST INTERNATIONAL, (365) (DEC 89), 15-16.
THE SECOND YEAR OF THE INTIFADA HAS SOMEWHAT OF AN
ANTICLIMAX. AFTER THE MAJOR ADVANCES IN THE FIRST YEAR,
PROGRESS HAS STALLED AND THREATENS TO STAGNATE COMPLETELY IN
A MAZE OF BUREAUCRATIC AND DIPLOMATIC COMPLEXITY. MEANWHILE,
THE LEVEL OF ISRAELI REPRESSION HAS INCREASED, AND
FACTIONALISM HAS ONCE AGAIN RESURFACED IN PALESTINE.
ALTHOUGH THE FUTURE OF THE MOVEMENT SEEMS BLEAK: THE
PALESTINIAN PEOPLE ARE UNABLE OR UNWILLING TO ESCALATE THE
MOVEMENT TO FULL SCALE CIVIL DISOBEDIENCE OR VIOLENCE, THE
RESOLVE OF THE PALESTINIANS SEEMS UNCHANGED.

05323 KUTTAB, D.
THE REASONS BEHIND SHAMIR'S ELECTION PLAN
MIDDLE EAST INTERNATIONAL, (348) (APR 89), 15.
THE ARTICLE ARGUES THAT THE ELECTION PLAN OF ISRAELI
PRIME MINISTER YITZHAK SHAMIR IS MERELY A DELAYING TACTIC
DESIGNED TO FURTHER POSTPONE ANY SORT OF DIALOGUE OR
NEGOTIATIONS BETWEEN ISRAEL AND THE PLO. CONTRARY TO POPULAR
BELIEF, ISRAEL'S REFUSAL TO SPEAK TO THE PLO HAS NOTHING TO
DO WITH THE ORGANIZATION'S CHARTER OR ITS STAND ON ISRAEL OR
TERRORISM. THE PAPER ARGUES THAT ISRAEL'S REFUSAL TO
ACKNOWLEDGE OR ACCEPT PALESTINIAN NATIONALISM IS THE
UNDERLYING CAUSE FOR ISRAEL'S REFUSAL TO NEGOTIATE DESPITE
INTERNATIONAL AND INTERNAL PRESSURE.

05324 KUTTAB, D.
THE RELIEF OF BEIT SAHUR
MIDDLE EAST INTERNATIONAL, (363) (NOV 89), 10-11.
THE ANNIVERSARY OF THE DECLARATION OF PALESTINIAN
INDEPENDENCE DEMONSTRATES HOW FAR ISRAEL AND PALESTINE ARE
FROM REACHING A SOLUTION TO THE THORNY OCCUPIED TERRITORIES
PROBLEM. THE ISRAELI "SIEGE" OF BEIT SAHUR HAS LIFTED AFTER
ISRAEL DECLARED THAT THE ARMY HAD CONFISCATED ENOUGH TO
COVER ALL TAXES OWED. HOWEVER, THE TOWN WAS DECLARED A
CLOSED MILITARY AREA FOUR DAYS LATER IN AN ATTEMPT TO BLOCK
ANY FURTHER DEMONSTRATION. ALL SCHOOLS IN THE OCCUPIED
TERRITORIES WERE PREMATURELY CLOSED IN ORDER TO AVOID ANY
PUBLIC CELEBRATION ON THE NOVEMBER 15 ANNIVERSARY OF THE
DECLARATION OF PALESTINIAN INDEPENDENCE.

05325 KUTTAB, D.
THE SUFFERING IN NABLUS
MIDDLE EAST INTERNATIONAL, (346) (MAR 89), 10-11.
MORE THAN 130,000 RESIDENTS OF NABLUS WERE CONFINED TO
THEIR HOMES FOR 11 DAYS DUE TO A TIGHT CURFEW PLACED ON THE
CITY FEBRUARY 24, 1989. THE CURFEW WAS ONE OF MANY
PUNISHMENTS IMPOSED ON THE RESIDENTS AFTER AN ISRAELI
SOLDIER WAS KILLED WHEN A CONCRETE SLAB WAS PUSHED ONTO HIM
FROM A ROOFTOP.

05326 KUTTNER, R.
SLOUCHING TOWARD PLURALISM
DISSENT, (SPR 89), 225-234.
THE WORLD SYSTEM IS EVOLVING FROM A BILATERAL ONE, WHERE
THE CAPITALIST HALF IS DOMINATED BOTH POLITICALLY AND
ECONOMICALLY BY THE UNITED STATES, INTO A MORE MULTILATERAL
ONE REMINISCENT OF THE NINETEENTH-CENTURY EUROPEAN CONCERT.
IDEOLOGY, DOMESTIC POLITICS, INTERNATIONAL ECONOMICS, AND
GLOBAL GEOPOLITICS NOW INTERACT IN COMPLEX AND POORLY
UNDERSTOOD WAYS. FOR THE FUTURE, A MORE PLURALIST WORLD
OFFERS BOTH RISKS AND GAINS. FOR NOW, THE ANOMALOUS
EMERGENCE OF JAPAN AND GERMANY AS ECONOMIC GIANTS WHILE
REMAINING GEOPOLITICAL PYGMIES AND THE CONVERSE POSITION OF
THE UNITED STATES AS HEGEMON-IN-DECLINE HAVE CREATED A KIND
OF GRIDLOCK.

05327 KUZMANIC, T.
POURING OIL ON THE FLAMES: INTERVIEW WITH AN ALBANIAN IN
KOSOVO
EAST EUROPEAN REPORTER, 4(1) (WIN 89), 90-91.
THE ARTICLE IS AN INTERVIEW WITH A 75-YEAR OLD ALBANIAN
LIVING IN THE YUGOSLAVIAN PROVINCE OF KOSOVO. HE OUTLINES
THE VARIOUS ETHNIC TENSIONS THAT ALBANIANS HAVE EXPERIENCED
OVER THE PAST SEVEN DECADES. ONE OF THE FEW CONSTANTS OVER
THAT PERIOD OF TIME IS THE PERSECUTION BY NEIGHBORING SERBS.
PERSECUTION AND OPPESSION HAS REACHED SUCH A LEVEL AS TO
MAKE CIVIL WAR ARE DISTINCT POSSIBILITY. THE INTERVIEWEE
CONCLUDES THAT THE ALABANIANS IN KOSOVO ARE RAPIDLY REACHING
THE DANGEROUS POINT OF HOPELESSNESS.

05328 KUZNETSOVA, G.
USSR-BRAZIL: PROSPECTS OF MUTUAL TRADE DEVELOPMENT
FOREIGN TRADE, 1 (1988), 12-15.
THIS ARTICLE EXAMINES THE STRONG TRADE RELATIONS BETWEEN
BRAZIL AND THE USSR. IT CONCLUDES THAT TRADITIONAL FORMS OF
COMMERCE DO NOT MEET THE TIMES AND REPORTS ON ATTEMPTS TO
REMEDY THIS. THE NEW INTERGOVERNMENTAL AGREEMENT IS
DISCUSSED AT LENGTH.

05329 KWABIA, K.
ALLOCATION AND DISTRIBUTION OF HEALTH RESOURCES IN WEST
AFRICA: POST WORLD WAR II EXPERIENCE
DISSERTATION ABSTRACTS INTERNATIONAL, 50(1) (JUL 89),
256-A.
BEFORE WORLD WAR II, HEALTH POLICIES IN WEST AFRICA
FAVORED HEALTH PROMOTION AND DISEASE PREVENTION. AFTER THE
WAR, HEALTH CARE BECAME MORE EXPENSIVE AND WAS DOMINATED BY
PROFESSIONAL MEDICAL EMPLOYEES IN THE PUBLIC SECTOR. WITH
THE EXPANDING SOCIAL RESPONSIBILITIES OF GOVERNMENT AND THE
HIGH COST OF MEDICAL CARE, THE LIMITED AVAILABLE RESOURCES
HAVE BEEN USED TO IMPROVE MEDICAL SERVICES FOR THE SOCIALLY
POWERFUL IN URBAN AREAS. THE ABSENCE OF ADEQUATE BASIC
HEALTH SERVICES FOR THE POOR AND FOR RURAL AREAS ILLUSTRATES
THE INEQUALITIES IN THE ALLOCATION AND DISTRIBUTION OF
HEALTH RESOURCES AND THE DECLINING IMPORTANCE OF SUCH
SERVICES AS COMMUNICABLE DISEASE PREVENTION, MATERNAL AND
CHILD CARE, AND HEALTH EDUCATION.

05330 KWAN-CHI, O.
THE REPUBLIC OF KOREA: ASIA'S NEW POWERHOUSE
NATO'S SIXTEEN NATIONS, 34(2) (APR 89), 41-45.
AFTER A DEVASTING WAR WHICH RUINED THE ECONOMY AND
CAUSED UNTOLD SUFFERING, THE REPUBLIC OF KOREA IS NOW
SURGING AHEAD. BUT THE ADJUSTMENT FROM A SIMPLE AGRARIAN
ECONOMY TO A MODERN INDUSTRIALISED STATE IS NOT BY ANY MEANS
PAINLESS. IN ADDITION, THE LONG CONFRONTATION WITH THE NORTH
REMAINS A PERMANENT CAUSE OF WORRY AND A DRAIN ON RESOURCES.
NEVERTHELESS, THE INDICATORS ARE FAVOURABLE AND THE
PROSPECTS FOR CONTINUED ECONOMIC, POLITICAL AND SOCIAL
DEVELOPMENT ARE GOOD.

05331 KWAN, Y.Y.
SOUTH PACIFIC AGENDA: A FRAMEWORK FOR ASEAN PARTICIPATION
AVAILABLE FROM NTIS, NO. AD-A208 221/2/GAR, MAR 89, 44.
RECENT EVENTS IN THE SOUTH PACIFIC HAVE SUGGESTED THAT
THIS QUIET PART OF THE WORLD HAS NOW BECOME AN ARENA FOR BIG
POWER COMPETITION AND INFLUENCE. THIS STUDY SEEKS TO REVIEW
THE CHANGES AND DEVELOPMENTS IN THE REGION AND TO EXAMINE
THE SOURCES OF FRICTION AND POTENTIAL AREAS OF INSTABILITY.
IT ALSO ATTEMPTS TO IDENTIFY THE INTERESTS OF BOTH THE BIG
POWERS, IN PARTICULAR THE SOVIET UNION AND THE US, AS WELL
AS THOSE OF THE SMALLER STATES IN THE REGION. THE MAIN
PURPOSE OF THIS STUDY IS TO PROPOSE THE CONTRIBUTION THAT
THE ASEAN, ESPECIALLY SINGAPORE, CAN MAKE TO ENSURE THAT THE
SOUTH PACIFIC WILL REMAIN A POLITICALLY STABLE AND
ECONOMICALLY VIABLE REGION, FULLY INTEGRATED INTO THE
AFFAIRS OF THE ASIA-PACIFIC REGION.

05332 KWANG, H.R.
THE CHARACTERISTICS OF THE PRAETORIAN MILITARY IN SOUTH
KOREA, 1961-1979
ASIAN PROFILE, 17(4) (AUG 89), 311-326.
THE PRAETORIAN ARMY AND MILITARY REGIME IN SOUTH KOREA
HAS BEEN A CENTRAL FACTOR IN KOREAN POLITICS SINCE 1961. THE

SECOND REPUBLIC WAS OVERTHROWN BY A MILITARY COUP LED BY
GENERAL PARK, WHO CREATED THE THIRD REPUBLIC. THE THIRD
REPUBLIC SUCCUMBED TO A "COUP IN OFFICE" ENGINEERED BY THE
INCUMBENT PRESIDENT, WHO INAUGURATED THE AUTHORITARIAN
YUSHIN SYSTEM OF THE FOURTH REPUBLIC. THE FIFTH REPUBLIC
EMERGED AS A RESULT OF AN INITIAL COUP IN 1979 LED BY A
MILITARY GROUP AND A SECOND COUP CARRIED OUT BY SUPPORTERS
OF GENERAL CHUN DOO-HWAN IN 1980.

05333 KWON, M.
    CAPITALIST GROWTH AND POLITICAL CHANGE IN SOUTH KOREA
    DISSERTATION ABSTRACTS INTERNATIONAL, 49(11) (MAY 89),
    3491-A.
    IMPORTANT FACTORS THAT HAVE LED TO RAPID CHANGE AND
    GROWTH IN SOUTH KOREA INCLUDE JAPANESE COLONIALISM, THE
    DEFEAT OF A SOCIAL REVOLUTION IN THE LATE 1940'S, THE
    FUNDAMENTAL CAPITALIST TRANSITION OF THE EARLY 1950'S, THE
    ESTABLISHMENT OF STATE CAPITALISM, AND THE RISE OF STATE
    MONOPOLY CAPITALISM.

05334 KY, D.K.; STROGANOV, A.
    WHAT IS IN STORE FOR MONGOLIA'S TWO MILLIONTH CITIZEN?
    WORLD MARXIST REVIEW, 32(8) (AUG 89), 25-29.
    THIS ARTICLE IS A REPORT OF A VISIT TO MONGOLIA,
    ORGANIZED IN RESPONSE TO AN INVITATION FROM THE SOCIALIST
    PARTY OF THAT COUNTRY. IT REPORTS ON A NEW SOCIETY WHICH IS
    BEING BUILT WITHOUT GOING THROUGH THE CAPITALIST STAGE OF
    DEVELOPMENT. AFTER THE 1921 REVOLUTION THE COUNTRY HAD NO
    INDUSTRY AND NO DEVELOPED AGRICULTURE. IT REPORTS ON
    IMPROVEMENTS SINCE THEN, AS WELL AS SOCIAL CHANGE. IT
    EXPLORES THE PEASANT'S LOT IN THE SPACE AGE, AND CHANGES
    AMONG THE WORKERS, IT CONCLUDES THAT MONGOLIAN CITIZENS WILL
    BENEFIT FROM THESE CHANGES.

05335 KYVIG, D.E.
    THE RAOD NOT TAKEN: FDR, THE SUPREME COURT, AND
    CONSTITUTIONAL AMENDMENT
    POLITICAL SCIENCE QUARTERLY, 104(3) (FAL 89), 463-482.
    DAVID E. KYVIG IDENTIFIES A TURNING POINT IN POLITICAL
    ATTITUDES TOWARD U.S. CONSTITUTIONAL AMENDMENTS, ENDING
    THREE DECADES OF SIGNIFICANT AMENDING ACTIVITY. HE DISCUSSES
    FDR'S EXPLORATION AND REJECTION OF PROPOSING AN AMENDMENT
    DURING HIS BATTLE WITH THE SUPREME COURT IN 1937.

05336 LACEFIELD, P.
    THE GENERAL DON'T REPENT
    COMMONWEAL, CXVI(19) (NOV 89), 583-584.
    ARGENTINE PRESIDENT MENEM HAS PARDONED NEARLY 280
    PERSONS CONVICTED OR ACCUSED IN CONNECTION WITH THE "DIRTY
    WAR" AND SUBSEQUENT MILITARY UPRISINGS AGAINST THE ALFONSIN
    GOVERNMENT. THE MOVE CONFIRMS THE CONTINUED POWER OF
    MILITARY CIRCLES OVER THE CIVILIAN GOVERNMENT AND PERONIST
    COMPLICITY IN THE EXERCISE OF THAT POWER.

05337 LACEFIELD, P.
    THE WAR CONTINUES
    COMMONWEAL, CXVI(7) (APR 89), 197-199.
    THE RIGHTIST ARENA PARTY WON THE 1988 ELECTIONS IN EL
    SALVADOR, BUT THE US EMBASSY REMAINS THE LEADING POWER,
    FOLLOWED BY THE MILITARY, AND ONLY THEN BY THE CIVILIAN
    GOVERNMENT. SINCE 1980, POWER HAS BEEN VESTED, WITH US
    BLESSING, IN THE CHRISTIAN DEMOCRATS. IN THE VIEW OF THE
    SALVADORAN RIGHT, THIS HAS AMOUNTED TO WASHINGTON-DIRECTED
    SOCIALISM AND REVOLUTION ON THE INSTALLMENT PLAN.

05338 LACHMANN, R.
    ELITE CONFLICT AND STATE FORMATION IN 16TH- AND 17TH-
    CENTURY ENGLAND AND FRANCE
    AMERICAN SOCIOLOGICAL REVIEW, 54(2) (APR 89), 141-162.
    CLASS CONFLICT, RELATIVE AUTONOMY, AND STATE-CENTERED
    THEORIES OF ABSOLUTISM ARE CRITIQUED FOR THEIR INABILITY TO
    ISOLATE CAUSAL FACTORS THAT COULD EXPLAIN THE DIFFERING
    PATTERNS OF STATE FORMATION IN ENGLAND AND FRANCE,
    CULMINATING IN THE CROWN'S DEFEAT IN THE ENGLISH CIVIL WAR
    OF 1640-46 AND THE FRENCH MONARCH'S VICTORY OVER
    ARISTOCRATIC REBELS IN THE FRONDES OF 1648-53. THIS ARTICLE
    ARGUES THAT CONFLICTS AMONG THE THREE PRINCIPAL ELITES--THE
    CLERGY, MONARCHS AND THEIR OFFICIALS, AND LAY LANDLORDS--ARE
    THE CRITICAL DYNAMIC THAT EXPLAINS THE CONTRASTING
    DEVELOPMENTS OF ABSOLUTISM IN THE TWO COUNTRIES. ENGLISH
    MONARCHS WON A HORIZONTAL NATIONAL-LEVEL HEGEMONY OVER RIVAL
    ELITES AT THE COST OF ACCESS TO RESOURCES AT THE POINT OF
    PRODUCTION, LEAVING THEM VULNERABLE TO A CLASS-BASED
    REBELLION BY LANDOWNERS. IN FRANCE, ELITES WERE AMALGAMATED
    INTO AN ABSOLUTIST STATE BY THEIR CONFLICTS AND THEREBY LOST
    THEIR SEPARATE IDENTITIES AS FEUDAL EXPLOITERS AS WELL AS
    THE OPPORTUNITY TO TRANSFORM AGRARIAN SOCIAL RELATIONS TO
    THEIR SOLE ADVANTAGE.

05339 LADD, E.C.
    THE 1988 ELECTIONS: CONTINUATION OF THE POST-NEW DEAL
    SYSTEM
    POLITICAL SCIENCE QUARTERLY, 104(1) (SPR 89), 1-18.
    FROM THE BEGINNING, THE 1988 PRESIDENTIAL CONTEST HAS

WAGED AGAINST A BACKDROP THAT FAVORED THE REPUBLICANS. ONE
ELEMENT OF THIS SETTING INVOLVED THE STATUS OF THE TWO-TERM
INCUMBENT PRESIDENT, RONALD REAGAN, WHO WAS MORE POPULAR IN
THE LAST MONTHS OF HIS PRESIDENCY THAN WHEN HE TOOK OFFICE.
A SECOND FACET OF THE SETTING WAS THE PUBLIC'S RESPONSE TO
CURRENT CONDITIONS IN THE ECONOMY, FOREIGN AFFAIRS, AND THE
LIKE.

05340 LADRECH, R.
    SOCIAL MOVEMENTS AND PARTY SYSTEMS: THE FRENCH SOCIALIST
    PARTY AND NEW SOCIAL MOVEMENTS
    WEST EUROPEAN POLITICS, 12(3) (JUL 89), 266-279.
    THIS ARTICLE EXAMINES THE APPARENT DIFFICULTY OF VARIOUS
    FRENCH 'NEW SOCIAL MOVEMENTS' OF THE 1970S AND 1980S TO
    COALESCE IN THE FORM OF A 'GREEN' OR 'NEW POLITICS' PARTY.
    IN ADDITION TO THE NATURE OF THE FRENCH ELECTORAL SYSTEM AND
    DOMINANT POLICY-MAKING APPARATUS, THIS ARTICLE FOCUSES UPON
    RELATIONS BETWEEN THE SOCIALIST PARTY AND FEMINIST AND
    ECOLOGY MOVEMENTS. THE MAJOR ARGUMENT IS THAT THE SOCIALISTS,
    IN THEIR BID FOR HEGEMONY AMONG THE LEFT THROUGHOUT THE
    1970S AND 1980S, EFFECTIVELY UNDERCUT POST-MATERIAL VALUE-
    ORIENTED SUPPORT FOR A 'NEW POLITICS' PARTY.

05341 LAFANTASIE, G.W.
    THE DISPUTED LEGACY OF ROGER WILLIAMS
    CHURCH AND STATE, 42(1) (JAN 89), 8-11.
    ALTHOUGH ROGER WILLIAMS IS ADMIRED FOR THE STEADFASTNESS
    WITH WHICH HE ESPOUSED THE PRINCIPLE OF RELIGIOUS FREEDOM IN
    NEW ENGLAND, SCHOLARS HAVE BEEN QUICK TO POINT OUT THAT THE
    AMERICAN TRADITION OF TOLERATION AND SEPARATION OF CHURCH
    AND STATE, AS ENSHRINED IN THE FIRST AMENDMENT, OWES MORE TO
    THE IDEAS OF THOMAS JEFFERSON AND JAMES MADISON THAN IT DOES
    TO THE RUGGED RELIGIOUS SEPARATISM OF WILLIAMS. IN THIS
    ARTICLE, THE AUTHOR EXAMINES THE QUESTION OF WILLIAMS'
    CONTRIBUTION TO MODERN RELIGIOUS FREEDOM IN THE USA.

05342 LAFFEY, J. F.
    FRENCH FAR EASTERN POLICY IN THE 1930S
    MODERN ASIAN STUDIES, 23(1) (FEB 89), 117-149.
    THE COMPLETION IN 1986 OF THE DOCUMENTS DIPLOMATIQUES
    FRANCAIS, 1932-1939 PERMITS A REVIEW OF FRENCH FAR EASTERN
    POLICY DURING THAT TROUBLED TIME. ALTHOUGH THIS MASSIVE
    DOCUMENTARY COLLECTION DOES NOT PROVIDE A FULL PICTURE OF
    THE FORCES WHICH SHAPED FRENCH EAST ASIAN POLICY IN THE
    YEARS BEFORE THE OUTBREAK OF THE PACIFIC WAR, THE DOCUMENTS
    DO SHED LIGHT AS THE AUTHOR HERE DESCRIBES, ON WHAT PASSED
    FOR FRENCH POLICY IN EAST ASIA DURING THAT TIME.

05343 LAGROYE, J.
    CHANGE AND PERMANENCE IN POLITICAL PARTIES
    POLITICAL STUDIES, 37(3) (SEP 89), 362-375.
    INCESSANT CHANGES ALTER POLITICAL PARTIES IN THEIR
    ORGANIZATION, STRUCTURE, RECRUITMENT AND ALL OTHER
    CHARACTERISTICS. NEVERTHELESS, THEY ARE USUALLY CREDITED
    WITH STABLE FEATURES BY WHICH THEY ARE IDENTIFIED, AND WHICH
    ENABLE THEM TO BE CLASSIFIED. IF WE CONSIDER FRENCH
    POLITICAL PARTIES, IT IS POSSIBLE TO DEMONSTRATE THAT BOTH
    CHANGE AND APPARENT STABILITY ARISE FROM INTERACTION WITHIN
    EACH PARTY AS WELL AS BETWEEN THEM AND BETWEEN THE SOCIAL
    ORGANIZATIONS TO WHICH THEY ARE LINKED. THESE INTERACTIONS
    AND THEIR EFFECTS MUST BE RELATED TO GENERAL PROCESSES, SUCH
    AS SOCIAL AND CULTURAL TRANSFORMATION; THEY CANNOT BE SOLELY
    EXPLAINED BY SPECIFICALLY POLITICAL COMPETITION.

05344 LAGUERRE, J.G.
    LEADERSHIP IN THE BRITISH AND FRENCH CARIBBEAN: SOME
    COMPARISONS
    SOCIAL AND ECONOMIC STUDIES, 38(1) (MAR 89), 133-156.
    THE AUTHOR EXAMINES SOME ASPECTS OF THE HISTORICAL AND
    CONTEMPORARY LEADERSHIP OF THE FRENCH AND BRITISH CARIBBEAN.
    MORE SPECIFICALLY, HE IS CONCERNED WITH THE INTELLIGENTSIA,
    WITH THE FORCES THAT SHAPED THEM, AND WITH THE ISSUES THAT
    PROPELLED THEM. HE CONCLUDES THAT, NOTWITHSTANDING THE
    PROCLAIMED DIFFERENCES IN THE FRENCH AND BRITISH EMPIRES,
    THEIR METHODS OF GOVERNMENT, AND THE AGENCIES OF
    SOCIALIZATION, THERE WAS A GREAT DEAL OF UNANIMITY IN THE
    RESPONSES OF THE INTELLIGENSIA AND THE WAYS IN WHICH THEY
    PERCEIVED THEIR RESPECTIVE ROLES.

05345 LAI, C.
    THE STRUCTURE AND CHARACTERISTICS OF THE CHINESE
    COOPERATIVE SYSTEM, 1928-1949
    INTERNATIONAL JOURNAL OF SOCIAL ECONOMICS, 16(2) (1989),
    59-66.
    HOW THE CHINESE NATIONALIST GOVERNMENT TRIED TO USE CO-
    OPERATIVES AS A SOCIO-ECONOMIC INSTRUMENT IN MAINLAND CHINA
    (1928-1949) BUT MET WITH LITTLE SUCCESS IS DISCUSSED. THE
    HISTORICAL BACKGROUND OF THE CHINESE CO-OPERATIVE MOVEMENT
    IS PRESENTED, THE STRUCTURE AND QUALITY OF DIFFERENT TYPES
    OF COOPERATIVES EXAMINED, THE PERFORMANCE OF CO-OPERATIVES
    AND THE BENEFITS OF BEING A CO-OPERATOR EVALUATED AND THE
    CHARACTERISTICS AND PROBLEMS OF THIS SYSTEM CONSIDERED.

05346 LAINGEN, B.
FUTURE U.S. POLICY AND ACTION
TERRORISM, 11(6) (1988), 550-552.
THIS IS A TALK GIVEN AT A CONFERENCE ON TERRORISM BY
BRUCE LAINGEN, EXECUTIVE DIRECTOR OF THE COMMISSION ON
PUBLIC SERVICE. HE SUGGESTS THAT TERRORISM PRESENTS ITS
ORIGINS IN MODERN TIMES. HE EXAMINES: INTELLIGENCE;
MULTILATERAL COOPERATION; THE MEDIA; PROTECTION; BUREAUCRACY;
THE APPLICATION OF FORCE; AND THE REASONS FOR TERRORISM

05347 LAIPSON, E.B.
THE "GREENING" OF WORLD POLITICS
CRS REVEIW, 10(7) (AUG 89), 22-23.
TO UNDERSTAND THE "GREENING" OF WORLD POLITICS, ONE HAS
TO LOOK BOTH AT THE ISSUE AS IT IS DEFINED BETWEEN AND AMONG
GOVERNMENTS AND AS IT HAS EVOLVED WITHIN SPECIFIC SOCIETIES.
GOVERNMENTS ADDRESS ENVIRONMENTAL PROBLEMS OFTEN BECAUSE OF
PRESSURES FROM GRASS-ROOTS EFFORTS AT THE LOCAL LEVEL AND
OFTEN FROM PEOPLE WHO MAY NOT BE POLITICALLY ACTIVE ON OTHER
ISSUES. ENVIRONMENTALLY ACTIVE CITIZENS OFTEN VIEW
GOVERNMENT AS BEING PART OF BOTH THE PROBLEM AND THE
SOLUTION.

05348 LAIRD, R.F. (ED.)
STRANGERS AND FRIENDS: THE FRANCO-GERMAN SECURITY
RELATIONSHIP
JOHN SPIERS PUBLISHING, BRIGHTON, SUSSEX, GB, 1989, 220.
THE AUTHORS PROVIDE AN OVERVIEW OF THE RECENT EVOLUTION
OF THE FRANCO-GERMAN SECURITY RELATIONSHIP BY ASSESSING IT
IN THREE DIMENSIONS: THE STRATEGIC ENVIRONMENT FROM THE WEST
GERMAN AND FRENCH NATIONAL PERSPECTIVES, THE CONVENTIONAL
ARMS DIMENSION, AND THE NUCLEAR DIMENSION.

05349 LAITIN, D.D.
LANGUAGE POLICY AND POLITICAL STRATEGY IN INDIA
POLICY SCIENCES, 22(3-4) (1989), 415-436.
THE OFFICIAL LANGUAGE POLICY OF INDIA IS DESCRIBED AS A
3 +/LANGUAGE OUTCOME. THE CENTRAL QUESTION THAT GUIDES THIS
PAPER IS TO EXPLAIN WHY, WHEN CONGRESS LEADERS ATTEMPTED TO
PROVIDE FOR INDIA A SINGLE INDIGENOUS LANGUAGE FOR OFFICIAL
COMMUNICATION, HAVE THEY SUFFERED MORE OPPOSITION THAN HAVE
RULERS OF STATES THAT CONSOLIDATED IN EARLIER CENTURIES?
STANDARD EXPLANATIONS FOR THE DIFFERENT OUTCOME, RELYING ON
SPECIAL ATTRIBUTES OF INDIAN CULTURE AND HISTORY, ARE FOUND
TO BE INADEQUATE. A GAME THEORETIC ANALYSIS POLITICAL
STRATEGY HELPS TO HIGH-LIGHT TWO VARIABLES THAT BEST INDIA'S
LANGUAGE OUTCOME: THE WORLD HISTORICAL TIME OF STATE
CONSOLIDATION, AND THE NATURE OF POLITICIAN/BUREAUCRAT
RELATIONS FOR POSTCOLONIAL STATES.

05350 LAITIN, D.D.
LINGUISTIC REVIVAL: POLITICS AND CULTURE IN CATALONIA
COMPARATIVE STUDIES IN SOCIETY AND HISTORY, 31(2) (APR 89),
297-317.
THE GAME THEORETIC ANALYSIS (WITH SOME CATALAN MATERIAL
USED FOR ILLUSTRATION) PROVIDES A SCRIPT FOR THE
INTERPRETATION OF LANGUAGE POLITICS. IT ALSO POINTS TO
ANOMALIES THAT REQUIRE RESEARCH ATTENTION. THE SCRIPT
INDICATES THAT RULERS OF HETEROGENEOUS (AND MULTILINGUAL)
TERRITORIES WILL BE ABLE TO LEGISLATE THE SOLE OFFICIAL USE
OF THEIR LANGUAGE WITHOUT GREAT DIFFICULTY. SECOND, THE
SCRIPT INDICATES THAT THE ESTABLISHMENT OF LINGUISTIC
HEGEMONY, WHEN RULERS AND RULED BOTH THINK IT OBVIOUS AND
NECESSARY THAT ALL CITIZENS SPEAK THE SAME LANGUAGE, DOES
NOT AUTOMATICALLY OR EASILY FOLLOW FROM STANDARDIZATION.
THIRD, THE SCRIPT REVEALS THAT THE POLITICS OF REGIONAL
REVIVAL REQUIRE INTRAGROUP COERCION, EVEN IF THE GREAT
MAJORITY OF THE PEOPLE IN THE REGION VOTE FOR THE OFFICIAL
REPLACEMENT OF THE CENTER'S LANGUAGE WITH THE LANGUAGE OF
THE REGION.

05351 LAKE, D.A.
EXPORT, DIE, ON SUBSIDIZE: THE INTERNATIONAL POLITICAL
ECONOMY OF AMERICAN AGRICULTURE, 1875-1940
COMPARATIVE STUDIES IN SOCIETY AND HISTORY, 31(1) (JAN 89),
81-105.
THE AGRICULTURAL POLICIES OF THE NEW DEAL PERSIST TO THE
PRESENT DAY AND ARE A PARTICULARLY IMPORTANT TURNING POINT
IN THE HISTORY OF THE AMERICAN FARM SECTOR. IN THE PERIOD
FROM 1875 TO 1940, AGRICULTURAL POLICY EVOLVED FROM A
STRATEGY OF EXPORTING THE DOMESTIC SURPLUS, TO SHRINKING
PRODUCTION THROUGH ATTRITION IN THE FARM POPULATION, TO
SUBSIDIZING PRODUCTION AND RESTRICTING ACREAGE. BECAUSE AN
INCREASE IN EXPORTS SUFFICIENT TO REMOVE THE SURPLUS IS
UNLIKELY, THE UNITED STATES IS LIMITED TO EITHER ALLOWING
MARKET FORCES TO SHRINK THE NUMBER OF AGRICULTURAL PRODUCERS
OR CONTINUING TO SUBSIDIZE PRODUCTION. WHILE THE FARM
POPULATION HAS DECLINED RAPIDLY SINCE WORLD WAR II, FARM
ORGANIZATIONS HAVE WAGED A VALIANT AND SUCCESSFUL EFFORT
OVER THE LAST SEVERAL DECADES TO MAINTAIN THE FARM SECTOR
AND FARM INCOMES THROUGH GOVERNMENT SUPPORT. ALL OF THIS MAY
EXPLAIN WHY AGRICULTURAL POLICY REFORM HAS PROVEN SO
DIFFICULT, AND WHY THE REAGAN ADMINISTRATION, DESPITE ITS
INTENTIONS, HAS ACTUALLY INCREASED FARM SUBSIDIES.

05352 LAKE, G.B.
BALD MAN ON A HORSE
NATIONAL REVIEW, XLI(4) (MAR 89), 38-39.
LITTLE MORE THAN A MONTH INTO HIS PRESIDENCY, SALINAS
HAS DECAPITATED A MONSTER THAT NONE OF HIS PREDECESSORS
DARED TO CONFRONT: THE PETROLEUM WORKERS' UNION, THE RICHEST
AND PROBABLY THE MOST CORRUPT UNION IN LATIN AMERICA. THE
UNION'S LEADERS HAVE BLACKMAILED A SUCCESSION OF MEXICAN
PRESIDENTS INTO GRANTING THEM UNCONSCIONABLE PRIVILEGES
UNDER THE THREAT OF CLOSING DOWN PEMEX, THE GOVERNMENT-OWNED
DRILLING, REFINING, AND MARKETING MONOPOLY.

05353 LAKE,C.
POLITICAL CONSULTANTS: OPENING UP A NEW SYSTEM OF
POLITICAL POWER
PS: POLITICAL SCIENCE AND POLITICS, XXII(1) (MAR 89),
26-29.
THE AUTHOR ADDRESSES THE QUESTION OF WHETHER HAVING
CONSULTANTS OPENS UP OR CLOSES THE POLITICAL SYSTEM,
ESPECIALLY FOR WOMEN AND MINORITY CONDIDATES.

05354 LAL, D.
A SIMPLE FRAMEWORK FOR ANALYSING VARIOUS REAL ASPECTS OF
STABILISATION AND STRUCTURAL ADJUSTMENT POLICIES
JOURNAL OF DEVELOPMENT STUDIES, 25(3) (APR 89), 291-313.
THIS ARTICLE SHOWS HOW A SIMPLE GEOMETRIC FRAMEWORK
CONTAINING A REAL MODEL BASED ON THE STANDARD TWO-GOOD THREE-
FACTOR TRADE THEORETIC MODEL AND A MONETARY MODEL OF THE
DOMESTIC BANKING SYSTEM CAN BE USED TO ANALYSE THE CHANGES
IN THE REAL AND NOMINAL VALUES OF VARIOUS ECONOMIC VARIABLES
OF CONCERN RESULTING FROM STABILISATION AND STRUCTURAL
ADJUSTMENT POLICIES

05355 LALLI, M.; THOMAS, C.
PUBLIC OPINION AND DECISION MAKING IN THE COMMUNITY.
EVALUATION OF RESIDENTS' ATTITUDES TOWARDS TOWN PLANNING
MEASURES
URBAN STUDIES, 26(4) (AUG 89), 435-447.
THE RELATIONSHIP BETWEEN POLITICAL DECISION-MAKING IN
THE COMMUNITY, LOCAL PUBLIC OPINION AND RESIDENTS' ATTITUDES
ARE EXAMINED WITH REFERENCE TO A CONCRETE LOCAL POLITICAL
ISSUE IN MANNHEIM (FEDERAL REPUBLIC OF GERMANY). THIS
INVOLVED TOWN PLANNING MEASURES WHICH WERE AIMED AT
ENHANCING URBAN QUALITY. THE FOCUS OF INTERESTS WERE
CONTROVERSIAL PLANS FOR AN UNDEVELOPED AREA OF THE INNER
CITY. THE AIM OF THE STUDY WAS TO INVESTIGATE THE ATTITUDES
OF RESIDENTS TOWARDS THIS PROBLEM AND THEIR PSYCHOLOGICAL
BACKGROUND. A QUASI-EXPERIMENTAL FIELD STUDY IN FORM OF A
TELEPHONE SURVEY WAS CARRIED OUT. IN TOTAL, 200 PEOPLE WERE
INTERVIEWED. IN EVALUATING THE DEVELOPMENT PLANS, PERCEIVED
URBAN QUALITY AND IDENTIFICATION WITH THE TOWN ARE IMPORTANT
PSYCHOLOGICAL VARIABLES. FURTHER RESULTS CONCERNING THE
DEGREE OF ACCEPTANCE AND SOCIAL IMPACT OF THE PLANS ARE
REPORTED. FINALLY, THE RELEVANCE OF SOCIAL SCIENTIFIC
EXAMINATION FOR LOCAL POLITICS IS EMPHASISED WHICH COULD BE
USED TO IMPROVE THE BASIS OF DECISION-MAKING IN THE
COMMUNITY.

05356 LALOR, P.
EUROPE AND THE PLO: AN APPOINTMENT WITH PEACE
MIDDLE EAST INTERNATIONAL, (343) (FEB 89), 10-11.
IN A SPEECH ON JAN. 25, 1989, BASSAM ABU SHARIF
CHALLENGED THE ISRAELI GOVERNMENT TO MAKE PEACE AND TO
ACCEPT UN RESOLUTION 242 AS THE PLO HAD DONE. BUT HE WAS NOT
OPTIMISTIC AND POINTED OUT THAT ISRAEL IS LED BY VETERANS OF
THE STERN GANG AND THE HAGANA, WHILE THE PLO REPRESENTS A
NEW GENERATION OF PALESTINIANS.

05357 LALOR, P.
PORTRAITS OF ABD RABO AND ABU SHARIF
MIDDLE EAST INTERNATIONAL, (363) (NOV 89), 19-21.
THE ARTICLE EXAMINES THE RISE TO POWER OF TWO KEY PLO
FIGURES: YASSER ABD RABO AND BASSAM ABU SHARIF. BOTH MEN ARE
REPRESENTATIVE OF HISTORIC DEVELOPMENTS OF THE PLO; BOTH ARE
CENTRAL TO CURRENT TRENDS WITHIN THE PALESTINIAN NATIONAL
MOVEMENT. COMBINED, THEY CREATE A MYTHICAL "YASSER ABU
SHARIF" WHO IS SECOND ONLY TO YASSER ARAFAT.

05358 LAMB, D.
EC PROJECT 1992: THE DYNAMICS OF CHANGE
DEPARTMENT OF STATE BULLETIN (US FOREIGN POLICY), 89(2143)
(FEB 89), 31-35.
THE AUTHOR, WHO IS THE US REPRESENTATIVE TO THE OECD,
DISCUSSES THE EUROPEAN COMMUNITY'S DRIVE TO ACHIEVE ECONOMIC
INTEGRATION BY 1992. HE CONSIDERS THE POTENTIAL IMPACT OF
THE MOVE, BOTH FOR THE EUROPEAN COMMUNITY AND FOR ITS
TRADING PARTNERS.

05359 LAMBERT, N.
THE ANONIMKA UNDER PERESTROIKA: A NOTE
SOVIET STUDIES, XLI(1) (JAN 89), 129-134.
THE ARTICLE EXAMINES THE ANGUISHED DEBATE THAT HAS TAKEN
PLACE IN THE USSR OVER ANONMKI, ANONYMOUS LETTERS SENT TO

GOVERNMENT OFFICIAL. IT OUTLINES THE USE OF ANONYMOUS LETTER IN EARLIER PERIODS TO DISCOVER AND PROSECUTE CORRUPTION AND SEDITION. HOWEVER, RECENT LAWS HAVE BEGUN TO CRACK DOWN ON THE USE OF ANONIMKA AND HAVE ATTEMPTED TO LIMIT THEIR INFLUENCE.

05360 LAMBERT, R.D.
DOD, SOCIAL SCIENCE, AND INTERNATIONAL STUDIES
PHILADELPHIA: ANLS OF AMER ACMY OF POLITICAL AND SOC SCIENCE, (502) (MAR 89), 94-107.
A GENERAL CYCLE OF RELATIONS BETWEEN THE DEPARTMENT OF DEFENSE (DOD) AND THE UNIVERSITY IS DESCRIBED WITH PARTICULAR REFERENCE TO THE SOCIAL SCIENCES AND INTERNATIONAL STUDIES: A GENERAL DECLINE IN AMITY SINCE WORLD WAR II, DECREASED SUPPORT FOR DOD OBJECTIVES, A CONCERN FOR THE EFFECT OF DOD PRIORITIES ON THE GENERAL RESEARCH PROFILE, THE GROWTH OF IN-HOUSE AND NONACADEMIC VENDORS IN RESEARCH AND TRAINING, AND THE ENCLAVING OF THE MILITARY-CONNECTED RESEARCH COMMUNITY WITHIN THE UNIVERSITY. THE PATTERN OF DOD SUPPORT FOR STRATEGIC STUDIES, LINGUISTICS, AND LANGUAGE AND AREA STUDIES IS EXAMINED.

05361 LAMBERTSON, D.F.
BURMA: POLITICAL SITUATION AND HUMAN RIGHTS
DEPARTMENT OF STATE BULLETIN (US FOREIGN POLICY), 89(2146) (MAY 89), 40-43.
THE AUTHOR REVIEWS THE POLITICAL SITUATION IN BURMA LEADING TO THE UPSURGE OF POLITICAL PROTEST IN 1988. SINCE THE MILITARY LEADERSHIP REASSERTED ITS CONTROL IN SEPTEMBER 1988, ARMY LOYALTY TO NE WIN HAS REMAINED STRONG AND MOST OBSERVERS SEE THE FORMER RULER'S HAND BEHIND THE FORCEFUL POLITICAL SUPPRESSION THAT QUELLED THE DEMONSTRATIONS. NEVERTHELESS, THE MILITARY LEADERSHIP HAS VOWED TO HOLD MULTI-PARTY ELECTIONS AND RELINQUISH POWER TO THE WINNERS.

05362 LAMBERTSON, D.F.
DEVELOPMENTS IN MALAYSIA AND SINGAPORE
DEPARTMENT OF STATE BULLETIN (US FOREIGN POLICY), 88(2140) (NOV 88), 23-27.
DEPUTY ASSISTANT SECRETARY FOR EAST ASIAN AND PACIFIC AFFAIRS DAVID LAMBERTSON GIVES A PROFILE OF SINGAPORE AND MALAYSIA. THIS PROFILE INCLUDES PEOPLE AND GOVERNMENT, ECONOMY, SHARED INTERESTS WITH THE US, THEIR ROLE IN REGIONAL STABILITY, AND THE CONDITION OF INTERNAL SECURITY. BOTH MALAYSIA AND SINGAPORE ARE OF GREAT STRATEGIC IMPORTANCE TO THE US.

05363 LAMBERTSON, D.F.
FUTURE PROSPECTS FOR THE PHILIPPINES
DEPARTMENT OF STATE BULLETIN (US FOREIGN POLICY), 89(2146) (MAY 89), 43-49.
A STABLE, DEMOCRATIC, AND PROSPEROUS PHILIPPINES WITH FRIENDLY TIES TO THE UNITED STATES IS CRITICALLY IMPORTANT TO THE PEACE AND STABILITY OF SOUTHEAST ASIA AND TO US INTERESTS. AMERICAN SUPPORT HAS HELPED THE AQUINO GOVERNMENT RE-ESTABLISH DEMOCRATIC POLITICAL INSTITUTIONS, PRESIDE OVER AN EMERGING POLITICAL CONSENSUS, AND RECOVER FROM A SEVERE ECONOMIC RECESSION.

05364 LAMBERTSON, D.F.
POLITICAL SITUATION IN BURMA
DEPARTMENT OF STATE BULLETIN (US FOREIGN POLICY), 89(2153) (DEC 89), 37-38.
THE BURMESE GOVERNMENT CONTINUES TO STATE THAT IT WILL HOLD A MULTIPARTY ELECTION IN 1990 AND THAT RESTRICTIONS ON POLITICAL ACTIVITY WILL BE RELAXED IN THE MONTHS LEADING UP TO THE ELECTION. BUT RECENT EVENTS HAVE NOT OFFERED REASON TO BE OPTIMISTIC THAT FREE AND FAIR ELECTIONS WILL TAKE PLACE IN BURMA. SINCE JULY 1989 THE MILITARY GOVERNMENT HAS ARRESTED THOUSANDS OF OPPOSITION PARTY MEMBERS, PRINCIPALLY FROM AUNG SAN SUU KYI'S NATIONAL LEAGUE FOR DEMOCRACY.

05365 LAMBERTSON, D.F.
SITUATION IN VIETNAM, CAMBODIA, AND LAOS
DEPARTMENT OF STATE BULLETIN (US FOREIGN POLICY), 88(2139) (OCT 88), 40-43.
THE ARTICLE EXAMINES THE CURRENT SITUATION IN SOUTHEAST ASIA, EMPHASIZING THE VIETNAMESE OCCUPATION OF CAMBODIA. ALTHOUGH RECENT DIPLOMATIC ACTIVITY MAY HAVE BEEN AN IMPORTANT FACTOR IN VIETNAM'S DECISION TO WITHDRAW 50,000 TROOPS FROM CAMBODIA, THE AUTHOR CAUTIONS THAT THERE STILL WOULD REMAIN OVER 50,000 TROOPS IN CAMBODIA AND VIETNAM IS SHOWING NO SIGNS OF WILLINGNESS TO TAKE AN ACTIVE AND DIRECT PART IN NEGOTIATIONS. THE AUTHOR THEREFORE ADVOCATES THE MAINTAINENCE OF CURRENT US POLICIES OF ECONOMIC AND DIPLOMATIC ISOLATION OF VIETNAM. THE ARTICLE ALSO DISCUSSES THE SITUATION IN LAOS AND THE DILEMMA PRESENTED BY THE NUMEROUS SOUTHEAST ASIAN REFUGEES.

05366 LAMBERTSON, D.F.
UPDATE ON CAMBODIA
DEPARTMENT OF STATE BULLETIN (US FOREIGN POLICY), 89(2146) (MAY 89), 37-40.
THE AUTHOR, WHO IS DEPUTY ASSISTANT SECRETARY FOR EAST

ASIAN AND PACIFIC AFFAIRS, DISCUSSES THE CURRENT SITUATION IN CAMBODIA AND US POLICIES IN SUPPORT OF EFFORTS TO ACHIEVE AN ACCEPTABLE CAMBODIAN SETTLEMENT.

05367 LAMDANY, R.
VOLUNTARY DEBT REDUCTION OPERATIONS: BOLIVIA, MEXICO, AND BEYOND
CONTEMPORARY POLICY ISSUES, VII(2) (APR 89), 66-82.
THIS PAPER DESCRIBES THE MAIN ASPECTS AND THE RESULTS OF VOLUNTARY DEBT REDUCTION OPERATIONS THAT OCCURRED RECENTLY IN BOLIVIA AND MEXICO. IT STUDIES THE MOTIVATIONS AND BEHAVIOR OF THE THREE MAIN AGENTS IN SUCH OPERATIONS: DEBTOR COUNTRIES, PARTICIPATING CREDITOR BANKS, AND NON-PARTICIPATING CREDITOR BANKS. THE PAPER ALSO DISCUSSES THE MAIN ISSUES THAT DEBTORS MUST ADDRESS IN DESIGNING FUTURE VOLUNTARY DEBT REDUCTION OPERATIONS.

05368 LAMENTOWICZ, W.
PARTNERS AROUND THE TABLE: AN INTERVIEW WITH WOJCIECH LAMENTOWICZ
EAST EUROPEAN REPORTER, 3(4) (SPR 89), 43-45.
WOJCIECH LAMENTOWICZ, A PROMINENT WARSAW LAWYER, SPEAKS OF THE RAPIDLY CHANGING SYSTEM IN POLAND. HE ARGUES THAT ALTHOUGH THERE HAS BEEN SIGNIFICANT CHANGE RECENTLY, POLAND STILL IS NOT ADVANCED TO THE STATE WHERE COLLECTIVE DISSENT IS "NO LONGER PUNISHABLE." HE CITES RECENT BEATINGS AND HARASSMENT OF ELECTION ACTIVISTS AS EXAMPLES OF THE CURRENT PROBLEMS IN THE THE SYSTEM. HE CONCLUDES THAT THE OVERALL PICTURE IS BRIGHT: THE ROUND TABLE IS A PROMISING SIGN THAT TRUE DEMOCRATIC REFORM IN POLAND IS POSSIBLE.

05369 LAMM, R.D.
THE BRAVE NEW WORLD OF PUBLIC POLICY
STATE LEGISLATURES, 15(7) (AUG 89), 31-34.
THE USA IS SAILING INTO A NEW WORLD OF PUBLIC POLICY WHERE INFINITE GOVERNMENT DEMANDS COLLIDE WITH FINITE RESOURCES. THE NEXT MAJOR GOVERNMENTAL REVOLUTION WILL BE THE REVOLUTION OF LOWERED EXPECTATIONS AS AMERICANS COME TO REALIZE THAT THE ECONOMY OF THE COUNTRY CANNOT CARRY THE EXPECTATIONS TRADITIONALLY ASSOCIATED WITH THE AMERICAN WAY, DUE TO INADEQUATE REVENUES.

05370 LAMPLAND, M.
UNTHINKABLE SUBJECTS: WOMEN AND LABOR IN SOCIALIST HUNGARY
EAST EUROPEAN QUARTERLY, XXIII(4) (WIN 89), 445-468.
THE AUTHOR ANALYZES A GROUP OF ESSAYS WRITTEN BY HUNGARIAN WOMEN FOR A CONTEST SPONSORED BY THE WOMEN'S COMMITTEE AND THE CULTURAL, AGITPROP DEPARTMENT OF THE NATIONAL COUNCIL OF TRADE UNIONS. HER PURPOSE IN ANALYZING THESE ESSAYS ON "WORK IS MY CALLING" IS TO REACH AN UNDERSTANDING OF THE SOCIALIST STATE'S DEFINITION OF WOMEN IN AND AT WORK. SHE USES THE ESSAYS TO CONSTRUCT A COHERENT PICTURE OF THE PREVAILING IDEOLOGICAL ASSUMPTIONS ABOUT WOMEN'S IDENTITY AS LABORERS WHICH INFORMS THE ACTIONS TAKEN BY PARTY OFFICIALS AND THE STATE BUREAUCRATS.

05371 LANC, E.
CONFIDENCE, NOT WEAPONS
WORLD MARXIST REVIEW, 32(7) (JUL 89), 38-40.
THIS ARTICLE SUGGESTS WAYS TO END THE FIFTY YEARS OF MILITARY CONFRONTATION IN EUROPE AND TO FIND PEACE. IT ADVOCATES AN END TO THE ARMS RACE. DETERRENCE, AND THE WARSAW PACT DOCTRINE ARE ANALYSED. THE ROLE OF THE US IN NATO IS EXAMINED, AS WELL AS THE CREATION OF A CENTER FOR CRISIS MANAGEMENT.

05372 LANCASTER, C.; SHATALOV, S.
A JOINT APPROACH TO AFRICA'S DEBT
AFRICA REPORT, 34(3) (MAY 89), 42-44.
WITH RECENT ECONOMIC REFORMS IN THE SOVIET UNION AND A NEW ERA IN U.S.-SOVIET RELATIONS, THERE ARE OPPORTUNITIES FOR COOPERATION IN ADDRESSING THE DEBT CRISIS PLAGUING MANY AFRICAN COUNTRIES. ALTHOUGH THE U.S. AND THE SOVIET UNION ARE NOT AFRICA'S MAJOR CREDITORS, COORDINATION OF DEBT RELIEF STRATEGIES COULD PROVIDE SOME MEASURE OF ASSISTANCE.

05373 LANCASTER, C.
ECONOMIC RESTRUCTURING IN SUB-SAHARAN AFRICA
CURRENT HISTORY, 88(538) (MAY 89), 213-216, 244.
ECONOMIC RESTRUCTURING HAS BECOME HIGH POLITICS IN SUB-SAHARAN AFRICA. NEARLY EVERY GOVERNMENT IN THE REGION HAS IN PLACE SOME FORM OF ECONOMIC RESTRUCTURING PROGRAM INTENDED TO REVERSE THE ECONOMIC DECLINE OF THE PAST DECADE. SUCH PROGRAMS ARE OFTEN CONTROVERSIAL BECAUSE THEY CHALLENGE LONG-ESTABLISHED AND WIDELY SHARED ECONOMIC BELIEFS AND PRACTICES AS WELL AS ENTRENCHED INTERESTS. AND SINCE THESE PROGRAMS TYPICALLY HAVE BEEN SHAPED AND FINANCED BY THE INTERNATIONAL MONETARY FUND (IMF) AND THE WORLD BANK WITH THE BACKING OF DEVELOPED COUNTRIES, THEY ARE OFTEN RESENTED BY AFRICANS AS HAVING BEEN IMPOSED BY OUTSIDERS IN YET ANOTHER ASSAULT ON SUB-SAHARAN AFRICA'S SOVEREIGNTY AND SELF-RELIANCE.

05374 LANCASTER, T.; LEWIS-BECK, M.
REGIONAL VOTE SUPPORT: THE SPANISH CASE

INTERNATIONAL STUDIES QUARTERLY, 33(1) (MAR 89), 29-44.
THE PAPER FOCUSES ON THE SPANISH CASE TO ASSESS THE
IMPORTANCE OF REGIONAL PARTIES IN EUROPEAN POLITICS. IT
BRIEFLY DESCRIBES THE REGIONAL PARTIES IN SPAIN. IN AN
EFFORT TO SYSTEMATICALLY EXPLAIN A VOTER'S GENERAL
PREFERENCE FOR A REGIONAL RATHER THAN A NATIONAL PARTY THE
PAPER PROPOSES AND TESTS WITH RECENT SURVEY DATA THREE
DIFFERENT HYPOTHESIS ABOUT REGIONAL VERSUS NATIONAL PARTY
SUPPORT. IT FINDS THAT CERTAIN SOCIOCULTURAL CLEAVAGES, PLUS
ECONOMIC ISSUES, DIRECTLY MOTIVATE REGIONAL VOTE INTENTION
IN SPAIN. IN ADDITION, IT CONCLUDES THAT POLITICAL
INVOLVEMENT IN GENERAL AND CONCERN OVER THE EUROPEAN
COMMUNITY IN PARTICULAR, INDIRECTLY INFLUENCE REGIONAL-
NATIONAL PARTY PREFERENCES.

05375 LAND, T.
MANAGING TOXIC WASTE
NEW LEADER, 72(18) (NOV 89), 4.
THIS IS A REPORT ON A TREATY TO REGULATE THE
INTERNATIONAL TRANSPORT AND DISPOSAL OF HAZARDOUS WASTE
MATERIALS WHICH WAS SIGNED RECENTLY BY SOME 50 COUNTRIES AT
A CEREMONY IN SWITZERLAND. THE ACCORD IS EXPECTED TO HAVE
ENORMOUS IMPACT ON GLOBAL PUBLIC HEALTH STANDARDS AND
POLUTION CONTROL, AS WELL AS ON THE SHIPPING, CHEMICALS AND
MANUFACTORING INDUSTRIES. AMONG OTHER CONTROVERSIAL
PRACTICES, IT SHOULD HELP PUT AN END TO THE DUMPING OF
DANGEROUS INDUSTRIAL CHEMICALS AND PESTICIDES IN THIRD WORLD
COUNTRIES.

05376 LANDAU, A.F.
WHY KAHANE WAS BANNED
NEW OUTLOOK, 32(1 (287)) (JAN 89), 51-52.
ON OCTOBER 5, 1988, THE CENTRAL ELECTION COMMITTEE OF
ISRAEL DECIDED NOT TO APPROVE THE KACH LIST FOR THE
ELECTIONS TO THE TWELFTH KNESSET. KACH THEN APPEALED TO THE
SUPREME COURT FOR REDRESS. ISRAELI LAW PERMITS THE
DISQUALIFICATION OF A POLITICAL PARTY ON THE BASIS OF (1)
THE REJECTION OF THE EXISTENCE OF THE STATE OF ISRAEL AS THE
STATE OF THE JEWISH PEOPLE; (2) THE REJECTION OF THE
DEMOCRATIC CHARACTER OF THE STATE; AND (3) INCITEMENT TO
RACISM.

05377 LANDAU, J.
IDEOLOGIES IN THE LATE OTTOMAN EMPIRE: A SOVIET PERSPECTIVE
MIDDLE EASTERN STUDIES, 25(3) (JUL 89), 405-406.
THE ARTICLE EXAMINES AN ANALYSIS OF IDEOLOGY IN THE
OTTOMAN EMPIRE WRITTEN BY A SOVIET SCHOLAR. REFLECTING THE
BROADENING AND LIBERAL TRENDS OF GLASNOST, THE ANALYSIS PAYS
SCANT LIP SERVICE TO COMMUNISM, BUT ON THE WHOLE CONSTITUTES
A SERIOUS SCHOLARLY WORK. THE ROLE OF RELIGION IN THE EMPIRE
IS ACCURATELY AND DISPASSIONATELY DISCUSSED AS IS THE
SIGNIFICANT INFLUENCE OF ETHNIC GROUPS.

05378 LANDAU, J. M.
SOME SOVIET WORKS ON MUSLIM SOLIDARITY
MIDDLE EASTERN STUDIES, 25(1) (JAN 89), 95-98.
THE GROWING NUMBER OF SOVIET PUBLICATIONS ON THE
INTERNATIONAL ORGANIZATIONS WHICH PROMOTE MUSLIM SOLIDARITY
NOT ONLY ADD SUBSTANTIALLY TO OUR KNOWLEDGE OF THE SUBJECT
BUT ALSO REFLECT A THINLYVEILED CONCERN OVER THE POSSIBLE
EFFECTS OF THE ACTIVITIES OF THESE ORGANIZATIONS ON SOVIET
GLOBAL INTERESTS AND - BY IMPLICATION, AT AT LEAST - ON
MUSLIM MINORITIES IN THE SOVIET UNION ITSELF. THIS ARTICLE
EXAMINES SOVIET PUBLICATIONS AND OTHER ACTIVITIES INTENDED
TO LOLSTE MUSLIM SOLIDARITY.

05379 LANDAU, S.
REMEMBER CENTRAL AMERICA?
TIKKUN, 4(6) (NOV 89), 52-55.
UNITED STATES POLICY THINKING REMAINS STUCK IN THE
ATTITUDE OF A PERMANENT COLD WAR. CENTRAL AMERICA OFFERS AN
ILLUSTRATION OF HOW REAL CHANGES IN WORLD AFFAIRS BEAR
LITTLE RELATION TO THINKING IN WASHINGTON. PRESIDENT REAGAN
AND HIS IDEOLOGUES INTERNATIONALIZED CENTRAL AMERICA IN THE
1980S BECAUSE THEY CHOSE TO MAKE IT "THE MOST IMPORTANT
PLACE IN THE WORLD." FOR A CENTURY CENTRAL AMERICA HAS BEEN
THE VICTIM OF GUNBOAT AND DOLLAR DIPLOMACY, THE GOOD
NEIGHBOR POLICY, AND DECADES OF CIA AND CONTRA FOUL PLAY-THE
REGION IS NOW HOME TO ITALIAN GEOTHERMAL ENERGY EXPERTS,
SCANDINAVIAN AND GERMAN FUEL EXPERIMENTERS, AND JAPANESE
ENGINEERS. BY THE MID 1980S, EUROPEAN SUPPORT FOR CONTRADORA,
A CENTRAL AMERICAN PEACE PLAN, EFFECTIVELY PUNCTURED THE
CENTURY-OLD DOGMA OF LEAVING THE WESTERN HEMISPHERE TO THE U.
S. THIS CLINGING TO THE COLD WAR GRAND STRATEGY HAS THROWN
THE U.S. OUT OF SYNCH-WITH THE DYNAMICS OF ITS OWN ECONOMY,
WITH THE POLITCAL TRAJECTORY OF EUROPE AND ASIA, AND EVEN
WITH THE LESS CENTRAL AFFAIRS OF CENTRAL AMERICA. IRONICALLY,
IT MAY BE WELL THAT BUSH WILL RECOGNIZE THE NEW
GEOPOLITICAL AND GEOENVIRONMENTAL RELATIONS PRECISELY
BECAUSE OF HIS ADMINISTRATION'S INABILITY TO ARRANGE EVEN
THE MOST APPARENTLY ROUTINE AFFAIRS IN CENTRAL AMERICA.

05380 LANDAU, S.
TOWARD A GLOBAL HIGH-DEFINITION TV PRODUCTION STANDARD

DEPARTMENT OF STATE BULLETIN (US FOREIGN POLICY), 89(2147)
(JUN 89), 48-51.
THE UNITED STATES STATE DEPARTMENT HAS BEEN INVOLVED IN
HIGH-DEFINITION TELEVISION (HDTV) ISSUES FOR 15 YEARS AND
HAS FOCUSED PRIMARILY ON THE STANDARD FOR PRODUCTION AND
INTERNATIONAL PROGRAM EXCHANGE. THE STATE DEPARTMENT, IN
CONJUNCTION WITH OTHER US GOVERNMENT AGENCIES AND THE
PRIVATE SECTOR, HAS SOUGHT TO PROMOTE AMERICAN INTERESTS
THROUGH THE ADOPTION OF A SINGLE, WORLDWIDE HDVT PRODUCTION
STANDARD. DURING THE PAST YEAR, THE DEPARMENT HAS
PARTICIPATED IN EXECUTIVE BRANCH DISCUSSIONS ON HDVT IN THE
ECONOMIC POLICY COUNCIL AND THE TRADE POLICY REVIEW GROUP.

05381 LANDAUER, C.
CURRENT DEBATE: JACKSON AND THE JEWS
TIKKUN, 4(1) (JAN 89), 47-48.
JESSE JACKSON'S ANTI-SEMITIC INCLINATIONS HAVE BEEN
UNMISTAKABLE AND NO OVERNIGHT CONVERSION CAN CONVINCINGLY
DEMONSTRATE HIS SINCERITY. ONLY A SUSTAINED RECORD WOULD
PROVE THAT HIS RECENT DENUNCIATIONS OF ANTI-SEMITISM
REPRESENT MORE THAN AN ARTIFICIAL GESTURE.

05382 LANDES, D.
ANTI-SEMITISM PARADING AS ANTI-ZIONISM
TIKKUN, 4(3) (MAY 89), 85-88.
MANY PEOPLE DISMISS HATEFUL CRITICISM AGAINST ISRAEL AS
OVERHEATED RHETORIC THAT WILL DISAPPEAR WHEN THE PALESTINIAN
CRISIS IS RESOLVED. BUT MANY ANTI-ISRAEL SENTIMENTS ARE NOT
PRODUCED BY THE CURRENT SITUATION NOR WILL THEY DISAPPEAR
ONCE THE PALESTINIAN ISSUE HAS BEEN RESOLVED. RATHER, THEY
SHOULD BE UNDERSTOOD FOR WHAT THEY ARE-AN EXTENSION OF
EARLIER FORMS OF ANTI-SEMITISM.

05383 LANE, C.
FROM 'WELFARE CAPITALISM' TO 'MARKET CAPITALISM'; A
COMPARATIVE REVIEW OF TRENDS TOWARDS EMPLOYMENT
FLEXIBILITY IN THE LABOUR MARKETS OF THREE MAJOR EUROPEAN
SOCIETIES
SOCIOLOGY, 23(4) (NOV 89), 583-610.
THE ARTICLE ADOPTS A SYSTEMATIC HISTORICAL AND CROSS-
NATIONAL PERSPECTIVE TO EXAMINE CHANGES IN EMPLOYMENT POLICY
AND PRACTICE FROM A PERIOD OF WELFARE CAPITALISM TO THE
CURRENT PERIOD OF MARKET CAPITALISM. THE TRENDS TOWARDS
EMPLOYMENT FLEXIBILITY IN BRITAIN, WEST GERMANY AND FRANCE
ARE DOCUMENTED IN SOME DETAIL, AND BOTH THE ROLE OF
STATE AND THE PRACTICES OF EMPLOYERS ARE EXAMINED. AN
ATTEMPT IS MADE TO ASSESS THE SIGNIFICANCE OF THE
FLEXIBILITY TRENDS IN THE THREE SOCIETIES AND TO EXPLAIN
THEIR EMERGENCE/ INTENSIFICATION IN THE 1980S. FINALLY, THE
ARTICLE CONSIDERS THE IMPACT OF FLEXIBLE EMPLOYMENT
PRACTICES ON THE QUANTITY AND QUALITY OF EMPLOYMENT OF
VARIOUS SOCIAL GROUPS.

05384 LANE, J.E.; ERSSON, S.
UNPACKING THE POLITICAL DEVELOPMENT CONCEPT
POLITICAL GEOGRAPHY QUARTERLY, 8(2) (APR 89), 123-744.
THE LITERATURE ON POLITICAL CHANGE HAS MUCH FOCUSED ON
POLITICAL DEVELOPMENT, IN PARTICULAR WITH REGARD TO THE
TRANSFORMATION OF THIRD-WORLD POLITIES. THE PURPOSE OF THE
ARTICLE IS TO TAKE A CLOSE LOOK AT THE MAIN CONCEPTIONS OF
POLITICAL DEVELOPMENT THEORETICALLY AND EMPIRICALLY. THESE
CONCEPTIONS INCLUDE: THE FUNCTIONAL APPROACH, THE SOCIAL
PROCESS APPROACH, THE CRISIS APPROACH AND THE RADICAL
APPROACH. VARIOUS DIMENSIONS OF POLITICAL DEVELOPMENT SUCH
AS A DEMOCRACY, BIG GOVERNMENT, MILITARY GOVERNMENT, PROTEST
AND VIOLENCE INDEX ARE UTILIZED IN THE ANALYSIS. THE ARTICLE
CONCLUDES THAT THE BASIC NOTIONS COVERED BY THE POLITICAL
DEVELOPMENT CONCEPT ARE REFERENTIALLY DIFFERENT TO SUCH AN
EXTENT THAT FUTURE RESEARCH SHOULD CONCENTRATE ON EACH OF
THE SEPARATE DIMENSIONS.

05385 LANE, R.
PROCEDURAL GOODS IN A DEMOCRACY: HOW ONE IS TREATED VERSUS
WHAT ONE GETS
SOCIAL JUSTICE RESEARCH, 2(3) (SEP 88), 177-192.
IT IS WELL ESTABLISHED THAT PEOPLE ARE AT LEAST AS
CONCERNED WITH PROCEDURAL JUSTICE AS WITH THE OUTCOMES OF
PROCEDURE, THAT IS, WITH DISTRIBUTIVE JUSTICE OR RETRIBUTIVE
JUSTICE. THERE ALSO IS SOME EVIDENCE THAT EVEN IN ECONOMIC
MATTERS PEOPLE ARE AS CONCERNED WITH FREEDOM OF OPPORTUNITY
AND EQUITABLE PROCEDURES AS WITH THE ACTUAL INCOMES THEY GET.
THE ARTICLE EXAMINES THE ESSENTIAL MORAL INGREDIENTS IN
PROCEDURAL JUSTICE AS ILLUSTRATED BY A VARIETY OF SOCIAL
INSTITUTIONS. IT CONCLUDES WITH SOME OBSERVATIONS ON THE
LACK OF PROTECTION OF THESE "PROCEDURAL GOODS" BY
CONVENTIONAL DEMOCRATIC INSTITUTIONS.

05386 LANGBEIN, L.I.; SIGELMAN, L.
SHOW HORSES, WORK HORSES, AND DEAD HORSES
AMERICAN POLITICS QUARTERLY, 17(1) (JAN 89), 80-95.
THIS STUDY BRINGS DATA ON HOUSE MEMBERS' USE OF TIME TO
BEAR ON THE TRADITIONAL DISTINCTION BETWEEN SHOW HORSES AND
WORK HORSES IN CONGRESS. ANALYSIS FAILS TO PRODUCE THE
HYPOTHESIZED TWO-DIMENSIONAL STRUCTURE IN THE TIME

ALLOCATIONS OF HOUSE MEMBERS, CALLING INTO QUESTION THE EMPIRICAL VALIDITY OF THE SHOW HORSE-WORK HORSE DISTINCTION.

05387 LANGE, D.
CALLING A DEAD LETTER A DEAD LETTER
NEW ZEALAND INTERNATIONAL REVIEW, 14(4) (JUL 89), 23-26.
THE AUTHOR EXPLAINS THE NEW ZEALAND GOVERNMENT'S STANCE ON NUCLEAR WEAPONS, BEGINNING BY SUMMARIZING THE HISTORY OF NEW ZEALAND'S FORMAL ALLIANCE WITH THE UNITED STATES, AND HIGHLIGHTING PERIODS OF RISING DIFFICULTIES IN THE RELATIONS DURING THE VIETNAM WAR. THE NUCLEAR ISSUE, WHICH BEGAN AS AN ENVIRONMENTAL ISSUES, BECAME AND REMAINS PART OF MAINSTREAM POLITICS. NEW ZEALAND REGARDS NUCLEAR TESTING AS VANDALISM BASED ON REACTIONS TO FRENCH TESTS IN THE AIR ABOVE MURUROA ATOLL. APPEALS TO THE UNITED NATIONS BY AUSTRALIA AND NEW ZEALAND SINCE 1972 ARE DISCUSSED. REGIONAL DEFENSE NEEDS ARE ASSESSED, AND ALLIANCE WITH AUSTRALIA IS EQUATED WITH THESE NEEDS.

05388 LANGE, K.
SOVIET AND OTHER PERSPECTIVES ON SOUTH AFRICA
SOUTH AFRICA INTERNATIONAL, 20(2) (OCT 89), 74-78.
SOVIET POLICY REGARDING SOUTH AFRICA HAS CHANGED CONSIDERABLY. SOVIET DECISION MAKERS NOW STRESS THE IMPORTANCE OF A NON-REVOLUTIONARY, POLITICAL EVOLUTION IN SOUTH AFRICA. THIS IS A DRAMATIC SHIFT FROM PREVIOUS SOVIET RHETORIC CONCERNING ARMED STRUGGLE AND THE EXPORT OF REVOLUTION. THE PRIMARY CAUSE OF THE SHIFT IS A SOVIET DESIRE TO REDUCE EXTERNAL PRESSURES SO AS TO PROMOTE PERESTROIKA. SECONDARY REASONS INCLUDE THE POSSIBILITY OF ACQUIRING TECHNOLOGY FROM SOUTH AFRICA AND CUTTING THE HUGE COSTS ASSOCIATED WITH THE EXPORT OF REVOLUTION.

05389 LANGLEY, W.
WHY DID THE US WITHDRAW FROM UNESCO?
SCANDINAVIAN JOURNAL OF DEVELOPMENT ALTERNATIVES, VIII(1) (MAR 89), 5-40.
THE OBJECTIVE OF THE PAPER IS TO LOOK AT THE REASONS WHY WASHINGTON CHOSE TO WITHDRAW FROM UNESCO. IT PRESENTS AN OUTLINE OF THE REASONS PRESENTED BY THE US FOR WITHDRAWING AND EXAMINES THOSE REASONS IN LIGHT OF AVAILABLE EVIDENCE. IT CONCLUDES THAT THE REASONS PUT FORWARD BY THE US DO NOT FIND SUPPORT IN AVAILABLE EVIDENCE, AND THAT THE UNSTATED BUT REAL REASONS FOR WITHDRAWAL REFLECT CONCERNS --ECONOMIC AND POLITICAL--WHICH, THOUGH TRANSCENDING UNESCO, CONVERGED IN CERTAIN ACTIVITIES OF THAT ORGANIZATION. THE PAPER ALSO ANALYZES THE IMPLICATIONS OF THE UNDERLYING CAUSE ESPECIALLY AS IT BEARS ON THE FUTURE OF UNESCO.

05390 LANGLOIS, J.P.
MODELING DETERRENCE AND INTERNATIONAL CRISES
JOURNAL OF CONFLICT RESOLUTION, 33(1) (MAR 89), 67-83.
THE CONTINUOUS PRISONER'S DILEMMA IS A REASONABLE MODEL FOR NUCLEAR CRISES (USUALLY REPRESENTED BY "CHICKEN"), AND FOR THE ARMS RACE. THIS ARTICLE ADDRESSES THE EXISTENCE OF CREDIBLE DETERRENCE STRATEGIES THAT PROMOTE COOPERATION AS A DYNAMICALLY STABLE STEADY STATE. DECISIONS MADE REPEATEDLY IN TIME ARE THE SELECTION BY EACH SIDE OF A LEVEL OF HOSTILITY. ASSESSMENT OF THE RESULTING SITUATION IS REPRESENTED BY A UTILITY FUNCTION FOR EACH PLAYER. AS THE GAME PROCEEDS, PLAYERS ARE CONCERNED WITH THE CURRENT SITUATION AS WELL AS WITH THE FUTURE CONSEQUENCES OF THEIR PRESENT DECISIONS. THUS EACH SIDE MUST FORMULATE INTENTIONS AND EXPECTATIONS OF EACH OTHER'S FUTURE BEHAVIOUR AND USE THEM TO INFER THEIR OWN PRESENT OPTIMAL DECISIONS. A FORMAL CONCEPT OF DETERRENCE STRATEGY IS INTRODUCED: IT PROMISES THE OTHER SIDE RETALIATION IN KIND TO PREVENT ANY GAIN FROM AGGRESSIVE PLAY, AND IT INFLICTS INCREASING LOSSES AS A RESULT OF ESCALATION. IF ONE SIDE ADOPTS SUCH A DETERRENCE STRATEGY, THE OTHER SIDE CANNOT DO BETTER THAN ACTING SIMILARLY, AND WHEN BOTH SIDES ADOPT IT, THEY BOTH ENJOY OPTIMAL DECISION RULES THAT CONFIRM INTENTIONS AND EXPECTATIONS. THE RESULTING DYNAMICAL SYSTEM ENDOWS COOPERATION WITH ASYMPTOTIC STABILITY PROVIDED THE THREATS OF RETALIATION CONTAIN A FAIR MIX OF FIRMNESS AND RESTRAINT.

05391 LANOU, D.
THE 'TEFLON' FACTOR: RONALD REAGAN AND COMPARATIVE PRESIDENTIAL POPULARITY
POLITY, XXI(3) (SPR 89), 481-501.
RONALD REAGAN WAS OFTEN CALLED THE "TEFLON PRESIDENT," BECAUSE CRITICISM AND BLAME NEVER SEEMED TO STICK TO HIM. HIS PERSONAL CHARM AND STYLE WERE SAID BY MANY TO FORM A PROTECTIVE COVERING THAT RESISTED PUBLIC DISPLEASURE AND EXPLAINED HIS HIGH POPULARITY RATINGS. THIS ARTICLE REJECTS THE TEFLON THESIS, ARGUING THAT PUBLIC AFFECTION FOR REAGAN WAS GOVERNED BY THE NORMAL LAWS OF PRESIDENTIAL POPULARITY RIGHTLY UNDERSTOOD. THESE LAWS, THE AUTHOR INSISTS, ARE, FIRST, THE GREAT ADVANTAGES IN POPULARITY ENJOYED BY REPUBLICAN PRESIDENTS IN GENERAL AND, SECOND, THE IMPORTANCE OF SHORT-TERM CRISES OR "RALLY" EVENTS ON PUBLIC AFFECTION FOR CHIEF EXECUTIVES. HE EXAMINES PRESIDENTIAL POPULARITY FROM DWIGHT EISENHOWER THROUGH REAGAN, IDENTIFIES PATTERNS COMMON TO ALL, AND CONCLUDES THAT THERE WAS REALLY NOTHING

THAT EXCEPTIONAL ABOUT PRESIDENT REAGAN'S STANDING WITH THE AMERICAN PEOPLE.

05392 LANOUE, D.J.; SCHROTT, P.R.
THE EFFECTS OF PRIMARY SEASON DEBATES ON PUBLIC OPINION
POLITICAL BEHAVIOR, 11(3) (SEP 89), 289-306.
THIS PAPER CONCERNS THE EFFECTS OF PRIMARY SEASON PRESIDENTIAL DEBATES ON PUBLIC OPINION. USING A QUASI-EXPERIMENTAL DESIGN, IT INVESTIGATES ONE OF THE DEMOCRATIC DEBATES CONDUCTED DURING THE 1988 CAMPAIGN. IT ATTEMPTS TO LINK THE ACTUAL STATEMENTS OF THE CANDIDATES WITH THE REACTIONS OF THE SUBJECTS. IT FINDS THAT VIEWERS' OPINIONS OF THE CANDIDATES CHANGED DRAMATICALLY AFTER WATCHING THE DEBATE, AND THAT THESE CHANGES ARE RELATED TO SUBJECTS' ASSESSMENTS OF THE CANDIDATES' IMAGES AND DEBATING "STYLES" (RATHER THAN THEIR PRESENTATIONS OF SUBSTANTIVE ISSUE POSITIONS). IT SPECULATES ON SOME OF THE REASONS FOR THE FINDINGS, AND DISCUSS THE DIFFERENCES BETWEEN PRIMARY SEASON AND GENERAL ELECTION DEBATES.

05393 LANOUE, D.J.; SCHROTT, P.R.
VOTERS' REACTIONS TO TELEVISED PRESIDENTIAL DEBATES: MEASUREMENT OF THE SOURCE AND MAGNITUDE OF OPINION CHANGE
POLITICAL PSYCHOLOGY, 10(2) (JUN 89), 275-285.
THIS PAPER REPRESENTS A PILOT STUDY, INVESTIGATING THE FIRST 1984 PRESIDENTIAL DEBATE BETWEEN RONALD REAGAN AND WALTER MONDALE. THE AUTHORS CONDUCTED SURVEYS OF DEBATE WATCHERS AND NONWATCHERS BEFORE AND AFTER THE OCTOBER ENCOUNTER, IN ORDER TO ASSESS THE EFFECTS OF THE DEBATE ON VOTERS' OPINIONS. A CONTENT ANALYSIS WAS EMPLOYED TO DETERMINE HOW WELL THE CANDIDATES DID IN DISCUSSING THE ISSUES OF GREATEST CONCERN TO OUR RESPONDENTS. THE AUTHORS FIND THAT MONDALE'S SUCCESS IN THE DEBATE WAS DUE LARGELY TO HIS SKILL AS A DEBATER (AS OPPOSED TO HIS ISSUE POSITIONS), WHILE REAGAN WAS ABLE TO EFFECTIVELY EXPLOIT THE TAXATION AND SPENDING ISSUES. THE AUTHORS DISCUSS THE IMPLICATIONS OF THIS STUDY FOR UNDERSTANDING THE 1984 ELECTION, AND SUGGEST WAYS IN WHICH THE FUTURE STUDY OF PRESIDENTIAL DEBATES MIGHT BE ENHANCED.

05394 LAPID, Y.
THE THIRD DEBATE: ON THE PROSPECTS OF INTERNATIONAL THEORY IN A POST-POSITIVIST ERA
INTERNATIONAL STUDIES QUARTERLY, 33(3) (SEP 89), 235-254.
THE DEMISE OF THE EMPIRICIST-POSITIVIST PROMISE FOR A CUMULATIVE BEHAVIORAL SCIENCE RECENTLY HAS FORCED SCHOLARS FROM NEARLY ALL THE SOCIAL DISCIPLINES TO REEXAMINE THE ONTOLOGICAL, EPISTEMOLOGICAL, AND AXIOLOGICAL FOUNDATIONS OF THEIR SCIENTIFIC ENDEAVORS. THE "THIRD DEBATE" IN THE FIELD OF INTERNATIONAL RELATIONS PARALLELS THIS INTELLECTUAL FERMENT AND CONSTITUTES A STILL MATURING DISCIPLINARY EFFORT TO RECONSIDER THEORETICAL OPTIONS IN A "POST-POSITIVIST" ERA. THIS ESSAY EXPLORES THE ETIOLOGY OF THIS DEBATE AND CRITICALLY ASSESSES ITS IMPLICATIONS FOR CURRENT AND FUTURE THEORETICAL PRACTICES. ALTHOUGH THE DEBATE HAS TRIGGERED MANY DIFFERENT RESPONSES, THE ANALYSIS FOCUSES ON ONLY ONE OF THEM--THE OPTIMISTIC RESPONSE--WHICH BOTH AFFIRMS AND CELEBRATES THE UNPARALLELED THEORETICAL POTENTIALITIES PRESUMABLY CREATED BY THE PRESENT INTELLECTUAL TRANSITION. WHILE ACKNOWLEDGING THE CONSIDERABLE PROMISE OF THE THIRD DEBATE, THE ESSAY NOTES THAT POST-POSITIVISM OFFERS NEARLY AS MANY DEAD ENDS AS IT OPENS PROMISING PATHS FOR FUTURE RESEARCH. THE ESSAY ISSUES SOME WARNINGS CONCERNING HAZARDS OF MISPLACED OR EXTRAVAGANT THEORETICAL HOPES, AND IT SINGLES OUT ENHANCED REFLEXIVITY IN THE SCHOLARLY COMMUNITY OF INTERNATIONAL RELATIONS AS THE NOTABLE CONTRIBUTION TO DATE OF THE CURRENT THEORETICAL RESTRUCTURING.

05395 LAPIDUS, G.W.
GORBACHEV'S NATIONALITIES PROBLEM
FOREIGN AFFAIRS, 68(4) (FAL 89), 92-108.
MIKHAIL GORBACHEV'S REFORMS HAVE UNLEASHED AN UNPRECEDENTED TIDE OF PROTESTS AND DEMONSTRATIONS ACROSS THE USSR, WITH NATIONAL GRIEVANCES OCCUPYING A CENTRAL PLACE. VIRTUALLY NO REGION OF THE SOVIET UNION APPEARS IMMUNE TO THE RISING TIDE OF NATIONAL SELF-ASSERTION. WHETHER IN THE FORM OF ANTI-RUSSIAN DEMONSTRATIONS OR IN THE EMERGENCE OF NEW SOCIOPOLITICAL MOVEMENTS DEMANDING GREATER ECONOMIC AND POLITICAL AUTONOMY OR IN VOLATILE OUTBURSTS OF COMMUNAL VIOLENCE, ALL THIS DOMESTIC TURMOIL POSES A THREAT TO GORBACHEV'S LEADERSHIP AND TO THE FUTURE OF HIS REFORMS.

05396 LAPIDUS, G.W.; DALLIN, A.
THE PACIFICATION OF RONALD REAGAN
BULLETIN OF THE ATOMIC SCIENTISTS, 45(1) (JAN 89), 14-17.
THIS ESSAY ANALYZES THE MILITARY AND ARMS CONTROL POLICIES AND ACTIONS DURING THE REAGAN YEARS. ALTHOUGH HE OPPOSED ARMS CONTROL AT THE BEGINNING OF HIS TERM AS PRESIDENT, HE ACHIEVED THE GREATEST ARMS CONTROL RESULTS SINCE THE COLD WAR BEGAN.

05397 LAPITAN, A.E.
THE RE-DEMOCRATIZATION OF THE PHILIPPINES: OLD WINE IN A NEW BOTTLE

ASIAN PROFILE, 17(3) (JUN 89), 235-242.
THE AUTHOR SURVEYS THE PROCESS OF RE-DEMOCRATIZATION IN
THE PHILIPPINES FOLLOWING THE SO-CALLED "EDSA" REVOLUTION
THAT ESTABLISHED THE GOVERNMENT OF PRESIDENT CORAZON AQUINO.
HE IDENTIFIES AND ANALYZES THE MAJOR STEPS UNDERTAKEN BY THE
AQUINO GOVERNMENT TO RESTORE DEMOCRACY IN THE PHILIPPINES
SINCE COMING TO POWER IN FEBRUARY 1986.

05398 LAPLANTE, J.M.
RESEARCH METHODS EDUCATION FOR PUBLIC SECTOR CAREERS: THE
CHALLENGE OF UTILIZATION
POLICY STUDIES REVIEW, 8(4) (SUM 89), 845-851.
AS THE WORLD RAPIDLY BECOMES MORE COMPLEX, THERE IS A
GREATER NEED FOR TOOLS OF RESEARCH AND DATA ANALYSIS TO
ASSIST THE PUBLIC ADMINISTRATOR. WHILE MANY UNIVERSITY
PROGRAMS RECOGNIZE THIS NEED AND INCLUDE SEVERAL METHODOLOGY
COURSES IN THEIR CURRICULUM, THERE IS LITTLE EVIDENCE THAT
STUDENTS ARE TAKING THIS KNOWLEDGE INTO THE FIELD. IN THIS
ARTICLE, THE NEED FOR USABLE METHODOLOGY COURSES ARE
STRESSED. THE FIRST SECTION OF THIS ARTICLE IS DEDICATED TO
IDENTIFYING THOSE FACTORS THAT MAKE METHODS CLASSES MORE
PRACTICAL. THE REMAINING PORTION CONCENTRATES ON TWO
APPROACHES TO TEACHING THAT THE AUTHOR ASSERTS WILL HELP
STUDENTS TO USE IN THE FIELD WHAT THEY HAVE LEARNED IN THE
CLASSROOM.

05399 LAPPE, F.M.
POLITICS FOR A TROUBLED PLANET
NATIONAL CIVIC REVIEW, 78(4) (JUL 89), 255-258.
IN SPITE OF HEALTHY GIVING AND VOLUNTEERING LEVELS--
REFLECTING COMMUNITY CONCERN AMONG AMERICANS--CITIZENS ARE
NOT LINKING THEIR CONCERNS WITH GOVERNMENT POLICIES AND
CITIZEN POLITICS. IF CITIZENS ARE TO VIEW INVOLVEMENT IN THE
POLITICAL PROCESS AS A MEANS TO BENEFICIAL SOCIAL CHANGE,
METHODS MUST BE INSTALLED THAT FOSTER GREATER IDENTIFICATION
OF PERSONAL WELFARE WITH COMMUNITY WELL-BEING AND DRAW UPON
THE CREATIVE CAPACITY OF CITIZENS TO SHAPE SOCIETY WITHIN
THE PARAMETERS OF OUR DEMOCRATIC INSTITUTIONS.

05400 LAPPER, R.
APARTHEID HEADS FOR A HARSH RECKONING
SOUTH, (108) (OCT 89), 26-27.
SOUTH AFRICA'S DEBT PROBLEM COULD PROVE THE ACHILLES
HEEL OF APARTHEID. IF THE WORLD BANKING COMMUNITY WOULD
EFFECTIVELY EXCLUDE SOUTH AFRICA FROM ITS INTERNATIONAL
TRADE AND PAYMENTS SYSTEMS, IT WOULD BE A MUCH MORE
EFFECTIVE SANCTIONS MEASURE THAN THE TRADE SANCTIONS APPLIED
BY GOVERNMENTS. WITH THE PRETORIA REGIME PREPARING FOR TOUGH
NEGOTIATIONS WITH ITS WESTERN BANK CREDITORS OVER THE
RESCHEDULING OF PAYMENTS ON ITS US$20 BILLION EXTERNAL DEBT,
THE OPPONENTS OF APARTHEID HAVE A PRIME OPPORTUNITY TO
TIGHTEN THE SCREWS ON SOUTH AFRICA.

05401 LAPPER, R.
PITFALLS OF A COVER DRIVE
SOUTH, (102) (APR 89), 29-30.
LIBERALIZATION OF THE WORLD'S FINANCE AND SERVICE
INDUSTRIES AND THEIR RAPID GROWTH IN THE DEVELOPING WORLD
SHOULD OFFER THE NORTH'S BIG INSURERS MAJOR EXPANSION
OPPORTUNITIES. BACKED BY US DIPLOMATIC PRESSURE, SOME NORTH
AMERICAN INSURANCE COMPANIES ARE MAKING INROADS INTO
SOUTHEAST ASIAN MARKETS. EUROPEAN COUNTRIES SEE MASSIVE
POTENTIAL IN CHINA, INDIA, AND BRAZIL. BUT THE PACE IS SLOW
AND THERE ARE PITFALLS.

05402 LAPPER, R.
SOMETHING HAS GOT TO GIVE
SOUTH, (99) (JAN 89), 11-12.
IN LATIN AMERICA, DEBT SERVICING HAS EATEN INTO TRADE
SURPLUSES AND STRAINED PUBLIC FINANCES. IN THE FUTURE, THE
CHOICE BETWEEN GROWTH AND DEBT SERVICE COULD BECOME EVEN
MORE STARK. POLITICIANS SUCH AS VENEZUELA'S CARLOS ANDRES
PEREZ AND ARGENTINA'S CARLOS MENEM ARE IDENTIFIED WITH THE
PRESSURE FOR A DEFAULT OR A MORATORIUM. BUT ANALYSTS
QUESTION WHETHER EITHER WILL HAPPEN BECAUSE DEBTORS WHO HAVE
REFUSED TO PAY, SUCH AS BRAZIL AND PERU, HAVE HAD LIMITED
SUCCESS. BRAZIL'S 11-MONTH MORATORIUM DID NOT ACHIEVE ANY
NOTABLE CONCESSIONS, AND PERU'S CHALLENGE TO THE
INTERNATIONAL BANKS AND THE IFM COLLAPSED UNDER 1,000
PERCENT INFLATION.

05403 LAPPER, R.
THE POVERTY OF EXPORT GROWTH
SOUTH, (99) (JAN 89), 13.
DESPITE THE STRONG PERFORMANCE OF LATIN AMERICA'S
EXPORTERS, THE REGION FACES ANOTHER YEAR OF STAGNATION.
BECAUSE ECONOMIC GROWTH IS PEGGED BELOW THE POPULATION
INCREASE, LATIN AMERICANS WILL PROBABLY BE POORER IN THE
COMING YEAR. ALTHOUGH THE TRADE SURPLUSES OF LATIN AMERICA'S
EIGHT BIGGEST ECONOMIES ARE EXPECTED TO INCREASE IN 1989,
DEBT REPAYMENTS AND INTEREST CHARGES WILL EAT UP THIS
SURPLUS AND MORE.

05404 LARIVIERE, R.W.
VIETNAMESE KINSHIP: STRUCTURAL PRINCIPLES AND THE
SOCIALIST TRANSFORMATION IN NORTHERN VIETNAM
JOURNAL OF ASIAN STUDIES, 48(4) (NOV 89), 741-757.
THIS ARTICLE EXPLORES THE DEBATE WHICH CENTERS ON THE
QUESTIONS OF HOW AND HOW MUCH INDIGENOUS TRADITIONS,
INCLUDING KINSHIP STRUCTURES, ARE TRANSFORMED BY THE MUCH
LARGER POLITICAL ECONOMIC FRAMEWORK. IT SUGGESTS THAT THE
TWO STRUCTURALLY OPPOSING MALE-ORIENTED ("PATRILINEAL") AND
NONMALE-ORIENTED ("BILATERAL") MODELS OF VIETNAMESE KINSHIP
STILL PERSIST AS THE FUNDAMENTAL PARAMETERS OF HOUSEHOLD
INFORMATION AND GENDER RELATIONS THROUGHOUT TWENTIETH-
CENTURY VIETNAM, DESPITE THE APPARENT CHANGE IN THE RELATION
OF STRUCTURAL DOMINANCE BETWEEN THESE TWO MODELS IN THE
SOCIALIST NORTH.

05405 LARKEY, P.D.; SMITH, R.A.
BIAS IN THE FORMULATION OF LOCAL GOVERNMENT BUDGET PROBLEMS
POLICY SCIENCES, 22(2) (MAY 89), 123-166.
GOVERNMENT BUDGETS ARE PREMISED ON FORECASTS OF REVENUES
AND EXPENDITURES. THESE FORECASTS ARE SUBJECT TO BOTH
STOCHASTIC ERROR AND STRATEGIC MANIPULATION. CIRCUMSTANTIAL
EVIDENCE IN THE BUDGETING LITERATURE AND IN THE POPULAR
MEDIA SUGGEST THAT GOVERNMENT OFFICIALS ROUTINELY BIAS THE
FORECASTS UNDERLYING BUDGETS. THE RESEARCH REPORTED HERE
ASKED THREE PRIMARY QUESTIONS: TO WHAT EXTENT ARE BUDGET
FORECASTS SYSTEMATICALLY BIASED? WHY? (ARE FISCAL AND
ELECTORAL VARIABLES SYSTEMATICALLY RELATED TO THE MAGNITUDE
AND DIRECTION OF THE BIASES?) WHAT POLITICAL AND ETHICAL
DIFFERENCE DO THE BIASES MAKE? FROM THE LITERATURE AND AN
ANALYSIS OF THE INCENTIVES FACING POLITICIANS AND
BUREAUCRATS, THE AUTHORS DEVELOPED HYPOTHESES ABOUT BUDGET
BIASES. THESE HYPOTHESES WERE TESTED USING TIME SERIES DATA
FOR THE CITY OF PITTSBURGH, PENNSYLVANIA (1941-1983); THE
CITY OF SAN DIEGO, CALIFORNIA (1950-1982); AND THE
PITTSBURGH (PENNSYLVANIA) SCHOOL DISTRICT (1946-1983). IN
THESE LOCALS OVER THE PERIODS EXAMINED, BUDGETS WERE
SYSTEMATICALLY PESSIMISTIC; REVENUES WERE UNDERESTIMATED AND
EXPENDITURES WERE OVERESTIMATED. THE FISCAL AND ELECTORAL
FACTORS HYPOTHESIZED TO ACCOUNT FOR THIS PESSIMISM ARE,
HOWEVER, VERY MIXED IN THEIR ABILITY TO EXPLAIN THE BIASES.

05406 LARMORE, C.
LIBERAL NEUTRALITY: A REPLY TO JAMES FISHKIN
POLITICAL THEORY, 17(4) (NOV 89), 580-581.
CHARLES LARMORE, THE AUTHOR OF THE BOOK PATTERNS OF
MORAL COMPLEXITY, REFUTES A REVIEW OF HIS BOOK BY JAMES
FISHKIN. (FISHKIN'S REVIEW APPEARED IN THE FEBRUARY ISSUE OF
POLITICAL THEORY, PAGES 153-156). LARMORE SAYS THAT FISHKIN
MADE SOME INSTRUCTIVE REMARKS ABOUT ONE OF THE PROBLEMS IN
THE BOOK, THE "NEUTRAL JUSTIFICATION OF POLITICAL NEUTRALITY.
" BUT HE BADLY REPRESENTS THE SOLUTION LARMORE PROPOSES.
SINCE LARMORE FEELS THE PROBLEM IS OF THE UPMOST IMPORTANCE,
AND BECAUSE HIS SOLUTION IS SO DIFFERENT FROM WHAT FISHKIN
DESCRIBES IT TO BE, HE FEELS BOUND TO OFFER THIS ARTICLE AS
RECTIFICATION. LARMORE CLAIMS THAT FISHKIN FAILS TO SEE THAT
THE NORM OF RATIONAL CONVERSATION IS ONLY ONE INGREDIENT
AMONG OTHERS IN HIS NEUTRAL JUSTIFICATION OF POLITICAL
NEUTRALITY.

05407 LARRABEE, F., S.
SOVIET POLICY TOWARD GERMANY: NEW THINKING AND OLD
REALITIES
WASHINGTON QUARTERLY, 12(3) (SUM 89), 33-52.
THE RELATIONS BETWEEN WEST GERMANY AND THE USSR ARE
MOVING INTO A NEW PHASE WHERE MANY LONG-HELD ASSUMPTIONS MAY
BE NO LONGER VALID. IN ORDER TO EXAMINE THESE ASSUMPTIONS
AND THEIR VALIDITY, THE ARTICLE EXAMINES THE EVOLUTION OF
SOVIET POLICY TOWARD GERMANY IN THE POSTWAR PERIOD. SOVIET
POLICY TOWARD GERMANY HAS RANGED FROM THE PUSH FOR
REUNIFICATION BY STALIN TO THE AGRESSIVE CAMPAIGN TO FORCE
GERMANY TO ACCEPT THE TERRITORIAL STATUS QUO BY KHRUSCHEV.
THE ARTICLE ANALYZES THE SOVIET POLICY UNDER MIKHAIL
GORBACHEV AND EXAMINES THE OPTIONS OPEN TO GORBACHEV WITH
REGARDS TO GERMANY IN THE FUTURE. THE ARTICLE CONCLUDES THAT
ALTHOUGH RELATIONS ARE LIKELY TO CONTINUE TO IMPROVE, NO
SIGNIFICANT POLICY SHIFT WILL TAKE PLACE IN THE NEAR FUTURE.

05408 LARSEN, F.; WATTLEWORTH, M.
STRUCTURAL POLICIES IN INDUSTRIAL COUNTRIES
FINANCE AND DEVELOPMENT, 26(3) (SEP 89), 20-23.
MANY COUNTRIES HAVE TRIED TO ELIMINATE OR REDUCE
DISTORTIONS AFFECTING DOMESTIC AND INTERNATIONAL MARKETS.
THIS ARTICLE DISCUSSES THE ISSUES BEHIND SUCH REFORMS, AND
IS BASED ON A LONGER PAPER, "THE ROLE OF STRUCTURAL POLICIES
IN INDUSTRIAL COUNTRIES," BY FELDMAN, HERNANDEZ-CATA, LARSEN,
AND WATTLEWORTH STRUCTURAL POLICIES AND MICROECONOMIC
POLICIES ARE DEFINED AND A DESCRIPTION OF HOW THEY WORK IS
GIVEN. IN ADDITION TO THEIR IMPACT ON POTENTIAL OUTPUT,
STRUCTURAL POLICIES CAN INFLUENCE THE WAY IN WHICH AN
ECONOMY REACTS TO ADVERSE DISTURBANCES AND THEREBY HELP TO
REDUCE THE COST OF ADJUSTMENT, THUS TIES WITH MACRO POLICIES
AND THE ISSUES OF IMPLEMENTATION ARE ANALYZED.

05409 LARSON, M.
PRESIDENTIAL NEWS COVERAGE AND "ALL THINGS CONSIDERED":
NATIONAL PUBLIC RADIO AND NEWS BIAS
PRESIDENTIAL STUDIES QUARTERLY, XIX(2) (SPR 89), 347-354.
SEVERAL STUDIES HAVE CONCLUDED THAT THERE IS A LIBERAL
BIAS IN THE PRESS, HOWEVER THE METHODOLOGY OF SEVERAL OF
THEM HAS BEEN SHARPLY CRITICIZED. THE STUDY HERE SEEKS TO
OVER COME THOSE PROBLEMS BY ANALYZING STORIES OVER A TIME
PERIOD OF SEVERAL YEARS AND BY ANALYZING ALL STORIES IN A
NEWSCAST RATHER THAN JUST THOSE RELATED TO A SPECIFIC TOPIC,
THERE ARE TWO CONCLUSIONS DISCUSSED: COVERAGE OF PRESIDENTS
HAS BECOME PROGRESSIVELY MORE NEGATIVE SINCE 1974 AND THE
ATC HAS SYSTEMATICALLY REPORTED THE ACTIVITIES OF
CONSERVATIVE PRESIDENTS LESS FAVORABLY THAN LIBERAL
PRESIDENTS.

05410 LASATER, M.L.
US POLICY TOWARDS CHINA'S REUNIFICATION, THE REAGAN YEARS:
1980-1986
DISSERTATION ABSTRACTS INTERNATIONAL, 49(7) (JAN 89),
1951-A.
AMERICAN INTERESTS ARE WELL SERVED BY THE PRESENT US
POLICY TOWARDS CHINA'S REUNIFICATION. ALTHOUGH SOME
FLEXIBILITY IN THAT POLICY HAS BEEN INTRODUCED IN RESPONSE
TO CHANGES IN THE REUNIFICATION PRONOUNCEMENTS OF BEIJING
AND TAIPEI, THE USA SHOULD CONTINUE TO VIEW THE ISSUE AS ONE
FOR THE CHINESE THEMSELVES TO RESOLVE.

05411 LASKIER, M.
JEWISH EMIGRATION FROM MOROCCO TO ISRAEL: GOVERNMENT
POLICIES AND THE POSITION OF INTERNATIONAL JEWISH
ORGANIZATIONS, 1949-56
MIDDLE EASTERN STUDIES, 25(3) (JUL 89), 323-362.
THE ARTICLE EXAMINES THE ISSUE OF JEWISH EMIGRATION FROM
MOROCCO TO ISRAEL. IT ANALYZES THE CHANGING POLICIES OF THE
FRENCH PROTECTORATE AUTHORITIES WITH REGARDS TO THE
EMIGRATION FROM 1949 WHEN THE FRENCH TOLERATED THIS PROCESS,
UNTIL 1956 WHEN THE NEWLY INDEPENDENT MOROCCAN GOVERNMENT
CURTAILED IT. THE ARTICLE ALSO EXAMINES THE REACTIONS TO AND
INITIATIVES TAKEN TOWARD THIS MASS MOVEMENT ON THE PART OF
SEVERAL INTERNATIONAL JEWISH ORGANIZATIONS ACTIVE IN MOROCCO
BETWEEN 1948 TO 1956. THESE GROUPS INCLUDE: THE ALLIANCE
ISRAELITE UNIVERSELLE (AIU), THE AMERICAN JEWISH JOINT
DISTRIBUTION COMMITTEE (AJDC), THE WORLD JEWISH CONFERENCE
(WJC), AND THE AMERICAN JEWISH COMMITTEE (AJC).

05412 LASSON, K.
FREE EXERCISE IN THE FREE STATE: MARYLAND'S ROLE IN
RELIGIOUS LIBERTY AND THE FIRST AMENDMENT
JOURNAL OF CHURCH & STATE, 31(3) (AUT 89), 419-449.
MARYLAND HOLDS THE DISTINCTION OF HAVING BEEN THE STATE
WHOSE EARLY HISTORY MOST DIRECTLY ENSURED, AND WHOSE
CITIZENRY WAS MOST DIRECTLY AFFECTED BY, THE FIRST
AMENDMENT'S GUARANTEE OF RELIGIOUS FREEDOM. BECAUSE OF ITS
RELATIVELY DIVERSE RELIGIOUS POPULATION, COLONIAL MARYLAND
STOOD OUT BOTH AS A CHAMPION OF TOLERANCE AND A HOTBED OF
DISCRIMINATION. THIS ESSAY FOCUSES ON THE IMPORTANT EVENTS
CONCERNING TOLERATION AND ITS DEVELOPMENT IN MARYLAND, FROM
RELIGIOUS PERSECUTION IN THE EARLY 1600'S TO THE ADOPTION OF
THE BILL OF RIGHTS.

05413 LATEY, M.
THE GENERAL CRISIS OF SOCIALISM
WORLD TODAY, 45(8-9) (AUG 89), 131-134.
WITHOUT THE BENEFIT OF AN OFFICIAL FUNERAL, THE IDEA OF
INTERNATIONAL CLASS WAR AND REVOLUTION HAS BEEN QUIETLY
BURIED BY MIKHAIL GORBACHEV, TO THE AUDIBLE GRIEF OF
COMMUNIST PARTY DIEHARDS, IN ITS PLACE, THE CONCEPT OF A
CRISIS IN WORLD SOCIALISM HAS CREPT INTO THE LANGUAGE AND
THINKING OF SOME COMMUNIST LEADERS. YUGOSLAVIA'S ANTE
MARKOVIC HAS PROCLAIMED THAT ALL SOCIALISM IS IN A STATE OF
CRISIS AND A NEW FORM OF SOCIALISM IS NEEDED. THE RACE
BETWEEN REFORM, REVOLUTIONARY OUTBURSTS, AND MILITARY-
FASCIST REACTION IS NOW AT A CRUCIAL STAGE. IT WILL DECIDE
WHETHER THE CRISIS OF SOCIALISM IS TERMINAL OR WHETHER A NEW
FORM OF SOCIAL DEMOCRACY WILL EMERGE.

05414 LATSIS, O.
PROGRESS OF ECONOMIC REFORM IN THE USSR
WORLD MARXIST REVIEW, 32(12) (DEC 89), 24-28.
IT IS HEARTENING THAT THE SOVIET GOVERNMENT HAS COME TO
GRIPS IN EARNEST WITH THE HUGE BUDGET DEFICIT, FOR THE MAIN
REASON BEHIND THE DESTRUCTION OF THE MARKET SEEMS TO BE THE
DRAMATICALLY SWOLLEN STATE BUDGET DEFICIT. THE AUTHOR
CONTENDS THAT THE RECENT IMPLEMENTATION OF CORRECTIVE
MEASURES WILL CREATE THE RIGHT CONDITIONS FOR THE HEALTHY
FUNCTIONING OF THE NEW ECONOMIC SYSTEM AND FOR RESOLVING
PRESSING SOCIAL PROBLEMS. ONLY THEN WILL A STABLE AND
DYNAMIC ECONOMIC GROWTH BECOME A REALITY.

05415 LATYSHEV, I.
USSR-JAPAN: WHY DISTORT HISTORY
REPRINTS FROM THE SOVIET PRESS, 48(10) (MAY 89), 24-26.
THE PEOPLES OF JAPAN AND THE SOVIET UNION HAVE BEEN
LIVING AS GOOD NEIGHBORS. OBJECTIVELY, THEY HAVE NOTHING TO
DIVIDE: THEIR TWO COUNTRIES HAVE A CLEARLY DEFINED BORDER.
THE PEOPLE LIVING ON BOTH SIDES OF THE BORDER ARE ENGAGED IN
PEACEFUL WORK. THE WAY TO THE LEGAL CODIFICATION OF SOVIET-
JAPANESE GOOD-NEIGHBORLINESS IS THE SOONEST POSSIBLE
COMPLETION OF THE DRAFTING OF A PEACE TREATY WHICH WILL DRAW
THE LINE BEHIND THE PAST, RATHER THAN FUTILE TERRITORIAL
DISPUTES.

05416 LAU, E.
AN EYE ON BIG BROTHER
FAR EASTERN ECONOMIC REVIEW, 141(38) (SEP 88), 36-37.
PERKING ANNOUNCED THE FORMATION OF THE MACAU SPECIAL
ADMINSTRATIVE REGION BASIC LAW DRAFTING COMMITTEE (BLDC)
CONSISTING OF 30 PEOPLE FROM CHINA AND 19 FROM MACAU.
ALTHOUGH THE PROCESS IS SIMILAR TO THE BLOC IN HONG KONG,
OBSERVERS NOTE THAT ALL OF MACAU'S BLOC MEMBERS TOE PEKING'S
LINE ON THE FUTURE OF MACAU, WHICH IS UNLIKELY TO SEE A
DEMOCRATIC SYSTEM OF GOVERNMENT. THE BASIC LAW IS LIKELY TO
BE SIMILAR TO THE ONE DRAFTED IN HONG KONG WHICH GENERALLY
HAS SEEN CHINESE DICTATING THE TERMS OF THE BASIC LAW WHICH
SERVES AS THE TERRITORY'S MINI-CONSTITUTION.

05417 LAU, E.
BASIC PROBLEMS OF LAW
FAR EASTERN ECONOMIC REVIEW, 141(32) (AUG 88), 18-19.
THE DRAFT BASIC LAW FOR HONG KONG HAS BROUGHT WIDESPREAD
CRITICISM FROM MANY SOURCES. THE BASIC LAW WILL SERVE AS A
MINI-CONSTITUTION FOR HONG KONG WHEN IT BECOME A SPECIAL
ADMINISTRATIVE REGION OF CHINA IN 1997. A LEADING BRITISH
CONSTITUTIONAL LAWYER, MEMBERS OF THE BRITISH PARLIAMENT,
THE HUMAN RIGHTS ORGANIZATION AMNESTY INTERNATIONAL AND THE
TERRITORY'S GOVERNOR HAVE ALL POINTED OUT FLAWS AND
INCONSISTENCIES IN THE BASIC LAW. THE MAJORITY OF THE
PROTESTS ARE CONCERNED WITH PROVISIONS THAT WOULD UNDERMINE
THE PROMISED "HIGH DEGREE OF AUTONOMY" OUTLINED IN THE SINO-
BRITISH JOINT DECLARATION IN HONG KONG IN 1984.

05418 LAU, E.
DEMOCRATIC MALAISE
FAR EASTERN ECONOMIC REVIEW, 142(50) (DEC 89), 38.
THE IS LITTLE EVIDENCE THAT HONG KONG'S PRO-DEMOCRACY
MOVEMENT IS SUCCEEDING IN MOVING TOWARDS A DEMOCRATIC
POLITICAL SYSTEM BEFORE CHINA TAKES OVER IN 1997. THE LOCAL
GOVERNMENT STILL MAINTAINS THAT DEVELOPMENTS WILL CONVERGE
WITH THE BASIC LAW, A MINI-CONSTITUTION FOR POST-1997 HONG
KONG, IMPLYING THAT ANY POLITICAL CHANGES MUST BE APPROVED
BY BEIJING. THE PRO-DEMOCRACY MOVEMENT HAS SUFFERED FORM A
LACK OF LEADERSHIP AND DIRECTION, AND THE FUTURE DIRECTION
OF THE LOBBY IS UNCLEAR.

05419 LAU, E.
NO MORE MR. NICE GUY
FAR EASTERN ECONOMIC REVIEW, 141(37) (SEP 88), 28-29.
HONG KONG'S REFUGEE POLICY IS INCREASINGLY COMING UNDER
LOCAL AND INTERNATIONAL FIRE FOR ALLEGED RACISM, BRUTALITY
AND ILLEGALITY, FORCING THE GOVERNMENT TO PROMISE A GRADUAL
OPEINING AND IMPROVEMENT OF CONDITIONS IN THE CLOSED CAMPS
IN WHICH VIETNAMESE REFUGEES ARE HELD. A REFUGEE SCREENING
POLICY WHICH PRESCRIBES THAT REFUGEES MUST PROVE THAT THEY
ARE POLITICAL RATHER THAN ECONOMIC REFUGEES IN ORDER TO BE
ALLOWED TO REMAIN IN HONG KONG, SQUALID CONDITIONS OF MANY
OF THE REFUGEE CAMPS, AND THE LACK OF EDUCATION FOR REFUGEE
CHILDREN BORN IN HONG KONG ARE ALL POINTS OF TENSION THAT
THE LEGISLATIVE COUNCIL IS NOW FACING.

05420 LAU, E.
POSITIONING FOR POWER
FAR EASTERN ECONOMIC REVIEW, 141(35) (SEP 88), 28-29.
THE CAMPAIGN FOR HONGKONG'S SECOND INDIRECT ELECTIONS
WERE LESS THAN INSPIRING AS CANDIDATES CONTESTING 13 OF THE
26 SEATS WERE RETURNED UNOPPOSED. UNDER THE PRESENT SYSTEM
OF INDIRECT ELECTIONS, ONLY 1% OF THE 5.6 MILLION IN
HONGKONG HAVE A VOTE. SOME OBSERVERS STATE THAT THE
UNOPPOSED VICTORIES WERE THE RESULT OF HORSETRADING AND
BEHIND-THESCENES CONSULTATION. OTHERS HAVE NOTED THAT THE
POLITICAL APATHY DOES NOT BODE WELL FOR THE INTRODUCTION OF
DIRECT ELECTIONS IN 1991.

05421 LAU, E.
RED CARDS ON THE TABLE
FAR EASTERN ECONOMIC REVIEW, 141(27) (JUL 88), 21-22.
THE CREATION OF "BASIC LAW" BY THE CENTRAL GOVERNMENT OF
CHINA HAS QUASHED ANY HOPES THAT HONG KONG WILL BE ALLOWED
TO ENJOY THE "HIGH DEGREE OF AUTONOMY" IT WAS ORIGINALLY
PROMISED BY PEKING AFTER THE PEOPLE'S REPUBLIC RECOVERS
SOVEREIGNTY IN 1997. THE ORIGINAL SINO-BRITISH JOINT
DECLARATION VESTED THE HONG KONG SPECIAL ADMINISTRATIVE
REGION WITH EXECUTIVE, LEGISLATIVE AND INDEPENDENT JUDICIAL
POWER WHILE THE CENTRAL GOVERNMENT WOULD ENJOY POWER OVER
FOREIGN AND DEFENSE AFFAIRS. HOWEVER, THE FORMULATORS OF THE
"BASIC LAW" FOR HONG KONG MAKE IT CLEAR THAT PEKING WILL
HAVE THE FINAL SAY IN HONG KONG'S EXECUTIVE, LEGISLATURE AND
JUDICIARY.

05422 LAU, R.
CONSTRUCT ACCESSIBILITY AND ELECTORAL CHOICE
POLITICAL BEHAVIOR, 11(1) (MAR 89), 5-32.
THIS PAPER ILLUSTRATES THE USEFULNESS OF STUDYING THE
CHRONIC ACCESSIBILITY OF POLITICAL CONSTRUCTS IN THE FIELD
OF POLITICAL BEHAVIOR. THE CHRONIC ACCESSIBILITY OF FOUR
GENERIC POLITICAL CONSTRUCTS ARE OPERATIONALIZED: CANDIDATES,
ISSUES, GROUPS, AND PARTIES. THE ACCESSIBILITY OF THESE
FOUR POLITICAL CONSTRUCTS IS SHOWN TO BE RELATIVELY STABLE
OVER TIME AND TO GUIDE THE PROCESSING OF INFORMATION ABOUT A
WIDE VARIETY OF POLITICAL OBJECTS. NEXT, A VOTING MODEL IS
TESTED THAT IDENTIFIES WHICH VOTERS WILL RELY CHIEFLY ON
ISSUE ORIENTATIONS, GROUP ORIENTATIONS, CANDIDATE
ORIENTATIONS, AND/OR PARTY ORIENTATIONS IN MAKING THEIR VOTE
DECISION. THE VOTING MODEL IS VALIDATED ACROSS TWO DISTINCT
WAYS OF OPERATIONALIZING THE POLITICAL CHRONICITIES AND
THREE DIFFERENT ELECTION STUDIES SPANNING A 28-YEAR PERIOD.
FINALLY, ALTHOUGH THIS PAPER HAS FOCUSED ON INDIVIDUAL
POLITICAL BEHAVIOR, SEVERAL WAYS THAT AN INFORMATION
PROCESSING APPROACH COULD SHED LIGHT ON MACROLEVEL POLITICAL
QUESTIONS ARE DISCUSSED.

05423 LAUFER, L.Y.
CHANGING PERSPECTIVES IN THE DISTRIBUTION OF US FOREIGN AID
JERUSALEM JOURNAL OF INTERNATIONAL RELATIONS, 11(3) (SEP
89), 26-39.
THIS OVERVIEW FINDS THAT US BILATERAL AID, WHICH BEGAN
AFTER WORLD WAR II LARGELY OUT OF SECURITY CONSIDERATIONS,
STILL RETAINS THAT ORIENTATION. THE CENTRALITY OF THE UNITED
STATES IN THE INTERNATIONAL DONOR COMMUNITY HAS, HOWEVER,
BEEN ERODED AS JAPAN AND OTHER COUNTRIES BECOME MORE
INVOLVED. ALSO DISCUSSED ARE THE RECENT EMERGENCY OF EGYPT
AND ISRAEL AS THE MAJOR RECIPIENTS OF US AID; AND AMERICA'S
USE OF AID LEVERAGE AS BOTH INDUCEMENT AND THREAT.

05424 LAURELL, A.
THE ROLE OF UNION DEMOCRACY IN THE STRUGGLE FOR WORKERS'
HEALTH IN MEXICO
INTERNATIONAL JOURNAL OF HEALTH SERVICES, 19(2) (1989),
279-294.
THE AUTHOR ANALYZES THE STRUGGLE FOR WORKERS' HEALTH IN
MEXICO, EMPHASIZING THE IMPORTANCE OF THE GENERAL AND
SPECIFIC POLITICAL CONTEXT. IN AN OVERVIEW OF THE
LEGISLATION ON INDUSTRIAL HEALTH AND SAFETY, THE AUTHOR
SHOWS THAT THE LIMITED ACTIVITIES RELATED TO WORKERS' HEALTH
HAVE MORE TO DO WITH THE RELATIVE POLITICAL WEAKNESS OF THE
MEXICAN WORKING CLASS THAN WITH THE FORMAL STRUCTURE OF
LEGISLATION, STATE INSTITUTIONS, AND UNIONS. THE ARTICLE
ALSO DEALS WITH THE FOUR MOST IMPORTANT STRUGGLES FOR HEALTH
AND SAFETY IN MEXICO DURING THE LAST TEN YEARS. IT CONCLUDES
THAT THESE STRUGGLES ARE LINKED TO PROCESSES OF UNION
DEMOCRATIZATION AND TEND TO DECLINE WHEN UNION DEMOCRACY IS
LOST.

05425 LAURENCE, D.; WYNNE, B.
TRANSPORTING WASTE IN THE EUROPEAN COMMUNITY: A FREE
MARKET?
ENVIRONMENT, 31(6) (JUL 89), 12-17, 34-35.
THIS ARTICLE EXPLORES THE FEAR BY SOME GROUPS, OF THE
IMPLICATIONS FOR HAZARDOUS WASTE TRANSPORT BETWEEN MEMBER
NATIONS AS THE EUROPEAN COMMUNITY MOVES TOWARD A FREE MARKET
IN 1992. EXAMINED ARE THE CONFLICTING DEFINITIONS FOR
HAZARDOUS WASTE WHICH MAY CAUSE THE REGULATORY STANDARDS OF
THE NATIONS WITH THE BEST DISPOSAL REGIMES TO BE UNDERMINED
BY THE NATIONS WITH THE WORST. IT GIVES THE REGULATORY
BACKGROUND AND EXPLORES THE EUROPEAN WASTE TRADE AND BREAKS
IN THE WASTE CHAIN, AS WELL AS PUBLIC REACTION TO THE WASTE
MANAGEMENT INDUSTRY. IT CONCLUDES WITH THE POLICY OPTIONS.

05426 LAURENCE, P.
NELSON MANDELA: PROSPECTS FOR HIS RELEASE
SOUTH AFRICA FOUNDATION REVIEW, 15(2) (FEB 89), 2-3.
ALTHOUGH THE SOUTH AFRICAN GOVERNMENT HAS BEEN CAUTIOUS
AND APPREHENSIVE ABOUT RELEASING NELSON MANDELA, IT DOES NOT
FOLLOW THAT IT HAS GROPED AROUND AIMLESSLY, WITH NO PLAN AT
ALL. THE DECISIVE LINE ON THE QUESTION OF FREEING MANDELA
HAS NOT BEEN CROSSED, BUT THERE HAS BEEN PROGRESS TOWARD IT
AND, TO SOME EXTENT, THE MOVEMENT HAS BEEN PURPOSEFUL.

05427 LAURENCE, P.
OPENING THE GATES
AFRICA REPORT, 34(6) (NOV 89), 23-26.
SOUTH AFRICA'S F.W. DEKLERK HAS UNDERTAKEN CAUTIOUS
STEPS TOWARD NEGOTIATIONS WITH THE BLACK MAJORITY BY
RELEASING VETERAN AFRICAN NATIONAL CONGRESS LEADERS FROM
PRISON. BUT HIS FOES MAINTAIN THAT HIS REFORMS ARE GROUNDED
ON THE PRINCIPLE OF DIVIDE-AND-RULE AND THAT HE IS NOT
PREPARING TO ADDRESS THE CENTRAL QUESTION OF BLACK POLITICAL
EMPOWERMENT.

05428 LAURENCE, P.
THE NATIONAL PARTY'S TRIAL OF STRENGTH
AFRICA REPORT, 34(5) (SEP 89), 20-23.
THE VICTORY OF SOUTH AFRICA'S NATIONAL PARTY BROUGHT F.W.
DEKLERK TO THE PRESIDENCY ON A MARGIN SLIMMER THAN ANY OF
HIS PREDECESSORS. FACING AN EROSION OF SUPPORT ON BOTH THE
RIGHT AND THE LEFT, THE SOUTH AFRICAN LEADER IS ALSO
CONFRONTING A GREATER CHALLENGE FROM EXTRA-PARLIAMENTARY
FORCES. WITH THE WANING OF POWER AMONG THE "SECUROCRATS,"
OBSERVERS ARE WONDERING IF THE DEKLERK PRESIDENCY WILL BRING
ABOUT A NEW ERA IN THE NATION'S HISTORY.

05429 LAURET, M.
SEIZING TIME AND MAKING NEW: FEMINIST CRITICISM, POLITICS,
AND CONTEMPORARY FEMINIST FICTION
FEMINIST REVIEW, (31) (SPR 89), 94-106.
THE AUTHOR CONSIDERS POSSIBLE REASONS WHY FEMINIST
CRITICISM HAS ABSENTED ITSELF FROM THE POLITICAL TERRAIN OF
FEMINIST FICTION AND SUGGESTS WAYS OF READING FEMINIST
FICTION THAT MIGHT ACTIVATE OR RE-ACTIVATE ITS POLITICAL
MEANINGS FOR A CONTEMPORARY READERSHIP. SHE USES AN
HISTORICAL DEFINITION OF FEMINIST FICTION AS WOMEN'S FICTION
THAT HAS ENGENDERED BY THE WOMEN'S LIBERATION MOVEMENT AND
THAT EXPLICITLY HAS FEMINISM AND FEMINIST CONCERNS AS ITS
CENTRAL FIELD OF SIGNIFICATION. FOR REASONS OF CLARITY AND
EXPEDIENCY, SHE CONFINES HER COMMENTARY TO AMERICAN FEMINIST
WRITING.

05430 LAURSEN, J.
SKEPTICISM AND INTELLECTUAL FREEDOM: THE PHILOSOPHICAL
FOUNDATIONS OF KANT'S POLITICS OF PUBLICITY
HISTORY OF POLITICAL THOUGHT, X(3) (FAL 89), 439-456.
IMMANUEL KANT'S POLITICS OF PUBLICITY IS FUNDAMENTALLY
THE POLITICS OF A RESPONSE TO THE TRADITION OF PHILOSPHICAL
SKEPTICISM. HIS CALLS FOR "PUBLIC" ENLIGHTENMENT AND
"PUBLICITY" MAKE UP, IN MODERN TERMS, A CALL FOR
INTELLECTUAL FREEDOM. THE ESSAY CONCENTRATES ON THIS ASPECT
OF KANT'S POLITICS AND SEEKS TO ESTABLISH ITS PHILOSOPHICAL
FOUNDATIONS AND ITS GENEALOGY IN KANT'S PHILOSOPHICAL
DEVELOPMENT. THE AUTHOR ALSO SEEKS TO EXPLORE, IN A LARGER
SENSE, THE IMPLICATIONS OF SKEPTICISM FOR POLITICAL THOUGHT.

05431 LAUTENBERG, L.
GLOBAL ECONOMIC DEVELOPMENTS: A VIEW FROM SWITZERLAND
STUDIES IN COMPARATIVE INTERNATIONAL DEVELOPMENT, 24(3)
(FAL 89), 62-69.
IN A FREE MARKET WORLD ECONOMY NOW CHARACTERIZED BY A
STRONG TREND TOWARDS INTEGRATED ECONOMIC AREAS DOMINATED BY
NORTH AMERICA, WESTERN EUROPE AND THE PACIFIC, EFFECTIVE
COOPERATION IS THE KEY TO SUSTAINED SUCCESS.

05432 LAV, E.
RETURN TO SENDER
FAR EASTERN ECONOMIC REVIEW, 142(49) (DEC 89), 33.
DESPITE PROTESTS BY THE U.S. GOVERNMENT AND THE UNITED
NATIONS HIGH COMMISSIONER FOR REFUGEES, THE BRITISH
GOVERNMENT IS DETERMINED TO REPATRIATE FORCIBLY VIETNAMESE
BOAT PEOPLE STRANDED IN HONGKONG. MORE THAN 40,000 MEN,
WOMEN AND CHILDREN ARE TO BE REPATRIATED AT A COST OF AT
LEAST US $600 PER PERSON. U.S. AND U.N. OFFICIALS CLAIM THAT
THE POLICY OF FORCED REMOVAL WILL JEOPARDIZE THE SYSTEM OF
VOLUNTARY REPATRAITION WHICH HAS BARELY BEGUN TO FUNCTION.

05433 LAV, E.
THE CHOSEN FEW
FAR EASTERN ECONOMIC REVIEW, 142(52) (DEC 89), 10-11.
AMID PROTESTS FROM MEMBERS OF PARLIAMENT AND HONG KONG
CRITICS, GREAT BRITAIN UNVEILED A POLICY OF GRANTING BRITISH
NATIONALITY TO ABOUT 225,000 HONG KONG CITIZENS. THE
BENEFICIARIES OF THE PACKAGE WILL BE A LIMITED NUMBER OF
"KEY" PEOPLE AND THEIR DEPENDENTS, INCLUDING PROFESSIONALS
AND BUSINESSMEN, PEOPLE IN THE EDUCATION AND HEALTH SERVICES,
THOSE WITH TECHNICAL AND MANAGERIAL SKILLS AND PUBLIC
SERVANTS. THE SCHEME IS VIEWED BY MANY AS INSUFFICIENT AND
ELITIST. IT'S INTRODUCTION IS LIKELY TO INCREASE TENSIONS
BETWEEN BRITAIN AND HONG KONG AS WELL AS BETWEEN BRITAIN AND
CHINA.

05434 LAVE, J.
BAND-AID SOLUTIONS
SOCIETY, 26(4) (MAY 89), 11-12.
THE AUTHOR COMMENTS THAT ANY ATTEMPTS TO SOLVE HEALTH
CARE PROBLEMS OF THE HOMELESS WITHOUT SOLVING THE UNDERLYING
PROBLEM OF LACK OF HOUSING ARE NOTHING MORE THAN BAND-AID
SOLUTIONS AND WILL NOT RESULT IN ANY LONG-TERM IMPROVEMENT
IN THE CONDITION OF THE HOMELESS IN THE US. HOWEVER, SIMPLY
ADVOCATING FAR-REACHING SOLUTIONS SUCH AS RAISING THE
MINIMUM WAGE WITHOUT CLEARLY ANALYZING THE IMPLICATIONS OF
SUCH A POLICY IS NOT ADVISABLE.

05435 LAVER, R.; CLARK, M.; TEDESCO, T.
BELT-TIGHTENING
MACLEAN'S (CANADA'S NEWS MAGAZINE), 102(7) (FEB 89), 10-12.
THE MULRONEY GOVERNMENT IS IMPLEMENTING PLANS DESIGNED
TO INCREASE AUSTERITY. NEW MINISTERS ARE BEING APPOINTED AND
THE ENTIRE STRUCTURE OF THE CABINET COMMITTEE SYSTEM IS
BEING REVAMPED. THE CANADIAN FEDERAL DEFICIT CURRENTLY

STANDS AT $29 BILLION; FEDERAL PLANS TO CUT SPENDING AND STREAMLINE OR CONSOLIDATE FEDERAL AGENCIES WILL DIRECTLY AFFECT NEARLY EVERY FEDERAL AGENCY AND INDIRECTLY AFFECT THE LIVES OF COUNTLESS CANADIANS.

05436 LAVER, R.; VAN DUSEN, L.
COOLING THE WELCOME
MACLEAN'S (CANADA'S NEWS MAGAZINE), 102(27) (JUL 89), 17-18.
CANADIAN LAWMAKERS ARE SENDING TO POTENTIAL REFUGEES THE MESSAGE THAT THERE ARE "LIMITS TO CANADIAN GENEROSITY." A SERIES OF LAWS HAVE BEEN ENACTED THAT ARE INTENDED TO SPEED UP THE REFUGEE SCREENING PROCESS AND LIMIT THE NUMBERS OF REFUGEES THAT WILL BE ALLOWED TO SETTLE IN CANADA. THE LAWS ARE ALREADY EXERTING INFLUENCE: OFFICIALS ESTIMATE THAT ONLY ABOUT 15,000 PEOPLE WILL SEEK REFUGE IN CANADA IN 1989, COMPARED WITH MORE THAN 35,000 IN 1988.

05437 LAVER, R.
FICKLE VOTERS, NEW LOYALTIES
MACLEAN'S (CANADA'S NEWS MAGAZINE), 102(1) (JAN 89), 14-17.
BRIAN MULRONEY, CANADIAN PRIME MINISTER AND CONSERVATIVE PARTY LEADER, OFTEN DISCUSSES HIS VISION OF THE FUTURE IN WHICH THE CONSERVATIVES WILL REPLACE THE LIBERALS IN THE MINDS OF THE MAJORITY OF CANADIANS AS CANADA'S NATURAL GOVERNING PARTY. A RECENT POLL INDICATES THAT SIGNIFICANTLY MORE CANADIANS IDENTIFY WITH THE CONSERVATIVES THAN WITH THE LIBERALS. HOWEVER, THE HIGH DEGREE OF VOTER VOLATILITY (ONE IN FOUR SAID THAT THEY CHANGED THEIR MINDS AT LEAST ONCE ABOUT HOW TO VOTE IN THE MOST RECENT FEDERAL CAMPAIGN), HAS CAUSED POLITICAL SCIENTISTS AND OTHER ANALYSTS TO DISAGREE ABOUT THE LONG-TERM IMPLICATIONS OF THE POLLS.

05438 LAVER, R.
IN SEARCH OF UNITY
MACLEAN'S (CANADA'S NEWS MAGAZINE), 102(10) (MAR 89), 12.
AS NATIONAL CHAIRMAN OF THE LIBERAL CAUCUS, BRIAN TOBIN HAS THE UNENVIABLE OF ATTEMPTING TO CREATE AN APPEARANCE OF UNITY AND SOLIDARITY FOR A PARTY THAT IS DIVIDED BY POLICY DIFFERENCES AND PREOCCUPIED BY THE EXPECTED RACE TO SUCCEED PARTY LEADER JOHN TURNER. HE CLAIMS THAT THE LAST ELECTION BROUGHT MUCH NEEDED "NEW BLOOD" TO CANADA'S ONCE DOMINANT PARTY, BUT SOME LIBERAL MPS ARE ALREADY TRYING TO DISTANCE THEMSELVES FROM SOME OF THE PARTY'S CENTRAL PLATFORMS.

05439 LAVER, R.
THE LEADERS IN WAITING
MACLEAN'S (CANADA'S NEWS MAGAZINE), 102(11) (MAR 89), 10-12.
RUMORS THAT LIBERAL PARTY LEADER JOHN TURNER MAY STEP DOWN BEFORE THE 1990 ELECTION ARE CAUSING JOSTLING AMONG LEADERSHIP CONTENDERS WITHIN THE PARTY. OPEN POLICY DIFFERENCES ON SOME MAJOR ISSUES SUCH AS FREE TRADE AND CONSTITUTIONAL REFORMS HAVE RISEN AMONG LIBERALS. AS OF YET HOWEVER, JOHN TURNER REMAINS SILENT ABOUT HIS FUTURE.

05440 LAVER, R.; BURKE, D.; LEWIS, P.; LOWTHER, W.; MATHER, I.
THE LOOKING-GLASS TRADE
MACLEAN'S (CANADA'S NEWS MAGAZINE), 102(29) (JUL 89), 12-14.
AFTER A ROCKY BEGINNING, THE CANADIAN SECURITY INTELLIGENCE SERVICE (CSIS) IS WINNING RESPECT AMONG INTERNATIONAL INTELLIGENCE CIRCLES. ESTABLISHED IN 1984, THE AGENCY HAS INITIALLY PLAGUED WITH PROBLEMS REGARDING MANAGEMENT, INTRA-GOVERNMENTAL SQUABBLES, INVESTIGATION PROCEDURES. HOWEVER, THE AGENCY HAS SEEMED TO PUT MANY OF THESE PROBLEMS BEHIND AND IS NOW EARNING INTERNATIONAL ACCLAIM. ONE KEY FACTOR IN THE TURNAROUND IS THE ESTABLISHMENT OF AN INDEPENDENT WATCHDOG AGENCY WHICH REVIEWS THE ACTIVITIES OF THE CSIS.

05441 LAVERS, A.
LOOKING TO A COMMERCIAL FUTURE
PACIFIC DEFENCE REPORTER, 16(1) (JUL 89), 61-62.
EXPORT SALES, A SEARCH FOR NEW OVERSEAS MARKETS, JOINT VENTURES WITH AUSTRALIAN AND FOREIGN COMPANIES - ARE NOW SOUGHT EAGERLY BY THE TWO LABOR GOVERNMENT MINISTERS CHARGED WITH AUSTRALIAN DEFENCE. THE AUTHOR OPINES THAT AUSTRALIAN GOVERNMENTS SHOULD BE USING THESE PRECIOUS YEARS OF PEACE TO ENSURE THAT IN ANY FUTURE CONFLICT AUSTRALIA CAN RELY TO A GREAT EXTENT ON ITS OWN ARMS PRODUCTION.

05442 LAVRENCIC, K.
CONGO: MORE PERESTROIKA MEANS MORE UNREST
AFRICAN BUSINESS, (FEB 89), 19-20.
THIS PAPER REVIEWS THE ECONOMIC PROBLEMS IN THE CONGO IN THE LAST DECADE. IT COVERS THE DRAMATIC REDUCTION OF REVENUES FROM OIL PRODUCTION, CUT-BACKS OF GOVERNMENTAL EXPENDITURES, INCREASED LOANS FROM THE IMF AND WORLD BANK, DRAINING INTEREST COSTS, AND THE NEED TO RETURN TO AGRICULTURE.

05443 LAW, J.
INTERVIEW WITH GEORGE HABASH
MIDDLE EAST INTERNATIONAL, (357) (AUG 89), 18.
THE ARTICLE IS AN INTERVIEW WITH THE FOUNDER AND LEADER OF THE POPULAR FRONT FOR THE LIBERATION OF PALESTINE (PLEP), GEORGE HABASH. HABASH COMMENTS ON THE CURRENT STATE OF THE INTIFADA, AND THE FUTURE COURSE OF THE PALESTINIAN INDEPENDENCE MOVEMENT. HE CONCLUDES THAT ALTHOUGH THE INTIFADA HAS BEEN SUCCESSFUL IN RALLYING PUBLIC SUPPORT, THE PALESTINIANS (NOTABLY TO PLO) NEED TO STEP UP THEIR EFFORTS IN OTHER SPHERES AS WELL. HE ALSO CRITICIZES SOME ANTI-DEMOCRATIC PRACTICES WITHIN THE PALESTINE NATIONAL COUNCIL.

05444 LAW, J.
IRAQ'S SPACE ROCKET
MIDDLE EAST INTERNATIONAL, (365) (DEC 89), 13.
IRAQ CAUGHT THE US INTELLIGENCE COMMUNITY BY SURPRISE BY ANNOUNCING THAT THEY HAD LAUNCHED A ROCKET CAPABLE OF PUTTING A SATELLITE INTO SPACE. CONFIRMATION OF IRAQ'S REPORT REVEALS THAT IRAQ IS NOW "AT THE FOREFRONT OF ALL THIRD WORLD COUNTRIES" IN THIS FIELD. IT ALSO IS A REFLECTION OF THE INCREASING NUMBER OF MIDEASTERN STATES POSSESSING BALLISTIC MISSILES. THESE INCLUDE: SAUDI ARABIA, ISRAEL, IRAN, AND SYRIA.

05445 LAW, J.; BARAM, H.
SHAMIR IN WASHINGTON
MIDDLE EAST INTERNATIONAL, (364) (DEC 89), 5-7.
ISRAEL'S PRIME MINISTER SHAMIR MADE AN UNOFFICIAL VISIT TO WASHINGTON TO MEET WITH US LEADERS. HE DISCOVERED THAT THE US WAS APPARENTLY MORE CONCERNED ABOUT ISRAEL'S RELATIONS WITH SOUTH AFRICA THAN WITH ISRAEL'S SUPPRESSION OF THE INTIFADA. US STATEMENTS WITH REGARDS OF THE OCCUPIED TERRITORIES WERE LIMITED TO EXPRESSIONS OF "CONCERN." THE US ALSO HAS BEEN SLOW IN RESPONDING TO YASSER ARAFAT'S PLEAS FOR SWIFTER DIALOGUE.

05446 LAW, J.
THE PEACE PROCESS: SAVING FACE
MIDDLE EAST INTERNATIONAL, (365) (DEC 89), 4-5.
THE ARTICLE OUTLINES THE FIVE POINT "BAKER PLAN" DESIGNED TO FACILITATE NEGOTIATIONS BETWEEN ISRAEL AND PALESTINE VIA EGYPT. IT DRAWS SEVERAL PARALLELS BETWEEN THE BAKER PLAN AND PRESIDENT CARTER'S CAMP DAVID INITIATIVE. IT CONCLUDES THAT THE PLAN WILL PROBABLY DO LITTLE MORE THAN REINFORCE THE IDEA THAT THE US IS ACTIVELY SEEKING A SOLUTION TO THE THORNY PROBLEM OF THE OCCUPIED TERRITORIES.

05447 LAW, J.
THE US AND THE PLO
MIDDLE EAST INTERNATIONAL, (364) (DEC 89), 16-17.
A YEAR AGO YASSER ARAFAT GAMBLED THAT REGOCNITION OF ISRAEL AND A RENUNCIATION OF TERRORISM WOULD CAUSE THE US TO APPLY PRESSURE ON ISRAEL TO COMPROMISE BY ALLOWING A PALESTINIAN STATE ON THE WEST BANK. HOWEVER, A YEAR OF LOW LEVEL NEGOTIATIONS HAS BROUGHT ABOUT LITTLE OR NO PROGRESS; ISRAEL, APPARENTLY, IS FEELING LITTLE PRESSURE TO ABANDON ITS POLICY OF REFUSING TO GIVE UP "ONE SQUARE INCH." THUS FAR, ARAFAT'S GAMBLE HAS YIELDED NO FRUIT.

05448 LAW, J.
US LEBANON POLICY
MIDDLE EAST INTERNATIONAL, (364) (DEC 89), 5.
US POLICY TOWARDS LEBANON HAS SHIFTED DRASTICALLY SINCE THE TIME WHEN US MARINES WERE STATIONED IN BERIUT. THE US HAS AGREED TO SUPPORT THE LEBANESE PARLIAMENT IN THEIR EFFORT TO REDUCE THE POWER OF THE MARONITE CHRISTIANS, ERSTWHILE ALLIES OF THE US. IN FACT THE US HAS THE FIRST NATION TO OFFICIALLY SUPPORT THE LEBANESE ACTION.

05449 LAW, J.
US MEDIA AND THE OBEID CASE
MIDDLE EAST INTERNATIONAL, (358) (SEP 89), 16-17.
THE ARTICLE EXAMINES US MEDIA COVERAGE OF THE ISRAELI KIDNAPPING OF SHAIKH AL-KARIM OBEID. IT CONCLUDES THAT THE COVERAGE HAS BEEN MYOPIC AND SINGULARLY ONE-SIDED. US JOURNALISTS CONSISTENTLY IGNORE THE POSSIBILITY OF US FOREIGN POLICY CHANGES LEADING TO BOTH SHORT AND LONG-TERM SOLUTIONS TO THE HOSTAGE CRISIS IN GENERAL. SPECIFIC PROBLEMS OUTLINED INCLUDE REFERENCES TO ISRAEL'S "SECURITY ZONE" IN SOUTHERN LEBANON, AND THE USE OF THE TERM "TERRORISTS" IN GENERAL.

05450 LAWLER, J.J.; PARLE, W.M.
EXPANSION OF THE PUBLIC TRUST DOCTRINE IN ENVIRONMENTAL LAW: AN EXAMINATION OF JUDICIAL POLICY MAKING BY STATE COURTS
SOCIAL SCIENCE QUARTERLY, 70(1) (MAR 89), 134-148.
THIS RESEARCH DOCUMENTS SUBSTANTIAL STATE COURT EXPANSION OF THE PUBLIC TRUST DOCTRINE IN ENVIRONMENTAL LAW SINCE 1970, AND EXPLORES THE RELATIONSHIP BETWEEN DOCTRINE EXPANSION AND A NUMBER OF POLITICAL, LEGAL INSTITUTIONAL, SOCIOECONOMIC, AND DEMOGRAPHIC FACTORS SUGGESTED BY THE LITERATURE ON JUDICIAL POLICY MAKING AND ENVIRONMENTAL POLICY. TWO OF THESE FACTORS, LEGAL PROFESSIONALISM AND "MORALISTIC" POLITICAL CULTURE, ARE FOUND TO EXERT IMPORTANT

INDEPENDENT INFLUENCES ON DOCTRINE EXPANSION.

05451 LAWLER, P.A.
THE LIMITS OF THE "SECULAR HUMANIST" INTERPRETATION OF THE
CONSTITUTION
JOURNAL OF POLITICAL SCIENCE, 16(1-2) (1988), 43-48.
TODAY'S SECULAR HUMANISTS AND FUNDAMENTALISTS REPRESENT
TWO EXTREMES OF THE AMERICAN POLITICAL SPECTRUM, BUT THERE
HAVE ALWAYS BEEN FACTIONS AND MOVEMENTS ROUGHLY COMPARABLE
TO THESE TWO GROUPS IN AMERICAN POLITICS. THIS IS PART OF
THE STRENGTH AND HEALTH OF LIBERAL DEMOCRACY.

05452 LAWLOR, S.
FUNDING THE ARTS
ENCOUNTER, LXXII(1) (JAN 89), 61-65.
GREAT BRITAIN'S MINISTER FOR THE ARTS, RICHARD LUCE, HAS
FORMULATED A POLICY IN LINE WITH PRIME MINISTER THATCHER'S
SOUND FINANCIAL PRINCIPLES. THE GOVERNMENT WILL CONTINUE TO
PAY FOR THE ARTS, BUT PUBLIC FUNDING MUST NOT SERVE AS A
DISINCENTIVE TO SELF-RELIANCE, WHICH WILL BE ENCOURAGED BY
COMPELLING INSTITUTIONS TO ATTRACT PRIVATE FUNDS. WHEN THEY
DO SO, THEY WILL BE REWARDED WITH PUBLIC MONEY. THIS POLICY
REFLECTS THE WIDER DIRECTION OF THATCHER'S ECONOMIC AND
SOCIAL POLICY. IT IS AN ARM'S LENGTH POLICY BECAUSE THE
GOVERNMENT SEEMS RESOLVED NOT TO INTERVENE IN THE MATTER OF
PRECISELY HOW, OR ON WHAT, MONEY FOR THE ARTS SHOULD BE
SPENT.

05453 LAWRENCE, H.
SOMALIA'S TROUBLED NORTH
AFRICAN BUSINESS, (JAN 89), 9-10.
THIS PIECE ANALYZES THE ECONOMIC AND POLITICAL
SITUATIONS IN SOMALIA. ISSUES REVIEWED INCLUDE THE CONFLICTS
BETWEEN THE FORMER BRITISH-RULED NORTH AND THE ITALIAN-
ADMINISTERED SOUTH, RELATIVE HEALTH IN THE NORTH AND SEVERE
UNEMPLOYMENT IN THE SOUTH, AND GOVERNMENT REPRESSION.

05454 LAWSON, F.H.
POLITICAL-ECONOMIC TRENDS IN BA'THI SYRIA: A
REINTERPRETATION
ORIENT, 29(4) (DEC 88), 579-594.
TO FORMULATE A CLASS PERSPECTIVE ON CONTEMPORARY
SYRIAIAN POLITICS, THIS ESSAY LAYS OUT A NEW PERIODIZATION
OF THE YEARS SINCE 1963. IT DIFFERENTIATES SUCCESSIVE PHASES
IN THE AGRARIAN AND INDUSTRIAL POLICIES ADOPTED BY THE
REGIME IN TERMS OF THE DEGREE TO WHICH THE STATE AND ITS
AGENCIES HAVE TAKEN A DIRECT ROLE IN RESTRUCTURING THE
COUNTRY'S ECONOMY.

05455 LAWSON, F.H.
THE IRANIAN CRISIS OF 1945-46 AND THE SPIRAL MODEL OF
INTERNATIONAL CONFLICT
INTERNATIONAL JOURNAL OF MIDDLE EAST STUDIES, 21(3) (AUG
89), 307-326.
THE AUTHOR ARGUES THAT THE IRANIAN CRISIS OF 1945-46
AROSE FROM A STRATEGIC SITUATION IN WHICH THE USA WAS
COMPETING WITH GREAT BRITAIN AS MUCH AS WITH THE SOVIET
UNION. THIS COMPETITION INVOLVED A PART OF THE WORLD IN
WHICH BOTH WESTERN ALLIES HAD SIGNIFICANT ECONOMIC INTERESTS
AND WAS CARRIED OUT IN THE CONTEXT OF GROWING INDIGENOUS
POLITICAL INSTABILITY. THE USA ADOPTED A FOREIGN POLICY
TOWARD THE GULF THAT INCLUDED A HEAVY MILITARY COMPONENT,
BOTH AS A MEANS OF GUARANTEEING THAT AMERICAN OFFICIALS
WOULD CONTINUE TO PLAY A LEADING ROLE IN REGIONAL AFFAIRS
WHEN THE WAR CAME TO AN END AND AS A WAY OF REASSURING LOCAL
RULER THREATENED BY SEVERE INTERNAL CHALLENGES AND SKEPTICAL
OF THE EFFICACY AND RELIABILITY OF AMERICAN DIPLOMATIC
SUPPORT.

05456 LAWTON, A.
THE INTERPRETATION OF POLITICAL ACTION: THE CASE OF CIVIL
DISOBEDIENCE
DISSERTATION ABSTRACTS INTERNATIONAL, 49(11) (MAY 89),
3492-A.
THE AUTHOR EXAMINES THE NATURE OF CIVIL DISOBEDIENCE AND
THE NATURE OF POLITICAL ACTIVITY IN GENERAL. CIVIL
DISOBEDIENCE IS CONCERNED WITH THE RELATIONSHIP BETWEEN THE
INDIVIDUAL AND THE STATE AND WITH THE SPECIFIC QUESTION OF
WHETHER OR NOT THE INDIVIDUAL CAN DISOBEY THE STATE. IN THIS
THESIS, THE AUTHOR CONSIDERS THE NATURE OF OBLIGATIONS AND
RIGHTS IN ADDRESSING THIS QUESTION. HE UTILIZES THE WORKS OF
HOBBES, LOCKE, HART, AND RAWLS IN ANALYZING POLITICAL
ACTIVITY.

05457 LAXER, G.
THE SCHIZOPHRENIC CHARACTER OF CANADIAN POLITICAL ECONOMY
CANADIAN REVIEW OF SOCIOLOGY AND ANTHROPOLOGY, 26(1) (FEB
89), 178-192.
THIS PAPER EXPLORES THE SCHIZOPHRENIC CHARACTER OF
CANADIAN POLITICAL ECONOMY. USE OF THE SAME MARXIST
VOCABULARY CANNOT HIDE THE EXISTENCE OF TWO VERY DIFFERENT
PERSPECTIVES UNDER THE RUBRIC 'POLITICAL ECONOMY.' ON ONE
SIDE ARE NATIONALIST IDIOGRAPHIC HISTORIANS WHO FOCUS ON
CANADA'S DEPENDENT POSITION IN THE WORLD ECONOMY AND ASSUME

THAT CANADIAN HISTORY IS LARGELY MADE OUTSIDE OF CANADA. ON
THE OTHER SIDE ARE NOMOTHETIC 'INTERNATIONALIST' THEORISTS
WHO ADDRESS ENTIRELY DIFFERENT ISSUES-THOSE OF SOCIAL ORDER
AND REVOLUTION. WHILE THE LATTER ASSUME THAT CANADA IS PART
OF AN INTERNATIONAL CAPITALIST ORDER, THEY ASSUME THE
CANADIAN BUSINESS CLASS IS LARGELY INDIGENOUS, AS IN OTHER
ADVANCED CAPITALIST COUNTRIES. BOTH PERSPECTIVES TEND TO BE
IDEOLOGICALLY CHARGED AND ENGAGE IN EPISTEMOLOGICAL AND
METHODOLOGICAL EXTREMISM. THE RESULT IS A DIALOGUE OF THE
DEAF. THE PAPER CONCLUDES BY SUGGESTING WAYS BY WHICH EACH
PERSPECTIVE CAN RENEW ITSELF AND LEAD IN MORE FRUITFUL
DIRECTIONS.

05458 LAYACHI, A.
IMAGES OF FOREIGN POLICY: THE UNITED STATES AND NORTH
AFRICA
DISSERTATION ABSTRACTS INTERNATIONAL, 50(1) (JUL 89),
252-A.
THE AUTHOR SEARCHES FOR THE PSYCHOLOGICAL UNDERPINNINGS
OF U.S. FOREIGN POLICY TOWARDS NORTH AFRICA FROM 1974 TO
1984. HE HYPOTHESIZES THAT (1) IMAGES PLAY AN IMPORTANT ROLE
AS INTERVENING VARIABLES IN THE FOREIGN POLICY MAKING
PROCESS; (2) BOTH PRIVATE IMAGES (INDIVIDUAL) AND OFFICIAL
IMAGES (COLLECTIVE) EXIST; (3) THE STRUCTURAL AND
SUBSTANTIVE NATURE OF IMAGES CORRELATES WITH EITHER A
GLOBALIST OR A NEUTRAL APPROACH TO FOREIGN POLICY ISSUES.

05459 LAYACHI, A.
TOWARDS PARLIAMENTARY DEMOCRACY
WORLD MARXIST REVIEW, 31(11) (NOV 88), 98-105.
THE PARTY OF PROGRESS AND SOCIALISM OF MOROCCO HAS
EMERGED FROM THE ELECTION CAMPAIGNS WITH A HEIGHTENED
AUTHORITY AND MORE SOLID ORGANISATION, AND THAT ESPECIALLY
BECAUSE IT DID NOT ENGAGE IN ELECTIONEERING AND DID NOT MAKE
ANY LAVISH PROMISES. WHAT IS MORE, IT HAD WARNED AGAINST ANY
ILLUSIONS CONCERNING THE 'RESULTS', WHICH ARE KNOWN TO BE
PATENTLY RIGGED. THE PPS USED ELECTION CAMPAIGNS NOT ONLY TO
DEMONSTRATE THE TOTAL FAILURE OF THE OFFICIAL POLICY IN
VARIOUS SPHERES, BUT ALSO TO CONVINCE THE PEOPLE THAT THE
PPS IS CAPABLE OF LEADING THE COUNTRY OUT OF THE CRISIS.

05460 LAYCOCK, D.
PEYOTE, WINE AND THE FIRST AMENDMENT
THE CHRISTIAN CENTURY, 106(28) (OCT 89), 876-879.
THIS ARTICLE EXPLORES THE FIRST AMENDMENT AND FREEDOM OF
RELIGION IN REGARDS TO THE USE OF PEYOTE IN A RITUAL OF THE
NATIVE AMERICAN CHURCH. THE U.S. SUPREME COURT WILL BE
CONSIDERING THIS FALL WHETHER THE STATE CAN PROHIBIT THIS
RELIGIOUS RITUAL. DOUGLAS LAYCOCK, WHO TEACHES AT THE
UNIVERSITY OF TEXAS IN AUSTIN, MAINTAINS THAT SUCH RITUALS
AS PRACTICED BY NATIVE AMERICANS SHOULD BE CONSTITUTIONALLY
PROTECTED.

05461 LAYNE, C.
REALISM REDUP: STRATEGIC INDEPENDENCE IN A MULTIPOLAR WORLD
SAIS REVIEW, 9(2) (SUM 89), 19-44.
THIS ARTICLE EXAMINES THE STRATEGIC SIGNIFICANCE OF
MULTI-POLARITY. COMPARING AND CONTRASTING THE JUDGEMENTS OF
REALIST AND COLD WAR INTERNATIONALIST THEORY AS IT APPLIES
TO TODAY'S POLITICAL CLIMATE.

05462 LAYNE, C.
SUPERPOWER DISENGAGEMENT
FOREIGN POLICY, (77) (WIN 89), 17-40.
THIS ARTICLE OUTLINES A DISENGAGEMENT PROPOSAL FOR
EUROPE WHICH WOULD LAST A LONG TIME BECAUSE IT WOULD BRING
ABOUT SYSTEMIC AND STRUCTURAL - NOT COSMETIC - CHANGES IN
EAST - WEST SECURITY RELATIONS, FOR BOTH SUPERPOWERS, AND
FOR ALL OF EUROPE. SUCH AN AGREEMENT WOULD END THE COLD WAR.
IT EXAMINES THE GERMAN QUESTION AND THE NATURE OF GERMAN
POWER AS WELL AS THE SOVIET AND UNITED STATES ROLE IN EUROPE.

05463 LAYS, J.
WHO'S IN CHARGE, ANYHOW?
STATE LEGISLATURES, 15(9) (OCT 89), 14-17.
RECENT SCHOOL REFORM HAS FOCUSED ON SHIFTING AUTHORITY
FROM THE STATE GOVERNMENT TO THE SCHOOL HOUSE. IN BOSTON,
FOR EXAMPLE, THE TEACHERS' UNION AND THE SCHOOL SYSTEM ARE
NEGOTIATING TO GIVE MORE CONTROL AND POWER TO SCHOOL
PERSONNEL INSTEAD OF SCHOOL BOARDS AND SUPERINTENDENTS. THE
BOSTON PLAN IS MODELED AFTER SIMILAR ONES IN ROCHESTER, N.Y.,
AND DADE COUNTY, FLA.

05464 LAYTNER, A.
CHINA'S ISRAEL POLICY REVIEWED
MIDDLE EAST REVIEW, XXI(4) (SUM 89), 54-60.
TIAN ZHONGQING'S ANALYSIS OF CHINA'S POLICY TOWARD
ISRAEL REFLECTS IDEOLOGICALLY-INSPIRED EMENDATION. HIS THREE-
STAGE FORMULATION OF THE POLICY IS DEFICIENT ON EACH LEVEL.
IN ANALYZING THE EARLY PERIOD, TIAN IGNORES THE SERIOUS
NEGOTIATIONS BETWEEN CHINA AND ISRAELI IN 1949 THROUGH 1955.
IN THE INTERMEDIATE PERIOD, HE GLOSSES OVER CHINA'S RADICAL
PRO-PALESTINIAN POLICIES OF THE CULTURAL REVOLUTION ERA. IN
THE CONTEMPORARY PERIOD, TIAN DISMISSES NOT ONLY THE

CONTACTS THAT ARE OCCURING BETWEEN CHINA AND ISRAEL BUT ALSO THEIR POLITICAL IMPLICATIONS. IT WOULD BE MORE ACCURATE TO PRESENT EARLY ISRAEL-CHINESE CONTACTS AS PHASE I; THE SINO-ARAB ALIGNMENT BEGINNING IN 1955 AND CULMINATING IN THE CULTURAL REVOLUTION AS PHASE II; AND DENG'S PRAGMATISM AS PHASE III.

05465 LAZAREV, B.
IMPROVEMENT OF THE ADMINISTRATIVE MACHINERY IN THE USSR: VITAL QUESTIONS
INTERNATIONAL REVIEW OF ADMINISTRATIVE SCIENCES, 55(1) (MAR 89), 7-14.
THE ARTICLE OUTLINES SOME OF THE OBJECTIVES OF PERESTROIKA WHICH INCLUDE THE IMPROVEMENT OF THE PARTY GUIDANCE SYSTEM AND ADMINISTRATIVE MACHINERY. IT DISCUSSES THE CURRENT EFFORTS BEING MADE TO FOSTER DECENTRALIZATION AND A PROPER DEMARCATION BETWEEN THE FUNCTIONS OF THE PARTY AND OF STATE BODIES.

05466 LEACH, B.
DISABLED PEOPLE AND THE IMPLEMENTATION OF LOCAL AUTHORITIES' EQUAL OPPORTUNITIES POLICIES
PUBLIC ADMINISTRATION, 67(1) (SPR 89), 65-78.
IN DEBATES ON EQUAL OPPORTUNITIES, DISABLED PEOPLE'S ISSUES ARE OFTEN IGNORED. DISABILITY IS TYPICALLY SEEN AS A MEDICALLY DEFINED CATEGORY POPULATED BY INDIVIDUALS 'WITH PROBLEMS'. THIS ARTICLE PRESENTS AN ALTERNATIVE PERSPECTIVE WHICH RE-DEFINES DISABILITY AND DEMANDS THAT THE AUTHENTICITY OF THE DISABLED PEOPLE'S MOVEMENTS BE ACKNOWLEDGED. SURVEYS ESTIMATING THE NUMBERS OF DISABLED PEOPLE IN THE UK ARE REVIEWED, AS ARE LOCAL AUTHORITY EQUAL OPPORTUNITIES STATEMENTS. TWO CASE STUDIES OF LOCAL AUTHORITIES, MANCHESTER AND LAMBETH, ARE USED TO SHOW HOW PROGRESS ON DISABLED PEOPLE'S ISSUES HAS BEEN ACHIEVED BY ACCOUNT BEING TAKEN OF THE DEMANDS OF THE DISABLED PEOPLE'S MOVEMENT. THE ARTICLE CONCLUDES BY LOOKING AT THE IMPLICATIONS OF RECENT LEGISLATION AND SUGGESTS THAT EQUAL OPPORTUNITIES POLICIES FOR DISABLED PEOPLE ARE MOST LIKELY TO BE IMPLEMENTED WHEN THEY ORGANIZE THEMSELVES EFFECTIVELY AND MAKE COALITIONS WITH OTHER DISADVANTAGED GROUPS.

05467 LEACH, B.
THE RIGHT OF NATIONS...': GORBACHEV S SOVIET UNION
ARENA, (89) (SUM 89), 25-31.
THE ARTICLE EXAMINES THE INCREASINGLY SIGNIFICANT PROBLEM OF SOVIET NATIONALISM. ALTHOUGH THE PROBLEM OF UNRULY ETHNIC MINORITIES HAS PLAGUED RUSSIANS SINCE THE DAYS OF THE TSARS, THE SOVIET LEADERS FACE NEW CHALLENGES. MIKHALL GORBACHEV MUST WALK THE FINE LINE BETWEEN LIBERAL REFORM AND THE BREAK-UP OF THE SOVIET UNION. THE ARTICLE CONCLUDES THAT HIS SOLUTION MUST BE A MIXTURE OF BOTH THE US FEDERALIST CORE/PERIPHERY CONSTITUTIONAL BALANCE AND THE EEC'S EMERGING ALLIANCE CONFEDERATION BUILT ON TRADE. FAILURE TO RESOLVE THE TENSIONS IN THE BALTIC, UKRAINE, BYELOUSSIA, AND THE CAUCASION REPUBLICS COULD RESULT IN GORBACHEV'S DEMISE.

05468 LEAHY, P.
REFLECTIONS ON FEDERAL JUDICIAL SELECTION
JOURNAL OF LAW & POLITICS, VI(1) (FAL 89), 25-30.
THE ARTICLE EXAMINES SEVERAL ISSUES CONNECTED WITH FEDERAL JUDICIAL SELECTION. THEY INCLUDE: THE PRESIDENT'S JUDICIAL APPOINTMENTS POWER, HOW THE SENATE HAS INTERPRETED ITS RESPONSIBILITY TO ADVISE AND CONSENT, THE APPOINTMENT OF MORE WOMEN AND MINORITIES TO THE FEDERAL BENCH, AND THE MEMBERSHIP OF JUDICIAL NOMINEES IN DISCRIMINATORY CLUBS. THE ARTICLE CONCLUDES THAT PARTICULAR JUDICIAL NOMINATION WILL CONTINUE TO INSPIRE FIERCE CONTROVERSY AND CONFLICT BETWEEN THE PRESIDENT AND THE SENATE. HOWEVER, IF THE PRESIDENT AND THE SENATE REMEMBER THE LEGACY KNOWN AS THE PHRASE "ADVICE AND CONSENT," THESE DISPUTES WILL INVIGORATE, NOT WEAKEN THE CONSTITUTIONAL SYSTEM THAT JUDGES, SENATORS, AND PRESIDENTS ARE ALL SWORN TO UPHOLD.

05469 LEATHERS, C.
SCOTLAND'S NEW POLL TAXES AS A HAYEKIAN POLICY
SCOTTISH JOURNAL OF POLITICAL ECONOMY, 36(2) (MAY 89), 194-201.
SCOTTISH LOCAL GOVERNMENTS WILL BE THE FIRST IN BRITAIN TO IMPLEMENT THE THATCHER GOVERNMENT'S PLAN TO SUBSTITUTE FLAT-SUM POLL TAXES FOR RATES ON DOMESTIC PROPERTY. ALTHOUGH THE PRIME MINISTER HAS DESCRIBED "THATCHERISM" AS A SCOTTISH INVENTION WITH ROOTS FROM THE WORKS OF ADAM SMITH AND DAVID HUME, A MUCH STRONGER ARGUMENT CAN BE MADE FOR THE CASE THAT THE THATCHERIST POLL TAX PLAN REFLECTS A PHILISOPHICAL/THEORETICAL KINSHIP WITH THE MODERN AUSTRIAN ECONOMIST F. A. HAYEK, RATHER THAN THE GREAT POLITICAL ECONOMISTS OF THE SCOTTISH ENLIGHTENMENT. THE ARTICLE BRIEFLY REVIEWS HUME AND SMITH'S OBJECTIONS TO POLL TAXES. IT ALSO DEMONSTRATES THAT THE GOVERNMENT'S RATIONALE FOR FLAT-SUM POLL TAXES IS CONSISTENT WITH HAYEK'S CRITICISMS OF CONVENTIONAL PUBLIC FINANCE THEORY.

05470 LEAVER, R.
RESTRUCTURING IN THE GLOBAL ECONOMY: FROM PAX AMERICANA TO PAX NIPPONICA?
ALTERNATIVES, 14(4) (OCT 89), 429-462.
THIS ARTICLE ADDRESSES QUESTIONS ABOUT THE EVOLVING STRUCTURE OF WORLD ORDER WHICH ARE BACK ON THE AGENDA OF CONTEMPORARY INTERNATIONAL STUDIES AFTER AN ABSENCE OF MORE THAN A DECADE. IT LOOKS AT THE CHANGING PATTERN OF JAPANESE 'THREATS' AND US 'RESPONSES' THAT HAVE BECOME MANIFEST IN TRANS-PACIFIC ECONOMIC RELATIONS DURING RECENT DECADES, IT THEN DISCUSSES THE BIASES OF INTERNATIONAL POLTIICAL ECONOMY LITERATURE AND THEN RETURNS TO THE THEME OF GEOPOLITICS.

05471 LEBLANC, J.
ANTI-COMMUNISM, LEFT UNITY, AND THE COMMUNIST PARTY
POLITICAL AFFAIRS, LXVIII(1) (JAN 89), 5-8.
ANTI-COMMUNISM PAINTS A FALSE PICTURE BASED ON THE IDEA THAT COMMUNISTS ARE UNPATRIOTIC, GODLESS, ANTI-FAMILY, FRINGE ELEMENTS. ANTI-COMMUNISM HAS ALWAYS BEEN USED TO DERAIL UNITY IN THE PEOPLE'S MOVEMENTS, DISARM THEIR MILITANCY, AND UNDERMINE THE STRUGGLE AGAINST CAPITALISM.

05472 LEBLANC, J.
FOR A BIGGER, BOLDER COMMUNIST PARTY AND PRESS IN 1989
POLITICAL AFFAIRS, LXVIII(3) (MAR 89), 34-39.
THERE SEEM TO BE TWO MAIN PROBLEMS AFFECTING THE GROWTH OF THE COMMUNIST PARTY IN THE UNITED STATES. ONE INVOLVES THE ADEQUACY OF THE PUBLIC ROLE OF THE PARTY AND THE IDEOLOGICAL ROLE OF THE COMMUNIST PRESS. THE SECOND INVOLVES THE CONSOLIDATION OF PARTY AND PRESS GROWTH.

05473 LEBLANC, J.
THE COMMUNIST PARTY AND ITS IDEOLOGY
POLITICAL AFFAIRS, LXVIII(8) (AUG 89), 13-19.
THE ARTICLE IS A REPORT TO THE IDEOLOGICAL CONFERENCE OF THE COMMUNIST PARTY, USA. IT EXAMINES THE IMPORTANCE OF A PROGRAM ROOTED IN MARXIST-LENINIST IDEOLOGY. IT ALSO ANALYZES SEVERAL OF THE CHALLENGES THE MOVEMENT FACES; THESE INCLUDE LIQUIDATIONISM, REFORMISM, FEAR, AND HOPELESSNESS. IT EXAMINES STRATEGIES DESIGNED TO BUILD AND INCREASE COALITIONS WITH PARTICULAR EMPHASIS ON THE USE OF CLUBS AS A RECRUITING TOOL.

05474 LEBLEBICI, H.; SALANCIK, G.R.
THE RULES OF ORGANIZING AND THE MANAGERIAL ROLE
ORGANIZATION STUDIES, 10(3) (1989), 301-326.
THIS PAPER IS AN ATTEMPT TO CLARIFY THE MEANING OF THE TERM 'AN ORGANIZATION' BASED ON THE WEBERIAN DISTINCTION BETWEEN CORPORATE GROUPS AND ORGANIZATIONS AND TO IDENTIFY THE MANAGERIAL ROLE IMBEDDED IN HIS DEFINITION. THIS IS DONE IN TWO STAGES. FIRST, WEBER'S DEFINITION IS THEORETICALLY ANALYZED AND ITS LOGICAL IMPLICATIONS ARE PRESENTED. IN THE SECOND STAGE, THE HYPOTHESES GENERATED FROM THESE IMPLICATIONS ARE EMPIRICALLY TESTED. BY UTILIZING DATA COLLECTED FROM 64 U.S. NATIONAL MANUFACTURING TRADE ASSOCIATIONS, WEBER'S ANALYTICAL DISTINCTIONS BETWEEN CORPORATE GROUPS AND ORGANIZATIONS ARE EXAMINED. THE PATTERNS OF FINDINGS ARE CONGRUENT WITH WEBER'S ARGUMENT THAT ORGANIZATIONS ARE A DISTINCT SUBSET OF CORPORATE GROUPS. IN ADDITION, FINDINGS SUGGEST THAT THE EXISTENCE OF A STAFF DISTINCT FROM THE MEMBERS OF THE GROUP IS CRITICAL FOR UNDERSTANDING THE NATURE OF ORGANIZATIONS.

05475 LEBOW, R.N.
MALIGN ANALYSTS OR EVIL EMPIRE? WESTERN IMAGES OF SOVIET NUCLEAR STRATEGY
INTERNATIONAL JOURNAL, XLIV(1) (WIN 89), 1-40.
ANALYSTS OPPOSED TO ARMS CONTROL AND SUPPORTIVE OF THE MILITARY BUILD-UP BY THE REAGAN ADMINISTRATION ARGUE THAT SOVIET STRATEGY IS OFFENSIVELY MOTIVATED. THEY INSIST THAT SOVIET LEADERS ARE DRIVEN NOT BY INSECURITY, BUT BY AMBITION. IN CONTRAST TO DEFENSIVE ANALYSTS WHO EMPHASIZE THE NUMEROUS INVASIONS OF RUSSIA AND THE INSECURITY THESE HAVE BRED, THE OFFENSIVE SCHOOL POINTS TO THE EQUALLY LONG HISTORY OF RUSSIAN EXPANSIONISM TO SUPPORT ITS CONTENTION THAT THE PRINCIPAL PURPOSE OF MOSCOW'S FOREIGN POLICY IS TO EXTEND SOVIET TERRITORIAL AND IDEOLOGICAL INFLUENCE. DIFFERENCES OF OPINION ABOUT SOVIET INTENTIONS CONSTITUTE THE FUNDAMENTAL CLEAVAGE IN THE FIELD OF SOVIET STUDIES, ALTHOUGH THE DEFENSIVE AND OFFENSIVE INTERPRETATIONS ARE BEST DESCRIBED AS GENERAL ORIENTATIONS, NOT FORMAL SCHOOLS OF THOUGHT.

05476 LECKIE, S.
THE UN COMMITTEE ON ECONOMIC, SOCIAL AND CULTURAL RIGHTS AND TO ADEQUATE HOUSING: TOWARDS AN APPROPRIATE APPROACH
HUMAN RIGHTS QUARTERLY, 11(4) (NOV 89), 522-560.
THIS ARTICLE EXPLORES THE HUMAN RIGHT TO ADEQUATE HOUSING WHICH HAS ITS LEGAL FOUNDATIONS THROUGHOUT THE BODY OF INTERNATIONAL HUMAN RIGHTS LAW, THE UN COMMITTEE ON ECONOMIC, SOCIAL AND CULTURAL RIGHTS HAS ADOPTED TWO CRUCIAL PROCEDURAL CHANGES THAT AT LEAST PARTIALLY PAVE THE WAY FOR HOUSING RIGHTS TO RECEIVE THE ATTENTION THEY DESERVE: (1) THE DECISION TO REFORMULATE GUIDELINES FOR REPORTS BY STATE

PARTIES TO THE COVENANT; AND (2) THE DECISION TO HAVE A GENERAL DISCUSSION ON ARTICLE 11 OF THE COVENANT WHICH ENSHRINES THE RIGHT TO HOUSING. THIS PAPER FOCUSES ON THESE DEVELOPMENTS AND ON THE COMMITTEE'S ROLE IN THE GLOBAL REALIZATION OF HOUSING RIGHTS.

05477 LEDBETTER, J.
REESE'S PIECES
CAMPAIGNS AND ELECTIONS, 10(4) (DEC 89), 27-32.
MATTHEW A. REESE REINVENTED POLITICS. HE BECAME THE QUINTESSENTIAL SALESMAN OF CANDIDATES AND CAUSES, PITCHING HIS INSTINCTS, SKILLS, AND SALESMANSHIP TO EVERY LIBERAL POLITICIAN WHO CAME DOWN THE PIKE, BEGINNING WITH JOHN F. KENNEDY. REESE CHANGED POLITICS FOREVER AND, IN THE PROCESS, TRANSFORMED POLITICAL CONSULTING FROM A BACKROOM FRATERNITY OF CUT-THROAT HACKS INTO A BONA FIDE BILLION-DOLLAR INDUSTRY.

05478 LEDEEN, M.
ENDGAME: PRESSURING GARBO
AMERICAN SPECTATOR, 22(5) (MAY 89), 29-31.
TODAY THE SOVIET EMPIRE IS FAR LESS CREDITWORTHY THAN THE LATIN AMERICAN (AND EVEN SOME AFRICAN) POOR CURRENTLY SEEKING OUR INVESTMENTS, CREDITS, AND TECHNOLOGY. ON SHEER BUSINESS GROUNDS, AMERICA IS LIKELY TO MAKE MORE MONEY IN THOSE AREAS THAN IN A FAILED SOVIET SYSTEM THAT HAS PROVED ITSELF UTTERLY INCAPABLE OF COMPETING IN THE WORLD MARKETPLACE. AND IF THE U.S. SUCCEEDS IN LATIN AMERICA AND AFRICA, IT IMPROVES ITS STRATEGIC POSITION, WHILE IF AMERICA SUCCEEDS IN THE EMPIRE, IT STRENGTHENS ITS HISTORIC ENEMIES. SO "SAVE GORBACHEV" HAS A TAG LINE: "AND INCREASE YOUR RISK."

05479 LEDEEN, M.
IRAN WITHOUT KHOMEINI
AMERICAN SPECTATOR, 22(8) (AUG 89), 12-13.
THIS ARTICLE EXPLORES THE FUTURE OF IRAN AFTER THE DEATH OF KHOMEINI. IT ANALYSES EACH OF THE POSSIBLE SUCCESSORS AND PREDICTS THE CHANCES OF EACH. IT DELVES INTO THE NEW BATTLEFRONT-THE DOMESTIC, AND PREDICTS THE POSSIBILITIES FOR THE U.S. TO HAVE A VOICE IN IRAN'S FUTURE.

05480 LEDEEN, M.
THE CURIOUS CASE OF CLEMICAL WARFARE
COMMENTARY, 88(1) (JUL 89), 37-41.
EVEN THOUGH GERMANY IS THE BIGGEST SINNER, HOWEVER, ALL WESTERN COUNTRIES BEAR A SHARE OF RESPONSIBILITY FOR THE CHEMICAL WARFARE THAT IS NOW ALMOST CERTAIN TO OCCUR AGAIN. FOR NO COUNTRY HAS FOUGHT WITH SUFFICIENT COURAGE AND TENACITY TO PREVENT THE WORLD FROM ARRIVING AT SO DANGEROUS A STATE. DESPITE AMPLE COVERAGE GIVEN TO THE STORY, THERE HAVE BEEN FEW CALLS FOR THE SORT OF ACTION THAT MIGHT PUT A STOP TO THE COMMERCE IN CHEMICAL WEAPONS. NOR HAS THERE BEEN ANY GREAT OUTCRY AGAINST THE USE BY SOVIET MILITARY FORCES OF SOME SORT OF POISON GAS AGAINST DEMONSTRATORS IN TBILISI, GEORGIA, THIS PAST APRIL, EVEN THOUGH (OR PERHAPS BECAUSE) THEIR WILLINGNESS TO GAS THEIR OWN CITIZENS SUGGESTS THEY WOULD BE WILLING TO USE CHEMICAL WEAPONS AGAINST US IN THE EVENT OF WAR. THERE IS ONLY ONE OPTION: THOSE COUNTRIES THAT HAVE TOLERATED THE MURDEROUS TRAFFIC MUST PUT AN IMMEDIATE END TO ANY FURTHER SUPPLIES, INCLUDING SERVICE AND SPARE PARTS. EVEN THE BEST HARDWARE WILL BREAK DOWN IN THE DESERTS OF THE MIDDLE EAST, ESPECIALLY IF EXPERT MAINTENANCE IS LACKING. THEREFORE, WHILE MUCH DAMAGE HAS ALREADY BEEN DONE, STOPPING THE TRAFFIC MIGHT STILL PRODUCE SOME SIGNIFICANT IMPROVEMENT IN THIS GRIM AND EXTRAORDINARILY DANGEROUS PICTURE.

05481 LEDEEN, M.
THE SUAVE GORBACHEV WEARS NO CLOTHES
AMERICAN SPECTATOR, 22(2) (FEB 89), 16-17.
GORBACHEV'S SOVIET EMPIRE IS DEAD BROKE, ABOUT TO ENTER THE INTERNATIONAL VERSION OF CHAPTER ELEVEN UNLESS AN EMERGENCY BAILOUT CAN BE ARRANGED. GORBACHEV'S DECEMBER 1988 SPEECH BEFORE THE UNITED NATIONS WAS AN ADMISSION OF FAILURE AND APPEAL TO CREDITORS FOR MORE MONEY AND MORE TIME, AND A GENERAL CRY FOR HELP. THE MAJOR FOREIGN-POLICY DEVELOPMENT THE BUSH ADMINISTRATION MUST DEAL WITH IS THE COLLAPSE OF THE SOVIET EMPIRE

05482 LEDOGAR, S.
A BREAK IN THE CLOUDS: THE TIME TABLE IS REALISTIC
WORLD MARXIST REVIEW, 32(9) (SEP 89), 35-36.
THIS ARTICLE BY US AMBASSADOR, STEPHEN LEDOGAR, ONE OF THE CHIEF NEGOTIATORS OF THE UNITED STATES IN THE VIENNA TALKS ON CONVENTIONAL ARMS IN EUROPE, GIVES HIS IMPRESSION OF THE PROGRESS SO FAR, AND THE PROSPECTS AHEAD IN THE TALKS. HE FEELS THAT MUCH PROGRESS HAS BEEN MADE IN SPECIFIC AREAS OF SIX DIFFERENT AREAS OF MILITARY ARMS AND EQUIPMENT AND PERSONEL REDUCTION AND THAT THE U.S. IS AHEAD OF SCHEDULE.

05483 LEDOGAR, S.
SECURITY AND ARMS CONTROL: PROSPECTS AND IMPLICATIONS
RUSI JOURNAL, 134(3) (FAL 89), 12-14.
THE ARTICLE OUTLINES CURRENT EFFORTS TO REDUCE CONVENTIONAL ARMS IN EUROPE. IT ARGUES THAT CLAIMS OF TOO MUCH CAUTION ON THE PART OF NATO ARE UNFOUNDED. IT CONCLUDES THAT ALTHOUGH PROGRESS IS BEING MADE, AND CAN CONTINUE, NATO MUST MAINTAIN A POLICY BASED ON THREE PRINCIPLES: REALISM, STRENGTH, AND DIALOGUE.

05484 LEDUC, L.
THE CANADIAN FEDERAL ELECTION OF 1988
ELECTORAL STUDIES, 8(2) (AUG 89), 163-168.
TO THE CASUAL FOREIGN OBSERVER, CANADA'S 34TH FEDERAL ELECTION HELD ON 21 NOVEMBER 1988 MIGHT HAVE SEEMED A PREDICTABLE AFFAIR. A PROGRESSIVE-CONSERVATIVE GOVERNMENT LED BY PRIME MINISTER BRIAN MULRONEY, WHICH HAD BEEN CONFIDENTLY PLANNING ITS POLITICAL AGENDA AROUND AN AUTUMN ELECTION CALL, WON A COMFORTABLE MAJORITY OF SEATS. A LIBERAL PARTY, WHICH HAD STUMBLED FROM DISASTER TO DISASTER UNDER THE UNEVEN LEADERSHIP OF JOHN TURNER, POLLED FEWER THAN A THIRD OF THE VOTES CAST. AND A RESURGENT NEW DEMOCRATIC PARTY, LED BY THE POPULAR AND SEASONED ED BROADBENT, ACHIEVED A RECORD TALLY OF 43 SEATS, EVEN THOUGH IT REMAINED A CLEAR THIRD IN OVERALL SUPPORT. THE FACT THAT THERE IS SO LITTLE THAT IS REMARKABLE ABOUT THESE RESULTS WOULD ENGENDER SHOCKED SURPRISE UPON LEARNING THAT THIS ELECTION WAS PERHAPS THE MOST DRAMATIC OF THE CENTURY, INVOLVING ISSUES OF OVERRIDING NATIONAL IMPORTANCE AND AN OUTCOME THAT REMAINED UNCERTAIN UNTIL THE VERY END. THE GREAT FREE TRADE ELECTION OF 1988, AS IT WILL ALMOST CERTAINLY BE REMEMBERED BY MANY OBSERVERS AND PARTICIPANTS, PROVIDED MOMENTS OF INCOMPARABLE POLITICAL DRAMA.

05485 LEE, A.R.
VALUE CLEAVAGES AND POLITICAL ATTITUDES: THE CASE OF KOREA
DISSERTATION ABSTRACTS INTERNATIONAL, 50(3) (SEP 89), 784-A.
THE AUTHOR STUDIES THE DISTRIBUTION OF FUNDAMENTAL SOCIAL VALUES IN KOREAN SOCIETY THAT FALL ALONG A TRADITIONAL/MODERN DIMENSION AND ANALYZES THE RELATIONSHIP BETWEEN THESE SOCIAL VALUES AND A VARIETY OF POLITICAL ATTITUDES. HE ALSO EXAMINES THE MAJOR CHARACTERISTICS OF KOREAN POLITICAL ORIENTATIONS AND EVALUATES THE EFFECTS OF KOREAN SOCIAL VALUES ON POLITICAL ORIENTATION.

05486 LEE, B.
JUSTIFYING POLITICAL OBLIGATION: AUTONOMY AND AUTHORITY
DISSERTATION ABSTRACTS INTERNATIONAL, 48(10) (APR 88), 2718-A.
IN ORDER TO JUSTIFY POLITICAL OBLIGATION WHICH APPEARS SELF-CONTRADICTORY, THE TWO CONCEPTS OF AUTONOMY AND AUTHORITY NEED TO BE RECONCILED. THE DISSERTATION ATTEMPTS A RECONCILIATION THROUGH THE USE OF "COMMON LEGISLATION" AND "COMMON RULES."

05487 LEE, C.K.
WAR IN THE CONFUCIAN INTERNATIONAL ORDER
DISSERTATION ABSTRACTS INTERNATIONAL, 49(11) (MAY 89), 3498-A.
USING DATA ON 131 WARS, INCLUDING THE DURATION, EXTENT, AND MAGNITUDE OF THE CONFLICT, THE AUTHOR PRESENTS A DESCRIPTIVE ANALYSIS OF THE INDIVIDUAL CHARACTERISTICS OF THE WARS. HE FINDS BOTH SIMILARITIES AND DIFFERENCES BETWEEN WARS IN THE CONFUCIAN AND WESTERN INTERNATIONAL SYSTEMS. HIS ANALYSIS SHOWS THAT WARS WERE WIDESPREAD AND NORMAL IN THE CONFUCIAN INTERNATIONAL SYSTEM, EVEN THOUGH IT WAS GUIDED BY A PACIFIC PHILOSOPHY.

05488 LEE, C.M.
PREVAILING IN A FUTURE CONFLICT: CONVENTIONAL DETERRENCE AND DEFENSE STRATEGIES WITH A SPECIAL REFERENCE TO THE DEFENSE PLANNING OF THE REPUBLIC OF KOREA
DISSERTATION ABSTRACTS INTERNATIONAL, 50(6) (DEC 89), 1795-A.
THE AUTHOR DISCUSSES THE IMPORTANCE OF MAINTAINING A CONVENTIONAL DETERRENT AND DEFENSE POSTURE IN THE REPUBLIC OF KOREA IN THE COMING DECADE, WITH SPECIAL REFERENCE TO THE ROLE OF DOCTRINES AND TECHNOLOGIES IN MODERN CONFLICT. HE BEGINS WITH A CRITICAL ASSESSMENT OF THE DEFENSE STRATEGIES OF SOUTH KOREA'S NEIGHBORS, INCLUDING THE USSR, JAPAN, NORTH KOREA, AND THE PEOPLE'S REPUBLIC OF CHINA. THEN HE CONSIDERS THE DEFENSE PLANNING OF SOUTH KOREA, WITH EMPHASIS ON THE ADAPTATION OF U.S. AIR-LAND BATTLE DOCTRINE, THE CHANGING CONDITIONS FOR MAINTAINING A CONVENTIONAL DETERRENT FORCE POSTURE, AND THE REQUIREMENTS FOR STRENGTHENING INTER-OPERABILITY WITHIN THE KOREAN-U.S. COMBINED FORCES COMMAND.

05489 LEE, C.S.
POLITICAL CHANGE, REVOLUTION, AND THE DIALOGUE IN THE TWO KOREAS
ASIAN SURVEY, 29(11) (NOV 89), 1033-1042.
THIS ARTICLE EXPLORES THE BEGINNING OF THE PROCESS OF ADJUSTMENT BETWEEN A MONOLITHIC OR UNITARY POLITICAL SYSTEM IN NORTH KOREA AND A NEW PLURALISTIC SYSTEM IN SOUTH KOREA. IT EXAMINES NEW DEVELOPMENTS IN SOUTH KOREA AND NORTH KOREA'S REACTION TO THEM. IT IDENTIFIES TASKS FOR THE FUTURE AND ENDS WITH A NOTE OF OPTIMISM.

05490 LEE, D.K.
A CAUSAL ANALYSIS OF MILITARY INTERVENTION IN POLISH
POLITICS
DISSERTATION ABSTRACTS INTERNATIONAL, 49(11) (MAY 89),
3492-A.
IN ORDER TO SYSTEMATICALLY INVESTIGATE THE CAUSES OF
MILITARY INTERVENTION IN POLISH POLITICS, THE AUTHOR
UTILIZES AN ANALYTICAL FRAMEWORK WITH THREE MAJOR CAUSAL
DIMENSIONS: (1) PRECIPITATING OPPORTUNITIES, THE PERFORMANCE
FAILURES OF THE CIVILIAN GOVERNMENT; (2) IDEOLOGICAL
JUSTIFICATIONS, THE PROTECTION OF NATIONAL INTERESTS; (3)
LATENT MOTIVATIONS, THE DEFENSE AND ENHANCEMENT OF THE
MILITARY'S CORPORATE INTERESTS. HE CONCLUDES THAT THE
GENERAL MODEL OF MILITARY INTERVENTION, DEVELOPED FROM
EXPERIENCES IN THIRD WORLD COUNTRIES IN AFRICA, ASIA, AND
LATIN AMERICA, CAN BE FRUITFULLY APPLIED TO A COMMUNIST
COUNTRY.

05491 LEE, D.R.
THE IMPOSSIBILITY OF A DESIRABLE MINIMAL STATE
PUBLIC CHOICE, 61(3) (JUN 89), 277-284.
THIS PAPER ARGUES THAT THE DESIRABLE SIZE OF GOVERNMENT
CAN BE EITHER POSITIVELY OR NEGATIVELY RELATED TO THE
CONTROL EXERTED OVER IT BY THE PUBLIC. THIS ARGUMENT COSTS
DOUBT ON THE POSSIBILITY OF A DESIRABLE MINIMUM STATE.

05492 LEE, D.T.
CONGRESS VERSUS PRESIDENT ON FOREIGN POLICY: A CASE STUDY
OF TAIWAN RELATIONS ACT
DISSERTATION ABSTRACTS INTERNATIONAL, 49(11) (MAY 89),
3498-A.
THE AUTHOR SURVEYS THE PROCESS BY WHICH THE TAIWAN
RELATIONS ACT WAS FORMULATED BY THE EXECUTIVE BRANCH AND THE
CONGRESS.

05493 LEE, J.
NURSING HOME ALTERNATIVES
FREE CHINA REVIEW, 39(3) (MAR 89), 28-31.
TAIWAN'S ECONOMIC DEVELOPMENT IS BRINGING SWEEPING
SOCIAL CONSEQUENCES, SOME OF WHICH ARE FORCING TRADITIONAL
VALUES INTO A NEW AND UNDESIRABLE SHAPE. IN THIS ARTICLE,
THE ARTHOR DISCUSSES THE PREDICAMENT OF TAIWAN'S ELDERLY AND
SOME GOVERNMENT PLANS TO PROVIDE HELP FOR SENIOR CITIZENS.

05494 LEE, J.K.
AN APPROACH TO THE PROBLEM OF JUSTICE THROUGH SOCIAL
CONTRACT THEORY
DISSERTATION ABSTRACTS INTERNATIONAL, 49(11) (MAY 89),
3492-A.
"GOOD" IS MERELY THE RATIONALIZATION OF SOME COMMITMENTS
ALREADY MADE BASED ON CUSTOM, WHEREAS "RIGHT" IS THE
JUSTIFICATION OF SOME PRINCIPLES WHOSE VALIDITY IS NOT
HYPOTHETICALLY SUPPOSED BUT UNQUESTIONABLY ACCEPTED. THE
CENTRAL QUESTION IS: WHAT IS THE NATURE AND CONTENT OF THE
PRINCIPLES WHICH LINK RIGHT WITH JUSTIFICATION? IN THIS
DISSERTATION, THE AUTHOR POSITS THE TERM "STATE OF NATURE"
FOR AN ANSWER. HIS EMPHASIS IS ON REFUTING HOBBES' STATE OF
NATURE, AND HE PROPOSES A NEW CLASSIFICATION OF A "NEGATIVE"
STATE OF NATURE AND A "POSITIVE" SOCIETY.

05495 LEE, K.
AFTER CHIANG, THE "LEE TENG-HUI ERA": POLITICAL
DEVELOPMENT IN TAIWAN
ASIAN PROFILE, 17(4) (AUG 89), 297-304.
FOUR HOURS AFTER PRESIDENT CHIANG CHING-KUO DIED,
TAIWAN'S VICE PRESIDENT LEE TENG-HUI WAS SWORN IN AS THE NEW
PRESIDENT. COMPARED TO THE BLOODY TRANSITIONS OF POLITICAL
POWER BY MILITARY COUPS IN SOME THIRD WORLD COUNTRIES, THIS
SMOOTH CHANGE DEMONSTRATED POLITICAL MATURITY IN TAIWAN.
HOWEVER, A POWER STRUGGLE AMONG POLITICAL FACTIONS WITHIN
THE RULING KUOMINTANG DID OCCUR DURING THE TRANSITIONAL
PERIOD. THIS PAPER ANALYZES THE TRANSITIONAL PROCESS AND THE
PROBLEMS FACED BY THE NEW TAIWANESE GOVERNMENT.

05496 LEE, K.
EXISTENCE OF ELECTORAL EQUILIBRIA WITH PROBABILISTIC VOTING
DISSERTATION ABSTRACTS INTERNATIONAL, 49(8) (FEB 89),
2344-A.
THE AUTHOR BEGINS WITH A CRITICAL SURVEY OF THE EXISTING
LITERATURE ON PROBABILISTIC VOTING MODELS. THEN HE DEVELOPS
AN ALTERNATE WAY OF MODELING AN ELECTION PROCESS, USING
INCOME REDISTRIBUTION. HE CONCLUDES THAT ELECTORAL
EQUILIBRIA DO NOT EXIST UNLESS ALL VOTERS HAVE IDENTICAL AND
LINEAR PROBABILITY DISTRIBUTION FUNCTIONS.

05497 LEE, M.
CHINA'S KOREAN POLICY WITHIN THE FRAMEWORK OF ANTI-
HEGEMONISM: 1969-1988
DISSERTATION ABSTRACTS INTERNATIONAL, 50(2) (AUG 89),
537-A.
THE AUTHOR REVIEWS THE HISTORICAL BACKGROUND THAT LINKS
CHINA AND KOREA, THE DYNAMIC EVOLUTION OF SINO-DPRK
RELATIONS SINCE THE LATE 1940'S COMMUNIST CHINA'S ANTI-
HEGEMONISM FOREIGN POLICY, SINO-KOREAN AND INTER-KOREAN

RELATIONS, BEIJING'S CURRENT FOREIGN POLICY AND ITS
IMPLICATIONS FOR THE SECURITY OF EAST ASIA, AND THE
INTERACTION OF CHINA WITH JAPAN, THE USA, AND THE USSR OVER
KOREAN AFFAIRS.

05498 LEE, M.
THE PRIME MINISTER
FAR EASTERN ECONOMIC REVIEW, 141(37) (SEP 88), 14-16.
THE ALL-BUT-ONE-SEAT SWEEP BY THE RULING PEOPLE'S ACTION
PARTY (PAP) IN SINGAPORE'S GENERAL ELECTION HAS BEEN
PORTRAYED AS A "RINGING ENDORSEMENT" OF THE YOUNGER LEADERS
POISED TO TAKE OVER FROM PRIME MINISTER LEE KUAN YEW. LEE
ANNOUNCED AFTER THE ELECTION THAT "THE TRANSITION IS
COMPLETE." THE MOST LIKELY CANDIDATE FOR SUCCESSOR TO LEE IS
47-YEAR OLD GOH CHOK TONG WHO HAS BEEN IN TRAINING FOR
NEARLY FOUR YEARS AS FIRST DEPUTY PRIME MINISTER. HE
DECLARED THAT HE WOULD BE READY TO ASSUME THE MANTLE WITHIN
TWO YEARS.

05499 LEE, R.W.
CHURCH PERSECUTION UNDER COMMUNISM
ASIAN OUTLOOK, 24(3) (MAY 89), 19-20.
THE AUTHOR LISTS INCIDENTS OF RELIGIOUS PERSECUTION
UNDER COMMUNIST REGIMES IN ANGOLA, CUBA, LAOS, LATVIA,
NICARAGUA, NORTH KOREA, VIETNAM, AND ELSEWHERE. HE ALSO
ENUMERATES SOME OF THE HEAVY RESTRICTIONS IMPOSED ON
CHRISTIANS IN COMMUNIST CHINA.

05500 LEE, R.W. III
SOUTH AMERICAN COCAINE: WHY THE U.S. CAN'T STOP IT
CURRENT, (313) (JUN 89), 22-31.
WASHINGTON WANTS TO ENCOURAGE STABLE, ECONOMICALLY
VIABLE GOVERNMENTS IN LATIN AMERICA, TO PROMOTE DEMOCRACY
THERE, AND TO SUPPRESS LEFTIST INSURGENT MOVEMENTS.
AMERICA'S WAR AGAINST DRUGS IS NOT NECESSARILY COMPATIBLE
WITH THESE PRIORITIES, AT LEAST IN THE SHORT RUN. IN FACT,
THE ARGUMENT CAN BE MADE THAT THE USA AND ITS LATIN AMERICAN
FRIENDS HAVE A COMMON INTEREST IN MINIMIZING THE INTENSITY
OF THE DRUG WAR.

05501 LEE, S.
DEMOCRACY, RIGHTS, AND CONFLICT IN THE SOVIET UNION
SOCIALISM AND DEMOCRACY, 6 (SPR 89), 89-114.
A NEW FLEXIBILITY EXISTS IN THE OFFICIAL SOVIET
ATTITUDES TOWARDS ISSUE OF HUMAN RIGHTS, INDIVIDUAL FREEDOM
AND RESPONSIBILITY, AND DEMOCRATIZATION. THE AUTHOR ARGUES
THAT THIS FLEXIBILITY CAN BE BETTER UNDERSTOOD BY ANALYZING
ARGUEMENTS MADE BY LENIN CONCERNING THE VITAL NEED FOR
BRINGING THE MASSES OF PEOPLE INTO FULL PARTICIPATION IN THE
ACTIVITIES OF A SOCIALIST GOVERNMENT. ON THE BASIS OF A
READING OF LENIN'S ARGUEMENTS IN THE STATE AND REVOLUTION, A
MORE THOROUGH UNDERSTANDING OF GORBACHEV'S CLAIMS THAT IF
SOVIET SOCIETY IS EVER TO ADVANCE THROUGH MATURE SOCIALISM
AND INTO COMMUNISM, THEN THE PROCESS OF DEMOCRATIZATION MUST
BEGIN IN EARNEST, CAN BE ACHIEVED.

05502 LEE, S.
JUDGES OR POLITICIANS?
CONTEMPORARY RECORD, 3(1) (FAL 89), 20-22.
SHOULD JUDGES KEEP OUT OF POLITICS? CAN THEY? HOW DO
THEY DECIDE CONTROVERSIAL CASES? SHOULD THEY BE GIVEN MORE
POWER AS THE INTERPRETERS OF A BILL OF RIGHTS? IN THIS
ARTICLE, THE AUTHOR CRITICIZES THE JUDGE'S CRITICS AND
EXPLAINS THE COMPLEX REALITY OF JUDICIAL LAW-MAKING.

05503 LEE, S.
REVOLUTIONARY MOBILIZATION: A STOCHASTIC PROCESS MODEL
DISSERTATION ABSTRACTS INTERNATIONAL, 50(5) (NOV 89),
1423-A.
THE AUTHOR USES A MATHEMATICAL MODEL TO DESCRIBE AND
ANALYZE THE PROCESS OF REVOLUTION. HE DEVELOPS A STOCHASTIC
PROCESS MODEL AS A FORM OF THE MASTER EQUATION, BASED ON THE
ASSUMPTIONS DERIVED FROM MOBILIZATION THEORIES. THEN HE
DERIVES AN APPROXIMATED DETERMINISTIC VERSION THAT PROVIDES
SEVEN QUALITATIVELY DIFFERENT CASES OF THE REVOLUTIONARY
PROCESS. FINALLY, HE USES TWO HISTORICAL CASE STUDIES TO
EVALUATE THE VALIDITY OF THE MODEL.

05504 LEEDS, R.S.
LEEDS: GENESIS OF A PRIVATIZATION TRANSACTION
WORLD DEVELOPMENT, 17(5) (MAY 89), 741-756.
THIS ESSAY TRACES THE EVOLUTION OF THE MALAYSIAN
GOVERNMENT'S DECISION TO UNDERTAKE A MAJOR PRIVATIZATION
INITIATIVE. A SPECIFIC TRANSACTION, THE PORT KELANG
CONTAINER TERMINAL, IS DESCRIBED AND ASSESSED. AS IN SEVERAL
OTHER DEVELOPING COUNTRIES THAT ARE UNDERGOING A SIMILAR
TRANSFORMATION, PRIVATIZATION WAS PART OF A BROADER PUBLIC
POLICY RESPONSE TO POOR PUBLIC ENTERPRISE PERFORMANCE,
MOUNTING DOMESTIC AND EXTERNAL DEBT LEVELS, UNSUSTAINABLE
PUBLIC SECTOR DEFICITS, AND POLITICAL CHANGE. THE CONTAINER
TERMINAL PRIVATIZATION ILLUSTRATES THE DIFFICULTIES INHERENT
IN IMPLEMENTATION, SUCH AS A SHORTFALL OF SKILLED GOVERNMENT
PERSONNEL, LEGAL OBSTACLES, PROTRACTED NEGOTIATIONS WITH
EMPLOYEES, AND DIFFERENCES ABOUT THE ACCEPTABLE TERMS AND

CONDITIONS OF SALE.

05505 LEEGE, D.C.; WELCH, M.R.
RELIGIOUS ROOTS OF POLITICAL ORIENTATIONS: VARIATIONS
AMONG AMERICAN CATHOLIC PARISHIONERS
THE JOURNAL OF POLITICS, 51(1) (FEB 89), 137-162.
SOCIAL SCIENTISTS HAVE FORMULATED SEVERAL THEORIES OR
PROTOTHEORIES TO ACCOUNT FOR PARTY IDENTIFICATION, POLITICAL
IDEOLOGY, AND ISSUE POSITIONS OF AMERICANS AND, BY EXTENSION,
OF AMERICAN CATHOLICS. THESE INCLUDE ETHNIC ASSIMILATION
AND COMMUNALISM, SOCIAL CLASS, REGIONAL POLITICAL CULTURE,
POLITICAL GENERATIONS, AND RECENTLY GENDER. AT THE SAME TIME,
SOME SCHOLARS HAVE ARGUED THAT RELIGIOUS VALUES PROFOUNDLY
AFFECT THESE POLITICAL VARIABLES. BUT THEIR MEASURES HAVE
NEVER BEEN CONVINCING OR THEIR FINDINGS STRONG. THIS PAPER
FORMULATES A NEW MEASURE OF FOUNDATIONAL RELIGIOUS BELIEFS
AND, CONTROLLING FOR MEASURES OF OTHER THEORETICALLY
RELEVANT VARIABLES, ESTIMATES THE IMPACT OF SUCH BELIEFS ON
POLITICAL VARIABLES. DATA ARE DRAWN FROM THE 2,667
REGISTERED CATHOLIC PARISHIONERS INCLUDED IN THE NOTRE DAME
STUDY OF CATHOLIC PARISH LIFE. THE OVERALL MODEL APPEARS
MODESTLY POWERFUL, BUT INDIVIDUAL FINDINGS ARE OF INTEREST.
INTERPRETING RESULTS THROUGH THEORIES OF PARTISANSHIP, THIS
PAPER ARGUES THAT THE TRADITIONAL MEASURE OF PARTISANSHIP
RESONATES TO SOCIAL STRUCTURAL CHARACTERISTICS OF CATHOLICS
BUT THAT NEWER THEORIES OF PARTISANSHIP MAY BE BETTER
PREDICTED BY A MEASURE OF FOUNDATIONAL RELIGIOUS BELIEFS.
POLITICAL IDEOLOGY AND MANY "CULTURAL POLITICS" ISSUES ARE
RESPONSIVE TO FOUNDATIONAL RELIGIOUS BELIEFS. POSITIONS ON
MORE TRADITIONAL PUBLIC POLICY CONCERNS - FOR EXAMPLE,
DEFENSE SPENDING, EQUAL OPPORTUNITY - ARE BETTER PREDICTED
BY DEMOGRAPHIC VARIABLES, BUT EVEN THESE ISSUES RESPOND TO
RELIGIOUS VALUES.

05506 LEES, M.
THE IMPACT OF EUROPE 1992 ON THE ATLANTIC PARTNERSHIP
WASHINGTON QUARTERLY, 12(4) (FAL 89), 171-182.
THIS ARTICLE FIRST OUTLINES THE CHANGES NOW IN PROGRESS
ACROSS THE WORLD AND PARTICULARLY IN THE KEY COMPONENTS OF
THE RELATIONSHIP BETWEEN THE UNITED STATES AND EUROPE. IT
THEN ARGUES THAT THESE PROBLEMS ARE MORE PROFOUND AND MORE
COMPLEX THAN MAY BE ACCOMMODATED BY SMALL ADJUSTMENTS TO
POLICIES AND ARRANGEMENTS. IT ALSO DESCRIBES THE CHALLENGE
FACING WESTERN GOVERNMENTS IF THEY ARE TO ENSURE THAT THE
CREATION OF THE UNIFIED MARKET IN EUROPE BY 1992 WILL
CONSTITUTE A SOURCE OF ADDED STRENGTH RATHER THAN A SOURCE
OF DISSENSION IN THE ATLANTIC PARTNERSHIP.

05507 LEGGE, M.
SHARING THE U.S. BURDEN: A BRITISH VIEW
CURRENT, (313) (JUN 89), 15-21.
THE AUTHOR DISCUSSES THE DEBATE OVER WHETHER THE
EUROPEAN MEMBERS OF NATO ARE CARRYING THEIR FAIR SHARE OF
THE BURDEN OF COMMON DEFENSE OR WHETHER THE USA HAS BEEN
UNFAIRLY SADDLED WITH TOO LARGE A RESPONSIBILTY.

05508 LEGRO, J.W.
THE MILITARY MEANING OF THE NEW SOVIET DOCTRINE
PARAMETERS, XIX(4) (DEC 89), 80-92.
THE CURRENT FERMENT IN SOVIET MILITARY DOCTRINE HAS LED
TO UNCERTAINTY AND DEBATE OVER ITS IMPLICATIONS. ON ONE HAND,
GORBACHEV'S PEACEFUL RHETORIC, BACKED BY FORCE REDUCTIONS,
IS COMPETING WITH THE BOLSHOI'S BALLERINAS FOR FAVORABLE
WESTERN PRESS REVIEWS. PUBLIC OPINION-AND MANY PUBLIC
OFFICIALS-PERCEIVE A REDUCED MILITARY THREAT FROM THE SOVIET
ARMY. ON THE OTHER HAND, SKEPTICS BELIEVE THAT RECENT
DOCTRINAL CHANGES ARE COMPATIBLE WITH A MODERNIZED, MORE
EFFICIENT SOVIET MILITARY MACHINE. IN THEIR VIEW, THE SOVIET
ARMY IS DEFINITELY CHANGING, BUT THE THREAT WILL NOT. A
REVIEW OF THE OPERATIONAL IMPLICATIONS OF THE NEW SOVIET
SECURITY THEMES INDICATES THAT NEITHER THE OPTIMIST NOR
PESSIMIST IS WHOLLY JUSTIFIED. THE EFFECT ON THE MILITARY
SITUATION IN EUROPE WILL BE MIXED: SOME CHANGES APPEAR TO
BENEFIT NATO'S POSITION, WHILE OTHERS SUGGEST NEW CHALLENGES.
UNDERSTANDING THE SPECIFICS OF THIS EVOLUTION IS CRUCIAL
FOR DETERMINING HOW THE WEST SHOULD RESPOND.

05509 LEGUM, C.
BLACK FUTURE FOR SOUTH AFRICA
NEW AFRICAN, (OCT 89), 36.
THIS ARTICLE EXAMINES BLACK INVOLVEMENT IN THE FUTURE
GOVERNING OF SOUTH AFRICA, HOW NEGOTIATIONS CAN BE STARTED
TO BRING BLACKS INTO THE POLITICAL PROCESS IS DISCUSSED. HOW
MANDELA, THE ANC AND THE MASS DEMOCRATIC MOVEMENT WILL BE
ENVOLVED IS DISCRIBED, THE COMPLEX DIPLOMACY FOR A BLACK
FUTURE IN SOUTH AFRICA BECOMES A POSSIBLITY.

05510 LEGUM, C.
EPLF'S PEACE OFFENSIVE
NEW AFRICAN, (262) (JUL 89), 11-13.
THE ERITREAN PEOPLE'S LIBERATION MOVEMENT IS NOT
DEMANDING OUTRIGHT INDEPENDENCE. WHAT IT WANTS IS A
REFERENDUM IN WHICH THE ERITREAN PEOPLE ARE GIVEN THE CHOICE
TO CHOOSE THE FUTURE OF THEIR COUNTRY. IF MENGISTU IS
CONVINCED THAT THE ERITREANS ARE HAPPY WITH PRESENT
ARRANGEMENTS WHY DOES HE NOT PUT IT TO THE TEST?

05511 LEGUM, C.
ETHIOPIA IN TURMOIL
NEW AFRICAN, (262) (JUL 89), 9-11.
MENGISTU HAILE MARIAM HAS SURVIVED THE IMMEDIATE
CHALLENGE TO HIS POWER, INDEED HE MAY HAVE ENGINEERED A PRE-
EMPTIVE COUP IN WHICH AT LEAST TEN GENERALS DIED AND
HUNDREDS OF OTHER OFFICERS PERISHED, BUT HE CANNOT SUSTAIN
THE WAR AGAINST ERITREA AND TIGRE FOREVER. THE SOVIETS ARE
HAVING SECOND THOUGHTS, AND NO ONE ELSE WILL PUT UP THE VAST
SUMS INVOLVED TO PAY HIS COSTLY WARS, HENCE THE RECENT
DECISION TO TALK. COLIN LEGUM ANALYSES THE NEW SITUATION.

05512 LEGUM, C.
POLICY FOR PEACE
NEW AFRICAN, (OCT 89), 22.
THIS ARTICLE ANALYSES PEACE TALKS BETWEEN THE ERITREAN
PEOPLE'S LIBERATION FRONT AND THE ETHIOPIAN GOVERNMENT. THE
GOAL IS TO SEE IF A LASTING FORMULA CAN BE NEGIOATED. AS THE
COMPLEX ISSUES WHICH ARE INVOLVED ARE EXAMINED THE
SUGGESTION THAT EVERYTHING DEPENDS ON THE ACCEPTANCE OF SOME
FORM OF FEDERALISM IS PUT FORTH.

05513 LEGUM, C.
THE WAY FORWARD
NEW AFRICAN, (OCT 89), 37.
THIS ARTICLE FOCUSES ON THE ATTEMPTS OF BLACK AND WHITE
AFRICANS TO NEGOTIATE SETTLEMENT RATHER THAN INTENSIFYING
THE ARMED STRUGGLE. CONDITIONS REQUIRED FOR NEGOTIATIONS
WITH THE PRETORIA REGIME ARE SET DOWN AND OBJECTIONS TO AN
INTERNATIONAL INITIATIVE BECAUSE OF FEAR OF GREAT BRITIAN
PRIME MINISTER MARGARET THATCHER'S SUPPORT OF APARTHEID ARE
DETAILED. IDEAS FOR CONDITIONS NEEDED FOR NEGOTIATIONS ARE
PRESENTED.

05514 LEHMAN-WILZIG, S.
ISRAEL: BETWEEN THE BOOK AND THE SWORD
MIDSTREAM, XXXV(1) (JAN 89), 15-19.
ISRAEL'S MILITARY CREED HAS ALWAYS BEEN BASED ON MAXIMUM
MILITARY POWER CIRCUMSCRIBED BY THE FORCE OF MAXIMAL
MORALITY. THE PRESENT UPRISING IN THE OCCUPIED TERRITORIES
AFFORDS NEITHER POSSIBILITY.

05515 LEHMAN-WILZIG, S.
ISRAEL: RED IS DEAD
MIDSTREAM, XXXV(8) (NOV 89), 9-12.
THE OVERALL TREND IN ISRAEL POINTS TO THE HISTORIC
DENOUEMENT OF THE COUNTRY'S ONCE PROUD AND PREDOMINANT
SOCIALIST ETHOS. PARADOXICALLY, THE DEMISE OF ISRAELI
SOCIALISM CAN BE TRACED TO THE EARLY SUCCESS OF THE
HISTADRUT AND THE LABOR PARTY. WITH VIRTUALLY NO NATURAL
RESOURCES, EXTREME MILITARY INSECURITY, AND A POPULATION
THAT HAD LITTLE EXPERIENCE IN MOST OF THE PROFESSIONS
NECESSARY FOR A MODERN STATE, THE HISTADRUT-LABOR PARTY
MANAGED TO PULL THE FLEDGLING COUNTRY INTO THE MODERN WORLD.
BUT THAT VERY SUCCESS MEANT THAT THEIR FORMER PROLETARIAN
SUPPORTERS BECAME DISTINCTLY MIDDLE CLASS IN BOTH
PROFESSIONAL AND SOCIO-ECONOMIC ORIENTATION.

05516 LEHMAN-WILZIG, S.
PROTEST, TELEVISION, NEWSPAPERS, AND THE PUBLIC: WHO
INFLUENCES WHOM?
POLITICAL COMMUNICATION AND PERSUASION, 6(1) (1989), 21-32.
THIS STUDY ANALYZES THREE RELATED QUESTIONS: TO WHAT
EXTENT DOES TV INFLUENCE ITS AUDIENCE, THE NEWPAPERS, AND
THE TACTICS OF PUBLIC PRESSURE GROUPS BASED ON THE EXISTENCE
AND AVAILABILITY OF TV IN GENERAL? THE STUDY IS BASED ON A
52-DAY NATIONAL TV STRIKE IN ISRAEL IN LATE 1987, WITH THE
FOLLOWING ASPECTS INVESTIGATED: THE CHANGE IN TRAFFIC
ACCIDENT AND PUBLIC PROTEST FREQUENCY DURING THE STRIKE
PERIOD; THE CHANGE IN NUMBER OF ARTICLES AND PHOTOS FOUND IN
THE NEWSPAPERS; THE COVERAGE OF ALL ISRAELI MEDIA REGARDING
PUBLIC PROTESTS OVER AN EXTENDED PERIOD OF TIME; AND LESS
QUANTITATIVELY, THE EFFECT OF PUBLIC SERVICE ANNOUNCEMENTS
(PSAS) ON TRAFFIC ACCIDENT RATES OVER THE YEARS.

05517 LEHMBRUCH, G.
INSTITUTIONAL LINKAGES AND POLICY NETWORKS IN THE FEDERAL
SYSTEM OF WEST GERMANY
PUBLIUS: THE JOURNAL OF FEDERALISM, 19(4) (FAL 89),
221-236.
WEST GERMAN FEDERALISM CAN BE UNDERSTOOD AS A SYSTEM OF
INTERLOCKING, BUT DISTINCT AND AUTONOMOUS, "POLICY NETWORKS.
" SECTORAL POLICY NETWORKS ARE INTEGRATED INTO OVERARCHING
NETWORKS. THE TRADITIONAL PLURI-CENTRISM OF STATE AND
SOCIETAL INSTITUTIONS IS CONTRASTED WITH AN INTEGRATED (BUT
NOT CENTRALIZED) ECONOMIC POLICY NETWORK ORIENTED TOWARD
NATIONAL HOMOGENEITY. WITH THE DECLINE OF KEYNESIAN
MACROECONOMIC POLICY, HOWEVER, REGIONAL POLICY NETWORKS ARE
BEING UPGRADED. AT THE SAME TIME, THE POLITICAL PARTY SYSTEM
AND THE POLITICIZATION OF ADMINISTRATIVE AGENCIES HAVE LED
TO THE DEVELOPMENT OF AN OVERARCHING NETWORK IN WHICH

BARGAINING AND ACCOMMODATION HAVE PRECEDENCE OVER
HIERARCHICAL CENTRALIZATION.

05518 LEIGH, W.A.
FEDERAL GOVERNMENT POLICIES AND THE "HOUSING QUOTIENT" OF
BLACK AMERICAN FAMILIES
REVIEW OF BLACK POLITICAL ECONOMY, 17(3) (WIN 89), 25-42.
THE "HOUSING QUOTIENT" -THE CONDITION OF AND ACCESS TO
HOUSING-IS DEFINED FOR BLACK AMERICAN FAMILIES AND IS
EXAMINED IN CONJUNCTION WITH THE MAJOR RELEVANT FEDERAL
POLICIES AND PROGRAMS. POLICIES CONSIDERED INCLUDE FAIR
HOUSING AND THE NATIONAL URBAN POLICY. PROGRAMS EXAMINED
INCLUDE PUBLIC HOUSING AND RENTAL ASSISTANCE. THE LACK OF
DATA CONSTRAINS THE COMPLETENESS OF THE ANALYSIS, ALTHOUGH
CERTAIN PROGRAMS SEEM TO ENROLL BLACKS IN DISPROPORTION TO
THE REST OF THE POPULATION. THE PAPER CONCLUDES THAT BLACKS
CURRENTLY ARE SERVED BY ALL FEDERAL PROGRAMS, EVEN THOUGH
MANY PROGRAMS HISTORICALLY HAVE FAILED TO LIVE UP TO THEIR
POTENTIAL TO ASSIST BLACKS.

05519 LEIGHLEY, J.E.
THE STRUCTURE AND CONSEQUENCES OF INDIVIDUAL POLITICAL
INVOLVEMENT
DISSERTATION ABSTRACTS INTERNATIONAL, 50(1) (JUL 89),
246-A.
USING DATA FROM AMERICAN NATIONAL ELECTION STUDIES, THE
AUTHOR STUDIES THE INTERRELATIONSHIPS OF THREE DIMENSIONS OF
POLITICAL INVOLVEMENT: COGNITION, AFFECT, AND PARTICIPATION.
SHE PROBES HOW ONE TYPE OF INVOLVEMENT ENHANCES ANOTHER TYPE,
HOW SOCIAL INTERACTION INFLUENCES INVOLVEMENT, AND HOW THE
PRESIDENTIAL CAMPAIGN INFLUENCES INDIVIDUAL POLITICAL
INVOLVEMENT.

05520 LEIKEN, R.S.
THE SOVIET UNION AND NICARAGUA
CURRENT HISTORY, 88(534) (JAN 89), 39-40, 57.
TO GATHER SUPPORT FOR ITS PROGRAMS, THE ADMINISTRATION
OF PRESIDENT RONALD REAGAN DEPICTED A COHESIVE, EXPANSIONIST
MOSCOW-HAVANA-MANAGUA AXIS. BUT ADMINISTRATION OPPONENTS
CLUNG TO THE IMAGE OF A NATIONALIST, NONALIGNED NICARAGUA,
WHOSE CONSPICUOUS TIES WITH MOSCOW HAD BEEN THRUST UPON IT.
THE TERMS OF THE AMERICAN DISPUTE OVER RELATIONS BETWEEN THE
SOVIET UNION AND THE SANDINISTA GOVERNMENT WERE SET BY THE
EXIGENCIES AND LIMITATIONS OF AMERICAN POLITICS.

05521 LEIULFSRUD, H.; WOODWARD, A.
CROSS-CLASS ENCOUNTERS OF A CLOSE KIND: CLASS AWARENESS
AND POLITICS IN SWEDISH FAMILIES
ACTA SOCIOLOGICA, 32(1) (MAR 89), 75-94.
THIS PAPER FOCUSES ON THE PROCESSES WITHIN AND AROUND
THE CROSS-CLASS FAMILY THAT CREATE CLASS AWARNESS AND
POLITICAL BEHAVIOUR. PREVIOUS THEORIES POSITING A PARTNER
EFFECT TO EXPLAIN FEMALE CLASS AWARENESS OFFER LITTLE BEYOND
A SURFACE DESCRIPTION OF SITUATIONS EVIDENT IN CLASS
HETEROGENEOUS HOUSEHOLDS. BOTH WOMEN AND TO SOME EXTENT MEN
DIFFER IN CLASS-MIXED PARTNERSHIPS AS COMPARED WITH
HOMOGENEOUS SITUATIONS, IN TERMS OF POLITICAL ACTIVITY AND
SOCIETAL IMAGES. THEY SHOW MORE AMBIVALENCE IN SOME WAYS AND
DEMONSTRATE A HIGHER AWARNESS OF THE NATURE OF CLASS SOCIETY
IN OTHERS. QUALITATIVE INTERVIEW MATERIAL HELPS EXPLORE THE
NATURE OF THE DYNAMICS THAT BRING ABOUT THESE DIFFERENCES.

05522 LEIVA, L.C.
THE IRONIES OF THE SPANISH-AMERICAN REVOLUTIONS
INTERNATIONAL SOCIAL SCIENCE JOURNAL, (119) (FEB 89),
53-68.
THE AUTHOR DISCUSSES THE SIGNIFICANCE OF THE IMPACT OF
THE FRENCH REVOLUTION ON THE ORIGINS AND CONSTRUCTION OF
SPANISH-AMERICAN LIBERAL REPUBLICANISM. SECONDLY, HE
CONSIDERS THE INTELLECTUAL MODE OF THOUGHT THAT FILTERED THE
ENLIGHTENMENT AND FRENCH PHILOSOPHICAL FORCE OF THE LANGUAGE
OF LIBERTY AND HUMAN RIGHTS. THEN HE FORMULATES SOME OF THE
CONCEPTUAL WEAKNESSES STEMMING FROM THIS STILL-ACTIVE SOURCE
OF POLITICAL LEGITIMACY.

05523 LEMANN, N.
LESSONS FORM THE POVERTY FRONT
WASHINGTON MONTHLY, 21(11) (DEC 89), 33-35.
THE OFFICE OF ECONOMIC OPPORTUNITY (OEO) IS OFTEN
POINTED TO AS EVIDENCE THAT POVERTY PROGRAMS ARE DESTINED TO
FAIL. HOWEVER, AN HONEST, INTELLECTUAL ANALYSIS OF THE
PERFORMANCE OF THE OEO REVEALS OTHERWISE. THE WAR ON POVERTY
DIDN'T FULLY SUCCEED, BUT THE OEO DID PROVIDE SIGNIFICANT
OPPORTUNITIES FOR MANY BLACKS. THE FACT THAT THE OEO TOUCHED
SENSITIVE NERVE ENDINGS: RACE RELATIONS AND THE CREED OF
SELF-RELIANCE DIMINISHED THE EFFECTIVENESS OF THE PROGRAM.
THE ARTICLE CONCLUDES THAT UNREALISTIC GOALS AND INEFFECTIVE
COMMUNITY ACTION ORGANIZATIONS LED TO THE OVERALL DEMISE OF
THE WAR ON

05524 LEMARCHAND, R.
THE GREEN AND THE BLACK: QADHAFI'S POLICIES IN AFRICA
INDIANA UNIVERSITY PRESS, BLOOMINGTON, IN, 1988, 198.
IN AN EFFORT TO MOVE BEYOND THE "MAD DOG" SYNDROME AS AN

EXPLANATION OF QADHAFI'S FOREIGN POLICY, THESE ESSAYS
EXAMINE THE HISTORICAL FORCES, ATTITUDES, INTERESTS, AND
PRIORITIES THAT HAVE SHAPED QADHAFI'S BEHAVIOR IN AFRICA.

05525 LEMIEUX, V,
LA COMMISSION ROCHON ET LA REALISATION DES POLITIQUES
PUBLIQUES
CANADIAN PUBLIC ADMINISTRATION, 32(2) (SUM 89), 261-273.
THE STUDY COMMISSION ON HEALTH AND SOCIAL SERVICES,
CREATED BY THE QUEBEC GOVERNMENT IN JUNE 1985, SUBMITTED ITS
REPORT IN EARLY 1988. THIS ARTICLE SHOWS THAT THE COMMISSION
ACTED AS A "PACKAGER," SPECIFYING THE RECOMMENDED ROLE OF
THE PARTIES INVOLVED AND THE POWER STRUCTURE FOR PUBLIC
POLICY ON HEALTH AND SOCIAL SERVICES. THE COMMISSION FAVOURS
A BUREAUCRATIC ALLIANCE COVERING THE SOCIAL/HEALTH AREA,
RATHER THAN A MEDICAL/MANAGERIAL ALLIANCE. THE LATTER
CURRENTLY SEEMS TO BE IN THE BEST POSITION TO STRUCTURE THE
POWER IN THE HEALTH/SOCIAL SERVICES SYSTEM IN ACCORDANCE
WITH ITS INTERESTS.

05526 LEMOYNE, J.
EL SALVADOR'S FORGOTTEN WAR
FOREIGN AFFAIRS, 68(3) (SUM 89), 105-125.
A GRUELING, VIOLENT PERIOD THAT WILL DEFY IDEAL
SOLUTIONS LIES AHEAD IN EL SALVADOR. AFTER A DECADE OF DEEP
INVOLVEMENT IN EL SALVADOR, IT SEEMS PAST TIME FOR A REVIEW
OF AN AMERICAN POLICY THAT HAS STRUGGLED TO ACHIEVE GOALS
THAT MAY STILL BE ATTAINABLE, BUT ONLY IF THEY ARE
FUNDAMENTALLY REORIENTED.

05527 LENART, S.; MCGRAW, K.M.
AMERICA WATCHES "AMERIKA:" TELEVISION DOCUDRAMA AND
POLITICAL ATTITUDES
THE JOURNAL OF POLITICS, 51(3) (AUG 89), 697-713.
THIS ARTICLE REPORTS THE RESULTS OF A PANEL STUDY
EXAMINING THE IMPACT OF THE 1987 TELEVISION MINISERIES
"AMERIKA" ON POLITICAL ATTITUDES AND STEROTYPES. VIEWING THE
DOCUDRAMA, WHICH OSTENSIBLY DEPICTED LIFE IN THE MIDWEST TEN
YEARS AFTER A SOVIET TAKEOVER OF THE UNITED STATES, WAS
ASSOCIATED WITH SIGNIFICANT CHANGES IN ATTITUDES CONCERNING
SOVIET-AMERICAN RELATIONS. THESE ATTITUDINAL CHANGES WERE
CONSISTENTLY IN THE DIRECTION OF GREATER CONSERVATISM (FOR
EXAMPLE, VIEWERS BECAME LESS TOLERANT OF COMMUNISM, AND
VOICED MORE SUPPORT FOR ENHANCED U.S. MILITARY STRENGTH).
THE MODERATING IMPACT OF PERCEIVED REALISM, EDUCATION, AND
IDEOLOGY, AS WELL AS THE INDEPENDENT IMPACT OF INDIRECT
EXPOSURE TO THE SERIES (THAT IS, INFORMAL PEER DISCUSSION
AND ATTENTION TO ASSOCIATED MEDIA COVERAGE), WERE ALSO
EXAMINED. THE IMPLICATIONS OF THE RESULTS FOR RESEARCH ON
THE POLITICAL IMPACT OF ENTERTAINMENT PROGRAMMING ARE
DISCUSSED.

05528 LENCZOWSKI, J.
THE SOVIET UNION AND THE UNITED STATES: MYTHS, REALITIES,
MAXIMS
GLOBAL AFFAIRS, 4(1) (WIN 89), 38-62.
THE AUTHOR OF THIS PAPER EXAMINES THE POLICIES OF THE
SOVIET UNION AND THE UNITED STATES IN THEIR DEALINGS WITH
EACH OTHER IN INTERNATIONAL POLITICS. SOME OF HIS GENERAL
CONCLUSIONS ARE THAT THE UNITED STATES' POSITIONS HAVE BEEN
AND ARE BASED ON WISHFUL THINKING AND A LACK OF
UNDERSTANDING, AND THAT THE SOVIETS STILL CONFORM TO THE
MARXIST-LENINIST DOCTRINE AND ARE TRYING TO CONVINCE OTHERS
THAT THEY ARE NO LONGER COMMUNIST.

05529 LENG,S.
A KEY TO CHINA'S FUTURE: RESPECT FOR THE LAW
ASIAN AFFAIRS, AN AMERICAN REVIEW, 16(2) (SUM 89), 77-82.
THE VIOLENT CRACKDOWN ON THE CHINESE DEMONSTRATORS IN
BEIJING ON 4 JUNE 1989 IS WIDELY BELIEVED TO HAVE UNDONE
MUCH OF WHAT DENG XIAOPING AND HIS REFORM-MINDED ASSOCIATES
HAD ACCOMPLISHED IN THE 80S. DENG HAS OFTEN EMPHASIZED
STABILITY AND UNITY AS ESSENTIAL TO CHINA'S DEVELOPMENT.
THUS, HIS STAND AGAINST THE PRODEMOCRACY MOVEMENT WAS NOT A
TOTAL SURPRISE. THE PROBLEM IS NOW, WHAT WILL BECOME OF
CHINA IN THE AFTERMATH OF THE STUDENT REVOLT? CHINESE
GOVERNMENT MUST REALISE THAT TO GOVERN EFFECTIVELY, IT
CANNOT RELY SOLEY ON GUNS. THEY MUST TRY TO RESTORE SOME
MEASURE OF MORAL LEGITIMACY BY SEEKING A RELATIONSHIP OF
ACCORD AND COOPERATION WITH THE ALIENATED POPULATION.

05530 LENGA, B.
AIDS SCANDAL ROCKS MINISTRIES
NEW AFRICAN, (258) (MAR 89), 26-27.
A NIGERIAN DOCTOR WHO CLAIMED HE COULD CURE AIDS USING A
COMBINATION OF TRADITIONAL AND WESTERN MEDICINE RECEIVED
OFFICIAL SPONSORSHIP FROM THE TANZANIAN GOVERNMENT. THE
DOCTOR WAS LATER EXPELLED FROM TANZANIA AMID RUMORS OF
BRIBERY AND CONSPIRACY AGAINST HIM. THE GOVERNMENT CLAIMED
THAT HIS WORK HAD PRODUCED POSITIVE RESULTS, RAISING
QUESTIONS ABOUT HIS EXPULSION.

05531 LENGA, B.
MIXED FEELINGS GREET "COSMETIC" BUDGET

AFRICAN BUSINESS, (AUG 88), 42-44.
THIS ARTICLE REPORTS ON ATTEMPTS OF THE TANZANIAN
GOVERNMENT TO REDUCE TAXES, RAISE WAGES AND REDUCE CUSTOMS
TARIFFS. REACTIONS OF SOME, INCLUDING MEMBERS OF PARLIAMENT
AND THE ACADEMICS HAVE BEEN NEGATIVE BECAUSE OF SPECIAL
INTERESTS.

05532 LENGA, B.
NYERERE STILL IN CHARGE
NEW AFRICAN, (JAN 88), 24.
THIS ARTICLE ANALYSES THE POSITION OF POWER HELD BY
JULIUS NYERERE, RECENTLY RE-ELECTED CHAIRMAN OF TANZANIA'S
SOLE POLITICAL PARTY. IT TALKS ABOUT THE POLITICAL CLIMATE
OF TANZANIA AT PRESENT (JAN 88) AND NAMES THOSE IN POWER.

05533 LENGYEL, P.
ELEMENTS OF CREATIVE SOCIAL SCIENCE: PART I--TOWARDS
GREATER AUTHORITY FOR THE KNOWLEDGE BASE
INTERNATIONAL SOCIAL SCIENCE JOURNAL, (122) (NOV 89),
567-583.
THE AUTHOR CONSIDERS SUCH QUESTIONS AS: WHY IS THE
SOCIAL SCIENTIFIC KNOWLEDGE OR COGNITIVE BASE LESS RESPECTED
IN ITS SPHERE THAN ARE OTHER KNOWLEDGE BASES IN THEIRS? WHY
IS THE COGNITIVE BASE OF MEDICINE OR ENGINEERING, FOR
EXAMPLE, TAKEN MUCH MORE SERIOUSLY WHERE IT MATTERS THAN IS
THAT WHICH THE SOCIAL SCIENCES HAVE PRODUCED IN RELATION TO
THE SOCIO-SPHERE? WHAT PREVENTS SOCIAL SCIENTIFIC FINDINGS,
EVEN WHEN REPEATEDLY CONFIRMED IN DIFFERENT SETTINGS AT
DIFFERENT TIMES, FROM ATTAINING THAT STATUS OF WEIGHTY
EXPERTISE THAT COMPARABLE FINDINGS OCCUPY IN OTHER FIELDS?

05534 LENT, J.A.
HUMAN RIGHTS AND FREEDOM OF EXPRESSION IN MALAYSIA AND THE
PHILIPPINES
ASIAN PROFILE, 17(2) (APR 89), 137-154.
MALAYSIA AND THE PHILIPPINES ARE USED AS CASE STUDIES IN
THIS ANALYSIS OF HUMAN RIGHTS FOR TWO MAJOR, CONTRASTING
REASONS. BOTH ARE DEMOCRACIES, MEMBERS OF THE ASSOCIATION OF
SOUTH EAST ASIAN NATIONS (ASEAN), MULTI-ETHNIC AND MULTI-
LINGUAL SOCIETIES, AND NEWLY DEVELOPED COUNTRIES. BUT THEY
DERIVE FROM DIFFERENT COLONIAL BACKGROUNDS-MALAYSIA FROM THE
BRITISH AND THE PHILIPPINES FROM THE UNITED STATES (AND
EARLIER, SPANISH). THE WAY HUMAN RIGHTS ISSUES ARE TREATED
CAN BE LINKED TO THOSE COLONIAL TRADITIONS, PARTLY BECAUSE
MANY OF THE OLD LAWS ARE STILL IN EFFECT. IN FACT,
MALAYSIANS SOMETIMES REACT TO CRITICISM OF THEIR LAWS
RESTRAINING HUMAN RIGHTS BY POINTING OUT THEY LEARNED THEIR
LESSONS WELL FROM THE BRITISH.

05535 LEON, D.
CREDO OF A LABOR DOVE
NEW OUTLOOK, 32(2 (288)) (FEB 89), 36-37.
CHAIM RAMON IS A LEADING LABOR PARTY DOVE WHO HAS BEEN
ELECTED TO HEAD THE LABOR FACTION IN ISRAEL'S THELFTH
KNESSET. ALTHOUGH HE IS YOUNG FOR AN ISRAELI LEADER, HE
EASILY DEFEATED SHIMON PERES' CANDIDATE FOR FACTION CHAIRMAN.
RAMON IS A FORCEFUL OPPONENT OF THE NEW UNITY GOVERNMENT
AND HAS PUBLICLY DECLARED THAT THE LABOR PARTY SHOULD JOIN
THE OPPOSITION.

05536 LEON, D.
NOT THE ONLY GAME IN TOWN
NEW OUTLOOK, 32(8 (294)) (AUG 89), 12-13.
ISRAEL'S LEFT-WING, DOVISH MAPAM PARTY IS PREPARED TO
ACCEPT ANY FRAMEWORK FOR NEGOTIATION THAT PROMISES DIALOGUE
BETWEEN THE ISRAELIS AND PALESTINIANS AND IS ORIENTED TOWARD
AN EVENTUAL AGREEMENT. BUT THERE ARE GRAVE DOUBTS ABOUT
PRIME MINISTER SHAMIR'S PROPOSAL BECAUSE THE PRE-CONDITIONS
ARE A "LAND MINE" AND ISRAEL CANNOT NEGOTIATE WITH THE
PALESTINIANS WITHOUT RECOGNIZING THE PLO. THE MAPAM PREDICTS
A NATIONAL CRISIS BETWEEN THE LABOR AND LIKUD COMPONENTS OF
THE UNITY COALITION GOVERNMENT.

05537 LEON, D.
PEACE PLAN OR GIMMICK?
NEW OUTLOOK, 32(5 (291)) (MAY 89), 8.
ISRAELI PRIME MINISTER SHAMIR AND DEFENSE MINISTER RABIN
HAVE PROPOSED THE ELECTION OF PALESTINIAN REPRESENTATIVES
FROM THE OCCUPIED TERRITORIES TO NEGOTIATE WITH ISRAEL TO
ESTABLISH AN INTERIM REGIME OF PALESTINIAN SELF-RULE. THE
ISSUE OF A FINAL SETTLEMENT OF THE STATUS OF THE TERRITORIES
WOULD BE LEFT FOR LATER NEGOTIATIONS. THE REACTIONS IN THE
ISRAELI PEACE CAMP TO THIS PROPOSAL ARE DIVIDED. SOME REJECT
THE PLAN AS A NON-STARTER, A PLOY BY SHAMIR TO PLAY FOR TIME
AND HOLD ONTO THE TERRITORIES. OTHERS BELIEVE THAT AN
OUTRIGHT REJECTION BY THE PLO WOULD PLAY INTO THE HANDS OF
THE REJECTIONISTS ON BOTH SIDES AND WOULD CERTAINLY LEAD TO
AN ESCALATION OF VIOLENCE.

05538 LEON, D.
THE ELECTION PLAN IS A NON-STARTER
NEW OUTLOOK, 32(8 (294)) (AUG 89), 16-17.
PALESTINIAN LEADER FAISAL HUSSEINI CLAIMS THAT THE
ISRAELI GOVERNMENT'S PROPOSAL FOR ELECTIONS IN THE OCCUPIED

TERRITORIES IS NOT AN HONEST ATTEMPT TO REACH A SOLUTION IN
TWO STAGES BUT IS A PROCESS DESIGNED TO INCREASE THE
DISTANCE BETWEEN THE PALESTINIANS LIVING UNDER OCCUPATION
AND THOSE IN EXILE. HE OPPOSES THE CONCEPT UNDERLYING THE
PROPOSALS BECAUSE THE PROBLEM MUST BE APPROACHED IN ITS
ENTIRETY.

05539 LEON, D.
THE GOVERNMENT INITIATIVE IS THE ONLY PRECONDITION
NEW OUTLOOK, 32(8 (294)) (AUG 89), 9-10.
IN THIS INTERVIEW, LIKUD MINISTER-WITHOUT-PORTFOLIO EHUD
OLMERT DISCUSSES PRIME MINISTER SHAMIR'S PEACE PROPOSAL AND
WHY HE OPPOSES THE CREATION OF A PALESTINIAN STATE.

05540 LEON, D.
THE INTIFADA AND ISRAELI ARABS
NEW OUTLOOK, 32(11-12 (297-298)) (NOV 89), 30-31.
THE INTIFADA HAS NOT FOSTERED POLITICAL EXTREMISM IN
ISRAEL'S ARAB SECTOR, AS SOME PROPAGANDISTS WOULD HAVE THE
PUBLIC BELIEVE. AS LONG AS THE PALESTINIANS IN THE OCCUPIED
TERRITORIES SUPPORT YASSER ARAFAT'S TWO-STATE SOLUTION, SO
WILL THE ISRAELI ARABS. TO THINK THAT THE ISRAELI ARABS ARE
GOING TO ADOPT A STANCE MORE EXTREME THAN THAT OF THE PLO IS
ABSURD. BUT THE INTIFADA HAS WIDENED THE GAP BETWEEN
ISRAEL'S JEWISH AND ARAB CITIZENS, BECAUSE THE ARAB REACTION
HAS BEEN ANGER AND PROTEST AGAINST THE ISRAELI POLICIES IN
THE OCCUPIED TERRITORIES.

05541 LEON, D.
THE ISRAELI WOMAN: MYTH AND REALITY
NEW OUTLOOK, 32(6-7 (292-293)) (JUN 89), 12-13.
DESPITE LEGISLATION IN THE AREA OF WOMEN'S RIGHTS, THE
PRESENT STATUS OF ISRAELI WOMEN IS UNSATISFACTORY IN MANY
RESPECTS. WOMEN ARE POORLY REPRESENTED IN POLITICS; THEY ARE
ALMOST NONEXISTENT IN THE HIGHER ECHELONS OF THE CIVIL
SERVICE AND BUSINESS; AND THEIR POSITION IN THE ACADEMIC
WORLD IS NOT MUCH BETTER. ISRAEL'S CONSCRIPTION LAW IS
UNIQUE IN THAT ALL WOMEN ARE CALLED UP FOR MILITARY SERVICE,
BUT EQUAL CONSCRIPTION DOES NOT MEAN EQUALITY IN THE ROLES
OF MEN AND WOMEN IN THE ARMED FORCES.

05542 LEON, D.
THE POLITICAL FACTOR REMAINS DECISIVE
NEW OUTLOOK, 32(6-7 (292-293)) (JUN 89), 23-24.
MORE AND MORE WOMEN ARE BECOMING INTEGRATED INTO THE
ISRAELI WORK FORCE AND AS WOMEN'S EDUCATIONAL LEVELS RISE,
THEY ARE GAINING HIGHER POSITIONS IN THEIR PROFESSIONS. BUT
THIS IS NOT REFLECTED IN THE POLITICAL STATUS OF THE ISRAELI
WOMAN. BECAUSE MANY WOMEN DEVOTE THEMSELVES FULLY TO THEIR
WORK, THEY UNDERESTIMATE THE IMPORTANCE OF POLITICS.

05543 LEON, D.
THERE IS NO VIABLE ALTERNATIVE
NEW OUTLOOK, 32(8 (294)) (AUG 89), 10-11.
LABOR PARTY MK SHEVAH WEISS BELIEVES THERE IS NO VIABLE
ALTERNATIVE TO THE ISRAELI PROPOSAL FOR ELECTIONS IN THE
OCCUPIED TERRITORIES. HE IS ALSO ADAMANT THAT THE LABOR
PARTY MUST REMAIN PART OF THE NATIONAL UNITY GOVERNMENT
COALITION.

05544 LEON, D.
UNLIKELY PEACE
NEW OUTLOOK, 32(6-7 (292-293)) (JUN 89), 43-44.
THE CONSENSUS THAT WOULD UNITE THE ISRAELI PEACE CAMP
IS BASED ON AN END TO THE OCCUPATION, NEGOTIATIONS WITH THE
PLO ON THE BASIS OF MUTUAL RECOGNITION, AND THE
ESTABLISHMENT OF AN INDEPENDENT PALESTINIAN STATE ALONGSIDE
ISRAEL. THIS PROGRAM HAS BEEN ACCEPTED BY THE PALESTINIANS,
BUT THE ISRAELI GOVERNMENT REJECTS IT. THE ISRAELI PEACE
MOVEMENT'S GOAL MUST BE TO BRING ISRAELIS FROM A BROAD
POLITICAL SPECTRUM INTO THIS CONSENSUS.

05545 LEONARD, D.
THE BELGIAN GENERAL ELECTION OF 1987
ELECTORAL STUDIES, 8(2) (AUG 89), 157-162.
THE BELGIAN GENERAL ELECTION OF 13 DECEMBER 1987 SAW A
REPLACEMENT OF A RIGHT-CENTER COALITION GOVERNMENT BY A LEFT-
CENTER COALITION WITH FLEMMISH NATIONALIST PARTICIPATION.
THE EXTENT OF THE CHANGE WAS CAMOUFLAGED BY THE FACT THAT
THE PRIME MINISTER OF BOTH THE OUTGOING AND THE INCOMING
GOVERNMENTS WAS WILFRIED MARTENS. THIS ARTICLE ATTEMPTS TO
EXPLAIN HOW THIS OCCURRED. IT DETAILS THE FOURONS AFFAIR AND
THE CAMPAIGN EVENTS. AFTER EXPLORING THE RESULTS IT DETAILS
THE AFTERMATH

05546 LEONARD, D.
VIEW FROM BRUSSELS
NATO'S SIXTEEN NATIONS, 34(6) (OCT 89), 9.
TWO CONTROVERSIAL ISSUES FACE THE GOVERNMENT OF
BELGIUM'S PRIME MINISTER WILFRIED MARTENS. THE FIRST IS
ABORTION, WHICH IS ILLEGAL. AFTER MANY YEARS OF AGITATION,
IT APPEARS THAT A BILL PERMITTING LEGAL ABORTIONS WILL BE
PASSED, ALTHOUGH THE PRIME MINISTER WILL VOTE AGAINST IT.
MORE THREATENING TO THE GOVERNMENT'S SURVIVAL IS THE ISSUE

OF CONSTITUTIONAL REFORM. THE PROPOSED CHANGES WOULD PROVIDE
FOR THE DIRECT ELECTION OF THE FLEMISH AND WALLOON REGIONAL
COUNCILS, SPECIFY THE PRECISE POWERS RESERVED FOR THE
CENTRAL GOVERNMENT, DEFINE THE RIGHT TO CONCLUDE TREATIES
AND BE REPRESENTED IN INTERNATIONAL ORGANIZATIONS, AND
DETERMINE THE FUTURE COMPOSITION AND POWERS OF THE SENATE.

05547 LEPAK, K.J.
PRELUDE TO CRISIS: LEADERSHIP DRIFT IN POLAND IN THE 1970S
STUDIES IN COMPARATIVE COMMUNISM, XXII(1) (SPR 89), 11-22.
POLAND IN THE 1970S WITNESSED A DYNAMIC BUT ULTIMATELY
FAILED EPISODE IN THE ONGOING EXPERIMENT OF COMMUNIST PARTY
RULE IN EASTERN EUROPE. IN THE EARLY PART OF THE DECADE, IT
WAS NOT UNCOMMON TO HEAR THE COUNTRY ANALYZED UNDER THE
RUBIC OF "GIEREK'S POLAND" IN REFERENCE TO EDWARD GIEREK,
THE POLISH FIRST SECRETARY. BUT BY THE CLOSE OF THE DECADE
IT APPEARED TO BE ANYBODY'S COUNTRY BUT HIS. THIS ARTICLE
CONSIDERS THAT EXPERIENCE AS A PARTICULAR CASE OF
"LEADERSHIP DRIFT;" IT ATTEMPTS TO ELABORATE A CONCEPT OF
LEADERSHIP DRIFT BY SUGGESTING A MULTI-DIMENSIONAL NOTION OF
LEADERSHIP AND CONSIDERING DRIFT AS A PATHOLOGICAL POLITICAL
CONDITION; IT THEN ATTEMPTS TO ASSESS THE POLISH CASE ON THE
BASIS OF SUCH A CONCEPTUALIZATION; AND FINALLY IT OFFERS A
TENTATIVE EVALUATION OF THE USEFULNESS OF LEADERSHIP DRIFT
IN THE STUDY OF CONTEMPORARY COMMUNIST SYSTEMS AND THE
JARUZELSKI REGIME.

05548 LERMAN, R.I.; LERMAN, D.L.
INCOME SOURCES AND INCOME INEQUALITY: MEASUREMENTS FROM
THREE U.S. INCOME SURVEYS
JOURNAL OF ECONOMIC AND SOCIAL MEASUREMENT, 15(2) (1989),
167-179.
THIS PAPER EXAMINES THE CONTRIBUTION OF INDIVIDUAL
INCOME SOURCES TO OVERALL INEQUALITY. IT PROVIDES NEW
EVIDENCE FROM THE SURVEY OF CONSUMER FINANCES (SCF) ON THE
MARGINAL EFFECTS OF EARNINGS OF FAMILY HEADS, CAPITAL INCOME,
SPOUSES' EARNINGS, AND HOUSING INCOME. THE RESULTS DIFFER
FROM AN EARLIER STUDY BASED ON THE CURRENT POPULATION SURVEY
(CPS). IN THE SCF, CAPITAL INCOME IS MORE DISEQUALIZING
WHILE SPOUSES' EARNINGS IS MORE EQUALIZING THAN IN THE CPS.
SCF MEASURES OF THE EFFECTS OF HOUSING INCOME ARE SIMILAR TO
THOSE BASED ON THE SURVEY OF RESIDENTIAL FINANCE.

05549 LERNER, M.
SURVIVING A BUSH PRESIDENCY
TIKKUN, 4(1) (JAN 89), 15-18, 86-87.
THE AUTHOR PRESENTS A STRATEGY FOR DRAMATICALLY CHANGING
AMERICAN POLITICS. HE ARGUES THAT THE BATTLE BETWEEN THE
"MODERATE CENTER" AND THE "LIBERAL WING" OF THE DEMOCRATIC
PARTY IS DISCOURAGING BECAUSE BOTH SIDES ARE WRONG. A
TRANSFORMATION OF LIBERALISM AND THE DEMOCRATIC PARTY IS
NEEDED.

05550 LERNER, R.; NAGAI, A.K.; ROTHMAN, S.
MARGINALITY AND LIBERALISM AMONG JEWISH ELITES
PUBLIC OPINION QUARTERLY, 53(3) (FAL 89), 330-352.
ALTHOUGH MUCH HAS BEEN WRITTEN ABOUT THE JEWISH
PROCLIVITY TOWARD LIBERALISM, LITTLE HAS BEEN WRITTEN ABOUT
ELITES WHO ARE JEWISH. THIS ARTICLE EXTENSIVELY COMPARES
AMERICAN ELITES, BOTH JEWISH AND NON-JEWISH, ON A WIDE
VARIETY OF SOCIAL, ECONOMIC, AND POLITICAL ATTITUDES. JEWISH
ELITES ARE FOUND TO BE CONSISTENTLY MORE LIBERAL THAN THEIR
NON-JEWISH COUNTERPARTS ON FOUR DIFFERENT MEASURES OF
LIBERALISM. THE DIFFERENCES BETWEEN JEWISH AND NON-JEWISH
ELITES PERSISTED AFTER CONTROLLING FOR A NUMBER OF
BACKGROUND VARIABLES INCLUDING CURRENT OCCUPATION. THESE
RESULTS ARE EXPLAINED AS A RESULT OF JEWISH SOCIALIZATION
INTO A TRADITION OF MARGINALITY WHICH HAS PERSISTED DESPITE
CHANGING CONDITIONS. THIS CONCLUSION IS SUPPORTED BY SHOWING
THAT PARENTAL IDEOLOGY CAN PARTIALLY PREDICT RESPONDENTS'
IDEOLOGICAL VIEWS.

05551 LERNOUX, P.
GRACE AND GLORY
CHURCH AND STATE, 42(7) (JUL 89), 4 (148)-9 (153).
THE AUTHOR LOOKS AT THE CATHOLIC RIGHT AS REPRESENTED BY
THE KNIGHTS OF MALTA, OR SMOM. SMOM HAS ENJOYED CONSIDERABLE
WEALTH AND POLITICAL CLOUT IN THE UNITED STATES SINCE A
BRANCH WAS ESTABLISHED ON THE EAST COAST IN 1927. IT HAS
BEEN ASSOCIATED WITH RICH, POWERFUL INDUSTRIAL FAMILIES,
INCLUDING THE KENNEDYS AND THE GRACES OF W.R. GRACE AND
COMPANY.

05552 LERNOUX, P.
THE STRUGGLE FOR NICARAGUA'S SOUL
SOJOURNERS, 18(5) (MAY 89), 14-23.
THE ARTICLE EXAMINES THE RELIGIOUS TENSIONS AND
CONFLICTS THAT HAVE BEEN INTENSIFIED BY THE CIVIL WAR IN
NICARAGUA. SOME HIGH-RANKING SANDINISTA OFFICIALS BELIEVE
THAT THE RELIGIOUS CONFLICT COULD CAUSE THE GOVERNMENT MORE
DAMAGE THAN THE CONTRAS EVER INFLICTED, BUT THE TRUE DAMAGE
IS TO THE PEOPLE OF NICARAGUA. A DEEPLY RELIGIOUS PEOPLE,
THE NICARAGUANS "DON'T KNOW TO WHOM TO GIVE THEIR LOYALTIES
ANYMORE."

05553 LESAGE, E.C. JR.
PUBLIC ADMINISTRATION CONTINUING EDUCATION IN CANADA
CANADIAN PUBLIC ADMINISTRATION, 32(4) (WIN 89), 585-611.
PUBLIC ADMINISTRATION PROFESSIONAL CONTINUING EDUCATION
HAS GAINED IMPORTANCE IN RECENT YEARS AS UNIVERSITIES,
GOVERNMENTS AND THE INSTITUTE OF PUBLIC ADMINISTRATION OF
CANADA HAVE TAKEN AN INTEREST IN IT. DESPITE INCREASED
INTEREST, LITTLE IN THE WAY OF HARD DATA OR INFORMED
COMMENTARY ON PUBLIC ADMINISTRATION CONTINUING EDUCATION HAS
FOUND ITS WAY INTO THE LITERATURE. THIS PAPER PROVIDES A
PARTIAL REMEDY FOR THIS LACUNA. RESULTS OF A 1985 STUDY OF
CANADIAN UNIVERSITY PUBLIC ADMINISTRATION CONTINUING
EDUCATION PROGRAMS ARE REPORTED AND ANALYSED TO ESTABLISH A
POINT OF DEPARTURE FOR FUTURE STUDIES AND DISCUSSION. PUBLIC
ADMINISTRATION CONTINUING EDUCATION'S PROPER PLACE WITHIN
THE UNIVERSE OF PUBLIC ADMINISTRATION PROFESSIONAL EDUCATION
IS EXPLORED, AS ARE REASONS FOR THE DIVERSITY OF CONTINUING
EDUCATION PROGRAMS. THE CHARACTER OF PROFESSIONAL EDUCATION,
AND THE NEED FOR PUBLIC ADMINISTRATION CONTINUING EDUCATION
PROGRAM STANDARDS. THE THEME RUNNING THROUGHOUT THE PAPER IS
THAT CONTINUING EDUCATION PLAYS A CENTRAL ROLE IN THE
PROFESSIONAL DEVELOPMENT OF PUBLIC ADMINISTRATORS.

05554 LESCH, A. M.
EGYPTIAN-ISRAELI BOUNDARY DESPUTES: THE PROBLEM OF TABA;
ISRAEL, EGYPT, AND THE PALESTINIANS: FROM CAMP DAVID TO
INTIFADA
INDIANA UNIVERSITY PRESS BLOOMINGTON, INDIANA, 1989, 43-60.
THIS ESSAY DESCRIBES EFFORTS TO RESOLVE THE QUESTION OF
TABA, A 250-ACRE TRIANGLE OF LAND WHICH PUTS INTO THE GULF
OF AQABA AND ADDS THREE-QUARTERS OF A MILE TO ISRAEL'S 5-
MILE WIDE COASTAL STRIP, MARGINALLY IMPROVING ITS SHIPPING
AND NAVAL ACTIVITIES IN THE GULF. ISRAEL HAD NEVER CLAIMED
TABA, AND HAD GIVEN UP SIGNIFICANTLY MORE VALUABLE ASSETS IN
SINAI BY VIRTUE OF THE 1979 PEACE TREATY, BUT JURISDICTION
OF THE LAND WAS DEMANDED BY ISRAEL IN DECEMBER 1981, JUST AS
WITHDRAWAL FROM THE SINAI WAS BEING FINALIZED.

05555 LESCH, A. M.
EGYPTIAN-ISRAELI RELATIONS: NORMALIZATION ON SPECIAL TIES?;
ISRAEL, EGYPT AND THE PALESTINIANS: FROM CAMP DAVID TO
INTIFADA
INDIANA UNIVERSITY PRESS BLOOMINGTON, INDIANA, 1989, 61-85.
EGYPTIAN OFFICIALS HAVE SEEN NORMALIZATION AS ADHERENCE
TO THE LETTER OF THE PEACE TREATY, IMPLEMENTATION OF VARIOUS
PROTOCOLS, AND THE MAINTENANCE OF A CORRECT- BUT NOT
PARTICULARLY WARM-RELATIONSHIP. THEY HAVE STRONGLY REJECTED
ANY IDEA THAT NORMALIZATION MEANS SPECIAL TIES TO OR A
PREFERENTIAL STATUS FOR ISRAEL. THAT THE ISRAELIS PRECEIVE
NORMALIZATION AS THE ESTABLISHMENT OF ESPECIALLY CLOSE,
REFERENTIAL BONDS WITH EGYPT HAS EXACERBATED AN ALREADY COOL
AND UNSATISFACTORY RELATIONSHIP BETWEEN THE TWO COUNTIES.

05556 LESCH, A. M.
GAZA: HISTORY AND POLITICS; ISRAEL, EGYPT AND THE
PALESTINIANS: FROM CAMP DAVID TO INTIFADA
INDIANA UNIVERSITY PRESS BLOOMINGTON, INDIANA, 1989,
223-237.
IN JUNE 1967 THE GAZA STRIP -- ALONG WITH SINAI, THE
WEST BANK, AND THE GOLAN HEIGHTS -- WAS OCCUPIED MILITARILY
BY ISRAEL. SINCE THEN, ONLY SINAI HAS RETURNED TO ARAB RULE,
AS A RESULT OF THE EGYPT-ISRAEL PEACE TREATY OF 1979. IN
CONTRAST, THE PROSPECTS FOR THE OTHER OCCUPIED TERRITORIES
TO BE FREED BECOME DAILY MORE REMOTE. IN THE GAZA STRIP, FOR
EXAMPLE, ISRAEL HAS TAKEN OVER A THIRD OF THE LAND, MOVED IN
1,400 SETTLERS, AND TIED THE PALESTINIAN ECONOMY TO ISRAEL.
NEVERTHELESS, THE PALESTINIANS STILL LONG FOR INDEPENDENCE,
AND THE REFUGEES CONTINUE TO DREAM OF RETURNING TO THEIR
HOMES. THIS ARTICLE DESCRIBES HOW THE WEAK STRATEGIC
POSITION OF THE ARAB WOULD VIS-A-VIS ISRAEL PROVIDES LITTLE
HOPE THAT A NEW ROAD WILL OPEN FOR THE PEOPLE OF GAZA AND
PALESTINIANS AS A WHOLE.

05557 LESCH, A. M.
GAZA: LIFE UNDER OCCUPATION; ISRAEL, EGYPT AND THE
PALESTINIANS: FROM CAMP DAVID TO INTIFADA
INDIANA UNIVERSITY PRESS BLOOMINGTON, INDIANA, 1989,
238-254.
THE CAMP DAVID ACCORD WITH EGYPT REQUIRED THE LIKUD
GOVERNMENT TO EVACUATE ALL THE SETTLEMENTS IN NORTHERN SINAI,
LEAVING THE PALESTINIANS IN THE GAZA STRIP DIRECTLY
ADJACENT TO THE EGYPTIANS IN RAFAH AND ELARISH. NO LONGER
ABLE TO SURROUND THE STRIP, THE GOVERNMENT DECIDED TO PLACE
SUBSTANTIAL SETTLEMENTS AMIDST THE ARAB RESIDENTS. THIS
POLICY SHIFT WAS PARALLELED IN THE WEST BANK, WHERE THE
GOVERNMENT BEGAN TO CONSTRUCT SETTLEMENTS NEAR MAJOR ARAB
TOWNS. IN BOTH TERRITORIES, THE AIM WAS TO CREATE SUCH AN
INTERLOCKING GRID OF JEWISH AND ARAB COMMUNITIES THAT THE
RESIDENTS COULD NOT BE DISENTANGLED IN ANY FUTURE DIPLOMATIC
NEGOTIATIONS. THE SETTLEMENTS WOULD THUS MAKE IT IMPOSSIBLE
FOR THE PALESTINIANS TO CARVE OUT A STATE IN THE WEST BANK
AND GAZA. MOREOVER, THE SETTLEMENTS WOULD ISOLATE THE ARAB
TOWNS FROM EACH OTHER, THUS PREVENTING COORDINATED POLITICAL

ACTION. THIS EASY DESCRIBES HOW THIS STRATEGY LED TO THE
CREATION OF SEVERAL BLOCS OF SETTLEMENTS WITHIN THE STRIP:
ONE BLOCK IN THE NORTH, ANOTHER IN THE SOUTH AND WEST, AND
SMALL CLUSTERS IN THE CENTER.

05558 LESCH, A. M.; TESSLER, M.
ISRAEL, EGYPT, AND THE PALESTINIANS: FROM CAMP DAVID TO
INTIFADA
INDIANA UNIVERSITY PRESS BLOOMINGTON, INDIANA, 1989, 298.
THE ESSAYS INCLUDED IN THIS BOOK DESCRIBE THE UNFOLDING
OBSTACLES TO PEACE BETWEEN EGYPT AND ISRAEL, WITH A CENTRAL
FOCUS ON THE PALESTINIAN ISSUE. CHAPTERS TREAT ISRAELI
POLICIES IN THE WEST BANK AND GAZA, THE IMPACT OF ISRAELI
POLITICS ON THE PEACE ISSUE, AND THE PALESTINIANS' RESPONSE
TO THE OCCUPATION. THE WRITINGS OF THE AUTHORS LEACH AND
TESSLER COVER THE PERIOD 1980-1986.

05559 LESCH, A. M.
PALESTINIAN WRITINGS: CLOSED BORDERS, DIVIDED LIVES;
ISRAEL, EGYPT AND THE PALESTINIANS: FROM CAMP DAVID TO
INTIFADA
INDIANA UNIVERSITY PRESS BLOOMINGTON, INDIANA, 1989,
125-139.
THIS ARTICLE PROVIDES SELECTIONS FROM THE WRITINGS OF AN
ARAB WOMAN FROM NAGARETH WHICH UNDERLINES THE DIFFICULTIES
OF LIFE FOR SECOND-CLASS CITIZENS IN ISRAEL. THAT SUCH
PEOPLE WERE UNHAPPY IN SPITE OF THE MODEST MATERIAL
ADVANTAGES OF LIVING IN ISRAEL AND THAT SUCH UNHAPPINESS
COULD HAVE EXPLOSIVE POTENTIAL IS THE IMPORT OF THESE
FICTIONAL STORIES.

05560 LESCH, A. M.; TESSLER, M.
THE WEST BANK AND GAZA: POLITICAL AND IDEOLOGICAL
RESPONSES TO OCCUPATION; ISRAEL, EGYPT AND THE
PALESTINIANS: FROM CAMP DAVID TO INTIFADA
INDIANA UNIVERSITY PRESS BLOOMINGTON, INDIANA, 1989,
255-271.
PALESTINIANS IN THE WEST BANK AND GAZA HAVE SUFFERED A
SERIOUS EROSION OF THEIR POLITICAL STATUS, A CONSTRICTION OF
THEIR EDUCATIONAL INSTITUTIONS, AND ALIENATION OF THEIR LAND.
NEVERTHELESS, THEIR SENSE OF NATIONAL IDENTITY REMAINS
STRONG, AND ITS MANIFESTATIONS CAN BE EXPECTED TO BECOME
MORE VEHEMENT IN RESPONSE TO EFFORTS TO REPRESS AND DENY ITS
EXISTENCE. AS ISRAEL ACCELERATES THE ABSORPTION AND
ANNEXATION OF THE WEST BANK AND GAZA, ISRAELI-PALESTINIAN
RELATIONS ARE BECOMING DANGEROUSLY EXPLOSIVE AND FATALLY
EMBITTERED. ONLY SUSTAINED AND CONCERTED DIPLOMATIC EFFORTS
FROM OUTSIDE CAN HALT THIS CATASTROPHIC PROCESS, AND EVEN
SUCH EFFORTS ARE UNLIKELY TO SUCCEED UNLESS SUPPORT FOR
TERRITORIAL COMPROMISE GROWS INSIDE ISRAEL. ACTING ALONE,
PALESTINIANS IN THE OCCUPIED TERRITORIES WILL BE UNABLE TO
HALT, AND PERHAPS NOT EVEN TO SLOW DOWN, ISRAEL'S DEEPENING
PENETRATION INTO THEIR HOMELAND.

05561 LESKOV, S.
SOVIET SPACE IN TRANSIT
SPACE POLICY, 5(3) (AUG 89), 183-185.
THE AUTHOR DISCUSSES THE IMPORTANCE - SYMBOLIC AND
TECHNICAL - OF SPACE SHUTTLES TO THE US AND SOVIET SPACE
PROGRAMS. CONTRARY TO VARIOUS CRITICS, HE BELIEVES THAT
BURAN-ENERGIA SYSTEM HAS RECAPTURED THE PUBLIC IMAGINATION
AND THAT THANKS TO GREATER VERSATILITY THAN ITS US
COUNTERPART, IT CAN ACCELERATE PROGRESS IN THE SOVIET SPACE
PROGRAM AND STIMULATE SPIN-OFFS. THE GROWING SPIRIT OF
GLASTNOST IN THE PROGRAM IS WELCOMED AND AN INCREASING
OPENNESS EXPECTED.

05562 LESSMANN, S.
GOVERNMENT, INTEREST GROUPS, AND INCREMENTALISM
EUROPEAN JOURNAL OF POLITICAL RESEARCH, 17(4) (JUL 89),
449-469.
THIS PAPER IS CONCERNED WITH THE TWO UNDERLYING
DIMENSIONS OF THE PEOPLE'S WELFARE ECONOMIC GROWTH AND
SOCIAL PROTECTION - AND THEIR REALIZATION IN THE THE DIVERSE
PROCESSES WHICH DETERMINE THE CHARACTER OF BUDGETING AND
BUDGETARY OUTCOMES. THESE CONFLICTING CONCEPTIONS OF WELFARE
AND THE DIVERSE AGENTS INVOLVED IN THE BUDGETARY PROCESS
GENERATE A GOVERNMENT FISCAL POLICY, WHICH EXPRESSES THE
CLASH BETWEEN IDEOLOGY AND POLITICAL FEASIBILITY AND BETWEEN
POLITICIANS' INTENTIONS AND ACTUAL OUTCOMES. THIS PAPER
FOCUSES PRIMARILY BUDGETARY PROCESS IN WEST GERMAN, BUT ALSO
MAKES SOME REFERENCE TO FISCAL POLICY IN THE UK AND THE USA.

05563 LESTER, J.P.; BOWMAN, A.O'M.
IMPLEMENTING ENVIRONMENTAL POLICY IN A FEDERAL SYSTEM: A
TEST OF THE SABATIER—MAZMANIAN MODEL
POLITY, 21(4) (SUM 89), 731-754.
IMPLEMENTATION RESEARCH HAS BEEN IMPEDED BY A VARIETY OF
CONCEPTUAL AND METHODOLOGICAL DIFFICULTIES, SOME OF WHICH
THIS ARTICLES HOPES TO REMEDY. IT EXAMINES THE REGULATION OF
HAZARDOUS WASTE IN THE FIFTY STATES AND, USING THE
CONCEPTUAL FRAMEWORK DEVELOPED BY SABATIER AND MAZMANIAN,
IDENTIFIES THE FACTORS THAT INHIBIT POLICY IMPLEMENTATION.
THE AUTHORS FOCUS SPECIFICALLY ON THE RESOURCE CONSERVATION

AND RECOVERY ACT OF 1976 AND FIND THAT STATE IMPLEMENTATION
IS A FUNCTION OF TECHNICAL UNCERTAINTY, AGENCY COMPETENCE,
AND THE ECONOMIC IMPORTANCE OF TARGET GROUPS. THEY ALSO FIND
THAT THERE ARE DIFFERENCES BETWEEN THE NONIMPLEMENTING
STATES.

05564 LETICH, L.
ABORTION: BAD CHOICES
TIKKUN, 4(4) (JUL 89), 22-25.
THE ARTICLE OUTLINES THE CONTINUED DEBATE OVER THE ISSUE
OF ABORTION AND ASSESSES THE REASONS WHY ABORTION IS STILL
AN ISSUE SOME SIXTEEN YEARS AFTER THE RIGHT TO A SAFE, LEGAL
ABORTION WAS GRANTED BY THE SUPREME COURT. THE ARTICLE
EXPLORES THE REASONS WHY THE PRO-ABORTION ARGUEMENTS OF
PROGRESSIVES HAVE NOT APPEALED TO LARGE SEGMENTS OF THE US
POPULATION. IT OUTLINES A SHIFT IN STRATEGY WITH EMPHASIS ON
A WOMAN'S NEED FOR (AS OPPOSED TO RIGHT TO) AN ABORTION AND
A REEXAMINATION OF THE HUMAN STATUS OF THE FETUS AT VARIOUS
STAGES OF DEVELOPMENT.

05565 LEUBE, K.R.
SOCIAL POLICY: HAYEK AND SCHMOLLER COMPARED
INTERNATIONAL JOURNAL OF SOCIAL ECONOMICS, 16(9-11) (1989),
106-116.
SCHMOLLER AND HIS SCHOOL NEVER OFFERED A PRECISE
DEFINITION OF THE TERMS "SOCIAL POLICY" AND "SOCIAL JUSTICE".
THEY WERE LOOSELY USED TO DESCRIBE A GRADUAL REPLACEMENT OF
CAPITALISM BY SOME KIND OF SYNDICALISM OR SOCIALISM. HAYEK'S
APPROACH CAN LEAD TO A "POLITICAL ORDER OF A FREE PEOPLE",
WHEREAS THE ALTERNATIVE APPROACHES OF SCHMOLLER, COMTE,
FEUERBACH AND MARX PAVED THE WAY TO TOTALITARIANISM.

05566 LEUENTHAL, P.; CHELLANEY, B.
NUCLEAR TERRORISM: THREAT, PERCEPTION, AND RESPONSE IN
SOUTH ASIA
TERRORISM, 11(6) (1988), 447-470.
THIS PAPER SEEKS TO ANSWER THE QUESTION: WHAT SHOULD BE
DONE IN SOUTH ASIA IN RESPONSE TO THE DANAGERS OF NUCLEAR
BLACKMAIL AND TERRORISM? THE RELEVANCE OF THE
RECOMMENDATIONS OF THE NUCLEAR CONTROL INSTITUTE'S
INTERNATIONAL TASK FORCE ON PREVENTION OF NUCLEAR TERRORISM
IS EXPLORED. THE AUTHORS EXAMINE CONVENTIONAL TERRORISM IN
THE CONTEXT OF INCREASED NUCLEAR ACTIVITIES AND PROVIDE AN
OVERVIEW OF RECENT NUCLEAR DEVELOPMENTS IN THE REGION.
POLICY RECOMMENDATIONS ARE GIVEN, AND SPECIFIC PROPOSALS ARE
MADE TO COUNTER THE THREATS OF NUCLEAR BLACKMAIL AND
TERRORISM.

05567 LEVADA, I.A.
THE DYNAMICS OF A SOCIAL TURNING POINT
SOVIET REVIEW, 30(6) (NOV 89), 12-30.
THE PERIOD NOW BEING EXPERIENCED BY SOVIET SOCIETY IS
CHARACTERIZED BY A PROFOUND BREAKDOWN OF SOCIAL STRUCTURES,
WHICH IS BRINGING TO LIGHT THE LATENT SPRINGS AND MECHANISMS
OF THE LIFE OF THE SOCIAL ORGANISM. IN SOME RESPECTS, THE
CURRENT SITUATION IS ANALOGOUS TO THAT OF THE SUMMER AND
FALL OF 1917. ONE OF THE FEATURES OF THE PRESENT SCENE IS
THAT IMPORTANT HISTORICAL FIGURES ARE LOSING THEIR AURA OF
INFALLIBILITY.

05568 LEVENDOSKY, C.
IN AMERICA BLASPHEMY IS NOT A CRIME, MR. KHOMEINI, BUT
THREATS TO LIFE ARE
CHURCH AND STATE, 42(4) (APR 89), 19 (91)-20 (92).
THE AYATOLLAH KHOMEINI'S THREATS AGAINST AUTHOR SALMAN
RUSHDIE ARE A GOOD EXAMPLE OF WHY THE THE UNITED STATES
PROHIBITS THE UNHOLY ALLIANCE BETWEEN THE GOVERNMENT AND A
CHURCH. POLITICS IS A MATTER OF COMPROMISE. POLITICAL
SOLUTIONS AND POLICIES REPRESENT THE OPINIONS OF DIVERSE
CITIZEN GROUPS AND EVEN INDIVIDUAL WITH SOME POWER OR
POLITICAL BASE. NOT SO IN RELIGION. RELIGION DEALS IN
ABSOLUTES. HISTORY HAS SHOWN THAT WHEN GOVERNMENT AND
RELIGION WED, POLITICS LOSES ITS DESIRE TO COMPROMISE AND
SEARCH FOR REAL CONSENSUS. "CONSENSUS" THEN COMES BY DIVINE
FIAT, RESTRICTION OF THOUGHT, THREAT OR TORTURE,
IMPRISONMENT, EXECUTION, OR MURDER.

05569 LEVETAK, S.
NATIONAL MINORITIES AND CULTURAL EDUCATIONAL COOPERATION
BETWEEN YUGOSLAVIA AND ITS NEIGHBOURS
PLURAL SOCIETIES, 18(2) (MAR 89), 87-91.
THIS ARTICLE DESCRIBES HOW YUGOSLAVIA CAN CLAIM CREDIT
FOR ACHIEVING IMPORTANT RESULTS NOT ONLY IN GENERAL EFFORTS
TOWARDS THE UNIVERSAL DEVELOPMENT OF CULTURAL COOPERATION,
BUT ALSO IN ITS ATTEMPTS, TOGETHER WITH ITS NEIGHBOURS, TO
DEVELOP AN INTERESTING FORM OF CULTURAL COOPERATION WHICH,
AMONG OTHER THINGS, ALSO AFFIRMS THE CULTURAL INHERITANCE
AND CONTEMPORARY CREATIVITY OF THE NATIONS OF YUGOSLAVIA AND
THE NATIONS OF YUGOSLAVIA WHO LIVE IN NEIGHBOURING STATES AS
MINORITIES.

05570 LEVIN-WALDMAN, O.M.
LIBERALISM AND PLANT SHUTDOWNS: THE CONSTRAINTS OF IDEOLOGY
DISSERTATION ABSTRACTS INTERNATIONAL, 50(4) (OCT 89),

1078-A.
THE ISSUE OF PLANT CLOSINGS POSES A SERIOUS CHALLENGE TO
LIBERAL PUBLIC PHILOSOPHY AS IT HAS EVOLVED IN THE USA.
BECAUSE MUCH OF THE POLICY DEBATE INVOLVES LEGISLATION
RESTRICTING A PROPERTY OWNER'S RIGHT TO FREELY DISPOSE OF
PRIVATE PROPERTY, A PLANT CLOSING POLICY IS NOT EASILY
RECONCILED WITH AN IDEOLOGICAL DOCTRINE THAT HAS ATTACHED
PRIMACY TO FEEDOM OF MARKETS AND INDIVIDUAL RIGHTS.
NOTIFICATION AND SEVERANCE SUGGEST THAT WORKERS MAY HAVE A
PROPERTY RIGHT IN THEIR JOBS. COMMUNITY ASSISTANCE MIGHT
IMPLY A SOCIAL CONTRACT BETWEEN FIRMS AND THEIR COMMUNITIES.
AND RESTRICTIVE LEGISLATION AS A PACKAGE SUGGESTS THAT THERE
OUGHT TO BE DEMOCRATIC CONTROL OVER THE LIBERTY OF CAPITAL.

05571 LEVIN, A.
"PEOPLE ARE NOT AFRAID ANYMORE"
ACROSS FRONTIERS, 5(2) (SUM 89), 1,36.
THIS ARTICLE IS AN INTERVIEW WITH MOSCOW ACTIVIST,
ANDREI FADIN, BY A RADIO JOURNALIST IMMEDIATELY FOLLOWING
THE FIRST ROUND ELECTIONS TO THE CONGRESS OF PEOPLES
DEPUTIES IN MARCH. IT EXPLORES THE UNEXPECTED ELECTION
RESUTS AND REACTION TO THESE RESULTS. IT EXPLORES THE
POPULARIZATION PROCESS AS WELL AS THE POSSIBILITY OF
MULTIPLE POLITICAL PARTIES IN THE USSR.

05572 LEVIN, B.; SILVER, E.
ENDING THE STALEMATE
MACLEAN'S (CANADA'S NEWS MAGAZINE), 102(1) (JAN 89), 48.
THE U.S. DECISION TO OPEN DIRECT TALKS WITH THE PLO WAS
THE FINAL IMPETUS THAT BROKE THE DEADLOCK IN ISRAELI
POLITICS THAT EXISTED SINCE THE NATIONAL ELECTION IN
NOVEMBER OF 1988. SPURRED BY THE SHOCK OF THE PLO'S ENHANCED
WORLD STATURE, THE RIGHT-WING LIKUD BLOC AND THE CENTER-LEFT
LABOUR PARTY AGREED TO TERMS FOR A NEW "NATIONAL GOVERNMENT--
AND REASSERTED THEIR COMMITMENT TO STAND FIRM AGAINST THE
PLO.

05573 LEVIN, B.; ELLWAND, G.; QUINN, M.
JAPAN AFTER HIROHITO
MACLEAN'S (CANADA'S NEWS MAGAZINE), 102(3) (JAN 89), 20.
THE DEATH OF JAPAN'S EMPEROR HIROHITO WAS MET WITH
REACTIONS RANGING FROM ABJECT GRIEF TO BITTER DENUNCIATION.
OLDER JAPANESE GENERALLY MOURNED THE LOSS OF "THE IMPERIAL
SON OF HEAVEN," BUT MANY OF THE YOUNGER GENERATION WERE
INDIFFERENT TO THE NEWS. SOME WERE EVEN OPENLY HOSTILE,
CRITICIZING THE LATE EMPEROR FOR HIS INVOLVEMENT IN WORLD
WAR TWO.

05574 LEVIN, B.
MUDDLING THROUGH
POLICY OPTIONS, 10(2) (MAR 89), 31-35.
THERE ARE NEW DEMANDS FOR SERVICES, AND, AT THE SAME
TIME, A DECLINE IN BOTH THE RESOURCES AVAILABLE AND THE
FAITH OF ORDINARY CANADIANS IN THE CAPACITY OF GOVERNMENTS
TO DEAL WITH MAJOR PROBLEMS. HOWEVER, GOVERNMENT IS ILL-
PREPARED TO MEET THESE CHALLENGES. THE NEED TO CUT BACK IS
MET, FOR EXAMPLE, BY THE FACT THAT POLITICIANS ARE ELECTED
AND MAINTAINED IN OFFICE FOR DOING THINGS. WITHIN THE
BUREAUCRACY, THERE ARE NO REWARDS FOR EFFICIENCY, BUT THERE
ARE PENALTIES FOR MAKING MISTAKES. THE RESULT IS AN
INEVITABLE COLLISION BETWEEN SHORT-TERM POLICIES AND LONG-
TERM NEEDS, ESPECIALLY IN THE AREA OF SOCIAL POLICY. JUST
THE SAME, THE AUTHOR REMAINS OPTIMISTIC THAT, DESPITE THE
TROUBLE THAT LOOMS AHEAD, WITH THE ADVANTAGES OF AN OPEN
DEMOCRACY AND WHAT HE CALLS "THE LARGELY ANARCHICAL
UNDERTAKING THAT IS GOVERNMENT", CANADA WILL ACHIEVE
SIGNIFICANT IMPROVEMENT, IF ONLY BY MUDDLING THROUGH.

05575 LEVIN, M.; FREEMAN, A.; HENKIN, J.; MENSCH, B.
CURRENT DEBATE: AFFIRMATIVE ACTION
TIKKUN, 4(1) (JAN 89), 50-60.
THE AUTHORS CONSIDER MAJOR ISSUES IN THE AFFIRMATIVE
ACTION DEBATE, INCLUDING THE CONSEQUENCES OF QUOTAS FOR
JEWISH MALES, JEWISH OPPOSITION TO AFFIRMATIVE ACTION,
MERITOCRACY, ADMISSION TO COLLEGES AND PROFESSIONAL SCHOOLS,
AND THE ROOTS OF EQUAL OPPORTUNITY THEORY IN UTILITARIANISM
AND KANTIANISM.

05576 LEVIN, R.; NEOCOSMOS, M.
THE AGRARIAN QUESTION AND CLASS CONTRADICTIONS IN SOUTH
AFRICA: SOME THEORETICAL CONSIDERATIONS
JOURNAL OF PEASANT STUDIES, 16(2) (JAN 89), 230-259.
THE ARTICLE FIRST CONSIDERS TWO DOMINANT APPROACHES TO
BLACK RURAL SOCIAL FORMATIONS IN SOUTH AFRICA, THOSE OF NEO-
CLASSICAL POPULISM AND RADICAL POLITICAL ECONOMY, EXAMINING
THEIR IDEOLOGY AND POLITICS AS WELL AS THEIR THEORETICAL
INADEQUACIES. THE MAJOR PART OF THE ARTICLE THEN PROVIDES A
GENERAL INTERPRETATION OF THE THEORY AND POLITICS OF THE
AGRARIAN QUESTION IN MARXISM, WHICH HAS STRATEGIC
IMPLICATIONS FOR THE CURRENT PHASE OF NATIONAL DEMOCRATIC
STRUGGLE IN SOUTH AFRICA, AS FOR DEMOCRATIC AND SOCIALIST
STRUGGLES ELSEWHERE. THIS DISCUSSION CONCENTRATES ON ISSUES
CONCERNING THE LAND QUESTION, THE AGRICULTURE/INDUSTRY
CONTRADICTION AND THE WORKER-PEASANT ALLIANCE, PETTY

COMMODITY PRODUCTION AND CLASS DIFFERENTIATION VS. A
HOMOGENISED RURAL MASS ('THE PEOPLE'), AND THE CENTRALITY OF
THE AGRARIAN QUESTION TO NATIONAL DEMOCRATIC STRUGGLES AND
THOSE FOR SOCIALIST TRANSFORMATION.

05577 LEVINE, B.B.
A RETURN TO INNOCENCE? THE SOCIAL CONSTRUCTION OF THE
GEOPOLITICAL CLIMATE OF THE POST-INVASIOIN CARIBBEAN
JOURNAL OF INTERAMERICAN STUDIES AND WORLD AFFAIRS, 31(3)
(FAL 89), 183-204.
THIS ARTICLE STUDIES HOW DIFFERENT VISIONS OF THE
CARRIBEAN HAVE BEEN SOCIALLY CONSTRUCTED. IT ANALYSES
SEVERAL DEFINITIONS, GEOPOLITICAL AND CULTURAL, THEN STUDIES
THE SOCIAL CONSTRUCTION OF DEFINITIONS. "CARRIBEAN
EXCELLENCE" IS EXAMINED AS IT PEAKED AND IS NOW IN SOME
DECLINE. MILITARIZATION, CENTRAL AMERICANIZATION, ANTI-
SOCIAL CHANGE, AND THE "ECIPSE OF WESTMINISTER" ARE EACH IN
TURN STUDIED.

05578 LEVINE, E.
POLICIES FOR THE ELECTRONIC INFORMATION AGE
STATE LEGISLATURES, 15(8) (SEP 89), 28-29.
IT IS POSSIBLE TO USE TECHNOLOGY TO MANAGE INFORMATION,
RATHER THAN HAVING TO MANAGE THE TECHNOLOGY ITSELF. FOR
STATE LEGISLATURES, THIS IS A CRITICAL DISTINCTION. IF THE
INFORMATION IS SEPARATED FROM THE TECHNOLOGY THAT STORES AND
PROCESSES IT, THE UNDERLYING POLICY ISSUES FOR STATE
LEGISLATURES ARE MUCH CLEARER: HOW WILL SCARCE RESOURCES BE
ALLOCATED? WHAT ARE THE EQUITY CONCERNS? WHAT IS THE PUBLIC
INTEREST?

05579 LEVINE, P.; CURRIE, D.; GAINES, J.
USE OF SIMPLE RULES FOR INTERNATIONAL POLICY AGREEMENTS
AVAILABLE FROM NTIS, NO. PB89-192801/GAR, NOV 88, 71.
THE PAPER HAS DEVELOPED AND APPLIED A GENERAL
METHODOLOGY FOR ANALYZING THE SUSTAINABILITY OF
INTERNATIONAL POLICY AGREEMENT IN THE FORM OF SIMPLE RULES.
A NUMBER OF OBJECTIONS TO THE USE OF FEEDBACK RULES FOR THE
PURPOSES OF MACROECONOMIC STABILIZATION HAVE BEEN ADDRESSED.
ABOVE ALL THE AUTHORS HAVE DEMONSTRATED EMPIRICALLY THAT
POLICY COORDINATION CAN BE EFFECTIVE UNDER THE CONSTRAINT
THAT RULES MUST BE SIMPLE. SECOND, THEY HAVE SHOWN THAT
THERE IS CONSIDERABLE SCOPE FOR USING AGREEMENTS IN THE FORM
OF SIMPLE RULES AS A SURROGATE FOR MORE FAR-REACHING
AGREEMENT ON INTERNATIONAL POLICY COORDINATION. FINALY, THE
AUTHORS HAVE SHOWN THAT SIMPLE RULES ARE SUSTAINABLE; INDEED
SIMPLICITY IN POLICY DESIGN MAY ACTUALLY IMPROVE THE
PROSPECTS OF SUSTAINABILITY.

05580 LEVINE, S.I.
THE UNCERTAIN FUTURE OF CHINESE FOREIGN POLICY
CURRENT HISTORY, 88(539) (SEP 89), 261-264, 295-296.
IN THE AFTERMATH OF THE BRUTAL SUPPRESSION OF THE
CHINESE DEMOCRACY MOVEMENT ON JUNE 4, 1989, A LARGE QUESTION
MARK HANGS OVER CHINA'S FOREIGN RELATIONS. MANY SUBSTANTIAL
FOREIGN POLICY ACCOMPLISHMENTS ACHIEVED DURING A DECADE OF
REFORM HAVE BEEN JEOPARDIZED. IT REMAINS TO BE SEEN WHETHER
INTERNATIONAL ASSISTANCE IN CHINA'S DRIVE TOWARD
MODERNIZATION WILL CONTINUE AT ITS PREVIOUS LEVEL OR WILL
SERIOUSLY DECLINE. CHINA'S MULTIFACETED RELATIONSHIP WITH
THE UNITED STATES; THE KEYSTONE OF BEIJING'S OPEN DOOR
POLICY TOWARD THE ADVANCED CAPITALIST WORLD. IS BOUND TO
SUFFER. THE QUESTION NOW IS WHETHER CHINA WILL PERSIST IN
ITS INTERNATIONALLY ORIENTED DEVELOPMENT STRATEGY OR REVERT
TO A MORE NARROWLY CIRCUMSCRIBED RELATIONSHIP WITH THE
OUTSIDE WORLD.

05581 LEVINSON, S.
ON CRITICAL LEGAL STUDIES
DISSENT, (SUM 89), 360-365.
THE CONFERENCE ON CRITICAL LEGAL STUDIES (CLS) CAME INTO
EXISTENCE IN MADISON, WISCONSIN, IN 1977 DURING A MEETING OF
LEGAL SCHOLARS AND PRACTITIONERS DISSATISFIED WITH
MAINSTREAM LAW. SINCE THEN THE MEMBERS HAVE BECOME ONE OF
THE MOST IMPORTANT AND CONTROVERSIAL GROUPS WITHIN THE LEGAL
ACADEMY. IN THIS ESSAY, THE AUTHOR FOCUSES ON SOME OF THE
MOST INTELLECTUALLY AND POLITICALLY CHALLENGING POSITIONS
ASSOCIATED WITH CLS.

05582 LEVITE, A.
CONTINUITY AND CHANGE IN ISRAEL'S OFFENSIVE MILITARY
DOCTRINE
IDF JOURNAL, (16) (WIN 89), 18-22.
THE AUTHOR RE-EVALUATES ISRAEL'S TRADITIONAL SECURITY
THINKING IN ORDER TO ASSESS HOW IT HAS STOOD THE TEST OF
TIME AND CHANGING CIRCUMSTANCES. HE CONSIDERS ISRAEL'S
POLITICAL ALLIANCES, THE REVISED ARAB MILITARY DOCTRINE, THE
GEOSTRATEGIC DISPOSITION, AND THE SOCIAL REALITIES.

05583 LEVITSKY, M.
CUBA AND NARCOTICS TRAFFICKING
DEPARTMENT OF STATE BULLETIN (US FOREIGN POLICY), 89(2151)
(OCT 89), 46-48.
IN AN UNPRECEDENTED MOVE ON JUNE 16, 1989, THE OFFICIAL

CUBAN PRESS ACCUSED GEN. ARNALDO OCHOA AND OTHER OFFICERS OF
NARCOTICS TRAFFICKING. THE PRESS STATED THAT AGREEMENTS HAD
BEEN CONCLUDED BETWEEN THE CUBAN OFFICERS AND COLOMBIAN DRUG
TRAFFICKERS AND THAT JOINT DRUG SMUGGLING OPERATIONS HAD
BEEN CARRIED OUT OVER A TWO-YEAR PERIOD. THIS WAS THE FIRST
TIME THE CUBAN GOVERNMENT HAD ADMITTED CUBAN INVOLVEMENT IN
THE DRUG TRADE. SOME OBSERVERS SPECULATED THAT OCHOA HAD
POSED A POLITICAL THREAT TO CASTRO AND THAT THE DRUG ISSUE
ALLOWED CASTRO TO TRY AND EXECUTE THE GENERAL.

05584 LEVITT, C.; SHAFFIR, W.
THE SWASTIKA AS DRAMATIC SYMBOL: A CASE STUDY OF ETHNIC
VIOLENCE IN CANADA
JEWISH JOURNAL OF SOCIOLOGY, XXXI(1) (JUN 89), 5-24.
THE PAPER EXAMINES THE ROLE OF THE SWASTIKA EMBLEM IN
FOMENTING THE VIRULENT ANTAGONISM BETWEEN CANADIAN JEWS AND
GENTILES WHICH CULMINATED IN THE CHRISTIE PITS RIOT IN THE
SUMMER OF 1933. IT FOCUSES SPECIFICALLY ON THE DRAMATIC
EVENT IN THE DEVELOPMENT OF THE RIOT--THE SUDDEN APPEARANCE
OF THE SWASTIKA SYMBOL ALONG TORONTO'S EASTERN BENCHES AND,
ABOUT TWO WEEKS LATER, AT A BASEBALL GAME IN WILLOWVALE PARK
(COMMONLY KNOWN AS CHRISTIE PITS). THE RIOT PROVIDED AMPLE
EXAMPLE THAT THE YOUNGER GENERATION OF TORONTO'S JEWRY WOULD
NOT MERELY TOLERATE EXCESSIVE FORMS OF ANTISEMITIC ABUSE
WITHOUT RESORTING TO VIOLENCE.

05585 LEVITT, W. K.
THE CHANGING ROLE OF THE PALESTINIAN POPULAR COMMITTEES
MIDDLE EAST INTERNATIONAL, 352 (JUN 89), 16-17.
ADJUSTING TO THE THE ECONOMIC HARDSHIPS OF THE INTIFADA
AND ITS CALL FOR MAXIMUM SELF-SUFFICIENCY HAS BECOME A WAY
OF LIFE TO WHICH PALESTINIANS ARE NOW THOROUGHLY ACCUSTOMED.
AS A CONSEQUENCE, AS THE POPULAR COMMITTEES HAVE DECLINED,
FAMILIES HAVE BEEN ABLE TO TAKE OVER THEIR OWN ORGANISATION,
INDIVIDUALLY AND WITH NEIGHBOURS. NOW, A SECOND GENERATION
OF POPULAR COMMITTEE IS IN THE MAKING. IT IS MORE
FACTIONALISED THAN ITS PREDECESSOR, AND MORE ADEQUATELY
FUNDED, IT IS WORKING IN FAR GREATER SECRECY, AND IT HAS
LONGTERM PLANNING AS ITS AIM. THE POPULAR COMMITTEE,
ORIGINALLY THE PRESERVE OF WILLING "AMATEURS", IS TAKING A
NEW TURN.

05586 LEVRAN, A.
CONSTRAINTS AND CHALLENGES
IDF JOURNAL, (18) (FAL 89), 35-42.
THIS ARTICLE EXPLORES THE STRATEGIC TURNING POINT
REGARDING ITS SECURITY THAT ISRAEL CURRENTLY FACES.
STRATEGIC THREATS AND CONSTRAINTS TO ISRAEL'S EXISTENCE FROM
THE ARABS ARE INVESTIGATED, ISRAEL'S TWO STRATEGIES
REGARDING THE SOLUTION TO THE CONFLICT ARE DEFINED.
SUPERPOWER INVOLVEMENT, ARAB MILITARY BUILD UP, ISRAEL'S
MILITARY DOCTRINE AND THE CHALLENGE OF MAINTAINING THE
BALANCE ARE EXAMINED THE ARTICLE CONCLUDES BY DEALING WITH
WAR RISKS.

05587 LEVY, B.
FOREIGN AID IN THE MAKING OF ECONOMIC POLICY IN SRI LANKA,
1977-1983
POLICY SCIENCES, 22(3-4) (1989), 437-461.
THE PAPER ANALYZES THE INTERACTION BETWEEN INFLOWS OF
FOREIGN AID AND THE CHARACTER OF THE ECOMOMIC POLICIES PURSUED
BY THE SRI LANKAN GOVERNMENT BETWEEN 1977 AND 1983. AID DID
NOT SUPPORT THE POLICIES OF LIBERALIZATION AND BALANCED
INVESTMENT THAT WAS PREFERRED BY DONORS. RATHER IT ENABLED
THE SRI LANKAN GOVERNMENT TO PUSH FORWARD WITH THE MAHAWELI
IRRIGATION SCHEME ON A SCALE THAT WORKED AGAINST BOTH
LIBVERALIZATION AND OTHER COMPONENTS OF PUBLIC INVESTMENT.
THE PROCESS THAT LED TO THE ADOPTION AND FUNDING OT THE
MAHAWELI SCHEME AND CONTINUED SUPPORT FOR THAT SCHEME EVEN
AFTER ITS IMPACT ON THE OVERALL ECONOMIC PROGRAM HAD BECOME
APPARENT IS EXAMINED IN DETAIL, WITH PARTICULAR EMPHASIS ON
THE DECISIONS AND BEHAVIOR OF BOTH SRI LANKAN GOVERNMENT AND
OF AID DONORS.

05588 LEVY, D.
WOMEN OF THE FRENCH NATIONAL FRONT
PARLIAMENTARY AFFAIRS, 42(1) (JAN 89), 102-111.
THE ARTICLE EXAMINES THE REASONS WHY THE MAJORITY OF
FRENCH WOMEN ARE ALIENATED BY JEAN-MARIE LE PEN AND HIS
NATIONAL FRONT PARTY AND WHY A STRIDENT MINORITY SUPPORT THE
NATIONAL FRONT. IRONICALLY, THE REASONS ARE OFTEN THE SAME:
THE MAJORITY OF FRENCH WOMEN VIEW THE NATIONAL FRONT"S
POSITION ON WOMEN TO BE "REGRESSION" AND A THREAT TO THE
RIGHTS THEY HAVE WON OVER THE PAST FEW DECADES; HOWEVER, IT
IS PRECISELY THE CONSERVATIVE VIEWS ON THE ROLE OF WOMEN
THAT APPEAL TO THE SMALL MINORITY OF LE PEN SUPPORTERS.
OTHER REASONS FOR SUPPORT OF THE NATIONAL FRONT ARE SIMILAR
TO THE REASONS MOST MEN GIVE: CONCERN WITH IMMIGRATION,
INSECURITY, UNEMPLOYMENT, DECADENCE, AND FRENCH NATIONALISM.

05589 LEVY, G.
SAMIHA KHALIL: FIRST LADY
NEW OUTLOOK, 32(6-7 (292-293)) (JUN 89), 37-39.
PALESTINIAN ACTIVIST SAMIHA KHALIL HEADS THE LARGEST

WOMEN'S ORGANIZATION IN THE WEST BANK. SHE IS CLOSE TO
GEORGE HABASH'S POPULAR FRONT FOR THE LIBERATION OF
PALESTINE, AND POLITICAL OBSERVERS BELIEVE HER PLACE AT THE
NEGOTIATING TABLE AS A REPRESENTATIVE OF WOMEN IS ASSURED.
KHALIL, WHO WAS FORMERLY MILITANTLY ANTI-ISRAEL AND ONCE
AVOIDED ALL CONTACT WITH ISRAELIS, SAYS THAT HER IDEAS HAVE
CHANGED, THAT SHE HAS BECOME MORE MODERATE, AND THAT SHE IS
READY FOR POLITICAL COMPROMISE.

05590 LEWELLEN, T.C.
HOLY AND UNHOLY ALLIANCES: THE POLITICS OF CATHOLICISM IN
REVOLUTIONARY NICARAGUA
JOURNAL OF CHURCH & STATE, 31(1) (WIN 89), 15-34.
IN 1983 THE NICARAGUAN EPISCOPAL CONFERENCE ISSUED
"GENERAL CONSIDERATIONS ON MILITARY SERVICE," WHICH ARGUES
THAT THE RIGHT TO CONSCRIPTION DOES NOT APPLY IF "A HIGHLY
POLITICIZED ARMY HAS BEEN CREATED AS A DEFENSE OF THE
GOVERNMENT'S OWN IDEOLOGY AND AT THE SAME TIME AS A MEANS TO
FORCE PEOPLE TO RECEIVE POLITICAL INDOCTRINATION." THE
DOCUMENT REPEATEDLY REFERS TO THE SANDINISTAS AS
"TOTALITARIAN," WHILE ADVISING CONSCIENTIOUS OBJECTION FOR
ALL WHO DO NOT SHARE SANDINISTA IDEOLOGY.

05591 LEWIN, M.
PERESTROIKA: A NEW HISTORICAL STAGE
JOURNAL OF INTERNATIONAL AFFAIRS, 42(2) (SPR 89), 299-316.
THE ARTICLE EXAMINES THE HISTORICAL ANTECEDENTS OF
PERESTROIKA IN AN ATTEMPT TO DETERMINE THE FUTURE DIRECT OF
THE LATEST ROUND OF SOVIET REFORMS. IT ANALYZES THE
IMPLICATIONS OF GLASNOST WITH EMPHASIS ON THE DEBATE OVER
PAST SOVIET HISTORY. IT ALSO ANALYZES THE INTERNATIONAL
IMPLICATIONS OF PERESTROIKA. MANY HISTORIANS VIEW
GORBACHEV'S REFORMS AS MERELY ANOTHER CYCLE OF REFORM THAT
IS DOOMED TO BE CUT SHORT; THE AUTHOR, HOWEVER, ARGUES THAT
PERESTROIKA IS MOVING THE SOVIET UNION TO A NEW STAGE IN ITS
HISTORY WHERE OLD MODELS OF ANALYSIS AND CRITICISM NO LONGER
APPLY.

05592 LEWIS-BECK, M.S.; LOCKERBIE, B.
ECONOMICS, VOTES, PROTESTS WESTERN EUROPEAN CASES
COMPARATIVE POLITICAL STUDIES, 22(2) (JUL 89), 155-177.
IN WESTERN EUROPEAN STUDIES, GENERAL INVESTIGATIONS OF
MASS POLITICAL PARTICIPATION ARE AN ESTABLISHED TRADITION.
HOWEVER, THESE EFFORTS HAVE NOT DRAWN FROM THE VIGOROUS
CURRENT OF RESEARCH ON ECONOMICS AND POLITICS. SPECIFICALLY
FOR WESTERN EUROPE, THERE EXISTS NO SYSTEMATIC WORK ON
ECONOMIC CONDITIONS AND POLITICAL PARTICIPATION
(CONVENTIONAL OR UNCONVENTIONAL). HERE THE AUTHORS INTEGRATE
THESE ECONOMIC ARGUMENTS INTO GENERAL EXPLANATIONS OF BOTH
PARTICIPATION MODES. FIRST VOTING TURNOUT IS EXAMINED, THEN
PROTEST ACTIVITY, BOTH AS MEASURED IN RECENT SURVEY DATA
FROM BRITAIN, FRANCE, GERMANY, AND ITALY. THE FINDINGS
UNCOVER SUPPORT FOR A GENERAL MODEL OF POLITICAL
PARTICIPATION WITHIN THESE NATIONS, AS WELL AS POINTING TO
PROVOCATIVE BETWEEN-NATION DIFFERENCES. THE ECONOMIC RESULTS
ARE ESPECIALLY STIMULATING. POCKETBOOK EFFECTS ARE ABSENT,
BUT COLLECTIVE EVALUATIONS OF ECONOMIC PERFORMANCE MAKE AN
IMPACT, AND DO SO IN INTRIGUING WAYS. FIRST, IT IS
PROSPECTIVE, NOT RETROSPECTIVE, EVALUATIONS THAT COUNT.
SECOND, THEY OPERATE ASYMMETRICALLY, WITH THE PROSPECT OF
GOOD TIMES HEIGHTENING TURNOUT, AND THE PROSPECT OF BAD
TIMES HEIGHTENING PROTEST. SUCH FINDINGS SUGGEST NOTEWORTHY
REVISIONS REGARDING THE THEORY OF ECONOMICS AND
PARTICIPATION.

05593 LEWIS, B.
STATE AND SOCIETY UNDER ISLAM
WILSON QUARTERLY, XIII(4) (AUT 89), 39-53.
THE CONFLICT BETWEEN WORLDLY AND SPIRITUAL AUTHORITY IS
AN IMPORTANT ONE IN ISLAM. THIS ARTICLE CONSIDERS THE
EVOLUTION OF CIVIC AND SOCIAL ARRANGEMENTS IN MUSLIM
POLITIES FROM THE TIME OF MUHAMMAD TO THE PRESENT. THE
AUTHOR ARGUES THAT SOME ISLAMIC LEADERS WHO TODAY CLAIM TO
BE RECREATING THE COMMUNITY AS IT WAS UNDER MUHAMMAD AND THE
EARLY CALIPHS ARE INVENTING SOMETHING QUITE NEW.

05594 LEWIS, E.A.
ROLE STRAIN IN AFRICAN-AMERICAN WOMEN THE EFFICACY OF
SUPPORT NETWORKS
JOURNAL OF BLACK STUDIES, 20(2) (DEC 89), 155-170.
USING THE EXISTING KNOWLEDGE OF TRADITIONAL STRATEGIES
USED BY AFRICAN-AMERICAN WOMEN, THIS STUDY EXAMINES THE
FOLLOWING QUESTIONS: 1. TO WHAT EXTENT DO AFRICAN-AMERICAN
MOTHERS USE EXTENDED KIN, FRIEND, CURRENT PARTNER, AND
RELIGIOUS COMMUNITY INFORMAL NETWORKS TO REDUCE THEIR ROLE
STRAIN? 2. HOW DOES THE PERCEPTION OF SUPPORT INFLUENCE
AFRICAN-AMERICAN MOTHERS' REPORTS OF ROLE STRAIN? 3. IS
THERE A RELATIONSHIP BETWEEN THE NUMBER OF CHILDREN AND
REPORTS OF ECONOMIC, HOUSEHOLD MAINTENANCE, AND PARENTAL
ROLE STRAIN? 4. WHAT OTHER DEMOGRAPHIC FACTORS MAY
CONTRIBUTE TO AFRICAN-AMERICAN MOTHERS' REPORTS OF ROLE
STRAIN?

05595 LEWIS, G.
FROM CARLTON TO BRYNTIRION: BUSINESS-GOVERNMENT SUMMITRY
SOUTH AFRICA FOUNDATION REVIEW, 15(1) (JAN 89), 1-3.
THE AUTHOR LOOKS AT RECENT SUMMITS THAT BROUGHT TOGETHER
SOUTH AFRICAN BUSINESS MEN AND GOVERNMENT OFFICIALS. HE
EVALUATES THE SUMMITS, INCLUDING THEIR IMPACT ON NATIONAL
POLICY MAKING, BASED ON A SURVEY OF BUSINESSMEN WHO ATTENDED.

05596 LEWIS, G.
MOVING A ROCK: BUSINESS AND CHANGE IN SOUTH AFRICA
SOUTH AFRICA INTERNATIONAL, 20(2) (OCT 89), 85-90.
THE ROLE OF BUSINESS IN PROMOTING POLITICAL CHANGE IN
SOUTH AFRICA HAS SIGNIFICANTLY SHIFTED. ACKNOWLEDGING THE
LIMITS OF BUSINESS POWER AND THE COUNTERPRODUCTIVE NATURE OF
"PROTEST POLITICS, MOST BUSINESSMEN HAVE ABANDONED TACTICS
OF APPLYING DIRECT PRESSURE ON THE PRETORIA. INSTEAD, THEY
HAVE ENGAGED IN POLICIES OF CORPORATE SOCIAL RESPONSIBILITY
AND DEVELOPMENT. THIS EMPHASIS ON BLACK ECONOMIC EMPOWERMENT
AND CHANGE FORM BELOW IS MORE LIKELY TO RESULT IN PERMANENT
CHANGE.

05597 LEWIS, G.
THE MAN IN THE MIDDLE: WHITE MANAGERS, BLACK ADVANCEMENT
AND CHANGE
SOUTH AFRICA FOUNDATION REVIEW, 15(5) (MAY 89), 1-3.
THIS ARTICLE PROVIDES AN ANALYSIS OF WHITE MIDDLE
MANAGEMENT ATTITUDES TOWARD CHANGE, AND TOWARD BLACK
ADVANCEMENT IN MANAGEMENT CIRCLES. THE AUTHOR REVEALS THAT
WHITE MIDDLE MANAGEMENT VIEWS ON BROADER SOCIOECONOMIC AND
POLITICAL ISSUES DO NOT DIFFER SUBSTANTIALLY FROM THOSE OF
MAINSTREAM WHITE OPINION, AND THERE IS CONSIDERABLE ACCORD
BETWEEN THEIR ATTITUDES AND THOSE OF SENIOR BUSINESS LEADERS
ON REFORMIST ISSUES. ONLY IN THEIR SHARPE HOSTILITY TO
ORGANIZED BLACK LABOUR DO WHITE MIDDLE MANAGERS EXHIBIT KEY
DIFFERENCES OF OPINION.

05598 LEWIS, G.B.
PROGRESS TOWARD RACIAL AND SEXUAL EQUALITY IN THE FEDERAL
CIVIL SERVICE?
PUBLIC ADMINISTRATION REVIEW, 48(3) (MAY 88), 700-707.
THIS PAPER REPORTS ON CHANGES BETWEEN 1976 AND 1986 IN
BOTH REPRESENTATIVENESS AND SALARY DIFFERENCES FOR ASIAN,
NATIVE AMERICAN, HISPANIC, BLACK NON-HISPANIC, AND WHITE NON-
HISPANIC MEN AND WOMEN. THE ANALYSIS OF REPRESENTATIVENESS
USES PUBLISHED DATA ON THE FEDERAL WORKFORCE IN GENERAL
SCHEDULE (GS), GS-EQUIVALENT PAY SYSTEMS, AND THE SENIOR
EXECUTIVE SERVICE TAKEN FROM THE CENTRAL PERSONNEL DATA FILE
(CPDF).

05599 LEWIS, G.B.; PARK, K.
TURNOVER RATES IN FEDERAL WHITE-COLLAR EMPLOYMENT: ARE
WOMEN MORE LIKELY TO QUIT THAN MEN?
AMERICAN REVIEW OF PUBLIC ADMINISTRATION, 19(1) (MAR 89),
13-28.
BETWEEN 1976 AND 1986, WOMEN'S GROSS TURNOVER RATES WERE
ABOUT ONE-THIRD HIGHER THAN MEN'S IN THE FEDERAL CIVIL
SERVICE. SUCH DIFFERENCES FREQUENTLY ARE CITED AS A
JUSTIFICATION FOR PREFERRING MEN FOR POSITIONS WITH HIGH
TRAINING COSTS OR AS ONE EXPLANATION WHY MEN EARN SO MUCH
MORE THAN WOMEN. USING A 1% SAMPLE OF FEDERAL PERSONNEL
RECORDS FOR 1976-86, THIS PAPER SHOWS HOW MISLEADING GROSS
TURNOVER RATES CAN BE. MALE-FEMALE DIFFERENCES SEEM TO BE
ALMOST ENTIRELY DUE TO DIFFERENCES IN AVERAGE AGE, SALARY,
AND LENGTH OF SERVICE. MEN AND WOMEN IN SIMILAR
CIRCUMSTANCES HAVE VERY SIMILAR TURNOVER PROBABILITIES.

05600 LEWIS, G.B.; STEIN, L.
UNIONS AND MUNICIPAL DECLINE UNION IMPACT ON SALARIES,
EMPLOYMENT, AND SERVICE LEVELS IN LARGE AND SMALL CITIES
AMERICAN POLITICS QUARTERLY, 17(2) (APR 89), 208-222.
THIS ARTICLE COMPARES THE IMPACT OF UNIONIZATION ON
CHANGES IN MUNICIPAL EMPLOYMENT, SALARIES, AND PERSONNEL
EXPENDITURES FOR GROWING AND DECLINING CITIES. BETWEEN 1974
AND 1984, UNIONS APPEAR TO HAVE HAD SIMILAR IMPACTS ON SMALL,
MEDIUM, AND LARGE CITIES EXPERIENCING EITHER STRESS OR
GROWTH. UNIONS ACCELERATED SALARY GROWTH BUT RETARDED THE
EXPANSION OF EMPLOYMENT.

05601 LEWIS, H.; CYGIELMAN, T.
ONLY THE INTIFADA ENSURES THE POLITICAL PROCESS
NEW OUTLOOK, 32(11-12 (297-298)) (NOV 89), 28-29.
THE INTIFADA HAS MADE IT CLEAR TO EVERYONE THAT THE
STATUS QUO THAT EXISTED BEFORE THE UPRISING CANNOT RETURN.
THE INTIFADA HAS PUSHED THE PALESTINIAN CAUSE TO THE TOP OF
THE MIDDLE EAST AGENDA, AND THERE ARE NOW SERIOUS EFFORTS
UNDERWAY BY THE USA AND THE EUROPEAN COMMUNITY TO HELP START
A PROCESS THAT WILL EVENTUALLY LEAD TO A POLITICAL SOLUTION.
ONLY THE CONTINUATION OF THE INTIFADA CAN GURANTEE THAT THE
PEACE PROCESS WILL BE PURSUED BECAUSE, WITHOUT THE INTIFADA,
EVERYONE WOULD FORGET THE PALESTINIANS.

05602 LEWIS, K.J.
WEBSTER AND THE FUTURE OF ABORTION
CRS REVEIW, 10(8) (SEP 89), 8-11.
WHILE NOT REVERSING ITS LANDMARK ABORTION DECISION (ROE
V. WADE) THE SUPREME COURT, IN A SPLINTERED OPINION,
RETURNED TO THE STATES GREATER LEEWAY IN REGULATING ABORTION.
FUTURE LITIGATION, INCLUDING THREE CASES ON THE DOCKET NEXT
TERM, MAY ELABORATE ON STATES' AUTHORITY WITH RESPECT TO
ABORTION AND PROVIDE OTHER OPPORTUNITIES FOR THE COURT TO
REVISIT ROE.

05603 LEWIS, N.
REGULATING NON-GOVERNMENT BODIES
CONSTITUTIONAL REFORM QUARTERLY REVIEW, 4(4) (WIN 89), 5.
WHILE THE PROBLEMS OF ACCOUNTABILITY EXIST ACROSS THE
WHOLE SPAN OF PUBLIC LIFE THERE ARE SPECIAL PROBLEMS
REGARDING NON-DEPARTMENTAL BODIES AND THE GOVERNMENT AT
LARGE. THE AUTHOR HERE DESCRIBES THE RELATIONSHIP OF TWO
SPECIFIC AGENCIES TO GOVERNMENT CONTROL: THE INTERNATIONAL
BROADCASTING AUTHORITY AND THE CIVIL AIRATION AUTHORITY IN
GREAT BRITAIN

05604 LEWIS, P.G.
POLAND - RENEWAL RENEWED
JOURNAL OF COMMUNIST STUDIES, 5(3) (SEP 89), 340-343.
ON 17 APRIL 1989 THE POLISH TRADE UNION SOLIDARITY WAS
REGISTERED AND PRONOUNCED LEGAL BY A WARSAW JUDGE. A SIMILAR
PROCESS HAD BEEN ENACTED EIGHT AND A HALF YEARS EARLIER.
THIS ARTICLE EXAMINES THE PERIOD BETWEEN THOSE DATES WHICH
HAD SEEN THE DEEPENING OF POLAND'S ECONOMIC AND POLITICAL
CRISIS DURING 1981; THE ANNOUNCEMENT OF MARTIAL LAW; AND
SEVERAL YEARS OF RELATIVELY STABLE BUT ECONOMICALLY AND
POLITICALLY UNPRODUCTIVE SEMI-NORMALIZATION.

05605 LEWIS, H.G.
TOWARD REPRESENTATIVE DEMOCRACY: AN ASSESSMENT OF BLACK
REPRESENTATION IN POLICE BUREAUCRACIES
DISSERTATION ABSTRACTS INTERNATIONAL, 49(9) (MAR 89),
2804-A.
THE AUTHOR MEASURES THE EXTENT TO WHICH POLICE
DEPARTMENTS IN LARGE AMERICAN CITIES ACHIEVED A LEVEL OF
RACIAL PARITY IN THE SWORN RANKS REFLECTIVE OF BLACKS IN THE
LABOR FORCE IN 1975 AND 1985. HE TESTS A SET OF HYPOTHESES
RELATING TO DEMOGRAPHIC, ORGANIZATIONAL, POLITICAL, AND
PUBLIC POLICY VARIABLES. HIS FINDINGS INDICATE THAT BLACK
MAYORS, BLACK POLICE CHIEFS, AFFIRMATIVE ACTION CONSENT
DECREES, AND BLACKS IN PROTECTIVE SERVICE RANKS WERE
POSITIVE VARIABLES IN BLACK REPRESENTATION.

05606 LEWIS, W.H.
GORBACHEV AND ETHNIC COEXISTENCE
COMPARATIVE STRATEGY, 8(4) (1989), 399-410.
ETHNIC GRIEVANCES ARE EXPRESSED IN A VARIETY OF MODES
THROUGHOUT THE SOVIET UNION. FROM THE PERSPECTIVE OF MOSCOW,
THE MOST SEVERE LONG-TERM CHALLENGE TO THE COHESION OF THE
SOVIET UNION EMANATES FROM THE SOUTHERN, PREDOMINANTLY
MOSLEM-POPULATED, REPUBLICS. THE SOVIET LEADERSHIP IS
COMPELLED TO ADDRESS A NUMBER OF DILEMMAS AS IT ATTEMPTS TO
PROVIDE COHERENCE AND SUBSTANCE TO THE CONCEPT OF
PERESTROIKA. THERE APPEAR TO BE NO FAIL-SAFE SOLUTIONS.

05607 LEYDEN, D. P.
INTERGOVERNMENTAL GRANTS AND THE ENDOGENOUS DETERMINATION
OF STATE AND LOCAL TAX RATES WITH AN APPLICATION TO
CONNECTICUT'S EDUCATION PROGRAM
DISSERTATION ABSTRACTS INTERNATIONAL, 49(7) (JAN 89),
1894-A.
THE AUTHOR EXAMINES THE EFFECT OF STATE GRANTS TO
LOCALITIES ON VOTER DECISION-MAKING. HE CONSTRUCTS AND
ANALYZES THEORETICALLY AND EMPIRICALLY AN EXPLICITLY MULTI-
JURISDICTIONAL MODEL OF STATE AND LOCAL GOVERNMENT IN WHICH
ALL TAXES AND EXPENDITURES, INCLUDING GRANTS, ARE ENDOGENOUS.

05608 LHO, K.
SEOUL-MOSCOW RELATIONS: LOOKING TO THE 1990S
ASIAN SURVEY, XXIX(12) (DEC 89), 1153-1166.
THE DECISION OF THE SOVIET UNION TO SEND A DELEGATION TO
THE 1988 OLYMPICS IN KOREA HAS RESULTED IN THE THAWING OF
RELATIONS BETWEEN SOUTH KOREA AND THE USSR. THIS CHANGE IN
FOREIGN POLICY IS LARGELY THE RESULT OF SEOUL'S ACTIVIST
"OPEN DOOR" POLICY DESIGNED TO OPEN DIPLOMATIC RELATIONS
WITH THE EASTERN BLOC AND TO REDUCE THE THREAT FROM NORTH
KOREA. THE ARTICLE EXAMINES THE CENTRAL FEATURES OF SOVIET
POLICY TOWARD THE ASIAN REGION BOTH BEFORE AND AFTER
GORBACHEV. IT ALSO LOOKS AT PRACTICAL DEVELOPMENTS IN SEOUL-
MOSCOW RELATIONS IN THE PAST SEVERAL YEARS AND OFFERS AN
INTERIM EVALUATION OF THE ACCOMPLISHMENTS AS WELL AS THE
CHALLENGES STILL FACING SEOUL'S DIPLOMACY TOWARD MOSCOW.

05609 LI, C.
THE INITIATION, PROCESSES, AND EFFECTS OF LINKAGE
DIPLOMACY: AN ANALYSIS OF ECONOMIC SANCTIONS, # 1947-1983
DISSERTATION ABSTRACTS INTERNATIONAL, 49(11) (MAY 89),
3498-A.
IN LINKAGE DIPLOMACY, A NATION'S POLICY-MAKING IN ONE
AREA IS CONTINGENT ON ANOTHER STATE'S BEHAVIOR IN OTHER
AREAS. BY USING LINKAGE DIPLOMACY, NATIONAL GOVERNMENTS CAN

PROJECT THEIR POWER IN AREAS OF STRENGTH TO OBTAIN
OBJECTIVES IN AREAS OF WEAKNESS. THIS STUDY IDENTIFIES THE
CONDITIONS UNDER WHICH SUCH A TECHNIQUE IS POSSIBLE AND
EFFECTIVE.

05610 LI, S.
    CHINA'S POPULATION CONTROL AND SOCIO-ECONOMIC REFORMS: THE
    CHINESE DILEMMA
    CHINA REPORT, 25(3) (JUL 89), 219-236.
    IN THE EARLY EIGHTIES THE CHINESE GOVERNMENT BEGAN TO
RELINQUISH SOME OF ITS POWER TO ITS CITIZENS UNDER THE SOCIO-
ECONOMIC REFORMS. THIS BRINGS CHINA'S POPULATION POLICY INTO
QUESTION. AMONG OTHERS, TWO CHALLENGES TO THE CURRENT POLICY
OF ONE-CHILD-PER-COUPLE ARE THE RISE OF PRIVATE
ENTREPRENEURS AND GREATER INDIVIDUAL FREEDOM. BECAUSE OF
THESE CHANGES, RECONSIDERING THE GOALS OF CHINA'S POPULATION
POLICY AND POPULATION PROBLEM IS NOW AN ISSUE. THIS ARTICLE
ATTEMPTS TO DISTINGUISH TWO KINDS OF POPULATION PROBLEMS, TO
ASSESS THE COST OF IMPLEMENTING POPULATION POLICY, AND TO
DISCUSS SOME POSSIBLE MEASURES WHICH MIGHT MITIGATE CHINA'S
POPULATION PROBLEMS.

05611 LI, V.
    THE STATUS OF TAIWAN
    ASIAN AFFAIRS, AN AMERICAN REVIEW, 16(3) (FAL 89), 167-171.
    ALTHOUGH IT IS CLEAR THAT THE U.S. NO LONGER RECOGNIZES
TAIWAN AS THE DE JURE GOVERNMENT OF THE STATE OF CHINA, IT
IS MUCH LESS CLEAR WHAT THE U.S. DOES CONSIDER TAIWAN TO BE.
THE ARTICLE EXPLORES A FEW POSSIBLE THEORIES THAT MAY GOVERN
U.S.-TAIWAN RELATIONS IN THE FUTURE. THESE INCLUDE: THE
SUCCESSOR-GOVERNMENT THEORY (THE MAINLAND PRC GOVERNMENT IS
THE SUCCESSOR GOVERNMENT TO THE ROC), RECOGNITION OF TAIWAN
AS A DE FACTO ENTITY WITH INTERNATIONAL PERSONALITY, AND THE
NOTION THAT "ACKNOWLEDGMENT" OF THE CHINESE POSITION IS NOT
TANTAMOUNT TO ACCEPTING IT. THE POSITION THAT THE U.S.
CHOOSES WILL LARGELY DETERMINE ITS FOREIGN POLICY TOWARDS
BOTH TAIWAN AND MAINLAND CHINA.

05612 LIBER, G.
    URBAN GROWTH AND ETHNIC CHANGE IN THE UKRAINIAN SSR, 1923-
    1933
    SOVIET STUDIES, 61(4) (OCT 89), 574-591.
    IN ORDER TO UNDERSTAND ARGUMENTS CONCERNING UKRAINIAN
NATIONAL COMMUNISM, THE PURGES IN THE UKRAINE AND THE FAMINE
OF 1932-33, ETHNIC CHANGES IN THE UKRAINIAN CITIES IN THE
1920S AND EARLY 1930S ARE INVESTIGATED IN THIS ARTICLE,
URBAN GROWTH IS TRACED, AS WELL AS, ETHNIC CHANGES DURING
THIS TIME PERIOD. AS THE CITIES ACQUIRED MORE UKRAINIAN
INHABITANTS, RUSSIAN POLITICAL CONTROL OVER THE URBAN AREAS
WAS THREATENED BY IMMINENT POLITICAL DE-RUSSIFICATION OF THE
MAJOR INDUSTRIAL AREAS. THIS ETHNIC TRANSFORMATION HAD
POLITICAL IMPLICATIONS. THESE INSTITUTIONS NOW REPRESENTED
UKRAINIAN, NOT NECESSARILY SOVIET, PREROGATIVES. FEARING THE
MANIFESTATION OF THESE TRENDS, STALIN HAD TO CHOOSE BETWEEN
ORDER AND LEGITIMACY. NOT SURPRISNGLY, HE EMBRACED THE FIRST.

05613 LIBERMAN, M.
    "ULSTER (STILL) SAYS NO!"
    FREEDOM AT ISSUE, (109) (JUL 89), 18-20.
    THE 1985 ANGLO-IRISH AGREEMENT, SIGNED AFTER MORE THAN A
YEAR OF SECRET NEGOTIATIONS BY PRIME MINISTERS MARGARET
THATCHER AND GARRET FITZGERALD, WAS IMMEDIATELY HAILED IN
THE USA AS "A PROMISE OF PEACE." BUT IN ULSTER THE AGREEMENT
WAS CONDEMNED BY BOTH PROTESTANTS AND CATHOLICS. ONLY AMONG
SOME MEMBERS OF THE CENTRIST SOCIAL DEMOCRATIC AND LABOR
PARTY AND THE TINY ALLIANCE PARTY DID THE AGREEMENT FIND
SUPPORT. THREE YEARS LATER, CONDITIONS IN NORTHERN IRELAND
ARE LESS, NOT MORE, SECURE THAN THEY WERE IN RECENT PRE-
AGREEMENT TIMES. IN FACT, 1988 WAS THE BLOODIEST YEAR IN
NEARLY A DECADE.

05614 LICHBACH, M.I.
    STABILITY IN RICHARDSON'S ARMS RACES AND COOPERATION IN
    PRISONER'S DILEMMA ARMS RIVALRIES
    AMERICAN JOURNAL OF POLITICAL SCIENCE, 33(4) (NOV 89),
    1016-1017.
    THIS PAPER FORMALLY DEVELOPS THE TIT-FOR-TAT (TFT)
SOLUTIONS, BASED ON REPEATED PLAY, TO DISCRETE AND
CONTINUOUS CHOICE VERSIONS OF ARMS RIVALRIES THAT ARE
INTEREATED (REPEATED) PRISONER'S DILEMMAS (IPDS). EARLIER
EFFORTS AT SOLVING A PRISONER'S DILEMMA (PD) ARMS RIVALRY
WITH TFT RELIED ON ARBITRARY PAYOFF FUNCTIONS. THE MODEL
USED HERE EMPLOYS RICHARDSON-TYPE UTILITY FUNCTIONS THAT
ALLOW A FASCINATING RESULT TO EMERGE: GIVEN THE ASSUMPTIONS
BEHIND CERTAIN RICHARDSON-TYPE UTILITY FUNCTIONS, THE
CONCLUSIONS ABOUT THE EXISTENCE AND STABILITY OF EQUILIBRIUM
IN RICHARDSON'S ARMS RACES, DERIVED FROM THE ADDITIONAL
ASSUMPTIONS OF NONRATIONALITY INHERENT IN RICHARDSON'S
DIFFERENTIAL EQUATIONS, AND THE CONCLUSIONS ABOUT THE
EMERGENCE OF COOPERATION IN IPD ARMS RIVALRIES, DERIVED FROM
THE ADDITIONAL ASSUMPTIONS OF RATIONALITY INHERENT IN GAME
THEORY, BEAR REMARKABLE SIMILARITIES YET SUBTLE DIFFERENCES.
MOREOVER, THE USE OF RICHARDSON-TYPE UTILITY FUNCTIONS IN
IPD GAMES PRODUCES FOUR FURTHER IMPROVEMENTS OVER PREVIOUS

TREATMENTS OF IPD ARMS RIVALRIES THAT USED ARBITRARY PAYOFF
FUNCTIONS: CONTINUOUS AS WELL AS BINARY CHOICE VERSIONS OF
THE IPD ARMS RIVALRY ARE NOW STUDIED; MORE SUBSTANTIVE
CONCLUSIONS ABOUT ARMS RIVALRIES ARE NOW PRODUCED;
CONNECTIONS BETWEEN THE CONDITIONS FOR A RICHARDSON-TYPE
ARMS RIVALRY TO BE A PD AND THE CONDITIONS FOR SOLVING A PD
ARMS RIVALRY WITH TFT ARE NOW ESTABLISHED; AND, SOME
FUNDAMENTAL FLAWS WITH THE TFT SOLUTION TO A PD ARMS RIVALRY
ARE NOW REVEALED.

05615 LICHFIELD, J.
    ANDRIESSEN, HILLS AIR THEIR VIEWS ON G.A.T.T., 1992
    EUROPE, 287 (JUN 89), 14-15.
    THIS YEAR'S EUROPEAN - AMERICAN JOURNALISTS CONFERENCE
IN ANNAPOLIS, MARYLAND, FOCUSED ON THE FUTURE OF
INTERNATIONAL TRADE FOLLOWING COMPLETION OF THE E.C.'S
SINGLE MARKET AND THE URUGUAY ROUND TALKS. CENSENSUS WAS
THAT THE MOST DISMAL THREAT TO WORLD TRADE RELATIONS IN THE
NEXT 18 MONTHS IS NOT THE U.S. OMNIBUS TRADE ACT, NOR THE E.
C. 1992 CAMPAIGN, NOR EVEN FEUDING IN THE GENERAL AGREEMENT
ON TARIFFS AND TRADE (GATT) URUGUAY ROUND. IT IS THE
PROSPECT OF A POLITICAL GRIDLOCK BETWEEN ALL THREE.

05616 LICHFIELD, J.
    RECENT TALKS DE-ESCALATE TRADE DISPUTES
    EUROPE, 284 (MAR 89), 16-17.
    AS THE EUROPEAN COMMUNITY'S LARGEST TRADING PARTNER, THE
UNITED STATES HAS HUGE, LEGITIMATE INTERESTS IN PREVENTING
THE E.C. FROM TURNING INTO AN INTROVERTED "FORTRESS EUROPE."
THERE ARE INFLUENTIAL VOICES WITHIN THE COMMUNITY WHO
BELIEVE THAT INTERNAL LIBERALIZATION SHOULD BE MATCHED BY
HIGHER EXTERNAL BARRIERS. A TOUGH AND VIGILANT AMERICAN
ATTITUDE WILL HELP THE E.C. FREE TRADERS--INTERNAL AND
EXTERNAL--TO HOLD THE LINE AGAINST THE PROTECTIONISTS.

05617 LICHFIELD, J.
    TRANS-ATLANTIC COMPANY ACQUISITIONS GAIN MOMENTUM
    EUROPE, (285) (APR 89), 24-25.
    COMPANIES IN THE US HAVE REVERSED RECENT TRENDS IN WHICH
EUROPEAN CAPITAL INVESTED IN THE US WAS 400 PERCENT HIGHER
THAN THE FLOW OR US INVESTMENT IN THE EUROPEAN COMMUNITY. IN
1989, US COMPANIES TOP THE LEAGUE TABLE FOR CROSSFRONTIER
ACQUISITIONS IN WESTERN EUROPE. IN THE FIRST TWO MONTHS OF
1989, US COMPANIES ANNOUNCED 23 EUROPEAN CORPORATE PURCHASES
WORTH $973 MILLION. IN RELATION TO THE SIZE OF THE US
ECONOMY, THE PURCHASES ARE SMALL, BUT MANY OBSERVERS SEE
RAPID EXPANSIONS IN THE NEAR FUTURE.

05618 LICHT, S.
    YUGOSLAVIA: THE FAILURE OF REFORM WITHOUT DEMOCRACY
    NEW POLITICS, 11(3) (SUM 89), 152-165.
    YUGOSLAVIA IS NOW CONFRONTED BY THE PARADOXICAL
SITUATION THAT, ALTHOUGH STILL A ONE-PARTY STATE WHICH WARNS
AGAINST POLITICAL PLURALISM AS THE HARBINGER OF NATIONAL
TENSIONS THAT COULD EVEN LEAD TO CIVIL WAR, THERE ARE SIX
NATIONAL COMMUNIST PARTIES IN EXISTENCE: EACH REPUBLIC HAS
ITS OWN CP WITH ITS OWN HIERARCHICAL STRUCTURE. THIS
INCREASED THE ISOLATION OF THE VARIOUS NATIONAL COMMUNITIES
FROM EACH OTHER. TO RESIST THE MOUNTING THREAT TO DEMOCRACY,
TO PLURALISM AND TO NATIONAL INTEGRITY, TO LIBERATE SOCIETY
FROM THE GROANING SOCIAL AND ECONOMIC BURDEN OF SUPPORTING
BLOATED, EXPLOITIVE STATE AND PARTY RULING ELITES, YUGOSLAV
DEMOCRATS AND SOCIALISTS NEED TO APPLY THEMSELVES TO
EXPANDING, IN SIZE AND INFLUENCE, EXISTING ALTERNATIVE
SOCIAL MOVEMENTS - WORKERS' STRIKE COMMITTEES, HUMAN RIGHTS
ORGANIZATIONS, PROFESSIONAL ASSOCIATIONS - AND BUILDING NEW
ONES.

05619 LICKLIDER, R.
    POLITICAL POWER AND THE ARAB OIL WEAPON: THE EXPERIENCES
    OF FIVE INDUSTRIAL NATIONS
    UNIVERSITY OF CALIFORNIA PRESS, BERKELEY, CA, 1988, 384.
    THE AUTHOR PROBES THE BEHAVIOR OF THE INDUSTRIAL
DEMOCRACIES TOWARD THE ARAB-ISRAELI DISPUTE DURING THE
1970'S, FOCUSING ON FIVE COUNTRIES THAT VARIED WIDELY IN
THEIR DEPENDENCE ON MIDDLE EASTERN OIL, THEIR RELATIONS WITH
THE ARAB STATES, AND THEIR POTENTIAL INFLUENCE ON ISRAEL. HE
THEN CONSTRUCTS A COMPARATIVE ANALYSIS OF ECONOMIC SANCTIONS
AND POLITICAL POWER IN INTERNATIONAL AFFAIRS.

05620 LICT, S.; NIKOLIC, M.
    ENDLESS CRISIS?
    ACROSS FRONTIERS, 5(2) (SUM 89), 25-26, 50-53.
    THIS IS THE SECOND PART OF AN ARTICLE OF WHICH PART ONE
WAS PUBLISHED IN ACROSS FRONTIER WINTER-SPRING 1989. IT
CONTINUES ON ABOUT RESURGENT NATIONALISM AND THE CRISIS OF
THE YUGOSLAV SYSTEM. IT ASKS THE QUESTION, "ARE SOME
NATIONALISMS MORE EQUAL THAN OTHERS?" IT TALKS ABOUT
RESURGENT NATIONALISM, THE VARIETIES OF YUGOSLAV NATIONALISM,
THE NEW "YUGOSLAVISM", AND EXAMINES THE SEEMINGLY ENDLESS
CRISIS.

05621 LIDDLE, A.M.
    FEMINIST CONTRIBUTIONS TO AN UNDERSTANDING OF VIOLENCE

AGAINST WOMEN - THREE STEPS FORWARD, TWO STEPS BACK
CANADIAN REVIEW OF SOCIOLOGY AND ANTHROPOLOGY, 26(5) (NOV
89), 759-775.
SOCIOLOGICAL WORK ON VIOLENCE HAS PROFITED IN RECENT
YEARS FROM A VARIETY OF INSIGHTS SUPPLIED BY FEMINIST
THEORISTS, CONCERNING BOTH THE PERVASIVENESS OF VIOLENCE
AGAINST WOMEN, AND THE IMPACT OF THIS VIOLENCE ON THE LIVES
OF INDIVIDUAL WOMEN. ON THE THEORETICAL PLANE THE FIELD HAS
ALSO BEEN ENRICHED BY EFFORTS TO DESCRIBE PARTICULAR KINDS
OF VIOLENCE AGAINST WOMEN AS BEING LINKED TO WIDER
STRUCTURES, AND AS BEING EMBEDDED IN GENDERED PATTERNS OF
SOCIAL CONTROL. THESE CONTRIBUTIONS HAVE BEEN BLUNTED BY
THEIR INCORPORATION OF AN IMPLAUSIBLE, ONE-DIMENSIONAL MODEL
OF MALE AGENCY, HOWEVER, AND BY A CONCEPTION OF 'INTERESTS'
WHICH STANDS IN NEED OF CLARIFICATION. IT IS SUGGESTED THAT
FEMINIST WORK ON VIOLENCE AGAINST WOMEN HAS ALSO TENDED TO
DISREGARD THE IMPORTANCE OF DEFINITIONAL MATTERS, AND THAT
THIS HAS DETRACTED FROM THE POWER OF THE FEMINIST CRITIQUE.

05622 LIEBL, P.
NATO AT 40
EUROPE, 287 (JUN 89), 28-29.
IF THE SOVIET MILITARY THREAT IS REALLY OVER--AND THE
NEXT FEW YEARS WILL TELL--THEN THE PROGRESSIVE DOWNSIZING OF
NATO SHOULD NOT BE FEARED AS AN UNWISE POLICY. AS FOR THE
ATLANTIC COMMUNITY, AMERICANS AND EUROPEANS ALIKE SHOULD
NEVER FORGET THE IDENTICAL SPIRITUAL ORIGINS OF THEIR
SOCIETIES. REGARDLESS OF GORBACHEV AND OF HIS CREATIVE
METAPHOR OF A "COMMON EUROPEAN HOUSE," EVEN IN THE BEST OF
CIRCUMSTANCES DECADES WILL PASS BEFORE THE SOVIET UNION HAS
ASSIMILATED AND FULLY UNDERSTOOD THE PRINCIPLES OF POPULAR
SOVEREIGNTY AND INDIVIDUAL RIGHTS THAT HAVE BEEN THE
FUNDAMENTAL PHILOSOPHICAL PRINCIPLES OF THE WEST. UNTIL THEN,
THERE WILL STILL BE A DISTINGUISHABLE COMMUNITY OF WESTERN
NATIONS.

05623 LIEBOVICH, L.W.
FAILED WHITE HOUSE PRESS RELATIONS IN THE EARLY MONTHS OF
THE TRUMAN ADMINISTRATION
PRESIDENTIAL STUDIES QUARTERLY, XIX(3) (SUM 89), 583-591.
THIS PAPER EXAMINES THE FIRST SEVENTEEN MONTHS OF THE
TRUMAN ADMINISTRATION AND TRACES THE STEPS THAT THE
PRESIDENT AND HIS PRESS AIDES TOOK IN DEALING WITH NEWSMEN,
PUBLISHERS, AND INCIDENTS THAT REFLECTED UPON THE
PRESIDENT'S PUBLIC IMAGE. THIS ILLUSTRATES HOW THEIR
DECISIONS EVENTUALLY LED TO POOR PRESS AND STRAINED
RELATIONS WITH THE WHITE HOUSE NEWS CORPS AND EDITORS AND
PUBLISHERS BACK HOME.

05624 LIEBSHUTZ, S.
TARGETING BY THE STATES: THE BASIC ISSUES
PUBLIUS: THE JOURNAL OF FEDERALISM, 19(2) (SPR 89), 1-16.
IN THIS INTRODUCTORY ARTICLE, THE AUTHOR EXPLORES THE
BACKGROUND TO THE EVER INCREASING PHENOMENON OF STATE
GOVERNMENTS TAKING ON RESPONSIBILITY FOR PROVIDING EQUITY
AND SERVICES FOR "DISTRESSED" PEOPLE. THE DIMENSIONS OF THE
PROBLEM OF THE GROWING "UNDERCLASS" ARE EXPLORED AS ARE THE
DIFFERENT METHODS STATES UTILIZE TO DEAL WITH THE PROBLEMO.

05625 LIESKE, J.
THE POLITICAL DYNAMICS OF URBAN VOTING BEHAVIOR
AMERICAN JOURNAL OF POLITICAL SCIENCE, 33(1) (FEB 89),
150-174.
THIS STUDY ANALYZES THE DYNAMICS OF URBAN VOTING
BEHAVIOR AND THE WORTH OF DIFFERENT POLITICAL CREDENTIALS IN
COUNCIL ELECTIONS. DATA FOR THE ANALYSIS ARE DRAWN FROM
CINCINNATI, OHIO, A CITY WHOSE ELECTORAL SYSTEM IS
REPRESENTATIVE OF THE MAJORITY OF AMERICAN CITIES OF OVER 25,
000 POPULATION THAT CURRENTLY EMPLOY NONPARTISAN, AT-LARGE
ELECTIONS. THE DATA CONSIST OF A SAMPLE OF 103 COUNCIL
CAMPAIGNS THAT WERE WAGED IN FIVE SUCCESSIVE ELECTIONS OVER
A TEN-YEAR TIME SPAN. THE RESULTS SUPPORT SEVERAL
CONCLUSIONS. FIRST, THEY DEMONSTRATE THE CRITICAL IMPORTANCE
OF POLITICAL LEGITIMACY IN URBAN ELECTIONS. THUS, THE MOST
IMPORTANT PREDICTORS OF ELECTORAL SUCCESS ARE THOSE THAT
MEASURE THE CANDIDATES' RELATIVE POLITICAL ACCEPTABILITY. IN
APPROXIMATE RANK ORDER, THEY ARE THE CANDIDATES' POLITICAL
FOLLOWING, POLITICAL RESOURCES, CIVIC ENDORSEMENTS, AND
PERSONAL ACHIEVEMENTS. SECOND, THE RESULTS SHOW THAT TWO
DIFFERENT VOTING MODELS ARE NECESSARY TO EXPLAIN THE
CALCULUS OF CANDIDATE CHOICE: ONE FOR FIRST-TIME CANDIDATES
AND A SECOND FOR INCUMBENTS AND FORMER LOSERS. FOR FIRST-
TIME CANDIDATES, THE KEY CREDENTIALS ARE THOSE THAT ENHANCE
THEIR NAME FAMILIARITY, ESPECIALLY PARTISAN AND NEWSPAPER
ENDORSEMENTS. IN SUBSEQUENT CAMPAIGNS, WHAT APPEARS TO BE
DECISIVE ARE THE SIZE OF THEIR POLITICAL FOLLOWING AND THE
RACIAL AND PARTISAN COALITIONS THAT COALESCE AROUND THEM.
FINALLY, THE RESULTS SUGGEST THAT A CANDIDATE'S POLITICAL
FOLLOWING MAY PLAY A ROLE IN LOCAL ELECTIONS SIMILAR TO THE
STABILIZING FUNCTION OF PARTY IDENTIFICATION IN NATIONAL
ELECTIONS.

05626 LIEVEN, A.
THE KINGDOM OF KABUL?

ENCOUNTER, LXXIII(5) (DEC 89), 57-60.
THE KABUL REGIME SEEMS TO BE GRADUALLY WINNING ITS
BATTLE FOR SURVIVAL, ON BOTH THE PROPAGANDA AND THE MILITARY
FRONTS. IT IS DOING SO LARGELY BECAUSE, IN THE MIDST OF THE
NEAR-ANARCHY THAT NOW OCCUPIES MOST OF AFGHANISTAN,
NAJIBULLAH AND HIS FOLLOWERS HAVE RETAINED A COMPLETE
MONOPOLY ON THE INSTITUTIONS OF STATE. THIS MEANS THAT THEY
CAN INCREASINGLY RELY ON THE ACQUIESCENCE OF THE STATE-
SUPPORTING CLASSES BECAUSE THE ONLY OTHER NATIONAL
"GOVERNMENT" (THAT OF THE MUJAHEDDIN IN PESHAWAR) IS A BAD
JOKE, AS ALMOST EVERYONE BUT, SEEMINGLY, THE U.S. STATE
DEPARTMENT NOW KNOWS.

05627 LIFTON, D.E.
THE INFLUENCE OF "FISCAL WILL": DETERMINANTS OF NEW YORK
COUNTIES' BUDGET PRIORITIES IN RESPONSE TO FISCAL STRESS
DISSERTATION ABSTRACTS INTERNATIONAL, 49(8) (FEB 89),
2415-A.
PUBLIC FINANCE THEORY DESCRIBES A LOCAL GOVERNMENT'S
FISCAL EFFORT IN RESPONSE TO THE FISCAL STRESS OF
REAGANOMICS IN TERMS OF THE AMOUNT OF LOCAL FISCAL CAPACITY
THAT IS AVAILABLE TO TAP. THIS STUDY OFFERS A SOMEWHAT
BROADER EXPLANATION THAT ADDS THE IMPORTANT INFLUENCE OF
POLITICAL IDEOLOGY IN INTERPRETING LOCAL FISCAL BEHAVIOR
UNDER STRESS. A MULTIPLE REGRESSION PATH MODEL REFLECTING
THIS VIEW COMBINES FISCAL WILL WITH CAPACITY, STRESS, AND
EFFORT TO PREDICT WHAT FUNDING PRIORITIES WILL BE EMPHASIZED
IN THE LOCAL BUDGETING PROCESS.

05628 LIGBER, R.
EAGLE REVISITED: A RECONSIDERATION OF THE REAGAN ERA IN US
FOREIGN POLICY
WASHINGTON QUARTERLY, 12(3) (SUM 89), 115-126.
THE ARTICLE ASSESSES BOTH THE REAGAN ERA IN FOREIGN
POLICY AND, MORE BROADLY, THE IMPLICATIONS OF THIS
EXPERIENCE FOR US FOREIGN POLICY IN GENERAL. TO DO SO, IT
BEGINS BY REVIEWING THE GLOBAL SETTING IN WHICH US FOREIGN
POLICY HAS BEEN CARRIED OUT DURING THE POSTWAR ERA. IT ALSO
REEXAMINES THE EXPERIENCE OF THE THREE PRESIDENCIES THAT
IMMEDIATELY PRECEDED REAGAN'S AS EACH GRAPPLED WITH PROBLEMS
OF ADJUSTMENT IN THE UNITED STATES' GLOBAL ROLE. IT THEN
REVIEWS THE WAY IN WHICH THE REAGAN ADMINISTRATION ITSELF
APPROACHES THE TASKS OF US FOREIGN POLICY--BOTH INITIALLY
AND IS ITS POLICIES EVOLVED OVER EIGHT YEARS. IT CONCLUDES
THAT NEITHER THE DIRE PREDICITIONS OF CRITICS NOR THE
COMPLACENT FORECASTS OF ADMINISTRATION OFFICIALS ARE
COMPLETELY ACCURATE. ALTHOUGH RELATIVE GLOBAL STANDING HAS
DIMINISHED FOR THE US, IT REMAINS THE ONLY ECONOMIC AND
MILITARY SUPERPOWER AND STILL HAS A GREAT DEAL OF ROOM TO
MANEUVER.

05629 LIGDEN, B.
BACKING SLOGANS WITH ACTION
WORLD MARXIST REVIEW, 31(2) (FEB 88), 48-50.
THIS ARTICLE DESCRIBES EFFORTS TO INCREASE THE ROLE OF
GRASSROOTS ORGANISATIONS AND TO MAKE THEM MORE ENERGETIC AND
COMBATIVE: THE CONSTITUTE THE POLITICAL CORE OF WORK
COLLECTIVES, WHICH PLAY THE DECISIVE PART IN FULFILLING THE
TASKS SET BY THE PARTY, CREATE MATERIAL, CULTURAL AND
INTELLECTUAL VALUES AND HELP TO A LARGE EXTENT TO SHAPE THE
PERSONALITY AND HIS OR HER ATTITUDES IN LIFE.

05630 LIGHT, P.
RESCUING AMERICA'S PUBLIC SERVICE
NATIONAL CIVIC REVIEW, 78(4) (JUL 89), 265-270.
MERELY RAISING THE SALARY OF PUBLIC EMPLOYEES WILL NOT
BE ADEQUATE TO ATTRACT YOUNG PEOPLE TO PUBLIC SERVICE.
POLITICAL SCANDAL AND CAMPAIGN RHETORIC CRITICAL OF
BUREAUCRATS AND PUBLIC SERVANTS NOT ONLY DEPRESS THE APPEAL
OF CAREER PUBLIC SERVICE, BUT ALSO DISCOURAGE YOUNG PEOPLE
FROM PUBLIC LIFE IN GENERAL. EVEN IF SALARIES ARE RAISED AND
RESPECT RESTORED, PUBLIC EMPLOYMENT MUST OFFER MEANINGFUL
CHALLENGE AND ROOM FOR ADVANCEMENT.

05631 LIGHTBODY, J.
WITH WHOM THE TOLLS DWELL: THE GREAT EDMONTON TELEPHONE
DISPUTE, 1984-87
CANADIAN PUBLIC ADMINISTRATION, 32(1) (SPR 89), 41-62.
THE RELATIVE WEAKNESS OF CANADIAN MUNICIPALITIES IN
THEIR BARGAINING POSITIONS WITH CENTRAL GOVERNMENTS MAY, IN
CERTAIN CIRCUMSTANCES, BE EFFECTIVELY SHORT-CIRCUITED. IN
THIS CASE STUDY OF THE 1984 ATTEMPT BY THE CITY OF EDMONTON
TO GARNER A LARGER PORTION OF LONG DISTANCE TOLLS FOR ITS
MUNICIPALLY-OWNED TELEPHONE SYSTEM FROM THE PROVINCIAL
MONOPOLY, IT IS DEMONSTRATED THAT A WELL-DEVELOPED CIVIC
CAMPAIGN ROOTED IN A STRATEGIC CONCEPT OF GAMESMANSHIP CAN
OUTFLANK CONSTITUTIONALLY DEFINED INSTITUTIONAL IMPOTENCE.
WHAT RISKS MUST BE TAKEN AND HOW THEY CAN BE MODERATED ARE
CONSIDERED. THE LESSON IS THAT, AS IN ANY CAMPAIGN, BOTH
TACTICS AND STRATEGY MUST BE CLEARLY DEFINED, UNDERSTOOD AND
ADHERED TO FOR A WINNING SCENARIO TO RESULT.

05632 LIH, L.T.
THE TRANSITION ERA IN SOVIET POLITICS

CURRENT HISTORY, 88(540) (OCT 89), 333-336, 353-354.
GORBACHEV WANTS TO EFFECT RADICAL CHANGES WITHOUT
REJECTING THE FOUNDATIONS OF THE SOVIET POLITICAL SYSTEM.
HIS AIM IS TO DISCREDIT THE STALINIST HERITAGE AND RETURN TO
THE ORIGINAL SOCIALIST IDEA OF A HIGHLY PRODUCTIVE, JUST
SOCIETY.

05633 LIJPHART, A.
FROM THE POLITICS OF ACCOMODATION TO ADVERSARIAL POLITICS
IN THE NETHERLANDS: A REASSESSMENT
WEST EUROPEAN POLITICS, 12(1) (JAN 89), 139-153.
MOST OBSERVERS OF POST-SECOND WORLD WAR DUTCH POLITICS
AGREE THAT THE BASIC PATTERN OF POLITICS HAS UNDERGONE
REVOLUTIONARY CHANGE FROM THE POLITICS OF ACCOMODATION TO
ADVERSARIAL POLITICS. IN THIS STUDY THE 1946-67 AND 1867-88
PERIODS ARE COMPARED WITH EACH OTHER AND WITH 20 OTHER
DEMOCRACIES IN TERMS OF THE EIGHT CRITERIA THAT DISTINGUISH
MAJORITARIAN FROM CONSENSUS DEMOCRACY. THE CONCLUSION IS
THAT, WHILE DUTCH DEMOCRACY HAS BECOME LESS CONSENSUAL AND
MORE ADVERSARIAL IN SOME RESPECTS, THE OVERALL CHANGE IS
RELATIVELY MODEST WHEN IT IS VIEWED IN A BROAD COMPARATIVE
PERSPECTIVE.

05634 LILLA, M.
GOD IS A FRENCH SOCIALIST
AMERICAN SPECTATOR, 22(5) (MAY 89), 27-28.
IN MANY WAYS MITTERRAND HAS KEPT HIS CAMPAIGN PROMISE TO
GOVERN FROM THE CENTER. BUT, IN IDEOLOGICAL TERMS, THE
POLITICAL CENTER IS NOT ALWAYS THE ECONOMIC CENTER. THE
FRENCH MAY HAVE ASSUMED THAT MITTERAND'S POLITICAL
TRANSFORMATION HAD BEEN ACCOMPANIED BY AN ECONOMIC
CONVERSATION TOO. IT MUST HAVE BEEN QUITE A SHOCK TO
DISCOVER THAT, WHEN IT COMES TO CAPITALISM, DIEU IS STILL A
SOCIALIST.

05635 LIM, G.; MOORE, R.J.
PRIVATIZATION IN DEVELOPING COUNTRIES: IDEAL AND REALITY
INTERNATIONAL JOURNAL OF PUBLIC ADMINISTRATION, 12(1)
(1989), 137-161.
IN THIS PAPER THE AUTHORS PRESENT A STUDY OF
PRIVATIZATION USING THE CASE OF HONDURAS. THEY EXAMINE THE
POLICY SHIFT FROM "DIRECT ADMINISTRATION" TO "CONTRACTING
OUT" FOR THREE CONSTRUCTION ACTIVITIES: URBAN UPGRADING FOR
HOUSING PROJECTS, RURAL PRIMARY SCHOOLS, AND RURAL ROADS.
THE PURPOSE OF THE STUDY IS THREEFOLD. FIRST, TO TEST KEY
HYPOTHESES PERTAINING TO THE EFFECTIVENESS OF PRIVATIZATION,
FOCUSING ON THREE ASPECTS: COST, TIME, AND QUALITY; SECOND,
TO IDENTIFY MAJOR FACTORS WHICH AFFECT THE PERFORMANCE OF
THIS PRIVATIZATION APPROACH. THIRD, THE AUTHORS DOCUMENT THE
IMPACT OF PRIVATIZATION AS IT INFLUENCES THE POLITICAL AND
INSTITUTIONAL SETTINGS OF HONDURAS. THE MAIN FINDING IS THAT
CONTRACTING OUT IN HONDURAS HAS NOT LED TO THE COMMON
EXPECTATIONS OF ITS PROPONENTS BECAUSE OF INSTITUTIONAL
BARRIERS AND LIMITED COMPETITIVENESS IN THE MARKET. THESE
FINDINGS SUGGEST THAT PRIVATIZATION CAN NOT PRODUCE GOODS
AND SERVICES EFFICIENTLY WITHOUT SUBSTANTIAL REFORM IN THE
MARKET AND REGULATORY PROCEDURES. POLICY MAKERS ALSO NEED TO
CONSIDER CAREFULLY MULTIPLE OBJECTIVES AT THE NATIONAL LEVEL
IN MAKING DECISIONS ABOUT PRIVATIZATION.

05636 LIN, C.
CHINA, THE U.S. AND THE SECURITY OF TAIWAN
DISSERTATION ABSTRACTS INTERNATIONAL, 50(1) (JUL 89),
252-A.
SINO-AMERICAN NORMALIZATION HAS BROUGHT DRASTIC CHANGES
IN THE TRIANGULAR RELATIONS AMONG CHINA, TAIWAN, AND THE
UNITED STATES. IN THIS DISSERTATION, THE AUTHOR REVIEWS THE
COURSE OF THESE RELATIONS SINCE NORMALIZATION, THE AMERICAN
ROLE IN TAIWANESE SECURITY, CHINA'S REUNIFICATION PROPOSALS,
AND TAIWAN'S NATIONAL SECURITY POLICY.

05637 LIN, C.
CHINA'S ECONOMY: THE ASPIRATIONS AND THE REALITY
WORLD TODAY, 45(1) (JAN 89), 4-7.
CHINA'S AIM IS MODERNIZATION. BUT IT ENCOMPASSES MORE
THAN ECONOMIC DEVELOPMENT. IT MEANS THE ACHIEVEMENT OF
ECONOMIC, TECHNOLOGICAL, POLITICAL, AND MILITARY PARITY WITH
THE WEST. IT IS INSPIRED BY A PROFOUND SENSE OF MISSION: A
HISTORICAL-NATIONALISTIC IMPERATIVE TO RECLAIM WHAT CHINESE
LEADERS BELIEVE TO BE THEIR COUNTRY'S RIGHTFUL PLACE IN THE
FRONT RANKS OF THE MOST ADVANCED NATIONS. THIS ASPIRATION IS
SHARED BY ALL CHINESE LEADERS, PAST AND PRESENT, OF ALL
IDEOLOGICAL PERSUASIONS ON BOTH SIDES OF THE TAIWAN STRAITS.

05638 LIN, C.
FROM PANDA TO DRAGON
NATIONAL INTEREST, (15) (SPR 89), 49-57.
THE ARTICLE EXAMINES THE NUCLEAR STRATEGY OF CHINA. IT
OUTLINES THE DEVELOPMENT OF CHINA'S NUCLEAR CAPACITY AND
EXAMINES THE BASIC TACTICAL WEAPON STRATEGY CURRENTLY
EMPLOYED BY CHINA. THIS STRATEGY IS BASED ON A "NO FIRST
USE" POLICY AND RELIES INSTEAD ON MINIMUM DETERRENCE. THE
ARTICLE ALSO INDICATES HOW CHINA'S NUCLEAR CAPACITY TAKES ON
ADDITIONAL SIGNIFICANCE IN LIGHT OF CHINA'S RAPIDLY

EXPANDING ECONOMY AND THE RECENT FLURRY OF ARMS CONTROL
AGREEMENTS.

05639 LIN, M.
ENGINE OF CHANGE
FREE CHINA REVIEW, 39(12) (DEC 89), 16-23.
THIS ARTICLE CONTAINS EXCERPTS FROM A PANEL DISCUSSION
THAT MET TO ASSESS THE IMPACT OF THE 1989 TAIWANESE
ELECTIONS AND THEIR SIGNIFICANCE FOR FUTURE POLITICAL
DEMOCRATIZATION.

05640 LIN, H.
THE 1980'S IN RETROSPECT
BEIJING REVIEW, 32(51) (DEC 89), 15-20.
DURING THE FIRST HALF OF THE 1980S, THE UNITED STATES
AND THE SOVIET UNION WERE LOCKED IN AN INTENSE ARMS RACE AND
REGIONAL CONTESTS, MAKING THE INTERNATIONAL SITUATION TENSE
AND TURBULENT. AFTER THE MID-1980S, THEY RESUMED TALKS,
"HOTSPOTS" GENERALLY COOLED DOWN, AND THE WORLD ENTERED A
NEW PERIOD OF RELAXATION AND DIALOGUE. UNDER THIS GENERAL
EASING OF TENSIONS, THE UNITED STATES STEPPED UP ITS
"PEACEFUL EVOLUTION" SCHEME IN AN ATTEMPT TO OVERTHROW THE
LEADERSHIP OF COMMUNIST PARTIES AND CHANGE THE SOCIALIST
SYSTEM IN SOCIALIST COUNTRIES.

05641 LINDBECK, A.
CONSEQUENCES OF THE ADVANCED WELFARE STATE
WORLD ECONOMY, 11(1) (MAR 88), 19-38.
THIS ARTICLE ADDRESSES THE ACHIEVEMENTS AND LIMITS OF
THE WELFARE STATE PRIMARILY IN NORTH WESTERN EUROPE, WITH
INCIDENTAL REFERENCES TO THE SITUATION IN THE UNITED STATES,
IT EXAMINES WHERE THE PUBLIC SPENDING IS 50-65 PERCENT OF
THE GNP IN NORTH-WESTERN EUROPE AND WHERE FOREIGN TRADE IS
ALSO A LARGE FRACTION OF GNP. IT SHOWS THAT THE WELFARE
STATE PROBLEMS IN NORTH-WESTERN EUROPE AND THE U.S. ARE
QUITE DIFFERENT.

05642 LINDENBERG, M.
MAKING ECONOMIC ADJUSTMENT WORK: THE POLITICS OF POLICY
IMPLEMENTATION
POLICY SCIENCES, 22(3-4) (1989), 359-394.
THIS ARTICLE IDENTIFIES TENTATIVE LESSONS ABOUT
SUCCESSFUL POLITICAL MANAGEMENT OF STABILIZATION AND
STRUCTURAL ADJUSTMENT POLICIES IN DEVELOPING COUNTRIES. IT
ADDRESSES THREE BASIC QUESTIONS: 1) WHAT IS THE PURPOSE OF
STABILIZATION AND STRUCTURAL ADJUSTMENT POLICIES AND WHAT
SPECIFIC MEASURES ARE USUALLY UNDERTAKEN? 2) WHO, IN THEORY,
IS SUPPOSED TO BENEFIT OR LOSE FROM SUCH POLICIES AND WHO,
IN ACTUAL PRACTICE, SUPPORTS OR OPPOSES THEM? 3) HOW HAVE
GOVERNMENTS IN DEVELOPING COUNTRIES SUCCESSFULLY MANAGED THE
SUPPORTS AND OPPONENTS OF ADJUSTMENT POLICIES? THE ARTICLE
CONCENTRATES IN DETAIL ON HOW GOVERNMENTS OF PANAMA, COSTA
RICA AND GUATEMALA MANAGED THE ACTUAL SUPPORTERS AND
OPPONENTS OF POLICIES BETWEEN 1982 AND 1987,

05643 LINDER, M.
TOWARDS UNIVERSAL WORKER COVERAGE UNDER THE NATIONAL LABOR
RELATIONS ACT: MAKING ROOM FOR UNCONTROLLED EMPLOYEES,
DEPENDENT CONTRACTORS, AND EMPLOYEE-LIKE PERSONS
UNIVERSITY OF DETROIT LAW REVIEW, 66(4) (SUM 89), 555-602.
THE REASONING IN THIS ARTICLE PROCEEDS THROUGH FOUR
STEPS. FIRST, THE POWERFUL NEW ECONOMIC REALITY OF
DEPENDENCE TEST THAT THE SUPREME COURT BROUGHT TO BEAR IN
THE PIVOTAL HEARST CASE IS SHOWN TO HAVE BEEN CAPACIOUS YET
UNNECESSARY TO THE DISPOSITION OF THE COVERAGE ISSUE. SECOND,
A CRITICAL CONFRONTATION OF THE FUNDAMENTAL GOALS OF THE
NLRA WITH THE PRESCRIPTION OF COMMON-LAW AGENCY PRINCIPLES
BY TAFT-HARTLEY REVEALS A CONFLICT: THE RESTRICTIVENESS AND
AMBIGUITY OF THOSE INTERPRETIVE GUIDELINES MAKE THEM AN
IRRATIONAL AND, HENCE, DYSFUNCTIONAL MEANS OF REALIZING THE
ACT'S EXPANSIVE ORGANIZATIONAL ENDS. THIRD, AN ANALYSIS OF
THE WORKING CONDITIONS OF THE JUDICIALLY MOST DISPUTED GROUP
OF WORKERS - LESSEE TAXICAB DRIVERS 11 - SHOWS THAT EVEN
UNDER PRE-NEW DEAL COMMON-LAW AGENCY FACTORS, SUCH WORKERS
ARE EMPLOYEES AND NOT INDEPENDENT CONTRACTORS. FOURTH, IT IS
CONCLUDED THAT, BECAUSE THE DISTINCTION BETWEEN IMMUNIZED
WAGE BARGAINING AND PRICE FIXING VIOLATIVE OF THE ANTITRUST
LAWS IS MERELY DERIVATIVE OF THE DISPOSITION OF THE
EMPLOYEEINDEPENDENT CONTRACTOR ISSUE, THAT DISTINCTION
CANNOT BE CONTROLLING. CONSEQUENTLY, IT IS PROPOSED THAT, IN
THE WAKE OF THE CONFUSION AND INEQUITY BRED BY THE EXCLUSION
OF INDEPENDENT CONTRACTORS FROM COVERAGE UNDER THE ACT, A
NEW CATEGORY OF STATUTORY OR CONSTRUCTIVE EMPLOYEE, MODELED
AFTER THOSE INTRODUCED IN OTHER JURISDICTIONS (E.G.,
"UNCONTROLLED EMPLOYEE," "DEPENDENT CONTRACTOR," OR
"EMPLOYEELIKE PERSON"), BE CREATED IN ORDER TO PREVENT
EMPLOYERS (AND COURTS) FROM DENYING HETERONOMOUS WORKERS THE
RIGHT TO SELF-ORGANIZATION BY VIRTUE OF UNILATERALLY IMPOSED
COSMETIC CONTRACTUAL CHANGES OF WORKING CONDITIONS.

05644 LINDSAY, C.M.; MALONEY, M.T.
PARTY POLITICS AND THE PRICE OF PAYOLA
ECONOMIC INQUIRY, 26(2) (APR 88), 203-222.
THIS ARTICLE EXPLORES THE NEED OF POLITICAL PARTIES FOR

UNITY AND TIGHT DISCIPLINE EXTENDING OVER LONG PERIODS OF TIME AND MANY VOTES. IT ARGUES THAT THIS IS FOUND NOT IN IDEOLOGY OR CONSTITUENT INTERESTS, BUT RATHER IN "POLITICAL INCOME." IT ASSERTS THAT THE STRUCTURE OF THE MARKET FOR VOTES EXPLAINS THE VIABILITY OF POLITICAL PARTIES.

05645 LINDSAY, M.
MONGOLIA'S PROSPECTS
WORLD TODAY, 45(11) (NOV 89), 183-184.
UNTIL NOW MONGOLIA HAS PURSUED AN ALMOST SLAVISH IMITATION OF SOVIET POLICIES, WITH A STRONG EMPHASIS ON INDUSTRIALIZATION AND AGRICULTURAL COLLECTIVISM. NOW THAT ECONOMIC AND POLITICAL REFORMS ARE TAKING PLACE IN THE USSR, MONGOLIANS HAVE BEGUN THEIR OWN PERESTROIKA AND GLASNOST. BUT MONGOLIA'S REFORMS ARE DECEPTIVELY SLOW AND LOW-KEY. ALTHOUGH THE CHANGES ARE OCCURRING QUIETLY, THEY ARE GATHERING MOMENTUM AND COULD RADICALLY CHANGE THE FACE OF MONGOLIA IN THE FUTURE.

05646 LINDSAY, R.
IDEOLOGICAL QUESTIONS RELATING TO AFRICAN AMERICAN EQUALITY
POLITICAL AFFAIRS, LXVIII(7) (JUL 89), 15-20.
BLACK-WHITE UNITY REMAINS AND HAS GROWN IN IMPORTANCE AS PIVOTAL TO THE BROAD DEMOCRATIC UNITY OF ALL THE PEOPLE'S FORCES. THIS IS NOT LIMITED TO ONE PARTICULAR SECTOR, OR THIS OR THAT ISSUE, OR UNDER THIS OR THAT CIRCUMSTANCE. AFRICAN AMERICANS HAVE MOVED TO THE FORE OF THE PEOPLE'S MOVEMENT AND BRING WITH THEM THE MOST PROGRESSIVE ELEMENTS OF THE STRUGGLE. FAILURE TO SEE THE IMPORTANCE OF THE FIGHT FOR EQUALITY AND THE ROLE OF AFRICAN AMERICANS IS LIMITING THE SCOPE AND EFFECTIVENESS OF THE PEOPLE'S FORCES.

05647 LING, C.
CHAI LING SOBS OUT: TIENANMEN SQUARE MASSACRE
ASIAN OUTLOOK, 24(4) (JUL 89), 10-13.
THIS ARTICLE IS A TRANSLATION OF AN EYEWITNESS ACCOUNT OF THE TIENANMEN SQUARE MASSACRE BROADCAST IN CHINESE ON A HONG KONG TELEVISION NETWORK. THE WITNESS, WHO WAS A LEADER OF THE PRO-DEMOCRACY STUDENT MOVEMENT, STATED THAT AS MANY AS FOUR THOUSAND DEMONSTRATORS MAY HAVE DIED BEFORE THE COMMUNIST GUNS AND UNDER THE TREADS OF THE ARMY TANKS.

05648 LINSENMEYER, W. S.
FOREIGN NATIONS, INTERNATIONAL ORGANIZATIONS, AND THEIR IMPACT ON HEALTH CONDITIONS IN NICARAGUA SINCE 1979
INTERNATIONAL JOURNAL OF HEALTH SERVICES, 19(3) (1989), 509-530.
THIS ARTICLE INVESTIGATES THE IMPACT OF FOREIGN NATIONS AND INTERNATIONAL ORGANIZATIONS ON NICARAGUA'S HEALTH CONDITIONS SINCE 1979. GIVEN OR PLEDGED ASSISTANCE, FOR HEALTH AND OTHER SOCIAL NEEDS, HAS BEEN FORTHCOMING, FOR EXAMPLE, FROM LATIN AMERICA, WESTERN EUROPE, SOCIALIST COUNTRIES, THE UNITED NATIONS, THE ORGANIZATION OF AMERICAN STATES, AND THE EUROPEAN ECONOMIC COMMUNITY. INTERNATIONAL FORCES, HOWEVER, HAVE ALSO HAD A NEGATIVE IMPACT ON NICARAGUA'S HEALTH CONDITIONS. SINCE 1981, COUNTER-REVOLUTIONARY GUERILLA FORCES, KNOWN AS CONTRAS, HAVE FOUGHT THE NICARAGUAN GOVERNMENT TROOPS IN A DISASTROUS CONFLICT, INVOLVING SUBSTANTIAL INTERNATIONAL ASSISTANCE FOR EACH SIDE. THE UNITED STATES AND SEVERALS OTHER NATIONS HAVE PROVIDED SOME FORM OF AID TO THE CONTRAS. THE WAR IN NICARAGUA HAS RESULTED IN ENORMOUS HUMAN AND MATERIAL LOSSES, AND, OF COURSE, HAS ADVERSELY AFFECTED HEALTH CONDITIONS.

05649 LINTNER, B.
AUNG GYI'S ANGUISH
FAR EASTERN ECONOMIC REVIEW, 141(30) (JUL 88), 16-19.
THE STUDENTS WHO PARTICIPATE IN DEMONSTRATIONS RANGHOOD BURMA HAVE LONG CLAIMED THAT THE NATIONALIST HERO AUNG SAN WHO WAS ASSASINATED IN 1947 WAS THEIR SYMBOLIC LEADER. NOW, SOME FEEL THAT AUNG GYI, A PROMINENT FORMER BRIGADIERGENERAL MAY BE THE NEW PROTEST LEADER FOR THIS GENERATION. AUNG GYI HAS WRITTEN A SERIOES OF LETTERS TO NE WIN, THE CHAIRMAN OF THE RULING BURMA SOCIALIST PROGRAMME PARTY CRITICIZING THE GOVERNMENT'S ECONOMIC POLICIES AND POLICE BRUTALITY. HOWEVER, HE CAREFULLY AVOIDED CRITICIZING NE WIN HIMSELF. AUNG GYI'S OWN POLITICAL AND MILITARY CARREER HAS BEEN CLOSELY CONNECTED WITH NE WIN'S RISE TO POWER.

05650 LINTNER, B.
BACK TO SQUARE ONE
FAR EASTERN ECONOMIC REVIEW, 141(39) (SEP 88), 16-17.
THE ARMY'S 18 SEPTEMBER TAKEOVER IN BURMA, AND SOME OF THE CHAOS THAT LED TO IT, APPEARS TO HAVE BEEN CAREFULLY ORCHESTRATED TO GIVE IT THE SEMBLANCE OF MILITARY INTERVENTION IN THE NATIONAL INTEREST. PREVIOUS EVENTS SUCH AS THE 16 SEPTEMBER ANNOUNCEMENT BY THE BURMESE GOVERNMENT THAT ALL 186,000 MEMBERS OF THE ARMED FORCES WERE NO LONGER MEMBERS OF THE RULING BSPP ARE NOW UNDERSTOOD IN THE CONTEXT OF THE MILITARY COUP. THE MILITARY WISHED TO DISTANCE ITSELF FROM THE BSPP WHO HAD PERMITTED THE KILLING OF MANY CIVILIANS IN DEMONSTRATIONS DURING THE LAST YEAR. IT SEEMS THAT NOW THE ARMY HAS MERELY DROPPED THE FACADE OF CIVILIAN LEADERSHIP IN THE FORM OF THE BSPP AND HAVE ASSUMED TITULAR

AS WELL AS DE FACTO CONTROL.

05651 LINTNER, B.
BACKDOWN OR BLOODBATH
FAR EASTERN ECONOMIC REVIEW, 141(38) (SEP 88), 14-16.
THE RULING BURMA SOCIALIST PROGRAM PARTY APPEARED TO MAKE A MAJOR CONCESSION TO ITS OPPOSITION AFTER WEEK OF ANTIGOVERNMENT PROTESTS. AN EXTRAORDINARY PARTY CONGRESS HAD PASSED A RESOLUTION TO HOLD MULTIPARTY GENERAL ELECTIONS WITHOUT FIRST HOLDING A REFERENDUM ON THE ISSUE AS HAD BEEN PREVIOUSLY PROPOSED. HOWEVER, OPPOSITION LEADERS REFUSED TO ACCEPT THE RESOLUTION ON THE GROUNDS THAT THE ELECTIONS WERE TO BE HELD UNDER A SPECIALLY APPOINTED FIVEMEMBER COMMISSION WITHIN THREE MONTHS. THEY DEMANDED MORE TIME TO ORGANIZE POLITICAL PARTIES AND THAT THE ELECTIONS BE HELD UNDER THE DIRECTION OF AN INTERIM GOVERNMENT THAT HAS ACCEPTABLE TO THE PUBLIC. THE DEMONSTRATIONS CONTINUE AND FOR THE FIRST TIME, THE PROTESTERS ARE BEING JOINED BY SMALL NUMBERS OF THE MILITARY.

05652 LINTNER, B.
BACKLASH IN THE MAKING
FAR EASTERN ECONOMIC REVIEW, 141(32) (AUG 88), 32-33.
THE HARD LINE OF THE GOVERNMENT IN BURMA IS SPURRING ANOTHER WAVE OF PROTESTS AMONG VARIOUS STUDENT GROUPS. ALTHOUGH OUTGOING CHAIRMAN NE WIN WARNED THAT SECURITY FORCES WOULD SHOOT TO KILL, THE DEMONSTRATIONS FLARED UP AFTER THE ARRESTS OF AUNG GYI, A RETIRED BRIGADIERGENERAL WHO WAS CRITICAL OF THE GOVERNMENT AND 24 OTHER WIN, THE HARDLINER SEIN LWIN. SEIN LWIN IS WIDELY UNPOPULAR EVEN AMONG THE MILITARY.

05653 LINTNER, B.
BURMA AT THE BREAKING POINT
FAR EASTERN ECONOMIC REVIEW, 141(34) (AUG 88), 10-11.
ALTHOUGH THE REASONS ARE UNKNOWN, THE RESIGNATION OF SEIN LWIN, BURMA'S LEADER OF LESS THAN THREE WEEKS, HAS EASED SLIGHTLY THE TENSION IN BURMA. SEIN LWIN IS WIDELY THOUGHT RESPONSIBLE FOR THE SUPRESSION OF ANTI-GOVERNMENT RIOTS IN WHICH AT LEAST 3,000 PEOPLE WERE KILLED. TENSION AND PROTEST ARE LIKELY TO CONTINUE AS SEIN LWIN'S SUCCESSOR IS CHOSEN.

05654 LINTNER, B.
COMMUNIST CLIMB-DOWN
FAR EASTERN ECONOMIC REVIEW, 142(52) (DEC 89), 11.
THE BURMESE GOVERNMENT HAS HELD SECRET POLICE TALKS WITH INSURGENT LEADERS, WHO EARLIER THIS YEAR LED TO A MUTINY AGAINST THE POLITICAL LEADERSHIP OF THE NOW DEFUNCT COMMUNIST PARTY OF BURMA (CPB). AUTHORITIES TOLD THE REBELS THAT THE GOVERNMENT WOULD ALLOW THEM TO CONVERT THEIR ARMY INTO GOVERNMENT-SUPERVISED MILITIA FORCES. EVIDENCE INDICATES THAT CHINA PLAYED AN IMPORTANT BEHIND-THE-SCENES ROLE IN THE TALKS.

05655 LINTNER, B.
KNIGHTS IN SHINING ARMOUR?
FAR EASTERN ECONOMIC REVIEW, 141(37) (SEP 88), 17.
AFTER THE POPULAR UPRISING IN RANGOON WAS PUT DOWN BY THE MILITARY KILLING PERHAPS AS MANY AS 3,000 CIVILIANS, THE POSITION OF THE COUNTRY'S ARMED FORCES HAS BECOME A HOTLY DEBATED QUESTION. THE ARMED FORCES HAVE ENJOYED A POSITION OF PRIVELEGE FOR THE 26 YEARS OF RULE BY FORMER BURMA SOCIALIST PROGRAMME PARTY CHAIRMAN NE WIN, AND MANY FEEL THAT THE MILITARY WILL BE UNWILLING TO GIVE UP THEIR PRIVELEGED STATUS. WHILE NEARLY THE ENTIRE COUNTRY HAS BEEN DEMONSTRATING AGAINST THE GOVERNMENT, THE MILITARY HAS REMAINED LOYAL TO THE GOVERNMENT AND IS SHOWING LITTLE SIGNS OF DISUNITY.

05656 LINTNER, B.
LESS THAN MEETS THE EYE
FAR EASTERN ECONOMIC REVIEW, 141(31) (AUG 88), 12-13.
WHEN THE EMERGENCY CONGRESS OF THE RULING BURMA SOCIALIST PROGRAM PARTY BEGAN, ITS FOUNDERM CHAIRMAN, AND SOLE GUIDING LIGHT, NE WIN SURPRISED THE DEGALATES WITH A SPEECH ANNOUNCING THE RESIGNATION OF FIVE TOP PARTY LEADERS AND NE WIN HIMSELF. THE SPEECH ALSO ADVOCATED FAR REACHING POLITICAL AND ECONOMIC REFORMS INCLUDING A NATIONAL REFERENDUM ON WHETHER BURMA SHOULD HAVE A SINGLE OR MULTI-PARTY SYSTEM. OBSERVERS THOUGHT THE THE 26 YEARS OF ONE-PARTY RULE HAD COME TO AN END. HOWEVER, WHEN THE CONGRESS ENDED, ONLY THE RESIGNATIONS OF NE WIN AND ONE OTHER PARTY OFFICIAL WAS ACCEPTED; ALL OTHER SUGGESTIONS OF REFORM WERE REJECTED. EVEN NE WIN'S RESIGNATION WILL PROBABLY NOT MEAN AN END TO HIS INFLUENCE ON THE GOVERNMENT OF BURMA AS HE WILL STILL CONTINUE TO OPERATE BEHIND THE SCENES.

05657 LINTNER, B.
NOT WHETHER, BUT WHEN
FAR EASTERN ECONOMIC REVIEW, 141(33) (AUG 88), 13-14.
BURMESE CITIZENS HAVE RISEN UP IN NUMBERS REMINISCENT OF THE ANTI-BRITISH DEMONSTRATIONS OF THE LATE 1930'S. THE PROTESTS WERE MET SWIFTLY AND HARSHLY BY GOVERNMENT TROOPS

AND AT LEAST 72 PROTESTERS HAVE BEEN KILLED. AN INCREASING
NUMBER OF BURMA-WATCHERS HAVE STOPPED ASKING WHETHER THE NEW,
HARDLINE WEIN LWIN REGIME WILL LAST, BUT WHEN IT WILL GO.

05658 LINTNER, B.
OPEN DOOR, CLOSED MINDS
FAR EASTERN ECONOMIC REVIEW, 142(50) (DEC 89), 90-91.
DESPITE PURPORTEDLY LIBERAL FOREIGN INVESTMENT LAWS,
FOREIGN BUSINESS INTEREST IN BURMA IS BEING STYMIED BY SHORT-
TERM UNCERTAINTIES, A MASSIVELY OVER-VALUED CURRENCY, AND
LONG-TERM DOUBTS ABOUT THE DURABILITY AND ACCEPTABILITY OF
THE BURMESE REGIME. THE CONDITIONS THAT PRODUCED LAST YEAR'S
UPHEAVAL ARE STILL PRESENT, AND ARE EVEN WORSENING. FOREIGN
INVESTORS ARE CLEARLY AWARE OF THAT, AND THE EVEN USUALLY
CAUTIOUS UNITED NATIONS DEVELOPMENT PROGRAM CONCLUDES THAT
FOREIGN INVESTMENT WILL BE UNLIKELY UNTIL A NATIONALLY
ELECTED DEMOCRATIC GOVERNMENT IS IMPLEMENTED.

05659 LINTNER, B.
SKIN-DEEP SOCIALISM
FAR EASTERN ECONOMIC REVIEW, 141(37) (SEP 88), 35.
AT FIRST GLANCE, BURMA'S POLITICAL SYSTEM APPEARS TO BE
MODELLED ON THE TOTALITARIAN SYSTEMS OF EASTERN EUROPE AND
OTHER COMMUNIST STATES. HOWEVER, BURMA'S "SOCIALIST WAY" WAS
A CLOAK TO DISGUISE THE REALITY THAT THE 1962 REVOLUTION WAS
JUST ANOTHER MILITARY COUP THAT DELIVERED POWER INTO THE
HANDS OF AN INNEFICIENT AND CORRUPT MILITARY ADMINISTRATION
AND BECAUSE IT DID NOT REVOLUTIONIZE SOCIETY, IT SOWED THE
SEEDS OF ITS OWN DOWNFALL.

05660 LINTNER, B.
STRIKING A BALANCE
FAR EASTERN ECONOMIC REVIEW, 141(36) (SEP 88), 30.
ANY NEW, REFORM-ORIENTED GOVERNMENT IN BURMA WILL HAVE
TO DEAL WITH THE "TWO" BURMAS: THE SPARSELY POPULATED, BUT
MINERAL RICH, PERIPHERAL AREAS WHICH ARE OCCUPIED PRIMARILY
BY ETHNIC MINORITIES, AND THE MORE POPULOUS, MAINLY
AGRICULTURAL REGIONS OF CENTRAL BURMA. THIS DIVISION HAS
EXISTED EVEN IN THE DAYS BEFORE INDEPENDENCE. THE CENTRAL
REGIONS ARE IN DIRE NEED OF AN OVERHAUL OF THEIR RICE-
GROWING AND SUPPLY STRUCTURE, AND THE GOVERNMENT WILL NEED
TO BE CAREFUL IN ITS DEALINGS WITH THE MINORITY DOMINATED
AREAS IN WHICH THE COUNTRY'S MOST IMPORTANT RESERVES ARE.

05661 LINTNER, B.
STUDENTS WHO ARE STEEPED IN TRADITION OF PROTEST
FAR EASTERN ECONOMIC REVIEW, 141(38) (SEP 88), 48-49.
THE ARTICLE ANALYZES THE RECENT HISTORY OF THE
INTELLECTUAL AND STUDENT MOVEMENTS IN BURMA. THE COUNTRY HAS
ENJOYED A LONG AND STRONG TRADITION OF WIDESPREAD LITERACY
AND EDUCATION WHICH HAS RESULTED IN AN INTENSE INTEREST IN
POLITICS AND JOURNALISM. STUDENTS HAVE TRADITIONALLY BEEN AT
THE FOREFRONT OF BURMESE POLITICS, LEADING MASS MOVEMENTS
AND STRIKES SINCE THE 1920'S. THE FUTURE OF EDUCATION IN
BURMA WILL LARGELY DEPEND ON THE RULING BURMESE SOCIALIST
PROGRAM PARTY

05662 LINTNER, B.
THE ELECTION CHARADE
FAR EASTERN ECONOMIC REVIEW, 142(51) (DEC 89), 22.
BURMA'S ELECTION COMMITTEE IS PREPARING FOR GENERAL
ELECTIONS ON 27 MAY 1990, AND THE RULING STATE LAW AND ORDER
RESTORATION COUNCIL (SLORC) HAS ATTEMPTED TO PUT A GUISE OF
NORMALCY ON THE ELECTIONS. HOWEVER, THE SLORC'S PRETENSE OF
NORMALCY HAS NOT FOOLED MANY, ESPECIALLY SINCE THE LAUNCHING
OF A WAVE OF ARRESTS-ESTIMATED AT 5-8,000--OF OPPOSITION
PARTY LEADERS AND MEMBERS. KEY OPPOSITION LEADERS INCLUDING
AUNG SAN SUU KYI, DAUGHTER OF BURMA'S INDEPENDENCE HERO AUNG
SAN, HAVE BEEN ARRESTED OR IMPRISONED. THE CONTRADICTION
BETWEEN THE SLORC'S PROMISES OF "FREE AND FAIR ELECTIONS"
AND THE DETERIORATING HUMAN RIGHTS SITUATION HAS CAUSED
INTERNATIONAL CONCERN.

05663 LINTNER, B.
THE RISE AND FALL OF BURMA'S COMMUNIST INSURGENCY
CULTURAL SURVIVAL QUARTERLY, 13(4) (1989), 21-24.
WHEN THE WA MUTINEERS STORMED THE PANGHSANG HEADQUARTERS
OF THE COMMUNIST PARTY OF BURMA ON APRIL 16, 1989, AND DROVE
THE OLD LEADERSHIP INTO EXILE IN CHINA, IT MARKED THE END OF
ONE OF THE LONGEST COMMUNIST REBELLIONS IN ASIA. SINCE ITS
FOUNDING IN 1939, THE CPB HAD ENJOYED PERIODS OF STRENGTH
AND PERIODS OF OBSCURITY. BEGINNING IN THE 1960'S, AN
ALLIANCE WITH CHINESE COMMUNISTS SUPPLIED THE CPB WITH
OUTSIDE ASSISTANCE IN ITS STRUGGLE AGAINST THE NE WIN REGIME.

05664 LINTNER, B.
THE WRATH OF THE CHILDREN
FAR EASTERN ECONOMIC REVIEW, 141(29) (JUL 88), 18-19.
THE MARCH AND JUNE RIOTS IN BURMA JOLTED THE NATION'S
RULERS BACK TO REALITY AFTER YEARS OF ISOLATION, DISASTROUS
ECONOMIC POLICIES AND AUTHORITARIAN RULE, AS DEMONSTRATING
STUDENTS WERE JOINED BY THE FIRST TIME BY THOUSANDS OF
ORDINARY CITIZENS, MAJOR CHANGES HAVE TO BE MADE TO PREVENT
FURTHER EROSION OF THE RAPIDLY DIMINISHING SUPPORT OF THE

REGIME. ALTHOUGH THE GOVERNMENT RELEASED A NUMBER OF
DETAINED STUDENTS IN AN EFFORT TO APPEASE THE STUDENTS, THE
DETAINEES' TALES OF POLICE BRUTALITY SEEMS TO HAVE UPSET THE
PUBLIC EVEN MORE.

05665 LIPIETZ, A.
THE DEBT PROBLEM, EUROPEAN INTEGRATION, AND THE NEW PHASE
OF WORLD CRISIS
NEW LEFT REVIEW, (178) (NOV 89), 37-50.
WHEN THE DEBT QUESTION IS EXAMINED ON A WORLD SCALE--
THAT IS, FROM THE POINT OF VIEW OF GLOBAL LIVING STANDARDS,
JOB SECURITY, WORLD PEACE, AND ECOLOGICAL PROTECTION--THE
LOGIC OF THE MACROECONOMY IMPLIES THE MAXIMUM DEVALORIZATION
OF THE DEBT. IN OTHER WORDS, AS MUCH OF THE DEBT AS POSSIBLE
SHOULD BE CANCELLED. BUT THIS PROCESS, WHICH HAS ALREADY
BEGUN, POSES A SERIES OF ETHICAL, TECHNICAL, AND POLITICAL
PROBLEMS.

05666 LIPP, S.
RACIAL AND ETHNIC PROBLEMS: PERU
INTERNATIONAL JOURNAL OF GROUP TENSIONS, 19(4) (WIN 89),
339-348.
THE ETHNIC FACTOR IS A MAJOR COMPONENT OF THE SOCIAL
STRATIFICATION EVIDENT IN PERU. THIS ARTICLE EXAMINES THE
DIFFICULTIES, HOWEVER, IN ANALYZING THE REASONS FOR THE
TENSION AND CONFLICT BETWEEN SO-CALLED RACIAL AND ETHNIC
GROUPS. THE AUTHOR DESCRIBES HOW THE LINES OF DEMARCATION
BETWEEN ONE RACE AND ANOTHER BASED ON PURELY GENETIC
CRITERIA ARE FAR FROM BEING WELL - DEFINED. ALSO, IT IS
DIFFICULT TO DETERMINE WHETHER RACIAL OR ECONOMIC FORCES
CARRY MORE WEIGHT IF ONE LOOKS FOR A CAUSAL RELATIONSHIP
BETWEEN TENSION AND CULTURAL IDENTIFICATION.

05667 LIPSCHUTZ, R.D.
ORE WARS: ACCESS TO STRATEGIC MATERIALS, INTERNATIONAL
CONFLICT, AND THE FOREIGN POLICIES OF STATES
DISSERTATION ABSTRACTS INTERNATIONAL, 49(7) (JAN 89),
1952-A.
CONFLICT OVER RESOURCES CAN BE DEFINED IN TERMS OF
CONFLICTING PERCEPTIONS OF RULES AND REGIMES THAT DEFINE NOT
ONLY THE TERMS OF A STATE'S ACCESS TO RESOURCES OUTSIDE ITS
NATIONAL TERRITORY BUT ALSO A STATE'S ELIGIBILITY TO
PARTICIPATE IN AN INTERNATIONAL RESOURCE DISTRIBUTION SYSTEM.
THE PROBLEM OF SECURING ACCESS TO STRATEGIC RESOURCES
ORDINARILY PLAYS ONLY A SUBSIDIARY ROLE IN THE BROADER
FOREIGN POLICIES OF STATES.

05668 LIPSON, L.
POWER, PRINCIPLES, AND DEMOCRACY
POLITICAL SCIENCE, 41(2) (DEC 89), 1-17.
WITHOUT POWER, NO GOVERNMENT CAN PERFORM ITS FUNCTIONS.
THEREFORE, ALL POLITICAL SYSTEMS INVOLVE THE ACQUISITION AND
EXERCISE OF POWER. DEMOCRATIC SYSTEMS INTRODUCE AN EXTRA
COMPONENT THAT IS OFTEN IN CONFLICT WITH THE FIRST: THE
ULTIMATE CONTROL OF THE POWERFUL BY THOSE WHOM THEY GOVERN.
DEMOCRACY SEEKS TO ACCOMPLISH THIS WITH INSTITUTIONS AND
PROCEDURES OF A SPECIAL CHARACTER. THEIR PURPOSE IS TO
CONFER AUTHORITY ON DESIGNATED PERSONS FOR ONLY A LIMITED
TIME AND THEN TO TRANSFER IT TO OTHERS BY AN ORDERLY, PRE-
ARRANGED METHOD.

05669 LIPTON, M.
AGRICULTURE, RURAL PEOPLE, THE STATE, AND THE SURPLUS IN
SOME ASIAN COUNTRIES: THOUGHTS ON SOME IMPLICATIONS OF
THREE RECENT APPROACHES IN SOCIAL SCIENCES
WORLD DEVELOPMENT, 17(10) (OCT 89), 1553-1571.
THE AUTHOR EXPLORES STATE-FARMER RELATIONSHIPS IN ASIA.
TO UNDERSTAND HOW STATES INTERACT WITH FARMING PEOPLE, HE
DISAGGREGATES THE STATE INTO ACTIVITIES AND INTO GROUPS WITH
DISTINCT FUNCTIONS OR GOALS. EACH ACTIVITY OR GROUP MAY (1)
INCREASE, TRANSFER, OR EXTRACT SURPLUS; (2) DO SO MAINLY
FROM URBAN OR RURAL PEOPLE; AND (3) RECIRCULATE SURPLUS
MAINLY TO URBAN OR RURAL PLACES. TO EXPLORE THIS, THE AUTHOR
EXAMINES THREE APPROACHES: THE THEORY OF RENT-SEEKING,
ANALYTICAL MARXISM, AND COALITION THEORY.

05670 LISTER, G.
GOOD NEWS: OUR HUMAN RIGHTS POLICY
DEPARTMENT OF STATE BULLETIN (US FOREIGN POLICY), 89(2142)
(JAN 89), 36-38.
THE AUTHOR DISCUSSES THE DEVELOPMENT OF THE UNITED
STATES' HUMAN RIGHTS POLICY, THE IMPACT OF HUMAN RIGHTS ON
US FOREIGN POLICY, AND THE KEY ROLES PLAYED BY CONGRESS AND
NONGOVERNMENTAL HUMAN RIGHTS ORGANIZATIONS.

05671 LITANI, Y.
MILITANT ISLAM IN THE WEST BANK AND GAZA
NEW OUTLOOK, 32(11-12 (297-298)) (NOV 89), 40-42.
THE NEXT YEAR OR TWO WILL BE DECISIVE IN THE ISRAELI-
PALESTINIAN CONFLICT. IF ISRAEL DOES NOT EXPLOIT THE PLO
OPTION FOR A POLITICAL SETTLEMENT, THE ISLAMIC EXTREMISTS IN
THE OCCUPIED TERRITORIES WILL TRIUMPH AND WITH THEM, NO
NEGOTIATION IS POSSIBLE--ONLY A WAR TO THE DEATH.

05672 LITTELL, F.H.
RELIGIOUS FREEDOM IN CONTEMPORARY AMERICA
JOURNAL OF CHURCH & STATE, 31(2) (SPR 89), 219-230.
THE AUTHOR LOOKS AT HOW THE RELIGIOUS COMPOSITION OF THE
UNITED STATES HAS CHANGED IN RECENT YEARS AND THE MEANING OF
RELIGIOUS FREEDOM IN CONTEMPORARY AMERICA.

05673 LITTLE, R.
DECONSTRUCTING THE BALANCE OF POWER: TWO TRADITIONS OF
THOUGHT
REVIEW OF INTERNATIONAL STUDIES, 15(2) (APR 89), 87-100.
THERE IS NOW AN AWARENESS THAT THE BALANCE OF POWER IS A
POLYSEMIC CONCEPT WHICH CAN EVOKE A WIDE RANGE OF DIFFERENT
AND INCOMPATIBLE MEANINGS. THERE HAVE BEEN TWO COMMON
REACTIONS TO THIS PROBLEM. ONE ARGUES THAT MANY OF THE
MEANINGS ASSOCIATED WITH THE CONCEPT CAN BE CAPTURED BY
ALTERNATIVE TERMINOLOGY. BY STRIPPING DOWN THE CONCEPT,
THEREFORE, IT BECOMES POSSIBLE TO EXPOSE AN IRREDUCIBLE AND
UNCONTESTED CENTRAL CORE OF MEANING. A SECOND REACTION COMES
TO A LESS CHARITABLE CONCLUSION. IT IS ARGUED THAT THE
CONCEPT IS SO RIDDLED WITH CONTRADICTIONS AND SO HOPELESSLY
CONTESTED THAT IT IS INCAPABLE OF SHEDDING ANY HELPFUL LIGHT
ON THE BEHAVIOUR OF STATES. IT IS RECOMMENDED THAT THE
CONCEPT BE ABANDONED. ALTHOUGH OPPOSED, THESE TWO REACTIONS
DERIVE FROM THE COMMON EPISTEMOLOGICAL PREMISE THAT SOCIAL
SCIENCE CAN ONLY ADVANCE ON THE BASIS OF UNIVOCAL CONCEPTS.
THE AIM OF THIS PAPER IS TO CONFRONT THE AMBIGUITY
SURROUNDING THE IDEA OF THE BALANCE OF POWER AND TO QUESTION
THE ASSUMPTION THAT THE CONCEPT CAN ONLY SERVE A USEFUL
FUNCTION IF IT IS SHORN OF ITS COMPETING MEANINGS.

05674 LITTLEJOHN, M.J.
BALANCING COMPETING HEALTH NEEDS
CRS REVIEW, 10(3) (MAR 89), 23-25.
WHEN CONSIDERING THE ALLOCATION OF FEDERAL FUNDS AMONG
COMPETING CLAIMS, THE QUESTION ARISES OF HOW TO DETERMINE AN
APPROPRIATE USE OF FUNDS. THE URGENCY OF NEED OR THE AMOUNT
OF LONG-TERM HEALTH IMPROVEMENT REALIZED FOR THE FEDERAL
DOLLARS SPENT ARE TWO MEASURES USED TO ASSESS
APPROPRIATENESS. WHATEVER THE MEASURE, SCIENTIFIC, ECONOMIC,
POLITICAL, AND MORAL JUDGMENTS ARE IMPLICIT IN MAKING AN
ALLOCATION. WITH HUMAN LIVES AT STAKE, THE ISSUE OF
DISTRIBUTIVE JUSTICE IS NOT MERELY AN ACADEMIC ISSUE THAT
CAN BE REMOVED FROM THE ARENAS OF POLICY AND POLITICS. WHEN
THE DEMAND FOR FEDERAL RESOURCES EXCEEDS THE SUPPLY, SOME OF
THE PUBLIC HEALTH NEEDS OF GROUPS AND THE MEDICAL NEEDS OF
INDIVIDUALS MAY BE DENIED.

05675 LITYNSKI, J.
AN HISTORIC TURNING POINT
NEW POLITICS, 11(3) (SUM 89), 119-128.
THE SOVEREIGNTY OF POLAND CANNOT BE ACCOMPLISHED BY
MAKING NOISY STATEMENTS ABOUT IT, BUT RATHER BY THE CREATION
OF APPROPRIATE CONDITIONS FOR ITS REALIZATION. THIS DEMANDS
A CAREFUL ELABORATION OF THE PRINCIPLES OF FOREIGN POLICY BY
POLES, ON THE ONE HAND, BUT ALSO A CAREFUL ANALYSIS OF THE
POLISH SITUATION IN THE WEST—BOTH WITHIN THE GOVERNMENTS AND
SOCIETIES AT LARGE. FOR IT IS INADMISSIBLE THAT IN THE
PERIOD OF GENERAL DETENTE, THERE SHOULD EXIST, RIGHT IN THE
CENTER OF EUROPE, A NEW INCENDIARY FOCUS.

05676 LIU, W.
IMPLICATIONS OF FOREIGN EXCHANGE CONTROL IN POST-MAO
ECONOMY
CHINA REPORT, 24(4) (OCT 88), 419-462.
SOCIALISM PUTS POST-MAO CHINA AT A DISADVANTAGE IN TRADE
WITH THE WEST ON THREE SCORES: ORGANIZATION OF FOREIGN TRADE,
WORLD PRICE AND EXCHANGE RATE. A CENTRALLY CONTROLLED AND
PLANNED FOREIGN TRADE LACKS THE FLEXIBILITY AND
COMPETITIVENESS OF THE CAPITALIST MULTINATIONAL CORPORATIONS.
BUT, GIVEN THE NATIONAL RESOURCES AT ITS DISPOSAL, AND WITH
GOOD MANAGEMENT THERE IS NO REASON WHY A CENTRALLY
CONTROLLED FOREIGN TRADE CANNOT BE TURNED INTO A FORCE TO BE
RECKONED WITH. THE REAL PROBLEM LIES NOT SO MUCH WITH A
SHIFT OF THE SOCIALIST BASE OF FOREIGN TRADE AS WITH AN
EFFICIENT ORGANIZATION OF THE SUPPLY AND DISTRIBUTION SYSTEM.

05677 LIVEZEY, L. W.
US RELIGIOUS ORGANIZATIONS AND THE INTERNATIONAL HUMAN
RIGHTS MOVEMENT
HUMAN RIGHTS QUARTERLY, 11(1) (FEB 89), 14-81.
THIS OVERVIEW OF THE IDEAS PRESENTED IN HUMAN RIGHTS
EDUCATION SUGGESTS THAT HUMAN RIGHTS ARE INTERPRETED BY US-
BASED RELIGIOUS ORGANIZATIONS IN THE HUMAN RIGHTS MOVEMENT
IN A WAY THAT IS LIBERAL, WESTERN, AND INDEED, AMERICAN.
THIS MAY NOT SEEM REMARKABLE IN VIEW OF THE DERIVATION OF
THE CENTRAL IDEAS OF HUMAN RIGHTS FROM LIBERAL POLITICAL
PHILOSOPHIES OF THE WEST. YET THE CONTENT OF THE
INTERNATIONAL HUMAN RIGHTS INSTRUMENTS DOES NOT SIMPLY
REPRESENT THAT TRADITION, AND INDEED THESE INSTRUMENTS ARE
BOTH PRAISED FOR GOING BEYOND THAT TRADITION AND CRITICIZED
FOR RETREATING FROM IT. THE RELIGIOUS HUMAN RIGHTS MOVEMENT
IS THE RECIPIENT OF THE SAME PRAISE AND BLAME, FOR IT
SUPPORTS AT LEAST IN GENERAL TERMS THE CONCEPTIONS OF RIGHTS

EXPRESSED IN UN INSTRUMENTS AND MANY OF ITS ORGANIZATIONS
TAKE A POSITIVE ATTITUDE TOWARD ARGUMENTS PRESENTED IN UN
MEETINGS. BUT THIS ANALYSIS OF RELIGIOUS GROUPS' PROGRAMS
SUGGESTS THAT THE RIGHTS THEY ACTUALLY PROMOTE ARE VIRTUALLY
ALL TO BE FOUND IN THE UNITED STATES CONSTITUTION.

05678 LIVINGSTONE, I.; ASSUNCAO, M.
GOVERNMENT POLICIES TOWARDS DROUGHT AND DEVELOPMENT IN THE
BRAZILIAN SERTAO
DEVELOPMENT AND CHANGE, 20(3) (JUL 89), 461-500.
BRAZILIAN GOVERNMENT POLICY TOWARD THE CHRONIC DROUGHT
IN THE SERTAO HAS BEEN PURSUED IN TWO PHASES. THE FIRST,
WHICH LASTED UNTIL THE MID-1970'S, EMPHASIZED THE
CONSTRUCTION OF VERY LARGE PUBLIC DAMS AND A LARGE NUMBER OF
SMALLER PRIVATE DAMS. THE SECOND, WHICH IS STILL BEING
PURSUED, FOCUSES MORE DIRECTLY ON IRRIGATION. IN BOTH CASES,
THE OSTENSIBLE PURPOSES HAVE BEEN THE SAME: TO REDUCE
POVERTY AND VULNERABILITY TO DROUGHT AND, THEREBY, STEM
RURAL-URBAN MIGRATION FROM THE REGION. THIS ESSAY ARGUES
THAT NEITHER POLICY HAS OR IS WELL DESIGNED TO ACHIEVE THE
PURPORTED AIMS, BECAUSE THE GOVERNMENT PLAN IS BASED ON
INADEQUATE APPRAISAL AND UNDERSTANDING OF THE ECONOMY OF THE
SERTAO.

05679 LIYU, N.
ON ZHOU ENLAI'S DIPLOMATIC THEORY
BEIJING REVIEW, 32(14) (APR 89), 15-19.
THE LATE PREMIER ZHOU ENLAI MADE GREAT CONTRIBUTIONS TO
THE DEVELOPMENT OF FRIENDSHIP BETWEEN THE CHINESE PEOPLE AND
THE PEOPLES OF OTHER COUNTRIES. IT WAS ZHOU WHO FIRST ISSUED
THE WELL-KNOWN FIVE PRINCIPLES OF COEXISTENCE: MUTUAL
RESPECT FOR SOVEREIGNTY AND TERRITORIAL INTEGRITY, MUTUAL
NON-AGGRESSION, NON-INTERFERENCE IN ANOTHER COUNTRY'S
INTERNAL AFFAIRS, EQUALITY AND MUTUAL BENEFIT, AND PEACEFUL
COEXISTENCE.

05680 LIZON, A.
THE SPANISH GENERAL STRIKE
CONTEMPORARY REVIEW, 254(1478) (MAR 89), 146-150.
THE ARTICLE EXAMINES THE GENERAL STRIKE THAT TOOK PLACE
IN SPAIN IN DECEMBER OF 1988. ALTHOUGH THE STRIKE WAS FILLED
WITH PARADOXES SUCH AS THE FACT THAT IT WAS LED BY A
SOCIALIST TRADE UNION AGAINST THEIR SOCIALIST GOVERNMENT,
THE FACT THAT THE SPANISH WORKING CLASS LED AND REPRESENTED
BY THE UNIONS STILL HOLD THE CAPACITY TO MOBILIZE AND MAKE
THEIR VOICE HEARD FLIES IN THE FACE OF THOSE WHO HAVE
DECLARED THE DEATH OF THE LABOR MOVEMENT.

05681 LLAMBI, L.
EMERGENCE OF CAPITALIZED FAMILY FARMS IN LATIN AMERICA
COMPARATIVE STUDIES IN SOCIETY AND HISTORY, 31(4) (OCT 89),
745-774.
THE ARTICLE EXAMINES THE CONSIDERABLE AMOUNT OF
DISAGREEMENT OVER THE EMERGING TRENDS IN THE AGRICULTURAL
STRUCTURE OF LATIN AMERICA. THE ONGOING DEBATE IS OVER
WHETHER A VIABLE SYSTEM OF FAMILY FARMS IS BEING DEVELOPED
IN LATIN AMERICA. THROUGH AN ANALYSIS OF THE CURRENT
INTERPRETATION OF THE PROCESSES BY WHICH A WHOLE VARIETY OF
PRODUCTIVE FORMS, BASED ON THE LABOR OF OWNER AND HIRED
WORKERS AND EMPLOYING A RELATIVELY HIGH TECHNOLOGY, WHICH
ARE EMERGING IN LATIN AMERICA, THE AUTHOR HOPES TO CONTRAST
THEORY AND REALITY. THE ARTICLE CONCLUDES WITH AN OUTLINE OF
THE DIFFERENT FARMER TRANSITIONS TO CAPITALISM IN LATIN
AMERICA AND RAISES SOME ISSUES FOR FURTHER THEORETICAL
DEVELOPMENT AND EMPIRICAL RESEARCH ON THIS SUBJECT.

05682 LLAMBI, L.; COUSINS, A.L.
PETTY - CAPITALIST PRODUCTION IN AGRICULTURE: LESSONS FROM
FIVE CASE STUDIES IN VENEZUELA, 1945-1983
LATIN AMERICAN PERSPECTIVES, 16(3) (SUM 89), 86-120.
THIS ARTICLE IS A COMPARATIVE HISTORICAL STUDY OF THE
DEVELOPMENT OF PETTY-CAPITALIST PRODUCTION IN VENEZUELA FROM
1945 TO 1983. THE AUTHORS ATTEMPT TO EXPLAIN FIVE HISTORICAL
PATTERNS OF PETTY-CAPITALIST FARMING, EMBRACING ALL
PRODUCTIVE FORMS BASED ON FAMILY AND WAGE LABOR WHICH
EXPERIENCE CAPITALIST ACCUMULATION AND EMPLOY SOPHISTICATED
TECHNOLOGY. THEY EXCLUDE FROM THEIR CONCEPTUAL FRAMEWORK
SUCH CATEGORIES AS "MODERN FAMILY FARM," A NONTHEORETICAL
AHISTORICAL NOTION, AND "SIMPLE COMMODITY PRODUCTION," A
THEORETICAL BUT HISTORICALLY MISPLACED CATEGORY. THEY
CONCLUDE THAT PETTY-CAPITALIST ACCUMULATION RESULTS FROM THE
DIFFICULTIES ENCOUNTERED BY CAPITALIST ACCUMULATION IN
OVERCOMING BIOLOGICAL AND CLIMATIC LIMITATIONS IN THE
PRODUCTIVE PROCESSES AND BY LEGAL AND INSTITUTIONAL BARRIERS.
THEY FIND NO THEORETICAL OR EMPIRICAL SUPPORT FOR THE
BELIEF IN THE "SUPERIORITY" OF PETTY-CAPITALIST PRODUCTION
OVER OTHER CAPITALIST FORMS OF PRODUCTION.

05683 LLAMBI, L.
THE VENEZUELA-COLOMBIA BORDERLANDS: A REGIONAL AND
HISTORICAL PERSPECTIVE
JOURNAL OF BORDERLAND STUDIES, IV(1) (SPR 89), 1-38.
THIS PAPER IS DIVIDED INTO TWO MAIN PARTS. IT GIVES AN
OVERVIEW OF THE COMPLEX RELATIONS AND PROCESSES THAT LINK

COLOMBIA AND VENEZUELA ALONG THEIR BORDER. SINCE 1941, THE
BOUNDARY HAS NOT CHANGED, BUT BORDERLAND RELATIONS HAVE BEEN
ALTERED DUE TO SHIFTING POLITICAL AND ECONOMIC FACTORS. IN
THE FIRST SECTION OF THE PAPER, A BROAD HISTORICAL VIEW OF
BORDERLAND RELATIONS BETWEEN COLOMBIA AND VENEZUELA IS
OFFERED. IN THE SECOND SECTION, THE AUTHOR TAKES A CLOSER
LOOK AT BORDERLAND RELATIONS ALONG THE VARYING GEOGRAPHICAL
AND ECOLOGICAL LANDSCAPES TRAVERSED BY THE BOUNDARY, TAKING
INTO CONSIDERATION THE LOCAL IMPACT OF NATIONAL AND
INTERNATIONAL EVENTS.

05684 LLOYD, J.; REID, M.; TAYLOR, R.
SYMPOSIUM: MRS. THATCHER AND THE ESTABLISHMENT
CONTEMPORARY RECORD, 2(6) (SUM 89), 18-26.
JOHN LLOYD'S THESIS, THAT A NEW ESTABLISHMENT IS
REPLACING THE OLD IN BRITISH SOCIETY, FORMS THE FIRST IN A
THREE-PART EXAMINATION OF MRS THATCHER'S IMPACT ON THE
ESTABLISHMENT OVER THE LAST 10 YEARS. IN HIS ARTICLE, LLOYD
RE-EXAMINES HIS THESIS AND DISCUSS THE ATTRIBUTES OF THE
'NEW ESTABLISHMENT'. THE OTHER TWO ARTICLES IN THE SYMPOSIUM
EXAMINE MRS THATCHER'S VERY DIFFERENT IMPACT ON TWO PARTS OF
THE OLD ESTABLISHMENT - THE CITY AND THE TRADES UNION
CONGRESS.

05685 LLOYD, R.
A WORLD DEMOCRACY DECADE, 1990-2000
FREEDOM AT ISSUE, (109) (JUL 89), 26-28.
THE 1980S HAVE WITNESSED SIGNIFICANT ADVANCES IN
DEMOCRACY AROUND THE WORLD, IN BOTH POLITICAL RIGHTS AND
CIVIL LIBERTIES. THE 1990S MUST SEE A DETERMINED EFFORT TO
CONSOLIDATE THOSE GAINS AND SHARE THEM WITH MORE OF THE
WORLD'S OPPRESSED PEOPLES. THIS WORK WOULD BE ENHANCED BY
THE FORMAL DESIGNATION OF THE PERIOD 19902000 AS A WORLD
DEMOCRACY DECADE.

05686 LO, A.
CONTROL BY ARRESTS AND FEAR
FREE CHINA REVIEW, 39(10) (OCT 89), 54-55.
ON JULY 3, 1989, HUANG TE-PEI, A TAIWANESE REPORTER, WAS
ARRESTED IN PEKING BY COMMUNIST AUTHORITIES FOLLOWING A
RENDEZVOUS WITH WANG TAN, ONE OF THE MOST ACTIVE STUDENT
LEADERS IN THE PRO-DEMOCRACY MOVEMENT. THE AUTHORITIES
CHARGED HUANG WITH PLOTTING TO HELP WANG TAN ESCAPE FROM THE
MAINLAND. NINE DAYS LATER, HUANG WAS RELEASED AND DEPORTED.

05687 LO, A.
THE CHALLENGES OF MEDICARE
FREE CHINA REVIEW, 39(3) (MAR 89), 22-27.
IN TAIWAN. MEDICAL CARE COSTS FOR SENIOR CITIZENS ARE
RISING STEADILY AND THOSE WHO CANNOT PAY HAVE NO CHOIE BUT
TO DEPEND ON GOVERNMENT ASSISTANCE. MANY DEVELOPED WESTERN
COUNTRIES HAVE YEARS OF EXPERIENCE WITH MEDICARE PROGRAMS,
BUT A COMPARABLE SYSTEM HAS YET TO BE FULLY DEVELOPED IN
TAIWAN. DESPITE THE ECONOMIC BOOM, GOVERNMENT FUNDING HAS
YET TO ADJUST FULLY TO THE RAPIDLY EXPANDING DEMANDS FOR
PUBLIC MEDICAL FACILITIES.

05688 LO, A.
TIME TO REFINE TRADE RELATIONS
FREE CHINA REVIEW, 39(4) (APR 89), 10-15.
IN THIS INTERVIEW, TAIWAN'S DIRECTOR-GENERAL OF THE
BOARD OF FOREIGN TRADE DISCUSSES TAIWAN'S TRADE RELATIONS
WITH THE USA, JAPAN, AND EUROPE. HE ALSO ANSWERS QUESTIONS
ABOUT THE IMPACT OF OTHER NATIONAL ECONOMIES ON TAIWANESE
IMPORTS, EXPORTS, MARKET DIVERSIFICATION, AND INDUSTRIAL
STRUCTURE.

05689 LO, L.N.
THE IRONY OF EDUCATIONAL REFORM IN CHINA
CHINA NEWS ANALYSIS, (1377) (JAN 89), 1-9.
A LITTLE MORE THAN A DECADE AGO, THE COMMUNIST PARTY OF
CHINA INITIATED A FULL-SCALE ATTEMPT TO SOLVE SOME OF THE
EDUCATIONAL PROBLEMS CREATED BY THE CULTURAL REVOLUTION. THE
1978 NATIONAL EDUCATION WORK CONFERENCE WAS USED TO RECTIFY
THE ANTI-INTELLECTUAL AND XENOPHOBIC EDUCATIONAL POLICIES OF
THE MAOIST REGIME AND TO CHART A DIRECTION FOR FUTURE
DEVELOPMENT. DESPITE OCCASIONAL INTERRUPTIONS CAUSED BY
IDEOLOGICAL BACKLASH AND STUDENT UNREST, THE CPC'S
EDUCATIONAL REFORM EFFORTS DURING THE PAST DECADE HAVE
BASICALLY EMBRACED THREE MAJOR THEMES: LEARNING FROM
ADVANCED INDUSTRIALIZED SOCIETIES, A RENEWED EMPHASIS ON
ACADEMIC EXCELLENCE AT ALL LEVELS OF SCHOOLING, AND THE
POPULARIZATION OF EDUCATION.

05690 LO, S.
COLONIAL POLICY-MAKERS, CAPITALIST CLASS AND CHINA:
DETERMINANTS OF ELECTORAL REFORM IN HONG KONG'S AND
MACAU'S LEGISLATURES
PACIFIC AFFAIRS, 62(2) (SUM 89), 204-218.
ONE-FIFTH OF THE MEMBERS IN HONG KONG'S LEGISLATIVE
COUNCIL WILL BE DIRECTLY ELECTED BY CITIZENS IN FUTURE
GEOGRAPHICAL CONSTITUENCIES IN 1991. HOWEVER, ONETHIRD OF
THE MEMBERS IN MACAU'S LEGISLATIVE ASSEMBLY WERE DIRECTLY
ELECTED BY CITIZENS IN 1976. IN COMPARISON WITH MACAU, THE

PACE OF INTRODUCING DIRECTLY ELECTED SEATS TO THE COLONIAL
LEGILSLATURE WAS SLOW IN HONG KONG FROM THE 1970S TO 1988.
UNLIKE THE PORTUGUESE ADMINISTRATORS IN MACAU, THE BRITISH
POLICY-MAKERS IN HONG KONG LACKED THE POLITICAL WILL AND
MISSED SEVERAL OPPORTUNITIES TO DEMOCRATIZE THE COLONIAL
LEGISLATURE. MOREOVER, THE SPLIT WITHIN THE CAPITALIST
CLASS ACCOUNTED FOR THE EARLY IMPLEMENTATION OF ELECTORAL
REFORM IN MACAU'S LEGISLATURE. IN BOTH HONG KONG AND MACAU,
A TRIPLE ALLIANCE BETWEEN THE COLONIAL POLICY-MAKERS, THE
CAPITALIST CLASS AND THE PEOPLE'S REPUBLIC OF CHINA
DETERMINED THE WAY IN WHICH ELECTORAL REFORM WAS INTRODUCED
TO THE COLONIAL LEGISLATURE.

05691 LOBINGIER, J.H.
NATIONALITY POLICY AND PRACTICE TOWARD MINORITIES IN THE
RUSSIAN AND SOVIET ARMED FORCES
DISSERTATION ABSTRACTS INTERNATIONAL, 50(4) (OCT 89),
1078-A.
RUSSIAN AND SOVIET NATIONALITY POLICIES AND PRACTICES
HAVE BEEN SHAPED BY RUSSIAN CHAUVINISM AND XENOPHOBIA, HAVE
HISTORICALLY TREATED THE NON-RUSSIAN AS A "COLONIAL," AND
HAVE EXHIBITED A PERVASIVE IGNORANCE OF NON-RUSSIAN PEOPLES
AND CULTURES. THE DRIVE TO ELIMINATE ETHNIC DIFFERENCES HAS
CONTRIBUTED TO LONG-STANDING ETHNIC TENSIONS, BOTH IN
SOCIETY AT LARGE AND IN THE MILITARY. THE GROWING RANKS OF
NON-RUSSIANS AND ESPECIALLY CENTRAL ASIANS IN THE DRAFT POOL
WILL ADVERSELY AFFECT FUTURE FORCE READINESS AND CAPABILITY.
BUT GORBACHEV IS RESHAPING NATIONALITY POLICY AND HIS
REFORMS COULD AMELIORATE THIS OUTLOOK IF THEY ARE POSITIVE,
FEASIBLE, AND TIMELY.

05692 LOCK, G.
THE 1689 BILL OF RIGHTS
POLITICAL STUDIES, XXXVII(4) (DEC 89), 540-561.
FOLLOWING THE DISASTROUS REIGN OF JAMES II. THE BILL OF
RIGHTS WAS INTRODUCED TO CURB FUTURE ARBITRARY BEHAVIOUR BY
THE CROWN. FIVE OF THE THIRTEEN ARTICLES ARE STILL ACTIVE
AND CASES ILLUSTRATING THEIR USE IN THE COURTS ARE DESCRIBED.
THE COURTS HAVE ENFORCED THE REQUIREMENT FOR PARLIAMENTARY
CONSENT TO TAXATION AND THE BAN ON THE EXECUTIVE'S POWER TO
SUSPEND STATUTES BUT HAVE BEEN LESS STRICT OVER THE
DISPENSING POWER. ARTICLE 9, ON PARLIAMENTARY FREEDOM OF
SPEECH, IS IN ACTIVE USE, AND DEVELOPMENTS IN AUSTRALIA AND
CANADA ARE REVIEWED. SCOTLAND'S OWN LEGISLATION - THE CLAIM
OF RIGHT - IS DISCUSSED BRIEFLY. MOST OF THE BILL PROBABLY
DOES NOT APPLY TO NORTHERN IRELAND. OPINIONS VARY ON THE
BILL'S IMPORTANCE BUT IN THE AUTHOR'S VIEW IT IS STILL A
POTENT FORCE.

05693 LOCK, J.
THE EFFECT OF IDEOLOGY IN GENDER ROLE DEFINITION: CHINA AS
A CASE STUDY
JOURNAL OF ASIAN AND AFRICAN STUDIES, XXIV(3-4) (JUL 89),
228-238.
MALE AND FEMALE ROLES ARE DEFINED BY SOCIETY IN
ACCORDANCE WITH CULTURAL VALUES AND DOMINANT IDEOLOGIES. BUT
GENDER-ROLE DEFINITIONS DO NOT REMAIN CONSTANT OVER TIME.
WHEN DOMINANT IDEOLOGIES CLASH WITH CULTURAL VALUES, GENDER-
ROLES MAY BE REDEFINED. TO ILLUSTRATE THIS, THE PRESENT
PAPER COMPARES GENDER-ROLE EXPECTATIONS IN CHINA BEFORE THE
REVOLUTION AND AFTER THE ESTABLISHMENT OF THE SOCIALIST
SYSTEM, ESPECIALLY DURING THE CULTURAL REVOLUTION (1966-76).
FAMILY ROLES, WORK ROLES, AND OTHER ROLE EXPECTATIONS FOR
FEMALES IN THESE TWO PERIODS ARE EXAMINED. THE STUDY
CONCLUDES THAT POLITICAL IDEOLOGY STRONGLY INFLUENCES GENDER-
ROLE DEFINITIONS AND EXPECTATIONS IN SOCIETY. THE
REDEFINITION OF GENDER-ROLES TENDS TO BE MORE EFFECTIVE WHEN
IT IS CONSISTENT WITH THE DOMINANT IDEOLOGY AND SOCIAL
VALUES. GENDER-ROLE EXPECTATIONS ARE AN IMPORTANT REFLECTION
OF THE DOMINANT IDEOLOGY OF SOCIETY AT ANY PARTICULAR PERIOD
OF TIME.

05694 LOCKARD, J.
U.S. AID: SUBSIDIZING COLLECTIVE PUNISHMENT OF PALESTINIANS
AMERICAN-ARAB AFFAIRS, (29) (SUM 89), 65-74.
THE UNITED STATES AGENCY FOR INTERNATIONAL DEVELOPMENT
(AID) IS SUBSIDIZING COLLECTIVE PUNISHMENT AGAINST
PALESTINIANS IN THE ISRAELI-OCCUPIED TERRITORIES. THIS
ARTICLE ARGUES THAT WHETHER THROUGH DEFAULT OR UNCONCERN IN
THE STATE DEPARTMENT, AID MONIES ARE BEING TWISTED FROM
THEIR ORIGINAL PURPOSES INTO A WEAPON IN THE ISRAELI ARMY'S
CONFRONTATION WITH PALESTINIAN NATIONALISM AND THE INTIFADA.
THE ARTICLE EXPLORES BOTH ISRAELI AND PALESTINIAN REACTION
TO AID SPONSORED PROGRAMS AND ALSO REPORTS ON BLOCKED AID-
ASSISTED PROJECTS. ISSUES OF CONCERN FOR U.S. LEGISLATIVE
INTEREST ARE IDENTIFIED.

05695 LOCKERBIE, B.
CHANGE IN PARTY IDENTIFICATION: THE ROLE OF PROSPECTIVE
ECONOMIC EVALUATIONS
AMERICAN POLITICS QUARTERLY, 17(3) (JUL 89), 291-311.
IN THE PAST FEW YEARS, A NEW DIRECTION HAS BEEN TAKEN IN
THE STUDY OF ECONOMICS AND POLITICS. RESEARCHERS HAVE BEGUN
TO FOCUS ON THE ROLE OF PROSPECTIVE ECONOMIC EVALUATIONS.

THE RESEARCH PRESENTED HERE APPLIES THE PROSPECTIVE MODEL TO
CHANGES IN PARTISANSHIP. REGARDLESS OF THE TIME PERIOD
EXAMINED, THESE PROSPECTIVE ECONOMIC EVALUATIONS EXERT AN
IMPORTANT INFLUENCE ON PARTY IDENTIFICATION. INDIVIDUALS
CHANGE THEIR PARTISANSHIP IN RESPONSE TO THEIR EXPECTATIONS
CONCERNING THE ABILITY OF THE PARTIES TO PROVIDE FINANCIAL
PROSPERITY. THESE FINDINGS INDICATE THAT PREVIOUS
EXAMINATIONS OF THE ELECTORATE HAVE UNDERSTATED THE
RATIONALITY OF THE POPULACE, AND, ACCORDINGLY, PREVIOUS
THEORIES OF POLITICAL BEHAVIOR ARE IN NEED OF REVISION.

05696 LOCKERBIE, B.; BORRELLI, S.A.
    GETTING INSIDE THE BELTWAY: PERCEPTIONS OF PRESIDENTIAL
    SKILL AND SUCCESS IN CONGRESS
    BRITISH JOURNAL OF POLITICAL SCIENCE, 19(1) (JAN 89),
    97-159.
    DIFFERENT METHODOLOGICAL APPROACHES MAY LEAD TO
DIFFERENT SUBSTANTIVE CONCLUSIONS. NOWWHERE IS THIS MORE
EVIDENT THAN IN STUDIES RELATING ASSESSMENTS OF PRESIDENTIAL
SKILL TO LEGISLATIVE SUCCESS.

05697 LOCKERBIE, B.E.
    THE VOTERS' DECISION: THE ROLE OF RETROSPECTIVE AND
    PROSPECTIVE ECONOMIC EVALUATIONS
    DISSERTATION ABSTRACTS INTERNATIONAL, 49(11) (MAY 89),
    3492-A.
    THE AUTHOR ASSESSES THE INFLUENCE OF PERSONAL ECONOMIC
EVALUATIONS OF POLITICAL PARTIES ON THE VOTING OF
INDIVIDUALS. PRESIDENTIAL, SENATE, AND HOUSE ELECTIONS FROM
1952 THROUGH 1986 ARE ANALYZED TO ASCERTAIN THE EXTENT TO
WHICH INDIVIDUALS EMPLOY BOTH PROSPECTIVE AND RETROSPECTIVE
ECONOMIC EVALUATIONS IN DECIDING HOW TO VOTE.

05698 LOCKHART, C.A.
    THE ARIZONA HEALTH CARE COST CONTAINMENT SYSTEM: A CASE
    STUDY OF POLITICAL INNOVATION AT THE STATE LEVEL
    DISSERTATION ABSTRACTS INTERNATIONAL, 49(8) (FEB 89),
    2416-A.
    THE AUTHOR ANALYZES WHY ARIZONA WAS THE LAST STATE TO
AGREE TO PARTICIPATE IN THE FEDERAL MEDICAID PROGRAM. SHE
TRACES THE INNOVATION FROM INITIATION THROUGH ENACTMENT,
IMPLEMENTATION, AND CONFIRMATION, FOCUSING ON THE CHANGE
PROCESS, INFLUENCES, AND LINKAGES.

05699 LOCKMAN, Z. (ED.); BEININ, J. (ED.)
    INTIFADA: THE PALESTINIAN UPRISING AGAINST ISRAELI
    OCCUPATION
    SOUTH END PRESS, BOSTON, MA, 1989, .
    THESE ESSAYS OFFER EYEWITNESS REPORTS OF THE INTIFADA,
ANALYSIS OF CURRENT EVENTS IN ISRAEL AND THE OCCUPIED
TERRITORIES, AND THE ROLE OF THE USA.

05700 LOCKWOOD, S.C.
    OF SMART HIGHWAYS AND SMART CARS
    AMERICAN CITY AND COUNTY, 104(9) (SEP 89), 78, 80-81.
    THE NATIONAL SURFACE TRANSPORTATION SYSTEM IS AT A CROSS-
ROADS. THE PHYSICAL DETERIORATION AND GROWING CONGESTION ON
STREETS AND HIGHWAYS ARE A MAJOR PUBLIC CONCERN. COMPETITION
FOR FUNDS AT ALL LEVELS OF GOVERNMENT, TOGETHER WITH
ENVIRONMENTAL CONCERNS, INHIBIT THE ADOPTION OF CONVENTIONAL
SOLUTIONS BY STATE AND LOCAL GOVERNMENTS. MEANWHILE, THE
ENTIRE FEDERAL-AID TRANSPORTATION PROGRAM FOR HIGHWAYS AND
TRANSIT, AS WELL AS THE USER-TAX SYSTEM THAT SUPPORTS IT, IS
SCHEDULED FOR RECONSIDERATION BY CONGRESS IN 1990.

05701 LODGE, M.; MCGRAW, K.M.; STROH, P.
    AN IMPRESSION-DRIVEN MODEL OF CANDIDATE EVALUATION
    AMERICAN POLITICAL SCIENCE REVIEW, 83(2) (JUN 89), 399-420.
    THE AUTHORS DESCRIBE AND TEST TWO PROCESS MODELS OF
CANDIDATE EVALUATION. THE MEMORY-BASED MODEL HOLDS THAT
EVALUATIONS ARE DEPENDENT ON THE MIX OF PRO AND CON
INFORMATION RETRIEVED FROM MEMORY. THE IMPRESSION-DRIVEN
MODEL HOLDS THAT EVALUATIONS ARE FORMED AND UPDATED "ON-
LINE" AS INFORMATION IS ENCOUNTERED. THE RESULTS PROVIDE
EVIDENCE FOR THE EXISTENCE OF STEREOTYPING AND PROJECTION
BIASES THAT RENDER THE MIX OF EVIDENCE AVAILABLE IN MEMORY A
NONVERIDICAL REPRESENTATION OF THE INFORMATION TO WHICH
SUBJECTS WERE EXPOSED. PEOPLE DO NOT RELY ON THE SPECIFIC
CANDIDATE INFORMATION AVAILABLE IN MEMORY. RATHER,
CONSISTENT WITH THE LOGIC OF THE IMPRESSION-DRIVEN
PROCESSING MODEL, AN "ON-LINE" JUDGMENT FORMED WHEN THE
INFORMATION WAS ENCOUNTERED BEST PREDICTS CANDIDATE
EVALUATION. THE RESULTS RAISE BOTH METHODOLOGICAL AND
SUBSTANTIVE CHALLENGES TO HOW POLITICAL SCIENTISTS MEASURE
AND MODEL THE CANDIDATE EVALUATION PROCESS.

05702 LOESCHER, G.
    THE EUROPEAN COMMUNITY AND REFUGEES
    INTERNATIONAL AFFAIRS, 65(4) (FAL 89), 617-636.
    THIS ARTICLE WILL FIRST BRIEFLY ANALYSE THE MAJOR
PERIODS IN REFUGEE PROTECTION IN EUROPE FROM THE END OF THE
SECOND WORLD WAR TO THE PRESENT. THAT THE 1980S HAVE SEEN
THE LARGE-SCALE ENTRY OF ASYLUM-SEEKERS INTO WESTERN EUROPE
HAS PRESENTED POLICYMAKERS WITH PROBLEMS BOTH QUALITATIVELY
AND QUANTITATIVELY DIFFERENT FROM THOSE OF EARLIER PERIODS.
IT THEN IDENTIFIES WHAT IS NEW ABOUT THIS PHENOMENON,
EXAMINE THE PUBLIC CONCERNS THAT THE ARRIVAL OF ASYLUM-
SEEKERS HAS GENERATED, AND EXPLAINS WHY EUROPEAN GOVERNMENTS
HAVE ADOPTED RESTRICTIVE PRACTICES AND DETERRENT MEASURES TO
CURB THE ENTRY OF NEW ARRIVALS. FINALLY, IT ANALYZES THE
INITIATIVES THAT ARE BEING TAKEN WITHIN THE EUROPEAN
COMMUNITY COUNTRIES TO FORMULATE A EUROPEAN ASYLUM POLICY,
AND SUGGESTS WHAT CONSIDERATIONS SHOULD BE UPPERMOST IN THE
MINDS OF EUROPEAN GOVERNMENTS WHEN FRAMING FUTURE POLICY
TOWARDS ASYLUM-SEEKERS AND REFUGEES.

05703 LOEWY, M.B.
    REAGANOMICS AND REPUTATION REVISITED
    ECONOMIC INQUIRY, 26(2) (APR 88), 253-264.
    THIS ARTICLE EXAMINES IN DETAIL THREE QUESTIONS RAISED
BY THE CALL FOR CHANGES IN MONETARY AND FISCAL POLICY BY
PRESIDENT REAGAN. THESE QUESTIONS ARE: 1) WHAT COMBINATION
OF POLICIES WILL ACTUALLY OCCUR? 2) WILL NEW POLICY PERSIST?
AND 3) WHAT IMPACT WILL THESE POLICIES HAVE ON THE STOCK OF
GOVERNMENT DEBT HELD BY THE PRIVATE SECTOR? TO ANSWER THESE
QUESTIONS A VERSION OF TABELLINI'S (1987) MODEL IS ANALYSED.
UTILITY FUNCTIONS FOR EACH AUTHORITY CITED THAT ARE
CONSISTENT WITH THE POLICY CHANGES. A CAVEAT ON INTERPRETING
THE MODEL'S EQUILIBRIUM IS GIVEN.

05704 LOGAN, B.; MENGISTEAB, K.
    THE POTENTIAL IMPACTS OF PRIVATIZATION ON HEALTH CARE
    DELIVERY IN SUB-SAHARAN AFRICA
    SCANDINAVIAN JOURNAL OF DEVELOPMENT ALTERNATIVES, VIII(1)
    (MAR 89), 133-152.
    THE GENERAL OBJECTIVE OF PRIVATIZATION IS TO INCREASE
THE EARNINGS OF AN ENTERPRISE BY IMPROVING OVERALL
MANAGEMENT EFFICIENCY. AS A RESULT, PRIVATIZATION IS SEEN AS
A MEANS BY WHICH A PRESUMABLY INNEFICIENT STATE OWNED
ENTERPRISE IS TRANSFORMED INTO AN EFFICIENT PROFIT-
GENERATING PRIVATE CONCERN THAT CONTRIBUTES TO A COUNTRY'S
ECONOMIC PERFORMANCE. THE STUDY USES THE CASE OF HEALTH CARE
DELIVERY TO DEMONSTRATE THAT, DESPITE ITS THEORETICAL APPEAL,
PRIVATIZATION HAS QUESTIONABLE UTILITY AS A STRATEGY TO
ENHANCE THE DEVELOPMENT PROCESS IN SUB-SAHARAN AFRICA.

05705 LOHR, S.
    PERESTROIKA ENTERS FINLAND, A BIT BUMPILY
    SCANDINAVIAN REVIEW, 77(3) (AUT 89), 21-26.
    PERESTROIKA HAS RIPPLED THROUGH FINLAND, THE WESTERN
NATION WITH THE LONGEST AND MOST EXTENSIVE TRADING
RELATIONSHIP WITH THE SOVIET UNION, CAUSING ALMOST AS MUCH
TURMOIL AND UNCERTAINTY IN BOARD ROOMS AND GOVERNMENT
OFFICES AS IT HAS CAUSED IN THE USSR. FINNISH EXECUTIVES SAY
THAT PERESTROIKA HAS BROUGHT A DIFFICULT TRANSITION IN THE
SOVIET APPROACH TO FOREIGN TRADE. THERE ARE NEW ATTITUDES
AND A NEW OPENNESS ABOUT AMBITIOUS PROJECTS, LIKE JOINT
VENTURES WITH WESTERN PARTNERS. AT THE SAME TIME, THE
DECENTRALIZATION OF DECISION-MAKING HAS BROUGHT A PERIOD OF
UNCERTAINTY IN WHICH WESTERN BUSINESSMEN ARE HARD PRESSED TO
FIND THOSE WITH REAL AUTHORITY. THE RESULT, IN MANY CASES,
IS TO INTENSIFY THE VERY STAGNATION PERESTROIKA HAS INTENDED
TO CURE.

05706 LOMAX, B.
    1989 IN HUNGARY: YEAR OF CHANGE
    JOURNAL OF COMMUNIST STUDIES, 5(3) (SEP 89), 344-348.
    THIS ARTICLE REPORTS ON UNEXPECTED POLITICAL CHANGES IN
HUNGARY AS THE MAY CONFERENCE OF THE HUNGARIAN SOCIALIST
WORKER'S PARTY OBSERVED THE DEPARTURE FROM POWER OF JANOS
KADAR AND HIS CLOSEST ASSOCIATES WHO HAD RULED HUNGARY SINCE
1956. IT NOTES THE RAPIDITY OF CHANGE THAT FOLLOWED, WHICH
SWEPT AWAY LONG-ESTABLISHED INSTITUTIONS AND PRINCIPLES, AND
RAISED THE PROSPECT OF THE COMMUNIST PARTY ABANDONING ITS
MONOPOLY OF POWER AND OF HUNGARY DETACHING ITSELF FROM THE
EASTERN BLOC'S MILITARY ALLIANCE, HISTORICAL BACKGROUND IS
OFFERED OF THE CONDITIONS LEADING TO THESE CHANGES.

05707 LOMBARDI, M.O.
    SUPERPOWER INTERVENTION IN SUB-SAHARAN AFRICA: A FRAMEWORK
    FOR ANALYZING THIRD WORLD CONFLICTS
    DISSERTATION ABSTRACTS INTERNATIONAL, 50(4) (OCT 89),
    1083-A.
    THIS DISSERTATION ATTEMPTS TO ADDRESS THE QUESTION OF
WHY THE SUPERPOWERS ARE SUCCESSFUL OR UNSUCCESSFUL IN THIRD
WORLD CONFLICTS BY FOCUSING EXPLICITLY ON THE LOCAL AND
REGIONAL FACTORS AND THEIR INTERACTION WITH SUPERPOWER
BEHAVIOR. THIS ENTAILS THE CREATION OF A FRAMEWORK THAT
OUTLINES THE PRINCIPAL CONFIGURATIONS OF THE LOCAL CONTEXT,
SUPERPOWER INTERVENTION AND OUTCOME. THROUGH THESE THREE
CONCEPTS, A COMPARATIVE CASE STUDY OF FOUR AFRICAN CONFLICTS
IS UNDERTAKEN: ANGOLA, SHABA II, THE OGADEN WAR AND RHODESIA-
ZIMBABWE.

05708 LONCAN, E.
    ARGENTINE PROSPECTS
    HEMISPHERE, 1(3) (SUM 89), 15.
    THE ECONOMIC POLICIES OF PRESIDENT CARLOS MENEM DO NOT

PROMISE QUICK RECOVERY FOR ARGENTINA, BUT THE INITIAL SIGNS
GIVE REASON FOR QUALIFIED OPTIMISM. MENEM'S MOST URGENT
CHALLENGE IS TO IMPLEMENT THE UNPOPULAR ECONOMIC MEASURES
THAT, WHILE NECESSARY TO STOP ARGENTINA'S HYPERINFLATION,
COULD QUICKLY ERODE HIS POLITICAL STANDING. MENEM'S EARLY
MOVES INDICATE THAT HE IS PREPARED TO TAKE THE POLITICAL
RISK.

05709 LONDON, B.; ROBINSON, T.D.
THE EFFECT OF INTERNATIONAL DEPENDENCE ON INCOME
INEQUALITY AND POLITICAL VIOLENCE
AMERICAN SOCIOLOGICAL REVIEW, 54(2) (APR 89), 305-308.
RECENT STUDIES OF COLLECTIVE POLITICAL VIOLENCE HAVE
OVERLOOKED INTERNATIONAL CASUAL FACTORS. THIS CROSS-NATIONAL
STUDY OF 46-51 NATIONS (INCLUDING ANALYSES OF INFLUENTIAL
CASES) EXPANDS EARLIER ANALYSES BY SIMULTANEOUSLY EXAMINING
BOTH THE "EXTERNAL" (INTERNATIONAL) AND THE "INTERNAL"
(INTRANATIONAL) DETERMINANTS OF COLLECTIVE POLITICAL
VIOLENCE. REGRESSION ANALYSIS SUGGESTS THAT TRANSNATIONAL
CORPORATE PENETRATION, AN INTERNATIONAL FACTOR, CONTRIBUTES
TO INCREASED POLITICAL VIOLENCE BOTH DIRECTLY AND INDIRECTLY,
THROUGH ITS EFFECT ON INCOME INEQUALITY. THEORETICAL AND
EMPIRICAL INTEGRATION OF INTRA- AND INTERNATIONAL FACTORS
YIELDS THE MOST COMPREHENSIVE EXPLANATION OF THE CAUSES OF
COLLECTIVE POLITICAL VIOLENCE.

05710 LONDON, M.
CHINA: THE ROMANCE OF REALPOLITIK
FREEDOM AT ISSUE, (110) (SEP 89), 9-14.
SINCE THE NIXON-KISSINGER OPENING GAMBIT ALMOST TWO
DECADES AGO, U.S. POLICY TOWARD THE PEOPLE'S REPUBLIC OF
CHINA HAS BEEN PREMISED ON A HARD-BOILED DEFINITION OF
POLITICAL REALISM--THAT OF SHREWD PLAYERS IN A GEOPOLITICAL
GAME. THIS POLICY HAS BEEN WIDELY APPROVED AS NECESSARY,
CLEVER, AND CORRECT. IT MAY BE ALL OF THESE THINGS BUT, EVEN
ON ITS OWN TERMS, IT HAS NEVER BEEN REALISTIC. FROM THE VERY
BEGINNING, IT HAS BEEN MARKED NOT ONLY BY EMOTIONALISM AND
SENTIMENTALITY BUT BY IGNORANCE AND FANTASY.

05711 LONG, N.V.
VIETNAM: THE REAL ENEMY
BULLETIN OF CONCERNED ASIAN SCHOLARS, 21(2 - 4) (APR 89),
6-34.
THIS PAPER CHARGES THAT IN THE VIETNAM WAR THE REAL
ENEMY OF THE UNITED STATES WAS THE VIETNAMESE PEOPLE
THEMSELVES. IT TRACES VIETNAMESE HISTORY FROM 1850 TO 1945
INCLUDING FRENCH CONQUEST AND CONSEQUENCES, AND ECONOMICS,
AND DETAILS THE FIRST THIRTY YEARS OF REVOLUTIONARY
STRUGGLES. IT THEN COVERS THE FOUR PHASES OF THE FIRST
INDOCHINA WAR AND THE RISE OF THE NATIONAL LIBERATION FRONT.
DIEM AND REPRESSION ARE DISCUSSED. THEN THE VIETNAM WAR 1965-
75 IS DETAILED AS WELL AS CHARGES MADE THAT NIXON TALKED
PEACE IN ORDER TO MAKE WAR. POSTWAR CONFLICT AND ECONOMIC
PERFORMANCE AND RECONSTRUCTION, REFORMS AND READJUSTMENTS
ARE EACH EXAMINED.

05712 LONG, S.
GORBACHEV AND TURMOIL IN CHINA
WORLD TODAY, 45(7) (JUL 89), 110-111.
THE SINO-SOVIET SUMMIT IN MAY 1989 WAS OVERSHADOWED BY
THE TUMULT IN THE STREETS OF PEKING AND OTHER CHINESE CITIES,
EVEN THOUGH IT WAS THE FIRST MEETING BETWEEN TOP CHINESE
AND SOVIET LEADERS FOR 30 YEARS. THE SUMMIT SET THE SEAL ON
ONE OF GORBACHEV'S MOST CHERISHED FOREIGN POLICY GOALS, THE
NORMALIZATION OF SINO-SOVIET RELATIONS. IT WAS ALSO AN
IMPORTANT MEETING FOR DENG XIAOPING. WITH THE SUMMIT, CHINA
CAME A STEP CLOSER TO REALIZING WHAT IT HAS LONG CLAIMED TO
BE ITS FOREIGN POLICY GOAL: INDEPENDENCE AND EQUIDISTANCE
BETWEEN THE SUPERPOWERS.

05713 LONG, T.
EL SALVADOR: CRACKDOWN
THIRD WORLD WEEK, 8(11) (MAY 89), 84-85.
HUMAN RIGHTS ORGANIZATIONS HAVE DENOUNCED A RASH OF
ARRESTS AND THE POLICE TORTURE OF LABOR UNION ACTIVISTS IN
EL SALVADOR. THE GOVERNMENT, WHICH LINKS THE UNION TO
GUERRILLA VIOLENCE, HAS INDICATED THAT IT WILL CONTINUE TO
TAKE STRICT MEASURES "TO ACHIEVE THE PROPER BALANCE BETWEEN
FREEDOM AND SECURITY." THE CRACKDOWN ON OPPOSITION
ORGANIZATIONS COINCIDED WITH THE ASSASSINATION OF SALVADORAN
ATTORNEY GENERAL ROBERTO GARCIA ALVARADO AND THE BOMBING OF
THE HOME OF VICE PRESIDENT-ELECT FRANCISCO MERINO.

05714 LONG, T.J.
EL SALVADOR: MODERATION?
THIRD WORLD WEEK, 8(5) (MAR 89), 33.
EL SALVADOR'S PRESIDENT-ELECT ALFREDO CRISTIANI IS A
RIGHT-WINGER, BUT THAT DOESN'T BOTHER MOST VOTERS, WHO ARE
EAGER FOR A CHANGE AND GAVE CRISTIANI FIFTY-FIVE PERCENT OF
THE VOTE. HIS VICTORY REFLECTS THE WIDESPREAD
DISILLUSIONMENT WITH PRESIDENT NAPOLEON DUARTE'S
ADMINISTRATION, WHICH HAS BEEN NOTED FOR ITS CORRUPTION. BUT
DUARTE'S MAJOR FAILURE HAS BEEN HIS INABILITY TO END THE
CIVIL WAR.

05715 LONGMIRE, L.A.
E.F. SCHUMACHER AND THE SEARCH FOR A POSTMODERN POLITICS
DISSERTATION ABSTRACTS INTERNATIONAL, 50(5) (NOV 89),
1423-A.
THE AUTHOR EXPLORES THE WORK OF E.G. SCHUMACHER IN ORDER
TO ASSESS HIS INFLUENCE ON THE THEORY AND PRACTICE OF
ECONOMIC DEVELOPMENT. SHE REVIEWS SHCUMACHER'S OWN LIFE AND
THE PROGRESSIVE TRANSFORMATION OF HIS WORLD VIEW AS HE MOVED
FROM AN UNDERSTANDING OF ECONOMICS TO POLITICS TO PHILOSOPHY
AND CULTURE. SHE SKETCHES HIS META-ECONOMICS, WHICH
ARTICULATED THE VALUES, PURPOSES, AND DIRECTIONS OF
POLITICAL AND ECONOMIC POLICY AS ENVISIONED BY SCHUMACHER.

05716 LONGSTAFF, S.A.
THE NEW YORK INTELLECTUALS AND THE CULTURAL COLD WAR: 1945-
1950
NEW POLITICS, 11(2) (WIN 89), 156-170.
BY 1948 INTELLECTUAL OPINION WAS RAPIDLY CONSOLIDATING
ITSELF BEHIND TRUMAN'S COLD WAR POLICIES. AN INCONSPICUOUS
SIGN OF THE TIMES COULD BE NOTED IN JANUARY OF THAT YEAR
WHEN THE NEW MASSES, HAVING SOMEHOW SURVIVED INTO THE
POSTWAR PERIOD, FINALLY GAVE UP THE GHOST. THE MARSHALL PLAN
MARKED A DECISIVE CHANGE IN THE OUTLOOK OF THE LIBERAL
WEEKLIES, TOWARD THE TRUMAN ADMINISTRATION AT ANY RATE.
INDEED, SO UNWAVERING WAS THE NATION'S AND THE NEW
REPUBLIC'S ENTHUSIASM FOR THIS GRAND "ROOSEVELTIAN" GESTURE
THAT NOT EVEN THE SOVIETS' VEHEMENT REFUSAL TO PARTICIPATE
MANAGED TO FAZE THEM. BY THE END OF 1947 BOTH PUBLICATIONS
WERE BACKING AWAY FROM HENRY WALLACE'S THIRD-PARTY RUN FOR
THE PRESIDENCY--A VENTURE WHICH IN THE COURSE OF THINGS THEY
HAD DONE MUCH TO ENCOURAGE--IN A LARGE PART BECAUSE OF
WALLACE'S PARTY-LINING HOSTILITY TO THE PLAN.

05717 LONGWORTH, R.
E.C. FOSTERS CHANGE IN EASTERN EUROPE
EUROPE, (291) (NOV 89), 24-26.
THE EUROPEAN COMMUNITY HAS BEEN GIVEN THE RESPONSIBILITY
OF DETERMINING AND COORDINATING WESTERN AID TO REFORMING
EAST EUROPE. ALTHOUGH THEY HAVE ALREADY RULED A FULL SCALE
NEW MARSHALL PLAN, THEY HAVE ALREADY PROPOSED A FIVE POINT
PLAN OF ACTION THAT CALLS FOR EASIER ACCESS TO WESTERN
MARKETS BY LOWERING TARIFFS; DIRECT GIFTS OF FARM MACHINERY
AND PESTICIDES TO HELP POLISH AND HUNGARIAN AGRICULTURE;
MORE FOREIGN INVESTMENT IN EASTERN EUROPE; PROFESSIONAL AND
MANAGEMENT TRAINING TO GIVE POLAND AND HUNGARY THE SKILLS TO
RUN A MARKET ECONOMY: AND ENVIRONMENTAL PROTECTION TO HELP
THE EAST EUROPEANS CLEAN UP AREAS OF OVER-INDUSTRIALIZATION
AND BAD MANAGEMENT.

05718 LONGWORTH, R. C.
TOWARD A EUROPE FROM THE ATLANTIC TO THE URALS?
EUROPE, (286) (MAY 89), 30-31.
AS EAST EUROPE CHANGES, THE REALIZATION IS GROWING AMONG
WESTERN EUROPEANS THAT THE EUROPEAN COMMUNITY CAN BE A
MAGNET DRAWING EAST EUROPE TOWARD MARKET ECONOMICS AND
WESTERN DEMOCRACIES.

05719 LOONEY, R.
HAVE THIRD-WORLD ARMS INDUSTRIES REDUCED ARMS IMPORTS?
CURRENT RESEARCH ON PEACE AND VIOLENCE, XII(1) (1989),
15-26.
IN 1945 ONLY ARGENTINA, BRAZIL, INDIA AND SOUTH AFRICA
IN THE THIRD WORLD POSSESSED DOMESTIC ARMS INDUSTRIES OTHER
THAN SMALL ARMS AND AMMUNITION. BY THE EARLY 1980S MANY OF
THE THIRD WORLD COUNTRIES BEGAN PRODUCING ADVANCED WEAPONS
SYSTEMS TO THE POINT WHERE THEY WERE COMPETING WITH
ESTABLISHED ARMS SUPPLIERS. THIS ARTICLE STATES THAT
INDIGENEOUS ARMS PRODUCTION IN THE THIRD WORLD HAS TENDED TO
REDUCE THE IMPORTATION OF ARMS. THE ARMS IMPORTS THEMSELVES
ARE LARGELY AFFECTED BY FOREIGN EXCHANGE AVAILABILITY,
RATHER THAN POLITICAL OR STRATEGIC FACTORS. IT CONCLUDES THAT
ARMS IMPORTS WILL MOST LIKELY NOT REACH LEVELS ATTAINED IN
THE LATE 1970S DUE NOT SO MUCH TO A GENERAL SPIRIT OF
CONSTRAINT, BUT TO LACK OF MONEY ON PART OF MANY OF THE
THIRD WORLD COUNTRIES AND THE DEVELOPMENT OF INDIGENOUS
PRODUCTION CAPABILITIES ON THE PART OF OTHERS.

05720 LOONEY, R.
THE INFLUENCE OF ARMS IMPORTS ON THIRD WORLD DEBT
JOURNAL OF DEVELOPING AREAS, 23(2) (JAN 89), 221-232.
DESPITE THE RATHER LOGICAL ASSERTION THAT CONSIDERABLE
AMOUNTS OF THIRD WORLD INDEBTEDNESS HAVE STEMMED FROM ARMS
IMPORTS, LITTLE EMPIRICAL TESTING OF THE LINK BETWEEN ARMS
IMPORTS AND THIRD WORLD DEBT HAS BEEN DONE. THE MAIN PURPOSE
OF THE STUDY IS TO DETERMINE THE ROLE PLAYED BY MILITARY
SPENDING IN GENERAL AND ARMS IMPORTS IN PARTICULAR IN
AFFECTING THE LEVEL OF THIRD WORLD DEBT. A SECONDARY
OBJECTIVE IS TO DETERMINE WHICH GROUPS OF DEVELOPING
COUNTRIES WERE MOST INCLINED TO FINANCE ARMS IMPORTS WITH
INCREASED EXTERNAL INDEBTEDNESS. IT CONCLUDES THAT THERE
GENERALLY IS NO LINK BETWEEN MILITARY EXPENDITURES AND DEBT,
BUT IN CERTAIN INSTANCES, CERTAIN LDCS HAVE SUFFERED FROM
HIGHER DEBT LEVELS DUE TO MILITARY SPENDING.

05721 LOONEY, R.E.
    IMPACT OF REGIME TYPE ON ARGENTINEAN CENTRAL GOVERNMENT
    BUDGETARY PRIORITIES 1961-82: A TEST OF THE O'DONNELL
    THESIS
    INTERNATIONAL JOURNAL OF PUBLIC ADMINISTRATION, 12(1)
    (1989), 45-77.
        A LARGE BODY OF LITERATURE ON ARGENTINA SUGGESTS THAT
    TRANSITIONS FROM MILITARY TO CIVILIAN REGIMES BRING ABOUT
    FUNDAMENTAL CHANGES IN POLICY-MAKING IN GENERAL AND IN
    ECONOMIC, SOCIAL, AND MILITARY PRIORITIES IN PARTICULAR.
    THIS VIEW HAS BEEN DEVELOPED BY O'DONNELL IN HIS PATH
    BREAKING THESIS ABOUT THE EMERGENCE OF NEW FORMS OF
    AUTHORITARIANISM IN LATIN AMERICA. ACCORDING TO O'DONNELL
    EACH SUCCESSIVE GOVERNMENT IS AN ALLIANCE OF VARIOUS
    DISTINCT INTEREST GROUPS. EACH ALLIANCE IS IMBUED WITH A
    DISTINCT SENSE OF WHAT SHOULD BE DONE AND AT WHOSE EXPENSE
    AND TRANSLATES THE GOALS AND INTERESTS OF THE MEMBERS OF THE
    COALITION INTO PUBLIC POLICIES. THE PURPOSE OF THIS PAPER IS
    TO TEST THE O'DONNELL THESIS I.E., TO DETERMINE THE POSSIBLE
    EXISTENCE AND NATURE OF STRUCTURAL CHANGES IN THE
    GOVERNMENT'S BUDGETARY PRIORITIES ASSOCIATED WITH REGIME
    CHANGE. THE EMPIRICAL RESULTS YIELD CONSIDERABLE SUPPORT TO
    THE GENERAL THESIS THAT REGIME TYPE IN ARGENTINA HAS A MAJOR
    IMPACT ON THE AMOUNT AND RELATIVE SHARE OF RESOURCES
    ALLOCATED TO DEFENSE AND SOCIOECONOMIC ACTIVITIES.

05722 LOONEY, R.E.
    MACROECONOMIC CONSEQUENCES OF THE SIZE OF THIRD WORLD
    NATIONS: WITH SPECIAL REFERENCE TO THE CARIBBEAN
    WORLD DEVELOPMENT, 17(1) (JAN 89), 69-83.
        THE MAIN PURPOSE OF THIS PAPER IS TO DETERMINE WHETHER,
    AND IF SO HOW, SMALL DEVELOPING COUNTRIES DIFFER FROM THEIR
    LARGER COUNTERPARTS WITH REGARD TO THE UNDERLYING
    DETERMINANTS OF KEY MACROECONOMIC VARIABLES. ANALYSIS
    INDICATES THAT MAJOR DIFFERENCES DO EXIST, PARTICULARLY WITH
    REGARD TO THE OVERALL RATE OF GROWTH, THE SHARE OF
    INVESTMENT AND SAVINGS IN GDP, EXTERNAL PUBLIC SECTOR DEBT,
    AND THE SHARE OF GOVERNMENT EXPENDITURES IN GDP. ULTIMATELY
    THESE DIFFERENCES APPEAR TO STEM FROM THE OBVIOUS FEATURE OF
    SMALL COUNTRIES RELATIVE OPENNESS AND SUSCEPTIBILITY TO
    EXTERNAL SHOCKS. GOVERNMENTS IN THIS ENVIRONMENT APPEAR MORE
    INCLINED TO INCREASE THEIR ECONOMIC ROLE THAN DO GOVERNMENTS
    IN LARGER COUNTRIES. THIS EXPANDED ROLE IS NOT WITHOUT COSTS,
    THE MOST IMPORTANT ONE BEING CONSISTENTLY NEGATIVE IMPACTS
    OF PUBLIC SECTOR EXPENDITURES ON THE MORE IMPORTANT MACRO
    AGGREGATES.

05723 LOPATKA, A.
    RENEWAL THROUGH DEMOCRATISATION
    WORLD MARXIST REVIEW, 31(12) (DEC 88), 45-52.
        SOCIALIST RENEWAL IS PROCEEDING IN A STRUGGLE ON TWO
    FRONTS, PRIMARILY AGAINST THOSE WHO, UNDER THE COVER OF
    REFORMIST PHRASES AND FROM A STANDPOINT ACTUALLY DESTRUCTIVE
    TO SOCIALIST POLAND, ARE SEEKING TO UNDERMINE THE ELEMENTARY
    CONDITIONS FOR EFFECTIVE REFORMS: ORDER, TRANQUILITY, WORK
    AND PUBLIC DIALOGUE. IT IS ALSO THE STRUGGLE AGAINST THOSE
    CONSERVATIVE ELEMENTS AT ALL LEVELS OF STATE POWER WHO ARE
    TRYING TO BLOCK, RETARD AND DISTORT THE RENEWAL PROCESS AND
    EVEN TO PARALYSE IT. SOCIALISM IS ADVANCING, DESPITE THE
    ACTIONS OF BOTH THESE CAMPS OF OPPONENTS.

05724 LOPEZ, A.M.
    CRISIS AND CINEMA IN LATIN AMERICA
    HEMISPHERE, 2(1) (FAL 89), 24-28.
        THE LATIN AMERICA CINEMA IS INTIMATELY LINKED TO THE
    REGION'S ECONOMIC AND SOCIOPOLITICAL DYNMICS. IT CURRENTLY
    FACES A DANGER THAT IS SIMULTANEOUSLY SOCIAL, POLITICAL, AND
    ECONOMIC BECAUSE IT IS LOSING ITS AUDIENCES. IN THIS ESSAY,
    THE AUTHOR REVIEWS THE RECENT HISTORY OF LATIN AMERICAN
    CINEMA AND SPECULATES ABOUT ITS FUTURE.

05725 LOPEZ, G.A.
    TRENDS IN COLLEGE CURRICULA AND PROGRAMS
    PHILADELPHIA: ANLS OF AMER ACMY OF POLITICAL AND SOC
    SCIENCE, (504) (JUL 89), 61-71.
        THIS ARTICLE EXPLORES TRENDS IN CURRICULUM DEVELOPMENT
    IN PEACE STUDIES OVER THE LAST TWO DECADES. IT ISOLATES
    THREE DIFFERENT TIME PERIODS AND THE CORRESPONDING THEMES
    THAT HAVE DOMINATED THEM, PAYING PARTICULAR ATTENTION TO THE
    DEVELOPMENT OF NEW SUBSTANTIVE AREAS OF INTEREST AND TO THE
    CHALLENGES THAT EACH ERA HAS FACED IN THE IMPLEMENTATION OF
    PEACE STUDIES. EACH ERA OF PEACE STUDIES DEVELOPMENT HAS
    BEEN STIMULATED BY THE LARGER SOCIOPOLITICAL DEBATES OF THE
    TIME, YET THE CONTINUITY OF SUBSTANTIVE THEMES AND
    PEDAGOGICAL CHALLENGES TESTIFIES THAT PEACE STUDIES IS NOT A
    TEACHING AND RESEARCH FIELD THAT MERELY PARODIES THE TRENDS
    OF THE TIME. THE ARTICLE CONCLUDES WITH A BRIEF STATEMENT
    ABOUT THE IMPORTANCE OF PEACE STUDIES TO UNIVERSITY
    EDUCATION.

05726 LOPEZ, T.S.
    COMMUNITY CONFLICT AND THE RETURN TO NEIGHBORHOOD SCHOOLS
    IN NORFOLK, VIRGINIA: SECESSION OF ANOTHER KIND

DISSERTATION ABSTRACTS INTERNATIONAL, 49(7) (JAN 89),
1989-A.
    THE AUTHOR ANALYZES THE COMMUNITY CONFLICT PROCESS FROM
THE TIME THE NORFOLK SCHOOL BOARD ANNOUNCED ITS INTENTION TO
RETURN TO NEIGHBORHOOD SCHOOLS UNTIL SHORTLY AFTER THE
FEDERAL HEARINGS. HE FINDS THAT: (1) HOSTILE ACTIVITIES WERE
RELATIVELY MODERATE DUE TO THE EXTERNAL PRESSURE APPLIED BY
THE COURTS; (2) THE CONFLICT SHOWED THE CONTINUANCE OF PAST
CLEAVAGES; AND (3) NEW ISSUES, RELATING TO CLASS INEQUITIES
AND MUNICIPAL POLITICAL DECISION MAKING, SURFACED.

05727 LORANC, W.
    STATE AND CHURCH IN POLAND
    WORLD MARXIST REVIEW, 32(6) (JUN 89), 21-24.
        THIS ARTICLE, ANALYZING THE CHURCH AND STATE IN POLAND,
    GIVES A HISTORY OF RELATIONS BETWEEN THE SOCIALIST STATE AND
    POLAND'S RELIGIONS. IT EXPLORES THE EFFECTIVENESS OF THE
    POLICY OF INTERACTION WITH THE CHURCH WHICH DEPENDS ON MANY
    FACTORS. MINORITIES; MARXISM AND RELIGION; AND POLICY ARE,
    IN TURN, DISCUSSED.

05728 LORANT, R.
    THE EUROPEAN WAR AGAINST DRUGS
    EUROPE, (289) (SEP 89), 24-25.
        DESPITE REGIONAL DIFFERENCES, THE DRUG MARKET IN EUROPE
    IS EXPANDING. DRUG DEALERS ALREADY VIEW EUROPE AS A SINGLE
    MARKET, BUT FULL-SCALE ECONOMIC INTEGRATION MAY BE THE ONLY
    WAY TO COMBAT THE PROBLEM. ALTHOUGH THERE REMAINS MUCH
    CONFLICT AND DEBATE OVER PROPOSED EUROPEAN JUDGES AND
    INVESTIGATORS DESIGNED TO COMBAT THE SPREAD DRUGS, CONCRETE
    STEPS ARE BEING TAKEN. HOWEVER MUCH REMAINS TO BE DONE.

05729 LORD, C.
    CHAPTER 1: THE PRESIDENCY AND THE PROBLEM OF BUREAUCRACY;
    THE PRESIDENCY AND THE MANAGEMENT OF NATIONAL SECURITY
    FREE PRESS, NEW YORK, NY, 1988, 15-34.
        THIS CHAPTER EXAMINES THE CONSTITUTIONAL OR POLITICAL
    LIMITATIONS ON THE PRESIDENT'S AUTHORITY WHICH HE FACES, AS
    WELL AS THE MANY CONSTRAINTS IN ATTEMPTING TO MAKE HIS WRIT
    RUN THROUGH THE BUREAUCRACY. THE DYNAMICS OF BUREAUCRACY ARE
    EXPLORED. PROBLEMS OF POLITICAL EXECUTIVES ARE DETAILED AS
    WELL AS THOSE OF THE PRESIDENT AND HIS OFFICE. THE CHAPTER
    CONCLUDES WITH THE PROBLEM OF PRESIDENTIAL GOVERNANCE.

05730 LORD, C.
    CHAPTER 2: NATIONAL SECURITY AND THE NATIONAL SECURITY
    AGENCIES; THE PRESIDENCY AND THE MANAGEMENT OF NATIONAL
    SECURITY
    FREE PRESS, NEW YORK, NY, 1988, 35-60.
        THIS CHAPTER DEFINES "NATIONAL SECURITY AND DELIMITS ITS
    SCOPE AND THE AGENCIES INVOLVED IN IT. IT EXAMINES THE
    CONSEQUENCE OF THE AMERICAN TENDENCY TO COMPARTMENTALIZE WAR
    AND PEACE AS A FAILURE TO APPROACH THE NATIONAL SECURITY
    BUREAUCRACY WITHIN A SINGLE FRAMEWORK OF ANALYSIS. EXPLORED
    ARE; THE POLITICAL - MILITARY FAULTLINE; THE DEFENSE
    ESTABLISHMENT, THE FOREIGN POLICY ESTABLISHMENT; THE
    INTELLIGENCE COMMUNITY AND PERIPHERAL AREAS.

05731 LORD, C.
    CHAPTER 3: THE NSC AND THE NSC SYSTEM; THE PRESIDENCY AND
    THE MANAGEMENT OF NATIONAL SECURITY
    FREE PRESS, NEW YORK, NY, 1988, 61-84.
        THIS CHAPTER GIVES THE BACKGROUND AND HISTORY OF THE
    NATIONAL SECURITY COUNCIL (NSC) AND EXAMINES HOW IT CAN BE
    USED BY THE PRESIDENT OF THE UNITED STATES. NSC FUNCTIONS
    ARE DETAILED AS FOLLOWED: 1) ROUTINE STAFF SUPPORT AND
    INFORMATION; 2) CRISIS MANAGEMENT; 3) POLICY DEVELOPMENT; 4
    POLICY IMPLEMENTATION; 5) POLICY ADVICE; AND 6) OPERATIONS.
    THEN, MANAGING NATIONAL SECURITY: FROM ROOSEVELT TO CARTER
    IS STUDIED. MUCH SPACE IS GIVEN TO THE NSC UNDER THE REAGAN
    ADMINISTRATION.

05732 LORD, C.
    CHAPTER 4: RETHINKING THE NSC ROLE; THE PRESIDENCY AND
    MANAGEMENT OF NATIONAL SECURITY
    FREE PRESS, NEW YORK, NY, 1988, 85-114.
        THIS CHAPTER EXPLORES THE QUESTION, "HOW SHOULD THE
    PRESIDENT EMPLOY THE NSC AND THE NSC SYSTEM?" SIX TYPES OF
    STRATEGIC PLANNING ARE IDENTIFIED FOR THE PURPOSE OF THIS
    ANALYSIS: 1) STRATEGIC INTELLIGENCE; 2) NET ASSESSMENT; 3)
    LONG-TERM PLANNING; 4) SHORT-TERM PLANNING; 5) RESOURCE
    ALLOCATION; AND 6) CRISIS PLANNING. POLICY DEVELOPMENT AND
    IMPLEMENTATION AS WELL AS OPERATIONS ARE STUDIED.
    OPERATIONAL ACTIVITIES ARE CHARACTERIZED IN THE FOLLOWING
    TERMS: 1) ROUTINE STAFF SUPPORT AND INFORMATION; 2)
    PERSONNEL MANAGEMENT; 3) SPEECH WRITING; 4) PERSONAL
    REPRESENTATION AND NEGOTIATION 5) STAFF SUPPORT FOR
    DIPLOMATIC REQUIREMENTS; 6) STAFF SUPPORT FOR MILITARY
    REQUIREMENTS; AND 7) CRISIS MANAGEMENT.

05733 LORD, C.
    CHAPTER 5: THE NSC AS AN ORGANIZATION; THE PRESIDENCY AND
    MANAGEMENT OF NATIONAL SECURITY
    FREE PRESS, NEW YORK, NY, 1988, 115-146.

THIS CHAPTER CLARIFIES THE ROLES AND MISSIONS THAT ARE ESSENTIAL FOR THE NSC TO PERFORM EFFECTIVELY. STAFFING FOR THE NSC IS CONSIDERED AND ITS ORGANIZATION IS EXPLORED IN REFERENCE TO: PLANNING, POLITICAL AFFAIRS, DEFENSE POLICY, POLITICAL-MILITARY AFFAIRS, ARMS CONTROL, ECONOMIC, SCIENTIFIC, AND TECHNOLOGICAL AFFAIRS AND INTELLIGENCE, PROCEDURES AND RELATIONSHIPS ARE EXAMINED.

05734 LORD, C.
CHAPTER 6: NATIONAL SECURITY AND PRESIDENTIAL GOVERNANCE; THE PRESIDENCY AND MANAGEMENT OF NATIONAL SECURITY
FREE PRESS, NEW YORK, NY, 1988, 147-176.
THIS CHAPTER CONCLUDES THE PRINCIPLE LINES OF ARGUEMENT IN THIS STUDY: THAT -PRESIDENTIAL MANAGEMENT OF NATIONAL SECURITY AFFAIRS CAN AND SHOULD BE STRENGTHENED BY A VARIETY OF INSTITUTIONAL MEANS. IT EXAMINES THE NSC AND THE INTERAGENCY SYSTEMS, COORDINATION AT THE OPERATIONAL LEVEL AND AGENCY ORGANIZATION AND CULTURE.

05735 LORD, C.
THE PRESIDENCY AND THE MANAGEMENT OF NATIONAL SECURITY
FREE PRESS, NEW YORK, NY, 1988, 198.
THIS BOOK EXAMINES THE MANAGEMENT OF NATIONAL SECURITY IN THE UNITED STATES AND TRACES THE HISTORY OF THN NSC ITSELF - ITS STAFF, AND ITS POLICY MAKING PROCESS FROM ITS CREATION IN THE IMMEDIATE POSTWAR PERIOD TO TODAY, SHOWING HOW IT HAS BEEN USED AND ABUSED BY EIGHT PRESIDENTIAL ADMINISTRATIONS. REVEALED IS HOW THE NSC STAFF AND SYSTEM HAS YET TO FULFILL THE PROMISE OF ITS EARLY YEARS TO PROVIDE A MECHANISM FOR THE DEVELOPMENT AND IMPLEMENTATION OF NATIONAL STRATEGY. IT SETS FORTH SUGGESTIONS FOR IMPROVING NSC'S OPERATIONS - RECOMMENDATIONS AFFECTING ITS INTERNAL ORGANIZATION, STAFFING, PROCEDURES, AND ITS EXTERNAL RELATIONS TO BOTH THE WHITE HOUSE AND THE CONGRESS. IT PROPOSES A REVAMPING OF THE SYSTEM AND EXPLORES THE IMPLICATIONS OF A STRENGTHENED NSC FOR THE PRESIDENT'S RELATIONS WITH HIS SENIOR CABINET OFFICIALS AN THE BUREAUCRACY AS A WHOLE.

05736 LORD, S. M.
SOVIET/VIETNAM RELATIONS, 1969 TO 1978
DISSERTATION ABSTRACTS INTERNATIONAL, 49(8) (FEB 89), 2382-A.
VIETNAM OCCUPIES AN AMBIGUOUS POSITION IN RELATION TO THE SOVIET UNION, CONFORMING NEITHER TO THE STATUS OF AN EASTERN BLOC STATE NOR TO THAT OF A DEVELOPING COUNTRY. MOREOVER, THE CLIENT-PATRON RELATIONSHIP HAS OFTEN BEEN REVERSED. THE SUBSTANTIAL POWER THE VIETNAMESE HAVE BEEN ABLE TO EXERT AT ANY GIVEN TIME SUGGESTS AN INTERPRETATION IN TERMS OF MUTUAL ADVANTAGE.

05737 LORD, W.
CHINA AND AMERICA: BEYOND THE BIG CHILL
FOREIGN AFFAIRS, 68(4) (FAL 89), 1-26.
IN THE RELATIVELY NEAR FUTURE, THERE WILL ONCE AGAIN BE A CHINESE REGIME COMPOSED OF LEADERS WITH WHOM THE USA CAN RESUME THE FORWARD MARCH OF SINO-AMERICAN RELATIONS. MEANWHILE, IT IS TO PRESIDENT BUSH'S CREDIT THAT HE IS SEEKING TO KEEP THE UNITED STATES' LONGER-TERM INTERESTS IN VIEW EVEN AS THE USA REGISTERS ITS REVULSION AT THE PRESENT STATE OF AFFAIRS IN COMMUNIST CHINA.

05738 LORRAIN, P.
JE ME SOUVIENS-QUEBEC: A VOYAGE INTO TWO CULTURES JOINED ON THE BANKS OF A GREAT RIVER
PARLIAMENTARIAN, 70(1) (JAN 89), 15-20.
THE AUTHOR TRACES THE DEVELOPMENT OF QUEBEC PARLIAMENT AS WELL AS THE LEGISLATIVE ASSEMBLY OF LOWER CANADA, BEGINNING WITH THE TRANSITION FROM THE LEGISLATIVE ASSEMBLY TO THE NATIONAL ASSEMBLY, AFTER WHICH QUEBEC EXPERIENCED SIX CONSTITUTIONAL REGIMES. PERIODS WHICH PRECEDED PARLIAMENT ARE ALSO SUMMARIZED ABSOLUTE MONARCHY OF THE FRENCH EMPIRE, PRIOR TO 1760, THE ROYAL PROCLAMATION OF THE REPLACEMENT BY THE BRITISH CROWN IN 1763, THE QUEBEC ACT, WHICH RECOGNIZED FRENCH INFLUENCE IN 1774, INTO THE CONSTITUTION ACT, WHICH SAW THE BEGINNINGS OF THE PARLIAMENTARY SYSTEM. THE ACT OF UNION OF 1840, WHICH ESTABLISHED MINISTERIAL RESPONSIBILITY AND THE CONFEDERATION OF QUEBEC IN 1867 WHICH PLACED QUEBEC IN A FEDERAL REGIME ARE ALSO DISCUSSED.

05739 LOSS, R.
THE POLITICAL THOUGHT OF PRESIDENT GEORGE WASHINGTON
PRESIDENTIAL STUDIES QUARTERLY, XIX(3) (SUM 89), 471-490.
THE AUTHOR'S THESIS IS THAT WASHINGTON'S POLITICAL THOUGHT MIXES CLASSICAL AND MODERN REPUBLICANISM. THE CLASSICAL ELEMENT IS INEGALITARIAN VIRTUE AND THE MOLDING OF POTENTIAL STATESMEN BY LIBERAL EDUCATION. THE MODERN ELEMENTS OF WASHINGTON'S REPUBLICANISM INCLUDE LIBERTY, EQUALITY, POPULAR SOVEREIGNTY AND MAJORITY RULE. THE AUTHOR FURTHER CONTENDS THAT WASHINGTON'S POLITICAL THOUGHT, THOUGH NOT STRICTLY POLITICAL PHILOSOPHY, IS STILL WORTHY OF ATTENTION. WASHINGTON DISTINCTLY BLENDED ELEMENTS OF CLASSICAL AND MODERN REPUBLICANISM AROUND THE IDEA OF A NATIONAL UNIVERSITY, AND THIS CONSTITUTES ON THE STATESMAN'S LEVEL A PROVOCATIVE CRITICISM OF THE MAINSTREAM SOLUTION TO THE POLITICAL PROBLEM IN THE FEDERALIST. WASHINGTON'S THOUGHT ON POLITICAL EDUCATION IS BETTER CONCEIVED THAN THE EDUCATIONAL THOUGHT OF HIS MORE RESPECTED CONTEMPORARIES, HAMILTON AND JEFFERSON. THIS ESSAY CALLS FOR A REAPPRAISAL OF WASHINGTON'S THOUGHT WHILE WARNING AGAINST UNDERSTANDING IT AS "THE CAUSE OF EVERYTHING" IN THE AMERICAN REGIME.

05740 LOTAN, Y.
WHAT KIND OF PEACE?
NEW OUTLOOK, 32(5 (291)) (MAY 89), 27-29.
NOBODY BELIEVES THE PRESENT STATE OF AFFAIRS IN THE MIDEAST CAN GO ON MUCH LONGER. THERE ARE MANY INDICATIONS THAT 1989 WILL SEE A TURNING-POINT IN THE ISRAELI-PALESTINIAN CONFLICT. UNFORTUNATELY, EVEN THE PEACE CAMP IN ISREAL IS UNCLEAR ABOUT THE KIND OF PEACE IT DESIRES.

05741 LOTT, J.; REED, W.
SHIRKING AND SORTING IN A POLITICAL MARKET WITH FINITE-LIVED POLITICIANS
PUBLIC CHOICE, 61(1) (APR 89), 75-96.
ABSTRACT. THIS PAPER ANALYZES PRINCIPAL-AGENT SLACK IN THE CONTEXT OF A POLITICAL MARKET COMPOSED OF VOTERS, CHALLENGERS, AND INCUMBENTS. THE INTRODUCTION OF A LAST PERIOD (VIA FINITE-LIVEDNESS) IN COMBINATION WITH VOTERS' IMPERFECT INFORMATION ABOUT POLITICIANS' PREFERENCES CAUSES TIME-VARYING SHIRKING BEHAVIOR ON THE PART OF POLITICIANS. POLITICAL MARKETS EVENTUALLY SORT OUT THOSE POLITICIANS WITH SIGNIFICANTLY DEVIANT POLICY PREFERENCES, POTENTIALLY PROVIDING A SOLUTION TO THE LAST PERIOD PROBLEM AND ENABLING POLITICIANS TO MAKE CREDIBLE COMMITMENTS. IN THE EXTREME, SORTING CAN INSURE THAT IT IS NOT WORTHWHILE FOR POTENTIAL SHIRKERS TO RUN FOR OFFICE. A SYSTEMATIC RELATIONSHIP BETWEEN POLITICAL SHIRKING AND NUMBER OF TERMS IN OFFICE MAY EXIST, AND DEPENDS ON HOW QUICKLY SORTING TAKES PLACE. THE EVIDENCE OF LITTLE IF ANY SHIRKING IS QUITE CONSISTENT WITH POLITICIANS HAVING DIVERSE AND STRONGLY HELD POLICY PREFERENCES.

05742 LOTT, J., R., JR.; REYNOLDS, M.O.
PRODUCTION COSTS AND DEREGULATION
PUBLIC CHOICE, 61(2) (MAY 89), 183-186.
THE ARTICLE STUDIES SOME OF THE RECENT THEORY AND RESEARCH ON DEREGULATION AND CONCLUDES THAT EITHER (1) REGULATION LOWERS PRODUCTION COSTS AND MAKES THE GAINS TO DEREGULATION RELATIVELY SMALL OR (2) REGULATION INCREASES PRODUCTION COSTS AND MAKES THE SOCIAL AND POLITICAL GAINS TO DEREGULATION RELATIVELY GREATER. WHILE SOME MAY NOT FIND ALTERNATIVE (1) CREDIBLE, ONE THING IS CLEAR: CLAIMING THAT THE DEREGULATORY GAINS ARE SMALL BECAUSE REGULATION INCREASES COSTS IS NOT AN ALTERNATIVE SOCIETY FACES.

05743 LOTT, J.R. JR.
RACIAL EMPLOYMENT AND EARNINGS DIFFERENTIALS: THE IMPACT OF THE REAGAN ADMINISTRATION--COMMENT
REVIEW OF BLACK POLITICAL ECONOMY, 17(4) (SPR 89), 83-84.
CHARLES REGISTER HAS CONCLUDED THAT "IN TERMS OF EMPLOYMENT SUCCESS, IT APPEARS THAT MR. REAGAN'S ELECTION HAS BEEN ASSOCIATED WITH A SIGNIFICANT WEAKENING IN THE POSITION OF BLACKS RELATIVE TO WHITES IN THE NEAR TERM." GIVEN THE CONTROVERSY OVER HOW BLACKS FARED UNDER THE REAGAN ADMINISTRATION, THE GENERAL QUESTION RAISED BY REGISTER IS OF INTEREST, BUT THE EMPIRICAL DATA HE PRESENTS DOES NOT JUSTIFY HIS CONCLUSION.

05744 LOVE, J.L.
MODELING INTERNAL COLONIALISM: HISTORY AND PROSPECT
WORLD DEVELOPMENT, 17(6) (JUN 89), 905-922.
THE STUDY CONSIDERS THE HISTORY OF THE CONCEPT OF INTERNAL COLONIALISM, SHOWS HOW IT HAS BEEN USED IN DIFFERENT IDEOLOGICAL TRADITIONS, AND OFFERS A DEFINITION BASED ON ECONOMIC RATHER THAN ETHNIC PROCESSES. IT COMPARES TWO EARLY QUANTITATIVE MODELS, THAT OF MIHAIL MANOILESCU FOR RUMANIA AND THAT OF CELSO FURTADO AND HANS SINGER FOR BRAZIL, RELATING THEM TO PREVIOUSLYEXISTING INTERNATIONAL TRADE THEORIES. IT CONCLUDES WITH THE SPECULATION THAT RECENT ECONOMETRIC EVIDENCE OF A DETERIORATION OF PRIMARY COMMODITIES' TERMS OF TRADE OVER THE LONG TERM HAS IMPLICATIONS FOR THE INTERNAL COLONIAL CONCEPT, AND NOT ONLY FOR STATES WITH A "CULTURAL DIVISION OF LABOR."

05745 LOVEJOY, D.C. JR.
UNCERTAIN OPENING: THE CATHOLIC CHURCH AND CHINA IN THE CONTEMPORARY INTERNATIONAL ORDER
DISSERTATION ABSTRACTS INTERNATIONAL, 50(4) (OCT 89), 1083-A.
THIS STUDY EXAMINES THE CONTEMPORARY RELATIONSHIP BETWEEN THE ROMAN CATHOLIC CHURCH AND THE GOVERNMENT OF THE PEOPLE'S REPUBLIC OF CHINA (PRC) WITHIN THE PERSPECTIVE OF INTERNATIONAL RELATIONS THEORY. IT IS THE THESIS OF THIS STUDY THAT CHINA'S CURRENT POLICY OF RELIGIOUS TOLERATION IS A NECESSARY RESPONSE TO THE STRATEGIC NEED TO PARTICIPATE IN THE CONTEMPORARY INTERNATIONAL MARKET SYSTEM.

05746 LOVENDUSKI, J.; NORRIS, P.
    SELECTING WOMEN CANDIDATES: OBSTACLES TO THE FEMINISATTION
    OF THE HOUSE OF COMMONS
EUROPEAN JOURNAL OF POLITICAL RESEARCH, 17(5) (SEP 89),
533-562.
    DESPITE CONCERN BY THEE MAJOR BRITISH POLITICAL PARTIES
TO INCREASE THE NUMBER OF WOMEN AT WESTMINISTER, PROGRESS
HAS BEEN SLOW, YIELDING ONLY JUST OVER 5 PER CENT OF WOMEN
MPS. THIS ARTICLE PRESENTS THE RESULTS OF AN INVESTIGATION
OF PARTY SELECTION PROCEDURES DESIGNED TO DETERMINE WHETHER
SELECTION PRACTICES WERE THEMSELVES THE EXPLANATION FOR THE
POOR SHOWING OF WOMEN. THE STUDY CONSISTED OF INTERVIEWS
WITH PARTY OFFICIALS AND A SURVEY OF THE CANDIDATES IN THE
1987 GENERAL ELECTION. IT WAS FOUND THAT SELECTION
PROCEDURES WERE IN A PROCESS OF CHANGE WHICH INCLUDED
EFFORTS BY CENTRAL LEADERSHIPS TO PROMOTE WOMEN'S
CANDIDACIES. BUT LOCAL SELECTORATES WERE NOT ALWAYS
COOPERATIVE. ALTHOUGH WOMEN DID NOT APPEAR TO BE SELECTED IN
THE PROPORTIONS IN WHICH THEY WERE COMING FORWARD, NO
EVIDENCE OF DIRECT DISCRIMINATION AGAINST ASPIRANT WOMEN
CANDIDATES WAS FOUND. BUT INDIRECT DISCRIMINATION MAY HAVE
TAKEN PLACE. BOTH THE WAY IN WHICH THE ROLE OF A CANDIDATES
IS DEFINED AND THE QUALITIES SELECTORATES SEEK PRODUCE IDEA
CANDIDATE PROFILES WHICH MAY PENALISE MANY WOMEN. THE
ARTICLE CONCLUDES THAT IF WOMEN ARE TO BE BETTER REPRESENTED
AT WESTMINISTER, PARTIES MUST GO BEYOND PROCEDURAL CHANGE
AND THE INTRODUCTION OF POSITIVE ACTION TO A RECONSIDERATION
OF THE CRITERIA FOR CHOOSING CANDIDATES.

05747 LOWE, G.; KRAHN, H.
    COMPUTER SKILLS AND USE AMONG HIGH SCHOOL AND UNIVERSITY
    GRADUATES
CANADIAN PUBLIC POLICY--ANALYSE DE POLITIQUES, XV(2) (JUN
89), 175-188.
    IN ORDER TO BETTER UNDERSTAND THE ADVANCE OF THE
MICROELECTRONICS REVOLUTION IN CANADA, THE ARTICLE EXAMINES
THE EXTENT OF COMPUTER TRAINING, SKILLS, AND ON-THE-JOB
COMPUTER USE REPORTED BY A SAMPLE OF 1985 HIGH SCHOOL AND
UNIVERSITY GRADUATES. THE ARTICLE FINDS THAT ON-THE-JOB
COMPUTER USE IS QUITE EXTENSIVE, BUT TENDS TO BE
CONCENTRATED IN ROUTINE TASKS SUCH AS DATA ENTRY AND WORD
PROCESSING. THE ARTICLE ALSO FOUND STRIKING GENDER
DIFFERENCES IN COMPUTER SKILLS AND USAGE WHICH REFLECT THE
SEGREGATION OF MEN AND WOMEN INTO DIFFERENT EDUCATIONAL
PROGRAMS AND OCCUPATIONS.

05748 LOWE, R.
    HAVE STAFFER, WILL TRAVEL
CAMPAIGNS AND ELECTIONS, 10(2) (AUG 89), 13.
    PARTICIPATION 2000, A POLITICAL ACTION COMMITTEE BASED
IN COLUMBUS, OHIO, CONTRIBUTES PERSONNEL INSTEAD OF MONEY TO
POLITICAL CAMPAIGNS. THE GROUP'S STAFF INTERNSHIP PROGRAM IS
DESIGNED TO PROVIDE HELP TO PROGRESSIVE DEMOCRATIC
CANDIDATES WHILE GIVING YOUNG ACTIVISTS ON-THE-JOB TRAINING
IN THE NITTY GRITTY OF RUNNING CAMPAIGNS.

05749 LOWERY, D.; GRAY, V.; HAGER, G.
    PUBLIC OPINION AND POLICY CHANGE IN THE UNITED STATES
AMERICAN POLITICS QUARTERLY, 17(1) (JAN 89), 3-31.
    THIS ARTICLE EXPLORES THE RELATIONSHIP BETWEEN PUBLIC
OPINION AND NONINCREMENTAL POLICY CHANGE BY EXTENDING THE
ANALYSIS OF WRIGHT ET AL. (1985, 1987). THE AUTHORS DEVELOP
A TWO-STEP MODEL IN WHICH THEY FIRST RELATE THE LEVEL OF A
RELEVANT OUTCOME MEASURE OF A POLICY TO THE DEGREE OF
OPINION LIBERALISM, THE STRATEGY OF WRIGHT AND HIS
COLLEAGUES. THEN THEY POSIT THAT POLICY SHOCKS WILL MOVE THE
POLICY SYSTEM INTO GREATER POLICY-OPINION CONGRUENCE. THE
MODEL IS TESTED FOR TWO POLICY AREAS THAT HAVE UNDERGONE
NONINCREMENTAL CHANGE OVER THE LATE 1970S AND EARLY 1980S:
TAX POLICY AND EDUCATION POLICY.

05750 LOWERY, D.; LYONS, W.E.
    THE IMPACT OF JURISDICTIONAL BOUNDARIES: AN INDIVIDUAL-
    LEVEL TEST OF THE TIEBOUT MODEL
THE JOURNAL OF POLITICS, 51(1) (FEB 89), 73-97.
    DESPITE THE CONSIDERABLE RESEARCH ATTENTION ACCORDED THE
TIEBOUT MODEL, ITS EMPIRICAL FOUNDATIONS ARE NOT ESPECIALLY
WELL DEVELOPED. THAT IS, EXISTING EMPIRICAL INVESTIGATIONS
OF THE TIEBOUT MODEL ONLY INDIRECTLY ADDRESS MANY OF ITS
CENTRAL ASSUMPTIONS, GIVEN THEIR NEARLY EXCLUSIVE FOCUS ON
AGGREGATE-LEVEL ANALYSES WHEN THE MODEL EVALUATES
INSTITUTIONAL ARRANGEMENTS ON THE BASIS OF A NUMBER OF
ASSUMPTIONS ABOUT INDIVIDUAL ATTITUDES AND BEHAVIORS. THIS
PAPER TAKES ONE STEP TOWARD IMPROVING THIS SITUATION BY
EXAMINING SURVEY DATA ON INDIVIDUAL POLITICAL BEHAVIOR UNDER
TWO POLAR CASES OF INSTITUTIONAL ARRANGEMENT WITHIN
METROPOLITAN AREAS. BY COMPARING THE RESPONSES OF FIVE
LOUISVILLE-AREA CITIES WITH THOSE OF THEIR MATCHED LEXINGTON
NEIGHBORHOODS, THE AUTHORS DIRECTLY ASSESS THE IMPACTS OF
JURISDICTIONAL ARRANGEMENTS ON A NUMBER OF ATTITUDES AND
BEHAVIORS THAT UNDERLIE THE TIEBOUT MODEL.

05751 LOWRY, W.R.
    FEDERALISM AND POLLUTION POLICIES

DISSERTATION ABSTRACTS INTERNATIONAL, 49(9) (MAR 89),
2796-A.
    THE AUTHOR COMPARES THE BEHAVIOR OF STATE GOVERNMENTS IN
THE IMPLEMENTATION OF AIR AND WATER POLLUTION CONTROL
POLICIES OVER THE LAST TWO DECADES. HE CONSIDERS HOW THE
FEDERAL STRUCTURE AFFECTS SYSTEM RESPONSIVENESS TO POLICY
DEMANDS.

05752 LOWTHER, W.; LEWIS, P.
    THE RIGHTS OF THE STATES
MACLEAN'S (CANADA'S NEWS MAGAZINE), 102(30) (JUL 89), 21.
    ABORTION HAS ENGENDERED CONTROVERSY IN THE US SINCE
CONNECTICUT FIRST OUTLAWED THE PRACTICE IN 1821. BUT A
SUPREME COURT DECISION ON JULY 3, STRENGTHENING THE RIGHT OF
STATES TO RESTRICT ABORTION, HAS BREATHED FRESH VIGOR INTO
THE DEBATE. THE BATTLE OVER ABORTION RIGHTS HAS BEEN CALLED
"AMERICA'S NEW VIETNAM" AND HAS PROVED INCREASINGLY DIVISIVE.
THE ULTIMATE OUTCOME OF THE BATTLE IS UNLIKELY TO BE
RESOLVED WITHOUT HIGH EMOTION.

05753 LOWY, M.
    THE POETRY OF THE PAST: MARX AND THE FRENCH REVOLUTION
NEW LEFT REVIEW, (177) (SEP 89), 111-124.
    THE AUTHOR TRACES THE IMPACT OF THE FRENCH REVOLUTION ON
THE THINKING OF KARL MARX AND ARGUES THAT THE REVOLUTION
CONTINUES TO HAVE A RELEVANCE FOR THE SOCIALIST MOVEMENT IN
WAYS PARTIALLY UNFORESEEN BY THE FOUNDERS OF HISTORICAL
MATERIALISM.

05754 LOYACONO, L.
    READY WITH WELFARE REFORM
STATE LEGISLATURES, 15(8) (SEP 89), 21-23.
    FIFTEEN STATES HAVE COMPLETED THEIR PLANS TO MEET
FEDERAL REQUIREMENTS FOR OVERHAULING THEIR WELFARE SYSTEMS,
CASHING IN ON $126 MILLION IN 1989 FEDERAL FUNDS. BUT
UNCERTAINTY ABOUT THE FINAL REGULATIONS AND FUTURE FUNDING
CLOUDS PROGRAMS IN OTHER STATES.

05755 LUBIN, N.
    UZBEKISTAN: THE CHALLENGES AHEAD
MIDDLE EAST JOURNAL, 43(4) (FAL 89), 619-634.
    THIS ARTICLE LOOKS AT A BROAD SPECTRUM OF CONCERNS IN
UZBEKISTAN, THE LARGEST AND MOST POPULOUS CENTRAL ASIAN
REPUBLIC. IT EXPLORES THE CATASTROPHIC DEVASTATION OF THE
ENVIRONMENT, LARGELY ATTRIBUTABLE TO THE IMPOSITION BY
MOSCOW OF A COTTON MONOCULTURE - AND ITS DOCUMENTED IMPACT
ON THE HEALTH AND LIFE EXPECTANCY OF THE PEOPLE LIVING THERE.

05756 LUBIN, P.
    HOW TO DISMANTLE COMMUNISM
NATIONAL REVIEW, 61(23) (DEC 89), 29-33.
    THIS ARTICLE IS AN INTERVIEW WITH 'EMIGRE' SOVIET
ECONOMIST, IGOR BIRMAN, WHOSE PAST PREDICTIONS ABOUT THE
SOVIET ECONOMY HAVE BEEN ACCURATE. IT EXAMINES THE CATCHZZ
THAT MIKHAIL GORBACHEV FINDS HIMSELF IN: HOW TO FREE THE
ENERGIES OF THE SOVIET ECONOMY WITHOUT FREEING THE PEOPLE,
AND HOW TO FREE THE PEOPLE WITHOUT GIVING UP POWER. THE
IDEOLOGICAL STRUGGLES INVOLVED ARE ADDRESSED.

05757 LUCAITES, J.L.; CHARLAND, M.
    THE LEGACY OF (LIBERTY): RHETORIC, IDEOLOGY, AND ASTHETICS
    IN THE POSTMODERN CONDITION
CANADIAN JOURNAL OF POLITICAL AND SOCIAL THEORY, 13(3)
(1989), 31-48.
    THE CONCERN IN THIS STUDY IS WITH (LIBERTY).
SPECIFICALLY, THE CONCERN IS WITH THE WAY IN WHICH THE
CONTEMPORARY IDEOLOGICAL RAISON D ETRE OF THE UNITED STATES
OF AMERICA IS LOCATED (LIBERTY) AS AN AESTHETIC OBJECT THAT
IS DETACHED FROM THE ACTUAL EXPERIENCE OF PUBLIC LIFE. TO
THAT END, IT PROBES THE 1986, NATIONALLY TELEVISED
CELEBRATION OF THE STATUTE OF LIBERTY'S CENTENNIAL AS A
MEANS OF IDENTFYING THE WAY(S) IN WHICH AESTHETIC VALUE IS
INSERTED INTO THE TERMS OF IDEOLOGICAL, REASON-GIVING
DISCOURSE.

05758 LUCAS, M.; EDGAR, A.
    GERMANY AFTER THE WALL
WORLD POLICY JOURNAL, (WIN 89), 189-214.
    THIS ARTICLE CONSISTS OF AN INTRODUCTION AND THEN
INTERVIEWS ABOUT GERMANY AFTER THE WALL, IT EXPLORES THE
CALLED-INTO-QUESTIONS ABOUT THE MOST FUNDAMENTAL FEATURES OF
THE POSTWAR EUROPEAN ORDER. IT ALSO EXAMINES THE ANXIETY
THAT THE REST OF THE WORLD HAS ABOUT THE POSSIBILITY OF THE
EUROPEAN BALANCE OF POWERS BEING UPSET, THE INTERVIEWS WERE
CONDUCTED AT THE INTERNATIONAL EAST-WEST WORKSHOP ON COMMON
SECURITY HELD IN DECEMBER IN FIVE CITIES IN THE FEDERAL
REPUBLIC OF GERMANY AND THE GERMAN DEMOCRATIC REPUBLIC.
INTERVIEWED ARE: BARBEL BOHLEY, HAROLD LANGE, KARSTEN VOIGHT
AND YURI DAVIDOV.

05759 LUCKEY, J.
    FLAG DESECRATION AND THE FIRST AMENDMENT
CRS REVEIW, 10(8) (SEP 89), 12-13.
    THE SUPREME COURT DECISION STRIKING DOWN A STATE LAW

CRIMINALIZING FLAG BURNING ON FIRST AMENDMENT GROUNDS SET
OFF PROTESTS IN MANY QUARTERS AND WAS ONE OF THE MOST
CONTROVERSIAL OPINIONS OF THE 1989 TERM. THE RULING PROMPTED
CALLS FOR A CONSTITUTIONAL AMENDMENT AND OTHER LEGISLATIVE
REMEDIES TO OVERCOME THE EFFECTS OF THE DECISION.

05760 LUCORE, R.E.
AMERICAN EXCEPTIONALISM AND THE ECONOMIC ROLE OF THE
PUBLIC SECTOR: CANADA AND THE US COMPARED
INTERNATIONAL JOURNAL OF SOCIAL ECONOMICS, 16(3) (1989),
34-43.
THE AMERICAN PUBLIC EXHIBITS AN EXCEPTIONALLY STRONG
BIAS AGAINST PUBLIC SECTOR ACTIVITY IN THE ECONOMY. WHY THIS
IS SO IS INVESTIGATED BY APPLYING THE TRADITIONAL LITERATURE
ON "AMERICAN EXCEPTIONALISM" AND THE COMPARATIVE METHOD. A
DEFENCE OF AN ACTIVE ROLE FOR GOVERNMENT IN THE ECONOMY IS
DEVELOPED, BASED ON SOCIAL AND INSTITUTIONAL ECONOMICS. THE
TRADITIONAL EXPLANATIONS FOR AMERICAN EXCEPTIONALISM GIVEN
BY SOMBART, COMMONS AND PERLMAN ARE OUTLINED. A COMPARISON
OF THE CANADIAN AND US POLITICOECONOMIC CULTURES IS EMPLOYED
AS A MEANS FOR EVALUATING THE VALIDITY OF THE ARGUMENTS IN
THE TRADITIONAL EXCEPTIONALIST LITERATURE. ALTHOUGH THOSE
INVESTIGATING AMERICAN EXCEPTIONALISM HAVE OFTEN COMPARED
THE US WITH EUROPE, IT IS ARGUED THAT CANADA MAKES A BETTER
SUBJECT FOR COMPARISON WITH THE US. THIS IS BECAUSE THE TWO
COUNTRIES ARE VERY SIMILAR, YET EXHIBIT DIFFERENT ATTITUDES
TOWARD THE PUBLIC SECTOR.

05761 LUDGIN, M.K.
THE POLITICS OR URBAN REDEVELOPMENT IN BOSTON, CHICAGO,
SAN FRANCISCO, AND DENVER: THE STRUCTURE OF THE
PUBLIC/PRIVATE PARTNERSHIP
DISSERTATION ABSTRACTS INTERNATIONAL, 49(11) (MAY 89),
3493-A.
DURING THE LATE 1970'S AND EARLY 1980'S, LOCAL URBAN
POLICY REGARDING REDEVELOPMENT BEGAN TO CHANGE. CITIES THAT
HAD ONCE ACTIVELY SOUGHT PRIVATE SECTOR INVESTMENT IN THEIR
CENTRAL BUSINESS DISTRICTS SHIFTED THEIR POSTURE. NEW
POLICIES REFLECTED CONCERN WITH MAXIMIZING PUBLIC AMENITIES
WHILE MINIMIZING PUBLIC COSTS. IN SOME CASES, CITIES WENT
EVEN FURTHER, PLACING RESTRICTIONS ON DEVELOPMENT AND
ADOPTING VIRTUAL NO-GROWTH POSITIONS.

05762 LUDLOW, P.M.
THE FUTURE OF THE INTERNATIONAL TRADING SYSTEM
WASHINGTON QUARTERLY, 12(4) (FAL 89), 157-171.
ANY DISCUSSION OF THE FUTURE OF THE INTERNATIONAL
TRADING SYSTEM MUST SOONER OR LATER DEAL WITH A PARADOX.
INTERNATIONAL TRADE CONTINUES TO GROW AT RATES THAT ARE BOTH
SUPRISING AND COMFORTING. AT THE SAME TIME, HOWEVER, MANY
INSIDERS OR WELL-INFORMED OBSERVERS BELIEVE THAT THE SYSTEM
IS UNDER THREAT, THAT THE DAYS OF NONDISCRIMINATORY FREE
TRADE ARE ALREADY PAST, AND THAT THE WORLD IS MOVING
INEXORABLY TOWARD AN ERA OF PROTECTIONISM, MANAGED TRADE,
AND REGIONAL BLOCS. THIS ARTICLE ATTEMPTS TO EXPLAIN THIS
PESSIMISM IN THE MIDST OF PLENTY, PARTICULARY WHEN STRONG
EVIDENCE SUPPORTS BOTH PESSIMISTS AND OPTIMISTS, IT
DESCRIBES A NEW INTERNATIONAL POLITICAL ECONOMY AND THE
CHARACTER OF THE NEW ORDER. THE SUCCESSFUL CONCLUSION OF THE
URUGUAY ROUND IS EXAMINED, AS WELL AS THE DEVELOPMENT OF
REGIONAL AND BILATERAL INITIATIVES, POLITICAL COOPERATION IN
THE WEST IS PROPOSED.

05763 LUGALLA, J.
PROSPECTS AND PROBLEMS OF REGIONAL COOPERATION IN AFRICA:
A CASE STUDY OF SADCC
SCANDINAVIAN JOURNAL OF DEVELOPMENT ALTERNATIVES, VIII(1)
(MAR 89), 101-116.
THE PAPER EXAMINES THE PROSPECTS AND PROBLEMS
CONFRONTING THE SOUTHERN AFRICAN DEVELOPMENT COORDINATION
CONFERENCE (SADCC) ORGANIZATION IN GENERAL AND THE MEMBER
STATES IN PARTICULAR. THE GOAL OF THE SADCC IS TO WORK
HARMONIOUSLY TOWARDS INTEGRATING THEIR ECONOMIES AND
GRADUALLY REDUCE THEIR DEPENDENCE, PARTICULARLY BUT NOT ONLY,
ON THE REPUBLIC OF SOUTH AFRICA. ALTHOUGH THE SADCC REGION
HAS A VARIETY OF ECONOMIC POTENTIALS, IDEOLOGICAL
DIFFERENCES AND STRUCTURAL LINKAGE OF SOME OF THE SADCC
ECONOMIES TO THE REPUBLIC OF SOUTH AFRICA POSES SOME
SIGNIFICANT PROBLEMS AND DIFFICULTIES IN THE IMPLEMENTATION
OF SADCC OBJECTIVES.

05764 LUGER, S.
PRIVATE POWER, PUBLIC POLICY, AND THE U.S. AUTOMOBILE
INDUSTRY
DISSERTATION ABSTRACTS INTERNATIONAL, 50(5) (NOV 89),
1423-A.
THE AUTHOR STUDIES THE CHANGING NATURE OF CORPORATE
POLITICAL POWER IN THE USA. HE SURVEYS GOVERNMENT POLICY
TOWARD THE AUTOMOBILE INDUSTRY TO ANALYZE HOW A CONTRACTING
ECONOMY AFFECTS THE POLITICAL LEVERAGE OF CONTENDING GROUPS
OVER PUBLIC POLICY. HE HYPOTHESIZES THAT THE VULNERABILITY
OF PUBLIC OFFICIALS TO CORPORATE INTEREST GROUPS INCREASES
WITH RECESSIONARY CONDITIONS. THIS CAN LARGELY BE EXPLAINED
BY THE STRUCTURAL DEPENDENCE OF GOVERNMENT ON PRIVATE

CORPORATIONS FOR TAX REVENUE AND ECONOMIC GROWTH. WITH
ECONOMIC CONTRACTION, POLICY-MAKERS ARE ATTRACTED TO THOSE
OPTIONS THAT FAVOR BUSINESS, IN THE HOPE OF STIMULATING
ECONOMIC GROWTH.

05765 LUHAN, J.M.
HOW THE CHINESE RULE TIBET
DISSENT, (WIN 89), 21-23.
EVENTS LIKE THE MARCH 1989 JOKANG MASSACRE ARE SWALLOWED
UP IN THE SILENCE THAT HAS SHROUDED TIBET'S FATE SINCE ITS
OCCUPATION BY THE PLA IN 1950. NEARLY FOUR DECADES AFTER
SIGNING THE FATEFUL "SEVENTEEN-POINT AGREEMENT ON MEASURES
FOR THE PEACEFUL LIBERATION OF TIBET," THE COUNTRY IS CLOSE
TO EXTINCTION AS A MEANINGFUL DEMOGRAPHIC AND CULTURAL
ENTITY. FAR FROM BEING SAVED FROM IMPERIALISM BY THE CHINESE
OCCUPATION, TIBET TODAY LOOKS LIKE THE VICTIM OF A
LIQUIDATION SALE AFTER AN UNFRIENDLY CORPORATE TAKEOVER.
NEARLY HALF OF ITS TERRITORY HAS BEEN CARVED UP AND
INCORPORATED INTO CONTIGUOUS CHINESE PROVINCES.

05766 LUKACS, J.
THE COMING OF THE SECOND WORLD WAR
FOREIGN AFFAIRS, 68(4) (FAL 89), 165-174.
THE START OF BOTH WORLD WARS INVOLVED MISCALCULATIONS.
IN 1914, THESE MISCALCULATIONS AND THE RESPONSIBILITY FOR
DECLARING WAR WERE SHARED BY ALL THE EUROPEAN GOVERNMENT AND
THEIR GENERAL STAFFS, WITH THE POSSIBLE EXCEPTION OF BELGIUM.
IN 1939, THE MISCALCULATIONS THAT STARTED THE WAR WERE
THOSE OF A SINGLE LEADER, ADOLF HITLER.

05767 LUKANOV, A.
A NEW STAGE OF CMEA COOPERATION TO COME
WORLD MARXIST REVIEW, 32(1) (JAN 89), 3-10.
THE AUTHOR DISCUSSES EFFORTS TO RESTRUCTURE THE COUNCIL
FOR MUTUAL ECONOMIC ASSISTANCE, BULGARIAN PARTICIPATION IN
CMEA, AND CMEA COOPERATION WITH DEVELOPING COUNTRIES OUTSIDE
THE COMMUNITY.

05768 LUKE, T.W.
CLASS CONTRADICTIONS AND SOCIAL CLEAVAGES IN
INFORMATIONALIZING POST-INDUSTRIAL SOCIETIES: ON THE RISE
OF NEW SOCIAL MOVEMENTS
NEW POLITICAL SCIENCE, (FAL 89), 125-154.
THE AUTHOR ARGUES THAT NEW SOCIAL MOVEMENTS ARE AN
IMPORTANT FORM OF ORGANIZED BUT WEAK OPPOSITION IN
INFORMATIONALIZING POST-INDUSTRIAL SOCIETIES, WITH THEIR
"NEWNESS" FOLLOWING FROM CHALLENGES BEING MADE AGAINST THE
CULTURAL CODES THROUGH RESISTANCE TO THE INSTRUMENTAL
COLONIZATION OF THE EVERYDAY LIFEWORLD AND THROUGH THE
PRESENTATION OF ALTERNATIVE CODES OF BEHAVIOR. GROUPS WHICH
ARE GIVEN CONSIDERATION IN THIS ARGUMENT INCLUDE FEMINIST,
SANCTUARY, CIVIL RIGHTS, PEACE, ECOLOGY, ANTI-NUCLEAR, ANTI-
ABORTION, AND COMMUNITY POWER GROUPS; THE SPECTRUM INCLUDES
CONSERVATIVE AND LIBERAL MOVEMENTS CATEGORIES ARE CREATED
FOR UNDERSTANDING THE NEW SOCIAL MOVEMENTS ON A
DEVELOPMENTAL LEVEL.

05769 LUKE, T.W.
POLITICAL SCIENCE AND THE DISCOURSES OF POWER: DEVELOPING
A GENEALOGY OF THE POLITICAL CULTURE CONCEPT
HISTORY OF POLITICAL THOUGHT, X(1) (SPR 89), 125-149.
THE IMPACT OF THE WORKS OF MICHAEL FOUCALT ON POLITICAL
SCIENCE ESPECIALLY IN THE US HAS BEEN NEGLIGIBLE. THE PAPER
AIMS AT POSSIBLY BROADENING HIS APPEAL TO CONTEMPORARY
POLITICAL SCIENCE BY ILLUSTRATING THE WORTH OF FOUCAULT'S
THINKING FOR FORMULATING A REFLEXIVE UNDERSTANDING OF
POLITICS AND POLITICAL ANALYSIS. IN PARTICULAR, IT EXPLORES
HOW THE PROBLEMATIC NOTIONS OF "POLITICAL CULTURE" AND
"INDIVIDUAL SUBJECTIVITY" MIGHT BE UNDERSTOOD MORE
CRITICALLY IN LIGHT OF FOUCAULT'S STYLE OF INTERPRETIVE
ANALYSIS.

05770 LUKES, I.
GREAT EXPECTATIONS AND LOST ILLUSIONS: SOVIET USE OF
EASTERN EUROPEAN PROXIES IN THE THIRD WORLD
INTERNATIONAL JOURNAL OF INTELLIGENCE AND
COUNTER-INTELLIGENCE, 3(1) (SPR 89), 1-13.
A WEAK, INEFFICIENT SOVIET ECONOMY AND THE STRENGTH OF
THE SOVIET ARMED FORCES VIRTUALLY PRE-DETERMINE THE NATURE
OF MOSCOW'S BEHAVIOR TOWARD THE THIRD WORLD. SOVIET LEADERS
CANNOT DELIVER SIGNIFICANT TECHNOLOGY, FOOD SUPPLIES,
EXPERTISE, OR HARD-CURRENCY LOANS. CONSEQUENTLY, THEY HAVE A
VESTED INTEREST IN FOMENTING CONFLICTS, MAINTAINING THEM,
AND EXPLOTING THEM. BOTH DIRECTLY AND INDIRECTLY, THE SOVIET
UNION PROVIDES POLITICAL AND MILITARY ASSISTANCE TO ANTI-
WESTERN MOVEMENTS IN THE THIRD WORLD. THIS PAPER FOCUSES ON
HOW THE SOVIETS USE EASTERN EUROPEAN PROXIES TO FURTHER
THEIR AIMS IN THE THIRD WORLD.

05771 LUKIANOV, A.
OUR COURSE: DEMOCRACY, SELF-GOVERNMENT, RULE OF LAW
WORLD MARXIST REVIEW, 31(11) (NOV 88), 14-23.
THE 19TH ALL-UNION CONFERENCE OF THE CPSU GAVE A NEW AND
POWERFUL IMPETUS TO SOVIET POLITICS. THE CONFERENCE

DEMONSTRATED THAT THE POLICY OF RENEWAL, ADOPTED AT THE APRIL 1985 PLENARY MEETING OF THE CPSU CENTRAL COMMITTEE AND AT THE 27TH PARTY CONGRESS, HAD PROVED ITS VIABILITY. PERESTROIKA'S STRATEGY AND TACTICS WERE WORKED OUT, AS HAS ITS IDEOLOGICAL, THEORETICAL AND ORGANISATIONAL BASIS, SHAPED BY MARXISM-LENINISM AND THE PRESENT REALITIES OF OUR SOCIETY. A NEW POLITICAL, MORAL AND PSYCHOLOGICAL CLIMATE HAS DEVELOPED IN THE USSR. GLASNOST AND CONSTRUCTIVE CRITICISM HAVE OPENED THE WAY TO SOCIETY'S MORAL RECOVERY.

05772 LUKYANOV, A.
SOVIET PARLIAMENT TODAY AND TOMORROW
REPRINTS FROM THE SOVIET PRESS, 49(7) (OCT 89), 8-13.
THIS IS AN INTERVIEW WITH ANATOLY LUKYANOV. MR. LUKYANOV EVALUATES THE RESULTS OF THE WORK OF THE NEW SOVIET PARLIAMENT; THE EFFECTIVENESS OF THE ACTIVITY OF THE DEPUTIES COMMISSIONS SET UP DURING THE SESSION WHICH VISITED THE SITE OF INTER-ETHNIC CONTROVERSIES AND MINER'S STRIKES; THE ROLE THAT DEPUTIES PLAY IN PARLIAMENT'S ACTIVITIES; AND DESCRIBES THE ISSUES SCHEDULED FOR DISCUSSION AT THE AUTUMN SESSION.

05773 LULEK, A.F.; PAGA, L.A.
THE SPHERES OF INEQUALITY IN A CENTRALLY PLANNED ECONOMY: THE CASE OF POLAND
INTERNATIONAL JOURNAL OF SOCIAL ECONOMICS, 16(1) (1989), 27-39.
ANALYSIS OF SELECTED SEGMENTS OF THE POLISH ECONOMY REVEALS SEVERAL SPHERES OF INEQUALITY. SOME OF THEM, SUCH AS INEQUALITIES IN WAGES OR HOUSEHOLD ASSETS, ARE FOUND IN EVERY TYPE OF ECONOMY. HOWEVER, SOME INEQUALITIES ARE SPECIFIC TO A CENTRALLY PLANNED ECONOMY, FOR EXAMPLE, THOSE IN THE SPHERE OF DECISION MAKING AND THOSE RESULTING FROM A TWOFOLD ATTITUDE TOWARDS VARIOUS FORMS OF OWNERSHIP.

05774 LUNA, C.J.
A GENERAL THEORY OF TWENTIETH CENTURY POLITICAL REVOLUTION
DISSERTATION ABSTRACTS INTERNATIONAL, 50(6) (DEC 89), 1788-A.
THE AUTHOR TESTS A GENERAL THEORY OF MODERN POLITICAL REVOLUTION, DERIVED FROM MARX'S ANALYSIS OF SOCIAL STRUCTURE, AGAINST FOUR ACTUAL REVOLUTIONS: THE RUSSIAN, CUBAN, GUATEMALAN, AND IRANIAN. HIS MODEL HYPOTHESIZES THAT REVOLUTION IS A FUNCTION OF THE DEGREE OF CONTRADICTION (STABILITY) BETWEEN THE LEVELS OF REWARDS AND SANCTIONS DISTRIBUTED ACROSS THE SOCIETY BY THE IDEOLOGICAL, ECONOMIC, AND SOCIAL SUB-SYSTEMS. THE PROBABILITY OF A REVOLUTION OCCURRING IN A GIVEN SOCIETY VARIES AS ITS STABILITY VARIES.

05775 LUNDAHL, M.
APARTHEID: CUI BONO?
WORLD DEVELOPMENT, 17(6) (JUN 89), 825-837.
ECONOMIC EXPLANATIONS OF RACIAL DISCRIMINATION IN SOUTH AFRICA TEND TO FALL EITHER INTO THE "LIBERAL" CATEGORY (CAPITALISM IS NOT RESPONSIBLE) OR INTO THE "RADICAL" ONE (THE CAPITALISTS BENEFIT FROM THE SYSTEM). THE PRESENT PAPER OFFERS A "RADIC-LIB" ANALYSIS OF APARTHEID. "RADICAL" (BASICALLY MARXIST) ASSUMPTIONS ARE COMBINED WITH A "LIBERAL" (NEOCLASSICAL) ANALYTICAL FRAMEWORK. THE MAIN ANALYTICAL RESULTS (PREDICTIONS) ARE SURVEYED. AN EXTENSION OF THE ANALYSIS -- THE APARTHEID BUREAUCRACY AS A DIRECTLY UNPRODUCTIVE, PROFIT-SEEKING ACTIVITY -- IS MADE. FINALLY, THE ANALYTICAL PREDICTIONS ARE COMPARED WITH THE HISTORY OF SOUTH AFRICA FROM THE MINERAL DISCOVERIES IN THE LATE 19TH CENTURY TO THE PRESENT. IT IS CONCLUDED THAT NEITHER THE "RADICAL' NOR THE "LIBERAL" APPROACH CAN EXPLAIN THE ENTIRE SEQUENCE. A COMBINATION OF THE TWO IS NEEDED.

05776 LUNDAHL, M.
HISTORY AS AN OBSTACLE TO CHANGE: THE CASE OF HAITI
JOURNAL OF INTERAMERICAN STUDIES AND WORLD AFFAIRS, 31(1, 2) (SPR 89), 1-21.
THIS ARTICLE ARGUES THAT HAITI HAS FUNCTIONED AS A PREDATORY AUTOCRACY SINCE 1843 AND THAT THE PREDATORY STATE HAS GAINED LEGITIMACY THROUGH ITS OWN SURVIVAL. THE FACT THAT LACK OF PRODUCTION OF BASIC HUMAN, POLITICAL, AND ECONOMIC RIGHTS IN ONE PERIOD HAS MADE IT LIKELY THAT THEY WILL NOT BE PRODUCED IN SUBSEQUENT PERIODS IS EXPLORED, IT CONCLUDES THAT THE PROSPECT FOR STABLE DEMOCRACY AND INTRODUCTION OF A MERITOCRATIC GOVERNMENT WHICH PRODUCES AND PROTECTS RIGHTS FOR ALL APPEAR REMOTE.

05777 LUNDBERG, S.J.
EQUALITY AND EFFICIENCY: ANTIDISCRIMINATION POLICIES IN THE LABOR MARKET
CONTEMPORARY POLICY ISSUES, VII(1) (JAN 89), 75-94.
SOME HAVE CRITICIZED GOVERNMENT ANTIDISCRIMINATION PROGRAMS FOR CAUSING EFFICIENCY LOSSES BOTH BY DEVOTING PUBLIC RESOURCES TO MONITORING AND ENFORCEMENT AND BY DISTORTING PERSONNEL DECISIONS. THIS PAPER EXAMINES THE EFFICIENCY CONSEQUENCES OF SUCH PROGRAMS WHEN DISCRIMINATION IS CAUSED BY A MARKET FAILURE AND WHEN REGULATORS ARE IMPERFECTLY INFORMED ABOUT INDIVIDUAL FIRMS' PERSONNEL POLICIES. THE PAPER OUTLINES A SIMPLE MODEL OF "STATISTICAL

DISCRIMINATION" AND SHOWS THAT AN EQUAL OPPORTUNITY RULE, WHICH CONSTRAINS EMPLOYERS FROM OFFERING DIFFERENT WAGE SCHEDULES TO DIFFERENT GROUPS, WILL IMPROVE THE EFFICIENCY OF THE ECONOMY. EMPLOYERS WILL ATTEMPT TO EVADE SUCH REGULATION, AND THE PAPER DESCRIBES AN EVASION STRATEGY IN WHICH EMPLOYERS SEARCH FOR WORKER "QUALIFICATIONS" THAT CAN ACT AS PROXIES FOR RACE OR SEX. THE PAPER DISCUSSES PROBLEMS INVOLVED IN MONITORING AND ENFORCING COMPLIANCE AND CONSIDERS TWO POSSIBLE RESPONSES BY THE REGULATORY AGENCY.

05778 LUNDBERG, T.A.
THIRD WORLD DEVELOPMENTAL ASSISTANCE: THE ENGINEER CONTRIBUTION
AVAILABLE FROM NTIS, NO. AD-A208 051/3/GAR, MAR 89, 80.
AS THE STRATEGIC IMPORTANCE OF THE THIRD WORLD INCREASES, MORE EMPHASIS IS BEING PLACED ON OPERATIONS SHORT OF WAR IN UNDERDEVLOPED NATIONS. ONE POTENTIAL INSTRUMENT FOR PROMOTING STABILITY IN A REGION, THEREBY ADVANCING U.S. INTERESTS, IS DEVELOPMENTAL ASSISTANCE IN THE FORM OF INFRASTRUCTURE PLANNING, DESIGN AND CONSTRUCTION. THIS STUDY SEEKS TO EXAMINE NATION BUILDING AS AN INSTRUMENT OF U.S. STRATEGY IN TERMS OF BENEFITS VERSUS LIABILITIES AND TO EXAMINE CONDITIONS THAT MUST EXIST FOR NATIONAL BUILDING TO BE SUCCESSFUL. IT PROVIDES A GENERAL OVERVIEW OF THE CURRENT U.S. NATION BUILDING POSTURE AND PLAYERS. THE PURPOSE FOR EXAMINING NATION BUILDING AS AN INSTRUMENT OF U.S. STRATEGY AND THE CURRENT U.S. POSTURE AND STRUCTURE IS TO IDENTIFY A SET OF PITFALLS THAT HAVE DERAILED PAST PROGRAMS; IDENTIFY THE CHALLENGES THAT MUST BE ADDRESSED TO INITIATE NEW PROGRAMS; A SET OF PRINCIPLES FOR SUCCESS IN NATION BUILDING PROGRAM; AND TO PUT FORWARD A GENERAL CONCEPT AND ORGANIZATIONAL STRUCTURE FOR FUTURE NATION BUILDING PROGRAMS WITH EMPHASIS ON THE ENGINEER CONTRIBUTION TO THIS EFFORT.

05779 LUNKOV, N.
THE EMBASSY IN THE ETERNAL CITY
INTERNATIONAL AFFAIRS (MOSCOW), (12) (DEC 89), 50-58.
DURING THE YEARS OF PERESTROIKA, THE SOVIET UNION'S PRESTIGE AND POPULARITY IN ITALY HAS GROWN UNPRECEDENTEDLY. THE ITALIAN STATE LEADERSHIP, MAJOR POLITICAL PARTIES, PUBLIC ORGANIZATIONS, AND MOST SEGMENTS OF THE POPULATION NOW OPENLY EXPRESS THEIR TRUST IN AND SUPPORT FOR THE USSR.

05780 LUSANE, C.
BLACK POLITICAL POWER IN THE 1990'S
BLACK SCHOLAR, 20(1) (JAN 89), 38-42.
ACKNOWLEDGEING THAT THE NEXT FIVE YEARS WILL SHAPE POLITICAL AND SOCIAL LIFE IN THE US WELL INTO THE 21ST CENTURY, THE ARTICLE EXAMINES CENSUS DATA AND DEMOGRAPHIC TRENDS TO ATTEMPT TO DETERMINE THE FUTURE OF BLACK POLITICAL POWER AND THE CHALLENGES THAT LIE AHEAD FOR THE MOVEMENT FOR EQUAL AND PROPORTIONAL REPRESENTATION. A KEY ISSUE WILL BE THE REAPPORTIONMENT OF CONGRESSIONAL DISTRICTS WHICH BOTH POLITICAL PARTIES WISH TO CONTROL IN ORDER TO DETERMINE A FAVORABLE OUTCOME.

05781 LUSCHEV, P.
THE SOVIET MILITARY DOCTRINE: SIGNIFICANCE, AIMS, AND REALISATION
NATO'S SIXTEEN NATIONS, 34(7) (DEC 89), 26-28.
IN SPITE OF IMPROVEMENTS IN THE INTERNATIONAL ATMOSPHERE, THERE HAS BEEN AS YET NO RADICAL CHANGE IN THE EAST-WEST CONFRONTATION. THE SOVIET UNION AND THE WARSAW PACT HAVE ANNOUNCED UNILATERAL FORCE REDUCTIONS TO CONFORM TO THEIR DEFENSIVE MILITARY DOCTRINE. BUT THIS HAS NOT BEEN RECOGNIZED NOR FOLLOWED BY NATO. ALTHOUGH THE VIENNA FORCE REDUCTION AND CONFIDENCE-BUILDING TALKS SHOW PROGRESS, NATO STILL NEEDS TO JOIN THE EFFORT OF ELIMINATING CONFRONTATION AND DEVELOPING EUROPEAN COOPERATION.

05782 LUSHEV, P.
SECURITY VERSUS DOGMA
WORLD MARXIST REVIEW, 32(12) (DEC 89), 14-17.
THIS ARTICLE OUTLINES THE POSITIONS AND ACTIVITIES OF THE WARSAW TREATY ORGANIZATION IN MILITARY MATTERS, AND COMPARES THEM TO THE SECURITY MEASURES TAKEN BY NATO. THE AUTHOR CONTENDS THAT THE ABOLITION OF NUCLEAR AND CHEMICAL WEAPONS AND DRASTIC CUTS IN CONVENTIONAL FORCES ARE THE MOST PRESSING TASK BEFORE HUMANITY TODAY, AND NATO COULD CONTRIBUTE MORE DECISIVELY TOWARDS ACHIEVING IT.

05783 LUSHEV, P.
SOVIET AND WARSAW PACT GOALS AND DEVELOPMENTS
RUSI JOURNAL, 134(3) (FAL 89), 3-8.
COMMANDER-IN-CHIEF OF THE JOINT ARMED FORCES OF THE WARSAW PACT PETR LUSHEV EXPRESSED HIS SURPRISE AT HAVING THE OPPORTUNITY TO VISIT LONDON, THE CAPITAL CITY OF NATO. HE THEN PROCEEDED TO DISCUSS VARIOUS MILITARY ISSUES INCLUDING CURRENT MILITARY DOCTRINE AND CHANGING TRENDS. HE OUTLINED THE EFFORTS OF THE WARSAW PACT NATIONS TO REDUCE CONVENTIONAL ARMS TO A LEVEL OF "SUFFICIENCY FOR DEFENSE." HE ALSO DISCUSSED THE EVER-PRESENT PROBLEM OF NUCLEAR WEAPONS AND THE CURRENT NEGOTIATIONS DESIGNED TO REDUCE THE NUMBER OF WEAPONS IN EUROPE. HE CONCLUDED THAT BOTH SIDES

ARE MOVING TOWARD A "LOWER EQUILIBRIUM" AND NEED TO CONTINUE
IN THIS POSITIVE DIRECTION.

05784 LUSK, G.
      BACK ON COURSE FOR PEACE
      MIDDLE EAST INTERNATIONAL, (347) (MAR 89), 13.
         KHARTOUM HAS A NEW GOVERNMENT, THE PRODUCT OF A MONTH OF
      INTENSE NEGOTIATIONS AMONG POLITICIANS OF EVERY POLITICAL
      COLOR. IT IS ALSO THE PRODUCT OF THE ARMY'S ULTIMATUM TO
      PRIME MINISTER SADIQ AL-MAHDI, DEMANDING THAT HE FORM A
      BROAD-BASED GOVERNMENT AND TALK PEACE.

05785 LUSK, G.
      GARANG MAKES A MARK
      MIDDLE EAST INTERNATIONAL, 353 (JUN 89), 13-14.
         GARANG'S SWING THROUGH EUROPE AND THE US HAS HELPED IN
      PRESENTING THE SPLA CHAIRMAN AS A SERIOUS POLITICIAN, AS
      WELL AS A SUCCESSFUL SOLDIER. THE TRIP WAS PUNCTUATED WITH
      ANNOUNCEMENTS CALCULATED TO KEEP UP THE PRESSURE ON SADIQ.
      IN BONN, GARANG DECLARED A TWO-WEEK EXTENSION OF HIS
      UNILATERAL CEASE-FIRE. IN GENEVA, HE OFFERED THE RED CROSS
      ACCESS TO PRISONERS. IN THE US, HE PROMISED TO OPEN A RELIEF
      OFFICE. IN LONDON, HE ANNOUNCED ANOTHER TWO-WEEK EXTENSION
      OF THE CEASE-FIRE AND AN OPEN-ENDED COMMITMENT TO LIFELINE'S
      "PEACE CORRIDORS". THIS WILL ENSURE NOT ONLY FOOD BUT
      CONTINUED FOREIGN PRESENCE IN THE SOUTH. THIS MAY NOT
      ENTIRELY PLEASE KHARTOUM BUT WILL REINFORCE THE PEACE
      PROCESS. OTHERWISE, THOUGH, HE SHOWED LITTLE CONCERN FOR THE
      PLIGHT OF CIVILIANS, WHOSE FATE WAS SECONDARY TO THE AIMS OF
      THE WAR.

05786 LUSK, G.
      MAKING MARTYRS IN SUDAN
      MIDDLE EAST INTERNATIONAL, (365) (DEC 89), 12-13.
         THE MILITARY GOVERNMENT OF SUDAN HAS RECENTLY ENGAGED IN
      A SERIES OF ARRESTS, BEATINGS, AND EVEN EXECUTIONS OF
      DOCTORS AND BUSINESSMEN. DISREGARDING THE LESSONS OF RECENT
      HISTORY (THE HANGING OF A "REPUBLICAN BROTHERS" LEADER IN
      1985 LED TO THE OVERTHROWS OF THE PREVIOUS REGIME), THE
      RULING REVOLUTIONARY COMMAND COUNCIL (RCC) HAS STATED THAT
      "ANYONE WHO BETRAYS THIS NATION DOES NOT DESERVE THE HONOR
      OF LIVING," AND HAS PROCEEDED TO ARREST CIVILIANS FOR SUCH
      CRIMES AS HOLDING FOREIGN CURRENCY.

05787 LUSK, G.
      MILITARY RULE AGAIN IN SUDAN
      MIDDLE EAST INTERNATIONAL, (354) (JUL 89), 3.
         THE LONG EXPECTED COUP D'ETAT FINALLY TOOK PLACE IN
      SUDAN. THE ARMY, FRUSTRATED BY ECONOMIC TURMOIL AND A LACK
      OF PROGRESS TOWARDS ENDING THE SIX YEAR CIVIL WAR OUSTED THE
      SADIQ GOVERNMENT IN A NEARLY BLOODLESS COUP. HOWEVER, THE
      MILITARY'S LOACK OF POLITICAL EXPERIENCE BECAME INSTANTLY
      OBVIOUS AS A SERIES OF CONFUSING AND OFTEN CONTRADICTING
      POLICY STATEMENTS EMERGED FROM THE GOVERNMENT. MOST OBSERVER
      HOWEVER, VIEW THE MOVE AS ONE THAT WILL INCREASE THE CHANCES
      OF NEGOTIATION AND PEACE. UNFORTUNATELY, SUDAN'S HARD-WON
      DEMOCRACY SEEMS DESTINED TO GET LOST IN THE SHUFFLE.

05788 LUSK, G.
      PEACE TALKS FOR SUDAN
      MIDDLE EAST INTERNATIONAL, (364) (DEC 89), 13-14.
         PEACE TALKS SCHEDULED TO OPEN ON DECEMBER FIRST WILL
      BRING BOTH THE GOVERNMENT AND THE SUDANESE PEOPLE'S
      LIBERATION ARMY (SPLA) TOGETHER, BUT THE CHANCES OF ANY REAL
      SOLUTION ARE SLIM. THE SPLA COMES TO THE TABLE IN AN
      UNPARALLELED POSITION OF MILITARY AND POLITICAL STRENGTH AND
      DOES NOT REALLY NEED PEACE. THE RULING REVOLUTIONARY COMMAND
      COUNCIL (RCC) IS FACING DECREASING DOMESTIC AND
      INTERNATIONAL SUPPORT, AN AILING ECONOMY, AND GRUMBLING
      ARMED FORCES. HOWEVER, THE RCC IS UNLIKELY TO ABANDON ITS
      TRADITIONAL HARD-LINE STANCE. ONLY THE ADVENT OF A COUP
      WOULD ALLOW THE POSSIBILITY OF COMPROMISE AND AN END TO THE
      BITTER SIX AND A HALF YEAR WAR.

05789 LUSK, G.
      SADIQ'S DIVISIVE PLAN
      MIDDLE EAST INTERNATIONAL, 352 (JUN 89), 12-13.
         SADIQ HAS BEEN QUOTED IN THE PRESS AS WANTING TO BRING
      15,000 MEN UNDER ARMS TO "CONFRONT REBELS". HOW THIS
      SCENARIO WOULD FIT IN WITH THE PEACE PROCESS REMAINS UNCLEAR.
      OPPONENTS ALL STRESS THAT SUCH A MOVE IS UNDEMOCRATIC AND
      UNCONSTITUTIONAL. YET MAINTAINING DEMOCRACY AND
      CONSTITUTIONALITY WERE THE ARMY'S EXPLICIT JUSTIFICATION FOR
      NOT OVERTHROWING SADIQ IN THE FEBRUARY-MARCH CRISIS, AND BY
      POLITICIANS AND UNIONS FOR ACCEPTING THE FORMATION OF A NEW
      GOVERNMENT WITH HIM AT ITS HEAD. THE "POPULAR DEFENCE"
      PROPOSAL THEREFORE BRINGS ALL THE LATENT TENSIONS BACK TO
      THE SURFACE. AND IT AGAIN CONCENTRATES POLITICIANS' MINDS ON
      EVENTS IN KHARTOUM, RATHER THAN ON THE PEACE PROCESS.

05790 LUSK, G.
      SUDAN: CONFUSED AND CONFUSING
      MIDDLE EAST INTERNATIONAL, 355 (JUL 89), 12-13.
         SUDAN'S NEW MILITARY GOVERNMENT HAS CONTINUED TO SEND

OUT CONFUSED AND CONFUSING SIGNALS. NEVERTHELESS, AS THIS
ARTICLE DESCRIBES, THE PICTURE THAT HAS BEEN GRADUALLY
EMERGING SINCE THE ARMY SEIZED POWER IS ONE THAT IS WORRYING
NORTHERNERS AND SOUTHERNERS ALIKE: THE PICTURE OF ISLAMIC
FUNDAMENTALIST INVOLVEMENT.

05791 LUSK, G.
      SUDAN: FEW OPTIONS OPEN
      MIDDLE EAST INTERNATIONAL, (357) (AUG 89), 13-14.
         THE RESPONSE OF THE SUDANESE PEOPLE'S LIBERATION ARMY
      (SPLA) TO THE JUNTA WHICH SEIZED POWER IN JUNE CAME AS NO
      SURPRISE. SPEAKING FROM A POSITION OF SIGNIFICANT POLITICAL
      AND MILITARY POWER, SPLA LEADER JOHN GARANG DENOUNCED THE
      NEW GOVERNMENT AS AN OBSTACLE TO PEACE. THE REVOLUTIONARY
      COMMAND COUNCIL (RCC) IMMEDIATELY SAW THAT ITS OPTIONS WERE
      FEW: WINNING AGAINST THE SPLA IS NEXT TO IMPOSSIBLE WITHOUT
      SIGNIFICANT FOREIGN INVOLVEMENT. THE FACT THAT THE RCC
      IMMEDIATELY CALLED FOR PEACE NEGOTIATIONS UNDERSCORED THE
      LACK OF CHOICES THE NEW GOVERNMENT FACES.

05792 LUSK, G.
      SUDAN: MORE PEACE TALKS
      MIDDLE EAST INTERNATIONAL, (359) (SEP 89), 12.
         SUDAN'S RULING REVOLUTIONARY COMMAND COUNCIL (RCC)
      FORMED A "NATIONAL PEACE COMMITTE" OSTENSIBLY DESIGNED TO
      SETTLE THE ONGOING CIVIL WAR. HOWEVER, THE 77-MEMBER (AND
      STILL GROWING) COMMITTEE IS UNWIELDY AND WIDELY VIEWED AS
      INEFFECTUAL AND MEANINGLESS. THE SUDANESE PEOPLE'S
      LIBERATION MOVEMENT (SPLM) ISSUED A NINE POINT PLAN DESIGNED
      TO ENCOURAGE A "CONDUCIVE ATMOSPHERE," BUT THESE REQUESTS
      WERE IGNORED. THE RCC AIMS TO PROJECT THE IMAGE OF BEING
      PEACE-MAKERS IN ORDER TO GAIN FOREIGN AID AND FUNDS TO
      ALLEVIATE SUDAN'S CRUMBLING ECONOMY AND AID THE BATTERED
      POPULATION. HOWEVER, MOST OBSERVERS FEEL THAT THE RCC'S
      INSINCERE OVERTURES WILL NOT IMPROVE THE CHANCES FOR PEACE.

05793 LUSK, G.
      SUDAN: NERO FIDDLES
      MIDDLE EAST INTERNATIONAL, (345) (MAR 89), 15-16.
         ALTHOUGH THE SUDANESE ARMY SEEMED SET TO OUST PRIME
      MINISTER SADIQ AL-MAHDI IN FEBRUARY 1989, THE BELEAGURED
      PREMIER MADE NO ATTEMPT TO ADDRESS THE PROBLEMS AT HAND.

05794 LUSK, G.
      SUDAN: PRESSURES MOUNT
      MIDDLE EAST INTERNATIONAL, (363) (NOV 89), 13.
         THE RESUMPTION OF HOSTILITIES BETWEEN THE SUDAN'S RULING
      REVOLUTIONARY COMMAND COUNCIL (RCC) AND THE SUDANESE
      PEOPLE'S LIBERATION ARMY (SPLA) CLEARLY DEMONSTRATES THAT
      SUDAN HAS FAR TO GO BEFORE A LASTING PEACE CAN BE ATTAINED.
      DESPITE PRESSURE FROM THE EUROPEAN COMMUNITY AND EGYPT TO
      NEGOTIATE A CEASE-FIRE, THE GOVERNMENT'S RESPONSE REMAINS
      UNCERTAIN. A RECENT SPATE OF SACKINGS BOTH ON THE MILITARY
      AND CIVILIAN LEVEL CAST FURTHER DOUBT ON THE ABILITY OF
      GENERAL BASHIR AND THE RCC TO SOLVE THE MYRIAD OF PROBLEMS
      AND CONFLICTS BESETTING THEM.

05795 LUSK, G.
      SUDAN: SADIQ HEADS FOR POLITICAL SUICIDE
      MIDDLE EAST INTERNATIONAL, (341) (JAN 89), 13-14.
         THE DECEMBER 21, 1988, DECISION BY PRIME MINISTER SADIQ
      AL MAHDI'S MAIN COALITION PARTNER TO QUIT THE GOVERNMENT AND
      THE PRIME MINISTER'S ATTEMPTS TO FORGE AHEAD WITH THE
      SUPPORT OF THE NATIONAL ISLAMIC FRONT OCCURRED AGAINST A
      BACKGROUND OF MASS PROTEST DIRECTED EXPLICITLY AGAINST SADIQ.
      SADIQ HAS RESPONDED TO EVENTS WITH WHAT CAN ONLY BE SEEN AS
      A DESIRE, PRESUMABLY UNCONSCIOUS, FOR POLITICAL SUICIDE.

05796 LUSK, G.
      SUDAN: SLOW MOTION NIGHTMARE
      MIDDLE EAST INTERNATIONAL, (346) (MAR 89), 13-14.
         SUDAN'S CONTINUING NIGHTMARE WAS PUNCTUATED BY THE
      FORMAL RESIGNATION OF THE GOVERNMENT ON MARCH 11, 1989, WITH
      THE PROMISE THAT A NEW, BROAD-BASED GOVERNMENT WOULD BE
      FORMED IN TWO DAYS. BUT, DESPITE PRESSURE FROM PARTIES AND
      TRADE UNIONS, THIS DID NOT HAPPEN.

05797 LUSK, G.
      SUDAN: TWO STEPS FORWARD
      MIDDLE EAST INTERNATIONAL, (350) (MAY 89), 13.
         THE UNILATERAL CEASE-FIRE ANNOUNCEMENT BY THE SUDANESE
      PEOPLE'S LIBERATION ARMY AND KHARTOUM'S IMMEDIATE ACCEPTANCE
      MARKED ANOTHER IMPORTANT STEP FORWARD IN THE PEACE PROCESS.

05798 LUSK, G.
      SUDAN'S ARMY DIVIDES?
      MIDDLE EAST INTERNATIONAL, (358) (SEP 89), 10-11.
         DIVISIONS WITHIN SUDAN'S GOVERNMENT AND ARMY LEAD
      OBSERVERS TO NOTE THAT AFRICA'S LARGEST NATION MAY BE MOVING
      TOWARDS A CRISIS. THE REVOLUTIONARY COMMAND COUNCIL (RCC)
      WHICH SEIZED POWER IN JUNE HAS SACKED ANY SENIOR OFFICER WHO
      MIGHT HAVE PROVIDED A FOCUS FOR THE ARMY AS A NATIONAL AND
      NATIONALIST BODY. THE RESULTING FRAGMENTATION IS QUITE
      CHAOTIC AS FUNDAMENTALIST ISLAMIC GROUPS VIE WITH DOZENS OF

OTHER FACTIONS FOR POWER. MEANWHILE, THE CIVIL WAR RAGES ON UNABATED.

05799 LUSK, G.
SUDAN'S CEASE-FIRE EXTENDED
MIDDLE EAST INTERNATIONAL, (360) (OCT 89), 11-12.
THE DECISION OF SUDAN'S RULING REVOLUTIONARY COMMAND COUNCIL (RCC) TO EXTEND THE CEASE-FIRE ANOTHER MONTH WILL GIVE THE CITIZENS OF SUDAN A FURTHER RESPITE FROM SUFFERING AND INCREASE THE POSSIBILITY OF A LASTING PEACE. THE LONGER THE CEASE-FIRE LASTS, THE MORE DIFFICULT IT WILL BE FOR THE RCC OR THE SUDANESE PEOPLE'S LIBERATION ARMY (SPLA) TO RESUME HOSTILITIES. HOWEVER, THE CEASE-FIRE BENEFITS THE SPLA FAR MORE THAN THE RCC. AS THE SPLA CONSOLIDATES POWER, THE RCC IS FACING INTERNAL STRIFE, A SLOWING OF FOREIGN MILITARY AID, AND CONFLICT OVER THE ROLE OF ISLAM IN THE REGIME.

05800 LUSK, G.
SUDAN'S REBEL SUCCESSES
MIDDLE EAST INTERNATIONAL, (362) (NOV 89), 15.
AFTER SIX MONTHS OF RELATIVE PEACE IN SUDAN'S WAR ZONE, THE SUDANESE PEOPLE'S LIBERATION ARMY (SPLA) RESUMED SERIOUS FIGHTING. ALTHOUGH CLAIMING THAT THE ACTIONS ARE MERELY RESPONSES TO GOVERNMENT AGGRESSION, THE SPLA CLEARLY HAS THE TAKEN THE INITIATIVE AND PLANS TO USE THEIR MILITARY POWESS TO BRING DOWN THE GOVERNMENT. THE RULING REVOLUTIONARY COMMAND COUNCIL (RCC) IS BECOMING INCREASINGLY ISOLATED INTERNATIONALLY AND SOON WILL HAVE LITTLE CHOICE THAN TO BARGAIN WITH THE SPLA.

05801 LUTHER, K.R.
DIMENSIONS OF PARTY SYSTEM CHANGE: THE CASE OF AUSTRIA
WEST EUROPEAN POLITICS, 12(4) (OCT 89), 3-27.
THIS ARTICLE EXAMINES THE SIX ELEMENTS THAT FIGURE PREDOMINENTLY IN DESCRIBING THE AUSTRIAN PARTY SYSTEM UP TO THE LATE 1970S. RECENT PUBLICATIONS HAVE IDENTIFIED CHANGES IN MANY OF THE SIX FEATURES. THE MAIN AIM OF THIS PAPER IS NOT MERELY TO INDICATE THE NATURE AND EXTENT OF THE MAJOR CHANGES THAT HAVE OCCURRED BUT TO ADVANCE A MODEL FOR THEIR DISCUSSION IN A SYSTEMATIC MANNER SO AS TO IDENTIFY AND EXPLAIN PARTY SYSTEM CHANGE. IT EXPLORES THE ELECTORAL, PARLIAMENTARY AND GOVERNMENTAL ARENAS AND THE FPO'S ROLE.

05802 LUTTWAK, E.
DO WE NEED A NEW GRAND STRATEGY?
NATIONAL INTEREST, (15) (SPR 89), 3-14.
THE ARTICLE EXPLORES THE VARIOUS CONDITIONS AND MOTIVATIONS THAT HAVE LED TO THE SOVIET MILITARY BUILD-UP OVER THE PAST FOUR DECADES. AGAINST THIS BACKDROP, THE AUTHOR EXPLORES THE IMPLICATIONS OF GORBACHEV'S REFORMS AND THE POSSIBLE FUTURE OF SOVIET POLICY. HE ARGUES THAT MOST OF THE ALTERNATIVES WILL RESULT IN A DECLINE ON SOVIET MILITARY POWER. LARGE CORRESPONDING REDUCTIONS IN WESTERN MILITARY MIGHT, HOWEVER, ARE NOT WARRANTED DUE TO THE FACT THAT US POLICY WILL HAVE TO CONTEND WITH THE CONTINUING REALITY OF SOVIET STRENGTH, NOT WITH THE HYPOTHESIS OF ITS TECHNOLOGICAL-DETERMINED DECLINE IN THE LONG TERM. HE ADVOCATES TAKING ADVANTAGE OF THE FLEXIBILITY OFFERED BY SOVIET REFORMS WHILE AT THE SAME TIME NOT ABANDONING GENERAL PRINCIPLES THAT HAVE GUIDED US FOREIGN AND MILITARY POLICY FOR DECADES.

05803 LUTTWAK, E. N.
GORBACHEV'S STRATEGY, AND OURS
COMMENTARY, 88(1) (JUL 89), 29-36.
THE ONLY VALID U.S. RESPONSE TO "PERESTROIKA" IS TO MAKE SOVIET DEMOCRATIZATION THE KEY DETERMINANT NOT ONLY OF OUR ARMS-CONTROL POLICIES, NUCLEAR AND NON-NUCLEAR, BUT OF ALL POLICIES TOWARD THE SOVIET UNION ACROSS THE BOARD, IN REGARD TO TECHNOLOGY TRANSFER, CAPITAL FLOWS, JOINT VENTURES, TRADE IN GENERAL, SPACE COOPERATION, AND MORE. INSTEAD OF ALLOWING EACH OF THESE TO UNFOLD IN A NARROW DEPARTMENTAL CONTEXT, WHEREIN EACH AGENCY OF GOVERNMENT IS APT TO PURSUE ITS OWN NARROW GOALS (E.G., NASA'S QUEST FOR MORE FUNDING UNDER JOINT U.S.-SOVIET SCHEMES), ALL RELEVANT ACTION SHOULD BE CLOSELY LINKED TO THE PROGRESS OF DEMOCRATIZATION, WITH SPECIFIC MOVES ON OUR PART MADE OR NOT MADE IN RESPONSE TO WHAT HAPPENS IN THE SOVIET UNION.

05804 LUTZ, D.
THE DECLARATION OF INDEPENDENCE AS PART OF AN AMERICAN NATIONAL COMPACT
PUBLIUS: THE JOURNAL OF FEDERALISM, 19(1) (WIN 89), 41-58.
THE DECLARATION OF INDEPENDENCE IS AN EFFICIENT, ABSTRACTED SUMMARY OF THE EIGHTEENTH-CENTURY AMERICAN MIND. VIEWED IN THIS CONTEXT, THE DECLARATION IS NOT ONLY AN EFFICIENT SUMMARY OF AMERICAN POLITICAL THOUGHT, BUT ALSO A CAREFUL RHETORICAL BALANCING OF CONTENDING VIEWS. THE DOCUMENT COULD BE READ WITH APPROVAL BY STUDENTS OF WHIG POLITICAL THOUGHT, OR THE ENLIGHTENMENT; RATIONALISTS, OR THE DEEPLY RELIGIOUS; THOSE JEALOUS OF STATE POWER, OR NATIONALISTS. INDEED, THE MANNER IN WHICH STATE AND NATIONAL PERSPECTIVES ARE BALANCED MAKE THIS THE FIRST NATIONAL

DOCUMENT TO LAY OUT FEDERALISM AS A CENTRAL ASPECT OF AMERICAN POLITICAL THOUGHT. THE DOCUMENT ALSO TURNS OUT TO BE PART OF A POLITICAL COVENANT OF THE KIND LONG USED IN AMERICA, AND ORIGINALLY DERIVED FROM COVENANT THEOLOGY. POLITICAL COVENANTS, CALLED COMPACTS IN THEIR SECULAR FORM, WOULD HAVE HAD THE DECLARATION SERVE AS A PREAMBLE AND BILL OF RIGHTS TO A CONSTITUTION. AS IT TURNS OUT, THE DECLARATION OF INDEPENDENCE SERVES PRECISELY SUCH A ROLE WITH RESPECT TO THE UNITED STATES CONSTITUTION, AND IS THUS PART OF A NATIONAL COVENANT/COMPACT.

05805 LUTZ, J.
EMULATION AND POLICY ADOPTIONS IN THE CANADIAN PROVINCES
CANADIAN JOURNAL OF POLITICAL SCIENCE, XXII(1) (MAR 89), 147-154.
ABSTRACT. PREVIOUS RESEARCH HAS ANALYZED THE VARIOUS CHARACTERISTICS ASSOCIATED WITH THE ADOPTION OF POLICIES BY THE CANADIAN PROVINCES. SINCE A NUMBER OF PROVINCES HAVE APPEARED AS REGIONAL LEADERS IN THE ADOPTION OF THESE POLICIES, THERE WOULD SEEM TO BE AN EMULATION EFFECT AMONG THE PROVINCES SIMILAR TO THAT FOUND FOR THE ADOPTION OF POLICIES BY STATES IN THE UNITED STATES. THE PROVINCES THAT DEMONSTRATED LEADERSHIP VARIED TO SOME EXTENT, DEPENDING UPON THE TYPES OF POLICIES IN QUESTION.

05806 LUTZ, J.; HUFF, D.
URBAN SPHERES OF INFLUENCE IN GHANA
JOURNAL OF DEVELOPING AREAS, 23(2) (JAN 89), 201-220.
THE PURPOSE OF THE STUDY IS TO DELINEATE THE SPHERES OF INFLUENCE OF 45 URBAN PLACES IN GHANA. THE DERIVATION OF THESE SPHERES OF INFLUENCE PROVIDES AN INDICATION OF THE EFFECT OF DIFFERENT URBAN CENTERS UPON THE GHANANIAN COUNTRYSIDE AND THE RELATIONSHIP BETWEEN THE LARGER URBAN PLACES. SUCH INFORMATION PERMITS THE GOVERNMENT TO MAKE DECISIONS ON WHERE TO LOCATE SERVICES OR ACTIVITIES IN EFFORTS TO DEVELOP OR INTEGRATE THE RURAL AREAS INTO THE NATIONAL URBAN NETWORK. THE NEED FOR SUCH SPATIAL, AS WELL AS ECONOMIC PLANNING IS CLEAR, PARTICULARLY FOR FORMER COLONIAL TERRITORIES WHERE THE URBAN NETWORK WAS ESTABLISHED AT THE WHIM OF THE COLONIZER AND SELDOM BASED ON LOCAL CONDITIONS AND CIRCUMSTANCES.

05807 LUZAN, S.
THE INDEPENDENTS' MOVEMENT: A VIEW FROM THE INSIDE
GLASNOST, (16-18) (JAN 89), 67-69.
IT IS IMPOSSIBLE TO COUNT THE TOTAL NUMBER OF PEOPLE INVOLVED IN THE INDEPENDENTS' MOVEMENT, BUT THERE ARE CLEARLY MILLIONS OF THEM. FOR THE FIRST TIME, THE SOVIET PEOPLE HAVE ROUSED THEMSELVES AND HAVE BEGUN TO OVERCOME THE APATHY OF DECADES. DEMOCRATIZATION IS BECOMING AN INALIENABLE PART OF EVERYDAY LIFE. FUNCTIONARIES AND APPARATCHIKS OF EVERY SHADE HERE UNPREPARED FOR THIS OUTBURST OF SOCIAL ACTIVISM AMONG THE PEOPLE. THE INDEPENDENTS HAVE BEEN PRECEIVED BY THE ESTABLISHMENT AS A DIRECT, IMMEDIATE DANGER THREATENING ITS VERY EXISTENCE.

05808 LYNCH, A.
THE CHANGING CONTOURS OF SOVIET-EAST EUROPEAN RELATIONS
JOURNAL OF INTERNATIONAL AFFAIRS, 42(2) (SPR 89), 423-434.
THE ARTICLE EXAMINES THE CHANGES THAT THE ADVENT OF MIKHAIL GORBACHEV HAVE CAUSED IN USSR-EASTERN EUROPEAN RELATIONS. ALTHOUGH MANY OBSERVERS ARE PREDICTING SIGNIFICANT CHANGE IN EASTERN EUROPE AS POLICIES OF PERESTROIKA AND GLASNOST TAKE HOLD IN THE USSR, THE ARTICLE CAUTIONS THAT MANY FACTORS COMBINE TO LIMIT THE INFLUENCE THAT REFORM IN THE USSR WILL HAVE ON ITS SATELLITES. AT THE HEART OF THE DIFFICULTIES IS THE UNDERLYING TENSION BETWEEN THE GOALS OF CREATING A POLITICALLY AND ECONOMICALLY VIABLE REGION AND MAINTAINING A MINIMUM DEGREE OF CONTROL THAT IS CONSISTENT WITH SOVIET IDEOLOGY. THIS AND OTHER FACTORS LIMIT THE ABILITY OF GORBACHEV TO REFORM HIS COMMUNIST ALLIES IN A FASHION SIMILAR TO THE USSR.

05809 LYNCH, T.D.
CONFRONTING THE BUDGET DEFICIT
BUREAUCRAT, 18(1) (SPR 89), 49-52.
THE CONTINUNING PROBLEM OF LARGE ANNUAL BUDGET DEFICITS IS A MATTER OF GROWING CONCERN TO MANY AMERICANS. SOME PROGRESS WAS MADE THROUGH JOINT LEGISLATIVE/EXECUTIVE BRANCH EFFORTS WITH RESPECT TO FISCAL YEAR 1989, BUT LONGER-TERM IMPROVEMENTS ARE NEEDEDX. THIS ARTICLE DEALS WITH SUGGESTED IMPROVEMENTS IN THE FEDERAL BUDGET PROCESS.

05810 LYON, P.
RAMPHAL'S NEO KANTIANISM
ROUND TABLE, (310) (APR 89), 201-206.
PETER LYON GIVES A REVIEW OF SHRIDATH SURENDRANATH RAMPHAL'S BOOK: INSEPERABLE HUMANITY: AN ANTHOLOGY OF REFLECTIONS OF SHRIDATH RAMPHAL. IT OUTLINES MANY OF THE SPEECHES AND WRITINGS OF THE 15-YEAR SECRETARY GENERAL OF THE COMMONWEALTH. THE EMPHASIS IS ON THE CARIBBEAN, BUT RAMPHAL ALSO DISCUSSES SUCH VARIOUS TOPICS AS APARTHEID AND POVERTY.

05811 LYONS, G.M.
REFORMING THE UNITED NATIONS
INTERNATIONAL SOCIAL SCIENCE JOURNAL, (120) (MAY 89),
249-272.
WHILE THE WORLD UNDERWENT PROFOUND POLITICAL,
DEMOGRAPHIC AND TECHNOLOGICAL CHANGES SINCE 1945, NEITHER
THE UNITED NATIONS ORGANIZATION NOR THE SPECIALIZED AGENCIES
WHICH CONSTITUTE THE 'UN FAMILY' HAVE BEEN ABLE TO ADJUST
PROPERLY TO SUCH CHANGES. THIS POLITICAL AND ORGANIZATIONAL
INERTIA CONTRIBUTED, WITH OTHER FACTORS, TO THE CRISIS OF
MULTILATERALISM.

05812 LYONS, W.E.; LOWERY, D.
CITIZEN RESPONSES TO DISSATISFACTION IN URBAN COMMUNITIES:
A PARTIAL TEST OF A GENERAL MODEL
THE JOURNAL OF POLITICS, 51(4) (NOV 89), 841-868.
THIS PAPER EVALUATES THE EXIT, VOICE, LOYALTY, AND
NEGLECT (EVLN) MODEL OF CITIZEN RESPONSES TO DISSATISFACTION
DEVELOPED BY LYONS AND LOWRY (1986), THE KEY PROPORTIONS ARE
SUMMARIZED, AND THE MODEL IS TESTED WITH DATA GATHERED FROM
10 SEPARATE SURVEYS OF CITIZENS LIVING IN MATCHED PAIRS OF
INDEPENDENT CITIES AND NEIGHBORHOODS. CONSIDERABLE SUPPORT
IS FOUND FOR A RESPECIFIED VERSION OF THE EVLN MODEL,
SUPPORT THAT IS THEN USED TO DEVELOP AN INTEGRATED
UNDERSTANDING OF CITIZEN RESPONSES TO DISSATISFACTION WITH
PUBLIC SERVICES IN URBAN COMMUNITIES.

05813 M'GONIGLE, M.
SUSTAINABILITY AND LOCAL GOVERNMENT: THE CASE OF THE
BRITISH COLUMBIA ISLANDS TRUST
CANADIAN PUBLIC ADMINISTRATION, 32(4) (WIN 89), 524-544.
IN RECENT YEARS ENVIRONMENTAL VALUES HAVE UNDERGONE A
POPULAR AND POLITICAL RESURGENCE, ONE OF THE CENTRAL
COMPONENTS OF WHICH IS A DEMAND FOR GREATER PUBLIC
PARTICIPATION, ESPECIALLY ENHANCED LOCAL CONTROL. THIS
DEVELOPMENT HAS IMPORTANT IMPLICATIONS FOR THEORETICAL
THINKING IN PUBLIC ADMINISTRATION. THE PRESENT ARTICLE
EXAMINES THE EXPERIENCE OF THE BRITISH COLUMBIA ISLANDS
TRUST, AN INNOVATIVE EXAMPLE OF LOCAL ADMINISTRATION WHICH
IS MOST RELEVANT TO THE QUEST FOR NEW ENVIRONMENTALLY
SUSTAINABLE FORMS OF ADMINISTRATION AS A RESULT OF ITS
UNUSUAL MANDATE ("TO PRESERVE AND PROTECT") AND ITS LOCALLY
BASED PLANNING APPROACH. THE ARTICLE DESCRIBES THE TRUST
AREA, REVIEWS THE GENESIS OF THE TRUST IN THE 1960S AND ITS
HISTORY TO THE PRESENT, DESCRIBES ITS STRUCTURE, AND
ASSESSES PUBLIC ATTITUDES TO IT.

05814 MA-CHI, C.
BITTER LIFE IN SOVIET UNION
ASIAN OUTLOOK, 24(3) (MAY 89), 33-34.
THE RECENT RATIONING OF SUGAR IN THE SOVIET UNION IS
RELATED TO GORBACHEV'S CAMPAIGN AGAINST ALCOHOLISM. AFTER
GORBACHEV UNLEASHED A NATIONWIDE ANTI-ALCOHOL CAMPAIGN THAT
INCLUDED SHARP CUTS IN THE PRODUCTION OF VODKA AND OTHER
ALCOHOLIC BEVERAGES, SOVIETS BEGAN BUYING LARGE QUANTITIES
OF SUGAR IN ORDER TO PRODUCE HOME BREW.

05815 MA, K. Y.
FOREIGN RELATIONS BETWEEN THE REPUBLIC OF CHINA AND THE
KINGDOM OF SAUDI ARABIA: THE PROCESS OF ESTABLISHING AND
SUSTAINING RELATIONSHIPS (1936-1986)
DISSERTATION ABSTRACTS INTERNATIONAL, 49(8) (FEB 89),
2382-A.
THE HALF-CENTURY OF ROC-KSA RELATIONS MAY BE DIVIDED
INTO THREE PERIODS: THE INITIAL ERA ENDING IN 1956, THE
PROMOTING PERIOD FROM 1957 TO 1971, AND THE MATURING AND
STRENGTHENING PERIOD SINCE 1971. BEFORE KING FAISAL'S STATE
VISIT TO THE ROC IN 1971, THE SCOPE OF CONTACTS BETWEEN THE
TWO WAS LIMITED TO RELIGIOUS ACTIVITIES AND AGRICULTURAL
ASSISTANCE; AFTER THAT, RELATIONS WERE BROADENED AND
STRENGTHENED.

05816 MA, S.K.
REFORM CORRUPTION: A DISCUSSION ON CHINA'S CURRENT
DEVELOPMENT
PACIFIC AFFAIRS, 62(1) (SPR 89), 40-52.
CORRUPTION AMONG CHINA'S BUREAUCRATS HAS ACCOMPANIED
RAPID REFORM. THIS PROBLEM REMAINS CHRONIC AND CONTAGIOUS.
THE PAPER ARGUES THAT BUREAUCRATIC CORRUPTION IN CHINA
DURING A PERIOD OF REFORM IS THE RESULT OF SEVERAL FACTORS,
INCLUDING IDEOLOGICAL CONFUSION, INCENTIVE HIATUS, LACK OF
DETERRENCE AND "MANAGEMENT GAP." THE PAPER ALSO EXAMINES
OPTIONS FOR REFORM.

05817 MAAITA, A.S.
POLITICAL LEADERSHIP AND MODERNIZATION: A CASE STUDY OF
JORDAN, 1921-1988
DISSERTATION ABSTRACTS INTERNATIONAL, 49(8) (FEB 89),
2387-A.
THE AUTHOR STUDIES THE ROLE, TYPE, AND STYLE OF JORDAN'S
MONARCHICAL POLITICAL LEADERSHIP IN THE MODERNIZATION OF THE
NATION. HE FINDS THAT KING ABDULLAH WAS DECISIVE IN
ESTABLISHING JORDAN BUT LESS IMPORTANT IN IMPLEMENTING
SOCIAL AND ECONOMIC CHANGE. KING HUSSEIN PRODUCED SOCIAL

CHANGE AND HAS ALSO RELATIVELY IMPORTANT IN THE ECONOMIC AND
POLITICAL ARENAS.

05818 MAASDORP, G.
ECONOMIC SYSTEMS IN A GLOBAL PERSPECTIVE
SOUTH AFRICA INTERNATIONAL, 20(1) (JUL 89), 14-23.
THIS BRIEF PROVIDES AN OVERVIEW OF THE BASIC SYSTEMIC
OPTIONS AND THE CURRENT INTERNATIONAL THINKING WITH REGARD
TO EACH. IT STARTS WITH THE PREMISE THAT THE BASIC CHOICE IS
BETWEEN TWO SYSTEMS, CENTRAL PLANNING AND THE MARKET. IT
EXAMINES CURRENT TRENDS OF THINKING AND PRACTICE IN THE
CENTRALLY PLANNED ECONOMIES AND THE INDUSTRIAL MARKET
ECONOMIES. THEN, TRENDS IN THE THIRD WORLD ARE CONSIDERED
BEFORE CONCLUDING WITH A BRIEF WORD ABOUT THE IMPLICATIONS
FOR SOUTH AFRICA.

05819 MABESOONE, W.
EUROPEAN COOPERATION: NAVAL LESSONS FROM THE GULF WAR
NATO'S SIXTEEN NATIONS, 34(1) (1989), 67-68, 70, 73-74.
THE AUTHOR REVIEWS THE RECORD OF EUROPEAN COOPERATION IN
PROTECTING WESTERN POLITICAL AND ECONOMIC INTERESTS IN THE
PERSIAN GULF DURING THE IRAN-IRAQ WAR. HE CONCLUDES THAT,
WHILE LOCAL NAVAL COMMANDERS SAW THE NEED FOR COOPERATION
AND WORKED TOGETHER TO THE EXTENT ALLOWED, THEIR GOVERNMENTS
WERE MORE CONCERNED WITH MAINTAINING THEIR NATIONAL
PREROGATIVES.

05820 MACDONALD, D.J.
"ADVENTURES IN CHAOS": REFORMISM IN U.S. FOREIGN POLICY
DISSERTATION ABSTRACTS INTERNATIONAL, 50(5) (NOV 89),
1429-A.
THE AUTHOR EXAMINES U.S. INTERVENTION TO PROMOTE
POLITICAL AND SOCIAL REFORM IN CLIENT STATES UNDERGOING
INTENSE POLITICAL INSTABILITY. HIS MAIN HYPOTHESIS CONCERNS
THE APPARENT INVERSE RELATIONSHIP BETWEEN COMMITMENTS TO THE
CLIENT GOVERNMENT AND BARGAINING LEVERAGE FOR REFORM WITHIN
THE CONTEXT OF STRATEGIC INTERDEPENDENCE. HE STUDIES THREE
AMERICAN DIPLOMATIC EPISODES: CHINA 1945-48, THE PHILIPPINES
1949-1953, AND VIETNAM 1960-63.

05821 MACDONALD, D.S.
SECURITY IN NORTHEAST ASIA: TWO KOREAS OR ONE?
WASHINGTON QUARTERLY, 12(4) (FAL 89), 139-153.
THIS ARTICLE EXPLORES THE TRAGEDY OF THE DIVISION OF
KOREA AND EXPLORES, ALSO, THE GENESIS OF THE REUNIFICATION
ISSUE. THE KOREAN SECURITY SITUATION IS DETAILED. THE
PROBLEM OF THE DIFFICULTY FOR ALL MAJOR POWERS OF ACCEPTING
A UNIFIED KOREA THAT IS NOT SOLIDLY IN THEIR IDEOLOGICAL
CAMP IS IDENTIFIED. THE CONCLUSION IS THAT THE REUNIFICATION
OF KOREA IS DESIRABLE AND THAT IT IS ATTAINABLE, ALTHOUGH
NOT WITHOUT GREAT DIFFICULTY AND NOT WITHOUT THE PASSAGE OF
CONSIDERABLE TIME.

05822 MACDONALD, M.
A FOLK HERO ON TRIAL
MACLEAN'S (CANADA'S NEWS MAGAZINE), 102(7) (FEB 89), 20.
JURY SELECTION FOR THE TRIAL OF OLIVER NORTH IS A
DIFFICULT PROCESS; THE EX-MARINE'S NOTORIETY IS WIDESPREAD.
HOWEVER, A JURY IS BEING GATHERED AND THE TRIAL TO DETERMINE
WHETHER THE CHARGES OF BLOCKING OR MISLEADING GOVERNMENT
INQUIRIES INTO THE IRAN/CONTRA AFFAIR, AND ACCEPTING GIFTS
AND MONEY WHILE ON GOVERNMENT PAYROLL IS SOON TO BEGIN.
ALTHOUGH OVERALL INTEREST IN THE TRIAL HAS DIMINISHED
SOMEWHAT, THE THEATRICAL POTENTIAL HAS NOT.

05823 MACDONALD, M.; CONNELLY, M.P.
CLASS AND GENDER IN FISHING COMMUNITIES IN NOVA SCOTIA
STUDIES IN POLITICAL ECONOMY: A SOCIALIST REVIEW, (30)
(FAL 89), 61-87.
THIS PAPER EXPLORES THE COMPLEXITY OF CLASS RELATIONS IN
NOVA SCOTIA FISHING COMMUNITIES, USING A CONCEPTION OF CLASS
WHICH TAKES INTO ACCOUNT GENDER AND HOUSEHOLD RELATIONS. THE
PURPOSE OF THE PAPER IS TO SHOW THAT A MORE COMPLEX, GENERED
CLASS ANALYSIS CAN ILLUMINATE OTHERWISE ANOMALOUS
CHARACTERISTICS OF THE PATTERN OF LABOR RELATIONS AND
CAPITAL ACCUMULATIONS IN AN INDUSTRY. IT USES A SPECIFIC
CASE STUDY OF THE FISHING INDUSTRY TO ILLUSTRATE THE GENERAL
POINT.

05824 MACDONALD, N.B.
WILL THE FREE TRADE DEAL DRIVE A GAPING HOLE THROUGH THE
AUTO PACT?
POLICY OPTIONS, 10(1) (JAN 89), 10-17.
UNDER THE FREE TRADE AGREEMENT, MAJOR CHANGES WILL OCCUR,
WITH EFFECTS THAT CANNOT BE MEASURED YET. IT IS LIKELY THAT
THE RATIONALIZATION OF THE MANUFACTURING PROCESS WILL LEAD
TO CLOSURES OF PLANTS IN CANADA RATHER THAN THE USA. THE
WINNERS WILL BE THE BIG THREE AMERICAN AUTOMAKERS, BECAUSE
THE CANADIAN NEGOTIATORS GAVE WAY TO AMERICAN PRESSURE.

05825 MACDONALD, S.B.
SLAYING THE DRUG HYDRA
SAIS REVIEW, 9(1) (WIN 89), 65-85.
THIS ARTICLE BRIEFLY OUTLINES THE KEY ELEMENTS OF A

COHERENT DRUG POLICY FOR THE NEW U.S. ADMINISTRATION. AS SUGGESTED BY THE ARGUMENT THAT CURRENT U.S. DRUG POLICY IS NEITHER WORKING NOR AN ENTIRE FAILURE, THE NEW POLICY SHOULD HAVE SOME CONTINUITY WITH PAST EFFORTS AND INNOVATIONS FOR THE FUTURE. FUNDAMENTALLY, CURRENT U.S. DRUG POLICY IS DISJOINTED, LACKING ANY CONSISTENT SUPPORT FROM THE REAGAN ADMINISTRATION AND CONGRESS (WITH SUCH EXCEPTIONS AS REPRESENTATIVE CHARLES RANGEL (D-NY) AND SENATOR JESSE HELMS (R-NC), AND IS IN BAD NEED OF AN OVERHAUL. THIS ARTICLE DOES NOT HAVE AN ACCUSATIVE FINGER AT EITHER THE EXECUTIVE OR THE LEGISLATIVE BRANCH-THERE IS PLENTY OF BLAME TO GO AROUND. THE NEED FOR ACTION IS TOO PRESSING TO WASTE TIME ON SOUL-SEARCHING INTROSPECTION AND THE EXCHANGE OF PARTISAN RECRIMINATIONS. RATHER, ACHIEVING A VIABLE DRUG POLICY MUST BE A BIPARTISAN AFFAIR INTERNALLY AND A QUESTION OF INTERNATIONAL COOPERATION EXTERNALLY.

05826 MACE, G.; HERVOUET, G.
CANADA'S THIRD OPTION: A COMPLETE FAILURE?
CANADIAN REVIEW OF SOCIOLOGY AND ANTHROPOLOGY, 15(4) (DEC 89), 387-404.
THIS PAPER ANALYSES THE DIVERSIFICATION ASPECTS OF CANADA'S THIRD OPTION STRATEGY FROM 1968 TO 1980. THE STUDY EXAMINES THE FEDERAL GOVERNMENT'S EFFORTS TO ENCOURAGE ECONOMIC DIVERSIFICATION AND FOCUSES AT THE SAME TIME ON A FEW DIMENSIONS OF THE PRIVATE SECTOR'S BEHAVIOUR. WE ANALYSE THE OVERALL EVOLUTION AND MAIN TARGETS OF SOME STRATEGIC FEDERAL PROGRAMS, SUCH AS THE PROMOTIONAL PROJECTS PROGRAM, THE EXPORT MARKET DEVELOPMENT PROGRAM AND SIMILAR PROGRAMS OF THE EXPORT DEVELOPMENT CORPORATION. WE ALSO ANALYSE PRIVATE SECTOR BEHAVIOUR THROUGH TRADE RELATIONS AND DIRECT INVESTMENT FLOWS. THE PAPER CONCLUDES THAT THE THIRD OPTION STRATEGY, IN ITS DIVERSIFICATION ASPECT, WAS NOT A FAILURE IN THE SENSE THAT THE FEDERAL GOVERNMENT ABANDONED ITS ORIGINAL OBJECTIVES. IT MIGHT BE CALLED A FAILURE IN THE SENSE THAT THE CANADIAN PRIVATE SECTOR'S FOLLOW-UP DID NOT MATERIALIZE PARTLY BECAUSE OF ADVERSE ECONOMIC CONDITIONS.

05827 MACEWAN, A.; TABB, W.K.
INSTABILITY AND CHANGE IN THE WORLD ECONOMY
MONTHLY REVIEW PRESS, NEW YORK, NY, 1989, 352.
THIS COLLECTION OF ESSAYS EXAMINES THE EVOLUTION AND IMPACT OF INSTABILITY AND CHANGE IN THE WORLD ECONOMY. THE AUTHORS FOCUS ON THE INTERACTIONS BETWEEN NATIONAL SOCIOPOLITICAL FORCES AND THE INCREASINGLY GLOBAL ECONOMY IN WHICH THOSE FORCES OPERATE. THEY EXAMINE THE CRISIS PRODUCED BY THE CURRENT INTERNATIONAL TURMOIL AND ARGUE THAT IT WILL BE A CONTINUING PHENOMENON, INVOLVING STAGNATION, RESTRUCTURING, CONFLICT AND DISRUPTION ON A WIDE SCALE. TOPICS OF SPECIAL CONCERN INCLUDE THE RISING INSTABILITY IN THE INTERNATIONAL FINANCIAL SYSTEM; THE CHANGING ROLE OF WOMEN IN THE INTERNATIONAL DIVISION OF LABOR; THE DECLINING POWER OF MACROECONOMIC POLICY IN THE FACE OF THE INTERNATIONAL CAPITAL MOBILITY; THE EMERGING IMPORTANCE OF "INFORMAL" ECONOMIC ACTIVITIES IN THE ADVANCED ECONOMIES AND IN THE UNDERDEVELOPED WORLD; AND THE CONTINUING EFFORTS OF THE WORLD BANK AND INTERNATIONAL MONETARY FUND TO SHAPE A WORLD SAFE FOR CAPITAL.

05828 MACEWAN, A.
INTERNATIONAL TRADE AND ECONOMIC INSTABILITY
MONTHLY REVIEW, 40(9) (FEB 89), 10-21.
THE UNITED STATES MAY CONTINUE THE LINE OF POLICY ITS HAS FOLLOWED FOR THE LAST SEVERAL YEARS, AND MAY THEN EXPERIENCE A MORE GENERALIZED CRASH OF FINANCIAL MARKETS, WITH THE CATACLYSMIC IMPACTS WHICH THIS IMPLIES. OR, THROUGH STANDARD MEASURES, THE GOVERNMENT COULD DROP ITS POLICIES OF STIMULATION WHICH HAVE GENERATED THE IMBALANCES, GREASING THE WAY FOR A SLIDE INTO DEEPER DEPRESSION. THE CATACLYSM MIGHT THEN BE AVOIDED, BUT THE PROGNOSIS WOULD HARDLY BE FAVORABLE. A REAL ALTERNATIVE WOULD GO BEYOND STANDARD POLICY AND FOCUS ON MORE BASIC STRUCTURAL CHANGES, CHANGES WHICH MIGHT DEAL IN ONE WAY OR ANOTHER WITH BOTH INTERNATIONAL POWER RELATIONS AND STAGNATION, THIS THIRD ALTERNATIVE ITSELF COULD HAVE MANY VARIANTS, RANGING FROM THE REACTIONARY TO THE PROGRESSIVE, BUT AT LEAST IT WOULD OPEN UP OPORTUNITIES AND REPRESENT A FOCUS FOR POSITIVE STRUGGLE.

05829 MACEWAN, A.; TABB, W.K.
THE ECONOMY IN CRISIS: NATIONAL POWER AND INTERNATIONAL INSTABILITY
SOCIALIST REVIEW, (MAR 89), 67-92.
THIS ARTICLE EXAMINES THE DEBATE ABOUT THE RELATIONSHIP BETWEEN THE NATIONAL AND THE INTERNATIONAL IN CONTEXT OF HOW THE ECONOMIC SYSTEM IS MOVING, IT ADDRESSES INTERNATIONAL-NATIONAL DUALITY; EXPANSION AND STAGNATION: DEBT AND DISORDER; TRADE; AND THE RELATION BETWEEN ECONOMICS AND POLITICS. IT ANALYSES THE DANGERS AND OPPORTUNITIES THAT ARISE FROM THE STRUGGLE OF SOCIALISTIC AND CAPITALISTIC IDEOLOGIES

05830 MACFARLANE, S.; NEL, P.
THE CHANGING SOVIET APPROACH TO REGIONAL CONFLICTS

JOURNAL OF COMMUNIST STUDIES, 5(2) (JUN 89), 148-172.
THE ARTICLE COMPARES THE SOVIET APPROACH TO REGIONAL CONFLICT UNDER BREZHNEV WITH CURRENT FOREIGN POLICY. GORBACHEV'S "NEW THINKING" SIGNALS SIGNIFICANT POLICY CHANGES IN SUCH AREAS AS "INTERNATIONAL SECURITY, POLITICAL SETTLEMENTS, REGIONAL CONFLICTS AND NUCLEAR WARS, DETENTE, RESISTANCE TO IMPERIALMISM, AND SUPPORT FOR NATIONAL LIBERATION MOVEMENTS. AFGHANISTAN AND ANGOLA ARE EXAMINED AS EXAMPLES OF CHANGING SOVIET POLICY. THE ARTICLE CONCLUDES THAT THE SOVIET LEADERSHIP HAS GONE A LONG WAY TOWARDS PROMOTING NEGOTIATED SETTLEMENTS. HOWEVER, THIS INCREASED FLEXIBILITY DOES NOT NECESSARILY SIGNAL AN END TO PATRON-CLIENT RELATIONSHIPS BETWEEN THE USSR AND THE DEVELOPING WORLD.

05831 MACFARLANE, S.N.
THE SOVIET UNION AND SOUTHERN AFRICAN SECURITY
PROBLEMS OF COMMUNISM, XXXVIII(2-3) (MAR 89), 71-89.
IN RECENT MONTHS, THE SOVIET UNION'S OUTLOOK ON REGIONAL SECURITY IN SOUTHERN AFRICA HAS SHIFTED FROM A POSTURE OF FOSTERING CONFLICT OVER ANGOLA AND NAMIBIA AND ENDORSING VIOLENT CHANGE IN SOUTH AFRICA PROPER TO CONTRIBUTING TO CONFLICT SETTLEMENT ON THE ANGOLA-NAMIBIA FRONT AND EVEN SOME MODERATION OF VIEWS ON SOCIAL CHANGE WITHIN SOUTH AFRICA ITSELF. THIS SHIFT BOTH REFLECTS AND INFORMS A BROADER GENERAL TREND IN SOVIET THIRD WORLD POLICY, A NEW RECEPTIVITY TO REGIONAL CONFLICT SETTLEMENT THAT IS ROOTED IN ADVERSE CONCRETE LOCAL EXPERIENCE RATHER THAN IN IDEOLOGICAL PRESCRIPTIONS.

05832 MACFIE, A. L.
THE TURKISH STRAITS IN THE SECOND WORLD WAR, 1939-45
MIDDLE EASTERN STUDIES, 25(2) (APR 89), 238-248.
IT IS EVIDENT THAT IN THE SECOND WORLD WAR, AS IN THE FIRST, THE TURKISH STRAITS PLAYED AN IMPORTANT PART IN DETERMINING THE COURSE OF EVENTS. THEIR CLOSURE, IN THE EARLY STAGES OF THE WAR IN PARTICULAR, ENABLED THE GERMANS TO PURSUE THEIR DESIGNS IN EASTERN EUROPE, SECURE IN THE KNOWLEDGE THAT BRITAIN AND FRANCE WOULD NOT BE ABLE TO LINK UP WITH GERMANY'S ENEMIES IN THE BLACK SEA. AT THE SAME TIME, PARTICULARLY IN 1940-41, WHEN THE PROSPECT OF A GERMAN MOVE AGAINST TURKEY LOOMED LARGE, THEY ACTED AS AN OBSTACLE, DISCOURAGING THE AXIS POWERS FROM UNDERTAKING AN ATTACK BY THAT ROUTE ON BRITAIN'S VITAL INTERESTS IN THE MIDDLE EAST. FINALLY, THEY FIGURED PROMINENTLY AS A COUNTER IN THE COMPLEX GAME OF DIPLOMACY PLAYED BY THE POWERS, PARTICULARLY IN THE RUSSO-GERMAN TALKS OF NOVEMBER 1940, WHEN RUSSIA'S DEMANDS REGARDING BULGARIA AND THE STRAITS, AND THEIR LONG-TERM STRATEGIC IMPLICATIONS, MAY WELL HAVE PERSUADED HITLER TO OPT NOT FOR WHAT NUMAN MENEMENCIOGLU REFERRED TO AS THE RUSSIAN 'OPTION' BUT FOR WAR.

05833 MACGREGOR, D.A.
DEMILITARIZING EAST-WEST CONFLICT: U.S. AND SOVIET MILITARY DISENGAGEMENT FROM GERMANY
COMPARATIVE STRATEGY, 8(4) (1989), 411-424.
THIS PAPER ARGUES THAT WASHINGTON SHOULD BILATERALLY NEGOTIATE A TREATY WITH MOSCOW TO GRADUALLY REMOVE ALL SOVIET AND AMERICAN FORCES FROM GERMANY. THE ESTABLISHMENT OF A BILATERALLY NEGOTIATED SECURITY REGIME IN GERMANY WOULD POSE MORE OF A CONSTRAINT OF FUTURE SOVIET BEHAVIOR THAN WOULD AN INFORMAL AND ILL-DEFINED EVOLUTION OF THE POLICIES OF THE TWO SUPERPOWERS IN EUROPE. THIS PROPOSAL WAS PRESENTED TO MEMBERS OF THE DEPARTMENT OF THE ARMY STAFF DURING A SEMINAR ON THE CONVENTIONAL STABILITY TALKS AT FT. LEAVENWORTH, KANSAS, IN FEBRUARY 1989.

05834 MACGREGOR, D.A.
THE SOVIET-EAST GERMAN MILITARY ALLIANCE
DISSERTATION ABSTRACTS INTERNATIONAL, 49(11) (MAY 89), 3498-A.
THE AUTHOR ENDEAVORS TO EXPLAIN THE EMERGENCE OF THE GDR AS THE SOVIET UNION'S PRIMARY MILITARY ALLY IN THE WARSAH PACT'S NORTHERN TIER. HE SURVEYS THE HISTORICAL RELATIONSHIP BETWEEN TSARIST-SOVIET RUSSIA AND PRUSSIA-GERMANY, THE SOVIET APPROACH TO THE DEVELOPMENT OF THE GDR'S ARMED FORCES, AND SOVIET SECURITY INTERESTS IN THE POSTWAR STRATEGIC NEXUS OF CENTRAL-EAST EUROPE. HE ALSO ASSESSES THE INCREASED RISKS TO SOVIET POWER AND INFLUENCE IN POLAND AND THE GDR'S ROLE IN THE EFFORT TO MANAGE OR SUPPRESS THE POLISH BID FOR GREATER INDEPENDENCE.

05835 MACHAN, T.R.
INDIVIDUAL VERSUS SUBJECTIVE VALUES
INTERNATIONAL JOURNAL OF SOCIAL ECONOMICS, 16(8) (1989), 49-59.
THE OBJECTIVE OF THIS ESSAY IS TO RECAST THE FAMILIAR SUBJECTIVE VALUE THEORY UNDERLYING NEO-CLASSICAL (INCLUDING AUSTRIAN) ECONOMICS AS MORE OF AN OBJECTIVIST ALBEIT INDIVIDUAL VALUE THEORY. THE BODY OF SCIENTIFIC ECONOMICS REMAINS INTACT, AS WELL AS THE POLITICAL ECONOMIC IMPLICATION OF VALUE DIVERSITY (WHICH THE PRICE SYSTEM OF THE MARKETPLACE ALONE CAN FULLY ACCOMMODATE). WHAT CHANGES IS THE VIEW THAT ECONOMIC SCIENCE MUST ASSUME THE META-

ETHICAL POSITION OF SUBJECTIVISM AND NONCOGNITIVISM, A
POSITION THAT CERTAINLY HAS NO PLACE WITHIN ECONOMICS PROPER
AND ONE THAT ASIDE FROM FACING MANY PHILOSOPHICAL
DIFFICULTIES IS ALSO INCREDIBLE FROM THE VIEWPOINT OF COMMON
SENSE (THUS POSING AS AN OBSTACLE TO THE PLAUSIBILITY OF NEO-
CLASSICAL ECONOMICS WHEN INTRODUCED INTO ORDINARY POLITICAL
DISCOURSE AND EVALUATED COMPARATIVELY, E.G. VIS-A-VIS
VARIETIES OF MARXIST ECONOMICS).

05836 MACHAN, T.R.
THE FANTASY OF GLASNOST
INTERNATIONAL JOURNAL OF SOCIAL ECONOMICS, 16(2) (1989),
46-53.
COMMUNISM APPEARS TO HAVE A "BETTER IMAGE" IN THE WEST
THAN FASCISM AND NAZISM. THE APPARENT REASONS FOR THIS ARE
REVEALED AND COMMENTED ON, AND THE CONCLUSION IS THAT THE
WEST SHOULD NOT BE MISLED INTO A COMPROMISE WITH SOVIET
COMMUNISM.

05837 MACHIN, H.
STAGES AND DYNAMICS IN THE EVOLUTION OF THE FRENCH PARTY
SYSTEM
WEST EUROPEAN POLITICS, 12(4) (OCT 89), 59-81.
DURING THE LAST DECADE THE FRENCH PARTY SYSTEM HAS
CHANGED CONTINUOUSLY AND DRAMATICALLY. IN THE LIGHT OF
RECENT FRENCH HISTORY THIS IS NEITHER NEW NOR SURPRISING;
INDEED, CHANGE APPEARS TO BE ONE OF THE FEW ENDURING
CHARACTERISTICS OF THAT PARTY SYSTEM. SINCE 1978, THE NUMBER
OF PARTIES, THEIR RELATIVE ELECTORAL STRENGTHS, THEIR
ALLIANCES OR DEALS WITH EACH OTHER AND THE IDEOLOGICAL
DIVERSITY OF PARTY POLITICAL COMPETITION HAVE ALL BEEN
MODIFIED. THERE HAS BEEN A TRANSFORMATION OF THE PARTY
SYSTEM, AND, IN THE FIRST SECTION OF THIS ANALYSIS, FOUR
MAIN STAGES IN THIS DEVELOPMENT ARE IDENTIFIED. IN THE THREE
SUBSEQUENT SECTIONS, THE DYNAMICS OF THE PROCESS OF PARTY
SYSTEM CHANGE ARE ANALYSED IN DIFFERENT WAYS. THE FIRST
APPROACH FOCUSES ON THE PARTIES THEMSELVES AND INTERNAL
PRESSURES FOR CHANGE. THIS UNDERLINES THE INHERENT TENSION
BETWEEN THE PARTIES AND THE PARTY SYSTEM IN WHICH THEY
OPERATE. THE SECOND APPROACH PLACES THE EMPHASIS ON THE
CHANGES IN THE IDEOLOGICAL CLIMATE AND DEMANDS OF THE
ELECTORATE AND THE SUCCESS OR FAILURE OF PARTIES TO MEET THE
CHALLENGES OF THEIR CHANGING ENVIRONMENT. THE RELATIVE
EFFECTIVENESS OF THE SOCIALISTS IN CREATING AND MAINTAINING
SOCIAL COALITIONS WITH NEW RADICAL LEFT FORCES, INCLUDING
GREENS, THE 1986 STUDENT MOVEMENT AND SOS-RACISME, CONTRASTS
WITH THE FAILURE OF THE CENTRE-RIGHT PARTIES TO CANALISE THE
PROTEST WHICH FED THE NATIONAL FRONT. THE THIRD APPROACH,
APPROPRIATE FOR 'DUVERGER'S COUNTRY', FOCUSES ON CHANGES IN
ELECTORAL SYSTEMS AND INSTITUTIONAL PATTERNS OF POWER. THIS
SHOWS HOW MODIFICATIONS IN PARTY STRATEGIES HAVE BEEN
INSPIRED BY THE CONFLICTING DEMANDS OF DIFFERENT ELECTORAL
RULES AND THE 'DE-COUPLING' OF THE PRESIDENCY FROM THE
PARLIAMENTARY MAJORITY, AND OF BOTH FROM LOCAL GOVERNMENTS.

05838 MACINTOSH, J.
NON-OFFENSIVE DEFENSE AND EUROPEAN ARMS CONTROL
INTERNATIONAL SPECTATOR, XXIV(1) (JAN 89), 39-49.
THE AUTHOR EXPLORES THE EXTENT TO WHICH THE ADOPTION OF
NEW CONVENTIONAL MILITARY DOCTRINES FEATURING A DEMONSTRABLY
"LESS OFFENSIVE" CHARACTER IN TERMS OF EQUIPMENT, DEPLOYMENT,
STRATEGY, AND TRAINING CAN BE PART OF THE EVOLVING
CONVENTIONAL ARMS CONTROL PROCESS AND THE OVERALL SECURITY
ENVIRONMENT IN EUROPE.

05839 MACKAY, J.
ZIMBABWE: BLACK AND WHITE, POOR AND RICH
NEW AFRICAN, (256) (JAN 89), 51-53.
ZIMBABWE'S POST-INDEPENDENCE GOVERNMENT EXTENDED A
GENEROUS OFFER OF RECONCILIATION TO ITS FORMER ENEMIES,
ENABLING IT TO AVOID THE MASS EXODUS AND ANIMOSITY AMONG
WHITES THAT OCCURRED IN MOZAMBIQUE IN 1975. BUT, DESPITE
CONCILIATORY EFFORTS, MANY WHITES REMAIN IN THEIR ECONOMIC
AND SOCIAL LAAGER, REFUSING TO PARTICIPATE FULLY IN THE LIFE
OF THE NEW STATE. ONE IMPEDIMENT TO INTEGRATION HAS BEEN THE
CONTINUING DEFECTION OF WHITE ZIMBABWEANS TO THE CAUSE OF
PRETORIA AND SOUTH AFRICAN DESTABILIZATION.

05840 MACKENZIE, G.W.
VOODOO AS A SOURCE OF POLITICAL CONTROL IN HAITI: 1959-1971
MICHIGAN JOURNAL OF POLITICAL SCIENCE, (11) (WIN 89),
88-96.
THIS ARTICLE EXAMINES ONE OF THE MOST BIZARRE SEGMENTS
IN HAITIAN HISTORY WHICH IS MARKED BY FRANCOIS DUVALIER'S
ELECTION AS PRESIDENT IN 1959, IT EXPLORES HOW DUVALIER
MANAGED EFFECTIVELY TO EXPLOIT AND CONTROL A NATION THROUGH
USE OF VOODOO AS A TACTIC OF SOCIAL CONTROL. IT ATTEMPTS TO
ANSWER TWO QUESTIONS: WHAT MAKES VOODOO AND ITS LEADERS
POWERFUL? AND HOW DID DUVALIER UTILIZE IT AS A MEANS OF
POLITICAL CONTROL? IT CONCLUDES THAT CURRENT POLITICAL
LEADERS ARE USING VOODOO TO CONTROL HAITI ONCE AGAIN.

05841 MACKENZIE, H.
FORGING NEW RELATIONS

MACLEAN'S (CANADA'S NEWS MAGAZINE), 102(4) (JAN 89), 32-33.
GEORGE BUSH DECLARED HIS INTENTION TO RENEW THE ANNUAL U.
S.-CANADIAN SUMMITS ESTABLISHED IN 1985. MANY CANADIANS
APPLAUD BUSH'S ELECTION, HOPING FOR HIS CONTINUED
SENSITIVITY TO IMPORTANT ISSUES SUCH AS ACID RAIN AND FREE
TRADE. HOWEVER, DOMESTIC ISSUES IN BOTH NATIONS THREATEN TO
OVERSHADOW U.S.-CANADIAN RELATIONS. THESE RANGE FROM THE
MEECH LAKE ACCORD AND THE DIVISIVE LANGUAGE DEBATE IN CANADA
TO THE FEDERAL BUDGET DEFICIT IN THE US.

05842 MACKENZIE, K.
FROM ANKARA: A VIEW
MIDDLE EAST INTERNATIONAL, 356 (AUG 89), 16.
THE HARDLINE STANCE OF THE TURKISH CYPRIOT LEADER, RAUF
DENKTASH, HAS BEEN WIDELY ENDORSED IN ANKARA, WHERE
OFFICIALS AND JOURNALISTS ALIKE HAVE FULMINATED NON-STOP
AGAINST THE GREEK WOMEN'S DEMONSTRATIONS - AND ALSO AGAINST
THE UN TROOPS IN CYPRUS FOR NOT HALTING THE PROTESTORS IN
THEIR TRACKS. RELATIONS BETWEEN TURKEY AND THE UN HAVE
BECOME ALMOST UNPRECEDENTEDLY STRAINED; APART FROM THE
HULLABALOO OVER THE WOMEN'S MARCH, TURKEY WILL NOT ACCEPT
THE LATEST UN PLAN, IN ITS PRESENT FORM, ON THE DEBATABLE
GROUND THAT THE TURKISH SIDE WAS NOT PROPERLY CONSULTED
ABOUT IT IN ADVANCE, AND THAT IT THEREFORE CONTAINS
PROVISIONS WHICH FAVOUR THE GREEKS.

05843 MACKENZIE, K.
OZAL AS TURKEY'S PRESIDENT
MIDDLE EAST INTERNATIONAL, (363) (NOV 89), 14-15.
FORMER TURKISH PRIME MINISTER TURGUT OZAL HAS BEEN
INSTALLED AS THE NATION'S NEW PRESIDENT. HE IMMEDIATELY MADE
IT CLEAR THAT, ALTHOUGH THE PRESIDENT'S CONSTITUTIONAL
POWERS ARE QUITE LIMITED, HE PLANS TO MAKE THE MOST OF HIS
SEVEN YEAR STAY IN THE PRESIDENTIAL PALACE. HE IMMEDIATELY
NAMED NEW MINISTERS OF STATE AND A NEW PRIME MINISTER WHO
ARE UNSWERVINGLY LOYAL. HIS ONLY CHALLENGE COMES FORM FORMER
SENIOR CABINET MINISTER, HASAN CELAL GUZEL; GUZEL IS VYING
FOR CONTROL OF THE RULING MOTHERLAND PARTY. IF HE IS ABLE TO
OVERCOME OZAL AND GAIN THE POST, TURKEY WILL BE FACED WITH
AN INTERESTING CONSTITUTIONAL CRISIS: ONE MAN WILL HEAD THE
GOVERNMENT, AND ANOTHER, THE PRESIDENT'S FIERCEST CHALLENGER,
WILL HEAD THE RULING PARTY.

05844 MACKENZIE, K.
TURKEY ROWS WITH SYRIA AND IRAQ
MIDDLE EAST INTERNATIONAL, (365) (DEC 89), 13.
INCREASING TENSION BETWEEN TURKEY AND ITS MIDEASTERN
NEIGHBORS, SYRIA AND IRAQ, HAS INCREASED THE LIKELIHOOD THAT
TURKEY MAY RESORT TO ITS TRUMP CARD: CONTROL OF THE
EUPHRATES RIVER. ANGERED OVER THE MASSACRE OF A TURKISH
VILLAGE BY A KURDISH GANG, AND OVER THE SHOOTING DOWN OF A
TURKISH CIVILIAN AIRCRAFT BY SYRIAN FIGHTERS HAS INCREASED
TENSION BETWEEN THE STATES. TURKEY HAS ALREADY DECLARED THAT
IT WILL CUT OFF THE FLOW OF VALUABLE WATER FOR A MONTH,
OSTENSIBLY FOR TECHNICAL REASONS, BUT THE MESSAGE TO IRAQ
AND SYRIA IS CLEAR: TURKEY HAS LONG REGARDED WATER AS THEIR
SECRET WEAPON IN THE MIDDLE EAST.

05845 MACKENZIE, K.
TURKEY: AMBIVALENCE REIGNS
MIDDLE EAST INTERNATIONAL, (345) (MAR 89), 16-17.
AS TURKEY'S BID TO JOIN THE EUROPEAN COMMUNITY NEARS THE
CRUCIAL POINT, TURKEY'S HUMAN RIGHTS RECORD IS COMING UNDER
INCREASED SCRUTINY. THE TURKS COMPLAIN THAT THE EUROPEANS
ARE "PICKING" ON THEM. BUT, IN EUROPEAN EYES, TURKEY'S
APPLICATION HAS JUSTIFIABLY FOCUSED ATTENTION ON SUBJECTS
LIKE TORTURE IN PRISONS AND THE TREATMENT OF THE KURDS.

05846 MACKENZIE, K.
TURKEY: FLAG FUSS
MIDDLE EAST INTERNATIONAL, 353 (JUN 89), 12-13.
IN DEATH, AYATOLLAH KHOMEINI HAS RENT THE TURKISH PEOPLE
APART MORE EFFECTIVELY THAN IN LIFE: THE SIGHT OF THE
TURKISH FLAG AT HALF-MAST, ALONE AMONG 16, WAS VIRTUALLY
INCOMPREHENSIBLE TO WESTERN SOLDIERS AND DIPLOMATS - AND AN
ALMOST UNBEARABLE EMBARRASSMENT TO TURKEY'S NATO
REPRESENTATIVES. THE IMPORTANCE OF THE AFFAIR SHOULD NOT BE
EXAGGERATED, BUT IT HAS INCREASED DOUBTS IN THE WEST ABOUT
THE GENUINENESS OF MR OZAL'S PROFESSED COMMITMENT TO EUROPE.
THOUGH TURKEY LOOKS UNITED AT THE MOMENT OVER THE CRISIS
WITH BULGARIA, THE COUNTRY WILL PROBABLY BE DIVIDED OVER THE
RELIGIOUS QUESTION FOR A LONG TIME.

05847 MACKENZIE, K.
TURKEY: ISLAMIC DILEMMAS
MIDDLE EAST INTERNATIONAL, (346) (MAR 89), 10.
TURKISH PRIME MINISTER TURGUT OZAL IS BELATEDLY TRYING
TO DISTANCE HIMSELF, VERY SLIGHTLY, FROM THE AYATOLLAH
KHOMEINI'S ATTACK ON SALMAN RUSHDIE. BUT CONSIDERABLE DAMAGE
HAS ALREADY BEEN DONE. OPPONENTS OF TURKEY'S ENTRY TO THE
EUROPEAN COMMUNITY ARGUE THAT OZAL'S STANCE ON THE RUSHDIE
AFFAIR PROVES THAT, IN MENTALITY, TURKEY IS NOT A EUROPEAN
COUNTRY.

05848 MACKENZIE, K.
TURKEY: MORTALLY WOUNDED
MIDDLE EAST INTERNATIONAL, (347) (MAR 89), 14-15.
TURKEY'S MARCH 1989 LOCAL ELECTIONS WERE AN UNMITIGATED
DISASTER FOR PRIME MINISTER TURGUT OZAL AND HIS PERSONAL
DOMINATION OF TURKISH POLITICS SEEMS NEAR THE END. IN THE
PROVINCIAL ASSEMBLY ELECTIONS, OZAL'S MOTHERLAND PARTY WON
ONLY ABOUT 21 PERCENT OF THE VOTE, DESPITE ITS TARGET OF 36
PERCENT.

05849 MACKENZIE, K.
TURKEY: OZAL'S BALANCING ACT
MIDDLE EAST INTERNATIONAL, (348) (APR 89), 12-13.
TURKEY'S PRIME MINISTER, TURGUT OZAL, IS DESPARATELY
TRYING TO REPAIR HIS IMAGE AFTER A RESOUNDING DEFEAT IN
LOCAL ELECTIONS. HE HAS RESHUFFLED THE CABINET AND TAKEN ON
A TOUGHER ANTI-IRANIAN STANCE WHICH HAS PLEASED THE
WESTERNIZED TURKS. HOWEVER, HIS UNPOPULARITY CONTINUES DUE
TO THE LAGGING ECONOMY; MANY OBSERVERS AND OPPOSITION
LEADERS ARE PREDICTING AN EARLY ELECTION, BUT AS OF YET,
OZAL HAS DEFIANTLY REFUSED TO CONSODER THE POSSIBILITY.

05850 MACKENZIE, K.
TURKEY: OZAL'S TRIBULATIONS
MIDDLE EAST INTERNATIONAL, (350) (MAY 89), 15.
PRIME MINISTER TURGUT OZAL'S MOTHERLAND PARTY IS RENT
WITH INTERNAL FEUDING, DUE TO ITS STAGGERING REVERSES IN THE
LOCAL ELECTIONS, FOREIGN BUSINESSMEN AND BANKERS ARE
HESITATING TO SINK MONEY INTO TURKEY BECAUSE OF THE NEW
POLITICAL UNCERTAINTIES. AND THE COUNTRY IS IN THE THROES OF
SERIOUS LABOR UNREST, WHICH COULD CRIPPLE OZAL'S GRANDIOSE
ECONOMIC PLANS.

05851 MACKENZIE, K.
TURKEY: SQUALID STORM
MIDDLE EAST INTERNATIONAL, (342) (JAN 89), 15.
PRIME MINISTER TURGUT OZAL'S GOVERNMENT HAS BEEN ROCKED
BY A FINANCIAL SCANDAL, WHICH HAS LED TO THE RESIGNATION OF
HIS DEPUTY PRIME MINISTER, KAYA ERDEM. OZAL HAS EMERGED IN
GOOD SHAPE, BUT MANY OBSERVERS FEEL THAT ERDEM HAS MADE A
SCAPEGOAT.

05852 MACKENZIE, K.
TURKEY'S KURDISH PROBLEM
MIDDLE EAST INTERNATIONAL, (360) (OCT 89), 12-13.
TURKEY'S PRIME MINISTER TURGUT ORZAL IS FACED WITH AN
EVER-INCREASING CONFLICT BETWEEN TURKS AND KURDS. THE DEATH
TOLL RESULTING FROM SUCH CONFLICTS HAS RISEN TO 70 A MONTH
AND HAS FORCED TURKEY TO BEGIN TO ACKNOWLEDGE THE EXISTENCE
OF A PROBLEM. HOWEVER, TURKISH ACTION HAS NOT GONE BEYOND A
TACIT ACKNOWLEDGEMENT OF THE KURDS' ETHNIC IDENTITY AND
CONTINUED FINGER POINTING AT SYRIA AND IRAN.

05853 MACKENZIE, O.
OZAL BIDS FOR PRESIDENT
MIDDLE EAST INTERNATIONAL, (361) (OCT 89), 13.
THE ANNOUNCEMENT OF PRIME MINISTER TURGUT OZAL THAT HE
WOULD SEEK THE OFFICE OF TURKEY'S PRESIDENCY HAS BROUGHT
WIDESPREAD CRITICISM UPON THE RULING MOTHERLAND PARTY.
ALTHOUGH HIS BEING ELECTED BY THE PARTY'S HUGE MAJORITY IN
PARLIAMENT IS NOT UNCONSTITUTIONAL, THE PARTY HAS LOST
SIGNIFICANT PUBLIC SUPPORT; OZAL WOULD HARDLY FUNCTION AS AN
IMPARTIAL SYMBOL OF NATIONAL UNITY. OPPOSITION GROUPS
THREATEN TO BOYCOTT THE BALLOTING AND NOT TO RECOGNIZE ITS
RESULTS, BUT IT REMAINS UNCERTAIN HOW THEY WILL IMPLEMENT
THEIR THREATS.

05854 MACKENZIE, S.P.
VOX POLULI: BRITISH ARMY NEWSPAPERS IN THE SECOND WORLD WAR
JOURNAL OF CONTEMPORARY HISTORY, 24(4) (OCT 89), 665-681.
BRITISH ARMY NEWSPAPERS IN WORLD WAR II WERE PRODUCED
UNDER OFFICIAL AUSPICES AND, THEREFORE, PRESUMABLY ONLY
PROVIDED INFORMATION AND VIEWS TO WHICH THE MILITARY
AUTHORITIES COULD NOT TAKE EXCEPTION. ON CLOSER EXAMINATION,
HOWEVER, THIS PROVES NOT TO BE THE CASE. MANY OF THE ARMY'S
PAPERS WERE QUITE OUTSPOKEN AND, AT TIMES, BECAME ALMOST AS
CONTROVERSIAL AS THEIR BETTER-KNOWN CIVILIAN COUNTERPARTS.
THIS ESSAY CHRONICLES THE DEVELOPMENT OF THE MORE
CONTROVERSIAL ARMY NEWSPAPERS AND EXPLAINS HOW AND WHY THEY
BECAME THE FOCUS OF SUSPICION IN OFFICIAL CIRCLES.

05855 MACKEUN, M.B.; ERICKSON, R.S.; STIMSON, J.A.
MACROPARTISANSHIP
AMERICAN POLITICAL SCIENCE REVIEW, 83(4) (DEC 89),
1125-1142.
FROM AN EARLY, INCORRECT CONSENSUS THAT PARTY
INDENTIFICATION WAS FREE OF THE SHORT-TERM INFLUENCES OF
POLITICAL LIFE, ITS AGGREGATE, MACROPARTISANSHIP, DREW
LITTLE SCHOLARY NOTICE. THOUGH MACROPARTISANSHIP, TYPICALLY
SEEN AS A BIENNIAL TIMES SERIES, APPEARS ESSENTIALLY
CONSTANT, THE QUARTERLY TREATMENT DEMONSTRATES SUBSTANTIAL
AND NOTABLY SYSTEMATIC MOVEMENT OF THIS CRUCIAL BAROMETER OF
THE U.S. PARTY SYSTEM. THE AUTHORS DEMONSTRATE THAT IT
VARIES SYSTEMATICALLY WITH RESPECT TO TIME, HAS ELECTORAL

CONSEQUENCES, AND CAN BE MODELED AS A FUNCTION OF ECONOMIC
EVALUATIONS AND APPROVAL OF THE INCUMBENT PRESIDENTIAL
ADMINISTRATION. MACROPARTISANSHIP IS A VARIABLE LIKE OTHERS,
SUBJECT TO ROUTINE EBB AND FLOW AS CITIZENS IN THE AGGREGATE
REFLECT THEIR EXPERIENCES OF POLITICS ONTO THE PARTIES. ITS
MEDIUM-TERM MOVEMENTS OF CONSIDERABLE MAGNITUDE ARE LASTING
ENOUGH TO MATTER BUT OCCUR WITHOUT CONNOTING SHIFTS IN THE
UNDERLYING PARTY SYSTEM AND CAN BE UNDERSTOOD WITHOUT
INVOKING THE CRISES AND CONVULSIONS OF REALIGNMENT THEORY.

05856 MACKIE, T.T.
GENERAL ELECTIONS IN WESTERN NATIONS DURING 1988
EUROPEAN JOURNAL OF POLITICAL RESEARCH, 17(6) (NOV 89),
747-752.
THIS ARTICLE GIVES THE RESULTS OF GENERAL ELECTIONS IN
CANADA, DENMARK, FRANCE, ICELAND, ISRAEL, SWEDEN, AND THE
UNITED STATES IN 1988.

05857 MACKINNON, C.A.
FEMINISM, MARXISM, METHOD, AND THE STATE
DISSERTATION ABSTRACTS INTERNATIONAL, 48(10) (APR 88),
2718-A.
FEMINISM AND MARXISM AS APPROACHES TO THE ANALYSIS OF
INEQUALITY ARE EVALUATED IN THE LIGHT OF THE OTHER AS ARE
UNSUCCESSFUL ATTEMPTS TO SYNTHESIZE THE TWO. THE LAWS OF
RAPE, ABORTION, SEX DISCRIMINATION, AND PORNOGRAPHY IN THE
US ARE EXAMINED TO SHOW HOW THE STATE ENFORCES THE SEXUAL
POLITICS OF MALE DOMINANCE.

05858 MACKINTOSH, M.
THE EVOLUTION OF THE WARSAW PACT
RUSI JOURNAL, 134(4) (WIN 89), 16-22.
THE ARTICLE TRACES THE DEVELOPMENT OF THE WARSAW PACT
SINCE ITS FORMATION IN 1955 TO THE PRESENT DAY. IT ANALYZES
ITS ROLE IN SOVIET POLITICAL AND MILITARY DECISION-MAKING IN
EASTERN EUROPE AND TOWARDS THE WEST. IT EXAMINES THE CRISES
IN WHICH MILITARY FORCES HAVE BEEN USED AND DESCRIBES THE
PACT'S POLITICAL AND MILITARY ORGANIZATION. IT CONCLUDES
WITH AN ANALYSIS OF THE EFFECT THAT FORCE REDUCTIONS AND
ATTEMPTS AT ARMS CONTROL, HAVE HAD ON THE WARSAW PACT.

05859 MACKOON, L.
GRENADA: TROUBLE AHEAD
THIRD WORLD WEEK, 7(11) (FEB 89), 81-82.
GRENADA'S PRIME MINISTER HERBERT A. BLAIZE, WHO HAS
HEADED THE GOVERNMENT SINCE 1984, MUST CALL AN ELECTION IN
1989 AND HIS CHANCES FOR WINNING ANOTHER TERM ARE
PRACTICALLY NIL. IN A HUMILIATING REBUFF, BLAIZE WAS VOTED
OUT OF LEADERSHIP OF HIS OWN NEW NATIONAL PARTY, LEAVING HIM
WITH NO POLITICAL BASE. EVEN WORSE FOR BLAIZE, FORMER PRIME
MINISTER ERIC M. GAIRY HAS COME OUT OF RETIREMENT TO GUIDE
HIS GRENADA UNITED LABOR PARTY IN THE ELECTION.

05860 MACLACHLAN, C. M.
SPAIN'S EMPIRE IN THE NEW WORLD: THE ROLE OF IDEAS IN
INSTITUTIONAL AND SOCIAL CHANGE
UNIVERSITY OF CALIFORNIA PRESS, BERKELEY, CA, 1988, 238.
THE AUTHOR EXAMINES BOTH THE THEORY AND THE PRACTICE OF
SPAIN'S EMPIRE IN THE NEW WORLD. HE ARGUES THAT LATIN
AMERICA'S COLONIAL HERITAGE, FAR FROM INSPIRING RIGID
CENTRALISM AND AUTHORITARIANISM, IS ONE OF POLITICAL
FLEXIBILITY AND COMPROMISE BASED ON WIDELY ACCEPTED
PHILOSOPHICAL NOTIONS. SPAIN'S STRUGGLE IN THE NEW WORLD WAS
NOT FOR JUSTICE BUT FOR THE ESTABLISHMENT OF AN ACCEPTABLE
SOCIOPOLITICAL BALANCE.

05861 MACLEAN, D.; MILLS, C.
LOVE AND JUSTICE
REPORT FROM THE INSTITUTE FOR PHILOSOPHY AND PUBLIC POLICY,
9(4) (FAL 89), 12-15.
LOVE AND JUSTICE HAVE COME TO BE ASSOCIATED WITH TWO
SPHERES AND WITH THE TWO GENDERS. LOVE IS THE PROVINCE OF
HEARTH AND HOME, OF THE DOMESTIC SPHERE, PRESIDED OVER BY
WOMEN. THE IDEAL OF JUSTICE REGULATES THE WORLD OF BUSINESS
AND POLITICS, THE MARKETPLACE AND THE PUBLIC FORUM, THE
WORLD OF MEN. BUT EVEN AS THE WORLD NOW CHALLENGES SUCH
GENDER-TYPING AND MANY ARGUE FOR A BLURRING, IF NOT
ERADICATION OF GENDER ROLES, MANY ALSO QUESTION THE
SEPARATENESS OF THE TWO SPHERES AND THE OPPOSITION BETWEEN
LOVE AND JUSTICE.

05862 MACLEAN, D.
NUCLEAR WASTE STORAGE: YOUR BACKYARD OR MINE?
REPORT FROM THE INSTITUTE FOR PHILOSOPHY AND PUBLIC POLICY,
9(2-3) (SPR 89), 5-8.
WHEN IT COMES TO THE SITING OF A NUCLEAR WASTE
REPOSITORY, IT IS FAIRLY EASY TO FIND REASONS WHY SOMEBODY
ELSE'S BACKYARD IS GEOGRAPHICALLY, TECHNOLOGICALLY,
POLITICALLY, AND MORALLY PREFERABLE TO ONE'S OWN. IN AN
IDEAL WORLD, THE RISKS OF NUCLEAR WASTE STORAGE WOULD BE
PARCELED OUT EQUALLY, SO THAT EVERYONE WOULD FACE THE SAME
CHANCE OF POSSIBLE HARM. BUT IN THE REAL WORLD, THESE RISKS
MUST BE DISTRIBUTED UNEQUALLY. GEOLOGY, DEMOGRAPHY, AND
DEMOCRACY ARE ALL RELEVANT TO THE PROCESS OF SITE SELECTION.

THE PROCEDURE MUST BE JUSTIFIED ON SCIENTIFIC, POLITICAL, AND MORAL GROUNDS. BUT A PROCEDURE THAT IS IDEALLY EQUITABLE, REASONABLE, AND SOCIALLY ACCEPTABLE HAS NOT YET BEEN FOUND.

05863 MACLELLAN, N.
POLICING THE ECONOMY IN PAPUA NEW GUINEA
ARENA, 86 (FAL 89), 37-44.
PAPUA NEW GUINEA HOVERS ON THE EDGE OF A NEW RESOURCES BOOM. ALTHOUGH THE PNG GOVERNMENT IS TAKING UP EQUITY IN SOME OF THESE PROJECTS, THE MINERALS SECTOR IS RELIANT ON OVERSEAS INVESTMENT, TECHNOLOGY AND EXPLORATION. FOREIGN INVESTORS ARE INCREASINGLY CALLING FOR POLITICAL AND INDUSTRIAL 'STABILITY' IN PAPUA NEW GUINEA, TO CREATE A SUITABLE CLIMATE FOR INVESTMENT. THE ALLOCATION OF INCREASED FUNDS FOR AN IMPROVEMENT IN POLICING COINCIDES WITH THESE CALLS FOR AN END TO LAWLESSNESS.

05864 MACMANAS, S.A.; BROWN, H. R. JR.; HICKEY, N.; O'DONNELL, S.; RATTLEY, J. M.; SHALMY, D. L.; UNGARO, P. J.
A DECADE OF DECLINE: A LONGITUDINAL LOOK AT BIG CITY AND BIG COUNTY STRATEGIES TO COPE WITH DECLINING REVENUES
INTERNATIONAL JOURNAL OF PUBLIC ADMINISTRATION, 12(5) (1989), 749-796.
MANY LOCAL GOVERNMENTS HAVE NOW ENDURED A DECADE OF FISCAL DECLINE DUE TO PERIODIC REDUCTIONS IN EXTERNAL FUNDING (FEDERAL AND STATE) AND SLOWDOWNS IN THE RATE OF GROWTH OF THE STATE AND LOCAL GOVERNMENT SECTOR. THIS RESEARCH EXAMINES THE EXTENT TO WHICH SIX LARGE JURISDICTIONS (THREE CITIES, THREE COUNTIES) UNDER FISCAL DURESS AVOIDED POLITICAL CONFLICT AND PREVENTED FURTHER FRAGMENTATION OF THEIR AUTHORITY BETWEEN 1978 AND 1987. THE RESULTS SHOWED THAT LOCAL OFFICIALS GENERALLY CHOSE RETRENCHMENT STRATEGIES (REVENUE, EXPENDITURE, AND BORROWING) WITH THE LEAST ANTICIPATED POLITICAL OPPOSITION; BUT WHERE HARD CHOICES HAD TO BE MADE (PERSONNEL REDUCTIONS), THEY WERE MADE WITHOUT HESITATION. THE TIMING OF POLITICALLY UNPOPULAR CHOICES TO COINCIDE WITH DOWNWARD TRENDS IN THE PRIVATE SECTOR REDUCED THE LEVEL OF POLITICAL FALLOUT, EVEN IN HEAVILY UNIONIZED, SOCIOECONOMICALLY DIVERSE COMMUNITIES. THE RESULTS ALSO SHOWED THAT LOCAL OFFICIALS STRONGLY ENDORSED, RATHER THAN OPPOSED, STRATEGIES THAT FURTHER FRAGMENTED THEIR AUTHORITY (PRIVATIZATION, INTERGOVERNMENTAL COOPERATIVE AGREEMENTS), BECAUSE THESE APPROACHES PRODUCE SIGNIFICANT PERSONNEL AND CAPITAL SAVINGS IN THE SHORT TERM. FINALLY, THE RESULTS INDICATED THAT THE LONG-TERM CUMULATIVE EFFECTS OF SHORT-TERM DECREMENTAL DECISIONMAKING ON THE QUALITY OF LIFE (AS MEASURED BY DROPS IN BOND RATINGS) WERE NEGATIVE IN ONLY ONE-THIRD OF THE JURISDICTIONS.

05865 MACMANUS, S.A.; BULLOCK, C.S. III
WOMEN ON SOUTHERN CITY COUNCILS: A DECADE OF CHANGE
JOURNAL OF POLITICAL SCIENCE, 17(1-2) (1989), 32-49.
THE AUTHORS EXAMINE THE INFLUENCES OF GOVERNMENTAL STRUCTURAL VARIABLES ON FEMALE REPRESENTATION ON SOUTHERN CITY COUNCILS. THE VARIABLES INCLUDE SINGLE MEMBER DISTRICT ELECTION SYSTEMS, COUNCIL SIZE, INCUMBENCY RETURN RATE, LENGTH OF TERM, STAGGERED TERMS, AND MAJORITY VOTE REQUIREMENTS. THE RESEARCH DATA ARE DRAWN FROM 211 CITIES IN ELEVEN SOUTHERN STATES.

05866 MACMILLAN, L.
NEW REPRODUCTIVE TECHNOLOGIES: THE FINAL SOLUTION OR NO SOLUTION?
COMMUNIST VIEWPOINT, 20(4) (WIN 88), 6-10.
THIS PAPER SEEKS TO EXPLORE THE RELATIONSHIP BETWEEN THE NEW REPRODUCTIVE TECHNOLOGIES, INCLUDING 'SURROGATE MOTHERHOOD' AND THE OTHER MAJOR TRANSFORMATIONS OVERTAKING THE WORLD NOW, IT AIMS TO DEVELOP THE INITIAL WORK OF MARXIST FEMINISTS IN UNITING CHANGES IN REPRODUCTION WITH CHANGES IN PRODUCTION FOR ONE OVERALL ANALYSIS OF THE MODE OF PRODUCTION OF A PARTICULAR EPOCH.

05867 MACNAIR, R
REVERSING A TREND
SOJOURNERS, 18(10) (NOV 89), 19.
ALTHOUGH ROE VS. WADE LEGALIZED ABORTION, IT DID NOT SOLVE MANY OF THE PROBLEMS ASSOCIATED WITH UNWANTED PREGNANCIES. A KEY PROBLEM HAS THE LACK OF INPUT INTO ABORTION POLICY BY WOMEN WHO HAD ABORTIONS, AND LATER REGRETTED THE DECISION. THE WEBSTER DECISION WILL ALLOW INCREASED INPUT AND A GENERAL EMPOWERING OF WOMEN.

05868 MACNEILL, J.
TOWARDS 2000
POLICY OPTIONS, 10(3) (APR 89), 3-6.
THE THREAT POSED TO GLOBAL SECURITY BY ENVIRONMENTAL DESTRUCTION RANKS JUST BEHIND THE THREAT OF GLOBAL NUCLEAR DESTRUCTION. BEHIND THE POLITICAL UPHEAVAL AND MILITARY VIOLENCE IN MANY COUNTRIES LIES THE DEPLETION OF FORESTS AND WATER AND THE INCAPACITY OF THE LAND TO SUPPORT THE PEOPLE. STEPS, INCLUDING THE TRANSFER OF SOME MILITARY SPENDING TO ENVIRONMENTAL PROJECTS, ARE NEEDED TO MEET THE ECOLOGICAL THREAT.

05869 MACQUEEN, N.
PAPUA NEW GUINEA'S RELATIONS WITH INDONESIA AND AUSTRALIA: DIPLOMACY ON THE ASIA-PACIFIC INTERFACE
ASIAN SURVEY, 22(5) (MAY 89), 530-541.
THIS ARTICLE REPORTS ON DIPLOMACY ON THE ASIA-PACIFIC INTERFACE. IT EXAMINES EVENTS FOLLOWING PAPUA NEW GUINEA'S (PNG) INDEPENDENCE AND EXAMINES THE RELATIONSHIP OF PNG TO INDONESIA AND AUSTRALIA. IT CONCLUDES THAT THERE MAY BE CONSIDERABLE IMPLICATIONS FOR AUSTRALIA-INDONESIA RELATIONS IN THE READJUSTMENTS IN THE DIPLOMATIC TRIANGLE ON THE SOUTH EAST ASIA-SOUTH PACIFIC INTERFACE.

05870 MACWILLIAM, S.
SMALLHOLDINGS, LAND LAW, AND THE POLITICS OF LAND TENURE IN PAPUA NEW GUINEA
JOURNAL OF PEASANT STUDIES, 16(1) (OCT 88), 77-109.
IT HAS BEEN ASSERTED OF PAPUA NEW GUINEA THAT THE NINETEENTH AND TWENTIETH CENTURY EXPANSION OF CAPITALISM INTO THAT COUNTRY OCCURRED WITHOUT THE COMMODIFICATION OF MORE THAN A SMALL AMOUNT OF LAND. THE VARIOUS ARGUMENTS SUPPORTING THIS VIEW ARE REJECTED, AND THE EVIDENCE TO THE CONTRARY IS PRESENTED. IT IS SHOWN THAT FROM THE 1950S SMALLHOLDER PRODUCTION INCREASES HAVE BEEN SUBSTANTIAL, MAINLY BUT NOT WHOLLY IN EXPORT CROPS. THE ROLE OF THE STATE IS EXAMINED, WITH PARTICULAR FOCUS UPON THE CHARACTERISTICS OF STATE POWER AND THE POLITICS OF LAND WHICH HAVE UNDERPINNED THE INCREASE IN SMALLHOLDER PRODUCTION. SIMILARITIES IN THE QUALITY AND APPLICATION OF STATE POWER ACROSS BOTH COLONIAL AND POST-COLONIAL REGIMES IS STRESSED.

05871 MADAR, D.
HEAVY TRAFFIC: TRUCKING DEREGULATION, FEDERALISM AND CANADIAN-US TRADE
PUBLIUS: THE JOURNAL OF FEDERALISM, 19(1) (WIN 89), 107-126.
TRUCKING DEREGULATION, IN THE INTEREST OF COMPETITION AND EFFICIENCY, REMOVES RATE CONTROLS AND GRANTS FREE ENTRY TO THE MARKET. WHEN THE UNITED STATES DEREGULATED TRUCKING IN 1980, IT OPENED THE INTERSTATE MARKET TO CANADIAN CARRIERS. HEAVY VOLUMES OF TRADE BY TRUCKING BETWEEN THE TWO COUNTRIES MAKE ENTRY CONDITIONS AN IMPORTANT BILATERAL ISSUE. DEREGULATORY SYMMETRY BETWEEN THE TWO COUNTRIES WOULD PRODUCE A DE FACTO REGIME OF FREE TRADE IN TRUCKING SERVICES. IN 1987 THE CANADIAN FEDERAL GOVERNMENT ADOPTED DEREGULATORY MEASURES SIMILAR TO THOSE OF THE UNITED STATES, BUT WITH MORE COMPLEX AND PROBLEMATIC RESULTS. THE REASONS, BROADLY CHARACTERISTIC OF THE EVOLUTION OF CANADIAN FEDERALISM, LIE IN THE ABILITY OF THE PROVINCES TO THWART FEDERAL INITIATIVES. REGULATORY RECIPROCITY IS ALSO A QUESTION OF THE PROVINCES AND STATES, WITH A MIXTURE OF STRICT AND EASY ENTRY POLICIES COMPLICATING THE ACHIEVEMENT OF BILATERAL BALANCE AND EQUITY. THE LARGER IMPLICATIONS OF DEREGULATION AND TRANSBORDER TRUCKING FOR CANADA LIE IN THE ABILITY OF A DECENTRALIZED FEDERAL SYSTEM TO PURSUE NECESSARY INITIATIVES COHERENTLY.

05872 MADDISON, A.
DUTCH INCOME IN AND FROM INDONESIA 1700-1938
MODERN ASIAN STUDIES, 23(4) (OCT 89), 645-670.
THE ARTICLE IS A QUANTITATIVE ANALYSIS OF DUTCH INCOME IN AND FROM INDONESIA. IT EXAMINES INCOME DERIVED IN SEVERAL PERIODS OF THE DUTCH COLONIZATION OF INDONESIA INCLUDING: THE MERCHANT CAPITALIST PERIOD (1602-1780); THE TRANSITION PERIOD (1780-1830); A PERIOD CHARACTERIZED BY FISCAL TRIBUTRE, BUREAUCRATIC RESTRICTIONS, AND FAVORITISM (1830-1870); COLONIAL CAPITALISM AND THE LIBERAL ORDER (1870-1928); AND THE DEPRESSION YEARS (1929-38). THE PRINCIPAL FINDINGS OF THE STUDY ARE THAT DUTCH INCOME IN AND FROM INDONESIA PROBABLY AMOUNTED TO ABOUT 1.4 PER CENT OF INDONESIAN DOMESTIC PRODUCT IN 1700 AND ROSE TO ABOUT 17 PER CENT IN 1921-38. THE ARTICLE CONCLUDES WITH AN ANALYSIS OF SOME PROBLEMS ASSOCIATED WITH MACROQUATIFICATION.

05873 MADING, H.
FEDERALISM AND EDUCATION PLANNING IN THE FEDERAL REPUBLIC OF GERMANY
PUBLIUS: THE JOURNAL OF FEDERALISM, 19(4) (FAL 89), .
IN 1969 DEMANDS FOR GREATER RATIONALITY IN EDUCATION PLANNING GAVE RISE TO NEW INSTITUTIONALIZED FORMS OF COOPERATION BETWEEN THE FEDERATION AND THE LANDER. CONFLICTS BETWEEN THE FEDERAL AND LAND GOVERNMENTS, PARTISAN CONFLICTS, AND FINANCIAL CONFLICTS OVERLAPPED THIS COOPERATION. DESPITE THE FACT THAT THE FORMAL CAPACITY FOR DEALING WITH CONFLICTS HAD MANY SHORTCOMINGS, A JOINT GENERAL PLAN FOR EDUCATION WAS ISSUED IN 1973 AS A RESULT OF FAVORABLE ECONOMIC AND POLITICAL CONDITIONS. HOWEVER, IN 1978 THE FEDERAL GOVERNMENT FAILED IN ITS ATTEMPT TO UTILIZE THE DISSATISFACTION WITH THE EXISTING SYSTEM OF COOPERATION TO EXTEND ITS RESPONSIBILITIES FOR EDUCATION. THE DETERIORATION IN ECONOMIC AND POLITICAL CONDITIONS LED TO AN END OF EFFORTS TO FORMULATE A GENERAL PLAN FOR EDUCATION IN 1982 AND REDUCED THE SCALE OF JOINT ACTIVITIES. FORMS OF EDUCATIONAL COOPERATION BETWEEN THE FEDERATION AND THE

LANDER STILL EXIST, BUT THEY NO LONGER FULFILL THEIR
ORIGINAL PURPOSE. THE CENTRALIZATION OF DECISIONMAKING,
WHICH WAS ORIGINALLY EXPECTED, NEVER CAME INTO BEING.

05874 MAGAGNA, V.V.
CONSUMERS OF PRIVILEGE: A POLITICAL ANALYSIS OF CLASS,
CONSUMPTION AND SOCIALISM
POLITY, 21(4) (SUM 89), 711-730.
THE TOTALITARIAN MODEL OF SOCIALISM IS NO LONGER
UNIVERSALLY ACCEPTED AS AN ANALYTIC FRAMEWORK IN THE STUDY
OF SOCIETIES THAT HAVE FOLLOWED THE SOVIET PATH OF
DEVELOPMENT. THERE IS, HOWEVER, NO ALTERNATIVE MODEL OF
AUTHORITARIAN SOCIALISM THAT SYSTEMATICALLY LINKS THE
POLITICAL AND ECONOMIC ASPECTS OF STATE SOCIALISM IN A
COMPREHENSIVE INTERPRETIVE FRAMEWORK. THIS ARTICLE, WHICH
EXPLORES THE RELATIONSHIP BETWEEN POLITICAL POWER, CENTRAL
PLANNING, AND SOCIAL INEQUALITY IN THE SOVIET UNION, SEEKS
TO FILL THIS VOID. THE AUTHOR ARGUES THAT CENTRALLY PLANNED
ECONOMIES GENERATE DISTINCTIVE PATTERNS OF CLASS HIERARCHY
IN THE SPHERE OF HOUSEHOLD AND INDIVIDUAL CONSUMPTION AND
THAT INEQUALITIES IN CONSUMPTION ARE PRODUCED BY THE
RESULTING BIFURCATION IN THE STRUCTURE OF CONSUMPTION
OPPORTUNITIES FOR THE PRIVILEGED AND THE MASSES. THE ARTICLE
LINKS THIS TO THE POLITICAL LOGIC OF "MARKETLESS" SOCIALISM
AND, ULTIMATELY, TO THE RISE OF NOVEL FORMS OF CLASS
DOMINATION.

05875 MAGAS, B.
YUGOSLAVIA: THE SPECTRE OF BALKANIZATION
NEW LEFT REVIEW, (174) (MAR 89), 3-32.
IN THE ABSENCE OF SOCIALIST DEMOCRACY AND COHERENT
POLITICAL DIRECTION IN YUGOSLAVIA, LAISSEZ-FAIRE ECONOMICS
WILL COMPOUND RATHER THAN REMEDY THE FUNDAMENTAL PROBLEMS OF
A POST-TITO ORDER BESET BY YAWNING REGIONAL AND SOCIAL
INEQUALITIES. THE AUTHOR FOCUSES ON THE POLITICAL CRUX OF
THE CRISIS: THE ASCENDANCE OF A REACTIONARY CURRENT IN
SERBIA BIDDING FOR HEGEMONY IN THE STATE AS A WHOLE. SHE
SHOWS HOW THE RISE OF MILOSEVIC HAS ACCOMPANIED BY A STATE-
SPONSORED CAMPAIGN AGAINST THE NATIONAL RIGHTS OF
YUGOSLAVIA'S ALBANIANS AND AGAINST FLEDGLING DEMOCRATIC
STIRRINGS. MILOSEVIC'S DEMAGOGIC INVOCATION OF AN "ANTI-
BUREAUCRATIC REVOLUTION" HIDES THE MOST SUSTAINED ONSLAUGHT
AGAINST DEMOCRACY IN YUGOSLAVIA SINCE THE WAR. HOWEVER,
MILOSEVIC HAS ENCOUNTERED DETERMINED RESISTANCE, WITH THE
ACTION OF STRIKING MINERS IN KOSOVO INSPIRING A NEW ATTEMPT
TO SALVAGE THE GAINS AND REPUTATION OF THE YUGOSLAV
REVOLUTION.

05876 MAGOCSI, P.R.
THE UKRAINIAN NATIONAL REVIVAL: A NEW ANALYTICAL FRAMEWORK
CANADIAN REVIEW OF STUDIES IN NATIONALISM, XVI(1-2) (1989),
45-62.
THE AUTHOR EXPLORES WHAT, IF ANY, FRAMEWORK HAS BEEN
USED IN PREVIOUS INVESTIGATIONS TO ANALYZE THE UKRAINIAN
NATIONAL REVIVAL AND PROPOSES A NEW ONE THAT WILL NOT ONLY
PLACE THE UKRAINIAN CASE IN THE LARGER EUROPEAN CONTEXT BUT
WILL ALSO RESPOND TO THE SPECIFIC CHARACTERISTICS OF THE
UKRAINIAN EXPERIENCE.

05877 MAH, H.
MARXISM'S TRUTH: RECENT INTERPRETATIONS OF MARXIST THEORY
JOURNAL OF MODERN HISTORY, 61(1) (MAR 89), 110-127.
AT THE CLOSE OF THE NINETEENTH CENTURY, THE VALIDITY OF
ORTHODOX MARXISM WAS CHALLENGED WITHIN THE MARXIST CAMP
ITSELF. EDUARD BERNSTEIN QUESTIONED MARX'S PREDICTIONS ABOUT
THE COLLAPSE OF CAPITALISM AND THE IMMINENCE OF PROLETARIAN
REVOLUTION. BERNSTEIN WAS, AND IS STILL, REVILED BY MANY
MARXISTS, BUT THE ISSUE OF MARXISM'S ABILITY TO EXPLAIN AND
PREDICT SOCIAL DEVELOPMENTS HAS NOT CEASED TO TROUBLE
INTERPRETERS OF MARX, INCLUDING THOSE SYMPATHETIC TO MARXISM.
INDEED, SINCE BERNSTEIN, THE GAP BETWEEN MARXIST THEORY AND
SOCIAL AND POLITICAL REALITY HAS ONLY SEEMED TO WIDEN AS
FURTHER DEVELOPMENTS HAVE TAKEN PLACE THAT HAVE BEEN
ENTIRELY OUTSIDE THE TERMS OF ANALYSIS OF CLASSICAL MARXISM.

05878 MAHALL, J.
1789 AND THE LIBERAL THEORY OF INTERNATIONAL SOCIETY
REVIEW OF INTERNATIONAL STUDIES, 15(4) (OCT 89), 297-308.
THIS ARTICLE DEALS WITH THE UNIQUENESS OF THE FRENCH
REVOLUTION AS THE BIRTHPLACE OF MODERNITY AND AS SOMETHING
WHICH HAS BOTH SHAPED AND BEEN ACCOMMODATED BY INTERNATIONAL
RELATIONS EVER SINCE. IT MAKES TWO CLAIMS: THE FIRST IS THAT
THE REVOLUTION WAS THE EVENT THAT SEPARATES THE MODERN WORLD
FROM THE OLD ORDER. THE SECOND CLAIM IS THAT THE COMBINATION
OF UNIVERSALEM AND NATIONALISM ALLOWED THE FRENCH REVOLUTION
TO ESTABLISH A FOUNDATION MYTH FOR CONTEMPORY INTERNATIONAL
SOCIETY.

05879 MAHAPATRA, U.K.
TIBET: DROPING TOWARDS A SOLUTION
CHINA REPORT, 24(3) (JUL 88), 213-220.
THIS ARTICLE EXAMINES THE HISTORIC STATUS OF TIBET TO
DETERMINE WHETHER OR NOT TIBET WAS EVEN A SOVEREIGN STATE
AND IF SO, WHEN DID IT LOSE ITS SOVEREIGNTY? FOCUS IS ON THE

PERIOD OF THE DALAI LAMA AND THE MARCHU EMPERORS. THE
CHINESE RECOGNIZE THAT THEY CANNOT WISH AWAY THE DALAI LAMA
AND THE TIBETANS ALSO RECOGNIZE THAT THEY CANNOT WISH THE
CHINESE OUT OF TIBET. BUT THE CHINESE AND TIBETANS ARE
PATIENT AND SKILLFUL NEGOTIATORS AND AN END TO THE
HISTORICALLY UNSETTLED RELATIONSHIP IS POSSIBLE.

05880 MAHIMER, S.M.
UNITED STATES - PHILIPPINES BASES AGREEMENTS: PROSPECT FOR
ITS RENEWAL
AVAILABLE FROM NTIS, NO. AD-A202 758/9/GAR, MAY 88, 93.
REMARKS ON THE PROBLEMS AND ISSUES RELATED TO THE UNITED
STATES-PHILIPPINES BASES AGREEMENT AND PROSPECT FOR ITS
RENEWAL. AN ANALYSIS OF THE PROVISIONS OF THE NEW PHILIPPINE
CONSTITUTION; ASEAN PERSPECTIVE ON THE BASES; US POLICY ON
NUCLEAR WEAPONS AND ITS INTEREST AND OPTIONS; PHILIPPINE
INTERESTS AND PRIORITIES, INCLUDING ALTERNATE PLANS TO
COMPENSATE FOR THE POSSIBLE WITHDRAWAL OF THE US FROM THE
PHILIPPINES; AND THEN AN ASSESSMENT OF THE EFFECTS OF THESE
FACTORS ON THE RENEWAL OF THE BASES AGREEMENT. THERE ARE
DIFFICULTIES AND BARRIERS TO THE RENEWAL OF THE SAID
AGREEMENT POSED BY CONFLICTING POLICIES OF BOTH PARTIES AND
ALSO DUE TO DIVERGENT VIEWS ON PRIORITIES, CONSTITUTIONAL
PROCESSES OF BOTH COUNTRIES, AND TIME CONSTRAINTS FOR
CONCLUDING AN AGREEMENT. HOWEVER THERE ARE OPTIONS FOR THE
UNITED STATES REGARDING THE PROBLEM, DEPENDING UPON THE
DESIRED LEVEL OF ITS PRESENCE IN ASIA/PACIFIC REGION AND HOW
CENTRAL THE PHILIPPINES BASES ARE TO US NATIONAL SECURITY
INTERESTS.

05881 MAHLER, V.A.
INCOME DISTRIBUTION WITHIN NATIONS PROBLEMS OF CROSS-
NATIONAL COMPARISON
COMPARATIVE POLITICAL STUDIES, 22(1) (APR 89), 3-32.
IN RECENT YEARS A LARGE NUMBER OF CROSS-NATIONAL STUDIES
HAVE EXAMINED THE CAUSES AND CONSEQUENCES OF INCOME
INEQUALITY WITHIN NATIONS. UNFORTUNATELY, FEW OF THESE
STUDIES HAVE ATTENDED VERY CAREFULLY TO PROBLEMS OF
MEASUREMENT AND DEFINITIONAL CONSISTENCY THAT CAN SERIOUSLY
UNDERMINE THE COMPARATIVE USE OF CURRENTLY AVAILABLE DATA ON
INCOME SHARES. THIS ARTICLE OFFERS A DISCUSSION OF THE MAJOR
THEORETICAL AND PRACTICAL PROBLEMS THAT CAN ARISE IN
MEASURING AND COMPARING PATTERNS OF INCOME DISTRIBUTION
ACROSS NATIONS, FOCUSING ON THE COMPLETENESS OF INCOME
COVERAGE, THE UNIT OF ANALYSIS, THE TIME PERIOD OVER WHICH
INCOME IS MEASURED, THE SCOPE OF POPULATION COVERAGE, THE
UNDERREPORTING OF INCOME, AND THE EFFECT OF PUBLIC SECTOR
FISCAL POLICIES. IT THEN ASSESSES MAJOR PUBLISHED SOURCES OF
CROSS-NATIONAL DATA ON THE SIZE DISTRIBUTION OF INCOME IN
LIGHT OF THESE PROBLEMS. FINALLY, THE ARTICLE OFFERS SEVERAL
SUGGESTIONS FOR MINIMIZING THE NEGATIVE CONSEQUENCES OF
MEASUREMENT PROBLEMS THAT REMAIN IN EVEN THE BEST AVAILABLE
DATA ON INCOME SHARES.

05882 MAHMOOD, C.
SIKH REBELLION AND THE HINDU CONCEPT OF ORDER
ASIAN SURVEY, XXIX(3) (MAR 89), 326-340.
ONE RELIGIOUS GROUP THAT HAS HAD DIFFICULTY IN BEING
ASSIMILATED INTO THE LARGER PREDOMINATELY HINDU INDIAN
SYSTEM IS THE SIKH. THE ARTICLE ANALYZES THE HISTORICAL
BEGININGS OF THE SIKH MOVEMENT IN AN ATTEMPT TO DETERMINE
THE REASON FOR THE MODERN SIKH SEPARATIST MOVEMENT WHICH HAS
BEEN RESPONSIBLE FOR MUCH OF INDIA'S COMMUNAL VIOLENCE. THE
REASONS WHY THE SIKH MOVEMENT HAS RESORTED TO VIOLENCE, WHEN
OTHER RELIGIOUS MINORITIES SUCH AS BUDDHISTS OR MUSLIM
ATTEMPTED TO MAINTAIN INDEPENDENCE THROUGH OTHER MEANS ARE
ALSO ANALYZED.

05883 MAHONEY, D.J. III
THE LIBERAL POLITICAL SCIENCE OF RAYMOND ARON:
"STATESMANLIKE PRUDENCE" AT THE "DAWN OF UNIVERSAL HISTORY"
DISSERTATION ABSTRACTS INTERNATIONAL, 50(4) (OCT 89),
1078-A.
THIS DISSERTATION INVESTIGATES ARON'S THOUGHT THROUGH AN
ANALYSIS OF HIS UNDERSTANDING AND PRACTICE OF POLITICAL
SCIENCE. THE INFLUENCES OF WEBER, ARISTOTLE, MONTESQUIEU AND
TOCQUEVILLE ON ARON'S WORK ARE ANALYZED. THE STUDY ALSO
INCLUDES AN EXEGESIS OF ARON'S "THE DAWN OF UNIVERSAL
HISTORY," A DISCUSSION OF HIS ANALYSIS OF MARX, AND AN
EVALUATION OF HIS CONTRIBUTION TO THE STUDY OF INTERNATIONAL
RELATIONS.

05884 MAHRDEL, C.
REFORM AND REVOLUTION IN THE THIRD WORLD
WORLD MARXIST REVIEW, 32(7) (JUL 89), 66-68.
WMR HAS PUBLISHED A SERIES OF CONTRIBUTIONS ON THE NEWLY-
FREE COUNTRIES CHOICE OF DEVELOPMENT, INCLUDING PROBLEMS OF
SOCIALIST ORIENTATION. THIS ARTICLE IS A RESPONSE TO AN
EARLIER ARTICLE ENTITLED "SOCIALISM AND THE DEMANDS FOR
DEVELOPMENT". IT SHARES ITS OWN VIEW OF THE PROBLEM AT HAND
AND THEN EXPLORES THE DANGER OF AN INSUFFICIENTLY
DIFFERENTIATED INTERPRETATION OF PAST HISTORICAL EXPERIENCE.
IT SUGGESTS THAT THE EXAMPLES OF REVOLUTIONS IN RUSSIA,
CHINA, VIETNAM, CUBA ETC CANNOT BE GROUPED TOGETHER BECAUSE

EACH CIRCUMSTANCE WAS DIFFERENT. IT THEN CLARIFIES FURTHER POINTS CONCERNING REFORM.

05885 MAHURKAR, U.
DEEP-ROOTED SCANDAL
INDIA TODAY, XIV(8) (APR 89), 34-35.
GUJARAT CHIEF MINISTER AMARSINH CHAUDHARY HAS NOT BEEN ABLE TO BURY THE CHARGE THAT, AS STATE FOREST MINISTER, HE ENCOURAGED THE PLUNDER OF THE FORESTS OF VYARA BY TRIBALS AND TIMBER CONTRACTORS IN ORDER TO BUY VOTES DURING THE 1985 ASSEMBLY ELECTION CAMPAIGN.

05886 MAHURKAR, U.
GUJARAT: DISSIDENT DISEASE
INDIA TODAY, XIV(5) (MAR 89), 33.
DISSIDENTS HAVE CHARGED GUJARAT'S CHIEF MINISTER CHAUDHARY WITH CORRUPTION AND WITH CRIMINALIZING POLITICS (TWO MLA'S AND THREE TALUKA PRESIDENTS HAVE BEEN MURDERED DURING HIS TENURE). THE CHIEF MINISTER WILL FIND IT HARD TO DEFEND HIMSELF AGAINST THESE ALLEGATIONS ESPECIALLY THOSE WHICH ARE SUPPORTED BY THE REPORT OF THE ESTIMATES COMMITTEE OF THE STATE ASSEMBLY.

05887 MAHURKAR, U.
HANGING IN THE BALANCE
INDIA TODAY, XIV(6) (MAR 89), 22-25.
CHIEF MINISTER AMARSINH CHAUDHARY OF GUJARAT IS IN DANGER OF BEING OUSTED BY DISSIDENTS WITHIN THE CONGRESS (I) PARTY.

05888 MAHURKAR, U.
MORE FISSURES
INDIA TODAY, XIV(1) (JAN 89), 39.
THE CONGRESS (I) HIGH COMMAND HAS GIVEN GUJARAT'S CHIEF MINISTER AMARSINH CHAUDHARY PERMISSION TO EXPAND HIS MINISTRY. THE PARTY OFFICIALS WERE MOTIVATED MORE BY A DESIRE TO STRENGTHEN THE PARTY THAN BY A WISH TO BACK CHAUDHARY AGAINST DISSIDENTS WITHIN HIS GOVERNMENT.

05889 MAIDAN, M.
ALIENATED LABOUR AND FREE ACTIVITY IN MARX'S THOUGHT
POLITICAL SCIENCE, 41(1) (JUL 89), 59-73.
THE YOUND MARX HELD TWO DIFFERENT THEORIES ABOUT FREE ACTIVITY, BOTH OF WHICH HE LATER REJECTED AND REPLACED WITH THE MORE PESSIMISTIC, DILUTED ACCOUNT IN THE THIRD VOLUME OF "DAS KAPITAL." THE GROUNDS FOR MARX'S DENIAL OF THE POSSIBILITY OF A SOCIETY BASED SOLELY ON FREE ACTIVITY ARE CLOSELY LINKED NOT TO THE REJECTION OF THE EARLIER IDEAL OF FREE ACTIVITY BUT TO HIS SCEPTICISM ABOUT THE POSSIBILITY OF ITS IMPLEMENTATION. IN ORDER TO RECONSTRUCT THIS FUNDAMENTAL ASPECT OF MARX'S THOUGHT, IT IS NECESSARY TO CONSIDER THE POSITION OF LABOR IN MARX'S SYSTEM AND THE CONCEPT OF FREE ACTIVITY UNDERLYING IT. THEN IT IS POSSIBLE TO UNDERSTAND THE PROBABLE GROUNDS FOR MARX'S REJECTION OF HIS EARLY THEORY OF NON-ALIENATED ACTIVITY AND THE MEANING OF THIS SHIFT.

05890 MAIDANAT, L.; MURSI, F.; SHOUKEIR, M.
THE POWER OF SOLIDARITY
WORLD MARXIST REVIEW, 32(7) (JUL 89), 74-76.
THE AFRO-ASIAN PEOPLE'S SOLIDARITY MOVEMENT HAS A GREAT POTENTIAL IN THE STRUGGLE AGAINST IMPERIALISM AND FOR PEACE, DEMOCRACY AND SOCIAL PROGRESS. THIS IS THE SUBJECT OF THIS ARTICLE. DEVELOPING COOPERATION IS EXPLORED BY THREE WRITERS FROM JORDON, EGYPT AND PALESTINE. ECONOMIC INDEPENDENCE IS SUGGESTED AS THE PREMIER TASK FOR THE NEWLY-FREE AFRO-ASIAN COUNTRIES. IT CONCLUDES THAT THE AFRO-ASIAN SOLIDARITY HAS ENTERED A NEW PERIOD AND THAT A STEP HAS BEEN TAKEN IN THE RIGHT DIRECTION.

05891 MAIER, K.
A PROGRAM FOR PEACE
AFRICA REPORT, 34(5) (SEP 89), 55-58.
ALTHOUGH FRELIMO'S IDEOLOGICAL TURNAROUND GRABBED HEADLINES DURING THE PARTY'S FIFTH CONGRESS, A MANDATE TO SEEK A NEGOTIATED SOLUTION TO THE WAR AGAINST RENAMO WAS THE MEETING'S MOST SIGNIFICANT OUTCOME. WITH PRESIDENTS MUGABE AND MOI ACTING AS INTERMEDIARIES, EFFORTS ARE UNDERWAY TO FIND COMMON GROUND WITH THE REBELS IN ORDER TO END THE LONG AND BRUTAL CONFLICT.

05892 MAIER, K.
THE BATTLE FOR ZAMBEZIA
AFRICA REPORT, 34(2) (MAR 89), 13-16.
COMMITTING ITS BEST TROOPS TO THE FIGHT FOR CONTROL OF ZAMBEZIA, PRESIDENT CHISSANO'S FRELIMO GOVERNMENT ARMY HAS GAINED SOME GROUND AGAINST THE INSURGENT MOZAMBIQUE NATIONAL RESISTANCE (RENAMO) IN THE ECONOMICALLY-VITAL PROVINCE. BUT THE WAR HAS COST THE REGION AND A THIRD OF ITS PEOPLE ARE NOW DEPENDENT ON FOOD AID FOR SURVIVAL.

05893 MAIN, J.
THIRD WORLD ECONOMIES: A NEW PROPOSAL
CURRENT, (314) (JUL 89), 38.

IN THE THIRD WORLD, THE UNDERGROUND ECONOMY IS MAINLY GOOD, NOT BAD. IT EMBODIES THE ENTREPRENEURIAL ENERGY OF ORDINARY PEOPLE STRIVING IN ADMIRABLE WAYS TO BREAK OUT OF POVERTY. IF THIS ENTREPRENEURIAL SPIRIT WERE LEGALIZED AND NURTURED RATHER THAN FETTERED AND SUPPRESSED, A BURST OF COMPETITIVE ENERGY WOULD BE RELEASED. LIVING STANDARDS WOULD START RISING. INTERNATIONAL TRADE WOULD INCREASE AND DEVELOPING COUNTRIES COULD SERVICE THEIR HUGE AND DEBILITATING EXTERNAL DEBTS MORE EASILY.

05894 MAINGOT, A.P.
ACCOUNTABILITY IN CUBA AND PUERTO RICO
HEMISPHERE, 1(3) (SUM 89), 2-3.
THE POLITICAL ACCOUNTABILITY OF THOSE IN POWER HAS BEEN THE GOAL OF POLITICAL MOVEMENTS SINCE AT LEAST THE MAGNA CARTA. IN THIS ESSAY, THE AUTHOR EXAMINES THE ISSUE OF ACCOUNTABILITY UNDER CASTRO IN CUBA AND THE ESTADO LIBRE ASOCIADO IN PUERTO RICO.

05895 MAINGOT, A.P.
NEW GEOPOLITICAL REALITIES
HEMISPHERE, 1(2) (WIN 89), 4-5.
GEOPOLITICS CONTINUES TO BE CENTRAL TO ANY ANALYSIS OF U. S.-CARIBBEAN BASIN RELATIONS. THE NATURE OF THE PROBLEMS AND OPPORTUNITIES PRESENTED BY GEOGRAPHICAL PROXIMITY DO CHANGE, HOWEVER. ONLY A DECADE AGO, THE CARIBBEAN BASIN HAS BLANKETED BY THE RHETORIC OF IDEOLOGICAL CONFRONTATION AND REVOLUTIONARY CHALLENGE, AS WELL AS BY THE PREDICTABLE GREAT POWER RESPONSES. NOW CARIBBEAN LEADERS ARE FOLLOWING A PRAGMATIC FOREIGN POLICY AND LOOKING FOR OPPORTUNITIES TO REDUCE REGIONAL TENSIONS, ALLOWING THEM TO ADDRESS THE FUNDAMENTAL CONCERNS SHARED BY NEARLY ALL WHO BORDER THE CARIBBEAN SEA. IN THE SHORT-TERM, TWO OF THESE CRITICAL ISSUES ARE IMMIGRATION AND CORRUPTION.

05896 MAINGOT, A.P.
THE DIFFICULT TRANSITION IN THE CARIBBEAN
HEMISPHERE, 2(1) (FAL 89), 6-9.
THE CARIBBEAN IS AN AREA IN IDEOLOGICAL AND ECONOMIC TRANSITION. THE TRANSITION APPEARS TO BE IRREVERSIBLE OVER THE SHORT TO MEDIUM-TERM AND IS ACCOMPANIED BY VERY REAL POLITICAL CONSEQUENCES. CLEARLY, ONE THE FACTORS BEHIND THIS TRANSITION IS THE FAILURE OF THE TRADITIONAL ECONOMIES. CARIBBEAN-BASED EXPERIMENTS WITH CENTRALIZED, STATE-DRIVEN STRATEGIES OF DEVELOPMENT HAVE FAILED. THE WORLDWID TREND TOWARD PRAGMATISM AND PLURALISM IS ANOTHER SOURCE OF CHANGE IN THE CARIBBEAN.

05897 MAIR, P.
CONTINUITY, CHANGE AND THE VULNERABILITY OF PARTY
WEST EUROPEAN POLITICS, 12(4) (OCT 89), 169-187.
DESPITE THE RECENT EVIDENCE OF WIDESPREAD ELECTORAL CHANGE IN WESTERN EUROPE, TWO FUNDAMENTAL FORCES FOR CONTINUITY CAN BE IDENTIFIED: FIRST, THE PERSISTENCE OF LEFT AND RIGHT AS ORGANISING PRINCIPLES IN POLITICAL PREDISPOSITIONS; AND SECOND, A PERSISTENCE AND STABILISATION OF THE AGGREGATE CLASS ELECTORAL ALIGNMENTS. IT IS AT THE LEVEL OF THE INDIVIDUAL PARTY THAT THE REAL CHANGE IS BEING FELT, AND IT IS ARGUED THAT MUCH OF THIS NEW VULNERABILITY OF PARTY MAY BE DUE TO FORMS OF ORGANISATIONAL ADAPTATION AND, IN PARTICULAR, TO THE DEVELOPMENT OF CATCH-ALL, TOP-DOWN STYLES OF MOBILISING SUPPORT.

05898 MAIR, P.
IRELAND: FROM PREDOMINANCE TO MODERATE PLURALISM, AND BACK AGAIN?
WEST EUROPEAN POLITICS, 12(4) (OCT 89), 129-142.
THIS ARTICLE SUGGESTS THAT ONLY IN CERTAIN SPECIFIC CIRCUMSTANCES CAN PARTY SYSTEM CHANGE BE SAID TO HAVE OCCURRED IT ALSO SUGGESTS THAT PARTY SYSTEM CHANGE, WHILE RARE, MAY OCCUR DESPITE AGGREGATE ELECTORAL CONTINUITY, DESPITE STABILITY IN SOCIAL ALIGNMENTS, OR DESPITE PERSISTENCE AT THE LEVEL OF THE INDIVIDUAL PARTY OR PARTIES. THE INTENTION OF THE THIS ANALYSIS IS TO EMPLOY THE IRISH CASE TO ILLUSTRATE THIS CONDITION AND TO SHOW THAT DESPITE LARGE-SCALE ELECTORAL STABILITY, A FUNDAMENTAL CHANGE OF THE IRISH PARTY SYSTEM OCCURRED IN THE EARLY 1970S; THAT THE SITUATION IN THE LATE 1980S NOW SUGGESTS THE POSSIBILITY FOR A FURTHER MAJOR CHANGE OF THE SYSTEM, ALBEIT THIS TIME IN THE CONTEXT OF PERVASIVE RECENT VOLATILITY; AND, ALBEIT MORE INCIDENTALLY, THAT THIS SHIFTING PATTERN IS PART OF A LARGER CYCLE OF CHANGE WHICH HAS CHARACTERISED IRISH POLITICS SINCE THE EARLY 1930S. FINALLY, SOME OF THE FACTORS WILL BE EXPLORED WHICH HAVE LED TO THE MORE RECENT CHANGES OF THE IRISH PARTY SYSTEM, FOCUSING PRIMARILY ON THE DISTINCTION BETWEEN ENDOGENOUS FACTORS, ON THE ONE HAND, AND EXOGENOUS FACTORS, ON THE OTHER.

05899 MAJESKI, S.
A RULE-BASED MODEL OF THE UNITED STATES MILITARY EXPENDITURE DECISION-MAKING PROCESS
INTERNATIONAL INTERACTIONS, 15(2) (1989), 129-154.
THE THEORETICAL FOUNDATIONS OF THE U.S. MILITARY EXPENDITURE DECISION-MAKING (MEDM) TRADITION, INCREMENTALISM

AND BOUNDED RATIONALITY, SUGGEST THAT POLICYMAKER'S BEHAVIOR IS RULE BASED. THE STANDARD WAY THAT THESE RULES ARE FORMALIZED. OUTPUTS ARE GENERATED BY A LINEAR AND ADDITIVE COMBINATION OF THE BASE AND RELEVANT INFORMATIONAL VARIABLES, IS NEITHER DESCRIPTIVELY ACCURATE NOR CONSISTENT WITH THE BASIC ASSUMPTIONS OF PROCEDURAL RATIONALITY, A RULE BASED MODEL CONSTRUCTED OF A SET OF HIERARCHICALLY AND CONDITIONALLY ORGANIZED "IF-THEN" RULES IS DEVELOPED AS AN ALTERNATIVE. MODELS OF THIS FORM PROVIDE AN OPPORTUNITY TO DEVELOP AND RIGOROUSLY TEST MORE DESCRIPTIVELY ACCURATE REPRESENTATION OF HOW INDIVIDUALS AND ORGANIZATIONS MAKE DECISIONS AND WHICH CAPTURE HIERARCHICAL AND CONDITIONAL RELATIONS OF THE MEDM PROCESS. AN EMPIRICAL ANALYSIS OF THE MODEL DEMONSTRATES BOTH ITS EXPLANATORY AND PREDICTIVE POWER.

05900 MAJOLI, S.
THE ITALIAN NAVY IN THE DEFENCE OF THE MEDITERRANEAN
NATO'S SIXTEEN NATIONS, 34(5) (SEP 89), 55-57.
THE MEDITERRANEAN LINKS EUROPE TO AFRICA AND THE MIDDLE EAST. IT IS A MOST IMPORTANT HIGHWAY ALONG WHICH MOST OF EUROPE'S RAW MATERIALS AND A GOOD DEAL OF ITS EXPORTS ARE CARRIED. IT IS ALSO A POLITICAL, STRATEGIC AND CULTURAL CONTACT AREA, EVEN MORE IMPORTANT IN TODAY'S CHANGING EAST-WEST RELATIONSHIP. THE ITALIAN NAVY PATROLS, SAFEGUARDS AND WATCHES IT AND ITS ADJACENT AREAS FOR ITALY AND FOR THE ALLIANCE. ITS PRESENCE ACTS AS A MAJOR STABILITY FACTOR IN THE REGION.

05901 MAKGETLA, N.S.; SEIDMAN, R.B.
THE APPLICABILITY OF LAW AND ECONOMICS TO POLICYMAKING IN THE THIRD WORLD
JOURNAL OF ECONOMIC ISSUES, 23(1) (MAR 89), 35-78.
THIS ARTICLE CONSIDERS THE USEFULNESS OF LAW AND ECONOMICS FOR POLICYMAKERS IN THE THIRD WORLD. EXAMINED IS ITS THEORY -- METHODOLOGY, PERSPECTIVES AND CONCEPTS -- IN LIGHT OF THIRD WORLD'S REALITY. IT CONCLUDES THAT THE PRESCRIPTIONS OF LAW AND ECONOMICS BECOME PART OF THE PROBLEM, NOT PART OF THE SOLUTION TO THIRD WORLD POVERTY AND POWERLESSNESS.

05902 MAKGOTHI, H.
THE PRETORIA REGIME IN CRISIS: INTERVIEW WITH HENRY MAKGOTHI
SECHABA, 23(8) (AUG 89), 10-11.
ANC DEPUTY SECRETARY GENERAL HENRY MAKGOTHI SPEAKS OF THE CRISIS THAT THE RULING REGIME IN SOUTH AFRICA IS FACING. HE POINTS OUT THAT SOUTH AFRICA'S USUAL FOREIGN POLICY BLUSTER IS BEING REPLACED BY AN EMPHASIS ON CONCILIATION. THIS IS A RESULT OF PRETORIA'S INCREASING ECONOMIC WOES AND THE STRENGTHENED POLITICAL RESOLVE OF SOUTH AFRICAN BLACKS. ALTHOUGH THE DE KLERK GOVERNMENT IS MAKING A FEW SMALL CONCESSIONS, NOTHING SHORT OF A COMPLETE ABOLITION OF APARTHEID WILL SAVE THE REGIME FROM COLLAPSE.

05903 MAKINEN, G.E.
SAVING TRENDS AND PRODUCTIVITY
CRS REVEIW, 10(5) (JUN 89), 5-7.
THE U.S. SAVINGS RATE HAS RECENTLY FALLEN TO VERY LOW LEVELS IN COMPARISON TO THE PAST AND TO OTHER COUNTRIES. SOME OBSERVERS SEE THIS DECLINE AS A SOURCE OF NATIONAL PROBLEMS RANGING FROM POOR PERFORMANCE IN INTERNATIONAL TRADE TO CRUMBLING DOMESTIC INFRASTRUCTURE AND BELOW-AVERAGE GROWTH IN PER CAPITA REAL INCOME. PUBLIC POLICY HAS NOT PROVED HIGHLY EFFECTIVE IN STIMULATING SAVING, IN PART BECAUSE COMPONENTS OF SAVING TEND TO MOVE IN OFFSETTING DIRECTIONS.

05904 MAKRAM-EBEID, M.
POLITICAL OPPOSITION IN EGYPT: DEMOCRATIC MYTH OR REALITY?
MIDDLE EAST JOURNAL, 43(3) (SUM 89), 423-436.
PUBLIC DEBATE IS A MAJOR LINK BETWEEN THOSE WHO GOVERN AND THE GOVERNED, AND A REQUISIT FOR AN EFFECTIVE POLICY-MAKING PROCESS. THIS PROPOSITION DOES NOT SEEM TO BE WIDELY UNDERSTOOD BY EITHER OBSERVERS OR PRACTIONERS OF POLITICS IN EGYPT. THIS ARTICLE LOOKS AT SOME OF THE PROBLEMS INHERENT IN A TRANSITION TO COMPETITIVE DEMOCRACY IN EGYPT BY EXAMINING THE ROLE AND POSITION OF OPPOSITION PARTIES, THE IMPORTANCE OF THE 1987 PARLIAMENTARY ELECTIONS, AND FINALLY, PROSPECTS FOR THE MULTIPARTY SYSTEM.

05905 MALASHENKO, I.
NON-MILITARY ASPECTS OF SECURITY
INTERNATIONAL AFFAIRS (MOSCOW), (1) (JAN 89), 40-51.
BUILDING NATIONAL SECURITY HAS TRADITIONALLY BEEN SEEN FIRST AND FOREMOST AS A MILITARY PROBLEM. BUT THE CHARACTER OF MODERN WEAPONS LEAVES A COUNTRY NO HOPE OF SAFE-GUARDING ITSELF SOLELY THROUGH MILITARY AND TECHNICAL MEANS. THE TASK OF ENSURING SECURITY IS INCREASINGLY SEEN AS A POLITICAL PROBLEM THAT MUST BE RESOLVED BY POLITICAL MEANS. THE TASK IS TO ACHIEVE A BALANCE OF INTEREST AMONG NATIONS AND, BY EXTENSION, SOUND INTERNATIONAL SECURITY. THE CONCEPT OF A COMPREHENSIVE SYSTEM OF INTERNATIONAL SECURITY IS NEEDED TO BIND TOGETHER MILITARY, POLITICAL, ECONOMIC, AND HUMANITARIAN FACTORS.

05906 MALCOM, N.
THE 'COMMON EUROPEAN HOME' AND SOVIET EUROPEAN POLICY
INTERNATIONAL AFFAIRS, 65(4) (FAL 89), 659-676.
THIS ARTICLE ATTEMPTS TO DRAW OUT THE LOGIC OF THE PROCESS OF CHANGE IN SOVIET THINKING ABOUT FOREIGN POLICY AND SOME OF ITS IMPLICATIONS, IT EXAMINES THE IDEA OF THE COMMON EUROPEAN HOME SINCE ITS FIRST APPEARANCE UNDER BREZHNEV IN 1981 AND ITS REAPPEARANCE UNDER GORBACHEV IN 1985, IT ATTEMPTS TO ESTABLISH WHETHER THE CONTENT OF THE IDEA HAS CHANGED SINCE 1985, AND ITS DEVELOPMENT INTO THE OUTLINE OF A FOREIGN POLICY PROJECT IS EXPLORED.

05907 MALEC, K.L.
UTILIZATION OF BENEFIT PROGRAMS BY SENIOR CITIZENS: A CASE STUDY
DISSERTATION ABSTRACTS INTERNATIONAL, 50(5) (NOV 89), 1424-A.
USING A CASE STUDY METHOD, THE AUTHOR EXAMINES THE UTILIZATION BEHAVIOR OF BENEFIT PROGRAMS FOR THE ELDERLY BY THE ELDERLY. BASED ON THE LITERATURE OF POLITICAL PARTICIPATION, CITIZEN-INITIATED CONTACTING OF GOVERNMENT OFFICIALS, AND THE SOCIOLOGY OF AGING, SHE SELECTED FOUR MODELS FOR ANALYSIS: THE SOCIO-ECONOMIC STATUS MODEL, THE NEED-AWARENESS MODEL, PERSONAL CHARACTERISTICS, AND DEPENDENT/INDEPENDENT ATTITUDES. THE DATA REVEALED THAT NONE OF THE MODELS WAS STRONGLY ASSOCIATED WITH THE KNOWLEDGE AND UTILIZATION OF GOVERNMENT PROGRAMS FOR THE ELDERLY BY THE ELDERLY.

05908 MALEK, M.H.
KURDISTAN IN THE MIDDLE EAST CONFLICT
NEW LEFT REVIEW, (175) (MAY 89), 79-94.
THE END OF THE IRAN-IRAQ WAR TRIGGERED A NEW ONSLAUGHT BY THE BAGHDAD REGIME ON THE KURDISH POPULATION OF NORTHERN IRAQ, INVOLVING THE MURDEROUS USE OF POISON-GAS WEAPONS AND THE FORCIBLE DEPOPULATION OF HUNDREDS OF VILLAGES. MOHAMMED MALEK TRACES THE VICISSITUDES OF THE KURDISH STRUGGLE IN IRAQ, TURKEY AND IRAN SINCE THE OUTBREAK OF THE REVOLT IN 1961 AND CRITICALLY ASSESSES THE POLICIES AND PERSPECTIVES OF THE NATIONALIST LEADERSHIPS. WHILE REGISTERING THE CULTURAL AND POLITICAL DEVELOPMENTS WHICH HAVE MADE THE IDEA OF A UNIFIED KURDISH STATE INCREASINGLY PROBLEMATIC, MALEK ENTERS AN APPEAL FOR RESPECT OF KURDISH NATIONAL RIGHTS BY THE MAJORITY NATIONS OF THE REGION.

05909 MALETZ, D.J.
HEGEL ON RIGHT AS ACTUALIZED WILL
POLITICAL THEORY, 17(1) (FEB 89), 33-50.
THE AUTHOR EXAMINES THE FORMAL STRUCTURE OF RIGHT, WHERE HEGEL'S METHOD OF LINKING EACH ASPECT OF RIGHT TO THE NEXT SHOWS SOMETHING IMPORTANT ABOUT THE EXPERIENCE OF RIGHT AND THE KNOWLEDGE OF RIGHT. SECOND, THE AUTHOR EXAMINES THE CRITIQUE OF ARBITRARINESS OR WILLFULNESS (WILLKUR) WITH WHICH HEGEL POSES A CRITICISM OF A CERTAIN DEFECTIVE UNDERSTANDING OF FREEDOM BY ARGUING FROM THE BASIS OF THE WILL CORRECTLY UNDERSTOOD. FINALLY, THE ARTICLE PROVIDES AN ANALYSIS OF HEGEL'S SPHERE OF "ABSOLUTE RIGHT," WHICH IS "WORLD HISTORY." HERE THE WILL REACHES A SORT OF CULMINATION IN WHICH IT DOES, IN A SENSE, ATTAIN A KIND OF COMPLETENESS.

05910 MALI, J.
THE POETICS OF POLITICS: VICO'S 'PHILOSOPHY OF AUTHORITY'
HISTORY OF POLITICAL THOUGHT, X(1) (SPR 89), 41-70.
THE AUTHOR ELABORATES SOME GENERAL ASPECTS OF "GIBBON'S DILEMMA", IN PARTICULAR THE PROBLEM OF POLITICAL MYTH IN THE ENLIGHTENMENT. ONE OF THE FIRST THINKER WHO WORKED OUT THE "NEW" THEORY OF POLITICAL MYTH HAS GIAMBATTUSTA VICO; HOWEVER, HIS THEORY OF POLITICAL MYTH HAS NOT BEEN EXTENSIVELY ANALYZED. THE MAIN TASK OF THE ARTICLE IS TO CLARIFY VICO'S CONCEPT OF AUTHORITY AND THEREBY MAKE CLEAR THE PECULIAR POLITICAL SENSIBILITIES AND AIMS OF HIS NEW SCIENCE.

05911 MALIK, A.R.
PAKISTAN'S RESPONSE TO THE POST-ZIA AFGHAN CRISIS
ASIAN PROFILE, 17(4) (AUG 89), 351-360.
THE AUTHOR SPECULATES ABOUT THE SHAPE OF PAKISTAN'S POLICY TOWARDS AFGHANISTAN IN THE POST-ZIA ERA. HE LOOKS AT HOW THE UNITED STATES HAS INFLUENCED PAKISTAN'S INVOLVEMENT IN AFGHANISTAN AND THE POSSIBILITY OF THE IMPLEMENTATION OF THE ACCORDS UNDER THE UNITED NATIONS' AEGIS.

05912 MALIK, G.P.
MALAYSIA
SOUTH, (103) (MAY 89), 55-61.
A SHARP UPTURN IN WORLD COMMODITY PRICES AND A SURGE IN MANUFACTURED EXPORTS FOLLOWING A DEPRECIATION OF THE RINGGIT HAVE PUT MALAYSIA ON THE ROAD TO ECONOMIC RECOVERY. THE ECONOMY HAS ALSO BENEFITED FROM CORRECTIVE MEASURES THAT HAVE HELD DOWN GOVERNMENT SPENDING AND FROZEN WAGES. WHILE POLITICAL UNCERTAINTIES CONTINUE, BUSINESS CONFIDENCE HAS BEEN LITTLE AFFECTED BY THE ILLNESS OF PRIME MINISTER MAHATHIR MOHAMAD OR THE JOSTLING FOR POWER WITHIN THE NEW

UNITED MALAYS NATIONAL ORGANISATION.

05913 MALIK, J.M.
CHINA AND SOUTH ASIAN NUCLEAR-FREE ZONE
CHINA REPORT, 25(2) (APR 89), 113-119.
THIS ARTICLE EXPLORES THE IDEA OF ESTABLISHING A NUCLEAR-
FREE ZONE IN SOUTH ASIA, IT EXAMINES CHINA'S RELATIONS WITH
INDIA AND PAKISTAN IN PARTICULAR. IT CONCLUDES THAT THE LACK
OF ANY SHARED SECURITY PERCEPTION, SHARP DIFFERENCES OVER
THE DELIMITATION OF THE ZONE, REGIONAL TENSIONS AND
RIVALRIES BETWEEN INDIA AND CHINA AND INDIA AND PAKISTAN
MEAN THAT THE PROSPECTS OF ESTABLISHING A SANFZ ARE REMOTE.

05914 MALIK, J.M.
HANDS ACROSS THE HIMALAYAS
PACIFIC DEFENCE REPORTER, 15(9) (MAR 89), 43-45.
INDIAN PRIME MINISTER RAJIV GANDHI'S FIVE-DAY OFFICIAL
VISIT TO CHINA FROM DECEMBER 19-23 LAST YEAR HAS AGAIN
RAISED FRESH HOPES ABOUT A POSSIBLE SETTLEMENT OF THE BORDER
DISPUTE WHICH LED TO A BRIEF BUT BLOODY WAR IN 1962 AND CAME
CLOSE TO ERUPTING INTO ANOTHER MILITARY CLASH IN 1987. THE
RELATIVE SIGNIFICANCE OF THE SINO-INDIAN SUMMIT LIES IN
STRENGTHENING THE ELEMENTS OF DETENTE BY CULTIVATING RAPPORT
WITH THE CHINESE LEADERSHIP ON MATTERS OF MUTUAL INTEREST,
INCLUDING THE TERRITORIAL DISPUTE. EVENTUALLY A MUTUALLY
ACCEPTABLE AGREEMENT ON THE BORDER QUESTION WILL GO A LONG
WAY IN EASING TENSIONS AND USHER IN AN ERA OF HEALTHY
COMPETITION BETWEEN INDIA AND CHINA. NONETHELESS, A SINO-
INDIAN RAPPROCHEMENT WOULD COME ONLY SLOWLY AND PAINFULLY,
BECAUSE, IN ADDITION TO THE COMPLEX BORDER DISPUTE, THERE
REMAIN SOME OTHER OUTSTANDING PROBLEMS. THE MOST NOTABLE ARE
TIBET, CHINA'S REFUSAL TO RECOGNIZE SIKKIM AS PART OF INDIA,
AND THE SINO-INDIAN RIVALRY FOR SPHERES OF INFLUENCE IN
SOUTH AND SOUTH-EAST ASIA.

05915 MALIK, M.
A WOLF IN WHITE CLOTHING
FAR EASTERN ECONOMIC REVIEW, 141(33) (AUG 88), 20-21.
OPPOSITION LEADER JOHN HOWARD HAS BROUGHT THE TABOO
ISSUE OF RACE BACK INTO AUSTRALIAN POLITICS. HIS DECISION TO
FOCUS ON WHAT HE BELIEVES IS PUBLIC DISQUIET OVER THE
PRESENT NUMBER OF ASIANS SETTLING IN AUSTRALIA MAY SIGNAL
THE END OF THE BIPARTISAN APPROACH ON NON-DICRIMINARY
IMMIGRATION WHICH GOVERNMENTS AND OPPOSITION HAVE HONOURED
SINCE THE 1960'S. HOWARD HAS BADLY DIVIDED HIS OWN PARTY AND
HAS CAUSED FEARS AMONG ETHNIC ORGANIZATIONS OF A NEW WAVE OF
RACISM IN AUSTRALIA. HE IS ALSO PUTTING HIS POLITICAL LIFE
ON THE LINE AS HIS POLITICAL FUTURE WILL LIKELY BE
DETERMINED BY THE SUCCESS OR FAILURE OF THE OPPOSITION TO
WIN USING THIS ISSUE.

05916 MALIK, M.
CHANGING PARTNERS
FAR EASTERN ECONOMIC REVIEW, 141(28) (JUL 88), 10-13.
IN PAPUA NEW GUINEA THERE ARE FEW SHADES OF IDEOLOGY
BETWEEN THE NINE POLITICAL PARTIES AND CHANGING CAMPS IS A
REGULAR EXERCISE. THE RECENT OUSTING OF PAIAS WINGTI WAS NO
EXCEPTION. THE VOTE OF NO-CONFIDENCE WAS LEAD BY OPPOSITION
LEADER RABBIE NAMAILU WHO WAS SUCCESSFUL IN DRAWING AWAY
MANY GOVERNMENT SUPPORTERS AND IN MANAGING THE POLITICAL
SHUFFLE THAT IS COMMONPLACE IN PORT MORESBY.

05917 MALIK, M.
THE MINISTER'S OTHER FACE
FAR EASTERN ECONOMIC REVIEW, 141(37) (SEP 88), 24,26.
AUSTRALIA HAS BEEN AMBARRASSED BY A LEAK OF OFFICIAL
DOCUMENTS CONTAINING SOME FRANK COMMENTS BY FORMER FOREIGN
MINISTER BILL HAYDEN ABOUT SEVERAL OF AUSTRALIA'S NEIGHBORS.
THE DOCUMENTS ALSO REVEAL HOW THE US VIRTUALLY DRAFTED A
STATEMENT FOR AUSTRALIA TO ISSUE WHEN NUCLEAR-ARMED SHIPS
VISITED THE COUNTRY. THE STATEMENTS BY HAYDEN, ALTHOUGH
ACERBIC, HARDLY DISCREDIT AUSTRALIAN FOREIGN POLICY OR
UNDERMINE LOCAL RELATIONSHIPS, BUT THE WILLINGNESS TO KOWTOW
TO THE US AND THE FACT THAT THE DOCUMENTS WERE LEAKED AT ALL
GIVES OPPOSITION POLITICIANS A GOOD DEAL OF AMMUNITION TO
USE AGAINST THE GOVERNMENT.

05918 MALIK, S.J.
LEGITIMIZING ISLAMIZATION - THE CASE OF THE COUNCIL OF
ISLAMIC IDEOLOGY IN PAKISTAN, 1962-1981
ORIENT, 30(2) (JUN 89), 251-268.
AS THIS ARTICLE DESCRIBES, THE DIFFERENT SCHOOLS OF
THOUGHT PREVALENT IN PAKISTAN AND THE RESULTING QUARRELS
BETWEEN THEM FINALLY HAMPERED A UNITED AND ORGANIZED
OPPOSITION. THIS REGIONALIZATION OF ISLAM ACTUALLY MAKES THE
UNIVERSALIZING ISLAMIZATION IMPOSSIBLE. SINCE THE UPHOLDERS
OF THE DIVERGING ISLAMIC TRADITIONS DISPOSE, HOWEVER, OF
CONSIDERABLE MASS SUPPORT, THEY HAVE TO BE TAKEN INTO
CONSIDERATION FOR FUTURE POLICIES OF THE STATE.

05919 MALIK, Y.; VAJPEYI, D.
THE RISE OF HINDU MILITANCY: INDIA'S SECULAR DEMOCRACY AT
RISK
ASIAN SURVEY, XXIX(3) (MAR 89), 308-325.

THE ARTICLE EXAMINES THE HISTORY, RISE AND EXTENT OF
HINDU MILITANCY IN INDIA AND ANALYZES ITS POTENTIAL EFFECTS
ON THE FABRIC OF INDIAN SOCIETY. IT EMPHASIZES THE
POSSIBILITY OF HINDU MILITANCY RESULTING IN THE DEMISE OF
THE SECULAR DEMOCRACY THAT EXISTS NOW. IT EXAMINES SOME OF
THE EXPRESSIONS OF THIS MILITANCY AND REASONS FOR THE
INCREASE.

05920 MALIK, Y.K.
POLITICAL FINANCE IN INDIA
POLITICAL QUARTERLY (THE), 60(1) (JAN 89), 75-94.
WITH THE INTRODUCTION OF UNIVERSAL FRANCHISE IN INDIA
AND THE CREATION OF LARGE ELECTORAL DISTRICTS THE COST OF
ELECTIONS BEGAN TO RISE. THEREFORE IT WAS NOT SURPRISING
THAT THE GOVERNMENT OF INDIA ENACTED NEW LAWS AND
REGULATIONS DEALING WITH ELECTORAL POLITICS. DESPITE THESE
DETAILED PROVISIONS THERE WERE AND STILL ARE A NUMBER OF
LOOPHOLES IN THE ELECTION FINANCE LAWS AND REGULATIONS. THIS
ARTICLE EXAMINES THE VARIOUS SOURCES OF PARTY FUNDS AND
LOOKS AT EACH ONE OF THESE IN DETAIL TO ASSESS THEIR
IMPORTANCE. THE AUTHOR CONSIDERS MAINLY THE ROLE OF SIX
NATIONAL POLITICAL PARTIES. THESE ARE: CONGRESS (I)
COMMUNIST PARTY OF INDIA (CPI), COMMUNIST PARTY OF INDIA
(MARXIST) (CPIM), BHARATIYA JANATA PARTY (BJP), JANATA PARTY,
AND LOK DAL.

05921 MALINA, S.
AN UNUSUAL TIME
WORLD MARXIST REVIEW, 32(8) (AUG 89), 34.
COMMUNISTS FROM VARIOUS COUNTRIES TOOK AN ACTIVE PART IN
ALLIED MILITARY OPERATIONS AGAINST FASCISM IN EUROPE, BUT
FEW REMEMBER THAT A LATIN AMERICAN COUNTRY LIKE BRAZIL ALSO
CONTRIBUTED TOWARDS THE VICTORY. SALOMAO MALINA WAS A MEMBER
OF THE EXPEDITIONARY CORPS SENT BY BRAZIL TO THE ITALIAN
FRONT AND HE SHARES HIS REMINISCENCES OF THAT HEROIC PERIOD
ON THE 50TH ANNIVERSARY OF THE OUTBREAK OF WORLD WAR II. HE
CONCLUDES BY SAYING THAT HE REGARDS WORLD WAR II AS HAVING
BEEN THE LAST WAR.

05922 MALKEVICH, V.
EAST-WEST ECONOMIC RELATIONS AND THEIR PROSPECTS.
FOREIGN TRADE, 1 (1989), 25-28.
THIS ARTICLE REVIEWS AND ANALYZES A WIDE RANGE OF
CHANGES UNDERWAY IN THE SOVIET UNION AND THROUGHOUT THE
WORLD, AND THEIR EFFECTS ON RELATIONS BETWEEN THE EASTERN
AND WESTERN NATIONS. THE CHANGES EVALUATED INCLUDE SUCH
MATTERS AS THE INCREASING GLOBAL INTERDEPENDENCE OF NATIONS,
DEVELOPING ECOLOGICAL DANGERS, DEMOCRATIZATION OF THE USSR'S
ECONOMIC MANAGEMENT, AND EFFORTS AMONG THE EASTERN NATIONS
FOR GREATER ECONOMIC COOPERATION AMONG COUNTRIES.

05923 MALKI, A.
LEGALITY WON - WHAT NEXT?
WORLD MARXIST REVIEW, 32(12) (DEC 89), 40-41.
SINCE SEPTEMBER 1989, THE PARTY OF THE SOCIALIST
VANGUARD, OF ALGERIA WITH 50 YEARS OF STRUGGLE FOR NATIONAL
LIBERATION AND THE INTERESTS OF THE WORKING PEOPLE BEHIND IT,
HAS BEEN OPERATING LEGALLY. THE AUTHOR CENTERALS TEST THIS
LEGALISATION OF THE PAGS IS A PRACTICAL EMBODIMENT OF THE
RIGHT OF THE WORKERS, AS OF THE OTHER CLASSES AND SOCIAL
GROUPS, TO HAVE THEIR OWN POLITICAL PARTY UNDER THE FEBRUARY
CONSTITUTION.

05924 MALLON, T.
THE PEOPLE NEXT DOOR
AMERICAN SPECTATOR, (DEC 89), 22-26.
THIS ARTICLE IS A DESCRIPTION OF THE "PERVERSE LOST
WORLD OF THE UNITED NATIONS," BY A RESIDENT OF NEW YORK
CITY'S TURTLE BAY. HE DESCRIBES THE DECOR, THE PRESS
FACILITIES, THE ARCHITECTUAL STYLE AS BEING "CLOAKED IN THE
ATMOSPHERE OF THE FIFTIES." MR MALLON ATTENDED U.N. PRESS
BRIEFINGS AS AN ACCREDITED CORRESPONDENT AND FROM HIS
PERSONAL EXPERIENCE AND OBSERVATION COMMENTS ON THE U.N
TREATMENT OF MEDIA COVERAGE, COMMITTEES, APARTHEID, PANAMA
CANAL TREATY, PALESTINE, TIANANMEN SQUARE, UN PROCEDURES,
AND THOUGHT.

05925 MALLORY, S.
ASAMOAH DEFENDS HIS REGIME
NEW AFRICAN, (267) (DEC 89), 12-13.
OBED ASAMOAH, GHANA'S FOREIGN MINISTER, IS INTERVIEWED
IN THIS ARTICLE. HE IS QUOTED AS SAYING THAT THE GOVERNMENT
IS STABLE. THE TWO REASONS HE GIVES FOR THIS ARE THAT, THERE
IS CONSIDERABLE CIVILIAN PARTICIPATION IN THE GOVERNMENT,
AND AT THE SAME TIME THERE IS ALSO MILITARY PARTICIPATION.
ALSO DISCUSSED ARE HUMAN RIGHTS IN GHANA, FREE PRESS, THE
ECONOMY AND THE CURRENT POLITICAL DIRECTION OF THE
GOVERNMENT. ASAMOAH CLAIMS THAT DURING HIS EIGHT YEAR REGIME,
GHANA'S GOVERNMENT HAS BROUGHT DISIPLINE INTO THE SOCIETY.
AMONG THE ACCOMPLISHMENTS THEY HAVE PUT AN END TO MUCH OF
THE CORRUPTION, FRAUD, NON-PAYMENT OF TAXES AND DISRESPECT
FOR CIVIL RESPONSIBILITIES.

05926 MALLOY, J.M.
POLICY ANALYSTS, PUBLIC POLICY AND REGIME STRUCTURE IN
LATIN AMERICA
GOVERNANCE, 2(3) (JUL 89), 315-338.
THIS ARTICLE FOCUSES ON THE ROLE OF TECHNICALLY-TRAINED
ANALYSTS IN THE DEVELOPMENT OF PUBLIC POLICY IN SOUTH
AMERICA. IN LATIN AMERICA, TECHNICALLY-TRAINED ANALYSTS OR
EXPERTS ARE USUALLY REFERRED TO AS TECHNOCRATS - TECNICOS -
AND THAT IS THE DESIGNATION THAT WILL BE USED THE ARTICLE IS
ORGANIZED IN THREE SECTIONS. THE FIRST LOOKS HISTORICALLY AT
TECHNOCRATS AND POLICY BY EXAMINING THEIR ROLE IN THE
DEVELOPMENT OF SOCIAL POLICY PARTICULARLY IN BRAZIL. PART
TWO WILL SHIFT FOCUS TO A COMPARATIVE ANALYSIS OF
MACROECONOMIC POLICY-MAKING IN THE POST WORLD WAR II PERIOD
IN A NUMBER OF SOUTH AMERICAN COUNTRIES. BOTH SECTIONS
EMPHASIZE THE CHANGING STRUCTURAL CONTEXT WITHIN WHICH
TECHNOCRATS OPERATED WITH EMPHASIS ON THE TYPES OF
STATECRAFT FOSTERED BY DIFFERENT REGIMES. IN A BRIEF
CONCLUDING SECTION, THE RELATIONSHIP BETWEEN TECHNOCRATIC
POLICY STYLES AND THE INSTITUTIONAL CONTEXT OF POLICY-MAKING
WILL BE EXAMINED.

05927 MALONEY, S. T.
FROM GLOBAL REFUSAL TO WORLD LEADERSHIP: AVANT - GARDE
MUSIC QUEBEC 1948-11988
AMERICAN REVIEW OF CANADIAN STUDIES, XIX(1) (SPR 89), 1-14.
IN 1948 THE VISUAL ARTIST PAUL-EMILE BORDUAS (1905-1960)
AND A NUMBER OF COLLEAGUES FROM THE WORLDS OF ART,
LITERATURE, DANCE AND JAZZ PUBLISHED THE RADICAL MANIFESTO
REFUS GLOBAL (GLOBAL OR TOTAL REFUSAL), WHICH CASTIGATED THE
STRICTURES THEY FELT WERE IMPOSED BY THE CONSERVATIVE,
CATHOLIC ESTABLISHMENT IN QUEBEC AND, IN PARTICULAR, BY THE
ALLEMBRACING AND, IN THEIR VIEW, SUFFOCATING INFLUENCE OF
THE CHURCH. THE TRANSFORMATION OF QUEBEC SOCIETY SINCE REFUS
GLOBAL HAS BEEN NOTHING SHORT OF REMARKABLE. FRENCH
CANADIANS HAVE MOVED INTO THE FOREFRONT OF MODERN ARTISTIC
EXPRESSION IN CANADA OVER THE PAST FORTY YEARS AND NUMEROUS
CANADIAN 'FIRSTS,' SOME MENTIONED HERE, HAVE BEEN RECORDED
BY QUEBEC ARTISTS AND COMPOSERS. THE COMMITMENT TO
MAINTAINING HIGH STANDARDS AND REMAINING ABREAST OF
INTERNATIONAL DEVELOPMENTS CONTINUES AS STRONGLY WITH THE
NEWEST GENERATION OF PROFESSIONAL COMPOSERS AS IT DID WITH
GARANT, TREMBLAY, AND MOREL IN THE EARLY DAYS OF THEIR
MOVEMENT. DENIS GOUGEON HAS BEEN APPOINTED ONE OF THREE
COMPOSERS-IN-RESIDENCE WITH THE CANADIAN OPERA COMPANY IN
TORONTO AND IS CURRENTLY WORKING ON A COMMISSIONED OPERA TO
BE PREMIERED IN MAY 1989, BASED ON CHEKHOV'S THE MARRIAGE
PROPOSAL. DENIS BOULIANE (B. 1955) HAS BECOME
INTERNATIONALLY ACCLAIMED IN THE PAST FEW YEARS AND NOW
LIVES IN

05928 MALTESE, J.A.
PRESIDENTIAL POWER AND THE MEDIA: THE ROLE OF THE WHITE
HOUSE OFFICE OF COMMUNICATIONS (1969-1988)
DISSERTATION ABSTRACTS INTERNATIONAL, 50(1) (JUL 89),
246-A.
THE AUTHOR TRACES THE DEVELOPMENT AND EVOLUTION OF THE
WHITE HOUSE OFFICE OF COMMUNICATIONS, WHICH WAS ESTABLISHED
IN 1969. HE ARGUES THAT THE OFFICE INSTITUTIONALIZED TWO
IMPORTANT ASPECTS OF THE MODERN PRESIDENCY: A WHITE HOUSE-
CENTERED SYSTEM FOR CONTROLLING THE INFORMATION POLICY OF
THE ENTIRE EXECUTIVE BRANCH AND A FORMAL MECHANISM FOR
MOBILIZING SUPPORT FOR PRESIDENTIAL POLICY THROUGH DIRECT
APPEALS TO THE PUBLIC.

05929 MAMA, A.
VIOLENCE AGAINST BLACK WOMEN: GENDER, RACE, AND STATE
RESPONSES
FEMINIST REVIEW, (32) (SUM 89), 30-48.
THE WOMEN'S REFUGE MOVEMENT IN BRITAIN BEGAN IN THE
1970'S TO MEET THE DESPERATE SITUATION OF WOMEN SEEKING TO
ESCAPE FROM VIOLENT ASSAULTS IN THEIR OWN HOMES, USUALLY AT
THE HANDS OF THEIR SPOUSES. IN THIS PAPER, THE AUTHOR
EXAMINES THE EXTENT TO WHICH THE FEMINIST DISCOURSES AND
PRACTICES REVOLVING AROUND SISTERHOOD, COLLECTIVISM, AND
SELF-HELP HAVE MET THE CHALLENGE OF RACISM WITHIN THE REFUGE
MOVEMENT. SHE ALSO LOOKS AT THE LOCAL AND CENTRAL GOVERNMENT
RESPONSES TO AUTONOMOUS WOMEN'S REFUGES. SHE FINDS THAT
LOCAL AUTHORITIES HAVE RESPONDED TO REFUGES IN
INTERVENTIONIST WAYS THAT HAVE SIGNIFICANT RACIAL
IMPLICATIONS. THE CENTRAL GOVERNMENT'S RESPONSES HAVE BEEN
LESS DIRECT, BUT BROAD CHANGES IN WELFARE HAVE HAD SOME
PARTICULAR CONSEQUENCES FOR WOMEN AND THE REFUGE MOVEMENT.

05930 MAMADOUH,V.D.; WUSTEN, H.H.V.
THE INFLUENCE OF THE CHANGE OF ELECTORAL SYSTEM ON
POLITICAL REPRESENTATION: THE CASE OF FRANCE IN 1985
POLITICAL GEOGRAPHY QUARTERLY, 8(2) (APR 89), 145-160.
FRANCE HAS EXPERIENCED NUMEROUS ELECTORAL SYSTEMS
CULMINATING WITH THE INTRODUCTION OF A PROPORTIONAL SYSTEM
IN 1985 WHICH REPLACED THE MAJORITY SYSTEM ESTABLISHED IN
1958. TAKING ADVANTAGE OF THIS OPPORTUNITY TO STUDY AND
COMPARE TWO ELECTORAL SYSTEMS, THE ARTICLE DESCRIBES BOTH
SYSTEMS AND FOLLOWS WITH A QUANTITATIVE STUDY OF THE IMPACT
OF THE ELECTORAL REFORM. TWO ASPECTS ARE STUDIES: THE
DISTRIBUTION OF SEATS AMONG POLITICAL PARTIES, AND THE RE-
ALLOCATIONS OF SEATS AMONG "DEPARTMENTS." THE ARTICLE
CONCLUDES THAT THE REPRESENTATION IN TERMS OF SEATS BECAME
MORE PROPORTIONAL TO THE REPRESENTATION IN TERMS OF VOTES
UNDER THE PROPORTIONAL SYSTEM. IN GENERAL, THE PROCESS
FAVORED THE LEFT-WING PARTIES THAT HAD BEEN UNDERREPRESENTED
UNDER THE MAJORITY SYSTEM. HOWEVER, THE ELECTORAL REFORM DID
NOT HAVE A CLEAR EFFECT ON THE STRATEGIES OF POLITICAL
PARTIES.

05931 MAMALAKIS, M.J.
SELECTED INTERAMERICAN PUBLIC POLICY ISSUES: THE NEED FOR
IMPROVED BASIC ECONOMIC RIGHTS
JOURNAL OF INTERAMERICAN STUDIES AND WORLD AFFAIRS, 31(1,
2) (SPR 89), 75-103.
THE MAIN THEME OF THIS ESSAY IS THAT THE LESS-THAN-
DESIRABLE ECONOMIC PERFORMANCE IN MOST OF LATIN AMERICA HAS
RESULTED FROM INADEQUATE PRODUCTION, BOTH QUANTITATIVELY AND
QUALITATIVELY, OF THE NEEDED COLLECTIVE COMMODITIES, BY THE
VARIOUS GOVERNMENTS. IT EXPLORES THE FACT THAT THE
COLLECTIVE COMMODITIES OF PUBLIC ADMINISTRATION AND DEFENSE
HAVE BEEN PRODUCED INSUFFICIENTLY TO GUARANTEE THE BASIC
ECONOMIC, POLITICAL, AND HUMAN RIGHTS OF ALL THEIR PEOPLE,
IT EXAMINES THE RESULTS OF THIS INADEQUATE PRODUCTION

05932 MANDA. P.H.M.
THE DECENTRALISATION OF GOVERNMENT IN ZAMBIA SINCE
INDEPENDENCE
DISSERTATION ABSTRACTS INTERNATIONAL, 50(6) (DEC 89),
1800-A.
THE AUTHOR STUDIES GOVERNMENT DECENTRALISATION IN ZAMBIA
AND EVALUATES IT AS AN INSTRUMENT FOR NATIONAL AND LOCAL
POLITICAL DEVELOPMENT. HE FOCUSES ON RELATIONS BETWEEN THE
CENTER AND THE LOCALITY, WHERE CHANGE IN LOCAL GOVERNMENT
OCCURS IN THE CONTEXT OF INTENSE POLITICAL COMPETITION
WITHIN THE RULING CENTRAL POLITICAL ELITE AND WHERE THERE IS
A TENDENCY FOR THE POLICY GOALS OF DECENTRALISATION AND THE
REALITY OF IMPLEMENTATION TO DIVERGE.

05933 MANDEL, S.
AVOIDING THE BURTONMANDER
NATIONAL REVIEW, 61(24) (DEC 89), 17.
THIS ARTICLE EXPLORES GERRYMANDERING AS "THE ONLY LEGAL
FORM OF VOTE-STEALING LEFT TODAY." IT EXAMINES
GERRYMANDERING IN CALIFORNIA IN 1983 WHEN DEMOCRATIC
CONGRESSMAN PHIL BURTON MASTERMINDED A REDISTRICTING PLAN
ESSENTIALLY THE SAME AS THE ONE VOTERS HAD REJECTED IN A
REFEREDUM, WHICH WAS SIGNED AN HOUR BEFORE JERRY BROWN
TURNED OVER HIS OFFICE TO A REPUBLICAN. IT ALSO EXAMINES
REDISTRICTING SOFTWARE WHICH GIVES LEGISLATORS ON THE
TECHNOLOGY TO REDRAW THEIR STATE DISTRICTS ON THE CALIFORNIA
MODEL.

05934 MANDEL, S.
DISABLING AMERICA
NATIONAL REVIEW, XLI(18) (SEP 89), 23-24.
THE AMERICANS WITH DISABILITIES ACT, IF AND WHEN PASSED,
COULD BECOME THE MOST DISRUPTIVE PIECE OF CIVIL RIGHTS
LEGISLATION IN AMERICAN HISTORY. THE BILL'S AMBIGUITY MAKES
IT CERTAIN THAT THE LEGAL EXPENSES OF COURT BATTLES TO
DETERMINE WHO IS DISABLED AND HOW FOR ONE MUST GO TO
ACCOMMODATE THEM WILL BE MAJOR.

05935 MANDEL, S.; MCGURN, W.
HOW THE DEMOCRATS HOLD ON TO CONGRESS
NATIONAL REVIEW, 62(22) (NOV 89), 37-40.
THIS ARTICLE EXPLORES THE PARADOX THAT ALTHOUGH THE
REPUBLICAN PARTY HAS PRESIDENTS IN OFFICE IT REMAINS A
MINORITY IN CONGRESS. IT CLAIMS THAT THE MINDSET OF ACTING
LIKE A MINORITY WILL KEEP THE GOP A MINORITY. THE SUCCESS OF
THE DEMOCRATIC PARTY IS ANALYSED AND THE CHALLENGE FOR THE
REPUBLICANS IN 1992 IS DEFINED.

05936 MANDEL, S.
JOBS WITH JUSTICE?
NATIONAL REVIEW, XLI(15) (AUG 89), 170.
THE SUPREME COURT RULED THAT UNION MEMBERS DON'T HAVE TO
PAY DUES TOWARD LABOR LOSSES PET POLITICAL CAUSES BUT, AS
THIS ARTICLE DESCRIBES, THE LEGISLATIVE BATTLE TO ENFORCE
THAT RULING HAS JUST BEGUN AND IS LIKELY TO BE BLOODY.

05937 MANDEL, S.
SUFFER THE LITTLE CHILDREN
NATIONAL REVIEW, XLI(16) (SEP 89), 20-21.
THE ACT FOR BETTER CHILD CARE WOULD SET UP A
LUREAUCRATIC DECISION - MAKING PROCESS THAT FAVORS LARGE,
SECULAR DAY-CARE CENTERS OVER OTHER LESS INSTITUTIONALIZED
CARE. ALTHOUGH THIS IS BEING DONE IN THE NAME OF "CHOICE"
THE IRONY IS THAT THE LARGE DAY CARE CENTERS SERVE ONLY 11
PERCENT OF THE POPULATION. THEIR ADVANTAGE IS PURELY
POLITICAL.

05938 MANDEL, S.
    UNHEALTY, UNHEALTHY, AND WORSE
    NATIONAL REVIEW, XLI(19) (OCT 89), 25-26.
        THE PROPOSED NATIONAL HEALTH CARE BILL WOULD BUILD ON
    THE PRESENT SYSTEM BY EXPANDING GOVERNMENT PROGRAMS AND
    FURTHER DISTORTING THE TAX SYSTEM WITH MORE INCENTIVES FOR
    EMPLOYERS TO OVER-INSURE, AGAIN EXACERLATING THE PROBLEM OF
    THIRD-PARTY PAYMENT. A SURPRISING DEVELOPMENT IN THIS ISSUE,
    AS DESCRIBED BY THE AUTHOR, IS THAT THE BUSINESS SECTOR,
    FROM SMALL BUSINESSES TO FORTUNE 500 COMPANIES IS JUMPING ON
    THIS GOVERNMENT-CURE-ALL LANDWAGON. NO ONE WANTS TO BE
    RESPONSIBLE FOR MOUNTINS COSTS AND OTHER HEALTH CARE
    PROBLEMS.

05939 MANDEL, S.T.
    THE PROBLEM AT HUD
    NATIONAL REVIEW, XLI(14) (AUG 89), 21-22.
        DESPITE ALL THE FUSS OVER POLITICAL ABUSE OF HUD
    SUBSIDIES, FEW CONGRESSMEN FAVOR VOUCHERS WHICH WOULD TAKE
    THE MONEY OUT OF EASILY INFLUENCED HANDS. THAT MOST
    CONGRESSMEN ARE INCLINED TO WAFFLE ON THE ISSUE IS NOT
    SURPRISING, GIVEN THE BENEFITS THAT RETAINING INFLUENCE WITH
    HUD GIVES THEM. BUT IT'S ENCOURAGING THAT OF THOSE WHO
    DECLARED ONE WAY OR THE OTHER, THERE ARE THICE AS MANY YEAS
    AS NAYS. IF MORE POLITICAL PRESSURE WERE BROUGHT TO BEAR ON
    THOSE WHO WAFFLED IT MIGHT NOT BE THAT DIFFICULT TO PUSH A
    VOUCHER PROGRAM THROUGH. DEPT/HUD CORRUPTION

05940 MANDELBAUM, M.
    ENDING THE COLD WAR
    FOREIGN AFFAIRS, 68(2) (SPR 89), 16-36.
        DUE TO GORBACHEV'S POLICIES, A MARKED IMPROVEMENT IN
    SOVIET-AMERICAN RELATIONS HAS ALREADY OCCURRED. EVEN MORE
    DRAMATIC IMPROVEMENT IS POSSIBLE. IT IS TIME TO THINK
    SERIOUSLY ABOUT WHAT IS REQUIRED TO END THE COLD WAR.

05941 MANDLER, P.
    THE "DOUBLE LIFE" IN ACADEMIA
    DISSENT, (WIN 89), 94-99.
        AMERICANS ARE NECK-DEEP IN A PERIOD OF COMPLACENCY,
    CONVENTIONALITY, AND NATIONALISM. FORTUNATELY ACADEMIA HAS
    NOT CONFORMED AS SUPINELY AS IT ONCE DID, ALTHOUGH IT HAS BY
    NO MEANS BEEN IMMUNE TO THE GENERAL RIGHTWARD DRIFT. YET
    THIS MODEST DISPLAY OF INDEPENDENCE IS NOT TO EVERYONE'S
    LIKING. TO SOME CONSERVATIVES, IT IS EVIDENCE THAT THE
    AMERICAN CAMPUS IS A HAVEN FOR A SIGNIFICANT POPULATION OF
    POLITICAL EXTREMISTS. THEY CONTEND THAT, INSTEAD OF
    OBEDIENTLY SHUFFLING RIGHTWARD, THE SPECTRUM OF RESPECTABLE
    ACADEMIC OPINION HAS MOVED DANGEROUSLY TO THE LEFT.

05942 MANFREDI, C.P.
    ADJUDICATION, POLICY-MAKING AND THE SUPREME COURT OF
    CANADA: LESSONS FROM THE EXPERIENCE OF THE UNITED STATES
    CANADIAN JOURNAL OF POLITICAL SCIENCE, XXII(2) (JUN 89),
    313-335.
        THIS ARTICLE EXPLORES THE RELEVANCE OF STUDIES OF
    JUDICIAL POLICY-MAKING IN THE UNITED STATES TO THE DECISION-
    MAKING OF THE SUPREME COURT OF CANADA UNDER THE CANADIAN
    CHARTER OF RIGHTS AND FREEDOMS. THE ARTICLE SUGGESTS THAT
    LITERATURE CONCERNING THE POLITICAL LEGITIMACY OF JUDICIAL
    POLICY-MAKING IS MINIMALLY RELEVANT, SINCE A BROAD FORM OF
    JUDICIAL REVIEW APPEARS TO BE WELL ESTABLISHED IN CHARTER
    JURISPRUDENCE. THE LITERATURE ON INSTITUTIONAL DECISION-
    MAKING CAPACITY HAS GREATER RELEVANCE, SINCE THE CANADIAN
    COURT FACES THE SAME INFORMATION-PROCESSING CONSTRAINTS AS
    ITS AMERICAN COUNTERPART. THE ARTICLE CONCLUDES BY
    SUGGESTING THAT ATTEMPTS TO OVERCOME PROBLEMS OF
    INSTITUTIONAL CAPACITY MAY PRODUCE ADDITIONAL QUESTIONS OF
    POLITICAL LEGITIMACY.

05943 MANGELS, J.C.
    MEXICO: THE ULTIMATE DOMINO
    AVAILABLE FROM NTIS, NO. AD-A202 070/9/GAR, MAY 88, 42.
        CRITICAL EXAMINATION OF CONGRESSIONAL TESTIMONY AND
    POPULAR PRESS ASSERTIONS THAT MEXICO'S FINANCIAL AND
    POLITICAL CONDITION MAKE IT RIPE FOR MARXIST EXPLOITATION
    AND THEREFORE A THREAT TO US SECURITY. REMARKS ON THE
    HISTORICAL RELATIONSHIP BETWEEN THE US AND MEXICO ARE
    FOLLOWED BY AN ANALYSIS OF FIVE KEY ISSUES CONFRONTING THE
    TWO COUNTRIES: FOREIGN DEBT, TRADE, MIGRATION, ILLEGAL DRUGS,
    AND FOREIGN POLICY. THE OUTLOOK FOR MEXICAN POLITICAL
    STABILITY IS EVALUATED. THE AUTHOR CONCLUDES THAT MEXICO'S
    FINANCIAL CONDITION PRESENTS NEAR-TERM CHALLENGES, BUT ITS
    PROGRESS TOWARD RECOVERY, ECONOMIC POTENTIAL, AND INHERENT
    DEMOCRATIC OUTLOOK MAKE PREDICTIONS OF POLITICAL COLLAPSE
    AND AN EMINENT THREAT TO US SECURITY OVERSTATED. SUGGESTED
    US ACTIONS TO FURTHER STRENGTHEN BILATERAL TIES ARE PROVIDED.
    KEYWORDS: INTERNATIONAL POLITICS, INTERNATIONAL RELATIONS.

05944 MANGO, A.
    HISTORIOGRAPHY BY POLITICAL COMMITTEE AND COMMITTED
    HISTORIANS
    MIDDLE EASTERN STUDIES, 25(4) (OCT 89), 531-562.
        THE ISSUE OF CULPABILITY AND COMPENSATION FOR THE

"GENOCIDE" OF ARMENIANS BY THE DYING OTTOMAN EMPIRE IN THE
    EARLY YEARS OF THE TWENTIETH CENTURY REMAIN UNRESOLVED. IN
    1987 THE EUROPEAN PARLIAMENT MET TO CONSIDER A "POLITICAL
    SOLUTION TO THE ARMENIAN QUESTION." THE WIDE VARIETY OF
    OPINIONS AND THE SOMETIMES HEATED DEBATE ILLUSTRATES MANY OF
    THE DECADES-OLD QUESTIONS THAT SURROUND THE INCIDENT. THE
    ARTICLE REPORTS THE DEBATES AND CONCLUSIONS OF THE EUROPEAN
    PARLIAMENT AS WELL AS THE WORKS OF MANY HISTORIANS.

05945 MANGO, A.
    TURKEY'S TEN-YEAR ITCH
    WORLD TODAY, 45(2) (FEB 89), 25-29.
        PRIME MINISTER TURGUT OZAL BELIEVES THAT TURKEY'S
    APPLICATION FOR FULL MEMBERSHIP IN THE EUROPEAN COMMUNITY
    HAS DEFINED TURKEY'S BASIC OPTIONS AND THAT EVEN THE
    PROSPECT OF MEMBERSHIP WILL ATTRACT FOREIGN INVESTORS TO HIS
    COUNTRY. THE SAME PROSPECT IS A STEADYING FACTOR IN TURKISH
    INTERNAL POLITICS, WHICH ARE ENTERING A TURBULENT PHASE.

05946 MANGO, A.
    TURKISH EXODUS FROM BULGARIA
    WORLD TODAY, 45(10) (OCT 89), 166-167.
        FROM LATE MAY TO LATE AUGUST 1989, MORE THAN 300,000
    ETHNIC TURKISH REFUGEES POURED INTO TURKEY FROM BULGARIA.
    THE EXODUS FOLLOWED MASS DEMONSTRATIONS BY BULGARIA'S
    TURKISH MINORITY DEMANDING HUMAN RIGHTS AND AN END TO THE
    BULGARIAN POLICY OF FORCIBLE ASSIMILATION. ON AUG. 22, 1989,
    THE TURKISH GOVERNMENT DEMANDED VISAS FROM BULGARIAN
    CITIZENS WISHING TO ENTER TURKEY--AN ACT TANTAMOUNT TO
    CLOSING THE FRONTIER TO REFUGEES FROM BULGARIA.

05947 MANIK, S.A.
    OURS IS A STRUGGLE FOR DEMOCRACY
    WORLD MARXIST REVIEW, 32(6) (JUN 89), 28-31.
        THIS ARTICLE EXAMINES THE STATUS OF THE COMMUNIST PARTY
    WHICH HAS REACHED A WATERSHED. A CALL FOR FRATERNAL PARTIES,
    OPERATING UNDER DIFFERENT CONDITIONS, TO DISCUSS NEW ASPECTS
    OF THEIR THEORETICAL AND PRACTICAL WORK, AND THE WAY THEY
    UNDERSTAND AND ASSERT THEIR ROLE AT NATIONAL AND
    INTERNATIONAL LEVELS WAS MADE BY WMR AND SEVERAL REPLIES
    WERE RECEIVED. THE BANGLADESH GENERAL SECRETARY REPLIED AND
    DISCUSSED PRESENT-DAY TASKS - TO BECOME A CATALYST OF
    PATRIOTIC UNITY AND TO ACHIEVE MORE GLASTNOST, MORE
    PLURALISM.

05948 MANN, A.J.; PASTOR, M. JR.
    ORTHODOX AND HETERODOX STABILIZATION POLICIES IN BOLIVIA
    AND PERU: 1985-1988
    JOURNAL OF INTERAMERICAN STUDIES AND WORLD AFFAIRS, 31(4)
    (WIN 89), 163-192.
        THIS PAPER COMPARES ORTHODOX AND HETERODOX STABILIZATION
    POLICY MEASURES IN BOLIVIA AND PERU. IT REVIEWS THE
    THEORETICAL DEBATE AND ISSUES OF POLICY SEQUENCING. IT
    SUGGESTS THAT DESPITE SEEMINGLY DIFFERENT OUTCOMES, THE
    EXPERIENCE OF EACH OF THE TWO COUNTRIES ILLUSTRATES ISSUES
    CENTRAL TO ANY STABILIZATION EXPERIENCE, THESE ISSUES ARE:
    THE NEED FOR POLICY-MAKERS TO SHIFT POLICY ONCE
    STABILIZATION IS ACHIEVED, THE IMPORTANCE OF NET EXTERNAL
    RESOURCE FLOWS, THE NEED TO COORDINATE BOTH SHORT-RUN AND
    LONG RUN POLICIES, AND THE DIFFICULTIES OF ACHIEVING, AND
    MAINTAINING, SOCIAL CONSENSUS ON THE DISTRIBUTION OF
    ADJUSTMENT BURDENS

05949 MANN, M.
    POWER AND KNOWLEDGE: THE CASE OF CONTEMPORARY SOUTH AFRICA
    PUBLIC ADMINISTRATION, 67(2) (SUM 89), 223-227.
        RECENT DEBATE HAS BEEN FOCUSED ON THE RELATIONSHIP
    BETWEEN POWER AND KNOWLEDGE; MANY ARGUE THAT EDUCATION IS
    FAR FROM NEUTRAL AND CAN HAVE A SIGNIFICANT EFFECT EITHER TO
    MAINTAIN OR CHANGE THE STATUS QUO. THE AUTHOR BRIEFLY
    EXAMINES THE ATTEMPTS OF THE SOUTH AFRICAN GOVERNMENT TO
    RELY ON A TECHNIST FORM OF KNOWLEDGE FOR THE LEGITIMATION OF
    ITS PRACTICES. THE GOVERNMENT'S POLICIES ARE JUSTIFIED, NOT
    BY THEIR SUBSTANTIVE ENDS OR THE VALUES THEY ENSHRINE, BUT
    BY THE EFFICIENCY OF THEIR MEANS. THE EFFECT IS TO
    DEPOLITICIZE POLITICS AND TO MAKE DECISIONMAKING CLOSED TO
    PUBLIC RATIFICATION AND DISCUSSION. THE AUTHOR EXAMINES SOME
    OF THE EFFECTS AND IMPLICATIONS OF SUCH A POLICY.

05950 MANN, T.E.; SCHULTZE, C.L.
    GETTING RID OF THE BUDGET DEFICIT: WHY WE SHOULD AND HOW
    WE CAN
    BROOKINGS REVIEW, 7(1) (WIN 89), 3-22.
        THE AUTHORS OFFER SEVERAL SUGGESTIONS ABOUT HOW
    PRESIDENT BUSH MIGHT GO ABOUT THE ESSENTIALLY POLITICAL TASK
    OF SECURING PUBLIC AND CONGRESSIONAL SUPPORT FOR THE
    MEASURES NEEDED TO ELIMINATE THE FEDERAL BUDGET DEFICIT.

05951 MANNS, E.K.; HAUGH, W.L.
    COMMUNICATION IN PUBLIC ADMINISTRATION: THE NEED FOR SKILL-
    BASED EDUCATION
    POLICY STUDIES REVIEW, 8(4) (SUM 89), 891-897.
        THIS ARTICLE NOTES THE TREMENDOUS SIGNIFICANCE OF
    COMMUNICATION SKILLS FOR PUBLIC ADMINISTRATORS WITH THE

AUTHORS EXAMINING THE ATTENTION THAT HAS BEEN GIVEN TO
TEACHING THESE SKILLS IN MPA PROGRAMS. THE AUTHORS HOLD THAT
BASIC COMMUNICATION SKILLS ARE THE ESSENTIAL BUILDING BLOCKS
ON WHICH MORE ADVANCED SKILLS (I.E., QUALITATIVE SKILLS AND
COMPUTER SKILLS) ARE CONSTRUCTED. THIS ARTICLE CONSIDERS THE
VARIOUS SKILLS OF COMMUNICATION THAT ARE MOST ESSENTIAL TO
PUBLIC ADMINISTRATORS AND THE MANNER IN WHICH COURSES
ADDRESSING THESE SKILLS ARE HANDLED IN MPA CURRICULUM. IN
CONCLUDING THE ARTICLE, THE AUTHORS OFFER SEVERAL OPTIONS
FOR TEACHING COMMUNICATION SKILLS TO STUDENTS OF THE
DISCIPLINE.

05952 MANOFF, R.
REPORTERS COVERING THE GOVERNMENT ALL TOO OFTEN SUCCUMB TO
THE URGE TO RUN IT
DEADLINE, IV(2) (MAR 89), 7-9.
THE ARTICLE EXAMINES THE "MANAGERIAL ETHOS" THAT IS
PREVALENT AMONG JOURNALISTS. SIMPLY PUT, ALTHOUGH MASS
PARTICIPATION IN FOREIGN AFFAIRS IS A RELATIVELY NEW AND
UNTESTED PHENOMENON, MANY JOURNALISTS HAVE GIVEN UP ON THIS
DEMOCRATIC APPROACH ENTIRELY AND HAVE CONCEDED FOREIGN
POLICYMAKING TO THE GOVERNMENT (AND TO THEMSELVES).

05953 MANOFF, R.K.
REPORTING THE NUCLEAR NEWS IN AN ERA OF U.S.-SOVIET ACCORD
DEADLINE, 3(4) (JUL 89), 1-2, 11.
THIS ARTICLE ANALYSES THE RESPONSIBILITY THAT
JOURNALISTS HAVE IN SHAPING PUBLIC OPINION. IT COMPARES THE
COVERAGE GIVEN IN 1963 AFTER THE LIMITED TEST BAN TREATY WAS
SIGNED TO WHAT IS HAPPENING NOW WITH THE INF. IT FOCUSES ON
THE FACT THAT THE INF STORY IS NOT OVER AND THE ATTENTION
THE PRESS PAYS TO THE NUCLEAR ISSUE WILL HAVE LONG TERM
CONSEQUENCES.

05954 MANOOCHEHRI, A.
ALI SHARI'ATI AND THE ISLAMIC RENAISSANCE
DISSERTATION ABSTRACTS INTERNATIONAL, 49(9) (MAR 89),
2797-A.
THE AUTHOR ANALYZES THE IDEAS OF ALI SHARI'ATI,
CONCENTRATING ON HIS THEORY OF REVOLUTIONARY PRAXIS.

05955 MANOOCHEHRI, H.
TOWARD AN EXPLANATION OF THE ISLAMIC IDEAL OF HUMAN
PERFECTION (WITH EMPHASIS ON THE DOCTRINE OF INNER JIHAD)
DISSERTATION ABSTRACTS INTERNATIONAL, 50(5) (NOV 89),
1424-A.
THE AUTHOR STUDIES SOME OF THE MAIN CURRENTS OF ISLAMIC
THOUGH ABOUT HUMAN PERFECTION IN THE CONTEXT OF POLITICAL
THEORY. HE DESCRIBES, EXPLAINS, AND ANALYZES THE MAIN
CURRENTS OF ISLAM REGARDING SUFISM (ISLAMIC MYSTICISM), THE
NEW WISDOM, AND THE ISLAMIC LAW. HE SKETCHES AN INTEGRATED
MODEL OF THE IDEAL ISLAMIC STATE AND DISCUSSES ITS FEATURES
IN THE CONTEXT OF WESTERN POLITICAL THOUGHT.

05956 MANOR, J.
INDIA: STATE AND SOCIETY DIVERGE
CURRENT HISTORY, 88(542) (DEC 89), 429-432, 447.
IF DYNASTIC DOMINANCE CEASES IN NEW DELHI, THE SUPPLY OF
SKILLED PEOPLE MAY FACILITATE CREATIVE REALIGNMENT OF
POLITICAL FORCES AND THE RECONSTITUTION OF COHERENT
GOVERNMENT AT THE STATE AND NATIONAL LEVELS. IF IT HAD TIME
TO TAKE ROOT, REALIGNMENT COULD ALSO PRODUCE A REASONABLY
RATIONAL, WORKABLE POLITICAL SYSTEM. THERE ARE MANY REASONS
WHY THIS MAY NOT OCCUR.

05957 MANSFIELD, H.C., JR.
ARISTOTLE: THE ABSENT EXECUTIVE IN THE MIXED REGIMES;
TAMING THE PRINCE: THE AMBIVALENCE OF MODERN EXECUTIVE
POWER
FREE PRESS, NEW YORK, NY, 1989, 45-71.
THE AUTHOR DESCRIBES ARISTOTLE'S ADVISE TO DEMOCRACIES
AND OLIGARCHIES ON HOW TO IMPROVE THEIR DELIBERATION BY
MIXING THEIR DELIBERATIVE PARTS. DELIBERATION IS "SEVEREIGN"
FOR ARISTOTLE, AN IDEA FOREIGN TO AN AMERICAN IDEOLOGY WHICH
HOLDS THAT LEGISLATIVE POWER IS SOVEREIGN, WHETHER IT
DECIDES AFTER DELIBERATING OR NOT.

05958 MANSFIELD, H.C., JR.
AUSTOTLE: THE EXECUTIVE AS KINGSHIP; TAMING THE PRINCE:
THE AMBIVALENCE OF MODERN EXECUTIVE POWER
FREE PRESS, NEW YORK, NY, 1989, 23-45.
THIS CHAPTER EXAMINES WHY THE CONCEPT OF EXECUTIVE POWER
DOES NOT APPEAR IN ARISTOTLE'S POLITICAL SCIENCE. FOCUS IS
ON ARISTOTLE'S ARGUMENT ABOUT KINGSHIP, HIS PREARRANGED
SUBSTITUTE DESIGNED TO FORESTALL EXECUTIVE POWER.

05959 MANSFIELD, H.C., JR.
CONSTITUTIONALIZING THE EXECUTIVE; TAMING THE PRINCE: THE
AMBIVALENCE OF MODERN EXECUTIVE POWER
FREE PRESS, NEW YORK, NY, 1989, 181-211.
JOHN LOCKE'S POLITICAL SCIENCE SHOWS THAT THE MODERN
CONSTITUTION AND THE MODERN EXECUTIVE ARE MUTUALLY DEPENDENT
AND YET ANTITHETICAL. THE AUTHOR HERE EXAMINES THE CONCEPT
OF THE CONSTITUTIONAL EXECUTIVE, AND THE RELATIONSHIP

BETWEEN THE CONSTITUTION AND EXECUTIVE POWER.

05960 MANSFIELD, H.C., JR.
HOBBES AND THE POLITICAL SCIENCE OF POWER; TAMING THE
PRINCE: THE AMBIVALENCE OF MODERN EXECUTIVE POWER
FREE PRESS, NEW YORK, NY, 1989, 151-178.
THE AUTHOR EXAMINES HOBBES CONTRIBUTION TO THE DOCTRINE
OF EXECUTIVE POWER IN LIGHT OF HOBBES MACHIAVELLIAN
INSPIRATION. WITH HIS SCIENCE OF POWER, HOBBES ABSTRACTED
FROM THE RICH DETAIL OF MACHIAVELLI'S EXAMPLES, BUT THE
MESSAGE HE SAVED WAS PROFOUNDLY MACHIAVELLIANTHE NECESSETY
OF ACQUISITION.

05961 MANSFIELD, H.C., JR.
MACHIAVELLI AND THE MODERN EXECUTIVE; TAMING THE PRINCE.
THE AMBIVALENCE OF MODERN EXECUTIVE POWER
FREE PRESS, NEW YORK, NY, 1989, 121-149.
MACHIAVELLI WAS THE FIRST WRITER ON POLITICS TO USE THE
WORD "EXECUTE" FREQUENTLY AND THEMATICALLY IN ITS MODERN
SENSE. THE AUTHOR HERE SETS FORTH MACHIAVELLI'S FUNDAMENTAL
STANCE ON CHRISTIANITY AND NATURE, CORRECTS IT TO HIS USE OF
"EXECUTE" AND TO HIS CONCEPTION OF ESECUZIONI AND THE
EXECUTIVE.

05962 MANSFIELD, H.C., JR.
PROTO - EXECUTIVES; TAMING THE PRINCE: THE AMBIVALENCE OF
MODERN EXECUTIVE POWER
FREE PRESS, NEW YORK, NY, 1989, 73-90.
IN THIS CHAPTER THE AUTHOR CONSIDERS THE ROMAN CONSULS
AS PRESENTED BY POLYBIUS TO SEE WHETHER THEY WERE REALY
EXECUTIVES OR MERELY "PROTO EXECUTIVES" - PSEUDO-EXECUTIVES
CONSTRAINED BY THE NOTION OF EMPIRE.

05963 MANSFIELD, H.C., JR.
THE AMERICAN ELECTION: ANOTHER REAGAN TRIUMPH
GOVERNMENT AND OPPOSITION, 24(1) (1989), 28-38.
ALTHOUGH THE REPUBLICANS HAVE THEIR FIFTH VICTORY IN SIX
PRESIDENTIAL ELECTIONS, THERE HAS BEEN NO PARTY REALIGNMENT.
THE LONG-TERM TREND FAVORING THE REPUBLICANS SINCE REAGAN'S
FIRST ELECTION HAS STALLED. THE PARTY OF ORDER (DEMOCRATS)
PRESIDES OVER SOCIAL PROGRAMS THAT ARE UNDERSTOOD, NOT AS
RIGHTS TO BE PROTECTED BY GOVERNMENT AND EXERCISED BY
PRIVATE INDIVIDUALS, BUT AS GOVERNMENT SERVICES TO WHICH
THEY ARE ENTITLED WITHOUT ANY ACTION ON THEIR PART. UNDER
THE AMERICAN SCHEME, THE PARTY OF ORDER IS SITUATED IN THE
LEGISLATURE, WHERE ADJUSTMENTS IN SOCIAL PROGRAMS MAY BE
EFFECTED. THE PARTY OF PROGRESS (REPUBLICANS) APPEALS TO
THOSE WHO DISLIKE THE STAGNATION AND DEPENDENCE CAUSED BY
AUTOMATIC ENTITLEMENTS, AND ITS HOME IS IN THE PRESIDENCY.

05964 MANSFIELD, H.C., JR.
THE THEOLOGICO - POLITICAL EXECUTIVE; TAMING THE PRINCE.
THE AMBIVALENCE OF MODERN EXECUTIVE POWER
FREE PRESS, NEW YORK, NY, 1989, 91-118.
THE THEOLOGICO - POLITICAL QUESTION WAS THE CONSTITUTIVE
ISSUE OF MEDIEVAL POLITICS, SETTING BISHOPS AGAINST KINGS
AND CULMINATING IN THE STRUGGLE BETWEEN THE POPE AND HIS
HOPED-FOR EXECUTIVE, THE EMPEROR. THE AUTHOR EXAMINES HOW
THREE PROMINENT ARISTOTELIANS - THOMAS AGUINAS, DANTE
ALIGLIERC AND MARSILIUS OF PADUA - DEAL WITH THE THREAT OF
THE THEOLOGICO - POLITICAL EXECUTIVE STRUGGLE.

05965 MANSFIELD, M.
THE U.S. AND JAPAN -- SHARING OUR DESTINIES
CURRENT, (316) (OCT 89), 27-33.
THE USA AND JAPAN, TWO NATIONS THAT HAVE HISTORICALLY
ACTED INDEPENDENTLY, HAVE BECOME INTERDENPENDENT. NEITHER
NATION CAN SURVIVE AT THE CURRENT LEVEL OF ECONOMIC WELFARE
AND SECURITY WITHOUT THE ACTIVE COOPERATION OF THE OTHER.
THIS FUNDAMENTAL ASPECT OF THE RELATIONSHIP HAS SOMETIMES
BEEN OVERSHADOWED BY A SEEMINGLY ENDLESS SERIES OF DISPUTES
OVER MARKET ACCESS AND UNFAIR TRADE PRACTICES, BUT THESE
FRICTIONS SHOULD BE ADDRESSED IN THE CONTEXT OF THE OVERALL
PARTNERSHIP.

05966 MANSFIELD, M.
THE US AND JAPAN: EXAMINING OUR DESTINIES
FOREIGN AFFAIRS, 68(2) (SPR 89), 3-15.
THE AUTHOR EXAMINES THE RECENT PAST HISTORY OF US-
JAPANESE RELATIONS AND EXPLAINS WHY THE INDIVIDUAL DESTINIES
OF JAPAN AND THE USA FORM A COMMON STRUCTURE VITAL TO THE
FUTURE OF BOTH, AS WELL AS THE REST OF THE WORLD.

05967 MANSINGH, S.; LEVINE, S.I.
CHINA AND INDIA: MOVING BEYOND CONFRONTATION
PROBLEMS OF COMMUNISM, XXXVIII(2-3) (MAR 89), 30-49.
RAJIV GANDHI'S VISIT TO CHINA IN DECEMBER 1988
REPRESENTS A CULMINATION OF RECENT ATTEMPTS BY CHINA AND
INDIA TO CLOSE THE BOOK ON 30 YEARS OF HOSTILITY AND TO
PROMOTE A BETTER ATMOSPHERE FOR THE RESOLUTION OF LONG-
STANDING CONTENTIOUS ISSUES. ALTHOUGH SUMMIT DIPLOMACY IS
UNLIKELY TO BRING ABOUT DRAMATIC CHANGES IN SINO-INDIAN
RELATIONS IN THE NEAR TERM, IT WILL CONTRIBUTE TO BUILDING
SUPPORT IN BOTH COUNTRIES FOR EXPANDED RELATIONS; AND IT HAS

CREATED A REGULAR MECHANISM FOR WORKING TOWARD THE
SETTLEMENT OF THE BORDER DISPUTE. THE GENERAL RELAXATION OF
INTERNATIONAL TENSION ALSO IS LIKELY TO ASSURE THAT SINO-
INDIAN DISPUTES WILL BE RESOLVED PEACEFULLY. HOWEVER, THE
DIVERGENT INTERESTS AND POSSIBLY INCOMPATIBLE REGIONAL
AMBITIONS OF CHINA AND INDIA WILL CONTINUE TO SHAPE
INTERSTATE RELATIONS IN SOUTH ASIA. THUS, THE NORMALIZATION
OF SINO-INDIAN RELATIONS CAN ONLY AMELICRATE, NOT ELIMINATE,
THE LONG-STANDING RIVALRY BETWEEN THESE TWO MAJOR POWERS.

05968 MANSINGH, S.
THE RELUCTANT DUO: WHAT INDIA EXPECTED OF AMERICA
ASIAN AFFAIRS, AN AMERICAN REVIEW, 15(4) (WIN 89), 204-211.
FROM A PERSONAL PERSPECTIVE THE AUTHOR DISCUSSES THE
EXPECTATIONS THAT INDIA HAD OF THE US IN THE 1950'S AND
1960'S. ALTHOUGH THE TWO NATIONS HAVE COOPERATED ON SEVERAL
ISSUES AND FRONTS, THE RESULTS HAVE OFTEN BEEN DISAPPOINTING
AND DID NOT MEET THE OFTEN HIGH EXPECTATIONS OF THE INDIAN
INTELLECTUAL ELITE. A KEY PROBLEM ON BOTH SIDES HAS THAT OF
INDIFFERENCE. NEITHER THE US NOR INDIA REGARDED THE OTHER
NATION AS BEING VITALLY IMPORTANT TO THEIR INTERESTS.

05969 MANSOUR, F.
THE EXTERNAL DEBT: ANATOMY OF THE PROBLEM
WORLD MARXIST REVIEW, 32(10) (OCT 89), 37-40.
THIS IS A DIALOGUE HELD IN CARIO BETWEEN TWO WELL KNOWN
EGYPTIAN ECONOMISTS: DR. FAWZI MANSOUR (U.N. EXPERT) AND DR.
IBRAHIM EL EISAWI (ADVISOR TO EGYPT'S NATIONAL PLANNING
INSTITUTE). IT CONCERNS THE LESS DEVELOPED COUNTRIES'
EXTERNAL DEBT AS AN INCREASINGLY COMPLEX AND ACUTE PROBLEM,
ONE THAT POLITICAL LEADERS, STATESMEN AND PUBLIC FIGURES IN
VARIOUS COUNTRIES ARE TRYING HARD TO FIND A SOLUTION TO.
THIS DISCUSSION ON THE PROBLEMS OF DEBT IS KEPT WITHIN THE
CAPITALIST SYSTEM AND EXAMINES THE ORIGINS OF THIS DEBT AND
POSSIBLE SOLUTIONS TO THE PROBLEMS INVOLVED.

05970 MANZETTI, L.
THE INTERNATIONAL MONETARY FUND AND THE ARGENTINE CASE
DISSERTATION ABSTRACTS INTERNATIONAL, 49(11) (MAY 89),
3493-A.
IN 1958, 1976, AND 1985, ARGENTINA EXPERIENCED SEVERE
IMBALANCES OF ITS EXTERNAL ACCOUNTS THAT LED TO ATTEMPTS AT
ECONOMIC STABILIZATION THROUGH STAND-BY AGREEMENTS WITH THE
INTERNATIONAL MONETARY FUND. IN THIS DISSERTATION, THE
AUTHOR APPRAISES THE SUCCESS OF THE IMF PROGRAMS AND HOW
SUCCESSFUL THE DIFFERENT POLITICAL REGIMES WERE IN THEIR
STABILIZATION EFFORTS. HE ALSO EXPLORES THE RELATIONSHIP
BETWEEN ECONOMIC STABILIZATION AND POLITICAL INSTITUTIONS
AND OFFERS AN EXPLANATION OF WHY IMF-SUPPORTED PROGRAMS
ENCOUNTER PROBLEMS.

05971 MANZO, K.A.
DEPENDENT DEVELOPMENT AND SOCIAL CHANGE IN SOUTH AFRICA
DISSERTATION ABSTRACTS INTERNATIONAL, 50(6) (DEC 89),
1795-A.
USING AN HISTORICAL-STRUCTURAL APPROACH POPULARIZED BY
LATIN AMERICAN DEPENDENCY SCHOLARS, THIS STUDY INVESTIGATES
THE NATURE OF CHANGES IN SOUTH AFRICAN APARTHEID OVER TIME.
IT DEMONSTRATES THE ENORMOUS INFLUENCE OF EXTERNAL
DEPENDENCE AND INTERNAL BLACK RESISTANCE ON WHITE POLITICS
AND ARGUES THAT ANY MOVEMENT IN THE DIRECTION OF WESTERN-
STYLE DEMOCRACY WILL DEPEND ON THE OUTCOME OF POLITICAL
STRUGGLES BETWEEN THE MASS OF THE PEOPLE AND THOSE WHO
OPPRESS THEM. SUCH AN OUTCOME IS POSSIBLE, BUT IT IS BY NO
MEANS INEVITABLE.

05972 MAOGUAN, L.
WHY LAWS GO UNENFORCED
BEIJING REVIEW, 32(37) (SEP 89), 17-19, 26.
MUCH HEADWAY HAS BEEN MADE IN THE ESTABLISHMENT OF
CHINA'S LEGAL SYSTEM. HOWEVER, FAILURE TO ENFORCE THE LAWS,
TO FOLLOW THEM STRICTLY WITHOUT RESERVATIONS, AND TO FOLLOW
THROUGH WITH PUNISHMENT OF LAW-BREAKERS IS A FAIRLY SERIOUS
PROBLEM IN SOME LOCALITIES AND DEPARTMENTS. THE AUTHOR OF
THE ARTICLE LISTS FACTORS LEADING TO THE DESULTORY
OBSERVANCE AND NON-ENFORCEMENT OF THE LAWS.

05973 MAOZ, Z.
JOINING THE CLUB OF NATIONS: POLITICAL DEVELOPMENT AND
INTERNATIONAL CONFLICT, 1816-1976
INTERNATIONAL STUDIES QUARTERLY, 33(2) (JUN 89), 199-231.
THIS STUDY EXAMINES THE RELATIONSHIPS BETWEEN REGIME
FORMATION, REGIME CHANGE, AND INTERNATIONAL CONFLICT. A
DISTINCTION IS MADE BETWEEN EVOLUTIONARY AND REVOLUTIONARY
STATE FORMATION PROCESSES AS WELL AS BETWEEN REVOLUTIONARY
AND EVOLUTIONARY CHANGES WITHIN EXISTING STATES. IT IS
HYPOTHESIZED THAT REVOLUTIONARY STATE FORMATIONS AND REGIME
CHANGES RESULT IN HIGH LEVELS OF POST-INDEPENDENCE OR POST-
REGIME CHANGE INVOLVEMENT IN INTERSTATE DISPUTES. ON THE
OTHER HAND, EVOLUTIONARY POLITICAL DEVELOPMENT AND REGIME
CHANGE RESULTS IN LOW LEVELS OF CONFLICT INVOLVEMENT. THESE
PATTERNS OF INDIVIDUAL STATE INVOLVEMENT IN INTERNATIONAL
CONFLICT PROVIDE NEW INSIGHTS INTO THE HIGH CORRELATIONS
BETWEEN THE SIZE OF THE INTERNATIONAL SYSTEM AND A VARIETY

OF INTERSTATE CONFLICT ATTRIBUTES. THE POLITICAL DEVELOPMENT
MODEL SUGGESTS THAT THE NUMBER OF INTERSTATE CONFLICTS IN
THE SYSTEM WILL INCREASE WHEN A LARGE NUMBER OF STATES ARE
UNDERGOING REVOLUTIONARY REGIME CHANGES, EVEN WHEN THERE IS
NO CHANGE IN THE NUMBER OF STATES IN THE SYSTEM. THESE
PROPOSITIONS ARE TESTED ON DATA COVERING NEARLY ALL
INTERSTATE SYSTEM MEMBERS IN THE 1816--1976 PERIOD. IN
ADDITION, THE EXTENT TO WHICH THE POLITICAL DEVELOPMENT
MODEL ACCOUNTS FOR PATTERNS OF CONTAGIOUS SPREAD OF
INTERNATIONAL CONFLICT IS EXAMINED. THE IMPLICATIONS OF THE
RELATIONS BETWEEN INTERNAL PROCESSES OF POLITICAL
DEVELOPMENT AND CHANGE AND INTERSTATE DISPUTES FOR THE STUDY
OF INTERNATIONAL POLITICS ARE EXAMINED.

05974 MAOZ, Z.; ABDOLALI, N.
REGIME TYPES AND INTERNATIONAL CONFLICT, 1816-1976
JOURNAL OF CONFLICT RESOLUTION, 33(1) (MAR 89), 3-35.
THIS STUDY REPLICATES AND EXTENDS PREVIOUS INQUIRES ON
THE RELATIONS BETWEEN REGIME TYPE AND CONFLICT INVOLVEMENT
OF STATES. IT EXAMINES THE ROBUSTNESS OF PREVIOUS FINDINGS
WITH RESPECT TO VARIOUS REGIME ATTRIBUTES, VARIOUS CONFLICT
INVOLVEMENT MEASURES, AND UNITS OF ANALYSIS. USING TWO
COMPREHENSIVE DATASETS ON POLITY CHARACTERISTICS AND
MILITARIZED INTERSTATE DISPUTES, THE EMPIRICAL ANALYSES
REVEAL: (1) THERE ARE NO RELATIONS BETWEEN REGIME TYPE AND
CONFLICT INVOLVEMENT MEASURES WHEN THE UNIT OF ANALYSIS IS
THE INDIVIDUAL POLITY (I.E., A STATE CHARACTERIZED BY A
CERTAIN REGIME TYPE OVER A GIVEN TIME SPAN); THIS FINDING IS
ROBUST IN THAT IT HOLDS OVER MOST REGIME CHARACTERISTICS AND
CONFLICT INVOLVEMENT MEASURES. (2) THERE IS A SIGNIFICANT
RELATIONSHIP BETWEEN THE REGIME CHARACTERISTICS OF A DYAD
AND THE PROBABILITY OF CONFLICT INVOLVEMENT OF THAT DYAD:
DEMOCRACIES RARELY CLASH WITH ONE ANOTHER AND NEVER FIGHT
ONE ANOTHER IN WAR. (3) BOTH THE PROPORTION OF DEMOCRATIC
DYADS AND THE PROPORTION OF AUTOCRATIC DYADS IN THE
INTERNATIONAL SYSTEM SIGNIFICANTLY AFFECT THE NUMBER OF
DISPUTES BEGUN AND UNDERWAY. BUT THE PROPORTION OF
DEMOCRATIC DYADS IN THE SYSTEM HAS A NEGATIVE EFFECT ON THE
NUMBER OF WARS BEGUN AND ON THE PROPORTION OF DISPUTES THAT
ESCALATE TO WAR.

05975 MARA, G.M.
VIRTUE & PLURALISM: THE PROBLEM OF THE ONE & THE MANY
POLITY, 22(1) (FAL 89), 25-48.
JOHN RAWLS AND OTHERS HAVE URGED THAT THE FACT OF
PLURALISM IN WESTERN DEMOCRACIES SHOULD BE ACCORDED
SUBSTANTIAL, IF NOT DOMINANT, SIGNIFICANCE WITHIN
CONTEMPORARY POLITICAL PHILOSOPHY. THIS IS REQUIRED IN ORDER
TO RESIST THE POLITICAL INFLUENCE OF CERTAIN SECTARIAN
VIRTUES OR WAYS OF LIFE. BUT THE OPTIONS OFFERED BY THESE
CHAMPIONS OF VIRTUE AND DEFENDERS OF PLURALISM, SUPPORTERS
OF THE ONE OR THE MANY AS THEY ARE PORTRAYED BY THE AUTHOR
OF THIS ESSAY, ARE NEITHER THE MOST DESIRABLE NOR THE ONLY
ALTERNATIVES AVAILABLE FOR PRACTICAL PHILOSOPHY. HE ARGUES
FOR A THIRD ALTERNATIVE, WHOSE PHILOSOPHICAL ROOTS TRACE TO
ARISTOTLE AND WHICH FOCUSES NOT ON MODEL LIVES BUT ON
PRAISEWORTHY MANNERS OF CONDUCT. AS SUCH, HE CONTENDS, IT
RECOGNIZES HUMAN DIVERSITY WITHOUT SURRENDERING THE
POSSIBILITY OF EVALUATING THE SUBSTANCE, AS DISTINCT FROM
SIMPLY THE CONSEQUENCES, OF HUMAN CHOICES.

05976 MARANOVA, H.; PAVUCEK, J.; PETROVA, P.
THE IDEALS OF AN INDEPENDENT CZECHOSLOVAKIA STILL LIVE ON
EAST EUROPEAN REPORTER, 3(4) (SPR 89), 52.
THE ARTICLE CONTAINS SHORTENED TEXTS THAT WERE WRITTEN
TO BE READ OUT BY REPRESENTATIVES OF CHARTER 77 AND THE
INDEPENDENT PEACE ASSOCIATION AT WENCESLAS SQUARE IN PRAGUE
ON OCTOBER 28, 1988. POLICE ACTION PREVENTED THE ACTUAL
READING, BUT BOTH TEXTS WERE PUBLISHED IN INDEPENDENT
JOURNALS. BOTH CALL FOR INCREASED DEMOCRACY AND CITIZEN
INVOLVEMENT.

05977 MARCUS, J.
ISRAEL: WHAT NOW?
WORLD TODAY, 45(2) (FEB 89), 22-25.
THE AUTHOR LOOKS AT THE CAMPAIGN ISSUES IN ISRAEL'S 1988
GENERAL ELECTION AND AT THE INCONCLUSIVE RESULTS OF THAT
ELECTION, WHICH PRODUCED A BROADLY-BASED COALITION
GOVERNMENT.

05978 MARCUS, J.
THE POLITICS OF ISRAEL'S SECURITY
INTERNATIONAL AFFAIRS, 65(2) (SPR 89), 233-246.
THE ARTICLE ANALYZES THE VARIOUS POLITICAL AND MILITARY
PRESSURES AND CHALLENGES THAT ISRAEL WILL FACE IN THE FUTURE.
IT CONCLUDES THAT ALTHOUGH IN PURELY MILITARY TERMS, ISRAEL
IS TODAY STRONGER THAN AT ANY TIME IN ITS 40-YEAR HISTORY.
HOWEVER, THE POSSIBILITY OF FUTURE MILITARY CONFLICT STILL
REMAINS. ON THE POLITICAL FRONT, THE ABSCENCE OF PROGRESS
TOWARDS PEACE IS BEGINING TO TAKE ITS TOLL AND ISRAEL IS
CAUGHT UP IN THE COSTLY OCCUPATION OF THE WEST BANK.

05979 MARDIN, S.
THE INFLUENCE OF THE FRENCH REVOLUTION ON THE OTTOMAN

EMPIRE
INTERNATIONAL SOCIAL SCIENCE JOURNAL, (119) (FEB 89),
17-32.
THE IMMEDIATE IMPACT OF THE FRENCH REVOLUTION ON THE
OTTOMAN EMPIRE WAS NOT DUE AS MUCH TO REVOLUTIONARY IDEOLOGY
AS TO THE POLICIES THE FRENCH GOVERNMENT IMPLEMENTED IN
THEIR RELATIONS WITH THE OTTOMANS. THE IDEOLOGICAL ELAN THT
FASCINATED EUROPE WAS MET WITH CONTEMPT BY OTTOMANS IN ELITE
POSITIONS ALTHOUGH THE REVOLUTIONARY IDEOLOGY DID PROMOTE
NEW IDEAS IN SOME OF THE NON-MUSLIM POPULATION OF THE EMPIRE.

05980 MARE, M.
PUBLIC GOODS, FREE RIDING, AND NATO DEFENCE BURDEN-SHARING
INTERNATIONAL SPECTATOR, XXIII(1) (JAN 88), 7-15.
IN PART ONE, THE AUTHOR DISCUSSES THE THEORY OF PUBLIC
GOODS AND, IN PARTICULAR, THE CHARACTERISTICS OF
INDIVISIBILITY AND EXTERNALITY OF THESE GOODS. IN PART TWO,
HE ENDEAVORS TO FIND A MORE DETAILED AND REALISTIC
DEFINITION OF THE INTERNATIONAL PUBLIC GOOD KNOWN AS
"COLLECTIVE DEFENSE." PART THREE INCLUDES A BRIEF DISCUSSION
OF "FREE RIDING" AND ITS THEORETICAL AND EMPIRICAL
CONSEQUENCES ON THE FUNCTIONING OF INTERNATIONAL
ORGANIZATIONS, ESPECIALLY NATO. FINALLY, HE DISCUSSES
DEFENSE BURDEN-SHARING AMONG THE NATO COUNTRIES AND DRAWS
SOME CONCLUSIONS ABOUT HIS SUBJECT MATTER.

05981 MAREN, M.
FORTRESS SOUTH AFRICA
AFRICA REPORT, 34(2) (MAR 89), 31-33.
THE SANCTIONS STRATEGIES BEING PROMOTED BY VARIOUS ANTI-
APARTHEID ORGANIZATIONS HAVE CONCENTRATED ON STOPPING
INVESTMENT IN SOUTH AFRICA AND BANNING SOUTH AFRICAN EXPORTS,
MEASURES AIMED AT SLOWLY SUFFOCATING THE REGIME. CURIOUSLY,
THEY HAVE NOT SPENT MUCH TIME DRAWING ATTENTION TO SOUTH
AFRICA'S OIL IMPORTS. BUT OIL IS THE REGIME'S ACHILLES HEEL--
THE ONE AREA IN WHICH SANCTIONS COULD BE EFFECTIVE. IF OIL
IMPORTS WERE STOPPED, IT WOULD DEAL A SUDDEN AND CRUSHING
BLOW TO THE NATION'S ECONOMY AND FORCE THE REGIME TO BARGAIN
FOR ITS LIFE.

05982 MAREN, M.
THE BACK PAGE
AFRICA REPORT, 34(1) (JAN 89), 66.
WITH THE POSSIBILITY OF A CUBAN WITHDRAWAL FROM ANGOLA
AND THE WARMING OF SUPERPOWER RELATIONS, THE BUSH
ADMINISTRATION HAS AN OPENING TO FREE ITSELF OF THE
IDEOLOGICAL CONSTRAINTS OF THE PAST AND ESTABLISH A MORE
RATIONAL POLICY IN AFRICA.

05983 MARENIN, O.
CONCEPTS OF NATIONAL UNITY: BUREAUCRATIC DECISION-MAKING
IN THE NATIONAL YOUTH SERVICE CORPS OF NIGERIA
JOURNAL OF COMMONWEALTH AND COMPARATIVE POLITICS, XXVII(3)
(NOV 89), 365-386.
THE MILITARY GOVERNMENT OF NIGERIA ESTABLISHED THE
NATIONAL YOUTH SERVICE CORPS (NYSC) IN MAY 1973 AS A MEANS
OF ENLISTING THE ENERGIES AND TALENTS OF ITS EDUCATED YOUNG
PEOPLE IN THE STRUGGLE FOR NATIONAL UNITY. THE FIRST SECTION
OF THE ARTICLE SKETCHES THE BACKGROUND AND BASIC STRUCTURE
OF THE PROGRAMME. SECTION TWO DISCUSSES THE INTERPRETATIONS
OF THE OBJECTIVES OF THE PROGRAMME AS THESE ARE REFLECTED IN
DEPLOYMENT OR POSTING POLICIES. SECTION THREE ARGUES THAT
OFFICIALS HAVE STUCK FAIRLY CLOSE TO THE MEANING OF NATIONAL
UNITY PREVALENT IN NIGERIA, AND THEREFORE HAVE NOT DISTORTED
THE GOALS OF THE PROGRAMME, BUT HAVE PROPERLY TRANSLATED
GOALS INTO POLICIES.

05984 MARGOLIS, R.J.
HOW THE WEST WAS LOST
NEW LEADER, 72(18) (NOV 89), 13-14.
THIS ARTICLE IS AN EXAMINATION OF THE REACTIONS OF
SEVERAL STATES AFTER BEING CALLED PART OF 'AMERICA'S
OUTBACK' BY NEWSWEEK AND BEING COMPLETELY LEFT OUT OF A RAND
MCNALLY ATLAS. BOTH DAKOTAS, OKLAHOMA, MINNESOTA, IOWA AND
KANSAS WERE OMITTED IN THE ATLAS. THE UPSETTING FACTOR TO
MANY OF THE CENTENNIALITES WAS THE MAGAZINE'S DISMISSIVE
TONE, ITS COMPLACENT ASSUMPTION THAT THE BATTLE FOR SURVIVAL
HAS ALREADY BEEN LOST. DETAILED, AS WELL AS PUBLIC RESPONSE,
ARE POSITIVE STEPS BEING TAKEN BY GOVERNMENT AND CITIZENS
ALIKE TO CORRECT THE MISPERCEPTION

05985 MARGOLIS, R.J.
RETURN OF THE HOMESTEAD
NEW LEADER, LXXII(2) (JAN 89), 15-16.
IN AN EFFORT TO ATTRACT SETTLERS TO AN AREA WITH A
DWINDLING POPULATION, THE MINNESOTA LEGISLATURE PASSED A
HOMESTEAD PROGRAM FOR KOOCHICHING COUNTY. BUT THE PROGRAM
HAS ATTRACTED ONLY THREE SERIOUS HOMESTEADING APPLICATIONS.

05986 MARGOLIS, R.J.
THIS IS MEXICO?
NEW LEADER, LXXII(8) (MAY 89), 11-12.
A VACATION IN MEXICO FOR THE AUTHOR AND HIS WIFE REVEALS
CULTURAL, HISTORICAL AND SOCIAL CHARACTERISTICS DIFFERENT

FROM AMERICAN EXPECTATION AND EXPERIENCE.

05987 MARGOUS, R.
A CERTAIN SPECIES OF HELPLESSNESS
NEW LEADER, LXXII(12) (AUG 89), 10-12.
THE ARTICLE ANALYZES AN INCREASINGLY APPARENT PROBLEM IN
THE UNITED STATES: CARE FOR THE ELDERLY. IT CONCLUDES THAT
ALTHOUGH THE UNITED STATES HAS THE RESOURCES TO PROVIDE
ADEQUATE CARE FOR THE ELDERLY OF TODAY AND OF THE FUTURE,
POLITICAL WILL IS SOMEWHAT LACKING. NOT ONLY ARE DEMOCRACIES
GENERALLY SLOW IN FORMULATING AND IMPLEMENTING REFORMS OF
THIS SCALE, BUT ASSUMPTIONS AND SENTIMENTS OF TODAY'S FAST
PACED, YOUTH ORIENTED SOCIETY ALSO SLOW REFORM EFFORTS.

05988 MARILLEY, S.M.
TOWARDS A NEW STRATEGY FOR THE ERA: SOME LESSONS FROM THE
AMERICAN WOMAN SUFFRAGE MOVEMENT
WOMEN AND POLITICS, 9(4) (1989), 23-42.
THIS ARTICLE COMPARES THE 1970S ERA MOVEMENT WITH THE
AMERICAN WOMAN SUFFRAGE MOVEMENT IN ORDER TO IDENTIFY A
POTENTIALLY MORE SUCCESSFUL STRATEGY FOR A FUTURE MOVEMENT.
THE SIMILARITIES AND DIFFERENCES IN THE NATURE OF THE
OPPOSITION, THE ISSUES ARTICULATED, AND THE ALLIANCES FORMED
BY BOTH MOVEMENTS ARE EXAMINED. IT IS ARGUED THAT THE
LEADERS OF A FUTURE ERA MOVEMENT MUST CELEBRATE WOMEN'S
DIFFERENCES, CHALLENGE MORE EFFECTIVELY THE NOTION THAT
WOMEN NEED MEN'S PROTECTION, SELECT ISSUES THAT CONCERN MOST
WOMEN, AND FORM FIRMER ALLIANCES.

05989 MARIOTTE, M.
THE RESURGENCE OF NUCLEAR POWER IN AMERICA
MULTINATIONAL MONITOR, 10(1-2) (JAN 89), 9-12.
DESPITE THE LONG NUCLEAR DROUGHT, THE NUCLEAR INDUSTRY
IN THE UNITED STATES IS MORE OPTIMISTIC NOW THAN IT HAS BEEN
SINCE ITS GLORY DAYS OF THE EARLY 1970'S. THE INDUSTRY IS
ACTIVELY PREPARING FOR A RESURGENCE. ITS APPROACH IS MULTI-
PRONGED AND RELIES HEAVILY ON ITS ALLIES IN CONGRESS AND THE
FEDERAL GOVERNMENT. THE KEY TO THE ANTICIPATED RESURRECTION
IS TO COUNTER ENVIRONMENTAL OPPOSITION BY PORTRAYING NUCLEAR
POWER AS A BENIGN SOLUTION TO THE GREENHOUSE EFFECT. THE
INDUSTRY STRATEGY INCLUDES EASING REGULATIONS TO VIRTUALLY
ELIMINATE PUBLIC PARTICIPATION IN THE LICENSING PROCESS,
REMOVING EMERGENCY EVACUATION PLANNING AS AN ISSUE IN
REACTOR SITING AND LICENSING, REDUCING THE COST OF
RADIOACTIVE WASTE DISPOSAL BY DEREGULATING SOME NUCLEAR
WASTE, AND FORCING TAXPAYERS TO PAY FOR THE DEVELOPMENT OF
"INHERENTLY-SAFE" REACTORS.

05990 MARIS, M.
THE ASSOCIATION OF SOUTHEAST ASIAN NATIONS (ASEAN):
POSSIBILITIES AND LIMITS OF REGIONAL INDUSTRIAL COOPERATION
DISSERTATION ABSTRACTS INTERNATIONAL, 50(1) (JUL 89),
257-A.
THE AUTHOR INVESTIGATES THE REASONS FOR THE FAILURE OF
ASEAN INDUSTRIAL COOPERATION. HE FINDS THAT THE ASEAN
COUNTRIES LACK A COMMON INTEREST THAT IS A PRECONDITION FOR
EFFECTIVE COOPERATION IN INDUSTRIAL DEVELOPMENT AND THAT
THEY HAVE FAILED TO USE THE TOOL OF INDUSTRIAL COOPERATION
TO INCREASE THEIR WELFARE.

05991 MARK, E.
OCTOBER OR THERMIDOR? INTERPRETATIONS OF STALINISM AND THE
PERCEPTION OF SOVIET FOREIGN POLICY IN THE UNITED STATES,
1927-1947
AMERICAN HISTORICAL REVIEW, 94(4) (OCT 89), 937-962.
AS STALIN EVER MORE DRAMATICALLY ALTERED THE BOLSHEVIK
HERITAGE, CONSERVATIVES INCREASINGLY PORTRAYED STALINISM AS
A THERMIDORIAN REACTION, THE FIRST STAGE OF AN INEVITABLE
CAPITALIST RESTORATION. PARTLY TO REBUT SUCH CLAIMS, MANY
AMERICAN LIBERALS EXPLAINED STALINISM AS AN EVOLUTIONARY
DEVELOPMENT OF BOLSHEVISM THAT, WHEN SHORN OF ITS WILDER
EXTREMES, REMAINED A PROGRAM OF SOCIAL BETTERMENT. MANY
NONCOMMUNIST RADICALS, ANXIOUS THAT STALINISM SHOULD NOT BE
TAKEN FOR SOCIALISM, HELPED TO PROPOUND THE THEORY OF
TOTALITARIANISM, WHICH HELD THAT STALINISM EXEMPLIFIED
NEITHER CAPITALISM OR SOCIALISM. THESE DIVERSE
INTERPRETATIONS OF STALINISM INFORMED AND DIVIDED AMERICAN
PERCEPTIONS OF SOVIET COMMUNISM DURING WORLD WAR II AND THE
COLD WAR.

05992 MARK, I.
DOUBTERS AMONG THE DEBTORS
SOUTH, (101) (MAR 89), 21.
FOREIGN BANKERS AND THE US TREASURY HAVE HAILED CHILE AS
A WORLD LEADER IN DEBT CONVERSION. BUT OPPOSITION ECONOMISTS
SAY THAT THE PROGRAM MERELY SWAPS ONE SET OF OBLIGATIONS FOR
ANOTHER. THE GOVERNMENT COUNTERS BY CLAIMING THAT THE DEBT
CONVERSION PLAN ATTRACTS NEW INVESTMENT.

05993 MARK, I.
VOTING ON THE BOTTOM LINE
SOUTH, (100) (FEB 89), 37.
IN THE OCTOBER 1988 PLEBISCITE, ALMOST 55 PERCENT OF
CHILE'S ELECTORATE VOTED AGAINST THE PLANS TO CONTINUE THE

TERM OF PRESIDENT AUGUSTO PINOCHET FOR EIGHT MORE YEARS.
MANY VOTED "NO" TO PROTEST THE BAD ECONOMIC SITUATION. IT IS
ESTIMATED THAT 40 PERCENT OF CHILEAN WORKERS EXIST ON THE
MINIMUM WAGE, AND THE MILITARY REGIME'S ECONOMIC POLICIES
HAVE BEEN ACCUSED OF SPLITTING CHILE INTO RICH AND POOR.

05994 MARK, S.M.; YUSHI, M.
PRICE POLICY AND PRICING REFORM IN CHINA'S ECONOMIC
MODERNIZATION
JOURNAL OF CONTEMPORARY ASIA, 18(3) (1988), 307-317.
THIS ARTICLE FOCUSES ON THE ROLE AND PERFORMANCE OF
PRICING IN A PLANNED REGIME, RATHER THAN ON THE QUALITY OF
THE PLANNING PROCESS. THE AUTHOR TRACES THE EVOLUTION OF
PRICE POLICY UNDER THE PLANDETERMINED PRICING REGIME PRIOR
TO THE RECENT MODERNIZATION INITIATIVES AND POINTS TO THE
CUMULATIVE EFFECTS OF PRICE INFLEXIBILITY IN THE PLANNING
PROCESS AS REPRESENTING A MAJOR CHALLENGE TO THE ENVISAGED
ECONOMIC REFORMS. THE CONCLUDING SECTION DISCUSSES SOME OF
THE CURRENT ISSUES IN PRICING REFORM AND SUGGESTS SOME
APPROACHES TO A MORE OPTIMAL SYSTEM.

05995 MARKAKIS, J.
NATIONALITIES AND THE STATE IN ETHIOPIA
THIRD WORLD QUARTERLY, 11(4) (OCT 89), 118-130.
THIS ARTICLE EXAMINES ETHNIC DIVERSITY IN ETHIOPIA AS
WELL AS THE VARIOUS LANGUAGES, AND CULTURES. AND POPULATIONS.
IT EXPLORES HAILE SALASSIE'S REIGN - THE IMPERIAL REGIME,
AND THE MILITARY REGIME. IT THEN DETAILS NATIONAL MOVEMENTS
AND THE LEFT. IT CONCLUDES THAT A MILITARY SOLUTION IS NOT A
REALISTIC OPTION FOR ETHIOPIA'S MANIFOLD NATIONAL CONFLICT.

05996 MARKS, C.
REACHING THE MILLIONS
POLITICAL AFFAIRS, LXVIII(9-10) (SEP 89), 6-9.
ENGELS AND MARX WROTE THAT "ONLY WHEN IDEOLOGY IS
GRASPED BY THE PEOPLE DOES IT BECOME A MATERIAL FORCE." THE
ARTICLE OUTLINES STRATEGIES FOR THE COMMUNIST PARTY USA TO
USE TO EFFECTIVELY UTILIZE THE MASS MEDIA RESOURCES IN THE
US. IT EXAMINES SOME CHALLENGES FACED BY A PROGRESSIVE
SOCIALIST PARTY ATTEMPTING TO WORK WITHIN A BOURGEOIS
DOMINATED SYSTEM, AND OUTLINES METHODS OF OVERCOMING THESE
BARRIERS. IT CONCLUDES THAT ALTHOUGH MEDIA COVERAGE IS
BECOMING INCREASINGLY FAVORABLE AND THE PARTY IS BECOMING
INCREASINGLY ADEPT AT USING THE MEDIA, MUCH REMAINS TO BE
ACCOMPLISHED.

05997 MARKS, G.
VARIATIONS IN UNION POLITICAL ACTIVITY IN THE UNITED
STATES, BRITAIN, AND GERMANY FROM THE NINETEENTH CENTURY
COMPARATIVE POLITICS, 22(1) (OCT 89), 83-104.
THE AUTHOR ANALYZES TWO BASIC SOURCES OF VARIATION IN
UNION POLITICAL STRATEGY. THE FIRST IS THE ORGANIZATIONAL
STRENGTH OF THE UNION. THE OTHER SET FACTORS ENCOMPASSES THE
ECONOMIC AND POLITICAL CONTEXT OF UNION ORGANIZATION IN THE
LABOR MARKET.

05998 MARKS, J.
COMMON PURSUIT
SOUTH, (103) (MAY 89), 21-22.
EFFORTS TO CREATE ECONOMIC UNITY IN NORTH AFRICA, WITH
STRUCTURES CAPABLE OF DEFUSING THE REGION'S POLITICAL
DISPUTES AND STIMULATING TRADE, HAVE CULMINATED IN THE
CREATION OF THE ARAB MAGHREB UNION. THE OCTOBER 1988 RIOTS
IN ALGERIA REINFORCED THE PRESSING NEED FOR THE MAGHREB
STATES TO FIND NEW WAYS OF STIMULATING GROWTH. MANY
OBSERVERS BELIEVE THAT REGIONAL ECONOMIC INTEGRATION AND THE
CREATION OF A GENUINE "MAGHREB EC" COULD OFFER A PARTIAL
SOLUTION.

05999 MARKS, L.
CSCE INFORMATION FORUM
DEPARTMENT OF STATE BULLETIN (US FOREIGN POLICY), 89(2150)
(SEP 89), 86-87.
IN DEMOCRATIC SOCIETIES, ALL POINTS OF VIEW ARE
PRESENTED TO THE PUBLIC BY INDEPENDENT JOURNALISTS. UNDER AN
AUTHORITARIAN GOVERNMENT, A JOURNALIST IS A SERVANT OF THE
STATE CHARGED WITH THE DUTY OF PRESENTING GOVERNMENTAL VIEWS,
NOT CHALLENGING THEM. WHILE THESE PRINCIPLES ARE PROFOUNDLY
DIFFERENT, THE INFORMATION FORUM OF THE CONFERENCE ON
SECURITY AND COOPERATION IN EUROPE IS COMMITTED TO REMOVING
BARRIERS TO THE FREE FLOW OF INFORMATION UNDER EITHER SYSTEM.
THERE IS GROWING RECOGNITION BY SOME EASTERN GOVERNMENTS
THAT CLOSING OFF THEIR SOCIETIES TO THE WORLD OF INFORMATION
MEANS CLOSING THE DOORS TO THE FUTURE.

06000 MARLO, M.L.; JOULFAIAN, P.
THE DETERMINANTS OF OFF-BUDGET ACTIVITY OF STATE AND LOCAL
GOVERNMENTS
PUBLIC CHOICE, 63(2) (NOV 89), 113-124.
THIS PAPER EXAMINES THE "OFF-BUDGET" SECTOR RELATION TO
OTHER LESS-HIDDEN FACETS OF THE PUBLIC SECTOR. IT STUDIES
THE SEMINAL WORK IN THIS AREA BY BENNETT AND DILORENZO
(1982). THAT THE TOTAL GOVERNMENT SPENDING IS INFLUENCED BY
RELATIVE PRICES AND POLITICAL CONSTRAINTS IS THE PRIMARY

THESIS. IT CONCLUDES THAT "BIG" ON-BUDGET SPENDERS TEND TO
BE "BIG" OFF-BUDGET SPENDERS AS WELL.

06001 MARMO, P.S.
A ONE-PARTY STATE-THE ROLE OF PARLIAMENT IN TANZANIA
PARLIAMENTARIAN, 70(2) (APR 89), 65-71.
THIS ARTICLE IS BASED ON A PAPER PRESENTED BY THE AUTHOR
AT A 1987 SEMINAR ON PARLIAMENT IN AFRICA HELD IN BOTSHANA.
A HISTORY OF TANZANIAN PARLIAMENT, WHICH LEGISLATES NOT ONLY
FOR MAINLAND TANZANIA BUT ALSO UPON MATTERS WHICH FALL UNDER
UNION JURISDICTION BUT EXTEND TO ZANZIBAR, IS PROVIDED. THE
RISE OF THE ONE-PARTY STATE IS TRACED AND THE MECHANICS OF
THE ELECTION PROCESS ARE EXPLAINED. THE AUTHOR ARGUES FOR A
CONTINUATION OF A ONE-PARTY STATE, CITING A HIGH DEGREE OF
LEADERSHIP CIRCULATION WITHOUT THE FORMALIZATION OF MULTIPLE
PARTIES. VOTER TURNOUT IS NOTED AS HIGH.

06002 MARMOR, T.R.; GILL, K.C.
THE POLITICAL AND ECONOMIC CONTEXT OF MENTAL HEALTH CARE
IN THE UNITED STATES
JOURNAL OF HEALTH POLITICS, POLICY AND LAW, 14(3) (FAL 89),
459-476.
SINCE THE MID-1970S, THE MENTAL HEALTH TREATMENT SYSTEM
IN THE U.S. HAS FACED BUDGETARY FAMINE. THIS IS IN STARK
CONTRAST TO THE GROWING CORNUCOPIA OF FISCAL RESOURCES
ENJOYED BY THE OVERALL HEALTH CARE SYSTEM. THIS PAPER
EXPLORES THE COMPLEX REASONS FOR THIS DISPROPORTIONATE
ALLOCATION IN HEALTH SPENDING. ON THE ONE HAND, MENTAL
HEALTH MAY SUFFER FROM THE PERCEPTION THAT ITS DIAGNOSES ARE
LARGELY "SUBJECTIVE" AND ITS TREATMENTS DO NOT FIT THE
TRADITIONAL "MEDICAL MODEL" THAT CAN BE DEFINED PRECISELY
AND PAID FOR BY THIRD-PARTY INSURERS. BUT MORE IMPORTANTLY,
THE DEARTH OF MENTAL HEALTH RESOURCES CAN BE ATTRIBUTED TO
THE PECULIAR NATURE AND CHARACTERISTICS INHERENT IN AMERICAN
POLITICS. THIS PAPER DESCRIBES THE AMERICAN POLITICAL
ENVIRONMENT, FROM BOTH A HISTORICAL AND A CONTEMPORARY
PERSPECTIVE, TO GIVE SOME INSIGHT INTO THE DEVELOPMENT OF
POLICIES AFFECTING THE MENTAL HEALTH SYSTEM IN THE U.S.
GIVEN THE CURRENT CLIMATE OF FISCAL CONSERVATISM IN THIS
COUNTRY TOWARD ANY INCREASES IN SOCIAL SPENDING, IT IS
LIKELY THAT THE PROFOUND MISMATCH IN NEED AND SPENDING FOR
MENTAL HEALTH PROGRAMS WILL CONTINUE INDEFINITELY.

06003 MARQUEZ, B.
THE POLITICS OF RACE AND ASSIMILATION: THE LEAGUE OF
UNITED LATIN AMERICAN CITIZENS 1929-40
WESTERN POLITICAL QUARTERLY, 42(2) (JUN 89), 355-376.
MINORITY CIVIL RIGHTS GROUPS ARE COMMONLY SEEN AS
VEHICLES THROUGH WHICH THE STRUGGLE AGAINST RACISM CAN BE
FOUGHT. WHILE SCHOLARS HAVE FOCUSED ON THEIR DEMAND FOR
EQUAL OPPORTUNITY, LITTLE ANALYSIS HAS BEEN FOCUSED ON THE
CONTENT OF THESE DEMANDS AND THEIR RELATIONSHIP TO OTHER
VALUES AND IDEALS. THIS PAPER ANALYZES THE WAY IN WHICH
CLASS INTEREST AND ECONOMIC PHILOSOPHY EXPRESSES ITSELF IN
THE POLITICAL PROGRAM OF THE LEAGUE OF UNITED LATIN AMERICAN
CITIZENS (LULAC), THE LARGEST AND OLDEST MEXICAN AMERICAN
CIVIL RIGHTS ORGANIZATION. THE FINDINGS INDICATE THAT WHILE
LULAC FOUGHT FOR EQUAL RIGHTS AND OPPORTUNITIES FOR ITS
PEOPLE, ITS DEMANDS WERE ANCHORED IN A WORLD VIEW THAT
EMBRACED LOYALTY TO THE UNITED STATES, INDIVIDUAL
ACHIEVEMENT, AND FREE MARKET CAPITALISM.

06004 MARQUEZ, J.
A HARVARD MAN TAKES CHARGE
REASON, 20(10) (MAR 89), 40-41.
MEXICO HAS SOME GOOD NEWS AND SOME BAD NEWS. THE GOOD
NEWS IS THE EMERGENCE OF A DEMOCRATIC TREND THAT PROMISES TO
HAVE GREAT POLITICAL SIGNIFICANCE IN THE NEAR FUTURE. AFTER
70 YEARS OF ONEPARTY RULE, THE 1988 PRESIDENTIAL ELECTIONS
WERE THE FIRST TO FEATURE THREE POWERFUL AND CHARISMATIC
CANDIDATES FROM THREE POLITICAL PARTIES SPANNING THE
IDEOLOGICAL SPECTRUM. THE BAD NEWS IS THAT THE ELECTORAL
PROCESS AND OUTCOME WERE RIDDLED WITH CORRUPTION AND FRAUD
AND THAT MISINTERPRETATION OF THE RESULTS BY THE MEXICAN
GOVERNMENT COULD SERIOUSLY HINDER THE COUNTRY'S ECONOMIC
PROGRESS.

06005 MARRA, R.F.; OSTROM, C.W. JR.
EXPLAINING SEAT CHANGES IN THE U.S. HOUSE OF
REPRESENTATIVES, 1950-86
AMERICAN JOURNAL OF POLITICAL SCIENCE, 33(3) (AUG 89),
541-569.
THIS PAPER DEVELOPS AN AGGREGATE-LEVEL MODEL THAT
EXPLAINS BOTH ON-YEAR AND MIDTERM HOUSE ELECTIONS. WHILE
TUFTE'S REFERENDUM VOTING MODEL PROVIDES A FOUNDATION. THIS
MODEL IS AUGMENTED BY ADDITIONAL HYPOTHESES DRAWN FROM
SUGGESTIONS IMPLICIT IN FIORINA'S (1981) INDIVIDUAL-LEVEL
RETROSPECTIVE VOTING MODEL AND JACOBSON AND KERNELL'S (1983)
STRATEGIC POLITICIAN MODEL. DATA ARE COLLECTED FOR THE 1950-
86 PERIOD AND MODEL PARAMETERS ARE ESTIMATED BASED ON BOTH
SUBSTANTIVE AND EMPIRICAL EVIDENCE THIS PAPER WILL (1)
EXPLAIN THE DIFFERENCES BETWEEN ON-YEAR AND MIDTERM
ELECTIONS WITHIN THE CONTEXT OF A SINGLE MODEL (WITHOUT
RECOURSE TO ONE OR MORE DUMMY VARIABLES) AND TO FORECAST

FAIRLY ACCURATELY THE 1946 AND 1948 CONGRESSIONAL ELECTIONS;
(2) PROVIDE AN INDICATION THAT THE DIRECT EFFECTS OF THE
ELECTORAL-ECONOMIC CYCLE ARE SOMEWHAT MUTED; (3) EXTEND THE
POSSIBLE WAYS IN WHICH THE PRESIDENT IS ABLE TO EXERCISE
SOME CONTROL OVER ELECTORAL OUTCOMES THROUGH USING
NONECONOMIC INCUMBENCY ADVANTAGES; AND (4) DEMONSTRATE THAT
VOTERS ARE, TO SOME DEGREE, RATIONAL GODS OF VENGEANCE AND
OF REWARD.

06006 MARSHALL, J.
    ISRAEL, THE CONTRAS AND THE NORTH TRIAL
    MIDDLE EAST REPORT, 19(5) (SEP 89), 34-35, 38.
        THE TESTIMONY OF OLIVER NORTH IN THE IRAN-CONTRA
    HEARINGS RECEIVED CONSIDERABLE PUBLIC ATTENTION AND SCRUTINY.
    ALTHOUGH THE ROLE OF ISRAEL IN CENTRAL AMERICA WAS REVEALED,
    IT RECEIVED LITTLE ATTENTION. DOCUMENTS FROM THE HEARINGS
    CONFIRM WHAT MANY HAVE LONG SUSPECTED: ISRAEL HAS BEEN A
    SIGNIFICANT THIRD-PARTY SUPPLIER OF AID, IN PARTICULAR ARMS,
    TO THE CONTRAS. MANY EXPERTS ARGUE THAT THE DOCUMENTS REVEAL
    ONLY THE TIP OF ISRAEL'S COVERT ICEBERG.

06007 MARSHALL, M.G.; ARESTIS, L.R.
    "REAGANOMICS" AND SUPPLY-SIDE ECONOMICS
    JOURNAL OF ECONOMIC ISSUES, 23(4) (DEC 89), 965-976.
        THIS ARTICLE IS AN ATTEMPT BY TWO OBSERVERS FROM ACROSS
    THE ATLANTIC TO EXPLAIN THE TRIUMPH IN THE UNITED STATES OF
    SUPPLY-SIDE IDEAS. IT ATTEMPTS TO REKINDLE DISCUSSION OF THE
    QUESTION: WHY DID SUPPLY-SIDE ECONOMICS GAIN A PRE-EMINENT
    POSITION DURING THE REAGAN PERIOD? THE ARTICLE IS CONCERNED
    WITH THE WAYS IN WHICH, AND THE REASONS WHY, SUPPLY-SIDE
    ECONOMICS CAME TO CONSTITUTE THE ECONOMIC CORE OF
    "REAGANOMICS." AND THE DECLINE OF THE "KEYNESIAN CONSENSUS.

06008 MARSHALL, T.J.
    NEW OPENINGS FOR CONVENTIONAL ARMS CONTROL
    PARAMETERS, XIX(2) (JUN 89), 75-85.
        THIS ARTICLE PROVIDES AN OVERVIEW OF THE CURRENT STATUS
    OF CONVENTIONAL ARMS CONTROL, EMPHASIZING THE PROSPECT OF A
    NEW NEGOTIATING FORUM KNOWN AS CONVENTIONAL FORCES IN EUROPE.
    SEVERAL RECENT EVENTS HAVE CONVERGED TO REDIRECT ATTENTION
    TO CONVENTIONAL ARMS CONTROL: CONCLUSION OF THE INTERMEDIATE-
    RANGE NUCLEAR FORCES TREATY; A LIBERALIZED SOVIET LEADERSHIP;
    PROSPECTS FOR STRATEGIC ARMS REDUCTION TALKS; HEIGHTENED
    AWARENESS AND RECEPTIVITY CONCERNING THIS ISSUE ON THE PART
    OF THE EUROPEAN PUBLICS; US BUDGET CONSTRAINTS AND CALLS FOR
    BURDENSHARING; AND PRESIDENTIAL POLITICS. AMONG THESE, A
    PRINCIPAL FACTOR IS THE RECENT SUCCESSFUL CONCLUSION OF THE
    INF NEGOTIATIONS, CAUSING MANY WITHIN EUROPEAN NATO AND THE
    UNITED STATES TO TURN THEIR ATTENTION NOW TOWARD THE LONG-
    STANDING IMBALANCE IN CONVENTIONAL FORCES.

06009 MARSHALL, T.R.
    POLICYMAKING AND THE MODERN COURT: WHEN DO SUPREME COURT
    RULINGS PREVAIL?
    WESTERN POLITICAL QUARTERLY, 42(4) (DEC 89), 493-508.
        MOST SUPREME COURT RULINGS SUCCESSFULLY WITHSTAND
    CHALLENGE, BUT A FEW RULINGS ARE OVERTURNED BY CONGRESS,
    CONSTITUTIONAL AMENDMENTS, OR BY LATER COURT DECISIONS. FOUR
    MODELS ARE IDENTIFIED, THEN TESTED, TO EXPLAIN WHY SOME
    COURT RULINGS PREVAIL, BUT OTHERS DO NOT. SINCE THE MID-
    1930S THE STRONGEST DETERMINANTS OF WHETHER A COURT RULING
    WILL PREVAIL OR BE OVERTURNED HAVE BEEN THE JUSTICES'
    UNANIMITY, THE RULING'S IDEOLOGICAL DIRECTION, AND THE
    PREVAILING CLIMATE OF PUBLIC OPINION.

06010 MARSHALL, P.
    HOW FARES THE WORLD IN 1989?
    ROUND TABLE, (311) (JUL 89), 266-671.
        THE UNITED NATIONS CONFERENCE ON TRADE AND DEVELOPMENT
    (UNCTAD) HAS BEEN CALLED THE FIRST INSTITUTIONAL RESPONSE IN
    THE ECONOMIC SPHERE TO THE ENTRY OF THE THIRD WORLD ON THE
    ECONOMIC SCENE. THIS PAPER SETS OUT THE INTERESTS OF
    DEVELOPING COUNTRIES AS EXPRESSED BY THEIR REPRESENTATIVES
    IN KEY MEETINGS BEFORE AND AFTER THE ESTABLISHMENT OF UNCTAD.
    THESE INTERESTS ARE EXAMINED IN THE CONTEXT OF THE CHANGING
    INTERNATIONAL ECONOMIC ENVIRONMENT AND THE INTERESTS OF THE
    WESTERN DEVELOPED STATES WHO WERE THE DOMINANT GROUP.
    UNCTAD'S EFFECTIVENESS, AS AN INSTRUMENT FOR PROMOTING THE
    INTERESTS OF DEVELOPING COUNTRIES, WILL THEN BE MEASURED BY
    THE EXTENT TO WHICH IT WAS ABLE TO ALTER THE PREVAILING
    INTERNATIONAL ECONOMIC SYSTEM TO ACHIEVE BENEFITS FOR
    DEVELOPING COUNTRIES.

06011 MARSTON, R. C.
    A REEVALUATION OF EXCHANGE RATE POLICY
    CANADIAN PUBLIC POLICY--ANALYSE DE POLITIQUES, XV (FEB 89),
    45-51.
        THIS PAPER DISCUSSES TWO DIFFERENT TYPES OF EXCHANGE
    RATE VARIABILITY: VOLATILITY AND MISALIGNMENT. VOLATILITY,
    THE SHORT-RUN MOVEMENT OF EXCHANGE RATES, LEADS TO GAINS AND
    LOSSES ON FINANCIAL AND TRADE TRANSACTIONS DENOMINATED IN
    FOREIGN CURRENCIES, BUT THESE GAINS AND LOSSES ARE NO
    GREATER THAN THOSE EXPERIENCED IN INDUSTRIES LIKE MINING AND
    FARMING WHERE PRICES ARE EVEN MORE VOLATILE. MISALIGNMENT,

IN CONTRAST, IMPOSES MORE SUBSTANTIAL LOSSES (OR GAINS) ON
INTERNATIONAL TRANSACTIONS. PLANT LOCATION DECISIONS, EXPORT
PROGRAMS, AS WELL AS LONG-TERM FINANCING MAY BE SERIOUSLY
AFFECTED BY MISALIGNMENT.

06012 MARTIN, B.
    POLITICS OF IRONY IN PAUL DE MAN
    CANADIAN JOURNAL OF POLITICAL AND SOCIAL THEORY, 13(3)
    (1989), 16-30.
        THIS ARTICLE ATTEMPTS TO HISTORICALLY AND POLITICALLY
    LOCATE THE CONCEPT OF IRONY WHICH IS A MAJOR THEME IN PAUL
    DE MAN'S WORK. THE DISCUSSION POSTULATES THAT WESTERN IRONY
    HAS POLITICAL-EPISTEMOLOGICAL ROOTS THAT ARE FAR MORE
    INDIVIDUALIST THAN COLLECTIVIST IN ORIENTATION AND THIS IS
    USED TO ARGUE FOR A POLITICS MORE OF THE LATTER INCLINATION.
    IT CONCLUDES THAT WHAT WE HAVE NOW IS QUITE THE OPPOSITE OF
    A WRITERLY POLITICS.

06013 MARTIN, C.J.
    BUSINESS INFLUENCE AND STATE POWER: THE CASE OF U.S.
    CORPORATE TAX POLICY
    POLITICS AND SOCIETY, 17(2) (JUN 89), 189-224.
        THE AUTHOR APPLIES A COALITION MODEL TO A SERIES OF
    CORPORATE TAX CASES, SHOWING THAT IN EACH CASE STATE
    FACTIONS UTILIZED A COALITION STRATEGY TO FURTHER THEIR
    POLICY AMBITIONS. THESE ALLIANCES CONTRIBUTED TO THE PASSAGE
    OF LEGISLATION AND TO THE ULTIMATE POLICY OUTCOMES. THE
    OBSERVED RELATIONS BETWEEN STATE AND SOCIETY ALSO ILLUSTRATE
    THE PATTERN OF MUTUAL DEPENDENCE, RECIPROCAL INFLUENCE, AND
    JOINT PARTICIPATION SUGGESTED BY THE COALITION MODEL.

06014 MARTIN, D.
    SPEAKING IN LATIN TONGUES
    NATIONAL REVIEW, XLI(18) (SEP 89), 30-35.
        THE PROTESTANT LOOM NOW GOING ON IN LATIN AMERICA IS A
    MASSIVE SHIFT IN PEOPLE'S IDENTIFICATIONS AND IN THEIR
    PRIORITIES. IN THE COURSE OF A GENERATION, ONE LATIN AMERICA
    IN TEN HAS BECOME AN EVAGELICAL "BELIEVER" MOST LIKELY A
    PENTACOSTAL. WHILE THIS DISCOMFITS ANGLO -- MARXISTS AND
    SOCIAL SCIENTISTS NO END, IT SIGNIFIES THAT LATIN AMERICA IS
    MATURING INDIGEROUSLY AND CONFIDENTLY.

06015 MARTIN, D. W.
    THE FADING LEGACY OF WOODROW WILSON
    PUBLIC ADMINISTRATION REVIEW, 48(2) (MAR 88), 631-636.
        THIS ARTICLE ATTEMPTS TO EVALUATE RECENT OPINIONS THAT
    WOODROW WILSON AS A FOUNDER IN THE FIELD OF PUBLIC
    ADMINISTRATION HAS IN ACTUALITY, UNKNOWN, UNCERTAIN, AND
    UNSKILLED. THE TWO POLITICS/ADMINISTRATION DICHOTOMIES,
    WILSON'S REVISION OF HIS DICHOTOMY AND THE BIRTH OF THE
    WILSON LEGEND ARE ALL EXPLORED.

06016 MARTIN, D.A.
    EFFECTS OF INTERNATIONAL LAW ON MIGRATION POLICY AND
    PRACTICE: THE USES OF HYPOCRISY
    INTERNATIONAL MIGRATION REVIEW, 23(3) (FAL 89), 547-578.
        CLASSICAL LEARNING RECOGNIZES NO ROLE FOR INTERNATIONAL
    LAW IN AFFECTING MIGRATION POLICY AND PRACTICE, BUT IN
    MODERN TIMES THE SALUTARY EFFECTS ARE INCREASING, ALTHOUGH
    THEY REMAIN MODEST. INTERNATIONAL LAW INFLUENCES MIGRATION
    POLICY PRIMARILY THROUGH EFFECTIVE INVOCATION OF VARIOUS
    FORMS OF "SOFT LAW" IN INTERNAL AND INTERNATIONAL POLITICAL
    FORUMS. MORE LIMITED PROSPECTS EXIST FOR BENEFICIAL CHANGES
    ENFORCED BY INTERNATIONAL INSTITUTIONS AND DOMESTIC COURTS.
    THE ARTICLE CAUTIONS AGAINST INFLATED EXPECTATIONS IN THE
    LATTER SETTINGS, HOWEVER, PARTICULARLY BECAUSE OVERLY
    AMBITIOUS CLAIMS CAN BE COUNTERPRODUCTIVE. IT THEN OFFERS A
    FEW PREDICTIONS ABOUT NEAR-TERM EFFECTS OF INTERNATIONAL LAW,
    HAVING TO DO WITH DEPARTURES FROM A COUNTRY, REFUGEE LAW
    AND THE INTEGRATION OF MIGRANTS INTO THEIR NEW HOMELANDS.

06017 MARTIN, F.E.
    DIFFERENCES IN MEN AND WOMEN JUDGES: PERSPECTIVES ON GENDER
    JOURNAL OF POLITICAL SCIENCE, 17(1-2) (1989), 74-85.
        THE AUTHOR ENDEAVORS TO IDENTIFY SOME DIFFERENT, GENDER-
    BASED PERSPECTIVES THAT MEN AND WOMEN MIGHT BRING TO THE
    BENCH. SHE EXAMINES THREE AREAS OF POTENTIAL ATTITUDINAL
    DIFFERENCES BETWEEN MEN AND WOMEN: PERCEPTIONS OF THE ROLE
    OF FEMALE JUDGES, PERCEPTIONS OF GENDER BIAS IN THE COURTS,
    AND DECISIONS ON FIVE HYPOTHETICAL CASES INVOLVING WOMEN'S
    RIGHTS ISSUES. A MAJOR UNDERLYING QUESTION IS WHETHER GENDER
    OR FEMINIST IDEOLOGY IS AN IMPORTANT INFLUENCE ON JUDICIAL
    ATTITUDES.

06018 MARTIN, G.
    KING HUSSEIN'S OPTIMISM
    MIDDLE EAST INTERNATIONAL, (362) (NOV 89), 8.
        JORDAN'S KING HUSSEIN RECEIVED INTERNATIONAL PRAISE FOR
    HIS RECENT REFORMS AND FOR HIS INCREASING PRESSURE ON
    NEIGHBORING ISRAEL TO CONSIDER SOME SORT OF COMPROMISE. HE
    HAS CALLED ON ISRAEL TO ACKNOWLEDGE THE PLO AS THE "SOLE
    LEGITIMATE REPRESENTATIVE OF THE PALESTINIAN PEOPLE."
    ALTHOUGH PERHAPS OVERLY OPTIMISTIC, THE KING OUTLINED FUTURE
    PROPOSALS REGARDING HUMAN RIGHTS, DEMOCRACY, AND ECOLOGY IN

BOTH JORDAN AND THE MIDDLE EAST.

06019 MARTIN, G.
THE "PRINCIPLE OF ALTERNATION" IN THE LEADERSHIP OF THE
LIBERAL PARTY OF CANADA: AN UNHELPFUL MYTH
ROUND TABLE, (310) (APR 89), 158-164.
MEMBERS OF THE LIBERAL PARTY IN CANADA SPEAK OF THE
TRADITION OF ALTERNATING BETWEEN ANGLOPHONE AND FRANCOPHONE
LEADERS. THE ARTICLE EXAMINES THIS TRADITION THAT ONCE MAY
HAVE HAD SOME VALIDITY, BUT NOW SEEMS TO HAVE OUTLIVED ITS
USEFULNESS. IT CONCLUDES THAT THE PRINCIPLE OF ALTERNATION
RESTS ON SIX CONTESTS SPREAD OVER ONE HUNDRED YEARS IN WHICH
FACTORS OTHER THAN ETHNIC ORIGIN HAD A LARGE ROLE IN THE
SELECTION OF PARTY LEADERS. CONTINUING TO CLING TO THIS
OUTWORN TRADITION MAY RESULT IN INCREASED DIVISION IN BOTH
THE PARTY AND THE NATION.

06020 MARTIN, J. M.
THE RECRUITMENT OF WOMEN TO CABINET AND SUBCABINET POSTS
WESTERN POLITICAL QUARTERLY, 42(1) (MAR 89), 161-172.
THERE HAS BEEN AN INCREASE IN THE NUMBERS OF WOMEN
APPOINTED TO CABINET AND SUBCABINET POSTS OVER THE PAST
FIFTEEN YEARS, AS WELL AS AN INCREASE IN THE RANGE OF
DEPARTMENTS TO WHICH WOMEN ARE APPOINTED. HOWEVER, THERE IS
AN APPARENT SYMBOLIC ATTACHMENT TO THE APPOINTMENT OF WOMEN:
WOMEN ARE MORE LIKELY TO BE SELECTED AS INITIAL THAN AS
REPLACEMENT APPOINTEES AND OVERWHELMINGLY FOR OUTER CABINET
POSTS. THERE IS A TENDENCY TO TURN TOWARD THE WASHINGTON
COMMUNITY FOR REPLACEMENTS. A DEARTH OF WOMEN IN CONGRESS
AND IN HIGH-LEVEL EXECUTIVE BRANCH POSTS DECREASES THE
LIKELIHOOD OF WOMEN BECOMING MIDTERM APPOINTMENTS. INTEREST
GROUPS PROVIDE WOMEN WITH A CAREER ROUTE DIFFERENT FROM THAT
OF MEN, BUT ALSO LIMIT THE RANGE OF DEPARTMENTS TO WHICH
WOMEN ARE APPOINTED. WOMEN APPEAR TO HAVE EXPERIENCES
SIMILAR TO THOSE OF MEN IN TERMS OF JOB SATISFACTIONS AND
FRUSTRATIONS. SOME DIFFERENCES REFLECT THE NATURE OF THE
POST TO WHICH THEY ARE APPOINTED.

06021 MARTIN, L.L.
MODERNISM PREFERENCES AND PARTICIPATION PATTERNS AMONG
AMERICAN INDIAN ADULTS, STAFF, AND BOARD MEMBERS IN TWO
TYPES OF COMMUNITY SERVICE AGENCIES IN MINNEAPOLIS
DISSERTATION ABSTRACTS INTERNATIONAL, 49(7) (JAN 89),
1958-A.
THE PURPOSE OF THIS STUDY WAS TWOFOLD: (1) TO DETERMINE
WHETHER THE MEAN MODERNISM SCORE OF AN AMERICAN INDIAN ADULT
COMMUNITY DIFFERS FROM THE MEAN MODERISM SCORES OF THE
STAFFS AND BOARDS OF TWO URBAN SERVICE PROGRAMS, ONE OF
WHICH EMPLOYS STRUCTURED APPROACHES WHILE THE OTHER USES
UNSTRUCTURED; AND (2) TO INVESTIGATE HOW SUCH DIFFERENCES
RELATE TO THE RATE OF PARTICIPATION OF AMERICAN INDIAN
ADULTS IN SERVICES PROVIDED BY THE PROGRAMS.

06022 MARTIN, M.
ON CULTURE, POLITICS, AND THE STATE IN NICARAGUA: AN
INTERVIEW WITH PADRE ERNESTO CARDENAL, MINISTER OF CULTURE
LATIN AMERICAN PERSPECTIVES, 16 (1989), 124-133.
THE MINISTER OF CULTURE IN NICARAGUA COMMENTS ON THE
RELATIONSHIP BETWEEN ART, CULTURE AND POLITICS IN THAT
NATION. HE COMPARES ART AND CULTURE OF THE PRE-REVOLUTION
PERIOD TO THAT OF TODAY. HE ALSO DISCUSSES THE POSITION OF
THE SANDINISTA GOVERNMENT TOWARDS ART AND CULTURE, INCLUDING
COUNTER-REVOLUTIONARY ART.

06023 MARTIN, P.M.
PEACE IN ANGOLA?
CURRENT HISTORY, 88(538) (MAY 89), 229-232, 246-248.
SUBSTANTIAL OBSTACLES STILL BLOCK THE PATH TO AN
INTERNAL ANGOLAN SETTLEMENT. PEACE IS IN SIGHT BUT REMAINS
ON THE DISTANT HORIZON.

06024 MARTINELLI, R.
TWO TYPES OF REALISM
WORLD MARXIST REVIEW, 32(12) (DEC 89), 47-50.
IN TODAY'S CONDITIONS, THE NEW INTERNATIONALISM, AS
UNDERSTOOD BY THE ITALIAN COMMUNIST PARTY, MUST RID ITSELF
OF ITS IDEOLOGICAL AND ORGANISATIONAL CHAINS. THE MOST
IMPORTANT THING IS NOT FORMAL PARTICIPATION IN A LEADING
CENTRE, BUT AN AUTONOMOUS AND CONSISTENT STRUGGLE FOR
SOLUTIONS TO THE DRAMATIC PROBLEMS OF THE AGE -- ABOVE ALL,
UNDERDEVELOPMENT.

06025 MARTINEZ, J.
LETTING THE PUBLIC IN ON THE PROCESS
STATE LEGISLATURES, 15(8) (SEP 89), 24-27.
TWENTY-ONE STATE LEGISLATURES PROVIDE ON-LINE PUBLIC
ACCESS TO LEGISLATIVE DATA BASES ON A SUBSCRIPTION BASIS.
THE TYPE OF INFORMATION AVAILABLE INCLUDES ADMINISTRATIVE
RULES, ATTORNEY GENERAL OPINIONS, BILL TEXT, LEGISLATIVE
CALENDAR, STATUTES, AND VOTING RECORDS. BILL STATUS IS THE
MOST WIDELY USED DATA BASE.

06026 MARTINEZ, M.D.
SUBERNATORIAL TICKETS IN PRIMARY ELECTIONS, 1983-1986

STATE AND LOCAL GOVERNMENT REVIEW, 21(2) (SPR 89), 84-87.
THE ROLE OF STATE PARTY ORGANIZATIONS IN FORMING TICKETS
OF CANDIDATES FOR GOVERNOR AND LIEUTENANT GOVERNOR IN
PRIMARY ELECTIONS IS INVESTIGATED IN THIS STUDY. THE
INVESTIGATION HAS IMPORT TO PARTY THEORISTS WHO ARE
CONCERNED THAT PRIMARY ELECTIONS ARE USURPING THE CLASSIC
FUNCTIONS OF PARTY, INCLUDING INTEREST AGGREGATION. A SURVEY
OF PARTY OFFICIALS SUGGESTS THAT PARTY ORGANIZATIONS DO
PRODUCE MORE GEOGRAPHICALLY, ETHNICALLY. AND GENDER BALANCED
TICKETS THAN DO CANDIDATES LEFT TO THEIR OWN DEVICES.

06027 MARTINO, A.
THE LEANING TOWER OF STATISM
REASON, 20(9) (FEB 89), 46.
GOVERNMENT IN ITALY HAS GROWN RAPIDLY IN THE PAST
QUARTER-CENTURY. BUT THE RESULTS OF THIS SPECTACULAR GROWTH
HAVE DISAPPOINTED ITS PROMOTERS, AND ITALIAN LEADERS ARE NOW
DISAVOWING STATISM.

06028 MARTINO, J.P.
POLITICAL SCIENCE: PORK INVADES THE LAB
REASON, 20(10) (MAR 89), 32-35.
OVER THE LAST SIX YEARS, CONGRESS HAS EXTENDED PORK-
BARREL POLITICS TO A NEW DOMAIN: SCIENCE. UNIVERSITIES HAVE
DISCOVERED THAT LOBBYING CAN BE AS PROFITABLE FOR THEM AS IT
IS FOR OTHERS. WITH HELP FROM THE RIGHT COMMITTEE MEMBERS,
COLLEGES THAT CAN'T COMPETE FOR MERIT-BASED RESEARCH FUNDS
CAN REAP MILLIONS IN "EARMARKED" APPROPRIATIONS.

06029 MARTY, W.R.
RELIGION, THE CONSTITUTION, AND MODERN RIVALS: OUR
FOUNDERS AND THEIRS
JOURNAL OF POLITICAL SCIENCE, 16(1-2) (1988), 79.
THE AUTHOR COMPARES THE VIEWS OF AMERICA'S FOUNDERS WITH
THOSE OF THE INTELLECTUAL FATHERS OF THE SOVIET UNION. HE
ARGUES THAT THE SUCCESS OF AMERICAN DEMOCRACY HAS BEEN
LARGELY DEPENDENT UPON THE APPLICATION OF PRINCIPLES
DEVELOPED BY THE FOUNDERS AND THAT THE SUCCESS OR FAILURE OF
THE SOVIET UNION MAY BE LARGELY ATTRIBUTED TO THE FOUNDING
PRINCIPLES OF MARX AND ENGELS.

06030 MARTZ, J.D.
COLOMBIA'S SEARCH FOR PEACE
CURRENT HISTORY, 88(536) (MAR 89), 125-128, 145-147.
DURING HIS 1986 PRESIDENTIAL CAMPAIGN, VIRGILIO BARCO
VARGAS PROMISED AN END TO SOCIAL CONFLICT AND POLITICAL
VIOLENCE IN COLOMBIA, BUT, BY LATE 1988, VARGAS' PROMISE
RANG HOLLOW AS THE PROSPECTS FOR A MODICUM OF DOMESTIC
TRANQUILITY SEEMED DIMMER THAN EVER.

06031 MARX, B.
WEST EUROPEAN INTEGRATION AND THE WORKING-CLASS MOVEMENT
WORLD MARXIST REVIEW, 32(1) (JAN 89), 78-82.
IN ORDER TO JUSTIFY THEIR INITIATIVES, THE LEADERS OF
THE EEC COUNTRIES WHICH SIGNED THE 1988 SINGLE EUROPEAN ACT
POINT TO THE DEMAND FOR INTERNATIONAL COOPERATION AND
DEVELOPMENT, THE INTERESTS OF PEACE, HUMANITARIAN IDEAS,
POPULAR ASPIRATIONS, AND THE NEED FOR A EUROPE WITHOUT
BORDERS OR CONFLICTS. THEIR ACTUAL PURPOSE IS TO CONSOLIDATE
THE BASIS OF THEIR DOMINATION AND INCREASE PROFITS FOR THE
MAJOR CAPITALIST GROUPS. THIS MEANS FURTHER SAVAGE ATTACKS
ON EMPLOYMENT, SOCIAL SECURITY AND RIGHTS, THE FURTHER
RENUNCIATION OF NATIONAL SOVEREIGNTY FOR THE BENEFIT OF
TRANSNATIONAL MONOPOLIES AND SUPRA-NATIONAL ETATIST BODIES,
AND GREATER EXPOITATION AND DIVISION OF THE PEOPLES.

06032 MASAMICHI, I.
CAN THE LDP RECOVER?
JAPAN ECHO, XVI(4) (WIN 89), 9-13.
THE AUTHOR REVIEWS THE HISTORY OF THE LIBERAL DEMOCRATIC
PARTY IN JAPAN AND SPECULATES ABOUT THE PARTY'S FUTURE IN
THE WAKE OF RECENT SCANDALS.

06033 MASANJA, P.
THE POLITICS OF WORKERS' PARTICIPATION: A STUDY OF
INDUSTRIAL RELATIONS IN TANZANIAN PUBLIC-SECTOR FACTORIES
DISSERTATION ABSTRACTS INTERNATIONAL, 50(6) (DEC 89),
1800-A.
THE AUTHOR LOOKS AT THE IMPACT OF "UJAMAA" ON THE
ORGANIZATION OF TANZANIAN PUBLIC-SECTOR FACTORIES. HE
FOCUSES ON THE ROLE PLAYED BY WORKERS' COUNCILS, PARTY
BRANCHES, AND OTHER WORKPLACE AGENCIES IN DECISION-MAKING.
HE UTILIZES CASE STUDIES OF TWO ENTERPRISES IN DAR ES SALAAM
AS WELL AS DATA OR A MORE GENERAL KIND.

06034 MASARU, Y.
TREATING AMERICA'S JAPANOPHOBIA
JAPAN ECHO, XVI(4) (WIN 89), 58-60.
THE AUTHOR DISCUSSES THE TREND TOWARD JAPAN-BASHING IN
THE UNITED STATES AS A GROWING NUMBER OF LEADERS AND EXPERTS
BLAME JAPAN FOR THE UNITED STATES' TRADE PROBLEMS. HE
REVIEWS RECENT ECONOMIC TRENDS AND SUGGESTS SOLUTIONS FOR
AMERICA'S JAPANOPHOBIA.

06035 MASATAKA, K.
     THE RULING PARTY LOSES ITS TOUCH
     JAPAN ECHO, XVI(3) (AUT 89), 7-13.
          THE LIBERAL DEMOCRATIC PARTY IS FACING THE WORST CRISIS
     IN ITS HISTORY. TWO DEVELOPMENTS BRING THE CRITICAL
     SITUATION INTO RELIEF: THE RECORD LOW LEVEL OF PUBLIC
     SUPPORT FOR THE NOBORU ADMINISTRATION AND THE CONTINUING
     PUBLIC RESISTANCE TO THE CONSUMPTION TAX.

06036 MASAYUKI, T.
     THE JAPANESE RIGHT WING
     JAPAN QUARTERLY, XXXVI(3) (JUL 89), 300-305.
          RIGHTISTS IN JAPAN TAKE A CONSERVATIVE, ANTI-COMMUNIST,
     ANTI-SOCIALIST STANCE AGAINST LEFTIST FORCES WHOSE
     IDEOLOGICAL BASE CONSISTS OF REVOLUTIONARY THEORY AND
     PRACTICE INTRODUCED FROM THE OUTSIDE, SUCH AS MARXISM-
     LENINISM. THE JAPANESE RIGHT IS DISTINCT FROM ITS
     COUNTERPARTS IN OTHER COUNTRIES IN THAT IT UPHOLDS THE
     IDEOLOGY OR REVERENCE FOR THE EMPEROR AND IMPERIAL
     ABSOLUTISM.

06037 MASLIN, V.
     THE SOVIET PEACE FUND: HOW THE MONEY IS SPENT
     REPRINTS FROM THE SOVIET PRESS, 48(8) (APR 89), 46-47.
          FIRST DEPUTY CHAIRMAN OF THE SOVIET PEACE FUND BOARD, V.
     MASLIN ANSWERS QUESTIONS AS TO THE SIZE AND USE OF THE MONEY
     DONATED TO THE FUND. THE MONEY HAS BEEN USED FOR
     INTERNATIONAL RELIEF AID, TO IMPROVE THE CONDITIONS OF AND
     PROVIDE MEDICAL CARE FOR WAR INVALIDS AND SENIOR CITIZENS,
     AS EMERGENCY RELIEF AID FOR EARTHQUAKE ROCKED ARMENIA AND
     PAKISTAN, AND FOR VARIOUS LOCAL SOCIAL PROGRAMS.

06038 MASLIYAH, S. H.
     ZIONISM IN IRAQ
     MIDDLE EASTERN STUDIES, 25(2) (APR 89), 216-237.
          THIS STUDY DESCRIBES AND EVALUATES THE RISE AND FALL OF
     THE VARIOUS ZIONIST SOCIETIES AND ORGANIZATIONS THAT EMERGED
     DURING THE FIRST HALF OF THE PRESENT CENTURY. THIS IS
     DIVIDED INTO THREE DISTINCT PERIODS: 1919-35, 1935-41 AND
     1942-51.

06039 MASLOVE, A.M.
     WHAT REALLY HAPPENED WITH TAX REFORM?
     POLICY OPTIONS, 10(1) (JAN 89), 18-24.
          THE DISTRIBUTIONAL IMPACT OF PRIME MINISTER MULRONEY'S
     TAX REFORMS SHOWS SOME GAINERS AND SOME LOSERS. THE BIGGEST
     GAINERS ARE PERSONS IN THE TOP ONE PERCENT INCOME GROUP; THE
     LOWEST TWENTY PERCENT IN TERMS OF INCOME AND MOST ELDERLY
     PEOPLE ALSO BENEFITTED. BUT THE MAJORITY OF FAMILIES ARE
     WORSE OFF IN TERMS OF DISPOSABLE INCOME THAN THEY WERE IN
     1984.

06040 MASLYUKOV, Y.
     DRAFT STATE PLAN FOR ECONOMIC AND SOCIAL DEVELOPMENT OF
     THE SOVIET UNION IN 1990: NEW APPROACHES AND PARAMETERS
     REPRINTS FROM THE SOVIET PRESS, 49(7) (OCT 89), 16-30.
          YURI MASIYUKOV ADDRESSES A SESSION OF THE USSR SUPREME
     SOVIET, AND DISCUSSES THE GENERAL OUTLINE OF THE DRAFT PLAN
     FOR 1990. HE EXPLAINS THAT THE BASIC APPROACHES TO IT, ITS
     PRINCIPAL PARAMETERS, PROPORTIONS AND PRIORITIES THAT ARE
     ALREADY CLEAR IN THE MAIN, AS ARE THE CENTRAL ISSUES, AND
     THE WAYS TO SOLVE THEM. HE THEN CONTINUES ON IN MORE DETAIL
     ON THE MOST PROBLEMATIC ASPECTS OF THE PLAN AND THE
     FORTHCOMING YEAR. HE INDICATES THAT THE DRAFT NATIONAL PLAN
     WILL CONTAIN A STRUCTURE AND INDICES IN FULL ACCORDANCE FOR
     THE NEW APPROACHES TO THE PLANS OF ECONOMIC AND SOCIAL
     DEVELOPMENT OF THE UNION REPUBLICS.

06041 MASON, D.S.
     SOLIDARITY AS A NEW SOCIAL MOVEMENT
     POLITICAL SCIENCE QUARTERLY, 104(1) (SPR 89), 41-58.
          THE AUTHOR STUDIES THE ORIGINS AND NATURE OF SOLIDARITY
     AND ITS IMPACT ON POLAND. ALTHOUGH SOLIDARITY IS FORMALLY
     IDENTIFIED AS A TRADE UNION, IT IS AS MUCH A SOCIAL MOVEMENT
     AS A TRADE UNION AND THE AUTHOR FOCUSES ON ITS SOCIAL
     MOVEMENT ASPECT.

06042 MASON, J.G.
     GORBACHEV, THE WESTERN FACE OF THE SOVIET PERIL: PARIS
     LOOKS AT PERESTROIKA, STRATEGIC ENTENTE, AND EUROPEAN
     SECURITY
     FRENCH POLITICS AND SOCIETY, 7(1) (WIN 89), 28-46.
          THE POLITICAL CONSENSUS FRENCH ELITES HAVE FORGED OVER
     THE PAST FIFTEEN YEARS HAS BECOME A FAMILIAR LANDMARK, BUT
     IT IS NOT AS SOLID AS IT SEEMS. THE CONSENSUS HAS ALWAYS
     BEEN IN MOTION BENEATH ITS CASING OF ORTHODOX DOCTRINE AND
     NOW APPEARS TO BE SHIFTING SIGNIFICANTLY. THIS ESSAY
     ANALYZES WHAT IS CHANGING AND WHAT REMAINS THE SAME ABOUT
     THIS CONSENSUS AND DISCUSSES SOME OF THE ISSUES THAT ARE
     LIKELY TO ARISE WHEN THE PUBLIC DEBATE TRULY OPENS UP ON THE
     MATTER, AS IT SOMEDAY MUST.

06043 MASON, J.H.
     INDIVIDUALS IN SOCIETY: ROUSSEAU'S REPUBLICAN VERSION

HISTORY OF POLITICAL THOUGHT, X(1) (SPR 89), 89-112.
          THERE IS A REASONABLE LEVEL OF AGREEMENT ABOUT THE
     MEANING OF ROUSSEAU'S THEORY OF SOCIAL DEVELOPMENT. WITH HIS
     POLITICAL THEORY, HOWEVER, THE OPPOSITE IS TRUE. THE DEBATE
     THAT HAS RAGED SINCE THE FRENCH REVOLUTION - - HIS POLITICAL
     THOUGHT BEING SEEN AS EITHER ARISTOCRATIC OR REVOLUTIONARY,
     ANCIENT OR MODERN, COLLECTIVIST OR INDIVIDUALIST,
     TOTALITARIAN OR LIBERAL -- SHOWS NO SIGN OF ENDING. THE
     AUTHOR ARGUES THAT MUCH OF THE ARGUEMENT IS MISCONCEIVED.
     THE FOCUS SHOULD BE ON WHY ROUSSEAU'S WRITINGS CONTAIN IDEAS
     OR STATEMENTS WHICH SEEM TO BE CONTRADICTORY, RATHER THAN
     WHETHER ROUSSEAU WAS EITHER ONE OR THE OTHER. THE AUTHOR
     SEEKS TO EXPLAIN THE APPARENT CONTRADICTIONS BY VIEWING HOW
     ROUSSEAU'S SOCIAL THEORY WAS INCORPORATED INTO HIS POLITICAL
     THOUGHT.

06044 MASON, R.
     NUCLEAR WEAPONS: NON-PROLIFERATION, TECHNOLOGIES, AND TEST-
     BAN TREATIES
     DISARMAMENT, XII(1) (WIN 89), 34-42.
          THE PROLIFERATION OF NUCLEAR WEAPONS MUST BE REGARDED AS
     THE END RESULT OF A GOVERNMENT'S ASSESSMENT OF THE
     INCENTIVES AND DISINCENTIVES FOR DEVELOPING THEM. ANY FUTURE
     NON-PROLIFERATION TREATY MUST CONTINUE TO INFLUENCE THE
     BALANCE OF INCENTIVES AND DISINCENTIVES AT THE MARGIN; THE
     REQUIREMENT CONTINUES TO BE FOR A SYSTEM OF MUTUAL
     CONFIDENCE-BUILDING BASED ON INTERNATIONAL SAFEGUARDS. THIS
     PAPER CONSIDERS WHETHER A COMPREHENSIVE NUCLEAR-TEST BAN,
     MENTIONED AS AN OBJECTIVE IN THE PREAMBLE TO THE NON-
     PROLIFERATION TREATY, WILL BE A SINGULARLY IMPORTANT AND
     ACHIEVABLE STEP TO DEMONSTRATE COMPLIANCE WITH ARTICLE VI OF
     THE TREATY.

06045 MASON, R.B.
     PRISONER OF SPEECH
     CANADIAN FORUM, 86(781) (SEP 89), 7-8.
          THIS ARTICLE WHICH IS AN INTERVIEW OF SALMAN RUSHDIE,
     AUTHOR OF "THE SATANIC VERSES" GIVES HIS REFLECTIONS ON THE
     BANNING OF HIS BOOK IN INDIA AND HIS OPTIMISM ABOUT THE
     EVENTUAL TRIUMPH OF ARTISTIC FREEDOM OVER THE STRUCTURES OF
     FUNDAMENTALISM. THE NATURE OF HIS EXILE HAS FRIGHTENING
     IMPLICATIONS FOR CITIZENS OF THE FREE WORLD. ALTHOUGH LIVING
     IN A WESTERN DEMOCRACY, RUSHDIE IS THE POLITICAL PRISONER OF
     A REGIME SITUATED THOUSANDS OF MILES AWAY.

06046 MASON, T.D.
     NON-ELITE RESPONSE TO STATE-SANCTIONED TERROR
     WESTERN POLITICAL QUARTERLY, 42(4) (DEC 89), 467-492.
          MUCH OF THE RESEARCH ON STATE-SANCTIONED TERRORISM AND
     DEATH SQUAD VIOLENCE FOCUSES ON THE DECISION CALCULUS OF
     RIVAL ELITES IN THE REGIME AND THE OPPOSITION AS THEY ENGAGE
     IN VIOLENT STRUGGLES OVER POLITICAL AUTHORITY AND LEGITIMACY.
     WHAT IS OFTEN IGNORED IN THIS LITERATURE IS THE IMPACT OF
     SUCH VIOLENCE ON THE BEHAVIORAL CALCULUS OF THE URBAN AND
     RURAL MASSES, WHOSE SUPPORT ULTIMATELY DETERMINES THE
     OUTCOME OF THE STRUGGLE BETWEEN RIVAL ELITES. THIS ARTICLE
     PRESENTS A RATIONAL CHOICE MODEL OF THE DECISION CALCULUS BY
     WHICH NONELITES CHOOSE BETWEEN SUPPORTING THE REGIME,
     SUPPORTING THE OPPOSITION, OR REMAINING UNINVOLVED. IT THEN
     EXAMINES THE IMPACT OF ESCALATING LEVELS OF STATE-SANCTIONED
     VIOLENCE ON THE OUTCOME OF THIS DECISION PROCESS AND,
     THEREFORE, ON THE LEVEL OF POPULAR SUPPORT FOR THE REGIME.
     FINALLY, IT PRESENTS AN ANALYSIS OF THOSE SOCIOECONOMIC AND
     DEMOGRAPHIC FACTORS WHICH RESTRAIN THE GOVERNMENT'S ABILITY
     TO COMPETE FOR POPULAR SUPPORT THROUGH PROGRAMS OF
     ACCOMMODATION AND, THEREFORE, MAKE THE ESCALATION OF
     REPRESSION ITS MORE LIKELY POLICY CHOICE WHEN FACED WITH
     CONTINUED OPPOSITION.

06047 MASON, T.D.; KRANE, D.A.
     THE POLITICAL ECONOMY OF DEATH SQUADS: TOWARD A THEORY OF
     THE IMPACT OF STATE-SANCTIONED TERROR
     INTERNATIONAL STUDIES QUARTERLY, 33(2) (JUN 89), 175-198.
          A CENTRAL THEORETICAL QUESTION IN THE LITERATURE ON
     STATE-SANCTIONED TERROR IS WHETHER, AND UNDER WHAT
     CONDITIONS, REPRESSIVE VIOLENCE DETERS OR STIMULATES A SHIFT
     IN POPULAR SUPPORT AWAY FROM THE REGIME AND TOWARD THE
     OPPOSITION. BY COMBINING A RATIONAL CHOICE MODEL OF THE
     NONELITE RESPONSE TO ESCALATING LEVELS OF DEATH SQUAD
     VIOLENCE WITH A STRUCTURAL ANALYSIS OF THE GLOBAL AND
     DOMESTIC CONDITIONS UNDER WHICH THE ESCALATION OF
     STATESANCTIONED TERROR CAN BE EXPECTED, THE AUTHORS
     DEMONSTRATE THEORETICALLY THAT CAREFULLY TARGETED REPRESSIVE
     VIOLENCE MAY IN FACT REDUCE THE LEVEL OF ACTIVE POPULAR
     SUPPORT FOR THE OPPOSITION, AT LEAST TEMPORARILY. HOWEVER,
     AS THE LEVEL OF REPRESSIVE VIOLENCE ESCALATES AND ITS
     APPLICATION BECOMES MORE INDISCRIMINATE, IT MAY IN FACT
     PRODUCE INCREASES IN ACTIVE SUPPORT FOR THE OPPOSITION
     BECAUSE NONELITES CAN NO LONGER ASSURE THEMSELVES OF
     IMMUNITY FROM REPRESSION BY SIMPLY REMAINING POLITICALLY
     INERT. THUS, THEY TURN TO THE REBELS IN SEARCH OF PROTECTION
     FROM INDISCRIMINATE VIOLENCE BY THE STATE.

06048 MASRY, A.H.
DEVELOPING THE ARCHAELOGY OF SAUDI ARABIA
AMERICAN-ARAB AFFAIRS, (30) (FAL 89), .
THIS ARTICLE IS INTENDED AS A BRIEF BUT COMPREHENSIVE
STATEMENT ON THE CONTEMPORARY STATUS OF, AND THE DEVELOPING
INTEREST IN, ARCHAELOGY WITHIN THE KINGDOM OF SAUDI ARABIA
AND OF ASPECTS OF SCHOLARSHIP AND RESEARCH RELATED TO IT. IT
OFFERS A VERY GENERALIZED AND SKETCHY OUTLINE OF A FEW OF
THE PROJECTS WHICH HAVE BEEN SPONSORED AND UNDERTAKEN BY THE
DIRECTORATE GENERAL OF ARCHAELOGY AND MUSEUMS IN THE LAST
FEW YEARS.

06049 MASSALA, F.N.
ANGOLA: STOP SOUTH AFRICAN AGGRESSION AGAINST OUR COUNTRY
WORLD TRADE UNION MOVEMENT, 1 (1988), 15-17.
THIS ARTICLE REPORTS ON SOUTH AFRICAN ATTEMPTS TO
DESTABILISE ANGOLA SINCE 1975. IT ACCUSES THE PRETORIA
REGIME OF SUPPORT FOR THE UNITA TERRORISTS, AND THE UNITED
STATES OF ENCOURAGING THE AGGRESSION, TERRORIST ATTACKS ARE
DETAILED

06050 MASSARI, O.
CHANGES IN THE PSI LEADERSHIP: THE NATIONAL EXECUTIVE
COMMITTEE AND ITS MEMBERSHIP (1976-1987)
EUROPEAN JOURNAL OF POLITICAL RESEARCH, 17(5) (SEP 89),
563-582.
THIS PAPER DEALS WITH THE ROLE AND COMPOSITION OF THE
ITALIAN SOCIALIST PARTY'S NATIONAL EXECUTIVE COMMITTEE
DURING THE 1976-1987 PERIOD. THESE YEARS SAW THE ADVENT, THE
STRENGTHENING AND THE UNCHALLENGED SUPREMACY OF CRAXI'S
LEADERSHIP FIRST WITHIN THE PSI AND THEN WITHIN THE ITALIAN
POLITICAL SYSTEM. WHILE IN OTHER POLITICAL PARTIES THE ROLE
OF THE NATIONAL EXECUTIVE COMMITTEE AS A DECISION-MAKING
BODY HAS REMAINED CRUCIAL, IN THE PSI THIS ROLE SEEMS TO
HAVE BEEN IMPAIRED BOTH BY CRAXI'S EXTREMELY PERSONAL AND
STRONG LEADERSHIP AND BY THE WEAKNESS OF THE PARTY
ORGANIZATION. HOWEVER, THE LOSS OF DECISION-MAKING POWER BY
THE COLLECTIVE LEADERSHIP HAS ACCOMPAINED BY AN INCREASE IN
MEMBERSHIP, WHICH FAVOURED THE RISE OF NEW MEMBERS TO
LEADING POSITIONS. THE SOCIAL AND POLITICAL CHARACTERISTICS
OF THIS NEW POLITICAL CLASS ARE ANALYSED AND EVALUATED
THROUGH A NUMBER OF EMPIRICAL INDICATORS. THE RESULTS ALLOW
A BETTER UNDERSTANDING OF THE ACTUAL CHANGES THAT OCCURRED
IN THE PARTY AS A CONSEQUENCE OF THE INNOVATIONS BROUGHT
ABOUT BY CRAXI'S LEADERSHIP. THIS, IN TURN, SHEDS LIGHT ON
AN IMPORTANT SECTION OF THE ITALIAN RULING CLASS.

06051 MASTANDUNO, M.; IKENBERRY, G.J.; LAKE, D.A.
TOWARD A REALIST THEORY OF STATE ACTION
INTERNATIONAL STUDIES QUARTERLY, 33(4) (DEC 89), 457-474.
THE REALITIES OF INTERDEPENDENCE DICTATE THAT THE
ABILITY OF GOVERNMENTS TO PURSUE DOMESTIC POLICIES
EFFECTIVELY IS INFLUENCED AND CONSTRAINED BY DEVELOPMENTS IN
THE INTERNATIONAL SYSTEM. IT IS EQUALLY EVIDENT THAT THE
REALIZATION OF INTERNATIONAL OBJECTIVES DEPENDS MEANINGFULLY
ON DOMESTIC POLITICS ANC ECONOMICS. THE PURPOSE OF THIS
PAPER IS TO LAY THE FOUNDATION FOR A REALIST THEORY OF STATE
ACTION WHICH BRIDGES DOMESTIC AND INTERNATIONAL POLITICS. IT
PROCEEDS BY POSITING ASSUMPTIONS ABOUT STATE OBJECTIVES AND
DEDUCING STRATEGIES RELEVANT TO THEIR PURSUIT. FIRST, IT
EXAMINES CONCEPTIONS OF THE STATE FOUND IN CLASSICAL AND
STRUCTURAL REALISM. SECOND, IT PRESENTS TWO MODELS OR
"FACES" OF STATE ACTION WHICH RELATE THE GOALS OF STATE
OFFICIALS IN ONE ARENA TO THE STRATEGIES AVAILABLE IN THE
PURSUIT OF SUCH GOALS IN THE OTHER. THIRD, BUILDING UPON
THESE TWO MODELS, IT PUTS FORTH SEVERAL HYPOTHESES WHICH
EXPLORE THE TYPES OF CHALLENGES TO THE STATE THAT ARISE IN
ONE ARENA THAT MAY TRIGGER RESPONSES IN THE SECOND. FOURTH,
IT INTRODUCES VARIATIONS IN DOMESTIC AND INTERNATIONAL
STRUCTURES AND PREDICT THE CHOICE OF STRATEGY MADE BY THE
STATES ACROSS VENUES. FINALLY, A CONCLUDING SECTION EXAMINES
THE IMPLICATIONS OF THIS EFFORT FOR FUTURE REALIST INQUIRY
AND THE STUDY OF DOMESTIC AND INTERNATIONAL POLITICS.

06052 MASTERS, R.D.; SULLIVAN, D.G.
NONVERBAL DISPLAYS AND POLITCAL LEADERSHIP IN FRANCE AND
THE UNITED STATES
POLITICAL BEHAVIOR, 11(2) (JUN 89), 123-156.
BECAUSE CONTEMPORARY THEORIES OF POLITICS DISCUSS THE
APPEAL OF LEADERS PRIMARILY IN VERBAL TERMS, IT IS OFTEN
DIFFICULT TO GO BEYOND ANECDOTES WHEN EXPLANING THE EFFECTS
OF TELEVIZED APPEARANCES OF LEADERS AND CANDIDATES.
EXPERIMENTAL STUDIES OF THE WAY AMERICAN VIEWERS RESPOND TO
TELEVIZED EXCERPTS OF LEADERS WERE REPLICATED IN FRANCE
SHORTLY BEFORE THE LEGISLATIVE ELECTIONS OF MARCH 1986,
USING COMPARABLE EXPRESSIVE DISPLAYS OF LAURENT FABIUS (THEN
SOCIAL PRIME MINISTER), JACQUES CHIRAC (GAULLIST MAYOR OF
PARIS WHO BECAME PRIME MINISTER), AND JEAN MARIE LEPEN (HEAD
OF THE FRONT NATIONALE). ALTHOUGH THE RESULTS SHOW STRIKING
SIMILARITIES IN THE SYSTEM OF NONVERBAL BEHAVIOR IN FRANCE
AND THE UNITED STATES, THERE ARE CULTURAL DIFFERENCES IN THE
ROLE OF ANGER/THREAT (WHICH ELICITS MORE POSITIVE RESPONSES
FROM FRENCH VIEWERS THAN AMERICAN) AS WELL AS VARIATIONS IN
THE EVOCATIVE CHARACTER OF THE FACIAL DISPLAYS OF INDIVIDUAL

LEADERS. THESE EXPERIMENTAL FINDINGS CLARIFY RECENT
DISCUSSIONS CONCERNING THE EVOLUTION OF THE FRENCH PARTY
SYSTEM, PROVIDING INSIGHTS INTO THE ROLE OF POLITICAL
CULTURE AS WELL AS LEADERSHIP "STYLE" IN THE MEDIA AGE.

06053 MASUMI, I.
RECKONING WITH RECRUIT
JAPAN QUARTERLY, XXXVI(2) (APR 89), 135-140.
RECRUIT COMPANY, A TOKYO CONGLOMERATE, IS AT THE CENTER
OF AN INSIDER TRADING SCANDAL THAT HAS PREMEATED THE HIGHER
ECHELONS OF JAPANESE GOVERNMENT AND BUSINESS. THE RECRUIT
REVELATIONS MAY BE STRONG ENOUGH TO LOOSEN THE LIBERAL
DEMOCRATIC PARTY'S STRANGLEHOLD ON THE GOVERNMENT, TO PROMPT
ENACTMENT OF STRICTER LAWS GOVERNING STOCK MARKET
TRANSACTIONS AND POLITICAL FUNDRAISING, AND TO STIR ENOUGH
PUBLIC OUTRAGE TO MAKE POLITICIANS REALIZE THAT THEY ARE
ACCOUNTABLE TO THE JAPANESE PEOPLE.

06054 MASUMI, I.
WHY THE LDP DEBACLE?
JAPAN QUARTERLY, XXXVI(4) (OCT 89), 386-391.
ALTHOUGH IT SUFFERED A SETBACK IN THE JULY 23, 1989,
ELECTION, JAPAN'S LIBERAL DEMOCRATIC PARTY REMAINS IN POWER.
ALTHOUG IT IS WOUNDED, IT IS NOT DEAD. IN THIS ARTICLE, THE
AUTHOR ANALYZES THE SOURCES OF THE LIBERAL DEMOCRATIC
PARTY'S DECLINE.

06055 MASUNAGA, R.
MACROECONOMIC COORDINATION AND THE SUMMIT: INTERNATIONAL
MONETARY REFORM
CANADIAN PUBLIC POLICY--ANALYSE DE POLITIQUES, XV (FEB 89),
55-57.
IN ORDER TO REDUCE FURTHER THE EXISTING IMBALANCES, THE
STRUCTURAL ADJUSTMENT OF DOMESTIC ECONOMIES SHOULD OR COULD
BE PROMOTED BOTH IN DEFICIT AND SURPLUS COUNTRIES. ON A
MACROECONOMIC BASIS, MUCH MORE SHOULD BE DONE ON THE US SIDE
TO MAKE ITS ECONOMY BOTH MORE EXPORTORIENTED AND TO INCREASE
DOMESTIC SAVINGS RATES. EFFORTS TO REDUCE LABOUR RIGIDITY
SHOULD BE PURSUED MORE VIGOROUSLY IN EUROPE. FOR THE BETTER
FUNCTIONING OF INTERNATIONAL ADJUSTMENT, THE ASIAN NICS
SHOULD BE ENCOURAGED TO PLAY A GREATER ROLE IN THE
ADJUSTMENT PROCESS, ALTHOUGH THE MEANS TO REALIZE THAT
OBJECTIVE HAD BETTER BE LEFT TO THE DISCRETION OF THE
COUNTRIES CONCERNED AND NONE OF THEM SHOULD BE PENALIZED
BECAUSE OF THEIR SUCCESS IN ECONOMIC MANAGEMENT.

06056 MATHES, R.; DAHLEM, S.
CAMPAIGN ISSUES IN POLITICAL STRATEGIES AND PRESS COVERAGE:
THE RENTAL LAW CONFLICT IN THE 1982-1983 ELECTION
CAMPAIGN IN THE FEDERAL REPUBLIC OF GERMANY
POLITICAL COMMUNICATION AND PERSUASION, 6(1) (1989), 33-48.
ELECTION CAMPAIGNS ARE INSTITUTIONALIZED CONFLICTS WHICH
ARE CARRIED OUT IN AND THROUGH THE MASS MEDIA. SUCCESS AND
DEFEAT IN THESE CONFLICTS DEPEND UPON THE COMMUNICATION
STRATEGIES OF THE PARTIES AND ON THE REACTIONS OF THE
JOURNALISTS. IN THE ELECTION CAMPAIGN OF 1982-1983, THE
CAMPAIGN MANAGER OF THE CHRISTIAN DEMOCRATS SUCCEEDED IN
ALTERING THE CONFLICT OVER THE NEW RENTAL LAW INTO A
CONFLICT OVER THE CREDIBILITY OF THE SPD-OPPOSITION. THUS,
HE CREATED A COUNTERPART TO THE CRITICISM DIRECTED AGAINST
THE FEDERAL GOVERNMENT. THE NEWSPAPERS AND WEEKLY NEWS
MAGAZINES DID NOT TAKE SIDES IN THE CONFLICT THROUGH
EXPLICIT EVALUATIONS, BUT RATHER BY EMPHASIZING OR
NEGLECTING ISSUES IN FAVOR OF ONE PARTY. THE CONFLICT
CARRIED OUT IN THE MASS MEDIA OVER THE RENTAL LAW WAS NOT A
RATIONAL DISCOURSE IN WHICH THE CONFLICT PARTIES MUTUALLY
REFERRED TO EACH OTHER AND ACCEPTED EACH OTHER'S
COMMUNICATIVE CLAIMS. RATHER, THE NATURE OF THE CONFLICT
COMMUNICATION WAS RHETORICAL; IT HAS A "BATTLE FOR PUBLIC
OPINION."

06057 MATHEWS, D.
THE POLITICS OF COMMUNITY
NATIONAL CIVIC REVIEW, 78(4) (JUL 89), 271-278.
IN THIS ADAPTATION OF HIS PLENARY REMARKS TO THE 94TH
NATIONAL CONFERENCE ON GOVERNMENT, DAVID MATHEWS, PRESIDENT
AND CHIEF EXECUTIVE OFFICER OF THE KETTERING FOUNDATION,
INDENTIFIES UNIQUE POLITICAL INSTINCTS DEMONSTRATED BY
PEOPLE WHO APPROACH PUBLIC INVOLVEMENT IN UNCONVENTIONAL
WAYS, WHO HAVE FAITH IN THE POWER OF THE COMMUNITY, AND WHO
WORK FOR THE ENGAGEMENT OF CITIZENS IN PUBLIC DECISION
MAKING.

06058 MATHEWS, J.T.
REDEFINING SECURITY
FOREIGN AFFAIRS, 68(2) (SPR 89), 162-177.
THE 1990S WILL DEMAND A REDEFINITION OF WHAT CONSTITUTES
NATIONAL SECURITY. IN THE 1970S THE CONCEPT WEAS EXPANDED TO
INCLUDE INTERNATIONAL ECONOMICS AS IT BECAME CLEAR THAT THE
U.S. ECONOMY WAS NO LONGER THE INDEPENDENT FORCE IT HAD ONCE
BEEN, BUT WAS POWERFULLY AFFECTED BY ECONOMIC POLICIES IN
DOZENS OF OTHER COUNTRIES. GLOBAL DEVELOPMENTS NOW SUGGEST
THE NEED FOR ANOTHER ANALOGOUS, BROADENING DEFINITION OF
NATIONAL SECURITY TO INCLUDE RESOURCE, INVIRONMENTAL AND

DEMOGRAPHIC ISSUES.

06059 MATHUR, A.B.
MAHATMA GANDHI'S RELEVANCE TODAY
INDIAN JOURNAL OF POLITICAL SCIENCE, L(2) (APR 89),
145-156.
TO MAHATMA GANDHI, POLITICS HAS NOT AN UGLY STRUGGLE FOR
POWER, BUT IT HAS UNFORTUNATELY BECOME SO IN THE HANDS OF
THOSE WHO SWEAR BY HIM BUT HAVE ABANDONED HIS IDEAS. TO
GANDHI, POLITICS HAS THE MORAL MEANS AND THE ETHICAL NORMS
ACCORDING TO WHICH THE LIVES OF THE PEOPLE SHOULD AND COULD
BE ARRANGED. THE NORMS ACCORDING TO WHICH LIFE IN A SOCIETY
SHOULD BE ARRANGED FORMED PART OF THE ETERNAL, UNCHANGEABLE
VALUES LAID DOWN BY THE GREAT RELIGIO-MORAL SYSTEMS FOR THE
BENEFIT OF MANKIND. GANDHI LOOKED FOR LEGITIMACY OF
AUTHORITY NOT IN LAWS AND CONSTITUTIONS, NOT IN PARLIAMENTS
AND COURTS, BUT IN THE CONSCIENCE OF MAN.

06060 MATHUR, G.B.
THE CURRENT IMPASSE IN DEVELOPMENT THINKING: THE
METAPHYSIC OF POWER
ALTERNATIVES, 14(4) (OCT 89), 463-480.
THIS PAPER HIGHLIGHTS THE EXACT NATURE AND THE LIKELY
SEQUEL OF THE IMPASSE THAT SEEMS TO BE UNFOLDING IN THE
FRONTLINE SOCIOLOGICAL THOUGHT ON WORLD DEVELOPMENT, IT
DESCRIBES THE NATURE OF THE IMPASSE AND OFFERS PROPOSALS FOR
OVERCOMING THE IMPASSE, IT THEN EXAMINES THE IMPLICATIONS OF
THE PROPOSED RESOLUTION FOR CHANGING OUR UNDERSTANDING OF
THE KIND OF NEXUS USUALLY POSITED BETWEEN THE ROLE OF POWER
IN HUMAN DEVELOPMENT AND A PARTICULAR VERSION OF THE THEORY
OF EVOLUTION.

06061 MATLARY, J.H.
GAS TRADE IN SCANDINAVIA: WILL POLITICAL FACTORS MATTER?
SCANDINAVIAN REVIEW, 77(1) (SPR 89), 23-28.
MUCH OF THE POLITICAL DEBATE ABOUT THE STRATEGIC ASPECTS
OF NATURAL GAS HAS CENTERED ON THE QUESTION OF WHETHER
SOVIET GAS IMPORTS INTO EUROPE POSE A SECURITY THREAT. WHILE
THERE WAS LITTLE OR NO POLITICAL INTEREST IN NATURAL GAS
TRADE DURING ITS FIRST TWENTY YEARS IN EUROPE, THE TRADE
BECAME THE SUBJECT OF CONTROVERSY WHEN THE U.S. GOVERNMENT
ATTEMPTED TO HINDER THE EUROPEAN EXPORT OF GAS TECHNOLOGY TO
THE USSR IN CONNECTION WITH THE BUILDING OF THE YAMAL
PIPELINE. SINCE THEN, GAS TRADE WITH THE SOVIETS HAS BEEN
DISCUSSED WITHIN THE CONTEXT OF SECURITY POLICY AND EUROPEAN
GOVERNMENTS HAVE OBSERVED A LIMITATION ON IMPORTS. EUROPEAN
NATURAL GAS TRADE HAS BECOMED POLITICIZED IN ANOTHER FASHION
AS COUNTER-TRADE IN CONNECTION WITH GAS TRADE HAS INCREASED
OVER THE LAST SEVERAL YEARS.

06062 MATSUBARA, N.
CONFLICT AND LIMITS OF POWER
JOURNAL OF CONFLICT RESOLUTION, 33(1) (MAR 89), 113-141.
SINCE DAHL'S DEFINITION, EVERY EFFORT TO MEASURE POWER
HAS AIMED SIMULTANEOUSLY TO CONCEPTUALIZE AND TO
SUBSTANTIATE THE MEANING OF POWER. HOWEVER, THERE IS A
SUBSTANTIAL LACK OF RIGOROUS AND CONCRETE MODELS OF POWER AS
A BASIS TO DISCUSS VARIOUS CHARACTERISTICS OF POWER IN
INTERNATIONAL POLITICS. IN THIS MODEL, THE "LIMIT OF POWER"
IS DEFINED AND MEASURED. AXELROD'S MODEL OF A "BULLY"
SUGGESTS A PROTOTYPE OF POWER SEEKER, BUT RAPOPORT AND
CHAMMAH'S EMPIRICAL DATA ON INTRINSIC DEFECTION PROBABILITY
PLAY THE CRITICAL ROLE IN MAKING IT MEASURABLE IN DAHL'S
SENSE. THE DISTRIBUTION OF POWER AS RELATED TO AXELROD'S
CONFLICT OF INTEREST IS NEITHER DIRECTLY NOR INVERSELY
PROPORTIONAL TO C.I. THREE PHASE OF C.I.--MILD, MODERATE,
AND SEVERE--ARE SHOWN TO CHARACTERIZE THREE IMPORTANT TYPES
OF INTERNATIONAL POLITICAL AND POLITICAL ECONOMY SYSTEMS:
ALLIANCE, INTERDEPENDENCE, AND BIPOLARITY, RESPECTIVELY.
OTHER IMPORTANT CHARACTERISTICS OF POWER ARE FORMULATED, AS
THE RATE OF COLLECTIVE GOODS CONSUMED, CREDIBILITY, THE
ACQUISITIVE AND PUNITIVE EFFICACIES OF POWER, AND
CHARACTERISTICS OF THE LIMIT OF POWER ARE REVIEWED IN
COMPARISON WITH THE SHAPLEY-SHUBIK POWER INDEX.

06063 MATTAR, P.
THE CRITICAL MOMENT FOR PEACE
FOREIGN POLICY, (76) (FAL 89), 141-159.
THIS PAPER EXPRESSES THE FEAR THAT THE U.S. IS AGAIN IN
DANGER OF MISSING AN OPPORTUNITY FOR PEACE IN THE MIDDLE
EAST. IT CONTENDS THAT NO SETTLEMENT IS LIKELY WITHOUT U.S.
BROKERING. THE PLO IS ANALYSED AS WELL AS THE BUSH POSITION.
IT IS SUGGESTED THAT THE PALESTINIANS NEED TO LOOK AT
ISRAEL'S PROBLEMS FROM ISRAELI PERSPECTIVE. IT ALSO SUGGESTS
THAT SECURITY FOR THE ISRAELIS AND SELF-DETERMINATION FOR
THE PALESTINIANS ARE NOT MUTUALLY EXCLUSIVE. WITH SECURITY
AND SELF-DETERMINATION AS THE BASIS FOR A NEW PEACE POLICY,
ACHIEVING PEACE WILL AT LEAST BE POSSIBLE.

06064 MATTHEE, R.
JAMAL AL-DIN AL-AFGHANI AND THE EGYPTIAN NATIONAL DEBATE
INTERNATIONAL JOURNAL OF MIDDLE EAST STUDIES, 21(2) (MAY
89), 151-169.
THE AUTHOR FOCUSES ON JAMAL AL-DIN AL-AFGHANI'S

CONTINUING ROLE IN EGYPT, THE COUNTRY WHERE HIS LEGACY IS
MOST STRONGLY FELT. IT IS IN EGYPT THAT THE INTERPRETATION
AND REINTERPRETATION OF AFGHANI HAS BEEN MOST CONTROVERSIAL
BECAUSE HIS STORY IS INTERWOVEN WITH A CRUCIAL EPISODE IN
EGYPTIAN HISTORY. THIS ESSAY ACCEPTS THE FACT THAT AFGHANI
WAS BORN AND RAISED IN IRAN BUT FOCUSES MORE ON THE
POLITICAL CONTEXT OF THE CONTROVERSY SURROUNDING AFGHANI
THAN ON THE ACCURACY OF PARTICULAR BIOGRAPHICAL FACTS.

06065 MATTHEWS, B.
SINHALA CULTURAL AND BUDDHIST PATRIOTIC ORGANIZATIONS IN
CONTEMPORARY SRI LANKA
PACIFIC AFFAIRS, 61(4) (WIN 89), 620-632.
A RECENT INCREASE IN THE NUMBER OF SINHALA "PATRIOTIC
ORGANIZATIONS" IS DIRECTLY RELATED TO COMMUNAL TENSIONS IN
SRI LANKA. MANY OF THESE INVOKE BUDDHISM IN ONE WAY OR
ANOTHER TO DEFINE THEIR PURPOSE, REFLECTING THE RELIGIO-
CULTURAL DIMENSION OF THE CURRENT CONFLICT. THIS PAPER
EXAMINES THIS PHENOMENON FROM TWO PERSPECTIVES. FIRST IT
INVESTIGATES THE ORIGINS OF THESE ORGANIZATIONS AND TRACES
THEIR IDEOLOGIES. THE QUESTION OF THEIR LEADERSHIP IS ALSO
RAISED. BY WAY OF EXAMPLE, TWO PROMINENT LEADERS (ONE A
MONK, ONE A LAY PERSON) ARE ISOLATED FOR REVIEW. A SECOND
ISSUE IS THE IMPORTANCE OF THESE ORGANIZATIONS IN THE
POLITICS OF SRI LANKA TODAY. IT IS ARGUED THAT THE THIRY-ODD
RELATIVELY SIGNIFICANT SINHALA GROUPS HAVE NO CENTRALIZED
LEADERSHIP, ARE IDEOLOGICALLY FICKLE, AND SO FAR HAVE
INSUFFICIENT ROOTS AT THE VILLAGE LEVEL. NONETHELESS,
PARTICIPATION IN THEM (OR EMPATHY FOR THEIR AIMS) REFLECTS A
WIDE RANGE OF CLASSES AND CASTES. THE ORGANIZATIONS ARE
VISIBLE REMINDERS OF THE DISTRESS AND STRAIN THE SINHALESE
COMMUNITY ENDURES.

06066 MATTHEWS, B.
SRI LANKA IN 1988: SEEDS OF THE ACCORD
ASIAN SURVEY, XXIX(2) (FEB 89), 229-235.
1988 MARKED THE FIRST ANNIVERSARY OF THE INDO-LANKAN
ACCORD WHICH IS DESIGNED TO ENSURE PEACE IN SRI LANKA.
ALTHOUGH THERE HAS A MARKED INCREASE IN TERRORISM AND
ANARCHY, THE ARTICLE ARGUES THAT THE "POSITIVE" ASPECTS OF
THE ACCORD SHOULD NOT BE OVERLOOKED. THE ARTICLE EXAMINES
SRI LANKA MAINLY FROM THREE PERSPECTIVES, EACH CLOSELY
RELATED TO THE ACCORD: THE DEVOLUTION OF POWER THROUGH THE
PROVINCIAL COUNCILS, THE PRESERVATION OF THE UNITARY NATURE
OF THE STATE, AND THE MILITARY AND ECONOMIC IMPACT OF THE
ACCORD. IT ALSO BRIEFLY EXAMINES THE 1988 PRESIDENTIAL
ELECTION.

06067 MATTHEWS, B.
THE JANATHA VIMUKTHI PERAMUNA AND THE POLITICS OF THE
UNDERGROUND IN SRI LANKA
ROUND TABLE, (312) (OCT 89), 425-439.
THIS PAPER SEEKS TO ANALYSE THE UNDERGROUND CHALLENGE TO
THE DESTINY OF SRI LANKA FROM THREE PERSPECTIVES. FIRST, IT
REVIEWS THOSE RECENT EVENTS IN SRI LANKA THAT HAVE MADE IT
POSSIBLE FOR THE JVP TO RETURN TO A POSITION OF INFLUENCE
AFTER YEARS OF LOW VISIBILITY. SECOND, THE PAPER DESCRIBES
THE PRESENT JVP IDEOLOGY AND CONSTITUENCY. THIRD, IT REPLIES
TO THE QUESTION OF HOW SERIOUS A PRESENT THREAT THE JVP IS
TO SOCIETY AND STATE, AND WHAT STRATEGIES ARE INVOLVED IN AN
ATTEMPT TO CHECK OR DEFEAT THEM.

06068 MATTHEWS, M.
PATTERNS OF DEPRIVATION IN THE SOVIET UNION UNDER BREZHNEV
AND GORBACHEV
HOOVER INSTITUTION PRESS, STANFORD, CA, 1989, 220.
BECAUSE THE WORD "POVERTY" CANNOT BE USED IN OFFICIAL
SOURCES TO REFER TO ANY SOCIAL CONDITION IN THE USSR AND NO
OFFICIAL STATISTICS ARE AVAILABLE, THE AUTHOR OF THIS STUDY
RELIED ON INFORMATION FROM SOVIET EMIGRANTS. HE CLEARLY
ILLUSTRATES THAT SOME OF THE CENTRAL AIMS OF THE BOLSHEVIK
REVOLUTION, INCLUDING THE ERADICATION OF WANT, HAVE NOT BEEN
ACHIEVED.

06069 MATTHEWS, W.; BOSIN, M.
THE PUBLIC ADMINISTRATOR ENGAGES BIOTECHNOLOGY: A CASE OF
MULTIPLE ROLES
POLICY STUDIES REVIEW, 8(2) (WIN 89), 455-467.
ONE OF THE MOST PERPLEXING DILEMMAS FACING PUBLIC
ADMINISTRATORS IS HOW TO ADDRESS EMERGING TECHNOLOGIES THAT
HOLD GREAT PROMISE FOR IMPROVING THE QUALITY OF LIFE BUT
ALSO HAVE POTENTIAL ADVERSE CONSEQUENCES THAT MUST BE
UNDERSTOOD AND MANAGED BY THE PUBLIC SECTOR. IN THIS ARTICLE,
THE AUTHOR EXAMINES THE PUBLIC ADMINISTRATOR'S ROLE FROM
TWO DISTINCT PERSPECTIVES: THE FUNCTIONAL AND THE
INTERPRETIVE. THE FUNCTIONALIST PERSPECTIVE IS CHARACTERIZED
BY A BELIEF THAT ORGANIZATIONS, ENVIRONMENTS, PRODUCTS, AND
PROCESSES ARE CONCRETE, OBJECTIVE ENTITIES. THESE ENTITIES
CAN BE DEALT WITH THROUGH AN INSTRUMENTAL LOGIC OR VIA
POLITICAL MANEUVERING. IN THE INTERPRETIVE PERSPECTIVE, ALL
MEANINGS ARE SOCIALLY CONSTRUCTED.

06070 MATTHEWS, W.A.
A MULTI-LEVEL DRAMATURGIC MODEL OF DECISION-MAKING

DISSERTATION ABSTRACTS INTERNATIONAL, 49(7) (JAN 89),
1958-A.
THE AUTHOR DEVELOPS A MODEL OF DECISION-MAKING IN PUBLIC
ORGANIZATIONS BY VIEWING IT AS A DRAMA. THE RESULTS SHOW
THAT MEETING OUTCOMES MAY BE PREDICTED ON THE BASIS OF
WHETHER BRIEFING MATERIAL HAS BEEN PROVIDED, SINCE MEETING
PARTICIPANTS CHOOSE ROLES AND FOLLOW SCRIPTS THEY HAVE
REHEARSED BEFORE COMING TO THE MEETING. MEETINGS WHERE
BRIEFING MATERIALS HAVE BEEN PROVIDED ARE MORE LIKELY TO END
WITH THE DECISION-MAKER ASSIGNING SPECIFIC ACTIONS TO
IMPLEMENT THE DECISION OR DECISIONS AGREED UPON DURING THE
MEETING.

06071 MAURO, F.; YAGO, G.
STATE GOVERNMENT TARGETING IN ECONOMIC DEVELOPMENT: THE
NEW YORK EXPERIENCE
PUBLIUS: THE JOURNAL OF FEDERALISM, 19(2) (SPR 89), 63-82.
THE ARTICLE EXAMINES THE TYPES OF TARGETING MEASURES
THAT THE STATE OF NEW YORK HAS USED IN THE ALLOCATION OF
ECONOMIC DEVELOPMENT AID. IN NEW YORK'S WIDE ARRAY OF
ECONOMIC DEVELOPMENT PROGRAMS, TARGETING IS THE RULE NOT THE
EXCEPTION BUT DISTRESSED COMMUNITIES AND DISTRESSED
INDIVIDUALS HAVE NOT BEEN THE ONLY, OR EVEN THE MOST COMMON,
TARGETS. NEW YORK HAS FOCUSED MORE FREQUENTLY ON DISTRESSED
INDUSTRIES, BUT IT HAS ALSO TARGETED HIGH TECHNOLOGY AND
OTHER PERCEIVED "GROWTH INDUSTRIES." THE ARTICLE CONCLUDES
THAT THE TARGETING MEASURES OFTEN MISSED THEIR MARK AND WHAT
ECONOMIC GROWTH THAT DID OCCUR OFTEN OCCURRED IN SPITE OF,
NOT BECAUSE OF NEW YORK'S TARGETING POLICIES.

06072 MAXFIELD, S.
INTERNATIONAL FINANCE, THE STATE AND CAPITAL ACCUMULATION:
MEXICO IN COMPARATIVE PERSPECTIVE
DISSERTATION ABSTRACTS INTERNATIONAL, 49(12) (JUN 89),
3858-A.
DESPITE ARGUMENTS THAT THE GLOBALIZATION OF FINANCE AND
FOREIGN BORROWING STRENGTHEN THE STATE, EVIDENCE FROM LATIN
AMERICA INDICATES THAT INTERNATIONAL FINANCIAL INTEGRATION
ENCOURAGES SHORT-TERM FINANCIAL ACTIVITY AND CAPITAL FLIGHT,
WHICH LIMITS STATE CAPACITY TO FOSTER NATIONAL INDUSTRIAL
DEVELOPMENT. ANALYSIS OF THE MEXICAN EXPERIENCE SUGGESTS
THAT GOVERNMENTS CAN MITIGATE THE POTENTIALLY NEGATIVE
ASPECTS OF FINANCIAL INTERDEPENDENCE WITH CERTAIN MACRO-
ECONOMIC POLICIES, INCLUDING FLEXIBLE EXCHANGE RATES WITH
CONTROLLED CONVERTIBILITY, DOMESTIC FINANCIAL REGULATION TO
REDUCE MARKET IMPERFECTIONS AN ENCOURAGE COUNTER-CYCLICAL
LENDING, PROGRESSIVE TAX POLICY, AND SELECTIVE PROTECTIONISM.

06073 MAY, A. M.
THE PRESIDENCY AND THE POLITICAL BUSINESS CYCLE, 1956-1984
DISSERTATION ABSTRACTS INTERNATIONAL, 49(8) (FEB 89),
2336-A.
THE POLITICAL BUSINESS CYCLE STATES THAT POLITICIANS
MANIPULATE THE ECONOMY TO ENHANCE THEIR REELECTION PROSPECTS
BY ENGAGING IN CONTRACTIONARY POLICIES IN THE EARLY YEARS OF
A PRESIDENT'S TERM AND EXPANSIONARY POLICIES BEFORE THE
PRESIDENTIAL ELECTION. THIS DISSERTATION EXAMINES THE
POLITICAL BUSINESS CYCLE HYPOTHESIS IN THE U.S. FROM 1956 TO
1984.

06074 MAY, L.
PHILOSOPHERS AND POLITICAL RESPONSIBILITY
SOCIAL RESEARCH, 56(4) (WIN 89), 877-902.
THE AUTHOR CONSIDERS THE POLITICAL RESPONSIBILITY OF
PROFESSIONAL PHILOSOPHERS. BY COMPARING MANY EXAMPLES FROM
THE HISTORY OF PHILOSOPHY WITH THE ACKNOWLEDGED
RESPONSIBILITIES OF OTHER PROFESSIONAL GROUPS (SUCH AS
JOURNALISTS, PHYSICIANS, AND LAWYERS), THE AUTHOR SUGGESTS
THAT THE PUBLIC EXPECTATION THAT PHILOSOPHERS SHOULD
STIMULATE THEIR SOCIETIES IN POSITIVE WAYS IS NOT IRRELEVANT
TO THEIR ACKNOWLEDGED OBLIGATION TO PURSUE WISDOM. HE ARGUES
THAT PHILOSOPHERS SHOULD HAVE A HEIGHTENED SENSE OF
POLITICAL RESPONSIBILITY AND MINIMIZE THE LIKELIHOOD THAT
HARM MIGHT BE PRODUCED BY THEIR WRITINGS. PHILOSOPHY IS A
POLITICIZED DOMAIN, AND THE GREATER A PHILOSOPHER'S
REPUTATION, THE GREATER IS HIS RESPONSIBILITY TO PREVENT THE
ABUSE OF PHILOSOPHY.

06075 MAY, R. JR.; JOHAL, D.; RAMACHDRAN, A.
CHAPTER 2: HUMAN SETTLEMENTS IN NATIONAL DEVELOPMENT
POLICY: THE YEAR 2000 AGENDA; THE URBANIZATION REVOLUTION
PLENUM PRESS, NEW YORK, NY, 1989, 10-18.
THIS CHAPTER PROJECTS FUTURE POPULATION GROWTH AND
HOUSING AND SETTLEMENT NEEDS UP TO THE YEAR 2000. IT DETAILS
A PROGRAM OF THREE PHASES WHICH WAS BEGUN IN 1983 AND
STRETCHES TO THE YEAR 2000. DESCRIBED IS THE UN ROLE IN
COORDINATING ACTION IN THE FIELD OF HUMAN SETTLEMENTS. THE
DESIGNATED PROJECTS ARE EXPLORED AS WELL AS THE "NEW AGENDA"
AND ITS GOALS. THE NEED FOR INDIVIDUAL GOVERNMENTAL SUPPORT
OF "NATIONAL DEVELOPMENT" IS STRESSED. LASTLY, THE NECESSARY
STEPS AND EMPHASIZED POINTS FOR GUIDELINES ARE LISTED.

06076 MAY, R. JR.
THE URBANIZATION REVOLUTION

PLENUM PRESS, NEW YORK, NY, 1989, 259.
THIS VOLUME ILLUSTRATES SOME OF THE NEW APPROACHES THAT
WILL FORM THE BASIS FOR PLANNING AND DEVELOPMENT ASSISTANCE
DURING THE COMING DECADE. IT SHARES INFORMATION DRAWN FROM
EXPERIENCE IN DIFFERENT COUNTRIES THAT ARE PLANNING FOR THE
INTERLOCKING COMPLEXITIES OF ECONOMY, CULTURE, AND
ENVIRONMENT. THE AUTHORS HAVE PUT MANY IDEAS TO WORK AND ARE
HERE REFLECTING WITH CARE ON HOW WELL THEY MAY BE WORKING.
IT STUDIES HOUSING, EDUCATION, EMPLOYMENT, TRANSPORTATION,
WATER SUPPLY, NUTRITION, AND METROPOLITAN CONCENTRATION.

06077 MAYALL, J.
THE COMMONWEALTH AT KUALA LUMPUR
WORLD TODAY, 45(12) (DEC 89), 201-202.
THE MEETING OF COMMONWEALTH HEADS OF GOVERNMENT IN
OCTOBER 1989 OPENED IN A MOOD OF SELF-CONGRATULATION AND
OPTIMISM BECAUSE THE MODERN COMMONWEALTH HAS SURVIVED FOR 40
YEARS AND REPRESENTS ONE OF EVERY THREE NATIONS. BUT BEHIND
THE BRAVADO AND EVIDENT COMMITMENT LURKED FAMILIAR DOUBTS
ABOUT THE IDENTITY OF THE ASSOCIATION AND ITS FUTURE ROLE.
THE MEETING ENDED IN THE KIND OF BLAZING ROW BETWEEN BRITAIN
AND THE OTHER MEMBERS THAT HAS BECOME A FEATURE OF
COMMONWEALTH GATHERINGS IN RECENT YEARS.

06078 MAYBURY-LEWIS, D.
INDIANS IN BRAZIL: THE STRUGGLE INTENSIFIES
CULTURAL SURVIVAL QUARTERLY, 13(1) (1989), 2-5.
SINCE 1911 BRAZILIAN LAW HAS GUARANTEED THE INDIAN
PEOPLES THEIR LANDS AND THE RIGHT TO MAINTAIN THEIR OWN
CUSTOMS. THE NATIONAL INDIAN FOUNDATION (FUNAI) EXISTS TO
HELP THE INDIANS AND DEFEND THEIR INTERESTS--AT LEAST IN
THEORY. BUT FUNAI IS A GOVERNMENT AGENCY AND, SINCE THE
1960'S, BRAZILIAN GOVERNMENT POLICY HAS EMPHASIZED A KIND OF
DEVELOPMENT THAT HAS HAD TERRIBLE CONSEQUENCES FOR THE
INDIANS AND ALSO FOR THE NON-INDIAN POOR.

06079 MAYER, F.
THE REALISM OF DREAMERS
WORLD MARXIST REVIEW. 32(5) (MAY 89), 34-35.
A PROGRESSIVE IDEOLOGY ALWAYS REQUIRES A CREATIVE
APPROACH, NOT RIGID ADHERENCE TO SOMETHING IMMUTABLE. IN THE
SOVIET UNION MANY BUREAUCRATS HAD AN EXCELLENT OPPORTUNITY
NOT TO THINK, NOT TO CHANGE ANYTHING AND TO AVOID SELF-
EXAMINATION AND CRITICISM IN ORDER TO UPHOLD OBSOLETE,
MOSSBACK PRINCIPLES. AN ESSENTIALLY PARASITIC WAY OF LIFE
PROLIFERATED. BUREAUCRATIC SOCIAL ORGANISATION SOONER OR
LATER LEADS TO SOCIAL DEGRADATION. PERESTROIKA WILL ENABLE
THE SOVIET UNION TO OVERCOME ITS PROBLEMS, BECOME A TRULY
DYNAMIC SOCIETY AND GIVE THE GREEN LIGHT TO THE DEVELOPMENT
OF THE PERSONALITY AND ITS TALENT.

06080 MAYER, F.W.
BARGAINS WITHIN BARGAINS: DOMESTIC POLICTICS AND
INTERNATIONAL NEGOTIATION
DISSERTATION ABSTRACTS INTERNATIONAL, 49(10) (APR 89),
3142-A.
ALMOST EVERY NEGOTIATION BETWEEN TWO PARTIES IS REALLY
THREE NEGOTIATIONS, ONE ACROSS THE TABLE AND TWO MORE ON THE
SIDE. THIS IS PARTICULARLY TRUE IN INTERNATIONAL
NEGOTIATIONS, WHERE THE INTERNAL NEGOTIATIONS AMONG DOMESTIC
FACTIONS ARE OFTEN MORE SPIRITED THAN THE EXTERNAL
NEGOTIATIONS AMONG NATIONS. THUS, IN ORDER TO UNDERSTAND
WHAT HAPPENS IN INTERNATIONAL NEGOTIATIONS AND TO PRESCRIBE
HOW TO ACT IN THEM, ONE MUST ATTEND TO BOTH THE INTERNAL AND
EXTERNAL BARGAINS.

06081 MAYER, T.F.
IN DEFENSE OF ANALYTICAL MARXISM
SCIENCE AND SOCIETY, 53(4) (WIN 89), 416-441.
THIS PIECE IS PARTICULARLY USEFUL IN SORTING OUT PRECISE
MEANINGS OF TERMS AND ARGUMENTS AND ATTEMPTS TO SHED LIGHT
ON THE QUESTION OF THE NATURE OF CAPITALIST EXPLOITATION. IT
EXPLORES THE STRUGGLE TO CONTROL THE MEANING OF MARXISM.
DEFINED IS WHO ARE THE ANALYTICAL MARXISTS, AND WHAT IS
ANALYTICAL MARXISM. THEN, CRITIQUES OF ANALYTICAL MARXISM
ARE PRESENTED, AND THE PAPER ATTEMPTS TO SHOW THAT THE
CRITICISMS ARE NOT WELL FOUNDED.

06082 MAYHEW, A.
POLANYI'S DOUBLE MOVEMENT AND VEBLEN ON THE ARMY OF THE
COMMONWEAL
JOURNAL OF ECONOMIC ISSUES, XXIII(2) (JUN 89), 555-562.
THIS ARTICLE IS ABOUT THE ARMY OF THE COMMONWEAL, THAT
GROUP OF UNEMPLOYED MEN WHO MARCHED TO WASHINGTON IN THE
SPRING OF 1984 TO PROTEST THEIR INABILITY TO FIND JOBS. IN
LARGER PART IT IS ABOUT THE WAY IN WHICH KARL POLANYI MIGHT
HAVE ANALYZED THE ARMY AND ABOUT THE WAY IN WHICH THORSTEIN
VEBLEN DID ANALYZE IT; AND FROM THIS LARGER PART OF THE
ARTICLE THE AUTHOR DRAWS A FEW SUGGESTIONS FOR INSTITUTIONAL
ANALYSIS.

06083 MAYHEW, D.; RUSSETT, B.
HOW THE DEMOCRATS CAN WIN IN '92
NEW LEADER, LXXII(1) (JAN 89), 13.

THE 1988 ELECTION RESULTS SHOW THAT A DEMOCRATIC PRESIDENTIAL CANDIDATE CAN WIN IN 1992 BY CAPTURING AN ADDITIONAL FOUR PERCENT OF THE VOTE. IN TERMS OF GAINING ELECTORAL VOTES, THE MOST EFFICIENT DEMOCRATIC STRATEGY WOULD BE TO CONCENTRATE ON THE STATES THE PARTY CARRIED IN 1988 AND ON THOSE WITHIN THE FOUR PERCENT RANGE. FOR INSURANCE, A FEW OTHER INDUSTRIAL STATES SHOULD ALSO BE TARGETED.

06084 MAYNARD, E.
THE BUREAUCRACY AND IMPLEMENTATION OF US HUMAN RIGHTS POLICY
HUMAN RIGHTS QUARTERLY, 11(2) (MAY 89), 175-248.
THE ARTICLE OUTLINES THE BUREAUCRACY IN THE US THAT DEALS WITH HUMAN RIGHTS ISSUES. IT EXAMINES THE BUREAU OF HUMAN RIGHTS AND HUMANITARIAN AFFAIRS, AN ORGANIZATION WHICH IS UNDER THE AUSPICES OF THE STATE DEPARTMENT. IT ALSO EXAMINES THE WORKINGS OF INTER-AGENCY GROUPS SUCH AS THE CHRISTOPHER GROUP AND THE "REAGAN WORKING GROUP", AS WELL AS OTHER FEDERAL AGENCIES, THE IMPORTANCE AND EFFECT OF COUNTRY REPORTS AND HUMAN RIGHTS TRAINING IS ALSO EXAMINED. THE ARTICLE ALSO ISSUES POLICY RECOMMENDATIONS FOR ALL OF THE BUREAUCRATIC AGENCIES INVOLVED IN THE HUMAN RIGHTS PROCESS.

06085 MAYNES, C.
COPING WITH THE 90'S
FOREIGN POLICY, (74) (SPR 89), 42-62.
THE AUTHOR EXPLORES THE REASONS WHY THE UNITED STATES WAS PRE-EMINENT IN THE WORLD AND THE FACTORS THAT HAVE LED TO ITS DECLINE. HE ARGUES THAT THE DEFERENCE GIVEN TO THE US IN THE DECADES FOLLOWING WORLD WAR II WAS BASED ON A RESPECT OF THE AMERICAN SYSTEM AND THAT CONTINUED RELAINCE ON FORCE AND ARMS HAS ERODED THAT WORLD-WIDE RESPECT. HE ALSO EXAINES SOME OF THE CHALLENGES THAT THE US WILL FACE IN THE NEXT DECADE. THESE INCLUDE ECONOMIC, SECURITY AND ENVIRONMENTAL CHALLENGES. THE INCREASE IN POWERS WITH NUCLEAR OR CHEMICAL WEAPONS, THE INCREASINGLY SHAKY WORLD ECONOMY, CHANGING GEOSTRATEGIC CONDITIONS, THE SPREAD OF AIDS AND INCREASING POLLUTION WILL ALL TRY US LEADERSHIP THROUGHOUT THE 1990'S.

06086 MAYNTZ, R.; DERLIEN, H-U.
PARTY PARTRONAGE AND POLITICZATION OF THE WEST GERMAN ADMINISTRATIVE ELITE 1970-1987 - TOWARD HYBRIDIZATION
GOVERNANCE, 2(4) (OCT 89), 384-404.
THIS ARTICLE EXPLORES EXECUTIVE CONTROL OF THE BUREAUCRACY WHICH IT DESCRIBES AS A PERENNIAL PROBLEM IN THEORY AS WELL AS IN PRACTICE. IT ANALYZES THE EXTENT THAT PARTY-POLITICIZATION HAS CHANGED FROM 1970 TO 1987. IT ALSO ANALYZES WHETHER AND TO WHAT EXTENT THE SUBJECTIVE ROLE DEFINITION OF CIVIL SERVANTS HAS CHANGED. THE FINDINGS TOUCH ON THE HYBRIDIZATION THESIS AND IT IS ASKED WHETHER OR NOT THE ADMINISTRATIVE ELITE IN BONN IS IN FACT CHANGING IN THE HYPOTHESIZED DIRECTION.

06087 MAZA, S.
DOMESTIC MELODRAMA AS POLITICAL IDEOLOGY: THE CASE OF THE COMTE DE SANOIS
AMERICAN HISTORICAL REVIEW, 94(5) (DEC 89), 1249-1264.
IT IS CUSTOMARY TO IMPOSE A SHARP DISTINCTION BETWEEN "PUBLIC" AND "PRIVATE" MATTERS IN THE UNDERSTANDING OF THE QUESTION OF IDEOLOGICAL ORIGINS. BUT PRE-MODERN WESTERN SOCIETIES DISTINGUISHED NOT SO MUCH BETWEEN INTIMATE MATTERS AND AFFAIRS OF STATE AS BETWEEN SUBJECTS OF GENERAL INTEREST AND CONCERN AND THOSE WITH "PARTICULAR" RELEVANCE. IN SUCH SOCIETIES, A PERSONAL OR INTIMATE MATTER COULD EASILY BE UNDERSTOOD AS A "PUBLIC" ISSUE IF ITS GENERAL RELEVANCE WERE MADE CLEAR. THIS ARTICLE ATTEMPTS TO ILLUSTRATE THIS THROUGH THE EXAMPLE OF THE COMTE DE SANOIS, WHO IN 1786 BROUGHT SUIT AGAINST HIS WIFE AND OTHER MEMBERS OF HIS IMMEDIATE FAMILY. ANALYSIS OF THE TRIAL BRIEFS SUGGESTS THE LIMITATIONS OF THE USUAL DISTINCTIONS BETWEEN FICTIONAL AND POLITICAL WRITING, BETWEEN EMOTIONAL PERSUASION AND RATIONAL ARGUMENT, AND BETWEEN THE PUBLIC AND PRIVATE SPHERES.

06088 MAZA, S.
POLITICS, CULTURE, AND THE ORIGINS OF THE FRENCH REVOLUTION
JOURNAL OF MODERN HISTORY, 61(4) (DEC 89), 704-723.
"REVISIONIST" INTERPRETATIONS OF THE FRENCH REVOLUTION NO LONGER DESERVE THAT LABEL. SINCE ALFRED COBBAN PUBLISHED "THE SOCIAL INTERPRETATION OF THE FRENCH REVOLUTION," THE REJECTION OF MARXIAN CATEGORIES AND, IN MOST CASES, OF ANY SOCIOECONOMIC EXPLANATION FOR THE UPHEAVAL HAS BECOME THE NEW ORTHODOXY. BEFORE THE EARLY 1960'S, THE EXPLANATORY POWER OF A CLASS-STRUGGLE MODEL FOR THE REVOLUTION SEEMED AS OBVIOUS TO HISTORIANS AS THE SUN'S MOTION AROUND THE EARTH DID TO PRE-COPERNICANS. BUT, IN BOTH CASES, THE ESTABLISHED PARADIGM EVENTUALLY COLLAPSED UNDER THE PRESSURE OF AN ACCUMULATED MASS OF NEW EMPIRICAL EVIDENCE THAT CONTRADICTED IT.

06089 MAZARR, M.J.
ON STRATEGIC NUCLEAR POLICY
SAIS REVIEW, 9(1) (WIN 89), 157-181.
THIS ARTICLE ASSESSES THE POSSIBLE EFFECTS ON STABILITY

OF THE START TREATY NOW UNDER CONSIDERATION. IT CONCLUDES THAT THE STABILITY OF A START REGIME RESTS MOST CRITICALLY ON THE WILLINGNESS OF THE UNITED STATES TO MODERNIZE ITS STRATEGIC NUCLEAR FORCE; SUCH MODERNIZATION COULD ALSO REINTRODUCE COHERENCE INTO THE U.S. STRATEGIC PROGRAM. BIPARTISAN RECOGNITION OF THESE FACTS -- AND AN EMPHASIS ON ARMS CONTROL AS A USEFUL TOOL TO MAXIMIZE THE BENEFITS OF THE U.S. STRATEGIC NUCLEAR PROGRAM, RATHER THAN AS A SELF-CONTAINED PANACEA -- WILL BE NECESSARY TO SELL A STRATEGIC ARMS TREATY TO A WARY SENATE. THE RATIFICATION PROCESS IS CRUCIAL, FOR ANOTHER SALT II-LIKE DEBACLE WOULD BE DISASTROUS FOR THE FUTURE OF ARMS CONTROL.

06090 MAZARR, M.J.
PROSPECTS FOR REVOLUTION IN POST-CASTRO CUBA
JOURNAL OF INTERAMERICAN STUDIES AND WORLD AFFAIRS, 31(4) (WIN 89), 60-90.
THIS ESSAY EXPLORES THE FUTURE OF CUBA AFTER THE DEATH OF FIDEL CASTRO. IT ADDRESSES A TWO-PART QUESTION: WHAT ARE THE CHANCES FOR A REVOLUTION IN POST-CASTRO CUBA?; AND, IF ONE OCCURRED: WHAT FORM WOULD IT TAKE? THE GENERAL ECONOMIC SITUATION, THE SOCIO-ECONOMIC MOTIVATIONS, HUMAN RIGHTS, AND CLASS ARE EACH EXAMINED. THE LIKELY NATURE OF THE OPPOSITION IS DETAILED AND IMPLICATIONS FOR U.S. POLICY ARE DETAILED.

06091 MBAKU, J.; PAUL, C.
POLITICAL INSTABILITY IN AFRICA: A RENT-SEEKING APPROACH
PUBLIC CHOICE, 63 (1989), 63-72.
THE CENTRAL THESIS OF THIS STUDY IS THAT RENT-SEEKING ON THE PART ON HETEROGENEOUS GROUPS OF POLITICAL ENTREPRENEURS IS RESPONSIBLE FOR THE POLITICAL INSTABILITY IN AFRICAN GOVERNMENTS. IN ORDER TO DEVELOP THIS LINE OF INQUIRY TWO EXISTING VEINS OF ECONOMIC RESEARCH ARE COMBINED. THE FIRST IS THE BY-PRODUCT THEORY OF REVOLUTION (TULLOCK, 1974). THE SECOND IS THE THEORY OF RENT-SEEKING INTRODUCED BY TULLOCK (1967) AND EXTENDED AND FURTHER DEVELOPED IN BUCHANAN, TOLLISON AND TULLOCK (1980).

06092 MBAKU, J. M.
POLITICAL INSTABILITY AND ECONOMIC DEVELOPMENT IN SUB-SAHARAN AFRICA: SOME RECENT EVIDENCE
REVIEW OF BLACK POLITICAL ECOMOMY, 17(1) (SUM 88), 89-112.
THIS ARTICLE EXPLORES HOW POLITICAL INSTABILITY AFFECTS THE AFRICAN ECONOMY. POLITICAL INSTABILITY IS DEFINED AS A CONDITION IN POLITICAL SYSTEMS IN WHICH THE INSTITUTIONALIZED PATTERNS OF AUTHORITY BREAK DOWN AND THE EXPECTED COMPLIANCE TO POLITICAL AUTHORITIES IS REPLACED BY POLITICAL VIOLENCE. THE HISTORY OF AFRICAN POLITICAL INSTABILITY IS TRACED.

06093 MBEKI, T.
THE CAMPAIGN FOR SANCTIONS
SECHABA, 23(12) (DEC 89), 12.
THIS ARTICLE IS PART OF A SPEECH THAT COMRADE THABO MBEKI, HEAD OF THE AFRICAN NATIONAL CONGRESS INTERNATIONAL DEPARTMENT MADE TO THE SOUTHERN AFRICA COALITION IN LONDON IN OCTOBER. HE DEALS WITH THE SITUATION IN SOUTH AFRICA AND THE URGENT NEED FOR SANCTIONS HE CALLS THE RELEASE OF POLITICAL PRISONERS A RETREAT BY DEKLERK - A CHANGE OF DIRECTION RATHER THAN A CHANGE OF HEART AND ANALYZES THE SITUATION IN ANGOLA AND NAMBIA. HE CALLS FOR AN INCREASE IN THE STRUGGLE.

06094 MC LEAN, D.; BALL, D.
CO-OPERATION ENHANCES NATIONAL DEFENCE
PACIFIC DEFENCE REPORTER, 16(3) (SEP 89), 60-62.
THE FUNDAMENTAL STRATEGIC INTEREST OF BOTH NEW ZEALAND AND AUSTRALIA IS TO PROTECT AND, SO FAR AS POSSIBLE, TO MAINTAIN THE ADVANTAGE IN THE ZONES CRITICAL TO THEIR SEA AND AIR APPROACHES. TWO VERY ISOLATED COUNTRIES ARE MORE HEAVILY DEPENDENT THAN MOST ON THEIR EXTERNAL COMMUNICATIONS AND SEA/AIR LINKS. SELF-SUFFICIENCY MAY HAVE ITS APPEAL TO SOME. THE REALITY IS THAT BOTH COUNTRIES ARE EQUALLY -- IF INDEPENDENTLY -- TIED INTO THE GREAT INTERNATIONAL SYSTEMS OF TRADE AND EXCHANGE. ALTHOUGH IT MAY SOMETIMES SEEM THAT THE EXCHANGE OF CHEAP JIBES AT ONE ANOTHER IS THE MAIN ELEMENT OF TRANS-TASMAN COMMERCE, THE FACTS ARE THAT AUSTRALIA AND NEW ZEALAND ARE CLOSELY LINKED TOGETHER BY TRADE, BUSINESS PRACTICE, FINANCIAL AND TECHNICAL EXCHANGE AT ALL LEVELS AND BY A GROWING HABIT OF CONSULTATION.

06095 MCADAM, D.
THE BIOGRAPHICAL CONSEQUENCES OF ACTIVISM
AMERICAN SOCIOLOGICAL REVIEW, 54(5) (OCT 89), 744-760.
USING SURVEY DATA COLLECTED IN 1983-84 ON 212 PARTICIPANTS IN THE 1964 MISSISSIPPI FREEDOM SUMMER PROJECT AND 118 INDIVIDUALS WHO APPLIED, WERE ACCEPTED, BUT DID NOT TAKE PART IN THE PROJECT, THE AUTHOR SEEKS TO ASSESS THE SHORTAND LONG-TERM POLITICAL AND PERSONAL CONSEQUENCES OF HIGH-RISK ACTIVISM. USING BOTH DESCRIPTIVE AND INFERENTIAL STATISTICS, THE AUTHOR DEMONSTRATES A STRONG EFFECT OF PARTICIPATION ON THE SUBSEQUENT LIVES OF THE VOLUNTEERS AND "NO-SHOWS." THE VOLUNTEERS WERE MORE POLITICALLY ACTIVE THROUGHOUT THE SIXTIES THAN THE NO-SHOWS AND REMAIN SO TODAY.

IN ADDITION, THE VOLUNTEERS ARE MUCH LESS LIKELY TO BE MARRIED AND TO HAVE SIGNIFICANTLY LOWER INCOMES AT PRESENT THAN ARE THE NO-SHOWS. BESIDES REPORTING THESE BASIC FINDINGS, THE AUTHOR SEEKS THROUGH PATH ANALYSIS TO EXPLORE THE SPECIFIC FACTORS AND PROCESSES THAT MEDIATE THE IMPACT OF PARTICIPATION IN FREEDOM SUMMER ON THE LATER LIVES OF THE VOLUNTEERS.

06096 MCALISTER, E.
THE LAW OF CONSCIENCE
SOJOURNERS, 18(10) (NOV 89), 20.
THE AUTHOR ARGUES THAT GOVERNMENT SANTIONED ABORTION DELEGITIMIZES THE UNITED STATES GOVERNMENT. SHE CALLS FOR AN ALTERNATIVE LAW BASED ON THE INDIVIDUAL CONSCIENCE AND COOPERATION BETWEEN PRO-CHOICE AND PRO-LIFE FACTIONS.

06097 MCALLISTER, E.
THE UNITED STATES LOOKS AT 1992
EUROPE, (289) (SEP 89), 16-17.
US ASSISTANT SECRETARY OF STATE, EUGENE MCALLISTER, GIVES THE "WASHINGTON" VIEW ON THE PROPOSED 1992 ECONOMIC INTEGRATION OF EUROPE. HE STATES THAT, ON BALANCE, THE PROPOSED CHANGES WILL BE BENEFICIAL TO ALL INVOLVED. HOWEVER, HE EXPRESSED CONCERNS WITH REGARDS TO RECIPROCITY; RULES OF ORIGIN; QUOTAS; AND THE STANDARDS, CERTIFICATION, AND TESTING PROCESS.

06098 MCAULIFF, J.; MCDONNELL, M.B.
ENDING THE CAMBODIAN STALEMATE
WORLD POLICY JOURNAL, 7(1) (WIN 89), 71-105.
THIS ARTICLE EXPLORES AMERICA'S DECADE LONG CAMBODIAN POLICY PREMISED ON PROVIDING POLITICAL, FINANCIAL, AND LOGISTICAL SUPPORT TO THE NONCOMMUNIST RESISTANCE. IT EXAMINES LAST SUMMER'S INTERNATIONAL CONFERENCE ON CAMBODIA WHICH BEGAN ON A NOTE OF HOPE, AND YET ENDED WITHOUT BREAKING THE 11-YEAR OLD STALEMATE IN INDOCHINA, AND DETAILS REASONS FOR THE FAILURE. IT CONCLUDES WITH REASONS FOR SETTLING THE CAMBODIA QUESTION AND NORMALIZING RELATIONS WITH INDOCHINA.

06099 MCBEATH, G.A.
DEVELOPMENT OF TAIWAN'S YOUTH POLITICAL CULTURE THROUGH SCHOOLS AND THE MEDIA
ASIAN PROFILE, 17(5) (OCT 89), 385-396.
THIS ARTICLE REVIEWS TWO CHANGES IN THE SCHOOL SYSTEM WHICH HAVE AN IMPACT ON SOCIOPOLITICAL VALUES AND ATTITUDES OF YOUTH: THE STRUCTURE OF AUTHORITY IN THE CLASSROOM, PARTICULARLY CHANGES IN INFLUENCE OVER TIME, AND THE "APPRENTICESHIP" OF YOUTH TO PARTICIPATORY POLITICS THROUGH THEIR INVOLVEMENT IN SELECTION OF CLASS LEADERS. THE ARTICLE ALSO CONSIDERS THE RATE OF MEDIA USE OF ADOLESCENTS AND THE CHANGES IN NEWSPAPER READING AND TELEVISION WATCHING HABITS OVER A TEN-YEAR PERIOD. FINALLY, THE ARTICLE CONSIDERS THE RELATIONSHIPS BETWEEN TYPES OF SCHOOL AUTHORITY SYSTEM AND RATES OF YOUTH APPRENTICESHIP TO POLITICS, ON THE ONE HAND, AND A SERIES OF VALUES WHICH ARE RELATED TO THE GLOBAL MARKETPLACE.

06100 MCBEATH, J.
CLEANING OUT THE BARRACKS
FAR EASTERN ECONOMIC REVIEW, 141(37) (SEP 88), 23.
SOUTH KOREAN PRESIDENT ROH TAE WOO IS BECOMING A GOOD DEAL MORE ASSERTIVE IN HIS OWN POLITICAL HOUSEHOLD. OVER THE PAST FEW MONTHS HE HAS RESHUFFLED A NUMBER OF SENIOR OFFICERS AND ANALYSTS ARE PREDICTING MORE BY THE END OF THE YEAR. EVEN THE POWERFUL MILITARY IS NOT EXEMPT FROM ROH'S BEHIND THE SCENES MOVES. SEVERAL CHANGES IN TOP MILITARY RANKS HAVE QUIETLY AND OFTEN UNPUBLICIZED TAKEN PLACE.

06101 MCBEATH, J.
GHOSTS FROM THE PAST
FAR EASTERN ECONOMIC REVIEW, 141(27) (JUL 88), 27.
FOUR MONTHS AFTER HE LEFT OFFICE, CHUN DOO HWAN REMAINS UNDER TIGHT PROTECTION AND IN VIRTUAL SECLUSION AS OPPOSITION LEADERS GATHER EVIDENCE TO ACCUSE HIM OF WIDESPREAD CORRUPTION, INFLUENCE PEDDLING, AND ABUSE OF POWER DURING THE FORMER GENERAL'S SEVEN YEARS IN POWER. SPECIAL LEGISLATIVE PANELS ARE ALSO EXAMINING OTHER CORRUPT AND ILLEGAL PRACTICES OF THE FIFTH REPUBLIC INCLUDING THE CIRCUMSTANCES BEHIND THE BLOODY 1980 KWANGJU UPRISING, ALLEGATIONS OF COMPUTER FRAUD IN LAST DECEMBER'S PRESIDENTIAL ELECTION, AND SEVERAL UNDEMOCRATIC LAWS.

06102 MCBETH, J.
GUNNING FOR CORY
FAR EASTERN ECONOMIC REVIEW, 142(50) (DEC 89), 12-13.
THE LATEST COUP ATTEMPT AGAINST PHILIPPINES PRESIDENT CORAZON AQUINO'S GOVERNMENT HAS PLUNGED THE NATION INTO POLITICAL AND ECONOMIC CRISIS. COMPARED WITH THE FIVE PREVIOUS ATTEMPTS TO OVERTHROW AQUINO, THE REBELLION THAT BEGAN ON 1 DECEMBER APPEARS TO BE MORE DETERMINED, BETTER PLANED, AND MORE WIDELY SUPPORTED BY SENIOR MILITARY OFFICERS, CIVILIAN POLITICIANS, AND FINANCIERS. RELATIONS WITH THE U.S. WILL ALSO BE AFFECTED, AS THE AIR COVER GIVEN TO GOVERNMENT FORCES BY THE U.S. HAS STIRRED UP THE LATENT NATIONALISTIC EMOTIONS OF POLITICIANS IN MANILA.

06103 MCBETH, J.
PRODDING PYONGYANG
FAR EASTERN ECONOMIC REVIEW, 141(29) (JUL 88), 26-28.
PRESIDENT ROH TAE WOO OF SOUTH KOREA HAS UNVEILED A BROAD DECLARATION IN WHICH HE HOLDS OUT THE PROSPECT OF INTERKOREA TRADE AND SEOUL'S ASSISTANCE TO PYONGYANG IN ENDING ITS INTERNATIONAL ISOLATION. OBSERVERS BELIEVE THAT PYONGYANG IS MORE LIKELY TO TAKE THIS OVERTURE MORE SERIOUSLY THAN PREVIOUS ONES.

06104 MCBETH, J.
REUNIFICATION REVIVED
FAR EASTERN ECONOMIC REVIEW, 141(28) (JUL 88), 19.
IN AN EFFORT TO PUT MORE SUBTANCE INTO ITS AVOWED POLICY OF APPEASING THE COMMUNIST NORTH AND TO APPEASE THE GROUPS OF STUDENT DEMONSTRATORS, SOUTH KOREAN PRESIDENT ROH TAE WOO HAS SUGGESTED A SOCCER MATCH BETWEEN NORTH AND SOUTH KOREA AS A MEANS TO BREAK THE ICE THAT EXISTS BETWEEN THE TWO NATIONS. HE ALSO HAS FOLLOWED UP ON A PROPOSAL TO EXCHANGE STUDENTS. MOST SOUTH KOREANS ACCEPT UNIFICATION AS A LONG TERM GOAL, BUT IT IS A HIGHLY EMOTIONAL ISSUE AND HAS BEEN UTILIZED BY STUDENT GROUPS WHO ARE PLAYING ON ANTI-AMERICAN SENTIMENT BY BLAMING THE US FOR THE ORIGINAL PARTITION OF THE KOREAN PENINSULA.

06105 MCBETH, J.
TIME FOR TOUGHNESS
FAR EASTERN ECONOMIC REVIEW, 142(51) (DEC 89), 11-13.
WHILE THE POLITICIZATION OF THE PHILIPPINES' MILITARY BEGAN UNDER MARCOS, THE RECENT COUP ATTEMPT DEMONSTRATED THE MILITARY'S DISGRUNTLEMENT--FROM THE LOWER RANKS TO SENIOR GENERALS--WITH THE COUNTRY'S CORRUPT POLITICAL STRUCTURE AND INEFFECTIVE GOVERNMENT. PRESIDENT AQUINO NOW FACES THE DAUNTING TASK OF INTRODUCING POLITICAL REFORMS AND REINING IN CORRUPTION AND CRONYISM, WHILE KEEPING AN EYE ON A MILITARY THAT IS INCREASINGLY CERTAIN THAT ONLY RADICAL CHANGE WILL BEGIN TO SOLVE THE PHILIPPINES' MANY PROBLEMS.

06106 MCBETH, J.
WITHDRAWAL SYMPTONS
FAR EASTERN ECONOMIC REVIEW, 141(39) (SEP 88), 35.
FOR DECADES, THE US HAS REFUSED TO CONFIRM OR DENY THE PRESENCE OF NUCLEAR WEAPONS IN SOUTH KOREA. THEY CONSIDERED THE UNCERTAINTY TO BE VITAL FOR DETERRENCE. RECENTLY, HOWEVER, TWO AMERICAN GENERALS ADMITTED TO THE PRESENCE OF CLAIMED THAT THEY ARE NO LONGER AN INTEGRAL PART OF THEY CLAIMED THAT THEY ARE NO LONGER AN INTEGRAL PART OF SOUTH KOREAN DEFENSE AND ARE BECOMING A POLITICAL LIABILITY AS DISSIDENTS ARE BEGINING TO MAKE THEM THEIR MAIN TARGET WITH WHICH TO INCREASE THE ANTI-AMERICAN SENTIMENT IN SOUTH KOREA.

06107 MCBRIDGE, W.L.
THE CASE OF SARTRE
SOCIAL RESEARCH, 56(4) (WIN 89), 849-876.
SARTRE WAS PERHAPS THE MOST POLITICALLY ACTIVE OF TWENTIETH-CENTURY PHILOSOPHERS. HE WAS AN ACTIVIST IN THE SENSE THAT CAN BE MEASURED BY THE QUANTITY OF PHYSICAL ACTIVITY EXERTED ON SPECIFIC OCCASIONS, BUT HE WAS FIRST AND FOREMOST A WRITER, WHO IN A VARIETY OF GENRES POLITICALLY INFLUENCED THE PUBLIC. THIS ESSAY ARGUES THAT, IN A CHANGING WORLD, THE FACT THAT SARTRE'S THOUGH CHANGED DOES NOT ENTAIL AN ALTERNATION IN HIS BASIC POLITICAL PROJECTS NOR ANY KIND OF REVISIONISM OR OPPORTUNISM. BY RAISING THE QUESTION OF THE LINES OF DEMARCATION BETWEEN A WRITER'S THEORY AND HIS OPINION, THE AUTHOR SUGGESTS THAT CONVENTIONAL BARRIERS BETWEEN PHILOSOPHY AND POLITICAL WRITING BECAME ERODED IN THE CASE OF SARTRE.

06108 MCCAIN, J.
BEYOND THE INF TREATY: THE NEXT STEP IN ARMS CONTROL
RUSI JOURNAL, 134(2) (SUM 89), 7-14.
THIS ARTICLE STATES THAT THE PRESENT CLIMATE FOR ARMS CONTROL IS ONE WHICH CREATES A PECULIAR MIX OF HOPE AND FEAR. THE REASON FOR THE HOPE: THE RATIFICATION OF THE INF TREATY MARKS THE FIRST MAJOR NUCLEAR ARMS CONTROL TREATY THAT ACHIEVES REAL REDUCTIONS IN NUCLEAR ARMS, RATHER THAN ANY EXERCISE IN POLITICAL SYMBOLISM. THE FEAR IS THAT IT IS ALL TO EASY FOR THE WEST TO GIVE IN TO FALSE HOPES AND EXPECTATIONS REGARDING ARMS CONTROL. IN SPITE OF THE LONG DEBATE OVER THE INF TREATY, MANY IN THE WEST ARE FAR MORE AVARE OF ITS STREGTHS THAN ITS LIMITATIONS. WITH CARE, THE NEXT STEP IN ARMS CONTROL COULD BE A START TREATY THAT WOULD BOTH REDUCE THE RISK OF ANY KIND OF NUCLEAR ATTACK OR ESCALATION. THE PROBLEM HERE LIES IN THE FACT THAT THERE IS LITTLE UNDERSTANDING OF THE FACT THAT THE WEST FACES NEGOTIATIONS IN START, CONVENTIONAL ARMS REDUCTIONS, AND THEATRE ARMS REDUCTIONS WHICH COULD ALL END IN EITHER INCREASING THE RISK OF CONFLICT OR ANOTHER SET OF TREATIES WHICH REDIRECT THE ARMS RACE, RATHER THAN REDUCE ITS COSTS AND DANGERS.

06109 MCCALLUM, J. S.
  WANTED: A ZERO INFLATION RATE POLICY
  POLICY OPTIONS, 10(3) (APR 89), 20-22.
    CANADIANS ARE WILLING TO ACCEPT AN ANNUAL INFLATION RATE
  OF THREE TO FIVE PERCENT BECAUSE THEY HAVE BEEN TOLD THAT A
  LOW RATE IS HARMLESS. IN FACT, THE DIFFERENCE BETWEEN A LOW
  RATE AND DOUBLE-DIGIT INFLATION IS ONE OF DEGREE, NOT KIND.
  SUSTAINED INFLATION WILL DO A GREAT DEAL OF HARM OVER TIME,
  EVEN IF IT IS NOT AT A SPECTACULARLY HIGH LEVEL.

06110 MCCARTHY, A.
  AN UPHILL BATTLE
  COMMONHEAL, CXVI(11) (JUN 89), 329-330.
    THE AUTHOR DISCUSSES THE CONTROVERSY SURROUNDING BETTY
  WRITHT'S JOB, WHICH ERUPTED DURING THE ETHICS INVESTIGATION
  OF SPEAKER OF THE HOUSE JIM WRIGHT, AND THE ROLE OF
  CONGRESSIONAL WIVES IN GEMERAL.

06111 MCCARTHY, A.
  CONGRESS HAS A BIRTHDAY
  COMMONHEAL, CXVI(7) (APR 89), 203.
    THE AUTHOR DISCUSSES THE ACCOMPLISHMENTS OF THE FIRST
  CONGRESS AND THE NEED FOR REFORM IN THE PRESENT CONGRESS.

06112 MCCARTHY, A.
  HANDLING THE HANDLERS
  COMMONHEAL, CXVI(1) (JAN 89), 7.
    THE 1988 PRESIDENTIAL CAMPAIGN TRIVIALIZED OR IGNORED
  VITAL NATIONAL ISSUES. NEGATIVE PERSONAL ATTACKS AND
  DISTORTIONS REPLACED SERIOUS DEBATE. UNLESS AMERICANS BESTIR
  THEMSELVES TO DO SOMETHING, THE PRECIOUS HERITAGE OF SELF-
  GOVERNMENT MAY EVENTUALLY SLIP AHAY.

06113 MCCARTHY, E.P.
  GLASNOST AND PERESTROIKA: CAMPAIGN OR DECEPTION
  AVAILABLE FROM NTIS, NO. AD-A207 900/2/GAR, MAR 89, 31.
    WHAT ARE THE STRATEGIC IMPLICATIONS OF GLASNOST AND
  PERESTROIKA. IS MIKHAIL GORBACHEV EMBARKED ON A CAMPAIGN OF
  STRATEGIC DECEPTION, OR ON A CRUSADE TO LEAD THE USSR INTO
  THE AGE OF MODERN TECHNOLOGY. MUST THE ANSWER BE ONE OR THE
  OTHER, OR IS IT POSSIBLE HE IS DOING BOTH. WHAT KIND OF
  SUPPORT DOES HE NEED BOTH AT HOME AND ABROAD. HOW MUCH TIME
  DOES HE HAVE TO SUCCEED. AND, IF HE DOES, WHAT WILL BE THE
  IMPACT ON WORLD ORDER. THESE QUESTIONS REPRESENT A
  SIGNIFICANT CHALLENGE. GORBACHEV HIMSELF PROBABLY CANNOT
  PROVIDE ACCURATE ANSWERS. HE MAY PERSONALLY BE ON A CRUSADE;
  HOWEVER, THE 'SYSTEM' MAY BE EXECUTING THE GREATEST
  STRATEGIC DECEPTION THE WEST HAS EVER SEEN.

06114 MCCARTHY, M. (ED.)
  THE NEW POLITICS OF WELFARE
  LYCEUM BOOKS, CHICAGO, IL, 1989, 420.
    THE ECONOMIC POLICIES OF RONALD REAGAN AND MARGARET
  THATCHER DIMINISHED OR DISMANTLED MANY SOCIAL WELFARE
  INSTITUTIONS IN THE UNITED STATES AND GREAT BRITAIN. THEIR
  POLICIES HELPED TO CHANGE THE PHILOSOPHICAL VALUES AND
  CONSUMER EXPECTATIONS THAT UNDERPIN SOCIAL PROGRAMS IN BOTH
  COUNTRIES. THESE ARTICLES IDENTIFY KEY EVENTS AND POLICY
  DEVELOPMENTS THAT HAVE SHAPED -- AND CONTRACTED -- THE
  WELFARE STATES OF THE 1980S AND ANALYZE HOW THESE EVENTS AND
  DEVELOPMENTS WILL DETERMINE THE AGENDA FOR THE 1990S.

06115 MCCARTHY, T.G.
  REBIRTH OF CIVIL SERVICE IN CHINA
  BUREAUCRAT, 18(2) (SUM 89), 24-26.
    CHINA FACES A WIDE ARRAY OF HISTORICAL AND CURRENT
  PROBLEMS AS IT STRUGGLES TO DESIGN AND IMPLEMENT A NEW CIVIL
  SERVICE SYSTEM. IT IS WRESTLING WITH THE ISSUES OF HOW BEST
  TO HIRE, DEVELOP, TRAIN, AND MOTIVATE CIVIL SERVANTS FOR A
  BETTER GOVERNMENT.

06116 MCCAUGHEY, E.
  MARBURY V. MADISON: HAVE WE MISSED THE REAL MEANING?
  PRESIDENTIAL STUDIES QUARTERLY, XIX(3) (SUM 89), 491-528.
    AMERICANS HAVE BEEN TAUGHT TO REMEMBER MARBURY V.
  MADISON (1803) AS THE LANDMARK CASE IN WHICH CHIEF JUSTICE
  JOHN MARSHALL MADE JUDICIAL REVIEW PART OF THE AMERICA
  SYSTEM OF GOVERNMENT. MARSHALL'S OPINION IN THAT CASE ALWAYS
  HAS BEEN ACCLAIMED AS AN INVENTIVE, ASSERTIVE DECLARATION
  THAT IN THE FUTURE THE FEDERAL COURTS WOULD STRIKE DOWN ANY
  LAW OR ACTION THAT CONFLICTED WITH THE UNITED STATES
  CONSTITUTION. BUT THE SAMPLING OF EVIDENCE PRESENTED IN THIS
  ARTICLE SUGGESTS THAT IN 1803 MARSHALL WAS RETREATING, NOT
  BOLDLY PUTTING FORWARD THE COURT'S REVIEW POWER. IN AN
  ATTEMPT TO QUIET POPULAR HOSTILITY TO THE FEDERAL COURTS
  FOLLOWING A LONG, NOISY CONTROVERSY, MARSHALL MOVED TO REIN
  IN JUDICIAL POWER. HE CAREFULLY CIRCUMSCRIBED JUDICIAL
  REVIEW BY DEFINING IT ENTIRELY IN TERMS OF THE JUDGE'S DUTY
  TO UPHOLD THE WRITTEN CONSTITUTION.

06117 MCCGWIRE, M.
  ABOUT FACE: HOW THE SOVIETS STOPPED PLANNING FOR WORLD WAR
  TECHNOLOGY REVIEW, 92(8) (NOV 89), 32-41.
    ACCORDING TO THE OLD ADAGE, "IF YOU WANT PEACE, PREPARE

FOR WAR," BUT GORBACHEV'S NEW MILITARY DOCTRINE HOLDS THAT
AVOIDING WORLD WAR IN THE NUCLEAR AGE MEANS RENOUNCING THE
ABILITY TO WAGE IT. THIS ARTICLE EXAMINES THE SOVIET
APPROACH TO WAR, THE EVOLUTION OF SOVIET MILITARY DOCTRINE,
PRECURSORS TO CHANGE, THE STEPS FOR CHANGE: 1) DEFENSIVE
DOCTRINE; AND 2) RENOUNCING WORLD WAR, AND A NEW POLITICAL
FRAMEWORK FOR EUROPE.

06118 MCCHESNEY, R.W.
  THE POLITICAL ECONOMY OF THE MASS MEDIA: AN INTERVIEW WITH
  EDWARD S HERMAN
  MONTHLY REVIEW, 40(8) (JAN 89), 35-45.
    IN THIS INTERVIEW, HERMAN ANSWERS A SERIES OF QUESTIONS
  CONCERNING SOME OF THE IMPLICATIONS AND ISSUES ARISING FROM
  HIS BOOK, WITH NOAM CHEMISTRY, MANUFACTURING CONSENT: THE
  POLITICAL ECONOMY OF THE MASS MEDIA. THE BOOK PROVIDES A
  "SYSTEMATIC" PROPOGANDA MODEL" TO ACCOUNT FOR THE BEHAVIOUR
  OF THE CORPORATE NEWS MEDIA IN THE UNITED STATES

06119 MCCLELLAN, E.F.
  THE POLITICS OF AMERICAN INDIAN SELF-DETERMINATION, 1958-
  75: THE INDIAN SELF-DETERMINATION AND EDUCATION ASSISTANCE
  ACT OF 1975
  DISSERTATION ABSTRACTS INTERNATIONAL, 50(3) (SEP 89),
  785-A.
    THE AUTHOR STUDIES THE FACTORS THAT PRODUCED PASSAGE OF
  THE INDIAN SELF-DETERMINATION AND EDUCATION ASSISTANCE ACT
  OF 1975, WHICH ENABLED INDIAN TRIBES TO ASSUME CONTROL OF
  FEDERAL PROGRAMS. THE FINDINGS REVEAL SEVERAL FEATURES OF
  THE AGENDA-BUILDING PROCESS IN THE 1960'S: (1) THE EMERGENCE
  OF INDIAN POLITICAL ACTIVISM, (2) FEDERAL PROGRAM EXPANSION
  FOR INDIANS, INCLUDING TRIBALLY-ADMINISTERED COMMUNITY
  ACTION PROGRAMS, (3) POLICY ENTREPRENEURSHIP IN CONGRESS,
  AND (4) PRESIDENTIAL INTERVENTION.

06120 MCCLENNEN, E.F.
  JUSTICE AND THE PROBLEM OF STABILITY
  PHILOSOPHY AND PUBLIC AFFAIRS, 18(1) (WIN 89), 3-30.
    THE AUTHOR HERE ARGUES FOR TWO THINGS. FIRST, THAT
  WITHIN A SOCIETY IN WHICH THERE IS PLURALISM WITH RESPECT TO
  FINAL ENDS, AND SOCIETY IS PERCEIVED AS A COMMON MEANS TO
  THOSE PERSONAL ENDS, A STABLE AND HENCE TRULY EFFICIENT
  SOCIAL CONTRACT WILL BE POSSIBLE ONLY INSOFAR AS
  PARTICIPANTS CAN DEVELOP AND EFFECTIVELY EXPRESS TO ONE
  ANOTHER A COMMUNITARIAN COMMITMENT TO THEIR MUTUAL WELL-
  BEING. SECOND, THAT FOR THOSE WHO HAVE ACHIEVED SUCH A SENSE
  OF COMMUNITY, PERHAPS THE MOST EFFECTIVE WAY TO EXPRESS IT
  WILL BE TO REGULATE THEIR AFFAIRS BY REFERENCE TO RAWLS'S
  PRINCIPLE OF JUSTICE AS FAIRNESS, INTERPRETED AS AN
  EGALITARIAN-EFFICIENCY PRINCIPLE, WHILE FOR THOSE WHO SEEK
  TO DEVELOP SUCH A SENSE OF COMMUNITY, THAT SAME PRINCIPLE
  OFFERS THE MOST PROMISING PLACE TO MAKE THEIR STAND.

06121 MCCLINTOCK, C.
  THE PROSPECTS FOR DEMOCRATIC CONSOLIDATION IN A "LEAST
  LIKELY" CASE: PERU
  COMPARATIVE POLITICS, 21(2) (JAN 89), 127-148.
    ACCORDING TO CONVENITONAL SOCIAL SCIENCE WISDOM, THE
  PROSPECTS OF DEMOCRATIC CONSOLIDATION IN PERU ARE BLEAK AND
  PERU IS A "LEAST LIKELY" CASE. HOWEVER, THERE IS A FAIR
  CHANCE FOR DEMOCRATIC CONSOLIDATION IN PERU. PREVIOUS
  THEORIES ABOUT DEMOCRATIC CONSOLIDATION UNDERESTIMATE THE
  POTENTIAL FOR THE EMERGENCE OF A DEMOCRATIC POLITICAL
  CONSENSUS DESPITE ADVERSE ECONOMIC CONDITIONS AND GUERRILLA
  MOVEMENTS. IN PARTICULAR, WHEREAS PREVIOUS THEORIES PERCEIVE
  GUERRILLA ACTION EXCLUSIVELY AS A THREAT TO DEMOCRACY, UNDER
  CERTAIN CIRCUMSTANCES A GUERRILLA MOVEMENT CAN UNITE KEY
  POLITICAL ACTORS BEHIND DEMOCRACY AS THE ONLY ALTERNATIVE TO
  CIVIL WAR.

06122 MCCONNELL, M.W.
  WHY "SEPARATION" IS NOT THE KEY TO CHURCH-STATE RELATIONS
  THE CHRISTIAN CENTURY, 106(2) (JAN 89), 43-47.
    IN RECENT CHURCH-STATE CONTROVERSIES, THE IDEAL OF
  SEPARATION HAS COME INTO CONFLICT WITH THE WIDER AND MORE
  IMPORTANT IDEAL OF RELIGIOUS FREEDOM. IN THIS ARTICLE, THE
  AUTHOR REVIEWS SOME SUPREME COURT DECISIONS THAT HAVE
  GRAPPLED WITH CONSTITUTIONAL RELIGIOUS ISSUES.

06123 MCCOOL, D.
  SUBGOVERNMENTS AND THE IMPACT OF POLICY FRAGMENTATION AND
  ACCOMMODATION
  POLICY STUDIES REVIEW, 8(2) (WIN 89), 264-287.
    FOR MANY YEARS POLITICAL SCIENTISTS HAVE UTILIZED THE
  SUBGOVERNMENT MODEL OF POLICY-MAKING TO EXPLAIN CERTAIN
  TYPES OF POLICY OUTPUT. RECENTLY A NUMBER OF SCHOLARS HAVE
  ARGUED THAT THE TRADITIONAL CONCEPTUALIZATION OF
  SUBGOVERNMENTS HAS SIMPLISTIC AND INCOMPLETE. THEY VIEW
  SUBGOVERNMENTS AS A COMPLEX AND INTEGRAL PART OF THE LARGER
  POLICY-MAKING ENVIRONMENT. THIS PAPER EXAMINES THIS "NEW"
  SUBGOVERNMENT BY ANALYZING ITS ROLE IN CONTEMPORARY PUBLIC
  POLICY-MAKING. IF SUBGOVERNMENTS HAVE LOST THEIR AUTONOMY
  AND BEEN EXPOSED TO THE COMPLEX DEMANDS OF THE LARGER
  POLITICAL SYSTEM, WHAT IMPACT DOES THIS HAVE ON POLICY

OUTPUTS? RELYING UPON THE LITERATURE ON SUBGOVERNMENTS AND
THEIR PRINCIPAL COMPONENTS, THE PAPER OFFERS AN
INTERPRETATION OF HOW SUBGOVERNMENTS HAVE POTENTIALLY
EXPANDED THEIR INFLUENCE ON PUBLIC POLICY AS A RESULT OF TWO
CONTEMPORARY DEVELOPMENTS: POLICY-MAKING FRAGMENTATION AND
THE ACCOMMODATION OF POLICY OUTPUTS.

06124 MCCORD, W.
EXPLAINING THE EAST ASIAN "MIRACLE"
NATIONAL INTEREST, 16 (SUM 89), 74-82.
IN EAST AND SOUTHEAST ASIA, GROWTH IN THE SUCCESSFUL
COUNTRIES IMPROVED ONLY AFTER THEIR GOVERNMENTS ADOPTED NEW
ECONOMIC STRATEGIES: LAND REFORM (IN JAPAN, KOREA, AND
TAIWAN), FINANCIAL MEASURES TO ENCOURAGE INVESTMENT,
MECHANISMS TO HOLD DOWN INFLATION, INCENTIVES FOR LABOR-
INTENSIVE, OUTWARD-LOOKING INDUSTRIES, GOVERNMENT
INTERVENTION TO CORRECT DISTORTIONS IN FREE MARKET
OPERATIONS, AND HEAVY INVESTMENT IN EDUCATION. THEIR ANCIENT
CULTURES REMAINED ESSENTIALLY UNCHANGED THROUGH STAGNATION
AND GROWTH. THE AUTHOR HERE CONCLUDES THAT CERTAIN SOCIO-
ECONOMIC POLICIES--COMBINED WITH POLITICAL STABILITY--HAVE
PLAYED A MORE DECISIVE ROLE THAN CULTURE IN PROMOTING
MODERNIZATION. AT MOST, PRE-EXISTING CULTURAL TENDENCIES
STRESSING ACTIVISM AND SELF-DISCIPLINE MAY HAVE BEEN
"MOBILIZED" IN A NEW ECONOMIC ENVIRONMENT.

06125 MCCORKLE, G.
PROBLEMS FOR POLISARIO
MIDDLE EAST INTERNATIONAL, (358) (SEP 89), 12-13.
THE DEFECTION OF A LEADING POLISARIO MEMBER TO MOROCCO
LEAD SOME TO SPECULATE THAT THE FRONT FOR AN INDEPENDENT
SAHRAWI STATE IN THE WESTERN SAHARA WAS CRUMBLING. HOWEVER,
A CLOSER ANALYSIS REVEALS OTHERWISE. POLISARIO REMAINS
UNITED AND COMMITTED TO THE IDEAL OF COMPLETE SEPARATION
FROM MOROCCO. THE BREAKDOWN OF PEACE NEGOTIATIONS WILL MOST
LIKELY MEAN THAT HOSTILITIES WILL CONTINUE.

06126 MCCORKLE, G.
THE WESTERN SAHARA CONFLICT
MIDDLE EAST INTERNATIONAL, (361) (OCT 89), 16-17.
INTENSE FIGHTING HAS INCREASED ATTENTION ON THE ONGOING
WESTERN SAHARA-MOROCCO COFLICT. MOROCCO'S CLAIM OF HISTORIC
TIES TO THE DISPUTED REGION IS CHALLENGED BY THE POLISARIO
WHO CLAIM TO REPRESENT THE SEPARATE AND DISTINCT SAHRAWI
PEOPLE. ALTHOUGH NEGOTIATIONS DESIGNED TO ENCOURAGE A
REFERRENDUM ON NATIONAL IDENTITY HAVE BEEN UNDERWAY, IT
REMAINS UNLIKELY THAT EVEN THE BEST OF REFERRENDUMS WILL
LEAD TO A SOLUTION. MANY OBSERVERS FEEL THAT SEMI-AUTONOMY
WITHIN THE MOROCCAN STATE MAY BE THE BEST THE SAHRAWIS MAY
GET.

06127 MCCORMACK, G.
MULTI FUNCTION POLIS: JAPAN - AUSTRALIA CO - PROSPERITY?
ARENA, 86 (FAL 89), 10-18.
AT THE CORE OF THE MFP PROJECT IS THE NOTION OF
CONSTRUCTING IN AUSTRALIA A NEW CITY (TO COST AROUND $1
BILLION), A PROTOTYPE TWENTY-FIRST CENTURY CITY IN WHICH
RESIDENCE, WORK, LEISURE, HEALTH AND EDUCATION NEEDS FOR A
POPULATION OF ABOUT 100,000 PEOPLE WOULD BE MET IN A SINGLE,
INTEGRATED PHYSICAL LOCATION. THERE ARE DEEP CONTRADICTIONS
EMBEDDED IN THE MFP IDEA, BUT THIS IS NOT TO SAY IT SHOULD
BE UTTERLY REJECTED. JAPAN'S PRODUCTIVE TECHNOLOGY HAS
LIBERATING POTENTIAL AND A CLOSE AND FRIENDLY RELATIONSHIP
BETWEEN AUSTRALIA AND JAPAN CAN AND SHOULD BE DEVELOPED.
BOTH PEOPLES HAVE MUCH TO LEARN FROM EACH OTHER, AND EACH
COULD HELP THE OTHER TO DEFINE THROUGH SUCH A RELATIONSHIP A
PATH OF SELF-INTEREST, MUTUAL BENEFIT, AND SERVICE TO
HUMANITY.

06128 MCCORMICK, J.M.; MITCHELL, N.J.
HUMAN RIGHTS AND FOREIGN ASSISTANCE: AN UPDATE
SOCIAL SCIENCE QUARTERLY, 70(4) (DEC 89), 969-979.
THE COMMITMENT TO HUMAN RIGHTS GOALS IS AN EXPLICIT AND
WELL-PUBLICIZED FEATURE OF U.S. FOREIGN POLICY. U.S. HUMAN
RIGHTS POLICY PERFORMANCE IS EVALUATED BY EXAMINING THE
RELATIONSHIP BETWEEN THE DISTRIBUTION OF U.S. FOREIGN
ASSISTANCE AND THE HUMAN RIGHTS RECORDS OF RECIPIENT
COUNTRIES. THIS STUDY, IN ADDITION TO INCLUDING MORE RECENT
DATA FOR A LARGER NUMBER OF COUNTRIES, GOES BEYOND EARLIER
STUDIES BY COMPARING THE DEGREE OF HUMAN RIGHTS VIOLATIONS
BETWEEN RECIPIENTS AND NONRECIPIENTS OF U.S. AID AND BY
COMPARING THE PERFORMANCE OF THOSE COUNTRIES THAT RECEIVE A
LARGE AMOUNT OF U.S. ASSISTANCE AND THOSE THAT DO NOT. THE
CONSISTENT FINDING OF THE VARIOUS ANALYTICAL APPROACHES USED
IN THIS PAPER IS THAT STATED HUMAN RIGHTS POLICY GOALS ARE
NOT BEING ACHIEVED.

06129 MCCORMICK, R.A.; BALCH, B.J.; CALLAHAN, D.; CALLAHAN, S.;
DIONNE, E.J.; GLENDON, M.A.; MILHAVEN, A.L.; SEGERS, M.C.;
SIEGEL, F.; WILEY, J.L.
ABORTION: WHAT DOES "WEBSTER" MEAN?
COMMONWEAL, CXVI(14) (AUG 89), 425-428.
THE AUTHORS EVALUATE THE IMPACT OF THE SUPREME COURT
DECISION IN WEBSTER V. REPRODUCTIVE HEALTH SERVICES.

06130 MCCRAY, S.B.
RENEGOTIATING SOVIET FEDERALISM: GLASNOST' AND REGIONAL
AUTONOMY
PUBLIUS: THE JOURNAL OF FEDERALISM, 19(3) (SUM 89),
129-144.
THE CURRENT EXPANSION OF FREE POLITICAL ASSOCIATION
UNDER GLASNOST' HAS FOCUSED THE POLITICAL ENERGIES OF
MOBILIZED NATIONAL MOVEMENTS ON DEMANDS FOR REPUBLICAN
AUTONOMY. REFORM-MINDED ELEMENTS IN THE GORBACHEV LEADERSHIP
HAVE ENCOURAGED THESE MOVEMENTS, SEEING THEM AS
COUNTERWEIGHTS TO CENTRAL GOVERNMENTAL BUREAUCRACY.
ASPIRATIONS FOR NATIONAL STATEHOOD HAVE REACHED FULLEST
EXPRESSION IN THE BALTIC REPUBLICS, WHERE THE REPUBLICAN
PARLIAMENTS HAVE EXPRESSED OVERWHELMING SUPPORT FOR ECONOMIC
AND CULTURAL SOVEREIGNTY, BUT SUCH SENTIMENTS ARE VOICED BY
NATIONAL INTELLIGENTSIAS IN EACH REPUBLIC. MOSCOW HAS
ADOPTED A PROGRAM OF REPUBLICAN DECENTRALIZATION AS A
SOLUTION TO THE GROWING PROBLEM OF THE FEDERAL BUDGET
DEFICIT, BUT THE IMPLICATIONS OF REPUBLICAN ECONOMIC
AUTONOMY FOR THE COHESIVENESS OF THE FEDERAL UNION ARE
FUNDAMENTAL AND FAR-REACHING.

06131 MCCREA, F. B.; MARKLE, G. E.
MINUTES TO MIDNIGHT: NUCLEAR WEAPONS PROTEST IN AMERICA
SAGE PUBLICATIONS, NEWBURY PARK, CA, 1989, 240.
MCCREA AND MARKLE EXPLORE THE DYNAMICS OF SOCIAL
MOVEMENTS BEHIND ANTINUCLEAR WEAPONS CAMPAIGNS IN AMERICA --
FROM THE EARLIEST POST-WAR "BAN THE BOMB" EFFORTS TO THE ILL-
FATED FREEZE MOVEMENT OF THE 1980S. THE AUTHORS NOTE THAT
THIS SOCIAL MOVEMENT WAS THE FIRST ATTEMPT BY SCIENTISTS -AS
SCIENTISTS -- TO PROTEST THE USES OF THEIR OWN CREATION.
THEY LOCATE CONTEMPORARY PROBLEMS IN THEIR HISTORICAL
CONTEXT BY EXPLORING THE WAYS IN WHICH TRADITIONAL PACIFIST
GROUPS PROVIDED THE INFRASTRUCTURE AND DIRECTLY PRESAGED --
IN STRATEGY, TACTICS, AND ORGANIZATIONAL DILEMMAS -- THE
FREEZE MOVEMENT.

06132 MCCUAIG, K.
SOVIET WOMEN: RE-OPENING THE BOOK
COMMUNIST VIEWPOINT, 20(4) (WIN 88), 20-22.
THIS ARTICLE EXAMINES THE CURRENT POSITION OF WOMEN IN
THE SOVIET UNION, AS GLASTNOST HAS RESULTED IN THE
RECOGNITION THAT THERE IS A WOMEN'S QUESTION IN THAT COUNTRY.
IT EXAMINES THE STATUS OF THE FAMILY, WOMEN REPRESENTATION,
WORKING WOMEN AND THE STRESS OF SINGLE PARENTING. DISCUSSED
IS A MOVEMENT TOWARDS FULL TIME HOMEMAKING.

06133 MCCUBBIN, P.R.
CONSENSUS THROUGH MEDIATION: A CASE STUDY OF THE
CHESAPEAKE BAY LAND USE ROUNDTABLE AND THE CHESAPEAKE BAY
PRESERVATION ACT
JOURNAL OF LAW & POLITICS, 5(4) (SUM 89), 827-863.
THIS NOTE EXPLORES THE IMPLICATIONS OF USING A MEDIATED
POLICY DIALOGUE TO CREATE CONSENSUS FOR LEGISLATION. IT WILL
BRIEFLY DESCRIBE MEDIATION GENERALLY, RECOUNT THE
DELIBERATIONS OF THE ROUNDTABLE, RETRACE THE LEGISLATIVE
HISTORY OF THE BAY ACT, AND COMPARE AND CONTRAST IN SOME
DETAIL THE ROUNDTABLE PROCESS TO MORE TRADITIONAL MEANS OF
CREATING PUBLIC POLICY AND BUILDING A CONSENSUS FOR
LEGISLATION. THE NOTE CONCLUDES THAT MEDIATION BUILDS
CONSENSUS MORE EFFECTIVELY THAN THE TRADITIONAL LEGISLATIVE
PROCESS FOR COMPLEX AND POLITICALLY DIVISIVE PUBLIC POLICY
ISSUES.

06134 MCDONAGH, E.L.
ISSUES AND CONSTITUENCIES IN THE PROGRESSIVE ERA: HOUSE
ROLL CALL VOTING ON THE NINETEENTH AMENDMENT, 1913-1919
THE JOURNAL OF POLITICS, 51(1) (FEB 89), 119-136.
THIS PAPER EXAMINES HOUSE ROLL CALL VOTING PATTERNS ON
THE NINETEENTH AMENDMENT IN THE CONTEXT OF PROGRESSIVE ERA
LEGISLATION, PARTICULARLY PROHIBITION, IMMIGRATION, BLACK
CIVIL RIGHTS, LABOR, AND MILITARY PREPAREDNESS. THOUGH
HISTORICAL ACCOUNTS OFTEN HAVE LINKED WOMAN SUFFRAGE WITH
ARGUMENTS OF "EXPEDIENCY" RATHER THAN "RIGHTS," THIS
ANALYSIS FINDS ROLL CALL VOTING PATTERNS ON SUFFRAGE
ASSOCIATED WITH SOCIAL JUSTICE AND CIVIL RIGHTS RATHER THAN
WITH STATUS CONSISTENCY ISSUES, SUCH AS PROHIBITION AND
IMMIGRATION. IN ADDITION, IT IS ESTABLISHED THAT PARTISAN
AND REGIONAL VOTING PATTERNS ON WOMAN SUFFRAGE ARE NOT AS
EXPLANATORY AS ARE STATE-LEVEL CONSTITUENCY INFLUENCES: THE
DRAMATIC INCREASE IN HOUSE SUPPORT FOR THE NINETEENTH
AMENDMENT FROM 1915 TO 1919 IS BEST UNDERSTOOD AS A RESULT
OF THE CORRESPONDING INCREASE IN THE NUMBER OF MEMBERS
REPRESENTING STATES WITH STATE-LEVEL WOMAN SUFFRAGE. THIS
FINDING POINTS TO THE IMPORTANCE OF LINKAGES BETWEEN STATE
AND NATIONAL LEGISLATURES IN THE PROGRESSIVE ERA AS AN
EXPLANATION OF HOW RESPONSIBILITY FOR SOCIAL POLICY HAS
TRANSFERRED FROM STATE TO FEDERAL LEVELS OF GOVERNMENT.

06135 MCDONALD, A.K.
TURKEY: A BRIDGE TO THE MIDDLE EAST
AVAILABLE FROM NTIS, NO. AD-A209 190/8/GAR, MAR 31 89, 56.
TURKEY'S GEOSTRATEGIC IMPORTANCE TO THE NORTH ATLANTIC

TREATY ORGANIZATION (NATO) IS WIDELY RECOGNIZED IN THE WEST. SHARING A COMMON BORDER WITH THE SOVIET UNION AND MAINTAINING THE SECOND LARGEST STANDING ARMY IN NATO, TURKEY IS POSITIONED ASTRIDE THE MAIN SOUTHERN ROUTE OF ADVANCE INTO WESTERN EUROPE FROM THE EAST. IT IS THIS NATO ROLE THAT IS MOST OFTEN USED AS THE RATIONALE FOR UNITED STATES MILITARY AND ECONOMIC AID. OFTEN NEGLECTED IS THE CRITICAL ROLE TURKEY PLAYS AS A BARRIER TO SOVIET EXPANSION AND INFLUENCE IN THE MIDDLE EAST. RECENT IMPROVEMENT OF ECONOMIC AND DIPLOMATIC RELATIONS WITH OTHER ISLAMIC NATIONS HAS ADDED A NEW DIMENSION TO THIS EQUATION. TODAY, TURKEY IS ENJOYING THE MOST PROSPEROUS PERIOD IT HAS EXPERIENCED SINCE THE DECLINE OF THE OTTOMAN EMPIRE. SINCE 1980, RAPID ECONOMIC GROWTH HAS RESULTED IN A SIGNIFICANT INCREASE IN TRADE WITH ARAB STATES AND THIS HAS LED TO CORRESPONDING INCREASES IN CULTURAL AND DIPLOMATIC RELATIONS. INCREASED INFLUENCE CONNOTES A STRONGER VOICE IN ISSUES AFFECTING THE REGION. THE GOVERNMENT'S FOREIGN POLICY OBJECTIVES ARE A DIRECT REFLECTION OF TURKEY'S GEOGRAPHICAL LOCATION, HISTORICAL TIES, AND EXPANDING ARAB RELATIONS.

06136 MCDONALD, F.; ZIS, G.
THE EUROPEAN MONETARY SYSTEM: TOWARDS 1992 AND BEYOND
JOURNAL OF COMMON MARKET STUDIES, XXVII(3) (MAR 89), 183-202.
THE AUTHORS BEGIN WITH A BRIEF STATEMENT OF THE ACHIEVEMENTS OF THE EUROPEAN MONETARY SYSTEM (EMS), FOLLOWED BY AN ASSESSMENT OF PROPOSITIONS REGARDING THE VIABILITY OF THE SYSTEM. THE NEXT SECTION OF THE ESSAY CONSIDERS THE OBJECTIVES OF THE SYSTEM THAT HAVE YET TO BE ACHIEVED. THEN THE AUTHORS EVALUATE THE IMPLICATIONS OF THE PROJECTED ABOLITION OF ALL CAPITAL CONTROLS AND DISCUSS CURRENCY SUBSTITUTION.

06137 MCDONALD, L.
CAN THE NDP BECOME THE GREEN PARTY OF CANADA?
CANADIAN FORUM, LXVIII(784) (DEC 89), 13-14.
THE AUTHOR ARGUES THAT BOTH SOCIALISM AND CAPITALISM HAVE FAILED WITH REGARDS TO THE ENVIRONMENT. CANADA'S NEW DEMOCRATIC PARTY IS PRESENTED AS AN ENVIRONMENTALLY AWARE ALTERNATIVE TO CANADA'S CURRENT POLITICAL LEADERS. THE ARTICLE OUTLINES A STRATEGY DESIGNED TO TRANSFORM THE NDP INTO A "GREEN" PARTY, ONE THAT IS THOROUGHLY COMMITTED TO A RADICAL ENVIRONMENTAL POLICY AND USING ALL REASONABLE MEANS AT ITS DISPOSAL TO ADVANCE IT.

06138 MCDONALD, M.
A CELEBRATION OF POWER
MACLEAN'S (CANADA'S NEWS MAGAZINE), 102(5) (JAN 89), 20-22.
ALTHOUGH GEORGE BUSH ASSUMED THE PRESIDENCY IN "THE FRIENDLIEST TRANSFER OF POWER IN RECENT AMERICAN HISTORY," HE WASTED NO TIME MAKING IT CLEAR THAT THE REAGAN ERA, WITH ITS SCRIPTED HOLLYWOOD POMP AND STARK IDEOLOGICAL BATTLE LINES, HAD COME TO AN END. THE STYLE OF ADMINISTRATION IS DESTINED TO BE SIGNIFICANTLY DIFFERENT FROM THAT OF HIS PREDECESSOR, BUT WHAT THE ACTUAL SUBSTANCE WILL AMOUNT TO IS STILL UNCERTAIN IN THE EYES OF MOST OBSERVERS.

06139 MCDONALD, M.
BUSH AT THE HELM
MACLEAN'S (CANADA'S NEWS MAGAZINE), 102(6) (FEB 89), 18-19.
GEORGE BUSH TOOK STEPS TO SUBTLY, BUT SURELY, REMOLD THE ADMINISTRATION TO HIS LIKING. HE MADE IT CLEAR THAT HE INTENDS TO PLAY THE ROLE OF AN ACCESSIBLE, ACTIVIST PRESIDENT. HE ALSO BEGAN MOVING TOWARDS FULFILLMENT OF CAMPAIGN PROMISES REGARDING DRUGS, THE ENVIRONMENT, AND THE BUDGET DEFICIT. MANY OBSERVERS FEEL THAT THE HONEYMOON ON CAPITOL HILL WILL BE SHORT-LIVED BECAUSE THE POLITICAL REALITIES THAT BUSH WILL HAVE TO FACE MUST BE MET BY DIFFICULT DECISIONS, NOT CAMPAIGN RHETORIC.

06140 MCDONALD, M.
FIELDS OF FORCE
MACLEAN'S (CANADA'S NEWS MAGAZINE), 102(26) (JUL 89), 26-30.
THE ESSAY EXAMINES THE RELATIONSHIP BETWEEN THE US AND CANADA. ALTHOUGH IT IS DIFFICULT TO DETERMINE THE PHYSICAL DIFFERENCES BETWEEN THE TWO NATIONS ALONG THEIR LONG, UNDEFENDED COMMON BORDER, THERE EXISTS A DIFFERENCE OF PERCEPTION. CANADA VIEWS THE US AS A MILITARY AND ECONOMIC SUPERPOWER THAT OCCASIONALLY ACKNOWLEDGES THE EXISTENCE OF THE NEIGHBOR TO THE NORTH, BUT USUALLY ADOPTS A POLICY OF "BENIGN NEGLECT." ALTHOUGH DIFFERENCES ON TRADE AND NUCLEAR WEAPONS ARE CLEAR, THE TWO NATIONS REMAIN INEXTRICABLY LINKED BY ECONOMY, GEOGRAPHY, AND CULTURE.

06141 MCDONALD, M.
OF GUNS AND A GURU
MACLEAN'S (CANADA'S NEWS MAGAZINE), 102(13) (MAR 89), 28-29.
THE ARTICLE EXAMINES THE WHEELINGS AND DEALINGS OF GLOBE-TROTTING INDIAN GURU NAMED SHRI CHANDRA SHAMIJI MAHARAJ. THE GURU HAS ASSOCIATED WITH THE LIKES OF FERDINAND AND IMELDA MARCOS; JEAN-CLAUDE DUVALIER; BRITISH INDUSTRIALIST ROLAND

ROWLAND; SAUDI ARMS DEALER ADNAN KHASHOGGI; AND WALTER MILLER, WHO HAS BEEN NAMED AS A SECRET FINANCIER BEHIND US COVERT ARMS SHIPMENTS TO IRAN. MONEY, ARMS, AND SCANDAL HAVE FOLLOWED THE GURU AND A GROUP OF CLOSE FOLLOWERS AROUND THE GLOBE. HOWEVER, THEY HAVE NOT BEEN VISIBLE SINCE THE IRAN/CONTRA SCANDAL.

06142 MCDONALD, M.
THE NEW LOOK
MACLEAN'S (CANADA'S NEWS MAGAZINE), 102(4) (JAN 89), 26-29.
GEORGE BUSH IS OFTEN PORTRAYED AS REPRESENTING THE ESTABLISHMENT, OLD MONEY, AND BIG BUSINESS. HOWEVER, AFTER HIS MASSIVE VICTORY IN NOVEMBER IT HAS BECOME INCREASINGLY CLEAR THAT THE ONLY CLEAR THING ABOUT BUSH'S IDEOLOGY IS THAT HE HAS LITTLE OR NONE. THE NEW ERA IS FORESEEN--BARRING ANY MAJOR INTERNATIONAL CRISIS-AS A QUIET TIME OF IDEOLOGICAL DRAFT AND PRAGMATISM, OVERSHADOWED BY THE CONSTRICTING REALITY OF A PROJECTED $185-BILLION BUDGET DEFICIT.

06143 MCDONALD, R.
GREECE'S YEAR OF POLITICAL TURBULENCE
WORLD TODAY, 45(11) (NOV 89), 194-197.
AS THE PANHELLENIC SOCIALIST MOVEMENT (PASOK) BEGAN THE LAST YEAR OF ITS SECOND TERM, IT APPEARED TO HAVE AN UNASSAILABLE HOLD ON POWER. THEN, IN RAPID SUCCESSION, THE SOCIALISTS SUFFERED A SERIES OF MAJOR REVERSES. FIRST, PRIME MINISTER ANDREAS PAPANDREOU FELL GRAVELY ILL AND SPENT NEARLY SIX WEEKS IN A BRITISH HOSPITAL. HE TRIED TO GOVERN FROM HIS SICKBED, BUT THE PARTY SEEMED INEFFECTIVE WITHOUT HIM. THEN HIS AFFAIR WITH A YOUNG AIRLINE STEWARDESS BECAME PUBLIC KNOWLEDGE, LEADING TO AN ACRIMONIOUS DIVORCE. THE MOVE COST PASOK DEARLY AMONG FEMALE VOTERS WHO LOOKED UPON MRS. PAPANDREOU AS A CHAMPION OF WOMEN'S RIGHTS. FINALLY, THE OWNER OF THE BANK OF CRETE ABSCONDED TO AMERICA, LEAVING BEHIND LARGE DEBTS AND ALLEGATIONS OF CORRUPT DEALINGS WITH SENIOR GOVERNMENT OFFICIALS.

06144 MCDONALD, R.
GUARDING THE LINE
MACLEAN'S (CANADA'S NEWS MAGAZINE), 102(13) (MAR 89), 24.
UN PEACEKEEPING FORCES MARKED THEIR 25TH ANNIVERSARY OF MEDIATING BETWEEN TURKISH AND GREEK CYPRIOTS. THE ARRIVAL OF THE UN CONTINGENT TO CYPRUS 25 YEARS AGO IS CREDITED WITH PROMPTING TURKEY TO CALL OFF A THREATENED INVASION AND HAS UNDOUBTEDLY HELPED AVOID MANY CONFLICTS AND SAVE MANY LIVES SINCE THEN. HOWEVER, THE EXTENDED COST AND DURATION OF THE OPERATION HAS SOME UN MEMBERS GRUMBLING. FINLAND, IRELAND, AND SWEDEN HAVE ALREADY CUT REPRESENTATION TO THE HEADQUARTERS. HOWEVER, THE CONFLICT ON CYPRUS SEEMS NO NEARER RESOLUTION WHICH VIRTUALLY GUARANTEES THAT THE UN WILL BE AROUND FOR MANY YEARS TO COME.

06145 MCDONNELL, A.
THE 1918 GENERAL ELECTION IN ULSTER AND THE BIOGRAPHY OF A CANDIDATE, DENIS HENRY
DISSERTATION ABSTRACTS INTERNATIONAL, 49(12) (JUN 89), 3858-A.
THE DECLINING FORTUNES OF THE IRISH PARTY AND THE RISE OF SINN FEIN WERE THE MAIN THEMES IN IRISH POLITICS IN THE MONTHS BEFORE THE 1918 GENERAL ELECTION. THE SINN FEIN MOVEMENT WAS BOOSTED BY THE CULT OF DEAD LEADERS THAT GREW AFTER THE RISING, THE CONTINUATION OF MARTIAL LAW, THE FAILURE OF THE LLOYD GEORGE NEGOTIATIONS, THE DEATH OF THOMAS ASNE, AND THE NAGGING FEAR OF CONSCRIPTION. THE MOST TANGIBLE EVIDENCE OF THE GROWING SUPPORT FOR SINN FEIN CAME IN THEIR BY-ELECTION VICTORIES AT NORTH ROSCOMMON, SOUTH LONGFORD, EAST CLARE, AND KILKENNY CITY IN 1917.

06146 MCDOUGALL, D.
THE HAWKE GOVERNMENT'S POLICIES TOWARDS THE USA
ROUND TABLE, (310) (APR 89), 165-176.
THE ARTICLE EXAMINES THE RELATIONSHIP BETWEEN AUSTRALIA'S GOVERNMENT LED BY LABOR PARTY LEADER BOB HAWKE AND THE GOVERNMENT OF THE USA. IT OUTLINES VARIOUS ISSUES INCLUDING: THE NEW ZEALAND CRISIS, VARIOUS SECURITY-RELATED MATTERS, REGIONAL AND NON-REGIONAL QUESTIONS, AND TRADE. IT ALSO ANALYZES THE GENERAL DIRECTION OF THE POLICIES PURSUED BY THE LABOR GOVERNMENT TOWARDS THE REPUBLICAN REAGAN ADMINISTRATION.

06147 MCDOWALL, D.
THE KURDS: ASYLUM SEEKERS
MIDDLE EAST INTERNATIONAL, 353 (JUN 89), 14.
THE 1,400 TURKISH KURD ASYLUM SEEKERS IN GREAT BRITAIN ARE VIRTUALLY ALL ALEVI, A CENTRAL ANATOLIAN SECT OF APPROXIMATELY TWO MILLION TURKISH AND ONE MILLION KURDISH ADHERENTS. THIS ARTICLE EXAMINES WHY IT IS SO SPECIFICALLY KURDISH ALEVIS AND NOT KURDISH MUSLIMS ON TURKISH ALEVIS WHO HAVE BEEN FLEEING THEIR TERRITORY FOR "GREENER PASTURES".

06148 MCDOWELL, D.
START AND U.S. STRATEGIC FORCES
PARAMETERS, XIX(1) (MAR 89), 100-108.

THE PROSPECTIVE REDUCTIONS IN STRATEGIC OFFENSIVE ARMS
PROVIDED BY THE START TREATY WILL PERMIT SUFFICIENT US
FORCES AND FORCE FLEXIBILITY TO RETAIN A VIABLE, ROBUST
TRIAD THAT IS SURVIVABLE AND CAPABLE OF CARRYING OUT ITS
MISSION OF DETERRENCE BASED ON THE THREAT OF OFFENSIVE
RETALIATION. STRATEGIC MODERNIZATION WILL CONTINUE TO BE
NECESSARY, BUT THE PROBLEMS FACING THE UNITED STATES IN
MAINTAINING AN EFFECTIVE AND STABLE DETERRENT SHOULD BE
EASED AFTER 50-PERCENT REDUCTIONS. THE PROSPECTIVE START
TREATY EMBRACING ALL ELEMENTS OF THE US PROPOSAL, IF
CONCLUDED EARLY IN THE BUSH ADMINISTRATION, COULD SERVE AS A
BENCHMARK FOR PLANNING AND MODERNIZING US STRATEGIC FORCES,
THUS MAKING A SIGNIFICANT CONTRIBUTION TO FUTURE US SECURITY.

06149 MCDOWELL, M.A.
DEVELOPMENT AND THE ENVIRONMENT IN ASEAN
PACIFIC AFFAIRS, 62(3) (FAL 89), 307-329.
THIS ESSAY PROVIDES AN OVERVIEW OF THE ENVIRONMENTAL
ISSUE IN THE ASEAN STATES, EMPHASIZING THE INTERRELATIONSHIP
OF ECONOMIC, POLICAL, LEGAL, ADMINISTRATIVE, AND
GEOGRAPHICAL FACTORS, WITH A FOCUS ON DEFORESTATION AND THE
COMPLEX OF PROBLEMS SURROUNDING IT. A BROADER CROSS SECTION
OF ENVIRONMENTAL PROBLEMS WILL BE DISCUSSED IN A CASE STUDY
OF MALAYSIAN RESPONSES, BOTH GOVERNMENTAL AND POPULAR, TO
ENVIRONMENTAL CHALLENGES. THE PAPER EXAMINES THE ROLE OF
ASEAN ITSELF AS A VEHICLE FOR ENVIRONMENTAL MANAGEMENT, AND
THE FUTURE OF THE ENVIRONMENT IN THE CONTEXT OF THE ASIA-
PACIFIC REGIONAL ECONOMY. IT IS ARGUED THAT THE ABILITY OF
THE ASEAN STATES TO DEAL WITH ENVIRONMENTAL PROBLEMS WILL BE
AN IMPORTANT FACTOR IN DETERMINING THE SUCCESS OR FAILURE OF
THE REGION'S FUTURE DEVELOPMENT.

06150 MCDOWELL, S.D.
HEGEMONY AND INTERNATIONAL ORGANIZATIONS: A HISTORY OF
TRANSBORDER DATA FLOW RESEARCH PROGRAMMES
DISSERTATION ABSTRACTS INTERNATIONAL, 49(12) (JUN 89),
3862-A.
THIS DISSERTATION EXAMINES THE ORIGINS, DEVELOPMENT, AND
DEMISE OF TRANSBORDER DATA FLOW AS A QUESTION GUIDING POLICY
RESEARCH PROGRAMS IN INTERNATIONAL ORGANIZATIONS FROM 1975
TO 1985. IT IS ORGANIZED BY A THREE-PART HEGEMONY FRAMEWORK
THAT LINKS IDEOLOGY, THE RELATIONSHIP OF MATERIAL FORCES,
AND INSTITUTIONS. IT STUDIES PROGRAMS UTILIZED BY THE
ORGANIZATION FOR ECONOMIC COOPERATION AND DEVELOPMENT, THE
INTERGOVERNMENTAL BUREAU FOR INFORMATICS, CANADA-UNITED
STATES INTERSTATE RELATIONS, AND THE UNITED NATIONS CENTER
ON TRASNATIONAL CORPORATIONS.

06151 MCEVOY, J.
THE SOCIAL SIDE OF "EUROPE 1992"
EUROPE, (289) (SEP 89), 26-28.
THE ARTICLE EXAMINES THE DRAFT CHARTER OF BASIC SOCIAL
RIGHTS WHICH WAS PROPOSED BY THE EUROPEAN COMMISSION IN 1989.
THE CHARTER IS A RESPONSE TO FEARS THAT THE BENEFITS OF THE
EUROPEAN ECONOMIC INTEGRATION WILL BE FELT ONLY BY BUSINESS
AND WILL TAKE PLACE AT THE EXPENSE OF WORKERS. IT OUTLINES
SPECIFIC RIGHTS OF WORKERS AND OFFERS WORKERS PROTECTION
FROM SOCIAL DUMPING, OR COMPANY RELOCATION TO AREAS WHERE
SOCIAL CONDITIONS, SUCH AS WAGES, ARE LOWER. A MAJOR BARRIER
TO THE DRAFT PROPOSAL'S PASSAGE IS THE RESISTANCE OF BRITISH
PRIME MINISTER MARGARET THATCHER. LACK OF COMPROMISE ON THIS
ISSUE COULD UNDERMINE THE ENTIRE INTEGRATION EFFORT.

06152 MCFARLANE, A.
THE "REBELLION OF THE BARRIOS": URBAN INSURRECTION IN
BOURBON QUITO
HISPANIC-AMERICAN HISTORICAL REVIEW, 69(2) (MAY 89),
283-330.
THE AUTHOR RE-EXAMINES QUITO'S REBELLION OF THE BARRIOS,
INCLUDING ITS CAUSES, THE POLITICAL CULTURE SURROUNDING IT,
AND THE POPULAR DIMENSION OF THE REVOLT.

06153 MCFARLANE, D.R.
TESTING THE STATUTORY COHERENCE HYPOTHESIS: THE
IMPLEMENTATION OF FEDERAL FAMILY PLANNING POLICY IN THE
STATES
ADMINISTRATION AND SOCIETY, 20(4) (FEB 89), 395-422.
THIS ARTICLE TESTS THE STATUTORY COHERENCE HYPOTHESIS,
DERIVED FROM THE SABATIER AND MAZMANIAN FRAMEWORK FOR POLICY
IMPLEMENTATION, WITHIN THE CONTEXT OF THE NATIONAL FAMILY
PLANNING PROGRAM. THE STATUTORY COHERENCE HYPOTHESIS STATES
THAT EFFECTIVE IMPLEMENTATION IS A FUNCTION OF THE EXTENT TO
WHICH A STATUTE COHERENTLY STRUCTURES THE IMPLEMENTATION
PROCESS. THE EQUITABLE DISTRIBUTION OF STATUTORY BENEFITS IS
DEFINED AS A CONDITION OF EFFECTIVE IMPLEMENTATION. DURING
THE PERIOD OF STUDY (FISCAL YEARS 1976-1981), NATIONAL
FAMILY PLANNING POLICY WAS EMBEDDED IN FOUR SEPARATE
STATUTES. IMPLEMENTATION WAS OPERATIONALIZED IN TERMS OF
INTERSTATE VARIATION IN PER CAPITA FAMILY PLANNING
EXPENDITURES UNDER EACH OF THE FOUR GRANT PROGRAMS.
STATUTORY COHERENCE SCORES WERE DEVELOPED FOR EACH OF THE
FOUR ENACTMENTS. THE FINDINGS OF THIS STUDY SUPPORT THE
STATUTORY COHERENCE HYPOTHESIS. BOTH THE THEORETICAL
SIGNIFICANCE AND THE POLICY IMPLICATIONS OF THESE RESULTS

ARE DISCUSSED.

06154 MCFAUL, M.
RETHINKING THE "REAGAN DOCTRINE" IN ANGOLA
INTERNATIONAL SECURITY, 14(3) (WIN 89), 99-135.
PROPONENTS OF THE "REAGAN DOCTRINE" HAVE DECLARED THE
1988 PEACE SETTLEMENT BETWEEN ANGOLA, CUBA, AND SOUTH AFRICA
TO BE A DIRECT RESULT OF REAGAN'S POLICY OF ASSISTING THE
"FREEDOM FIGHTERS" IN ANGOLA. THE ARTICLE EXAMINES THIS
CLAIM AND SEEKS TO EVALUATE THE APPLICATION OF THE REAGAN
DOCTRINE TO ANGOLA IN THE CONTEXT OF OTHER LOCAL, REGIONAL,
AND INTERNATIONAL FACTORS AFFECTING THE COURSE OF EVENTS
THERE. THESE OTHER VARIABLES INCLUDE: CHANGES AND
CONTINUITIES IN THE ANGOLAN GOVERNMENT'S APPROACH TO
NEGOTIATIONS, THE IMPACT OF "NEW THINKING" IN THE SOVIET
UNION, AND THE IMPORTANCE OF RECENT SHIFTS IN THE MILITARY
BALANCE IN SOUTHERN AFRICA. THE ARTICLE CONCLUDES THAT THE
SETTLEMENT BETWEEN ANGOLA, CUBA, AND SOUTH AFRICA, WAS
ACHIEVED DESPITE, NOT BECAUSE OF, THE REAGAN DOCTRINE.

06155 MCGEE CROTTY, P.
ASSESSING THE ROLE OF FEDERAL ADMINISTRATIVE REGIONS: AN
EXPLORATORY ANALYSIS
PUBLIC ADMINISTRATION REVIEW, 48(2) (MAR 88), 642-648.
THIS ARTICLE EXPLORES THE RELATIONSHIP BETWEEN THE
NATIONAL AND STATE GOVERNMENTS WHICH IS DEFINED AS
PERMISSIVE, MANAGERIAL, AND REGULATORY, THIS STUDY
CONCENTRATES ON THE CHALLENGE FACED BY NATIONAL AGENCIES IN
COORDINATING INTERGOVERNMENTAL POLICIES AND PROPOSES A
GENERAL FRAMEWORK TO MEASURE THE IMPACT THAT FEDERAL
ADMINISTRATIVE REGIONS HAVE ON POLICY IMPLEMENTION BY THE
STATES.

06156 MCGIFFERT,C.; GOODMAN, E.; GOODMAN, M.
GORBACHEV'S "NEW DIRECTIONS" IN AISA
JOURNAL OF NORTHEAST ASIAN STUDIES, VIII(3) (FAL 89), 3-24.
THE GORBACHEV REGIME HAS MADE A DRAMATIC ATTEMPT TO
ALTER THE POLITICAL ENVIRONMENT FOR SOVIET POLICY IN ASIA
AND TO SHIFT REGIONAL PERCEPTIONS IN ITS FAVOR. AS ELSEWHERE,
THE MAJOR COMPONENTS OF THIS NEW APPROACH ARE THE
DOWNPLAYING OF THE UTILITY OF MILITARY INSTRUMENTS OF POWER,
AN EMPHASIS ON THE PEACEFUL RESOLUTION OF REGIONAL DISPUTES,
A DEEMPHASIZING OF THE ROLE OF IDEOLOGY, AND A STEPPED-UP
EFFORT TO PURSUE RELATIONS WITH REGIONAL STATES THROUGH
TRADITIONAL DIPLOMACY. THE VARIOUS ELEMENTS OF "NEW
THINKING" AS APPLIED TO ASIA HAVE CONTRIBUTED TO IMPROVED
SOVIET RELATIONS WITH CHINA, SOUTH KOREA, AND SEVERAL NON-
COMMUNIST STATES OF SOUTHEAST ASIA, AND CREATED AN
OPPORTUNITY FOR IMPROVED RELATIONS WITH JAPAN.

06157 MCGILL, W.D.
GUATEMALAN COUNTERINSURGENCY STRATEGY
AVAILABLE FROM NTIS, NO. AD-A208 050/5/GAR, MAR 89, 39.
FOR MORE THAN TWO DECADES, THE GOVERNMENT OF ANOTHER
CENTRAL AMERICAN COUNTRY, GUATEMALA, HAS BEEN FIGHTING AN
INSURGENCY. IN THE LATE 1960S AND EARLY 1970S, WITH SOME
ASSISTANCE FROM THE UNITED STATES, GUATEMALA WAS ABLE TO
QUASH THE INSURGENTS. HOWEVER, THE INSURGENCY REKINDLED IN
THE MID 1970S. YET, EVEN WHILE THE INSURGENCY GAINED
STRENGTH, IN 1977 THE GOVERNMENT OF GUATEMALA REJECTED
FURTHER UNITED STATES AID BECAUSE IT CONSIDERED PRESIDENT
CARTER'S DEMANDS TO IMPROVE HUMAN RIGHTS TO BE MEDDLING IN
THE COUNTRY'S INTERNAL AFFAIRS. BECAUSE THE GUATEMALAN
GOVERNMENT HAS ABLE TO EFFECTIVELY COUNTER THE INSURGENCY
WITH LITTLE OUTSIDE AID, THIS STUDY REVIEWS THE POLITICAL,
SOCIAL AND ECONOMIC EVENTS AROUND WHICH THE INSURGENCY
DEVELOPED, EXAMINES THE GUATEMALAN STRATEGY TO COUNTER THE
INSURGENCY, AND RECOMMENDS THE STRATEGIES THAT OTHERS MIGHT
USE TO COUNTER FUTURE INSURGENCIES.

06158 MCGILLIVRAY, M.
THE ALLOCATION OF AID AMONG DEVELOPING COUNTRIES: A MULTI-
DONOR ANALYSIS USING A PER CAPITA AID INDEX
WORLD DEVELOPMENT, 17(4) (APR 89), 561-568.
THIS PAPER SEEKS TO MEASURE THE RELATIVE AID GIVING
PERFORMANCE OF AID DONORS IN TERMS OF INTER-RECIPIENT
DISTRIBUTION OF THEIR AID. "PERFORMANCE" IS TAKEN TO BE THE
EXTENT TO WHICH A DONOR BASES ITS AID ALLOCATION ON THE
RELATIVE NEEDS OF RECIPIENT COUNTRIES. DONOR PERFORMANCE IS
MEASURED BY AN INCOME-WEIGHTED PER CAPITA AID INDEX,
FORMULATED IN THIS PAPER. THIS INDEX WAS CALCULATED USING
THE PER CAPITA ALLOCATIONS TO A SAMPLE OF 85 RECIPIENT
COUNTRIES IN THE YEARS 1969-84. THE PERFORMANCE OF 17 DAC
MEMBERS, PLUS THAT OF A NUMBER OF MULTILATERAL AGENCIES, AND
THAT OF THE DAC AND THESE AGENCIES COMBINED IS IDENTIFIED.
RESULTS INDICATE THAT THE PERFORMANCE OF FOUR COUNTRIES -
BELGIUM, FINLAND, DENMARK AND NORWAY - HAS GENERALLY
SUPERIOR TO THAT OF OTHER DONORS.

06159 MCGINNIS, M.D.; WILLIAMS, J.T.
CHANGE AND STABILITY IN SUPERPOWER RIVALRY
AMERICAN POLITICAL SCIENCE REVIEW, 83(4) (DEC 89),
1101-1124.
THE AUTHORS INVESTIGATE THE DYNAMICS OF SUPERPOWER

RIVALRY. PARTICIPANTS IN POLICY DEBATES WITHIN EACH STATE USE INFORMATION ABOUT EXPECTED FUTURE THREATS AND ECONOMIC COSTS TO INFLUENCE OTHER POLICY ACTORS, AND THIS PROCESS OF SOPHISTICATED REACTION LINKS THE SECURITY POLICIES OF THESE TWO STATES INTO A SINGLE RIVALRY SYSTEM. ANALYSIS OF VECTOR AUTOREGRESSION MODELS OF U.S. AND SOVIET MILITARY EXPENDITURES AND DIPLOMATIC HOSTILITY AND U.S. GROSS NATIONAL PRODUCT SUPPORTS THE HYPOTHESIS THAT THESE POLICIES APPROXIMATE THE BEHAVIOR OF UNITARY RATIONAL STATES CAPABLE OF FORMING RATIONAL EXPECTATIONS OF EACH OTHER'S FUTURE BEHAVIOR. THE DYNAMIC RESPONSE OF THIS SYSTEM TO A WIDE RANGE OF EXOGENOUS SHOCKS (OR INNOVATIONS) REVEALS THE UNDERLYING STABILITY OF THIS RIVALRY SYSTEM. THE MILITARY EXPENDITURES OF BOTH STATES EXHIBIT A CYCLICAL RESPONSE TO INNOVATIONS, WITH A SHORTER U.S. CYCLE. THIS LACK OF SYNCHRONIZATION CREATES SEVERAL PROBLEMS FOR ANALYSIS AND FOR POLICY CHANGE.

06160 MCGLINN, T.
SDI: THE CLOUDED VISION
JOURNAL OF LEGISLATION, 15(2) (1989), 151-170.
THE ARTICLE GIVES AN OVERVIEW ON SDI AND THE HISTORY OF BALLISTIC MISSILE DEFENSES. IT ALSO EXPLORES THE TECHNICAL ASPECTS OF SDI INCLUDING DIRECTED ENERGY WEAPONS, SPACEBASED INTERCEPTORS, AND COMMAND, CONTROL, AND COMMUNICATIONS FEATURES OF THE PROPOSED SYSTEMS. IT ALSO EXPLORES THE POLITICAL SUPPORT THAT SDI ENJOYS, MUCH OF WHICH IS BASED ON FALSE OR BIASED ASSUMPTIONS. IT CONCLUDES THAT SDI ENJOYS LITTLE PRACTICAL UTILITY AND FULL DEPLOYMENT WOULD BE A COSTLY MISTAKE.

06161 MCGOUGH, M.
THE LEFEBVRITE-FEMINIST COALITION?
AMERICAN SPECTATOR, (AUG 89), 28-29.
THIS ARTICLE EXAMINES THE AUTHENTICITY OF ORDINATION OF PRIESTS AND BISHOPS IN THE CATHOLIC CHURCH. IT DISCUSSES THE RAMIFICATIONS OF ORDINATIONS OF WOMEN BY THE ANGLICAN CHURCH AS WELL AS BY EXCOMMUNICATED MARCEL LEFEBVRE OF FOUR BISHOPS FOR HIS BREAKAWAY CHURCH. IT DISCUSSES THE DEBATE OVER THE TRADITIONAL APOSTIOLIC SUCCESSION AND A MORE UP TO DATE METHOD OF ORDAINING MINISTERS.

06162 MCGOVERN, A.F.
LIBERATION THEOLOGY ADAPTS AND ENDURES
COMMONWEAL, (CXVI 19) (NOV 89), 587-590.
LIBERATION THEOLOGY HAS PROFOUNDLY AFFECTED THE LIFE OF THE CHURCH IN LATIN AMERICA, EVEN THOUGH THE POLITICAL INVOLVEMENT OF THE CHURCH REMAINS CONTROVERSIAL. LATIN AMERICAN LIBERATION THEOLOGY GREW OUT OF THE SAME HISTORICAL CONTEXT BUT THEY HAVE DIFFERENT PERSPECTIVES ON ISSUES AND SOLUTIONS.

06163 MCGOWAN, R. A.
BUSINESS, POLITICS, AND CIGARETTES: AN ANALYSIS OF PUBLIC POLICY INTERVENTION ON CIGARETTE SALES
DISSERTATION ABSTRACTS INTERNATIONAL, 49(9) (MAR 89), 2727-A.
THE AMERICAN CIGARETTE INDUSTRY IS FACING A THIRD WAVE OF REGULATION, SPARKED BY THE PASSIVE SMOKING ISSUE. THE PROPOSED RESTRICTIONS ARE THOSE EMPLOYED IN THE PREVIOUS WAVES OF REGULATION: ADVERTISING BANS, SMOKING BANS, AND EXCISE TAX INCREASES. BUT THE CURRENT PROPOSALS ARE MUCH MORE SEVERE THAN THOSE PREVIOUSLY ENACTED AT THE FEDERAL LEVEL AND ARE BEING SUPPORTED AT LOCAL, STATE, AND NATIONAL LEVELS OF GOVERNMENT.

06164 MCGRATH, A.
ABORTION RIGHTS IN CANADA
COMMUNIST VIEWPOINT, 21(1) (SPR 89), 1-2.
THIS ARTICLE SUMMARIZES THE STATUS OF THE ABORTION DEBATE IN CANADA. IT DETERMINES THAT IT SEEMS CERTAIN THAT THE FEDERAL GOVERNMENT WILL CONTINUE IN ATTEMPTS TO 'RESOLVE" THE ISSUE THROUGH SOME FORM OF RESTRICTIVE LEGISLATION. IT EXAMINES THE GROWING MILITANCY IN THE ANTI-CHOICE FORCES. IT DETAILS THE NEED FOR A CONTINUING TWOFOLD STRATEGY OF THE MOVEMENT FOR REPRODUCTIVE CHOICE.

06165 MCGREGOR, E. B.
THE PUBLIC SECTOR HUMAN RESOURCE PUZZLE: STRATEGIC MANAGEMENT OF A STRATEGIC RESOURCE
PUBLIC ADMINISTRATION REVIEW, 48(6) (NOV 88), 941-950.
THIS ARTICLE EXAMINES THE GROWING AWARENESS OF THE STRATEGIC ROLE OF HUMAN RESOURCES IN POST. INDUSTRIAL SOCIETIES AND ORGANIGATIONS. ALSO, THE RESOURCE ITSELF AND THE PRACTICES WHICH MANAGE THAT RESOURCE WHICH HAS BECOME PIVOTAL TO THE SUCCESS OF MANY PUBLIC SECTOR ENTERPRISES IS EXPLORED.

06166 MCGREGOR, J.
ECONOMIC REFORM AND PUBLIC OPINION
SOVIET STUDIES, XLI(2) (APR 89), 215-227.
PUBLIC SUPPORT FOR REFORM MEASURES PLAYS A CENTRAL ROLE IN THE LIKELIHOOD OF THEIR SUCCESS AND CENTRALLY-DIRECTED ECONOMIES SUCH AS POLAND'S ARE NO EXCEPTION TO THIS PRINCIPLE THE PAPER USES OFFICIAL PUBLIC OPINION POLLS PUBLISHED BETWEEN 1983 AND 1988 TO EXAMINE THE ATTIDUNAL ENVIRONMENT IN WHICH POLAND'S REFORM PLANNERS MUST OPERATE. IT CONCLUDES THAT THE DATA INDICATES THAT THE POLISH GOVERNMENT MUST ATTEMPT TO IMPLEMENT ITS PLAN IN A NEAR-HOSTILE ENVIRONMENT AND THAT THE LIKELIHOOD OF SUCCESS IS DIMINISHED EVEN FARTHER THAN IS INDICATED BY THE MASSIVE "OBJECTIVE" OBSTACLES THAT IT CONFRONTS.

06167 MCGUIRE, P.
INSTRUMENTAL CLASS POWER AND THE ORIGIN OF CLASS-BASED STATE REGULATION IN THE U.S. ELECTRIC UTILITY INDUSTRY
CRITICAL SOCIOLOGY, 16(2-3) (SUM 89), 181-203.
THIS PAPER ANALYZES THE CREATION OF STATE GOVERNMENTREGULATED ELECTRIC UTILITIES IN THE UNITED STATES BEFORE 1915. ANALYZING HOW CLASS ACTORS REACTIVELY MOBILIZED POWER, CREATED POLICY, AND DIRECTLY AND INDIRECTLY INFLUENCED STATES TO CREATE A CLASSBIASED REGULATORY STRUCTURE AND UNDERMINE PUBLIC OWNERSHIP, THE AUTHOR ARGUES THE NEED FOR A MODIFIED INSTRUMENTALIST THEORY OF THE STATE, WHICH HE CALLS THE THEORY OF INSTRUMENTAL CLASS POWER. THE STUDY DEMONSTRATES THAT CLASS POWER: (1) CAN BE CREATED OUTSIDE OF THE STATE; (2) IS A REACTION TO CLASS CHALLENGE AND NOT NECESSARILY AN ATTEMPT TO RATIONALIZE THE ECONOMY; AND (3) CAN BE EXERCISED AT VARIOUS LEVELS OF THE U.S. FEDERALIST STATE SYSTEM.

06168 MCGURK, J.J.N.
THE SIEGE, DEFENCE AND RELIEF OF DERRY: APRIL - JULY 1689
CONTEMPORARY REVIEW, 254(1481) (JUN 89), 304-312.
THE SIEGE, DEFENCE AND RELIEF OF DERRY WOULD BECOME THE GREAT EPIC OF PROTESTANT HISTORY, FOLK-LORE AND MYTHOLOGY IN WHICH, TIME, AND THE RE-TELLING IN SONG AND STORY, WOULD IRON OUT THE CONTRADICTIONS, SIMPLIFY A COMPLEX SERIES OF EPISODES AND LEAVE A HEIGHTENED DRAMATIC VERSION OF EVENTS REMOTE FROM ACTUALITY. IN ORANGE TRADITION IT IS OF COURSE DERRY'S WALLS, NOT LONDONDERRY'S THAT BECAME THE SYMBOL OF THE 'NO SURRENDER'. TO UNDERSTAND WHY THERE WAS A SIEGE THERE IN THE SUMMER OF 1689 IN THE FIRST PLACE AND ITS HISTORICAL SIGNIFICANCE IN THE SECOND PLACE THIS ARTICLE LOOKS AT THE BACKGROUND TO THE EVENTS AND PLACES THEM IN THEIR PROPER CONTEXT.

06169 MCGURK, J.N.N.
BI-CENTENARY REFLECTIONS: THE FRENCH REVOLUTION AND IRELAND
CONTEMPORARY REVIEW, 255(1483) (AUG 89), 84-91.
THE DRAMATIC EVENTS WHICH UNFOLDED IN FRANCE FROM 1789 UNTIL THE END OF THE CENTURY AND THE FERMENT OF IDEAS WHICH PRECEEDED AND ACCOMPANIED THEM ARE COLLECTIVELY CALLED THE FRENCH REVOLUTION. IN IRELAND THE IMPETUS FROM FRENCH REVOLUTIONARY IDEAS WOULD EVENTUALLY BRING DIRECTION TO REVOLUTIONARY AND REPUBLICAN ENDS. THIS ARTICLE EXPLORES THE RADICAL AGITATION FOR REFORM IN IRELAND AND FOLLOWS ACTIVITIES OF YOUNG DUBLIN PROTESTANT BARRISTER, THEOBALD WOLFE TONE WHO BECAME MOUTHPIECE OF IRISH ASPIRATIONS AND THE CATALYST OF POLITICAL AND MILITARY ACTION.

06170 MCGURN, W.
ABORTION: THE POLITICS: WHAT PEOPLE REALLY SAY
NATIONAL REVIEW, 61(24) (DEC 89), 26-29.
THIS ARTICLE CONTENDS THAT THE MAJORITY OF AMERICAN VOTERS ARE OPPOSED TO "ABORTION ON DEMAND," MR. MCGURN, THE WRITER, FEELS THAT THE GOP WOULD BE INVIGORATED BY TAKING A PRINCIPLED STAND ON THE QUESTION. HE ARGUES THAT NOTHING HAS BEEN TRANSCRIBED ON THE MATTER OF WILL OF THE AMERICAN PEOPLE, AND THAT MOST AMERICANS WOULD LOOK ASKANCE AT A CANDIDATE WHO OPPOSED GIVING AMERICAN WOMEN THE SAME EXTENSIVE INFORMATION ABOUT ABORTION THAT THEY CAN GET ON EVERY OTHER OPERATION.

06171 MCGURN, W.
ADVANCE AUSTRALIA FAIR
NATIONAL REVIEW, XLI(17) (SEP 89), 45.
CURRENT SENTIMENT IN AUSTRALIA IS THAT THE NEW WAVE OF NON-EUROPEAN IMMIGRANT THREATENS THE "AUSTRALIAN WAY OF LIFE. " THIS SIGNIFIES A CHANGE IN AUSTRALIA'S POLICY OF MULTICULTURALISM, AT A TIME WHEN AUSTRALIA IS BENEFITING MOST FROM THE MORAL AND ECONOMIC DYNAMISM THE ASEANS BRING. THE FAILURE TO DEFINE MULTICULTURALISM HAS MEANT THAT THE SCAMS IT HAS SPAWNED HAVE BECOME LINKED UNTS IMMIGRATION ITSELF. RESOLUTION OF THIS DILEMMA IS THE PROJECT FOR THE CURRENT ADMINISTRATION.

06172 MCGURN, W.
CUTTING THE CORD IN HONDURAS
NATIONAL REVIEW, XLI(18) (SEP 89), 22-23.
UNITED STATES' FAILURE TO SUPPORT THE CONTRAS TODAY GUARANTEES GREATER REGIONAL INSTABILITY IN CENTRAL AMERICA IN THE FUTURE, TO THE POINT WHERE ANOTHER U.S. ADMINISTRATION MIGHT HAVE NO CHOICE BUT TO SEND IN TROOPS.

06173 MCGURN, W.
DRUG CZAR IN SEARCH OF A THRONE
NATIONAL REVIEW, XLI(11) (JUN 89), 22-24.

THERE HAS BEEN AN IMMENSE AMOUNT OF DEBATE ON THE
NATION'S DRUG PROBLEMS: MANY SOLUTIONS TO THE PROBLEM HAVE
BEEN PROPOSED AND MANY FINGERS HAVE BEEN POINTED IN BLAME AT
VARIOUS POSSIBLE CAUSES OF THE PROBLEM. WILLIAM BENNETT THE
DIRECTOR OF THE OFFICE OF NATIONAL DRUG CONTROL POLICY,
BLAMES GOVERNMENT HESITANCY AND ITS FAILURE TO BACK UP
SOCIETAL STATEMENTS THAT DRUG USE WAS WRONG AS A KEY FACTOR
IN THE PROLIFERATION OF THE PROBLEM. HE ADVOCATES HOLDING
THE MORAL LINE AND ENCOURAGING AMERICAN INSTITUTIONS: THE
FAMILY, CHURCH, AND SCHOOL TO STAND UP AND FIGHT AGAINST THE
PROBLEM AS THE OPTIMAL SOLUTION.

06174 MCGURN, W.
EXIT STAGE WRIGHT
NATIONAL REVIEW. XLI(12) (JUN 89), 23.
THE ACCUSATORY SPOTLIGHT HAS BEEN TURNED ON CONGRESS
ITSELF, AND IT FINDS HOUSE DEMOCRATS SCURRYING FOR THE
CORNERS WITH ALL THE GRACE OF COCKROACHES CAUGHT HAVING A
MIDNIGHT SNACK ON THE KITCHEN COUNTER. AS THE GUN WRIGHT
AFFAIR DEMONSTRATES, THE FORM OF JUSTICE NOW RACING THROUGH
THE CORRIDORS OF CONGRESS IS STREET JUSTICE: ALWAYS HARSH,
FREQUENTLY TARNISHED, BUT USUALLY WELL DESERVED.

06175 MCGURN, W.
GUESS WHO'S (NOT) COMING TO DINNER?
NATIONAL REVIEW, XLI(16) (SEP 89), 18-19.
WHEN THE SENATE JUDICIARY COMMITTEE REFUSED TO ENDORSE
WILLIAM LUCAS AS ASSISTANT ATTORNEY GENERAL FOR CIVIL RIGHTS
IT DID SO BECAUSE HE WAS A THREAT TO THE DEMOCRATIC AND
BLACK-ESTABLISHMENT AGENDA. HAD THE WHITE HOUSE UNDERSTOOD
THIS, IT WOULD NOT HAVE LABELED LUCAS' DEFEAT AS RACISM.

06176 MCGURN, W.
HIGH NOON FOR NEWT
NATIONAL REVIEW, XLI(15) (AUG 89), 21-23.
NEWT GINGRICH, THE NEW CONSERVATIVE HOUSE HERO HAS TAKEN
ANY NUMBER OF POSITIONS THAT GIVE MOST CONSERVATIVES PAUSE,
PARTICULARLY BUT NOT EXCLUSIVELY IN THE AREA OF FREE TRADE.
WHETHER HE SURVIVES THE SCRUTINY OF HIS OWN ALLIES WILL BE A
GOOD TEST OF WHETHER CONSERVATISM HAS GOTTEN OVER ITS
DESTRUCTIVE TENDENCY TO INSIST ON 100 PER CENT PURITY, WHICH
EFFECTIVELY MAKES A "GOVERNING CONSERVATISM" IMPOSSIBLE.

06177 MCGURN, W.
LOSING WELL IS THE BEST REVENGE
NATIONAL REVIEW, 61(23) (DEC 89), 16.
THIS ARTICLE ANALYSES SOME OF THE REASONS THAT SOME
REPUBLICAN CANDIDATES LOST IN THE '89 ELECTIONS. IT EXAMINES
HOW A CANDIDATE'S POSITION ON ABORTION AND RIGHT TO LIFE
AFFECTED THE ELECTION RESULTS AND POSTULATES THAT LOSING
WELL IS THE BEST REVENGE, LOSING WOULDN'T BE SO BAD IF THE
GOP HAD STOOD FOR IDEALOGY RATHER THAN COMPETENCE.

06178 MCGURN, W.
NO ROOM AT THE INN
NATIONAL REVIEW, XLI(12) (JUN 89), 26.
THE VERY ORGANIZATION SET UP TO LOOK OUT FOR REFUGEE
RIGHTS IS NOW GIVING ITS IMPRIMATUR TO EFFORTS TO CUT BACK
ON ASYLUM. THE UNHCR ARGUES THAT THE GOVERNMENTS ARE GOING
TO DO THIS ANYWAY AND THAT IT IS BETTER FOR THE COMMISSION
TO HAVE SOME INFLUENCE RATHER THAN BE SHUT OUT ALTOGETHER.
THIS ARGUMENT WOULD BE MORE PERSUASIVE IF THE UNHCR COULD
SHOW HOW WELL ITS INFLUENCE WORKED IN THE PAST. FOR THIS IS
THE SAME ORGANIZATION THAT "SOLVED" THE THAILAND PUSH-OFF
PROBLEM BY SIGNING AWAY THE RIGHT OF RESETTLEMENT FOR
REFUGEES ARRIVING IN THAILAND AFTER JANUARY 1988.

06179 MCGURN, W.
THAT MEMO
NATIONAL REVIEW, 110(21) (NOV 89), 22-23.
THIS ARTICLE DEALS WITH A MEMO ON TOM FOLEY, THE MAN WHO
SEEMED MOST LIKELY TO BECOME SPEAKER OF THE HOUSE AFTER JIM
WRIGHT. THE MEMO GREW OUT OF A CONCERN THAT EVEN THOUGH THE
DEMOCRATS WERE PUTTING IN A MORE LIBERAL LEADERSHIP THEY
WERE BEING HAILED AS MORE MODERATE. IT EXPLORES THE
CIRCUMSTANCES UNDER WHICH THE MEMO WAS RELEASED AND THE
RESPONSES TO IT.

06180 MCGURN, W.
THE DODD DOCTRINE
NATIONAL REVIEW, XLI(17) (SEP 89), 27-28.
THE AUTHOR DESCRIBES WHAT MIGHT BE THE FINAL TRAGEDY OF
NICARAGUAN RESISTANCE - DEFEATED NOT BY THE SANDINISTAS ON
THE BATTLEFIELD BUT BY THE DEMOCRATS IN THE AMERICAN
CONGRESS. THE "BI-PARTISAN" AID PACKAGE EFFECTIVELY SANK THE
CONTRAS - DEMOCRATIC LEADERS IN KEY POSITIVE PROUDLY BOAST
PERFECT ANTI-CONTRA RECORDS.

06181 MCGURN, W.
WASHINGTON SHOWS SOLIDARITY
NATIONAL REVIEW, 61(20) (OCT 89), 24-25.
THE AUTHOR ASKS, "WHY DO DEMOCRATS THINK BAILING OUT
POLISH STATE INDUSTRIES IS ANTI-COMMUNIST?" AS HE REPORTS ON
US INVOLVEMENT WITH THE NEW POLISH SOLIDARITY GOVERNMENT.

THE ARTICLE EXPLORES PARTY SUPPORT AND OPPOSITION TO HELP TO
POLAND.

06182 MCILHAIN, J.
REGIONAL APPROACHES GAINING GROUND
AMERICAN CITY AND COUNTY, 104(8) (AUG 89), 38-41.
JOINT VENTURES BETWEEN UNITS OF LOCAL GOVERNMENTS OR
BETWEEN LOCAL GOVERNMENTS AND BUSINESS GROUPS ARE POPPING UP
ALL OVER THE UNITED STATES, AS AMERICAN CITIES AND COUNTRIES
TRY TO GRAPPLE WITH COMPLEX PROBLEMS. WHILE NOT READY TO
GIVE UP THEIR RESPECTIVE BAILIWICKS AND COMPLETELY COMBINE
FORCES, MANY LOCAL GOVERNMENTS ARE DISCUSSING OR ARE
ACTIVELY INVOLVED IN JOINT VENTURES. THE SQUEEZE IMPOSED ON
LOCAL GOVERNMENTS BY THE REAGAN ADMINISTRATION'S DRASTIC
CUTBACKS IN FEDERAL AID IS THE PRIMARY MOTIVATION FOR THESE
NEW JOINT VENTURES.

06183 MCINTOSH, J.
BACKPACK SOCIALISM
REASON, 21(2) (JUN 89), 40-41.
IN MARCH 1989, BERNARD SANDERS OF BURLINGTON, VERMONT,
THE NATION'S ONLY ADMITTED SOCIALIST MAYOR, LEFT OFFICE
AFTER DECLINING TO SEEK A FIFTH TERM. SANDERS CLAIMS HIS
POLICIES MADE BURLINGTON THRIVE, BUT OPPONENTS SAY THAT THE
CITY PROSPERED IN SPITE OF HIM AND THAT BURLINGTON'S
ECONOMIC SUCCESS WAS DUE MORE TO REAGANOMICS AND INCREASED
DEFENSE SPENDING THAN TO LOCAL LEADERSHIP.

06184 MCINTOSH, M.K.
AUSTRALIA AND THE UNITED STATES: PARTNERS IN DEFENCE
NATO'S SIXTEEN NATIONS, 34(6) (OCT 89), 6-7 (SPECIAL
SECTION).
AUSTRALIA REGARDS THE UNITED STATES AS ITS MOST
IMPORTANT ALLY BUT RECOGNIZES THAT IT MUST HAVE THE CAPACITY
TO DEFEND ITSELF WITH ITS OWN RESOUREECES WITHIN THE
FRAMEWORK OF ITS ALLIANCES WITH THE USA AND OTHER COUNTRIES.
AUSTRALIA'S ALLIANCE WITH THE USA ALLOWS IT TO PURSUE A
POLICY OF SELF-RELIANCE BY SHARING INTELLIGENCE INFORMATION,
ACCESS TO ADVANCED TECHNOLOGY, THE EXCHANGE OF PERSONNEL,
AND RECEIPT OF PREFERRED BUYER OF MILITARY EQUIPMENT STATUS.
COLLABORATIVE ARRANGEMENTS, ESPECIALLY WITH THE USA, AND
ACCESS TO MILITARY TECHNOLOGY ARE ESSENTIAL ELEMENTS IN
ACHIEVING AUSTRALIA'S GOAL OF SELF-RELIANT DEFENCE.

06185 MCINTYRE, R.
ECONOMIC CHANGE IN EASTERN EUROPE: OTHER PATHS TO
SOCIALIST CONSTRUCTION
SCIENCE AND SOCIETY, 53(1) (SPR 89), 5-28.
WESTERN OBSERVERS GENERALLY POINT TO HUNGARY AND ITS NEW
ECONOMIC MECHANISM AS PROOF OF THE IMMUTABILITY OF
SOVIETTYPE ECONOMIC INSTITUTIONS. THEY ARGUE THAT IT IS ONLY
WHEN HUNGARY MOVED AWAY FROM CENTRALIZATION AND SOVIET STYLE
ECONOMICS THAT IT WAS ABLE TO SUSTAIN ECONOMIC GROWTH. THEY
ARGUE THAT RECENT CHANGES IN THE USSR BEAR OUT THE CLAIM.
THE ARTICLE LOOKS AT THE EXPERIENCE OF BULGARIA AND THE
GERMAN DEMOCRATIC REPUBLIC WHO HAVE ALSO ENJOYED SIGNIFICANT
ECONOMIC PROGRESS, BUT HAVE ACHIEVED IT THROUGH THE ADOPTION
OF TACTICS NEARLY THE OPPOSITE OF HUNGARY'S. THE AUTHOR
ARGUES THAT THE EXPERIENCE OF THESE OTHER EUROPEAN ECONOMIES
HOLDS MUCH MORE INTERESTING LESSONS FOR SOVIET REFORMERS AND
FOR ANYONE CONCERNED WITH DETERMINING THE RANGE OF FEASIBLE
SOCIALIST INSTITUTIONAL EVOLUTION.

06186 MCINTYRE, R.
ECONOMIC RHETORIC AND INDUSTRIAL DECLINE
JOURNAL OF ECONOMIC ISSUES, XXIII(2) (JUN 89), 483-491.
IN THIS ARTICLE THE AUTHOR CONSIDERS THE RECENT DEBATE
OVER INDUSTRIAL POLICY IN THE UNITED STATES. BOTH SIDES IN
THIS DEBATE WERE INTERESTED IN INFLUENCING THE "KING"--THE
NON-ECONOMISTS WHO WOULD EVENTUALLY MAKE POLICY. ONE SIDE
THOUGHT THAT INFLUENCE OVER THE KING COULD BE MADE TO DEPEND
ON MEMBERSHIP IN THE "PRIESTHOOD"-THE OFFICIALLY SANCTIONED
ECONOMICS ESTABLISHMENT. THUS THE OPPONENTS OF INDUSTRIAL
POLICY ARGUED THAT THE PRO-INDUSTRIAL POLICY FORCES WERE
UNQUALIFIED TO PASS JUDGMENT ON THE ISSUES AT HAND. THIS
DEBATE, WHILE OSTENSIBLY ABOUT THE INTERPRETATION OF A GIVEN
REALITY, WAS JUST AS MUCH ABOUT WHO GETS TO DEFINE THAT
REALITY. THE AUTHOR DOCUMENTS THIS ASSERTION THROUGH A CLOSE
READING OF THE TEXTS OF THE NEO-KEYNESIAN CRITICS OF
INDUSTRIAL POLICY.

06187 MCIVOR, C.
MNR BANDITS TERRORISE NORTH EAST ZIMBABWE
NEW AFRICAN, 263 (AUG 89), 20.
THIS IS A REPORT ON THE NORTH EAST FARMING AREA OF
ZIMBABWE WHERE MNR BANDITS CONTINUE TO WAGE WAR AGAINST
CIVILIAN TARGETS. THE INHABITANTS SUFFER CONTINUAL MAIMING
AND ROBBERY AND DEATH AS THE DEPLOYMENT OF TROOPS FAIL TO DO
MUCH OTHER THAN SOMEWHAT CURB THE INCIDENTS. CONTROVERSIAL
IS THE GOVERNMENT POLICY OF RIGOROUS SCREENING OF MOZAMBICAN
CASUAL FARM WORKERS SINCE THE LOCAL FARMERS HAVE
TRADITIONALLY DEPENDED ON THEM FOR HARVEST.

06188 MCIVOR, C.
SOUTH AFRICAN CONNECTION
NEW AFRICAN, (263) (AUG 89), 19.
THIS ARTICLE EXAMINES THE GROWING DEPENDENCE OF LESOTHO
UPON SOUTH AFRICA. IT EXPLORES THE SECURITY LIASON AND
CONCERNS ABOUT SA LINKS, AS WELL AS FACILITIES PROVIDED,
POLICE HELP WITH SECURITY MATTERS AND HELP TO BREAK BOYCOTTS-
ALL FROM SOUTH AFRICA. IT QUESTIONS WHETHER THE DEPENDENCE
IS JUSTIFIED.

06189 MCKAY, D.
PRESIDENTIAL STRATEGY AND THE VETO POWER: A REAPPRAISAL
POLITICAL SCIENCE QUARTERLY, 104(3) (FAL 89), 447-462.
DAVID MCKAY SHOWS THAT SINCE THE 1960S A MAJOR CHANGE
HAS OCCURRED IN THE WAY IN WHICH THE PRESIDENTIAL VETO HAS
BEEN WIELDED. IN WHAT IS NOW A MUCH MORE CONFRONTATIONAL
EXECUTIVE/LEGISLATIVE ENVIRONMENT, THE VETO HAS BEEN
INCREASINGLY APPLIED TO MAJOR BILLS. EVIDENCE EXISTS TO
SUGGEST THAT THIS CHANGE IS NOT MERELY A SYMPTOM OF DIVIDED
PARTY CONTROL.

06190 MCKAY, D.
U.S. VOTING BEHAVIOR
CONTEMPORARY RECORD, 2(5) (SPR 89), 24-25.
THIS ARTICLE EXAMINE AMERICAN CAMPAIGN COALITIONS IN THE
LIGHT OF THE 1988 ELECTIONS. BARRING SOME SORT OF ECONOMIC
COLLAPSE WHICH COULD PRODUCE A NEW CLASS-BASED POLITICS, ALL
THE INDICATIONS ARE THAT THE ELECTORAL FRAGMENTATION OF
RECENT DECADES WILL CONTINUE. IF SO, AMERICANS MUST EXPECT
EVEN LOWER LEVELS OF PUBLIC INTEREST IN POLITICS AND EVEN
MORE CANDIDATE-CENTERED POLITICS. THE ONLY REASSURING FACTOR
IS THE CONTINUING CONSENSUS IN THE UNITED STATES ON THE
FUNDAMENTALS OF HOW THE SOCIETY AND ECONOMY SHOULD BE
ORGANISED. FEW IMPORTANT SOCIAL GROUPS CHALLENGE THE NEED
FOR A FREE-ENTERPRISE ECONOMY AND THE DEMOCRATIC VALUES
REPRESENTED BY THE CONSTITUTION.

06191 MCKAY, F.
A DRACONIAN MEASURE
MIDDLE EAST INTERNATIONAL, 353 (JUN 89), 8-9.
IT HAD BEEN RUMOURED FOR SOME TIME THAT THE ISRAELI
GOVERNMENT WAS PLANNING TO INTRODUCE LEGISLATION AIMED AT
HALTING THE FLOW OF CASH FROM THE PLO TO ISRAEL AND THE
OCCUPIED TERRITORIES. NOW IT HAS INTRODUCED AN AMENDMENT TO
THE PREVENTION OF TERROR ORDINANCE OF 1948, WHICH INCLUDES
MEASURES EVEN MORE DRACONIAN THAT HAD BEEN EXPECTED, AND
WHICH IT IS IN THE PROCESS OF RUSHING THROUGH THE KNESSET.
THE MOST IMPORTANT QUESTION IS OBVIOUSLY HOW THIS LAW IS
GOING TO BE APPLIED, BUT THERE SEEMS LITTLE DOUBT THAT IT
WILL CONSTITUTE YET ANOTHER MEANS OF DISCRIMINATION AGAINST
THE PALESTINIAN POPULATION OF ISRAEL AND WILL BE USED TO
CLOSE AND LIMIT THE ACTIVITIES OF PALESTINIAN ASSOCIATIONS.

06192 MCKEE, D.L.
SCHUMPETER AND THE POLITICAL ECONOMY OF INTERNATIONAL
CHANGE
INTERNATIONAL JOURNAL OF SOCIAL ECONOMICS, 16(12) (1989),
26-33.
THE ARTICLE ATTEMPTS TO REASSESS THE WORLD ECONOMY WITH
AN EYE TO UNDERSTANDING WHAT IS AUTOMATIC ABOUT IT AND THUS
BEYOND THE CONTROL OF NATIONAL ECONOMIES. TOWARDS THAT END,
SCHUMPETERIAN ANALYSIS IS APPLIED IN AN EFFORT TO ILLUSTRATE
HOW CHANGES OCCUR AND HOW SUCH CHANGES AFFECT DISCRETE UNITS
OR SUBSETS OF INTERNATIONAL CAPITALISM. THE DISCUSSION
SUGGESTS THAT FIRMS WITH LEADERSHIP ROLES IN NATIONAL
ECONOMIES MAY BRING THOSE ECONOMIES DOWN WITH THEM IF THEY
LOSE THEIR POSITION IN THE WORLD ECONOMY. IT ALSO SUGGESTS
THAT THE INTERNATIONAL ECONOMY MAY PROVIDE FIRMS WITH A MORE
FLEXIBLE CLIMATE WHICH IN TURN MAY PROLONG THEIR EFFECTIVE
LIVES. THE MAJOR POLICY IMPLICATION FOR GOVERNMENTS IS THAT
SUCH INSTITUTIONS MAY NO LONGER HAVE IT WITHIN THEIR
PRESERVES TO CONTROL ECONOMIC ACTIVITIES SPAWNED IN THE
INTERNATIONAL ARENA.

06193 MCKEE, K.
MICROLEVEL STRATEGIES FOR SUPPORTING LIVELIHOODS,
EMPLOYMENT, AND INCOME GENERATION OF POOR WOMEN IN THE
THIRD WORLD: THE CHALLENGE OF SIGNIFICANCE
WORLD DEVELOPMENT, 17(7) (JUL 89), 993-1006.
PROGRAMS THAT SUPPORT POOR WOMEN'S INCOME ARNING CAN USE
FOUR MEASURES OF EFFECTIVENESS. THESE ARE: MEANINGFUL,
SUSTAINABLE INCREASE IN INCOME LEVELS FOR LARGE NUMBERS OF
PARTICIPANTS; POLICY AND REGULATORY CHANGES THAT EXPAND
ECONOMIC CHOICES FOR THE POOR; INCREASES IN AGGREGATE
EMPLOYMENT, ECONOMIC GROWTH, AND DIVERSIFICATION OF THE
LOCAL ECONOMY; AND "EMPOWERMENT" - EVIDENCE THAT WOMEN
MOBILIZE AND GAIN MORE CONTROL OVER THEIR SOCIAL, POLITICAL,
AND ECONOMIC LIVES. USING THESE CRITERIA, THE PAPER ANALYZES
THE STRENGTHS AND WEAKNESSES OF THREE STRATEGIES FOR
ADDRESSING THE PROBLEMS OF SELF-EMPLOYED INDIVIDUALS AND
MICROENTERPRISES: THE AREA-, SECTOR-, AND FUNCTION-FOCUSED
APPROACHES. IT CONCLUDES THAT THE SECTOR- AND
FUNCTIONFOCUSED STRATEGIES OFFER THE MOST PROMISE FOR
HELPING WOMEN TO MAKE SIGNIFICANT ECONOMIC GAINS AND DESERVE

FURTHER EXPERIMENTATION AND DONOR SUPPORT.

06194 MCKEE, V.
CONSERVATIVE FACTIONS
CONTEMPORARY RECORD, 3(1) (FAL 89), 30-32.
THIS ARTICLE ADDRESSES THE FACT THAT THE HIERARCHICAL
NATURE OF THE PARTY IS THAT LEADERSHIP CHANGES ARE A
PREREQUISITE FOR MAJOR POLICY REVISION. OVER WHICH GROUPS OF
ALL THREE MAINSTREAM TENDENCIES COMPETE. IT EXPLORES
CONSERVATIVES IN TRANSITION; CHURCHILL -- THATCHER. THE
THREE GROUPS, PROGRESSIVES, NEW RIGHT, AND NATIONALISTS/NEO-
IMPERIALISTS ARE COMPARED IN AREAS OF INTELLECTUAL GURUS,
CONTEMPORARY ADVOCATES, PREVIOUS ADVOCATES, CAUSES,
ORGANIZATIONS, SPHERES OF INFLUENCE 1989, PUBLICATIONS AND
JOURNALS.

06195 MCKEE, V.
FACTIONALISM IN THE SOCIAL DEMOCRATIC PARTY 1981-1987
PARLIAMENTARY AFFAIRS, 42(2) (APR 89), 165-179.
THE SOCIAL DEMOCRATIC PARTY ACTIVELY CULTIVATED THE
IMAGE OF UNITY AND HOMOGENITY. THE ARTICLE EXAMINES THE
CLAIMS OF DAVID OWEN AND OTHER PARTY LEADERS AND FIND THEM
TO BE SOMEWHAT FALLACIOUS AND SHORT-TERM. THE ARTICLE
EXPLORES THE ORIGINS AND ACTIVITIES OF VARIOUS FACTIONS
WITHIN THE SDP AS WELL AS THE ORGANIZATIONS THAT THEY WERE
INVOLVED WITH.

06196 MCKENZIE, R.
THE DECLINE OF AMERICA: MYTH OR FATE?
SOCIETY, 27(1) (NOV 89), 41-48.
THE ARTICLE EXAMINES THE WIDELY HELD NOTION THAT THE
AMERICAN ECONOMY IS ON THE DECLINE. IT CONCLUDES THAT
ALTHOUGH DATA SERIES USED TO TEST THE DECLINE THESIS ARE NOT
ALWAYS IN AGREEMENT, CAREFUL REVIEW OF THE FACTS REVEALS
THAT A RELATIVE DECLINE OF THE UNITED STATES IN THE WORLD
ECONOMY HAS OCCURRED, BUT IT APPEARS TO HAVE OCCURRED IN THE
1960'S AND 1970'S, NOT IN THE 1980'S. RECENTLY, AMERICA'S
GLOBAL STATUS HAS IMPROVED. THE ARTICLE CONCLUDES THAT THE
PRIMARY EXPLANATION FOR THIS SHARPLY CONTRASTING VIEW IS
THAT THE PROPONENTS OF THE DECLINE THESIS OFTEN ENDED THEIR
RESEARCH EFFORTS IN THE EARLY 1980'S AND THAT UPDATED DATA
DRAWS INTO QUESTION THE ACTUAL DIRECTION OF RECENT TRENDS.

06197 MCKENZIE, R.B.
CAPITAL FLIGHT: THE HIDDEN POWER OF TECHNOLOGY TO SHRINK
BIG GOVERNMENT
REASON, 20(10) (MAR 89), 22-26.
BECAUSE TECHNOLOGY IS CHANGING THE NATURE OF CAPITALISM,
THE SMALL PERSONAL COMPUTER REPRESENTS PEOPLE POWER. CAPITAL
IS BEING FREED FROM THE STRICT CONFINES OF ARBITRARY
NATIONAL BOUNDARIES; IT IS BECOMING INTERNATIONALIZED TO AN
EXTENT NEVER BEFORE IMAGINED. AS A CONSEQUENCE, THE POWER OF
GOVERNMENT TO TAX AND REGULATE MAY BE IN ITS TWILIGHT YEARS.

06198 MCKEOWN, T.J.
THE POLITICS OF CORN LAW REPEAL AND THEORIES OF COMMERCIAL
POLICY
BRITISH JOURNAL OF POLITICAL SCIENCE, 19(3) (JUL 89),
353-380.
THE LARGE SHIFT IN VOTING IN THE HOUSE OF COMMONS ON
REPEAL OF THE CORN LAWS IN THE 1842-46 PERIOD HAS LED MANY
ANALYSTS TO FOCUS ON THE POLITICAL CALCULUS OF PEEL'S
GOVERNMENT AND ON THE ROLE OF IDEOLOGY IN SHAPING THIS
POLICY CHANGE. WHILE THE CLAIM THAT IDEOLOGY WAS AN
INDEPENDENT SOURCE OF CHANGE LACKS SUBSTANTIATION. THE
CLAIMS ABOUT PEEL'S CHANGING POLITICAL CALCULUS ARE AN
IMPORTANT PART OF A LARGER EXPLANATION FOR THE CHANGE IN
VOTING. HOWEVER, SHOWING THAT PEEL HAD HIS OWN REASONS FOR
PREFERRING REPEAL IS NOT THE SAME AS SHOWING WHY PEEL WAS
SUCCESSFUL. AN ANALYSIS OF THE POLITICAL AND ECONOMIC
INTERESTS OF CONSTITUENTS AND MEMBERS OF PARLIAMENT REVEALS
THAT THESE INTERESTS WERE SYSTEMATICALLY RELATED TO MEMBERS'
VOTES ON REPEAL. REPEAL IS THUS MORE APPROPRIATELY
UNDERSTOOD AS THE RESULT OF THE INTERACTION OF PEEL'S
IMMEDIATE OBJECTIVES WITH A MORE CONGENIAL POLITICAL
ENVIRONMENT THAT HAD ARISEN DUE TO THE CHANGES INDUCED BY
BRITISH ECONOMIC DEVELOPMENT.

06199 MCKINLEY, M.
DISCOVERING THE PRINCIPLE OF INVERSE RELEVANCE:
AUSTRALIA'S STRATEGIC DILEMMAS IN THE INDIAN OCEAN
CONFLICT, 9(3) (1989), 213-250.
AUSTRALIA, AS AN INDIAN OCEAN LITTORAL STATE, HAS AN
OBVIOUS AND LEGITIMATE INTEREST IN THE AFFAIRS OF THE REGION
DEFINED BY THAT SEA. FOR MUCH OF ITS HISTORY, THOUGH, ITS
GOVERNMENTS IGNORED OR NEGLECTED THEM IN TERMS OF ANY
SUBSTANTIVE POLICY. NOW, JUST WHEN THE REALIZATION THAT SUCH
AN ATTITUDE IS ENTIRELY INAPPROPRIATE IS TAKING HOLD IN
CANBERRA, AUSTRALIA FINDS THAT IT IS POWERLESS TO INFLUENCE
SIGNIFICANTLY THE FORCES AT WORK IN THE REGION. INDEED,
AUSTRALIA IS ALMOST IRRELEVANT TO THE PROCESSES THEREIN,
WHILE THESE PROCESSES THEMSELVES IMPOSE THEIR OWN BURDEN OF
RELEVANCE UPON AUSTRALIA. ESSENTIALLY, AUSTRALIA'S CHOICE IS
BETWEEN BASELESS SELF-ASSERTION AND BEFITTING HUMILITY.

06200 MCKNIGHT, B.
    OUTLOOK FOR CANADIAN DEFENCE
    NATO'S SIXTEEN NATIONS, 34(4) (AUG 89), 75, 77-78, 80, 82.
        ALONG WITH ALL THE MAIN CANADIAN GOVERNMENT DEPARTMENTS,
    NATIONAL DEFENCE MUST TIGHTEN ITS BELT. AS A CONSEQUENCE,
    SEVERAL IMPORTANT PROJECTS WILL HAVE TO BE CANCELLED OR
    DELAYED. BUT INTERNATIONAL COMMITMENTS, ESPECIALLY THOSE
    INVOLVING NATO, WILL REMAIN INTACT. COST-EFFECTIVE PLANNING
    AND MANAGEMENT WILL HELP TO MAINTAIN A REAL GROWTH OF 4.4
    PERCENT IN DEFENCE SPENDING OVER THE NEXT FIVE YEARS.

06201 MCLANAHAN, S.; GARFINKEL, I.
    SINGLE MOTHERS, THE UNDERCLASS, AND SOCIAL POLICY
    PHILADELPHIA: ANLS OF AMER ACMY OF POLITICAL AND SOC
    SCIENCE, (501) (JAN 89), 92-104.
        THIS ARTICLE FOCUSES ON THE QUESTION OF WHETHER MOTHER-
    ONLY FAMILIES ARE PART OF AN EMERGING URBAN UNDERCLASS. AN
    UNDERCLASS IS DEFINED AS A POPULATION EXHIBITING THE
    FOLLOWING CHARACTERISTICS: WEAK LABOR FORCE ATTACHMENT,
    PERSISTENCE OF WEAK ATTACHMENT, AND RESIDENTIAL ISOLATION IN
    NEIGHBORHOODS WITH HIGH CONCENTRATIONS OF POVERTY AND
    UNEMPLOYMENT. ONLY A SMALL MINORITY OF SINGLE MOTHERS FIT
    THE DESCRIPTION OF AN UNDERCLASS: LESS THAN 5 PERCENT. BUT A
    SMALL AND GROWING MINORITY OF BLACK, NEVER-MARRIED MOTHERS
    MEET ALL THREE CRITERIA. WELFARE PROGRAMS ARE NECESSARY BUT
    TOO HEAVY A RELIANCE ON WELFARE CAN FACILITATE THE GROWTH OF
    AN UNDERCLASS. IN CONTRAST, UNIVERSAL PROGRAMS SUCH AS CHILD
    SUPPORT ASSURANCE, CHILD CARE, HEALTH CARE, CHILDREN'S
    ALLOWANCES, AND FULL EMPLOYMENT WOULD DISCOURAGE SUCH A
    TREND AND PROMOTE ECONOMIC INDEPENDENCE AMONG SINGLE MOTHERS.

06202 MCLAREN, R.I.
    ORGANIZING GOVERNMENT DEPARTMENTS: EXPERIENCE FROM
    SASKATCHEWAN
    CANADIAN PUBLIC ADMINISTRATION, 32(3) (FAL 89), 462-469.
        THERE ARE TWO MAJOR ASPECTS OF ORGANIZING GOVERNMENT
    DEPARTMENTS IN CANADA. FIRST, THE CABINET CHOOSES WHICH
    POLICIES IT WILL PURSUE AND WHICH INSTRUMENTS AND
    DEPARTMENTS IT WILL UTILIZE. THEN THE CABINET MUST DECIDE
    HOW THOSE DEPARTMENTS WILL BE ORGANIZED AND HOW THE PUBLIC
    EMPLOYEES WILL BE GROUPED WITHIN THOSE DEPARTMENTS. THIS
    SECOND ASPECT, WHICH IS REFERRED TO AS "DEPARTMENTALIZATION,
    " IS THE SUBJECT OF THIS RESEARCH NOTE.

06203 MCLAUGHLIN, D. L.
    THE PICK SLOAN PLAN, LOCAL LAND-USE CONTROLS, AND LOCAL
    GROWTH: A LONGITUDINAL STUDY
    DISSERTATION ABSTRACTS INTERNATIONAL, 49(8) (FEB 89),
    2377-A.
        THE AUTHORITY TO REGULATE LAND USE IS ONE OF THE MOST
    POWERFUL TOOLS AVAILABLE TO LOCAL GOVERNMENTS TO ATTRACT AND
    CONTROL ECONOMIC DEVELOPMENT. THIS STUDY FOCUSES ON THE
    ECONOMIC GROWTH RELATED TO THE FEDERAL RESERVOIRS CREATED BY
    THE PICK SLOAN PLAN IN NORTH AND SOUTH DAKOTA AND HOW LOCAL
    LAND-USE REGULATION HAS INFLUENCED THIS GROWTH.

06204 MCLENNAN, G.
    GREAT BRITAIN: WHO WILL DEFEAT THE TORIES?
    WORLD MARXIST REVIEW, 32(4) (APR 89), 13-16.
        COMMUNISTS ARE CONVINCED THAT, GIVEN A GREATER DEGREE OF
    COMMON PURPOSE BETWEEN THE POLITICAL PARTIES WHICH OPPOSE
    TORY POLICIES, THE PRESENT GOVERNMENT CAN BE DEFEATED AT THE
    NEXT GENERAL ELECTION. THERE IS NO DOUBT THAT THE DIVISION
    OF THE FORCES OPPOSED TO THE CONSERVATIVES IS A GREAT FACTOR
    IN STRENGTHENING THEIR (THE TORIES') HAND. OPPOSITION FORCES
    HAVE FAILED TO COORDINATE IN EXTRAPARLIAMENTARY ACTIONS AND
    CONTESTED ELECTIONS IN A WAY THAT HELPED THE RIGHT MAINTAIN
    ITS MAJORITY IN PARLIAMENT. HOWEVER, THERE IS A RANGE OF
    ISSUES AND THEMES ON WHICH IT SHOULD BE POSSIBLE TO REACH
    BROAD AGREEMENT. THESE INCLUDE: GREATER DEMOCRACY IN SOCIETY;
    A NEW FOREIGN POLICY AND A NEW ROLE FOR BRITAIN IN THE
    WORLD; THE EXPANSION AND IMPROVEMENT OF PUBLIC SERVICES;
    ECONOMIC AND INDUSTRIAL MODERNISATION; GREATER EQUALITY IN
    SOCIETY. THE IMPORTANCE OF PREVENTING ANOTHER TORY VICTORY
    IS SO GREAT THAT IT SHOULD DETERMINE THE APPROACH TO BRITISH
    POLITICS IN 1989 OF ALL POLITICAL PARTIES AND DEMOCRATIC
    FORCES WHO WANT A DIFFERENT COURSE FOR BRITAIN.

06205 MCLEOD, I.
    FIT TO BE TIED
    CANADIAN FORUM, 68(782) (OCT 89), 7-9.
        THIS ARTICLE EXPLORES THE ELECTORAL MISFORTUNES OF THE
    GETTY GOVERNMENT WHICH HAVE CAST DARK SHADOWS OVER THE
    FUTURE FOR ALBERTA TORIES. WHEN PREMIER DON GETTY FIRST TOOK
    OFFICE THE TORIES LOOKED TO BE UNBEATABLE. SINCE THEN THEY
    HAVE LOST EDMONTON AND ARE LOSING CALGARY, AND IT IS NOT
    CLEAR THAT THEY CAN REVERSE THEIR DECLINE, JOURNALIST IAN
    MCLEOD EXAMINES THE RECENT POLITICS OF ROPING VOTES IN
    ALBERTA.

06206 MCLOUGHLIN, G.J.
    TECHNOLOGY POLICY IN JAPAN AND THE UNITED STATES
    CRS REVEIW, 10(6) (JUL 89), 8-10.

TECHNOLOGY POLICY IS VIEWED WITH INCREASING IMPORTANCE
BY U.S. POLICYMAKERS AND INDUSTRY LEADERS. FOR MANY, JAPAN
HAS SET THE STANDARD FOR INNOVATIVE, HIGH-QUALITY GOODS SOLD
IN GLOBAL MARKETS. THESE PRODUCTS OFTEN ARE THE RESULT OF
TECHNOLOGICAL ADVANCEMENTS, USUALLY INCREMENTAL, WITH
GOVERNMENT-COORDINATED INDUSTRY COOPERATION.

06207 MCMENAMIN, M.
    CLEANING UP THE TEAMSTERS
    REASON, 21(1) (MAY 89), 26-31.
        THE ARTICLE EXAMINES THE TEAMSTERS UNION AND THEIR
    CONNECTION WITH ORGANIZED CRIME. IT ANALYZES THE FACTORS
    THAT MADE THE WORLD'S LARGEST UNION SO SUSCEPTIBLE TO
    INFILTRATION BY THE MOB. IT ALSO OUTLINES THE EFFORTS OF
    TEAMSTERS LEADERS AND THE FEDERAL GOVERNMENT TO REDUCE THE
    INFLUENCE OF ORGANIZED CRIME. A KEY ELEMENT IN THE
    GOVERNMENT STRATEGY WAS A CIVIL ACTION FILED BY THE JUSTICE
    DEPARTMENT THAT SEEKS TO PLACE THE ENTIRE UNION UNDER
    TRUSTEESHIP. WHILE SOME BRAND THE MEASURE AS TOTALITARIAN,
    OTHERS SEE IT AS THE ONLY WAY TO CLEAN THE UNION UP.

06208 MCMICHAEL, S.R.
    THE SOVIET ARMY, COUNTERINSURGENCY, AND THE AFGHAN WAR
    PARAMETERS, XIX(4) (DEC 89), 21-35.
        THE MILITARY SITUATION THAT CONFRONTED THE SOVIET ARMY
    IN AFGHANISTAN DURING ITS INVOLVEMENT THERE DIFFERED
    SIGNIFICANTLY FROM ITS PRE-WAR EXPECTATIONS. THIS ESSAY
    STUDIES HOW THE SOVIET ARMY RESPONDED TO THE UNEXPECTED
    DILEMMAS IT MET. IT ALSO ANALYZES HOW THE SOVIET GROUND
    FORCES ADAPTED AND FAILED TO ADAPT TO THE PECULIAR
    CONDITIONS OF COUNTERINSURGENCY WARFARE IN A LARGE, DRY,
    MOUNTAINOUS REGION AND EVALUATES THE SUITABILITY OF THE
    SOVIET ARMY FOR SUCH OPERATIONS.

06209 MCMURTRY, J.
    THE LANGUAGE OF POLITICS
    CANADIAN FORUM, LXVIII(780) (APR 89), 13-15.
        THE ARTICLE DISCUSSES THE PHENOMENON IN WHICH CERTAIN
    CONCEPTS OR IDEAS ARE A PRIORI CONSIDERED TO BE UNSPEAKABLE.
    THE TOPICS OF DISCUSSION WHICH ARE THUSLY RULED OUT ARE
    THOSE WHICH CHALLENGE THE BASIC SOCIAL-STRUCTURAL FACT
    (BSSF) OF THE SOCIAL ORDER. THE EXCLUSION OF SUCH POSITIONS
    FROM PUBLIC DISCOURSE DOES NOT DEPEND AT ALL ON CRITERIA OF
    TRUTH OR FALSITY. THE ARTICLE ALSO ANALYZES THE WAYS IN
    WHICH THESE IDEALS ARE RULED OUT, OMITTED, SELECTED OUT, AND
    MARGINALIZED.

06210 MCNAIR, B.
    GLASNOST AND RESTRUCTURING IN THE SOVIET MEDIA
    MEDIA, CULTURE, AND SOCIETY, 11(2) (APR 89), 327-349.
        SINCE THE APRIL 1985 PLENUM, THE SOVIET GOVERNMENT HAS
    DEVELOPED AN INFORMATION POLICY THAT PROMISES FREEDOM OF
    SPEECH, PLURALISM OF OPINIONS, THE OPEN EXCHANGE OF IDEAS,
    AND LEGAL GUARANTEES FOR THE RIGHTS OF THE MINORITY. THIS
    ARTICLE EXAMINES THE SIGNIFICANCE OF THE NEW POLICIES AND
    THE CONCEPT OF GLASNOST THAT UNDERLIES THEM, WITH PARTICULAR
    REFERENCE TO THE SOVIET NEWS MEDIA. GLASNOST IS DISCUSSED AS
    IT APPEARS IN THE WORKS OF LENIN, AS IT WAS APPLIED BY
    SUCCESIVE SOVIET LEADERSHIPS, AND AS IT HAS AFFECTED THE
    ORGANIZATION AND PRACTICE OF THE SOVIET NEWS MEDIA SINCE THE
    APRIL PLENUM.

06211 MCNALLY, D.
    LOCKE, LEVELLERS AND LIBERTY: PROPERTY AND DEMOCRACY IN
    THE THOUGHT OF THE FIRST WHIGS
    HISTORY OF POLITICAL THOUGHT, X(1) (SPR 89), 17-40.
        A RECENT NUMBER OF STUDIES HAVE REDEFINED HOW MANY VIEW
    JOHN LOCKE. SOME OF THE CHANGES INCLUDE A GROWING BODY OF
    EVIDENCE THAT LOCKE'S POLITICAL PRINCIPLES AND THOSE OF THE
    LEVELLERS WERE SIMILAR, MORE SIMILAR THAN PREVIOUSLY THOUGHT.
    ANOTHER "ILLUMINATION" WAS LOCKE'S DEBT TO ANTHONY ASHLEY
    COOPER, THE FIRST EARL OF SHAFTESBURY. THE ARTICLE ARGUES
    THAT IF THE SECOND IDEA IS VALID, THEN THE FIRST BECOMES
    INVALID. IT ANALYZES THE WRITINGS OF LOCKE AND CONCLUDES
    THAT LOCKE WAS CLOSER TO SHAFTESBURY AND THE FIRST WHIGS
    THAN HE WAS TO THE LEVELLERS.

06212 MCNAUGHT, K.
    CANADA'S EUROPEAN AMBIENCE
    ROUND TABLE, (310) (APR 89), 144-157.
        FOR DECADES, EVEN CENTURIES, CANADIANS HAVE WRESTLED
    WITH THEIR IDENTITY. SOME CALLED THEMSELVES AMERICANS, SOME
    CLAIM THAT CANADA HAS REMAINED EUROPEAN, SOME ARGUE THAT
    THEY ARE NEITHER. THE ARTICLE EXAMINES THE EVIDENCE AND
    CONCLUDES THAT, ON BALANCE, CANADA HAS MAINTAINED A WORLD
    VIEW THAT IS SUBSTANTIVELY MORE EUROPEAN THAN AMERICAN. A
    MAJOR DIFFERENCE IS THAT CANADA SUBSCRIBES THE "FUNCTIONAL"
    FOREIGN RELATIONS WHILE THE US IS OFTEN MORE MOTIVATED BY
    "DOCTRINES" OR IDEOLOGY.

06213 MCNAUGHT, K.
    REFLECTIONS ON LEADERSHIP: J.S. WOODSWORTH
    CANADIAN FORUM, LXVIII(779) (MAR 89), 14-17.
        THE AUTHOR ANALYZES THREE ASPECTS OF J.S. WOODWORTH'S

LEADERSHIP: HIS MOTIVATION, HIS PRATICAL ACHIEVEMENTS, AND
HIS NOTIONS ABOUT THE COMMINGLING OF TRUTH AND COMPROMISE.

06214 MCNELLY, T.
GENERAL MACARTHUR'S PACIFISM
INTERNATIONAL JOURNAL ON WORLD PEACE, VI(1) (JAN 89),
41-60.
THE ARTICLE EXAMINES AN APPARENT CHANGE IN PHILOSOPHY
REFLECTED IN THE POLICIES OF GENERAL DOUGLAS MACARTHUR. HIS
FIRING BY PRESIDENT TRUMAN FOR PUBLICLY ADVOCATING
ENLARGEMENT OF THE KOREAN WAR CONTRARY TO AMERICAN POLICY
OVERSHADOWS HIS SHIFT FROM MILITARISM OF PACIFISM AFTER
WORLD WAR TWO. THE ARTICLE EXAMINES MACARTHUR'S AIMS AND
CONCLUDES THAT THE CONSTITUTIONAL OUTLAWRY OF WAR WOULD NOT
MEAN PEACE AT ANY PRICE OR A BAN ON DEFENSIVE FORCES.

06215 MCNOWN, L.H.
THE EVOLUTION OF THE MANAGERIAL PRESIDENCY: THE ROLE OF
THE ASH COUNCIL AND REORGANIZATION PLAN NO. 2 OF 1970
DISSERTATION ABSTRACTS INTERNATIONAL, 49(8) (FEB 89),
2388-A.
THE PRESIDENT'S ADVISORY COUNCIL ON EXECUTIVE
ORGANIZATION (PACEO) STUDIED THE EXECUTIVE OFFICE OF THE
PRESIDENT AND RECOMMENDED THE ESTABLISHMENT OF A DOMESTIC
COUNCIL AND THE TRANSFORMATION OF THE BUREAU OF THE BUDGET
INTO AN UPGRADED OFFICE OF MANAGEMENT AND BUDGET. THIS
DISSERTATION EVALUATES REORGANIZATION PLAN NO. 2, WHICH
IMPLEMENTED THESE REFORMS.

06216 MCPHEE, P.
THE FRENCH REVOLUTION, PEASANTS, AND CAPITALISM
AMERICAN HISTORICAL REVIEW, 94(5) (DEC 89), 1265-1280.
ONLY RECENTLY HAVE HISTORIANS BEGUN TO RE-EXAMINE THE
GENERAL NATURE OF THE PEASANT MOVEMENT AND THE IMPACT OF THE
FRENCH REVOLUTION ON RURAL LIFE. YET THESE ISSUES ARE AT THE
HEART OF UNDERSTANDING THE FRENCH REVOLUTION. WAS IT A
CLASSIC BOURGEOIS REVOLUTION OR A UNIQUE CASE OF THE
TRANSFORMATION FROM FEUDALISM TO CAPITALISM?

06217 MCQUARIE, D.; SPAULDING, M.
THE CONCEPT OF POWER IN MARXIST THEORY: A CRITIQUE AND
REFORMULATION
CRITICAL SOCIOLOGY, 16(1) (SPR 89), 3-28.
THE DOMINANT MODEL OF POWER IN MARXIST THEORY CONTAINS A
NUMBER OF PROBLEMATIC ASSUMPTIONS. THESE INCLUDE: (1) THE
ASSUMPTION OF OBJECTIVE CLASS INTERESTS; (2) THE ASSUMPTION
THAT CLASSES ARE COLLECTIVE SOCIAL ACTORS; (3) THE
ASSUMPTION THAT CLASSES HAVE A POLITICAL "CONSCIOUSNESS,"
AND (4) THE ASSUMPTION THAT THE STATE IS THE LOCUS OF CLASS
POWER. THE CENTRAL ERROR WHICH UNDERLIES THESE FOUR
ASSUMPTIONS OF THE DOMINANT MODEL IS A CONFUSION OF THE
THEORETICAL LEVELS OF AGENCY AND STRUCTURE IN MARXIST THEORY.
THE UNCRITICAL ACCEPTANCE OF THESE ASSUMPTIONS HAS BEEN
HARMFUL TO THE DEVELOPMENT OF MARXIST THEORY AND POLITICAL
PRACTICE.

06218 MCWHIRTER, J.A.
SELF-INFLICTED WOUND: THE U.S. IN LEBANON 1982-1984
AVAILABLE FROM NTIS, NO. AD-A210 097/2/GAR, APR 89, 25.
THIS DOCUMENT DESCRIBES SOME OF THE ASSUMPTIONS
UNDERLYING THE DIPLOMATIC-MILITARY DECISION-MAKING OVER THE
EIGHTEEN-MONTH PERIOD IN WHICH THE U.S. WAS INVOLVED IN
LEBANON. THE MARINE HEADQUARTERS DISASTER ON OCTOBER 23,
1983, SIGNALLED THE END OF U.S. INVOLVEMENT IN LEBANON. THE
CAUSES OF THE DISASTER HAD THEIR ROOTS IN THE UNREALISTIC
ASSUMPTIONS MADE BY THE U.S. FOLLOWING THE ISRAELI INVASION,
NONE OF WHICH WERE REALIZED OVER THE FOLLOWING MONTHS.
PERSONALITIES OF POLICYMAKERS, OVER-CONFIDENCE LEADING TO
UNREALISTIC ASSUMPTIONS, DISREGARD OF LOCAL REALITIES,
INCONSISTENCIES DUE TO CRITICAL TURNOVERS OF KEY U.S.
DECISION MAKERS, FRUSTRATIONS IN FAILURE CAUSING THE
RECKLESS USE OF FORCE AND SIMPLE NEGLIGENCE, WERE ALL
INGREDIENTS IN THE LEBANON FIASCO. THESE THREADS ARE HEREIN
TRACED FROM THE ORIGINAL OVEROPTIMISM FOLLOWING THE
SUCCESSFUL EVACUATION OF P.L.O. FORCES FROM BEIRUT, THROUGH
THE UNSUCCESSFUL ATTEMPTS TO PRESSURE AND CAJOLE A U.S.-
BROKERED PEACE PLAN, AND FINALLY TO THE REALIZATION THAT THE
DIPLOMATIC-MILITARY EFFORTS ON BEHALF OF THE LEBANESE
GOVERNMENT COULD NOT PROP UP AN OTHERWISE HOPELESS REGIME.

06219 MCWILLIAMS, R.; MESSICK, R.E.
KEMP'S OPPORTUNITY
REASON, 20(11) (APR 89), 40-41.
JACK KEMP BELIEVES THAT TRADITIONAL POVERTY PROGRAMS
SUPPRESS THE VERY ATTRIBUTES THAT SHOULD BE REWARDED,
INCLUDING INDIVIDUAL INITIATIVE, SELF-RELIANCE, AND PRIVATE
ENTERPRISE. AS HUD SECRETARY, KEMP WANTS TO FOSTER SELF-
RELIANCE BY SELLING PUBLIC HOUSING TO RESIDENTS AT PRICES
THEY CAN AFFORD. HE ALSO WANTS TO ENCOURAGE PRIVATE
ENTERPRISE BY GIVING TAX BREAKS, REGULATORY RELIEF, AND
OTHER INCENTIVES TO BUSINESSES THAT WILL CREATE JOBS IN
GHETTOS AND BY REINSTATING TAX DEDUCTIONS FOR BUILDERS OF
LOW-INCOME HOUSING.

06220 MCHILLIAMS, W.C.
A REPUBLIC OF COUCH POTATOES
COMMONWEAL, CXVI(5) (MAR 89), 138-140.
THE ELECTION OF 1988 SENT AN URGENT SIGNAL THAT
SOMETHING IS WRONG WITH THE POLITICAL SOUL OF AMERICAN
DEMOCRACY. THE CAMPAIGN WAS MORE THAN NEGATIVE. THE
ELECTRONIC MEDIA GAVE GREATER FORCE AND CURRENCY TO
SCURRILITIES THAN WAS POSSIBLE BEFORE VOTERS BECAME SO
DEPENDENT ON THE MASS MEDIA.

06221 MEAD, L.M.
THE LOGIC OF WORKFARE: THE UNDERCLASS AND WORK POLICY
PHILADELPHIA: ANLS OF AMER ACMY OF POLITICAL AND SOC
SCIENCE, (501) (JAN 89), 156-169.
MUCH OF TODAY'S ENTRENCHED POVERTY REFLECTS THE FACT
THAT POOR ADULTS SELDOM WORK CONSISTENTLY. THE PROBLEM
CANNOT BE BLAMED PREDOMINANTLY ON LACK OF JOBS OR OTHER
BARRIERS TO EMPLOYMENT, AS THE CHANCE TO WORK SEEMS WIDELY
AVAILABLE. MORE LIKELY, THE POOR DO NOT SEE WORK IN MENIAL
JOBS AS FAIR, POSSIBLE, OR OBLIGATORY, THOUGH THEY WANT TO
WORK IN PRINCIPLE. GOVERNMENT HAS EVOLVED POLICIES
EXPLICITLY TO RAISE WORK LEVELS AMONG THE POOR. WORKFARE
PROGRAMS, LINKED TO WELFARE, SHOW THE MOST PROMISE BUT STILL
REACH ONLY A MINORITY OF EMPLOYABLE RECIPIENTS. WELFARE
REFORM SHOULD, ABOVE ALL, RAISE PARTICIPATION IN THESE
PROGRAMS, AS THE SHARE OF CLIENTS INVOLVED LARGELY GOVERNS
THEIR IMPACT. WELFARE SHOULD ALSO COVER MORE NONWORKING MEN
TO BRING THEM UNDER WORKFARE. WHILE WORK ENFORCEMENT MAY
SEEM PUNITIVE, THE POOR MUST BECOME WORKERS BEFORE THEY CAN
STAKE LARGER CLAIMS TO EQUALITY.

06222 MEAD, W.R.
THE UNITED STATES AND THE NEW EUROPE
WORLD POLICY JOURNAL, 7(1) (WIN 89), 35-70.
THIS ARTICLE ATTEMPTS TO DESCRIBE BRIEFLY AMERICA'S
INTERESTS, THE DANGERS IN ITS PATH, AND A POLICY ORIENTATION
THAT COULD MAKE THE MOST OF ITS OPPORTUNITIES WHILE
MINIMIZING THE RISKS. THE WORLD SITUATION IS CHANGING TOO
RAPIDLY FOR ANY SUCH TREATMENT TO BE MORE THAN A SKETCH, BUT
THE WRITER DECIDES THAT THE SPEED OF CHANGE MAKES EVEN A
SKETCHY ACCOUNT OF AMERICA'S GRAND STRATEGY IN THE POST-COLD
WAR ERA WORTH ATTEMPTING. HE DECLARES THAT THE RECOVERY OF
THE PRINCIPLES GROUNDED IN THE HISTORY OF FOREIGN POLICY
WILL HELP IT NEGOTIATE THE DIFFICULT TIMES AHEAD.

06223 MEADE, T.
"LIVING WORSE AND COSTING MORE": RESISTANCE AND RIOT IN
RIO DE JANEIRO, 1890-1917
JOURNAL OF LATIN AMERICAN STUDIES, 21(2) (MAY 89), 241-266.
BECAUSE THE TRANSITION PROCESS IN BRAZIL HAS BEEN SO
UNEVEN, POPULAR PROTEST CANNOT BE DIVIDED INTO THE NEAT
CATEGORIES OF PRE-MODERN STREET RIOTS AND MODERN TRADE
UNIONISM. IN FACT, IT IS ARGUABLE WHETHER RIO DE JANEIRO HAS
EVER UNDERGONE A COMPLETE TRANSITION FROM PRE-MODERN TO
MODERN PROTEST IN EITHER FORM OR IDEOLOGY. RIOTS AND
PROTESTS IN RECENT YEARS INDICATE THAT THE FORM OF PROTEST
THAT STUDENTS OF EUROPEAN COMMUNAL VIOLENCE HAVE LABELLED
"PRE-MODERN" IS STILL COMMON IN RIO AND OTHER BRAZILIAN
CITIES. BY CONTRAST, THE CARIOCA STREET PROTESTS PRIOR TO
1917 WERE PART OF A DEVELOPING SYSTEM OF POLITICAL IDEOLOGY,
REPRESENTING A FACET OF THE POPULAR CLASSES' CULTURE THAT
WAS NO LESS "MODERN" THAN THE TRADE UNION MOVEMENT THAT HAS
DEVELOPING ALONGSIDE IT.

06224 MEADOR, D.
UNACCEPTABLE DELAYS IN JUDICIAL APPOINTMENTS
JOURNAL OF LAW & POLITICS, VI(1) (FAL 89), 7-14.
THE ARTICLE EXAMINES A "GLARING FLAW" IN THE FEDERAL
JUDGE APPOINTMENT PROCESS: THE EXTRAORDINARILY LONG PERIOD OF
TIME THAT IT TAKES TO FILL A VACANCY ON THE FEDERAL BENCH.
THE AUTHOR ARGUES THAT THIS TIME LAPSE IS A DEFECT IN THE
ADMINISTRATION OF FEDERAL JUSTICE THAT SHOULD BE SERIOUSLY
ADDRESSED WITH A VIEW TOWARD REDUCING DELAY. HE OUTLINES THE
TIME LAPSE BOTH BETWEEN VACANCY AND NOMINATION AND BETWEEN
NOMINATION AND CONFIRMATION OF FEDERAL JUDGES. HE CONCLUDES
THAT THE CREATION OF AN APPROPRIATELY-STAFFED PERMANENT
JUDICIAL APPOINTMENTS OFFICE WITHIN THE DEPARTMENT OF
JUSTICE WOULD SIGNIFICANTLY REDUCE DELAY.

06225 MEADWELL, H.
ETHNIC NATIONALISM AND COLLECTIVE CHOICE THEORY
COMPARATIVE POLITICAL STUDIES, 22(2) (JUL 89), 139-154.
THIS ARTICLE ASSESSES HOW DIFFERENT KINDS OF DIVISIONS
OF LABOR CONSTRAIN AND ENABLE ETHNIC COLLECTIVE ACTION. THE
ARGUMENT BEGINS FROM THE ISSUE OF THE COMPLETENESS OF THE
GROUP'S DIVISION OF LABOR AND PURSUES THE CONTRADICTION
BETWEEN HECHTER'S AND ROGOWSKI'S POSITION ON THE IMPORTANCE
OF THE SKILL DISTRIBUTION AMONG CULTURAL GROUP MEMBERS. THE
ARTICLE DEMONSTRATES THAT EACH OF THESE POSITIONS DRAWS ON A
DIFFERENT THEORY OF INTERNATIONAL TRADE. THE ARGUMENT
EMPHASIZES THE IMPORTANCE OF "TRADING FOR INDEPENDENCE," AS
A CONDITION FOR THE EMERGENCE OF ETHNIC COLLECTIVE ACTION,
WHEN THE GROUP IS INCOMPLETE. THE ARGUMENT ALSO EMPHASIZES
THE IMPORTANCE OF PREFERENCE AGGREGATION WITHIN A GROUP, AND

THUS REINTERPRETS THE CONVENTIONAL TREATMENT OF ETHNIC
NATIONALISM AS A SINGLE-ISSUE MOVEMENT.

06226 MEANEY, C.S.
MARKET REFORM IN A LENINIST SYSTEM: SOME TRENDS IN THE
DISTRIBUTION OF POWER, STATUS, AND MONEY IN URBAN CHINA
STUDIES IN COMPARATIVE COMMUNISM, 22(2/3) (SUM 89),
203-220.
THIS ARTICLE POSTULATES THAT MARKET REFORM HAS NOT
CREATED A TRUE MARKET IN CHINA. IT EXAMINES THE ENORMOUS
UPSURGE IN THE FREQUENCY AND SEVERITY OF ECONOMIC CORRUPTION
IN URBAN INDUSTRY AND COMMERCE. FRESH INSIGHT IS OFFERED
INTO THE MANY OBSTACLES AND PITFALLS THAT CONFRONT
STRUCTURAL REFORMERS IN ALL COMMUNIST SYSTEMS.

06227 MEARSHEIMER, J.
ASSESSING THE CONVENTIONAL BALANCE: THE 3:1 RULE AND ITS
CRITICS
INTERNATIONAL SECURITY, 13(4) (SPR 89), 54-89.
THE CONVENTIONAL BALANCE IN EUROPE HAS LATELY BECOME THE
FOCUS OF INTENSE DEBATE AS EVEN THE THEORIES CONSIDERED
FUNDAMENTAL TO STRATEGIC DEFENSE PLANNING ARE EXAMINED AND
CRITICIZED. ONE OF THESE THEORIES IS THE 3:1 RULE OF
CONVENTIONAL DEFENSE WHICH STATES THAT AN ATTACKER MUST HAVE
AT LEAST A 3:1 SUPERIORITY TO BREAKTHROUGH A DEFENDERS FRONT
AT A SPECIFIC POINT. THE PAPER OUTLINES THE CASE FOR THE 3:1
RULE, EXPLAINS HOW THE RULE SHOULD BE USED IN ANALYSIS AND
ATTEMPTS TO ANSWER CRITICISM OF THE RULE.

06228 MEDEMA, S.G.
DISCOURSE AND THE INSTITUTIONAL APPROACH TO LAW AND
ECONOMICS: FACTORS THAT SEPARATE THE INSTITUTIONAL
APPROACH TO LAW AND ECONOMICS FROM ALTERNATIVE APPROACHES
JOURNAL OF ECONOMIC ISSUES, XXIII(2) (JUN 89), 417-425.
THIS ARTICLE EXPLORES THE RHETORIC OF THE INTERRELATIONS
BETWEEN LEGAL AND ECONOMIC PROCESSES AS EXPOUNDED IN
NEOCLASSICAL LAW AND ECONOMICS, CRITICAL LEGAL STUDIES, AND
NEO-INSTITUTIONAL LAW AND ECONOMICS. ECONOMICS IS SEEN TO
ADVOCATE A POINT OF VIEW OR IDEOLOGY, AS DISCOURSE AND NOT
NECESSARILY TRUTH. RECOGNITION OF THE CHANNELING,
OBFUSCATION, SELECTIVE PERCEPTION, AND FICTIONS INVOLVED IN
ECONOMIC DISCOURSE IS NECESSARY FOR A COMPLETE ANALYSIS OF
ECONOMIC MODELS AND THEIR POLICY PRESCRIPTIONS.

06229 MEDHURST, K.; MOYSER, G.
THE CHURCH OF ENGLAND AND POLITICS: THE POLITICS OF
ESTABLISHMENT
PARLIAMENTARY AFFAIRS, 42(2) (APR 89), 230-249.
THE CHURCH OF ENGLAND WAS ONCE POPULARLY KNOWN AS "THE
CONSERVATIVE PARTY AT PRAYER." HOWEVER, PUBLICLY VOICED
OPPOSITION BY THE CHURCH TO A RELATIVELY WIDE RANGE OF
OFFICIAL CONSERVATIVE POLICIES HAS ATTRACTED A DEGREE OF
PUBLIC ATTENTION AND RAISED ONCE AGAIN THE QUESTION OF
POLITICAL INVOLVEMENT. THE ARTICLE SEEKS TO EXPLAIN THE
DEVELOPMENT OF THE CURRENT CONDITIONS AND EVALUATES THE
GENERAL CONDITION OF CHURCH-STATE RELATIONSHIPS.

06230 MEDOFF, M.H.
CONSTITUENCIES, IDEOLOGY, AND THE DEMAND FOR ABORTION
LEGISLATION
PUBLIC CHOICE, 60(2) (1989), 185-192.
IN A STUDY ON THE POLITICAL IMPLICATIONS OF THE RECENT
FUROR OVER ABORTION, THE PAPER IDENTIFIES THE VARIOUS
CONSTITUENCIES WHICH SIGNIFICANTLY AFFECTED THE VOTE ON THE
HATCH/EAGLETON (ANTI-ABORTION) AMENDMENT. IT DEVELOPS AND
TESTS A MODEL TO INVESTIGATE: WHICH SPECIAL INTEREST GROUPS
ARE DEMANDERS OF LEGISLATION ALLOWING OR ABOLISHING LEGAL
ABORTIONS; AND ARE IDEOLOGICAL ATTITUDES REGARDING THE
APPROPRIATE ROLE OF WOMEN RELATED TO THE DEMAND FOR LEGAL
ABORTIONS?

06231 MEDVEDEV, R.
THE SOURCES OF POLITICAL TERROR
DISSENT, (SUM 89), 318-322.
THE AUTHOR, WHO IS A WELL-KNOWN SOVIET HISTORIAN,
DISCUSSES THE HISTORY OF THE SOLOVETSK ISLANDS IN THE WHITE
SEA, WHERE SOME OF THE FIRST CAMPS FOR SOVIET POLITICAL
PRISONERS WERE LOCATED.

06232 MEEHAN, M.
ARGENTINA: EARLY EXIT?
THIRD WORLD WEEK, 8(13) (MAY 89), 98-99.
ARGENTINA'S FINANCIAL CRISIS IS SO BADLY OUT OF CONTROL
THAT PRESIDENT RAUL ALFONSIN MAY RESIGN BEFORE HIS TERM ENDS.
PERONIST PRESIDENT-ELECT CARLOS SAUL MENEM HAS DECLARED
THAT, IF THE PRESIDENCY IS OFFERED EARLY, HE WILL ACCEPT IT.
MENEM'S PERONIST PARTY TROUNCED ALFONSIN'S RADICAL PARTY IN
THE MAY 1989 GENERAL ELECTIONS, WINNING THE PRESIDENCY AND
CONTROL OF BOTH HOUSES OF CONGRESS.

06233 MEEHAN, M.
ARGENTINA: RAIL PERONIST
THIRD WORLD WEEK, 8(8) (APR 89), 58-59.
ARGENTINES VIEW PERONISM AS THE MOST POWERFUL MOVEMENT

IN THEIR NATIONAL HISTORY. FOR SOME, CARLOS SAUL MENEM
REPRESENTS THE SPIRITUAL RETURN OF PERON, WHO RULED
ARGENTINA FROM 1946 TO 1955 AND FROM 1973 TO 1974. MENEM,
WHO IS RUNNING FOR PRESIDENT IN THE MAY 1989 ELECTION, SAYS
THAT PERON'S MESSAGE IS STILL VALID BUT NEEDS TO BE UPDATED.
MENEM'S POPULIST IMAGE IS QUITE DIFFERENT FROM THAT OF HIS
MORE BUSINESSLIKE OPPONENT, EDUARDO ANGELOZ, THE CANDIDATE
OF THE RADICAL CIVIC UNION PARTY.

06234 MEEKS, C.
TO RESPECT LIFE
SOJOURNERS, 18(10) (NOV 89), 22.
THE WILLINGNESS OF THE UNITED STATES TO SANCTION
ABORTION DEMONSTRATES ITS DISREGARD FOR THE SANCTITY OF
HUMAN LIFE. THE AUTHOR MAINTAINS THAT SUCH POLICIES ARE
NOTHING NEW: GENOCIDE OF NATIVE AMERICANS, PARTICIPATION IN
WAR, AND ADHERENCE TO CAPITAL PUNISHMENT ALL CHEAPEN THE
VALUE OF HUMAN LIFE. HOWEVER, A BLANKET BAN OF ABORTION IS
NOT A SOLUTION BECAUSE IT DOES NOT RESPECT THE RIGHTS AND
LIFE OF THE MOTHER. THE AUTHOR CALLS FOR INCREASED
INVOLVEMENT OF THOSE IN THE MIDDLE GROUND BETWEEN PRO-LIFE
AND PRO-CHOICE CAMPS.

06235 MEIDER, R.
THE SWEDISH LABOUR MOVEMENT AT THE CROSSROADS
STUDIES IN POLITICAL ECONOMY: A SOCIALIST REVIEW, (28)
(SPR 89), 7-32.
THIS PAPER IS AN INTERVIEW IN WHICH MEIDNER DISCUSSES
RECENT CRITICAL DEVELOPMENTS IN RELATIONS AMONG LABOR,
CAPITAL, AND THE STATE IN SWEDEN, AS WELL AS A MORE GENERAL
STRATEGIC QUESTIONS OF INTEREST TO SOCIALISTS, THREATS TO
EQUALITY, SOLIDARITY, POLARISATION, TAXES, WORK HOURS, WAGES
ARE DISCUSSED.

06236 MEISSNER, B.
"NEW THINKING" AND SOVIET FOREIGN POLICY
AUSSEN POLITIK, 40(2) (1989), 101-118.
IF GORBACHEV INTENDS TO EFFECT AN ECONOMIC AND SOCIAL
RESTRUCTURING OF THE SOVIET UNION, HE NEEDS MORE THAN A
BRIEF PERIOD OF QUIET ON THE FOREIGN AND SECURITY POLICY
FRONT. THE CHANGES IN THESE AREAS AMOUNT TO A CHANGE OF
COURSE: MORE THAN JUST A CHANGE OF TACK AS HAD BEEN MADE
BEFORE HIM, BUT LESS THAN A CONCEPT THAT COULD CLAIM TO BE
COMPLETE AND CONSISTENT. THIS ARTICLE DESCRIBES THE FOUR
PHASES IN WHICH THE "NEW THINKING", THE DRIVING FORCE BEHIND
THE CURRENT POLITICAL THEORY, HAS BEEN INJECTED INTO FOREIGN
POLICY, CULMINATING IN THE SHAKE-UP OF THE SOVIET LEADERSHIP
LAST FALL.

06237 MEJAK, H.
YUGOSLAVIA: SERB CRUSADE
THIRD WORLD WEEK, 7(9) (JAN 89), 75-76.
SLOBODAN MILOSEVIC, THE COMMUNIST PARTY CHIEF OF SERBIA,
IS GATHERING POWER AT AN EVER-FASTER PACE. MILOSEVIC SEEMS
INTENT ON REINVENTING THE WHOLE COUNTRY, AND HIS ASCENT
WORRIES MANY YUGOSLAVS.

06238 MELANSON, R.A.
ACTION HISTORY, DECLARATORY HISTORY, AND THE REAGAN YEARS
SAIS REVIEW, 9(2) (SUM 89), 225-246.
THIS ARTICLE POINTS OUT THE OFTEN WIDE GAPS BETWEEN
ACTUAL AND STATED HISTORY USED OF THE REAGON ADMINISTRATION
TO JUSTIFY ITS FOREIGN POLICY. THE AUTHOR'S ANALYSIS CENTERS
AROUND THE IMPORTANCE OF THE VIETNAM WAR TO THE
DECISIONMAKERS IN THE REAGAN WHITE HOUSE. THIS IDEA OF A
VIETNAM PERSON, THROUGH WHICH PAST AND FUTURE
ADMINISTRATIONS LOOK WHEN DELIBERATING OVER POLICY FURTHER
CERTIFIES THE LONG-RANGE IMPACT OF THIS WAR ON THE AMERICAN
PUBLIC AND POLICYMAKER.

06239 MELCHIOR, L.
SCHOOL SELF-GOVERNMENT IN SOCIALIST POLAND: THEORY AND
PRACTICE
SOCIALISM AND DEMOCRACY, (8) (SPR 89), 45-88.
THIS EXAMINATION OF EDUCATION IN POLAND DESCRIBES
ATTEMPTS IN RECENT YEARS TO IMPROVE THE PRACTICAL
IMPLEMENTATION OF THE IDEALS OF SOCIALIST DEMOCRACY. IT
ARGUES THAT LIMITATIONS ON DEMOCRATIZATION OF SCHOOLS HAVE
CREATED A DEGREE OF SKEPTICISM ABOUT THE DEMOCRATIC
POTENTIAL OF SELF-GOVERNMENT. IT CONCLUDES THAT THIS HAS LED
TO ACTIVISM AS WELL AS APATHY AMONG YOUNG PEOPLE.

06240 MELDRUM, A.
A GOLDEN HANDSHAKE?
AFRICA REPORT, 34(4) (JUL 89), 34-35.
MUCH TO THE SURPRISE OF ANGOLA WATCHERS AROUND THE WORLD,
PRESIDENT DOS SANTOS AND JONAS SAVIMBI MET IN GBADOLITE,
ZAIRE, AGREEING TO A CEASE-FIRE IN THE LONG AND COSTLY WAR.
BUT THE REAL TASK LIES AHEAD IN NEGOTIATING THE TERMS OF
PEACE, INCLUDING THE FUTURE ROLE OF UNITA AND ITS REBEL
LEADER.

06241 MELDRUM, A.
CAMPUS CRITICISM

AFRICA REPORT, 34(6) (NOV 89), 42-44.
AS ROBERT MUGABE'S GOVERNMENT CONTINUES ITS CAMPAIGN FOR
A ONEPARTY STATE IN 1990, STUDENTS AND OTHER GOVERNMENT
CRITICS ARE WORRIED THAT ZIMBABWE IS BACKTRACKING ON FREEDOM
OF POLITICAL ASSOCIATION AND THE ANTI-CORRUPTION DRIVE BY
USING IAN SMITERA EMERGENCY POWERS TO CLAMP DOWN ON
PERCEIVED OPPONENTS.

06242 MELDRUM, A.
FINDING A MEETING POINT
AFRICA REPORT, 34(2) (MAR 89), 38-40.
INTERNAL AND EXTERNAL PRESSURE ON THE PRETORIA
GOVERNMENT TO BEGIN NEGOTIATIONS TO END APARTHEID HAS THE
FOCUS OF TWO CONFERENCES RECENTLY HELD IN HARARE. THE FIRST
BROUGHT TOGETHER 30 SOUTH AFRICAN LAWYERS AND TOP MEMBERS OF
THE AFRICAN NATIONAL CONGRESS (ANC) TO DISCUSS THE SHAPE OF
A NEW CONSTITUTION FOR A POST-APARTHEID SOUTH AFRICA. THE
SECOND GATHERED EIGHT FOREIGN MINISTERS FROM COMMONWEALTH
COUNTRIES TO EXAMINE HOW TO INCREASE PRESSURE ON SOUTH
AFRICA THROUGH ECONOMIC SANCTIONS AND A TIGHTENED ARMS
EMBARGO.

06243 MELDRUM, A.
MUGABE'S MANEUVERS
AFRICA REPORT, 34(3) (MAY 89), 38-41.
ZIMBABWE'S POLITICAL LANDSCAPE HAS BEEN ALTERED BY THE
LAUNCHING OF A NEW PARTY, THE CORRUPTION SCANDAL WHICH COST
EIGHT TOP OFFICIALS THEIR JOBS, AND THE RECENT INTRODUCTION
OF ECONOMIC REFORMS. PRESIDENT MUGABE'S ADEPT HANDLING OF
THE CHALLENGES FACING THE NATION HAS STRENGTHENED HIS HAND,
TAKING THE STING OUT OF CRITICS ATTACKS.

06244 MELDRUM, A.
THE BUSH AGENDA IN SOUTHERN AFRICA
AFRICA REPORT, 34(1) (JAN 89), 16-17.
ZIMBABWE'S FOREIGN MINISTER HAS CALLED ON GEORGE BUSH TO
ABANDON THE REAGAN ADMINISTRATION'S POLICY OF CONSTRUCTIVE
ENGAGEMENT TOWARD SOUTH AFRICA. BUT MANY OBSERVERS BELIEVE
THE BUSH ADMINISTRATION'S POLICIES WILL DIFFER ONLY SLIGHTLY
FROM ITS PREDECESSORS.

06245 MELDRUM, A.
THE CORRUPTION CONTROVERSY
AFRICA REPORT, 34(1) (JAN 89), 36-37.
ALTHOUGH LAST YEAR, THE MUGABE GOVERNMENT SEEMED AT THE
PEAK OF ITS POLITICAL STRENGTH WITH THE CONCLUSION OF A
UNITY AGREEMENT WITH ZAPU, A SUCCESSFUL AMNESTY FOR
DISSIDENTS, AND A HEALTHY ECONOMIC OUTLOOK, CORRUPTION
SCANDALS IMPLICATING PARTY LEADERS MAY MAKE 1989 A TOUGH
YEAR FOR THE PRESIDENT.

06246 MELDRUM, A.
THE GBADOLITE DEBACLE
AFRICA REPORT, 34(5) (SEP 89), 30-31.
FOLLOWING THE COLLAPSE OF THE PEACE PLAN NEGOTIATED IN
ZAIRE IN JUNE 1989, ANGOLA IS ONCE AGAIN ENGULFED IN WAR.
THIS ARTICLE EXPLAINS THE BACKGROUND TO THE COLLAPSE OF THE
GBADOLITE AGREEMENT AND THE RESUMPTION OF FIGHTING AND
REPORTS ON THE FLOUNDERING EFFORTS OF ZAIRIAN PRESIDENT
MOBUTU TO FIND A SETTLEMENT.

06247 MELDRUM, A.
THE NEGOTIATING PLATFORM
AFRICA REPORT, 34(5) (SEP 89), 24-26.
IN THE EXPECTATION THAT A SETTLEMENT OF THE CRISIS IN
SOUTH AFRICA WILL BE BROUGHT ABOUT THROUGH NEGOTIATION, THE
AFRICAN NATIONAL CONGRESS HAS PREPARED A DOCUMENT OUTLINING
ITS POSITION ON DISCUSSIONS WITH THE PRETORIA GOVERNMENT.
DESPITE THE SETBACKS DUE TO ANC PRESIDENT TAMBO'S ILLNESS
AND QUESTIONS REGARDING ITS EXILE HEADQUARTERS IN LUSAKA,
THE ANC'S STATURE IS RISING AND IT HAS WON ENDORSEMENTS FOR
ITS POSITION FROM THE OAU AND THE NON-ALIGNED MOVEMENT.

06248 MELLY, P.
TOKYO SPREADS IT AROUND
SOUTH, (105) (JUL 89), 20-21.
JAPAN HAS CONFOUNDED ITS CRITICS BY HONORING ITS US$30
BILLION CASH PLEDGE TO THE DEVELOPING WORLD WITHOUT IMPOSING
TRADE TIES. BUT JAPAN WILL NOT COME OUT OF THE PROCESS EMPTY-
HANDED. ITS BIG TRADING HOUSES ARE SURE TO WIN A SHARE OF
THE DEALS FINANCED BY TOKYO. AND JAPAN'S IMPROVED STANDING
IN THE THIRD WORLD IS CERTAIN TO BRING LONG-TERM BENEFITS IN
TERMS OF TRADE AND POLITICAL INFLUENCE.

06249 MELODY, W.
EFFICIENCY AND SOCIAL POLICY IN TELECOMMUNICATION: LESSONS
FROM THE US EXPERIENCE
JOURNAL OF ECONOMIC ISSUES, XXIII(3) (SEP 89), 657-688.
THE ARTICLE EXAMINES PUBLIC POLICY WITH REGARDS TO THE
RAPIDLY CHANGING FIELD OF TELECOMMUNICATION. IT CONCENTRATES
ON THE DEBATE BETWEEN PROPONENTS OF GOVERNMENT REGULATION OF
THE "NATURAL MONOPOLY" AND THOSE WHO FAVOR DEREGULATION AND
MARKET COMPETITION. IT CONCLUDES THAT CURRENT DEBATE IS
SIMPLISTIC AND AVOIDS THE REAL ISSUES. EACH SIDE TO THE

DEBATE COMPARES AN ABSTRACT IDEAL OF ITS PREFERRED POSITION
WITH PERCEIVED WEAKNESSES IN THE REALITY THAT PURPORTEDLY
REPRESENTS THE OPPOSING VIEW. A CLOSE EXAMINATION OF THE
LAST 80 YEARS OF US TELECOMMUNICATIONS POLICY REVEALS THAT
NEITHER MONOPOLY, NOR COMPETITION PROVIDES THE ULTIMATE
SERVICE AT THE BEST PRICE.

06250 MELOSSI, D.
POLITICAL BUSINESS CYCLES AND IMPRISONMENT RATES IN ITALY:
REPORT ON WORK IN PROGRESS
REVIEW OF BLACK POLITICAL ECOMOMY, 16(1) (SUM 87), 211-218.
THIS ARTICLE STUDIES IMPRISONMENT AND SOCIAL CONTROL IN
ITALY FROM 1896-1965. THE HYPOTHESIS OF THE ARTICLE IS THAT
THE OBSERVED ASSOCIATION BETWEEN CHANGE IN IMPRISONMEN RATES
AND CHANGE IN ECONOMIC INDICATORS DEPENDS ON AN INTERVENING
VARIABLE CALLED VOCABULARIES OF PUNITIVE MOTIVES. "LAW IN
ACTION" IS EXPLORED.

06251 MEMON, A.
A FAILING GAMBIT
INDIA TODAY, XIV(14) (JUL 89), 38.
THE APPOINTMENT OF M. CHENNA REDDY AS ANDHRA PRADSH
CONGRESS (I) COMMITTEE PRESDIENT REFLECTS THE DEPERATION OF
THE PARTY. REDDY, ONCE A WELL RESPECTED POLITICIAN WITH A
REPUTATION FOR ORGANIZATION AND THE ABILITY TO MINIMALIZE
FACTIONALISM HAS SINCE BEEN TARNISHED WITH SCANDAL AND
CORRUPTION. MOST OBSERVERS CONCEDE THAT REDDY'S TASK IS A
NEXT TO IMPOSSIBLE ONE.

06252 MENARD, J.C.
REGENERATION AND POLITICS: BUBER'S IDEA OF NATIONHOOD
DISSERTATION ABSTRACTS INTERNATIONAL, 50(5) (NOV 89),
1424-A.
THE AUTHOR STUDIES MARTIN BUBER'S CONCEPT OF JEWISH
NATIONHOOD AND, IN PARTICULAR, HIS IDEA OF REGENERATION.
WHEN APPLIED TO ISRAEL, BUBER'S CONCEPTION OF REGENERATION
INVOLVES DIVINE AND UNIVERSAL DIMENSIONS AS WELL AS SECULAR
AND PARTICULAR DIMENSIONS. IT INCLUDES THE BIBLICAL IDEA OF
COSMIC MISSION AND CHOSEN NATIONHOOD, ON ONE HAND, AND
RETURN TO LABOR ON THE LAND AND THE FORMATION OF COMMUNAL
SOCIALISM, ON THE OTHER.

06253 MENDE, J.
EDUCATION - FOR WHOM?
WORLD MARXIST REVIEW, 31(2) (FEB 88), 136-141.
A DEBATE ON AUSTRIAN EDUCATION HAS DEMONSTRATED THAT
RIGID DIVIDES BETWEEN EDUCATIONAL CYCLES AS WELL AS THE
TRADITIONAL 'CRAMMING' ARE OUTDATED. PEOPLE TRAINED TO TAKE
ORDERS AND OBEY WILL BE UNABLE TO SHOW INITIATIVE IN
TECHNOLOGICAL INNOVATION, IN OPERATION OF MACHINERY OR IN
THE SOCIAL SPHERE. THE DEMAND OF THE COMMUNIST PARTY FOR THE
DEVELOPMENT OF A GENERAL POLYTECHNICAL SCHOOL IS THEREFORE
INSEPARABLE FROM THE GOAL OF THE DEMOCRATISATION OF THE
ACADEMIC PROCESS, FROM THE INTEGRATION OF RESEARCH,
TECHNOLOGICAL AND INDUSTRIAL PROJECTS INTO IT, AND FROM
STUDIES OF PRACTICAL PROBLEMS IN THE LIFE OF SOCIETY.

06254 MENDELSOHN, J.
SDI: DREAM OR FANTASY?
NATO'S SIXTEEN NATIONS, 34(4) (AUG 89), 54-56.
DREAMS CAN BECOME REALITIES, BUT FANTASIES ARE DELUSIONS.
IF THE ORIGINAL INTENTION OF SDI HAS TO CREATE A WEAPONS
SYSTEM TO ELIMINATE THE THREAT OF NUCLEAR WARFARE FOREVER,
THEN IT WAS A FANTASY. BY THE SAME TOKEN, THE PRESENT SOVIET
CAMPAIGN TO ELIMINATE SUCH WARFARE MUST BE CLASSIFIED IN
THIS CATEGORY. NOW AND IN THE FORESEEABLE FUTURE, STABILITY
MUST REST ON AN EVEN BALANCE, ALBEIT AT THE LOWEST POSSIBLE
LEVELS, OF THE DETERRENT FORCES OF THE SUPERPOWERS.

06255 MENDLOVITZ, S.H.
STRUGGLES FOR A JUST WORLD PEACE: A TRANSITION STRATEGY
ALTERNATIVES, 64(3) (JUL 89), 363-370.
OVER THE LAST 20 YEARS, THE AUTHOR HAS BEEN ACTIVELY
ENGAGED IN RESEARCH, TEACHING, DIALOGUE, ADVOCACY, AND
POLITICAL ACTION IN THE STRUGGLES FOR A JUST WORLD PEACE,
RECENTLY HE HAS BEEN INVOLVED IN A NEW PROJECT CALLED "THE
COMING GLOBAL CIVILIZATION: CHALLENGES TO POLITY." THE
PROJECT SEEKS TO DEVELOP CROSS-CULTURAL AND
MULTIDISCIPLINARY PERSPECTIVES ON THE COMING GLOBAL
CIVILIZATION, TO ANALYZE THE CONSEQUENT CHALLENGES TO
EXISTING FORMS OF POLITY AND TO ARTICULATE BOTH A NORMATIVE
VISION AND PRACTICAL GUIDELINES FOR ACTION IN A PERIOD OF
RAPID TRANSITION. THIS ESSAY IS A RESULT OF THESE VARIOUS
ENGAGEMENTS. IT DESCRIBES SETTING UP A PROCESS WHICH
ARTICULATES CONCRETE POLITICAL GOALS AND PARTICULAR KINDS OF
ACTIONS TO ACHIEVE THOSE GOALS.

06256 MENG-CHI, T.
MAINLAND INTELLECTUALS SPARK DISSIDENT MOVEMENT
ASIAN OUTLOOK, 24(2) (MAR 89), 29-31.
ON FEBRUARY 13, 1989, THIRTY-THREE MAINLAND CHINESE
INTELLECTUALS SIGNED A PETITION CALLING FOR A GENERAL
AMNESTY FOR POLITICAL PRISONERS AND SENT IT TO HIGH-RANKING
COMMUNIST PARTY OFFICIALS, INCLUDING TENG HSIAO-PING. IN

THIS RARE SHOW OF UNITED DISSENT, THE PETITIONERS UNLEASHED
A POWERFUL MOVEMENT FOR FREEDOM, HUMAN RIGHTS, AND DEMOCRACY.
THEY MAY HAVE SPARKED A BRUSH FIRE THAT COULD GET OUT OF
HAND AND CONSUME THE COMMUNIST PARTY ITSELF.

06257 MENG, W.
    THE PRINCIPAL CONTRADICTION IN CULTURE
    BEIJING REVIEW, 32(20) (MAY 89), 31.
        WHAT IS THE PRINCIPAL CONTRADICTION IN CULTURE AT THE
    PRIMARY STAGE OF SOCIALISM? SOME SAY THAT ANTI-FEUDALISM IS
    THE PRINCIPAL CONTRADICTION. OTHERS SAY ANTI-CAPITALISM.
    SOME EVEN SAY IT IS BOTH FEUDALISM AND CAPITALISM AND THEN
    POINT TO SOME REMNANTS OF FEUDAL THOUGHT AND DECADENT
    CAPITALISM PRESENT IN SOCIETY. IN FACT, THE PRINCIPAL
    CONTRADICTION FACING CHINESE SOCIALISM AT PRESENT LIES
    BETWEEN CIVILIZATION AND IGNORANCE. IGNORANCE AND BARBARISM
    MUST BE ELIMINATED.

06258 MENGISTEAB, K.
    THE NATURE OF THE STATE AND AGRICULTURAL CRISIS IN POST-
    1975 ETHIOPIA
    STUDIES IN COMPARATIVE INTERNATIONAL DEVELOPMENT, 24(1)
    (SPR 89), 20-38.
        ETHIOPIA'S AGRICULTURE IS IN SERIOUS CRISIS EVEN AFTER
    THE 1975 RADICAL REDISTRIBUTION OF LAND. A LARGE NUMBER OF
    INTERNAL AND EXTERNAL FACTORS WHICH ARE OFTEN INTRICATELY
    INTERRELATED ARE INVOLVED IN GENERATING THIS CRISIS. THIS
    PAPER CONTENDS THAT MANY OF THESE FACTORS ARE CLOSELY
    ASSOCIATED WITH THE NATURE OF THE STATE. IN AN ATTEMPT TO
    ESTABLISH THIS ASSOCIATION, THE PAPER ANALYZES THE CHANGES
    BOTH IN THE NATURE OF THE STATE AND IN THE TYPES OF PROBLEMS
    THE COUNTRY'S AGRICULTURE HAS ENCOUNTERED SINCE THE EARLY
    17TH CENTURY WHEN AGRICULTURAL STAGNATION BECAME MORE
    APPARENT. EMPHASIS IS, HOWEVER, PLACED ON THE POST 1975 ERA.

06259 MENON, A.
    A TOUGH ROLE
    INDIA TODAY, XIV(13) (JUL 89), 18-20.
        N.T. RAMA RAO'S FILM, BRAHMARISHI VISHAMITRA, HAS
    SPARKED OFF A STIFF LEGAL AND POLITICAL BATTLE BETWEEN THE
    TELUGU DESAM PARTY AND THE CONGRESS (I). THE FILM IS THE
    LATEST IN A GROWING SERIES OF ALLEGATIONS OF CORRUPTION AND
    LITIGATION. THIS ARTICLE EXPLORES RAMA RAO'S TOUGHEST
    POLITICAL BATTLE YET.

06260 MENON, A.
    N.T. RAMA RAO: FACING THE RECOIL
    INDIA TODAY, XIV(7) (APR 89), 24-27.
        RAMA RAO'S DECISION TO SACK HIS 31-MEMBER CABINET WAS,
    EVEN BY HIS OWN MELODRAMATIC STANDARDS, A STUNNING MOVE. NOW
    THE DUMPED MINISTERS ARE REGROUPING, AND FOR THE FIRST TIME
    RAMA RAO FACES A BREWING CHALLENGE TO HIS AUTOCRATIC
    LEADERSHIP.

06261 MENON, A.K.
    A CASTE WAR ERUPTS
    INDIA TODAY, XIV(2) (JAN 89), 30-32.
        THE RIVALRY BETWEEN THE KAMMA AND KAPU COMMUNITIES HAS
    GIVEN A NEW DIMENSION TO POLITICS IN ANDHRA PRADESH. IN LATE
    DECEMBER 1988 THE MURDER OF RANGA RAO, A CONGRESS (I) MLA
    AND LEADER OF THE KAPU COMMUNITY, TRIGGERED CASTE VIOLENCE
    IN FOUR COASTAL DISTRICTS. THE OUTBREAK WAS THE CULMINATION
    OF AN ONGOING CONFLICT THAT HAS BEEN FUELED BY THE CONGRESS
    (I) PARTY AND TELUGU DESAM.

06262 MENON, A.K.; CHAWLA, P.; DILEEP, L.; MENON, R.
    A CLOSE RACE
    INDIA TODAY, XIV(2) (JAN 89), 14-20.
        TAMIL NADU, MIZORAM, AND NAGALAND ARE BELLWETHER STATES
    WHERE THE POLITICAL FUTURES AND PRESTIGE OF RAJIV GANDHI, M.
    KARUNANIDHI, AND JAYALALITHA WILL BE TESTED IN THE 1989
    ASSEMBLY ELECTIONS. TOGETHER, THE THREE STATES WILL
    DETERMINE WHETHER THE ERA OF THE REGIONAL PARTIES HAS
    DEFINITELY ARRIVED. EACH OF THE 334 ASSEMBLY SEATS AT STAKE
    WILL BE KEENLY CONTESTED.

06263 MENON, A.K.
    ANDHRA PRADESH: SWEEPING CLOUT
    INDIA TODAY, XIV(5) (MAR 89), 30-31.
        EXACTLY ONE WEEK AFTER HE COLLECTED THE RESIGNATIONS OF
    ALL HIS 31 MINISTERS, ANDHRA PRADESH CHIEF MINISTER N.T.
    RAMA RAO MADE HISTORY OF SORTS BY USHERING IN A 23-PERSON
    TEAM OF NEW FACES, RETAINING NOT A SINGLE MEMBER FROM THE
    EARLIER MINISTRY. NEVER BEFORE HAD ANY CHIEF MINISTER --
    FEARING THE POLITICAL FALL-OUT -- EFFECTED SUCH A COMPLETE
    SWEEP. THE UNDAUNTED RAMA RAO OF COURSE DID IT WITH
    CUSTOMARY ELAN TO SHOW HIS MINISTERS AND THE WORLD AT LARGE
    THAT NONE CAN STAND IN THE WAY OF HIS HONEYMOON WITH THE
    ELECTORATE. THIS ARTICLE EXAMINES POTENTIAL FALLOUT FROM
    THIS POLITICAL CABINET SHUFFLE.

06264 MENON, A.K.
    DISSENT DRAMA
    INDIA TODAY, XIV(6) (MAR 89), 34.
        THE SIMMERING DISCONTENT IN THE TELUGU DESAM LEGISLATURE
    PARTY HAS BURST INTO THE OPEN. THE DISGRUNTLED PARTY MEMBERS
    HAVE RALLIED BEHIND SPEAKER G. NARAYANA RAO, WHO HAS
    DEMANDED INNER-PARTY DEMOCRACY.

06265 MENON, A.K.
    PUBLICITY PITFALLS
    INDIA TODAY, XIV(8) (MAY 89), 29-31.
        WITH HIS PENCHANT FOR PUBLICITY, RAMA RAO HAS ALWAYS
    KEPT IN THE PUBLIC SPOTLIGHT. BUT NOW THE BLATANT MISUSE OF
    A GOVERNMENT JOURNAL FOR SELF-PROMOTION IS BREWING CHARGES
    OF WASTING PUBLIC FUNDS.

06266 MENON, A.K.
    RAISING AN ALARM
    INDIA TODAY, XIV(3) (FEB 89), 49-50.
        IN JANUARY 1989, HEADLINES IN A HYDERABAD NEWSPAPER
    SUGGESTED THAT THE ANDHRA PRADESH GOVERNMENT WAS ON THE
    VERGE OF COLLAPSE. BUT CHIEF MINISTER N.T. RAMA RAO, ALREADY
    UNDER ATTACK FOR THE HANDLING OF THE RIOTS THAT FOLLOWED THE
    MURDER OF MLA RANGA RAO, LAUGHED AT THE REPORTS THAT HIS
    ADMINISTRATION WAS IN DANGER.

06267 MENON, K.U.
    BRUNEI DARUSSALAM IN 1988: AGING IN THE WOOD
    ASIAN SURVEY, XXIX(2) (FEB 89), 140-144.
        1988 WAS A YEAR OF POLITICAL STABILITY FOR BRUNEI. THE
    ARTICLE ASSESSES THIS STABILITY IN THREE AREAS: THE REGIME
    (CONTINUITY OF GOVERNMENT STRUCTURES); AUTHORITY HOLDERS
    (SUSTAINED TENURE IN TOP POSITIONS WITH NO COUP D'ETAT OR
    ABRUPT DISMISSALS); AND PUBLIC ORDER (NO RIOTS OR TURMOIL IN
    THE STREETS). THE ARTICLE ALSO ANALYZES BRUNEI'S EFFORTS TO
    MAINTAIN EXTERNAL SECURITY AND CONTINUE ITS ECONOMIC GROWTH
    THROUGH NON-OIL VENTURES.

06268 MENON, R.
    A HARD-BOUGHT VICTORY
    INDIA TODAY, XIV(3) (FEB 89), 21-22.
        THE CONGRESS (I) PARTY RETURNED TO POWER IN NAGALAND IN
    JANUARY 1989, AMID ALLEGATIONS THAT ITS VICTORY WAS ASSURED
    BY ITS FORMIDABLE MONEY POWER. THE VICTORY WAS LED BY S.
    CHUBATOSHI JAMIR. EVEN THOUGH JAMIR HAS ONCE FORCED OUT OF
    THE CHIEF MINISTERSHIP BY CHARGES OF CORRUPTION AND ANTI-
    INDIAN RHETORIC, CONGRESS (I) LEADERS BELIEVED THAT HE WAS
    THE ONLY PERSON WHO COULD STEER THE PARTY TO VICTORY IN THE
    INSURGENCY-RIDDEN STATE.

06269 MENON, R.
    ASSAM: ROLE REVERSAL
    INDIA TODAY, XIV(5) (MAR 89), 34-35.
        AFTER FIGHTING FOREIGN NATIONALS AND IMMIGRANTS FOR
    NEARLY A DECADE IN ORDER TO SAFEGUARD THE ETHNIC, ECONOMIC,
    CULTURAL AND POLITICAL IDENTITY OF THE ORIGINAL INHABITANTS
    OF ASSAM, THE GOVERNMENT IS NOW FACING AN UPRISING FROM THE
    MOST ORIGINAL SETTLERS OF ALL, THE TRIBALS, WHO ARE
    AGITATING FOR A SEPARATE STATE. THE LATEST PHASE OF
    AGITATION, WHICH IS CONTINUING UNCHECKED, LEFT 32 DEAL AND
    40 INJURED.

06270 MENON, R.
    KERALA NAXALITES: RELICS OF A REBELLION
    INDIA TODAY, XIV(14) (JUL 89), 78-81.
        THE ARTICLE EXAMINES THE RELICS OF THE NAXALITE MOVEMENT,
    A SERIES OF ATTACKS ON LANDED GENTRY BY MARXIST EXTREMISTS
    THAT TOOK PLACE SOME TWENTY YEARS PREVIOUSLY. IT CONCLUDES
    THAT MOST OF THOSE INVOLVED HAVE LEFT REVOLUTION BEHIND AND
    ARE NOW MORE OR LESS ORDINARY CITIZENS. JAIL, TORTURE AND
    THE PASSAGE OF TIME SEEMS TO HAVE HAD A MELLOWING EFFECT;
    THE NAXALITES STILL EXIST, BUT ONLY IN SMALL SPLINTER GROUPS
    THAT ARE A FRACTION OF THEIR EARLIER SIZE.

06271 MENON, R.
    LEFT IS RIGHT
    INDIA TODAY, XIV(8) (MAY 89), 40-41.
        SINCE THE CPI(M) LEFT DEMOCRATIC FRONT GAINED POWER IN
    KERALA IN 1987, UNDESERVING MARXIST FILMMAKERS, WRITERS, AND
    ARTISTES HAVE BEEN CATAPULTED INTO POSITIONS OF PROMINENCE.
    THE MOST RECENT INSTANCE OF THE GOVERNMENT TRYING TO
    INFLUENCE THE STATE'S CULTURAL ETHOS CAME WHEN THE LEFTIST
    PRODUCTION "ORE THUVAL PAKSHIKAL" WON FIRST PLACE IN THE
    STATE FILM AWARDS.

06272 MENON, R.
    NEW THINKING AND NORTHEAST ASIAN SECURITY
    PROBLEMS OF COMMUNISM, XXXVIII(2-3) (MAR 89), 1-29.
        IN LINE WITH HIS "NEW THINKING" IN FOREIGN POLICY,
    MIKHAIL GORBACHEV HAS ATTEMPTED TO EFFECT SUBSTANTIAL CHANGE
    IN SOVIET RELATIONSHIPS WITH THE NORTHEAST ASIAN STATES.
    THUS, THE USSR HAS OFFERED PROPOSALS ON MILITARY BASES, ARMS
    CONTROL, AND ECONOMIC COOPERATION IN NORTHEAST ASIA TO ALLAY
    THE CONCERNS IN CHINA, JAPAN, AND, TO A LESSER EXTENT, SOUTH
    KOREA THAT STEMMED FROM THE BREZHNEV-ERA'S MILITARY BUILDUP
    IN THE FAR EAST. ATTEMPTS TO EXPLORE COMMON GROUND WITH
    CHINA AND JAPAN IN PROMOTING TRADE AND OTHER KINDS OF TIES

HAVE ALSO MARKED BILATERAL SOVIET RELATIONS WITH THESE
COUNTRIES. TO ENHANCE THE CREDIBILITY OF THE NEW APPROACH,
GORBACHEV HAS APPOINTED NEW OFFICIALS TO BE RESPONSIBLE FOR
THE OVERALL DIRECTION OF FOREIGN POLICY AS WELL AS DIFFERENT
SPECIALISTS AND DIPLOMATS TO DEAL WITH THE NORTHEAST ASIAN
COUNTRIES. HOWEVER, THESE COUNTRIES ARE NOT CONVINCED OF
SOVIET GOOD INTENTIONS, AND MANY PROBLEMS BETWEEN THEM AND
MOSCOW REMAIN UNRESOLVED.

06273 MENON, R.
     NO SCRUPLES
     INDIA TODAY, XIV(1) (JAN 89), 28.
        AS THE JANUARY 21, 1989, ELECTION APPROACHED, THERE WERE
     TWO STRIKING FEATURES IN THE POLITICAL SCENE IN NAGALAND:
     THE OPPOSITION'S ANTI-INDIA RHETORIC AND THE FACTIONAL
     INFIGHTING WITHIN THE CONGRESS (I) PARTY.

06274 MENON, R.
     REJECTING THE REBEL
     INDIA TODAY, XIV(3) (FEB 89), 23-24.
        LESS THAN TWO YEARS AFTER HE WAS TRIUMPHANTLY ELECTED
     MIZORAM'S CHIEF MINISTER, LALDENGA AND HIS MIZO NATIONAL
     FRONT WERE REDUCED TO IGNOMINY IN THE STATE ASSEMBLY
     ELECTIONS. REPLACING HIM WAS CONGRESS (I) PARTY LEADER
     LALTHANHAWLA, WHO HAD PREVIOUSLY STEPPED ASIDE VOLUNTARILY
     TO MAKE WAY FOR LALDENGA FOLLOWING THE MIZORAM PEACE ACCORD.

06275 MENON, R.
     THE BUBBLE BURSTS
     INDIA TODAY, XIV(1) (JAN 89), 27-28.
        MANY VOTERS FEEL THAT THE MIZO NATIONAL FRONT, UNDER
     LALDENGA'S LEADERSHIP, HAS BETRAYED THE ASPIRATIONS OF THE
     MIZOS. LADLENGA FACES A TOUGH BATTLE BECAUSE MOST OF HIS
     SUPPORTERS HAVE JOINED THE OPPOSITION CAMP, THE CHURCH
     OPPOSES HIM BECAUSE OF HIS POLICY ON LIQUOR, AND CONGRESS
     (I) IS MAKING INROADS IN THE STATE.

06276 MENSHIKOV, S.
     THE STRUGGLE FOR THE SOVIET CENTRE
     SOUTH, (99) (JAN 89), 26.
        THE MAIN THRUST OF THE SOVIET ECONOMIC REFORMS HAS BEEN
     TO PROVIDE WIDE AUTONOMY TO THE STATE-OWNED ENTERPRISES THAT
     DOMINATE INDUSTRY, TRANSPORT, CONSTRUCTION, AND TRADE AND
     ACCOUNT FOR A LARGE PART OF FARM PRODUCTION. SINCE JANUARY
     1988, LEGISLATION HAS GIVEN PLANTS MORE FREEDOM TO PLAN
     THEIR OUTPUT AND USE THEIR INCOME, BUT IT HAS ALSO PRESERVED
     THE AUTHORITY OF THE MINISTRIES, ENABLING THEM TO CONTINUE
     TO PASS ORDERS DOWN THE LINE AS IF NOTHING MUCH HAD CHANGED.
     MANY PLANT MANAGERS AND WORKERS HAVE DEMANDED THAT THE
     MINISTRIES' ROLE BE REDUCED TO ADVICE AND CONSULTATION. THE
     BIG QUESTION IS WHETHER THIS DEMAND WILL BE HEEDED IN 1989.

06277 MENY, YVES
     THE NATIONAL AND INTERNATIONAL CONTEXT OF FRENCH POLICY
     COMMUNITIES
     POLITICAL STUDIES, 37(3) (FAL 89), 387-399.
        THERE ARE NUMEROUS, WELL-ORGANIZED POLICY COMMUNITIES IN
     FRANCE, BASED UPON SPECIALIZED CORPS OF SENIOR
     ADMINISTRATIVE OFFICIALS IN SYMBIOSIS WITH THE ENVIRONMENT
     THEY ARE RESPONSIBLE FOR REGULATING AND MANAGING. THEY ALSO
     DERIVE THEIR STRENGTH FROM THE INTEGRATION OF THE GROUPS
     CONCERNED IN THE POLICY PROCESS, ALLOWING THEM TO COMPENSATE
     FOR THE WEAKNESS OF THEIR ORGANIZATION AND SOCIAL BASE BY
     THE PRIVILEGED ACCESS AND LEGITIMACY THEY ACQUIRE.
     NEVERTHELESS, THE TRADITIONAL WAY IN WHICH THE POLICY
     PROCESS IS STRUCTURED IS MODIFIED BY THE TERRITORIAL SHIFT
     (BOTH LOCAL AND INTERNATIONAL) IN THE ARENAS IN WHICH PUBLIC
     POLICIES ARE MADE.

06278 MENZEL, D.C.
     INTERGOVERNMENTAL IMPLEMENTATION MANDATES: A STUDY OF TWO
     LAND USE REGULATORY POLICIES
     POLICY STUDIES REVIEW, 9(1) (AUT 89), 160-167.
        THIS PAPER EXAMINES THE IMPLEMENTATION MANDATES AND
     EXPERIENCES ASSOCIATED WITH TWO INTERGOVERNMENTAL REGULATORY
     POLICIES, ONE AT THE FEDERAL-STATE LEVEL AND THE OTHER AT
     THE STATE-CONTROL LEVEL. THE POLICIES ARE THE FEDERAL
     SURFACE MINING CONTROL AND RECLAMATION ACT OF 1977 AND THE
     FLORIDA GROWTH MANAGEMENT ACT OF 1985. THESE EXPERIENCES
     SUGGEST THAT IMPLEMENTATION MANDATES, AT LEAST WITH RESPECT
     TO INTERGOVERNMENTAL REGULATORY POLICIES, ARE NOT AS
     EFFECTIVE AS LOGIC AND RATIONAL ARGUMENT MIGHT DICTATE.

06279 MENZLER-HOKKANEN, I.
     GROUPS, ENTREPRENEURSHIP AND ECONOMIC DEVELOPMENT
     SCANDINAVIAN JOURNAL OF DEVELOPMENT ALTERNATIVES, VIII(1)
     (MAR 89), 47-60.
        IN THE 1960'S AND EARLY 1970'S THE NEWLY INDUSTRIALIZING
     COUNTRIES (NICS) WERE PREFERRED WHEN MOVING LABOR-INTENSIVE
     STAGES OF BIG PRODUCTION PROCESSES OVERSEAS, WHILE MANY LESS
     DEVELOPED COUNTRIES (LDC'S) REMAINED PERIPHERAL TO GLOBAL
     ECONOMIC ACTIVITY. THE PAPER ARGUES THAT THE KEY TO
     UNDERSTANDING THE DIFFERENCES BETWEEN COUNTRIES IN ACHIEVING
     ECONOMIC DEVELOPMENT THROUGH FOREIGN DIRECT INVESTMENT IS A

COMBINATION OF CULTURAL AND GEOGRAPHICAL FACTORS. SOCIAL
GROUPS BASED AT ENTREPOT CENTERS DEVELOP OUTWARD-LOOKING
ATTITUDES, WHEREAS THOSE IN REMOTE AREAS DEVELOP
INWARDLOOKING ATTITUDES WHICH ENCOURAGE HOSTILITY TOWARDS
FOREIGN GROUPS.

06280 MEOW, S.C.
     RELATIONS THE TAICHI WAY
     FREE CHINA REVIEW, 39(5) (MAY 89), 10-17.
        THE AUTHOR REVIEWS SINGAPORE'S BASIC FOREIGN POLICY
     REGARDING TAIWAN AND COMMUNIST CHINA. AFTER ASSESSING ITS
     APPROACH TO THE CHINA QUESTION, HE EXAMINES THE IMPACT OF
     TAIWANESE PRESIDENT LEE'S 1989 VISIT TO SINGAPORE.

06281 MERCADO-MONT, M.I.
     ORIGINS OF STATE FORMATION IN MEXICO
     DISSERTATION ABSTRACTS INTERNATIONAL, 50(5) (NOV 89),
     1424-A.
        THE AUTHOR EXAMINES AND ANALYZES THE SALIENT ELEMENTS
     THAT INFLUENCED THE NATURE OF THE STATE WHICH EVOLVED IN
     MEXICO FROM THE PERIOD OF SPANISH COLONIZATION TO THE
     FORMULATION OF THE MEXICAN CONSTITUTION OF 1917. THE
     POLITICAL EXPERIENCES RELATIVE TO THE EVOLUTION OF THE
     NATURE OF THE STATE IN MEXICO REFLECT A PERVASIVE
     AUTHORITARIAN ORIENTATION IN POLITICAL AFFAIRS, WHICH IS A
     PRODUCT OF POLITICAL HISTORY AND PHILOSOPHICAL COSMOLOGY.
     TAKEN AS A WHOLE, THESE SALIENT ELEMENTS BOTH INFLUENCED THE
     NATURE OF STATE FORMATION IN MEXICO AND DIRECTED THE PROCESS
     OF STATE FORMATION.

06282 MERDAD, J.M.
     SAUDI-AMERICAN BILATERAL RELATIONS: A CASE STUDY OF THE
     CONSEQUENCES OF INTERDEPENDENCE ON INTERNATIONAL RELATIONS
     DISSERTATION ABSTRACTS INTERNATIONAL, 50(6) (DEC 89),
     1795-A.
        THE AUTHOR STUDIES THE CONSEQUENCES OF INTERDEPENDENCE
     BETWEEN SAUDI ARABIA AND THE UNITED STATES FROM 1960 TO 1978
     AS IT RELATES TO THE CONCEPTS OF COOPERATION AND CONFLICT.
     HE CONCLUDES THAT INCREASED BILATERAL INTERDEPENDENCE
     BETWEEN THE TWO COUNTRIES PRODUCED BOTH INCREASED
     COOPERATION AND CONFLICT.

06283 MERELMAN, R.M.
     ON CULTURE AND POLITICS IN AMERICA: A PERSPECTIVE FROM
     STRUCTURAL ANTHROPOLOGY
     BRITISH JOURNAL OF POLITICAL SCIENCE, 19(4) (OCT 89),
     465-493.
        THIS ARTICLE PROPOSES A STRUCTURALIST ALTERNATIVE TO
     MAINSTREAM BEHAVIOURAL STUDIES OF POLITICAL CULTURE IN THE
     UNITED STATES. AFTER FIRST DESCRIBING THE DEFICIENCIES IN
     THE MAINSTREAM APPROACH, THE ARTICLE SUGGESTS THAT POLITICAL
     CULTURE AS ATTITUDES AND VALUES SHOULD BE SEEN AS SURFACE
     ELEMENTS OF A DEEP CULTURAL STRUCTURE. THE STRUCTURALIST
     ALTERNATIVE IS PRESENTED IN SOME DETAIL, WITH EMPHASIS UPON
     CULTURAL NARRATIVES. BUILDING UPON STRUCTURALIST THEORY,
     AMERICAN POLITICAL CULTURE EMERGES AS 'MYTHOLOGIZED
     INDIVIDUALISM', THE RAMIFICATIONS OF WHICH ARE DESCRIBED IN
     TERMS OF AMERICAN IDEOLOGICAL COGNITION AND IN TERMS OF
     AMERICAN CAPACITIES TO USE CULTURE AS A MEANS OF REALIZING
     DEMOCRATIC IDEALS. IN THESE LATTER RESPECTS, MYTHOLOGIZED
     INDIVIDUALISM IS FOUND WANTING.

06284 MERIROWITZ, M.J.
     U.S. COASTAL FISHERY INTERESTS IN DOMESTIC AND
     INTERNATIONAL POLITICS
     DISSERTATION ABSTRACTS INTERNATIONAL, 50(5) (NOV 89),
     1424-A.
        IN THE DOMESTIC DEBATE OVER FISHERIES LEGISLATION AND IN
     THE FORMATION OF U.S. FISHERIES POLICY AT THE THIRD UNITED
     NATIONS CONFERENCE ON THE LAW OF THE SEA, CONGRESS AND
     INTEREST GROUPS PLAYED A SIGNIFICANT ROLE. COASTAL FISHERY
     INTERESTS AND THEIR ALLIES IN CONGRESS WERE ABLE TO ENSURE
     THE PASSAGE OF THE 1976 FISHERY CONSERVATION AND MANAGEMENT
     ACT. THESE COASTAL FISHERY INTERESTS PREVAILED OVER DISTANT
     WATER FISHERY INTERESTS, EVEN THOUGH THE LATTER HAD MORE
     FUNDING AND BETTER CONTACTS WITH CONGRESS, AND OVER THE
     OPPOSITION OF THE U.S. DEPARTMENTS OF STATE AND DEFENSE. AS
     A RESULT, U.S. POLICY MOVED IN A COASTAL DIRECTION, AWAY
     FROM THE SPECIES APPROACH.

06285 MERKX, G.W.
     BORDERING ON CONSENSUS: U.S. POLICY
     HEMISPHERE, 1(3) (SUM 89), 38-41.
        WITH THE ADVENT OF THE BUSH ADMINISTRATION, SEVERAL U.S.
     POLICY ASSOCIATIONS HAVE AUTHORED PROPOSALS TO ALTER
     WASHINGTON'S RELATIONS WITH ITS SOUTHERN NEIGHBORS. THE
     SURPRISING FEATURE OF THESE PROPOSALS IS THAT, DESPITE
     DIVERSE POLITICAL POINTS OF DEPARTURE, THEY SUBSTANTIALLY
     CONVERGE IN THEIR RECOMMENDATIONS FOR A NEW U.S. AGENDA IN
     LATIN AMERICA. IN THIS ARTICLE, THE AUTHOR SUMMARIZES SOME
     OF THESE RECOMMENDATIONS, INCLUDING THOSE MADE BY POLICY
     ALTERNATIVES FOR THE CARIBBEAN AND CENTRAL AMERICA (PACCA)
     AND THE INTER-AMERICAN DIALOGUE OF THE ASPEN INSTITUTE.

06286 MERLINI, C.
A CONCISE HISTORY OF NUCLEAR ITALY
INTERNATIONAL SPECTATOR, XXIII(3) (JUL 88), 135-152.
THE AUTHOR LOOKS AT INTERNATIONAL NUCLEAR NON-
PROLIFERATION EFFORTS AND AT THE STATUS OF NUCLEAR POWER IN
ITALY.

06287 MERRICK, J.C.
FEDERAL INTERVENTION IN THE TREATMENT OF HANDICAPPED
NEWBORNS: BABY DOE REGULATIONS AND THE 1984 CHILD ABUSE
AMENDMENTS
POLICY STUDIES REVIEW, 8(2) (WIN 89), 405-419.
THE BABY DOE DEBATE PROVIDES INTERESTING INSIGHTS INTO
INTEREST GROUP ACTIVITY AND ESPECIALLY INTO SINGLE-ISSUE
POLITICS. IN THIS ARTICLE, THE AUTHOR DISCUSSES HOW THE
ISSUE OF TREATING HANDICAPPED NEWBORNS EVOLVED AND HOW HHS
AND THE FEDERAL COURTS BECAME ENTANGLED IN THE LEGAL
STRUGGLE. THEN SHE ANALYZES THE ROLE OF CONGRESS AND
CONCLUDES WITH A LOOK AT NEONATAL CARE IN THE POST-BABY DOE
PERIOD.

06288 MERRIDALE, C.
THE RELUCTANT OPPOSITION: THE RIGHT 'DEVIATION' IN MOSCOW,
1928
SOVIET STUDIES, 61(3) (JUL 89), 382-400.
THIS ARTICLE EXPLORES THE 'RIGHT DEVIATION' THE
COUNTERWEIGHT TO TROTSKY'S 'SO-CALLED "LEFT" OPPOSITION,'
WHICH LOOKS SET FOR A NEW IMAGE IN THE NEXT GENERATION OF
SOVIET HISTORY TEXTBOOKS. IN THIS STUDY THE RIGHT'S
ORGANIZATION AND CAMPAIGN IS EXAMINED BY LOOKING AT ONE CITY,
MOSCOW. IF THE RIGHT COULD NOT HOLD ON TO MOSCOW, THERE HAS
LITTLE HOPE FOR IT IN OTHER RUSSIAN CITIES. THE CONTEST IN
THE CAPITOL WAS A TURNING POINT IN THE WHOLE AFFAIR. IT
CONCLUDES THAT RIGHTISM WAS MORE A STATE OF MIND THAN AN
ACTIVE POLITICAL MOVEMENT, AND THAT THEY WERE SO USEFUL THAT
IF THEY HAD NOT EXISTED ALREADY, IT WOULD HAVE BEEN
NECESSARY TO INVENT THEM AS STALIN USED THE RIGHT IN 1928
AND SUBSEQUENTLY AS A MEANS OF CONTAINING OPPOSITION TO HIS
POLICIES.

06289 MERSHON, C.A.
BETWEEN WORKERS AND UNION: FACTORY COUNCILS IN ITALY
COMPARATIVE POLITICS, 21(2) (JAN 89), 215-236.
THIS ARTICLE LOOKS AT UNIONS FROM THE INSIDE,
CONCENTRATING ON THE CONSTRAINTS AND OPPORTUNITIES FACING
WORKPLACE UNIONS IN ITALY. WITH THE FOUNDING OF FACTORY
COUNCILS IN THE LATE 1960S, ITALIAN UNIONS ACQUIRED THE
ORGANIZATIONAL BASES FOR PROMOTING REFORM WITHIN AND BEYOND
THE WORKPLACE. THESE WORKPLACE BODIES, HOWEVER, HAVE POSED
DILEMMAS FOR THE UNION MOVEMENT. IN PROBING FACTORY
COUNCILS' CAPACITIES TO BARGAIN WITH EMPLOYERS, REPRESENT
WORKERS, AND BUILD CONSENT OR DISSENT BEFORE NATIONAL UNION
POLICY, THIS ARTICLE SHOWS THAT SHOP FLOOR OUTCOMES HAVE SET
LIMITS ON NATIONAL UNION POWER. THE FIRST SECTION ASSESSES
CROSS-NATIONAL COMPARISONS OF UNION ACTION IN LIGHT OF THE
RECENT EVOLUTION OF ITALIAN UNIONISM. THE SECOND SECTION
PRESENTS SEVERAL HYPOTHESES ABOUT WORKPLACE UNIONS. THE
THIRD PART INVESTIGATES UNION REPRESENTATION AND NEGOTIATION
IN MILANESE FACTORIES. THE ARTICLE CLOSES WITH REFLECTIONS
ON THE STUDY OF UNIONS.

06290 MERVIN, D.
RONALD REAGAN'S PLACE IN HISTORY
JOURNAL OF AMERICAN STUDIES, 23(2) (AUG 89), 269-286.
THE AUTHOR CONSIDERS THE ARGUMENTS THAT RONALD REAGAN
WAS A FAILURE AS PRESIDENT AND THAT REAGAN WAS UNUSUALLY
SUCCESSFUL IN THE OFFICE. HE CONCLUDES, THAT DESPITE RONALD
REAGAN'S SHORTCOMINGS, REAGAN WAS MORE EFFECTIVE THAN MOST
MEN WHO HAVE HELD THE PRESIDENCY IN THE LAST FIFTY YEARS.

06291 MESA-LAGO, C.
CUBA'S ECONOMIC COUNTER-REFORM (RECTIFICACION): CAUSES,
POLICIES AND EFFECTS
JOURNAL OF COMMUNIST STUDIES, 5(4) (DEC 89), 98-139.
CUBA HAS EXPERIENCED MORE FREQUENT SHIFTS IN ITS TYPES
OF ECONOMIC ORGANIZATION THAN MOST POST-REVOLUTIONARY
REGIMES. THE CURRENT 'RECTIFICATION PROCESS' CAN BE
EXPLAINED PRINCIPALLY BY IDEOLOGICAL AND POLITICAL FACTORS:
A DESIRE TO 'RESCUE' THE REVOLUTION AND TO RETAIN CASTRO'S
OWN POWER. THIS POLICY IS IN PART AN ATTEMPT TO COPE WITH
SOME ECONOMIC PROBLEMS, ALTHOUGH ITS EFFECT TO DATE IS
NEGATIVE RATHER THAN POSITIVE. MOREOVER, ITS GENERAL THRUST
IS IN THE OPPOSITE DIRECTION TO THE CURRENT REFORMS IN
EASTERN EUROPE, AND THIS HAS LED TO FRICTION BETWEEN HAVANA
AND MOSCOW. IF SOVIET PERESTROIKA SUCCEEDS, IT IS BOUND TO
LEAD TO FURTHER SHIFTS IN CUBAN ECONOMIC POLICY.

06292 MESKEL, Y. G.
NEW HOPE IN THE HORN
NEW AFRICAN, (262) (JUL 89), 14.
YEMANE G. MESKEL, DIRECTOR OF INFORMATION OF THE EPLF,
SAYS THAT RECENT DEVELOPMENTS IN THE HORN OF AFRICA ARE FULL
OF HOPE. THE VICTORY OF THE LIBERATION FORCES AND ETHOPIA'S
RECENT ATTEMPTED COUP ARE BOTH SIGNS THAT TIMES ARE CHANGING.

ALL THAT IS NEEDED IS THE POLITICAL WILL TO GRASP THE NEW
OPPORTUNITIES.

06293 MESZAROS, I.
THE DECREASING RATE OF UTILIZATION AND THE CAPITALIST STATE
JOURNAL OF CONTEMPORARY ASIA, 18(3) (1988), 265-306.
WHAT IS TRULY ADVANTAGEOUS TO CAPITAL-EXPANSION IS NOT
THE INCREASE IN THE RATE AT WHICH (OR IN THE DEGREE TO
WHICH) A COMMODITY--FOR INSTANCE A SHIRT--IS UTILIZED BUT,
ON THE CONTRARY, THE DECREASE IN THE HOURS OF ITS DAILY USE.
FOR SO LONG AS SUCH DECREASE IS ACCOMPANIED BY A SUITABLE
EXPANSION IN SOCIETY'S PURCHASING POWER, IT CREATES THE
DEMAND FOR ANOTHER SHIRT. THE CAPITALIST STATE MUST NOW
ASSUME A DIRECT INTERVENTIONIST ROLE AT ALL PLANES OF SOCIAL
LIFE, ACTIVELY PROMOTING AND MANAGING THE DESTRUCTIVE
CONSUMPTION AND DISSIPATION OF SOCIAL HEALTH ON A MONUMENTAL
SCALE. FOR WITHOUT SUCH DIRECT INTERVENTION IN THE SOCIAL
METABOLIC PROCESS, NO LONGER ONLY IN A SITUATION OF
EMERGENCY BUT ON A CONTINUOUS BASIS, THE EXTREME
WASTEFULNESS OF THE CONTEMPORARY CAPITALIST SYSTEM COULD NOT
BE MAINTAINED IN EXISTENCE.

06294 MESZAROS, T.
CHANGES IN ECONOMIC MANAGEMENT SYSTEMS IN HUNGARY AND
OTHER EAST EUROPEAN COUNTRIES
FUTURES, 21(6) (DEC 89), 632-639.
TAKING HUNGARY AS AN EXAMPLE, THIS ARTICLE EXAMINES
CHANGES TAKING PLACE IN ECONOMIC MANAGEMENT SYSTEMS IN
EASTERN EUROPE. DEVELOPMENTS IN THE POLITICAL, INSTITUTIONAL
AND ECONOMIC SECTORS OF HUNGARIAN SOCIETY ARE ANALYSED, AND
CURRENT TRENDS AND PROBLEMS ARE PRESENTED. COUNTRIES OF
EASTERN EUROPE ARE CLASSIFIED INTO THREE CATEGORIES IN ORDER
TO SHOW HOW A NEED FOR CHANGE EMERGES UNDER DIFFERENT
CONSTRAINTS.

06295 METHVIN, E.H.
THE UNQUIET GHOSTS OF STALIN'S VICTIMS
NATIONAL REVIEW, XLI(16) (SEP 89), 24-25.
ALL OVER THE USSR TODAY INTRESSES ARE STEPPING FORWARD
TO TESTIFY FOR THE UNQUIET GHOSTS OF STALIN'S GREAT TERROR.
THE REALITY IS DAWNING THAT THE STALIN REGIME WAS A MURDER
MACHINE WHOSE KILLINGS EXCEEDED EVEN THOSE OF THE NAZIS AND
THEIR DEATH CAMPS. GORBACHEV'S POLICY OF "NO BLANK PAGES" IN
THE HISTORY OF THE PEOPLE HAS FORCED REEXAMINATION OF STALIN
AND AN ENTIRE CHAPTER IN SOVIET HISTORY.

06296 METZ, S.
FOUNDATION FOR A LOW-INTENSITY CONFLICT STRATEGY
COMPARATIVE STRATEGY, 8(2) (1989), 265-274.
THE ARTICLE EXAMINES LOW-INTENSITY CONFLICT WHICH HAS
BEEN PERVASIVE IN THE LATE 20TH CENTURY. IT OUTLINES THE
NATURE OF LOW INTENSITY CONFLICT, EXISTING US CAPABILITIES
AND SEEKS TO ESTABLISH A WORKABLE FRAMEWORK FOR THE
APPLICATION OF US CAPABILITIES. THIS "GRAND" OR "TOTAL"
STRATEGY SEEKS TO INCORPORATE AND INTEGRATE MILITARY,
POLITICAL, PSYCHOLOGICAL, IDEOLOGICAL AND ECONOMIC FACTORS.

06297 METZ, S.
THE CASE FOR SUPERPOWER COOPERATION IN SOUTHERN AFRICA
SAIS REVIEW, 9(1) (WIN 89), 199-212.
CONDITIONS ARE RIPE FOR SUPERPOWER COOPERATION IN
SOUTHERN AFRICA, BUT SUCH A RADICAL BREAK WITH THE PAST
REQUIRES A DEGREE OF POLITICAL COURAGE UNCHARACTERISTIC OF U.
S. FOREIGN POLICY. IT IS ALWAYS SAFE TO CLING TENACIOUSLY TO
PAST POLICY, EVEN WHEN ONE KNOWS THAT THIS WILL LEAD TO A
SLOW SLIDE INTO IRRELEVANCE IN A VITAL REGION. POLICY
INNOVATION ENTAILS RISKS, ESPECIALLY WHEN IT REQUIRES THE
UNITED STATES TO TAKE THE SOVIETS AT THEIR WORD. BASED ON
PAST SOVIET BEHAVIOR AND THE TENETS OF MARXISMLENINISM,
PLEAS FOR COOPERATION MAY SIMPLY BE A RUSE TO EXPAND
MOSCOW'S INFLUENCE IN AN UNDERHANDED WAY. THE ONLY WAY TO
KNOW IS TO TEST SOVIET COMMITMENT. BECAUSE SOUTHERN AFRICA
IS A REGION WHERE SUCCESSFUL SUPERPOWER COOPERATION COULD
HAVE A LONG-TERM IMPACT AND WHERE THE UNITED STATES COULD
RECOUP ITS LOSSES IF MOSCOW PROVED TO BE INSINCERE ABOUT
COOPERATION. THE RISKS INVOLVED ARE WORTH TAKING. WHAT IS
REQUIRED IS THE POLITICAL WILL TO DO SO.

06298 MEVORACH, B.
THE POLITICAL MONETARY BUSINESS CYCLE: POLITICAL REALITY
AND ECONOMIC THEORY
POLITICAL BEHAVIOR, 11(2) (JUN 89), 175-188.
THIS PAPER ADDRESSES THE ISSUE OF EXPECTATIONS
INCORPORATED INTO POLITICAL BUSINESS CYCLE MODELS. RATIONAL
AGENTS ANTICIPATE DEMOCRATIC EFFORTS TO STIMULATE THE
ECONOMY VIA MONETARY POLICY, DISCOUNTING MONEY SUPPLY FROM
THE CALCULATIONS FOR DETERMINING OUTPUT VARIANCE, SO THAT
OUTPUT UNDER DEMOCRATS IS WHOLLY UNAFFECTED BY CHANGES IN
THE MONEY SUPPLY. RATIONAL AGENTS APPEAR TO BE NAIVE ABOUT
REPUBLICANS, INCORPORATING MONEY SUPPLY INTO THE
CALCULATIONS FOR DETERMINING OUTPUT VARIANCE, SO THAT OUTPUT
UNDER REPUBLICANS IS SIGNIFICANTLY RELATED TO MONEY SUPPLY.

06299 MEYER, C.A.
    AGRARIAN REFORM IN THE DOMINICAN REPUBLIC: AN ASSOCIATIVE
    SOLUTION TO THE COLLECTIVE/INDIVIDUAL DILEMMA
    WORLD DEVELOPMENT, 17(8) (AUG 89). 1255-1267.
        THE DILEMMA OF APPROPRIATE ORGANIZATIONAL STRUCTURE FOR
    AGRARIAN REFORM PROJECTS IS PERVASIVE IN ALL OF LATIN
    AMERICA. COLLECTIVES OR PRODUCTION COOPERATIVES PROVIDE
    SUPERIOR VEHICLES FOR NECESSARY CREDIT AND TECHNICAL
    ASSISTANCE. BUT, UNLIKE FAMILY PLOTS, THEY ARE WROUGHT WITH
    ADMINISTRATIVE PROBLEMS AND LOW WORKER INCENTIVE. THIS CASE
    STUDY OF LAND REFORM PROJECTS IN THE DOMINICAN REPUBLIC
    PRESENTS THE LIMITATIONS OF COLLECTIVE AND INDIVIDUAL
    FARMING STRUCTURES AND CHARACTERIZES AN INTERMEDIATE
    "ASSOCIATIVE" PREFERRED BY THE DOMINICAN REFORM
    BENEFICIARIES. EMPIRICAL EVIDENCE SHOWS HIGHER PRODUCTIVITY
    AS THE REFORM PROJECTS ADOPT THE ASSOCIATIVE STRUCTURE.

06300 MEYER, M.A.
    ANTI-SEMITISM AND JEWISH IDENTITY
    COMMENTARY, 88(5) (NOV 89), 35-40.
        THIS ARTICLE EXPLORES THE ANTI-SEMITISM IN THE MODERN
    WORLD WHICH HAS BEEN A MAJOR INFLUENCE IN SHAPING JEWISH
    IDENTITY. IT EXAMINES THE HISTORY OF ANTI-SEMITISM IN THE
    19TH AND 20TH CENTURIES AND EVALUATES ITS EFFECTS ON JEWISH
    IDENTITY. IT CONCLUDES THAT ANTI-SEMITISM IN THE
    CONTEMPORARY JEWISH DIASPORA HAS CEASED TO BE AMBIGUOUS IN
    ITS EFFECTS AND THAT THE MEMORY OF THE HOLOCAUST HAS BECOME
    FOR MOST DIASPORA JEWS HAS BECOME THE FUNDAMENTAL
    CONSTITUENTS OF THEIR IDENTITY.

06301 MEYER, R.
    HOW DO INDIANS VOTE?
    ASIAN SURVEY, XXIX(12) (DEC 88), 1111-1122.
        BASED ON INDIA'S NINE GENERAL ELECTIONS, THE ARTICLE
    ANALYZES TRENDS AND UNDERLYING CAUSES OF INDIAN VOTER
    BEHAVIOR. ALTHOUGH POLICY AND PERFORMANCE, PERSONAL
    CHARACTERISTICS, CLASS, AND STRUCTURE ALL AFFECT ELECTORAL
    SUCCESS, THE ARTICLE CONCLUDES THAT OTHER FACTORS ARE ALSO
    SIGNIFICANT. IT EXAMINES SUCH FACTORS AS ECONOMIC INDICATORS,
    CLIMATE, AND A GENERAL SENSE OF WELL-BEING AND CONCLUDES
    THAT THEY ALL HAVE A SIGNIFICANT EFFECT ON VOTING BEHAVIOR.
    IN ADDITION, MANY CITIZENS OF INDIA TEND TO VOTE
    RETROACTIVELY RATHER THAN PROSPECTIVELY.

06302 MEYER, W.H.
    DEPENDENCY AND NEOIMPERIALISM
    COMPARATIVE POLITICAL STUDIES, 22(3) (OCT 89), 243-264.
        THIS ARTICLE SEEKS TO TEST CERTAIN HYPOTHESES DRAWN FROM
    STRUCTURAL COMMUNICATIONS THEORY, HYPOTHESES THAT TEND TO
    SUPPORT THE CALL FOR A NEW WORLD INFORMATION ORDER (NWIO).
    STRUCTURAL THEORISTS SUCH AS JOHAN GALTUNG AND NWIO
    ADVOCATES FROM THE THIRD WORLD HAVE CHARGED THAT DEVELOPING
    NATIONS ARE DEPENDENT UPON THE WEST FOR INTERNATIONAL NEWS.
    NEWS DEPENDENCY, IN TURN, IS SAID TO LEAD TO THE ADOPTION OF
    WESTERN NEWS VALUES AND SUBSEQUENT CULTURAL IMPERIALISM IN
    THE SOUTH. FINALLY, NEWS DEPENDENCY IS SAID TO BE
    NEOCOLONIAL IN THE SENSE THAT INFORMATION FLOWS THROUGH
    "VERTICAL" CHANNELS (FROM NORTH TO SOUTH) AND WITHIN
    DISTINCT SPHERES OF COMMUNICATION HEGEMONY. THESE CLAIMS ARE
    TESTED WITH A NEWS FLOW STUDY DRAWN FROM AFRICAN AND LATIN
    AMERICAN DAILIES. RESULTS OF THE EMPIRICAL TESTS SHOW THAT
    THIRD WORLD IS DEPENDENT ON WESTERN AGENCIES FOR THE BULK OF
    ITS INTERNATIONAL NEWS, AND THAT THIRD WORLD NEWSPAPERS
    REFLECT THE NEWS VALUES OF WESTERN PRESTIGE DAILIES.
    NONALIGNED NEWSWIRES, HOWEVER, ARE SHOWN TO BE MORE
    RESISTANT TO JOURNALISTIC WESTERNIZATION, AS THEIR COVERAGE
    IS MARKEDLY DIFFERENT FROM THAT OF THE WESTERN WIRE SERVICES.
        FINALLY, NEWS FLOW PATTERNS DO EXHIBIT A PRONOUNCED
    NEOIMPERIAL CHARACTER. AGENCIES FROM THE UNITED STATES,
    GREAT BRITIAN, AND FRANCE EACH HOLD SWAY OVER THEIR OWN
    REGIONAL DOMAINS WITHIN THE THIRD WORLD.

06303 MEYERS, E.M.
    AN EVALUATION OF FURTHER REFORMS IN THE DEMOCRATIC PARTY'S
    PRESIDENTIAL NOMINATION PROCESS
    POLICY STUDIES REVIEW, 8(4) (SUM 89), 812-830.
        BY 1992. THE PARTY OF THE MAJORITY, THE DEMOCRATIC PARTY,
    WILL HAVE BEEN OUT OF POWER FOR TWENTY YEARS OF A TWENTY-
    FOUR YEAR SPAN. SINCE 1968, NUMEROUS REFORMS IN THE
    PRESIDENTIAL NOMINATING PROCESS HAVE BEEN CONSIDERED AND
    ADOPTED BY THE DEMOCRATS. THESE REFORMS HAVE HAD THE EFFECT
    OF OPENING THE NOMINATING PROCESS TO RANK-AND-FILE DEMOCRATS
    THROUGH STATE PRIMARIES AND PARTICIPATORY CAUCUSES. WHILE
    THE REFORMS ACHIEVE THIS PURPOSE, THE END RESULT IS A MIXED
    SYSTEM THAT HAS BEEN DESCRIBED AS A DISJOINTED HODGEPODGE OF
    RULES. THIS ARTICLE PRESENTS TEN CRITERIA OF A SOUND
    NOMINATION SYSTEM. THEN A PANEL OF RESEARCHERS AND
    PRACTITIONERS WEIGHS SEVEN OPTIONS FOR FURTHER REFORM
    AGAINST THE TEN CRITERIA. SEVERAL POLICY OPTIONS ARE
    CONSIDERED BY THE PANEL AS IMPROVEMENTS OVER THE CURRENT
    PRESIDENTIAL NOMINATION SYSTEM.

06304 MEYERS, G.
    THE FRESH WINDS IN LABOR BLOW STRONGER

POLITICAL AFFAIRS, LXVIII(5) (MAY 89), 7-12.
    PRESIDENT GEORGE BUSH'S ACTIONS PROVE THAT ORGANIZED
LABOR WAS CORRECT IN OPPOSING HIS ELECTION. HIS ROLE IN THE
EASTERN AIRLINES STRIKE QUICKLY SHATTERED ANY ILLUSION THAT
HE MIGHT MODERATE THE BITTERLY ANTI-LABOR POSTURE OF THE
REAGAN ADMINISTRATION.

06305 MEYERS, R.T.
    MICROBUDGETARY STRATEGIES AND OUTCOMES
    DISSERTATION ABSTRACTS INTERNATIONAL, 50(1) (JUL 89),
    247-A.
        MICROBUDGETING IS THE PROCESS OF ALLOCATING BUDGET
    RESOURCES TO INDIVIDUAL PROGRAMS. POLITICAL SCIENTISTS HAVE
    COMMONLY PERCEIVED MICROBUDGETING TO BE AN INCREMENTAL
    PROCESS. BUT EMPIRICAL AND THEORETICAL CRITIQUES OF THE
    INCREMENTAL MODEL, AS WELL AS RECENT EXPERIENCES IN THE
    FEDERAL GOVERNMENT, INDICATE THAT THE INCREMENTAL THEORY
    DESCRIBES NEITHER THE BUDGETARY PROCESS NOR BUDGETARY
    RESULTS PARTICULARLY WELL. THUS, THE GOAL OF THIS
    DISSERTATION IS TO DEVELOP A MORE ACCURATE MODEL OF
    MICROBUDGETING.

06306 MEYERSON, H.
    WHY THE DEMOCRATS KEEP LOSING
    DISSENT. (SUM 89), 305-310.
        ONE OF THE DIFFERENCES BETWEEN THE TWO POLITICAL PARTIES
    OVER THE PAST TEN YEARS IS THAT THE REPUBLICAN PRESIDENTIAL
    CANDIDATES FORGET MANY THINGS; THE DEMOCRATS ONLY ONE. ON A
    RANGE OF QUESTIONS SMALL AND LARGE-THE DATE OF PEARL HARBOR
    DAY, WHETHER NUCLEAR MISSILES CAN BE RECALLED, THEIR OWN
    WHEREABOUTS IN THE SHIPPING OF ARMS TO IRAN - THE
    REPUBLICANS ARE REMARKABLY UNRETENTIVE. DEMOCRATIC
    CANDIDATES, BY COMPARISON, ARE MASTERS OF DETAIL. THEIR
    MEMORY LAPSES ARE OF A HIGHLY RAREFIED TYPE. THEY FORGET
    ONLY THE RAISON D'ETRE FOR THEIR CANDIDACY - WHY THEY WISH
    TO BE PRESIDENT.

06307 MEYNEN, W.
    FISHERIES DEVELOPMENT, RESOURCES DEPLETION, AND POLITICAL
    MOBILIZATION IN KERALA: THE PROBLEM OF ALTERNATIVES
    DEVELOPMENT AND CHANGE, 20(4) (OCT 89), 735-770.
        THE PAPER IS ORGANISED AS FOLLOWS: SECTION 1 GIVES A
    BACKGROUND TO THE KERALA FISH ECONOMY WITH SPECIAL ATTENTION
    TO THE NATURE OF ARTISANAL FISHERIES AND FISHING COMMUNITIES.
    SECTION 2 DISCUSSES THE SPECIFIC FORMS AND IMPACTS OF
    CAPITALIST PENETRATION WITHIN FISHERIES. SECTION 3 REVIEWS
    AND ASSESSES MOBILIZATION STRATEGIES FOR EMPOWERING THE
    ARTISANAL FISH WORKERS VIS-A-VIS THE NEWLY EMERGED FORCES
    WITHIN THE FISHING INDUSTRY. FINALLY, SECTION 4 BRIEFLY
    REVIEWS SOME ALTERNATIVE DEVELOPMENT PROPOSITIONS FOR
    FISHERIES MANAGEMENT AND DEVELOPMENT AND CONSIDERS THEIR
    VIABILITY WITHIN THE KERALA CONTEXT.

06308 MEZEY, S.
    THE BURGER COURT AND YOUNGER ABSTENTION: ENHANCING THE
    ROLE OF STATE COURTS IN CONSTITUTIONAL ADJUDICATION
    PUBLIUS: THE JOURNAL OF FEDERALISM, 19(1) (WIN 89), 25-40.
        AN IMPORTANT DETERMINANT OF FEDERAL BALANCE IS THE
    DEGREE OF STATE COURT AUTHORITY TO DECIDE FEDERAL
    CONSTITUTIONAL ISSUES. THIS STUDY TRACES THE DEVELOPMENT OF
    THE YOUNGER ABSTENTION DOCTRINE, ONE OF THE PRIMARY VEHICLES
    BY WHICH THE BURGER COURT RESTRICTED FEDERAL COURT
    JURISDICTION AND ENHANCED THE AUTHORITY OF STATE COURTS IN
    CONSTITUTIONAL ADJUDICATION. THE YOUNGER DOCTRINE WAS
    ADOPTED BY THE SUPREME COURT IN 1971 FOR REASONS OF COMITY
    AND EQUITABLE RESTRAINT. THROUGHOUT THE BURGER COURT YEARS,
    YOUNGER WAS EXPANDED FROM AN INITIAL DENIAL OF JURISDICTION
    TO LITIGANTS SEEKING INJUNCTIVE RELIEF IN STATE CRIMINAL
    PROCEEDINGS, TO LITIGANTS IN CASES "AKIN" TO CRIMINAL
    PROCEEDINGS, AND THEN TO LITIGANTS IN CASES "IMPORTANT TO
    STATE INTERESTS." BY RELYING ON YOUNGER ABSTENTION, THE
    BURGER COURT HAS REDUCED THE ROLE OF THE FEDERAL COURTS AS
    THE PRIMARY ENFORCEMENT OF U.S. CONSTITUTIONAL RIGHTS.

06309 MHANGO, M.
    BANDA BANGS THE BANKERS
    NEW AFRICAN, (256) (JAN 89), 44-45.
        KAMUZU BANDA HAS PUBLICLY SCOLDED MALAWIAN BANKERS AND
    PLEDGED SWIFT RETRIBUTION AGAINST THEM FOR ALLEGEDLY
    COLLABORATING WITH EXILED DISSIDENTS IN NEIGHBORING
    COUNTRIES. BANDA'S ACCUSATIONS LEND CREDENCE TO THE
    DISSIDENTS' CLAIMS THAT THEY HAVE SUCCEEDED IN CONVINCING
    MALAWIAN PEASANTS AND WORKERS AND OTHER SEGMENTS OF SOCIETY
    TO REPUDIATE THE ENTIRE BANDA SYSTEM AND PREPARE FOR A
    SOCIALIST REVOLUTION.

06310 MICAH, B.
    "PACIFIC" ISLANDS?
    WORLD MARXIST REVIEW, 31(11) (NOV 88), 50-51.
        THE PRINCIPLE OF NATIONAL SOVEREIGNTY AND SECURITY IN
    THE RAROTONGA TREATY, SIGNED, AMONG OTHERS, BY PAPUA NEW
    GUINEA AND OPERATIVE SINCE THE END OF 1986, HAS ACQUIRED AN
    ANTI-NUCLEAR THRUST. THE GOAL IS SOUTH PACIFIC WITHOUT
    NUCLEAR WEAPONS, EXPLOSIONS AND RADIOACTIVE WASTE, AND THE

TREATY HAS PROVIDED AN EXAMPLE OF A RESPONSIBLE COLLECTIVE
ATTITUDE TO THE ISSUE OF A DENUCLEARISED WORLD.

06311 MICHAELY, M.; CHOKSI, A.; PAPAGEORGIU, D.
THE DESIGN OF TRADE LIBERALIZATION
FINANCE AND DEVELOPMENT, 26(1) (MAR 89), 2-5.
SOME PATHS TO LIBERALIZATION ARE MORE SUSTAINABLE AND
INVOLVE SMALLER SHORT-TERM COSTS THAN OTHERS. IT WOULD BE
ONLY AN ACCIDENT IF THE SAME PATH HERE EQUALLY GOOD, AND
SIMILARLY SUSTAINABLE, IN TWO DIFFERENT ECONOMIES, OR EVEN
IN THE SAME ECONOMY IN TWO DIFFERENT PERIODS. YET, CERTAIN
CRUCIAL ELEMENTS OF A SUCCESSFUL LIBERALIZATION PROCESS MAY
BE COMMON TO A LARGE NUMBER OF COUNTRIES, OVER DIFFERENT
PERIODS, AND AT DIFFERENT STAGES OF DEVELOPMENT. THIS
ARTICLE ATTEMPTS TO IDENTIFY SUCH MAJOR ELEMENTS THROUGH THE
STUDY OF THE EXPERIENCE WITH LIBERALIZATION IN 19 COUNTRIES
LOCATED IN ASIA, LATIN AMERICA, AND THE MEDITERRANEAN AREA.

06312 MICHALSKI
STRIKES AND THE ROUND TABLE
ACROSS FRONTIERS, 5(2) (SUM 89), 15-21.
THIS IS A COLLECTION OF WRITINGS AS SOLIDARITY IN POLAND
DEBATES STRATEGY AMIDST A WILDCAT STRIKE WAVE. IT COVERS
RADICAL MINIMALISM, THE BELCHATOW STRIKE, A DEBATE OVER
BASIC PRINCIPLES, AND WAGE DEMANDS. IT EXAMINES DECISIONS
THAT SOLIDARITY MUST NOW MAKE NOW THAT IT HAS BEEN MADE
LEGAL, AND THE ISSUES AND CHALLENGES NOW FACED.

06313 MICHALSKI, F.
PRIVATIZATION AND ITS DISCONTENTS
ACROSS FRONTIERS, 5(3) (FAL 89), 14.
THIS ARTICLE EXAMINES SEVERAL CHANGES IN POLAND AND
THEIR SOCIAL CONSEQUENCES IT OFFERS A BRIEF SUMMARY OF
SEVERAL OBSERVATIONS BY DIFFERENT WRITERS ON THE SOCIAL
CONSEQUENCES OF MARKETIZATION. THEY COVER THE SCHOOL SYSTEM,
PUBLICATIONS, ORANGE ALTERNATIVE, THE DISMANTLING OF THE
COMMAND ECONOMY, AND EMIGRATION.

06314 MICHAUD, M.
DETECTION OF ETI--AN INTERNATIONAL AGREEMENT
SPACE POLICY, 5(2) (MAY 89), 103-106.
THE AUTHOR ARGUES THAT THE CHANCES OF DETECTING SIGNALS
FROM EXTRATERRESTRIAL INTELLIGENCE ARE INCREASING. IN ORDER
TO REACT APPROPRIATELY IF CONTACT IS MADE, HE ADVOCATES
ADOPTION OF THE AGREEMENTS MADE AT THE 1987 CONGRESS OF THE
INTERNATIONAL ASTRONAUTICAL FEDERATION REGARDING DETECTION
OF AND REPLIES TO SIGNS OF EXTRATERRESTRIAL INTELLIGENCE.
THE AGREEMENTS ARE REPRODUCED IN THE ARTICLE AND THE AUTHOR
EXPLAINS THEIR IMPORTANT PROVISIONS.

06315 MICHAUD, P.
AFTER ACHIEK, CDR CHOOSES NEW LEADERS
NEW AFRICAN, 261 (JUN 89), 22.
THIS ARTICLE DESCRIBES THE NEW LEADERS CHOSEN BY THE
CONSEIL DEMOCRATIQUE REVOLUTIONNAIRE OF CHAD IN THE WAKE OF
ACHIEK'S RETURN TO CHAD AS FOREIGN MINISTER IN HISSINE
HABRE'S GOVERNMENT.

06316 MICHAUD, P.
MILITARY RUMBLES
NEW AFRICAN, (MAR 88), 14.
THIS ARTICLE REPORTS ON THE GROWING DISCONTENT THAT
GENERAL MATHIEU KEREKOU IS FACING AMONG THE RANKS OF HIS OWN
SOLDIERS. IT EXPLORES THE FACT THAT ALTHOUGH THEY HAVE
ALWAYS ENJOYED A PRIVILEGED STATUS, THAT THEY OBJECT TO THE
GROWING CILIVAN CORRUPTION.

06317 MICHAUD, P.
NEW CONSTITUTION
NEW AFRICAN, 263 (AUG 89), 21-22.
THIS ARTICLE REPORTS ON CHAD'S NEW CONSTITUTION WHICH
WILL HAVE A NUMBER OF US-STYLE CHECKS AND BALANCES TO A
BASICALLY PRESIDENTIAL SYSTEM. THIS IS DESPITE CONFIRMATION
THAT THE RECENT ATTEMPTED COUP, ROCKING THE COUNTRY'S
FRAGILE EQUILIBRIUM HAS LOST PRESIDENT HABRE MANY OF HIS
MAIN SUPPORTERS. IT EXPLORES THE FEATURES OF THE
CONSTITUTION AS WELL AS THE POLITICAL CLIMATE IN CHAD - COUP
ATTEMPTS AND ATTEMPTED ASSASSINATION OF THE PRESIDENT.

06318 MICHAUD, P.; MISSER, F.
OPPOSITION IN TATTERS
NEW AFRICAN, (257) (FEB 89), 17-18.
ACHIEK IBN OUMAR'S DEFECTION, WITH MANY OF HIS TROOPS,
TO HABRE HAS PLUNGED THE CHADIAN OPPOSITION INTO CHAOS. A
FIGHT IS ON FOR CONTROL OF THE DEMOCRATIC REVOLUTIONARY
COUNCIL, WHILE A NEW PARTY IS TRYING TO ATTRACT MEMBERS FROM
GOUKOUNI OUEDDEI'S GUNT ORGANIZATION.

06319 MICHAUD, P.
SEYBOU'S INHERITANCE
AFRICAN BUSINESS, (JAN 88), 45.
THIS ARTICLE EXAMINES THE SITUATION OF NIGER AS NEW
PRESIDENT ALI SEYBOU TAKES THE LEADERSHIP ROLE. IT DISCUSSES
THE PROBLEMS OF AGRICULTURE, CLIMATE, MORE DESERTIFICATION,

AND FALLING PRICES OF URANIUM, THE PRINCIPAL EXPORT. THE
CONDITION OF EMPTY COFFERS AFTER A BUDGET INCREASE IS
EXPLORED AS WELL AS POSSIBLE MEANS TO RAISE THE NECESSARY
FUNDING.

06320 MICHAUD, P.
WAR OVER BENIN SUCCESSION
NEW AFRICAN, (266) (NOV 89), 18.
THIS ARTICLE EXPLORES THE POSSIBLE CANDIDATES FOR
SUCCESSION TO BENIN'S HEAD OF STATE. IT EXAMINES, IN
PARTICULAR, ADABOU KOSSA, AS THE MOST LIKELY SUCCESSOR TO
KEREKOU. IT ALSO EXAMINES FRANCE'S INVOLVEMENT IN THE
AFFAIRS OF BENIN.

06321 MICHAUD, P.
ZINZOU SPEAKS OUT ON BENIN'S PROBLEMS
NEW AFRICAN, (266) (NOV 89), 18.
THIS ARTICLE REPORTS AN INTERVIEW WITH DR. EMILE ZINZOY,
FORMER PRESIDENT OF BENIN, WHO IS NOW IN EXILE IN PARIS. IT
REVEALS THAT HE IS NOW LEADER OF AN OPPOSITION PARTY AS HE
AT LAST BREAKS SILENCE ON THE AFFAIRS OF BENIN.

06322 MICHELETTI, M.
THE SWEDISH ELECTIONS OF 1988
ELECTORAL STUDIES, 8(2) (AUG 89), 169-174.
THE RESULTS OF THE AUTUMN ELECTIONS CAN BE SUMMARIZED
UNDER FOUR MAIN HEADINGS: (1) VOTER TURNOUT WAS LOWER THAN
IN THE 1985 ELECTIONS; (2) THE ECOLOGICAL, GREEN, PARTY
ENTERED THE RIKSDAG AND GAINED STRENGTH IN THE
MUNICIPALITIES; (3) THE SOCIAL DEMOCRATS STAYED IN OFFICE AT
THE NATIONAL LEVEL, BUT THEIR STRENGTH CONTINUED TO DECLINE;
AND (4) A MUNICIPALITY IN SOUTHERN SWEDEN RECEIVED NATIONAL
ATTENTION BY EXERCISING ITS RIGHT TO HOLD A REFERENDUM,
REGARDING PUBLIC POLICY ON REFUGEES. AN ANALYSIS OF THE FOUR
POINTS FOLLOWS A STATISTICAL PRESENTATION OF THE NATIONAL,
REGIONAL AND LOCAL ELECTION RESULTS.

06323 MICHENER, H.A.; RICHARDSON, G.D.; SALZER, M.S.
EXTENSIONS OF VALUE SOLUTIONS IN CONSTANT-SUM NON-
SIDEPAYMENT GAMES
JOURNAL OF CONFLICT RESOLUTION, 33(3) (SEP 89), 530-553.
THIS ARTICLE DEFINES TWO NEW SOLUTION CONCEPTS FOR NON-
SIDEPAYMENT GAMES--THE LAMBDA-TRANSFER NUCLEOLUS AND THE
LAMBDA-TRANSFER DISRUPTION VALUE--AND REPORTS THE RESULTS OF
AN EXPERIMENT TESTING THEIR PREDICTIVE ACCURACY AGAINST THAT
OF A THIRD SOLUTION CONCEPT, THE WELL-KNOWN LAMBDA-TRANSFER
VALUE (SHAPLEY, 1969). THE TEST WAS BASED ON DATA FROM A
LABORATORY EXPERIMENT UTILIZING FIVE-PERSON, TWO-CHOICE
GAMES THAT WERE CONSTANT-SUM IN NORMAL FORM. GOODNESS-OF-FIT
RESULTS SHOW THAT THE LAMBDA-TRANSFER VALUE AND THE LAMBDA-
TRANSFER DISRUPTION VALUE WERE ABOUT EQUALLY ACCURATE IN
PREDICTING THE OBSERVED PAYOFFS TO PLAYERS IN THESE GAMES;
BOTH OF THESE SOLUTIONS WERE MORE ACCURATE THAN THE LAMBDA-
TRANSFER NUCLEOLUS.

06324 MICHITOSHI, T.
THE LIBERAL-DEMOCRATIC PARTY IN CRISIS
JAPAN QUARTERLY, XXXVI(3) (JUL 89), 244-251.
JAPAN IS IN THE MIDST OF POLITICAL UPHEAVAL. THE RULING
LIBERAL DEMOCRATIC PARTY, IN POWER FOR MORE THAN THREE
DECADES, FACED ITS MOST SERIOUS CRISIS EVER WHEN POPULAR
SUPPORT FOR LDP PRESIDENT AND PRIME MINISTER TAKESHITA
NOBORU PLUMMETED TO SINGLE-DIGIT PERCENTAGES IN EARLY 1989.
EVEN AFTER TAKESHITA FINALLY ANNOUNCED HIS DECISION TO
RESIGN, PARTY EXECUTIVES FOLUNDERED OVER HIS REPLACEMENT

06325 MICHNIK, A.
AFTER THE ELECTIONS: NOTHING SHALL REMAIN AS IT WAS BEFORE
EAST EUROPEAN REPORTER, 3(4) (SPR 89), 40.
THE ELECTIONS IN POLAND ARE VIEWED AS A SIGNIFICANT
FIRST STEP TOWARDS DEMOCRATIZATION. THE ARTICLE STATES THAT
THE EFFECT OF THE ELECTION IS DESTINED TO BE SIGNIFICANT AND
FAR-REACHING. IT ALSO DECRIES ANY RESORT TO VIOLENCE OR
VIGILANCE DESIGNED TO FOSTER REFORM.

06326 MICHNIK, A.
THE ELECTION CAMPAIGN A SPECTRE IS HAUNTING EUROPE
EAST EUROPEAN REPORTER, 3(4) (SPR 89), 35-36.
THE ARTICLE, WRITTEN BY A SOLIDARITY JOURNALIST AND
POLITICAL CANDIDATE, ARGUES THAT DEVELOPMENTS IN POLAND,
SUCH AS THE ROUND TABLE NEGOTIATIONS, AS WELL AS OTHER
EVENTS IN EASTERN EUROPE AND THE USSR, SIGNAL THE BEGINNING
OF THE END FOR TOTALITARIANISM AND MILITARY COMMUNISM. HE
ADVOCATES CONTINUED REFORM AND PROGRESS TOWARDS DEMOCRACY
WITH THE ULTIMATE GOAL OF THE REPLACEMENT OF TOTALITARIANISM.

06327 MICHNIK, A.
THE FIRST STEP TOWARDS DEMOCRACY: AN INTERVIEW WITH ADAM
MICHNIK
EAST EUROPEAN REPORTER, 3(4) (SPR 89), 36.38, 39.40.
SOLIDARITY CANDIDATE ADAM MICHNIK SPEAKS OF POLAND'S
FUTURE. HE DISCUSSES SUCH ISSUES AS FACTIONALISM AMONG
OPPOSITION GROUPS, THE SIGNIFICANCE OF THE ROUND TABLE TALKS,
THE FUTURE OF POLAND'S ECONOMY, AND THE IMPORTANCE OF THE

CURRENT ELECTIONS. HE CONCLUDES THAT THERE IS NO CERTAINTY IN THIS TIME OF DRASTIC CHANGE, AND THAT THERE ARE NO EASY ANSWERS TO POLAND'S MULTI-FACETED POLITICAL AND ECONOMIC PROBLEMS. HOWEVER, HE SEES THE CURRENT REFORMS AS STEPS IN THE RIGHT DIRECTION.

06328 MICKIEWICZ, E.
MOBILIZATION AND REFORM: POLITICAL COMMUNICATION POLICY UNDER GORBACHEV
PS: POLITICAL SCIENCE AND POLITICS, XXII(2) (JUN 89), 199-207.
FROM THE BEGINNING OF GORBACHEV'S TENURE IN POWER, AN OBSERVER OF SOVIET POLITICS COULD DETECT IN THE USE OF THE MEDIA THE OPERATION OF A KEY MECHANISM IN EFFECTING MAJOR CHANGE. GLASNOST, THE NEW OPENNESS AND PUBLIC DISCUSSION, IS A IS A MEDIA PHENOMENON. THE NEW ROLE ACCORDED IN THE MEDIA IS IN MANY WAYS A REVOLUTIONARY ONE. THE EXPANDED FUNCTIONS OF THE MEDIA IN THE GORBACHEV ADMINISTRATION REQUIRE THEM TO PRECIPITATE INSTITUTIONAL CHANGE IN THE SOVIET POLITICAL SYSTEM. MOBILIZATION WILL BE TEMPORARY IF THERE IS INSUFFICIENT STRUCTURAL CHANGE TO SUPPORT IT, AND THE MEDIA SYSTEM ITSELF HAS BECOME A PRINCIPAL FACTOR IN BREAKING DOWN DYSFUNCTIONAL INSTITUTIONS INHERITED FROM PREVIOUS REGIMES, STRENGTHENING WEAK INSTITUTIONS (SUCH AS THE SOVIETS) AND DEVELOPING NEW TYPES OF INSTITUTIONS. AS A CONSEQUENCE OF THIS DYNAMIC, SYSTEMIC CHANGE IN THE MEDIA SYSTEM PRECEEDS OTHER LARGE-SCALE CHANGE.

06329 MIDDENDORF, J.; HEATHERLY, C., (ED.); PINES, B., (ED.)
INTERNATIONAL ECONOMIC DEVELOPMENT; MANDATE FOR LEADERSHIP III: POLICY STRATEGIES FOR THE 1990S
THE HERITAGE FOUNDATION, WASHINGTON, DC, 1989, 665-684.
THE ARTICLE EXAMINES THE EFFORTS OF THE US TO PROMOTE ECONOMIC DEVELOPMENT IN LESSER DEVELOPED COUNTRIES (LDC). IT EMPHASIZES THE EFFORTS OF THE US AGENCY FOR INTERNATIONAL DEVELOPMENT (AID) TO PROMOTE GROWTH AND ANALYZES THE SUCCESS AND FAILURE OF AID MEASURES. FUTURE POLICY GOALS ARE ADVOCATED INCLUDING: SPURRING GROWTH BY ENHANCING ECONOMIC FREEDOM, ENCOURAGING EMPLOYEE OWNERSHIP, REWRITING THE FOREIGN ASSISTANCE ACT TO EMPHASIZE FREE MARKET PRINCIPLES, CURBING THE EXCESSES OF PRIVATE VOLUNTARY ORGANIZATIONS, AND MASTERING THE DEBT CRISIS.

06330 MIDDENDORP, C.P.
MODELS FOR PREDICTING THE DUTCH VOTE ALONG THE LEFT-RIGHT AND THE LIBERTARIANISM-AUTHORITARIANISM DIMENSIONS
INTERNATIONAL POLITICAL SCIENCE REVIEW, 10(4) (OCT 89), 279-308.
THERE ARE TWO "FUNDAMENTAL DIMENSIONS OF IDEOLOGICAL CONTROVERSY" IN THE NETHERLANDS WHICH ARE STABLE THROUGH THE PERIOD 1970-85: SOCIO-ECONOMIC LEFT-RIGHT, WITH EGALITARIAN IMPLICATIONS, AND LIBERTARIANISM-AUTHORITARIANISM WITH THE UNDERLYING VALUE OF FREEDOM. BOTH DIMENSIONS ARE "BELIEF SYSTEMS" BASED ON HIGHLY INTERRELATED ATTITUDE SCALES, AND BOTH ARE "SUSTAINED" BY STABLE PHILOSOPHICAL DIMENSIONS: SOCIALISM AND LIBERALISM FOR THE LEFT-RIGHT DIMENSION, CONSERVATISM AND AUTHORITARIANISM FOR THE LIBERTARIAN-AUTHORITARIAN DIMENSION. THE ORDERING OF POLITICAL PARTIES BY MEANS OF AVERAGE SCORES OF THEIR SUPPORTERS IS DIFFERENT ON EACH DIMENSION. THEN, OBVIOUSLY, TWO SETS OF CAUSAL MODELS CAN BE DEVELOPED, WITH PARTY PREFERENCE ALONG EACH DIMENSION AS THE DEPENDENT VARIABLE. THE MODELS DEVELOPED IN THIS STUDY CONTAIN SOCIAL CHARACTERISTICS (AGE, EDUCATION, INCOME, CLASS AND RELIGION), PHILOSOPHICAL DIMENSIONS, IDEOLOGICAL DIMENSIONS AND, IN ADDITION, LEFT-RIGHT AND PROGRESSIVE-CONSERVATIVE SELF-IDENTIFICATIONS. THE LEFT-RIGHT VOTE IS BEST PREDICTED BY LEFT-RIGHT SELFIDENTIFICATION FOLLOWED BY A MIXTURE OF OTHER DETERMINANTS OF ABOUT EQUAL STRENGTH: LEFT-RIGHT IDEOLOGICAL POSITION, SOCIALISM, LIBERALISM, CONSERVATISM, RELIGION, SOCIAL CLASS AND INCOME. THE AUTHORITARIAN VOTE IS PREDOMINANTLY DETERMINED BY RELIGION, FOLLOWED AT SOME DISTANCE BY LEFT-RIGHT SELFIDENTIFICATION, LIBERTARIAN-AUTHORITARIAN IDEOLOGY, CONSERVATISM, SOCIALISM, LEFT-RIGHT IDEOLOGICAL POSITION AND SOCIAL CLASS. INCOME AND LIBERALISM DO NOT PLAY AN IMPORTANT ROLE HERE. AGE AND EDUCATIONAL LEVEL HAVE NEGLIGIBLE EFFECTS AS PREDICTORS OF EITHER VOTE. THE ROLE OF IDEOLOGY AS A DETERMINANT OF THE VOTE IN A EUROPEAN CONTEXT IS CONTRASTED WITH AMERICAN EVIDENCE AND THE CONTENT VALIDITY OF IDEOLOGICAL SELF-IDENTIFICATION IN TERMS OF LEFT-RIGHT IS QUESTIONED.

06331 MIDDLEBROOK, K.J.
THE SOUNDS OF SILENCE: ORGANISED LABOR'S RESPONSE TO ECONOMIC CRISIS IN MEXICO
JOURNAL OF LATIN AMERICAN STUDIES, 21(2) (MAY 89), 195-220.
THIS ARTICLE BEGINS WITH AN ASSESSMENT OF THE ECONOMIC AND POLITICAL PROBLEMS FACING THE MEXICAN LABOUR MOVEMENT IN THE 1980S AND ORGANISED LABOUR'S RESPONSES TO THEM. THE SECOND SECTION CONSIDERS DIFFERENT EXPLANATIONS OF LABOUR STRATEGY DURING THIS PERIOD, FOCUSING SPECIFICALLY ON STATE CONTROLS ON LABOUR'S ORGANISATIONAL AND MOBILISATIONAL ACTIVITIES, ORGANISATIONAL WEAKNESSES WITHIN THE LABOUR MOVEMENT ITSELF, AND LABOUR LEADERS' POLITICAL BELIEFS. THE

CONCLUSION EXAMINES POSSIBLE FUTURE STRATEGIES FOR THE ORGANISED LABOUR MOVEMENT DURING A PERIOD OF FARREACHING ECONOMIC AND POLITICAL CHANGE.

06332 MIDDLETON, A.
THE CHANGING STRUCTURE OF PETTY PRODUCTION IN ECUADOR
WORLD DEVELOPMENT, 17(1) (JAN 89), 139-155.
THIS ARTICLE DEALS WITH THE EXTENT TO WHICH THE ECONOMIC ACTIVITIES OF THE URBAN POOR IN THIRD WORLD CITIES WILL DISAPPEAR, STAGNATE OR INCREASE AS CAPITALISM DEVELOPS. FIRST, IT SEEKS TO DEVELOP A THEORETICAL FRAMEWORK TO MAKE SENSE OF THE ECONOMIC CHANGES WHICH ARE TAKING PLACE IN THE CITIES OF THE DEVELOPING WORLD. THIS IS FOLLOWED BY AN EMPIRICAL ANALYSIS WHICH SHOWS THAT WHILE THE NUMBER OF PETTY MANUFACTURING WORKSHOPS IN KEY AREAS OF QUITO REMAINED REMARKABLY CONSTANT OVER A SEVEN-YEAR PERIOD OF RAPID ECONOMIC GROWTH, THIS STAGNATION WAS THE NET RESULT OF GROSS CHANGES IN THE STRUCTURE OF PRODUCTION WHEREBY PRODUCTION OF THE MEANS OF SUBSISTENCE DECLINED AND PRODUCTION OF THE MEANS OF PRODUCTION INCREASED. IN ADDITION, THE NATURE OF THE LATTER HAS MODIFIED IN TERMS OF THE TYPE OF WORK UNDERTAKEN. THE CHANGES WHICH TOOK PLACE VARIED ACROSS THE CITY AND WERE INADVERTENTLY AFFECTED BY GOVERNMENT HOUSING POLICY.

06333 MIDDLETON, B.S.; CORY, E.F.
AUSTRALIAN SPACE POLICY
SPACE POLICY, 5(1) (FEB 89), 41-46.
BY THE MID-1980S AUSTRALIA'S SPACE INDUSTRY WAS CONCENTRATED IN THE AREAS OF TRACKING ACTIVITIES, ASSEMBLY OF SPACECRAFT AND GROUND STATION EQUIPMENT, AND ACTIVE REMOTE SENSING APPLICATIONS. IN 1986 THE GOVERNMENT ANNOUNCED A POLICY AIMED AT INCREASING THE COUNTRY'S INVOLVEMENT IN SPACE RESEARCH AND DEVELOPMENT AND THE DEVELOPMENT OF COMMERCIALLY VIABLE INDUSTRIAL ACTIVITIES BASED ON SPACE TECHNOLOGIES. THE MAIN CURRENT COMPONENT OF THE NATIONAL SPACE PROGRAM IS THE PROVISION OF A DIGITAL ELECTRONICS UNIT AND FAST DELIVERY PROCESSOR FOR THE ERS-1 REMOTE SENSING SPACECRAFT. FUTURE PRIORITY AREAS ARE SATELLITE-BASED COMMUNICATIONS, REMOTE SENSING, SPACECRAFT GROUND SUPPORT, AN AUSTRALIAN ROCKET LAUNCHING SITE, AND SCIENTIFIC RESEARCH SUPPORTING SPACE INDUSTRY DEVELOPMENT.

06334 MIDDLETON, J.
THE DRAINING OF NAMIBIA'S WEALTH
SECHABA, 23(9) (SEP 89), 10-16.
NAMIBIA HAS EXPERIENCED EXPLOITATION AT THE HANDS OF VARIOUS COLONIAL POWERS: GERMANY, GREAT BRITAIN, AND SOUTH AFRICA. ON THE EVE OF INDEPENDENCE, OUTSIDE INVESTORS ARE WORKING IN ALLIANCE WITH THE SOUTH AFRICAN ADMINISTRATION TO GAIN FINANCIAL CONTROL OF NATURAL RESOURCES AND OTHER ASSETS. ALTHOUGH FORBIDDEN BY A UNITED NATIONS DECREE, ILLEGAL EXPORTS ARE ON THE INCREASE. POWERFUL INTERESTS IN THE WEST COOPERATE WITH A "CAMPAIGN OF DISINFORMATION" WHICH KEEPS THE INTERNATIONAL COMMUNITY IGNORANT OF ACTUAL EVENTS.

06335 MIECZKOWSKI, S.
THE RISE AND FALL OF THE JAPANESE STUDENT FEDERATION (ZENGAKUREN)
ASIAN THOUGHT AND SOCIETY, XIV(40) (JAN 89), 53-58.
THE ALL-JAPAN STUDENT SELF-GOVERNING FEDERATION (ZENGAKUREN) WAS FORMED IN SEPTEMBER, 1948. THIS "SELF-GOVERNING JAPANESE STUDENT ASSOCIATION" AS IT WAS CALLED AT THE TIME, SUCCEEDED IN FORCING THE JAPANESE MINISTRY OF EDUCATION TO WITHDRAW THE DRAFT OF A BILL TO ESTABLISH A BOARD OF TRUSTEES IN EVERY INSTITUTION OF HIGHER EDUCATION. THE MOST IMPORTANT LESSON THE STUDENT ASSOCIATION LEARNED WAS THAT A UNITED EFFORT COULD LEAD TO A CHANGE OF THE ESTABLISHMENT. CHANCES ARE THAT, WITH THE GROWING PLURALISM IN JAPANESE POLITICS AND ECONOMY--WITH MORE EVEN STRENGTH OF THE MAJOR POLITICAL PARTIES, AND WITH MORE SERVICE ENTERPRISES OUTSIDE THE ZAIKAI BIG BUSINESS GROUPS--THERE WILL BE SOME FUTURE CAUSES FOR THE EXPRESSION OF MASS OR GROUP DISCONTENT. THE JAPANESE ECONOMY IS GETTING INCREASINGLY MORE DIVERSIFIED, IT FEATURES MORE DIVERGENT INTEREST GROUPS, AND IT MAY WITNESS MORE OPEN CLASHES AMONG PARTISAN GROUPS. IT IS LIKELY, HOWEVER, THAT SUCH DEMONSTRATIONS WILL ASSUME A LESS RADICAL AND LESS VIOLENT CHARACTER THAN IN THE PAST.

06336 MIES, H.
TURN FROM CONFRONTATION TO COOPERATIVE COEPISTENCE IS POSSIBLE
INFORMATION BULLETIN, 26(19-20) (OCT 88), 13-14.
MIES DESCULIES HOW ALL THE SIGNIFICANT POLITICAL FORCES IN THE FRG ARE UNITED IN THEIR POSITIVE ASSESSMENT OF THE MOSCOW SUMMIT, OF ITS RESULTS AND ITS IMPULSES TO DISARMAMENT AND THE IMPROVEMENT OF THE INTERNATIONAL SITUATION. FROM THAT ONE COULD DRAW THE FOLLOWING CONCLUSION: IN THAT CASE, NEW POTENTIALITIES FOR DIALOGUE AND COOPERATION ARE EVIDENTLY ALSO OPENED UP IN THE RELATIONS BETWEEN THE VARIOUS POLITICAL AND SOCIAL FORCES, ESPECIALLY IN ORDER THAT PEACE ALONE -- AND WAR NEVER AGAIN -- SHOULD COME FROM GERMAN SOIL, AND THIS MEANS, IN PARTICULAR,

IMPULSES FOR DISARMAMENT.

06337 MIGLANI, S.
THE BATTLE CONTINUES IN THE NORTHEAST
CULTURAL SURVIVAL QUARTERLY, 13(2) (1989), 40-42.
THE WAR IN THE INDIAN NORTHEAST HAS BEEN GOING ON SINCE
INDIA BECAME AN INDEPENDENT COUNTRY. SEVERAL ETHNIC GROUPS
HAVE BEEN INVOLVED AT VARIOUS TIMES. SOME GROUPS HAVE FOUGHT
FOR A SOCIALIST STATE, SOME FOR CHRISTIANITY, AND SOME FOR A
SEPARATE TRIBAL STATE. THE GROUPS HAVE FOUGHT THE NATIONAL
ARMY AND THEY HAVE ALSO FOUGHT ONE ANOTHER. NOW, FOR THE
FIRST TIME, THE GUERRILLAS ARE TALKING OF JOINT ACTION
AGAINST THE UNION. THEIR BATTLE CRY IS NOW "A SEPARATE STATE
FOR PEOPLE OF MONGOLOID ORIGIN."

06338 MIGRANIAN, A.M.
INTERRELATIONS OF THE INDIVIDUAL, SOCIETY, AND THE STATE
IN THE POLITICAL THEORY OF MARXISM: THE PROBLEM OF THE
DEMOCRATIZATION OF SOCIALIST SOCIETY
SOVIET REVIEW, 30(1) (JAN 89), 40-63.
THE AUTHOR USES COMPARATIVE ANALYSIS TO DETERMINE HOW
THE PROBLEM OF THE INTERRELATIONS BETWEEN THE INDIVIDUAL,
SOCIETY, AND THE STATE HAVE BEEN INTERPRETED IN THE
POLITICAL THEORY OF LIBERAL DEMOCRACY; WHAT IS QUALITATIVELY
NEW ABOUT THE WAY MARXIST POLITICAL THEORY DEALS WITH THE
PROBLEM; AND WHAT REAL LIFE FACTORS CAN HAVE A NEGATIVE
EFFECT ON THE PROCESS OF ACHIEVING THE IDEAL OF POLITICAL
THEORY IN PERFECTING SOCIALIST SOCIETY.

06339 MIKHEYEV, V.
THE KOREAN PROBLEM IN FUTURE
INTERNATIONAL AFFAIRS (MOSCOW), (9) (SEP 89), 138-147.
IN THE 1990'S, THE KOREAN PENINSULA AND THE KOREAN
PROBLEM WILL BE THE CAUSE OF DYNAMIC CLASHES BETWEEN THE NEW
TENDENCIES IN INTERNATIONAL RELATIONS AND THE OLD
STEREOTYPES AND AMBITIONS. SUCCESS WILL HINGE LARGELY ON THE
CONSISTENT APPLICATION OF THE PRINCIPLES OF NEW POLITICAL
THINKING, EXISTING REALITIES, AND THE INTERESTS OF ALL SIDES
INVOLVED IN THE CONFLICT.

06340 MIKMAILOV, L.
USSR-YUGOSLAVIA: COOPERATION PROBLEMS
FOREIGN TRADE, 3 (1988), 8-11.
THIS ARTICLE EXAMINES THE ECONOMIC RELATIONSHIP BETWEEN
YUGOSLAVIA AND THE USSR AS TRADE PARTNERS. IT EXPLORES THE
ECONOMIES OF BOTH COUNTRIES AND THE FACTORS WHICH AFFECT THE
BALANCE OF TRADE BETWEEN THEM. IT ANALYSES THE CURRENT (1985-
1990) FIVE YEAR PLAN WHICH HAS RESULTED IN HIGH TRADE
TURNOVER GROWTH RATES.

06341 MIKO, F.T.
THE EVOLVING SOVIET CHALLENGE
CRS REVEIW, 10(4) (APR 89), 4-6.
SOVIET POLICIES UNDER GORBACHEV PRESENT NEW
OPPORTUNITIES AND PROBLEMS FOR THE WESTERN ALLIANCE. THE
TASK AT HAND FOR NATO LEADERS WILL BE TO REAP THE POTENTIAL
BENEFITS WITHOUT PREMATURELY SACRIFICING ALLIANCE COHESION
AND RESOLVE.

06342 MILBURN, T.W.; CHRISTIE, D.J.
REWARDING IN INTERNATIONAL POLITICS
POLITICAL PSYCHOLOGY, 10(4) (DEC 89), 625-646.
THE RELATIONSHIP BETWEEN THE SUPERPOWERS IS POTENTIALLY
THE MOST DESTRUCTIVE TO MANKIND OF ANY THAT HAS EXISTED
THROUGH HISTORY. MOREOVER, IT IS, THROUGH THE CONTINUING
ARMS RACE, ITSELF BASED ON MUTUAL DETERRENCE AND WEAPONS
MODERNIZATION, EXTREMELY COSTLY TO BOTH COUNTRIES. THE TIME
MAY HAVE COME TO CONSIDER SYSTEMATICALLY AN ALTERNATIVE
APPROACH TO THE CONFLICT THAT PERVADES THE RELATIONSHIP
BETWEEN THE SUPERPOWERS, AN ALTERNATIVE WITHOUT THE MAJOR
DISADVANTAGES OF THREAT WITH ITS POTENTIAL IMPLICATIONS FOR
INSTABILITY, DISTRUST, AND MUTUAL DISLIKE. THE ALTERNATIVE
DESCRIBED INVOLVES USING POSITIVE INDUCEMENTS TO INFLUENCE
ONE ANOTHER, POTENTIALLY A POWERFUL ADDITION AND EVENTUALLY
A POWERFUL SUBSTITUTE FOR MUTUAL THREAT. MUTUAL REWARDING AS
A MODE OF INFLUENCE CAN PROVE LESS DANGEROUS AND LESS
EXPENSIVE. AT THE SAME TIME, THE USE OF REWARDS IS A COMPLEX
MATTER, OFTEN SUBTLE, AND CERTAINLY NOT READILY ACCEPTED BY
EVERYONE. BECAUSE OF OBSTACLES OF VARIOUS KINDS, REWARDS ARE
RARELY USED BY ADVERSARIES. THESE OBSTACLES ARE DESCRIBED,
TOGETHER WITH CRITERIA IN TERMS OF WHICH ANY SYSTEMATIC AND
SUCCESSFUL USE OF REWARDING BETWEEN THE SUPERPOWERS MUST
OCCUR.

06343 MILENKOVITCH, M.M.
WHAT SOVIET CARTOONS REVEAL
FREEDOM AT ISSUE, (108) (MAY 89), 11-14.
THERE ARE MANY WAYS OF EVALUATING THE DEGREE OF
CONTINUITY OR CHANGE IN SOVIET BEHAVIOR UNDER GORBACHEV'S
COMBINATION OF PERESTROIKA AND GLASNOST, BUT THERE IS ONE
THAT IS USUALLY OVERLOOKED OR UNDERESTIMATED. THE SOVIET
CARICATURE AS IT REFLECTS SOVIET FOREIGN AND DOMESTIC
POLICIES CAN STRENGTHEN WESTERN ANALYSIS AND ADD INSIGHTS.
FOR EXAMPLE, AN ANALYSIS OF SOVIET CARTOONS BEFORE AND AFTER

THE BEGINNING OF THE GORBACHEV ERA REVEALS THAT SOVIET
ATTITUDES TOWARD THE USA HAVE CHANGED IN WAYS THAT ARE BOTH
NUANCED AND STRIKING.

06344 MILES, I.
MASCULINITY AND ITS DISCONTENTS
FUTURES, 21(1) (FEB 89), 47-59.
THE EMERGENCE OF SEXUAL POLITICS AND WOMEN'S MOVEMENTS
IS GENERALLY VIEWED IN TERMS OF THE PROBLEMS OF WOMEN - OR
OF WOMEN AS PROBLEMS. HOWEVER, WHILE IT IS WOMEN WHO
EXPERIENCE SEXUAL OPPRESSION, IT IS THE SYSTEM OF GENDER
RELATIONS THAT IS THE PROBLEM, AND MASCULINITY IN ITS
CONTEMPORARY FORMS IS A MAJOR CONTRIBUTOR TO THIS SYSTEM.
MASCULINITY IS CHALLENGED BY THE NEW MOVEMENTS, AND IN THIS
ARTICLE IT IS ARGUED THAT IT IS IN CRISIS DUE TO THESE AND
TO CHANGES IN SOCIAL STRUCTURES. THIS CRISIS IS REFLECTED IN
THE BACKLASH AGAINST WHAT ARE OFTEN LABELLED '1960S' DEMANDS
FOR WOMEN'S AND GAY RIGHTS. BUT IT CREATES OPPORTUNITIES FOR
MEN TO RECOGNIZE THAT MASCULINITY LIMITS THEIR HUMANITY TOO,
AND TO BEGIN TO EXAMINE WAYS IN WHICH THEY CAN CONTRIBUTE TO
DEFINING NEW SEX ROLES.

06345 MILES, S.; OSTERTAG, B.
FRANCISCO JOVEL: WE'RE NOT TALKING ABOUT SOCIALISM
NACLA REPORT ON THE AMERICAS, XXIII(3) (SEP 89), 30.
FRANCISCO JOVEL, A MEMBER OF THE FMLN GENERAL COMMNAND,
SPEAKS OF THE CONFLICT BETWEEN THE FMLN AND GOVERNMENT
FORCES ON THE MARCH 19 ELECTIONS. ALTHOUGH MANY EXPECTED A
SIGNIFICANT AND IMPORTANT CLASH BETWEEN THE FMLN AND THE
ARMY, THE FMLN DID NOT VIEW IT AS A MATTER OF VICTORY OR
DEATH AND ACCORDINGLY ACTED PRUDENTLY. JOVEL ALSO DISCUSSES
THE FUTURE OF EL SALVADOR SHOULD THE FMLN TAKE POWER. HE
STATES THAT THE FMLN WILL NOT INSTALL A SOCIALIST REGIME,
BUT SIMPLY PROPOSE THE ESTABLISHMENT OF AN AUTHENTICALLY
DEMOCRATIC SOCIETY.

06346 MILES, S.; OSTERTAG, B.
HECTOR RECINOS: PUSHING FROM BEHIND
NACLA REPORT ON THE AMERICAS, XXIII(3) (SEP 89), 20-21.
FOUNDER OF THE NATIONAL FEDERATION OF SALVADORAN WORKERS
(FENASTRAS) HECTOR RECINOS DISCUSSES EL SALVADOR'S FUTURE
AND THE CHANGING ROLE OF UNIONS IN THE ANTI-GOVERNMENT
MOVEMENT. HE STATES THAT THE UNION STRUGGLES IN THE 1970'S
WAS AGAINST ECONOMISM, BUREAUCRATISM, AND LEGALISM. ALTHOUGH
FENASTRAS WAS AT THE FOREFRONT OF THE MOVEMENT IN THE 1970'S,
RECINOS STATES THAT ITS ROLE IS NOW TO SUPPORT AND "PUSH
FROM BEHIND" THE MORE RADICAL MOVEMENTS SUCH AS THE FMLN.

06347 MILES, S.; OSTERTAG, B.
JACKLOOT DEMOCRACY
NACLA REPORT ON THE AMERICAS, XXIII(2) (JUL 89), 28-38.
AN IMMEDIATE MOVE TOWARD DEATH SQUAD RAMPAGES LIKE THOSE
OF THE EARLY 1980S OR A GUATEMALA-STYLE "TOTAL WAR" SEEM NOT
TO BE IN THE CARDS, EVEN THOUGH CERTAIN OFFICERS CHAMP AT
THE BIT AND THE THREE MASS MURDERERS FINGERED BY GEORGE BUSH
IN 1983 ARE BACK FROM EXILE. TO CRUSH DISSENT IN EL SALVADOR,
ARENA IS MORE LIKELY TO ERECT A "LEGAL" POLICE STATE, ONE
WHICH COULD BE SOLD BY WASHINGTON AS A HUMAN RIGHTS
IMPROVEMENT.

06348 MILES, S.; OSTERTAG, B.
LEO CABRAL: OUR STRATEGIC TIME IS SHORT
NACLA REPORT ON THE AMERICAS, XXIII(3) (SEP 89), 28-29.
LEO CABRAL, A MEMBER OF THE POLITICAL COMMISSION OF THE
GENERAL COMMAND OF THE FMLN, OUTLINES THE UNIQUE NATURE OF
THE "INSURRECTION" THE ORGANIZATION SEEKS TO SPARK. UNLIKE A
CLASSIC MODEL, WHICH CALLS FOR A GENERAL UPRISING OF THE
MASSES AT THE SAME TIME, THE FMLN'S BRAND OF INSURRECTION IS
IRREGULAR, BOTH IN TACTICS AND IN WEAPONRY. THIS IRREGULAR
STYLE ALLOWS THE FMLN TO RESPOND TO SITUATIONS WITH
FLEXIBILITY AND SPEED. CABRAL PREDICTS SIGNIFICANT CHANGES
WITHIN A YEAR AND A HALF.

06349 MILES, S.; OSTERTAG, B.
MARCHING ORDERS
NACLA REPORT ON THE AMERICAS, XXIII(2) (JUL 89), 24-27.
ARENA MOBILIZED ON A SCALE UNPRECEDENTED IN SALVADORAN
ELECTORAL POLITICS. ITS MEDIA CAMPAIGN FEATURED SLICK
TELEVISION SPOTS THAT WOULD HAVE BEEN THE ENVY OF A U.S.
PRESIDENTIAL CAMPAIGN AND A RADIO BLITZ THAT RAN UP TO FIVE
SPOTS IN A ROW SEVERAL TIMES DURING THE SAME PROGRAM.
ARENA'S FREE MARKET PROGRAM AND ITS DRACONIAN "ANTI-
TERRORIST" PLANS ARE CERTAIN TO BE IMPLEMENTED. NOT ONLY
DOES THE PARTY DOMINATE ALL BRANCHES OF GOVERNMENT, IT IS
UNLIKELY TO FACE OPPOSITION FROM EITHER THE ARMED FORCES OR
THE BUSINESS COMMUNITY. AND WHILE ARENA MAY HAVE EARNED THE
ANTIPATHY OF WASHINGTON LIBERALS, ITS RELATIONSHIP TO THE
REPUBLICANS HAS BEEN LONG AND COZY.

06350 MILES, S.; OSTERTAG, B.
RETHINKING PEACE
NACLA REPORT ON THE AMERICAS, XXIII(3) (SEP 89), 24-37.
THE STRATEGY ADOPTED BY THE FARABUNDO MARTI NATIONAL
LIBERATION FRONT (FMLN) SEEMS QUITE INCONGRUOUS. ON ONE HAD,

THEY ARE STEPPING UP THE EFFORTS TO "INVOLVE ALL KINDS OF
PEOPLE IN ALL KINDS OF POPULAR VIOLENCE" BY INCREASING URBAN
ACTIONS, RECONCENTRATING REBEL FORCES, AND LINKING WITH MANY
GRASS ROOTS, RURAL ORGANIZATIONS. ON THE OTHER HAND, THEY
ARE ALSO PURSUING A NEGOTIATED SOLUTION TO THE CONFLICT.
HOWEVER, FMNL LEADERS ARE CONFIDENT THAT THIS STRATEGY WILL
UNITE THE COUNTRY'S REFORMISTS AND REVOLUTIONARIES INTO A
MAJORITY COALITION CAPABLE OF MOVING THE STRUGGLE TO A LESS
VIOLENT TERRAIN.

06351 MILES, S.; OSTERTAG, B.
RETHINKING WAR
NACLA REPORT ON THE AMERICAS, XXIII(3) (SEP 89), 16-22.
THE MILITARY PROWESS OF EL SALVADOR'S FARABUNDO MARTI
NATIONAL LIBERATION FRONT (FMLN) HAS INCREASED AS FIGHTING
HAS REACHED ALL CORNERS OF THE COUNTRY. THE AUTHORS TRACE
THE DEVELOPMENT OF FMLN STRATEGY FROM THE ESTABLISHING OF
"ZONES OF CONTROL" IN 1981-1984 TO THE AMBIGUOUS "WAR OF
RESISTANCE" THAT FOLLOWED. THE SUCCESS OF THE FMLN IS
LARGELY DUE TO ITS EFFORTS TO FOSTER RURAL COMMUNITY
ORGANIZATIONS AND WORK AT A GRASS ROOTS LEVEL. AS ONE
OBSERVER NOTED, "THE KID ON THE CORNER WITH A MOLOTOV
COCKTAIL HAS BECOME THE KEY."

06352 MILES, S.; OSTERTAG, B.
THE LEFT DEBATES INSURRECTION
NACLA REPORT ON THE AMERICAS, XXIII(3) (SEP 89), 23.
THE ABILITY OF THE LEFT TO SPARK A WIDESPREAD
INSURRECTION IS STILL HOTLY DEBATED AMONG THE VARIOUS
FACTIONS. THE FARABUNDO MARTI NATIONAL LIBERATION FRONT
(FMLN) SPEAKS WITH CONFIDENCE OF ITS "FIRE PLAN" DESIGNED TO
PROVOKE A WIDESPREAD POPULAR INSURRECTION. HOWEVER, A SERIES
OF POLLS REVEAL THAT ONLY 30% OF THE POPULATION HAS ADOPTED
EXPLICITLY "RADICALIZED" POLITICS, AND MANY DOUBT THE FMLN'S
ABILITY TO GAIN WIDESPREAD POPULAR SUPPORT.

06353 MILES, S.; OSTERTAG, B.
THE RISE OF THE REEBOK RIGHT
NACLA REPORT ON THE AMERICAS, XXIII(2) (JUL 89), 15-23.
REPUTED DEATH SQUAD LEADER ROBERTO D'AUBUISSON EL
SALVADOR'S NATIONALIST REPUBLICAN ALLIANCE ON THE MODEL OF
GERMANY'S NAZI PARTY. ORIGINALLY THE VOICE OF A SMALL BUT
VOCAL ULTRA-RIGHT, IT GREW TO BECOME THE CONSENSUS POLITICAL
INSTRUMENT OF THE ENTIRE BUSINESS COMMUNITY. THEN WITH AN
ARMY OF REEBOK-CLAD FOOT SOLDIERS -- SALVADORAN YOUTH FRESH
FROM REPUBLICAN PARTY CAMPAIGNING IN THE UNITED STATES -
D'AUBUISSON FORGED A MULTI-CLASS ALLIANCE TO MAKE ARENA "THE
ENVY OF THE LATIN AMERICAN RIGHT."

06354 MILES, W.F.S.
THE RALLLY AS RITUAL: DRAMATURGICAL POLITICS IN NIGERIAN
HAUSALAND
COMPARATIVE POLITICS, 21(3) (APR 89), 323-338.
THE DRAMATIC ASPECTS OF POLITICS AND ELECTORAL CAMPAIGNS
HAVE INCREASINGLY DRAWN THE ATTENTION OF STUDENTS OF THE
POLITICAL SCENE. THIS ESSAY LOOKS AT THE INSTITUTION OF THE
RALLY IN NIGERIAN HAUSALAND.

06355 MILIBAND, R.
REFLECTIONS ON THE CRISIS OF COMMUNIST REGIMES
NEW LEFT REVIEW, (177) (SEP 89), 27-36.
IN VIEW OF RECENT EVENTS IN THE COMMUNIST WORLD, THE
AUTHOR CONSIDERS WHAT KIND OF POLITICAL PERSPECTIVE REMAINS
VIABLE. HE IS FUNDAMENTALLY CONCERNED WITH BRINGING
DEMOCRATIC CHECKS AND SAFEGUARDS INTO THE HEART OF SOCIALIST
RENEWAL IN THE EAST.

06356 MILJAN, T.
PERESTROIKA: AN INTERIM REVIEW OF ITS OBJECTIVES, PROGRAMS,
AND PROSPECTS
JOURNAL OF BALTIC STUDIES, XX(2) (SUM 89), 109-126.
THE AUTHOR EXAMINES THE BACKGROUND TO PERESTROIKA AND
THE PROSPECTS FOR ITS SUCCESS.

06357 MILJAN, T.
THE PROPOSAL TO ESTABLISH ECONOMIC AUTONOMY IN ESTONIA
JOURNAL OF BALTIC STUDIES, XX(2) (SUM 89), 149-164.
AFTER THE PUBLICATION OF THE DOCUMENTS OF THE JUNE 1987
PLENUM OF THE CENTRAL COMMITTEE, ECONOMISTS AND PLANNERS IN
ESTONIA BEGAN TO DRAW UP A PLAN FOR AN ESTONIAN VERSION THAT
WOULD ADAPT PERESTROIKA TO THEIR PARTICULAR LOCAL CONDITIONS.
THE ESTONIANS ADOPTED THREE MAJOR GOALS: TO PURSUE THE
ESTABLISHMENT OF REGIONAL ECONOMIC AUTONOMY FOR ESTONIA, TO
STOP THE ECOLOGICAL RAPE OF NORTHEAST ESTONIA, AND TO HASTEN
THE DEMOCRATIZATION OF POLITICAL, ECONOMIC, AND CULTURAL
LIFE IN ESTONIA.

06358 MILLAN, B.
DEVELOPING EUROPE'S PERIPHERY
EUROPE, (290) (OCT 89), 26-28.
THE ARTICLE ANALYZES THE PROBLEMS PRESENTED BY THE
INCREASINGLY APPARENT GAP BETWEEN RICH AND POOR NATIONS IN
THE EUROPEAN COMMUNITY. IF THE SINGLE MARKET IS TO BECOME A
REALITY, THE DISPARITIES OF WEALTH AND DEVELOPMENT IN THE E.

C. MUST BE DEALT WITH. THE E.C. IS SHIFTING EMPHASIS FORM A
LARGE NUMBER OF "ONE-OFF" PROJECTS TO CONTINUING PROJECTS,
WHOSE IMPLEMENTATION WILL ALSO INVOLVE LOCAL AND NATIONAL
AUTHORITIES.

06359 MILLARD, W.J.
THE USIA CENTRAL AMERICAN SURVEYS
PUBLIC OPINION QUARTERLY, 53(1) (SPR 89), 134-135.
THE AUTHOR RESPONDS TO CRITICISM OF THE 1985 USIA-
SPONSORED SURVEY IN CENTRAL AMERICA, INCLUDING THE PLACEMENT
OF QUESTIONS AND THE FINDING THAT THE PUBLIC WISHES UNITED
STATES INVOLVEMENT IN CENTRAL AMERICA TO CONTINUE.

06360 MILLER, A.D.
PALESTINIANS AND THE INTIFADA: ONE YEAR LATER
CURRENT HISTORY, 88(535) (FEB 89), 73-76, 106-107.
THE INTIFADA HAS INTRODUCED A GREAT DEAL OF UNCERTAINTY
INTO TRADITIONAL THINKING ABOUT THE ARAB-ISRAELI CONFLICT;
IT HAS CHANGED PALESTINIAN PERCEPTIONS AND HAS FORCED KEY
PARTIES TO ADJUST THEIR CALCULATIONS. THE VIOLENCE HAS
FORCED THE PLO TO EMBARK ON A NEW POLITICAL STRATEGY, BUT IT
IS TOO SOON TO TELL WHETHER THIS WILL LEAD TO A POLITICAL
PROCESS ABLE TO CHANGE THE STATUS QUO.

06361 MILLER, A.H.; ROBBINS, J.S.
WHO DID VOTE FOR HITLER? A REANALYSIS OF THE LIPSET/BENDIX
CONTROVERSY
POLITY, 21(4) (SUM 89), 655-678.
THIS ARTICLE ADDRESSES TWO OF THE LEADING EXPLANATIONS
OF HITLER'S SUCCESS, ONE ADVANCED BY SEYMOUR MARTIN LIPSET
AND THE OTHER BY RHEINHARD BENDIX. THE AUTHORS ADDRESS BOTH
EVIDENTARY AND METHODOLOGICAL QUESTIONS IN THEIR ANALYSES
AND CONCLUDE THAT, ON THE WHOLE, BENDIX'S MASS SOCIETY
EXPLANATION IS THE MORE PERSUASIVE, THIS MAY NOT SETTLE THE
CONTROVERSY BUT IT PRESENTS A NEW CHALLENGE FOR THOSE WHO
WOULD ARGUE TO THE CONTRARY.

06362 MILLER, A.M.
DISARMAMENT AND ECONOMIC RESTRUCTURING: A QUANTITATIVE
ANALYSIS OF MILITARY PROCUREMENT IN LOS ANGELES COUNTY
DISSERTATION ABSTRACTS INTERNATIONAL, 49(8) (FEB 89), 2319.
THIS DISSERTATION ANALYZES THE ECONOMIC PROBLEMS
ASSOCIATED WITH DISARMAMENT AND THE TRANSFER OF RESOURCES
FROM MILITARY TO CIVILIAN USE, USING THE POTENTIAL IMPACT ON
LOS ANGELES COUNTY AS A CASE STUDY. EMPHASIS IS PLACED ON
ANALYZING THE MICROECONOMIC PROBLEMS OF DISARMAMENT LIKELY
AT THE REGIONAL LEVEL.

06363 MILLER, B.
CAN OPPONENTS COOPERATE: EXPLAINING GREAT POWER
COOPERATION IN MANAGING THIRD AREA CONFLICTS
DISSERTATION ABSTRACTS INTERNATIONAL, 50(4) (OCT 89),
1084-A.
MODERATE AND SIMILAR POWERS CAN SOMETIMES FIND
THEMSELVES IN UNINTENDED WARS WHILE IMMODERATE AND
DISSIMILAR STATES CAN MANAGE CRISES EFFECTIVELY. AT THE SAME
TIME, SOME STATES ARE ABLE TO COOPERATE IN NORMAL DIPLOMACY
BETTER THAN OTHERS, EVEN IS MORE ACTORS PARTICIPATE IN THE
COOPERATIVE CASE. IN THIS DISSERTATION, THE AUTHOR EXPLAINS
THESE PUZZLES BY INTRODUCING A THEORETICAL MODEL WHICH
ARGUES THAT WHEREAS CRISIS COOPERATION DEPENDS ON STRUCTURAL
ELEMENTS, COOPERATION IN NORMAL DIPLOMACY DEPENDS ON STATE
ATTRIBUTES AND COGNITIVE FACTORS. HE UTILIZES A FOCUSED
COMPARISON OF U.S.-SOVIET TACIT COOPERATION IN MIDDLE
EASTERN CRISES AS A CASE STUDY.

06364 MILLER, C.A.
THE NEED FOR A NATIONAL HEALTH PROGRAM: THOUGHTS ON
EXAMINING THE JACKSON NATIONAL HEALTH PROGRAM
INTERNATIONAL JOURNAL OF HEALTH SERVICES, 19(3) (1989),
553-556.
IN THE DISCUSSION OF THE PROPOSED "JACKSON NATIONAL
HEALTH PROGRAM" THE AUTHOR STRONGLY ADVOCATES ITS ADOPTION.
HE OUTLINES "ESSENTIAL" ISSUES WHICH INCLUDE UNIVERSALITY
WITHOUT FINANCIAL BARRIERS, GOVERNMENT MANAGEMENT AND
NATIONAL CONSISTENCY. HE ALSO ANALYZES SEVERAL ISSUES THAT,
DUE TO STRONG POLITICAL RESISTANCE WILL PROBABLY BE
COMPORMISED SUCH AS THE SHRINKING OF THE PRIVATE INSURANCE
INDUSTRY. THE AUTHOR CONCLUDES THAT ALTHOUGH THE JACKSON
PROGRAM STRIVES TO CORRECT THE DEFECTS OF EARLIER PROPOSALS,
IT STILL HAS PROBLEMS THAT NEED TO BE DEALT WITH.

06365 MILLER, J.
REINVENTING THE BRAKE
COMMONWEAL, CXVI(4) (FEB 89), 105-107.
DESPITE THE PHILIPPINES' OVERPOPULATION CRISIS,
PRESIDENT AQUINO HAS BEEN RELUCTANT TO SPEAK OUT ON THE
ISSUE, GIVING THE IMPRESSION THAT SHE DOESN'T TAKE THE
PROBLEM SERIOUSLY. THERE IS DISAGREEMENTWITHIN HER
GOVERNMENT ON HOW AGGRESSIVE THE PHILIPPINES' FAMILY
PLANNING PROGRAM SHOULD BE, BECAUSE 85 PERCENT OF FILIPINOS
ARE CATHOLICS.

06366 MILLER, J.E.
A SHORT HISTORY OF NATO
DEPARTMENT OF STATE BULLETIN (US FOREIGN POLICY), 89(2149)
(AUG 89), 1-10.
THE AUTHOR BRIEFLY RECOUNTS THE HISTORY OF NATO,
INCLUDING ITS ORIGINS AND THE CREATION OF THE ALLIANCE
STRUCTURE.

06367 MILLER, J.N. JR.
APPROACHING ZERO: AN EVALUATION OF RADICAL REDUCTIONS IN
SUPERPOWER NUCLEAR ARSENALS
DISSERTATION ABSTRACTS INTERNATIONAL, 50(4) (OCT 89),
1084-A.
THIS DISSERTATION EXAMINES THE EFFECTS ON THE LIKELIHOOD
OF NUCLEAR WAR IF SUPERPOWER NUCLEAR ARSENALS WERE REDUCED
TO ONE THOUSAND OR FEWER WARHEADS. IT INVESTIGATES THE
SENSITIVITY OF THESE FINDINGS TO ASSUMPTIONS ABOUT THE
STRUCTURE OF REMAINING NUCLEAR FORCES, VERIFICATION AND
LIMITS ON BREAKOUT, THE EXTENT OF STRATEGIC DEFENSES, AND
SUPERPOWER NUCLEAR DOCTRINES.

06368 MILLER, L.B.
BUSH'S FOREIGN POLICY: OLD BOTTLES, NEW WINE?
WORLD TODAY, 45(4) (APR 89), 59-61.
THE GENERAL TENOR OF PRESIDENT BUSH'S FOREIGN POLICY
APPOINTMENTS HAS REINFORCED THE APPEARANCE OF PRAGMATISM AS
THE PREVAILING CHARACTERISTIC OF HIS ADMINISTRATION.
EXPERIENCED REPUBLICAN STALWARTS LIKE JAMES BAKER AND BRENT
SCOWCROFT ARE UNLIKELY TO RIDE IDEOLOGICAL HOBBY-HORSES OR
ALARM ALLIES WITH ZIGZAGS IN POLICY FORMULATION OR
IMPLEMENTATION. CAUTION TOWARD THE SOVIET UNION LOOKS LIKE
THE HALLMARK OF THE GROUP.

06369 MILLER, M.
"MA'AM, WHAT YOU NEED IS A NEW, IMPROVED HOOVER"
WASHINGTON MONTHLY, 20(12) (JAN 89), 10-18.
THE AUTHOR LOOKS AT CHARGES THAT THE FBI HAS PERMITTED
RACIAL HARASSMENT OF MINORITY EMPLOYEES AND HAS ABUSED ITS
SURVEILLANCE AUTHORITY.

06370 MILLER, M. H.
PLANS TO SOLVE THE PROBLEM OF THE TWIN US DEFICITS
CANADIAN PUBLIC POLICY--ANALYSE DE POLITIQUES, XV (FEB 89),
58-62.
THE ORTHODOX SOLUTION TO THIS PROBLEM OF THE TWIN
DEFICITS' IS, IN PRINCIPLE, STRAIGHTFORWARD - A DEVALUATION
OF THE DOLLAR COMBINED WITH FISCAL CONTRACTION. THE FALL OF
THE DOLLAR IS DESIGNED TO PRICE THE US BACK INTO WORLD
MARKETS AND RESTORE EXTERNAL BALANCE; WHILE THE FISCAL
CONTRACTION IS INTENDED TO PREVENT THE SWITCHING OF DEMAND
TOWARDS THE US FROM UPSETTING THE 'INTERNAL BALANCE,' I.E.
THE NON-INFLATIONARY FULL EMPLOYMENT ALREADY ATTAINED. THIS
ARTICLE EXAMINES THE PRACTICAL PROBLEMS AND BENEFITS OF THIS
ORTHODOX SOLUTION.

06371 MILLER, R.
A POLITICAL ECONOMY PORTRAIT OF THE CANADIAN ECONOMY FROM
1926 TO 1983: THE CHANGING DIVISION OF LABOR AND
ESTIMATION OF MARXIAN VARIABLES
DISSERTATION ABSTRACTS INTERNATIONAL, 49(7) (JAN 89),
1894-A.
THE AUTHOR DEVELOPS AN EMPIRICAL PICTURE OF THE CANADIAN
ECONOMY SINCE 1926, USING POLITICAL ECONOMY CONCEPTS. HE
TRANSLATES NATIONAL INCOME AND EXPENDITURE ACCOUNTS DATA
INTO MARXIAN CATEGORIES.

06372 MILLER, R.
IMPLEMENTING A PROGRAM OF COOPERATIVE FEDERALISM: THE
SURFACE MINING CONTROL AND RECLAMATION ACT OF 1977
POLICY STUDIES REVIEW, 9(1) (AUT 89), 79-87.
THIS ARTICLE OUTLINES THE LEGISLATIVE HISTORY OF THE
SURFACE MINING CONTROL AND RECLAMATION ACT OF 1977 AND
DESCRIBES THE FORCES THAT PROMOTED A FEDERALIST ARRANGEMENT
OF SHARED POWERS AND RESPONSIBILITY FOR IMPLEMENTING THE
ENVIRONMENTAL RECLAMATION PROVISIONS OF THE ACT. THE MAJOR
COMPONENTS OF THE ACT ARE REVIEWED AND THE ACT IS EXAMINED
IN TERMS OF ITS GENERAL EFFECTIVENESS IN PROMOTING
RECLAMATION AS WELL AS ITS CONTRIBUTION TO THE PRACTICE OF
AMERICAN FEDERALISM AND THE CAPACITY OF STATE GOVERNMENT TO
IMPLEMENT COMPLEX REGULATORY PROGRAMS. THE ARTICLE CONCLUDES
THAT SMCRA HAS HAD A POSITIVE IMPACT IN TERMS OF IMPROVING
STATE CAPABILITIES, EXPANDING PUBLIC INVOLVEMENT IN DECISION
MAKING, AND ENHANCING FEDERAL AND STATE COOPERATION.

06373 MILLER, R.B.
INDUSTRIAL STRUCTURE, POLITICAL POWER, AND UNIONIZATION:
THE UNITED STATES IN COMPARATIVE PERSPECTIVE
DISSERTATION ABSTRACTS INTERNATIONAL, 49(8) (FEB 89),
2412-A.
THE AUTHOR IDENTIFIES THE CAUSES OF PRIVATE AND PUBLIC
SECTOR UNIONISM IN THE USA AND COMPARES THE US EXPERIENCE TO
OTHER INDUSTRIALIZED WESTERN COUNTRIES. HE TESTS SEVERAL
VARIABLES: ECONOMIC FACTORS, POPULATION CHARACTERISTICS,
INDUSTRIAL INFRASTRUCTURE CHARACTERISTICS, AND POLITICAL
FACTORS.

06374 MILLER, R.F.
DEVELOPMENTS IN YUGOSLAV AGRICULTURE: BREAKING THE
IDEOLOGICAL BARRIER IN A PERIOD OF GENERAL ECONOMIC AND
POLITICAL CRISIS
EASTERN EUROPEAN POLITICS AND SOCIETIES, 3(3) (FAL 89),
500-533.
THIS ARTICLE ADDRESSES THE QUESTION OF WHETHER THE
YUGOSLAV AUTHORITIES HAVE THE ECONOMIC SENSE AND POLITICAL
COURAGE TO ACTIVATE THE ROLE OF THE PRIVATE SECTOR, LARGELY
TAKING ADVANTAGE OF THE TRADITIONAL LABOR-INTENSIFYING
BEHAVIOR OF PEASANT FARMERS. IT LOOKS AT THE PHASES OF
POSTWAR YUGOSLAV AGRICULTURAL POLICY AND MAKES OBSERVATIONS
ABOUT YUGOSLAV AGRICULTURE IN THE EIGHTIES PROSPECTS FOR THE
FUTURE ARE EXPLORED.

06375 MILLER, R.F.
ECHOES OF PERESTROIKA
PACIFIC DEFENCE REPORTER, 16(6) (DEC 89), 7-9.
IT HAS BECOME A COMMONPLACE IN THE WEST, AND IN MORE
CANDID CIRCLES IN THE SOVIET ELITE AS WELL, THAT THE SOVIET
UNION NEEDS PEACE AND DETENTE IN ORDER TO BE ABLE TO DIVERT
FUNDS FROM MILITARY TO CIVILIAN PURPOSES AND THAT HEAVY
DEFENCE EXPENDITURES ARE A MAJOR CAUSE OF INFLATION AND
BUDGETARY SHORTFALLS. BUT THE REVERSE RELATIONSHIP IS ALSO
IMPORTANT: A VISIBLY UNSTABLE AND PROBLEMRIVEN SOVIET STATE
IS IN A WEAKENED POSITION TO CARRY OUT ITS FOREIGN POLICY
OBJECTIVES. EVEN SO, NON-COMMUNIST STATESMEN WILL HAVE TO
EXERCISE A GOOD DEAL MORE POLITICAL CIRCUMSPECTION AND
INSIGHT INTO THEIR OWN VITAL INTERESTS IF THEY ARE TO BE
ABLE TO COPE EFFECTIVELY WITH THE NEW SOVIET CHALLENGES TO
REGIONAL STABILITY IN THE COMING YEARS.

06376 MILLER, S.
TOTALITARIANISM, DEAD AND ALIVE
COMMENTARY, 88(2) (AUG 89), 28-32.
NOTHING IS MORE LIKELY TO PROLONG THE PROCESS OF CHANGE
THAN TO OPERATE UNDER THE ASSUMPTION THAT THE COLD WAR IS
OVER. IT WAS, AFTER ALL, THE WEST'S POLICY OF CONTAINMENT
THAT CONTRIBUTED SIGNIFICANTLY TO MOVING THE SOVIET UNION IN
THE DIRECTION OF POST-TOTALITARIAN COMMUNISM.

06377 MILLER, S. E.
THE LIMITS OF MUTUAL RESTRAINT: ARMS CONTROL AND THE
STRATEGIC BALANCE
DISSERTATION ABSTRACTS INTERNATIONAL, 49(8) (FEB 89),
2382-A.
THE AUTHOR EXAMINES THE ORIGINS AND CONTENT OF THE
MODERN THEORY OF NUCLEAR ARMS CONTROL AND EXPLAINS WHY THIS
THEORY HAS PROVEN SO DIFFICULT TO IMPLEMENT. ARMS CONTROL
HAS COME TO PLAY AN IMPORTANT POLITICAL ROLE BUT HAS NOT
SERVED AS A MAJOR DETERMINANT OF THE STRATEGIC BALANCE, AS
THE ARMS CONTROL THEORISTS ORIGINALLY HOPED IT MIGHT,
BECAUSE OF THE CONSTRAINTS IMPOSED BY THE STRATEGIC
DOCTRINES OF THE SUPERPOWERS.

06378 MILLER, S.M.; RUSSEK, F.S.
ARE THE TWIN DEFICITS REALLY RELATED?
CONTEMPORARY POLICY ISSUES, VII(4) (OCT 89), 91-115.
THIS PAPER EXAMINES WHETHER POST-WORLD WAR II DATA FOR
THE UNITED STATES REVEAL A LONG-RUN SECULAR RELATIONSHIP
BETWEEN THE TRADE DEFICIT AND THE FISCAL DEFICIT. THE FOCUS
IS ON THE SECULAR RELATIONSHIP SINCE THAT IS THE ONE MOST
RELEVANT TO LONG-RUN POLICY CONCERNS. THE AUTHORS EMPLOY
THREE DIFFERENT STATISTICAL TECHNIQUES: (I) A DETERMINISTIC
TECHNIQUE FOR SEPARATING THE SECULAR COMPONENTS FROM THE
CYCLICAL COMPONENTS TO DERIVE SECULAR MEASURES OF THE TWIN
DEFICITS, (II) A STOCHASTIC PROCEDURE TO ISOLATE THE SECULAR
COMPONENTS, (III) COINTEGRATION ANALYSIS TO TEST FOR A LONG-
RUN EQUILIBRIUM RELATIONSHIP.

06379 MILLER, W.L.; BROUGHTON, D.; SONNTAG, N.
TELEVISION IN THE 1987 BRITISH ELECTION CAMPAIGN: ITS
CONTENT AND INFLUENCE
POLITICAL STUDIES, XXXVII(4) (DEC 89), 626-651.
THE MAIN PURPOSE IN THIS PAPER IS TO LOOK AT THE CONTENT
OF TELEVISION NEWS DURING THE MONTH OF THE OFFICIAL ELECTION
CAMPAIGN IN 1987, AND THEN USE BRITISH ELECTION CAMPAIGN
STUDY PANEL SURVEY TO SEE WHAT INFLUENCE TELEVISION HAD ON
THE ELECTORATE IN THAT SHORT SPAN OF TIME. IN THE SHORT SPAN
OF A FOUR- OR FIVE-WEEK ELECTION CAMPAIGN THE AUTHORS'
CONCLUSION IS THAT TELEVISION FAILED TO SET THE PUBLIC
AGENDA AND THE PUBLIC FAILED TO SET THE TELEVISION AGENDA.
EACH INFLUENCED THE OTHER TO A VERY MODEST EXTENT, BUT THEY
REMAINED POLES APART.

06380 MILLNER, E.L.; PRATT, M.D.
AN EXPERIMENTAL INVESTIGATION OF EFFICIENT RENT-SEEKING
PUBLIC CHOICE, 62(2) (AUG 89), 139-152.
IT IS THE PURPOSE OF THIS PAPER TO PRESENT A LABORATORY
INVESTIGATION OF TULLOCK'S MODEL OF EFFICIENT RENT-SEEKING.
THE ARTICLE EXAMINES THE EFFECTS OF CHANGES IN THE
PROBABILITY FUNCTION THAT DETERMINES WHETHER OR NOT AN

INDIVIDUAL IS THE RECIPIENT OF THE MONOPOLY PROFIT. IT PRESENTS TULLOCK'S MODEL AND FOLLOWS IT WITH A DESCRIPTION OF THE EXPERIMENTAL PROCEDURES AND AND ANALYSIS OF THE RESULTS.

06381 MILLS, M.K.
STRAINED MERCY: HOSPITAL STRUCTURE, DRG'S, AND PUBLIC POLICY
POLICY STUDIES REVIEW, 8(2) (WIN 89), 432-440.
IN 1983, A SIGNIFICANT CHANGE HAS ENACTED IN MEDICARE. CONGRESS APPROVED A SYSTEM OF PAYMENTS FOR HOSPITAL INPATIENT SERVICES WHEREBY HOSPITALS RECEIVED A FIXED SUM PER CASE ACCORDING TO A PRE-ESTABLISHED SCHEDULE OF DIAGNOSIS RELATED GROUPINGS (DRG'S). THIS ESSAY EXAMINES THE EFFECT OF THIS MEDICARE CHANGE ON THE HEALTH DELIVERY SYSTEM AND CONSIDERS ITS PUBLIC POLICY IMPLICATIONS.

06382 MILLS, O.H.
U.S. STRATEGY FOR THE FAR EAST: TOWARD THE 21ST CENTURY
AVAILABLE FROM NTIS, NO. AD-A208 608/0/GAR, MAR 31 89, 62.
THE UNITED STATES POST-WORLD WAR II SECURITY MEASURES FOR THE FAR EAST HAVE RESULTED IN DYNAMIC REGIONAL ECONOMIC AND POLITICAL CHANGE. IRONICALLY, AMERICA MUST NOW MEET NEW CHALLENGES RESULTING FROM ITS SUCCESSFUL SECURITY POLICIES. SOME OBSERVES PREDICT THE TWENTY-FIRST CENTURY WILL BE THE PACIFIC CENTURY. THE STRONG EXPORT-LED REGIONAL ECONOMIES - NOTABLY JAPAN ARE THE PRIMARY CAUSE FOR THIS PERCEIVED SHIFT IN POWER. FURTHERMORE, WE'VE BECOME INCREASINGLY AWARE OF THE IMPORTANCE OF ECONOMICS AS AN ASPECT OF NATIONAL SECURITY AND ITS IMPACT ON AMERICANS' QUALITY OF LIFE. ANALYZING THE SOVIET REGIONAL THREAT AND AMERICA'S MILITARY, ECONOMIC, POLITICAL AND SOCIOPSYCHOLOGICAL REGIONAL INTERESTS AND IDENTIFYING CURRENT AND FUTURE ISSUES, THIS PAPER DEVELOPS A GENERAL FRAMEWORK FOR DESIGNING A REGIONAL U.S. STRATEGY FOR THE FAR EAST IN THE NEXT CENTURY.

06383 MILLHARD, W.G.
RUSHDIE, ISLAM, AND US
INTERNATIONAL PERSPECTIVES, 18(4) (JUL 89), 15-18.
ISLAM IS NOW GETTING THE SHARE OF ATTENTION THAT ONE BILLION PEOPLE - A FIFTH OF THE WORLD'S POPULATION - DESERVE. THIS ARTICLE EXAMINES THE FUROR THAT FOLLOWED THE PUBLICATION OF SALMAN RUSHDIE'S BOOK, "THE SATANIC VERSES." THE PAPER CONCLUDES THAT THE FUROR WON'T GO AWAY AND TELLS WHY. IT EXPLORES THE EFFECT OF THE BOOK IN CANADA AND THE REASONS WHY THE BOOK IS A SOCIAL DOCUMENT. INTERNATIONAL ACTION IS EXAMINED.

06384 MILNE, R.S.
THE RELEVANCE OF ETHNICITY
POLITICAL SCIENCE, 41(2) (DEC 89), 30-50.
THE AUTHOR DISCUSSES ETHNICITY, BOTH IN A GENERAL SENSE AND IN REFERENCE TO THE MAORIS AND CANADIAN ABORIGINALS. HE CONSIDERS THE CHANGES IN THE PERCEPTIONS OF ETHNICITY IN THE PAST THIRTY YEARS AND PROPOSES POSSIBLE STRATEGIES FOR DEALING WITH SOME DISRUPTIVE EFFECTS OF ETHNICITY.

06385 MILNER, H.
DOMESTIC AND INTERNATIONAL SOURCES OF COOPERATION: OIL POLITICS IN THE 1940'S AND 1970'S
INTERNATIONAL SPECTATOR, XXIV(3-4) (JUL 89), 141-152.
THIS PAPER HAS THREE TASKS. FIRST, IT EXAMINES VARIOUS SALIENT THEORIES ABOUT THE INTERNATIONAL FACTORS THAT INFLUENCE COOPERATION AMONG STATES. SECOND, IT SUGGESTS WHY THESE THEORIES ARE INADEQUATE AND WHY CERTAIN DOMESTIC SOURCES MUST BE CONSIDERED. THIRD, IT EXAMINES THE CASES OF INTERNATIONAL COOPERATION OVER THE CONTROL OF OIL IN THE 1940S TO SEE THE ROLE DOMESTIC FACTORS PLAYED. IT CONCLUDES BY SUGGESTING HOW SUCH AN EXPLANATION CAN AID IN UNDERSTANDING CONTEMPORARY OIL POLITICS.

06386 MILNER, H.V.; YOFFIE, D.B.
BETWEEN FREE TRADE AND PROTECTIONISM: STRATEGIC TRADE POLICY AND A THEORY OF CORPORATE TRADE DEMANDS
INTERNATIONAL ORGANIZATION, 43(2) (SPR 89), 239-272.
THIS ARTICLE SEEKS TO EXPLAIN THE EMERGENCE OF NEW CORPORATE TRADE DEMANDS AND THEREBY BROADEN THEORIES OF THE POLITICAL ECONOMY OF TRADE. THE ARTICLE BEGINS WITH THE WIDELY SUPPORTED POSITION THAT MULTINATIONAL AND EXPORT-ORIENTED FIRMS PREFER UNCONDITIONAL FREE TRADE. BUILDING ON CONCEPTS FROM THEORIES OF INDUSTRIAL ORGANIZATION AND INTERNATIONAL TRADE, THE ARTICLE THEN HYPOTHESIZES THAT RISING ECONOMIES OF SCALE AND STEEP LEARNING CURVES WILL NECESSITATE THAT THESE FIRMS HAVE ACCESS TO GLOBAL MARKETS VIA EXPORTS. IF GROWING DEPENDENCE ON WORLD MARKETS IS COMBINED WITH FOREIGN GOVERNMENT SUBSIDIES OR PROTECTION, THE TRADE PREFERENCES OF FIRMS WILL SHIFT FROM UNCONDITIONAL FREE TRADE TO DEMANDS THAT OPENNESS AT HOME BE CONTINGENT ON OPENNESS OVERSEAS. THE MANNER IN WHICH FIRM DEMANDS THEN GET TRANSLATED INTO INDUSTRY DEMANDS WILL VARY WITH THE INDUSTRY'S STRUCTURE. IF THE INDUSTRY CONSISTS OF FIRMS WITH SYMMETRIC STRATEGIES, IT WILL SEEK STRATEGIC TRADE POLICY; BUT IF THE INDUSTRY IS HIGHLY SEGMENTED, IT WILL TURN TOWARD PROTECTIONISM. THE ARTICLE CONCLUDES WITH A PRELIMINARY

TEST OF THESE HYPOTHESES IN FOUR BRIEF STUDIES OF THE POLITICS OF TRADE IN THE SEMICONDUCTOR, COMMERCIAL AIRCRAFT, TELECOMMUNICATIONS EQUIPMENT, AND MACHINE TOOL INDUSTRIES.

06387 MIN, C.
CHINA AND EASTERN EUROPE: A NEW RELATIONSHIP BASED ON REALISTIC NEEDS
JERUSALEM JOURNAL OF INTERNATIONAL RELATIONS, 11(1) (MAR 89), 12-36.
CHINA'S RELATIONS WITH EASTERN EUROPE HAVE GREATLY EXPANDED IN THE POST-MAO PERIOD. THE PAST FEW YEARS HAVE SEEN FREQUENT, HIGHRANKING OFFICIAL EXCHANGE BETWEEN CHINA AND MOST EAST EUROPEAN COUNTRIES, SOMETIMES AT THE LEVEL OF TOP LEADERS OF PARTY AND STATE. 1 WHAT HAS MOTIVATED CHINA TO WARM UP AGAIN, AND AT SUCH A TEMPO, ITS LONG COOLED-OFF RELATIONS WITH THESE COUNTRIES, AND WHAT HAS MOTIVATED THE EAST EUROPEAN COUNTRIES TO PROMOTE THEIR RELATIONS WITH CHINA? THIS ARTICLE EXPLORES THE EXISTING SITUATION, AND ATTEMPTS TO PREDICT THE GENERAL TREND OF DEVELOPMENT IN THE COMING DECADES.

06388 MINDLE, G.B.
LIBERALISM, PRIVACY, AND AUTONOMY
THE JOURNAL OF POLITICS, 51(3) (AUG 89), 575-598.
THE PROMINENCE THE RIGHT TO PRIVACY NOW COMMANDS IN AMERICAN PUBLIC LAW IS LARGELY ATTRIBUTABLE TO THE EFFORTS OF ONE MAN: LOUIS D. BRANDEIS. HIS ROLE IN THE FORMULATION AND DEVELOPMENT OF THIS RIGHT, AND ITS RELATIONSHIP TO THE LIBERALISM OF THE FRAMERS AND THE CONTEMPORARY DOCTRINE OF AUTONOMY AS EXPOUNDED BY LAURENCE TRIBE ARE RECONSIDERED; BRANDEIS'S OWN UNDERSTANDING OF THE RIGHT TO PRIVACY IS CONTRARY TO THE FORMER, AND DISTINGUISHABLE FROM THE LATTER, A VARIANT OF THE RIGHT TO PRIVACY MORE SOCIAL THAN PRIVATE.

06389 MING
CHINESE INTELLECTUALS AND THE UNITED STATES
ASIAN SURVEY, 29(7) (JUL 89), 645-654.
THIS ARTICLE OFFERS A PRELIMINARY ANAYSIS OF CONTEMPORARY MAWLAND CHINESE INTELLECTUALS WHO REGARD THE U.S. AS A POINT OF REFERENCE FOR THEIR OWN CONCERNS WITH THE PROCESS OF CHINESE MODERNIZATION. IT EXAMINES THREE GENERATIONS OF CHINESE MAINLAND INTELLECTUALS AND THE DEVELOPMENT OF NEGATIVE ATTITUDES TOWARDS THE UNITED STATES, AS WELL AS CHANGES WHICH HAVE BEEN TAKING PLACE BOTH ON THE SUBJECT AND THE OBJECT, ON THE PERCEIVERS AND ON THE WORLD, IT EXPLORES THE SEARCH FOR A SATISFACTORY ANSWER TO THE QUESTION OF WHAT KIND OF A COUNTRY IS THE UNITED STATES?

06390 MING, Z.
BEIJING CONTINUES TO OPEN THE DOOR
BEIJING REVIEW, 32(30) (JUL 89), 19-20.
PUBLIC ORDER IN BEIJING HAS RETURNED TO NORMAL AND ITS FOREIGN TRADE ACTIVITIES HAVE ALSO BEEN QUICKLY RESTORED FOLLOWING THE QUELLING OF THE COUNTER-REVOLUTIONARY REBELLION IN JUNE 1989. THE DOOR TO BEIJING AS WELL AS TO THE WHOLE COUNTRY CONTINUES TO REMAIN OPEN TO THE OUTSIDE WORLD,

06391 MING, Z.
BUSH'S ASIAN AND PACIFIC STRATEGY
BEIJING REVIEW, 32(37) (SEP 89), 31-34.
THERE ARE FIVE MAJOR POWERS IN THE ASIAN-PACIFIC AREA: THE UNITED STATES, THE SOVIET UNION, JAPAN, CHINA, AND INDIA. THERE WILL BE NO DIRECT, LARGE-SCALE MILITARY CONFRONTATION IN THE REGION IN THE NEAR FUTURE. BUT THE SOVIET UNION AND THE USA ARE RIVALS AND NORTHEAST ASIA IS A MAJOR OBJECT OF CONTENTION, AS IS EVIDENCED BY THE CONCENTRATION OF SUPERPOWER MARINE FORCES IN THE REGION.

06392 MINGYI, Z.
CHINA'S WORKING CLASS WANTS REFORMS
WORLD MARXIST REVIEW, 32(10) (OCT 89), .
THIS ARTICLE DEALS WITH MAJOR ASPECTS OF BUILDING SOCIALISM IN PEOPLE'S CHINA. IT EXAMINES THE CONCRETE ROLE OF THE WORKING CLASS IN EFFECTING THE SOCIALIST REFORM, AND HOW IT CAN BE ENHANCED, IT EXPLORES THE ALL-AROUND REVOLUTIONARY REFORM OF CHINA'S ECONOMIC, POLITICAL, AND IDEOLOGICAL SYSTEM. IT EXAMINES SOCIAL STATISTICS AND THE NEED FOR INTERNATIONAL SOLIDARITY.

06393 MINNEY, T.
CHURCHES IN FIRING LINE
NEW AFRICAN, (256) (JAN 89), 21-23.
WITH THE INCREASING REPRESSSION OF POLITICAL LEADERS, TRADE UNIONISTS, AND YOUTH, THE CHURCHES OF SOUTH AFRICA ARE ASSUMING A GREATER ROLE IN THE ANTI-APARTHEID STRUGGLE. THE REFUSAL OF THE MAINSTREAM CHURCHES TO SUPPORT DISCRIMINATION HAS BEEN A THORN IN THE SIDE OF SOUTH AFRICA'S NOMINALLY CHRISTIAN GOVERNMENT FOR YEARS, BUT IN 1988 THE GOVERNMENT FOUND ITSELF CONFRONTING THE CHURCHES MORE DIRECTLY.

06394 MINNS, D.; WILLIAMS, C.
AGENT INFLUENCE IN POLITICAL LEARNING: AN EXPERIMENTAL STUDY

SOCIAL SCIENCE JOURNAL, 26(2) (1989), 173-188.
THIS EXPERIMENTAL STUDY INVESTIGATES THE ROLE OF THREE
AGENTS--PARENT, TEACHER, AND FRIEND--IN THE SOCIALIZATION OF
ISSUE BELIEFS OF FIFTH- AND SIXTH-GRADE CHILDREN. THE
AUTHORS STUDIED 164 PUPILS BY ASKING THEM TO COMPLETE
STORIES ABOUT NUCLEAR ENERGY, REFUGEES, SPACE EXPLORATION,
AND SO FORTH. TWO DIMENSIONS ARE THE LEVEL OF ISSUE SALIENCE
(HIGH VERSUS LOW STIMULUS), AND THE ISSUE AGREEMENT AMONG
AGENTS (HOMOGENEOUS VERSUS HETEROGENEOUS CUES). IT FINDS
THAT OPINION CHANGE IS GREATEST IN THE HOMOGENEOUS CUE
CONDITION AND LEAST IN THE HETEROGENEOUS CUE CONDITION.

06395 MINOGUE, K.
FREEDOM UNDER MRS. THATCHER
CONTEMPORARY RECORD, 3(1) (FAL 89), 27-28.
THIS ARTICLE EXPLORES THATCHERITE CRITICISM OF ARBITRARY
AND IRRESPONSIBLE LOCAL GOVERNMENT WITH COUNTER-CRITICISMS
OF THE THATCHER GOVERNMENT OF GREED, PREVENTION OF FREEDOM
OF SPEECH, WRONG ADMINISTRATION OF THE LAW-SUMMED UP AS
'ELECTIVE DICTATORSHIP'. IT EXPLORES THE REAL INTELLECTUAL
CONFUSION ON THE QUESTION OF FREEDOM ENCOURAGED BY CIVIL
RIGHTS ORGANIZATIONS AND OPPORTUNIST IDEOLOGUES.

06396 MINOGUE, K.
JOURNALISM AND THE PUBLIC MIND
GOVERNMENT AND OPPOSITION, 24(4) (AUT 89), 473-488.
THE JOURNALIST SUPPLIES CITIZENS WITH MOST OF WHAT THEY
KNOW AND ALSO IS AN IMPORTANT SOURCE OF INFORMATION FOR
GOVERNMENT OFFICIALS. CITIZENS, POLITICIANS, AND GOVERNMENT
ADVISERS BELONG TO WHAT MIGHT BE CALLED "THE PUBLIC MIND" OF
THE MODERN STATE AND JOURNALISTS ARE THE MOST ACTIVE
INFLUENCE UPON THAT MIND.

06397 MINORU, H.
THE CHANGING IMPERIAL FAMILY: PRINCE AYA'S LOVE MATCH
JAPAN ECHO, XVI(4) (WIN 89), 85-88.
THE AUTHOR DISCUSSES THE LEGAL RAMIFICATIONS OF THE
MARRIAGE OF A MALE MEMBER OF THE JAPANESE IMPERIAL FAMILY,
WHAT IS EXPECTED OF A HEISEI PRINCESS, THE PROPER PEDIGREE
FOR A PRINCESS, HER ROLES AND DUTIES, AND THE PRACTICALITY
OF A LOVE MATCH IN THE JAPANESE IMPERIAL FAMILY.

06398 MINOWITZ, P. I.
RELIGION AND POLITICAL ECONOMY IN ADAM SMITH
DISSERTATION ABSTRACTS INTERNATIONAL, 49(8) (FEB 89),
2377-A.
RECOGNIZING THE CENTRALITY OF RELIGION IN SMITH'S CORPUS,
THE AUTHOR ANALYZES SMITH'S PRONOUNCEMENTS ON RELIGION AND
HIS QUIET BUT UNEQUIVOCAL REJECTION OF CHRISTIANITY'S
CENTRAL TENETS IN "THE HEALTH OF NATIONS."

06399 MINSHULL, P.; RAMSAMY, S.
APARTHEID'S LAST STAND
SOUTH, (99) (JAN 89), 94.
IN 1989, WHITE SOUTH AFRICA WILL LAUNCH ITS BIGGEST
CAMPAIGN SO FAR TO SMASH THE INTERNATIONAL SPORTS BOYCOTT OF
APARTHEID. THE FOCAL POINT OF ITS OFFENSIVE WILL BE THE
CELEBRATIONS SURROUNDING THE CENTENARIES OF SOUTH AFRICAN
RUGBY AND SOUTH AFRICA'S INTERNATIONAL CRICKET DEBUT.

06400 MINTER, W.
AN ARMY OF ABDUCTORS
AFRICA REPORT, 34(3) (MAY 89), 17-20.
THE MOTIVES OF THE RENAMO FIGHTERS AND THE EXTENT OF
SOUTH AFRICAN INVOLVEMENT ARE SHROUDED IN MYSTERY AND
SPECULATION. SOME OBSERVERS BELIEVE THAT RENAMO IS A
COLLECTION OF DISPERSED BANDS OF MEN, THRIVING IN THE
CHAOTIC, DESPERATE CONDITIONS OF RURAL MOZAMBIQUE. MANY
ACKNOWLEDGE THE LIKELIHOOD OF CONTINUING SOUTH AFRICAN
INVOLVEMENT BUT SAY THAT, NEVERTHELESS, THE GROUP HAS A
LARGELY SELF-SUSTAINING MOMENTUM.

06401 MINTZ, A.
GUNS VERSUS BUTTER: A DISAGGREGATED ANALYSIS
AMERICAN POLITICAL SCIENCE REVIEW, 83(4) (DEC 89),
1285-1296.
PRIOR STUDIES OF THE GUNS-VERSUS-BUTTER TRADE-OFF HAVE
FOCUSED ON TOTAL MILITARY EXPENDITURES AND SUB-COMPONENTS OF
WELFARE SPENDING (EDUCATION, HEALTH, AND HOUSING). IN THIS
ARTICLE, THE AUTHOR EXTENDS THE ANALYSIS TO INCLUDE THE
MAJOR SUB-COMPONENTS OF THE DEFENSE BUDGET. THE RESULTS ARE
CONSISTENT WITH PREVIOUS FINDINGS THAT SHOW A LACK OF
DEFENSE-WELFARE TRADE-OFF IN THE 1947-80 ERA BUT REVEAL VERY
SPECIFIC TRADE-OFFS DURING THE REAGAN YEARS.

06402 MINTZ, A.; WARD, M.D.
THE POLITICAL ECONOMY OF MILITARY SPENDING IN ISRAEL
AMERICAN POLITICAL SCIENCE REVIEW, 83(2) (JUN 89), 521-534.
THE AUTHORS PRESENT A MATHEMATICAL MODEL INCORPORATING
SECURITY THREATS AS WELL AS ELECTORAL CYCLES AND CORPORATE
PROFITS IN AN ANALYSIS OF ISRAELI MILITARY SPENDING. THE
RESULTS SUPPORT THE HYPOTHESIS THAT THE ISRAELI MILITARY
BUDGET AT THE MARGINS IS ALSO EMPLOYED AS A POLITICAL-
ECONOMIC INSTRUMENT TO HELP MANAGE THE ECONOMY AND PROVIDE A

FAVORABLE ELECTION CLIMATE FOR INCUMBENTS.

06403 MINTZ, S.W.
THE FOREFATHERS OF CRACK
NACLA REPORT ON THE AMERICAS, XXII(6) (MAR 89), 31-32.
STIMULANTS HAVE PLAYED A KEY ROLE IN THE HISTORY OF
CAPITALISM. THE ARTICLE ASSESSES THE IMPACT OF COCAINE ON
THE CAPITALIST SYSTEM. UNLIKE ITS PREDECESSORS, COFFEE, TEA,
SUGAR, AND TOBACCO, COCAINE IS COUNTERPRODUCTIVE TO THE
SYSTEM FOR THREE REASONS. THEY ARE: IT INTERFERES WITH LABOR
PRODUCTIVITY, THE PROFITS IT GARNERS ARE NOT MADE BY
RESPECTABLE CAPITALISTS, AND THE STATE HAS TROUBLE CLAIMING
ITS SHARE.

06404 MIRANTE, E.T.
BURMA UPDATE: URBAN UPRISING AND FRONTIER REBELLION
CULTURAL SURVIVAL QUARTERLY, 13(1) (1989), 52-54.
FROM AUGUST TO OCTOBER 1988, MASS UPRISINGS IN BURMESE
TOWNS AND CITIES BROUGHT BURMA TO WORLD ATTENTION. MILLIONS
OF CITY DWELLERS FROM EVERY STRATUM OF SOCIETY MARCHED IN
THE STREETS. LED BY STUDENTS AND BUDDHIST MONKS, THEY CALLED
FOR DEMOCRACY. THEIR PROTESTS CAME AS A SHOCK TO MUCH OF THE
OUTSIDE WORLD, WHICH HAD LONG REGARDED BURMA AS A TRANQUIL,
PEACEFUL LAND WITH A DOCILE POPULATION CONTENT TO FOREGO THE
LUXURY OF DEMOCRACY. IN ACTUALITY, BURMA HAS BEEN IN A STATE
OF CIVIL WAR SINCE ITS INDEPENDENCE JUST AFTER WORLD WAR II.

06405 MIRANTE, E.T.
INDIGENOUS PEOPLE MIRED IN "FOREIGN MUD"
CULTURAL SURVIVAL QUARTERLY, 13(4) (1989), 18-20.
THE FRONTIER AREAS OF BURMA HAVE NOT KNOW PEACE SINCE
WORLD WAR II BECAUSE IT FANNED A BLAZE OF ETHNIC ANIMOSITY
BETWEEN MINORITY GROUPS AND THE BURMESE, WHO GAINED AN UPPER
HAND IN POST-INDEPENDENCE BURMA. IN SHAN STATE, WHERE MOST
OF BURMA'S OPIUM IS GROWN, INSTABILITY INCREASED IN 1949
WITH THE ARRIVAL OF KUOMINTANG ARMY REMNANTS FLEEING THE
COMMUNIST TAKEOVER IN CHINA. KMT FORCES BECAME INVOLVED IN
THE LUCRATIVE OPIUM TRADE, AS DID GENERAL NE WIN'S
FRANCHISED MILITIAS (THE KA KWE YE) IN THE 1960'S. THE
BURMESE COMMUNIST PARTY ALSO BECAME ENMESHED IN NARCOTICS
TRADE. ALTHOUGH THE BURMESE GOVERNMENT HAS OFFICIALLY
CURTAILED ITS INVOLVEMENT, THE LIAISONS HAVE CONTINUED TO
THIS DAY.

06406 MISCHE, P.M.
ECOLOGICAL SECURITY AND THE NEED TO RECONCEPTUALIZE
SOVEREIGNTY
ALTERNATIVES, 14(4) (OCT 89), 389-428.
THIS ARTICLE SUGGESTS SOME PREMISES AND PRINCIPLES FOR A
SYSTEM OF GLOBAL ECOLOGICAL SECURITY AND RESPONSIBILITY. IT
DETAILS: 1) SOVEREIGNTY OF THE EARTH, 2) INDIVISIBILITY OF
THE EARTH, 3) BIOREGIONAL ALLIANCES: 4) ECO-VALUES FOR
ECOLOGICAL SECURITY, AND: 5) INTENTIONALITY. VALUES EXPLORED
INCLUDE: REVERENCE FOR ALL LIFE, INTERGENERATIONAL EQUITY,
RESPECT FOR DIVERSITY, AND COMMUNION,

06407 MISCHKE, A.
A NEW ERA LOOMING
SOUTH AFRICA FOUNDATION REVIEW, 15(7) (JUL 89), 3,8.
THE ARTICLE EXAMINES SOUTH AFRICA'S APPROACHING 6
SEPTEMBER NATIONAL ELECTIONS. IT OUTLINES THE VARIOUS
PARTICIPANTS INCLUDING THE RIGHT-WING CONSERVATIVE PARTY,
THE RULING NATIONAL PARTY, AND THE LEFT-LEANING DEMOCRATIC
PARTY. ALTHOUGH FW DE KLERK AND THE RULING NATIONAL PARTY
ARE EXPECTED TO WIN THE MAJORITY OF SOUTH AFRICA'S VOTE
ELECTIONS, THEY FACE SIGNIFICANT CHALLENGES BOTH BEFORE AND
AFTER THE ELECTIONS. THE RESOLUTION OF THE NAMIBIAN CONFLICT,
GROWING UNREST IN SOUTH AFRICAN TOWNSHIPS, ECONOMIC WOES,
AND POLITICAL COMPETITION ALL GUARANTEE THAT THE "NEW ERA"
OF FW DE KLERK (OR HIS CONSERVATIVE OR LIBERAL COUNTERPART)
WILL NOT BEGIN EASILY.

06408 MISHLER, W.; FITZGERALD, R.; HOSKIN, M.
BRITISH PARTIES IN THE BALANCE: A TIME-SERIES ANALYSIS OF
LONG-TERM TRENDS IN LABOUR AND CONSERVATIVE SUPPORT
BRITISH JOURNAL OF POLITICAL SCIENCE, 19(2) (APR 89),
211-236.
THE ELECTORAL DOMINATION OF THE CONSERVATIVE PARTY
DURING THE PAST DECADE HAS BEEN INTERPRETED BY MANY AS
EVIDENCE OF A LONG-TERM SHIFT IN THE BALANCE OF PUBLIC
SUPPORT FROM LABOUR TO THE CONSERVATIVES. THIS ARTICLE
ARGUES THAT SUCH A SHIFT HAS NOT OCCURRED. RATHER, THE
STABILITY APPARENT IN RECENT ELECTION RESULTS DISGUISES
CONSIDERABLE UNDERLYING VOLATILITY. THE BALANCE OF PUBLIC
SUPPORT BETWEEN THE MAJOR PARTIES TO BE HIGHLY UNSTABLE AND
SUBJECT TO LARGE AND PRECIPITOUS FLUCTUATIONS IN RESPONSE TO
RELATIVELY SMALL ECONOMIC CHANGES AND ORDINARY POLITICAL
EVENTS. RECENT CONSERVATIVE VICTORIES APPEAR TO BE THE
RESULTS MORE OF GOOD TIMING AND LUCK THAN OF ANY FUNDAMENTAL,
LONG-TERM DYNAMIC IN BRITISH POLITICS.

06409 MISIUNAS, R.J.; TAAGEPERA, R.
THE BALTIC STATES: YEARS OF DEPENDENCE, 1980-86
JOURNAL OF BALTIC STUDIES, XX(1) (SPR 89), 65-88.

THE AUTHORS REVIEW THE HISTORY OF THE BALTIC STATES FROM
1980 TO 1986, INCLUDING EVENTS AFFECTING PUBLIC
ADMINISTRATION, DOMESTIC POLITICS, AND POLITICAL IDEOLOGY.

06410 MISSER, F.
BURUNDI: DRIVE FOR RECONCILIATION
NEW AFRICAN, (262) (JUL 89), 18.
THE COMMITTEE FOR NATIONAL UNITY IN BURUNDI HAS MADE
SPECIFIC RECOMMENDATIONS FOR NATIONAL RECONCILIATION, AND
THE GOVERNMENT HAS ACCEPTED THESE PROPOSALS. PRESIDENT
PIERRE BUYOYA HAS ASKED FOR A CHARTER OF NATIONAL UNITY FROM
THE COMMITTEE, WHICH HAS AN EQUAL NUMBER OF HUTUS AND TUTIS
MEMBERS; AND PROMISES THAT A PARLIMENT AND CONSTITUTION WILL
BE ESTABLISHED.

06411 MISSER, F.
BUYOYA'S GLASNOST
NEW AFRICAN, (267) (DEC 89), 25.
PRESIDENT PIERRE BUYOYA'S OF BURUNDI, AFRICA, HAS
INTRODUCED A NEW POLICY OF "TRANSPARENCE", LIKE A LOCAL
GLASNOST, IN WHICH HIS PEOPLE ARE ENCOURAGED TO SPEAK OPENLY
AND THUS OVERCOME THEIR ETHNIC DIFFICULTIES. HE IS ALSO
INTRODUCING A CHARTER OF NATIONAL UNITY. THE TUTSI AND HUTUS
TRIBES OF THIS COUNTRY HAVE BEEN FEUDING, WHICH PROVOKED 5,
OOO DEATHS IN MASSACRES IN AUGUST/SEPTEMBER 1989. DESPITE
EFFORTS TO OVERCOME THIS ETHNIC RIVALARY, NOT ALL THE
CITIZENS ACCEPT BUYOYA'S MEASURES.

06412 MISSER, F.
HOUPHOUET VS MOBUTU BATTLE FOR PEACE PRIZE
NEW AFRICAN, (OCT 89), 20.
THIS ARTICLE REPORTS ON THE AFTERMATH OF A
RECONCILIATION MEETING BETWEEN UNITA AND THE MPLA. DETAILED
ARE ACCUSATIONS BY SUPPOSEDLY EXILED MPLA LEADER, SAVIMBI,
AND COUNTER RESPONSE BY THE STATE OWNED NEWS AGENCY, AZAP.
RIVALRY BETWEEN MOBUTU AND HOUPHOUET IS EXAMINED.

06413 MISSER, F.
LOME IV - THE ACP STATES AND THE EEC ARE SET FOR SOME
TOUGH TALKING
AFRICAN BUSINESS, (OCT 88), 12-13.
THIS ARTICLE REPORTS ON ISSUES WHICH WILL BE ADDRESSED
AT THE FOURTH LOME CONVENTION DUE TO BE SIGNED IN 1989.
DISCUSSED WILL BE INTERNATIONAL TRADE, THE DEBT CRISIS,
RURAL DEVELOPMENT. IMPORT PROGRAMS, ENCOURAGEMENT TO THE
PRIVATE SECTOR IN THE ACP COUNTRIES, THE BEST WAY TO
MOBILISE LOCAL SAVINGS, AND EEC AID.

06414 MISSER, F.
MAKING THE ENEMY MAD
NEW AFRICAN, (APR 88), 10-11.
THIS ARTICLE REPORTS ON WHAT IS APPARENTLY A NEW
TECHNIQUE TO GET RID OF THE OPPOSITION LEADER, ETIENNE
TSHISEKEDI, BY ZAIREAN AUTHORITIES. IT REPORTS ON HIS
CONFINEMENT TO A MENTAL INSTITUTION AFTER BEING ACCUSED OF
DELIRIUM FOLLOWING A RIOT IN KINSHAMA AND HIS ARREST.

06415 MISSER, F.
MOBUTU KIDNAPS OPPONENTS
NEW AFRICAN, (267) (DEC 89), 19.
THE MOBUTU REGIME IN ZAIRE IS REACHING OUTSIDE THE
COUNTRY AND KIDNAPPING ITS ENEMIES IN EXILE. ACCORDING TO
CONFIDENTIAL DOCUMENTS, A NUMBER OF ZAIREAN REFUGEES IN
NEIGHBORING COUNTRIES HAVE BEEN KIDNAPPED BY AGENTS OF THE
ZAIREAN AGENCE NATIONALE DE DOCUMENTATION. SEVERAL INCIDENTS
OF THIS NATURE ARE REPORTED IN THIS ARTICLE. APPARENTLY, THE
VICTIMS OF THIS KIDNAPPING ARE TREATED WITH CRUELITY, AND
THEIR LIVES ARE IN DANGER.

06416 MISSER, F.; RAKE, A.
MOBUTU'S BOOMERANG BOUNCES BACK
NEW AFRICAN, (258) (MAR 89), 17-19.
THE BELGIAN PRESS AND PARLIAMENT HAVE EXPOSED THE GROSS
CORRUPTION OF PRESIDENT MOBUTU OF ZAIRE, A FORMER BELGIAN
COLONY.

06417 MISSER, F.
PICKING UP THE PIECES
NEW AFRICAN, (256) (JAN 89), 19-21.
IN A MOVE TO SOOTHE HUTU SENSIBILITIES, PRESIDENT PIERRE
BUYOYA RESHUFFLED HIS CABINET IN OCTOBER 1988, BRINGING IN
12 HUTU MINISTERS TO ROUND OUT HIS TUTSI-DOMINATED
GOVERNMENT. BUT EVIDENCE SUGGESTS THAT THE TACTIC FAILED TO
WIN OVER THE EMBITTERED HUTUS.

06418 MISSER, F.
PLANNERS MEND THE RIFT WITH THE IMF
AFRICAN BUSINESS, (DEC 88), 32-34.
THIS ARTICLE EXAMINES THE CAUSES OF AND THE MENDING OF
THE RIFT BETWEEN ZAIRE AND THE INTERNATIONAL MONETARY FUND.
IT EXPLORES LIVING STANDARDS, DEBT RELIEF, AND ILL WILL, AS
WELL AS THE RAMIFICATIONS OF DIAMOND FRAUD, ALL WHICH HAVE
BEEN FACTORS IN THE RECONCILIATION.

06419 MISSER, F.
ZAIRE: OPPOSITION GOES UNDERGROUND
NEW AFRICAN, (258) (MAR 89), 23.
ZAIRE'S OPPOSITION PARTY HAS DECIDED TO CHANGE TACTICS,
REORGANIZING ITSELF AS AN UNDERGROUND MOVEMENT. THE ONLY
VISIBLE FACE OF THE PARTY WILL BE ITS MILITANTS ABROAD.
MARCEL LIHAU EBUA LIBANA HAS BEEN ELECTED TO LEAD THE GROUP.

06420 MISSER, F.
ZALRE: RIFT WITH BELGIUM HALTS LOANS AND REPAYMENTS
AFRICAN BUSINESS, (FEB 89), 34-35.
THIS PIECE DESCRIBES THE CONFLICTS BETWEEN ZAIRE AND
BELGIUM WHICH CULMINATED IN ZAIRE HALTING LOAN REPAYMENTS TO
BELGIUM AND IN THE STOPPING OF AID FROM BELGIUM. THE EVENTS
DESCRIBED WHICH LET UP TO THIS RIFT INCLUDE CRITICISM OF THE
PRESIDENT'S LAVISH EXPENDITURES WHILE POVERTY AND SEVERE
HEALTH CONDITIONS EXIST THROUGHOUT THE COUNTRY, AND ORDERS
FOR ZAIRE STUDENTS AND BUSINESS TO LEAVE BELGIUM. THE AUTHOR
CONJECTURES THAT ZAIRE'S PRESIDENT MOBUTU MAY BE PLAYING
POKER WITH BELGIUM TO STRENGTHEN HIS POSITION WITH OTHER
FINANCIAL SOURCES.

06421 MISZLIVETZ, F.
"DIALOGUE" -- AND WHAT IS BEHIND IT
ACROSS FRONTIERS, 5(2) (SUM 89), 30-33.
THIS ARTICLE EXAMINES THE "ERA OF TRANSITION" TAKING
PLACE IN HUNGARY WHICH SEEMS TO BE LEADING TO DEMOCRATIC
TRANSFORMATIONS THERE. IT DESCRIBES THE NUMEROUS GROUPS
FORMING TO PROTEST THE PRESENT GOVERNMENT, WHICH IS MAKING A
NUMBER OF VISIBLE CONCESSIONS WHILE EMPLOYING MORE REFINED
METHODS OF MANIPULATION TO TRY TO THWART COALITION OF THE
OPPOSING GROUPS. THE ELITE WANTS TO RETAIN POWER AND IS
WILLING TO INTEGRATE THE NEW AND WEAK POLITICAL
ORGANIZATIONS INTO THE STILL-PREVALING POLITICAL STRUCTURE.

06422 MITCHELL, C.
DISARMAMENT AND CHANGING THOUGHT PATTERNS
POLITICAL AFFAIRS, LXVIII(7) (JUL 89), 24-27.
IT IS NOT ENOUGH TO BE SATISFIED THAT PEOPLES' ATTITUDE
TOWARD THE SOVIET UNION IS CHANGING. THE PEACE MOVEMENT MUST
BE DIRECTED TOWARDS: WINNING MASSES THROUGH DEMONSTRATIONS,
MASS LOBBYING INCLUDING PICKETING, PETITIONING, SITTING IN
TO PASS LEGISLATION SUCH AS THE WEISS BILL CALLING FOR
CONVERSION; THE OUTER SPACE PROTECTION ACT (ANTI-STAR WARS
TECHNOLOGY); THE DELLUMS BILL, INCREASING SANCTIONS AGAINST
SOUTH AFRICA; THE WEISS BILL, LIFTING THE TRADE EMBARGO
AGAINST NICARAGUA; OR THE KASTENMEIER BILL CUTTING ALL
MILITARY AID TO EL SALVADOR; OR ANY NUMBER OF BILLS THAT
SHOULD BE INTRODUCED OUTLAWING TRIDENT, CRUISE, STEALTH AND
ANY OTHER NUCLEAR WEAPONS DEVELOPMENT AND DEPLOYMENT.

06423 MITCHELL, C.
FAMILY AND PERSONAL NETWORKS IN INTERNATIONAL MIGRATION:
RECENT DEVELOPMENTS AND NEW AGENDAS
INTERNATIONAL MIGRATION REVIEW, 23(3) (FAL 89), 681-708.
FAMILY, FRIENDSHIP AND COMMUNITY NETWORKS UNDERLIE MUCH
OF THE RECENT MIGRATION TO INDUSTRIAL NATIONS. CURRENT
INTEREST IN THESE NETWORKS ACCOMPANY THE DEVELOPMENT OF A
MIGRATION SYSTEM PERSPECTIVE AND THE GROWING AWARENESS OF
THE MACRO AND MICRO DETERMINANTS OF MIGRATION. THIS ARTICLE
PRESENTS AN OVERVIEW OF RESEARCH FINDINGS ON THE
DETERMINANTS AND CONSEQUENCES OF PERSONAL NETWORKS. IN
ADDITION, IT CALLS FOR GREATER SPECIFICATION OF THE ROLE OF
NETWORKS IN MIGRATION RESEARCH AND FOR THE INCLUSION OF
WOMEN IN FUTURE RESEARCH.

06424 MITCHELL, C.
MADELEINE PELLETIER (1874-1939): THE POLITICS OF SEXUAL
OPPRESSION
FEMINIST REVIEW, (33) (AUT 89), 72-92.
MADELEINE PELLETIER WAS ONE OF THE MOST SIGNIFICANT
EARLY FEMINIST THINKERS IN FRANCE. SHE BROKE WITH NINETEENTH-
CENTURY FEMINISM TO DEVELOP A CULTURAL THEORY OF SEXUAL
DIFFERENCE. THIS PAPER EXAMINES PELLETIER'S WORK AND THE
HISTORICAL-POLITICAL BACKGROUND THAT HELPED FROM HER
FEMINIST THEORY.

06425 MITCHELL, J.
EXPECTATIONS OF THE BUSH PRESIDENCY
AMERICAN CITY AND COUNTY, 104(5) (MAY 89), 83-86.
LOCAL GOVERNMENT WILL FARE BETTER UNDER PRESIDENT BUSH
THAN IT DID IN THE REAGAN FEND-FOR-YOURSELVES YEARS.
ALTHOUGH BUSH HAS NOT COME FORWARD WITH AN URBAN AGENDA,
MANY LOCAL LEADERS FEEL BUSH'S CABINET CHOICES AND OTHER TOP-
LEVEL ADVISORY APPOINTMENTS INDICATE THAT THE PRESIDENT WILL
WORK TOWARD A PARTNETSHIP BETWEEN LOCAL AND FEDERAL
GOVERNMENTS.

06426 MITCHELL, N.
EUROPEAN CORPORATE CONCERNS ON SOUTH AFRICA
SOUTH AFRICA INTERNATIONAL, 20(2) (OCT 89), 85-90.
POLITICS AND ECONOMICS IN SOUTH AFRICA ARE INEXTRICABLY
INTERDEPENDENT TO A FAR GREATER EXTENT THAN FOR MOST OTHER
MARKETS. THE AUTHOR EXAMINES THE FUTURE POTENTIAL FOR

CONTINUED TRADE WITH AND INVESTMENT IN SOUTH AFRICA BY
EUROPEAN MULTI-NATIONAL CORPORATIONS. ALTHOUGH THE OUTLOOK
IS BY NO MEANS BRIGHT, HE CONCLUDES THAT CONTINUED
INVESTMENT IS JUSTIFIED. HE CITES THE CHANGE OF LEADERSHIP,
ATTITUDE, AND ACTION IN SOUTH AFRICA, AS WELL AS SUPERPOWER
COOPERATION, AS REASONS JUSTIFYING HIS CONCLUSION.

06427 MITCHELL, P.
ECONOMY KEY IN PHILIPPINES' STRUGGLE
PACIFIC DEFENCE REPORTER, 16(9) (MAR 90), 14-16.
THE SURVIVAL OF DEMOCRACY IN THE PHILIPPINES DEPENDS IN
NO SMALL MEASURE ON THE SUCCESS OF THE ECONOMY. GENUINE LAND
REFORM WOULD HAVE SIGNIFICANT IMPACT IN IMPROVING CONDITIONS
IN THE IMPORTANT SUGAR-PRODUCING AREAS AND WOULD DECREASE
THE INFLUENCE OF DISSIDENT OPPOSITION PARTIES. THE QUESTION
OF U.S. BASES IS NOT ONE OF VITAL IMPORTANCE TO THE
IMPOVERISHED OF THE PHILIPPINES; THAT IS MAINLY THE PRESERVE
OF THE EDUCATED. SERIOUS REFORM IS NEEDED IN RURAL AREAS,
WHICH ARE THE MOST ECONOMICALLY NEGLECTED AREAS OF THE
PHILIPPINES.

06428 MITCHELL, T.
THE WORLD AS EXHIBITION
COMPARATIVE STUDIES IN SOCIETY AND HISTORY, 31(2) (APR 89),
217-236.
THE CASE OF ORIENTALISM SHOWS HOW THE SUPPOSED
DISTINCTION BETWEEN THE INTERIOR REPRESENTATION AND AN
EXTERNAL REALITY CORRESPONDS TO ANOTHER APPARENT DIVISION OF
THE WORLD, INTO THE WEST AND ITS ORIENTAL EXTERIOR.
ORIENTALISM, IT FOLLOWS, IS NOT JUST A NINTEENTH-CENTURY
INSTANCE OF SOME GENERAL HISTORICAL PROBLEM OF HOW ONE
CULTURE PORTRAYS ANOTHER, NOR JUST AN ASPECT OF COLONIAL
DOMINATION, BUT PART OF A METHOD OF ORDER AND TRUTH
ESSENTIAL TO THE PECULIAR NATURE OF THE MODERN WORLD.

06429 MITCHELL, W.
THE CALCULUS OF CONSENT: ENDURING CONTRIBUTIONS TO PUBLIC
CHOICE AND POLITICAL SCIENCE
PUBLIC CHOICE, 60(3) (MAR 89), 201-210.
WHEN THE CALCULUS OF CONSENT WAS PUBLISHED IN 1962, ITS
TENETS WHICH WERE BASED ON METHODOLOGICAL INDIVIDUALISM OR
RATIONAL UTILITY MAXIMIZATION FLEW IN THE FACE OF THE
HIGHFLYING BEHAVIORALISM THAT WAS THEN THE RAGE AMONG
POLITICAL ANALYSISTS. THE AUTHOR RE-EXAMINES THE CALCULUS
AND ANALYZES THE LONG-TERM EFFECTS IT HAS HAD ON POLITICAL
SCIENCE.

06430 MITCHELL, W.D.
THE "NEW" MIDDLE MANAGER: UNLEASHING ENTREPRENEURIAL
POTENTIAL
CANADIAN PUBLIC ADMINISTRATION, 32(2) (SUM 89), 234-243.
THE AUTHOR OUTLINES STRATEGIES FOR UNLEASHING
ENTREPRENEURIAL POTENTIAL WITHIN THE BUREAUCRACY, ESPECIALLY
AT THE MIDDLE-MANAGEMENT LEVEL. TO INCORPORATE THESE
STRATEGIES SUCCESSFULLY WILL DEMAND CHANGE IN TRADITIONAL
WAYS OF THINKING AND WILL INVOLVE TAKING RISKS--SOMETHING
THAT IS ANATHEMA TO TRADITIONAL BUREAUCRACY.

06431 MITSUHARU, I.
SHODDY TAXES, SHADY POLITICS
JAPAN ECHO, XVI(2) (SUM 89), 52-57.
THE CORRECTION OF MAJOR INEQUITIES SHOULD HAVE BEEN THE
FIRST PRIORITY IN JAPANESE TAX REFORM. HOWEVER, IT APPEARS
THAT THE LATEST CHANGES IN THE JAPANESE TAX SYSTEM NOT ONLY
FAIL TO ADDRESS THESE PROBLEMS BUT COULD ACTUALLY MAKE THEM
WORSE. THE WORST OFFENDER IS THE NEW CONSUMPTION TAX. THE
TAX TREATMENT OF CAPITAL GAINS IS SIMILARLY DEFECTIVE.

06432 MIZRUCHI, M. S.
SIMILARITY OF POLITICAL BEHAVIOR AMONG LARGE AMERICAN
CORPORATIONS
AMERICAN JOURNAL OF SOCIOLOGY, 95(2) (SEP 89), 401-424.
POLITICAL SOCIOLOGISTS HAVE DEBATED FOR DECADES, WITHOUT
RESOLUTION, WHETHER ELITES IN ADVANCED CAPITALIST SOCIETIES
ARE INTEGRATED. RATHER THAN ASK WHETHER ELITES ARE
INTEGRATED, THIS STUDY EXAMINES THE CONDITIONS UNDER WHICH
CONVERGENCE OF POLITICAL BEHAVIOR OCCURS, FOCUSING ON
CAMPAIGN CONTRIBUTIONS OF POLITICAL ACTION COMMITTEES IN THE
AMERICAN BUSINESS COMMUNITY. A MODEL OF SIMILARITY IN
CORPORATE POLITICAL BEHAVIOR IS PROPOSED THAT DRAWS ON
PRINCIPLES DEVELOPED BY RESOURCE-DEPENDENCE AND SOCIAL CLASS
THEORISTS OF INTERCORPORATE RELATIONS. THE MODEL WAS
SUPPORTED BY AN EXAMINATION OF THE 1,596 DYADS CREATED BY
RELATIONS AMONG 57 LARGE U.S. MANUFACTURING FIRMS IN 1980.
MEMBERSHIP IN THE SAME PRIMARY INDUSTRY OR SEVERAL SIMILAR
INDUSTRIES, GEOGRAPHICAL PROXIMITY OF HEADQUARTERS LOCATIONS,
MARKET CONSTRAINT, AND COMMON RELATIONS WITH FINANCIAL
INSTITUTIONS WERE POSITIVELY ASSOCIATED WITH THE SIMILARITY
OF POLITICAL BEHAVIOR BETWEEN FIRMS. MARKET CONSTRAINT
AFFECTED THE SIMILARITY OF POLITICAL BEHAVIOR PRIMARILY
BECAUSE IT INCREASED THE LIKELIHOOD THAT FIRMS WOULD PRODUCE
IN THE SAME INDUSTRIES. THE EFFECT OF INDIRECT BOARD
INTERLOCKING THROUGH FINANCIAL INSTITUTIONS HAS A STRONGER
PREDICTOR OF SIMILARITY OF POLITICAL BEHAVIOR THAN HAS

DIRECT INTERLOCKING BETWEEN MANUFACTURING FIRMS.

06433 MKHONDO, L.
SOUTH AFRICA: TRIBAL CONFLICT
THIRD WORLD WEEK, 8(3) (MAR 89), 10-11.
TRANSKEI AND CISKEI HAVE NOT BECOME THE TWO IDYLLIC
BLACK TRIBAL HOMELANDS THEY WERE INTENDED TO BE UNDER SOUTH
AFRICA'S PLAN FOR SEPARATION OF THE RACES. NOW THEY HAVE HIT
A NEW LOW. A LONG-STANDING DISPUTE BETWEEN THEM HAS GROWN
INTO A KIND OF WAR. THE DISORDERS ARE EMBARRASSING THE SOUTH
AFRICAN GOVERNMENT AND THREATENING THE REGIONAL ECONOMY.

06434 MLADENKA, K.R.
BLACKS AND HISPANICS IN URBAN POLITICS
AMERICAN POLITICAL SCIENCE REVIEW, 83(1) (MAR 89), 165-192.
ARE LOCAL POLITICAL INSTITUTIONS RESPONSIVE TO THE
DEMANDS OF RACIAL MINORITIES FOR A MORE EQUITABLE SHARE OF
SCARCE PUBLIC RESOURCES? DOES AN ENHANCED POLITICAL PRESENCE
IMPROVE BLACK AND HISPANIC PROSPECTS IN THE STRUGGLE FOR
PUBLIC JOBS? BASED UPON DATA FOR 1200 CITIES, ANALYSIS
REVEALS THAT WHILE MINORITY COUNCIL MEMBERS MAKE A
SUBSTANTIAL CONTRIBUTION TO EMPLOYMENT SUCCESS, MINORITY
MAYORS DO NOT. FOR BLACKS, AN INTERACTIVE EFFECT WAS ALSO
DISCOVERED FOR THE RELATIONSHIP BETWEEN THE LEVEL OF
POLITICAL REPRESENTATION, GOVERNMENTAL STRUCTURE, AND
EMPLOYMENT OUTCOMES. THIS RESEARCH REVEALS THAT THE
POLITICAL PROCESS DOES WORK. HOWEVER, ITS EFFECTIVENESS FOR
MINORITIES IS MEDIATED BY A COMPLEX OF FACTORS THAT INCLUDES
AN INTERACTION BETWEEN POLITICAL POWER, RACIAL POLARIZATION,
AND THE NATURE OF LOCAL POLITICAL INSTITUTIONS.

06435 MLADENKA, K.R.
THE DISTRIBUTION OF AN URBAN PUBLIC SERVICE: THE CHANGING
ROLE OF RACE AND POLITICS
URBAN AFFAIRS QUARTERLY, 24(4) (JUN 89), 556-583.
THE RESEARCH ON THE DISTRIBUTION OF URBAN PUBLIC
SERVICES HAS MADE A VALUABLE CONTRIBUTION IN ENHANCING
UNDERSTANDING OF URBAN POLITICS. HOWEVER, THIS LITERATURE IS
CRITICIZED BECAUSE THE AUTHORS EMPLOYED CROSS-SECTIONAL
RATHER THAN LONGITUDINAL DESIGNS, RELIED UPON SINGLE RATHER
THAN MULTIPLE INDICATORS OF THE DISTRIBUTIONAL PATTERN, AND
EMPHASIZED BUREAUCRATIC RATHER THAN POLITICAL EXPLANATIONS
OF DISTRIBUTIONAL OUTCOMES. IN THIS ARTICLE, THE
DISTRIBUTION OF PARK AND RECREATION SERVICES IN CHICAGO IS
ANALYZED FOR A 22-YEAR PERIOD, REVEALING THAT A
REDISTRIBUTION OF RESOURCES BETWEEN WHITE AND BLACK WARDS
OCCURRED DURING THIS TIME. ONE CONCLUSION IS THAT CLASS HAS
REPLACED RACE AS THE PRIMARY DETERMINANT OF THE SERVICE
DISTRIBUTION PATTERN.

06436 MMBAGA, C.
FRIENDS IN NEED
NEW AFRICAN, (256) (JAN 89), 21.
KENYA AND TANZANIA ARE OLD IDEOLOGICAL RIVALS, BUT
NATIONAL LEADERS HAVE RECENTLY HELD A SERIES OF FRIENDLY
MEETINGS. A PROBABLE EXPLANATION FOR THE NEW ATMOSPHERE IS
THE WISH OF EACH COUNTRY'S PRESIDENT TO PREVENT SUBVERSIVE
GROUPS FROM TAKING REFUGE IN NEIGHBORING STATES.

06437 MNANGAGWA, E.D.
BUILDING ON A FIRM FOUNDATION--CONSTITUTIONAL DEVELOPMENTS
IN ZIMBABWE, 1987 TO 1990
PARLIAMENTARIAN, 70(3) (JUL 89), 127-131.
THE AUTHOR COVERS THE CONSTITUTIONAL DEVELOPMENTS THAT
HAVE TAKEN PLACE IN ZIMBABWE SINCE 1987. IN 1980 THE
ZIMBABWEAN POLITICAL LEADERS ACCEPTED A CONSTITUTION
CONTAINING CERTAIN WESTMINSTER-TYPE PROVISIONS THEY DID NOT
REALLY WANT. CONSTITUTIONAL AMENDMENTS WHICH TOOK PLACE
BETWEEN 1980 AND 1987 ARE SUMMARIZED, AND THE AUTHOR
FORECASTS UPCOMING CHANGES. RACIAL REPRESENTATION IS
HIGHLIGHTED, SINCE IT WAS ABOLISHED, WITH MUCH DEBATE, IN
TERMS OF THE RELEVANT CONSTITUTIONAL PROVISIONS FOR ACCURATE
REPRESENTATION.

06438 MOADDEL. M.
STATE-CENTERED VS. CLASS-CENTERED PERSPECTIVES ON
INTERNATIONAL POLITICS: THE CASE OF U.S. AND BRITISH
PARTICIPATION IN THE 1953 COUP AGAINST PREMIER MOSADDEQ IN
IRAN
SOUTHERN CALIFORNIA LAW REVIEW, 24(2) (SUM 89), 3-23.
TWO ALTERNATIVE PERSPECTIVES--STATE-CENTERED AND CLASS-
CENTERED--ON STATE ACTIONS ARE CONSIDERED. THE EXPLANATORY
POWER OF EACH OF THESE PERSPECTIVES IS EXAMINED BY ANALYZING
THE BEHAVIOR OF THREE MAJOR POLITICAL ACTORS IN THE IRANIAN
OIL DISPUTES-THE IRANIAN, THE BRITISH, AND THE U.S.
GOVERNMENTS--USING THE EXISTING HISTORICAL EVIDENCE. THE
ARTICLE SUPPORTS A CLASS-CENTERED EXPLANATION BY
DEMONSTRATING THE SIGNIFICANCE OF THE INTERNATIONAL
PETROLEUM CARTEL IN DETERMINING U.S. AND BRITISH POLICY
TOWARDS IRAN IN THIS PERIOD AND THE FAILURE OF THE IRANIAN
BOURGEOISIE TO CONTINUE THEIR SUPPORT OF MOSADDEQ IN THE
FACE OF ECONOMIC DIFFICULTIES RESULTING FROM THE
NATIONALIZATION OF THE OIL INDUSTRY. PARTIAL SUPPORT FOR A
STATE-CENTERED EXPLANATION IS ALSO NOTED. FOR FUTURE

RESEARCH, THE UTILITY OF CONSIDERING THE STATE AND CLASS AS INTERDEPENDENT ACTORS WITH THE SPECIFICATION THAT THE NATURE OF THIS INTERDEPENDENCE IS ASYMMETRICAL IS SUGGESTED.

06439 MOBERLY, P.
TOWARDS AN INDEPENDENT NAMIBIA
WORLD TODAY, 45(10) (OCT 89), 168-171.
ALTHOUGH THE ROAD TO NAMIBIAN INDEPENDENCE IS STILL STREWN WITH HAZARDS, TOO MUCH HAS BEEN INVESTED IN IT TO TURN BACK. A STUDY GROUP AT CHATHAM HOUSE HAS IDENTIFIED THREE DISTINCT PHASES IN THE PROCESS OF INDEPENDENCE FOR NAMIBIA: THE RUN-UP TO THE NOVEMBER ELECTIONS FOR THE CONSTITUENT ASSEMBLY; DRAWING UP A CONSTITUTION AND PREPARING FOR THE ACTUAL MOMENT OF INDEPENDENCE; AND MEETING THE DOMESTIC AND REGIONAL CHALLENGES THAT WILL FACE THE NEW NAMIBIA.

06440 MOCK, A.
A VIEW FROM VIENNA
INTERNATIONAL AFFAIRS (MOSCOW), (2) (FEB 89), 15-19.
THE PRESENT INCIPIENT STAGE OF EUROPEAN COOPERATION CAN AND SHOULD BE SUCCEEDED BY A PERIOD OF EUROPEAN INTEGRATION. IT IS UTOPIAN TO SPEAK ABOUT SUCH A PERIOD NOW. BUT IN THE FUTURE THE INTER-DEPENCENCE OF STATES ON THE EUROPEAN CONTINENT SHOULD REACH A LEVEL AT WHICH THE SOLUTION OF CONFLICTS BETWEEN THEM IN A MILITARY WAY WILL BECOME IMPOSSIBLE. POOLING THEIR CULTURAL HERITAGE AND ECONOMIC POTENTIALS, THE EUROPEAN PEOPLES SHOULD BE IN A POSITION TO REACH POLITICAL UNDERSTANDING AS WELL. IN THIS EUROPEAN PROCESS, AUSTRIA CAN PLAY AN ACTIVE ROLE THROUGH ITS NEUTRALITY AND ITS TRADITIONAL ABILITY TO CONDUCT DIALOGUE BETWEEN PARTIES.

06441 MOCK, A.
THE ROAD AWAY FROM "COEXISTENCE"
AUSTRIA TODAY, (1) (1989), 4-6.
THE THIRD FOLLOW-UP MEETING OF THE CONFERENCE ON SECURITY AND COOPERATION IN EUROPE WAS NO LIGHT UNDERTAKING. EXPECTATIONS WERE HIGH, SOMETIMES TOO HIGH. IT WAS PARTICULARLY DIFFICULT TO TRANSLATE THE "NEW THINKING" OF SOME COUNTRIES INTO CONCRETE, BINDING AGREEMENTS THAT COULD FUNCTION AS THE BASIS FOR INTERNATIONAL COOPERATION IN EUROPE. THE NEGOTIATIONS WERE OFTEN LABORIOUS; MANY A SETBACK, AND MANY A DISAPPOINTMENT, COULD BE OVERCOME ONLY WITH A GREAT DEAL OF PATIENCE. BUT IN THE END THE RESULTS JUSTIFIED THE EFFORT.

06442 MODENA, G.N.
THE COURTS AND THE DIFFICULT ROAD TO INDEPENDENCE
ITALIAN JOURNAL, III(4) (1989), 23-27.
THE AUTHOR EXAMINES THE RELATIONSHIP OF THE ITALIAN JUDICIARY TO THE POLITICAL POWER STRUCTURE. HE USES AN HISTORICAL APPROACH, BEGINNING WITH THE ERA OF NATIONAL UNIFICATION.

06443 MODIGLIANI, F.; JAPPELLI, T.
THE DETERMINANTS OF INTEREST RATES IN THE ITALIAN ECONOMY
REVIEW OF ECONOMIC CONDITIONS IN ITALY, 1 (JAN 88), 9-34.
THIS PAPER PROVIDES NEW EVIDENCE BETWEEN FISCAL POLICY AND INTEREST RATES AND AIMS AT IMPROVING ON MOST OF THE PREVIOUS ANALYSES IN ONE OR MORE OF THE FOLLOWING ASPECTS: 1) THE ESTIMATED EQUATION IS DERIVED FROM THE LIFE-CYCLE HYPOTHESIS, 2) THE SEPARATION OF THE EFFECT OF CUTTING TAXES FROM THAT OF INCREASING GOVERNMENT EXPENDITURE, 3) DIFFERENT EFFECTS ON INTEREST RATES ON THE FLOW OF THE GOVERNMENT DEFICIT, AND 4) A DEFINITION OF THE DEFICIT WHICH SUBSTRACTS FROM THE BUDGET THE DEPRECIATION OF THE STOCK OF GOVERNMENT DEBT OWNED BY THE PRIVATE SECTOR.

06444 MOENS, A.A.
THE MULTIPLE ADVOCACY STRATEGY AND THE ROLE OF THE CUSTODIAN: THE CARTER YEARS
DISSERTATION ABSTRACTS INTERNATIONAL, 50(2) (AUG 89), 537-A.
THE INCREASING COMPLEXITY AND HIGH STAKES OF FOREIGN POLICY DECISIONS HAVE GENERATED SPECIALIZED STUDIES OF DECISION-MAKING. ONE APPROACH, CALLED "MULTIPLE ADVOCACY," MAPS A STRATEGY OF ROLE TASKS AND PROCESS NORMS TO GUIDE THE PARTICIPANTS IN THE DECISION-MAKING PROCESS. A CRUCIAL ACTOR IN THIS PROCESS IS THE NATIONAL SECURITY ADVISOR, WHO MUST ACT AS PROCESS MANAGER OR CUSTODIAN WHILE ABSTAINING FROM PERSONAL INVOLVEMENT IN THE SUBSTANCE OF POLICY ADVICE AND EXECUTION. THIS THESIS EXAMINES THE INTERNAL COHERENCE AND USEFULNESS OF THIS STRATEGY, FOCUSING ON THE CARTER ADMINISTRATION AND FOUR POLICY ISSUES: THE DEEP CUTS PROPOSALS IN SALT II, THE WAR IN THE HORN OF AFRICA, SINO-AMERICAN NORMALIZATION, AND THE FALL OF THE SHAH OF IRAN.

06445 MOERAN, B.
LAST DAYS OF THE EMPEROR
ENCOUNTER, LXXII(2) (FEB 89), 58-62.
THE AUTHOR LOOKS AT THE IMPACT OF THE EMPEROR HIROHITO'S LAST ILLNESS AND DEATH UPON THE JAPANESE PEOPLE AND JAPANESE PUBLIC LIFE.

06446 MOFID, K.
AFTER THE GULF WAR II: THE COST OF RECONSTRUCTION
WORLD TODAY, 45(3) (MAR 89), 49.
GIVEN THE MAGNITUDE OF THEIR LOSSES IN THE GULF WAR, IRAN AND IRAQ BOTH FACE A GIGANTIC TASK OF RECONSTRUCTION. EVEN IF OIL PRICES REMAIN STABLE AND DO NOT FALL, THEIR EXPECTED FUTURE INCOMES WILL BE HARDLY ENOUGH TO FINANCE THE NECESSARY IMPORTS OF FOOD AND OTHER COMMODITIES, LET ALONE TO PURSUE THE HUGE TASK OF RECONSTRUCTION. IN ORDER TO OVERCOME THIS PROBLEM, THE POST-WAR RECONSTRUCTION OF IRAN AND IRAQ SHOULD BECOME AN INTERNATIONAL RESPONSIBILITY, IN THE INTERESTS OF THE WORLD COMMUNITY AS A WHOLE.

06447 MOGHADAM, V.
AGAINST EUROCENTRISM AND NATIVISM: A REVIEW ESSAY ON SAMIR AMIN'S EUROCENTRISM AND OTHER TEXTS
SOCIALISM AND DEMOCRACY, (FAL 89), 81-104.
THIS ARTICLE IS A REVISED AND EXPANDED VERSION OF A PAPER PRESENTED AT THE SOCIALIST SCHOLARS CONFERENCE IN APRIL 1989. THE PAPER REPRESENTS A TRANSITION IN SAMIR AMIN'S WORK FROM A CONCENTRATION ON ECONOMIC RELATIONS AND STRUCTURES TO A NEW FOCUS ON CULTURAL, INTELLECTUAL, AND EPISTEMOLOGICAL PROBLEMS. IT OFFERS A REVIEW OF AMIN'S BOOK AND AN EXTENDED ARGUMENT OF MOGHADAM'S ON PROBLEMS ARISING FROM THE INDISCRIMINATE REJECTION OF MODERNITY, SECULARISM, AND MARXISM.

06448 MOGULL, R.G.
DETERMINANTS OF STATE PUBLIC WELFARE EXPENDITURES: AN ANALYTICAL SURVEY
MANKIND QUARTERLY, 30(1/2) (FAL 89), 39-64.
THERE HAS BEEN AN ABUNDANCE OF RESEARCH WHICH HAS ATTEMPTED TO EXPLAIN LEVELS AND FLUCTUATIONS IN JURISDICTIONAL WELFARE OUTLAYS. THE PURPOSE OF THIS PAPER IS TO SURVEY THE ACCOMPLISHMENTS OF THOSE STUDIES. A MODEL IS SPECIFIED AND PRIMARY SOCIOECONOMIC AND POLITICAL FACTORS ARE REVIEWED WITH RESPECT TO THEIR EXPLANATORY ASSOCIATION WITH PUBLIC WELFARE SPENDING AT THE LEVEL OF STATES. THE ANALYSIS PRESENTS THE HYPOTHESIS AND THE FINDINGS.

06449 MOISEYEV, M.
REDUCTION OF ARMED FORCES AND ARMAMENTS: A GUARANTEE OF SECURITY FOR ALL
INTERNATIONAL AFFAIRS (MOSCOW), (9) (SEP 89), 3-12.
THE SOVIET UNION AND ITS WARSAW TREATY ALLIES ARE PURSUING A CHANGE IN THE WAY INTERNATIONAL PROBLEMS ARE SOLVED--A CHANGE FROM MILITARY CONFRONTATION TO DEMILITARIZATION OF INTERNATIONAL RELATIONS, FROM THE ARMS RACE AND SUPER-ARMAMENT TO A REDUCTION OF ARSENALS. THE SOVIET UNION AND ITS ALLIES HAVE ADOPTED A PURELY DEFENSIVE MILITARY DOCTRINE, HAVE ADVANCED A SERIES OF CONSTRUCTIVE PROPOSALS, AND HAVE TAKEN UNILATERAL STEPS TOWARD DISARMAMENT, THEREBY DEMONSTRATING TO THE WORLD THEIR FIRM ADHERENCE TO AN ENTIRELY NEW SECURITY MODEL.

06450 MOJTAHED, A.; ESFAHANI, H.S.
AGRICULTURAL POLICY AND PERFORMANCE IN IRAN: THE POST-REVOLUTIONARY EXPERIENCE
WORLD DEVELOPMENT, 17(6) (JUN 89), 839-860.
THE AGRICULTURAL SECTOR OF IRAN HAS EXPERIENCED LOW GROWTH RATES SINCE THE 1979 REVOLUTION. THIS HAS HAPPENED DESPITE REMARKABLE INCREASES IN THE USE OF INPUTS, SUCH AS FERTILIZERS AND FARM MACHINERY, AND DESPITE THE POST-REVOLUTIONARY GOVERNMENT'S PROCLAIMED EMPHASIS ON AGRICULTURAL DEVELOPMENT AND SELF-SUFFICIENCY IN FOOD. ANALYSIS OF THE AVAILABLE DATA SHOWS THAT INCREASED LABOR COSTS HAVE REDUCED THE PROFITABILITY OF AGRICULTURAL PRODUCTION AS A WHOLE AND THAT THE GOVERNMENT'S LOPSIDED CONTROL OF AGRICULTURAL PRICES HAS TURNED PRODUCTION INCENTIVES AGAINST FOOD GRAINS. ALSO, BETWEEN 1978 AND 1982 AGRICULTURAL INVESTMENT AND RESEARCH AND DEVELOPMENT EXPENDITURES, ESPECIALLY THE INFRASTRUCTURAL AND BASIC RESEARCH PARTS, WERE SIGNIFICANTLY CUT. THESE SHORTCOMINGS IMPEDED AGRICULTURAL GROWTH IN THE EARLY 1980S. THE MORE RECENT CHANGES IN THE INVESTMENT AND RESEARCH POLICIES OF THE GOVERNMENT SEEM TO BE FAVORABLE; HOWEVER, THE WAR AND THE DECLINE OF OIL REVENUES HAVE SEVERELY RESTRAINED THE OVERALL AVAILABILITY OF DEVELOPMENT FUNDS IN THE IRANIAN ECONOMY.

06451 MOL, N.
CONTRACT-BASED MANAGEMENT CONTROL IN GOVERNMENT ORGANIZATIONS
INTERNATIONAL REVIEW OF ADMINISTRATIVE SCIENCES, 55(3) (SEP 89), 365-381.
THE CONTENTION THAT GOVERNMENT BUREAUCRACIES SHOULD ADOPT MORE DECENTRALIZED TYPES OF MANAGEMENT CONTROL MAY BE CONSIDERED ONE OF THE CONVENTIONAL WISDOMS OF OUR TIMES. THE IDEA THAT ADMINISTRATION IS FRUSTRATED, IF NOT PARALYSED, BY A PROFUSION OF INTERNAL DIRECTIVES IS WIDELY ACCEPTED IN THE EAST AND WEST. IN THIS ARTICLE ONE OF THE MANY RECENT ATTEMPTS AT SUCH A DECENTRALIZATION WILL BE DISCUSSED: THE EXPERIENCE WITH A REFORM COINED 'SELF-MANAGEMENT',

INTRODUCED IN THE PAST FEW YEARS IN THE DUTCH CENTRAL
GOVERNMENT. THIS REFORM HAS MANAGED TO GAIN THE SUPPORT
NECESSARY TO MAKE ITS WAY TO THE IMPLEMENTATION STAGE.
NOTWITHSTANDING INITIAL EXPECTATIONS, THE IMPACT OF
SELFMANAGEMENT SEEMS TO BE RATHER LIMITED. THIS ARTICLE
TRIES TO IDENTIFY THE CAUSES OF THESE OUTCOMES, TO DERIVE
THE LESSONS TO BE DRAWN FROM THEM AND POSSIBLY TO SUGGEST
SOLUTIONS FOR SOME OF THE PROBLEMS ENCOUNTERED IN THE
ATTEMPTED REFORM.

06452 MOLANA, H.
HEALTH ALLOCATION, CAPITAL GAINS AND PRIVATE EXPENDITURE
IN THE UK
SCOTTISH JOURNAL OF POLITICAL ECONOMY, 36(3) (AUG 89),
209-237.
THE MAIN OBJECTIVE OF THE PAPER IS ONE OF SPECIFYING A
DYNAMIC RELATIONSHIP BETWEEN PERSONAL NONDURABLE CONSUMPTION
AND EXPLANATORY VARIABLES SUCH AS PERSONAL DISPOSABLE INCOME,
THE CONSUMERS' PRICE INDEX, PERSONAL WEALTH AND A PRICE
INDEX AND RATE OF RETURN FOR PERSONAL WEALTH. THE AUTHOR
ALSO BRIEFLY EXPLAINS THE RECENT MODELS OF THE AGGREGATE
CONSUMPTION FUNCTION AND LOOKS AT THE BEHAVIOR OF THE SERIES
WHICH ARE THOUGHT TO AFFECT CONSUMERS' EXPENDITURE DECISIONS.
THE AUTHOR CONCLUDES BY OUTLINING A SIMPLE--BUT
SUFFICIENTLY GENERAL--SPECIFICATION OF THE LONG-RUN
FUNCTIONAL FORM OF THE CONSUMPTION FUNCTION. THIS
SPECIFICATION USES THE ECONOMETRIC MODELING TECHNIQUES TO
CAPTURE THE DYNAMICS INHERENT IN THE SHORT-RUN RELATIONSHIP.
THE EMPIRICAL RESULTS ARE PRESENTED AND DISCUSSED.

06453 MOLE, V.C.
TECHNOLOGICAL INNOVATION AND LOCAL AUTHORITIES: A CASE
STUDY OF THE GREATER LONDON COUNCIL (GLC)
DISSERTATION ABSTRACTS INTERNATIONAL, 50(4) (OCT 89),
1086-A.
THIS IS A CASE STUDY OF A SOCIALLY-DIRECTED TECHNOLOGY
POLICY FORMULATED AND IMPLEMENTED BY THE GREATER LONDON
COUNCIL BETWEEN 1981 AND 1986. THE GLC ENDEAVORED TO
DIRECTLY LINK TECHNOLOGICAL INNOVATION AND SOCIAL NEEDS BY
CREATING THE FACILITIES, IN THE FORM OF FIVE TECHNOLOGY
NETWORKS, FOR USER INVOLVEMENT IN SOCIALLY-USEFUL PRODUCT
DESIGN AND DEVELOPMENT.

06454 MOLINARO, I.C.
CONQUEST AND RECONQUEST: A READING OF QUEBEC POLITICAL
CULTURE
DISSERTATION ABSTRACTS INTERNATIONAL, 50(5) (NOV 89),
1425-A.
THE AUTHOR ANALYZES THE NEXUS BETWEEN POLITICAL IDENTITY
AND LEGITIMATE AUTHORITY AND EXPLAINS THE CONTEMPORARY
LANGUAGE DISPUTES THAT HAVE REVISED RELATIONS AMONG MEMBERS
OF QUEBEC SOCIETY. ALTHOUGH THE LANGUAGE DISPUTES ARE
COUCHED IN TERMS OF INDIVIDUAL RIGHTS, THE CONTROVERSY IS A
CONTEMPORARY EXPRESSION OF THE HISTORICAL RIVALRY BETWEEN
FRENCH CANADA AND ENGLISH CANADA.

06455 MOLNAR, T.
RECENTRALIZING EUROPE
NATIONAL REVIEW, 62(22) (NOV 89), 34, 36.
THIS ARTICLE EXAMINES THE PROSPECT OF A REUNIFIED,
NEUTRALIZED GERMANY WHICH IS FRIGHTENING TO WESTERN
EUROPEANS. THE POSSIBILITIES FOR THE NATIONS WHO USED TO BE
CALLED CENTRAL EUROPE, AND ARE UNDER SOVIET RULE, ARE
EXPLORED. IT CONCLUDES THAT THE COMING IMBALANCE AND SEARCH
FOR EQUILIBRIUM MAY AGAIN TURN EUROPE INTO AN AREA OF
ADVENTURE.

06456 MONAKREOV, V.
USSR-CZECHOSLOVAKIA: ECONOMIC AND TECHNICAL COOPERATION
FOREIGN TRADE, 1 (1988), 2-4.
THIS ARTICLE TRACES THE POSTWAR SOCIO-ECONOMIC
DEVELOPMENT OF CZECHOLOVAKIA AND THE USSR. IT REPORTS ON THE
INCREASE OF MUTUAL GOODS EXCHANGE FROM 1948-1986. IT
EXAMINES COOPERATION IN THE FIELDS OF METALLURGY,
TRANSPORTATION, FOREST RESOURCES, AUTOMATED CONTROL SYSTEMS,
WITH SPECIAL EMPHASIS ON THE FIELDS OF CHEMICAL PROJECTS AND
ATOMIC ENERGY. COOPERATION OF THE TWO NATIONS IN
CONSTRUCTION OF PROJECTS IN THIRD WORLD COUNTRIES CONTINUES.

06457 MONTEIRO, T.
AFRICAN-AMERICAN EQUALITY AND THE STRUGGLE AGAINST RACISM
POLITICAL AFFAIRS, LXVIII(8) (AUG 89), 24-30.
THE ARTICLE PRESENTS FIFTEEN PROPOSITIONS REGARDING
RACISM IN THE US. IT ALSO ANALYZES FOUR MAJOR CURRENTS IN
THE IDEOLOGICAL ARSENAL OF MONOPOLY CAPITAL ON THE ISSUE OF
RACISM. THESE ARE: THE CONCEPT OF RACISTS WHITE WORKING-
CLASS MAJORITY; THE UNDERCLASS THEORY; THE "PLURAL BUT
EQUAL" IDEA; AND THE "ETHNICITY REPLACES CLASS AND RACE"
IDEA. IT CONCLUDES THAT RACISM IS STILL PREVALENT IN THE US
AND THAT THE BOURGEOIS THEORIES REGARDING RACISM PERPETUATE
THE OPPRESSION AND WEAKEN THE ANTI-RACISM MOVEMENT.

06458 MONTERO, A.C.; GONZALEZ, P.M.
CUBA'S EXTERNAL ECONOMIC CONSTRAINTS IN THE 1980S: AN
ASSESSMENT OF THE POTENTIAL ROLE OF THE UNITED STATES
JOURNAL OF COMMUNIST STUDIES, 5(4) (DEC 89), 84-97.
THE POTENTIAL FOR THE EXPANSION OF ECONOMIC RELATIONS
BETWEEN CUBA AND THE UNITED STATES HINGES ON THE INITIAL
RENEWAL OF ECONOMIC TIES, WHICH IN TURN DEPENDS ON THE PRIOR
RENEWAL OF POLITICAL RELATIONS BETWEEN THE TWO COUNTRIES.
THE ESTABLISHMENT AND CONSOLIDATION OF COMMERCIAL TIES WOULD
FOSTER ADDITIONAL FORMS OF ECONOMIC CO-OPERATION OF NEW
TYPES, AND WOULD REPRESENT AN IMPORTANT STEP TOWARDS MEETING
THE ASPIRATIONS FOR PEACE OF THE PEOPLES OF BOTH COUNTRIES.

06459 MONTERO, S.S.
HOW TO OPEN THE DOOR
WORLD MARXIST REVIEW, 32(11) (NOV 89), 13-16.
THE COMMUNISTS' INFLUENCE IN SPAIN DEPENDS ON THEIR
ACTIONS, ON THEIR ABILITY TO PUT FORWARD CORRECT IDEAS IN
WORKING OUT ALTERNATIVE SOLUTIONS AND CHOOSING FORMS OF
STRUGGLE, AND ON THEIR ENTHUSIASM AND MILITANCY. TO DO THIS,
PARTY MUST JETTISON THE DOGMATISM OF IDEOLOGICAL FORMULAS,
WHICH NOT ONLY RESOLVE NOTHING, BUT ALSO SEPARATE SPAIN FROM
MANY PEOPLE, INCLUDING THOSE WHO ARE READY TO JOIN THE PARTY.
THE PCE MUST GIVE UP THE SPECIOUSLY THEORETICAL AND OVERLY-
FORMAL DISCUSSIONS OF THE WORKING CLASS AS THE SUBJECT OF
REVOLUTION, OF THE PCE'S LEADERSHIP ROLE AS A SPECIAL
PRIVILEGE, AND OF THE COMMUNISTS' HEGEMONY IN A FUTURE
PROGRESSIVE BLOC.

06460 MONTES, M.F.
OVERCOMING PHILLIPINE UNDERDEVELOPMENT: AN ALTERNATIVE
PROGRAMME
THIRD WORLD QUARTERLY, 11(3) (JUL 89), 107-119.
THE INSTALLATION OF THE AQUINO GOVERNMENT IN FEBRUARY
1986, AFTER THE OVERTHROW OF THE MARCOS DICTATORSHIP, RE-
IGNITED THE DEBATE OVER DEVELOPMENT STRATEGY IN THE
PHILIPPINES. THIS ARTICLE AIMS TO ANALYSE PHILIPPINE
UNDERDEVELOPMENT AND TO SKETCH AN ALTERNATIVE DEVELOPMENT
PROGRAMME. THE MODEL PROPOSED HERE SUMMARISES PREVIOUS
RESEARCH DISCUSSED IN FERRER (1987), FERRER AND MONTES
(1987), AND MONTES (1988).

06461 MONTI, D.J.
THE ORGANIZATIONAL STRENGTHS AND WEAKNESSES OF RESIDENT-
MANAGED PUBLIC HOUSING SITES IN THE UNITED STATES
JOURNAL OF URBAN AFFAIRS, 11(1) (1989), 39-52.
THE FEDERAL GOVERNMENT HAS INITIATED AN EFFORT TO
ENCOURAGE PUBLIC HOUSING RESIDENTS TO MANAGE AND OWN THEIR
DEVELOPMENTS. NOTWITHSTANDING THE PUBLIC ATTENTION RESIDENT
MANAGEMENT HAS RECEIVED, THERE HAS BEEN LITTLE RESEARCH
DEALING WITH THIS SUBJECT. REVIEWED IN THIS ARTICLE ARE THE
EXPERIENCES OF 11 DEVELOPMENTS THAT HAVE RESIDENT MANAGEMENT
OR WHOSE RESIDENTS WOULD LIKE TO HAVE IT. FOUR MAJOR
FINDINGS ARE DISCUSSED: (1) GOOD HOUSING AUTHORITY AND
TENANT RELATIONS DO NOT NECESSARILY PRODUCE EFFECTIVE
RESIDENT MANAGEMENT CORPORATIONS (RMCS); (2) A FEW STRONG
RESIDENT LEADERS DO NOT PRODUCE EFFECTIVE RMCS; (3) SITES
WITH GOOD TIES TO OUTSIDE INSTITUTIONS ARE LIKELY TO FARE
BETTER; AND (4) SITES WITH GOOD COMMUNITY ORGANIZATIONS TEND
TO HAVE MORE EFFECTIVE RMCS.

06462 MONTIAS, J.M.
NATIONAL VALUES AND ECONOMIC REFORMS IN SOCIALIST ECONOMIES
WORLD DEVELOPMENT, 17(9) (SEP 89), 1433-1442.
MAJOR ECONOMIC REFORMS IN PREREVOLUTIONARY AND SOVIET
RUSSIA HAVE ONLY BEEN CARRIED OUT TO RESOLVE POLITICAL OR
MILITARY PROBLEMS TRANSCENDING THE ECONOMIC REALM. THE
PROMOTION OF EFFICIENCY THROUGH SYSTEM CHANGE HAS
TRADITIONALLY CONFLICTED WITH THE PRESERVATION OF
EGALITARIAN VALUES (OPPOSITION TO INCOME DISPARITIES), THE
DESIRE TO MAINTAIN STABILITY (INCLUDING THE AVOIDANCE OF
UNEMPLOYMENT), AND XENOPHOBIA (FOREIGNERS SHOULD NOT ENRICH
THEMSELVES AT RUSSIAN EXPENSE). VARIOUS EPISODES OF RUSSIAN
HISTORY SHOW THAT REFORMS HAVE ALWAYS MET WITH RIGOROUS
OPPOSITION FROM AN ENTRENCHED BUREAUCRACY. THE PROSPECTS FOR
CURRENT REFORM IN THE SOVIET UNION AND IN EASTERN EUROPE ARE
EXAMINED IN THE LIGHT OF THESE AND SIMILAR CONSIDERATIONS.

06463 MOODIE, M.
BURDEN-SHARING IN NATO: A NEW DEBATE WITH AN OLD LABEL
WASHINGTON QUARTERLY, 12(4) (FAL 89), 61-72.
AT THE HEART OF ANY RESOLUTION OF TODAY'S BURDEN-SHARING
DEBATE ARE THE FUNDAMENTAL QUESTIONS OF NATO'S APPROPRIATE
RESPONSES TO THE CHANGES UNLEASHED IN EASTERN EUROPE AND THE
SOVIET UNION AND THE REQUIREMENTS FOR IMPLEMENTING NATO'S
STRATEGY OF FLEXIBLE RESPONSE IN THE 1990S. THIS ARTICLE
EXPLORES THE DEBATE'S CHANGING CONTEXT, ITS OLD LABELS AND
ITS NEW ISSUES. CHANGING THE TERMS OF THE DEBATE IS
NECESSARY SO THAT ALLIES CAN EXPLOIT GREATER AWARENESS OF
THE ISSUE AND CHANNEL IT TOWARDS A POSITIVE OUTCOME FOR THE
ENTIRE ALLIANCE.

06464 MOORE, C.M.
OBSCURE HEROES
NATIONAL CIVIC REVIEW, 78(6) (NOV 89), 411-420.
HEROIC LEADERSHIP MAY HAVE MORE NOSTALGIC APPEAL THAN

CONSTRUCTIVE RELEVANCE TO MODERN SOCIETY. AFTER BRIEFLY
IDENTIFYING THE ORIGIN, EVOLUTION AND COMPONENTS OF THE HERO,
THIS ARTICLE ARGUES THAT WHAT HAS BECOME KNOWN AS HEROIC
LEADERSHIP IS NOT DESIRABLE BECAUSE IT IS ANTITHETICAL TO
DEMOCRACY, UNREALISTIC IN A NUCLEAR AGE, AND CAN ENCOURAGE
US TO "WAIT FOR SALVATION." IT WOULD BE MORE APPROPRIATE TO
RECOGNIZE AND ENCOURAGE "OBSCURE HEROES," WHO ARE
CHARACTERIZED PRIMARILY BY SOUND JUDGEMENT AND MORAL COURAGE.

06465 MOORE, J.
    ACTIVATING THE STUDENTS
    FAR EASTERN ECONOMIC REVIEW, 141(28) (JUL 88), 20.
        STUDENTS IN TAIWAN ARE BREAKING FREE FROM DECADES OF
    EFFICIENT CONTROL OF STUDENT LIFE AT ALL LEVELS BY THE PARTY
    ESTABLISHMENT AND ARE BECOMING INCREASINGLY POLITICALLY
    ACTIVE. THE NATIONAL TAIWAN UNIVERSITY ELECTED AS HEAD OF
    THE STUDENT ASSOCIATION A CANDIDATE THAT WAS NOT BACKED BY
    THE RULING KOUMINTANG. STUDENTS ARE PUSHING FOR UNIVERSITY
    REFORM AND ARE TENTATIVELY BRANCHING OUT INTO OTHER POLITICAL
    ISSUES.

06466 MOORE, J.
    CONFRONTING REALITIES OF REFUGEE ASSISTANCE
    DEPARTMENT OF STATE BULLETIN (US FOREIGN POLICY), 89(2149)
    (AUG 89), 85-86.
        THE RECORD AND COMMITMENT OF THE UNITED STATES'
    WORLDWIDE PROGRAM FOR REFUGEES IS IN JEOPARDY. INCREASES IN
    REFUGEE FLOWS AND REFUGEE NEEDS AREN'T BEING MET WITH
    ADEQUATE FUNDING. INCONSISTENCIES IN AMERICAN POLICIES AMONG
    REGIONS AND REFUGEE GROUPS THREATEN THE EVEN-HANDED
    CHARACTER OF THE PROGRAM. ADMISSIONS REQUIREMENTS FOR
    THOUSANDS OF REFUGEES EAT UP FUNDING NEEDED TO ASSIST
    MILLIONS OF REFUGEES IN LIFE-THREATENING SITUATIONS.

06467 MOORE, J.
    DEVELOPING SOLUTIONS FOR CENTRAL AMERICAN REFUGEE PROBLEMS
    DEPARTMENT OF STATE BULLETIN (US FOREIGN POLICY), 89(2149)
    (AUG 89), 87-88.
        THE AUTHOR, WHO IS THE UNITED STATES COORDINATOR FOR
    REFUGEE AFFAIRS, DISCUSSES ASPECTS OF THE REFUGEE PROBLEM IN
    CENTRAL AMERICA, INCLUDING THE DEFINITION OF REFUGEE STATUS
    AND UNITED STATES AID PROGRAMS FOR CENTRAL AMERICAN REFUGEES.

06468 MOORE, J.
    FY 1990 ASSISTANCE REQUEST FOR REFUGEE PROGRAMS
    DEPARTMENT OF STATE BULLETIN (US FOREIGN POLICY), 89(2146)
    (MAY 89), 72-73.
        THE AUTHOR SUMMARIZES THE DEPARTMENT OF STATE'S FY 1990
    REQUEST FOR MIGRATION AND REFUGEE ASSISTANCE, EMERGENCY
    REFUGEE MIGRATION AND ASSISTANCE, AND THE DEPARTMENT'S
    AUTHORIZATION BILL. HE STATES THAT THE GOVERNMENT'S REFUGEE
    PROGRAM IS AN ESSENTIAL EXPRESSION OF AMERICAN COMMITMENT TO
    HUMANITARIAN PRINCIPLES AND A MEANS OF SUPPORTING FOREIGN
    POLICY OBJECTIVES.

06469 MOORE, J.
    SUMMER OF DISCONTENT
    FAR EASTERN ECONOMIC REVIEW, 141(36) (SEP 88), 116-117.
        TAIWAN'S RAPID SOCIAL AND ECONOMIC DEVELOPMENT IS
    CREATING STRAINS WITHIN THE LABOUR MARKET AND CAUSING
    UNCERTAINTY AMONG GOVERNMENT POLICYMAKERS. SOME OF THE
    TENSION HAS BEEN MANIFESTED IN A SERIES OF STRIKES INCLUDING
    TAIWAN'S FIRST TECHNICALLY LEGAL STRIKE. CONFUSION IS HIGH
    IN THE ONE-YEAR-OLD, CABINET LEVEL COUNCIL OF LABOR AFFAIRS
    (CLA). IT FINDS ITSELF CAUGHT BETWEEN GOVERNMENT TRADITION
    WHICH DEMANDS REPRESSION OF LABOR UNREST AND ITS STATED ROLE
    AS A CHAMPION OF WORKER'S RIGHTS. THE RESULT HAS A SERIES OF
    CONFLICTING SIGNALS TO TAIWAN'S 7.7 MILLION INDUSTRIAL
    WORKERS.

06470 MOORE, J.
    TAIWAN TECHNOCRATS PROMOTED
    FAR EASTERN ECONOMIC REVIEW, 141(31) (AUG 88), 45.
        THE ARTICLE EXAMINES THE YOUNGER, REFORM-MINDED
    TECHNOCRATS WHO HAVE TAKEN MINISTERIAL POSITIONS AS A RESULT
    OF TAIWAN'S CABINET SHUFFLE. IT GIVES A BRIEF PROFILE OF
    EACH ONE OF THE CHALLENGES THAT THEY WILL FACE FROM AN
    IMPATIENT PRIVATE SECTOR WHICH IS EAGER TO SEE REFORMS
    IMPLEMENTED QUICKLY.

06471 MOORE, J.
    U.S. RESPONDS TO SOUTHERN AFRICA REFUGEE CRISIS
    DEPARTMENT OF STATE BULLETIN (US FOREIGN POLICY), 88(2140)
    (NOV 88), 46-48.
        THE ARTICLE ANALYZES THE SITUATION IN SOUTHERN AFRICA
    WITH SPECIAL CONCERN FOR THE GROWING NUMBER OF REFUGEES FROM
    MOZAMBIQUE AND OTHER SOUTH AFRICAN NATIONS. IT EXPLORES THE
    EXTENT OF THE PROBLEM AND THE EFFORTS THAT ARE BEING MADE TO
    ALLEVIATE IT. THE ARTICLE ALSO OUTLINES SOME POSSIBLE FUTURE
    POLICY OPTIONS DESIGNED TO COPE WITH THIS INCREASINGLY
    SIGNIFICANT PROBLEM.

06472 MOORE, J.
    UPDATE ON IMMIGRATION AND REFUGEE ISSUES
    DEPARTMENT OF STATE BULLETIN (US FOREIGN POLICY), 89(2148)
    (JUL 89), 59-62.
        THE AUTHOR, WHO IS THE UNITED STATES COORDINATOR FOR
    REFUGEE AFFAIRS, REVIEWS THE MAJOR REFUGEE ISSUES IN AFRICA,
    EAST ASIA, CENTRAL AMERICA, EUROPE, AND THE NEAR EAST AND
    SOUTH ASIA. THEN HE EXPLAINS THE POLICY INITIATIVES THE BUSH
    ADMINISTRATION IS TAKING IN RESPONSE TO THE CURRENT,
    UNPRECEDENTED RATE OF APPLICATION BY SOVIET EMIGRANTS FOR
    RESETTLEMENT IN THE USA.

06473 MOORE, K.
    SOLIDARITY'S MANY FACES
    COMMONWEAL, CXVI(13) (JUL 89), 391-392.
        ALTHOUGH SOLIDARITY WON CONVINCINGLY IN THE 1989 POLISH
    ELECTIONS, IT WILL NOT ASSUME CONTROL OF THE GOVERNMENT,
    BECAUSE IT HAS AGREED BEFOREHAND THAT THE ELECTION WOULD BE
    NO MORE THAN ONE STEP IN THE DIRECTION OF PARLIMENTARY
    DEMOCRACY.

06474 MOORE, M.
    ANDREW JACKSON: "PRETTY NEAR 'TREASON' TO CALL HIM DOCTOR!"
    NEW ENGLAND QUARTERLY, LXII(3) (SEP 89), 424-435.
        THE ARTICLE BRIEFLY EXAMINES THE CONTROVERSY SURROUNDING
    THE GRANTING OF AN HONORARY LAW DEGREE FROM HARVARD COLLEGE
    TO PRESIDENT ANDREW JACKSON. THE PRESIDENT OF HARVARD,
    JOSIAH QUINCY, FACED A CONSIDERABLE DILEMMA: HE DESIRED TO
    FOLLOW THE TRADITION THAT HAD GRANTED HONORARY DEGREES TO
    WASHINGTON, LAFAYETTE, MONROE, AND OTHERS, BUT WAS UNEASY
    DUE TO JACKSON'S OBVIOUS LACK OF QUALIFICATIONS. IN THE END,
    TRADITION WON OUT, BUT QUINCY WAS SUBJECT TO MUCH RIDICULE
    FROM THE BOSTON COMMUNITY.

06475 MOORE, M.
    EUROPE: AN OPPORTUNITY?
    NEW ZEALAND INTERNATIONAL REVIEW, 14(3) (MAY 89), 2-6.
        THE MINISTER OF EXTERNAL RELATIONS AND TRADE IN NEW
    ZEALAND SUGGESTS THAT THE EUROPEAN COMMUNITY'S SINGLE MARKET
    WILL HAVE A SUBSTANTIAL IMPACT ON GLOBAL ECONOMIC AND TRADE
    PATTERNS AND THAT ALERT NEW ZEALAND EXPORTERS STAND TO GAIN
    LUCRATIVE BUSINESS. THE DIVERSIFICATION OF NEW ZEALAND'S
    TRADE BASE IS SUGGESTED AS BEING AT THE FOREFRONT ALONG WITH
    THE POLITICAL EFFORT WHICH HAS OCCURRED IN TRADE RELATIONS,
    SPECIFICALLY THE GATT ROUND FOR TRADE LIBERALIZATION. THE
    CREATION OF THE SINGLE EUROPEAN MARKET IS BROUGHT INTO
    QUESTION.

06476 MOORE, P.
    GENERAL-PURPOSE AID IN NEW YORK STATE: TARGETING ISSUES
    AND MEASURES
    PUBLIUS: THE JOURNAL OF FEDERALISM, 19(2) (SPR 89), 17-32.
        THE ARTICLE EXPLORES KEY QUESTIONS ABOUT TARGETED VERSUS
    DISTRIBUTIVE AID POLICIES WITHIN THE CONTEXT OF NEW YORK'S
    GENERAL-PURPOSE STATE AID PROGRAM. DEVELOPMENT OF THAT
    PROGRAM OVER THE PAST FORTY YEARS SHOWS EBBS AND FLOWS OF
    SUPPORT FOR BOTH TARGETED AND DISTRIBUTIVE APPROACHES
    INTENSE POLICY DEBATES CONCERNING LOCAL FISCAL POLICIES AS
    PART OF ANNUAL STATE BUDGET NEGOTIATIONS. ALTHOUGH RECENTLY,
    NEW YORK POLICYMAKERS HAVE FAVORED TARGETED APPROACHES YET
    THE TRADITIONAL MEASURES OF TARGETING GOVERNMENTAL NEEDS,
    SUCH AS DIFFERENCES IN FISCAL CAPACITY AND EFFORT, HAVE BEEN
    EXPANDED TO EMPHASIZE DIFFERENCES IN SERVICE
    RESPONSIBILITIES. STRONG, AND PERHAPS IRONIC, PARALLELS ARE
    ALSO EVIDENT BETWEEN NEW YORK'S PROGRAM AND THE NOW DEFUNCT
    FEDERAL REVENUE SHARING PROGRAM.

06477 MOORE, Z.L.
    OUT OF THE SHADOWS: BLACK AND BROWN STRUGGLES FOR
    RECOGNITION AND DIGNITY IN BRAZIL, 1964-1985
    JOURNAL OF BLACK STUDIES, 19(4) (JUN 89), 394-410.
        THIS ARTICLE WILL ATTEMPT TO RETRACE THE TRIALS AND
    TRAVAILS OF AFRO-BRAZILIANS UNDER THE AUTHORITARIAN "REGIME
    MILITAR APO'S 64" (AFTER 1964). IN ORDER TO UNDERSTAND THE
    POSITION OF AFRO-BRAZILIANS IN SOCIETY IT IS NECESSARY TO
    UNDERSTAND THE MEANING OF THE 1964 MILITARY COUP FOR ALL
    BRAZILIANS. THE SITUATION OF AFRO-BRAZILIANS AND OTHER POOR
    WORKERS IS STUDIED IN TERMS OF THE WORK FORCE, POPULATION
    STUDIES DISCRIMINATION, EDUCATION, THE CHURCH, MIXED
    MARRIAGES, ATHELETICS, RACISM, POVERTY AND POLITICS. IT
    CONCLUDES THAT A NEW CIVILIAN ADMINISTRATION GIVES AFRO-
    BRAZILIANS YET ANOTHER OPPORTUNITY TO INTENSIFY THEIR
    EFFORTS TO OVERCOME RACIAL BARRIERS IN EDUCATION, ECONOMICS
    AND POLITICS.

06478 MORAIHED, T.; DJEBBAR, S.; ESES, R.
    JORDAN
    SOUTH, (102) (APR 89), 53-61.
        SINCE APRIL 1985, WHEN PRIME MINISTER ZAID RIFAI TOOK
    OFFICE, JORDAN HAS BEEN EXPLORING WAYS OUT OF ITS RECESSION,
    INCLUDING A FIVE-YEAR PLAN (1991-1995). ONE PROBLEM HAS BEEN
    THE DROP IN FOREIGN AID FROM THE OTHER ARAB NATIONS, AS
    SAUDI ARABIA HAS BEEN THE ONLY ONE OF THE DONORS TO PAY ITS
    FULL SHARE OF PROMISED AID TO JORDAN. JORDANIAN PLANNERS
    HAVE TRIED TO LIBERLIZE THE ECONOMY AND MAKE IT MORE EXPORT-
    ORIENTED TO COMPENSATE FOR THE LOSS OF FOREIGN EXCHANGE

EARNINGS.

06479 MORALES, W.Q.
THE WAR ON DRUGS: A NEW U.S. NATIONAL SECURITY DOCTRINE?
THIRD WORLD QUARTERLY, 11(3) (JUL 89), 147-169.
THE U.S. WAR ON DRUGS IS EMERGING AS A POWERFUL NEW
POLITICAL DOCTRINE THAT MESHES WITH ANTI-COMMUNIST IDEOLOGY,
THE LOW INTENSITY CONFLICT STRATEGY, AND THE REASSERTION OF
COVERT ACTION. THE U.S. INTELLIGENCE SERVICES HAVE LONG HAD
AN INTIMATE RELATIONSHIP WITH THE DRUG UNDERWORLD, AND THIS
INTIMACY COULD FACILITATE THE MANIPULATION OF THE WAR
AGAINST DRUGS IN THE INTERESTS OF THE NATIONAL SECURITY
STATE.

06480 MORAN, C.
ECONOMIC STABILIZATION AND STRUCTURAL TRANSFORMATION:
LESSONS FROM THE CHILEAN EXPERIENCE, 1973-87
WORLD DEVELOPMENT, 17(4) (APR 89), 491-502.
THIS PAPER EVALUATES THE EXPERIENCE OF ECONOMIC REFORMS
AND STABILIZATION EFFORTS IN CHILE DURING 1973-87. THE PAPER
PRESENTS A BRIEF HISTORICAL BACKGROUND AND THEN REVIEWS THE
MAIN GOALS, POLICY TOOLS, AND RESULTS OF THE ECONOMIC
PROGRAM IMPLEMENTED SINCE THE MILITARY GOVERNMENT CAME TO
POWER IN SEPTEMBER 1973. THE PAPER DISCUSSES IN DETAIL THE
STABILIZATION AND STRUCTURAL TRANSFORMATION ASPECTS OF THE
ECONOMIC PROGRAM INCLUDING THE PRIVATIZATION OF THE ECONOMY
AND THE TRADE AND FINANCIAL LIBERALIZATION. THE MAIN
CONCLUSION IS THAT, DESPITE A HEALTHY IMPROVEMENT IN THE
ECONOMIC SITUATION DURING 1985-87, THE FUTURE OF THE CHILEAN
ECONOMY REMAINS UNCERTAIN AND VULNERABLE TO EXTERNAL SHOCKS.
THE PAPER CONCLUDES BY SUMMARIZING THE MAIN POLICY LESSONS
OF THE CHILEAN EXPERIENCE.

06481 MORAVCSIK, A. M.
DISCIPLINING TRADE FINANCE: THE OECD EXPORT CREDIT
ARRANGEMENT
INTERNATIONAL ORGANIZATION, 43(1) (WIN 89), 173-205.
THE SALIENCE OF TARIFFS, QUOTAS, AND OTHER IMPORT
RESTRICTIONS IN CURRENT DISCUSSIONS OF TRADE POLICY OBSCURES
WHAT MAY WELL BECOME A MORE SIGNIFICANT FORM OF GOVERNMENT
INTERVENTION: SUBSIDIZED EXPORT PROMOTION. OVER THE PAST TWO
DECADES, SUBSIDIZED TRADE FINANCE HAS BEEN ONE OF THE MOST
WIDELY USED INSTRUMENTS OF EXPORT PROMOTION. THIS ARTICLE
OFFERS AN HISTORICAL DESCRIPTION AND A THEORETICAL
EXPLANATION FOR THE SUCCESS OF THE ORGANIZATION FOR ECONOMIC
COOPERATION AND DEVELOPMENT (OECD) EXPORT CREDIT ARRANGEMENT,
AN INTERNATIONAL REGIME RESTRICTING THE PROVISION OF
SUBSIDIZED TRADE FINANCE. THE EXPLANATION EMPHASIZES THREE
FACTORS: THE STRUCTURE OF GOVERNMENT INSTITUTIONS, THE
RELATIVE POWER OF STATES, AND THE FUNCTIONAL VALUE OF
INFORMATION. MORE GENERALLY, THE ANALYSIS DEMONSTRATES THE
INHERENT WEAKNESSES OF MONOCAUSAL EXPLANATIONS OF
INTERNATIONAL COOPERATION AND THE ADVANTAGES OF EXPLANATIONS
BASED ON A CONCEPTION OF INTERNATIONAL COOPERATION AS A
MULTISTAGE PROCESS, EACH STAGE OF WHICH MAY BE EXPLAINED BY
A SEPARATE THEORY.

06482 MORAWSKA, E.
LABOR MIGRATIONS OF POLES IN THE ATLANTIC WORLD ECONOMY,
1880-1914
COMPARATIVE STUDIES IN SOCIETY AND HISTORY, 31(2) (APR 89),
237-272.
THIS PAPER OFFERS AN INTERPRETATION OF MASS LABOR
MIGRATIONS OF POLES TO WESTERN EUROPE AND THE UNITED STATES
BETWEEN 1880 AND 1914, BY EXTENDING THE HISTORICAL-
COMPARATIVE SCOPE OF SOCIOLOGICAL ANALYSIS OF IMMIGRATION
AND INTEGRATING THE COMPETING MACRO- AND MICRO-EXPLANATORY
FRAMEWORKS: FIRST, IN TERMS OF THE CIRCULAR PUSH-AND-PULL
FORCES THAT OPERATED WITHIN THE EXPANDING ATLANTIC ECONOMIC
SYSTEM OF RECIPROCAL EXCHANGES OF GOODS, CAPITAL, AND LABOR;
AND SECOND, WITHIN THIS STRUCTURAL CONTEXT, IN TERMS OF THE
LOCAL CONDITIONS FROM WHICH MILLIONS OF PEOPLE FROM ALL
CORNERS OF THE POLISH COUNTRYSIDE WERE SET IN MOTION.

06483 MOREL, P.
THE PARIS CONFERENCE ON THE PROHIBITION OF CHEMICAL WEAPONS
DISARMAMENT, XII(2) (SUM 89), 127-144.
THE AUTHOR DISCUSSES THE NEED FOR PROHIBITING CHEMICAL
WEAPONS AND THE CIRCUMSTANCES SURROUNDING THE 1989 PARIS
CONFERENCE, WHICH ADOPTED A SHORT BUT COMPREHENSIVE DOCUMENT
THAT LAYS DOWN SPECIFIC GUIDELINES FOR MATTERS PERTAINING TO
CHEMICAL WEAPONS.

06484 MORELLO, T.
CAUSE FOR CONCERN
FAR EASTERN ECONOMIC REVIEW, 141(38) (SEP 88), 27.
A RECENT UN FUND-RAISING CONFERENCE BROUGHT ACCUSATIONS
OF HUMAN-RIGHTS VIOLATIONS BY THE KHMER ROUGE, THE COMMUNIST
FACTION OF THE ANTI-VIETNAM RESISTANCE IN CAMBODIA. CHARGES
OF TORTURE, MURDER AND THE "DISAPPEARANCE" OF 7,000 REFUGEES
IN CAMPS CONTROLLED BY THE KHMER ROUGE WERE COMPUNDED BY THE
FACTIONS "TOTAL LACK OF COOPERATION" AND BARRING OF
INTERNATIONAL ACCESS TO THE CAMPS IN QUESTION.

06485 MOREMI, B.
DO WE NEED PERESTROIKA IN THE LIBERATION MOVEMENT?
SECHABA, 23(7) (JUL 89), 28-30.
PERESTROIKA IS HAVING A POSITIVE EFFECT ON LIBERATION
MOVEMENTS BY ENCOURAGING AND ENSURING FREE DIALOGUE,
CRITICISM, SELF-CRITICISM AND SELF-ASSESSMENT OF MOTIVE AND
METHOD. LET PERESTROIKA PREVAIL.

06486 MORGAN, C. JR.
THE SUPREME COURT AND FREEDOM'S FUTURE
FREEDOM AT ISSUE, (107) (MAR 89), 5-6.
THE SUPREME COURT RULING ON A RICHMOND, VIRGINIA,
ORDINANCE THAT REQUIRED A MINORITY QUOTA ON CITY-AWARDED
CONSTRUCTION CONTRACTS IS AN IMPORTANT DISCLOSURE ABOUT THE
COURT AND ITS ROLE IN FREEDOM'S FUTURE. THE REAGAN-APPOINTED
JUSTICES HAVE WRITTEN THEIR VIEWS OF RACE AND THE
CONSTITUTION ACROSS THE PAGES OF HISTORY. IN DOING SO, THEY
HAVE ADDED QUALIFICATIONS TO THE "EQUAL JUSTICE UNDER LAW"
SIGN ABOVE THE SUPREME COURT'S DOOR AND HAVE SET THEIR
COURSE. THEY ACTED NOT WITH MALICE BUT IN IGNORANCE.

06487 MORGAN, D.R.; HIRLINGER, M.W.
SOCIOECONOMIC DIMENSIONS OF THE AMERICAN STATES: AN UPDATE
SOCIAL SCIENCE QUARTERLY, 70(1) (MAR 89), 184-192.
THE TWO PRINCIPAL FACTORS DEFINING THE SOCIOECONOMIC
CONTEXT OF THE AMERICAN STATES-AFFLUENCE AND
INDUSTRIALIZATION-ARE UPDATED FOR 1980. THE TWO DIMENSIONS
REFLECT SOME CHANGES FROM 1970 AND 1960 BUT IN GENERAL SEEM
TO REPRESENT THE SAME TWO BASIC CHARACTERISTICS THAT
HOFFERBERT IN 1968 IDENTIFIED AS EXISTING FOR THE STATES AT
PERIODS AS EARLY AS 1890. USING PATH ANALYSIS, A LIMITED
TEST IS OFFERED OF THE CONTINUED USEFULNESS OF THE TWO
DIMENSIONS IN PREDICTING POLICY VARIATIONS AMONG THE STATES.
THE TWO FACTORS ARE CONSISTENTLY POWERFUL EXPLANATORY
MEASURES.

06488 MORGAN, D.R.; ENGLAND, R. E.
THE TWO FACES OF PRIVATIZATION
PUBLIC ADMINISTRATION REVIEW, 48(6) (NOV 88), 979-987.
THIS ARTICLE ADDRESSES TWO PRENNIAL ISSUES VITAL TO THE
AMERICAN POLICY - CITIZENSHIP AND COMMUNITY, WHICH HAVE BEEN
REFERRED TO AS THE "SECOND FACE" OF PRIVATIZATION. THE
BETTER-KNOWN FACE OF PRIVATIZATION - THE QUEST FOR
EFFECIENCY IS EXPLORED AS WELL. AN ELABORATION OF THE
ECONOMIC UNDERPINNINGS OF THE PRIVATIZATION MOVEMENT IS
OFFERED RELYING HEAVILY ON URBAN SERVICE DELIVERY LITERATURE.

06489 MORGAN, J.A.
DIALECTICAL POLITICAL SYSTEM: SELF-DETERMINATION AS THE
BASIS OF A SOCIAL FORMATION
DISSERTATION ABSTRACTS INTERNATIONAL, 50(1) (JUL 89),
247-A.
THIS DISSERTATION IS A THEORETICAL ANALYSIS OF YUGOSLAV
SOCIALIST SELF-MANAGEMENT. IT FOCUSES ON THE PROBLEM OF HOW
TO ESTABLISH THE FREE AND MUTUALLY AFFIRMATIVE SELF-
DETERMINATION OF INDIVIDUALS AND COMMUNITIES AS MOMENTS OF A
CONCRETE ETHICAL TOTALITY.

06490 MORGAN, J.G. JR.; STAVRIDIS, J.G.
EXAMINING RISK IN U.S. MILITARY OPERATIONS
COMPARATIVE STRATEGY, 8(2) (1989), 241-248.
THE PAPER ARGUES THAT THE CURRENT EMPHASIS ON "RISK-
FREE" OPERATIONS IN US MILITARY CIRCLES IS INEFFICIENT AND
COUNTERPRODUCTIVE. TO COMBAT THIS TREND, THE PAPER OFFERS A
BASIC EQUATION OF RISK ASSESSMENT AND MANAGEMENT. IT SEEKS
TO ENCOMPASS BOTH MILITARY AND POLITICAL SENSITIVITIES, AS
WELL AS ECONOMIC, PSYCHOLOGICAL, AND INFORMATIONAL RISKS. IT
OFFERS FOUR RISK-ORIENTED QUESTIONS WHICH FORM A "FILTER"
THAT PLANNERS MUST APPLY AFTER THE COMMITMENT TO USE FORCE
HAS BEEN MADE.

06491 MORGAN, L.
IN FLORIDA A COALITION SAVES SPEAKER-DESIGNEE
STATE LEGISLATURES, 15(4) (APR 89), 22-23.
POLITICAL OBSERVERS EXPECTED A COALITION BETWEEN
DEMOCRATS AND REPUBLICANS TO DECIDE THE RACE FOR SPEAKER OF
THE FLORIDA HOUSE IN 1989, BUT THE COMPOSITION OF THAT
COALITION WAS A SURPRISE.

06492 MORGAN, S.
IDEOLOGY ON THE BLOCK
FAR EASTERN ECONOMIC REVIEW, 141(28) (JUL 88), 22, 24-26.
FOR THE FIRST TIME SINCE 1949, LAND WAS SOLD BY PUBLIC
AUCTION IN CHINA. THE SHIFT IN POLICY BY THE CHINESE
GOVERNMENT PROMISES TO HAVE FAR-REACHING IMPLICATIONS FOR
THE CHINESE COMMUNIST PARTY. ALTHOUGH TECHNICALLY, THE LAND
"SALE" DOES NOT CONSTITUTE FREEHOLD OWNERSHIP, MANY FEEL
THAT THE CONCEPT OF SELLING OR LEASING LAND INFRINGED ON THE
BASIC PRINCIPLES OF MARXISM.

06493 MORGENTHAU, H.J.
U.S. MISADVENTURE IN VIETNAM
CURRENT HISTORY, 88(534) (JAN 89), 32-34, 56.
THE MOST DISASTROUS EVENT FOR THE UNITED STATES IN THE

POSTWAR PERIOD WAS THE VIETNAM WAR, AN ACTION TAKEN IN THE
NAME OF CONTAINING THE EXPANSION OF COMMUNISM. IN THIS
ARTICLE, THE AUTHOR DISCUSSES THE AMERICAN INVOLVEMENT IN
SOUTHEAST ASIA IN THE 1950'S AND 1960'S.

06494 MORLEY, J.; BYRNE, M.
THE DRUG WAR AND "NATIONAL SECURITY"
DISSENT, (WIN 89), 39–46.
TO UNDERSTAND WHY THE U.S. DRUG WAR HAS FAILED, IT IS
NECESSARY TO GO BACK TO ITS EARLIEST DAYS, FROM 1969 TO 1973,
WHEN THE CURRENT STRATEGY WAS ESTABLISHED AND FAILURE WAS
INSTITUTIONALIZED. THEN, AS NOW, CONVENTIONAL LAW
ENFORCEMENT AGENCIES WERE JUDGED INCAPABLE OF HANDLING THE
EFFORT; THE WHITE HOUSE ORGANIZED (AND REORGANIZED) THE ANTI-
DRUG CAMPAIGN; BETTER INTELLIGENCE WAS DEMANDED FROM THE CIA;
INVESTIGATIONS INTO THE DRUG TRADE WERE LAUNCHED BY
CONGRESS AND RESISTED BY THE EXECUTIVE. MOST IMPORTANTLY,
DRUG ENFORCEMENT BECAME A MATTER OF U.S. NATIONAL SECURITY.

06495 MORNA, C.
MOZAMBIQUE: EMERGENCY DONORS' CONFERENCE
AFRICAN BUSINESS, (JUN 88), 16–17.
THIS ARTICLE REPORTS ON ECONOMIC, LIVING, AND POLITICAL
CONDITIONS IN MOZAMBIQUE. IT EXPLORES THE RAMIFICATIONS OF
AID THAT HAS BEEN PLEDGED AS A RESULT OF A U.N.-SPONSORED
EMERGENCY CONFERENCE FOR MOZAMBIQUE HELD IN GENEVA APRIL
1987. THE NEED TO LINK EMERGENCY AND ECONOMIC REFORM
PROGRAMS IN THE COUNTRY'S LONGTERM INTEREST IS ANALYSED.

06496 MORNA, C.L.
A FRESH BID TO BYPASS APARTHEID
SOUTH, (102) (APR 89), 41.
THE JANUARY 1989 AGREEMENT BETWEEN ANGOLA AND SOUTH
AFRICA NOT ONLY PAVED THE WAY FOR NAMIBIA'S INDEPENDENCE BUT
ALSO LED THE WEST TO PLEDGE MONEY TO HELP REOPEN SOUTHERN
AFRICA'S GATEWAY TO THE ATLANTIC, THE BENGUELA RAILWAY. BUT
SECURITY CONCERNS AND COMPLICATIONS REGARDING THE OWNERSHIP
OF THE LINE, WHICH HAS BEEN CLOSED FOR 13 YEARS DUE TO UNITA
ATTACKS, HAVE YET TO BE RESOLVED.

06497 MORNA, C.L.
A GRASSROOTS DEMOCRACY
AFRICA REPORT, 34(4) (JUL 89), 17–20.
VOTER TURNOUT WAS HIGH FOR GHANA'S 1989 DISTRICT
ASSEMBLY ELECTIONS, INTENDED AS THE FIRST STEP IN BUILDING
GRASSROOTS POLITICAL PARTICIPATION. UNLIKE PAST ELECTIONS
ORGANIZED ON PARTY LINES, THE CONTESTS REVOLVED AROUND THE
CANDIDATES' PROBITY AND COMPETENCE, PROVIDING A HOPEFUL SIGN
FOR THE GROWTH OF DEMOCRATIC PRACTICE.

06498 MORNA, C.L.
AN EXERCISE IN EDUCATIONAL REFORM
AFRICA REPORT, 34(6) (NOV 89), 34–37.
IN WHAT IS CONSIDERED A TEST CASE FOR AFRICA, GHANA'S
PROGRAM TO REFORM THE EDUCATIONAL SECTOR IS PAYING OFF. WITH
PAST EFFORTS AND FUNDING FOCUSED ON HIGHER EDUCATION, THE
NEW THRUST IS ON PRIMARY AND SECONDARY SCHOOLING. REDUCING
SUBSIDIES TO UNIVERSITY STUDENTS, HOWEVER, IS PROVING
CONTROVERSIAL.

06499 MORNA, C.L.
ANGOLA: RAIL PROJECT OK'D
THIRD WORLD WEEK, 8(1) (MAR 89), 2–3.
ENCOURAGED BY THE DECEMBER 1988 PEACE ACCORD REACHED BY
SOUTH AFRICA, ANGOLA, AND CUBA, THE DONARS GROUP OF SADCC
HAS APPROVED AN AID PACKAGE AIMED AT EVENTUALLY REOPENING
THE BENGUELA RAILWAY. THE RAILWAY HAS BEEN ABLE TO PROVIDE
ONLY SPORADIC SERVICE SINCE ANGOLA WAS PLUNGED INTO CIVIL
WAR IN 1975. DESPITE THE PEACE AGREEMENT, THE SECURITY OF
THE RAIL LINE IS STILL A MAJOR CONCERN. SAVIMBI'S UNITA
REBELS ARE NOT A PARTY TO THE PACT AND U.S. PRESIDENT GEORGE
BUSH HAS PROMISED TO CONTINUE MILITARY AID TO SAVIMBI'S
MOVEMENT, WHICH ALSO RECEIVES SUPPORT FROM SOUTH AFRICA.

06500 MORNA, C.L.
ASHES AND DIAMONDS
AFRICA REPORT, 34(1) (JAN 89), 21–23.
AN ARDENT OPPONENT OF APARTHEID AND A STRONG SADCC AND
FRONTLINE SPOKESMAN, BOTSWANA IS NONETHELESS CLOSELY LINKED
TO ITS SOUTHERN NEIGHBOR. TWO AREAS CRITICAL TO BOTSWANA'S
ECONOMIC DEVELOPMENT, DIAMONDS AND A SALT-SODA ASH COMPLEX-
IN WHICH SOUTH AFRICAN CAPITAL PLAYS A MAJOR ROLE-PRESENT
GABORONE WITH A DILEMMA OF WHERE TO DRAW THE LINE WHERE
SANCTIONS BUSTING IS CONCERNED.

06501 MORNA, C.L.
BANDA'S QUARTER-CENTURY
AFRICA REPORT, 34(5) (SEP 89), 66–70.
ALTHOUGH MALAWI HAS ONE OF THE OLDEST STRUCTURAL
ADJUSTMENT PROGRAMS IN AFRICA AND HAS MADE IMPRESSIVE GAINS
IN AGRICULTURAL PRODUCTION, THE NATION'S TIES TO SOUTH
AFRICA, STRAINED RELATIONS WITH ITS NEIGHBORS, AND A MASSIVE
REFUGEE BURDEN ARE PROVIDING INCREASING CAUSE FOR CONCERN.
WITH THE LIFE PRESIDENT'S HUMAN RIGHTS RECORD BEING CALLED

INTO QUESTION, MALAWI'S FUTURE REMAINS UNCERTAIN.

06502 MORNA, C.L.
BEYOND THE DROUGHT
AFRICA REPORT, 34(6) (NOV 89), 30–33.
FROM 1981 TO 1987, WHEN BOTSWANA SUFFERED THE WORST
DROUGHT IN ITS HISTORY, PRESIDENT QUETT MASIRE'S DROUGHT
RELIEF PROGRAM COUPLED WITH NUTRITIONAL SURVEILLANCE AND AN
EARLY WARNING SYSTEM ENSURED THAT ADEQUATE FOOD SUPPLIES
WERE DISTRIBUTED THROUGHOUT THE COUNTRY. NOW THAT THE
DROUGHT SEEMS TO HAVE FINALLY BROKEN, BOTSWANA IS TURNING
ITS ATTENTION TO THE LONGER-TERM PROSPECTS FOR AGRICULTURE
WITH THE GOAL OF IMPROVING ITS SELF-SUFFICIENCY IN FOOD AND
ADOPTING NEW FARMING METHODS.

06503 MORNA, C.L.
DAMAS MBOGORO: THE BUSINESS OF DEVELOPMENT
AFRICA REPORT, 34(2) (MAR 89), 43–44.
TANZANIA'S MINISTER OF STATE FOR FINANCE, ECONOMIC
PLANNING, AND DEVELOPMENT, DAMAS MBOGORO ASSESSES THE IMF,
THE ACHIEVEMENTS OF TANZANIA'S ECONOMIC REFORM PROGRAM, AND
THE CHALLENGES THAT LIE AHEAD.

06504 MORNA, C.L.
ELECTION AFTERMATH
NEW AFRICAN, (259) (APR 89), 24–25.
IN DECEMBER 1988 GHANA EXPERIENCED THEIR FIRST
DEMOCRATIC ELECTIONS FOR NEARLY A DECADE. THE FACT THAT THE
DISTRICT COUNCIL ELECTION WERE HELD ON A NON-PARTISAN BASIS
AND WERE STAGGERED OVER A THREE MONTH PERIOD MADE THE
ELECTIONS A "NONSENSICAL EXERCISE" BY WESTERN STANDARDS.
HOWEVER, GHANA VIEWS THEM AS AN IMPORTANT FIRST STEP IN A
GRADUAL PROCESS OF MOVING AWAY FROM A CENTRALIZED,
AUTHORITARIAN GOVERNMENT.

06505 MORNA, C.L.
GOING HOME
AFRICA REPORT, 34(4) (JUL 89), 40–42.
SEVERAL THOUSAND MOZAMBICAN REFUGEES ARE EXPECTED TO
REPATRIATE THIS YEAR, AND EACH IS OF CONSIDERABLE POLITICAL
IMPORTANCE TO THE GOVERNMENT, WHICH IS ENCOURAGING THEM TO
COME HOME. BUT THE NUMBER OF REFUGEES WILL CONTINUE TO
EXCEED THE RETURNEES, SOME OF WHOM ARE FORCIBLY SENT BACK BY
SOUTH AFRICA OR ZIMBABWE.

06506 MORNA, C.L.
HARVEST IN THE KILLING GROUNDS
SOUTH, (105) (JUL 89), 42–43.
ALTHOUGH MOZAMBIQUE HAS YET TO SPELL OUT HOW IT INTENDS
TO END THE WAR ON ITS HOME FRONT, HOPES THAT THE CIVIL WAR
IS DRAWING TO A CLOSE ARE ENCOURAGING FOREIGN INVESTORS TO
START VENTURES IN THE WAR-TORN COUNTRY. OVER THE LAST TWO
YEARS, AN IMF-SPONSORED ECONOMIC REFORM PROGRAM AND A REVIEW
OF A DECADE OF RIGID ECONOMIC STATE CONTROL HAVE MADE
MOZAMBIQUE MORE ATTRACTIVE TO POTENTIAL INVESTORS. THE FOCUS
IS ON THE RESUSCITATION OF THE STATE-RUN AGRIBUSINESS.

06507 MORNA, C.L.
HOW DOES GHANA'S "ECONOMIC MIRACLE" LOOK FROM THE INSIDE?
AFRICAN BUSINESS, (NOV 88), 10–11.
THIS ARTICLE EXAMINES THE INTERNATIONAL MONETARY FUND'S
ECONOMIC REFORM PROGRAM IN GHANA. IT EXAMINES THE STANDARD
OF LIVING OF THE AVERAGE GHANAIAN CITIZEN AND THE EXODUS OF
GHANAIANS TO FIND WORK IN OTHER COUNTRIES. IT DESCRIBES
THIEVERY IN EVERY SECTOR OF EVERY ENTERPRISE AND GOVERNMENT
BUREAUCRACY AS WELL AS THE IMAGINATIVE EFFORTS TO EARN EXTRA
INCOME, AND THE DISCOURAGEMENT WHICH IS BECOMING WIDESPREAD
AMONG THE PEOPLE.

06508 MORNA, C.L.
LETTER FROM LUSAKA: KAUNDA'S CHALLENGES
AFRICA REPORT, 34(1) (JAN 89), 24.
KENNETH KAUNDA HAS WON A SIXTH TERM AS ZAMBIA'S
PRESIDENT. BUT THE BIGGER BATTLE LIES AHEAD AS KAUNDA MUST
GRAPPLE WITH AN ECONOMIC CRISIS. THE NEW ECONOMIC RECOVERY
PROGRAMME, INTRODUCED AFTER ZAMBIA BROKE WITH THE IMF IN
LATE 1986, IS WIDELY ACKNOWLEDGED TO BE INADEQUATE.

06509 MORNA, C.L.
REVOLUTION CHANGES ITS COURSE
SOUTH, (105) (JUL 89), 33–34.
AFTER YEARS OF AMBIVALENCE AND IDEOLOGICAL SOUL-
SEARCHING, ZIMBABWE HAS LAUNCHED ITS FIRST SERIOUS EFFORT TO
WOO LOCAL AND FOREIGN INVESTORS. FACED WITH AN AVERAGE
ECONOMIC PERFORMANCE AND RISING UNEMPLOYMENT, ROBERT
MUGABE'S GOVERNMENT HAS PRODUCED NEW GUIDELINES TO BOOST
INVESTMENT, WHICH HAS BEEN DISAPPOINTINGLY LOW SINCE 1980.

06510 MORNA, C.L.
SCHOOLED TO JOIN THE JOB QUEUES
SOUTH, (100) (FEB 89), 26–27.
SINCE AN INCREASING NUMBER OF AFRICANS BOAST SOME LEVEL
OF EDUCATION, UNEMPLOYMENT IS LIKELY TO BE THE KEY POLITICAL
AND ECONOMIC ISSUE IN THE 1990'S. ZAMBIA, ZIMBABWE, AND

BOTSWANA HAVE AS MANY PEOPLE UNEMPLOYED AS ARE EMPLOYED. EACH HAS OPTED FOR A DIFFERENT ECONOMIC APPROACH, THE SUCCESS OF WHICH WILL BE MEASURED BY THE NUMBER OF JOBS CREATED.

06511 MORNA, C.L.
STUDENTS DIG IN
NEW AFRICAN, (256) (JAN 89), 17-18.
GHANA'S UNIVERSITIES ABRUPTLY CLOSED AT MID-YEAR, DUE TO STUDENT UNREST. AT THE CENTER OF THE CONTROVERSY LAY A DISPUTE OVER GOVERNMENT SUBSIDIES TO HIGHER EDUCATION. THE WORLD BANK HAS RECOMMENDED THAT AFRICAN GOVERNMENTS SPEND LESS ON HIGHER EDUCATION, SO THE GHANAIAN GOVERNMENT WANTS TO ABOLISH ALL EDUCATION, FOOD, AND LODGING SUBSIDIES. BUT THE STUDENTS HAVE DEMANDED THAT THE PRESENT FOOD SUBSIDY BE TRIPLED.

06512 MORNA, C.L.
SURVIVING STRUCTURAL ADJUSTMENT
AFRICA REPORT, 34(5) (SEP 89), 45-48.
WHILE THE EFFECTIVENESS OF STRUCTURAL ADJUSTMENT IN PROMOTING AFRICA'S ECONOMIC GROWTH CONTINUES TO BE A POINT OF CONTROVERSY AMONG GOVERNMENT OFFICIALS AND THE INTERNATIONAL COMMUNITY, WHAT IS NOT IN DISPUTE IS THE OFTEN HEAVY IMPACT OF THE PROGRAMS ON THE NATION'S AVERAGE CITIZENS. THE HUMAN SIDE OF ECONOMIC REFORM IS EVIDENT ACROSS THE CONTINENT.

06513 MOROZIUK, R.P.
POLITICS AND ECUMENICS OF THE MILLENNIUM OF CHRISTIANITY IN KYIVAN RUS
UKRAINIAN QUARTERLY, XLV(3) (FAL 89), 318-331.
THE RUSSIAN ORTHODOX CHURCH HAS CLAIMED THE MILLENNIUM OF CHRISTIANITY IN KYIVAN RUS AS ITS OWN AND HAS MUCH OF THE WORLD BELIEVING THE LEGITIMACY OF THAT CLAIM. CONSEQUENTLY, WHAT HAS PREVAILED THROUGHOUT THE COMMEMORATIONS OF THE MILLENNIUM IS NOT THE TRUTH OF HISTORY, RELIGION, CULTURE, AND LEAST OF ALL CHRISTIANITY BUT OF POLITICS, ECCLESIASTICAL ASPIRATIONS, AND INSTITUTIONALISM. THE UKRAINIAN COMMUNITY FINDS THE INSTITUTIONAL, NATIONAL, AND POLITICAL IMPLICATIONS OF THE RUSSIAN ORTHODOX CHURCH'S CLAIM MOST DISTURBING. THE CLAIM IMPLIES THAT THE RUSSIAN ORTHODOX CHURCH HAS EXISTED INSTITUTIONALLY FOR 1000 YEARS. THIS IMPLIES THAT MODERN RUSSIANS ARE ETHNICALLY IDENTICAL TO THE PEOPLE OF KYIVAN RUS, WHICH LEADS TO THE CONCLUSION THAT THE MODERN RUSSIAN STATE HAS ALSO POLITICALLY EXISTED FOR 1000 YEARS.

06514 MORRIS, B.
NEW ADMINISTRATION FACES CHANGING EUROPE
EUROPE, (285) (APR 89), 16-17.
THE COMPLAINTS OF MANY PRIVATE GROUPS ABOUT THE POTENTIAL DANGERS TO US INTERESTS OF THE EUROPEAN INTEGRATION IN 1992 THREATENS TO PERCOLATE UP THROUGH THE SYSTEM AND POLLUTE THE BROADER POLITICAL RELATIONSHIP BETWEEN THE US AND THE EUROPEAN COMMUNITY. IN ORDER TO HEAD OFF THIS POTENTIAL CONFLICT, THE BUSH ADMINISTRATION IS CONSIDERING THE CREATION OF A SPECIAL UNIT THAT WOULD BE DEVOTED TO ALL ASPECTS OF A NEWLY INTEGRATED EUROPE. THE EMPHASIS WOULD PROBABLY BE ON A MULTIPOLAR, RATHER THAN BIPOLAR WORLD.

06515 MORRIS, C.T.: ADELMAN, I.
NINETEENTH-CENTURY DEVELOPMENT EXPERIENCE AND LESSONS FOR TODAY
WORLD DEVELOPMENT, 17(9) (SEP 89), 1417-1432.
IN SPITE OF IMPORTANT DIFFERENCES IN THE INTERNATIONAL AND TECHNOLOGICAL CONTEXTS OF GROWTH BETWEEN TODAY AND THE 19TH CENTURY, FUNDAMENTAL SIMILARITIES REMAIN. NOW AS THEN GOVERNMENT POLICIES DETERMINE THE NATURE OF MARKET SYSTEMS PROPERTY RIGHTS, AND THE DISTRIBUTION OF ASSETS, AND THUS HOW FAR DOMESTIC ECONOMIC GROWTH SPREADS. BUT FAVORABLE IMPACTS OF GOVERNMENT POLICIES ON THE STRUCTURE OF ECONOMIC GROWTH CAN BE EXPECTED ONLY WHERE POLITICAL INSTITUTIONS LIMIT ELITE CONTROL OF ASSETS. LAND INSTITUTIONS SPREAD A SURPLUS OVER SUBSISTENCE WIDELY, AND DOMESTIC EDUCATION AND SKILLS ARE WELL DIFFUSED.

06516 MORRIS, F.B.
WHAT CAN CENTRAL AMERICA EXPECT FROM THE BUSH ADMINISTRATION?
THE CHRISTIAN CENTURY, 106(15) (MAY 89), 472-475.
THE AUTHOR LOOKS AT THE SITUATION IN CENTRAL AMERICA AND SPECULATES ABOUT PRESIDENT BUSH'S POLICY THERE.

06517 MORRIS, J.
JUST SAY "YES" TO INFRASTRUCTURE
AMERICAN CITY AND COUNTY, 104(11) (NOV 89), 31-32, 34.
LOCAL GOVERNMENT OFFICIALS REPORT THAT THEIR OVERALL INFRASTRUCTURE IS INCREASINGLY DETERIORATING. THEIR STATEMENTS REFUTE THE FEDERAL GOVERNMENT'S CONTENTION THAT MUNICIPALITIES AND STATES HAVE THE CAPACITY TO REPAIR THEIR FACILITIES WITHOUT OUTSIDE HELP. LOCAL OFFICIALS, FACED WITH DWINDLING FUNDS AND ANGRY TAXPAYERS, SAY THAT THE PROBLEM OF

FINANCING REPAIRS AND NEW INFRASTRUCTURE IS A SERIOUS ONE. THEY ADD THAT BOTH FEDERAL AND STATE GOVERNMENTS MUST LOOK MORE CLOSELY AT THE COST OF WHAT THEY MANDATE AT THE LOCAL GOVERNMENT LEVEL.

06518 MORRIS, M.
SRI LANKA VOTES-OBSERVER TEAM MONITORS THE ELECTION IN BESIEGED ISLAND
PARLIAMENTARIAN, 70(3) (JUL 89), 136-139.
THE AUTHOR DISCUSSES FEBRUARY 1989 PARLIAMENTARY ELECTIONS IN SRI LANKA, FOCUSING ON THE MONITORING EFFORTS WHICH WERE CARRIED OUT BY AN INTERNATIONAL TEAM COMPRISED OF EIGHTEEN OBSERVERS FROM TEN COUNTRIES. WHO WERE INVITED BY ALL THE SRI LANKAN POLITICAL PARTIES. AID GIVEN BY THE SOUTH ASIAN ASSOCIATION FOR REGIONAL COOPERATION (SAARC) WHICH HAD CONDUCTED MONITORING OF THE NOVEMBER 1988 PRESIDENTIAL ELECTIONS, IS RECOGNIZED. THE CREATION OF NINE TEAMS EACH OF WHICH WERE HAD DIFFERENT NATIONALITIES REPRESENTED, METHODS WHICH WERE USED TO DEAL WITH ALLEGATIONS BY COMPETING PARTIES, AND THE EVENTS OF THE POLLING DAY ARE DETAILED.

06519 MORRIS, P.
UNIVERSITY CHALLENGE
NEW AFRICAN, (JAN 88), 21-22.
THIS ARTICLE EXAMINES THE SOUTH AFRICAN ATTEMPT TO CLAMP DOWN ON ANY INSTITUTIONS WHICH MIGHT POSSIBLY UNDERMINE ITS AUTHORITY. IT DEALS SPECIFICALLY WITH ITS THREAT TO WITHDRAW STATE SUBSITIES FROM UNIVERSITIES IF THEY DO NOT ADHERE TO STRICT NEW POLICING REGULATIONS OVER THEIR STAFF AND STUDENTS. IT DESCRIBES THE REACTION ON THE UNIVERSITIES WHICH IS TO FIGHT BACK, RATHER THAN SUPPORT GOVERNMENT POLICY.

06520 MORRIS, S.D.
THE CAUSES, CONSEQUENCES, AND DYNAMICS OF POLITICAL CORRUPTION IN MEXICO
DISSERTATION ABSTRACTS INTERNATIONAL, 49(11) (MAY 89), 3493-A.
THE OVERWHELMING POWER OF THE STATE AND THE RELATIVE WEAKNESS OF SOCIAL ORGANIZATIONS CREATE THE INCENTIVES FOR WIDESPREAD EXTORTION IN MEXICO. CORRUPTION ACTUALLY CONTRIBUTES TO POLITICAL STABILITY THERE BY INTEGRATING THE POLITICAL ELITE, CUSHIONING THE IMPACT OF POLICY, DISPLACING POLITICAL ACCOUNTABILITY, AND SERVING AS A SYMBOLIC DEVICE TO MOBILIZE SOCIETY. ALTHOUGH CORRUPTION HAS FOSTERED WIDESPREAD DISTRUST OF THE GOVERNMENT AND OFFICIALS AMONG THE PUBLIC, IT IS SEEN AS A NON-SYSTEMIC PROBLEM AND HENCE DOES NOT ERODE DIFFUSE SYSTEMS SUPPORT.

06521 MORRIS, S.J.
HO CHI MINK, POL POT, AND CORNELL
NATIONAL INTEREST, 16 (SUM 89), 49-62.
THE PARTISAN ROLE PLAYED BY CORNELL ACADEMICS IN THE PROPAGANDA AND COUNTERPROPAGANDA SURROUNDING THE 1965 COUP AND ITS AFTERMATH RESULTED IN THE NEW INDONESIAN GOVERNMENT DECLARING CORNELL AFFILIATES PERSONAE NON GRATA IN INDONESIA. THIS POLITICAL DEVELOPMENT COINCIDED WITH THE INTENSIFICATION OF THE AMERICAN MILITARY INVOLVEMENT IN THE WAR IN SOUTH VIETNAM, A PROCESS WHICH INCREASINGLY AGITATED MANY AMERICAN ACADEMICS. ALTHOUGH CORNELL COULD NOT BOAST RECOGNIZED SCHOLARS ON VIETNAMESE AFFAIRS, ITS SOUTHEAST ASIA PROGRAM BECAME INCREASINGLY FOCUSED ON VIETNAM, AND SOON BEGAN TO ATTRACT GRADUATE STUDENTS AND OTHERS WHO HAD BECOME PROGRESSIVELY MORE ABSORBED IN THE POLITICS OF THE WAR.

06522 MORRIS, S.R.
BUDGET CUTBACK: AN EMPIRICAL TEST OF BUDGETING THEORY IN CONDITIONS OF FINANCIAL STRESS
DISSERTATION ABSTRACTS INTERNATIONAL, 49(10) (APR 89), 3151-A.
THE AUTHOR TESTS THE APPLICABILITY OF INCREMENTALISM TO THE BUDGET PROCESS WHEN CHANGES OCCUR IN FINANCIAL AND POLITICAL STABILITY, LEADING TO SLOWER GROWTH. SHE ASSESSES THE RESPONSE OF BUDGETARY DECISION-MAKERS UNDER CONDITIONS OF CYCLICAL AND PROTRACTED FISCAL STRESS. HER STUDY USES DATA DRAWN FROM MICHIGAN STATE GOVERNMENT FROM 1963 TO 1984.

06523 MORRIS, T.M.
REFUGEE RESETTLEMENT: THE ROLE OF PUBLIC ASSISTANCE
DISSERTATION ABSTRACTS INTERNATIONAL, 49(11) (MAY 89), 3501-A.
USING ALAMEDA COUNTY, CALIFORNIA, AS A CASE STUDY, THE AUTHOR PROBES THE INTERACTION BETWEEN PROGRAM RESPONSES TO REFUGEE RESETTLEMENT AND THE REFUGEES' RESETTLEMENT PROBLEMS. SHE USES A THEORETICAL FRAMEWORK THAT DESCRIBES REFUGEE RESETTLEMENT AS THE INTERACTION AMONG THE CONTEXT OF MIGRATION, THE ORIENTATION OF THE HOST SOCIETY, AND THE ORIENTATION OF THE REFUGEE GROUP. THEN SHE PROCEEDS TO AN EMPIRICAL STUDY FOCUSING ON THE SECOND AND THIRD FACTORS OF THE THEORETICAL FRAMEWORK.

06524 MORRISON, M.
PRESCRIPTIONS FOR THE MIDDLE EAST

AMERICAN SPECTATOR, 22(1) (JAN 89), 16-18.
THE AUTHOR RECOMMENDS FROM GUIDELINES FOR A CREATIVE,
SENSIBLE U.S. ROLE IN THE ARAB ISRAELI DISPUTE: 1)
REACTIVATE THE OFFICE OF SPECIAL MIDDLE EAST ENVOY; 2) SEND
A DIRECT MESSAGE TO MODERATE PALESTIANIANS; 3) OPERATE IN
THE POLITICAL CULTURE OF THE MIDDLE EAST, NOT HE WEST; 4) BE
REALISTIC ABOUT TIME REQUIRED FOR FINAL SETTLEMENT.

06525 MORRISON, M.
THE ROAD TO REVOLT IN CHINA
AMERICAN SPECTATOR, (NOV 89), 14-16.
THIS ARTICLE RECOUNTS VICTORY AND DEFEAT IN TIANANMEN
SQUARE IN CHINA, JUNE 1989. TOLD BY THE DEMOCRACY MOVEMENT'S
INTELLIGENCE CHIEF, XIN KU, IT RECOUNTS HIS RISE TO POWER IN
STUDENT LEADERSHIP. IT GIVES THE BACK GROUND LEADING TO THE
DEMONSTRATIONS, DETAILS GORBACHEV'S VISIT, THE HORROR OF THE
TANKS IN JUNE, AND RECAPS KU'S PRESENT FEELINGS ABOUT THE
ATTEMPT.

06526 MORRISON, M.
THE YELLOWSTONE SCAM
AMERICAN SPECTATOR, 22(8) (AUG 89), 17-20.
THIS ARTICLE REPORTS ON THE CONNING OF THE PRESIDENT,
THE PRESS AND THE PUBLIC BY THE NATIONAL PARK SERVICE. IT
FOCUSES ON THE FIRES OF '88 IN YELLOWSTONE PARK AND THEIR
POLITICAL AND ECONOMIC REPERCUSSIONS. IT PREDICTS THAT A
COVERUP COULD RESHAPE THE TRADITIONAL CULTURE OF THE
AMERICAN WEST.

06527 MORROW, J.D.
A TWIST OF TRUTH: A REEXAMINATION OF THE EFFECTS OF ARMS
RACES ON THE OCCURRENCE OF WAR
JOURNAL OF CONFLICT RESOLUTION, 33(3) (SEP 89), 500-529.
THIS ARTICLE CONSIDERS THE EFFECTS OF ARMS RACES ON THE
OCCURRENCE OF WARS. EXISTING EVIDENCE ON THE LINK BETWEEN
ARMS RACES AND WARS SUGGESTS THAT ARMS RACES DO NOT
NECESSARILY CAUSE WARS, BUT THAT SOME ARMS RACES END IN WAR
AND OTHERS DO NOT. WHY? THIS ARTICLE PROPOSES AN ANSWER TO
THIS QUESTION BY EXAMINING THE MOTIVATIONS OF EACH RACING
NATION TO GO TO WAR BY EXPRESSING THOSE MOTIVATIONS IN
UTILITY TERMS. SWINGS IN MILITARY SUPERIORITY BETWEEN THE
RACING POWERS PROVOKED BY THE RACE CREATE A MOTIVATION FOR
WAR TO EXPLOIT TEMPORARY ADVANTAGES. RISK-ACCEPTANT ACTORS
ARE MORE LIKELY TO INITIATE ARMS RACE WARS, AND RISK-AVERSE
ACTORS ARE MORE LIKELY TO RESIST THEIR THREATS. THE
CONCLUSIONS OF THE ARGUMENT ARE TESTED AND SUPPORTED
ROBUSTLY BUT NOT STRONGLY.

06528 MORROW, J.D.
CAPABILITIES, UNCERTAINTY, AND RESOLVE: A LIMITED
INFORMATION MODEL OF CRISIS BARGAINING
AMERICAN JOURNAL OF POLITICAL SCIENCE, 33(4) (NOV 89),
941-972.
THIS PAPER PRESENTS AND SOLVES A CRISIS BARGAINING GAME
UNDER LIMITED INFORMATION. THE SIDES ALTERNATE OFFERS FROM
THREE POSSIBLE OFFERS, WITH WAR AND ITS COSTS STARTING IF
THE TARGET'S COUNTEROFFER IS REJECTED. THE EQUILIBRIUM OF
THE MODEL FALLS INTO FOUR DIFFERENT CASES. THESE FOUR CASES
ARE ANALYZED TO DETERMINE HOW THE SIDES COMMUNICATE THROUGH
THEIR OFFERS AND HOW THE COSTS OF WAR, INITIAL BELIEFS,
MISPERCEPTIONS, AND DISTRIBUTION OF CAPABILITIES DRIVE THE
PROBABILITIES OF A CRISIS AND WAR. THE MODEL DEMONSTRATES A
JOINT SELECTION BIAS-MISSPECIFICATION PROBLEM IN EMPIRICAL
STUDIES OF CRISES ARISING FROM THE UNOBSERVABLE NATURE OF
BELIEFS. SEVERAL EMPIRICAL STUDIES OF CRISIS BARGAINING ARE
DISCUSSED IN THE LIGHT OF THIS METHODOLOGICAL PROBLEM, NEW
PATTERNS OF EVIDENCE ARE FOUND THAT SUPPORT THE PRESENCE OF
THE SELECTION PROBLEM, AND THEIR CONCLUSIONS ARE REEXAMINED.

06529 MORSE, S.W.
THE ROLE OF COLLEGES AND UNIVERSITIES IN DEVELOPING A NEW
KIND OF PUBLIC LEADER
NATIONAL CIVIC REVIEW, 78(6) (NOV 89), 439-455.
PREVAILING CYNICAL ATTITUDES TOWARD POLITICS AS IT IS
TOO COMMONLY PRACTICED--A "WIN/LOSE" GAME, BASED MORE ON
PERSONALITIES THAN POLICIES--HAVE MADE CITIZENS, ESPECIALLY
YOUTHFUL ONES, SUSPICIOUS OF PUBLIC LIFE AND ACTIVE
LEADERSHIP. THIS ARTICLE PRESENTS AN INNOVATIVE WAKE FOREST
UNIVERSITY (WINSTON-SALEM, N.C.) PROGRAM DESIGNED TO
SUPPLEMENT TRADITIONAL POST-SECONDARY EDUCATION WITH
PREPARATION FOR PUBLIC LIFE AND FIRST-HAND PARTICIPATION IN
COMMUNITY ISSUES.

06530 MORSY, L. A.
BRITAINS WARTIME POLICY IN EGYPT, 1940-42
MIDDLE EASTERN STUDIES, 25(1) (JAN 89), 64-94.
ANGLO-EGYPTIAN RELATIONS DURING THIS PERIOD CANNOT BE
DISCUSSED WITHOUT CONSIDERATION OF THE PAST HISTORY OF
BRITISH RELATIONS WITH EGYPT. THESE RELATIONS HAD BEEN TO
TWO KINDS: RELATIONS WITH EGYPT ITSELF AND RELATIONS WITH
OTHER EUROPEAN POWERS SEEKING INFLUENCE THERE. FOR EGYPT HAS
SERVED AS BOTH A HIGHWAY OF TRADE AND A PASSAGE FOR CONQUEST,
AND ON BOTH ACCOUNTS, GREAT BRITAIN EVENTUALLY BECAME
INVOLVED. THE ANGLO-EGYPTIAN TREATY DID NOT ALTER THE BASES

ON WHICH ANGLO-EGYPTIAN RELATIONS WERE POISED. MOREOVER THE
OUTBREAK OF THE SECOND WORLD WAR EMPHASIZED THE STRATEGIC
IMPORTANCE OF THE SUEZ CANAL, THE NODAL POINT IN BRITISH
DEFENCE PLANS. WHILE THE WAR LASTED, POLITICAL AND MILITARY
CONTROL OVER EGYPT WAS VITAL TO BRITAIN.

06531 MORTIMER, J.
IKIBINE DOGRU: THE THORN IN THE TURKISH GOVERNMENT'S SIDE
MIDDLE EAST INTERNATIONAL, (344) (FEB 89), 19-20.
IN LESS THAN TWO YEARS OF PUBLICATION, "IKIBINE DOGRU"
HAS BECOME TURKEY'S MOST INFLUENTIAL MAGAZINE. LIBERALS
RESPECT IT FOR ITS REVELATIONS ABOUT CORRUPTION AND HUMAN
RIGHTS WHILE RIGHT-WINGERS LAMBAST IT FOR WAGING COMMUNIST
PSYCHOLOGICAL WARFARE THROUGH ATTACKS ON TURKISH
INSTITUTIONS. THE GOVERNMENT OF PRIME MINISTER TURGUT OZAL
TOOK THE PUBLISHERS TO COURT 21 TIMES IN 18 MONTHS.

06532 MORTIMER, R.A.
MAGHREB MATTERS
FOREIGN POLICY, (76) (FAL 89), 160-175.
THIS PAPER EXAMINES A STRING OF EXTRAORDINARY
DEVELOPMENTS IN NORTH AFRICA CAPPED BY THE FEBRUARY 1989
CREATION OF THE ARAB MAGHREB UNION WHICH CALLS FOR NEW
THINKING ABOUT U.S. POLICY TOWARDS THIS KEY REGION OF THE
ARAB WORLD. IT DESCRIBES THE RISING REGIONALISM AND THE
FACTORS INVOLVED IN THE FORMING OF THE UNION. EXPLORED IS
THE POSSIBILITY TO RESOLVE CRUCIAL POLICY PROBLEMS IN THE
ARAB EAST, INCLUDING THE PALESTINIAN QUESTION.

06533 MOSHER, S.
THE CHINA SYNDROME
REASON, 21(5) (OCT 89), 22-25; 27-28.
THE MASSACRE AT TIANANMEN SQUARE REVEALED THE
CONTRADICTION AT THE HEART OF THE UNITED STATES POLICY WITH
REGARDS TO CHINA: THE US HAS TRIED TO WEAN COMMUNIST STATES
AWAY FROM THEIR MARXIST-LENINIST EXTREMES, BUT THE
DEMOCRATIC MOVEMENT THAT WAS INSPIRED BY THE EXAMPLE OF THE
US WAS CRUSHED BY ORTHODOX MARXISTS WHOSE ECONOMY THE US
HELPED STRENGTHEN AND WHOSE ARMY THE US HELPED TO MODERNIZE.
THE ARTICLE EXPLORES THE US REACTION TO THE PRO-DEMOCRACY
MOVEMENT IN CHINA AND TO ITS REPRESSION. IT CONCLUDES THAT
US POLICYMAKERS ARE MORE CONCERNED WITH BILATERAL RELATIONS
THAN FOSTERING DEMOCRACY.

06534 MOSHER, S.W.
PEKING'S POPULATION PROGRAM: STILL COERCIVE?
ASIAN OUTLOOK, 24(4) (JUL 89), 27-28.
IN RECENT MONTHS, THE CHINESE GOVERNMENT HAS MADE
STRENUOUS EFFORTS TO IMPROVE THE IMAGE OF ITS POPULATION
CONTROL PROGRAM. COMMUNIST OFFICIALS HAVE ADMITTED THAT
"OVERZEALOUS" CADRES IN THE PAST FORCED WOMEN TO HAVE
ABORTIONS AGAINST THEIR WILL BUT CLAIM THAT SUCH ABUSES HAVE
NOW BEEN CURBED. FEMALE INFANTICIDE IS ALSO DECLINING
BECAUSE RURAL COUPLES ARE ALLOWED TO HAVE A SECOND CHILD IF
THEIR FIRST IS A GIRL.

06535 MOSHER, S.W.
THE TRAGEDY OF AMERICA'S COMMUNIST CHINA POLICY
ASIAN OUTLOOK, 24(4) (JUL 89), 30-31.
IN THE WAKE OF THE BLOODY ASSAULT BY THE PEOPLE'S
LIBERATION ARMY ON THE CITIZENS OF PEKING, THE REACTION OF
THE FOREIGN POLICY ESTABLISHMENT OF THE UNITED STATES HAS
BEEN LIMP ACQUIESCENCE. THE FAILURE OF THE BUSH
ADMINISTRATION TO RESOLUTELY CONDEMN COMMUNIST CHINA'S
ACTIONS AND FOLLOW THAT WITH STRICT SANCTIONS IS PUZZLING.
BUT THE BUSH ADMINISTRATION IS NOT THE FIRST TO TREAT
COMMUNIST CHINA AS THE HUMAN RIGHTS EXCEPTION. GROSS
VIOLATIONS OF HUMAN RIGHTS BY THE CHINESE COMMUNISTS HAVE
BEEN GLOSSED OVER OR IGNORED IN SUCCESSIVE ADMINISTRATIONS,
FROM NIXON TO REAGAN.

06536 MOSIKARE, N.
TODAY'S GENERATION: THE UDF TREASON TRIAL
SECHABA, 23(2) (FEB 89), 24-26.
THE ARTICLE RECOUNTS THE RECENT TRIAL OF FOUR PROMINENT
LEADERS OF THE UNITED DEMOCRATIC FRONT (UDF). IT ARGUES THAT
THE BIAS EVIDENT IN THE COURT PROCEEDINGS IS PROOF THAT
PRETORIA'S CLAIMS OF REFORM ARE HOLLOW. THE SENTENCES WERE
GENERALLY THOUGHT TO BE MORE LENIENT THAN EXPECTED, BUT THE
ENTIRE PROCESS WAS VIEWED AS A "TRAVESTY OF JUSTICE."

06537 MOSKIN, J.R.
A TALK WITH YITZHAK SHAMIR
PRESENT TENSE, 16(4) (MAY 89), 29-33.
YITZHAK SHAMIR FIRST SAT BEHIND THE DESK OF THE PRIME
MINISTER OF ISRAEL IN 1983 AFTER THE RESIGNATION OF MENACHEM
BEGIN. FROM 1955 TO 1965 SHAMIR HELD A SENIOR POST IN
ISRAEL'S INTELLIGENCE SERVICE, THE MOSSAD. IN 1970 HE BECAME
ACTIVE IN POLITICS AND WAS ELECTED TO THE KNESSET IN 1973.
WHEN THE LIKUD FIRST WON POWER IN 1977, HE WAS ELECTED
SPEAKER OF THE KNESSET AND IN 1980 BECAME FOREIGN MINISTER.
IN THIS INTERVIEW SHAMIR TOUCHES ON THE CONFLICT BETWEEN
ARAB AND JEW, THE INTIFADA, THE QUESTION OF WHO IS A JEW,
THE SPREAD OF FUNDAMENTALISM AND THE ROLE OF AMERICAN JEWS.

06538 MOSSE, G.L.
FASCISM AND THE FRENCH REVOLUTION
JOURNAL OF CONTEMPORARY HISTORY, 24(1) (JAN 89), 5-26.
THE FRENCH REVOLUTION AS A HISTORICAL EVENT DID NOT PLAY
A CRUCIAL ROLE IN FASCIST THOUGHT OR IMAGINATION, AT LEAST
ON A CONSCIOUS LEVEL. BUT THE REVOLUTION DID PROVIDE AN
IMPORTANT BACKGROUND FOR THE FASCIST CONCEPTION OF POLITICS.
IT CREATED A CIVIL RELIGION THAT MODERN NATIONALISM MADE ITS
OWN, AND FASCISM HAS, ABOVE ALL, A NATIONALIST MOVEMENT.
MOREOVER, SOME FASCISMS, ALMOST IN SPITE OF THEMSELVES, DID
SHOW SOME CONTINUITY OF MIND WITH THE FRENCH REVOLUTION. THE
RELATIONSHIP BETWEEN FASCISM AND THE REVOLUTION INVOLVED A
GENERAL REORIENTATION OF POST-REVOLUTIONARY EUROPEAN
POLITICS, RATHER THAN SPECIFIC POINTS OF CONTACT.

06539 MOTE, M.E.
ELECTING THE USSR CONGRESS OF PEOPLE'S DEPUTIES
PROBLEMS OF COMMUNISM, XXXVIII(6) (NOV 89), 51-56.
THE SPRING 1989 ELECTIONS TO THE CONGRESS OF PEOPLE'S
DEPUTIES IN THE SOVIET UNION DID NOT SHIFT POWER AWAY FROM
THE COMMUNIST PARTY AND THE EXISTING ADMINISTRATIVE
APPARATUS, BUT THEY DID ENHANCE THE POWER OF GENERAL
SECRETARY MIKHAIL GORBACHEV. THE ELECTION CAMPAIGN WAS SEEN
AS A WAY TO CULTIVATE NEW PATTERNS OF POLITICAL BEHAVIOR,
WITH THE STORMY DEBATES IN THE NEW CONGRESS BEING THE MOST
SALIENT RESULT SO FAR.

06540 MOTOHARU, O.
CHINA'S ECONOMIC REFORM ON TRIAL
JAPAN QUARTERLY, XXXVI(3) (JUL 89), 256-262.
THE AUTHOR ASSESSES THE STATUS OF CHINA'S ECONOMIC
REFORM AND LIBERALIZATION PROGRAM, WHICH HAD BEEN IN
PROGRESS FOR ONE WHOLE DECADE AT THE END OF 1988.

06541 MOTOO, A.
FOREIGN AID: A DISSENTER'S VIEW
JAPAN ECHO, XVI(1) (SPR 89), 19-22.
THE AUTHOR, WHO IS A MEMBER OF THE JAPANESE HOUSE OF
REPRESENTATIVES, QUESTIONS THE WISDOM OF JAPAN'S OVERSEAS
DEVELOPMENT AID PROGRAM.

06542 MOTT, J. C.
THE FATE OF AN ALLIANCE: THE ROOSEVELT COALITION, 1932-1952
DISSERTATION ABSTRACTS INTERNATIONAL, 49(8) (FEB 89),
2367-A.
THE AUTHOR TRACES THE HISTORY OF THE ROOSEVELT COALITION
IN PRESIDENTIAL ELECTIONS. BY ANALYZING THE VOTING PATTERNS
OF DEMOCRATIC VOTERS ALONG DEMOGRAPHIC AND IDEOLOGICAL LINES,
HE SEEKS TO DISCOVER HOW THEY PERCEIVED EVENTS AROUND THEM
AND HOW THEY CHANGED OVER TIME.

06543 MOTYL, A.J.
REASSESSING THE SOVIET CRISIS: BIG PROBLEMS, MUDDLING
THROUGH, BUSINESS AS USUAL
POLITICAL SCIENCE QUARTERLY, 104(2) (SUM 89), 269-280.
SOVIETOLOGISTS COMMONLY PERCEIVE THE SOVIET UNION TO BE
IN THE THROES OF WHAT THEY CALL "CRISIS." THEIR RESULTING
ANALYSIS OF THE CURRENT SITUATION IN THE USSR AND THE
PROGNOSIS FOR THE FUTURE SUFFERS FROM THE CONCEPTUAL
CONFUSION SURROUNDING THE WORD "CRISIS" AND IS BASED ON FOUR
METHODOLOGICAL ERRORS: CIRCULARITY OF REASONING,
SUBSTITUTION OF PROJECTION FOR PREDICTION, AHISTORICITY, AND
LACK OF COMPARATIVE PERSPECTIVE. BY DISTORTING CONCEPTS, BY
ASSUMING WHAT THEY INTEND TO PROVE, BY PROJECTING CURRENT
TRENDS INTO THE FUTURE, BY IGNORING LONG-TERM DEVELOPMENTS,
AND BY OVERLOOKING THE INTERNATIONAL CONTEXT, SCHOLARS
INEVITABLY SKEW THEIR UNDERSTANDING OF CONTEMPORARY
DEVELOPMENTS IN THE USSR.

06544 MOUDDEN, A.M.
MALTHUSIAN DEVELOPMENT AND POLITICAL WEAKNESS OF MOROCCO'S
INDUSTRIAL BOURGEOISIE
DISSERTATION ABSTRACTS INTERNATIONAL, 49(8) (FEB 89),
2378-A.
THE AUTHOR ASSESSES THE SOCI-POLITICAL IMPACT OF LATE
MODERNIZATION ON MOROCCO BY FOCUSING ON THE RELATIONSHIP
BETWEEN THE STATE AND THE INDUSTRIAL BOURGEOISIE. THIS
RELATIONSHIP HAS BEEN CHARACTERIZED BY THE INCREASE OF THE
CORPORATE POWER OF THE BOURGEOISIE, THE EXPANSION OF ITS
CAPITAL, ITS HISTORICAL PREDOMINANCE OVER THE ECONOMIC
SPHERE, AND ITS INABILITY TO TRANSLATE THIS CORPORATE POWER
INTO POLITICAL POWER.

06545 MOUGHRABI, F.
PUBLIC OPINION: PUBLIC POLICY AND THE ISREALI-PALESTINIAN
CONFLICT
AMERICAN-ARAB AFFAIRS, (30) (FAL 89), 40-51.
THIS ARTICLE EXAMINES THE EFFECT OF THE INTIFADA ON
INTERNATIONAL AND AMERICAN PUBLIC OPINION WHICH HAS BEEN SO
GREAT THAT A WIDE GAP NOW SEPARATES PUBLIC ATTITUDES, WHICH
ARE CRITICAL OF ISRAEL'S BEHAVIOR, AND U.S. GOVERNMENT
POLICY IN THE REGION. IT EXPLORES MASS-PUBLIC AND ELITE
OPINION AND THE GAP BETWEEN PUBLIC SENTIMENT AND POLICY

DECISIONS, AS WELL AS SHIFTS IN JEWISH-AMERICAN ATTITUDES.
IT THEN EXPLORES THE OPTIONS FOR AMERICAN SUPPORT IN THE
FUTURE.

06546 MOUGHRABI, F.; EL-NAZER, P.
WHAT DO PALESITINIAN AMERICANS THINK? RESULTS OF A PUBLIC
OPINION SURVEY
JOURNAL OF PALESTINE STUDIES, XVIII(4) (SUM 89), 91-101.
THE ARTICLE SUMMARIZES THE RESULTS OF A PUBLIC OPINION
POLL OF PALESTINIAN-AMERICANS RESIDING IN THE UNITED STATES.
THE PURPOSE OF THE SURVEY IS THE DISCOVER THE OPINIONS OF
RESPONDENTS ON A HOST OF ISSUES: THE EXTENT OF SUPPORT FOR
THE PALESTINE LIBERATION ORGANIZATION; ATTITUDES TOWARDS
KNOWN PALESTINIAN LEADERS; THE RANGE OF ACTIVITIES THAT
REINFORCE POLITICAL VIEWS; ATTITUDES TOWARD VARIOUS
SCENARIOS FOR A SETTLEMENT OF THE ISRAELI-PALESTINIAN
CONFLICT; ATTITUDES TOWARD AMERICA'S ROLE IN THE CONFLICT;
AND POLITICAL ASPIRATIONS. THE SURVEY REVEALS THAT
PALESTINIANS IN AMERICA ARE A HIGHLY EDUCATED AND
POLITICALLY ACTIVE COMMUNITY WHICH HOVERS AROUND THE MIDDLE
OF THE POLITICAL SPECTRUM AND SUPPORTS THE PLO AND ARAFAT AS
ITS LEADER. THEY PREFER POLITICAL NEGOTIATIONS AND CIVIL
DISOBEDIENCE TO ARMED STRUGGLE AND EXPECT THE U.S. TO PLAY A
KEY ROLE IN RESOLVING THE PROBLEM.

06547 MOUHAMMED, A.
TOWARD A DEVELOPMENTAL APPROACH TO THE BALANCE OF PAYMENTS
FOR LDC'S: SOME GENERAL CONSIDERATIONS
SCANDINAVIAN JOURNAL OF DEVELOPMENT ALTERNATIVES, VIII(2)
(JUN 89), 111-122.
IN ECONOMIC LITERATURE THERE HAVE BEEN SEVERAL BASIC
THEORETICAL MODELS OF ANALYZING THE PROBLEMS OF THE BALANCE
OF PAYMENTS. THE STUDY EXAMINES SEVERAL OF THESE INCLUDING
THE CLASSICAL, KEYNESIAN, AND "ABSORPTION" EXPENDITURE
APPROACH AND ANALYZES THEIR UTILITY WITH REGARDS TO LESSER
DEVELOPED COUNTRIES (LDC'S). THE STUDY FINDS ALL OF THE
CURRENT METHODS LACKING AND COUNTERPRODUCTIVE AND ATTEMPTS
TO ESTABLISH A COMPREHENSIVE DEVELOPMENTAL MODEL CAPABLE OF
RESOLVING LDC BALANCE OF PAYMENT PROBLEMS AS WELL AS FOSTER
RAPID GROWTH AND STRUCTURAL TRANSFORMATION OF LDC'S.

06548 MOUL, W. B.
MEASURING THE "BALANCES OF POWER": A LOOK AT SOME NUMBERS
REVIEW OF INTERNATIONAL STUDIES, 15(2) (APR 89), 101-121.
THE PURPOSE OF THIS PAPER IS TO EXAMINE CRITICALLY SOME
MEASURES OF POWER CAPABILITIES USED IN SYSTEMATIC EMPIRICAL
STUDIES OF GREAT POWER CONFLICT SINCE THE CONGRESS OF VIENNA,
AND TO SUGGEST WHY SOME ARE BETTER THAN OTHERS. THE FIRST
STEP IS TO DEFINE 'BALANCE OF POWER'. THAT DEFINITION
PROVIDES TWO BASIC PRINCIPLES TO BE USED TO DISTINGUISH GOOD
MEASURES FROM POORER ONES, AND TWO MORE GENERAL PRINCIPLES
EMERGE EASILY FROM THE DISCUSSION. PUT BRIEFLY, THESE
PRINCIPLES OF MEASUREMENT ARE: (1) CONTEXT IS CRUCIAL; (2)
DIRECT MEASURES ARE SIMPLE, VALID AND RARE; (3), WHEN, AS IS
MORE OFTEN THAN NOT THE CASE, MEASUREMENT IS INDIRECT,
SIMPLE INFERENCES ARE BETTER THAN COMPLEX ONES; (4) IT IS
BETTER TO CONSERVE THAN DISREGARD HISTORICAL INFORMATION.

06549 MOUL, W.B.
GREAT POWER NONDEFENSE ALLIANCES AND THE ESCALATION TO WAR
OF CONFLICTS BETWEEN UNEQUALS, 1815-1939
INTERNATIONAL INTERACTIONS, 15(1) (1988), 25-43.
ESTIMATES OF HOW OTHER GREAT POWERS WOULD ACT IF WAR
WERE TO OCCUR ARE FUNDAMENTAL TO A DECISION BY A PREDATORY
GREAT POWER TO WAGE WAR AGAINST A MUCH WEAKER STATE. AN
ENTENTE OR NEUTRALITY AGREEMENT WITH A RIVAL GREAT POWER IS
MEANT TO REDUCE DECISIONAL UNCERTAINTY CONCERNING THE THE
SCOPE OF THE CONFLICT WITH A NONGREAT POWER. THE FIRMNESS OF
THE ALLIANCE OF RESTRAINT (NEUTRALITY PACT; ENTENTE; NO
ALLIANCE) VARIES WITH GEOPOLITICAL LOCATION OF THE NONGREAT
POWER TARGET. DURING 1815-1939 NONDEFENSE ALLIANCE
COMMITEMENTS BETWEEN GREAT POWERS ENCOURAGED THE ESCALATION
TO WAR OF UNEQUAL INTERSTATE CONFLICTS.

06550 MOURITZEN, P.E.
CITY SIZE AND CITIZENS' SATISFACTION: TWO COMPETING
THEORIES REVISITED
EUROPEAN JOURNAL OF POLITICAL RESEARCH, 17(6) (NOV 89),
661-688.
THE REFORM THEORY AND THE POLITICAL ECONOMY THEORY
POSTULATE CONTRADICTORY EFFECTS OF GOVERNMENT SIZE ON
CITIZENS' SATISFACTION WITH URBAN SERVICES. THE FORMER
ASSERTS THAT CITIZENS' SATISFACTION INCREASES WITH
INCREASING SIZE OF URBAN GOVERNMENTS BECAUSE LARGE UNITS ARE
MORE EFFICIENT AND ALLOW CITIZENS TO PARTICIPATE EFFECTIVELY
IN PUBLIC POLICY-MAKING. THE LATTER POSTULATES THAT CITIZENS
ARE MORE SATISFIED IN THE SMALLER JURISDICTIONS BECAUSE
SMALL UNITS ARE MORE HOMOGENEOUS, EFFICIENT AND DEMOCRATIC.
A SERIES OF TESTS PERFORMED IN THIS STUDY OVERWHELMINGLY
SUPPORTS THE POLITICAL ECONOMY THEORY: CITIZENS IN SMALL
JURISDICTIONS HOLD MORE FAVOURABLE ATTITUDES TOWARDS
PARTICIPATION AND DEMOCRACY, AND THE SMALLER UNITS ARE MORE
HOMOGENEOUS AND MORE EFFICIENT IN THE PROVISION OF SERVICES.
THIS IN TURN LEADS TO MORE FAVOURABLE EVALUATIONS OF PUBLIC

SERVICES.

06551 MOUW, C.J.
CONGRESSIONAL ELECTIONS AND THE STRATEGIC BEHAVIOR OF
ELITES: THE ROLE OF PARTY ORGANIZATION
DISSERTATION ABSTRACTS INTERNATIONAL, 50(3) (SEP 89),
785-A.
THE AUTHOR PROBES THE ROLE OF AMERICAN POLITICAL PARTY
ORGANIZATIONS IN THE US HOUSE OF REPRESENTATIVE ELECTIONS.
HE USES AS THIS BASE JOSEPH SCHLESINGER'S THEORY OF PARTY
ORGANIZATION, WHICH PORTRAYS PARTIES AS RATIONAL
ORGANIZATIONS THAT DEVELOP CALCULI BASED UPON INDIVIDUAL AND
COLLECTIVE DECISION-MAKING.

06552 MOUZELIS, N.
POLITICAL TRANSITIONS IN GREECE AND ARGENTINA TOWARD A
REORIENTATION OF MARXIST POLITICAL THEORY
COMPARATIVE POLITICAL STUDIES, 21(4) (JAN 89), 443-466.
IN THIS ARTICLE AN ATTEMPT IS MADE BOTH TO UTILIZE THE
ECONOMISTIC, REDUCTIONIST FEATURES OF MARXIST POLITICAL
THEORY AND TO SUGGEST CONCEPTUAL TOOLS FOR OVERCOMING SUCH
FEATURES. THE UTILITY OF THE CONCEPTUAL FRAMEWORK PROPOSED
IS DEMONSTRATED BY APPLYING IT TO THE ANALYSIS OF POLITICAL
DEVELOPMENTS IN TWO LATE-INDUSTRIALIZING SOCIETIES:
ARGENTINA AND GREECE.

06553 MOWBRAY, A.R.
ADMINISTRATIVE GUIDANCE: A PUBLIC LAW STUDY
DISSERTATION ABSTRACTS INTERNATIONAL, 49(10) (APR 89),
3515-A.
THIS DISSERTATION EXAMINES THE CHARACTERISTICS OF
ADMINISTRATIVE GUIDANCE AND NOTES THE SIGNIFICANCE OF THESE
PROVISIONS FOR OFFICIAL DECISION-MAKING AFFECTING
INDIVIDUALS AND GROUPS; CONSIDERS THE ORGANIZATIONAL CONTEXT
WITHIN WHICH ADMINISTRATIVE GUIDANCE IS CREATED AND UTILIZED;
PLACES THE ADVOCACY OF ADMINISTRATIVE RULEMAKING AS A
STRATEGY FOR CONTROLLING ADMINISTRATIVE DISCRETION WITHIN
ITS AMERICAN CONSTITUTIONAL FRAMEWORK THROUGH AN EXAMINATION
OF THE FEDERAL JUDICIAL AND LEGISLATIVE REACTIONS TO SUCH
PROVISIONS; ANALYZES THE RESPONSES OF THE PARLIAMENTARY
COMMISSIONER FOR ADMINISTRATION, THE COURTS, AND V.A.T.
TRIBUNALS TOWARDS ADMINISTRATIVE GUIDANCE; AND SCRUTINIZES
THE DEGREE OF HARMONY EXISTING BETWEEN THE RESPONSES OF THE
VARIOUS BRITISH GRIEVANCE-HANDLING AGENCIES AND THE
COMPATIBILITY OF THOSE REACTIONS WITH THE ORGANIZATIONAL
NEEDS OF CENTRAL GOVERNMENT DEPARTMENTS.

06554 MOXON,J
EUROPE'S AIR AND SPACE INDUSTRY
EUROPE, (289) (SEP 89), 30-32.
THE ARTICLE EXAMINES THE PROGRESS MADE BY EUROPE'S AND
SPACE INDUSTRIES. INTRA-EUROPEAN COOPERATION IN THIS AREA
OVER THE PAST FEW DECADES HAS CREATED INDUSTRIES THAT ARE
COMPETING WITH AEROSPACE COMPANIES OF THE US AND OTHER
NATIONS OTHER NATIONS. MANY OBSERVERS GIVE EUROPE THE EDGE
IN CIVIL, AND MILITARY AEROSPACE TECHNOLOGY

06555 MOYNIHAN, D.P.
END OF THE MARXIST EPOCH
NEW LEADER, LXXII(2) (JAN 89), 9-11.
THE AUTHOR LOOKS AT THE FAILURE OF SOCIALIST ECONOMICS
AND AT ETHNIC CONFLICT IN THE USSR.

06556 MOYNIHAN, D.P.
TOWARD A POST-INDUSTRIAL SOCIAL POLICY
PUBLIC INTEREST, (96) (SUM 89), 16-27.
THE AUTHOR SURVEYS THE UNITED STATES' EFFORT TO COPE
WITH INDUSTRIAL POVERTY AND DIVIDES IT INTO THREE PERIODS:
THEODORE ROOSEVELT TO WOODROW WILSON (1901-1921), FRANKLIN
ROOSEVELT TO HARRY TRUMAN (1933-1953), AND JOHN KENNEDY TO
RICHARD NIXON (1961-1974). THEN HE LOOKS AT THE NEW POST-
INDUSTRIAL SOCIETY AND THE TYPE OF SOCIAL DISTRESS THAT
ACCOMPANIES IT.

06557 MOZHAEV, P.
HOW SOVIET PEOPLE ABROAD VOTE
INTERNATIONAL AFFAIRS (MOSCOW), (8) (AUG 89), 78-81.
AT PRESENT, APPROXIMATELY 170,000 SOVIET CITIZENS ARE ON
BUSINESS TRIPS ABROAD AT ANY GIVEN TIME AND SOME 100,000
SOVIET CITIZENS PERMANENTLY RESIDE ABROAD. WITH EFFORTS
TOWARD GREATER DEMOCRATIZATION HAS COME THE QUESTION OF HOW
THESE SOVIETS CAN PARTICIPATE IN ELECTIONS AT HOME. THE
MINISTRY OF FOREIGN AFFAIRS ORGANIZED ONE EXPERIMENT TO
ENABLE SOVIET CITIZENS TO VOTE ABROAD.

06558 MRAZ, G.
HUNGARY AND AUSTRIA
AUSTRIA TODAY, (3) (1989), 21-32.
THE ECONOMIC AND POLITICAL DEVELOPMENT OF HUNGARY HAS
GAINED THE SPOTLIGHT OF INTERNATIONAL ATTENTION WITHIN
RECENT YEARS. AS HUNGARY EMERGES FROM BEHIND THE IRON
CURTAIN AND FOLLOWS A DOMESTIC POLICY OF "AUSTRIFICATION,"
IT IS NATURAL TO LOOK BACK AT THE IMPERIAL AND ROYAL AUSTRO-
HUNGARIAN DOUBLE MONARCHY. LITERATURE, FILMS AND TELEVISION

HAVE ENDOWED THE MONARCHY WITH A SUGAR COATING OF NOSTALGIA.
IN FACT, THE UNION WAS MORE LIKE A MARRIAGE CHARACTERIZED BY
TENSIONS IN AN EMANCIPATORY STRUGGLE FOR PERSONAL FREEDOM.
THE DIVORCE AFTER WORLD WAR I WAS INEVITABLY FOLLOWED BY
DISPUTES ABOUT THE DIVISION OF PROPERTY. THE CONSEQUENCES OF
WORLD WAR II UNITED BOTH PEOPLES OVER THE BARBED WIRE OF THE
IDEOLOGICAL FRONTIER. NOW HUNGARY HAS BECOME THE VENUE FOR
AN EXPERIMENT IN REGAINING INDEPENDENCE.

06559 MRAZ, G.
HUNGARY AND AUSTRIA: SCENES FROM A "MARRIAGE," PART II
AUSTRIA TODAY, (4) (1989), 25-30.
THE HISTORIC RELATIONSHIP BETWEEN AUSTRIA AND HUNGARY IS
REGARDED AS THE CLASSIC EXAMPLE OF A "MARRIAGE" BETWEEN TWO
FUNDAMENTALLY DIFFERENT NATIONS. THE MARRIAGE ENDED IN 1918
AND WAS FOLLOWED BY A BITTER DISPUTE OVER THE DISTRIBUTION
OF THE PROPERTY. ONCE THE DIVORCE SETTLEMENT WAS REACHED,
AUSTRIA AND HUNGARY LEARNED TO LIVE AS NEIGHBORS IN PEACE
AND FRIENDSHIP.

06560 MRAZEK, R.
RETHINKING NATIONAL AND GLOBAL SECURITY
SPACE POLICY, 5(2) (MAY 89), 155-163.
IN 1955 US PRESIDENT EISENHOWER MADE HIS OPEN SKIES
PROPOSAL TO THE USSR, SUGGESTING AN EXCHANGE OF BLUEPRINTS
SHOWING THE LOCATION OF MILITARY INSTALLATIONS IN THE TWO
COUNTRIES. THE PROPOSAL WAS REJECTED AT THE TIME, BUT TODAY
THE PROLIFERATION OF REMOTE SENSING TECHNOLOGY, ALONG WITH
INTERRELATED SECURITY CONCERNS, SUGGESTS THAT THE TIME HAS
COME TO RETHINK AND UPDATE THE CONCEPT. IN THIS PAPER THE
AUTHOR EXPLAINS HIS RECENT PROPOSAL TO THE US CONGRESS THAT
A NATIONAL COMMISSION BE ESTABLISHED TO EXPLORE HOW
INFORMATION GATHERED BY CIVILIAN REMOTE SENSING SATELLITES
COULD INCREASE INTERNATIONAL SECURITY AND STABILITY WITHOUT
JEOPARDIZING NATIONAL DEFENCE.

06561 MUDGAL, V.
PUNJAB: ANGUISHED CRY
INDIA TODAY, XIV(5) (MAR 89), 32.
FOR THE HARRIED PEOPLE OF THE BORDER DISTRICTS OF PUNJAB
THEIR LIVES ARE THREATENED BY EITHER TERRORISTS OR THE
POLICE. THIS ARTICLE DESCRIBES HOW, IN RECENT MONTHS, POLICE
TOOK CENTER-STAGE ONCE AGAIN AS BATALA, A SMALL-INDUSTRY
TOWN IN GURDASPUR DISTRICT HIT THE HEADLINES WITH MORE THAN
40 SARPANCHES OF THE AREA RESIGNING THEIR POSTS TO PROTEST
"STATE TERRORISM". GRASSROOTS DEMOCRACY STRUCK BACK WITH A
VENGEANCE AS IN THE FOLLOWING DAYS HUNDREDS OF AGITATED
VILLAGERS MET THE DISTRICT AUTHORITIES WITH COMPLAINTS
RANGING FROM ILLEGAL AND UNREGISTERED ARRESTS TO GROSS
MISBEHAVIOUR BY POLICEMEN.

06562 MUDGAL, V.
RETURN OF THE PRODIGAL
INDIA TODAY, XIV(2) (JAN 89), 46-47.
IN JANUARY 1988, SURJIT SINGH BARNALA WAS READMITTED TO
THE SIKH FAITH, AND THEN HIS PARTY DELEGATES REFUSED TO
ACCEPT HIS RESIGNATION FROM THE PARTY PRESIDENCY. BARNALA'S
RETURN TO SIKH POLITICS REOPENS THE QUESTION OF POLITICAL
EQUATIONS AMONG THE VARIOUS AKALI FACTIONS.

06563 MUDGAL, V.
WHIPPING UP PASSIONS
INDIA TODAY, XIV(3) (FEB 89). 44-46.
TRILOK SINGH AND SUCHA SINGH HAVE ARRAYED THEMSELVES
BEHIND BABA JOGINDER SINGH OF THE SIMRANJIT SINGH MANN
FACTION OF THE AKALI DAL. THEY ENJOY A SPECIAL IDENTITY
AMONG HARDLINE SIKHS, AND OBSERVERS SAY THEY ARE THE NEW MEN
TO WATCH IN EXTREMIST POLITICS.

06564 MUELLER, E.N.; FU, H.; MIDLARSKY, M.I.; SELIGSON, M.A.
LAND INEQUALITY AND POLITICAL VIOLENCE
AMERICAN POLITICAL SCIENCE REVIEW, 83(2) (JUN 89), 577-602.
CONSIDERABLE RESEARCH EFFORT HAS BEEN INVESTED IN
ESTABLISHING THE APPROPRIATE RELATIONSHIP BETWEEN PATTERNS
OF LAND DISTRIBUTION AND POLITICAL VIOLENCE. MANUS I.
MIDLARSKY PROPOSED AND TESTED A NEW MEASURE OF THE
DISTRIBUTION OF LAND, WHICH HE CALLED "PATTERNED INEQUALITY.
" HE PRESENTED SUPPORTING EVIDENCE WITH DATA FROM LATIN
AMERICAN AND MIDDLE EASTERN COUNTRIES. IN THIS CONTROVERSY,
MIDLARSKY'S ANALYSIS IS CHALLENGED BY EDWARD N. MULLER,
MITCHELL A. SELIGSON, AND HUNG-DER FU. THEY ADVOCATE AN
ALTERNATIVE MEASURE OF LAND INEQUALITY, TEST ITS EFFECT ON
LEVELS OF POLITICAL VIOLENCE IN LATIN AMERICA, AND FIND IT
WANTING.

06565 MUELLER, J.
A NEW CONCERT OF EUROPE
FOREIGN POLICY, (77) (WIN 89), 3-16.
THIS ARTICLE SUGGESTS THAT IT MIGHT BE TIME TO TAKE
PEACE SERIOUSLY AND ADVANCES TWO PROPOSITIONS. FIRST, UNDER
PRESENT CIRCUMSTANCES ARMS REDUCTION IS MORE LIKELY TO
PROCEED EFFECTIVELY IF IT IS ALLOWED TO EVOLVED WITHOUT
EXPLICIT AGREEMENT, SECOND, THE BEST WAY TO RESOLVE THE
DIVIDED AND STILL-CONTENTIOUS CONDITION OF EUROPE WOULD NOT

BE TO FRAGMENT OR EVISCERATE NATO AND THE WARSAW PACT BUT
RATHER TO COMBINE THEM, SPECIFICALLY, THEREFORE, IT IS
PROPOSED THAT ARMS REDUCTION TALKS BE ABANDONED AND THAT
EUROPEAN ALLIANCES BE CONFEDERATED.

06566 MUELLER, K.J.
THE NATIONAL ORGAN TRANSPLANT ACT OF 1984: CONGRESSIONAL
RESPONSE TO CHANGING BIOTECHNOLOGY
POLICY STUDIES REVIEW, 8(2) (WIN 89), 346-356.
THE ENACTMENT OF THE NATIONAL ORGAN TRANSPLANT ACT OF
1984 SHOWS HOW IDIOSYNCRATIC THE AGENDA-SETTING PROCESS CAN
BE IN CONGRESS AND ILLUSTRATES THE ROLE OF PROFESSIONAL
POLICY ANALYSIS IN SHAPING PUBLIC POLICY. THE BLEND OF
CONCERNS FROM PARTICULAR GROUPS PUSHING FOR THE LEGISLATION
AND THE REACTIONS OF OTHER ENTRENCHED INTERESTS HAS
REFLECTED IN THE EVENTUAL SPECIFICS OF THE LEGISLATION.

06567 MUGABE, R.
THE WORLD IS ONE FAMILY
WORLD MARXIST REVIEW, 31(12) (DEC 88), 39-44.
THE NON-ALIGNED DEVELOPING COUNTRIES APPEAL TO THE
WESTERN AND EASTERN BLOCS TO CREATE A NEW INTERNATIONAL
ECONOMIC ORDER, HOPING THAT WITHIN THE CONTEXT OF THIS ORDER,
THE ECONOMIC RESOURCES AVAILABLE TO THE DEVELOPED NATIONS
COULD BE MADE TO SOME EXTENT AVAILABLE TO THE DEVELOPING
COUNTRIES TOO -- BY WAY OF GRANTS, SOFT LOANS, INVESTMENT,
TRANSFER OF TECHNOLOGY AND THE LIKE. BUT BECAUSE QUITE A
GREAT PART OF MATERIAL, FINANCIAL AND OTHER RESOURCES IS
BEING UTILISED FOR MILITARY PURPOSES (PRIMARILY, FOR THE
MANUFACTURE OF NUCLEAR ARMS), THE OPPORTUNITIES FOR
ASSISTANCE TO THE DEVELOPING WORLD ARE CONSIDERABLY LIMITED.
THE SOVIET-AMERICAN SUMMIT TALKS HAVE PRODUCED SOME MEASURE
OF AGREEMENT. EVEN THOUGH THE PROCESS HAS NOT GONE FAR
ENOUGH, HOPEFULLY THINGS WILL ADVANCE TOWARDS COMPLETE
DENUCLEARISATION, TOWARDS A WORLD WITHOUT THESE TERRIBLE
WEAPONS. THE DESTRUCTION OF SOVIET AND US MEDIUM AND SHORTER-
RANGE MISSILES IS A GOOD BEGINNING.

06568 MUHRI, F.
AUSTRIA: TAKING A COMMON STAND AGAINST CAPITAL'S OFFENSIVE
INFORMATION BULLETIN, 25/26(1-2) (JAN 88), 12-14.
THE AUTHOR, AUSTRIA'S COMMUNIST PARTY CHAIRMAN, AFFERS
AN EIGHT - POINT ALTERNATIVE PLAN FOR EMPLOYMENT ON THE
FEDERAL, LAND AND COMMUNITY LEVELS. FOCUS IS ON PRESERVATION
AND EXPANSION OF THE NATIONALIZED INDUSTRY THROUGH A SWITCH
TO THE OUTPUT OF NEW TYPES OF AUSTRIAN FINAL PRODUCTS.

06569 MUIR, J.
AOUN BLAZES THE TRAIL
MIDDLE EAST INTERNATIONAL, (345) (MAR 89), 8-9.
THE LATEST UPHEAVALS IN CHRISTIAN EAST BEIRUT HAVE
PRODUCED A BIZARRE AND IMPORTANT TURNAROUND. THE VIOLENT
BATTLE OF FEB. 15, 1989, BETWEEN SAMIR GEAGEA'S LEBANESE
FORCES MILITIA AND GENERAL MICHEL AOUN'S LOYALIST ARMY UNITS
ENDED IN A MAJOR SETBACK FOR THE MILITIA. THE RESULT IS A
MAJOR BOOST TO THE PRESTIGE AND CREDIBILITY OF GENERAL AOUN,
WHO HAS ESTABLISHED HIMSELF AS THE STRONGMAN AND SPOKESMAN
FOR THE CHRISTIANS.

06570 MUIR, J.
AOUN'S BLOODY CHALLENGE TO ASAD
MIDDLE EAST INTERNATIONAL, (347) (MAR 89), 3-4.
THE CEASE-FIRE ANNOUNCED BY GENERAL AOUN IN MARCH 1989
GOT OFF TO A PREDICTABLY SHAKY START. SHELLS FIRED BY THE
SYRIANS OR THEIR ALLIES CONTINUED TO FALL IN THE CHRISTIAN
AREA HOURS AFTER THE ANNOUNCEMENT, BUT AOUN'S LOYALIST ARMY
UNITS REFRAINED FROM SHELLING BACK. WITH NO POLITICAL
AGREEMENT UNDERPINNING THE CEASE-FIRE AND THE ISSUE OF THE
MILITIA-RUN PORTS UNRESOLVED, THE SITUATION WAS HARDLY
STABLE.

06571 MUIR, J.
LEBANESE PARLIAMENTARIANS MEET IN TAIF
MIDDLE EAST INTERNATIONAL, (360) (OCT 89), 6-7.
DEPUTIES OF LEBANON'S PARLIAMENT MET IN TAIF, SAUDI
ARABIA, TO ARGUE PROPOSED REFORMS OF THE CONSTITUTION. THE
REFORMS CALLED FOR THE REDUCTION OF THE TRADITIONAL
PRIVILEGES ENJOYED BY THE CHRISTIANS, A SYRIAN PULL BACK,
AND THE ELECTION OF A NEW PRESIDENT. GENERAL MICHEL AOUN,
THE CHIEF CRITIC OF THE REFORMS RELUCTANTLY ACCEPTED THE
PLAN WHICH ALLOWED FOR THE FIRST PROPER CEASE-FIRE SINCE
MARCH. HOWEVER, THE CONFLICT BETWEEN CHRISTIANS AND MUSLIMS
IS LIKELY TO CONTINUE IN THE POLITICAL ARENA.

06572 MUIR, J.
LEBANON NO NEARER PEACE
MIDDLE EAST INTERNATIONAL, (358) (SEP 89), 6-8.
DESPITE CONSIDERABLE DIPLOMATIC ACTIVITY ON THE PART OF
ARAB AND OTHER INTERNATIONAL ORGANIZATIONS, A CEASE-FIRE IN
LEBANON HAS YET TO MATERIALIZE. AS THE FORCES OF BOTH SYRIA
AND OF CHRISTIAN GENERAL MICHEL AOUN CONTINUE TO DEVASTATE
THE LEBANON, OBSERVERS ARE BEGINNING TO FEAR THAT THE
CONFLICT COULD CONTINUE INDEFINITELY, AND ACT ACCORDINGLY.

06573 MUIR, J.
LEBANON ON A KNIFE-EDGE
MIDDLE EAST INTERNATIONAL, (364) (DEC 89), 3-5.
THE NEXT FEW WEEKS WILL BE CRITICAL FOR LEBANON'S FUTURE.
FORCES LOYAL TO GENERAL MICHEL AOUN ARE HOLED UP IN THE
BAABDA PRESIDENTIAL PALACE. FACING THEM ARE THE FORCES OF
NEWLY ELECTED ELIAS HRAWI AND SYRIAN FORCES. HRAWI HAS
REPLACED AOUN AS COMMANDER OF THE LEBANESE ARMY, WHICH PUTS
AOUN AND HIS LOYALIST TROOPS IN A STATE OF MUTINY. HOWEVER,
AOUN CONTINUES TO ENJOY HUGE POPULARITY AMONG THE GENERAL
POPULATION. THE CONFLICT WILL PROBABLY NOT BE RESOLVED UNTIL
EITHER AUON, OR THE SYRIANS ARE GONE.

06574 MUIR, J.
LEBANON: AOUN THE STUMBLING BLOCK
MIDDLE EAST INTERNATIONAL, (363) (NOV 89), 4-6.
GENERAL MICHEL AOUN"S REACTION TO THE ELECTION OF
MARONITE CHRISTAIN RENE MUAWAD TO LEBANON'S PRESIDENTIAL
OFFICE WAS SWIFT AND CERTAIN: UTILIZING "PEOPLE POWER," HE
TOOK CONTROL OF THE PRESIDENTIAL PALACE AND EFFECTIVELY
REMOVED MUAWAD FROM POWER. THIS MOVE INCREASES TENSION IN
LEBANON TO A STILL HIGHER LEVEL AS SYRIAN, CHRISTIAN, AND
OTHEE FORCES FACE EACH OTHER IN AN UNTENABLE STALEMATE.
MUAWAD IS SEEKING FOR A GOVERNMENT THAT WILL DRAW POPULAR
SUPPORT AWAY FROM THE GENERAL, BUT MANY OBSERVERS FEEL THAT
HIS CHANCES ARE NOT GOOD.

06575 MUIR, J.
LEBANON: AOUN V. ASAD
MIDDLE EAST INTERNATIONAL, (357) (AUG 89), 3-4.
DESPITE A FLURRY OF INTERNATIONAL DIPLOMATIC ACTIVITY,
HOSTILITIES BETWEEN THE CHRISTIAN FORCES OF GENERAL MICHEL
AOUN AND THE SYRIAN "INVADERS" SHOWED NO SIGN OF CEASING.
SYRIA REJECTED THE CEASE-FIRE PROPOSED BY THE UN SECURITY
COUNCIL, BUT ITS OPTIONS ARE LIMITED. A MILITARY WITHDRAWAL
APPEARS TO BE OUT OF THE QUESTION. BUT DAMASCUS WOULD LIKE
TO AVOID FURTHER ESCALATION IF AT ALL POSSIBLE. BOTH SIDES
SEEM CONTENT TO CONTINUE HOSTILITIES ON BEIRUT AND OTHER
AREAS AS THEY JOCKEY FOR THE BEST POSITION IN INTERNATIONAL
CIRCLES.

06576 MUIR, J.
LEBANON: FRATRICIDAL BLOODLETTING
MIDDLE EAST INTERNATIONAL, (342) (JAN 89), 6-7.
THE INTER-SHI'ITE CONFLICT BETWEEN AMAL AND HIZBULLAH IS
MADE UP OF SEVERAL INTERTWINED STRANDS THAT GIVE IT DEPTH
AND MAKE IT DIFFICULT TO SETTLE OR SUPPRESS. BOTH FACTIONS
ARE LINKED TO OUTSIDE POWERS: HIZBULLAH TO IRAN AND AMAL TO
SYRIA. THE PROSPECTS FOR A SOLID SETTLEMENT ARE DIM BECAUSE
THE SYRIANS DO NOT CARE IF THE CONFLICT CONTINUES, PROVIDED
IT DOES NOT GET OUT OF CONTROL.

06577 MUIR, J.
LEBANON: MONTHS OF USELESS DEATH AND DESTRUCTION
MIDDLE EAST INTERNATIONAL, (350) (MAY 89), 6-7.
GENERAL MICHEL AOUN HAS BEEN OBLIGED TO AGREE TO
SOMETHING VERY CLOSE TO THE STATUS QUO ANTE WHICH HE HAD SO
OFTEN AND SO STRENUOUSLY REJECTED. WITH BOTH THE ARAB LEAGUE
AND THE INTERNATIONAL COMMUNITY INSISTING THAT HE MUST DROP
HIS NAVAL BLOCKADE OF THE MUSLIM MILITIA PORTS AS PART OF A
CEASE-FIRE PACKAGE, HE ENDED UP WITH NO REAL OPTION BUT TO
DO SO, IN THE FULL KNOWLEDGE THAT IT RISKED MAKING NONSENSE
OF THE PREVIOUS TWO MONTHS OF DEATH AND DESTRUCTION.

06578 MUIR, J.
LEBANON: THE FUSE BURNS SHORT
MIDDLE EAST INTERNATIONAL, (351) (MAY 89), 11.
THE ONLY AGREEMENT IN LEBANON IS THAT ONLY A MIRACLE
FROM THE ARAB LEAGUE SUMMIT COULD AVERT ANOTHER EXPLOSION OF
VIOLENCE. SUCH A MIRACLE IS UNLIKELY AS NEITHER THE SYRIANS
NOR THE FORCES OF GENERAL MICHEL AOUN SEEM WILLING TO BUDGE
FROM THEIR POLITICAL AND MILITARY POSITIONS. THE RECENT
ASSASINATION OF THE SUNNI MUSLIM MUFTI, SHAIKH HASSAN KHALED
AND A FRESH INFLUX OF IRANIAN REVOLUTIONARY GUARDS HAS
SERVED ONLY TO INCREASE TENSION ALMOST TO THE BREAKING POINT.

06579 MUIR, J.
LEBANON: THE STRUGGLE AOUN CANNOT WIN
MIDDLE EAST INTERNATIONAL, (348) (APR 89), 7-9.
THE CONFLICT BETWEEN THE CHRISTIAN FACTIONS LED BY
GENERAL AOUN AND THE SYRIANS CONTINUES AS BEIRUT CONTINUE
TO BE SHELLED BY THE SYRIANS. GENERAL AOUN REFUSES TO END
HIS BLOCKADE OF ILLEGAL, MILITIA-RUN PORTS IN THE SYRIAN
CONTROLLED AREAS AND THE SYRIANS, IN THEIR CHARACTERISTIC
STUBBORNNESS REFUSE TO BUDGE FROM THEIR POSITION. AN
OBSERVER STATED THAT "THERE IS LITERALLY NO POWER ON EARTH
THAT CAN BUDGE THE SYRIANS IF THEY DO NOT WANT TO MOVE."
INSTEAD, THE CHRISTIANS ARE BEGINING TO LEAVE BEIRUT IN
DROVES, TAKING THE ONLY ROUTE LEFT TO AVOID THE CONTINUAL
BOMBARDMENT: THE BOAT TO CYPRUS.

06580 MUIR, J.
LEBANON: VERY GUARDED OPTIMISM
MIDDLE EAST INTERNATIONAL, (354) (JUL 89), 6.

THE ARAB INITIATIVE FOR PEACE IN LEBANON IS BEING
RECEIVED WITH "GUARDED OPTISMISM" IN MOST CIRCLES. ALTHOUGH
SYRIA ANNOUNCED ITS READINESS TO GO ALONG WITH THE PROPOSALS,
SHELLING IN BERIUT CONTINUED. IN ADDITION CHRISTIAN GENERAL
MICHEL AOUN SEEMS UNLIKELY TO ACCEPT THE PROPOSAL FOR
POLITICAL REFORM DUE TO THE FACT THAT IT ALLOWS A CONTINUED
SYRIAN PRESENCE IN LEBANON. BOTH THE US AND THE USSR SUPPORT
THE ARAB LEAGUE'S INITIATIVE, BUT WITHOUT COOPERATION
BETWEEN THE TWO MAIN ANTAGONISTS, THE SYRAINS AND THE
CHRISTIANS, THE CHANCES OF LASTING PEACE SEEM SLIM.

06581 MUIR, J.
    LEBANON: VICIOUS CIRCLES
    MIDDLE EAST INTERNATIONAL, (349) (APR 89), 9-10.
        GEN. MICHEL AOUN WILL NOT, PERHAPS CANNOT, TURN BACK
    FROM THE ALL-OR-NOTHING COURSE HE HAS TAKEN IN JORDAN. HE
    BELIEVES THAT, IF HE ALLOWS THE SITUATION TO REVERT TO THE
    "STATUS QUO ANTE," HIS WAR OF LIBERATION WILL FIZZLE OUT IN
    AN ENDLESS ROUND OF FRUITLESS TALKS. HE IS DETERMINED TO BE
    LEBANON'S SAVIOR AND HAS REPEATEDLY DEMANDED THAT THE
    SYRIANS WITHDRAW BEFORE THERE CAN BE ANY SERIOUS POLITICAL
    EFFORT TO END LEBANON'S INTERNAL CRISIS.

06582 MUIR, J.
    LEBANON'S POST-TAIF REACTIONS
    MIDDLE EAST INTERNATIONAL, (362) (NOV 89), 3-5.
        THE SITUATION IN BERIUT IN THE WAKE OF THE TAIF
    AGREEMENT FOR PEACE AND REUNIFICATION HAS ONE OF UNDENIABLE
    TENSION. A COLLISION COURSE BETWEEN OPPOSING FORCES SEEMED
    INEVITABLE, BUT NEITHER SIDE SEEMED WILLING TO COMPROMISE.
    THE KEY FIGURE IS GENERAL MICHEL AOUN. IF HE DOESN'T REVISE
    HIS UNCONDITIONAL REJECTION OF THE TAIF ACCORDS, LEBANON
    COULD BE THROWN INTO ADDITIONAL TURMOIL AND VIOLENCE. LESS
    THAN A WEEK BEFORE THE SCHEDULED PRESIDENTIAL ELECTION, ALL
    PARTIES INVOLVED ARE ANXIOUSLY WATCHING AOUN AND HOLD THEIR
    COLLECTIVE BREATH.

06583 MUIR, J.
    LEBANON'S SHI'ITES FORCED TO CALL A TRUCE
    MIDDLE EAST INTERNATIONAL, (343) (FEB 89), 3-4.
        THE AGREEMENT BETWEEN THE FEUDING SHI'ITE FACTIONS HAS
    THE RESULT OF PRESSURES BY THE SYRIANS AND IRANIANS, WHOSE
    FOREIGN MINISTERS PLAYED A KEY ROLE IN NEGOTIATING THE
    ACCORD. IN BROAD TERMS, THE AGREEMENT LEAVES THE REGIONAL
    ALLIANCE BETWEEN IRAN AND SYRIA INTACT, DESPITE THE BLOOD
    LETTING BETWEEN THEIR LEBANESE SHI'ITE ALLIES. THE FACT THAT
    THE ACCORD IS BASICALLY A HOLDING OPERATION PROVIDES ONE
    REASON FOR SKEPTICISM ABOUT ITS LONG-TERM EFFECTIVENESS.

06584 MUIR, J.
    NEW ARAB PLAN FOR LEBANON
    MIDDLE EAST INTERNATIONAL, (359) (SEP 89), 9-10.
        THE NEW PEACE PLAN FOR LEBANON PROPOSED BY THE ARAB
    LEAGUE OFFERS GENERAL MICHEL AOUN LITTLE WITH WHICH TO
    PERSUADE HIS DWINDLING FOLLOWERS THAT HIS "WAR OF
    LIBERATION" HAD PAID OFF. THE PROSPECT OF A SYRIAN
    WITHDRAWAL, AUON'S OVERRIDING CONCERN, HAS NOT EVEN
    MENTIONED IN THE SEVEN-POINT PLAN. MEANWHILE, THE EVACUATION
    OF ALL US DIPLOMATIC PERSONNEL FROM AOUN'S CHRISTIAN ENCLAVE
    SIGNALS STRONG US DISAPPROVAL OF AOUN'S TACTICS AND AN
    ALMOST CERTAIN LACK OF US SUPPORT IN THE FUTURE. ALTHOUGH
    AOUN IS APPARENTLY ON THE ROAD TO DEFEAT (HE IS INCAPABLE OF
    EXPELLING THE SYRIANS WITHOUT OUTSIDE HELP), HE IS UNLIKELY
    TO GIVE IN WITHOUT FURTHER STRUGGLE.

06585 MUIR, J.
    SHEVARDNADZE'S TOUR: DOING WHAT THE AMERICANS COULDN'T
    MIDDLE EAST INTERNATIONAL, (345) (MAR 89), 3-5.
        THE SOVIETS SEEM CONFIDENT THAT THE NEW ERA OF
    SUPERPOWER COOPERATION CAN BE EXTENDED TO THE CONTENTIOUS
    MIDDLE EAST. EDWARD SHEVARDNADZE'S TOUR OF SYRIA, JORDAN,
    EGYPT, IRAN, AND IRAQ SIGNALLED CLEARLY THAT THE RUSSIANS
    ARE SERIOUSLY INTERESTED IN DOING ALL THEY CAN TO FACILITATE
    AND ENCOURAGE A MIDDLE EAST SETTLEMENT, PROVIDED IT IS A
    BALANCED SOLUTION ACHIEVED THROUGH THE BALANCED MECHANISM OF
    AN INTERNATIONAL CONFERENCE SPONSORED BY THE UNITED NATIONS.
    MEANWHILE, THE BUSH ADMINISTRATION HAS BEEN VERY SLOW TO
    FORMULATE A COURSE OF ACTION.

06586 MUIR, J.
    SOUTH LEBANON: "TERRORISM" UNDER THE MICROSCOPE
    MIDDLE EAST INTERNATIONAL, (346) (MAR 89), 7-8.
        IN THE SPRING OF 1989, TWO LARGELY UNRELATED EVENTS
    FOCUSED ATTENTION ON THE HILLS OF SOUTH LEBANON: AN UPSURGE
    IN ATTEMPTS BY PALESTINIAN GUERRILLAS TO MOUNT CROSS-BORDER
    ATTACKS ON ISRAEL AND INCREASED FRICTION BETWEEN THE
    ISRAELIS AND THE UNITED NATIONS FORCES AT THE EASTERN END OF
    THE BORDER ZONE.

06587 MUIR, J.
    STAND-OFF IN LEBANON
    MIDDLE EAST INTERNATIONAL, (365) (DEC 89), 7-8.
        THOUSANDS OF SYRIA'S BEST TROOPS ALMOST QUASHED
    CHRISTIAN GENERAL MICHEL AOUN'S REBELLION, BUT HALTED AT THE

LAST MOMENT. OBSERVERS SPECULATE THAT AOUN'S UTILIZATION OF
THOUSANDS OF CIVILIAN SUPPORTERS AS A HUMAN WALL CAUSED US,
LEBANESE, AND ISRAELI AUTHORITIES, WHO ORIGINALLY GAVE TACIT
APPROVAL TO THE OPERATION, TO APPLY PRESSURE ON THE SYRIANS
TO ABORT IT. FORCES IN LEBANON NOW MAINTAIN AN UNEASY
STALEMATE.

06588 MUIR, J.
    THE ATTEMPTS TO BREAK THE VICIOUS CIRCLE
    MIDDLE EAST INTERNATIONAL, (344) (FEB 89), 6-8.
        IT IS UNREALISTIC TO EXPECT THE ARAB LEAGUE INITIATIVE
    ALONE TO BREAK THE VICIOUS CIRCLE IN LEBANON. BUT THAT DOES
    NOT MEAN THE ARAB MOVE IS USELESS BECAUSE THE LEAGUE MAY BE
    ABLE TO PLAY AN IMPORTANT RESTRAINING ROLE.

06589 MUIR, J.
    THE CLOUDS DARKEN OVER LEBANON
    MIDDLE EAST INTERNATIONAL, 355 (JUL 89), 3-4.
        ANY OPTIMISM ENGENDERED BY THE ANNOUNCEMENT FROM SYRIA'S
    ALLIES THAT THE LAND PASSAGES TO THE EMBATTLED CHRISTIAN
    ENCLAVE HAD BEEN REOPENED WAS SHORTLIVED. WITH THE FAILURE
    OF THE LATEST ARAB LEAGUE MISSION TO BREAK THE VICIOUS
    CIRCLE AND ESTABLISH A PROPER CEASE-FIRE, THE PREDICTIONS
    ARE UNIVERSALLY DIRE, WITH SOME VERY DARK CLOUDS LOOMING ON
    THE NEAR HORIZON. THE DAILY SHELLINGS GO ON, DISRUPTING ALL
    ACTIVITY AND CLAIMING A STEADY TOLL OF LIVES, WITH THE
    SYRIANS INVARIABLY STARTING IT OFF. POWER SUPPLIES HAVE BEEN
    CUT TO ONE HOUR PER DAY, AND OFTEN NONE AT ALL. EVERYTHING
    ELSE IS BREAKING DOWN. SCHOOLS, UNIVERSITIES AND MANY
    BUSINESSES HAVE BEEN PARALYSED SINCE MARCH. EVERYBODY WITH
    CHILDREN IS IN A STATE OF PERMANENT CONSTERNATION OVER THEIR
    FUTURE. AND OVER ALL HANGS THE BLACK CERTAINTY THAT, UNLESS
    THE ARABS CAN SOMEHOW PULL IT OFF, IT CAN ONLY GET WORSE.

06590 MUIR, J.
    THE DANGEROUS FALLOUT FROM ISRAELIS ABDUCTION
    MIDDLE EAST INTERNATIONAL, 356 (AUG 89), 3-4.
        IT MAY BE HARD TO BELIEVE THAT THE ISRAELI LEADERSHIP
    COULD HAVE BEEN SO BLINKERED AS TO THINK THAT THE FALL-OUT
    FROM THEIR ABDUCTION OF A LEADING HIZBULLAH CLERIC COULD BE
    KEPT AT A LOCAL LEVEL, AND THAT HIZBULLAH WOULD QUIETLY FALL
    INTO LINE AND AGREE TO RELEASE THE TWO OR THREE ISRAELI
    SERVICEMEN IT IS HOLDING IN EXCHANGE FOR SHAIKH OBEID AND
    OTHER SHI'ITES HELD PRISONER BY THE ISRAELIS. ALTHOUGH SUCH
    A SWAP WAS IMMEDIATELY RULED OUT IN LEBANESE SHI'ITE CIRCLES,
    THEY, LIKE MANY ISRAELIS, BELIEVED IT TO BE ISRAEL'S MOST
    LIKELY INSPIRATION. IF RAFSANJANI COULD DEFUSE THE HOSTAGE
    CRISIS, IT COULD SERVE BOTH TO BOLSTER HIS POSITION
    INTERNALLY AND TO PREPARE THE FOUNDATIONS FOR FUTURE
    RELATIONS WITH THE ALIENATED WEST. BUT IF HE FAILED, THE
    WHOLE NEW REGIME IN TEHRAN RISKED BEING TARRED WITH THE
    KIDNAPPERS' BRUSH, WITH ALL THAT THAT IMPLIED.

06591 MUIR, J.
    THE GENERAL OVERPLAYS HIS HAND
    MIDDLE EAST INTERNATIONAL, (346) (MAR 89), 6-7.
        IN MARCH 1989, THE SHELLS WERE FALLING ON BEIRUT AGAIN,
    THE AIRPORT WAS CLOSED, AND THE ARAB LEAGUE'S PEACE EFFORT
    IN LEBANON WAS IN SERIOUS TROUBLE. THE ABRUPT DETERIORATION
    THERE WAS THE PREDICTABLE RESULT OF A CHAIN OF EVENTS SET IN
    MOTION BY GENERAL AOUN.

06592 MUIR, J.
    THE TAIF CONFERENCE
    MIDDLE EAST INTERNATIONAL, (361) (OCT 89), 3-4.
        THE ARTICLE FOLLOWS THE LABORIOUS PEACE NEGOTIATIONS
    TAKING PLACE IN TAIF, SAUDI ARABIA. REPRESENTATIVES OF
    VARIOUS LEBANESE FACTIONS ARE WRANGLING OVER PLAN DRAWN UP
    BY A TRIPARTITE ARAB COMMITTEE MADE UP OF REPRESENTATIVES OF
    SAUDI ARABIA, ALGERIA, AND MOROCCO. ALTHOUGH MANY OBSERVERS
    FEEL THAT THE CHRISTIAN REPRESENTATIVES MAY ACCEPT THE
    PROPOSALS RATHER THAN GO HOME EMPTY HANDED, THE VERBAL
    ASSULT BY GENERAL MICHEL AOUN HAS KEPT ALL SIDES GUESSING.
    IF AOUN FAILS TO BACK THE PROPOSAL, THE ENTIRE PEACE PROCESS
    WOULD BE STYMIED AND THE SIX-MONTH OLD CEASE-FIRE WOULD BE
    PLACE IN A PRECARIOUS POSITION.

06593 MUJICA, H.
    A NEW HUMANISM
    WORLD MARXIST REVIEW, 32(4) (APR 89), 31-33.
        WITHOUT FURTHER ADVANCING MARXISM-LENINISM, WE CANNOT
    EXPECT TO TACKLE TODAY'S COMPLEX PROBLEMS SUCCESSFULLY. THE
    DEVELOPMENT OF A NEW HUMANISM IS ONE OF THESE TASKS. WHILE
    RAMAINING, LIKE THE HUMANISM OF THE PAST, A SYSTEM OF VIEWS
    UPHOLDING THE VALUE OF THE INDIVIDUAL, THE NEW HUMANISM
    SHOULD BE VERY BROAD AND EXTENSIVE SINCE IT IS BASED ON THE
    ENTIRE HUMANISTIC HERITAGE OF ALL MANKIND, ON THE GREAT
    HUMANITARIAN TRADITIONS OF ART, LITERATURE AND CULTURE. ON
    THE OTHER HAND, THE NEW HUMANISM EXPRESSES UNIVERSAL HUMAN
    INTERESTS AND ABANDONS PREJUDICES WHICH, IN THE PAST,
    DISTORTED THE IDEAS OF SOCIALISM AND DEMOCRACY. FINALLY, THE
    NEW HUMANISM REMAINS LINKED WITH SOCIETY'S REALITIES AND
    CHAMPIONS THE WORKING PEOPLE AND ALL THOSE OPPRESSED AND
    HUMILIATED.

06594 MUJICA, H.
    THE ANATOMY OF DOGMATISM
    WORLD MARXIST REVIEW, 31(12) (DEC 88), 93-96.
        IT IS NOW IMPERATIVE NOT ONLY TO RAISE THE OVERALL
    CULTURAL LEVEL OF THE PARTY CADRES OR TO INVOLVE NEW
    SECTIONS OF THE INTELLIGENTSIA IN THE ACTIVITIES AND
    POLICIES OF COMMUNIST PARTIES BUT ALSO TO LOOK FOR WAYS OF
    OVERCOMING CONSERVATIVE TRENDS IN CREATIVE ENDEAVOURS.
    WITHOUT IT, THE INFLUENCE OF THE MOVEMENT AS THE LEADING
    FORCE CANNOT GROW. COMMUNISTS MUST NOT PRODUCE THE
    IMPRESSION OF LECTURING OTHERS. THE POLITICAL ROLE THEY PLAY
    IN SOCIETY SHOULD HELP LIBERATE ITS INTELLECTUAL POTENTIAL,
    REVISE TRADITIONAL CLASS-BASED VALUES AND STEREOTYPED
    THOUGHT PATTERNS WHICH HOLD US BACK, AND PUT THIS POTENTIAL
    INTO THE EFFORT OF CHANGING THE WORLD.

06595 MUK, Y. H.
    POLITICAL METHODS FOR ECONOMIC MANAGEMENT
    WORLD MARXIST REVIEW, 32(1) (JAN 89), 11-13.
        THE WORKERS' PARTY OF KOREA DEVOTES MUCH OF ITS
    ATTENTION TO THE EFFICIENT ADMINISTRATION OF THE NATIONAL
    ECONOMY. IT SEEKS TO ATTAIN ITS OBJECTIVES NOT BY
    ADMINISTRATIVE COMMAND BUT EXCLUSIVELY BY POLITICAL WORK
    WITH THE PEOPLE.

06596 MUKERJEE, D.
    THE GULF WAR LESSON
    FAR EASTERN ECONOMIC REVIEW, 141(36) (SEP 88), 38,41.
        THE ARTICLE EXAMINES SOME OF THE LESSONS THAT CAN BE
    LEARNED FROM THE EIGHT-YEAR IRAN-IRAQ CINFLICT. THEY INCLUDE:
    THE INCREASING ROLE OF MODERN TECHNOLOGY IN DEFENSE WHICH
    ALMOST ENSURES THAT MOST THIRD WORLD CONFLICTS WILL END IN
    STALEMATE; THE EFFECT THAT TECHNOLOGY HAS ON INSURGENTS,
    MAKING THEM MUCH MORE EFFECTIVE; MOST NATIONS CAN NOT COUNT
    ON MAINTAINING A MONOPOLY ON ANY TYPE OF MILITARY HARDWARE,
    SUCH AS IRAQ EXPECTED WITH MUSTARD GAS; ANY WAR THAT
    THREATENS TO TIP THE REGIONAL BALANCE WILL INVITE OUTSIDE
    INTERVENTION AGAINST THE SIDE THAT SEEMS TO BE GAINING AN
    UPPER HAND.

06597 MUKERJEE, D.
    ZIA'S MILITARY LEGACY
    ROUND TABLE, (310) (APR 89), 179-191.
        THE ARTICLE ANALYZES GENERAL ZIA-UL HAQ'S USE OF THE
    MILITARY TO AMALGAMATE POWER DURING HIS 11-YEAR TENURE AS
    PRESIDENT OF PAKISTAN. IT ALSO EXAMINES THE LEGACY HE HAS
    LEFT TO FUTURE LEADERS OF PAKISTAN. SOME SIGNIFICANT
    EXAMPLES OF THE LEGACY ARE THE ARMED FORCES PERCEPTION,
    APPARENTLY NOW ACCEPTED BY CIVILIANS AS WELL, OF THEIR ROLE
    IN NATIONAL LIFE AND THE ROLE OF THE AREMD FORCES IN
    PRESERVING ISLAM. THE ARTICLE ALSO EXAMINES SEVERAL POLICIES
    AND PRACTICES OF ZIA AND THEIR FUTURE IMPLICATIONS INCLUDING
    HIGH LEVELS OF MILITARY SPENDING AND THE PRESENCE OF NUCLEAR
    WEAPONS IN PAKISTAN.

06598 MUKHERJEE, R.
    THE QUALITY OF LIFE: VALUATION IN SOCIAL RESEARCH
    SAGE PUBLICATIONS NEW DELHI, INDIA, 1989, 248.
        THIS ARTICLE EXAMINES THE METHODS UTILIZED BY THE TWO
    PERSPECTIVES OF QUALITY OF LIFE RESEARCH: SOCIAL INDICATORS
    RESEARCH WHICH CONSIDERS THE ELITES' VALUATION OF WHAT THE
    PEOPLE NEED SO AS TO ATTAIN A BETTER QUALITY OF LIFE; AND
    CONVENTIONAL QUALITY OF LIFE RESEARCH WHICH IS MEANT TO
    ASCERTAIN WHAT THE PEOPLE WANT IN ORDER TO IMPROVE THEIR
    QUALITY OF LIFE. THE AUTHOR FORMULATES A NEW METHODOLOGY IN
    AN EFFORT TO SYNCHRONIZE THESE TWO PERSPECTIVES AND REMOVE
    THE CONSTRAINTS FACING QUALITY OF LIFE RESEARCH. HE
    HIGHLIGHTS THE IMPORTANCE OF TREATING VALUE AS AN ANALYTIC
    VARIABLE FOR THE APPRAISAL OF SOCIAL REALITY, AGAINST THE
    APPARENTLY INSOLUBLE CONTROVERSY ON SUBJECTIVISM,
    OBJECTIVISM AND EMPIRICISM, BY EXAMINING THE EXTENT OF
    OBJECTIVITY FROM SUBJECTIVITY OF PERCEPTION OF THE
    PHENOMENON OF QUALITY OF LIFE.

06599 MUKONOWESHURO, E.G.
    SOCIO-ECONOMIC AND POLITICAL CAUSES OF THE FAILURE OF
    PUBLIC ENTERPRISE IN AFRICA: A CASE STUDY
    JOURNAL OF SOCIAL, POLITICAL AND ECONOMIC STUDIES, 14(2)
    (SUM 89), 215-225.
        IN THE MAJORITY OF AFRICAN COUNTRIES, NO VIABLE
    ENTREPRENEURIAL GROUP HAD DEVELOPED AS A DOMINANT SOCIO-
    ECONOMIC FORCE AT THE TIME OF INDEPENDENCE. THE COLONIAL
    PETTY TRADERS HAD NOT MANIFESTED THEMSELVES OR HAD NOT
    ESTABLISHED A MEANINGFUL GRIP ON INDUSTRY, TRADE, OR THE
    STATE APPARATUS OF THE COLONIAL SYSTEM. THEY HAD NOT REACHED
    A LEVEL OF DEVELOPMENT WHERE THEY COULD ASSUME EFFECTIVE
    CONTROL OF THE POST-COLONIAL STATE AND TAKE OVER THE
    ECONOMIC FUNCTIONS PREVIOUSLY FULFILLED BY EXPATRIATE
    COMMERCIAL INTERESTS. BECAUSE THE COLONIAL ENTREPRENEURIAL
    GROUPS HAD COMPLETELY OVERSHADOWED AND FRUSTRATED THE GROWTH
    OF AN INDIGENOUS ENTREPRENEURIAL GROUP, THE NEW GOVERNMENTS
    GENERALLY RESORTED TO POLITICAL METHODS TO WREST ECONOMIC
    DOMINANCE FROM THE HANDS OF EXPATRIATE COMMERCIAL INTERESTS.

THE DEVELOPMENT OF A GOVERNMENT SECTOR IN THE ECONOMY
THROUGH PUBLIC ENTERPRISE WAS THOUGHT TO BE THE ANSWER.

06600 MUKONOWESHURO, E.G.
    THE HISTORICAL BASIS OF THE POLITICS OF INDIGENOUS
    "CAPITALISM" IN SIERRA LEONE
    JOURNAL OF ASIAN AND AFRICAN STUDIES, XXIV(3-4) (JUL 89),
    213-227.
        ONE OF THE MAJOR PROBLEMS FACED BY NEWLY-INDEPENDENT
    AFRICAN GOVERNMENTS HAS BEEN HOW TO DEVISE AN ECONOMIC
    STRATEGY THAT WOULD SIMULTANEOUSLY REDUCE FOREIGN DOMINATION
    OF THE ECONOMY WHILE CREATING A VIABLE INDIGENOUS
    ENTREPRENEURIAL CLASS. IN SIERRA LEONE, THE GOVERNMENT
    ATTEMPTED TO OVERCOME THIS DILEMMA THROUGH A THREE -PRONGED
    STRATEGY: THE CREATION OF PARASTATALS; THE INTRODUCTION OF
    LEGISLATION DESIGNED TO CARVE OUT AND PROTECT LUCRATIVE
    ECONOMIC NICHES FOR INDIGENOUS ENTREPRENEURS IN THE ECONOMY;
    AND THE CREATION OF FINANCIAL INSTITUTIONS TO STRENGTHEN
    INDIGENOUS CAPITAL. ALL THESE STRATEGIES FAILED AND BY THE
    1980S THE ECONOMY FACED AN UNPRECEDENTED CRISIS.

06601 MULCAHY, F.D.
    GYPSY/NON-GYPSY CONFLICT IN SPAIN
    INTERNATIONAL JOURNAL OF GROUP TENSIONS, 19(4) (WIN 89),
    349-363.
        DURING THE COURSE OF THIS ANALYSIS, THE AUTHOR DISCUSSES
    HOW, IN THE COURSE OF THE LAST TWO DECADES, PROFOUND CHANGES
    IN SPANISH POLITICAL AND SOCIAL ORGANIZATION HAVE BEGUN TO
    AFFECT THE WAY SPANIARDS MANAGE CONFLICT BETWEEN THEMSELVES
    AND THEIR MARGINAL COMMUNITIES. THE AUTHOR DESCRIBES TWO
    MODERN CASES OF CONFLICT BETWEEN GYPSIES AND NON-GYPSIES IN
    SPAIN. ONE CASE WHICH UNFOLDED IN THE BARCELONA SUBURB OF LA
    VERNEDA IN 1972 WILL BE COMPARED WITH ANOTHER AND MORE
    RECENT CASE WHICH BEGAN IN THE NEARBY MUNICIPALITY OF
    RIPOLLET IN 1987 AND DEVELOPED INTO CRISIS PROPORTIONS IN
    1988.

06602 MULGAN, R.
    CAN THE TREATY OF WAITANGI PROVIDE A CONSTITUTIONAL BASIS
    FOR NEW ZEALAND'S POLITICAL FUTURE?
    POLITICAL SCIENCE, 41(2) (DEC 89), 51-68.
        FOR MANY MAORI PEOPLE, THE TREATY OF WAITANGI HAS ALWAYS
    HAD SIGNIFICANCE AS A FOCUS OF THEIR LONG-STANDING
    GRIEVANCES AGAINST THE CROWN. FOR MOST PAKEHA, HOWEVER, THE
    TREATY WAS OF LITTLE RELEVANCE UNTIL 1985, WHEN THE LANGE
    GOVERNMENT EXTENDED THE SCOPE OF THE WAITANGI TRIBUNAL BACK
    TO 1840. SINCE THEN THERE HAVE BEEN HIGHLY PUBLICIZED CLAIMS
    BEFORE THE TRIBUNAL AND A NUMBER OF HIGHLY CONTROVERSIAL
    RECOMMENDATIONS. THE MAIN SOURCE OF CONFLICT AND CONFUSION
    OVER THE TREATY IS A CRISIS OF LEGITIMACY, WHICH IS
    AFFLICTING ALL STATES WHOSE ORIGINS LIE IN COLONIAL CONQUEST
    AND SETTLEMENT. THE TREATY PROVIDES THE FOCUS OF DISCUSSION
    BUT IT IS NOT THE ORIGIN OF THE DEBATE. THAT ORIGIN IS TO BE
    FOUND IN CHANGING ATTITUDES TO COLONIALISM.

06603 MULHOLLAN, D.P.
    CONGRESS AND THE DELIBERATIVE PROCESS: STAYING INFORMED
    CRS REVEIW, 10(7) (AUG 89), 30-31.
        THROUGHOUT THE HISTORY OF THE CONGRESS, DELIBERATION HAS
    PLAYED A CRUCIAL ROLE IN GETTING AND KEEPING MEMBERS
    INFORMED IN MATTERS OF PUBLIC POLICY.

06604 MULLER, E.N.
    DEMOCRACY AND INEQUALITY
    AMERICAN SOCIOLOGICAL REVIEW, 54(5) (OCT 89), 868-871.
        THE AUTHOR REPLIES TO CRITICISM OF HIS ARGUMENT THAT
    THERE IS A THEORETICALLY AND STATISTICALLY SIGNIFICANT
    RELATIONSHIP BETWEEN THE AGE OF A DEMOCRACY AND INCOME
    REDISTRIBUTION.

06605 MULLER, E.N.
    DISTRIBUTION OF INCOME IN ADVANCED CAPITALIST STATES:
    POLITICAL PARTIES, LABOR UNIONS AND THE INTERNATIONAL
    ECONOMY
    EUROPEAN JOURNAL OF POLITICAL RESEARCH, 17(4) (JUL 89),
    367-400.
        HYPOTHESES ABOUT DETERMINANTS OF INCOME INEQUALITY IN
    ADVANCED CAPITALIST SOCIETIES ARE TESTED WITH DATA FROM THE
    WORLD BANK FOR 1975-80 ACROSS VIRTUALLY THE COMPLETE
    POPULATION. THE RESULTS SUPPORT MOST OF THE PROPOSITIONS OF
    A MODEL THAT TAKES INTO ACCOUNT DIFFERENCES IN PARTISAN
    CONTROL OF GOVERNMENT, THE ORGANIZATION STRENGTH OF LABOUR,
    AN THE OPENNESS OF THE ECONOMY TO INTERNATIONAL MARKET
    FORCES. HYPOTHESES DERIVED FROM GLOBAL MODELS OF INCOME
    DISTRIBUTION ARE NOT SUPPORTED. THE MAJOR FINDINGS ARE (1)
    THAT LABOR ORGANIZATION HAS NO DIRECT EFFECT ON INCOME
    INEQUALITY; (2) THAT STRONG SOCIALIST PARTIES HAVE A
    NEGATIVE EFFECT ON THE SIZE OF THE GAP BETWEEN THE RICH AND
    THE POOR BUT NO EFFECT ON THE GAP BETWEEN THE RICH AND THE
    MIDDLE CLASS; (3) THAT THE GOVERNMENTAL STRENGTH OF
    CONSERVATIVE PARTIES IS UNRELATED TO THE SIZE OF THE GAP
    BETWEEN THE RICH AND THE POOR BUT HAS A VERY STRONG POSITIVE
    EFFECT ON THE GAP BETWEEN THE RICH AND THE MIDDLE CLASS; AND
    (4) THAT, REGARDLESS OF PARTISAN CONTROL OF GOVERNMENT,

RELATIVELY SMALL TRADE DEPENDENT ECONOMICS ARE MORE
EGALITARIAN THAN RELATIVELY LARGE ECONOMIES WHICH ARE LESS
DEPENDENT ON INTERNATIONAL TRADE.

06606 MULLER, S.
THE VIEW OF THE BIG PERFORMERS
PHILADELPHIA: ANLS OF AMER ACMY OF POLITICAL AND SOC
SCIENCE, (502) (MAR 89), 120-129.
THE APPLIED PHYSICS LABORATORY (APL) OF THE JOHNS
HOPKINS UNIVERSITY SERVES AS AN ILLUSTRATIVE EXAMPLE OF A
LARGE LABORATORY SPONSORED BY A MILITARY SERVICE-THE U.S.
NAVY-THAT IS OWNED AND OPERATED BY A MAJOR RESEARCH
UNIVERSITY. AFTER AN EXAMINATION OF HOW APL FUNCTION WITHIN
JOHNS HOPKINS, THE POSITIVE SIDE OF THE RELATIONSHIP IS
EXAMINED. IT IS FOUND PRIMARILY IN THE COMBINATION OF
NATIONAL SERVICE AND RESEARCH AND TEACHING COLLABORATION
WITH THE UNIVERSITY'S ACADEMIC DIVISIONS. THE PRIMARY
NEGATIVES ARE PUBLIC CONTROVERSY AND THE RISKS AND BURDENS
OF THE UNIVERSITY'S OBLIGATION. THE POSITION OF THE JOHNS
HOPKINS UNIVERSITY HAS BEEN AND REMAINS THAT CLASSIFIED
RESEARCH IS NOT NECESSARILY INCONSISTENT WITH THE PURPOSES
OF THE UNIVERSITY AND THAT A MAJOR PUBLIC SERVICE IS
LEGITIMATELY RENDERED BY THE CONTRIBUTIONS TO NATIONAL
DEFENSE MADE BY APL TO THE NAVY, WITHIN LIMITS SET BY THE
UNIVERSITY.

06607 MUNGER, M.C.
A SIMPLE TEST OF THE THESIS THAT COMMITTEE JURISDICTIONS
SHAPE CORPORATE PAC CONTRIBUTIONS
PUBLIC CHOICE, 62(2) (AUG 89), 181-186.
STUDIES OF PAC CONTRIBUTION PATTERNS HAVE BEEN CONDUCTED
AT HIGH LEVELS OF AGGREGATION SUCH AS 'LABOR' OR
'CORPORATIONS,' AND AT THE MORE DISAGGRAGATED LEVEL OF
INDIVIDUAL PACS OR SMALL SPECIFIC GROUPS. REGRESSION
ANALYSIS HAS DEMONSTRATED THAT PACS RESPOND TO CANDIDATES
SENIORITY, COMMITTEE ASSIGNMENTS, REPUTATION BUILT ON VOTING
RECORD, AND EXPECTED ELECTORAL MARGIN. THIS NOTE DETERMINES
THE ROBUSTNESS OF THESE RESULTS BY EXAMINING CORPORATE PAC
BEHAVIOR USING A NON-PARAMETRIC (CHI-SQUARE) TEST.

06608 MUNI, S.D.
PEACE THROUGH CONFIDENCE-BUILDING: PROSPECTS IN THE INDIAN
OCEAN
DISARMAMENT, XII(3) (AUT 89), 129-139.
ALTHOUGH INITIATIVES FOR CONFIDENCE-BUILDING MEASURES
MAY PLAY A CONSTRUCTIVE ROLE IN THE PEACE PROCESS IN THE
INDIAN OCEAN REGION, THEY WILL NOT REDUCE ITS COMPLEXITY. IT
IS NECESSARY THAT THE CONFIDENCE-BUILDING MEASURES ADVANCE
AND FACILITATE THE PEACE PROCESS RATHER THAN HALTING OR
FREEZING THE PROCESS IN THE FORM OF JUST CONFIDENCE-BUILDING
MEASURES. THEREFORE, THE QUESTION OF CONFIDENCE-BUILDING
MUST BE HANDLED WITH GREAT CARE AND CIRCUMSPECTION.

06609 MUNRO, G.
ONTARIO'S URBAN TRANSPORTATION DEVELOPMENT CORPORATION: A
CASE STUDY IN PRIVATIZATION
CANADIAN PUBLIC ADMINISTRATION, 32(1) (SPR 89), 25-40.
THE PRIVATIZATION OF GOVERNMENT-OWNED CORPORATIONS
REFLECTS BOTH THE TREND TOWARDS A GREATER RELIANCE ON THE
MARKET AND ATTEMPTS TO BETTER MANAGE THE PUBLIC SECTOR. BUT
WHILE ADVOCATES OF PRIVATIZATION ASSUME THAT IT WILL READILY
YIELD GAINS IN EFFICIENCY, A NUMBER OF PROBLEMS ARISE IF
GOVERNMENTS SEEK TO PURSUE PUBLIC POLICY GOALS FOLLOWING
PRIVATIZATION. THE ONTARIO LIBERAL GOVERNMENT'S
PRIVATIZATION OF THE URBAN TRANSPORTATION DEVELOPMENT
CORPORATION ILLUSTRATES THE DIFFICULTY IN COMPLETELY
DISENTANGLING THE GOVERNMENT AND THE CORPORATION.
COMPLICATED LINKS BETWEEN THE UTDC AND THE GOVERNMENT HAVE
EVOLVED SINCE ITS CREATION WHICH WERE ESSENTIAL TO THE
PERFORMANCE OF THE UTDC EITHER AS A PUBLIC OR AS A PRIVATE
CORPORATION. FURTHERMORE, THE GOVERNMENT SOUGHT TO CONTINUE
TO PROTECT EMPLOYMENT USING THE UTDC AFTER PRIVATIZATION IN
ADDITION TO THE UTDC'S ORIGINAL GOAL OF PROMOTING HIGH
TECHNOLOGY IN THE FIELD OF URBAN MASS TRANSIT. THE RESULTING
AGREEMENT BETWEEN THE GOVERNMENT AND THE BUYER, LAVALIN, IS
A COMPLEX DEAL IN WHICH THE GOVERNMENT RETAINS A SUBSTANTIAL
INTEREST IN THE NEW FIRM. RATHER THAN A SHARP BREAK BETWEEN
THE GOVERNMENT AND THE FIRM, WHAT OCCURRED WAS A CHANGE IN
THE MIX OF INSTRUMENTS USED BY THE GOVERNMENT.

06610 MUNRO, G.E.
PAYING FOR POLAND'S PARTITIONS
JOURNAL OF BALTIC STUDIES, XX(4) (WIN 89), 327-336.
BENEATH THE POLITICAL AND DIPLOMATIC ENTANGLEMENTS
INVOLVED IN POLAND'S PARTITIONS LAY THE FINANCIAL
ARRANGEMENTS WITHOUT WHICH THE PARTITIONS WOULD HAVE BEEN
IMPOSSIBLE. BY HAVING TO BORROW ABROAD, POLAND CREATED YET
ANOTHER OPENING THROUGH WHICH NON-POLISH INTERESTS,
POLITICAL AND FINANCIAL, MIGHT INTERFERE IN POLAND'S AFFAIRS.
IF EVENTS IN OTHER PARTS OF EUROPE, SUCH AS THE FRENCH
REVOLUTION, FRIGHTENED POTENTIAL INVESTORS IN POLISH BONDS
INTO HOLDING ONTO THEIR MONEY RATHER THAN PUTTING IT TO USE,
POLAND WOULD FIND IT HARD TO RENEGOTIATE ITS LOANS WHEN THEY
FELL DUE. ON THE OTHER HAND, POLAND COULD RISK THE IRE OF

ITS NEIGHOR RUSSIA ONLY AT GREAT PERIL TO ITSELF, FOR RUSSIA
GUARANTEED MANY OF THE LOANS TO POLAND AND COULD, THEREFORE,
USE ITS FINANCIAL INTERST TO FURTHER ITS POLITICAL DESIGNS.

06611 MUNROE, T.
CONTEMPORARY MARXIST MOVEMENTS ASSESSING WPJ PROSPECTS IN
JAMAICA
SOCIAL AND ECONOMIC STUDIES, 36(3) (SEP 87), 1-36.
THE AIM OF THIS PAPER IS TO SITUATE THE WORKERS PARTY OF
JAMAICA (WPJ) IN THE CONTEXT OF THE POSITION OF PARTIES AND
MOVEMENTS OF SIMILAR ORIENTATION OUTSIDE OF JAMAICA. THE
ROLE AND PROSPECTS OF THE WPJ ARE EXAMINED.

06612 MUNROE, T.
JAMAICA: NEW THINKING INSPIRING PRACTICAL STEPS
INFORMATION BULLETIN, 27 (MAR 89), 9-12.
THESE EXCERPTS FROM A REPORT BY THE GENERAL SECRETARY OF
THE WORKERS' PARTY OF JAMAICA CALL FOR DOMESTIC POLITICAL
REFORM AND NEW POLITICAL THINKING WITHIN THE PARTY, JAMAICA,
AND BEYOND.

06613 MUNTEANU, A.
A PROMINENT WRITER RESIGNS FROM THE COMMUNIST PARTY
EAST EUROPEAN REPORTER, 3(4) (SPR 89), 25.
THE ARTICLE CONTAINS THE RESIGNATION LETTER OF AUREL-
DRAGOS MUNTEANU, A PROMINENT INTELLECTUAL ELITE AND EDITOR,
FROM THE ROMANIAN COMMUNIST PARTY. HIS SPECIFIC REASONS FOR
THE BREAK WITH THE PARTY INCLUDE DISAGREEMENT WITH PARTY
LEADER CEAUSESCU'S DENUNCIATION OF GOD, THE GOVERNMENT-
SPONSORED PROGRAM OF VILLAGE DESTRUCTION, AND REPRESSION OF
HIS OWN ARTICLES.

06614 MURADYAN, I.
GLASNOST AND NAGORNO-KARABAKH: THE PUBLIC SPEAKS
GLASNOST, (16-18) (JAN 89), 19-20.
THE AUTHOR CHRONICLES GRASSROOTS ACTION BY ARMENIANS
FROM 1985 TO 1987, INCLUDING PETITIONS AND APPEALS TO THE
CPSU CENTRAL COMMITTEE TO TAKE THE LEADERSHIP IN RESOLVING
THE NAGORNO-KARABAKH QUESTION QUICKLY AND FAIRLY.

06615 MURAVCHIK, J.
WHY THE DEMOCRATS LOST AGAIN
COMMENTARY, 87(2) (FEB 89), 13-22.
THE AUTHOR LOOKS AT SOME OF THE FACTORS IN THE 1988
PRESIDENTIAL CAMPAIGN, INCLUDING CHARGES OF DIRTY TACTICS
AND RACISM.

06616 MURAVHIK, J.
US POLITICAL PARTIES OVERSEAS
WASHINGTON QUARTERLY, 12(3) (SUM 89), 91-100.
THE ARTICLE EXAMINES THE INEXPERIENCED, YET INCREASING
EFFORTS OF US POLITICAL PARTIES TO "INTERNATIONALIZE".
UTILIZING SUCH MECHANISMS AS THE NATIONAL ENDOWMENT FOR
DEMOCRACY (NED), THE FREE TRADE UNION INSTITUTE (FTUI), THE
NATIONAL REPUBLICAN INSTITUTE FOR INTERNATIONAL AFFAIRS
(NRI), AND THE NATIONAL DEMOCRATIC INSTITUTE FOR
INTERNATIONAL AFFAIRS (NDI) THE US IS MOVING INTO POLITICAL
TERRITORY THAT HAS ONCE THE SOLE DOMAIN OF COMMUNIST
MOVEMENTS. ALTHOUGH PHILOSOPHY AND METHODS OF EACH
ORGANIZATION DIFFER, THEY ARE RELATIVELY UNITED IN A COMMON
DESIRE TO FOSTER THE GROWTH OF DEMOCRACY IN THE THIRD WORLD
AND EVENTUALLY IN SOCIALIST NATIONS AS WELL.

06617 MURAY, L.
A NEW ROLE FOR JAPAN
CONTEMPORARY REVIEW, 254(1478) (MAR 89), 127-131.
THE ARTICLE EXPLORES THE FUTURE OF JAPAN IN LIGHT OF THE
RECENT DEATH OF EMPEROR HIROHITO. THE NEW EMPEROR, AKIHITO
WILL FACE THE CHALLENGE OF CONFLICT BETWEEN TRADITIONALISTS
WHO WANT A RETURN TO JAPAN'S ANCIENT POWER STRUCTURE AND
THOSE WHO FAVOR THE CONTEMPORARY CONSTITUTION AND SYSTEM OF
GOVERNMENT. HE ALSO FACES THE CHALLENGE OF A POSSIBLE
"FORTRESS EUROPE" IN 1992, INCREASED PRESSURE FROM THE US
AND OTHER ALLIES TO INCREASE JAPAN'S SHARE OF SPENDING ON
DEFENSE AND FOREIGN AID, AND THE OPENING UP OF RELATIONS
WITH CHINA, LATIN AMERICA, AND AFRICA.

06618 MURAY, L.
CHINA - THE PUZZLING UNCERTAINTY
CONTEMPORARY REVIEW, 255(1483) (AUG 89), 63-67.
THE MASSACRE ON PEKING'S MAIN SQUARE ON 4 JUNE AND THE
REPRESSION THAT HAS FOLLOWED HAS CHANGED THE INTERNATIONAL
SCENE CRITICALLY, MORE THAN HAD BEEN ORIGINALLY EXPECTED.
THIS ARTICLE EXPLORES ITS IMPACT ON CHINESE POLITICS AND THE
RESULTANT FACT THAT IT ILLUSTRATES THAT CHINA IS STILL
DEEPLY TROUBLED AND UNSTABLE. CHINA HAS CEASED TO BE
CONSIDERED A SUPERPOWER. THE OBJECTIVES OF THE DENG
GOVERNMENT, THEIR DEFINITION OF DEMOCRATISATION, THEIR BASIC
IDEOLOGY AND ALSO THE ECONOMIC ASPECTS OF THE CRISIS ARE
EXPLORED, AS WELL AS THE EFFECT OF THIS ON THE HONG KONG
SITUATION.

06619 MURAY, L.
NO MORE TITOSLAVIA?

CONTEMPORARY REVIEW, 254(1476) (JAN 89), 7-11.
THE ARTICLE EXAMINES THE SERIOUS ETHNIC TENSIONS AND
DIFFICULTIES THAT CURRENTLY EXIST IN YUGOSLAVIA. ALTHOUGH
ETHNIC DIFFERENCES WERE PREVALENT THROUGHOUT THE REIN OF
MARSHAL TITO, HE MANAGED TO WEATHER MOST OF THE CRISES WITH
AN ADEPT MIX OF COMMUNIST IDEOLOGY AND PRAGMATIC COMPROMISE.
HOWEVER TITO LEFT A SIGNIFICANT VACUUM NOT BE FILLED.
ECONOMIC PROBLEMS COMPOUND THE ALREADY TENSE RELATIONS
BETWEEN SERBS, CROATS, SLOVENES, MACEDONIANS, AND THE DOZENS
OF OTHER ETHNIC GROUPS IN YUGOSLAVIA.

06620 MURAY, L.
REFLECTIONS ON SOME CONSEQUENCES OF THIRD SEPTEMBER 1939
CONTEMPORARY REVIEW, 255(1484) (SEP 89), 130-134.
THIS ARTICLE SUGGESTS THAT WORLD WAR II STARTED 50 YEARS
AGO IN AN ATMOSPHERE OF CONFUSION. THE GLOBAL NATURE OF THE
WAR FORCED A DECISIVE CHANGE ON WARFARE AND ON THE NATURE OF
FUTURE RELATIONS BETWEEN COUNTRIES. A CONSEQUENCE OF THIS
WAS THAT WARFARE WAS INDUSTRIALISED. OTHER CONSEQUENCES
EXAMINED ARE THE DISAPPEARANCE OF THE WESTERN EMPIRE, THE
YALTA AGREEMENT, AND THE POSSIBILITIES OF DE-STALINISATION
GORBACHEV CAN ENGAGE IN. THE FINAL CONSEQUENCE EXAMINED IS
THAT THE U.S. IS NOW ABLE TO LOOK WITH INCREASING CONCERN TO
THE FAR EAST, THE PACIFIC, CHINA, JAPAN, AND INDIA.

06621 MURAY, L.
TAKING NOTICE OF SPAIN
CONTEMPORARY REVIEW, 254(1480) (MAY 89), 225-230.
THE GONZALEZ GOVERNMENT HAS SHOWN THAT THE 10 YEAR OLD
DEMOCRATIC CONSTITUTION WORKS. THE GENUINE AND FRIENDLY
COOPERATION BETWEEN THE KING AND THE SOCIALIST PREMIER AND
HIS GOVERNMENT HAS MADE AN IMPACT. IT HAS CREATED THE
IMPRESSION THAT, FOR THE FIRST TIME IN ITS TROUBLED HISTORY,
DEMOCRACY IS THERE TO STAY. THE ROMAN CATHOLIC HIERARCHY,
THOUGH DISTURBED BY THE RAPID SECULARISATION OF SOCIETY, HAS
ADJUSTED ITSELF WHILE MILITANT ANTICLERICALISM IS ON THE
WANE. THE CONSTITUTION PROVIDES A FAIR SCOPE FOR REGIONAL
SELF-GOVERNMENT. THIS IS A POWERFUL STABILISING FACTOR, EVEN
IN THE BASQUE COUNTRY, WHEN ONE RECALLS THAT ONCE THE USE OF
CATALAN LANGUAGE, FOR EXAMPLE, HAS BEEN BANNED.

06622 MURAY, L.
THE HUNGARIAN ELEMENT
CONTEMPORARY REVIEW, 254(1481) (JUN 89), 292-297.
HUNGARY'S PRESENT LEADERSHIP WANTS FREEDOM OF CHOICE TO
INTRODUCE A WORKING 'SOCIALIST MARKET SYSTEM' WITHOUT HAVING
TO OBEY THE RULES OF THE SOVIET BLOC. ANY SUCCESS, EVEN A
MODEST ONE, WILL PUT NEW FORCE AND NEW ARGUMENTS INTO THE
MOVEMENT OF REFORMERS IN ALL OTHER SOVIET BLOC COUNTRIES,
JUST AS FAILURE WILL HARDEN THE LINE OF THE RULING
TRADITIONALISTS, SAY IN CZECHOSLOVAKIA OR EAST GERMANY, NOT
TO MENTION THE ARGUMENTS IT WILL PRODUCE ONE WAY OR THE
OTHER IN THE CONSTANT IN-FIGHTING IN THE KREMLIN.

06623 MURFETT, M.
THE PERILS OF NEGOTIATING FROM AN EXPOSED POSITION: JOHN
SIMON KERANS AND THE YANGTSE TALKS OF 1949
CONFLICT, 9(3) (1989), 271-300.
THIS ARTICLE DETAILS THE CAPTURE AND DARING ESCAPE OF
THE H.M.S. AMETHYST FROM MAO'S PEOPLE'S LIBERATION ARMY IN
1949. THE AMETHYST'S CAPTURE AND SUBSEQUENT ESCAPE SERVED TO
SEVER THE ALREADY STAINED POLITICAL AND COMMERCIAL RELATIONS
BETWEEN THE BRITISH AND CHINESE. A DETAILED ACCOUNT OF THE
INCIDENT IS FORTHCOMING IN MALCOLM MURFETT'S BOOK HOSTAGE ON
THE YANGTSE: BRITAIN, CHINA AND THE AMETHYST CRISIS OF 1949
(U.S. NAVAL INSTITUTE PRESS, 1990).

06624 MURPHY, C.A.
LIBERATION THEOLOGY AS POLITICAL IDEOLOGY
DISSERTATION ABSTRACTS INTERNATIONAL, 50(6) (DEC 89),
1789-A.
AN ANALYSIS OF THE PUBLISHED MATERIALS OF LIBERATION
THEOLOGY AND THE STATEMENTS OF ITS ADHERENTS DEMONSTRATES
THAT THE MOVEMENT IS IN REALITY AN IDEOLOGY IN THE POLITICAL
SENSE, RATHER THAN A THEOLOGY. THAT THE THEORY AND ITS
POLITICAL INSTITUTIONS ARE MARXIST IS READILY ACKNOWLEDGED
BY BOTH PROPONENTS AND OPPONENTS. THUS FAR, LIBERATION
THEOLOGY HAS FAILED TO REACH ITS POTENTIAL AS A POLITICAL
MOVEMENT BECAUSE IT HAS FAILED TO ADEQUATELY EXPLAIN OR
ADDRESS THE REAL CAUSES OF LATIN AMERICA'S ECONOMIC AND
POLITICAL BACKWARDNESS.

06625 MURPHY, E.
ISRAELI SETTLERS: AN OBSTACLE TO PEACE
MIDDLE EAST INTERNATIONAL, 355 (JUL 89), 15-16.
THE PALESTINIAN INTIFADA IS NOT JUST A QUESTION OF STONE-
THROWERS VERSUS SOLDIERS. THERE IS A THIRD, QUASI-MILITARY
FORCE TO BE RECKONED WITH, ONE WHICH IS SEEKING TO PLAY AN
INCREASINGLY ACTIVE AND VIOLENT ROLE. THEY ARE THE JEWISH
SETTLERS WHO HAVE BUILT THEIR IDEOLOGICAL FORTRESSES HIGH IN
THE JUDEAN AND SAMARIAN HILLS, AN EVER PRESENT REMINDER TO
THE VILLAGES BELOW OF THE ISRAELI VISION OF ERETZ ISRAEL.
SINCE 1967 OVER 52,000 ISRAELIS HAVE MOVED TO THE WEST BANK
AND THE OWNERSHIP OF 52 PER CENT OF WEST BANK LAND AND 30

PER CENT OF THE GAZA STRIP HAS BEEN TRANSFERRED (ILLEGALLY)
TO ISRAELI HANDS. THIS HAS CREATED A TRICKY SITUATION FOR
THE ISRAELI GOVERNMENT. ANY REALISTIC NEGOTIATIONS FOR PEACE
MUST INCLUDE THE RETURN OF SOME OR ALL OF THESE LANDS.

06626 MURPHY, R.W.
MIDDLE EAST PEACE: FACING REALITIES AND CHALLENGES
DEPARTMENT OF STATE BULLETIN (US FOREIGN POLICY), 88(2138)
(SEP 88), 44-47.
THE ARTICLE EXAMINES DEMOGRAPHIC, ECONOMIC, AND MILITARY
TRENDS IN THE MIDDLE EAST AND ASSESSES THE IMPACT OF EACH ON
THE MIDDLE EAST PEACE PROCESS. IT CONCLUDES THAT THE CHANGES
AFFECT THE ABILITY OF COUNTRIES TO COMPETE POLITICALLY AND
ECONOMICALLY IN THE INCREASINGLY INTERDEPENDENT WORLD OF THE
20TH CENTURY. IT ALSO CONCLUDES THAT EXTREMISM IS ON THE
RISE AND THE RISK OF A MAJOR ARABISRAELI MILITARY CONFLICT
IS INCREASING. UNFORTUNATELY, MANY OF THE PARTIES INVOLVED
ARE STILL CLINGING TO "OLD VISIONS AND DREAMS" THAT ARE NO
LONGER FEASIBLE IN THE MIDDLE EAST OF TODAY.

06627 MURPHY, R.W.
THE SEARCH FOR MIDDLE EAST PEACE
DEPARTMENT OF STATE BULLETIN (US FOREIGN POLICY), 89(2143)
(FEB 89), 57-60.
THE AUTHOR LOOKS AT WHAT THE PALESTINIANS HAVE BEEN
DOING TO AFFECT THEIR FUTURE, HOW THE INTIFADA FITS INTO THE
SEARCH FOR MIDDLE EAST PEACE, AND WHAT THE INTIFADA MAY
PORTEND IF THERE IS NO RESOLUTE EFFORT TO ACHIEVE A
NEGOTIATED SETTLEMENT.

06628 MURPHY, R.W.
UPDATE ON THE SITUATION IN THE MIDDLE EAST
DEPARTMENT OF STATE BULLETIN (US FOREIGN POLICY), 88(2141)
(DEC 88), 41-45.
THE ARTICLE OUTLINES SOME OF THE RECENT DEVELOPMENTS IN
THE MIDDLE EAST WHICH INCLUDE THE SITUATION IN LEBANON WHERE
THE FAILURE TO ELECT A NEW PRESIDENT INCREASES THE RISK OF
THAT NATION'S PARTITION BETWEEN LEBANESE CHRISTIANS AND
LEBANESE MUSLIMS, THE IRAN-IRAQ WAR AND THE CEASE-FIRE, AND
THE PEACE PROCESS WITH REGARDS TO THE OCCUPIED TERRITORIES
WHICH HAS CHANGED SIGNIFICANTLY WITH THE ANNOUNCEMENT BY
JORDAN'S KING HUSSEIN THAT HE WOULD END ADMINISTRATIVE AND
LEGAL TIES WITH THE WEST BANK. THE ISSUES OF ARMS SALES,
BALLISTIC MISSILES, AND CHEMICAL WARFARE WERE ALSO EXAMINED.

06629 MURRAY, C.
THE BEST THINGS IN LIFE
REASON, 21(7) (DEC 89), 35-37.
THIS ARTICLE IS A BOOK REVIEW OF "THE EXAMINED LIFE:
PHILOSOPHICAL MEDITATIONS," BY ROBERT NOZICK, THE CONNECTING
THEME OF THE BOOK IS ROUGHLY: LIFE SHOULD BE INTIMATELY
BOUND UP WITH REALITY. IT COVERS AREAS SUCH AS DYING,
PARENTS AND CHILDREN, CREATING, SEXUALITY, EMOTIONS, THE
HOLOCAUST, ETC. THE POINT OF THE BOOK IS TO EVOKE FROM THE
READER WHAT HE THINKS, AND IN DOING SO ENABLE THE READER TO
THINK BETTER AND MORE CLEARLY ON THESE TOPICS.

06630 MURRAY, G.; CROTHERS, C.
CORPORATE DECISION-MAKING: SOME NEW ZEALAND SURVEY EVIDENCE
CRITICAL SOCIOLOGY, 16(2-3) (SUM 89), 75-89.
USING DATA FROM A NEW ZEALAND SURVEY OF TOP BUSINESS
LEADERS, THE AUTHORS EXPLORE THE RELEVANCE OF INTERVIEW DATA
FOR ILLUMINATING THE STRUCTURES AND PROCESSES OF THE
CAPITALIST CLASS. THE AUTHORS ARE ABLE TO SHOW FROM THIS
SURVEY THAT FAMILY GROUPS ARE STILL VERY IMPORTANT UNITS OF
CORPORATE POWER ANALYSIS; DIRECTORS, NOT MANAGERS, TEND TO
MAKE THE LARGER DECISIONS; BOARD MEMBERS ARE MORE CONCERNED
WITH THE DEVELOPMENT OF POLICY THAN ITS IMPLEMENTATION;
DIRECTORS MAJOR CONCERN IN DECISION MAKING IS TO MAJOR
SHAREHOLDERS; AND DIRECTORS HAVE FREQUENT CONTACT WITH MAJOR
SHAREHOLDERS AND OTHER BUSINESS INTERESTS.

06631 MURRAY, L.
GORBACHEV - THE 12 MONTH'S TEST
CONTEMPORARY REVIEW, 255(1486) (NOV 89), 237-241.
GORBACHOV HAS 11 MONTHS UNTIL THE NEXT PARTY CONGRESS TO
CONSOLIDATE HIS AUTHORITY AND PUT INTO EFFECT HIS
'PERESTROIKA REVOLUTION'. THIS ARTICLE ANALYZES THE CHANGES
THAT HAVE OCCURRED AND WHAT YET NEEDS TO BE ACCOMPLISHED.
THE CRITICAL PERIOD FOR FOOD AND FUEL BEING MADE AVAILABLE
(WINTER); DISARMAMENT TALKS; FOREIGN RELATIONS; RESHUFFLING
THE POLITBURO; THE PARTY; CENTRALIZATION; REFORMS; TRADE;
THE BALANCE BETWEEN THE REFORMERS AND THE TRADITIONALISTS;
AND THE NATIONALITY ISSUE ARE EACH, IN TURN, DISCUSSED.

06632 MURRAY, M.J.
THE POPULAR UPSURGE IN SOUTH AFRICA, 1984-1986
CRITICAL SOCIOLOGY, 16(1) (SPR 89), 55-76.
THIS PAPER EXAMINES THE POPULAR REVOLT IN SOUTH AFRICA
BETWEEN 1984 AND 1986. IT SURVEYS THE COURSE OF THIS REVOLT
IN DIFFERENT REGIONS OF SOUTH AFRICA. SPECIAL ATTENTION IS
GIVEN TO THE EMERGENCE DURING THIS PERIOD OF A MORE POWERFUL
INDEPENDENT BLACK TRADE UNION MOVEMENT. IT ALSO CONSIDERS
THE NATURE OF THE WHITE MINORITY REGIME AND ITS RESPONSE TO

THE POPULAR UPSURGE. FINALLY, IT NOTES THE EMERGENCE OF NEW
FORMS OF POPULAR RESISTANCE THAT POINT TOWARD A NEW STAGE IN
THE STRUGGLE AGAINST APARTHEID.

06633 MURRAY, P.
EDGAR TEKERE: FIGHTING TOOTH AND CLAW
AFRICA REPORT, 34(1) (JAN 89), 38-39.
EDGAR TEKERE, ONE-TIME SECRETARY-GENERAL OF ZIMBABWE'S
RULING PARTY ZANU, WAS EXPELLED FROM THE CENTRAL COMMITTEE
AND THE PARTY DURING A MEETING HELD IN HARARE ON OCTOBER 21
1988 FIVE DAYS LATER, FOLLOWING A PUBLIC MEETING ATTENDED BY
SOME 600 PEOPLE FROM TEKERE'S MUTARE CONSTITUENCY, THE
OUTSPOKEN POLITICIAN GAVE A LONG PRESS CONFERENCE AT HIS
HOME, ATTENDED BY A SMALL GROUP OF FOREIGN REPORTERS. THIS
ARTICLE CONTAINS EXTRACTS FROM THAT PRESS CONFERENCE.

06634 MURTHY, K. V.
INDUSTRIALISATION STRATEGY IN SOUTH ASIA
SOUTH ASIA JOURNAL, 2(4) (APR 89), 373-393.
THE CURRENT DEBATE PIVOTS AROUND THE POSSIBILITY OF A
RAPID INDUSTRIALISATION WITH ESSENTIALLY CAPITALISTIC
INSTITUTIONS OF PRIVATE PROPERTY, MARKET MECHANISM AND
CONSONANT POLICIES OF FREE TRADE. THE SACS ARE BEING TOLD
THAT THEIR PROBLEMS WOULD VANISH IF THEY WERE TO ADOPT THE
SEAWICS' EXPORT-ORIENTED INDUSTRIALISATION AS A ROUTE TO
SUCCESS. THE CENTRAL QUESTION THEN IS AS TO WHETHER ANY OF
THE EXISTING MODELS CAN BE ADOPTED WITH LITTLE MODIFICATION
OR WHETHER INDUSTRIALISATION WOULD EVOLVE IN THE SACS IN THE
MANNER OF THE WESTERN EUROPEAN COUNTRIES. IN THE ABSENCE OF
THE ABOVE TWO POSSIBILITIES, THE SACS WOULD HAVE TO DO SOME
INTROSPECTION AND WOULD HAVE TO EVOLVE INDEPENDENT
INDUSTRIALISATION STRATEGIES.

06635 MUSA, A.
JAPAN AND SUB-SAHARAN AFRICA: A STUDY OF CONTEMPORARY AND
DIPLOMATIC HISTORY, 1960-1984
DISSERTATION ABSTRACTS INTERNATIONAL, 49(9) (MAR 89),
2757-A.
THE AUTHOR OUTLINES THE MAJOR ECONOMIC AND DIPLOMATIC
TRENDS IN JAPANESE-SUB-SAHARAN RELATIONS SINCE 1960, WHEN
MOST AFRICAN COUNTRIES EMERGED FROM COLONIAL RULE. TOPICS
INCLUDE JAPAN'S POLITICAL AND ECONOMIC CONTACTS WITH AFRICA
BEFORE 1960, THE RECENT HISTORY OF AFRICA'S DEVELOPMENT
CRISES, AND THE PATTERNS OF JAPANESE TRADE WITH SUB-SAHARAN
AFRICA.   .

06636 MUSOKE, D.
MUSEVENI WANTS ONE PARTY STATE
NEW AFRICAN, 263 (AUG 89), 21.
THIS IS A REPORT ON THE POLITICAL ACTIVITIES OF UGANDA
PRESIDENT, MUSEVENI, SINCE HE ASSUMED POWER EARLY 1986. IT
FOCUSES ON THE DEMOCRATIC PARTY RESPONSE TO MUSEVENI'S
DESIRE FOR A ONE PARTY STATE. DETAILED IS THEIR 11 PAGE
CIRCULAR AND ITS RECOUNTING OF MUSEVENI'S FAILURE TO KEEP
HIS EARLIER PROMISES AND THE CONTINUATION OF VIOLENCE AND
POLITICAL PROBLEMS.

06637 MUTWIRA, R.
A QUESTION OF CONDONING GAME SLAUGHTER: SOUTHERN RHODESIAN
WILD LIFE POLICY 1890-1953
JOURNAL OF SOUTHERN AFRICAN STUDIES, 15(2) (JAN 89),
250-262.
THE ARTICLE EXAMINES THE POLICY OF COLONISTS AND LATER
THE GOVERNMENT OF RHODESIA TOWARDS WILDLIFE AND HUNTING.
INITIALLY WANTON SLAUGHTER WAS ALLOWED UNDER THE EXCUSE OF
ELIMINATING RABIES, "VERMIN", OR THE TSETSE FLY. LATER
HUNTING FOR SPORT INCREASED IN POPULARITY. AROUND THE TURN
OF THE CENTURY, THE ATTITUDES OF COLONIAL GOVERNMENTS AND
SOME SETTLERS CHANGED WITH REGARDS TO THE SHRINKING AMOUNT
OF WILDLIFE IN RHODESIA. ALTHOUGH HUNTING RESTRICTIONS WERE
LEGISLATED, THEY GENERALLY WERE NOT ENFORCED. THE ARTICLE
CONCLUDES THAT THE INTERESTS OF SETTLER FARMERS AND
MINEOWNERS DOMINATED THE WAY THAT HUNTING LEGISLATION HAS
APPLIED AND IMPLEMENTED, EVEN AFTER THE CURTAILMENT OF
PRIVATE HUNTING.

06638 MUTZ, D.C.
YOURS, MINE, AND OURS: INFORMATION SOURCES, PERCEPTIONS OF
UNEMPLOYMENT, AND THEIR POLITICAL CONSEQUENCES
DISSERTATION ABSTRACTS INTERNATIONAL, 49(9) (MAR 89),
2797-A.
THE AUTHOR INVESTIGATES HOW MEDIATED AND UNMEDIATED
INFORMATION ABOUT UNEMPLOYMENT INFLUENCES PERCEPTIONS OF
THIS ISSUE AS A PROBLEM AT PERSONAL AND SOCIAL LEVELS AND
HOW THESE PERCEPTIONS, IN TURN, AFFECT EVALUATIONS OF
INCUMBENT POLITICAL LEADERS. SHE ALSO PROBES THE
IMPLICATIONS FOR DEPENDENCY THEORIES OF MEDIA EFFECTS AND
FOR THE STUDY OF ECONOMIC INFLUENCES ON VOTING.

06639 MWEMBE, K.
KENYA'S CHALLENGE: POPULATION GROWTH AND THE ECONOMY
MULTINATIONAL MONITOR, 10(5) (MAY 89), 10-12.
LIKE MUCH OF SUB-SAHARAN AFRICA, KENYA FACES SEVERE
ECONOMIC PROBLEMS. A RISING EXTERNAL DEBT, A DECLINING

CURRENCY, A LOW PER CAPITA INCOME AND A TROUBLESOME
INTERNATIONAL FINANCIAL CLIMATE REPRESENT SOME OF THE MOST
SIGNIFICANT CHALLENGES TO THE COUNTRY SINCE ITS INDEPENDENCE.
KENYA'S POPULATION GROWTH RATE, THE HIGHEST IN THE WORLD,
INTENSIFIES THESE PROBLEMS. DESPITE ALL THIS, MANY KENYANS
BOAST THAT THEIR ECONOMY IS STRONGER THAN THOSE IN
NEIGHBORING EAST AFRICAN COUNTRIES.

06640 MWEMBE, K.
KENYAN LABOR: THE POST-COLONIAL ERA
MULTINATIONAL MONITOR, 10(5) (MAY 89), 13-15.
FOR MORE THAN A QUARTER-CENTURY, THE LABOR MOVEMENT IN
KENYA HAS MADE SIGNIFICANT STRIDES. THE TRANSITION FROM
COLONIAL RULE TO INDEPENDENCE SAW THE INSTALLATION OF
IMPORTANT LABOR LAWS THAT WERE PROGRESSIVE BY THIRD WORLD
STANDARDS. IN RECENT YEARS, HOWEVER, THESE RIGHTS HAVE BEEN
GRADUALLY ERODED BECAUSE OF THE EVER-GROWING POPULATION AND
AN ECONOMY WHERE JOB CREATION SIMPLY CANNOT KEEP PACE WITH
THE NUMBERS LOOKING FOR WORK. THE KENYAN GOVERNMENT HAS
CREATED A NEW MINISTRY OF MANPOWER DEVELOPMENT AND
DEPLOYMENT TO ADDRESS THE PROBLEM, BUT THE TASK OF CREATING
JOBS WITH LITTLE CAPITAL IN A TIGHT WORLD ECONOMY MAY BE
IMPOSSIBLE.

06641 MYASNIKOV, A.
WHY SOVIET MINERS REFUSE TO BE RAKED OVER THE COALS
GLASNOST, II(4) (SEP 89), 4-7, 17.
THE NATIONWIDE STRIKE BY COAL MINERS IN JULY 1989 WAS
THE LARGEST WORK STOPPAGE IN THE SOVIET UNION SINCE THE
1920'S. THIS ARTICLE DESCRIBES EVERYDAY LIFE IN THE COAL-
MINING REGION OF VORKUTA AND EXPLAINS THE CONDITIONS THAT
LED TO THE SHUTDOWNS AND PROMPTED THE VORKUTA WORKERS TO BE
AMONG THE LAST TO RETURN TO THE MINES.

06642 MYERS, J.T.
CHINA: MODERNIZATION AND "UNHEALTHY TENDENCIES"
COMPARATIVE POLITICS, 21(2) (JAN 89), 193-214.
THE CHINESE PRESS HAS REVEALED A PERSISTENT CONCERN ON
THE PART OF THE LEADERSHIP OF THE CPC WITH "UNHEALTHY
TENDENCIES" ARISING IN THE WAKE OF RECENT ECONOMIC REFORMS.
THE CAMPAIGN AGAINST THESE TENDENCIES HAS BEEN AIMED AT
UNDESIRABLE BEHAVIOR ON THE PART OF PARTY AND GOVERNMENT
CADRES AND OFFICIALS, BUT THE LEADERS OF THE CPC APPEAR TO
HAVE LITTLE REAL UNDERSTANDING OF THE UNDERLYING CAUSES OF
THE PROBLEM.

06643 MYERS, N.
ENVIRONMENT AND SECURITY
FOREIGN POLICY, (74) (SPR 89), 23-41.
ENVIRONMENTAL ISSUES PRESENT A NOVEL AND INCREASINGLY
IMPORTANT SET OF CHALLENGES FOR US FOREIGN POLICY. THE
AUTHOR EXPLORES LINKAGES BETWEEN ENVIRONMENTAL AND SECURITY-
RELATED ISSUES AND THEIR IMPLICATIONS FOR FUTURE US FOREIGN
POLICY. ISSUES ANALYZED INCLUDE: DECADES-LONG DEFORESTATION
IN THE PHILIPPINES, WATER DEFICITS IN THE MIDDLE EAST, LAND
DEGRADTION IN EL SALVADOR, AND RAPID POPULATION GROWTH IN
NEW MEXICO.

06644 MYERS, S.L.
URUGUAY: THE TRAUMATIC YEARS, 1967-1987
DISSERTATION ABSTRACTS INTERNATIONAL, 49(9) (MAR 89),
2784-A.
A COUNTRY FIRMLY ESTABLISHED IN THE DEMOCRATIC TRADITION,
URUGUAY HAS RECENTLY BEEN RACKED BY BY ECONOMIC RECESSION,
LABOR STRIFE, EXTREMIST SUBVERSION, AND MILITARY
DICTATORSHIP. IN THIS DISSERTATION, THE AUTHOR STUDIES
URUGUAY'S POLITICAL COMPLEXITIES, ECONOMIC FAILURES,
MILITARY COMPLEX, AND EXTREMIST ORGANIZATIONS TO UNDERSTAND
HOW THEY HAVE SHAPED RECENT GOVERNMENTAL UPHEAVALS.

06645 MYLROIE, L.
IRAQ'S CHANGING ROLE IN THE PERSIAN GULF
CURRENT HISTORY, 88(535) (FEB 89), 89-92, 98-99.
KEY ELEMENTS OF IRAQI FOREIGN POLICY CHANGED DUE TO THE
IRAN-IRAQ WAR, AND TODAY THE COUNTRY'S POSITIONS ARE
CONTRADICTORY. DICTATORSHIP REIGNS AT HOME, BUT IRAQ'S
REGIONAL POLICY IS NOT RADICAL AND THERE ARE AMBIGUITIES IN
ITS DEALINGS WITH THE SUPERPOWERS.

06646 MYLROIE, L. A.
AFTER THE GUNS FELL SILENT: IRAQ IN THE MIDDLE EAST
MIDDLE EAST JOURNAL, 43(1) (WIN 89), 51-67.
MIDDLE EAST GENERALLY WELCOMED THE CEASE-FIRE IN THE
IRAN-IRAQ WAR, IF ONLY BECAUSE THE BLOODY CONFLICT
THREATENED TO ENGULF NEIGHBORING STATES. THERE ARE ALSO
OTHER BENEFITS FROM THE CEASE-FIRE THAT ARE NOT WIDELY
RECOGNIZED. ON THE REGIONAL LEVEL, IRAQ HAS NOW MODERATED
ITS POSITION. IT HAS STRENGTHENED TIES WITH ITS FRIENDS,
EGYPT AND JORDAN, AND HAS MOVED TO WEAKEN SYRIA IN PART BY
BACKING ANTI-SYRIAN ELEMENTS IN LEBANON. MOREOVER, SYRIA
LOST THE CARD IT LONG USED TO BLACKMAIL THE ARAB GULF STATES
-- ITS PRESUMED ABILITY TO MEDIATE WITH IRAN ON THEIR BEHALF.
THE WEAKENING OF SYRIA, THE MOST REJECTIONIST OF ISRAEL'S
NEIGHBORS, AND THE PROMOTION OF AN EGYPTIAN-JORDANIAN-IRAQI

TRIANGLE ENHANCES PROSPECTS FOR ARAB-ISRAELI NEGOTIATIONS.

06647 MYSAK, J.
THE BEAUTY OF MUNICIPAL BONDS
AMERICAN SPECTATOR, 22(6) (JUN 89), 18-20.
THE AUTHOR DISCUSSES THE GROWING MUNICIPAL BOND MARKET,
AND THE GROWING ATTEMPTS OF CONGRESS TO TAX MUNICIPAL BONDS.
MOST OF THE "BOND BASHING", THE AUTHOR MAINTAINS, IS DUE TO
IGNORANCE ON THE PART OF CONGRESS. ONLY A DETERMINED
CAMPAIGN DESIGNED TO INFORM CONGRESS OF THE BENEFITS OF
MUNICIPAL BONDS IS LIKELY TO SAVE THEM FROM LOSING THEIR
CURRENTLY TAX-EXEMPT STATUS.

06648 MYTELKA, L.K.
THE UNFULFILLED PROMISE OF AFRICAN INDUSTRIALIZATION
AFRICAN STUDIES REVIEW, 32(3) (DEC 89), 77-137.
THIS PAPER REVIEWS THE THEORETICAL DEBATE ABOUT THE
MEANS TO INDUSTRIALIZATION IN UNDERDEVELOPED COUNTRIES AND
THE PRAXIS TO WHICH IT GAVE RISE, FOCUSING ON THE COUNTRIES
OF SUB-SAHARAN AFRICA. WHILE RECOGNIZING THE CONSIDERABLE
GEOGRAPHICAL, ETHNIC, AND ECONOMIC DIVERSITY THAT
CHARACTERIZES THESE COUNTRIES, IT POINTS TO THE BROAD
SIMILARITY OF HISTORICAL EXPERIENCES AMONG THEM WITH REGARD
TO THE PROCESS OF INDUSTRIALIZATION AND TO THE ROLE OF
TECHNOLOGY IN THAT PROCESS.

06649 MZALA
NEGOTIATIONS AND PEOPLE'S POWER
SECHABA, 23(8) (AUG 89), 20-26.
THE ARTICLE EXAMINES THE ISSUE OF WHETHER THE CURRENT
STRUGGLE IN SOUTH AFRICA WILL GO ON TO THE COMPLETE
OVERTHROW OF THE CURRENT REGIME AND THE ESTABLISHMENT OF A
DEMOCRATIC GOVERNMENT OR WHETHER IT WILL BE FORCED INTO A
PREMATURE COMPROMISE, A NEGOTIATED SETTLEMENT, WHOSE
ULTIMATE EFFECT WOULD BE TO CURTAIL APARTHEID AND ESTABLISH
A POWER-SHARING GOVERNMENT. ALTHOUGH THIS QUESTION HAS BEEN
THE SUBJECT OF CONSIDERABLE DEBATE IN THE MEDIA, THE AFRICAN
NATIONAL CONGRESS REMAINS FIRM IN ITS RESOLVE THAT THE ONLY
NEGOTIATIONS ALLOWED WILL BE ABOUT THE TRANSFORMATION OF
APARTHEID TO A ONE-PERSON-ONE-VOTE SYSTEM OF GOVERNMENT.

06650 NABLI, M.K.; NUGENT, J.B.
THE NEW INSTITUTIONAL ECONOMICS AND ITS APPLICABILITY TO
DEVELOPMENT
WORLD DEVELOPMENT, 17(9) (SEP 89), 1333-1347.
THE SEVERAL REMARKABLE DEVELOPMENTS IN THE SOCIAL
SCIENCES WHICH HAVE COME TO BE KNOWN AS THE NEW
INSTITUTIONAL ECONOMICS (NIE) HAVE NOT YET BEEN FULLY
EXPLOITED FOR ANALYZING THE DETERMINANTS AND EFFECTS OF
INSTITUTIONAL CHANGE IN THE CONTEXT OF DEVELOPMENT. THIS
PAPER IDENTIFIES TWO IMPORTANT COMPONENTS OF THE NIE AND
ILLUSTRATES BOTH (A) POTENTIAL COMPLEMENTARITIES BETWEEN
THEM AND (B) THEIR APPLICABILITY TO VARIOUS PROBLEMS AND
POLICIES IN THE LONGTERM DEVELOPMENT OF DEVELOPING COUNTRIES.

06651 NABOUS, H.G.
THE IMPACT OF THE CHANGE IN EGYPT'S SUPERPOWER ALLEGIANCE
ON THE MIDDLE EASTERN SUB-SYSTEM
DISSERTATION ABSTRACTS INTERNATIONAL, 49(11) (MAY 89),
3498-A.
THE AUTHOR SEEKS TO APPLY THE SUB-SYSTEM CONCEPT TO
INTERNATIONAL POLITICS IN THE MIDDLE EAST. HE FOCUSES ON THE
IMPACT THAT THE CHANGE IN EGYPT'S SUPERPOWER ALLEGIANCE HAD
ON THE MIDEAST SUB-SYSTEM FROM 1972 TO 1980 IN THREE MAIN
DIMENSIONS: THE ARAB-ISRAELI SITUATION, THE INTER-ARAB
DIMENSION, AND THE SUPERPOWER DIMENSION.

06652 NADELMANN, E. A.
THE CASE FOR LEGALIZATION
PUBLIC INTEREST, 92 (SUM 88), 3-31.
THIS ARTICLE EXAMINES THE ABUNDANT EVIDENCE WHICH
SUGGESTS THAT LEGALIZATION OF DRUG USE MAY WELL BE THE
OPTIMAL STRATEGY FOR TACKLING THE DRUG PROBLEM. HOW
LEGALIZATION BEGAN TO BE SERIOUSLY CONSIDERED AS A POLICY
OPTION IS EXPLORED. VARIOUS LEGALIZATION STRATEGIES ARE
EXPLORED AS WELL AS POLITICIAN AND PUBLIC REACTION TO THE
CONCEPT.

06653 NADKARNI, V.
SOVIET PERCEPTIONS OF THE CORRELATION OF FORCES
DISSERTATION ABSTRACTS INTERNATIONAL, 49(8) (FEB 89),
2382-A.
FOCUSING ON THE KHRUSHCHEV AND BREZHNEV REGIMES, THE
AUTHOR TRACES EVOLVING SOVIET PERCEPTIONS OF THE CORRELATION
OF FORCES BETWEEN THE SOCIALIST AND CAPITALIST WORLDS, IN
GENERAL, AND THE USSR AND USA, IN PARTICULAR. A ROUGH SOVIET
EQUIVALENT OF THE WESTERN CONCEPT OF THE "BALANCE OF POWER,"
"CORRELATION OF FORCES" ENCOMPASSES ECONOMIC, POLITICAL AND
MILITARY DIMENSIONS.

06654 NADLER, R.; DONELSON, T.
AFFIRMATIVE REACTION
NATIONAL REVIEW, XLI(17) (SEP 89), 28-29.
THE CENTRAL PARADOX IN THE COURT-ORDERED PLAN FOR

DESEGREGATING THE KANSAS CITY, MISSOURI, METROPOLITAN SCHOOL
DISTRICT (KCMSD) WAS THAT JUDICIAL TAXATION AND COERCIRE
SOCIAL ENGINEERING WERE APPLIED TO FASHION A REMEDY WHOSE
SUCCESS DEPENDED UPON ITS VOLUNTARY ACCEPTANCE BY THE PUBLIC.
THE PUBLIC HAS NOT CONVINCED, AND APPEALS TO THE COURT ARE
STILL BEING BROUGHT.

06655 NAGAHARU, H.
A TAX REFORM FRAUD?
JAPAN QUARTERLY, XXXVI(2) (APR 89), 127-134.
JAPAN'S NEW CONSUMPTION TAX WILL BE THE FIRST OF ITS
KIND FOR THE COUNTRY. TO SMOOTH THE WAY FOR ITS INTRODUCTION,
THE ADMINISTRATION OF PRIME MINISTER TAKESHITA NOBORU
MOBILIZED THE MINISTRY OF FINANCE, THE MINISTRY OF
INTERNATIONAL TRADE AND INDUSTRY, THE NATIONAL TAX
ADMINISTRATION AGENCY, AND THE SMALL- AND MEDIUM-SIZED
ENTERPRISE AGENCY TO CONDUCT ORIENTATION MEETINGS AT MORE
THAN 10,000 LOCATIONS. TAKESHITA'S ENERGETIC PRONOUNCEMENTS
ABOUT THE NEW TAX, WHICH IS SIMILAR TO THE VALUE-ADDED TAXES
LEVIED IN THE EUROPEAN COMMUNITY, REFLECT EXTREME
NERVOUSNESS OVER ITS SUCCESS.

06656 NAGEL, T.
WHAT MAKES A POLITICAL THEORY UTOPIAN?
SOCIAL RESEARCH, 56(4) (WIN 89), 903-920.
WHILE THERE IS A NOTION OF TRUTH RELEVANT TO POLITICAL
THEORIES, IT DIFFERS FROM THAT OF SCIENCE, FOR WHAT HUMAN
BEINGS SHARE THAT PERMITS A POLITICAL ARGUMENT TO BE
ADDRESSED TO THEM IS NOT ONLY RATIONALITY BUT ALSO CERTAIN ·
MORAL VALUES, SUCH AS MUTUAL RESPECT AND EQUAL REGARD. BUT
NO POLITICAL THEORY CAN IGNORE INDIVIDUAL MOTIVES. WHILE
MUTUALITY AND INDIVIDUALITY OVERLAP, POLITICAL INSTITUTIONS
OFFER BOTH MORE PROTECTION AND GREATER THREATS TO THE
INDIVIDUAL THAN PRINCIPLES OF INDIVIDUAL MORALITY, AND
POLITICAL THEORY IS DISTINCTIVE IN PRESENTING AN ETHICAL AND
PRACTICAL DEMAND. THE THEORIES OF A CLASSLESS SOCIETY AND OF
A LIBERAL SYSTEM OF INDIVIDUAL RIGHTS ILLUSTRATE THE PROBLEM
OF DOUBLE JUSTIFICATION. WHEREAS THE IDEAL OF MORAL EQUALITY
IN THE FORMER SEEMS HOPELESSLY UTOPIAN, THE PERSUASIVE
FUNCTION OF THE LATTER APPEARS LESS THAN ADEQUATE IN TERMS
OF REALIZING ANY SORT OF EGALITARIAN IDEAL.

06657 NAGLER, J.
STRATEGIC IMPLICATIONS OF CONFEREE SELECTIONS IN THE HOUSE
OF REPRESENTATIVES: "IT AIN'T OVER TIL IT'S OVER"
AMERICAN POLITICS QUARTERLY, 17(1) (JAN 89), 54-79.
IN THIS ARTICLE THE AUTHOR EXAMINES THE PROCEDURE USED BY
THE HOUSE TO SELECT CONFEREES, AND DESCRIBE THE IMPLICATIONS
OF THIS PROCESS FOR LEGISLATIVE OUTCOMES. THE AUTHOR SHOWS
THAT COMMITTE INFLUENCE DEPENDS ON THE BEHAVIOR OF THE
SPEAKER OF THE HOUSE. HE ANALYSES THE DEBATE OVER MINIMUM
WAGE LEGISLATION IN THE HOUSE DURING 1972, 1973, AND 1977.

06658 NAGLER, J.D.
AN EXAMINATION OF STRATEGIC OPPORTUNITIES PROVIDED BY THE
CONFERENCE COMMITTEE PROCEDURE IN THE U.S. CONGRESS
DISSERTATION ABSTRACTS INTERNATIONAL, 50(5) (NOV 89),
1425-A.
THE AUTHOR TESTS THE HYPOTHESIS THAT BECAUSE CONFERENCE
REPORTS IN THE SENATE AND HOUSE OF REPRESENTATIVES ARE
CONSIDERED UNDER A RULE THAT DOES NOT ALLOW AMENDMENTS, THE
CONFEREES ENJOY AGENDA-SETTING POWER. HE UTILIZES A RANDOM-
UTILITY MODEL TO ESTIMATE LEGISLATORS' IDEAL POINTS ON
APPROPRIATIONS BILLS FROM 1973 THROUGH 1980. HE CONCLUDES
THAT COMMITTEE DEFERENCE CANNOT BE SAID TO BE A RESULT OF
THE CONFERENCE PROCEDURE AND THAT, IN FACT, COMMITTEE
DEFERENCE DOES NOT APPEAR TO EXIST AT ALL.

06659 NAGO, M.C.
CAN AFRICA FEED ITSELF: RESOURCES MUST BE USED TO MEET
REAL NEEDS
WORLD MARXIST REVIEW, 32(9) (SEP 89), 76-77.
THIS ARTICLE ADDRESSES THE EXISTING FOOD SUPPLY IN BENIN,
AS WELL AS AFRICA AS A WHOLE. IT EXPLORES THE REASONS FOR
SHORTAGES, AMONG THEM CIVIL WARS, CHARGING GOVERNMENTS WITH
THE BUYING OF WEAPONS INSTEAD OF BUILDING UP NATIONAL
ECONOMIC POTENTIAL. THAT THERE MUST BE NO WARS IN AFRICA IS
THE CONCLUSION DRAWN.

06660 NAGORNY, A.; TSYPLAKOV, S.
THE PRC: THE FIRST DECADE OF THE POLICY OF REFORMS
INTERNATIONAL AFFAIRS (MOSCOW), (1) (JAN 89), 22-30.
TEN YEARS AGO THE THIRD CPC CC PLENARY MEETING OF THE
ELEVENTH CONVOCATION USHERED IN A NEW STAGE IN THE HISTORY
OF THE PEOPLE'S REPUBLIC OF CHINA. SINCE THAT TIME, CHINA
HAS FOLLOWED A POLICY OF REFORM THAT HAS TRANSFORMED THE
POLITICAL, ECONOMIC, AND IDEOLOGICAL ATMOSPHERE IN THE
COUNTRY.

06661 NAGPAUL, H.
SECULARISM IN INDIA: UNRESOLVED CONFLICTS AND PERSISTENT
PROBLEMS
INTERNATIONAL JOURNAL OF POLITICS, CULTURE AND SOCIETY,
2(2) (WIN 88), 201-216.

THIS STUDY EXAMINES THE CONCEPTION OF SECULARISM AS VIEWED IN THE CONSTITUTION OF INDIA IN THE CONTEXT OF A LOCAL COMMUNITY. THOUGH THIS CONCEPT ITSELF IS NOT FORMALLY DEFINED, THE CONSTITUTION DOES SET UP INDIA AS A SECULAR STATE BASED UPON CULTURAL PLURALISM WHICH EMPHASIZES (1) SEPARATION OF CHURCH AND STATE; (2) ACCEPTANCE OF ALL RELIGIONS BY PROVIDING SOME BASIC FUNDAMENTAL RIGHTS, AND FREEDOM OF RELIGION, BOTH INDIVIDUAL AND COLLECTIVE; (3) INTRODUCTION OF REFORMS OF SOME OUTDATED AND UNJUST TRADITIONAL ELEMENTS ESPECIALLY IN HINDUISM THROUGH SOCIAL WELFARE LEGISLATION AND (4) PROMOTION OF NATIONAL LOYALTIES AND INTEGRATION REPLACING RELIGIOUS AND COMMUNAL LOYALTIES. THIS CONCEPTION STARTS ON A DIFFERENT FOOTING THAN THE ONE WHICH IS USUALLY PRACTICED IN MOST WESTERN SOCIETIES. IT HAS COME TO BE CALLED A REFORMIST BRAND OF SECULARISM.

06662 NAHAYLO, B.
THE CASE OF NIKOLAI BUKHARIN
ENCOUNTER, LXXII(1) (JAN 89), 54-60.
POLITICAL AND ECONOMIC EXIGENCIES HAVE LED THE GORBACHEV REGIME TO EMBARK ON A FAR-REACHING CAMPAIGN OF DE-STALINIZATION. THE PRESENT DENUNCIATION OF STALIN AND HIS METHODS, AS WELL AS THE DENIGRATION OF LEONID BREZHNEV, HAS OPENED A LIVELY DEBATE IN THE SOVIET PRESS ABOUT THE WHOLE NATURE OF THE SOVIET EXPERIENCE. ONE OF THE CENTRAL FIGURES IN THIS RE-EVALUATION IS NIKOLAI BUKHARIN, THE CELEBRATED PARTY THEORETICIAN AND IDEOLOGIST WHO BECAME THE MOST FAMOUS VICTIM OF STALIN'S TRIALS AGAINST "OLD BOLSHEVIKS."

06663 NAIDU, A.G.
PAKISTAN AFTER ZIA-UL-HAQ: ISLAMABAD'S POLICY OPTIONS
INDIAN JOURNAL OF POLITICAL SCIENCE, L(3) (JUL 89), 321-334.
THE AUTHOR CONSIDERS HOW THE MILITARY AND RELIGIOUS FACTORS WILL AFFECT PAKISTANI POLICY-MAKING UNDER PRIME MINISTER BENAZIR BHUTTO. HE ALSO DISCUSSES PAKISTAN'S POLICY OPTIONS REGARDING RELATIONS WITH INDIA, NUCLEAR WEAPONS, RELATIONS WITH THE UNITED STATES, AND THE WAR IN AFGHANISTAN.

06664 NAIDU, M.V.
RELIGIONISM, RATIONALISM AND VIOLENCE: A STUDY IN RELIGIOUS TERRORISM
PEACE RESEARCH, 21(2) (MAY 89), 1-12.
THE PRESENT MUSLIM PERSECUTION OF THE ISLAMIC CRITICS COMPLETES THE VICIOUS CIRCLE OF RELIGIOUS PERSECUTIONS BY THE THREE MIDDLE EASTERN RELIGIONSJUDAISM, CHRISTIANITY AND ISLAM. HISTORICALLY, CHRISTIAN PERSECUTION OF THE JEWS WAS FOLLOWED BY THE CATHOLIC PERSECUTION OF THE PROTESTANTS, THE JEWISH PERSECUTION OF THE ANTI-ZIONISTS, AND THE PLO PERSECUTION OF THE ANTI-PALESTINIANS. THE THREE RELIGIONS HAVE COMMON CULTURAL ROOTS, SHARE SIMILAR SUCCESSES IN THEIR EXPANSION AND HAVE WEAVED SIMILAR TRAGIC TALES OF TERRORISM. THIS ARTICLE PROVIDES AN ANALYSIS OF THE FUROR GENERATED IN ISLAMIC CIRCLES OVER THE PUBLICATION OF SALMAN RUSHDIE'S NOVEL THE SATANIC VERSES.

06665 NAIDU, M.V.
SSHRCC & PEACE STUDIES
PEACE RESEARCH, 21(1) (JAN 89), 1-12.
SOCIAL SCIENCES AND HUMANITIES RESEARCH COUNCIL OF CANADA (SSHRCC) IS THE LARGEST SINGLE GRANTING AGENCY OF THE CANADIAN GOVERNMENT IN THE FIELDS OF SOCIAL SCIENCES AND HUMANITIES. THIS ARTICLE FOCUSES UPON SSHRCC SUPPORT TO PEACE STUDIES. OUT OF 783 PROJECTS ONLY 13 ARE RELATED, DIRECTLY OR INDIRECTLY, TO PEACE THEMES - FIVE HISTORY PROJECTS, FIVE ECONOMICS PROJECTS, TWO LAW PROJECTS, AND ONE POLITICAL SCIENCE PROJECT. TOGETHER THESE 13 PROJECTS (1.6% OF THE TOTAL) RECEIVED $310,576 WHICH CONSTITUTES ABOUT 1.3% OF THE TOTAL OF $22.5 MILLION DOLLARS.

06666 NAITAO, W.
CHINA HITS HARD AT CORRUPTION
BEIJING REVIEW, 32(52) (DEC 89), 23-27.
FOLLOWING THE DICTATES OF THE CPC CENTRAL COMMITTEE AND THE STATE COUNCIL, CHINA HAS LAUNCHED A CRACKDOWN ON GRAFT AND CORRUPTION. THE ANTI-CORRUPTION DRIVE DEMONSTRATES THE FIRM DETERMINATION OF THE PARTY AND GOVERNMENT TO PROVIDE CLEAN GOVERNMENT AND PUNISH WRONGDOERS. IN ACCORDANCE WITH "THE CIRCULAR ON CRIMINALS GUILTY OF GRAFT, BRIBERY, AND SPECULATION WHO MUST SURRENDER THEMSELVES WITHIN A SPECIFIED TIME LIMIT," THOSE OFFICIALS WHO SURRENDERED BEFORE OCTOBER 31, 1989, WILL BE GIVEN LENIENT TREATMENT. OTHERS WILL BE SEVERELY PUNISHED.

06667 NAITAO, W.
ICE MELTING ON THE SINO-SOVIET BORDER
BEIJING REVIEW, 32(20) (MAY 89), 21-26.
TWENTY YEARS AGO, THE BOOM OF GUNS BURST THE SILENCE OF ZHENBAO ISLAND AS STRAINED SINO-SOVIET RELATIONS REACHED A BREAKING-POINT. ALONG THE CLOSED BOUNDARY, TROOPS OF THE TWO COUNTRIES PATROLLED IN FULL BATTLE ARRAY. BUT NOW ALL THIS HAS BEEN SUPERCEDED BY AN ATMOSPHERE OF PEACE, FRIENDSHIP AND BRISK TRADE TRANSACTIONS.

06668 NAJIBULLAH
AFGHANISTAN: OUR GOAL IS NATIONAL RECONCILIATION
INFORMATION BULLETIN, 25/26(1-2) (JAN 88), 17-20.
THIS DESCRIPTION OF THE GENERAL CONFERENCE OF THE PEOPLE'S DEMOCRATIC PARTY OF AFGLANISTAN DETAILS HOW THE DELEGATES HEARD AND CONSIDERED REPORTS ON THE WAYS TO ADVANCE THE ECONOMY, IMPLEMENT AFGLANISTAN'S NEW CONSTITUTION, AND PARTICIPANT IN WORLD ECONOMIC AFFAIRS. THE PARTY DESCRIBED ITS GOAL TO BECOME A COMMUNIST VANGUARD PARTY.

06669 NAJIBULLAH
THE HUMANE IDEA OF RECONCILIATION
WORLD MARXIST REVIEW, 31(1) (JAN 88), 34-39.
THE POLICY OF NATIONAL RECONCILIATION DECLARED BY THE PEOPLE'S DEMOCRATIC PARTY OF AFGHANISTAN (PDPA) HAS THE SIMPLE AND CONCRETE AIM TO PUT AN END TO THE FRATRICIDAL WAR, WHICH HAS BEEN AFFLICTING OUR LAND, THE BODIES AND SOULS OF MILLIONS OF THE AFGHAN PEOPLE FOR NEARLY TEN YEARS NOW. THE IDEA OF RECONCILIATION HAS IMBIBED THE HISTORICAL EXPERIENCE OF THE REVOLUTIONARY TRANSFORMATION OF SOCIETY AND REFLECTS PEOPLE'S ETERNAL STRIVING FOR ERADICATING WARS, FOR PROGRESS AND HUMANISM. IT REFLECTS AN ATTEMPT AT MASTERING A NEW POLITICAL THINKING WHICH HAS DECLARED HUMAN LIFE AND PEACE ON EARTH TO BE THE HIGHEST VALUES.

06670 NAJJAR, F.
ELECTIONS AND DEMOCRACY IN EGYPT
AMERICAN-ARAB AFFAIRS, (29) (SUM 89), 96-113.
HOSNI MUBARAK, WHO LED EGYPT AFTER THE DEATH OF SUDAT, RELAXED STATE CONTROL, RELEASED POLITICAL PRISONERS, AND GRANTED GREATER FREEDOM TO POLITICAL PARTIES AND THE PRESS, HIS OFTEN REPEATED COMMITMENT TO DEMOCRACY MUST BE ASSESSED IN LIGHT OF TWO NATIONAL ELECTIONS HELD ON MAY 27, 1984, AND ON APRIL 6, 1987. THIS PAPER EXAMINES BOTH ELECTIONS IN ORDER TO DETERMINE THE PROGRESS OF DEMOCRACY IN EGYPT SINCE MUBARAK ASSUMED THE PRESIDENCY.

06671 NAKARADA, R.
THE PRINCIPLES OF BALANCED DEVELOPMENT
ALTERNATIVES, 14(4) (OCT 89), 517-522.
THIS ARTICLE CONTINUES IN THE SEARCH FOR SOLUTIONS TO PROBLEMS OF DEVELOPMENT, AND EXAMINES HOW CRITICAL THOUGHT ASSESES THE SOURCES OF PROBLEMS. IN ORDER TO ILLUSTRATE THE IMPORTANCE OF A HISTORICALLY BALANCED ASSESSMENT OF PROBLEMS THE WRITER REFERS TO THE EXPERIENCES OF EXISTING SOCIALIST SOCIETIES. IT EXPLORES TRADITION AND MODERNITY AND EXAMINES THE NATURE OF SOCIAL AGENTS.

06672 NAKHLEH, E.
THE PALESTINIANS AND THE FUTURE: PEACE THROUGH REALISM
JOURNAL OF PALESTINE STUDIES, XVIII(2) (WIN 89), 3-15.
THE ARTICLE EXAMINES THE ISSUES UNDERLYING THE PALESTINIAN QUEST FOR INDEPENDENCE, ESPECIALLY IN LIGHT OF THE RECENT DECLARATION OF PALESTINIAN INDEPENDENCE BY THE PLO AND THE APPARENT ACKNOWLEDGEMENT OF ISRAEL'S EXISTENCE AND THEIR REJECTION OF TERRORISM. THE ARTICLE PROPOSES A PROGRAM OF ACTION FOR THE PLO IN ORDER TO BE A GENUINE NEGOTIATING PARTNER. IT ALSO REFLECTS ON RECENT POLITICAL DEVELOPMENTS IN THE OCCUPIED TERRITORIES, ANALYZES THE PRESENT REALITIES OF THE PALESTINIAN-ISRAELI CONFLICT, AND PROPOSES A COURSE OF ACTION FOR RESOLVING THE CONFLICT.

06673 NALBANDIAN, J.
THE CONTEMPORARY ROLE OF CITY MANAGERS
AMERICAN REVIEW OF PUBLIC ADMINISTRATION, 19(4) (DEC 89), 261-278.
A GROWING BODY OF RECENT LITERATURE DOCUMENTS THE CITY MANAGER'S POLITICALLY ACTIVE ROLE IN TODAY'S COMMUNITIES. THIS ROLE CHALLENGES THE NORMATIVE ASSUMPTION UPON WHICH THE COUNCILMANAGER PLAN OF GOVERNMENT IS BASED: NAMELY, THAT THE CITY MANAGER IS A POLITICALLY NEUTRAL, ADMINISTRATIVE EXPERT SUBORDINATE TO A GOVERNING BODY. ON THE BASIS OF IN-DEPTH INTERVIEWS AND THE PUBLISHED WORK OF TODAY'S CITY MANAGERS, THE WAY CITY MANAGERS EXPLAIN AND JUSTIFY THEIR ROLE IS IDENTIFIED AND EXAMINED.

06674 NAM, K.G.
RELYING ON THE PEOPLE'S ENTHUSIASM AND CREATIVE EFFORT
WORLD MARXIST REVIEW, 32(9) (SEP 89), 16-17.
THIS ARTICLE, FROM THE WORKER'S PARTY OF KOREA (WPK), PROPAGANDA DEPARTMENT, IS AN ANALYSIS OF WHAT IS NEEDED FOR SOCIALIST CONSTRUCTION TO PROCEED SUCCESSFULLY IN NORTH KOREA. IT SUGGESTS A PRIORITY OF POLITICAL METHODS TO RELEASE, STIMULATE AND DEVELOP THE REVOLUTIONARY ENTHUSIASM AND CREATIVE ACTIVITY OF THE MASSES. IT STRESS THE ATTENTION THAT THE PARTY GIVES TO IDEOLOGICAL EDUCATION OF THE WORKING PEOPLE AND ADDRESSES THE CHOLLIM MOVEMENT. IT ILLUSTRATES HOW ENTHUSIASM AND CREATIVITY IS SUCCEEDING IN AGRICULTURE AND CONSTRUCTION AND IS OPTIMISTIC FOR THE FUTURE.

06675 NAMENWIRTH, J.Z.; WEBER, R.P.
CYCLES OF THE FOURTH KIND: A REPLY TO MOHLER'S CYCLES OF VALUES

EUROPEAN JOURNAL OF POLITICAL RESEARCH, 17(1) (JAN 89),
115-119.
MOHLER ARGUES THAT GERMAN CULTURE DOES NOT DISPLAY
THEMATIC CYCLES LIKE THOSE FOUND BY NAMENWIRTH AND WEBER IN
AMERICA AND GREAT BRITAIN. IN THIS ESSAY, THE AUTHORS ARGUE
THAT MOHLER'S CLAIM IS NOT SUPPORTED BY THE EMPIRICAL
EVIDENCE HE PRESENTS. THEY ALSO FIND HIS CLAIM TO BE
CONCEPTUALLY AND THEORETICALLY FLAWED.

06676 NAMSRAY, T.
THE PARTY IS RESPONSIBLE FOR THE FATE OF RENEWAL
WORLD MARXIST REVIEW, 32(4) (APR 89), 34-37.
ALTHOUGH SOCIALISM IN MONGOLIA IS FIRMLY ON ITS FEET AND
HAS PROVED ITS VIABILITY, IT HAS NOT YET REVEALED ITS FULL
POTENTIAL. THIS, OF COURSE, CANNOT BE EXPLAINED BY THE
SYSTEM'S COMPARATIVE YOUTH, NOR FOR THAT MATTER, BY ANY SUCH
CLAIMS AS "OUTDATEDNESS" OR "INCONSISTENCIES" IN THE
DOCTRINE OF MARX, ENGLES AND LENIN. SOCIALISM HAS NOT BEEN
ABLE TO PROVE ITS SUPERIORITY SO FAR BECAUSE IN PRACTICE IT
HAS RUN UP AGAINST MANY DIFFICULTIES, AND SUFFERED
DEFORMATIONS WHICH HAVE NOTHING IN COMMON WITH ITS ESSENCE.
RESTRUCTURING IN MONGOLIA IS BOTH A COMPONENT AND A SPECIFIC
PART OF THE RADICAL POLITICAL AND ECONOMIC CHANGES NOW
OCCURRING IN FRATERNAL SOCIALIST COUNTRIES. THIS IS NOT A
CASE OF SIMPLY FOLLOWING FASHION, STILL LESS BLIND IMITATION.
THE POLICY OF RENEWAL MUST NOT BE UNDERSTOOD AS A SHORT-
TERM OR AD HOC ACTION. IT IS AN INEXORABLE DEMAND OF LIFE, A
DEEPLY CONSCIOUS LONG-TERM STRATEGIC LINE.

06677 NAOKI, T.
THE DOLLAR'S FINE DE SIECLE, THE YEN'S DEBUT
JAPAN QUARTERLY, XXXVI(2) (APR 89), 120-126.
INDISPUTABLY, THE 20TH CENTURY HAS BEEN THE AMERICAN
CENTURY. BUT THE APPROACHING ERA IS OFTEN BILLED AS THE
JAPANESE CENTURY. THE RISE OF JAPANESE ECONOMIC DOMINANCE
SHOULD BE VIEWED IN TERMS OF JAPAN'S POTENTIAL FOR
GENERATING AN ECONOMIC ORDER THAT CAN SERVE THE NEXT
GENERATION. ALTHOUGH NO COMPARISON BETWEEN THE UNITED STATES
AND JAPAN SHOULD FAIL TO TAKE BOTH MILITARY AND CIVILIAN
SPENDING INTO ACCOUNT, ASSESSMENT OF THESE EXPENDITURES IS
FRAUGHT WITH DIFFICULTIES. THEREFORE, IT IS BEST TO FOCUS ON
THE CAPACITIES OF AMERICA'S AND JAPAN'S PRIVATE SECTORS TO
PROVIDE A FRAMEWORK FOR TOMORROW'S ECONOMY.

06678 NAPLES, N.A.
WOMEN AGAINST POVERTY: COMMUNITY WORKERS IN ANTI-POVERTY
PROGRAMS, 1964-1984
DISSERTATION ABSTRACTS INTERNATIONAL, 49(9) (MAR 89),
2833-A.
THE STUDY DRAWS UPON THE SOCIOLOGICAL THEORIES OF WORK
AND OCCUPATIONS, THE SOCIOLOGY OF COMMUNITY, POLITICAL
SOCIOLOGY, AND FEMINIST THEORY TO UNDERSTAND THE EXPERIENCE
OF INDIGENOUS COMMUNITY WORKERS. SEVERAL AVENUES OF INQUIRY
ARE EXPLORED: (1) SOCIALIZATION; (2) COMMUNITY WORK AS
"WOMEN'S WORK"; (3) THE EFFECT OF PAY ON INDIGENOUS WOMEN'S
COMMUNITY WORK; (4) COMMUNITY WORK AND POLITICAL
PARTICIPATION; (5) EMPOWERMENT AND RADICALIZATION; (6) THE
IMPORTANCE OF COMMUNITY FOR LOW INCOME WOMEN; (7) THE ROLE
OF THE STATE IN SOCIAL REFORM.

06679 NAPOLITANO, G.
FOR NEW POLITICAL AND MILITARY EQUILIBRIA BETWEEN EAST AND
WEST, A NEW ROLE FOR EUROPE
INTERNATIONAL SPECTATOR, XXIII(3) (JUL 88), 153-159.
IT IS WITH REFERENCE TO THE REALITY OF NATO THAT THE
QUESTION OF EUROPE'S ROLE IN INTERNATIONAL POLITICS TAKES ON
MEANING. THE REAL ISSUE CONCERNS THE CREATION OF A EUROPEAN
ENTITY, DISTINCT AND INDEPENDENT OF THE USSR AND
SUFFICIENTLY AUTONOMOUS FROM THE UNITED STATES TO PLAY A
LEADING ROLE AND KEEP THE TWO SUPERPOWERS FROM BEING THE
ONLY ARBITERS ON THE WORLD POLITICAL SCENE.

06680 NARJES, K.
SPACE AND THE EUROPEAN COMMUNITY
SPACE POLICY, 5(1) (FEB 89), 59-64.
EUROPE IS TODAY THE THIRD MOST IMPORTANT SPACE POWER,
THANKS TO THE WORK OF THE EUROPEAN SPACE AGENCY. BUT THERE
REMAIN MAJOR WEAKNESSES, IN PARTICULAR THE LACK OF A COGENT
AND COMPREHENSIVE EUROPEAN SPACE POLICY. THE EUROPEAN
COMMUNITY IS ALREADY PLAYING A MAJOR ROLE IN FACILITATING
DEVELOPMENT, AND THE COMMISSION IS PROPOSING SIX ACTION
LINES AIMED AT PROVIDING A COHERENT FRAMEWORK FOR THE
COMMUNITY'S FUTURE INVOLVEMENT IN SPACE ACTIVITIES. THESE
ARE RESEARCH AND TECHNOLOGICAL DEVELOPMENT,
TELECOMMUNICATIONS, EARTH OBSERVATION, INDUSTRIAL
DEVELOPMENT, THE LEGAL ENVIRONMENT, AND TRAINING. PROPOSALS
HAVE BEEN SENT TO MEMBER STATES FOR CONSIDERATION BEFORE A
DEBATE IN THE COUNCIL OF MINISTERS AND EUROPEAN PARLIAMENT.

06681 NARPATI, B.
COUNTERTRADE
CONTEMPORARY REVIEW, 254(1481) (JUN 89), 289-291.
THE TERM 'COUNTERTRADE' COVERS A WIDE RANGE OF
INTERNATIONAL TRANSACTIONS IN WHICH EXPORTING IS LINKED

CONTRACTUALLY TO IMPORT COMMITMENTS. THESE MECHANISMS
INCLUDE BARTER, COUNTERPURCHASE, OFFSET, BUYBACK, EVIDENCE
ACCOUNTS AND SWITCH TRADING. UNDER COUNTERTRADE ARRANGEMENTS,
EXPORT SALES TO A PARTICULAR MARKET ARE MADE CONDITIONAL
UPON UNDERTAKINGS TO ACCEPT IMPORTS FROM THAT MARKET. SUCH
OPERATIONS ARE SET UP BY NEGOTIATION AND THERE ARE HARDLY
ANY INTERNATIONAL REGULATIONS WHICH GOVERN THEM.

06682 NASH, B.E.
VOLUNTARISM IN LAW ENFORCEMENT
DISSERTATION ABSTRACTS INTERNATIONAL, 49(10) (APR 89),
3152-A.
THIS IS A LONGITUDINAL STUDY OF VOLUNTARISM IN LOCAL LAW
ENFORCEMENT IN THE UNITED STATES, UNDERTAKEN IN COOPERATION
WITH THE AMERICAN ASSOCIATION OF RETIRED PERSONS. THE AUTHOR
SELECTED AGENCIES OF VARIOUS SIZES ACROSS THE UNITED STATES
FOR STUDY. HE FOUND THAT VOLUNTEERS ARE NOW INVOLVED IN LAW
ENFORCEMENT AGENCY WORK IN FAR GREATER NUMBERS AND IN A
LARGER VARIETY OF FUNCTIONS THAN PREVIOUSLY ASSUMED.

06683 NASH, M.L.
A CONSTITUTIONAL MONARCHY
CONTEMPORARY REVIEW, 254(1479) (APR 89), 205-208.
THIS ESSAY DESCRIBES THE BEGINNINGS OF BRITAIN'S
CONSTITUTIONAL MONARCHY ON FEBRUARY 13, 1689 WITH THE
SIGNING BY WILLIAM AND MANY OF THE CONSTITUTIONAL BILL OF
RIGHTS.

06684 NASH, M.L.
THE ENLARGEMENT OF THE COMMUNITY: PART 1: AUSTRIA AND THE
EASTERN BLOC
CONTEMPORARY REVIEW, 255(1486) (NOV 89), 225-231.
THIS ARTICLE SUGGESTS THAT A SET OF UNOFFICIAL CRITERIA
HAVE GROWN UP IN THE COMMUNITY WITH REGARD TO THE APPLICANT
STATES. IT THEN EXAMINES THE SITUATION OF AUSTRIA WHERE NOT
ONLY DOES SHE BELONG TO THE EUROPEAN FREE TRADE AREA, BUT
SHE IS NEUTRAL. THE ARGUEMENT ABOUT NON-ALIGNED COUNTRIES IS
EXPLORED. AUSTRIA HAS A SPECIAL POSITION IN THIS. NO
CONSIDERATION CAN REALLY BE GIVEN TO THE FACTORS INVOLVED
WITHOUT GOING BACK TO THE BREAK-UP OF THE HOLY ROMAN EMPIRE
BY NAPOLEON IN 1806, AND THE VACUUM WHICH ALWAYS SEEMS TO
EXIST IN CENTRAL EUROPE UNLESS THERE IS SOME COHESION AMONG
THE STATES THERE: WHAT OTTO VON HABSBURG SUCCINCTLY SUMMED
UP AS 'THE PLACE WHERE THE WORLD FEELS NEURALGIA'. THE
ARTICLE EXPLORES TWO POSSIBLE INITIATIVES AND CONCLUDES THAT
THE IDEA OF CONFEDERATION OF THE OLD DOMINIONS BEFORE 1918
WILL NOT GO AWAY.

06685 NASHIF, T.
PLO MOVES ARE GENUINE
NEW OUTLOOK, 32(5 (291)) (MAY 89), 14-15.
RECENT PLO STATEMENTS AND PNC RESOLUTIONS ARE
SIGNIFICANT AND GENUINE MOVES, NOT TACTICAL RUSES. THE
ENORMITY OF THE SUFFERING OF THE PALESTINIAN PEOPLE ON THE
WEST BANK AND THE GAZA STRIP LENDS WEIGHT TO THE ARGUMENT
THAT THE PLO MOVES ARE GENUINE. UNDER THE PREVAILING
CONDITIONS OF ISRAELI OCCUPATION, THE VERY PHYSICAL
EXISTENCE OF PALESTINIANS IN THE TERRITORIES IS AT STAKE. IN
THIS CONTEXT, THE PLO HAS CONCLUDED THAT IT IS BEYOND ITS
POWER TO ACHIEVE ONE DEMOCRATIC STATE IN THE LAND LOCATED
WEST OF THE JORDAN RIVER. THUS, THE PLO ACKNOWLEDGES
ISRAEL'S EXISTENCE AND THAT PALESTINIAN NATIONAL ASPIRATIONS
MUST BE LIMITED TO THE ESTABLISHMENT OF AN INDEPENDENT
PALESTINIAN STATE IN GAZA AND THE WEST BANK.

06686 NASRALLAH, F.
SYRIA PAYS THE PRICE OF ISOLATION
MIDDLE EAST INTERNATIONAL, (347) (MAR 89), 17-18.
THERE ARE INDICATIONS THAT SYRIA WANTS TO EMERGE FROM
ITS GROWING ISOLATION AND MARGINALIZATION. A LONG SERIES OF
FOREIGN POLICY MISHAPS HAS SIGNALLED THE NEED FOR A CHANGE
IN TACTICS. PRESIDENT HAFIZ AL-ASAD HAS BEGUN SLOWLY
PLOTTING THE RETURN OF SYRIA INTO THE ARAB MAINSTREAM.

06687 NASRALLAH, F.
SYRIA'S FOREIGN STRATEGY
MIDDLE EAST INTERNATIONAL, (359) (SEP 89), 17-18.
THE ARTICLE ANALYZES THE HISTORY OF SYRIA'S MILITARY
INTERVENTION IN LEBANON. IT BEGINS WITH THE INITIAL SYRIAN
INVASION OF 1976 AND FOLLOWS THE CHANGES IN POLICY AS SYIRA
CONFRONTED A CHANGE IN ALLIES, INCREASING WESTERN
INVOLVEMENT, AND THE ISRAELI INVASION OF 1982. IT CONCLUDES
WITH AN ANALYSIS OF THE CURRENT MILITARY AND POLITICAL
SITUATION. SYRIA CURRENTLY FACES THE FORCES OF CHRISTIAN
GENERAL MICHEL AOUN WHO HAS DECLARED A "WAR OF LIBERATION"
ON SYRIA. SYRIA MUST NOW WALK THE FINE LINE BETWEEN
MAINTAINING POLITICAL INFLUENCE AND BECOMING ENTRAPPED IN A
VIET NAM-LIKE CONFLICT.

06688 NASRALLAH, F.
THE ARAB COOPERATION COUNCIL
MIDDLE EAST INTERNATIONAL, (357) (AUG 89), 19-20.
THE ARTICLE DISCUSSES THE CREATION OF ARAB REGIONAL
ORGANIZATIONS. IT CONCENTRATES ON THE NEWLY-FORMED ARAB

COOPERATION COUNCIL (ACC) WHICH CONSISTS OF EGYPT, JORDAN,
IRAQ, AND NORTH YEMEN. THE ORGANIZATION HAS FORMED
OSTENSIBLY FOR SOLELY ECONOMIC REASONS; ALL MEMBERS OF THE
NEW FORUM HAVE SIGNIFICANT ECONOMIC PROBLEMS ASSOCIATED WITH
SIZABLE DEBT. HOWEVER, DESPITE ITS ECONOMIC EMPHASIS, IT IS
MOSTLY FOR POLITICAL REASONS THAT THE ACC HAS CREATED.
HOWEVER, PROPOSED SOLUTIONS TO PROBLEMS IN SUDAN, PALESTINE,
AND LEBANON HAVE YET TO YIELD FRUIT.

06689 NASRALLAH, F.
    THE INTERNATIONAL AND REGIONAL DIMENSIONS OF THE LEBANESE
    CRISIS
    MIDDLE EAST INTERNATIONAL, (350) (MAY 89), 16-17.
        THE ERUPTION OF VIOLENCE IN LEBANON HAS BEEN
    PRECIPITATED BY THE REGIONAL AND INTERNATIONAL FORCES AT
    PLAY IN THE MIDDLE EAST. ON THE INTERNATIONAL LEVEL, IT IS
    AN INDICATION THAT THE TREND IN SUPERPOWER COOPERATION FOR
    RESOLVING REGIONAL CONFLICTS HAS NOT EXTENDED TO THE MIDDLE
    EAST. ON THE REGIONAL LEVEL, LEBANON'S CONSTITUTIONAL CRISIS
    HAS PREOCCUPIED THE ARAB WORLD FOR MOST OF 1989. THIS
    ARABIZATION OF THE CRISIS HAS EXACERBATED THE INTERNAL
    SITUATION AS IT PUTS LEBANON AT THE MERCY OF INTER-ARAB
    RIVALRIES AND COMPETITION.

06690 NASS, K.O.
    THE FOREIGN AND EUROPEAN POLICY OF THE GERMAN LANDER
    PUBLIUS: THE JOURNAL OF FEDERALISM, 19(4) (FAL 89),
    165-184.
        ALTHOUGH THE GERMAN FEDERAL GOVERNMENT IS RESPONSIBLE
    UNDER THE BASIC LAW FOR FOREIGN AFFAIRS, THE LANDER MAY,
    UNDER CERTAIN CIRCUMSTANCES, CONCLUDE TREATIES WITH THE
    CONSENT OF THE FEDERATION. THE LANDER HAVE ALSO BECOME
    INVOLVED DIRECTLY AND INDIRECTLY IN OTHER INTERNATIONAL
    ACTIVITIES. EUROPEAN INTEGRATION, ESPECIALLY THROUGH THE
    EUROPEAN COMMUNITIES (EC), PRESENTS THE LANDER WITH NEW
    CHALLENGES. THE LANDER HAVE SOUGHT MEANS TO INFLUENCE THE
    FEDERAL GOVERNMENT AND THE EC COMMISSION AND COUNCIL OF
    MINISTERS IN ORDER TO PROTECT THEIR SPHERE OF AUTONOMOUS
    DECISIONMAKING, BUT EC PROCEDURES AND THE REALITIES OF
    FEDERAL GOVERNMENT INVOLVEMENT DO NOT PLACE THE LANDER IN A
    STRONG NEGOTIATING POSITION.

06691 NASSAR, A.
    THE ATOMIC BOMB, THE COLD WAR, AND THE SOVIET THREAT
    MONTHLY REVIEW, 41(7) (DEC 89), 1-8.
        THIS ARTICLE CONTRASTS THE TRADITIONAL AMERICAN VERSION
    OF THE ATOMIC BOMB THE COLD WAR, AND THE SOVIET THREAT WITH
    "WHAT ACTUALLY HAPPENED" BY EXTENSIVE QUOTING OF GAR
    ALPEROVITZ, AUTHOR OF THE UPDATED EDITION OF "ATOMIC
    DIPLOMACY," ORIGINALLY PUBLISHED IN 1965. ALPEROVITZ OFFERS
    CONSIDERATIONS MEANT TO EXPOSE ATOMIC DIPLOMACY AS THE
    "CUTTING EDGE OF U.S. IMPERIALISM AFTER THE SECOND WORD WAR,
    " IT CONCLUDES THAT THE SOVIET THREAT IS A MYTH AND SUGGESTS
    THAT EDUCATION IS NEEDED TO UNDERSTAND THE TRUTH.

06692 NASSAR, J. R.
    THE MESSAGE OF THE INTIFADA
    MIDDLE EAST INTERNATIONAL, (344) (FEB 89), 18-19.
        THE POLITICS OF THE ARAB-ISRAELI CONFLICT CANNOT BE
    UNDERSTOOD WITHOUT COMING TO GRIPS WITH THE PALESTINIAN
    UPRISING. THE INTIFADA REPRESENTS THE ACCELERATION OF AN
    ONGOING PROCESS OF RESISTANCE. AS SUCH, IT IS NOT THE
    INTERRUPTION OF AN ORDER BUT THE CULMINATION. IT IS THE
    NATURAL REACTION TO AN UNNATURAL OCCUPATION.

06693 NATAN, Y.B.
    PEACEFUL INITIATIVE: DOUBTFUL PROGNOSIS
    NEW OUTLOOK, 32(8 (294)) (AUG 89), 7-8.
        IN THIS OVERVIEW OF THE PLO AND ISRAELI GOVERNMENT
    POSITIONS ON THE PLAN FOR ELECTIONS IN THE WEST BANK AND
    GAZA, YAACOV BAR NATAN ARGUES THAT WHILE BOTH SIDES HAVE
    THEIR OWN REASONS FOR MAINTAINING THE INITIATIVE, THE
    PROSPECTS FOR ANY GENUINE PROGRESS ARE SLIM.

06694 NATHAN, A.J.
    CHINESE DEMOCRACY IN 1989: CONTINUITY AND CHANGE
    PROBLEMS OF COMMUNISM, XXXVIII(5) (SEP 89), 16-29.
        BY 1989, WHAT HAD STARTED AS SMALL CONGERIES OF SMALL,
    ISOLATED, CLANDESTINE GROUPS THAT DID NOT KNOW OF EACH
    OTHER'S EXISTENCE HAD GRADUALLY GROWN INTO A NATIONAL FORCE
    THAT APPARENTLY HAD THE PARTICIPATION OR SYMPATHY OF ALMOST
    ALL URBAN CHINESE COMMUNISTS. THE TIANANMEN SQUARE INCIDENT
    OF 1976, THE DEMOCRACY WALL MOVEMENT OF 1978-79, AND THE
    STUDENT DEMONSTRATIONS OF 1985 AND 1986-87 HAD BEEN
    IMPORTANT STEPS IN THE CONSOLIDATION OF THE DIFFERENT
    RESISTANCE GROUPS. IN THIS PROCESS, THE MOVEMENT FOR CHINESE
    DEMOCRACY HAD BECOME MORE COMPLEX IN ITS SOCIAL COMPOSITION
    AND IN ITS POLITICAL GOALS AND TACTICS.

06695 NATHAN, J.A.
    DECISIONS IN THE LAND OF THE PRETEND: U.S. FOREIGN POLICY
    IN THE REAGAN YEARS
    VIRGINIA QUARTERLY REVIEW, 65(1) (WIN 89), 1-31.
        THE GREAT REAGAN DEPARTURE FROM THE COLD WAR SEEMED AT

ODDS WITH ITS OWN INCLINATIONS AND PURPOSES. REAGAN'S LAST
18 MONTHS HERE MARKED BY A SELF-CONSCIOUS STRUGGLE WITH A
STUNNING TRANSFORMATION IN SOVIET-AMERICAN RELATIONS. BY THE
LAST MONTHS OF THE REAGAN YEARS, AN OCEAN OF OBSTACLES HAD
BEEN TRAVERSED. THE REAGAN ADMINISTRATION HAD MEANDERED LIKE
SOME WEARY HOBO TO A PLACE, IN MATTHEW ARNOLD'S WORDS,
"BETWEEN TWO WORLDS, ONE NOT YET DEAD, AND THE OTHER STILL
UNBORN."

06696 NATHAN, K.S.
    MALAYSIA IN 1988: THE POLITICS OF SURVIVAL
    ASIAN SURVEY, XXIX(2) (FEB 89), 129-139.
        1988 WAS A YEAR OF SIGNIFICANT POLITICAL CHANGE IN
    MALAYSIA. THE DOMINANT UNITED MALAYS NATIONAL ORGANIZATION
    (UNMO) SUFFERED FROM FACTIONALISM AND COURT CHALLENGES TO
    ITS LEGITIMACY. PRIME MINISTER DR. MAHATHIR MOHAMAD'S
    LEGITIMACY WAS REPEATEDLY CHALLENGED AND OPPOSITION PARTIES
    JOCKEYED FOR POSITION IN THE ENSUING CONFUSION. ON THE
    ECONOMIC FRONT, THINGS FARED BETTER THAN PREVIOUS YEARS WITH
    A PREDICTED 7.4% GROWTH RATE. PRIME MINISTER MAHATHIR'S
    TRAVELS IN AN ATTEMPT TO PROMOTE FOREIGN INVESTMENT WAS THE
    CHIEF FOREIGN POLICY EMPHASIS IN 1988. MALAYSIA HAS ALSO
    SUCCESSFUL IN ITS EFFORTS TO SECURE A SECURITY COUNCIL SEAT
    IN THE UN.

06697 NATHAN, R.P.; ADAMS, C.F. JR.
    FOUR PERSPECTIVES ON URBAN HARDSHIP
    POLITICAL SCIENCE QUARTERLY, 104(3) (FAL 89), 483-508.
        THE AUTHORS FOCUS ON 55 LARGE AMERICAN CITIES TO STUDY
    DEVELOPMENTS IN URBAN HARDSHIP CONDITIONS IN THE 1970'S.
    THEIR ANALYSIS INDICATES THAT DURING THE DECADE THESE CITIES
    LOST GROUND RELATIVE TO THEIR SUBURBS, THAT THE MOST
    DISTRESSED CITIES LOST GROUND RELATIVE TO OTHER CITIES, AND
    THAT THE PROBLEM OF CONCENTRATED POVERTY INCREASED AND IS
    CORRELATED WITH THE WORSENING PROBLEMS OF THE MOST
    DISTRESSED LARGE CITIES. THEY ALSO PRESENT MORE RECENT DATA
    SUGGESTING THAT THE HARDSHIP CONDITIONS OF LARGE CITIES
    PERSISTED IN THE 1980'S AND ARE, IN FACT, WORSENING.

06698 NATHAN, R.P.
    INSTITUTIONAL CHANGE AND THE CHALLENGE OF THE UNDERCLASS
    PHILADELPHIA: ANLS OF AMER ACMY OF POLITICAL AND SOC
    SCIENCE, (501) (JAN 89), 170-181.
        THIS ARTICLE CALLS FOR GREATER EMPHASIS ON THE
    INSTITUTIONAL CHALLENGE OF THE URBAN UNDERCLASS,
    PARTICULARLY ON IMPLEMENTATION STUDIES OF NEW SOCIAL
    PROGRAMS. THE NEED FOR SUCH A SHIFT IN EMPHASIS IS EXAMINED
    IN HISTORICAL CONTEXT, STRESSING THE PLURALISTIC AND
    COMPETITIVE NATURE OF THE AMERICAN POLICY PROCESS, THE
    STRUCTURE OF AMERICAN FEDERALISM, AND THE CRITICAL ROLE OF
    STATE GOVERNMENTS IN CHARTERING AND OVERSEEING THE MAJOR
    INSTITUTIONS THAT PROVIDE SOCIAL SERVICES. TWO TYPES OF
    ACTION ARE PROPOSED TO GIVE GREATER ATTENTION TO
    INSTITUTIONAL DIMENSIONS OF THE CHALLENGE OF THE URBAN
    UNDERCLASS: (1) EVALUATION RESEARCH THAT INCORPORATES
    INSTITUTIONAL, ATTITUDINAL, AND COMMUNITY VARIABLES; AND (2)
    NEW CONSULTATIVE ARRANGEMENTS INVOLVING PANELS OF ACADEMICS
    AND EXPERTS TO ASSIST GOVERNMENT AGENCIES IN THE
    IMPLEMENTATION OF SOCIAL POLICIES FOCUSED ON THE URBAN
    UNDERCLASS.

06699 NATHANSON, R.
    ISREAL, THE ARMS RACE AND INTERNATIONAL COMPETITION
    IDF JOURNAL, (18) (FAL 89), 3-7.
        THIS ARTICLE EXPLORES ROLE THAT THE EXPANSION OF
    ISRAEL'S ARMS INDUSTRIES HAS PLAYED IN THE COUNTRY'S
    ECONOMIC DEVELOPMENT AGAINST THE BACKGROUND OF THE SECURITY
    SITUATION IN THE MIDDLE EAST SINCE THE BEGINNING OF THE
    1970S. THIRD WORLD EXPANSION IS EXPLORED IN TERMS OF WORLD
    ARMS EXPORTS; LEADING EXPORTERS OF MAJOR WEAPONS PERCENT OF
    TOTAL ARMS EXPORTS, 1983-1987; AND, WEAPONS IMPORTERS. HOW A
    COUNTRY BECOMES AN EXPORTER OF ARMS AND TECHNOLOGY IS
    EXAMINED.

06700 NATION, J.E.
    GERMAN, BRITISH, AND FRENCH MILITARY REQUIREMENTS AND
    RESOURCES TO THE YEAR 2005
    DISSERTATION ABSTRACTS INTERNATIONAL, 50(6) (DEC 89),
    1795-A.
        THE AUTHOR EXAMINES PLANNED MILITARY MODERNIZATION
    PROGRAMS IN WEST GERMANY, BRITAIN, AND FRANCE AND COMPARES
    THESE REQUIREMENTS WITH A RANGE OF DEFENSE BUDGET RESOURCES
    THAT ARE LIKELY TO BE AVAILABLE. HE ESTIMATED FUTURE
    RESOURCES IN TWO STEPS. FIRST, A RANGE OF PLAUSIBLE DEFENSE
    BUDGET GROWTH WAS ESTABLISHED. SECONDLY, HE USED HISTORICAL
    DATA TO CONSTRUCT A RESIDUAL MODEL OF EACH NATION'S DEFENSE
    BUDGET.

06701 NAUGHTON, B.
    INFLATION AND ECONOMIC REFORM IN CHINA
    CURRENT HISTORY, 88(539) (SEP 89), 269-272, 289-291.
        CHINA STUMBLED INTO AN ECONOMIC CRISIS DURING 1988 THAT
    PREPARED THE WAY FOR A MORE PROFOUND POLITICAL AND SOCIAL
    CRISIS IN 1989. THE ECONOMIC CRISIS CAN BE SUMMED UP IN A

SINGLE WORD: INFLATION. ACCELERATING INFLATION WAS
EXACERBATED AT MIDYEAR BY A MISHANDLED ATTEMPT AT PRICE
REFORM. BY SEPTEMBER, 1988, DISCONTENT WITH INFLATION AMONG
THE CENTRAL LEADERSHIP WAS INTENSIFIED BY THE NEWS THAT THE
YEAR'S HARVEST WOULD BE MEDIOCRE. IN AN ATMOSPHERE OF CRISIS,
A NEW GROUP TOOK OVER THE MANAGEMENT OF THE ECONOMY AND
DRASTICALLY SHIFTED THE DIRECTION OF ECONOMIC POLICY. THIS
NEW GROUP WAS HEADED BY PRIME MINISTER LI PENG.

06702 NAVARI, C.
THE GREAT ILLUSION REVISITED: THE INTERNATIONAL THEORY OF
NORMAN ANGELL
REVIEW OF INTERNATIONAL STUDIES, 15(4) (OCT 89), 341-358.
THIS ARTICLE EXAMINES NORMAN ANGELL'S PLACE IN TWENTIETH
CENTURY INTERNATIONAL THEORY AND THE THEORY HE WAS
ATTEMPTING TO DEVELOP. ALSO EXAMINED IS ANGELL'S ANTI-WAR
TRACT, "THE GREAT ILLUSION." HIS ROLE AS THE FIRST MODERN
THEORIST OF CHANGE WHO PAID PARTICULAR ATTENTION TO THE
CONSEQUENCES OF CHANGE FOR INTERNATIONAL RELATIONS IS
EXPLORED.

06703 NAVARRO, V.
HISTORICAL TRIUMPH: CAPITALISM OR SOCIALISM?
MONTHLY REVIEW, 41(6) (NOV 89), 37-50.
THIS ARTICLE IS BASED ON A PRESENTATION TO THE STUDENT-
SPONSORED SEMINAR ON ECONOMIC DEVELOPMENT AND INTERNATIONAL
HEALTH OF THE JOHNS-HOPKINS UNIVERSITY ON MAY 30, 1989. THE
SPEAKER COMMENTS ON THE WIDELY DEBATED ISSUE OF THE ASSUMED
SUPERIORITY OF CAPITALISM OVER SOCIALISM. HE COMMENTS ON THE
CHAUVINISM OF THE U.S. MEDIA AND THEN FOCUSES ON WHY
SOCIALISM BETTER RESPONDS TO THE NEEDS OF THE MAJORITY OF
WORLD POPULATIONS. USING CUBA AND CHINA AS EXAMPLES HE
COMPARES COUNTRIES WITH SIMILAR LEVELS OF DEVELOPMENT OF THE
FORCES OF PRODUCTION AND DISCUSSES RECENT EVENTS IN
SOCIALIST COUNTRIES. HE FOCUSES PRIMARILY BUT NOT
EXCLUSIVELY ON HEALTH INDICATORS AS INDEXES OF THE QUALITY
OF LIFE.

06704 NAVARRO, V.
RACE OR CLASS, OR RACE AND CLASS
INTERNATIONAL JOURNAL OF HEALTH SERVICES, 19(2) (1989),
311-314.
IN A RESPONSE TO AN ARTICLE ON RACISM AND THE HEALTH
STATUS OF BLACKS IN THE US, DR VICENTE NAVARRO ARGUES THAT
DIVIDING THE US POPULATION ALONG RACIAL LINES IS BOTH
INACCURATE AND COUNTERPRODUCTIVE. BOTH BLACK AND WHITE
MEMBERS OF THE "WORKING CLASS" HAVE MORE IN COMMON WITH EACH
OTHER THAN WITH MEMBERS OF THE "VERY RICH". UNTIL THE
PROBLEMS THAT CONFRONT THE WORKING CLASS ARE VIEWED IN THE
PROPER PERSPECTIVE, NO LONG-TERM SOLUTIONS WILL BE POSSIBLE.

06705 NAVARRO, V.; HIMMELSTEIN, D.U.; WOOLHANDLER, S.
THE JACKSON NATIONAL HEALTH PROGRAM
INTERNATIONAL JOURNAL OF HEALTH SERVICES, 19(1) (1989),
19-44.
IN THIS POSITION PAPER THE AUTHORS OUTLINE THE MAJOR
PROBLEMS THAT EXIST IN THE U.S. HEALTH CARE SYSTEM AND
PRESENT A PROPOSAL FOR ADDRESSING THEM. THIS PAPER CONTAINS
THE MAJOR HEALTH PROPOSAL PUT FORWARD BY THE JESSE JACKSON
1988 CAMPAIGN, CALLING FOR THE ESTABLISHMENT IN THE UNITED
STATES OF A UNIVERSAL AND COMPREHENSIVE NATIONAL HEALTH
PROGRAM (NHP) THAT WILL BE FEDERALLY FUNDED AND ADMINISTERED
AND BE EQUITABLY FINANCED. THE AUTHORS ALSO DISCUSS HOW THE
NHP WILL AFFECT PATIENTS, UNIONS, CORPORATIONS AND EMPLOYERS,
PRACTITIONERS AND OTHER HEALTH WORKERS, HOSPITALS, AND THE
INSURANCE INDUSTRY. SPECIFIC PROPOSALS ARE MADE FOR THE
TRANSITION FROM THE CURRENT SYSTEM TO THE PROPOSED NHP, WITH
A DISCUSSION OF THE MAJOR DIFFERENCES BETWEEN NATIONAL
HEALTH PROPOSALS PUT FORWARD BY THE TWO MAJOR DEMOCRATIC
CONTENDERS FOR THE U.S. PRESIDENCY. THIS POSITION PAPER ALSO
INCLUDES A BRIEF APPENDIX SKETCHING SOME OF THE MAJOR
DIFFERENCES BETWEEN THE U.S. AND THE CANADIAN MEDICAL CARE
SYSTEMS.

06706 NAVARRO, V.
THE REDISCOVERY OF THE NATIONAL HEALTH PROGRAM BY THE
DEMOCRATIC PARTY OF THE UNITED STATES: A CHRONICLE OF THE
JESSE JACKSON 1988 CAMPAIGN
INTERNATIONAL JOURNAL OF HEALTH SERVICES, 19(1) (1989),
1-18.
THIS REPORT CHRONICLES THE MAJOR DEVELOPMENTS IN THE
JESSE JACKSON 1988 CAMPAIGN AND THEIR CONSEQUENCES FOR THE
ESTABLISHMENT OF A NATIONAL HEALTH PROGRAM IN THE UNITED
STATES. IT DESCRIBES THE CHARACTERISTICS OF THE JACKSON 1988
CAMPAIGN, AND THE SET OF EVENTS THAT LED TO THE REDISCOVERY
OF THE NATIONAL HEALTH PROGRAM BY THE DEMOCRATIC PARTY OF
THE UNITED STATES.

06707 NAVARRO, V.
WHY SOME COUNTRIES HAVE NATIONAL HEALTH INSURANCE, OTHERS
HAVE NATIONAL HEALTH SERVICES, AND THE UNITED STATES HAS
NEITHER
INTERNATIONAL JOURNAL OF HEALTH SERVICES, 19(3) (1989),
383-404.

THIS ARTICLE PRESENTS A DISCUSSION OF WHY SOME
CAPITALIST DEVELOPED COUNTRIES HAVE NATIONAL HEALTH
INSURANCE SCHEMES, OTHERS HAVE NATIONAL HEALTH SERVICES, AND
THE UNITED STATES HAS NEITHER. THE FIRST SECTION PROVIDES A
CRITICAL ANALYSIS OF SOME OF THE MAJOR ANSWERS GIVEN TO
THESE QUESTIONS BY AUTHORS BELONGING TO THE SCHOOLS OF
THOUGHT DEFINED AS "PUBLIC CHOICE," "POWER GROUP PLURALISM,"
AND "POSTINDUSTRIAL CONVERGENCE." THE SECOND SECTION PUTS
FORWARD AN ALTERNATIVE EXPLANATION ROOTED IN A HISTORICAL
ANALYSIS OF THE CORRELATION OF CLASS FORCES IN EACH COUNTRY.
THE DIFFERENT FORMS OF FUNDING AND ORGANIZATION OF HEALTH
SERVICES, STRUCTURED ACCORDING TO THE CORPORATE MODEL OR TO
THE LIBERAL-WELFARE MARKET CAPITALISM MODEL, HAVE APPEARED
HISTORICALLY IN SOCIETIES WITH DIFFERENT CORRELATIONS OF
CLASS FORCES. IN ALL THESE SOCIETIES THE MAJOR SOCIAL FORCE
BEHIND THE ESTABLISHMENT OF A NATIONAL HEALTH PROGRAM HAS
BEEN THE LABOR MOVEMENT (AND ITS POLITICAL INSTRUMENTS-THE
SOCIALIST PARTIES) IN ITS PURSUIT OF THE WELFARE STATE. IN
THE FINAL SECTION THE DEVELOPMENTS IN THE HEALTH SECTOR
AFTER WORLD WAR II ARE EXPLAINED. IT IS POSTULATED THAT THE
GROWTH OF PUBLIC EXPENDITURES IN THE HEALTH SECTOR AND THE
GROWTH OF UNIVERSALISM AND COVERAGE OF HEALTH BENEFITS THAT
HAVE OCCURRED DURING THIS PERIOD ARE RELATED TO THE STRENGTH
OF THE LABOR MOVEMENT IN THESE COUNTRIES.

06708 NAVIAS, M.S.
TERMINATING CONSCRIPTION? THE BRITISH NATIONAL SERVICE
CONTROVERSY 1955-56
JOURNAL OF CONTEMPORARY HISTORY, 24(2) (APR 89), 195-208.
IN APRIL 1957, THE BRITISH DEFENCE WHITE PAPER MADE
PUBLIC THE MACMILLAN GOVERNMENT'S INTENTION OF EMPHASIZING
NUCLEAR DETERRENCE AT THE EXPENSE OF CONVENTIONAL FORCE
LEVELS. MANY COMMENTATORS ON THIS POLICY HAVE TRACED ITS
ROOTS TO TENDENCIES LONG PREVALENT IN DEFENCE THINKING AND,
INDEED, OBJECTIONS TO CONSCRIPTION HAD BEEN A CONSTANT
FACTOR IN BRITISH POLITICS SINCE THE BEGINNING OF
DISCUSSIONS PRECEDING THE NATIONAL SERVICE ACT IN 1949. BUT
THE CONTENTS OF RECENTLY RELEASED DOCUMENTS INDICATE THAT IN
THE PERIOD IMMEDIATELY PRIOR TO THE 1957 WHITE PAPER THE
ARMED SERVICES REMAINDED STRONGLY OPPOSED TO THE TOTAL END
OF CONSCRIPTION, WHILE LITTLE EFFORT WAS MADE BY THE
PROPONENTS OF AN ALL-VOLUNTEER FORCE TO LINK THE TERMINATION
OF NATIONAL SERVICE TO A FOCUS ON NUCLEAR DETERRENCE.

06709 NDUBISI, V. M.
AUTHORITATIVE DECISION AS A FUNCTION OF FEEDBACK AND ITS
RELEVANCE FOR DEMOCRACY: A NIGERIAN CASE STUDY
DISSERTATION ABSTRACTS INTERNATIONAL, 49(8) (FEB 89),
2378-A.
FOR MORE THAN A DECADE, A SIGNIFICANT NUMBER OF OBOSI
HAVE NOT ACCEPTED THE LEGITIMACY OF THEIR KING, CLAIMING
THAT HE CAME TO POWER THROUGH ILLEGAL AND UNDEMOCRATIC MEANS.
THE ISSUES INVOLVED ARE THE POLITICS OF LEADERSHIP
SELECTION AND SUCCESSION, LEGITIMACY, POLITICAL DECISION-
MAKING, AND THE PERCEPTION OF A TRADITIONAL RULER.

06710 NDURU, M.K.
FEAR IN THE SOUTH
NEW AFRICAN, (OCT 89), 13, 16.
THIS ARTICLE ADDRESSES THE CONCERN IN THE SOUTH SUDAN
ABOUT THEIR FUTURE AS A PART OF THE COUNTRY. THE LONG
STANDING UNEASE OF THE STATUS OF THE SOUTH AND THE REASONS
FOR THEIR ALARM IS DETAILED.

06711 NEAR, J.P.
ORGANIZATIONAL COMMITMENT AMONG JAPANESE AND U.S. WORKERS
ORGANIZATION STUDIES, 10(3) (1989), 281-300.
THE 'PSYCHOLOGICAL MODEL' OF ORGANIZATIONAL COMMITMENT
HAS BEEN WIDELY INVESTIGATED WITH RESPECT TO U.S. WORKERS,
BUT LESS FREQUENTLY APPLIED IN CROSS-CULTURAL STUDIES.
RESULTS FROM A SURVEY OF 7,000 JAPANESE AND U.S. PRODUCTION
WORKERS, REPORTED HERE, INDICATED THAT THE JAPANESE
RESPONDENTS EXPRESSED LOWER LEVELS OF ORGANIZATIONAL
COMMITMENT THAN U.S. RESPONDENTS. THE VARIANCE EXPLAINED IN
COMMITMENT BY SO-CALLED 'JAPANESE MANAGEMENT SYSTEM'
VARIABLES -- ORGANIZATION STRUCTURE AND CONTEXT, PERCEIVED
JOB CHARACTERISTICS AND PERSONAL PRACTICES -- WAS ALSO LOWER
FOR JAPANESE RESPONDENTS THAN FOR U.S. RESPONDENTS.
IMPLICATIONS FOR CURRENT MODELS OF COMMITMENT ARE CONSIDERED;
A NEW HEURISTIC FOR STUDYING COMMITMENT IS PROPOSED.

06712 NEAVE, E.H.
CANADA'S APPROACH TO FINANCIAL REGULATION
CANADIAN PUBLIC POLICY--ANALYSE DE POLITIQUES, XV(1) (MAR
89), 1-11.
THIS PAPER DISCUSSES ASPECTS OF DESIGNING APPROPRIATE
FINANCIAL REGULATION FOR CANADA. IT OUTLINES A THEORY OF
FINANCIAL SYSTEM ORGANIZATION AND USES IT TO ASSESS RECENT
LEGISLATIVE ACTIONS AND PROPOSALS. IT ARGUES THAT CURRENT
AND PROPOSED REGULATION INCORPORATES TOO MANY CONSTRAINTS
AND DOES NOT PROVIDE FOR SUFFICIENT INFORMATION
DISSEMINATION, NOR DOES IT IN ALL CASES PROVIDE APPROPRIATE
INCENTIVES FOR IMPROVED SYSTEM FUNCTIONING.

06713 NEFF, D.
    A STRANGE AND DANGEROUS GAME
    MIDDLE EAST INTERNATIONAL, (341) (JAN 89), 3.
        THE REAGAN ADMINISTRATION HAS A HISTORY OF BULLYING
    BEHAVIOR TOWARD LIBYA, AND REAGAN SUFFERS FROM A NEUROTIC
    FEAR OF QADHAFI. THE REAGAN ADMINISTRATION HAS BEEN
    CONDUCTING A MEDIA CAMPAIGN AGAINST LIBYA'S POISON GAS
    FACILITY, BUT THE USA SEEMS UNCONCERNED THAT SIX OTHER
    MIDEAST COUNTRIES ALREADY HAVE CHEMICAL WEAPONS. THE REAGAN
    CAMPAIGN MAY BE JUST ANOTHER EFFORT TO DIVERT ATTENTION FROM
    ISRAEL TO SCREEN THE ESCALATED BRUTALITY IN ITS EFFORTS TO
    SUPPRESS THE PALESTINIAN UPRISING.

06714 NEFF, D.
    BAKER GRASPS THE NETTLE
    MIDDLE EAST INTERNATIONAL, (351) (MAY 89), 6-7.
        IN A SPEECH TO THE AMERICAN ISRAELI POLITICAL ACTION
    COMMITTEE, SECRETARY OF STATE BAKER WAS BLUNT IN HIS CALL
    FOR RESTRAINT AND COMPROMISE ON BOTH SIDES OF THE ARAB-
    ISRAELI CONFLICT. HE ADVISED ARABS TO TAKE CONCRETE STEPS
    TOWARDS ACCOMODATION WITH ISRAEL AS A "CATALYST" FOR PEACE.
    HE ADMONISHED ISRAEL TO RELINQUISH ITS DREAM OF A GREATER
    ISRAEL AND TO EASE UP ON ISRAEL'S HARSH REPRESSION IN THE
    OCCUPIED TERRITORIES.

06715 NEFF, D.
    BAKER'S BAG OF TRICKS
    MIDDLE EAST INTERNATIONAL, 355 (JUL 89), 7-8.
        FOREMOST AMONG SECRETARY OF STATE JAMES BAKER'S BAG OF
    TRICKS IS THE RECOGNITION THAT AMERICAN JEWS OR WASHINGTON -
    WORKING SEPARATELY OR TOGETHER - CAN PRESSURE ISRAEL AT ANY
    TIME THEY FEEL LIKE. THIS WAS AMPLY PROVED LAST YEAR BY THE
    SUDDEN DROPPING OF WHO'SA-JEW QUESTIONS AMONG ISRAEL'S
    POLITICAL PARTIES AFTER FURIOUS PROTESTS FROM AMERICAN JEWS.
    SIMILAR GOVERNMENT PRESSURE SAVED THE EGYPTIAN THIRD ARMY IN
    1973 DESPITE ISRAEL'S INTENT TO DESTROY IT. THE REASON FOR
    ISRAEL'S VULNERABILITY IS OBVIOUS: WITHOUT THE US ISRAEL
    SIMPLY COULD NOT EXIST IN ITS PRESENT STATE OF WELL-BEING.
    ISRAELIS MAINTAIN THEIR RELATIVELY HIGH LIFESTYLE SOLELY
    BECAUSE OF GENEROUS CONTRIBUTIONS FROM AMERICAN JEWS AND AN
    ANNUAL DONATION OF $3 BILLION IN US AID, ALL OF IT EXEMPT
    FROM REPAYMENT. BUT THAT IS A BASIC FACT THAT ISRAELI
    LEADERS TRY TO IGNORE AND WASHINGTON IS CONTENT TO PRETEND
    DOESN'T EXIST, LEST IT BE FORCED TO APPLY PRESSURE THAT
    COULD CAUSE SEVERE GRIEF AT THE BALLOT BOX. AND SO THE
    SECRET PERSISTS.

06716 NEFF, D.
    BUSH LEFT FLOUNDERING
    MIDDLE EAST INTERNATIONAL, (345) (MAR 89), 7-8.
        THE BUSH ADMINISTRATION IS OFF TO AN UNUSUALLY SLOW
    START. IT WAS CAUGHT FLAT-FOOTED BY THE CENTRAL AMERICAN
    DEMOCRACIES' PLAN TO BRING NICARAGUA BACK INTO THE FOLD. IT
    HASN'T FIGURED OUT WHAT TO DO IN POST-SOVIET AFGHANISTAN,
    AND IN THE MIDDLE EAST THE ADMINISTRATION DOESN'T SEEM TO
    HAVE AN IDEA IN ITS COLLECTIVE HEAD.

06717 NEFF, D.
    BUSH NO MATCH FOR SHAMIR
    MIDDLE EAST INTERNATIONAL, (363) (NOV 90), 7-8.
        GEORGE BUSH AND JAMES BAKER ATTEMPTED TO PRESSURE
    ISRAEL'S PRIME MINISTER, YITZHAK SHAMIR, TO ADOPT A MORE
    FLEXIBLE STANCE TOWARDS PALESTINE. HOWEVER, THE US EFFORTS,
    WHICH AMOUNTED TO THE DENIAL TO SHAMIR OF AN INVITATION TO
    THE WHITE HOUSE, DISPLAY THE NAIVETE OR INEPTITUDE OF US
    POLICYMAKERS. SHAMIR IS AN EXPERIENCED AND SOMEWHAT HARDENED
    POLITICAL FIGURE, AND IS UNLIKELY TO BE DAUNTED BY A SOCIAL
    SNUB.

06718 NEFF, D.
    CRACKS IN THE SUPPORTING WALL
    MIDDLE EAST INTERNATIONAL, 353 (JUN 89), 5-6.
        GEORGE BUSH AND JAMES BAKER ARE NO CLONES OF RONALD
    REAGAN AND GEORGE SHULTZ WHEN IT COMES TO A VISCERAL
    ADMIRATION OF THE JEWISH STATE. BUSH AND BAKER HAVE GIVEN
    THE PUBLIC NO EVIDENCE OF BEING ANYTHING BUT TOTALLY
    DEDICATED TO ISRAEL. BUT THERE'S A CERTAIN COOLNESS AND
    DISTANCE ABOUT THEIR ATTITUDE THAT SHOULD GIVE ISRAEL NO
    ILLUSIONS OF HAVING ANOTHER ADMINISTRATION THAT IS "THE BEST
    FRIEND ISRAEL EVER HAD". THE DIFFERENCE IS ALREADY STARK.
    BAKER'S PLAIN WORDS TO ISRAEL IN HIS AIPAC SPEECH LAST MONTH
    MARKED A SEA-CHANGE IN WASHINGTON'S DEALINGS WITH ISRAEL.
    THE BASIC POLICY IS NOT DIFFERENT BUT THE POLICY OF THE
    ADMINISTRATION IN CARRYING IT OUT IS DRAMATICALLY SO. THE
    UNDERLYING MESSAGE OF BAKER'S AIPAC SPEECH WAS THAT THE DAYS
    OF SUGAR-COATING DIFFERENCES ARE CHANGING, IS NOT YET OVER.
    IF BUSH AND BAKER CONTINUE TO ACT IN THE SAME WAY, ISRAEL
    WILL BE HEARING SOME TOUGH LANGUAGE FROM WASHINGTON IN THE
    FUTURE.

06719 NEFF, D.
    ISRAEL'S SUCCESS IN WASHINGTON
    MIDDLE EAST INTERNATIONAL, (361) (OCT 89), 5-6.
        THE ARTICLE EXAMINES RECENT EVENTS THAT HAVE SLOWED THE
PACE OF NEGOTIATIONS BETWEEN ISRAEL AND PALESTINE. ISRAEL
HAS ENGAGED IN ITS LONG-USED TACTIC OF CONFUSING ISSUES TO
THE POINT WHERE A SIMPLE SOLUTION SEEMS IMPOSSIBLE. THE
AUTHOR NOTES YITZHAK SHAMIR'S REJECTION OF BAKER'S "FIVE
POINTS" AS WELL AS HIS REJECTION OF MUBARAK'S SUGGESTIONS
REGARDING ISRAEL"S ELECTION PLAN AS EVIDENCE OF ISRAEL'S
CONFUSION AND DELAYING TACTICS. THE END RESULT IS LITTLE OR
NO PROGRESS.

06720 NEFF, D.
    SHULTZ'S VOLTE FACE
    MIDDLE EAST INTERNATIONAL, (341) (JAN 89), 8-9.
        SECRETARY OF STATE SHULTZ INADVERTENTLY PAINTED HIMSELF
    INTO A CORNER WITH HIS REPEATED REJECTIONS OF ARAFAT'S
    COMMITMENTS TO RECOGNITION OF ISRAEL, RENUNCIATION OF
    TERRORISM, AND ACCEPTANCE OF UN RESOLUTIONS 242 AND 338. TWO
    DAYS BEFORE ARAFAT'S DECEMBER 13 ADDRESS TO THE UN GENERAL
    ASSEMBLY, IT WAS CLEAR THAT SHULTZ HAD BEEN TOTALLY OUT-
    MANOEUVRED AND HAD COMPLETELY HUMILIATED HIS COUNTRY.

06721 NEFF, D.; KIDRON, P.
    THE STATE DEPARTMENT FLAYS ISRAELI REPRESSION
    MIDDLE EAST INTERNATIONAL, (344) (FEB 89), 3-6.
        AN AMERICAN STATE DEPARTMENT REPORT ON HUMAN RIGHTS
    CONTAINS AN INDICTMENT OF ISRAELI TRANSGRESSIONS SO
    INCLUSIVE AND AUTHORITATIVE AS TO MARK A NEW ERA IN AMERICAN-
    ISRAELI RELATIONS. THE INTIFADA HAS PREVENTED ISRAEL FROM
    SUCCESSFULLY DENYING HUMAN RIGHTS VIOLATIONS BECAUSE THE
    TELEVISION COVERAGE HAS MADE THEM DAILY NEWS.

06722 NEFF, D.
    THE UNITED STATES: KEEPING EVERYONE GUESSING
    MIDDLE EAST INTERNATIONAL, (349) (APR 89), 8-9.
        PRESIDENT BUSH AND SECRETARY OF STATE BAKER ARE PLAYING
    A SUBTLE GAME-PERHAPS TOO SUBTLE-IN THE MIDEAST. THEY HAVE
    STREWN THE HORIZON WITH ENOUGH AMBIGUITIES TO MAKE ALMOST
    ANY ANALYSIS OF THEIR POLICY BELIEVABLE.

06723 NEFF, D.
    THE UNITED STATES: WARNING SIGNALS
    MIDDLE EAST INTERNATIONAL, (343) (FEB 89), 11.
        HENRY KISSINGER'S ENEMIES VIEW HIS WARM WELCOME IN THE
    BUSH WHITE HOUSE AS A WARNING SIGNAL OF THE RESURRECTION OF
    HIS INFLUENCE. ALREADY KISSINGER'S POWER BASE HAS BEEN LAID
    BY THE APPOINTMENTS OF HIS FORMER AIDE, BRENT SCOWCROFT, TO
    HEAD THE NATIONAL SECURITY COUNCIL AND HIS PROTEGE, LAWRENCE
    EAGLE BURGER, TO A TOP JOB AT THE STATE DEPARTMENT.

06724 NEFF, D.
    THE US AND THE IRANIAN MUJAHEDIN
    MIDDLE EAST INTERNATIONAL, (359) (SEP 89), 13.
        A RECENT INCREASE IN US HARASSMENT OF IRANIAN MUJAHEDIN
    IS BELIEVED TO BE DUE TO THE EFFORTS OF THE BUSH
    ADMINISTRATION TO CURRY THE FAVOR OF IRAN'S NEW RAFSANJANI
    REGIME. ALTHOUGH THE MUJAHEDIN HAVE GAINED WORLD SYMPATHY
    AND US FAVOR FOR THEIR EXPOSING OF HUMAN RIGHTS ATROCITIES
    IN IRAN, SOME OBSERVERS FEEL THAT THE DETENTION OF A SENIOR
    MUJAHEDIN OFFICIAL IN LOS ANGELES AND OTHER CASES OF
    "HARASSMENT" ARE MERELY A BID BY THE US TO ENCOURAGE THE
    RELEASE OF US HOSTAGES HELD BY PRO-IRANIAN GROUPS IN LEBANON.

06725 NEFF, D.
    THE US, ISRAEL, AND SHAIKH OBEID
    MIDDLE EAST INTERNATIONAL, (357) (AUG 89), 7-9.
        THE ISRAELI KIDNAPPING OF SHAIKH ABD AL-KARIM OBEID
    SIGNIFICANTLY INCREASED TENSIONS BETWEEN ISRAEL AND THE
    UNITED STATES. THE QUICK RELEASE BY SH'ITE TERRORISTS OF TV
    FOOTAGE SHOWING THE HANGING BODY OF US MARINE LT. COL.
    WILLIAM HIGGINS COMPOUNDED THE MATTER BY DEMONSTRATING THAT
    ISRAELI DISREGARD OF THE LIVES OF US HOSTAGES DOES HAVE
    CONSEQUENCES. THE BUSH ADMINISTRATION RESPONDED WITH
    STRONGLY WORDED STATEMENTS CONDEMNING ALL KIDNAPPINGS AND AN
    INCREASED SHOW OF FORCE IN THE MEDITERRANEAN. ISRAELI
    ATTEMPTS TO ASSUAGE US CONCERNS HAVE BEEN UNSUCCESSFUL.

06726 NEFF, D.
    THE WIDER IMPLICATIONS OF US ARMS SALES TO THE ARABS
    MIDDLE EAST INTERNATIONAL, (341) (JAN 89), 18-19.
        ARMS SALES TO THE ARABS IS AMONG THE TOUCHIEST ISSUES
    FACING THE BUSH ADMINISTRATION. BUSH AND JAMES BAKER FAVOR
    SUCH SALES AS AN ECONOMIC STIMULANT AND A BOOST TO AMERICA'S
    STRATEGIC POSITION IN THE MIDDLE EAST. BUT THE ISSUE HAS
    ACQUIRED SUCH EXAGGERATED SYMBOLISM THAT BOTH ARABS AND JEWS
    HAVE COME TO REGARD AMERICA'S ARMS POLICY AS THE LITMUS TEST
    OF WASHINGTON'S TRUE INTENTIONS IN THE MIDEAST.

06727 NEFF, D.
    UNITED STATES: JAMES BAKER'S TROUBLES
    MIDDLE EAST INTERNATIONAL, (344) (FEB 89), 10.
        THE BUSH ADMINISTRATION HAS SIGNALLED THAT IT REMAINS
    ISRAEL'S FRIEND BUT, AT THE SAME TIME, IT DEPLORES ISRAELI
    BRUTALITY IN THE INTIFADA AND PLANS TO CONTINUE TALKS WITH
    THE PLO. ON THE DOMESTIC FRONT, BUSH'S CHOICE FOR SECRETARY
    OF STATE, JAMES BAKER, HAS ENCOUNTERED PROBLEMS IN

ASSEMBLING HIS STAFF. HIS CHOICES FOR DEPUTY SECRETARY AND
ASSISTANT SECRETARY FOR THE MIDDLE EAST COULD ENCOUNTER
CONFIRMATION DIFFICULTIES.

06728 NEFF, D.; HAERI, S.
US AND IRAN
MIDDLE EAST INTERNATIONAL, (363) (NOV 89), 11-12.
THE US RELEASE OF $567 MILLION IN IRANIAN ASSETS FROZEN
SINE THE 1979 HOSTAGE CRISIS AND US EFFORTS TO SECURE THE
RELEASE OF 17 IRANIAN CITIZENS TAKEN PRISONER IN BEIRUT BY
THE LEBANESE FORCES MILITIA ARE SIGNS THAT PRESIDENT BUSH IS
SERIOUS ABOUT NORMALIZING RELATIONS WITH THE US'S ERSTWHILE
ENEMY. US MOTIVES FOR THIS POLICY SHIFT INCLUDE CONCERN OVER
THE WELFARE OF EIGHT AMERICAN HOSTAGES HELD IN LEBANON,
GEOPOLITICAL CONCERNS, AND BUSINESS: IRAN WILL SPEND AN
ESTIMATED $40 BILLION ON POST WAR RECONSTRUCTION.

06729 NEFF, D.
US AND ISRAEL: SMALL STICK AND LARGE CARROT
MIDDLE EAST INTERNATIONAL, (347) (MAR 89), 4-5.
IN NORMAL CIRCUMSTANCES, THE BUSH ADMINISTRATION'S
OPENING MOVES IN THE MIDEAST MIGHT SERVE AS THE BASIS FOR
OPTIMISM ABOUT ITS POLICIES IN THE ISRAELI-PALESTINIAN
CONFLICT. BUT IT IS OBVIOUS THAT WASHINGTON IS PLAYING THE
OLD GAME OF CARROT AND STICK WITH ISRAEL. THIS IS A GAME
THAT ISRAEL KNOWS WELL AND ENJOYS, SINCE IT INVARIABLY GETS
MORE THAN IT GIVES. THE BUSH ADMINISTRATION HAS ALREADY
FALLEN VICTIM TO ISRAELI SHREWDNESS IN THIS LITTLE GAME.

06730 NEFF, D.
WASHINGTON IN FAVOUR
MIDDLE EAST INTERNATIONAL, (359) (SEP 89), 6-7.
THE "TEN POINTS" OF EGYPTIAN PRESIDENT MUBARAK DOESN'T
FULLY SATISFY EITHER ISRAEL OR THE PALESTINIANS. HOWEVER,
THE US SEEMS MORE THAN HAPPY WITH THE PROSPECT OF THE
POSSIBILITY OF REVIVING THE STAGNANT NEGOTIATING PROCESS. ON
ANOTHER FRONT, THE US WITHDRAWAL FROM ITS EMBASSY IN BEIRUT
IS EVIDENCE OF ITS NEARLY COMPLETE FAILURE TO RESOLVE THE
CONFLICT IN LEBANON. THE AMERICANS LEAVE BEHIND A NATION
THAT IS BECOMING INCREASINGLY VIOLENT AND CHAOTIC.

06731 NEIER, A.
HUMAN RIGHTS IN THE REAGAN ERA: ACCEPTANCE IN PRINCIPLE
PHILADELPHIA: ANLS OF AMER ACMY OF POLITICAL AND SOC
SCIENCE, (506) (NOV 89), 30-41.
OVER EIGHT YEARS, THE REAGAN ADMINISTRATION'S POLICY ON
HUMAN RIGHTS SHIFTED DRAMATICALLY. AT THE OUTSET, SOME IN
THE ADMINISTRATION REPUDIATED PROMOTING HUMAN RIGHTS
INTERNATIONALLY AS A FOREIGN POLICY GOAL OF THE UNITED
STATES; OTHERS ARGUED THAT THE UNITED STATES SHOULD CONDEMN
ABUSES BY HOSTILE TOTALITARIAN GOVERNMENTS BUT NOT FRIENDLY
AUTHORITARIAN GOVERNMENTS. BY THE TIME THE REAGAN
ADMINISTRATION LEFT OFFICE, IT ACCEPTED THAT PROMOTING HUMAN
RIGHTS WAS A MAJOR GOAL AND THAT THE UNITED STATES SHOULD BE
EVENHANDED IN CONDEMNING ABUSES. DESPITE THE SEEMING HEADWAY,
MUCH REMAINS TO BE DONE.

06732 NEILD, R.
FORGIVE AND FORGET?
COMMONWEAL, CXVI(12) (JUN 89), 358-360.
IN APRIL 1989 URUGUAY UPHELD ITS 1986 IMPUNITY LAW
GIVING AMNESTY TO MILITARY PERSONNEL RESPONSIBLE FOR GROSS
VIOLATIONS OF HUMAN RIGHTS DURING THE 1973-1984 REGIME. THE
VICTORY REFLECTED A LOSS OF FAITH IN THE ABILITY OF
POLITICIANS AND DEMOCRATIC INSTITUTIONS AND FEAR THAT
OVERTURNING THE LAW WOULD PRECIPITATE A CONSITUTIONAL CRISIS.

06733 NEIMAN, M.
GOVERNMENT DIRECTED CHANGE OF EVERYDAY LIFE AND
COPRODUCTION: THE CASE OF HOME ENERGY USE
WESTERN POLITICAL QUARTERLY, 42(3) (SEP 89), 365-390.
IN RECENT YEARS A NUMBER OF INDIVIDUALS HAVE ARGUED FOR
THE USEFULNESS OF "COPRODUCTION" AS AN ALTERNATIVE TO
TRADITIONAL, HIERARCHICAL SYSTEMS OF POLICY DESIGN AND
IMPLEMENTATION. COPRODUCTION HAS BEEN TOUTED AS A MEANS OF
REDUCING GOVERNMENT INTRUSIVENESS, INCREASING SERVICE
DELIVERY, AND ENCOURAGING CITIZEN PARTICIPATION AND
EDUCATION BY MAKING SOCIETY'S MEMBERS SERVE AS PARTNERS IN
THE CREATION OF SERVICES, NOT MERELY OBJECTS ON WHICH
GOVERNMENT AGENTS ACT. BY FOCUSING ON THE RESIDENTIAL
CONSERVATION SERVICE (A HIGHLY DECENTRALIZED, FEDERAL
GOVERNMENT EFFORT TO ENCOURAGE HOUSEHOLD ENERGY EFFICIENCY)
AND BY USING UNIQUE DATA ON HOME ENERGY USE, THIS STUDY
EXAMINED THE OPERATION OF A ARCHETYPAL COPRODUCTION POLICY.
THE RESULTS INDICATE SOME MIXED FINDINGS REGARDING THE
PROMISE OF COPRODUCTION, AND THE STUDY CONCLUDES WITH A
PRESENTATION OF SOME QUALIFICATIONS ON "THE PROMISE" OF
COPRODUCTION.

06734 NELLIS, J.; KIKERI, S.
PUBLIC ENTERPRISE REFORM: PRIVATIZATION AND THE WORLD BANK
WORLD DEVELOPMENT, 17(5) (MAY 89), 659-672.
THE OBJECTIVES OF THIS PAPER ARE: (I) TO REVIEW THE
IMPORTANCE AND PERFORMANCE OF PUBLIC ENTERPRISES IN

DEVELOPING COUNTRIES; (II) TO EXAMINE THE QUESTIONS OF
WHETHER AND WHY PERFORMANCE IMPROVEMENTS SHOULD RESULT FROM
PRIVATIZATION; AND (III) TO DISCUSS, IN LIGHT OF THE
PRECEDING ANALYSIS, THE APPROACH USED BY THE WORLD BANK
CONCERNING PRIVATIZATION.

06735 NELSON, B.J.
WOMEN AND KNOWLEDGE IN POLITICAL SCIENCE: TEXTS, HISTORIES,
AND EPISTEMOLOGIES
WOMEN AND POLITICS, 9(2) (1989), 1-25.
THIS ARTICLE EXAMINES THE GENDERED NATURE OF THE
ASSUMPTIONS AND TRADITIONS OF POLITICAL SCIENCE. THE
DISCUSSION COVERS THE ASSUMPTIONS ABOUT WOMEN'S ROLES
PRESENT AT THE FOUNDING OF POLITICAL SCIENCE IN THE LATE
NINETEENTH CENTURY, THE COVERAGE OF WOMEN AND GENDER IN THE
EARLIEST TEXTBOOKS IN THE DISCIPLINE, THE COVERAGE OF WOMEN
AND GENDER IN CURRENT TEXTBOOKS, AND THE GENDER ASSUMPTIONS
OF CONTEMPORARY ANALYSES OF POLITICAL SCIENCE. THE
THEORETICAL CONCERN OF THE ARTICLE IS TO DETERMINE WHICH
EPISTEMOLOGIES UNDERPIN THE INTRODUCTORY AND SELF-REFLEXIVE
LITERATURE AND TO ASSESS THE AWARENESS OF THE AUTHORS OF
THESE WORKS CONCERNING THE LINKAGES BETWEEN GENDER AND
EPISTEMOLOGIES.

06736 NELSON, C.
THE PARADOX OF THE EXCLUSIONARY RULE
PUBLIC INTEREST, (96) (SUM 89), 117-130.
CIVIL LIBERTARIANS SHOULD JOIN LAW-AND-ORDER ADVOCATES
IN DEMANDING THE ABOLITION OF THE EXCLUSIONARY RULE.
EVIDENCE SUGGESTS THAT THE EXCLUSIONARY RULE, IN ADDITION TO
FREEING CRIMINALS, ENCOURAGES JUDGES TO UNDERMINE INDIVIDUAL
RIGHTS. A CLOSE LOOK AT SUPREME COURT CASES OVER THE PAST
TWO DECADES INDICATES THAT THE RULE IS CAUSING A STEADY
CONSTRICTION IN THE EFFECTIVE SCOPE OF THE FOURTH AMENDMENT,
AS THE COURT CONDONES QUESTIONABLE POLICE BEHAVIOR RATHER
THAN SUPPRESS CRUCIAL EVIDENCE. JUST AS THE 1914 COURT
TWISTED THE CONSTITUTION TO INVENT THE EXCLUSIONARY RULE, SO
THE MODERN COURT INVENTS LEGAL THEORIES TO CIRCUMVENT THE
RULE, UNINTENTIONALLY BUT INEVITABLY ERODING THE VERY RIGHTS
THAT THE RULE HAS CREATED TO PROTECT.

06737 NELSON, C.J.; MAGLEBY, D.B.
CONGRESS AND CAMPAIGN MONEY: THE PROSPECTS FOR REFORM
BROOKINGS REVIEW, 7(2) (SPR 89), 34-41.
ALMOST EVERY ELECTION BRINGS CALLS FOR FINANCE REFORM,
AND THE 1988 ELECTIONS ARE NO EXCEPTION. THE ENORMOUS
QUANTITIES OF "SOFT MONEY" SPENT BY GEORGE BUSH AND MICHAEL
DUKAKIS ARE ONE AREA OF CONTENTION, AND CAMPAIGN FINANCE
COULD BECOME PART OF THE LARGER DEBATE ABOUT ETHICS IN THE
101ST CONGRESS.

06738 NELSON, J.
MULTINATIONAL FREE LUNCH
CANADIAN FORUM, 68(782) (OCT 89), 10-14.
THIS ARTICLE EXAMINES FREE TRADE ZONES AND EXPORT
PROCESSING ZONES WHICH HAVE BEEN A BOON TO MULTINATIONAL
CORPORATIONS -- AND A BLIGHT ON THIRD WORLD ECONOMIES. THE
DEVASTATION, BOTH HUMAN AND ECONOMIC, CAUSED BY THESE TRADE
PRACTICES IS NOW BEING FELT IN COUNTRIES LIKE BRITAIN AND
THE U.S. AS WELL. IT ASKS THE QUESTION, "UNDER FREE TRADE,
COULD CANADA BECOME ONE BIG FREE TRADE ZONE?" JOYCE NELSON
SHOWS HOW THE NEO-CONSERVATIVE POLICY OF ENCOURAGING FREE
TRADE IS SENDING WESTERN SOCIETY BACK TO THE MID-19TH
CENTURY.

06739 NELSON, J.
THE NEW GLOBAL SWEATSHOP
CANADIAN FORUM, 86(781) (SEP 89), 10-15.
IN THE FIRST OF A TWO PART SERIES, JOYCE NELSON EXPOSES
THE CONDITIONS THAT HAVE ALLOWED FINANCIAL INSTITUTIONS OF
THE WEST TO MAINTAIN A VIRTUAL STRANGLEHOLD ON THIRD WORLD
COUNTRIES, EXPLOITING THEIR LAND AND WORKERS, AND HOLDING
THEIR GOVERNMENTS HOSTAGE TO THE INFAMOUS DEBT CRISIS. IT
DISCOVERS THAT EXPORT PROCESSING ZONES ARE A THIRD WORLD
HAVEN FOR MULTINATIONAL CORPORATIONS AND THAT INSIDE THE
ZONES, COMPANIES ARE EXEMPT FROM ENVIRONMENT REGULATIONS,
TAX RESTRICTIONS, EMPLOYMENT STANDARDS-VIRTUALLY EVERYTHING
THAT MIGHT HINDER THEM FROM MAKING A PROFIT.

06740 NELSON, R.
LIBERALISM, REPUBLICANISM AND THE POLITICS OF THERAPY:
JOHN LOCKE'S LEGACY OF MEDICINE AND REFORM
REVIEW OF POLITICS, 51(1) (WIN 89), 29-54.
THE CURRENT HISTORIOGRAPHICAL DEBATE OVER THE RELATION
OF JOHN LOCKE'S PHILOSOPHY TO THE REPUBLICAN POLITICAL
TRADITION HAS IGNORED THE MEDICAL ORIENTATION WHICH LOCKE
BROUGHT TO HIS POLITICAL WRITINGS. RECOGNIZING THAT LOCKE
WROTE WITHIN A MEDICAL PARADIGM, WHICH HE DERIVED FROM
CALVINIST RELIGIOUS THOUGHT, PERMITS US TO SEE THAT LOCKE
HAS WORKING WITHIN A VARIATION OF REPUBLICANISM AND NOT IN
OPPOSITION TO IT. LOCKE ATTEMPTED TO "CURE" POLITICAL
CORRUPTION, MUCH AS PURITANS HAD TRIED TO CURE THEIR SOCIETY
OF SIN'S CORRUPTION. THE FAILURE OF LOCKE'S THERAPEUTIC
APPROACH TO POLITICAL VIRTUE HAS PROVIDED THE BASIS FOR

RECENT CRITICISMS OF LIBERALISM AND A CHALLENGE TO THE
CONVENTION THAT LOCKE WAS AN ORIGINAL AND CENTRAL FIGURE IN
CREATING ANGLO-AMERICAN POLITICAL CULTURE.

06741 NEMCOVA, D.; HRADILEK, T.; VONDRA, S.
    JAN PALACH'S SACRIFICE: A LIVING CHALLENGE
    EAST EUROPEAN REPORTER, 3(4) (SPR 89), 52-53.
        THE ARTICLE IS A SHORTENED VERSION OF A CHARTER 77
    DOCUMENT INTENDED TO BE READ ON JANUARY 15, 1989 (POLICE
    ACTION PREVENTED THE ACTUAL READING). IT COMMEMORATES THE
    SACRIFICE OF JAN PALACH, A STUDENT WHO KILLED HIMSELF AS A
    PROTEST OF GOVERNMENTAL COMPROMISE THAT ROBBED CITIZENS OF
    THEIR FREEDOM.

06742 NEMEM, M.
    A CITY UNDER SIEGE
    MACLEAN'S (CANADA'S NEWS MAGAZINE), 102(6) (FEB 89), 22.
        AFTER SEVERAL YEARS OF REMAINING RELATIVELY UNSCATHED,
    AFGHANISTAN"S CAPITAL CITY, KABUL, IS UNDER SEIGE. AS THE
    SOVIET WITHDRAWS ITS FINAL 50,000 TROOPS, MUJAHEDEEN REBELS
    ARE POISED TO TAKE THE CAPITAL AND SWEEP THE NAJIBULLAH
    GOVERNMENT FROM POWER. FLEEING FOREIGNERS ARE BEING JOINED
    BY AFGHANS WHO CAN AFFORD IT. EVEN IF THE REBELS TOPPLE THE
    GOVERNMENT, THE FUTURE OF AFGHANISTAN REMAINS UNCERTAIN; THE
    MUJAHEDEEN ARE FACTION-RIDDEN AND DISORGANIZED AND ARE
    UNLIKELY TO BE ABLE COME UP WITH A UNIFIED GOVERNMENT.

06743 NEMETH, L.
    DOE'S DISGRACE
    MULTINATIONAL MONITOR, 10(1-2) (JAN 89), 26-27.
        IN LATE 1988, DISCLOSURES THAT DEPARTMENT OF ENERGY
    NUCLEAR WEAPONS FACILITIES AROUND THE COUNTRY HAD RELEASED
    HUGE QUANTITIES OF RADIOACTIVE PARTICLES INTO THE AIR AND
    DUMPED TONS OF RADIOACTIVE AND HAZARDOUS WASTE INTO THE
    GROUND SHOOK THE NATION. ESTIMATES OF THE COST OF CLEANING
    UP THE MESS RUN AS HIGH AS $175 BILLION. BUT THAT FIGURE
    DOES NOT INCLUDE OTHER, LESS QUANTIFIABLE COSTS. MORE ACUTE
    AMONG THESE IS THE HEALTH RISK FOR WORKERS AT DOE FACILITIES
    AND RESIDENTS WHO LIVE NEAR THOSE FACILITIES.

06744 NEMETH, M.; ERASMUS, C.
    BOTHA'S UNTIMELY STROKE
    MACLEAN'S (CANADA'S NEWS MAGAZINE), 102(5) (JAN 89), 28.
        SOUTH AFRICAN PRESIDENT, PIETER BOTHA SUFFERED A STROKE
    THAT THREATENED TO END HIS 40-YEAR POLITICAL CAREER AND
    PLUNGE THE SOUTH AFRICAN GOVERNMENT INTO THE PRETORIA
    GOVERNMENT FACES NOT ONLY THE ONGOING BLACK STRUGGLE, BUT
    ALSO SOARING INFLATION AND A GENERAL ELECTION FOR WHITES.
    BOTHA IS LIKELY TO STEP DOWN, AND THE ENSUING STRUGGLE FOR
    SUCCESSION COULD SPLIT THE CONSERVATIVE AND REFORMIST
    FACTIONS OF THE RULING NATIONAL PARTY WIDE OPEN.

06745 NEMETH, M.; COLLETT, M.
    FIRES OF DISCONTENT
    MACLEAN'S (CANADA'S NEWS MAGAZINE), 102(11) (MAR 89), 28.
        RIOTING AND UNREST SHEPT VENEZUELA KILLING MORE THAN 300
    PEOPLE AND INJURING OVER 2,000. THE CAUSE OF THE VIOLENCE
    WAS A GOVERNMENT AUSTERITY PROGRAM THAT INCREASED PRICES ON
    FUEL, BUS FARES AND OTHER NECESSITIES OF LIFE BY OVER 90
    PERCENT. VENEZUELA, GENERALLY CONSIDERED ONE OF LATIN
    AMERICA'S MOST STABLE DEMOCRACIES, HAS EXPERIENCED A STEADY
    DECLINE IN THE STANDARD OF LIVING OVER THE PAST DECADE AND A
    DRAMATIC INCREASE IN FOREIGN DEBT. GOVERNMENT OFFICIALS
    WARNED FOREIGN BANKS THAT IF LENIENCY IS NOT DEMONSTRATED,
    THE NATION COULD BE PLUNGED INTO FURTHER CHAOS.

06746 NEMETH, M.; BRANSON, L.
    LEGACY OF REPRESSION
    MACLEAN'S (CANADA'S NEWS MAGAZINE), 102(28) (JUL 89), 22.
        THE CRACKDOWN FOLLOWING THE TIANANMEN SQUARE MASSACRE
    CONTINUED AS CHINESE POLICE ARRESTED MORE PROTESTERS,
    CONFISCATED FILM OF JAPANESE TOURISTS, AND LAUNCHED A SERIES
    OF VERBAL ATTACKS ON ZHAO ZIYANG, FORMER PARTY GENERAL
    SECRETARY. US-CHINESE RELATIONS CONTINUED TO DETERIORATE AS
    THE US EMBASSY IN BEIJING FORMALLY PROTESTED WHAT IT CALLED
    A "PREMEDITATED" MILITARY ATTACK ON A COMPOUND IN BEIJING
    HOUSING FOREIGN DIPLOMATS. THE GOVERNMENT IS ENGAGED IN
    EFFORTS TO RETURN TO NORMALCY, BUT IT REMAINS UNCERTAIN
    WHETHER THEIR EFFORTS WILL BE SUCCESSFUL.

06747 NEMETH, M.; ERASMUS, O.G.
    SHOWDOWN IN CAPE TOWN
    MACLEAN'S (CANADA'S NEWS MAGAZINE), 102(13) (MAR 89), 30.
        SOUTH AFRICAN PRESIDENT PIETER BOTHA IS, ONCE AGAIN,
    BATTLING TO REMAIN IN POWER. HOWEVER, HIS CHIEF OPPONENTS
    ARE MEMBERS OF HIS OWN PARTY. AFTER SUFFERING A STROKE,
    BOTHA RELINQUISHED LEADERSHIP OF THE RULING NATIONAL PARTY,
    BUT HELD ON TO THE POWERFUL POST OF PRESIDENT. THERE IS AN
    INCREASING PRESSURE FOR BOTHA'S RESIGNATION COMING FROM ALL
    SIDES, BUT THE MOST STRIDENT OPPOSITION COMES FROM BOTHA'S
    OWN NATIONAL PARTY. WHETHER THE "GREAT CROCODILE" WILL QUIT
    OR NOT REMAINS UNKNOWN.

06748 NEMETH, M.; LAVER, R.; MACKENZIE,H.
    TEST OF WILLS: FREE TRADE'S TAXING DETAILS
    MACLEAN'S (CANADA'S NEWS MAGAZINE), 102(26) (JUL 89),
    63-64.
        ALTHOUGH THE US-CANADA FREE TRADE AGREEMENT HAS ALREADY
    TAKEN EFFECT, THERE REMAIN A NUMBER OF ISSUES TO BE RESOLVED
    OVER THE NEXT FEW YEARS. THE NEGOTIATIONS WILL BE CONDUCTED
    PRIMARILY BY CANADIAN INTERNATIONAL TRADE MINISTER JOHN
    CROSBIE AND US TRADE REPRESENTATIVE CARLA HILLS, ALTHOUGH
    BOTH NEGOTIATORS ARE KNOWN FOR THEIR TENACITY AND WILL,
    NEITHER FORESEE INSURMOUNTABLE DIFFICULTIES IN THE YEARS
    AHEAD. ISSUES THAT WILL BE DISCUSSED INCLUDE THE DEFINITION
    OF SUBSIDIES, THE FUTURE OF THE AUTOMOTIVE INDUSTRY, AND
    SPECIFIC IMPORTS/EXPORTS SUCH AS STEEL AND PLYWOOD.

06749 NEMETH, M.; KOPPEL, T.
    THE DIRT ON "MR CLEAN"
    MACLEAN'S (CANADA'S NEWS MAGAZINE), 102(27) (JUL 89), 32.
        TWO DAYS AFTER PRIME MINISTER SOSUKO UNO, "MR CLEAN,"
    ASSUMED OFFICE, AN ARTICLE IN A RESPECTED MAGAZINE BROUGHT
    ALLEGATIONS OF SEX SCANDAL OUT IN THE OPEN. ALTHOUGH IT IS
    UNUSUAL FOR PRIVATE AFFAIRS TO BE BLOWN INTO A FULL-SCALE
    POLITICAL SCANDAL, THE INTERNATIONAL ATTENTION THAT HAS
    CENTERED ON UNO HAS SHAKEN THE GOVERNMENT AND BROUGHT CALLS
    FOR THE PRIME MINISTER'S RESIGNATION.

06750 NEMETH, M.; SEBASTIAN, R.
    VOTING FOR PEACE
    MACLEAN'S (CANADA'S NEWS MAGAZINE), 102(1) (JAN 89), 44-45.
        DESPITE A POWERFUL DISINCENTIVE: MARXIST RADICALS HAD
    VOWED TO KILL VOTERS AND POLLING OFFICIALS, MORE THAN FIVE
    MILLION SRI LANKANS STREAMED TO THE POLLING GROUPS TO CAST
    THEIR BALLOTS IN THE COUNTRY'S PRESIDENTIAL ELECTIONS.
    ALTHOUGH THE VICTOR, PRIME MINISTER RANASINGHE PREMADASA,
    HAS AN INCREDIBLE ARRAY OF CHALLENGES AS HE ATTEMPTS TO
    BRING PEACE TO THE STRIFE-TORN ISLAND, HE HAS GOOD REASON TO
    DECLARE THAT "THE BALLOTS OF THE PEOPLE HAVE TRIUMPHED OVER
    THE BULLETS OF BRUTALITY."

06751 NESTER, W.
    JAPAN'S MAINSTREAM PRESS: FREEDOM TO CONFORM?
    PACIFIC AFFAIRS, 62(1) (SPR 89), 29-39.
        THE NATURE OF JAPAN'S POLITICAL SYSTEM REMAINS
    CONTROVERSIAL. IS JAPAN RULED BY CORPORATIST RULING ELITE OR
    IS THE SYSTEM ESSENTIALLY PLURALISTIC? A RECENT SURVEY
    INDICATES THAT MOST JAPANESE NOT ONLY BELIEVE THEIR SYSTEM
    IS CORPORATIST BUT IDENTIFY THE MASS MEDIA AS THE MOST
    INFLUENTIAL ACTOR IN THE SYSTEM. ALTHOUGH FREEDOM OF THE
    PRESS IS CONSTITUTIONALLY GUARANTEED, AN ANSLYSIS OF JAPAN'S
    MAINSTREAM PRESS REVEALS A RELATIVELY COHESIVE NEWS CARTEL
    THAT TENDS TO SUPPORT THE GOVERNMENT POSITION ON MOST
    CENTRAL ISSUES. EVEN NEWS OF SCANDALS IS PICKED UP BY THE
    MAINSTREAM PRESS ONLY AFTER IT HAS BROKEN ELSEWHERE. YET, IN
    CONTRAST TO THE COMMON JAPANESE PERCEPTION THAT THE PRESS IS
    THE MOST IMPORTANT ACTOR IN THE SYSTEM, THE NEWSPAPERS
    ACTUALLY TEND TO BE EASILY MANIPULATED BY LDP, MINISTRIES,
    OR CORPORATE WORLD. THIS STUDY ANALYZES THE PRESS STRUCTURE
    AND ROLE IN JAPAN'S POLITICAL SYSTEM.

06752 NESTER, W.; AMPIAH, K.
    JAPAN'S OIL DIPLOMACY: TATEMAE AND HONNE
    THIRD WORLD QUARTERLY, 11(1) (JAN 89), 72-88.
        JAPAN'S POLICY TOWARD THE MIDDLE EAST CAN BE EXPLAINED
    BY TWO WORDS: "TATEMAE" AND "HONNE." "TATEMAE" IS THE MASK
    OF IDEALISTIC RHETORIC AND SYMBOLIC ACTIONS THAT HIDE "HONNE,
    " ONE'S TRUE FEELINGS AND ACTIONS. IN PRINCIPLE, TOKYO
    RESPONDED TO THE 1973 OIL EMBARGO BY ABANDONING ITS NEUTRAL
    POSITION IN THE ARAB-ISRAELI CONFLICT TO SIDE WITH THE
    PALESTINIANS, WHILE EMBARKING ON A POLICY OF DIVERSIFYING
    ITS FOREIGN OIL SOURCES. IN REALITY, JAPAN'S MIDDLE EAST
    POLICY SHIFTED ONLY RHETORICALLY.

06753 NESVISKY, M.
    BROKEN PROMISES: WHY ISRAEL IS LOSING SOVIET JEWISH
    IMMIGRANTS
    PRESENT TENSE, 16(3) (MAR 89), 20-25.
        WITH THE ADVENT OF GLASNOST, A WAVE OF JEWISH IMMIGRANTS
    ARE EXPECTED TO LEAVE THE USSR. HOWEVER, UNLIKE TIMES PAST,
    FULLY 80 PERCENT OF THESE IMMIGRANTS DO NOT SETTLE DOWN IN
    ISRAEL, BUT IN OTHER NATIONS. MANY OF THOSE WHO INITIALLY
    COME TO ISRAEL WILL EVENTUALLY LEAVE. THE MAJOR CAUSE OF
    THIS PHENOMENON IS ECONOMICS: THE ISREALI ECONOMY AND
    GOVERNMENT IS UNABLE TO PROVIDE EMPLOYMENT, HOUSING, AND
    OTHER NECESSITIES FOR THE IMMIGRANTS. WHAT SOVIET JEWS HEAR
    ABOUT ISRAEL'S ECONOMIC SITUATION SUGGESTS THAT THEY MIGHTS
    AS WELL STAY IN RUSSIA, OR GO TO THE US.

06754 NETEROWICZ, E.M.
    TIBET AFTER MAO ZEDONG
    JOURNAL OF SOCIAL, POLITICAL AND ECONOMIC STUDIES, 13(4)
    (WIN 88), 405-427.
        ASIDE FROM THE DIVISION OF TIBET, TWO MAJOR CRISES FACE
    THE TIBETANS: (1) THE CHINESE MILITARY FORCES THAT BRUTALLY
    SUPPRESS ANY SIGN OR HOPE OF TIBETAN FREEDOM AND (2) THE

CHINESE POLICY OF POPULATION TRANSFER, WHICH THREATENS THE
TIBETANS WITH BECOMING A MINORITY IN THEIR OWN COUNTRY.

06755 NETTE, A.; TEMPANT, K.; WILSON, I.
NURRUNGAR: GIVING WARNING
ARENA, (89) (SUM 89), 38-43.
A PEACE CAMP AT NURRUNGAR, A KEY US NUCLEAR WARNING BASE
IN SOUTH AUSTRALIA, DEMONSTRATED THAT THE CLAIMS OF THE
DEATH OF THE PEACE MOVEMENT TO BE PREMATURE. HOWEVER,
ACTIONS AND DEBATE BY SEVERAL OF THE PARTICIPATING GROUPS
RAISED SOME SIGNIFICANT ISSUES. THESE INCLUDE: THE
AUSTRALIAN PEACE MOVEMENT'S LACK OF A COHERENT CRITIQUE OF
IMPERIALISM AND THE STATE; THE ROLE OF VIOLENCE IN A
PRIMARILY NON-VIOLENT MOVEMENT; AND THE RELATIVE VALUE OF
"SYMBOLIC" AND "REAL" PROTEST. THE ARTICLE CONCLUDES THAT
ALTHOUGH THESE ISSUES WERE NOT RESOLVED AT NURRUNGAR, A RE-
ASSESSMENT OF THE SITUATION IS NECESSARY.

06756 NEUHAUS, R. J.
AFTER ROE
NATIONAL REVIEW, XLI(6) (APR 89), 38-42.
AS THE SUPREME COURT DISMANTLES THE ABORTION RIGHTS OF
AMERICAN WOMEN, THE ABORTION DEBATE WILL SHIFT FROM THE
JUDICIAL REALM INTO THE POLITICAL ARENA.

06757 NEUHOUSER, K.
THE RADICALIZATION OF THE BRAZILIAN CATHOLIC CHURCH IN
COMPARATIVE PERSPECTIVE
AMERICAN SOCIOLOGICAL REVIEW, 54(2) (APR 89), 233-244.
THE ORGANIZATIONAL TRANSFORMATION LITERATURE
TRADITIONALLY HAS FOCUSED ON THE PROCESSES BY WHICH
ORGANIZATIONS BECOME POLITICALLY MORE CONSERVATIVE. RECENT
CHANGES IN THE BRAZILIAN CATHOLIC CHURCH, HOWEVER, PROVIDE
THE OPPORTUNITY FOR EXAMINING THE CONDITIONS UNDER WHICH
ORGANIZATIONAL TRANSFORMATION CAN TAKE A POLITICALLY RADICAL
DIRECTION. THE CHURCH'S RADICALIZATION CAN BE UNDERSTOOD
ONLY BY EXAMINING THE INTERACTION OF THE ORGANIZATIONAL
VALUE SET AND ELITE RESPONSE TO ENVIRONMENTAL CHANGES.
OPPORTUNITY FOR ORGANIZATIONAL TRANSFORMATION IS CREATED BY
ENVIRONMENTAL CHANGES, BUT THE FORM THAT TRANSFORMATION
TAKES IS CONSTRAINED BY THE VALUE-DEFINED TERMS OF
LEGITIMATE DISCOURSE. THIS INTERPLAY OF OPPORTUNITY AND
CONSTRAINT EXPLAINS BOTH THE TRANSFORMATION OF THE BRAZILIAN
CHURCH AND THE DIRECTION OF THAT TRANSFORMATION.

06758 NEUMAN, R.
POLITICAL PUNCH LINES
CAMPAIGNS AND ELECTIONS, (10 2) (AUG 89), 17-20.
THE AUTHOR LOOKS AT THE IMPORTANCE OF HUMOR IN POLITICAL
CAMPAIGNS, USING THE 1976 CAMPAIGNS OF U.S. REP. MORRIS
UDALL AND SEN. HENRY JACKSON AS EXAMPLES.

06759 NEUSNER, J.
POLISH MEMORIES
NATIONAL REVIEW, 61(20) (OCT 89), 27-28.
THIS ARTICLE IS A REFLECTION ON CATHOLIC-JEWISH
RELATIONS BY THE WRITER AFTER A VISIT TO AUSCHWITZ. THE
WRITER, A RABBI, WAS ATTENDING A MEETING OF RELIGIOUS GROUPS
ASSEMBLED BA A COMMUNITY ORGANIZED BY THE VATICAN TO DO GOOD
WORKS. HE CONCLUDES THAT POLAND MUST NOT DEFAULT TO
COMMUNISM BY ANY ACTION THE JEWS TAKE OR FAIL TO TAKE.

06760 NEVILLE, S.R.
POTENTIAL FOR CONFLICT IN SOUTH AMERICA
AVAILABLE FROM NTIS, NO. AD-A200 345/7/GAR, JUN 88. 116.
BETWEEN 1978 AND 1983, A NUMBER OF VIOLENT INTERSTATE
CONFRONTATIONS IN SOUTH AMERICA, INCLUDING THE
FALKLANDS/MALVINAS WAR, INDICATED THAT THE CONTINENT WAS
EXPERIENCING A PERIOD OF TENSION AND INSTABILITY, WITH A
STRONG POSSIBILITY OF ADDITIONAL INTERSTATE WAR. SEVERAL
SOUTH AMERICAN NATIONS WERE ENGAGED IN ARMAMENTISM, WERE
INTERNALLY UNSTABLE, AND DISPLAYED CONSIDERABLE ANIMOSITY
TOWARDS EACH OTHER. MEANWHILE, U.S. ABILITY TO PLAY A
CONSTRUCTIVE SECURITY ROLE APPEARED GREATLY DIMINISHED. THIS
THESIS EXAMINES CONFLICT IN SOUTH AMERICA FROM A HISTORICAL
AND CONTEMPORARY VIEWPOINT, ANALYZING THE FACTORS WHICH HAVE
LED TO WARS IN THE PAST AND MAY (OR MAY NOT) DO SO IN THE
FUTURE. GEOPOLITICS, MILITARISM, ARMS RACES AND BOUNDARY
DISPUTES ARE DISCUSSED, AS IS THE U.S. ROLE IN THE REGION IN
THE PAST AND PRESENT; A PERSPECTIVE ON A BROADENED U.S.
MILITARY AND POLICY OPTION IS INCLUDED. THE CONCLUSION OF
THE WORK IS THAT INTERSTATE WAR IS NOT LIKELY IN THE
FORESEEABLE FUTURE, ESPECIALLY WHILE DEMOCRATIC REGIMES
REMAIN IN POWER.

06761 NEVITTE, N.; BAKVIS, H.; GIBBINS, R.
THE IDEOLOGICAL CONTOURS OF "NEW POLITICS" IN CANADA:
POLICY, MOBILIZATION AND PARTISAN SUPPORT
CANADIAN JOURNAL OF POLITICAL SCIENCE, 22(3) (SEP 89),
475-504.
THIS ARTICLE EXPLORES COMPARATIVELY THE IDEOLOGICAL
"PURCHASE" OF THE LEFT/RIGHT AND MATERIALIST/ POST
MATERIALIST DIVIDES WITHIN AN IDEOLOGICALLY ARTICULATE
SEGMENT OF THE CANADIAN POPULATION YOUTH ELITES. IT EMPLOYS

ATTITUDINAL SURVEY DATA AND STUDIES THREE STAGES. IT
CONCLUDES THAT POST MATERIALISM IS LINKED TO GREATER
MOBILIZATION POTENTIAL AND IS SHOWN TO PREDICT NEW
DEMOCRATIC PARTY VERSUS LIBERAL PARTY SUPPORT.

06762 NEWBERG, P.
PAKISTAN AT THE EDGE OF DEMOCRACY
WORLD POLICY JOURNAL, VI(3) (SUM 89), 563-588.
SINCE ASSUMING OFFICE, PRIME MINISTER BENAZIR BHUTTO AND
HER RULING PAKISTAN PEOPLE'S PARTY (PPP) ARE MAKING GREAT
PROGRESS TOWARD DEMOCRACY. BHUTTO FACES CHALLENGES ON THREE
DIFFERENT FRONTS: DOMESTIC LEGITIMACY, ECONOMIC SOVEREIGNTY,
AND EXTERNAL RELATIONS. MOREOVER, SHE MUST CONFRONT THEM ALL
AT ONCE AND ALTOGETHER. THESE CHALLENGES WILL NOT ONLY TEST
THE PPPS ABILITY TO GOVERN EFFECTIVELY BUT THEY WILL ALSO
INFLUENCE THE FUTURE COURSE OF PAKISTAN'S DEMOCRACY. THE PPP
MUST TRANSFORM ITSELF FROM A PARTY OF OPPOSITION TO THE
MAJORITY PARTY OF THE GOVERNMENT, LEARN TO USE THE
MECHANISMS OF THE STATE TO PROMOTE ITS PROGRAMS, AND
ENFRANCHISE THE ENTIRE POLICY. THESE REFORMS ARE DISCUSSED
HERE, ALONG WITH THE EFFECT U.S. INTERVENTION ON THE
PAKISTAN SITUATION WOULD HAVE.

06763 NEWELL, R.S.
POST SOVIET-AFGHANISTAN: THE POSITION OF THE MINORITIES
ASIAN SURVEY, 29(11) (NOV 89), 1090-1108.
THIS ARTICLE EXAMINES ATAVISTIC PROCESSES IN AFGHANISTAN
WHICH HAVE TAKEN TWO PREDOMINANT FORMS: REPUDIATION OF THE
STATE AND A SHARP WIDENING OF CULTURAL/IDEOLOGICAL DISTANCE
BETWEEN THE CITIES AND THE COUNTRYSIDE. MAJOR ETHNIG GROUPS
ARE DETAILED - PUSHTUNS, TAJIKS, TURKOMAN, AIMAQ, NURISTANS
AND BALUCHI, HAZARAS, FARSIWANS, AND QIZILBASHS. CHANGES
INDUCED BY THE SOVIET WAR ARE EXPLORED AND IT CONCLUDES THAT
PUSHTUN ACCEPTANCE OF THE CLAIMS OF THE MINORITIES TO FULL
CITIZENSHIP AND POLITICAL PARTNERSHIP WILL BE THE OUTCOME OF
AN AMAZING VICTORY IN A DEVASTATING WAR.

06764 NEWLAND, C.A.
SHARED RESPONSIBILITY AND THE RULE OF LAW
BUREAUCRAT, 18(1) (SPR 89), 37-42.
FIFTY YEARS AGO THE PUBLIC ADMINISTRATION COMMUNITY WAS
CONCERNED WITH MAKING GOVERNMENT WORK WITHIN THE SHARED
POWERS SYSTEM OF THE CONTITUTION AND WITH THE RULE OF LAW
WITHIN THAT SYSTEM. THE ISSUES OF THE 1980S ARE SIMILAR, BUT
THERE ARE SOME IMPORTANT DIFFERENCES, NOTABLY A REDUCED
LEVEL OF CONFIDENCE IN GOVERNMENT. A KEY LESSON IS THAT SUCH
CONSTITUTIONAL PRINCIPLES AS SHARED RESPONSIBILITY AND THE
RULE OF LAW PREVAIL ONLY WHEN ACTIVE CITIZENS INTERACT WITH
RESPONSIBLE LEADRES TO COMPEL POLITICIANS TO OBSERVE SUCH
STANDARDS.

06765 NEWLAND, S.J.
PERSPECTIVES ON THE FEDERAL REPUBLIC OF GERMANY: PAST,
PRESENT AND FUTURE
AVAILABLE FROM NTIS. NO. AD-A201 340/7/GAR, SEP 88, 57.
THIS INDIVIDUAL STUDY EXAMINES THE CHANGING POLITICAL
SPECTRUM IN THE FEDERAL REPUBLIC OF GERMANY (FRG), A SUBJECT
CHOSEN BECAUSE OF THE IMPORTANCE OF THE FRG TO THE U.S.
DEFENSE EFFORT AND ITS KEY POSITION IN NATO. THE REPORT
PROVIDES A BRIEF SURVEY OF SOME ISSUES FROM THE PAST WHICH
IMPACT ON CURRENT GERMAN ATTITUDES, A REVIEW OF THE ISSUES
WHICH APPEAR TO BE AFFECTING THE RELATIONSHIP BETWEEN
GERMANY AND THE UNITED STATES, AND SCENARIOS WHICH FORESEE
THREE DIFFERENT GERMANIES IN THE WORLD OF 2013. SOME
FISSURES HAVE BEEN DEVELOPING BETWEEN THE UNITED STATES AND
ITS STRONG ALLY OF SOME 40 YEARS. HOWEVER, THE AUTHOR OF
THIS REPORT CONCLUDES THAT THERE IS NO IMMEDIATE DANGER OF A
RUPTURE IN THE CLOSE RELATIONSHIP. THE STUDY ENCOURAGES
READERS TO RECOGNIZE THESE CHANGES AND TO ILLUSTRATE THEIR
POSSIBLE EFFECTS, THE AUTHOR CONSTRUCTS THREE DIFFERENT
GERMANIES WHICH COULD EMERGE BY 2013, EACH BASED ON THE
EXISTENT TRENDS. TO PRESERVE THE STRONG RELATIONSHIP BETWEEN
WEST GERMANY AND THE UNITED STATES, IT IS NECESSARY TO NOT
ONLY UNDERSTAND THAT CHANGES ARE OCCURRING BUT TO PLAN TO
MANAGE CHANGES IN THE FUTURE.

06766 NEWMAN, D.
CIVILIAN AND MILITARY PRESENCE AS STRATEGIES OF
TERRITORIAL CONTROL: THE ARAB-ISRAEL CONFLICT
POLITICAL GEOGRAPHY QUARTERLY, 8(3) (JUL 89), 211-214.
THE ARTICLE EXAMINES THE ISRAELI EFFORT TO MAINTAIN
SOVEREIGNTY AND EFFECTIVE TERRITORIAL CONTROL THROUGH A
VARIETY OF CIVILIAN AND MILITARY METHODS. IT OUTLINES THE
GENERAL ISRAELI STRATEGY OF TERRITORIAL CONTROL THAT HAS
BEEN IN EFFECT OVER THE PAST 40 YEARS AND SEEKS TO ASSESS
ITS EFFECTIVENESS, WITH SPECIAL EMPHASIS ON THE USE OF
CIVILIAN SETTLEMENTS. IT CONCLUDES THAT CIVILIAN SETTLEMENTS
FAIL TO FULLY MEET THEIR OBJECTIVES AND, IN SOME CASES,
EXACERBATE ETHNIC TENSIONS WHICH NECESSITATE AN INCREASED
MILITARY PRESENCE IN THE AREA.

06767 NEWMAN, D.
NEW ISRAELI GOVERNMENT AND PEACE
INTERNATIONAL PERSPECTIVES, XVIII(2) (MAR 89), 15-16.

THE ARTICLE EXAMINES THE "NEW" BROAD-BASED NATIONAL
UNITY ADMINISTRATION AND THE OPTIONS OPEN TO IT WITH REGARDS
TO THE EVER PRESENT PROBLEM OF THE OCCUPIED TERRITORIES.
ALTHOUGH THE NEW GOVERNMENT IS PRIMARILY AN EXTENSION OF THE
OLD COALITION, THE NEW ADMINISTRATION HAS MORE FLEXIBILITY
WITH REGARDS TO THEIR DECISIONS. FLEXIBILITY WILL BE
NECESSARY TO DEAL WITH THE CHANGING SUPERPOWER POSITIONS
WITH REGARDS TO ISRAEL, THE PLO, AND THE OCCUPIED TERRITORIES

06768 NEWMAN, F.
NATIONAL POLICIES TO ENCOURAGE SERVICE
CHANGE, 21(5) (SEP 89), 8-17.
THIS INTERVIEW WITH CHARLES MOSKOS AND DAVID EVANS, TWO
KEY FIGURES IN THE "NATIONAL SERVICE" DEBATE, IS INDEED
ABOUT THE ISSUES INVOLVED IN NATIONAL MILITARY AND CIVILIAN
SERVICE. IT GETS THE POSITIONS OF THESE TWO PEOPLE ON THE
RECORD, AND EXPLORES HOW ANY NATIONAL SERVICE PROGRAM FITS
WITH ENCOURAGED VOLUNTEERISM. IT TALKS ABOUT THE NEEDED
FINANCING FOR HIGHER EDUCATION AND THE SOCIAL CONTRACT
INVOLVED-THE COUNTRY HELPS YOU, AND YOU HELP THE COUNTRY IN
RETURN. WHICH SERVICES OUGHT TO BE PERFORMED ARE DETAILED
AND THE EFFECT ON COLLEGES AND UNIVERSITIES IS EXAMINED.

06769 NEWMAN, P.
APARTHEID AND THE CANADA CONNECTION
MACLEAN'S (CANADA'S NEWS MAGAZINE), 102(7) (FEB 89), 29.
CONTROVERSY SURROUNDS AN INDIRECT LOAN OF BY THE BANK OF
NOVA SCOTIA TO SOUTH AFRICA'S LEADING RESOURCE CONGLOMERATE,
MINORCO SA OF LONDON. ALTHOUGH NOT DIRECTLY INVOLVED WITH
THE SOUTH AFRICAN COMPANY, THE LOAN HELPS MINORCO IN A BID
FOR LONDON'S GIANT CONSOLIDATED GOLD FIELDS PLC. ANTI-
APARTHEID ACTIVISTS CLAIM THAT SUCH MOVES ARE PART OF A
STRATEGY TO CREATE CORPORATE STRUCTURES THAT ARE
INTERNATIONAL AND CAN COUNTER THE THREAT OF FUTURE BOYCOTTS
AND ALLEVIATE THE IMPACT OF EXISTING SANCTIONS.

06770 NEWMAN, P.
CANADA'S GROWING ECONOMIC OUTLOOK
MACLEAN'S (CANADA'S NEWS MAGAZINE), 102(4) (JAN 89), 42.
CANADIAN FINANCIAL INSTITUTIONS ARE ESTABLISHING
SIGNIFICANT OUTPOSTS IN EUROPE AND THE PACIFIC BASIN AND AS
A RESULT ARE INCREASING IN INTERNATIONAL INFLUENCE. THEY ARE
LED BY THE TORONTO-BASED ROYAL TRUST WHICH HAS ESTABLISHED
BRANCHES IN SWITZERLAND, AUSTRIA, TOKYO, HONG KONG,
SINGAPORE, AMSTERDAM, LUXEMBOURG, AND LONDON. THE MOVE TO
EXPAND INTERNATIONAL BRANCHES IS SEEN AS A MEANS BY WHICH
SMART OPERATORS PROTECT THEIR FLANKS IN A GROWING ATMOSPHERE
OF US-CANADIAN FREE TRADE.

06771 NEWMAN, P.
DOLLAR SIGNS FLOATING IN THE CRYSTAL BALL
MACLEAN'S (CANADA'S NEWS MAGAZINE), 102(1) (JAN 89), 52.
DESPITE DIRE PREDICTIONS BY ECONOMISTS, THERE IS SIMPLY
TOO MUCH MOMENTUM IN CANADA'S ECONOMIC SYSTEM FOR A SERIOUS
RECESSION. HOWEVER, SIGNIFICANT CHANGES SUCH AS THE CANADA-U.
S. FREE TRADE AGREEMENT INTERGRATES CANADA MORE FULLY IN THE
INTERNATIONAL ECONOMY; IN THE FUTURE, CANADA WILL BE MORE
SUSCEPTIBLE TO WORLDWIDE ECONOMIC CHANGES AND FLUCTUATIONS.
HOWEVER, THE OVERALL OUTLOOK FOR CANADA'S ECONOMY IS GOOD:
AMONG THE INDUSTRIALIZED WESTERN NATIONS, ONLY JAPAN IS
EXPANDING MORE QUICKLY THAN CANADA.

06772 NEWMAN, P.
NEW BROOMS AGAINST DEADLY WEAPONS
MACLEAN'S (CANADA'S NEWS MAGAZINE), 102(2) (JAN 89), 28.
ALTHOUGH MINES ARE SELDOM MENTIONED IN DISARMAMENT TALKS,
THEY ARE A PROFOUNDLY POTENT THREAT AND HAVE BEEN USED IN
ALMOST EVERY MAJOR NAVAL CONFLICT IN THE 20TH CENTURY.
CANADA, A PEACEABLE NATION DEPENDENT FOR ONE-THIRD OF ITS
GROSS NATIONAL PRODUCT ON EXPORTS, WITH THE WORLD'S LONGEST
COASTLINE IS ESPECIALLY VULNERABLE TO MINES. HOWEVER, NEW
TECHNOLOGY, DEVELOPED BY A CANADIAN ENTERPRISE, PROMISE A
SOLUTION.

06773 NEWMAN, P.
THE HONEYMOON WILL END ON BUDGET NIGHT
MACLEAN'S (CANADA'S NEWS MAGAZINE), 102(10) (MAR 89), 33.
THE MULRONEY ADMINISTRATION WILL FACE SIGNIFICANT
CHALLENGES ON BUDGET NIGHT. WORRIES ABOUT THE DEFICIT WILL
NECESSITATE INCREASED TAXES OR SIGNIFICANT CUTS IN SPENDING.
A RISE IN CORPORATE TAXES, A TEMPORARY EXCESS-PROFITS TAX,
AND EVEN POSSIBLY A CUT IN CANADA'S UNIVERSAL WELFARE SYSTEM
ARE BEING CONSIDERED. WHATEVER THE RESULT, THE BUDGET
DECISIONS ARE SURE TO BE PAINFUL.

06774 NEWMAN, S.L.
LIBERAUSM AND THE DIVIDED MIND OF THE AMERICAN RIGHT
POLITY, 22(1) (FAL 89), 75-96.
THE U.S. IS WITHOUT A BURKEAN TRADITION OF CONSERVATION,
AND INSTEAD, AS LOUIS HARTZ AND OTHERS HAVE SAID, HAS A
CONSERVATISM GROUNDED IN LOCKEAN LIBERALISM. THE RECENT
REVIVAL OF POLITICAL CONSERVATISM, MARKED BY THE THWICE
SUCCESSFUL CANDIDACY OF RONALD REAGAN FOR PRESIDENT, POINTS
UP THE DILEMMAS IN THIS CONSERVATISM: IT MUST EITHER REACH

BACK TO ITS LIBERAL HERITAGE FOR INTELLECTUAL SUSTENANCE, OR
IT MUST REJECT THAT PAST. THE FIRST STRATEGY, THIS ARTICLE
ARGUES, IS POTENTIALLY SELF-DEFEATING, WHILE THE SECOND
BREEDS CONTRADICTION BY MAKING CONSERVATIVES INTO RADICAL
INNOVATORS. THE NEW CONSERVATIVES, THE ESSAY CONTINUES, HAVE
TRIED TO HAVE IT BOTH WAYS. THEY HAVE SOUGHT AT ONCE TO
EMBRACE A LIBERTARIANISM FOR WHICH THE MODERN STATE IS
ANATHEMA AND A MORALISM DRAWN LARGELY FROM AN ILLIBERAL
RELIGIOUS FUNDAMENTALISM. IN THE END, THE AUTHOR CONCLUDES,
THE NEW CONSERVATISM'S PURSUIT OF A MORALLY REGENERATE
REPUBLIC NEITHER TRANSCENDS NOR RESOLVES THE DILEMMA THAT
PLAGUES CONSERVATIVES IN AMERICAN POLITICS.

06775 NGANDA, B.M.
SUPERPOWERS INFLUENCE IN THE HORN OF AFRICA
AVAILABLE FROM NTIS, NO. AD-A209 507/3/GAR, MAY 19 89, 78.
THIS PAPER ATTEMPTS TO COMBINE HISTORICAL, SOCIAL AND
POLITICAL VARIABLES WHICH MAKE UP THE REGIONAL SYSTEM THAT
IS THE HORN OF AFRICA. THIS WORK PRESENTS AN EVALUATION AND
ANALYSIS THAT THROWS SOME LIGHT INTO EVENTS AND EXTERNAL
INTRUSIONS WHICH CONTRIBUTE TO THE SITUATION AS IT GENERALLY
EXISTS TODAY. THE REGION IS VIEWED FROM FOUR PERSPECTIVES--
INTERNAL ASPECTS, REGIONAL LINKAGES, STRATEGIC AND A
HISTORICAL INTERPRETATION. THESE FOUR ARE INTEGRATED TO FORM
AN INFLUENTIAL CONSIDERATION AND CONCLUSIONS REGARDING THE
REGION AND THE POTENTIAL AREAS OF CONFLICT OR COOPERATION
BETWEEN THOSE INVOLVED DURING THE NEXT TEN TO FIFTEEN YEARS
OR SO.

06776 NGUON, C.
THE FLEXIBILITY OF OUR CONCEPT
WORLD MARXIST REVIEW, 31(12) (DEC 88), 8-10.
THE KAMPUCHEAN CONCEPT OF NATIONAL RECONCILIATION COVERS
AND ACCOMMODATES A WIDE RANGE OF FACTORS AND PURSUES LONG-
TERM GOALS. IT STIPULATES JOINT EFFORTS OF ALL KAMPUCHEANS
FOR THE SAKE OF THE COUNTRY'S PROSPERITY. IRRESPECTIVE OF
THEIR CLASS OR ETHNIC BACKGROUND, IDEOLOGICAL OR RELIGIOUS
BELIEFS, ALL CITIZENS CAN TAKE PART IN THE DRIVE TO BUILD AN
INDEPENDENT, PEACEFUL AND NON-ALIGNED KAMPUCHEA.

06777 NGWENYA, S.
BRAIN DRAIN
NEW AFRICAN, 263 (AUG 89), 20.
THIS IS A REPORT ON THE INCREASING NUMBER OF SWAZILAND'S
YOUNG ADULTS MOVING TO THE SOUTH AFRICAN HOMELANDS. THE
RESIGNATION OF TEACHERS, NURSES, ARMY, POLICE AND SOCCER
STARS TO JOIN THE HOMELANDS HAS REACHED ALARMING PROPORTIONS.
IT EXPLORES THE MAJOR CONCERNS WHICH RESULT IN THE BRAIN
DRAIN AND THE BETTER INCENTIVES OFFERED IN THE HOMELANDS.

06778 NGWENYA, S.
SWAZILAND: KING TAKES CONTROL
NEW AFRICAN, (262) (JUL 89), 19.
ACCOUNT IS GIVEN OF THE CONFIRMATION OF KING MSWATI III,
AGE 21, WHO NOW HAS FULL SIGNING POWERS OVER INSTRUMENTS OF
STATE. THE INDICATION THAT HE WILL USE THESE NEW POWERS TO
ASSERT HIS OWN AUTHORITY AND SHOW HIS OPPONENTS THAT HE
MEANS TO RULE WITHOUT FEAR OR FAVOR IS EXPLORED.

06779 NIANLU, W.
SINO-U.S. FINANCIAL CONTACTS GROW
BEIJING REVIEW, 32(14) (APR 89), 37-39.
SINCE 1979, ECONOMIC, TRADE, AND FINANCIAL RELATIONS
BETWEEN COMMUNIST CHINA AND THE UNITED STATES HAVE DEVELOPED
RAPIDLY. THE EXPANSION OF ECONOMIC AND TRADE RELATIONS
BETWEEN THE TWO COUNTRIES HAS PROPELLED THE DEVELOPMENT OF
FINANCIAL RELATIONS. AMERICAN PRIVATE FINANCIAL INSTITUTIONS
HAVE SHOWN THEIR WILLINGNESS TO ESTABLISH CONTACTS WITH THE
BANK OF CHINA, AS HAVE GOVERNMENTAL FINANCIAL BODIES. THE
TWO COUNTRIES HAVE COOPERATED AND HELD A VARIETY OF
EXCHANGES, BRINGING SINO-AMERICAN FINANCIAL RELATIONS TO A
NEW PHASE OF DEVELOPMENT.

06780 NICHOLSON, N.K.; CONNERLY, E.F.
THE IMPENDING CRISIS IN DEVELOPMENT ADMINISTRATION
INTERNATIONAL JOURNAL OF PUBLIC ADMINISTRATION, 12(3)
(1989), 385-425.
TWO QUESTIONS ARE POSED ABOUT DEVELOPMENT ADMINISTRATION
THEORY AND PRACTICE. DOES IT OFFER APPARENT, PLAUSIBLE
SOLUTIONS TO THE RECENT AND CURRENT CRISES OF DEVELOPING
COUNTRIES? IS IT BASED UPON A KNOWLEDGE OF THE
ORGANIZATIONAL TERMS AND CONDITIONS WHICH ARE NECESSARY TO
ADVANCE HUMAN WELFARE? CURRENT THEORY AND PRACTICE ARE FOUND
TO BE WANTING IN BOTH RESPECTS. AN EMPHASIS ON COMPARATIVE
INSTITUTIONAL ANALYSIS IS SUGGESTED AS ONE POTENTIAL REMEDY
FOR THESE WEAKNESSES.

06781 NIELSEN, D.A.
RATIONALIZATION IN MEDIEVAL EUROPE: THE INQUISITION AND
SOCIOCULTURAL CHANGE
INTERNATIONAL JOURNAL OF POLITICS, CULTURE AND SOCIETY,
2(2) (WIN 88), 217-241.
THIS PAPER FOCUSES ON THE ORIGINS OF THE INQUISITION. AS
THE AUTHOR DESCRIBES, ITS ORIGIN AND SUBSEQUENT HISTORY AS A

SPECIALIZED AND DIFFERENTIATED RELIGIOUS JURIDICAL INSTITUTION DEPENDED UPON A PECULIAR COMBINATION OF CHANGES BOTH AT THE LEVEL OF THE CIVILIZATIONAL STRUCTURE OF WESTERN EUROPE, AS WELL AS THE MORE LOCAL EVENTS AND PROCESSES WITHIN THE SOCIOCULTURAL SETTINGS OF THE VARIOUS EUROPEAN NATIONS.

06782 NIELSEN, D.A.
SECTS, CHURCHES AND ECONOMIC TRANSFORMATIONS IN RUSSIA AND WESTERN EUROPE
INTERNATIONAL JOURNAL OF POLITICS, CULTURE AND SOCIETY, 2(4) (SUM 89), 493-522.
IN RUSSIA, RELIGIOUS SECTS NOT ONLY FAILED TO SUSTAIN "LIBERAL" POLITICAL IDEAS OR RATIONALIZED AND UNIVERSALISTIC SOCIAL, ECONOMIC AND CULTURAL ORIENTATIONS, THEY BOTH REFLECTED AND REINFORCED TRADITIONAL CULTURAL IDEALS AND SOCIAL STRUCTURES. AS THIS ARTICLE DEMONSTRATE THIS HISTORICAL FACT HAS SIGNIFICANT IMPLICATIONS FOR THE UNDERSTANDING OF 20TH CENTURY SOCIAL AND POLITICAL ORGANIZATION IN THE SOVIET UNION.

06783 NIELSEN, K.
A MORAL CASE FOR SOCIALISM
CRITICAL REVIEW, 3(3) (SUM 89), 542-553.
A MORAL CASE FOR SOCIALISM IS MADE, ESCHEWING EFFICIENCY ARGUMENTS-AS CRUCIAL AS THEY ARE IN OTHER CONTEXTS. THE BEST FEASIBLE MODELS OF SOCIALISM AND CAPITALISM ARE COMPARED WITH RESPECT TO SUCH FUNDAMENTAL VALUES AS WELL-BEING, RIGHTS, AUTONOMY, EQUALITY AND JUSTICE. IT IS ARGUED THAT A FEASIBLE DEMOCRATIC SOCIALISM IS SUPERIOR IN ALL THESE DIMENSIONS TO EVEN THE BEST FEASIBLE FORMS OF CAPITALISM.

06784 NIELSEN, K.
MARXISM AND ARGUING FOR JUSTICE
SOCIAL RESEARCH, 56(3) (AUT 89), 713-740.
BASED ON MARX'S CENTRAL VIEWS ABOUT HISTORY, ABOUT HOW CAPITALISM IS STRUCTURED, AND ABOUT THE NATURE OF SOCIETY, THE AUTHOR ENDEAVORS TO DISCERN IMPLICIT PRINCIPLES OF JUSTICE THAT CAN BE OF SOME VALUE IN THE CRITIQUE OF CAPITALISM AND OTHER WHOLE SOCIAL FORMATIONS. HE INVESTIGATES WHETHER MARXISTS, OPERATING WITH CORE MARXIST BELIEFS, CAN CONSISTENTLY MAKE TRANS-HISTORICAL ASSESSMENTS OF THE JUSTICE OR INJUSTICE OF WHOLE SOCIAL SYSTEMS AND, IF THEY CAN, WHETHER THEY SHOULD DO SO. CAN THEY REASONABLY CLAIM THAT CAPITALISM IS UNJUST AND SOCIALISM IS JUST, OR AT LEAST LESS UNJUST THAN CAPITALISM, AND THAT THE COMMUNIST SOCIETY OF THE FUTURE WILL BE THROUGH AND THROUGH JUST, OR WILL IT BE BEYOND JUSTICE?

06785 NIELSON, D.
SURFACE MINING CONTROL AND RECLAMATION ACT: A UTAH PERSPECTIVE
POLICY STUDIES REVIEW, 9(1) (AUT 89), 153-159.
THE AUTHORITY TO REGULATE THE COAL INDUSTRY AT THE STATE LEVEL UNDER STATE STATUTE AND RULES, THE IMPORTANCE OF THE COAL INDUSTRY TO THE STATE, THE IMPORTANCE OF AN ENVIRONMENTALLY SOUND REGULATORY PROGRAM, AND THE BENEFIT OF A STATE-MANAGED ABANDONED MINE RECLAMATION PROGRAM (IN SHORT, THE ABILITY OF THE STATE TO MANAGE ITS OWN NATURAL RESOURCES) MAKE STATE PRIMACY A NECESSITY, NOT AN OPTION.

06786 NIEROP, T.
MACRO-REGIONS AND THE GLOBAL INSTITUTIONAL NETWORK 1950-1980
POLITICAL GEOGRAPHY QUARTERLY, 8(1) (JAN 89), 43-66.
ABSTRACT. THE ARTICLE PRESENTS AN ANALYSIS OF POST-WAR DEVELOPMENTS IN THE INTERNATIONAL NETWORK OF INTERGOVERNMENTAL ORGANIZATIONS (IGOS), AND IDENTIFIES AND DELINEATES INSTITUTIONALLY COHESIVE SUBSYSTEMS OF STATES BELOW THE WORLD LEVEL. IT LINKS UP WITH AND, FOR IGOS, TESTS APPROACHES THAT STRESS THE INCREASING SALIENCE OF (MOSTLY REGIONAL) SUBSYSTEMS WITHIN WORLD POLITICS. AFTER A BRIEF OVERVIEW OF EXISTING LITERATURE AND THEORETICAL ISSUES AND CHOICES, THE GROWTH OF THE NUMBER OF ORGANIZATIONS, THEIR CHARACTER, AND THE LEVEL OF INSTITUTIONAL INVOLVEMENT OF STATES IN DIFFERENT PARTS OF THE WORLD IS DESCRIBED.

06787 NIGUDKAR, A.
SEA POWER, SEA CONTROL AND SEA DENIAL
PACIFIC DEFENCE REPORTER, 16(4) (OCT 89), 22-23, 30-31.
WHEN INDIA BECAME INDEPENDENT IN 1947, THE NAVY INHERITED THE ASSETS OF THE ROYAL INDIAN MARINE, CONSISTING OF A FEW OLD FRIGATES, MINESWEEPERS AND TRAINING ESTABLISHMENTS, TOTALLING ABOUT 800 OFFICERS AND 6000 SAILORS. TODAY IT IS A FORMIDABLE FORCE OF SOME 150 SHIPS, INCLUDING TWO AIRCRAFT CARRIERS, BEAR F LONG-RANGE RECONNAISSANCE AIRCRAFT AND 17 SUBMARINES. WITH ANOTHER 50 SHIPS IN THE PIPELINE, IT HAS THE CAPABILITY, TO PLAY A ROLE IN THE LITTORAL STATES OF THE INDIAN OCEAN. THE AUTHOR EXAMINES THE POTENTIAL FOR THIS OUTCOME OF THE EXPANSION OF THE INDIAN NAVY.

06788 NIKITIN, V.
SOVIET-AUSTRIAN ECONOMIC TIES' NEW DIRECTION

FOREIGN TRADE, 5 (1988), 34-35.
THIS ARTICLE REPORTS ON THE 19TH REGULAR SESSION OF THE JOINT SOVIET-AUSTRIAN COMMISSION ON ECONOMIC, SCIENTIFIC AND TECHNICAL COOPERATION. DISCUSSED IN DETAIL WAS THE REALIZATION OF UNDERSTANDING IN THE FIELD OF ECONOMIC COOPERATION DURING THE VISIT OF N.I. RYZHOV TO AUSTRIA. MEASURES TO STABILIZE TRADE BETWEEN THE TWO COUNTRIES WERE ENCOURAGED. RESULTS ON THE SESSION REAFFIRMED BOTH SIDE'S DESIRE TO DEVELOP SOVIET-AUSTRIAN ECONOMIC RELATIONS.

06789 NIKOLAYEV, V.
USSR-CYPRUS: DEVELOPMENT OF TRADE AND ECONOMIC TIES.
FOREIGN TRADE, 11 (1988), 32-33.
TRADE RELATIONS BETWEEN USSR AND CYPRUS WERE ESTABLISHED IMMEDIATELY AFTER THE PROCLAMAION OF CYPRUS' INDEPENENCE IN 1960. THIS ARTICLE TRACES THE HISTORY OF THEIR TRADE TIES AND SUGGESTS WAYS TO EXPAND THE TWO COUNTRIES' GOODS EXCHANGE. IT EXAMINES THE FAVORABLE IMPACT OF SOVIET PARTICIPATION IN NICOSIA'S INTERNATIONAL FAIRS ON THE DEVELOPMENT OF SOVIET-CYPRIAN BUSINESS TIES AND PREDICTS THAT PROSPECTS FOR FURTHER TRADE AND ECONOMIC COOPERATION ARE FAVORABLE.

06790 NIKOLIC, M.
1968 PROTEST IN YUGOSLAVIA
NEW POLITICS, 11(2) (WIN 89), 66-70.
THE "REFORMS" INTRODUCED IN 1965 CREATED WHAT COULD BE DESCRIBED AS A MARKET ECONOMY (WITH ALL ITS EVILS) ON THE ONE HAND, AND A NEO-STALINIST ONE-PARTY POLITICAL MONOPOLY (WITH ALL ITS EVILS) ON THE OTHER. AS A RESULT, IN THE 1960S YUGOSLAVIA WAS FACED WITH RISING UNEMPLOYMENT, INFLATION, THE GROWTH OF THE SECOND ECONOMY, AND AN INCREASING NATIONAL DEBT. GIVEN THESE DOMESTIC FAILURES AND THE PERSONAL MISERIES THEY INDUCED, IT IS SMALL WONDER THAT THE STUDENT REVOLT OCCURRED NEAR THE END OF THE DECADE. IN YUGOSLAVIA, STUDENTS WERE AGAINST: THE CONSERVATIVE NEO-STALINIST LEADERSHIP, STALINIST HARD-LINERS, OFFICIAL CONTROL AND MANIPULATION OF THE MEDIA, IDEOLOGICAL CONTROL OF THE SCHOOL SYSTEM, REPRESSION OF THE STUDENT AND YOUTH PRESS, THE SUPPRESSION OF THE ROCK AND OTHER YOUTH SUBCULTURES, THE MANIPULATION OF EXISTING POLITICAL INSTITUTIONS, AND THE U.S. WAR IN VIETNAM.

06791 NIKSCH, L.A.
BURDEN SHARING AND POWER SHARING
CRS REVEIW, 10(6) (JUL 89), 19-22.
THE UNITED STATES IS ENGAGED IN NEGOTIATIONS WITH JAPAN OVER THE DIVISION OF RESPONSIBILITIES AND FINANCIAL COSTS FOR DEFENSE AND OTHER SECURITY-RELATED POLICIES. THIS ISSUE EMERGED BECAUSE OF NEW DEFENSE AND STRATEGIC CONSIDERATIONS FOLLOWING THE 1979 SOVIET INVASION OF AFGHANISTAN. SUBSEQUENT ECONOMIC DISPUTES BETWEEN JAPAN AND THE UNITED STATES MAKE FUTURE AGREEMENT ON EQUITABLE BURDEN SHARING ARRANGEMENTS MORE COMPLEX.

06792 NIKSCH, L.A.
JAPAN-U.S. RELATIONS
CRS REVEIW, 10(6) (JUL 89), 1-2.
DESPITE A GENERALLY CORDIAL RELATIONSHIP, KEY ELEMENTS OF U.S.-JAPANESE RELATIONS, ESPECIALLY BILATERAL TRADE, ARE COMPETITIVE. THE RESULTING TENSIONS HAVE PRODUCED ATTITUDES AND PERCEPTIONS OF CONFLICT AND ANTAGONISM IN BOTH COUNTRIES. RECENT PUBLIC OPINION POLLS SHOW THAT A MAJORITY OF AMERICANS VIEW JAPAN AS AN ECONOMIC COMPETITOR AND A THREAT TO AMERICAN ECONOMIC SECURITY. NEARLY ONE IN THREE JAPANESE PERCEIVES RELATIONS WITH THE USA AS UNFRIENDLY.

06793 NIKSCH, L.A.
THAILAND IN 1988: THE ECONOMIC SURGE
ASIAN SURVEY, XXIX(2) (FEB 89), 165-173.
THAILAND IN 1988 EXPERIENCED IMPORTANT POLITICAL CHANGES AS A RESULT OF THE JULY PARLIAMENTARY ELECTION, WITH AN ELECTED CIVILIAN PRIME MINISTER TAKING OFFICE FOR THE FIRST TIME SINCE THE 1973-1976 PERID. THERE ALSO WAS IMPORTANT DIPLOMATIC MOVEMENT ON THE CAMBODIAN ISSUE. BUT THESE DEVELOPMENTS WERE OVERSHADOWED BY THAILAND'S RAPID ECONOMIC GROWTH, THE EXPANSION OF THE INDUSTRIAL BASE, AND THE BROADERBASED SURGE IN EXPORTS. PREDICTIONS IN 1987 THAT THAILAND WOULD JOIN THE RANKS OF THE NEWLY INDUSTRIALIZED COUNTRIES IN THE EARLY 1990S GAINED ADDITIONAL SUPPORT FROM THE ECONOMY'S PERFORMANCE IN 1988.

06794 NILSON, K.A.
TAKING STOCK OF THE TOTALITY OF CONTRADICTIONS
WORLD MARXIST REVIEW, 32(9) (AUG 89), 3-7.
THIS ARTICLE EXAMINES THE INTERNATIONAL COMMUNIST MOVEMENT. THE WORLD MARXIST REVIEW COMMISSION ON THE INTERNATIONAL COMMUNIST MOVEMENT AND EXCHANGES OF PARTY EXPERIENCE ASKS THIS QUESTION: HOW ARE SISTER PARTIES RESTRUCTURING THEIR ACTIVITY IN FACE OF RAPIDLY CHANGING NATIONAL AND WORLD REALITIES? THE LEADER OF THE NORWEGIAN COMMUNISTS ANSWERS IN THE ARTICLE. HE EXAMINES SOCIAL PROGRESS, CAPITALISM, MARXISM, THE TECHNICAL EXPLOSION, SOCIALISM AND PARTY STRATEGY.

06795 NILSSON, A.
    SWEDISH FOREIGN POLICY IN THE POST - PALME ERA
    WORLD AFFAIRS, 151(1) (SUM 88), 25-33.
        NO SURPRISES OR MAJOR CHANGES SHOULD, THEREFORE, BE
    EXPECTED IN THE DIRECTION OF SWEDISH FOREIGN POLICY IN THE
    FORESEEABLE FUTURE. THE IMPACT OF NON-SOCIALIST GOVERNMENTS
    ON FOREIGN POLICY IS LIKELY TO BE RATHER LIMITED. A MAJOR
    CHANGE IN SWEDISH FOREIGN POLICY WOULD REQUIRE BOTH A
    SIGNIFICANT CONSERVATIVE PARLIAMENTARY MAJORITY AND A SHIFT
    IN THE BROADER POLITICAL PERSPECTIVE AND TRADITION IN SWEDEN.
    WITH A STRONG POPULAR SUPPORT FOR THE SOCIAL DEMOCRATIC
    PARTY AS WELL AS FOR AN ACTIVE FOREIGN POLICY, SWEDISH
    NEUTRALITY WILL REMAIN ACTIVE AND ENGAGED FOR A LONG TIME
    POST PALME.

06796 NIQUET-CABESTAN, V.
    THE SINO-SOVIET SUMMIT
    CHINA NEWS ANALYSIS, (1388) (JUL 89), 1-9.
        THE SINO-SOVIET SUMMIT OF MAY 1989 CONCLUDED TEN YEARS
    OF PROGRESSIVE RAPPROCHEMENT BETWEEN CHINA AND THE SOVIET
    UNION. AS THE FINAL JOINT COMMUNIQUE EMPHASIZED, THE TWO
    COUNTRIES AGREED THAT STATE-TO-STATE RELATIONS WILL BE
    SEPARATED FROM PARTY-TO-PARTY ONES AND WILL BE BASED ON THE
    PRINCIPLE OF PEACEFUL COEXISTENCE. THE SUMMIT FAILED TO
    PRODUCE AGREEMENT ON CAMBODIA OR THE DEMARCATION OF THE
    COMMON BORDER. IT IS ALSO NOTEWORTHY THAT CHINA REJECTED THE
    NOTION OF SOCIALIST SOLIDARITY AND SEEMINGLY REMAINS
    UNCONVINCED OF THE PEACEFUL INTENTIONS OF THE USSR.

06797 NIRK, E.
    VIEWPOINT: ACCIDENTAL ERRORS?
    UKRANIAN QUARTERLY, XLV(1) (SPR 89), 71-74.
        THE ESTONIANS HAVE FOR A LONG TIME BEEN IN THE POSITION
    OF AN ETHNIC MINORITY IN THEIR OWN HOME COUNTRY NOT ONLY IN
    EVERYDAY LIFE BUT ALSO IN PSYCHOLOGICAL TERMS. ESTONIA, AN
    AGRARIAN SCANDINAVIAN-TYPE COUNTRY, HAS BEEN PRESSED INTO A
    DEVELOPMENT PATTERN THAT IS NOT IN HARMONY WITH ITS SOCIAL
    STRUCTURE, POLITICAL TRADITIONS, NATURAL ECONOMIC PRE-
    CONDITIONS, OR THE WAY OF LIFE OF THE MAJORITY OF ITS PEOPLE.

06798 NISKANEN, W.; ENGLAND, C.
    TOO LITTLE, TOO LATE
    NATIONAL REVIEW, XLI(9) (MAY 89), 38-39.
        THE BUSH ADMINISTRATION DESERVES CREDIT FOR MOVING
    QUICKLY TO ADDRESS THE SAVINGS AND LOAN CRISIS. BUT THE
    PROPOSED CHANGES IN BANK REGULATION AND DEPOSIT INSURANCE
    ARE TOO LITTLE TO PREVENT A REPETITION OF THE PROBLEM.
    MOREOVER, THE PROPOSED SCHEDULE FOR CLOSING OR MERGING THE
    INSOLVENT SAVINGS BANKS IS TOO SLOW TO MINIMIZE THE COSTS TO
    TAXPAYERS AND OTHER BANKS.

06799 NISSAN, E.
    A MEASUREMENT OF ECONOMIC GROWTH FOR SELECTED CARIBBEAN
    NATIONS
    REVIEW OF BLACK POLITICAL ECONOMY, 18(2) (FAL 89), 61-79.
        THIS ARTICLE EXPLORES ECONOMIC GROWTH PERFORMANCE OF
    VARIOUS CARIBBEAN COUNTRIES OVER A TWENTY-YEAR PERIOD.
    ASPECTS OF GROWTH OR DECLINE OF AGRICULTURAL, INDUSTRIAL AND
    SERVICE SECTORS ARE EXAMINED. IN PARTICULAR, THE ARTICLE
    SEEKS TO PROVIDE AN ASSESSMENT OF THE IMPACT OF THE
    AGRICULTURAL SECTOR ON ECONOMIC GROWTH AS MEASURED BY SIMON
    KUZNETS' MODELS AND PROPOSITIONS IN RELATION TO AGRICULTURAL
    PRODUCT AND LABOR CONTRIBUTION. GENERAL COMPARISONS BETWEEN
    THE CARIBBEAN COUNTRIES AND A SAMPLE OF ECONOMIES ARE
    PROVIDED. A CENTRAL FINDING IS THAT ECONOMIC GROWTH HAS
    MINOR DURING THE PERIOD UNDER CONSIDERATION.

06800 NITZE, P.H.
    SECURITY CHALLENGES FACING NATO IN THE 1990'S
    DEPARTMENT OF STATE BULLETIN (US FOREIGN POLICY), 89(2145)
    (APR 89), 44-48.
        THE AUTHOR, WHO IS A SPECIAL ADVISOR TO THE PRESIDENT
    AND THE SECRETARY OF STATE ON ARMS CONTROL, DISCUSSES THE
    SECURITY CHALLENGES FACING THE NORTH ATLANTIC ALLIANCE AND
    LESSONS NATO CAN LEARN FROM ITS RECENT EXPERIENCE IN MEETING
    SUCH CHALLENGES.

06801 NIVA, S.
    THE BUSH TEAM
    MIDDLE EAST REPORT, 19(158) (MAY 89), 31.
        THE AUTHOR BRIEFLY PROFILES SECRETARY OF STATE JAMES
    BAKER AND OTHER BUSH ADMINISTRATION STAFFERS WHO ARE
    RESPONSIBLE FOR MIDDLE EAST POLICY.

06802 NJURURI, B.
    DETAINEES RELEASED
    NEW AFRICAN, (263) (AUG 89), 17-18.
        THIS ARTICLE EXAMINES RECENT EVENTS IN KENYA AS
    PRESIDENT MOI RELEASES POLITICAL DETAINEES AND PROMISES
    AMNESTY TO EXILES RETURNING TO KENYA. THE PUBLIC,
    INTERNATIONAL, AND CHURCH REACTION TO THIS IS REPORTED AS
    POSITIVE, BUT CONCERN FOR THE MANY DETAINEES WHO REMAIN
    INSIDE IS EXPRESSED. PRESSURE FROM THE WESTERN DEMOCRACIES
    IS DETAILED.

06803 NJURURI, B.
    GEORGE SAITOTI IN THE HOT SEAT
    NEW AFRICAN, 261 (JUN 89), 17.
        THIS ARTICLE PROFILES KENYA'S SIXTH VICE-PRESIDENT,
    GEORGE SAITOTI. LARGELY A TECHNOCRAT WHO ROSE FROM THE
    UNIVERSITY ELITE, SAITOTI IS WELL CONNECTED IN BOTH ACADEMIC
    AND FINANCIAL CIRCLES.

06804 NJURURI, B.
    KARANJA'S FALL
    NEW AFRICAN, 261 (JUN 89), 16-17.
        THIS ARTICLE EXAMINES THE CIRCUMSTANCES BEHIND THE
    SUDDEN ECLIPSE OF DR. JOSEPHAT KARANJA, FORMER RISING STAR
    IN THE RULING KENYA AFRICAN NATIONAL UNION. CAUGHT IN THE
    COILS OF KENYA'S INTERNECINE POLITICS, KARANJA WAS THE
    VICTIM OF A "NO-CONFIDENCE" VOTE, WHICH FORCED HIS
    RESIGNATION FROM GOVERNMENT AND FUELLED HIS POLITICAL
    ASPIRATIONS.

06805 NJURURI, B.
    MAJOR SHAKE UP IN KANU
    NEW AFRICAN, (263) (AUG 89), 17.
        THIS IS A REPORT ON CHANGES IN KENYA LEADERSHIP JUST
    NINE MONTHS AFTER THE LAST ELECTIONS. IT DETAILS THE NEWLY
    FILLED POSITIONS OF VICE-PRESIDENT, SECRETARY-GENERAL, AND
    TREASURER AND NOTES THAT FOR THE FIRST TIME BOTH THE
    PRESIDENT AND THE VICE-PRESIDENT ARE FROM THE SAME
    GEOGRAPHICAL AREA, AS WELL AS THE SECRETARY-GENERAL. DETAILS
    ARE GIVEN ON EACH OF THESE MEN.

06806 NJURURI, B.
    PARTIAL PRIVATISATION
    AFRICAN BUSINESS, (JUN 88), 33-34.
        THIS ARTICLE EXPLORES THE ECONOMICS OF KENYA'S MOST
    IMPORTANT FOOD CROP, MAIZE. IT DISCUSSES THE IMPACT THAT THE
    PARTIAL PRIVATISATION OF THE PURCHASE, DISTRIBUTION AND
    IMPORT OF MAIZE IS EXPECTED TO HAVE ON MARKETING EFFICIENCY.
    THE NCPB'S MONOPOLY AND THE WORLD BANK GRANT ARE DETAILED.

06807 NKALA, C.
    SPY SCARES
    NEW AFRICAN, (266) (NOV 89), 19.
        THIS ARTICLE REPORTS ON SOUTH AFRICAN INTELLIGENCE. IT
    EXPLORES THE PRESENT USAGE OF BLACKS AS SPIES TO GATHER
    INFORMATION ABOUT THE ACTIVITIES OF THE OUTLAWED AFRICAN
    NATIONAL CONGRESS IN ZIMBABWE, AS WHITES ARE NO LONGER
    EFFECTIVE AS UNDERCOVER AGENTS.

06808 NKALA, C.
    ZIMBABWE: NOW SCANDAL IN THE ARMY
    NEW AFRICAN, (262) (JUL 89), 16.
        THE RECENT MURDER OF AN ARMY CAPTIAN WHO HAD THREATENED
    EXPOSURE, HIGHLIGHTS THE CONTINUING SCANDAL IN THE
    ZIMBABHEAN ARMY, ALLEGATIONS OF MISUSE OF FUNDS, SLAUGHTER
    OF INDANGERED SPECIES OF ANIMALS BY MEMBERS OF THE ARMY, AND
    MISUSE OF ARMY EQUIPMENT HAVE SURFACED.

06809 NOAH, T.
    BORN TO BE MILD
    WASHINGTON MONTHLY, 21(11) (DEC 89), 10-14, 16-18.
        THE ARTICLE EXAMINES THE LIFE AND RISE TO POWER OF
    SENATOR SAM NUNN. NUNN IS UNIVERSALLY RECOGNIZED AS ONE OF
    THE LEADING SENATE AUTHORITIES ON DEFENSE ISSUES. HIS
    REPUTATION LEADERSHIP IN THE DRIVE TO BLOCK THE NOMINATION
    OF JOHN TOWER TO THE POSITION OF SECRETARY OF DEFENSE
    INCREASED HIS VISIBILITY AND OVERALL POPULARITY. DESPITE
    WIDESPREAD RUMORS, NUNN DENIES ANY PRESIDENTIAL ASPIRATIONS.

06810 NOBLE, G.W.
    BETWEEN COMPETITION AND COOPERATION: COLLECTIVE ACTION IN
    THE INDUSTRIAL POLICY OF JAPAN AND TAIWAN
    DISSERTATION ABSTRACTS INTERNATIONAL, 50(2) (AUG 89),
    535-A.
        THE AUTHOR EXAMINES MATCHED CASE STUDIES OF INDUSTRIAL
    POLICY-MAKING IN JAPAN AND TAIWAN SINCE THE FIRST OIL SHOCK.
    THE CASES ARE STANDARDIZATION OF PRODUCT FORMATS IN THE
    JAPANESE CONSUMER VIDEO INDUSTRY, COPING WITH SURPLUS
    CAPACITY IN THE STEEL MINI-MILL INDUSTRIES OF BOTH COUNTRIES,
    AND STANDARDIZATION AND JOINT RESEARCH IN THE PERSONAL
    COMPUTER INDUSTRY IN TAIWAN.

06811 NOBUAKI, T.
    SUPERPOWER JAPAN, THE CLOSET PAUPER
    JAPAN ECHO, XVI(2) (SUM 89), 47-51.
        JAPAN IS NOT AS MIGHTY NOR THE JAPANESE AS RICH, AS THE
    STATISTICS SUGGEST. UNCRITICAL ACCEPTANCE OF STATISTICS HAS
    CAUSED THE JAPANESE TO TURN THEIR ATTENTIN TO OVERSEAS
    RESPONSIBILITIES AND, IN DOING SO, THEY HAVE LOST SIGHT OF
    THE POVERTY AND INEQUITIES AT HOME. INCOME DIFFERENTIALS
    REMAIN RELATIVELY SMALL IN JAPAN, BUT HEALTH DIFFERENTIALS
    HAVE BEEN WIDENING. THE LEVELING OF JAPANESE SOCIETY HAS
    REVERSED DIRECTION, AND THE GROWING DISPARITIES IN HEALTH

ARE PRODUCING A NEW, MORE SHARPLY DEFINED CLASS STRUCTURE.
JAPAN'S RECENT TAX REFORM IS INDICATIVE OF THE GOVERNMENT'S
STANCE AND THE INADEQUACIES IN ITS APPROACH TO HEALTH
REDISTRIBUTION.

06812 NODJOMI, M.
       FROM POPULAR REVOLUTION TO THEOCRATIC ABSOLUTISM: IRAN
       1979-1981
       SOCIALISM AND DEMOCRACY, 6 (SPR 89), 31-56.
       THE PURPOSE OF THE ESSAY IS TO TRACE THE PROCESS THROUGH
       WHICH THE IRANIAN POPULAR REVOLUTION OF 1979, WHICH SEEMED
       TO HOLD THE PROMISE OF A LIBERALIZATION OF IRANIAN SOCIETY,
       ENDED IN AN OVERTHROW OF A MODERNIZING DICTATORSHIP AND ITS
       REPLACEMENT BY AN ABSOLUTIST THEOCRATIC STATE. IT EXAMINES
       THE ACTORS INVOLVED INCLUDING THE ISLAMIC CLERGY, THE
       DEMOCRATIC OPPOSITION, THE LIBERAL BOURGEOISIE, AND THE FAR
       LEFT.

06813 NOEL, E.
       THE SINGLE EUROPEAN ACT
       GOVERNMENT AND OPPOSITION, 24(1) (1989), 3-14.
       THE AUTHOR OFFERS SOME GENERAL REFLECTIONS ON THE SINGLE
       EUROPEAN ACT, THE CONDITIONS IN WHICH IT WAS NEGOTIATED, AND
       ITS INITIAL CONSEQUENCES.

06814 NOLAN, C.J.
       PRINCIPLED INTERVENTION: NATIONAL SECURITY AND THE IDEAL
       OF LIBERTY IN THE DIPLOMACY OF THE UNITED STATES AND CANADA
       DISSERTATION ABSTRACTS INTERNATIONAL, 50(6) (DEC 89),
       1796-A.
       THE UNITED STATES AND CANADA HAVE NUMEROUS COMMON
       SECURITY CONCERNS AND JOINTLY PARTICIPATE IN AN EXTENSIVE
       NETWORK OF SECURITY ARRANGEMENTS. BUT THEY HAVE NOT ALWAYS
       AGREED ON HOW TO ESTABLISH LASTING INTERNATIONAL SECURITY,
       ON THE EXTENT OF THEIR OBLIGATION TO PROMOTE LIBERTY ABROAD,
       OR ON THE NATURE OF THE RELATIONSHIP BETWEEN NATIONAL
       SECURITY AND THE SUPPRESSION OF LIBERTY IN FOREIGN LANDS.
       THESE CONFLICTING VIEWS HAVE OFTEN BEEN APPARENT IN THEIR
       APPROACHES TO THE UNITED NATIONS AND IN THEIR RELATIONS WITH
       THE SOVIET UNION.

06815 NOLAN, D.F.
       IS THE PARTY OVER?
       REASON, 20(10) (MAR 89), 30-31.
       THE CONDITIONS THAT LED TO THE FORMATION OF THE
       LIBERTARIAN PARTY NO LONGER PREVAIL AND THE ROLE OF A THIRD
       PARTY AS A VEHICLE FOR ACHIEVING FREEDOM NEEDS TO BE
       REEXAMINED. THE PARTY IS THE ONLY MAJOR NETWORK OF
       CONSISTENT FREEDOM ADVOCATES AND LIBERTARIANS WOULD BE
       FOOLISH TO DISMANTLE IT. BUT PERHAPS THEY SHOULD CONSIDER
       TRANSFORMING IT INTO SOMETHING OTHER THAN A POLITICAL PARTY.

06816 NOMAN, O.
       PAKISTAN AND GENERAL ZIA: ERA AND LEGACY
       THIRD WORLD QUARTERLY, 11(1) (JAN 89), 28-54.
       THE AUTHOR SURVEYS PAKISTAN'S ECONOMIC AND POLITICAL
       DEVELOPMENT FROM 1977 TO 1988. HE BEGINS BY PROVIDING A
       CHRONOLOGY OF EVENTS, PLACING THEM WITHIN THE FRAMEWORK OF
       THE THREE PHASES INTO WHICH THE ZIA PERIOD CAN BE DIVIDED.
       THEN HE EXAMINES THE MAJOR THEMES THAT EMERGED DURING THE
       COURSE OF ZIA'S RULE.

06817 NOONE, M.F. JR.
       MILITARY SOCIAL SCIENCE RESEARCH AND THE LAW
       ARMED FORCES AND SOCIETY, 15(2) (WIN 89), 193-206.
       FEDERAL COURTS ARE CALLED UPON TO DECIDE CLAIMS BY
       INDIVIDUAL MEMBERS OF THE ARMED FORCES THAT THEY HAVE BEEN
       MISTREATED BY THEIR SUPERIORS. A COURT'S DECISION WILL OFTEN
       DEPEND ON THE JUDGE'S PERCEPTION OF THE NECESSITY OF THE
       ACTION IN MAINTAINING MORALE AND DISCIPLINE. RECENTLY,
       GOVERNMENT LAWYERS HAVE BEGUN TO JUSTIFY COMMANDERS' ACTIONS
       ON THE GROUNDS OF UNIT COHESION. THIS ARTICLE EXAMINES THOSE
       JUSTIFICATIONS BY APPLYING MODELS DEVELOPED TO EVALUATE THE
       USE OF SOCIAL SCIENCE FINDINGS IN LAW SUITS AND CONCLUDES
       THAT COHESION ARGUMENTS HAVE NO PLACE IN THE COURTROOM.

06818 NORBU, D.
       CHANGES IN TIBETAN ECONOMY, 1959-76
       CHINA REPORT, 24(3) (JUL 88), 221-236.
       THIS ARTICLE EXAMINES THE QUESTION OF WHETHER THE
       TIBETAN RULING CLASS WOULD HAVE CARRIED OUT LONG OVERDUE
       ECONOMIC CHANGES, INCLUDING INDUSTRIALIZATION, HAD THE
       CHINESE NOT "LIBERATED" TIBET IN 1950. THE AUTHOR CONCLUDES
       THAT, ALTHOUGH TIBET ON HER OWN COULD NOT HAVE CARRIED ON
       DEVELOPMENT ON THE SCALE THAT CHINA INITIATED, SHE CERTAINLY
       COULD NOT HAVE REMAINED A "CLOSED" COUNTRY BECAUSE OF THE
       REVOLUTIONARY CHANGES TAKING PLACE ALL AROUND HER. NOR WOULD
       TIBET HAVE PAID SUCH A HIGH PRICE FOR DEVELOPMENT AS SHE HAS
       DONE UNDER CHINESE RULE.

06819 NORD, P.
       MANET AND RADICAL POLITICS
       JOURNAL OF INTERDISCIPLINARY HISTORY, XIX(3) (WIN 89),
       447-480.

REVISIONIST INTERPRETATIONS OF MANET'S POLITICS ARE
WRONG. MANET WAS NEVER A COMMUNARD NOR A VISIONARY OF THE
WORKING CLASS. HE WAS A BOURGEOIS, BUT A RADICAL NOT A
LIBERAL BOURGEOIS. MANET FIXED HIS SYMPATHIES ON A NARROW
STRETCH OF FRANCE'S POLITICAL SPECTRUM EXTENDING FROM HENRI
ROCHEFORT, AN INTRANSIGENT AND RADICAL JOURNALIST ON THE
LEFT, TO LEON GAMBETTA, A CI-DEVANT RADICAL ON THE RIGHT.
THE ARTIST WAS BOUND BY TIES OF FAMILY AND SOCIABILITY TO
THE RADICAL REPUBLICAN CAMP, AND HE PRODUCED A BODY OF WORK
RESONANT WITH THEMES CONGENIAL TO RADICALS.

06820 NORMAN, M.A.
       CHANGE IN THE FEDERAL BUDGET: PUBLIC OPINION AS A
       CONGRUENT CHANGE VARIABLE
       DISSERTATION ABSTRACTS INTERNATIONAL, 50(1) (JUL 89),
       257-A.
       THE RESEARCH EMPLOYS COVARIATIONAL ANALYSIS AND PRECISE
       TIME SERIES MODELS TO STUDY ASSOCIATION BETWEEN THE BUDGET
       AND PUBLIC OPINION FOR NINE POLICY DOMAINS: NATIONAL DEFENSE,
       SOCIAL SECURITY, SOCIAL WELFARE (PUBLIC ASSISTANCE), HEALTH,
       SPACE EXPLORATION, EDUCATION, ENVIRONMENTAL PROTECTION,
       FOREIGN AID, AND FEDERAL INCOME TAX. DESCRIPTIVE AND
       STATISTICAL ANALYSES ARE PERFORMED. A QUALITIATIVE ANALYSIS
       IS PROVIDED FOR THE SOCIAL SECURITY TAX.

06821 NORMANDY, E.L.
       BLACK AMERICANS AND U.S. POLICY TOWARD AFRICA: TWO CASE
       STUDIES FROM THE PRE-WORLD WAR II PERIOD
       DISSERTATION ABSTRACTS INTERNATIONAL, 48(8) (FEB 88),
       2155-A.
       THE STUDY ATTEMPTS TO DETERMINE WHETHER OR NOT BLACK
       AMERICANS EXERTED SIGNIFICANT INFLUENCE IN US POLICY TOWARDS
       AFRICA IN TWO CASES FROM THE PRE-WORLD WAR II PERIOD: THE
       CONGO FROM 1904 TO 1907 AND LIBERIA FROM 1908 TO 1912. IT
       ANALYZES WHAT FACTORS ACCOUNTED FOR THEIR SUCCESS OR FAILURE
       AND CONCLUDES THAT BLACK AMERICANS, IN SEEKING TO EXERCISE
       INFLUENCE ON POLICY SHOULD PAY ATTENTION TO THE SELECTION OF
       ISSUES, THE ESTABLISHMENT OF LEGITIMACY AND TO THE
       LIMITATIONS IMPOSED BY THE STRUCTURE OF THE DECISIONMAKING
       SYSTEM.

06822 NORRANDER, B.
       IDEOLOGICAL REPRESENTATIVENESS OF PRESIDENTIAL PRIMARY
       VOTERS
       AMERICAN JOURNAL OF POLITICAL SCIENCE, 33(3) (AUG 89),
       570-587.
       CONTRARY TO CONVENTIONAL WISDOM AND PREVIOUS RESEARCH,
       THIS ARTICLE FINDS LITTLE EVIDENCE THAT PRESIDENTIAL PRIMARY
       VOTERS ARE IDEOLOGICALLY UNREPRESENTATIVE. IN DRAWING THIS
       CONCLUSION, TWO ASSERTIONS ARE MADE. FIRST, THE ARTICLE
       ARGUES THE APPROPRIATE COMPARISON GROUP FOR PRIMARY VOTERS
       IS GENERAL ELECTION VOTERS WHO FAIL TO VOTE IN PRIMARIES,
       NOT ALL PRIMARY NONVOTERS. THE LATTER GROUP INCLUDES
       HABITUAL NONVOTERS WHOSE DIFFERENCES FROM PRIMARY VOTERS
       WOULD BE ATTRIBUTABLE NOT TO THE PRIMARY PROCESS BUT TO
       GENERAL PATTERNS OF PARTICIPATION IN THE UNITED STATES.
       SECOND, THE ARTICLE ARGUES IDEOLOGY MUST BE DEFINED AS MORE
       THAN EXTREMISM. IDEOLOGY CAN BE CONSTRUED AS A SOPHISTICATED
       BELIEF SYSTEM OR A PSYCHOLOGICAL IDENTIFICATION. ONLY ON
       THESE LATTER TWO DEFINITIONS DO A FEW MINOR DIFFERENCES
       ARISE BETWEEN PRESIDENTIAL PRIMARY VOTERS AND GENERAL
       ELECTION VOTERS.

06823 NORRIS, P.; FEIGERT, F.
       GOVERNMENT AND THIRD-PARTY PERFORMANCE IN MID-TERM BY-
       ELECTIONS: THE CANADIAN, BRITISH AND AUSTRALIAN EXPERIENCE
       ELECTORAL STUDIES, 8(2) (AUG 89), 117-130.
       THE RESULTS OF MID-TERM BY-ELECTIONS OFTEN ATTRACT
       CONSIDERABLE MEDIA COVERAGE BUT, EXCEPT FOR THE SUCCESSFUL
       CANDIDATES, DO BY-ELECTIONS REALLY MATTER? ARE THEY LARGELY
       IDIOSYNCRATIC AND EPHEMERAL POLITICAL PHENOMENA OR CAN AN
       ANALYSIS OF THE RESULTS PROVIDE INSIGHTS INTO TRENDS IN
       ELECTORAL BEHAVIOUR? IN THIS ANALYSIS WE ATTEMPT TO ANSWER
       THESE QUESTIONS, FOCUSING INITIALLY ON THE BROAD FEATURES OF
       BY-ELECTIONS AND THEN MORE CLOSELY ON THE RELATIONSHIP
       BETWEEN GOVERNMENT AND THIRD PARTY ELECTORAL PERFORMANCE AND
       EFFECTS. INCLUDED IS A CONSIDERATION OF THE IMPACT OF THIRD
       OR MINOR PARTY INTERVENTION IN BY-ELECTIONS AND THE
       CONTRIBUTION THIS MAKES TO ELECTORAL VOLATILITY. TO PROVIDE
       A COMPARATIVE BASIS FOR THE ANALYSIS WE EXAMINE ALMOST SIX
       HUNDRED CONTESTED BY-ELECTIONS IN AUSTRALIA, CANADA AND
       BRITAIN FROM 1945 TO 1987.

06824 NORTH, D.C.
       INSTITUTIONS AND ECONOMIC GROWTH: AN HISTORICAL
       INTRODUCTION
       WORLD DEVELOPMENT, 17(9) (SEP 89), 1319-1332.
       THE AUTHOR EXAMINES THE INTERDEPENDENCE OF POLITICAL AND
       ECONOMIC INSTITUTIONS AGAINST PREMISES IN NEOCLASSICAL
       THEORIES OF ECONOMIES, WHICH MAINTAIN THAT POPULATION AND
       SAVINGS ARE THE PRINCIPAL DETERMINANTS OF ECONOMIC GROWTH.
       HE LOOKS AT THE INSTITUTIONAL FRAMEWORKS THAT PRECEDED
       ADOPTION OF THE UNITED STATES CONSTITUTION AND THE NORTHWEST
       ORDINANCE IN EARLY AMERICA. THEN HE TRACES THE PRECEDENTS OF

THESE AMERICAN INSTITUTIONS TO THE EVOLUTION OF COMMON LAW
IN ENGLAND. WHERE INTERESTS UNCONCERNED WITH THE CROWN
COALESCED TO FORM COMPETING POLITICAL UNITS. FINALLY, HE
CONTRASTS ENGLAND'S INSTITUTIONAL DEVELOPMENT WITH THE
COMPARATIVELY CENTRALIZED ENFORCEMENT MECHANISMS OF SPAIN TO
EVALUATE THE HYPOTHESIS THAT INSTITUTIONAL DIFFERENCES
PRODUCE ECONOMIC CONSEQUENCES.

06825 NORTON, A. R.; WEISS, T. G.
TURNING AGAIN TO UN PEACEKEEPERS
NEW LEADER, LXXII(6) (MAR 89), 12-14.
WITH THE CHANGED INTERNATIONAL CLIMATE OF 1988 AND 1989,
THE UN HAS BEGUN TO SHOW A NEW VITALITY IN PERFORMING WHAT
MAY BE ITS MOST IMPORTANT ROLE, THE PEACEFUL RESOLUTION OF
INTERNATIONAL CONFLICT. BUT THE UN HAS NOT ACTED ALONE. A
KEY ELEMENT HAS BEEN THE DRAMATIC IMPROVEMENT IN RELATIONS
BETWEEN MOSCOW AND WASHINGTON.

06826 NORTON, B.T.
THE MAKING OF A FEMALE MARXIST: E.D. KUSKOVA'S CONVERSION
TO RUSSIAN SOCIAL DEMOCRACY
INTERNATIONAL REVIEW OF SOCIAL HISTORY, 34(2) (1989),
227-248.
HISTORIANS HAVE TRADITIONALLY OVERLOOKED THE ROLE OF
WOMEN IN RUSSIAN SOCIAL DEMOCRACY. THIS ARTICLE, BASED ON
ARCHIVAL AS WELL AS PUBLISHED SOURCES, EXAMINES THE
RADICALIZATION OF E.D. KUSKOVA (1860-1958), A LONG NEGLECTED
PARTICIPANT IN THE RUSSIAN MARXIST MOVEMENT DURING ITS
FORMATIVE YEARS. KUSKOVA WAS ATTRACTED TO RADICALISM BY ITS
PROMISE OF A FULFILLING LIFE OF SERVICE TO SOCIETY, AND AS
AN ESCAPE FROM THE TRADITIONAL, CONFINING ROLES FOR WOMEN IN
PREREVOLUTIONARY RUSSIA. SHE CAME TO SOCIAL DEMOCRACY AFTER
CONCLUDING THAT IT PROVIDED A MORE SATISFACTORY
WELTANSCHAUUNG AND A MORE ACCURATE DIAGNOSIS OF RUSSIA'S
SOCIOECONOMIC ILLS THAN DID ITS IDEOLOGICAL ALTERNATIVES.

06827 NORTON, G.
GEORGE BUSH'S CARIBBEAN BACKYARD
WORLD TODAY, 45(7) (JUL 89), 124-127.
THE AUTHOR OFFERS A QUICK SURVEY OF THE FOREIGN POLICY
ISSUES FACING THE BUSH ADMINISTRATION IN THE CARIBBEAN
COUNTRIES, INCLUDING PUERTO RICO, THE VIRGIN ISLANDS, THE
DOMINICAN REPUBLIC, HAITI, AND PANAMA.

06828 NORTON, P.
THE CHANGING CONSTITUTION
CONTEMPORARY RECORD, 3(1) (FAL 89), 9-12.
IN THIS SURVEY ARTICLE, PHILIP NORTON REVIEWS 25 YEARS
OF CHANGE TO THE BRITISH CONSTITUTION AND EXAMINES THE
THESES WHICH HAVE BEEN ADVANCED TO EXPLAIN IT. HE GIVES
BROAD AND NARROW DEFINITIONS FOR A CONSTITUTION AND DEFENDS
THE BRITISH 'FLEXIBLE' CONSTITUTION. CIVIL RIGHTS, LOCAL
GOVERNMENT, MEMBERSHIP IN THE EUROPEAN COMMUNITY ARE THREE
OF THE CHANGES IN THE CONSTITUTION THAT ARE EXAMINED.

06829 NORTON, P.
THE CHANGING CONSTITUTION - PART 2
CONTEMPORARY RECORD, 3(2) (NOV 89), 9-10.
THE SECOND PART OF A REVIEW OF THE BRITISH CONSTITUTION,
THIS ARTICLE EXPLORES THE PRESENT DEBATE FOR A NEW
CONSTITUTIONAL SETTLEMENT, AND THE ELECTIVE DICTATORSHIP
THESIS, AS WELL AS THE THESIS OF CONSTITUTIONAL
FRAGMENTATION. DYNAMIC PLURALISM IS CHARGED WITH MAKING IT
INCREASINGLY DIFFICULT FOR THE GOVERNMENT TO GOVERN. IT
CONCLUDES THAT THE CONSTITUTION IS THE SUBJECT OF DISCUSSION,
BUT RECEIVES LITTLE PRAISE. REFORM IS CALLED FOR.

06830 NORTON, P.
THE GLORIOUS REVOLUTION OF 1688 AND 1689: ITS CONTINUING
RELEVANCE
PARLIAMENTARY AFFAIRS, 42(2) (APR 89), 135-147.
THE ARTICLE EXAMINES THE EVENTS THAT CAME TO BE KNOWN AS
THE "GLORIOUS REVOLUTION" THAT TOOK PLACE IN 1688 AND 1689.
IT OUTLINES THE CONTINUING RELEVANCE AND INFLUENCE THAT THE
EVENTS THAT MADE UP THE GLORIOUS REVOLUTION HAVE ON BRITISH
POLITICS TODAY. IT ALSO EXAMINES THE RELATIONSHIP BETWEEN
"THE ONE FUNDAMENTAL LAW OF THE BRITISH CONSTITUTION" AND
THE CONTEMPORARY CONSTITUTIONAL DEBATE THAT IS TAKING PLACE.

06831 NORTON, S.W.
REGULATION, THE OPEC OIL SUPPLY SHOCK, AND WEALTH EFFECTS
FOR ELECTRIC UTILITIES FURTHER EVIDENCE ON THE
RELATIONSHIP BETWEEN FEDERAL GOVERNMENT DEBT AND INFLATION
ECONOMIC INQUIRY, 26(2) (APR 88), 223-238.
THIS PAPER EXAMINES THE IMPACT OF REGULATION ON
SHAREHOLDER WEALTH FOR FIRMS FACING PRICE-ENTRY OR PUBLIC
UTILITY TYPE REGULATION. THE TOPIC ADDRESSES TWO IMPORTANT
ISSUES. FIRST IS WHETHER SHAREHOLDER WEALTH EFFECTS IN
REGULATED INDUSTRIES ARE ENDOGENOUS TO THE REGULATORY
PROCESS ITSELF, AN ISSUE RAISED BY MARSHALL, YAWITZ, AND
GREENBERG (1981). SECOND IS WHETHER THE REGULATORY PROCESS
RETARDS PRICE ADJUSTMENTS WHEN COSTS RISE UNEXPECTEDLY,
THEREBY DIMINISHING FINANCIAL PERFORMANCE FOR REGULATED
FIRMS AS ISSUE RAISED BY NUMEROUS SCHOLARS. THE POSITIVE

THEORY OF REGULATION PIONEERED BY STIGLER (1971) AND REFINED
BY PELTZMAN (1976) OFFERS SOME TESTABLE PROPOSITIONS
REGARDING BOTH ISSUES. MORE SPECIFICALLY, THIS PAPER FOCUSES
ON THE PROPOSITION SUGGESTED BY THE COMPARATIVE STATICS OF
PELTZMAN'S PRICE-ENTRY EQUILIBRIUM - THAT THE REGULATORY
PROCESS WILL "BUFFER" A FIRM FROM EXOGENOUS DEMAND AND COST
SHOCKS. BECAUSE U.S. ELECTRIC UTILITIES ARE HIGHLY SENSITIVE
TO ENERGY PRICES, THE SEVERE OIL PRICE SHOCKS INDUCED BY THE
OPEC'S FIRST LARGE PRICE INCREASE AND OIL EMBARGO IN OCTOBER
1973 OFFER AN OPPORTUNITY TO TEST THESE PROPOSITIONS IN THE
EXTREME. THE THEORETICAL AND EMPIRICAL BACKGROUND OF THE
STUDY IS REVIEWED BRIEFLY IN THE NEXT SECTION. THE EMPIRICAL
METHOD AND SAMPLE ARE DESCRIBED IN THE THIRD SECTION, WHILE
SECTION IV CONTAINS THE EMPIRICAL RESULTS AND SECTION V
CONTAINS THE SUMMARY AND CONCLUSIONS.

06832 NOSSAL, K.R.
INTERNATIONAL SANCTIONS AS INTERNATIONAL PUNISHMENT
INTERNATIONAL ORGANIZATION, 43(2) (SPR 89), 301-322.
THIS ARTICLE EXPLORES PUNISHMENT AS BOTH A USEFUL AND AN
EFFECTIVE PURPOSE OF INTERNATIONAL SANCTIONS. IT ARGUES NOT
ONLY THAT SANCTIONS SHOULD BE DISTINGUISHED FROM OTHER FORMS
OF HURTFUL STATECRAFT BUT ALSO THAT THEY ARE A FORM OF
"INTERNATIONAL PUNISHMENT" FOR WRONGDOING, DESPITE THE
DIFFICULTIES OF APPLYING THE TERM "PUNISHMENT" IN THE
CONTEXT OF INTERNATIONAL RELATIONS. THE ARTICLE THEN
EXAMINES THE PURPOSES OF PUNISHMENT AND REVEALS THAT ONLY
SOME ARE UNDERSTANDABLE WHEN A MODEL OF MEANS-END
RATIONALITY IS USED, SUGGESTING THAT THE ELEMENT OF THE
NONRATIONAL ALSO PLAYS AN IMPORTANT ROLE IN INTERNATIONAL
SANCTIONS. THE ARGUMENT IS THEN APPLIED TO THE CASE OF U.S.
SANCTIONS IMPOSED AFTER THE SOVIET UNION'S INVASION OF
AFGHANISTAN TO DEMONSTRATE THE DIFFERENT PURPOSES OF
PUNISHMENT AT WORK IN THIS CASE. THE ARTICLE CONCLUDES THAT
JUST AS WE CANNOT UNDERSTAND PUNISHMENT AS A PURPOSIVE HUMAN
ACTIVITY SOLELY BY REFERENCE TO A RATIONAL MODEL OF A MEANS
TO A CLEARLY DELINEATED END, SO TOO WE CANNOT ENTIRELY
UNDERSTAND SANCTIONS AS A FORM OF INTERNATIONAL PUNISHMENT
BY AN ATTACHMENT TO A RATIONAL MODEL OF POLICY BEHAVIOR.
HOWEVER, SOME FORMS OF PUNISHMENT ARE EXCEEDINGLY EFFECTIVE,
AND THIS MAY EXPLAIN WHY SANCTIONS CONTINUE TO BE A POPULAR
INSTRUMENT OF STATECRAFT.

06833 NOSSAL, K.R.
KNOWING WHEN TO FOLD: WESTERN SANCTIONS AGAINST THE USSR,
1980-83
INTERNATIONAL JOURNAL, XLIV(3) (SUM 89), 698-724.
THE AUTHOR STUDIES THE USE OF WESTERN SANCTIONS AGAINST
THE USSR IN THE EARLY 1980'S. THE SANCTIONS IMPOSED IN
RESPONSE TO THE SOVIET INVASION OF AFGHANISTAN, THE
IMPOSITION OF MARTIAL LAW IN POLAND, AND THE SHOOTING DOWN
OF KOREAN AIR LINES FLIGHT 007 DEMONSTRATE AN INTERESTING
RELATIONSHIP BETWEEN THE DECISIONS MADE AT THE TIME
SANCTIONS ARE IMPOSED AND THE CALCULUS MADE ABOUT
TERMINATION ONCE THE SANCTIONS ARE IN PLACE. SANCTIONS ARE
MOST USEFUL AS RETRIBUTIVE PUNISHMENTS, AND THEY SHOULD BE
IMPOSED IN A DISCRETE WAY AND FOR DEFINITE, STRICTLY LIMITED
PERIODS OF TIME.

06834 NOSSAL, K.R.
THE IMPERIAL CONGRESS: THE SEPARATION OF POWERS AND
CANADIANAMERICAN RELATIONS
INTERNATIONAL JOURNAL, XLIV(4) (AUG 89), 863-883.
THE AUTHOR STUDIES THE POWER OF CONGRESS, HOW THE
CONSTITUTION DEFINES THE POWER OF CONGRESS, HOW FOREIGN
GOVERNMENTS DEAL WITH THE U.S. CONGRESS, LOBBYING, AND HOW
THE POWER OF CONGRESS AFFECTS U.S.-CANADIAN DIPLOMATIC
RELATIONS.

06835 NOSSOV, M.
THE USSR AND THE SECURITY OF THE ASIA-PACIFIC REGION: FROM
VLADIVOSTOK TO KRASNOYARSK
ASIAN SURVEY, XXIX(3) (MAR 89), 252-267.
THE ARTICLE EXAMINES THE CHANGING SITUATIONS AND
CONDITIONS IN THE ASIA-PACIFIC REGION AND OUTLINES SOVIET
ATTEMPTS TO INCREASE THE SECURITY AND STABILITY OF THE
REGION. SOME KEY SOVIET POLICIES INCLUDE: DEBLOCKING THE
KOREAN CONFLICT; MOVING TOWARD A KAMPUCHEAN SETTLEMENT,
PROGRESS IN USSRJAPAN RELATIONS; DECREASING TENSION BETWEEN
THE USSR AND CHINA; AND DEVELOPING THE SOVIET FAR EAST.

06836 NOTZOLD, J.
SEVERAL EUROPEAN ECONOMIC BLOCS? THE FUTURE SIGNIFICANCE
OF THE COMECON
AUSSEN POLITIK, 40(3) (1989), 277-292.
THE EUROPEAN COMMUNITY (EC) HOPES THAT THE CREATION OF
AN INTERNAL MARKET BY THE END OF 1992 WILL INTENSIFY ITS
INTEGRATION. THE COUNCIL OF MUTUAL ECONOMIC ASSISTANCE
(COMECON) IS MARKED BY VARYING REFORMS AND SIGNS OF
DISINTEGRATION. INDIVIDUAL COMECON MEMBERS HAVE GAINED
GREATER AUTONOMY THROUGH SOVIET PERESTROIKA: TRADE BETWEEN
COMECON COUNTRIES, HOWEVER, STILL ACCOUNTS FOR 60 PERCENT OF
THEIR TOTAL FOREIGN TRADE. DR. JURGEN NOTZOLD FROM THE
STIFTUNG WISSENSCHAFT UND POLITIK (RESEARCH INSTITUTE FOR

INTERNATIONAL AFFAIRS) IN EBENHAUSEN TAKES THE VIEW THAT THE ACCELERATION OF THE PROCESS OF INTEGRATION WITHIN THE EC RAISES THE QUESTION OF ITS IMPLICATIONS FOR THE COMECON BLOC. WESTERN EUROPE ACCOUNTS FOR ALMOST 90 PERCENT OF THE EXPORTS AND ROUGHLY 75 PERCENT OF THE IMPORTS OF THE COMECON FROM WESTERN INDUSTRIAL COUNTRIES; THE EC ACCOUNTS FOR OVER 15 PERCENT OF THE TOTAL FOREIGN TRADE OF COMECON MEMBERS AND FOR ALMOST 60 PERCENT OF COMECON TRADE WITH THE WEST. THE ENTIRE EAST-WEST TRADE, THEREFORE, CONCENTRATES ON THE CONTINENT OF EUROPE. IT THUS HAS A PRIMARILY EUROPEAN CHARACTER AND SERVES EUROPEAN INTERESTS. THE FUTURE DEVELOPMENT OF THESE ECONOMIC TIES IS NOT A PROBLEM OF TERRITORIAL FRONTIERS, BUT OF THE FRONTIERS OF THE DIFFERING SYSTEMS. LAST YEAR THE COMECON ALSO SET ITSELF THE OBJECTIVE OF ESTABLISHING A COMMON MARKET. IT INTENDS ORIENTATING THIS GOAL TO THE REQUIREMENTS OF A MARKET ECONOMY. INDIVIDUAL MEMBERS, HOWEVER, HAVE INITIATED COMPLETELY DIFFERENT STRUCTURAL POLICIES. THE TECHNOLOGICAL GAP HAS NOT BEEN REDUCED AND COMPETITIVENESS HAS NOT IMPROVED. PROSPECTS FOR AN EXTENDED FOREIGN TRADE WITH WESTERN EUROPE HAVE ONLY AMELIORATED IN THOSE COUNTRIES IN WHICH ECONOMIC REFORMS HAVE BEGUN AND ARE CONTINUING - SUCH AS IN THE SOVIET UNION, POLAND AND HUNGARY. THIS WOULD INDICATE THAT THE DECISIVE FACTOR IS THE GRADUAL ELIMINATION OF THE DIFFERENCES BETWEEN THE SYSTEMS IN EASTERN AND WESTERN EUROPE. THE FUTURE PARTNER OF THE EUROPEAN COMMUNITY WOULD THEN BE A TRANSFORMED COMECON. THE TWO EUROPEAN ECONOMIC INTEGRATIONS WOULD PRESENT THEMSELVES AS CONTRIBUTORY FACTORS TOWARDS ESTABLISHING A NEW ECONOMIC ORDER IN EUROPE.

06837 NOURU, M. K.
SUDAN: NEW MINISTER; NEW IMAGE
NEW AFRICAN, 261 (JUN 89), 21.
IN A RECENT CABINET RESHUFFLE, ABDULLAH MOHAMED AHMED HAS REMOVED AS INFORMATION MINISTER AND REASSIGNED AS MINISTER OF EXTERNAL TRADE. OBSERVERS SUGGEST THAT AHMED WILL HAVE TO QUICKLY DEVELOP A SENSE OF DIPLOMACY TO HEAD THAT SENSITIVE MINISTRY, A TRAIT HE SORELY LACKED AS INFORMATION MINISTER.

06838 NOVAK, J.A.
WHAT ARE THE STRATEGIC IMPLICATIONS FOR THE UNITED STATES OF THE 1977 PANAMA CANAL TREATIES
AVAILABLE FROM NTIS, NO. AD-A209 530/5/GAR, MAR 31 89, 30.
UNDER THE PROVISIONS OF THE 1977 CARTER-TORRIJOS PANAMA CANAL TREATIES, U.S. CONTROL OF THE CANAL OPERATION AND ALL U.S. MILITARY BASING RIGHTS CEASE/EXPIRE ON 31 DECEMBER 1999. THE TITLE SUGGESTS THAT THE UNITED STATES MIGHT HAVE TO MAKE SOME SIGNIFICANT DECISIONS IN ITS MILITARY AND POLITICAL STRATEGY IN ORDER TO PROVIDE FOR A SMOOTH TRANSITION TO POST-1999 CANAL ZONE/PANAMA OPERATIONS/RELATIONS. THIS MILITARY STUDY PROJECT STUDIES THE EFFECT OF THE TREATIES IMPACT ON U.S. NATIONAL SECURITY INTERESTS/OBJECTIVES AND HOW THESE INTERESTS/OBJECTIVES MAY DRIVE DEFENSE/MILITARY STRATEGY. THE WHAT/HOW CHANGES AFTER 1999 WILL BE ADDRESSED IN CHAPTER III FOLLOWED BY CONCLUSIONS AND RECOMMENDATIONS. THIS STUDY WILL ATTEMPT TO ISOLATE WHAT AREAS OF NATIONAL SECURITY INTEREST MAY IMPACT ON NATIONAL STRATEGY, HOW PANAMA RELATIONS COULD BE AFFECTED, WHAT AREAS WILL CHANGE AND WHAT USE/RIGHTS WILL REMAIN FOR MILITARY PLANNING PURPOSES.

06839 NOVAK, M.
LIBERALS AND CATHOLICS: POLITICAL ECONOMY IN OUR TIME
CURRENT, (311) (MAR 89), 20-23.
CATHOLICS HAVE BEEN TAUGHT A CERTAIN AMBIVALENCE CONCERNING LIBERAL PHILOSOPHY. ON THE ONE HAND, THEY HAVE LEARNED TO LOVE LIBERAL INSTITUTIONS AS THEY HAVE COME TO SHARE IN THE UNITED STATES AND A FEW OTHER PLACES ON EARTH. ON THE OTHER HAND, VATICAN DOCUMENTS AND MANY POLEMICAL OR CATECHETICAL WRITINGS HARSHLY CRITICIZE LIBERAL PHILOSOPHIES AND TEND TO USE THE WORD "LIBERAL" PEJORATIVELY.

06840 NOVAK, R.
DINING IN MOSCOW
NATIONAL REVIEW, 61(23) (DEC 89), 30-31.
THIS ARTICLE CONTRASTS RESTAURANTS IN MOSCOW - AND CONTINUES ON TO CONTRAST THE UKRAINE AND U PERSOMANY. HE CONCLUDES THAT THEY ARE DIFFERENT IN KIND AND THAT THEREIN LIES THE CONTRADICTION OF PERESTROIKA. AS PRIVATE - SECTOR ENTERPRISES (CAPITALISM) PROLIFERATES, THE SOCIALIST SECTOR IS ALL THE MORE UNACCEPTABLE.

06841 NOVAK, R.D.
THE SHIFTY RICHARD GEPHARDT
AMERICAN SPECTATOR, 22(8) (AUG 89), 14-16.
THIS ARTICLE EXAMINES THE SHIFT TOWARDS THE LEFT MADE BY RICHARD GEPHARDT SINCE 1977. IT ANALYSES THE POSSIBILITIES FOR FURTHER CHANGE AND CONCLUDES THAT IT IS NOT LIKELY, IT EXAMINES HIS ETHICS AND FINDS HIM CLEAN.

06842 NOVAK, R.D.
THE UNFINISHED REAGAN AGENDA
AMERICAN SPECTATOR, 22(3) (MAR 89), 14-15.

THIS ARTICLE DESCRIBES HOW GEORGE BUSH - IF HE IS TO MEET CONSERVATIVE EXPECTATION - MUST PAY MORE THAN LIP SERVICE TO SUCH INCENDIARY TOPICS AS GOVERNMENT SPENDING, THE CONTRAS AND ABORTION.

06843 NOVICKI, M.A.
A PERMANENT EMERGENCY
AFRICA REPORT, 34(2) (MAR 89), 17-22.
FACING YET ANOTHER FOOD EMERGENCY THIS YEAR, THE MOZAMBICAN GOVERNMENT IS LAUNCHING ITS THIRD APPEAL TO THE INTERNATIONAL COMMUNITY FOR SUPPORT. WHILE THE DONOR RESPONSE HAS BEEN GENEROUS, THE CRISIS WILL BE ONGOING UNTIL ITS ROOT CAUSE-RENAMO'S WAR AND CONTINUING SOUTH AFRICAN BACKING--IS ENDED.

06844 NOVICKI, M.A.
EDWARD V.K. JAYCOX: A NEW SCENARIO FOR AFRICA
AFRICA REPORT, 34(6) (NOV 89), 17-22.
"SUB-SAHARAN AFRICA: FROM CRISIS TO SUSTAINABLE GROWTH," THE WORLD BANK'S MOST COMPREHENSIVE ASSESSMENT TO DATE OF DEVELOPMENT OPTIONS FOR THAT REGION, CALLS FOR A DOUBLING OF EXPENDITURES ON HUMAN RESOURCE DEVELOPMENT AS PART OF A NEW EFFORT TO STRENGTHEN AFRICAN SKILLS AND INSTITUTIONS, IN ORDER TO REVERSE THE CONTINENT'S ECONOMIC DECLINE. IN THIS ARTICLE, THE WORLD BANK'S VICE PRESIDENT FOR AFRICA SUMMARIZES THE NEW PERSPECTIVES OF THE REPORT AND EXPLAINS THE NEED FOR AN INTERNATIONAL CONSENSUS ABOUT AFRICA'S LONG-TERM DEVELOPMENT OBJECTIVES.

06845 NOVICKI, M.A.
FREDERIK VAN ZYL SLABBERT: A VOICE OF OPPOSITION
AFRICA REPORT, 34(1) (JAN 89), 33-35.
HAVING REPRESENTED THE PROGRESSIVE FEDERAL PARTY IN THE SOUTH AFRICAN PARLIAMENT FOR 12 YEARS, FREDERIK VAN ZYL SLABBERT RESIGNED AS MP AND LEADER OF THE OFFICIAL OPPOSITION IN 1986 AND FOUNDED THE INSTITUTE FOR DEMOCRATIC ALTERNATIVES IN SOUTH AFRICA (IDASA). AN EFFORT TO BRING TOGETHER WHITES WITH THE DEMOCRATIC MOVEMENTS INSIDE AND OUTSIDE THE COUNTRY TO DEBATE OPTIONS FOR THE FUTURE, IDASA ORGANIZED THE CONTROVERSIAL MEETING OF 50 WHITE SOUTH AFRICANS AND REPRESENTATIVES OF THE AFRICAN NATIONAL CONGRESS IN DAKAR, SENEGAL, IN 1987.. RECENTLY IN THE UNITED STATES, SLABBERT TALKED ABOUT THE ROLE HE AND HIS INSTITUTE PLAY IN THE SOUTH AFRICAN POLITICAL SPECTRUM, THE RECENT ELECTIONS AND THE RISE OF THE RIGHT-WING, AND THE GOVERNMENT'S "REFORM" STRATEGIES.

06846 NOVICKI, M.A.
HERMAN J. COHEN: FORGING A BIPARTISAN POLICY
AFRICA REPORT, 34(5) (SEP 89), 13-19.
THIS ARTICLE CONTAINS AN INTERVIEW WITH HERMAN J. COHEN, US ASSISTANT SECRETARY OF STATE FOR AFRICAN AFFAIRS. COHEN EXPLAINS THE BUSH ADMINISTRATION'S AFRICA POLICY PERSPECTIVES, HIGHLIGHTING THE DIFFERENCES IN APPROACH FROM THE REAGAN ERA. HE EMPHASIZES THAT THE BUSH ADMINISTRATION IS SEEKING TO ACHIEVE A DOMESTIC BIPARTISAN CONSENSUS IN SUPPORT OF ITS POLICIES.

06847 NOVICKI, M.A.
JOHN GARANG: A NEW SUDAN
AFRICA REPORT, 34(4) (JUL 89), 43-47.
ON JUNE 30, 1989, THE GOVERNMENT OF PRIME MINISTER SADIQ AL-MAHDI WAS OVERTHROWN IN A MILITARY COUP LED BY LT.-GEN. OMAR HASSAN AL-BASHIR. IN THE WEEKS PRECEDING THE COUP, THE SUDANESE GOVERNMENT, FACED WITH AN ARMY ULTIMATUM TO NEGOTIATE AN END TO THE WAR IN THE SOUTH, INITIATED DISCUSSIONS WITH THE SUDAN PEOPLE'S LIBERATION MOVEMENT (SPLM) IN ADDIS ABABA. WHILE THOSE MEETINGS WERE TAKING PLACE, COL. JOHN GARANG, LEADER OF THE SPLM, WAS IN THE UNITED STATES, MEETING WITH GOVERNMENT, CHURCH, FOUNDATION, AND UN OFFICIALS TO EXPLAIN THE OBJECTIVES FOR WHICH HIS MOVEMENT IS FIGHTING.

06848 NOVICKI, M.A.
MARCELINO DOS SANTOS: OPENING NEW FRONTS
AFRICA REPORT, 34(3) (MAY 89), 21-23.
IN THIS INTERVIEW, THE PRESIDENT OF THE MOZAMBICAN PEOPLE'S ASSEMBLY DISCUSSES THE EVOLUTION OF HIS COUNTRY'S POLITICAL AND ECONOMIC TIES WITH THE UNITED STATES. EXPLAINING THE GOVERNMENT'S STRATEGY REGARDING RENAMO, HE ALSO OUTLINES CURRENT MILITARY NEEDS.

06849 NOVICKI, M.A.
PEDRO DE CASTRO VAN-DUNEM LOY: CREATING CONDITIONS FOR PEACE
AFRICA REPORT, 34(2) (MAR 89), 23-25.
IN THIS ARTICLE, ANGOLA'S NEW MINISTER OF EXTERNAL RELATIONS EXPLAINS HIS GOVERNMENT'S CONCERNS REGARDING THE IMPLEMENTATION OF THE NEW YORK ACCORDS ON NAMIBIAN INDEPENDENCE AND CUBAN TROOP WITHDRAWAL. DISCUSSING ANGOLA'S EFFORTS TO RESOLVE ITS INTERNAL PROBLEMS, HE OUTLINES OPTIONS FOR UNITA AND ITS LEADERSHIP, IN ORDER FOR PEACE TO BE ATTAINED.

06850 NOVICKI, M.A.
THABO MBEKI: SHINING A SPOTLIGHT ON SOUTH AFRICA
AFRICA REPORT, 34(2) (MAR 89), 34-37.
WITH INTERNATIONAL ATTENTION FOCUSED ON THE NAMIBIAN
INDEPENDENCE PROCESS, THE ANC MUST ENSURE THAT THE SPOTLIGHT
ON APARTHEID DOES NOT DIMINISH AND THAT ACTION AGAINST IT,
PARTICULARLY SANCTIONS, IS STRENGTHENED.

06851 NOVICKI, M.A.
THE BACK PAGE
AFRICA REPORT, 34(2) (MAR 89), 70.
A CONVERGENCE OF INTERESTS ON THE PART OF THE
SUPERPOWERS IN SOLVING REGIONAL PROBLEMS HAS CONTRIBUTED TO
CLEARING THE AIR OF FAILED POLICIES AND TIRED FORMULAS.
THOUGH PEACE HASN'T YET BROKEN OUT IN SOUTHERN AFRICA, IT
MAY HAVE A FIGHTING CHANCE. FEW AFRICAN LEADERS EXPECT THE
BUSH ADMINISTRATION TO BE A CARBON COPY OF ITS PREDECESSOR
AND THEY ANTICIPATE A MORE SYMPATHETIC EAR FROM BUSH'S
FOREIGN POLICY-MAKERS.

06852 NOVICKI, M.A.
WILLEM DE KLERK: A VIEW OF THE FUTURE
AFRICA REPORT, 34(4) (JUL 89), 36-39.
WILLEM DE KLERK IS THE BROTHER OF SOUTH AFRICAN
PRESIDENT F.W. DE KLERK. IN THIS INTERVIEW, HE DISCUSSES HIS
BROTHER'S PRESIDENCY AND HOW IT WILL DIFFER FROM THAT OF P.W.
BOTHA.

06853 NOVICKI, M.A..
BACHIR MUSTAPHA SAYED: POLISARIO'S POLICIES FOR PEACE
AFRICA REPORT, 34(3) (MAY 89), 57-60.
DIPLOMATIC EFFORTS TO END THE WAR IN THE WESTERN SAHARA
HAVE ACCELERATED IN 1989, THANKS TO THE EFFORTS OF THE UN
AND THE OAU. HOWEVER, THE DIALOGUE BEGUN IN JANUARY BETWEEN
MOROCCAN KING HASSAN AND POLISARIO HAS RUN AGROUND FOR THE
MOMENT, ACCORDING TO THE HEAD OF THE MOVEMENT'S EXTERNAL
RELATIONS COMMITTEE, AND RENEWED EFFORTS ARE REQUIRED TO
BRING THE PEACE PROCESS BACK ON TRACK.

06854 NOVIKOV, M.
BEING ABLE "TO GET AWAY FROM IT ALL" IS THE ULTIMATE
GUARANTEE OF FREEDOM
GLASNOST, II(3) (MAY 89), 44-46.
FOR THOSE WHO WISH TO EMIGRATE FROM THE SOVIET UNION,
BEING ABLE TO LEAVE IS THE ULTIMATE GUARANTEE OF FREEDOM AND
THE ONLY REALISTIC ALTERNATIVE TO BONDAGE. IN THIS ARTICLE,
THE AUTHOR REVIEWS THE HISTORY OF SOVIET EMIGRATION
LEGISLATION AND THE TRADITIONAL SOVIET RESPONSE TO THE
DESIRE TO EMIGRATE.

06855 NOWAK, L.
THE POWER OF LOST REVOLUTIONS
POLISH PERSPECTIVES, XXXII(3) (1989), 51-54.
IN 1956, 1970, 1980-81, AND 1988, POLAND UNDERWENT
REFORMS THAT WERE INTRODUCED BY THE POWER ELITES OF THE TIME.
BUT BEHIND THESE REFORMS LAY MASS SOCIAL MOVEMENTS THAT
BROKE FREE OF THE ESTABLISHED SCHEME OF THINGS. GRASSROOTS
MOVEMENTS THAT GO BEYOND THE BOUNDS OF THE ORDER IMPOSED
FROM ENDED IN FAILURE BECAUSE NONE OF THEM MANAGED TO
OVERTHROW THE SYSTEM. BUT SOCIAL PROGRESS CAME ABOUT DUE TO
REFORMS THAT WERE THE RESPONSE TO THE FAILED REVOLUTIONS.
CONTRARY TO MARXIST REVOLUTIONARY THEORY, IT IS NOT
VICTORIOUS BUT FAILED REVOLUTIONS THAT ARE THE DRIVING FORCE
OF PROGRESS.

06856 NOWAK, L.
THE POWER OF THE LOST REVOLUTION
SOCIALISM AND DEMOCRACY, (FAL 89), 35-41.
THIS IS WRITTEN FROM WITHIN THE STRUGGLE FOR A
REDEFINITION OF THE SOCIALIST PROJECT IN POLAND AND OFFERS
SOME NEW THINKING ON THE SUBJECT OF REFORM, REVOLUTION,
CIVIL SOCIETY, AND MARXISM. THE SUBJECT OF THIS ARTICLE IS
THE HISTORIC NECESSITY FOR COMPROMISE IN POLAND AND IN OTHER
SOCIALIST COUNTRIES. IT ADDRESSES: A SHORT LESSON FROM
HISTORY: NON-MARXIAN HISTORICAL MATERIALISM; PRESSURE TO
COMPROMISE; WHAT IS HAPPENING TODAY IN POLAND; AND OFFERS
FACTORS OF HOPE.

06857 NOWELS, L.K.
JAPAN'S EMERGENCE AS A LEADING FOREIGN AID DONOR
CRS REVEIW, 10(6) (JUL 89), 14-16.
JAPAN IS REPLACING THE UNITED STATES AS THE WORLD'S
LEADING BILATERAL AID DONOR. HOW TOKYO ASSUMES ITS NEW
POSITION AND WHAT IT MEANS FOR THE UNITED STATES,
PARTICULARLY IN TERMS OF ECONOMIC AND POLITICAL INFLUENCE,
ARE ISSUES FACING POLICYMAKERS TODAY.

06858 NOWOTNY, K.
THE GREENHOUSE EFFECT AND ENERGY POLICY IN THE UNITED
STATES
JOURNAL OF ECONOMIC ISSUES, 23(4) (DEC 89), 1075-1084.
THIS ARTICLE SUMMARIZES THE NATURE OF THE PHYSICAL
CHARACTERISTICS OF THE GREENHOUSE EFFECT AND THEN DEVELOPS
ITS IMPLICATIONS FOR MARKET STRUCTURES IN VARIOUS SECTORS OF

THE ECONOMY CURRENTLY BASED ON THE USE OF FOSSIL FUELS. THE
CONCLUSIONS ARE THAT "FREE RIDER" PROBLEMS COMMON TO PUBLIC
GOOD ANALYSIS ALLOWS THE CONCLUSION THAT FREELY OPERATING
MARKETS CAN NO LONGER BE RELIED UPON TO ALLOCATE FOSSIL FUEL
RESOURCES TO ENERGY USERS AND THAT ANY ATTEMPT TO ALLOW
COMPETITION INTO THE MARKET FOR ELECTRICITY GENERATION WILL
ONLY EXACERBATE THE PROBLEMS OF THE GREENHOUSE EFFECT.

06859 NOYES, J.H.
THROUGH THE GULF LABYRINTH: NAVAL ESCORT AND U.S. POLICY
AMERICAN-ARAB AFFAIRS, (29) (SUM 89), 1-19.
OVER A YEAR HAS PASSED SINCE THE IRAN-IRAQ CEASE-FIRE.
SINCE EVEN THE MOST BASIC DISPUTES BETWEEN THE COMBATANTS
REMAIN NOT ONLY UNSETTLED BUT UNADDRESSED, THIS ARTICLE
PROVIDES AN ASSESSMENT OF U.S. POLICY DURING THE LAST PHASES
OF THE WAR. IT EXAMINES U.S. PURPOSES IN REFLAGGING AND
ESCORTING KUWAITI TANKERS, AND ADDRESSES WHETHER THESE
PURPOSES WERE ACHIEVED. IT ALSO EXPLORES WHETHER THIS MAJOR
NAVAL COMMITMENT WAS CONSISTENT WITH U.S. WIDER MIDDLE EAST
POLICY AND IF THERE WAS ADEQUATE PUBLIC UNDERSTANDING OF THE
ISSUES. IT OFFERS A CLEAR PERSPECTIVE ON U.S. POLICY.

06860 NSOULI, S.
STRUCTURAL ADJUSTMENT IN SUB-SAHARAN AFRICA
FINANCE AND DEVELOPMENT, 26(3) (SEP 89), 30-33.
IN THE AREA OF STRUCTURAL ADJUSTMENT, THIS ARTICLE
OFFERS A PREVIEW OF POLICY ISSUES AND CHALLENGES FOR THE
1990S IN SUB-SAHARAN AFRICA. PROGRAMS HAVE BEEN IMPLEMENTED
SINCE THE EARLY 1980S AIMED AT REDUCING PROGRAMS HAVE BEEN
IMPLEMENTED SINCE THE EARLY 1980S AIMED AT REDUCING ECONOMIC
DISTORTIONS AND FINANCIAL IMBALANCES. IT SUGGESTS THAT FOR
THE REGION AS A WHOLE IT WILL BE NECESSARY TO STRENGTHEN THE
ADJUSTMENT PROCESS TO REACH THE ROOTS OF THE STRUCTURAL
PROBLEMS; SUSTAIN THE ADJUSTMENT EFFORTS; AND INCREASE THE
NUMBER OF COUNTRIES PURSUING STRUCTURAL REFORM PROGRAMS, IT
OFFERS THE BACKGROUND IN THE 1980S, THE ADJUSTMENT IN THE
1990S, FINANCIAL AND FISCAL MEASURES, POLICY-BASED FINANCIAL
ASSISTANCE AND CONCLUDES WITH A DESCRIPTION OF THE LONG TERM
PROCESS.

06861 NUNEZ, O.
"WE HAVE NEVER HAD SUCH A CONGRESS"
WORLD MARXIST REVIEW, 32(9) (SEP 89), 46-48.
THIS IS A REPORT OF THE 15TH CONGRESS OF THE BANNED
COMMUNIST PARTY IN CHILI. PROGRESS MADE BY THE CONGRESS IS
DETAILED, AND ITS HALLMARK WHICH WAS A CRITICAL LOOK AT
PARTY LIFE IS REVIEWED. THE CONGRESS REAFFIRMED AND
EXPOUNDED THE PARTY'S POLICY LINE NOW KNOWN AS THE COURSE
TOWARDS A MASS POPULAR UPRISING. THE NEED OF THE RESTORATION
OF DEMOCRACY IN CHILI IS EXAMINED AND SUPPORT WAS GIVEN TO
RENEWAL IN THE USSR AS "A REVOLUTION WITHIN A REVOLUTION."
FOLLOW UP ACTIONS ARE EXPLORED.

06862 NUSSEIBEH, S.
A PEOPLE'S REVOLUTION
MIDDLE EAST INTERNATIONAL, (365) (DEC 89), 16-18.
THE ARTICLE RECOUNTS THE SUCCESSES AND FAILURES OF THE
INTIFADA. IT OUTLINES THE BIRTH OF THE MOVEMENT, THE
FORMATION OF THE UNIFIED COMMAND, AND THE DECLARATION OF
INDEPENDENCE. HOWEVER, THE MOMENTUM OF THE MOVEMENT HAS
SLACKENED SOMEWHAT IN THE SECOND YEAR, AND ISRAEL HAS
SKILLFULLY PLAYED ON FACTIONALIST TENSIONS AND CONFLICT. THE
AUTHOR CALLS FOR THE FORMATION OF A PROVISIONAL GOVERNMENT
TO REGAIN MOMENTUM AND WORK TOWARDS UNITY.

06863 NUSSEIBEH, S.
OCCUPIED PALESTINE: AN OFFENSIVE THAT OFFENDS
MIDDLE EAST INTERNATIONAL, (345) (MAR 89), 11-13.
THE PALESTINIAN CAUSE CANNOT BE ADVANCED UNLESS THE
PALESTINIAN PEOPLE CONTINUE TO PRESS THEIR OFFENSIVE ON TWO
COMPLEMENTARY FRONTS: THE INTIFADA AND THE PR CAMPAIGN AIMED
AT THE ISRAELI PUBLIC. BUT THERE ARE BUILT-IN LIMITATIONS TO
WHAT THE PALESTINIANS CAN DO. THE PALESTINIANS MUST OVERCOME
NOT ONLY ISRAEL'S PUNITIVE, REPRESSIVE MEASURES BUT ALSO THE
WORSENING ECONOMIC AND PSYCHOLOGICAL SUFFERING CAUSED BY
THEIR DISOBEDIENCE CAMPAIGN.

06864 NUSSEIBEH, S.
OCCUPIED PALESTINE: THE INTIFADA'S NEW DIRECTION?
MIDDLE EAST INTERNATIONAL, (344) (FEB 89), 9-10.
IN WHAT MANY OBSERVERS REGARDED AS A SIGN OF NEW
DEVELOPMENTS IN THE INTIFADA, THE UNIFIED NATIONAL COMMAND
SET ASIDE FEB. 19-21 FOR A TOTAL STRIKE ASSERTING THE
PALESTINIAN COMMITMENT TO THE RIGHT OF RETURN, SELF-
DETERMINATION, AND INDEPENDENCE.

06865 NUSSEIBEH, S.
THE INTIFADA?
MIDDLE EAST INTERNATIONAL, 352 (JUN 89), 9.
ONE OF THE MAIN STRENGTHS OF THE INTIFADA HAS BEEN THE
AMAZING SELF-CONTROL EXERCISED BY THE PALESTINIAN PEOPLE
DESPITE THE VIOLENCE PERPETRATED AGAINST THEM BY THE ISRAELI
ARMY OVER THE PAST 18 MONTHS. THE VOICE OF VIOLENCE ON THE
PALESTINIAN SIDE IS STILL PERIPHERAL, REGARDLESS OF REPORTED

STATEMENTS BY SOME PLO MEMBERS TO THE EFFECT THAT
PALESTINIANS SHOULD NOW RESORT TO THE USE OF FIREARMS. THE
PALESTINIANS UNDER OCCUPATION WILL SIMPLY NOT RESORT TO THE
USE OF FIREARMS, WHETHER NOW OR IN THE FUTURE. BECAUSE,
APART FROM ANY OTHER REASON, THE PALESTINIANS WILL NOT
DELIVER TO THEIR ENEMY THE JUSTIFICATION REQUIRED FOR THE
EXPECTED CRACK-DOWN. IF AND WHEN THE CRACK-DOWN BEGINS,
ISRAEL'S ACTS WILL BE UNDER THE SCRUTINY OF WORLD OPINION.

06866 NVQUD, M.I.
BREAKING THE VICIOUS CIRCLE
WORLD MARXIST REVIEW, 31(2) (FEB 88), 108-116.
THIS ARTICLE ATTEMPTS TO CLARIFY SOME OF THE SPECIFIC
ASPECTS WHICH, DESPITE THEIR SIMILARITY WITH PROCESSES IN
OTHER THIRD WORLD COUNTRIES, MAY SHED LIGHT ON THE
DISTINCTIVE AND UNIQUE FEATURES OF THE SUDANESE EXPERIENCE.

06867 NWAKA, G.I.
DOUBTS AND DIRECTIONS IN NIGERIAN URBAN POLICY
PUBLIC ADMINISTRATION AND DEVELOPMENT, 9(1) (JAN 89),
49-63.
THE PAPER DISCUSSES URBAN POLICY AND PERFORMANCE IN
NIGERIA AGAINST THE BACKGROUND OF THE DEVELOPMENT OF IDEAS
AND INSTITUTIONS AFFECTING THE CITIES SINCE THE EARLY
COLONIAL PERIOD. IT CRITICALLY EXAMINES THE PATTERNS OF
RURAL-URBAN RELATIONS, THE POLICIES FOR URBAN LAND-USE
CONTROL, TOWN PLANNING AND MUNICIPAL GOVERNMENT, POINTING
OUT THE INADEQUACIES, ESPECIALLY THE INEFFICIENCY OF THE
MACHINERY FOR IMPLEMENTING OTHERWISE WELL-INTENTIONED
POLICIES AND PROGRAMMES. THE PAPER IS ESPECIALLY CRITICAL OF
THE LACK OF COORDINATION AND IMAGINATION IN URBAN MANAGEMENT,
AS WELL AS THE ELITIST ORIENTATION IN URBAN PLANNING AND
HOUSING. IT EXPLORES THE POTENTIAL VALUE, AS WELL AS THE
LIMITATIONS, OF COMMUNITY SELF-HELP PROGRAMMES FOR HOUSING
AND SANITATION IN TOWNS, IN CIRCUMSTANCES OF WORSENING
ECONOMIC DIFFICULTIES AND DRASTIC CUTBACKS IN PUBLIC FUNDING
AND PRIVATE INVESTMENTS. FINALLY, WHILE ENDORSING THE
VIGOROUS PROGRAMMES NOW UNDER WAY FOR RURAL DEVELOPMENT, THE
PAPER POINTS OUT THE FUTILITY OF THE CURRENT AGGRESSIVE ANTI-
URBAN BACK-TO-LAND CRUSADE, EVEN IN THE LEGITIMATE CONCERN
TO MEET THE BASIC NEEDS OF THE PREDOMINANTLY RURAL MAJORITY.

06868 NWANKWO, P.N.
FRANCO-AFRICAN RELATIONS: THE CASE OF CAMEROON IN THE
POSTCOLONIAL PERIOD, 1960-1985
DISSERTATION ABSTRACTS INTERNATIONAL, 50(1) (JUL 89),
252-A.
FRENCH INTERESTS IN CAMEROON HAVE FLOURISHED OVER AND
ABOVE ALL OTHER FOREIGN INTERESTS IN THE PERIOD FROM 1960 TO
1985 DUE TO THE FOLLOWING FACTORS: (1) THE SUCCESSFUL
ELIMINATION OF RADICAL NATIONALISM FROM THE CAMEROONIAN
POLITICAL SCENE; (2) AHIDJO'S LONG TENURE IN OFFICE AS A PRO-
FRENCH LEADER WHO FAVORED THE CONTINUATION OF A FRENCH-STYLE
CAPITALIST ECONOMIC SYSTEM WITH AN OPEN-DOOR POLICY FOR
FOREIGN INVESTMENT; AND (3) THE BILATERAL ACCORDS THAT
PROVIDED CAMEROON WITH ECONOMIC AND MILITARY AID IN RETURN
FOR FRANCE'S PROMINENT ROLE AS A KEY PLAYER IN CAMEROON'S
POST-COLONIAL DEVELOPMENT.

06869 NYANDAK, T.
TIBET: THE UNDYING NATION
FREEDOM AT ISSUE, (108) (MAY 89), 25-27.
IN MARCH 1989, CHINA IMPOSED MARTIAL LAW ON LHASA AFTER
A PEACEFUL PROTEST TURNED VIOLENT. THE DEMONSTRATION BEGAN
WITH MONKS, NUNS, AND YOUNG PEOPLE CHANTING PRO-INDEPENDENCE
SLOGANS, DISPLAYING THE BANNED TIBETAN NATIONAL FLAG, AND
MARCHING AROUND THE JOKHANG TEMPLE. THIS DEMONSTRATION AND
VIOLENT RESPONSE WERE JUST ANOTHER EPISODE IN THE PATTERN OF
TIBETAN PROTESTS AND CHINESE REPRESSION.

06870 NYANG'ORO, J.
THE STATE OF POLITICS IN AFRICA: THE CORPORATIST FACTOR
STUDIES IN COMPARATIVE INTERNATIONAL DEVELOPMENT, 24(1)
(SPR 89), 5-19.
IN THE PAST DECADE, STUDIES OF THE STATE IN AFRICA HAVE
EITHER SUGGESTED ITS PERVASIVENESS IN BOTH POLITICAL AND
ECONOMIC LIFE OR HAVE CONCENTRATED ON ITS NONREPRESENTATIVE
(I.E., UNDEMOCRATIC) NATURE AND ITS DEPENDENCE ON FOREIGN
CAPITAL FOR ITS SURVIVAL. THIS STUDY ADOPTS A DIFFERENT
REASONING. IT SUGGESTS THAT THE STATE IN AFRICAN COUNTRIES
SHOULD BE VIEWED AS GRAPPLING WITH PROBLEMS OF MANAGING
SOCIETY WITHIN THE CONTEXT OF UNDERDEVELOPMENT, A TASK THAT
IS INCREASINGLY BECOMING MORE DIFFICULT GIVEN THE RECURRING
ECONOMIC CRISES ON THE CONTINENT. POLITICS OF CORPORATIST
ORGANIZATION THUS BECOME AN ATTRACTIVE OPTION FOR THE STATE
TO EXPRESS ITS AUTHORITY AND ATTEMPT TO LEGITIMIZE ITS
EXISTENCE.

06871 NYE, J.S. JR.
ARMS CONTROL AFTER THE COLD WAR
FOREIGN AFFAIRS, 68(5) (WIN 90), 42-64.
GEOPOLITICAL ANALYSTS WARN ABOUT THE DIFFUSION OF POWER
IN WORLD POLITICS AS THE SPREAD OF CHEMICAL AND BALLISTIC
MISSILE TECHNOLOGIES TO MORE COUNTRIES WILL POSE A NEW TYPE

OF SECURITY THREAT IN THE FUTURE. SOME CRITICS ASSAIL THE
BUSH ADMINISTRATION FOR MOVING TOO SLOWLY ON THE BIPOLAR
STRATEGIC ARMS CONTROL AGENDA; OTHERS CALL FOR GIVING A
HIGHER PRIORITY TO PROLIFERATION AND MULTILATERAL MEASURES.
STILL OTHERS WARN THAT ALL ARMS CONTROL AGREEMENTS ARE A
SNARE AND A DELUSION. THE NEW TWIST IS THAT THE USA AND THE
USSR, THOUGH REMAINING ANTAGONISTS ON THE TRADITIONAL AGENDA,
WILL BE PARTNERS IN SOME OF THE EMERGING PROBLEMS OF ARMS
CONTROL IN THE FUTURE.

06872 NYE, M.A.
ROLL CALL VOTES ON CIVIL RIGHTS IN THE HOUSE OF
REPRESENTATIVES: 1963-1982
DISSERTATION ABSTRACTS INTERNATIONAL, 49(11) (MAY 89),
3493-A.
THE AUTHOR ANALYZES ROLL CALL VOTES ON CIVIL RIGHTS IN
THE HOUSE OF REPRESENTATIVES TO DETERMINE IF CIVIL RIGHTS
ISSUES ARE BEST VIEWED FROM A UNIDIMENSIONAL OR A
MULTIDIMENSIONAL PERSPECTIVE. HER RESULTS LEND SUPPORT TO
PREVIOUS RESEARCH INDICATING THAT CIVIL RIGHTS IS
MULTIDIMENSIONAL. DISTINCT DIMENSIONS RELATED TO VOTING
RIGHTS, SCHOOL DESEGREGATION, FAIR HOUSING, AND EQUAL
EMPLOYMENT ARE IDENTIFIED.

06873 NYONG'O, P.A.
AFRICA: THE CASE FOR DISARMAMENT
DISARMAMENT, XII(2) (SUM 89), 1-5.
IT IS QUITE CLEAR THAT CONFLICTS, BOTH REGIONAL AND
INTERNAL, HAVE LED TO AN INCREASE IN MILITARY SPENDING IN
AFRICA, WHICH IS SPENDING TOO MUCH ON DEFENSE AT A TIME WHEN
SOCIO-ECONOMIC DEVELOPMENT SHOULD COMMAND ALL OF ITS
RESOURCES. THE ARMS RACE CAN BE ENDED ONLY THROUGH THE
POLITICAL RESOLUTION OF REGIONAL AND INTERNAL CONFLICTS.
DISARMAMENT IN AFRICA WOULD NOT MEAN DESTROYING SUPERFLUOUS
OR COSTLY WEAPONS BECAUSE THE ARMS ARE NOT SUPERFLUOUS OR
COSTLY BY INTERNATIONAL STANDARDS. BUT THEY ARE COSTLY IN
THE SENSE THAT THEY WASTE MEAGER RESOURCES THAT AFRICAN
ECONOMIES CAN ILL AFFORD TO SPEND.

06874 NZO, A.
THE SOVIET UNION SUPPORTS OUR STRUGGLE
SECHABA, 23(5) (MAY 89), 2-4.
THE ARTICLE DISCUSSES THE IMPLICATIONS OF THE RECENT
VISIT OF AN ANC DELEGATION TO THE USSR. MEMBERS OF THE
DELEGATION STATE THAT THERE IS NO TRUTH TO THE RUMOR THAT
THE SOVIETS ARE ON THE VERGE OF ESTABLISHING DIPLOMATIC
RELATIONS WITH THE REPUBLIC OF SOUTH AFRICA AND THAT THE
SOVIETS ARE TRYING TO CONVINCE THE ANC TO RENOUNCE ITS
INTENTION OF VICTORY THROUGH ARMED STRUGGLE. ALTHOUGH
CULTURAL EXCHANGES BETWEEN ACADEMICS OF THE USSR AND SOUTH
AFRICA SEEM TO ON THE INCREASE SUCH A POLICY DOES NOT
CONFLICT WITH THE STATED GOALS OF THE ANC.

06875 O'BRIEN, D.J.
JOIN IT, WORK IT, FIGHT IT
COMMONWEAL, CXVI(20) (NOV 89), 624-630.
AMERICAN CATHOLICS ARE DEEPLY DIVIDED ABOUT POLITICAL
PARTIES, POLICIES, AND CANDIDATES AS WELL AS THE MOST BASIC
QUESTIONS OF THE CHURCH'S PUBLIC ROLE. SIGNS ARE ALREADY
APPEARING THAT INTERNAL CATHOLIC DIVISIONS WILL BE EVEN MORE
EVIDENT IN THE UPCOMING STATE-BY-STATE BATTLES OVER ABORTION.

06876 O'BRIEN, J.
SUDAN'S KILLING FIELDS
MIDDLE EAST REPORT, 19(6) (NOV 89), 32-35.
THIS ARTICLE DETAILS THE PRESENT SITUATION IN UDAN AS
THE COUNTRY HAS LURCHED FROM ONE DOMINANT PATTERN OF CAPITAL
ACCUMULATION TO ANOTHER AND BACK AGAIN, PRODUCING A GENERAL
CRISIS OF SUBSISTENCE THROUGHOUT THE SOCIETY. IT EXPLORES
THE RULING CLASS CONFLICT AND THE CIVILIAN POLITICIAN'S
ACTIONS OF CORRUPTION IN AN EFFORT TO ACCUMULATE WEALTH.

06877 O'BRIEN, J.C.
GUSTAV VON SCHMOLLER: SOCIAL ECONOMIST
INTERNATIONAL JOURNAL OF SOCIAL ECONOMICS, 16(9-11) (1989),
17-46.
THE AUTHOR'S PURPOSE IS TO SHOW BY REFERENCE TO
SCHMOLLER'S OWN WRITINGS THAT HE CAN BE CLASSIFIED AS A
SOCIAL ECONOMIST. SCHMOLLER REJECTED THE STUDY OF ECONOMICS
IN ISOLATION, BUT PREFERRED A HOLISTIC APPROACH. HE ESCHEWED
LAISSEZ-FAIRE AND THOUGHT LITTLE OF SELFSEEKING
ENTREPRENEURS WHO MADE NO CONTRIBUTION TO THE COMMON GOOD.

06878 O'BRIEN, K.J.
LEGISLATIVE DEVELOPMENT AND CHINESE POLITICAL CHANGE
STUDIES IN COMPARATIVE COMMUNISM, XXII(1) (SPR 89), 57-75.
THIS STUDY FOCUSES ON THE LATEST ROUND OF LEGISLATIVE
CHANGE IN CHINA - THE RENEWAL UNDERWAY SINCE 1978. THE
AUTHOR EXAMINES NATIONAL PEOPLE'S CONGRESS (NPC) INVOLVEMENT
IN FOUR COMMON LEGISLATIVE ACTIVITIES (LAWMAKING,
SUPERVISION, REPRESENTATION, REGIME SUPPORT) AND SHOWS HOW
LEGISLATIVE ROLE EXPANSION IS ONE COMPONENT OF SYSTEMIC,
POLITICAL CHANGE. BY FOCUSING ON ONE INSTITUTION AND ONE SET
OF POLITICAL FUNCTIONS, THE AUTHOR TRACES THE TRAJECTORY OF

CHINESE POLITICAL DEVELOPMENT, FINDING CONTINUING WARINESS
TOWARD LIBERALIZATION, COMBINED WITH A GROWING COMMITMENT TO
NATIONALIZATION AND INCLUSION.

06879 O'BRIEN, P.
THE PARADOXICAL PARADIGM: TURKISH MIGRANTS AND GERMAN
POLICIES
DISSERTATION ABSTRACTS INTERNATIONAL, 49(11) (MAY 89),
3494-A.
THE AUTHOR CONCEPTUALIZES AND EXAMINES LANGUAGE AS A
CONCRETE SOCIAL STRUCTURE WITH THE POWER TO DETERMINE SOCIAL
REALITY. HE ANALYZES THE IMPACT OF THE POLITICAL LANGUAGE
USED TO DISCUSS POLICIES CONCERNING MIGRATION TO WEST
GERMANY ON GERMAN POLICY-MAKERS AND ON TURKISH MIGRANTS. THE
COMMON TERMINOLOGY OF THE POLICY LANGUAGE IS TRACED TO
STUDIES OF SOCIAL SCIENTISTS COMMISSIONED BY THE GERMAN
GOVERNMENT TO RESEARCH MIGRANTS. THEIR FINDINGS HAVE
PRODUCED A PARADIGMATIC IMAGE OF THE "TURK IN GERMANY."

06880 O'CONNOR, J. S.
WELFARE EXPENDITURE AND POLICY ORIENTATION IN CANADA IN
COMPARATIVE PERSPECTIVE
CANADIAN REVIEW OF SOCIOLOGY AND ANTHROPOLOGY, 26(1) (FEB
89), 127-150.
THIS PAPER EXAMINES WELFARE EFFORT IN CANADA IN THE 1960-
83 PERIOD IN THE CONTEXT OF CROSS-NATIONAL PATTERNS. WELFARE
EFFORT IS CONSIDERED ON FOUR DIMENSIONS: DECOMMODIFICATION,
SOLIDARITY, REDISTRIBUTION AND FULL EMPLOYMENT. CANADA HAS
RELATIVELY HIGH GOVERNMENT CIVIL CONSUMPTION EXPENDITURE BY
OECD STANDARDS BUT THIS CONSISTS MOSTLY OF HEALTH AND
EDUCATIONAL EXPENDITURE. GENERAL AND PREVENTIVELY ORIENTED
EXPENDITURE IS LOW, REFLECTING THE LOW EXPENDITURE ON
HOUSING AND EMPLOYMENT CREATION. IN TERMS OF THE FULL
EMPLOYMENT DIMENSION CANADA IS ONE OF THE LEAST SUCCESSFUL
OF THE OECD WELFARE STATES. DESPITE CONSISTENTLY HIGH
UNEMPLOYMENT, SOCIAL TRANSFER EXPENDITURE IS LOW BUT DOES
CONTRIBUTE TO THE REDUCTION OF INEQUALITY OF PRIMARY INCOME
AND IS CONSISTENTLY MORE IMPORTANT IN THIS REGARD THAN THE
TAX SYSTEM. THERE IS CONSIDERABLE EVIDENCE TO INDICATE THAT
THE CANADIAN WELFARE STATE IS BEING RESTRUCTURED TOWARDS A
DISTRIBUTION OF BENEFITS BASED ON CLASS RATHER THAN
CITIZENSHIP.

06881 O'DONNELL, W.M.
PRIME TIME HOSTAGES: A CASE STUDY OF COVERAGE DURING
CAPTIVITY
POLITICAL COMMUNICATION AND PERSUASION, 5(4) (1988),
237-248.
MEDIA COVERAGE OF THE HIJACKING AND DIVERSION OF TO
BEIRUT OF TWA FLIGHT 847 ON 14 JUNE 1985 BY MEMBERS OF THE
SHI'ITE MUSLIM ISLAMIC JIHAD WAS CHARACTERIZED BY SEVERAL
UNIQUE ASPECTS. FOR THE FIRST TIME DURING REPORTING OF SUCH
AN EVENT, THE HOSTAGES, THEIR CAPTORS, AND MIDDLE EASTERN
POLITICAL LEADERS WERE INTERVIEWED LIVE ON AMERICAN
TELEVISION. THE MEDIA WERE DRAWN DIRECTLY INTO THE
NEGOTIATIONS TO FREE THE HOSTAGES WHEN THE HIJACKERS AND
AMAL MEDIATORS DELIVERED A LETTER FROM THE CAPTIVES TO
PRESIDENT REAGAN VIA THE CREW OF REPORTERS AT BEIRUT AIRPORT.
THE HIJACKERS' AWARENESS OF THE IMPORTANCE OF NEWS COVERAGE
WAS INDICATED BY THEIR CONTINUING USE OF THE MEDIA TO
COMMUNICATE THEIR POLITICAL VIEWS AND DEMANDS TO GOVERNMENT
OFFICIALS AND THE PUBLIC. THIS PAPER TRACES THE EFFORTS OF
THE HIJACKERS TO MAKE USE OF THE MEDIA AND DETAILS THE
COVERAGE OF THE EVENT BY THE THREE MAJOR U.S. NETWORKS AND
OTHER MAJOR NEWS ORGANIZATIONS FROM THE BEGINNING OF THE
CRISIS UNTIL THE RELEASE OF THE HOSTAGES ON 30 JUNE.

06882 O'HARA, T.J.
RELIGIOUS LOBBY GROUPS: THE PLURALISM OF THE CATHOLIC
COMMUNITY
DISSERTATION ABSTRACTS INTERNATIONAL, 49(12) (JUN 89),
3859-A.
THE CATHOLIC LOBBY IN WASHINGTON, D.C., IS NOT
MONOLITHIC. THE EXISTENCE OF AT LEAST 31 DIFFERENT CATHOLIC
LOBBY GROUPS HAS BEEN DOCUMENTED. THIS STUDY DISCUSSES LOBBY
GROUP FORMATION, MAINTENANCE, AND STRATEGY AS ILLUSTRATIVE
OF THE PLURALISM WITHIN THE CATHOLIC LOBBY.

06883 O'HEARN, D.
THE IRISH CASE OF DEPENDENCY: AN EXCEPTION TO THE
EXCEPTIONS?
AMERICAN SOCIOLOGICAL REVIEW, 54(4) (AUG 89), 578-596.
THE DEPENDENCY APPROACH HAS RECENTLY BEEN CRITICIZED BY
AUTHORS WHO QUOTE THE "EXCEPTIONAL" EAST ASIAN CASES. THE
IRISH CASE IS USED TO REFUTE THESE NEW MODERNIZATIONIST
ARGUMENTS ON TWO COUNTS. (1) COUNTRIES SUCH AS IRELAND, NOT
THE EAST ASIAN COUNTRIES, HAVE REGIMES WITH CHARACTERISTICS
THAT TEND TO SET DEPENDENCY RELATIONS IN MOTION. THESE
CHARACTERISTICS INCLUDE RADICAL FREE TRADE, FREE ENTERPRISE,
AND FOREIGN INDUSTRIAL DOMINATION. (2) BECAUSE OF THESE
CHARACTERISTICS, IRELAND HAS ENDURED ECONOMIC STAGNATION AND
TENDENCIES TOWARD HIGHER INEQUALITY. IRISH ECONOMIC GROWTH
UNDER FOREIGN-DOMINATED INDUSTRIALIZATION WAS SLOWED BY
DECAPITALIZATION AND BY THE ABSENCE OF LINKAGES BETWEEN

FOREIGN AND DOMESTIC INDUSTRY. TIME-SERIES MODELS SHOW THAT
FOREIGN PENETRATION AND FREE TRADE ARE RELATED TO SLOWER
ECONOMIC GROWTH, BECAUSE OF SLOWER INVESTMENT-GROWTH AND
OTHER REASON. INEQUALITY INCREASED PRIMARILY BECAUSE OF
RISING UNEMPLOYMENT. ALTHOUGH SOCIAL WELFARE PROGRAMS
REDUCED THE EFFECTS OF DIRECT-INCOME INEQUALITY, THEIR
EFFECTS HAVE BEEN REDUCED BY REGRESSIVE TAXATION AND
AUSTERITY PROGRAMS.

06884 O'KANE, G.
A DIPLOMATIC SOLUTION?
NEW AFRICAN, (JAN 88), 18.
THIS ARTICLE ANALYSES ANGOLA'S PROSPECTS FOR A SOLUTION
TO ITS PROBLEMS. POSSIBLE DIPLOMATIC MANOEUVRINGS ARE
EXPLORED WITH THE USSR, THE EUROPEAN STATES, AND THE USA.
THE BENGUELA PROBLEM IS DISCUSSED.

06885 O'KANE, R.H.T.
MILITARY REGIMES: POWER AND FORCE
EUROPEAN JOURNAL OF POLITICAL RESEARCH, 17(3) (MAY 89),
333-350.
IT IS GENERALLY HELD THAT COUPS ARE THE START OF FULL
MILITARY INTERVENTION. AS A CONSEQUENCE, STUDIES INTENT ON
CONTRASTING THE PERFORMANCE OF 'MILITARY' AS OPPOSED TO
'CIVILIAN' GOVERNMENTS HAVE USED THE EVENT OF A MILITARY
COUP AS THE ESSENTIAL CRITERION FOR DISTINCTION. THE
EVIDENCE CLEARLY SHOWS, HOWEVER, THAT THE DISTINCTION IS NOT
SO EASILY DRAWN. FURTHER, CONSIDERATION OF THE ONLY
SYSTEMATIC ATTEMPT TO DELINEATE TYPES OF MILITARY REGIMES IN
RESPECT OF CIVILIAN INVOLVEMENT SUGGESTS THAT THE
DICHOTOMISED VIEW OF MILITARY AND CIVILIAN REGIMES SHOULD
BE REPLACED BY ATTENTION BEING DRAWN TO POWER AND FORCE IN
ALL POLITICAL SYSTEMS. THIS VIEW IS SUPPORTED BY A
CLASSIFICATION OF THIRD WORLD POLITICAL SYSTEMS WHICH
REFLECTS THESE TWO DIMENSIONS. IRONICALLY, THE STUDY OF
MILITARY GOVERNMENTS INSTALLED BY COUPS D'ETA HAS ACTUALLY
SERVED TO OBSCURE THE IMPORTANCE OF FORCE IN POLITICS.

06886 O'KEEFE, J.
THE GOP WHISTLES DIXIE
CAMPAIGNS AND ELECTIONS, 10(2) (AUG 89), 10-11.
IT MAY NOT BE THE MASSIVE REALIGNMENT THE NATIONAL
REPUBLICAN PARTY HAD HOPED FOR, BUT IT HAS BECOME CLEAR THAT
THE GOP'S PRESIDENTIAL SUCCESS OVER THE PAST DECADE IS
REACHING THE GRASSROOTS IN THE SOUTH. SINCE THE FALL OF 1988,
MORE THAN SEVENTY ELECTED OFFICIALS IN SEVEN SOUTHERN
STATES HAVE DESERTED THE DEMOCRATIC PARTY FOR THE GOP. WHILE
THE CURRENT WAVE OF CROSS-OVERS BEARS SOME RESEMBLANCE TO
THE MOVEMENT IN 1981 AND 1985 AFTER REAGAN'S LANDSLIDES, GOP
STRATEGISTS SAY THE CURRENT SWEEP IS WIDER AND DEEPER.

06887 O'LEARY-ARCHER, L.M.
THE CONTENTIOUS COMMUNITY: THE IMPACT OF INTERNECINE
CONFLICT ON THE NATIONAL WOMAN'S PARTY, 1920-1947
DISSERTATION ABSTRACTS INTERNATIONAL, 49(7) (JAN 89),
1995-A.
THE NATIONAL WOMEN'S PARTY BEGAN AS A RADICAL SUFFRAGE
ORGANIZATION AND LATER ESTABLISHED THE PASSAGE OF THE EQUAL
RIGHTS AMENDMENT AS ITS SINGLE GOAL. IN THIS DISSERTATION,
THE AUTHOR STUDIES THE INTERNECINE CONFLICT THAT ULTIMATELY
LED TO THE DISRUPTION OF THE PARTY IN 1947.

06888 O'LEARY, B.
THE LIMITS TO COERCIVE CONSOCIATIONALISM IN NORTHERN
IRELAND
POLITICAL STUDIES, XXXVII(4) (DEC 89), 562-588.
THE MERITS OF CONSOCIATION AS A MEANS OF SOLVING THE
NORTHERN IRELAND CONFLICT ARE PRESENTED THROUGH CONTRASTING
IT WITH OTHER WAYS OF STABILIZING HIGHLY DIVIDED POLITICAL
SYSTEMS. WHY VOLUNTARY CONSOCIATION HAS BEEN UNSUCCESSFUL IN
NORTHERN IRELAND AND UNFORTUNATELY IS LIKELY TO REMAIN SO IS
EXPLAINED. THE SIGNING OF THE ANGLO-IRISH AGREEMENT (AIA)
MUST BE UNDERSTOOD AGAINS THE BACKGROUND OF THE FAILURE OF
PREVIOUS CONSOCIATIONAL EXPERIMENTS. THE AIA PARTLY
REPRESENTED A SHIFT IN BRITISH STRATEGY FROM VOLUNTARY TO
COERCIVE CONSOCIATIONALISM. THE PROSPECTS FOR THIS COERCIVE
CONSOCIATIONAL STRATEGY AND VARIANTS ON IT ARE EVALUATED.

06889 O'LEARY, R.
THE IMPACT OF FEDERAL COURT DECISIONS ON THE POLICIES AND
ADMINISTRATION OF THE UNITED STATES ENVIRONMENTAL
PROTECTION AGENCY
DISSERTATION ABSTRACTS INTERNATIONAL, 50(1) (JUL 89),
258-A.
THE AUTHOR ANALYZES THE IMPACT OF FEDERAL COURT
DECISIONS ON THE UNITED STATES ENVIROMENTAL PROTECTION
AGENCY IN ALL SEVEN OF ITS STATUTORY AREAS, APPLYING
THEORIES OF THE "JUDGE AS ADMINISTRATOR" AND "THE EXTERNAL
CONTROL OF ORGANIZATIONS" TO EPA CASES. SHE FINDS THAT
JUDICIAL INTERVENTION INTO DISPUTES CONCERNING THE EPA CAN
BE CATEGORIZED INTO FIVE GROUPS AND THAT THE EPA HAS
RESPONDED TO FEDERAL COURT DECISIONS IN TEN DISTINCT WAYS.
SHE ALSO CONCLUDES THAT COURT DECISIONS HAVE PROMPTED A
REDISTRIBUTION OF BUDGETARY AND STAFF RESOURCES WITHIN THE

EPA, REDUCED THE DISCRETION AND AUTONOMY OF EPA
ADMINISTRATORS, INCREASED THE POWER OF THE EPA LEGAL STAFF,
DECREASED THE POWER AND AUTHORITY OF EPA SCIENTISTS, AND
SELECTIVELY EMPOWERED CERTAIN ORGANIZATIONAL UNITS WITHIN
THE EPA.

06890 O'MEARA, P.
POLITICS IN SOUTH AFRICA
CURRENT HISTORY, 88(538) (MAY 89), 217-220, 248.
AS SOUTH AFRICA MOVES INTO THE 1990'S, THE IMPORTANT
QUESTIONS CONCERN THE MOBILIZATION OF THE BLACK POLITICAL
OPPOSITION, THE ROLE OF THE BLACK TRADE UNIONS IN BRINGING
ABOUT A NEW POLITICAL ORDER, AND THE VIABILITY OF THE
PREVAILING WHITE POLITICAL AND ECONOMIC SYSTEMS. IN MANY
WAYS, THESE ISSUES ARE MORE SIGNIFICANT THAN THE ISSUE OF
WHO WOULD SUCCEED P.W. BOTHA AS PRESIDENT OF SOUTH AFRICA.

06891 O'NEILL, R,
ANZUS AND FUTURE AUSTRALIAN-AMERICAN RELATIONS
ROUND TABLE, (310) (APR 89), 177-178.
THE ARTICLE BRIEFLY OUTLINE THE HISTORY OF THE ANZUS
TREATY AND THE EFFECTS IT HAS HAD ON THE PACIFIC REGION. IT
CONCLUDES THAT IN AN ERA OF DECREASING TENSION AND THAWING
EAST-WEST RELATIONS THAT ANZUS WILL NOT BE VIEWED AS
STRATEGICALLY IMPORTANT, AT LEAST NOT AS IMPORTANT AS
PREVIOUSLY. THE RESULT WILL BE USE PRESSURE ON AUSTRALIA TO
SHOULDER MORE OF THE REGIONAL DEFENSE BURDENS THAT ARE
CURRENTLY SHARED WITH THE US.

06892 O'RANE, G.
AMNESTY INTERNATIONAL
NEW AFRICAN, (MAR 88), 27-28.
THIS ARTICLE REPORTS ON THE WORK OF AMNESTY
INTERNATIONAL TO BRING PRISONERS OF CONSCIENCE OUT OF
PRISONS. IT DESCRIBES HOW AMNESTY WORKS IMPARTIALLY AND
PEACEFULLY TO HELP FREE PEOPLE IMPRISONED FOR THEIR SINCERE
BELIEFS DESPITE CRITICISMS FROM GOVERNMENTS OF EVERY
POLITICAL AND RACIAL COLOR. IT DOCUMENTS THAT INDIVIDUALS
CAN CHANGE THE WORLD.

06893 O'RANE, G.
WHAT MRS THATCHER DID NOT SEE
NEW AFRICAN, (FEB 88), 18-19.
THIS ARTICLE REPORTS ON A RECENT VISIT BY MARGARET
THATCHER TO KENYA. IT SPECULATES THAT MRS. THATCHER REFUSED
TO ACKNOWLEDGE AN ENTIRE RANGE OF POLITICAL PROBLEMS
BESETTING THE KENYAN GOVERNMENT. IT DESCRIBES CALMING
ACTIONS AS OCCURING ONLY TO MAKE MRS. THATCHER'S PASSAGE
EASIER. IT ANALYSES THE NEED BY PRESIDENT MOI OF SCAPEGOATS.

06894 O'RANE, G.
ZIMBABWE COMPLETES ITS REVOLUTION
NEW AFRICAN, (FEB 88), 28.
THIS ARTICLE REPORTS ON RECENT ELECTIONS IN ZIMBABWE.
THE MERGING OF TWO OPPOSING POLITICAL PARTIES IS EXAMINED AS
THE UNITY AGREEMENT IS SIGNED. ZIMBABWE'S NEW CABINET IS
LISTED.

06895 O'RIORDAN, M.
THE SPIRIT AND THE LETTER OF THE OCTOBER REVOLUTION
WORLD MARXIST REVIEW, 31(11) (NOV 88), 5-13.
THE OCTOBER REVOLUTION EXPRESSED AND EFFECTIVELY MET
SOCIETY'S PROFOUND DEMAND FOR THE EMANCIPATION OF MAN FROM
SOCIAL EXPLOITATION AND OTHER FORMS OF OPPRESSION. WITH
HINDSIGHT WE CAN SEE THAT THE SYSTEM THAT EMERGED WAS FAR
FROM IDEAL. HOWEVER, IT IS THE OVERALL RESULT THAT IS
IMPORTANT -- THE FACT THAT THE 1.5 BILLION PEOPLE CURRENTLY
LIVING UNDER SOCIALISM HAVE EFFECTIVELY PROVED THE
POSSIBILITY OF CREATING A SOCIETY WHICH IS NOT TORN APART BY
ANTAGONISTIC INTERNAL CONTRADICTIONS AND WHICH ENSURES
EVERYONE'S RIGHT TO EMPLOYMENT, MEETS OTHER VITAL HUMAN
NEEDS AND GUARANTEES INVOLVEMENT IN GOVERNMENT. WITHOUT
THESE ACCOMPLISHMENTS, MANKIND'S FURTHER PROGRESS IS SIMPLY
UNTHINKABLE.

06896 O'RIORDAN, T.; WEALE, A.
ADMINISTRATIVE REORGANIZATION AND POLICY CHANGE: THE CASE
OF HER MAJESTY'S INSPECTORATE OF POLLUTION
PUBLIC ADMINISTRATION, 67(3) (FAL 89), 277 - 294.
ENVIRONMENTAL PROTECTION NOWADAYS IS A MAJOR ISSUE OF
POLICY AND ADMINISTRATION. IT IS WELL RECOGNIZED THAT AN
EFFECTIVE APPROACH TO POLLUTION CONTROL REQUIRES IT TO BE
INTEGRATED, BUT UK GOVERNMENTS HAVE BEEN SLOW TO RESPOND TO
THIS NEED. THE CREATION OF A NEW UNIFIED POLLUTION
INSPECTORATE IN ENGLAND AND WALES MUST BE SET IN THE CONTEXT
OF A GENERAL TRANSITION IN BRITISH POLLUTION CONTROL
PRACTICE, WHERE THE INCORPORATION OF MORE FORMAL PROCEDURES
IS TAKING PLACE WITHIN A TRADITION OF EMITTER SELF-POLICING,
CLIENT-REGULATOR MUTUAL RESPECT, AND REGULATORY ADAPTABILITY.
THIS ARTICLE EXAMINES THE CIRCUMSTANCES THAT LED TO THE
FORMATION OF THE NEW POLLUTION INSPECTORATE AND CONSIDERS
THE CHALLENGES THAT IT FACES.

06897 O'ROURKE, P.J.
A CALL FOR A NEW MCCARTHYISM
AMERICAN SPECTATOR, 22(7) (JUL 89), 14-15.
THE WORST PUNISHMENT FOR DUPES, PINK-WIENERS, AND
DIALECTICAL IMMATERIALISTS MIGHT BE A KIND OF REVERSE
BLACKLIST. DON'T PREVENT THEM FROM WRITTING, SPEAKING,
PERFORMING, AND OTHERWISE BEING THEIR USUAL NUISANCE SELVES.
INSTEAD, HANG ON THEIR EVERY WORD, BEG THEM TO WORK, DRAG
THEM ONTO ALL AVAILABLE TV AND RADIO CHAT SHOWS, AND WRITE
HUNDREDS OF FAWNING NEWSPAPER AND MAGAZINE ARTICLES ABOUT
THEIR WONDERFUL SWELLNESS. IN OTHER WORDS, SUBJECT THEM TO
THE MONSTROUS, GROSS, AND IRREVERSIBLE LATE TWENTIETH-
CENTURY PHENOMENON OF MEDIA OVER-EXPOSURE SO THAT A
SURFEITED PUBLIC REBELS IN DISGUST. THIS IS THE BURT
REYNOLDS/LONI ANDERSON TREATMENT, AND, FOR CONDEMNING PEOPLE
TO OBSCURITY, IT BEATS THE SMITH ACT HOLLOW.

06898 O'SULLIVAN, J.
BRITAIN: UNDER THE IRON (HIGH) HEEL?
COMMENTARY, 88(3) (SEP 89), 47-52.
THIS ARTICLE EXAMINES CHARGES AGAINST BRITISH PRIME
MINISTER, MARGARET THATCHER THAT "THE GAME WAS RIGGED, THE
PRESS BOUGHT, THE TELEVISION NETWORKS INTIMIDATED,
INTELLIGENCE SCANDALS SUPPRESSED, OFFICIAL SECRECY BLANKETED
ON LAND, AND THE VOTERS LED LIKE LAMBS TO THE POLLING BOOTHS.
" IT CONCLUDES THAT THESE CHARGES REFLECT AN IMPOTENT RAGE
AT THE LASTING DEFEAT MRS. THATCHER HAS INFLICTED ON
SOCIALISM: THAT THESE CHARGES ARE A COMBINATION OF
MISREPRESENTATION, DISTORTION AND PARANOID FANTASIES.

06899 O'TOOLE, J.
THE ECONOMICS OF THE IMPLEMENTATION OF SOCIAL POLICY:
SEARCHING FOR THE MISSING LINK
SOCIAL SCIENCE JOURNAL, 26(2) (1989), 115-130.
IMPLEMENTATION OF PUBLIC POLICY IS THE MISSING LINK IN
MUCH SOCIAL SCIENCE. PUBLIC AGENCIES MUST CONVERT "POLICY"
AS DEFINED BY LAW INTO CLEANER WATER OR CLEANER AIR OR SAFER
WORKPLACES OR EQUAL OPPORTUNITY, AND SO FORTH. USING
TECHNIQUES OF PUBLIC CHOICE, THIS ARTICLE ANALYZES THE
CHOICES OF THE BUREAUCRATIC DECISION-MAKER AS HE REACTS TO
INTEREST GROUP PRESSURE. HE OPERATES WITH INCOMPLETE AND
ASYMMETRIC INFORMATION. THE ARTICLE DRAWS ON BOTH ECONOMICS
AND POLITICAL SCIENCE. POLLUTION CONTROL BY THE UNITED
STATES ENVIRONMENTAL PROTECTION AGENCY SERVES AS AN EXAMPLE.

06900 OAKERSON, R.J.; PARKS, R.B.
LOCAL GOVERNMENT CONSTITUTIONS: A DIFFERENT VIEW OF
METROPOLITAN GOVERNANCE
AMERICAN REVIEW OF PUBLIC ADMINISTRATION, 19(4) (DEC 89),
279-294.
METROPOLITAN GOVERNANCE IN MOST METROPOLITAN AREAS OF
THE UNITED STATES CAN BEST BE UNDERSTOOD BY REFERENCE TO THE
CONCEPT OF A "LOCAL GOVERNMENT CONSTITUTION." A LOCAL
GOVERNMENT CONSTITUTION IS FRAMED BY CHOICES MADE AT TWO
LEVELS: (1) AN ENABLING LEVEL COMPOSED OF STATE
CONSTITUTIONAL AND STATUTORY PROVISIONS THAT LOCAL CITIZENS
AND PUBLIC OFFICIALS MAY USE TO CREATE AND MODIFY LOCAL
GOVERNMENTS AND (2) A CHARTERING LEVEL THAT DETERMINES THE
SPECIFIC CHARTER OF A LOCAL GOVERNMENT THROUGH CITIZEN
ACTION. THE RULES OF A LOCAL GOVERNMENT CONSTITUTION INCLUDE
THOSE OF ASSOCIATION, BOUNDARY ADJUSTMENT, FISCAL RULES, AND
RULES GOVERNING INTERJURISDICTIONAL ARRANGEMENTS. CITIZENS
AND THEIR OFFICIALS CAN AND DO USE THESE CONSTITUTIONAL
RULES TO CONSTRUCT COMPLEX LOCAL PUBLIC ECONOMIES THAT TEND
TO EXHIBIT STRONG PATTERNS OF CITIZEN GOVERNANCE.
RECOGNITION OF THESE PHENOMENA YIELDS A DIFFERENT VIEW OF
LOCAL GOVERNMENTS FROM THAT OF "CREATURES OF THE STATE."

06901 OBERST, R.C.
POLITICAL DECAY IN SRI LANKA
CURRENT HISTORY, 88(542) (DEC 89), 425-428, 448-449.
THE FUTURE OF SRI LANKA MAY WELL LIE IN THE HANDS OF THE
INDIAN GOVERNMENT, AND IF IT CONTINUES TO DESTABILIZE THE
SRI LANKAN GOVERNMENT, SRI LANKA MAY BE ON THE ROAD TO A
COMPLETE BREAKDOWN OF CIVIL RULE AND STABILITY.

06902 OCANA, J.
THE SOCIALIST STATE AND THE CHURCH
WORLD MARXIST REVIEW, 31(1) (JAN 88), 113-120.
THE COMMUNIST PARTY OF CUBA HAS ALWAYS UPHELD THE
PRINCIPLE OF RESPECT FOR THE RELIGIOUS BELIEFS OF ANY
CITIZEN AND FOR THE CULT. THE REVOLUTIONARY POWER HAS NOT
TAKEN OVER OR CLOSED DOWN ANY CHURCHES, AND HAS NOT HINDERED
THE ACTIVITY OF ANY CLERGYMAN WISHING TO EXERCISE HIS PROPER
RELIGIOUS FUNCTIONS. THE CONSISTENT APPLICATION OF THIS
POLICY WITH RESPECT TO RELIGION, THE CHURCH AND BELIEVERS
HAS BECOME THE CRUCIAL FACTOR IN MAINTAINING NORMAL
RELATIONS WITH THE IMMENSE MAJORITY OF RELIGIOUS
INSTITUTIONS IN THE COUNTRY. AS FOR THE CATHOLIC CHURCH,
FOLLOWING THE CONFRONTATION OF THE EARLY POSTREVOLUTIONARY
YEARS THERE HAS RECENTLY BEEN AN EVOLUTIONARY PROCESS WHICH,
FOR ALL ITS NUANCES, SHOWS THAT THE RELIGIOUS INSTITUTIONS
HAVE BEEN ADAPTING THEMSELVES TO THE CUBAN REALITY.

06903 OCASIO, J.A.; ZORRILLA, L.C.
LATIN AMERICAN REACTION TO THE UNITED STATES INVOLVEMENT
IN LATIN AMERICAN AFFAIRS
AVAILABLE FROM NTIS, NO. AD-A209 784/8/GAR, MAY 89, 77.
WHAT ARE THE LATIN AMERICAN REACTIONS TO THE UNITED
STATES INVOLVEMENT IN LATIN AMERICAN AFFAIRS. ARE SUCH
REACTIONS EXPRESSED IN A SUPPORTIVE, INDIFFERENT, HOSTILE,
OR COOPERATIVE ATTITUDE. THROUGHOUT ITS HISTORY, THE UNITED
STATES HAS BEEN INVOLVED CONSTANTLY IN LATIN AMERICAN
AFFAIRS. THESE INVOLVEMENTS RANGE FROM ECONOMIC ASSISTANCE
TO DIRECT MILITARY INTERVENTION, INCLUDING THE USE OF
AMERICAN TROOPS. EACH TIME THE UNITED STATES GETS INVOLVED,
THE LATIN AMERICAN COUNTRIES EXPRESS THEIR VIEWS AND
OBSERVATIONS BASED ON THE NATURE OF THE EVENT. TO
DEMONSTRATE SUCH REACTION AND DETERMINE IF A TREND OF LATIN
AMERICAN OPINION TOWARDS THE UNITED STATES HAS BEEN
ESTABLISHED, IT IS BEST TO EXAMINE SEVERAL INCIDENTS IN
WHICH THE UNITED STATES HAS DIRECTLY INTERVENED IN LATIN
AMERICAN AFFAIRS. THIS ANALYSIS OF HISTORICAL EVENTS WILL
ANSWER THE QUESTIONS POSED ABOVE. SUCH EXAMINATION WILL BE
THE BASIS FOR A COMPARISON OF LATIN AMERICAN RESPONSES TO
SEVERAL EXAMPLES OF UNITED STATES INTERVENTION IN LATIN
AMERICA. KEYWORDS: CUBAN MISSILE CRISIS, MILITARY
INTERVENTION. DOMINICAN REPUBLIC.

06904 OCCHETTO, A.
POLICIES AND IDEALS OF THE ITALIAN COMMUNIST PARTY: NEW
VENUES
ITALIAN JOURNAL, III(2-3) (1989), 9-13.
BASED ON INDEPENDENCE AND PLURALISM FIRMLY ANCHORED TO
THE DEMOCRATIC PRINCIPLES OF THE EUROPEAN LEFT. GLOBAL
PROBLEMS ARE NOW EMERGING THAT CANNOT BE DEALT WITH BY
EMPLOYING OLD APPROACHES. IF MANKIND DOES NOT CONFRONT VITAL
WORLD ENERGY PROBLEMS IN A SPIRIT OF SOLIDARITY, IF THE POOR
ARE COMPELLED TO DESTROY THEIR ENVIRONMENT IN ORDER TO EARN
A LIVING, IF THE ENVIRONMENTAL PROTECTION OF THE PLANET
COUPLED WITH AN IMPROVED AND BALANCED ECONOMIC DEVELOPMENT
DO NOT BECOME COMMON IMPERATIVES, THE VERY SURVIVAL OF THE
HUMAN RACE WILL BE IN JEOPARDY. WITH THESE COMMON GLOBAL
PROBLEMS IN MIND, THE PCI ADVOCATES A POLICY OF COOPERATION
AND FRIENDSHIP WITH THE UNITED STATES AND OTHER WESTERN
COUNTRIES.

06905 ODAH, O. S.
SAUDI-AMERICAN RELATIONS, 1968-1978: A STUDY IN AMBIGUITY
DISSERTATION ABSTRACTS INTERNATIONAL, 49(8) (FEB 89),
2383-A.
THE AUTHOR EXAMINES SAUDI-AMERICAN RELATIONS FROM THE
SIX DAY WAR TO THE CAMP DAVID AGREEMENT AND THE COLLAPSE OF
THE SHAH'S REGIME IN IRAN, FOCUSING ON SAUDI SECURITY
INTERESTS, AMERICAN ARMS SALES, AND THE TENSIONS PRODUCED BY
THE ARAB-ISRAELI CONFLICT.

06906 ODOM, W.E.
THE FUTURE OF THE SOVIET POLITICAL SYSTEM
PS: POLITICAL SCIENCE AND POLITICS, XXII(2) (JUN 89),
193-198.
THE AUTHOR REVIEWS THE HISTORICAL LEGACY OF THE SOVIET
POLITICAL SYSTEM AND ISOLATES PRACTICAL DILEMMAS FACING
SOVIET REFORMERS.

06907 OHN, C.
THE BASIC NATURE OF U.S.-KOREA ALLIANCE RELATIONS
KOREA OBSERVER, XX(4) (WIN 89), 479-506.
THE AUTHOR ENDEAVORS TO DETERMINE THE BEST METHOD FOR
ENDING THE FIGHTING IN KOREA, TO IDENTIFY THE MEASURES
NECESSARY TO SECURE THE END-OF-FIGHTING ARRANGEMENT, AND TO
EXPLAIN THE SIGNIFICANCE OF THESE MEASURES IN TERMS OF THE
BASIC NATURE OF THE RELATIONS BETWEEN THE UNITED STATES AND
THE REPUBLIC OF KOREA.

06908 OI, J.C.
MARKET REFORMS AND CORRUPTION IN RURAL CHINA
STUDIES IN COMPARATIVE COMMUNISM, 22(2/3) (SUM 89),
221-234.
THIS ARTICLE EXTENDS THE ANALYSIS OF POST-MAO
CLIENTELISM AND CORRUPTION FROM THE CITIES TO THE CHINESE
COUNTRYSIDE WHERE IS FOUND INCREASE IN THE FREQUENCY AND
MAGNITUDE OF ILLEGAL ACTIVITIES SINCE THE INITIATION OF
RURAL MARKET REFORMS IN THE LATE 1970S. THIS UPSURGE OF
MALFEASANT BEHAVIOUR IS TRACED TO PARTIAL DEREGULATION WHICH
HAVE GIVEN LOCAL OFFICIALS AUTHORITY OVER ALLOCATION OF
VILLAGE RESOURCES. IT IS SUGGESTED THAT RISING RESENTMENT TO
THIS COULD ULTIMATELY JEOPARDIZE THE PROGRESS OF RURAL
REFORMS.

06909 OJO, L.
NIGERIA: HALF A BILLION
THIRD WORLD WEEK, 8(8) (APR 89), 60-61.
WORRIED BY PROJECTIONS THAT ITS POPULATION WILL GROW TO
AT LEAST A HALF-BILLION PEOPLE WITHIN THE NEXT FIFTY YEARS,
THE GOVERNMENT OF NIGERIA IS TRYING TO SHRINK THE SIZE OF
THE AVERAGE FAMILY. IT HAS ADOPTED A NATIONAL POPULATION
POLICY THAT RECOMMENDS THAT A WOMAN HAVE NO MORE THAN FOUR

CHILDREN. SO FAR, THE POLICY REMAINS LITTLE MORE THAN WORDS
ON A DOCUMENT, AS MOST NIGERIANS CONTINUE THE AFRICAN
TRADITION OF HAVING AS MANY CHILDREN AS POSSIBLE. BUT, WITH
THE INTRODUCTION OF NEW ECONOMIC EXPECTATIONS, THERE ARE
SOME SIGNS THAT YOUNGER NIGERIANS MAY BE READY TO LIMIT THE
SIZE OF THEIR FAMILIES.

06910 OJULU, E.
GRINDING TOWARDS VICTORY
NEW AFRICAN, (257) (FEB 89), 21.
THERE ARE SIGNS THAT THE NATIONAL RESISTANCE ARMY IS
GRADUALLY WINNING THE GRUELLING WAR IN NORTHERN UGANDA.
THOUGH IT IS OFTEN A CASE OF TWO STEPS FORWARD AND ONE STEP
BACK, THE NRA APPEARS TO BE INCHING TOWARD SUCCESS.

06911 OJULU, E.
MADHVANI'S EMPIRE CRUMBLES AWAY
NEW AFRICAN, 263 (AUG 89), 29.
THIS IS A REPORT ON MULTIBHAI MADHVANI AND COMPANY, EAST
AFRICA'S INDUSTRIAL EMPIRE WHICH IS CRUMBLING DUE TO A
FAMILY ROW IT TRACES THE HISTORY OF THE CONGLOMERATE SINCE
ITS ORIGIN IN 1890- ITS RISE TO ULTIMATE SUCCESS IN THE
1970S SINCE ITS DECLINE BY 1957. IT DETAILS FAMILY
DISAGREEMENTS AND THE PROBLEMS CAUSED BY THEM FOR THE
COMPANY. THE ULTIMATE SOLUTION HAS YET TO BE FOUND.

06912 OKITA, S.
JAPAN'S QUITE STRENGTH
FOREIGN POLICY, (75) (SUM 89), 128-145.
THE RISE OF JAPAN AFTER WORLD WAR II IS WELL KNOWN AND
WELL DOCUMENTED. THE ARTICLE EXAMINES THE CURRENT
INTERNATIONAL ECONOMY TO PROVIDE A FRAMEWORK IN WHICH THE
ECONOMICALLY STRONG, MILITARILY WEAK, AND INTERNATIONALLY
PASSIVE POPULATION OF JAPAN MUST OPERATE. IT EXAMINES THE
BILATERAL AND REGIONAL RELATIONSHIPS OF JAPAN TO ANALYZE
JAPAN'S FUTURE OPTIONS. THESE RELATIONS INCLUDE RELATIONS
WITH THE UNITED STATES, THE ASIA-PACIFIC REGION, THE SOVIET
UNION, WESTERN EUROPE, AND THE DEVELOPING WORLD.

06913 OKOLO, J.E.
MORALITY AND REALISM IN NIGERIAN FOREIGN POLICY
WORLD AFFAIRS, 151(2) (FAL 88), 67-83.
NIGERIA'S FOREIGN POLICY PROCESS IS COMPOUNDED BY
MORALITY AND POWER; ITS FOREIGN POLICY CANNOT BE EXPLAINED
IN TERMS OF ABSOLUTE MORALITY OR ABSOLUTE POWER. SOME
POLICIES JUSTIFIED ON MORAL GROUNDS HAVE ALSO BEEN JUSTIFIED
ON THE GROUNDS OF NATIONAL INTEREST AND POWER. CONSIDER THE
POLICY THAT FAVORED NUCLEAR NONPROLIFERATION IN THE LATE
1960S AND THE CURRENT ATTITUDE TOWARD NUCLEAR TECHNOLOGY. IN
SUM, AS THIS STUDY OF NIGERIA SHOWS, ONE CANNOT EXPLAIN A
STATE'S FOREIGN POLICY, ONE OF THE AIMS OF WHICH IS THE
PROMOTION OF WORLD ORDER, BY USING THE CONCEPT OF MORALITY
TO THE EXCLUSION OF REALISM, OR VICE VERSA.

06914 OKOLO, J.E.
OBSTACLES TO INCREASED INTRA-ECOWAS TRADE
INTERNATIONAL JOURNAL, XLIV(1) (WIN 89), 171-214.
THIS PAPER ASSERTS THAT AN UNDERSTANDING OF THE
INABILITY OF ECOWAS TO FOSTER TRADE LIBERALIZATION CAN ONLY
BE GAINED FROM A CRITICAL EXAMINATION OF THE OBSTACLES
FACING THE COMMUNITY IN THIS AREA OF ACTIVITY. EFFORTS HAVE
BEEN MADE TO ENCOURAGE INTRAREGIONAL TRADE THROUGH THE
PROGRESSIVE ELIMINATION OF BARRIERS. BUT AN EXAMINATION OF
ACTUAL INTRA-REGIONAL TRADE SHOWS THAT IT REMAINS AT A LOW
LEVEL. AS WELL, A NUMBE OF SUBREGIONAL AND INTERNATIONAL
FORCES HAVE INTERACTED WITH DOMESTIC FORCES PARTICULAR TO
WEST AFRICA TO CREATE OTHER SERIOUS OBSTACLES TO THE
ASPIRATIONS OF ECOWAS TO FOSTER TRADE LIBERALIZATION. THIS
PAPER SEEKS TO EXPLAIN THE PROBLEMS FACED BY THE COMMUNITY
AND TO CONSIDER WAYS OF OVERCOMING THEM.

06915 OKONKWO, J.
THE ECONOMIC QUESTION AND THE AFRICAN NOVEL
BLACK SCHOLAR, 20(3/4) (SUM 89), 18-24.
THE ARTICLE EXPLORES THE ROLE OF AFRICAN NOVELS IN
PORTRAYING ECONOMIC PROBLEMS IN AFRICA AS WELL AS POTENTIAL
REFORMS. AFRICAN NOVELISTS HAVE VIVIDLY PORTRAYED THE
CORRUPTION, BRIBERY, FRAUD, NEPOTISM, AND THEFT THAT
CHARACTERIZES MANY OF THE "KLEPTOCRACIES" IN AFRICA. IN
ADDITION, THEY PRESENT IDEAS ON THE RESTRUCTURING OF AFRICAN
ECONOMIC ORDERS. THE ARTICLE CONCLUDES THAT ALTHOUGH AFRICAN
NOVELS ARE NOT NECESSARILY SCHOLARLY WORKS, THEY DO PROVIDE
A BROAD RANGE OF STIMULATING IDEAS THAT SCHOLARS CAN
CONSIDER.

06916 OKONOGI, M.
THE KOREAN PENINSULA: THE REVIVAL OF THE OLD EQUILIBRIUM
IN THE NEW CONTEXT
JOURNAL OF NORTHEAST ASIAN STUDIES, 8(1) (SPR 89), 56-69.
SINCE CHAIRMAN KIM II-SUNG'S VISIT TO THE SOVIET UNION
IN MAY 1984, MOSCOW-PYONGYANGBEIJING RELATIONS HAVE TAKEN AN
EXTRAORDINARY TURN. THIS ARTICLE EXPLORES THE DEVELOPMENT OF
SOVIET-NORTH KOREAN COOPERATION, CHINA'S "LINKAGE" POLICY,
NORTH KOREA'S "INDEPENDENT FOREIGN POLICY," AS WELL AS, THE

AMERICAN FACTOR AND SOVIET POLICY. IT OFFERS THE FUTURE
PERSPECTIVE AND JAPAN'S POSITION. IT CONCLUDES WITH
SUGGESTIONS ON HOW TO CONTROL THE BIPOLAR TENDENCY THAT
GIVES PRIORITY TO MILITARY POWER WITHIN A CERTAIN LIMIT AND
TO FURTHER THE EQUILIBRIUM OF POWER.

06917 OKUN, H.S.
US REPORTS TO UNITED NATIONS ON DOWNING OF LIBYAN PLANES
DEPARTMENT OF STATE BULLETIN (US FOREIGN POLICY), 89(2144)
(MAR 89), 90-91.
THE AUTHOR, WHO IS THE ACTING US PERMANENT
REPRESENTATIVE TO THE UN, REVIEWS THE EVENTS PRECEDING THE
US DOWNING OF LIBYAN PLANES ON JAN. 4, 1989. HE STATES THAT
THE ACTION BY THE AMERICAN NAVAL AIRCRAFT IN RESPONSE TO
PROVOCATION BY TWO ARMED LIBYAN AIRCRAFT HAS FULLY
CONSISTENT WITH INTERNATIONALLY ACCEPTED PRINCIPLES OF SELF-
DEFENSE.

06918 OLCOTT, M.
GORBACHEV'S NATIONAL DILEMMA
JOURNAL OF INTERNATIONAL AFFAIRS, 42(2) (SPR 89), 399-422.
GORBACHEV'S POLICIES OF GLASGNOST AND PERESTROIKA HAVE
INADVERTENTLY REOPENED THE "NATIONAL' QUESTION IN THE USSR.
GORBACHEV'S POLICY OF OPENNESS HAS ALLOWED THE NON-RUSSIAN
POPULATION IN THE USSR TO EXAMINE MANY LAWS, STATUTES, AND
POLICIES THAT SEEM TO FURTHER RUSSIAN DOMINATION. THE
OPENNESS HAS MERELY WHETTED THE NATIONALIST APPETITES OF
MANY GROUPS AND INCREASED TENSION SEEMS A CERTAINTY IN THE
FUTURE. THE ARTICLE EXAMINES THE "NATIONAL POLICY" OF THE
USSR AND THE OPTIONS OPEN TO GORBACHEV AS HE FACES INCREASED
PROBLEMS IN THE BALTIC STATES, THE CAUCUS AND OTHER AREAS.

06919 OLDENBURG, F.S.
CORRELATIONS BETWEEN SOVIET AND GDR REFORMS
STUDIES IN COMPARATIVE COMMUNISM, XXII(1) (SPR 89), 77-91.
IT IS CLEAR THAT AT PRESENT THERE IS NO DIRECT "
CORRELATION BETWEEN SOVIET AND GDR REFORMS." BUT EVEN BEFORE
GORBACHEV TOOK POWER AND EVEN BEFORE THE ECONOMIC CRISES IN
THE USSR, THE STRATEGIES OF THE SED LEADERSHIP COULD NOT
SERVE AS A MODEL FOR THE USSR. AFTER GORBACHEV'S REFORMS HAD
GAINED MOMENTUM, THE GDR IN TURN HAS REFUSED TO COPY THE
SOVIET APPROACH AND HAS CONTINUED TO BE ONE OF THE MOST
TRADITIONAL COMMUNIST SYSTEMS IN EUROPE, TAKING SIDES WITH
THE ROMANIANS, CZECHOSLOVAKS, AND CUBANS. ONLY IF THE SOVIET
REFORMS SUCCEED IN CREATING A NEW AUTOCRATIC-PARTICIPATIVE
SYSTEM WILL A CORRELATION OF POLITICAL AND ECONOMIC
DEVELOPMENTS AND SYSTEMS BETWEEN THE USSR AND THE GDR BE
MORE THAN PROBABLE.

06920 OLDENBURG, P.
INDIA AND THE UNITED STATES: ACCIDENTAL OR INEVITABLE
ANTAGONISTS?
ASIAN AFFAIRS, AN AMERICAN REVIEW, 15(4) (WIN 89), 220-229.
THE ARTICLE EXAMINES THE MANY LAYERS TO THE INDIA-US
RELATIONSHIP INCLUDING THE GEOPOLITICAL, ECONOMIC, AND
SOCIOCULTURAL/PERSONAL FACETS OF THE OVERALL RELATIONS. IT
CONCLUDES THAT THERE ARE FUNDAMENTAL DIVERGENCES OF
INTERESTS AND WORLD-VIEW THAT KEEP INDIA AND THE US APART
AND EXPLAIN THE SURFACE-LEVEL, OFTEN TRIVIAL, DISAGREEMENTS
AND CONFLICTUAL POLICIES.

06921 OLDFIELD, D.M.; WILDAVSKY, A.
RECONSIDERING THE TWO PRESIDENCIES
SOCIETY, 26(5) (JUL 89), 54-59.
VARIOUS STUDIES CAST SERIOUS DOUBT ON THE CONCLUSIONS OF
"THE TWO PRESIDENCIES" OUTSIDE OF THE PERIOD IN WHICH THE
THESIS WAS PROPOSED. ONLY DWIGHT EISENHOWER WAS CLEARLY MORE
SUCCESSFUL IN FOREIGN POLICY. PRESIDENTS CANNOT COUNT UPON
BIPARTISAN SUPPORT WHEN THEY FIND A WORKABLE POLICY. FROM
RICHARD NIXON'S VIETNAM POLICIES AND GERALD FORD'S ATTEMPTS
TO INTERVENE IN ANGOLA TO RONALD REAGAN'S DIFFICULTIES
GAINING SUPPORT FOR THE CONTRAS AND THE STRATEGIC DEFENSE
INITIATIVE (SDI), IT HAS BECOME CLEAR THAT PRESIDENTIAL
CONTROL OF FOREIGN POLICY IS NOT SO COMPLETE AS WILDAVSKY
CLAIMED.

06922 OLESZEK, W.J.
THE HOUSE: STABILITY AND DISCONTENT
CRS REVEIW, 10(1) (JAN 89), 6-7.
THE MODERN HOUSE OF REPRESENTATIVES DIFFERS IN AT LEAST
ONE IMPORTANT RESPECT FROM WHAT THE FOUNDING FATHERS
ENVISIONED. THE HOUSE, RATHER THAN THE SENATE, HAS BECOME
THE CHAMBER THAT EPITOMIZES MEMBERSHIP STABILITY AND
CONTINUITY IN OFFICE-HOLDING. ONCE ELECTED, AN INCUMBENT
HOUSE MEMBER IS DIFFICULT TO UNSEAT. FOR 34 YEARS DEMOCRATS
HAVE CONTROLLED THE HOUSE AND WILL DO SO AGAIN IN THE 101ST
CONGRESS.

06923 OLIVER, D.
LAW, CONVENTION AND ABUSE OF POWER
POLITICAL QUARTERLY (THE), 60(1) (JAN 89), 38-49.
THERE SEEMS TO BE A TREND TOWARDS MORE FREQUENT, MORE
BLATANT AND MORE PUBLICLY CONTROVERSIAL ABUSES OF POWER; AND
THERE IS CERTAINLY A BELIEF THAT THIS IS SO ON THE PART OF

THE PRESS AND POLITICAL ACTIVISTS, WHO REGULARLY ACCUSE
THEIR POLITICAL OPPONENTS OF BREAKING WITH CONVENTION,
ABUSING THEIR POWERS AND ACTING IN AN AUTHORITARIAN AND
UNDEMOCRATIC WAY. THIS ARTICLE CONSIDERS WHAT THE REASONS
ARE FOR THESE TRENDS AND THE IMPLICATIONS FOR THE FUTURE
ROLE OF THE LAW IN EMPOWERING AND CONTROLLING THE STATE.

06924 OLUGBADE, K.
STATE OF THE STATE IN THE THIRD WORLD
ROUND TABLE, 309 (JAN 89), 16-32.
THIS ESSAY PROVIDES AN EXPLORATION OF THE DYNAMICS OF
STATE FORMATION AND DEVELOPMENT IN THIRD WORLD COUNTRIES
WITH PARTICULAR EMPHASIS ON THE SITUATION IN LATIN AMERICA
AND AFRICA. IT IS NOTED THAT MOST OF THE THEORIES THAT
ADEQUATELY EXPLAIN STATE FORMATION IN DEVELOPED SOCIETIES DO
NOT FULLY HELP WITH THE THIRD WORLD COUNTRIES. THIS DUE TO
HISTORICAL, POLITICAL, CULTURAL AND ECONOMIC DIFFERENCES OF
THE SOCIETIES CONCERNED. ANY DISCUSSION OF THE STATE IN THE
THIRD WORLD THEREFORE, SHOULD NOT USE THE SAME YARDSTICK OF
ASSESSMENT AS ADVANCED SOCIETIES. THE STATES IN THESE
SOCIETIES ARE STILL IN GESTATION. THEY ARE INCOMPLETE AND
LITTLE DIFFERENTIATED FROM CIVIL SOCIETY, THE FORMATION OF
WHICH DEPENDS ON THE ACTION OF THE STATE. THE FORMATION OF
STATES IN THE THIRD WORLD IS UNIQUELY COMPLICATED BY THE
DISARTICULATING IMPACT OF DOMINATION EXERCISED BY THE CENTRE
OF THE WORLD SYSTEM ON ITS PERIPHERY. THE COUNTRIES OF THE
THIRD WORLD DO NOT HAVE THE ADVANTAGES CONFERRED BY THE
HISTORICAL CIRCUMSTANCES ENJOYED BY WESTERN EUROPE WHEN 'THE
MODERN STATE' WAS FIRST FORMED SIMULTANEOUSLY WITH THE WORLD
CAPITALIST SYSTEM.

06925 OLUJIC, M.B.
ECONOMIC AND DEMOGRAPHIC CHANGE IN CONTEMPORARY YUGOSLAVIA:
PERSISTENCE OF TRADITIONAL GENDER IDEOLOGY
EAST EUROPEAN QUARTERLY, XXIII(4) (WIN 89), 477-485.
YUGOSLAVIA HAS LONG HAD AN IDEOLOGICAL COMMITMENT TO
EQUALITY AMONG ITS CONSTITUENT NATIONAL GROUPS AS WELL AS TO
GENDER EQUALITY. POST-WORLD WAR II CHANGES GUARANTEED
YUGOSLAV WOMEN POLITICAL, ECONOMIC, AND SOCIAL EQUALITY WITH
MEN. WOMEN WERE GIVEN THE RIGHT TO VOTE, TO HOLD PUBLIC
OFFICE, TO BE EDUCATED, AND TO ENTER PUBLIC EMPLOYMENT
WITHOUT DISCRIMINATION. YET GENDER ASYMMETRY STILL PERSISTS
IN YUGOSLAVIA DESPITE THE SOCIALIST RHETORIC PROCLAIMING
SEXUAL EQUALITY.

06926 OMAAR, R.
A QUESTION OF HUMAN RIGHTS
AFRICA REPORT, 34(3) (MAY 89), 31-33.
ACCORDING TO AFRICA WATCH, JONAS SAVIMBI'S UNITA
MOVEMENT HAS SYSTEMATICALLY COMMITTED GROSS VIOLATIONS OF
THE HUMAN RIGHTS OF ANGOLAN CIVILIANS, WITH THE OBJECTIVE OF
INTIMIDATING THEM INTO SUPPORTING THE REBEL MOVEMENT. FORCED
CONSCRIPTION, STARVATION, SABOTAGE, AND MURDER ARE AMONG ITS
TACTICS--ABUSES WHICH SHOULD BE EXAMINED BY AMERICAN POLICY-
MAKERS WHO SUPPORT IT WITH MILITARY AID.

06927 OMAR, D.A.
HEADS OF GOVERNMENT-MALAYSIA AND THE KUALA LUMPUR
COMMONWEALTH MEETING
PARLIAMENTARIAN, 70(3) (JUL 89), 132-135.
THE AUTHOR DISCUSSES THE 1989 COMMONWEALTH HEADS OF
GOVERNMENT MEETING AND THE SIGNIFICANCE IT MAY HOLD FOR THE
REGION. THE CHOGM'S ROLE IN THE PAST WHICH INCLUDES
CONTRIBUTIONS TO THE ECONOMIC DEVELOPMENT OF MEMBER
COUNTRIES AND SIGNIFICANT IMPACT ON THE INTERNATIONAL SCENE,
IS DISCUSSED. OTHER REGIONAL GROUPINGS WHICH INVOLVE MEMBERS
CHOGM'S ARE HIGHLIGHTED. THE AUTHOR PROJECTS THAT A
SIGNIFICANT TOPIC OF DISCUSSION-THE ISSUE OF SOUTH AFRICA
AND APARTHEID--WILL IMPACT HEAVILY ON THE MEETING'S FORM.
ENVIRONMENTAL ISSUES AND THE COMMONWEALTH EQUITY FUND ARE
ALSO DISCUSSED.

06928 OMESTAD, T.
SELLING OFF AMERICA
FOREIGN POLICY, (76) (1989), 119-141.
THIS ARTICLE ANALYSES THE PROBLEMS, AS WELL AS THE
BENEFITS, OF FOREIGN INVESTMENT. IT DESCRIBES THE
TRADITIONAL LAISSEZ FAIRE APPROACH THAT THE U.S. HAS TAKEN
AND ANSWERS THE VARIOUS CLAIMS OF THE CRITICS THAT FOREIGN
INVESTMENT IS BECOMING TOO INTRUSIVE. IT EXAMINES THE
RESTRICTIONS ON FOREIGN INVESTMENT IMPOSED BY CANADA, FRANCE,
JAPAN, AND WEST GERMANY. IT ADDRESSES THE EFFECT OF FOREIGN
INVESTMENT ON THE ECONOMY, JOBS, AND POLITICAL ATONOMY.
SUGGESTED IS A REFINEMENT OF U.S. INVESTMENT POLICY.

06929 OMOLE, T.
THE SENEGAMBIA CONFEDERATION 1982-1987: VISION AND REALITY
CONTEMPORARY REVIEW, 254(1480) (MAY 89), 258-264.
WHEN THE SENEGAMBIA CONFEDERATION WAS ESTABLISHED IN
FEBRUARY 1982, FIVE MAJOR PRINCIPLES WERE ENUNCIATED AS THE
OBJECTIVES OF THE CONFEDERATION. THESE WERE, THE INTEGRATION
OF THE ARMED FORCES AND OF THE SECURITY OF THE TWO STATES,
THE DEVELOPMENT OF AN ECONOMIC AND MONETARY UNION, CO-
ORDINATION OF POLICY IN THE FIELD OF EXTERNAL RELATIONS, CO-

ORDINATION OF POLICY IN THE FIELD OF COMMUNICATIONS AND LASTLY THE ESTABLISHMENT OF JOINT INSTITUTIONS. THE MAIN OBJECTIVE OF THIS ARTICLE IS TO EXAMINE, WITH THE AID OF UNFOLDED EVIDENCE, HOW FAR THE VISIONS THAT INFORMED THE ESTABLISHMENT OF THE CONFEDERATION IN 1982 HAVE BEEN MATCHED WITH REALITIES IN THE PAST SEVEN YEARS. GIVEN THE FACT, HOWEVER, THAT THE CONFEDERATION IS JUST SEVEN YEARS OLD, A PERIOD THAT COULD BE SAID TO BE SHORT FOR ANY BROAD-BASED ASSESSMENT OF A POLITICO-ECONOMIC ORGANISATION LIKE THAT OF THE SENEGAMBIA CONFEDERATION. THIS ARTICLE WILL CONCERN ITSELF WITH MID-TERM CONCLUSIONS. FOR THE PURPOSES OF ANALYSIS, FOUR ISSUE-AREAS, VIZ: SECURITY MATTERS, FOREIGN RELATIONS, ECONOMIC/MONETARY UNION AND COMMUNICATION MATTERS WILL BE EXAMINED.

06930 OMOLEHINWA, E.
PPBS IN NIGERIA: ITS ORIGIN, PROGRESS AND PROBLEMS
PUBLIC CHOICE, 9(4) (SEP 89), 395-404.
ONE OF THE NORMATIVE MODELS OF BUDGETING PRESCRIBED FOR THE THIRD WORLD COUNTRIES IS PPBS. THIS PAPER EXAMINES THE ATTEMPTS MADE BY THE NIGERIAN FEDERAL GOVERNMENT TO MAKE PPBS PART OF ITS BUDGETING SYSTEM. ALTHOUGH THE IDEA OF PPBS WAS FIRST HIGHLIGHTED BY THE 1974 UDOJI PUBLIC SERVICE REVIEW COMMISSION, IT HAS ONLY IN 1980 THAT A SERIOUS ATTEMPT WAS MADE TO START EXPERIMENTING WITH PPBS. IT WAS HOPED THAT, BY THE END OF THE 1983, PPBS WOULD BE FULLY UTILIZED IN ALL THE GOVERNMENT MINISTRIES AND DEPARTMENTS. IT WAS THE INTENTION OF THE GOVERNMENT TO USE PPBS TO ACHIEVE A 'COORDINATED AND COMPREHENSIVE' BUDGETARY SYSTEM THAT RELATES COST WITH OUTPUT IN ORDER TO ACHIEVE 'QUICK RESULTS' IN THE IMPLEMENTATION OF ITS PROGRAMME. HOWEVER, AS AT THE END OF 1986, APART FROM DOCUMENTARY REFORM (THAT IS IMPROVEMENT IN CLASSIFICATION OF EXPENDITURE CATEGORIES IN THE BUDGET DOCUMENTS), NOT MUCH WAS ACHIEVED IN NIGERIA. IN ADDITION TO THE GENERAL DIFFICULTIES ENCOUNTERED WITH PPBS IN OTHER PLACES WHERE IT WAS TRIED, THE EFFECTIVENESS OF PPBS WAS CIRCUMSCRIBED BY A VARIETY OF INSTITUTIONAL, ECONOMIC AND POLITICAL FACTORS. THE PAPER CONCLUDES BY ASKING WHETHER THE EXERCISE WAS NOT A RETREAT FROM THE REALITY FACING THE COUNTRY.

06931 OMUOREH, U.
INTERNATIONAL LAW AND THE HUMAN RIGHTS OF MIGRANT WORKERS IN AFRICA WITH PARTICULAR REFERENCE TO NIGERIA
DISSERTATION ABSTRACTS INTERNATIONAL, 50(4) (OCT 89), 1084-A.
PART I OF THIS DISSERTATION DEALS WITH THE DEFINITION AND DESCRIPTION OF THE MIGRANT WORKER IN THE INTERNATIONAL ARENA, THE STATE OF INTERNATIONAL LAW REGARDING THE ADMISSION OF ALIENS, THE RIGHTS ACCORDED ALIENS WHO ARE LAWFULLY IN FOREIGN TERRITORY, AND EXPULSION OF ALIENS. PART II SURVEYS ILO PROVISIONS REGARDING THE WELFARE OF MIGRANT WORKERS. PART III TRACES MIGRATION HISTORY IN AFRICA.

06932 ONEAL, F.H.
THE POLITICAL CONSEQUENCES OF PUBLIC SECTOR GROWTH
DISSERTATION ABSTRACTS INTERNATIONAL, 50(6) (DEC 89), 1789-A.
THE AUTHOR EXAMINES THE CAUSES OF PUBLIC SECTOR GROWTH AND DEVELOPS A THEORY LINKING IT TO DOMESTIC POLITICAL PROTEST. A REGRESSION ANALYSIS SHOWS A POSITIVE RELATIONSHIP BETWEEN PUBLIC SECTOR GROWTH AND DOMESTIC POLITICAL PROTEST, PARTICULARLY FOR THOSE OECD COUNTRIES WITH SMALLER BUT RAPIDLY GROWING PUBLIC SECTORS. BUT NO STATISTICALLY SIGNIFICANT RELATIONSHIP IS FOUND BETWEEN PUBLIC SECTOR GROWTH AND PROTEST. ECONOMIC GROWTH IS FOUND TO BE NEGATIVELY RELATED TO DOMESTIC POLITICAL PROTEST, BUT THE RELATIONSHIP IS STATISTICALLY WEAK.

06933 ONEAL, J.R.
MEASURING THE MATERIAL BASE OF THE CONTEMPORARY EAST-WEST BALANCE OF POWER
INTERNATIONAL INTERACTIONS, 15(2) (1989), 177-196.
THERE HAS BEEN CONSIDERABLE PROGRESS IN ESTIMATING THE POWER OF NATIONS, PARTICULARLY WITH REGARD TO THE MATERIAL CAPABILITIES THAT INFLUENCE CONFLICTUAL SITUATIONS. TWO MEASURES HAVE DOMINATED THE FIELD: THE INDEX OF THE CORRELATES OF WAR (COW) AND THE GROSS NATIONAL PRODUCT (GNP THESE INDICATORS ARE CONSISTENT IN THE MAJORITY OF CASES BUT NOT FOR THE USA AND THE USSR AFTER 1971. GNP SEEMS MORE VALID FOR CONTEMPORARY COMPARISON, PRIMARILY BECAUSE THE COW INDEX NO LONGER ACCURATELY MEASURES INDUSTRIALIZATION AND TECHNOLOGICAL SOPHISTICATION FOR THE ECONOMICALLY ADVANCED COUNTRIES. IN THIS ESSAY, THE MOST IMPORTANT ESTIMATES OF THE US AND SOVIET GNP'S ARE SURVEYED TO DETERMINE THE RELATIVE CAPABILITIES OF THE SUPERPOWERS.

06934 ONEAL, J.R.; ELROD, M.A.
NATO BURDEN SHARING AND THE FORCES OF CHANGE
INTERNATIONAL STUDIES QUARTERLY, 33(4) (DEC 89), 435-456.
THIS ARTICLE IS A POLICY-RELEVANT ELABORATION OF THE THEORY OF COLLECTIVE ACTION, PARTICULARLY REGARDING THE EFFECTS OF DECLINING HEGEMONY ON INTERNATIONAL REGIMES. ANALYSIS OF THE DISTRIBUTION OF DEFENSE EXPENDITURES IN NATO

INDICATES THAT THIS THEORY STILL PROVIDES VALUABLE INSIGHTS INTO THE OPERATION OF THE ALLIANCE, PARTICULARLY REGARDING THE ROLE OF THE UNITED STATES. CONTRARY TO THE CONCLUSION OF A SERIES OF INFLUENTIAL ARTICLES, NATO STILL SEEMS IN ESSENCE A UNIQUELY PRIVILEGED GROUP SEEKING AN INCLUSIVE PUBLIC GOOD: REGIONAL SECURITY THROUGH DETERRENCE. BUT, AS THEORETICALLY EXPECTED, AMERICA'S CONTRIBUTION TO COLLECTIVE SECURITY HAS BEEN SENSITIVE TO ITS DECLINING ECONOMIC PREPONDERANCE. THE IMPLICATIONS OF THESE FINDINGS FOR THE FUTURE OF THE ALLIANCE ARE CONSIDERED.

06935 ONGKILI, J.F.
SABAH'S ENTRY INTO MALAYSIA: THE NORTH BORNEO RESPONSE
ASIAN PROFILE, 17(1) (FEB 89), 39-60.
THE AUTHOR EXAMINES THE DEVELOPMENT OF POLITICS IN NORTH BORNEO PRIOR TO THE INCEPTION OF INDEPENDENCE AND NORTH BORNEO'S REACTION TO THE PROPOSAL TO FORM MALAYSIA.

06936 ONTIVEROS, E.
AS SPAIN RUSHES TOWARD '92
NEW LEADER, LXXII(15) (OCT 89), 10-11.
SPAIN'S SOCIALIST PRIME MINISTER FELIPE GONZALEZ IS ATTEMPTING TO MOVE SPAIN IN SOME VERY NON-SOCIALIST DIRECTIONS. HIS ATTEMPTS TO REVITALIZE SPAIN'S ECONOMY HAS LEGITIMIZED THE ONCE-SCORNED ENTERPRENEUR AND HAS INCREASED PRIVATIZATION AT AN ASTOUNDING RATE. HIS ATTEMPTS TO INTEGRATE SPAIN WITH THE REST OF THE EUROPEAN COMMUNITY HAVE BEEN SOMEWHAT SUCCESSFUL, BUT HAVE LARGELY HURT SPAIN'S ECONOMY IN THE SHORT-RUN. THE RESULT IS INCREASING ALIENATION OF GONZALEZ'S ERSTWHILE ALLIES ON THE LEFT.

06937 ONUF, N.; KLINK, F.F.
ANARCHY, AUTHORITY, RULE
INTERNATIONAL STUDIES QUARTERLY, 33(2) (JUN 89), 149-173.
INTERNATIONAL RELATIONS AND POLITICAL SCIENCE ARE CONSTITUTED AS DISCIPLINES ON THE HOBBESIAN OPPOSITION OF ANARCHY AND AUTHORITY. THE AUTHORS REJECT THIS OPPOSITION AND THE PARADIGMS OF ANARCHY AND AUTHORITY IT HAS COME TO AUTHORIZE, AND PROPOSE INSTEAD A SINGLE PARADIGM OF RULE TO ACCOUNT FOR THE PERVASIVE ASYMMETRIES OF INTERNATIONAL RELATIONS. THE AUTHORS SHOW THAT IN GERMAN SOCIAL THOUGHT FROM HEGEL TO WEBER POLITICAL SOCIETY CONSISTS IN RELATIONS OF SUPER- AND SUBORDINATION--RELATIONS MAINTAINED THROUGH RULES AND OBTAINING IN RULE. THEY REFORMULATE WEBER'S THREE IDEAL TYPES OF RULE, SHOW THEIR RELATION TO INDEPENDENTLY ESTABLISHED TYPES OF RULE, AND APPLY THEM TO POLITICAL SOCIETY GENERALLY. THE AUTHORS THEN EXAMINE DIVERSE EFFORTS IN THE RECENT LITERATURE OF INTERNATIONAL RELATIONS TO CHALLENGE THE ASSUMPTION OF ANARCHY, USING THE PARADIGM OF RULE TO CLEAR UP NUMEROUS TERMINOLOGICAL AND CONCEPTUAL CONFUSIONS. FINALLY, THEY SHOW HOW THE PARADIGM OF RULE FACILITATES AND UNDERSTANDING OF SUCH CONTEMPORARY ASYMMETRIES AS SOVIETEAST EUROPEAN AND NORTH-SOUTH RELATIONS.

06938 ONYANGO, W.
KENYA TO TOUGHEN DRUG LAW
NEW AFRICAN, (269) (DEC 89), 14.
KENYA HAS BEEN HOST TO A WORKSHOP OF THE UNITED NATIONS INTERNATIONAL NARCOTICS CONTROL BOARD (INCB). POLICE THINK THAT KENYA IS BECOMING THE CENTER OF THE DRUG TRADE ON THE AFRICAN CONTINENT. HEROIN IS FINDING ITS WAY INTO THE COUNTRY IN INCREASING QUANITIES. THE KENYA ATTORNEY GENERAL SAID THAT EXISTING PENALTIES AGAINST DRUG TRAFFICKERS WERE FAR TOO LENIENT, THE INCB WORKSHOP TAUGHT MANY WAYS TO INTERCEPT DRUGS AT EUROPEAN AIRPORTS.

06939 ONYANGO, W.
MAJOR OKELLO KOLO ASSASSINATED
NEW AFRICAN, (267) (DEC 89), 35.
MAJOR OKELLO KOLO A FORMER MEMBER OF THE NATIONAL RESISTANCE COUNCIL AND NATIONAL RESISTANCE ARMY (NRA) HIGH COMMAND, WHO DEFECTED LAST YEAR, WAS ASSASSINATED. THE PRECISE DATE OF HIS MURDER BY SECURITY PERSONNEL FROM PRESIDENT YOWERI MUSEVENI'S ARMY HAS NOT YET BEEN ESTABLISHED. (IT HAPPENED BETWEEN 18-19 SEPTEMBER 1989.)

06940 ONYANGO, W.
TOURIST SHOCK
NEW AFRICAN, (OCT 89), 21.
THIS ARTICLE ANALYSES THE CONCERN OF THE KENYAN GOVERNMENT AND THE TOURIST INDUSTRY AFTER MANY INCIDENTS IN THE KENYA GAME PRESERVES CULMINATED IN THE ASSASSINATION OF WORLD FAMOUS CONSERVATIONIST, GEORGE ADAMSON.

06941 OPANSETS, N.
MORE PLATONISM
REVIEW OF POLITICS, 51(3) (SUM 89), 412-434.
RAPHAEL HYTHLODAEUS, THE PHILOSOPHER OF THOMAS MORE'S UTOPIA, IS GENERALLY CONSIDERED TO BE AN UNCOMPROMISING AND INFLEXIBLE POLITICAL IDEALIST. HOWEVER, RAPHAEL MAY BE MORE SUBTLE AND COMPLEX THAN HE IS USUALLY THOUGHT TO BE. RAPHEAL MAY BE CAPABLE OF PRACTICAL, PRUDENT POLITICAL ADVICE, AND MAY EVEN DESIRE TO GIVE SUCH ADVICE IN SOME WAY, AS LONG AS HIS ACTIVE PARTICIPATION IN POLITICS IS NOT REQUIRED. IF

THIS IS TRUE, THEN HIS REAL FAULT OR BLINDNESS COULD BE HIS LACK OF AWARENESS OF HOW VULNERABLE HE IS TO THE ACCUSATION THAT HE IS AVOIDING HIS PUBLIC DUTY AND NOT POLITICAL IDEALISM. MORE (THE CHARACTER IN THE DIALOGUE) IN BOOK 1 COMPELS AND/OR GUIDES RAPHAEL TO AN AWARENESS OF HIS VULNERABILITY AND TO A RESPONSE TO IT. THAT RESPONSE, INVOLVING THE EXTREME DENIGRATION OF POLITICAL LIFE, THE DENIAL THAT ANY GOOD CAN POSSIBLY BE ATTAINED THROUGH POLITICAL ACTIVITY, AND CULMINATING IN THE STORY OF UTOPIA LEAVES RAPHAEL OPEN TO THE CHARGE OF BLIND IDEALISM BUT SUCCEEDS IN DISCHARGING HIS DEBT TO SOCIETY IN A WAY THAT DOES NOT ACTUALLY REQUIRE HIM TO ENTER POLITICAL SERVICE, OR IN A WAY THAT PUSHES INTO THE BACKGROUND HIS AVOIDANCE OF POLITICAL ACTIVITY. THE KEY TO THIS UNDERSTANDING OF MORE'S UTOPIA MAY BE FOUND IN PLATO'S PRESENTATION OF SOCRATES AND ORDINARY POLITICAL LIFE.

06942 OPPENHEIM, C.T.
    TALKING PEACE
    PRESENT TENSE, 16(6) (SEP 89), 32-38.
        THE ARTICLE EXPLORES THE PUSH BEING GIVEN BY AMERICAN JEWS, ISRAELI DOVES AND PALESTINIANS FOR A POLITICAL SETTLEMENT, THE STEADILY GROWING AMOUNT OF "FEELING OUT" BY THE JEWISH COMMUNITY, OF THE POSSIBILITIES FOR A NEW, PEACEFUL RELATIONSHIP WITH THE PALESTINIANS AFTER 40 YEARS IS DETAILED. THE VIEWS OF THE MAJORITY OF AMERICAN JEWS TOWARD ISRAELI POLICY IS EXAMINED, AS WELL AS THEIR EFFORTS TO RESOLVE THE DIFFERENCES.

06943 OPPENHEIMER, B.I.
    SPLIT PARTY CONTROL OF CONGRESS, 1981-86; EXPLORING ELECTORAL AND APPORTIONMENT EXPLANATIONS
    AMERICAN JOURNAL OF POLITICAL SCIENCE, 33(3) (AUG 89), 653-669.
        THIS RESEARCH INVESTIGATES WHY THE DEMOCRATIC AND REPUBLICAN PARTIES ACHIEVED DIFFERENT LEVELS OF SUCCESS IN SENATE AND HOUSE ELECTIONS FOR THE 97TH-99TH CONGRESSES, A PERIOD OF SPLIT PARTY CONTROL. FIVE POTENTIAL EXPLANATIONS ARE EXAMINED. OF THESE, TWO APPORTIONMENT EXPLANATIONS, THE DISPROPORTIONATE SUCCESS OF REPUBLICANS IN SMALL-POPULATION STATE SENATE CONTESTS AND TURNOUT DIFFERENCES IN HOUSE DISTRICTS WITHIN STATES, ACCOUNTED FOR MUCH OF THE DIFFERENCE IN PARTY SUCCESS IN HOUSE AND SENATE ELECTIONS. SURPRISINGLY, AN EXPLANATION BASED ON THE INCUMBENCY ADVANTAGE OF DEMOCRATS IN THE HOUSE OF REPRESENTATIVES MADE ONLY A SMALL CONTRIBUTION TO THE DIFFERENCE IN SUCCESS. THE RESULTS OF THIS ANALYSIS SUGGEST THAT, WITHOUT A MAJOR PARTISAN UPHEAVAL, REPUBLICANS WILL BE UNABLE TO CHALLENGE DEMOCRATS FOR CONTROL OF THE HOUSE BUT SHOULD REMAIN COMPETITIVE FOR CONTROL OF THE SENATE.

06944 OPPENHEIMER, M.
    THE YEAR OF DANGEROUS LIVING
    NEW POLITICS, 11(2) (WIN 89), 15-25.
        THE YEAR 1968 HAS BECOME A SYMBOL FOR THE ENTIRE DECADE OF '60S ACTIVISM IN THE VARIOUS DEBATES ABOUT THE SUCCESSES AND FAILURES OF THE NEW LEFT. BUT 1968 IS A DISTORTED STAND-IN FOR THE '60S. HIGH TIDES HELP IN UNDERSTANDING THE MOTION OF THE OCEAN, BUT ARE NOT SYNONYMOUS WITH IT. 1968 SHOULD THEREFORE BE APPROACHED AS A SYMPTOM RATHER THAN AS A SYMBOL. THE EVENTS OF THAT YEAR RADICALIZED HUNDREDS OF THOUSANDS THROUGHOUT THE WORLD, EVEN THOUGH THEIR FORCES WERE FREQUENTLY DEFEATED AND THEIR ORGANIZATIONS LEFT IN SHAMBLES. THE CRUEL RESISTANCE OF THE STATUS QUO WAS ITSELF PART OF THE RADICALIZATION PROCESS. ROMANTICIZING THOSE HEADY TIMES, HOWEVER, CAN BE AS DANGEROUS AS AN OVERLY DEFEATIST INTERPRETATION FOR THOSE SEEKING GUIDANCE TO FUTURE STRATEGIES.

06945 OPUKRI, C. O.
    AFRICA AND THE SUPERPOWERS: THE CONTEXTUAL BASIS OF AFRICAN POLICY IN THE UNITED NATIONS
    DISSERTATION ABSTRACTS INTERNATIONAL, 49(8) (FEB 89), 2383-A.
        THIS STUDY INVESTIGATES WESTERN ALLEGATIONS OF AFRICAN-SOVIET FOREIGN POLICY COLLUSION IN THE UN GENERAL ASSEMBLY. IT BEGINS BY TRACING THE EVOLUTION OF AFRICAN GLOBAL POLITICAL PERCEPTIONS. THEN IT EXAMINES AFRICA'S UN MEMBERSHIP. IT CONCLUDES THAT AFRICA HAS NO CONSCIOUSLY FORMULATED FOREIGN POLICY AT THE AGGREGATE LEVEL, EITHER PRO-EAST OR ANTI-WEST.

06946 OREFICE, G.O.
    NEW TRENDS IN THE TRADITIONAL BALANCE OF THE ITALIAN POLITICAL SYSTEM
    ITALIAN JOURNAL, III(1) (1989), 19-22.
        THE ITALIAN POLITICAL SYSTEM MAY BE ENTERING AN ENTIRELY NEW EVOLUTIONARY STAGE IN ITS LONG-STANDING BALANCE. THERE IS A PREVAILING TENDENCY TO FORM NEW POLITICAL ORGANIZATIONS DESTINED TO BECOME TRUE POLITICAL PARTIES WITH AGENDAS THAT ARE NOT DERIVED FROM TRADITIONAL IDEOLOGIES BUT FROM NEW POSITIONS, SUCH AS ECOLOGICAL CONCERNS OR THE INTERESTS OF PARTICULAR GROUPS OF CITIZENS.

06947 OREN, M.B.
    A DECADE OF EGYPT-ISRAEL PEACE, 1979-1989
    MIDSTREAM, XXXV(7) (OCT 89), 6-9.
        THE AUTHOR LOOKS AT WHAT THE DECADE OF PEACE (1979-1989) BETWEEN EGYPT AND ISRAEL HAS ACCOMPLISHED AND WHAT IT HAS FAILED TO ACCOMPLISH. IN TERMS OF EGYPT-ISRAELI RELATIONS, THE TEN YEARS HAVE BROUGHT NOTHING EXTRAORDINARY, NOTHING TO REFLECT THE GREAT OPTIMISM AND EXCITEMENT THAT CHARACTERIZED THE SIGNING OF THE PEACE AGREEMENT.

06948 ORLOVSKY, Z.
    IT'S TIME TO DOMESTICATE SOVIET FOREIGN POLICY
    GLASNOST, II(4) (SEP 89), 43-44.
        TREATIES AMONG SOVEREIGN STATES GRANT RIGHTS TO AND IMPOSE PROHIBITIONS ON ORDINARY CITIZENS. HENCE, IT IS IMPORTANT FOR CITIZENS TO KNOW THEIR RIGHTS AND RESPONSIBILITIES UNDER SUCH AGREEMENTS. BUT SOVIET CITIZENS ARE OFTEN DENIED KNOWLEDGE OF INTERNATIONAL LAWS AND AGREEMENTS THAT PERTAIN TO THEM.

06949 ORNSTEIN, M.
    THE SOCIAL ORGANIZATION OF THE CANADIAN CAPITALIST CLASS IN COMPARATIVE PERSPECTIVE
    CANADIAN REVIEW OF SOCIOLOGY AND ANTHROPOLOGY, 26(1) (FEB 89), 151-177.
        THIS PAPER ASSESSES CLAIMS ABOUT THE CHARACTER OF CANADIAN CAPITALIST CLASS BY COMPARING THE NETWORK OF INTERLOCKING DIRECTORATES AMONG THE LARGEST 256 CANADIAN CORPORATIONS TO THE CORRESPONDING NETWORKS IN THE U.S. AND NINE EUROPEAN NATIONS. THE ANALYSIS INDICATES THAT THE CANADIAN INTER-CORPORATE NETWORK IS NOT UNUSUALLY FRAGMENTED, THAT THERE ARE NO PRONOUNCED CLEAVAGES BETWEEN INDUSTRIAL AND FINANCIAL CAPITAL OR BETWEEN FOREIGN AND DOMESTIC CAPITAL, AND THAT INDUSTRIAL CAPITAL IS NEITHER SUBORDINATED NOR PERIPHERAL TO FINANCE. THE CANADIAN NETWORK IS QUITE SIMILAR TO THE NETWORKS OF A NUMBER OF EUROPEAN NATIONS, SUCH AS GERMANY AND FRANCE, ABOUT WHICH IT IS IMPOSSIBLE TO ADVANCE ARGUMENTS ABOUT DEPENDENCY AND UNDERDEVELOPMENT. IN COMPARISON, THE NETWORKS OF THE U.S. AND BRITISH ARE UNUSUALLY FRAGMENTED.

06950 OROPESA, R.S.
    THE SOCIAL AND POLITICAL FOUNDATIONS OF EFFECTIVE NEIGHBORHOOD IMPROVEMENT ASSOCIATIONS
    SOCIAL SCIENCE QUARTERLY, 70(3) (SEP 89), 723-743.
        FEW PREVIOUS STUDIES HAVE SYSTEMATICALLY EXAMINED THE SOCIAL AND POLITICAL FACTORS THAT AFFECT THE ABILITY OF NEIGHBORHOOD IMPROVEMENT ASSOCIATIONS TO ACCOMPLISH THEIR OBJECTIVES. IN AN ATTEMPT TO FILL THIS GAP, DATA COLLECTED FROM LEADERS OF 82 NEIGHBORHOOD IMPROVEMENT ASSOCIATIONS IN SEATTLE AND BELLEVUE, WASHINGTON, ARE ANALYZED. THE RESULTS INDICATE THAT ASSOCIATION EFFECTIVENESS IS A COMPLICATED PHENOMENON; THE CORRELATES DEPEND ON THE ISSUES ADDRESSED. COMMUNITY HEALTH AND STABILITY ARE WEAKLY RELATED TO OVERALL EFFECTIVENESS. THE FORMER EFFECT IS MEDIATED MORE BY THE PRESENCE OF SKILLED LEADERSHIP THAN THE NUMBER OF ACTIVE RANK-AND-FILE MEMBERS FROM THE NEIGHBORHOOD. THE EMPIRICAL EVIDENCE SUGGESTS THAT MEMBER ACTIVITY IS MORE IMPORTANT FOR EXPLAINING THE GENERAL EFFECTIVENESS OF DEMOCRATIC TYPES OF ASSOCIATIONS.

06951 ORR, E.L.
    SHAPING PUBLIC SERVICE VISION
    BUREAUCRAT, 18(2) (SUM 89), 17-23.
        AFTER OFFERING SOME GENERAL INFORMATION ABOUT PUBLIC SERVICE IN SEVERAL COUNTRIES, THIS ARTICLE PRESENTS SOME NATIONAL EXPERIENCES IN PUBLIC SERVICE COMPENSATION, PREPARATION FOR THE PUBLIC SERVICE, PUBLIC PERCEPTIONS, POLITICS VERSUS ADMINISTRATION, DECENTRALIZING GOVERNMENT FUNCTIONS, INFORMATION TECHNOLOGY, PRIVATIZATION, AND COMPETITIVENESS AND INTERNATIONALIZATION OF PUBLIC SECTION ISSUES, ESPECIALLY AS THEY RELATE TO "EUROPE 1992."

06952 ORR, R.
    STRAIGHTENING OUT THE WORLD STARTS WITH THE HOME FIRST
    FAR EASTERN ECONOMIC REVIEW, 141(32) (AUG 88), 20-21.
        JAPAN HAS INCREASED THE PERCENTAGE OF ITS GNP SPENT ON DEFENSE AND FOREIGN AID IN RESPONSE TO PRESSURE FROM THE US AND ITS WESTERN ALLIES. HOWEVER, THERE ARE STILL SIGNIFICANT PROBLEMS WITH JAPAN'S FOREIGN AID EFFORT. A LACK OF QUALIFIED JAPANESE WHO CAN IMPLEMENT AID PLANS, FEW DEVELOPMENT SPECIALISTS, THE COMPLEXITIES OF THE DECISION-MAKING PROCESS, AND BUREAUCRATIC RED TAPE ALL COMBINE TO DECREASE THE QUALITY AND EFFECTIVENESS OF JAPANESE FOREIGN AID. BEFORE JAPAN INCREASES THE AMOUNT OF MONEY SPENT ON FOREIGN AID, A RESTRUCTURING OF THE PROCESS SEEMS TO BE A NECESSITY.

06953 ORTEGA, D.
    NICARAGUA: FIGHTING FOR PEACE WITHOUT SACRIFICING THE REVOLUTION
    INFORMATION BULLETIN, 26(19-20) (OCT 88), 22-25.
        ORTEGA AFFIRMS THAT NICARAGUA HAS MANAGED TO INFLICT A SERIOUS MILITARY AND, THEREFORE, POLITICAL DEFEAT ON THE

STRATEGY OF REAGAN AIMED AT DESTROYING THE NICARAGUAN
REVOLUTION. THIS WILL BE A FUNDAMENTAL BASE FOR CREATING
FAVORABLE CONDITIONS FOR A PEACEFUL RESOLUTION OF THE
CONFLICT. IT IS CLEAR THAT IF REAGAN WERE TAKING THE UPPER
HAND, IT WOULD ENABLE HIM TO PURSUE A POLICY OF LARGE-SCALE
WAR, ALWAYS WITH THE DANGER OF U.S. TROOPS BEING SENT INTO
NICARAGUA. THIS THREAT WILL BE PRESENT SO LONG AS
IMPERIALISM EXISTS. NICARAGUA HAS MORE THAN ONCE BEEN THE
TARGET OF U.S. MILITARY INTERVENTION.

06954 ORTIZ, A.A.
DANIEL JAMES: A COLD WAR CORRESPONDENT IN LATIN AMERICA
DISSERTATION ABSTRACTS INTERNATIONAL, 49(12) (JUN 89),
3839-A.
DANIEL JAMES DEDICATED HIS CAREER TO EXPOSING COMMUNIST
THREATS AND TAKEOVERS IN LATIN AMERICA AND ARGUING BEFORE
THE U.S. GOVERNMENT THAT IT SHOULD GIVE GREATER RECOGNITION
TO THE STRATEGIC AND ECONOMIC IMPORTANCE OF LATIN AMERICA.
ALTHOUGH JAMES WAS SLOW TO COMPREHEND THE IMPORTANCE OF THE
CASTRO REVOLUTION, HE SOON BECAME AN ARCHENEMY OF THE NEW
REGIME AND BECAME AN ACTIVIST IN CUBAN EXILE ORGANIZATIONS.
AFTER THE DEATH OF CHE GUEVARA, JAMES ACQUIRED A COPY OF THE
LEADER'S DIARY AND PUBLISHED A CRITICAL EDITION OF IT AND A
BIOGRAPHY OF GUEVARA.

06955 ORTIZ, E.
TWO PLANS, NO SOLUTION
HEMISPHERE, 1(3) (SUM 89), 13-14.
THE DEBT-RELIEF PLAN PROPOSED BY U.S. TREASURY SECRETARY
NICHOLAS BRADY IS A PALLIATIVE TO TWO KINDS OF LATIN
AMERICAN THREATS: WIDESPREAD DEBT REPUDIATION AND POLITICAL
INSTABILITY. THE ELECTORIAL VICTORIES OF POPULISTS CARLOS
ANDRES PEREZ IN VENEZUELA AND CARLOS MENEM IN ARGENTINA
UNDERSCORE SUCH THREATS. THE SPECTER OF SUCH CHALLENGES IN
NIEGHBORING MEXICO IS PARTICULARLY TROUBLING TO U.S.
POLICYMAKERS. BUT THE BRADY PLAN IS FUNDAMENTALLY FLAWED
BECAUSE NO DEBT-RELIEF PROGRAM CAN BE SUCCESSFUL UNLESS IT
FOCUSES ON THE STRUCTURAL CAUSES OF THE HEMISPHERE'S DEBT
CRISIS.

06956 ORWA, D.K.
KENYA'S RELATIONS WITH ITS NEIGHBORS: THE SEARCH FOR A
REGIONAL EQUILIBRIUM
JERUSALEM JOURNAL OF INTERNATIONAL RELATIONS, 11(4) (DEC
89), 106-128.
SINCE THE 1960S KENYA HAS HAD TO GUIDE ITS FOREIGN
POLICY WITHIN EASTERN AFRICA THROUGH THREE STAGES IN THE
REGION'S DEVELOPMENT. THE DECADE OF THE 1960S WAS MARKED BY
A STATE OF GENERAL EQUILIBRIUM; THE 1970S SAW A SHARP
DECLINE INTO INSTABILITY; IN THE 1980S THE REGION RETURNED
TO EQUILIBRIUM. THIS ARTICLE EXAMINES KENYA'S FOREIGN POLICY
IN PERSPECTIVE, ITS POLICY OF NONALIGNMENT, ITS INTERSTATE
RELATIONS IN EASTERN AFRICA AND THE MILITARY FACTOR.

06957 ORWIN, C.
THUCYDIDES' CONTEST: THUCYDIDEAN "METHODOLOGY" IN CONTEXT
REVIEW OF POLITICS, 51(3) (SUM 89), 345-364.
THUCYDIDES IS FAMOUS FOR THE SPEECHES IN HIS WORK, SO
RICH IN ARRESTING GENERALITIES. YET HIS HANDLING OF THESE
SPEECHES HAS BEEN OFTEN QUESTIONED AND SELDOM UNDERSTOOD.
THIS ARTICLE ILLUMINATES HIS PROCEDURES BY CONSIDERING THEM
WITHIN THE CONTEXT, TOO OFTEN IGNORED, OF THUCYDIDES'
EQUALLY FAMOUS "ARCHAEOLOGY," OR ACCOUNT OF ANCIENT TIMES,
WHICH EXPRESSES HIS CRITICISM OF PREVIOUS WRITERS. IT
ATTEMPTS TO VINDICATE HIS OWN METHODS, AND IN PARTICULAR HIS
OWN CONTRIBUTION TO THE SPEECHES THAT HE PRESENTS IN THE
MOUTHS OF HIS CHARACTERS, WITH REFERENCE TO THE POLITICAL
CHARACTER OF THE SPEECHES AS ORIGINALLY DELIVERED AS WELL AS
OF THUCYDIDES' PURPOSE IN REPRODUCING THEM.

06958 ORZECH, Z.B.; GROLL, S.
STAGES IN THE DEVELOPMENT OF A MARXIAN CONCEPT: THE
COMPOSITION OF CAPITAL
HISTORY OF POLITICAL ECONOMY, 21(1) (SPR 89), 57-76.
THE AUTHORS STUDY THE WRITINGS OF MARX, INCLUDING
"GRUNDRISSE DER KRITIK DER POLITISCHEN OKONOMIE," TO
UNDERSTAND THE STAGES IN THE DEVELOPMENT OF MARX'S CONCEPT
OF THE COMPOSITION OF CAPITAL.

06959 OSA, M.
RESISTANCE, PERSISTENCE, AND CHANGE: THE TRANSFORMATION OF
THE CATHOLIC CHURCH IN POLAND
EASTERN EUROPEAN POLITICS AND SOCIETIES, 3(2) (SPR 89),
268-299.
THE ARTICLE ANALYZES THE CATHOLIC CHURCH'S CONTINUED
EXISTENCE AND VITALITY IN POLAND IN THE FACE OF DAUNTING
CONSTRAINTS. IT OUTLINES THE ORGANIZATIONAL AND CULTURAL
FACTORS DEEMED IMPORTANT BY OTHER ANALYSTS. IT ALSO ARGUES
THAT THE CHURCH IN POSTWAR POLAND IS FUNDAMENTALLY A
DIFFERENT ENTITY THAN THAT WHICH EXISTED DURING THE SECOND
REPUBLIC. FACED WITH A RADICALLY ALTERED ENVIRONMENT AND A
NOVEL SET OF ORGANIZATIONAL TASKS, THE CHURCH INSTITUTION
CHANGED ITS ECONOMIC BASE, ITS RECRUITMENT AND PROMOTION
POLICIES, THE RELATIONS BETWEEN THE CLERGY AND LAITY, AND

THE SCOPE OF CHURCH ACTIVITY.

06960 OSAGHAE, E.E.
THE STRENTHENING OF LOCAL GOVERNMENTS AND THE OPERATION OF
FEDERALISM IN NIGERIA
JOURNAL OF COMMONWEALTH AND COMPARATIVE POLITICS, XXVII(3)
(NOV 89), 347-364.
THE AUTHOR EXAMINES THE OPERATION OF 'AUTONOMOUS' LOCAL
GOVERNMENTS IN RELATION TO THE FEDERAL AND STATE GOVERNMENTS
AND, ON THE BASIS OF THIS, ANALYSE THE IMPLICATIONS OF THE
PRESENT TREND FOR THE FUTURE DEVELOPMENT OF NIGERIAN
FEDERALISM. THE AUTHOR NOTES THAT, IN SPITE OF THEIR
STRENGTHENING SINCE THE 1976 REFORMS, LOCAL GOVERNMENTS IN
NIGERIA REMAIN A SUBORDINATE RATHER THAN AN AUTONOMOUS THIRD
TIER OF GOVERNMENT. APART FROM THE FACT THAT THEY DEPEND
ALMOST ENTIRELY ON THE FEDERAL AND STATE GOVERNMENTS FOR
THEIR REVENUE, LOCAL 'AUTONOMY' IS NOT DERIVED FROM ANY
CONSTITUTIONALLY GUARANTEED NON-CENTRALISATION AS IS THE
CASE WITH FEDERAL AUTONOMY AND STATE AUTONOMY.

06961 OSAGHAE, M.O.F.
MASS MEDIA USE AND POLITICAL INTEGRATION IN NIGERIA
DISSERTATION ABSTRACTS INTERNATIONAL, 50(6) (DEC 89),
1789-A.
THE AUTHOR STUDIES THE HISTORY OF ETHNIC CONFLICT IN
NIGERIA, THE ROLE OF THE MEDIA IN POLITICS, AND THE
HYPOTHESIS THAT MEDIA REPORTING STIMULATES PARTICIPATION IN
POLITICS AND INTEGRATIONIST ATTITUDES.

06962 OSANAKPO, T.C.
THE EEC AND ECOWAS: SOME COMPARATIVE LEGAL PERSPECTIVES
DISSERTATION ABSTRACTS INTERNATIONAL, 50(1) (JUL 89),
244-A.
THE AUTHOR COMPARES THE EEC AND ECOWAS, WITH A VIEW
TOWARD PROVIDING BACKGROUND FOR PROMOTING DISCUSSION ON
ECOWAS, ESPECIALLY IN TERMS OF THE GENERAL LEGAL PRINCIPLES
APPLICABLE TO AN ECONOMIC COMMUNITY AND THE BASIC CONCEPTS
OF LAW GOVERNING ECONOMIC FREEDOMS. TOPICS INCLUDE THE
HISTORICAL DEVELOPMENT OF THE EEC AND ECOWAS, THE
INSTITUTIONAL FRAMEWORK, METHODS OF SETTLING INTER-STATE
DISPUTES INVOLVING COMMUNITY LAW, AND THE LAW GOVERNING FREE
MOVEMENT OF GOODS, PERSONS, SERVICES, AND CAPITAL.

06963 OSBAND, K.
REFORMING THE SOVIET CARTEL
CONTEMPORARY POLICY ISSUES, VII(1) (JAN 89), 53-69.
THE KEY TO SOVIET ECONOMIC REFORM IS COMPETITION.
CULTURAL INERTIA, IDEOLOGY, AND VESTED PRIVILEGE DISCOURAGE
COMPETITION. THE ATTEMPTS AT REFORM HAVE ACHIEVED NO
SIGNIFICANT BREAKTHROUGH IN THE STATE SECTOR. IN THE NON-
STATE SECTOR THE SITUATION IS MORE PROMISING. TO THE EXTENT
THAT THE NEW LAW ON COOPERATIVES IS IMPLEMENTED, IT MAY MARK
A TURNING POINT FOR PERESTROIKA.

06964 OSBORN, A.
BRUSSELS: AN EXECUTIVES'S PARADISE
EUROPE, (285) (APR 89), 34, 47.
THE ARTICLE EXAMINES THE FACTORS THAT IS TRANSFORMING
BRUSSELS INTO A "MECCA FOR INTERNATIONAL BUSINESS." THE CITY
IS HOME TO THE E.C. COMMISSION, THE E.C. COUNCIL OF
MINISTERS, THE E.C.'S ECONOMIC AND SOCIAL COMMITTEE AND, TO
A LARGE AND GROWING EXTENT, THE EUROPEAN PARLIAMENT.
BRUSSELS HAS PROVED TO BE A LUSH BREEDING GROUND FOR
LOBBYISTS, CONSULTANTS, ADVISORS, AND GENERAL "EXPERTS." NOT
ONLY ARE MEMBERS OF THE EUROPEAN COMMUNITY HEAVILY INVOLVED
IN THE EVENTS THAT TAKE PLACE IN THE BELGIAN CAPITAL, BUT
OTHER NATIONS INCLUDING THE US AND JAPAN, AND EVEN
INDIVIDUAL STATES IN THE US ARE ESTABLISHING THEIR PRESENCE
TO OBSERVE CURRENT TRENDS AND IMPROVE TRADE AND INVESTMENT.

06965 OSBORN, A.
MEMBER STATE REPORT: BELGIUM
EUROPE, (290) (OCT 89), 34-37, 46.
WITH REGARDS TO BELGIUM, THE BIG NEWS IS THAT THERE HAS
BEEN NO NEWS. AFTER YEARS OF ETHNIC, LINGUISTIC, AND
POLITICAL INFIGHTING, PRIME MINISTER WILFRIED MARTENS HAS
SOOTHED TENSIONS CONSIDERABLY BY MOVING BELGIUM AS CLOSE TO
FEDERALISM AS A COUNTRY THAT SIZE COULD REALISTICALLY
SUSTAIN. THE ECONOMIC PICTURE IS AS EQUALLY BRIGHT: AFTER
YEARS OF AUSTERITY AND PAINFUL DECISIONS, REAL GROWTH IS UP,
INFLATION IS DOWN, AND BUSINESS INVESTMENT IS RISING.
OBSERVERS PREDICT AN EVEN BRIGHTER FUTURE FOR BELGIUM.

06966 OSHIKOYA, W.T.
FOREIGN BORROWING, AGRICULTURAL PRODUCTIVITY, AND THE
NIGERIAN ECONOMY: A MACRO-SECTORAL ANALYSIS
JOURNAL OF POLICY MODELING, 11(4) (WIN 89), 531-546.
THIS PAPER INVESTIGATES THE SECTORAL AND ECONOMYWIDE
EFFECTS OF INCREASED FOREIGN BORROWING IN THE EMPIRICAL
CONTEXT OF NIGERIA. AN INTEGRATED MACROECONMETRIC AND INPUT-
OUTPUT MODEL IS USED TO SIMULATE THE BEHAVIOR OF THE
NIGERIAN ECONOMY TO AN EXOGENOUS INCREASE IN FOREIGN CAPITAL
INFLOW. THE FOCUS OF THE ANALYSIS IS ON THE IMPACT OF THE
INCREASED DOMESTIC SPENDING OF EXTERNALLY BORROWED FUNDS

DIRECTED TOWARD INCREASING THE TECHNOLOGICAL EFFICIENCY OF THE AGRICULTURAL SECTOR. SECTION 2 OF THE PAPER DESCRIBES THE POLICY CONTEXT OF THE STUDY, FOCUSING ON THE EXTENT TO WHICH NIGERIAN GOVERNMENT INCREASINGLY RESORTED TO EXTERNAL BORROWING. THE STRUCTURE AND ESTIMATION OF THE MACRO-SECTORAL MODEL ARE DESCRIBED IN SECTIONS 3 AND 4, RESPECTIVELY. SECTION 5 EXAMINES THE IMPACTS OF INCREASED FOREIGN BORROWING THROUGH MODEL SIMULATION. SECTION 6 CONCLUDES THE PAPER AND SUGGESTS OPERATIONAL POLICY RECOMMENDATIONS.

06967 OSHUNBIYI, S.O.
THE ROLE OF ECOWAS IN THE PEACEFUL SETTLEMENT OF DISPUTES: THE ECOWAS PROTOCOL ON NON-AGGRESSION AND THE PROTOCOL ON MUTUAL ASSISTANCE IN DEFENCE MATTERS
DISARMAMENT, XII(1) (WIN 89), 67-72.
THE AIM OF ECOWAS IS TO PROMOTE COOPERATION AND DEVELOPMENT IN ALL FIELDS OF ECONOMIC ACTIVITY FOR THE PURPOSE OF RAISING THE STANDARD OF LIVING FOR WEST AFRICANS, INCREASING AND MAINTAINING ECONOMIC STABILITY, FOSTERING CLOSER RELATIONS, AND CONTRIBUTING TO THE PROGRESS AND DEVELOPMENT OF THE AFRICAN CONTINENT. BUT THESE GRAND GOALS CANNOT BE ATTAINED WITHOUT AN ATMOSPHERE OF PEACE AND HARMONIOUS UNDERSTANDING AMONG THE COMMUNITY'S MEMBER STATES. THE RECOGNITION OF THIS LINK LED TO THE ADOPTION BY ECOWAS OF COLLECTIVE MEASURES GEARED TOWARD SECURITY AND A PEACEFUL, POLITICALLY STABLE ENVIRONMENT IN THE SUB-REGION.

06968 OSMOND, W.
DEATH IN THE AFTERNOON
FAR EASTERN ECONOMIC REVIEW, 141(35) (SEP 88), 26.
THE DEATH BY GUNSHOT OF PALAU PRESIDENT LAZARUS SALII IS LIKELY TO THROW THE POLITICS OF THE TINY MICRONESIAN REPUBLIC INTO GREATER TURMOIL. PALAU IS IN THE STAGES OF BECOMING "INDEPENDENT IN FREE ASSOCIATION WITH THE US" AND SALII WAS VIEWED AS A STAUNCH US ALLY. THE FUTURE COURSE OF THE REPUBLIC NOW BECOMES MORE UNCERTAIN.

06969 OSSENBRUGGE, J.
TERRITORIAL IDEOLOGIES IN WEST GERMANY 1945-1985: BETWEEN GEOPOLITICS AND REGIONALIST ATTITUDES
POLITICAL GEOGRAPHY QUARTERLY, 8(4) (OCT 89), 387-400.
RECENT FORMS OF TERRITORIAL IDEOLOGIES IN WEST GERMANY, MAINLY NATIONALISM AND REGIONALISM, ARE USED TO ANALYSE THE SOCIAL USE OF A SYMBOLIC ARGUMENT WITHIN A HISTORICAL CONTEXT WHICH HAS FEW COUNTERPARTS IN MODERN WORLD HISTORY. CONCEPTS SUCH AS A REUNIFIED GERMANY, A CENTRAL EUROPE CONSCIOUSNESS AND REGIONAL IDENTITY ARE ILLUSTRATED ALONG A LEFT-RIGHT POLITICAL AXIS RANGING FROM NEOFASCIST ACTIVITIES TO IDEAS PROMOTED BY THE PEACE MOVEMENT. THOUGH A HYPOTHESIS OF A UNIQUE HISTORICAL EXPERIENCE IS EMPHASIZED, THE DESCRIPTIVE ELEMENTS ARE INCORPORATED IN A GENERAL APPROACH TO TERRITORIAL IDEOLOGIES WITH AN EMPHASIS ON CRITICAL THEORY AT THE END.

06970 OST, D.
TOWARD A CORPORATIST SOLUTION IN EASTERN EUROPE: THE CASE OF POLAND
EASTERN EUROPEAN POLITICS AND SOCIETIES, 3(1) (WIN 89), 152-174.
THIS PAPER EXPLORES THEORETICALLY, THE NATURE OF THE RELATIONSHIP BETWEEN TOTALITARIAN AND REFORM TENDENCIES IN CONTEMPORARY STATE SOCIALISM. THEN, WITH A FOCUS ON POLAND AND SOLIDARITY, A "NEOCORPORATIST" SOLUTION WILL BE PRESENTED. SOLIDARITY WAS PUSHING IN THE DIRECTION OF NEOCORPORATISM, AND, DESPITE THE IMPOSITION OF MARTIAL LAW IN DECEMBER 1981, BOTH GOVERNMENT AND OPPOSITION FORCES APPEAR TO BE PUSHING IN A SIMILAR DIRECTION TODAY. THIS CONCEPTUALIZATION OF THE INHERENT TENDENCIES OF THE SYSTEM WILL PROVIDE A FRUITFUL WAY OF THINKING ABOUT CURRENT POLITICAL CHANGES IN CONTEMPORARY STATE SOCIALIST SOCIETIES.

06971 OSTERFELD, D.
ANARCHISM AND THE PUBLIC GOODS ISSUE: LAW, COURTS, AND THE POLICE
JOURNAL OF LIBERTARIAN STUDIES, IX(1) (WIN 89), 47-68.
THE AUTHOR ENDEAVORS TO USE WHAT IS ESSENTIALLY PUBLIC CHOICE ANALYSIS (WHICH ASSUMES THAT INDIVIDUALS WILL MAKE RATIONAL CHOICES BASED ON SELF-INTEREST) TO SHOW HOW THE PRIMARY COLLECTIVE GOOD (SECURITY) MIGHT BE PROVIDED NON-COERCIVELY IN THE ABSENCE OF A STATE. FOR PURPOSES OF PRESENTATION, THE BROAD CONCEPT OF SECURITY IS DIVIDED INTO THREE COMPONENTS: (1) LAW, (2) THE COURTS, AND (3) THE POLICE.

06972 OSTROM, C.W. JR.; SIMON, D.M.
THE MAN IN THE TEFLON SUIT: THE ENVIRONMENTAL CONNECTION, POLITICAL DRAMA, AND POPULAR SUPPORT IN THE REAGAN PRESIDENCY
PUBLIC OPINION QUARTERLY, 53(3) (FAL 89), 353-387.
AN EXAMINATION OF PUBLIC SUPPORT DURING THE PRESIDENCY OF RONALD REAGAN REVEALS A UNIQUE PATTERN. THE MAJOR FEATURES INCLUDE TWO INSTANCES OF RAPIDLY DECLINING SUPPORT FOLLOWED BY HISTORICALLY UNPRECEDENTED AND SUSTAINED

RECOVERIES. THE RECOVERY OF SUPPORT IS PARTICULARLY SURPRISING GIVEN THAT THE LITERATURE OF THE EARLY 1980S EMPHASIZES THE IRRECOVERABLE EROSION OF PUBLIC SUPPORT AND A RESULTING "NO WIN" PRESIDENCY. IN THIS SENSE, THE PATTERN OF PUBLIC SUPPORT FROM 1981 TO 1987 RAISES A SIGNIFICANT QUESTION ABOUT THE "NO WIN" PRESIDENCY. DOES THE REAGAN CASE CONTRADICT RECENT ASSERTIONS ABOUT THE INABILITY OF MODERN PRESIDENTS TO MAINTAIN PUBLIC SUPPORT OR IS REAGAN AN EXCEPTION THAT "PROVES THE RULE"?

06973 OSTROWITZ, R.
DANGEROUS WOMEN: THE ISRAELI WOMEN'S PEACE MOVEMENT
NEW OUTLOOK, 32(6-7 (292-293)) (JUN 89), 14-15.
THE INTIFADA HAS GIVEN ISRAELI WOMEN THE CHANCE TO RE-EVALUATE THEIR THOUGHTS ABOUT THE OCCUPATION, ABOUT THEIR MILITARISTIC SOCIETY, AND ABOUT THE FACT THAT THEIR VOICE IS MISSING IN GOVERNMENT AND POLICY DECISIONS. A SOCIETY THAT PLACES STRONG EMPHASIS ON ITS MILITARY STRENGTH AND THE HEROISM OF SOLDIERS INEVITABLY MARGINALIZES WOMEN. THE INTIFADA HAS SPURRED WOMEN TO RETHINK THE RULES OF THE GAME THAT DIVIDES THE WORLD INTO VICTIMS AND OPPRESSORS, THE VICTORIOUS AND THE VANQUISHED. AS A RESULT, MANY ISRAELI WOMEN HAVE BEEN MOTIVATED TO RE-ENTER THE POLITICAL WORLD AND TO JOIN GROUPS OF FEMALE ACTIVISTS.

06974 OTANI, I.; VILLANUEVA, D.
MAJOR DETERMINANTS OF LONG TERM GROWTH IN LDCS
FINANCE AND DEVELOPMENT, 26(3) (SEP 89), 41-43.
COMPARED WITH THE RECORD OF THE POST-WAR PERIOD UP TO 1970, THE GROWTH PERFORMANCE OF DEVELOPING COUNTRIES IN THE 1970S AND THE 1980S HAS BEEN RATHER DISAPPOINTING. THIS ARTICLE OFFERS A QUANTITATIVE ANALYSIS OF LONG-TERM GROWTH PERFORMANCE, WITH POLICY IMPLICATIONS FOR IMPROVING HUMAN CAPITAL, MOBILIZING DOMESTIC SAVINGS, AND PROMOTING EXPORTS. IT DRAWS ON "DETERMINANTS OF LONG TERM GROWTH PERFORMANCE IN DEVELOPING COUNTRIES," IMF WORKING PAPER (WP/88/97) AVAILABLE FROM THE AUTHORS. IT EXPLORES THE FRAMEWORK FOR ANALYSIS AND SUGGESTS WHAT THE FINDINGS MEAN FOR GROWTH-ORIENTED ADJUSTMENT POLICIES.

06975 OTERO, G.
THE NEW AGRARIAN MOVEMENT; SELF-MANAGED, DEMOCRATIC PRODUCTION
LATIN AMERICAN PERSPECTIVES, 16(63) (FAL 89), 28-59.
THIS ESSAY FOCUSES ON SOUTHERN SONORA WHERE CAPITALISM HAS DEVELOPED MOST THOROUGHLY IN MEXICAN AGRICULTURE. IT FOLLOWS A COMPLEX SET OF CLASS TRAJECTORIES FOR BOTH THE SUBORDINATE AND DOMINATE AGRARIAN CLASSES. IT SHOWS, THROUGH A COALITION OF COLLECTIVES, EXAMPLES OF ORGANIZATIONAL LESSONS, BOTH POLITICAL AND ECONOMIC TERMS FOR THE AGRARIAN MOVEMENT IN MEXICO.

06976 OTIS, P.J.
POLICIES AND PRECIPITANTS OF ETHNIC CONFLICT: CASE STUDY, SRI LANKA
DISSERTATION ABSTRACTS INTERNATIONAL, 50(3) (SEP 89), 787-A.
THE AUTHOR ARGUES THAT ETHNIC CONFLICT IN SRI LANKA IS DIRECTLY ATTRIBUTABLE TO: (1) THE POLICIES OF THE STATE THAT AFFECT THE STRUCTURE OF ETHNIC RELATIONSHIPS AND (2) SPECIFIC BEHAVIORS OF THE STATE THAT PRECIPITATE VIOLENCE.

06977 OVERHOLT, W. H.
BURMA: THE WRONG ENEMY
FOREIGN POLICY, (77) (WIN 89), 172-191.
BURMA IS THE SOURCE OF MUCH OF ASIAN DRUG TRAFFICKING AND AS SUCH, REMAINS A FORMIDABLE OBSTACLE TO THE U.S. FIGHT AGAINST DRUGS. THIS ARTICLE EXPLORES THE BURMESE GOVERMENTS DESTRUCTION OF THE ECONOMY AND ALSO THE MASSACRES OF ITS OWN PEOPLE. IT SUGGESTS THAT THE U.S. TOP PRIORITIES IN BURMA SHOULD BE ANTICOMMUNISM AND DRUG SUPPRESSION. THE BURMESE LINK WITH THAILAND IS EXPLORED, AND SUGGESTIONS ARE MADE FOR METHODS BY BURMA AND THE U.S. TO DEAL WITH THESE PROBLEMS.

06978 OVINNIKOV, R.
TO OVERCOME THE INTOLERANCE
INTERNATIONAL AFFAIRS (MOSCOW), (12) (DEC 89), 10-20.
ARMS CONTROL AND THE TASK OF ESTABLISHING PROPER, CIVILIZED RELATIONS AMONG STATES ARE BOTH FUNDAMENTAL TO THE NEW THINKING IN THE SOVIET UNION. WEAPONS STOCKPILING IS THE RESULT OF POLITICAL TENSION. WORLD PEACE REQUIRES EFFORTS TO REDUCE POLITICAL TENSIONS AS WELL AS ARMS CONTROL.

06979 OVITT, G., JR.
APPROPRIATE TECHNOLOGY: DEVELOPMENT AND SOCIAL CHANGE
MONTHLY REVIEW, 40(9) (FEB 89), 22-32.
"TECHNOLOGY FROM ABOVE" HAS LITTLE TO OFFER THE MASSES OF MEN AND WOMEN WHOSE DAILY LIVES ARE A SUGGLE FOR POTABLE WATER, NOURISHING FOOD, AND SUFFICIENT FUEL. MULTINATIONAL CORPORATIONS AND U.S. BANKS FUND MASSIVE IRRIGATION PROJECTS FOR AGRO-EXPORT FIRMS, NOT WATER SYSTEMS FOR REMOTE VILLIAGES. THE PROMISE OF APPROPRIATE TECHNOLOGY (AT) IS THAT IT CAN HELP PROVIDE THE NECESSITIES OF LIFE TO THOSE LIVING IN RURAL COMMUNITIES AND ON THE MARGINS OF URBAN

CENTERS. AT HAS THE POTENTIAL TO TRANSFORM "DEVELOPMENT" INTO A PROCESS THAT RESPECTS LOCAL NEEDS, RESOURCES, AND CULTURE. WHILE AT CANNOT BRING HEALTH TO THE WORLD'S POOR, IT CAN BRING THE ESSENTIAL STRUCTURE UPON WHICH A DECENT LIFE IS BUILT: FOOD, SHELTER, CLEAN WATER AND ENERGY.

06980 OWEN, B.
THE PARTY AT THE WALL
NATIONAL REVIEW, 61(24) (DEC 89), 20-21.
THE WRITER CAPTURES THE SUDDEN JOY AND REMEMBERED SORROWS OF A WHOLE BERLIN. IT DESCRIBES SCENES OF EAST GERMAN BERLINERS CROSSING THROUGH THE WALL; THE CELEBRATION; THE REJOICING; AND THE REFLECTION OF SUFFERING CAUSED BY THE WALL, LATE ESCAPE ATTEMPTS ARE DETAILED AND THE POIGNANT OCCASION WHEN THE WALL FELL AT POTSDAMER PLATZ IS RECOUNTED

06981 OWEN, H.; MEYER, E.C.
CENTRAL EUROPEAN SECURITY
FOREIGN AFFAIRS, 68(3) (SUM 89), 22-40.
THE AUTHORS EXAMINE INTERNATIONAL POLITICAL AND ECONOMIC TRENDS THAT AFFECT CENTRAL EUROPEAN SECURITY. THEN THEY REVIEW CHANGES IN THE MILITARY ENVIRONMENT AND THE COURSES OF ACTION THAT SEEM MOST LIKELY TO ADVANCE AMERICAN INTERESTS IN REGARD TO CENTRAL EUROPEAN SECURITY.

06982 OWENS, M.T.
A NUCLEAR TEST BAN AS ARMS CONTROL
COMPARATIVE STRATEGY, 8(2) (1989), 205-220.
ABSTRACT THE TRADITIONAL GOALS OF ARMS CONTROL ARE TO REDUCE THE RISKS OF WAR, TO REDUCE THE COST OF PREPARING FOR WAR, AND TO REDUCE THE CONSEQUENCES OF WAR IN THE EVENT THAT DETERRENCE FAILS. ADVOCATES OF A NUCLEAR TEST BAN CLAIM THAT SUCH A BAN WOULD ACHIEVE THE GOALS OF ARMS CONTROL. THIS ARTICLE EXAMINES THE CLAIMS OF TEST BAN PROPONENTS, AND THE UNINTENDED, AS WELL AS THE INTENDED, CONSEQUENCES OF A TEST BAN, DEMONSTRATING THAT IN FACT SUCH A STEP, FAR FROM ENHANCING ARMS CONTROL, ACTUALLY UNDERMINES IT.

06983 OWENS, M.T.
DOE'S UNILATERAL DISARMAMENT
NATIONAL REVIEW, XLI(3) (FEB 89), 42-43.
PRESIDENT REAGAN'S FAILURE TO ELIMINATE THE DEPARTMENT OF ENERGY HAS HAD AN ADVERSE IMPACT ON NATIONAL SECURITY, AS MANIFESTED IN THE PROBLEMS WITH THE AGING NUCLEAR-WEAPONS-PRODUCTION COMPLEX, ESPECIALLY THE REACTORS AT HANFORD, WASHINGTON AND SAVANNAH RIVER, SOUTH CAROLINA. THE PROBLEMS AT THESE SITES HAVE THEIR GENESIS IN THE ORGANIZATION AND BUREAUCRATIC PRIORITIES OF DOE.

06984 OWENS, R. H.
PEACEFUL WARRIOR: HORACE PORTER (1837-1921) AND UNITED STATES FOREIGN RELATIONS
DISSERTATION ABSTRACTS INTERNATIONAL, 49(8) (FEB 89), 2368-A.
REPRESENTATIVE OF EASTERN REPUBLICANS PROMINENT IN AMERICA BETWEEN THE CIVIL WAR AND WORLD WAR 1, HORACE PORTER REFLECTED THE CONFLICTING FORCES OF WAR AND PEACE IN HIS CAREER AS SOLDIER, STATESMAN, AND POLITICAL LEADER. HIS DIPLOMATIC CAREER SPANNED A PERIOD OF TRANSITION IN COMMUNICATIONS, TECHNOLOGY, AMERICA'S ROLE IN THE WORLD, AND THE INTERNATIONAL BALANCE OF POWER.

06985 OWUSU, M.
REBELLION, REVOLUTION, AND TRADITION: REINTERGRETING COUPS IN GHANA
COMPARATIVE STUDIES IN SOCIETY AND HISTORY, 31(2) (APR 89), 372-397.
IT IS THE AUTHOR'S CONTENTION THAT, PARTICULARLY IN AFRICAN STATES LIKE GHANA, WHERE COMMUNAL VALUES AND TIES ARE HIGHLY RESPECTED, THE RITUALS OF REBELLION, LIKE COUPS, SYMBOLICALLY STATE AND TRY TO RESOLVE THE PERENNIAL CONFLICT AND CONTRADICTIONS BETWEEN THE IDEALS OF LEADERSHIP AND THE REALITIES OF THE EXERCISE OF POWER--THE COMMON "FRAILTY OF AUTHORITY." THE SEEMINGLY ENDLESS CYCLES OF COUPS AND COUNTER-COUPS THAT PROVIDE CLEAR INSTANCES OF THE INTRACTABLE PROBLEM OF SUCCESSION TO HIGH OFFICE COULD BE SHOWN TO BE HISTORICALLY AND CULTURALLY CONNECTED, ACCORDING TO THE PECULIAR INSTITUTIONAL CHARACTERISTICS OF AFRICAN POLITIES. THESE INCLUDE A PERSISTENT TRADITION OF POPULISM, AND AFRICAN CONCEPTIONS OF THE ROLE OF THE STATE, OF POWER AND ITS LEGITIMATE EXERCISE.

06986 OZACKY-LAZAR, S.
A NEW APPROACH TO THE QUESTION OF ISRAELI ARABS
NEW OUTLOOK, 32(9-10 (295-296)) (SEP 89), 36-37.
THE AUTHOR OUTLINES A NEW WAY OF THINKING ABOUT THE ISSUE OF ISRAELI ARABS. SHE PROPOSES A CONCEPTUAL CHANGE IN THE JEWISH MAJORITY'S APPROACH TO THE ARAB MINORITY AND SUGGESTS PRACTICAL STEPS TO ACHIEVE THIS CHANGE. THE STATUS OF THE ARAB MINORITY MUST BE CONCEIVED AS BEING PARALLEL TO THE STATUS OF THE JEWISH MINORITY IN THE WESTERN DEMOCRACIES. THE PERCEPTION OF ISRAELI ARABS AS "THE ENEMY" AND AS A POTENTIAL FIFTH COLUMN MUST BE ABANDONED. WHILE ACKNOWLEDGING THAT ISRAELI ARABS ARE A PART OF THE PALESTINIAN PEOPLE, THE DIFFERENCE IN STATUS AND INTERESTS BETWEEN ISRAELI ARABS AND THE RESIDENTS OF THE TERRITORIES MUST BE CLARIFIED. ISRAELI JEWS MUST UNDERSTAND THAT ISRAELI ARAB SOLIDARITY WITH THEIR BRETHREN IN THE TERRITORIES IS LEGITIMATE--JUST AS ISRAELI JEWISH ACTIVITY FOR DISTRESSED JEWS THROUGHOUT THE WORLD IS LEGITIMATE.

06987 OZAWA, M.N.; KIM, T.S.
DISTRIBUTIVE EFFECTS OF SOCIAL SECURITY AND PENSION BENEFITS
SOCIAL SERVICE REVIEW, 63(3) (SEP 89), 335-358.
AS THE PUBLIC DEBATES THE DANGER OF THE INCREASING FEDERAL DEFICIT, SOCIAL SECURITY IS ONCE AGAIN RECEIVING PUBLIC ATTENTION. SHOULD THE GOVERNMENT DE-EMPHASIZE SOCIAL SECURITY AND EMPHASIZE EMPLOYER-PROVIDED PENSIONS AS A VEHICLE FOR PROVIDING RETIREMENT INCOME? BEFORE POLICYMAKERS FACE THIS QUESTION, IT IS IMPORTANT TO EVALUATE THE ROLE OF THESE PROGRAMS IN SHAPING THE LEVEL AND THE DISTRIBUTION OF INCOME AMONG THE RETIRED. THIS ARTICLE PRESENTS FINDINGS FROM A STUDY BASED ON THE 1982 NEW BENEFICIARY SURVEY. THE STUDY FOUND THAT, COMPARED WITH EMPLOYER-PROVIDED PENSION BENEFITS, SOCIAL SECURITY BENEFITS NOT ONLY ASSURE A RELATIVELY HIGHER LEVEL OF INCOME TO ECONOMICALLY DISADVANTAGED DEMOGRAPHIC GROUPS OF RECENT RETIREES BUT ALSO ARE SIGNIFICANTLY MORE EFFECTIVE IN EQUALIZING INCOME DISTRIBUTION AMONG A RECENT COHORT OF RETIREES. POLICY IMPLICATIONS ARE DRAWN FROM THE STUDY'S FINDINGS.

06988 PAALBERG, H.
ON THE ORIGINS OF SOVIET ECONOMIC MECHANISMS AND THE NEED FOR RACIAL REFORM: AN ESSAY
JOURNAL OF BALTIC STUDIES, XX(2) (SUM 89), 191-195.
IT IS GENERALLY RECOGNIZED THAT THE SOVIET ECONOMY IS IN CRISIS, OR AT LEAST A STATE OF STAGNATION BORDERING ON CRISIS. BUT ANY POSSIBLE SOLUTION TO THE PRESENT ECONOMIC CRISIS REQUIRES A THOROUGH ANALYSIS OF THE SEVENTY YEARS THAT BROUGHT THE SOVIET UNION TO ITS PRESENT PLIGHT, BECAUSE IT CANNOT BE BLAMED SOLELY ON THE MISTAKES OF THE LAST FIFTEEN OR TWENTY YEARS. THE THEORETICAL MISTAKES AND POLICY ERRORS THAT PRODUCED THE CRISIS MUST BE IDENTIFIED AND PUBLICIZED. THE ROOTS OF THE CURRENT ECONOMIC PROBLEMS LIE IN THE HISTORY OF THE 1920'S AND 1930'S WHEN THE FOUNDATION WAS LAID FOR THE SOVIET UNION'S SOCIAL ORDER AND ECONOMIC SYSTEM.

06989 PAASIO, P.
ACTIONS SPEAK LOUDER THAN WORDS
WORLD MARXIST REVIEW, 31(11) (NOV 88), 28-34.
THIS ARTICLE IS THE TEXT OF THE FIRST INTERVIEW WITH PERTTI PAASIO, CHAIR OF THE FINNISH SOCIAL DEMOCRATIC PARTY, WHO DESCRIBES THE VIEW TAKEN BY THIS INFLUENTIAL SOCIALIST INTERNATIONAL PARTY OF CURRENT PROCESSES IN WESTERN EUROPE, AND THE ROLE OF THE SOCIAL DEMOCRATS IN THEM.

06990 PACHAURI, P.
AKALI POLITICS: ON A COLLISION COURSE
INDIA TODAY, XIV(7) (APR 89), 47.
AKALI POLITICS ON PUNJAB HAS LONG ALTERNATED BETWEEN PERIODS OF FISSION AND OF FUSION. FACTIONS HAVE SHIFTED FROM ATTACKS ON THE CENTRAL GOVERNMENT TO ATTACKS ON EACH OTHER AND BACK AGAIN. A RECENT ATTEMPT AT UNITY HAS TORPEDOED BY THE SMALLEST FACTION, BUT THE ACTIONS OF THE AKALI DAL WERE ENOUGH TO SPARK ANOTHER ROUND OF FACTIONAL STRIFE AND CONFLICT.

06991 PACHAURI, P.
ANOTHER STEP BACKWARD
INDIA TODAY, XIV(8) (MAY 89), 36-37.
PRIME MINISTER RAJIV GANDHI HAS DECLARED THAT THE ANANDPUR SAHIB RESOLUTION SMACKS OF SEPARATISM AND DISINTEGRATION. BASICALLY, THE RESOLUTION DEMANDS GREATER AUTONOMY FOR PUNJAB AND A PREDOMINANT ROLE FOR SIKHS. IT ALSO SEEKS TO LIMIT THE POWERS OF THE CENTRE TO DEFENSE, FOREIGN AFFAIRS, CURRENCY, AND COMMUNICATIONS.

06992 PACHAURI, P.
BLUNDERING ON
INDIA TODAY, XIV(2) (JAN 89), 42-43.
FOUR LEADERS OF THE JANATA PARTY HAVE REFUSED TO ACCEPT THE MERGER OF THEIR PARTY INTO THE JANATA DAL AND HAVE ATTACKED ITS PRESIDENT, V.P. SINGH. THEY HAVE VOWED TO CONVENE A NATIONAL CONVENTION TO RECONSIDER THE MERGER.

06993 PACHAURI, P.
BOOMERANGING SCANDALS
INDIA TODAY, XIV(1) (JAN 89), 52-53.
THE AUTHOR REVIEWS THE BOFORS SCANDAL AND ITS IMPACT ON RAJIV GANDHI'S PUBLIC IMAGE.

06994 PACHAURI, P.
CLASHING EGOS
INDIA TODAY, XIV(1) (JAN 89), 44-45.
ALWAYS FIGHTING, EVER BACK-STABBING, INDIA'S MAJOR OPPOSITION LEADERS CONTINUED TO VIE AMONG THEMSELVES AND

FAILED TO FORM A UNITED FRONT IN 1988. IN THIS ARTICLE, THE AUTHOR BRIEFLY TRACES THE RISE AND FALL OF SEVERAL OPPOSITION POLITICIANS.

06995 PACHAURI, P.
HALFWAY HOUSE
INDIA TODAY, XIV(1) (JAN 89), 93.
THE RULING CONGRESS (I) PARTY HAS PROPOSED TWO NEW LAWS TO INTRODUCE ELECTORAL REFORMS THE REPRESENTATION OF THE PEOPLE (AMENDMENT) AND THE CONSTITUTION (62ND AMENDMENT) BILL WILL LOWER THE VOTING AGE, INTRODUCE ELECTRONIC VOTING MACHINES, INCREASE PENALTIES FOR ELECTION FRAUD, AND GIVE MORE POWER TO THE ELECTION COMMISSION.

06996 PACHAURI, P.; AWASTHI, D.
JANATA DAL: CONTINUING CONFLICTS
INDIA TODAY, XIV(5) (MAR 89), 26-27.
THE PARLIAMENTARY BOARD MEETING HELD JUST AFTER THE TRIUMPH OF THE DMK -WHICH IS PART OF THE NATIONAL FRONT -- IN TAMIL NADU SHOULD HAVE BEEN THE RIGHT TIME FOR THE JANATA DAL TO PUT A STOP TO THE EGO-CLASHES AND PRESENT ITSELF AS A UNIFIED PARTY CAPABLE OF TAKING ON THE CONGRESS(I). INSTEAD ITS LEADERS WHO HAVE COME TOGETHER UNDER THE SAME UMBRELLA TO CHALLENGE RAJIV GANDHI HERE TRYING TO EDGE EACH OTHER OUT. IN THE PROCESS, THE JANATA DAL IS BEING RIVEN FROM WITHIN.

06997 PACHAURI, P.
LONE RANGER
INDIA TODAY, XIV(6) (MAR 89), 26-28.
THE AUTHOR PROFILES AND INTERVIEWS RAM JETHMALANI, AN OPPOSITION LEADER DETERMINED TO TOPPLE RAJIV GANDHI.

06998 PACHAURI, P.
STALL SQUALL
INDIA TODAY, XIV(3) (FEB 89), 47-48.
CONGRESS(I) HAS POSTPONED ELECTIONS TO THE DELHI METROPOLITAN COUNCIL AND THE MUNICIPAL CORPORATION. THE MCD WILL ENJOY AN UNPRECEDENTED SEVEN-YEAR TENURE, INSTEAD OF THE NORMAL FOUR-YEAR TERM, WHILE THE COUNCIL WILL SERVE TWO YEARS BEYOND ITS NORMAL FIVE. THE OPPOSITION HAS CHARGED THE RULING PARTY WITH EVADING ELECTIONS IN THE FACE OF SCANDALS AND INEFFICIENCY.

06999 PACHAURI, P.
YOUTH POWER
INDIA TODAY, XIV(8) (APR 89), 54-56.
WITH THE LOWERING OF THE VOTING AGE TO 18, THE YOUNG HAVE SUDDENLY BECOME POLITICALLY IMPORTANT. IN A SIZEABLE NUMBER OF CONSTITUENCIES, THEY CAN SWING THE RESULT. NOT SURPRISINGLY, EVERY POLITICAL PARTY IS GOING ALL OUT TO WOO THEM.

07000 PACINI, M.
INTERNATIONAL CULTURAL RELATIONS: ITALY AND THE EURO-AMERICAN UNIVERSE
ITALIAN JOURNAL, III(1) (1989), 23-30.
INTERNATIONAL CULTURAL RELATIONS ARE ONE WAY IN WHICH THE POLITICAL CULTURE OF A COUNTRY IS EXPRESSED. CULTURAL INITIATIVES ORGANIZED ABROAD ARE FILTERED, SELECTED, AND DECIDED UPON BY REAL PEOPLE STEEPED IN THEIR OWN PARTICULAR CULTURAL CLIMATE. INTERNATIONAL CULTURAL RELATIONS ARE STRICTLY CONDITIONED BY THE CONTEXT AND THE ENVIRONMENT SURROUNDING THEM. THEY ARE INFLUENCED NOT ONLY BY CULTURAL BODIES, BE THEY GOVERNMENTAL OR PRIVATE, BUT ALSO BY POLITICAL BALANCES, ECONOMIC TRENDS, AND TECHNOLOGICAL CHANGES.

07001 PACK, J.R.
PRIVATIZATION AND COST REDUCTION
POLICY SCIENCES, 22(1) (MAR 89), 1-25.
IN THIS PAPER SEVERAL EXAMPLES OF GOVERNMENT CONTRACTS WITH PRIVATE FIRMS ARE EXAMINED TO SEE HOW EXPERIENCE CONFORMS TO A PRINCIPAL-AGENT MODEL OF COST MINIMIZATION VIA COMPETITIVE BIDDING AND HOW IMPORTANT ARE THE MANY QUALIFICATIONS TO THE MODEL. FIFTEEN CASES OF LOCAL GOVERNMENT CONTRACTING ARE EXAMINED.

07002 PADDOCK, J.W.
THE CHANGING SUBSTANCE OF PARTISAN CONFLICT: INTER- AND INTRA-PARTY VARIATIONS IN DEMOCRATIC AND REPUBLICAN PLATFORMS, 1956-1980
DISSERTATION ABSTRACTS INTERNATIONAL, 49(11) (MAY 89), 3494-A.
THE AUTHOR ANALYZES PLATFORMS FROM ELEVEN STATES AND THE NATIONAL PARTIES FROM 1956 TO 1980 TO DETERMINE THE NATURE AND DEGREE OF INTER- AND INTRA-PARTY VARIATION IN THE ARTICULATION OF POLICY ALTERNATIVES. GENERALLY, DIFFERENCES BETWEEN STATE PARTIES RELATE TO DIFFERENCES IN THE NATURE OF PARTY ORGANIZATIONS AND POLITICAL CULTURE. STATES WITH TRADITIONS OF WEAK PARTY ORGANIZATIONS AND MORALISTIC CULTURES TEND TO HAVE MORE PROGRAMMATIC PARTIES THAN THOSE WITH STRONG PARTY ORGANIZATIONS AND INDIVIDUALISTIC CULTURES.

07003 PADDOCK, R.C.
FIRST IN THE NATION
STATE LEGISLATURES, 15(7) (AUG 89), 26-29.
THE CALIFORNIA LEGISLATURE HAS OVERCOME THE OPPOSITION OF THE POLITICALLY POWERFUL NATIONAL RIFLE ASSOCIATION AND ADOPTED A PRECEDENT-SETTING LAW THAT WILL MAKE IT ILLEGAL TO MANUFACTURE OR SELL 60 DIFFERENT TYPES OF MILITARY-STYLE SEMIAUTOMATIC WEAPONS.

07004 PADOAN, P.C.
INTERNATIONAL FINANCIAL INSTABILITY AND COLLECTIVE ACTION: IMPLICATIONS FOR DEVELOPED COUNTRIES
INTERNATIONAL SPECTATOR, XXIV(1) (JAN 89), 8-20.
THIS PAPER OFFERS A THEORETICAL FRAMEWORK FOR THE DISCUSSION OF INTERNATIONAL FINANCIAL INSTABILITY, BASED ON THE THEORY DEVELOPED BY HYMAN MINSKY. BY APPLYING RESULTS REACHED BY THE LITERATURE ON INTERNATIONAL POLITICAL ECONOMY, THE AUTHOR MODIFIES MINSKY'S CLOSED-ECONOMY MODEL TO FIT THE INTERNATIONAL SITUATION. HE DRAWS IMPLICATIONS FOR DEVELOPED COUNTRIES IN THE CONTEXT OF THE COLLECTIVE ACTION PROBLEMS THAT ARISE IN THE DEVELOPMENT OF THE INTERNATIONAL FINANCIAL CYCLE.

07005 PAGANO, M.A.; BOWMAN, A.O'M.
THE STATE OF AMERICAN FEDERALISM - 1988-1989
PUBLIUS: THE JOURNAL OF FEDERALISM, 19(3) (SUM 89), 1-18.
THIS ARTICLE DEFINES FEDERALISM AND THEN TRACES THE HISTORY AND IMPACT OF PRESIDENT REAGAN'S PROPOSALS TO DESIGN A NEW FEDERALISM. IT EXPLORES THE RELATIONSHIP BETWEEN THE PRESIDENT AND CONGRESS, CONSTITUTIONAL FEDERALISM, STATE ACTIVITY, AND COMPARATIVE FEDERALISM, IT THEN EXAMINES THE METAMORPHOSIS FROM REAGAN TO BUSH.

07006 PAI, M.
AFGHANISTAN'S UNCERTAIN FUTURE
NEW ZEALAND INTERNATIONAL REVIEW, 14(2) (MAR 89), 26-27.
THE AUTHOR SUGGESTS THE NEED FOR A POPULAR INTERIM GOVERNMENT IN AFGHANISTAN FOLLOWING THE SOVIET WITHDRAWAL AFTER NINE YEARS OF CONFLICT. THE REVIVAL OF THE TRADITIONAL NATIONAL ASSEMBLY, THE LOYA JIRGEH WHICH INVOLVES REPRESENTATION OF THE DIFFERENT TRIBES AND PROVINCES WHO WOULD FUNCTION UNDER THIS ELECTED LEADER IS ALSO SUGGESTED. SOCIAL PROBLEMS SUCH AS A COMPLETE LACK OF SCHOOLS, INADEQUATE MEDICAL FACILITIES, A HIGH RATE OF OPIUM ADDICTION, AND THE WIDESPREAD DEPENDENCE ON PERSONAL FIREARMS TO KEEP ONE'S FAMILY SAFE, ARE EXAMINED.

07007 PAI, S.
TOWARDS A THEORETICAL FRAMEWORK FOR THE STUDY OF STATE POLITICS IN INDIA: SOME OBSERVATIONS
INDIAN JOURNAL OF POLITICAL SCIENCE, L(1) (JAN 89), 94-109.
THE AUTHOR REVIEWS THE LITERATURE ON STATE POLITICS IN INDIA, DIVIDING THE PERIOD SINCE INDEPENDENCE INTO THREE PHASES. HE EMPHASIZES THE NEED FOR A THEORETICAL FRAMEWORK FOR THE STUDY OF INDIAN STATE POLITICS. SUCH A FRAMEWORK WOULD PROVIDE A DIRECTION, A FOCUS, AND A FOUNDATION FOR ANALYSIS OF THE INCREASING RESEARCH ON STATE POLITICS.

07008 PAIL, M.
DANGER--SABOTEURS
NEW OUTLOOK, 32(8 (294)) (AUG 89), 14-15.
THE SHAMIR-RABIN PLAN FOR ELECTIONS IN THE OCCUPIED TERRITORIES IS INTENDED TO LEAD TO LIMITED PALESTINIAN SELF-RULE, WHICH WILL LEAD TO PARTIAL INDEPENDENCE, WITH THE ESTABLISHMENT OF A PALESTINIAN STATE ALONGSIDE ISRAEL AND JORDAN (OR INDEPENDENCE WITHIN A PALESTINE-JORDAN FEDERATION AND MAYBE LATER EVEN A CONFEDERATION BETWEEN ISRAEL, PALESTINE, AND JORDAN). THE PROCESS WILL LAST 15-20 YEARS. BUT THOSE IN POWER--INCLUDING SHAMIR, ARENS, THE LIKUD, THE LABOR PARTY HAWKS, THE RELIGIOUS PARTIES, AND THE EXTREME RIGHT WING--WILL DO EVERYTHING IN THEIR POWER TO ACT OUT AN ENTIRELY DIFFERENT SCENARIO. THE IDEA IS TO DRAG OUT THE PROCESS AS LONG AS POSSIBLE, IN ORDER TO SINK ALL PROSPECTS OF PEACE IN THE QUICKSAND OF DELAYING TACTICS.

07009 PAINE, S.C.
PERSUASION, MANIPULATION AND DIMENSION
THE JOURNAL OF POLITICS, 51(1) (FEB 89), 36-49.
MANIPULATION OF DIMENSIONS, A HERESTHETIC STRATEGY ADVANCED BY RIKER (1986), IS DESCRIBED AS A DETERMINISTIC STRATEGY. THE DIMENSIONS OF A POLITICAL DECISION, ONCE ESTABLISHED, CANNOT BE IGNORED. THIS ARTICLE EXPLORES CONCEPTUALLY THE FACTORS THAT MIGHT MAKE IT IMPOSSIBLE TO IGNORE NEW OR FIXED DIMENSIONS. TWO FACTORS, THE EXISTENCE OF AN AUDIENCE THAT COULD BE PERSUADED TO ACCEPT THE DIMENSION AS RELEVANT AND THE BELIEFS OF MANIPULATED ACTORS ABOUT THAT AUDIENCE, ARE CLAIMED TO PLAY AN IMPORTANT ROLE IN EFFECTIVE MANIPULATION. POTENTIAL CHANGES IN THE AUDIENCE'S SUPPORT OR OPPOSITION ARE THE FACTORS THE MANIPULATOR SEEKS TO AFFECT BY CONTROLLING THE DIMENSIONS UNDER CONSIDERATION. PERSUASION THUS MAY PLAY A ROLE IN MANIPULATION OF DIMENSIONS, BOTH BY FACILITATING A CHANGE IN AUDIENCE OPINION AND BY INFLUENCING OTHER ACTORS' PERCEPTIONS OF AUDIENCE OPINION. RIKER'S CENTRAL CLAIM,

HOWEVER, THAT MANIPULATION OF DIMENSIONS AS A FORM OF
HERESTHETIC IS DISTINCT FROM PERSUASION IS SUPPORTED.

)7010 PAINTER, C.
     THATCHERITE RADICALISM AND INSTITUTIONAL CONSERVATISM
     PARLIAMENTARY AFFAIRS, 42(4) (OCT 89), 463-484.
         THIS ARTICLE CONTENDS THAT INSTITUTIONAL INERTIA IN
     CENTRAL GOVERNMENT IS ONE OF THE MAJOR PARADOXES OF THATCHER
     ADMINISTRATIONS. IT RE-EXAMINES THE INSTITUTIONAL RECORD OF
     THE CONSERVATIVES IN OFFICE 1979 AND ALSO DEALS WITH THE
     WIDER INSTITUTIONAL SIGNIFICANCE OF A PARALLEL CONSERVATISM.
     CONSIDERATION IS GIVEN TO WHETHER THE THATCHER GOVERNMENTS
     HAVE SPEARHEADED A MAJOR PROGRAM OF ADMINISTRATIVE REFORM
     AND TO THE FRAGMENTATION OF THE UNIFIED CIVIL SERVICE. IT
     CONCLUDES THAT MRS. THATCHER DOMINATED WHITEHALL BUT DID NOT
     REFORM IT.

)7011 PAINTON, P.H.
     TROUBLE ON THE RIGHT IN FRANCE
     NEW LEADER, LXXII(8) (MAY 89), 5-6.
         THE BASIC PROBLEM OF THE RIGHT AT THE MOMENT IS THE NEED
     TO RE-EXAMINE WHAT IT STANDS FOR. THE SOCIALISTS HAVE
     COOPTED MUCH OF ITS OLD IDEOLOGICAL TERRITORY AT THE CENTER.
     TO COUNTER THIS, CHIRAC IN HIS DRIVE FOR THE PRESIDENCY
     INITIALLY ESPOUSED SUCH REAGANESQUE POLICIES AS DEREGULATION,
     PRIVATIZATION, AND A SHRINKING ROLE FOR THE STATE. YET
     DESPITE EVIDENCE THAT THE CURRENT BUOYANT ECONOMY HAS
     BENEFITED TO SOME DEGREE FROM INCREASED ECONOMIC FREEDOM,
     THE FRENCH ARE NOT COMFORTABLE WITH THE IDEA OF TRUE LAISSEZ
     FAIRE. THAT WOULD DISMANTLE THE COUNTRY'S LONG-ESTABLISHED
     ENTITLEMENT PROGRAMS AND CUT BACK ITS GENEROUS HEALTH CARE
     AND RETIREMENT PLANS. THE CONSERVATIVES FINALLY RETREATED.

)7012 PAKENDORF, H.
     NEW PERSONALITY, OLD POLICIES?
     AFRICA REPORT, 34(3) (MAY 89), 24-26.
         SINCE HIS ELECTION AS PARTY LEADER, F. W. DE KLERK HAS
     BEEN SIGNALLING THAT HE INTENDS TO INSTITUTE POLITICAL
     REFORM. BUT A CLOSE LOOK AT DE KLERK REVEALS A SOLID
     NATIONAL PARTY MAN, WITH LEANINGS TO THE RIGHT OF THE
     POLITICAL SPECTRUM.

)7013 PAL, L.A.
     IDENTITY, CITIZENSHIP, AND MOBILIZATION: THE NATIONALITIES
     BRANCH AND WORLD WAR TWO
     CANADIAN PUBLIC ADMINISTRATION, 32(3) (FAL 89), 407-426.
         A PERENNIAL THEME OF CANADIAN POLITICAL DEBATES IS THE
     NATURE OF CANADA'S NATIONAL IDENTITY. IT IS BECOMING
     INCREASINGLY CLEAR THAT THIS ISSUE IS INTIMATELY BOUND UP
     WITH THE QUESTION OF CITIZENSHIP, SINCE CONTEMPORARY
     IDENTITY CLAIMS ARE OFTEN COUCHED IN THE LANGUAGE OF RIGHTS
     AND THE CONTEMPORARY CANADIAN STATE ACTIVELY ENCOURAGES
     IDENTITY THROUGH CITIZENSHIP DEVELOPMENT. THE FEW EXISTING
     STUDIES ON MODERN CANADIAN CITIZENSHIP POLICY TEND TO LOCATE
     ITS ORIGINS IN THE 1960S, OR AT BEST IN THE 1946 CITIZENSHIP
     ACT. THIS ARTICLE SHOWS THAT THE QUESTIONS OF IDENTITY,
     CITIZENSHIP AND MOBILIZATION WERE ADDRESSED FIRST DURING
     WORLD WAR TWO IN AN AGENCY CALLED THE NATIONALITIES BRANCH
     OF THE DEPARTMENT OF NATIONAL WAR SERVICES. WHILE
     CONTEMPORARY POLICY CERTAINLY DIFFERS FROM THESE ORIGINS,
     THE NATIONALITIES BRANCH NONETHELESS WAS THE PARENT OF ALL
     SUBSEQUENT ADMINISTRATIVE ORGANS DEVOTED EXPLICITLY TO
     CITIZENSHIP DEVELOPMENT. THE ARTICLE SHOWS THAT CITIZENSHIP
     POLICY FIRST DEVELOPED AROUND THE QUESTION OF ETHNIC
     IDENTITY, THAT "IDENTITY FORMATION" THROUGH CITIZENSHIP
     POLICY IS A COHERENT FIELD OF GOVERNMENT ACTIVITY THAT PRE-
     DATES THE CITIZENSHIP ACT, AND THAT MOBILIZATION IS AN
     EQUALLY COHERENT FIELD OF GOVERNMENT PRACTICE, EVEN IN A
     LIBERAL-DEMOCRATIC STATE SUCH AS CANADA.

07014 PALACIO, J.O.
     CARIBBEAN INDIGENOUS PEOPLES JOURNEY TOWARD SELF-DISCOVERY
     CULTURAL SURVIVAL QUARTERLY, 13(3) (1989), 49-51.
         THROUGHOUT THE CARIBBEAN, INDIGENOUS PEOPLES ARE RAISING
     A RESOUNDING CRY FOR LAND AND THE EXTENSION OF LAND RIGHTS.
     BUT CLEAR GOVERNMENTAL POLICY GUIDELINES ADDRESSING THE
     SPECIFIC CONCERNS OF THE CARIBBEAN'S INDIGENOUS PEOPLES ARE
     LACKING. EXCESSIVE GOVERNMENTAL CENTRALIZATION, BOTH IN THE
     ELECTORAL AND ADMINISTRATIVE STRUCTURES, PRECLUDES
     REPRESENTATIVE LOCAL GOVERNMENT IN MOST CASES. DESPITE
     VEILED REFERENCES TO THE NEED FOR SOCIAL AND CULTURAL
     PLURALISM, NATIONAL GOVERNMENTS HAVE YET TO TRANSLATE THE
     OCCASIONAL SYMBOLIC REPRESENTATION INTO A PERMANENT AGENDA
     FOR INDIGENOUS WELL-BEING.

07015 PALANITHURAI, G.
     ROLE ORIENTATION OF THE MEMBERS OF VIII LEGISLATIVE
     ASSEMBLY OF TAMIL NADU
     INDIAN JOURNAL OF POLITICAL SCIENCE, L(2) (APR 89),
     169-190.
         IN ADDITION TO PARTICIPATING IN THE DECISION-MAKING AND
     POLICY-MAKING PROCESS, A LEGISLATOR MUST ATTEND TO A NUMBER
     OF DUTIES RELATING TO HIS CONSTITUENTS, PARTY MEMBERS.
     INTEREST GROUPS, AND SO FORTH. A LEGISLATOR MUST WORK AS A

REPRESENTATIVE. A LIAISON OFFICER, A REFLECTOR, A MESSENGER,
AND A SERVANT. THIS ARTICLE ANALYZES THE ROLE ORIENTATION OF
THE LEGISLATORS OF THE TAMIL NADU LEGISLATIVE ASSEMBLY AND
THE FACTORS THAT SHAPE ROLE ORIENTATION.

07016 PALAT, R.A.
     FROM WORLD EMPIRE TO WORLD ECONOMY: SOUTHEASTERN INDIA AND
     THE EMERGENCE OF THE INDIAN OCEAN WORLD ECONOMY (1350-1650)
     DISSERTATION ABSTRACTS INTERNATIONAL, 49(7) (JAN 89),
     1990-A.
         THE AUTHOR CORRELATES PROCESSES OF AGRARIAN EXPANSION TO
     CHANGING CONFIGURATIONS OF POLITICAL AUTHORITY ON THE
     SUBCONTINENT. HE ARGUES THAT AN EXPANSION OF SEDENTARY
     SETTLEMENTS STRETCHED THE LIMITED COMPETENCIES OF THE EARLY
     MEDIEVAL POLITIES AND LED ULTIMATELY TO THEIR DEMISE. THOUGH
     THE TRANSMISSION OF NEW TECHNOLOGIES OF RULE AND
     ADMINISTRATIVE FORMS FROM THE ISLAMIC WEST ENABLED SOUTH
     ASIAN RULERS TO TRANSCEND SOME OF THE LIMITATIONS IMPOSED BY
     THE CONTINUED ABSENCE OF REGULARIZED PROCEDURES OF
     BUREAUCRATIC RECRUITMENT, THESE TECHNOLOGIES WERE NOT
     SUFFICIENT TO SUSTAIN A PAN-INDIAN POLITY. THE CONSEQUENT
     EMERGENCE OF AN INTER-STATE SYSTEM WAS CRUCIAL TO THE
     FORMATION OF THE INDIAN OCEAN WORLD-ECONOMY.

07017 PALM, T.
     PERESTROIKA IN ESTONIA: THE COOPERATIVES
     JOURNAL OF BALTIC STUDIES, XX(2) (SUM 89), 127-148.
         THIS STUDY DISCUSSES THE ORIGINS, NATURE, AND POTENTIAL
     FOR ESTONIAN COOPERATIVES IN THE CONTEXT OF PERESTROIKA IN
     THE SOVIET UNION. THE PAPER FOCUSES SPECIFICALLY ON THE
     IMPLICATIONS OF THE LAW ON COOPERATIVES ADOPTED BY THE
     SUPREME SOVIET IN MAY 1988. AT THE MEETING OF THE COMMUNIST
     PARTY PRECEDING THE ADOPTION OF THE LEGISLATION, ESTONIA'S
     DELEGATES EXHIBITED AN UNPRECEDENTED DISPLAY OF INDEPENDENCE,
     ALONG WITH SPOKESMEN FOR OTHER SOVIET MINORITIES, IN
     PREVENTING THE RUBBER-STAMPING OF THE ORIGINAL DRAFT
     PUBLISHED IN MARCH 1988. AFTER THREE DAYS OF DEBATE. THE LAW
     WAS ADOPTED, WITH AMENDMENTS EXPANDING REGIONAL AUTONOMY AND
     INCREASING FREEDOM FROM STATE INTERFERENCE.

07018 PALMA, H.
     CO-OPERATION AND CONFIDENCE-BUILDING MEASURES IN LATIN
     AMERICA AND THE CARIBBEAN
     DISARMAMENT, XII(3) (AUT 89), 83-94.
         THE AUTHOR LOOKS AT THE RELEVANCE OF CONFIDENCE-BUILDING
     MEASURES TO LATIN AMERICA AND AT SOME AGREEMENTS PROMOTING
     COOPERATION AND INTERGRATION IN THE LATIN AMERICA-CARIBBEAN
     REGION.

07019 PALMER, M.; ABDELRAHMAN, M.B.; AL-HEGELAN, A.; LEILA, A.;
     YASSIN, E.S.
     BUREAUCRATIC INNOVATION AND ECONOMIC DEVELOPMENT IN THE
     MIDDLE EAST: A STUDY OF EGYPT, SAUDI ARABIA, AND THE SUDAN
     JOURNAL OF ASIAN AND AFRICAN STUDIES, XXIV(1-2) (1989),
     12-27.
         ECONOMIC POLICY IN THE ARAB WORLD IS DOMINATED BY THE
     BUREAUCRACY WHICH PLANS, COORDINATES, AND IMPLEMENTS
     DEVELOPMENT PLANS; CONTROLS THE ALLOCATION OF THE STATE'S
     NATURAL RESOURCES; AND IS INCREASINGLY USED BY ARAB STATES
     TO REGULATE THE ECONOMIC ACTIVITIES OF THEIR CITIZENS. THIS
     PAPER PROVIDES AN EMPIRICAL ASSESSMENT OF BUREAUCRATIC
     INNOVATION AND ITS RELATIONSHIP TO ECONOMIC DEVELOPMENT IN
     EGYPT, SAUDI ARABIA, AND THE SUDAN. THE DATA ARE DERIVED
     FROM PARALLEL SURVEYS OF SENIOR PUBLIC OFFICIALS IN SUDAN
     AND SAUDI ARABIA, AS WELL AS FROM A GENERAL SURVEY OF THE
     EGYPTIAN BUREAUCRACY. IT CONCLUDES THAT PUBLIC SERVANTS IN
     THOSE COUNTRIES ARE NOT INNOVATIVE ON THE JOB, NOR INCLINED
     TO TRY NEW IDEAS AND TAKE RISKS. THEIR APATHY DOES NOT AUGUR
     WELL FOR ECONOMIC DEVELOPMENT IN THE COUNTRIES WHICH SERVE
     AS A FOCUS FOR THIS STUDY.

07020 PALMER, M.
     MACHIAVELLIAN "VIRTU" AND THUCYDIDEAN "ARETE": TRADITIONAL
     VIRTUE AND POLITICAL WISDOM IN THUCYDIDES
     REVIEW OF POLITICS, 51(3) (SUM 89), 365-385.
         THIS ARTICLE INVESTIGATES AN OFT-ALLEGED KINSHIP BETWEEN
     THE POLITICAL THOUGHT OF MACHIAVELLI AND THUCYDIDES
     CONCERNING "VIRTUE". IN THE BACKGROUND IS THE CURRENT DEBATE
     OVER WHETHER OR NOT MACHIAVELLI INITIATES "MODERN" THOUGHT
     WITH (AMONG OTHER THINGS) A RADICALLY NEW TEACHING ON
     "VIRTUE." MACHIAVELLIAN VIRTU IS REPRISED: THUCYDIDEAN
     ATTRIBUTIONS OF ARETE, CATALOGUED; OBSERVATIONS PROFFERED.
     THEN THUCYDIDES' ASSESSMENT OF THE CAREER OF NICIAS IS
     DISCUSSED; THIS, TO SUPPORT THE CONTENTION THAT WHEN READ IN
     THEIR PROPER CONTEXTS, CONTEXTS CAREFULLY CRAFTED BY
     THUCYDIDES, THUCYDIDEAN ATTRIBUTIONS OF ARETE DO NOT SUPPORT
     THE APPARENT KINSHIP BETWEEN THUCYDIDES AND MACHIAVELLI:
     THUCYDIDES IS NOT A "MACHIAVELLIAN."

07021 PALMER, M. J.
     CIVIL ADOPTION IN CONTEMPORARY CHINESE LAW: A CONTRACT TO
     CARE
     MODERN ASIAN STUDIES, 23(2) (MAY 89), 373-410.
         ADOPTION LAW IN THE PRC INVOLVES A RIGOROUS ATTEMPT TO

ENSURE THAT CIVIL ADOPTION RELATIONS FUNCTION TO FURNISH
CARE FOR ELDERLY PERSONS. CUSTOMARY ADOPTIONS MAY BE
CHARACTERIZED AS LEGAL ADOPTIONS IF, IN PARTICULAR, THEY
MANIFEST RECIPROCAL OBLIGATIONS OF CARE. THE MUTUAL DUTIES
CREATED BETWEEN THE ADOPTANT AND THE ADOPTED PERSON IN MANY
CASES INVOLVE A LONG-TERM TRANSFER OF CARE RESPONSIBILITIES
WHICH CAN ONLY TAKE PLACE IF THE ADOPTED PERSON HONOURS HER
OR HIS OBLIGATIONS TOWARDS THE ADOPTANTS. THIS EXCHANGE OF
RIGHTS AND PRIVILEGES OF CARE IS A POTENTIAL SOURCE OF
CONFLICT BECAUSE OVER SUCH AN EXTENDED PERIOD OF TIME THE
TWO PRINCIPAL PARTIES MAY WELL DEVELOP THEIR OWN IDEAS ON
WHAT CONSTITUTES APPROPRIATE OBLIGATIONS AND RIGHTS OF CARE
AND FINANCIAL SUPPORT IN RELATIONS BETWEEN THE ADOPTED CHILD
AND ITS NATURAL PARENTS.

07022 PALMER, N.D.
    UNITED STATES POLICY IN EAST ASIA
    CURRENT HISTORY, 88(537) (APR 89), 161-164, 191-192.
        THE REMARKABLE CHANGES THAT ARE OCCURRING IN EAST AND
    SOUTHEAST ASIA CONFRONT THE BUSH ADMINISTRATION WITH A
    MULTITUDE OF PROBLEMS AND OPPORTUNITIES. THE USA MUST
    DEVELOP A MORE COHERENT, MORE REALISTIC, AND MORE POSITIVE
    POLICY TOWARD THIS INCREASINGLY IMPORTANT PART OF THE WORLD

07023 PALMQUIST, R.D.
    FACTORS INFLUENCING SMALL CITY BUDGET POLICIES
    DISSERTATION ABSTRACTS INTERNATIONAL, 49(7) (JAN 89),
    1959-A.
        THE AUTHOR ENDEAVORS TO DETERMINE THE CAUSE OF THE WIDE
    VARIANCES IN SMALL CITY EXPENDITURES FOR CITY SERVICES. HE
    ANALYZES THE BUDGETS FOR FIRE PROTECTION, POLICE, PARKS AND
    RECREATION, STREET MAINTENANCE, AND ADMINISTRATION IN 60
    CITIES OVER A FIVE-YEAR PERIOD.

07024 PALOS, D.; SOELDNER, T.
    THE ILLUSION OF REFORM IN SOUTH AFRICA
    THE CHRISTIAN CENTURY, 106(14) (APR 89), 447-450.
        MANY OBSERVERS, INSIDE AND OUTSIDE SOUTH AFRICA, ARE
    SUGGESTING THAT THE REFORMS OF RECENT YEARS REPRESENT A MOVE
    AWAY FROM APARTHEID. BUT SOUTH AFRICA'S NEW CONSTITUTION
    FIRMLY ENTRENCHES APARTHEID IN THE GOVERNING STRUCTURES AND
    MAKES MEANINGFUL REFORM IMPOSSIBLE.

07025 PANDAY, D.R.
    ADMINISTRATIVE DEVELOPMENT IN A SEMIDEPENDENCY: THE
    EXPERIENCE OF NEPAL
    PUBLIC ADMINISTRATION AND DEVELOPMENT, 9(3) (JUN 89),
    301-314.
        THE ARTICLE EXAMINES THE ATTEMPTS OF NEPAL TO MODERNIZE
    ITS ADMINISTRATIVE SYSTEM AND ENACT REFORMS DESIGNED TO LIFT
    THE COUNTRY OUT OF ITS "SEMI-DEPENDENT" STATE. IT ANALYZES
    THE POLITICO-ECONOMIC BACK AGAINST WHICH PAST REFORMS WERE
    ATTEMPTED. IT ALSO ASSESSES THE RELATIVE SUCCESSES AND
    FAILURES OF CURRENT EFFORTS TO EXPAND ADMINISTRATION BEYOND
    MERE MAINTENANCE OF LAW AND ORDER. THE ARTICLE CONCLUDES
    THAT NEPAL'S INABILITY TO DETERMINE OBJECTIVES OF
    MODERNIZATION THAT ARE CONSISTENT WITH THE "PREVAILING
    VALUES" IS THE MAIN CAUSE FOR THE FAILURE OF MOST ATTEMPTS
    AT REFORM.

07026 PANKIN, B.
    IN SWEDEN
    INTERNATIONAL AFFAIRS (MOSCOW), (7) (JUL 89), 54-64.
        IN THIS INTERVIEW, THE SOVIET AMBASSADOR TO SWEDEN
    ANSWERS QUESTIONS ABOUT HIS POST AS AMBASSADOR AND ABOUT
    SOVIET-SWEDISH RELATIONS.

07027 PANKRASHOVA, M.
    TALKS BETWEEN GREAT BRITAIN, FRANCE, AND THE USSR IN 1939
    INTERNATIONAL AFFAIRS (MOSCOW), (9) (SEP 89), 27-37.
        ON MARCH 18, 1939, THE SOVIET GOVERNMENT PROPOSED
    CONVENING A CONFERENCE OF THE MOST INTERESTED STATES TO
    AGREE ON A JOINT POSITION IN THE EVENT OF NEW GERMAN
    AGGRESSION. FROM THE VERY BEGINNING, THE POLITICAL
    NEGOTIATIONS RAN INTO DIFFICULTIES BECAUSE OF THE DUAL
    POSITION OF LONDON AND PARIS, WHO DID NOT WANT TO BIND
    THEMSELVES WITH RIGID OBLIGATIONS IN RELATION TO THE SOVIET
    SIDE. THE TRUE MOTIVES OF THE BRITISH GOVERNMENT ARE CLEARLY
    REVEALED IN THE MINUTES OF THE GOVERNMENT'S COMMITTEE ON
    FOREIGN POLICY, WHICH SERVE AS THE BASIS FOR THIS ESSAY.

07028 PANTOJAS-GARCIA, E.
    PUERTO RICAN POPULISM REVISITED: THE PPD DURING THE 1940'S
    JOURNAL OF LATIN AMERICAN STUDIES, 21(3) (OCT 89), 521-558.
        THIS ARTICLE ANALYSES THE REFORMIST PROJECT FROM ITS
    ORIGINS AROUND 1934, WHEN THE ARCHETYPE OF THE PPD'S
    REFORMIST PROGRAMME-THE 'CHARDON PLAN' - WAS PROPOSED, UNTIL
    ITS IMPLEMENTATION DURING THE 1940S. THE POINT OF DEPARTURE
    OF THIS ANALYSIS IS THE POLITICO-ECONOMIC CRISIS OF THE
    1930S, ITS IMPACT UPON THE PUERTO RICAN SOCIO-ECONOMIC
    STRUCTURE AND CLASS RELATIONS, PARTICULARLY IN TERMS OF ITS
    IMPACT ON THE CLASS ALIGNMENTS WITHIN THE COLONIAL POWER
    BLOC. THE ARTICLE THEN PROCEEDS TO EXAMINE THE IMPACT OF THE
    PPD'S REFORMS PROGRAMME, IN TERMS OF THE REARRANGEMENT OF

THE SOCIO-ECONOMIC STRUCTURE AND CLASS RELATIONS THAT IT
EFFECTED. IT CONCLUDES WITH AN ASSESSMENT OF HOW THE PPD
REFORMS RELATED TO THE PRESERVATION OF CAPITALISM AND
COLONIALISM IN PUERTO RICO AND WITH A BRIEF DISCUSSION OF
THE PARALLELS AND DIFFERENCES BETWEEN PUERTO RICAN AND LATIN
AMERICAN POPULISM.

07029 PAOLINI, J.
    THE GAULLIST MODEL REVISITED: LONG-RANGE STRATEGIC VISION
    AND SHORT-TERM POLITICAL IMPLEMENTATION IN FRENCH DEFENSE
    POLICY
    FRENCH POLITICS AND SOCIETY, 7(4) (FAL 89), 16-23.
        FRENCH DEFENSE POLICY HAS EVOLVED CONTINUOUSLY SINCE THE
    TIME OF ITS CONCEPTUAL INCEPTION UNDER GENERAL DEGAULLE
    (1958-1969). THE PATTERN FOR THE CONTEMPORARY EVOLUTION OF
    FRANCE'S DEFENSE POLICIES WAS CONTAINED BOTH IN THE LONG-
    TERM POLITICAL VISION AND THE STRATEGIC FRAMEWORK LAID
    DURING THE GAULLIST ERA. THESE TRANSFORMATIONS ARE
    OSTENSIBLE SIGNS OF AN HISTORICAL AND GEOSTRATEGIC
    CONTINUITY, A PROGRESSIVE FULFILLMENT OF THE STRATEGIC
    FRAMEWORK OF FRENCH DEFENSE DOCTRINE AND FOREIGN POLICY.

07030 PAPADOPOULOS, Y.
    PARTIES, THE STATE AND SOCIETY IN GREECE: CONTINUITY
    WITHIN CHANGE
    WEST EUROPEAN POLITICS, 12(2) (APR 89), 55-71.
        THE NEW GREEK PARTY SYSTEM WHICH EMERGED AFTER THE
    RESTORATION OF DEMOCRACY IN 1974 IS CHARACTERIZED BY A
    COMBINATION OF FEATURES INDICATIVE OF BOTH CONTINUITY AND
    CHANGE IN COMPARISON WITH T THE PARTY SYSTEM THAT EXISTED
    BEFORE THE MILITARY COUP OF 1967. THIS ARTICLE CONCLUDES
    THAT IN THE PRESENT PHASE THE CONTRIBUTION OF PARTIES TO
    INSTITUTIONAL CONSOLIDATION AND THE STABILITY OF PARTY
    IDENTIFICATION, THOUGH NOT NEGLIGIBLE, REMAINS UNCERTAIN. IT
    IS LIKELY TO BE INFLUENCED BY VARIABLES BOTH INTERNAL AND
    EXTERNAL TO THE POLITICAL SYSTEM, RELATING TO PARTY
    INTERACTION AND TO THE RELATIONSHIP OF PARTIES WITH STATE
    AND SOCIETY.

07031 PAPANTHIMOS, A.
    THE STRATEGY OF COALITION
    WORLD MARXIST REVIEW, 32(10) (OCT 89), 70-73.
        THIS ARTICLE EXPLORES THE COALITION OF LEFT AND
    PROGRESSIVE FORCES. IT ANALYSES IT SOMETHING OTHER THAN A
    TEMPORARY ALLIANCE MOTIVATED BY PLOITICAL EXPEDIENCY, BUT
    RATHER TO WIN POWER AND TO TRANSFORM GREECE ALONG DEMOCRATIC
    AND SOCIALIST LINES. AS THE COALITION IS GROWING STRONGER
    WITH TIME, THE REASONS FOR ITS RAPID PROCESS OF RAPPROCHMENT
    AND WHAT HAS CEMENTED THE LEFT FORCES ARE EXAMINED.

07032 PAQUET, G.
    THE UNDERGROUND ECONOMY
    POLICY OPTIONS, 10(1) (JAN 89), 3-6.
        THE AUTHOR OUTLINES SOME OF THE PROBLEMS THE UNDERGROUND
    ECONOMY PRESENTS TO THE GOVERNMENT. HE SUGGESTS A NUMBER OF
    REFORMS, INCLUDING ABOLISHING INCOME TAXES AND SWITCHING TO
    SOME FORM OF VALUE ADDED TAX OR BUSINESS TRANSFER TAX.

07033 PARENTI, M.
    SAYING "NO" TO LEGALIZED DRUGS
    POLITICAL AFFAIRS, LXVIII(11) (NOV 89), 8-10.
        THE ARTICLE ANALYZES THE GROWING MOVEMENT FOR THE
    LEGALIZATION OF NARCOTICS. IT ARGUES THAT THE REAL PROBLEM
    IS NOT THE UNLAWFUL CONSUMPTION OF DRUGS, BUT THE
    CONSUMPTION OF DRUGS IN GENERAL. LEGALIZATION MIGHT HAVE THE
    BENEFICIAL EFFECT OF INCREASING GOVERNMENT REVENUE THROUGH
    TAXATION, BUT, AS THE MULTI-BILLION DOLLAR ALCOHOL AND
    TOBACCO INDUSTRIES REVEAL, CONSUMPTION IS UNLIKELY TO
    DECREASE.

07034 PARHAM, L.
    ENTERPRISE ZONES RENEWED
    AMERICAN CITY AND COUNTY, 104(6) (JUN 89), 16.
        LOCAL GOVERNMENT'S ROLE IN ENCOURAGING BUSINESS
    REDEVELOPMENT IN POOR NEIGHBORHOODS IS COMING UNDER SCRUTINY
    AS CONGRESS BEGINS TO RE-EXAMINE FEDERAL ENTERPRISE ZONE
    PROGRAMS. JACK KEMP, SECRETARY OF THE U.S. HOUSING AND URBAN
    DEVELOPMENT (HUD) DEPARTMENT, IS CAREFULLY PRODDING
    LAWMAKERS TOWARD SUPPORTING THE FEDERAL PROGRAM, WHICH
    LANGUISHED THROUGHOUT MOST OF THE REAGAN ADMINISTRATION.

07035 PARHAM, L.
    EQUAL RIGHTS FOR HANDICAPPED SOUGHT
    AMERICAN CITY AND COUNTY, 104(10) (OCT 89), 16.
        THE AMERICANS WITH DISABILITIES ACT IS DESIGNED TO
    PROHIBIT DISCRIMINATION AGAINST THE HANDICAPPED. STATE AND
    LOCAL GOVERNMENTS ARE BARRED FROM DENYING THE DISABLED
    ACCESS TO PUBLIC SERVICES. EMPLOYMENT AND ACCESS TO PUBLIC
    ACCOMMODATIONS, TRANSPORTATION, AND TELECOMMUNICATIONS, AS
    WELL AS EMPLOYMENT IN THE PUBLIC AND PRIVATE SECTORS, MUST
    BE OPEN TO THE DISABLED. THE EXPENSE THAT WILL COME WITH
    RENOVATING BUILDINGS AND RESTRUCTURING SERVICES HAS LOCAL
    GOVERNMENTS WORRIED.

07036 PARHAM, L.
   FEDERAL GAS TAXES RE-EXAMINED
   AMERICAN CITY AND COUNTY, 104(7) (JUL 89), 16.
      CONGRESSIONAL SOURCES SAY THAT RECENT HOUSE AND SENATE
   VOTES DEMONSTRATE FIRM COMMITMENTS AGAINST A FEDERAL GAS TAX
   INCREASE, BUT THOSE DETERMINED TO PRESERVE FUEL EXCISE TAXES
   AS A REVENUE SOURCE FOR LOCAL ROAD-BUILDING ARE NOT
   REASSURED. LOCAL GOVERNMENTS ARE CONCERNED THAT FEDERAL
   EFFORTS TO BALANCE THE NATIONAL BUDGET WITH INCREASED GAS
   TAX REVENUE WOULD UNBALANCE THEIR LOCAL BUDGETS.

07037 PARHAM, L.
   NIBBLING AT MUNICIPAL BOND TAX-EXEMPTION
   AMERICAN CITY AND COUNTY, 104(8) (AUG 89), 16.
      EXTENDING THE CORPORATE ALTERNATIVE MINIMUM TAX BITE ON
   MUNICIPAL BONDS WOULD DRY UP THE POOL OF POTENTIAL MUNICIPAL
   BOND INVESTORS. FULL LOSS OF MUNICIPAL BOND TAX-EXEMPT
   STATUS WOULD MEAN THAT CORPORATIONS SUBJECT TO THE
   ALTERNATIVE MINIMUM TAX WOULD PROBABLY AVOID BUYING NEW
   BONDS AND EVEN SELL BONDS OUT OF THEIR PORTFOLIOS IN
   COMPETITION WITH ANY NEW ISSUES. IN ORDER TO ATTRACT
   INVESTORS, LOCAL GOVERNMENTS WOULD BE FORCED TO PAY THE SAME
   INTEREST RATES AS PRIVATE PROFIT BONDS. THE COST OF PAYING
   INVESTORS HIGHER INTEREST RATES WOULD FALL TO THE TAXPAYERS.

07038 PARHAM, L.
   TORT REFORM WOULD REDUCE LOCAL LIABILITY
   AMERICAN CITY AND COUNTY, 104(9) (SEP 89), 16.
      DURING THE PAST THIRTY YEARS, FEDERAL COURTS HAVE SEEN
   AN EXPLOSION OF LAWSUITS FILED AGAINST LOCAL GOVERNMENTS
   UNDER THE CIVIL RIGHTS ACT OF 1871. LOCAL GOVERNMENT
   OFFICIALS COMPLAIN THAT BUSINESSMEN ARE USING THE CIVIL
   RIGHTS LAW TO RECOVER PROPERTY DAMAGES IN ZONING CASES,
   FRANCHISE AWARDS, AND CONTRACT DISPUTES. DISMISSED WORKERS
   WHO CLAIM A PROPERTY INTEREST IN LOST JOBS ARE ALSO SUING
   THEIR FORMER LOCAL GOVERNMENT EMPLOYERS. SENATOR MITCH
   MCCONNELL OF KENTUCKY HAS INTRODUCED LEGISLATION THAT WOULD
   CURTAIL THIS LAWSUIT EXPLOSION.

07039 PARK, J.
   REGIONAL CLEAVAGES AND ORIENTATIONS TOWARD THE POLITICAL
   SYSTEM IN SOUTH KOREA
   DISSERTATION ABSTRACTS INTERNATIONAL, 50(4) (OCT 89),
   1079-A.
      TERRITORIAL STRAINS, RESULTING MAINLY FROM UNEVEN
   PROGRESS AMONG REGIONS IN THE PROCESS OF MODERNIZATION, HAVE
   WORKED TO UNDERMINE SOCIAL UNITY IN KOREA. MANY SOCIAL AND
   POLITICAL PROBLEMS ARE DUE TO TERRITORIAL CLEAVAGES BETWEEN
   YUNGNAM AND HONAM. THIS STUDY PROBES THE EXTENT TO WHICH AND
   THE WAYS IN WHICH REGIONAL CONFLICTS BETWEEN HONAM AND
   YUNGNAM HAVE AFFECTED THE OPERATION OF THE CONTEMPORARY
   KOREAN POLITICAL SYSTEM.

07040 PARK, J.Y.
   KOREA'S RETURN TO ASIA: AN ANALYSIS OF NEW MOVES IN SOUTH
   KOREAN DIPLOMACY IN THE 1960'S AND 1970'S
   DISSERTATION ABSTRACTS INTERNATIONAL, 49(12) (JUN 89),
   3863-A.
      FOLLOWING THE MILITARY REVOLUTION IN 1961, SOUTH KOREA'S
   NEW LEADERSHIP TRANSFORMED THE COUNTRY'S PASSIVE DIPLOMATIC
   POSTURE INTO AN ACTIVE, OUTWARD-DIRECTED FOREIGN POLICY. TO
   EXPLAIN THE CHANGING ASPECTS OF SOUTH KOREAN FOREIGN POLICY,
   THIS DISSERTATION USES THREE THEORIES OF INTERNATIONAL
   RELATIONS: THE SECURITY-PROSPERITY-PRESTIGE PARADIGM, THE
   ALLIANCE POLITICS THEORY, AND THE SMALL-POWER POLITICS
   THEORY. IT IDENTIFIES SIX MAJOR DETERMINANTS THAT LED SOUTH
   KOREA TO PRACTICE ACTIVE DIPLOMACY IN ASIA.

07041 PARK, K.
   AMERICAN FOREIGN POLICY TOWARD EAST ASIA # (CHINA, KOREA,
   AND JAPAN)
   DISSERTATION ABSTRACTS INTERNATIONAL, 49(11) (MAY 89),
   3499-A.
      THE AUTHOR EXAMINES THREE CASE STUDIES OF UNITED STATES
   FOREIGN POLICY IN THE EMERGING ERA OF THE COLD WAR: US-CHINA
   POLICY FROM 1946 TO 1949, US POLICY TOWARD KOREA FROM 1945
   TO 1948, AND US POLICY TOWARD JAPAN'S LABOR MOVEMENT FROM
   1945 TO 1947.

07042 PARK, K.U.
   FUTURE OF NORTH - SOUTH KOREAN RELATIONS AND DESIRABLE
   ROLES OF THE UNITED STATES
   AVAILABLE FROM NTIS, NO. AD-A202 749/8/GAR, APR 88, 44.
      SINCE THE END OF THE KOREAN WAR, BOTH NORTH AND SOUTH
   KOREA HAVE BEEN BUILDING UP THEIR MILITARY POWER. THE ARMS
   RACE AND PRECARIOUS MILITARY BALANCE HAVE INCREASED THE RISK
   OF A MILITARY CONFLICT BETWEEN THE NORTH AND SOUTH WHICH
   COULD RESULT IN THE MAJOR POWERS' INVOLVEMENT. IN RECENT
   YEARS, VARIOUS PLANS FOR DEESCALATION AND CONFLICT
   RESOLUTION HAVE BEEN ATTEMPTED TO ENHANCE STABILITY ON THE
   KOREAN PENINSULA WITHOUT AVAIL. THE GEOPOLITICAL LOCATION OF
   THE KOREAN PENINSULA AND HISTORY OF THE SUPERPOWER
   INTERVENTION IN INTER-KOREAN RELATIONS MAKE IT IMPOSSIBLE TO
   ATTEMPT ANY PROGNOSIS OF FUTURE INTER-KOREAN RELATIONS

WITHOUT ASSESSING EXPECTED ACTIONS OF THE CONCERNED POWERS,
NAMELY THE U.S., SOVIET UNION, CHINA, AND JAPAN. THE U.S. IS
THE ONLY NATION AMONG THE FOUR THAT HAS NOT SHOWN ANY
TERRITORIAL INTEREST IN THE KOREAN PENINSULA, AND ALSO HAS
DIVERSE AND MULTI-PRONGED COOPERATIVE RELATIONS WITH ALL
CONCERNED POWERS. THE U.S. CAN INITIATE AN EFFORT TO KEEP
PEACE ON THE KOREAN PENINSULA. THIS PAPER REVIEWS PRESENT
SITUATIONS BETWEEN THE NORTH AND SOUTH KOREA AND DISCUSSES
THE SECURITY ENVIRONMENT ON THE KOREAN PENINSULA AND
SUGGESTS SEVERAL DESIRABLE ROLES OF THE UNITED STATES FOR
SUSTAINING PEACE ON THE KOREAN PENINSULA.

07043 PARK, S.
   THE STATE, REVOLUTION, AND DEVELOPMENT: A COMPARATIVE
   STUDY OF TRANSFORMATION OF THE STATE IN INDONESIA AND THE
   PHILIPPINES
   DISSERTATION ABSTRACTS INTERNATIONAL, 49(12) (JUN 89),
   3867-A.
      IN THE CLASSIC MARXIST AND PLURALIST PERSPECTIVES
   DERIVED FROM THE HISTORICAL CONTEXT OF METROPOLITAN
   CAPITALISM, THE STATE TENDS TO LACK AUTONOMY FROM SOCIAL
   FORCES SUCH AS THE ECONOMICALLY DOMINANT CLASS OR INTEREST
   GROUPS. THIS STUDY QUESTIONS THE VALIDITY OF THE BASICALLY
   SOCIETY-CENTERED PERSPECTIVES OF THE STATE IN DEPENDENT
   CAPITALISM BY CONCEPTUALIZING THE STATE AS A COHERENT
   INSTITUTIONAL STRUCTURE WITH ITS OWN INTERESTS AND BY
   COMPARING HISTORICAL TRANSFORMATION OF THE POLITICAL FORM
   AND ECONOMIC ROLE OF THE STATE IN INDONESIA AND THE
   PHILIPPINES.

07044 PARK, S.B.
   MODERN SPATIAL THEORY AND IDEOLOGICAL DIMENSIONS OF
   POLITICAL CONFLICTS: THE KOREAN PRESIDENTIAL ELECTION OF
   1987
   DISSERTATION ABSTRACTS INTERNATIONAL, 50(6) (DEC 89),
   1789-A.
      THIS THESIS WAS PREDICATED ON THE ASSUMPTION THAT MODERN
   SPATIAL THEORY HAS A PROMISING FUTURE IN ELECTION STUDIES OF
   NON-WESTERN DEMOCRACIES AND IN THE COMPARATIVE STUDY OF
   POLITICS THROUGH AN EMPIRICAL STUDY OF IDEOLOGY. TO TEST
   THIS ASSUMPTION, THE AUTHOR USES THREE SURVEYS OF THE 1987
   KOREAN ELECTORATE.

07045 PARK, T.H.
   THE POSITIVE ANALYSIS OF HIERARCHICAL BEHAVIOR AND
   DECISION IN ORGANIZATIONS
   DISSERTATION ABSTRACTS INTERNATIONAL, 50(6) (DEC 89),
   1800-A.
      THE AUTHOR UTILIZES A POSITIVE ANALYSIS OF
   ORGANIZATIONAL HIERARCHY TO PROVIDE A NEW PERSPECTIVE ON
   BUREAUCRATIC PATHOLOGIES: INEFFICIENCY, UNRESPONSIVENESS,
   INHUMANITY, AND IMMORALITY. THE ANALYSIS YIELDS SOME
   IMPLICATIONS FOR ORGANIZATIONAL DESIGN AND MANAGEMENT IN
   SOLVING THESE CHRONIC PATHOLOGIES.

07046 PARK, W.
   ALLIANCE, INDEPENDENCE, AND SECURITY: AN ANALYSIS OF
   BRITISH DEFENSE POLICY
   JOHN SPIERS PUBLISHING, BRIGHTON, SUSSEX, GB, 1989, 256.
      THE AUTHOR ANALYZES THE OPTIONS OPEN TO BRITISH DEFENSE
   POLICY MAKERS. SUBJECTS INCLUDE THE PROS AND CONS OF THE
   INDEPENDENT NUCLEAR DETERRENT. THE NAVAL CONTRIBUTION IN THE
   EASTERN ATLANTIC, THE OUT-OF-AREA ROLE, HOME DEFENSE, AND
   THE COMMITMENTS ON THE CENTRAL FRONT AND THE NORTHERN FLANK.

07047 PARK, Y.H.
   STATE, SOCIETY, AND AUTHORITARIAN DEVELOPMENT: THE CASE OF
   KOREA
   DISSERTATION ABSTRACTS INTERNATIONAL, 50(2) (AUG 89),
   536-A.
      THE AUTHOR CONSTRUCTS A STATE-CENTERED FRAMEWORK TO TEST
   THE PROPOSITION THAT UNDERSTANDING POLITICAL CHANGE IN SOUTH
   KOREA REQUIRES THE EXAMINATION OF THE RELATIONSHIP BETWEEN
   THE STATE AND SOCIETY IN A MACROSCOPIC MANNER. HE ARGUES
   THAT, GIVEN THE NATURE OF ITS POLITICAL AND ECONOMIC
   SITUATION, THE KOREAN STATE HAS PLAYED A KEY ROLE IN
   DIRECTING THE COURSE OF ECONOMIC DEVELOPMENT AND POLITICAL
   CHANGE IN THE PROCESS OF RAPID INDUSTRIALIZATION.

07048 PARKER, A.
   DAVID DUKE'S SHORT JOURNEY FROM KKK TO GOP
   SOJOURNERS, 18(5) (MAY 89), 6.
      THE ELECTION OF FORMER GRAND WIZARD OF THE KU KLUX KLAN,
   DAVID DUKE, TO THE LOUISIANA STATE LEGISLATURE IS MERELY A
   SYMPTOM OF THE UNDERLYING INSECURITY AND RACIAL TENSION FELT
   BY WHITES IN THE SOUTH AND USED BY THE REPUBLICAN PARTY TO
   GAIN VOTES. THE REPUBLICAN PARTY'S DENUNCIATION OF DUKE IS
   VIEWED AS HYPOCRITCAL IN LIGHT OF THE RECENT USE OF THE
   WILLIE HORTON ISSUE--A BLACK CONVICTED MURDERED WHO RAPED A
   WHITE WOMEN WHILE ON PRISON FURLOUGH--TO WIN VOTES IN THE
   SOUTH.

07049 PARKER, A.
   WHEN ANY BLACK WILL DO

SOJOURNERS, 18(10) (NOV 89), 4-5.
THE RACIALLY MOTIVATED MURDER OF YUSEF HAWKINS, A BLACK
NEW YORK YOUTH, AND THE LABOR DAY RACIAL UNREST AT VIRGINIA
CLEARLY REVEAL THAT AMERICA HAS FAR TO GO BEFORE IT BECOMES
A "COLOR BLIND" SOCIETY. STATEMENTS THAT BLACKS ARE AN
UNDERCLASS NOT DUE TO THEIR RACE, BUT DUE TO POVERTY OR
WIDESPREAD DRUG USAGE ONLY INCREASE THE PROBLEM AND STYMIE
EFFORTS AT SOLUTIONS.

07050 PARKER, A.A.
BOTHA'S SMOKESCREEN OF REFORM
SOJOURNERS, 18(2) (FEB 89), 5-6.
AN EXAMINATION OF THE CONFLICT BETWEEN SOUTH AFRICA'S
PRESIDENT P.W. BOTHA AND THE CONSERVATIVE PARTY REVEALS THAT
BOTH ARE PRO-APARTHEID. BOTHA CRITICIZES THE CONSERVATIVES
FOR ENFORCING STRICT APARTHEID LAWS IN THE MUNICIPAL
GOVERNMENTS THEY CONTROL, BUT THE NATIONAL PARTY ALSO
OBSERVES APARTHEID LAWS IN COMMUNITIES THEY DOMINATE.

07051 PARKER, A.A.
TRAGEDY IN CHINA
SOJOURNERS, 18(8) (AUG 89), 4-5.
CHINA'S ALREADY DAMAGED CREDIBILITY IN WORLD OPINION
WILL WORSEN IF THE REPRESSION CONTINUES. THE PEOPLE WHO ARE
MOST ABLE TO DELIVER ON DENG'S DESIRE TO MAKE CHINA MORE
ECONOMICALLY COMPETITIVE WILL NOT DO IT WITHOUT THE BASIC
FREEDOMS OF PRESS, SPEECH, ASSEMBLY, AND A MORE DEMOCRATIC
STYLE OF GOVERNMENT. BY NEUTRALIZING THEM, DENG THREATENS
CHINA'S FUTURE.

07052 PARKER, G.R.
LOOKING BEYOND REELECTION: REVISING ASSUMPTIONS ABOUT THE
FACTORS MOTIVATING CONGRESSIONAL BEHAVIOR
PUBLIC CHOICE, 63(3) (DEC 89), 237-252.
THIS PAPER CHALLENGES THE ASSUMPTION WHERENT IN MOST
MODELS OF LEGISLATIVE BEHAVIOR - NAMELY THAT CONGRESSMEN ARE
DRIVEN BY THE DESIRE FOR REFLECTION, DRIVEN BY THE DESIRE
FOR REELECTION. IT OFFERS AN ALTERNATIVE PERSPECTIVE:
INCUMBENTS SEEK TO MAXIMIZE THEIR DISCRETIONARY INVESTMENTS
AND THE INCOME GENERATED BY THE JOB. THE ONLY CONSTRAINT ON
THIS BEHAVIOR IS THAT LEGISLATORS PROVIDE A SATISFACTORY
LEVEL OF CONSTITUENCY SERVICE - A PRODUCT THAT THE AUTHOR
SUGGESTS ENTAILS SLIGHT OPPORTUNITY, AND FEW MANUFACTURING,
COSTS FOR CONGRESSMEN, AND ONE THAT IS UNLIKELY TO LOSE ITS
VALUE WITH INCREASED PRODUCTION. IT ALSO DEMONSTRATES THAT
INCREASES IN SALARY AND DISCRETIONARY INVESTMENTS HAVE
LENGTHENED CONGRESSIONAL CAREERS.

07053 PARKER, G.R.
THE ROLE OF CONSTITUENT TRUST IN CONGRESSIONAL ELECTIONS
PUBLIC OPINION QUARTERLY, 53(2) (SUM 89), 175-196.
THE PURPOSE OF THIS INQUIRY IS TO INTRODUCE A NEW
VARIABLE INTO THE STUDY OF CONGRESSIONAL ELECTIONS--
CONSTITUENT TRUST. CONSTITUENT TRUST IS DEFINED AS THE LEVEL
OF CONFIDENCE THAT CONSTITUENTS HAVE IN THEIR ELECTED
REPRESENTATIVE. THIS ANALYSIS SUGGESTS A STRATEGY FOR
MEASURING CONSTITUENT TRUST AND DEVELOPS A MODEL THAT
RELATES CONSTITUENT TRUST DIRECTLY AND INDIRECTLY TO
ELECTORAL SUPPORT. WHEN CONSTITUENT TRUST IS SALIENT IN
VOTER COGNITIONS, IT HAS A SIGNIFICANT DIRECT INFLUENCE ON
ELECTORAL SUPPORT AND IS A BETTER PREDICTOR OF ELECTORAL
SUPPORT THAN THE INCUMBENT'S PARTY IDENTIFICATION. IN
ADDITION TO ITS DIRECT EFFECTS, CONSTITUENT TRUST INDIRECTLY
INFLUENCES ELECTORAL SUPPORT BECAUSE OF ITS CAUSAL
RELATIONSHIP TO INCUMBENT POPULARITY.

07054 PARKER, R.
ASSESSING PERESTROIKA
WORLD POLICY JOURNAL, VI(2) (SPR 89), 265-296.
AFTER A FIVE WEEK VISIT TO THE SOVIET UNION, THE AUTHOR
ASSESSES THE ONGOING PHENOMENON OF PERESTROIKA. HE CONCLUDES
THAT CONTRARY TO POPULAR OPINION IN THE WEST, THE FAILURE OF
PERESTROIKA IS NOT A FOREGONE CONCLUSION AND THAT
GORBACHEV'S ECONOMIC REFORMS ARE MAKING SIGNIFICANT AND
MEASURABLE PROGRESS. HE ALSO FOUND EVIDENCE OF A STANDARD OF
LIVING AMONG SOVIET CITIZENS THAT IS HIGHER THAN GENERALLY
BELIEVED IN THE WEST. HE DISCUSSES IN DETAIL THE VARIOUS
STAGES OF THE PLANNED REFORMS AND THE CHALLENGES THAT SOVIET
REFORMERS ARE FACING AND WILL FACE IN THE FUTURE.

07055 PARKER, R.S.
THE QUEST FOR ADMINISTRATIVE LEADERSHIP
POLITICAL SCIENCE, 41(2) (DEC 89), 18-29.
THE AUTHOR BRIEFLY TRACES HOW THE IDEA OF AN
ADMINISTRATIVE CADRE SEEMS AT LAST TO HAVE TRIUMPHED OVER
THE POWERFUL FORCES OF INERTIA, EXPEDIENCE, AND VESTED
INTEREST IN AUSTRALIA AND NEW ZEALAND. THEN HE EXPLORES SOME
OF THE IMPLICATIONS FOR THE ADMINISTRATIVE CADRE OF THE
DRAMATIC CHANGES IN GOVERNMENT AND ADMINISTRATION IN
AUSTRALIA AND NEW ZEALAND OVER THE PAST DECADE.

07056 PARKS, R.B.; OAKERSON, R.J.
METROPOLITAN ORGANIZATION AND GOVERNANCE: A LOCAL PUBLIC
ECONOMY APPROACH

URBAN AFFAIRS QUARTERLY, 25(1) (SEP 89), 18-29.
NEW CONCEPTUALIZATIONS ARE NEEDED TO ENCOMPASS
CUMULATING RESEARCH FINDINGS THAT COMPLEX,
MULTIJURISDICTIONAL, MULTILEVEL ORGANIZATION IS A PRODUCTIVE
ARRANGEMENT FOR METROPOLITAN AREAS. A LOCAL PUBLIC ECONOMY
APPROACH RECOGNIZES (1) THE DISTINCTION BETWEEN PROVISION
AND PRODUCTION, AND THE DIFFERENT CONSIDERATIONS THAT BEAR
ON EACH; (2) THE DISTINCTION BETWEEN GOVERNANCE AND
GOVERNMENT, AND THE MULTIPLE LEVELS OF GOVERNANCE; (3) THE
DIFFERENCE BETWEEN METROPOLITAN FRAGMENTATION AND COMPLEX
METROPOLITAN ORGANIZATION, AND THE PREVALENCE OF THE COMPLEX
ORGANIZATION OVER FRAGMENTATION; AND (4) THE NECESSITY FOR
CITIZEN CHOICE AND PUBLIC ENTREPRENEURSHIP IN CRAFTING
PRODUCTIVE ORGANIZATIONAL AND GOVERNANCE ARRANGEMENTS. IT
MAY CONTRIBUTE TO A RETHINKING WITH RESPECT TO GOVERNANCE
STRUCTURES ADAPTED TO THE DIVERSITY CHARACTERISTIC OF
AMERICAN METROPOLITAN AREAS.

07057 PARMET, W.E.
LEGAL RIGHTS AND COMMUNICABLE DISEASE: AIDS, THE POLICE
POWER, AND INDIVIDUAL LIBERTY
JOURNAL OF HEALTH POLITICS, POLICY AND LAW, 14(4) (WIN 89),
741-772.
THE POLICY DEBATE OVER AIDS HAS FOCUSED ON HOW TO
BALANCE THE RIGHTS OF INDIVIDUALS WHO HAVE THE DISEASE
AGAINST THE RIGHTS OF THE PUBLIC. THIS PAPER EXAMINES THE
NATURE OF BOTH SETS OF RIGHTS BY ANALYZING THE DEVELOPMENT
OF PUBLIC HEALTH LAW AND ITS DOMINANT VISIONS TODAY. THE
ARTICLE ARGUES THAT WHILE ONCE PUBLIC HEALTH RIGHTS IMPLIED
A VAST RESERVE OF COMMUNITY AUTHORITY AND OBLIGATION TO
PREVENT ILLNESS, TODAY THE RIGHTS OF THE PUBLIC AND THOSE OF
INDIVIDUALS ARE SEEN AS BEING IN OPPOSITION. PUBLIC HEALTH
JURISPRUDENCE NOW PRESUPPOSES THAT ILLNESS IS PRIMARILY A
MATTER OF INDIVIDUAL CONCERN. IN THIS VIEW, THE SCIENCE OF
MEDICINE MEDIATES THE RELATIONSHIP BETWEEN THE INDIVIDUAL
AND THE PUBLIC. THIS UNDERSTANDING OF RIGHTS PROTECTS SOME
OF THE INTERESTS OF INFECTED INDIVIDUALS, BUT IS INADEQUATE
FOR ADDRESSING MANY OF THE MAJOR PROBLEMS RAISED BY THE AIDS
EPIDEMIC, PARTICULARLY THE SPREAD OF INFECTION AMONG THE
UNINFECTED.

07058 PARRI, L.
TERRITORIAL POLITICAL EXCHANGE IN FEDERAL AND UNITARY
COUNTRIES
WEST EUROPEAN POLITICS, 12(3) (JUL 89), 197-219.
THIS ARTICLE CONSIDERS TERRITORIAL POLITICS IN ITALY,
FRANCE, SWITZERLAND AND THE FEDERAL REPUBLIC OF GERMANY. ITS
PURPOSE IS TO DEMONSTRATE THAT THESE WHICH JUDGE BOTH
UNITARY-REGIONALISED AND FEDERAL CO-OPERATIVE SYSTEMS AS
HAVING BECOME CENTRALISED REST ON STATIC AND FORMAL
JURIDICAL ANALYSES. A BROADER APPROACH, GROUNDED ON THE
DYNAMICS OF INTERGOVERNMENTAL PUBLIC POLICIES AND UTILISING
AN EXCHANGE-BASED CONCEPT OF POWER, IS PROPOSED. IN SUCH A
FRAMEWORK, A GOVERNMENT LEVEL IS CONSIDERD AS A COMPLEX
ORGANISATION POSSESSING JURIDICO-INSTITUTIONAL, FINANCIAL,
ADMINISTRATIVE AND POLITICO-REPRESENTATIVE POWER RESOURCES.
IN THE FOUR COUNTRIES CONSIDERED, THE NATIONAL GOVERNMENT
DOES NOT POSSESS ENOUGH RESOURCES HIERARCHICALLY TO CONTROL
THE SUBNATIONAL GOVERNMENTS. THE LATTER, ON THE BASIS OF THE
MOBILISATION OF RESOURCES, FORCE THE FORMER TO NEGOTIATE THE
CONTENT OF DECISIONMAKING AND IMPLEMENTATION OF NATIONWIDE
INTEGRATED POLICIES. THIS NEGOTIATION PROCESS IS DEFINED AS
TERRITORIAL POLITICAL EXCHANGE.

07059 PARRY, G.
DEMOCRACY AND AMATEURISM: THE INFORMED CITIZEN
GOVERNMENT AND OPPOSITION, 24(4) (AUT 89), 489-502.
THE AUTHOR FOCUSES ON ONE ASPECT OF THE PROBLEM OF
POLITICAL KNOWLEDGE WHICH IS IMPORTANT TO AN UNDERSTANDING
OF MODERN DEMOCRACY. THIS IS THE KNOWLEDGE ATTRIBUTED TO THE
CITIZEN, WHICH RAISES QUESTIONS ABOUT THE INFLUENCE OF
CITIZENS VERSUS THE INFLUENCE OF EXPERTS.

07060 PARSONS, A.
IRAN AND WESTERN EUROPE
MIDDLE EAST JOURNAL, 43(2) (SPR 89), 218-229.
THE ARTICLE EXAMINES THE RELATIONS BETWEEN IRAN AND THE
NATIONS OF WESTERN EUROPE AFTER THE ISLAMIC REVOLUTION. IT
OUTLINES THE EFFORTS OF THE EUROPEAN COMMUNITY OVER THE PAST
10 YEARS TO TRY AND COME TO TERMS WITH THE REVOLUTION AND TO
PROTECT THEIR INTERESTS, AND SETS FORTH A BALANCE SHEET OF
THEIR SUCCESSES AND FAILURES. IT MAKES SPECIAL REFERENCE TO
BRITAIN, FRANCE, WEST GERMANY, AND ITALY AND STUDIES THE
EFFECTS OF THE HOSTAGE CRISIS AND THE IRAN-IRAQ WAR ON
IRAN'S FOREIGN RELATIONS.

07061 PARSONS, A.
THE CASE FOR DIRECT NEGOTIATIONS
MIDDLE EAST INTERNATIONAL, (341) (JAN 89), 17-18.
THE DIPLOMATIC ASPECT OF THE PALESTINIAN PROBLEM HAS
RECENTLY CHANGED SHAPE MORE RADICALLY THAN AT ANY TIME SINCE
THE ISRAELI OCCUPATION OF JUNE 1967. ISRAEL NOW APPEARS TO
HAVE NO VALID ALTERNATIVE BETWEEN A CONTINUED REFUSAL TO
NEGOTIATE OR NEGOTIATING WITH THE PLO AS PROPOSED. ALL

ISRAELIS MUST BE CONSCIOUS THAT THEY WILL BE UNDER GREAT
PRESSURE, EVEN FROM THE USA, TO NEGOTIATE.

07062 PARSONS, E.
SOME INTERNATIONAL IMPLICATIONS OF THE 1918 ROOSEVELT-
LODGE CAMPAIGN AGAINST WILSON AND A DEMOCRATIC CONGRESS
PRESIDENTIAL STUDIES QUARTERLY, XIX(1) (WIN 89), 141-158.
THE STANCE OF THEODORE ROOSEVELT AND HENRY CABOT LODGE
AGAINST WOODROW WILSON DURING WORLD WAR I IS USUALLY
ATTRIBUTED TO PARTISAN POLITICAL BIAS. THE ESSAY ARGUES THAT
THEIR HATRED OF WILSON ALSO STEMMED FROM THEIR APPREHENSION
THAT THE PRESIDENT, DURING AMERICA'S PARTICIPATION IN THE
WAR, SOUGHT A COMPROMISE PEACE WHICH WOULD LEAVE GERMANY
WITH SUBSTANTIAL POWER AND WITH HER KAISER ON THE THRONE. IT
ALSO ARGUES THAT THEIR LOVE OF GREAT BRITAIN AND THEIR FEAR
THAT WILSON PEACE TERMS WOULD WEAKEN HER LED THEM TO
ENCOURAGE THE BRITISH LEADERS TO STAND FAST AGAINST THE
PRESIDENT'S PERCEIVED INTENTIONS TOWARD THE SUPREMACY OF THE
ROYAL NAVY. AND THE PRE-EMINENCE OF THE EMPIRE. THE ESSAY
ATTEMPTS TO INDICATE THE EXTENT TO WHICH THEIR PERCEPTIONS
OF WILSON'S INTENTIONS WERE ACCURATE.

07063 PARSONS, H.
COOPERATION BETWEEN MARXISTS AND RELIGIOUS BELIEVERS
POLITICAL AFFAIRS, LXVIII(11) (NOV 89), 11-17.
THE ARTICLE EXAMINES THE IDEOLOGICAL DIFFERENCES THAT
HAS TRADITIONALLY PLACED RELIGIOUS GROUPS AND MARXIST GROUPS
IN OPPOSITION. THE HISTORICAL DISTRUST IS EXACERBATED BY THE
INCREASING SEPARATION OF RELIGION AND STATE IN THE MODERN
SECULAR WORLD. HOWEVER, BOTH GROUPS SHARE A COMMON FEAR OF
GLOBAL ANNIHILATION AND BOTH DESIRE TO IMPROVE THE HUMAN
CONDITION. THE ARTICLE CONCLUDES THAT COOPERATION BETWEEN
THE TWO GROUPS IS FEASIBLE AND DESIRABLE.

07064 PARSONS, H. L.
CREATIVE INTERACTION IN THE STRUGGLE FOR PEACE
POLITICAL AFFAIRS, LXVIII(1) (JAN 89), 20-27.
FACTORS IN THE CREATIVE INTERACTION BETWEEN PERSONS IN
THE STRUGGLE FOR PEACE INCLUDE WILLINGNESS TO INTERACT,
ACKNOWLEDGEMENT OF INTERDEPENDENCE, RESPECT FOR DIFFERENCES,
RENUNCIATION OF CENTRIC CLAIMS, COMMUNICATION, TRUST, AND
RENUNCIATION OF WAR.

07065 PASCAL, N.S.
EAST EUROPEAN-SOVIET RELATIONS IN A CHANGING ECONOMIC
ENVIRONMENT
EAST EUROPEAN QUARTERLY, XXIII(1) (MAR 89), 99-107.
THIS PAPER EXAMINES CHANGES IN TRADE RELATIONS BETWEEN
THE USSR AND CMEA IN THE 1980'S AND CHANGES IN THE COMMODITY
COMPOSITION OF USSR-CMEA TRADE, ESPECIALLY IN MACHINERY AND
ENERGY.

07066 PASOUR, E.C. JR.
NONCONVENTIONAL COSTS OF RENT-SEEKING: X-INEFFICIENCY IN
THE POLITICAL PROCESS
PUBLIC CHOICE, 63(1) (OCT 89), 87-92.
THIS ARTICLE DEPARTS FROM THE TRADITIONAL DEFINITION OF
RENT SEEKING WHICH REFERS TO RESOURCE-WASTING ACTIVITIES OF
INDIVIDUALS IN SEEKING TRANSFERS OF WEALTH THROUGH THE AEGIS
OF THE STATE. SOURCES OF INNEFFICIENCY IN THE POLITICAL
PROCESS MAY RESULT FROM VOTERS VOTING IN TERMS OF THEIR
SPECIAL INTEREST OR BECAUSE THEY LACK INFORMATION ABOUT THE
EFFECTS OF THE POLICIES. THE ARTICLE SHOWS THAT APPARENT
MISTAKES BECAUSE OF A LACK OF INFORMATION ABOUT POLITICAL
CONDITIONS IS EQUIVALENT TO "X-INEFFICIENCY IN THE MARKET
BUT IS DIFFERENT THAN THE CONVENTIONAL RENT-SEEKING ACTIVITY
DEFINITION.

07067 PASQUINO, G.
THAT OBSCURE OBJECT OF DESIRE: A NEW ELECTORAL LAW FOR
ITALY
WEST EUROPEAN POLITICS, 12(3) (JUL 89), 280-294.
THIS ARTICLE ANALYSES THE MOST IMPORTANT REASONS THAT
MIGHT MAKE IT NECESSARY TO REVISE THE ITALIAN ELECTORAL
SYSTEM. THE TYPE OF PROPORTIONAL REPRESENTATION UTILISED IN
THE ITALIAN SYSTEM (IMPERIALI WITH THE HIGHEST REMAINDER)
HAS ALLOWED THE FRAGMENTATION OF THE PARTY SYSTEM AND
PRODUCED A PRIVILEGED SITUATION FOR SOME PARTIES, PREVENTING
ALTERNATION IN POWER. THE MAJOR REFORM PROPOSALS ARE
REVIEWED AND EVALUATED ACCORDING TO THEIR PARTISAN
OBJECTIVES AND SYSTEMIC CONSEQUENCES. FEW PROPOSALS SEEM TO
PASS THIS TEST. THE ISSUE OF AN ELECTORAL REFORM IS ON THE
POLITICAL AGENDA, AND ALTHOUGH SCEPTICISM AS TO ITS
FEASIBILITY IS IN ORDER, THE TIME FOR INSTITUTIONAL AND
ELECTORAL REFORM SEEMS TO BE APPROACHING.

07068 PASSIN, H.
TWENTY YEARS ON
ENCOUNTER, LXXII(5) (MAY 89), 64-67.
DURING THE PAST TWO DECADES, THE US-JAPANESE
RELATIONSHIP HAS CHANGED DRAMATICALLY. JAPAN HAS GROWN
LARGER, THE UNITED STATES SMALLER, AND THE FUNDAMENTAL
STRUCTURE OF THE WORLD ORDER HAS BEEN ALTERED. THE UNITED
STATES' GNP IS NOW ABOUT TWICE THE SIZE OF JAPAN'S, WHICH

MEANS THAT PER CAPITA GNP IS ABOUT THE SAME. THE USA REMAINS
THE MOST POWERFUL SINGLE COUNTRY IN THE WORLD BUT IT NO
LONGER EXCELS IN ALL INDICATORS AND IS NO LONGER AS
OVERWHELMINGLY DOMINANT AS BEFORE.

07069 PASTOR, M. JR.
LATIN AMERICA, THE DEBT CRISIS, AND THE INTERNATIONAL
MONETARY FUND
LATIN AMERICAN PERSPECTIVES, 16(1) (WIN 89), 79-110.
IN THIS ARTICLE THE AUTHOR EXAMINES THE ROLE OF THE IMF
IN MANAGING THE LATIN AMERICA DEBT CRISIS. THE ARTICLE
PROVIDES A BRIEF REVIEW OF VARIOUS EXPLANATIONS OF THE
CAUSES OF THE CRISIS, SUGGESTING VARIOUS INADEQUACIES IN
BOTH THE FUND'S ORTHODOX APPROACH AND THE APPROACH OF ITS
MAINSTREAM LIBERAL CRITICS. THIS ARTICLE BRIEFLY DISCUSSES
SOME ELEMENTS OF A LEFT ANALYSIS OF THE CRISIS. NEXT THE
AUTHOR EXAMINES THE ENTRANCE OF THE FUND INTO THE CRISIS AND
SUGGEST THAT THE FUND'S ABILITY TO ENFORCE ITS VISION OF
APPROPRIATE POLICY HAS DRAMATICALLY ENHANCED IN THE CAPITAL-
SCARCE WORLD OF THE 1980S. COORDINATING PRIVATE CAPITAL
FLOWS AND STEERING MACROECONOMIC POLICY IN ALMOST EVERY
COUNTRY IN LATIN AMERICA, THE IMF HAS ACTED ALMOST AS A
GLOBAL CAPITALIST PLANNER.

07070 PASTOR, R.A.
FORGING A HEMISPHERIC BARGAIN: THE BUSH OPPORTUNITY*
JOURNAL OF INTERNATIONAL AFFAIRS, 43(1) (SUM 89), 69-82.
THIS ARTICLE EXPLORES THE SITUATION IN THE WESTERN
HEMISPHERE WHERE CONFLICT IN CENTRAL AMERICA, THE DEBT AND
DRUG CRISIS, AND THE FRAGILITY OF THE NEW DEMOCRACIES HAS
REACHED THE POINT OF CRISIS AND SOLUTIONS ARE URGENTLY
NEEDED. IT EXAMINES BUSH'S OPPORTUNITY TO CONSTRUCT A
BIPARTISAN CONSENSUS AT HOME AND TO FORGE A COMMON APPROACH
AMONG THE DEMOCRACIES OF THE HEMISPHERE TO SOLVE THESE
PROBLEMS, IT EXPLORES THE POSSIBILITY OF ENLISTING EUROPEAN
AID.

07071 PATERNEK, M.A.
THE CLASSICAL LIBERAL CONCEPT OF LAW AND PUNISHMENT:
HOBBES, BENTHAM, AND FOUCAULT
DISSERTATION ABSTRACTS INTERNATIONAL, 50(6) (DEC 89),
1784-A.
THE AUTHOR JUXTAPOSES MICHEL FOUCAULT'S HISTORY OF
MODERN PUNITIVE PRACTICES WITH THE THEORETICAL JUSTIFICATION
OF THE STATE'S RIGHT TO PUNISH PROVIDED BY THOMAS HOBBES AND
JEREMY BENTHAM. THE PURVIEW OF CLASSICAL LIBERALISM IS
TANTAMOUNT TO THE ENDORSEMENT OF JURIDICAL SOVEREIGNTY,
WHILE THAT OF FOUCAULTIAN POST-MODERNIST ADVANCES FROM THE
EXPLICIT REJECTION OF LEGAL FICTION. HOBBES AND BENTHAM ARE
THE BEST REPRESENTATIVES OF THE JURIDICAL MODEL OF POWER
THAT FOUCAULT IS ATTEMPTING TO DESCRIBE, TO CRITICIZE, AND
ULTIMATELY TO OVERCOME. IT IS FROM BENTHAM'S UTILITARIAN
THEORY OF LAW AND PUNISHMENT THAT THE METAPHOR OF
PANOPTICISM, WHICH FORMS THE CORE OF FOUCAULT'S CRITIQUE, IS
DERIVED.

07072 PATERSON, T.
THE SECULAR CONTROL OF SCIENTIFIC POWER IN THE POLITICAL
PHILOSOPHY OF FRANCIS BACON
POLITY, XXI(3) (SPR 89), 457-480.
THIS ARTICLE IS A SEQUEL TO ONE PUBLISHED IN THE SPRING
1987 ISSUE OF POLITY BY THE SAME AUTHOR. THE FIRST ESSAY
ARGUED THAT FRANCIS BACON DID NOT SEE CHRISTIANITY AS THE
ULTIMATE GUIDE OF APPLIED SCIENCE. THIS ESSAY FOCUSES ON THE
PURELY SECULAR FACTORS WHICH BACON THOUGHT MIGHT SERVE AS
SUCH A GUIDE AND, IN PARTICULAR, ON HIS APPARENT SUGGESTION
THAT A POWER-GENERATING SCIENCE WOULD BE BENEFICIAL TO
MANKIND BECAUSE SCIENTISTS WOULD IN THE FUTURE PARTICIPATE
IN POLITICAL RULE. THE CENTRAL ARGUMENT HERE IS THAT WHILE
ANY SUCH SOLUTION TO THE PROBLEM OF THE MORAL AND POLITICAL
CONTROL OF SCIENTIFIC POWER NECESSARILY RESTS UPON A BELIEF
THAT SCIENTISTS AS SCIENTISTS WILL BE GOOD MEN, BACON'S
PSYCHOLOGY OF THE SCIENTIST SEEMS TO BE IN PROFOUND TENSION
WITH ANY SUCH SUGGESTION. THE AUTHOR CONCLUDES THAT BACON
RESOLVED THIS TENSION BY FINDING AN AMORAL SUBSTITUTE FOR
MORALITY IN THE DESIRE OF SCIENTISTS FOR FAME; THIS PURELY
SELFISH IMPULSE COULD LEAD SCIENTISTRULERS OF THE FUTURE TO
ACT AS IF THEY WERE IN FACT THE HUMANE AND CHARITABLE
SCIENTIST-SAINTS OF BACONIAN LEGEND.

07073 PATNAIK, L.K.
MODEL BUILDING IN POLITICAL SCIENCE
INDIAN JOURNAL OF POLITICAL SCIENCE, L(2) (APR 89),
234-250.
THE AUTHOR PRESENTS A SUMMARY OF THE WHOLE PROCESS OF
USING MODELS IN POLITICAL SCIENCE TO INTRODUCE THE CONCEPT,
THE HISTORY, TECHNIQUES, AND TYPES TO THE BEGINNER IN THE
FIELD.

07074 PATON, R.
MIDDLE MANAGERS: UPSCALE SUPERVISORS OR EMERGING EXECUTIVES
CANADIAN PUBLIC ADMINISTRATION, 32(2) (SUM 89), 244-260.
THE REQUIREMENTS FOR THE JOBS OF MIDDLE MANAGERS IN
GOVERNMENT ARE INCREASINGLY SIMILAR TO THE CHALLENGES THAT

FACE SENIOR EXECUTIVES. THIS IS DUE TO THE INCREASING RATE
OF CHANGE AND UNCERTAINTY IN THE PUBLIC SECTOR AND THE
GROWING INTERDEPENDENCE OF FUNCTIONS IN GOVERNMENT
ORGANIZATIONS. IT IS ALSO A RESULT OF THE CHANGING ROLE OF
SENIOR EXECUTIVES IN THE PUBLIC SECTOR. TO RESPOND TO CHANGE
MIDDLE MANAGERS WILL HAVE TO BROADEN THEIR SKILLS AND THEIR
UNDERSTANDING OF THEIR DEPARTMENTS AND THE GOVERNMENT
ENVIRONMENT. IN SHORT, THEIR JOBS WILL BECOME A LOT MORE
LIKE THOSE OF SENIOR EXECUTIVES AND A LOT LESS LIKE THE JOBS
OF SUPERVISORS.

07075 PATTERSON, H.
IRELAND: A NEW PHASE IN THE CONFLICT BETWEEN NATIONALISM
AND UNIONISM
SCIENCE AND SOCIETY, 53(2) (SUM 89), 192-218.
AGAINST THE BACKGROUND OF CHANGING ECONOMIC FORTUNES IN
BOTH THE REPUBLIC AND NORTHERN IRELAND, PATTERSON DISCUSSES
THE COMPLEX POLITICAL SITUATION OF CONTEMPORARY NORTHERN
IRELAND. REJECTING THE POPULAR INTERNATIONAL IMPRESSION THAT
IT IS A "RELIGIOUS" WAR FUELED BY THE BRITISH STATE,
PATTERSON FOCUSES ON DIVISIONS WITHIN NATIONALISM AND
UNIONISM, THE ROLE OF SOUTHERN NATIONALISTS AND THE BRITISH
STATE. ON THE POSSIBILITIES FOR POLITICAL PROGRESS, HE
CONCLUDES THAT THE RECENT ANGLO-IRISH AGREEMENT HAS
UNINTENTIONALLY INTENSIFIED SECTARIAN CONFLICT BETWEEN
PROTESTANTS AND CATHOLICS.

07076 PATTERSON, S.C.
PARTY LEADERSHIP IN THE U.S. SENATE
LEGISLATIVE STUDIES QUARTERLY, 14(3) (AUG 89), 393-414.
THE FIRST STEPS IN UNDERSTANDING U.S. SENATE PARTY
LEADERSHIP REQUIRE MAPPING AND ANALYZING ITS PROPERTIES AND
PROBLEMATICS. HERE, SENATE LEADERSHIP IS CHARACTERIZED AS
SITUATIONAL, PERSONALIZED, PARTISAN, COLLEGIAL, AND
MEDIATING. SENATE LEADERS FACE PERPLEXING INSTITUTIONAL
PROBLEMS -- PROBLEMS OF CONTEXT, MANAGEMENT, PARTY,
SUCCESSION, THE LEADER'S ROLE, AND EXTERNAL RELATIONS.
INVESTIGATING THE SALIENT FEATURES OF SENATE LEADERSHIP AND
THE INSTITUTIONAL PROBLEMS LEADERS CONFRONT WILL CONTRIBUTE
TO ANALYSES OF LEADERS' BEHAVIOR.

07077 PATTERSON, W.; BHATIA, S.; GLICKMAN, P.; HAYES, D.; PERERA,
J.; PINGPING, F.; QINGHUA, W.; STAUBUS, J.
POWER GENERATION
SOUTH, (102) (APR 89), 63-72.
UNTIL RECENTLY, INTERNATIONAL AID AGENCIES, SUCH AS THE
WORLD BANK AND THE EXPORT CREDIT BRANCHES OF NATIONAL
GOVERNMENTS IN THE INDUSTRIALIZED COUNTRIES, PARTICIPATED IN
MAJOR THIRD WORLD POWER-GENERATION PROJECTS. WITHIN THE PAST
TWO YEARS, HOWEVER, MANY OF THEM HAVE HAD SECOND THOUGHTS
ABOUT SUPPORTING PROJECTS THAT MIGHT DAMAGE THE ENVIRONMENT
AND LOCAL POPULATIONS, DUE TO PRESSURE FROM SCIENTISTS,
ENVIRONMENTALISTS, AND HUMAN RIGHTS GROUPS. THIRD WORLD
NUCLEAR POWER COULD BE ONE CASUALTY OF THE NEW TREND TOWARD
ENVIRONMENTAL AWARENESS.

07078 PATTON, P.
TAYLOR AND FOUCAULT ON POWER AND FREEDOM
POLITICAL STUDIES, XXXVII(2) (JUN 89), 260-276.
THE ARGUMENT OF THIS PAPER IS THAT FOUCAULT USES
CONCEPTS OF BOTH POWER AND FREEDOM WHICH ARE BASED UPON A
CONCEPT OF POWER WHICH IS NEITHER EVALUATIVE NOR
ANTITHETICAL TO FREEDOM. TO SHOW THIS, THE AUTHOR TAKES AS A
BASIS FOR COMPARATIVE DISCUSSION CHARLES TAYLOR'S ARTICLE,
'FOUCAULT ON FREEDOM AND TRUTH'. THIS PROVIDES A POINT OF
COMPARISON BECAUSE TAYLOR IS SUCH A STRONG EXPONENT OF THE
HUMANIST APPROACH WHICH FOUCAULT ESCHEWS. HE ALSO GOES
FURTHER THAN MOST CRITICS IN TURNING THE DIFFERENCES BETWEEN
FOUCAULT'S APPROACH AND HIS OWN INTO CRITICISMS, CHARGING
HIM WITH AN INCOHERENT THEORY OF POWER. OTHERS HAVE ARGUED
THAT TAYLOR'S CRITICISMS DO NOT ALWAYS FULLY ADDRESS
FOUCAULT'S POSITION. IN THIS ARTICLE THE AUTHOR TRIES TO
ADVANCE THIS ARGUMENT BY BRINGING TO THE SURFACE SOME OF THE
UNDERLYING DIFFERENCES IN THEIR RESPECTIVE CONCEPTS OF POWER,
FREEDOM AND SUBJECTIVITY.

07079 PAUL, J.C.N.
INTERNATIONAL DEVELOPMENT AGENCIES, HUMAN RIGHTS AND
HUMANE DEVELOPMENT PROJECTS
ALTERNATIVES, XIV(1) (JAN 89), 77-106.
THE DUTY TO PROTECT AND PROMOTE RIGHTS SHOULD BE SEEN AS
A MANDATORY OBLIGATION IMPOSED BY LAW; IT CANNOT BE IGNORED,
BUT SHOULD ALSO BE ASSUMED BY INTERNATIONAL DEVELOPMENT
AGENCIES (IDAS) AS A MATTER OF SOUND POLICY--POLICY BASED ON
BOTH LESSONS OF EXPERIENCE AND A GENERAL, INTERNATIONAL
CONSENSUS REGARDING THE OBJECTIVES OF "DEVELOPMENT." THIS
PAPER EXPLORES THE LEGAL BASES FOR THE OBLIGATION;
RELATIONSHIPS BETWEEN PARTICULAR KINDS OF DEVELOPMENT
PROJECTS AND PARTICULAR RIGHTS; THE KINDS OF HARMS CAUSED
WHEN THESE RIGHTS ARE IGNORED; AND STRATEGIES WHICH IDAS CAN
ADOPT TO PROTECT AND PROMOTE THEM.

07080 PAULS, F.H.
GOVERNANCE IN AMERICA: ENDURING BUT ESSENTIAL TENSIONS

CRS REVIEW, 10(1) (JAN 89), 2-3.
THE FRAMEWORK AND SAFEGUARDS DEVISED BY THE FOUNDING
FATHERS HAVE CREATED TENSIONS AND PROBLEMS THAT HAVE HAD TO
BE RESOLVED IN ORDER FOR THE AMERICAN SYSTEM OF DISPERSED
GOVERNMENT TO WORK WELL. THE DIVISION OF POWER BETWEEN
NATIONAL AND STATE GOVERNMENTS HAS REQUIRED ARTFUL EFFORT TO
ENSURE MUTUAL SUPPORT AND TO ALLOW FOR NATIONAL GOVERNMENT
INTERVENTION WHEN PROMOTION OF THE GENERAL WELFARE REQUIRES
FEDERAL FINANCIAL RESOURCES AND A COMMON APPROACH TO
PROBLEMS. THE EBB AND FLOW OF AUTHORITY IN THESE POWERS,
WHICH IS DIVIDED BUT FREQUENTLY OVERLAPS, MARK THIS AS ONE
OF THE ENDURING TENSIONS IMPLICIT IN THE CONSTITUTION.

07081 PAULS, F.H.; SAYLER, J.
THE CONGRESS AT 200
CRS REVIEW, 10(4) (APR 89), 30-32.
THE BUILDING OF AMERICA'S POLITICAL CULTURE OVER THE
PAST TWO CENTURIES HAS BEEN EXTRAORDINARY AND IS LIKELY TO
REMAIN SO. THE BUILDING OF THE STABILITY AND CONTINUITY OF
AMERICAN POLITICS DERIVES PARTLY FROM THE ABILITY OF
CONGRESS TO ACT DECISIVELY AND WITH DISPATCH WHEN NECESSARY,
AS AN EXPRESSION OF POLITICAL CULTURE.

07082 PAULSEN, G.E.
THE FEDERAL TRADE COMMISSION VERSUS THE NATIONAL RECOVERY
ADMINISTRATION: FAIR TRADE PRACTICES AND VOLUNTARY CODES,
1935
SOCIAL SCIENCE QUARTERLY, 70(1) (MAR 89), 149-163.
THIS STUDY EXAMINES THE FAILURE OF THE ROOSEVELT
ADMINISTRATION TO MAINTAIN "FAIR LABOR STANDARDS" THROUGH A
VOLUNTARY PROGRAM OF INDUSTRIAL REGULATION AFTER THE SUPREME
COURT VOIDED THE NRA CODES IN 1935. IT REVEALS THE HOSTILITY
OF THE FEDERAL TRADE COMMISSION AND THE JUSTICE DEPARTMENT
TOWARD THE PROGRAM, AND EXPLAINS WHY CONGRESS PREFERRED
TRADITIONAL ENFORCEMENT OF THE ANTITRUST LAWS.

07083 PAULY, L.
CHANGING INTERNATIONAL FINANCIAL MARKETS
FINANCE AND DEVELOPMENT. 26(4) (DEC 89), 34-37.
BASED PRINCIPALLY ON A BOOK CALLED "INTERNATIONAL
CAPITAL MARKETS: DEVELOPMENTS AND PROSPECTS," THIS IS A LOOK
AT THE FORCES CURRENTLY RESHAPING THE WORLD'S FINANCIAL
MARKETS AND THE CONSEQUENCES FOR BANKING IN BOTH INDUSTRIAL
AND DEVELOPING NATIONS. IT EXAMINES A VARIETY OF FACTORS
CHANGING CONTEMPORARY FINANCIAL MARKETS, NEW CAPITAL
ADEQUACY STANDARDS, MARKET INTEGRATION, AND ITS IMPACT ON
DEVELOPING COUNTRIES, A LISTING OF CAPITAL/ASSETS RATIOS OF
BANKS IN SELECTED INDUSTRIAL COUNTRIES 1980-1988 IS GIVEN.

07084 PAUS, E.
THE POLITICAL ECONOMY OF MANUFACTURED EXPORT GROWTH:
ARGENTINA AND BRAZIL IN THE 1970'S
JOURNAL OF DEVELOPING AREAS, 23(2) (JAN 89), 173-200.
ALTHOUGH THERE IS WIDESPREAD AGREEMENT AS TO THE
BENEFITS OF NONTRADITIONAL EXPORT GROWTH (NTEG), THERE IS NO
GENERALLY ACCEPTED THEORY CONCERNING WHICH GROUP OF FACTORS
IS MOST BENEFICIAL FOR ACHIEVING IT. THE PURPOSE OF THE
ARTICLE IS TO CONTRIBUTE THROUGH A CASE STUDY ANALYSIS TO AN
UNDERSTANDING OF THE FACTORS AND FORCES BEHIND NTEG. IT
ANALYZES AND COMPARES THE RATHER DIFFERENT EXPERIENCES OF
NTEG IN BRAZIL AND ARGENTINA IN THE 1970'S. IT DEMONSTRATES
THE IMPORTANCE OF UNDERSTANDING THE UNDERLYING
POLITICALECONOMIC STRUCTURE AND OF THE KEY ROLE THAT
POLITICAL FORCES PLAY IN THE FORMULATION OF ECONOMIC POLICY.

07085 PAVALKO, E.K.
STATE TIMING OF POLICY ADOPTION: WORKMEN'S COMPENSATION IN
THE UNITED STATES, 1909-1929
AMERICAN JOURNAL OF SOCIOLOGY, 95(3) (NOV 89), 592-615.
USING EVENT-HISTORY ANALYSIS, THIS STUDY OF WORKMEN'S
COMPENSATION ANALYZES HOW FAST AMERICAN STATE LEGISLATORS
RESPONDED TO THE WORKACCIDENT PROBLEM. STATES WERE QUICKER
TO ADOPT LEGISLATION WHEN PRODUCTIVITY AND WORK-ACCIDENT
LITIGATION WERE HIGH AND WHEN NONAGRICULTURAL WORKERS
OUTNUMBERED AGRICULTURAL ONES. DESPITE THE INFLUENCE OF
CAPITAL AND LABOR IN SHAPING WORKMEN'S COMPENSATION IN OTHER
ANALYSES, THE SPEED OF STATE LEGISLATION HAS UNAFFECTED BY
THE PRESENCE OF INTERESTS OF CAPITAL AND LABOR GROUPS. THIS
SUGGESTS THAT THE SPEED OF ADOPTION WAS SHAPED BY A
DIFFERENT ASPECT OF CAPITAL-LABOR RELATIONS THAN IS SEEN
WHEN STUDIES FOCUS ON THE ACTIVITIES OF SPECIFIC ACTORS OR
GROUPS.

07086 PAVLAK, T.J.; POPS, G.M.
ADMINISTRATIVE ETHICS AS JUSTICE
INTERNATIONAL JOURNAL OF PUBLIC ADMINISTRATION, 12(6) (NOV
89), 931-949.
THIS PAPER PRESENTS AN ETHICAL FRAMEWORK FOR DECISION-
MAKING IN PUBLIC ADMINISTRATION BASED ON THE PREEMINENT
VALUE OF JUSTICE. IN DISCUSSION OF THIS FRAMEWORK, THE PAPER
DEALS WITH THREE MAJOR ISSUES. THE FIRST OF THESE IS THE
CHARACTER OF THE JUST ADMINISTRATIVE DECISION, THE SECOND IS
THE CHARACTER OF OF THE JUST PUBLIC ORGANIZATION, AND THE
THIRD IS THE IMPACT OF A JUSTICE-BASED ADMINISTRATIVE ETHIC

ON THE ROLE OF THE RESPONSIBLE ADMINISTRATOR.

07087 PAYIND, A.
SOVIET-AFGHAN RELATIONS FROM COOPERATION TO OCCUPATION
INTERNATIONAL JOURNAL OF MIDDLE EAST STUDIES, 21(1) (FEB
89), 107-128.
A CAREFUL REVIEW OF SOVIET POLICY TOWARD AFGHANISTAN
FROM 1919, AND ESPECIALLY AFTER BRITAIN'S RETREAT FROM INDIA
IN 1947, REVEALS THAT THE KREMLIN'S POLICIES HAVE BEEN MORE
THAN JUST REACTIONS TO DANGERS AND THREATS. THE SOVIETS
OFTEN CREATED OPPORTUNITIES AND CAPITALIZED ON THEM. THEN,
WHEN THE KREMLIN RAN OUT OF OPTIONS AND COULD NOT EASILY
INFLUENCE THE DIRECTION OF AFGHAN DOMESTIC DEVELOPMENTS AND
FOREIGN POLICY, IT RESORTED TO RISKIER MEASURES. THESE RISKY
POLICIES HAVE GRADUALLY ESCALATED SOVIET INVOLVEMENT IN
AFGHANISTAN'S AFFAIRS. BUT A STRONG LOVE OF ISLAM, A LONG
HISTORY OF INDEPENDENCE, AND AND A TRADITION OF FIERCE
RESISTANCE TO FOREIGN INVADERS HAVE PRESENTED MAJOR BARRIERS
TO THE SOVIETS.

07088 PAYNE, A.
UNIVERSITY STUDENTS AND POLITICS IN JAMAICA
ROUND TABLE, (310) (APR 89), 207-222.
THE ARTICLE FOCUSES ON A CONFLICT BETWEEN UNIVERSITY
STUDENTS AND THE GOVERNMENT OF JAMAICA OVER FUNDING OF
HIGHER EDUCATION IN THE CARIBBEAN ISLAND. THE AFFAIR RAISED
A WIDE SET OF CONSIDERATIONS INCLUDING THE STRUCTURE OF THE
POLITICAL ECONOMY IN JAMAICA, THE ROLE OF STUDENTS IN
CARIBBEAN SOCIETY AND THE NATURE OF THE RELATIONSHIP BETWEEN
THE UNIVERSITY AND ITS SUPPORTING GOVERNMENTS. THE ARTICLE
EXAMINES THESE DIMENSIONS BY EXAMINING THE POSITIONS OF THE
DIFFERENT PARTIES INVOLVED INCLUDING THE STUDENTS, THE
UNIVERSITY, THE GOVERNMENT, AND A SPECIAL TASK FORCE CREATED
TO STUDY THE PROBLEM.

07089 PAYNE, A.J.
BRITAIN AND THE CARIBBEAN'S FUTURE
HEMISPHERE, 2(1) (FAL 89), 38-39.
SINCE OCTOBER 1983, THE BRITISH FOREIGN OFFICE HAS
DEVOTED CONSIDERABLE EFFORT TO REASSESSING BRITISH POLICY
TOWARDS THE CARIBBEAN AND TO WIDENING ITS FOCUS BEYOND A
NARROW PREOCCUPATION WITH COLD WAR ISSUES. FOLLOWING THE
GRENADA CRISIS, BRITAIN INCREASED ITS ASSISTANCE IN
PROVIDING EQUIPMENT AND TRAINING TO THE POLICE AND MILITARY
FORCES OF THE CARIBBEAN. OTHER NEW POLICY INITIATIVES HAVE
CONCERNED THE REMAINING BRITISH DEPENDENCIES AND THE GROWING
PROBLEM OF DRUGS.

07090 PAYNE, A.J.
THE FIJI EFFECT: A REVIEW OF TRENDS IN SOUTH PACIFIC
POLITICS
ROUND TABLE, (312) (OCT 89), 440-446.
THE MILITARY INTERVENTION IN FIJI GAVE RISE TO A LINE OF
ANALYSIS WHICH EMPHASIZED ITS GROWING POLITICAL INSTABILITY.
THE ARGUMENT OF THIS SHORT ESSAY IS THAT THE THRUST OF MUCH
RECENT ANALYSIS HAS BEEN MISLEADING. THE WRITER SUGGESTS
THAT WHAT IS CLEAR IS THAT THE GENERAL PATTERN OF CHANGE
WILL NOT MERELY REPLICATE THE FIJIAN EXAMPLE. FIJI IS AN
UNUSUAL SOCIETY AND EVENTS THERE HAVE BEEN MORE EXCEPTIONAL
THAN NORMAL. THE ESSAY ATTEMPTS TO UNRAVEL EVENTS AND THEN
INDICATES THAT FIJI IS NOT TO BE CONSIDERED A PARADIGM.

07091 PAYNE, D.W.
LATIN AMERICA: CRISIS OF DEMOCRACY
FREEDOM AT ISSUE, (106) (JAN 89), 9-12.
AS A RESULT OF THE DEMOCRATIC TREND THAT BEGAN AT THE
OUTSET OF THE DECADE, LATIN AMERICANS ARE FREER NOW THAN AT
ANY TIME IN THEIR HISTORY. BUT THEY ARE ALSO INCREASINGLY
POORER, AND IN 1988 DEMOCRACY WAS BEGINNING TO BE IDENTIFIED
MORE WITH HARDSHIP THAN WITH FREEDOM. THE CONSOLIDATION OF
DEMOCRACY IN THE REGION WILL REQUIRE AT LEAST ANOTHER
GENERATION FOR DEMOCRATIC INSTITUTIONS TO BECOME FIRMLY
ROOTED. BUT ECONOMIC TURMOIL IS TODAY CRIPPLING THE PROCESS
AND TURNING ONCE HOPEFUL POLITICAL TRANSFORMATION INTO
OMINOUS POLITICAL DECAY.

07092 PAYNE, D.W.
SCRAP IRONY IN NICARAGUA
FREEDOM AT ISSUE, (110) (SEP 89), 8.
THE NICARAGUAN PEOPLE ARE STRUGGLING TO MAINTAIN THEIR
SENSE OF IRONY. A CONFIDENTIAL STUDY, PREPARED BY AN
INTERNATIONAL TEAM OF EXPERTS AT THE REQUEST OF THE ORTEGA
GOVERNMENT, HAS REVEALED THAT NICARAGUA MAY BE THE POOREST
COUNTRY IN THE WESTERN HEMISPHERE, BEATING OUT HAITI FOR THE
DUBIOUS HONOR. THE SANDINISTAS HAVE RESPONDED WITH A SEVERE
AUSTERITY PROGRAM DESCRIBED BY FOREIGN DIPLOMATS AS A
TEXTBOOK LESSON IN CAPITALIST ECONOMICS. OF COURSE,
NICARAGUAN TEXTBOOKS CONTINUE TO TEACH THAT CAPITALISM IS
EVIL.

07093 PAYNE, D.W.
THE DRUG "SUPER STATE" IN LATIN AMERICA
FREEDOM AT ISSUE, (107) (MAR 89), 7-10.
THE HEMISPHERIC NARCOTICS TRADE HAS SPAWNED A BORDERLESS

DRUG STATE WHOSE POLITICAL POWER NOW THREATENS THE
SOVEREIGNTY OF THE LATIN AMERICAN NATIONS IN WHICH IT
OPERATES. WILLIAM BENNETT, WASHINGTON'S FIRST DRUG CZAR,
SHOULD KNOW ABOUT THE DRUG STATE; THAT'S WHAT HE'S FIGHTING
ON THE SO-CALLED SUPPLY SIDE OF THE ISSUE. PRESIDENT BUSH,
HAVING SINGLED OUT DRUG ABUSE AS A NATIONAL "SCOURGE" IN HIS
INAUGURAL ADDRESS, SHOULD BE AWARE TOO; THE DRUG STATE IS A
MAJOR NATIONAL SECURITY THREAT. THE WAY TO START IS BY
LISTENING TO LATIN AMERICAN LEADERS WHO CONFRONT DIRECTLY
WHAT HAS BECOME A MENACE OF GEOPOLITICAL MAGNITUDE.

07094 PAYNE, J. G.
SHAPING THE RACE ISSUE: A SPECIAL KIND OF JOURNALISM
POLITICAL COMMUNICATION AND PERSUASION, 5(3) (1988),
145-160.
THE PAPER EXAMINES THE PRESS COVERAGE OF THE LOS ANGELES
TIMES IN THE 1982 GUBERNATORIAL ELECTION BETWEEN MAYOR TOM
BRADLEY AND GEORGE DEUKMEJIAN IN TERMS OF THE PROCLIVITY TO
HIGHLIGHT BRADLEY'S RACE IN CAMPAIGN NEWS STORIES. THE PAPER
FOCUSES ON THE STATEMENT MADE BY DEUKMEJIAN CAMPAIGN MANAGER,
BILL ROBERTS, IN THE EARLY DAYS OF OCTOBER, WITH HIS
CANDIDATE TRAILING BADLY IN THE POLLS, THAT "THERE WAS A
HIDDEN ANTI-BLACK VOTE" THAT WOULD AID DEUKMEJIAN ON
ELECTION DAY. THE AUTHORS DETAIL THE LOS ANGELES TIMES
COVERAGE OF THIS STATEMENT AND THE TENDENCY OF THE TIMES TO
FOCUS ON THIS STORY DURING THE ENTIRE MONTH OF OCTOBER
RATHER THAN TO REPORT ON THE ISSUES ADDRESSED BY THE
CANDIDATES. THE ANALYSIS NOTES THAT AS CAMPAIGN COVERAGE
ZEROED IN ON THE RACE ISSUE, SO DID POLLS AND VOTER INTEREST.
AFTER EXAMINING THE COVERAGE AND DEUKMEJIAN'S NARROW
VICTORY, THE AUTHORS POSE QUESTIONS OF ETHICS TO REPORTERS
ENGAGED IN THIS WRITING AND OUTLINE CONCERNS FOR SUCH
PRACTICES IN FUTURE ELECTIONS AND CAMPAIGNS.

07095 PAYNE, J. G.; BAUKUS, R. A.
TREND ANALYSIS OF THE 1984 GOP SENATORIAL SPOTS
POLITICAL COMMUNICATION AND PERSUASION, 5(3) (1988),
161-177.
THE PAPER PRESENTS A QUANTITATIVE AND QUALITATIVE
ANALYSIS OF 101 SENATORIAL SPOTS OF THE 1984 NATIONAL
CAMPAIGN. EXAMINING THE ADVERTISEMENTS ACCORDING TO THE
CLASSIFICATION SYSTEM OUTLINED BY DIAMOND AND BATES IN THE
SPOT, THE AUTHORS NOTE THE EMERGENCE OF NEGATIVE ATTACK
SPOTS AS THE MOST PREDOMINANT TYPE OF ADVERTISEMENT AMONG
INCUMBENTS AND CHALLENGERS AND PRESENT NOTABLE TRENDS
ACCORDING TO REGION AND OTHER CHARACTERISTICS OF THE SPOTS
OF THE 1984 GOP SENATORIAL TELEVISION BLITZ.

07096 PAYNE, K.
ICBMS, ARMS CONTROL, AND THE SDI
COMPARATIVE STRATEGY, 8(1) (1989), 55-71.
THE CONDITIONS THAT WILL LIKELY BE NECESSARY TO MOVE THE
SOVIET UNION TOWARD A "DEFENSIVE TRANSITION" WILL BE SOVIET
CONVICTIONS THAT, 1) COUNTERFORCE OFFENSE CAN NOT SUPPORT
SOVIET DAMAGE-LIMITATION GOALS; AND, 2) THE U.S. OFFENSIVE
THREAT WILL NOT BE REDUCED WITHOUT OFFENSIVE CONCESSIONS ON
THE PART OF THE SOVIET UNION. CONSEQUENTLY, U.S. OFFENSIVE
MODERNIZATION PROGRAMS, INCLUDING THOSE FOR ICBMS, WILL BE
ESSENTIAL LEVERAGE TO MOVE THE SOVIET UNION TOWARD A
"COOPERATIVE TRANSITION." THIS PLACES THE U.S. IN THE
POLITICALLY UNENVIABLE POSITION OF ENDORSING A DEFENSIVE
TRANSITION AND DEEP OFFENSIVE REDUCTIONS, BUT NEEDING TO
SUSTAIN DYNAMIC OFFENSIVE FORCES PROGRAMS IF A COOPERATIVE
TRANSITION IS EVER TO BE A POSSIBILITY.

07097 PAYNE, R.A.
THE POLITICS OF DEFENSE POLICY COMMUNICATION: THE "THREAT"
OF SOVIET STRATEGIC DEFENSE
POLICY STUDIES REVIEW, 8(3) (SPR 89), 505-526.
SCHOLARS HAVE FOUND THAT POLITICAL LEADERS MANIPULATE
THREAT ASSESSMENTS TO ACHIEVE DESIRED DEFENSE POLICY
OUTCOMES. YET CONTEMPORARY COMMUNICATION ABOUT THREATS IS
NOT EASILY STUDIED, LEADING SOME WRITERS TO CALL FOR NEW
STUDIES OF CLAUSEWITZ'S SOCALLED "SOCIAL" DIMENSION OF
STRATEGY -- THE EFFORTS BY GOVERNMENTS TO ASSURE DOMESTIC
SUPPORT FOR DEFENSE POLICIES. TO APPLY THE SUGGESTED
TECHNIQUE, THIS PAPER EXAMINES THE REAGAN ADMINISTRATION'S
CLAIM THAT THE THREATS FROM SOVIET STRATEGIC DEFENSES
JUSTIFY THE U.S. STRATEGIC DEFENSE INITIATIVE. THE
ADMINISTRATION'S ARGUMENTS ARE FOUND TO BE UNCLEAR AND
INTERNALLY INCONSISTENT. DESPITE SOME FEAR APPEALS ABOUT
SOVIET THREATS, REAGAN OFFICIALS TYPICALLY NOTED THAT
AMERICAN OFFENSIVE FORCES WILL CONTINUE TO RENDER SOVIET
DEFENSES IMPOTENT AND OBSOLETE FOR THE FORSEEABLE FUTURE.
INDEED, VAGUE AND INCONSISTENT STATEMENTS ABOUT SOVIET
FORCES MAY HAVE UNDERMINED ADMINISTRATION EFFORTS TO FULFILL
SDI FUNDING GOALS, TO CODIFY EARLY DEPLOYMENT PLANS, AND
EVEN TO ESTABLISH MANHATTAN OR APOLLO-TYPE POLICY
PREEMINENCE.

07098 PAZOS, F.
THE NEED TO DESIGN AND APPLY MORE EFFECTIVE ANTI-
INFLATIONARY PLANS IN LATIN AMERICA
JOURNAL OF INTERAMERICAN STUDIES AND WORLD AFFAIRS, 31(1,

2) (SPR 89), 105-123.
THIS ARTICLE ARGUES THAT LATIN AMERICAN INFLATIONS ARE
MAINTAINED BY THEIR INERTIAL MOMENTUM AND ACCELERATED BY
ECONOMIC AND FINANCIAL DISEQUILIBRIA. AS A CONSEQUENCE, IT
CONTINUES, ANTI-INFLATIONARY PLANS MUST ATTACK BOTH FACTORS
AND TAKE MEASURES TO BREAK THE INERTIAL INFLATIONS AN
BALANCE THE BASIC ACCOUNTS OF THE COUNTRIES, IT EXPLORES
WAGE AND PRICE CONTROLS, TAXES, AND REDUCED EXPENDITURES AS
WAYS TO RESTORE ECONOMIC AND FINANCIAL BALANCE.

07099 PAZOS, L.
IS FOREIGN DEBT THE REAL PROBLEM?
MEXICO-UNITED STATES REPORT, II(6) (FEB 89), 4-6.
UNDER MEXICO'S PRESENT JUDICAL, ECONOMIC, AND POLITICAL
SYSTEM, ITS ECONOMIC PROBLEMS WOULD REMAIN UNSOLVED EVEN IF
ITS FOREIGN DEBT WERE TOTALLY FORGIVEN AND OIL ROSE TO $40
PER BARREL. MEXICO'S PROBLEM HAS NOT BEEN THE LACK OF
ECONOMIC RESOURCES BUT THE MISMANAGEMENT OF THEM BY
SUCCESSIVE GOVERNMENTS.

07100 PEAL, D.
THE POLITICS OF POPULISM: GERMANY AND THE AMERICAN SOUTH
IN THE 1890'S
COMPARATIVE STUDIES IN SOCIETY AND HISTORY, 31(2) (APR 89),
340-362.
THIS ARTICLE SEEKS TO PLACE THE MOVEMENT LAUNCHED BY
OTTO BOCKEL, GERMANY'S FIRST ANTI-SEMITIC REICHSTAG DEPUTY,
IN ITS BROAD CONTEMPORARY CONTEXT, INSTEAD OF VIEWING IT IN
LIGHT OF ITS IMPUTED NAZI OUTCOME. THE AIM IS TO CLARIFY THE
CONDITIONS IN WHICH ANTI-SEMITIC SLOGANS AND PROGRAMS
ENTERED POLITICAL LIFE IN GERMANY AND TO THROW LIGHT ON THE
FAILURE AND LEGACY OF THE BOCKEL MOVEMENT. POPULISM IN THE
AMERICAN SOUTH (THE COTTON STATES FROM TEXAS TO THE
CAROLINAS) LENDS ITSELF WELL TO COMPARISON. BOTH MOVEMENTS
ACQUIRED INSTITUTIONAL FORM IN THE LATE 1880S, MOBILIZED
SMALL FARMERS ON THE MARGINS OF POLITICAL AND ECONOMIC LIFE,
ADOPTED SIMILAR SCHEMES OF COOPERATIVE ORGANIZATION, AND
BROUGHT FORTH CHARISMATIC LEADERS SKILLFUL AT PLAYING ON
POPULAR GRIEVANCES AND RANGING "THE PEOPLE" AGAINST THEIR
ALLEGED ENEMIES. BOTH FAILED WITHIN A DECADE. RACISM
PERVADED BOTH MOVEMENTS AND WAS PERHAPS THEIR PRINCIPAL
LEGACY.

07101 PEARCE, J.
COLOMBIA
MONTHLY REVIEW PRESS, NEW YORK, NY, 1989, 150.
THE AUTHOR TRACES THE HISTORICAL DEVELOPMENT OF
COLOMBIA'S TWO-PARTY SYSTEM AND THE ORIGINS OF ITS WEAK
STATE. SHE FOCUSES ON THE GROWING POLITICAL VIOLENCE AGAINST
AN INCREASINGLY UNIFIED POPULAR MOVEMENT, THE ROLE PLAYED BY
GUERRILLA FORCES, AND THE DEEPENING CRISIS OF COLOMBIA'S
POLITICAL AND SOCIAL ORDER.

07102 PEARSON, M.M.
THE CONTROL OF FOREIGN DIRECT INVESTMENT IN A SOCIALIST
STATE: THE CASE OF EQUITY JOINT VENTURES IN THE PEOPLE'S
REPUBLIC OF CHINA
DISSERTATION ABSTRACTS INTERNATIONAL, 48(10) (APR 88),
2719-A.
TO ANSWER THE QUESTION "CAN A CENTRALIZED SOCIALIST
STATE AVOID PROBLEMS ASSOCIATED WITH FOREIGN DIRECT
INVESTMENT THAT HAVE PLAGUED MANY CAPITALIST NATIONS?" THE
STUDY EXAMINES THE CHINESE GOVERNMENT'S EFFORT FROM 1979 TO
MID-1986 BOTH TO ATTRACT FOREIGN CAPITALAND TO GUARD AGAINST
WHAT IT BELIEVES ARE POTENTIAL RISKS OF JOINT VENTURES. THE
STUDY CONCLUDES THAT ALTHOUGH CHINA'S ATTEMPTS AT CONTROLS
WERE SOMEWHAT SUCCESSFUL, IT ALSO FACED MANY SIGNIFICANT
PROBLEMS.

07103 PEASE, P.; KANFER, R.; LIND, E.
PROCEDURAL FAIRNESS AND WORK GROUP RESPONSES TO
PERFORMANCE EVALUATION SYSTEMS
SOCIAL JUSTICE RESEARCH, 2(3) (SEP 88), 193-206.
IN A VARIETY OF SETTINGS, PROCEDURES THAT PREMIT
PREDICISION INPUT BY THOSE AFFECTED BY THE DECISION IN
QUESTION HAVE BEEN FOUND TO HAVE POSITIVE EFFECTS ON
FAIRNESS JUDGEMENTS. TWO MAJOR MODELS OF THE PSYCHOLOGY OF
PROCEDURAL JUSTICE MAKE CONTRARY PREDICTIONS ABOUT WHETHER
REPEATED NEGATIVE OUTCOMES ATTENTUATE SUCH INPUT EFFECTS.
THE STUDY EXAMINES THE PROCEDURAL AND DISTRIBUTIVE FAIRNESS
JUDGEMENTS PRODUCED BY HIGH AND LOW INPUT PERFORMANCE
EVALUATION PROCEDURES UNDER CONDITIONS OF REPEATED NEGATIVE
OUTCOMES. MEASURES OF PROCEDURAL AND DISTRIBUTIVE FAIRNESS
SHOWED THAT THE HIGH-INPUT PROCEDURE LED TO JUDGEMENTS OF
GREATER PROCEDURAL AND DISTRIBUTIVE FAIRNESS. THE ARTICLE
ALSO DISCUSSES THE IMPLICATIONS OF THESE FINDINGS FOR THE
THEORIES OF PROCEDURAL JUSTICE AND FOR THE APPLICATIONS OF
PROCEDURAL JUSTICE TO ORGANIZATIONAL SETTINGS.

07104 PECKHAM, R.S.
GREECE AND THE EUROPEAN COMMUNITY
CONTEMPORARY REVIEW, 255(1487) (DEC 89), 281-285.
THE DOUBLE-HEADED EAGLE WHICH DESCRIBES MID-NINETEENTH
CENTURY RUSSIA IS STILL PERTINENT FOR THE SOVIET UNION AND

ALSO GREECE OF THE 1980S. THIS ARTICLE EXPLORES THE
'DOUBLENESS' THAT CHARACTERIZES GREECE WHICH IS CULTURAL AS
WELL AS GEOGRAPHICAL AND HISTORICAL. IT EXAMINES THE
AMBIGUITY OF GREECE'S HISTORICAL IDENTITY, AND THEN THE
IMPACT OF THE EUROPEAN COMMUNITY (EC) ON GREECE, PLUS THE
ECONOMIC DISCREPANCY BETWEEN GREECE AND THE EC. THE BENEFITS
OF GREECE'S ACCESSION ARE WEIGHED AGAINST THE PROBLEMS IT
HAS CREATED.

07105 PECORELLA, R.F.
MEASURED DECENTRALIZATION: THE NEW YORK CITY COMMUNITY
BOARD SYSTEM
NATIONAL CIVIC REVIEW, 78(3) (MAY 89), 202-208.
IN 1975, DURING A PERIOD WHEN A NUMBER OF AMERICAN
CITIES PROVIDED FOR INCREASED COMMUNITY PARTICIPATION IN THE
POLICY-MAKING PROCESS, NEW YORK CITY'S EXISTING COMMUNITY
PLANNING BOARDS WERE STRENGTHENED, USHERING IN A PERIOD OF
"MEASURED DECENTRALIZATION." WITH MORE THAN A DECADE HAVING
PASSED SINCE THE COMMUNITY BOARDS' ENHANCED EMPOWERMENT, WE
MAY BEGIN TO ASSESS THEIR IMPACT ON CITY POLITICS.

07106 PEDEN, E.A.; BRADLEY, M.D.
GOVERNMENT SIZE, PRODUCTIVITY, AND ECONOMIC GROWTH: THE
POSTWAR EXPERIENCE
PUBLIC CHOICE, 61(3) (JUN 89), 229-245.
IN THIS PAPER, THE AUTHORS EXAMINE THE RELATIONSHIP
BETWEEN THE SIZE OF THE GOVERNMENT SECTOR RELATIVE TO THE
ECONOMY AND THE LEVELS OF PRODUCTIVITY AND THUS ECONOMIC
GROWTH. A NEGATIVE LINK BETWEEN GOVERNMENT SIZE AND
PRODUCTIVITY AND OUTPUT GROWTH IS, POTENTIALLY, AN IMPORTANT
PIECE OF THE GROWTH-SLOWDOWN PUZZLE. TRADITIONAL FACTORS, BY
THEMSELVES, DO NOT SUFFICIENTLY EXPLAIN THE SLOWDOWN AND AN
UNDERSTANDING OF THELINK BETWEEN GOVERNMENT SIZE AND
ECONOMIC ACTIVITY MAY HELP RESOLVE THE PRODUCTIVITY MYSTERY.
THE AUTHORS FIND THAT INCREASES IN THE SCALE OF GOVERNMENT
LEAD TO STATISTICALLY SIGNIFICANT REDUCTIONS IN BOTH THE
ECONOMIC BASE AND THE ECONOMIC GROWTH RATE. IN ADDITION,
THEY FIND THAT MOST OF THIS GOVERNMENTINDUCED RETARDATION OF
ECONOMIC ACTIVITY ARISES FROM REDUCTIONS IN PRODUCTIVITY
RATHER THAT REDUCTIONS IN THE EMPLOYMENT OF FACTORS.

07107 PEDLER, J.
CAMBODIA: DANGER AND OPPORTUNITY FOR THE WEST
WORLD TODAY, 45(2) (FEB 89), 19-21.
THE AUTHOR REVIEWS EFFORTS TO NEGOTIATE A POLITICAL
SOLUTION TO THE CAMBODIAN SITUATION. HE LOOKS AT THE
POSSIBLE ROLE OF THE KHMER ROUGE AND THE RELATIVE POSITIONS
OF PRINCE SIHANOUK AND PRIME MINISTER HUN SEN ON KHMER ROUGE
INVOLVEMENT IN A NEW GOVERNMENT.

07108 PEETERS, Y.J.
MINORITY PROVISIONS IN THE HELSINKI PROCESS
PLURAL SOCIETIES, 18(2) (MAR 89), 95-119.
THIS ARTICLE PROVIDES THE TEXT OF PRINCIPLE VII OF THE
FINAL ACT OF THE CONFERENCE ON SECURITY AND COOPERATION IN
EUROPE WHICH WAS SIGNED IN HELSINKI IN 1975. PRINCIPLE VII
DEALS WITH THE COMMITMENT OF THE SIGNATORIES TO RESPECT
FUNDAMENTAL FREEDOMS AND HUMAN RIGHTS FOR ALL WITHOUT
DISTINCTION BETWEEN RACE, SEX, LANGUAGE OR RELIGION.

07109 PEHE, J.
HUMAN RIGHTS VS. COMMUNIST SYSTEMS
FREEDOM AT ISSUE, (108) (MAY 89), 5, 7-8.
IN THE PAST TWO YEARS, SOME OF THE COMMUNIST STATES IN
EASTERN EUROPE HAVE APPEARED INCREASINGLY READY TO EMBRACE
THE INTERNATIONALLY RECOGNIZED NORMS OF HUMAN RIGHTS AS
PRESENTED IN THE UNIVERSAL DECLARATION OF HUMAN RIGHTS AND
THE HELSINKI ACCORDS. MOSCOW IS PREPARED TO HOST A
CONFERENCE ON SECURITY AND COOPERATION IN EUROPE FOLLOW-UP
MEETING IN 1991. THE SOVIET LEADERSHIP HAS ALSO PROMISED TO
CHANGE SOVIET LAWS SO THAT SOME BASIC HUMAN RIGHTS, SUCH AS
FREEDOM OF ASSEMBLY AND FREEDOM OF OPINION, ARE BETTER
PROTECTED.

07110 PEHE, J.
ON TOTALITARIAN LANGUAGE TODAY
FREEDOM AT ISSUE, (110) (SEP 89), 29-31.
THERE ARE HUNDREDS OF BASIC TERMS USED FREQUENTLY BY
"COMMUNIST SPEAK," INCLUDING AN ENTIRE ECONOMIC AND
POLITICAL VOCABULARY DERIVED FROM MARXIST THEORY. THE
STARTLING CHANGES NOW OCCURRING IN THE SOVIET EMPIRE ARE
REFLECTED IN, AND FURTHERED BY, CHANGES TAKING PLACE IN THE
LANGUAGE OF TOTALITARIAN COUNTRIES.

07111 PEIJUN, S.
RURAL INDUSTRIES IN CHINA AND INDIA: ACHIEVEMENTS AND
PROBLEMS
CHINA REPORT, 24(2) (APR 89), 147-1.
THIS ARTICLE ADDRESSES THE NEED FOR CHINA AND INDIA TO
DEVELOP RURAL INDUSTRIES IN AN EFFORT TO MODERNISE. IT
ATTEMPTS A PRELIMINARY COMPARISON BETWEEN THE TWO COUNTRIES
IN TERMS OF THE ROADS THEY HAVE BEEN PASSING THROUGH IN
DEVELOPING THEIR OWN RURAL INDUSTRIES, AND ALSO IN TERMS OF
THE DIFFICULTIES AND PROBLEMS THEY HAVE BEEN FACING IN THE

PROCESS OF DOING SO.

07112 PEIRCE, L.P.
THE IMPERIAL HAREM: GENDER AND POWER IN THE OTTOMAN EMPIRE,
1520-1656
DISSERTATION ABSTRACTS INTERNATIONAL, 49(8) (FEB 89),
2362-A.
THIS DISSERTATION TRACES THE EMERGENCE OF THE IMPERIAL
HAREM OF THE OTTOMAN EMPIRE AS A SIGNIFICANT POLITICAL FORCE
AND ARGUES THAT THE HAREM'S RISE TO POWER WAS LARGELY THE
RESULT OF A TRANSFORMATION OF THE IMAGES OF SOVEREIGNTY
PROJECTED BY THE OTTOMAN SULTANATE. DURING A PERIOD WHEN THE
DYNASTY FOUND IT NECESSARY TO EMPHASIZE NEW BASES OF
POLITICAL LEGITIMACY, THE ROLE OF WOMEN WAS CRUCIAL.

07113 PEKIC, V.
THE LATIN AMERICAN COMMUNITY OF PEOPLES
REVIEW OF INTERNATIONAL AFFAIRS, (JAN 88), 13-18.
THIS ARTICLE DESCRIBES HOW THE MEETING OF THE PRESIDENTS
OF ARGENTINA, BRAZIL, COLOMBIA, MEXICO, PANAMA, PERU,
URUGUAY AND VENEZUELA, HELD FROM THE 27TH TO THE 29TH OF
NOVEMBER 1987, INDICATED A DECLINE IN U.S. INFLUENCE IN THE
REGION AND HIGHLIGHTED A NEW LATIN AMERICAN SPIRIT OF
INDEPENDENCE. IT WAS THE FIRST MEETING OF LATIN AMERICAN
PRESIDENTS CONVENED BY THEIR OWN DECISION AND WITHOUT THE
PARTICIPATION OF THE PRESIDENT OF THE U.S.A. FOR THE PURPOSE
OF AGREEING ON A COMMON POLICY OF DEALING WITH THE MOST
IMPORTANT PROBLEMS OF THEIR REGION. BY AN AGREED POLICY AND
ACTION THE "EIGHT" HOPE TO STRENGTHEN LATIN AMERICA'S
NEGOTIATING POSITION IN WORLD AFFAIRS AND IN THE WORLD
ECONOMY.

07114 PELED, M.
THE INTERNATIONAL PEACE CONFERENCE ON THE MIDDLE EAST
REVIEW OF INTERNATIONAL AFFAIRS, (JAN 88), 22-25.
THE CONCEPT OF AN INTERNATIONAL PEACE CONFERENCE IS BEST
SUITED FOR MEETING THE IMMENSELY COMPLICATED PROBLEMS
INVOLVED IN ESTABLISHING PEACE BETWEEN ISRAEL AND ITS ARAB
NEIGHBORS. ANY OTHER PROCEDURE IS BOUND TO FAIL AND
SUPPORTING IT SHOULD BE TAKEN AS CLEAR INDICATION THAT THE
ULTIMATE GOAL OF ITS ADVOCATES IS RATHER TO AVOID THAN TO
REACH PEACE. IT IS THEREFORE IMPERATIVE THAT ALL EFFORTS
SHOULD BE MADE TO PRESUADE THE USA AND ISRAEL TO REMOVE
THEIR OBJECTION TO IT AND COOPERATE WITH THE VAST MAJORITY
OF IMPLEMENTING THE GENERAL ASSEMBLY'S RESOLUTION CALLING
FOR SUCH A CONFERENCE.

07115 PELISSERO, J.P.; GRANATO, J.S.
LOCAL OFFICIALS' EVALUATIONS OF STATE-ADMINISTERED
COMMUNITY DEVELOPMENT PROGRAMS
STATE AND LOCAL GOVERNMENT REVIEW, 21(1) (WIN 89), 31-37.
IN THE EARLY 1980S, STATES ASSUMED ADMINISTRATIVE
CONTROL OF FEDERAL FUND ALLOCATIONS TO THE SMALL CITIES
COMMUNITY DEVELOPMENT BLOCK GRANT (CDBG) PROGRAM PREVIOUSLY
FUNDED AND MANAGED BY THE DEPARTMENT OF HOUSING AND URBAN
DEVELOPMENT (HUD). EXAMINING ISSUES RAISED BY THE EVOLVING
STATE-CENTERED FEDERALISM, THIS STUDY NOTES THE REACTIONS TO
THIS CHANGE OF TWO GROUPS OF TEXAS LOCAL OFFICIALS INVOLVED
WITH CDBG PROJECTS--APPOINTED PROFESSIONAL ADMINISTRATORS
AND ELECTED OFFICIALS OR "POLITICOS." TWO ASPECTS OF THESE
REACTIONS ARE EXPLORED: THE OFFICIALS' VIEWS AS TO THE
CAPACITY OF THE STATE TO MANAGE CDBG AND THEIR OPINIONS AS
TO THE IMPACT OF STATE POLITICS ON THE MANAGEMENT STRUCTURE.
THE STUDY FINDS THAT BOTH GROUPS ARE SATISFIED WITH THE
STATE'S MANAGEMENT CAPACITY, BUT THAT PROFESSIONAL
ADMINISTRATORS PERCEIVE HUD TO HAVE BEEN A BETTER PROGRAM
MANAGER THAN THE STATE, WHILE POLITICOS PREFER THE STATE'S
MANAGEMENT PERFORMANCE.

07116 PELLETIERE, J.C.
PUBLIC VS. PRIVATE: A WAVERING LINE
BUREAUCRAT, 18(2) (SUM 89), 57-60.
THERE ARE MANY FORCES THAT MAKE IT DIFFICULT TO DRAW
CLEAR-CUT LINES BETWEEN PUBLIC AND PRIVATE RESPONSIBILITIES
IN A CIVIL SOCIETY. IN OMB CIRCULAR A-76, THE OFFICE OF
MANAGEMENT AND BUDGET SEPARATED ACTIVITIES INTO "INHERENTLY
GOVERNMENTAL" AND "COMMERCIAL" CAUSES. IT IS APPROPRIATE
ALSO TO CONSIDER WHICH MIGHT BE THE REASONABLE
RESPONSIBILITY OF WHICH GOVERNMENTAL, POLITICAL, OR ECONOMIC
GROUP.

07117 PENG, L.
RESOLUTELY CARRY OUT THE PRINCIPLES OF IMPROVEMENT,
RECTIFICATION, AND DEEPENDED REFORM
BEIJING REVIEW, 32(16) (APR 89), I-XXIV.
CHINESE PREMIER LI PENG HAS CALLED FOR THE CHINESE
PEOPLE TO CONCENTRATE ON THE IMPROVEMENT AND RECTIFICATION
OF THE GOVERNMENT'S REFORM POLICIES, TO CURB DEMAND, TO
CORRECT THE ECONOMIC ORDER, AND TO READJUST THE COUNTRY'S
ECONOMIC STRUCTURE.

07118 PENG. W.; XIAOBING, Y.
TIBETAN DEPUTIES ON "HUMAN RIGHTS"
BEIJING REVIEW, 32(17) (APR 89), 27-29.
ALTHOUGH SOME PEOPLE ADVOCATE THE INDEPENDENCE OF TIBET,
THE CHINESE CENTRAL GOVERNMENT CANNOT AGREE TO THIS AND
NEITHER CAN THE CHINESE PEOPLE, INCLUDING THE TIBETANS. OVER
THE PAST THIRTY YEARS, TIBET'S ECONOMY HAS GRADUALLY
IMPROVED WITH THE SUPPORT OF THE CENTRAL GOVERNMENT.
PROGRESS HAS BEEN MADE TOWARDS IMPLEMENTING NATIONAL
AUTONOMY FOR TIBET BUT IT MUST REMAIN PART OF CHINA, BECAUSE
HISTORICALLY IT HAS BEEN CHINESE TERRITORY SINCE THE YUAN
DYNASTY. FROM A HUMAN RIGHTS STANDPOINT, THE TIBETAN PEOPLE
ENJOY DEMOCRATIC FREEDOM WITHIN THE FRAMEWORK OF THE
CONSTITUION.

07119 PEPALL, L.M.; SHAPIRO, D.M.
THE MILITARY-INDUSTRIAL COMPLEX IN CANADA
CANADIAN PUBLIC POLICY--ANALYSE DE POLITIQUES, 15(3) (SEP
89), 265-284.
THIS PAPER HAS TWO OBJECTIVES. THE FIRST IS TO PROVIDE
NEW EVIDENCE ABOUT CANADIAN FIRMS WHICH RECEIVE MILITARY
CONTRACTS, AND THUS TO DEFINE THE EXTENT AND NATURE OF THE
MILITARY-INDUSTRIAL COMPLEX (MIC) IN CANADA. THE SECOND IS
TO EXAMINE SOME ASPECTS OF THE PUBLIC POLICY ISSUES RELATED
TO THE MIC. THE EVIDENCE INDICATES THAT THE CANADIAN MIC
MIRRORS THE STRUCTURE OF CANADIAN INDUSTRY IN GENERAL TO A
LARGE EXTENT. IT IS HIGHLY CONCENTRATED, EXPORT-ORIENTED AND
HAS SIGNIFICANT DEGREES OF FOREIGN CONTROL. THE RESULTS ALSO
SUGGEST THAT DOMESTIC MILITARY PROCUREMENT MAY HAVE BEEN
USED TO PROMOTE NON-MILITARY OBJECTIVES, PARTICULARLY
REGIONAL EQUALITY, BUT NOT IN A CONSISTENT WAY.

07120 PEPPER, D.
HELSINKI, CSCE AND VIENNA
INTERNATIONAL PERSPECTIVES, 18(4) (JUL 89), 19-22.
THE "HELSINKI PROCESS" HAS BEEN RE-INVIGORATED BY
GLASTNOST, AND ITS MAIN INSTITUTION, THE CONFERENCE ON
SECURITY AND COOPERATION (CSCE) IN EUROPE, IS GETTING
HEALTHIER. IT IS NOT JUST IN HUMAN RIGHTS, ALTHOUGH THAT
SEEMS TO MONOPOLIZE POPULAR ATTENTION. THIS ARTICLE
EVALUATES THE PROGRESS SO FAR AND EXPLORES NEW LIFE FOR CSCE
AND THE CONTINUING PROBLEMS IT FACES, SECURITY, ECONOMICS,
SCIENCE, TECHNOLOGY AND THE ENVIRONMENT; PRINCIPLES, HUMAN
DIMENSION AND THE MEDITERRANEAN ARE EACH EXAMINED.

07121 PERAMUNETILLEKE, T.B.
SRI LANKA: WAR ON POVERTY
THIRD WORLD WEEK, 8(3) (MAR 89), 20-21.
RANASINGHE PERMADASA, SRI LANKA'S FIRST LOW-CASTE
PRESIDENT, HAS DECLARED WAR ON POVERTY TO MAKE GOOD ON HIS
CAMPAIGN PROMISE. THE ESSENCE OF HIS POVERTY ALLEVIATION
PROGRAM IS A PROMISE OF 2500 RUPEES A MONTH FOR EVERY FAMILY
BELOW THE POVERTY LEVEL. THE FAMILY IS ALLOWED TO SPEND A
PORTION IMMEDIATELY, WITH THE BALANCE BEING HELD IN A
SAVINGS ACCOUNT. THE SAVINGS MAY LATER BE WITHDRAWN FOR
INVESTMENT IN BUSINESS VENTURES.

07122 PERCIVAL, R.
MALTHUS AND HIS GHOST
NATIONAL REVIEW, XLI(15) (AUG 89), 30-33.
BOTH THE PROPHETS OF DOOM AND SOBER PESSIMISTS HAVE
FOUNDERED ON THE ROCKS OF SCIENTIFIC RESEARCH. IT IS NOW
TIME TO LAY TO REST BOTH MALTHUS AND HIS TROUBLED GHOST, IN
THE KNOWLEDGE THAT POPULATION GROWTH DOES NOT IMPEDE BUT
ACTUALLY CONTRIBUTES TO MAN'S RISE FROM POVERTY AND HARDSHIP.
THE MORE PEOPLE THERE ARE, FREE TO EXPLOIT THEIR OWN AND
THE EARTH'S RESOURCES, THE EASIER IT IS TO FEED THEM.

07123 PEREIRA, A.W.
BRAZIL: FIRE IN THE FOREST
HEMISPHERE, 1(3) (SUM 89), 20-23.
MUCH HAS BEEN SAID ABOUT THE DIMENSIONS AND CONSEQUENCES
OF THE RAPID DEFORESTATION OF THE BRAZILIAN AMAZON, BUT
LITTLE DISCUSSION HAS ADDRESSED ITS FUNDAMENTAL CAUSES.
RARELY MENTIONED ARE THE ORIGINS OF THE PROBLEM IN BRAZIL'S
AGRARIAN POLICIES OF THE LAST 50 YEARS. UNDERSTANDING THE
POLICY ORIGINS OF AMAZONIA'S DEFORESTATION IS CRUCIAL TO THE
SEARCH, IN BRAZIL AND WORLDWIDE, FOR WAYS OF HARMONIZING
DEMANDS ON THE ENVIRONMENT WITH THE NEED TO IMPLEMENT
PROGRAMS OF SUSTAINABLE DEVELOPMENT. THE MATTER OF AGRARIAN
POLICY IS EQUALLY IMPORTANT IN DRAWING ATTENTION TO ANOTHER
OVERLOOKED ISSUE: THE ROLE OF CONFLICT OVER LAND REFORM IN
BRAZIL'S CONTINUING TRANSITION FROM AUTHORITARIAN TO
DEMOCRATIC GOVERNANCE.

07124 PERERA, J.
TEST TUBE PERESTROIKA
SOUTH, (100) (FEB 89), 82-83.
STIFLED BY BUREAUCRACY AND DEADWOOD AT THE TOP, SOVIET
SCIENCE HAS LANGUISHED IN THE PAST, FALLING BEHIND THE WEST
IN SEVERAL KEY AREAS. BUT FUNDAMENTAL CHANGES IN SOVIET
SCIENCE FUNDING, RESEARCH, AND ADMINISTRATION UNDER
GORBACHEV ARE BEGINNING TO HAVE THEIR INITIAL IMPACT. THE
FUTURE REPERCUSSIONS WILL BE WORLDWIDE.

07125 PERERA, J.
THE MISSILE RACE HOTS UP

SOUTH, (106) (AUG 89), 102-106.
THE SPREAD OF BALLISTIC MISSILES TO THIRD WORLD
COUNTRIES HAS BECOME A CAUSE FOR CONCERN IN THE WEST, ALMOST
ON A PAR WITH NUCLEAR PROLIFERATION. DESPITE TRADE
RESTRICTIONS IMPOSED IN 1987, THE SPREAD OF THESE WEAPONS IS
CONTINUING UNABATED. SECRET DEALS ABOUND, AND THE WEST'S
MISSILE TECHNOLOGY CONTROL REGIME HAS BEEN A RANK FAILURE.

07126 PERETZ, D.
THE MIDDLE EAST: BREAKTHROUGHS AND BREAKDOWNS
FREEDOM AT ISSUE, (106) (JAN 89), 27-32.
EVENTS IN THE MIDDLE EAST PRESENTED A MIXED PICTURE IN
1988, WITH BOTH ENCOURAGING AND DISCOURAGING SIGNS OF
STABILITY. THERE SEEMED TO BE A MAJOR BREAKTHROUGH TOWARD
ENDING THE GULF WAR, AND PROSPECTS FOR RESOLVING THE ARAB-
ISRAEL CONFLICT SEEMED TO IMPROVE AS A RESULT OF MAJOR
CHANGES IN PLO POLICIES AND IN U.S. RELATIONS WITH THAT
ORGANIZATION. IT WAS A BAD YEAR FOR HUMAN RIGHTS IN THE
REGION. NEARLY EVERY COUNTRY FROM MOROCCO TO IRAN WAS CITED
BY AMNESTY INTERNATIONAL FOR VIOLATIONS THAT INCLUDED,
THROUGHOUT THE MIDDLE EAST, TENS OF THOUSANDS OF PEOPLE
IMPRISONED FOR POLITICAL REASONS (THOUSANDS OF THEM
PRISONERS OF CONSCIENCE) AND WIDESPREAD USE OF SYSTEMATIC
TORTURE.

C7127 PEREZ-LOPEZ, J.F.
SUGAR AND STRUCTURAL CHANGE IN THE CUBAN ECONOMY
WORLD DEVELOPMENT, 17(10) (OCT 89), 1627-1646.
DIVERSIFICATION OF THE ECONOMY AWAY FROM SUGAR HAS HIGH
AMONG THE ECONOMIC PRIORITIES OF THE CUBAN REVOLUTIONARY
GOVERNMENT IN POWER SINCE 1959. THIS ESSAY EXPLORES WHETHER
SUGAR'S ROLE IN THE STRUCTURE OF THE ECONOMY HAS IN FACT
CHANGED SIGNIFICANTLY IN THE LAST 25 YEARS OR SO BY
EXAMINING THREE ASPECTS OF STRUCTURAL CHANGE: SPECIALIZATION
IN PRODUCTION, EXPORT CONCENTRATION, AND EFFECTS OF CHANGES
IN WORLD SUGAR MARKET PRICES ON ECONOMIC GROWTH. THE
ANALYSIS SUGGESTS THAT POLICIES OF THE REVOLUTIONARY
GOVERNMENT HAVE HAD A MARGINAL IMPACT IN REDUCING SUGAR'S
ROLE. PLANS TO INCREASE SUGAR PRODUCTION AND EXPORTS THROUGH
THE END OF THE CENTURY VIRTUALLY ASSURE THAT SUGAR WILL
CONTINUE TO PLAY A PREDOMINANT ROLE IN THE ECONOMY.

07128 PEREZ, E.M.
"THROUGH HER LOVE AND SWEETNESS": WOMEN, REVOLUTION, AND
REFORM IN YUCATAN, 1910-1918
DISSERTATION ABSTRACTS INTERNATIONAL, 49(9) (MAR 89),
2784-A.
MEXICAN FEMINISTS IN YUCATAN FORGED THEIR OWN SOCIAL
MOVEMENT WITH THE HELP OF AN OUTSIDER, GOVERNOR SALVADOR
ALVARADO. IN THIS DISSERTATION, THE AUTHOR FOCUSES ON
FEMINIST EFFORTS IN THREE AREAS: EDUCATION, WORK, AND
POLITICS. YUCATAN'S FEMINISTS TOOK ADVANTAGE OF ALVARADO'S
SOCIALIST REFORMS TO IMPROVE THEIR LIVES, BUT THE LIMITS OF
THE GOVERNOR'S IDEOLOGY ALSO LIMITED THEIR TRUE LIBERATION.

07129 PEREZ, L.
CUBA AND THE AMERICAN LEFT
HEMISPHERE, 2(1) (FAL 89), 13-14.
THE AMERICAN COUNTER-CULTURAL MOVEMENT OF THE 1960'S HAD
A NATURAL AFFINITY WITH THE CUBAN REVOLUTION LED BY YOUNG
REBELS WHO INSTITUTED SWEEPING SOCIAL REFORMS IN DEFIANCE OF
THE U.S. MILITARY-INDUSTRIAL COMPLEX. THE CUBAN REVOLUTION
HAS AN IMPORTANT SYMBOL AND CAUSE FOR THE AMERICAN REBELS OF
THE TIME. NOW AT THE THRESHOLD OR IN THE THROES OF MIDDLE
AGE, THOSE RADICAL IDEALISTS OF THE 1960'S ARE RE-EVALUATING
THEIR SUPPORT OF CUBA UNDER FIDEL CASTRO. WITHOUT ABANDONING
THEIR SOCIALIST AND REVOLUTIONARY STANCES, MANY ARE
NEVERTHELESS VOICING CRITICISMS OF THE STATE OF AFFAIRS IN
CUBA.

07130 PERI, Y.
THE REVERSAL OF 1988
NEW OUTLOOK, 32(1 (287)) (JAN 89), 31-32.
THE TRUE STORY OF THE ELECTIONS TO THE TWELFTH KNESSET
IS THE DIZZYING RISE OF THE RELIGIOUS BLOC AND, IN
PARTICULAR, ITS COMPOSITION. SINCE THE ESTABLISHMENT OF THE
STATE, THE RELIGIOUS ZIONISTS HAVE COMPRISED TWO-THIRDS OF
THE RELIGIOUS CAMP WHILE THE ULTRA-ORTHODOX WERE ONLY ONE-
THIRD. THIS HAS NOW BEEN REVERSED. AN EXAMINATION OF THE
POLLING AREAS THAT SHOWED A STEEP INCREASE IN VOTES FOR SHAS
AND AGUDAT YISRAEL REVEALS TWO PHENOMENA. THE ULTRA-ORTHODOX
"BLACKS" ARE ENTERING POLITICS, AND HUNDREDS OF THOUSANDS OF
ORIENTAL JEWS AND THEIR ISRAELI-BORN OFFSPRING LEFT THE
ALIGNMENT FOR THE LIKUD.

07131 PERITORE, N.P.
BRAZILIAN PARTY LEFT OPINION: A Q-METHODOLOGY PROFILE
POLITICAL PSYCHOLOGY, 10(4) (DEC 89), 675-702.
THE BRAZILIAN SOCIALIST AND COMMUNIST LEFT HAS FOR
HISTORICAL REASONS DIVIDED INTO 12 PARTIES OF FACTIONS,
SPANNING THE LEFT IDEOLOGICAL SPECTRUM. THIS FIELD RESEARCH
UTILIZED A Q-METHOD PROTOCOL OF 54 STATEMENTS ADMINISTERED
TO 43 PROMINENT MEMBERS OF THE 12 PARTIES TO ASCERTAIN THE
DEEP STRUCTURE OF OPINION UNDERLYING SURFACE ORGANIZATIONAL

DIVERSITY. FACTORAL ROTATION PRODUCED THREE OPINION TYPES:
(1) SOCIALISTS PROPOSING A RADICAL MASS MOVEMENT WITH
EMPHASIS ON PARTICIPATORY DEMOCRACY, ECOLOGICAL AND FEMINIST
ISSUES; (2) MILITANT MARXIST-LENINISTS COMMITTED TO CREATION
OF A VANGUARD PARTY BUT WITH LEANINGS TOWARD PLURALISM AND
INTERNAL DEMOCRACY; AND (3) EUROCOMMUNISTS STRIVING FOR A
PEACEFUL, DEMOCRATIC, AND LEGAL ROAD TO SOCIALISM. THESE
OPINION TYPES ARE EXPLICATED AND COMPARED ACROSS A SET OF
MAIN ISSUE CLUSTERS, AND PROVIDE A MODEL OF UNDERLYING
ATTITUDINAL COHERENCE.

07132 PERKINS, E.J.
REVIEW OF US-SOUTH AFRICA RELATIONS
DEPARTMENT OF STATE BULLETIN (US FOREIGN POLICY), 89(2150)
(SEP 89), 69-73.
THE SOUTH AFRICA OF 1989 CANNOT BE EXPLAINED AWAY BY A
FEW WELL-CHOSEN CLICHES. THE LAND, THE SOCIETY, AND THE
PEOPLES ARE TWO COMPLEX FOR THAT. BUT THERE IS HOPE.
PRESIDENT ALBERTINA SISULU OF THE UNITED DEMOCRATIC FRONT IS
FIGHTING FOR CHANGE, EVEN THOUGH SHE IS RESTRICTED BY THE
GOVERNMENT. THE GOOD WILL OF BLACK SOUTH AFRICANS IS STILL
EVIDENT DESPITE THEIR BITTER EXPERIENCE UNDER APARTHEID. AND
GROWING NUMBERS OF WHITE SOUTH AFRICANS ARE ATTEMPTING TO
MAKE A DIFFERENCE. OFFICIAL REPRESENTATIVES OF THE USA ARE
ALSO VISIBLE, MANIFESTING THE VALUES THAT AMERICA STANDS FOR.

07133 PERKINS, E.J.
THE SEEDLINGS OF HOPE: US POLICY IN AFRICA
DEPARTMENT OF STATE BULLETIN (US FOREIGN POLICY), 89(2149)
(AUG 89), 69-72.
AFRICA IS ON THE BRINK OF SOME DRAMATIC AND FUNDAMENTAL
SHIFTS. THE CHANGES WILL BE NO LESS REVOLUTIONARY THAN THOSE
THAT ALTERED THE FACE OF THE CONTINENT IN THE 1950'S AND
1960'S. MORE AND MORE AFRICAN GOVERNMENTS ARE LOOKING AT
LIBERALIZED PRICING POLICIES, INCENTIVES TO FARMERS AND
BUSINESSMEN, MORE REALISTIC EXCHANGE RATES, REDUCED
GOVERNMENT DEFICITS, PRIVATIZATION, AND INCREASED INVESTMENT
IN EDUCATION. AT THIS CRITICAL JUNTURE, THE UNITED STATES
MUST INTENSIFY ITS COMMITMENT TO AFRICA'S FUTURE WITH A
THOUGHTFUL FOREIGN POLICY.

07134 PERKINS, R.S.
A STUDY OF THE IMPACT OF THE 1970 ILLINOIS CONSTITUTIONAL
CHANGE ON THE OFFICE OF COOK COUNTY TREASURER
DISSERTATION ABSTRACTS INTERNATIONAL, 49(8) (FEB 89),
2388-A.
IN 1970, AN ILLINOIS CONSTITUTIONAL CHANGE REMOVED THE
PROHIBITION AGAINST SUCCESSIVE TERMS BY A TREASURER, IN
ORDER TO ENCOURAGE PROFESSIONALISM IN THIS OFFICE. THIS
STUDY EXAMINES THE IMPACT OF THIS CHANGE, THE IMPLEMENTATION
OF THE CONSTITUTIONAL CONVENTION'S POLICY GOALS, THE
LITERATURE ON THE FUNCTION OF THE CONSTITUTION, AND ITS
ABILITY TO DIRECT THE COURSE OF PUBLIC POLICY.

07135 PERKOVICH, G.
WINDOW OF OPPORTUNITY
PRESENT TENSE, 16(4) (MAY 89), 12-17.
TO MAKE UNITED STATES FOREIGN POLICY AN ALSO THE WESTERN
SOVIET JEWRY MOVEMENT MORE RELEVANT TO THE NEEDS AND
REALITIES OF JEWS IN THE U.S.S.R., IT IS NECESSARY TO SHIFT
AWAY FROM COLD WAR-INTENSIFIED IMAGERY AND ALLEGIANCES. A
MORE FORTHCOMING AND THOUGHTFUL RESPONSE TO THE ECONOMIC,
ARMS CONTROL AND FOREIGN POLICY INITIATIVES OF THE CURRENT
SOVIET LEADERSHIP IS REQUIRED. ULTIMATELY, IN THE ERA OF
GLASNOST AND PERESTROIKA, THE U.S. CAN BEST AID SOVIET JEWRY
BY CONCEPTUALIZING AND COMMUNICATING HUMAN RIGHTS CONCERNS
AS PART OF A GENUINE WESTERN ENDEAVOR TO CREATE AN
INTERNATIONAL ENVIRONMENT THAT SATISFIES THE NEEDS OF BOTH
SUPERPOWERS FOR SECURITY, NORMAL TRADE AND DIPLOMATIC
PRESTIGE.

07136 PERL, R.F.
INTERNATIONAL ASPECTS OF U.S. DRUG-CONTROL EFFORTS
CRS REVEIW, 10(10) (NOV 89), 17-19.
BUSH'S NEW NATIONAL DRUG STRATEGY EMPHASIZES ECONOMIC
AND MILITARY ASSISTANCE TO THE ANDEAN DRUG-PRODUCING
COUNTRIES. WITH LIMITED FUNDS, POLICY-MAKERS MUST EXAMINE
THE ADEQUACY AND USES OF RESOURCES FOR FOREIGN DRUG PROGRAMS,
THE PUBLIC WILLINGNESS TO COMMIT THEM, AND THE PROSPECTS
FOR THEIR SUCCESS.

07137 PERLA, S.
ISRAEL-JORDAN ARMISTICE TALKS IN 1949: A CASE STUDY OF
ISRAEL'S PREDILECTION FOR DIRECT NEGOTIATION WITH THE ARABS
MIDDLE EAST REVIEW, XXII(1) (FAL 89), 26-34.
THE ISRAELI DECISION TO INITIATE PEACE TALKS WITH THE
ARABS WAS ADOPTED AS A CABINET RESOLUTION ON NOVEMBER 3,
1948. THIS ESSAY OFFERS A CASE STUDY OF THOSE NEGOTIATIONS.

07138 PERLMAN, B.J.
MODERNIZING THE PUBLIC SERVICE IN LATIN AMERICA: PARADOXES
OF LATIN AMERICAN PUBLIC ADMINISTRATION
INTERNATIONAL JOURNAL OF PUBLIC ADMINISTRATION, 12(4)
(1989), 671-704.

THIS ARTICLE PRESENTS IMPEDIMENTS TO THE MODERNIZATION
OF THE PUBLIC BUREACRACY IN THE LATIN AMERICAN REGION. THESE
IMPEDIMENTS ARE PRESENTED AS PARADOXES IN ORDER TO EMPHASIZE
BOTH THE CONTRADICTIONS FOUND IN, AND THE DIFFICULTY OF ALL
DEVELOPMENT EFFORTS IN LATIN AMERICA. THE ARTICLE PRESENTS
EXAMPLES FROM VARIOUS CASES IN CENTRAL AND SOUTH AMERICA IN
ORDER TO SHOW THE LACK OF A PUBLIC SERVICE TRADITION, THE
OBSTACLES OF PATRONAGE AND CORRUPTION, THE OPPORTUNITY COSTS
OF BUREACRATIC DEVELOPMENT, THE DIFFICULTY OF REFORM, AND
THE DRAWBACKS OF PROFESSIONALIZATION. IT CONCLUDES WITH SOME
SUGGESTIONS, GROUPED UNDER THE GENERAL STRATEGIES OF
INSULATION AND FORTIFICATION, ABOUT HOW TO OVERCOME THESE
IMPEDIMENTS.

07139 PERLMUTTER, A.
ISRAEL'S DILEMMA
FOREIGN AFFAIRS, 68(5) (WIN 90), 119-132.
THE PROTRACTED AND UNRESOLVED PALESTINE QUESTION HAUNTS
THE STATE OF ISRAEL. ITS LIBERAL CULTURE IS THREATENED BY
THE STATE'S CONTINUING ROLE AS AN OCCUPIER OF A FOREIGN
PEOPLE. AS A COUNTRY WEARY FROM FIGHTING, ISRAEL NOW FINDS
THE PALESTINE PROBLEM TO BE ITS PRINCIPAL THREAT, BOTH TO
ITS EXTERNAL SECURITY AND ITS INTERNAL UNITY.

07140 PERLO, V.
BEWARE THE POISONED ECONOMIC PROPAGANDA
POLITICAL AFFAIRS, LXVIII(4) (APR 89), 2-9.
GOVERNMENT OFFICIALS, CAPITALISTS, AND THEIR ECONOMISTS
ARE TRYING TO PERSUADE THE AMERICAN PEOPLE TO ACCEPT LOWER
LIVING STANDARDS TO ELIMINATE WEAKNESSES IN THE AMERICAN
ECONOMY. BUT THEIR REAL MOTIVES ARE TO INCREASE THEIR OWN
PROFITS AND IMPROVE THE INTERNATIONAL COMPETITIVE POSITION
OF AMERICAN CAPITAL AT THE EXPENSE OF THE WORKING CLASS,
FARMERS, AND THE MIDDLE CLASS.

07141 PERLO, V.
CURRENT ANTI-SOVIETISM: STALE ITEMS ON A NEW SHOPPING LIST
POLITICAL AFFAIRS, LXVIII(11) (NOV 89), 21-26.
THE ARTICLE ANALYZES THE PROPAGANDA OFFENSIVE WAGED BY
THE CAPITALIST POWERS (ESPECIALLY IN THE US) DESIGNED TO
UNDERMINE THE SUCCESS OF THE COMMUNIST SYSTEMS. FIVE
PRINCIPLE INMGRREDIENTS OF CAPITALIST PROPAGANDA ARE:
COMMUNISM IS BANKRUPT; THE USA IS THE WORLD'S LEADER; THE
COUNTRIES OF AFRICA, LATIN AMERICA AND ASIA NEED CULTURAL
LIFE IS BECOMING INTERNATIONAL-BUT NOT AN INTERNATIONALISM
OF EQUAL PARTNERS, AND ANTI-SOVIETISM MUST PERSIST AS A
FEATURE OF CAPITALIST PROPAGANDA. THE ARTICLE CONCLUDES THAT
THESE CAPITALIST CLAIMS ARE HOLLOW AND INACCURATE.

07142 PERLO, V.
RECIPROCAL MEASURES ARE NEEDED FOR PEACE AND DISARMAMENT
INFORMATION BULLETIN, 27 (MAR 89), 4-5.
THE AUTHOR DISCUSSES AMERICAN RESPONSE TO GORBACHEV'S
PROPOSALS FOR ARMS REDUCTION.

07143 PERRITT, H.H. JR.
GOVERNMENT INFORMATION GOES ON-LINE
TECHNOLOGY REVIEW, 92(8) (NOV 89), 60-67.
INFORMATION TECHNOLOGIES ARE CREATING A NEW PUBLIC-
POLICY QUESTION: SHOULD THE FEDERAL GOVERNMENT BECOME AN
ELECTRONIC PUBLISHER? THIS ARTICLE EXAMINES: THE CENSUS ON A
CD-ROM; THE ROLE FOR THE PRIVATE SECTOR: THE ROLE FOR
GOVERNMENT; AND PRESENTS A CASE BY CASE APPROACH.

07144 PERRT, B.
THE LIFE AND DEATH OF THE "CATHOLIC SEAT" ON THE UNITED
STATES SUPREME COURT
JOURNAL OF LAW & POLITICS, VI(1) (FAL 89), 55-92.
THE CONFIRMATION OF JUDGE ANTHONY KENNEDY TO THE U.S.
SUPREME COURT MADE HIM THE THIRD ROMAN CATHOLIC TO SIT ON
THE CURRENT COURT. HIS APPOINTMENT MADE THE QUESTIONS
CONCERNING THE RELATIONSHIP BETWEEN RELIGION AND NOMINATIONS
TO THE SUPREME COURT ASSUME A MORE URGENT CHARACTER. THE
ARTICLE EXAMINES THE NOMINATIONS OF THE EIGHT CATHOLICS WHO
HAVE SERVED ON THE HIGH TRIBUNAL IN THE PAST TWO CENTURIES.
IT CONCLUDES THAT RELIGIOUS AFFILIATION WAS A FACTOR, TO
VARYING DEGREES, IN ALL BUT TWO OF THE APPOINTMENTS. AN
ANALYSIS OF THE DEMOGRAPHIC, SOCIOLOGICAL, GEOGRAPHIC, AND
ELECTORAL CONTEXTS IN WHICH THE CATHOLIC NOMINATIONS
OCCURRED REVEALS THAT AS CATHOLICS EMERGED AS A POTENTIALLY
SIGNIFICANT VOTING BLOC, PRESIDENTS ATTEMPTED TO WOO THEIR
VOTES THROUGH SUPREME COURT APPOINTMENTS.

07145 PERRY, B.A.
JUSTICE HUGO BLACK AND THE "WALL OF SEPARATION BETWEEN
CHURCH AND STATE"
JOURNAL OF CHURCH & STATE, 31(1) (WIN 89), 55-72.
THE PHRASE "WALL OF SEPARATION BETWEEN CHURCH AND STATE"
COINED BY THOMAS JEFFERSON AS AN INTERPRETIVE METAPHOR FOR
THE ESTABLISHMENT CLAUSE OF THE FIRST AMENDMENT. JUSTICE
HUGO BLACK, THE FOREMOST JURISPRUDENTIAL INTERPRETER OF THE
METAPHOR IN THE SUPREME COURT'S MODERN ERA, IS RESPONSIBLE
FOR THE PUBLIC'S FAMILIARITY WITH THE "WALL" DOCTRINE.

07146 PERRY, D.
FRANCE IN AFRICA
ENCOUNTER, LXXII(4) (APR 89), 62-64.
THIRTY YEARS AFTER INDEPENDENCE, THE AMIABLE TIES
BETWEEN FRANCE AND FRENCH WEST AFRICA CONTINUE TO EXIST.
FRANCE HAS INVESTED HEAVILY IN WEST AFRICA, TO THE POINT
WHERE MANY AFRICANS WONDER WHETHER THEIR NATIONAL INTEGRITY
HAS BEEN COMPROMISED AND THE IDEA OF GENUINE INDEPENDENCE
FROM PARIS SOMETIMES SEEMS STILLBORN.

07147 PERRY, G.E.
PERESTOROIKA AND GLASTNOST IN THE SOVIET SPACE PROGRAMME
SPACE POLICY, 5(4) (NOV 89), 279-287.
FOR MANY YEARS THE WORLD-FAMOUS KETTERING GROUP OF
AMATEUR SATELLITE OBSERVERS HAVE CONFOUNDED MANY MORE
'OFFICIAL' ORGANIZATIONS IN THEIR ACCURACY IN TRACKING
SOVIET SPACE LAUNCHES. IN THIS ARTICLE THE GROUP'S FOUNDER,
GEOFFREY E. PERRY, MBE, PRESENTS HIS PERSONAL PERSPECTIVE ON
CURRENT DEVELOPMENTS IN THE SOVIET SPACE PROGRAM. THE USSR'S
INCREASED OPENNESS ABOUT NON-SENSITIVE ISSUES IS TO BE
WELCOMED, HE CONCLUDES, BUT THE KETTERING GROUP HAS WORK YET
TO DO.

07148 PERRY, M.J.
NEUTRAL POLITICS?
REVIEW OF POLITICS, 51(4) (FAL 89), 479-509.
IN AMERICAN SOCIETY MORAL DISSENSUS IS DEEP, PERVASIVE,
AND PERSISTENT. DIFFERENT MORAL COMMUNITIES WITHIN THE
SOCIETY, SECULAR AS WELL AS RELIGIOUS, ADHERE TO DIFFERENT
CONCEPTIONS OF HUMAN GOOD AND OF HOW IT IS FITTING FOR SOME
OR ALL HUMAN BEINGS TO LIVE THEIR LIVES. ACCORDING TO THE
LIBERAL VISION OF THE PROPER RELATION OF MORALITY TO
POLITICS, THE POLITICS OF A PLURALISTIC SOCIETY SHOULD AIM
TO BE NEUTRAL. THE PRINCIPAL CONCEPTIONS OF MORALITY AND
POLITICS EXAMINED IN THIS ESSAY EACH IN ITS OWN WAY PURPORTS
TO PORTARY A NEUTRAL POLITICS, IN THE SENSE OF A POLITICS IN
WHICH THE PRACTICE OF JUSTIFYING POLITICAL INSTITUTIONS,
PRACTICES, AND POLICIES IS NEUTRAL OR IMPARTIAL.

07149 PERRY, W.J.
DEFENSE INVESTMENT STRATEGY
FOREIGN AFFAIRS, 68(2) (SPR 89), 72-92.
A NEW AMERICAN NATIONAL SECRUITY POLICY MUST TAKE
ACCOUNT OF THE NEW COMPLEXITIES IN INTERNATIONAL RELATIONS.
THIS ARTICLE DEALS WITH ONE ASPECT OF SUCH A POLICY: NAMELY,
HOW TO STRUCTURE A DEFENSE INVESTMENT STRATEGY THAT
RECOGNIZES BOTH THE OPPORTUNITIES AND THE RISKS IN THE NEW
POLITICAL AND ECONOMIC DYNAMICS.

07150 PERSAUD, B.
THE SIGNIFICANCE OF ESTABLISHING A COMMONWEALTH EQUITY FUND
ROUND TABLE, (312) (OCT 89), 363-370.
THIS ARTICLE EXAMINES THE INITIATIVE BEING NOW
CONSIDERED - THE ESTABLISHMENT OF A COMMONWEALTH EQUITY FUND
(CEF). IT EXPLORES THE SIGNIFICANCE OF THIS MOVE FOR
COMMONWEALTH ECONOMIC COOPERATION, AND WHAT IT IMPLIES FOR
THE COMMONWEALTH IN RELATION TO INNOVATIVENESS, CHANGE AND
ADAPTATION. IT GIVES THE RATIONALE, THE BENEFITS, THE CASE
FOR ACTION AND LONGTERM OBJECTIVES.

07151 PERSKY, J.
BLACK ECONOMIC THOUGHT AND THE SOUTHERN ECONOMY
REVIEW OF BLACK POLITICAL ECONOMY, 17(4) (SPR 89), 27-44.
FROM EARLY IN THE NINETEENTH CENTURY SOUTHERN WHITES
OFTEN ANALYZED THE ILLS OF THE SOUTH AS ORIGINATING IN THE
REGION'S COLONIAL RELATION TO THE NORTH. A SURVEY OF BLACK
ECONOMIC THOUGH-ACADEMIC, JOURNALISTIC AND POLITICAL-
SUGGESTS THAT THIS NOTION WAS NEVER STRONGLY ENDORSED BY
BLACK INTELLECTUALS. THE OUTSTANDING EXCEPTIONS HERE WORKS
BY BLACK SOCIOLOGISTS COLLABORATING WITH WHITE COLLEAGUES IN
THE 1930S. FOR THE MOST PART. HOWEVER, BLACK WRITERS
SUBSCRIBED TO A VIEW THAT EMPHASIZED THE DEPENDENT NATURE,
NOT OF THE SOUTH, BUT OF THE ECONOMY OF THE BLACK COMMUNITY
IN ITS RELATIONS WITH THE SOUTH.

07152 PERUCCI, G.; SANDERSON, S.E.
PRESIDENTIAL SUCCESSION, ECONOMIC CRISIS, AND POPULIST
RESURGENCE IN BRAZIL
STUDIES IN COMPARATIVE INTERNATIONAL DEVELOPMENT, 24(3)
(FAL 89), 30-49.
LATIN AMERICAN POPULISM HAS BEEN CHARACTERIZED AS A TIME-
BOUND PHENOMENON, PART OF THE POLITICAL REVOLUTION AGAINST
THE OLD AGRICULTURAL OLIGARCHY AND ACCOMPANYING IMPORT-
SUBSTITUTION INDUSTRIALIZATION. IT HAS BEEN ASSERTED THAT
POPULISM DIED WITH THE "EXHAUSTION" OF THE "EASY PHASE" OF
IMPORT-SUBSTITUTION, AND THAT BUREAUCRATIC AUTHORITARIAN
REGIMES HERE PREDICTED ON THAT DEMISE. BRAZIL, ARGENTINA,
MEXICO, AND PERU ARE REGULARLY CITED AS EVIDENCE. THIS
ARTICLE EXAMINES THESE DEFINITIONAL PREMISES IN LIGHT OF THE
APPARENT RESURGENCE OF POPULIST POLITICS IN THE DEMOCRATIC
TRANSITION IN BRAZIL. IT IS ARGUED THAT POPULISM IS NOT A
PRE-1964 ANACHRONISM, BUT IS PREDICTABLY APPEALING IN THE
1980S. DISTINCTIONS AMONG POPULIST APPEALS, CONTENTION FOR
POWER, AND SUCCESSFUL POPULIST ORDER SUGGEST THAT POPULISM

AND ITS LEADERS OFFER A VERY LIMITED ALTERNATIVE TO THE
FUTURE OF BRAZILIAN POLITICS.

07153 PERUMAL, C.A.; THANDAVAN, R.
ETHNIC VIOLENCE IN SRI LANKA: CAUSES AND CONSEQUENCES
INDIAN JOURNAL OF POLITICAL SCIENCE, L(1) (JAN 89), 1-17.
THE AUTHORS DISCUSS THE THEORETICAL BACKGROUND TO ETHNIC
VIOLENCE AND EXAMINE THE ONGOING ETHNIC CRISIS IN SRI LANKA.

07154 PESCHEK, J.G.
"FREE THE FORTUNE 500!" THE AMERICAN ENTERPRISE INSTITUTE
AND THE POLITICS OF THE CAPITALIST CLASS IN THE 1970S
CRITICAL SOCIOLOGY, 16(2-3) (SUM 89), 165-180.
DURING THE 1980S CONSERVATIVE U.S. POLICIES WERE SHAPED
BY THE PRIOR WORK OF A WELL-FUNDED NETWORK OF PRIVATE POLICY-
PLANNING ORGANIZATIONS, NOTABLY THE AMERICAN ENTERPRISE
INSTITUTE. DURING THE 1970S THE AEI BECAME A FAVORED
RECIPIENT OF POLICY-ORIENTED BUSINESS FUNDING, RECRUITED
PROMINENT NEOCONSERVATIVE INTELLECTUALS, AND REFORMULATED
CONSERVATIVE IDEOLOGY TO MAKE CRITICS OF CAPITALISM APPEAR
UNDEMOCRATIC. IT IS ARGUED THAT WIDESPREAD BUSINESS SUPPORT
FOR CONSERVATIVE POLICY ORGANIZATIONS LIKE THE AEI WERE
CONSISTENT WITH CAPITALIST DRIVES TO ATTACK LABOR,
REGULATION, AND SOCIAL WELFARE PROGRAMS IN THE SPECIFIC
CONTEXT OF THE ECONOMIC CRISIS OF THE 1970S.

07155 PETEMAN, C.
"GOD HATH ORDAINED TO MAN A HELPER": HOBBES, PATRIARCHY,
AND CONJUGAL RIGHT
BRITISH JOURNAL OF POLITICAL SCIENCE, 19(4) (OCT 89),
445-464.
THERE ARE TWO CONFLICTING AND EQUALLY MISLEADING
INTERPRETATIONS OF HOBBES: EITHER HE IS A PATRIARCHSLIST
LIKE FILMER -- BUT THE PREMISE OF HOBBES'S THEORY IS THAT
POLITICAL RIGHT ORIGINATES IN MATERNAL NOT PATERNAL LORDSHIP;
OR HE IS AN ANTIPATRIARCHALIST -- BUT HE ENDORSE THE
SUBJECTION OF WIVES TO HUSBANDS IN CIVIL SOCIETY. TO
APPRECIATE HOW HOBBES TURNS MOTHER RIGHT INTO A SPECIFICALLY
MODERN, NON-PATERNAL FORM OF PATRIARCHY, AN UNDERSTANDING IS
REQUIRED OF HIS PECULIAR VIEW OF THE FAMILY AS A PROTECTIVE
ASSOCIATION OF MASTER AND SERVANTS THAT ORIGINATES IN
CONQUEST (CONTRACT). SECONDLY, A CONJECTURAL HISTORY OF THE
DEFEAT OF WOMEN BY MEN IN THE NATURAL CONDITION AND THEIR
INCORPORATION INTO 'FAMILIES' HAS TO BE PROVIDED. THE
OVERTHROW OF MOTHER RIGHT ENABLES MEN TO ENTER THE ORGINAL
CONTRACT, TO CREATE LEVIATHAN IN THEIR OWN IMAGE, AND TO
SECURE THE FRUITS OF THEIR CONQUEST BY ESTABLISHING
PATRIARCHAL POLITICAL RIGHT, EXERCISED IN LARGE PART AS
CONJUNGAL RIGHT.

07156 PETER, K.B.
THE PATHOLOGY OF DEMOCRATIC DOMINATION: THE CORRUPTION OF
DEMOCRACIES THAT DOMINATE FOREIGN PEOPLES
DISSERTATION ABSTRACTS INTERNATIONAL, 49(7) (JAN 89),
1952-A.
A DEMOCRACY THAT DOMINATES FOREIGN PEOPLES WILL FIND
IMPORTANT ELEMENTS OF THAT DOMINATION RETURNING HOME TO
COMPROMISE ITS OWN DEMOCRACY. IN EXPLORING THIS THESIS, THE
AUTHOR EXAMINES THE RELEVANT TREATISES BY THUCYDIDES AND
MACHIAVELLI. THEN HE IDENTIFIES FOUR SPECIFIC MECHANISMS
THAT HAVE LINKED AMERICAN INFLUENCE OVERSEAS WITH PARTIAL
CORRUPTION OF AMERICAN DEMOCRACY SINCE WORLD WAR II.

07157 PETERS, T.
NOT IN MY BACKYARD! THE WASTE-DISPOSAL CRISIS
THE CHRISTIAN CENTURY, 106(5) (FEB 89), 175-177.
THE AUTHOR PROPOSES SEVEN PRINCIPLES TO HELP TRANSLATE
THE ABSTRACT WHOLE-PART DIALECTIC INTO PUBLIC POLICY
REGARDING WASTE DISPOSAL.

07158 PETERSEN, J.
THE FUTURE OF INFRASTRUCTURE NEEDS
AMERICAN CITY AND COUNTY, 104(4) (APR 89), 10.
THE NEED TO REPLENISH AND EXPAND PUBLIC WORKS IN THE
UNITED STATES HAS BEEN LARGELY IGNORED, RESULTING IN THE
DETERIORATION OF FACILITIES AND THE LACK OF CAPITAL INFUSION.
STATE AND LOCAL GOVERNMENT SPENDING ON FIXED INVESTMENT
NEEDS TO INCREASED SIGNIFICANTLY TO REPLACE EXISTING CAPITAL
STOCK, MEET PERFORMANCE STANDARDS, AND ACCOMMODATE NEW
GROWTH. BUT, OVER THE NEXT DECADE, STATE AND LOCAL
GOVERNMENTS WILL FACE CONSIDERABLE FINANCIAL CONSTRAINTS IN
RAISING THEIR LEVELS OF CAPITAL SPENDING.

07159 PETERSEN, P.A.
NEW TECHNOLOGICAL AND ECONOMICS OF DEFENCE: ITALY IN
SOVIET MILITARY STRATEGY
INTERNATIONAL SPECTATOR, XXIII(1) (JAN 88), 16-27.
IN THE EYES OF SOVIET STRATEGIC PLANNERS, ITALY OCCUPIES
A VITAL MILITARY-GEOGRAPHIC POSITION FOR THE CONDUCT OF
COMBAT OPERATIONS AGAINST THE SOUTHERN FLANK OF WARSAW PACT
FORCES IN THE WESTERN TSMA, AS WELL AS AGAINST PACT FORCES
OPERATING IN THE SOUTHWESTERN TSMA. THESE TWO FACTORS ARE
CRITICAL ELEMENTS OF THE ROLE OF ITALY IN SOVIET MILITARY
STRATEGY. THIS DISCUSSION FOCUSES ON SOVIET ASSESSMENTS OF

ITALY IN THE CONTEXT OF SOVIET STRATEGIC OFFENSIVES IN THE
WESTERN AND SOUTHWESTERN TSMA'S.

07160 PETERSMANN, E.U.
STRENGTHENING GATT PROCEDURES FOR SETTLING TRADE DISPUTES
WORLD ECONOMY, 11(1) (MAR 88), 55-90.
THIS ARTICLE BEGINS WITH A FEW INTRODUCTORY COMMENTS ON
THE DIFFICULTIES OF UNDERSTANDING THE GENERAL AGREEMENT ON
TARIFFS AND TRADE (GATT) LEGAL SYSTEM AND OF ENSURING ITS
CONSISTENT INTERPRETATION AND APPLICATION. IT GOES ON TO
DESCRIBE THE CONTRIBUTION OF GATT DISPUTE-SETTLEMENT
PROCEDURES TO THE MAINTENANCE OF LEGAL CERTAINTY AND OVERALL
CONSISTENCY IN THE GATT LEGAL SYSTEM, THEN LISTS A NUMBER OF
REMAINING PROCEDURAL WEAKNESSES AND DISCUSSES SOME PROPOSALS
FOR FOR IMPROVEMENTS IN THE GATT DISPUTE-SETTLEMENT SYSTEM.

07161 PETERSON, J.
HORMONES, HEIFERS AND HIGH POLITICS-BIOTECHNOLOGY AND THE
COMMON AGRICULTURAL POLICY
PUBLIC ADMINISTRATION, 67(4) (WIN 89), 455-471.
THE RECENT EC BAN ON IMPORTS OF HORMONE-TREATED BEEF AND
THE CENTRAL PLACE OF AGRICULTURAL REGIME LIBERALIZATION IN
THE URUGUAY ROUND OF GATT (GENERAL AGREEMENT ON TRADE AND
TARIFFS) NEGOTIATIONS HAVE COMBINED TO MAKE AGRICULTURAL
REFORM A MATTER OF 'HIGH POLITICS' IN INTERNATIONAL TRADE.
BUT DEBATES ON MEDIUM-TERM REFORM OF THE COMMON AGRICULTURAL
POLICY FAIL TO CONSIDER THE IMPACT OF FUTURE DEVELOPMENTS IN
BIOTECHNOLOGY, WHICH THREATEN TO OVERWHELM THE EC'S ABILITY
TO COPE WITH AGRICULTURAL SURPLUS. MEANWHILE, THE EC HAS
BEGUN TO ACCELERATE ITS EFFORTS TO PROMOTE EUROPE'S
COMPETITIVENESS IN GLOBAL BIOTECHNOLOGY MARKETS THROUGH NEW
COLLABORATIVE RESEARCH PROGRAMMES. THE CLASH OF INTERESTS
BETWEEN THE EC'S AGRICULTURAL AND TECHNOLOGY POLICY
COMMUNITIES HAS PRODUCED CONTRADICTORY POLICIES AND NEW
OBSTACLES TOWARD THE CRITICAL GOAL OF REFORMING THE CAP. THE
EC'S EFFORTS TO PROMOTE BIOTECHNOLOGY MUST BE RECONCILED
WITH BIOTECHNOLOGY'S FUTURE IMPACTS ON EUROPEAN AGRICULTURE
THROUGH MORE RIGOROUS TECHNOLOGY ASSESSMENT AND REFORM OF
AGRICULTURAL POLICY-MAKING MECHANISMS.

07162 PETERSON, J. E.
THE POLITICAL STATUS OF WOMEN IN THE ARAB GULF STATES
MIDDLE EAST JOURNAL, 43(1) (WIN 89), 34-50.
A REQUISITE STEP TO INCREASING POLITICAL PARTICIPATION
BY WOMEN IN THE GULF IS EXTENDING (OR BREAKING THROUGH) THE
TRADITIONAL BOUNDARIES OF THE "WOMEN'S DOMAIN." WIDESPREAD
DIRECT POLITICAL PARTICIPATION MAY NOT BE ATTAINED UNTIL
THIS HAS OCCURRED AND MORE EQUALITY BETWEEN THE SEXES HAS
BEEN ACHIEVED IN THE PUBLIC ARENA. THE NATURE AND EXTENT OF
THAT PARTICIPATION WILL BE DETERMINED, FOR MEN AS WELL AS
FOR WOMEN, BY THE STRUCTURE OF GCC POLITICAL SYSTEMS
PREVAILING IN THE NEXT FEW DECADES.

07163 PETERSON, M.R.
EARTHQUAKE PREPAREDNESS IN MISSOURI COUNTIES: EFFECTS OF
PROBLEM DEFINITION ON AGENDA BUILDING
DISSERTATION ABSTRACTS INTERNATIONAL, 50(3) (SEP 89),
790-A.
EARTHQUAKES PRESENT A DANGER FOR MISSOURI AND OTHER
STATES, BUT ATTENTION DEVOTED TO THIS PROBLEM BY LOCAL
OFFICIALS IS SPORADIC. IN THIS DISSERTATION, THE AUTHOR
ENDEAVORS TO DISCOVER HOW COUNTY COMMISSIONS REACT TO
PROCESS AGENDA-SETTING INFORMATION AND TO DETERMINE HOW THIS
PROCESS OCCURS FOR LOW-SALIENCE ISSUES, ESPECIALLY
EARTHQUAKE PREPAREDNESS.

07164 PETERSON, P.E.; ROM, M.
AMERICAN FEDERALISM, WELFARE POLICY, AND RESIDENTIAL
CHOICES
AMERICAN POLITICAL SCIENCE REVIEW, 83(3) (SEP 89), 711-728.
THE RELATIONSHIP BETWEEN WELFARE BENEFIT LEVELS AND THE
RESIDENTIAL CHOICES OF THE POOR RAISES TWO ISSUES FOR
FEDERALISM IN THE UNITED STATES. DO STATE BENEFIT LEVELS
AFFECT THE RESIDENTIAL CHOICES OF THE POOR? DO RESIDENTIAL
CHOICES OF THE POOR AFFECT THE LEVEL AT WHICH A STATE SETS
ITS BENEFIT LEVELS? EMPIRICAL STUDIES HAVE SELDOM STUDIED
THE INTERCONNECTION BETWEEN THESE TWO ISSUES. THIS RESEARCH
ESTIMATES SIMULTANEOUSLY THE MUTUAL EFFECTS OF WELFARE
BENEFITS AND POVERTY RATES CONTROLLING FOR OTHER ECONOMIC
AND POLITICAL VARIABLES. WHEN BENEFIT LEVELS BECOME HIGH,
THE SIZE OF THE POVERTY POPULATION INCREASES. CONVERSELY,
WHEN POVERTY RATES BECOME HIGH, BENEFIT LEVELS ARE CUT. THE
FINDINGS ARE CONSISTENT WITH THE CLAIM THAT STATE-DETERMINED
BENEFIT LEVELS DISTORT POLICY AND RESIDENTIAL CHOICES.

07165 PETERSON, S.A.; LAWSON, R.
RISKY BUSINESS: PROSPECT THEORY AND POLITICS
POLITICAL PSYCHOLOGY, 10(2) (JUN 89), 325-339.
PROSPECT THEORY SUGGESTS THAT INDIVIDUALS' ORIENTATIONS
TOWARD RISK AFFECT PEOPLE'S BEHAVIOR. THIS ESSAY CONSIDERS
POLITICAL IMPLICATIONS, EXPLORING THE EXTENT TO WHICH
PEOPLE'S VIEWS ABOUT RISK INFLUENCE STATUS QUO ORIENTATIONS,
POLITICAL PARTICIPATION, AND POLITICAL INVOLVEMENT. DATA
FROM A STUDENT SAMPLE ARE USED TO TEST THESE EXPECTED

RELATIONSHIP.

07166 PETERSON, V.S.
AN ARCHEOLOGY OF DOMINATION: HISTORICIZING GENDER AND
CLASS IN EARLY WESTERN STATE FORMATION
DISSERTATION ABSTRACTS INTERNATIONAL, 50(5) (NOV 89),
1425-A.
THE AUTHOR PRESENTS A THEORETICAL FRAMEWORK FOR AND
HISTORICAL DISCUSSION OF THE CONSTRUCTION, LEGITIMATION, AND
INSTITUTIONALIZATION OF DOMINATION RELATIONS IN EARLY
WESTERN STATE FORMATION. PROCESSES OF SOCIAL DIFFERENTIATION
ARE EXAMINED WITHIN THREE SOCIETAL CONFIGURATIONS:
COMMUNAL/EGALITARIAN, KIN CORPORATE/LINEAGE, AND
ARCHAIC/CIVIL STATE. SOCIETAL TRANSFORMATIONS ARE SHOWN TO
RESULT FROM SYSTEMIC AND PROCESSUAL INTERACTIONS AMONG
ECOLOGICAL, CULTURAL, AND TECHNOLOGICAL VARIABLES--
PARTICULARLY THE POLITICS OF SEXUALITY, KINSHIP, AND
CITIZENSHIP; MILITARISM; TRADE/EXCHANGE RELATIONSHIPS; AND
COSMOLOGICAL/IDEOLOGICAL TRANSFORMATIONS.

07167 PETKOV, K.
THE CAUSES OF ALIENATION
WORLD MARXIST REVIEW, 32(10) (OCT 89), 51-52.
THIS ARTICLE ADDRESSES THE ALIENATION OF CITIZENS FROM
SOCIALIST SOCIETY AND QUESTIONS SUCH AS HOW LONG CAN THE
BLAME BE PUT ON CAPITALISM? EXAMINED ARE OTHER CAUSES SUCH
AS DISTORTIONS IN THE SYSTEM OF ADMINISTRATION AND
GOVERNMENT. FINALLY, EXPLORES THE SPHERE OF OWNERSHIP AND
HOW IT CAUSES ALIENATION.

07168 PETKOVIC, R.
WHAT IS CHANGING IN YUGOSLAVIA'S FOREIGN POLICY
INTERNATIONAL AFFAIRS (MOSCOW), (3) (MAR 89), 75-82.
IN THE POST-WAR DECADES, JOSIP BROZ TITO'S FOREIGN
POLICY CARVED OUT A REASONABLY IMPORTANT INTERNATIONAL ROLE
FOR YUGOSLAVIA. NOW THE DEMOCRATIZATION OF POLITICAL LIFE IN
YUGOSLAVIA IS CREATING NEW OPPORTUNITIES FOR FOREIGN POLICY
DEVELOPMENT. IN THIS ARTICLE, THE AUTHOR REVIEWS
YUGOSLAVIA'S PAST FOREIGN POLICY AND HOW IT IS CHANGING.

07169 PETRACCA, M.P.
POLITICAL CONSULTANTS AND DEMOCRATIC GOVERNANCE
PS: POLITICAL SCIENCE AND POLITICS, XXII(1) (MAR 89),
11-14.
THE USA FACES A MONUMENTAL CHALLENGE TO THE PRACTICE OF
DEMOCRATIC GOVERNANCE. THIS CHALLENGE STEMS, IN PART, FROM
CHANGES IN THE CONCEPTUALIZATION AND PRACTICE OF POLITICAL
CAMPAIGNING AND FROM THE REVOLUTIONARY EFFECTS OF THE
TECHNOLOGY DEPLOYED IN RECENT CAMPAIGNS. TWO MAJOR FORCES
BEHIND THIS TRANSFORMATION ARE THE RISE OF POLITICAL
CONSULTANTS AND THE TECHNOLOGY THAT THEY UTILIZE.

07170 PETRAEUS, D.H.
MILITARY INFLUENCE AND THE POST-VIETNAM USE OF FORCE
ARMED FORCES AND SOCIETY, 15(4) (SUM 89), 489-505.
THE CARICATURE OF AMERICA'S MILITARY LEADERS AS CIGAR-
CHOMPING, TABLE-POUNDING WARMONGERS REFLECTS A COMMON
ASSUMPTION THAT DURINC CRISIES, THE MILITARY URGE THE USE OF
ARMS. SUCH STEREOTYPES, HOWEVER, HAVE SELDOM HELD TRUE; THEY
ARE PARTICULARLY UNSUPPORTED BY THE EVIDENCE IN THE POST-
VIETNAM ERA. AN EXAMINATION OF THE CASES SINCE 1973 IN WHICH
THE USE OF FORCE WAS CONSIDERED REVEALS THAT THE MILITARY'S
VOICE IN PRESIDENTIAL COUNSELS OF WAR HAS BEEN NEITHER THE
MOST BELLICOSE NOR THE MOST COMMANDING. ON THE OTHER HAND,
AMERICA'S SENIOR SOLDIERS HAVE NOT BEEN DOVES IN UNIFORM OR
OF INSIGNIFICANT INFLUENCE. THE MILITARY FREQUENTLY HAVE
INFLUENCED INTERVENTION DECISION-EVEN WHEN THEY HAVE SOUGHT
TO AVOID THE ISSUE OF WHETHER FORCE SHOULD BE USED. AND WHEN
THE DISCUSSION HAS TURNED TO CONSIDERATION OF HOW TO USE
FORCE IN A PARTICULAR SITUATION, SENIOR MILITARY LEADERS
HAVE EXERTED CONSIDERABLE INFLUENCE.

07171 PETRAEUS, D.H.
THE AMERICAN MILITARY AND THE LESSONS OF VIETNAM: A STUDY
OF MILITARY INFLUENCE AND THE USE OF FORCE IN THE POST-
VIETNAM ERA
DISSERTATION ABSTRACTS INTERNATIONAL, 48(8) (FEB 88),
2155-A.
THE FOCUS OF THE DISSERTATION IS THE IMPACT OF VIETNAM
ON AMERICA'S SENIOR MILITARY WITH RESPECT TO THEIR MOST
IMPORTANT TASK--ADVISING THE NATION'S LEADERSHIP ON THE USE
OF AMERICAN MILITARY FORCES IN POTENTIAL COMBAT SITUATIONS.
IT CONCLUDES THAT THE GREATEST LEGACY OF VIETNAM IS THE
CAUTION THAT HAS CHARACTERIZED THE MILITARY EVER SINCE AND
IS LIKELY TO CONTINUE FOR SOME TIME IN THE FUTURE.

07172 PETRAS, J.
STATE TERROR AND SOCIAL MOVEMENTS IN LATIN AMERICAN
POLITICS
INTERNATIONAL JOURNAL OF POLITICS, CULTURE AND SOCIETY,
3(2) (WIN 89), 179-212.
JAMES PETRAS UNCOVERS THE DILEMMAS AND CONTRADICTIONS OF
GOVERNANCE AND RESISTANCES TO IT, POINTING OUT THE CENTRAL
ROLES OF MASS MOVEMENTS AND STATE TERROR IN THE SOCIAL

DISORDERS THAT HAVE PLAGUED THE COUNTRIES OF SOUTH AMERICA.
HE STUDIES THE SIGNIFICANCE OF SOCIAL MOVEMENTS AND
CONCLUDES THAT OVER THE PAST 30 YEARS SOCIAL MOVEMENTS HAVE
BEEN A MAJOR POLITICAL FORCE IN LATIN AMERICAN POLITICS,
BOTH AS AGENTS OF SOCIAL TRANSFORMATIONS AND AS OBJECTS OF
UNPRECEDENTED VIOLENCE.

07173 PETRAS, J.
STATE, REGIME AND THE DEMOCRATIZATION MUDDLE
JOURNAL OF CONTEMPORARY ASIA, 9(1) (1989), 26-32.
THIS ARTICLE SUGGESTS THAT IN ANALYZING THE PROCESS OF
POLITICAL CHANGE IT IS IMPORTANT TO RECOGNIZE THE DIFFERENT
LEVELS AT WHICH TRANSFORMATION TAKES PLACE IN ORDER TO
DETERMINE THE SCOPE AND DIRECTION OF POLICY AS WELL AS TO BE
ABLE TO ADEQUATELY CHARACTERIZE THE PROCESS. IT USES FOR AN
EXAMPLE, A NUMBER OF POLITICAL CHANGES IN LATIN AMERICA THAT
HAVE BEEN DUBBED A "DEMOCRATIZATION" PROCESS WHICH PRODUCED
"DEMOCRATIC STATES," THE ARTICLE CONCLUDES THAT THOSE
POLITICAL CHANGES HAVE NOT CHANGED THE NATURE OF STATE, BUT
RATHER HAVE LED TO CHANGES AT THE LEVEL OF GOVERNMENT OR
REGIME.

07174 PETRITSCH-HOLADAY, M.
WOMEN AND DECISION-MAKING
AUSTRIA TODAY, (4) (1989), 6-9, 62.
THE ISSUE OF EQUALITY IN POLITICAL PARTICIPATION AND
DECISION-MAKING, AS IT RELATES TO AUSTRIA, HAS A WIDE RANGE
OF ASPECTS. THESE INCLUDE WOMEN AS MEMBERS OF PARLIAMENT, AS
CABINET MEMBERS AND ADVISERS, AS SENIOR FEDERAL CIVIL
SERVANTS, AND AS MEMBERS OF THE PROVINCIAL GOVERNMENTS. AN
IMPORTANT ADDITIONAL ELEMENT IS THE PARTICIPATION, OR NON-
PARTICIPATION, OF WOMEN IN DECISION-MAKING POSITIONS IN THE
INSTITUTIONS OF THE "SOCIAL AND ECONOMIC PARTNERSHIP." THESE
INCLUDE SUCH GROUPS AS THE TRADE UNIONS AND EMPLOYERS'
ASSOCIATIONS THAT REPRESENT THE ORGANIZED ECONOMIC INTERESTS
IN NEGOTIATIONS THAT REGULATE VARIOUS ASPECTS OF ECONOMIC
LIFE.

07175 PETROCIK, J.R.
AN EXPECTED PARTY VOTE: NEW DATA FOR AN OLD CONCEPT
AMERICAN JOURNAL OF POLITICAL SCIENCE, 33(1) (FEB 89),
44-66.
AT ITS INTRODUCTION THE NORMAL VOTE WAS A POWERFUL
CONCEPT AND A USEFUL TOOL. WITHIN THE LAST DECADE IT HAS
BECOME A SUSPECT IDEA AND A FLAWED MEASUREMENT. THIS PAPER
USES A NEW AND EXTENSIVE DATA SET TO REOPERATIONALIZE THE
CONCEPT. THE SPECIFICATION BY WHICH IT IS DERIVED AVOIDS
MOST OF THE PROBLEMS INHERENT IN THE INITIAL FORMULATION.
THE PAPER ILLUSTRATES THE USEFUL ANALYTIC INSIGHTS PROVIDED
BY THE CONCEPT, AND IT DOCUMENTS ITS UTILITY AS AN ANALYTIC
TOOL.

07176 PETROVICH, R.
PERMANENT NEUTRALITY FOR ISRAEL?
REVIEW OF INTERNATIONAL AFFAIRS, (JAN 88), 25-28.
THE AUTHOR ARGUES THAT THE ARAB-ISRAELI CONFLICT CANNOT
BE SOLVED COMPREHENSIVELY AND ON A LASTING BASIS WITHOUT
RECOURSE TO A RECOGNIZED INTERNATIONAL SOLUTION:
ESTABLISHING PERMANENT NEUTRALITY FOR ISRAEL. THE AUTHOR
EVALUATES WHAT EACH COUNTRY INVOLVED IN THE MIDDLE EAST
CRISIS WOULD GAIN OR LOSE BY SUCH A SOLUTION.

07177 PETROVSKY, V.
A DIALOGUE ON COMPREHENSIVE SECURITY
INTERNATIONAL AFFAIRS (MOSCOW), (11) (NOV 89), 3-13.
INTERNATIONAL POLITICAL DEVELOPMENTS SHOULD STIMULATE A
LASTING INTEREST IN THE IDEA OF COMPREHENSIVE INTERNATIONAL
SECURITY. DIALOGUE ON ALL-EMBRACING SECURITY IS ESSENTIALLY
A FRANK EXCHANGE OF VIEWS ON HOW TO PUT THE IDEAS OF NEW
POLITICAL THINKING INTO PRACTICE, HOW TO BUILD INTERNATIONAL
INTERCOUSE ON THE PRINCIPLE OF GIVING PRIORITY TO UNIVERSAL
VALUES, AND HOW TO SEARCH IN COLLABORATION WITH OTHER
MEMBERS OF THE INTERNATIONAL COMMUNITY FOR AN OVERALL
STRATEGY OF GUARANTEED SURVIVAL. THE TASK OF PRESERVING AND
ADVANCING CIVILIZATION INCLUDES ESTABLISHING A DURABLE
SECURITY SYSTEM AND ORGANIZING INTERNATIONAL RELATIONS ON
THE BASIS OF A BALANCE OF THE INTERESTS OF ALL COUNTRIES AND
ON JUST, REASONABLE, AND RATIONAL PRINCIPLES.

07178 PETROVSKY, V.
SECURITY AND DISARMAMENT
DISARMAMENT, XII(3) (AUT 89), 40-44.
NEW POLITICAL THINKING, THE ELIMINATION OF
CONFRONTATIONAL STEREOTYPES, AND A SEARCH FOR A BALANCE OF
INTERESTS HAVE MADE IT POSSIBLE TO ENHANCE CONFIDENCE,
IMPROVE THE INTERNATIONAL SITUATION, AND MAKE PROGRESS IN
STRENGTHENING GLOBAL SECURITY IN ITS PRINCIPAL AREA, THAT OF
DISARMAMENT. THE DYNAMIC REDUCTIONS IN MILITARY ARSENALS
HAVE MADE IT POSSIBLE TO WARD OFF THE MILITARY THREAT AND
REDIRECT THE COURSE OF WORLD AFFAIRS AWAY FROM CONFRONTATION
AND TOWARDS COOPERATION, UNDERSTANDING, AND NEGOTIATION. THE
WORLD HAS BEGUN TO BUILD A NEW SECURITY MODEL, NOT THROUGH
MILITARY BUILDUP AS HAS ALWAYS BEEN THE CASE IN THE PAST,
BUT THROUGH ARMS REDUCTION ON A MUTUALLY ACCEPTABLE BASIS.

THE SECURITY THROUGH DISARMAMENT PRINCIPLE IS GAINING
CURRENCY.

07179 PETTERSEN, P.A.
COMPARING NON-VOTERS IN THE USA AND NORWAY: PERMANENCE
VERSUS
EUROPEAN JOURNAL OF POLITICAL RESEARCH, 17(3) (MAY 89),
351-359.
TRANSIENCE VOTER TURNOUT FOR THE 1984 PRESIDENTIAL
ELECTION IN THE USA WAS 30 PERCENT LOWER THAN THE LAST
PARLIAMENTARY ELECTION IN NORWAY (1985). SIMILARITIES AMONG
THE FACTORS WHICH EXPLAINS NON-VOTING IN THE TWO NATIONS ARE
APPARENT, BUT THE FACTORS UNIQUE TO EACH COUNTRY ARE
IMPORTANT FOR UNDERSTANDING THE DIFFERENCE IN TURNOUT LEVEL
AS WELL AS PATTERNS OF NON-PARTICIPATION. WHILE THE
NORWEGIAN NON-VOTERS ARE IN A TRANSIENT SITUATION WHERE
YOUTH AND LIMITED LIFE-CYCLE EXPERIENCE DETERMINE NON-VOTING,
FACTORS EFFECTING AMERICAN NON-VOTERS ARE MORE PERMANENT.
IN PARTICULAR, IF SOCIO-ECONOMIC RESOURCES ARE NOT ACQUIRED
IN YOUTH, THE DEVELOPMENT OF POLITICAL INVOLVEMENT AND
PARTICIPATION WILL BE OBSTRUCTED.

07180 PETZOLDT, D.M.
EXAMINATION OF THE UNITED STATES' ROLE IN THE DEVELOPMENT
OF THE ISRAELI LAVI FIGHTER AIRCRAFT PROGRAM
AVAILABLE FROM NTIS, NO. AD-A201 537/8/GAR, SEP 88, 72.
FOR THE PURPOSE OF THIS RESEARCH, SECURITY ASSISTANCE
WAS EXAMINED THROUGH AN ANALYSIS OF THE U.S. ROLE IN THE
DEVELOPMENT OF THE ISRAELI LAVI FIGHTER AIRCRAFT PROGRAM.
THE METHODOLOGY INCLUDED AN OVERVIEW OF ISRAEL'S HISTORICAL
DEPENDENCE ON U.S. AID. THIS RESEARCH ADDRESSED THE
FOLLOWING OBJECTIVE QUESTIONS: (1) WHY DID ISRAEL WANT TO
BUILD THE LAVI WHEN THERE WERE SEVERAL ADVANCED FIGHTERS
ALREADY AVAILABLE; (2) WHY DID THE UNITED STATES FUND THE
LAVI; AND (3) WHAT DID THE LAVI PROJECT ACCOMPLISH IN TERMS
OF U.S. FOREIGN POLICY. THE EXAMINATION OF THE LAVI ANALYZED
HOW ISRAEL DEVELOPED THE INITIAL PROPOSAL FOR THE AIRCRAFT,
HOW THEY ACQUIRED THE FUNDS AND TECHNOLOGY FROM THE U.S.,
HOW THE PROGRAM COSTS ESCALATED, WHY THE PROJECT WAS
CANCELLED, AND HOW ISRAEL WILL MEET FUTURE THREATS TO ITS
SECURITY. ALSO EXAMINED WERE THE EFFECTS THE LAVI HAD ON
PROMOTING U.S. FOREIGN POLICY GOALS IN THE MIDDLE EAST AND
IF THOSE GOALS WERE MET. KEYWORDS: THESES.

07181 PEZESHKAN, F.
IRAN: FREEDOM MOVEMENT
THIRD WORLD WEEK, 8(3) (MAR 89), 13-14.
IRAN'S FREEDOM MOVEMENT PARTY IS PREPARED TO ACCEPT THE
GOVERNMENT'S INVITATION TO RETURN TO THE POLITICAL ARENA AS
AN ACTIVE PARTY. THE FREEDOM MOVEMENT PARTY IS DEMANDING
THAT THE GOVERNMENT REMOVE THE PADLOCKS FROM ITS OFFICES,
LIFT THE BAN ON ITS DAILY NEWSPAPER, AND GUARANTEE THE
SAFETY OF THE MOVEMENT'S LEADERS. THE PARTY WANTS SIMILAR
RIGHTS EXTENDED TO SOME 35 OTHER GROUPS THAT HAVE ALSO
APPLIED FOR PERMISSION TO OPERATE AS POLITICAL PARTIES.

07182 PEZESHKAN, F.
IRAN: MOSCOW OVERTURE
THIRD WORLD WEEK, 8(10) (MAY 89), 75-76.
IRANIAN GOVERNMENT SOURCES SAY THAT THE SOVIET UNION
HELPED TO UNCOVER A U.S. SPY RING OPERATING IN IRAN. AS A
RESULT, IRAN AND THE SOVIET UNION ARE PLANNING CLOSER
MILITARY TIES. HOUSE SPEAKER ALI AKBAR HASHEMI RAFSANJANI
WILL VISIT THE SOVIET UNION TO SIGN AN AGREEMENT FOR THE
PURCHASE OF SOVIET WEAPONS, INCLUDING MISSILES, TANKS, AND
ARTILLERY. HIGH-LEVEL TALKS BETWEEN IRAN AND THE USSR ARE
ALSO LAYING THE GROUNDWORK FOR COOPERATION IN INDUSTRIAL AND
TECHNICAL AREAS.

07183 PEZESHKAN, F.
IRAN: POWER STRUGGLE
THIRD WORLD WEEK, 8(9) (APR 89), 65-66.
CONCERN HAS GROWN STEADILY OVER THE UNWIELDINESS OF THE
IRANIAN GOVERNMENT UNDER ITS PRESENT CONSTITUTION. THE
AYATOLLAH KHOMEINI HAS APPOINTED A COMMITTEE TO RECOMMEND
CONSTITUTIONAL CHANGES. THE REVIEW COMMITTEE IS COMPOSED OF
CLERICS FROM THE ASSEMBLY OF EXPERTS AND THE THREE BRANCHES
OF GOVERNMENT. THE REVIEW PROCESS MAY PROVE TO BE A
BATTLEFIELD FOR COMPETITION AMONG LEADERS WHO WANT TO BE
KHOMEINI'S SUCCESSOR.

07184 PEZESHKAN, F.
IRAN: RAFSANJANI
THIRD WORLD WEEK, 8(11) (MAY 89), 85-86.
WITH HIS CALL FOR THE MURDER OF AMERICAN, BRITISH, AND
FRENCH CITIZENS IN RETALIATION FOR THE DEATHS OF
PALESTINIANS, ALI AKBAR HASHEMI RAFSANJANI STRENGTHENED HIS
BID TO BE THE AYATOLLAH KHOMEINI'S SUCCESSOR. ALTHOUGH
RAFSANJANI LATER RETRACTED HIS REMARKS, POLITICAL OBSERVERS
SAY THAT THE COMMENTS WERE MEANT TO INGRATIATE RAFSANJANI
WITH RADICALS IN THE GOVERNMENT AND THE ISLAMIC CLERGY.

07185 PEZESHKAN, F.
IRAN: STRONG PRESIDENCY?

THIRD WORLD WEEK, 7(9) (JAN 89), 67-68.
IRAN APPEARS TO BE MOVING TOWARD THE ADOPTION OF A
STRONG-PRESIDENT FORM OF GOVERNMENT IN PLACE OF ITS PRESENT
MODIFIED PARLIAMENTARY SYSTEM OF GOVERNMENT. THE CHANGE HAS
BEEN PROPOSED BY THE SPEAKER OF THE IRANIAN PARLIAMENT,
HOJATOLISLAM ALI AKBAR HASHEMI RAFSANJANI, WHO IS THE MOST
LIKELY CHOICE FOR PRESIDENT IN THE ELECTION SCHEDULED FOR
JUNE 1989.

07186 PEZESHKAN, F.
IRAN: TO RUSSIA, WITH LOVE
THIRD WORLD WEEK, 8(13) (MAY 89), 97-98.
FOLLOWING THE DETERIORATION OF RELATIONS WITH THE WEST
CAUSED BY THE SALMAN RUSHIDE AFFAIR, IRAN APPEARS TO BE
MAKING SWIFT MOVES TO STRENGTHEN ITS TIES WITH COMMUNIST
NATIONS. PARLIAMENTARY SPEAKER HASHEMI RAFSANJANI IS
EXPECTED TO SIGN SEVERAL AGREEMENTS AND LETTERS OF
UNDERSTANDING ON IRAN-SOVIET COOPERATION IN MANY FIELDS,
INCLUDING JOINT INFRASTRUCTURE DEVELOPMENT PROJECTS AND
MILITARY AFFAIRS.

07187 PEZESHKAN, F.
IRAN: TRADE THREATENED
THIRD WORLD WEEK, 8(4) (MAR 89), 28.
HAVING BROKEN DIPLOMATIC RELATIONS WITH GREAT BRITAIN,
IRAN'S RADICALS ARE NOW PRESSING FOR AN ECONOMIC BOYCOTT.
THE RADICAL DEPUTIES ARE BEING ENCOURAGED BY LEADERS OF
POWERFUL POLITICAL-RELIGIOUS GROUPS, WHO SHARE THEIR RAGE
OVER BRITAIN'S REFUSAL TO BAN SALMAN RUSHDIE'S "THE SATANIC
VERSES."

07188 PEZESHKAN, F.
IRAN: USSR MOVES CLOSER
THIRD WORLD WEEK, 8(1) (MAR 89), 6.
SOVIET FOREIGN MINISTER EDUARD SHEVARDNADZE HAS BEEN
CULTIVATING CLOSER RELATIONS WITH IRAN. IRAN AND THE USSR
ARE PUTTING ASIDE THEIR IDEOLOGICAL DIFFERENCES AND FINDING
COMMON GROUND IN TERMS OF NATIONAL INTERESTS.

07189 PFLUGER, F.
HUMAN RIGHTS UNBOUND: CARTER'S HUMAN RIGHTS POLICY
REASSESSED
PRESIDENTIAL STUDIES QUARTERLY, 19(4) (FAL 89), 705-716.
DR. FRIEDBERT PFLUGER, PRESS SECRETARY TO THE PRESIDENT
OF WEST GERMANY, RE-EXAMINES PRESIDENT CARTERS HUMAN RIGHTS
POLICIES. HE OBSERVES THAT EVERYWHERE THE FORCE OF THE IDEA
OF HUMAN RIGHTS IS MAKING ITSELF FELT-MOVING REPRESSED AND
REPRESSOR ALIKE. HE EXAMINES REACTIONS OF DEMOCRATIC NATIONS
TO CARTER'S STATEMENTS REGARDING EASTERN EUROPE AND ALSO
RIGHTIST DICTATORSHIPS IN OTHER PARTS OF THE WORLD. CARTER
IS CREDITED WITH ADVANCING HUMAN RIGHTS IN LATIN AMERICA BUT
WAS UNABLE TO ACHIEVE NATIONAL CONSENSUS REGARDING FOREIGN
POLICY GOALS. PFLUGER CONCLUDES THAT REAGAN CONTINUED THE
HUMAN RIGHTS PURSUIT BUT MORE PRIVATELY AND DIPLOMATICALLY
THAN HIS PREDECESSOR.

07190 PHARAND, D.
INTERNATIONAL LAW PROBLEMS IN THE ARCTIC
ETUDES INTERNATIONALES, XX(1) (MAR 89), 131-186.
THE TERRITORIAL SOVEREIGNTY OVER ALASKA, THE ARCTIC
ISLANDS OF THE SOVIET UNION, SVALBARD, GREENLAND AND THE
CANADIAN ARCTIC ARCHIPELAGO POSES NO PROBLEM, BUT THE
CONTINENTAL SHELF OFF THOSE TERRITORIES AND ISLANDS HAS YET
TO BE DELIMITED BETWEEN THE FIVE ARCTIC STATES: ALASKA, THE
SOVIET UNION, NORWAY, DENMARK AND CANADA. THE ARCTIC OCEAN
BEING A SEMI-ENCLOSED SEA, BORDERING STATES SHOULD COOPERATE
UNDER THE NEW LAW OF THE SEA CONVENTION IN THE EXPLOITATION
OF THE LIVING RESOURCES, THE PROTECTION OF THE MARINE
ENVIRONMENT AND THE CONDUCT OF SCIENTIFIC RESEARCH. THIS
COOPERATION COULD BEST BE ATTAINED BY THE CREATION OF AN
ARCTIC BASIN COUNCIL COMPOSED OF ALL ARCTIC STATES AND,
POSSIBLY, THE NORDIC COUNTRIES. NOTE: ARTICLE IS PRINTED IN
FRENCH

07191 PHARES, D.
BIGGER IS BETTER, OR IS IT SMALLER? RESTRUCTURING LOCAL
GOVERNMENT IN THE ST. LOUIS AREA
URBAN AFFAIRS QUARTERLY, 25(1) (SEP 89), 5-17.
ST. LOUIS HAS A LONG-STANDING TRADITION AS AN URBAN
WORKSHOP FOR ACADEMIC ANALYSIS IN PART BECAUSE SMALL LOCAL
GOVERNMENTS IN ST. LOUIS COUNTY HAVE PROVIDED UNITS OF
ANALYSIS FOR A WIDE RANGE OF TOPICS RELATED TO URBAN SERVICE
PROVISION AND URBAN DEVELOPMENT. RECENTLY, A FEDERAL
COMMISSION AND A BOARD AUTHORIZED BY THE MISSOURI
CONSTITUTION SEPARATELY STUDIED GOVERNMENTAL FRAGMENTATION
AND HOW IT RELATES TO THE LONG-TERM VIABILITY OF ST. LOUIS
COUNTY. THE FEDERAL COMMISSION PRAISED THE EXISTING
ARRANGEMENT AS A MODEL FOR URBAN AMERICA TO CONSIDER. THE
MISSOURI BOARD PROPOSED DRAMATIC CHANGES IN LOCAL GOVERNMENT
STRUCTURE AND FINANCE. REORGANIZATION FOR THE ST. LOUIS AREA
IS DISCUSSED IN THE CONTEXT OF THESE TWO STARKLY CONTRASTING
STUDIES.

07192 PHARR, A.E.
EFFECTS OF STRESS ON WOMEN MANAGERS IN WASHINGTON, D.C.
GOVERNMENT
DISSERTATION ABSTRACTS INTERNATIONAL, 49(11) (MAY 89),
3502-A.
THE AUTHOR STUDIES HOW STRESS, JOB SATISFACTION, AND
OTHER INDEPENDENT VARIABLES AFFECT PSYCHOSOMATIC DISORDERS
AMONG MANAGERS IN THE WASHINGTON, D.C., GOVERNMENT. HER
FINDINGS SHOW THAT THE EFFECTS OF STRESS IN THE DEVELOPMENT
OF VARYING LEVELS OF PSYCHOSOMATIC DISORDERS VARY AMONG
DIFFERENT MANAGEMENT SUBGROUPS AND POINT TO A POSSIBLE
EXPLANATION FOR WHY BLACK FEMALE MANAGERS HAVE EXTREMELY
HIGH LEVELS OF PSYCHOSOMATIC DISORDERS.

07193 PHELPS, G.A.
GEORGE WASHINGTON AND THE PARADOX OF PARTY
PRESIDENTIAL STUDIES QUARTERLY, 19(4) (FAL 89), 733-746.
THIS ESSAY PORTRAYS THE DEVELOPMENTS DURING THE FIRST
YEARS OF AMERICAN INDEPENDENCE. NATIONAL AUTHORITY REMAINED
TO BE PUT IN PLACE AND WASHINGTON HOPED THAT THIS COULD BE
ACCOMPLISHED WITHOUT PARTY FACTION. IT SUGGESTS THAT THE
CHARACTERIZATION OF WASHINGTON AS A KIND OF REFEREE IN THE
GREAT HAMILTON-JEFFERSON STRUGGLE LACKING ANY STRONG
IDEALOGICAL CONVICTIONS OF HIS OWN, SIMPLY IS NOT TRUE.
WASHINGTON WAS A STAUNCH FEDERALIST. FINALLY, IT CONCLUDES
THAT WASHINGTON WAS OUR FIRST PARTISAN PRESIDENT.

07194 PHILIPSON, I.
THE ANTI-COMMUNIST PAST OF THE NEOCONSERVATIVE PRESENT
TIKKUN, 4(2) (MAR 89), 70-72.
THE AUTHOR SEEKS THE ORIGINS OF CONTEMPORARY
NEOCONSERVATISM IN THE UNIQUE EXPERIENCE OF NEW YORK CITY'S
JEWISH INTELLECTUALS, PARTICULARLY THEIR CONFLICTUAL,
EMOTIONALLY SCARRING RELATIONSHIP TO COMMUNISM.

07195 PHILLIPS, A.
A NATION DIVIDED
MACLEAN'S (CANADA'S NEWS MAGAZINE), 102(7) (FEB 89), 16-18.
YUGOSLAVIA IS PLAGUED BY ECONOMIC WOES AND GROWING
RIVALRIES BETWEEN MUTUALLY SUSPICIOUS ETHNIC GROUPS AS WELL
AS THE SHARPEST DIVISIONS AMONG THE LEADERS OF ITS RULING
COMMUNIST PARTY IN DECADES. NEWLY APPOINTED PRIME MINISTER
ANTE MARKOVIC HAS GONE FURTHER THAN ANY PREVIOUS YUGOSLAV
LEADER IN CALLING FOR A MARKET-DRIVEN ECONOMY, FOREIGN
INVESTMENT, AND POLITICAL PLURALISM, BUT HE HAS HIS WORK CUT
OUT FOR HIM. YUGOSLAVIA'S FOREIGN DEBT IS ESTIMATED AT $25
BILLION AND INFLATION CONTINUES TO SOAR.

07196 PHILLIPS, A.; CLARK, M.
A POISONOUS THREAT
MACLEAN'S (CANADA'S NEWS MAGAZINE), 102(4) (JAN 89), 20-22.
REPRESENTATIVES OF 149 NATIONS MET IN PARIS AND AFFIRMED
THEIR DESIRE TO CREATE A TREATY THAT WOULD BAN THE
"DEVELOPMENT, PRODUCTION, STOCKPILING AND USE OF ALL
CHEMICAL WEAPONS." ALTHOUGH THE CONFERENCE GAVE MUCH-NEEDED
POLITICAL MOMENTUM TO TALKS THAT HAVE BEEN DRAGGING ON FOR
20 YEARS IN GENEVA, SIGNIFICANT OBSTACLES REMAIN. THESE
INCLUDE: RELUCTANCE OF ARAB NATIONS TO ABANDON CHEMICAL
STOCKPILES IN THE FACE OF ISRAEL'S NUCLEAR CAPABILITY, THE
DIFFICULTY OF VERIFICATION OF WEAPONS PRODUCTION, AND THE
LACK OF EFFECTIVE SANCTIONS AGAINST OFFENDERS.

07197 PHILLIPS, A.; CLARK, M.; NEMETH, M.
DEADLY DEFIANCE
MACLEAN'S (CANADA'S NEWS MAGAZINE), 102(10) (MAR 89),
18-19.
CANADA JOINED 16 OTHER NATIONS IN WITHDRAWING
REPRESENTATIVES FROM IRAN TO EMPHASIZE THEIR OPPOSITION TO
THE AYATOLLAH KHOMEINI'S DEATH ORDER ON BRITISH AUTHOR
SALMAN RUSHDIE. IT IS BECOMING INCREASINGLY CLEAR THAT
KHOMEINI USED THE RUSHDIE AFFAIR TO SHIFT THE BALANCE OF
POWER AWAY FROM THOSE WHO WERE FAVORING MODERATION AND
INCREASING OPENNESS WITH THE WEST. IT IS LIKELY THAT THE
SEVERAL MONTHS OF QUIET AND GRADUAL PROGRESS THAT HAS BEING
MADE IN RELATIONS BETWEEN IRAN AND THE WEST HAS BEEN
COMPLETELY NEGATED.

07198 PHILLIPS, A.
THATCHER'S COMPROMISE
MACLEAN'S (CANADA'S NEWS MAGAZINE), 102(27) (JUL 89), 28.
MANY OBSERVERS HERE READY FOR A MAJOR CONFRONTATION AT
THE ECONOMIC SUMMIT OF THE EUROPEAN COMMUNITY (EC) OVER THE
ISSUE OF MONETARY UNION. HOWEVER, UNLIKE PREVIOUS OCCASIONS,
MARGARET THATCHER ADOPTED A REMARKABLY CONCILIATORY ATTITUDE
TOWARD THE ISSUE. REASONS FOR HER "CHANGE OF HEART" INCLUDE
A DESIRE TO ENSURE THAT BRITAIN IS NOT POLITICALLY ISOLATED
AND AN INCREASING UNSURE BASE OF SUPPORT AT HOME. WHATEVER
THE CAUSE, IT BECAME CLEAR THAT "EVEN THE IRON LADY KNOWS
WHEN IT IS WISE TO BEND."

07199 PHILLIPS, A.
TOLERATING DISSENT
MACLEAN'S (CANADA'S NEWS MAGAZINE), 102(13) (MAR 89),
20-23.
POLITICAL CHANGES IN HUNGARY HAVE TAKEN PLACE SO QUICKLY
THAT IT IS DIFFICULT FOR THE AVERAGE CITIZEN TO KEEP UP.
HUGE STREET DEMONSTRATIONS ARE TOLERATED, SOVIET/COMMUNIST
HOLIDAYS AND SYMBOLS ARE SHED IN FAVOR OF OLDER HUNGARIAN
ONES, AND GOVERNMENT OFFICIALS ARE NOW DRAFTING A NEW
WESTERN-STYLE CONSTITUTION. THERE ARE MANY OBSTACLES TO
REFORM, BUT MANY OBSERVERS FEEL THAT HUNGARY HAS THE BEST
CHANCE OF ANY COMMUNIST COUNTRY OF INTEGRATING SUCCESSFUL
ECONOMIC AND POLITICAL REFORMS.

07200 PHILLIPS, A.; MART, J.
TROUBLE AT THE SOURCE
MACLEAN'S (CANADA'S NEWS MAGAZINE), 102(7) (FEB 89), 38,40.
THROUGHOUT BRITAIN, WHERE STATE OPERATED HEALTH WAS
BORN 40 YEARS AGO, THE GAP BETWEEN PUBLIC AND PRIVATE
MEDICINE IS GROWING. ALTHOUGH THE GOVERNMENT FUNDED HEALTH
SERVICE IS ALMOST ENTIRELY FREE UNIVERSALLY. RISING COSTS
HAVE RESULTED IN DECREASING TECHNOLOGY AND INCREASED
COMPETITION FROM A GROWING PRIVATE SECTOR. THE NUMBER OF
PEOPLE CHOOSING PRIVATE HEALTH CARE HAS DOUBLED OVER THE
PAST TEN YEARS AND IS CONTINUING TO GROW. PLANS FOR
ABOLITION OF PRIVATE HEALTH CARE ARE SCRAPPED AS IT OCCUPIES
AND INCREASINGLY LARGE AND IMPORTANT ROLE IN KEEPING BRITONS
HEALTHY.

07201 PHILLIPS, C.S.
POLITICAL VERSUS ADMINISTRATION DEVELOPMENT: WHAT THE
NIGERIAN EXPERIENCE CONTRIBUTES
ADMINISTRATION AND SOCIETY, 20(4) (FEB 89), 423-445.
A CONFLICT IN POLITICAL SCIENCE OF 25 YEARS' DURATION
REVOLVES AROUND THE RELATIONSHIP OF BUREAUCRATIC DEVELOPMENT
TO POLITICAL DEVELOPMENT. ONE SCHOOL ARGUES THAT IN THE
PRESENCE OF WEAK POLITICAL SYSTEMS, IT IS NECESSARY TO
STRENGTHEN THE BUREAUCRACY IF ECONOMIC DEVELOPMENT IS TO
OCCUR. ANOTHER SCHOOL ARGUES THAT WHILE BUREAUCRATIC
INSTITUTIONS MUST BE STRENGTHENED TO PROMOTE ECONOMIC
DEVELOPMENT, IT IS NECESSARY ALSO TO STRENGTHEN POLITICAL
INSTITUTIONS TO CONTROL THE TENDENCY OF BUREAUCRATS TO
PROMOTE THEIR OWN INTERESTS IN THE ABSENCE OF POLITICAL
CONTROL. NIGERIA'S PERIOD OF MILITARY RULE, 1966-1979,
PROVIDES A TEST FOR THE TWO POSITIONS. UNDER MILITARY RULE,
THE CIVIL SERVICE BECAME EXTREMELY POWERFUL, CONTROLLED ONLY
SLIGHTLY BY THE UNCERTAIN POLICIES OF MILITARY RULERS.
UNTRAMMELED BY POLITICAL CONTROL, AND FAVORED WITH A BONANZA
OF OIL MONEY, THE BUREAUCRACY SHOULD HAVE DEMONSTRATED
CONSIDERABLE ECONOMIC DEVELOPMENT, IF ONE SCHOOL IS CORRECT.
THE OPPOSITE SCHOOL SAID AN UNCONTROLLED BUREAUCRACY WOULD
PROMOTE ITS OWN, RATHER THAN THE NATIONAL, INTEREST. THIS
ARTICLE MARSHALS EVIDENCE THAT THE BUREAUCRACY OF 1966-1979
DID NOT PROMOTE ECONOMIC DEVELOPMENT THAT COULD BE
ATTRIBUTED TO THE BUREAUCRACY, AND INDEED PURSUED POLICIES
THAT ENHANCED THE BUREAUCRACY RATHER THAN NIGERIA. FURTHER
EVIDENCE IS PRESENTED THAT SHOWS THAT THE PERIOD OF
UNCONTROLLED BUREAUCRATIC POWER ACTUALLY WEAKENED ANY
MEASURABLE POLITICAL DEVELOPMENT, AS REVEALED IN THE EVENTS
AFTER 1979. THE NIGERIAN EXPERIENCE SUPPORTS THE POSITION
THAT POLITICAL INSTITUTIONS MUST BE STRENGTHENED AT THE SAME
TIME BUREAUCRATIC INSTITUTIONS ARE BEING STRENGTHENED.

07202 PHILLIPS, J.A.
GORBACHEV'S "NEWTHINK" ON THE MIDDLE EAST
MIDSTREAM, XXXV(6) (AUG 89), 12-15.
MIKHAIL GORBACHEV HAS INJECTED A NEW DYNAMISM INTO
SOVIET MIDDLE EAST POLICY. GORBACHEV'S NEW THINKING
EMPHASIZES POLITICAL SETTLEMENT OF REGIONAL CONFLICTS AND
DOWNGRADES THE IDEOLOGICAL BASIS OF SOVIET FOREIGN POLICY.
HIS NEW TACTICS MASK THE FACT THAT THE MAJOR SOVIET GOALS IN
THE MIDEAST HAVE REMAINED CONSTANT. THEY INCLUDE THE
EXPANSION OF SOVIET INFLUENCE AND THE EROSION OF WESTERN,
ESPECIALLY AMERICAN, INFLUENCE. THESE UNCHANGING SOVIET
GOALS NOTWITHSTANDING, GORBACHEV'S BOLD PRAGMATISM AND FLAIR
FOR PUBLIC RELATIONS HAVE COMBINED TO GIVE A NEW, LESS
THREATENING LOOK TO SOVIET POLICY IN THE MIDDLE EAST.

07203 PHILLIPS, R.F.
EUROPEAN RESERVE FORCES AND THE CONVENTIONAL DEFENSE OF
EUROPE
DISSERTATION ABSTRACTS INTERNATIONAL, 49(12) (JUN 89),
3863-A.
THE AUTHOR ANALYZES THE CONTRIBUTION THAT CURRENTLY
UNUSED OR UNDER-UTILIZED EUROPEAN RESERVISTS COULD MAKE TO
CONVENTIONAL NATO DEFENSE. HE CONCLUDES THAT THE ADDITIONAL
MANPOWER AND BUDGETARY REQUIREMENTS NECESSARY TO REALIZE THE
"RESERVE OPTION" WOULD REPRESENT A SIGNIFICANT POLITICAL
CHALLENGE FOR NATO. BUT, WHEN COMPARED TO OTHER ALTERNATIVES
CURRENTLY BEING CONSIDERED FOR IMPROVING NATO'S CONVENTIONAL
CAPABILITIES, THE RESERVE OPTION COMPARES VERY FAVORABLY.

07204 PICKAR, C.K.
EVOLVING ARMS TRANSFER RATIONALES: THE CASE OF ITALY
AVAILABLE FROM NTIS. NO. AD-A210 688/8/GAR, JUN 87, 133.
CONVENTIONAL WISDOM ABOUT EUROPEAN ARMS SUPPLIERS HOLDS
THAT THEY ARE MOTIVATED PRIMARILY BY FINANCIAL
CONSIDERATIONS WHEN FACED WITH A DECISION TO SELL ARMS. THIS

PAPER ARGUES THAT THE ECONOMIC RATIONALE IS BECOMING LESS IMPORTANT IN THE ITALIAN CASE. EVIDENCE SUGGESTS THAT AS ITALY MOVES INTO THE NEXT DECADE, THE POLITICAL RATIONALE WILL BECOME MORE IMPORTANT. ITALY IS USING ARMS TRANSFERS FOR REASONS OF POLICY RATHER THAN ECONOMICS. THERE ARE THREE REASONS FOR THIS CHANGE: 1) THE ITALIAN GOVERNMENT HAS RECENTLY INSTITUTED A NUMBER OF CHANGES IN THE ARMS TRANSFER MECHANISM DESIGNED TO INCREASE CONTROL OVER THE EXPORT PROCESS; 2) THE NEW AND STILL DEVELOPING DEFENSE POLICY OFFERS ITALY AN OPPORTUNITY TO USE ARMS SALES TO INCREASE ITALY'S POWER IN THE MEDITERRANEAN; AND 3) THE ITALIAN NATION, LONG THE OBJECT OF SCORN FROM ITS NORTHERN EUROPEAN NEIGHBORS, IS GAINING A SENSE OF PRIDE IN ITS ACCOMPLISHMENTS. ITALY'S GROSS NATIONAL PRODUCT EXCEEDS THAT OF GREAT BRITAIN AND ITALIAN TECHNOLOGY IS BECOMING INCREASINGLY IN DEMAND. THESE DEVELOPMENTS HAVE RESULTED IN ITALY BEING TREATED AS A SERIOUS MIDDLE-LEVEL POWER AND IN REFLECTED IN THE ARMS TRANSFER AREA. KEYWORDS: DEFENSE INDUSTRIES; FOREIGN POLICY; DEFENSE POLICY.

07205 PICKEL, A.
NEVER ASK WHO SHOULD RULE: KARL POPPER AND POLITICAL THEORY
CANADIAN JOURNAL OF POLITICAL SCIENCE, XXII(1) (MAR 89), 83-106.
ABSTRACT. THE PHILOSOPHY OF KARL POPPER HAS RARELY BEEN EXAMINED WITH RESPECT TO ITS FRUITFULNESS AND RELEVANCE FOR POLITICAL THEORY. WHILE HIS CONTRIBUTIONS TO THE PHILOSOPHY OF SCIENCE MAY APPEAR TO BE OF ONLY MARGINAL SIGNIFICANCE FOR THE FUNDAMENTAL CONCERNS OF POLITICAL THEORY HIS OWN FORAYS INTO THE FIELD, PARTICULARLY IN THE OPEN SOCIETY AND ITS ENEMIES, HAVE BEEN POLEMICAL IN TONE AND EXPLICITLY POLITICAL IN MOTIVATION. THIS ARTICLE RE-EXAMINES POPPER'S CRITIQUE OF THE THEORY OF SOVEREIGNTY AND HIS OWN APPROACH TO POLITICAL THEORY BY EMPLOYING A LARGELY NEGLECTED ELEMENT OF HIS CRITICAL APPROACH, NAMELY HIS PROBLEM-ORIENTED METHOD.

07206 PICRURGIN, O.
USSR-FRANCE: PRESENT STAGE OF ECONOMIC COOPERATION
FOREIGN TRADE, 6 (1988), 11-13.
THIS ARTICLE INVESTIGATES THE COMPLICATED CONDITIONS IN WHICH TRADE AND ECONOMIC TIES BETWEEN THE USSR AND FRANCE PROCEEDED IN 1986-1987. IT EXAMINES THE CONTENT OF TALKS BETWEEN SOVIET LEADERSHIP AND FRENCH PRIME MINISTER JACQUES CHIRAC IN MAY 1987. RESULTS OF THEIR EFFORTS, WHICH ARE ATTRIBUTED TO A REVERSAL OF DECLINING TRADE, ARE REVIEWED. GOALS SET BY THE SOVIET-FRENCH JOINT COMMISSION IN MOSCOW JANUARY 1988 ARE DETAILED.

07207 PIDDINGTON, K.W.
SOVEREIGNTY AND THE ENVIRONMENT: PART OF THE SOLUTION OR PART OF THE PROBLEM?
ENVIRONMENT, 31(7) (SEP 89), 18-20; 35-39.
DEBT-FOR-NATURE SWAPS AND "GREEN CONDITIONALITY" ON DEVELOPMENT AID OFTEN ARE SEEN AS INFRINGEMENTS OF DEVELOPING NATION'S SOVEREIGNTY. THUS, MANY ENVIRONMENTALISTS HAVE COME TO VIEW SOVERIGNTY AS AN OBSTACLE. THIS ARTICLE SUGGESTS THAT ACTUALLY, SOVEREIGNTY CAN BE A CRITICAL TOOL IN THE PROMOTION OF ECOLOGICALLY SOUND, SUSTAINABLE DEVELOPMENT.

07208 PIERCE, D.C.
RESETTLEMENT AS A FOREIGN POLICY EXTERNALITY: THE EFFECTS OF AND LOCAL GOVERNMENT RESPONSES TO THE SECOND WAVE OF INDOCHINESE REFUGEES INTO ORANGE COUNTY, CALIFORNIA, 1979-1982
DISSERTATION ABSTRACTS INTERNATIONAL, 48(8) (FEB 88), 2156-A.
THE STUDY ANALYZES THE EFFECTS OF A LARGE AND RAPID INFLUX OF INDOCHINESE REFUGEES FROM 1979 AND 1982 INTO A FEW HOST COMMUNITIES IN SOUTHERN CALIFORNIA, AND OF EFFORTS BY LOCAL GOVERNMENTS TO COPE WITH THESE EFFECTS. IT EXAMINES THE ROOT CAUSES OF THE INTER-ETHNIC TENSIONS IN ORANGE COUNTY AND PROVIDES POLICY RECOMMENDATIONS FOR AVOIDING FUTURE PROBLEMS REGARDING REFUGEES.

07209 PIERCE, P.A.
GENDER ROLE AND POLITICAL CULTURE: THE ELECTORAL CONNECTION
WOMEN AND POLITICS, 9(1) (1989), 21-46.
ONE OF THE DIFFICULTIES FACED BY WOMEN CANDIDATES IS HOW TO PRESENT THEMSELVES AS WOMEN TO THE ELECTORATE. CAMPAIGNING, AS WELL AS GOVERNING, IS REGARDED AS STEREOTYPICALLY MALE; HENCE, WOMEN CANDIDATES AT LEAST PERCEIVE THAT THE PRESENTATION OF THEIR GENDER ROLE DURING A CAMPAIGN IS PROBLEMATIC. RESEARCH ON WOMEN CANDIDATES, HOWEVER, HAS ONLY EXAMINED THE EFFECTS OF THEIR SEX OR THEIR SELF ROLE, I.E., THE WAY THEY SEE THEMSELVES. THIS STUDY EXAMINES HOW WOMEN CANDIDATES FOR CONGRESS IN 1984 PRESENTED THEMSELVES TO THE ELECTORATE, AND HOW THAT PRESENTATION WAS AFFECTED BY THE CULTURAL AND POLITICAL CONTEXT OF THE DISTRICT.

07210 PIKE, D.
CULTURAL POLITICS IN SOVIET-OCCUPIED GERMANY, 1945-46
JOURNAL OF CONTEMPORARY HISTORY, 24(1) (JAN 89), 91-123.

CULTURAL POLITICS IN SOVIET-OCCUPIED GERMANY WERE AN AMALGAM OF STALIN'S GERMAN POLICY AND THE POLITICAL PROGRAM THAT THE LOCAL COMMUNISTS PURSUED IN CLOSE CONSULTATION WITH OFFICERS OF THE OCCUPATION ADMINISTRATION (SMAD). THUS, THE LOCAL POLITICAL AND CULTURAL PROCESSES MAKE MOST SENSE WHEN THE IMMEDIATE POST-WAR OBJECTIVES OF THE USSR ARE KEPT IN MIND. SOVIET POLICY-MAKING WITH RESPECT TO GERMANY GENERALLY AND THE EASTERN ZONE SPECIFICALLY COMBINED WITH THE WORSENING OF INTERNATIONAL TENSIONS TO INFLUENCE THE DIRECTION OF CULTURAL-POLITICAL AND POLITICAL DEVELOPMENT IN THE ZONE.

07211 PILIAWSKY, M.
RACIAL POLITICS IN THE 1988 PRESIDENTIAL ELECTION
BLACK SCHOLAR, 20(1) (JAN 89), 30-37.
THE ARTICLE ANALYZES THE INFLUENCE THAT RACISM HAD ON THE PROCESS AND OUTCOME OF THE 1988 PRESIDENTIAL ELECTION. IT CONCLUDES THAT A MAJOR FACTOR IN THE VICTORY OF BUSH WAS SOCIAL AND CULTURAL CONSERVATISM WHICH INCLUDES WHITE RACISM AS A KEY ELEMENT. BUSH'S USE OF WILLIE HORTON AND DUKAKIS'S STRATEGY OF TREATING JACKSON AS SOMETHING HE "HAD TO COPE WITH, KEEP A HEALTHY DISTANCE FROM..." ARE EVIDENCES OF THE UNDERLYING RACISM THAT IS STILL PERVASIVE IN THE US AND STILL HAS A GREAT INFLUENCE ON POLITICS.

07212 PILLAI, K.R.
TENSIONS WITHIN REGIONAL ORGANIZATIONS: A STUDY OF SAARC
INDIAN JOURNAL OF POLITICAL SCIENCE, L(1) (JAN 89), 18-27.
REGIONAL COOPERATION AMONG SOUTH ASIAN NATIONS WAS INSTITUTIONALIZED WITH THE FORMATION OF SAARC ON DECEMBER 8, 1985. THE HEADS OF THE SEVEN SOUTH ASIAN COUNTRIES AGREED THAT SAARC WOULD PLAY AN IMPORTANT ROLE IN ACCELERATING ECONOMIC AND SOCIAL DEVELOPMENT, PROMOTING NATIONAL AND COLLECTIVE SELF-RELIANCE, AND FURTHERING THE CAUSE OF PEACE, PROGRESS, AND STABILITY IN THE REGION AND THE WORLD. BUT SINCE THE BEGINNING SAARC HAS BEEN PLAGUED BY TENSIONS FROM WITHIN. POLITICAL, ECONOMIC, RELIGIOUS, AND ETHNIC FACTORS HAVE CONTRIBUTED TO THESE TENSIONS.

07213 PILLAI, K.R.
THE SIGNIFICANCE OF THE 1987 ELECTIONS
INDIAN JOURNAL OF POLITICAL SCIENCE, L(3) (JUL 89), 293-306.
AS A RESULT OF THE EVOLUTION OF ELECTORAL POLITICS, TWO MAJOR FRONTS HAVE EMERGED IN KERALA: THE UNITED DEMOCRATIC FRONT LED BY THE CONGRESS (I) PARTY AND THE LEFT DEMOCRATIC FRONT LED BY THE COMMUNIST PARTY OF INDIA (MARXIST). THESE FRONTS HAVE MORE OFTEN THAN NOT BEEN PLAGUED BY INTER-PARTY AND INTRA-PARTY RIVALRIES THAT HAVE RESULTED IN THE FALL OF MINISTRIES LONG BEFORE THEIR NORMAL TERM COULD BE COMPLETED. THE YEARS 1957, 1967, 1977, AND 1987 WERE ESPECIALLY IMPORTANT IN THE ELECTORAL HISTORY OF KERALA. IN THIS ESSAY, THE AUTHOR FOCUSES ON THE BACKGROUND TO THE 1987 ELECTION AND ITS RESULTS.

07214 PILLAI, S.
LAVISH SHOW
INDIA TODAY, XIV(1) (JAN 89), 40.
THE COMMUNIST PARTY OF INDIA SPARED NO EXPENSE IN STAGING ITS 13TH PARTY CONGRESS IN KERALA IN DECEMBER 1988. UNLIKE THE SOVIET COMMUNISTS, INDIA'S COMMUNISTS STILL REVERE STALIN AND DO NOT GIVE PRIORITY TO PERESTROIKA AND GLASNOST.

07215 PILLAI, S.
VOTE FOR CONTINUITY
INDIA TODAY, XIV(2) (JAN 89), 27-29.
THE 13TH PARTY CONGRESS OF THE COMMUNIST PARTY OF INDIA (MARXIST), HELD IN TRIVANDRUM IN DECEMBER 1988, WAS ONE OF THE MOST SIGNIFICANT IN ITS HISTORY. IT BROUGHT INTO THE OPEN THE CONTRADICTIONS WITHIN THE PARTY ON THE QUESTION OF ELECTORAL ALLIANCES. EQUALLY IMPORTANT, IT REVEALED THAT THE INDIAN PARTY HAS SO FAR REFUSED TO GO ALONG WITH THE RAPID CHANGES IN THE COMMUNIST MOVEMENT ELSEWHERE IN THE WORLD.

07216 PIMLOTT, B.; KAVANAGH, D.; MORRIS, P.
CONTROVERSY: IS THE "POSTWAR CONSENSUS" A MYTH?
CONTEMPORARY RECORD, 2(6) (SUM 89), 12-15.
SINCE PRIME MINISTER THATCHER TOOK OFFICE AND BEGAN TO INTRODUCE MAJOR CHANGES, IT HAS BEEN WIDELY ACCEPTED THAT BRITISH POLITICS WAS FORMERLY CHARACTERIZED BY A CONSENSUS, BUT THIS NATION-UNITING MOOD NO LONGER EXISTS. IN THIS SYMPOSIUM, THE AUTHORS DISAGREE OVER THE REALITY OF THE CONSENSUS.

07217 PIN-SUNG, H.
FINE-TUNING FAIRNESS
FREE CHINA REVIEW, 39(9) (SEP 89), 20-22.
TAIWAN'S OPEN AND COMPETITIVE EXAMINATIONS FOR RECRUITING CIVIL SERVANTS HAVE GIVEN SPECIAL FORM AND CONTENT TO THE GOVERNMENT. WITH AN EFFECTIVE, FAIR, AND COMPETITIVE EXAMINATION SYSTEM IN PLACE, CIVIL SERVICE POSTS ARE GRANTED NOT BY A SINGLE LEADER OR INTEREST GROUP. THEREFORE, THE GOVERNMENT EMPLOYEES ARE LOYAL TO THE

GOVERNMENT AND CITIZENS AT LARGE, NOT TO A POLITICIAN OR AN INTEREST GROUP.

07218 PINCHUKOV, Y.E.
1963 MOSCOW TREATY: ACHIEVEMENTS AND FUTURE PROSPECTS
DISARMAMENT, XII(2) (SUM 89), 81-89.
THE 1963 MOSCOW TREATY BANNING NUCLEAR WEAPON TESTS IN
THE ATMOSPHERE, IN OUTER SPACE, AND UNDER WATER IS RIGHTLY
CONSIDERED A MAJOR INTERNATIONAL AGREEMENT. ITS HISTORICAL
SIGNFICANCE RESIDES IN THE FACT THAT IT WAS THE FIRST
INTERNATIONAL TREATY IN WHICH THE TASK OF REACHING AGREEMENT
ON GENERAL AND COMPLETE DISARMAMENT UNDER INTERNATIONAL
CONTROL WAS ENUNCIATED AS A MAJOR GOAL. ITS IMPORTANCE AND
THE POWER OF ITS POSITIVE INFLUENCE ON THE DIFFICULT PROCESS
OF RIDDING THE PLANET OF THE NUCLEAR THREAT ARE BECOMING
MORE OBVIOUS AS THE YEARS GO BY.

07219 PINDER, J.
ECONOMIC INTEGRATION VERSUS NATIONAL SOVEREIGNTY:
DIFFERENCES BETWEEN EASTERN AND WESTERN EUROPE
GOVERNMENT AND OPPOSITION, 24(3) (SUM 89), 309-326.
PERESTROIKA COULD BE THE START OF A LONG MARCH AWAY FROM
THE TRADITION OF ABSOLUTIST POWER MONOPOLY AND TOWARDS A
DISTRIBUTION OF POLITICAL AND ECONOMIC POWER THAT IS A MORE
PROPER FRAMEWORK FOR A MODERN ECONOMY AND SOCIETY, AS WELL
AS A MORE PROMISING BASIS FOR THE ECONOMIC INTEGRATION THAT
IS ALREADY URGENT FOR THE EAST EUROPEANS AND WILL BECOME
INCREASINGLY NECESSARY FOR THE SOVIET UNION. OTHER
INDUSTRIAL COUNTRIES WILL BE ABLE TO SHARE IN MUTUAL
BENEFITS IF THE COMECON COUNTRIES BECOME MORE OPEN TO
INTERNATIONAL COOPERATION. IF THIS CAN TAKE PLACE IN A LONG-
TERM PERSPECTIVE OF EVENTUAL INTEGRATION AMONG ALL THE GREAT
INDUSTRIAL ECONOMIES, THE EUROPEAN COMMUNITY EXPERIENCE
SHOWS THAT POLITICAL AND SECURITY RELATIONSHIPS CAN ALSO BE
TRANSFORMED.

07220 PINDER, J.
THE EUROPEAN COMMUNITY AND THE GAULLIST FALLACY
WORLD TODAY, 45(4) (APR 89), 55-56.
UNLESS EUROPEAN COMMUNITY LEGISLATION IS TO BECOME LESS
IMPORTANT IN THE FUTURE, IT IS QUESTIONABLE HOW LONG WESTERN
EUROPE'S LIBERAL DEMOCRACIES CAN TOLERATE A LEGISLATIVE
PROCESS THAT GIVES PARLIAMENTARY REPRESENTATIVES SUCH A
SECONDARY ROLE. AND IT SEEMS LIKELY THAT GROWING
INTERDEPENDENCE, FAR FROM BYPASSING THE EC INSTITUTIONS,
WILL REQUIRE THE FRAMEWORK OF LAW AND, HENCE, THE
LEGISLATIVE PROCESS TO BE STRENGTHENED, NOT WEAKENED OR
IGNORED.

07221 PINES, A.M.
ISRAELI BURNOUT AND THE INTIFADA
NEW OUTLOOK, 32(11-12 (297-298)) (NOV 89), 34-36.
BURNOUT IS A STATE OF PSYCHOLOGICAL EXHAUSTION CAUSED BY
LONG-TERM INVOLVEMENT IN EMOTIONALLY DEMANDING SITUATIONS.
IN THIS STUDY AN ATTEMPT WAS MADE TO EXTEND THE CONCEPT TO
THE NATIONAL LEVEL AND TO INVESTIGATE "NATIONAL BURNOUT" IN
ISRAELI SOCIETY AS AFFECTED BY THE PALESTINIAN INTIFADA. THE
STUDY WAS CONDUCTED DURING THE PERIOD FROM DECEMBER 1988
UNTIL THE MIDDLE OF 1989. THREE METHODS OF INVESTIGATION
WERE UTILIZED: INDEPTH INTERVIEWS, QUESTIONNAIRES, AND GROUP
DISCUSSIONS. SIX GROUPS RESPONDED TO THE QUESTIONNAIRES: (1)
A RANDOM STREET SAMPLE; (2) PEOPLE WITH A LEFT-WING
POLITICAL ORIENTATION ASSOCIATED WITH THE SOCIALIST MAPAM
PARTY; (3) PEOPLE WITH A RIGHT-WING POLITICAL ORIENTATION
ASSOCIATED WITH THE NATIONALIST HERUT (LIKUD) PARTY; (4)
ORTHODOX JEWS; (5) HIGH-RANKING IDF CAREER OFFICERS; AND (6)
ISRAELI ARABS.

07222 PINES, B., (ED.); ARON, L.; HEATHERLY, C., (ED.); HOLMES,
K.; PIPES, R.; ROBINSON, R.
THE DEPARTMENT OF STATE; MANDATE FOR LEADERSHIP III:
POLICY STRATEGIES FOR THE 1990S
THE HERITAGE FOUNDATION, WASHINGTON, DC, 1989, 487-632.
THE ARTICLE EXPLORES THE VARIOUS FUNCTIONS OF THE US
DEPARTMENT OF STATE. THE RECORD OF THE REAGAN ADMINISTRATION
IS EXAMINED AND FUTURE POLICY RECOMMENDATIONS ARE GIVEN.
SPECIFIC AREAS EXAMINED INCLUDE: US-SOVIET RELATIONS,
CENTRAL/EUROPE, WESTERN ECONOMIC SECURITY, WESTERN EUROPE,
MEXICO, CENTRAL AMERICA, THE CARIBBEAN, SOUTH AMERICA, ASIA,
AFGHANISTAN, THE MIDDLE EAST, THE PERSIAN GULF, AFRICA, THE
LIBERATION DOCTRINE, HUMAN RIGHTS, AND STATE-SPONSORED
TERRORISM.

07223 PING-LUN, J.
COMPETITION MIXED WITH CONSENSUS
FREE CHINA REVIEW, 39(10) (OCT 89), 36-39.
TAIWAN FORMALLY ENTERED THE ERA OF COMPETITIVE POLITICS
IN JANUARY 1989 WITH THE PASSAGE OF THREE KEY LAWS BY THE
LEGISLATIVE YUAN: THE CIVIC ORGANIZATION LAW, WHICH PROVIDES
FOR THE LEGALIZATION AND REGISTRATION OF POLITICAL PARTIES;
THE ELECTION AND RECALL LAW; AND THE LAW ON THE VOLUNTARY
RETIREMENT OF SENIOR PARLIAMENTARIANS.

07224 PING, L.
INITIAL SUCCESS FOR ECONOMIC RECTIFICATION AND IMPROVEMENT
BEIJING REVIEW, 32(48) (NOV 89), 20-22.
FROM JANUARY TO SEPTEMBER 1989, CHINA MADE DEFINITE
ACHIEVEMENTS IN ITS EFFORTS TO RECTIFY AND CONSOLIDATE THE
NATIONAL ECONOMY. HOWEVER, THE IMBALANCES IN SUPPLY AND
DEMAND CONTINUED, AS DID THE STRUCTURAL CONTRADICTION.

07225 PINK, G.H.
GOVERNMENT RESTRICTION ON FOREIGN INVESTMENT BY PENSION
FUNDS: AN EMPIRICAL EVALUATION
CANADIAN PUBLIC POLICY--ANALYSE DE POLITIQUES, 15(3) (SEP
89), 300-312.
UNDER THE INCOME TAX ACT, REGISTERED PENSION FUNDS,
INCLUDING REGISTERED RETIREMENT SAVINGS PLANS (RRSPS), MAY
INVEST NO MORE THAN 10 PER CENT OF THEIR ASSETS IN FOREIGN
SECURITIES AND PROPERTY. FINANCIAL THEORY STATES THAT
RESTRICTING THE OPPORTUNITY FOR DIVERSIFICATION SHOULD
RESULT IN INFERIOR INVESTMENT PERFORMANCE. THIS STUDY TESTS
THE EFFECTS OF THE 10 PER CENT RESTRICTION ON THE INVESTMENT
PERFORMANCE OF A SAMPLE OF CANADIAN MUTUAL FUNDS, SOME OF
WHICH ARE SUBJECT TO THE RESTRICTION (RRSP ELIGIBLE), AND
THE REMAINDER OF WHICH ARE NOT (RRSP INELIGIBLE). RESULTS
SHOW THAT INVESTMENT PERFORMANCE OF RRSP INELIGIBLE FUNDS IS
SUPERIOR TO THAT OF RRSP ELIGIBLE FUNDS OF A CANADIAN STOCK
MARKET INDEX. THEY ALSO INDICATE THAT AN RRSP INELIGIBLE
FUND INVESTMENT HAS A SUBSTANTIALLY HIGHER TERMINAL VALUE
THAN AN RRSP ELIGIBLE FUND INVESTMENT. THE STUDY CONCLUDES
THAT THE 10 PER CENT RESTRICTION IS NOT IN THE BEST
FINANCIAL INTERESTS OF PENSION PLAN PARTICIPANTS.

07226 PINTO-DUSCHINSKY, M.
TRENDS IN BRITISH PARTY FUNDING 1983-1987
PARLIAMENTARY AFFAIRS, 42(2) (APR 89), 197-212.
THE PURPOSE OF THE ARTICLE IS TO ANALYZE THE MAIN
DEVELOPMENT IN THE FUNDING OF BRITISH PARTIES IN THE
PARLIAMENTARY CYCLE 1983-7. FACED BY THE CONSERVATIVE
GOVERNMENT'S DOMINANCE IN THE POLITICAL ARENA, THE LABOUR
PARTY'S HEAD OFFICE MOUNTED A STRONG CHALLENGE TO
CONSERVATIVE CENTRAL OFFICE IN TERMS OF ORGANIZATION AND
FUNDRAISING. THE MAJOR UNIONS, DESPITE LOSS OF MEMBERS,
CONTINUED TO GIVE INCREASING FINANCIAL SUPPORT TO THE LABOUR
PARTY. THE CONSERVATIVES ALSO RAISED THEIR LEVEL OF CENTRAL
INCOME AND MAINTAINED THEIR EDGE OVER LABOUR. THE ALLIANCE
PARTIES ON THE OTHER HAND, FAILED TO BUILD ON THEIR
POLITICAL SUCCESS IN THE 1983 GENERAL ELECTION.

07227 PION-BERLIN, D.
LATIN AMERICAN NATIONAL SECURITY DOCTRINES: HARD- AND SOFT-
LINE THEMES
ARMED FORCES AND SOCIETY, 15(3) (SPR 89), 411-429.
CONVENTIONAL WISDOM HAS IT THAT THE LATIN AMERICAN
MILITARIES OF THE 1960S AND 1970S WERE UNDER THE STRONG
INFLUENCE OF A SINGLE, COHESIVE, SELF-REINFORCING, AND
CONSERVATIVE NATIONAL SECURITY DOCTRINE. THIS DOCTRINE, ONCE
PLACED IN THE HANDS OF MILITARY GOVERNMENTS, PROVIDED THEM
WITH A JUSTIFICATION TO STOP PROGRESSIVE SOCIAL AND
POLITICAL CHANGE MOVEMENTS AND TO ENFORCE THEIR VERSION OF
THE NATIONAL SECURITY STATE. THIS ARTICLE CONTENDS THAT THE
NSD IS MULTITHEMATIC, LACE WITH BOTH CONSERVATIVE AND
PROGRESSIVE IDEOLOGY. CLEAR "HARDLINE" AS WELL AS "SOFTLINE"
POSITIONS CAN BE FOUNDWITH DIFFERENT ASSUMPTIONS AND
ARGUMENTS ABOUT THE STATE, NATIONAL SECURITY, AND STRATEGY.
MOREOVER, THESE POSITIONS ARE SUFFICIENTLY COHERENT TO
SUGGEST THAT THERE REALLY ARE TWO DISTINCT DOCTRINES.
COMPARISONS BETWEEN THE SOUTHERN CONE, ON THE ONE HAND, AND
BRAZIL AND PERU, ON THE OTHER HAND, DEMONSTRATE HOW THESE
VIEWS GAVE SHAPE TO DIFFERING MILITARY PERCEPTIONS AND
POLICIES.

07228 PIPA, A.
THE POLITICAL SITUATION OF THE ALBANIANS IN YUGOSLAVIA,
WITH PARTICULAR ATTENTION TO THE KOSOVO PROBLEM: A
CRITICAL APPROACH
EAST EUROPEAN QUARTERLY, XXIII(2) (JUN 89), 159-181.
THE KOSOVO PROBLEM IS BASICALLY AN ETHNIC ONE. THE
PROVINCE IS INHABITED BY A MAJORITY OF ALBANIANS, WITH SERBS
AND MONTENEGRINS AS MINORITIES. THE KOSOVARS (ALBANIAN
ETHNICS) ARE UNHAPPY WITH THE STATUS OF THE PROVINCE, WHICH
IS INFERIOR TO THAT OF A REPUBLIC AND THEREFORE INVOLVES
LESSER REPRESENTATIVE AND PARTICIPATORY POWER. THEY RESENT
SERBIA'S CONTROL AND WANT THE PROVINCE TO BE FULLY
EMANCIPATED, CLAIMING THE RIGHT TO HAVE THEIR OWN REPUBLIC.

07229 PIPES, D.
CHAPTER ONE: FUNDAMENTAL MUSLIMS BETWEEN AMERICA AND
RUSSIA; THE LONG SHADOW
TRANSACTION PUBLISHERS, NEW BRUNSWICK, NJ, 1989, 3-26.
THIS CHAPTER IN, THE LONG SHADOW, BY DANIEL PIPES
EXPLORES FUNDAMENTALIST MUSLIMS BETWEEN AMERICA AND RUSSIA,
AS IT EXAMINES ISLAM AND PUBLIC LIFE. IT STUDIES THE
SIMILARITIES OF RUSSIA AND AMERICA AND THEN DETAILS FOUR
APPROACHES TO ISLAM AS FUNDAMENTALIST MUSLIMS BASE THEIR
VIEWS ON LIFE ON THE SACRED LAW OF ISLAM. U.S. POLICY TOWARD

FUNDAMENTAL MUSLIMS AND MUSLIM OPPOSITION TO PRO-AMERICAN
AND PRO-SOVIET GOVERNMENTS ARE DETAILED.

07230 PIPES, D.
CHAPTER SIX: THE CURSE OF OIL WEALTH; THE LONG SHADOW
TRANSACTION PUBLISHERS, NEW BRUNSWICK, NJ, 1989, 91-101.
THIS CHAPTER EXPLORES THE RAMIFICATIONS OF THE GREAT
WEALTH OFFERED TO THE ARAB WORLD BY OIL. THE NEED FOR
DIVERSITY IS EMPHASIZED AND THE "TALENT FOR SPENDING MONEY"
IS EXPLORED, AS WELL AS THE VESTED INTERESTS. IT CONCLUDES
THAT THE OIL BOOM HAS HARMED THE INDUSTRIAL NATIONS AND
BROUGHT SUFFERING TO POOR COUNTRIES, AND THAT ITS MOST
DEVASTATING IMPACT, NOT YET FELT, IS RESERVED FOR THE
APPARENT BENEFICIARIES.

07231 PIPES, D.
CHAPTER THREE: TRADITIONAL JEWISH AND MUSLIM WAYS OF LIFE;
THE LONG SHADOW
TRANSACTION PUBLISHERS, NEW BRUNSWICK, NJ, 1989, 33-41.
THIS CHAPTER EXPLORES THE DIFFERENCES AND RESEMBLANCES
BETWEEN JUDIASM AND ISLAM. THE LAW IS EXAMINED AS IT AFFECTS
MIDEASTERNERS. SIMILARITIES IN THEIR WAYS OF LIFE IS
DETAILED, AS WELL AS HOW THEY COPE WITH MODERN LIFE.

07232 PIPES, D.
CHAPTER 10: ARAB VS. ARAB OVER PALESTINE; THE LONG SHADOW
TRANSACTION PUBLISHERS, NEW BRUNSWICK, NJ, 1989, 130-144.
THIS CHAPTER EXPLORES ARAB CLAIMS TO PALESTINE.
PALESTINIAN SEDARATISTS AND ARAB NATIONALISTIC VIEWS
INTRODUCE THIS SECTION OF THE BOOK. CLAIMS BY JORDAN, SYRIA,
EGYPT AND THEIR DIFFERING PLANS FOR FOR PALESTINE ARE
ENUMERATED, AND THEN CONCLUSIONS ARE DRAWN AND POLITICAL
IMPLICATIONS ARE DETAILED.

07233 PIPES, D.
CHAPTER 11: HOW IMPORTANT IS THE PLO?; THE LONG SHADOW
TRANSACTION PUBLISHERS, NEW BRUNSWICK, NJ, 1989, 145-162.
THIS CHAPTER EXPLORES THE ANOMALIES OF THE PLO
TERRORIZING PALESTINIANS AS WELL AS OTHER NATIONS AND HOW IT
HAS FAILED TO ACHIEVE EVEN ONE OF ITS MILITARY OBJECTIVES
AGAINST ISRAEL INSPITE OF ITS MASSIVE INTERNATIONAL ACCLAIM.
PAN-ARABISM, AND PAN-ISLAM ARE EXPLORED AND THE RESULTANT
PLO. ALSO DETAILED IS ITS EXTREMIST IDEOLOGY, INEFFICACY,
AND HATRED BY THE PALESTINIANS. THE IMPLICATIONS OF ALL THIS
CONCLUDES THE CHAPTER.

07234 PIPES, D.
CHAPTER 12: SYRIA: THE CUBA OF THE MIDDLE EAST; THE LONG
SHADOW
TRANSACTION PUBLISHERS, NEW BRUNSWICK, NJ, 1989, 163-184.
THIS CHAPTER OF THE LONG SHADOW EXAMINES SYRIA. EXPLORED
IS ITS ALLIANCE WITH RUSSIA, MILITARY OBJECTIVES, AND
TERRORISM, AS WELL AS ITS HOSTILITY TOWARDS THE UNITED
STATES AND AGGRESSION AGAINST ITS NEIGHBORS. DOMESTIC
SOVIETIZATION, U.S. HOSTAGES, AND U.S. ATTITUDES TOWARD
SYRIA ARE EACH STUDIED.

07235 PIPES, D.
CHAPTER 16: "DEATH TO AMERICA" IN LEBANON; THE LONG SHADOW
TRANSACTION PUBLISHERS, NEW BRUNSWICK, NJ, 1989, 215-226.
THIS CHAPTER FOCUSES ON RADICAL FUNDAMENTALISM IN
LEBANON. IT EXPLORES THE INFLUENCE OF THIS IDEOLOGY WHICH
INITIALLY WAS ONLY IN IRAN. ATTACKS ON AMERICANS WITH AN EYE
ON EXTIRPATION OF WESTERN CIVILIZATION FROM THE MIDDLE EAST
ARE RECOUNTED. THE SPREAD OF RADICAL FUNDAMENTALIST MUSLIM
THOUGHT TO LEBANON IS TRACED. THE CHALLENGE FOR AMERICANS
AND THE WEST TO FIND DIPLOMATIC SOLUTIONS IS EXAMINED AND
THE USE OF RETALIATION MEASURED IS ASSESSED.

07236 PIPES, D.
CHAPTER 17: A DANGEROUS WHITEHOUSE OBSESSION; THE LONG
SHADOW
TRANSACTION PUBLISHERS, NEW BRUNSWICK, NJ, 1989, 227-236.
THIS CHAPTER EXPLORES THE REACTION OF THE AMERICAN
PEOPLE TO THE HOSTAGE SITUATION IN TEHRAN IN 1979. IT THEN
FOCUSES ON GOVERNMENT REACTION AND DETAILS THE AMOUNT OF
TIME AND ATTENTION SPENT ON DEALING WITH THE SITUATION. THE
ARTICLE CALLS THIS "AN EXTREME PERVERSION OF PRIORITIES";
RECOUNTS NEGLECTED ISSUES DURING THE TIME PERIOD; ANALYSES
THE REASONS FOR THE OBSESSION WITH THIS PARTICULAR SITUATION
AND SUGGESTS WAYS TO LEARN FROM MISTAKES MADE BY THE
GOVERNMENT IN DEALING WITH THE HOSTAGE SITUATION.

07237 PIPES, D.
CHAPTER 18: BREAKING ALL RULES: AMERICAN DEBATE OVER THE
MIDDLE EAST; THE LONG SHADOW
TRANSACTION PUBLISHERS, NEW BRUNSWICK, NJ, 1989, 237-262.
THIS CHAPTER ASSESSES THE AMERICAN DEBATE OVER THE
MIDDLE EAST, WHICH STANDS OUTSIDE THE USUAL AMERICAN FOREIGN
POLICY STANCE, AS CONSERVATIVE AND LIBERAL VIEWPOINTS TURN
TOWARD PRACTICAL MATTERS IN THAT REGION OF THE WORLD. THE
PRO-ARAB AND THE PRO-ISRAEL CAMPS ARE ANALYSED AND IT IS
NOTED THAT ISRAEL AND ARAB SYMPATHIZERS ARE FOUND ACROSS THE
MAINSTREAM OF AMERICAN POLITICAL LIFE. REASONS FOR POLITICS

IN THE MIDDLE EAST ARE AN ISSUE APART ARE EXPLORED AS WELL
AS SPECIAL INTERESTS FOR AMERICANS

07238 PIPES, D.
CHAPTER 19: PRESIDENTS AND MIDDLE EAST POLICY; THE LONG
SHADOW
TRANSACTION PUBLISHERS, NEW BRUNSWICK, NJ, 1989, 263-270.
THIS CHAPTER ANALYSES A STUDY ENTITLED "THE OTHER ARAB-
ISRAELI CONFLICT" BY STEVEN SPIEGEL, PROFESSOR OF POLITICAL
SCIENCE AT THE UNIVERSITY OF CALIFORNIA. IT FOCUSES ON HOW
AMERICAN POLICY TOWARD THE ARAB-ISRAEL DISPUTE IS MADE, AND
WHO MAKES IT. EACH PRESIDENT SINCE WWI IS DETAILED IN HIS
MIDDLE EAST POLICY AND WHO ACTUALLY MAKES THE DECISIONS IS
ANALYSED. THE STUDY CONCLUDES WITH A NEGATIVE ASSESSMENT OF
U.S. POLICY IN THE MIDDLE EAST.

07239 PIPES, D.
CHAPTER 20: THE MEDIA AND THE MIDDLE EAST
TRANSACTION PUBLISHERS, NEW BRUNSWICK, NJ, 1989, 271-282.
THIS CHAPTER ANALYSES AMERICAN PRESS COVERAGE OF THE
MIDDLE EAST WHICH COVERED MOSTLY THE ARAB-ISRAEL CONFLICT
AND THE U.S. ROLE IN THAT REGION. THE PREOCCUPATION WITH
JUST TWO PARTS OF A MUCH LARGER WHOLE GIVES TO AN EXTREME
NARROWNESS OF VISION, WHICH IN TURN ACCOUNTS FOR THE GREAT
NUMBER OF DISTORTIONS AND MISTAKES OF AMERICAN JOURNALISM
WITH REGARD TO THE MIDDLE EAST. ISRAEL IN AMERICAN EYES IS
EXAMINED FROM THE VIEWPOINT OF MEDIA INTEREST, AS WELL AS, U.
S. INTERESTS THERE. INTERNATIONAL REPERCUSSIONS ARE EXPLORED.

07240 PIPES, D.
IS THE WEST BANK A VITAL AMERICAN INTEREST
COMMENTARY, 88(5) (NOV 89), 19-24.
THIS ARTICLE EXAMINES THE ARAB-ISRAELI CONFLICT AND ITS
STATUS QUO AND SCHEMES TO SOLVE THE DIFFICULTIES BY ISRAEL,
EGYPT, THE PLO AND THE JAFFEE CENTER AS WELL AS THE UNITED
STATES. IT REVIEWS THE ROLE ASSIGNED TO THE U.S. IN THE
RESOLUTION OF THE CONFLICT. THE CHOICES ARE FIRST DELINEATED
AS THEY APPEAR IN THE MIDEAST WITH EMPHASIS ON THE
STANDPOINT OF THE ISRAELI ELECTORATE THEN SOVIET AND US
INTERESTS ARE EXAMINED. THE WRITER SUGGESTS THREE GUIDELINES
FOR THE US: 1) US SHOULD DOWNGRADE THE IMPORTANCE ATTACHED
TO THE TERRITORIES, 2) US SHOULD PAY MORE ATTENTION TO
MODERATE ARAB STATES, 3) US SHOULD STOP EXPECTING THE
CONFLICT TO PLAY AN IMPORTANT ROLE IN EITHER THE SOVIET
PRESENCE IN THE AREA OR IN THE FREE FLOW OF OIL.

07241 PIPES, D.
PLURALISM IN PERIL
REASON, 21(3) (JUL 89), 42-43.
THE MOBILIZATION OF MUSLIMS IN GREAT BRITAIN AND WESTERN
EUROPE AROUND THE ISSUE OF SALMAN RUSHDIE'S THE SATANIC
VERSES BROUGHT THE ISSUE OF WHETHER THEIR GROWING POLITICAL
POWER WILL BE USED TO CHANGE SOME FUNDAMENTAL ASPECTS OF
WESTERN LIFE INCLUDING FREEDOM OF SPEECH AND SECULARISM. THE
RESPONSE TO POTENTIAL ENCROACHMENTS ON FREEDOM OF SPEECH AND
OTHER ISSUES IS LIKELY TO DETERMINE THE NEAR FUTURE OF THE
INCREASING POLITICAL MUSCLE OF MUSLIMS IN THE WEST.

07242 PIPES, D.
TERRORISM: THE SYRIAN CONNECTION
NATIONAL INTEREST, (15) (SPR 89), 15-28.
THE ARTICLE EXAMINES SYRIAN SPONSORED TERRORISM. IT
OUTLINES THE MOTIVATIONS AND METHODS OF DAMASCUS AND
EXPLORES THE REASONS WHY SYRIA HAS BEEN MORE EFFECTIVE IN
SPONSORING TERRORISM AND AVOIDING THE CONSEQUENCES OF ITS
ACTIONS. IT EXAMINES THE ORGANIZATIONS THAT COOPERATE WITH
SYRIA AND THE VICTIMS OF THIS COOPERATION. THE ARTICLE
CONCLUDES THAT TERRORISM IS WAR AND THAT UNTIL IT IS FULLY
RECOGNIZED AS SUCH, IT WILL CONTINUE UNABATED.

07243 PIPES, D.
THE ALAWI CAPTURE OF POWER IN SYRIA
MIDDLE EASTERN STUDIES, 25(4) (OCT 89), 429-450.
FOR MANY CENTURIES, THE ALAWIS WERE THE WEAKEST, POOREST,
MOST RURAL, MOST DESPISED AND MOST BACKWARD PEOPLE IN SYRIA.
IN RECENT YEARS, HOWEVER, THEY HAVE TRANSFORMED THEMSELVES
INTO THE RULING ELITE OF DAMASCUS. TODAY ALAWIS DOMINATE THE
GOVERNMENT, HOLD KEY MILITARY POSITIONS, ENJOY A
DISPROPORTIONATE SHARE OF THE EDUCATIONAL RESOURCES, AND ARE
BECOMING WEALTHY. THIS ARTICLE EXPLORES HOW THIS DRAMATIC
CHANGE OCCURRED AND HOW THE ALAWIS MANAGED TO ESCAPE THEIR
TRADITIONAL CONFINES, AND WHAT THE MECHANISM OF THEIR RISE
HAS.

07244 PIPES, D.
THE AYATOLLAH, THE NOVELIST, AND THE WEST
COMMENTARY, 87(6) (JUN 89), 9-17.
THE ARTICLE EXAMINES THE FUROR THAT HAS ERUPTED OVER
SALMAN RUSHDIE'S THE SATANIC VERSES. IT EXPLORES THE
SECTIONS OF THE BOOK THAT ARE OBJECTIONABLE TO MUSLIMS AND
TRACES THE DEVELOPMENT OF THE EFFORTS OF MUSLIMS TO PROTEST
THE BOOK CULMINATING IN THE DEATH SENTENCES ISSUED BY THE
AYATOLLAH KHOMEINI. IT EXAMINES THE WESTERN WORLD'S REACTION
TO THE MUSLIM UPROAR AND STUDIES THE IMPLICATIONS FOR THE

FUTURE OF FREE SPEECH AND FREE EXPRESSION IN THE WEST.

07245 PIPES, D.
THE LONG SHADOW
TRANSACTION PUBLISHERS, NEW BRUNSWICK, NJ, 1989, 291.
THIS IS A BOOK ABOUT POLITICS BY A HISTORIAN. IT
CONCENTRATES ON FIVE VIVID AND CRITICAL TOPICS OF THE MIDDLE
EAST: 1) ISLAM AND PUBLIC LIFE. 2) THE PERSIAN GULF; WHERE
THE ORIGINS OF THE IRAQ-IRAN WAR & THE CURSE OF OIL HEALTH
IS DISCUSSED. 3) THE ARAB - ISRAELI CONFLICT; WHERE THE
CONFLICT IS LIKELY TO BE PERMANENT, 4) IRANIAN, LEBANESE AND
LIBYAN TERRORISM - THEIR DIFFERENCES AND WHY THE IRANIANS
POSE THE GREATEST THREAT TO THE UNITED STATES. 5) THE UNITED
STATES IN THE MIDDLE EAST - WHERE U.S. POLICY TOWARD THE
AREA, AND AMERICAN MEDIA COVERAGE ARE DETAILED.

07246 PIPES, D.
THE YEAR THE ARABS DISCOVERED PALESTINE
MIDDLE EAST REVIEW, XXI(4) (SUM 89), 37-44.
THE IDEA OF AN ARAB STATE RESTING BETWEEN THE JORDAN
RIVER AND THE MEDITERRANEAN SEA IS A TWENTIETH-CENTURY
CONCEPT. IN FACT, ITS ORIGINS CAN BE TRACED WITH SURPRISING
PRECISION TO A SINGLE YEAR. IN JANUARY 1920, PALESTINIAN
NATIONALISM HARDLY EXISTED; BY DECEMBER OF THAT SAME YEAR,
IT HAD BEEN BORN. THE EVENTS OF 1920 PROVIDE INSIGHT INTO
THE MOST WIDELY SUPPORTED, BUT POSSIBLY THE LEAST SUCCESSFUL,
NATIONALIST CAUSE OF THIS CENTURY.

07247 PITNART, P.
SOCIAL AND ECONOMIC DEVELOPMENTS IN CZECHOSLOVAKIA IN THE
1980S
EAST EUROPEAN REPORTER, 4(1) (WIN 89), 42-45.
THE ARTICLE EXAMINES SOCIAL AND ECONOMIC TRENDS IN
CZECHOSLOVAKIA OVER THE PAST DECADE. IT CONCLUDES THAT THE
DECADE IS CHARACTERIZED BY AN EVER-INCREASING CRISIS. A
DECLINING STANDARD OF LIVING, ETHNIC TENSIONS, CORRUPTION,
SCARCITY, AND ORGANIZED CRIME ARE ALL EVIDENCE OF THE
MISMANAGEMENT (OR NON-MANAGEMENT) BY THE RULING GOVERNMENT.
THE RESULT OF THESE PROBLEMS HAS BEEN INCREASING UNREST IN
THE GENERAL POPULATION AND GROWING CALLS FOR REFORM.

07248 PITNEY, J. J. JR.
BUDGET BALANCING ACT
REASON, 20(8) (JAN 89), 28-31.
THE AUTHOR CONSIDERS THE PROS AND CONS OF CALLING A
CONSTITUTIONAL CONVENTION TO WRITE A BALANCED BUDGET
AMENDMENT.

07249 PIVEN, F.F.; CLOWARD. R.A.
GOVERNMENT STATISTICS AND CONFLICTING EXPLANATIONS OF
NONVOTING
PS: POLITICAL SCIENCE AND POLITICS, XXII(3) (SEP 89),
580-588.
WHEN VOTER TURNOUT FELL TO A NEAR-HISTORIC LOW IN THE
1988 ELECTIONS, THE TWO SOURCES OF GOVERNMENT STATISTICS
SUGGESTED OPPOSITE REASONS. ONE INDICATED THAT FEWER PEOPLE
ARE REGISTERED TO VOTE. THE OTHER SUGGESTED THAT VOTERS ARE
REGISTERED BUT GOING TO THE POLLS LESS.

07250 PLACHER, W.C.
AFTER BABEL: THE VIRTUES OF LIBERALISM
THE CHRISTIAN CENTURY, 106(24) (AUG 89), 753-754.
THIS ARTICLE REVIEWS JEFFREY STOUT'S "ETHICS AFTER
BABEL" WHERE HE REFLECTS ON THE MORAL CLIMATE OF
CONTEMPORARY LIBERALISM. IT EXAMINES THE THREE DIVISIONS OF
THE BOOK: THE FIRST ARGUES THAT THERE IS NO UNIVERSAL HUMAN
LANGUAGE FOR MAKING OR DEFENDING ETHICAL JUDGEMENTS; THE
SECOND EXPLORES THE IMPLICATIONS OF THAT THESIS FOR
RELIGIOUS ETHICS; AND THE THIRD DEFENDS A LIBERALISM
SUITABLY CHASTENED IN THE FACE OF THE ARGUMENTS OF THE FIRST
PART. THE WRITER OF THE ARTICLE WONDERS WHAT DISTINCTIVE
ROLE STOUT WOULD ALLOW FOR THEOLOGIANS.

07251 PLANT, R.
FRONTIERS OF INJUSTICE
SOUTH, (103) (MAY 89), 79.
ABOUT 300 MILLION PEOPLE WORLDWIDE ARE CLASSIFIED AS
INDIGENOUS PEOPLES. THE GOVERNMENTS THAT SHOULD BE
PROTECTING THEM ARE WATERING DOWN THE PROVISIONS OF AN
INTERNATIONAL CONVENTION DESIGNED TO PROTECT THEIR RIGHTS
AND SCHEDULED FOR ADOPTION BY THE INTERNATIONAL LABOUR
ORGANISATION IN JUNE 1989.

07252 PLATT, H. L.
THE COST OF ENERGY: TECHNOLOGICAL CHANGE, RATE STRUCTURES,
AND PUBLIC POLICY IN CHICAGO, 1880-1920
URBAN STUDIES, 26(1) (FEB 89), 32-44.
A REVIEW OF THE HISTORICAL RECORD REVEALS THAT PUBLIC
POLICY HAS HAD MAJOR IMPACTS ON BOTH THE COST OF ENERGY AND
THE PATH OF TECHNOLOGICAL CHANGE. THE CASE OF GAS AND
ELECTRIC SERVICES IN CHICAGO BETWEEN 1900 AND 1920 WARRANTS
CLOSE SCRUTINY BECAUSE THE CITY ESTABLISHED AN EARLY
LEADERSHIP IN THE FORMATION OF PUBLIC POLICY. A COMPARISON
OF THE POLITICS OF RATE MAKING FOR GAS AND ELECTRIC SERVICES

UNDERSCORES THE IMPORTANCE OF GOVERNMENT-BUSINESS RELATIONS
IN DETERMINING THE PRICE OF ENERGY AND THE PACE OF
TECHNOLOGICAL INNOVATION, AS WELL AS THE PROFITS OF THE
UTILITY COMPANIES.

07253 PLATTEAU, J.
PENETRATION OF CAPITALISM AND PERSISTENCE OF SMALL-SCALE
ORGANIZATIONAL FORMS IN THIRD WORLD FISHERIES
DEVELOPMENT AND CHANGE, 20(4) (OCT 89), 621-651.
THIS PAPER ANALYSES THE CONCRETE MECHANISMS, CONTRACTUAL
ARRANGEMENTS AND ECONOMIC PROCESSES THROUGH WHICH SMALL-
SCALE FISHERMEN COMMUNITIES HAVE BEEN INCORPORATED INTO THE
MARKET SYSTEM AT THE NATIONAL, REGIONAL AND INTERNATIONAL
LEVELS. THE CENTRAL QUESTION IS HOW CAPITAL PENETRATED INTO
THE FISHING SECTOR OF MOST DEVELOPING COUNTRIES AND HOW THE
LATTER WAS MADE FUNCTIONAL TO THE OBJECTIVE NEEDS OF CAPITAL
ACCUMULATION AND OUTPUT EXPANSION WHICH NEW MARKET
OPPORTUNITIES DETERMINED DURING THE POST-WAR PERIOD. SUCH AN
ANALYSIS OF THE PRECISE MODES OF ARTICULATION BETWEEN THE
TRADITIONAL DIRECT PRODUCERS OR DEALERS OF FISH AND THE
LARGER ECONOMIC SYSTEM INTENDED TO ACHIEVE TWO MAJOR
OBJECTIVES. IT AIMS AT FILLING AN IMPORTANT GAP IN THE
LITERATURE, WHICH EITHER ASSUMES THAT COUNTRIES ARE SUDDENLY
'OPENED UP' TO INTERNATIONAL TRADE AS THOUGH THE CONCRETE
WAYS IN WHICH THIS PROCESS OF 'OPENING-UP' COMES ABOUT AND
IS EFFECTED DO NOT MATTER (AS IN NEOCLASSICAL ECONOMIC
THEORIES) OR, ALTERNATIVELY, DEPICTS THE SAME PROCESS AT A
MUCH TOO ABSTRACT LEVEL (AS IN MANY NEO-MARXIST ANALYSES).

07254 PLEMMONS, R.N.
ASSESSING SOVIET-AMERICAN ARMS RACE INTERACTION IN THE
ACCUMULATION OF STRATEGIC NUCLEAR WEAPONS, 1955-1984
DISSERTATION ABSTRACTS INTERNATIONAL, 50(6) (DEC 89),
1796-A.
THE AUTHOR PRESENTS AN EMPIRICAL ANALYSIS OF SOVIET-
AMERICAN ARMS RACING USING LAUNCHER, WARHEAD, AND EQUIVALENT
MEGATONNAGE DATA. THE ANALYSIS UTILIZES A REGRESSION
METHODOLOGY, CORRELATIONS, COEFFICIENTS OF DETERMINATION, T-
TESTS, AND A GEARY TEST FOR AUTOCORRELATION.

07255 PLESKOV, V.
ON FRG'S SOVEREIGNTY
INTERNATIONAL AFFAIRS (MOSCOW), (2) (FEB 89), 78-81.
WEST GERMANS HAVE BEEN RAISING QUESTIONS ABOUT THE
EXTENT OF THEIR OWN SOVEREIGNTY, DUE TO WHAT SOME SEE AN
INFRINGEMENT ON THEIR SOVEREIGNTY BY FRANCE, GREAT BRITAIN,
AND THE UNITED STATES. THE HOME POLICY AND DEFENSE
COMMITTEES OF THE BUNDESTAG AND THE WEST GERMAN GOVERNMENT
HAVE BEEN INVOLVED IN THE LARGER-SCALE DEBATE ON THE
SOVEREIGNTY QUESTION.

07256 PLOOG, W.H.
A RESPONSE TO RATIONALISM: EDMUND BURKE AND THE
CONTEMPORARY TURN TO TRADITIONS
DISSERTATION ABSTRACTS INTERNATIONAL, 50(5) (NOV 89),
1425-A.
THE CONTEMPORARY TURN TO TRADITIONS IN SOCIAL AND
POLITICAL THEORY, EXEMPLIFIED BY THE WORKS OF ALASDAIR
MACINTYRE AND MICHAEL WALZER, CAN BE DISTINGUISHED FROM
OTHER FORMS OF TRADITIONALISM BY ITS EMPHASIS ON A CRITICAL
ENGAGEMENT WITH TRADITIONS. IN THIS DISSERTATION, THE AUTHOR
ARGUES THAT A TURN TO TRADITIONS OFFERS THE POSSIBILITY OF A
POLITICS IN WHICH THE HISTORY AND EXPERIENCE OF PAST
GENERATIONS MATTERS. BUT NEITHER WALZER NOR MACINTYRE
ADEQUATELY CONCERN THEMSELVES WITH THE ISSUE OF HOW
CONTEMPORARY MAN IS RELATED TO TRADITIONS AND TO THE PAST.
EDMUND BURKE'S CONCEPT OF INHERITANCE OFFERS AN ARTICULATE
VIEW OF HOW ONE MIGHT UNDERSTAND ONESELF AS PART OF A
TRADITION.

07257 PLOTKE, D.
MARXISM AND DEMOCRATIC THEORY
DISSENT, (SUM 89), 343-349.
FAILED EFFORTS AT A NEW MARXIST ORTHODOXY HAVE OPENED
THE WAY TO A CREATIVE INTERACTION AMONG THEORIES OFTEN
CONSIDERED INCOMPATIBLE. AS MARXISM HAS BECOME MORE
LEGITIMATE, ITS ORTHODOXIES HAVE DECAYED. THE PROMISE OF
THIS LOGIC IS A FRUITFUL CONVERGENCE AMONG MARXIST,
DEMOCRATIC, AND LIBERAL THEORIES CONCERNED WITH A DEMOCRATIC
POLITICS IN ADVANCED INDUSTRIAL SOCIETIES.

07258 PLUMB, L.
BUILDING A DEMOCRATIC COMMUNITY: THE ROLE OF THE EUROPEAN
PARLIAMENT
WORLD TODAY, 45(7) (JUL 89), 112-117.
THERE HAVE ALWAYS BEEN TWO DRIVING FORCES BEHIND THE
EUROPEAN IDEA: IDEALISM AND PRAGMATISM. THE IDEALISM STEMMED
FROM THE EXPERIENCES OF WORLD WAR II, INSPIRING THOSE WHO
WERE DETERMINED TO ESTABLISH A SYSTEM OF BINDING COOPERATION
AMONG THE EUROPEAN STATES THAT WOULD MAKE CONFLICTS BETWEEN
THEM INCONCEIVABLE. THE PRAGMATISM STEMMED FROM THE GROWING
INTER-DEPENDENCE OF EUROPEAN COUNTRIES AND THE NEED TO FIND
COMMON SOLUTIONS TO COMMON PROBLEMS. THE SINGLE EUROPEAN ACT
HAS ENLARGED THE EUROPEAN COMMUNITY'S FORMAL

RESPONSIBILITIES, IMPROVED ITS DECISION-MAKING PROCEDURES, AND ASSOCIATED THE EUROPEAN PARLIAMENT MORE CLOSELY WITH THE ADOPTION OF COMMUNITY LEGISLATION.

07259 PLUMMER, S.B.
EGYPTIAN AIR FORCE: INSURANCE FOR U.S. NATIONAL INTEREST IN THE MIDDLE EAST
AVAILABLE FROM NTIS, NO. AD-A202 133/5/GAR, APR 88, 67.
A SYNOPSIS OF HISTORY MAKING EVENTS IN EGYPT FROM THE OVERTHROW OF KING FAROUK IN 1952 UNTIL 1988; REMARKS ON THE CONTRASTING LEADERSHIP STYLES OF NASSER, SADAT AND MUBARAK; A BRIEF HISTORY OF THE EGYPTIAN AIR FORCE AS WELL AS LESSONS LEARNED FROM PAST WARS; AN ANALYSIS OF PROS AND CONS OF BEING A SOVIET PROTEGE AND THE RATIONALE BEHIND THE SWITCH FROM EAST TO WEST; A COMPARATIVE ANALYSIS OF THE EGYPTIAN AND THE ISRAELI AIR FORCES OF 1988; AN ASSESSMENT OF EGYPTIAN FOREIGN POLICY IN 1988 AND AS AN ASSERTION OF SIMILARITIES BETWEEN IT AND U.S. NATIONAL INTERESTS WITHIN THE REGION; THE AUTHOR BELIEVES THAT BY CONTINUING TO SUPPLY EGYPT WITH VAST AMOUNTS OF MILITARY AND ECONOMIC AID, THE U.S. WILL ACHIEVE A BALANCE OF POWER BETWEEN ISRAEL AND THE MODERATE ARAB STATES, INCREASING REGIONAL STABILITY AND SERVING U.S. INTERESTS IN THE REGION.

07260 POCKRASS, R.M.
BUILDING A CIVIL POLICE COUNTERTERRORIST TEAM
CONFLICT, 8(4) (1988), 327-332.
THIS ARTICLE IS BASED ON DISCUSSIONS HELD WITH EXPERIENCED LAW-ENFORCEMENT OFFICERS AT THE FEDERAL, STATE, COUNTY, AND MUNICIPAL LEVELS, AND WITH CONCERNED CIVILIANS. IT PROPOSES GUIDELINES FOR THE CREATION OF A CIVIL POLICE TEAM TO COMBAT TERRORISM AND PRESENTS AN APPROACH THAT DESERVES STUDY AND DISCUSSION.

07261 POCOCK, J.G.A.
CONSERVATIVE ENLIGHTENMENT AND DEMOCRATIC REVOLUTIONS: THE AMERICAN AND FRENCH CASES IN BRITISH PERSPECTIVE
GOVERNMENT AND OPPOSITION, 24(1) (1989), 81-105.
THE AUTHOR CONSIDERS THE SUBJECT OF CONSERVATIVE ENLIGHTENMENT AND DEMOCRATIC REVOLUTIONS IN THE USA AND FRANCE FROM A BRITISH PERSPECTIVE.

07262 PODHORETZ, N.
ISRAEL: A LAMENTATION FROM THE FUTURE
COMMENTARY, 87(3) (MAR 89), 15-21.
THE AUTHOR FORECASTS THAT A NEW PLO STATE COULD BE INEVITABLE IF THE WAR-WEARY, INTERNALLY DIVIDED, AND ISOLATED JEWS OF ISRAEL AND JEWS OF AMERICA DO NOT OFFER THE MOST DETERMINED RESISTANCE POSSIBLE.

07263 POHLMAN, H.L.
AMERICAN POLITICAL THOUGHT: AN INTERPRETATION
TEACHING POLITICAL SCIENCE, 16(4) (SUM 89), 166-173.
IT IS THE AUTHOR'S HOPE THAT THIS PAPER WILL PROVOKE DISCUSSION CONCERNING THE OBJECTIVES AND TECHNIQUES OF TEACHING AMERICAN POLITICAL THOUGHT. IT OFFERS AN INTERPRETATION OF WHAT SUCH A COURSE IS ALL ABOUT. IT ADDRESSES THE QUESTIONS OF: WHAT DOES THE STUDY OF POLITICAL THOUGHT HAVE TO DO WITH HOW AMERICAN POLITICAL INSTITUTIONS OPERATE; WHAT IS THE OBJECTIVE OF SUCH A COURSE: WHAT ARE THE BEST MEANS OF OBTAINING IT; AND, HOW WILL IT FIT INTO AN UNDERGRADUATE EDUCATION? THE WRITER'S INTERPRETATION RESTS ON THE ASUMPTION THAT VALUES PLAY AN IMPORTANT PART IN OUR SOCIOPOLITICAL WORLD AND THAT AN UNDERGRADUATE EDUCATION SHOULD HELP STUDENTS ACHIEVE IDEOLOGICAL MATURITY.

07264 POHLMANN, M.
CONSTRAINING PRESIDENTS AT THE BRINK: THE CUBAN MISSLE CRISIS
PRESIDENTIAL STUDIES QUARTERLY, XIX(2) (SPR 89), 337-346.
IN THE FALL OF 1962, THE WORLD STOOD ON THE BRINK OF A NUCLEAR HOLOCAUST AS THE UNITED STATES AND THE SOVIET UNION ATTEMPTED TO RESOLVE THE CUBAN MISSLE CRISIS HIGH-LEVEL ADVISERS MET IN SECLUSION AND ULTIMATELY MADE THE CRITICAL DECISIONS FOR MORE THAN 200 MILLION UNITED STATES CITIZENS WHOSE LIVES HUNG IN THE BALANCE. THIS ARTICLE EXAMINES THE ROLE PLAYED BY THE GENERAL PUBLIC IN SUCH FOREIGN POLICY CRISES AND HOW THAT ROLE COULD BE STRENGTHENED, GIVEN THEIR TREMENDOUS STAKE IN THESE DECISIONS.

07265 POIS, A. M.
THE POLITICS AND PROCESS OF ORGANIZING FOR PEACE: THE UNITED STATES SECTION OF THE WOMEN'S INTERNATIONAL LEAGUE FOR PEACE AND FREEDOM, 1919-1939
DISSERTATION ABSTRACTS INTERNATIONAL, 49(8) (FEB 89), 2369-A.
THE AUTHOR STUDIES THE DEVELOPMENT OF THE USWILPF AS A WOMEN'S INTERNATIONAL, PACIFIST, REFORM GROUP, EXPLORING ITS NATURE BY EXAMINING THE INTER-RELATED FACTORS OF IDEOLOGY, REFORM METHODS, AND ORGANIZATIONAL PROCESS. SHE PROVIDES INSIGHT INTO THE GROUP'S POLITICAL AND ORGANIZATIONAL CHOICES AS IT ENDEAVORED TO REFORM A WORLD DIVIDED BY NATIONALISM AND VIOLENCE.

07266 POLANYI-LEVITT, K.; MENDELL, M.
THE ORIGINS OF MARKET FETISHISM
MONTHLY REVIEW. 41(2) (JUN 89), 11-32.
THE ARTICLE TRACES THE DEVELOPMENT OF THE ECONOMIC THEORIES OF FRIENDRICH HAYEK AND ANALYZES THE EFFECT THAT THEY HAVE HAD ON WORLD ECONOMICS. IT EXPLORES THE BACKGROUND IN EUROPE AND ESPECIALLY IN HAYEK'S NATIVE AUSTRIA THAT INFLUENCED THE DEVELOPMENT OF HIS "FAITH": THE BELIEF IN THE FREE MARKET OR 'PRICE MECHANISM' -- THAT A COMPETITIVE SYSTEM FREE OF ALL INTERFERENCES BY GOVERNMENT WOULD EASILY FIND AN "EQUILIBRIUM"

07267 POLESE. M.; VERREAULT, R.
TRADE IN INFORMATION-INTENSIVE SERVICES: HOW AND WHY REGIONS DEVELOP EXPORT ADVANTAGES
CANADIAN REVIEW OF SOCIOLOGY AND ANTHROPOLOGY, 15(4) (DEC 89), 376-386.
STARTING FROM THE OBSERVATION THAT CANADA IS A NET EXPORTER OF ENGINEERING CONSULTING SERVICES, LARGELY ATTRIBUTABLE TO A SINGLE PROVINCE, QUEBEC, THIS PAPER ATTEMPTS TO EXPLAIN HOW REGIONS DEVELOP EXPORT ADVANTAGES IN INFORMATION INTENSIVE SERVICES. THE AUTHORS CONTEND THAT TRADE IN SERVICES IS BASED ON COMPARATIVE ADVANTAGE JUST AS TRADE IN GOODS, THAT THE DEVELOPMENT OF COMPETITIVE ADVANTAGE IN THE SERVICE SECTOR IS NOT FUNDAMENTALLY DIFFERENT FROM THAT IN THE MANUFACTURING SECTOR. SERVICES DO NOT OFFER A SHORT-CUT TO DEVELOPING EXPORT ADVANTAGES. THE AUTHORS SPECIFICALLY EXAMINE THE ROLE OF TECHNOLOGY (KNOWLEDGE), WORK EXPERIENCE, R & D, EXTERNAL ECONOMIES AND PUBLIC POLICY IN THE DEVELOPMENT OF EXPORT ADVANTAGES IN INFORMATION INTENSIVE SERVICES.

07268 POLGAR, T.
POLITICS: CONTRADICTIONS AND ALTERNATIVES
WORLD MARXIST REVIEW, 31(12) (DEC 88), 52-58.
DURING THE PAST TEN OR FIFTEEN YEARS SOCIAL DEVELOPMENT IN SOME SOCIALIST COUNTRIES HAS SLOWED DOWN, AND SEVERAL HAVE BEEN IN A STATE OF PRE-CRISIS OR EVEN OF CRISIS. ADVERSE TRENDS HAVE ACCUMULATED IN THE ECONOMY, IN EDUCATION, CULTURE, SCIENCE, PUBLIC HEALTH, AND EVEN IN POLITICS, THE RESULT OF INHERENT CONTRADICTIONS WHICH, AS HUNGARY'S EXPERIENCE SHOWS, CANNOT BE RESOLVED BY HALF-MEASURES. SOCIALIST SOCIETY CAN BE RENEWED ONLY BY A CONSISTENT AND RADICAL PROCESS, DIRECTED TOWARDS THE DIALECTICAL NEGATION OF EXISTING STRUCTURES. THE EVOLUTION OF DEMOCRACY WILL PAVE THE WAY FOR THE ACTIVE PARTICIPATION OF EVERYONE IN AFFECTING THE REFORMS, THEREBY PROMOTING THE SIMULTANEOUS IMPLEMENTATION OF TWO HISTORICAL TRENDS: THE NATIONAL DEVELOPMENT OF THE SOCIALIST COUNTRIES, AND THEIR POLITICAL INTEGRATION BASED ON ECONOMIC COOPERATION.

07269 POLLACK, B.
THE DILEMMAS FACING THE CHILEAN LEFT FOLLOWING THE PLEBISCITE OF 1988.
JOURNAL OF COMMUNIST STUDIES, 5(2) (JUN 89), 222-227.
THE VICTORY OF THE OPPOSITION FORCES IN THE CHILEAN PLEBISCITE IN OCTOBER OF 1988 SIGNALED THE END OF THE PINOCHET REGIME. HOWEVER, THE 16-STRONG ALLIANCE OF SOCIAL MOVEMENTS AND POLITICAL PARTIES WERE UNITED ONLY BY THEIR DESIRE TO OUST PINOCHET. THE ARTICLE EXAMINES THE UNCERTAIN FUTURE OF THE PARTIES OF THE CHILEAN LEFT. IT OUTLINES SEVERAL OF THE PROBLEMS THEY FACE INCLUDING ORGANIZATION, IMAGE, FEAR, AND MOST SIGNIFICANTLY SECTARIANISM. IT CONCLUDES THAT ALTHOUGH THE PROBLEMS ARE SIGNIFICANT, THE OUTLOOK IS, ON THE WHOLE, POSITIVE.

07270 POLLACK, J.D.
MOSCOW TAKES A HARD LOOK AT TIES WITH VIETNAM
FAR EASTERN ECONOMIC REVIEW, 141(38) (SEP 88), 26-27.
BY CONSENTING TO VISIT BEIJING FOR TALKS FOCUSED EXCLUSIVELY ON CAMBODIA, SOVIET VICE-FOREIGN MINISTER IGOR ROGACHEV HAS WEAKENED MOSCOW'S LONG STANDING INSISTENCE THAT IT WOULD NOT ALLOW THE INJECTION OF "THIRD PARTY" ISSUES INTO ITS DIALOGUE WITH BEIJING. SOME LEADERS IN HANOI FEAR THAT VIETNAMESE INTERESTS WILL AGAIN BE COMPROMISED FOR MUCH LARGER POLITICAL STAKES. ALTHOUGH MOSCOW DOES SEEM TO BE TAKING A CLOSER LOOK AT THE BENEFITS AND DISADVANTAGES OF ITS RELATIONS WITH VIETNAM, MOST OBSERVERS FEEL THAT A MAJOR DIVERGENCE FROM THE USSR'S CURRENT POLICY IS UNLIKELY.

07271 POLLINS, B.M.
CONFLICT, COOPERATION, AND COMMERCE: THE EFFECT OF INTERNATIONAL POLITICAL INTERACTIONS ON BILATERAL TRADE FLOWS
AMERICAN JOURNAL OF POLITICAL SCIENCE, 33(3) (AUG 89), 737-761.
THE PUBLIC CHOICE APPROACH TO POLITICAL ECONOMY IS EMPLOYED TO GAIN INSIGHT INTO THE CONNECTION BETWEEN INTERNATIONAL POLITICS AND TRADE FLOWS. A MODEL IS CONSTRUCTED IN WHICH IMPORTERS ARE ASSUMED TO BE RATIONAL UTILITY MAXIMIZERS WHO SEEK TO SATISFY INTERNATIONAL SECURITY AS WELL AS ECONOMIC WELFARE OBJECTIVES. THIS MODEL OF BILATERAL TRADE FLOWS REFLECT CONTEMPORARY THEORY IN THE FIELD OF INTERNATIONAL ECONOMICS, AND IT EXPLICITLY

INCORPORATES THE GENERAL FOREIGN POLICY ORIENTATION OF
IMPORTERS AMONG ITS DETERMINANTS. THE MODEL IS TESTED IN 16
ANNUAL CROSSSECTIONAL ESTIMATIONS (1960-75) FOR A COMPLETE
NETWORK OF 25 COUNTRIES. THE FINDINGS SHOW CONSIDERABLE
SUPPORT FOR THE HYPOTHESIS THAT TRADE FLOWS ARE
SIGNIFICANTLY INFLUENCED BY BROAD POLITICAL RELATIONS OF
AMITY AND ENMITY BETWEEN NATIONS. THE AUTHOR CONCLUDES THAT
NATIONS ADJUST TRADE TIES TO SATISFY SECURITY AS WELL AS
ECONOMIC WELFARE GOALS AND THAT A FORMAL POLITICAL ECONOMY
OF TRADE SHOULD REFLECT THIS FACT.

07272 POLLINS, B.M.
DOES TRADE STILL FOLLOW THE FLAG?
AMERICAN POLITICAL SCIENCE REVIEW, 83(2) (JUN 89), 465-480.
THE OBJECTIVE OF THIS STUDY IS TO MAP ONE OF THE MANY
CONNECTIONS BETWEEN INTERNATIONAL POLITICS AND COMMERCIAL
TIES. SPECIFICALLY, THE AUTHOR SEEKS TO IDENTIFY AND MEASURE
THE EFFECT OF CHANGES IN STATE-TO-STATE DIPLOMATIC RELATIONS
ON TRADE FLOWS BETWEEN THOSE NATIONS. THEORETICAL
UNDERPINNINGS OF HIS EFFORT ARE IN THE TRADITION OF "PUBLIC
CHOICE" POLITICAL ECONOMY BECAUSE HE TREATS IMPORTERS AS
RATIONAL UTILITY MAXIMIZERS AND THEIR BEHAVIOR AS DETERMINED
BY PREFERENCES PURSUED WITHIN A CONTEXT OF SPECIFIED
CONSTRAINTS.

07273 POLYAKOV, G.
WHAT SHALL WE BUY IN AFRICA?
INTERNATIONAL AFFAIRS (MOSCOW), (10) (OCT 89), 68-73.
ECONOMIC COOPERATION BETWEEN THE SOVIET UNION AND THE
AFRICAN COUNTRIES HAS ENTERED A NEW, COMPLEX STAGE MARKED BY
A DROP IN THE GROWTH RATE AND ABSOLUTE VOLUME OF DELIVERIES.
WHAT WAS ONCE BELIEVED TO BE A TEMPORARY DOWNWARD TREND IN
SOVIET-AFRICAN TRADE HAS PROVED TO BE VERY DURABLE AND WILL
REQUIRE A LOT OF EFFORT, TIME, AND RESOURCES TO REMEDY. IN
THIS ARTICLE, THE AUTHOR LOOKS AT THE PAST ECONOMIC
COOPERATION AND THE PROSPECTS FOR THE FUTURE OF TRADE
BETWEEN THE SOVIET UNION AND AFRICA.

07274 POLYAKOV, V.
OPTIONS FOR THE PERSIAN GULF
INTERNATIONAL AFFAIRS (MOSCOW), (9) (SEP 89), 126-130.
THE SOVIET UNION SUPPORTS THE IDEA OF NORMALIZING THE
SITUATION IN THE PERSIAN GULF. IT SUPPORTS A TRANSITION TO
MUTUAL RELATIONS BASED ON PEACEFUL COEXISTENCE, WHICH WOULD
PROMOTE BOTH THE SOVIET UNION'S NATIONAL INTERESTS AND THE
INTERESTS OF THE INTERNATIONAL COMMUNITY AT LARGE. TO ENSURE
SECURITY IN THE GULF AREA, THE SOVIET UNION ADVOCATES A
BROAD INTERNATIONAL AGREEMENT THAT WOULD PROVIDE A RELIABLE
SYSTEM OF SAFEGUARDS BY THE UN SECURITY COUNCIL. THE USSR
BELIEVES THAT IT IS IMPERATIVE TO WITHDRAW FOREIGN WARSHIPS
OF NON-LITTORAL STATES FROM THE PERSIAN GULF AND EXPRESSES
ITS READINESS TO WITHDRAW ITS OWN SHIPS.

07275 POLYAKOV, Y.
THE YEAR 1789 AND 1917
INTERNATIONAL AFFAIRS (MOSCOW), (12) (DEC 89), 3-9.
GREAT REVOLUTIONS, ALTHOUGH THEY SEEM TO BREAK OUT
UNEXPECTEDLY, TAKE A LONG TIME TO COME TO A HEAD. A COMMON
CHARACTERISTICS OF THE FRENCH AND RUSSIAN REVOLUTIONS WAS
THAT THE REVOLUTIONARY PROCESS WAS COMPLEX AND PROTRACTED.
THE STRUGGLE GRADUALLY DREW IN THE MASS OF THE PEOPLE,
CHARACTERIZED BY A PARTICULARLY STRONG ASPIRATION FOR
DECISIVE CHANGE, THE GREATEST RESOLVE, AND AN INTENSE HATRED
FOR THE RULING POWERS.

07276 POMERANTS, G.
OUR ATOMIC AGE, OUR STONE AGE
GLASNOST, II(2) (MAR 89), 70-71.
THE AUTHOR CONSIDERS WHY CERTAIN RUSSIAN DISSIDENT
WRITERS AND THEIR WORKS REMAIN TABOO IN THE SOVIET UNION
WHILE OTHER FORMERLY TABOO WRITERS ARE BEGINNING TO BE
PUBLISHED AND DISCUSSED.

07277 PONOMAREV, B.
FROM ARMS-BRISTLINGECONOMIES TO DISARMAMENT ECONOMIES,
REPRINTS FROM THE SOVIET PRESS, 48(5) (MAR 89), 22-27.
THE ARTICLE RECOUNTS MIKHAIL GORBACHEV'S ADDRESS TO THE
UNITED NATIONS. HE STRESSED THE IMPORTANCE OF GIVING UP
"ARMS-BRISTLING ECONOMIES" FOR THE ECONOMIES OF DISARMAMENT.
HE OUTLINED PAST AND CURRENT SOVIET EFFORTS AT DISARMAMENT
AND AT CONVERSION OF MILITARY INDUSTRIES OVER TO CIVILIAN
ONES. HE CALLED UPON THE NATIONS OF THE WEST TO FOLLOW THE
LEAD OF THE USSR BY SUBMITTING DISARMAMENT AND CONVERSION
PLANS TO THE UN.

07278 POOLE, W.; DARBY, M.R.; EISNER, R.; SINAI, A.L.
CHALLENGES OF MACRO POLICY IN THE OPEN U.S. ECONOMY
CONTEMPORARY POLICY ISSUES, VII(1) (JAN 89), 1-34.
THIS SYMPOSIUM DISCUSSES THE PROBLEMS THE U.S. ECONOMY
FACES AND WHAT U.S. MACROECONOMIC POLICY SHOULD BE. AMONG
THE TOPICS ARE EMPLOYMENT, REAL OUTPUT, AND INVESTMENT.

07279 POOLE, W.T.
HOW BIG BUSINESS BANKROLLS THE LEFT

NATIONAL REVIEW, XLI(4) (MAR 89), 34-37.
SURVEYS OF PATTERNS OF CORPORATE PHILANTHROPY INDICATE-
IN CLEAR VIOLATION OF WHAT WOULD APPEAR TO BE COMMON SENSE
AND SIMPLE SELF INTEREST-A PATTERN OF PREFERENCE FOR CAUSES
OF THE MODERATE TO LESS-MODERATE LEFT RATHER THAN FOR
ORGANIZATIONS AND PROGRAMS DEDICATED TO THE PERPETUATION OF
ECONOMIC FREEDOM UNDER CAPITALISM.

07280 POPE, D.H.
PERSONALITY AND JUDICIAL PERFORMANCE: A PSYCHOBIOGRAPHY OF
JUSTICE JOSEPH P. BRADLEY
DISSERTATION ABSTRACTS INTERNATIONAL, 49(10) (APR 89),
3142-A.
THE PERSONALITY OF ASSOCIATE JUSTICE JOSEPH P. BRADLEY
IS ANALYZED IN RELATION TO HIS JUDICIAL PERFORMANCE DURING
HIS SERVICE ON THE U.S. SUPREME COURT FROM 1870 TO 1892. THE
MAJOR HYPOTHESIS OF THIS STUDY IS THAT BRADLEY'S OBSESSIVE-
COMPULSIVE PERSONALITY PLAYED AN IMPORTANT ROLE IN THE
EXECUTION OF HIS JUDICIAL DUTIES.

07281 POPOV, G.
ANTI-SOCIALISM BEHAVIOR: EITHER RESTRUCTURE PERESTROIKA OR
WATCH THE REBUILDING COLLAPSE
GLASNOST, II(3) (MAY 89), 11-18.
THE SOVIET UNION NEEDS RADICAL CHANGE BECAUSE THE
COUNTRY IS APPROACHING A CRISIS. AND THEIR CRISIS WILL
ENTAIL MORE THAN ECONOMIC TRAVAIL BECAUSE NO MAJOR CRISIS
CAN EVER BE PURELY ECONOMIC. IT WILL ALSO BE A MORAL CRISIS,
AN IDEOLOGICAL CRISIS, AND A POLITICAL CRISIS.

07282 POPOV, G.
THE RESTRUCTURING OF PERESTROIKA: TEN THESES ON THE SECOND
STAGE OF PERESTROIKA
GLASNOST, (16-18) (JAN 89), 48-49.
IN THE FIRST STAGE OF PERESTROIKA, THE KEY ISSUE WAS THE
BASIC CONCEPT. THE VERSION OF PERESTROIKA DEVELOPED FROM THE
DECISIONS OF THE 27TH CONGRESS OF THE CPSU PROVIDED FOR A
TRANSITION TO ECONOMIC METHODS OF INDUSTRIAL MANAGEMENT AND
TO A HIGH LEVEL OF DEMOCRACY IN PUBLIC LIFE. THE SOVIET
UNION NOW FACES THE CRUCIAL MOMENT WHEN THIS CONCEPT MUST BE
CARRIED OUT. BUT IT IS INCORRECT TO REDUCE THE SECOND STAGE
OF PERESTROIKA TO THE PROBLEMS OF IMPLEMENTING THE CONCEPT.
TO DO SO WOULD VASTLY OVERSIMPLIFY THE ISSUES.

07283 POPP, G.; ANWAR, S.
FROM PERESTROIKA TO ETHNIC NATIONALISM
INTERNATIONAL PERSPECTIVES, XVIII(2) (MAR 89), 21-23.
THE ARTICLE EXPLORES WHAT IT ARGUES WILL BE THE MOST
FUNDAMENTAL AND VITAL ISSUE OF RUSSIAN SOCIETY IN THE FUTURE:
THE RISE IN ETHNO-NATIONALISM IN THE USSR. IT EXAMINES THE
DEMOGRAPHICS THAT INDICATE THAT RUSSIANS WILL BE A MINORITY
IN THE USSR BY THE YEAR 2000. THE USSR IS ALREADY FEELING
THE TENSION BETWEEN SOME OF ITS 120 NATIONALITIES AND ETHNIC
GROUPS. IT CONCLUDES THAT FUTURE EVENTS WILL SEVERELY TEST
THE ABILITY OF THE TOTALITARIAN SYSTEM AND OF CENTRALIZED
PLANNING TO COPE WITH THE COMPLEXITIES OF A POLYETHNIC
SOCIETY.

07284 POPP, G.E.; ANWAR, S.T.
CHINA'S PRAGMATIC MODERNISATION
CONTEMPORARY REVIEW, 254(1476) (JAN 89), 19-24.
THE ARTICLE OUTLINES THE CHANGES THAT OCCURRED IN THE
13TH PARTY CONGRESS OF THE CHINESE COMMUNIST PARTY. IT
EXAMINES THE INCREASING TREND TOWARDS MODERATION AND REFORM.
IT ALSO EXAMINES THE ECONOMIC CHANGES AND REFORMS TAKING
PLACE IN THE PEOPLE'S REPUBLIC. WRITTEN BEFORE TIANAMMEN
SQUARE, IT CONCLUDES THAT THE NEAR FUTURE WILL SEE REFORMERS,
LED BY ZHAO ZIYANG, MAKING GRADUAL BUT SIGNIFICANT CHANGES
IN CHINA'S POLITICAL AND ECONOMIC STRUCTURE.

07285 PORADO, P.
FINDING FASTER FEEDBACK
CAMPAIGNS AND ELECTIONS, 10(4) (DEC 89), 34-36.
INTERACTIVE RESEARCH, A TECHNOLOGY THAT COMBINES
RESPONSE TABULATION SOFTWARE AND A REMOTE-CONTROL DATA ENTRY
TOOL, HAS RESTORED THE INTEGRITY OF FOCUS GROUP EVALUATIONS
OF POLITICAL ADVERTISEMENTS. INTRODUCED IN THE EARLY 1980'S,
IT HAS GROWN IN POPULARITY SINCE CAMPAIGN MEDIA EXPERTS
PICKED UP ON IT DURING THE 1986 CONGRESSIONAL CYCLE.

07286 PORADO, P.
LET THEIR FINGERS DO THE TALKING
CAMPAIGNS AND ELECTIONS, 10(4) (DEC 89), 41-44.
A TENNESSEE CONGRESSMAN HAS BEEN USING A COMPUTER-DRIVEN
KIOSK POLLING SYSTEM TO COLLECT CONSTITUENT FEEDBACK. THE
KIOSKS HAVE BEEN INSTALLED IN SHOPPING MALLS AND GROCERY
STORES. SHOPPERS CAN STOP AND COMPLETE A SIX-MINUTE SURVEY
GIVING THE CONGRESSMAN THEIR OPINIONS ON BOTH LOCAL AND
NATIONAL ISSUES.

07287 PORK, A.
THE CONCEPT OF 'IDEOLOGICAL STRUGGLE': SOME SOVIET
INTERPRETATIONS
GOVERNMENT AND OPPOSITION, 24(3) (SUM 89), 283-293.

THE AUTHOR LOOKS AT SOME PHASES IN THE DEVELOPMENT OF THE SOVIET PERCEPTION OF WESTERN NON-SOCIALIST POLITICAL IDEAS OVER THE PAST FEW YEARS. HE ALSO ATTEMPTS TO TRACE SOME ELEMENTS OF CONTINUITY AND CHANGE IN THE SOVIET DOCTRINE OF IDEOLOGICAL STRUGGLE DURING THE AGE OF PERESTROIKA.

07288 PORPORA, D.V.; LIM, M.H.; PROMMAS, U.
THE ROLE OF WOMEN IN THE INTERNATIONAL DIVISION OF LABOR: THE CASE OF THAILAND
DEVELOPMENT AND CHANGE, 20(2) (APR 89), 269-294.
THE PURPOSE OF THIS PAPER IS TO SHOW HOW THE MARXIST FEMINIST MODEL REGARDING THE DIVISION OF LABOR NEEDS TO BE QUALIFIED IN THE CASE OF THAILAND. DATA INDICATE THAT IN THAILAND MANAGEMENT'S PREFERENCE FOR FEMALE LABOR DOES NOT ALWAYS REFLECT A CONSCIOUS STRATEGY TO SECURE DOCILE WORKERS. INSTEAD, MANAGEMENT OFTEN HIRES WOMEN FOR JOBS IN THE TEXTILE FACTORIES BECAUSE SUCH WORK HAS TRADITIONALLY BEEN PERFORMED BY WOMEN AND MANAGERS UNCRITICALLY ASSUME THAT SUCH JOBS ARE MORE PROPERLY DONE BY WOMEN. FAR FROM BEING MORE DOCILE THAN MEN, FEMALE THAI WORKERS ARE ACTUALLY MORE MILITANT THAN THEIR MALE CO-WORKERS AND FORM THE BACKBONE OF THE UNION MOVEMENT.

07289 PORRONI, A.
EHTICAL SELF-POLICING: SERVING INSTITUTIONS AND INDIVIDUALS
JOURNAL OF STATE GOVERNMENT, 62(5) (SEP 89), 199-201.
NEW JERSEY'S JOINT LEGISLATIVE COMMITTEE ON ETHICAL STANDARDS IS AN EXPERIMENT IN PROVIDING A MEANS OF ADJUDICATION OF ETHICAL CONDUCT QUESTIONS INVOLVING MEMBERS OF THE LEGISLATURE. HISTORICALLY, SUCH MATTERS HAVE BEEN COMMITTED TO THE HOUSE OF THE LEGISLATURE IN WHICH A MEMBER SITS, OFTEN THROUGH COMMITTEES CONTROLLED BY THE MAJORITY PARTY. THE JOINT LEGISLATIVE COMMITTEE IS INTENDED AS A MEANS FOR LEGISLATORS TO POLICE THEIR OWN ETHICAL CONDUCT IN A MANNER THAT MERITS PUBLIC TRUST AND LEGISLATIVE CONFIDENCE.

07290 PORTEOUS, S.D.; VERBEKE, A.C.
THE IMPLEMENTION OF STRATEGIC EXPORT CONTROLS IN CANADA
CANADIAN PUBLIC POLICY--ANALYSE DE POLITIQUES, XV(1) (MAR 89), 12-24.
THIS ARTICLE DESCRIBES THE INSTITUTIONAL CHARACTERISTICS OF CANADA'S EXPORT CONTROLS SYSTEM AND ASSESSES ITS IMPACT ON BUSINESS FIRMS. THE AUTHORS EXAMINE WHETHER OR NOT UNNESSARY CONSTRAINTS ARE IMPOSED ON THE ACTIVITIES OF BUSINESS FIRMS, I.E. CONTRAINTS THAT DO NOT CONTRIBUTE TO THE ACHIEVEMENT OF NATIONAL GOALS. THE RESULTS OF A SURVEY CONDUCTED AMONGST CANADIAN FIRMS DEMONSTRATE THAT A NUMBER OF UNNESSARY CONSTRAINTS CURRENTLY RESULT FROM THE CANADIAN EXPORT CONTROLS SYSTEM. THE USE OF EXPORT CONTROLS IN CANADA IS COMPARED WITH THE SYSTEM PREVAILING IN THE UNITED STATES. THE MAIN CONCLUSION OF THIS COMPARISON IS THAT THE EXOGENOUS NATURE OF THE CANADIAN EXPORT CONTROL SYSTEM LEADS TO HIGH UNCERTAINTY FOR THE AFFECTED FIRMS, POLICY RECOMMENDATIONS ARE PRESENTED THAT WOULD ALLOW THE REDUCTION OR ELIMINATION OF UNNESSARY CONSTRAINTS ON BUSINESS.

07291 PORTER, B.
DAVID DAVIES : A HUNTER AFTER PEACE
REVIEW OF INTERNATIONAL STUDIES, 15(1) (JAN 89), 27-36.
TODAY WE ARE MUCH MORE CONSCIOUS THAN WAS LORD DAVIES'S GENERATION OF THE FEROCIOUS IDEOLOGICAL AND NATIONALISTIC MAELSTROM THAT THE WORLD IN FACT IS; AND IF WE ARE MORE SOPHISTICATED THAN WE WERE ABOUT UNDERSTANDING AND HAVING TO COPE WITH IT, FOR THAT WE HAVE IN PART TO THANK DAVID DAVIES- NOT FOR HIS IDEAS ABOUT PEACE, BUT FOR BEQUEATHING US THE VALUABLE RESEARCH INSTITUTE WHICH BEARS HIS NAME, AND ABOVE ALL FOR HAVING PIONEERED, IN 1919, THE SYSTEMATIC AND SCIENTIFIC STUDY OF INTERNATIONAL POLITICS. IT IS A FITTING LEGACY OF ONE WHO TIRELESSLY AND SINGLE-MINDEDLY PURSUED THE IDEAL, WHETHER ONE SEES HIM AS A LATTER-DAY DON QUIXOTE, OR AS THE LAST WELSH PALADIN IN HIGH QUEST OF THE GRAIL. PERHAPS HE WAS SOMETHING OF BOTH.

07292 PORTER, R.C.
RECENT TRENDS IN LDC MILITARY EXPENDITURES
WORLD DEVELOPMENT, 17(10) (OCT 89), 1573-1584.
SEVERAL ALARMING AND LARGELY IGNORED TRENDS IN THE SIZE AND STRUCTURE OF MILITARY EXPENDITURE OF LESS DEVELOPED COUNTRIES (LDCS) HAVE APPEARED DURING THE PAST QUARTER CENTURY. NEW, FULLER, AND BETTER DATA SERIES PERMIT US TO DISCERN FOUR OF THESE RECENT TRENDS SUFFICIENTLY CLEARLY TO CALL THEM "STYLIZED FACTS" OF THE CONTEMPORARY DEVELOPMENT PROCESS: (1) LDC DEFENSE EXPENDITURES HAVE BEEN RISING AS A FRACTION OF GDP; (2) THE CAPITAL COST COMPONENT OF THIS SPENDING APPEARS TO HAVE BEEN RISING RELATIVE TO THE OPERATING COST COMPONENT; (3) THE PORTION OF THE LDC POPULATION SERVING IN THE ARMED FORCES HAS BEEN INCREASING; AND (4) LDC MILITARY WAGES APPEAR TO HAVE BEEN RISING RELATIVE TO CIVILIAN WAGES.

07293 PORTER, V.
THE RE-REGULATION OF TELEVISION: PLURALISM, CONSTITUTIONALITY, AND THE FREE MARKET IN THE USA, WEST

GERMANY, FRANCE, AND THE UK
MEDIA, CULTURE, AND SOCIETY, 11(1) (JAN 89), 5-27.
IN RECENT YEARS, THERE HAVE BEEN MAJOR DEBATES RELATING TO THE RE-REGULATION OF TELEVISION IN THE USA, WEST GERMANY, FRANCE, AND GREAT BRITAIN. THE DEBATE HAS OFTEN BEEN COMPLEX BECAUSE IT HAS RAISED AGRUMENTS NOT SIMPLY BETWEEN TRADITIONAL POLITICAL OPPONENTS ON THE RIGHT AND THE LEFT BUT ALSO BETWEEN DIFFERENT GROUPS WITHIN THE SAME POLITICAL PARTY. SOME OF THESE GROUPS HAVE WANTED TO SEIZE THE ECONOMIC AND EMPLOYMENT OPPORTUNITIES OFFERED BY NEW TECHNOLOGY WHILE OTHERS HAVE ARGUED FOR CAUTION, BECAUSE THEY ARE CONCERNED ABOUT THE IMPACT THAT TECHNOLOGICAL EXPANSIONISM IS LIKELY TO HAVE ON THE POLITICAL, CULTURAL, AND INFORMATIONAL ECOLOGIES OF THEIR COUNTRY.

07294 PORTES, A.; BOROCZ, J.
CONTEMPORARY IMMIGRATION: THEORETICAL PERSPECTIVES ON ITS
INTERNATIONAL MIGRATION REVIEW, 23(3) (FAL 89), 606-630.
DETERMINANTS AND MODES OF INCORPORATION 1 THIS ARTICLE REVIEWS CONVENTIONAL THEORIES ABOUT DIFFERENT ASPECTS OF LABOR MIGRATION: ITS ORIGINS, STABILITY OVER TIME, AND PATTERNS OF MIGRANT SETTLEMENT. FOR EACH OF THESE ASPECTS, WE PROVIDE ALTERNATIVE EXPLANATORY HYPOTHESES DERIVED FROM THE NOTIONS OF INCREASING ARTICULATION OF THE INTERNATIONAL SYSTEM AND THE SOCIAL EMBEDDEDNESS OF ITS VARIOUS SUBPROCESSES, INCLUDING LABOR FLOWS. A TYPOLOGY OF SOURCES AND OUTCOMES OF CONTEMPORARY IMMIGRATION IS PRESENTED AS AN HEURISTIC DEVICE TO ORGANIZE THE DIVERSITY OF SUCH MOVEMENTS AS DESCRIBED IN THE EMPIRICAL LITERATURE.

07295 POSNER, M.V.
SUPPORTING RESEARCH IN THE SOCIAL SCIENCES
GOVERNMENT AND OPPOSITION, 24(1) (1989), 15-27.
THE AUTHOR CONSIDERS QUESTIONS REGARDING RESEARCH IN THE SOCIAL SCIENCES: WHAT IS ITS PURPOSE? SHOULD IT BE FINANCED BY THE STATE? HOW SHOULD IT BE ORGANIZED? WHERE SHOULD IT TAKE PLACE?

07296 POST, J.M.; EZEKIEL, R.
WORLDS IN COLLISION, WORLDS IN COLLUSION: THE UNEASY RELATIONSHIP BETWEEN THE COUNTERTERRORISM POLICY COMMUNITY AND THE ACADEMIC COMMUNITY
TERRORISM, 11(6) (1988), 503-510.
THIS PAPER EXPLORES THE TENSION AND BARRIERS TO COOPERATION BETWEEN THE GOVERNMENT AND ACADEMIC COMMUNITIES IN POLICY-RELEVANT AREAS. IN THE FIELD OF POLITICAL TERRORISM, THE TIME URGENCY OF DEALING WITH VIOLENCE OR THE THREAT OF VIOLENCE CHARACTERIZES THE GOVERNMENT PROFESSIONAL'S APPROACH. WHILE THE ACADEMIC VIEWS TERRORISM WITH A LONG-RANGE PERSPECTIVE. OTHER DIFFERENCES IN MISSIONS, ROLE REQUIREMENTS, AND ATTITUDES WITHIN THE TWO COMMUNITIES CONTRIBUTE TO THE GAP BETWEEN THEM. EXCHANGES OF PERSONNEL, ONGOING PROGRAMS FOR THE EXCHANGE OF INFORMATION, AND INCREASING THE NUMBER OF ACADEMIC ADVISORS WITH SECURITY CLEARANCES ARE AMONG THE RECOMMENDATIONS FOR NARROWING THE GAP.

07297 POSTHUMA, M.A.
RICHARDSON'S MODEL OF AN ARMS RACE
MICHIGAN JOURNAL OF POLITICAL SCIENCE, (11) (WIN 89), 76-87.
LEWIS F. RICHARDSON DEVELOPED THE FIRST MODEL OF AN ARMS RACE BETWEEN TWO COUNTRIES. MATHEW POSTHUMA EXPLAINS THE THEORIES THAT ARE THE BASIS FOR THE MODEL; THEN DEVELOPES THE ACTUAL MATHEMATICS. HE THEN TRIES TO DISCOVER IF THE MODEL CAN ACCURATELY PREDICT THE GROWTH IN MILITARY EXPENDITURES BETWEEN THE U.S. AND THE U.S.S.R. HE ALSO TRIES TO INFER FROM THE MODEL WHETHER THIS ARMS RACE, IF IT EXISTS, IS STABLE OR HEADED FOR WAR. IN CONCLUSION, HE OFFERS HIS OWN ANALYSIS OF THE MODEL AND DISCUSSES THE VALUE OF RICHARDSON'S MODEL TO POLITICAL SCIENCE TODAY.

07298 POSTREL, V.I.
WHO'S BEHIND THE CHILD CARE CRISIS?
REASON, 21(2) (JUN 89), 20-27.
EVERYONE IN WASHINGTON SEEMS TO AGREE THAT DAY CARE IS A PRESSING ISSUE THAT DEMANDS THAT THE FEDERAL GOVERNMENT DO SOMETHING, BUT THERE IS DISAGREEMENT ABOUT WHAT THE GOVERNMENT SHOULD DO. THE ACT FOR BETTER CHILD CARE (ABC) WOULD ESTABLISH AN ELABORATE $2.5 BILLION PROGRAM TO FUNNEL MONEY THROUGH THE STATES TO HELP LOW-INCOME FAMILIES PAY FOR DAY CARE IN APPROVED HOMES AND CENTERS. BUT PRESIDENT BUSH IS PUSHING A TAX CREDIT FOR LOW-INCOME FAMILIES.

07299 POTEMKINA, I.
USSR-MONGOLIA: COURSE FOR MORE EFFECTIVE TIES
FOREIGN TRADE, 7 (1988), 4-6.
THIS ARTICLE EXAMINES THE IMPACT OF ECONOMIC COOPERATION WITH THE SOVIET UNION ON MONGOLIA'S SOCIAL PRODUCTION. ANALYSED IS THE PURPOSEFUL AND EFFECTIVE USE OF SOVIET CREDITS AND OTHER TYPES OF ASSISTANCE, AS WELL AS THE TRANSITION FROM STRICTLY TRADE RELATIONS TO WIDE SPECIALIZATION AND COOPERATION IN PRODUCTION, AND DEEPER SCIENTIFIC, TECHNICAL AND ECONOMIC INTEGRATION. SPECIFIC

JOINT ENTERPRISES ARE DISCUSSED.

07300 POTTER, C.; PORTER, J.
AMERICAN PERCEPTIONS OF THE BRITISH NATIONAL HEALTH
SERVICE: FIVE MYTHS
JOURNAL OF HEALTH POLITICS, POLICY AND LAW, 14(2) (SUM 89),
341-365.
THIS ARTICLE EXPLORES FIVE STRONG BELIEFS, OR MYTHS,
HELD BY AMERICANS ABOUT THE BRITISH NATIONAL HEALTH SERVICE:
(1) THE NHS IS SOCIALIZED MEDICINE; (2) WIDESPREAD RATIONING
OCCURS; (3) NHS PATIENTS HAVE TO FACE LONG WAITING TIMES;
(4) THE NHS DOES NOT OFFER FREE CHOICE OF PROVIDER; AND (5)
PRIVATE MEDICINE IS TAKING OVER. THE AUTHORS EXPLORE HOW
ETHNOCENTRICITY AND AMERICAN VALUES HAVE SHAPED THESE FIVE
MYTHS, AND ARGUE THAT THESE CULTURAL BIASES LIMIT THE
ABILITY OF AMERICANS TO OBJECTIVELY EVALUATE THE NHS AND
PREVENT THEM FROM LEARNING FROM THE BRITISH SYSTEM.

07301 POTTINGER, B.
THE UNIONS AND DISINVESTMENT
SOUTH AFRICA FOUNDATION REVIEW, 15(6) (JUN 89), 7.
THE RECENT DISINVESTMENT OF MOBIL OIL COMPANY IN SOUTH
AFRICA HAS RAISED ANEW THE QUESTIONS OF WHO DO SANCTIONS
REALLY HURT, AND WHAT ROLE HAVE UNIONS PLAYED IN THE PROCESS.
A CLOSE ANALYSIS OF THE ENTIRE SANCTIONS AND DISINVESTMENT
PROCESS WILL REVEAL THAT IT IS THE POOR, WHO MAKE UP THE
MAJORITY OF UNION MEMBERSHIP THAT ARE HURT THE MOST BY THE
MEASURES THAT THEIR UNIONS ONCE FERVENTLY SUPPORTED. "THE
UNIONS, HAVING HELPED SCUTTLE THE SHIP, ARE NOW FIGHTING FOR
THE LIFE RAFTS.

07302 POULDERS, J.; MSETEKA, B.; RASHID, A.
TANZANIA
SOUTH, (99) (JAN 89), 55-59.
TWO DECADES AFTER THE ARUSHA DECLARATION OF SOCIALISM
AND SELF-RELIANCE, TANZANIA IS WELL INTO AN ECONOMIC
RECOVERY PROGRAMME PRESCRIBED BY THE IMF AND THE WORLD BANK.
UNDER IMF PRESSURE, PRESIDENT ALL HASSAN MWINYI DEVALUED THE
SHILLING BY 22 PERCENT IN NOVEMBER 1988. MWINYI INSISTS THE
UNPALATABLE RECOVERY PLAN WILL ONE DAY LIFT TANZANIA OUT OF
ITS ECONOMIC MALAISE, BUT SO FAR IT'S ALL PROMISES AND
THERE'S A LONG WAY TO GO.

07303 POULSON, B.W.
THE MEXICAN DEBT CRISIS: A CASE STUDY IN PUBLIC SECTOR
FAILURE
JOURNAL OF SOCIAL, POLITICAL AND ECONOMIC STUDIES, 13(4)
(WIN 88), 371-394.
MUCH OF THE LITERATURE ON THE DEBT CRISIS HAS FOCUSED ON
THE VOLATILE CONDITIONS IN INTERNATIONAL CAPITAL MARKETS,
FLUCTUATIONS IN ENERGY PRICES, AND THE INSTABILITY RESULTING
FROM WORLDWIDE RECESSION. THIS HAS DIVERTED ATTENTION FROM
THE MORE FUNDAMENTAL SOURCE OF FINANCIAL INSTABILITY
EMPHASIZED BY FRIEDRICH HAYEK: THE VARIABLE AND
UNPREDICTABLE FISCAL AND MONETARY POLICIES PURSUED BY BOTH
THE CREDITOR AND DEBTOR NATIONS. THIS STUDY EXPLORES THE
MEXICAN DEBT CRISIS IN THE AUSTRIAN PERSPECTIVE. IT SHOWS
THAT ITS ORIGINS CAN BE TRACED TO FISCAL AND MONETARY
EXPANSION BEGINNING WITH THE MEXICAN GROWTH MIRACLE IN THE
1950'S AND 1960'S. THE FISCAL AND MONETARY INSTITUTIONS
ESTABLISHED IN THAT PERIOD SET THE STAGE FOR FINANCIAL
INSTABILITY AND ULTIMATELY FOR THE DEBT CRISIS.

07304 POURNELLE, J.R.
KONRAD ADENAUER'S MILITARY ADVISORS
AVAILABLE FROM NTIS, NO. AD-A205 786/7/GAR, FEB 13 89, 79.
THIS THESIS POSES THE QUESTION: WHY DID KONRAD ADENAUER
APPOINT FORMER WEHRMACHT GENERALS HANS SPEIDEL AND ADOLF
HEUSINGER AS HIS MILITARY ADVISORS. THE QUESTION IS USED TO
EXAMINE THE POLITICAL RELATIONSHIPS BETWEEN THE ARMY OFFICER
CORPS, STATE, AND SOCIETY IN WESTERN-OCCUPIED GERMANY
IMMEDIATELY FOLLOWING THE SECOND WORLD WAR, AND TO DRAW
CONCLUSIONS ABOUT THE NATURE OF THE RELATIONSHIP BETWEEN
POLITICAL AND MILITARY POWER. TO ANSWER THIS QUESTION, I
HAVE CONSIDERED HISTORIGRAPHY OF THE GERMAN POSTWAR PERIOD;
GERMAN TWENTIETH-CENTURY MILITARY HISTORIOGRAPHY; HISTORICAL
AND SOCIOLOGICAL EXAMINATIONS OF POLITICO-MILITARY
RELATIONSHIPS IN GENERAL; AND POLITICAL SCIENCE ANALYSES OF
POSTWAR GERMAN DOMESTIC AND FOREIGN POLICY ISSUES,
ESPECIALLY AS THEY RELATE TO THOSE OF THE WESTERN OCCUPYING
POWERS. IN THE NARROWEST SENSE, I CONCLUDE THAT ADENAUER
PICKED THESE PARTICULAR MEN TO BE HIS MILITARY ADVISORS
BECAUSE THEY WERE TECHNICALLY COMPETENT AND HIGHLY QUALIFIED;
TRUSTED BY AND ACCEPTABLE POLITICALLY TO THE UNITED STATES,
FRANCE, AND KEY MEMBERS OF HIS OWN AND THE OPPOSITION
POLITICAL PARTIES; AND SHARED AN INTERRELATED SET OF
POLITICAL AND MORAL CONVICTIONS WHICH WERE NEARLY IDENTICAL
TO HIS OWN.

07305 POWELL, C.L.
AMERICAN FOREIGN POLICY: OPPORTUNITIES AND CHALLENGES
DEPARTMENT OF STATE BULLETIN (US FOREIGN POLICY), 88(2139)
(OCT 88), 51-53.
WITH REGARDS TO FOREIGN POLICY THERE HAS EMERGED A
CONSIDERABLE AMOUNT OF CONSENSUS IN THE US OVER A WIDE
VARIETY OF ISSUES. HOWEVER THE NEXT PRESIDENT OF THE US WILL
FACE MANY PROBLEMS AND CHALLENGES. THE ARTICLE OUTLINES US
FOREIGN POLICY GOALS AND THE CHALLENGES THE US FACES IN
EUROPE, EAST ASIA AND THE PACIFIC, LATIN AMERICA, AFRICA,
THE MIDDLE EAST, AND IN EAST-WEST RELATIONS. IT DEMONSTRATES
THE NEED FOR UNITY AND LEADERSHIP IN THE COMING YEARS.

07306 POWELL, C.L.
THE NSC ADVISOR: PROCESS MANAGER AND MORE
BUREAUCRAT, 18(2) (SUM 89), 45-47.
THE GENERAL WISDOM IS THAT TWO MODELS CAN APPLY TO THE
ROLE OF THE NATIONAL SECURITY COUNCIL ADVISOR AND THE
OPERATION OF THE NATIONAL SECURITY COUNCIL STAFF. ZBIGNIEW
BREZINSKI DESCRIBES THEM AS THE PRESIDENTIAL MODEL AND THE
SECRETARIAL MODEL. THE PRESIDENTIAL MODEL HOLDS THAT THE NSC
ADVISOR IS A POWERFUL PERSON WORKING WITH A PRESIDENT WHO
HAS DECIDED TO DRIVE THE DAY-TO-DAY FOREIGN POLICY OF THE
USA DIRECTLY FROM THE WHITE HOUSE. IN THE SECRETARIAL MODEL,
THE SECRETARY OF STATE IS THE MAJOR FOREIGN POLICY DRIVER IN
THE ADMINISTRATION.

07307 POWELL, C.L.
U.S. FOREIGN POLICY IN A TIME OF TRANSITION
DEPARTMENT OF STATE BULLETIN (US FOREIGN POLICY), 89(2142)
(JAN 89), 30-32.
THE AUTHOR, WHO IS ASSISTANT TO PRESIDENT REAGAN FOR
NATIONAL SECURITY AFFAIRS, DISCUSSES THE LESSONS REGIONAL
CONFLICTS HAVE TAUGHT US ABOUT INTERNATIONAL RELATIONS,
CHANGES IN THE USSR UNDER GORBACHEV, AND THE EXPANDING ROLE
OF THE UNITED NATIONS IN PEACEKEEPING. HE ALSO LOOKS AT HOW
US FOREIGN POLICY MUST ADAPT TO THIS TIME OF TRANSITION IN
WORLD AFFAIRS.

07308 POWELL, L.W.
ANALYZING MISINFORMATION: PERCEPTIONS OF CONGRESSIONAL
CANDIDATES' IDEOLOGIES
AMERICAN JOURNAL OF POLITICAL SCIENCE, 33(1) (FEB 89),
272-293.
THIS ANALYSIS EXAMINES THE ERRORS IN RESPONDENT'S
CANDIDATES' POSITIONS AS MEASURED BY THE AMERICAN NATIONAL
ELECTION STUDY SEVEN-POINT IDEOLOGICAL SCALES. A METHODOLOGY
IS DEVELOPED THAT PARTITIONS THE ERROR INTO TWO TYPES. ONE
TYPE IS STRONGLY CORRELATED WITH POLITICAL SOPHISTICATION
AND THUS CONSISTS OF ERROR LARGELY ATTRIBUTABLE TO THE
RESPONDENT; THE REMAINDER ROUGHLY CORRESPONDS TO MEASUREMENT
ERROR IN THE INSTRUMENT. THESE RESULTS EXTEND AND CONTRIBUTE
TO THE DEBATE BETWEEN CONVERSE, ACHEN, AND ERIKSON ON THE
NATURE OF ERROR IN RESPONDENT SELF-PLACEMENTS ON THE SEVEN-
POINT IDEOLOGICAL AND ISSUE SCALES. THE TECHNIQUE DEVELOPED
HERE CAN BE USED TO MEASURE THE EFFECT OF CONTEXTUAL AND
INDIVIDUAL RESPONDENT CHARACTERISTICS ON THE ACCURACY OF
INDIVIDUAL'S PERCEPTIONS OF CANDIDATES' IDEOLOGIES.

07309 POWELL, M.
THE SLIDE TOWARD SLOW GROWTH
AMERICAN CITY AND COUNTY, 104(4) (APR 89), 61-62.
AMERICAN CITIES AND COUNTIES ARE REELING FROM CITIZEN
INITIATIVES DESIGNED TO LIMIT NEW HOUSING AND HIGH-RISE
COMMERCIAL BUILDINGS. THESE INITIATIVES ARE MOTIVATED BY
OUTDATED AND INADEQUATE ROADS, POOR PUBLIC SCHOOLS, WANING
WATER SUPPLIES, AND INEFFICIENT WASTE DISPOSAL. ALL THESE
PROBLEMS HAVE BEEN EXACERBATED BY MASSIVE REVENUE REDUCTIONS
FOR PUBLIC SERVICES AND INCREASED COSTS FOR THOSE SERVICES.
NOWHERE ARE CITIZEN-LED MOVEMENTS TOWARD SLOW GROWTH MORE
VISIBLE THAN IN CALIFORNIA.

07310 POWELL, M.
UK OPPOSITION TO EC TOBACCO TAX
CONTEMPORARY REVIEW, 254(1477) (FEB 89), 77-82.
THE UK GOVERNMENT HAS TAKEN A FIRM STAND AGAINST
EUROPEAN COMMUNITY (EC) PROPOSALS TO HARMONISE VAT AND
EXCISE DUTIES. DESPITE MAKING AN INITIAL COMMITMENT ON
SIGNING THE SINGLE EUROPEAN ACT (1986), THE GOVERNMENT NOW
CITES THE NEED FOR NATIONAL TAXED-BASED HEALTH POLICY AS A
MAJOR REASON FOR OPPOSING THE HARMONISATION OF ALCOHOL AND
TOBACCO DUTIES. HOWEVER, EVIDENCE FROM PAST BUDGETS
INDICATES THAT THE UK GOVERNMENT IS RELUCTANT TO ADOPT THIS
TYPE OF HEALTH POLICY. GOVERNMENT RELIANCE ON INDIRECT
(EXPENDITURE) TAX REVENUE AND FLEXIBLE, LOW COST REVENUE
ADJUSTERS SUGGESTS THAT THE UK HEALTH ARGUMENT IN OPPOSITION
TO HARMONISATION IS A SMOKESCREEN, BEHIND WHICH THE
GOVERNMENT HOPES TO RETRIEVE FISCAL SOVEREIGNTY. COMMON/MKT

07311 POWELL, R.
CRISIS STABILITY IN THE NUCLEAR AGE
AMERICAN POLITICAL SCIENCE REVIEW, 83(1) (MAR 89), 61-76.
IN THE LOGIC OF CRISIS STABILITY, FIRST-STRIKE
ADVANTAGES MAY STILL BE DESTABILIZING, ALTHOUGH EVEN A
SUCCESSFUL FIRST STRIKE CANNOT PROTECT A STATE FROM A
TERRIBLY COSTLY RETALIATORY SECOND STRIKE. IF THERE IS AN
ADVANTAGE TO STRIKING FIRST AND IF WAR SEEMS SUFFICIENTLY
LIKELY, LAUNCHING A PREEMPTIVE FIRST STRIKE MAY SEEM TO BE
THE LEAST OF EVILS. THE AUTHOR RECONSIDERS THE LOGIC OF

CRISIS STABILITY BY STUDYING GAMES THAT ARE COMPLETELY
STABLE. ALTHOUGH THERE ARE FIRST-STRIKE ADVANTAGES. FOUR
GENERAL CONDITIONS ENSURE STABILITY. IDENTIFYING THESE
CONDITIONS REFINES OUR UNDERSTANDING OF CRISIS STABILITY BY
ALSO IDENTIFYING THE POTENTIAL SOURCES OF INSTABILITY, AND
THIS MORE REFINED UNDERSTANDING SHOWS THAT THE LOGIC OF
CRISIS STABILITY FOCUSES ATTENTION TOO NARROWLY ON FIRST-
STRIKE ADVANTAGES. STABILITY RESULTS FROM A MORE SUBTLE
INTERACTION OF SEVERAL FACTORS OF WHICH A FIRST-STRIKE
ADVANTAGE IS ONLY ONE.

07312 POWELL, R.
    NUCLEAR DETERRENCE AND THE STRATEGY OF LIMITED RETALIATION
AMERICAN POLITICAL SCIENCE REVIEW, 83(2) (JUN 89), 503-520.
    RECENT FORMAL WORK IN NUCLEAR DETERRENCE THEORY HAS
FOCUSED ON BRINKMANSHIP CRISES IN WHICH STATES EXERT
COERCIVE PRESSURE BY MANIPULATING THE RISK OF AN UNLIMITED
NUCLEAR EXCHANGE. THIS ESSAY EXTENDS THE FORMAL ANALYSIS OF
DETERRENCE THEORY TO THE STRATEGY OF LIMITED RETALIATION IN
WHICH STATES EXERT COERCIVE PRESSURE BY INFLICTING LIMITED
AMOUNTS OF DAMAGE IN ORDER TO MAKE THE THREAT OF FUTURE
PUNISHMENT MORE CREDIBLE. THIS STRATEGY IS MODELED AS A GAME
OF SEQUENTIAL BARGAINING WITH INCOMPLETE INFORMATION. THE
EQUILIBRIA SUGGEST THAT STATES PREFER RELATIVELY SMALLER,
LESSDESTRUCTIVE LIMITED OPTIONS; THAT COUNTERFORCE OPTIONS
ARE DESIRABLE EVEN IF THEY CANNOT LIMIT THE TOTAL AMOUNT OF
DAMAGE AN ADVERSARY CAN INFLICT; THAT SMALLER, LESS-
DESTRUCTIVE LIMITED NUCLEAR OPTIONS MAY MAKE A NUCLEAR
EXCHANGE MORE LIKELY; AND THAT UNCERTAINTY AND INCOMPLETE
INFORMATION MAY SIGNIFICANTLY ENHANCE DETERRENCE.

07313 POWER, G.; BOLFEK, M.; BRUN, M.; SVETLICIC, M.
    YUGOSLAVIA
SOUTH, (107) (SEP 89), 41-52.
    YUGOSLAV PRIME MINISTER ANTE MARKOVIC SEEMS TO HAVE AN
IMPOSSIBLE JOB: HE MUST DEAL WITH THE COUNTRY'S WORST
ECONOMIC CRISIS SINCE 1945 BUT IS HINDERED BY AN OSSIFIED
AND INTRICATE POLITICAL STRUCTURE. IN ORDER TO CURB RUNAWAY
INFLATION AND REACTIVATE INDUSTRIAL PRODUCTION, MARKOVIC IS
HASTENING THE INTRODUCTION OF MARKET FORCES INTO
YUGOSLAVIA'S UNIQUE BRAND OF SOCIALISM. THE DOORS TO THE
WEST ARE BEING OPENED AND BUREAUCRATIC RED TAPE CUT, BUT THE
SOCIAL CONSEQUENCES COULD BE DIRE.

07314 POWERS, D.S.
    ORIENTALISM, COLONIOLISM, AND LEGAL HISTORY: THE ATTACK ON
    MUSLIM FAMILY ENDOWMENTS IN ALGERIA AND INDIA
COMPARATIVE STUDIES IN SOCIETY AND HISTORY, 31(3) (JUL 89),
535-571.
    THIS STUDY PROBES THE RELATIONSHIP BETWEEN EUROPEAN
COLONIAL BEHAVIOR AND THE STUDY OF ISLAMIC LAW BY FOCUSING
ON THE SPECIFIC HISTORICAL CONTEXT OF FRENCH ALGERIA. THE
AUTHOR ARGUES THAT THE COLONIAL EXPERIENCE EXERTED A SUBTLE
BUT SIGNIFICANT INFLUENCE ON THE EMERGING DISCIPLINE OF
ISLAMIC LEGAL STUDIES. SPECIFICALLY, THE COLONIZATION OF
ALGERIA CREATED AN INEVITABLE CONFLICT BETWEEN ISLAMIC LAW
AND THE COLONS (FRENCH SETTLERS). EFFORTS BY THE LATTER TO
PURCHASE LAND WERE REPEATEDLY FRUSTRATED BY THE FACT THAT
MUCH OF THE LAND IN ALGERIA HAD BEEN DESIGNATED AS RELIGIOUS
ENDOWMENTS AND THEREFORE COULD NOT LEGALLY BE BOUGHT OR SOLD
ON THE OPEN MARKET. THE FRENCH EXPERIENCE WITH FAMILY
ENDOWMENTS WILL BE CONTRASTED WITH THE NEARLY
CONTEMPORANEOUS BRITISH EXPERIENCE WITH THE SAME INSTITUTION
IN INDIA.

07315 POYNTING, S.
    A NEW LEFT PARTY?
ARENA, (88) (SPR 89), 41-49.
    A NAMELESS NEW LEFT PARTY WAS LAUNCHED IN SYDNEY,
AUSTRALIA WITH THE INTENT TO BE FOUNDED IN THE SPRING WHEN
POLICIES, CONSTITUTION AND NAME WILL BE FINALIZED. THIS
ARTICLE EXAMINES THE THE QUESTION: IS THE COMMUNIST PARTY
BEING SACRIFICED OR REBORN? IT DETAILS THE GOALS OF THE NEW
PARTY AND ITS DETERMINATION TO COURT THE NON-ALIGNED LEFT AS
PARTY MEMBERS. THE HOPE OF THE AUTHOR IS THAT THE NEW PARTY
WILL NOT BECOME A SOCIAL DEMOCRATIC CLONE BUT RATHER WILL BE
A GENUINELY SOCIALIST NEW LEFT PARTY.

07316 POZDNYAKOV, E.
    FOREIGN AND HOME POLICY: PARADOXES OF INTERCONNECTION
INTERNATIONAL AFFAIRS (MOSCOW), (11) (NOV 89), 38-48.
    THE AUTHOR QUESTIONS THE CLASSIC CLICHE THAT DOMESTIC
POLICY DETERMINES FOREIGN POLICY, THAT THE FORMER FUNCTIONS
AS AN EXTERNAL NECESSITY WITH REGARD TO THE LATTER. THIS CAN
ONLY MEAN THAT THE LAWS OF FOREIGN POLICY SHOULD BE
SUBORDINATED TO THE LAWS OF DOMESTIC POLICY AND, IF THEY
CONFLICT, THE FORMER IS FORCED TO GIVE WAY TO THE LATTER.

07317 PRABHAKARAN, M.P.
    THE HISTORICAL ORIGIN OF INDIA'S UNDERDEVELOPMENT: A WORLD-
    SYSTEM PERSPECTIVE
DISSERTATION ABSTRACTS INTERNATIONAL, 49(7) (JAN 89),
1952-A.
    THE AUTHOR REVIEWS THE PROCESSES BY WHICH INDIA WAS

INCORPORATED IN THE WORLD SYSTEM AND WHAT THIS INCORPORATION
MEANT TO INDIA'S ECONOMY AND ITS SOCIAL STRUCTURE. THE
UNDERLYING THEME IS THAT THE ORIGINS OF INDIA'S
UNDERDEVELOPMENT CAN BE TRACED TO THE BEGINNING OF THE
EXTRACTION OF SURPLUS VALUE FROM INDIA BY THE WEST. THE
LATTER, IN TURN, CAN BE TRACED TO THE ADVENT OF CAPITALISM
OR THE WORLD SYSTEM ITSELF.

07318 PRASAD, G.
    AIADMK: A NEW MOOD OF AGRESSION
INDIA TODAY, XIV(7) (APR 89), 28-29, 31.
    FOLLOWING ITS ROUT IN THE TAMIL NADU ELECTIONS THE
AIADMK SEEMED TO HAVE LOST THE WILL TO FIGHT. BUT AFTER THE
DRAMA WHICH SURROUNDED PARTY LEADER JAYALALITHAS'S LETTER OF
RESIGNATION FROM THE ASSEMBLY, WHICH INCLUDED A ALL OUT
BRAWL THAT SENT MANY ASSEMBLY MEMBERS TO THE HOSPITAL, THE
PARTY HAS BEEN GALVANIZED. AS THE PANDEMONIUM IN THE
ASSEMBLY SHOWED, THE AIADMK IS ALL SET TO TAKE THE DMK HEAD
ON.

07319 PRASAD, G.
    MISSED MISSION
INDIA TODAY, XIV(6) (MAR 89), 38.
    V. GOPALASAMY SLIPPED INTO SRI LANKA FOR A CLANDESTINE
MEETING WITH VELUPILLAI PIRABHAKARAN IN FEBRUARY 1989. BUT
THE SECRET TALKS BETWEEN THE INDIAN MP AND THE CHIEF OF THE
LIBERATION TIGERS OF TAMIL EELAM FAILED TO BRING THE TIGERS
TO THE NEGOTIATING TABLE.

07320 PRASAD, G.
    TAMIL NADEE: CASTE RUMBLES
INDIA TODAY, XIV(10) (MAY 89), 29.
    THIS ARTICLES DESCRIBES THE SPECTRE OF A CASTE WAR WHICH
IS HAUNTING TAMIL NADEE IN THE SOUTH ARCOT DISCRICT. THE
MAIN AGITATION IS COMING FROM THE VANNIARS, A MOVEMENT WHICH
HAS BEEN AGITATING FOR 20 PERCENT RESERVATIONS AT THE STATE
LEVEL AND 2 PERENT AT THE CENTRAL LEVEL. INTENSIFICATION IS
LIKELY TO PROLONG THE ALREADY VOLATILE CASTE UPRISING.

07321 PRASAD, G.
    THE GREAT FALL
INDIA TODAY, XIV(8) (MAY 89), 32-34.
    WHEN PRIME MINISTER RAJIV GANDHI CHOSE V.K. RAMAMURTHY
AS THE TAMIL NADU CONGRESS (I) COMMITTEE CHIEF, IT WAS
OBVIOUS THAT G.K. MOOPANAR HAD LOST HIS EXALTED STATUS IN
THE PARTY. AS IF TO RUB SALT INTO HIS ARCHRIVAL'S WOUND,
RAMAMURTHY BEGAN HIS NEW JOB WITH A BLISTERING ATTACK ON
MOOPANAR.

07322 PRATT, E.K.
    WEAPONS SPONSORSHIP: PROMOTING STRATEGIC DEFENSE IN THE
    NUCLEAR ERA
DISSERTATION ABSTRACTS INTERNATIONAL, 50(5) (NOV 89),
1429-A.
    USING THE CONCEPT OF WEAPONS SPONSORSHIP, THE AUTHOR
DEVELOPS A FRAMEWORK FOR AN ELITE NETWORK ANALYSIS AND
TRACES THE EVOLUTION OF U.S. POLICY REGARDING BALLISTIC
MISSILE DEFENSE, INCLUDING RONALD REAGAN'S DECISION TO
INITIATE THE STRATEGIC DEFENSE INITIATIVE. HE FINDS
RELATIONS AMONG THE MAJOR NETWORKS OF BALLISTIC MISSILE
DEFENSE SPONSORS TO BE LARGELY UNCOORDINATED, OFTEN
COMPETITIVE, AND SOMETIMES ANTAGONISTIC.

07323 PREECE, C.P.
    NATO FORCES AND STRATEGY: POST-INF ISSUES
CRS REVEIW, 10(4) (APR 89), 7-8.
    PUBLIC PRESSURE TO REDUCE DEFENSE SPENDING AND RESPOND
TO GENERAL SECRETARY GORBACHEV'S "PEACE INITIATIVES" WILL
REQUIRE THAT ALLIANCE POLICYMAKERS BALANCE DECISIONS ON
NUCLEAR AND CONVENTIONAL FORCE MODERNIZATION WITH A CAUTIOUS,
BUT FORWARD-LOOKING, ARMS CONTROL AGENDA.

07324 PREEG, E.H.
    THE GATT TRADING SYSTEM IN TRANSITION: AN ANALYTICAL
    SURVEY OF RECENT LITERATURE
WASHINGTON QUARTERLY, 12(4) (FAL 89), 201-213.
    THIS BRIEF REVIEW DOES NOT ATTEMPT TO ASSESS THE
LITERATURE IN AN EXHAUSTIVE WAY BUT RATHER SURVEYS IT
SELECTIVELY, CONCENTRATING ON A FEW KEY AREAS WHERE IT HAS
PLAYED A SIGNIFICANT ROLE OR WHERE MORE IN-DEPTH AND
CREATIVE RESEARCH SHOULD BE ENCOURAGED. FIRST, HOWEVER,
SEVERAL COMPREHENSIVE WORKS NEED TO BE CITED, WHICH HAVE HAD
A CUMULATIVE IMPACT ON THE UNDERSTANDING OF GATT-RELATED
TRADE ISSUES, AND WHICH CONTAIN A WEALTH OF REFERENCES FOR
THE MORE SPECIALIZED READER. THESE VARIOUS WORKS OF BROADER
OR NARROWER SCOPE HAVE HAD CONSIDERABLE IMPACT IN PROVIDING
THE INTELLECTUAL GROUNDWORK FOR THE AMBITIOUS URUGUAY ROUND
AGENDA. THE REMAINDER OF THIS ARTICLE, HOWEVER, IS DIRECTED
TO A CRITIQUE OF FIVE ISSUES WHEREIN ATTITUDES ABOUT THE
FUTURE ROLE OF THE GATT HAVE BEEN LESS WELL DEFINED OR
ANALYZED, AT LEAST UNTIL RECENTLY, AND THUS WHERE THE
PROFESSIONAL LITERATURE HAS PLAYED OR CAN PLAY AN ESPECIALLY
USEFUL ROLE. THEY ARE (1) THE THREE SOCALLED NEW AREAS,
NAMELY TRADE IN SERVICES, PROTECTION OF INTELLECTUAL

PROPERTY, AND TRADE-RELATED INVESTMENT MEASURES; (2) INTEGRATION OF DEVELOPING COUNTRIES AND CENTRALLY PLANNED ECONOMIES INTO THE GATT SYSTEM OF COMMITMENTS; (3) THE CONCEPT OF MANAGED TRADE AS A CHALLENGE TO THE MARKET-ORIENTED GATT SYSTEM; (4) REGIONAL FREE TRADE AND ITS RELATION TO THE MOST-FAVORED-NATION GATT PRINCIPLE; AND (5) THE IMPACT ON THE GATT SYSTEM OF THE INCREASINGLY INTEGRATED RELATIONSHIP BETWEEN INTERNATIONAL TRADE, INVESTMENT, AND FINANCE.

07325 PREEG, E.H.
TRADE, AID, AND CAPITAL PROJECTS
WASHINGTON QUARTERLY, 12(1) (WIN 89), 173-185.
THE TRADE-AID RELATIONSHIP HAS BEEN SLIPPING BETWEEN THE CRACKS IN TERMS OF A COHERENT POLICY RESPONSE, TO THE DETRIMENT OF U.S. EXPORT INTERESTS AS WELL AS OF THE MOST EFFICIENT DELIVERY OF FOREIGN ECONOMIC ASSISTANCE. TO ADDRESS THE SITUATION, THE STAKES MUST BE CLARIFIED AND SUGGESTIONS BE MADE FOR RESTRUCTURING U.S. FOREIGN ECONOMIC ASSISTANCE AND RELATED EXPORT FINANCE PROGRAMS. A MORE FRUITFUL BALANCE BETWEEN U.S. TRADE AND DEVELOPMENT INTERESTS MUST BE FOUND.

07326 PREISLER, B.E.
LEBANON: THE RATIONALITY OF NATIONAL SUICIDE
DISSERTATION ABSTRACTS INTERNATIONAL, 40(4) (OCT 89), 1080-A.
THE AUTHOR ENDEAVORS TO EXPLAIN THE BREAKDOWN OF POLITICAL ORDER IN LEBANON IN 1975 BY ANALYZING THE SPECIAL NATURE OF ITS STABILITY IN THE YEARS PRIOR TO THE 1975 CIVIL WAR. HE DEVELOPS A GENERAL MODEL THAT EXPLAINS THIS STABILITY BY USING THE POLITICAL DOMINANCE OF THE ZU'AMA AS THE STARTING POINT OF THE ANALYSIS. THEN HE TRACES THE GENERAL BREAKDOWN IN LEBANESE POLITICAL STABILITY TO THE DEGENERATION OF THE ZU'AMA-BASED STABILITY.

07327 PRENTICE, S.
WORKERS, MOTHERS, REDS: TORONTO'S POSTWAR DAYCARE FIGHT
STUDIES IN POLITICAL ECONOMY: A SOCIALIST REVIEW, (30) (FAL 89), 115-142.
THIS ARTICLE EXPLORES THE CONTINUOUS STRUGGLE BY AND FOR CANADIAN WOMEN TO IMPROVE THEIR ECONOMIC, POLITICAL AND SOCIAL CONDITION. ONE EXAMPLE OF FEMINIST ORGANIZING WAS THE FIGHT TO ENSURE THAT POST-WAR RECONSTRUCTION ADDRESSED WOMEN'S NEEDS FOR CHILD CARE. THIS ARTICLE DISCUSSES THE RISE AND FALL OF DAYCARE, USING FRENCH REGULATION ECONOMIC THEORY AND THE SOCIAL REPRODUCTION LITERATURE TO ANLYZE THE COMPLICATED INTERACTIONS OF THE STATE AND THE OLD 'NEW' SOCIAL MOVEMENT OF WOMEN IN THE POLITICS, HISTORY AND ORGANIZATION OF DAYCARE.

07328 PREST, M.
OPEC'S UNCERTAIN FUTURE
MIDDLE EAST INTERNATIONAL, (365) (JAN 89), 14.
SOME OF OPEC'S SENIOR MINISTERS HAVE EXPOUNDED THE VIEW THAT GROWING WORLD DEMAND FOR OIL WILL SOON MAKE THE ORGANIZATION'S QUOTAS REDUNDANT. THIS VIEW IS A REFLECTION OF THE INCREASING POWER OF IRAN, IRAQ, KUWAIT, AND SAUDI ARABIA; THEY ARE SIMPLY SAYING TO OTHER OPEC NATIONS SUCH A VENEZUELA, ECUADOR, AND THE UNITED ARAB EMIRATES, "YOU MUST GIVE UP SOME OF YOUR QUOTA TO US BECAUSE YOU CANNOT PRODUCE ANY MORE OIL." IF THIS VIEW IS VALID, THAN OPEC IS FACT BECOMING A REDUNDANT, IF NOT DECEASED, ORGANIZATION.

07329 PREST, M.
THE OUTLOOK FOR COMMODITY PRODUCERS
ROUND TABLE, (312) (OCT 89), 371-382.
THIS ARTICLE SUGGESTS THAT A MORE OPEN TRADING SYSTEM SHOULD SMOOTH THE WAY FOR THE INVESTMENT FLOWS DESPERATELY NEEDED BY DEVELOPING COUNTRY COMMODITY PRODUCERS. IT EXPLAINS DEPENDENCE ON COMMODITY EXPORTS, THE SOURCE OF THIS DEPENDENCY, AND THE COMMODITY CYCLE. IT ALSO EXAMINES HOW THE TERMS OF TRADE HAS AFFECTED COMMODITY GROWERS AND CONCLUDES THAT FOR DEVELOPING COUNTRY COMMODITY PRODUCERS THE AUGURIES ARE DISCOURAGING.

07330 PREST, P.
OPEC'S UNEDIFYING MEETING
MIDDLE EAST INTERNATIONAL, (360) (OCT 89), 13.
A MEETING OF OPEC MINISTERS IN GENEVA CONCLUDED WITH LITTLE OR NO SEMBLANCE OF THE CAREFULLY MAINTAINED UNITY OF THE PAST YEAR. EACH MEMBER ADVOCATED QUOTA REDISTRIBUTION INVOLVING EVERY QUOTA SAVE ITS OWN. THE AGREEMENT TO RAISE THE OVERALL QUOTA WAS LARGELY IRRELEVANT DUE TO THE SIGNIFICANT OVER-PRODUCTION OF MANY OPEC MEMBERS. THE POSSIBILITY OF A UNIFYING SOLUTION IS BECOMING INCREASINGLY SMALL.

07331 PRETEL, D.
MARX'S PHILOSOPHY: FROM A DOGMATIC INTERPRETATION TO CREATIVE DEVELOPMENT
WORLD MARXIST REVIEW, 32(1) (JAN 89), 42-46.
MARXIST THEORY WAS LONG DOMINATED BY DOGMATISM, THE ANTITHESIS OF DIALECTICS. DUE TO DOGMATISM, THEORY AND

REVOLUTIONARY STRATEGY LAGGED CONSIDERABLY BEHIND THE TIMES. NEW POLITICAL THINKING IS CHANGING THIS SITUATION RADICALLY, OPENING FAVORABLE PROSPECTS FOR CREATIVE RESEARCH.

07332 PRIANI, C.G.; CUNNINGHAM, A.M.
DRUGS IN THE AMERICAS: THEIR INFLUENCE ON INTERNATIONAL RELATIONS
AVAILABLE FROM NTIS, NO. AD-A207 462/3/GAR, MAR 89, 31.
WITH THE INCREASING DRUG PROBLEM IN THE AMERICAS, IT IS NECESSARY TO ANALYZE THE SOCIAL IMPACT OF PRODUCTION, TRAFFICKING, AND DEMAND FOR DRUGS. FURTHER, WE SHOULD EXAMINE HOW THIS PROBLEM HAS DAMAGED THE RELATIONS BETWEEN THE UNITED STATES AND LATIN AMERICA. THIS STUDY SEEKS, BY MEANS OF AN APPRAISAL OF THE DRUG CHALLENGE'S HISTORICAL BACKGROUND, TO UNDERSTAND WHY LATIN AMERICAN COUNTRIES ARE USED FOR SOWING AND PRODUCTION: WHY TRAFFICKING IS SO DIFFICULT TO INTERDICT; AND HOW THE US DEMAND INFLUENCES THIS PHENOMENON. THE PAPER ALSO WILL SHOW THE EFFECT OF THIS ON US - LATIN AMERICAN RELATIONS. FINALLY, RECOMMENDATIONS WILL BE MADE CONCERNING STEPS THAT BOTH THE UNITED STATES AND LATIN AMERICA MIGHT TAKE TO DIMINISH DAMAGES TO HEMISPHERIC SOCIETIES CAUSED BY ILLEGAL DRUGS.

07333 PRICE, J.C.
MARXISM AND ETHICS
DISSERTATION ABSTRACTS INTERNATIONAL, 49(10) (APR 89), 3143-A.
THE AUTHOR PRESENTS A VERSION OF HISTORICAL MATERIALISM THAT ALLOWS FOR THE POSSIBILITY OF DEVELOPING A MARXIST ETHIC. TWO FAMILIAR OBJECTIONS TO SUCH A POSSIBILITY ARE REFUTED: THAT ETHICS MUST BE REJECTED AS A FORM OF IDEOLOGY AND THAT IT MUST BE REJECTED AS AN EXAMPLE OF UTOPIAN THINKING.

07334 PRICE, M.F.
GLOBAL CHANGE: DEFINING THE ILL DEFINED
ENVIRONMENT, 31(8) (OCT 89), 18-20; 42-43.
THIS ARTICLE EXPLORES THE EVOLVING DEFINITION OF GLOBAL CHANGE WHICH HAS REFLECTED THE SHIFTING CONCERNS OF POLICY MAKERS, PHILOSOPHERS, AND SCIENTISTS. ALTHOUGH THE MOST RECENT VERSION FOCUSES ON EARTH'S NATURAL PROCESSES, A NEW TWIST IN THE DEFINITION INCLUDES HUMAN ACTIVITIES AS AN INTEGRAL PART OF THESE PROCESSES. HISTORICAL BACKGROUND IS GIVEN, GLOBAL CHANGE IN THE 1980S IS EXAMINED AND A HOLISTIC DEFINITION IS MADE.

07335 PRICE, P. G.
IDEOLOGY AND ETHNICITY UNDER BRITISH IMPERIAL RULE: BRAHMANS , LAWYERS AND KIN-CASTE RULES IN MADRAS PRESIDENCY
MODERN ASIAN STUDIES, 23(1) (FEB 89), 151-177.
IN MAKING AN ARGUMENT ABOUT THE DEVELOPMENT OF ETHNIC ANTAGONISM THE AUTHOR INTRODUCES SEVERAL POINTS IN BRIEF BASED ON RECENT INTERPRETATIONS OF THE IDEOLOGY OF CASTE AND OF THE NATURE OF THE PRE-COLONIAL STATE IN SOUTH INDIA. THE AUTHOR PROVIDES A SETTING FOR CHANGES IN LEGAL CULTURE WHICH ATTENDED THE CONSOLIDATION OF MADRAS PRESIDENCY AFTER 1800. IN ORDER TO CONVEY SOMETHING OF THE PERSONAL POWER AND ENERGY OF THE LEADERS OF THE LEGAL PROFESSION, INCLUDED ARE THREE BIOGRAPHICAL SKETCHES. A DISCUSSION OF SOCIAL RELATIONS AMONG MEMBERS OF THE LEGAL PROFESSION IN THE LATE NINETEENTH CENTURY AND EARLY TWENTIETH CENTURY FOLLOWS. THE AUTHOR ENDS WITH A DISCUSSION OF THE TENSIONS EXISTENT IN CONFLICTING POLITICAL CLAIMS EXPLICIT AND IMPLICIT, OF LEADING BRAHMAN LAWYERS AND HOW THESE CONTRADICTIONS SET THEM APART AND COULD MAKE THEM A FOCUS FOR NON-BRAHMAN ELITE ANTAGONISM IN THE EARLY TWENTIETH CENTURY.

07336 PRICE, P. G.
KINGLY MODELS IN INDIAN POLITICAL BEHAVIOR: CULTURE AS A MEDIUM OF HISTORY
ASIAN SURVEY, XXIX(6) (JUN 89), 559-572.
THE ARTICLE CONCENTRATES ON THE UNDERLYING REASONS FOR THE APPARENT LACK OF IDEOLOGICAL COMMITMENT IN INDIA. IT OUTLINES THE ROOTS OF THIS PHENOMENON IT THE "OLD REGIME" OF PRE-INDEPENDENCE INDIA. IT TRACES THE DEVELOPMENT AND CONTINUANCE OF THIS POLITY THROUGH THE BRITISH IMPERIAL RULE AND BEYOND. IT ANALYZES THE STRUCTURES OF WEST BENGAL AND TAMIL NADU FOR A CONTEMPORARY LOOK AT THESE ISSUES. IT CONCLUDES THAT THE TENSION THAT EXISTS BETWEEN MODELS OF AUTHORITATIVE LEADERSHIP THAT DERIVE FROM THE OLD REGIME AND THE DISCIPLINE DEMANDED BY POLITICAL PARTIES AND PRINCIPLES IS THE UNDERLYING CAUSE OF THE APPARENT LACK OF IDEOLOGICAL STEADFASTNESS. THE RESULT IS THE CHAOTIC FACTIONALISM THAT IS PREVALENT IN INDIA TODAY.

07337 PRIEST, G.
DIALECTIC AND DIALETHEIC
SCIENCE AND SOCIETY, 53(4) (WIN 89), 388-415.
THIS ESSAY ARGUES FOR AN INTIMATE CONNECTION BETWEEN DIALECTICS AND DIALETHEISM. ITS BURDEN IS THAT ALTHOUGH THE NAME MAY BE NOVEL, THE VIEW ITSELF IS BY NO MEANS SO, IT EXPLORES DIALETHIC LOGIC AND USES MOTION AS AN ILLUSTRATION. AS THE HISTORY OF HEGEL'S DIALECTIC IS GIVEN, THE CONTRADICTIONS IN BOTH HEGEL'S AND MARX'S THEORIES ARE

POINTED OUT. AFTER THE ROLE AND FORM OF CONTRADICTION ARE
DISCUSSED, THE WRITER CONCLUDES THAT HIS APPLICATION OF
DIALECTICS SHOWS VERY CLEARY THE DIALETHEIC NATURE OF
DIALECTICS.

07338 PRIESTLY, T.M.S.
CULTURAL CONSCIOUSNESS AND POLITICAL NATIONALISM: LANGUAGE
CHOICE AMONG SLOVENES IN CARINTHIA (AUSTRIA)
CANADIAN REVIEW OF STUDIES IN NATIONALISM, XVI(1-2) (1989),
79-97.
THE AREA OF AUSTRIAN CARINTHIA WHERE SLOVENE IS SPOKEN
IS IDEAL FOR STUDYING THE MANIFESTATIONS OF NATIONALISM
BECAUSE IT MOST FERVENTLY EMBRACED NATIONAL SOCIALISM IN THE
1930'S AND NOW APPEARS TO HOUSE A DISPROPORTIONATE NUMBER OF
RIGHTWING ORGANIZATIONS THAT EQUATE LANGUAGE WITH
NATIONALISM. THIS PAPER EXAMINES THE ROLE DIFFERENT KINDS OF
ETHNIC CONSCIOUSNESS PLAY IN LANGUAGE BEHAVIOR AND THE
VARIOUS TYPES OF SITUATIONS WHERE DIFFERENT KINDS OF
LINGUISTIC BEHAVIOR OCCUR. THEN SITUATIONS WHERE LANGUAGE
CHOICE IS AUTOMATIC ARE DISTINGUISHED FROM THOSE WHERE IT IS
DELIBERATE, AND LANGUAGE CHOICE MOTIVATED BY POLITICAL
FACTORS ARE COMPARED TO THOSE BASED ON NON-POLITICAL FACTORS.

07339 PRIMAKOV, Y.
A NEW STAGE OF POLITICAL REFORM
WORLD MARXIST REVIEW, 32(9) (SEP 89), 13-15.
THIS PAPER EXPLORES THE PROGRESS AND POLITICAL CHANGE
THAT PERESTROIKA HAS BROUGHT ABOUT IN THE USSR. IT ADDRESSES
FREEDOM AND PLURALISM OF OPINION AND PROGRESS MADE TOWARDS A
HUMANE AND DEMOCRATIC SOCIALISM. IT INSISTS THAT THE PARTY
IS NOT GIVING UP ITS VANGUARD ROLE AND ANALYSES PERESTROIKA
AND THE OUTSIDE WORLD

07340 PRINCE, J.
IS THERE A ROLE FOR INTELLIGENCE IN COMBATING TERRORISM?
CONFLICT, 9(3) (1989), 301-317.
THIS PAPER BEGINS WITH AN ANALYSIS OF THE MANY
DEFINITIONS OF TERRORISM DELINEATED BY THE VARIOUS U.S.
GOVERNMENT AGENCIES, AND HOW THE DISPOSITION TO DEBATE THE
SUBJECT BECOMES SELF-DEFEATING. IT CONTINUES WITH A LOOK AT
THE ROLE OF THE CIA AND LAW ENFORCEMENT AGENCIES IN
COMBATING INTERNATIONAL TERRORISM. FINALLY, GUIDELINES FOR
RESTRUCTURING AMERICAN COUNTERTERRORISM FORCES ARE PRESENTED.

07341 PRINCEN, T.E.
INTERMEDIARY INTERVENTION: A MODEL OF INTERVENTION AND A
STUDY OF THE BEAGLE CHANNEL CASE
DISSERTATION ABSTRACTS INTERNATIONAL, 49(8) (FEB 89),
2383-A.
THE AUTHOR LOOKS AT HOW INTERMEDIARIES INTERVENE
EFFECTIVELY IN DISPUTES. THROUGH THE EXPOSITION OF A
DEDUCTIVE MODEL AND THE ANALYSIS OF A CASE, HE PROBES
INTERMEDIARY INTERVENTIONS IN TERMS OF THEIR DECISION
PROCESSES. AS A CASE STUDY, HE USES THE BEAGLE CHANNEL
DISPUTE INVOLVING ARGENTINA AND CHILE, WITH POPE JOHN PAUL
II AND A VATICAN TEAM AS INTERVENORS

07342 PRISCO, S.
THE AMERICAN FRIENDS SERVICE COMMITTEE AND NIXON'S CHINA
POLICY
POLITICAL COMMUNICATION AND PERSUASION, 5(3) (1988),
203-210.
THIS STUDY INVESTIGATES THE INFLUENCE OF THE AMERICAN
FRIENDS SERVICE COMMITTEE (A QUAKER LOBBYING GROUP) ON THE
POLICY OF DETENTE PURSUED BY THE NIXON ADMINISTRATION IN
DEALING WITH THE PEOPLE'S REPUBLIC OF CHINA. NIXON'S QUAKER
FAMILY BACKGROUND IS VIEWED AS A LINK BETWEEN A.F.S.C.
LOBBYING EFFORTS AFTER 1965 AND PRESIDENT NIXON'S DECISION
TO CHANGE U.S. POLICY TOWARD MAINLAND CHINA. THE QUAKERS
WERE NOT DIRECTLY RESPONSIBLE FOR THE NIXON-KISSINGER
INITIATIVE, BUT THROUGH ITS LOBBYING ACTIVITIES IN
WASHINGTON, AT HARVARD UNIVERSITY, AND ELSEWHERE, THEY DID
HELP TO CREATE A CLIMATE OF OPINION WHICH MADE ACCEPTABLE A
SHIFT IN U.S. CHINA POLICY.

07343 PRITCHARD, K.
POLITICAL SCIENCE AND THE TEACHING OF HUMAN RIGHTS
HUMAN RIGHTS QUARTERLY, 11(3) (AUG 89), 459-475.
EFFORTS IN THE AREA OF EDUCATION ABOUT HUMAN RIGHTS HAVE
BEEN LIMITED. THE PAPER PRESENTS THE RESULTS OF A SURVEY ON
THE INTERNATIONAL TEACHING OF HUMAN RIGHTS WITHIN THE
DISCIPLINE OF POLITICAL SCIENCE. FINDINGS OF THE SURVEY
INCLUDE: POLITICAL SCIENCE IS CONSIDERED AN APPROPRIATE
DISCIPLINARY BASE FOR HUMAN RIGHTS TEACHING, BUT THE TOPIC
IS STILL PRIMARILY TAUGHT ONLY IN LAW SCHOOLS; HUMAN RIGHTS
TEACHING SHOULD BE INTEGRATED INTO EXISTING COURSES AT THE
UNDERGRADUATE LEVEL, BUT ALSO TAUGHT AS A SPECIALIZED COURSE
OR TOPIC FOR ADVANCED AND GRADUATE LEVEL STUDENTS; STUDENTS
NEED TO LOOK AT SPECIFIC LOCAL OR NATIONAL PROBLEMS TO MAKE
INTERNATIONAL STANDARDS RELEVANT; AND CURRICULUM DEVELOPMENT
IS THE MOST PRESSING NEED IN THE FIELD.

07344 PRIZEL, I.
CASTRO'S QUARREL WITH MOSCOW

SAIS REVIEW, 9(2) (SUM 89), 151-163.
THE RISE TO AND CONSOLIDATION OF POWER BY GORBACHEV HAS
REFOCUSED THE SPOTLIGHT ON FIDEL CASTRO'S SUPERPOWER QUANDRY.
THIS ARTICLE DISCUSSES THE POTENTIAL FOR GORBACHEV AND
CASTRO TO HEAD DOWN DIFFERENT IDEOLOGICAL READS.

07345 PROKHOROV, Y.; SHEVCHUK, L.
JAPAN'S TERRITORIAL CLAIMS TO THE USSR
INTERNATIONAL AFFAIRS (MOSCOW), (2) (FEB 89), 42-47.
ALTHOUGH PROGRESS HAS BEEN MADE IN IMPROVING RELATIONS
BETWEEN JAPAN AND THE SOVIET UNION, THE PRESENT LEVEL IS NOT
YET WHAT IT SHOULD BE. THE PRIMARY REASON IS THE GENERAL
TREND IN TOKYO'S POLICY TOWARD BUILDING UP ITS MILITARY-
POLITICAL ALLIANCE WITH THE UNITED STATES. ALONG WITH THAT,
JAPANESE CLAIMS ON A PORTION OF SOVIET TERRITORY ARE PLAYING
A NEGATIVE ROLE. THE DISPUTED TERRITORY ENCOMPASSES THE
SOUTHERN PART OF THE KURIL ISLANDS AND THE MINOR KURILE
RANGE, CONSISTING OF THE SHIKOTAN ISLAND AND A GROUP OF
ISLETS AND ROCKS CALLED THE "HABOMAI ISLANDS."

07346 PRYBYLA, J.S.
CHINA'S ECONOMIC EXPERIMENT: BACK FROM THE MARKET?
PROBLEMS OF COMMUNISM, XXXVIII(1) (JAN 89), 1-18.
CHINA'S ECONOMIC REFORMS HAVE PROCEEDED FROM AN
INITIALLY SUCCESSFUL EFFORT IN AGRICULTURE, TO A MUCH LESS
SUCCESSFUL EFFORT IN THE URBAN INDUSTRIAL ECONOMY, TO A
THIRD STAGE OF RETRENCHMENT IN THE FACE OF AN OVERHEATED
INDUSTRIAL ECONOMY, INFLATION, AND WIDENING INCOME
DIFFERENTIALS. THE CHINESE LEADERSHIP HAS FAILED TO APPLY
MARKETIZATION AND PRIVATIZATION WITH SUFFICIENT VIGOR AND
CONSISTENCY AND FINDS ITSELF WITH THE WORST OF BOTH WORLDS--
INADEQUATE PLAY OF MARKET FORCES AND A DIMINISHED CAPABILITY
OF THE CENTER TO APPLY OLD ADMINISTRATIVE MEANS TO CORRECT
ECONOMIC MALADJUSTMENTS. BY REINSTITUTING CENTRALIZED
CONTROLS RATHER THAN BOLDLY PUSHING AHEAD WITH THE
APPLICATION OF MARKET MECHANISMS AND THE PRIVATIZATION OF
ECONOMIC RELATIONSHIPS, THE REGIME ALMOST CERTAINLY WILL
BRING ON ECONOMIC STAGNATION.

07347 PRYBYLA, J.S.
THE POLISH ECONOMY: A CASE STUDY IN THE STRUCTURE AND
STRATEGY OF DISASTER
COMPARATIVE STRATEGY, 8(2) (1984), 191-204.
THE ARTICLE ANALYZES THE DECLINE OF THE POLISH ECONOMY
AND ITS CAUSES AND IMPLICATIONS. IT EXAMINES BOTH THE
MEASURABLE ECONOMIC FACTORS SUCH AS RATE OF INVESTMENT,
WAGES, AND NET MATERIAL PRODUCT, AND THE UNDERLYING
POLITICAL APATHY AND ESTRANGEMENT THAT EXACERBATES THE
PROBLEM. IT OUTLINES THE STEPS THE POLISH GOVERNMENT HAS
TAKEN THAT HAS LED TO THE CURRENT SAD STATE OF AFFAIRS. IT
CONCLUDES WITH AN ANALYSIS OF WHAT CORRECTIVE MEASURES ARE
REQUIRED TO ALLEVIATE CURRENT PROBLEMS AS WELL AS WHAT CAN
REALISTICALLY BE EXPECTED FROM THE GOVERNMENT.

07348 PRYBYLA, J.S.
WHY CHINA'S ECONOMIC REFORMS FAIL
ASIAN SURVEY, 29(11) (NOV 89), 1017-1032.
IN THIS ARTICLE THE WRITER EXAMINES WHY ECONOMIC REFORMS
FAIL IN CHINA (AS THEY OTHER SOCIALIST COUNTRIES), FOCUSING
ON SYSTEMIC REASONS. PART ONE CONSIDERS THESE GENERAL
CONCEPTS: (A) CHINA'S ECONOMIC PROBLEMS CA. 1978; (B) THE
ORIGINS OF THESE PROBLEMS; (C) POSSIBLE POLICY AND
STRUCTURAL REMEDIES FOR THE PROBLEMS (E.G., ADJUSTMENT,
REFORM); (D) IF REFORM, WHAT KIND OF REFORM? (E)
REQUIREMENTS FOR MARKET-TYPE REFORM; AND (F) REQUIREMENTS
FOR A SUCCESSFUL MARKET SYSTEM. PART TWO CONSIDERS CHINA'S
REFORMS SINCE 1979, SPECIFICALLY (A) THE CHRONOLOGY AND
POSITIVE OR NEGATIVE RESULTS; (B) GENERAL REASONS FOR
NEGATIVE RESULTS; AND (C) SPECIFIC REASONS FOR NEGATIVE
RESULTS (I.E., VIOLATIONS IN VARIOUS DEGREES OF THE
REQUIREMENTS FOR A SUCCESSFUL MARKET SYSTEM). THE FINAL
SECTION DRAWS CONCLUSIONS AND SUGGESTS POSSIBLE POINTERS TO
THE FUTURE.

07349 PRYCE-JONES, D.
SELF-DETERMINATION, ARAB STYLE
COMMENTARY, 87(1) (JAN 89), 39-46.
WESTERNERS, PROJECTING THEIR OWN POLITICAL AND MORAL
ATTITUDES WHERE THESE CANNOT APPLY, HABITUALLY AND
IGNORANTLY MISCONCEIVE THE RESPONSES THEY ARE LIKELY TO
ENCOUNTER FROM THE ARABS. IT IS DIFFICULT FOR A WESTERNER TO
JETTISON HIS DECEPTIVE SLOGAN-METAPHORS AS WORTHLESS, TO
MAKE THE IMAGINATIVE LEAP OF ABANDONING HIS UNIVERSE AND HIS
INSTITUTIONS, AND SO ENTER THE ARAB COLLECTIVITY OF TRIBE
AND KIN AND RELIGIOUS AFFILIATION.

07350 PRYSBY, C.L.
ATTITUDES OF SOUTHERN DEMOCRATIC PARTY ACTIVISTS TOWARD
JESSE JACKSON: THE EFFECTS OF THE LOCAL CONTEXT
THE JOURNAL OF POLITICS, 51(2) (MAY 89), 305-318.
THIS ARTICLE EXAMINES THE EFFECT OF THE RACIAL
COMPOSITION OF THE LOCAL CONTEXT ON THE ATTITUDES OF
SOUTHERN DEMOCRATIC PARTY ACTIVISTS TOWARD THE 1984 JESSE
JACKSON PRESIDENTIAL CANDIDACY. REDEMOCRATIC PARTY STATE

CONVENTION, THE ANALYSIS FINDS THAT WHITE ACTIVISTS WERE MORE LIKELY TO HAVE A NEGATIVE ATTITUDE TOWARD THE JACKSON CANDIDACY WHEN THEY WERE FROM A COUNTY THAT HAD A HIGHER PROPORTION OF BLACKS. THIS RELATIONSHIP OCCURS BECAUSE THE RACIAL COMPOSITION OF THE LOCAL CONTEXT AFFECTS BOTH THE CONSERVATISM OF WHITE ACTIVISTS, ESPECIALLY ON RACIALLY RELATED ISSUES, AND THE ASSESSMENT THESE ACTIVISTS HAVE OF THE LIKELY EFFECTS OF THE JACKSON CANDIDACY. MOST IMPORTANT ARE BELIEFS THAT WHITE ACTIVISTS HAVE ABOUT THE IMPACT OF THE JACKSON CANDIDACY ON THE MOBILIZATION OF BLACK VOTERS AND ON THE GENERATION OF INTRA-PARTY CONFLICT.

07351 PRYSBY, C.L.
THE STRUCTURE OF SOUTHERN ELECTORAL BEHAVIOR
AMERICAN POLITICS QUARTERLY, 17(2) (APR 89), 163-180.
THE DISTINCTIVENESS OF SOUTHERN ELECTORAL BEHAVIOR HAS BEEN A WELL-STUDIED ASPECT OF POLITICS IN THE REGION. WHILE DISTINCTIVENESS CAN REFER TO ABSOLUTE DIFFERENCES IN ATTITUDES AND BEHAVIOR, IT ALSO CAN REFER TO THE STRUCTURE OF ELECTORAL BEHAVIOR, AND THAT IS THE FOCUS OF THIS ARTICLE. DEVELOPMENTS IN THE REGION AND IN THE NATION SUGGEST THAT THE STRUCTURE OF ELECTORAL BEHAVIOR MAY NO LONGER BE DIFFERENT IN THE NORTH AND THE SOUTH. THIS POSSIBILITY IS EXAMINED USING DATA FROM SEVERAL RECENT GENERAL SOCIAL SURVEYS, MERGED TO YIELD LARGE NS FOR THE REGIONS. THE ANALYSIS RESULTS SHOW LITTLE DIFFERENCE BETWEEN THE REGIONS IN BOTH THE SOCIAL AND THE ATTITUDINAL SOURCES OF PARTISAN CHOICE.

07352 PUDDINGTON, A.
LIFE UNDER COMMUNISM TODAY
COMMENTARY, 87(2) (FEB 89), 32-38.
THE QUESTION FACING MIKHAIL GORBACHEV AND HIS EAST EUROPEAN ACOLYTES IS NOT SIMPLY WHETHER THE SOVIET EMPIRE CAN BE MADE COMPETITIVE WITH MARKET-ORIENTED SOCIETIES BUT WHETHER A CATASTROPHIC EROSION OF MATERIAL CONDITIONS CAN BE FORESTALLED. THE USSR AND EAST EUROPE ARE EXHIBITING DISTURBING SIMILARITIES WITH CRISIS-RIDDEN THIRD WORLD COUNTRIES, INCLUDING POVERTY, HOMELESSNESS, HIGH INFLATION, DECLINING HEALTH CARE, AND HIGH EXTERNAL DEBT.

07353 PUDDINGTON, A.
THE HOUNDS OF GLASTNOST
NATIONAL REVIEW, 62(22) (NOV 89), 26 - 28.
THIS ARTICLE EXAMINES THE ISSUES FACING THE AMERICAN LEFT AS GLASTNOST BECOMES A REALITY. IT EXPLORES BOTH: THE REACTION OF RELIEF AS A CHOICE BETWEEN INTELLECTUAL INTEGRITY AND SUPPORT FOR MOSCOW IS NO LONGER NECESSARY, AND THE PROBABILITY OF THE CONCLUSION OF THE MARXIST ENTERPRISE. IT CONCLUDES THAT OTHER POLITICAL ISSUES WILL REPLACE THOSE THAT HAVE EXISTED.

07354 PUDDINGTON, A.
THESE WERE THE DAYS: THE SDS REVISITED
AMERICAN SPECTATOR, 22(3) (MAR 89), 18-20.
THIS ARTICLE POSITS THAT IF THE NEW LEFT FAILED POLITICALLY, IT WAS BECAUSE STUDENTS WERE NO SUBSTITUTE FOR AN EXPLOITED PROLETARIST - AND THE UNITED STATES NEVER HAD AN EXPLOITED PROLETARIAT.

07355 PUGH, J.
CHURCH AND STATE IN AMERICA: A VETERAN REPORTER'S WARNING
CHURCH AND STATE, 42(9) (OCT 89), 16 (208)-18 (210).
RELIGION AND RELIGIOUS PEOPLE HAVE BEEN SHAMELESSLY USED IN THE LAST DECADE BY POLITICIANS PLAYING ON THE THEME OF RESTORING "TRADITIONAL VALUES" TO THE NATION. AND VICE VERSA. IN MANY CASES, CONSERVATIVE OR FUNDAMENTALIST RELIGION HAS BEEN USED AS A SMOKE SCREEN FOR AN OMINOUS RESURGENCE OF ETHNIC BIGOTRY, RACISM, SEXISM, AND SECTARIAN PREJUDICES. WORSE YET, THERE ARE MILLIONS OF WELL-MEANING BUT MISGUIDED AMERICANS WHO, GIVEN THE OPPORTUNITY, WOULD CHEERFULLY SCRAP THE FIRST AMENDMENT TO THE U.S. CONSTITUTION IN ORDER TO IMPOSE THEIR PARTICULAR BRAND OF RELIGION UPON THE WHOLE NATION. IN RECENT YEARS, THE RELIGIOUS RIGHT HAS HAD A GREATER IMPACT ON POLITICS, GOVERNMENT, AND THE ECONOMY THAN ITS NUMBERS WARRANT.

07356 PUGH, M.
NUCLEAR WARSHIP VISITING: STORMS IN PORTS
WORLD TODAY, 45(10) (OCT 89), 180-183.
IN THE MID-1980'S, NAVAL DEPLOYMENT ISSUES ACHIEVED A HIGHER PROFILE THAN HITHERTO, BOTH WITH REGARD TO NUCLEAR WEAPONRY AND NUCLEAR PROPULSION. OPPOSITION TO WARSHIP VISITS SURFACED IN MANY PORTS AROUND THE WORLD. THE U.S. NAVY'S PLANS FOR HOMEPORTING BATTLESHIP TASK GROUPS NEAR MAJOR CITIES STIMULATED ENVIRONMENTAL OBJECTIONS IN BOSTON, NEW YORK, AND SAN FRANCISCO. THIS ARTICLE ASSESSES THE SIGNIFICANCE OF DISPUTES ABOUT PORT VISITS, PARTICULARLY IN THE CONTEXT OF WESTERN ALLIANCE LOYALTY.

07357 PULKINGHAM, J.
FROM PUBLIC PROVISION TO PRIVATISATION: THE CRISIS IN WELFARE REASSESSED
SOCIOLOGY, 23(3) (AUG 89), 387-408.
PRIVATISATION POLICIES. PURSUED BY A GOVERNMENT INFORMED BY NEOCLASSICAL ECONOMIC THEORY AND INTENT ON 'ROLLING BACK THE FRONTIERS OF THE WELFARE STATE', HAVE BEEN WIDELY CRITICISED AS TURNING THE TIDE AGAINST BOTH THE 'WELFARE STATE' AND 'WELFARE' MORE BROADLY. THE POLICY TO PRIVATISE PUBLIC INDUSTRIES AND SERVICES IS, IN EFFECT, BOTH AN EMPLOYMENT AND WAGE POLICY: THE INTENTION IS TO GOVERN, NOT SIMPLY THE GENERAL TYPE OF SERVICE PROVISION BUT ALSO, THE METHOD OF WAGE DETERMINATION ITSELF. THE ARGUMENT IN THIS PAPER IS THAT THE PRIVATISATION STRATEGY IS THE CULMINATION OF, RATHER THAN A DIGRESSION FROM, POST-WAR POLICIES IN THE PUBLIC SECTOR CONCERNING WAGE DETERMINATION. IN ARGUING THAT PRIVATISATION REPRESENTS THE CULMINATION OF PUBLIC SECTOR WAGE POLICIES IN THE POST-WAR PERIOD, IT IS BEING SUGGESTED THAT PRIVATISATION DENOTES THE MOST CATEGORICAL STATEMENT AND EXTENSION OF SUCCESSIVE POLICY DEVELOPMENTS PROMOTING THE SALIENCE OF SO-CALLED 'MARKET' PRINCIPLES IN THE DETERMINATION OF WAGES. IT IS CONTENDED, FURTHERMORE, THAT THE LEGITIMACY OF AND INCREASING EMPHASIS GIVEN TO CRITERIA SUCH AS EFFICIENCY AND PRODUCTIVITY IN THE NAME OF 'ECONOMIC NECESSITY', HAS BEEN CULTIVATED AS A RESULT OF THE POWER GIVEN TO ECONOMIC, AS AGAINST SOCIAL EXPLANATIONS, RATHER THAN EMANATING FROM ANY INTRINSIC 'ECONOMIC' LOGIC. POLITICAL AND SOCIAL RESEARCH CONCERNING THE PRIVATISATION OF PUBLIC SERVICES, THOUGH OFTEN HIGHLY CRITICAL OF THE GOVERNMENT'S PHILOSOPHICAL AND ECONOMIC BELIEFS, NEVERTHELESS HAS PERPETUATED AND ULTIMATELY REINFORCED THESE BELIEFS BY FAILING TO CHALLENGE FULLY THE PRINCIPLES UNDERLYING THE PRIVATISATION AGENDA. THE PRIVATISATION DEBATE IS PREMISED UPON THE ASSUMPTION THAT 'THE LOGIC OF THE MARKET' PROVIDES A SALIENT DESCRIPTION OF THE OVERALL PROCESS OCCURING. IT SUGGESTS THAT THIS NEEDS TO BE RECONSIDERED AND AN ALTERNATIVE CONCEPTION ESTABLISHED TO FURTHER OUR PRACTICAL AND ANALYTICAL UNDERSTANDING OF THE PROCESSES OBSERVED.

07358 PULLEY, R.V.
MAKING THE POOR CREDITWORTHY: A CASE STUDY OF THE INTEGRATED RURAL DEVELOPMENT PROGRAM IN INDIA
AVAILABLE FROM NTIS, NO. PB89-220321/GAR, 1989, 107.
INDIA'S INTEGRATED RURAL DEVELOPMENT PROGRAM (IRDP) IS AMONG THE WORLD'S MOST AMBITIOUS EFFORTS AT CREDITBASED POVERTY ALLEVIATION. THE IRDP WAS INITIATED A DECADE AGO AND HAS REACHED 27 MILLION POOR HOUSEHOLDS THROUGH COMMERCIAL BANKS WHICH PROVIDE FINANCE FOR INVESTMENT IN INCOME GENERATING ASSETS. CREDIT IS MATCHED BY CAPITAL SUBSIDIES OF 33-50% ON HOUSEHOLD INVESTMENT. THE PAPER SHOWS THAT PROVIDING SOME POOR HOUSEHOLDS WITH CAPITAL TO INVEST IN INCOME GENERATING ASSETS CAN BE AN EFFECTIVE MEANS OF RAISING THEIR INCOMES. THE PAPER POINTS OUT THAT GAINS IN PRODUCTIVITY OF INVESTMENT AND CREDIT RECOVERY CAN BE MADE BY ALTERING CERTAIN DELIVERY FEATURES OF IRDP, BUT ARGUES THAT THE EXISTING STRUCTURE OF INCENTIVES FACING BANKS AND BORROWERS ARE RESPONSIBLE FOR CRITICAL SHORTCOMINGS. TO OVERCOME THESE PROBLEMS, FLEXIBLE INSTRUMENTS ARE NEEDED.

07359 PUNCOG, G.G.; JIANQUN, P.
FROM PEACEFUL LIBERATION TO DEMOCRATIC REFORM
CHINA RECONSTRUCTS, XXXVIII(4) (APR 89), 8-12, 28.
THIS ARTICLE INCLUDES AN ACCOUNT OF IMPORTANT TURNING POINTS IN TIBET'S HISTORY SINCE 1950 AS RECALLED BY THE VICE-CHAIRMAN OF THE PEOPLE'S POLITICAL CONSULTATIVE CONFERENCE OF THE TIBET AUTONOMOUS REGION. THE VICE-CHAIRMAN SHARES HIS OWN MEMORIES OF SIGNIFICANT EVENTS BOTH BEFORE AND AFTER THE 1959 REBELLION.

07360 PUNZO, V.A.
THREE MOVES FOR PEACE
COMMONWEAL, CXVI(14) (AUG 89), 422-423.
THE MARKING OF AUGUST, 1989, AS THE BEGINNING OF THE THIRD DECADE OF BRITISH TROOPS PATROLLING THE STREETS OF NORTHERN IRELAND PORTENDS LITTLE MORE THAN THE DISTURBING REALIZATION THAT OLD WOUNDS, FAR FROM HEALING, CONTINUE TO FESTER. SEEMINGLY INSURMOUNTABLE OBSTACLES REMAIN, BUT THERE ARE GLIMMERS OF HOPE FOR THE FUTURE.

07361 PURVER, R.
ARCTIC SECURITY: THE MURMANSK INITIATIVE AND ITS IMPACT
CURRENT RESEARCH ON PEACE AND VIOLENCE, 11(4) (1989), 147-158.
WHAT HAS COME TO BE KNOWN AS THE 'MURMANSK INITIATIVE' WAS LAUNCHED BY MIKHAIL GORBACHEV IN A SPEECH IN THAT CITY ON 1 OCTOBER 1987. THIS ARTICLE TRACES THE STIMULUS TO THE INITIATIVE AND THEN ANALYZES THE SPEECH AND REPORTS ON THE REACTION AND FOLLOW-UP. ASSESSMENTS AND A PROGNOSIS ARE OFFERED. IT SUGGESTS THAT THE INITIATIVES GREATEST SIGNIFICANCE MAY LIE IN THE ACT OF COOPERATION IN NONMILITARY FIELDS IN THE ARCTIC WHICH MAY PAVE THE WAY FOR FORMAL ARMS CONTROL AGREEMENTS IN THE FUTURE.

07362 PUSIC, E.
PUBLIC ADMINISTRATION AND SELF-MANAGEMENT IN YUGOSLAVIA
INTERNATIONAL REVIEW OF ADMINISTRATIVE SCIENCES, 55(1) (MAR 89), 25-28.

THE ARTICLE EXPLORES THE DEVELOPMENT OF SELF-MANAGEMENT, A CONCEPT THAT IMPLIES GREATER DIRECT PARTICIPATION OF PEOPLE IN THE REGULATIVE ACTIVITIES OF THE STATE AS WELL AS THEIR EXPANDING RESPONSIBILITIES AS USERS, CONSUMERS, AND CLIENTS OF THE PUBLIC SERVICES, IN YUGOSLAVIA. IT OUTLINES THE LEGAL FRAMEWORK ON WHICH SELF-MANAGEMENT RESTS AND ATTEMPTS A BRIEF ASSESSMENT OF EFFORTS TO MOVE TOWARDS SELFMANAGEMENT AND THE AUTHORITARIAN INERTIA THAT THEY ENCOUNTER.

07363 PUTTERMAN, L.
ENTERING THE POST-COLLECTIVE ERA IN NORTH CHINA: DAHE TOWNSHIP
MODERN CHINA, 15(3) (JUL 89), 275-320.
THE AUTHOR USES DAHE TOWNSHIP AS A CASE STUDY OF THE EFFECTS OF DECOLLECTIVIZATION AND OTHER ASPECTS OF SYSTEMIC AND STRUCTURAL CHANGE IN POST-MAO RURAL CHINA. HE DISCUSSES THE PROBLEM OF GRAIN PRODUCTION AT DAHE, CHANGES IN THE STRUCTURE OF INCOME SOURCES AND LABOR DEPLOYMENT, INSTITUTIONAL AND ORGANIZATIONAL CHANGE IN THE SPHERE OF PRODUCTION, AND THE EFFECT OF REFORM ON THE DISTRIBUTION OF INCOME.

07364 PYPER, R.
THE DOCTRINE OF INDIVIDUAL MINSTERIAL RESPONSIBILITY IN BRITISH GOVERNMENT: THEORY AND PRACTICE IN A NEW REGIME OF PARLIAMENTARY ACCOUNTABILITY
DISSERTATION ABSTRACTS INTERNATIONAL, 49(7) (JAN 89), 1959-A.
BY 1966 IT HAD BECOME CLEAR THAT THE DOCTRINE OF INDIVIDUAL MINISTERIAL RESPONSIBILITY, WHICH LAY AT THE HEART OF THE BRITISH CONSTITUTION, HAD FAILED TO EVOLVE IN ORDER TO MEET THE REQUIREMENTS OF MODERN GOVERNMENT. THIS THESIS PUTS FORWARD A REVIEW OF THE DOCTRINE'S OPERATION AND THEORETICAL BASIS OVER A SEVENTEEN YEAR PERIOD, STARTING WITH THE ADVENT OF NEW ORGANS OF PARLIAMENTARY SCRUTINY UNDER THE SECOND WILSON GOVERNMENT.

07365 QI, J.
ANTI-CORRUPTION AND PUBLIC SUPERVISION
BEIJING REVIEW, 32(23) (JUN 89), 7, 9.
IN RECENT YEARS, THE CHINESE STATE HAS ADOPTED MANY MEASURES DESIGNED TO CURTAIL CORRUPTION AMONG PUBLIC OFFICIALS. BUT THE PHENOMENON OF CORRUPTION IS FAR FROM BEING ERADICATED. IN FACT, IT HAS WORSENED IN SOME PLACES. OFFICIAL PROFITEERING, IN WHICH OFFICIALS AND BUSINESSMEN COLLABORATE TO FURTHER THEIR PRIVATE INTERESTS, IS THE MOST HARMFUL FORM OF CORRUPTION AND HAS EVOKED THE GREATEST POPULAR INDIGNATION. A MORE OPEN POLITICAL SYSTEM, WITH GREATER PUBLIC SUPERVISION, SEEMS TO PROMISE LESS CORRUPTION.

07366 QI, J.
WHY CHINA WILL NOT PRACTICE PRIVATIZATION
BEIJING REVIEW, 32(36) (SEP 89), 7.
IN AUGUST 1989, PREMIER LI PENG SAID THAT CHINA WOULD GIVE PROPER CONSIDERATION TO THE REGULATORY ROLE OF THE MARKET IN THE PROCESS OF ECONOMIC REFORM, BUT THE CHINESE ECONOMY IS BASED ON SOCIALIST PUBLIC OWNERSHIP AND MUST NEVER BE TURNED COMPLETELY INTO A MARKET ECONOMY. IF CHINA ABANDONED ITS ECONOMIC FOUNDATION BASED ON PUBLIC OWNERSHIP AND PRACTISED PRIVATIZATION, SERIOUS POLARIZATION WOULD INEVITABLY EMERGE BETWEEN THE RICH AND THE POOR. NATIONWIDE POLITICAL TURMOIL WOULD OCCUR AND THE COUNTRY'S INDEPENDENT INTERNATIONAL STATUS WOULD BE LOST. MOREOVER, THE REFORM OF THE PAST DECADE HAS INJECTED FRESH VIGOR INTO PUBLICLY-OWNED ENTERPRISES, GIVING THEM A PROMISING FUTURE.

07367 QICHEN, Q.
CHINA URGES TOTAL BAN ON CHEMICAL WEAPONS
BEIJING REVIEW, 32(4) (JAN 89), 14-15.
CHINA HAS ALWAYS OPPOSED THE ARMS RACE IN ALL ITS FORMS AND ADVOCATED THE COMPLETE PROHIBITION AND DESTRUCTION OF NUCLEAR, CHEMICAL, AND SPACE WEAPONS, ALONG WITH A DRASTIC REDUCTION OF CONVENTIONAL ARMAMENTS. CHINA NEITHER POSSESSES NOR PRODUCES CHEMICAL WEAPONS BECAUSE THE CHINESE PEOPLE WERE ONCE SUBJECTED TO THE SCOURGE OF CHEMICAL WARFARE.

07368 QICHEN, Q.
CURRENT INTERNATIONAL SITUATION AND SINO-US RELATIONS
BEIJING REVIEW, 32(41) (OCT 89), 7-9.
PROFOUND CHANGES HAVE TAKEN PLACE IN SINO-US RELATIONS SINCE THE ESTABLISHMENT OF DIPLOMATIC TIES IN 1979. MARKED PROGRESS HAS BEEN MADE IN BILATERAL EXCHANGES AND COOPERATION IN MANY FIELDS. BUT DIFFICULTIES HAVE EMERGED SINCE THE POLITICAL TURMOIL IN JUNE 1989, AND RELATIONS HAVE BEEN STRAINED SINCE THAT TIME.

07369 QICHEN, Q.
NEW CHINA'S DIPLOMACY: 40 YEARS ON
BEIJING REVIEW, 32(39) (SEP 89), 15-19.
UPON ITS FOUNDING IN 1949, NEW CHINA BURIED THE HUMILIATING DIPLOMACY OF OLD CHINA AND EMBARKED ON A NEW DIPLOMACY OF INDEPENDENCE. OVER THE PAST 40 YEARS, CHINESE DIPLOMACY HAS UNDERGONE MANY ADJUSTMENTS IN RESPONSE TO THE

CHANGEABLE INTERNATIONAL SITUATION AND THE DEVELOPMENT OF DOMESTIC SOCIALIST CONSTRUCTION. LOOKING BACK OVER THE COURSE OF NEW CHINA'S DIPLOMATIC PRACTICE, THE MOST FUNDAMENTAL LESSON IS THAT EACH COUNTRY MUST MAINTAIN STATE SOVEREIGNTY AND NATIONAL DIGNITY AND UPHOLD ITS INDEPENDENT FOREIGN POLICY.

07370 QIMEN, C.
NATO SAFEGUARDS UNITY WITH SNF COMPROMISE
BEIJING REVIEW, 32(28) (JUL 89), 14-16.
THE 40TH ANNIVERSARY SUMMIT OF NATO REACHED A COMPROMISE ON SHORT-RANGE NUCLEAR FORCES IN THE INTEREST OF UNITY, THEREBY ENDING A SERIOUS DISPUTE WITHIN THE ORGANIZATION. ON MAY 30, 1989, NATO LEADERS ISSUED A FINAL DOCUMENT AND A "COMPREHENSIVE CONCEPT." THE FINAL DOCUMENT GAVE A DETAILED EXPLANATION OF THE POLITICAL CONCEPT BEHIND THE ATLANTIC LEAGUE, WHILE THE COMPREHENSIVE CONCEPT CONCENTRATED ON NATO STRATEGY FOR DISARMAMENT.

07371 QING, C.
CHINESE FOREIGN MINISTER TOURS AFRICA
BEIJING REVIEW, 32(35) (AUG 89), 14-15.
TO PROMOTE FRIENDSHIP, DEEPEN UNDERSTANDING, AND STRENGTHEN COOPERATION BETWEEN CHINA AND SOUTHERN AFRICAN COUNTRIES, CHINESE FOREIGN MINISTER QIAN QICHEN VISITED BOTSWANA, LESOTHO, ZIMBABWE, ANGOLA. ZAMBIA, AND MOZAMBIQUE IN THE SUMMER OF 1989. QIAN EXCHANGED VIEWS WITH AFRICAN LEADERS ON BILATERAL RELATIONS AND INTERNATIONAL ISSUES, ESPECIALLY THE SITUATION IN SOUTHERN AFRICA. HE ALSO EXPLAINED THE SITUATION IN CHINA FOLLOWING THE SUPPRESSION OF THE COUNTER-REVOLUTIONARY REBELLION IN JUNE 1989.

07372 QING, Y.
MONEY POLITICS PRODUCES RECRUIT SCANDAL
BEIJING REVIEW, 32(30) (JUL 89), 16.
THE RECRUIT STOCK SCANDAL INVOLVING JAPANESE GOVERNMENT OFFICIALS REFLECTS THE RELATIONSHIP BETWEEN MONEY AND POLITICS. REMOVING MONEY FROM POLITICS IS THE KEY TO PREVENTING SIMILAR POLITICAL SCANDALS.

07373 QINGCHANG, Z.
SINO-SOVIET SUMMIT IN SIGHT
BEIJING REVIEW, 32(7-8) (FEB 89), 11-12.
SOVIET FOREIGN MINISTER EDUARD SHEVARDNADZE PAID AN OFFICIAL VISIT TO CHINA IN FEBRUARY 1989. DURING A VISIT WITH SHEVARDNADZE, DENG XIAOPING STATED THAT IT IS IMPERATIVE TO REMOVE THE OBSTACLES TO THE NORMALIZATION OF SINO-SOVIET RELATIONS. THE TWO ISSUED A JOINT STATEMENT ON THE KAMPUCHEAN ISSUE, STRESSING THE IMPORTANCE OF A VIETNAMESE TROOP WITHDRAWAL.

07374 QUADAGNO, J.
GENERATIONAL EQUITY AND THE POLITICS OF THE WELFARE STATE
POLITICS AND SOCIETY, 17(3) (SEP 89), 353-376.
AMERICANS FOR GENERATIONAL EQUITY (AGE) HAS BEEN VERY SUCCESSFUL IN SHAPING THE PARAMETERS OF PUBLIC POLICY DEBATES CONCERNING SOCIAL BENEFITS FOR THE ELDERLY. AGE, IN FACT, CREATED THE NOTION THAT THE PROBLEM OF INADEQUATE SOCIAL RESOURCES FOR CHILDREN IS A PRODUCT OF EXCESSIVE BENEFITS FOR THE AGED. THIS ARTICLE TRACES THE DEVELOPMENT OF THE ORGANIZATION, EXAMINES ITS TACTICS, AND ANALYZES THE UNDERLYING POLICY AGENDA OF THE GENERATIONAL EQUITY MESSAGE.

07375 QUADAGNO, J.; MEYER, M.H.
ORGANIZED LABOR, STATE STRUCTURES, AND SOCIAL POLICY DEVELOPMENT: A CASE STUDY OF OLD AGE ASSISTANCE IN OHIO, 1916-1940
SOCIAL PROBLEMS, 36(2) (APR 89), 181-196.
IN ATTEMPTING TO EXPLAIN THE RELATIVE UNDERDEVELOPMENT OF THE AMERICAN WELFARE STATE, ONE THEORY, BASED ON A CLASS CONFLICT MODEL, ATTRIBUTES THE LACK OF COMPREHENSIVE SOCIAL BENEFITS TO THE WEAKNESS OF THE LABOR MOVEMENT. THE STATE-CENTERED APPROACH, BY CONTRAST, LOCATES SOCIAL PROGRAM DEVELOPMENT IN ASPECTS OF STATE STRUCTURES: PARTY COMPETITION, AUTONOMOUS ACTIVITY OF PARTY OFFICIALS AND STATE BUREAUCRATS, AND STATE ORGANIZATIONAL STRUCTURE. THIS HISTORICAL CASE STUDY OF THE INITIATION AND IMPLEMENTATION OF OLD AGE ASSISTANCE IN OHIO DEMONSTRATES THAT NEITHER A CLASS CONFLICT NOR A STATE-CENTERED MODEL CAN ADEQUATELY EXPLAIN THE DEVELOPMENT OF AMERICAN WELFARE PROGRAMS. OLD AGE ASSISTANCE WAS SHAPED THROUGH THE COMPLEX INTERSECTION OF CLASS AND POLITICAL FACTORS INVOLVING DIFFERENT FACTIONS OF THE LABOR MOVEMENT, PARTY POLITICS, AND AN EXPANDING FEDERAL BUREAUCRACY.

07376 QUAYLE, D.
AMERICAN LEADERSHIP IN THE PACIFIC
DEPARTMENT OF STATE BULLETIN (US FOREIGN POLICY), 89(2149) (AUG 89), 52-55.
IN THIS ADDRESS TO THE AMERICAN BUSINESS COUNCIL IN SINGAPORE, VICE PRESIDENT QUAYLE REVIEWED AMERICAN POLICY IN THE PACIFIC AND DISCUSSED WHAT ROLE THE USA MIGHT PLAY IN THE REGION IN THE FUTURE.

07377 QUBING, Z.
A REVIEW OF THE DEVELOPMENT OF U.S.-SOVIET RELATIONS
BEIJING REVIEW, 32(49) (DEC 89), 34-35.
AS SOON AS GEORGE BUSH MOVED INTO THE WHITE HOUSE, HE
INITIATED A NEW POLICY TOWARD THE SOVIET UNION. MOVING
BEYOND CONTAINMENT, BUSH'S POLICY IS INTENDED TO USHER THE
USSR BACK INTO THE INTERNATIONAL COMMUNITY. RECENT
DEVELOPMENTS IN THE SOVIET DOMESTIC SITUATION AND IN EASTERN
EUROPE HAVE ENCOURAGED THE AMERICAN PRESIDENT TO GO EVEN
FURTHER. CLOSER RELATIONS BETWEEN THE USA AND THE USSR ARE
IN THE INTEREST OF BOTH COUNTRIES.

07378 QUBING, Z.
BUSH'S FOREIGN POLICY: A CHINESE VIEW
BEIJING REVIEW, 32(44) (OCT 89), 33-34.
THE UNITED STATES' NEW POLICY ON RELATIONS WITH THE
SOVIET UNION, ANNOUNCED BY PRESIDENT GEORGE BUSH IN MAY 1989,
HAS STIMULATED LIVELY DEBATE IN THE INTERNATIONAL COMMUNITY.
IN THIS ARTICLE, A CHINESE EXPERT ON INTERNATIONAL
RELATIONS OFFERS AN ANALYSIS OF THE NEW POLICY FROM A
CHINESE VIEWPOINT.

07379 QUESTER, G.H.
INTERNATIONAL-SECURITY CRITICISMS OF PEACE RESEARCH
PHILADELPHIA: ANLS OF AMER ACMY OF POLITICAL AND SOC
SCIENCE, (504) (JUL 89), 98-105.
THE INTELLECTUAL COMMUNITY THAT ADDRESSES ARMS CONTROL
OR INTERNATIONAL SECURITY HAS A NUMBER OF CRITICISMS TO
OFFER OF ITS COLLEAGUES WORKING ON PEACE RESEARCH OR PEACE
STUDIES. THE LATTER ARE SEEN AS BEING TOO OPTIMISTIC AND
UNREALISTIC, TENDING TO ASSUME THAT GOOD THINGS MUST GO
TOGETHER, THAT DOMESTIC AND INTERNATIONAL IMPROVEMENTS ARE
ALWAYS LINKED, AND THAT DISARMAMENT SERVES ALL THE PURPOSES
OF HUMANKIND. PEACE STUDIES TEACHERS ARE MOREOVER SEEN AS
ENGAGED TOO OFTEN IN CONSCIOUSNESS RAISING, ON THE MISTAKEN
ASSUMPTION THAT MANY OF US DO NOT UNDERSTAND THE
DESIRABILITY OF PEACE. FINALLY, PEACE RESEARCHERS ARE
SOMETIMES SEEN AS REDEFINING PEACE TO INCLUDE JUSTICE AND
SOCIAL IMPROVEMENT AND WHATEVER OTHER CAUSES THEY FAVOR, SO
THAT MAJOR CONFUSIONS CAN RESULT AS TO WHICH PARTICULAR
PROBLEM WE ARE TRYING TO SOLVE AT ANY PARTICULAR TIME.

07380 QUIGLEY, J.
AGGRESSION AS A WAR CRIME
LINK, 22(4) (SEP 89), 2-6.
THIS ARTICLE ATTEMPTS TO HIGHLIGHT ILLEGAL ACTS FOR
WHICH INDIVIDUAL ISRAELI OFFICIALS ARE RESPONSIBLE. ONE
EXAMPLE OF THIS IS THE INITIATION OF AN AGGRESSIVE WAR AS AN
ACT WHICH IS A WAR CRIME. IT DETAILS THE AGGRESSION
COMMITTED BY ISRAEL ON A NUMBER OF OCCASIONS OVER ITS YEARS
OF EXISTENCE. IT STARTS WITH 1947-48 WHEN ZIONIST MILITARY
FORCES UNDERTOOK A CAMPAIGN OF ATTACKS ON PALESTINIAN
VILLAGES WITH THE AIM OF TAKING OVER PALESTINE. IT THEN
COVERS AGGRESSIVE WAR IN 1955, 1966, 1982 AND OTHER YEARS.
IT ALSO DETAILS THE SERIES ON SECURITY COUNCIL UN
CONDEMNATIONS OF ISRAEL'S ATTACKS.

07381 QUIGLEY, J.
THE INTERNATIONAL CRIMES OF ISRAELI OFFICIALS
LINK, 22(4) (SEP 89), 1-2.
THIS ARTICLE EXPLORES THE LEGALITY OF MANY OF THE
ACTIONS OF THE GOVERNMENT OF ISRAEL TOWARDS THE PALESTINIAN
ARABS. UN CRITICISM OF ISRAEL FOR VIOLATING THE LEGALLY
PROTECTED INTERESTS OF ARABS ARE DETAILED. IT EXAMINES WAR
AS AN AREA OF INTER-COUNTRY ACTION WHICH HAS BECOME A
SUBJECT OF INTERNATIONAL LAW. IT DISCUSSES INTERNATIONAL LAW
WHICH WAS DEVELOPED WITH THE CONCEPT OF INDIVIDUAL
RESPONSIBILITY IN AN EFFORT BRING ABOUT A MORE HUMANE WORLD,
IN WHICH INDIVIDUALS WOULD NOT HAVE TO FEAR BECOMING THE
VICTIMS OF ATROCITIES.

07382 QUIGLEY, K.E.F.; LONG, W.J.
EXPORT CONTROLS: MOVING BEYOND ECONOMIC CONTAINMENT
WORLD POLICY JOURNAL, (WIN 89), 166-188.
THIS ARTICLE EXPLORES THE U.S. SYSTEM OF EXPORT CONTROLS
AND SUGGESTS THAT IT IS SERIOUSLY OUT OF STEP WITH TODAY'S
INTERNATIONAL REALITIES. THE EFFECTS OF THE COORDINATING
COMMITTEE ON MULTILATERAL EXPORT CONTROLS (COCOM) ARE
DETAILED, AND PRINCIPLES THAT POLICYMAKERS MUST FOLLOW TO
CRAFT A VIABLE NEW EXPORT-CONTROL POLICY ARE OFFERED IT
CONCLUDES THAT WESTERN SECURITY INTERESTS, COCOM HARMONY,
AND U.S. COMPETITIVENESS WOULD ALL BE SERVED BY A LESS
EXTENSIVE REGIME THAT REGULATED ONLY THE MOST CRITICAL
MILITARY-RELATED ITEMS.

07383 QUIJANO, A.
PARADOXES OF MODERNITY IN LATIN AMERICA
INTERNATIONAL JOURNAL OF POLITICS, CULTURE AND SOCIETY,
3(2) (WIN 89), 147-178.
ANIBAL QUIJANO REOPENS THE CLASSIC DEBATE ON INDIGENISMO
IN A NEW FRAMEWORK, POSING THE QUESTION OF WHETHER EURO-
AMERICAN POLITICAL AND ECONOMIC THOUGHT CAN COMPREHEND THE
ACTUALITIES OF POST-CONQUEST SOUTH AMERICAN SOCIETIES, THE
AUTHOR LOOKS AT MODERNITY AND "MODERNIZATION" IN LATIN

AMERICA, AND EXAMINES THE PARADOXES. THEN STUDIES THE BASIS
OF ANOTHER MODERNITY-PRIVATE AND PUBLIC. HE SEES IN LATIN
AMERICA, ANOTHER OPTION FOR ANOTHER RATIONALITY.

07384 QUIMBY, E.; FRIEDMAN, S.R.
DYNAMICS OF BLACK MOBILIZATION AGAINST AIDS IN NEW YORK
CITY
SOCIAL PROBLEMS, 36(4) (OCT 89), 403-415.
BLACKS HAVE BEEN DISPROPORTIONATELY LIKELY TO GET AIDS
THROUGH MALE/MALE SEX, INTRAVENOUS DRUG USE, AND
HETEROSEXUAL TRANSMISSION. IN SPITE OF THE LONG HISTORY OF
BLACK MOBILIZATION, THERE HAS BEEN LITTLE MOBILIZATION
AROUND AIDS, EVEN THOUGH COLLECTIVE EFFORT COULD REDUCE THE
EXTENT OF HIV SPREAD, PROVIDE CARE AND SERVICES FOR SICK
PEOPLE WHO NOW DIE IN ISOLATED LONELINESS, AND CREATE A
VOICE IN BUDGETARY AND POLICY DECISIONS THAT HAVE SO FAR
FAILED TO DEAL ADEQUATELY WITH AIDS AMONG MINORITIES.
ATTEMPTS AT BLACK AIDS MOBILIZATION IN NEW YORK CITY ARE
DESCRIBED AND ASSESSED ON THE BASIS OF FIELD RESEARCH
CONDUCTED IN 1987-88. REASONS FOR THE FAILURE OF THESE
ATTEMPTS TO PRODUCE SIZABLE MOBILIZATION INCLUDE SOCIALLY
STRUCTURED DIVISIONS AMONG BLACKS; IDEOLOGICAL PARALYSIS OF
KEY ACTORS SUCH AS CHURCHES AND POLITICIANS CONFRONTED BY
EPIDEMIC SPREAD BY RISK BEHAVIORS THEY OPPOSE; POVERTY; THE
INHERENT CONTRADICTIONS OF ATTEMPTED MOBILIZATION BY ELITES
WHOSE INTERESTS DIFFER FROM THOSE OF THE THREATENED
POPULATION; AND THE WEAKENING OF ORGANIZATIONAL TIES AND
EXPERIENCE FROM THE 1960S.

07385 QUINN-JUDGE, S.
A PLANNER'S DREAM, BUT IT IS NOT THE WHOLE STORY
FAR EASTERN ECONOMIC REVIEW, 141(33) (AUG 88), 64-65,68.
AT FIRST GLANCE, THE CITY OF TASHKENT SEEMS TO BE THE
PICTURE OF SOVIET BROTHERHOOD AND PROGRESS THAT HAS BEEN
PREDICTED FOR DECADES. THE BUILDINGS ARE LARGE AND MODERN,
SPACE IS LARGE, AND THE POPULATION IS DIVERSE: UZBEKS,
TADZHIKS, RUSSIANS, KOREANS. JEWS, AND CRIMEAN TATARS ALL
LIVE TOGETHER IN APPARENT HARMONY. HOWEVER A SCRATCH BENEATH
THE SURFACE REVEALS WIDESPREAD PARTY CORRUPTION AND AN
UNDERLYING DISSATISFACTION AMONG THE POPULATION WHO SEEM TO
LONG, NOT FOR MODERN CITIES, BUT A ONE STORY HOME IN THE
COUNTRY "WITH A COURTYARD WHERE THEY CAN GROW GRAPES."

07386 QUINN-JUDGE, S.
GLASNOST'S ASIAN FRONTIER
FAR EASTERN ECONOMIC REVIEW, 141(31) (AUG 88), 24-25.
SINCE MIKHAIL GORBACHEV'S 1986 STATEMENT IN VLADIVOSTOK
THAT HIS COUNTRY WOULD PARTICIPATE CONSTRUCTIVELY IN ASIAN
AFFAIRS, A SLOW PROCESS OF DETENTE HAS BEGUN IN THE ASIA
PACIFIC REGION. MORE PROGRESS HAS BEEN MADE TOWARDS SOLVING
REGIONAL CONFLICTS THAN THOUGHT POSSIBLE BY MANY OBSERVERS
IN 1986. SINO-SOVIET RELATIONS ARE THAWING SOMEWHAT AS THE
USSR IS BEGINING TO GRANT SOME CONCESSIONS TO CHINA WITH
REGARDS TO TROOPS ON THE BORDER AND WITH REGARDS TO THE
VIETNAMESE OCCUPATION OF CAMBODIA.

07387 QUINN, B.
PUBLIC SERVICES IN AGING AMERICA
AMERICAN CITY AND COUNTY, 104(11) (NOV 89), 78-80, 82.
THE GRADUAL AND INEVITABLE AGING OF THE AMERICAN
POPULATION IS RESTRUCTURING AND REDEFINING AMERICAN SOCIETY,
ITS NEEDS, AND THE WAYS THOSE NEEDS WILL BE MET. AMERICAN
CITY AND COUNTY GOVERNMENTS ARE BEGINNING TO GRAPPLE WITH A
NEW SET OF ISSUES CONCERNING PUBLIC SERVICES TO THE ELDERLY.

07388 QUINN, D.P.; JACOBSON, R.
INDUSTRIAL POLICY THROUGH THE RESTRICTION OF CAPITAL FLOWS:
A TEST OF SEVERAL CLAIMS MADE ABOUT INDUSTRIAL POLICY
AMERICAN JOURNAL OF POLITICAL SCIENCE, 33(3) (AUG 89),
700-736.
THIS ARTICLE EXAMINES THE EXTENT AND EFFECT OF AN
INTEREST RATE-BASED INDUSTRIAL POLICY IN SELECTED EUROPEAN
COUNTRIES AND JAPAN WHILE USING THE UNITED STATES AS A
CONTROL CASE. IT ARGUES THAT SOME GOVERNMENTS HAVE
UNDERTAKEN INDUSTRIAL POLICIES THAT ACHIEVE A "BLOW
COMPETITIVE MARKET" INTEREST RATE, THEREBY ALLOWING THE
REDIRECTION OF FINANCIAL FLOWS TO FIRMS IN THE FORM OF
CHEAPER CAPITAL. THE RELATIONSHIP BETWEEN DOMESTIC INTEREST
RATES AND EUROCURRENCY RATES IS ASSESSED. THE RELATIVE
INFLUENCES OF DOMESTIC AND EXTERNAL INTEREST RATES ON STOCK
PRICES ARE EVALUATED. PARTISAN POLITICAL CHANGES IN
GOVERNMENT POLICIES WERE TESTED FOR.

07389 QUINN, K.M.
SOVIET OIL TRADE FROM 1950 TO 1976 IN THE CONTEXT OF THE
REGIME PERSPECTIVE
DISSERTATION ABSTRACTS INTERNATIONAL, 50(2) (AUG 89),
538-A.
THE AUTHOR APPLIES AN INTERNATIONAL POLITICAL ECONOMY
PERSPECTIVE, "REGIME THEORY," TO THE SOVIET OIL TRADE. SHE
FOCUSES ON THE INTERACTION OF THE SOVIET UNION WITH A REGIME
THAT HAD ALREADY BEEN ESTABLISHED AND WAS CONTROLLED BY
WESTERN ACTORS. SHE ARGUES THAT THE SOVIET UNION--IN VIEW OF
ITS POSITION IN THE INTERNATIONAL SYSTEM, ITS PLANNING

SYSTEM, AND ITS MARXIST IDEOLOGY--ADHERED TO A VERY
DIFFERENT VIEW OF THE PROPER STRUCTURING OF INTERNATIONAL
TRADE RELATIONS THAN THAT EMBODIED IN THE WESTERN OIL TRADE
REGIME.

07390 QUINN, W.S.
ACTIONS, INTENTIONS, AND CONSEQUENCES: THE DOCTRINE OF
BOUBLE EFFECT
PHILOSOPHY AND PUBLIC AFFAIRS, 18(4) (FAL 89), 334-351.
THIS ARTICLE EXPLORES THE DOC OF DOUBLE EFFECT (DDE).
THE AUTHOR EXAMINES THE CONTROVERSIAL IDEA THAT THE PURSUIT
OF A GOOD TENDS TO BE LESS ACCEPTABLE WHERE A RESULTING HARM
IS INTENDED AS A MEANS THAN WHERE IT IS MERELY FORESEEN. IT
DEALS WITH THE MAJOR PROBLEMS WITH THE DDE AND SUGGESTS A
RATIONALE WITH CLEAR KANTIAN ECHOES.

07391 QUINT, J.C.
DECISION-MAKING IN PUBLIC WELFARE BUREAUCRACIES
DISSERTATION ABSTRACTS INTERNATIONAL, 49(8) (FEB 89),
2417-A.
THE AUTHOR TESTS THE HYPOTHESIS THAT STREET-LEVEL
BUREAUCRACIES ARE INEVITABLY CHARACTERIZED BY A HIGH DEGREE
OF DISCRETIONARY DECISION-MAKING ON THE PART OF LOWER-LEVEL
STAFF. SHE UTILIZES CASE STUDIES OF TWO PROGRAMS AIMED AT
INCREASING EMPLOYABILITY AND WORK EFFORT AMONG AFDC WELFARE
RECIPIENTS IN BALTIMORE AND CHICAGO.

07392 QUIRK, P. J.
THE COOPERATIVE RESOLUTION OF POLICY CONFLICT
AMERICAN POLITICAL SCIENCE REVIEW, 83(3) (SEP 89), 905-922.
THE AUTHOR DEVELOPS AN APPROACH FOR ANALYZING THE
CONDITIONS FOR COOPERATIVE RESOLUTION OF POLICY CONFLICT. HE
ANALYZES CERTAIN POLICY CONFLICTS AS BARGAINING SITUATIONS
WITH OPPORTUNITY FOR COOPERATION, AMONG OPPOSING ISSUE
FACTIONS. AS A FRAMEWORK FOR ANALYSIS, HE PRESENTS AN
INFORMAL GAME-THEORETIC INTERPERTATION OF NONZERO-SUM POLICY
CONFLICT. WITH THAT FOUNDATION, HE DERIVES IMPLICATIONS
ABOUT THE CONDITIONS FOR COOPERATIVE OUTCOMES WITH RESPECT
TO SEVERAL ASPECTS OF THE POLICY PROCESS: ISSUE CONTENT, THE
STRUCTURE OF CONFLICT, LEADERSHIP, PARTY POLITICS, AND
POLITICAL INSTITUTIONS.

07393 QURAISHI, Z.M.
LIBYA'S EXPERIMENT IN DEMOCRATIC TELETHON
INDIAN JOURNAL OF POLITICAL SCIENCE, L(3) (JUL 89),
343-356.
THE CURRENT POLITICAL EXPERIMENT IN LIBYA CLOSELY
FOLLOWS ITS TRADITIONAL ROLE IN HUMAN CIVILIZATION. LIBYA'S
EXPERIMENT IN "JAMAHIRIYA" IS UNIQUE BECAUSE IT PROMISES TO
MOBILIZE THE INARTICULATE POPULATION OF A DEVELOPING COUNTRY
INTO THE PROCESS OF DIRECT PARTICIPATION IN LEGISLATIVE
DECISION MAKING AND EXECUTIVE IMPLEMENTATION. THE MODEL
OFFERS AN ALTERNATIVE TO THE PREVAILING FORMS OF DEMOCRACY
AND INCORPORATES IN A SYSTEMATIC WAY SEVERAL INNOVATIVE
DEVICES UTILIZED IN THE EMERGENT NATIONS OF ASIA AND AFRICA.

07394 RAACK, R.C.
HISTORY AS PAST AND CURRENT POLITICS: THE GENSEK, STALIN,
AND THE BEGINNINGS OF THE COLD WAR
EAST EUROPEAN QUARTERLY, XXIII(2) (JUN 89), 129-144.
GENSEK (GENERAL SECRETARY) MIKHAIL GORBACHEV HAS
PUBLICLY REOPENED THE DISCUSSION OF STALIN'S ROLE IN THE
BEGINNINGS OF WORLD WAR II. HIS AIM IS TO STABILIZE POLITICS
NOW AND FOR THE FUTURE ON THE BASIS OF AN AGREED HISTORY: TO
FIX THE IDEA THAT THE SOVIET UNION, LED BY STALIN, WAS
FORCED BY FOREIGN DANGER BEFORE 1939 INTO A SELF-PROTECTIVE
ROLE AND WAS FORCED TO MAKE THE INFAMOUS "NON-AGGRESSION
PACT" WITH HITLER IN AUGUST 1939.

07395 RABBANI, M.
THE PALESTINIAN ECONOMY
MIDDLE EAST INTERNATIONAL, (359) (SEP 89), 16-17.
AS THE SECOND ANNIVERSARY OF THE INTIFADA NEARS, IT IS
BECOMING INCREASINGLY CLEAR THAT THE PALESTINIANS CURRENTLY
LACK THE ECONOMIC FOUNDATION TO CONTINUE TO SUPPORT ITS
SOPHISTICATED POLITICAL ORGANIZATION. THE DEVALUATION OF
BOTH ISRAELI AND JORDANIAN CURRENCY; THE DISRUPTION OF
PALESTINIAN AGRICULTURE; AND THE FREQUENT CURFEWS, SIEGES,
AND MILITARY REPRESSION HAVE ALL STRAINED THE ECONOMY TO THE
BREAKING POINT. HOWEVER, SOME OBSERVERS FEEL THAT THE
INCREASED ECONOMIC DEPRIVATION WILL ONLY INCREASE THE
PALESTINIAN RESOLVE FOR INDEPENDENCE.

07396 RABBANI, M.
THE PLO AND THE INTIFADA: A COMPLEX RELATIONSHIP
MIDDLE EAST INTERNATIONAL, (347) (MAR 89), 20-21.
THE ROLE AND INFLUENCE OF THE PALESTINE LIBERATION
ORGANISATION IN THE DEVELOPMENT, INSTITUTIONALISATION AND
DIRECTION OF THE CURRENT POPULAR UPRISING IN THE WEST BANK
AND GAZA STRIP HAS BEEN FIERCELY CONTESTED SINCE ALMOST THE
MOMENT IT BEGAN BY PALESTINIAN, ARAB AND FOREIGN OBSERVERS
ALIKE. WHILE FEW CONTINUE TO DENY THE LEADING ROLE WHICH HAS
BEEN AND CONTINUES TO BE EXERCISED BY THE PALESTINIAN
NATIONAL MOVEMENT IN THE OCCUPIED TERRITORIES, CHANGING

POLITICAL CIRCUMSTANCES HAVE AT THE SAME TIME TRANSFORMED
THE NATURE OF THE DEBATE.

07397 RABE, B.G.
CROSS-MEDIA ENVIRONMENTAL REGULATORY INTEGRATION: THE CASE
OF CANADA
AMERICAN REVIEW OF CANADIAN STUDIES, 29(3) (FAL 89),
261-274.
THIS ARTICLE EXPLORES THE NEED FOR CROSS-MEDIA
ENVIRONMENTAL REGULATION AS IT APPLIES TO CANADIAN
DECENTRALIZATION WHICH CONSTRAINS THE FEDERAL GOVERNMENT'S
CAPACITY TO INTEGRATE PROVINCIAL POLICY. IT EXAMINES THE
ROLE OF THE FEDERAL GOVERNMENT; THE PROVINCES; AND BILATERAL
ORGANIZATIONS IN CROSS MEDIA INTEGRATION. IT CONCLUDES THAT
THE MOST PRESSING PROBLEMS IN CANADA MAY BE BEYOND THE
CAPACITY OF ANY CANADIAN REGULATORY SYSTEM BUT THAT CANADA
MAY BE POSITIONED TO BEGIN TO TAKE MORE SIGNIFICANT STEPS IN
FUTURE YEARS.

07398 RABESAHALA, G.
MADAGASCAR: FOR POPULAR UNITY
WORLD MARXIST REVIEW, 32(5) (MAY 89), 51-52.
THE MADAGASCAR INDEPENDENCE PARTY (AKFM) HELD
ITS 11TH CONGRESS IN SEPTEMBER 1988. THE CONGRESS NOTED IN
ITS RESOLUTION THAT THE DECISIONS TAKEN BY SEVERAL
CAPITALIST GOVERNMENTS TO WRITE OFF THE DEVELOPING
COUNTRIES' DEBTS EITHER FULLY (CANADA) OR PARTIALLY (FRANCE)
DID NOT SIGNIFICANTLY EASE THE DEBT BURDEN. THE TERMS OF
TRADE ARE EVEN WORSE NOW FOR THE YOUNG STATES, AND THEIR
NATIONAL CURRENCIES ARE DECLINING. ACOORDINATED EFFORT IS
NEEDED TO DEFEND COMMON INTERESTS. AT A NON-ALIGNED SUMMIT
DIDIER RATSIRAKA, PRESIDENT OF THE DEMOCRATIC REPUBLIC OF
MADAGASCAR, PROPOSED THE ESTABLISHMENT OF THREE FUNDS FOR
DEVELOPMENT, AND THIS OUGHT TO BE EXAMINED. THE PROBLEM IS
VERY URGENT BECAUSE MADAGASCAR IS NOT THE ONLY COUNTRY
SUFFERING FROM IMMENSE FINANCIAL HARDSHIPS CAUSED BY UNFAIR
RATES OF EXCHANGE AND IMPORTED INFLATION. NATURALLY, ALL
THIS ADVERSELY AFFECTS NATIONAL ECONOMIC GROWTH AND LIVING
STANDARDS.

07399 RABIE, M.
TOWARD A PALESTINIAN-ISRAELI PEACE
NEW OUTLOOK, 32(8 (294)) (AUG 89), 18-20.
MORE THAN FORTY YEARS OF BITTER ENMITY AND VIOLENT
CONFRONTATION SEEM TO HAVE CONVINCED MOST PEOPLES ON BOTH
SIDES THAT ARAB-ISRAELI PEACEFUL COEXISTENCE IN PALESTINE IS
INEVITABLE. BUT FOR PEACEFUL COEXISTENCE TO BE REALIZED,
EACH PARTY MUST ACKNOWLEDGE THE EXISTENCE OF THE OTHER,
RECOGNIZE ITS LEGITIMATE RIGHTS, AND ACCEPT ITS DEFINITION
OF ITSELF. OFFICIAL PALESTINE, REPRESENTED BY THE PLO, HAS
ALREADY RECOGNIZED ISRAEL'S EXISTENCE AND ACCEPTED ITS
DEFINITION OF ITSELF. IN CONTRAST, OFFICIAL ISRAEL,
REPRESENTED BY THE ISRAELI GOVERNMENT, HAS CONTINUED TO
REJECT RECOGNIZING THE PLO AND TO RESIST ACCEPTING THE
PALESTINIANS' DEFINITION OF THEMSELVES.

07400 RABIE, M.
US AID TO ISRAEL
LINK, 22(2) (MAY 89), 1.
THE ARTICLE GIVES AN OVERVIEW OF THE US AID TO ISRAEL.
IT BEGINS WITH THE DIPLOMATIC RECOGNITION OF THE JEWISH
STATE BY TRUMAN AND TRACES THE EXPANSION OF US AID AND
SUPPORT THROUGH THE FOLLOWING DECADES. THE US HAS
CONSISTENTLY PROVIDED ISRAEL WITH THE MORAL, ECONOMIC
POLITICAL, AND MILITARY SUPPORT NECESSARY FOR ISRAEL TO
MAINTAIN ITS EVER EXPANDING BORDERS.

07401 RABINOVICH, I.
SYRIA AND LEBANON IN 1988
CURRENT HISTORY, 88(535) (FEB 89), 77-80, 103-104.
THE AUTHOR SURVEYS SYRIA'S FOREIGN POLICY, INCLUDING ITS
RELATIONS WITH IRAN, IRAQ, AND LEBANON.

07402 RABINOVITZ, F.
WHAT SHOULD BE DONE?
SOCIETY, 26(4) (MAY 89), 12-13.
THE AUTHOR ADVOCATES AN EXTENSIVE TEN-YEAR PROGRAM TO
UPGRADE THE CONDITION OF THE HOMELESS WHICH INCLUDES
SPECIFIC ECONOMIC AND SOCIAL OBJECTIVES. THESE OBJECTIVES
INCLUDE: MONEY INCOME FOR 90 PERCENT OF CURRENTLY HOMELESS
HOUSEHOLDS, AVAILABLE AND ACCESSIBLE EMPLOYMENT, PRICE
LEVELS ON ESSENTIALS CONSISTENT WITH PREVAILING INCOME
TRENDS, "STREET HOMELESSNESS" EXISTING ONLY BY CHOICE, AND
NEW HOUSING FACILITIES FOR VERY LOW INCOME PEOPLE. ONLY A
COMPREHENSIVE AND COMPELLING POLICY WILL BE ABLE TO MOBILIZE
COMMITMENT NECESSARY TO ACHIVE THESE GOALS.

07403 RABINOWITZ, G.; MACDONALD, S.E.
A DIRECTIONAL THEORY OF ISSUE VOTING
AMERICAN POLITICAL SCIENCE REVIEW, 83(1) (MAR 89), 93-122.
BASED ON THE IDEAS OF SYMBOLIC POLITICS, THE DIRECTIONAL
THEORY OF ISSUE VOTING ASSUMES THAT MOST PEOPLE HAVE A
DIFFUSE PREFERENCE FOR A CERTAIN DIRECTION OF POLICY-MAKING
AND THAT PEOPLE VARY IN THE INTENSITY WITH WHICH THEY HOLD

THOSE PREFERENCES. IN THIS PAPER, THE AUTHORS TEST TWO
COMPETING THEORIES AT THE INDIVIDUAL LEVEL WITH NATIONAL
ELECTION STUDY DATA AND FIND THE DIRECTIONAL THEORY MORE
STRONGLY SUPPORTED THAN THE TRADITIONAL SPATIAL THEORY. THEN
THEY EXPLORE THE IMPLICATIONS OF THE DIRECTIONAL THEORY FOR
CANDIDATE BEHAVIOR AND ASSESS THE PREDICTIONS IN LIGHT OF
EVIDENCE FROM THE U.S. CONGRESS.

07404 RABITOY, N.
   BRITISH SOVEREIGNTY AND THE PRINCELY STATES OF SOUTH ASIA,
   THE BHAVANAGAR RETROCESSION, 1860-66
   ASIAN PROFILE, 17(1) (FEB 89), 91-100.
      THIS ESSAY EXAMINES A CASE OF BRITISH RETROCESSION (THE
   RETURN OF TERRITORY TO THE THAKUR OF BHAVNAGAR BY THE
   GOVERNMENT OF BOMBAY DURING 1860-66) AND DEMONSTRATES THAT
   EVEN A POLICY OF DELIBERATE CONCILIATION COULD BE FRUSTRATED
   BY THE LACK OF A CLEAR OPERATIONAL DEFINITION OF BRITISH
   SOVEREIGNTY. IT BECAME OBVIOUS DURING THE RETROCESSION
   DELIBERATIONS THAT THE BRITISH COULD NOT AGREE ON WHAT
   CONSTITUTED BRITISH INDIA AND BRITISH SOVEREIGNTY. IT BECAME
   EQUALLY OBVIOUS THAT, IN THE ABSENCE OF SUCH AN AGREEMENT,
   BRITISH RELATIONS WITH THE SOUTH ASIAN PRINCELY STATES WERE
   BOUND TO BE INCONSISTENT AND MUTUALLY FRUSTRATING.

07405 RABLE, G.
   PATRIOTISM, PLATITUDES, AND POLITICS: BASEBALL AND THE
   AMERICAN PRESIDENCY
   PRESIDENTIAL STUDIES QUARTERLY, XIX(2) (SPR 89), 355-362.
      THE COMPLEX RELATIONSHIP BETWEEN BASEBALL AND AMERICAN
   PRESIDENCY FROM WILLIAM HOWARD TAFT TO RICHARD NIXON IS
   DISCUSSED. THE EMPHASIS IS ON HOW PRESIDENTS USED BASEBALL
   TO REAFFIRM THE IMPORTANCE OF CERTAIN AMERICAN VIRTUES WHILE
   AT THE SAME TIME IDENTIFYING THEMSELVES WITH A POPULAR SPORT.
   EACH PRESIDENT BROUGHT HIS OWN STYLE, PERSONALITY, AND
   PURPOSES TO THE BALLPARK, BUT PUBLIC EXPECTATIONS FOR
   PRESIDENTIAL BEHAVIOR ALSO EVOLVED. PUBLIC CEREMONIES --
   SUCH AS THROWING OUT THE FIRST PITCH-OFTEN BECAME ELABORATE
   AND POLITICALLY BENEFICIAL RITUALS. THE ARTICLE DESCRIBES
   THE CHANGING RELATIONSHIP BETWEEN BASEBALL AND AMERICAN
   PRESIDENTS AND AT THE SAME TIME ANALYZES THE HISTORICAL
   REASONS FOR CHANGE.

07406 RABY, D.
   THE TWELFTH CONGRESS OF THE PORTUGUESE COMMUNIST PARTY
   JOURNAL OF COMMUNIST STUDIES, 5(2) (JUN 89), 220-221.
      OBSERVERS OF THE TWELFTH CONGRESS OF THE PORTUGUESE
   COMMUNIST PARTY LARGELY DECLARE THE CONGRESS TO SIGNAL
   CONTINUED UNITY AND ORTHODOXY. IT WAS LARGELY A
   REAFFIRMATION OF THE LEADERSHIP OF 75-YEAR-OLD ALVARO CUNHAL
   AND OF TRADITIONAL POSITIONS. HOWEVER, CLOSE OBSERVERS NOTE
   THAT DISCONTENT AND CRITICISM IS INCREASING AND THAT PARTY
   WILL HAVE TO DEAL WITH INCREASINGLY VOCAL AND MILITANT
   FACTIONS IN THE FUTURE.

07407 RACHWALD, A.R.
   SOVIET-EAST EUROPEAN RELATION
   CURRENT HISTORY, 88(541) (NOV 89), 377-380, 408-409.
      THE SOVIET EMPIRE IS SLOWLY DISINTEGRATING. BUT THIS
   DEVELOPMENT HAS NOT YET CHANGED THE FACT THAT THE SOCIALIST
   COMMONWEALTH CONTINUES TO OPERATE AND DECIDE THE MOST VITAL
   NATIONAL SECURITY ISSUES OF THE EAST EUROPEAN STATES.

07408 RACZ, B.
   THE PARLIAMENTARY INFRASTRUCTURE AND POLITICAL REFORMS IN
   HUNGARY
   SOVIET STUDIES, XLI(1) (JAN 89), 39-66.
      THE HUNGARIAN EXPERIMENTATION WITH ECONOMIC AND
   POLITICAL REFORMS SO FAR HAS BEEN LARGELY DIFFERENT FROM
   WHAT HAS HAPPENED IN OTHER SOCIALIST STATES. THE 1985
   PARLIAMENTARY AND LOCAL ELECTIONS WERE HELD ON THE BASIS OF
   AN ELECTORAL LAW UNKNOWN IN OTHER SOCIALIST COUNTRIES AT
   THAT TIME AND CITIZENS WERE ABLE TO NOMINATE CANDIDATES OF
   THEIR OWN CHOOSING. THE HUNGARIAN SOCIALIST WORKERS PARTY
   AND THE GOVERNMENT ALSO ENGAGED IN A POLICY OF ENLARGING THE
   FUNCTION OF THE LEGISLATURE. PERMANENT COMMITTEES APPEAR TO
   PLAY A KEY ROLE IN THE MORE ACTIVE WORK OF THE LEGISLATURE.
   THIS ROLE IS STUDIED BY THE AUTHOR AS IS THE NATURE AND
   EXTENT OF THE COMMITTEES' FUNCTIONING, THEIR PARTICIPATION
   IN POLITICAL AND LEGISLATIVE POLICIES, AND HOW THE
   COMMITTEES' ROLE INTERFACES WITH POLITICAL REFORMS.

07409 RADCLIFFE, J.
   THE REORGANISATION OF THE CENTRAL GOVERNMENT, 1970-1976
   DISSERTATION ABSTRACTS INTERNATIONAL, 50(1) (JUL 89),
   247-A.
      THE WHITE PAPER, CMND 4506 (1970), ON THE REORGANISATION
   OF CENTRAL GOVERNMENT DECLARED ITS INTENTION OF CREATING A
   NEW STYLE OF GOVERNMENT. THIS THESIS EXAMINES THE
   IMPLEMENTATION OF THIS INTENTION PRIMARILY THROUGH CASE-
   STUDIES OF THE DEPARTMENT OF THE ENVIRONMENT AND THE
   DEPARTMENT OF TRADE AND INDUSTRY, THE ORGANISATIONAL
   FLAGSHIPS OF THE NEW STYLE.

07410 RADENKOV, R.
   THE TURKISH MINORITY IN BULGARIA
   EAST EUROPEAN REPORTER, 3(4) (SPR 89), 26-28.
      THE ARTICLE CONCENTRATES ON THE SIGNIFICANT TURKISH
   MINORITY IN BULGARIA. IT TRACES THE HISTORY OF THE MINORITY,
   AND LOOKS AT THE CHANGING FACE OF GOVERNMENT POLICY TOWARDS
   THEM, CULMINATING UNDER TODOR ZHIVKOV, IN THE "CAMPAIGN" OF
   1984-85, THE "PROMOTION AND CONSOLIDATION OF AN EMPHATIC
   BULGARIAN NATIONAL SELF-CONSCIOUSNESS." THE CAMPAIGN, WHICH
   INCLUDED THE DENIAL OF TURKISH LANGUAGE, RELIGIONS, AND
   NAMES, HAS SPARKED OFF DEMONSTRATIONS AND THE DEPARTURE OF
   SOME 12,000 TURKS FROM BULGARIA.

07411 RADIVILOV, B.
   USSR-ICELAND: TRADE AND COOPERATION.
   FOREIGN TRADE, 10 (1988), 30-31.
      THIS ARTICLE EXPLORES SEVERAL FACTORS WHICH ACCOUNT FOR
   THE GROWING SOVIET-ISLANDIC TRADE. IT FOLLOWS THE GROWTH
   BETWEEN 1953 AND 1987 AND DESCRIBES THE COOPERATION AND
   CONTACTS WHICH HAVE CONTRIBUTED TO THIS GROWTH, THE ARTICLE
   CONCLUDES BY SUGGESTING THAT THE SEARCH FOR POSSIBLE FORMS
   OF CONTINUALLY MUTUALLY PROFITABLE COOPERATION REQUIRES
   GREATER JOINT EFFORTS BY SOVIET AND ISLANDIC COMPANIES AND
   MUCH WORK TO MAKE THEM A FACT.

07412 RADNER, E.
   FROM 'LIBERATION' TO 'EXILE' A NEW IMAGE FOR CHURCH MISSION
   THE CHRISTIAN CENTURY, 106(30) (OCT 89), 931-933.
      DESPITE THE PREVALENCE OF LIBERATION RHETORIC IN MANY
   CIRCLES, CHURCHES IN THE U.S. ARE DRIFTING SO FAR FROM
   ACTUAL LIVED CONTACT WITH THE POOR THAT THEY RISK PERMANENT
   IRRELEVANCE ARGUES THIS ARTICLE. IT SUGGESTS AN ALTERNATIVE
   TO TOTALISTIC LIBERATION REMEDIES, WHICH IT FEELS CARRY AN
   UNACKNOWLEDGED SANCTIONING OF COERCIVE GOVERNMENT ACTION

07413 RAEHN, R.V.
   TRADITIONAL AMERICAN CONSERVATISM AND "NEO-CONSERVATISM"
   JOURNAL OF SOCIAL, POLITICAL AND ECONOMIC STUDIES, 14(4)
   (WIN 89), 485-509.
      THE CONSERVATIVES OF AMERICA, ONCE A POWERFUL FORCE,
   HAVE BEEN SET BACK BY FUNDAMENTAL DIVISIONS WITHIN THEIR
   RANKS. ON THE ONE HAND, THERE ARE THE TRADITIONAL
   CONSERVATIVES WHOSE PRIMARY EMPHASIS LIES IN LOYALTY TO
   AMERICA AS A NATION OF PEOPLE PROUD OF THEIR CULTURAL AND
   SCIENTIFIC ACHIEVEMENTS. ON THE OTHER HAND, THE NEW BREED OF
   "NEO-CONSERVATIVES" CORRESPONDS MORE CLOSELY TO NINETEENTH
   CENTURY LIBERALS. THE LATTER PLACE ECONOMIC INDIVIDUALISM
   ABOVE THE INTERESTS OF THE NATION AND OFTEN LOOK FOR
   FINANCIAL PROSPERITY NOT IN STRENGTH AT HOME BUT IN
   UNFETTERED WORLDWIDE TRADE. THE "NEO-CONSERVATIVES" THINK
   NOT OF NATIONS BUT OF INDIVIDUALS AND THEY CHAFF AT THE OLD
   TRADITION OF MERCANTILISM.

07414 RAFIULLA, S.
   THE EFFECT OF SOCIAL STRUCTURE ON JAPANESE SUCCESS.
   MICHIGAN JOURNAL OF POLITICAL SCIENCE, (11) (WIN 89),
   22-45.
      THIS ARTICLE EXPLORES THE REASONS BEHIND JAPAN'S
   ECONOMIC SUCCESS, WHILE AMERICA FACES DECLINE. UNDERSTANDING
   JAPANESE SOCIAL STRUCTURE IS OF KEY IMPORTANCE IN
   UNDERSTANDING ITS ECONOMIC GROWTH; AND THEIR FOCUS ON GROUP
   ORIENTATION, HIERARCHY, AND NON-CONFORNTATIONAL APPOACH ARE
   EACH EXAMINED IN DETAIL. THE EFFECT OF THE FACT THAT THE
   JAPANESE SOURCE OF HONOR AND PRIDE IS SOCIAL POSITION; THE
   SUBSERVIENT POSITION OF WOMEN; THE AMBIGUOUS LANGUAGE; AND
   EDUCATION ARE EACH JAPAN'S WEAKNESSES AND DEPENDENCE ARE
   EXAMINED. ANALYZED. IT CONCLUDES THAT AMERICA COULD ADAPT
   WHAT IS MOST APPROPRIATE FROM THEIR SYSTEM TO CREATE OUR OWN
   UNIQUE SYSTEM.

07415 RAGHAVAN, C.
   THE THIRD WORLD TAKES A STAND AT GATT-MONTREAL
   MULTINATIONAL MONITOR, 10(1-2) (JAN 89), 7-8.
      AT THE GATT MEETING IN DECEMBER 1988, THE THIRD WORLD
   MEMBERS THREW A MONKEY WRENCH IN THE WORKS. THEY DERAILED
   INITIATIVES ON TEXTILES AND SAFEGUARDS FOR INTELLECTUAL
   PROPERTY THAT HAD BEEN NEGOTIATED BY THE USA AND THE
   EUROPEAN ECONOMIC COMMUNITY. THE USA AND EEC HAD "AGREED TO
   DISAGREE" ON AGRICULTURE AND PROCEED WITH NEGOTIATIONS TO
   CONCLUDE EARLY ACCORDS IN OTHER AREAS WHERE THE TWO WERE IN
   AGREEMENT WITH EACH OTHER BUT IN CONFLICT WITH THIRD WORLD
   MEMBERS. SOME THIRD WORLD MEMBERS, HOWEVER, REFUSED TO GO
   ALONG. THE REJECTION CAME FROM THE CAIRNS GROUP (AGRENTINA,
   BRAZIL, CHILD, COLOMBIA, AND URUQUAY).

07416 RAGSDALE,H.
   THE CHALLENGE OF RUSSIAN NATIONALIST TO SOVIET STABILITY
   VIRGINIA QUARTERLY REVIEW, 65(3) (SUM 89), 377-389.
      ALTHOUGH ECONOMIC PROBLEMS AND ETHNIC CONFLICTS BETWEEN
   MINORITIES ARE CHALLENGES TO MIKHAIL GORBACHEV AND HIS
   REFORM POLICIES, PERHAPS THE GREATEST THREAT TO PERESTROIKA
   AND GLASNOST IS THE SPECTER OF RUSSIAN NATIONALISM. IF
   GORBACHEV PUSHES TOO FAR INTO THE DOMAIN OF RUSSIAN CULTURE
   AND IDENTITY, IT COULD RESULT IN A CONSERVATIVE BACKLASH

THAT WOULD NOT ONLY OVERTHROW GORBACHEV AND END HIS
RELATIVEL MODERATE REFORMS, BUT PLUNGE ASIA INTO AN ENORMOUS
CONFLICT.

07417 RAHMAN, A.B.M.S.
THE MATRIX OF INSTITUTIONAL COMMUNICATION IN DEVELOPMENT
PROJECTS: A CASE STUDY OF THE BARISAL IRRIGATION PROJECT,
BANGLADESH
DISSERTATION ABSTRACTS INTERNATIONAL, 50(4) (OCT 89),
1086-A.
THE AUTHOR ANALYZES COMMUNICATION RELATIONS AMONG
NATIONAL PARASTATAL DEVELOPMENT INSTITUTIONS AND THEIR LOCAL
EXTENSIONS IN BANGLADESH. HE STUDIES THE WORLD BANK-FUNDED
BARISAL IRRIGATION PROJECT, ITS FOUR MANAGING PARASTATAL
BUREAUCRACIES, AND ITS LOCAL INSTITUTIONS, USING LONG-TERM
EMPIRICAL FIELD METHODS TO UNDERSTAND THE INSTITUTIONAL
MATRIX AND ITS CONSEQUENCES.

07418 RAHMAN, M.
GOA: JOINING HANDS
INDIA TODAY, XIV(14) (JUL 89), 37.
TWO OLD POLITICAL FOES IN THE FORMER PORTUGUESE COLONY
OF GOA HAVE OVERCOME DIFFERENCES AND APPEAR TO BE WORKING IN
UNISON. MUCH TO THE DELIGHT OF CONGRESS (I) PARTY LEADERS IN
NEW DELHI DR. WILFRED DE SOUZA, THE LEADER OF THE GOA
CONGRESS, AND STATE CHIEF MINISTER PRATAPSINH RANE HAVE
AGREED TO BURY THE HATCHET AND MERGE THEIR FACTIONS. DE
SOUZA WAS IN OPPOSITION TO RANE DUE TO THE FACT THAT DE
SOUZA'S DEMANDS FOR STATEHOOD FOR GOA AND OFFICIAL LANGUIAGE
STATUS FOR KONKANI WERE NOT BEING MET; NOW BOTH DEMANDS HAVE
BEEN MET, MANY FELT THAT DE SOUZA'S RETURN TO THE FOLD WAS
INEVITABLE.

07419 RAHMAN, M.
GROWING SWAY
INDIA TODAY, XIV(2) (JAN 89), 39-40.
ALTHOUGH IT PRESENTLY HAS ONLY TWO MLA'S, THE SHIV SENA
CLAIMS THAT IT WILL WIN THE MAJORITY OF SEATS IN THE NEXT
STATE ASSEMBLY ELECTIONS IN MAHARASHTRA. THE PRESENCE OF 40,
000 DELEGATES AT THE NEW YEAR'S EVE SHIV SENA CONVENTION HAS
CLEAR EVIDENCE THAT THE MILITANT HINDU ORGANIZATION HAS
BECOME A POTENT FORCE IN STATE POLITICS.

07420 RAHMAN, M.
MAHARASHTRA: BOOMING SCANDAL
INDIA TODAY, 19(13) (JUL 89), 30-31.
THIS ARTICLE EXAMINES THE HOUSING SCANDAL IN MAHARASHTRA
AS THE GOVERNMENT FAVORS PRIVATE BUILDERS WITH PRIZE
CONTRACTS. IT REPORTS ON THE OFFICIAL DEBATE OVER BUILDING
MATERIALS AND PREFAB CONSTRUCTION.

07421 RAHMAN, M.
MIFFED MINORITIES
INDIA TODAY, XIV(6) (MAR 89), 67.
WITH PAKISTAN'S RETURN TO DEMOCRACY, MANY EXPECTED THE
RESTORATION OF THE RIGHTS OF WOMEN AND MINORITIES. BUT IT IS
DIFFICULT FOR BELEAGURED PRIME MINISTER BENAZIR BHUTTO TO
RISK THE WRATH OF FUNDAMENTALISTS BY RESTORING SUCH RIGHTS.

07422 RAHMAN, M.
THE TRUCE ENDS
INDIA TODAY, XIV(1) (JAN 89), 35.
DURING THE WINTER SESSION OF THE MAHARASHTRA ASSEMBLY,
CHIEF MINISTER SHARAD PAWAR CAME UNDER ATTACK FROM TWO
PROMINENT LEADERS OF THE CONGRESS (I) PARTY. TWO UNLIKELY
ALLIES, FORMER DEPUTY CHIEF MINISTER NASIKRAO TIRPUDE AND
FORMER CHIEF MINISTER SHIVAJIRO PATIL-NILANGEKAR, WERE
UNITED BY A COMMON GRUDGE BECAUSE BOTH HAVE BEEN DENIED A
SHARE OF POWER BY PAWAR.

07423 RAHMAN, M.; CHAHLA, P.; DHAR, R.N.
WADIA-AMBANI WAR: CRIME, MONEY AND POLITICS
INDIA TODAY, 14(16) (AUG 89), 14-21.
THIS ARTICLE IS A REPORT ON THE BOMBAY DYING - RELIANCE
INDUSTRIES FEUD. THIS FEUD TOOK A STARTLING TWIST WITH THE
ARREST ON SENIOR RELIANCE EXECUTIVE, KIRTI AMBANI, ON THE
CHARGE OF CONSPIRING TO KILL BOMBAY DYEING CHAIRMAN, NUSLI
WADIA. THE CASE IS A VOLATILE MIX OF POLITICS, CRIME AND
BUSINESS AND THIS REPORT FINDS THE POLITICAL DIMENSION THE
MOST INTRIGUING. THE CLAIMS AND COUNTER CLAIMS OF BOTH CAMPS
ARE DETAILED AND THE DRAWN POLITICAL BATTLE LINES ARE
DESCRIBED.

07424 RAHMAN, S.
BANGLADESH IN 1988: PRECARIOUS INSTITUTION BUILDING AMID
CRISIS MANAGEMENT
ASIAN SURVEY, XXIX(2) (FEB 89), 216-222.
THE ARTICLE EXAMINES THE EVENTS THAT SHAPED BANGLADESH
IN 1988. ALTHOUGH POLITICAL AND ECONOMIC POLICIES WERE MANY
AND SIGNIFICANT, ONE OF THE MOST DISASTROUS FLOODS IN
HISTORY OVERSHADOWED ALL OTHER CONCERNS. IT CRIPPLED THE
ECONOMY AND PARALYZED THE POLITICAL STRUCTURE. CLEVER
MANEUVERING BY THE RULING ERSHAD REGIME ALLOWED IT TO REMAIN
IN POWER DESPITE CONCERTED EFFORTS BY THE OPPOSITION. THE

ARTICLE CONCLUDES THAT NATURAL DESTRUCTION NEGATES THE
ACCURACY OF MOST CONVENTIONAL ECONOMIC AND POLITICAL
ANALYSES; HOWEVER, IT IS CLEAR THAT A GREATER CONSENSUS IS
NECESSARY FOR FUTURE POLITICAL AND ECONOMIC PROGRESS.

07425 RAHO, S.A.
KOREA AND UNITED STATES: NATIONAL SECURITY
AVAILABLE FROM NTIS, NO. AD-A209 501/6/GAR, MAR 9 89, 50.
THE KOREAN PENINSULA STILL REMAINS A POTENTIAL FLASH
POINT WHICH COULD LEAD TO MAJOR EAST-WEST CONFRONTATION.
UNITED STATES POLICY TOWARD THE REPUBLIC OF KOREA HAS OFTEN
BEEN CHARACTERIZED BY VACILLATION AND UNCERTAINTY. IT IS
IMPERATIVE THAT U.S. STRATEGIES TAKE INTO ACCOUNT THE
CURRENT FRICTIONS BETWEEN THE U.S. AND SOUTH KOREA, AND
ESTABLISH A POLICY WHICH PROTECTS THE REGIONAL INTERESTS OF
OUR ALLIES WHILE MAINTAINING AMERICAN INFLUENCE IN THE
PACIFIC. AS NATIONALISM SWEEPS THROUGH SOUTH KOREA, IT IS
VITAL FOR THE U.S. TO ADDRESS IMPORTANT ISSUES CAUSING
FRICTION BETWEEN OUR COUNTRIES: FORWARD DEPLOYMENT OF U.S.
MILITARY FORCES ON THE PENINSUAL; THE ALLEGED BASING OF
NUCLEAR WEAPONS ON KOREAN SOIL; CONTINUANCE OF A MILITARY
COMMAND STRUCTURE WHICH PLACES A U.S. GENERAL OFFICER IN
CONTROL OF A SIGNIFICANT PORTION OF SOUTH KOREA'S MILITARY
FORCES. THROUGH A VISIONARY ASSESSMENT OF OUR ROLE IN AN
EMERGING MULTIPOLAR WORLD, THE U.S. CAN DEVELOP AN
APPROPRIATE FORCE STRUCTURE AND INTEGRATED STRATEGY WHICH
WILL ENSURE REGIONAL STABILITY WHILE PROVIDING FOR CONTINUED
ECONOMIC AND POLITICAL GROWTH THROUGHOUT SOUTH KOREA, THE
ASIA-PACIFIC REGION AND THE WORLD.

07426 RAHO, S.A. III
KOREA AND AMERICAN NATIONAL SECURITY
PARAMETERS, XIX(3) (SEP 89), 69-80.
THROUGHOUT THE 20TH CENTURY, U.S. POLICY WITH RESPECT TO
KOREA HAS LACKED CONTINUITY AND CONSISTENCY. IN 1954, THE
USA CONCLUDED A MUTUAL DEFENSE TREATY WITH THE REPUBLIC OF
KOREA TO DEMONSTRATE ITS COMMITMENT TO THE ASIAN REGION, BUT
IN 1969 THE NIXON DOCTRINE SEEMED TO PULL THE RUG OUT FROM
UNDER THE TREATY OBLIGATION. UNDER PRESIDENT CARTER, THE USA
FLIRTED WITH THE NOTION OF WITHDRAWING ALL GROUND FORCES
FROM KOREA. BUT BY 1981, THE STRATEGY WAS REVERSED AND THE
AMERICAN MILITARY FORCE STRUCTURE WAS INCREASED. IN 1989,
THE USA IS ONCE AGAIN CONSIDERING A WITHDRAWAL OF TROOPS
FROM THE PENINSULA TO ASSIST IN BALANCING THE FEDERAL BUDGET.

07427 RAI, S.
MARKET ECONOMY AND GENDER PERCEPTION IN POST-MAO CHINA
CHINA REPORT, 24(4) (OCT 88), 463-467.
THE EMERGENCE OF THE 'WOMAN' FROM BEHIND THE
'REVOLUTIONARY WORKER' CAN BE LINKED TO THE MANY CHANGES
THAT HAVE OCCURRED AND HAVE BEEN INTRODUCED IN THE POST-
CULTURAL REVOLUTIONARY PERIOD. THIS ESSAY LOOKS AT THE
ECONOMIC REFORMS PRIMARILY AND THEIR IMPACT ON THE STATUS OF
WOMEN AT HOME AND AT WORK. THE AUTHOR SUGGESTS THAT THE
LOGIC OF MARKET MECHANISM IS NOT AN UNMIXED BLESSING FOR THE
STATUS OF WOMEN IN CHINA; THAT PROBLEMS ARE EMERGING FROM
THE RETREAT OF THE STATE AND OF RADICAL POLITICAL AND SOCIAL
RHETORIC FROM THE PUBLIC SPHERE AND HAVE TO BE RECOGNISED
AND CONFRONTED.

07428 RAIKLIN, E.
ON PEOPLE'S WELFARE IN AGANBEGYAN'S "THE ECONOMIC
CHALLENGE OF PERESTROIKA"
INTERNATIONAL JOURNAL OF SOCIAL ECONOMICS, 16(7) (1989),
16-33.
THE MAJOR OBJECTIVE OF AGANBEGYAN'S BOOK IS TO ENHANCE
ARGUMENTS MADE BY GORBACHEV IN THE LATTER'S "PERESTROIKA:
NEW THINKING FOR OUR COUNTRY AND THE WORLD." LIKE HIS LEADER,
AGANBEGYAN ASSERTS THAT THE ULTIMATE PURPOSE OF PERESTROIKA
IS PEOPLE'S WELFARE AND THAT THE POLICY OF THE ACCELERATION
OF THE SOVIET ECONOMIC DEVELOPMENT IS THE PRINCIPAL MEANS TO
ACHIEVE THE GOAL. THIS ARTICLE CHALLENGES AGANBEGYAN'S CLAIM.
IT ARGUES THAT: (1) GIVEN THE INEFFICIENT AND WASTEFUL
CHARACTER OF THE SOVIET SYSTEM, THE PROJECTED INCREASE IN
THE STANDARD OF LIVING OF THE SOVIET POPULATION COULD BE
ACCOMPLISHED NOW AND NOT IN THE FUTURE; (2) THE ACCELERATION
OF THE ECONOMIC GROWTH AND RESTRUCTURING OF SOVIET SOCIETY
CONTRADICT ONE ANOTHER AND, THUS, MAKE THE ATTAINMENT OF THE
PROCLAIMED GOAL IMPOSSIBLE EVEN IN THE FUTURE, AND (3) THE
FORTHCOMING REFORM OF RETAIL PRICES MORE THAN ANYTHING ELSE
REVEALS THE TRUE, ANTI-CONSUMERIST NATURE OF THE POLICIES OF
THE SOVIET LEADERSHIP.

07429 RAIKLIN, E.
REFLECTIONS ON ECONOMIC ASPECTS OF GORBACHEV'S BOOK
"PERESTROIKA": WISHFUL THINKING FOR A MAKE-BELIEVE WORLD?
INTERNATIONAL JOURNAL OF SOCIAL ECONOMICS, 16(3) (1989),
9-33.
GORBACHEV'S BOOK "PERESTROIKA" IS USED TO EXPLAIN WHY
THE AUTHOR BELIEVES THE NEW POLICY OF RESTRUCTURING OF THE
SOVIET ECONOMY CANNOT AND WILL NOT WORK. THE POLICIES OF
"PERESTROIKA" ARE INTRODUCED AND EVALUATED AND THE EXISTING
SOCIO-ECONOMIC SYSTEM PRESENTED. IT IS CONCLUDED THAT THE
POLICY IS COSMETIC RESTRUCTURING AND GORBACHEV'S DOWNFALL,

LIKE KHRUSCHEV'S, IS ASSURED.

07430 RAIKLIN, E.; MCCORMICK, K.
THE CONDITIONAL VIEW OF THE NEOCLASSICAL AND MARXIST
APPROACHES TO THE CONCEPT OF PRODUCTIVE LABOR
INTERNATIONAL JOURNAL OF SOCIAL ECONOMICS, 16(1) (1989),
13-26.
THE MAJOR REASON FOR THE DIVERGENCE OF VIEWS REGARDING
THE DEFINITION OF PRODUCTIVE LABOUR IS THE FACT THAT THE
CONCEPT IS VIEWED FROM DIFFERENT PERSPECTIVES. FOR EXAMPLE,
NEOCLASSICAL ECONOMISTS SEE A WORLD COMPRISED OF ATOMISTIC
AND SELFISH INDIVIDUALS. IN THIS WORLD, ANY KIND OF LABOUR
PRODUCING ANY GOOD OR SERVICE IS CONSIDERED PRODUCTIVE IF IT
CREATES UTILITY FOR ANYBODY. MARXISTS, ON THE OTHER HAND, DO
NOT REJECT THIS BROAD RELATIONSHIP BETWEEN LABOUR AND
UTILITY BUT DENY THAT ALL ACTIVITIES CREATING UTILITY ARE
PRODUCTIVE. GROUPING INDIVIDUALS INTO SOCIAL CLASSES,
MARXISTS INSIST THAT LABOUR IS PRODUCTIVE ONLY IF IT
CONTRIBUTES TO THE HISTORICAL DEVELOPMENT OF THE DOMINANT
MODE OF PRODUCTION. IN THIS ERA, LABOUR IS PRODUCTIVE ONLY
IF IT GENERATES PROFITS FOR THE CAPITALIST. THE TWO
VIEWPOINTS DO NOT CONTRADICT ONE ANOTHER, BUT ACTUALLY
COMPLEMENT EACH OTHER.

07431 RAIKLIN, E.
THE SOVIET BUDGET DEFICIT: REALITY OR MYTH?
JOURNAL OF SOCIAL, POLITICAL AND ECONOMIC STUDIES, 14(3)
(FAL 89), 299-349.
THE RECENT ADMISSION BY SOVIET FINANCE MINISTER BORIS
GOSTEV THAT THE SOVIETS HAVE A BUDGET DEFICIT PROBLEM RAISES
THE FOLLOWING QUESTIONS: HOW IS THE SOVIET BUDGET
DETERMINED? WHAT IS THE MEANING OF ITS NEGATIVE OR POSITIVE
RESIDUAL? WHAT HAVE BEEN THE LATTER'S ACTUAL SIZES DURING
THE LAST DECADE? WHY DID THE TIMING OF THE GOSTEV REVELATION
FALL AT THE END OF THE YEAR 1988?

07432 RAIS, RASUL B
PAKISTAN IN 1988: FROM COMMAND TO CONCILIATION POLITICS
ASIAN SURVEY, XXIX(2) (FEB 89), 199-208.
1988 SIGNALED A SIGNIFICANT SHIFT IN PAKISTANI POLITICS.
FOLLOWING THE DEATH OF GENERAL ZIA UL-HAQ AND THE ENSUING
GENERAL ELECTIONS GALVANIZED THE NATION. BENAZIR BHUTTO AND
THE PAKISTAN PEOPLE'S PARTY WERE THE OVERALL WINNERS IN THE
ELECTIONS, BUT THEY DO NOT WIELD ENOUGH POLITICAL POWER TO
IMPLEMENT THEIR POLICIES AT WILL. OPPOSITION GROUPS LED BY
THE POWERFUL ISLAMIC DEMOCRATIC ALLIANCE WILL HAVE DEMANDS
THAT REQUIRE COMPROMISE AND CONSENSUS POLITICS. THE BEST
HOPE FOR DEMOCRACY AND CONSTITUTIONAL LAW DEPEND ON THE
GROUP'S ABILITY TO COMPROMISE AND OVERCOME POLITICAL
DIFFERENCES.

07433 RAJ, S.L.
A MAN-CENTERED PHILOSOPHY: REFLECTIONS ON JP'S CONCEPT OF
MAN
INDIAN JOURNAL OF POLITICAL SCIENCE, L(1) (JAN 89), 74-93.
THIS ESSAY EXAMINES THE CONCEPT OF MAN AS THE FOUNDATION
OF JAYAPRAKASH NARAYAN'S PHILOSOPHY AND PROVIDES THE
NECESSARY MATRIX FOR A CORRECT UNDERSTANDING OF HIS SOCIAL,
ECONOMIC, POLITICAL, AND MORAL PHILOSOPHY. THE FIRST SECTION
DEALS WITH THE NATURE OF MAN. THE SECOND PART ANALYZES THE
RELATIONSHIP BETWEEN THE INDIVIDUAL AND SOCIETY, INCLUDING
THE BASIC RIGHTS OF THE INDIVIDUAL THAT ARISE IN THE CONTEXT
OF HIS SOCIAL NATURE. THE FINAL SECTION EXAMINES NARAYAN'S
VIEWS ON THE SPIRITUAL DIMENSION OF MAN AND HIS ORIENTATION
TOWARDS TRANSCENDENTAL MATTERS.

07434 RAJAB, A.; GREENING, J.; MINSHULL, P.; MSETEKA, B.
SOUTH SURVEY: TANZANIA
SOUTH, (110) (DEC 89), 89-100.
THE DISMANTLING OF "UJAMAA," TANZANIA'S BRAND OF
SOCIALISM, SEEMS TO BE WELL UNDERWAY AS PRESIDENT ALI HASSAN
MWINYI SLOWLY GAINS THE UPPER HAND IN THE NATIONAL
IDEOLOGICAL DEBATE. RESULTS FROM THE 1986 IFM-BACKED
ECONOMIC REFORM PROGRAM ARE BEGINNING TO BE EVIDENT, WITH
INCREASING EXPORTS AND ECONOMIC GROWTH. BUT WESTERN DONORS
ARE STILL ASKING FOR MORE LIBERALIZATION, INCLUDING A
FURTHER DEVALUATION OF THE SHILLING.

07435 RAJGHATTA, C.
BACK FROM THE BRINK
INDIA TODAY, 14(15) (AUG 89), 26-29.
THIS REPORT IS ABOUT THE MAJOR BREAKTHROUGH ACHIEVED BY
INDIA AND SRI LANKA IN THE DEADLOCK OVER IPKE WITHDRAWAL
WITH NEW DELHI AGREEING FOR A TOKEN PULL-OUT AND COLOMBO
CONSENTING TO SEND A HIGH-LEVEL DELEGATION FOR TALKS ON
OTHER DETAILS. IT IS AN ON THE SPOT REPORT PLUS AN INTERVIEW
WITH J.R. JAYEWARDENE.

07436 RAJGHATTA, C.
KARNATAKA: CLAMBERING FOR THE CROWN
INDIA TODAY, XIV(10) (MAY 89), 24-25.
IN KARNSTAKA, DESPITE THE FRATRICIDAL NATURE OF THE
STATE CONGRESS (I), THE INCUMBENT, PATIL, APPEARS TO HAVE
EMERGED UNSCATHED SO FAR. IN UPCOMING ELECTIONS OF

PHENOMENAL STAKES THIS RELATIVE STABILITY MAY PROVE THE
TRUMP CARD IN CONGRESS (I) S' PLAY FOR JANATA DAL
CONSTITUENCY.

07437 RAJGHATTA, C.
KARNATAKA: PEOPLE POWER
INDIA TODAY, XIV(11) (JUN 89), 27.
THIS ARTICLE DESCRIBES THE SUCCESS OF PANCHAYATI RAY.
SINCE ITS INCEPTION IN EARLY 1987, VILLAGES ARE NOT RULED BY
REMOTE CONTROL BY MLA'S, MINISTERS OF BUREACRATS BUT BY
ELECTED OFFICIALS IN DISTRICT HEADQUARTERS. THE STATE
GOVERNMENT HAS DIVESTED NEARLY THIRTY PERCENT OF ITS FUNDS
TO THEM, AND PLANNING IS CLOSER TO THE PEOPLE THAN EVER
BEFORE. WITH ELECTIONS DRAWING NEAR, EACH PARTY IS
CLAMOURING TO JUMP ON THE BANDWAGON OF SUCCESS AND CLAIM
CREDIT.

07438 RAJGHATTA, C.
PARTING WAYS
INDIA TODAY, XIV(3) (FEB 89), 40-43.
DISSIDENT LEADER H.D. DEVE GOWDA HAS QUIT KARNATAKA'S
JANATA DAL GOVERNMENT, SIGNALLING THE BIRTH OF NEW POLITICAL
TURMOIL IN THE STATE. DEVE GOWDA'S DECISION BROUGHT THE
FIRST SPLIT IN THE GOVERNMENT SINCE 1985, BUT IT DOES NOT
POSE AN IMMEDIATE THREAT TO THE BOMMAI MINISTRY.

07439 RAKE, A.
A RAY OF HOPE?
NEW AFRICAN, (257) (FEB 89), 16-17.
AFTER THE AGREEMENT-IN-PRINCIPLE FOR A UN-SUPERVISED
SETTLEMENT IN WESTERN SAHARA WAS REACHED IN AUGUST 1988,
EVERYTHING SEEMED TO COME TO A HALT. POLISARIO FOUND THAT
THE TERMS WERE STACKED HEAVILY AGAINST IT AND MOROCCO
REFUSED DIRECT NEGOTIATIONS WITH A REBEL GROUP THAT IT DID
NOT RECOGNIZE. BUT, UNDER INTENSE INTERNATIONAL PRESSURE,
KING HASSAN HAS RELENTED AND PROPER NEGOTIATIONS ARE
EXPECTED TO BE FORTHCOMING.

07440 RAKE, A.
BENGUELA LIFELINE OF HOPE
NEW AFRICAN, (263) (AUG 89), 13.
THIS IS A REPORT OF THE PROGRESS BEING MADE TOWARD THE
REOPENING OF THE MAIN RAILWAY LINE RUNNING ACROSS THE CENTER
OF ANGOLA. SINCE IT DEPENDS ON THE FUTURE OF THE GBADOLITE
AGREEMENT, THIS IS OF GREAT IMPORTANCE TO ANGOLA.
THE HISTORY OF THIS LINE IS DETAILED, AS WELL AS THE ATTEMPTS TO
REOPEN THE LINE.

07441 RAKE, A.
ELECTION FEVER
NEW AFRICAN, (260) (MAY 89), 21-23.
THE INDEPENDENCE ELECTIONS ARE NOT DUE UNTIL NOVEMBER,
BUT THE GLOVES ARE ALREADY OFF IN THE NAMIBIAN CAMPAIGN,
WITH SWAPO TRYING TO CONSOLIDATE ITS POPULARITY AND THE
POLICE TRYING TO SMASH THE SWAPO RALLIES. AS ELECTION FEVER
MOUNTS WITH ACCUSATIONS BY BOTH SIDES OVER INTIMIDATION AND
IRREGULARITIES, THE UNITED NATIONS IS TRYING TO GET A GRIP
ON THE SITUATION, AND THE SMALL POLITICAL PARTIES ARE
SCRAMBLING TO FORM NEW ALLIANCES.

07442 RAKE, A.
IDI AMIN: "I DID NOT KILL"
NEW AFRICAN, (256) (JAN 89), 9-13.
IDI AMIN IS TRYING TO CLEAR HIS NAME, PARTICULARLY
AGAINST EVIDENCE PRESENTED AT THE UGANDA HUMAN RIGHTS
COMMISSION. THERE, WITNESSES HAVE SAID THAT HE WAS
RESPONSIBLE FOR THE DEATH OF THE ANGLICAN ARCHBISHOP JANAN
LUWUM AND TWO OTHER MINISTERS. BUT AMIN IS ADAMANT THAT HE
HAD NO PART IN THE MURDERS.

07443 RAKE, A.
MARADONA'S DRIBBLE TO DEMOCRACY
NEW AFRICAN, (267) (DEC 89), 21.
PRESIDENT BABANGIDA OF NIGERIA, SHOCKED HIS COUNTRY IN A
SPEECH IN OCTOBER 1989. HE BANNED ALL OLD POLITICAL PARTIES,
SEALED THEIR OFFICES, AND CONFISCATED THEIR ASSETS. THE
OBJECTIVE IS TO ALLOW ORDINARY PEOPLE AND NON-DISQUALIFIED,
NEW STYLE POLITICANS TO EMERGE THROUGH THE NEW SYSTEM.
EVERYONE WILL HAVE TO JOIN THE NEW PARTIES IN THEIR LOCAL
GOVERNMENT AREAS.

07444 RAKE, A.
PEACE BLOOMS IN AFRICA
NEW AFRICAN, (263) (AUG 89), 10-12.
THIS ARTICLE REPORTS ON THE NEW HOPE FOR PEACE IN AFRICA.
IT EXAMINES ANGOLA, NAMIBIA, ETHIOPIA, MOZAMBIQUE, SOUTH
AFRICA AND SUDAN WHERE PROMISES HAVE BEEN MADE TO SETTLE
WARS AND DISPUTES, AND DEFINITE PROGRESS HAS BEEN MADE.
DETAILED ARE THE REASONS FOR THIS CHANGE IN POLICY AND HOPES
FOR THE FUTURE, ALSO THE RECENT AGREEMENTS AND THE NEWLY
ESTABLISHED MEDIATION COMMISSION.

07445 RAKE, A.
PROMISES, PROMISES

NEW AFRICAN, (258) (MAR 89), 20-21.
GENERAL MOHAMED ALI SAMATAR HAS ANNOUNCED A TOTAL CHANGE
IN SOMALI POLICIES. HE HAS PROMISED COMPLETE AMNESTY FOR ALL
POLITICAL PRISONERS. THE RECONSTRUCTION AND RESTORATION OF
THE WAR TORN NORTHERN REGION, AND REVOLUTIONARY CHANGES IN
ECONOMIC POLICY TOWARDS A FREE MARKET SYSTEM.

07446 RAKE, A.
SAVIMBI WINS ROUND 13
NEW AFRICAN, (JAN 88), 16-17.
THIS ARTICLE REPORTS ON THE ONGOING WAR BETWEEN JONAS
SAVIMBI AND THE ANGOLAN FAPLA ARMY. IT EXAMINES THE RECENT
VICTORY BY SAVIMBI, POSSIBLE ONLY THROUGH THE SUPPORT OF HIS
SOUTH AFRICAN ALLIES, AS BEING ONLY A STALEMATE, WITH THE
WAR BY NO MEANS WON YET.

07447 RAKE, A.
TIMETABLE FOR NAMIBIAN INDEPENDENCE
NEW AFRICAN, (256) (JAN 89), 26.
WHEN NAMIBIA GAINS ITS FREEDOM, 500 YEARS OF COLONIALISM
IN AFRICA WILL END. NAMIBIAN INDEPENDENCE WILL FOLLOW SEVEN
MONTHS AFTER THE IMPLEMENTATION OF RESOLUTION 435 AND IS
EXPECTED BY 1990.

07448 RAKE, A.
WHAT NEXT NAMIBIA?
NEW AFRICAN, (257) (FEB 89), 9-11.
NAMIBIA IS ON ITS WAY TO INDEPENDENCE, BUT MANY CHANGES
ARE REQUIRED. THERE MUST BE A CEASE-FIRE BETWEEN SOUTH
AFRICA AND SWAPO, THE WITHDRAWAL OF SOUTH AFRICAN TROOPS,
FREE AND FAIR ELECTIONS, AND THE ESTABLISHMENT OF A
CONSTITUTIONAL ASSEMBLY.

07449 RAKE, A.
WILL SWAPO WIN?
NEW AFRICAN, (266) (NOV 89), 36-37.
THIS ARTICLE REPORTS ON THE IMMINENT ELECTIONS IN NAMBIA
WHERE SWAPO WILL UNDOUBTEDLY WIN. IT ASKS THE QUESTION, "BY
HOW MUCH?", AS IT WONDERS IF THE EVIDENCE OF TERRIBLE
TREATMENT AT SWAPO CAMPS WILL HAVE ANY EFFECT,

07450 RAKE, M.
WAR WORSENS, FAMINE WORSENS
AFRICAN BUSINESS, (JUN 88), 21-22.
THIS ARTICLE EXPLORES THE POLITICAL RAMIFICATIONS OF
ETHOPIA'S REFUSAL TO ALLOW OUTSIDE RELIEF EFFORTS TO
CONTINUE THERE. THE CONCLUSION THAT STARVATION AND SCORCHED
EARTH ARE BEING USED AS WEAPONS TO DEFEAT THE REBELLION IS
DRAWN. SUDAN'S REFUGEE POLICY IS EXAMINED.

07451 RAKOWSKI, M.F.
EXPOSE OF GOVERNMENT POLICY
POLISH PERSPECTIVES, XXXII(1) (1989), 5-13.
POLAND IS A COUNTRY OF MILLIONS OF PEOPLE DESIRING TO
WORK HARD AND PRODUCTIVELY. IT IS THE CONCERN OF THE
GOVERNMENT TO CREATE CONDITIONS CONDUCIVE TO PREVENTING ANY
PHYSICAL OR MENTAL EFFORT FROM GOING TO WASTE. THE
GOVERNMENT'S MISSION INCLUDES BREAKING DOWN BARRIERS,
OBSTACLES, AND BUREAUCRATIC CONSTRAINTS TO CREATE CONDITIONS
FOR INITIATIVE AND ENTREPRENEURSHIP.

07452 RAKOWSKI, M.F.
OUR ACTIONS ARE DEFINED BY THE WELL-BEING OF POLAND
CONTEMPORARY POLAND, XXII(10) (1989), 1-5.
M.F. RAKOWSKI, THE FIRST SECRETARY OF THE POLISH UNITED
WORKERS' PARTY CC, ADDRESSED THE POLISH PEOPLE ON SEPT. 13,
1989, ONE DAY AFTER THE APPOINTMENT OF THE NEW NATIONAL
GOVERNMENT. HE PRESENTED HIS VIEW OF THE CURRENT POLITICAL
SITUATION AND THE STATUS OF THE PUWP.

07453 RAMATI, Y.
A PLO STATE AND ISRAEL'S SECURITY
MIDSTREAM, XXXV(3) (APR 89), 3-6.
SOVIET AND ARAB PROPAGANDA-MASSIVELY FINANCED, EXPERTLY
EXECUTED, AND REINFORCED BY THE POLITICAL DIVISIONS AMONG
ISRAELI AND AMERICAN JEWS-HAS ACCOMPLISHED ITS MAIN
OBJECTIVE: THE ARAB-ISRAELI CONFLICT HAS BEEN TRANSMOGRIFIED
INTO A CONFLICT BETWEEN "PALESTINIANS" AND "ISRAELIS." THE
GENERAL ACCEPTANCE OF ARAB AND SOVIET PROPAGANDA IN THE WEST
HAS DISTORTED ATTITUDES TOWARDS ISRAEL'S SECURITY PROBLEMS,
EXAGGERATING THE DANGER FROM THE PLO. THE REAL THREAT TO
ISRAEL'S EXISTENCE COMES FROM THE ARAB STATES IN GENERAL AND
FROM SYRIA, JORDAN, IRAQ, AND EGYPT IN PARTICULAR.

07454 RAMATI, Y.
JEWISH DESTINY AND MR. BAKER
MIDSTREAM, XXXV(6) (AUG 89), 3-6.
U.S. SECRETARY OF STATE JAMES BAKER'S CONTROVERSIAL
SPEECH TO AIPAC ON MAY 22, 1989, EVOKED A FLURRY OF CRITICAL
COMMENT FROM ISRAEL AND ISRAEL'S FRIENDS. THE ISRAELIS
BELIEVED THAT THE POLICY EXPOUNDED IN THE SPEECH WOULD PRE-
DETERMINE THE OUTCOME OF FUTURE NEGOTIATIONS IN THE ARABS'
FAVOR. THEY FELT THAT THEY WERE NOW DEALING WITH AN
UNFRIENDLY AMERICAN ADMINISTRATION, WHICH HAD EMBARKED ON A

COURSE OF GRADUALLY ABANDONING ISRAEL'S INTERESTS. BUT A
CAREFUL EXAMINATION OF BAKER'S SPEECH REVEALS THAT THIS
EVALUATION IS SUPERFICIAL AND PROBABLY INCORRECT.

07455 RAMAZANI, R., K.
IRAN'S FOREING POLICY: CONTENDING ORIENTATIONS
MIDDLE EAST JOURNAL, 43(2) (SPR 89), 202-217.
THE US VIEWS OF IRAN'S FOREING POLICY HAVE GENERALLY
BEEN RATHER SIMPLISTIC. SOME VIEW IT AS IF IT WERE A MIRROR
IMAGE OF ITS DOMESTIC POLITICS, OTHERS SEE IT MAINLY IN
TERMS OF GEOPOLITICS. AN EXAMINATION OF IRAN'S WORDS AND
DEEDS AND ITS THOERIES AND PRACTICES MAKES CLEAR THAT
TEHRAN'S FOREIGN POLICY HAS BEEN SHAPED LARGELY BY AN ACUTE
INTERPLAY BETWEEN ITS DOMESTIC SITUATION, NOT MERELY
FACTIONAL POLITICS, AND ITS EXTERNAL ENVIRONMENT, NOT MERELY
SUPERPOWER BEHAVIOR. THE ARTICLE ATTEMPTS TO IDENTIFY THE
MAIN ORIENTATIONS OF IRAN'S FOREIGN POLICY AND SHED SOME
FRESH LIGHT ON SOME OLDER INTERPRETATIONS AS TO WHY IRAN
TOOK US HOSTAGES. AND WHY IT CONTINUED THE WAR WITH IRAQ
WHEN BOTH SITUATIONS COULD HAVE BEEN AVERTED OR ENDED FAR
EARLIER THAN THEY WERE.

07456 RAMELSON, B.; DRAGANOV, D.
INTERNATIONALISM TODAY: THE DEBATE CONTINUES
WORLD MARXIST REVIEW, 32(8) (AUG 89), 58-61.
THE ARTICLE "THE NEW INTERNATIONALISM: A DRAMA WITH A
HAPPY ENDING," BASED ON A DIALOGUE BETWEEN ANTONIO RUBBI, A
MEMBER OF LEADERSHIP OF THE ITALIAN COMMUNIST PARTY, AND
GRIGORY VODOLAZOV, PUBLISHED IN THE APRIL 1989 ISSUE OF WMR
ELICITED RESPONSES FROM TWO READERS. BERT RAMELSON FROM
GREAT BRITAIN PROTESTS THAT THE CASE OF PROLETARIAN
INTERNATIONALISM AND NEW NATIONALISM SHOULD NOT BE AN
"EITHER OR" SITUATION. DRAGOMIR DRAGA OF FROM BULGARIA
SUPPORTS NEW NATIONALISM AND TELLS WHY.

07457 RAMESH, M.
THE POLITICS OF INDUSTRIAL ADJUSTMENT IN CANADA: THE CASE
OF THE FOOTWEAR INDUSTRY
DISSERTATION ABSTRACTS INTERNATIONAL, 49(12) (JUN 89),
3867-A.
THE AUTHOR DESCRIBES THE CANADIAN GOVERNMENT'S POLICY
REGARDING THE DOMESTIC FOOTWEAR INDUSTRY FROM 1970 TO 1985
AND ENDEAVORS TO EXPLAIN THE FORCES THAT SHAPED IT. HE
POSTULATES THAT THE RELATIONSHIPS WITHIN AND AMONG STATE,
SOCIETAL, AND INTERNATIONAL POLITICAL-ECONOMIC INSTITUTIONS
ARE THE KEY DETERMINANTS OF ECONOMIC POLICY. HE ARGUES THAT
THE CANADIAN POLICY WAS SHAPED BY THE CONFLICTS WITHIN AND
AMONG THE STATE, MANUFACTURING, AND TRADING INTERESTS
CONDITIONED BY THE INTERNATIONAL POLITICAL ECONOMY.

07458 RAMET, P.
CATHOLICS UNDER COMMUNISM: THE CASE OF CZECHOSLOVAKIA
THE CHRISTIAN CENTURY, 106(6) (FEB 89), 202-205.
COMMUNIST STRATEGY TOWARD THE CATHOLIC CHURCH IN
CZECHOSLOVAKIA HAS HAD FIVE CENTRAL FEATURES. (1) THE
COMMUNISTS SMASHED THE CHURCH INFRASTRUCTURE. (2) THEY
SOUGHT TO CONTROL THE REMAINING CHURCH INSTITUTIONS AND, AT
THE SAME TIME, TO CREATE A SERIES OF BOGUS CATHOLIC
INSTITUTIONS. (3) THE COMMUNIST PARTY LAUNCHED A DRIVE TO
UNDERCUT POPULAR SUPPORT FOR THE CLERGY AND THE CHURCH. (4)
THE COMMUNISTS FOSTERED DISTRUST BETWEEN CATHOLICS AND NON-
CATHOLICS. (5) THEY ASPIRED TO SOW DIVISION WITHIN THE RANKS
OF THE CLERGY ITSELF.

07459 RAMET, P.
KOSOVO AND THE LIMITS OF YUGOSLAV SOCIALIST PATRIOTISM
CANADIAN REVIEW OF STUDIES IN NATIONALISM, XVI(1-2) (1989),
227-250.
SINCE THE TURBULENT DAYS OF APRIL 1981, WHEN KOSOVO WAS
SHAKEN BY WIDESPREAD RIOTING, THE PROVINCE HAS DEEPLY
TROUBLED PARTY LEADERS IN BELGRADE AND AROUSED FEARS THAT
THE OLD POLITICAL FORMULAS. DEVELOPED IN THE 1960'S, MAY BE
DISSOLVING. IN THE RESULTING UNCERTAINTY, THE AUTHORITIES
HAVE ABANDONED THEIR ONCE-CONCILIATORY POSTURE VIS-A-VIS THE
DISSATISFIED ALBANIAN RESIDENTS OF KOSOVO AND ADOPTED A NEW
HARD LINE, EVEN WHILE THE SITUATION SLIPS FURTHER OUT OF
CONTROL.

07460 RAMIREZ, M. D.
THE COMPOSITION OF GOVERNMENT SPENDING AND THE ASSIGNMENTS
OF INSTRUMENTS TO TARGETS IN A SMALL OPEN ECONOMY
SOUTHERN ECONOMIC JOURNAL, 55(2) (OCT 88), 432-442.
THIS PAPER INVESTIGATES THE RELATIONSHIP BETWEEN POLICY
INSTRUMENTS AND DESIRED TARGET LEVELS IN A SMALL OPEN
ECONOMY WHEN GOVERNMENT AND PRIVATE SPENDING ARE DEPENDENT
ON ONE ANOTHER. FIRST, THE CONCEPTUAL BASIS FOR THE
INCLUSION OF GOVERNMENT SPENDING AS AN ARGUMENT IN THE
PRIVATE CONSUMPTION AND INVESTMENT FUNCTIONS IS EXAMINED FOR
BOTH A FIXED AND FLEXIBLE EXCHANGE RATE REGIME. NEXT, IT IS
SHOWN THAT IN THE LIMITING CASE OF PERFECT CAPITAL MOBILITY,
THE SIGNS AND/OR MAGNITUDES OF THE MULTIPLIERS OF INTEREST
ARE NO LONGER UNAMBIGUOUS. IN VIEW OF THIS, HE SHOW THAT A
GAP ARISES BETWEEN THE PERCEIVED AND ACTUAL MODELS UNDER
WHICH THE MONETARY AUTHORITIES OPERATE. THUS, THE PAPER

OUTLINES HOW THE ASSIGNMENT PROBLEM IS MODIFIED UNDER
CONDITIONS OF POLICY INSTRUMENT IN THE FORM OF THE
UNCERTAINTY. IT IS SHOWN THAT THE PRESENCE OF AN ADDITIONAL
COMPOSITION OF GOVERNMENT SPENDING MAY RENDER THE ASSIGNMENT
PROBLEM MORE TRACTABLE IN AN OPEN ECOMOMY SETTING.

07461 RAMIREZ, S.
THE KID FROM NIQUINOHOMO
LATIN AMERICAN PERSPECTIVES, 16(3) (SUM 89), 48-82.
THIS ARTICLE DESCRIBES THE ORIGINS OF SANDINISMO
NATIONALISM IN A DETAILED ACCOUNT OF THE CONDITIONS THAT
SPAWNED THIS REVOLUTIONARY MOVEMENT. IT IS THE STORY OF THE
STRUGGLES OF GENERAL AUGUSTO CESAR SANDINO AGAINST NORTH
AMERICAN IMPERIALISM.

07462 RAMNARINE, D. J.
THE POLITICAL SIGNIFICANCE OF THE UNITED STATES CARIBBEAN
BASIN INITIATIVE
DISSERTATION ABSTRACTS INTERNATIONAL, 49(9) (MAR 89),
2799-A.
CHAPTERS ONE AND TWO OUTLINE THE PROVISIONS AND
DEVELOPMENTAL PHILOSOPHY OF THE CBI. CHAPTER THREE EXAMINES
THE CBI'S PERFORMANCE CHAPTER FOUR PRESENTS AN OVERVIEW OF
US CONTINENTAL AND EXTRACONTINENTAL EXPANSION. CHAPTER FIVE
EXAMINES THE WORLD VIEW OF THE REAGAN ADMINISTRATION AND ITS
MANIFESTATIONS IN THE CARIBBEAN BASIN. CHAPTER SIX
DEMONSTRATES THE POLITICAL REALITIES OF THE CBI.

07463 RAMOS, V.
BANNER YEAR FOR AQUINO IN FIGHTING COMMUNIST INSURGENCY
PACIFIC DEFENCE REPORTER, 16(5) (NOV 89), 47-49.
DESPITE THE FACT THAT THE PHILIPPINES FACES THE MOST
FORMIDABLE INTERNAL THREATS, IT CONTINUES TO HAVE ONE OF THE
MOST THINLY SPREAD ARMED FORCES AMONG THE ASEAN COUNTRIES -
ALLOTTED THE LOWEST AMOUNT BUDGETED PER SOLDIER IN THE
REGION. THIS ARTICLE DESCRIBES HOW, EVEN IN THE FACE OF
HIGHLY STRINGENT FISCAL CONSTRAINTS, THE ARMED FORCES OF THE
PHILIPPINES (AFP), HAVE INCREASED THE MOMENTUM, PURSUED THE
INITIATIVE, AND KEPT THEIR FIGHTING SPIRIT IN THE STRUGGLE
AGAINST THE ENEMIES OF THE REPUBLIC, PROPELLED BY WHAT
PRESIDENT AQUINO DESCRIBES AS "A LONG HISTORY OF VALOR AND A
STEEP LOYALTY TO THE CONSTITUTION."

07464 RAMPHAL, S.
SOVEREIGN DEFAULT: A BACKWARD GLANCE
THIRD WORLD QUARTERLY, 11(2) (APR 89), 63-75.
THE THIRD WORLD DEBT CRISIS HAS RAISED THE SPECTRE OF
SOVEREIGN DEFAULT AS ONE WAY OUT. THIS ESSAY REVIEWS THE
MASS OF HISTORICAL MATERIAL ON THE CONSEQUENCES OF
DEFAULTING, FOCUSING ON MAJOR PHASES OF LENDING AND DEFAULT
IN THE NINETEENTH CENTURY AND IN THE INTER-WAR PERIOD OF THE
TWENTIETH CENTURY.

07465 RAMPHELE, M.
THE DYNAMICS OF GENDER POLITICS IN THE HOSTELS OF CAPETOWN:
ANOTHER LEGACY OF THE SOUTH AFRICAN MIGRANT LABOUR SYSTEM
JOURNAL OF SOUTHERN AFRICAN STUDIES, 15(3) (APR 89),
393-414.
THIS PAPER EXAMINES THE DYNAMICS OF GENDER POLITICS AS
PLAYED OUT IN THE CHALLENGING ENVIRONMENT OF SUPPOSEDLY
SINGLE-SEX HOSTELS IN THE WESTERN CAPE. IN PARTICULAR, IT
FOCUSES ON HOW THIS DYNAMIC IS SHAPED BY THE EXPLOITATIVE
SYSTEM OF RACIAL DISCRIMINATION, ECONOMIC DEPRIVATION AND
THE MANIPULATION OF 'TRADITION' AS A RESOURCE FOR THE SOCIAL
CONTROL OF WOMEN BY MEN. 'TRADITION' HERE DENOTES A
RECONSTRUCTION OF THE PAST AS REPRESENTING A REALITY THAT IS
UNCHALLENGEABLE AND USED TO LEGITIMATE THE PERPETUATION OF
CERTAIN BEHAVIOURAL PATTERNS FAVOURABLE TO MEN.

07466 RAMSAY, W.M.
THE WALL OF SEPARATION: WHY CHURCHES SHOULD SUPPORT IT
CHURCH AND STATE, 42(7) (JUL 89), 19 (163)-20 (164).
THE AUTHOR PRESENTS SIX ARGUMENTS EXPLAINING WHY
RELIGIOUS PEOPLE WHO WANT THE UNITED STATES TO BE A GODLY
NATION SHOULD SEEK TO PRESERVE THE WALL OF SEPARATION
BETWEEN CHURCH AND STATE.

07467 RAMSDEN, J.; WORCESTER, R.W.
ADAPTING TO THE POSTWAR CONSENSUS: CONSERVATIVE
CONTEMPORARY RECORD, 3(2) (NOV 89), 11-13.
THIS SYMPOSIUM FOCUSES ON THE TWO CANADIAN RADICAL
GOVERNMENTS SINCE 1945: THE LABOUR GOVERNMENT OF 1945-51
WHICH ESTABLISHED POSTWAR CONCENSUS; AND THE CONSERVATIVE
GOVERNMENT SINCE 1979, WHICH HAS LARGELY DISMANTLED IT. JOHN
RAMSDEN EXAMINES HOW THE CONSERVATIVES ADAPTED THEMSELVES TO
THE LABOR CONSENSUS. IT EXPLORES FOREIGN POLICY PROBLEMS FOR
THE CONSERVATIVES AND HOW THE FOREIGN LEGACY WAS OVERCOME.
IT ALSO EXAMINES DOMESTIC POLICY PROBLEMS, THE REFORMATION
AND MODERNIZATION OF CONSERVATIVE ORGANIZATION AND POLICY.

07468 RAN, N.; RAN, B.
CUT IN CONVENTIONAL ARMS HOPEFUL IN EUROPE
BEIJING REVIEW, 32(47) (NOV 89), 9-11.
NEGOTIATORS HAVE ENTERED THE ALL-IMPORTANT FOURTH ROUND

OF TALKS TO REDUCE CONVENTIONAL WEAPONS IN EUROPE. THE TALKS
COME AT A TIME WHEN THE INTERNATIONAL SITUATION IS
EXPERIENCING MANY CHANGES. MILITARY HOSTILITY BETWEEN THE
EAST AND WEST HAS EASED, BUT POLITICAL UNREST AND ECONOMIC
HARDSHIPS HAVE INCREASED IN SOME COUNTRIES. NATO AND THE
WARSAW PACT ARE ATTEMPTING TO IMPROVE SECURITY CONDITIONS
AND CUT THE HUGE COST OF THE ARMS RACE.

07469 RANADE, S.
A COMMUNIST PERSPECTIVE ON DEVELOPMENT STRATEGY FOR RURAL
INDIA
JOURNAL OF PEASANT STUDIES, 16(4) (JUL 89), 542-574.
THIS ARTICLE EXAMINES THE STRATEGY OF THE COMMUNIST
PARTY OF INDIA (MARXIST) FOR DEVELOPING RURAL INDIA. IT
ORIGINATED IN AN EXPLORATION OF SOME OF THE EFFORTS BEING
MADE BY THE GOVERNMENT OF INDIA TO REDISTRIBUTE INCOME
OPPORTUNITIES IN RURAL INDIA, SPECIFICALLY THROUGH RURAL
WORK PROGRAMS AND THE INTEGRATED RURAL DEVELOPMENT PROGRAM.

07470 RAND, R.
PERESTROIKA UP CLOSE
WILSON QUARTERLY, XIII(2) (SPR 89), 51-58.
THE FAILURE OF PERESTROIKA JUMPS OUT AND TOUCHES THE
AVERAGE MOSCOW RESIDENT DAY IN AND DAY OUT, LIKE AN ITCH
THAT WON'T GO AWAY. AS THE SOVIET CITIZENS LIKE TO SAY,
PERESTROIKA IS "ALL ON PAPER. "THEY CAN READ ABOUT IT IN THE
NEWSPAPER OR FOLLOW ITS PURPOTED COURSE ON TELEVISION, BUT
THE PLAIN TRUTH IS THEY HAVEN'T SEEN ANY BENEFIT YET. THIS
MAKES PERESTROIKA, IN THE VIEW OF MANY MUSCOVITES, YET
ANOTHER IN A LONG SERIES OF EMPTY POLITICAL SLOGANS
PROMULGATED FROM ON HIGH.

07471 RANDALL, M.
WHEN THE IMAGINATION OF THE WRITER IS CONFRONTED BY THE
IMAGINATION OF THE STATE
LATIN AMERICAN PERSPECTIVES, 16(2) (SPR 89), 115-123.
MARGARET RANDALL WRITES OF HER EXPERIENCE OF BEING
DENIED THE STATUS OF PERMANENT RESIDENCY IN THE US ON THE
BASIS OF HER WRITTEN OPINIONS. SHE SEEKS TO DISPEL THE MYTH
OF COMPLETE FREEDOM OF EXPRESSION IN THE UNITED STATES.

07472 RANDALL, R.; WILSON, C.
THE IMPACT OF FEDERALLY IMPOSED STRESS UPON LOCAL-
GOVERNMENT AND NONPROFIT ORGANIZATIONS
ADMINISTRATION AND SOCIETY, 21(1) (MAY 89), 3-19.
THE REAGAN ADMINISTRATION'S DOMESTIC BUDGET CUTS HAVE
IMPOSED SEVERE FISCAL STRESS UPON LOCAL-GOVERNMENT AND
NONPROFIT AGENCIES. THE RESPONSES TO THIS STRESS BY
ORGANIZATIONS IN NORTHWEST OHIO ARE ANALYZED IN THIS STUDY.
COMPARED TO LOCAL-GOVERNMENT AGENCIES, THE FEDERAL FISCAL
CHANGES HAD THE GREATER IMPACT UPON NONPROFIT AGENCIES,
WHICH SEARCHED MORE ACTIVELY FOR ALTERNATIVE FUNDING SOURCES,
VARIED INTERNAL PROCESS MORE DRAMATICALLY, MADE PROGRAMS
MORE READILY, AND CAST ABOUT FOR MORE EFFECTIVE MANAGEMENT
TECHNIQUES.

07473 RANDALL, S.
DEBATING ABORTION
STATE LEGISLATURES, 15(9) (OCT 89), 26-28.
THE SUPREME COURT'S WEBSTER VS. REPRODUCTIVE HEALTH
SERVICES DECISION HAS TOSSED THE ABORTION ISSUE BACK TO THE
STATES, SIGNALING THE START OF A MAJOR STRUGGLE ON STATE
LEGISLATIVE FLOORS AND AT THE POLLS.

07474 RANDALL, S.
SENSIBLE SENTENCING
STATE LEGISLATURES, 15(1) (JAN 89), 14-18.
WITH CRIMINAL JUSTICE COSTS THE FASTEST-GROWING SEGMENT
OF MOST STATE BUDGETS, LEGISLATORS ARE SEARCHING FOR WAYS TO
RESPOND TO THE SHORTCOMINGS OF THEIR CURRENT SYSTEMS IN WAYS
THAT SAVE MONEY. ONE WAY IS TO RESERVE SCARCE AND EXPENSIVE
PRISON SLOTS FOR VIOLENT AND DANGEROUS OFFENDERS WHILE
PUNISHING LESS-DANGEROUS LAWBREAKERS IN OTHER WAYS.

07475 RANIS, G.
THE ROLE OF INSTITUTIONS IN TRANSITION GROWTH: THE EAST
ASIAN NEWLY INDUSTRIALIZING COUNTRIES
WORLD DEVELOPMENT, 17(9) (SEP 89), 1443-1453.
THIS PAPER REJECTS BOTH THE CLAIMS OF THOSE WHO SEE THE
EAST ASIAN STORY AS ONE OF THE APPLICATION OF PURE LAISSEZ-
FAIRE AND THE MORE RECENT REVISIONIST VIEW THAT IT ALL
RESULTED FROM THE ACTIVITY OF A HIGHLY INTRUSIVE GOVERNMENT.
INSTEAD, THIS PAPER EMPHASIZES THE ROLE OF
INSTITUTIONAL/ORGANIZATIONAL CHANGES ORCHESTRATED BY A
GOVERNMENT WHICH WAS BOTH SENSITIVE TO THESE SYSTEMS'
INITIAL CONDITIONS AND TO THE IMPORTANCE OF SETTING THE
STAGE FOR THE FULLEST POSSIBLE PARTICIPATION, THROUGH
MARKETS, OF LARGE NUMBERS OF DISPERSED PRIVATE ACTORS.
SPECIFICALLY, THE SUCCESS OR FAILURE OF GOVERNMENT ACTIONS
IN THE DIMENSION OF ORGANIZATIONAL/ INSTITUTIONAL CHANGE IS
RELATED TO THREE INGREDIENTS -SECULARISM, EGALITARIANISM AND
NATIONALISM. THE PAPER CONCLUDES BY DEMONSTRATING THE
APPLICABILITY OF THESE NOTIONS TO THE EAST ASIAN CASE,
ESPECIALLY TAIWAN DURING ITS POSTWAR PERIOD OF SPECTACULAR

DEVELOPMENT SUCCESS.

07476 RANLY, E.
PERU IN PERIL
THE CHRISTIAN CENTURY, 106(21) (JUL 89), 657-659.
FROM HIS VIEWPOINT AS A CATHOLIC PRIEST AND A PHILOSOPHY
PROFESSOR WHO HAS SPENT MANY YEARS IN PERU, THE AUTHOR
OUTLINES THE EVENTS THAT HAVE LED TO THE CURRENT STATE OF
AFFAIRS. PERU IS CURRENTLY GRAPPLING WITH ECONOMIC PROBLEMS
OF HUGE PROPORTIONS, ARMED INSURGENCY, AND NARCOTICS
TRAFFICKING. THE AUTHOR ALSO ANALYZES THE ROLE OF THE
CATHOLIC CHURCH IN ONE OF THE FEW STATES THAT HAS RETAINED
CATHOLICISM AS A STATE RELIGION.

07477 RANSON, S.; STEWART, J.
CITIZENSHIP AND GOVERNMENT: THE CHALLENGE FOR MANAGEMENT
IN THE PUBLIC DOMAIN
POLITICAL STUDIES, XXXVI(1) (MAR 89), 5-24.
THE PAPER ARGUES THAT ANALYSIS OF MANAGEMENT THAT
OBSCURES THE DISTINCTIVE CHARACTERISTICS OF THE PUBLIC AND
PRIVATE DOMAIN WILL MISS THE SIGNIFICANCE OF EACH. TO REMEDY
THIS PROBLEM, THE PAPER SEEKS TO ANALYZE THE VALUES,
INSTITUTIONAL CONDITIONS AND MANAGEMENT TASKS WHICH ARE
UNIQUE TO THE PUBLIC DOMAIN. IT ARGUES THAT THE DISTINCTIVE
CHALLENGE FOR THE PUBLIC DOMAIN DERIVES FROM THE DUALITY OF
PUBLICNESS: THE NEED TO ENABLE CITIZENS IN THEIR PLURALITY
TO EXPRESS THEIR CONTRIBUTION TO THE LIFE OF THE COMMUNITY
AND OUT OF THAT PLURALITY, TO ENABLE A PROCESS OF COLLECTIVE
CHOICE AND THE GOVERNMENT OF ACTION IN THE PUBLIC INTEREST
TO TAKE PLACE.

07478 RAO, C. V.
INDO-OPEC TRADE RELATIONS
OPEC REVIEW, 12(4) (WIN 88), 387-412.
THE PRINCIPAL OBJECTIVES OF THIS STUDY ARE: 1. TO
ANALYZE THE TRENDS IN OPEC'S EXTERNAL TRADE AND TO EXAMINE
THE ORIGIN AND STRUCTURE OF OPEC'S IMPORTS, SO AS TO
IDENTIFY THEIR REQUIREMENTS AND THE POTENTIAL COMPETITORS TO
INDIA. 2. TO STUDY THE AGGREGATE TRENDS IN INDO-OPEC TRADE,
AND TO ANALYZE THE STRUCTURAL CHANGES THAT HAVE TAKEN PLACE
IN THE COMMODITY COMPOSITION OF INDIA'S EXPORTS TO, AND
IMPORTS FROM, OPEC. 3. TO MAKE AN IN-DEPTH STUDY OF INDIA'S
TRADE RELATIONS WITH FIVE OPEC COUNTRIES.

07479 RAO, C.R.
INDIA: SOVIET REFORMS TO ENRICH THE IDEAL OF SOCIALISM
INFORMATION BULLETIN, 26(21-22) (NOV 88), 4-5.
IN THIS ARTICLE, THE GENERAL SECRETARY OF THE COMMUNIST
PARTY OF INDIA OFFERS HIS ASSESSMENT OF PERESTROIKA AND THE
NEW POLITICAL THINKING IN THE SOVIET UNION. OF PARTICULAR
INTEREST TO RAO IS THE PROPOSED SEPARATION OF THE FUNCTIONS
OF THE PARTY AND THE SOVIETS. THE PARTY WOULD GIVE GENERAL
GUIDANCE AND WOULD NOT INTERFERE IN THE DAY TO DAY
ADMINISTRATION AND THE SOVIETS WOULD RUN THE ADMINISTRATION.

07480 RAO, C.R.
THE PEOPLE WANT THE COMMUNISTS TO BE UNITED
WORLD MARXIST REVIEW, 32(7) (JUL 89), 47-51.
THIS ARTICLE SUMMARIZES THE POLITICAL LINE THAT HAS
EMERGED AT THE 14TH PARTY CONGRESS IN INDIA AND CONCLUDES
THAT THE RAJIV GANDI GOVERNMENT HAS FAILED AND MUST BE
REPLACED; THAT THE FIGHT AGAINST THE COMMUNAL, SUCCESSIONIST
AND CHAUVINIST FORCES SHOULD BE INTENSIFIED. IT SUGGESTS A
STRATEGY TO OBTAIN A BETTER ALTERNATIVE TO THE CONGRESS-1
GOVERNMENT.

07481 RAO, J.M.
TAXING AGRICULTURE: INSTRUMENTS AND INCIDENCE
WORLD DEVELOPMENT, 17(6) (JUN 89), 809-823.
THIS PAPER ANALYZES THE WAYS IN WHICH INDIVIDUAL
INSTRUMENTS OF TAX/SUBSIDY POLICY INVOLVING AGRICULTURE
AFFECT INCOME DISTRIBUTION, PRODUCTION, AND TRADE IN
DEVELOPING COUNTRIES. IT HIGHLIGHTS THE INTERACTIONS AMONG
POLICY INSTRUMENTS IN EFFECTING INCOME TRANSFERS AMONG
GOVERNMENT, FARMERS, AND NONAGRICULTURAL SECTORS. THESE
INTERACTIONS AND INDIRECT EFFECTS BECOME INTELLIGIBLE ONLY
WHEN THE MULTIPLICITY AND CHARACTERISTIC FORMS OF GOVERNMENT
INTERVENTIONS IN INTERNATIONAL TRADE AND DOMESTIC ECONOMY
ARE EXPLICITLY RECOGNIZED. IN DEVELOPING COUNTRIES, TERMS-OF-
TRADE TAXES ON AGRICULTURE CANNOT BE EASILY REPLACED. HENCE,
ATTEMPTS TO REMOVE TRADE "DISTORTIONS" WITH HYPOTHETICALLY
NONDISTORTING TAXES CAN BE COUNTERPRODUCTIVE.

07482 RAO, P. V.
FOREIGN INVOLVEMENT IN SURI LANKA
ROUND TABLE, 309 (JAN 89), 88-100.
WHILE ACKNOWLEDGING INDIAN INVOLVEMENT IN SRI LANKA AS
AN UNAVOIDABLE REGIONAL COMPULSION, BUT NOT NECESSARILY AN
ACCEPTABLE ONE AT THAT, THIS PAPER EXAMINES THE NATURE OF
OUTSIDE INVOLVEMENT IN SRI LANKA'S ETHNIC CONFLICT. THE
DISCUSSION IS AN ANALYSIS OF THE NATURE AND EXTENT OF
FOREIGN INVOLVEMENT IN THE ISLAND'S CRISIS, INDIAN REACTION
TO SUCH INVOLVEMENT AND THE REACTION OF EXTERNAL POWERS TO
INDIA'S OWN ROLE IN SRI LANKA.

07483 RAO, R.
NEW DELHI SETS OFF A FIRE ALARM
SOUTH, (106) (AUG 89), 106.
INDIAN OFFICIALS CLAIM THAT THE SUCCESSFUL TEST OF ITS
MEDIUM-RANGE AGNI MISSILE IN MAY 1989 WAS JUST A
"TECHNOLOGICAL DEMONSTRATION" AND THAT THEIR AMBITIOUS
MISSILE DEVELOPMENT PROGRAM HAS NO OFFENSIVE INTENTIONS.
THEY CITE NATIONAL SECURITY AND DEFENSE AGAINST PAKISTAN AND
CHINA AS THEIR MOTIVES FOR THE PROGRAM. BUT CRITICS SAY THE
DEFENSE ARGUMENT IS SPURIOUS BECAUSE THE AGNI WILL NOT DETER
CHINA AND PAKISTAN'S MISSILES ARE NO MATCH FOR INDIA'S
CAPABILITIES.

07484 RAPOPORT, A.; BORNSTEIN, G.
SOLVING PUBLIC GOOD PROBLEMS IN COMPETITION BETWEEN EQUAL
AND UNEQUAL SIZE GROUPS
JOURNAL OF CONFLICT RESOLUTION, 33(3) (SEP 89), 460-479.
FORTY-EIGHT GROUPS PARTICIPATED ONCE IN AN INTERGROUP
CONFLICT IN WHICH TWO GROUPS OF EQUAL OR UNEQUAL SIZE
COMPETED FOR THE PROVISION OF STEP-LEVEL (BINARY) PUBLIC
GOODS. THE STUDY INCLUDED A TWO-FACTORIAL DESIGN WITH
PREPLAY COMMUNICATION VERSUS NO PREPLAY COMMUNICATION
DEFINING ONE DIMENSION, AND EQUAL GROUP SIZE VERSUS UNEQUAL
GROUP SIZE DEFINING THE OTHER. THE DECISION TO CONTRIBUTE OR
NOT TOWARD THE PROVISION OF THE GOOD WAS MADE PRIVATELY AND
ANONYMOUSLY. BOTH THE RELATIVE GROUP SIZE AND COMMUNICATION
CONDITIONS AFFECTED THE LEVEL OF CONTRIBUTION. THE FINDINGS
SUPPORT A MODEL PREDICTING THAT WITHIN-GROUP DISCUSSION
RESULTS IN A TWO-PERSON GAME BETWEEN THE TWO GROUPS, EACH OF
WHICH USES THE MAXIMIN CRITERION TO DESIGNATE A NUMBER OF
CONTRIBUTORS. THIS CRITERION DOES NOT NECESSARILY MAXIMIZE
GROUP REWARD, ENCHANCE CONTRIBUTION, OR GUARANTEE EFFICIENT
PROVISION OF THE GOOD.

07485 RAPOPORT, L.
THE HOSKINS AFFAIR
MIDSTREAM, XXXV(8) (NOV 89), 17-22.
THOSE WHO MAINTAIN THAT AMERICAN JEWS WERE COMPLETELY
POWERLESS IN THE WARTIME ERA USUALLY CHOOSE TO IGNORE A
CHAPTER IN THE HISTORY OF THOSE YEARS, THE HOSKINS AFFAIR,
WHICH SHOWS THAT AMERICAN JEWS COULD AND DID EXERT POWER
WHEN THE OCCASION CALLED FOR IT. IN 1943, THE ESTABLISHMENT
ZIONISTS, ANTI-ZIONIST JEWS, NON-ZIONIST JEWS, AND THE
BERGSONITES MANAGED TO TORPEDO A SINISTER ATTEMPT BY THE
STATE DEPARTMENT TO ISSUE A JOINT DECLARATION WITH THE
BRITISH THAT WOULD HAVE DISAVOWED COMMITMENT TO A JEWISH
STATE IN PALESTINE AND PREVENTED FREEDOM OF EXPRESSION TO A
MINORITY IN THE UNITED STATES.

07486 RAPOPORT, L.
THE OSSETIAN CONNECTION
ENCOUNTER, LXXIII(1) (JUN 89), 42-46.
JOSEPH STALIN WAS THE FIRST SOVIET COMMISSAR OF
NATIONALITIES, CHARGED WITH DEALING WITH THE PROBLEMS OF A
POPULATION WITH MORE THAN 100 DISTINCT PEOPLES. LENIN SENT
STALIN TO CRUSH THE GEORGIAN INDEPENDENT STATE. STALIN'S
TREATMENT OF HIS FELLOW CAUCASIANS, INCLUDING THE DECIMATION
AND DEPORTATION OF EIGHT NATIONALITIES, SHOWED HIM TO BE THE
QUINTESSENTIAL ASSIMILATIONIST, WHO TOTALLY IDENTIFIED WITH
THE GREAT RUSSIANS.

07487 RAPOPORT, R.B.; HARTMAN, J.A.; METCALF, K.L.
CANDIDATE TRAITS AND VOTER INFERENCES: AN EXPERIMENTAL
STUDY
THE JOURNAL OF POLITICS, 51(4) (NOV 89), 917-932.
THIS PAPER EXAMINES TO WHAT EXTENT, AND IN WHAT WAYS,
VOTERS ARE WILLING TO GO BEYOND THE INFORMATION GIVEN--WHEN
THAT INFORMATION CONSISTS OF EITHER A CANDIDATE'S PERSONAL
TRAITS OR HIS ISSUE POSITIONS--TO MAKE BROADER CANDIDATE
ASSESSMENTS. BASED ON AN EXPERIMENT IN WHICH STUDENTS WERE
GIVEN EITHER PERSONAL TRAIT OR ISSUE INFORMATION ABOUT
CANDIDATES FOR PRESIDENT. IT FINDS STRONG EVIDENCE FOR VOTER
INFERENCES FROM TRAITS TO ISSUES AND VICE VERSA (ALTHOUGH
THERE IS GREATER INFERENCE FROM ISSUES THAN FROM TRAITS).
FINALLY, IT FINDS THAT ALTHOUGH INFERENCES ARE FREQUENTLY
MADE, THEY ARE OFTEN IDIOSYNCRATIC. ONLY IN PARTICULAR CASES
(I.E., RELATING CANDIDATE'S COMPASSION WITH HIS SUPPORT OF
GOVERNMENT PROVIDING JOBS), DO DIFFERENT TYPES OF
RESPONDENTS MAKE THE SAME INFERENCES (A FINDING WHICH IS
ALSO BORNE OUT BY THE 1984 NES).

07488 RARE, A.
TPLF VICTORY LIBERATES TIGRE
NEW AFRICAN, (259) (APR 89), 27.
THE TIGREAN PEOPLES' LIBERATION FRONT (TPLF) CLAIM TO
HAVE LIBERATED THE WHOLE OF THEIR TIGREAN PROVINCE FROM THE
ETHIOPIAN GOVERNMENT. THIS ACTION, ALTHOUGH STILL DENIED BY
THE GOVERNMENT, WOULD MEAN THAT THE TPLF, IN CONCERT WITH
THEIR NEW FOUND ALLIES THE ERITREAN PEOPLES' LIBERATION
FRONT, ARE MUCH CLOSER TO THEIR ULTIMATE AIM OF OUSTING THE
MENGISTU RETGIME THAN EVER BEFORE.

07489 RASHID, A.
THE CORDOVEZ COMPROMISE
FAR EASTERN ECONOMIC REVIEW, 141(29) (JUL 88), 28-29.
UN MEDIATOR DIEGO CORDOVEZ, HAS PROPOSED A CEASEFIRE AND
THE CREATION OF A NEUTRAL GOVERNMENT WHICH COULD HOLD A
TRIBAL COUNCIL TO ELECT A BROAD-BASED GOVERNMENT FOR
AFGHANISTAN. THIS IS THE FIRST CONCRETE PROPOSAL TO BRING AN
END TO THE CIVIL WAR AND IS BACKED BY MODERATES IN KABUL AND
AMONG THE MUJAHIDEEN. THE CRITICAL FACTORS WILL BE THE
WILLINGNESS OF AFGHAN PRESIDENT NAJIBULLAH TO STEP DOWN AND
THE ABILITY OF THE DIFFERENT FACTIONS AMONG THE MUJAHIDEEN
TO MAINTAIN UNITY.

07490 RASHISH, P.
E.C. MOVES TO DIPLOMATIC CENTER STAGE
EUROPE, (290) (OCT 89), 14-15.
THE DECISION TAKEN AT THE SEVEN-NATION ECONOMIC SUMMIT
TO ENTRUSTS THE EUROPEAN COMMUNITY COMMISSION WITH THE JOB
OF COORDINATING A LONG-TERM ECONOMIC AID PROGRAM FOR POLAND
AND HUNGARY SIGNALS A CHANGE IN U.S.-E.C. RELATIONS. GEORGE
BUSH SEEMS MORE THAN WILLING TO ALLOW, AND EVEN ENCOURAGE
THE E.C. TO TAKE ON A GREATER ROLE IN INTERNATIONAL AFFAIRS
AND DIPLOMACY. THUS FAR, THE EMPHASIS HAS BEEN ON EAST-WEST
AFFAIRS.

07491 RASHISH, P.
RACING INTO THE HI-TECH FUTURE
EUROPE, (292) (DEC 89), 14-15.
THE UNITED STATES AND EUROPEAN COMMUNITY (EC) SEEK NEW
WAYS TO CHALLENGE JAPAN'S IMPRESSIVE ECONMIC PERFORMANCE.
EMPHASIS IS INCREASINGLY BEING PLACED ON COLLABORATIVE
EFFORTS TO GAIN AN EDGE IN TWO VITAL TECHNOLOGIES:
SEMICONDUCTORS AND HIGH-DEFINITION TELEVISION (HDTV). JAPAN
CURRENTLY HAS THE LEAD IN HDTV. THE FIRST STEPS HAVE BEEN
TAKEN TO EXPLORE COLLABORATION BETWEEN THE U.S. AND E.C.
FIRMS TO COMBAT THIS LEAD. THE SAME MOMENTUM TOWARD
COLLABORATION CAN BE DISCERNED IN THE AREA OF SEMICONDUCTORS.

07492 RASINSKI, K.A.
THE EFFECT OF QUESTION WORDING ON PUBLIC SUPPORT FOR
GOVERNMENT SPENDING
PUBLIC OPINION QUARTERLY, 53(3) (FAL 89), 388-394.
ANALYSES OF QUESTION WORDING EXPERIMENTS ON THE GENERAL
SOCIAL SURVEY SPENDING ITEMS SHOWED CONSISTENT WORDING
EFFECTS FOR SEVERAL ISSUES ACROSS THREE YEARS. AN
EXAMINATION OF TYPES OF WORDING CHANGE INDICATE THAT EVEN
MINOR CHANGES CAN AFFECT RESPONSES. HOWEVER, AN EXAMINATION
OF INTERACTIONS WITH RESPONDENT INDIVIDUAL DIFFERENCES
SHOWED NO CONSISTENT PATTERN.

07493 RASMID, A.
THE CREDIBILITY GAP
FAR EASTERN ECONOMIC REVIEW, 142(49) (DEC 89), 19.
ALTHOUGH THE UNITED STATES AND PAKISTAN ADMIT THAT
AFGHANISTAN'S MUJAHIDEEN-LED INTERIM GOVERNMENT HAS FAILED
TO BROADEN ITS BASE OF PUBLIC SUPPORT, BOTH COUNTRIES
CONTINUE TO POUR IN MILITARY AID, PREFERRING TO GIVE THE
MUJAHIDEEN "ONE MORE CHANCE" TO REGAIN CREDIBILITY BY TAKING
THE BORDER CITY OF KHOST. ALTHOUGH A MILITARY VICTORY WOULD
PROVIDE SHORT-TERM CREDIBILITY, CONSTANT BICKERING AMONG
VARIOUS FACTIONS OF THE MUJAHIDEEN AND CLAIMS OF
MANIPULATION OF AFGHAN REFUGEES ARE SERIOUS LONG-TERM
PROBLEMS. MANY OBSERVERS NOTE THAT WITHOUT POLITICAL, AS
WELL AS MILITARY SOLUTIONS, THE CHANCES FOR RESOLUTION OF
THE CONFLICT ARE SLIM.

07494 RATFORD, D.
DEVELOPMENTS IN THE SOVIET UNION AND EASTERN EUROPE
RUSI JOURNAL, 134(1) (SPR 89), 15-18.
THE AUTHOR DISCUSSES GORBACHEV'S POLICIES CONCERNING
GLASNOST, HUMAN RIGHTS, INTERNATIONAL RELATIONS, AND EASTERN
EUROPE.

07495 RATHJENS, G.W.
GLOBAL SECURITY: APPROACHING THE YEAR 2000
CURRENT HISTORY, 88(534) (JAN 89), 1-4, 48-50.
A NUMBER OF DEVELOPMENTS ARE INDICATIVE OF CHANGE IN THE
INTERNATIONAL SECURITY ENVIRONMENT. THESE INCLUDE CHANGING
PERSPECTIVES ON THE RELATIVE IMPORTANCE OF MILITARY AND
ECONOMIC FACTORS AS INDICES AND INSTRUMENTS OF POWER; SOME
DISCREDITING OF NUCLEAR DETERRENCE ON MORAL GROUNDS IN THE
USA; AND THE REFORM MOVEMENT INVOLVING GLASNOST AND
PERESTROIKA IN THE USSR. THE ULTIMATE RESULT OF ALL THESE
CHANGES IS THAT THE DEMISE OF THE BIPOLAR WORLD MUST
EVENTUALLY COME, ALTHOUGH IT MIGHT BE DELAYED FOR A WHILE.

07496 RATNER, M.
SOME REFLECTIONS ON THE GROWING U.S. - INDOCHINA
FRIENDSHIP MOVEMENT
BULLETIN OF CONCERNED ASIAN SCHOLARS, 21(2-4) (APR 89),
176-178.
IN AN EFFORT TO UNDERSTAND THE NEW VIETNAM FRIENDSHIP
MOVEMENT AND ANSWER CHARGES THAT PARTICIPANTS IN THE ANTIWAR
MOVEMENT BECAME DISAFFECTED WITH THEIR ANTIWAR STANCES AND

VIETNAM, THIS ARTICLE LOOKS AT THE NATURE OF THE ANTIWAR
MOVEMENT AND THE REASONS FOR THE DISAPPEARANCE OF A LARGE
VIETNAM RELATED MOVEMENT AFTER THE WAR. IT DETAILS THE
NUMBER OF NATIONAL AND LOCAL GROUPS DOING EDUCATIONAL AND
ORGANIZING WORK AIMED AT BUILDING PUBLIC SENTIMENT FOR BOTH
PEOPLE-TO-PEOPLE AND GOVERNMENT TO GOVERNMENT RELATIONS WITH
VIETNAM AND CAMBODIA.

07497 RATTAN, K.
A WAR WITHIN
INDIA TODAY, XIV(3) (FEB 89), 50-51.
AFTER ONLY THREE MONTHS AS PRESIDENT OF THE WEST BENGAL
PCC(I), ABU BARKAT ATAUL GHANI KHAN CHOUDHURY HAS BEGUN TO
REALIZE THAT HIS WORST ENEMIES RESIDE NOT IN THE LEFT FRONT
GOVERNMENT BUT IN HIS OWN PARTY. PRIYA RANJAN DAS MUNSHI
LEADS THE INTERNAL OPPOSITION, AND CHOUDHURY'S EFFORTS TO
REORGANIZE THE PARTY HAVE BEEN SERIOUSLY HAMPERED BY THE
CENTRE'S FAILURE TO STATE UNAMBIGUOUSLY THAT IT STANDS BY
HIM.

07498 RATTAN, K.
HOPE OF PEACE
INDIA TODAY, XIV(1) (JAN 89), 38-39.
THE GORKHA NATIONAL LIBERATION FRONT SWEPT THE ELECTIONS
TO THE NEW DARJEELING GORKHA HILL COUNCIL, WINNING 26 OF 28
SEATS. GORKHA LEADER SUBHAS GHISING HAILED THE ELECTION AS
THE BEGINNING OF A NEW ERA IN DARJEELING, BUT INDEPENDENT
OBSERVERS EXPRESSED DOUBT ABOUT HOW LONG THE AUGUST 22
ACCORD WILL LAST AND GHISING'S ABILITY TO MOVE FROM A
VIOLENT REVOLUTIONARY TO A PEACEFUL LEADER.

07499 RATTAN, K.
POWERFUL PROBLEM
INDIA TODAY, XIV(8) (APR 89), 40-41.
IN 1988, WEST BENGAL'S LEFT FRONT GOVERNMENT DECLARED
THAT, BECAUSE THE CENTRE SEEMED DETERMINED TO BLOCK THE
BAKRESHWAR THERMAL POWER PROJECT, THE STATE WOULD IMPLEMENT
IT. BUT THE STATE IS HAVING TROUBLE FUNDING THE PROJECT.

07500 RATTAN, K.
REVOLT WITHIN
INDIA TODAY, XIV(2) (JAN 89), 50.
THE GHISING-LED DARJEELING GORKHA HILL COUNCIL HAS RUN
INTO ROUGH WEATHER BEFORE IT COULD EVEN TAKE OFF.
DIFFERENCES AMONG GORKHA NATIONAL LIBERATION FRONT LEADERS
ARE THREATENING TO TEAR APART THE DARJEELING ACCORD. ON THE
DAY THE HILL COUNCIL MEMBERS WERE TO HAVE BEEN SWORN IN, THE
REGION WAS RIDDLED WITH INCIDENTS OF VIOLENCE AND THE
BURNING OF VEHICLES.

07501 RATTAN, K.
STERN MESSAGE
INDIA TODAY, (JUL 89), 32-33.
THIS ARTICLE REPORTS ON RECENT ELECTION RESULTS WHICH
HAVE PROVIDED A SETBACK FOR CONGRESS (I). IT EXAMINES THE
RAMIFICATIONS OF PRESENT LEADERSHIP ACTIONS WHICH LEADS
OPPOSITION LEADERS TO MAKE PROGRESS.

07502 RATTAN, K.
STRIKING A SEPARATIST STANCE
INDIA TODAY, XIV(6) (MAR 89), 29-30.
THE BODOS' AGITATION FOR A SEPARATE STATE TOOK A GRIM
TURN IN MARCH 1989 AS VIOLENT PROTESTS LEFT 30 PEOPLE DEAD.
THE BODOS THREATENED TO ISOLATE ASSAM FROM THE REST OF THE
COUNTRY AND SINGLED OUT TRAINS FOR ATTACK, THROWING THE
RAILWAYS INTO DISARRAY.

07503 RATTAN, K.
WEST BENGAL: BORDER CHAOS
INDIA TODAY, XIV(7) (APR 89), 53-54.
THE REFUGEES THAT HAVE MOVED ACROSS THE INDIAN BORDER
FROM BANGLADESH HAVE RECENTLY BEEN TAKING ON A NEW LOOK. IN
THE PAST THEY WERE PREDOMINATELY MUSLIMS, BUT AFTER THE
PROCLAMATION OF ISLAM AS THE STATE RELIGION IN BANGLADESH,
THE EXODUS HAS BEEN COMPRISED LARGELY OF HINDUS. ETHNIC AND
RELIGIOUS CONFLICT AND TENSIONS ARE INCREASING AS THE HINDUS
MOVE INTO REGIONS THAT ARE COMPRISED MAINLY OF MUSLIM
REFUGEES. THE GOVERNMENT IS ATTEMPTING TO INCREASE BORDER
CONTROLS, BUT THE EFFECT OF THEIR EFFORTS HAS BEEN MINIMAL.

07504 RAUSCHENBACH, B.S.
POLICY CHANGE IN THE UNITED STATES: THE DIFFUSION OF STATE
LEGISLATION
DISSERTATION ABSTRACTS INTERNATIONAL, 49(7) (JAN 89),
1959-A.
THE AUTHOR EXAMINES POLICY CHANGE IN THE USA FROM THE
PERSPECTIVE OF A MODEL OF POLICY-MAKING WHERE BOTH INTERNAL
AND EXTERNAL INFLUENCES AFFECT THE TIMING AND PATTERNING OF
ADOPTIONS OF POLICY INNOVATIONS. SHE ANALYZES THE ADOPTION
OF 55 LAWS BY STATES WITHIN THE USA.

07505 RAVALLION, M.
LAND-CONTINGENT POVERTY ALLEVIATION SCHEMES
WORLD DEVELOPMENT, 17(8) (AUG 89), 1223-1233.

TARGET GROUPS FOR RURAL POVERTY ALLEVIATION SCHEMES IN SOUTH ASIA AND ELSEWHERE HAVE OFTEN BEEN IDENTIFIED IN TERMS OF THEIR LANDHOLDING CLASS, WITH LANDLESS OR NEAR LANDLESS HOUSEHOLDS BEING THE INTENDED BENEFICIARIES. THIS PAPER OFFERS A QUANTITATIVE APPROACH TO THE ANALYSIS AND DESIGN OF LAND-CONTINGENT POVERTY ALLEVIATION SCHEMES. AN APPLICATION TO BANGLADESH SUGGESTS THAT, WHEN INCOME IS GENERALLY UNOBSERVED, LANDHOLDING CLASS IS A GOOD INSTRUMENT FOR TARGETING POVERTY RELIEF. IT IS, HOWEVER, FAR FROM BEING A PERFECT INSTRUMENT. EVEN UNDER OTHERWISE IDEAL CONDITIONS, THE MAXIMUM FEASIBLE REDUCTION IN POVERTY WHICH IS ATTAINABLE BY RELYING SOLELY ON LAND-BASED TARGETING IS SUBSTANTIALLY LESS THAN THAT ATTAINABLE WITH PERFECT INCOME INFORMATION. INDEED, THE POVERTY ALLEVIATION IMPACT OF DOMESTICALLY FINANCED AND REVENUE-NEUTRAL TRANSFERS ACROSS 10 LANDHOLDING CLASSES IN RURAL BANGLADESH COULD ALSO BE ACHIEVED WITHOUT TARGETING BY SIMPLY GIVING EVERY HOUSEHOLD A LUMPSUM PAYMENT EQUIVALENT TO 10% OF MEAN RURAL INCOME. POLITICAL RESTRICTIONS ON TAX POWERS OR ERRORS IN ADMINISTRATION WILL FURTHER REDUCE THE GAINS FROM LAND-CONTINGENT TARGETING.

07506 RAVALLION, M.; CHAO, K.
TARGETED POLICIES FOR POVERTY ALLEVIATION UNDER IMPERFECT INFORMATION: ALGORITHMS AND APPLICATIONS
JOURNAL OF POLICY MODELING, 11(2) (SUM 89), 213-224.
A METHODOLOGY IS PROPOSED FOR SOLVING THE TARGETING PROBLEM OF POVERTY ALLEVIATION WITH IMPERFECT INFORMATION ON RECIPIENTS' INCOMES. A MEASURE OF THE GAIN FROM TARGETING IS ALSO PROPOSED. THE PROBLEM OF ALLOCATING A FIXED BUDGET FOR POVERTY RELIEF AMONG SECTORS AND REGIONS OF AN LDC IS USED AS AN EXAMPLE, AND CALCULATIONS OF THE POVERTY MINIMIZING ALLOCATIONS ARE PRESENTED FOR BANGLADESH, INDONESIA, THE PHILIPPINES, AND SRI LANKA. THE GAINS FROM OPTIMAL TARGETING CAN BE CONSIDERABLE, ALTHOUGH THEY VARY WIDELY ACCORDING TO THE DISTRIBUTIONAL CIRCUMSTANCES OF PARTICULAR COUNTRIES AND THE AMOUNT OF TARGETING INFORMATION AVAILABLE TO THE POLICYMAKER.

07507 RAY, J. L.
THE ABOLITION OF SLAVERY AND THE END OF INTERNATIONAL WAR
INTERNATIONAL ORGANIZATION, 43(5) (SUM 89), 405-440.
SLAVERY AND WAR HAVE BOTH HISTORICALLY BEEN CONSIDERED INEVITABLE CONSEQUENCES OF HUMAN NATURE. YET SLAVERY HAS BEEN ABOLISHED, AND MORAL PROGRESS MAY HAVE CONTRIBUTED TO SLAVERY'S DISAPPEARANCE. BOTH REALISTS AND MARXISTS ARE SKEPTICAL ABOUT THE IMPACT OF ETHICAL CONSTRAINTS ON POLITICAL DECISIONS, WHILE IDEALISTS AS WELL AS AT LEAST SOME REGIME ANALYSTS EMPHASIZE THE ROLE OF THOSE CONSTRAINTS. HOWEVER, ELEMENTS OF ALL OF THESE APPROACHES SUPPORT THE PROPOSITION THAT MORAL PROGRESS MAY BRING AN END TO INTERNATIONAL WAR. SOME HISTORICAL TRENDS DO NOT SUPPORT THE IDEA THAT INTERNATIONAL WAR IS ON THE VERGE OF DISAPPEARANCE, BUT THERE HAS NOT BEEN A WAR BETWEEN MAJOR POWERS SINCE 1945. IN ADDITION, NORMS AGAINST COLONIALISM ARE STRONG. NO WAR HAS OCCURED BETWEEN DEMOCRATIC STATES, NOR DOES A WAR APPEAR LIKELY AMONG THE RATHER SIZABLE NUMBER OF INDUSTRIALIZED DEMOCRATIC STATES IN THE INTERNATIONAL SYSTEM TODAY. EXPLANATIONS OF THESE POCKETS OF PEACE BASED ON CAUTION INDUCED BY NUCLEAR WEAPONS OR ON ECONOMIC INTERDEPENDENCE, FOR EXAMPLE, ARE CERTAINLY NOT BEYOND QUESTION. THEREFORE, IT MAY BE THAT NORMS INHIBITING THE INITIATION OF INTERNATIONAL WAR HAVE ALREADY MADE OBSOLETE NOT ONLY WARS BETWEEN THE RICHEST AND MOST POWERFUL STATES IN THE WORLD BUT ALSO SOME FORMS OF DEPRADATION BY THE STRONG AGAINST THE RELATIVELY WEAK STATES.

07508 RAZVI, S.
INDIA AND THE SECURITY OF INDIAN OCEAN/SOUTH ASIAN STATES
ROUND TABLE, (311) (JUL 89), 317-322.
THE INDIAN OCEAN IS SUBSTANTIALLY LINKED WITH THE POLITICAL SITUATION IN SOUTH ASIA. INDIA IS THE MAJOR ACTOR IN SOUTH ASIA, WITH AN ABITION TO BE A MINI-SUPERPOWER AND THE SECURITY MANAGER OF THE INDIAN OCEAN REGION. SO DOMINANT IS ITS POSITION IN THE REGION THAT ALL THE RESTBANGLADESH, BHUTAN, MALDIVES, NEPAL, PAKISTAN, AND SRI LANKA-PERCEIVE THEIR STRATEGIC AND POLITICAL ACTIONS MOSTLY IN RELATION TO WHAT INDIA DOES. THIS ACTION-REACTION ORIENTATION OF RELATIONSHIPS BETWEEN INDIA AND ITS NEIGHBOURS DOMINATES THE SECURITY ENVIRONMENT OF SOUTH ASIA. TWO OTHER ISSUES OF GREAT RELEVANCE TO SOUTH ASIAN SECURITY ARE FIRST, THE CONTINUOUS SEARCH BY THREE POWERS-THE US, THE SOVIET UNION AND CHINA- TO FIND DURABLE FRIENDSHIPS IN SOUTH WEST ASIA. SECOND, SOVIET INTERVENTION IN AFGHANISTAN HAS A DIRECT BEARING ON THE SECURITY ENVIRONMENT OF SOUTH WEST ASIA, THEREBY INCREASING THE SUPERPOWERS' RIVALRY IN THE REGION.

07509 READ, J.H.
SCARCITY, CONFLICT, DESIRE: AN INQUIRY INTO THE POSSIBILITY OF A UNIVERSAL INCREASE IN POWER
DISSERTATION ABSTRACTS INTERNATIONAL, 49(10) (APR 89), 3143-A.
THIS DISSERTATION IS AN INQUIRY INTO THE POSSIBILITY OF A UNIVERSAL INCREASE IN POWER. THE AUTHOR CRITICALLY

EXAMINES THE ZERO-SUM CONCEPTION OF POWER WHEREBY ONE'S GAIN IS ASSUMED TO EQUAL ANOTHER'S LOSS. HE ARGUES THAT A UNIVERSAL INCREASE IN POWER IS POSSIBLE IN PRINCIPLE AND AT LEAST APPROACHABLE IN PRACTICE. THE PURPOSE OF HIS INQUIRY IS TO DEFEND THE PLAUSIBILITY OF THE IDEAL OF UNIVERSAL FREEDOM OR UNIVERSAL LIBERATION.

07510 REAGAN, D.J.
AMBITION, CHARACTER, AND REPRESENTATION: AN INQUIRY INTO RETIREMENT FROM THE U.S. HOUSE OF REPRESENTATIVES
DISSERTATION ABSTRACTS INTERNATIONAL, 50(4) (OCT 89), 1080-A.
IN THE 1970'S, RETIREMENT FROM THE U.S. CONGRESS ROSE DRAMATICALLY, REACHING LEVELS NOT SEEN SINCE THE TURN-OF-THE-CENTURY. THIS DISSERTATION EXPLORES WHETHER CHANGING PROFESSIONAL INCENTIVES OFFERED BY THE INSTITUTION CAN EXPLAIN THIS CAREER PATTERN. IT CONCLUDES THAT THE INSTITUTIONAL IMPACT OF CONTEMPORARY RETIREMENT LEVELS SEEMS TO HAVE DRAINED THE HOUSE OF ITS MEMBERS MOST WILLING TO DO THE KIND OF WORK NEEDED TO PASS BROAD LEGISLATIVE PACKAGES. THIS, IN TURN, MAY HAVE DIMINISHED ITS CAPACITY TO SEE BEYOND THE SPECIAL NEEDS OF SPECIFIC INTEREST GROUPS AND ISSUES AND MAY HAVE IMPAIRED ITS ABILITY TO GOVERN IN THE LARGER, PUBLIC INTEREST.

07511 REAGAN, R.
FLATTENING HIERARCHIES IN THE AMERICAN FEDERAL SYSTEM
BUREAUCRAT, 18(2) (SUM 89), 15-16.
AMERICA'S STRENGTH AND WISDOM HAVE NEVER COME FROM THE POWER AND CLEVERNESS OF THOSE ON TOP, BUT FROM THE STRENGTH AND WISDOM OF THE AMERICAN PEOPLE. AND AFTER YEARS OF SKEPTICISM, THE WISDOM OF OUR FOUNDERS IS ONCE MORE THE ACCEPTED GUIDE IN WASHINGTON. THE FEDERAL GOVERNMENT HAS BEEN BROKEN OF ITS COMPULSION TO CONTROL EVERY BREATH THE STATES TAKE.

07512 REAGAN, R.
U.S.-SOVIET RELATIONS
DEPARTMENT OF STATE BULLETIN (US FOREIGN POLICY), 89(2143) (FEB 89), 3-4.
MANY FUNDAMENTAL DIFFERENCES ON MATTERS SUCH AS HUMAN RIGHTS AND REGIONAL TENSIONS REMAIN UNSETTLED BETWEEN EAST AND WEST. BUT THERE IS HOPE OF AN ERA IN WHICH THE TERRIBLE NIGHTMARES OF THE POSTWAR ERA, TOTALITARIANISM AND NUCLEAR TERROR, MAY DIMINISH SIGNIFICANTLY AND SOMEDAY FADE AWAY. TOWARD THIS END, THE USA AND ITS ALLIES HAVE PURSUED A COURSE OF PUBLIC CANDOR AND MILITARY STRENGTH BUT ALSO A COURSE OF VIGOROUS DIPLOMATIC ENGAGEMENT WITH THE SOVIETS.

07513 REDD, M.D.
INTERNATIONAL TECHNOLOGY TRANSFER AS PRACTISED IN THE USSR: IMPLICATIONS FOR U.S. NATIONAL SECURITY
AVAILABLE FROM NTIS, NO. AD-A208 010/9/GAR, FEB 89, 28.
IN ITS BROADEST SENSE, TECHNOLOGY TRANSFER ENCOMPASSES THE COLLECTION, DOCUMENTATION AND DISSEMINATION OF SCIENTIFIC AND TECHNICAL INFORMATION, INCLUDING DATA ON THE PERFORMANCE AND COSTS OF USING THE TECHNOLOGY; THE TRANSFORMATION OF RESEARCH AND TECHNOLOGY INTO PROCESSES, PRODUCTS, AND SERVICES THAT CAN BE APPLIED TO PUBLIC OR PRIVATE NEEDS; AND THE SECONDARY APPLICATION OF RESEARCH OR TECHNOLOGY DEVELOPED FOR A PARTICULAR MISSION THAT FILLS A NEED IN ANOTHER ENVIRONMENT. THE ABOVE PERSPECTIVE OF TECHNOLOGY TRANSFER IS A BENIGN ONE; ONE WHICH TAKES PLACE AMONG AND BETWEEN AMICABLE AND COOPERATING SOCIOPOLITICAL, CULTURAL AND/OR NATIONAL FRIENDS. THE FOLLOWING PAPER EXAMINES THE MORE NOTORIOUS SIDE OF THE TECHNOLOGY TRANSFER ISSUE, WITH ESPECIAL EMPHASIS ON ITS PRACTICE BY THE SOVIET UNION, WHO THROUGH COPYING, ESPIONAGE, AND BLATANT THIEVERY, SOONER OR LATER ACQUIRES WESTERN TECHNOLOGY FOR THEMSELVES AND WARSAW PACT NATIONS. FORMS OF TECHNOLOGY TRANSFER ARE SCRUTINIZED THROUGH THE USE OF SEVERAL CASE STUDIES AND FINALLY THE EFFORTS USED BY THE U.S. AT DETERRING THIS LEACHING AWAY OF ONE OF THE BULWARKS OF WESTERN-NATION NATIONAL SECURITY ARE SURVEYED.

07514 REDDAWAY, P.
THE GOOD, THE BAD, AND THE OUTSTANDING
DEADLINE, 3(5) (SEP 88), 1-2, 8-10.
THIS ARTICLE DETAILS HOW AMERICAN CORRESPONDENTS COVERED THE COMMUNIST PARTY CONFERENCE IN MOSCOW IN JUNE 1988. IT ESPECIAL FOCUSES ON THE MONITOR'S PAUL QUINN-JUDGE WHO PROVIDED THE MOST SOPHISTICATED POLITICAL ANALYSIS OF THE CONFERENCE, WHICH HE DESCRIBED AS "A PARADOXICAL VICTORY" FOR GORBACHEV FORCES; AND MICHAEL PARKS OF THE LOS ANGELES TIMES WHO WAS MORE OPTIMISTIC ABOUT THE PROSPECTS FOR CHANGE THAN GORBACHEV HIMSELF.

07515 REDDY, E. S.
NEHRU AND AFRICA
SECHABA, 23(7) (JUL 89), 22-27.
PANDIT NEHRU PLAYED AN HISTORIC ROLE IN ASSISTING THE AFRICAN PEOPLE TO ENSURE THAT THE COLONIAL REVOLUTION IN ASIA WOULD SOON BE FOLLOWED BY THE RESURGENCE OF AFRICA, CONFOUNDING THOSE WHO HOPED TO KEEP THAT CONTINENT IN

PERPETUITY AS THEIR PRESERVE. HE WAS, IN A SENSE, ONE OF THE
ARCHITECTS OF THE UNITED FRONT DETERMINED TO DESTROY THE
ABOMINATION OF APARTHEID IN SOUTH AFRICA. THE DECISION OF
THE AFRICAN STATES IN 1963 TO JOIN THE MOVEMENT OF NON-
ALIGNED COUNTRIES EN BLOC, MAKING AFRICA THE ONE CONTINENT
THAT IS TOTALLY NONALIGNED, HAS, IN A SENSE, THE BEST
TRIBUTE TO THE VISION AND THE LABOURS OF PANDIT NEHRU, AS IT
IS TO THAT OF AFRICAN LEADERS. THE CO-OPERATION OF INDIA AND
THE AFRICAN NATIONS - AND, INDEED, OF ALL NONALIGNED AND
LIKE-MINDED COUNTRIES - TO SECURE A WORLD WITHOUT ARMS, AND
GENUINE INTERNATIONAL COOPERATION IN THE INTERESTS OF
HUMANITY IS THE ABIDING MONUMENT TO HIS MEMORY.

07516 REDDY, L.
PRACTICAL NEGOTIATING LESSONS FROM INF
HASHINGTON QUARTERLY, 12(2) (SPR 89), 71-81.
THE UNITED STATES SHOULD NEGOTIATE FROM A POSITION OF
BOTH MILITARY STRENGTH AND ALLIANCE COHESION. IT MUST BE
ABLE TO RECOGNIZE WHEN IT IS IN A POSITION OF RELATIVE
STRENGTH-POLITICAL, ECONOMIC. AND MILITARY-VIS-A-VIS THE
SOVIET UNION AND TO ACT ON THAT RECOGITION. IT IS IN SUCH A
POSITION TODAY, BUT ITS DECLINING LEAD IN COMPARISON TO 1985-
1987 SUGGESTS THAT 1989 AND 1990 HOULD BE MORE ADVANTAGEOUS
YEARS FOR GAINING FAVORABLE TERMS THAN LATER YEARS. STRONG
PRESIDENTIAL LEADERSHIP AND INVOLVEMENT HILL BE NEEDED TO
CONSUMMATE ARMS-CONTROL AGREEMENTS. WITHOUT CENTRAL
DIRECTION, A SINGLE AGENCY CAN BLOCK THE FORMULATION OF
TIMELY U.S. NEGOTIATING POSITIONS. DIPLOMACY INT/REL

07517 REDEKOP, M.
THE LITERARY POLITICS OF THE VICTIM
CANADIAN FORUM, 68(783) (NOV 89), 14-17.
THIS ARTICLE IS AN INTERVIEW OF NOVELIST, JOY KOGAHA,
WHO WROTE, "OBASAN," THE EXPERIENCE OF THE JAPANESE-
CANADIANS INTERNED BY CANADA DURING WORLD WAR II. THE BOOK
TELLS OF HER FAMILIE'S EXPERIENCE DURING THE WAR AND OF THE
INJUSTICES AND DEPRIVATIONS SUFFERED BY THEM. IT DEALS HITH
THE PSYCHOLOGY OF BEING A VICTIM.

07518 REDING, A.
MEXICO UNDER SALINAS
WORLD POLICY JOURNAL, 6(4) (FAL 89), 685-729.
THIS ARTICLE EXPLORES THE GAP BETWEEN SALINA'S REFORMIST
IMAGE ABROAD AND THE REALITY WITHIN MEXICO BY LOOKING AT HIS
RECORD. IT EXAMINES ELECTORAL DEMOCRACY AND THE NEED FOR THE
ELIMINATION OF ELECTORAL FRAUD, AND EXPLORES ELECTIONS IN
DETAIL. IT THEN EXAMINES UNION DEMOCRACY AND SALINA'S
ATTITUDE TOWARD THE LABOR MOVEMENT. NEXT THE MEXICAN POLICE
STATE IS STUDIED AND THEN THE TRAGIC RESULTS OF SALINA'S
ECONOMIC MODERNIZATION. IT CONCLUDES THAT NOW IS A HISTORIC
OPPORTUNITY FOR U.S. POLICY TOHARDS MEXICO TO HELP THAT
COUNTRY,

07519 REED, F.
A NATION IN TURMOIL
MACLEAN'S (CANADA'S NEHS MAGAZINE), 102(3) (JAN 89), 23-25.
A DECADE AFTER THE OVERTHROW OF THE SHAH OF IRAN, IRAN'S
ISLAMIC REVOLUTION HAS FAILED TO LIVE UP TO ITS PROMISES.
THE DESERT WAR HITH IRAQ LEFT 300,000 IRANIANS DEAD AND
ENDED IN A DISMAL STALEMATE. IRAN REMAINS POLITICALLY AND
ECONOMICALLY ISOLATED FROM OTHER COUNTRIES, HHILE INTERNALLY
IT IS TORN BY PUBLIC DISSATISFACTION OVER SOCIAL INEQUALITY,
SOARING PRICES AND CORRUPTION. HOWEVER, THE END OF THE WAR
IS SEEN BY MANY AS A SIGN OF THE DECLINING INFLUENCE OF THE
AYATOLAH KHOMEINI. PARLIAMENT SPEAKER RAFSANJANI, THE HEIR
APPARENT, IS ALREADY MAKING OVERTURES TO THE WEST IN AN
ATTEMPT TO GAIN MUCH-NEEDED FOREIGN AID AND TRADE. HOWEVER,
IRAN FACES AN IMMENSE UPHILL BATTLE AS IT ATTEMPTS TO
OVERCOME THE RAVAGES OF REVOLUTION AND WAR.

07520 REED, I.W.
THE LIFE AND DEATH OF UDAG: AN ASSESSMENT BASED ON EIGHT
PROJECTS IN FIVE NEH JERSEY CITIES
PUBLIUS: THE JOURNAL OF FEDERALISM, 19(3) (SUM 89), 93-110.
THE FEDERAL URBAN DEVELOPMENT ACTION GRANT PROGRAM,
BEGUN IN 1977, PROVIDED $5 BILLION OVER ELEVEN YEARS
REVITALIZING SEVERELY DISTRESSED URBAN PLACES THROUGH THE
ENCOURAGEMENT OF PRIVATE SECTOR INVESTMENT. DESIGNED TO
ASSIST COMMERCIAL, INDUSTRIAL, AND HOUSING PROJECTS THAT
"BUT FOR" THE FEDERAL GRANT HOULD NOT BE BUILT, THE PROGRAM
WAS CHARACTERIZED BY A STREAMLINED GRANT-MAKING PROCESS
ADMINISTERED BY FINANCE AND DEVELOPMENT EXPERTS. EIGHT UDAG
PROJECTS IN FIVE NEH JERSEY CITIES, FIRST STUDIED IN THE
PROPOSAL STAGE IN 1979 AND REVISITED IN 1987, SHOH THAT THE
UDAGS SUCCEEDED IN ATTRACTING DEVELOPMENT TO THESE HARD-
PRESSED CITIES. ALTHOUGH THE PROJECTS SUCCEEDED, THE PROGRAM
HAS UNABLE TO ARREST THE MORE GENERAL DISTRESSED CONDITIONS
OF THE CITIES. DURING THE REAGAN YEARS, THE ADMINISTRATION
SOUGHT TO END THE PROGRAM. CONGRESS SUPPORTED IT, BUT
REDUCED THE FUNDING EACH YEAR. IN AN EFFORT TO GAIN SUPPORT
FOR THE PROGRAM, ELIGIBILITY REQUIREMENTS HERE BROADENED TO
INCLUDE MORE LOCALITIES. THESE EFFORTS FAILED, AND IN 1988
CONGRESS DID NOT FUND THE PROGRAM. DESPITE ITS DEMISE, UDAG
IS RECOGNIZED AS HAVING STIMULATED URBAN REVITALIZATION AND

HAVING CREATED A NEH MODEL FOR PRIVATE SECTOR AND PUBLIC
SECTOR COLLABORATION IN ECONOMIC DEVELOPMENT.

07521 REED, M. C.
AN ETHMOHISTORICAL STUDY OF THE POLITICAL ECONOMY OF
NDJOLE, GABON
DISSERTATION ABSTRACTS INTERNATIONAL, 49(9) (MAR 89),
2709-A.
THIS DISSERTATION'S OBJECTIVE IS TO EXPLAIN WHY THE
VIGOROUS NDJOLE FANG ENTREPRENEURIAL ACTIVITY OF THE LATE-
NINETEENTH CENTURY HAS BEEN NEGLIGIBLE EVER SINCE. PARTIAL
EXPLANATIONS ARE THE LACK OF INDIGENOUS MARKET TRADITION,
THE RESTRAINTS IMPOSED BY FRENCH COLONIALISM, FOCUS ON
CAPITAL-INTENSIVE MINERAL EXPORTS, AND THE TOWNSPEOPLE'S
RELIANCE UPON PUBLIC SECTOR EMPLOYMENT. THIS SUBJECT IS
CLARIFIED BY POLITICAL ECONOMY, DEFINED AS "RADICAL" (I.E.
CRITICAL OF MAINSTREAM ECONOMICS), MARXIST-INSPIRED,
MATERIALIST ECONOMIC ANALYSIS EMPHASIZING THE "FORCES OF
(COMMODITY) PRODUCTION."

07522 REES, G.J.
SCOURGE OR PLOT?
NATIONAL REVIEW, XLI(14) (AUG 89), 34-35.
IN THIS ARTICLE THE AUTHOR ATTEMPTS TO CLARIFY THE
CONTRADICTORY AND CONFUSING POSITION OF THE SUPREME COURT IN
WEBSTER VS. REPRODUCTIVE HEALTH SERVICES. FOR THE FIRST TIME
IN 16 YEARS, THE COURT REFUSED A REQUEST TO EXPAND THE
ABORTION RIGHT. THIS IS NOT INSIGNIFICANT. FOR A
CONSTITUTIONAL RIGHTAT LEAST FOR A RIGHT DRAHING ITS
STRENGTH PRIMARILY FROM JUDICIAL ASSESSMENT OF FUNDAMENTAL
PRINCIPLE OR DEEP SOCIAL CONSENSUS RATHER THAN FROM THE
EXPLICIT TEXT OR CONTEXT OF A PARTICULAR CONSTITUTIONAL
PROVISION-MOMENTUM IS EVERYTHING. WHEN THE COURT STOPS
EXTENDING A CONSTITUTIONAL DOCTRINE. IT OFTEN PROCEEDS TO
CONTRACT OR EVEN TO DISCARD THE DOCTRINE.

07523 REES, H.
THE 1957 SANDYS WHITE PAPER: NEH PRIORITIES IN BRITISH
DEFENCE POLICY?
JOURNAL OF STRATEGIC STUDIES, 12(2) (JUN 89), 215-229.
THREE MAIN QUESTIONS ARE ADDRESSED IN THIS ARTICLE. THE
FIRST IS THE EXTENT TO WHICH ECONOMIC CONSTRAINT HAS THE
DRIVING FORCE BEHIND THE 1957 SANDYS DEFENCE WHITE PAPER.
THE SECOND QUESTION MEASURES THE IMPORTANCE ATTACHED BY
SANDYS TO THE CHIEFS OF STAFF COMMITTEE'S ASSESSMENT OF THE
NATURE OF THE THREAT TO THE UNITED KINGDOM. FINALLY, THE
QUESTION OF SANDYS' ULTIMATE AIM FOR DEFENCE POLICY IS
EXAMINED TO DETERMINE WHETHER HE SOUGHT A MORE INDEPENDENT
STANCE FOR BRITAIN OR ONE MORE CLOSELY TIED TO THE ALLIES.
TO ANSWER THESE QUESTIONS, IT IS NECESSARY TO STUDY THE
HHITE PAPER IN RELATION TO THE MILITARY POLICY GOALS
ESTABLISHED BY THE CHIEFS OF STAFF: PREVENTING GLOBAL WAR,
HINNING THE COLD WAR, AND MAINTAINING BRITAIN'S ABILITY TO
FIGHT A LIMITED WAR.

07524 REES, H.E.
NORMAN HELLS IMPACT FUNDING: BOON OR BUST?
CANADIAN PUBLIC ADMINISTRATION, 32(1) (SPR 89), 104-123.
THE NORMAN HELLS PROJECT INVOLVED A TEN-FOLD EXPANSION
OF THE NORMAN HELLS OILFIELD AND CONSTRUCTION OF A PIPELINE
EXTENDING UP THE MACKENZIE VALLEY TO NORTHERN ALBERTA.
BECAUSE OF ITS HIGHLY INNOVATIVE APPROACH TO PROJECT
MANAGEMENT, NORMAN HELLS HAS BEEN HERALDED AS A MODEL FOR
FUTURE DEVELOPMENT PROJECTS. CONSTRUCTION HAS DELAYED
SEVENTEEN MONTHS FROM THE TIME OF PROJECT APPROVAL, PARTLY
TO PERMIT EFFECTIVE PLANNING AND THE USE OF SPECIAL MEASURES
DURING THE CONSTRUCTION PHASE. A MAJOR COMPONENT OF THESE
MEASURES HAS THE UNIQUE FUNDING IMPACT PROGRAM SET TO HELP
MANAGE NEGATIVE EFFECTS AND ENCOURAGE NATIVE INVOLVEMENT IN
THE PROJECT. THIS PAPER ASSESSES THE PLANNING AND
ADMINISTRATION OF TWO SOCIOECONOMIC COMPONENTS OF THE IMPACT
FUNDING PROGRAM.

07525 REESE, R.
A NOT ON A CONSEQUENCE OF THE EXPANSION OF THE RED ARMY ON
THE EVE OF WORLD WAR II
SOVIET STUDIES, XLI(1) (JAN 89), 135-140.
THE ARTICLE EXAMINES THE RAPID EXPANSION OF THE RED ARMY
DURING THE PERIOD 1935-41 AS ONE CAUSE FOR THE EARLY DEFEATS
IN THE CONFLICT HITH GERMANY. IT OUTLINES THE REASONS FOR
THE EXPANSION AND ANALYZES THE STRAIN THAT IT PUT ON SOVIET
RESOURCES AND LEADERSHIP. INSUFFICIENT LEADERSHIP HAS A
PRIMARY CAUSE OF THE RED ARMY'S UNPREPARED STATE MHEN THE
GERMAN'S INVADED, AND, ALTHOUGH THE PROBLEMS OF LEADERSHIP
ARE GENERALLY ATTRIBUTED TO STALIN'S PURGES, THE EXPANSION
HAS ALSO A FACTOR IN THAT IT SPREAD HHAT GOOD LEADERSHIP
THAT EXISTED TOO THIN.

07526 REEVES, M.M.
STATE ACTIVISM AS A BALANCE IN PRESERVING FEDERALISM
JOURNAL OF STATE GOVERNMENT, 62(1) (JAN 89), 20-24.
STATES ARE LEADING THE FEDERAL GOVERNMENT IN DOMESTIC
POLICY, FORGING AHEAD IN SOCIAL HELFARE, EDUCATION, AND
CONSUMER AFFAIRS. HITHOUT THE FREEDOM AND FLEXIBILITY

AFFORDED STATES UNDER FEDERALISM, HOWEVER, STATE INNOVATIONS
WOULD BE HAMPERED.

07527 REGATO, J.
A LATIN AMERICAN PEACE ZONE
WORLD MARXIST REVIEW, 31(11) (NOV 88), 47-50.
THE ATTEMPTS BY THE US MILITARY TO SET UP BASES IN
ECUADOR'S AMAZONIA WITH THE CONNIVANCE OF THE FORMER RIGHT-
WING PRESIDENT FEBRES CORDERO, WERE THWARTED BY THE
ECUADORANS, WHO ACHIEVED A SIGNIFICANT VICTORY IN THE
STRUGGLE AGAINST IMPERIALISM WHEN SOCIAL DEMOCRAT RODRIGO
BORJA, SUPPORTED BY THE COMMUNISTS AND OTHER LEFT-WING
FORCES, WAS ELECTED PRESIDENT.

07528 REGELSBERGER, E.
SPAIN AND THE EUROPEAN POLITICAL COOPERATION: NO ENFANT
TERRIBLE
INTERNATIONAL SPECTATOR, XXIV(2) (APR 89), 118-124.
THE AUTHOR DISCUSSES SPAIN'S MEMBERSHIP IN THE EUROPEAN
COMMUNITY. IN 1989 SPAIN HELD THE PRESIDENCY OF THE EC AND
EPC FOR THE FIRST TIME. WHILE THIS WAS NOT AN ESPECIALLY
SIGNIFICANT EVENT FOR THE COMMUNITY, FOR SPAIN IT WAS THE
CROWING ACHIEVEMENT OF THE LONG MARCH TOWARDS REAL
ACCEPTANCE IN THE COMMUNITY OF WESTERN EUROPEAN DEMOCRACIES.

07529 REGELSBERGER, E.
THE DIALOGUE OF THE EC/TWELVE WITH OTHER GROUPS OF STATES
INTERNATIONAL SPECTATOR, XXIII(4) (OCT 88), 252-269.
WHILE THE CREATION OF A SINGLE EUROPEAN MARKET BY 1992
OCCUPIES THE PUBLIC'S ATTENTION, EUROPEAN POLITICAL
COOPERATION (EPC) CONTINUES TO OPERATE SILENTLY. IN THIS
ARTICLE, THE AUTHOR SURVEYS THE RELATIONS OF THE EC AND ITS
MEMBER STATES WITH OTHER GROUPS OF STATES.

07530 REGENS, J.A.; RYCROFT, R.W.
FUNDING FOR ENVIRONMENTAL PROTECTION: COMPARING
CONGRESSIONAL AND EXECUTIVE INFLUENCES
SOCIAL SCIENCE JOURNAL, 26(3) (1989), 289-302.
EXAMINING THE BUDGET OF THE U.S. ENVIRONMENTAL
PROTECTION AGENCY PROVIDES A UNIQUE OPPORTUNITY TO TEST THE
RELATIVE IMPORTANCE OF EXECUTIVE AND LEGISLATIVE INFLUENCES
ON FUNDING. IN GENERAL SINCE ESTABLISHMENT OF EPA IN 1970,
CONGRESS HAS ADVOCATED MORE PROGRAMS AND THE PRESIDENT HAS
TRIED TO RESTRAIN SPENDING. IN PARTICULAR DURING THE REAGAN
ADMINISTRATION, THE EXECUTIVE AND LEGISLATIVE BRANCHES
DIFFERED SHARPLY IN THEIR PRIORITIES THIS ARTICLE COMPARES
BUDGETARY PATTERNS OVER TIME AND OFFERS AN ANALYSIS OF THE
BUDGET. IT CONCLUDES THAT DOING MORE WITH LESS IS QUITE
LIKELY TO CHARACTERIZE THE EPA'S NEAR-TERM FUTURE IN THE
POST-REAGAN ERA.

07531 REGENS, J.L.
ACID RAIN POLICYMAKING AND ENVIRONMENTAL FEDERALISM:
RECENT DEVELOPMENTS, FUTURE PROSPECTS
PUBLIUS: THE JOURNAL OF FEDERALISM, 19(3) (SUM 89), 75-92.
ACID RAIN CONTROLS ARE ONE OF THE MORE SALIENT POLICY
ISSUES FOR CONTEMPORARY ENVIRONMENTAL FEDERALISM. AGENDA
PROMINENCE, HOWEVER, DOES NOT GUARANTEE AGREEMENT ON THE
COMPONENTS OF A REGULATORY PROGRAM. DEPENDING ON HOW MANY
TONS OF EMISSIONS REDUCTION ONE WANTS, WHEN ONE WANTS THEM,
AND HOW ONE PERMITS EMITTERS TO ACHIEVE COMPLIANCE, A
CONTROL PROGRAM'S COSTS CAN VARY BY BILLIONS OF DOLLARS
ANNUALLY. THIS ARTICLE PROVIDES A SUMMARY OF SIGNIFICANT
STATE AND NATIONAL POLICY INITIATIVES AS WELL AS AN
EXAMINATION OF THE BARRIERS AND INCENTIVES FOR SUCH ACTION.

07532 REGISTER, C.A.
RACIAL EMPLOYMENT AND EARNINGS DIFFERENTIALS: THE IMPACT
OF THE REAGAN ADMINISTRATION--REPLY
REVIEW OF BLACK POLITICAL ECONOMY, 17(4) (SPR 89), 85-87.
THE AUTHOR DEFENDS AN EARLIER PAPER IN WHICH HE
CONCLUDED THAT, IN TERMS OF EMPLOYMENT SUCCESS, THE POSITION
OF BLACKS RELATIVE TO WHITES WEAKENED SIGNIFICANTLY DURING
THE ADMINISTRATION OF RONALD REAGAN.

07533 REHBEIN, R.E.
THE JAPAN-SOVIET FAR EAST TRADE RELATIONSHIP: A CASE OF
THE CAUTIOUS BUYER AND THE OVERCONFIDENT SELLER
JOURNAL OF NORTHEAST ASIAN STUDIES, 8(2) (SUM 89), 38-64.
GIVEN JAPAN'S RESOURCE SCARCITY, THE EASTERN SOVIET
UNION'S WEALTH OF NATURAL RESOURCES AND DIRE NEED FOR LARGE
INFUSIONS OF INVESTMENT CAPITAL AND TECHNOLOGY, AND THE
CLOSE DISTANCE BETWEEN THE TWO, ONE WOULD BELIEVE THAT TRADE
BETWEEN THE TWO COUNTRIES WOULD BE QUITE SIZABLE. HOWEVER,
THE CONVERSE IS THE CASE, WITH EACH COUNTRY PROVIDING NO
MORE THAN 2 PERCENT OF THE OTHER'S FOREIGN TRADE. TO EXPLAIN
THIS PHENOMENON, IT IS NECESSARY TO EXPLORE THE INTRINSIC
AND SELF-IMPOSED OBSTACLES TO EXPANDED JAPANESE-USSR TRADE.
IT TURNS OUT THAT BOTH COUNTRIES DO NOT PURSUE TRADE FOR
MUTUAL ADVANTAGE BUT RATHER SEEK AN ENTIRELY DIFFERENT SET
OF ULTERIOR ZERO-SUM MOTIVES. THE ARTICLE DISCUSSES WHAT
WOULD APPEAR TO BE A NATURAL "FIT" BETWEEN THE TWO
COUNTRIES' NEEDS AND ABILITIES, EXPLORES THE EXTENSIVE JOINT
SIBERIAN DEVELOPMENT PROJECTS OF THE 1960S AND 1970S TO

EXPLAIN THE UNDESIRED SIDE EFFECTS OF JAPANESESOVIET TRADE,
DETAILS JAPANESE AND SOVIET BUSINESS, GOVERNMENT, AND
ECONOMIST ARGUMENTS FOR AND AGAINST EXPANDED ECONOMIC
RELATIONS, EXPLAINS THE MALDEVELOPMENT OF A RESOURCE-
EXTRACTIVE VERSUS COMMODITY-PRODUCING EASTERN USSR AS A
PRODUCT OF CLIMATE, LABOR SHORTAGES, INVESTMENT POLICIES,
AND A STALINIST-PLANNED SYSTEM OUTLINES JAPANESE DESIRES TO
ACCRUE POLITICAL ADVANTAGES FROM ITS TRADE WITH THE SOVIET
UNION, AND PREDICTS THE INABILITY OF GORBACHEV'S ECONOMIC
REFORMS TO TRULY EXPAND JAPANESE-SOVIET TRADE AT A LOW COST
TO ITS LARGER POLITICAL CONCERNS. ALTHOUGH CONTINUING
PRIVATE JAPANESE EFFORTS ARE BEING MADE TO WORK OUT JOINT
VENTURE DEALS WITH THE USSR (THUS BELYING THE NOTION OF A
COMPLETELY CONSENSUS-UNIFIED "JAPAN, INC."), THEY ARE STILL
ANOMALIES. ULTIMATELY, IF EXPANDED TRADE TIES ARE TO OCCUR
(AND INDEED IT IS THIS ARTICLE'S CONTENTION THAT THEY MUST
FOR THE USSR TO SURVIVE AS A SUPERPOWER), THEN THEY MUST BE
MADE ON JAPAN'S TERMS.

07534 REHEIS, F.
THE JUST STATE: OBSERVATIONS ON GUSTAV VON SCHMOLLER'S
POLITICAL THEORY
INTERNATIONAL JOURNAL OF SOCIAL ECONOMICS, 16(9-11) (1989),
93-100.
THE AUTHOR ATTEMPTS TO RECONSTRUCT THE POLITICAL WAY OF
THINKING PERVADING SCHMOLLER'S WORKS. SCHMOLLER'S PLEADING
FOR A PRIMARILY ARISTOCRATIC CONSTITUTION RESULTS FROM A
THEORY OF JUSTICE IN WHICH EACH MEMBER OF THE COMMUNITY IS
REWARDED ACCORDING TO HIS OR HER CONTRIBUTION TO THE
COMMUNITY. THE EPISTEMOLOGICAL PRECONDITION FOR THIS IS
SCHMOLLER'S AXIOM ON THE FORMATION OF COMMUNITIES.

07535 REICH, S.
ROADS TO FOLLOW: REGULATING FOREIGN INVESTMENT
INTERNATIONAL ORGANIZATION, 43(4) (FAL 89), 543-584.
THIS ARTICLE DRAWS ON DATA RELATING TO THE TREATMENT OF
SUBSIDIARIES OF AMERICAN AUTOMOBILE MANUFACTURERS BY
EUROPEAN GOVERNMENTS WITH COMPETING INDIGENOUS PRODUCERS IN
SPECIFYING TWO VARIABLES CRITICAL TO IDENTIFYING POLICY
ALTERNATIVES: FIRST, THE DEGREE OF ACCESS GRANTED BY THE
STATE TO FOREIGN FIRMS (LIMITED OR UNLIMITED ACCESS) AND
SECOND, THE TYPE OF SUPPORT PROVIDED BY THE STATE TO
DOMESTIC FIRMS (DISCRIMINATORY OR NONDISCRIMINATORY
INTERVENTION). THE ANALYSIS SUGGESTS THAT THERE ARE FOUR
POSSIBLE POLICY COMBINATIONS, WHICH GENERALLY REFLECT THE
FOUR DIFFERENT POSTWAR STATE POLICIES PURSUED BY WEST
GERMANY, FRANCE, BRITIAN AND THE UNITED STATES. OF THESE
FOUR, THE COMBINATION EMPLOYED BY WEST GERMANY HAS PROVED
MOST EFFECTIVE IN PURSUING POLICIES CONSISTENT WITH LIBERAL
TRADE PRINCIPLES WHILE RECONCILING SHORT-TERM EMPLOYMENT AND
FISCAL GOALS WITH THE BROADER LONG-TERM OBJECTIVES OF
SUSTAINING STATE AUTONOMY AND BALANCE-OF-PAYMENTS SURPLUSES
IN THE FACE OF FOREIGN COMPETITION. BRITISH POLICIES, WHICH
HAVE CONSISTENTLY PROVED THE MOST INEFFECTIVE, HAVE
SACRIFICED LONG-TERM OBJECTIVES FOR SHORT-TERM ONES. AS A
RESULT OF STRUCTURAL CHANGES DURING THE 1970S, THE AMERICAN
STATE'S CHOSEN POLICY COMBINATION HAS ALTERED AND NOW
REPLICATES THE TRADITIONAL BRITISH FORMULA. THE UNITED
STATES THEREFORE RISKS COMPARABLE ECONOMIC AND POLITICAL
CONSEQUENCES.

07536 REICHLEY, A.J. (ED.)
ELECTIONS, AMERICAN STYLE
BROOKINGS INSTITUTION, WASHINGTON, DC, 1987, 291.
STRONGER POLITICAL PARTIES WOULD REDUCE MANY OF THE MOST
TROUBLESOME PROBLEMS WITH THE PRESENT PROCESS OF ELECTING A
PRESIDENT. STRONGER PARTIES WOULD LEND MORE STRUCTURE TO THE
SELECTION SYSTEM, INCREASE VOTER TURNOUT, AND ALLEVIATE SOME
PROBLEMS OF CAMPAIGN FINANCING.

07537 REID, J.; KURTH, M.
PUBLIC EMPLOYEES IN POLITICAL FIRMS: PART B, CIVIL SERVICE
AND MILITANCY
PUBLIC CHOICE, 60(1) (JAN 89), 41-54.
THE AUTHORS CONTINUE THEIR EXPLANATION OF THE EVOLUTION
OF PUBLIC EMPLOYEES' ORGANIZATION. THEY ANALYZE THE
EVOLUTION FROM PATRONAGE TO CIVIL SERVICE, NOW CHARACTERIZED
BY THE MILITARY, THE OCCURRED OVER THE PAST CENTURY.
CONTRARY TO THE COMMON BELIEF THAT EACH TRANSFORMATION IS
RELATED ONLY TO SOME FAILURE IN THE PRECEDING FORM, THE
AUTHORS OFFER THE SAME EXPLANATION FOR EACH CHANGE: THAT THE
NEW ORGANIZATIONAL FORM MORE EFFICIENTLY MAXIMIZED THE
MIXTURE OF VOTES, POWER, AND INCOME THAT POLITICIANS SEEK.

07538 REID, M.
PERU UNIONS FEEL THE SQUEEZE
SOUTH, (102) (APR 89), 42.
KILLINGS OF UNION LEADERS HAVE BECOME COMMON IN PERU IN
THE PAST FEW MONTHS. THE RIPPLE EFFECT OF A WIDER
POLARIZATION, PROVOKED IN PART BY THE VIOLENT INSURGENCY OF
THE HARD-LINE MAOIST GUERRILLAS OF SENDERO LUMINOSO, REACHED
THE UNIONS AND SET OFF A SERIES OF MURDERS AND
DISAPPEARANCES. A COLLAPSE IN LIVING STANDARDS ON A SCALE
THAT ALMOST DEFEIES DESCRIPTION HAS SPARKED LABOR UNREST AND

NUMEROUS STRIKES. GOVERNMENT AUSTERITY MEASURES HAVE
COMBINED WITH INFLATION AND RECESSION TO PRODUCE THE BLEAK
ECONOMIC PICTURE.

07539 REINHOLD, O.
THE BASIS OF THE STRATEGY FOR THE 1990S
WORLD MARXIST REVIEW, 32(8) (AUG 89), 19-23.
THIS ARTICLE EXAMINES SED POLICY (GDR SOCIALIST UNITY
PARTY) BASED ON THE FUNDAMENTAL IDEA THAT THERE IS UNITY OF
CONTINUITY AND RENEWAL WHICH REQUIRES DYNAMISM WHICH
REQUIRES CHANGE. IT EXPLORES THE MODERN IMAGE OF SOCIALISM
AND THE FACT THAT THERE IS NOW EVIDENCE OF TWO CONCEPTS OF
SCIENTIFIC AND TECHNOLOGICAL PROGRESS IN THE SOCIALIST
COUNTRIES. IT RECOGNIZES THAT PERESTROIKA IS NECESSARY IN
THE USSR AND SUPPORTS THE PROCESS. IT ALSO RECOGNIZES THAT
THERE CAN BE NO SINGLE MODEL FOR SOCIALISM FOR ALL THE
COUNTRIES.

07540 REISCHAUER, R.D.
IMMIGRATION AND THE UNDERCLASS
PHILADELPHIA: ANLS OF AMER ACMY OF POLITICAL AND SOC
SCIENCE, (501) (JAN 89), 120-131.
THE SIZE AND NATURE OF RECENT IMMIGRATION TO THE UNITED
STATES HAVE RAISED THE POSSIBILITY THAT IMMIGRANTS HAVE
DIMINISHED THE LABOR MARKET OPPORTUNITIES OF LOW-SKILLED,
NATIVE MINORITY WORKERS AND, THEREBY, MIGHT HAVE CONTRIBUTED
TO THE EMERGENCE OF THE URBAN UNDERCLASS. TO THE EXTENT THAT
IMMIGRANTS AND NATIVE WORKERS ARE SUBSTITUTE FACTORS OF
PRODUCTION, IMMIGRANTS MAY REDUCE THE WAGE RATES OF NATIVE
LABOR, INCREASE THEIR UNEMPLOYMENT, LOWER THEIR LABOR FORCE
PARTICIPATION, UNDERMINE WORKING CONDITIONS, AND REDUCE
RATES OF INTERNAL MOBILITY. WHILE CASUAL EMPIRICISM WOULD
SEEM TO SUPPORT THE NOTION THAT IMMIGRANTS HAVE DEPRESSED
THE OPPORTUNITIES OF LOW-SKILLED NATIVE WORKERS, CAREFUL AND
SOPHISTICATED ANALYSES BY A NUMBER OF SOCIAL SCIENTISTS
PROVIDE LITTLE EVIDENCE THAT IMMIGRANTS HAVE HAD ANY
SIGNIFICANT NEGATIVE IMPACTS ON THE EMPLOYMENT SITUATION OF
BLACK AMERICANS. THUS COMPETITION FROM UNSKILLED IMMIGRANTS
SHOULD NOT BE INCLUDED ON THE LIST OF FACTORS THAT HAVE
FACILITATED THE GROWTH OF THE UNDERCLASS.

07541 REITSMA, R.
AFTER 40 YEARS DOES NATO HAVE TO CHANGE (A EUROPEAN
PERSPECTIVE)
AVAILABLE FROM NTIS, NO. AD-A208 016/6/GAR, APR 89, 53.
NATO HAS UNDERWRITTEN AN UNPRECEDENTED PERIOD OF PEACE
IN EUROPE. MANY DEVELOPMENTS, HOWEVER, INDICATE THAT NATO
SHOULD HAVE TO CHANGE TO SUSTAIN ITS SUCCESS. THIS STUDY
SEEKS TO FIND AN ANSWER ON THE NEED FOR CHANGE. IT EXPLORES
THE KIND OF POSSIBLE CHANGES AND CONCENTRATES ON ISSUES LIKE:
NATO AFTER THE INF-TREATY, EAST-WEST RELATIONS, BURDEN-
SHARING AND POLITICAL AND ECONOMICAL DEVELOPMENTS IN EUROPE.
THE ROLE OF EUROPE IN RELATION TO THE INTERESTS AND THE
POSITION OF THE UNITED STATES IS STUDIED IN PARTICULAR. THE
STUDY ALSO EXPLORES THE MORE FUNDAMENTAL QUESTION IF IN THE
LONG TERM NATO ITSELF WILL SURVIVE. THE STUDY CONCLUDES WITH
A LONG TERM OUTLOOK ON NATO'S POSSIBLE STRUCTURE AND
INTERNAL RELATIONSHIPS.

07542 REJALI, D.M.
DISCIPLINE AND TORTURE, OR HOW IRANIANS BECAME MODERNS
DISSERTATION ABSTRACTS INTERNATIONAL, 48(10) (APR 88),
2719-A.
THE DISSERTATION INCLUDES AN EMPIRICAL ANALYSIS OF
IRANIAN PUNITIVE PRACTICES OVER THE LAST CENTURY. IT ALSO
EXAMINES SEVERAL CLAIMS MADE BY MODERN PHILOSPHERS AND
OTHERS REGARDING CORPORAL PUNISHMENTS, TORTURE, THE
"DISCIPLINARY PROCESS" AND THEIR RELATIONSHIP TO DEVELOPING
AND MODERN SOCIETIES WITHIN THE IRANIAN CONTEXT.

07543 REJANTE, C.R.
LOCAL GOVERNMENT PARTICIPATION IN AN INTEGRATED AREA
PROGRAM
DISSERTATION ABSTRACTS INTERNATIONAL, 49(11) (MAY 89),
3502-A.
USING THE BICOL RIVER BASIN DEVELOPMENT PROGRAM IN THE
PHILIPPINES AS A CASE STUDY, THE AUTHOR EXAMINES LOCAL
GOVERNMENT PARTICIPATION IN AN INTEGRATED AREA PROGRAM. SHE
FINDS THAT LOCAL GOVERNMENT PARTICIPATION IS MOST HEAVILY
INFLUENCED BY THE EXPECTATIONS OF LOCAL OFFICIALS,
SUBJECTIVE VALUATIONS OF RESOURCES, AND DOMINANT SOCIAL
VALUES REGARDING COMPLIANCE AND SOCIAL ACCEPTANCE.

07544 REKHESS, E.
THE ARAB NATIONALISM CHALLENGE TO THE ISRAELI COMMUNIST
PARTY, 1970-1985
STUDIES IN COMPARATIVE COMMUNISM, XXII(4) (WIN 89),
337-350.
THE ARTICLE OUTLINES THE CONFLICTS AND CHALLENGES
PRESENTED TO THE ARAB-JEWISH ISRAELI COMMUNIST PARTY BY
RADICAL ARAB NATIONALIST ORGANIZATIONS SUCH AS THE SONS OF
THE VILLAGE AND THE NATIONAL PROGRESSIVE MOVEMENT. THE
ARTICLE CONCENTRATES ON THE IDEOLOGICAL DIFFERENCES BETWEEN
THE TWO CAMPS, PARTICULARLY THE CONFLICT BETWEEN THOSE WHO

FAVOR MILITANT ACTIVISM AND THOSE WHO SUPPORT REVOLUTIONARY
STRUGGLE. THE FIFTEEN YEAR CONFLICT CULMINATED IN TOTAL
VICTORY BY THE MORE MODERATE COMMUNISTS. THE COMMUNIST
PARTY'S VICTORY IS ATTRIBUTED TO ITS IDEOLOGICAL, TACTICAL,
ORGANIZATIONAL, AND NUMERICAL SUPERIORITY.

07545 REMDE, A.; MORNA, C.L.
SAVIMBI STATES HIS CASE
NEW AFRICAN, (258) (MAR 89), 11-13, 16.
DESPITE THE ANGOLAN PEACE AGREEMENT, UNITA LEADER JONAS
SAVIMBI HAS VOWED TO CONTINUE FIGHTING UNLESS THE MPLA
GOVERNMENT IS PREPARED TO SHARE POWER WITH HIM. BUT THE
ANGOLAN GOVERNMENT REMAINS DETERMINED NOT TO SPEAK TO
SAVIMBI.

07546 REMDE, A.
WEST GERMANY REDISCOVERS AFRICA
NEW AFRICAN, (FEB 88), 27.
THIS ARTICLE REPORTS ON A VISIT OF WEST GERMAN
CHANCELLOR HELMUT KOHL TO KENYA. IT DESCRIBES THE PREVIOUS
LOW PROFILE WEST GERMAN GOVERNMENTS HAVE TRIED TO KEEP WITH
AFRICA AND THE FAVORABLE RESPONSE OF THE PRESENT WEST GERMAN
GOVERNMENT, AND THE POSSIBILITIES OF AFRICA BEING AN
IMPORTANT FIELD OF FOREIGN POLICY FOR THEM.

07547 REMINGTON, T.F.
SOVIET SOCIETY UNDER THE OLD REGIME
PROBLEMS OF COMMUNISM, XXXVIII(6) (NOV 89), 78-83.
THE QUALITY OF WESTERN LITERATURE ON SOVIET SOCIETY IN
THE PRE-GORBACHEV ERA ULTIMATELY DEPENDED ON THE RESTRICTED
NATURE OF THE AVAILABLE SOURCE MATERIAL. BUT BIASES AND
CONTROL ALSO CHARACTERIZE THE FLOOD OF PUBLISED INFORMATION
EMANATING FROM THE USSR IN THE AGE OF GLASNOST. MOREOVER,
GLASNOST HIGHLIGHTS THE NEED TO ADDRESS THE NEW SOCIAL
FORCES THAT HAVE EMERGED IN A SOCIETY UNDERGOING PERESTROIKA.
SPECIFICALLY, SCHOLARS MUST NOW TURN TO SUCH TOPICS AS THE
ROLE OF THE INTELLIGENTSIA, THE RISE OF THE ENVIRONMENTAL
MOVEMENT, AND THE BURGEONING NATIONAL MOVEMENTS WITHIN THE
USSR.

07548 REMMER, A.
A NOTE ON POST-PUBLICATION CENSORSHIP IN POLAND 1980-1987
SOVIET STUDIES, 61(3) (JUL 89), 415-425.
ONE POLITICAL REPERCUSSION OF SOLIDARITY IN POLAND HAS
BEEN IN CHANGES WHICH OCCURRED IN THE CONTROL OF INFORMATION
BY AUTHORITIES. THE CENSORSHIP LAW OF 31 JULY 1981 HAS
REMAINED ON THE BOOKS AS A LEGACY OF THE SOLIDARITY ERA,
PROVIDING SOME LEGAL PROTECTION FROM OVER-ZEALOUS CENSORS.
THE CENSORSHIP LAW WAS A DOCUMENT FOCUSED MOSTLY ON
REGULATING PREVENTIVE CENSORSHIP, EXERCISED PRIOR TO THE
PUBLICATION, BROADCASTING, PERFORMANCE AND/OR EXHIBITING OF
MATERIAL IN POLAND. IT DID NOT REGULATE POST-PUBLICATION
CENSORSHIP IN THE FORM OF RESTRICTING PRINTED MATTER IN
SPECIAL LIBRARY COLLECTIONS FOR POLITICAL REASONS, AND IT
BARELY TOUCHED ON ONE OF THE LEAST KNOWN FORMS OF THAT
CENSORSHIP: THE CONTROL OF THE IMPORT OF FOREIGN
PUBLICATIONS TO POLAND. THIS ARTICLE EXPLORES RESTRICTED
LIBRARY HOLDINGS, CONTROL OF THE IMPORT OF FOREIGN
PUBLICATIONS, LEGAL CHANGES AND JURISPRUDENCE AND CONCLUDES
THAT NOW PERHAPS MORE INDIVIDUAL POLES WILL HAVE ACCESS TO
FOREIGN PUBLICATIONS PREVIOUSLY LABELLED AS 'HARMFUL' TO THE
STATE.

07549 REMMER, K.L.
NEOPATRIMONIALISM: THE POLITICS OF MILITARY RULE IN CHILE,
1973-1987
COMPARATIVE POLITICS, 21(2) (JAN 89), 149-170.
THE DICTATORSHIP OF GENERAL AUGUSTO PINOCHET HAS
EXHIBITED THREE DISTINCTIVE CHARACTERISTICS. FIRST, POWER
HAS BEEN CONCENTRATED IN THE HANDS OF A SINGLE INDIVIDUAL AT
THE EXPENSE OF RULE BY THE MILITARY AS AN INSTITUTION.
SECONDLY, CHILEAN AUTHORITARIANISM HAS DEMONSTRATED
SURPRISING DURABILITY. THIRDLY, IT HAS BEEN DISTINGUISHED BY
ITS DETERMINED PURSUIT OF ORTHODOX ECONOMIC POLICIES.

07550 REMMER, K.L.
STATE CHANGE IN CHILE, 1973-1988
STUDIES IN COMPARATIVE INTERNATIONAL DEVELOPMENT, 24(3)
(FAL 89), 5-29.
ALL OF THE SOUTHERN CONE MILITARY REGIMES OF THE 1970S
ARTICULATED A COMMITMENT TO A NEOCONSERVATIVE PROGRAM OF
STATE CHANGE. NOWHERE, HOWEVER, WAS THE COMMITMENT
TRANSLATED INTO POLICY WITH GREATER ZEAL, SPEED, AND
CONSISTENCY THAN IN CHILE. WHAT DIFFERED IN CHILE WAS LESS A
LACK OF RESISTANCE TO NEOCONSERVATISM THAN THE CAPACITY OF
THE ECONOMIC TEAM TO IGNORE OR OVERRIDE THAT RESISTANCE DUE
TO THE EXTREME CONCENTRATION OF POLITICAL POWER ACHIEVED BY
GENERAL AUGUSTO PINOCHET. THE CHILEAN EXPERIENCE
CONSEQUENTLY UNDERLINES THE IMPORTANCE OF INSTITUTIONAL
ARRANGEMENTS FOR UNDERSTANDING VARIATIONS IN POLICY OUTCOMES.

07551 REN, Z.
BUSH, GORBACHEV TO MEET IN DECEMBER
BEIJING REVIEW, 32(47) (NOV 89), 11-12.

WITH A VIEW TO PREVENTING THE RAPIDLY CHANGING WORLD
SITUATION FROM AFFECTING SOVIET-AMERICAN RELATIONS, GEORGE
BUSH AND MIKHAIL GORBACHEV HAVE SCHEDULED AN INFORMAL SUMMIT
ON DECEMBER 2-3, 1989. EARLIER THE TWO COUNTRIES HAD AGREED
TO HOLD A FORMAL SUMMIT MEETING IN THE USA IN 1990. THE
DIFFERENCE BETWEEN THE TWO SUMMITS IS THAT THE FORMAL ONE
WILL CONCENTRATE ON ARMS CONTROL AND REGIONAL CONFLICTS. THE
INFORMAL MEETING WILL HAVE NO FIXED AGENDA.

07552 RENARD, C.
THE DEMOCRATIC DIMENSIONS OF A EUROPE OF THE TWELVE
WORLD MARXIST REVIEW, 32(8) (AUG 89), 12-14.
THIS ARTICLE EXPLORES WEST EUROPEAN INTEGRATION AND THE
WORKING-CLASS MOVEMENT. THE PROSPECTIVE CREATION OF THE
EEC'S SINGLE MARKET IN 1992 ALSO RAISED THE QUESTION OF A
POLITICAL EUROPE. THIS ARTICLE EXPLORES THE NEED FOR PEACE
AND DEMOCRACY AND SEARCHES FOR A LEFT STRATEGY. IT FAVORS A
POLITICAL APPROACH TO SECURITY OVER A MILITARY APPROACH AND
DESIRES A 12-NATION EUROPE RATHER THAN A WEST EUROPEAN UNION.

07553 RENBERG, D.
JUST SAY "NO": JUDICIAL RESTIANT IN CONGRESSIONAL
EXPULSION CASES
JOURNAL OF LAW & POLITICS, V(3) (SPR 89), 657-683.
THIS NOTE SUMMARIZES BOTH THE RECENT HISTORY OF HOUSE
EXPULSIONS AND THE PROCEDURES INVOLVED. IT ALSO DISCUSSES
THE POWER OF JUDICIAL REVIEW AND THE CONSIDERATIONS WHICH
HAVE LED TO CONSTRAINTS ON THAT POWER. THE AUTHOR EXAMINES
THE "POLITICAL QUESTION" DOCTRINE, ARGUING THAT A COURT
SHOULD APPLY IT TO HOUSE EXPULSION PROCEEDINGS TO FIND THE
ISSUE NONJUSTICIABLE. FURTHERMORE, THE POWER OF CONGRESS TO
EXPEL A MEMBER SHOULD BE DISTINGUISHED FROM ITS POWER TO
EXCLUDE, WHICH HAS REVIEWED IN POWELL. THE AUTHOR ELABORATES
UPON THE REMEDAIL DISCRETION DOCTRINE AND RECOMMENDS THAT A
COURT COULD ALSO DENY REVIEW BASED ON "PRUDENTIAL CONCERNS."
THE ARTICLE CONCLUDES THAT EXISTING DISCIPLINARY PROCEDURES
IN THE HOUSE ADEQUATELY SAFEGUARD A CONGRESSMAN'S RIGHTS
DURING THE EXPULSION PROCESS.

07554 RENZCH, W.
GERMAN FEDERALISM IN HISTORICAL PERSPECTIVE: FEDERALISM AS
A SUBSTITUTE FOR A NATIONAL STATE
PUBLIUS: THE JOURNAL OF FEDERALISM, 19(4) (FAL 86), 17-34.
RENZSCH ARGUES THAT DESPITE A LONG HISTORY OF
CONSTITUTIONAL EXPERIENCE WITH FEDERAL INSTITUTIONS, THE OLD
GERMAN REICH WAS NOT A TRUE FEDERAL STATE, HE EXPLORES THE
HISTORY OF THE CREATION AND DEVELOPMENT OF A UNITED GERMAN
NATIONAL STATE, ITS FAILURE, AND REESTABLISHMENT, HE
CONCLUDES THAT BASIC LAW HAS PRESERVED THE GERMAN TRADITION
OF COOPERATION OF THE FEDERAL AND STATE GOVERNMENTS THROUGH
THE JOINT EXERCISE OF PUBLIC AUTHORITY IN MOST FIELDS OF
DOMESTIC POLITICS.

07555 RESZLER, A.
LATENT PLURALISM IN CENTRAL EUROPE.
PLURAL SOCIETIES, 18(2) (MAR 89), 30-44.
THIS ARTICLE EXAMINES THE RENEWAL OF ACTIVE CENTRAL
EUROPEAN IDENTITY SENTIMENTS FOUNDED ON NOSTALGIA TOWARDS AN
OPEN AND PLURALIST EUROPE, DRAWING ITS STRENGHT FROM THE
RENAISSANCE ON A SPIRITUAL LEVEL FROM AN AFFIRMED CENTRAL
EUROPEAN CONSCIOUSNESS. NUMEROUS HISTORICAL STUDIES,
ESPECIALLY IN HUNGARY, CONTRIBUTE TO THE "PARTICULARISM" OF
AN INTERMEDIARY EUROPE, DETACHED SINCE THE MIDDLE AGES FROM
THE WEST EUROPEAN FAMILY OF NATIONS AS FAR AS CERTAIN
DECISIVE ASPECTS OF ITS POLITICAL CULTURE ARE CONCERNED.

07556 RETI, T.
DEPENDENCE AND CENTRALIZATION IN ROMANIA 1944 TO 1956
EASTERN EUROPEAN POLITICS AND SOCIETIES, 3(3) (FAL 89),
465-499.
THIS ARTICLE CONCLUDES THAT RUMANIA ENTERS THE 1990S
WITH ALL THE PROBLEMS CREATED IN THE EARLY 1950S MAGNIFIED
BY FOUR EXTRA DECADES OF ADHERENCE TO THE SAME MODEL. IT
BEGINS BY EXPLORING ANTECEDENTS TO THE PRESENT SITUATION.
EXAMINED IS ROMANIA ON THE SIDE OF THE ALLIES AND THEN THE
TASK OF ECONOMIC RESTORATION. ROMANIAN-SOVIET RELATIONS ARE
DETAILED AS WELL AS THE DEJ ERA, 1949-53, AGRICULTURE, THE
STANDARD OF LIVING AND CHANGES IN THE FIRST FIVE-YEAR PLAN
ARE DETAILED.

07557 RETTIG, R.
THE POLITICS OF ORGAN TRANSPLANTATION: A PARABLE OF OUR
TIME
JOURNAL OF HEALTH POLITICS, POLICY AND LAW, 14(1) (SPR 89),
191-228.
ABSTRACT. THIS PAPER REVIEWS THE HISTORICAL DEVELOPMENT
OF FEDERAL GOVERNMENT POLICY FOR KIDNEY, HEART, AND LIVER
TRANSPLANTATION. IT EXAMINES SEVERAL POLITICAL DIMENSIONS OF
WHOLE ORGAN TRANSPLANTATION: THE ROLE OF THE PRINT AND
BROADCAST MEDIA; THE MANAGEMENT OF ORGAN PROCUREMENT; THE
CERTIFICATION OF TRANSPLANT CENTERS; THE EVALUATION OF NEW
SURGICAL PROCEDURES; AND THE ISSUES OF FINANCING,
DISTRIBUTIVE JUSTICE, AND RATIONING OF SCARCE MEDICAL
RESOURCES. THE AUTHOR FINDS THAT THE MEDIA, THOUGH POWERFUL

IN AFFECTING TRANSPLANT POLICY, HAVE NOT BEEN SUBJECTED TO
CRITICAL ANALYSIS. ORGAN PROCUREMENT MODIFICATIONS, DRIVEN
BY A NEED ORIENTATION TOWARD CLOSING THE GAP BETWEEN ACTUAL
AND DESIRED LEVELS OF PERFORMANCE, MAY HAVE ADVERSELY
AFFECTED PERFORMANCE. THE CASE OF LIVER TRANSPLANTATION
SUGGESTS THE NEED FOR IMPROVED INSTITUTIONS AND MECHANISMS
FOR EVALUATING NEW SURGICAL PROCEDURES. FINALLY, STATES THAT
CONFRONT THE NEED TO MEET A BINDING BUDGET-BALANCING
REQUIREMENT MAY ALLOCATE FUNDS AWAY FROM EXPENSIVE MEDICAL
PROCEDURES THAT BENEFIT THE FEW TOWARD BASIC SERVICES THAT
BENEFIT THE MANY; THE OREGON AND VIRGINIA MEDICAID PROGRAMS
EXEMPIFY THIS POINT.

07558 REUSCH, J.
PEACE AND CAPITALISM
WORLD MARXIST REVIEW, 31(10) (OCT 88), 27-34.
THE URGE TO RESORT TO VIOLENCE NATURALLY SPRINGS FROM
THE VERY NATURE OF MONOPOLY CAPITAL. THE SPEARHEAD OF
MILITARISM IS DIRECTED PRIMARILY AGAINST WORLD SOCIALISM AND
ALSO AGAINST THE NATIONAL LIBERATION MOVEMENT. IT IS
IMPERIALISM, US IMPERIALISM IN THE FIRST PLACE, THAT IS
RESPONSIBLE FOR THE ARMS RACE AND THE NUCLEAR THREAT LOOMING
OVER MANKIND. CAPITALISM HAS CEASELESSLY WAGED WARS
THROUGHOUT ITS HISTORY, OVER 150 OF THEM IN THE LAST FOUR
DECADES. IMPERIALISM MUST BE MADE TO GIVE UP ITS USE OF
ARMED FORCE, AND TO 'SOFTEN' MILITARISM-WITHIN THE FRAMEWORK
OF THAT SYSTEM. THIS CANNOT BE DONE UNLESS CAPITALISM ITSELF
MAKES A CONSTRUCTIVE CONTRIBUTION TO PEACE AND DISARMAMENT.

07559 REUTER, P.
CAN THE BORDERS BE SEALED?
PUBLIC INTEREST, 92 (SUM 88), 51-65.
THIS ARTICLE EXAMINES THE TRADITIONAL METHODS OF
ENFORCEMENT OF DRUG POLICY, DRUG PROHIBITIONS, AND
INTERDICTION. OFFICIALS ARE AGREED UPON THE FACT THAT
ENFORCEMENT OF DRUG PROHIBITIONS HAS CLEAR LIMITS IN ITS
ABILITY TO REDUCE DRUG USE. A PROGRAM OF SEALING OFF U.S.
BORDERS IS CONSIDERED.

07560 REVEL, J.
IMMIGRATION: TELLING IT THE WAY IT IS
ENCOUNTER, LXXII(5) (MAY 89), 38-40.
THE DISPUTE OVER IMMIGRATION TO FRANCE IS CHARACTERIZED
BY A GREAT DEAL OF TALK ON THE BASIS OF VERY LITTLE
KNOWLEDGE. WITH AN ALIEN POPULATION OF SEVEN PERCENT, FRANCE
IS CLOSE TO THE EUROPEAN AVERAGE. BUT SEVERAL FACTORS
EXACERBATE THE TENSIONS, NOTABLY OVER-CONCENTRATION IN
CERTAIN DEPARTEMENTS AND URBAN AREAS. THE IMMIGRANT
POPULATION SUFFERS FROM OVERCROWDING, UNEMPLOYMENT,
INADEQUATE EDUCATION, AND A HIGH INCIDENCE OF DELINQUENCY.
THE PROBLEMS OF THE IMMIGRANTS NEED TO BE TAKEN AWAY FROM
THE SPEECHIFIERS OF EVERY POLITICAL PERSUASION AND PLACED
WHERE THEY BELONG--AT THE LEVEL OF HUMAN ECONOMIC AND
CULTURAL REALITY.

07561 REVEL, J.
IS COMMUNISM REVERSIBLE?
COMMENTARY, 87(1) (JAN 89), 17-24.
THE AUTHOR LOOKS AT RECENT REFORM EFFORTS IN THE
COMMUNIST WORLD AND CONSIDERS THE CAPACITY OF COMMUNIST
SYSTEMS TO TRANSFORM THEMSELVES.

07562 REVEL, J.
SOCIALIST-COMMUNIST PACTS: THE FRENCH EXCEPTION
ENCOUNTER, LXXIII(1) (JUN 89), 46-48.
THE COMMUNIST VOTE IS DECLINING ALL OVER EUROPE. APART
FROM THE TINY SWEDISH COMMUNIST PARTY, WHICH BACKS THE
SOCIALISTS IN PARLIAMENT, THE COMMUNISTS ARE OUT OF THE
RUNNING IN EUROPE. IN EVERY EEC COUNTRY EXCEPT FRANCE AND
SWEDEN, COLLABORATION WITH THE COMMUNISTS HAS BEEN A NON-
STARTER FOR YEARS AS FAR AS THE SOCIALIST PARTY IS CONCERNED.
ALTHOUGH THE COMMUNIST PARTY IS STILL VERY STRONG IN ITALY,
IT IS MARGINAL AS FAR AS THE PARLIAMENTARY MAJORITY IS
CONCERNED AND HAS LOST STRENGTH IN THE LAST TEN YEARS.

07563 REVEL, J.
THE LE PEN SYNDROME
ENCOUNTER, LXXIII(2) (JUL 89), 42.
THE SHORT-LIVED POLITICAL SUCCESS OF LE PEN IN FRANCE
HAS DUE IN PART TO A REFUSAL TO ANALYZE THE REAL SOCIAL AND
CULTURAL CAUSES BEHIND HIS POPULAR APPEAL. THE CAUSES OF THE
ELECTORAL SUCCESSES OF THE REPUBLICAN PARTY IN BERLIN ARE
THE SAME: FRICTION BETWEEN IMMIGRANT AND HOST POPULATIONS IN
A POVERTY-STRIKEN URBAN MILIEU, EXACERBATED BY THE SPECTRE
OF DRUGS, AIDS, AND INSECURITY.

07564 REVEL, J-F.
HASTENING THE DEATH OF COMMUNISM
COMMENTARY, 88(4) (OCT 89), 19-23.
THIS ARTICLE EXPLORES THE QUESTIONS: WHAT POLICY SHOULD
THE DEMOCRACIES ADOPT TOWARD THE COMMUNIST WORLD AT THIS
STAGE OF ITS EVOLUTION? AND, TOWARD WHAT END SHOULD SUCH A
POLICY BE DIRECTED? IT SUGGESTS THAT IT IS FALSE THAT
COMMUNISM HAS PASSED OUT OF ITS STALINIST PHASE AND HAS

ENTERED DEFINITELY THE STAGE OF "POST - TOTALITARIAN"
SOCIETY. IT SUGGESTS THAT ONE'S DUTY IS TO IMPROVE THE
PROSPECTS OF DEMOCRACY AND PEACE IN THE WORLD AND THAT THIS
IS INCOMPATIBLE WITH THE VERY STRUCTURES OF COMMUNIST
SOCIETY. IT CONCLUDES THAT HE MUST HASTEN THE DEATH OF
COMMUNISM.

07565 REYES-BARAONA, C.O.; WITTER, J.A.
EVALUATION OF UNITED STATES STRATEGY IN CENTRAL AMERICA
AVAILABLE FROM NTIS, NO. AD-A209 464/7/GAR, MAR 89, 112.
THE PURPOSE OF THIS STUDY IS TO EVALUATE THE
EFFECTIVENESS OF RECENT U.S. STRATEGY IN CENTRAL AMERICA.
OBVIOUSLY, THE SCOPE IS BROAD; HOWEVER, THE FACT THAT ONE
AUTHOR IS HONDURAN AND THE OTHER RECENTLY SERVED TWO YEARS
IMPLEMENTING U.S. MILITARY POLICY IN HONDURAS BRINGS SOME
DEPTH OF EXPERIENCE TO THE TASK. IN OFFERING RECOMMENDATIONS
FOR U.S. STRATEGY AT THE CONCLUSION, THE AUTHORS DO SO WITH
A SENSE OF HUMILITY AS MANY DISTINGUISHED GOVERNMENT
OFFICIALS AND ANALYSTS OF U.S. STRATEGY AND CENTRAL AMERICAN
AFFAIRS HAVE BEEN WORKING ON THIS EFFORT FOR MANY YEARS. IF
THE STUDY PROMPTS CRITICAL THINKING AND RAISES QUESTIONS FOR
FURTHER RESEARCH, IT HAS ACCOMPLISHED ITS PURPOSE. THE STUDY
BEGINS WITH A SHORT BACKGROUND OF HISTORICAL U.S. INTERESTS
AND INVOLVEMENTS IN CENTRAL AMERICA CONCLUDING WITH A REVIEW
OF CURRENT INTERESTS AND THREATS TO THOSE INTERESTS. THEN,
THE CARTER AND REAGAN ADMINISTRATION STRATEGIES ARE
DESCRIBED AND EVALUATED. THE STUDY CONCLUDES WITH THE
AUTHORS' RECOMMENDATIONS FOR U.S. STRATEGY IN CENTRAL
AMERICA. KEYWORDS: INTERNATIONAL RELATIONS, EL SALVADOR,
NICARAGUA, LATIN AMERICA, NATIONAL INTERESTS.

07566 REYKOWSKI, J.
HERE IS POLAND GOING?
WORLD MARXIST REVIEW, 32(11) (NOV 89), 17-20.
THIS ARTICLE EXAMINES THE ABILITY AND INCLINATION OF
POLAND TO UPHOLD SOCIALIST PRINCIPLES. COMMUNIST IN ORDER TO
REBUILD THE PARTY'S AUTHORITY AND WIN BACK PUBLIC SUPPORT,
IT IS VERY IMPORTANT TO FORMULATE A PROGRAMME FOR THE
RENEWAL OF SOCIALISM AND TO MAKE IT CLEAR WHOSE INTERESTS
THE PARTY WILL WORK FOR, AND HOW. AN EQUALLY CRUCIAL TASK IS
TO DECIDE ON CORRECT METHODS. IN THE PAST THE PUMP BECAME AN
ADMINISTRATOR, A TOOL OF GOVERNMENT. BUT IN THE NEW
SITUATION THE PARTY SHOULD BECOME A POLITICAL FORCE CAPABLE
OF MAKING CONTACT WITH PEOPLE, WINNING THEM OVER TO ITS SIDE
AND INFLUENCING THEIR MINDS. IN SHORT, THE PARTY HAS TO
LEARN THE ART OF PERSUASION.

07567 REYLES, F.
ISRAEL AND THE PLO: THE INPACT OF THE INTIFADA
INTERNATIONAL SPECTATOR, XXIII(4) (OCT 88), 215-229.
ISRAELI ILLUSIONS ABOUT THE POSSIBILITY OF BYPASSING THE
PLO AND SATISFYING PALESTINIAN ASPIRATIONS WITH SOME
SUBSTITUTE FOR NATIONAL INDEPENDENCE HAVE BEEN CHALLENGED,
IF NOT DISPELLED, BY THE INTIFADA, KING HUSSEIN. AND THE USA.
ARAB ILLUSIONS ABOUT DISMANTLING THE ZIONIST STATE SAND
RECOVERING DTHE WHOLE OF PALESTINE ARE ALSO VANISHING. YET,
CONDITIONS FOR DIRECT NEGOTIATIONS BETWEEN ISRAEL AND THE
PLO SEEM FAR FROM RIPE.

07568 REYMARS, S. H.; WOLFE, J. C.
THE U.S. ECONOMIC OUTLOOK FOR 1989-90
ECONOMIC OUTLOOK USA, 15(3) (WIN 88), 3-10.
THIS ARTICLE REVIEWS THE ECONOMIC FORECAST FOR 1987 AND
ANALYZES THE CAUSES FOR ERROR IN PREDICTING THE OUTLOOK IT
THEN LOOKS FORWARD TO 1989-90 AND EXAMINES THE GNP. CONSUMER
PURCHASING, CAPITAL PURCHASES, RESIDENTIAL CONSTRUCTION, OUR
EXPORT POSITION, UNEMPLOYMENT AND GROWTH RATE. IT ALSO
DISCUSSES THE FEDERAL BUDGET AND FISCAL POLICY.

07569 REYNOLDS, D.E.
ANARCHY AND ORDER: A SOCIAL PHYSICS OF INTERNATIONAL
RELATIONS
DISSERTATION ABSTRACTS INTERNATIONAL, 50(6) (DEC 89),
1796-A.
THE AUTHOR LOOKS AT THE CONSTRUCTION OF BOTH ANCIENT AND
MODERN SCIENTIFIC EXPLANATIONS OF GLOBAL POLITICS, THEIR
UNDERLYING LOGIC AND AXIOMS, AND THE AGE-OLD LOVE-HATE
RELATIONSHIP BETWEEN SCIENCE, PHILOSOPHY, AND SOCIAL SCIENCE.
SHE EXPLORES THE IMPLICATIONS OF APPLYING NEW
SUPERCOMPUTING-BASED METHODOLOGIES TO GLOBAL POLITICS AND
ARGUES IN SUPPORT OF A TYPE OF "COMPUTATIONAL SYNERGETICS"
THAT MIGHT PROVIDE NEW INSIGHTS IN THE STUDY OF GLOBAL
POLICTICS.

07570 REYNOLDS, M.O.
THE CAMBODIAN EXPERIMENT IN RETROSPECT
ASIAN OUTLOOK, 25(1) (NOV 89), 13-16.
SOCIALISM IN ALL ITS VARIANTS HAS BEEN WIDELY ASSOCIATED
WITH ECONOMIC FAILURE, BUT TWO EPISODES STAND OUT AS VIRTUAL
LABORATORY EXPERIMENTS IN THE PERENNIAL WAR ON COMMERCIAL
ACTIVITY: LENIN'S EFFORT OF 1918-1921 AND THE CAMBODIAN
DISASTER OF 1975-1979. THIS ARTICLE CONSIDERS THE PARALLELS
BETWEEN THE TWO ECONOMIC POLICIES AND THE FAILURE OF THE
CAMBODIAN EXPERIMENT IN SOCIALISM.

07571 REYNOLDS, M.R.
MEMBERS OF PARLIAMENT AND THEIR CONSTITUENCIES: A
COMPARATIVE STUDY OF BRITAIN AND CANADA
DISSERTATION ABSTRACTS INTERNATIONAL, 49(7) (JAN 89),
1946-A.
IN BOTH BRITAIN AND CANADA, BACKBENCH MP'S ARE SHOWING A
GROWING AWARENESS OF THE POTENTIAL "PERSONAL VOTE" AMONG THE
ELECTORATE. INDIVIDUAL MP'S GO ABOUT DEVELOPING A PERSONAL
FOLLOWING IN DIFFERENT WAYS, OR "HOME STYLES." THE STRONGER
THE BELIEF IN THE PERSONAL VOTE, THE MORE LIKELY IT IS THAT
AN MP WILL DEVELOP A DISTINCTIVE HOME STYLE.

07572 REZUN, M.
AFGHANISTAN'S AGONY
INTERNATIONAL PERSPECTIVES, XVIII(2) (MAR 89), 17-20.
THE ARTICLE EXAMINES THE FUTURE OF AFGHANISTAN AS THE
SOVIET UNION WITHDRAWS ITS TROOPS AND LEAVES THE COMMUNIST
REGIME LED BY NAJIBULLAH TO FIGHT THE REBEL MUJAHEDEEN ON
ITS OWN. THE ARTICLE EXPLORES THE ROLE THAT IRAN, PAKISTAN
THE USSR, THE VARIOUS REBEL GROUPS, AND THE AFGHAN SECRET
POLICE WILL PLAY IN FUTURE EVENTS. IT CONCLUDES THAT
PARTITION ALONG THE LINES OF THE HINDU KUSH MOUNTAINS IS A
DISTINCT POSSIBILITY, BUT WHATEVER THE OUTCOME, THE
SUFFERING IN AFGHANISTAN IS FAR FROM OVER.

07573 RHODEBECK, L.A.
THE INFLUENCE OF GROUP IDENTIFICATION ON POLITICAL
PREFERENCES
DISSERTATION ABSTRACTS INTERNATIONAL, 48(10) (APR 88),
2719-A.
WITHIN THE CONTEXT OF GROUP BEHAVIOR, THE DISSERTATION
DEVELOPS AN INTEGRATED THEORETICAL FRAMEWORK BASED ON
CONCEPTS FROM COGNITIVE PSYCHOLOGY FOR UNDERSTANDING THE
PROCESS THROUGH WHICH SOCIO-DEMOGRAPHIC GROUPS TAKE ON
PSYCHOLOGICAL AND POLITICAL SIGNIFICANCE. IT FOCUSES ON
GROUP IDENTIFICATION AS ONE OF THE FORCES THAT MOTIVATES
GROUP ACTION.

07574 RHODES, C.
RECIPROCITY IN TRADE: THE UTILITY OF A BARGAINING STRATEGY
INTERNATIONAL ORGANIZATION, 43(2) (SPR 89), 273-300.
RECENT WORKS IN INTERNATIONAL RELATIONS THEORY HAVE
FOCUSED ON THE VALUE OF RECIPROCITY AS A MEANS OF ACHIEVING
COOPERATION IN INTERNATIONAL POLITICS. THEY ARGUE THAT EVEN
IN AN ANARCHIC SETTING IN WHICH SELF-HELP TYPIFIES THE
BEHAVIOR OF SOVEREIGN NATION STATES, THE STRATEGY OF
MATCHING COMPARABLE RESPONSES TO THE ACTIONS OF OTHER
NATIONS MAY EDUCATE THEM OVER TIME TO COOPERATE. THIS
ARTICLE EMPIRICALLY CONFIRMS THAT THIS ASSUMPTION IS CORRECT.
IT EXAMINES THE USE OF FLEXIBLE RECIPROCAL BARGAINING
STRATEGIES BETWEEN THE UNITED STATES AND ITS MAJOR TRADING
PARTNERS IN KEY SECTORS IN WHICH SURPLUS CAPACITY AND
DOMESTIC ADJUSTMENT DIFFICULTIES HAVE MADE COMMERCIAL
CONFLICTS APPARENT. THE OUTCOMES OF MOST OF THE DISPUTES
DEMONSTRATE THAT RECIPROCITY IS AN EFFECTIVE MEANS OF
ELICITING COOPERATION FROM TRADING PARTNERS. RESULTS ALSO
ILLUSTRATE THAT THIS COOPERATION IS USUALLY CONSISTENT WITH
THE GENERAL AGREEMENT ON TARIFFS AND TRADE (GATT) NORMS OF
LIBERAL TRADE AND DISPUTE SETTLEMENT, EVEN WHEN IT IS
INCONSISTENT WITH THE GATT PRINCIPLE OF NONDISCRIMINATION.

07575 RIBANSZKI, R.; POGANT, S.
INTERVIEW WITH ROBERT RIBANSZKI
WORLD AFFAIRS, 151(4) (1989), 220-223.
ROBERT RIBANSZKI, A LEADING ORGANIZED VOICE WITHIN
HUNGARY'S RULING PARTY THAT OPPOSES REFORM, SPEAKS OF THE
EVENTS OF 1956 SORTED A SAMPLE OF 86 OPINION STATEMENTS ON
DEFINITIONS OF HUNGARY'S FUTURE. HE DEFENDS THE RULING
PARTY'S STANCE THAT IT, ITS CAUSES AND EFFECTS, AND SOCIAL
POLICY RECOMMENDATIONS. THE MOVEMENT IN 1956 HAS A
COUNTERREVOLUTION. NOT A POPULAR UPRISING. HE CRITICIZES
CURRENT REFORM ADVOCATES FOR ACCEPTING THE STIGMA OF
STALINISM AND IGNORING THE SIGNIFICANT REFORMS BROUGHT ABOUT
LABELED RELIGIOUS-CONSERVATIVE, LIBERAL, AND ANTIPORNOGRAPHY
RULING SOCIALIST WORKERS PARTY. HE ALSO DENOUNCES THE
INCREASING PLURALISM IN HUNGARY AND DECLARES IT TO BE NOT A
MULTI-PARTY SYSTEM, BUT A WELL-ORGANIZED ANTISOCIALIST,
ANTICOMMUNIST MOVEMENT.

07576 RIBEIRU, A.
BRAZIL: PAGES OF HISTORY
WORLD MARXIST REVIEW, 32(5) (MAY 89), 76-78.
THE ROAD TRAVELLED OVER THE PAST THREE DECADES BY THE
BRAZILIAN COMMUNIST PARTY HAS BEEN DIFFICULT AND PAINFUL,
BUT ALSO INSTRUCTIVE, AND RICH IN LESSONS AND ACHIEVEMENTS
FOR THE REVOLUTIONARY PROCESS, ALL OF WHICH HAS HELPED
PROMOTE NEW THINKING AMONG THE PARTY CADRES. THE CENTRAL
COMMITTEE HAS ADMITTED TO DEVIATIONS FROM THE GENERAL
PRINCIPLES OF LENINISM AND DISREGARD FOR THE EXPERIENCE OF
THE WORLDWIDE WORKING-CLASS MOVEMENT. THIS COULD HAVE LED TO
THE PARTY LOSING ITS CLASS CHARACTER AND DEGENERATING INTO
REVISIONISM. IT WAS ALSO ADMITTED THAT THE PARTY RISKED
RAVELLING ITSELF IN SECTARIANISM AND DOGMATISM AND BECOMING

UNABLE TO EXERCISE ITS POLITICAL ROLE BECAUSE OF AN
INADEQUATE SCIENTIFIC ANALYSIS OF BRAZILIAN REALITIES AND
IGNORANCE OF THE SPECIFIC CIRCUMSTANCES IN ITS OWN COUNTRY.
FINALLY, THE NEED TO GET RID OF DEEP-SEATED ILLS AND EMBRACE
A QUALITATIVELY NEW WORLD VIEW WAS CLEARLY REALISED. THE
MARCH 1958 RESOLUTION READ, INTER ALIA: "DOGMATIC AND
SECTARIAN CONCEPTS, THE MAIN DANGER THE PARTY SHOULD FIGHT
TODAY, ARE ABSOLUTELY AT ODDS WITH THE CHARACTER OF THE
HISTORICAL TASKS SET BEFORE THE COMMUNISTS". 1

07577 RICE, C.
    IS GORBACHEV CHANGING THE RULES OF DEFENSE DECISION-MAKING?
    JOURNAL OF INTERNATIONAL AFFAIRS, 42(2) (SPR 89), 377-398.
    IN AN ATTEMPT TO DETERMINE THE CHANGES THAT THE SOVIET
    MILITARY STRUCTURE IS UNDERGOING, THE ARTICLE EXAMINES THE
    CHANGES IN LEADERSHIP, NUCLEAR STRATEG, ARMS CONTROL, AND
    CONVENTIONAL STRATEGY AND POSTURE. IT ALSO EXAMINES THE
    INCREASING AMOUNT OF DEBATE THAT IS OCCURRING IN THE SOVIET
    UNION ABOUT THE MILITARY STRUCTURE. IT CONCLUDES THAT
    GORBACHEV IS ATTEMPTING TO CREATE A NATIONAL SECURITY LAYER
    BETWEEN THE PURELY POLITICAL AND THE PURELY MILITARY.
    HOWEVER, THIS CHANGE IS NOT VIEWED AS A MAJOR RESTRUCTURING
    OF THE DEFENSE SYSTEM.

07578 RICE, C.
    PARTY RIVALRY IN THE CAUCASUS: SR'S, ARMENIANS AND THE
    BAKU UNION OF OIL WORKERS, 1907-08
    SLAVONIC AND EAST EUROPEAN REVIEW, 67(2) (APR 89), 228-243.
    ON 11 JANUARY 1909 TWO HUNDRED MEMBERS AND INVITED
    GUESTS OF THE BAKU UNION OF OIL WORKERS GATHERED FOR A LONG
    OVERDUE GENERAL MEETING. THE MAIN ITEM ON THE AGENDA WAS THE
    ELECTION OF A NEW BOARD. THOSE OPPOSED TO THE EXISTING BOARD
    PACKED THE LEFT-HAND SIDE OF THE ROOM, SIGNALLING THEIR
    DETERMINATION TO EFFECT A CHANGE. IN THIS THEY WERE
    SUCCESSFUL. AFTER THE VOTE WAS TAKEN ONLY THREE MEMBERS OF
    THE ORIGINAL, BOLSHEVIK-DOMINATED BOARD REMAINED; THE NEW
    BOARD WAS DOMINATED BY THE SOCIALIST REVOLUTIONARY PARTY.
    THE OUTCOME OF THE ELECTION WAS NO SURPRISE; ON THE CONTRARY,
    IT WAS THE ALMOST INEVITABLE END PRODUCT OF A PERSISTENT
    AND RUTHLESS CAMPAIGN TO WREST CONTROL FROM THE BOLSHEVIKS
    WHICH HAD BEEN GOING ON FOR MORE THAN A YEAR. THE STORY OF
    THIS STRUGGLE, IS WORTH RECOUNTING FOR ITS RELEVANCE TO ONE
    OF THE CENTRAL PROBLEMS AFFLICTING THE RUSSIAN LEGAL LABOUR
    MOVEMENT IN THE PRE-WAR PERIOD: NAMELY, THAT OF RECONCILING
    THE IDEOLOGICAL INDEPENDENCE OF THE TRADE UNIONS WITH THE
    INFLUENCE OF POLITICAL PARTIES CLAIMING TO STAND IN THE
    VANGUARD OF THE WORKING CLASS. INTER-PARTY CONFLICT WITHIN
    THE UNIONS (ALMOST ENDEMIC IN THIS PERIOD) DISCREDITED BOTH
    TYPES OF ORGANIZATION (UNIONS AND PARTIES) IN THE EYES OF
    MANY FAIR-MINDED WORKERS, DISTRACTED THE UNIONS FROM
    IMPORTANT LONG-TERM GOALS, AND CAST GRAVE DOUBTS ON THEIR
    CLAIM TO SPEAK AUTHORITATIVELY ON BEHALF OF ALL WORKERS IN
    THEIR DAY-TO-DAY RELATIONS WITH MANAGEMENT.

07579 RICE, J.
    AN OPEN AND SHUT-DOWN CASE
    SOJOURNERS, 18(9) (OCT 89), 4-5: 8.
    THIS ARTICLE EXAMINES WRONG DOINGS BY THE DEPARTMENT OF
    ENERGY IN THEIR PRODUCTION OF THE U.S. NUCLEAR ARSENAL. IT
    GIVES, BY WAY OF EXAMPLE, EVIDENCE OF ILLEGAL WASTE DISPOSAL
    PRACTICES AND A MASSIVE PUBLIC COVER-UP AT THE NUCLEAR
    WEAPONS TRIGGER FACTORY AT ROCKY FLATS, COLORADO. IT
    SUGGESTS THAT THE PRODUCTION OF WEAPONS IS NOT MERELY IN
    NEED OF PROPER MANAGEMENT, BUT RATHER, THE NUCLEAR FACTORIES
    SHOULD BE SHUT DOWN.

07580 RICE, J.
    BACK TO THE KILLING FIELDS
    SOJOURNERS, 18(10) (NOV 89), 5-6.
    US POLICY WITH REGARDS TO CAMBODIA SEEMS SINGULARLY
    CONFUSED. ALTHOUGH US OFFICIALS PROCLAIM THEIR AVERSION TO
    THE KHMER ROUGE FORCES, THEY ALSO SUPPORT PRINCE NORODOM
    SIHANOUK, WHO HEADS A COALITION THAT INCLUDES THE KHMER
    ROUGE. FEARING THE RETURN OF THE GENOCIDAL KHMER ROUGE, SOME
    CAMBODIANS RESENT US CONTINUED INTRUSION IN THEIR AFFAIRS.
    US POLICY SEEMS MOTIVATED PRIMARILY BY A CONTINUED ENMITY
    AGAINST VIET NAM.

07581 RICE, J.
    STAR WARS: THE MYTH UNFOLDS
    SOJOURNERS, 18(4) (APR 89), 5-6.
    FOR SIX YEARS, THE GOVERNMENT HAS SOLD THE AMERICAN
    PUBLIC A FALSE BILL OF GOODS- SOIAND AT A PRICE TAG OF
    BILLIONS OF DOLLARS IN A TIME WHEN PROGRAMS FOR THE SURVIVAL
    OF THE POOR HAVE BEEN SLASHED. IT IS NOW BECOMING CLEAR
    THAT MANY POLITICAL AND MILITARY LEADERS WERE AWARE FROM THE
    BEGINNING THAT THE ORIGINAL CONCEPT OF PROTECTING THE ENTIRE
    NATION WAS UNATTAINABLE, BUT IT WAS KEPT ALIVE FOR THE
    PURPOSE OF SELLING THE SNAKE OIL OF MISSILE DEFENSE TO
    SKEPTICAL PUBLIC.

07582 RICE, J.
    THE WINDS OF DEMOCRACY
    SOJOURNERS, 18(6) (JUN 89), 4.

THE ELECTIONS HELD IN THE USSR DRAMATICALLY DEMOSTRATE
THE EXTENT OF THE REFORMS THAT ARE TAKING PLACE THERE.
MIKHAIL GORBACHEV'S POLICIES OF PERESTROIKA AND GLASNOST
SEEM TO BE TAKING HOLD ON THE SOVIET PEOPLE; FOR THE FIRST
TIME IN SOVIET HISTORY, THE PEOPLE ARE ACTING AS IF THEY ARE
NO LONGER AFRAID. ALTHOUGH THE USSR IS STILL FAR FROM BEING
A DEMOCRACY, A HUNGER FOR LIBERTY AND DEMOCRACY HAS BEEN SET
LOOSE AND WILL BE DIFFICULT TO CONTROL.

07583 RICH, D.
    EMBARGO ECONOMICS KEEPING CUBA AT BAY
    MULTINATIONAL MONITOR, 10(4) (APR 89), 10-13.
    THE U.S. GOVERNMENT BELIEVES THAT TRADING WITH CUBA IS
    DIFFERENT FROM TRADING WITH THE SOVIETS OR THE CHINESE.
    SINCE 1964, THE U.S. GOVERNMENT HAS ENFORCED A TOTAL EMBARGO
    ON ALL DIRECT TRADE BETWEEN THE UNITED STATES AND CUBA. THE
    COST OF THE EMBARGO HAS BEEN HIGH FOR AMERICAN BUSINESS,
    WHICH COULD EARN $750 MILLION ANNUALLY FROM TRADING WITH THE
    CUBANS. CONGRESSMAN BILL ALEXANDER HAS PROPOSED A BILL TO
    EXEMPT U.S. AGRICULTURAL PRODUCTS FROM THE CUBAN TRADE
    EMBARGO.

07584 RICH, M.J.
    DISTRIBUTIVE POLITICS AND THE ALLOCATION OF FEDERAL GRANTS
    AMERICAN POLITICAL SCIENCE REVIEW, 83(1) (MAR 89), 193-216.
    UNDERSTANDING THE DYNAMICS OF POLICY DISTRIBUTION
    REQUIRES AN APPRECIATION OF FEDERAL GRANT PROGRAMS THAT HAVE
    ACHIEVED A PROMINENT PLACE IN NEARLY ALL AREAS OF DOMESTIC
    POLICY. THE THEORETICAL LITERATURE ON DISTRIBUTIVE POLITICS,
    HOWEVER, FOCUSES ALMOST EXCLUSIVELY ON A CENTRALIZED, TOP-
    DOWN VIEW OF POLICY DISTRIBUTION. BY EXAMINING THE ROLE OF
    PRESIDENTS, LEGISLATORS, AND BUREAUCRATS, SCHOLARS HAVE
    IGNORED PARTICIPANTS WHO HAVE BECOME KEY ACTORS IN THE
    DISTRIBUTION OF FEDERAL EXPENDITURES-THE RECIPIENT
    JURISDICTIONS. THIS ANALYSIS OF THE ALLOCATION PATTERNS
    UNDER SIX FEDERAL PROGRAMS SHOWS THAT LOCAL GOVERNMENTS
    EXERT IMPORTANT INFLUENCES ON THE DISTRIBUTION OF FEDERAL
    GRANTS AND THAT THE DISTRIBUTIONAL PATTERNS AND THEIR
    DETERMINANTS VARY OVER TIME. THE ANALYSIS ALSO POINTS OUT
    THE IMPORTANCE OF DISAGGREGATION BY FOCUSING ON PROGRAMS AND
    RECIPIENT JURISDICTIONS, AS OPPOSED TO TOTAL FEDERAL
    EXPENDITURES AND REGIONS, STATES, OR CONGRESSIONAL DISTRICTS.

07585 RICH, W.C.
    MINORITIES AND PUBLIC SERVICE: A FUTURE PERSPECTIVE
    INTERNATIONAL JOURNAL OF PUBLIC ADMINISTRATION, 12(4)
    (1989), 651-670.
    THIS PAPER ANALYZES THE FUTURE PROSPECTS OF BLACKS AND
    OTHER MINORITIES IN THE PUBLIC SERVICE. IT EXAMINES STUDIES
    ON RACE/ROLE EXPECTATIONS OF MINORITY ADMINISTRATORS,
    TOKENISM AND MARGINALITY TO DISCERN TRENDS IN INTERETHNIC
    RELATIONS. IT ALSO DISCUSSES FUTURE DEMOGRAPHIC PROJECTIONS
    AND THEIR IMPLICATIONS FOR MAJORITY/MINORITY RELATIONS.
    FINALLY, THE ESSAY EXPLAINS WHY PUBLIC SERVICE CAREERS ARE
    PARTICULARLY SIGNIFICANT FOR BLACKS AND OTHER MINORITIES.

07586 RICHARD, P.B.
    ALTERNATIVE ABORTION POLICIES: WHAT ARE THE HEALTH
    CONSEQUENCES?
    SOCIAL SCIENCE QUARTERLY, 70(4) (DEC 89), 941-955.
    THIS ARTICLE OFFERS AN ANALYSIS OF ONE DOMAIN OF
    ABORTION POLICY CONSEQUENCES, THE HEALTH IMPACTS OF
    ALTERNATIVE ABORTION POLICIES. AFTER OUTLINING THE LEGAL AND
    PRACTICAL CRITERIA BY WHICH ABORTION POLICIES CAN BE
    ASSESSED, IT DETAILS THE HEALTH CONSEQUENCES OF COMPLETELY
    PROHIBITED ABORTION AND OF COMPLETELY ELECTIVE ABORTION,
    CONCLUDING THAT THE FORMER PRODUCES HIGHER HEALTH COSTS THAN
    THE LATTER.

07587 RICHARD, Y.
    THE RELEVANCE OF "NATIONALISM" IN CONTEMPORARY IRAN
    MIDDLE EAST REVIEW, XXI(4) (SUM 89), 27-36.
    FAR FROM BEING THE PRODUCT OF A NATURAL EVOLUTION, BOTH
    ISLAMISM AND NATIONALISM ARE EMOTIONAL RESPONSE TO AN
    EXTERNAL CHALLENGE. THIS IS OBVIOUS IN IRAN, WHERE THE MAJOR
    CHANGES SINCE THE 19TH CENTURY (THE OVEREVALUATION OF THE
    NATIONAL IDENTITY BY THE NEW SECULAR ELITES AND THE
    OVEREVALUATION OF THE RELIGIOUS IDENTITY) OCCURRED IN
    SPECIFIC FORMS CONNECTED WITH EXTERNAL INTRUSION.

07588 RICHARDS, C.
    SHUFFLING THE GENERALS
    MIDDLE EAST INTERNATIONAL, 353 (JUN 89), 8.
    ISRAEL'S GENERALS ARE IN THE LINE OF FIRE. THEY ARE
    BEING SNIPED AT BY THE ISRAELI RIGHT WHO SUSPECT THEY ARE
    INSUFFICIENTLY DETERMINED TO SNUFF OUT THE UPRISING. CRITICS
    CHARGE THAT THE GENERALS, MOST OF THEM LEFTWARD LEANING
    KIBBUTZNIKS, ARE HOLDING FIRE IN PUTTING DOWN THE UPRISING
    OUT OF THEIR IDEOLOGICAL CONVICTION THAT THERE IS ONLY A
    POLITICAL, NOT A MILITARY SOLUTION TO THE UPRISING. THIS
    ARTICLE EXAMINES THE CRITICISM LEVELED AGAINST TWO GENERALS
    IN PARTICULAR: THE CHIEF OF STAFF LIEUTENANT GENERAL DAN
    SHOMRON AND MAJOR-GENERAL AMRAM MITZRA.

07589 RICHARDS, M.
THEORY AND ATTITUDE IN NIETZSCHE'S POLITICAL THOUGHT
DISSERTATION ABSTRACTS INTERNATIONAL, 49(10) (APR 89),
3143-A.
IN THIS DISCUSSION OF NIETZSCHE'S PHILOSOPHY, THE AUTHOR
FOCUSES ON THREE THESES: (1) NIETZSCHE'S THOUGHT CONSTITUTES
A UNIFIED WHOLE AND FORMS A SYSTEM OF IDEAS; (2) NIETZSCHE'S
SYSTEM OF IDEAS CONSTITUTES A CONCEPTION OF HISTORY THAT
SHOULD BE UNDERSTOOD IN THE CONTEXT OF GERMAN HISTORICISM;
(3) NIETZSCHE'S PHILOSOPHY IS INTRINSICALLY POLITICAL.

07590 RICHARDSON, B.
CONCEALED CONTEMPT
CANADIAN FORUM, LXVIII(784) (DEC 89), 15-20.
THE ARTICLE EXAMINES RECENT CANADIAN POLICY TOWARDS
CANADA'S NATIVE INDIAN POPULATION. IT CONCLUDES THAT THE
RECORD OF THE MULRONEY GOVERNMENT HAS BEEN ONE OF CYNICISM
AND CALCULATED INSULT. CANADA'S NATIVES ARE PUSHING FOR
FREEDOM FROM THE SUFFOCATING BUREAUCRACY OF THE MINISTRY OF
INDIAN AFFAIRS; HOWEVER, THEY STILL DO NOT WISH TO BE
ABANDONED ENTIRELY BY THE FEDERAL GOVERNMENT.

07591 RICHARDSON, B.
MANUFACTURING OUR CONSENT
CANADIAN FORUM, 68(781) (SEP 89), 5-6.
THIS ARTICLE EXAMINES THE MASS MEDIA AS AN INSTRUMENT OF
SOCIAL MANIPULATION WHICH SERVES THE INTERESTS OF THE
POWERFUL. IT EXPLORES THE IDEAS BROUGHT FORTH IN A BOOK
CALLED "MANUFACTURING WITH CONSENT BY NORM CHOMSKY AND
EDWARD S. HERMAN. THEIR ANALYSIS ACCUSES THE MEDIA OF
SERVING SPECIAL. POWERFUL INTERESTS AND OUTLINE A
"PROPAGANDA MODEL" AND DEMONSTRATES WITH MANY EXAMPLES THAT,
FOR THE MOST PART, THE U.S. MEDIA FULFILL THE EXPECTATIONS
OF THAT PROPAGANDA.

07592 RICHARDSON, K.
EUROPE'S INDUSTRIALISTS HELP SHAPE THE SINGLE MARKET
EUROPE, (292) (DEC 89), 18-20.
THE EUROPEAN ROUND TABLE OF INDUSTRIALISTS (ERT) IS ONE
ORGANIZATION THAT HAS GREATLY CONTRIBUTED TO THE RAPID
BUSINESS PROGRESS IN THE EUROPEAN COMMUNITY (E.C.). THE
CHALLENGE IN EUROPE IS TO BUILD A NEW ENVIRONMENT IN WHICH
BUSINESS CAN FLOURISH AND HOLD IT'S OWN IN WORLD-WIDE
COMPETITION, SO THAT PROSPERITY CAN BE SPREAD ACROSS THE
CONTINENT. THE OBJECTIVE OF THE ERT IS TO STRENGTHEN
EUROPE'S ECONOMY AND TO IMPROVE ITS GLOBAL COMPETITIVENESS,
WHICH IT PURSUES BY INDENTIFYING THE MOST IMPORTANT ISSUES,
ANALYZING THE CRITICAL FACTORS, AND MAKING ITS VIEWS KNOWN
TO THE POLITICAL DECISION MAKERS. THE ERT'S WORK AIMS TO
ENSURE THAT EUROPE REMAINS A MEMBER OF THE WORLD TRADING
SYSTEM. ABOVE ALL THE ERT SEEKS TO PRESERVE THE HIGHEST
POSSIBLE LINKS OF FRIENDSHIP AND BUSINESS COOPERATION WITH
THE UNITED STATES.

07593 RICHARDSON, M.
"SYMBOL OF GOOD GOVERNMENT"
PACIFIC DEFENCE REPORTER, 16(1) (JUL 89), 18.
IN THIS ARTICLE PRESIDENT LEE TENG-HUI OF TAIWAN
DISCUSSES HOW THE ISLAND'S ECONOMIC STENGTH IS BEING USED TO
WIN FRIENDS AND INFLUENCE. HE DESCRIBES THE TAIWANESE
GOVERNMENT'S ESTABLISHMENT OF A ONE BILLION DOLLAR
INTERNATIONAL ECONOMIC COOPERATION AND DEVELOPMENT FUND
WHICH PROVIDES LOANS AND TECHNICAL ASSISTANCE TO THIRD WORLD
NATIONS. FOCUS IS ALSO ON RELATIONS WITH CHINA, AND
DIPLOMATIC EFFORTS TO IMPROVE RELATIONS WITH THAT COUNTRY.

07594 RICHARDSON, M.
ARE THE VIETS BACK IN CAMBODIA?
PACIFIC DEFENCE REPORTER, 16(10) (APR 90), 19-20.
REPORTS HAVE BEEN CIRCULATING THAT VIETNAMESE REGULAR
SOLDIERS WEARING CAMBODIAN UNIFORMS HAVE BEEN IN THE THICK
OF THE FIGHTING TO STRENGTHEN HUN SEN'S BARGAINING POSITION
IN NEGOTIATIONS WITH OPPOSITION FORCES. THE AUTHOR CONCLUDES,
AFTER AN INVESTIGATION, THAT THIS IS, IN FACT, PROBABLY THE
CASE. THE STABILITY OF SOUTH-EAST ASIA MAY BE THREATENED BY
THIS DEVELOPMENT.

07595 RICHARDSON, M.
ASEAN CAUTIOUS ABOUT PACIFIC PARTNERSHIP
PACIFIC DEFENCE REPORTER, 16(3) (SEP 89), 19-21.
A US PROPOSAL FOR ESTABLISHING "A NEW PACIFIC
PARTNERSHIP", WAS REGARDED AS A MAJOR INITIATIVE BY
COUNTRIES THAT TOOK PART IN TALKS ON CLOSER CO-OPERATION
BETWEEN KEY ASIAN AND PACIFIC TRADING NATIONS. HOWEVER, SOME
MEMBERS OF ASEAN. THE ASSOCIATION OF SOUTH-EAST ASIAN
NATIONS, REMAIN WARY OF THE PROPOSAL WHICH AUSTRALIA, AND
MORE RECENTLY THE US AND JAPAN, ARE PUSHING. THIS ARTICLE
DESCRIBES HOW SOME ASEAN MEMBERS FEAR THAT IF WIDER ASIA-
PACIFIC CO-OPERATION MOVES AHEAD AND LEADS TO THE
ESTABLISHMENT OF A NEW ORGANIZATION, IT MAY OVERSHADOW AND
EVENTUALLY DOMINATE ASEAN.

07596 RICHARDSON, M.
BIG ECONOMIC ROLE FOR JAPAN

PACIFIC DEFENCE REPORTER, 16(1) (JUL 89), 39-43.
ESSENTIAL ELEMENTS OF JAPAN'S POLICIES TOWARDS SOUTH-
EAST ASIA - REGARDED BY TOKYO AS A REGION OF KEY STRATEGIC
IMPORTANCE - ARE UNLIKELY TO BE AFFECTED BY THE POLITICAL
TURMOIL IN JAPAN THAT FORCED MR TAKESHITA TO ANNOUNCE HIS
RESIGNATION IN APRIL. HOWEVER, GROWING JAPANESE ECONOMIC
POWER HAS RAISED EXPECTATIONS OF PARTNERSHIP WHICH MR
TAKESHITA WAS UNABLE TO SATISFY DURING A TOUR OF THAILAND,
MALAYSIA, SINGAPORE, INDONESIA AND THE PHILIPPINES IN MAY
ALSO THERE IS CONCERN IN ASEAN, THE ASSOCIATION OF SOUTH-
EAST ASIAN NATIONS, THAT JAPAN MAY BE ENTERING A PERIOD OF
CHRONICALLY WEAK LEADERSHIP THAT WILL REDUCE POLITICAL
IMPETUS BEHIND THE PROGRAM OF GRADUAL ECONOMIC
LIBERALIZATION ENDORSE BY THE JAPANESE GOVERNMENT IN RECENT
YEARS. JAPAN IS THE MAIN SOURCE OF AID, INVESTMENT AND
IMPORTS FOR ASEAN.

07597 RICHARDSON, M.
CRACKS IN THE MOSCOW-HANOI ALLIANCE
PACIFIC DEFENCE REPORTER, 16(5) (NOV 89), 38.
AS DEBATE INTENSIFIES IN THE COMMUNIST WORLD OVER
POLITICAL CHANGES IN THE SOVIET UNION AND EASTERN EUROPE,
VIETNAM HAS DENOUNCED POLAND AND HUNGARY, FOR LETTING NON-
COMMUNISTS GAIN A SHARE OF POWER AND VOWED TO CRUSH ANY
ATTEMPT TO PROMOTE WESTERN-STYLE DEMOCRACY. IMPLICIT IN
RECENT STATEMENTS BY VIETNAM'S COMMUNIST LEADERS AND
OFFICIAL MEDIA IS A WARNING THAT LONG-STANDING CLOSE TIES
BETWEEN SOCIALIST STATES IN EUROPE AND INDO-CHINA WILL BE
UNDERMINED IF IDEOLOGICAL DISUNITY DEEPENS.

07598 RICHARDSON, M.
MAJOR CHANGES IN POWER BALANCE AS SOVIETS WITHDRAW FROM
CAM RANH
PACIFIC DEFENCE REPORTER, 16(9) (MAR 90), 13-14.
THE SOVIET UNION IS UNILATERALLY WITHDRAWING MOST OF ITS
OFFENSIVE FORCES FROM VIETNAM IN A MAJOR INITIATIVE THAT
WILL RESHAPE THE BALANCE OF POWER AND POLTICAL ALIGNMENTS IN
ASIA AND THE PACIFIC. THIS ARTICLE EXAMINES HOW SUCH
REDUCTIONS IN SOVIET MILITARY AID IS LIKELY TO INCREASE
HANOI'S INTEREST IN REDUCING RELIANCE ON THE SOVIET BLOC FOR
TRADE AND AID. IT WILL ALSO PROVIDE AN ADDED INCENTIVE FOR
VIETNAM TO IMPROVE ECONOMIC AND POLITICAL RELATIONS WITH
OTHER ASIAN COUNTRIES AND WESTERN NATIONS.

07599 RICHARDSON, M.
NEW FEARS OF CHINA'S MILITARY POWER
PACIFIC DEFENCE REPORTER, 16(2) (AUG 89), 15-18.
THE RUTHLESS ATTACKS BY CHINESE ARMY UNITS AGAINST
SUPPORTERS OF THE PRO-DEMOCRACY MOVEMENT IN BEIJING HAVE
REVIVED FEARS IN MANY EAST ASIAN COUNTRIES ABOUT CHINA'S
GROWING MILITARY POWER IN THE REGION AND ITS READINESS TO
USE FORCE AS AN INSTRUMENT OF FOREIGN POLICY. THIS ARTICLE
EXAMINES HOW THE TURMOIL IS ALSO LIKELY TO REWRITE THE
ECONOMIC MAP OF EAST ASIA IN STRATEGICALLY SIGNIFICANT WAYS,
ENHANCING INDUSTRIAL AND FINANCIAL GROWTH IN SOUTH-EAST ASIA,
ESPECIALLY IN LARGE NATIONS SUCH AS INDONESIA.

07600 RICHARDSON, M.
RELIGIOUS REVIVALISM CAUSES CONCERN
PACIFIC DEFENCE REPORTER, 16(1) (JUL 89), 44-45.
AN UPSURGE OF SPIRITUAL FERVOR IN SOUTH-EAST ASIA IS
FRACTURING LONG-ESTABLISHED RELIGIONS AND CREATING
CONDITIONS FOR FUTURE CONFLICT. OFFICIALS AND RELIGIOUS
LEADERS IN THE REGION WARN. THE CAUSES OF RELIGIOUS FERMENT
IN SOUTHEAST ASIA ARE COMPLEX AND VARY FROM COUNTRY TO
COUNTRY, BUT THE RENEWED APPEAL OF RELIGION, PARTICULARLY TO
YOUNG ASIANS, IS OFTEN LINKED TO CHANGES IN LIFE-STYLES AND
VALUES THAT HAVE ACCOMPANIED THE RAPID ECONOMIC GROWTH AND
INDUSTRIALIZATION SWEEPING OVER THE REGION IN THE PAST TWO
DECADES. MANY PEOPLE HAVE EMBRACED RELIGION TO COPE WITH, OR
ESCAPE FROM, THE CONSEQUENCES OF MODERNIZATION.

07601 RICHARDSON, M.
RENEWED SEARCH FOR SECURITY STRATEGIES
PACIFIC DEFENCE REPORTER, 16(6) (DEC 89), 25-26.
THIS ARTICLE EXAMINES HOW A PHASE-OUT OF AMERICAN
MILITARY BASES IN THE PHILIPPINES IS PROMPTING THE UNITED
STATES TO BEGIN RELOCATING SOME OF ITS FORCES AND FACILITIES
TO JAPAN, SINGAPORE AND OTHER COUNTRIES IN THE REGION. THE
REDEPLOYMENTS ARE PART OF A WIDER REVAMP OF SECURITY
ARRANGEMENTS LINKING THE UNITED STATES AND NON-COMMUNIST
NATIONS IN THE WESTERN PACIFIC. THEY HAVE SERVED TO
GALVANIZE ASEAN COUNTRIES INTO A RENEWED SEARCH FOR
STRATEGIES TO PREVENT DOMINATION OF SOUTH-EAST ASIA OF
OUTSIDE FORCES.

07602 RICHARDSON, M.
SIHANOUK'S PESSIMISTIC PERCEPTION
PACIFIC DEFENCE REPORTER, 15(10) (APR 89), 34.
IN THIS INTERVIEW, PRINCE SIHANOUK OFFERS A PESSIMISTIC
ASSESSMENT OF THE LIKELY OUTCOME OF THE MEETING OF SOUTHEAST
ASIAN NATIONS AND WARRING CAMBODIAN FACTIONS TO TRY TO END
THE CAMBODIAN CONFLICT.

07603 RICHARDSON, M.
   STORM CLOUDS GATHERING OVER PHILIPPINE BASES
   PACIFIC DEFENCE REPORTER, 16(3) (SEP 89), 16-17.
   IN THIS ARTICLE, LETICIA RAMOS SHAHANI, WHO CHAIRS THE
COMMITTEE ON FOREIGN RELATIONS OF THE PHILIPPINE SENATE,
DISCUSSES THE RISING TIDE OF NATURALISM IN THE PHILIPPINES.
SHE OPINES THAT PHILIPPINE PEOPLE MUST STOP THINKING LIKE
THE BEGGARS AMERICANS HAVE MADE OF THEM - ALWAYS WAITING FOR
LARGESSE. ECONOMIC GAINS CAN SURELY COME WITHOUT U.S. AID.

07604 RICHARDSON, M.
   THE ASEAN SCENE: CHINESE STOCKPILE FOR THAILAND CAUSES
   CONCERN
   PACIFIC DEFENCE REPORTER, 15(9) (MAR 89), 34-36.
   THIS ARTICLE EXAMINES HOW A PLAN TO SET UP A STOCKPILE
OF CHINESE ARMS IN THAILAND IS SEEN BY SEVERAL COUNTRIES IN
SOUTH-EAST ASIA AS AN UNWELCOME MEANS OF EXPANDING AND
ENTRENCHING CHINA'S INFLUENCE IN THE REGION. ARRANGEMENTS
FOR THE STOCKPILE ARE BEING WORKED OUT IN MEETINGS BETWEEN
THAI AND CHINESE MILITARY OFFICIALS. MAJOR PURCHASES OF
CHINESE WEAPONS BY THAILAND IN THE PAST FEW YEARS INCLUDE
TANKS, ARMORED PERSONNEL CARRIERS, ARTILLERY, ANTI-AIRCRAFT
GUNS AND, MOST RECENTLY, FOUR FRIGATES. MILITARY ANALYSTS IN
BANGKOK SAID THAT THAI OFFICERS WERE TRAVELLING TO CHINA TO
TRAIN AS INSTRUCTORS FOR THE NEW EQUIPMENT.

07605 RICHARDSON, M.
   TRADE RESTRICTIONS MAY REKINDLE CONFLICT
   PACIFIC DEFENCE REPORTER, 15(10) (APR 89), 31-33.
   TRADE-DEPENDENT NATIONS IN THE WESTERN PACIFIC FEAR
THERE WILL BE A DANGEROUS DETERIORATION IN THE SECURITY
ENVIRONMENT OF EAST ASIA IF THE US AND EUROPE CONTINUE TO
RAISE PROTECTIONIST BARRIERS AGAINST IMPORTS FROM ASIA.
OFFICIALS IN THE REGION AND WESTERN ANALYSTS WARN THAT
CONSTRICTION OF INTERNATIONAL TRADE WILL UNDERMINE ECONOMIC
GROWTH, REKINDLING CONFLICTS AND POLITICAL INSTABILITY THAT
CHARACTERIZED MUCH OF EAST ASIA IN THE 1950S AND 1960S
BEFORE MODERNIZATION TOOK HOLD. FUNDAMENTAL CHANGES TO BE
EXPECTED IN THE REGIONAL BALANCE OF POWER AS WESTERN
INFLUENCE IS SHARPLY REDUCED AND OPPORTUNITIES OPEN FOR
OTHER BIG NATIONS IN, OR CLOSE TO, ASIA TO APPLY LEVERAGE.
THEY INCLUDE JAPAN, CHINA AND THE SOVIET UNION.

07606 RICHARDSON, M.
   U.S. BASES MORE IMPORTANT AS GLOBAL THREAT RECEDES
   PACIFIC DEFENCE REPORTER, 16(8) (FEB 90), 12-14.
   AUSTRALIA AND THE UNITED STATES SEE EYE-TO-EYE OVER
MILITARY BASES IN THE SOUTH PACIFIC BUT THE TWO COUNTRIES
DIFFER ON NEW ZEALAND'S POLICY OF A NUCLEAR FREE ZONE.
CRITICS OF US OPPOSITION TO THE SOUTH PACIFIC NUCLEAR FREE
ZONE TREATY SAY THAT IT HAS CREATED UNNECESSARY FRICTION
WITH MANY COUNTRIES IN THE REGION, ALLOWED THE SOVIET UNION
TO EXTEND ITS INFLUENCE IN THE AREA AND CLOSED AN
OPPORTUNITY TO ENCOURAGE NEW ZEALAND TO MODIFY ITS ANTI-
NUCLEAR STAND AND RETURN TO ACTIVE PARTICIPATION IN ANZUS.

07607 RICHARDSON, M.
   VIETNAM: WHERE WILL ALL THE SOLDIERS GO?
   PACIFIC DEFENCE REPORTER, 15(9) (MAR 89), 36-38.
   PLANS TO REDUCE THE VIETNAMESE ARMY BY MORE THAN 25
PERCENT OF ITS STRENGTH IS SEEN AS AN EFFORT TO SAVE MONEY
AND FOCUS RESOURCES ON REVIVING THE ECONOMY. THE AUTHOR
NOTES THAT IT ALSO REFLECTS AN EASING OF TENSION BETWEEN
VIETNAM AND OTHER ASIAN COUNTRIES INCLUDING CHINA AND
THAILAND. HOWEVER, DEMOBILIZATION, UNLESS ACCOMPANIED OF
ECONOMIC GROWTH, WILL ONLY SERVE TO SWELL THE LARGE POOL OF
UNEMPLOYED AND UNDEREMPLOYED, LEADING TO SOCIAL DISCONTENT.

07608 RICHARDSON, R.C. III
   SECURITY, SPACE, AND COST: A NEW, AFFORDABLE, DEFENSE
   PROPOSAL
   JOURNAL OF SOCIAL, POLITICAL AND ECONOMIC STUDIES, 14(1)
   (SPR 89), 3-24.
   THE U.S. CONGRESS AND THE BUSH ADMINISTRATION FACE THREE
CRITICAL, INTERRELATED PROBLEMS: HOW TO PERPETUATE A
CREDIBLE U.S. AND NATO SECURITY POSTURE, HOW TO BEST ASSURE
ACCESS TO SPACE AND HOW TO EXPLOIT IT FOR THE BENEFIT OF THE
U.S. AND THE FREE WORLD, AND HOW TO COPE WITH THE BUDGET
DEFICIT. THE ABILITY TO HANDLE THE DEFICIT DEPENDS TO A
GREAT EXTENT ON THE SOLUTIONS ADOPTED FOR SPACE AND DEFENSE,
WHILE DEFENSE AND SPACE ISSUES ARE INCREASILY INTERDEPENDENT.
MOREOVER, WHAT MUST BE DONE IN BOTH SPACE AND DEFENSE
DEPENDS NOT ONLY ON U.S. DECISIONS BUT ALSO ON SOVIET
DECISIONS AND ACTIONS.

07609 RICHMAN, A.
   AMERICAN ATTITUDES TOWARD ISRAELI-PALESTINIAN RELATIONS IN
   THE WAKE OF THE UPRISING
   PUBLIC OPINION QUARTERLY, 53(3) (FAL 89), 415-430.
   THE PALESTINIAN UPRISING HAS SPARKED THE LARGEST AMOUNT
OF POLLING ON THE ISRAELI-PALESTINIAN DISPUTE SINCE THE
ISRAELI INVASION OF LEBANON AND THE MASSACRES OF
PALESTINIANS AT THE SABRA AND SHATILA CAMPS IN 1982. ABOUT A
DOZEN POLLS ON ISRAELI-PALESTINIAN RELATIONS, SOME OF THEM

CONTAINING A SUBSTANTIAL NUMBER OF QUESTIONS, APPEARED IN
THE FIRST HALF OF 1988. THEY HAVE SHOWED THAT THE AMERICAN
PUBLIC (1) IS CLOSELY DIVIDED ABOUT WHETHER THE ISRAELI
REACTION TO THE DISTURBANCES HAS BEEN "TOO HARSH," (2)
REMAINS CONSIDERABLY MORE PRO-ISRAEL THAN PRO-ARAB OR PRO-
PALESTINIAN IN ITS SYMPATHIES, (3) IS INCLINED TO APPROVE A
PALESTINIAN HOMELAND THAT DOES NOT THREATEN ISRAEL'S
SECURITY, AND (4) SUPPORTS AN ACTIVE U.S. DIPLOMATIC ROLE IN
THE MIDDLE EAST.

07610 RICHMAN, L.
   INCOME GROWTH: ARE WE BETTER OFF?
   CURRENT, (312) (MAY 89), 4-9.
   AFTER EIGHT YEARS OF REAGAN, WHO'S REALLY AHEAD AND
WHO'S BEHIND ECONOMICALLY? DEMOCRATS POINT TO THE DECLINING
AVERAGE HOURLY WAGE, WHICH HAS FALLEN 2.6 PERCENT IN REAL
TERMS SINCE 1981. ON THE OTHER HAND, REPUBLICANS REMIND
VOTERS THAT MEDIAN FAMILY INCOMES ARE UP. THE REPUBLICANS
HAVE THE BETTER CASE.

07611 RICHTER, M.
   MONTESQUIEU, THE POLITICS OF LANGUAGE, AND THE LANGUAGE OF
   POLITICS
   HISTORY OF POLITICAL THOUGHT, (X 1) (SPR 89), 71-88.
   THE AUTHOR TACKLES THE PROBLEM OF "POLITICAL VOCABULARY.
" SOME THEORISTS USED VOCABULARY THAT WAS CONTEMPORARY AND
COULD BE EASILY UNDERSTOOD BY THEIR AUDIENCE, WHILE OTHERS
MAY MODIFY OR REVOLUTIONIZE THE LINGUISTIC AND CONCEPTUAL
PRACTICES OF THEIR OWN OR A LATER TIME. THE PAPER ANALYZES
THE WORKS OF MONTESQUIEU AND CONCLUDES THAT HIS LANGUAGE WAS
A SHEWDLY CALCULATED COMPROMISE BETWEEN CONTEMPORARY
PRACTICES AND THE SORT OF CHANGES JUDGED NECESSARY TO CONVEY
THEORETICAL AND PRACTICAL INNOVATIONS.

07612 RICHTER, S.
   CLIMBING DOWN FROM THE HILL: THE DECLINE OF AMERICA AND
   THE NATIONAL CRISIS IN ECONOMIC POLICYMAKING
   PS: POLITICAL SCIENCE AND POLITICS, XXII(3) (SEP 89),
   600-605.
   THE ONE TANGIBLE RESULT OF THE 1988 OMNIBUS TRADE AND
COMPETITIVENESS ACT WAS THE PRESERVATION OF THE STATUS QUO
ANTE. THE PASSAGE OF THE BILL HAS THE PERFORMANCE OF A
NATIONAL RITE. THE RITUAL INVOLVED NUMEROUS PLAYERS WHO
INVESTED VAST POLITICAL ENERGY IN MAKING THE LAW. BUT THEIR
INPUTS TRAVELED ALONG LARGELY PREDETERMINED PATHS AND
PRIMARILY SATISFIED SYMBOLIC NEEDS WHILE OBSCURING A
NATIONAL POLICY ISSUE URGENTLY AWAITING RESOLUTION.

07613 RICHTER, W.L.
   PAKISTAN UNDER BENAZIR BHUTTO
   CURRENT HISTORY, 88(542) (DEC 89), 433-436, 449-451.
   ALTHOUGH BENAZIR BHUTTO HAS SOUGHT TO ASSOCIATE HERSELF
STRONGLY WITH HER FATHER, THE NEW BHUTTO ERA IS NOT A
RESTORATION OF THE EARLIER ONE. BENAZIR BHUTTO IS BY NO
MEANS A CARBON COPY OF HER FATHER, AND THE CIRCUMSTANCES SHE
FACES ARE SIGNIFICANTLY DIFFERENT FROM THOSE IN THE EARLY
1970'S. SHE HAS INHERITED A LARGE ARRAY OF POLITICAL,
ECONOMIC, AND FOREIGN POLICY PROBLEMS. BUT SHE APPEARS TO BE
PROVIDING PAKISTAN WITH THE LEADERSHIP IT NEEDS. SHE IS
AVOIDING THE MOST OBVIOUS PITFALLS AND BUILDING THE
FOUNDATION FOR A MORE ENDURING DEMOCRATIC SYSTEM.

07614 RICKETTS, R.
   THE SHAPE OF TRADE TO COME
   NEW ZEALAND INTERNATIONAL REVIEW, 14(3) (MAY 89), 11-14.
   THE AUTHOR DISCUSSES THE PROSPECTS FOR TRADE
LIBERALIZATION IN LIGHT OF THE FORTHCOMING ESTABLISHMENT OF
THE SINGLE MARKET IN EUROPE. THE PERSPECTIVE IS OFFERED FROM
NEW ZEALAND'S POSITION IN RELATION TO THESE CHANGES, IN
CONTRAST TO THE POSITIONS OF THE UNITED STATES AND JAPAN,
THE MAIN COMPETITORS WITH THE EUROPEAN COMMUNITY MARKET. THE
AGRICULTURAL SECTOR IS GIVEN PARTICULAR ATTENTION.

07615 RICKEY, C.
   THILIGHT OF THE REAGANAUNTS
   TIKKUN, 4(6) (NOV 89), 49-51.
   THIS ARTICLE EXPLORES THE CORRELATION BETWEEN AMERICAN
FILMS IN THE EIGHTIES AND AMERICAN CULTURE IN THE EIGHTIES.
THOUGH FILMS CAN BE A REFLECTION OF THE VALUES OF THE TIME
PERIOD, THE EIGHTIES, LIKE MOST DECADES, CONTRADICTS ITSELF.
ONCE A TREND IS SEEN AS HAVING A CULTURAL CORRELATIVE,
ANOTHER TREND CANCELS IT OUT. A DISTURBING TREND BEGAN IN
1981, WHEN THE NEWSPAPER USA TODAY BEGAN IMPLYING A
CORRELATION BETWEEN BOX-OFFICE SUCESS AND AESTHETIC WORTH.
THIS CONFLATION OF MARKET VALUE AND ACTUAL VALUE HAS
DEFORMED THE DISCOURSE ABOUT MOVIEMAKING OVER THE DECADE.
SUCH MARKETPLACE VALIDATION PROMPTED EIGHTIES MOVIE MAKERS
TO SPEAK WITH MORE PRIDE ABOUT THEIR PROFITS THAN ABOUT
THEIR PRODUCTS.

07616 RICKS, B.A.
   FUTURE DOMESTIC AND INTERNATIONAL TERRORISM: THE FBI
   PESPECTIVE
   TERRORISM, 11(6) (1988), 538-540.

THIS IS A TALK GIVEN AT A CONFERENCE ON TERRORISM BY BOB
RICKS, DEPUTY ASSISTANT DIRECTOR IN THE FBI. HE DEFINES
TERRORISM AND THEN DIFFERENTIATES BETWEEN DOMESTIC AND
INTERNATIONAL TERRORISM. HE DISCUSSES THE FBI'S PRIMARY GOAL
IN CONDUCTING COUNTERTERRORISM INVESTIGATIONS AND DETAILS
ITS SUCCESSES. HE EXPLORES INFRASTRUCTURES ESTABLISHED IN
THE UNITED STATES AND DETAILS INDIVIDUAL AS WELL AS STATE
SPONSORED THREATS OF TERRORISM. HE CONCLUDES THAT THE THREAT
FROM INTERNATIONAL GROUPS REMAINS VERY REAL AND MUST BE MET.

07617 RIDDELL, P.
    IN DEFENCE OF PARLIAMENT
    CONTEMPORARY RECORD, 3(1) (FAL 89), 6-9.
        PARLIAMENT HAS TOO OFTEN BEEN DISMISSED AS OF LITTLE
    IMPORTANCE, ESPECIALLY WITH THE COMFORTABLE SIZE OF
    CONSERVATIVE MAJORITIES SINCE 1979. IN THIS ARTICLE, PETER
    RIDDELL PROVIDES AN EXPANDED, MODIFIED AND UPDATED VERSION
    OF HIS FAREWELL PIECE AS POLITICAL EDITOR OF THE FINANCIAL
    TIMES. HE TALKS ABOUT THE IMPORTANCE OF PARTY DISCIPLINE AND
    DEFINES PARLIAMENT AS A FORUM FOR EXPRESSION OF INTERESTS;
    THE SCRUTINEER OF THE EXECUTIVE; AND THE MAKER OF REPUTATIONS

07618 RIDDLESPERGER, J.W. JR.; KING, J.D.
    ELITISM AND PRESIDENTIAL APPOINTMENTS
    SOCIAL SCIENCE QUARTERLY, 70(4) (DEC 89), 902-910.
        THE PRESIDENT'S APPOINTMENTS TO SENIOR-LEVEL
    ADMINISTRATIVE POSITIONS PROVIDE A MECHANISM THROUGH WHICH
    THE ECONOMIC AND POLITICAL ELITES IN THE UNITED STATES
    MAINTAIN CONTROL OF PUBLIC POLICY. THIS PAPER ANALYZES THE
    EXTENT TO WHICH SUCH APPOINTMENTS ARE GIVEN TO INDIVIDUALS
    WHO CAN BE DEFINED AS MEMBERS OF AN ELITE, BEGINNING WITH
    THE KENNEDY ADMINISTRATION AND CONTINUING THROUGH THE REAGAN
    ADMINISTRATION. THE RESULTS INDICATE THAT AN EXTRAORDINARY
    PROPORTION OF APPOINTEES MAY BE CONSIDERED MEMBERS OF AN
    ELITE AND SUPPORT THE NOTION THAT ELITES DOMINATE U.S.
    NATIONAL POLITICS.

07619 RIDGWAY, R.L.
    PERSPECTIVES ON CHANGE IN THE SOVIET UNION
    DEPARTMENT OF STATE BULLETIN (US FOREIGN POLICY), 88(2138)
    (SEP 88), 23-25.
        THAT THERE IS CHANGE OCCURING IN THE SOVIET UNION IS
    UNDENIABLE, BUT IT IS DIFFICULT TO GO BEYOND THAT STATEMENT.
    THE AUTHOR ATTEMPTS TO OUTLINE AND DIFFERENTIATE BETWEEN THE
    PROMISE OF CHANGE, THE PERCEPTION OF CHANGE, AND THE REALITY
    OF CHANGE. SHE EXAMINES THE INFLUENCE THAT CHANGE IN THE
    USSR HAS ON US INTERESTS AND FUTURE POLICY OPTIONS.

07620 RIDING, A.
    LATIN AMERICA'S CASTLES IN SPAIN
    HEMISPHERE, 2(1) (FAL 89), 32-33.
        AFTER MORE THAN A DECADE OF RENEWAL, RELATIONS BETWEEN
    SPAIN AND LATIN AMERICA ARE COOLING. MUCH TO LATIN AMERICA'S
    CHAGRIN, SPAIN'S DEMANDING NEW ASSOCIATION WITH THE EUROPEAN
    ECONOMIC COMMUNITY IS DIVERTING THE MOTHER COUNTRY'S
    ATTENTION FROM HER TRANSATLANTIC OFFSPRING. SPAIN WANTED TO
    END GENERATIONS OF ISOLATION FROM EUROPE BY JOINING THE
    EEC'S PROCESS OF ECONOMIC AND POLITICAL INTEGRATION. BUT
    SPAIN HAS IN NO POSITION TO MAKE CONDITIONS AND FELIPE
    GONZALEZ HAD TO DROP HIS OBJECTIONS TO SPAIN'S MEMBERSHIP IN
    NATO, LIFT THE BLOCKADE OF GIBRALTAR, AND AGREE TO A
    TRANSITION TO FULL EEC MEMBERSHIP IN SEVEN YEARS.
    SIMULTANEOUSLY, SPAIN HAD TO ABANDON ANY THOUGHTS OF
    EXTRACTING THE SAME TRADE-AND-AID PRIVILEGES FOR LATIN
    AMERICA THAT ARE ENJOYED BY FORMER BRITISH, BELGIAN, AND
    FRENCH COLONIES.

07621 RIEFE, R.H.
    CUBAN POLITICAL ACTION IN THE UNITED STATES
    JOURNAL OF SOCIAL, POLITICAL AND ECONOMIC STUDIES, 14(2)
    (SUM 89), 235-249.
        CONCERNED OVER DEVELOPMENTS IN MOSCOW THAT MIGHT LEAD TO
    A REDUCTION IN THE HUGE SOVIET SUBSIDIES TO HAVANA, FIDEL
    CASTRO HAS INITIATED A DIPLOMATIC OFFENSIVE DESIGNED, IN
    LARGE PART, TO PERSUADE THE U.S. GOVERNMENT TO RELAX ITS
    EMBARGO. CASTRO IS CONCENTRATING ON A CAMPAIGN OF POLITICAL
    ACTION AIMED AT SOFTENING U.S. HOSTILITY TO HIS GOVERNMENT.
    AND THERE ARE SIGNS THAT CASTRO'S EFFORTS ARE MAKING
    PROGRESS.

07622 RIEFE, R.H.
    GORBACHEV, CASTRO, AND NATIONAL LIBERATION IN LATIN AMERICA
    JOURNAL OF SOCIAL, POLITICAL AND ECONOMIC STUDIES, 14(3)
    (FAL 89), 259-282.
        IN THE PAST, THE ESSENTIAL DIFFERENCE BETWEEN THE
    SOVIETS AND THE CUBANS REGARDING SUPPORT TO RADICALS IN
    THIRD WORLD COUNTRIES HAS BEEN ONE OF DEGREE, NOT OF
    PRINCIPLE. THE SOVIETS HAVE MADE SERIOUS EFFORTS TO CONCEAL
    THEIR ROLE, WHILE CASTRO HAS OFTEN FLOUTED HIS. AS U.S.
    NEGOTIATORS EXPAND DISCUSSIONS WITH THEIR SOVIET
    COUNTERPARTS, WASHINGTON MUST INSIST ON TYING SOVIET
    BEHAVIOR IN THE THIRD WORLD, AND ESPECIALLY IN LATIN AMERICA,
    TO PROPOSALS TO FACILITATE ECONOMIC AND TECHNICAL EXCHANGES
    THAT MOSCOW IS ANXIOUS TO REALIZE. THIS INSISTENCE SHOULD BE

EXTENDED TO CUBA AND BEYOND, SPECIFICALLY TO NICARAGUA.

07623 RIEMER, N.
    RELIGIOUS LIBERTY AND CREATIVE BREAKTHROUGHS IN AMERICAN
    POLITICS: ROGER WILLIAMS AND JAMES MADISON
    JOURNAL OF POLITICAL SCIENCE, 16(1-2) (1988), 43-48.
        RELIGIOUS IDEAS--SUCH AS RELIGIOUS LIBERTY, SEPARATION
    OF CHURCH AND STATE, AND STATE AND RELIGIOUS PLURALISM--HAVE
    BEEN INVOLVED IN "CREATIVE BREAKTHROUGHS" AT KEY TIMES IN
    AMERICAN HISTORY. SUCH REFORM MOVEMENTS AS ANTI-SLAVERY,
    WOMEN'S SUFFRAGE, PEACE, ECONOMIC OPPORTUNITY, AND ANTI-
    DISCRIMINATION HAVE INCORPORATED PROMINENT RELIGIOUS IDEAS.

07624 RIGGIO, E.
    PLANNING AND DEVELOPMENT IN WESTERN SICILY: THE GRASSROOTS
    ORGANIC APPROACH OF DANILO DOLCI
    DISSERTATION ABSTRACTS INTERNATIONAL, 49(7) (JAN 89),
    1990-A.
        THIS RESEARCH ON GRSSSROOTS PLANNING AND COMMUNITY
    ORGANIZING FOCUSES ON DANILO DOLCI'S EXPERIENCE OF LOCAL
    DEVELOPMENT IN WESTERN SICILY SINCE 1952: PLANNING PROJECTS,
    SOCIAL WORK, CONSCIOUSNESS RAISING, EDUCATIONAL PROGRAMS,
    AND CIVIL AND HUMAN RIGHTS CAMPAIGNS. TRACING THE HISTORY OF
    DOLCI'S ROLE AS A POPULAR LEADER, THIS STUDY IS AN ATTEMPT
    TO UNDERSTAND HOW EFFECTIVELY THIS FIGURE HAS PUT INTO
    PRACTICE HIS THEORIES OF AUTHENTIC DEMOCRACY AND HOW
    POLITICAL AND/OR PROFESSIONAL LEADERSHIP IS RELATED TO
    GRASSROOTS DECISION-MAKING PROCESSES.

07625 RIGGS, F.W.
    THE POLITICAL ECOLOGY OF AMERICAN PUBLIC ADMINISTRATION A
    NEO-HAMILTONIAN APPROACH
    INTERNATIONAL JOURNAL OF PUBLIC ADMINISTRATION, 12(3)
    (1989), 355-384.
        PUBLIC ADMINISTRATION EVERYWHERE IS ROOTED IN POLITICS.
    PUBLIC OFFICIALS (MILITARY AND CIVIL) ARE NECESSARILY
    INVOLVED IN POLITICS AS WELL AS ADMINISTRATION. NORMAL
    THEORIES OF PUBLIC ADMINISTRATION RECOGNIZE THESE REALITIES.
    AN ABNORMAL, "CONVENTIONAL," THEORY OF PUBLIC ADMINISTRATION
    WHICH EVOLVED IN AMERICA SINCE THE 1880S PRESUPPOSES THAT
    POLITICS AND ADMINISTRATION CAN AND SHOULD BE SEPARATED. IT
    REPLACED THE "NORMAL" HAMILTONIAN TRADITION WHICH SAW PUBLIC
    ADMINISTRATION IN A POLITICAL CONTEXT. A REVIVED AND
    MODIFIED NEO-HAMILTONIAN PERSPECTIVE IS NOW NEEDED. IT COULD
    INTEGRATE THE NON-POLITICAL THEORIES OF PUBLIC
    ADMINISTRATION, CONNECT THEM WITH A NON-ADMINISTRATIVE VIEW
    OF BUREAUCRATIC POLITICS, AND FACILITATE RESEARCH IN
    COMPARATIVE AND DEVELOPMENT ADMINISTRATION. TO SUPPORT THESE
    PROPOSITIONS HE WILL IDENTIFY KEY DIMENSIONS OF BUREAUCRATIC
    POLITICS, SEE HOW THE CONVENTIONAL PUBLIC ADMINISTRATION
    AROSE IN RESPONSE TO THE AMERICAN CIVIL SERVICE REFORM
    MOVEMENT A CENTURY AGO, AND COMPARE EXISTING THEORIES WITH
    THE PROPOSED NEO-HAMILTONIAN PARADIGM.

07626 RIKHYE, R.
    THE INDO-TILETAN BORDER TODAY: SOME MILITARY IMPLICATIONS
    CHINA REPORT, 24(3) (JUL 88), 289-298.
        THIS ARTICLE IS AN ANALYSIS OF ROAD AND RAIL ACCESS INTO
    TIBET FROM CHINA AND INDIA SPECIFIC TOPOGRAPHIC DETAIL IS
    PROVIDED CONCLUSIONS FOR MILITARY STRATEGIES ARE PROVIDED

07627 RILEY, A.
    OVERCOMING FEDERAL WATER POLICIES: THE WILDCAT-SAN PABLO
    CREEKS CASE
    ENVIRONMENT, 31(10) (DEC 89), 12-20, 29-31.
        THE ARTICLE EXAMINES THE 33-YEAR HISTORY OF THE FLOOD-
    CONTROL PROJECT ON WILDCAT AND SAN PABLO CREEKS IN NORTH
    RICHMOND, CALIFORNIA. THE DETAILED ANALYSIS REVEALS A
    FEDERAL POLICY THAT IS DISCRIMINATORY, ENVIRONMENTALLY
    HARMFUL, AND PLAGUED BY A LONG AND COSTLY PLANNING SYSTEM.
    MULTI-OBJECTIVE PLANNING WITH GENUINE LOCAL AND NATIONAL
    BENEFITS IS EXTREMELY DIFFICULT TO IMPLEMENT UNDER CURRENT
    CONDITIONS.

07628 RILEY, J. V. JR.
    THE MEANING OF POLITICAL HISTORY: THE UNITY AND ARGUMENT
    OF THUCYDIDES'S BOOK I
    DISSERTATION ABSTRACTS INTERNATIONAL, 49(7) (JAN 89),
    1946-A.
        THE AUTHOR ENDEAVORS TO RECOVER THE MEANING OF POLITICAL
    HISTORY BY ANALYZING BOOK I OF THUCYDIDES' "THE WAR OF THE
    PELOPONNESIANS AND THE ATHENIANS."

07629 RIMANELLI, M.
    FROM ASHES TO RENEWAL: POST-WAR ITALY'S FOREIGN POLICY
    ITALIAN JOURNAL, III(4) (1989), 28-33.
        THE AUTHOR STUDIES HOW ITALY'S FOREIGN POLICY HAS BEEN
    INFLUENCED BY ITS GEO-STRATEGIC LOCATION AT THE CROSSROADS
    OF MEDITERRANEAN AND EUROPEAN AVENUES OF TRADE AND POLITICS.

07630 RINEHART, S.; PERKINS, J.
    THE INTERSECTION OF GENDER POLITICS AND RELIGIOUS BELIEFS
    POLITICAL BEHAVIOR, 11(1) (MAR 89), 33-56.
        TRADITIONAL UNDERSTANDING HAS PLACED CONSERVATISM AT THE

INTERSECTION OF RELIGION AND POLITICS AND HAS ASSUMED THAT
THIS RELATIONSHIP IS STRONGER FOR WOMEN THAN IT IS FOR MEN.
HOWEVER, THE RELATIONSHIPS HAVE NOT BEEN THOROUGHLY
DOCUMENTED. THE AUTHORS ANALYZES THE 1980 AND 1984 NATIONAL
ELECTION STUDY DATA AND FIND THAT RELIGION IS NOT A MORE
CONSERVATIZING INFLUENCE ON VOTING BEHAVIOR FOR WOMEN THAN
IT IS FOR MEN. ALTHOUGH WOMEN ARE MORE RELIGIOUS THAN MEN,
POLITICAL OBSERVERS ARE CAUTIONED THAT THIS FINDING CANNOT
BE TAKEN AS EVIDENCE OF WOMEN'S GREATER SUPPORT FOR
CONSERVATIVE CANDIDATES.

07631 RING, W.
    HONDURAS: CONTRA PLIGHT
    THIRD WORLD WEEK, 8(3) (MAR 89), 17.
    HONDURAS BROKE WITH U.S. POLICY IN FEBRUARY 1989, WHEN
IT SIGNED A REGIONAL AGREEMENT TO DRAW UP A PLAN TO
DEMOBILIZE THE CONTRAS AND REPATRIATE THEM TO NICARAGUA OR A
THIRD COUNTRY. HONDURAN PRESIDENT JOSE AZCONA HOYO SIGNED
THE AGREEMENT BECAUSE HE WAS CONFRONTING INCREASING PUBLIC
OPINION AGAINST THE CONTRAS AND LACK OF SUPPORT FROM THE
BUSH ADMINISTRATION. WITHOUT SOLID AMERICAN SUPPORT FOR THE
ANTI-SANDINISTA POLICY, THE HONDURAN ARMY AND GOVERNMENT
HAVE COME TO FEEL THAT THEY HAVE NO CHOICE BUT TO SEEK A
REGIONAL APPROACH TO THE CENTRAL AMERICAN PROBLEM.

07632 RIPY, T.B.; MORRIS, M.B.
    TAXATION OF RETIREMENT INCOME: RECENT DEVELOPMENTS
    CRS REVEIW, 10(7) (AUG 89), 28-29.
    TWO ISSUES INVOLVING STATE TAXATION OF RETIREMENT INCOME
HAVE DRAWN CONSIDERABLE ATTENTION IN RECENT MONTHS. ONE
ISSUE, STATE INCOME TAXATION OF FEDERAL PENSIONERS, WAS THE
SUBJECT OF A SIGNIFICANT SUPREME COURT DECISION IN MARCH
1989 (DAVIS V. MICHIGAN DEPARTMENT OF TREASURY). A SECOND
ISSUE, PART OF A LARGER CONTROVERSY, INVOLVES STATE TAXATION
OF NONRESIDENTS' PENSION INCOME. BOTH ARE LIKELY TO CONTINUE
TO ATTRACT INTEREST FOR SOME TIME.

07633 RIST, R.
    DECLINING OPTIONS/ INCREASING NEEDS
    SOCIETY, 26(6) (SEP 89), 39-45.
    THE ARTICLE ANALYZES THE CHANGES AND CHALLENGES THAT
AMERICA WILL FACE IN THE COMING YEARS. IT FOCUSES ON TWO
LONG-TERM TRENDS THAT WILL DETERMINE THE FUTURE COURSE OF
THE US: US INSTITUTIONAL VIABILITY TO SOLVE PRESSING
PROBLEMS SUCH AS HEALTH CARE, FINANCIAL MARKETS, AND
PROVERTY; AND THE OVERALL "DECLINE" OF THE US. IT CONCLUDES
BY DISCUSSING THE IMPLICATIONS OF THE TRENDS FOR FUTURE
POLICY STUDIES.

07634 RITCHIE, L.H.
    PRIVATIZATION PROSPECTS IN NEPAL
    AVAILABLE FROM NTIS, NO. PB89-159347/GAR, DEC 87, 100.
    THE STUDY BEGINS WITH A BRIEF CHAPTER DESCRIBING THE
CREATION OF PUBLIC ENTERPRISES OVER THE PAST 30 PLUS YEARS,
AND IS FOLLOWED BY A SECTION DEVOTED TO THE CURRENT
SITUATION. THE MANUFACTURING SECTOR RECEIVES PRIMARY
ATTENTION. THERE FOLLOW BRIEF DESCRIPTIONS OF FIVE PUBLIC
ENTERPRISES. THE OBJECT IN EACH INSTANCE IS TO RAISE A
SINGLE QUESTION: DOES THIS ENTERPRISE NOW BELONG IN THE
PUBLIC SECTOR. THERE FOLLOW SECTIONS ON VARIOUS CURRENT
CONSTRAINTS TO PRIVATIZATION GROUPED UNDER STATUTORY,
FINANCIAL, AND SEEMING HMG CONCERNS, AND, ULTIMATELY,
CONCLUSIONS AND RECOMMENDATIONS.

07635 RITCHIE, T. J.
    A LICENCE FOR THE TEACHER
    POLICY OPTIONS, 10(2) (MAR 89), 18-22.
    SCHOOLS ARE PRESENTLY RUN IN CANADA AS BUREAUCRATIC
HIERARCHIES WHERE POWER AND STATUS RESIDE IN AN
ADMINISTRATIVE OFFICE, ARGUES THOMAS RITCHIE. HE SUGGESTS
THAT THE PUBLIC, AND TEACHERS, WOULD BE BETTER SERVED IF WE
WERE TO MOVE TO A SYSTEM MUCH CLOSER TO THAT EMBRACED BY
SUCH PROFESSIONS AS MEDICINE AND LAW, COMPLETE WITH A
COLLEGE OF TEACHERS TO OVERSEE THE LICENSING, TRAINING,
INDOCTRINATION, CONTINUING EDUCATION AND DISCIPLINING OF
TEACHERS. HE SUGGESTS THAT THE PRESENT SYSTEM DOES NOT
IDENTIFY EITHER EXCELLENT OR SUBSTANDARD TEACHERS, AND THAT
THE PRESENT INSPECTION SYSTEM, WHICH IS SUPPOSED TO
SAFEGUARD STANDARDS, IS NO MORE THAN A PROCESS OF
"CEREMONIAL CONGRATULATION". USELESS WHEN REAL PROBLEMS TURN
UP. HE ACKNOWLEDGES THAT TRANSFERRING POWER AND
RESPONSIBILITY TO TEACHERS PRESENTS SOME DIFFICULTIES -THEY
DO NOT MEET ALL THE CRITERIA OF A TRUE PROFESSION -- BUT
ARGUE THAT THIS PROPOSAL WOULD LEAD TO A MUCH NEEDED BETTER
MANAGEMENT OF OUR EDUCATORS.

07636 RITTENBERG, L.
    ON THE PROBLEM OF IDENTIFYING THE ENGINES OF ECONOMIC
    GROWTH
    STUDIES IN COMPARATIVE INTERNATIONAL DEVELOPMENT, 24(3)
    (FAL 89), 51-61.
    THIS ARTICLE INVESTIGATES THE EMPIRICAL RELATIONSHIP
BETWEEN SECTORAL GROWTH AND INCOME GROWTH AND IN SO DOING
CASTS DOUBT ON PREVIOUS STUDIES WHICH HAVE ARGUED THAT

EITHER EXPORT OR AGRICULTURAL GROWTH ENHANCES TOTAL INCOME
GROWTH. IT IS SHOWN THAT THE EVIDENCE FROM THE CORRELATION
AND REGRESSION MODELS USED TO DATE IS INCONCLUSIVE AND THAT
MUCH OF THE MEASURED IMPACT OF SECTORAL GROWTH ON OVERALL
INCOME GROWTH MAY BE SPURIOUS IN THE SENSE THAT IT CAN BE
EXPLAINED BY GROWTH IN THE UNDERLYING INPUTS.

07637 RIVAGE-SEUL, D.M.
    GAUGING OPPOSITION AND RESOURCES IN NICARAGUA'S "THIRD WAR"
    THE CHRISTIAN CENTURY, 106(22) (JUL 89), 687-689.
    FACED WITH A REVITALIZED POLITICAL OPPOSITION
NICARAGUA'S SANDINISTA GOVERNMENT IS ENGAGED IN WHAT IT
CONSIDERS A "THIRD WAR" - ONE THAT MAY TEST IT AS SEVERELY
AS DID THE WARS AGAINST SAMOZA AND THE U.S. - BACKED CONTRAS.
THIS ARTICLE EXAMINES HOW THIS "THIRD WAR" IS LIKELY TO
PROCEED.

07638 RIVELAND, C.
    GUBERNATORIAL STYLES: IS THERE A RIGHT ONE?
    JOURNAL OF STATE GOVERNMENT, 62(4) (JUL 89), 136-139.
    THE AUTHOR COMPARES A GOVERNOR'S RESPONSIBILITIES WITH
THOSE OF A PRIVATE-SECTOR CHIEF EXECUTIVE. HE CONCLUDES THAT,
IN GOVERNING, A LEADER'S MANAGEMENT STYLE IS LESS IMPORTANT
THAN HIS ABILITY TO COMMUNICATE VALUES. THUS, THERE IS NO
SINGLE MANAGEMENT STYLE -THAT ENSURES A SUCCESSFUL
ADMINISTRATION FOR A GOVERNOR.

07639 RIVELES, S.
    DIPLOMATIC ASYLUM AS A HUMAN RIGHT: THE CASE OF THE DURBAN
    SIR
    HUMAN RIGHTS QUARTERLY, 11(1) (FEB 89), 139-159.
    THIS PAPER EXAMINES THE HISTORY OF DIPLOMATIC ASYLUM AND
ASYLUM PRACTICE AS IT HAS DEVELOPED IN LATIN AMERICA. THE
PAPER THEN ADDRESSES THE KEY ISSUE IN THIS CONTROVERSY, I.E.,
THE INTERNATIONAL LAW OBLIGATIONS OF THE SENDING STATE, E.G.
, BRITAIN OR FRANCE, AND THE RECEIVING STATE, E.G., SOUTH
AFRICA, IN RELATION TO THE PERSON SEEKING REFUGE. IF THE
EXISTENCE OF A DUTY TO GRANT ASYLUM COULD BE ESTABLISHED, IT
WOULD INDEED REPRESENT A FAR MORE DIRECT INVOLVEMENT OF
HUMAN RIGHTS LAW IN THE DECISION-MAKING PROCESS OF SENDING
STATES. HUMAN RIGHTS WOULD BECOME A MAJOR CONSIDERATION IN
FOREIGN POLICY DECISIONS.

07640 RIVERS, R.; VEST, G.
    GETTING INTO THE TAKEOVER BUSINESS
    EUROPE, (291) (NOV 89), 18-20.
    THE DRAMATIC RISE IN THE NUMBER OF TAKEOVER BIDS HAS LED
THE EUROPEAN COMMUNITY (EC) TO ADDRESS THE REGULATION OF
TAKEOVER BIDS. THE ARTICLE ANALYZES THE CONTENTS OF THE EC'S
PROPOSED DIRECTIVE ON "COMPANY LAW CONCERNING TAKEOVER AND
OTHER GENERAL BIDS." ALTHOUGH THE COMMISSION'S PROPOSAL ONLY
ESTABLISHES MINIMUM RULES AND GIVES MEMBER STATES FREEDOM TO
ENACT STRICTER REGULATIONS, IT HAS BEEN MET WITH
CONSIDERABLE RESISTANCE ON THE PART OF SOME MEMBER STATES.
THE EVENTUAL OUTCOME OF THIS AND OTHER PROPOSED LEGISLATION
WILL ULTIMATELY BE DETERMINED BY THE DEGREE OF WILLINGNESS
TO COMPROMISE ON THE PART OF MEMBER STATES.

07641 RIVERS, R.; VEST, G.
    MAKING DEALS IN POST-1992 EUROPE
    EUROPE, (290) (OCT 89), 18-20, 46.
    THE ARTICLE EXAMINES THE EFFECT THAT THE ECONOMIC
INTEGRATION OF EUROPE IN 1992 WILL HAVE ON THE HIGH STAKES
WORLD OF MERGERS AND ACQUISITIONS. IT OUTLINES VARIOUS
MERGER CONTROL PROPOSALS AND ANALYZES THEIR POTENTIAL
EFFECTS ON BOTH US AND EURPOPEAN BUSINESSESS. IT CONCLUDES
THAT BRUSSELS WILL PLAY THE DOMINANT ROLE IN SHAPING THE
FUTURE OF EUROPEAN INVESTMENT AND THAT US AND EUROPEAN
FINANCIAL COMMUNITIES MUST UNDERSTAND THE NEW E.C.
COMPETITION RULES TO PARTICIPATE FULLY IN POST-1992 EUROPE.

07642 RIZA, B. A.
    TURKISH PARTICIPATION IN MIDDLE EAST DEFENCE PROJECTS AND
    ITS IMPACT ON TURCO-ARAB RELATIONS, MAY 1950 - JUNE 1953
    DISSERTATION ABSTRACTS INTERNATIONAL, 49(8) (FEB 89),
    2383-A.
    THE AUTHOR OFFERS A CHRONOLOGICAL ACCOUNT OF TURKEY'S
INVOLVEMENT IN MIDDLE EAST DEFENSE PROJECTS BETWEEN 1950 AND
1953 WITHIN THE CONTEXT OF TURKEY'S GENERAL ALIGNMENT WITH
THE WEST. HE DISCUSSES TURKEY'S CAMPAIGN FOR NATO MEMBERSHIP,
HER INVOLVEMENT IN REGIONAL DEFENSE SCHEMES, AND THE
EFFECTS ON TURCO-ARAB RELATIONS.

07643 RIZZO, A.
    REFLECTIONS ON PUTTING THEORY IN PRACTICE INTO ACTION IN
    THE CLASSROOM
    POLICY STUDIES REVIEW, 8(4) (SUM 89), 840-844.
    EFFECTIVE LEARNING NECESSITATES A CHANGE OF BEHAVIOR ON
THE PART OF THE STUDENT. THE AUTHOR ASSERTS THAT THE
INTRODUCTION OF ABSTRACT THEORIES TO STUDENTS DOES LITTLE TO
ADVANCE THE STUDENTS' COMPETENCE OR EFFICIENCY. RATHER, A
CASE IS MADE FOR ALLOWING STUDENTS TO CREATE THEIR OWN
THEORIES OF ACTION BASED UPON THEIR INDIVIDUAL CIRCUMSTANCES
AND EXPERIENCES. THE CONCEPT OF AN "ACTION THEORY" IS

FORWARDED AS AN EFFECTIVE TOOL FOR TEACHING PUBLIC
ADMINISTRATION STUDENTS. THE ACTION THEORY RECOGNIZES THE
STUDENT'S NEED TO HAVE RELEVANT FRAMEWORKS AND PRACTICAL
GUIDELINES. FUTHERMORE, THE AUTHOR PREDICTS THAT THE ACTION
THEORY WILL GIVE PUBLIC ADMINISTRATORS GREATER CONTROL OVER
THEIR WORK ENVIRONMENTS INASMUCH AS IT ESTABLISHES MORE
HONEST ASSESSMENTS OF ORGANIZATIONAL CONDITIONS.

07644 ROBBINS, L.; FIENUP-RIORDAN, A.; MCNABB, S.; PETTERSON, J.;
   WARING, K.
   VILLAGE ECONOMICS IN RURAL ALASKA: SOCIAL AND ECONOMIC
   STUDIES
   AVAILABLE FROM NTIS, NO. PB89-189799/GAR, NOV 88, 348.
   THE ANALYSIS DESCRIBES HOW THE VILLAGE ECONOMIES
FUNCTION AND IDENTIFIES THE ECONOMIC DIFFERENCES THAT
DISTINGUISH THE STUDY COMMUNITIES OF ST. PAUL, GAMBELL, AND
ALAKANUK IN ALASKA. THE STUDY COMMUNITIES DISPLAYED A RANGE
OF IMPORTANT ECONOMIC CHARACTERISTICS. AS DIFFERENT AS THEY
WERE, THEY CAN ARGUABLY BE CONSIDERED ALASKAN ECONOMIC
'PROTOTYPES' THAT EXEMPLIFY ARRANGEMENTS OF GOVERNMENT
PROGRAMS AND SUBSIDIES, NATURAL RESOURCES HARVESTS FOR BOTH
HOUSEHOLD AND COMMERCIAL USE, AND LIMITED EXPORTS BASED ON
BOTH RAW AND WORKED (E.G., CRAFTS) RESOURCES SIMILAR TO
THOSE PATTERNS FOUND IN ANY OTHER RURAL ALASKA COMMUNITIES.
ALL THREE COMMUNITIES' RESOURCE BASES ARE SUBJECT TO
SIGNIFICANT REGULATIONS WHICH PROVIDED RAW MATERIAL FOR THE
POLITICAL-ECONOMIC ANALYSIS. EVEN THOUGH THE VILLAGES HAVE
MANY ECONOMIC ELEMENTS IN COMMON, THEY DIFFERED MOST
STRONGLY IN THEIR BLENDS OF THESE ELEMENTS.

07645 ROBERT, P.
   A CONTRADICTION: DEVELOPMENT V. ENVIRONMENT
   CHINA NEWS ANALYSIS, (1379) (FEB 89), 1-9.
   THE AUTHOR LOOKS AT CHINA'S SERIOUS INDUSTRIAL POLLUTION
PROBLEM AND AT THE MEASURES THE GOVERNMENT IS TAKING TO DEAL
WITH IT.

07646 ROBERT, P.
   INTELLECTUALS AND POLITICS
   CHINA NEWS ANALYSIS, (1387) (JUN 89), 3-10.
   THE TIANANMEN SQUARE MASSACRE HAS PRODUCED A TIME OF
RECKONING FOR MANY CHINESE INTELLECTUALS REGARDING THEIR
COMMITMENT TO THE PARTY AND OTHER INSTITUTIONS. THE
INTELLECTUALS ARE REASSESSING THEIR POSITION VIS-A-VIS
CHINA'S IDEOLOGY, MODERNIZATION, AND POLITICAL STRUCTURE.
THE UNEASY "MODUS VIVENDI" BETWEEN INTELLECTUALS AND THE
CHINESE LEADERSHIP HAS SHATTERED BY THE MILITARY VIOLENCE,
AND POLICE ACTION HAS ENSURED THAT THE DEBATES OF
INTELLECTUALS ARE EXCLUDED FROM THE NEWSPAPERS.

07647 ROBERTI, M.; STARR, P.
   SUCCESS WILL BRING ITS OWN HEADACHES
   SOUTH, (99) (JAN 89), 16-17.
   IN 1989, THE BIGGEST PROBLEM FOR ASIA'S NEWLY
INDUSTRIALIZING ECONOMIES WILL BE SUCCESS. TWO YEARS OF
BOOMING EXPORTS AND SURGING DOMESTIC DEMAND HAVE SPARKED
INFLATION, LABOR SHORTAGES, AND FEAR OF PROTECTIONISM.
ECONOMISTS ARE FORECASTING A YEAR OF RELATIVELY MODEST
GROWTH AND CONSOLIDATION FOR HONG KONG, SINGAPORE, TAIWAN,
AND SOUTH KOREA AS THEY STRUGGLE TO MAINTAIN THEIR EXPORT
COMPETITIVENESS.

07648 ROBERTS, A. R.
   THE SOUTH AFRICAN STRATEGY
   AFRICA REPORT, 34(1) (JAN 89), 29-30.
   THE SOUTH AFRICAN GOVERNMENT HAD REASON ENOUGH TO ENTER
INTO THE U.S. BROKERED TALKS TOWARD PEACE IN ANGOLA AND
NAMIBIAN INDEPENDENCE. HOWEVER, ALTHOUGH PRETORIA HAS
FINALLY INITIALLED THE AGREEMENT, THE CONCRETE DIFFICULTIES
THE UN WILL ENCOUNTER IN CARRYING OUT ITS MANDATE IN THE
TERRITORY DEMONSTRATE THAT FREEDOM NAMIBIA IS NOT AS CLOSE
AS IT APPEARS.

07649 ROBERTS, A.R.
   NAMIBIA: WHAT THEY DIDN'T TELL US
   AFRICA REPORT, 34(4) (JUL 89), 61.
   SINCE NAMIBIA'S TRANSITION TO INDEPENDENCE BEGAN ON
APRIL 1, 1989, THE SOUTH AFRICAN-LED KOEVOET PARAMILITARY
UNITS HAVE BROUGHT REPEATED AGGRESSION AND OCCASIONAL DEATH
TO THE PEOPLE OF NORTHERN NAMIBIA. THE KOEVOET'S MOST
STUNNING ACT OF VIOLENCE WAS THE EXECUTION OF 18 MEMBERS OF
SWAPO'S MILITARY ARM.

07650 ROBERTS, C.; WISHNICK, E.
   IDEOLOGY IS DEAD! LONG LIVE IDEOLOGY?
   PROBLEMS OF COMMUNISM, XXXVIII(6) (NOV 89), 57-69.
   EXAMINATION OF THE EVOLVING RELATIONSHIP BETWEEN
IDEOLOGY AND SOVIET FOREIGN POLICY REQUIRES THE ANALYSIS OF
SYSTEMATIC CONNECTIONS BETWEEN SOVIET DOMESTIC POLITICS AND
CHANGING FOREIGN POLICY CONCEPTS. THE NEW THINKING IN SOVIET
FOREIGN POLICY ADVOCATED BY MIKHAIL GORBACHEV AND HIS
ADVISORS CANNOT BE GRASPED WITHOUT AN UNDERSTANDING OF
SOVIET IDEOLOGICAL TERMS OF REFERENCE. NEW THINKING DOES NOT
DENOTE DE-IDEOLOGIZATION. RATHER, GORBACHEV'S FOREIGN POLICY

EFFORTS INDICATE A MODIFICATION OF THE FUNCTIONS PERFORMED
BY IDEOLOGY. THESE MODIFICATIONS HAVE BEEN PROMPTED BY
CHANGES IN THE INTERNATIONAL ENVIRONMENT AND BY A
REASSESSMENT OF DOMESTIC PRIORITIES.

07651 ROBERTS, G.K.
   PARTY SYSTEM CHANGE IN WEST GERMANY: LAND-FEDERAL LINKAGES
   WEST EUROPEAN POLITICS, 12(4) (OCT 89), 98-113.
   THIS STUDY FOCUSES ON BOTH THE FEDERAL AND LANDER PARTY
SYSTEMS, AND LINKAGES BETWEEN THEM. IT IS CONFINED TO WEST
GERMANY (WHAT FROM 1949 BECAME THE FEDERAL REPUBLIC OF
GERMANY, AND WEST BERLIN), AND HAS THEREFORE THE OBVIOUS
ADVANTAGES AND DISADVANTAGES OF A CASE-STUDY: CONTEXTUAL
SENSITIVITY, LONGITUDINAL WITHIN-SYSTEM COMPARISON, BUT
POSSIBLE OVER-EMPHASIS OF CONTEXTUALLY-SPECIFIC FACTORS, ETC.
   IT EMPHASIZES FIVE SPECIAL FEATURES OF THE WEST GERMAN
CONTEXT OF PARTY SYSTEMS SINCE THEY AFFECT THE PARAMETERS
AND PROCESSES OF PARTY SYSTEMS WHICH HAVE EXISTED AT FEDERAL
AND LANDER LEVELS SINCE THE REVIVAL OF POLITICAL LIFE AFTER
1945.

07652 ROBERTS, J.F.
   PROSPECTS FOR STATE-LOCAL RELATIONS
   NATIONAL CIVIC REVIEW, 78(5) (SEP 89), 356-361.
   IN SPITE OF A BURGEONING ERA OF "DO-IT-YOURSELF
FEDERALISM," STATE AND LOCAL OFFICIALS CONTINUE TO PLACE
EMPHASIS ON TRADITIONAL SERVICE-DELIVERY AND PROGRAM
RESPONSIBILITIES. THEY HAVE TAKEN THE LEAD IN A BROAD RANGE
OF ENTREPRENEURIAL ACTIVITIES AND ARE DEMONSTRATING PROGRESS
IN FORGING STRONGER STATE-LOCAL PARTNERSHIPS. WHEN VIEWED
TOGETHER, THESE DEVELOPMENTS PROVIDE HOPEFUL SIGNALS THAT
STATE AND LOCAL GOVERNMENTS ARE INDEED RESPONDING TO THE
CHALLENGES POSED BY A DECENTRALIZING FEDERAL SYSTEM AND AN
INCREASINGLY COMPLEX AND INTERNATIONALIZED FISCAL ORDER.

07653 ROBERTS, P.C.
   "SUPPLY-SIDE" ECONOMICS -- THEORY AND RESULTS
   PUBLIC INTEREST, 93 (FAL 88), 16-36.
   THIS ARTICLE CONTRASTS SUPPLY-SIDE AND KEYNESIAN
ECONOMIC POLICY AND TRACES THE HISTORY OF EACH. IT EXAMINES
THE THEORY OF SUPPLY-SIDE ECONOMICS WHICH RELIES MORE ON THE
MICROECONOMIC ANALYSIS OF MARKET BEHAVIOR THAN THE KEYNESIAN
APPROACH OF THE MACROECONOMIC ANALYSIS OF STATICAL AGGREGATES

07654 ROBERTS, P.C.
   PINBALL WIZARD AT THE FLIPPERS
   NATIONAL REVIEW, XLI(3) (FEB 89), 24-27.
   THE GIGANTIC EGO OF RICHARD DARMAN, BUSH'S DIRECTOR OF
THE OFFICE OF MANAGEMENT AND BUDGET, MAKES HIM A DANGER TO
EVERYONE IN THE ADMINISTRATION. DARMAN'S PUBLIC SERVICE
CAREER ILLUSTRATES THE AXIOM THAT ANYONE WHO CAN GET HIMSELF
INTO A REASONABLY HIGH POSITION IN WASHINGTON CAN CREATE HIS
OWN IMAGE BY APPROPRIATING THE IDEAS OF OTHERS AND
MANIPULATING LEAK-HUNGRY REPORTERS.

07655 ROBERTS, P.C.
   STOP PANICKING OVER INFLATION
   WASHINGTON MONTHLY, 21(4) (MAY 89), 26-30.
   THE AUTHOR CONSIDERS THAT ECONOMIC CONSEQUENCES OF THE
FEAR OF INFLATION.

07656 ROBERTS, R.A.
   IMAGES OF WOMEN IN THE FICTION OF ZHANG JIE AND ZHANG
   XINXIN
   CHINA QUARTERLY, (120) (DEC 89), 800-813.
   ZHANG XINXIN AND ZHANG JIE ARE CONTEMPORARY CHINESE
WOMEN WRITERS KNOWN FOR THEIR FICTIONAL DEPICTIONS OF THE
PROBLEMS OF URBAN, INTELLECTUAL WOMEN. ZHANG JIE PRESENTS
CHARACTERS STRONGLY INFLUENCED BY CONFUCIAN MORALITY AND
SOCIALIST IDEALS. ZHANG XINXIN DRAWS CHARACTERS WHO SHOW
LITTLE ENTHUSIASM FOR POLITICAL IDEALS AND ARE LESS
CONSTRAINED BY TRADITIONAL MORALITY. IN THIS ESSAY, THE
AUTHOR BEGINS WITH AN OVERVIEW OF THE DEVELOPMENT OF THE
IMAGES OF WOMEN IN THE FICTION OF THE TWO WRITERS. THEN SHE
CONSIDERS TO WHAT EXTENT THE IMAGES CHALLENGE TRADITIONAL
IDEALS OF FEMINITY AND WOMEN'S ROLES AND TO WHAT EXTENT THEY
PERPETUATE TRADITIONAL VALUES THAT, IN FACT, LIMIT WOMEN'S
PROGRESS TOWARDS A POSITION OF SOCIAL AND POLITICAL EQUALITY.

07657 ROBERTS, W.R.
   A NEW STATUS FOR EASTERN EUROPE?
   WORLD TODAY, 45(10) (OCT 89), 165-166.
   EVENTS IN POLAND APPEAR TO CONFIRM THAT MIKHALL
GORBACHEV HAS JETTISONED THE BREZHNEV DOCTRINE, UNDER WHICH
EAST EUROPEAN COUNTRIES WERE SUBJECT TO SOVIET INTERVENTION
IF THEIR ORTHODOX COMMUNIST REGIMES WERE ENDANGERED. THE NEW
NON-COMMUNIST-LED POLISH GOVERNMENT SUGGESTS THAT MOSCOW
WILL TOLERATE THE EMERGENCE OF MULTI-PARTY SYSTEMS AND NON-
COMMUNIST-LED GOVERNMENTS IF THE COUNTRIES REMAIN MEMBERS OF
THE WARSAW PACT. MOREOVER, THERE ARE INDICATIONS THAT SOVIET
THINKING ON EASTERN EUROPE IS STILL EVOLVING AND COULD IN
THE FUTURE GO EVEN BEYOND THE POLICY ADOPTED IN THE CASE OF
POLAND. IT IS POSSIBLE THAT IN THE FUTURE EAST EUROPEAN
COUNTRIES MIGHT BE ALLOWED TO LEAVE THE WARSAW PACT OR THE

PACT MIGHT BE REVAMPED ALONG NON-MILITARY LINES.

07658 ROBERTS, H.R.
THE INFORMATION REVOLUTION, I: A BREAKTHROUGH IN THE EAST?
WORLD TODAY, 45(6) (JUN 89), 95-96.
MIKHAIL GORBACHEV HAS ADMITTED THAT THE INFORMATION
REVOLUTION HAS BEEN A POWERFUL IMPETUS FOR CHANGES INSIDE
THE SOVIET UNION BECAUSE MASS COMMUNICATIONS MAKE IT
DIFFICULT TO PRESERVE A CLOSED SOCIETY. THE DISPARITY
BETWEEN THE INFORMATION-RICH WESTERN MEDIA AND THE
INFORMATION-STARVED SOVIET MEDIA EXERTED PRESSURE ON THE
SOVIET UNION FOR A LONG TIME AND WITH SUCH INTENSITY THAT
ALL EFFORTS TO KEEP INFORMATION OUT COLLAPSED IN THE END.
THE RISE OF TELEVISION PRESENTED A PROBLEM FOR THE SOVIETS
BECAUSE SPILLOVER SIGNALS FROM WESTERN STATIONS ATTRACTED
SIZEABLE AUDIENCES IN SOVIET BORDER REGIONS. OTHER WESTERN
MEDIA, SUCH AS FILMS, ALSO CHALLENGED THE SOVIET
AUTHORITIES' MONOPOLOY ON INFORMATION. THE INFLUX OF AUDIO
AND VIDEO CASSETTES FROM THE WEST WAS ANOTHER PROBLEM.

07659 ROBERTSON, D.B.
PLANNED INCAPACITY TO SUCCEED? POLICY STRUCTURE AND SOCIAL
POLICY FAILURE
POLICY STUDIES REVIEW, 8(2) (WIN 89), 241-263.
BY FAILING TO DISTINGUISH BETWEEN INEFFECTIVENESS AND
POLITICAL FAILURE, THE THREE MOST COMMON INTERPRETATIONS OF
THE WAR ON POVERTY AND THE COMPREHENSIVE EMPLOYMENT AND
TRAINING ACT (FAILURE OWING TO CENTRAL GOVERNMENT
INCOMPETENCE, FAILURE OWING TO PLURALISM, AND "HIDDEN"
SUCCESS) CANNOT ADEQUATELY ACCOUNT FOR THE GAP BETWEEN THEIR
AMBIGUOUS PERFORMANCE AND THEIR CLEAR POLITICAL FAILURE. TO
UNDERSTAND THESE DIFFERENCES, ONE MUST UNDERSTAND THE EFFECT
OF AMERICA'S FRAGMENTED POLITICAL STRUCTURE ON THE DESIGN
AND IMPLEMENTATION OF POVERTY AND UNEMPLOYMENT REMEDIES.
UNDER RESOURCE CONSTRAINTS AND GIVEN A LARGE DEGREE OF
POLICY DISCRETION, AMERICAN STATES IN THE AGGREGATE HAVE
RETAINED THEIR HISTORIC RESISTANCE TO SOCIAL POLICIES THAT
WOULD INCREASE SHORT-TERM EXPENDITURES AND REDUCE THE
ATTRACTIVENESS OF THEIR BUSINESS CLIMATE. THESE
JURISDICTIONS AND THEIR CONGRESSIONAL REPRESENTATIVES
OPPOSED NEW FULLY NATIONALIZED INITIATIVES, INSISTING ON
POLICY DESIGNS THAT PROMISED FISCAL RELIEF WHILE PROTECTING
STATE AND LOCAL POLICY CONTROL. NATIONAL POLICYMAKERS FOUND
THAT GRANT-IN-AID PROGRAMS OFFERED THE PATH OF LEAST
RESISTANCE IN THESE CIRCUMSTANCES. ALTHOUGH SOCIAL POLICY
GRANT PROGRAMS COULD WIN INITIAL APPROVAL IN CONGRESS, THESE
DESIGNS PROVED TO BE INCREASINGLY UNWIELDY, EXPENSIVE, AND
DIFFICULT TO CONTROL IN PRACTICE. THE PROGRAMS YIELDED
AMBIGUOUS OVERALL RESULTS BUT PROVIDED UNAMBIGUOUS EXAMPLES
OF WASTE, FRAUD AND ABUSE.

07660 ROBERTSON, G.
A BILL OF RIGHTS FOR BRITAIN?
CONSTITUTIONAL REFORM QUARTERLY REVIEW, 4(3) (FAL 89), 4.
THE AUTHOR ARGUES THAT THE IMPROVEMENTS IN CIVIL
LIBERTIES IN THE PAST DECADE HAVE BEEN MORE A RESULT OF
BRITAIN'S OBLIGATIONS UNDER THE EUROPEAN CONVENTION OF HUMAN
RIGHTS AND THE TREATY OF ROME THAN FROM INITIATIVES BY ITS
OWN GOVERNMENT. HE ADVOCATES THE "BRINGING OF THE EUROPEAN
CONVENTION BACK HOME" THROUGH THE ADOPTION ADOPTION OF A
BILL OF RIGHTS IN BRITAIN. SUCH AN ACTION WOULD PROVIDE
SYMBOLIC SUPPORT FOR THE FACT THAT INDIVIDUAL FREEDOM NEEDS
GREATER PROTECTION THAN GOVERNMENTS AND THEIR LEGISLATION.
IT WOULD ALSO ENCOURAGE MINISTERIAL ACCOUNTABILITY.

07661 ROBERTSON, G.
THE GLOBAL CHALLENGE AND CANADIAN FEDERALISM
CANADIAN PUBLIC ADMINISTRATION, 32(1) (SPR 89), 124-134.
IF THE MAIN GLOBAL CHALLENGE OF THE FUTURE IS ECONOMIC
AND THE SYSTEM BEST DESIGNED TO PRODUCE ECONOMIC EFFICIENCY
IS A FREE MARKET, A COUNTRY WITH A FEDERAL SYSTEM OF
GOVERNMENT HAS A DISADVANTAGE. THE DISADVANTAGE IS GREATER
IF THE SYSTEM, LIKE CANADA, IS CHARACTERIZED BY STRONG
PROVINCIAL GOVERNMENTS THAT FIGHT OVER THEIR REGIONAL
DIFFERENCES AND DEMAND ACTION TO REDUCE ANY PERCEIVED
DISPARITY. CLEARLY, CANADA IS NOT GOING TO ABOLISH ITS
FEDERAL SYSTEM OR EVEN UNDERTAKE MAJOR CONSTITUTIONAL
CHANGES THAT WILL AFFECT THE INTERNAL BALANCE OF POWER,
POLITICAL OR ECONOMIC. THUS, THE PROBLEM IS HOW TO RECONCILE
THE NATURE AND THE POLITICAL PRESSURES OF CANADIAN
FEDERATION WITH THE NEED FOR NATIONAL ECONOMIC EFFICIENCY IN
AN INCREASINGLY COMPETITIVE WORLD.

07662 ROBERTSON, H.
PATTIGATE AND THE POLITICS OF SCHMOOZE
CANADIAN FORUM, 68(783) (NOV 89), 3-5.
THIS ARTICLE DEALS WITH THE PATRONAGE SYSTEM THAT THE
PETERSON GOVERNMENT ENCOURAGED, THEN EXPLOITED. IT ZEROS IN
ON PATTI STARR, A MEMBER OF THE EXECUTIVE OF THE NATIONAL
COUNCIL OF JEWISH WOMEN WHO CHAIRED THE CHARITABLE
FOUNDATION THAT RAN A PROGRAM OF CONSTRUCTION OF HOUSING FOR
SENIORS AND USED THE MONEY RECIEVED IN REBATES TO PAY FOR
DINNERS, GIFTS, AND POLITICAL DONATIONS. IT EXPLORES HOW HER
WORK COULD TOPPLE FIVE ONTARIO CABINET MINISTERS AND CAST A

PALL OF SUSPICION OVER THE PETERSON GOVERNMENT.

07663 ROBERTSON, K.G.
CANADIAN INTELLIGENCE POLICY: THE ROLE AND FUTURE OF CSIS
INTERNATIONAL JOURNAL OF INTELLIGENCE AND
COUNTER-INTELLIGENCE, 3(2) (SUM 89), 225-248.
THE CREATION OF THE CANADIAN SECURITY INTELLIGENCE
SERVICE (CSIS) HAS PLACED THE ISSUE OF THE DEGREE OF
COORDINATION, CENTRALIZATION, AND INTEGRATION OF
INTELLIGENCE HIGH ON THE AGENDA IN CANADIAN INTELLIGENCE
POLICY. THE DEBATE HAS MOVED FAR BEYOND THE ORIGINAL CONCERN
WITH RULES AND GUIDELINES TO A NEW FOCUS ON INTEGRATING CSIS
INTO THE INTELLIGENCE COMMUNITY AND MANAGING THE NEWLY
ENLARGED COMMUNITY AND CAPACITIES EFFECTIVELY AND
EFFICIENTLY.

07664 ROBERTSON, M.
TWENTIETH CENTURY CONFLICT IN THE FOURTEENTH CENTURY:
INTERVENTION IN YEMEN
FLETCHER FORUM, 13(1) (WIN 89), 95-11.
EGYPTIAN MILITARY INTERVENTION IN NORTH YEMEN FROM 1962
TO 1967 ILLUSTRATES THE SELECTIVE AND OFTEN CREATIVE
APPLICATION OF CODIFIED INTERNATIONAL LAW (UNITED NATIONS
CHARTER, GENERAL ASSEMBLY RESOLUTIONS, TREATIES, AND
CONVENTIONS) TO JUSTIFY POLITICAL AND MILITARY ACTIONS.
EGYPT INITIALLY JUSTIFIED ITS MILITARY INTERVENTION ON THE
BASIS OF BILATERAL DEFENSE AGREEMENTS. THE AUTHOR EXPLAINS,
HOWEVER, HOW THE EGYPTIANS QUICKLY ABANDONED THIS RATIONALE
IN FAVOR OF INCHOATE PRINCIPLES OF ARAB UNITY, CAREFULLY
LEGITIMIZING ITS "ETHNIC INTERVENTION" WITH EXPLICIT
REFERENCES TO PRIMARY INTERNATIONAL LEGAL NORMS. HE
CONCLUDES THAT EGYPTIAN INTERVENTION IN YEMEN REMAINS A
PRECEDENT ON THE USE AND NON-USE OF INTERNATIONAL LAW AND ON
THE LEGITIMACY OF ETHNIC INTERVENTION.

07665 ROBERTSON, R.T.; TAMANISAU, A.
FIJI: RACE, CLASS, AND THE MILITARY
DEVELOPMENT AND CHANGE, 20(2) (APR 89), 203-234.
IN 1987 FIJI EXPERIENCED THREE COUPS, FOLLOWED BY AN
UNSUCCESSFUL COUP ATTEMPT IN EARLY 1988. THESE COUPS REFLECT
THE ISLAND'S ETHNIC COMPOSITION, WITH APPROXIMATELY EQUAL
NUMBERS OF ETHNIC FIJIANS AND INDIANS, AND THE ROLE OF THE
MILITARY IN FIJI'S CHRONIC POLITICAL INSTABILITY.

07666 ROBINSON, C.P.
THE JOINT VERIFICATION EXPERIMENT: A UNIQUE APPROACH TO
DEVELOPING VERIFICATION AGREEMENTS
DISARMAMENT, XII(2) (SUM 89), 90-95.
IN NOVEMBER 1987 THE USA AND THE USSR BEGAN FULL-SCALE
NEGOTIATIONS ON NUCLEAR TESTING. THE FIRST STEP WAS TO WORK
OUT AN AGREEMENT ON EFFECTIVE VERIFICATION MEASURES FOR USE
IN ESTABLISHING COMPLIANCE WITH THE 1974 THRESHOLD TEST-BAN
TREATY (TTBT) AND THE 1976 PEACEFUL NUCLEAR EXPLOSIONS
TREATY (PNET). THE SIDES AGREED TO PLAN AND CONCLUDE A JOINT
VERIFICATION EXPERIMENT, WHICH WOULD INVOLVE EXPLOSIONS AT
TEST SITES WITH THE OPPORTUNITY FOR EACH NATION TO MEASURE
THE YIELDS.

07667 ROBINSON, G.
AN OPPORTUNITY TO LOWER ARAB BARRIERS
SOUTH, (107) (SEP 89), 23.
OF THE ARAB WORLD'S THREE ECONOMIC GROUPINGS (THE GULF
COORDINATING COUNCIL, THE ARAB MAGHREB UNION, AND THE ARAB
COOPERATION COUNCIL), THE ACC IS THE LEAST LOGICAL AND
COHERENT. BUT DESPITE ITS FRAGILE BASE, IT IS SHOWING MORE
VIGOR THAN EXPECTED, BOTH AS A REGIONAL ECONOMIC BODY AND AS
A POLITICAL ENTITY.

07668 ROBINSON, G.
EASING TENSIONS AND CHANGING PARTNERS
PACIFIC DEFENCE REPORTER, 16(6) (DEC 89), 30-32.
DESPITE THE CONTINUATION OF LOW-LEVEL CONFLICT INSIDE
CAMBODIA AND ALONG THAILAND'S WESTERN AND EASTERN BORDERS,
THERE HAS BEEN A SIGNIFICANT REDUCTION IN TENSION IN THE
THAI/INDO-CHINA REGION OVER THE LAST YEAR. SETTING THE TREND
ARE THAILAND'S INCREASINGLY ACTIVE TRADE AND SECURITY LINKS
WITH FORMERLY HOSTILE NEIGHBORS SUCH AS CAMBODIA TO THE EAST,
LAOS TO THE NORTH AND BURMA TO THE WEST. THIS ARTICLE
DESCRIBES THAILAND'S CONTROVERSIAL POLICY OF TURNING
SURROUNDING BATTLEFIELDS INTO MARKETPLACES; ITS AMBITIOUS
MILITARY MODERNIZATION PROGRAM AND ITS SOCIAL AND ECONOMIC
INITIATIVES.

07669 ROBINSON, G.
JOINT SINO-THAI ARMS VENTURE
PACIFIC DEFENCE REPORTER, 15(10) (APR 89), 31.
THAILAND AND CHINA ARE UPGRADING THEIR EMERGING SECURITY
RELATIONSHIP WITH AN UNPRECEDENTED AGREEMENT JOINTLY TO
MANUFACTURE MILITARY HARDWARE IN THAILAND. THIS ARTICLE
EXAMINES HOW THE JOINT VENTURE, TO BE LAUNCHED WITHIN THE
YEAR, COULD EVENTUALLY SEE THAILAND SHARE IN CHINA'S GROWING
ROLE AS A KEY ARMS SUPPLIER IN THE REGION. IT ALSO WILL ALSO
BOOST CHINA'S EFFORTS TO ENLARGE THE REGIONAL MARKET FOR ITS
WEAPONRY.

07670 ROBINSON, G.
RAISING THE RISKS IN THE NAME OF ISLAM
SOUTH, (103) (MAY 89), 34.
CAIRO'S ISLAMIC INVESTMENT HOUSES, WHICH WERE FOUNDED TO
OFFER DEPOSITORS PROFITS THAT WOULD NOT CONTRAVENE ISLAMIC
USURY LAW, HAVE BEEN SUBJECTED TO TOUGH, NEW GOVERNMENT
REGULATIONS DUE TO SPECULATION THAT PRODUCED LARGE LOSSES
FOR SOME OF THE BANKS. NEW GOVERNMENT LEGISLATION DESIGNED
TO REFORM THE SYSTEM AND PROTECT DEPOSITORS GIVES EACH HOUSE
THE OPTION OF CONVERTING TO A JOINT STOCK COMPANY AND
ABIDING BY THE NEW REGULATIONS OR DISSOLVING ITSELF AND
RETURNING ALL DEPOSITS.

07671 ROBINSON, G.
RESISTANCE FORCES INCREASE PRESSURE IN CAMBODIA
PACIFIC DEFENCE REPORTER, 16(1) (JUL 89), 43-44.
CAMBODIAN RESISTANCE FORCES ARE INTENSIFYING THEIR
MILITARY CAMPAIGN AGAINST THE RECENTLY-RENAMED STATE OF
CAMBODIA, AMID REPORTS OF SIGNIFICANT NEW SOURCES OF
MILITARY ASSISTANCE FOR TWO GUERILLA FACTIONS. SUCH
DEVELOPMENTS ARE PROMPTING CONCERN IN SOME INTERNATIONAL
CIRCLES, THAT AN ESCALATION OF THE 10-YEAR MILITARY CONFLICT
IN CAMBODIA COULD UNDERMINE THE DELICATE PEACE PROCESS
BETWEEN OPPOSING KHMER FACTIONS.

07672 ROBINSON, G.
THAILAND'S BIG EQUIPMENT DEAL WITH CHINA
PACIFIC DEFENCE REPORTER, 16(4) (OCT 89), 20-22.
WHILE CROSS-BORDER TRADE AND UNPRECEDENTED MILITARY CO-
OPERATION HAVE STEADILY REPLACED TRADITIONAL TENSIONS ALONG
THAILAND'S BORDERS WITH LAOS, BURMA AND MALAYSIA, IT IS
THAILAND'S GROWING UNOFFICIAL RAPPROCHEMENT WITH CAMBODIA
WHICH IS UNDERPINNING THE MILITARY'S STRATEGIC THINKING. AS
THIS ARTICLE DESCRIBES ONE RESULT IS A SIGNIFICANT WARMING
OF RELATIONS BETWEEN THE THAI AND CAMBODIAN MILITARY
ORGANIZATIONS, WHICH NOW (UNOFFICIALLY) COMMUNICATE
REGULARLY WITH EACH OTHER AND CO-OPERATE ON MATTERS OF
BORDER SECURITY.

07673 ROBINSON, G.
VIETNAMESE GOING FROM CAMBODIA BUT NO LIGHT AT THE END OF
THE TUNNEL
PACIFIC DEFENCE REPORTER, 16(2) (AUG 89), 18-20.
THE VIETNAMESE WITHDRAWAL FROM CAMBODIA BRINGS WITH IT
THE STICKY QUESTION OF AN INTERNATIONAL PEACEKEEPING
MECHANISM. THERE IS WIDESPREAD INTERNATIONAL ACKNOWLEDGEMENT
THAT SUCH A MECHANISM IS ESSENTIAL TO OBSERVE AND MONITOR
NOT ONLY THE TROOP WITHDRAWAL, BUT ALSO A CEASEFIRE AND
ELECTIONS. IN VIEW OF RAPIDLY DIMINISHING PROSPECTS FOR
AGREEMENT AMONG THE FOUR WARRING CAMBODIAN FACTIONS ON A
POWER-SHARING FORMULA, THE SECURITY EQUATION COULD CHANGE
DRAMATICALLY. SPECULATION CENTRES IN PARTICULAR ON THE
FUTURE OF THE KHMER ROUGE, WHICH LOOKS INCREASINGLY AS
THOUGH THEY COULD BE ENTIRELY EXCLUDED FROM A POLITICAL
SETTLEMENT. THIS IS THE MAIN ISSUE ADDING URGENCY TO CURRENT
PROPOSALS FOR AN INTERNATIONAL PEACEKEEPING MECHANISM FOR
CAMBODIA.

07674 ROBINSON, H. B.
DIEFENBAKER'S WORLD: A POPULIST IN WORLD AFFAIRS
UNIVERSITY OF TORONTO PRESS, TORONTO, ONTARIO, CA, 1989,
384.
THE AUTHOR REVIEWS JOHN DIEFENBAKER'S ROLE IN SHAPING
CANADA'S FOREIGN POLICY. HE CONSIDERS DIEFENBAKER'S APPROACH
TO CANADIAN-US RELATIONS, HIS PART IN THE APPROVAL OF THE
NORTH AMERICAN AIR DEFENCE AGREEMENT, HIS ROLE IN THE
CONTROVERSY OVER THE STATIONING OF NUCLEAR WEAPONS ON
CANADIAN SOIL, AND RELATED EVENTS.

07675 ROBINSON, J.
WOMEN AND THE COLLECTIVE INTEREST IN CONTEMPORARY CHINA
POLICY STUDIES REVIEW, 8(3) (SPR 89), 648-662.
THIS PAPER ANALYZES MARRIAGE AND DIVORCE REFORM AND
FAMILY PLANNING POLICIES IN THE PEOPLE'S REPUBLIC OF CHINA
IN THE CONTEXT OF THE STATE-DEFINED COLLECTIVE INTEREST. A
THEORETICAL EXAMINATION OF THE CONTRADICTIONS BETWEEN
WOMEN'S LIBERATION AND THE MARXIST DEFINED ECONOMIC AND
POLITICAL CONCERNS OF THE STATE SHOWS THAT LIBERATION CANNOT
BE ACHIEVED UNTIL THE STATE ACKNOWLEDGES THE VALUES OF
SOCIAL REPRODUCTION AND FAMILY NURTURANCE. THE EMPIRICAL
DISCUSSION OF RECENT REFORMS IN FAMILY POLICIES IN CHINA
POINTS TO THE CONTINUING MANIPULATION OF WOMEN'S INTERESTS
BY THE STATE. THE TENDENCY OF THE PRC GOVERNMENT TO MAKE
POLICY BASED ON NARROW ECONOMIC CONSIDERATIONS RESULTS IN
THE MAINTENANCE OF A SYSTEM IN WHICH WOMEN'S SPECIAL
INTERESTS ARE EXCLUDE FROM THE COLLECTIVE INTEREST AND THUS
DENIED LEGITIMACY.

07676 ROBINSON, L.
DWINDLING OPTIONS IN PANAMA
FOREIGN AFFAIRS, 68(5) (WIN 90), 187-205.
EVEN THOUGH THE UNITED STATES HAS ESCALATED NORIEGA'S
RULE TO A MAJOR FOREIGN POLICY ISSUE, THE RANGE OF MEASURES
EMPLOYED TO DEAL WITH IT HAS BEEN LIMITED. THE PANAMA
PROBLEM NOW SEEMS LIKELY TO CONTINUE TO FESTER, WITH NO
CLEAR US STRATEGY IN PLACE TO DEAL WITH IT.

07677 ROBINSON, R.; SCHMITZ, L.
JAMAICA: NAVIGATING THROUGH A TROUBLED DECADE
FINANCE AND DEVELOPMENT, 26(4) (DEC 89), 30-33.
THIS ARTICLE EXPLORES HOW THE GOVERNMENT, THE FUND, AND
THE WORLD BANK COORDINATE EFFORTS TO HELP BRING THE ECONOMY
OF JAMAICA BACK ONTO A PATH OF SUSTAINABLE GROWTH. IT
EXAMINES THE DETERIORATION OF THE OVERALL ECONOMIC
PERFORMANCE IN MUCH OF THE 1970S, AND THE GOVERNMENT'S
ATTEMPTS AT ADJUSTMENT STRATEGY BY GEARING POLICIES TO THE
REVITALIZATION OF THE PRIVATE SECTOR. DETAILED IS EXTERNAL,
FISCAL, MONETARY, AND SECTORAL REFORMS. ECONOMIC RESULTS OF
THESE REFORMS, AND THE LESSONS LEARNED ARE RECOUNTED.

07678 ROBINSON, W.I.
MAKING THE ECONOMY SCREAM: U.S. ECONOMIC WARFARE AGAINST
NICARAGUA
MULTINATIONAL MONITOR, 11(12) (DEC 89), 22-26.
ECONOMIC WARFARE HAS LONG BEEN USED BY WASHINGTON AS A
POLITICAL INSTRUMENT AGAINST COUNTRIES CONSIDERED UNFRIENDLY
OR THREATENING TO U.S. INTERESTS. WHAT MAKES NICARAGUA
DIFFERENT FROM OTHER EMBARGOED COUNTRIES IS THAT THE UNITED
STATES HAS HISTORICALLY HAD NO SIGNIFICANT DIRECT ECONOMIC
STAKE THERE; NO MORE THAN TWO DOZEN U.S. COMPANIES HAVE EVER
MAINTAINED SUBSTANTIAL INVESTMENTS THERE AND NICARAGUA DOES
NOT SUPPLY THE USA WITH ANY STRATEGIC RESOURCES.
WASHINGTON'S INTEREST THERE HAS ALWAYS BEEN GEOPOLITICAL.
THE REAGAN/BUSH ECONOMIC SANCTIONS ARE ONE COMPONENT IN A
COMPLEX WAR STRATEGY DIRECTED AGAINST THE SANDINISTAS AND
DESIGNED TO GRIND AWAY AT THE COUNTRY'S PRODUCTIVE
INFRASTRUCTURE.

07679 ROCHA, J.
UNDER THE DEAD HAND OF PATRONAGE
SOUTH, (101) (MAR 89), 20-21.
MILITARY RULE MAY HAVE ENDED IN BRAZIL, BUT ITS LEGACIES
ENSURE THAT PATRONAGE AND SOCIAL INJUSTICE CONTINUE TO
PREVAIL. PRESIDENT JOSE SARNEY SAYS THAT BRAZIL WANTS TO BE
PART OF THE CURRENT REORGANIZATION OF THE WORLD, BUT SOME
OBSERVERS BELIEVE THAT, IF THE SOCIAL STRUCTURE IS LEFT
UNCHANGED, THE DEVELOPMENT OF THE WORLD'S EIGHTH-LARGEST NON-
COMMUNIST ECONOMY WILL REMAIN LIMITED. THE POLITICAL SYSTEM
MUST ALSO UNDERGO A REVOLUTION IF BRAZIL IS TO REALIZE ITS
POTENTIAL.

07680 ROCHE, J.P.
GUILTY OF WHAT?
NATIONAL REVIEW, XLI(18) (SEP 89), 47-48.
THE AUTHOR ARGUES THAT AMERICA WAS BORN WITHOUT A
HISTORICAL UMBILICAL CORD. THIS "INVINCIBLE AHISTORICISM" IS
DESCRIBED AS "TEMPORAL SOLIPSISM," OR, THE BLAND ASSUMPTION
THAT EVERY MOMENT IN TIME AND ITS EVENTS ARE INDEPENDENT
ENTITIES LACKING LOTS PRECEDENTS AND CONSEQUENCES. THAT
AMERICA COULD OR SHOULD FEEL GUILTY ABOUT NOT ENTERING WORLD
WAR II SOONER IS AN OZYMORON.

07681 ROCHE, J.P.
THE GREAT MAFIA WEDDING
NATIONAL REVIEW, XLI(16) (SEP 89), 23-24.
THE AUTHOR EXAMINES THE RELATIONSH BETWEEN WES HE
CONSIDERS TO BE THE TOP TWO IDEOLOGICAL GANGSTERS OF THE
CENTURY: ADOLPE HITLER AND JISEF STALIN. AS GLASNOST GERMITS
OPEN DISCUSSION OF THE THIRTIES PURGES FOR THE FIRST TIME,
STARLIN NOW TAKES HIS RIGHTFUL PLACE AHEAD OF HITLER ON THE
LIST OF TWENTIETS - CENTURY MASS MURDERERS.

07682 ROCHE, J.P.
THE NEW LEFT VIGILANTES
NATIONAL REVIEW, 61(23) (DEC 89), 34-37.
THIS ARTICLE EXAMINES THE SITUATION IN AMERICAN
UNIVERSITIES BY THE OLIN PROFESSOR OF CIVILIZATION AND
FOREIGN AFFAIRS AT THE FLETCHER SCHOOL OF LAW AND DIPLOMACY.
HE SUGGESTS THAT THROUGH THE CONCEPT OF ACADEMIC FREEDOM,
ACADEMIES ARE IGNORING A TRAGIC SITUATION. HOW LEFTOVER NEW
LEFTISTS ARE DOING THEIR BEST TO UNDERMINE TRUE ACADEMIC
DISCOURSE IS CAREFULLY EXAMINED. MR. ROCHE CALLS THIS THE
MOST SERIOUS THREAT TO ACADEMIC FREEDOM SINCE WORLD WAR II.

07683 ROCHON, T.R.; MITCHELL, M.J.
SOCIAL BASES OF THE TRANSITION TO DEMOCRACY IN BRAZIL
COMPARATIVE POLITICS, 21(3) (APR 89), 307-322.
THE MASS POLITICAL CULTURE OF BRAZIL HAS NOT ONLY BECOME
DISAFFECTED FROM THE AUTHORITARIAN REGIME BUT HAS ALSO
DEVELOPED TWO DISTINCT PATTERNS OF DEMOCRATIC ATTACHMENT
THAT PRESAGE FUNDAMENTAL CONFLICTS IN THE FUNCTIONING OF
BRAZILIAN DEMOCRACY. BRAZIL HAS AN EMERGING DEMOCRATIC
POLITICAL CULTURE THAT PARALLELS THE EXPERIENCE OF EUROPE,
IN WHICH ADVOCACY OF DEMOCRATIC INSTITUTIONS AND UNIVERSAL
SUFFRAGE HAD DISTINCTIVE CLASS BASES BEFORE BECOMING A
CONSENSUAL ELEMENT OF THE NATIONAL POLITICAL CULTURE.

07684 ROCKMAN, B.A.
    WHAT DIDN'T HE KNOW & SHOULD HE FORGET IT? POLITICAL
    SCIENCE & THE REAGAN PRESIDENCY
    POLITY, 21(4) (SUM 89), 777-792.
        THE REAGAN PRESIDENCY POSED MORE THAN THE USUAL NUMBER
    OF EXPLANATORY CHALLENGES FOR POLITICAL SCIENCE. HOW COULD
    AN IDEOLOGUE WIN THE WHITE HOUSE IN A POLITICAL SYSTEM AS
    RELENTLESSLY CENTRIST AS OURS? HOW WAS HE ABLE TO GIVE
    POLICY DIRECTION TO A DIVIDED GOVERNMENT? AND HOW WAS HE
    ABLE TO MAINTAIN HIS POPULARITY THROUGH EIGHT YEARS THAT
    SUBSTANTIALLY RECAST THE POLITICS OF THE NATION? THIS ESSAY
    SEEKS TO LINK CERTAIN ASPECTS OF THE REAGAN PRESIDENCY TO
    THE LITERATURE OF POLITICAL SCIENCE. THE AUTHOR LOOKS AT
    BOTH REAGAN THE CANDIDATE AND REAGAN THE PRESIDENT AND
    CONCLUDES THAT, AS A PROFESSION, POLITICAL SCIENCE IS RICHER
    IN DATA THAN THEORY AND RATHER MYOPIC IN ITS INCREMENTALIST
    VIEW OF CHANGE.

07685 RODENBECK, M.
    CRACKDOWN IN EGYPT
    MIDDLE EAST INTERNATIONAL, (358) (SEP 89), 10.
        EGYPTIAN POLICY IS STAGNATING IN THE MIDST OF ECONOMIC
    WOES, INTERNAL DISCONTENT, AND A DECREASING MOMENTUM FOR
    REGIONAL PEACE. THE ILL-HEALTH OF PRIME MINISTER ATIF SIDQI
    HAS CONTRIBUTED TO THE SLUGGISH PACE OF REFORMS. ACCUSATIONS
    OF ILLEGAL IMPRISONMENT AND POLICE BRUTALITY ABOUND AS THE
    GOVERNMENT ATTEMPTS TO DEAL WITH THE GROWING PROBLEM OF
    INTERNAL UNREST.

07686 RODENBECK. M.
    EGYPT AND SAUDI ARABIA: FANFARE FOR THE KING
    MIDDLE EAST INTERNATIONAL, (347) (MAR 89), 10-11.
        KING FAHD'S 1989 VISIT TO EGYPT WAS THE FIRST VISIT IN
    15 YEARS BY THE WEALTHIEST ARAB MONARCH TO THE MOST POPULOUS
    ARAB NATION. SIGNIFICANTLY, THE KING'S ARRIVAL FOLLOWED ON
    THE HEELS OF A TRIPARTITE MEETING BETWEEN PRESIDENT MUBARAK,
    KING HUSSEIN, AND PLO CHAIRMAN ARAFAT. AMIDST RUMORS OF A
    NEW JOINT ARAB PEACE PLAN, IT APPEARED THAT THE ARAB CENTRE
    WAS FINALLY BEGINNING TO DEVELOP A UNIFIED APPROACH TO SUCH
    ISSUES AS THE ISRAELI-PALESTINIAN CONFLICT AND THE LEBANON
    MORASS. BUT, DUE TO THE DISMAL EGYPTIAN ECONOMY, THE AVERAGE
    EGYPTIAN HAS FAR MORE INTERESTED IN TALKS ABOUT SAUDI AID.

07687 RODENBECK, M.
    EGYPT: ALIGNMENTS
    MIDDLE EAST INTERNATIONAL, (344) (FEB 89), 8-9.
        THE MIDEAST IS IN A STATE OF FERMENT. FOR THE TIME BEING,
    THE PEACE PROCESS IS ON THE BACK BURNER WHILE THE ARABS
    REALIGN, THE ISRAELIS DRAG THEIR HEELS, AND THE SUPERPOWERS
    PLOT NEW MOVES. EGYPT, IN PARTICULAR, IS CAUGHT UP IN ALL
    THE DIPLOMATIC MANUEVERING AS IT LOOKS TO BE MORE CLOSELY
    ALIGNED WITH THE OTHER ARAB STATES.

07688 RODENBECK, M.
    EGYPT: DOUBLE BLOW
    MIDDLE EAST INTERNATIONAL, (346) (MAR 89), 14-15.
        REPORTS OF AMERICAN CONCERN OVER EGYPT'S ECONOMY AND ITS
    PLANS TO PRODUCE CHEMICAL WEAPONS HAVE PUT A DENT IN
    PRESIDENT MUBARAK'S CAREFULLY NURTURED IMAGE. THE NEWS
    REPORTS MAY INDICATE THAT THE BUSH ADMINISTRATION WILL BE NO
    LESS INSENSITIVE TO ITS MAJOR ARAB ALLY THAN REAGAN'S.

07689 RODENBECK, M.
    EGYPT: LIMITED ACHIEVEMENTS
    MIDDLE EAST INTERNATIONAL, 353 (JUN 89), 10-11.
        THE FIRST REGULAR SUMMIT MEETING OF THE ORAB COOPERATION
    COUNCIL WAS ONE OF LIMITED ACHIEVEMENTS. WITH PROMISES TO
    WORK FOR GREATER ECONOMIC INTEGRATION, BUT FEW SOLID PLANS
    BEYOND A MUCH-TALKED-OF ELECTRICITY LINK BETWEEN EGYPT AND
    JORDAN, THE HEADS OF STATE ASSURED ONE ANOTHER THAT THEIR
    ORGANISATION IS TO PROVIDE THE CORNERSTONE FOR FURTHER ARAB
    UNITY. THE PRESS, MEANWHILE, WAS FULL OF PRAISE FOR THE
    SEEMINGLY SLOW PACE OF THINGS, NOTING THAT PAST EFFORTS AT
    CHARGING BLINDLY INTO UNIONS HAD SIGNALLY FAILED.

07690 RODENBECK, M.
    EGYPT: REVOLUTION OF GOOD WILL
    MIDDLE EAST INTERNATIONAL, (342) (JAN 89), 12-13.
        THE MUBARAK ADMINISTRATION SEEMS TO HAVE BEEN BELATEDLY
    INFECTED WITH A MOOD OF IMPATIENCE. KEY BILLS FOR CORRECTING
    PROBLEMS WITH HOUSING, THE JUDICIARY, FOREIGN INVESTMENT,
    AND THE ELECTORAL SYSTEM WILL BE CONSIDERED DURING THIS
    YEAR'S PARLIAMENT. ON THE INTERNATIONAL SCENE, EGYPT HAS
    REJOINED SEVERAL ARAB ORGANIZATIONS AND HOPES TO PLAY A
    GREATER ROLE IN ARAB AFFAIRS.

07691 RODENBECK, M.
    EGYPT: SENSE OF ANTI-CLIMAX
    MIDDLE EAST INTERNATIONAL, (351) (MAY 89), 10.
        THE RE-INTRODUCTION OF EGYPT INTO THE ARAB LEAGUE WAS
    SOMETHING OF AN ANTI-CLIMAX FOR MOST EGYPTIANS. THE MAJOR
    REASON FOR THIS SENTIMENT WAS THE RECOGNITION THAT ALTHOUGH
    EGYPT HAS BEEN OFFICIALLY ABSENT FROM THE LEAGUE, IT HAS
    FULLY SHARED IN TEN YEARS OF DECLINING ARAB FORTUNES.

DESPITE INTERNATIONAL SUCCESSES, EGYPT IS STRUGGLING
INTERNALLY WITH AN APATHETIC PUBLIC, POLICE DETENTION, AND
ALLEGATIONS OF HUMAN RIGHTS VIOLATIONS.

07692 RODENBECK, M.
    EGYPT: STAMPING ON EXTREMISTS
    MIDDLE EAST INTERNATIONAL, (341) (JAN 89), 12-13.
        AN ALL-OUT ASSAULT ON MILITANT ISLAMIC GROUPS IN
    DECEMBER 1988 CROWNED THE EGYPTIAN GOVERNMENT'S EFFORTS TO
    ERADICATE RELIGIOUS EXTREMISM AND BROUGHT A DEGREE OF
    SUCCESS, PARTICULARLY IN THE RADICAL GAMI'AT AL ISLAMIYA'S
    STRONGHOLD IN THE AIN SHAMS DISTRICT OF CAIRO. THE
    ENLISTMENT OF VOICES FROM THE RELIGIOUS MAINSTREAM HAS
    BECOME PART OF THE GOVERNMENT'S POLICY OF MULTI-FACETED
    CONFRONTATION WITH THE PHENOMENON OF MUSLIM EXTREMISM.

07693 RODENBECK, M.; NEFF, D.
    EGYPT: THE FALL OF ABU GHAZALA
    MIDDLE EAST INTERNATIONAL, (349) (APR 89), 12-13.
        IN A MOVE THAT SURPRISED MANY OBSERVERS, EGYPTIAN
    PRESIDENT HOSNI MUBARAK HAS REPLACED HIS POWERFUL DEFENSE
    MINISTER, ABD AL-HALIM ABU GHAZALA. THE MOVE HAS SPAWNED
    CONSIDERABLE DEBATE IN CAIRO'S DIPLOMATIC COMMUNITY BUT IS
    GENERALLY SEEN AS BOLSTERING MUBARAK'S OWN POSITION.

07694 RODENBECK, M.
    EGYPT: UNDISGUISED GLEE
    MIDDLE EAST INTERNATIONAL, (354) (JUL 89), 4.
        THE REACTION OF EGYPT TO THE COUP D'ETAT IN SUDAN WAS
    SWIFT AND NEARLY UNIVERSAL: THE GOVERNMENT OF PRESIDENT
    HOSNI MUBARAK WAITED BARELY 24 HOURS TO RECOGNIZE SUDAN'S
    MILITARY REGIME, AND THE STATE-CONTROLLED PRESS COULD BARELY
    CONTAIN ITS GLEE. OUSTED PRESIDENT SADIQ WAS STRIDENTLY ANTI-
    EGYPT; HIS FAILURE TO RESOLVE THE CIVIL WAR IN SUDAN DID NOT
    ENDEAR HIM TO THE HEARTS OF SUDAN'S POWERFUL NEIGHBOR TO THE
    NORTH.

07695 RODENBECK, M.
    EGYPT'S LABOUR TROUBLES
    MIDDLE EAST INTERNATIONAL, (357) (AUG 89), 13.
        A RECENT LABOR DISPUTE IN ONE OF EGYPT'S LARGEST STATE-
    OWNED INDUSTRIES ENDED IN VIOLENCE THAT LEFT ONE WORKER DEAD
    AND 16 SERIOUSLY WOUNDED. SUCH CONFLICTS ARE NOTHING NEW;
    EGYPT'S STATE INDUSTRIES ARE KNOWN TO SUFFER FROM MASSIVE
    DEBT, UNDERCAPITALIZATION, AND WORKER UNREST. ALTHOUGH
    PRESIDENT MUBARAK HAS PROPOSED SIGNIFICANT REFORMS OF THE
    STATE SECTOR, MANY OBSERVERS NOTE THAT EGYPT IS STILL IN THE
    "SOCIALIST DARK AGES."

07696 RODENBECK, M.
    EGYPTIAN IMPATIENCE
    MIDDLE EAST INTERNATIONAL, (362) (NOV 89), 7.
        EGYPT IS ON THE CENTER STAGE IN THE PALESTINIAN PEACE
    PROCESS. ITS LEADERS HAVE MANAGED TO PROJECT THE IMAGE OF
    COMPLETE IMPARTIALITY THAT IS FAR ABOVE THE SQUABBLING OF
    ISRAEL, THE US, AND THE PALESTINIANS. EGYPT IS ALSO
    PARTICIPATING IN MANY ARAB UNIFICATION PROJECTS. HOWEVER,
    EGYPT'S HUGE FOREIGN DEBT THREATENS TO REDUCE ITS
    INTERNATIONAL PRESTIGE AND WILL FORCE SOME DIFFICULT
    DECISIONS.

07697 RODENBECK, M.
    IRAN AND IRAQ
    MIDDLE EAST INTERNATIONAL, (364) (DEC 89), 10-11.
        A YEAR AFTER IRAN'S AYATOLLAH KHOMEINI ACCEPTED THE
    "BITTER POISON" OF A CEASE-FIRE WITH IRAQ, PREMANENT PEACE
    SEEMS LITTLE CLOSER. THE MAJOR OBSTACLE BETWEEN NEGOTIATION
    REMAINS THE SHATT AL-ARAB WATERWAY, ONE OF THE CHIEF CAUSES
    OF THE INITIAL CONFLICT. ARGUMENTS OVER THE FATE OF MORE
    THAN 200,000 PRISONERS OF WAR AND IRAQI TROOP WITHDRAWALS
    ALSO HAVE SLOWED DIPLOMATIC PROGRESS. WITHOUT A MAJOR
    CONCESSION ON ONE SIDE, PROGRESS TOWARDS PEACE IS LIKELY TO
    REMAIN PAINFULLY SLOW.

07698 RODENBECK, M.
    MUBARAK AND HIS CRITICS
    MIDDLE EAST INTERNATIONAL, (357) (AUG 89), 15-16.
        THE ARTICLE EXAMINES THE PRESIDENCY OF EGYPT'S HOSNI
    MUBARAK. IT CONCLUDES THAT ON BALANCE, MUBARAK HAS USED HIS
    WIDE PRESIDENTIAL POWERS LESS FREQUENTLY THAN HIS
    PREDECESSORS; HE HAS BEEN WILLING TO GIVE HIS SUBORDINATES
    SIGNIFICANT LEEWAY. HE ALSO HAS MANAGED TO WEATHER A SERIES
    OF DOMESTIC AND INTERNATIONAL CRISES. HOWEVER, OPPOSITION TO
    MUBARAK IS ON THE INCREASE. ALLEGATIONS OF WIDESPREAD
    CORRUPTION AND FRAUD IN THE RULING NATIONAL DEMOCRATIC PARTY
    AND THE CONTINUED ECONOMIC DECLINE HAVE CAUSED INCREASED
    CRITICISM AND HAVE GIVEN OPPOSITION PARTIES POINTS TO RALLY
    AROUND.

07699 RODENBECK, M.
    MUBARAK THE MEDIATOR
    MIDDLE EAST INTERNATIONAL, 356 (AUG 89), 12-13.
        THE KEY ISSUE ON MUBARAK'S AFRICAN AGENDA IS THE PROBLEM
    OF DEBT. INCREASINGLY, EGYPT HAS COME TO SEE ITS OWN

INDEBTEDNESS - TO THE TUNE OF $45 BILLION AS PART OF THE GLOBAL PATTERN OF THIRD WORLD DEPENDENCE RATHER THAN AS A UNIQUE PHENOMENON. MUBARAK HAS COME TO ADVOCATE A UNITED STAND ON THE PART OF DEBTOR NATIONS, AND TO THIS END TABLED A JOINT PROPOSAL WITH VENEZUELA, MEXICO AND INDONESIA AT THE PARIS BICENTENARY CELEBRATIONS. ON THE HOME FRONT, TALK OF PRIVATISING EGYPT'S COLOSSALLY INEFFICIENT PUBLIC SECTOR, OR AT LEAST PARTS OF IT, MUST WARM THE HEARTS OF AID DONORS WHO FOR YEARS HAVE BEEN TEARING THEIR HAIR OUT OVER THE OBSTINACY OF WHAT HAS COME TO BE KNOWN AS THE NASSERIST LOBBY, IE THOSE WHO REGARD THE DISMANTLING OF THE BLOATED STATE AS AN ACT OF TREASON.

07700 RODENBECK, M.
MUBARAKS TEN POINTS
MIDDLE EAST INTERNATIONAL, (359) (SEP 89), 3.
EGYPTIAN PRESIDENT HUSNI MUBARAK'S ANNOUNCEMENT OF TEN CLARIFYING POINTS DESIGNED TO FOSTER DIRECT PALESTINIAN-ISRAELI TALKS HAS CAUSED A FLURRY OF DIPLOMATIC ACTIVITY. ALTHOUGH MANY PALESTINIAN AND ISRAELI REPRESENTATIVES HAVE MET IN EGYPT TO DISCUSS OPTIONS, THEY HAVE MAINTAINED AN OFFICIAL SILENCE ON THE POSSIBLE OUTCOMES. ALTHOUGH SOME OBSERVERS FEEL THAT THE EGYPTIAN ANNOUNCEMENT MAY CAUSE ISRAEL TO SHAKE OFF ITS DIPLOMATIC LETHARGY, MANY FEEL THAT ISRAEL'S REJECTION OF THE "TEN POINTS" IS A FOREGONE CONCLUSION.

07701 RODENBECK, M.
SLAPS AND WIRE TAPS
MIDDLE EAST INTERNATIONAL, (345) (MAR 89), 16.
WHEN MINISTER OF INTERIOR ZAKI BADR WAS CALLED TO DEFEND HIS GOVERNMENT AGAINST CHARGES OF POLICE BRUTALITY, OBSERVERS ANTICIPATED A STORMY SESSION IN EGYPT'S PARLIAMENT. BUT THE OPPOSITION'S IMPATIENCE WITH HIS BLUSTERY SPEECH GAVE WAY TO FURIOUS INDIGNATION WHEN HE PLAYED COMPROMISING RECORDINGS OF OPPOSITION POLITICIANS. THE OUTRAGED OPPOSITION CLAIMED THE EAVESDROPPING WAS AN UNCONSTITUTIONAL INFRINGEMENT OF PARLIAMENTARY IMMUNITY.

07702 RODENBECK, M.
THE FRUITS OF CASABLANCA
MIDDLE EAST INTERNATIONAL, 352 (JUN 89), 5.
THE MOST IMMEDIATE AND DIRECT BONUS OF THE CASABLANCA SUMMIT HAS BEEN THE DRAMATIC IMPROVEMENT IN TIES WITH WHAT IS NOW FREQUENTLY REFERRED TO IN THE CAIRO PRESS AS "SISTERLY LIBYA". FOLLOWING A 13 YEAR HIATUS, THE REOPENING OF THE COUNTRIES' BORDER HAS BROUGHT AN ALMOST TANGIBLE RELEASE OF PRESSURE ON A CROWDED EGYPT, HEMMED IN IN RECENT YEARS BY STRIFE IN ADJACENT NATIONS. IN THE FIRST WEEK OF USE, A REPORTED 10,000 TRAVELLERS CROSSED THE NEWLY OPENED LAND BORDER. ALREADY, DAILY FLIGHTS FLY BETWEEN CAIRO, TRIPOLI AND BENGHAZI, SHORT-CIRCUITING THE TORTUOUS ROUTES THROUGH ATHENS AND MALTA THAT THE 200,000 EGYTIANS RESIDENT IN LIBYA HAVE HAD TO ENDURE FOR THE PAST DECADE.

07703 RODENBECK, M.
THE PLO IN CAIRO
MIDDLE EAST INTERNATIONAL, (363) (NOV 89), 8.
A RECENT MEETING OF THE PLO'S EXECUTIVE COMMITTEE IN CAIRO STIRRED UP MUCH SPECULATION, BUT GARNERED LITTLE OR NO SIGNIFICANT RESULTS. MOST OBSERVERS FEEL THAT THE PALESTINIANS ARE UNLIKELY TO ACCEPT THE US-SPONSORED BAKER PLAN; YASSER ARAFAT DECLARED THAT THE SOLE AIM OF THE US PEACE PLAN IS TO BUT TIME FOR THE SHAMIR GOVERNMENT. MEANWHILE, EGYPT FACES SOME INTERNAL PROBLEMS INCLUDING A GROWING ISLAMIC TREND. STRAINS IN RELATIONS WITH IRAQ ARE ALSO BECOMING EVIDENT.

07704 RODENBECK, M.
WARMING EGYPTIAN HEARTS
MIDDLE EAST INTERNATIONAL, (345) (MAR 89), 5-6.
IN A GESTURE THAT MARKED THE THAWING OF SOVIET-EGYPTIAN TIES, FOREIGN MINISTER SHEVARDNADZE VISITED EGYPT AND EXPRESSED "IDENTICAL VIEWS" WITH THE EGYPTIANS AND THE PALESTINIANS. IN A RELATED DEVELOPMENT, AN AMERICAN-BROKERED AGREEMENT RESULTED IN ISRAEL'S CEDING TABA BACK TO EGYPT.

07705 RODINA, C.
SOCIALIST-CAPITALIST JOINT VENTURES
FOREIGN TRADE, 10 (1988), 13-16.
THIS ARTICLE REPORTS ON JOINT VENTURES BETWEEN CMEA AND CAPITALIST COUNTRIES SINCE 1970. LEGISLATION IN MANY CMEA COUNTRIES WHICH PRESCRIBES BASIC PRINCIPLES OF JOINT VENTURE PERFORMANCE IS EXPLORED. OPERATIONS IN CHINA, HUNGARY, POLAND, KOREA, BULGARIA, ROMANIA AND CZECHOSLOVAKIA ARE EXPLORED. SOME OF THE DIFFICULTIES ARE NOTED.

07706 RODMAN, P. W.
IS THE COLD WAR OVER?
WILSON QUARTERLY, XIII(1) (JAN 89), 39-42.
WHILE MUCH HAS CHANGED IN EAST-WEST RELATIONS UNDER GOVBACHEV AND THE WEST SHOULD TAKE ADVANTAGE OF THE NEW OPPORTUNITIES TO SETTLE SOME OUTSTANDING ISSUES AND SCALE DOWN THE MILITARY DANGER, THE WEST SHOULD ALSO BE AWARE OF

THE CONTINUTIES THAT REMAIN IN SOVIET POLICY AND THE PERSISTENCE OF EAST-WEST COMPETITION IN AREAS THAT HAVE NOT BEEN BLESSED WITH DIPLOMATIC SOLUTIONS. FOREMOST AMONG THESE IS EUROPE. LIKE HIS PREDECESSORS, GORBACHEV HAS CONTINUED THE POLITICAL WARFARE AGAINST NATO COHESION AND NATO STRATEGIES WHILE REJECTING THE WESTERN CALL TO TEAR DOWN THE BERLIN WALL AND END THE ARTIFICIAL DIVISION OF THE CONTINENT. MOREOVER, IN NICARAGUA, THE SOVIETS CONTINUE TO PROVIDE A SUBSTANTIAL FLOW OF ARMS TO THE SANDINISTA MILITARY.

07707 RODMAN, S.
HAITI'S PROSPECTS UNDER PROSPER AVRIL
NEW LEADER, LXXII(13) (SEP 89), 5-7.
THE ARTICLE EXAMINES THE ATTITUDES AND POLICIES OF HAITI'S "INTERIM LEADER," PROSPER AVRIL. ARVIL SEEMS TO BE ONE OF THE RARE CASES OF A "BAD MAN TURNED GOOD." AN ADVISER TO THE TYRANNICAL DUVALIER DYNASTY FOR MANY YEARS, ARVIL WAS RUMORED TO KNOW MORE ABOUT THE DICTATORS' PERSONAL FINANCES THAN THEY DID. HOWEVER, AFTER BECOMING PRESIDENT IN A COUP INSTIGATED BY NONCOMISSIONED OFFICERS, ARVIL SEEMS DETERMINED TO GUARANTEE FREE ELECTIONS AND ECONOMIC REFORM.

07708 RODMAN, S.
LITTLE PRIEST, BIG GENERAL
NATIONAL REVIEW, XLI(18) (SEP 89), 24-25.
HAITI'S CLIMB FROM THE DEPTHS OF STAGNATION IN THE THREE YEARS OF COUPS AND COUNTER -- COUPS THAT FOLLOWED THE OUSTER OF THE DUVALIER DYNASTY HAS BEEN FAIRFULLY SLOW. BUT LAW AND ORDER NOW REIGNS IN THE STREETS WITH NO MILITARY PRESENCE, AND THE IMPROVEMENT IN THE POLITICAL CLIMATE SINCE THE TERM OF PRESIDENT PROSPER AVRIL IS MURACULOUS.

07709 RODMAN, S.
THE DILEMMA IN PUERTO RICO
NEW LEADER, LXXII(6) (MAR 89), 3-5.
AN INDEPENDENCE PLEBISCITE IS TENTATIVELY SCHEDULED FOR PUERTO RICO IN 1990 AND THE QUESTION OF STATEHOOD HAS MONOPOLIZED THE PUERTO RICAN PRESS FOR SEVERAL MONTHS. BY DECLARING THAT HE FAVORS GIVING THE PUERTO RICANS THE STATUS THEY CHOOSE, GEORGE BUSH HAS FIRED UP THE PRO-STATEHOOD FORCES. BUT GOVERNOR RAFAEL HERNANDEZ COLON SUPPORTS AN "ENHANCED COMMONWEALTH" AS THE ISLAND'S BEST OPTION.

07710 RODRIGO, N.
"THE DISCONTINUANCE OF ALL TEST EXPLOSIONS OF NUCLEAR WEAPONS FOR ALL TIME . . ."
DISARMAMENT, XII(2) (SUM 89), 109-116.
WHEN THE USA, THE UNITED KINGDOM, AND THE SOVIET UNION SIGNED THE TREATY BANNING NUCLEAR WEAPONS TESTS IN THE ATMOSPHERE, IN OUTER SPACE, AND UNDER WATER, THEY PROCLAIMED THAT THEIR PRINCIPAL AIM WAS "THE SPEEDIEST POSSIBLE ACHIEVEMENT OF AN AGREEMENT ON GENERAL AND COMPLETE DISARMAMENT UNDER STRICT INTERNATIONAL CONTROL." THEY ALSO SOUGHT "THE DISCONTINUANCE OF ALL TEST EXPLOSIONS OF NUCLEAR WEAPONS FOR ALL TIME." BUT PROGRESS TOWARD THESE GOALS HAS BEEN LIMITED, DESPITE INTERNATIONAL PRESSURE EXERTED THROUGH THE UNITED NATIONS, THE CONFERENCE ON DISARMAMENT, AND OTHER MULTILATERAL FORUMS, SUCH AS THE MOVEMENT OF NONALIGNED COUNTRIES.

07711 RODRIGUEZ, C.R.
CUBA: TRYING TO PAY THE DEBT IS A POLITICAL ERROR
INFORMATION BULLETIN, 26(19-20) (OCT 88), 27-29.
THIS ARTICLE IS THE TEXT OF A SPEED ON EXTERNAL DEBT DELIVERED BY RODRIQUEZ TO THE THIRD WORLD FOUNDATION. RODRIQUEZ NOTES THAT THE MAIN CONCLUSION THAT SHOULD BE DRAWN IN THE LIGHT OF THE EXPERIENCE OF MANY YEARS OF FUTILE EFFORTS AND THE STEADILY WORSENING LATIN AMERICAN DEBT SITUATION IS TO ADMIT THAT THE ATTEMPTS TO NEGOTIATE SEPARATELY ARE STERILE AND NEGATIVE. IT IS NECESSARY TO WORK OUT A JOINT APPROACH, AND NOT ONLY A LATIN AMERICAN ONE, BUT ONE THAT IS COMMON TO ALL THE DEBTOR COUNTRIES. CONSIDERING THAT THE CREDITORS HAVE THEIR OWN CLUB, THE DEBTORS SHOULD, AT LEAST, HAVE THEIR GROUP TO ELABORATE JOINT SOLUTIONS.

07712 RODRIGUEZ, E.
UNITY AND STRUGGLE IN THE POLICY OF ALLIANCES
WORLD MARXIST REVIEW, 32(9) (SEP 89), 78-81.
THIS ARTICLE REPORTS ON PREPARATIONS FOR THE UPCOMING GENERAL ELECTIONS IN URUGUAY. IT DETAILS THE COMMUNIST PARTY PRIORITY TO UNITE ALL SOCIAL GROUPS, PARTIES AND PUBLIC MOVEMENTS IN ORDER TO RID THE COUNTRY OF ITS DEPENDENCE ON FOREIGN POWERS AND TO CREATE THE CONDITIONS FOR THE FREE DEVELOPMENT OF URUGUAY. SINCE PRACTICE SHOWS THAT UNITY NEVER OCCURS SPONTANEOUSLY, THE NEED TO ACCURATELY DEFINE THE THEORETICAL BASIS AND PRACTICAL FOUNDATIONS OF THE POLICY OF ALLIANCES IS DETAILED. THE FACTORS INVOLVED IN DEVELOPING THIS ALLIANCE ARE EXPLORED.

07713 ROE, E.M.
UNCOMMON GROUNDS FOR COMMONS MANAGEMENT: MAKING SENSE OF LIVESTOCK RANGELAND PROJECTS SOUTH OF THE SAHARA
DISSERTATION ABSTRACTS INTERNATIONAL, 49(11) (MAY 89), 3502-A.

THE AUTHOR ASSESSES WHY MANY DONOR-FUNDED, GOVERNMENT-SPONSORED LIVESTOCK RANGELAND PROJECTS HAVE FAILED IN SUB-SAHARAN AFRICA AND DETAILS A NEW MODEL OF COMMON PROPERTY RESOURCE MANAGEMENT THAT COULD IMPROVE THE DESIGN OF FUTURE PROJECTS.

07714 ROEDER, P.G.
ELECTORAL AVOIDANCE IN THE SOVIET UNION
SOVIET STUDIES, 61(3) (JUL 89), 462-483.
ELECTORAL AVOIDANCE--THE DELIBERATE ACT OF NOT VOTING IN A MOBILISATIONAL POLITY THAT DEMANDS NEARLY UNANIMOUS AFFIRMATION OF ITS OFFICIAL CANDIDATES--HAS BEEN GROWING AS AN EVER MORE COMMON FEATURE OF SOVIET POLITICAL LIFE. THE RESULTS OF THE 1987 ELECTIONS TO LOCAL SOVIETS REPORT THE FIRST ABSOLUTE DECLINE IN THE NUMBER OF VOTERS IN NEARLY A QUARTER OF A CENTURY. MORE SIGNIFICANTLY, THIS COMES AFTER A SLIDE IN THE PROPORTION OF ADULTS VOTING IN EACH ELECTION THAT HAS NOW LASTED THREE DECADES. THE PURPOSE OF THIS ARTICLE IS TO EXPLORE THE DIMENSIONS OF THIS MASS POLITICAL BEHAVIOUR. SPECIFICALLY, IT SEEKS TO ESTIMATE THE MAGNITUDE OF THIS BEHAVIOUR, ITS TRENDS OVER TIME, AND PATTERNS IN ITS INCIDENCE IN THE MAJOR CONSTITUENT TERRITORIES OF THE SOVIET UNION, AND IT SEEKS TO IDENTIFY CORRELATES OF ELECTORAL AVOIDANCE THAT MAY HELP TO EXPLAIN ITS INCIDENCE. IF, AS IT IS ARGUED, ELECTORAL AVOIDANCE IS ITSELF SIGNIFICANT POLITICAL BEHAVIOUR, UNDERSTANDING OF SOVIET POLITICS IS ADVANCED BY MEASURES OF ITS INCIDENCE. BUT MORE IMPORTANTLY, ELECTORAL AVOIDANCE APPEARS TO BE PART OF A LARGER 'SYNDROME' OF KINDS OF NON-CONFORMIST BEHAVIOUR AND TO BE STRONGLY CORRELATED WITH THE PROPENSITY TO ENGAGE IN THESE OTHER ACTS. THUS, ESTIMATES OF THE VARIATION OF ELECTORAL AVOIDANCE ACROSS SEGMENTS OF SOCIETY AND OVER TIME PROVIDE ONE OF OUR BEST INDICATORS (IN THE SOCIAL SCIENCE SENSE OF THAT TERM) OF THE PATTERNS OF DISAFFECTION AND DISSIDENCE IN SOVIET SOCIETY.

07715 ROEDER, P.G.
MODERNIZATION AND PARTICIPATION IN THE LENINIST DEVELOPMENTAL STRATEGY
AMERICAN POLITICAL SCIENCE REVIEW, 83(3) (SEP 89), 859-884.
THE SOVIET UNION ACHIEVED ITS STABILITY IN THE EARLY STAGES OF DEVELOPMENT NOT BY INSTITUTIONALIZING PARTICIPATION BUT BY FORCING DEPARTICIPATION AND SUBSTITUTING A FUNCTIONALLY DISTINCT FORM OF POLITICAL ACTIVITY--INVOLVEMENT IN COPRODUCTION. THESE POLICIES CONSTITUTE ESSENTIAL COMPLEMENTS IN THE LENINIST DEVELOPMENTAL STRATEGY. THE ABILITY OF ENLISTED INVOLVEMENT TO BLOCK THE GROWTH OF PARTICIPATORY PRESSURES TENDS TO DECLINE IN LATER STAGES OF DEVELOPMENT, HOWEVER. THE RESULT IS SPONTANEOUS WITHDRAWAL FROM THE INSTITUTIONS OF COPRODUCTION AND THE RISE OF PARTICIPATORY PRESSURES. THIS PATTERN IS DOCUMENTED WITH EVIDENCE FROM SOVIET ELECTORAL AND MEMBERSHIP STATISTICS, SOVIET REPORTS OF OPINION SURVEYS, WESTERN INTERVIEWS OF SOVIET EMIGRES, AND CROSS-NATIONAL ESTIMATES OF POLITICAL DISSIDENCE. THE LENINIST CRISIS OF PARTICIPATION REQUIRES A POLICY RESPONSE TO CLOSE THE PARTICIPATION-INSTITUTION GAP ONCE AGAIN. THE ALTERNATIVE POLICY RESPONSES OF SOVIET GENERAL SECRETARIES ARE CHARACTERIZED AS TOTALITERON, AUTHORITARIAN, LIBERAL, AND SOCIALIST.

07716 ROEMER, C.E. III
A GOVERNOR'S EXAMPLE: PUTTING HONESTY IN POLITICS
JOURNAL OF STATE GOVERNMENT, 62(5) (SEP 89), 171-172.
THE AUTHOR, WHO IS GOVERNOR OF LOUISIANA, DISCUSSES HIS EFFORTS TO BRING A NEW STANDARD OF PERSONAL ETHICS TO THAT STATE. HE STATES THAT ETHICS IN STATE GOVERNMENT DEMANDS A GOOD EXAMPLE FROM THE CHIEF EXECUTIVE ALONG WITH STRONG CAMPAIGN CONTRIBUTIONS AND DISCLOSURE LAWS THAT ARE ENFORCED.

07717 ROEMER, J.
DEMOCRACY AND PRODUCTION SERIES: VISIONS OF CAPITALISM AND SOCIALISM
SOCIALIST REVIEW, (MAR 89), 93-102.
THIS ARTICLE SUPPORTS THE CLAIM BY THE AUTHOR THAT EXPLOITATION IS BROUGHT ABOUT BY AN UNEQUAL DISTRIBUTION OF PROPERTY IN THE MEANS OF PRODUCTION AND COMPETITIVE MARKETS. IT ARGUES THAT DOMINATION OF THE WORKER BY THE BOSS AT THE POINT OF PRODUCTION NEED NOT PLAY A ROLE, THIS VIEW MAINTAINS THAT PROPERTY RELATIONS ARE THE KEY TO EXPLOITATION, NOT SOCIAL RELATIONS AT THE POINT OF PRODUCTION.

07718 ROEMER, M.
THE MACROECONOMICS OF COUNTERPART FUNDS REVISITED
WORLD DEVELOPMENT, 17(6) (JUN 89), 795-807.
SUMMARY. - USE OF AID-GENERATED COUNTERPART FUNDS HAS BECOME AN IMPORTANT ISSUE AGAIN, ESPECIALLY IN AFRICA. THIS PAPER EXPLAINS WHY THE MONETARY IMPACT OF COUNTERPART FUNDS IS NOT INHERENTLY INFLATIONARY. WHEN THE IMPORT OF AID-FUNDED COMMODITIES AND THE MONETARY BALANCEOF-PAYMENTS IMPACT ARE INCORPORATED INTO THE ANALYSIS, HOWEVER, THE EXPENDITURE OF COUNTERPART FUNDS HAS A STRONG TENDENCY TO CAUSE INFLATION, EVEN THOUGH THE MONETARY AUTHORITIES

COUNTERACT ANY INCREASES IN THE MONEY SUPPLY. BUT IF AID-FUNDED COMMODITIES PERMIT OUTPUT TO GROW, THEN THE JOINT EFFECT OF ADDITIONAL IMPORTS AND COUNTERPART OUTLAYS CAN BE DEFLATIONARY. FURTHER, THE DRAWDOWN OF COUNTERPART ACCOUNTS DOES NOT REDUCE GOVERNMENT DEFICITS, BUT MERELY FINANCES THEM. DONORS AND RECIPIENT GOVERNMENTS NEED TO RECOGNIZE THAT COUNTERPART ACCOUNTS DO NOT REPRESENT REAL RESOURCES AND HAVE EXTREMELY LIMITED USE IN DEVELOPMENT FINANCING.

07719 ROEMER, M.I.
THE FEASIBILITY OF A NATIONAL HEALTH PROGRAM
INTERNATIONAL JOURNAL OF HEALTH SERVICES, 19(3) (1989), 531-548.
THE ARTICLE IS A RESPONSE TO THE PROPOSED "JACKSON HEALTH PROGRAM" WHICH ADVOCATES A NATIONAL HEALTH PROGRAM. THE AUTHOR APPLAUDS THE PROGRAM'S AIMS, BUT CAUTIONS THAT POLITICAL REALITIES MUST NOT BE IGNORED. HE DRAWS UPON THE EXPERIENCE OF OTHER NATIONS TO ILLUSTRATE THE NECESSITY OF INCORPORATING EXISTING VOLUNTARY HEALTH INSURANCE PLANS, THE MAINTENANCE OF A SEPARATE TRUST FUND FOR BUDGETARY PURPOSES AND THE IMPORTANCE OF COOPERATION AT THE STATE AND LOCAL LEVEL.

07720 ROETT, R.
BRAZILS TRANSITION TO DEMOCRACY
CURRENT HISTORY, 88(356) (MAR 89), 117-120,149-151.
IN 1988, BRAZIL APPEARED TO BE IN SUSPENDED ANIMATION. THE ECONOMY HAD DETERIORATED DRAMATICALLY, AND PROTESTS HAD ESCALATED. ALL EYES WERE TURNED TO THE NOVEMBER 1989 PRESIDENTIAL ELECTION, WITH THE EXPECTATION THAT IT WOULD RESTORE LEGITIMACY TO THE BADLY TATTERED DEMOCRATIC SYSTEM

07721 ROETT, R.
PARAGUAY AFTER STROESSNER
FOREIGN AFFAIRS, 68(2) (SPR 89), 124-142.
GENERAL ALFREDO STROESSNER'S REPLACEMENT, GENERAL ANDRES RODRIGUEZ, IS CUT FROM THE SAME CLOTH. THE SUCCESSION RAISES THE QUESTION OF WHETHER FORCES WILL BE UNLEASHED IN THE FORESEEABLE FUTURE TO CHANGE THE EQUATION OF POWER IN PARAGUAY OR WHETHER A GERIATRIC POLITICAL ELITE CAN CONTINUE TO CONVINCE THE MAJORITY THAT THE ABSENCE OF DEMOCRACY IS A NECESSARY PRICE TO BE PAID FOR CONTINUED SOCIAL PEACE AND POLITICAL STABILITY.

07722 ROGERS, J.M.
SOCIAL SCIENCE DISCIPLINES AND POLICY RESEARCH: THE CASE OF POLITICAL SCIENCE
POLICY STUDIES REVIEW, 9(1) (AUT 89), 13-28.
IT HAS BEEN ARGUED THAT SOCIAL SCIENCE DISCIPLINES INFLUENCE THEIR MEMBERS POLICY RESEARCH VIA THEORETICAL FOCUS, METHODS, NORMS, AND SYSTEM MAINTENANCE MECHANISMS AND THAT THESE FORCES INHIBIT THE USEFULNESS OF POLICY RESEARCH FOR POLICY-MAKING. POLITICAL SCIENCE IS FOUND TO INFLUENCE SUBSTANTIALLY ITS MEMBERS POLICY RESEARCH OUTPUT AND TO DECREASE ITS POLICY USEFULNESS, PRIMARILY BY PROMOTING EXPLANATIONS OF POLICY, ALTHOUGH THE EXTENT OF INFLUENCE AND LACK OF USEFULNESS ARE LESS THAN STUDIES OF OTHER DISCIPLINES SUGGEST. WHEREAS HIGHLY USEFUL OUTCOME ANALYSES ARE PRODUCED LESS FREQUENTLY THAN MANY ADVOCATES OF POLICY RESEARCH WOULD HOPE, A SUBSTANTIAL BODY OF POLICY RESEARCH UNDERTAKES OBJECTIVES THAT WHEN SATISFIED, PARTICULARLY IN THE AREA OF PROBLEM DEFINITION, PROVIDE MODERATELY USEFUL OUTPUT TO DECISION MAKERS. IN ADDITION, POLICY RESEARCH OUTPUT IS REMARKABLY DIVERSE SUBSTANTIVELY, BUT LESS SO IN TERMS OF THE PURPOSES IT SERVES.

07723 ROGERS, M.L.
PATTERNS OF CHANGE IN RURAL MALAYSIA: DEVELOPMENT AND DEPENDENCE
ASIAN SURVEY, 29(8) (AUG 89), 764-785.
THIS ARTICLE ANALYZES THE SOCIAL AND ECONOMIC CHANGES THAT TOOK PLACE IN THE RURAL MALAY VILLIAGE OF SUNGAI RAYA IN THE SOUTH WESTERN PART OF PENINSULAR MALAYSIA BETWEEN 1966 AND 1988. THE LOGITUDINAL STUDY DOCUMENTS DRAMATIC SOCIAL CHANGES AND DESCRIBES STRIKING ECONOMIC IMPROVEMENTS. IT ALSO EXAMINES THE RISING INCOME EQUALITY AMONG THE RURAL MALAYS, THEIR GROWING DEPENDENCE ON GOVERNMENT PROGRAMS AND SERVICES, AND THEIR INCREASING VULNERABILITY TO PRESSURE FROM POLITICIANS

07724 ROGGE, J.; AKOL, J.
REPATRIATION: ITS ROLE IN RESOLVING AFRICA'S REFUGEE DILEMMA
INTERNATIONAL MIGRATION REVIEW, XXIII(2) (SUM 89), 184-200.
THE LITERATURE ON AFRICA'S REFUGEES HAS GROWN DRAMATICALLY OVER THE PAST DECADE. TWO ISSUES, HOWEVER, REMAIN RELATIVELY UNRESEARCHED AND POORLY UNDERSTOOD - THE PLIGHT OF URBAN REFUGEES AND THE PROBLEMS ASSOCIATED WITH REPATRIATION. THIS ARTICLE EXAMINES THE DIMENSIONS OF THE LATTER. AFTER PLACING REPATRIATION INTO THE CONTEXT OF CONTEMPORARY DURABLE SOLUTIONS APPLIED TO THE AFRICAN REFUGEE DILEMMA, THE ARTICLE EXAMINES SOME OF THE PROBLEMS, CONCERNS AND FRUSTRATIONS ASSOCIATED WITH AFRICAN REPATRIATION EXERCISES IN TERMS OF CULTURAL, ECONOMIC AND

POLITICAL OBSTACLES ENCOUNTERED IN THE PROCESS OF
REPATRIATION AND THE CONCOMITANT REHABILITATION OF REFUGEES
IN THEIR AREAS OF ORIGIN. THE ARTICLE IS ILLUSTRATED WITH
EXAMPLES DRAWN FROM THE SOUTHERN SUDANESE REPATRIATION OF
THE EARLY 1970S.

07725 ROGOV, S.
DETENTE IS NOT ENOUGH
FOREIGN POLICY, (74) (SPR 89), 86-102.
THE AUTHOR ARGUES THAT US-SOVIET CONFRONTATION IS NOT
INEVITABLE AND THAT A POLICY OF MUTUAL PARITY IS NOT A SOUND
FOUNDATION FOR RELATIONS OR REDUCING TENSIONS. HE OUTLINES
AND EXAMINES SEVERAL AREAS WHICH THE US AND THE SOVIET UNION
COULD REDUCE COMPETITION AND INCREASE COOPERATION. THESE ARE
ESPECIALLY IMPORTANT IN LIGHT OF THE REFORMS OF MIKHAIL
GORBACHEV; THEY INCLUDE: COOPERATION IN THE AREA OF ARMS
CONTROL, REDUCTION OF REGIONAL CONFLICTS AND TENSIONS,
ECONOMIC COOPERATION, JOINT SPACE EXPLORATION AND EFFORTS TO
COMBAT HUNGER, EPIDEMICS, AND ENVIRONMENTAL DEGRADATION.
WILLINGNESS TO ABANDON HOSTILE MILITARY STANCES AND THE
ABILITY TO COMPROMISE ARE VIEWED AS VITAL RECONDITIONS TO
THIS COOPERATION.

07726 ROHN, L.L.
CONVENTIONAL FORCES IN EUROPE: A NEW APPROACH TO THE
BALANCE, STABILITY, AND ARMS CONTROL
DISSERTATION ABSTRACTS INTERNATIONAL, 49(12) (JUN 89),
3863-A.
THE DEBATE SURROUNDING THE BALANCE OF CONVENTIONAL
FORCES IN CENTRAL EUROPE IS SOMEWHAT CONFUSED. THIS PAPER
SUGGESTS A DEFINITION OF CONVENTIONAL STABILITY AND
DESCRIBES SEVERAL TECHNIQUES FOR ASSESSING CONVENTIONAL
BALANCE. IT OFFERS A NEW FRAMEWORK THAT RELATES MEASURES OF
MILITARY CAPABILITIES, BALANCE ASSESSMENT METHODOLOGIES, AND
DEFENSE OBJECTIVES TO CONVENTIONAL STABILITY. IT ALSO
PROVIDES AN ANALYTIC METHODOLOGY THAT RELATES FORCE PLANNING,
ARMS CONTROL POLICY, AND DEFENSE GOALS.

07727 ROHRSCHNEIDER, R.
THE GREENING OF PARTY POLITICS IN WESTERN EUROPE:
ENVIRONMENTALISM, ECONOMICS, AND PARTISAN ORIENTATIONS IN
FOUR NATIONS
DISSERTATION ABSTRACTS INTERNATIONAL, 50(6) (DEC 89),
1789-A.
EUROPEAN PUBLICS GIVE CONSIDERABLE SUPPORT TO
ENVIRONMENTAL ORGANIZATIONS IN WEST GERMANY, FRANCE, GREAT
BRITAIN, AND THE NETHERLANDS. POST-MATERIAL VALUE PRIORITIES
AND THE PERCEPTION OF NATIONAL POLLUTION PROBLEMS ARE TWO
FACTORS THAT ARE VERY STRONGLY RELATED TO ENVIRONMENTAL
GROUP SUPPORT. IN ADDITION, ENVIRONMENTALISM IN THESE
COUNTRIES IS INTEGRATED INTO A WELL STRUCTURED SCHEMA THAT
GUIDES THE EVALUATION OF ENVIRONMENTALLY RELATED INFORMATION.

07728 ROJO, S.V.
THE BASIS OF OLD THINKING
WORLD MARXIST REVIEW, 32(10) (OCT 89), 46-48.
THIS ARTICLE IS THE FIRST IN A SERIES OF CONTRIBUTIONS
STRESSING THE RELEVANCY OF LENIN'S IDEAS AND URGING THAT
THEY BE CLEARED OF ALL VULGAR INTERPRETATIONS. IT STUDIES
THE DEVELOPMENT OF MARXIST THEORY NOT ONLY AS A RESPONSE TO
THE NEW REALITIES OF THE MODERN WORLD, BUT AS A BRINGING OUT
THE THEORETICAL WEALTH CONTAINED WITHIN THE CORE OF MARXISM,
THE IDEAS OF ALSO ENGELS AND LENIN. IT REFUTES THE VIEW THAT
MARXISM IS NO LONGER RELEVANT TO OUR DAY.

07729 ROLFE, J.
TRIMMING THE DEFENCE FAT
NEW ZEALAND INTERNATIONAL REVIEW, 14(4) (JUL 89), 13-17.
THE AUTHOR PROVIDES A SUMMARY OF THE REPORT ON THE
DEFENCE MANAGEMENT RESOURCE REVIEW CARRIED OUT BY FORMER
CABINET MINISTER DEREK QUIGLEY. HE COVERS SUCH TOPICS,
ADDRESSED BY THE REPORT. AS DEFENCE OBJECTIVS, FORCE
STRUCTURE, AND RESOURCE MANAGEMENT FOR THE NEW ZEALAND
DEFENCE FORCES. STRUCTURAL AND ATTITUDINAL MANAGEMENT
PROBLEMS ARE IDENTIFIED, AND SHOWN TO BE DIRECTLY RELATED TO
RESOURCE COSTS. THE TOP THREE PRIORITIES FOR NEW ZEALAND'S
DEFENCE ARE OUTLINED AND SPECIFIC RECOMMENDATIONS BY QUIGLEY
ARE DETAILED.

07730 ROLLER, C.G.; MAJOR, D.M.
RAMIFICATIONS OF ILLEGAL U.S. ARMS EXPORTS
AVAILABLE FROM NTIS, NO. AD-A208 410/1/GAR, MAR 89, 150.
THIS THESIS EXAMINES THE IMPACT OF ILLEGAL U.S. ARMS
TRANSFERS UPON RECIPIENT NATIONS' WAR FIGHTING CAPABILITIES
AND UPON THE AMERICAN NATIONAL SECURITY. DATA WERE GATHERED
PRIMARILY FROM U.S. DISTRICT COURT RECORDS AND INTERVIEWS
WITH U.S. GOVERNMENTAL OFFICIALS FROM INTELLIGENCE SERVICES
AND THE DEPARTMENTS OF COMMERCE, JUSTICE AND STATE. AN
INVESTIGATION OF THE ILLICIT ARMS TRANSFERS TO IRAN FORMED
THE BASIS OF CONCLUSIONS REACHED. ADDITIONALLY, POLICY
RECOMMENDATIONS ARE PROVIDED TO ENHANCE THE GOVERNMENTAL
DETECTION AND INVESTIGATION OF ILLEGAL EXPORT VIOLATIONS.
THE VIABILITY OF UTILIZING COURT DOCUMENTS AS INTELLIGENCE
TOOLS FOR MEASURING MILITARY CAPABILITIES IS ASSESSED.

07731 ROLLY, M.
THE KARENNI AND PA-OH: REVOLUTION IN BURMA
CULTURAL SURVIVAL QUARTERLY, 13(4) (1989), 15-17.
WHEN THE BRITISH GAVE BURMA ITS INDEPENDENCE IN 1948,
THEY ALLOWED THE KARENNI TO BE INCORPORATED INTO THE STATE;
THIS, HOWEVER, WAS DONE WITHOUT THE CONSENT OF THE KARENNI
PEOPLE. WHEN THE KARENNI REFUSED TO COOPERATE WITH THE NEW
GOVERNMENT, THE PRIME MINISTER SENT HIS MILITARY POLICE TO
OCCUPY THEIR LAND. ON AUG. 9, 1948, THE MILITARY POLICE
ATTACKED THE KARENNI NATIONAL ORGANIZATION HEADQUARTERS,
WHICH IGNITED A WAR BETWEEN THE KARENNI AND THE BURMESE
GOVERNMENT THAT CONTINUES TO THIS DAY. THE PA-OH, UNDER THE
COMMAND OF CHAN ZONE, JOINED RANKS WITH THE KARENNI TO
RESIST THE GOVERNMENT.

07732 ROM, M.
THE FAMILY SUPPORT ACT OF 1988: FEDERALISM, DEVELOPMENTAL
POLICY, AND WELFARE REFORM
PUBLIUS: THE JOURNAL OF FEDERALISM, 19(3) (SUM 89), 57-74.
REVISING THE USUAL DISTINCTION BETWEEN DEVELOPMENTAL AND
REDISTRIBUTIVE POLICIES, THIS ARTICLE THAT STATE AND FEDERAL
GOVERNMENTS EACH SEEK PROGRAMS THEY BELIEVE WILL HELP THEM
GAIN THEIR DEVELOPMENTAL GOALS. BUT THERE IS LITTLE
CONSENSUS ON THE TYPES OF WELFARE PROGRAMS THAT ACTUALLY DO
CREATE ECONOMIC DEVELOPMENT. STATE AND FEDERAL PARTICIPANTS
IN WELFARE REFORM CONSEQUENTLY PROMOTE THE KIND OF FEDERAL
ARRANGEMENTS THAT ARE LIKELY TO PRODUCE THE POLICIES THEY
FAVOR. THE DEVELOPMENTAL POLITICS OF THE FAMILY SUPPORT ACT
OF 1988 ARE SHOWN THROUGH FIVE MAIN REFORM ISSUES: CHILD
SUPPORT; NATIONAL MINIMUM BENEFITS; TRANSITIONAL BENEFITS;
WELFARE FOR FAMILIES HAVING BOTH PARENTS PRESENT; AND
EDUCATION, TRAINING, AND EMPLOYMENT PROGRAMS.

07733 ROMALIS, A.; CLARK, M.
FORMING THE TORONTO DISARMAMENT NETWORK
PEACE RESEARCH, 21(1) (JAN 89), 33-36.
THIS REPORT DEALS WITH THE FORMATION OF THE TORONTO
DISARMAMENT NETWORK (TDN), ONE OF CANADA'S PRINCIPAL ANTI-
WAR ORGANIZATIONS. THE AUTHOR TRACES THE ORIGINS OF TDN BACK
THROUGH SIMILAR GROUPS OF THE 1960'S, TO THE 1980'S WHEN
DURING A PLANNED SURVIVAL AND DISARMAMENT WEEK, VARIOUS ANTI-
WAR/ANTI-NUCLEAR GROUPS CAME TOGETHER TO DRAFT A STATEMENT
OF PURPOSE FOR TDN.

07734 ROMANI, F.
ANTI-TRUST LEGISLATION IN A FREE SOCIETY
REVIEW OF ECONOMIC CONDITIONS IN ITALY, 1 (JAN 88), 35-48.
THIS PAPER EXAMINES THE PARADOX IN PROPOSING IN A FREE
SOCIETY LEGISLATION (HENCE STATE INTERVENTION) IN DEFENCE OF
COMPETITION. IT CONSIDERS THE FORMS OF COMPETITION
CONSIDERED UNACCEPTABLE WITHIN A LIBERAL JURIDICAL FRAMEWORK,
AS WELL AS THE IMPLICATIONS FOR ECONOMIC LEGISLATION IN A
FREE SOCIETY. POSSIBLE SOLUTIONS TO SPECIFIC PROBLEMS ARE
CONSIDERED.

07735 ROMDHANI, O.
THE ARAB MAGHREB UNION: TOWARD NORTH AFRICAN INTEGRATION
AMERICAN-ARAB AFFAIRS, (28) (SPR 89), 42-47.
THE ARTICLE FOCUSES PRIMARILY ON THE ARAB MAGHREB UNION
(AMU) OF MOROCCO, LIBYA, TUNISIA, MAURITANIA AND ALGERIA. IT
EXAMINES THE HISTORICAL EVENTS AND TRENDS THAT LED TO THE
CREATION OF THE AMU IN 1989. IT ANALYZES THE CHIEFLY
ECONOMIC FACTORS THAT LED TO THE UNION AND THE IMPLICATIONS
THAT THE AMU WILL HAVE ON THE AILING NATIONS' ECONOMIES AND
POLITICAL SYSTEMS. HAVING SHAKEN OFF COLONIAL CHAINS SOME
THREE DECADES PREVIOUSLY, MANY NORTH AFRICAN LEADERS SEE
MAGHREB UNION AS THE NEXT LOGICAL STEP TOWARDS ECONOMIC
INDEPENDENCE AND THE REALIZATION OF A COMMON DESTINY.

07736 ROME, J.
REGULATING THE DEREGULATED
SOCIETY, 27(1) (NOV 89), 11-12.
THE ARTICLE DISCUSSED THE EFFECTS OF REGULATION AND
DEREGULATION ON SAFETY. IT CONCLUDES THAT GOVERNMENTAL
REGULATION, ALTHOUGH MISTAKE-RIDDEN, HAS THE BEST CHANCE FOR
IMPROVING THE SAFETY OF US CITIZENS. THE AUTHOR OUTLINES
EXAMPLES FROM TRAFFIC SAFETY AND REGULATION AND FROM
ATTEMPTS TO DEREGULATE THE TRUCKING INDUSTRY TO SUPPORT HIS
THESIS THAT GOVERNMENTAL REGULATION INCREASES OVERALL LEVELS
OF SAFETY.

07737 ROMERO, D.W.
THE CHANGING AMERICAN VOTER REVISITED; CANDIDATE
EVALUATIONS IN PRESIDENTIAL ELECTIONS, 1952 TO 1984
AMERICAN POLITICS QUARTERLY, 17(4) (OCT 89), 409-421.
THE STATE OF KNOWLEDGE REGARDING THE RELATIVE INFLUENCE
OF ISSUES, PARTIES, AND CANDIDATES ACROSS TIME IN
PRESIDENTIAL ELECTIONS IS CONFOUNDED BECAUSE RESEARCHERS
HAVE TYPICALLY EMPLOYED STANDARDIZED CORRELATION
COEFFICIENTS. EMPLOYING UNSTANDARDIZED COEFFICIENTS ON
OPENENDED PRESIDENTIAL CANDIDATE EVALUATIONS FOR THE 1952 TO
1984 ELECTIONS, THIS ARTICLE EXAMINES THE MANNER AND EXTENT
TO WHICH THE RELATIONSHIP BETWEEN ISSUES, PARTY, CANDIDATES,

AND THE VOTE HAVE FLUCTUATED OVER TIME. THE RESULTS SUGGEST, AS HAVE OTHERS, THAT PARTY INFLUENCE ON THE VOTE HAS DECLINED. HOWEVER, NO EVIDENCE IS FOUND TO SUPPORT THE ASSERTION OF AN INCREASE IN ISSUE INFLUENCE ON THE VOTE DECISION. CANDIDATE INFLUENCE ON THE VOTE IS FOUND TO BE STABLE OVER TIME.

07738 RONDINELLI, D.A.; JOHNSON, R.W.; MCCULLOUGH, J.S.
ANALYZING DECENTRALIZATION POLICIES IN DEVELOPING COUNTRIES: A POLITICAL-ECONOMY FRAMEWORK
DEVELOPMENT AND CHANGE, 20(1) (JAN 89), 57-87.
THE AUTHORS OFFER AN INTEGRATED POLITICAL-ECONOMY FRAMEWORK FOR ANALYSING DECENTRALIZATION POLICIES AND PROGRAMMES THAT DRAWS ON THE MOST USEFUL CONCEPTS IN BOTH APPROACHES AND IDENTIFIES THE FACTORS THAT SHOULD BE CONSIDERED BY POLICY ANALYSTS. THE FRAMEWORK ADDRESSES THE NEEDS OF RESEARCHERS INTERESTED IN EXPLORING THE POLITICAL, ECONOMIC AND SOCIAL DIMENSIONS OF DECENTRALIZATION POLICIES IN DEVELOPING COUNTRIES FOR AN INTERDISCIPLINARY APPROACH TO ANALYSIS; THE NEEDS OF POLICY DESIGNERS FOR A COMPREHENSIVE FRAMEWORK FOR ASSESSING POTENTIAL INTERVENTION STRATEGIES; AND THE NEEDS OF THOSE ENGAGED IN TECHNICAL ASSISTANCE AND TRAINING TO IDENTIFY THE FACTORS AFFECTING SUCCESSFUL POLICY AND PROGRAMME IMPLEMENTATION.

07739 RONDINELLI, D.A.
DECENTRALIZING PUBLIC SERVICES IN DEVELOPING COUNTRIES: ISSUES AND OPPORTUNITIES
JOURNAL OF SOCIAL, POLITICAL AND ECONOMIC STUDIES, 14(1) (SPR 89), 77-98.
IN MOST DEVELOPING COUNTRIES, THE PROVISION, FINANCING, AND MAINTENANCE OF PUBLIC SERVICES AND INFRASTRUCTURE PLAY A CRUCIAL ROLE IN NATIONAL DEVELOPMENT AND ACCOUNT FOR A SUBSTANTIAL PORTION OF THE EXPENDITURES IN NATIONAL BUDGETS. INCREASINGLY, HOWEVER, THE ABILITY OF CENTRAL GOVERNMENT MINISTRIES, AGENCIES, AND ENTERPRISES TO PROVIDE PUBLIC SERVICES AND INFRASTRUCTURE EFFICIENTLY AND EFFECTIVELY IS BEING QUESTIONED. GOVERNMENTS ARE SEARCHING FOR ALTERNATIVE WAYS OF PROVIDING PUBLIC SERVICES, IN ORDER TO RELIEVE THE GROWING FINANCIAL BURDENS ON CENTRAL TREASURIES. DECENTRALIZING ADMINISTRATIVE AND FINANCIAL RESPONSIBILITIES IS ONE POSSIBLE OPTION.

07740 RONFELDT, D.
A NEW DARK AGE FOR LATIN AMERICA?
HEMISPHERE, 2(1) (FAL 89), 34-35.
ALTHOUGH THE SCENARIO OF A DEMOCRATIC FUTURE FOR LATIN AMERICA HAS BEEN ADJUSTED PERIODICALLY, IT REMAINS WIDELY ACCEPTED. NEVERTHELESS, MUCH OF LATIN AMERICA SEEMS HEADED TOWARD THE FAILURE OF DEMOCRACY AND A PLUNGE INTO A NEW DARK AGE. THIS GRIM POSSIBILITY HAS GROWN MORE LIKELY WITH ONE EVENT AFTER ANOTHER SINCE 1986. THE PATH TO DARKNESS WILL NOT FOLLOW ONE FACTOR BUT WILL BE DUE TO A VARIETY OF GLOBAL, REGIONAL, AND INTERNAL TRENDS THAT WEAKEN MODERATE LEADERS, AROUSE ANTIDEMOCRATIC FORCES, AND LESSEN THE CONSTRAINTS ON VIOLENCE. MOST LATIN AMERICAN COUNTRIES WILL REMAIN WEAK DUE TO ECONOMIC STAGNATION AND POLITICAL DISARRAY; DOUBTS ABOUT THE SUPERIORITY OF DEMOCRACY WILL RESURFACE; AND DICTATORS AND DEMAGOGUES WILL TAKE OVER.

07741 RONGGUANG, S.
A CIVIL SERVICE SYSTEM CREEPS IN
BEIJING REVIEW, 32(23) (JUN 89), 30-33.
WITH A HISTORY OF RENZHI (ADMINISTRATION BY MAN) AND A LACK OF FAZHI (ADMINISTRATION BY LAW), CORRUPTION SEEMS TO HAVE BECOME AN INTEGRAL PART OF CHINESE POLITICS. REFORMING THE POLITICAL STRUCTURE, INCLUDING THE PERSONNEL SYSTEM, HAS BECOME AN URGENT DEMAND IN CHINA. BOTH THE GOVERNMENT AND THE PEOPLE KNOW THAT THE ON-GOING ECONOMIC REFORM WILL INEVITABLY BE HAMPERED UNLESS POLITICAL REFORM PARALLELS IT.

07742 RONGGUANG, S.
MODERNIZATION AND CORRUPTION: A FOREIGN CPC MEMBER'S VIEW
BEIJING REVIEW, 32(36) (SEP 89), 32-34.
IN THIS INTERVIEW, A JOURNALIST WHO HAS REPORTED ON CHINA AND WRITTEN SEVERAL BOOKS ABOUT ITS HISTORY COMMENTS ON CHINA TODAY AND THE OUTLOOK FOR THE FUTURE. HE WARNS THAT SOME OLD THINKING PERSISTS IN CHINESE SOCIETY AND SOME FEATURES OF THE OLD CHINA ARE REAPPEARING, LIKE CORRUPTION AND PROSTITUTION.

07743 RONGGUANG, S.
VETERAN DIPLOMAT TALKS ABOUT REBELLION
BEIJING REVIEW, 32(42) (OCT 89), 34-35.
CHAI ZEMIN, PRESIDENT OF THE CHINESE DIPLOMATIC SOCIETY, WAS THE FIRST CHINESE AMBASSADOR TO THE UNITED STATES AFTER THE NORMALIZATION OF DIPLOMATIC RELATIONS BETWEEN THE TWO COUNTRIES. FOLLOWING THE JUNE 1989 UNREST IN BEIJING, HE SUPPORTED THE GOVERNMENT'S ACTIONS AS A NECESSARY STEP TO RESTORE ORDER IN THE CAPITAL CITY. HE STATED THAT IT WAS OBVIOUS THAT THE MAJORITY OF THE STUDENTS WERE BEING MANIPULATED BY A HANDFUL OF PLOTTERS AGAINST THE GOVERNMENT, THE COMMUNIST PARTY, AND SOCIALISM. FANG LIZHI, YAN JIAQI, AND OTHER CONSPIRATORS TRIED TO USE THE STUDENTS' ANGER OVER

CORRUPTION IN GOVERNMENT TO ESCALATE THE DEMONSTRATIONS INTO A FULL-SCALE REVOLT.

07744 RONGGUANG, S.
WOMEN'S EMANCIPATION: A LONG WAY TO GO
BEIJING REVIEW, 32(18) (MAY 89), 32-34.
IN THE NOVEL "SPRING MOON," BETTE BAO LORD CREATED A TYPICAL CHINESE WOMAN WHO WAS BORN IN THE LATE QING DYNASTY AND LIVED THROUGH THE HUNDRED DAY REFORM, THE 1911 REVOLUTION, THE WAR OF RESISTANCE AGAINST THE JAPANESE, THE CIVIL WARS, AND THE CULTURAL REVOLUTION. THE NOVEL MIRRORS THE STRUGGLE OF CHINESE WOMEN FOR EMANCIPATION AND EQUALITY IN THE SOCIALIST ERA AND BEFORE.

07745 RONGXIA, L.
ADHERING TO THE OPEN POLICY
BEIJING REVIEW, 32(17) (APR 89), 30-31.
CHINA HAS NOW APPROVED MORE THAN 15,000 FOREIGN-FUNDED ENTERPRISES. SOME FORTY PERCENT ARE ALREADY OPERATIONAL, AND EIGHTY PERCENT ARE LOCATED IN COASTAL REGIONS. ECONOMIC RESTRUCTURING AND THE CHANGES IN CHINA'S ECONOMIC SITUATION WILL HAVE BOTH BENEFICIAL AND ADVERSE EFFECTS ON FOREIGN BUSINESSES.

07746 RONGXIA, L.; XIAOBIN, Y.
QIAN QICHEN ON CHINA'S FOREIGN POLICY
BEIJING REVIEW, 32(15) (APR 89), 15-18.
ACCORDING TO CHINESE FOREIGN MINISTER QIAN QICHEN, THE SIGNIFICANCE OF THE UPCOMING SINO-SOVIET SUMMIT WILL NOT LIE IN THE SIGNING OF ANY AGREEMENTS BUT IN THE NORMALIZATION OF RELATIONS BETWEEN CHINA AND THE USSR. KAMPUCHEA WILL A KEY TOPIC DURING THE SUMMIT MEETINGS. GORBACHEV WILL MEET WITH ZHAO ZIYANG BECAUSE BOTH ARE LEADERS OF THEIR RESPECTIVE PARTIES, BUT DIFFERENCES BETWEEN THE SOVIET AND CHINESE COMMUNIST PARTIES ARE NOT LIKELY TO BE ERADICATED AS A RESULT OF THE TALKS.

07747 RONGXIA, L.
THE NEED FOR MACRO-ECONOMIC REGULATION
BEIJING REVIEW, 32(16) (APR 89), 25-27.
THE MAJOR TOPICS OF DISCUSSION AT THE SECOND SESSION OF THE SEVENTH NPC AND THE SECOND SESSION OF THE SEVENTEENTH CPPC NATIONAL COMMITTEE WERE HOW TO CONTROL INFLATION AND RECTIFY THE ECONOMIC ORDER BY RESOLVING THE PROBLEMS OF ECONOMIC IMBALANCE AND THE LACK OF CONTROLS OVER THE MACRO-ECONOMY. MANY NPC DEPUTIES WERE CONCERNED BECAUSE MAJOR ECONOMIC PROBLEMS PRODUCED DOUBLE-DIGIT INFLATION AND PRICE HIKES IN 1988. DEPUTIES SINGLED OUT SERIOUS ECONOMIC IMBALANCES AND THE LACK OF CONTROL OVER THE MACRO-ECONOMY AS THE PRINCIPAL CAUSES OF THE PROBLEMS.

07748 RONNOW, H.
THE INFORMATION REVOLUTION, II: SATELLITES AND PEACE
WORLD TODAY, 45(6) (JUN 89), 97-99.
THE AUTHOR DISCUSSES THE USE OF SURVEILLANCE SATELLITES TO VERIFY COMPLIANCE WITH ARMS CONTROL AGREEMENTS. HE FOCUSES ON THE PROPOSED SWEDISH TELLUS SATELLITE PROJECT.

07749 ROPP, S.C.
A POLITICAL OBITUARY: ARNULFO ARIAS OF PANAMA
HEMISPHERE, 1(2) (WIN 89), 16-17.
FOR HALF A CENTURY, ARNULFO ARIAS WAS PANAMA'S LEADING POLITICAL FIGURE. THERE IS LITTLE QUESTION THAT THE IMPOSITION OF A MILITARYDOMINATED REGIME IN 1968 STEMMED FROM DOMESTIC RESISTANCE TO THE POSSIBILITY OF AN ARIAS PRESIDENCY. JUST AS CURRENT DEVELOPMENTS IN ARGENTINA CANNOT BE UNDERSTOOD WITHOUT REFERENCE TO THE LEGACY OF JUAN PERON, ANALYSIS OF PANAMANIAN POLITICS MUST START WITH THE LEGACY OF "EL HOMBRE."

07750 RORTY, R.
EDUCATION WITHOUT DOGMA
DISSENT, (SPR 89), 198-204.
WHEN PEOPLE ON THE POLITICAL RIGHT TALK ABOUT EDUCATION, THEY IMMEDIATELY START TALKING ABOUT TRUTH. TYPICALLY, THEY ENUMERATE WHAT THEY TAKE TO BE FAMILIAR AND SELF-EVIDENT TRUTHS AND REGRET THAT THESE ARE NO LONGER BEING INCLUCATED IN THE YOUNG. WHEN PEOPLE ON THE POLITICAL LEFT TALK ABOUT EDUCATION, THEY TALK FIRST ABOUT FREEDOM. THE LEFT TYPICALLY VIEWS THE OLD FAMILIAR TRUTHS CHERISHED BY THE RIGHT AS A CRUST OF CONVENTION, VESTIGES OF OLD-FASHIONED MODES OF THOUGH FROM WHICH THE NEW GENERATION SHOULD BE FREED.

07751 ROSARDO, L.
NEIGHBORLY DISPUTE
FAR EASTERN ECONOMIC REVIEW, 142(51) (DEC 89), 55.
IN THE WAKE OF THE TIANANMEN MASSACRE, THE JAPANESE GOVERNMENT JOINED OTHER INDUSTRIAL NATIONS IN IMPOSING SANCTIONS ON CHINA. AS A RESULT, ECONOMIC RELATIONS BETWEEN CHINA AND JAPAN ARE AT A LOW POINT, DESPITE AN APPARENT DESIRE BY BOTH SIDES, PARTICULARLY JAPANESE BANKS, TO GET BACK TO BUSINESS. UNCERTAINTY ABOUT CHINA'S ECONOMIC FUTURE IS HEIGHTENED BY THE COMEBACK OF CONSERVATIVE LEADERS AND FREQUENT SHIFTS IN PEKING'S ECONOMIC POLICY. THE SURPRISE

VISIT OF U.S. NATIONAL SECURITY ADVISER BRENT SCOWCROFT TO
CHINA IS THE ONLY GLIMMER OF HOPE IN AN OTHERWISE DISMAL
PICTURE OF CHINA'S INTERNATIONAL ECONOMIC FUTURE.

07752 ROSCOW, S.
NUCLEAR DETERRENCE, STATE LEGITIMATION, AND LIBERAL
DEMOCRACY
POLITY, XXI(3) (SPR 89), 563-586.
THE AUTHOR ATTEMPTS A HOLISTIC EXAMINATION OF THE
REASONS BEHIND THE MASSIVE BUILD-UP OF NUCLEAR WEAPONS OVER
THE PAST FOUR DECADES. HE ARGUES THAT NUCLEAR PROLIFERATION
SHOULD BE VEIWED NOT ONLY IN STRATEGIC CONTEXTS, BUT ALSO IN
SOCIAL, POLITICAL AND ECONOMIC CONTEXTS. HE ATTRIBTUES THE
RECNT MILITARY BUILD-UP TO THE CRISIS IN THE WELFARE STATE
AND OF AMERICAN HEGEMONY. THE AUTHOR CONCLUDES THAT
CONTINUED BUILD-UP OF ADVANCED WILL ONLY EXACERBATE THE
CRISIS OF THELIBERAL DEMOCRATIC, ADVANCED CAPITALISTIC STATE.

07753 ROSE, C.
THE SOVIET PROPAGANDA NETWORK
JOHN SPIERS PUBLISHING, BRIGHTON, SUSSEX, GB, 1988, 298.
THE AUTHOR SURVEYS THE NETWORK OF ORGANIZATIONS THAT
DISSEMINATES SOVIET PROPAGANDA. ESSENTIALLY, THESE
ORGANIZATIONS ARE INSTRUMENTS OF SOVIET FOREIGN POLICY,
OPERATING UNDER THE GENERAL DIRECTION OF THE CENTRAL
COMMITTEE OF THE SOVIET COMMUNIST PARTY.

07754 ROSE, H.
NUCLEAR-TEST BAN AND VERIFICATION
DISARMAMENT, XII(3) (AUT 89), 16-23.
SO FAR, THE ISSUE OF STOPPING NUCLEAR WEAPONS TESTING
HAS BEEN ONLY PARTIALLY AFFECTED BY THE RECENT POSITIVE
DEVELOPMENTS IN ARMS CONTROL. DESPITE SEVERAL APPEALS BY THE
UNITED NATIONS TO STOP THEM, NUCLEAR EXPLOSIONS HAVE
CONTINUED. PROPOSALS FOR A COMPREHENSIVE BAN CONTINUE TO
MEET PERSISTENT OPPOSITION FROM SOME STATES, EVEN THOUGH THE
GREAT MAJORITY OF COUNTRIES BELIEVE THAT A COMPREHENSIVE
TEST BAN WOULD BE AN ESSENTIAL STEP TOWARDS THE PROMOTION OF
NUCLEAR DISARMAMENT AND UNIVERSAL CONFIDENCE-BUILDING.

07755 ROSE, M.
WHEN THE BOUGH BREAKS
MACLEAN'S (CANADA'S NEWS MAGAZINE), 102(2) (JAN 89), 42.
DENMARK'S EXTENSIVE WELFARE SYSTEM HAS BEEN A MODEL FOR
SIMILAR, BUT OFTEN LESS COSTLY, SYSTEMS IN OTHER
INDUSTRIALIZED NATIONS. HOWEVER, IN SPITE OF THE BILLIONS
SPENT, MOUNTING SOCIAL PROBLEMS ARE AN INTRACTABLE PART OF
DANISH LIFE. INCREASING NUMBER OF "DOWN AND OUTS" AND LONG-
TERM UNEMPLOYED ARE STRAINING THE GOVERNMENT'S BUDGET TO THE
LIMIT. THE RULING CONSERVATIVE GOVERNMENT IS EXPLORING JOB
TRAINING AND OTHER ALTERNATIVES IN AN ATTEMPT TO GET AT THE
ROOTS OF MANY OF DENMARK'S SOCIAL PROBLEMS.

07756 ROSE, R.
HOW EXCEPTIONAL IS THE AMERICAN POLITICAL ECONOMY?
POLITICAL SCIENCE QUARTERLY, 104(1) (SPR 89), 91-116.
THE AUTHOR TESTS WHETHER OR NOT THE USA HAS A BIG
GOVERNMENT AND WHETHER ITS POSTWAR GROWTH HAS BEEN NORMAL OR
EXCEPTIONAL AMONG ADVANCED INDUSTRIAL NATIONS. HE BEGINS BY
REVIEWING THEORIES ABOUT THE GROWTH OF GOVERNMENT. THEN HE
SHOWS THAT, BY COMPARISON WITH OTHER ADVANCED INDUSTRIAL
NATIONS, THE USA IS EXCEPTIONAL IN TOTAL PUBLIC EXPENDITURE,
IN MAJOR PRIORITIES, AND IN THE VALUE OF PUBLIC BENEFITS.
BUT GOVERNMENT IN THE USA HAS BEEN GROWING MORE SLOWLY THAN
THE AVERAGE IN THE OECD.

07757 ROSE, R.
PRIVATIZATION AS PROBLEM OF SATISFICING AND DISSATISFICING
AMERICAN REVIEW OF PUBLIC ADMINISTRATION, 19(2) (JUN 89),
97-118.
PRIVATIZATION HAS FOUR DISTINGUISHING QUALITIES: AN
INCREASE IN PRIVATE OWNERSHIP, COMPETITION, DEREGULATION,
AND REDUCING RELIANCE UPON PUBLIC FUNDS. IT IS A
MULTIDIMENSIONAL CONCEPT INVOLVING TRADE-OFFS BETWEEN
COMPETING OBJECTIVES IN A CONTINUING PROCESS OF
DISSATISFACTION AND SATISFACTION. THUS, TO UNDERSTAND THE
DYNAMICS OF PRIVATIZATION ONE MUST CONSIDER IN WHICH
DIRECTION GOVERNMENT IS MOVING. THE EXTENSIVE BRITISH
EXPERIENCE SHOWS THAT THERE CAN BE A LARGE REDUCTION IN
PUBLIC OWNERSHIP AND PUBLIC SUBSIDIES WITHOUT PROMOTING
COMPETITION AND EVEN INTRODUCING NEW FORMS OF REGULATION.
THREE EXTREME "SATISFICING" GOALS ARE CONSIDERED:
RENATIONALIZATION THROUGH THE BACK DOOR OF REGULATION AND
SUBSIDY; FURTHER PRIVATIZATION OF PUBLIC ENTERPRISES SELLING
GOODS AND SERVICES; AND THE PRIVATIZATION OF SOCIAL PROGRAMS.
THE MOST LIKELY POLITICAL EQUILIBRIUM INVOLVES A MIXTURE OF
BOTH STATE AND MARKET CALCULATIONS RATHER THAN A RIGID
SEPARATION OF ACTIVITIES INTO PURELY PRIVATE OR PURELY
PUBLIC.

07758 ROSEN, J.
DILEMMA FOR NATIONAL SECURITY REPORTERS: IS ANYBODY
LISTENING?
DEADLINE, III(6) (NOV 88), 3-5.

THE ARTICLE DISCUSSES THE "TRAGIC PARADOX" OF NUCLEAR
WEAPONS POLICY AND PUBLIC OPINION: ALTHOUGH NUCLEAR WEAPONS
AND THE DECISION TO USE THEM IS PROBABLY THE MOST FATEFUL
DECISION FOR AMERICANS, THEY REMAIN IGNORANT ABOUT US
NUCLEAR POLICY, AND ARE SLIPPING INTO APATHY. THE AUTHOR
ARGUES THAT IT IS THE RESPONSIBILITY OF THE PRESS TO
"AWAKEN" THE PUBLIC THROUGH THE USE OF "ADVOCACY JOURNALISM."

07759 ROSEN, J.
THE CAMPAIGN PRESS AND NUCLEAR ISSUES
DEADLINE, 3(4) (JUL 89), 6-8.
THIS ARTICLE ANALYSES THE NEED FOR JOURNALISTS AND THE
PRESS TO RECOGNIZE WHERE IGNORANCE EXISTS AND TO RESIST THE
TEMPTATION TO EXPLOIT IT. IT USES AS AN EXAMPLE, DURING THE
1988 POLITICAL CAMPAIGN FOR PRESIDENT, THAT PUBLIC IGNORANCE
OF NUCLEAR POLICY ALLOWED AN INNOCUOUS REMARK BY DUKAKIS TO
BECOME A CAMPAIGN EVENT. IT DESCRIBES "TWO PUBLICS", THE
INFORMED INSIDERS AND POLITICAL ANALYSTS, AND THE OTHER
PUBLIC, THE MASS OF UNINFORMED VOTERS.

07760 ROSEN, L.
RELEVANCE OF INTERNATIONAL RESEARCH FACILITIES TO
INTERNATIONAL STABILITY
AVAILABLE FROM NTIS, NO. DE89009400/GAR, MAR 89, 14.
INTERNATIONAL FACILITIES HAVE PLAYED AN IMPORTANT PLAY
IN EXPANDING AND KEEPING OPEN A DIALOGUE BETWEEN EAST AND
WEST. THE ADVENT OF GLASNOST HAS DRAMATICALLY REDUCED
INHIBITIONS ON COMMUNICATIONS AND OPENED NEW OPPORTUNITIES
FOR INTERNATIONAL FACILITIES TO FACILITATE THE UNDERSTANDING
AND APPRECIATION OF COMMON GOALS AND COMMON THREATS. THIS IS
ACCOMPLISHED THROUGH FRANK DISCUSSIONS IN WHICH REAL
PROBLEMS ARE IDENTIFIED AND ASSESSED WHILE FICTITIOUS ONES
ARE LAID REST.

07761 ROSEN, S.
PUBLIC OPINION AND REFORM IN THE PEOPLE'S REPUBLIC OF CHINA
STUDIES IN COMPARATIVE COMMUNISM, 22(2/3) (SUM 89),
153-170.
THIS ARTICLE EXAMINES CHINA'S PUBLIC OPINION POLLS AND
ATTITUDINAL STUDIES. IT TRACES THE RECENT UPSURGE IN
ATTEMPTS TO MEASURE PUBLIC REACTION TO GOVERNMENT REFORM
POLICIES. IT STUDIES THE TWO-EDGED NATURE OF SURVEY RESEARCH
IN ITS ABILITY TO EITER MEASURE OR MANIPULATE PUBLIC
ATTITUDES. PREDICTED ARE TROUBLE TIMES AHEAD FOR CHINA'S
PUBLIC OPINION-SENSITIVE REFORMERS.

07762 ROSENBERG, A.
FY 1990 ASSISTANCE REQUEST FOR SUB-SAHARAN AFRICA
DEPARTMENT OF STATE BULLETIN (US FOREIGN POLICY), 89(2148)
(JUL 89), 39-42.
THE AUTHOR REVIEWS THE OBJECTIVES OF AMERICAN FOREIGN
AID IN SUB-SAHARAN AFRICA, RECENT REDUCTIONS IN AID LEVELS,
AND THE BUSH ADMINISTRATION'S BUDGET REQUESTS FOR ECONOMIC
ASSISTANCE TO SUB-SAHARAN AFRICA IN FY 1990.

07763 ROSENBERG, M.
CONGRESS, THE AGENCIES, AND SEPARATION OF POWERS
CRS REVEIW, 10(5) (JUN 89), 25-27.
A DECADE OF INTENSE SEPARATION OF POWERS LITIGATION
BEFORE THE SUPREME COURT HAS NOW ESTABLISHED THAT CONGRESS'
PREROGATIVE OVER THE ORDERING AND ARRANGEMENTS OF THE
ADMINISTRATIVE BUREAUCRACY, WHILE NOT UNLIMITED, IS BROAD
AND FAR-REACHING, ENCOMPASSING THE POWER TO CREATE, ABOLISH,
AND LOCATE AGENCIES AND TO DEFINE THE POWERS, DUTIES, TENURE,
COMPENSATION, AND OTHER INCIDENTS OF ITS OFFICES WITHIN
THEM.

07764 ROSENBERG, M.B.
FORGING CONSENSUS
HEMISPHERE, 1(2) (WIN 89), 6-7.
THE BUSH ADMINISTRATION FACES A MYRIAD OF TACTICAL
DECISIONS IN LATIN AMERICAN FOREIGN POLICY. THESE DECISIONS
ARE COMPLICATED BY LATIN AMERICAN IMPATIENCE AND FRUSTRATION
OVER PAST U.S. POLICY. COMPLIANTS FOCUS ON WASHINGTON'S
PENCHANT FOR PATERNALISM AND ITS INATTENTION TO BASIC
MATTERS OF ECONOMIC RECOVERY AND MULTILATERAL CONSULTATION.
WHAT IS NEEDED IS A FRESH, MORE RESPONSIVE U.S. APPROACH TO
LATIN AMERICAN AFFAIRS. THE KEY IS TO FORGE A CONSENSUS IN
WASHINGTON AROUND THREE CRITICAL ISSUES: NATIONAL SECURITY,
DRUG POLICY, AND THE DEBT CRISIS.

07765 ROSENBERG, M.B.
LIFE (AND DEATH): AN ANDEAN SAGA
HEMISPHERE, 1(3) (SUM 89), 4.
PERU'S INSTITUTIONS ARE GIVING WAY TO VIOLENCE IN THE
CONDUCT OF POLITICS. DEMOCRACY AFFORDS THE POSSIBILITY FOR
PLURALIST DIALOGUE, EVEN AMONG THE MOST CONTENTIOUS OF
FORCES. BUT IS PREMISES ARE UNITY OF PURPOSE AMONG GROUPS
AND CONSENSUS ABOUT THE RULES OF THE GAME. IN PERU, THERE IS
NEITHER UNITY OF PURPOSE OR CONSENSUS. THE ADMINISTRATION OF
ALAN GARCIA IS IN DISARRAY, ITS POLICIES HAVING LED TO THE
BREAKDOWN OF THE ECONOMY AND THE DISPERSION OF POLITICAL
POWER.

07766 ROSENBERG, S.
CHAPTER 1: LABOR MARKET RESTRUCTURING IN EUROPE AND THE
UNITED STATES: THE SEARCH FOR FLEXIBILITY; THE STATE AND
THE LABOR MARKET
PLENUM PRESS, NEW YORK, NY, 1989, 3-22.
THIS CHAPTER BY EDITOR SAMUEL ROSENBERG INTRODUCES THE
REST OF THE BOOK WRITTEN BY EIGHTEEN INTERNATIONAL
ECONOMISTS AND SOCIOLOGISTS ABOUT THE STATE AND THE LABOR
MARKET. THIS CHAPTER ADDRESSES FLEXIBILITY IN U.S. AND
EUROPEAN LABOR MARKETS. IT EXPLORES LABOR MARKET
SEGMENTATION; DEFINES LABOR MARKET FLEXIBILITY, AND GIVES
THE RATIONALES FOR IT. THE CHAPTER CONCLUDES WITH AN OUTLINE
FOR THE BOOK, WHICH COVERS INDUSTRIAL RELATIONS, EMPLOYMENT
POLICIES, EVALUATIONS OF SPECIFIC POLICIES, AND DRAWS SOME
LESSONS TO BE LEARNED FROM THE SEARCH FOR MARKET FLEXIBILITY.

07767 ROSENBERG, S.; POWER, M.
CHAPTER 10: THE REAGAN ADMINISTRATION AND THE REGULATION
OF LABOR: THE CURIOUS CASE OF AFFIRMATIVE ACTION THE STATE
AND THE LABOR MARKET
PLENUM PRESS, NEW YORK, NY, 1989, 197-206.
THIS CHAPTER GIVES A BRIEF DESCRIPTION OF THE HISTORY
AND EFFECTIVENESS OF THE AFFIRMATIVE ACTION EXECUTIVE ORDER,
AND CHRONICLE THE REAGAN ADMINISTRATION'S ATTEMPTS TO
DISMANTLE IT. IT THEN FOCUSES ON THE USE OF GOALS AND
TIMETABLES. IT ARGUES THAT CORPORATE COMMITMENT TO GOALS
AND TIMETABLES HAVE A PROTECTIVE AND A POSITIVE ASPECT. IT
SHOWS, IN BRIEF, HOW FEDERALLY MANDATED AFFIRMATIVE ACTION
MAY BE USED BY CAPITAL TO PROTECT ITSELF FROM MORE MILITANT
CIVIL RIGHTS PRESSURE.

07768 ROSENBERG, S.
CHAPTER 13 THE STATE AND THE LABOR MARKET: AN EVALUATION;
THE STATE AND THE LABOR MARKET
PLENUM PRESS, NEW YORK, NY, 1989, 235-250.
THIS CHAPTER IS DIVIDED INTO FOUR MAIN SECTIONS. THE
FIRST WILL SUMMARIZE THE POLICIES UNDERTAKEN BY GOVERNMENTS
IN THE UNITED STATES AND SUCH EUROPEAN COUNTRIES AS THE
UNITED KINGDOM, THE FEDERAL REPUBLIC OF GERMANY, SPAIN, AND
ITALY TO FOSTER LABOR MARKET FLEXIBILITY. THE SECOND WILL
INVESTIGATE WHETHER INCREASED WAGE AND NUMERICAL FLEXIBILITY
SHOULD BE EXPECTED TO INCREASE EMPLOYMENT AND DECREASE
UNEMPLOYMENT. THE THIRD WILL ANALYZE THE DARK SIDE OF LABOR
MARKET FLEXIBILITY. THE FOURTH WILL DISCUSS SOME QUESTIONS
FOR FURTHER RESEARCH REGARDING THE IMPLICATIONS OF THE PUSH
FOR LABOR MARKET FLEXIBILITY.

07769 ROSENBERG, S.; BRUSCO, S.; VILLA, P.
CHAPTER 7 THE STATE, THE UNIONS, AND THE LABOR MARKET: THE
ITALIAN CASE, 1969-1985; THE STATE AND THE LABOR MARKET
PLENUM PRESS, NEW YORK, NY, 1989, 127-150.
AN ANALYSIS OF RECENT ITALIAN INDUSTRIAL RELATIONS MUST
BEGIN WITH THE EVENTS OF 1968-1969. THIS PERIOD WAS OF
SPECIAL IMPORTANCE IN THE HISTORY OF ALL WESTERN COUNTRIES
AS WELL AS OF THE EASTERN BLOC, BUT PERHAPS NOWHERE WAS IT
IMPACT AS WIDELY AND LASTINGLY FELT AS IN ITALY. THE
INDUSTRIAL RELATIONS SYSTEM, THE RELATIONS BETWEEN UNIONS
AND POLITICAL PARTIES, AND BETWEEN UNIONS AND GOVERNMENT
WERE DRAMATICALLY MODIFIED. THE CHANGES IN THE ITALIAN
INDUSTRIAL RELATIONS SYSTEM IN THE PAST TWO DECADES HAVE
THEREFORE TO BE ANALYZED AS A CONTINUOUS PROCESS OF
ADJUSTMENT, INTERRELATED WITH THE MODIFICATIONS IN THE
SOCIAL, ECONOMIC, AND POLITICAL FRAMEWORK, DATING BACK TO
THE EVENTS OF THE LATE 1960S. WITHIN THE ELEMENTS OF
CONTINUITY THAT CHARACTERIZE THE WHOLE PERIOD UNDER
CONSIDERATION, THIS CHAPTER IDENTIFIES THREE MAIN THEMES
COMING TO PROMINENCE AT DIFFERENT TIMES: "PANSYNDICALISM" IN
THE YEARS 1968-1975; "NATIONAL SOLIDARITY GOVERNMENT" IN THE
YEARS 1975-1980; AND "TRILATERAL BARGAINING" IN THE PERIOD
1980-1985.

07770 ROSENBERG, S.; GALASI, P.; SZIRACZKI, G.
CHAPTER 8: STATE REGULATION, ENTERPRISES BEHAVIOR, AND THE
LABOR MARKET IN HUNGARY, 1963-1983; THE STATE AND THE
LABOR MARKET
PLENUM PRESS, NEW YORK, NY, 1989, 151-174.
THIS CHAPTER ANALYSES STATE REGULATION, ENTERPRISE
BEHAVIOR, AND THE OPERATION AND CHARACTERISTICS OF THE
LABOUR MARKET IN THE FOLLOWING THREE PERIODS OF LABOR MARKET
CHARACTERISTICS IN HUNGARY. THE FIRST PERIOD WAS
CHARACTERIZED BY A RAPID INCREASE IN NATIONAL INCOME AND IN
LIVING STANDARDS AND A SLIGHT INCREASE IN THE PRICE LEVEL,
THE SECOND PERIOD WAS ACCOMPANIED BY AN ACCELERATING RATE OF
INFLATION, A SLOWDOWN IN THE RISE OF LIVING STANDARDS. WHILE
LABOR SHORTAGES BECAME GENERAL, THE THIRD PERIOD HAS BEEN
CHARACTERIZED BY HIGH INFLATION, SLOW GROWTH, AND DECLINING
REAL WAGES.

07771 ROSENBERG, S.; BOSCH, G.; SENGENBERGER, W.
EMPLOYMENT POLICY, THE STATE AND THE UNIONS IN THE FEDERAL
REPUBLIC OF GERMANY
PLENUM PRESS, NEW YORK, NY, 1989, 87-106.
THE CHAPTER IS DIVIDED INTO FIVE MAIN SECTIONS. THE
FIRST DESCRIBES THE SUBSTANTIAL CUTBACKS IN UNEMPLOYMENT

COMPENSATION THAT HAVE OCCURRED IN RECENT YEARS. THE SECOND
INVESTIGATES THE GOVERNMENTAL ASSAULT ON LEGAL RULES AND
REGULATIONS GOVERNING EMPLOYMENT SECURITY AND WORKER
PROTECTION. THE THIRD DISCUSSES THE EMPLOYER DEMAND FOR
INCREASED FLEXIBILITY IN THE WAGE LEVEL AND THE WAGE
STRUCTURE. ALTHOUGH MANAGEMENT HAS STRIVED FOR GREATER
FLEXIBILITY AND COST RELIEF FROM WAGE AND SOCIAL POLICIES,
ORGANIZED LABOR HAS TRIED TO DEFEND EXISTING RULES AND
REGULATIONS. BUT, IN THE AREA OF WORK-TIME REDUCTION,
TREATED IN THE FOURTH SECTION, LABOR HAS BEEN ON THE
OFFENSIVE. A SCHEME FOR ANALYZING AND INTERPRETING RECENT
CHANGES IN WEST GERMAN EMPPLOYMENT AND LABOR MARKET POLICIES
IS PRESENTED IN THE FIFTH SECTION.

07772 ROSENBERG, S.; PIORE, M.J.
FISSURE AND DISCONTINUITY IN U.S. LABOR MANAGEMENT
RELATIONS; THE STATE AND THE LABOR MARKET
PLENUM PRESS, NEW YORK, NY, 1989, 47-62.
DEVELOPMENTS IN LABOR AND MANAGEMENT MARK FUNDAMENTAL
CHANGE IN THE VERY STRUCTURE OF THE SYSTEM ITSELF. STRAINS
ON INDUSTRIAL RELATIONS SYSTEM HAVE BEEN ACCOMODATED IN A
WAY THAT PRESERVES THE OUTLINE OF THE ORIGINAL FRAMEWORK AND
WOULD PERMIT ITS RESTORATION IN A MORE FAVORABLE ECONOMIC
AND POLITICAL CLIMATE. THIS CHAPTER ADDRESSES THIS THOUGH
ITS EVALUATION OF THE INSTITUTIONAL BACKGROUND, WAGE CONTROL
POLICY, AND REGULATION OF LAYOFFS AND JOB SECURITY.

07773 ROSENBERG, S.; RUBERY, J.; TARLING, R.; WILKINSON, F.
GOVERNMENT POLICY AND THE LABOR MARKET:; THE STATE AND THE
LABOR MARKET
PLENUM PRESS, NEW YORK, NY, 1989, 23-46.
THIS CHAPTER DESCRIBES AND ASSESSES THE THATCHER
GOVERNMENT'S POLICY TOWARD SPECIFIC ASPECTS OF THE LABOR
MARKET AGAINST A BACKGROUND OF PREVIOUS GOVERNMENT'S
POLICIES AND CHANGING ECONOMIC, POLITICAL, AND SOCIAL
CONDITIONS. FOUR AREAS OF POLICY ARE IDENTIFIED:
MACROECONOMIC. INDUSTRIAL AND LABOR MARKET, INDUSTRIAL
RELATIONS, AND SOCIAL SECURITY AND FAMILY. IT THEN CONSIDERS
THE POLITICAL AND INDUSTRIAL RESPONSE TO THESE POLICIES AND
CONCLUDES BY CONSIDERING THEIR IMPACT ON LABOR MARKET
ORGANIZATION IN THE UNITED KINGDOM.

07774 ROSENBERG, S.; FINA, L.; MEIXIDE, A.; TOHARIA, L.
REREGULATING THE LABOR MARKET AMID AN ECONOMIC AND AND
POLITICAL CRISIS: 1975 - 1986
PLENUM PRESS, NEW YORK, NY, 1989, 107 - 126.
THIS CHAPTER IS DIVIDED INTO FOUR MAIN SECTIONS. THE
FIRST SERVES AS A BACKGROUND FOR DISCUSSING THE NEW
REGULATORY REGIME FOR THE LABOR MARKET BY PROVIDING SOME
INSTITUTIONAL INFORMATION ON WORKER AND EMPLOYER
ORGANIZATIONS. THE SECOND TRACES THE CHANGES IN WAGE CONTROL
POLICY FROM THE OLD FRANCOIST PERIOD TO THE NEW SYSTEM. THE
THIRD DOES THE SAME FOR JOB SECURITY AND EMPLOYMENT POLICIES.
THE CHAPTER ENDS WITH SOME GENERAL CONCLUSIONS PRESENTED IN
THE FOURTH SECTION.

07775 ROSENBERG, S.
THE STATE AND THE LABOR MARKET
PLENUM PRESS, NEW YORK, NY, 1989, 250.
A MAJOR THEME OF THIS BOOK IS THAT DEFLATIONIST
MACROECONOMIC POLICY AND POLICIES AIMED AT DIRECTLY
INCREASING 'FLEXIBILITY' IN WAGE DETERMINATION AND THE
DEPLOYMENT OF LABOR BY THE FIRM HAVE NOT BEEN EFFECTIVE IN
COMBATING THE HIGH RATES OF UNEMPLOYMENT WHICH HAS BEEN
PREVALENT IN MOST OF THE COUNTRIES OF WESTERN EUROPE SINCE
THE LATE 1970S. THE WRITERS OF THIS BOOK ARE REPEATING IN
CONCRETE TERMS THE KEYNESIAN THEORY OF ECONOMICS. IT
IDENTIFIES AN IMPORTANT TURNING POINT IN THE MAKING OF LABOR
MARKET POLICIES IN THE 80S: AND, EMPHASIZES THE
REDISTRIBUTIONAL ASPECTS OF POLICIES DESIGNED TO MAKE WAGES
AND LABOR MARKETS MORE RESPONSIVE TO ADVERSE CHANGES IN
DEMAND AND SUPPLY.

07776 ROSENBERG, T.
WILL DEMOCRACY COME TO CHILE?
DISSENT, (SUM 89), 295-300.
MOST LATIN AMERICAN COUNTRIES HAVE RETURNED TO DEMOCRACY
IN THE LAST TEN YEARS. CHILE'S PLEBISCITE OF OCTOBER 1988
STARTED THAT COUNTRY BACK ON THE ROAD TO A DEMOCRATIC
GOVERNMENT. BUT LATIN AMERICA'S "DEMOCRACIES" HAVE A BAD
RECORD IN HUMAN RIGHTS. THOUSANDS OF POLITICAL ACTIVISTS ARE
KILLED OR "DISAPPEAR" EVERY YEAR IN LATIN AMERICA.

07777 ROSENBERGER, L.
TOWARD A U.S.-SOVIET AGREEMENT IN THE PHILIPPINES
SAIS REVIEW, 9(1) (WIN 89), 213-226.
THE MOST IMPORTANT FOREIGN POLICY ISSUE FACING THE NEW U.
S. ADMINISTRATION WILL BE THE ARCHITECTURE AND MAINTENANCE
OF A HEALTHY U.S.-SOVIET RELATIONSHIP. SOVIET THREATS TO
VITAL U.S. SECURITY INTERESTS IN THE THIRD WORLD, PERCEIVED
OR REAL, UNDERMINE THE PROSPECTS FOR THE STEADY IMPROVEMENT
OF THIS RELATIONSHIP. IN THE CONTEXT OF A WARMING TREND IN
SUPERPOWER RELATIONS, RECENT MOVEMENT TOWARD RESOLUTION OF
SEVERAL REGIONAL CONFLICTS, AND "NEW THINKING" IN BOTH THE

KREMLIN AND THE WHITE HOUSE. THE ALLEVIATION OF TENSIONS THROUGH JOINT U.S.-SOVIET EFFORTS IN THE THIRD WORLD IS BOTH FEASIBLE AND TIMELY. THIS ARTICLE'S EXAMINATION OF THE CURRENT PHILIPPINE SITUATION AND ITS SUPERPOWER COMPONENT SERVES AS A YARDSTICK BY WHICH TO MEASURE THE POSSIBILITIES AND PROSPECTS FOR GENERAL SUPERPOWER COOPERATION IN THE THIRD WORLD.

07778 ROSENBLATH, M.
PALESTINIAN WORKERS FACE RACISM
MIDDLE EAST INTERNATIONAL, (362) (NOV 89), 17-19.
THE ARTICLE EXAMINES THE COVERT AND OVERT DISCRIMINATION THAT PALESTINIANS WHO WORK IN ISRAEL FACE. PALESTINIANS, ALREADY HAMPERED BY CURFEWS, BANS ON TRANSPORTATION, AND STRIKES, ARE NOW FACING ADDITIONAL EFFORTS BY THE ISRAELI GOVERNMENT, THE HISTADRUT (THE ISRAELI TRADE UNION FEDERATION), AND PRIVATE EMPLOYERS TO COMPLETELY EXCLUDE THEM FROM ISRAEL'S LABOR POOL. SUCH EFFORTS BENEFIT ISRAEL BOTH BY PUTTING ADDITIONAL PRESSURE ON THE INTIFADA, AND BY ALLEVIATING THE CURRENT HIGH RATE IF UNEMPLOYMENT AMONG ISRAELI CITIZENS.

07779 ROSENBLUM, S.; ROBINSON, B.
MODERNING THE CRUISE
INTERNATIONAL PERSPECTIVES, 18(4) (JUL 89), 13-14.
THE US CRUISE MISSILE ALWAYS SEEMS TO NEED CANADA FOR ITS TESTING. NOW THAT A MUCH ADVANCED VERSION IS IN EXISTENCE, CANADIAN RANGES HAVE AGAIN MADE THEIR CONTRIBUTION TO FIRE-POWER GROWTH. EXPLORED IS WHETHER THE ADVANCED CRUISE MISSILE (ACM) CAN BE USED FOR FIRST STRIKE OR RETALIATION AND ACM'S USE IN NUCLEAR WAR-FIGHTING. THE INCREASED RISK OF WAR AND THE FACT THAT THE DECISION TO PERMIT ACM TESTS IN CANADA HAS MADE IN SECRET ARE EXAMINED.

07780 ROSENBLUM, V.G.
LETTING THE STATES SET ABORTION POLICY
THE CHRISTIAN CENTURY, 106(8) (MAR 89), 252-253.
THE ABORTION QUESTION IS BETTER VIEWED AS A MATTER OF PUBLIC POLICY THAN AS ONE FOR JUDICIAL DETERMINATION. THE SUPREME COURT WOULD HONOR THE DEMOCRATIC PROCESS BY UPHOLDING THE MISSOURI REGULATIONS. THIS WOULD ENHANCE CONSTITUTIONAL PRINCIPLES OF SEPARATION OF POWERS AND FEDERALISM AND ALLOW THE "ONE PERSON, ONE VOTE" ELECTORAL SYSTEM OPERATIVE IN EVERY STATE TO DETERMINE HOW TO APPLY THE PRINCIPLE OF RESPECT FOR LIFE AT ALL ITS STAGES.

07781 ROSENFIELD, B.B.; ROSENFIELD, S.S.
SOVIET JEWRY AT THE CROSSROADS
PRESENT TENSE, 16(6) (SEP 89), 24-31.
THIS ARTICLE ADDRESSES THE QUESTION: IS THE JEWISH EXPERIENCE COMING TO AN END IN RUSSIA? THE NEW OPENNESS HAS IN MANY RESPECTS BEEN POSITIVE FOR JEWS, HOWEVER, THE POSSIBILITIES FOR A NEW PUBLIC ROLE FOR ANTI-SEMITISM IS EXPLORED. WITH EMMIGRATION NOW A CHOICE, THE DECISIONS WHICH JEWS IN RUSSIA NOW HAVE TO MAKE, AND THE RAMIFICATIONS OF THE POSSIBLE OF FAILURE OF PERESTROIKA ARE EXAMINED

07782 ROSENGARTEN, F.
A U.S. SOCIALIST LOOKS AT THE SOVIET UNION
SOCIALISM AND DEMOCRACY, (8) (SPR 89), 119-142.
THIS ESSAY ATTEMPTS TO RECOVER THE SENCE OF THE PROBLEM INVOLVED IN THE MORAL AND POLITICAL OUTLOOK OF SOCIALIST SCHOLARSHIP. IT RECOUNTS THE AUTHOR'S REFLECTIONS ON HIS OWN COMING TO BE A SOCIALIST AND ATTEMPTS TO RECAPTURE THE EXISTENTIAL CONDITIONS OF POLITICAL AND INTELLECTUAL COMMITMENT. THE ESSAY PROMOTES APPRECIATION AND THE NECESSITY OF UNDERSTANDING THE RELATIONSHIP BETWEEN SOCIALISTS IN NONSOCIALIST SOCIETIES.

07783 ROSENSTEIN, A.; BURGESS, P.
U.S. COMPETITIVENESS IN GLOBAL MARKETS
BUREAUCRAT, 18(3) (FAL 89), 21-29.
THE USA MUST ADDRESS SOME BASIC AND MASSIVE INSTITUTIONAL DEFICIENCIES IF IT IS GOING TO REGAIN ITS ECONOMIC AND LIFE-QUALITY LEADERSHIP. THE USA DOES NOT POSSES THE INSTITUTIONAL MEANS FOR CREATING THE COHERENT NATIONAL POLICIES NECESSARY TO PROVIDE AN ENVIRONMENT CONDUCIVE TO INDUSTRIAL GROWTH AND COMPETITIVENESS. MOREOVER, IT HAS A VERY INEFFICIENT RESEARCH AND DEVELOPMENT POLICY.

07784 ROSENTHAL, D.; HOEFLER, J.
COMPETING APPROACHES TO THE STUDY OF AMERICAN FEDERALISM AND INTERGOVERNMENTAL RELATIONS
PUBLIUS: THE JOURNAL OF FEDERALISM, 19(1) (WIN 89), 1-24.
THE DEVELOPMENT OF THEORY IN THE STUDY OF AMERICAN FEDERALISM AND INTERGOVERNMENTAL RELATIONS HAS LONG BEEN MARKED BY DIVERGENT APPROACHES. THIS ARTICLE REVIEWS THE LITERATURE PRODUCED BY FIVE "SCHOOLS" WITHIN THE FIELD: (1) DUAL FEDERALISM, (2) COOPERATIVE FEDERALISM, (3) PROGMATIC FEDERALISM, (4) NONCENTRALIZED FEDERALISM, AND (5) NATION-CENTERED FEDERALISM. AS DIFFERENT AS THESE APPROACHES ARE, SCHOLARLY WORK IN THIS FIELD HAS MADE ONLY SPARING USE OF TWO OTHER POTENTIALLY USEFUL APPROACHES: DISTRIBUTIVE JUSTICE AND PUBLIC CHOICE THEORY. THIS ARTICLE SUGGESTS HOW

THESE ALTERNATE APPROACHES MIGHT CONTRIBUTE TO REINVIGORATING A FIELD THAT APPEARS TO BE OTHERWISE AT AN INTELLECTUAL IMPASSE.

07785 ROSENTHAL, G.
SOME THOUGHTS ON POVERTY AND RECESSION IN LATIN AMERICA
JOURNAL OF INTERAMERICAN STUDIES AND WORLD AFFAIRS, 31(1, 2) (SPR 89), 63-74.
THIS ARTICLE GIVES A DETAILED ACCOUNT OF THE MAJOR DIFFICULTIES FACED BY GOVERNMENTS IN TRYING TO PURSUE, SIMULTANEOUSLY, THE TWIN GOALS OF ECONOMIC DEVELOPMENT AND REDUCED INEQUALITY IN POVERTY AND INCOME. IT ARGUES THAT A STRATEGY FOR OVERCOMING POVERTY IS ESSENTIALLY A STRATEGY FOR ECONOMIC GROWTH AND DEVELOPMENT, IN THE SENSE THAT IT CANNOT BE ISOLATED FROM THE DEBT PROBLEM, THE EFFICIENCY OF PRODUCTION ISSUES, THE SAVING CONSTRAINT, AND MANY OTHER STRUCTURAL ECONOMIC DEFECTS.

07786 ROSHWALD, A.
THE POLITICS OF STATELESSNESS: JEWISH REFUGEES IN AUSTRIA AFTER THE SECOND WORLD WAR
JEWISH JOURNAL OF SOCIOLOGY, XXXI(1) (JUN 89), 47-52.
THE ARTICLE IS A REVIEW OF THOMAS ALBRICH'S WORK EXODUS DURCH OESTERREICH--DIE JUEDISCHEN FLEUCHTLINGE 1945-1948 (EXUDES THROUGH AUSTRIA--THE JEWISH REFUGEES, 1945-1948). IT CONCLUDES THAT ALBRICH'S BOOK SOUNDS AN UNUSUAL NOTE OF CRITICAL SELF-APPRAISAL ON THE PART OF AN AUSTRIAN HISTORIAN. THE FOCUS OF ALBRICH'S STUDY CAN BE TERMED THE POLITICS OF STATELESSNESS. THE PROBLEM OF JEWISH REFUGEES IN WAR-RAVAGED EUROPE WAS POLITICIZED FROM THE VERY BEGINNING, AND NOWHERE WAS THIS MORE THE CASE THAN IN AUSTRIA.

07787 ROSS, D.A.
"CASUALTIES OF WAR": MYTH AND MISPERCEPTION IN THE AMERICAN DEBATE ON VIETNAM--WHY IT MATTERS TO CANADA
INTERNATIONAL JOURNAL, XLIV(4) (AUT 89), 884-920.
THE VIETNAM CONFLICT CONTINUES TO HOLD IMPORTANT IMPLICATIONS FOR CANADIAN FOREIGN POLICY: HOW CANADIANS RESPOND, OR FAIL TO RESPOND, TO THE EFFORTS OF AMERICANS TO COME TO TERMS WITH THEIR 'LONGEST WAR' WILL UNDOUBTEDLY HAVE DEEP AND PERHAPS LASTING EFFECTS ON CANADIANS' OWN UNDERSTANDING OF THEIR ROLE IN THE WORLD AND THEIR CAPACITY TO ACT FOR GOOD OR ILL. THE AMERICAN DEBATE ABOUT THE VIETNAM CONFLICT MATTERS TO CANADIANS BECAUSE THE CONCLUSIONS FROM THAT DEBATE ARE LIKELY EITHER TO SET THE STAGE FOR A NEW ERA OF RESTRAINT AND COMMON SENSE IN AMERICAN INTERNATIONAL SECURITY POLICY OR TO PAVE THE WAY FOR A NEW ROUND OF ALLEGEDLY 'WISER,' MORE MEASURED, BUT PROBABLY NO LESS BLOODY INTERVENTIONS IN COUNTRIES DEEMED TO BE GEOPOLITICALLY VITAL TO AMERICAN NATIONAL INTERESTS (MOST NOTABLY THE STATES OF LATIN AMERICA).

07788 ROSS, G.; JENSON, J.
"QUEL JOLI CONSENSUS!" STRIKES AND POLITICS IN AUTUMN 1988
FRENCH POLITICS AND SOCIETY, 7(1) (WIN 89), 1-13.
IN THE FALL OF 1988, A MOVEMENT OF PUBLIC-SECTOR STRIKES IN FRANCE SENT THOSE WHO DREAMED OF A NEW SOCIAL CONSENSUS BACK TO THE DRAWING BOARD. THE AUTUMN OF DISCONTENT STARTED IN AN UNEXPECTED PLACE AND CAME IN UNLIKELY WAYS, LED BY A NURSES' STRIKE. THE NURSES' MOVEMENT PROVED POPULAR DESPITE GRUMBLING THAT IT SPOKE EXCLUSIVELY TO THE INTERESTS OF A NARROW OCCUPATIONAL GROUP (AS OPPOSED TO THE WORKING CLASS) AND DESPITE REPEATED EFFORTS TO DEPICT PUBLIC-SECTOR WORKERS AS PRIVILEGED BECAUSE OF THEIR JOB SECURITY.

07789 ROSS, J.I.; GURR, T.R.
WHY TERRORISM SUBSIDES: A COMPARATIVE STUDY OF CANADA AND THE UNITED STATES
COMPARATIVE POLITICS, 21(4) (JUL 89), 405-426.
THE AUTHOR DOCUMENTS AND EXAMINES IN DETAIL THE DECLINING INCIDENCE OF TERRORISM BY DOMESTIC OPPOSITION GROUPS IN CANADA AND THE USA. USA+45 CANADA

07790 ROSS, M.L.
DISARMAMENT AT SEA
FOREIGN POLICY, (77) (WIN 89), 94-112.
THIS ARTICLE SUGGESTS THAT IT IS TIME TO RESTRUCTURE THE SUPERPOWER NAVIES AND THAT THE DECLINE OF THE ARMS RACE AT SEA HAS, THUS FAR, ATTRACTED LITTLE NOTICE, IT EXPLORES TRADITIONAL MARITIME STRATEGY AND THE PROBLEMS FOR THE NAVY THAT NUCLEAR WEAPONS RAISED. IT ALSO EXAMINES SOVIET PROPOSAL FOR BILATERAL AND MULTILATERAL NAVAL CUTBACKS AND THE FOUR TYPES OF NAVAL ARMS CONTROL AVAILABLE TO SUPER POWER NAVIES.

07791 ROSS, R.S.
FROM LIN BIAO TO DENG XIAOPING: ELITE INSTABILITY AND CHINA'S U.S. POLICY
CHINA QUARTERLY, (118) (JUN 89), 265-299.
DESPITE CHINESE DOMESTIC INSTABILITY, THERE HAS BEEN GREAT CONTINUITY IN U.S.-CHINA STRATEGIC RELATIONS OVER THE PAST 15 YEARS BECAUSE CHINA'S INTERNATIONAL CIRCUMSTANCES HAVE ESTABLISHED HER STRATEGIC ORIENTATION. WITHIN THIS CONTEXT, POLICY EVOLUTION HAS PRIMARILY BEEN A FUNCTION OF

THE PRE-EMINENT LEADER'S EVALUATION OF CHINA'S APPROPRIATE
RESPONSE TO INTERNATIONAL CIRCUMSTANCES. NEVERTHELESS, WHEN
THE LEADER IS INCAPACITATED OR WHEN THERE IS NO STRONG PRE-
EMINENT LEADER, AS AT THE HEIGHT OF A SUCCESSION CRISIS,
PAROCHIAL POLITICAL CONSIDERATIONS WILL INFLUENCE THE WEAK
LEADER'S CHOICES. EVEN THESE CIRCUMSCRIBED CHANGES OCCURRING
IN THE MIDST OF LEADERSHIP CHANGE DIMINISH WHEN A PRE-
EMINENT LEADER EMERGES AND ESTABLISHES AUTHORITY OVER THE
FOREIGN POLICY-MAKING PROCESS.

07792 ROSSIA, S.
    LEARNING FROM THE PAST
    REPRINTS FROM THE SOVIET PRESS, 49(5) (SEP 89), 44-47.
    THE HEAD OF THE INTERNATIONAL DEPARTMENT OF THE SOVIET
COMMUNIST PARTY CENTRAL COMMITTEE, VALENTIN FALIN, SUMS UP
THE RESULTS OF THE BUCHAREST SUMMIT IN THIS ARTICLE. FALIN
ANSWERS QUESTIONS ABOUT THE OUTSTANDING FEATURES OF THE
SUMMIT, THE CONCENSUS ACHIEVED AT IT, AND HIS VIEWS ON
INTERNATIONAL EVENTS IN 1989. HE COMMENTS ON MIKHAIL
GORBACHEV'S SERIES OF VISITS TO BRITIAN, WEST GERMANY, AND
FRANCE. FINALLY, HE CONCLUDES BY STATING THAT THE SOVIET
UNION IS OPTIMISTIC ABOUT POLITICS IN THE FUTURE.

07793 ROSTOW, E.
    NOW, ABOUT THOSE BALTIC REPUBLICS
    NEW LEADER, LXXII(16) (OCT 89), 8-9.
    THE DISCONTENTED RUMBLINGS IN THE BALTIC STATES
UNDERSCORE ONE OF THE RESULTS OF MIKHAIL GORBACHEV'S REFORMS.
HE UNEQUIVOCALLY DECLARED HIS COMMITMENT TO THE RULE OF LAW
WHICH INCLUDES THE RIGHT TO SUCCESSION. HOW THE USSR WILL
DEAL WITH THE POSSIBILITY OF SUCCESSION OF THE BALTIC STATES
OR OTHER SOVIET REPUBLICS WILL HAVE A TREMENDOUS IMPACT ON
THE FUTURE OF PERESTROIKA AND GLASNOST. THE RESPONSE OF THE
US AND OTHER WESTERN NATIONS IS EQUALLY AS IMPORTANT.

07794 ROSTOW, E.V.
    A FALSE START IN THE MIDDLE EAST
    COMMENTARY, 88(4) (OCT 89), 24-27.
    THIS ARTICLE ANALYSES A SPEECH MADE BY SECRETARY OF
STATE, JAMES BAKER, TO AIPAC, MAY 1989. THIS, TO DATE, IS
THE ONLY GENERAL STATEMENT OF MIDDLE EAST POLICY THE BUSH
ADMINISTRATION HAS MADE SINCE TAKING OFFICE. BAKER REPEATS
WHAT HAS BEEN THE MAJOR BIPARTISAN PREMISE OF AMERICAN
POLICY IN THE REGION SINCE 1967, BUT AS THE ARTICLE POINTS
OUT, THE SPEECH ITSELF CONTAINS A NUMBER OF STATEMENTS
FUNDAMENTALLY INCONSISTANT WITH UN RESOLUTIONS 242 AND 338,
IT CONCLUDES THAT BAKER HAS MADE A FALSE START.

07795 ROSTOWSKI, J.
    THE DECAY OF SOCIALISM AND THE GROWTH OF PRIVATE
    ENTERPRISE IN POLAND
    SOVIET STUDIES, XLI(2) (APR 89), 194-214.
    THE ARTICLE EXAMINES THE RATE OF PRIVATE ECONOMIC
ACTIVITY IN POLAND AND ITS ORIGINS AND FUTURE IMPLICATIONS.
IT CONCLUDES THAT PRIVATE ECONOMIC ATIVITY CAN NO LONGER BE
CONSIDERED A MARGINAL PHENOMENON AND IS DESTINED TO INCREASE
IN THE FUTURE. IT ATTEMPTS TO EXPLAIN WHY THESE EVENTS HAVE
OCCURRED AND DISCUSSES THE POLICY AND SYSTEMIC IMPLICATIONS
IF CURRENT DEVELOPMENTS CONTINUE.

07796 ROTFELD, A.D.
    A STRATEGY FOR EUROPE
    POLISH PERSPECTIVES, XXXII(3) (1989), 19-26.
    THE WATERSHED IN OVERCOMING THE INTELLECTUAL BARRIERS
AND STEREOTYPES IN EAST-WEST RELATIONS CAME WITH THE
PROCEEDINGS OF THE INDEPENDENT DISARMAMENT AND SECURITY
COMMISSION PRESIDED OVER BY OLOF PALME AND THE COMMISSION
REPORT, "COMMON SECURITY: A PROGRAMME FOR DISARMAMENT."
ALTHOUGH ONLY SIX YEARS HAVE PASSED SINCE THE PUBLICATION OF
THE PALME REPORT, MANY OF ITS ARGUMENTS HAVE INFLUENCED THE
POLICIES OF GOVERNMENTS IN BOTH EAST AND WEST. SOME OF ITS
SPECIFIC IDEAS AND PROPOSALS HAVE BEEN INCORPORATED IN
ACCORDS, WHILE OTHERS ARE THE SUBJECT OF CURRENT TALKS.

07797 ROTH, K.H.
    THE INTERNATIONAL INSTITUTE OF SOCIAL HISTORY AS A DAWN OF
    NAZI SOCIAL RESEARCH
    INTERNATIONAL REVIEW OF SOCIAL HISTORY, 39 (1989), 3-24.
    THIS ARTICLE DRAWS FROM NEW DOCUMENTS ON THE HISTORY OF
THE AMSTERDAM INTERNATIONAL INSTITUTE OF SOCIAL HISTORY
(IISH) DURING GERMAN OCCUPATION RULE FROM 1940 TO 1944. IN
ORDER TO MAKE IT CLEAR WHY THE CONFISCATED AMSTERDAM
INSTITUTE HAS MADE INTO A PAWN OF INTERNAL NAZI POWER
CONFLICTS OVER SOCIAL POLICY AND SOCIAL SCIENCE POSTWAR
PLANNING, THE HISTORY OF THE INTRIGUES SPUN BY EBERHARD
KAUTTER ON ALFRED ROSENBERG'S ORDERS IS RECONSTRUCTED. IT
CONCLUDES THAT THE REASON THE ATTEMPT TO INSTRUMENTALIZE THE
IISH FAILED WAS BECAUSE OF THE POLITICAL, MORAL, AND
INTELLECTUAL INTEGRITY OF THE MEN AND WOMEN WORKING AT THE
IISH AND TO THE PROCESS OF ALIGNMENT OF THE OPPOSITION.

07798 ROTHBARD, M.N.
    WORLD WAR I AS FULFILLMENT: POWER AND THE INTELLECTUALS
    JOURNAL OF LIBERTARIAN STUDIES, IX(1) (WIN 89), 81-125.

WORLD WAR I BROUGHT THE FULFILLMENT OF SEVERAL
PROGRESSIVE TRENDS. MILITARISM, CONSCRIPTION, MASSIVE
INTERVENTION AT HOME AND ABROAD, AND A COLLECTIVIZED WAR
ECONOMY ALL CAME ABOUT DURING THE WAR AND CREATED A MIGHTY
CARTELIZED SYSTEM THAT MOST OF ITS LEADERS SPENT THE REST OF
THEIR LIVES TRYING TO RECREATE, IN PEACE AS IN WAR. THIS
PAPER STUDIES EXAMPLES OF INDIVIDUAL AND GROUPS OF
PROGRESSIVE INTELLECTUALS, WHO EXULTED IN THE TRIUMP OF
THEIR CREED AND THEIR OWN PLACE IN IT, AS A RESULT OF
AMERICA'S ENTRY INTO WORLD WAR I.

07799 ROTHCHILD, D.; GYIMAH-BOADI, E.
    POPULISM IN GHANA AND BURKINA FASO
    CURRENT HISTORY, 88(538) (MAY 89), 221-224, 241-244.
    IN THE 1980'S, THE WEST AFRICAN COUNTRIES OF BURKINA
FASO (FORMERLY UPPER VOLTA) AND GHANA, MIRED IN POVERTY AND
DEPENDENCY, TURNED IN DESPAIR TO EXPERIMENTS WITH HOME-GROWN
POPULIST REGIMES. RADICAL, OFTEN AFRO-MARXIST IN TONE, THESE
LEFTIST POPULIST REGIMES SEARCHED FOR AUTHENTIC AFRICAN
SOLUTIONS TO THE PROBLEMS FACING THEIR COUNTRIES. IN
PRINCIPLE, THEY REJECTED THE INDIVIDUALISM, ACQUISITIVENESS,
AND TRANSNATIONAL LINKAGES THEY ASSOCIATED WITH CAPITALISM;
AND WHILE ACCEPTING MANY OF THE TENETS OF THE
MARXISTLENINIST WORLDVIEW, THEY FAILED IN PRACTICE TO BUILD
DISCIPLINED VANGUARD PARTIES BASED ON THE PRINCIPLE OF
DEMOCRATIC CENTRALISM.

07800 ROTHENBERG, L.
    PUTTING THE PUZZLE TOGETHER: WHY PEOPLE JOIN PUBLIC
    INTEREST GROUPS
    PUBLIC CHOICE, 60(3) (MAR 89), 241-258.
    ABSTRACT. WHY PEOPLE JOIN ORGANIZATIONS, ESPECIALLY
PUBLIC INTEREST GROUPS, HAS BEEN AN UNSOLVED PUZZLE. IN THIS
ANALYSIS, CHOICE-BASED PROBABILITY METHODS ARE EMPLOYED TO
COMBINE DATA FROM THE 1980 NATIONAL ELECTION STUDY WITH
COMPARABLE INFORMATION ABOUT COMMON CAUSE MEMBERS AND TO
ESTIMATE MODELS OF THE PARTICIPATION CALCULUS THAT PUT THE
PIECES OF THE PUZZLE TOGETHER. THE RESULTS DEMONSTRATE THE
PRIMARY IMPORTANCE OF POLITICAL INTEREST AND POLICY
PREFERENCES FOR THE MEMBERSHIP CHOICE.

07801 ROTHENBERG, S.
    THE INVISIBLE SUCCESS STORY
    NATIONAL REVIEW, XLI(17) (SEP 89), 43-46.
    DEMOGRAPHERS AND POLITICAL ANALYSTS ARE FOCUSING ON THE
INCIEASED IMPORTANCE OF AMERICANS OF ASIAN DESCENT, AN
ETHNIC GROUP WHICH HAS CONSISTENTLY DEMONSTRATED ITS ABILITY
TO OPERATE URTLIN THE POLITICAL SYSTEM. THIS ARTICLE REPORTS
HOW POLITICAL PARTIES ARE SCRAMBLING TO BE THE FIRST TO TAP
THE YET UNTOUCHED RESERVOIR OF ENERGY AND TALENT.

07802 ROTHMAN, J.
    SUPPLEMENTING TRADITION: A THEORETICAL AND PRACTICAL
    TYPOLOGY FOR INTERNATIONAL CONFLICT MANAGEMENT
    NEGOTIATION JOURNAL, 5(3) (JUL 89), 265-278.
    THE ARTICLE EXAMINES THE GROWING LIBRARY OF THEORETICAL
AS WELL AS PRACTICAL GUIDES TO NEGOTIATION AND CONFLICT
MANAGEMENT THAT SEEK TO ACCOMMODATE CHANGING GLOBAL
CONDITIONS. IT COMPARES THE POWER POLITICS CONFLICT
MANAGEMENT APPROACH WITH NEW ALTERNATIVES. USING THE EXAMPLE
OF CONFLICT IN THE MIDDLE EAST, IT DEVELOPS A "COMPARATIVE
CONFLICT MANAGEMENT TYPOLOGY" THAT SEEKS TO MEET NEW
GEOPOLITICAL CHALLENGES PRESENTED BY CHANGING CONDITIONS.

07803 ROTHMAN, J. M.
    ANALYSES AND STRATEGIES FOR PEACE -- A METHODOLOGY FOR
    ININTERNATIONAL CONFLICT MANAGEMENT TRAINING AND
    EVALUATION (A CASE STUDY WITH ARABS AND JEWS IN ISRAEL)
    DISSERTATION ABSTRACTS INTERNATIONAL, 49(9) (MAR 89),
    2799-A.
    THIS DISSERTATION AIMS TO INCREASE THE CONCEPTUAL
PRECISION AND PRACTICAL DEVELOPMENT OF INTERNATIONAL
CONFLICT MANAGEMENT. IT PRESENTS METHODS AND PROCEDURES THAT
PROVIDE A CLEAR, SYSTEMATIC DESIGN FOR INTERNATIONAL
CONFLICT MANAGEMENT TRAINING WORKSHOPS, A SCRIPT FOR GUIDING
THIRD PARTY INTERVENTIONS, AND A METHODOLOGY FOR EVALUATING
PARTICIPANTS' SKILL ATTAINMENT. ARAB AND JEWISH STUDENT
LEADERS IN ISRAEL ARE USED AS A CASE STUDY.

07804 ROTHMAN, S.; LERNER, R.
    POLITICS AND THE MEDIA: A TV REVOLUTION
    CURRENT, (311) (MAR 89), 4-11.
    THE AUTHORS EXAMINE THE IMPLICATIONS OF THE MEDIA
REVOLUTION FOR AMERICAN POLITICS AND POLITICAL CANDIDATES.

07805 ROTHSTEIN, R.L.
    ADAPTATION TO CHANGE: THE CHALLENGE TO THE NICS
    JERUSALEM JOURNAL OF INTERNATIONAL RELATIONS, 11(3) (SEP
    89), 1-26.
    THIS DISCUSSION OF THE NEW INDUSTRIALIZING COUNTRIES
(NIC) FOCUSES ESPECIALLY ON THE EAST ASIAN NICS, WHOSE
SUCCESS IN THE PAST TWO DECADES MAKES THEM AN INTERESTING
TEST CASE AND WHOSE FATE IS INCREASINGLY CONSEQUENTIAL FOR
THE ENTIRE INTERNATIONAL SYSTEM. THE RISE OF THE NICS IS

EXAMINED, AS WELL AS THE STRUCTURAL CHANGE AND THE SEARCH FOR A NEW FORMULA.

07806 ROTUNDO, L.
STALIN AND THE OUTBREAK OF WAR IN 1941
JOURNAL OF CONTEMPORARY HISTORY, 24(2) (APR 89), 277-299.
THE QUESTION OF WHY STALIN ALLOWED THE SOVIET ARMED FORCES TO BE SURPRISED ON JUNE 22, 1941, IS A SUBJECT OF CONTINUING CONTROVERSY IN SOVIET HISTORIOGRAPHY. IN VIEW OF THE DIVERSITY OF OPINION AND THE CONTINUING DEBATE CONCERNING STALIN'S PROMINENCE AS A WAR LEADER, THIS PAPER OFFERS A FRESH LOOK AT THE QUESTION OF SOVIET PREPAREDNESS IN 1941 AND STALIN'S ROLE REGARDING THE EVENTS OF THAT SUMMER.

07807 ROUHANA, N.
THE POLITICAL TRANSFORMATION OF THE PALESTINIANS IN ISRAEL: FROM ACQUIESCENCE TO CHALLENGE
JOURNAL OF PALESTINE STUDIES, XVIII(3) (SPR 89), 38-59.
THIS ARTICLE REVIEWS THE MAJOR CHANGES THAT ARAB SOCIETY IN ISRAEL HAS WITNESSED. IT SHOWS HOW THESE CHANGES ESTABLISHED NEW MODES OF INTERACTION WITH ISRAEL AND WITH THE PALESTINIAN PEOPLE, BUT IT EMPHASIZES THE INFLUENCE OF THESE CHANGES--ACTUAL AND POTENTIAL--ON ISRAEL. THE INTERACTION BETWEEN DEVELOPMENTS IN ARAB SOCIETY IN ISRAEL AND THE UNFOLDING OF ISRAEL'S FATAL CONTRADITION--BEING THE STATE OF THE JEWISH PEOPLE AND BEING A DEMOCRACY WITH EQUALITY FOR ITS CITIZENS--IS ANALYZED; AND THE RESULTING INFLUENCE OF THIS CONTRADICTION ON THE NATURE OF ISRAEL AS A NATION-STATE, AND ON ITS FORM OF GOVERNMENT IS ADDRESSED.

07808 ROULSTON, C.
WOMEN ON THE MARGIN: THE WOMEN'S MOVEMENT IN NORTHERN IRELAND 1973-1988
SCIENCE AND SOCIETY, (SUM 89), 219-236.
THIS ARTICLE ADDRESSES THE LINK BETWEEN NATIONAL INDEPENDENCE AND SOCIALISM FOR THE IRISH LEFT IN CONTEXT OF THE WOMEN'S MOVEMENT IN NORTHERN IRELAND. THE IMPACT OF THE PARADIGM OF THE NECESSARY INCLUSION OF THE NATIONALIST STRUGGLE WITHIN THE SOCIALIST AGENDA IS LOOKED AT. ILLUSTRATED IS HOW POSSIBILITIES FOR REAL PROGRESS FOR WOMEN HAS BEEN HAMPERED BY RELIGIOUS AND POLITICAL DIFFERENCES.

07809 ROURKE, F.; SHULMAN, P.
ADHOCRACY IN POLICY DEVELOPMENT
SOCIAL SCIENCE JOURNAL, 26(2) (1989), 131-142.
THE ARTICLE EXAMINES "ADHOCRACY": THE USE OF AD HOC ORGANIZATIONS SUCH AS THE SOCHCROFT COMMISSION OR THE TOWER COMMISSION TO BUILD AGENDAS, EVALUATE MAJOR BLUNDERS, RESOLVE DEADLOCKS, AND SOMETIMES OPERATE LIKE REGULAR AGENCIES. THE ARTICLE TRACES THE DEVELOPMENT OF THE THEORY OF ADHOCRACY AND OF THE USE OF AD HOC ORGANIZATIONS AND EXAMINES THE POTENTIAL DANGERS OF CONTINUED ADHERING TO A POLICY OF ADHOCRACY. IT ARGUES THAT THE GROWTH OF ADHOCRACY IS A SYMPTON OF FAILURE OF THE REGULAR GOVERNMENT AND PRESENTS DANGERS OF INADEQUACY, LACK OF ACCOUNTABILITY, AND THREATS TO DEMOCRACY.

07810 ROUSE, J.W.; HARVEY, B. III
PUBLIC-PRIVATE PARTNERSHIPS
BUREAUCRAT, 18(3) (FAL 89), 30-32.
AS FEDERAL SPENDING FOR HOUSING HAS DECLINED, A NUMBER OF OTHER ACTORS (STATE AND LOCAL GOVERNMENTS, PRIVATE-SECTOR GROUPS, AND NONPROFIT INSTITUTIONS) HAVE STEPPED UP THEIR INVOLVEMENT. ALTHOUGH THEIR RESOURCES AREN'T ADEQUATE TO THE TASK OF SHELTERING ALL THE HOMELESS OR HOUSING ALL THOSE PRICED OUT OF THE MARKET, THEIR WORK HAS SUGGESTED THE KINDS OF PUBLIC-PRIVATE PARTNERSHIPS THAT MIGHT BE MOST EFFECTIVE AT CREATING MORE AFFORDABLE HOUSING IN THE FUTURE.

07811 ROUYER, A.R.
THE EFFECTS OF POLITICAL STRUCTURE ON FERTILITY IN POOR COUNTRIES
SCANDINAVIAN JOURNAL OF DEVELOPMENT ALTERNATIVES, 8(3) (SEP 89), 19-36.
THIS ARTICLE EXAMINES THE EFFECTS OF STATE AUTONOMY, REGIME TYPE, AND THE CAPACITY OF GOVERNMENTS ON THE FORMULATION AND IMPLEMENTATION OF SOCIAL DEVELOPMENT AND FAMILY PLANNING POLICIES WHICH IN TURN AFFECT PATTERNS OF FERTILITY BEHAVIOR IN POOR THIRD WORLD COUNTRIES. THE ARTICLE EXAMINE THE "STATE-CENTERED" APPROACH AND DEFINE THE KEY CONCEPTS OF STATE AUTONOMY AND STATE CAPACITY. IN SO DOING, IT HIGHLIGHTS THE CONNECTION BETWEEN THE STRENGTH OF STATES AND EFFECTIVE SOCIAL DEVELOPMENT POLICY IN POOR COUNTRIES. SECTION TWO EXAMINES THE FERTILITY TRANSITION MODEL AND HOW IT HELPS EXPLAIN THE RELATIONSHIP OF UNDERDEVELOPMENT TO RAPID POPULATION GROWTH IN MANY THIRD WORLD COUNTRIES. IT WILL ATTEMPT TO SHOW WHY THE STATE MUST BECOME A SIGNIFICANT PLAYER IF THIS GROWTH RATE IS TO BE BROUGHT UNDER CONTROL. THE LAST SECTION OF THIS ESSAY OUTLINES THE PARAMETERS FOR A NEW FIELD OF POLITICAL DEMOGRAPHY AND SUGGEST A RESEARCH AGENDA TO BE FOLLOWED.

07812 ROWE, J.
DOWN AND OUT IN WASHINGTON ON $89,500 A YEAR
WASHINGTON MONTHLY, 21(6) (JUL 89), 12-14, 16-17.
THE RECENT PROPOSED CONGRESSIONAL PAY RAISE BROUGHT CRIES OF OUTRAGE FROM ACROSS THE US. THE AVERAGE AMERICAN WORKER, EARNING UNDER $21,000 COULDN'T UNDERSTAND WHY THE POLITICIANS COULDN'T LIVE ON FOUR TIMES THAT MUCH. HOWEVER, WHEN VIEWED IN PURELY "BELTWAY" TERMS, CONGRESSMEN ARE AT THE BOTTOM OF THE SALARY LADDER. THEY ARE SURROUNDED BY LOBBYISTS, BUSINESSMEN, AND JOURNALIST WHO MAKE FAR MORE THAN THEY DO. BRIEFLY PUT, CONGRESS ISN'T UNDERPAID, THE REST OF WASHINGTON IS OVERPAID.

07813 ROWLEY, A.
APOCALYPSE SOON
FAR EASTERN ECONOMIC REVIEW, 142(51) (DEC 89), 59.
THE ORGANIZATION FOR ECONOMIC COOPERATION AND DEVELOPMENT (OEC) HAS DECLARED THAT POPULATION PRESSURES ARE BUILDING UP TO THE POINT WHERE WORLD POPULATION COULD REACH NEARLY 15 BILLION IN THE 21ST CENTURY. THEIR CONCLUSION IS THAT "WE ARE NOT ON A COURSE TOWARDS A SUSTAINABLE CIVILIZATION." A KEY FACTOR IS THE EXTENT AND NATURE OF FOREIGN AID PROVIDED TO THE THIRD WORLD; TRADITIONAL FORMS OF AID HAVE FAILED TO ELIMINATE POVERTY AND PROVIDE BALANCED DEVELOPMENT. THE OECD EMPHASIZES THE VITAL ROLE THAT EDUCATION MUST PLAY IN RAISING POLITICAL AND SOCIAL AWARENESS AND TO MORE DEMANDS FOR DEMOCRACY AND PUBLIC ACCOUNTABILITY.

07814 ROWLEY, A.
RAISING A LOW PROFILE
FAR EASTERN ECONOMIC REVIEW, 141(27) (JUL 88), 14-15.
THE RECENT ECONOMIC SUMMIT IN TORONTO REVEALED THAT JAPAN HAS BEGUN TO SPEAK FOR A HOST OF OTHER ASIAN ANATIONS AND SEEMS TO BE ON THE ROAD TO CREATING A NEW "CO-PROSPERITY ZONE" IN THE PACIFIC REGION. WESTERN NATIONS SEEM OBLIVIOUS TO THE IMPLICATIONS FOR WORLD TRADE AND CONTINUE TO TREAT JAPAN AS AN "HONORARY WESTERNER" AND A RELATIVELY INSIGNIFICANT ONE AT THAT.

07815 ROWLEY, A.
TWO CHEERS FROM GATT
FAR EASTERN ECONOMIC REVIEW, 142(52) (DEC 89), 56.
AUSTRALIA RECEIVED A NEEDED BOOST FROM THE GENEVA-BASED GENERAL AGREEMENT ON TARIFFS AND TRADE (GATT); GATT DECLARED THAT AUSTRALIA'S LONG-TERM TRADE AND ECONOMIC PROSPECTS ARE GOOD. GATT PRAISED AUSTRALIA FOR ITS INCREASINGLY OPEN ECONOMY AND FOR ITS LIBERALIZATION OF ITS TRADE POLICIES. THE DECLARATION CAME AT A GOOD TIME FOR AUSTRALIA, WHOSE ECONOMIC POLICIES WERE COMING UNDER OUTSIDE CRITICISM AND WHOSE EXTERNAL DEBT RATING WAS BEING DOWNGRADED.

07816 ROWLEY, A.
WANING OF THE NIC'S ?
FAR EASTERN ECONOMIC REVIEW, 141(33) (AUG 88), 79.
15 YEARS AFTER THE NEWLY INDUSTRIALIZED COUNTRIES (NIC) BURST ONTO THE INTERNATIONAL TRADING SCENE, THEIR PHENOMENAL GROWTH APPEARS TO BE SLOWING SOMEWHAT. THE FOREIGN MANUFACTURING INVESTMENT THAT WAS AN IMPORTANT FACTOR IN THEIR GROWTH IS BEGINING TO RETURN TO NATIONS IN THE WEST DUE TO INCREASING LABOR COSTS AND COST-SAVING INNOVATIONS. ALL IN ALL, THE NICS WILL CONTINUE TO GROW, BUT AT A SLOWER RATE AS THE WEST REGAINS THE COMPETETIVE EDGE.

07817 ROWNY, E.L.
NEGOTIATING WITH THE SOVIET UNION: THEN AND NOW
DEPARTMENT OF STATE BULLETIN (US FOREIGN POLICY), 88(2138) (SEP 88), 26-28.
AMBASSADOR EDWARD ROWNY DISCUSSES THE "NEW JUNTURE" IN US-SOVIET RELATIONS AND GIVES SUGGESTIONS TO FUTURE NEGOTIATORS WHO WILL DEAL WITH THE USSR. HE CAUTIONS THAT GLASNOST IS NOT ANALOGOUS TO THE FIRST AMMENDMENT AND DEMOCRATIZATION DOES NOT MEAN THE SAME THING IN THE USSR AS IT DOES IN THE WEST. HE POINTS OUT THAT TO THE SOVIETS, FORM IS SUBSTANCE AND THAT THE SOVIETS ARE CONCERNED WITH DENYING THE US THE IMAGE OF AN ENEMY. ALL IN ALL, THE ADVENT OF MIKHAIL GORBACHEV AND HOS FAR-REACHING REFORMS SHOULD BE VIEWED WITH GUARDED OPTOMISM, NOT UNCONDITIONAL ACCEPTANCE.

07818 ROWNY, E.L.
SDI:ENCHANCING SECURITY AND STABILITY
DEPARTMENT OF STATE BULLETIN (US FOREIGN POLICY), 88(2134) (MAY 88), 24-26.
AMBASSADOR EDWARD ROWNY DISCUSSES THE IMPORTANCE OF STRATEGIC DEFENSES, NOTABLY THE SDI. HE DEMONSTRATES THE IMPORTANCE OF INHIBITING SOVIET FIRST-STRIKE PLANNING AND ENCOURAGING A COOPERATIVE TRANSITION TO DEFENSE. HE ARGUES THAT THE SOVIET RHETORIC WHICH BRANDS SDI AS BEING "DESTABILIZING" IS NOT IN KEEPING WITH SOVIET ACTIONS, AMONG WHICH IS THE SPENDING OF SOME $20 BILLION ANNUALLY ON A STRATEGIC DEFENSE PROGRAM OF THEIR OWN. HE ADVOCATES SDI AS A WAY TO AVOID BOTH THE CHANCES AND THREAT OF WAR.

07819 ROY, A.
WHEN THE GREEN REVOLUTION FAILS TO REACH ITS GOAL
WORLD MARXIST REVIEW, 31(12) (DEC 88), 103-107.
THE ADOPTION OF NEW TECHNOLOGIES IN A NUMBER OF AREAS OF
BANGLADESH HAS LED TO AN INCREASE IN PRODUCTION AND INCOME
WHICH IS REAPED MORE BY THE RICH FARMERS, AND ITS ALSO
EXPANDS THE SCOPE OF EMPLOYMENT FOR THE LANDLESS OR NEAR-
LANDLESS IN AGRICULTURE. BUT THE TOTAL EFFECT OF THE CHANGES
BROUGHT ON BY THE GREEN REVOLUTION IS A STILL GREATER
DIFFERENTIATION AMONG THE PEASANTRY, MORE WEALTH FOR THE
PARASITISING SECTIONS AND DEEPER POVERTY FOR THE WORKING
PEOPLE. THE CAPITALIST WAY FOR WHICH EFFORTS HAVE BEEN MADE
DURING THE PAST TWENTY YEARS OR MORE WILL NOT BE ABLE TO
SOLVE THE PROBLEMS OF RURAL BANGLADESH OR FEED THE PEOPLE.
LIMITATIONS OF THE CAPITALIST WAY HAVE BEEN EXPRESSED. WHAT
BANGLADESH NEEDS IS A SOCIAL TRANSFORMATION ORIENTED TOWARDS
SOCIALISM. THE MORE THIS TRANSFORMATION WILL BE DELAYED, THE
MORE PROLONGED WILL BE THE PERPETUATION OF PRESENT
BACKWARDNESS AND THE EVER INCREASING POVERTY OF THE MASSES.

07820 ROY, B.
BALRAM JAKHAR: FODDER FOR CONTROVERSY
INDIA TODAY, XIV(10) (MAY 89), 22-23.
A REPORT ON ALLEGED IRREGULARITIES IN THE IMPORT OF 50
FODDER - MAKING MACHINES BY THE BOMBAY-BASED SANJEEVANI
FODDER PRODUCTIONS HAS EMBROILED TOK SABHA SPEAKER BALRAM
JAKHAR IN CHARGES OF AIDING AND ABETTING CUSTOMS DUTY
EVASION. IN AN ELECTION YEAR, JAKHAR'S DISCOMFITURE IS NOT
GOING TO BE EASY TO DIGEST FOR THE CONGRESS (I).

07821 ROY, B.; AHMED, F.
CAUGHT IN A BIND
INDIA TODAY, (JUL 89), 31-32.
THIS ARTICLE REPORTS ON THE PRESENT POLITICAL SITUATION
IN INDIA AS COMMUNIST PARTIES FIND THEMSELVES IN A BIND,
WHERE THEY PONDER THEIR OPTIONS AS PRESIDENT JANATA DAL AND
BJP BEGIN TALKS, IT EXPLORES THE RAMIFICATIONS OF AN
ADJUSTMENT OF SEATS WITH THE BJB FOR THE COMMUNIST PARTY.

07822 ROY, D.
DEVELOPMENT POLICY AND LABOR MIGRATION IN THE SUDAN
MIDDLE EASTERN STUDIES, 25(3) (JUL 89), 301-322.
THE ARTICLE FOCUSES ON LABOR MIGRATION FROM SUDAN TO
OTHER NATIONS. IT EXAMINES THE DEMOGRAPHY OF THE FLEEING
MASSES AS WELL AS THE UNDERLYING CAUSES OF THE MIGRATION.
BOTH PUSH FACTORS--A HIGH RATE OF INTERNAL INFLATION,
REDUCED CIVIL SERVICE BENEFITS AND PRIVILEGES AND THE
DISENCHANTMENT OF PROFESSIONAL ELITES WITH THE POLICIES OF
AN INEPT GOVERNMENT--AND PULL FACTORS--A TREMENDOUS INCREASE
OF VERY LUCRATIVE EXTERNAL EMPLOYMENT OPPORTUNITIES ARE
CONSIDERED RESPONSIBLE FOR THE MIGRATION. IN ADDITION,
DROUGHT, FAMINE, AND CIVIL WAR COMPOUNDED THE PROBLEM.

07823 ROY, D.
INDOCTRINATION VERSUS INFORMATION: CHINESE NEWS COVERAGE
OF POLAND, 1980-83
ASIAN PROFILE, 17(1) (FEB 89), 15-24.
THIS PAPER STUDIES CHINESE NEWS COVERAGE OF EVENTS IN
POLAND, FOCUSING ON THE CHANGE IN CHINESE ATTITUDES TOWARD
POLISH LABOR. WHEN POLISH WORKERS WENT ON STRIKE IN THE
SUMMER OF 1980, THE CHINESE NEWS MEDIA SUPPORTED THEIR CAUSE.
YET LESS THAN THREE YEARS LATER, THE SAME MEDIA CONDEMNED
THE SOLIDARITY UNION AND EXPRESSED COMPLETE SUPPORT FOR THE
WARSAW REGIME'S POLICIES FOR BRINGING THE DISCONTENTED
WORKERS UNDER CONTROL. THE EXPLAANATION FOR THIS REVERSAL IS
FOUND IN THE DYNAMIC RELATIONSHIP BETWEEN UNFOLDING EVENTS
AND THE INTERPRETIVE FRAMEWORKS DESIGNED TO EXPLAIN THEM.

07824 ROY, D.A.; IRELAN, W. T.
LAW AND ECONOMICS IN THE EVOLUTION OF CONTEMPORARY EGYPT
MIDDLE EASTERN STUDIES, 25(2) (APR 89), 163-185.
THE RELATIONSHIP BETWEEN LAW AND ECONOMICS IS AN
INTIMATE ONE IN ALL SOCIETIES. IN MODERN EGYPT RADICAL
CHANGES IN ECONOMIC POLICY HAVE OCCASIONED SIMILAR CHANGES
IN THE LEGAL SYSTEM AND VICE VERSA. UNDER THE STATIST
ECONOMIC POLICIES OF NASSER, THE INDEPENDENT LEGAL SYSTEM
HAS NEARLY DESTROYED. SADAT'S RETURN TO A RULE OF LAW
PRESAGED LIBERAL ECONOMIC REFORM. IN THIS ARTICLE, THE
EVOLUTION, AND TO A LESSER EXTENT THE INTERACTION, OF LAW
AND ECONOMICS IN EGYPT FROM THE TIME OF THE REVOLUTION OF
1952 IS GENERALLY EXAMINED AND ANALYSED.

07825 ROY, O.
AFGHANISTAN: BACK TO TRIBALISM OR ON TO LEBANON?
THIRD WORLD QUARTERLY, 11(4) (OCT 89), 70-82.
NOW THAT THE SOVIET TROOPS HAVE WITHDRAWN FROM
AFGHANISTAN, THE DOMESTIC AND REGIONAL FACTORS ARE SLOWLY
OVERSHADOWING THE EAST-WEST IDEOLOGICAL DIMENSION OF THE WAR.
BUT THE CURRENT FIGHTING DOES NOT DEMONSTRATE A SIMPLE
RETURN TO THE TRADITIONAL PRE-WAR TRIBAL RIVALRIES. THE
IDEOLOGICAL DIMENSION, ALTHOUGH IT HAS DIMINISHED, HAS NOT
DISAPPEARED; IT WILL REMAIN AS LONG AS NAJIBULLAH IS IN
CHARGE IN KABUL. THE WAR HAS POLITICIZED TRADITIONAL SOCIETY;
THERE ARE NOW POLITICAL PARTIES INSIDE AFGHANISTAN AND THEY

EXPRESS, TO A CERTAIN EXTENT, TRADITIONAL SEGMENTATION. THE
CONFLICT HAS ALSO PRODUCED NEW LEADERSHIP, WHICH IS ALTERING
THE SECULAR TRIBAL STRUCTURES, AND ETHNIC IDENTITIES HAVE
BEEN RESHAPED BY THE WAR. WHATEVER HAPPENS, THE FUTURE
AFGHANISTAN WILL DIFFER FROM THE OLD.

07826 ROY, S.
M.N. ROY AND CHINA: A TESTING GROUND FOR GLOBAL REVOLUTION
CHINA REPORT, 24(4) (OCT 88), 395-403.
IN ORDER TO PROMOTE REVOLUTION IN THE UNDERDEVELOPED
WORLD, ROY PROPOSED FIRST, THAT IT SHOULD BE BASED ON A
PROGRAMME OF AGRARIAN REFORMS, AND SECOND, THAT IT SHOULD BE
LED BY THE COMMUNIST PARTIES AS THE MILITANT REVOLUTIONARY
VANGUARD OF THE NATIONAL LIBERATION MOVEMENT. THIS ARTICLE
EXAMINES THE "CORRECTNESS" OF ROY'S CONCEPT AND CONCLUDES
THAT, AS WITH ANY OTHER THEORIST OF COMMUNISM, EVENT PROVED
ROY ONLY PARTIALLY CORRECT.

07827 ROZEK, S.
THE FIRST DAUGHTER OF THE LAND: ALICE ROOSEVELT AS
PRESIDENTIAL CELEBRITY, 1902-1906
PRESIDENTIAL STUDIES QUARTERLY, XIX(1) (WIN 89), 51-70.
THE POPULAR OBSESSION WITH THE ODORE ROOSEVELT SPILLED
OVER INTO A RELATED FASCINATION WITH THE PRESIDENT'S FAMILY.
IT WAS THE PRESIDENT'S DAUGHTER BY HIS FIRST MARRIAGE, ALICE
LEE ROOSEVELT, WHO DOMINATED THE HEADLINES UNTIL HER WEDDING
TO CONGRESSMAN NICHOLAS LONGWORTH IN 1906. PRESIDENT
ROOSEVELT FOUND HIS DAUGHTER BOTH A DISTRACTION AND A
POLITICAL ASSET. THEIR RELATIONSHIP OFFERS AN INSIGHTFUL
PERSPECTIVE ON THEODORE ROOSEVELT'S CHARACTER. THE ARTICLE'S
EXAMINATION OF ALICE ROOSEVELT ALSO UNDERSCORES THE ANALYTIC
POSSIBILITIES OF THE STUDY OF PRESIDENTS AS PARENTS

07828 RUBANOV, V.
FROM THE "CULT OF SECRECY" TO THE INFORMATION CULTURE
SOVIET REVIEW, 30(5) (SEP 89), 18-35.
THE VIEW OF INFORMATION AS BOTH A MEDIUM AND AN OBJECT
OF POLITICAL CONTROL SERVES AS A GUIDE FOR IDENTIFYING
SOVIET SOCIETY'S VITAL NEEDS FOR KNOWLEDGE AND FOR
DETERMINING THE POTENTIAL OF STATE ORGANS AND SOCIAL
INSTITUTIONS TO SATISFY THESE NEEDS IN ACCORDANCE WITH THE
GOALS OF SOCIALIST MODERNIZATION AND DEVELOPMENT. THUS, THE
POINT AT ISSUE IS THE DEVELOPMENT OF A UNIFORM
ORGANIZATIONAL-LEGAL MECHANISM FOR CONTROLLING INFORMATION
PROCESSES. THIS MECHANISM MUST OVERCOME THE FACTORS THAT
INHIBIT THE DEVELOPMENT OF GLASNOST AND THE WIDESPREAD
PROVISION OF INFORMATION TO SOCIETY, MUST INTENSIFY
PROGRESSIVE TRANSFORMATIONS OF SOCIAL CONSCIOUSNESS, MUST
CREATE FAVORABLE CONDITIONS FOR DEMOCRATIZATION, AND MUST
ACTIVELY PROMOTE NEW POLITICAL THOUGHT IN INTERNATIONAL
AFFAIRS.

07829 RUBENSTEIN, E.
DIVIDENDS OF PEACE
NATIONAL REVIEW, 61(25) (DEC 89), 20.
THIS ARTICLE EXPLORES DEFENSE SPENDING WHICH HAS BEEN
DECLINING FOR MORE THAN A QUARTER OF A CENTURY. IT CLAIMS
THAT THIS DECLINE DID NOT PREVENT THE ONSET OF HIGHER
INFLATION AND CHRONICALLY POOR ECONOMIC PERFORMANCE. IT
EXAMINES 16 STATES THAT RECEIVE MORE IN MILITARY SPENDING
THAN THEY CONTRIBUTE TO THE DEFENSE BUDGET IN TAXES. IT
SUGGESTS THAT A SHARP CUTBACK WOULD HAVE OMINOUS ECONOMIC
IMPLICATIONS.

07830 RUBENSTEIN, E.
THE ECONOMIC WALL
NATIONAL REVIEW, 61(24) (DEC 89), 22.
THE WRITER CONSIDERS WHAT ECONOMIC DIFFERENCE A WALL
MAKES. HE COMPARES THE TWO SYSTEMS OF EAST AND WEST GERMANY,
PLUS THE INTERNATIONAL TRADE DATA INFLATION, THE BUDGET
DEFICIT AND GNP OF EAST GERMANY IS EXPLORED, AND A
COMPARISON IS MADE OF EAST GERMANY AND OTHER COUNTRIES AT
EASTERN EUROPE.

07831 RUBENSTEIN, E.
THE PRIVATIZATION POTENTIAL
NATIONAL REVIEW, 110(21) (NOV 89), 24.
THIS BRIEF REPORT ON THE GLOBAL TREND TOWARD
PRIVATIZATION AND THE FACT THAT THE U.S. IS VIRTUALLY ALONE
IN HAVING NO SERIOUS NATIONAL COMMITMENT TO PRIVATIZATION.
PRIVATIZATION POSSIBILITIES WHICH INCLUDE NAVAL PETROLEUM
RESERVES, SPECTRUM LICENSE FEES, HELIUM PROCESSING, AND
ALASKA POWER ADMINISTRATION ARE DETAILED AS WELL AS THE
OBSTACLES THESE INITIATIVES MAY FACE.

07832 RUBENSTEIN, E.
THE RISING TIDE
NATIONAL REVIEW, 61(23) (DEC 89), 20.
THIS ARTICLE EXAMINES CENSUS BUREAU DATA FOR 1988 THAT
SHOWS THAT THE NUMBER OF POOR PERSONS IS LOWER THAN IT HAS
BEEN SINCE 1981. THE WASHINGTON POST DEFINED THE REPORT AS
"BAD NEWS" BUT THIS ARTICLE TAKES EXCEPTION TO THAT ANALYSIS.
THE RICH ARE GETTING RICHER, BUT RUBENSTEIN DEMONSTRATES
THAT THE POOR ABE ALSO.

07833 RUBIN, A.A.
THE CASE FOR PRIVATE DIPLOMACY
FLETCHER FORUM, 13(1) (WIN 89), 25-30.
THE PUBLIC CONDUCT OF INTRASTATE RELATIONS OFTEN
OBSCURES THE MULTITUDE OF NONGOVERNMENTAL INTERNATIONAL
CONTACTS. THESE EXCHANGES SERVE AMERICAN NATIONAL INTEREST
BY FOSTERING UNDERSTANDING AT HOME AND ABROAD. ALAN RUBIN
SUGGESTS THAT GREATER COORDINATION OF PRIVATE DIPLOMACY,
ESPECIALLY AT THE STATE LEVEL, WILL HEIGHTEN AMERICAN WORLD
PERFORMANCE. THE NEW ADMINISTRATION SHOULD SEIZE THE
OPPORTUNITY TO IMPROVE PRIVATE DIPLOMATIC EFFORTS.

07834 RUBIN, B.
KOOR: ISRAEL'S ECONOMIC CRISIS OF FAITH
MIDSTREAM, XXXV(8) (NOV 89), 3-8.
KOOR, ISRAEL'S LARGEST INDUSTRIAL CONGLOMERATE AND A
CORNERSTONE OF THE "WORKERS' ECONOMY," TEETERS ON THE VERGE
OF BANKRUPTCY. THE IDEOLOGICAL AND SOCIOPOLITICAL
SIGNIFICANCE OF KOOR'S INSOLVENCY IS GREAT BECAUSE KOOR IS
THE INCARNATION OF ISRAEL'S ORTHODOX SOCIALIST IDEOLOGY.
KOOR PROVIDES THE NON-COMMUNIST WORLD'S ONLY EXAMPLE OF A
GIGANTIC ECONOMIC EMPIRE CONTROLLED BY A POLITICAL PARTY.

07835 RUBIN, B.R.
AFGHANISTAN: "BACK TO FEUDALISM"
CURRENT HISTORY, 88(542) (DEC 89), 421-424, 444-446.
NEITHER AFGHAN PRESIDENT NAJIBULLAH NOR THE MUJAHIDEEN
LEADERS HAVE SUFFICIENT LEGITIMACY TO RE-ESTABLISH EVEN THE
WEAK STATE STRUCTURE AFGHANISTAN HAD DEVELOPED BEFORE 1978.
AS LONG AS THE USSR, THE USA, PAKISTAN, SAUDI ARABIA, AND
IRAN ALL BACK THEIR CLIENTS, AFGHANISTAN WILL REMAIN A
FRAGEMENTED SOCIETY WITH FOREIGN-SUPPLIED FIREPOWER.

07836 RUBIN, B.R.
AFGHANISTAN: THE NEXT ROUND
ORBIS, 33(1) (WIN 89), 57-72.
THE ACCORDS ON AFGHANISTAN, SIGNED IN GENEVA ON APRIL 14,
1988, HAVE AT BEST BEGUN, NOT ENDED, THE RESOLUTION OF THAT
COUNTRY'S CONFLICT. IT IS NOT ONLY THAT THE DEPARTURE OF ALL
UNIFORMED SOVIET TROOPS REMAINS INCOMPLETE AND UNCERTAIN. IT
IS, FAR MORE IMPORTANT, THAT A CIVIL WAR RAGES ON, AND
MILLIONS OF AFGHAN REFUGEES STILL CANNOT RETURN HOME TO
REBUILD THEIR LAND AND THEIR LIVES. WHAT THE APRIL ACCORDS
DID NOT ATTEMPT TO ACHIEVE DIRECTLY WAS INTERNAL PEACE. THAT
IS THE NEXT STEP. AND IT WILL COME TO AFGHANISTAN ONLY WITH
THE ESTABLISHMENT OF A BROAD-BASED GOVERNMENT ENJOYING BOTH
GENERAL DOMESTIC SUPPORT AND GOOD RELATIONS WITH ITS
NEIGHBORS.

07837 RUBIN, B.R.
THE FRAGMENTATION OF AFGHANISTAN
FOREIGN AFFAIRS, 68(5) (WIN 90), 150-168.
THE WITHDRAWAL OF SOVIET FORCES FROM AFGHANISTAN HAS
REVEALED THAT THE CRISIS THERE WAS NOT ONLY ONE OF FOREIGN
INTERVENTION BUT ALSO OF THE BREAKDOWN AND FRAGMENTATION OF
THE STATE. HAVING SACRIFICED MORE THAN A MILLION LIVES, THE
PEOPLE OF AFGHANISTAN FACE THE UNHAPPY ALTERNATIVES OF A
GOVERNMENT THEY REJECT AND A RESISTANCE THEY FEAR.

07838 RUBIN, C.T.
ENVIRONMENTAL POLICY AND ENVIRONMENTAL THOUGHT: COMMONER
AND RUCKELSHAUS
ENVIRONMENTAL ETHICS, 11(1) (SPR 89), 27-52.
BARRY COMMONER IS ACKNOWLEDGED AS BEING A "FOUNDING
FATHER" OF ENVIRONMENTALISM. COMMONER'S VIEWS ON TECHNOLOGY
AND ITS ROLE WITH REGARDS TO THE ENVIRONMENT HAVE HAD A
GREAT EFFECT ON PRINCIPLES AND POLICIES OF CURRENT
ENVIRONMENTALISTS INCLUDING TWO-TIME EPA DIRECTOR WILLIAM
RUCKELSHAUS. THE ARTICLE EXAMINES COMMONER'S VIEWS AND
CONCLUDES THAT THEY OFTEN DEPEND ON A UTOPIAN VISION OF
TECHNOLOGY THAT IS NOT COMPATIBLE WITH LIBERALISM AND
CAPITALISM. THIS THINKING, OFTEN STILL PREVALENT TODAY, HAS
HAMPERED MANY EFFORTS TO SERIOUSLY CONSIDER ENVIRONMENTAL
ISSUES.

07839 RUBIN, D.
IDEOLOGY AND NATIONAL OPPRESSION
POLITICAL AFFAIRS, LXVIII(9-10) (SEP 89), 10-14.
THE ARTICLE EXAMINES THE IDEOLOGICAL BACKGROUND OF THE
CURRENT OPPRESSION OF NATIONAL AND ETHNIC GROUPS IN THE US.
THE AUTHORS ARGUE THAT ONE IN EVERY FOUR PEOPLE IN THE US IS
NATIONALLY OPPRESSED; THEY IDENTIFY CAPITALISM AND THE CLASS
INTERESTS OF THE MONOPOLY CAPITALISTS AS THE ROOT CAUSE OF
THIS INEQUALITY. THEY OUTLINE MULTI-LEVEL STRATEGIES FOR THE
COMMUNIST PARTY USA TO ATTACK THIS DISCRIMINATION.

07840 RUBIN, D.M.
INF INSPECTIONS: U.S. AND U.S.S.R. QUIETLY LIMIT PRESS
ACCESS
DEADLINE, 3(5) (SEP 88), 3-4, 10.
THIS ARTICLE EXPLORES AN IRONIC BY-PRODUCT OF THE INF
TREATY WHICH IS THAT THE US AND USSR HAVE TEAMED UP TO KEEP
THEIR RESPECTIVE PUBLICS UNINFORMED ABOUT THE DETAILS OF THE
INSPECTIONS. IT DETAILS THE SITUATION AND CONCLUDES THAT IF
JOURNALISTS CAN DEVELOP SOURCES BEYOND OSIA, AS WELL AS
RESIST THE VIEW THAT ONLY A POTENTIAL SUPER-POWER CONFLICT
OVER VERIFICATION IS NEWS, THEN A REAL CONTRIBUTION TO
PUBLIC EDUCATION IS POSSIBLE.

07841 RUBIN, H.J.
SYMBOLISM AND ECONOMIC DEVELOPMENT WORK: PERCEPTIONS OF
URBAN ECONOMIC DEVELOPMENT PRACTITIONERS
AMERICAN REVIEW OF PUBLIC ADMINISTRATION, 19(3) (SEP 89),
233-248.
TO ELABORATE THEMES SUGGESTED BY EDELMAN'S MODEL OF
SYMBOLIC POLITICS, DATA FROM A NATIONAL SURVEY OF ECONOMIC
DEVELOPMENT PRACTITIONERS ARE EXAMINED. IN RESPONSE TO THE
UNCERTAINTY OF MUNICIPAL ECONOMIC DEVELOPMENT EFFORTS,
ECONOMIC DEVELOPMENT PRACTITIONERS CLAIM THEY UNDERTAKE
FORMALISTIC ACTIVITIES AND INDICATE THAT CITY LEADERS
ENCOURAGE SYMBOLIC ECONOMIC DEVELOPMENT PROJECTS. CONCERNS
WITH FORMALISM AND SYMBOLISM ARE MOST PREVALENT AMONG THOSE
ECONOMIC DEVELOPMENT PRACTITIONERS WHO WORK IN CITIES WITH A
LARGER NUMBER OF ECONOMIC PROBLEMS, THOSE WHO FEEL THEIR OWN
TASK IS HARD TO DEFINE, AND AMONG THOSE FEELING MOST
PRESSURED BY LOCAL POLITICIANS OR ECONOMIC DEVELOPMENT
BOARDS TO "DO SOMETHING." IMPLICATIONS OF SYMBOLIC EFFORTS
FOR THE PRACTICE OF ECONOMIC DEVELOPMENT ARE EXAMINED.

07842 RUBIN, I. S.
MUNICIPAL ENTERPRISES: EXPLORING BUDGETARY AND POLITICAL
IMPLICATIONS
PUBLIC ADMINISTRATION REVIEW, 48(1) (JAN 88), 542-550.
THIS PAPER EXPLORES THE POLITICAL IMPLICATIONS OF THE
USE OF PUBLIC ENTERPRISES AT THE MUNICIPAL LEVEL, IT
PROVIDES A PRELIMINARY LOOK AT HOW MUNCIPALITIES ARE USING
PUBLIC ENTERPRISES. ITS AIMS ARE TO SKETCH AND ANALYSE
PRACTICES IN ILLINOIS AND TO OFFER SOME PROMISING AVENUES
FOR RESEARCH.

07843 RUBIN, J.
START FINISH
FOREIGN POLICY, (76) (FAL 89), 96-118.
THIS ARTICLE CONTENDS THAT THE RELUCTANCE OF THE BUSH
ADMINISTRATION TO ENGAGE IN "START" (STRATEGIC ARMS
REDUCTION TALKS) IS UNJUSTIFIED. EXAMINED IS THE STATUS QUO
OF STRATEGIC NUCLEAR WEAPONS AND EFFORTS SINCE PRESIDENT
JOHNSON TO CONTROL THEM. CLAIMS BY CRITICS OF "START" ARE
ANSWERED AND ENDGAME COMPROMISES ARE OFFERED. OPTIONS FOR
VERIFICATION ARE GIVEN.

07844 RUBLACK, S.
CONTROLLING TRANSBOUNDARY MOVEMENTS OF HAZARDOUS WASTE:
THE EVOLUTION OF A GLOBAL CONVENTION
FLETCHER FORUM, 13(1) (WIN 89), 113-125.
THE DISPOSAL AND MANAGEMENT OF HAZARDOUS WASTE IS ONE OF
THE WORLD'S MOST PROBLEMATIC ISSUES. SHIPMENT OF HAZARDOUS
WASTE BETWEEN OECD COUNTRIES IS EXTENSIVE AND HAS BEEN GOING
ON FOR YEARS. UNTIL RECENTLY, HOWEVER LITTLE HAS BEEN KNOWN
ABOUT HAZARDOUS WASTE SHIPMENTS FROM THE INDUSTRIALIZED
NORTH TO THE LESS DEVELOPED SOUTH. SOME THIRD WORLD LEADERS
POINT TO THE LACK OF BINDING INTERNATIONAL LAW, CALLING THE
ISSUE "TOXIC TERRORISM" AND "GARBAGE IMPERIALISM." IN THIS
ARTICLE THE AUTHOR SUMMARIZES INTERNATIONAL REGULATORY
EFFORTS TO CONTROL SUCH MOVEMENTS AND TRACES THE EVOLUTION
OF AN UPCOMING UN-SPONSORED INTERNATIONAL CONVENTION ON
TRANSFRONTIER SHIPMENT OF HAZARDOUS WASTE.

07845 RUDD, C.
NEWSPAPER COVERAGE OF THE NEW ZEALAND 1987 GENERAL ELECTION
POLITICAL SCIENCE, 41(1) (JUL 89), 35-47.
THE AUTHOR EXAMINES THE ROLE NEWSPAPER COVERAGE PLAYED
IN FORMING PUBLIC OPINION AND INFLUENCING VOTING IN THE 1987
GENERAL ELECTION IN NEW ZEALAND.

07846 RUETHER, R.R.
THE CHRISTIAN CHURCHES AND THE INTIFADA
AMERICAN-ARAB AFFAIRS, (30) (FAL 89), 72-76.
THIS ARTICLE BRIEFLY SUMMARIZES THE POSITION OF KEY
CHRISTIAN GROUPS AND THEN SUGGESTS SOME DIRECTIONS THAT
CHRISTIAN LEADERSHIP SHOULD GO TO GIVE TO THE INTIFADA
QUESTION A TOP PRIORITY ON THE EDUCATIONAL AGENDA OF THE
CHURCHES. IT CONCLUDES THAT THE CHRISTIAN CHURCHES HAVE
ENORMOUS POTENTIAL FOR SHAPING AND MOBILIZING PUBLIC OPINION
AND THAT THEY HAVE YET TO MAKE USE OF THIS POWER ON BEHALF
OF JUSTICE FOR THE PALESTINIANS.

07847 RUETHER, R.R.
TO PRESERVE AND PROTECT DEMOCRACY
SOJOURNERS, 18(2) (FEB 89), 19.
THE AUTHOR ADVOCATES MAJOR REFORM FOR THE AMERICAN
POLITICAL SYSTEM. SHE COMPARES THE US ELECTORAL PROCESS TO
THAT OF CUBA, WHICH EMPHASIZES GRASSROOTS POLITICAL
PARTICIPATION. SHE BELIEVES GREATER EMPHASIS SHOULD BE
PLACED ON PARTY PLATFORMS.

07848 RUGUMAMU, S. M.
STATE REGULATION OF FOREIGN INVESTMENT: A CASE OF TANZANIA, 1961-1985
DISSERTATION ABSTRACTS INTERNATIONAL, 49(8) (FEB 89), 2384-A.
TANZANIA HAS EXPERIENCED A CONTRADICTION BETWEEN THE INCREASINGLY INTERNATIONAL NATURE OF CAPITAL AND THE CONTINUING NATIONAL BASIS OF THE STATE. THE CONFLICTING PRESSURES HAVE LED TO STATE POLICY RESPONSES THAT HAVE BEEN GENERALLY CONTRADICTORY TOWARD FOREIGN INVESTMENT. A LOOSELY CONSOLIDATED RULING CLASS AND FRAGILE SUPPORTING STATE INSTITUTIONS HAVE BEEN LARGELY THE CAUSE OF TANZANIA'S POOR PERFORMANCE RECORD.

07849 RUHALA, K.
PROSPECTS FOR CONVENTIONAL ARMS REDUCTION AND CONFIDENCE- AND SECURITY-BUILDING MEASURES IN EUROPE
DISARMAMENT, XII(2) (SUM 89), 60-69.
THE VIENNA CSCE FOLLOW-UP MEETING ESTABLISHED TWO NEGOTIATING PROCESSES: ONE FOR REDUCING CONVENTIONAL ARMED FORCES IN EUROPE AND ONE FOR CONFIDENCE- AND SECURITY- BUILDING MEASURES. IN THIS ARTICLE, THE AUTHOR DISCUSSES THE PROSPECTS FOR ARMS LIMITATION AND CSBM'S BY EXAMINING SOME OF THE ISSUES LIKELY TO BE RAISED IN EACH OF THE TWO FORUMS.

07850 RUHLE, H.
NATO STRATEGY: BACK TO BASICS
CURRENT, (312) (MAY 89), 34.
NATO URGENTLY NEEDS TO RETHINK ITS STRATEGY, IN THE BROADEST MEANING OF THAT TERM. IN ORDER TO MUSTER SUCH A RETHINKING, LET ALONE TO BID FOR PUBLIC UNDERSTANDING AND SUPPORT OF THE COMMON DEFENSE, THE ALLIANCE MUST RETURN TO A CONSIDERATION OF THE MOST BASIC ELEMENTS OF ITS STRATEGY.

07851 RUICHANG, L.
SUMMIT PLANS NICARAGUAN PEACE
BEIJING REVIEW, 32(10) (MAR 89), 14-16.
THE FOURTH CENTRAL AMERICAN SUMMIT MEETING WAS HELD IN FEBRUARY 1989 IN A BID TO PROMOTE PEACE IN THE REGION. THE MEETING REACHED AN AGREEMENT ON NICARAGUA THAT CALLS FOR GENERAL ELECTIONS IN 1990, EXPANDED DEMOCRACY, AMNESTY FOR ALL POLITICAL PRISONERS, AND FREEDOM OF THE PRESS.

07852 RUIZ, G.
THE IDEOLOGICAL CONVERGENCE OF THEODORE ROOSEVELT AND WOODROW WILSON
PRESIDENTIAL STUDIES QUARTERLY, XIX(1) (WIN 89), 159-178.
THEODORE ROOSEVELT AND WOODROW WILSON, THE TWO EXPOSITORS OF PROGRESSIVISM IN THE EXECUTIVE BRANCH OF THE UNITED STATES GOVERNMENT, TRAVELLED REMARKABLY DIFFERENT PATHS IN ARRIVING AT A COMMON CONCEPTION OF SOCIETAL ILLS AND THE APPROPRIATE WAY TO REMEDY THOSE ILLS. ON THE ONE HAND, THEODORE ROOSEVELT WAS CONSISTENT IN HIS LIFELONG ATTACHMENT TO A LIBERAL POLITICAL PHILOSOPHY. CONVERSELY, WOODROW WILSON EVENTUALLY MOVED FROM BEING A STATES'-RIGHTS CONSERVATIVE TO BECOMING A PROPONENT OF ROOSEVELTIAN ECONOMIC PROGRESSIVISM. THE GREATER PURPOSE OF THIS PAPER IS TO EXAMINE AND ANALYZE THE EVOLUTION OF WOODROW WILSON'S POLITICAL THOUGHT. IN THE COURSE OF THIS STUDY, TWO COMPONENTS OF AN EXPLANATION ARE POSTULATED FOR THE RADICAL CHANGE IN HIS IDEOLOGY, ONE HAVING TO DO WITH THE INTRINSIC NATURE OF THE PROBLEMS CONFRONTING THE UNITED STATES IN THE EARLY TWENTIETH CENTURY, THE OTHER RELATED TO WILSON'S DEVOTION TO AN INDIVIDUALIST ETHIC.

07853 RUMER, B.; SCHOENFELD, G.
THE PERILS OF PERESTROIKA
NEW LEADER, LXXII(12) (AUG 89), 7-9.
MIKHAIL GORBACHEV'S SWEEPING CHANGES (GLASNOST AND PERESTROIKA) ARE DESIGNED TO SAVE THE COMMUNIST SYSTEM. HOWEVER, INCREASING INTERNAL DISSENT AND VIOLENCE, AS WELL AS THE CONTINUED DECLINE OF THE ECONOMY HAS INCREASED THE RATE AND SCOPE OF CRITICISM OF THE STATE AND OF COMMUNISM ITSELF. SOVIET INTELLECTUALS HAVE ABANDONED THE LONG-HELD POLICY OF CRITICIZING ONLY STALIN AND THE "CULT OF PERSONALITY" AND HAVE MOVED TO ATTACK THE FOUNDER OF SOVIET COMMUNISM, VLADIMIR LENIN. INTERNAL DISCONTENT IS ON THE RISE AND MANY SOVIET CITIZENS HAVE FOREBODINGS OF SIGNIFICANT CRISES IN THE NEAR FUTURE.

07854 RUML, J.
WHAT IS WRONG WITH THE CZECHOSLOVAK OPPOSITION
EAST EUROPEAN REPORTER, 4(1) (WIN 89), 46-48.
THE ARTICLE EXAMINES THE ACTIVITIES OF THE CZECHOSLOVAK OPPOSITION IN 1989. IT CONCENTRATES ON THE PLANNED DEMONSTRATIONS COMMEMORATING THE ANNIVERSARY OF THE WARSAW PACT INVASION OF 1968. IT CONCLUDES THAT THE OPPOSITION GROUPS REMAIN DIVIDED AND UNSURE OF THEIR AIMS AND GOALS. A DIVIDED OPPOSITION ALLOWS THE CENTRALIZED, TOTALITARIAN GOVERNMENT TO PREY ON INDIVIDUAL WEAKNESSES IN A FRANTIC BID TO RETAIN POWER. HOWEVER, THE DEMONSTRATIONS REVEALED A RESERVE OF PERSONAL COURAGE IN MANY CITIZENS OF CZECHOSLOVAKIA.

07855 RUMLEY, D.
CONFLICT AND COMPROMISE: POLITICAL GEOGRAPHY AT THE IGU CONGRESS IN SYDNEY, AUSTRALIA, AUGUST 1988
POLITICAL GEOGRAPHY QUARTERLY, 8(2) (APR 89), 181-196.
THE ARTICLE IS A BRIEF REPORT ON THE PAPERS DELIVERED AT THE 26TH CONGRESS OF THE INTERNATIONAL GEOGRAPHICAL UNION IN SYDNEY, AUSTRALIA IN AUGUST 1988. MOST OF THE PAPERS WERE CONCERNED WITH ASPECTS OF CONFLICT AND THEIR ACTUAL OR LIKELY RESOLUTION EITHER WITHIN OR BETWEEN STATES. HOWEVER, THE SUBJECT MATTER WAS DIVERSE, RANGING FROM DISCUSSION ON ELECTORAL MATTERS, GOVERNMENT STRUCTURES AND DEFENSE TO COLONIALISM, WAR, REGIONAL CONFLICT, NATIONALISM AND THE LIKELY CAUSES OF POLITICAL CONFLICT.

07856 RUMMEL, R.
MODERNIZING TRANSATLANTIC RELATIONS: WEST EUROPEAN SECURITY COOPERATION AND THE REACTION IN THE UNITED STATES
WASHINGTON QUARTERLY, 12(4) (FAL 89), 83-92.
THIS ARTICLE EXAMINES THE TYPE OF MODERNIZATION THE WESTERN SECURITY SYSTEM NEEDS IN ORDER TO ADAPT TO THE POLITICAL DYNAMICS IN EUROPE, EAST AND WEST. IT DETAILS THE CHALLENGES IN EAST-WEST RELATIONS AND THE TRENDS IN WEST EUROPEAN INTEGRATION. IT THEN EXPLORES NATIONAL TRENDS AND FOCUSES ON THE CASE OF WEST GERMANY. THE ISOLATIONIST AND UNILATERALIST, MULTIPOLARIST, AND TRADITIONALIST APPROACHES IN THE U.S. ARE EXPLORED, AND THEN WAYS TO MODERNIZE TRANSATLANTIC RELATIONS ARE SUGGESTED.

07857 RUMMEL, R.
THE POLITICS OF COLD BLOOD
SOCIETY, 27(1) (NOV 89), 32-40.
THE AUTHOR EXAMINES THE RELATIONSHIP BETWEEN POLITICAL SYSTEMS AND COLLECTIVE VIOLENCE AND WAR. HE CONCLUDES THAT THOSE POLITICAL SYSTEMS THAT MAXIMIZE AND GUARANTEE INDIVIDUAL FREEDOMS (DEMOCRACIES) ARE LEAST VIOLENCE-PRONE; THOSE THAT MAXIMIZE THE SUBORDINATION OF ALL INDIVIDUAL BEHAVIOR (TOTALITARIAN SYSTEMS) ARE THE MOST VIOLENT. HE ACKNOWLEDGES THAT MUCH OF CURRENT POLITICAL THOUGHT IS CONTRARY TO HIS CONCLUSIONS AND ANALYZES SOME OF THE METHODOLOGICAL BLINDERS RESPONSIBLE FOR THE PREVAILING OPINION THAT SOCIALIST OR OTHER CENTRALIZED SYSTEMS ARE LESS VIOLENCE-PRONE.

07858 RUNDLE, G.
NOTES FROM THE UNDERGROWTH: THEORY AND THE GREEN MOVEMENT
ARENA, (89) (SUM 89), 55-69.
THE AUTHOR SEEKS TO ADDRESS GREEN ISSUES IN A PRACTICAL POLITICAL CONTEXT. HE BEGINS BY CRITICALLY EXAMINING TWO THEMES PROMINENT IN GREEN CIRCLES--THOSE OF THE "THIRD WAY" THESIS AND THE DEEP ECOLOGY PHILOSOPHY--AND THEIR RELATION TO MORE MATERIAL POLITICAL APPROACHES. HE ALSO OUTLINES A NUMBER OF FUNDAMENTAL PRINCIPLES ON WHICH A GREEN POLITICS MIGHT BE BASED. THESE INCLUDE: SUSTAINABILITY, HEALTH, AND THE "CULTURAL VALUE" OF NATURE. HE CONCLUDES WITH AN ANALYSIS OF SOME OF THE TENSIONS AND CONTRADICTIONS WHICH MIGHT OCCUR IN ANY ATTEMPT TO IMPLEMENT GREEN PRINCIPLES WITHIN A VARIETY OF POSSIBLE POLITICAL FORMS.

07859 RUNDQUIST, P.S.
CONGRESS AND PARLIAMENTS
CRS REVEIW, 10(3) (MAR 89), 31-32.
NATIONAL LEGISLATURES VARY WIDELY IN SIZE AND PARTISAN COMPOSITION, IN THE EXTENT OF LINKAGE BETWEEN THE EXECUTIVE AND THE LEGISLATURE, AND IN THE SCOPE OF THE LEGISLATURE'S POWER, AMONG OTHER CHARACTERISTICS. THIS ARTICLE SPOTLIGHTS THREE AREAS THAT CLEARLY HIGHLIGHT THE DIFFERENCES BETWEEN THE AMERICAN CONGRESS AND MOST PARLIAMENTS: THE POWER OF THE INDIVIDUAL MEMBER, THE POWER OF PARTIES, AND THE POWER OF BICAMERALISM.

07860 RUNYAN, A.S.
FEMINISM, PEACE, AND INTERNATIONAL POLITICS: AN EXAMINATION OF WOMEN ORGANIZING INTERNATIONALLY FOR PEACE AND SECURITY
DISSERTATION ABSTRACTS INTERNATIONAL, 49(11) (MAY 89), 3499-A.
THE AUTHOR ASSESSES FEMINIST CLAIMS ABOUT THE RELATIONSHIPS BETWEEN WOMEN AND PEACE AND MEN AND WAR AGAINST THE BACKDROP OF FEMALE ROLES IN ORGANIZING FOR PEACE AND PARTICIPATING IN WARS. SHE ARGUES THAT IT IS NECESSARY TO MOVE BEYOND BOTH ANDROCENTRIC AND GYNOCENTRIC CONSTRUCTIONS OF REALITY, WHICH ARE PRODUCTS OF PATRIARCHAL IDEOLOGIES AND RELATIONS THAT GIVE RISE TO THE DUALISTIC, POLEMICAL, AND INTRANSIGENT POLITICS OF WAR AND PEACE.

07861 RUPERT, J.
AFGANISTAN'S SLIDE TOWARD CIVIL WAR
WORLD POLICY JOURNAL, 6(4) (FAL 89), 759-786.
THE ALLIANCE PARTIES, BASED IN PESHAWAR, PAKISTAN HAVE BEEN ALMOST THE ONLY RECOGNIZABLE ORGANIZATION IN THE RESISTANCE. THIS ARTICLE SUGGESTS THAT THE KEY TO UNDERSTANDING THE AFGHAN CONFLICT--AND TO FORMULATING AN INTELLIGENT U.S. POLICY TOWARD ITIS REALIZING THAT THE ALLIANCE IS AT THE MARGIN, RATHER THAN AT THE CENTER, OF

AFGHAN POLITICS, IT EXPLORES AFGHANISTAN'S COMPLICATED JIHAD, THE CHANGING COURSE OF THE WAR, THE FAILURE OF U.S. POLICY, AND THE DILPOMATIC OPTION. IT CONCLUDES THAT THE COMPLEX AND CHANGING REALITIES OF AFGHANISTAN, AND ESPECIALLY THE RECENT TRANSFORMATION IN THE CHARACTER OF THE WAR THERE, SUGGEST THAT THE U.S. POLICY OF SEEKING A MILITARY VICTORY BY THE PESHAWAR ALLIANCE RISKS DAMAGING THE MOST IMPORTANT AMERICAN INTERESTS IN THE REGION. THE DANGER TO PAKISTAN'S FRAGILE CIVILIAN DEMOCRACY IS PARTICULARLY ACUTE, BUT NO LESS REAL ARE THE THREATS TO AFGHANISTAN'S LONG-TERM POLITICAL VIABILITY AND TO THE STABILITY OF THE REGION AS A WHOLE. CLEARLY, A FUNDAMENTAL SHIFT IN POLICY IS REQUIRED TO PROTECT THOSE INTERESTS.

07862 RUPESINGHE, K.
THE INDO-SRI LANKAN AGREEMENT 1987, AND CONFLICT RESOLUTION IN SRI LANKA
SOUTH ASIA JOURNAL, 2(3) (JAN 89), 271-294.
THE ARTICLE EXAMINES THE BACKGROUND OF THE INDO-SRI LANKAN AGREEMENT OF 1987 AND ITS FUTURE IMPLICATIONS. IT ARGUES THAT THE CONCEPT OF A UNITARY SINHALA-BUDDHIST STATE, WITH STRONG CENTRALIZATION OF POWER, AND THE SECESSIONIST DEMAND FOR "TAMIL EELAM" ARE BOTH CONTRARY TO THE PREREQUISITES OF A MULTI-ETHNIC SOCIETY BASED ON PLURALISM AND EQUALITY. HOWEVER, THE INDO-SRI LANKAN AGREEMENT THEORETICALLY PROVIDES A FRAMEWORK FOR OPENING UP A NATIONAL DIALOGUE ON THE SPECIFICS OF A MULTI-ETHNIC SOCIETY. IN PRACTICE, HOWEVER, THE ACTUAL PROCESS WOULD BE DETERMINED BY WHICH POLITICAL FORCE OR TENDENCY CAPTURES THE POLITICAL SPACE PROVIDED UNDER THE ACCORD.

07863 RUSH, M.
THE WAR DANGER IN SOVIET POLICY AND PROPAGANDA
COMPARATIVE STRATEGY, 8(1) (1989), 1-9.
ASSESSMENTS OF THE DANGER OF WAR ARE CRUCIAL FOR MILITARY PLANNING ("THREAT ASSESSMENT"). WHEN PUBLICLY EXPRESSED, THEY ARE ALSO IMPORTANT DEVICES FOR JUSTIFYING THE IMPOSITION OF HEAVY ECONOMIC BURDENS ON SOCIETY, AS WELL AS FOR INTIMIDATING FOREIGN STATES. THE DISTINCT OBJECTIVES SERVED BY STATEMENTS ON THE LIKELIHOOD OF WAR OFTEN HAVE GIVEN RISE IN SOVIET POLITICS TO A DIVERGENCE BETWEEN THE LEADERS' REAL ASSESSMENT AND THE ONE PROCLAIMED PUBLICLY. THIS ESSAY IS CONCERNED CHIEFLY WITH DISTINGUISHING BETWEEN SOVIET MANIPULATION OF THE WAR DANGER AND THE LEADERS' REAL FEARS AND INTENTIONS REGARDING THE OUTBREAK OF WAR. FOR THIS PURPOSE, CERTAIN DISTINCTIONS ARE IMPORTANT: BETWEEN IMMINENT WAR AND WAR THAT IS INEVITABLE (OR PROBABLE) SOME YEARS IN THE FUTURE; BETWEEN WAR LIMITED TO THE CAPITALIST STATES AND WAR INVOLVING THE USSR; AND BETWEEN WAR IMPOSED ON THE SOVIET LEADERS AND WAR CHOSEN BY THEM. PART ONE PROVIDES A BRIEF HISTORICAL SURVEY, PART TWO, A CASE STUDY OF THE ASCENDENCY OF THE WAR-DANGER THEME AFTER JUNE 1980.

07864 RUSH, R.P.
HANDURAS: PREVENT A FLOUTING OF THE DIGNITY OF THE PEOPLE AND THE SOVEREIGNTY OF OUR COUNTRY
INFORMATION BULLETIN, 26(13-14) (JUL 88), 20-21.
THE HANDURAN GOVERNMENT HAS NOW FOUND ITSELF IN SUCH ISOLATION IN WHICH IT HAS NEVER BEEN BEFORE. NOTHING REMAINS FOR IT BUT EITHER CHANGE ITS POLICY AND TAKE A CONSISTENT STAND ON THE ISSUE OF IMPLEMENTING THE GUATEMALAN ACCORD AND THE PLAN FOR A PEACEFUL SETTLEMENT IN CENTRAL AMERICA, OR TO FACE THE THREAT OF BEING OVERTHROWN BY THE PEOPLE WHO WILL NO LONGER PUT UP WITH A FLOUTING OF THEIR DIGNITY AND THE SOVEREIGNTY OF HONDURAS.

07865 RUSSELL, C.
FAMINE IN AFRICA: A CHALLENGE TO THE WEST
CONTEMPORARY REVIEW, 254(1479) (APR 89), 196-200.
BY WAY OF THE LOME CONVENTIONS THE EUROPEAN ECONOMIC COMMUNITY IS A PARTNER OF ITS AFRICAN ASSOCIATES IN THE SEARCH FOR FOOD SECURITY. THIS ARTICLE DESCRIBES THE CHALLENGE TO THE COMMUNITY AND THE WEST WITH ITS SUBSTANTIAL FOOD SURPLUS, AS PERMANENT A FEATURE OF CONTEMPARARY ECONOMIC AS FAMINE IN AFRICA.

07866 RUSSELL, C.
GORBACHEV AT STRASBOURG
CONTEMPORARY REVIEW, 255(1487) (DEC 89), 286-287.
THIS ARTICLE IS A REPORT ON A TALK GIVEN BY MIKHAIL GORBACHOV TO THE PARLIAMENTARY ASSEMBLY OF THE 23 NATION COUNCIL OF EUROPE. IT REPORTS ON RUSSIAN WILLINGNESS TO SCALE DOWN MILITARY CONFRONTATION AS WELL AS SOVIET ACCEPTANCE OF THE INVITATION TO TAKE PART IN A WIDE VARIETY OF COUNCIL ACTIVITIES. MR. GORBACHOV ADDRESSED THE WISH FOR COOPERATION IN THE ADVANCE OF NEW TECHNOLOGY; HE LISTED PROJECTS OF EQUAL INTEREST TO THE EAST AND WEST; AND EXPRESSED CONCERN FOR THE ENVIRONMENT.

07867 RUSSELL, C.
THE COUNCIL OF EUROPE - OLD LOOK AND NEW ROLE
CONTEMPORARY REVIEW, 255(1484) (SEP 89), 143-145.
THIS ARTICLE LOOKS BACK FORTY YEARS AFTER THE FIRST MEETINGS OF THE COUNCIL OF EUROPE IN STRASBOURG, IT EXAMINES

THE ASSEMBLY DRAWN FROM EXISTING MEMBERS OF NATIONAL PARLIAMENTS, CHURCHILL'S ARRIVAL AND HIS EUROPEAN ARMY SPEECH, AND THE ACHIEVEMENTS IN 1949 AND 1950 IN THE AREA OF HUMAN RIGHTS, THE NOTION OF 'REAL POWERS' FOR THE COUNCIL IS EXPLORED AS WELL AS THE TOPICS COVERED BY CONVENTIONS. IT LOOKS TO THE FUTURE WHEN THE COUNCIL OF EUROPE WILL WELCOME ADDITIONAL MEMBERS.

07868 RUSSELL, F.
TRADING AWAY THE WHEAT BOARD
CANADIAN FORUM, 68(783) (NOV 89), 5-7.
THIS ARTICLE ANALYSES THE COMBINATION OF FREE TRADE AND THE TORIES WHICH SPELL TROUBLE FOR CANADA'S FUTURE AS A GRAIN TRADING NATION. IT EXPLORES THE REGULATIONS SET BY THE GRAIN BOARD AND FARMERS REACTIONS TO THEM. IT QUESTIONS HOW MUCH LONGER FARMERS WILL REMAIN LOYAL TO THE CROWN GRAIN SELLING AGENCY.

07869 RUSSELL, L.B.
PROPOSED: A COMPREHENSIVE HEALTH CARE SYSTEM FOR THE POOR
BROOKINGS REVIEW, 7(3) (SUM 89), 13-20.
THE AUTHOR PROPOSES A UNIFIED, UNIFORM, COMPREHENSIVE PROGRAM THAT WOULD PROVIDE HEALTH CARE DIRECTLY TO THE POOR. IT WOULD BE A JOINT FEDERAL-STATE SYSTEM, WITH THE FRAMEWORK ESTABLISHED BY FEDERAL LEGISLATION, ADMINISTRATION CARRIED OUT BY THE STATES, AND FINANCING PROVIDED BY BOTH. CARE WOULD BE GIVEN IN EXISTING FEDERAL FACILITIES OR IN HOSPITALS AND CLINICS UNDER CONTRACT TO THE GOVERNMENT. IT WOULD END THE CATEGORICAL APPROACH TO PROVIDING MEDICAL SERVICES TO THE POOR AND WOULD OFFER A TRUE SAFETY NET TO ALL CITIZENS WHO ARE OR BECOME POOR.

07870 RUSSELL, S.S.
POLITICS AND IDEOLOGY IN MIGRATION POLICY FORMULATION: THE CASE OF KUWAIT
INTERNATIONAL MIGRATION REVIEW, 23(1) (SPR 89), 24-47.
THEORETICAL APPROACHES TO INTERNATIONAL MIGRATION FOR EMPLOYMENT LARGELY IGNORE THE ROLE OF GOVERNMENT POLICIES IN SHAPING BOTH MIGRATORY FLOWS AND THE FUNCTIONING OF INTERNATIONAL LABOR MARKETS, DESPITE EMPIRICAL EVIDENCE THAT SUCH POLICIES EXIST. TO FACILITATE CONSIDERATIONS OF POLICY IN MIGRATION THEORY, THIS ARTICLE EXAMINES POLITICS AND IDEOLOGY IN THE EVOLUTION OF MIGRATION POLICY IN KUWAIT. POLICY DETERMINANTS ARE FOUND TO INCLUDE NOT ONLY CHANGES IN ECONOMIC CONDITIONS, BUT ALSO SHIFTS IN POWER AMONG POLITICAL ACTORS AND THE SALIENCE OF ISSUES ON THE POLITICAL AGENDA: SECURITY ISSUES, REGIONAL POLITICAL EVENTS, DEMOGRAPHIC CHANGES AND PERCEIVED SOCIAL COSTS OF IMMIGRATION. FUTURE PROSPECTS FOR THE GULF ARE ALSO CONSIDERED.

07871 RUSSETT, B.
NO STICKS, NO ASPIRINS
COMMONWEAL, CXVI(11) (JUN 89), 336-337.
FOR THE PAST DECADE, AMERICAN POLICY IN THE MIDDLE EAST HAS ESSENTIALLY CONSISTED OF SUPPORTING WHATEVER BROAD POLICY HAS BEEN PURSUED BY THE ISRAELI GOVERNMENT. THERE HAVE BEEN SOME DISAGREEMENTS ON THE MARGIN, BUT THOSE WERE BASICALLY ON MATTERS OF WHAT THE USA SHOULD DO RATHER THAN WHAT ISRAEL SHOULD DO. THE USA SHOULD NOT TELL ISRAEL WHAT IT MUST DO BUT NEITHER SHOULD IT, FIGURATIVELY OR LITERALLY, GIVE ISREAL A BLANK CHECK THAT IMPOSES COSTS ON THE UNITED STATES.

07872 RUSTIN, M.
THE POLITICS OF POST-FORDISM: OR, THE TROUBLE WITH "NEW TIMES"
NEW LEFT REVIEW, (175) (MAY 89), 54-78.
IN RECENT YEARS, THE CHANGING FORMS OF CAPITALIST REGULATION HAVE GIVEN RISE ON THE LEFT TO A HYPOTHETICAL MODEL OF 'POST-FORDIST' FLEXIBLE ACCUMULATION, ANALOGOUS TO THE FORDIST SYSTEM OF RELATIONS EXTENSIVELY ANALYSED BY THE REGULATION SCHOOL. MICHAEL RUSTIN SUBJECTS THE CLAIMS OF THIS NEW MODEL TO A CRITIQUE, RECOGNIZING ITS SYNTHETIC AMBITIONS BUT ARGUING THAT IT DOES NOT ADEQUATELY COMPREHEND THE VARIEGATED NATURE OF CAPITALIST STRATEGIES IN THE EIGHTIES. THOSE WHO SEEK TO GROUND SOCIALIST POLITICS ON POST-FORDIST 'NEW TIMES' ARE, IN RUSTIN'S VIEW, IN DANGER OF CONFUSING THE INTERESTS AND WORLD-VIEW OF THE TECHNICAL INTELLIGENTSIA WITH THOSE OF THE WORKING POPULATION AS A WHOLE-AND OF MAKING THE LATTER IN PRACTICE SUBORDINATE TO THE FORMER.

07873 RUTKUS, D.S.
THE CONGRESS AND THE PRESS
CRS REVEIW, 10(6) (JUL 89), 26-27.
THE FIRST AMENDMENT TO THE U.S. CONSTITUTION EXPLICITY PROVIDES FOR FREEDOM OF THE PRESS THAT CONGRESS MAY NOT ABRIDGE BY LAW. THUS, THE CONSTITUTION NOT ONLY CREATED A SYSTEM OF CHECKS AND BALANCES AMONG THE THREE BRANCHES OF GOVERNMENT BUT ALSO PROVIDED FOR A PRESS INDEPENDENT OF THOSE BRANCHES. OVER THE YEARS, PRESS COVERAGE OF CONGRESS HAS EVOLVED THROUGH FOUR HISTORIC PHASES: THE PHASE OF PARTISAN TRANSCRIBERS; THE DEVELOPMENT OF A MORE OBJECTIVE

BUT EDITORIALLY SELECTIVE FORM OF PRINT JOURNALISM; THE
ARRIVAL OF ELECTRONIC PRESS COVERAGE; AND THE CURRENT PHASE,
IN WHICH THE PUBLIC IS INFORMED ABOUT CONGRESS THROUGH BOTH
PRESS ACCOUNTS AND LIVE TELECASTS.

07874 RUTLAND, P.
THE ROLE OF THE SOVIET COMMUNIST PARTY IN ECONOMIC
DECISION-MAKING (VOLUMES I AND II)
DISSERTATION ABSTRACTS INTERNATIONAL, 49(10) (APR 89),
3152-A.
THE AUTHOR EXPLORES THE ECONOMIC ROLE PLAYED BY LOCAL
ORGANIZATIONS OF THE SOVIET COMMUNIST PARTY. THE NATURE OF
PARTY INTERVENTION IN ECONOMIC MANAGEMENT IS EXAMINED FROM
1976 TO 1985, DRAWING UPON A RANGE OF SOVIET JOURNALS,
NEWSPAPERS, AND ACADEMIC PUBLICATIONS. THE AUTHOR STUDIES
THE ROLE OF PARTY ORGANIZATIONS IN RUNNING INDUSTRY,
AGRICULTURE, ENERGY, TRANSPORT, CONSTRUCTION, AND CONSUMER
INDUSTRIES.

07875 RUTTAN, V.W.
INSTITUTIONAL INNOVATION AND AGRICULTURAL DEVELOPMENT
WORLD DEVELOPMENT, 17(9) (SEP 89), 1375-1387.
THIS PAPER ELABORATES A THEORY OF INSTITUTIONAL
INNOVATION IN WHICH SHIFTS IN THE DEMAND FOR INSTITUTIONAL
CHANGE ARE INDUCED BY CHANGES IN RELATIVE RESOURCE
ENDOWMENTS AND BY TECHNICAL CHANGE. THE SUPPLY OF
INSTITUTIONAL INNOVATIONS RESPONDS TO ADVANCES IN SOCIAL
SCIENCE KNOWLEDGE AND CHANGES IN CULTURAL ENDOWMENTS. CASE
STUDIES DRAWING ON (1) INNOVATIONS IN LAND TENURE AND LABOR
RELATIONS IN THE PHILIPPINES; (2) EXPORT PROMOTION AND
IMPORT SUBSTITUTION OF AGRICULTURAL COMMODITIES IN EAST ASIA;
AND (3) FARM COMMODITY POLICY IN THE UNITED STATES ARE
PRESENTED. ELEMENTS OF A GENERAL INSTITUTIONAL INNOVATION
MODEL ARE OUTLINED.

07876 RUWEI, C.; WEIJIAN, F.
A MIDEAST PEACE BREAKTHROUGH
BEIJING REVIEW, 32(1) (JAN 89), 19-21.
THE FIRST ROUND OF U.S.-PLO TALKS ENDED ON DECEMBER 16,
1988. THE HEADS OF THE TWO DELEGATIONS TOLD THE PRESS THAT
THEIR DIALOGUE WAS "PRACTICAL, FRANK, AND SERIOUS." THE
OPENING OF DIRECT DIALOGUE BETWEEN THE UNITED STATES AND THE
PLO MARKS A BREAKTHROUGH IN THE LONG-STALLED MIDDLE EAST
PEACE PROCESS.

07877 RYAN, B.
IDEOLOGICAL PURITY AND FEMINISM: THE U.S. WOMEN'S MOVEMENT
FROM 1966 TO 1975
GENDER AND SOCIETY, 3(2) (JUN 89), 239-257.
THROUGH A REINTERPRETATION OF PUBLICATIONS, INTERVIEWS
WITH LONG-TERM ACTIVISTS, AND AN ANALYSIS OF CHANGE IN THE
SOCIAL ENVIRONMENT, THIS ARTICLE EXPLAINS WHY FEMINIST
IDEOLOGY FAILED TO CREATE UNITY AMONG FEMINIST WOMEN IN THE
UNITED STATES DURING THE PERIOD 1966-1975. IN SPITE OF THE
DESIRE TO CREATE A COMMUNITY OF WOMEN TO CHALLENGE THE
EXISTING SOCIOCULTURAL STRUCTURE, SCHISMS WITHIN THE
MOVEMENT OFTEN CREATED DIVISIVE AND ANTAGONISTIC FEMINIST
GROUP RELATIONS. IN CONTRAST TO EARLIER RESEARCH THAT
ATTRIBUTED THIS LACK OF UNITY TO COMPETING IDEOLOGIES, THIS
ARTICLE ARGUES THAT, IN MANY CASES, FEMINIST LEADERS USED
IDEOLOGY AND THEORY TO PROMOTE RADICAL SELF-IDENTITIES THAT
MAINTAINED EXISTING SOCIAL STRUCTURAL DIVISIONS. THUS, WHILE
FEMINISM ESTABLISHED A PRINCIPLE OF UNITY FOR WOMEN AS A
GROUP, DISPUTES OVER IDEOLOGICAL PURITY CREATED DIVISIONS
WITHIN THE MOVEMENT BASED ON DIFFERENCES AMONG WOMEN.

07878 RYAN, J.E.
THE BRITISH SOCIAL DEMOCRATS: A CASE STUDY OF FACTIONALISM
IN LEFT-OF-CENTER PARTIES, 1964-1981
DISSERTATION ABSTRACTS INTERNATIONAL, 49(8) (FEB 89),
2378-A.
THE AUTHOR EXAMINES THE DEVELOPMENT OF BRITISH SOCIAL
DEMOCRATIC FACTIONALISM FROM 1964 TO 1981, INCLUDING THE
RELEVANCE OF EXISTING TERMS AND MODELS OF FACTIONALISM IN
THE BRITISH CASE. HE FINDS THAT EXISTING TERMS AND MODELS OF
FACTIONALISM DO APPLY TO THE BRITISH CASE, BUT THERE IS A
NEED TO REFINE THEIR USE TO ACCOUNT FOR SUCH PHASES OF
FACTIONAL DEVELOPMENT AS THE PRE-FACTIONAL TENDENCY AND THE
PRE-PARTY FACTION.

07879 RYAN, M.A.
EARLY CHINESE ATTITUDES TOWARD CIVIL DEFENCE AGAINST
NUCLEAR ATTACK
AUSTRALIAN JOURNAL OF CHINESE AFFAIRS, (21) (JAN 89),
81-109.
CHINESE DEFENCES AGAINST NUCLEAR ATTACK BECAME COMMON
KNOWLEDGE IN THE 1960'S WHEN, IN REACTION TO THE LOOMING
NUCLEAR THREAT FROM THE SOVIET UNION, MAO ZEDONG ORDERED
MASSIVE SHELTER SYSTEMS CONSTRUCTED UNDER MAJOR CHINESE
CITIES. BUT IT CAN BE ARGUED THAT THE BLUEPRINTS AND
FOUNDATIONS FOR THE NATIONWIDE CIVIL DEFENCE NETWORK WERE
ACTUALLY COMPLETED DURING THE KOREAN WAR PERIOD IN REACTION
TO THE AMERICAN NUCLEAR THREAT. THIS PAPER PRESENTS EVIDENCE
OF SIGNIFICANT CHINESE INTEREST IN CIVIL DEFENCE DURING THE

KOREAN WAR AND CONCLUDES WITH COMMENTS CONCERNING THE
STRIKING CONTRASTS BETWEEN CHINESE AND AMERICAN ATTITUDES
REGARDING CIVIL DEFENCE IN THE 1950'S.

07880 RYCZKOWSKI, M.
POLISH REALITIES
CONTEMPORARY POLAND, XXII(4) (1989), 8-11.
THIS ARTICLE CONTAINS EXCERPTS FROM A SEMINAR FOR THE
FOREIGN PRESS ON THE SYSTEMIC REFORMS UNDERWAY IN ALL
SPHERES OF POLAND'S ECONOMIC AND POLITICAL LIFE. IT INCLUDES
ANSWERS TO QUESTIONS THE CORRESPONDENTS SUBMITTED TO PRIME
MINISTER MIECZYSLAW F. RAKOWSKI AND MEMBERS OF HIS CABINET.

07881 RYDON, J.
THE FEDERAL STRUCTURE OF AUSTRALIAN POLITICAL PARTIES
PUBLIUS: THE JOURNAL OF FEDERALISM, 18(1) (WIN 88),
159-172.
AUSTRALIAN PARTIES REFLECT THE COMBINATION OF BRITISH
RESPONSIBLE GOVERNMENT AND ELEMENTS OF AMERICAN FEDERALISM
EMBODIED IN THE CONSTITUTION. DESPITE CONSIDERABLE SYMMETRY
IN PARTY COMPETITION FOR ALL SEVEN PARLIAMENTS, PARTY
ORGANIZATIONS MUST FUNCTION WITHIN ELECTORAL SYSTEMS
COMPLICATED BY STATE DIFFERENCES AND BICAMERALISM. THE EXTRA-
PARLIAMENTARY FEDERAL ORGANIZATIONS, WHICH BEGAN AS WEAK
CONFEDERATIONS, HAVE GRADUALLY GAINED ASCENDANCY OVER STATE
PARTIES, PARTICULARLY WITHIN THE LABOR PARTIES. YET THIS
SHIFT OF POWER TO NATIONAL PARTY ORGANIZATIONS IS LESS
MARKED THAN THE INCREASE IN COMMONWEALTH GOVERNMENT
ACTIVITIES. SUCH DEVELOPMENTS HAVE NOT MADE FOR COMPLETE
COMMONWEALTH DOMINATION BUT THE INTERMESHING OF STATE AND
FEDERAL RESPONSIBILITIES HAS INCREASED THE NEED FOR
BARGAINING BETWEEN THE TWO PLANES OF GOVERNMENT AND
DECREASED THE AREAS IN WHICH INDEPENDENT DECISIONS BY EITHER
ARE POSSIBLE. FREQUENT ELECTIONS, IN WHICH FEDERAL AND STATE
ISSUES CAN RARELY BE SEPARATED, STRENGTHEN THESE TRENDS AND
MAKE BARGAINING BETWEEN FEDERAL AND STATE LEADERS WITHIN
EACH PARTY AS IMPORTANT AS BARGAINING BETWEEN GOVERNMENTS.

07882 RYDZKOWSKI, W.; ZAOLADKIEWICZ, K.
POLISH INTERNATIONAL DEBT: PROSPECTS FOR REPAYMENT
EAST EUROPEAN QUARTERLY, XXIII(2) (JUN 89), 211-224.
THE AUTHOR REVIEWS THE COURSE OF POLISH INTERNATIONAL
DEBT IN THE POSTWAR ERA AND EVALUATES THE PROSPECTS FOR
REPAYMENT.

07883 RYN, C.G.
THE DEMOCRACY BOOSTERS
NATIONAL REVIEW, XLI(5) (MAR 89), 30.
WHAT IS DISTURBING ABOUT THE BURST OF DEMOCRATISM IS NOT
THAT IT IS FAVORABLE TO DEMOCRACY. THE TROUBLE IS THE
BLATANTLY UNCRITICAL AND UTOPIAN NATURE OF THE ENDORSEMENTS
OF DEMOCRACY. ALTHOUGH DEMOCRACY CAN BE UNDERSTOOD IN VASTLY
DIFFERENT WAYS, SO THAT CAREFUL DEFINITIONS ARE URGENTLY
NEEDED, MOST OF THE CHAMPIONS OF DEMOCRACY SEEM VIRTUALLY
OBVIOUS TO THAT NEED. THEY GIVE THE IMPRESSION THAT IN ORDER
TO EXTEND THE BLESSINGS OF DEMOCRACY TO COUNTRIES PREVIOUSLY
DEPRIVED OF THEM, ALL THAT IS NEEDED TO PROCLAIM DEMOCRACY
IN THE PARTICULAR COUNTRY. THIS SIMPLISTIC APPROACH DENIES
ACCESS TO THE FULL RANGE OF DEMOCRACY'S REQUIRMENTS.
POL/CULTUR

07884 RYOO, J.
THE REPUBLIC OF KOREA'S POLICY TOWARD JAPAN: AN ANALYSIS
OF MAJOR DETERMINANTS
DISSERTATION ABSTRACTS INTERNATIONAL, 49(11) (MAY 89),
3499-A.
THE AUTHOR IDENTIFIES THE MAJOR DETERMINANTS AFFECTING
RELATIONS BETWEEN THE REPUBLIC OF KOREA AND JAPAN,
CONCENTRATING ON THE 1980'S, WITHIN THE CONTEXT OF THE
CHANGING INTERNAL AND EXTERNAL ENVIRONMENT. MAJOR FACTORS
INCLUDE THE REGIME CHANGE IN 1980, THE GENERATIONAL CHANGE
IN POLITICAL LEADERSHIP, AND KOREA'S ECONOMIC PERFORMANCE.

07885 RYSIN, V.
MIDTERM REPORT CARD FOR PERESTROIKA
GLASNOST, (16-18) (JAN 89), 50-51.
THE AUTHOR EVALUATES THE ECONOMIC, SOCIAL, AND POLITICAL
RESULTS OF PERESTROIKA IN THE SOVIET UNION.

07886 RYZHKOV, N.
NIKOLAI RYZHKOV ADDRESSES SESSION OF USSR COUNCIL OF
MINISTERS
REPRINTS FROM THE SOVIET PRESS, 49(1) (JUL 89), 27-32.
NIKOLAI RYZHKOV DISCUSSES THE SWEEPING REFORMS INITIATED
IN APRIL, 1985 AND THEIR IMPLICATIONS. HE CONCENTRATES ON
THE ECONOMIC ASPECTS OF PERESTROIKA AND OUTLINES ISSUES SUCH
AS THE STATE OF THE CONSUMER MARKET, MONEY CIRCULATION, AND
FINANCE. HE CONCLUDES THAT ALTHOUGH ALL OF THE GOALS OF
PERESROIKA HAVE YET TO BE MET, THE GROUNDWORK HAS BEEN LAID
AND FURTHER EFFORTS AIMED AT DEEPENING THE ECONOMIC REFORM
WILL BE SUCCESSFUL.

07887 RZEMIENIECKI, K.
ON MOST SIGNIFICANT ISSUES

CONTEMPORARY POLAND, XXII(10) (1989), 6-7.
   IT IS ESTIMATED THAT THE CONTINUATION OF CURRENT TRENDS
IN THE POLISH ECONOMY WOULD YIELD A FOUR THOUSAND PERCENT
HYPER-INFLATION RATE WITHIN A YEAR. TO STEM THIS TIDE, PRIME
MINISTER TADEUSZ MAZOWIECKI HAS PRESENTED A NEW ECONOMIC
PROGRAM AND IT HAS BEEN PASSED BY THE SEJM. THE PROGRAM
INCLUDES A PACKAGE OF AUSTERITY MEASURES AND CUTS IN THE
STATE BUDGET, BUT THE REDUCTIONS WILL NOT AFFECT HEALTH
SERVICES, EDUCATION, CULTURE, AND SOCIAL WELFARE.

07888 SAAD, A.M.
   IRAQ AND ARAB POLITICS: THE NURI AS-SAID ERA, 1941-1958
   DISSERTATION ABSTRACTS INTERNATIONAL, 48(12) (JUN 88),
   3182-A.
   WITH SPECIAL ATTENTION GIVEN TO THE DOMINANT FIGURE ON
THE IRAQI POLITICAL SCENE, NURI AS-SAID, THE DISSERTATION
STUDIES THE ROLE OF IRAQ AND ITS ATTITUDES TOWARDS ARAB
INDEPENDENCE, THE ARAB LEAGUE, ARAB UNITY, AND THE
PALESTINIAN PROBLEM.

07889 SABATIER, P. A.; HUNTER, S.
   THE INCORPORATION OF CAUSAL PERCEPTIONS INTO MODELS OF
   ELITE BELIEF SYSTEMS
   WESTERN POLITICAL QUARTERLY, 42(3) (SEP 89), 229-262.
   MOST STUDIES OF ELITE BELIEFS--PARTICULARLY THOSE
RELYING ON SURVEY DATA--HAVE FOCUSED ON THE RELATIONSHIP
BETWEEN GENERAL NORMATIVE (AND/OR PARTISAN) ORIENTATION AND
OPINIONS ON SPECIFIC POLICY PROPOSALS. THIS PAPER ARGUES
THAT ELITES' PERCEPTIONS OF CAUSAL RELATIONSHIPS AND OF
VALUES OF SYSTEM VARIABLES WITHIN THEIR AREAS OF POLICY
SPECILIZATION SHOULD BE ADDED TO MODELS OF THEIR BELIEF
SYSTEMS. SURVEY DATA FROM AN ENVIRONMENTAL POLICY ELITE
INDICATES THAT CAUSAL PERCEPTIONS ADD SIGNIFICANTLY TO THE
VARIANCE ACCOUNTED FOR BY TRADITIONAL NORMATIVE MODELS, WITH
THE AMOUNT DEPENDING UPON WHICH OF TWO SOCIALIZATION MODELS
ARE EMPLOYED.

07890 SABATO, L.
   POLITICAL INFLUENCE, THE NEWS MEDIA, AND CAMPAIGN
   CONSULTANTS
   PS: POLITICAL SCIENCE AND POLITICS, XXII(1) (MAR 89),
   15-17.
   THE AUTHOR ANALYZES THE EFFECT OF POLITICAL CONSULTANTS
ON THE 1988 PRESIDENTIAL CAMPAIGN AND SPECULATES THAT
CONSULTANTS WERE ULTIMATELY RESPONSIBLE FOR DAN QUAYLE'S
EMERGENCE AS THE VICE PRESIDENTIAL CANDIDATE ON THE
REPUBLICAN TICKET.

07891 SABEL, C.F.; DEEG, R.; HERRIGEL, G.B.; KAZIS, R.
   REGIONAL PROPERITIES COMPARED: MASSACHUSETTS AND BADEN-
   WURTTEMBERG IN THE 1980'S
   ECONOMY AND SOCIETY, 18(4) (NOV 89), 374-404.
   THIS ARTICLE COMPARES THE RELATIONSHIP BETWEEN ECONOMIC
DEVELOPMENT AND PUBLIC POLICY IN TWO OF THE MOST PROSPEROUS
REGIONS OF THE 1980S: MASSACHUSETTS IN THE UNITED STATES AND
BADEN-WURTTEMBERG IN WEST GERMANY. BEGINNING WITH A CRITIQUE
OF THE THEORY OF THE PRODUCT LIFE-CYCLE, THE ARTICLE
EXAMINES THE RISE AND FALL OF TRADITIONAL INDUSTRIES IN
MASSACHUSETTS AND THEIR SURVIVAL IN BADENWURTTEMBERG. IT
THEN GOES ON TO CONSIDER THE RISE - BUT ALSO THE
VULNERABILITY - OF THE HIGH-TECH AND FINANCIAL FIRMS IN
MASSACHUSETTS, AS WELL AS THE MORE ROBUST, THOUGH ALMOST
INVISIBLE GROWTH OF THESE SECTORS IN BADEN-WURTTEMBERG. THE
BURDEN OF THE ARGUMENT IS THAT THERE ARE, STRICTLY SPEAKING,
NO 'MATURE' INDUSTRIES AND PUBLIC POLICIES AIMED AT
STIMULATING INNOVATION ARE MOST SUCCESSFUL WHEN THE LATTER
IS INTEGRATED INTO THE LOCAL INDUSTRIAL STRUCTURE AS A WHOLE
RATHER THAN ISOLATED INTO A DISTINCT HIGH-TECH SECTOR.

07892 SABET, M.G.
   PUBLIC PERSONNEL DIRECTORS' PROFESSIONALISM AND AGENCY
   DRUG/ALCOHOLIC TESTING POLICIES: AN INNOVATION MODEL
   DISSERTATION ABSTRACTS INTERNATIONAL, 50(6) (DEC 89),
   1801-A.
   THE AUTHOR EXAMINES THE RELATIONSHIP BETWEEN THE DEGREE
OF PROFESSIONALISM OF PUBLIC PERSONNEL DIRECTORS AND THE
ADOPTION OF DRUG/ALCOHOL TESTING POLICIES. HE ALSO
INVESTIGATES THE RELATIONSHIP BETWEEN THE DEGREE OF
PROFESSIONALISM OF PUBLIC PERSONNEL DIRECTORS AND DIFFERENT
DRUG/ALCOHOL TESTING PROGRAM CHARACTERISTICS.

07893 SABROSKY, A.N.
   BORDER WARS
   JOURNAL OF SOCIAL, POLITICAL AND ECONOMIC STUDIES, 14(4)
   (WIN 89), 433-442.
   THE UNITED STATES IS CONFRONTED SIMULTANEOUSLY WITH
THREE TYPES OF CHALLENGES TO THE INTEGRITY OF ITS BORDERS,
EACH OF WHICH HAS HISTORICAL PRECEDENTS. ONE IS THE
BURGEONING WAVE OF ILLEGAL IMMIGRATION, WHICH IS LIKELY TO
HAVE ENORMOUS SOCIOECONOMIC CONSEQUENCES OVER THE LONG TERM.
A SECOND IS INTERNATIONAL TERRORISM, THE MODERN EQUIVALENT
OF PIRACY AND CROSS-BORDER RAIDS. THE THIRD IS THE THREAT
POSED BY ILLEGAL NARCOTICS TRAFFICKERS, THE MODERN VERSION
OF SMUGGLERS AND BOOTLEGGERS.

07894 SABROSKY, A.N.
   OF SMOKE AND MIRRORS: GRAND STRATEGY BY COMMISSION
   PARAMETERS, XIX(1) (MAR 89), 41-48.
   "DISCRIMINATE DETERRENCE," THE REPORT OF THE COMMISSION
ON INTEGRATED LONG-RANGE STRATEGY, IS THE MOST RECENT
OFFICIAL GOVERNMENT ATTEMPT TO CRAFT AN APPROPRIATE MILITARY
STRATEGY FOR THE UNITED STATES. THE OBJECTIVE OF THE REPORT
IS TO DEVISE AN INTEGRATED STRATEGY "DESIGNED FOR THE LONG
TERM, TO GUIDE FORCE DEVELOPMENT, WEAPONS PROCUREMENT, AND
ARMS NEGOTIATIONS." THE REPORT SURVEYS THE CHANGING SECURITY
ENVIRONMENT, THIRD WORLD CONFLICTS AND U.S. INTERESTS, WARS
ON THE SOVIET PERIPHERY, EXTREME THREATS, HOW TO INFLUENCE
SOVIET ARMS POLICY, MANAGING TECHNOLOGY, AND MANAGING THE
DEFENSE BUDGET.

07895 SABROSKY, A.N.; SLOANE, R.L.
   RECOURSE TO WAR: AN APPRAISAL OF THE WEINBERGER DOCTRINE
   AVAILABLE FROM NTIS, NO. AD-A209 757/4/GAR, JUN 89, 65.
   IN RECENT YEARS, A DEBATE BETWEEN THE SECRETARIES OF
STATE AND DEFENSE FOCUSED ON THE MORAL JUSTIFICATION
NECESSARY FOR THE CRITICAL APPLICATION OF U.S. MILITARY
FORCE. HISTORICALLY, THOSE CHARGED WITH THE RESPONSIBILITY
FOR MAINTAINING THE DIPLOMATIC AFFAIRS OF STATE HAVE BEEN
MOST RELUCTANT TO RESORT TO THE USE OF SUCH FORCE. ONLY
AFTER ALL OTHER RECOURSES HAVE BEEN EXHAUSTED WOULD THEY
AGREE TO CONSIDER THE COMMITMENT OF MILITARY FORCES. ON THE
OTHER HAND, THOSE MORE DIRECTLY CHARGED WITH THE DEFENSE OF
THE COUNTRY TRADITIONALLY HAVE BEEN FAR MORE WILLING TO
EXERCISE MILITARY POWER IN THE DISCHARGE OF THEIR
RESPONSIBILITIES. WITHIN THE RECENT QUEST FOR VIABLE
CRITERIA UPON WHICH TO BASE SUCH A DECISION THERE WAS,
HOWEVER, AN UNUSUAL REVERSAL. KEYWORDS: WEINBERGER DOCTRINE;
DEFENSE ESTABLISHMENT; U.S. MILITARY FORCE; MILITARY
INTERVENTION; SECRETARY OF DEFENSE CASPAR WEINBERGER.

07896 SACHDEVA, P.
   COMBATING POLITICAL CORRUPTION: A CRITIQUE OF ANTI-
   DEFECTION LEGISLATION
   INDIAN JOURNAL OF POLITICAL SCIENCE, L(2) (APR 89),
   157-168.
   THE WORST FORM OF POLITICAL CORRUPTION IN INDIA HAS BEEN
THE PERNICIOUS AND OUTRAGEOUS PHENOMENON OF DEFECTIONS.
SINCE THE 1967 GENERAL ELECTIONS, MORE THAN FOUR THOUSAND
AYA RAMS AND GAYA RAMS HAVE CHANGED PARTIES IN THE VARIOUS
STATES, MAINLY TO BECOME CHIEF MINISTERS, MINISTERS, AND
CHAIRMEN OF PUBLIC SECTOR CORPORATIONS. THE DEBASING
PRACTICE, WHICH PUTS A PRICE TAG ON LEGISLATORS, IS USED AS
MUCH TO CAPTURE POWER AS TO TOPPLE GOVERNMENTS AND SUBVERT
THE ELECTORAL MANDATE.

07897 SACHS, A.
   POST-APARTHEID IN SOUTH AFRICA: A CONSTITUTIONAL FRAMEWORK
   WORLD POLICY JOURNAL, VI(3) (SUM 89), 589-608.
   THIS ARTICLE IS BASED ON AN ADDRESS BY ALBIE SACHS AT
NEW YORK UNIVERSITY ON MAY 4, 1989. HE IS A MEMBER OF THE
AFRICAN OF THE AFRICAN NATIONAL CONGRESS'S LEGAL AND
CONSTITUTIONAL COMMITEE. SACHS CLAIMS THAT APARTHEID IS JUST
NOW BECOMING A REAL, CONCRETE ISSUE IN SOUTH AFRICA. HIS
ADDRESS IS CONCERNED MAINLY WITH A BILL OF RIGHTS BEING
ADDED TO THE SOUTH AFRICAN CONSTITUTION. HE BELIEVES THAT A
BILL OF RIGHT IS A NECESSARY STEP. AFFIRMATIVE ACTION, AND
WOMEN'S RIGHTS ARE BRIEFLY DISCUSSED. THE PAPER ENDS WITH A
QUESTION AND ANSWER SESION BETWEEN SACHS AND HIS AUDIENCE.

07898 SACHS, J.
   MAKING THE BRADY PLAN WORK
   FOREIGN AFFAIRS, 68(3) (SUM 89), 87-104.
   THE AUTHOR EXAMINES THE BRADY PLAN FOR DEALING WITH
THIRD WORLD INDEBTEDNESS.

07899 SACHS, R.C.
   CONGRESSIONAL LEADERSHIP AND INSTITUTIONAL CHANGE
   CRS REVEIW, 10(9) (OCT 89), 27-28.
   THE CONSTITUTION CALLS FOR THREE CONGRESSIONAL OFFICES:
THE SPEAKER OF THE HOUSE, THE VICE PRESIDENT, AND A SENATE
PRESIDENT PRO TEMPORE. EACH HOUSE IS ALSO PERMITTED TO
CHOOSE OTHER OFFICERS, ALTHOUGH THE CONSTITUTION OFFERS NO
DIRECTION ON HOW TO SELECT THEM OR WHAT THEIR DUTIES SHOULD
BE. BECAUSE OF THIS, LEADERSHIP DEVELOPED DIFFERENTLY IN THE
HOUSE AND THE SENATE.

07900 SACHS, R.C.
   THE FIRST AND 101ST CONGRESSES: THE LEGISLATURE THEN AND
   NOW
   CRS REVEIW, 10(1) (JAN 89), 12-13.
   THE AUTHOR DISCUSSES THE SIMILARITIES AND DIFFERENCES
BETWEEN THE FIRST U.S. CONGRESS AND THE 101ST CONGRESS.

07901 SADKOVICH, J.J.
   UNDERSTANDING DEFEAT: REAPPRAISING ITALY'S ROLE IN WORLD
   WAR II
   JOURNAL OF CONTEMPORARY HISTORY, 24(1) (JAN 89), 27-61.
   FOR MOST READERS AND WRITERS OF ENGLISH, THE ITALIAN WAR

EFFORT IS STILL VIEWED AS VACILLATING BETWEEN TRAGEDY AND
FARCE. MUSSOLINI IS SEEN AS A NASTY LITTLE DICTATOR AND A
MENTAL FEATHERWEIGHT INCAPABLE OF FATHOMING THE INDUSTRIAL
AND ECONOMIC EXIGENCIES OF WAR OR OF MATCHING HITLER'S
TACTICAL GENIUS. BUT TO DISCOUNT ITALY AS INSIGNIFICANT IS
TO DISTORT THE REALITY OF THE 1930'S AND 1940'S. TO PLAY
DOWN THE THREAT ITALY POSED TO BRITAIN IS TO MISUNDERSTAND
THE IMPORTANCE OF THE EMPIRE AND THE MIDDLE EAST TO LONDON
AND, THEREBY, TO PRETEND THAT THE ELIMINATION OF FASCIST
ITALY WAS NOT AS CRUCIAL TO THE SECURITY OF THE EMPIRE AS
THE DESTRUCTION OF NAZI GERMANY AND MILITARIST JAPAN.

07902 SADOFF, L.R.
      AT THE CROSSROADS OF THE NATO BURDERSHARING DEBATE
      AVAILABLE FROM NTIS, NO. AD-A207 340/1/GAR, MAR 89, 68.
      THIS STUDY FOCUSES ON THE FUTURE OF THE UNITED STATE'S
BURDEN-SHARING RESPONSIBILITIES WITHIN NATO. IT EXAMINES AN
ALLIANCE IN TRANSITION -- ASSESSING THE FUTURE ALLOCATION OF
ROLES, RISK, AND RESPONSIBILITIES. THE FIRST SEGMENT
CONCENTRATES ON POLITICAL, ECONOMIC, SOCIAL AND TECHNICAL
IMPACTS -- CONCLUDING THAT: EUROPE MUST MAINTAIN PRIMACY IN
U.S. DEFENSE PLANNING; THE SOVIET UNION WILL CONTINUE TO BE
THE U.S.'S MOST FORMIDABLE ADVERSARY; NATO MUST RECOGNIZE
ITS GLOBAL RESPONSIBILITIES; AND THE U.S. AND ITS ALLIES
MUST STRENGTHEN COHESIVENESS THROUGH COMPROMISE. THE SECOND
SEGMENT BUILDS UPON THESE JUDGEMENTS -- PROPOSING TEN
GUIDELINES FOR USE IN ALLOCATING BURDEN WITHIN NATO. THE
ANALYSIS DEMONSTRATES THAT WHILE MANY FACTORS IMPACT UPON
THE BURDENSHARING DEBATE, ECONOMIC ASSESSMENTS ARE THE MOST
CONTENTIOUS. SEVERAL ECONOMIC ASSESSMENTS ARE CONDUCTED --
EACH SHOWING THAT THE U.S. CONTRIBUTES A DISPROPORTIONATELY
HIGH SHARE OF THE FINANCIAL SUPPORT TO THE ALLIANCE. THE
AUTHOR THEN IDENTIFIES FACTORS WHICH DICTATE A
REDISTRIBUTION OF COSTS, DEMONSTRATING THAT FAILURE TO
REALLOCATE EXPENSES WILL NEUTRALIZE THE REMAINING NINE
FINDINGS. SPECIFIC RECOMMENDATIONS INCLUDE: SELECTED
IMPLEMENTATION OF ROLE SPECIALIZATION; INCREASED
STANDARDIZATION; RECOGNITION OF INDIRECT COSTS;
INCORPORATION OF NON-QUANTITATIVE COMMITMENTS; BETTER USE OF
MULTILATERAL AGREEMENTS; AND A REVIEW OF THE CURRENT FORCE
STRUCTURE WITHIN NATO. THE STUDY CONCLUDES BY WARNING THAT
ALTHOUGH A REDISTRIBUTION OF U.S. COMMITMENTS IS WARRANTED,
ANY REDUCTION OF U.S. RESPONSIBILITIES WILL BRING WITH IT A
CORRESPONDING REDUCTION IN THE UNITED STATE'S DOMINANT
LEADERSHIP ROLE WITHIN NATO.

07903 SADRI, S.; RAMASAMY, B.
      SOCIALIST REFORM IN CHINA
      INTERNATIONAL SOCIAL SCIENCE REVIEW, 64(4) (AUT 89),
      158-164.
      THIS BRIEF PAPER EXAMINES THE POSITION IN WHICH CHINESE
SOCIALISM FINDS ITSELF 12 YEARS AFTER THE DEATH OF ITS
FOUNDING FATHER MAO ZEDONG AND 11 YEARS AFTER THE CONTROL OF
STATE PASSED INTO THE HANDS OF DENG ZIAOPING. AN ANALYSIS OF
THE HISTORICAL ANTECEDENTS OF THE PRESENT ADMINISTRATION IS
ATTEMPTED IN ORDER TO DEMONSTRATE THE TRANSITION OF THOUGHT
IN OFFICIAL PARTY CIRCLES OVER THE 40-YEAR HISTORY OF THE
PEOPLE'S REPUBLIC OF CHINA. IT ARGUES THAT POWER HAS SHIFTED
AWAY FROM THE RADICAL TENDENCY WITHIN THE PARTY AND IS
LODGED IN THE HANDS OF THE REVISIONIST TENDENCY IN THE PARTY.
      FUTURE PLANS, AS WELL AS CHINA'S ROLE IN THE ASIAN
CONTINENT, WILL VERY MUCH DEPEND ON WHETHER THE PRESENT
REFORMIST TENDENCY WILL CONTINUE TO HOLD POWER OR WHETHER
CHINA WILL WITNESS A RETURN OF THE GHOST OF MAO. THE PAPER
POINTS OUT THAT NO REAL EXPECTATIONS CAN BE MADE UNLESS THIS
CENTRAL QUESTION IS RESOLVED AND ONLY TIME WILL PROVIDE THE
ANSWER TO WHERE CHINESE SOCIALISM IS HEADED.

07904 SADUNAITE, N.
      THE WAR AGAINST THE CHURCH
      GLASNOST, II(2) (MAR 89), 26-28, 30.
      THE CURRENT STATUS OF THE LITHUANIAN CATHOLIC CHURCH
REVEALS HOW THE RIGHTS OF BELIEVERS ARE VIOLATED BY THE
SOVIET STATE. RESTRICTIONS AND LIMITATIONS ON THE LITHUANIAN
CATHOLIC CHURCH INCLUDE A SCARITY OF BIBLES AND CHURCH
LITERATURE, ANTI-RELIGIOUS PROGRAMMING ON STATE RADIO AND
TELEVISION, A PROHIBITION AGAINST RELIGIOUS SCHOOLS, AND
PERSECUTION OF CHURCH LEADERS WHO ATTEMPT TO ORGANIZE
RELIGIOUS GROUPS FOR CHILDREN AND TEENAGERS.

07905 SAGASTI, F.
      CRISIS AND CHALLENGE: SCIENCE AND TECHNOLOGY IN THE FUTURE
      OF LATIN AMERICA
      FUTURES, 21(2) (APR 89), 161-168.
      A TURBULENT INTERNATIONAL ARENA AND DIFFICULT
CIRCUMSTANCES WITHIN LATIN AMERICAN ITSELF PRESENT BOTH A
CRISIS AND CHALLENGE FOR THE REGION. SOCIAL PRESSURES,
ECONOMIC CONSTRAINTS, POLITICAL UNCERTAINTY, CULTURAL CHANGE
AND VULNERABLE ECOSYSTEMS WOULD SEEM TO INDICATE A
PESSIMISTIC VIEW OF THE REGION'S FUTURE--BUT WITHIN THESE
SAME ISSUES LIE POSSIBILITIES FOR POSITIVE ADVANCE,
PARTICULARLY IF ECONOMIC, AND SCIENTIFIC AND TECHNOLOGICAL
OPPORTUNITIES ARE GRASPED.

07906 SAGDEYEV, R.; KOKOSHIN, A.; VELIKHOV, Y.
      STRATEGIC AND POLITICAL ASPECTS OF THE STRATEGIC DEFENSE
      INITIATIVE: A SOVIET VIEWPOINT
      JOURNAL OF LEGISLATION, 15(2) (1989), 179-198.
      THE AUTHORS EXAMINE SDI AND OTHER BALLISTIC MISSILE
DEFENSE (BMD) MECHANISMS FROM A SOVIET VIEWPOINT. THEY
ANALYZE THE STRATEGIC BALANCE AND HOW SDI WOULD EFFECT THAT
BALANCE AS WELL AS THE EFFECT OF SDI ON EUROPEAN SECURITY.
THEY CONCLUDE THAT THE UNCERTAINTY THAT IS INHERRENT IN
SPACE-BASED DEFENSE SYSTEMS WOULD MEAN THAT THE DESIRED US
SHIFT FROM MUTUAL ASSURED DESTRUCTION TO MUTUAL ASSURED
SURVIVAL WOULD BE IMPOSSIBLE. IN ADDITION, THE FACT THAT THE
US REFUSES TO RENOUNCE FIRST STRIKE OPTIONS AND CONTINUES TO
DEVELOP ADVANCED STRATEGIC OFFENSIVE ARMS WOULD MEAN THAT
THE DEVELOPMENT AND DEPLOYMENT OF SDI WOULD MERELY INCREASE
GLOBAL INSTABILITY AND THE RISK OF WAR.

07907 SAGVE, C.
      NEITHER MURDER NOR LIBERATION
      SOJOURNERS, 18(10) (NOV 89), 21.
      CITIZENS OF THE UNITED STATES HAVE HISTORICALLY SOUGHT
LEGAL REMEDIES FOR MANY SOCIAL ILLS. HOWEVER, THE ISSUE OF
ABORTION IS SIGNIFICANTLY DIFFERENT FROM OTHER ISSUES. THE
AUTHOR ARGUES THAT A LEGAL SOLUTION TO ABORTION WILL NOT
RESULT IN ANY SIGNIFICANT PROGRESS. ONLY WHEN ABORTION
BECOMES UNTHINKABLE, NOT MERELY ILLEGAL, WILL GENUINE
PROGRESS BE MADE. THE AUTHOR ARGUES THAT UNTIL THIS TIME,
ABORTION SHOULD REGARDED AS NEITHER A CRIME NOT A
CONSTITUTIONAL RIGHT.

07908 SAHAGUN, V. M.
      THE FOREIGN DEBT AND BEYOND: ALTERNATIVES TO THE LATIN
      AMERICAN ECONOMIC CRISIS
      LATIN AMERICAN PERSPECTIVES, 16(1) (WIN 89), 111-126.
      THIS ARTICLE SUMMARIZES THE CENTRAL ELEMENTS FOR A NEW
TECHNICOPOLITICAL PROGRAM OF ACTION. FIRST, IT IS CLEAR THAT
THE RISING ACCUMULATION OF FORCES RESULTING FROM STRUCTURAL
DEPENDDENCY IS SHAPING THE ONLY JUSTIFIABLE ALTERNATIVE AT
PRESENT: THE TOTAL OR PARTIAL CANCELLATION OF THE FOREIGN
DEBT OF THE THIRD WORLD AND THE SUSPENSION OF INTEREST
PAYMENTS. SECOND, VARIOUS FORMS OF LIQUIDATION SHOULD BE
ESTABLISHED FOR DEBTS CONTRACTED UNDER "SOFT" SCHEDULES WITH
RESPECT TO TERMS OF INTEREST THAT WOULD BE APPLIED TO
PROJECTS THAT ARE PRODUCTIVE IN THE BROADEST POSSIBLE SOCIAL
SENSE. THESE WOULD COME UNDER THE CATEGORY OF "PAYABLE DEBT.
" THIRD, THE DEBT WILL HAVE TO BE RENEGOTIATED UNDER
MULTILATERAL AGREEMENTS AND ON NEW BASES, TAKING INTO
ACCOUNT EACH COUNTRY'S CAPACITY TO PAY. THIS SHOULD BE
DETERMINED BY THE POSITIVE NET BALANCE OF PAYMENTS AND NOT
BY A PERCENTAGE OF TOTAL EXPORTS.

07909 SAICH, T.
      HARSH END TO CHINA'S SPRING
      JOURNAL OF COMMUNIST STUDIES, 5(4) (DEC 89), 184-188.
      THE STUDENT DEMONSTRATIONS OF APRIL-JUNE 1989 AND THEIR
VIOLENT SUPPRESSION HIGHLIGHTED IN TRAGIC FASHION THE
CENTRAL PROBLEM OF THE REFORM MOVEMENT DURING THE 1980S.
THERE HAS BEEN A CONSISTENT REFUSAL BY CHINA'S TOP LEADERS
TO COME TO TERMS WITH THE PROCESS OF CHANGE WHICH THEIR OWN
ECONOMIC REFORM PROGRAMMES HAD SET IN MOTION. THE REPRESSION
HAS BROUGHT BACK TO POWER A GROUP OF VETERAN REVOLUTIONARIES
WHO HAVE REFUSED TO SEE THAT THE ECONOMIC DIVERSITY AND
CHANGE WHICH IS TAKING PLACE IS CREATING NEW INTERESTS AND
GROUPS IN SOCIETY THAT HAVE TO BE ACCOMMODATED BY REFORMS OF
THE AUTHORITARIAN POLITICAL SYSTEM. THE LACK OF POLITICAL
REFORM DURING THE LAST DECADE WAS SEEN BY MANY AS A CLEAR
FAILING AND AS AN ESSENTIALLY DESTABIZING FACTOR. THE BRUTAL
MURDER OF SO MANY OF BEIJING'S CITIZENS WAS A CRUEL PROOF OF
THIS VIEW.

07910 SAID, A.A.
      DEMOCRACY AND THE SULTANATE
      WORLD MARXIST REVIEW, 32(11) (NOV 89), 67-69.
      THIS ARTICLE DESCRIBES HOW THE CHANGES IN OMAN'S FOREIGN
POLICY ARE LARGELY THE RESULT OF THE POPULAR MAN STRUGGLE.
RECOGNIZING THE OPINION OF THE POPULAR MASSES, THE SULTANATE
OF OMAN HAS ANNOUNCED A NEW FOREIGN POLICY WHICH ESTABLISHES
DIPLOMATIC RELATIONS UNITS THE USSR. THIS TREND GIVES HOPE
THAT OTHER SOCIALIST STATES MAY SOON OPEN EMBASSIES IN THE
CAPITAL.

07911 SAID, E.H.
      FROM INTIFADAH TO INDEPENDENCE
      MIDDLE EAST REPORT, 19(158) (MAY 89), 12-16.
      THE AUTHOR REPORTS ON THE 19TH SESSION OF THE PALESTINE
NATIONAL COUNCIL, HELD NOVEMBER 1988 IN ALGIERS.

07912 SAID, E.H.
      THE SATANIC VERSES AND DEMOCRATIC FREEDOMS
      BLACK SCHOLAR, 20(2) (MAR 89), 17-18.
      THIS PAPER EXPLORES THE IMPACT THAT SALMAN RUSHDIE'S,
"THE SATANIC VERSES" HAS HAD UPON THE QUESTION OF AND
PRESERVATION OF DEMOCRATIC FREEDOM. IT QUOTES RUSHDIE,
HIMSELF, SAYING, "THE MODERN WORLD LACKS NOT ONLY HIDING

PLACES BUT CERTAINTIES", AND APPLIES THOSE WORDS TO
RUSHDIE'S BOOK AND TO HIS SITUATION TODAY. IT CONCLUDES THAT
THOSE FROM THE MOSLEM PART OF THE WORLD CANNOT ACCEPT THE
NOTION THAT DEMOCRATIC FREEDOMS SHOULD BE ABROGATED TO
PROTECT ISLAM.

07913 SAIDEL, R.G.
THE ROLE OF THE HOLOCAUST IN THE POLITICAL CULTURE OF
ISRAEL
MIDSTREAM, XXXV(7) (OCT 89), 17-21.
THE CENTRALITY OF THE HOLOCAUST IN ISRAEL'S POLITICAL
CULTURE SERVES BOTH AS A BARRIER TO ISRAEL'S ACHIEVING
MODERN NATIONALISM AND AS AN EXCUSE FOR SUCH NATIONALISM. IF
ISRAEL IS TO TRULY BECOME A NATION AMONG NATIONS, THIS
PARADOX MUST BE RESOLVED. THE CENTRALITY OF THE HOLOCAUST IN
ISRAEL'S POLITICAL CULTURE IS ALSO REFLECTED IN ISRAEL'S AND
ISRAELI'S ATTITUDES ABOUT THEIR ARAB NEIGHBORS. AS THE NEW
ENEMY OF THE JEWS, THE ARABS ARE CONSIDERED A THREAT THAT
MUST NOT BE ALLOWED TO LAUNCH A NEW HOLOCAUST AND DESTROY
THE JEWISH STATE.

07914 SAIKAL, A.
AFGHANISTAN: THE END-GAME
WORLD TODAY, 45(3) (MAR 89), 37-39.
DESPITE VALIANT EFFORTS, THE SOVIET UNION WAS UNABLE TO
NEGOTIATE A COALITION SETTLEMENT OF THE AFGHAN PROBLEM,
PRIOR TO ITS TROOP WITHDRAWAL. A NUMBER OF FACTORS WORKED
AGAINST THE SOVIET EFFORTS, INCLUDING TIME AND GROWING
SOVIET WEAKNESS ON THE GROUND IN AFGHANISTAN. ALTHOUGH
NAJIBULLAH HAS PUT ON A BRAVE FACE IN PUBLIC AND SUPPORTED
THE SOVIET WITHDRAWAL, HE HAS NOT BEEN ABLE TO ARREST
GROWING DISCONTENT WITH HIS LEADERSHIP AND THE MUJAHIDIN ARE
WELL PLACED FOR A FINAL ASSAULT ON KABUL WHEN THE
APPROPRIATE TIME COMES.

07915 SAINBURY, D.
THE 1988 SWEDISH ELECTION: THE BREAKTHROUGH OF THE GREENS
WEST EUROPEAN POLITICS, 12(2) (APR 89), 140-143.
THE PARTY LANDSCAPE IN SWEDEN WAS ALTERED BY THE 1988
ELECTION FOR THE FIRST TIME IN NEARLY SEVEN DECADES A NEW
PARTY SUCCEEDED IN BEING ELECTED TO THE RIKSDAG. IN THEIR
THIRD BID TO CROSS THE 4 PERCENT THRESHOLD ENTITLING
PARLIAMENTARY REPRESENTATION, THE ENVIRONMENTALIST PARTY,
THE GREENS WON 5.5 PERCENT OF THE VOTES COMPARED WITH LESS
THAN 2 PERCENT IN THE 1982 AND 1985 ELECTIONS. THIS ARTICLE
EXPLORES WHAT ACCOUNTED FOR THE SUCCESS OF THE GREENS IN
THIS ELECTION.

07916 SAINT-GERMAN, M.A.
DOES THEIR DIFFERENCE MAKE A DIFFERENCE? THE IMPACT OF
WOMEN ON PUBLIC POLICY IN THE ARIZONA LEGISLATURE
SOCIAL SCIENCE QUARTERLY, 70(4) (DEC 89), 956-968.
THROUGH A LONGITUDINAL ANALYSIS OF BILLS INITIATED IN
THE ARIZONA STATE LEGISLATURE BETWEEN 1969 AND 1986, THIS
STUDY INVESTIGATES QUALITATIVE AND QUANTITATIVE CHANGES IN
THE EFFECTS OF GENDER ON PUBLIC POLICY. WOMEN LEGISLATORS
GENERALLY INITIATED MORE PROPOSALS THAN MEN IN TRADITIONAL
WOMEN'S INTEREST AREAS AND ON FEMINIST ISSUES. DIFFERENCES
CAN BE SEEN IN THE NUMBER, SUBJECT MATTER, AND ENACTMENT
RATE OF WOMEN'S BILLS AS THE PROPORTION OF WOMEN IN THE
STATE LEGISLATURE INCREASED. THIS STUDY SUGGESTS THAT
PROPORTIONAL GROUP SIZE MAY BE AN IMPORTANT CONSIDERATION IN
THE EVALUATION OF THE IMPACT OF GENDER ON PUBLIC POLICY.

07917 SAISUNTHORN, J.
FISHERIES OF THE ASEAN STATES: TRANSITION IN THE 200-MILE
EEZ REGIME
DISSERTATION ABSTRACTS INTERNATIONAL, 49(11) (MAY 89),
3487-A.
THE AUTHOR STUDIES THE FISHERIES OF THE ASEAN STATES
UNDER THE NEW 200-MILE EXCLUSIVE ECONOMIC ZONE (EEZ) IN THE
CONTEXT OF INDIVIDUAL STATE FISHERIES POLICIES AND
LEGISLATION AS WELL AS THE 1982 UNITED NATIONS CONVENTION ON
THE LAW OF THE SEA. ALTHOUGH PART V OF THE UN CONVENTION HAS
NOT YET ENTERED INTO FORCE, FOUR ASEAN STATES (INDONESIA,
MALAYSIA, THE PHILIPPINES, AND THAILAND) HAVE ALREADY
CLAIMED THEIR EEZ AND FORMULATED FISHERIES POLICIES.

07918 SAITO, N.
"STAR WARS" DEBATE: STRATEGIC DEFENSE INITIATIVE AND ANTI-
SATELLITE WEAPONS
DISSERTATION ABSTRACTS INTERNATIONAL, 48(10) (APR 88),
2723-A.
SDI IS ASSESSED BY SEVERAL CRITERIA: TECHNOLOGICAL
FEASIBILITY; COMPATIBILITY WITH THE ABM TREATY; SOVIET
RESPONSES TO SDI; IMPICATIONS FOR DETEREENCE AND ARMS
CONTROL PROSPECTS; AND IMPLICATIONS FOR THE SECURITY OF NATO
EUROPE. THE CONCLUSION IS THAT SDI WOULD ENHANCE THE
PROBABILITY OF CONFRONTATION BETWEEN THE US AND THE USSR.

07919 SAITO, S.
JAPAN'S SPACE POLICY
SPACE POLICY, 5(3) (AUG 89), 193-200.
JAPAN HAS BEEN ACTIVE IN THE DEVELOPMENT OF SPACE

SCIENCE AND TECHNOLOGY, FOR PEACEFUL PURPOSES ONLY, SINCE
1955. THIS ARTICLE DESCRIBES THE FORMATION OF THE SPACE
ACTIVITIES COMMISSION AS THE COUNTRY'S PRIMARY SPACE-POLICY
MAKING BODY, AND OF THE NATIONAL SPACE DEVELOPMENT AGENCY,
WHICH OVERSEES THE DEVELOPMENT OF SPACE TECHNOLOGY. THE
FUNDAMENTAL GUIDELINES GOVERNING SPACE ACTIVITIES ARE ARE
EXPLAINED, AND A DETAILED BREAKDOWN IS GIVEN OF PROJECTS
AGREED FOR THE COMING YEARS.

07920 SAIVETZ, C.
ISLAM AND GORBACHEV'S POLICY IN THE MIDDLE EAST
JOURNAL OF INTERNATIONAL AFFAIRS, 42(2) (SPR 89), 435-444.
THE ARTICLE EXAMINES THE POLICY CHANGES THAT MIKHAIL
GORBACHEV HAS MADE IN THE AREA OF FOREIGN POLICY WITH
REGARDS TO THE MIDDLE EAST. THESE INCLUDE AN OVERALL
ACKNOWLEDGEMENT OF THE LINKAGE BETWEEN REGIONAL AND
BILATERAL RELATIONS, ATTEMPTS TO INCREASE DIPLOMATIC TIES
WITH ISRAEL, THE WITHDRAWAL OF TROOPS FROM AFGHANISTAN, AND
ATTEMPTS TO MEDIATE THE IRAN-IRAQ CONFLICT. THE ARTICLE ALSO
ANALYZES THE CHALLENGES THAT ISLAMIC FUNDAMENTALISM POSES TO
THE USSR BOTH OUTSIDE OF ITS BORDERS AND FROM WITHIN. THE
IRANIAN REVOLUTION AND THE MUSLIM COUNTERINSURGENCY IN
AFGHANISTAN BOTH HAVE HAD SPILLOVER EFFECTS IN THE USSR AS
ISLAMIC NATIONALISM INCREASES.

07921 SAIVETZ, C.R.
"NEW THINKING" AND SOVIET THIRD WORLD POLICY
CURRENT HISTORY, 88(540) (OCT 89), 325-328, 354-357.
EARLY IN THE GORBACHEV REGIME, IT BECAME CLEAR THAT
MOSCOW'S THIRD WORLD POLICY HAD CHANGED. HE INDICATED THAT
HE HOPED TO CUT SOVIET LOSSES IN THE THIRD WORLD AND
ELIMINATE, WHEREVER POSSIBLE, AREAS OF POTENTIAL
CONFRONTATION WITH THE USA. YET HIS POLICIES HAVE MADE IT
CLEAR THAT MOSCOW INTENDS TO REMAIN INVOLVED IN THE THIRD
WORLD, TO SOME EXTENT.

07922 SAJOO, A.B.
INTERNATIONAL HUMAN RIGHTS AND CANADIAN FOREIGN POLICY:
PRINCIPLES, PRIORITIES, AND PRACTICES IN THE TRUDEAU ERA
AND BEYOND
DISSERTATION ABSTRACTS INTERNATIONAL, 48(10) (APR 88),
2723-A.
THE ROLE OF HUMAN RIGHTS CRITERIA IN CANADIAN
POLICYMAKING IS ASSESSED. CENTRAL AMERICA AND SOUTH AFRICA
ARE UTILIZED AS CASE STUDIES TO EXAMINE THE DECLARED ROLE OF
HUMAN RIGHTS AND THE ACTUAL ROLE IT PLAYED. THEREFORE, AN
"OVERVIEW" OF RIGHTS-OREINTATION THROUGH THE TRUDEAU ERA AND
BEYOND IS FORMULATED.

07923 SAKWA, R.
COMMUNE DEMOCRACY AND GORBACLEV'S REFORMS
POLITICAL STUDIES, XXXVII(2) (JUN 89), 224-243.
THE PROCESS OF DEMOCRATIC RESTRUCTING IN THE SOVIET
UNION SINCE 1986 CAN BE UNDERSTOOD IN TERMS OF A REVIVAL OF
THE DEMOCRATIC IDEAL OF A PARTICIPATORY AND SELFMANAGING
SOCIETY. THE CONCEPT OF COMMUNE DEMOCRACY ESPOUSED BY MARX
AND LENIN, HOWEVER, IS PROBLEMATICAL, NOT LEAST BECAUSE OF
AMBIGUITIES IN ITS RELATIONSHIP TO THE STATE, THE ROLE OF
THE DICTATORSHIP OF THE PROLETARIAT AND THE DIRIGISME OF THE
PARTY. GORBACHEV'S REFORMS ARE DEVELOPING WITHIN THE CONTEXT
OF AN ATTEMPT TO REGENERATE COMMUNE DEMOCRACY, AND SOME OF
THE HESITANCIES OF THE REFORM PROCESS CAN BE ATTRIBUTED TO
THE CONTRADICTIONS IN THE THEORY. THE SCOPE FOR A
RECONSTITUTED CIVIL SOCIETY IS LIMITED BY THE INCLUSIVE
TENDENCIES OF TRADITIONAL COMMUNE DEMOCRACY. THE REFORM
PROCESS MAY ULTIMATELY BE ABLE TO EXPLOIT THE AMBIGUITIES IN
COMMUNE DEMOCRACY SUFFICIENTLY TO ALLOW THE DEVELOPMENT OF A
LAW-GOVERNED STATE.

07924 SALAMONE, S.D.
THE DIALECTICS OF TURKISH NATIONAL IDENTITY: ETHNIC
BOUNDARY MAINTENANCE AND STATE IDEOLOGY
EAST EUROPEAN QUARTERLY, XXIII(1) (MAR 89), 33-61.
THE AUTHOR OFFERS A BRIEF SOCIO-HISTORICAL ANALYSIS OF
TURKEY'S FIVE MOST PROMINENT ETHNIC MINORITY GROUPS WITH A
DISTINCT OTTOMAN HERITAGE: THE KURDS, ARABS, JEWS, ARMENIANS,
AND GREEKS. THEN HE CONSIDERS THE CONSTITUTIONAL AND
POLITICAL STRUCTURE OF THE TURKISH REPUBLIC FROM ITS
IDEOLOGICAL ORIGINS TO ITS INSTANTIATION IN 1924. HE
CONCLUDES WITH A REFORMULATION OF THE OUTSTANDING, BASIC
ISSUES OF SOCIAL, POLITICAL, AND CULTURAL PLURALISM
CONFRONTING THE EVOLUTION OF TURKEY'S NATIONAL IDENTITY.

07925 SALAMONE, S.D.
THE DIALECTICS OF TURKISH NATIONAL IDENTITY: ETHNIC
BOUNDARY MAINTENANCE AND STATE IDEOLOGY
EAST EUROPEAN QUARTERLY, XXIII(2) (JUN 89), 225-248.
THE IDEOLOGY OF ATATURKISM APPLIES CONSTITUTIONALLY TO
ALL TURKISH CITIZENS REGARDLESS OF THEIR NATIONAL ORIGINS,
AND THE PRINCIPLES OF ATATURKISM PERMEATE THE TURKISH
CONSTITUTION. THUS, THE TURKISH CONSTITUTIONAL MOVEMENT SET
IN MOTION BY MUSTAFA KEMAL ATATURK CONTINUES TO CONFLICT
WITH SOCIAL REALITY SINCE THE OVERRIDING QUESTION REMAINS
WHETHER OR NOT THE GOALS OF TURKEY'S REPUBLICAN MANDATE CAN

ANNUAL SUPPLEMENT - 1989 07926-07938

INSURE THE CONDITIONS FOR STRUCTURAL PLURALISM THAT ARE
ESSENTIAL TO THE FORMATION OF A MODERN MULTI-ETHNIC
DEMOCRACY.

07926 SALANT, T.J.
COUNTY HOME RULE: CHALLENGING THE TENETS OF REFORM WITH
EMPHASIS ON COUNTIES IN ARIZONA
DISSERTATION ABSTRACTS INTERNATIONAL, 49(7) (JAN 89),
1960-A.
THE EXPERIENCE OF STATES WITH COUNTY HOME RULE REFORM IS
CHRONICLED IN THIS DISSERTATION. ACTUAL RESULTS ARE FOUND TO
BE AT VARIANCE WITH THE PROCLAMATIONS OF REFORMERS. EVIDENCE
FROM EXPERIENCE IN ARIZONA AND CALIFORNIA IS HIGHLIGHTED.

07927 SALEM, A.H.K.
THE SUPERPOWERS' INVOLVEMENT IN THE MIDDLE EAST AND ITS
IMPACT ON SELF-DETERMINATION FOR THE PALESTINIAN PEOPLE
DISSERTATION ABSTRACTS INTERNATIONAL, 50(6) (DEC 89),
1796-A.
THE AUTHOR SURVEYS THE INVOLVEMENT OF THE TWO
SUPERPOWERS IN THE MIDDLE EAST AND THEIR IMPACT ON THE
PALESTINIANS' QUEST FOR SELF-DETERMINATION. HE ATTEMPTS TO
ANSWER THREE MAJOR QUESTIONS: HOW DO UNITED STATES INTERESTS
IN THE MIDDLE EAST AFFECT THE SELF-DETERMINATION OF THE
PALESTINIAN PEOPLE? HOW DO SOVIET INTERESTS AFFECT THE
ASPIRATIONS OF THE PALESTINIANS? HOW DOES SUPERPOWER
INVOLVEMENT IN THE ARAB-ISRAELI CONFLICT AFFECT THE SEARCH
FOR A LASTING PEACE IN THE REGION?

07928 SALEM, E
WHAT PRICE REFORM?
FAR EASTERN ECONOMIC REVIEW, 141(38) (SEP 88), 70-71.
CHINESE LEADERS ARE EFFECTIVELY SCRAPPING THEIR
EXPERIMENT WITH PRICE REFORM. RAPANT INFLATION HAVE CAUSED
CHINESE LEADERS TO PUT OFF PRICE REFORM FOR "FIVE YEARS OR
MORE" AS THE PLOT A COURSE THAT WILL REQUIRE INCREASED
SUBSIDIES FOR FOOD AND EVENTUALLY INCREASE BUDGET DEFICTS.
THE FAILURE OF PRICE REFORM WAS A POLITICAL ONE FOR ZHAO
ZIYANG AND OTHER REFORMERS IN CHINA'S COMMUNIST PARTY. ZHAO
WAS ONCE CONSIDERED TO BE THE SUCCESSOR OF DENG XIAOPING,
BUT IS FALLING FROM FAVOR.

07929 SALIH,M.
THE EUROPEANIZATION OF WAR IN AFRICA: FROM TRADITIONAL TO
MODERN WARFARE
CURRENT RESEARCH ON PEACE AND VIOLENCE, XII(1) (1989),
27-37.
THE MAIN PROPOSITION OF THIS ARTICLE IS THAT THERE WERE
SEVERAL WORLD WARS BEFORE THE FIRST AND SECOND EUROPEAN
WORLD WARS. THE PENETRATING EFFECT OF THE EARLIER WARS HAS
STAGGERING IMPACTS ON AFRICA TODAY. THE PRESENT WARS IN
AFRICA CANNOT BE DISCUSSED WITHOUT REFERENCE TO DIRECT OR
INDIRECT EUROPEAN INVOLVEMENT. EUROPE HAS MEDIATED AND
TRANSFORMED WAR IN AFRICA FROM LIMITED TRIBAL WARFARE TO THE
USE OF MACHINEHUNS AND MODERN WEAPON SYSTEMS. THIS ARTICLE
PROPOSES THAT THE END OF THE COLONIAL WARS HAS MARKED THE
BEGINNING OF CONVENTIONAL INTER-STATE. INTERNAL AND INTER-
ETHNIC WARS AS WELL AS SILENT WARS. POLITICAL INSTABILITY
CAUSED BY AUSTERITY MEASURES, DE DEVALUATION OF CURRENCIES,
MONETARY PRESSURES, AND TRADE RESTRICTIONS REPRESENT THE
MOST VISIBLE FORM OF SILENT WAR BETWEEN AFRICA AND EUROPE.
THE EUROPEANIZATION OF WAR IN AFRICA IS BOTH MILITARY AND
NON-MILITARY ADDING ONE MISERY TO ANOTHER AND DEVELOPING THE
WHOLE CONTINENT INTO ECONOMIC, POLITICAL AND SOCIAL
BANKRUPTCY.

07930 SALISBURY, R.H.; HEINZ, J.P.; JOHNSON, P.; LAUMANN, E.O.;
NELSON, R.L.
WHO YOU KNOW VERSUS WHAT YOU KNOW: THE USES OF GOVERNMENT
EXPERIENCE FOR WASHINGTON LOBBYISTS
AMERICAN JOURNAL OF POLITICAL SCIENCE, 33(1) (FEB 89),
175-195.
PRIVATE INTEREST REPRESENTATIVES IN WASHINGTON ARE OFTEN
SAID TO EXPLOIT PRIOR EXPERIENCE WITH THE FEDERAL GOVERNMENT,
ESPECIALLY THEIR CONTACTS WITH OFFICIALS, TO GAIN ADVANTAGE
FOR THEIR CLIENT GROUPS. DATA ON 776 INTEREST
REPRESENTATIVES ARE EXAMINED TO ESTIMATE THE FREQUENCY AND
INSTITUTIONAL LOCATION OF PRIOR GOVERNMENTAL EXPERIENCE.
JUST OVER HALF OF THE RESPONDENTS HAD HAD SOME SUCH SERVICE;
THICE AS MANY IN THE EXECUTIVE BRANCH AS IN THE MILIEU OF
CAPITOL HILL. FOR THOSE WITH EXPERIENCE, THE EXTENT AND
CHARACTER OF ITS ADVANTAGES FOR THEIR WORK AS LOBBYISTS ARE
ASSESSED. IN GENERAL, REPRESENTATIVES ASSIGN GREATER VALUE
TO THE KNOWLEDGE GAINED OF BOTH SUBSTANTIVE POLICY AND
DECISION-MAKING PROCESSES THAN TO CONTACTS WITH OFFICIALS OR
OTHER LOBBYISTS.

07931 SALLINGER-MCBRIDE, J.; PICARD, L.A.
RURAL DEVELOPMENT AREAS IN SWAZILAND: THE POLITICS OF
INTEGRATED RURAL DEVELOPMENT
COMPARATIVE POLITICS, 22(1) (OCT 89), 1-22.
THE AUTHORS EXPLAIN INTEGRATED RURAL DEVELOPMENT (IRD)
AND ITS APPLICATION IN SWAZILAND. THEY ARGUE THAT, IN ORDER
TO UNDERSTAND THE SOCIAL AND TECHNICAL CONSTRAINTS THAT

LIMIT THE EFFECTIVENESS OF IRD PROGRAMS, ONE MUST ALSO
EXAMINE THE FUNDAMENTAL POLITICAL CONTRADICTIONS BETWEEN THE
IRD APPROACH AND THE NATURE OF NATIONAL AND LOCAL POLITICAL
ELITES WHO ARE AFFECTED BY IRD ACTIVITIES.

07932 SALMAN, H.D.
TECHNOLOGY PLANNING FOR THE POST-OIL ERA IN THE UNITED
ARAB EMIRATES (UAE): A STUDY OF TECHNOLOGY POLICY OPTIONS
OPEN TO THE UNITED ARAB EMIRATES (UAE)
DISSERTATION ABSTRACTS INTERNATIONAL, 49(7) (JAN 89),
1960-A.
THE AUTHOR SURVEYS TECHNOLOGY POLICY OPTIONS OPEN TO THE
UNITED ARAB EMIRATES AS IT PLANS FOR CONTINUED ECONOMIC
DEVELOPMENT WHILE, AND AFTER, ITS OIL IS DEPLETED.

07933 SALOKAR, R.M.
THE SOLICITOR GENERAL: BALANCING THE INTERESTS OF THE
EXECUTIVE AND JUDICIAL BRANCHES, 1959-1982
DISSERTATION ABSTRACTS INTERNATIONAL, 50(4) (OCT 89),
1080-A.
THE ROLE OF THE SOLICITOR GENERAL OF THE UNITED STATES
EPITOMIZES THE TENSIONS INHERENT IN A SYSTEM OF SEPARATE AND
SHARED POWER. THE SOLICITOR GENERAL SERVES BOTH THE
EXECUTIVE AND JUDICIAL BRANCHES, EVEN THOUGH THEIR
PERSPECTIVES ON LAW AND POLICY DIFFER AND SOMETIMES CONFLICT.
THIS DISSERTATION CONSIDERS HOW THE SOLICITOR GENERAL
ADJUSTS THE PRIORITIES OF THE EXECUTIVE BRANCH TO THE
TRADITIONS OF THE JUDICIAL BRANCH.

07934 SALPETER, E.
ARAFAT'S CHALLENGE: AGONIZING REAPPRAISAL IN ISRAEL
NEW LEADER, LXXII(1) (JAN 89), 5-6.
ISRAEL'S INTERNAL POLITICS ARE OFTEN SHAPED BY EXTERNAL
EVENTS. REACTIONS TO THE INTIFADA RANGE FROM HAWKS, WHO
INSIST ON IRREVERSIBLE ANNEXATION OF THE OCCUPIED
TERRITORIES, TO THE DOVES, WHO WANT ISRAEL TO NEGOTIATE WITH
ARAFAT. ALTHOUGH SHIMON PERES AGREES WITH YITZCHAK SHAMIR
THAT ISRAEL SHOULD NOT TALK TO THE PLO, HE HAS PROPOSED FREE
ELECTIONS OF PALESTINIAN REPRESENTATIVES, WITH WHOM ISRAEL
WOULD NEGOTIATE.

07935 SALPETER, E.
BENEATH THE SURFACE IN ISRAEL
NEW LEADER, LXXII(3) (FEB 89), 5-6.
EVENTS ON THE ISRAELI SIDE IN THE PALESTINIAN CONFLICT
MAY SOON ACQUIRE A MOMENTUM THAT COULD INDUCE SOME
FLEXIBILITY, EVEN AMONG THE MAJORITY OF THE RIGHT. SEVERAL
FACTORS ARE CONTRIBUTING TO THIS TREND, INCLUDING THE
INTIFADA, AMERICAN WILLINGNESS TO TALK TO THE PLO, AND
WARNINGS THAT THE INTIFADA CANNOT BE ENDED BY MILITARY MEANS
ALONE.

07936 SALPETER, E.
ISRAEL'S NEXT TEST: SHAMIR GEST SET FOR WASHINGTON
NEW LEADER, LXXII(5) (MAR 89), 6-8.
THE RESOLUTION OF THE DISPUTE OVER THE TABA ENCLAVE,
INCREASING CONTACTS WITH THE USSR, AND A HUGE VICTORY IN
MUNICIPAL ELECTIONS HAVE ALL BOOSTED THE CONFIDENCE OF
ISRAEL'S LIKUD PARTY AND ITS LEADER YITZHAK SHAMIR. THE
PRIME MINISTER IS PREPARING FOR A MEETING WITH PRESIDENT
BUSH IN WASHINGTON AND SPECULATION ON SHAMIR'S STRATEGY
TOWARDS THE US IS RUNNING WILD. SOME OBSERVERS NOTE THAT THE
LIKUD PARTY'S SUCCESS IN THE MUNICIPAL ELECTIONS GIVE THE
PARTY A MANDATE FOR A CONTINUATION OF THEIR HAWKISH POLICIES.
HOWEVER, OTHERS FEEL THAT SHAMIR IS SLOWLY BEGINNING TO
ACCEPT POLITICAL REALITY WHICH INCLUDES THE NECESSITY OF
MAKING CONCESSIONS TO THE US IN ORDER TO MAINTAIN FRIENDLY
RELATIONS AND THE ALL IMPORTANT FINANCIAL AID FROM THE US.

07937 SALPETER, E.
THE MIDEAST ON THE BACK BURNER
NEW LEADER, 72(18) (NOV 89), 5-6.
THIS ARTICLE EXAMINES THE EFFECT THAT THE RUSH OF
DEVELOPMENTS IN EASTERN EUROPE IS HAVING ON WORLD INTEREST
IN THE PERENNIAL DISPUTES IN THE MIDDLE EAST. IT IS ASSUMED
THAT IF DETENTE BECOMES A PERMANENT FEATURE OF SUPERPOWER
RELATIONS, THE MIDDLE EAST WILL BE LESS IMPORTANT AND THE
STRATEGIC VALUE OF ISRAEL FOR THE U.S. WILL DIMINISH
SIGNIFICANTLY. HOWEVER, ISRAEL WELCOMES INDICATIONS THAT
MOSCOW WILL BE LESS WILLING TO LAVISH ARMS ON THE ARABS.
ISRAEL'S RELATIONS WITH BOTH THESE SUPERPOWERS IS EXPLORED
IN LIGHT OF RECENT EVENTS.

07938 SALPETER, E.
THE POLITICS OF PEACE IN THE MIDEAST
NEW LEADER, LXXII(15) (OCT 89), 5-7.
THE INTRODUCTION OF EGYPTIAN PRESIDENT MUBRAK'S "TEN
POINTS" INTO THE ISRAEL-PALESTINIAN NEGOTIATING SCENE CAUSED
NO SMALL STIR IN ISRAELI AND INTERNATIONAL CIRCLES. IN
ISRAEL IT THREATENED TO SPLIT THE ALREADY SHAKY LABOUR-LIKUD
RULING COALITION; MUCH TO THE CHAGRIN OF PRIME MINISTER
YITZHAK SHAMIR AND HIS LIKUD FOLLOWERS, DEFENSE MINISTER
YITZHAK RABIN ACCEPTED MUBARAK'S PROPOSAL INCLUDING THE
CONCEPT OF "LAND FOR PEACE." IN INTERNATIONAL CIRCLES, THE

PLAN RECEIVED SUPPORT FROM THE US AND USSR, BUT WAS REJECTED BY THE PLO.

07939 SALPETER, E.
THE VIEW FROM THE WEST BANK
NEW LEADER, LXXII(10) (JUN 89), 5-6.
THE JEWISH SETTLEMENTS ON THE WEST BANK ARE BOTH A SYMBOL OF AND THE ESSENCE OF THE DAILY DEBATE HERE OVER PAST, PRESENT AND FUTURE ISRAELI-PALESTINIAN RELATIONS. FOR THOSE CALLING THEMSELVES THE NATIONAL CAMP, THE RIGHT OF EVERY JEW TO LIVE IN ANY PART OF PALESTINE IS NO MORE OPEN TO DISPUTE THAN AN AMERICAN JEW'S RIGHT TO RESIDE IN NEW YORK, HOUSTON OR OSHKOSH. BUT MANY ISRAELIS, POSSIBLY THE MAJORITY, SEE THIS VIEW AS CREATING AN UNNECESSARY SOURCE OF IRRITATION AMONG LOCAL ARABS AND SOME WESTERN GOVERNMENTS. IN ADDITION, IT IS ARGUED, THE VAST SUMS DEVOTED TO INFRASTRUCTURE AND TO PROVIDING SECURITY COULD BE BETTER SPENT IN THE GALILEE OR IN THE NEGEV.

07940 SALT, J.
A COMPARATIVE OVERVIEW OF INTERNATIONAL TRENDS AND TYPES, 1950-80
INTERNATIONAL MIGRATION REVIEW, 23(3) (FAL 89), 431-456.
THIS ARTICLE PROVIDES A GENERAL OVERVIEW OF INTERNATIONAL MIGRATION TRENDS AND TYPES DURING THE POSTWAR PERIOD. ITS THESIS IS THAT INTERNATIONAL MIGRATION CONSISTS OF A SET OF SPATIAL NETWORKS WHICH SHARE MANY OF THE PROCESSES THAT CREATE THEM, BUT THAT THE NETWORKS ARE CHARACTERIZED BY FACTORS WHICH VARY GEOGRAPHICALLY AND DISTINGUISH ONE FROM ANOTHER. FULLER ANALYSIS OF THESE REQUIRES A SYSTEMS APPROACH TO PROVIDE A FRAMEWORK WITHIN WHICH TO STUDY THE PROCESSES THAT PRODUCE FLOW PATTERNS. IT CONCLUDES THAT OUR ABILITY TO FORECAST FUTURE WORLD PATTERNS OF INTERNATIONAL MIGRATION MUST BE BASED ON AN ASSESSMENT OF THE LIKELY BEHAVIOR OF THE COMPONENT MACRO-REGIONAL SYSTEMS WE CAN RECOGNIZE.

07941 SALT, J.
SUNBELT CAPITAL AND CONSERVATIVE POLITICAL REALIGNMENT IN THE 1970S AND 1980S
CRITICAL SOCIOLOGY, 16(2-3) (SUM 89), 145-163.
ELITE THEORISTS DISAGREE OVER WHETHER THE RECENT CONSERVATIVE SHIFT IN U.S. POLITICS RESULTS FROM A RIGHTWARD SHIFT OF THE CAPITALIST CLASS AS WHOLE OR FROM THE POLITICAL ASCENDANCE OF AN ULTRACONSERVATIVE SUNBELT SEGMENT. USING DATA ON CORPORATE POLITICAL ACTION COMMITTEE CONTRIBUTIONS BETWEEN 1978 AND 1986, THE AUTHOR FINDS EVIDENCE OF GREATER CONSERVATISM AMONG SUNBELT CORPORATIONS THAN AMONG NORTHEASTERN CORPORATIONS, AS WELL AS EVIDENCE LINKING CONSERVATISM TO KEY SUNBELT INDUSTRIES AND FAMILY-OWNED COMPANIES. SURPRISINGLY, MIDWESTERN CAPITAL WAS ALSO A STRONG SUPPORTER OF THE NEW RIGHT'S RISE IN 1978 AND 1980, BUT SIGNIFICANTLY REDUCED ITS CONTRIBUTIONS AFTER 1980.

07942 SALTZSTEIN, G.H.
BLACK MAYORS AND POLICE POLICIES
THE JOURNAL OF POLITICS, 51(3) (AUG 89), 525-544.
THIS STUDY EXAMINES THE IMPACT OF BLACK MAYORS ON POLICE DEPARTMENT POLICIES OF INTEREST TO BLACK CITIZENS IN 105 MUNICIPAL GOVERNMENTS IN THE UNITED STATES. THE CORRELATES OF COMMUNITY-ORIENTED POLICING, MINORITY RECRUITMENT, BLACK REPRESENTATION AMONG SWORN OFFICERS, CITIZEN CONTROLS OVER DEPARTMENT POLICIES, AND DEPARTMENTAL RESPONSES TO PUBLIC DISORDER INCIDENTS ARE EXAMINED, AND THE PRESENCE OF A BLACK MAYOR DURING THE TIME FRAME IN QUESTION IS FOUND TO BE ASSOCIATED WITH BOTH BLACK REPRESENTATION AMONG SWORN OFFICERS AND ADOPTION OF CITIZEN CONTROLS OVER THE DEPARTMENT. THE IMPLICATIONS OF THESE FINDINGS FOR THE STUDY OF BLACK MAYORAL INFLUENCE ARE EXPLORED.

07943 SALWEN, M.B.; LEE, J.-S.
NEWS OF TERRORISM: A COMPARISON OF THE US. AND SOUTH KOREAN PRESS
TERRORISM, 11(4) (1988), 309-322.
THIS STUDY COMPARED U.S. AND SOUTH KOREAN NEWSPAPER COVERAGE OF THE NOVEMBER 1987 CRASH OF KOREAN AIRLINES (KAL) FLIGHT 858 OVER THE THAI-BURMA BORDER. COMPARISONS HERE MADE BEFORE AND AFTER EVIDENCE OF NORTH KOREAN TERRORIST INVOLVEMENT IN THE CRASH WAS UNCOVERED. THE FINDINGS DID NOT SUGGEST EVIDENCE SUPPORTING THE NOTION THAT THE PRESS PLAYS UP OR SENSATIONALIZES REPORTS OF TERRORISM WITH LITTLE OR NO EVIDENCE. EVEN THOUGH THE U.S. AND SOUTH KOREAN PRESS WERE AWARE OF RUMORS OF NORTH KOREAN TERRORIST INVOLVEMENT IN THE CRASH BEFORE EVIDENCE OF NORTH KOREAN INVOLVEMENT WAS AVAILABLE, THE PRESS OF BOTH NATIONS DID NOT STRESS THE TERRORIST ANGLE OR NORTH KOREAN INVOLVEMENT UNTIL AFTER EVIDENCE SUPPORTING NORTH KOREAN TERRORISM WAS UNCOVERED. IT WAS ALSO FOUND THAT SOUTH KOREAN PUBLIC OFFICIALS EXERCISED AT LEAST A DEGREE OF "AGENDA CONTROL" IN DIRECTING PRESS COVERAGE TO STRESS NORTH KOREAN INVOLVEMENT IN THE CRASH.

07944 SAMANDARY, A.B.
BY POLITICAL MEANS, NOT BY FORCE
WORLD MARXIST REVIEW, 31(12) (DEC 88), 5-8.

IN THIS ARTICLE, THE PRAGUE - BASED AMBASSADOR OF AFGHANISTAN EXPLAINS THE MECHANICS, OBJECTIVES, MOTIVE FORCES AND PRINCIPLES OF THE NATIONAL RECONCILIATION POLICY IN AFGHANISTAN.

07945 SAMAYOA, S.
NEGOTIATIONS OR TOTAL WAR
WORLD POLICY JOURNAL, VI(2) (SPR 89), 321-356.
THE ARTICLE INITIALLY ANALYZES THE POLITICAL AND MILITARY SITUATION IN EL SALVADOR ESPECIALLY WITH REGARDS TO THE MARCH, 1989 ELECTIONS IN WHICH AN UNPRECEDENTED 50 PERCENT OF THE ELIGIBLE ELECTORATE DID NOT CAST BALLOTS. IT ALSO CONTAINS AN INTERVIEW WITH SALVADOR SAMAYOA, THE OFFICIAL SPOKESMAN FOR THE REBEL COALITION, THE FARABUNDO MARTI NATIONAL LIBERATION FRONT (FMLN). SAMAYOA DISCUSSES THE RECENT ELECTION AND THE EFFECT THAT FMLN CALLS FOR A BOYCOTT HAD ON THE OUTCOME AND ALSO THE PEACE PLAN INITIATED BY THE FMLN. HE ALSO DISCUSSES THE MILITARY SITUATION IN EL SALVADOR AS WELL AS HUMAN RIGHTS.

07946 SAMHOUN, R.
CONTROVERSIAL INTERDEPENDENCE: WHAT NEXT?
WORLD MARXIST REVIEW, 32(6) (JUN 89), 50-54.
THIS ARTICLE EXAMINES CONTROVERSIAL INTERDEPENDENCE IN RELATION TO MARXIST-LENINIST TRADITION. THIS INVOLVES AN ANALYSIS OF THE CO-EXISTENCE OF THE TWO SOCIAL AND POLITICAL SYSTEMS AT A TIME OF GLOBAL PROBLEMS, PRIMARILY THE RISK OF NUCLEAR AND ECOLOGICAL CATASTROPHES AND A CRISIS OF CIVILISATION, WHICH CAN BE RESOLVED ONLY BY THE JOINT EFFORTS OF ALL HUMANITY. THE RELATIONS BETWEEN THE "CAPITALIST CENTER" AND THE "DEVELOPING PERIPHERY" FIGURE PROMINENTLY AMONG THESE PROBLEMS AND ARE DISCUSSED BY RAFIC SAMHOUN.

07947 SAMOFF, J.
POPULAR INITIATIVES AND LOCAL GOVERNMENT IN TANZANIA
JOURNAL OF DEVELOPING AREAS, 24(1) (OCT 89), 1-18.
POST-COLONIAL AFRICAN LEADERSHIPS ASSUMED POWER WITH AN IDEOLOGY THAT EMPHASIZED DEMOCRACY AND CITIZEN PARTICIPATION. OVER TIME, THE PRESSURES FOR CENTRALIZATION OF AUTHORITY PREVAILED OVER THE COMMITMENT TO LOCAL PARTICIPATION. THE ARTICLE EXAMINES THE EXPERIENCE OF LOCAL GOVERNMENT IN TANZANIA, A NATION WHERE LOCAL AUTONOMY WAS VIRTUALLY ABOLISHED, THEN SUBSEQUENTLY RE-CREATED. THE ARTICLE CONCLUDES THAT ALTHOUGH TANZANIA'S SINGLE PARTY SUPREMACY WAS NEVER DIRECTLY CHALLENGED, LOCAL GOVERNMENTS AND ORGANIZATIONS WERE OFTEN TAKING THE INITIATIVE IN THE FORM OF AGRICULTURAL COOPERATIVES, SCHOOL ORGANIZING COMMITTEES, AND OTHER ORGANIZATIONS.

07948 SAMPHEL, T.
A CULTURE IN EXILE: TIBETAN REFUGEES IN INDIA
CHINA REPORT, 24(3) (JUL 88), 237-242.
THIS ARTICLE EXAMINES THE CULTURAL CHANGES EXPERIENCED BY THE TIBETAN PEOPLE WHEN, AFTER THE CHINESE COMMUNIST OCCUPATION OF TIBET, AND THE CRUSHING DEFEAT OF THE TIBETAN PEOPLE'S POPULAR UPRISING OF 10 MARCH, THE DALAI LAMA, FOLLOWED BY 75,000 TIBETANS, SOUGHT POLITICAL ASYLUM IN INDIA IN 1959.

07949 SAMSTAG, T.
SEAL SCANDALS AND SCARES
SCANDINAVIAN REVIEW, 77(3) (AUT 89), 5-13.
A SWEDISH-MADE TELEVISION DOCUMENTARY ON THE ANNUAL NORWEGIAN SEAL-CULL ELICITED STRONG PUBLIC RESPONSE, INCLUDING DEMONSTRATIONS AT THE NORWEGIAN EMBASSY IN SWEDEN AND CANCELLATIONS OF FISH IMPORTS. SWEDISH KING CARL XVI GUSTAF CRITICIZED THE REFUSAL OF NORWEGIAN PRIME MINISTER BRUNDTLAND TO COMMENT ON THE AFFAIR, BUT BRUNDTLAND WAS NOT ABLE TO IGNORE THE PUBLIC UPROAR FOR LONG. TERRIFIED THAT EUROPEAN COUNTRIES OR THE UNITED STATES MIGHT BOYCOTT NORWEGIAN PRODUCTS DUE TO PRESSURE FROM ENVIRONMENTALISTS, BRUNDTLAND URGENTLY CONFERRED WITH HER FISHERIES MINISTER. SEVERAL COMMISSIONS WERE SET UP TO INVESTIGATE THE AFFAIR, AND THE NORDIC COUNCIL PUT THE SEAL PROBLEM ON ITS AGENDA.

07950 SAMUELS, R.J.
CONSUMING FOR PRODUCTION: JAPANESE NATIONAL SECURITY, NUCLEAR FUEL PROCUREMENT, AND THE DOMESTIC ECONOMY
INTERNATIONAL ORGANIZATION, 43(4) (FAL 89), 625-646.
ONE OF THE MOST INTRIGUING ASPECTS OF POSTWAR JAPAN IS A REVERSAL OF ECONOMIC ROLES IN WHICH CONSUMERS SERVE PRODUCERS RATHER THAN VICE VERSA. BY ACQUIESCING TO "CONSUMER UNFRIENDLY" PRICE AND DISTRIBUTION SYSTEMS, JAPANESE CONSUMERS HAVE SUBSIDIZED JAPANESE INDUSTRY AND WESTERN CONSUMERS AS WELL. ALTHOUGH MUCH OF THE RECENT THEORIZING ABOUT JAPANESE PRODUCTION AND CONSUMPTION HAS FOCUSED ON JAPANESE CONSUMERS AS END USERS. IT HAS SELDOM ADDRESSED THE QUESTION OF HOW JAPANESE PRODUCERS THAT PAY MORE THAN OTHERS FOR FACTOR INPUTS REMAIN COMPETITIVE IN WORLD MARKETS. THIS ARTICLE USES THE CASE OF NUCLEAR FUEL PRICE INSENSITIVITY, DERIVED FROM SECURITY CONCERNS, TO EXPLORE HOW THIS BEHAVIOR IS INSTITUTIONALIZED THROUGH REGULATORY POLICY IN THE LARGER JAPANESE ECONOMIC CULTURE.

07951 SAMUELS, H.J.
SOME FUNDAMENTALS OF THE ECONOMIC ROLE OF GOVERNMENT
JOURNAL OF ECONOMIC ISSUES, XXIII(2) (JUN 89), 427-433.
THE CONVENTIONAL DISTINCTION BETWEEN GOVERNMENT AND
ECONOMY, AND BETWEEN PRIVATE AND PUBLIC, SEEMS BOTH
ANALYTICALLY FALSE AND NORMATIVELY MISLEADING AND SUBJECT TO
SELECTIVE PERCEPTION AND PUTATIVE ABUSE. FOR LAW-GOVERNMENT
IS NOT EXOGENOUS TO THE ECONOMIC SYSTEM AND THE ECONOMIC
SYSTEM CANNOT EXIST INDEPENDENT OF LAW AND GOVERNMENT. THERE
IS A LEGAL-ECONOMIC NEXUS IN WHICH IT MAY APPEAR THAT
GOVERNMENT AND ECONOMY INTERACT AS SEPARATE SOCIAL PROCESSES
BUT IN WHICH EACH IS ACTUALLY FUNDAMENTALLY INVOLVED IN THE
(RE)DETERMINATION OF THE OTHER AND THEREBY OF SOCIAL REALITY.

07952 SANCHEZ, A.L.
THE CONTRIBUTION OF PERSONALITY TYPE (PREFERENCE) AND
SELECTED SITUATIONAL FACTORS TO VISIONARY LEADERSHIP
BEHAVIOR
DISSERTATION ABSTRACTS INTERNATIONAL, 50(3) (SEP 89),
790-A.
THE AUTHOR INVESTIGATES THE RELATIVE CONTRIBUTION OF
PERSONALITY TYPE/PREFERENCE TO VISIONARY LEADERSHIP BEHAVIOR.
SHE ALSO CONSIDERS SITUATIONAL FACTORS AND ANALYZES TO WHAT
EXTENT PERSONALITY VARIABLES AND SITUATIONAL FACTORS
INTERACT TO IMPACT VISIONARY LEADERSHIP BEHAVIOR.

07953 SANDERS, A.
BRITISH COLONIAL POLICY AND THE ROLE OF AMERINDIANS IN THE
POLITICS OF THE NATIONALIST PERIOD IN BRITISH GUIANA, 1945-
68
SOCIAL AND ECONOMIC STUDIES, 36(3) (SEP 87), 77-98.
THIS PAPER ANALYZES THE POLITICAL BEHAVIOR OF GUYANA'S
AMERIDIAN POPULATION DURING THE PERIOD OF THE SECOND WORLD
WAR TO THE PEOPLES NATIONAL CONGRESS VICTORY OF 1968. THE
THESIS THAT THEIR BEHAVIOUR WAS LARGELY A CONSEQUENCE OF THE
SPECIAL COLONIAL POLICIES ADOPTED TOWARDS AMERIDIANS DURING
GUYANA'S LONG COLONIAL HISTORY IS EXPLORED.

07954 SANDERS, A.
IDEOLOGICAL SYMBOLS
AMERICAN POLITICS QUARTERLY, 17(3) (JUL 89), 227-255.
PREVIOUS STUDIES OF CITIZENS' UNDERSTANDING AND USE OF
THE CONCEPTS OR SYMBOLS OF LIBERALISM AND CONSERVATISM HAVE
FOUND THAT MOST PEOPLE DO NOT HAVE COHERENT, CONSTRAINED
IDEOLOGICALLY LIBERAL OR CONSERVATIVE BELIEF SYSTEMS, BUT
ARE ABLE TO PLACE THEMSELVES RELATIVELY ACCURATELY ON A
LIBERAL-CONSERVATIVE SCALE. FURTHERMORE, THEIR FEELINGS OF
LIKE OR DISLIKE TOWARD LIBERALS AND/OR CONSERVATIVES HELP
THEM TO SORT OUT THE WORLD OF POLITICS. A SERIES OF IN-DEPTH
INTERVIEWS WITH 26 RANDOMLY CHOSEN PEOPLE SHOW THAT THERE
ARE TWO DIFFERENT WAYS THAT PEOPLE RELATE TO THESE CONCEPTS,
A POLICY OR A STYLISTIC ORIENTATION. EDUCATION AND POLITICAL
INTEREST SEEM TO AFFECT WHICH TYPE OF ORIENTATION ONE HAS,
WITH BETTER EDUCATED AND MORE INTERESTED CITIZENS DEVELOPING
POLICY ORIENTATIONS, BUT EITHER TYPE OF ORIENTATION CAN LEAD
TO THE USE OF THESE SYMBOLS AS EVALUATIVE TOOLS. RECOGNIZING
THE DIFFERENT WAYS IN WHICH PEOPLE RELATE TO THESE COMMON
POLITICAL SYMBOLS CAN IMPROVE OUR ABILITY TO UNDERSTAND THE
WAYS IN WHICH THE PUBLIC THINKS ABOUT POLITICS.

07955 SANDERS, ALAN J.K.
MONGOLIA IN 1988: YEAR OF RENEWAL
ASIAN SURVEY, XXIX(1) (JAN 89), 46-53.
IN 1988 MONGOLIA SAW ATTEMPTS AT REFORMS EMBRACING
IDEOLOGY, EDUCATION, MORALITY, AND ECONOMICS. SIGNIFICANT
AMONG THESE WERE THE POLICY OF "IL TOD", THE MONGOLIAN
EQUIVALENT OF GLASNOST, ECONOMIC REFORM AIMED AT SEPARATING
FOOD INDUSTRY PLANTS FROM OTHER LIGHT INDUSTRY ENTERPRISES,
AND AN ATTEMPT TO INCREASE RELATIONS WITH NON-SOCIALIST
NATIONS. ALTHOUGH MONGOLIA'S LEADERS ATTEMPTED TO BE
PRAGMATIC AND FLEXIBLE IN THEIR REFORMS, CONTINUING
INEFFICIENCY ENSURED THE LACK OF ANY REAL, LONG-TERM SUCCESS.

07956 SANDERS, D.
THE UN WORKING GROUP ON INDIGENOUS POPULATIONS
HUMAN RIGHTS QUARTERLY, 11(3) (AUG 89), 406-433.
THE ARTICLE EXAMINES THE UN WORKING GROUP ON INDIGENOUS
POPULATIONS, ITS HISTORY, MEMBERSHIP, AND GUIDING PRINCIPLES.
IT ALSO EXAMINES THE ORGANIZATION'S ACTIVITIES IN LATIN
AMERICA, WESTERN AND EASTERN EUROPE, ASIA, AND AFRICA. TEN
OTHER INDIGENOUS NONGOVERNMENTAL ORGANIZATIONS ARE BRIEFLY
OUTLINED. BANGLADESH IS USED AS A CASE STUDY OF THE
ORGANIZATIONS' CURRENT MONITORING ABILITY.

07957 SANDERS, D.G.
WATERGATE REMINISCENCES
JOURNAL OF AMERICAN HISTORY, 75(4) (MAR 89), 1228-1233.
THE AUTHOR REVIEWS THE WATERGATE SCANDAL AND HOW IT
ALTERED THE SCOPE OF PRESIDENTIAL POWER AND ENLARGED THE
POWER OF THE LEGISLATIVE BRANCH TO INVESTIGATE MATTERS
CONCERNING THE EXECUTIVE BRANCH.

07958 SANDERS, R.
THE RELEVANCE AND FUNCTION OF DIPLOMACY IN INTERNATIONAL
POLITICS FOR SMALL CARIBBEAN STATES
ROUND TABLE, (312) (OCT 89), 413-424.
THIS ARTICLE BEGINS WITH SPECIFIC DEFINITIONS, ADOPTED
FOR THIS DISCUSSION, OF "SMALL STATES," "DIPLOMACY," AND
"INTERNATIONAL POLITICS". THE FOCUS OF THIS PAPER IS THE
STATE AND SUCH POLITICAL ENTITIES AND INTERNATIONAL
ORGANIZATIONS WHICH INTERACT WITH THE STATE, DIPLOMACY AS AN
INSTRUMENT OF FOREIGN POLICY; THE PURPOSE AND FUNCTION OF
DIPLOMACY; AND ASSOCIATIVE DIPLOMACY AND ITS LIMITS ARE
EXPLORED. THE CARIBBEAN, AS A SMALL STATE, IS EXAMINED IN
REGARDS TO THE ECONOMIC DIMENSION, THE GEO-POLITICAL SETTING
AND THE MILITARY DIMENSION.

07959 SANDERS, R.J.
PERMANENT NEUTRALITY AND THE PANAMA CORAL AFTER 1999
AVAILABLE FROM NTIS, NO. AD-A207 385/6/GAR, MAR 89, 45.
THE TRANSFER OF ALL RESPONSIBILITY FOR THE OPERATION AND
MAINTENANCE OF THE PANAMA CANAL TO THE REPUBLIC OF PANAMA ON
31 DECEMBER 1999 MARKS THE END OF AN ERA AND THE BEGINNING
OF A NEW CHAPTER IN U.S.-PANAMAINIAN RELATIONS. UNDER THE
TERMS OF THE TREATY CONCERNING THE PERMANENT NEUTRALITY AND
OPERATION OF THE PANAMA CANAL, THE U.S. AND PANAMA AGREED
THAT THE CANAL WOULD BE OPERATED IN ACCORDANCE WITH A REGIME
OF PERMANENT NEUTRALITY. THE U.S. RETAINS THE RIGHT TO
EXPEDITIOUS TRANSIT AND UNILATERAL ACTION IN DEFENSE OF THE
CANAL IF DEEMED NECESSARY. THIS STUDY SEEKS TO EXAMINE THE
HISTORICAL EXAMPLE OF NEUTRALITY WITH RESPECT TO THE PANAMA
CANAL. A BRIEF COMPARATIVE LOOK AT THE SUEZ CRISIS OF 1956
IS PROVIDED. THE STUDY ANALYZES THE 1977 NEUTRALITY TREATY,
THEN POSTULATES SEVERAL SCENARIOS FOR CONSIDERATION OF
APPROPRIATE U.S. RESPONSES.

07960 SANDMAN, J.
WINNING THE PRESIDENCY: THE VISION AND VALUES APPROACH
PRESIDENTIAL STUDIES QUARTERLY, XIX(2) (SPR 89), 259-266.
THE PRESIDENTIAL ELECTION CONTEST IS DISCUSSED. BASED ON
RESEARCH ON THE PRESIDENTIAL ELECTION PROCESS, THE
PRESIDENTIAL CANDIDATE WHO BEST ARTICULATES, VERBALLY AND
SYMBOLITICALLY, THE VISIONS AND VALUES MOST TRADITIONAL TO
AMERICAN SOCIETY, OF THE BROADEST SECTION OF MIDDLE CLASS,
WILL WIN THE PRESIDENTIAL ELECTION. THE VISION AND VALUES
CONCEPT, HAS BECOME A DECISIVE ELEMENT IN THE PRESIDENTIAL
CONTEST.

07961 SANTAMARIA, U.
THEORIES OF REVOLUTION: THE AGE OF SUSPICION
NEW POLITICAL SCIENCE, (FAL 89), 111-124.
THE AUTHOR'S PREMISE IS THAT CONTEMPORARY POLITICAL
THOUGHT SEEMS TO BE MOVING TOWARD A CONDEMNATION OF THE IDEA
THAT REVOLUTION IS A REFLECTION OF MYTH, A MYSTIFICATION AND
UTOPIAN PROJECT FOUNDED ON THE KIND OF METAPHYSICS THAT
CARRIES WITHIN IT A PROJECT FOR INSTITUTIONAL ORDER WHICH IS
ULTIMATELY TOTALITARIAN: TOTAL REVOLUTION=TOTALITARIANISM.
HE PUTS THIS STATEMENT TO THE TEST BY APPLYING A SERIES OF
THEORETICAL QUESTIONS, ONE OF WHICH IS: IS IT POSSIBLE TO
CONCEIVE OF A REVOLUTION THAT IS NOT CONDEMNED TO THE SELF-
CONTRADICTION THAT HAS PLAGUED ITS CONCEPTION UP UNTIL THE
PRESENT?

07962 SANTERRE, R.E.
REPRESENTATIVE VERSUS DIRECT DEMOCRACY: ARE THERE ANY
EXPENDITURE DIFFERENCES?
PUBLIC CHOICE, 60(2) (1989), 145-154.
THE ARTICLE EXMINES MUNICIPAL AND SCHOOL EXPENDITURE
DIFFERENCES IN A SAMPLE OF 90 JURISDICTIONS IN CONNECTICUT
WITH TWO DIFFERENT GOVERNMENT FORMS: REPRESENTATIVE AND
DIRECT DEMOCRATIC SYSTEMS. IT CONCLUDES THAT ALTHOUGH THE
UNDERLYING REASONS ARE UNCLEAR, THE SYSTEM OF LOCAL
GOVERNMENT HAS A SIGNIFICANT EFFECT ON THE LEVEL OF
EXPENDITURES.

07963 SANTILLI, M.
NOTES ON THE CONSTITUTIONAL RIGHTS OF THE BRAZILIAN INDIANS
CULTURAL SURVIVAL QUARTERLY, 13(1) (1989), 13-15.
BRAZIL'S NEW CONSTITUTION PROPOSES A CURIOUS ETHNIC PACT:
RECOGNITION OF CULTURAL DIFFERENCES AND THE CONCLUSION OF
THE STATE'S CEDING OF DIRECT USUFRUCT TO THE INDIANS. THE
PACT IS BASED ON A NEW CONCEPTUAL FRAMEWORK AND MAKES
EXPLICIT THE SET OF RELATIONSHIPS OF THE INDIANS WITH THE
NATIONAL SOCIETY IN THEIR CONDITION AS FULL CITIZENS.

07964 SANTILLI, M.
THE CALHA NORTE PROJECT: MILITARY GUARDIANSHIP AND
FRONTIER POLICY
CULTURAL SURVIVAL QUARTERLY, 13(1) (1989), 42-43.
THE CALHA NORTE IS A PROJECT OF A STRATEGIC NATURE,
FORMULATED AND EXECUTED BY BRAZIL'S GENERAL SECRETARIAT OF
THE NATIONAL SECURITY COUNCIL. ITS OBJECTIVE IS TO PROMOTE
THE OCCUPATION OF THE FRONTIER STRIP ALONG BRAZIL'S NORTHERN
BORDERS. THE PROJECT WAS FORMULATED IN A SERIES OF OFFICIAL,
CONFIDENTIAL DOCUMENTS AND IS DEVELOPING OUTSIDE THE CONTROL
OF BOTH THE LEGISLATIVE AND JUDICIARY POWERS. IT INVOLVES

ASPECTS OF INDIGENOUS POLICY, REGIONAL DEVELOPMENT, THE
ENVIRONMENT, DEFENSE, AND INTERNATIONAL RELATIONS. THE
PERSPECTIVE OF THE MILITARY SEGMENT OF THE NATIONAL SECURITY
COUNCIL DOMINATES THE PROJECT, TO THE POTENTIAL DETRIMENT OF
THE INDIANS AND THE ENVIRONMENT.

07965 SANTOS, J.E.D.
THERE WILL BE PEACE IN SOUTHERN AFRICA
WORLD MARXIST REVIEW, 32(10) (OCT 89), 13-15.
THIS ARTICLE IS A REPLY TO WORLD MARXIST REVIEW'S
QUESTIONS ABOUT THE SITUATION IN THE SOUTH OF AFRICA,
PROGRESS TOWARDS SETTLING THE REGIONAL CONFLICT, AND THE
STATE OF AFFAIRS IN THE PARTY AND THE COUNTRY. IT IS WRITTEN
BY THE CHAIRMAN, MPLA - PARTY OF LABOR, PRESIDENT OF THE
PEOPLE'S REPUBLIC OF ANGOLA. HE DESCRIBES THE ECONOMIC
DEVELOPMENT CONCEPT, THE ROLE OF THE MPLA-PARTY OF LABOR,
AND PREDICTS THAT RACIAL HARMONY IS POSSIBLE.

07966 SANTOSO, M.P.
AN EVALUATION OF ADMINISTRATIVE PROCEDURES AND TAXPAYERS'
COMPLIANCE: A CASE STUDY OF THE INDONESIAN URBAN PROPERTY
TAX
DISSERTATION ABSTRACTS INTERNATIONAL, 50(4) (OCT 89),
1087-A.
THE AUTHOR INVESTIGATES THE PROBLEM OF LOW PROPERTY
TAXPAYERS' COMPLIANCE IN THE INDONESIAN URBAN SECTOR. HE
FINDS THAT THERE IS A STRONG POSITIVE CORRELATION BETWEEN
THE PERCEPTION OF FAIRNESS AND THE INDIVIDUAL'S TAX
KNOWLEDGE AND THE LEVEL OF TAX COMPLIANCE. LACK OF
COMPLIANCE OFTEN RESULTS FROM PROBLEMS WITH THE TAX
COLLECTION PROCEDURE. STANDARD ENFORCEMENT PROCEDURES, SUCH
AS PENALTIES AND INCARCERATION, ARE NECESSARY BUT ARE
UNLIKELY TO DRAMATICALLY IMPROVE THE LEVEL OF COMPLIANCE.

07967 SANUSSL,M.
SIERRA LEONE SCANDAL OVER TOXIC WASTE SCANDLE
NEW AFRICAN, (OCT 89), 33-.
THIS ARTICLE REPORTS ON THE EUROPEAN ATTEMPT TO GIVE ITS
LOW GRADE TOXIC WASTE TO FUEL SIERRA LEONE'S POWER STATIONS,
REPORTED IS THE SIERRA LEONE GOVERNMENTAL INVOLVEMENT IN
BRIBERY AND THE RESULTANT EXPOSURE OF IT.

07968 SAOTOME, M.
THE 1988 PRESIDENTIAL ELECTION AND THE FUTURE OF U.S.
POLITICS
JOURNAL OF AMERICAN AND CANADIAN STUDIES, (3) (SPR 89),
75-88.
UNDER GEORGE BUSH, THE GOVERNING PARTY REMAINS THE SAME
AND THE POLICIES SIMILAR, YET THE IMAGE THE PARTY LEADER
PROJECTS HAS CHANGED. THE INTERNATIONAL ENVIRONMENT
STABILITY AND THE LOW UNEMPLOYMENT RATE HAS BEEN A PLUS
FACTOR FOR THE REPUBLICAN PARTY. THIS ARTICLE ANALYZES THE
FUTURE OF U.S. POLITICS AND CONCLUDES THAT PUBLIC OPINION
SHOULD NOT CHANGE DRASTICLY AS LONG AS THE ECONOMY STAYS
HEALTHY.

07969 SARABI-KIA, F.
POLITICAL ECONOMY OF INTERVENTION: IMPERIALISM,
UNDERDEVELOPMENT, AND REVOLUTION IN IRAN, #1953-1979
DISSERTATION ABSTRACTS INTERNATIONAL, 49(10) (APR 89),
3143-A.
THE AUTHOR DEMONSTRATES THE THEORETICAL INADEQUACIES IN
THE STUDIES OF INTERVENTION AS A POLITICAL TOOL OF ECONOMIC
IMPERIALISM. HE FOCUSES ON THEIR WEAKNESSES IN EXPLAINING
THE STRUCTURAL IMPACT OF INTERVENTION ON THE INTERVENED
PARTY AND FORMULATES A NEW, STRUCTURAL APPROACH, WHICH
DEMONSTRATES THAT FORCEFUL INTEGRATION INTO THE WORLD
CAPITALIST SYSTEM DEPRIVES THE PERIPHERY OF INTERNAL
DEVELOPMENT AND FORCES IT INTO A PATTERN OF OUTWARD-ORIENTED,
DEPENDENT GROWTH. THE EXTERNAL DEPENDENCY OF THE
PERIPHERY'S ECONOMY DISTORTS INTERNAL STRUCTURES AND RETARDS
DEVELOPMENT. THESE CONTRIBUTIONS ARE UTILIZED TO ILLUSTRATE
THE CAUSAL EFFECT OF INTERVENTION IN IRAN.

07970 SARASWATHI, S.
PARTICIPATIVE CENTRALIZATION: SARAKARIA COMMISSION'S
PRESCRIPTION FOR UNION-STATE RELATIONS IN INDIA
INDIAN JOURNAL OF POLITICAL SCIENCE, L(2) (APR 89),
191-208.
THE SARKARIA COMMISSION WAS APPOINTED TO STUDY RELATIONS
BETWEEN THE STATE AND CENTRAL GOVERNMENTS IN INDIA AND TO
MAKE RECOMMENDATIONS FOR IMPROVING THOSE RELATIONS. IN THIS
ARTICLE, THE AUTHOR REVIEWS THE COMMISSION REPORT AND THE
WAYS THAT CENTRE-STATE INTERACTION SHOULD BE MODIFIED.

07971 SAREEN, R.
IN THE NAME OF RELIGION
FAR EASTERN ECONOMIC REVIEW, 141(29) (JUL 88), 28-29.
A CONTROVERSY SURROUNDING A MOSQUE BUILT IN THE 16TH
CENTURY HAS EXACERBATED THE HINDU-MUSLIM EMNITY AND IS
INCREASING COMMULIZATION OF BROAD SECTIONS OF BOTH
COMMUNITIES. THE MOSQUE IS BUILT ON THE SITE OF THE
LEGENDARY BIRTHPLACE OF THE HINDU GOD RAMA. A RECENT COURT
DECISION HAS REVIVED THE ISSUE AND THE BATTLE LINES ARE

BEGINING TO BE DRAWN. BOTH SIDES FEAR A RECURRENCES OF ETHNIC
VIOLENCE THAT HAS ROCKED INDIA IN THE PAST.

07972 SAREEN, R.
MUSICAL CHAIRS
FAR EASTERN ECONOMIC REVIEW. 141(28) (JUL 88), 38.
AS CONGRESS AND OPPOSITION PARTIES SCRAMBLE TO FIND
FORMULAS THAT WILL WORK IN THE APPROACHING GENERAL ELECTION,
THE UNDERLYING POLITICAL PROBLEMS OF ATROPHY AT THE GRASS
ROOTS AND "BOSSISM" ARE NEGLECTED. THE OPPOSITION IS
ATTEMPTING TO FORM A WORKABLE COALITION AND CONGRESS IS
WORKING TO DECREASE INTERNAL STRIFE, BUT UNTIL THE
UNDERLYING PROBLEMS ARE MORE FULLY RECOGNIZED AND DEALT WITH,
A WINNING FORMULA IS UNLIKELY TO BE FOUND.

07973 SAREEN, R.
PICKING UP THE PIECES
FAR EASTERN ECONOMIC REVIEW, 141(36) (SEP 88), 35-37.
AS THE IRAN-IRAQ CONFLICT CEASES, IRAN LOOKS TO EMERGE
FROM ITS SELF-IMPOSED ISOLATION FROM NEARLY ALL OF THE WORLD.
IN AN EFFORT TO SEEK AID TO REBUILD THE NATION, IRANIAN
LEADERS ARE PURSUING DIPLOMATIC AND ECONOMIC TIES WITH
SEVERAL NATIONS INCLUDING JAPAN, SOUTH KOREA, INDIA, AND
EVEN ON A LOW LEVEL, THE US. ALTHOUGH ISLAMIC FUNDAMENTALISM
IS STILL THE MOST POTENT POLITICAL FORCE IN IRAN, ECONOMIC
REALITY IS BEGINING TO TAKE ITS TOLL.

07974 SARID, Y.; ZUCKER, D.
A YEAR OF INTIFADA
NEW OUTLOOK, 32(1 (287)) (JAN 89), 48-50.
AFTER A YEAR OF THE INTIFADA. IN DIRECT CONTRADICTION TO
OFFICIAL APPRAISALS FROM THE ISRAELI MINISTER OF DEFENSE,
THE UPRISING IN THE TERRITORIES IS NOT WEAKENING BUT IS
GAINING STRENGTH AND ESTABLISHING ITSELF EVEN MORE FIRMLY.
THE INTIFADA KEEPS CHANGING FORM AND DISCOVERING NEW
CONDUITS THROUGH WHICH IT CHANNELS RESISTANCE AND REBELLION.
THERE ARE NO MASS DEMONSTRATIONS, AS THERE WERE IN THE FIRST
DAYS OF THE UPRISING. BUT THERE IS MASS PARTICIPATION IN THE
STRUGGLE AGAINST ISRAELI OCCUPATION--EVIDENCE THAT THE ROOTS
OF THE INTIFADA HAVE TAKEN HOLD AND ARE PROSPERING.

07975 SARID, Y.
CROSS THE NARROW BRIDGE
NEW OUTLOOK, 32(5 (291)) (MAY 89), 9-12.
THE AUTHOR, WHO IS A CITIZENS' RIGHTS MOVEMENT MK, SAYS
THAT THE ISRAELI OCCUPATION OF GAZA AND THE WEST BANK IS
BASED ON A LIE AND THAT THOSE WHO SEEK A COMPROMISE ARE THE
MOST DANGEROUS ENEMIES OF THE STATUS QUO. HE CALLS UPON
AMERICAN JEWS TO SUPPORT A POLITICAL SOLUTION TO THE ISRAELI-
PALESTINIAN CONFLICT.

07976 SARKAR, D.K.
MUNICIPAL REFORMS IN THE STATE OF WEST BENGAL: AN ATTEMPT
OF INSTITUTIONAL PARTNERSHIP
INDIAN JOURNAL OF POLITICAL SCIENCE, L(1) (JAN 89), 49-63.
THE GOVERNMENT OF WEST BENGAL HAS CREATED THREE NEW
INSTITUTIONS DESIGNED TO IMPROVE THE OPERATIONAL EFFICIENCY
OF THE MUNICIPAL ADMINISTRATION: THE CENTRAL VALUATION BOARD,
THE DIRECTORATE OF LOCAL BODIES (AND DIRECTORATE OF
MUNICIPAL ENGINEERING), AND THE INSTITUTE OF LOCAL
GOVERNMENT AND URBAN STUDIES. IN THIS ESSAY, THE AUTHOR
LOOKS AT THESE NEW INSTITUTIONS AND THE PHILOSOPHY BEHIND
THEM.

07977 SARKAR, J.
A HUNDRED FLOWERS
FAR EASTERN ECONOMIC REVIEW, 141(38) (SEP 88), 38-39.
OVER TWO DECADES AFTER THEOR FOUNDING, THE NAXALITE
MOVEMENT IS HIGHLY FRAGMENTED AND SUFFERING FROM IDEOLOGICAL
AND INTELLECTUAL EXHAUSTION. THE DECLINE OF THE ONCE
POWERFUL COMMUNIST MOVEMENT BEGAN WITH THE DEATH OF ITS
FOUNDER IN 1972 AND HAS NOT BEEN CHECKED. NOW SOME 25 GROUPS
AND FACTIONS FIGHT ONE ANOTHER AND THEIR POLITICAL INFLUENCE
IS NEGIGIBLE.

07978 SAROYAN, M.
THE ARMENIAN PROTESTS: IS IT PASSION OR POLITICS?
DEADLINE, 3(4) (JUL 89), 8-11.
THIS ARTICLE CONTRASTS THE MEDIA COVERAGE OF THE
ARMENIAN PROTESTS BY FRENCH AND AMERICAN JOURNALISTS,
AMERICAN COVERAGE FAILED TO EXPLORE IN DEPTH A RANGE OF
SOCIAL, ECONOMIC, AND POLITICAL FACTORS THUS SIMPLIFYING THE
ISSUES, FRENCH REPORTERS TOOK SOVIET POLITICS SERIOUSLY ON
ITS OWN TERMS AND SKETCHED THE OUTLINE OF INTEREST-GROUP
POLITICS.

07979 SARTI, C.
THE PANORAMA OF BRAZILIAN FEMINISM
NEW LEFT REVIEW, (173) (JAN 89), 75-92.
THE AUTHOR EXAMINES THE FATE OF CONTEMPORARY FEMINISM IN
BRAZIL. ORIGINATING IN THE MID SEVENTIES, IN A PERIOD MARKED
BY THE HEIGHTENING OF DEMOCRATIC STRUGGLE. FEMINIST GROUPS
INITIALLY COLLABORATED WITH AN OLDER TRADITION OF WOMEN'S
NEIGHBOURHOOD AND OCCUPATIONAL ASSOCIATIONS TO BUILD A

POWERFUL MOVEMENT FOR CRECHES. THE OPENING OF NEW POLITICAL
SPACE IN THE PAST DECADE, HOWEVER, HAS LED TO A CERTAIN
FRAGMENTATION OF THE MOVEMENT-A PROCESS WHICH HAS QUITE
DISTINCTIVE ASPECTS BUT WILL NEVERTHELESS APPEAR FAMILIAR TO
MANY IN EUROPE AND NORTH AMERICA.

07980 SARTORI, G.
    UNDERCOMPREHENSION
    GOVERNMENT AND OPPOSITION, 24(4) (AUT 89), 391-400.
        AS POLITICS BECOMES MORE AND MORE COMPLICATED, KNOWLEDGE
    BECOMES MORE AND MORE THE PROBLEM. THE GROWING COMPLEXITY OF
    POLITICS RESULTS NOT ONLY FROM INCREASING AND GLOBAL
    INTERDEPENDENCIES, BUT FROM THE VERY EXPANSION OF THE SPHERE
    OF POLITICS. THE MORE POLITICAL ENGINEERING DISPLACES THE
    INVISIBIBLE HAND OF ADJUSTMENT (AND MALADJUSTMENT) AND THE
    MORE THE INFLUENCE OF POLITICS SPREADS, THE LESS MANKIND IS
    IN CONTROL OF WHAT IS HAPPENING. MAN IS LIVING ABOVE AND
    BEYOND HIS INTELLIGENCE IN THE REALM OF POLITICS.

07981 SARTORI, G.
    VIDEO-POWER
    GOVERNMENT AND OPPOSITION, 24(1) (1989), 39-53.
        MUCH RHETORIC TODAY IS GLOBALISTIC. BUT MANKIND IS
    CONFRONTED WITH A FORCEFUL COUNTER-PULL THAT IS GENERALLY
    GLOSSED OVER OR SEALED AWAY AS IF IT BELONGED TO ANOTHER
    PLANET: LOCALISM. LOCALISM IS A SURGING DRIVE THAT COUNTERS
    GLOBALISM ON A PAR, AS A COUNTER-PULL OF EQUAL LEGITIMACY,
    BECAUSE "REAL DEMOCRACY" CAN ONLY BE, AND MUST BE,
    PARTICIPATORY DEMOCRACY.

07982 SARTORIUS. R.H.; RUTTAN, V.W.
    THE SOURCES OF THE BASIC HUMAN NEEDS MANDATE
    JOURNAL OF DEVELOPING AREAS, 23(3) (APR 89), 331-362.
        THIS ARTICLE EXAMINES THE EVOLUTION OF THE U.S. BASIC
    HUMAN NEEDS (BHN) MANDATE AND OF THE DEVELOPMENT ASSISTANCE
    POLICY FROM THE MID-1960'S TO THE EARLY 1970'S. THE MOST
    DISTINCTIVE FEATURE OF BHN POLICY WAS THAT IT PROPOSED TO
    CONCENTRATE ASSISTANCE ON FOOD PRODUCTION RURAL DEVELOPMENT
    AND NUTRITION, POPULATION PLANNING AND HEALTH, AND EDUCATION.
    THIS MARKED A DEPARTURE FROM THE DEVELOPMENT ASSISTANCE
    PROGRAMS OF THE 1960'S WHICH HAD EMPHASIZED GENERAL PURPOSE
    RESOURCE TRANSFER.

07983 SASANKAN, R.
    A LACK OF GOOD HOUSEKEEPING
    SOUTH, (106) (AUG 89), 71, 73.
        RADICAL GOVERNMENT ACTION IS NEEDED TO DEAL WITH THE
    HOUSING CRISIS IN INDIA. THE NATIONAL COMMISSION ON
    URBANIZATION SAYS THAT ONE IN TWO INDIAN CITY DWELLERS WILL
    BE LIVING IN A SLUM BY 2000. DESPITE THE GOVERNMENT'S POLICY
    PRONOUNCEMENTS AND CLAIMS OF ERADICATING SHORTAGES IN THE
    NEXT DECADE, ITS CURRENT CONSTRUCTION STRATEGIES WILL FALL
    FAR SHORT OF WHAT IS NEEDED.

07984 SASSEN, S.
    AMERICA'S IMMIGRATION PROBLEM
    WORLD POLICY JOURNAL, 6(4) (FAL 89), 811-832.
        THIS ARTICLE SUGGESTS THE "REAL CAUSES" FOR AMERICA'S
    IMMIGRATION PROBLEM AND THAT UNTIL WE BETTER UNDERSTAND THE
    POWERFUL POLITICAL AND ECONOMIC FORCES THAT DRIVE THESE
    INTERNATIONAL FLOWS, AND OUR OWN ROLE IN CREATING THEM, U.S.
    IMMIGRATION POLICIES WILL CONTINUE TO BE MISGUIDED AND
    FRUSTRATINGLY INEFFECTIVE, IT EXAMINES THE NEW IMMIGRATION,
    THE INADEQUACY OF CLASSICAL EXPLANATIONS, THE
    INTERNATIONALIZATION OF PRODUCTION, AND THE NEW LABOR DEMAND
    IN THE UNITED STATES. IT CONCLUDES WITH A WORKABLE
    IMMIGRATION POLICY.

07985 SATLOFF, R.
    JORDAN AND REVERBERATIONS OF THE UPRISING
    CURRENT HISTORY, 88(535) (FEB 89), 85-88, 97, 104-106.
        AS THE INTIFADA MARKED ITS FIRST ANIVERSARY, JORDAN WAS
    AT A CRITICAL CROSSROADS. KING HASSEIN'S INTENTIONS IN
    SEVERING LINKS WITH THE WEST BANK WERE UNKNOWN, AS WAS
    JORDAN'S FUTURE ROLE IN THE ARAB-ISRAELI CONFLICT.

07986 SATOW, Y.
    PEACE STUDIES IN CANADIAN UNIVERSITIES
    JOURNAL OF AMERICAN AND CANADIAN STUDIES, (3) (SPR 89),
    25-42.
        PEACE STUDIES PROGRAMS IN CANADIAN UNIVERSITIES HAVE
    MADE REMARKABLE PROGRESS DURING THE PAST TWO DECADES,
    BUILDING ON THE RAPID DEVELOPMENT OF COURSES WHICH BEGAN IN
    THE 1970S. THIS PAPER INTRODUCES THE PRESENT SITUATION OF
    PEACE STUDIES IN LEADING CANADIAN UNIVERSITIES, WITH
    EMPHASIS ON THE PROGRAMS AS BOTH VEHICLES FOR RESEARCH AND
    EDUCATION. INFORMATION IS DRAWN FROM THE 1987-1988 PEACE
    STUDIES CIRRICULAR THE AUTHOR SURVEYED WITH THE ASSISTANCE
    OF THE CANADIAN GOVERNMENT.

07987 SATZEWICH, V.
    UNFREE LABOUR AND CANADIAN CAPITALISM: THE INCORPORATION
    OF POLISH WAR VETERANS
    STUDIES IN POLITICAL ECONOMY: A SOCIALIST REVIEW, (28)
(SPR 89), 89-110.
        THIS ISSUE DEALS WITH UNFREE LABOR IN THE CASE WHERE
    POLISH WAR VETERANS WERE BROUGHT TO CANADA TO WORK AS FARM
    LABORERS AFTER WWII. IT DOCUMENTS THE POLISH VETRANS'
    RESISTANCE TO THEIR LABOR ASSIGNMENTS AND SHOWS HOW THE
    IMAGE OF A FREE MARKET IN LABOR IN 20TH CENTURY CANADA MUST
    BE REVISED.

07988 SAUNG, A.
    AUTOBIOGRAPHY OF A BURMESE REBEL
    CULTURAL SURVIVAL QUARTERLY, 13(4) (1989), 25-26.
        THE AUTHOR, WHO IS THE SON OF A BURMESE POLITICIAN AND
    THE SPOKESMAN FOR THE DEMOCRATIC ALLIANCE OF BURMA,
    DESCRIBES SOME OF HIS EXPERIENCES AMONG THE BURMESE REBEL
    FORCES.

07989 SAVAGE, D.
    SUPREME COURT: LET STATES DECIDE
    STATE LEGISLATURES, 15(8) (SEP 89), 10-14.
        THE AUTHOR REVIEWS THE RECORD OF THE SUPREME COURT IN
    1989.

07990 SAVAGE, J.D.
    POPULISM, DECENTRALIZATION, AND ARTS POLICY IN CALIFORNIA:
    THE JERRY BROWN YEARS AND AFTERWARD
    ADMINISTRATION AND SOCIETY, 20(4) (FEB 89), 446-464.
        ARTS POLICY IN CALIFORNIA REFLECTS THE DIVISION
    SEPARATING THE "ELITE" AND "POPULIST" ARTS. THE STATE ARTS
    AGENCY, THE CALIFORNIA ARTS COUNCIL, FAVORS THE POPULIST OR
    COMMUNITY ARTS. THE COUNCIL'S SUCCESS IN PRESERVING AND
    EXPANDING ITS POPULIST ARTS POLICY IN A SOMETIMES HOSTILE
    POLITICAL ENVIRONMENT HAS DEPENDED ULTIMATLEY UPON ITS
    ABILITY TO ALTER ITS ORGANIZATIONAL STRUCTURE IN A FASHION
    THAT MINIMIZES ADMINISTRATIVE STRESS AND MAXIMIZES ITS
    POLITICAL ASSETS. IN THIS REGARD, THE 10-YEAR HISTORY OF
    THIS PUBLIC ORGANIZATION WITH ITS RATHER UNORTHODOX ORIGINS
    CONFIRMS SOME OF THE CONVENTIONAL WISDOM THAT HAS
    ACCUMULATED IN THE STUDY OF PUBLIC ADMINISTRATION AND PUBLIC
    POLICY.

07991 SAVAS, D.J.
    INTEREST GROUP LEADERSHIP AND GOVERNMENT FUNDING: THE
    FEDERATION DES FRANCO-COLOMBIENS--COMMUNITY ORGANIZATION
    OR GOVERNMENT POLICY AGENT?
    DISSERTATION ABSTRACTS INTERNATIONAL, 49(12) (JUN 89),
    3867-A.
        THE AUTHOR INVESTIGATES THE IMPACT OF STATE SUPPORT
    PROGRAMS ON INTEREST GROUP LEADERSHIP AND PROVIDES INSIGHTS
    INTO HOW THE STATE USES INTEREST GROUPS AS AGENTS FOR SOCIAL
    INTERVENTION. STATE-INTEREST GROUP RELATIONS CAN BE AFFECTED
    BY STATE FUNDING PROGRAMS IN TWO FUNDAMENTAL WAYS: (1) AS
    POLICY AGENTS AND POLITICAL ACTORS, INTEREST GROUP LEADERS
    CAN BE CAPTURED IN A VICIOUS CIRCLE OF FINANCIAL AND POLICY
    DEPENDENCY THAT ALLOWS A MINIMUM AMOUNT OF FREEDOM IN
    COMMUNITY DEVELOPMENT ACTIVITIES; (2) THE STATE CAN
    UNDERMINE THE LINK BETWEEN AN INTEREST GROUP ORGANIZATION
    AND ITS INTEREST COMMUNITY, THEREBY HINDERING ITS OWN
    ABILITY TO PURSUE EFFECTIVE POLICY ACTION. AS A CASE STUDY,
    THIS DISSERTATION USES THE FEDERATION DES FRANCO-COLOMBIENS
    AND THE OFFICIAL LANGUAGES POLICY.

07992 SAVOT, P.
    WHEN CRIMINAL RIGHTS GO WRONG
    WASHINGTON MONTHLY, 21(11) (DEC 89), 36-41, 44-45.
        THE ARTICLE EXAMINES THE CONTROVERSIAL ISSUE OF CRIMINAL
    RIGHTS. IT CONCLUDES THAT THERE IS CONSIDERABLE VALIDITY TO
    THE PROFOUND, THOUGH POORLY ARTICULATED, INTUITION OF THE
    PUBLIC AT LARGE THAT THE PROCEDURAL GUARANTEES OF THE
    CONSTITUTION ARE NOT TO BE USED TO UNDERMINE A DEFENDANT'S
    RESPONSIBILITY FOR HIS CRIMINAL ACTS. THE ARTICLE
    CONCENTRATES ON TRADITIONAL FOURTH AMENDMENT RIGHTS (THE
    EXCLUSIONARY RULE) AND THE FAMOUS MIRANDA DECISION. IT
    CONCLUDES THAT THE WIDESPREAD PROTECTION OF THE RIGHTS OF
    CRIMINALS, OFTEN AT THE EXPENSE OF THE VICTIMS, IS NOT WELL
    GROUNDED IN PERCEDENT AND IS NOT JUSTIFIED.

07993 SAWARD. M.
    CO-OPTION AND LEGITIMACY: THE VARIETIES AND CONSEQUENCES
    OF FORMAL INCORPORATION
    DISSERTATION ABSTRACTS INTERNATIONAL, 50(2) (AUG 89),
    536-A.
        THIS DISSERTATION PRESENTS A THREE-PART TYPOLOGY OF
    INSTITUTIONAL CO-OPTION (VALUE, EXPERTISE, AND PRODUCER)
    ILLUSTRATED BY NINE CASE STUDIES (THREE CASES FOR EACH TYPE).
    A SET OF INTERMEDIATE PRINCIPLES OF MORAL LEGITIMACY,
    INCLUDING PROCEDURAL AND SUBSTANTIVE CRITERIA, ARE APPLIED
    TO EACH CASE. THIS REVEALS A WIDE RANGE OF MORAL COSTS AND
    BENEFITS ACCRUING DIFFERENTIALLY FOR EACH TYPE OF
    INSTITUTIONAL CO-OPTION. THESE COSTS AND BENEFITS INVOLVE
    POTENTIALLY LEGITIMATING OR POTENTIALLY DE-LEGITIMATING
    EFFECTS FOR GOVERNMENT OR GOVERNMENT AGENCIES.

07994 SAWYER, C.H.
    LEADERS' USE OF CHANGE STRATEGIES IN THE IMPLEMENTATION OF

PUBLIC POLICY
DISSERTATION ABSTRACTS INTERNATIONAL, 50(5) (NOV 89),
1434-A.
     NO ONE ELEMENT, CONDITION, OR FACTOR IS MORE IMPORTANT
TO THE SUCCESSFUL IMPLEMENTATION OF POLICY THAN THAT OF
LEADERSHIP. ADMINISTRATORS RESPONSIBLE FOR THE
IMPLEMENTATION OF POLICY NEED TO ASSUME RESPONSIBILITY FOR
THEIR OWN LEADERSHIP SKILLS AND ACTIONS, AS WELL AS THE
DEVELOPMENT OF LEADERSHIP SKILLS AND THE PROVISION OF
OPPORTUNITIES FOR THE EXERCISE OF LEADERSHIP FOR OTHERS AT
MULTIPLE LEVELS IN THEIR ORGANIZATIONS. ADMINISTRATORS MUST
RECOGNIZE THE SIGNIFICANCE OF TWO LEADERSHIP SKILL AREAS IN
PARTICULAR: THE ABILITY TO COMMUNICATE A VISION IN WAYS THAT
ENABLE OTHERS TO EMBRACE IT AND THE ABILITY TO GIVE
ATTENTION TO THE INITIAL PLANNING TO PROVIDE A FOUNDATION
FOR SUCCESS.

07995 SAXENIAN, A.L.
     THE CHESHIRE CAT'S GRIN: INNOVATION, REGIONAL DEVELOPMENT,
AND THE CAMBRIDGE CASE
ECONOMY AND SOCIETY, 18(4) (NOV 89), 448-477.
     THE PREVAILING APPROACH TO HIGH-TECH REGIONS LOCATES THE
DETERMINANTS OF GROWTH IN ATTRIBUTES OF THE REGIONAL
ENVIRONMENT. THE CASE OF CAMBRIDGE, ENGLAND IS USED TO
ILLUSTRATE THE WEAKNESSES OF THIS APPROACH AND TO HIGHLIGHT
THE IMPORTANCE OF THE BROADER POLITICAL AND ECONOMIC CONTEXT.
IN BRITAIN, THE INSTITUTIONAL LEGACIES OF A CENTURY OF
INDUSTRIAL DECLINE AND A PATTERN OF CLIENTELISTIC RELATIONS
BETWEEN THE STATE AND THE BIG ELECTRONICS FIRMS CONSTRAIN
THE GROWTH OF INNOVATIVE ENTERPRISES AND THE DEVELOPMENT OF
REGIONS SUCH AS CAMBRIDGE. FUTURE RESEARCH SHOULD CONSIDER
HOW POLITICAL RELATIONSHIPS AT BOTH NATIONAL AND THE LOCAL
LEVELS AFFECT INNOVATION AND REGIONAL DEVELOPMENT.

07996 SAYEED, A.
     A LESSON FROM NEW ZEALAND
POLICY OPTIONS, 10(1) (JAN 89), 27-29.
     NEW ZEALAND HAS BEEN THROUGH SOME OF THE SAME POLICY
DEBATES ABOUT INCOME SECURITY AND TAXATION AS IN CANADA, BUT
HAS COME TO DIFFERENT -- AND MUCH MORE DEFINITE -- DECISIONS
AND ACTED ON THEM. ADIL SAYEED OUTLINES THE WAY IN WHICH THE
LANGE GOVERNMENT HAS IMPLEMENTED A GUARANTEED INCOME PLAN
FOR FAMILIES WITH CHILDREN, REDUCED TRANSFER PAYMENTS TO OLD
AGE PENSIONERS WHO ARE HEALTHY, AND INTRODUCED A REFORMED
SALES TAX, MUCH LIKE THE ONE PROPOSED IN CANADA, INTEGRATED
WITH THE INCOME TRANSFER SYSTEM. THE GOVERNMENT MANAGED TO
DO THIS WHILE REDUCING THE DEFICIT AND, DESPITE RAISING
TAXES, GETTING RE-ELECTED.

07997 SAYIGH, Y.
     STRUGGLE WITHIN, STRUGGLE WITHOUT: THE TRANSFORMATION OF
PLO POLITICS SINCE 1982
INTERNATIONAL AFFAIRS, 65(2) (SPR 89), 247-271.
     THE ARTICLE TRACES THE DEVELOPMENTS THAT LED TO THE
DRAMATIC REVERSAL BY YASSER ARAFAT AND THE PLO BY THEIR
ACCEPTANCE OF THE AMERICAN CONDITIONS FOR HOLDING OFFICIAL
TALKS. IT ANALYZES THE INTERNAL PRESSURES AND EXTERNAL
PRESSURE FROM SYRIA AND JORDAN THAT LED TO THE DECISION.
SOME CRITICAL FACTORS THAT LED TO THE REVERSAL INCLUDE:
CHANGE AMONG THE PLO GEURRILLA GROUPS; THE EMERGENCE OF
ARAFAT AS THE SOLE DECISION-MAKER FOR THE PALESTINIAN
MOVEMENT; AND THE OCCUPIED TERRITORIES' RISE TO PREEMINENCE
ON THE WORLD STAGE.

07998 SAYIGH, Y.
     THE INTIFADAH CONTINUES: LEGACY, DYNAMICS, AND CHALLENGES
THIRD WORLD QUARTERLY, 11(3) (JUL 89), 20-49.
     THE PALESTINIANS HAVE UNDENIABLY COME A LONG WAY TOWARDS
ACHIEVING THEIR GOAL OF SELF-DETERMINATION, IN THE FORM OF
AN INDEPENDENT STATE. THE ROLE OF THE INTIFADAH IS EQUALLY
EVIDENT, WHETHER IN TRANSFORMING INTERNATIONAL OPINION OR IN
PROVIDING THE PLO WITH BOTH THE INCENTIVE AND THE
OPPORTUNITY TO UNDERTAKE A BASIC SHIFT IN DECLARED STRATEGY.
THIS ARTICLE STUDIES THE FEATURES THAT HAVE MADE THE
PALESTINIAN UPRISING SO REMARKABLE, WITH A REVIEW OF ITS
HISTORICAL LEGACY, ITS IMPACT, AND THE CHALLENGES FACING ITS
FUTURE DEVELOPMENT.

07999 SAYIGH, Y.A.
     THE INTIFADA AND THE BALANCE OF POWER IN THE REGION
INTERNATIONAL SPECTATOR, XXIII(4) (OCT 88), 203-214.
     THE AUTHOR CONSIDERS THE FOLLOWING QUESTIONS ABOUT THE
BALANCE OF POWER IN THE MIDEAST: HAS THE BALANCE OF POWER IN
THE REGION TANGIBLY ALTERED AS A RESULT OF THE INTIFADA? IF
NOT, WHY NOT? IF IT HAS ALTERED, IN WHAT WAYS AND WITHIN
WHAT TIME FRAME WILL THE CHANGE IN THE PATTERN OF POWER
DISTRIBUTION BE SEEN? WHAT ARE THE PALESTINIANS' OBJECTIVES?

08000 SAYLE, M.
     THE POWERS THAT MIGHT BE
FAR EASTERN ECONOMIC REVIEW, 141(31) (AUG 88), 38-43.
     WRITER MURRAY SAYLE TAKES A LOOK AT THE RISE AND FALL OF
GREAT POWERS BY PAUL KENNEDY. HE CONCENTRATES ON THE PART OF
KENNEDY'S THESIS THAT STATES THAT AS THE US DECLINES, JAPAN

IS RISING AS THE NEXT GREAT POWER. HE POINTS OUT THAT
ALTHOUGH THE INTERNATIONAL SCENE CERTAINLY HAS CHANGED, THE
ASCENT OF JAPAN TO WORLD SUPREMACY IS BY NO MEANS A GIVEN.

08001 SAYLE, M.
     TROUBLE ON THE ORIENTAL EXPRESS THE CRISES IN CHINA AND
JAPAN
NATIONAL INTEREST, (18) (WIN 89), 29-45.
     THIS ARTICLE EXPLORES THE FACT THAT THOUGH CHINA AND
JAPAN SEEM TO BE, AT FIRST, INCOMPATIBLE UNIVERSES, BUT AT
CLOSER EXAMINATION THE POLITICAL CRISIS IN TOKYO AND THE
VIOLENT EVENTS IN BEIJING, HAVE MUCH THE SAME PLOT: THE
FAILURE OF OBSOLETE SYSTEMS OF GOVERNMENT TO RESPOND TO
CHANGING ECONOMIC AND SOCIAL CONDITIONS, THE REFLEXIVE
APPLICATION OF OLD REMEDIES WHICH HAVE MADE THE MALADIES
WORSE, THIS DIAGNOSIS DEPENDS ON A READING OF TWO CASE
HISTORIES WHICH ARE COMPLEX AND WIDELY CONTESTED. THE AUTHOR
OFFERS SOME VALIANT SIMPLICATION, WITH APOLOGIES TO
SPECIALISTS, WHICH MAY HELP TO MAKE THE PARALLEL CLEARER.

08002 SAYLER, J.
     POLITICALLY DIVIDED GOVERNMENT: AN ENDURING U.S. PROBLEM?
CRS REVIEW, 10(5) (JUN 89), 28-29.
     DOES POLITICALLY DIVIDED GOVERNMENT CREATE EXTRAORDINARY,
PERHAPS INSURMOUNTABLE, PROBLEMS FOR FEDERAL RULE IN THE
UNITED STATES? SOME OBSERVERS BELIEVE IT DOES, THAT
DISCIPLINE AND POLITICAL PARTY INFLUENCE IN CONGRESS ARE
WEAKENING. THEY DEPLORE WHAT THEY SEE AS AN INCREASED
RELIANCE BY THE CONGRESS AND THE PRESIDENT ON TEMPORARY,
CROSS-PARTY COALITIONS THAT INHIBIT THE FORMULATION OF
DURABLE SOLUTIONS TO PROBLEMS. BUT AMERICA'S POLITICAL
HISTORY SUGGESTS THAT OMINOUS CONCLUSIONS ABOUT THE PARTISAN
DIVISION OF THE FEDERAL GOVERNMENT ARE DIFFICULT TO
SUBSTANTIATE. SUCH POLITICAL DIVISIONS, IN ONE FORM OR
ANOTHER, HAVE EXISTED AND EVEN FLOURISHED LONG ENOUGH TO BE
A NORMAL PART OF AMERICAN POLITICS AND GOVERNMENT.

08003 SAYRS, L.W.
     TRADE AND CONFLICT REVISITED: DO POLITICS MATTER?
INTERNATIONAL INTERACTIONS, 15(2) (1989), 155-175.
     THIS PAPER RE-EXAMINES THE RELATIONSHIP BETWEEN TRADE
AND CONFLICT. IT IS ARGUED THAT THE CURRENT FINDINGS ON THE
TRADE-CONFLICT HYPOTHESIS OMIT POLITICAL EFFECTS GERMANE TO
A FULLY SPECIFIED EXPLANATION OF INTERNATIONAL CONFLICT. IN
PARTICULARY, CONFLICT IS GREATLY INFLUENCED BY THE PATTERNS
OF EXCHANGE WHICH CONSTRAIN TRADING ACTIVITY: THE DYNAMICS
OF THE CONFLICT PROCESS WHICH MAY OVERSHADOW THE PEACEFUL
EFFECTS FROM TRADE; AND THE SOURCES OF RISK AND UNCERTAINTY
WHICH HAVE A POLITICAL AS WELL AS ECONOMIC COMPONENT. BY
INCLUDING THESE EFFECTS, SEVERAL ANOMALIES IN THE LITERATURE
ARE MORE SATISFYINGLY EXPLAINED AND SOME COUNTERINTUITIVE
RESULTS MAY BE PREDICTED FROM THE GENERAL MODEL OF TRADE AND
CONFLICT. A RETEST OF THE HYPOTHESIS THAT TRADE LOWERS THE
LEVEL OF CONFLICT IS MADE VIA A POOLED REGRESSION MODEL. THE
RESULTS CONFIRM EARLIER FINDINGS BUT AS ANTICIPATED. SEVERAL
IMPORTANT EXCEPTIONS EMERGE. FIRST, TRADE DOES NOT PROVIDE
AN ECONOMIC INCENTIVE TO COOPERATE EVEN THOUGH IT MAY SRVE
TO DIMINISH THE OVERALL LEVEL OF CONFLICT. SECOND, TRADE MAY
DIMINISH CONFLICT EVEN IN THE ABSENCE OF THE THREAT OF
RECIPROCAL ACTION ON THE PART OF THE TRADING PARTNER. THIRD,
TRADE MAY DIMINSH COOPERATION IN THE ECONOMIC ARENA WHERE
NORMS OF COMPETITION DOMINATE OR WHERE THE U.S. AS A TRADING
PARTNER EXERTS EXTRAORDINARY INFLUENCE.

08004 SCALAPINO, R.A.; BAOLIN, M.
     SINO-U.S. DECADE: AN AMERICAN SCHOLAR LOOKS BACK
BEIJING REVIEW, 32(2) (JAN 89), 32-34.
     IN THIS INTERVIEW, AN AMERICAN EXPERT ON CHINA REVIEWS
THE EVOLUTION OF SINO-AMERICAN RELATIONS FROM 1979 TO 1989.

08005 SCANLAN, J.P.
     STRATEGIC DEFENSE CAN BE DANGEROUS
NEW LEADER, LXXII(10) (JUN 89), 13-14.
     GIVEN THE U.S.' TECHNOLOGICAL SUPERIORITY, THE USSR
CANNOT WIN A RACE TO NUCLEAR INVULNERABILITY WITHOUT
COMPLETELY SINKING ITS BADLY LISTING ECONOMY. THE SOVIET
UNION MAY ALSO RECOGNIZE--IN CONTRAST, APPARENTLY, TO THE
UNITED STATES--THE DANGERS NOT SO MUCH OF WINNING THE RACE
BUT OF LEADING IN IT. THE KREMLIN LEADERS SEEM LIKELY TO
DECIDE, THEREFORE, THAT THEIR BEST--AND PERHAPS THE ONLY
AVAILABLE-STRATEGY WOULD BE TO CONCENTRATE ON DEVELOPING PRE-
EMPTIVE WEAPONS. THIS WOULD ALLOW A REASONABLE PROSPECT OF
SUCCESSFULLY CARRYING OUT A FIRST STRIKE PRIOR TO THE
DEPLOYMENT OF THE UNITED STATES' DEFENSIVE SYSTEM. THE
SOVIETS MUST RESPOND TO DANGERS, NOT MERELY TO CERTAINTIES.
WHATEVER THE COST OR PERIL, THEY WILL NEVER PERMIT
THEMSELVES TO BE PLACED AT THE MERCY OF AN INVULNERABLE
UNITED STATES.

08006 SCANNELL, P.
     PUBLIC SERVICE BROADCASTING AND MODERN PUBLIC LIFE
MEDIA, CULTURE, AND SOCIETY, 11(2) (APR 89), 135-166.
     THE AUTHOR ARGUES THAT BROADCASTING IN ITS PRESENT FORM
IS A PUBLIC GOOD THAT HAS UNOBTRUSIVELY CONTRIBUTED TO THE

DEMOCRATIZATION OF EVERYDAY LIFE, IN PUBLIC AND PRIVATE
CONTEXTS, FROM ITS BEGINNINGS UNTIL THE PRESENT TIME. HE
DEFENDS THIS PROPOSITION BY DEVELOPING AN EXPLANATION OF
BROADCASTING AS A PUBLIC GOOD AND THEN CONSIDERING THE WIDER
IMPLICATIONS OF THIS IN RELATION TO POSSIBLE OBJECTIONS AND
CRITICISMS. HE CONSTRUCTS HIS ARGUMENTS WITH REFERENCE TO
THE WORK OF JURGEN HABERMAS, ESPECIALLY HABERMAS' CONCEPTS
OF THE PUBLIC SPHERE AND OF COMMUNICATIVE RATIONALITY.

08007 SCANZONI, J.
ALTERNATIVE IMAGES FOR PUBLIC POLICY: FAMILY STRUCTURE
VERSUS FAMILIES STRUGGLING
POLICY STUDIES REVIEW, 8(3) (SPR 89), 599-609.
A CONSTRAST IS DRAWN BETWEEN PUBLIC POLICY AND
PROGRAMMATIC IMPLEMENTATIONS OF POLICY. THE ARGUMENT IS MADE
THAT CONSERVATIVES POSSESS A COHERENT AND THOUGHTFUL FAMILY
POLICY, WHEREAS PROGRESSIVES ARE DEVOID OF SUCH A POLICY.
LACKING ANY "HIGH MORAL GROUND" PROGRESSIVES FIND THEMSELVES
ON THE DEFENSIVE WHEN PROPOSING SPECIFIC PROGRAMS.
CONSEQUENTLY GUIDELINES FOR A PROGRESSIVE POLICY FOR
FAMILIES IS PROPOSED, ALONG WITH EXAMPLES OF PROGRAMS THAT
MIGHT DERIVE FROM IT.

08008 SCARBOROUGH, J.W.
AN EXAMINATION OF THE FEDERAL ROLE IN THE DEVELOPMENT OF
COMMERCIAL SPACE TRANSPORTATION
DISSERTATION ABSTRACTS INTERNATIONAL, 49(8) (FEB 89),
2388-A.
THIS RESEARCH EXAMINES THE CONTENT OF PUBLIC POLICY AND
AND MANAGEMENT OF THE POLICY PROCESS REGARDING SPACE
TRANSPORTATION, AS IT SERVES THE LARGER OBJECTIVE OF
COMMERCIALIZATION OF SPACE. IT IDENTIFIES VALID BUT
SOMETIMES CONFLICTING NATIONAL GOALS FOR SPACE PROGRAMS AND
POLITICAL FORCES ALIGNED WITH THE CONTENDING VIEWS. IT DOES
SO IN LIGHT OF HUGE CAPITAL NEEDS AND AN IMPOSING ARRAY OF
TECHNOLOGICAL, FINANCIAL AND POLITICAL OBSTACLES AND MARKET
RISKS.

08009 SCHABERT, T.
CHAPTER 1: THE AUTOCRACY, CONDITION OF CREATIVITY; BOSTON
POLITICS: THE CREATIVITY OF POWER
BERLIN: WALTER DEGRVYER, 1989, 9-44.
THE PARADOX OF POWER PERSISTS. IT IS THE PARADOX OF
LIBERTY, CONSTITUTIONALLY TRANSFIGURED. THE BOOK BEGINS WITH
A PHILOSOPICAL ARGUMENT ABOUT THE PARADOX OF LIBERTY. IT
CONTINUES ON TO EXPLORE THE ARCHITECTURE AND POTENTIAL OF
POWER, THEN-THE CONSTRUCTION, STRATEGY, AND PRINCIPLES OF
THE AUTOCRACY. BOSTON MAYOR, KEVIN WHITE, IS STUDIED THROUGH
AN INVESTIGATION OF POLITICS VERSUS GOVERNMENT; THE EXERCISE
OF AUTHORITY; THE GOVERNMENT AND ITS PERSONNEL, AND
CONCLUDES WITH AN EXPLANATION OF THE CHAOS OF POWER.

08010 SCHABERT, T.
CHAPTER 2: THE COURT, LOCUS OF CREATIVITY
BERLIN: WALTER DEGRUYER, 1989, 45-98.
POLITICS IS THE PROCESS OF CREATIVITY FROM WHICH HUMAN
SOCIETIES EMERGE. CHAPTER 2 STUDIES THE CITY OF BOSTON AS AN
EXTREMELY DIFFERENTIATED AND UNIQUE CITY, FROM THE
PHILOSOPICAL ARGUMENT OF THE FEW AND THE MANY. IT CONTINUES
ON TO THE FIELD OF POLITICAL CREATIVITY AS A PHENOMENON TO
BE SEEN BY THE SECOND GOVERNMENT THAT IS FORMED BY THE COURT.
PHENOMENA OF POLITICS STUDIED INCLUDES THE REALITY THAT IS
HISTORY, AND THE RHYTHM OF ORGANIZATIONAL CREATIVITY. THE
ALTER EGO, THE COURT THEOLOGIAN, THE POLITICS PRO, AND THE
ENTREPRENEUR ARE DETAILED AS PERSONS WHO DEFINE PLACES OF
POLITICS. AFTER ADDRESSING THE POSITIONS OF MAYOR, VICE AND
DEPUTY MAYORS, STAFF AND CABINET AND COMMITTEES IN RELATION
TO CREATIVITY AND EFFICIENCY THE PROCESS OF ALTERNATING
PERCEPTIONS AS A PHENOMENON OF CREATIVITY IS EXAMINED.

08011 SCHABERT, T.
CHAPTER 3: THE PARTY, CARRIER OF CREATIVITY; BOSTON
POLITICS: THE CREATIVITY OF POWER
BERLIN: WALTER DEGRUYER, 1989, 99-212.
THE PHILOSOPHICAL ARGUEMENT INTRODUCING CHAPTER THREE,
CONCERNS TIME, HISTORY, AND SOCIETY. IT THEN ANALYZES THE
KEVIN WHITE INTEREST IN THE PARTY AND IN ITS LEGITIMACY. THE
STRUCTURE OF THE PARTY IS EXAMINED IN TERMS OF MEMBERS,
METAMORPHOSES AND METASTASES AS THE UNREFLECTIVE CREATION OF
A POLITICAL BODY, THE JUNCTURES OF CREATIVITY, AS WELL AS
ITS CONFIGURATION. INGRESSION, TRANSPLANTATION, IMPLANTATION,
CONFIGURATION AND FOUNDATION ARE EACH RELATED TO THE
EFFECTIVENESS OF PARTY CREATIVITY.

08012 SCHABERT, T.
CHAPTER 4: THE GOVERNMENT, MOVEMENTS OF CREATIVITY; BOSTON
POLITICS: THE CREATIVITY OF POWER
BERLIN: WALTER DEGRUYER, 1989, .
THE POLITICIAN'S PROGRESS; THE "NEW" AND THE "OLD;" THE
DISCOVERY OF THE POLITICIAN; AND THE REVELATION OF POWER:
COMPRISE THE PHILOSOPHICAL ARGUMENT INTRODUCING THIS CHAPTER.
IT CONTINUES ON TO STUDY PERSONS AND INSTITUTIONS,
INCLUDING THE PRIMACY OF PERSONS. POWER IS ANALYZED IN TERMS
OF ITS APPEARANCE, LIMITS, REPRESENTATION, AND ASSUMPTION.

IT CONCLUDES THAT THE WHITE GOVERNMENT ACHIEVED BOSTON'S
CREATO CONTINUA AND MADE BOSTON A CITY IN CREATIVITY.

08013 SCHABERT, T.
CHAPTER 5: THE CITY: SPACE OF CREATIVITY; BOSTON POLITICS:
THE CREATIVITY OF POWER
BERLIN: WALTER DEGRUYER, 1989, .
THIS CHAPTER CONTRASTS THE SPATIAL PROCESS OF SOCIETY
WITH THE PROCESS OF SPATIAL CREATIVITY. THE CONSTRUCTION OF
SOCIETY IS STUDIED IN TERMS OF CITIES AND URBAN ARCHITECTURE.
MOVEMENTS OF PLANNING IS STUDIED IN TERMS OF INSTITUTIONAL
HISTORY, "PLANS," SHIFTS OF FUNCTIONS AND ACTIVITY, PEOPLE,
AND THE RISE OF CREATIVITY. IT CONCLUDES WITH AN ANALYSIS OF
POLITICS, SPACE, AND CREATIVITY.

08014 SCHACHT, W.H.
TECHNOLOGY, PRODUCTIVITY, AND PUBLIC POLICY
CRS REVEIH, 10(5) (JUN 89), 11-16.
TECHNOLOGY DEVELOPMENT RESPONDS TO ECONOMIC FORCES. IT
IS ALSO INFLUENCED BY ADVANCES IN SCIENCE AND ENGINEERING,
THE ORGANIZATION AND MANAGEMENT OF FIRMS, GOVERNMENT
ACTIVISM, AND SERENDIPITY. TECHNOLOGICAL ADVANCES CAN AFFECT
ECONOMIC GROWTH, PRODUCTIVITY, AND COMPETITIVENESS OVER THE
LONG TERM INDEPENDENTLY OF ECONOMIC FACTORS, SUCH AS CHANGES
IN THE COST OF LABOR OR CAPITAL. DUE TO THE IMPORTANCE OF
TECHNOLOGICAL PROGRESS TO GROWTH IN PRODUCTIVITY AND LIVING
STANDARDS, THE FEDERAL GOVERNMENT IS EXPANDING EFFORTS TO
ACCELERATE IT.

08015 SCHACHTER, H.L.
FREDERICK WINSLOW TAYLOR AND THE IDEA OF WORKER
PARTICIPATION A BRIEF AGAINST EASY ADMINISTRATIVE
DICHOTOMIES
ADMINISTRATION AND SOCIETY, 21(1) (MAY 89), 20-30.
THE PUBLIC ADMINISTRATION LITERATURE TENDS TO DEPICT
FREDERICK TAYLOR AS PROMULGATING A "MEN-AS-MACHINES"
APPROACH TO MOTIVATION. THE LITERATURE CONTRASTS TAYLOR AND
MAYO/MASLOW, LEADING TO ANALYSIS THAT DICHOTOMIZES
ENGINEERING AND PSYCHOLOGICAL THEORIES OF MOTIVATION. THIS
DICHOTOMIZATION SERIOUSLY DISTORTS THE THRUST OF TAYLOR'S
WORK, WHICH ACTUALLY PREFIGURES MANY HUMAN RELATIONS
INSIGHTS CURRENTLY ATTRIBUTED TO ELTON MAYO OR ABRAHAM
MASLOW. THE PARTIALIZATION OF TAYLOR'S WORK RAISES QUESTIONS
ABOUT THE WAY THE DISCIPLINE PASSES ON KNOWLEDGE.

08016 SCHAFFER, A.
THE HOUSTON GROWTH COALITION IN "BOOM" AND "BUST"
JOURNAL OF URBAN AFFAIRS, 11(1) (1989), 21-38.
ALTHOUGH GROWTH MACHINE THEORY EMPHASIZES THE
COALITION'S TACTICS AND ORGANIZATION, IT NEGLECTS ADJUSTMENT
TO CHANGING ECONOMIC CONDITIONS. THIS ARTICLE EXPLORES THE
CHANGES IN THE STRATEGY AND ORGANIZATION OF HOUSTON'S GROWTH
COALITION DURING THE PEAK GROWTH OF THE 1970S AND THE
DECLINE OF THE 1980S. DURING THE BOOM, THE COALITION FOCUSED
NOT ON ADDITIONAL GROWTH BUT ON EASING THE CITY'S
INFRASTRUCTURE PROBLEMS. THE COALITION UNDERWENT SEVERAL
MAJOR CHANGES DURING DECLINE AS IT STRUGGLED TO COMPETE
AGGRESSIVELY WITH OTHER CITIES FOR VARIOUS ENTERPRISES AND
TO DEVISE STRATEGIES FOR DIVERSIFYING THE ECONOMY. A GROWTH
COALITION HAS THE OPPORTUNITY TO ESTABLISH THE ECONOMIC
BASIS FOR FUTURE GROWTH WHEN THE CITY'S DOMINANT INDUSTRIES
REACH MATURITY AND DECLINE.

08017 SCHAFFER, T.
PROPOSAL TO SELL F-16S TO PAKISTAN
DEPARTMENT OF STATE BULLETIN (US FOREIGN POLICY), 89(2151)
(OCT 89), 65-66.
THE BUSH ADMINISTRATION'S DECISION TO SELL SIXTY F-16
A/B FIGHTER AIRCRAFT TO PAKISTAN WAS BASED ON THE IMPACT OF
THE SALE ON PAKISTAN'S SECURITY AND DEVELOPMENT, ON
PAKISTAN'S IMPROVING RELATIONS WITH INDIA, ON THE RISKS OF
CONVENTIONAL AND NUCLEAR ARMS PROLIFERATION IN THE REGION,
ON THE NEW DEMOCRATIC GOVERNMENT IN PAKISTAN, AND ON
AMERICAN RELATIONS WITH PAKISTAN.

08018 SCHALK, A.
THE SWISS DEBATE THEIR ARMY'S FUTURE
COMMONHEAL, CXVI(11) (JUN 89), 331-333.
IN LATE 1989, SWISS VOTERS WILL DECIDE WHETHER TO
ABOLISH THEIR ARMY. SINCE SWITERZERLAND'S POLICY OF ARMED
NEUTRALITY HAS BEEN IN FORCE FOR NEARLY TWO CENTURIES, IT IS
ASTONISHING THAT THE SWISS WOULD EVEN CONSIDER THE PROPOSAL.
THE VOTE IS MADE POSSIBLE BY THE COUNTRY'S UNIQUE SYSTEM OF
DIRECT DEMOCRACY.

08019 SCHEB, J. M. II; HAYES, A. L.; UNGS, T. D.
JUDICIAL ROLE ORIENTATIONS, ATTITUDES AND DECISION MAKING.
A RESEARCH NOTE
WESTERN POLITICAL QUARTERLY, 42(3) (SEP 89), 427.
"JUDICIAL ROLE ORIENTATIONS" REFER TO JUDGES'
PERCEPTIONS OF THE NORMS GOVERNING JUDICIAL DECISION MAKING.
IN THIS STUDY, THE ROLE ORIENTATIONS OF A SAMPLE OF FLORIDA
APPELLATE JUDGES ARE MEASURED USING A SURVEY INSTRUMENT THAT
ASKS RESPONDENTS TO EVALUATE A SERIES OF STATEMENTS ABOUT

JUDICIAL DECISION MAKING. FACTOR ANALYSIS REVEALS THAT THESE
STATEMENTS DISCRIMINATE NICELY BETWEEN COMPETING ROLE
ORIENTATIONS LABELED "JUDICIAL ACTIVISM" AND "JUDICIAL
RESTRAINT." THESE ROLE ORIENTATIONS ARE FOUND TO INFLUENCE
RESPONDENTS' DECISION MAKING IN CRIMINAL APPEALS BY
INTERACTING WITH THEIR POLITICAL ATTITUDES. THE RESULTS
BUTTRESS THE FINDINGS OF OTHER STUDIES THAT INDICATE THAT
JUDICIAL ROLE ORIENTATIONS ARE AS IMPORTANT AS POLITICAL
ATTITUDES IN EXPLAINING JUDICIAL BEHAVIOR.

08020 SCHECHTER, H.E.
    IN DEFENSE OF DEMOCRACY: ABRAHAM LINCOLN AND PERICLES
    DISSERTATION ABSTRACTS INTERNATIONAL, 49(11) (MAY 89),
    3494-A.
    ABRAHAM LINCOLN AND PERICLES BOTH LED THEIR DEMOCRACIES
    INTO AND DURING WARS THAT WERE CRITICAL TO THE FUTURE OF
    THEIR RESPECTIVE POLITIES. BOTH HAD TO USE A RHETORICAL
    DEFENSE OF DEMOCRACY IN ORDER TO INSPIRE PATRIOTISM AND
    WILLINGNESS TO FIGHT AND DIE. THE DIFFERING RESULTS THAT
    LINCOLN AND PERICLES ACHIEVED WERE DUE TO THE PLACE MORAL
    PRINCIPLES OCCUPIED IN EACH MAN'S APPEAL AND IN THE
    POLITICAL ARRANGEMENTS OF EACH POLITY.

08021 SCHEELE, H.Z.
    RESPONSE TO KENNEDY ADMINISTRATION: THE JOINT SENATE-HOUSE
    REPUBLICAN PRESS CONFERENCE
    PRESIDENTIAL STUDIES QUARTERLY, 19(4) (FAL 89), 825-846.
    THIS ESSAY POINTS OUT THAT REPUBLICAN OPPOSITION TO THE
    KENNEDY ADMINISTRATION WAS AN EXTENSION OF EISENHOWER'S
    LEADERSHIP. HE PROPOSED THE JOINT SENATE-HOUSE REPUBLICAN
    LEADERSHIP, A NEW POLICY MAKING GROUP AND THE NEWS
    CONFERENCES WHICH FOLLOWED ITS WEEKLY MEETINGS. IT TRACES
    ITS ACTIVITIES, DEMOCRATIC PARTY RESPONSE, AND DETAILS ITEMS
    MOST DISCUSSED IT CONCLUDES THAT THESE PRESS CONFERENCES
    EMERGED AS A SIGNIFICANT VEHICLE FOR POLITICAL DISSEMINATION
    AND SERVED AS AN EFFECTIVE COMMUNICATIVE RESPONSE TO THE
    KENNEDY ADMINISTRATION.

08022 SCHEFFER, D.J.
    NOUVEAU LAW AND FOREIGN POLICY
    FOREIGN POLICY, (76) (FAL 89), 44-65.
    THIS ARTICLE EXAMINES THE PRACTICE OF JUSTIFYING FOREIGN
    POLICY BY REINTERPRETING TREATIES AND NATIONAL SECURITY LAWS.
    REINTERPRETATION OF THE ORIGINAL MEANING OF THE LAW WHICH
    IS SANCTIONED BY NEITHER INTERNATIONAL NOR FEDERAL LAW IS
    TRACED TO ITS RECENT OCCURANCE IN THE REAGAN ERA. METHODS OF
    INTERPRETATION ARE DETAILED. EXAMINED ARE BOTH TREATY AND
    NATIONAL SECURITY REINTERPRETATION EXAMPLES. SOLUTIONS ARE
    SUGGESTED FOR BOTH THE U.S. AND THE U.N. TO PREVENT THIS
    PRACTICE TO CONTINUE

08023 SCHEINMAN, L.
    LAYMAN'S GUIDE TO CONSTITUTIONAL ASPECTS OF INTERNATIONAL
    ARMS CONTROL AGREEMENTS INVOLVING THE UNITED STATES
    AVAILABLE FROM NTIS, NO. DE89006331/GAR, DEC 88, 11.
    AN INITIAL ASSESSMENT HAS BEEN CONDUCTED TO EXAMINE THE
    LEGAL IMPLICATIONS AND COMPLEXITIES THAT MUST BE UNDERSTOOD
    AND EVALUATED SHOULD THE FACILITIES AND CONTRACTORS OF THE
    US DEPARTMENT OF ENERGY (DOE) NOT BE EXEMPTED FROM ON-SITE
    INSPECTIONS (OSIS) CONDUCTED BY THE SOVIET UNION UNDER THE
    PENDING STRATEGIC ARMS REDUCTION TALKS (START) TREATY OR
    UNDER FUTURE ARMS CONTROL TREATIES. THE ASSESSMENT LOOKS AT
    THE FOURTH AMENDMENT RIGHTS (RIGHT TO BE SECURE FROM
    UNREASONABLE SEARCHES AND SEIZURES) OF PARTIES AT GOVERNMENT-
    OWNED; GOVERNMENT-OWNED, CONTRACTOR-OPERATED (GOCO); AND
    PRIVATE SECTOR FACILITIES THAT ARE CANDIDATES FOR SOVIET
    SUSPECT SITE INSPECTIONS (SSIS). IN PARTICULAR, THE
    ASSESSMENT EXAMINES THE LEGAL CONSEQUENCES OF PUTTING AT
    RISK CLASSIFIED INFORMATION DESIGNATED AS EITHER NATIONAL
    SECURITY INFORMATION (NSI), AS CITED IN RELEVANT EXECUTIVE
    ORDERS, AND/OR RESTRICTED DATA (RD), WHICH IS DEFINED IN THE
    ATOMIC ENERGY ACT OF 1954 AS AMENDED. GIVEN THE POTENTIAL
    RISK OF INADVERTENT LOSSES OF RD AND OTHER CLASSIFIED
    INFORMATION AT DOE SITES DURING OSIS, THE DIVISION OF POLICY
    AND TECHNICAL ANALYSIS OF DOE'S OFFICE OF ARMS CONTROL (OAC)
    COMMISSIONED THIS STUDY TO AID IN UNDERSTANDING SOME OF THE
    LEGAL ASPECTS THAT MUST BE CONSIDERED TO PREPARE DOE
    FACILITIES FOR POSSIBLE FUTURE OSIS.

08024 SCHEMAN, L.R.; BAILEY, N.A.
    PUTTING LATIN AMERICAN DEBT TO WORK: A POSITIVE ROLE FOR
    THE US
    JOURNAL OF INTERAMERICAN STUDIES AND WORLD AFFAIRS, 31(4)
    (WIN 89), 1-21.
    THIS ARTICLE EXPLORES THE ANTICIPATED COLLAPSE OF THE
    ECONOMIES OF LATIN AMERICA WHICH IS UNDERWAY. DETAILED ARE
    THE ROOTS OF THE PRESENT DOWNFALL AND THE PART THAT
    PRESIDENT KENNEDY'S "ALLIANCE FOR PROGRESS PLAYS IN ALL OF
    THIS. IT EXAMINES THE ROLE THAT THE U.S. GOVERNMENT AND
    OTHER NATIONS OF THE WORLD WILL PLAY TO ENABLE THE COUNTRIES
    TO REGENERATE THEIR ECONOMIES. THE PSYCHOLOGICAL ASPECT OF
    THE PROBLEM IS ALSO NOTED.

08025 SCHENKER, H.
    EGYPT IS IN A UNIQUE POSITION
    NEW OUTLOOK, 32(8 (294)) (AUG 89), 21-22.
    THE EGYPTIAN GOVERNMENT IS NOT OPPOSED TO THE ISRAELI
    PROPOSAL FOR ELECTIONS IN THE OCCUPIED TERRITORIES BUT WOULD
    LIKE TO KNOW WHERE THE ELECTIONS WILL LEAD. THE EGYPTIAN
    AMBASSADOR TO ISRAEL, MOHAMMAD BASSIOUNI, BELIEVES THAT THE
    CONFLICT COULD BE SOLVED IF ISRAEL WOULD AGREE TO THE
    PRINCIPLE OF LAND FOR PEACE. THE ISRAELI LABOR PARTY HAS
    AGREED TO ACCEPT THIS PRINCIPLE, BUT THE LIKUD HAS NOT.

08026 SCHENKER, H.
    I AM VERY OPTIMISTIC
    NEW OUTLOOK, 32(8 (294)) (AUG 89), 23-26.
    IN THIS INTERVIEW, RITA HAUSER, WHO CHAIRS THE AMERICAN
    SECTION OF THE INTERNATIONAL CENTER FOR PEACE IN THE MIDDLE
    EAST, DISCUSSES THE BACKGROUND TO THE ISRAELI GOVERNMENT'S
    PROPOSAL FOR ELECTIONS IN THE OCCUPIED TERRITORIES AND THE
    PROSPECTS FOR PEACE THERE.

08027 SCHENKER, H.
    ON THE ROAD TO ISRAELI-PALESTINIAN PEACE
    AMERICAN-ARAB AFFAIRS, (28) (SPR 89), 1-8.
    THE ARTICLE RECOUNTS THE RECENT "ROAD TO PEACE"
    CONFERENCE HELD AT COLUMBIA UNIVERSITY. THE CONFERENCE WAS A
    LANDMARK DUE TO THE FACT THAT BOTH MEMBERS OF ISRAEL'S
    KNESSET AND SENIOR PLO OFFICIALS MET PUBLICLY AND DISCUSSED
    THE FUTURE OF THEIR PEOPLES. THE DIFFICULTIES ENCOUNTERED BY
    THE SPONSORS OF THE CONFERENCE IN THE PROCESS OF ARRANGING,
    PLANNING, AND EXECUTING ARE INDICATIVE OF THE TENSIONS THAT
    STILL REMAIN BETWEEN THE TWO GROUPS. HOWEVER, THERE WAS A
    SURPRISING DEGREE OF AGREEMENT BETWEEN BOTH SIDES ON THE
    NEED FOR PEACE AND SELF-DETERMINATION FOR BOTH ISRAEL AND
    PALESTINE.

08028 SCHENKER, H.
    STOCKHOLM ENCOUNTER
    NEW OUTLOOK, 32(3-4 (289-290)) (MAR 89), 29-31.
    STANLEY SHEINBAUM WAS ONE OF FIVE AMERICAN JEWS TO MEET
    WITH YASSER ARAFAT IN STOCKHOLM IN DECEMBER 1988, PRIOR TO
    THE ISSUANCE OF THE PLO STATEMENT CLARIFYING ITS POSITION ON
    THE THREE CONDITIONS SET BY THE U.S. GOVERNMENT FOR THE
    BEGINNING OF TALKS. IN THIS INTERVIEW, SHEINBAUM DISCUSSES
    THE MEETING WITH ARAFAT AND THE BACKGROUND TO IT.

08029 SCHENKER, H.
    THE ART AND SCIENCE OF ELECTION OBSERVATION
    NEW OUTLOOK, 32(8 (294)) (AUG 89), 29-31.
    THE PALESTINIANS VIEW INTERNATIONAL SUPERVISION AS A
    NECESSARY COMPONENT OF ANY ELECTION IN THE WEST BANK AND THE
    GAZA STRIP. THE ISRAELIS OPPOSE THE IDEA OF EXTENSIVE
    INTERNATIONAL SUPERVISION, BUT THERE COULD BE AN AD HOC BODY
    ESTABLISHED AT THE INVITATION OF THE ISRAELIS OR AS A RESULT
    OF AN AGREEMENT WITH THE PALESTINIANS ON THE MODALITIES OF
    THE ELECTIONS. THE UNITED NATIONS MIGHT BE AN APPROPRIATE
    BODY.

08030 SCHENKER, H.
    THE QUEST FOR PEACE: AN ISRAELI PERSPECTIVE
    AMERICAN-ARAB AFFAIRS, (30) (FAL 89), 84-88.
    MR. SCHENKER GIVES THE BACKGROUND OF THE INTIFADA, WHICH
    HE DESCRIBES AS A CONFLICT BETWEEN TWO LEGITIMATE NATIONAL
    CLAIMS. HE EXPLORES THE PARTITION PLAN; THE OLD STATUS QUO;
    THE PRESENT POLARIZATION OF ISRAELI SOCIETY; AND THE
    POSITION OF THE PLO. THE PROPOSALS FOR ENDING THE CONFLICT
    ARE EXAMINED AND IT IS SUGGESTED THAT EGYPT'S TEN-POINT
    FORMULA HAS A POSSIBILITY OF BEING ACCEPTED BY BOTH THE
    ISRAELIS AND PALESTINIANS. THE KEY IS THE ACTIVE INVOLVEMENT
    OF THIRD-PARTY MEDIATORS AND SHOULD BE BASED ON AN EMPATHY
    FOR BOTH ISRAELIS AND PALESTINIANS

08031 SCHENKER, H.
    TIME WAITS FOR NO ONE
    NEW OUTLOOK, 32(8 (294)) (AUG 89), 27-28.
    HAROLD SAUNDERS, THE FORMER U.S. ASSISTANT SECRETARY OF
    STATE FOR NEAR EASTERN AND SOUTH ASIAN AFFAIRS, IS
    INTERVIEWED IN THIS ARTICLE. HE DISCUSSES THE PEACE PROCESS
    AND THE ISRAELI GOVERNMENT'S PROPOSAL FOR ELECTIONS IN THE
    OCCUPIED TERRITORIES AS A FIRST STEP TOWARD RESOLVING THE
    CONFLICT THERE.

08032 SCHERZER, K. A.
    THE POLITICS OF DEFAULT: FINANCIAL RESTRUCTURE AND REFORM
    IN DEPRESSION ERA FALL RIVER, MASSACHUSETTS
    URBAN STUDIES, 26(1) (FEB 89), 164-176.
    THE SURVIVAL OF AN UNUSUALLY COMPLETE SET OF RECORDS
    (INCLUDING INTERNAL FILES FROM THE BANK THAT UNDERWROTE
    DEFAULTED SECURITIES, MEMOS FROM THE CHIEF FIRM REPRESENTING
    LOCAL BUSINESS LEADERS IN THE MIDST OF THE FISCAL CRISIS,
    AND ORAL HISTORIES FORM SEVERAL OF THE KEY PARTICIPANTS)
    MAKE THE DEFAULT OF FALL RIVER, MASSACHUSETTS, ESPECIALLY
    IMPORTANT TO THE STUDY OF URBAN FINANCE IN GENERAL AND
    DEPRESSION ERA MUNICIPAL DEFAULT IN PARTICULAR. ALTHOUGH
    RELATIVELY FEW CITIES IN THE 1930S HAD TO FACE SUCH HARSH

SOLUTIONS AS VIRTUAL RECEIVERSHIP FOR TEN YEARS UNDER THE WATCHFUL EYES OF A STATE-APPOINTED FINANCE BOARD. THIS ESSAY ARGUES THAT FALL RIVER, LIKE NEW YORK IN 1975, PROVIDES IMPORTANT INSIGHTS ON THE CRITICAL LINK BETWEEN THE OUTWARD POLITICS OF MUNICIPAL REFORM AND THE INWARD PROCESS OF DEFAULT.

08033 SCHICK, A.
MICRO-BUDGETARY ADAPTATIONS TO FISCAL STRESS IN INDUSTRIALIZED DEMOCRACIES
PUBLIC ADMINISTRATION REVIEW, 48(1) (JAN 88), 523-533.
THIS ARTICLE ADDRESSES A KEY QUESTION: WHY HAVE DEMOCRATIC GOVERNMENTS FAILED TO SEEK MORE FAR-REACHING INNOVATIONS IN BUDGETING? IT EXTENDS A PREVIOUS DISCUSSION WHICH EXAMINED THE MANNER IN WHICH INDUSTRIALIZED DEMOCRACIES HAVE ADAPTED THEIR MACRO-BUDGETARY PRACTICES TO FISCAL STRESS. THIS ARTICLE IDENTIFIES SOME OF THE PROBLEMS ARISING OUT OF EFFORTS TO HARMONIZE MACRO AND MICRO BUDGETING. A SECTION ON CUTBACK BUDGETING EXAMINES THIS ADAPTATION.

08034 SCHICK, A.
THE WAYS AND MEANS OF LEADING WAYS AND MEANS
BROOKINGS REVIEW, 7(4) (FAL 89), 16-23.
THE DEBACLES SUFFERED BY THE CHAIRMAN OF THE HOUSE WAYS AND MEANS COMMITTEE IN 1981 AND 1982 CAN BE SEEN AS FORMATIVE EXPERIENCES IN THE EMERGENCE OF NEW PATTERNS OF LEADERSHIP THAT HAVE RESTORED THE COMMITTEE TO ITS POSITION OF PREEMINENCE. SINCE 1983, THE COMMITTEE HAS PRODUCED A STEADY FLOW OF SIGNIFICANT LEGISLATION, INCLUDING THE RESCUE OF THE SOCIAL SECURITY SYSTEM, THE 1986 TAX REFORM, AND FOUR MAJOR BUDGET RECONCILIATION BILLS.

08035 SCHIFF, B. N.
BETWEEN OCCUPIER AND OCCUPIED:UNRWA IN THE WEST BANK AND THE GAZA STRIP
JOURNAL OF PALESTINE STUDIES, XVIII(3) (SPR 89), 60-75.
THIS ARTICLE EXAMINES THE TRADITIONAL ROLE OF THE UNITED NATIONS RELIEF AND WORKS AGENCY FOR PALESTINE REFUGEES IN THE NEAR EAST (UNRWA), AND DEMONSTRATES HOW UNRWA'S RECENT ACTIONS IN RESPONSE TO THE INTIFADA CONSTITUTE IMPORTANT CHANGES IN ITS MISSION. WHILE THE AGENCY IS NOW BECOMING AN ADJUNCT TO AMELIORATING OR SOLVING THE ISRAELI-PALESTINIAN CONFLICT IT WILL MORE LIKELY COME UNDER INCREASING PRESSURE TO RETURN TO ITS TRADITIONAL, LESS POLITICAL ROLE.

08036 SCHIFTER, R.
GLASNOST - THE DAWN OF FREEDOM
WORLD AFFAIRS, 151(1) (SUM 88), 17-23.
AS WE ENTER YEAR FIVE OF THE GORBACHEV ERA THE FUTURE OF REFORM IN THE SOVIET UNION REMAINS IN DOUBT, THOUGH THE REFORMERS ARE NOW CLEARLY IN THE ASCENDANCY. WE HAVE IN THE PAST BEEN TOLD OF SHARP DIVISIONS IN THE SOVIET LEADERSHIP, BETWEEN "DOVES" AND "HAWKS," WHEN IT WAS LIKELY THAT THESE REPORTS WERE DISINFORMATION. BUT IT DOES NOT STAND TO REASON THAT THE DIVISIONS OF OPINION NOW IN EVIDENCE ARE A CHARADE. CRITICISM OF THE BASIC TENETS ON WHICH THE SYSTEM RESTS IS NO LONGER THE PROVINCE SOLELY OF THE DISSIDENT MOVEMENT. THERE ARE NOW REFORMERS IN THE SOVIET ESTABLISHMENT WHO HAVE CONCLUDED THAT THE DOCTRINES OF THE PAST MUST BE PUT ASIDE AND THAT OTHER STANDARDS DEFINING THE RELATIONSHIP BETWEEN THE GOVERNING AND THE GOVERNED MUST TAKE THEIR PLACE. INCREASINGLY, THEY LOOK TO THE STANDARDS WHICH ARE THE PRODUCT OF THE ENLIGHTENMENT OF THE 18TH CENTURY, THE STANDARDS TO WHICH THE WESTERN DEMOCRACIES SUBSCRIBE.

08037 SCHIFTER, R.
GLASNOST: THE DAWN OF FREEDOM?
PHILADELPHIA: ANLS OF AMER ACMY OF POLITICAL AND SOC SCIENCE, (506) (NOV 89), 85-97.
THE FAILURE OF THE COMMUNIST ECONOMIC MODEL BROUGHT ABOUT IN THE SOVIET UNION A CRISIS OF FAITH IN THE ECONOMIC PROGRAM AND THE POLITICAL PRECEPTS ASSOCIATED WITH LENINISM. AS A RESULT, THERE HAVE COME TO THE FORE A GROUP OF REFORMERS WHO, OPERATING WITHIN THE SYSTEM, ARE SEEKING TO CREATE A MORE OPEN SOCIETY. THE REFORMERS ARE OPPOSED BY HARD-LINE ELEMENTS WHOSE PRINCIPAL PURPOSE IS TO MAINTAIN THEIR POSITIONS OF POWER AND PRIVILEGE. THE OUTCOME OF THE STRUGGLE BETWEEN THESE TWO GROUPS IS IN DOUBT. THE REFORMIST TENDENCIES HERE NOT IN EVIDENCE IMMEDIATELY UPON GORBACHEV'S ELECTION TO THE POST OF GENERAL SECRETARY IN FEBRUARY 1985. THE FIRST SIGNIFICANT INDICATIONS OF CHANGE HERE NOTED IN DECEMBER 1986. EVIDENCE OF PROFOUND, SYSTEMIC CHANGES STARTED TO ACCUMULATE ONLY AS RECENTLY AS THE SPRING OF 1988.

08038 SCHIFTER, R.
HUMAN RIGHTS SITUATION IN CUBA
DEPARTMENT OF STATE BULLETIN (US FOREIGN POLICY), 89(2151) (OCT 89), 41-43.
BECAUSE FIDEL CASTRO IS NOT THE GARDEN-VARIETY HUMAN RIGHTS VIOLATOR BUT OCCUPIES A UNIQUE POSITION AMONG THE WORLD'S TYRANTS, THE CUBAN HUMAN RIGHTS SITUATION DESERVES SPECIAL ATTENTION. BECAUSE WORLD ATTENTION HAS BEEN FOCUSED ON CUBAN HUMAN RIGHTS CONDITIONS, CASTRO HAS OSTENTATIOUSLY

RELEASED SOME POLITICAL PRISONERS, IMPROVED SOME PRISON CONDITIONS, ALLOWED SOME DISSIDENTS TO LEAVE, AND TOLERATED A FEW MUTED VOICES OF DISSENT. BUT NONE OF THESE GESTURES HAVE HAD THE SLIGHTEST IMPACT ON THE TOTALITARIAN CHARACTER OF THE CASTRO REGIME BECAUSE OTHER MOVES HAVE CANCELED OUT THESE MINOR IMPROVEMENTS.

08039 SCHIFTER, R.; REAGAN, R.; WALTERS, V.A.; WHITEHEAD, J.C.; WILLIAMSON, R.S.
US COMMERORATES 40TH ANNIVERSARY OF THE UNIVERSAL DECLARATION OF HUMAN RIGHTS
DEPARTMENT OF STATE BULLETIN (US FOREIGN POLICY), 89(2144) (MAR 89), 59-70.
THE AUTHORS REVIEW WHAT HAS BEEN ACCOMPLISHED IN THE FIELD OF HUMAN RIGHTS DUE TO THE UNIVERSAL DECLARATION OF HUMAN RIGHTS. THEY ALSO TAKE STOCK OF THE REAGAN ADMINISTRATION'S ACHIEVEMENTS IN HUMAN RIGHTS AND SUGGEST GOALS FOR THE IMMEDIATE FUTURE.

08040 SCHIRMER, J.G.
"THOSE WHO DIE FOR LIFE CANNOT BE CALLED DEAD:" WOMEN AND HUMAN RIGHTS PROTEST IN LATIN AMERICA
FEMINIST REVIEW, (32) (SUM 89), 3-29.
USING THE LANGUAGE OF SACRIFICE AND THE TRADITIONAL VALUES ASSOCIATED WITH MOTHERHOOD AS BOTH POLITICAL PROTECTION AND POLITICAL TOOL, WOMEN HAVE TAKEN PUBLIC ACTION DURING THE WORST YEARS OF REPRESSION IN ARGENTINA, GUATEMALA, AND CHILE. THEIR PRESISTENCE RAISES THE FOLLOWING QUESTIONS: WHAT IS IT ABOUT FORCED DISAPPEARANCE THAT STIMULATES MOBILIZATION OF WOMEN WHO, FOR THE MOST PART, WERE PREVIOUSLY APOLITICAL? MOREOVER, GIVEN THE IMPORTANCE OF RELIGION IN LATIN AMERICAN SOCIETIES, HOW HAS THE RELIGIOUS LANGUAGE OF OBEDIENCE AND SUBMISSION BEEN TRANSFORMED INTO THESE WOMEN'S FORM OF POLITICAL EXPRESSION?

08041 SCHISSEL, H.
AFRICA'S UNDERGROUND ECONOMY
AFRICA REPORT, 34(1) (JAN 89), 43-46.
WITH OFFICIAL ECONOMIC CIRCUITS CHOKED BY BUREAUCRATIC RED TAPE, NEPOTISM, INEFFICIENCY, AND CORRUPTION, THE UNDERGROUND ECONOMY PLAYS AN ESSENTIAL COMMERCIAL ROLE IN AFRICA. IT ALSO HAS AN IMPORTANT POLITICAL FUNCTION: PROVIDING MILLIONS OF JOBS AND UPWARD MOBILITY FOR THOSE WHO CANNOT BE INTEGRATED INTO THE OFFICIAL JOB MARKET, THEREBY REPRESENTING AN INVALUABLE SAFETY VALVE FOR THE OFTEN-INEPT RULING CLASSES.

08042 SCHIWDING, K.
FOREIGN PRESSURE AND CHANGE IN SOUTH AFRICA
SOUTH AFRICA INTERNATIONAL, 20(2) (OCT 89), 91-101.
IN HIS ANALYSIS OF THE ABILITY OF INTERNATIONAL PRESSURE TO CAUSE CHANGE IN SOUTH AFRICA THE AUTHOR EMPHASIZES SOUTH AFRICA'S DEPENDENCE ON THE WEST. HOWEVER, HE ARGUES THAT INTERNATIONAL PRESSURE CAN NEVER PLAY A DECISIVE ROLE IN SOUTH AFRICA; IT CAN ONLY WORSEN THE ECONOMIC SITUATION IN THE ENTIRE SUBCONTINENT. THE AUTHOR CALLS FOR INTELLIGENT SUPPORT RATHER THAN MORAL POSTURING FROM THE WEST.

08043 SCHLACK, R.F.
ECONOMIC CHANGE IN THE PEOPLE'S REPUBLIC OF CHINA
JOURNAL OF ECONOMIC ISSUES, 23(1) (MAR 89), 155-188.
THIS ARTICLE BEGINS WITH A SUMMARY OF ECONOMIC DEVELOPMENT IN THE PRC CONTRASTING THE NEARLY THIRTY YEARS OF MADIST LEADERSHIP WITH THE POLICIES OF THE LAST DECADE. CONSIDERED ARE: 1) CAPITAL AND THE PROCESS OF ACCUMULATION, 2) CONSUMPTION AND INCOME DISTRIBUTION, 3) EDUCATION AND THE ROLE OF HUMAN RESOURCE DEVELOPMENT, 4) FOREIGN TRADE AND INVESTMENT, AND 5) ECONOMIC PLANNING AND POLITICAL REFORMS. IT CONCLUDES BY OFFERING A HEURISTIC MODEL OF INSTITUTIONAL ADJUSTMENT AND ECONOMIC PROGRESS.

08044 SCHLEMMER, L.
INTERNATIONAL STRATEGIES FOR CHANGE IN SOUTH AFRICA
SOUTH AFRICA INTERNATIONAL, 19(3) (JAN 89), 130-139.
PRESSURE WITHIN THE INTERNATIONAL COMMUNITY FOR ACTION THAT WILL INFLUENCE CHANGE IN SOUTH AFRICA ARE STILL QUITE HIGH. THE ARTICLE EXAMINES SOME OF THE OPTIONS THAT EXTERNAL POWERS HAVE USED TO ATTEMPT TO INFLUENCE INTERNAL CHANGE IN SOUTH AFRICA. THEY INCLUDE: PERSUASION AND MORAL EXHORTATION, CONCRETE PRESSURES SUCH AS SANCTIONS, AND SUPPORT FOR THE ARMED STRUGGLE, INSURRECTION AND REVOLUTION. THE ARTICLE CONCLUDES THAT ALL OF THESE METHODS ARE OF LIMITED UTILITY AND OFFERS A FEW ALTERNATIVES FOR FUTURE POLICY CONSIDERATION.

08045 SCHLEMMER, L.
SOUTH AFRICA'S FUTURES: PROBABLE DEVELOPMENTS IN THE MEDIUM TERM
SOUTH AFRICA INTERNATIONAL, 20(2) (OCT 89), 63-73.
THIS ARTICLE OUTLINES A RANGE OF FUTURE SCENARIOS FOR SOUTH AFRICA IN THE 1990S. IT PRESENTS THE BACKGROUND TO ASSESSING THE FUTURE AND THEN DETAILS SEVEN POLITICAL PATHWAYS TO THE FUTURE. FOUR SCENARIOS OF POSSIBILITIES WITHIN THE PATHWAYS ARE DESCRIBED. THEN, THE TENTATIVE

PROBABILITIES ARE GIVEN. IT CONCLUDES THAT THE PATHS ARE ALL BUMPY, BUT THAT THERE ARE NO COMPLETE DEAD-ENDS OR CRATERS IN THE ROADS THAT LIE AHEAD.

08046 SCHLESINGER, A., JR.
THE LEGISLATIVE - EXECUTIVE BALANCE IN INTERNATIONAL AFFAIRS: THE INTENTIONS OF THE FRAMERS
WASHINGTON QUARTERLY, 12(1) (WIN 89), 99-107.
NO ONE CAN DOUBT THAT THE ORIGINAL INTENT OF THE FRAMERS WAS TO DENY THE EXECUTIVE BRANCH OF THE GOVERNMENT THE POWER TO BRING THE COUNTRY INTO WAR. THEIR ORIGINAL INTENT WAS TO REJECT THE HERESY THAT FOREIGN POLICY WAS THE PRIVATE PRESERVE AND PROPERTY OF THE PRESIDENT. NEITHER BRANCH OF GOVERNMENT HAS A DIVINE RIGHT TO PREVAIL OVER THE OTHER. CONGRESS MUST UNDERSTAND THAT IT CANNOT CONDUCT DAY-TO-DAY FOREIGN POLICY. THE PRESIDENT MUST UNDERSTAND THAT NO FOREIGN POLICY CAN LAST THAT IS NOT FOUNDED ON POPULAR UNDERSTANDING AND CONGRESSIONAL CONSENT. THE SEARCH FOR WAYS TO MAKE THE PARTNERSHIP REAL IS THE TRUEST FIDELITY TO THE DEEPER INTENTIONS OF THE FRAMERS.

08047 SCHLESINGER, M.
LEGISLATIVE GOVERNING COALITIONS IN PARLIAMENTARY DEMOCRACIES THE CASE OF THE FRENCH THIRD REPUBLIC
COMPARATIVE POLITICAL STUDIES, 22(1) (APR 89), 33-65.
THIS ARTICLE EXAMINES THE RELATIONS BETWEEN THE TWO COALITIONS IN THE PRIMORDIAL PARLIAMENTARY DEMOCRACY, THE FRENCH THIRD REPUBLIC. USING CORRELATION ANALYSIS, THE AUTHOR FOUND A WEAK PARTISAN RELATION BETWEEN THE TWO COALITIONS DURING THE FIVE LEGISLATURES OF THE INTERWAR YEARS. USING TWO MEASURES OF STABILITY, DURABILITY AND THE CONTINUITY OF COALITIONS BEYOND FORMAL TENURE, THE AUTHOR FOUND THE LEGISLATIVE COALITION ALWAYS MORE STABLE. INSTITUTIONAL RULES AND THE MULTIPARTY SYSTEM HELPED ACCOUNT FOR THESE DIFFERENCES. NEVERTHELESS, THERE WAS ENOUGH VARIATION FROM LEGISLATURE TO LEGISLATURE TO SHOW THAT ELECTORAL RULES AND RESULTS HAD AN IMPACT. VARIATIONS RESEMBLED THOSE IN THE AMERICAN REPUBLIC. PERIODS OF GREATER SIMILARITY IN PARTISAN COMPOSITION COINCIDED WITH GREATER EFFECTIVENESS OR STABILITY FOR THE EXECUTIVE; PERIODS OF DIVIDED CONTROL COINCIDED WITH LESSER EXECUTIVE STABILITY. THIS WAS OF CONSEQUENCE FOR THE MAKING OF POLICY.

08048 SCHLICHTING, K.C.
DEMOCRATIC INCUMBENTS AND THE 1984 PRESIDENTIAL ELECTION
PUBLIC OPINION QUARTERLY, 53(1) (SPR 89), 83-97.
THIS ARTICLE EXAMINES THE ADVANTAGES A SINGLE DEMOCRATIC INCUMBENT UTILIZED TO WIN REELECTION IN 1984 DESPITE AN OVERWHELMING VICTORY BY RONALD REAGAN AT THE TOP OF THE TICKET IN THE CONGRESSIONAL DISTRICT. THE INCUMBENT WON REELECTION BECAUSE OF TWO TYPES OF TICKET SPLITTING: REPUBLICAN-INCLINED VOTERS WHO VOTED FOR REPUBLICAN CANDIDATES FOR PRESIDENT AND U.S. SENATE AND SPLIT TO VOTE FOR THE DEMOCRATIC INCUMBENT FOR CONGRESS, AND DEMOCRATIC VOTERS WHO SUPPORTED DEMOCRATIC CANDIDATES FOR U.S. SENATE AND CONGRESS BUT SPLIT TO VOTE FOR RONALD REAGAN FOR PRESIDENT. TICKET SPLITTING WAS FOUND TO BE ASSOCIATED WITH BASIC POLITICAL ORIENTATION—WEAK REPUBLICAN AND INDEPENDENT VOTERS SPLIT IN FAVOR OF THE DEMOCRATIC INCUMBENT AND WERE FAR LESS LIKELY TO VOTE A STRAIGHT TICKET FOR EITHER PARTY. SUPPORT FOR THE DEMOCRATIC INCUMBENT WAS EXPLAINED IN NONIDEOLOGICAL TERMS AND WAS BASED UPON HIGH RECOGNITION AND FAVORABILITY, CONSTITUENT SERVICE, VOTING RECORD, AND PERSONAL FAMILIARITY.

08049 SCHMAHLING, E.
GERMAN SECURITY POLICY BEYOND AMERICAN HEGEMONY
WORLD POLICY JOURNAL, VI(2) (SPR 89), 371384.
THE AUTHOR EXAMINES THE CONTINUED "OCCUPATION" OF THE FEDERAL REPUBLIC OF GERMANY BY THE US AND OTHER NATO ALLIES. HE OUTLINES THE IMPORTANCE OF FULL SOVEREIGNTY IN GERMANY ESPECIALLY WITH REGARDS TO MILITARY DECISIONS SUCH AS THE PLACEMENT OF TACTICAL NUCLEAR WEAPONS ON GERMAN SOIL. HE OUTLINES SEVERAL MAJOR DIFFERENCES IN OPINION BETWEEN THE US AND GERMANY ON KEY MILITARY AND ECONOMIC ISSUES. THE IMPORTANCE OF CONTINUED EFFORTS FOR RENIFICATION IS ALSO EMPHASIZED.

08050 SCHMANDT, J.
SCIENCE AND TECHNOLOGY: ITS FUTURE IN THE US
CURRENT, (309) (JAN 89), 7-13.
IN THE PAST FEW YEARS, MANY AMERICANS HAVE BECOME CONCERNED ABOUT THE SEEMING FAILURE OF AMERICAN TECHNOLOGY AND THE END OF AMERICAN ECONOMIC LEADERSHIP. MANAGEMENT EXPERTS SAY THE PROBLEM IS NOT WITH RESEARCH IN THE USA, BUT THAT THE COUNTRY LACKS MANAGEMENT SKILLS. ECONOMISTS POINT TO THE ADVANTAGES ENJOYED BY LOW-WAGE COUNTRIES TO EXPLAIN THE LOSS OF AMERICAN MANUFACTURING CAPACITY. SOME POLITICIANS BLAME EXCESSIVE REGULATION OF AMERICAN INDUSTRY WHILE OTHERS ADVOCATE PROTECTIONISM. IN THIS ARTICLE, THE AUTHOR LOOKS AT HISTORY TO GAIN A PERSPECTIVE ON THE CURRENT SITUATION AND MAKE SOME PREDICTIONS FOR THE FUTURE, REGARDING GOVERNMENT SPENDING FOR R+D AND GOVERNMENT ACTION THAT COULD REVERSE THE PRESENT TREND.

08051 SCHMID, G.
LOCAL GOVERNMENT IN THE 21ST CENTURY
AMERICAN CITY AND COUNTY, 104(9) (SEP 89), 30-32.
FIFTY YEARS FROM NOW, LOCAL GOVERNMENT PROBLEMS WILL BE SOMEWHAT SIMILAR TO THOSE OF TODAY. BUDGETS WILL STILL NEED BALANCING, SOME PROMISING NEW PROGRAMS WILL BE ADDED WHILE OTHERS ARE CUT, IRATE CITIZENS WILL NEED TO BE MOLLIFIED, PERSONNEL MATTERS WILL REQUIRE TOO MUCH TIME, AND PLANNING WILL BE ALLOCATED TOO LITTLE. BUT SOME STRIKING DIFFERENCES IN ORGANIZATION AND OPERATIONS ARE ALSO LIKELY.

08052 SCHMIDT, G.D.
POLITICAL VARIABLES AND GOVERNMENTAL DECENTRALIZATION IN PERU, 1949-1988
JOURNAL OF INTERAMERICAN STUDIES AND WORLD AFFAIRS, 31(1, 2) (SPR 89), 193-232.
THIS ARTICLE EXAMINES THE CONCEPTUAL, INSTITUTIONAL, POLITICAL, ECONOMIC, AS WELL AS POLICY ASPECTS OF DECENTRALIZATION OF STATE PRODUCTION— NOT ONLY OF COLLECTIVE AND SEMI-PUBLIC, BUT ALSO OF PRIVATE COMMODITIES. AFTER DEMONSTRATING THAT DECENTRALIZATION IS A MULTIDIMENTIONAL CONCEPT, IT DESCRIBES HOW THE DIFFERENT DIMENTIONS OF DECENTRALIZATION HAVE BEEN (AND ARE) AFFECTED BY INTERNAL OR EXTERNAL AGENTS, AND BY ECONOMIC AND POLITICAL VARIABLES.

08053 SCHMIDT, M.G.
SOCIAL POLICY IN RICH AND POOR COUNTRIES: SOCIO-ECONOMIC TRENDS AND POLITICAL-INSTITUTIONAL DETERMINANTS
EUROPEAN JOURNAL OF POLITICAL RESEARCH, 17(6) (NOV 89), 641-659.
TO WHAT EXTENT CAN THE DRAMATIC DIFFERENCES IN SOCIAL POLICY EFFORTS IN RICH AND POOR COUNTRIES BE ACCOUNTE FOR BY GENUINELY POLITICAL EXPLANATIONS? THE HYPOTHESIS ADVANCED IN THIS ARTICLE RESTS UPON THE COMBINATION OF TWO SCHOOLS OF THOUGHT IN COMPARATIVE SOCIAL POLICY ANALYSIS: SOCIOECONOMIC MODELS WHICH FOCUS ATTENTION ON LEVELS OF ECONOMIC WEALTH, NEED, AND DEMAND FOR SOCIAL SECURITY AND MODELS OF A COMPARATIVE-HISTORIOGRAPHIC AND POLITICAL-INSTITUTIONALIST NATURE. EMPIRICAL APPLICATIONS OF SOCIO-ECONOMIC MODELS WITH LAGGED DEPENDENT VARIABLES REVEAL THE EXISTENCE OF TWO DEVIANT FAMILIES OF NATIONS: OVERSPENDERS IN SOCIAL POLICY (SUCH AS OVERSPENDERS OF SOCIAL DEMOCRATIC COMPLEXION AND OF CHRISTIAN DEMOCRATIC COMPOSITION) AND UNDERSPENDERS (SUCH AS THE SUPERPOWERS IN EAST AND WEST AS WELL AS JAPAN AND EAST GERMANY. THE RESIDUALS THAT CAN BE DERIVED FROM THESE MODELS ARE AMENABLE TO AN EXPLANATION WHICH RESIDES IN COMPARATIVE-HISTORIOGRAPHIC POLITICAL ANALYSIS OF SOCIAL POLICY.

08054 SCHMIDT, P.
THE FRANCO-GERMAN DEFENCE AND SECURITY COUNCIL
AUSSEN POLITIK, 40(4) (1989), 360 - 371.
THIS ARTICLE DEALS WITH THE PROTOCOL ESTABLISHING A DEFENCE AND SECURITY COUNCIL FIFTEEN YEARS AFTER THE ELYSEE TREATY BETWEEN THE FEDERAL REPUBLIC OF GERMANY AND FRANCE WAS SIGNED. THE REASONS FOR THIS TURNABOUT AFTER YEARS OF DISSONANCE ARE EXPLORED. THE WORK OF THE COUNCIL IS DETAILED, AND THE OPTIMISM FOR CONTINUING SUCCESS IS EXPLAINED.

08055 SCHMIEGELOW, H.
IDEALISM AND REALISM IN US FOREIGN POLICY
AUSSEN POLITIK, 40(1) (JAN 89), 15-29.
THE 1989 CHANGE OF PRESIDENCY IN THE US CALLS FOR AN APPRAISAL OF AMERICAN FOREIGN POLICY FROM ITS OWN PHILOPHICAL PERSPECTIVE. THE AUTHOR ANALYZES THE "REAGAN REVOLUTION" AND ITS BLEND OF IDEALISM AND REALISM. THE CLEAVAGES BETWEEN IDEALISM AND REALISM CUT ACROSS PARTY LINES AND DIVIDED PARTIES, GOVERNMENT AGENCIES, AND THE WHITE HOUSE ITSELF. AND YET, AT THE BEGINNING OF REAGAN'S SECOND TERM, SECRETARY OF STATE SHULTZ MANAGED TO PREVAIL WITH ANOTHER BLEND OF DOCTRINES: PRAGMATISM. WHILE NEO-CONSERVATIVE CRUSADERS PREVAILED IN LATIN AMERICAN POLICY, SHULTZ WAS ABLE TO DEMONSTRATE THE VALUE OF PRAGMATISM IN THE GENEVA TALKS, WITH CHINA, IN THE PHILIPPINES, AND IN AFRICA.

08056 SCHMITT, G.
WHY COMMISSION DON'T WORK
NATIONAL INTEREST, (15) (SPR 89), 58-67.
THE ARTICLE ANALYZES THE USE OF PRESIDENTIAL COMMISSIONS TO SOLVE TOUGH POLITICAL PROBLEMS. CONVENTIONAL WISDOM ARGUED THAT IF COMMISSIONS WERE NOT THE SOLUTIONS TO SUCH PROBLEMS, THEY AT LEAST WERE A CONVENIENT WAY OF DELAYING JUDGEMENT AND SOLVING THE "POLITICS OF THE SITUATION." THE ARTICLE ANALYZES THE SCOWCROFT COMMISSION WHICH DEALT WITH THE MODERNIZATION OF THE NATION'S LAND-BASED NUCLEAR FORCES AND THE KISSINGER COMMISSION WHICH DEALT WITH CENTRAL AMERICA. IT CONCLUDES THAT NEITHER COMMISSION HAD THEIR INTENDED EFFECT AND THAT COMMISSIONS GENERALLY DO NOT SOLVE THE STRUCTURAL PROBLEMS THAT MARK CURRENT CONGRESSIONAL POLICY AND ARE A POOR SUBSTITUTE FOR FOR PRESIDENTIAL LEADERSHIP.

08057 SCHMITT, H.
ON PARTY ATTACHMENT IN WESTERN EUROPE AND THE UTILITY OF
EUROBAROMETER DATA
WEST EUROPEAN POLITICS, 12(2) (APR 89), 122-140.
AN ANALYSIS OF 25 EUROBAROMETER SURVEYS CONDUCTED
BETWEEN 1974 AND 1988 IN EACH OF THE EUROPEAN COMMUNITY
MEMBER-COUNTRIES SHOWS THAT THERE IS NO SINGLE TREND
DISCERNIBLE THROUGHOUT WESTERN EUROPE. ALTHOUGH LEVELS OF
PARTY ATTACHMENT ARE DECREASING IN MOST MEMBER-STATES, FOUR
DIFFERENT PATTERNS HAVE EMERGED, AND THEY CLOSELY RELATE TO
MORE GENERAL DEVELOPMENTS IN THE RESPECTIVE PARTY SYSTEMS.
THESE PATTERNS ARE: STRONG DEALIGNMENT (IRELAND); PERIPHERAL
DEALIGNMENT (UNITED KINGDOM AND ITALY); POST-REALIGNMENT
(DENMARK, FRANCE, THE NETHERLANDS, GREECE, BELGIUM); AND
STABLE ALIGNMENT (WEST GERMANY).

08058 SCHMITT, H.
THEATER OF WAR OR THEATER OF COOPERATION
WORLD MARXIST REVIEW, 31(10) (OCT 88), 5-10.
IN DENSELY POPULATED EUROPE, STATES' RELATIONS BASED ON
PEACEFUL COEXISTENCE, DIALOGUE AND MUTUAL CONFIDENCE ARE
EVER MORE IMPERATIVE. THE IDEA OF A COMMON EUROPEAN HOME,
PUT FORWARD BY MIKHAIL GORBACHOV, CPSU CC GENERAL SECRETARY,
MEETS TODAY'S OBJECTIVE NEED TO WIDEN AND IMPROVE
CONTINENTAL TEAMWORK. THE COMMUNIST PARTY CONSIDERS IT
EXPEDIENT TO SAFEGUARD, BY 2000, THE VIABILITY OF EUROPE,
AND PEACE AND PROSPERITY FOR FUTURE GENERATIONS.

08059 SCHMITT, R.
ORGANIZATIONAL INTERLOCKS BETWEEN NEW SOCIAL MOVEMENTS AND
TRADITIONAL ELITES: THE CASE OF THE WEST PEACE MOVEMENT.
EUROPEAN JOURNAL OF POLITICAL RESEARCH, 17(5) (SEP 89),
583-598.
THIS PAPER DEALS WITH THE QUESTION OF WHETHER THE
CONCEPT OF OF ELITES IS A FRUITFUL CATEGORY FOR THE ANALYSIS
OF NEW SOCIAL MOVEMENTS. IT IS PROPOSED THAT MOBILIZATIONS
OF NEW SOCIAL MOVEMENTS ARE TO BE UNDERSTOOD AS DYNAMIC
INTERACTION PROCESSES BETWEEN MASS CONSTITUENCIES AND
MOVEMENT ENTREPRENEURS, MEDIATED BY ORGANIZATIONAL
COMMUNICATION NETWORKS. TAKING THE CASE OF THE WEST GERMAN
PEACE MOVEMENT, IT IS SHOWN THAT SUCH LEADERSHIP ROLES CAN
BE IDENTIFIED AS PARTS OF THE MOVEMENT'S INTERNAL DIVISION
OF LABOUR. FURTHERMORE, IS SHOWN THAT MOVEMENT ENTREPRENEURS
OF THE PEACE MOVEMENT ARE ALSO LINKED TO ESTABLISHED ELITE
SECTOR.

08060 SCHMITTER, P.C.
CORPORATISM IS DEAD! LONG LIVE CORPORATISM!
GOVERNMENT AND OPPOSITION, 24(1) (1989), 54-73.
READING ANDREW SHONFIELD'S "MODERN CAPITALISM" REVEALS
WHY, WHEN CORPORATISM HAS RESTORED TO ACADEMIC
RESPECTABILITY BY POLITICAL SCIENTISTS AND SOCIOLOGISTS IN
THE MID-1970'S, SHONFIELD HAS DENIED HIS SHARE OF THE
PATERNAL RIGHTS TO THE CONCEPT. MOST OF THE THEMES THAT
SUBSEQUENT HORDES OF NEO-CORPORATISTS TOOK SEVERAL YEARS TO
DISCOVER CAN BE FOUND THERE, BUT THEY ARE SCATTERED ABOUT IN
THE DISCUSSION OF SEVERAL CASES. CAUSES, DEFINING CONDITIONS,
AND CONSEQUENCES ARE JUMBLED TOGETHER.

08061 SCHNAPP, C.G.
ASEAN AND THE UNITED STATES IN THE TWENTY FIRST CENTURY
AVAILABLE FROM NTIS, NO. AD-A209 546/1/GAR, FEB 9 89, 40.
FOR 21 YEARS THE ASSOCIATION OF SOUTHEAST ASIAN NATIONS
(ASEAN) HAS BEEN A MODEL ORGANIZATION FOR REGIONAL
COOPERATION AMONG DEVELOPING NATIONS. IT HAS PROVIDED AN
EXAMPLE TO ALL SOUTH ASIAN NATIONS WHOM ARE THEMSELVES
MOVING TOWARD CLOSER TIES OF COOPERATION AS IN SAARC -- THE
SOUTH ASIAN ASSOCIATION FOR REGIONAL COOPERATION. IMPORTANT
ASPECTS OF THIS TREND ARE THE DEVELOPMENT OF ECONOMIC AND
SECURITY COOPERATION AGREEMENTS THAT WILL LIKELY HAVE GREAT
IMPACT ON THE POLITICAL ALIGNMENTS OF THE 21ST CENTURY.
GIVEN ITS NON-COMMUNIST STANCE, ASEAN SHOULD BE A KEY
ELEMENT IN THE LONG RANGE SECURITY PLANS OF THE UNITED
STATES. ECONOMICALLY, THE RAPIDLY RISING IMPORTANCE OF ALL
OF THE PACIFIC RIM COUNTRIES, WITH ASEAN REPRESENTING NEARLY
300 MILLION PEOPLE, WILL BE ECONOMICALLY INVOLVED TO A GREAT
DEGREE IN THE INTERNATIONAL ECONOMIC BATTLEGROUNDS OF THE
21ST CENTURY. THE COMBINATION OF THE POLITICAL AND ECONOMIC
LEVERAGE THAT COULD BE EXERTED BY ASEAN MAY MAKE THEM A
FORMIDABLE ALLY, OR ADVERSARY. RECOGNIZING THIS, JAPAN IS
ALREADY COURTING ASEAN WITH A STRATEGIC (ECONOMICALLY
SPEAKING) EYE TO THE FUTURE. GREAT DEVELOPMENTAL INTERPLAY
BY THE UNITED STATES HAS NOT BEEN AS STRONG AS SOME ASEAN
MEMBER COUNTRIES WOULD HAVE.

08062 SCHNECK, S.
CONNOLLY'S POSTMODERN LIBERALISM
REVIEW OF POLITICS, 51(2) (SPR 89), 281-291.
CONNOLLY ARGUES THAT AMERICAN LIBERALISM'S UNDERSTANDING
OF THE COMMON GOOD, ITS IDOL OF LIBERATION, IS BEING
DEFROCKED BEFORE THE AMERICAN PEOPLE. AT SOME UNARTICULATED
LEVEL, AMERICANS PERCEIVE THAT THE OLD DREAM OF PROGRESSIVE
ECONOMIC GROWTH AND INDIVIDUAL PROSPERITY IS ONLY AN IDOL.
ACCORDINGLY, THERE IS A GROWING RESENTMENT OF THE INCREASING

DISCIPLINE IMPOSED UPON THEM FOR THE SUPPOSED PURPOSE OF
ATTAINING THIS END. THE UPSHOT IS A HEDONISTIC TURNING FROM
THE OLD IDOL OF THE COMMON GOOD TOWARD IMMEDIATE SELF-
GRATIFICATION.

08063 SCHNEIDER, B.
CREATIVE INSTABILITY: SOURCE OF INSPIRATION FOR A NEW WORLD
FUTURES, 21(2) (APR 89), 199-200.
ON 24-28 OCTOBER 1988, THE CLUB OF ROME CELEBRATED THE
20TH ANNIVERSARY OF ITS CREATION BY HOLDING A CONFERENCE IN
PARIS. THE THEME OF THE CONFERENCE WAS 'THE GREAT TRANSITION:
REASONS TO LIVE AND HOPE IN A NEW GLOBAL SOCIETY'. THIS
ARTICLE OFFERS SOME REFLECTIONS ON THIS THEME AND ON THE
CHALLENGES AND HOPE REPRESENTED BY THE PRESENT AGE OF
TRANSITION AND UNCERTAINTY.

08064 SCHNEIDER, J.
ARGENTINA: THE ENIGMA OF LA TABLADA
NACLA REPORT ON THE AMERICAS, XXIII(3) (SEP 89), 9-13.
SIX MONTHS AFTER GUERRILLAS OF THE LEFTIST ALL FOR THE
FATHERLAND MOVEMENT (MTP) ATTACKED AN ARGENTINE ARMY
BARRACKS AT LA TABALADA, THE EVENT REMAINS AN ENIGMA. THE
LEFTISTS BELIEVE THAT THEY WERE STOPPING A MILITARY COUP.
THE ARMED FORCES CLAIMED THAT THE MTP WAS ACTING ON BEHALF
OF AN INTERNATIONAL TERRORIST NETWORK LINKED TO NICARAGUA
AND CUBA. THE LA TABALADA INCIDENT DEMONSTRATES THE TENSION
BETWEEN OPPOSITES THAT MEMBERS OF THE REVOLUTIONARY MOVEMENT
IN LATIN AMERICA MUST DEAL WITH: VIOLENCE OR NONVIOLENCE;
MASS STRUGGLE OR VANGUARDISM; AND REFORM OR REVOLUTION.
HOWEVER, THE INCIDENT DOES NOT PROVIDE ANY ANSWERS TO THESE
QUESTIONS.

08065 SCHNEIDER, M.
INTERCITY COMPETITION AND THE SIZE OF THE LOCAL PUBLIC
WORK FORCE
PUBLIC CHOICE, 63(3) (DEC 89), 253-266.
THE NEED TO LIMIT THE SIZE OF GOVERNMENT IS A CONSTANT
THEME IN CONTEMPORARY RESEARCH. MOST, IF NOT ALL, OF THE
THEORETICAL INSIGHTS INTO RESTRAINING THE SIZE OF GOVERNMENT
REST ON THE USE OF COMPETITION TO LIMIT ITS EXPANSION. IN
THIS PAPER, IT IS SHOWN HOW COMPETITION BETWEEN LOCAL
GOVERNMENTS LIMITS THE LABOR INPUTS USED IN PROVIDING LOCAL
PUBLIC GOODS AND SERVICES. THIS RESULT IS IMPORTANT BECAUSE
PROVIDING LOCAL PUBLIC GOODS AND SERVICES IS LABOR INTENSIVE
AND THE BULK OF LOCAL EXPENDITURES ARE LABOR RELATED.

08066 SCHNEIDER, M.
INTERMUNICIPAL COMPETITION, BUDGET-MAXIMIZING BUREAUCRATS,
AND THE LEVEL OF SUBURBAN COMPETITION
AMERICAN JOURNAL OF POLITICAL SCIENCE, 33(3) (AUG 89),
612-628.
THIS ARTICLE IDENTIFIES SEVERAL SOURCES OF INTERMUNCIPAL
COMPETITION IN POLYCENTRIC METROPOLITAN REGIONS. THE EFFECTS
OF SUCH COMPETITION IS TESTED EMPIRICALLY ON THE SIZE OF
SUBURBAN MUNCIPAL BUDGETS. IT FINDS THAT COMPETITION DOES
ACT AS A CONSTRAINT ON THE SIZE OF GOVERNMENT BY INCREASING
THE ABILITY AND INCENTIVES FOR RESIDENTS AND POLITICIANS TO
CONTROL THE BUDGET-MAXIMIZING TENDENCIES OF LOCAL
BUREAUCRATS.

08067 SCHOEPFLE, G.K.; PEREZ-LOPEZ, J.F.
EXPORT ASSEMBLY OPERATIONS IN MEXICO AND THE CARIBBEAN
JOURNAL OF INTERAMERICAN STUDIES AND WORLD AFFAIRS, 31(4)
(WIN 89), 131-161.
THIS PAPER FOCUSES ON OFFSHORE-ASSEMBLY OPERATIONS IN
MEXICO AND THE CARIBBEAN, TWO AREAS THAT HAVE BEEN MAJOR
BENEFICIARIES OF US MANUFACTURERS WHO HAVE TAKEN ADVANTAGE
OF THIS TREND. PART II OF THE PAPER DESCRIBES BRIEFLY THE
INSTITUTIONAL ARRANGEMENTS WHICH HAVE CREATED EXPORT-
ORIENTED ASSEMBLY FACILITIES IN MEXICO AND SELECTED NATIONS
OF THE CARIBBEAN. PART III DISCUSSES THE BENEFICIAL IMPACT
ON HOST COUNTRIES IN TERMS OF EMPLOYMENT CREATION,
CONTRIBUTION TO EXPORT EARNINGS, AND ECONOMIC
DIVERSIFICATION. THE PAPER CLOSES WITH SOME GENERAL
OBSERVATIONS ABOUT THE GROWTH IN EXPORT-ASSEMBLY OPERATIONS
AND THE IMPLICATIONS OF THESE OPERATIONS FOR HOST COUNTRY
DEVELOPMENT AND EMPLOYMENT.

08068 SCHORR, D.
A SLOW START FOR BUSH
NEW LEADER, LXXII(3) (FEB 89), 3-4.
ALTOGETHER, PRESIDENT BUSH HAS BEEN SLOW IN GETTING OFF
THE MARK IN PROGRAMMATIC TERMS, BOTH IN DOMESTIC PROGRAMS
AND FOREIGN POLICY.

08069 SCHORR, D.
REACTING TO CHINA'S "RED TERROR
NEW LEADER, LXXII(10) (JUN 89), 3-4.
IN THE BRUTAL CRACKDOWN ON PRODEMOCRACY DEMONSTRATIONS,
CHINA EMPLOYED A POLICY THAT LENIN TERMED "RED TERROR" FOR
THE USE OF UNSPARING VIOLENCE NOT ONLY TO CRUSH ANY
REBELLION BUT TO WIPE OUT THE WILL TO RESIST. UNDER PRESENT
CONDITIONS, THE COST OF RED TERROR IS HIGH--THE SACRIFICE OF
SOME OF THE GAINS MADE IN 20 YEARS OF EFFORT TO OPEN CHINA'S

DOOR TO TRADE AND IMPROVE THE COUNTRY'S IMAGE IN THE WORLD.
BUT WHEN REGIME AND SYSTEM ARE PERCEIVED TO BE IN DANGER,
THE PRICE IS ACCEPTABLE. DENG XIAOPING SAID IN HIS APRIL 25
STATEMENT THAT SET THE STAGE FOR THE CRACKDOWN, "WE MUST NOT
BE AFRAID OF PEOPLE CURSING US, OF A BAD REPUTATION OR OF
INTERNATIONAL REACTION."

08070 SCHORR, D.
REVISING THE US-SOVIET DIALOGUE
NEW LEADER, LXXII(15) (OCT 89), 3-4.
GEORGE BUSH HAS MOVED BEYOND HIS "WAIT-AND-SEE" ATTITUDE
TOWARDS NEGOTIATION WITH THE SOVIETS; A SERIES OF SUMMITS
AND MEETINGS PROMISE TO RESULT IN SOLID, IF MODEST, ARMS
CONTROL PROGRESS. BOTH SIDES ARE ALSO FIGHTING AN INTENSE
PUBLIC RELATIONS BATTLE; BOTH WISH TO BE PERCEIVED AS TAKING
THE MOST INITIATIVE ON ARMS CONTROL ISSUES WHILE
SIMULTANEOUSLY HOLDING ON TO DEAR WEAPONS SYSTEMS AND
POLICIES.

08071 SCHORR, D.
TACKLING THE TERRORISTS
NEW LEADER, LXXII(1) (JAN 89), 3-4.
ALTHOUGH RONALD REAGAN PROMISED SWIFT, EFFECTIVE
RETRIBUTION AGAINST TERRORISTS, HIS RECORD WAS SPOTTY, AT
BEST. HE HANDED THE OVAL OFFICE OVER TO GEORGE BUSH, WHO
BEGAN ON A NOTE OF ANTI-TERRORIST IMPOTENCE BY VOWING "TO
PUNISH FIRMLY" THE BOMBERS OF PAN AMERICAN FLIGHT 103 "IF
YOU CAN EVER FIND THEM."

08072 SCHORR, D.
THE BATTERED BUSH PRINCIPLES
NEW LEADER, LXXII(5) (MAR 89), 3.
ONE OF THE THEMES ENUNCIATED BY NEWLY ELECTED PRESIDENT
GEORGE BUSH WAS ETHICS IN GOVERNMENT. HOWEVER, LONG BEFORE
THE LEGENDARY HUNDRED DAYS HAD ELAPSED, SEVERAL OF THE
FRIENDS AND NOMINEES OF BUSH FACED ALLEGATIONS OF ACTIONS OF
QUESTIONABLE ETHICS. THE MOST NOTABLE OF THE ALLEGATIONS
INVOLVES THE NOMINEE FOR SECRETARY OF DEFENSE, JOHN TOWER.

08073 SCHORR, D.
WHAT THE PEOPLE SAID
NEW LEADER, LXXII(17) (NOV 89), 3-4.
THE FIRST ANNIVERSARY OF PRESIDENT BUSH'S ELECTION
REVEALED CHANGES IN THE US POPULACE, SOME SUBTLE AND SOME
OBVIOUS. SOME OF THE APPARENT TRENDS INCLUDE: A MOVEMENT
AWAY FROM POLARIZATION AND THE "CYNICAL MANIPULATION OF
RACIAL ANTIPATHIES"; AND A CALL FOR A CEASE-FIRE IN THE
POLITICAL WAR OVER ABORTION. ALTHOUGH THE DECISION OF THE US
SUPREME COURT TO BROADEN THE POWER OF STATES TO RESTRICT
ABORTION GALVANIZED THE PRO-CHOICE MOVEMENT, POLITICAL
EMPHASIS ON ABORTION, AS WELL AS OTHER "SINGLE-ISSUES," HAS
DECLINED. PRESIDENT BUSH HAS CONTINUED TO TAKE SYMBOLIC
ACTION AGAINST ABORTION, BUT HIS STRIDENT ANTI-ABORTION
RHETORIC HAS DIMINISHED.

08074 SCHOUTEN, R.
VIEW FROM THE HAGUE
NATO'S SIXTEEN NATIONS, 34(3) (JUN 89), 17.
AT THE END OF APRIL 1989, THE COLLAPSE OF THE CENTRE-
RIGHT DUTCH GOVERNMENT HEADED BY RUUD LUBBERS BEGAN TO LOOK
INEVITABLE. THE CRISIS WAS TRIGGERED BY LUBBERS' ADOPTION OF
THE ENVIRONMENTAL CAUSE AND HIS INTRODUCTION OF A SWEEPING
NATIONAL ENVIRONMENTAL PLAN. THE STRAW THAT BROKE THE
CAMEL'S BACK WAS LUBBERS' PROPOSAL TO ABOLISH A TAX BREAK
FOR COMMUTERS, WHICH HAD BEEN INTRODUCED WHEN THE GOVERNMENT
WAS ENCOURAGING PEOPLE TO MOVE TO THE COUNTRY TO ALLEVIATE
CROWDING IN WESTERN CITIES. ENCOURAGING COMMUTERS TO DRIVE
THEIR OWN CARS INSTEAD OF TAKING MASS TRANSIT HAS AN OBVIOUS
NEGATIVE EFFECT ON THE ENVIRONMENT. THE MOST LIKELY OUTCOME
OF THE ELECTIONS, SCHEDULED FOR SEPTEMBER 6, IS A COALITION
OF CHRISTIAN DEMOCRATS AND SOCIAL DEMOCRATS.

08075 SCHQARTZ, R.
US INTEREST IN EUROPE'S 1992 PROCESS: AN ANALYTIC SURVEY
WASHINGTON QUARTERLY, 12(3) (SUM 89), 205-213.
THE ARTICLE EXAMINES THE IMPLICATIONS OF THE EUROPEAN
COMMUNITY'S INTERNAL MARKET PROGRAM FOR THE US. IT OUTLINES
POTENTIAL EFFECTS ON US INTERESTS BOTH COMMERCIAL AND
POLITICAL, AS WELL AS THE EFFECT ON OVERALL US GLOBAL
ECONOMIC STRATEGY. IT ALSO EXAMINES THE CURRENT STATE OF
LITERATURE IN THE FIELD.

08076 SCHRAM, A.; VAN WINDEN, F.
REVEALED PREFERENCES FOR PUBLIC GOODS: APPLYING A MODEL OF
VOTER BEHAVIOR
PUBLIC CHOICE, 60(3) (MAR 89), 259-282.
ABSTRACT. MOST ANALYSES OF PREFERENCES FOR GOVERNMENT-
SUPPLIED GOODS DISREGARD THE FACT THAT IN A DEMOCRATIC
SOCIETY, THESE PREFERENCES ARE REVEALED BY AN INDIVIDUAL
CHOICE: THE VOTE. IN THIS PAPER THIS IS TAKEN ACCOUNT OF IN
A MODEL, EXPLAINING THE DYNAMICS IN VOTING BEHAVIOR IN A
MULTI-PARTY SYSTEM. THE MODEL ALLOWS ONE TO ESTIMATE PARTY
IDENTIFICATION, SENSITIVENESS TO ECONOMIC PERFORMANCES, TIME
PREFERENCE, AND RELATIVE PREFERENCES FOR PUBLIC VERSUS

PRIVATE GOODS, ALL FOR EACH OF THE GROUPS. FURTHERMORE, THE
MODEL ALLOWS FOR AN ESTIMATION OF THE LEVEL TO WHICH VARIOUS
PARTIES ARE HELD RESPONSIBLE FOR GOVERNMENT POLICIES. AN
EMPIRICAL APPLICATION OF THE MODEL TO THE NETHERLANDS IS
PRESENTED.

08077 SCHRAMM, G.; WARFORD, J.J.
ENVIRONMENTAL MANAGEMENT AND ECONOMIC DEVELOPMENT
AVAILABLE FROM NTIS, NO. PB89-217210/GAR, 1989, 220.
CONTENTS: ENVIRONMENTAL MANAGEMENT AND ECONOMIC POLICY
IN DEVELOPING COUNTRIES; ENVIRONMENTAL AND NATURAL RESOURCE
ACCOUNTING; MARGINAL OPPORTUNITY COST AS A PLANNING CONCEPT
IN NATURAL RESOURCE MANAGEMENT; THE ENVIRONMENTAL BASIS OF
SUSTAINABLE DEVELOPMENT; ECONOMIC INCENTIVES FOR SUSTAINABLE
PRODUCTION; DEFORESTATION IN BRAZIL'S AMAZON REGION:
MAGNITUDE, RATE, AND CAUSES; AN ECONOMIC JUSTIFICATION FOR
RURAL AFFORESTATION: THE CASE OF ETHIOPIA; MANAGING THE
SUPPLY OF AND DEMAND FOR FUELWOOD IN AFRICA; ECONOMIC
ASPECTS OF AFFORESTATION AND SOIL CONSERVATION PROJECTS;
MULTILEVEL RESOURCE ANALYSIS AND MANAGEMENT: THE CASE OF
WATERSHEDS.

08078 SCHROEDER, L.
A COMPARATIVE ANALYSIS OF GRANTS TO LOCAL GOVERNMENTS IN
SOUTHEAST AND SOUTH ASIA
INTERNATIONAL REVIEW OF ADMINISTRATIVE SCIENCES, 55(1)
(MAR 89), 59-84.
IN ORDER TO STUDY THE ROLES THAT TRANSFERS TO LOWER
LEVELS OF GOVERNMENTS PLAY, THE ARTICLE ANALYZES STUDIES THE
TRANSFER OF FUNDS IN BANGLADESH, PAKISTAN, INDONESIA, AND
THE PHILIPPINES. IT FOCUSES PARTICULARLY ON THE USE OF
GRANTS TO PROMOTE DECENTRALIZED DECISIONMAKING. IT REVIEWS
HOW FUND TRANSFERS ARE ACCOMPLISHED IN THE FOUR COUNTRIES
AND EVALUATES THEIR PROGRAMS FROM A COMPARATIVE PERSPECTIVE
WHILE RECOGNIZING THE FACT THAT GRANTS ARE OFTEN INTENDED TO
ACCOMPLISH A VARIETY OF OBJECTIVES.

08079 SCHROEDER, P. W.
THE NINETEENTH CENTURY SYSTEM: BALANCE OF POWER OR
POLITICAL EQUILIBRIUM
REVIEW OF INTERNATIONAL STUDIES, 15(2) (APR 89), 135-153.
INSTEAD OF ARGUING OVER THE EXACT MEANING OF 'BALANCE OF
POWER' THE AUTHOR ADVOCATES SUBSTITUTING A PHRASE APPARENTLY
JUST AS VAGUE AND SUBJECT TO MISUNDERSTANDING AND
MANIPULATION, NAMELY, 'POLITICAL EQUILIBRIUM'. THE ARGUMENT
TO BE SKETCHED OUT IS THAT THE NINETEENTH CENTURY
INTERNATIONAL SYSTEM, AS ANY STABLE INTERNATIONAL SYSTEM
MUST DO IN THE TWENTIETH CENTURY AS WELL, DEPENDED MAINLY
NOT ON BALANCING POWER AGAINST OTHER POWER BUT ON BALANCING
OTHER VITAL FACTORS IN INTERNATIONAL POLITICS, AND THAT PURE
BALANCE OF POWER POLITICS DESTROYS POLITICAL EQUILIBRIUM
RATHER THAN SUSTAINS IT.

08080 SCHUBERT, W.
UNEMPLOYMENT INSURANCE COSTS: ISSUES AND DILEMMAS
INTERNATIONAL JOURNAL OF SOCIAL ECONOMICS, 16(8) (1989),
60-67.
THIS ARTICLE FOCUSES ON A SET OF ISSUES CONCERNING
UNEMPLOYMENT INSURANCE COSTS. THE EFFECT ON UNEMPLOYMENT
INSURANCE COSTS OF VARIABLES UNDER THE CONTROL OF THE STATE
LEGISLATURE, SUCH AS THE MAXIMUM BENEFIT AMOUNT PAID PER
WEEK TO UNEMPLOYED WORKERS, IS ANALYSED, AS ARE THE PROBLEMS
OF ABUSING THE SYSTEM THROUGH "LAY-OFF" MANAGEMENT AND THE
TOPIC OF UNDEREMPLOYMENT. THE MAIN POLICY THRUST OF THE
ARTICLE IS TO ARGUE THAT THERE ARE LIKELY TO BE IMPORTANT
TRADE-OFFS BETWEEN LIBERAL BENEFIT POLICIES WHICH TYPICALLY
INCREASE BUSINESS COSTS, AND LONG-TERM EMPLOYMENT
OPPORTUNITIES THEREFORE, LIBERAL POLICIES TOWARDS THE
UNEMPLOYED NEED TO BE OFFSET BY OTHER BUSINESS COST
REDUCTIONS IN ORDER TO ALLOW INDIVIDUAL STATES TO REMAIN
DESIRABLE LOCATIONS FOR NEW BUSINESS CAPACITY. THE
LEGISLATURE'S ROLE IN THIS PROCESS IS ARGUED TO BE OF
CRUCIAL IMPORTANCE.

08081 SCHUCK, P.
GOVERNMENT FUNDING FOR ORGAN TRANSPLANTS
JOURNAL OF HEALTH POLITICS, POLICY AND LAW, 14(1) (SPR 89),
169-190.
THIS PAPER EXAMINES THE ROLE OF THE FEDERAL AND STATE
GOVERNMENTS IN PAYING FOR ORGAN TRANSPLANTS. THE FIRST
SECTION, DESCRIPTIVE IN NATURE, PRESENTS DATA ON THE PAST,
CURRENT AND PROJECTED PAYMENT PATTERNS FOR DIFFERENT KINDS
OF ORGAN TRANSPLANTS UNDER VARIOUS FEDERAL AND STATE
PROGRAMS. THE SECOND SECTION, WHICH IS NORMATIVE, CONSIDERS
THE THREE PRINCIPAL ARGUMENTS FOR AND AGAINST GOVERNMENT
PAYMENT FOR ORGAN TRANSPLANTS. THESE ARGUMENTS REVOLVE
AROUND EFFICIENCY, EQUITY AND COMMUNITARIAN CLAIMS, AND NONE
OF THEM IS WHOLLY SATISFACTORY. THE FINAL SECTION, WHICH IS
POLICYORIENTED, ASSUMES THAT GOVERNMENT FINANCING OF ORGAN
TRANSPLANTS WILL CONTINUE BUT WILL BE FISCALLY CONSTRAINED,
AND GOES ON TO ANALYZE A NUMBER OF IMPORTANT PAYMENT POLICY
ISSUES IN THE LIGHT OF BROADER PRINCIPLES. THESE ISSUE
RELATE TO ELIGIBILITY, COMPREHENSIVENESS OF BENEFITS,
REIMBURSEMENT FORMULAS, ENTITLEMENT, AND LEVEL OF GOVERNMENT.

THE PAPER CONCLUDES BY PREDICTING THAT AS TRANSPLANT
PROCEDURES BECOME LESS CONSTRAINED BY ORGAN SUPPLY AND MORE
ROUTINELY PERFORMED, THEY WILL LOSE THE PRIVILEGED POLITICAL
POSITION THAT THEY NOW ENJOY AND WILL INSTEAD BE OBLIGED TO
COMPETE FOR SCARCE GOVERNMENTAL RESOURCES WITH OTHER SOCIAL
GOODS ON MORE EQUAL TERMS. GOVERNMENT POLICY SHOULD BE
DESIGNED TO ENCOURAGE THIS COMPETITION.

08082 SCHUCK, P. M.
THE NEW IDEOLOGY OF TORT LAW
PUBLIC INTEREST, 92 (SUM 88), 93-109.
THIS ARTICLE EXAMINES THE EXPANSION OF LIABILITY IN
AMERICAN TORT LAW, AND STUDIES THE REASONS FOR THE LONG
PERIOD OF LIABILITY GROWTH. A CHANGE IN THE IDEOLOGY THAT
COURTS BRING TO TORT CASES IS EMPHASIZED AS AN ALTERNATIVE
CAUSE FOR THE EXPANSION OF LIABILITY. IT IDENTIFIES THE
NATURE OF THIS IDEOLOGY; EXAMINES HOW IT LEADS TO EXPANDED
LIABILITY; AND CONSIDERS WHETHER THE TORT LAW CAN SATISFY
ITS OWN CRITERIA OF LEGITIMACY.

08083 SCHUESSLER, R.
EXIT THREATS AND COOPERATION UNDER ANONYMITY
JOURNAL OF CONFLICT RESOLUTION, 33(4) (DEC 89), 728-749.
A STRATEGY CONTEST IN AN ITERATED PRISONER'S DILEMMA
WITH AN EXIT OPTION AFTER EACH GAME IS DEVELOPED. THE WHOLE
MODEL IS ASSUMED TO REPRESENT THE CONDITIONS FOR EGOISTICAL
COOPERATION IN A LARGE AND ANONYMOUS SOCIETY, WHICH IS BASED
MAINLY ON EXCHANGE RELATIONSHIPS AND VOLUNTARY COOPERATION
BETWEEN INDIVIDUALS; THEREFORE, IT IS APPROPRIATE FOR
STUDYING THE SOCIAL STABILITY OF FREE MARKETS. THE
STRATEGIES HAVE NO MEMORY, EFFECTS OF REPUTATION DO NOT
EXIST, AND DEFECTORS CANNOT BE IDENTIFIED, TRACED, AND HELD
RESPONSIBLE FOR THEIR ACTIONS. THIS SCENARIO ABANDONS THE
PRECONDITIONS USUALLY REGARDED AS NECESSARY FOR ESTABLISHING
COOPERATION. NEVERTHELESS, EGOISTICAL COOPERATION MAY EMERGE
IN THIS MODEL. IT TURNS OUT THAT EGOISTICAL COOPERATION IS
MUCH MORE ROBUST THAN REALIZED BY MOST GAME-THEORETICAL AND
SOCIOLOGICAL ANALYSES.

08084 SCHULMAN, P.R.
THE "LOGIC" OF ORGANIZATIONAL IRRATIONALITY
ADMINISTRATION AND SOCIETY, 21(1) (MAY 89), 31-53.
THIS ARTICLE EXAMINES THE STABILITY OF RATIONAL DECISION
MAKING IN COMPLEX, TIGHTLY COUPLED ADMINISTRATIVE
ORGANIZATIONS. IN PARTICULAR, IT ANALYZES A PROCESS OF
DECISIONAL "TUNNELING" IN WHICH MEMBERS OF A SET OF
DECISIONS PROGRESSIVELY UNDERMINE THE RATIONALITY OF ONE
ANOTHER, DEGRADING ORGANIZATIONAL MEANS-ENDS CALCULATIONS.
UNDER THESE CIRCUMSTANCES, THE PURSUIT OF EVEN BOUNDEDLY
RATIONAL DECISION MAKING IS DISPLACED BY "PATHOLOGY"--
BEHAVIOR THAT IS LOGICALLY SELF-DEFEATING, BOTH
ORGANIZATIONALLY AND IN RELATION TO THE SELF-INTEREST OF
INDIVIDUAL PARTICIPANTS. THE IMPLICATIONS OF THIS PHENOMENON
ARE ANALYZED, BOTH FOR ORGANIZATION THEORY AND FOR EXERCISES
IN ORGANIZATIONAL DESIGN.

08085 SCHULT, R.
"THE TIME IS RIPE": THE NEW OPPOSITION
ACROSS FRONTIERS, 5(3) (FAL 89), 1-2.
THIS IS BY REINHARD SCHULT, A BRICKLAYER AND FOUNDING
MEMBER OF NEW FORUM, THE UMBRELLA GROUP WHICH PROVIDED A
CRUCIAL CATALYST FOR THE WAVE OF PROTEST IN THE GDR. HE
DETAILS THE PROGRAM AND GOALS OF THIS NEW MASS MOVEMENT. HE
DISCUSSES THE LOW MORALE OF THE EAST GERMAN PEOPLE AND
POINTS OUT THAT REUNIFICATION IS NOT AN ISSUE FOR THEM. HE
ALSO ADDRESSES THE PROBLEM OF ECONOMIC REFORM AND DESCRIBES
THE HARDLINE RESPONSE FROM THE GOVERNMENT TO NEW FORUM.

08086 SCHULTHEIS, M.J.
REFUGEES IN AFRICA: THE GEOPOLITICS OF FORCED DISPLACEMENT
AFRICAN STUDIES REVIEW, 32(1) (APR 89), 3-29.
THE PAPER IS DEVELOPED IN FIVE SECTIONS. THE FIRST MAPS
THE PRINCIPAL AREAS OF DISPLACEMENT IN AFRICA AND REVIEWS
SOME OF THE THEORIES OF FORCED DISPLACEMENT. SECTION TWO
LOOKS MORE SPECIFICALLY AT REFUGEES, HOW INTERNATIONAL
DOCUMENTS DEFINE THEM AND SOME LIMITATIONS OF THIS
DEFINITION IN THE AFRICAN SETTING. SECTION THREE FOCUSES ON
THE CONTEXT OF DISPLACEMENT AND ANALYZES THE CAUSAL FACTORS
OF DISPLACEMENT. SECTION FOUR LOOKS AT SOUTHERN AFRICA AND
THE DYNAMICS OF DISPLACEMENT IN ANGOLA AND MOZAMBIQUE. THE
CONCLUSION CONSIDERS SOME IMPLICATIONS OF THIS ANALYSIS,
ESPECIALLY FOR NON-GOVERNMENTAL ORGANIZATIONS (NGOS)-
UNIVERSITIES, CHURCHES AND OTHERS-BOTH IN PROVIDING
ASSISTANCE AND PROTECTION FOR DISPLACED PEOPLES AND IN
COLLABORATING WITH THEM TO TRANSFORM THE UNDERLYING
CONDITIONS WHICH CAUSED THEM TO FLEE.

08087 SCHULTZE, C.L.
OF WOLVES, TERMITES, AND PUSSYCATS: OR, WHY WE SHOULD
WORRY ABOUT THE BUDGET DEFICIT
BROOKINGS REVIEW, 7(3) (SUM 89), 26-33.
THE CONSEQUENCES OF PERPETUATING LARGE FEDERAL BUDGET
DEFICITS WILL BE NEITHER EXPLOSIVE NOR HARMLESS. RATHER, BY
SHARPLY REDUCING THE NATION'S ALREADY LOW RATES OF SAVING

AND INVESTMENT, THE DEFICITS WILL SLOWLY AND ALMOST
IMPERCEPTIBLY BUT INEXORABLY DEPRESS THE POTENTIAL GROWTH OF
AMERICAN LIVING STANDARDS.

08088 SCHULZ, N.; WEIMANN, J.
COMPETITION OF NEWSPAPERS AND THE LOCATION OF POLITICAL
PARTIES
PUBLIC CHOICE, 63(2) (NOV 89), 125-148.
THIS PAPER SUGGESTS A MODEL FOR AN ANALYSIS OF HOW
NEWSPAPERS AND POLITICAL PARTIES DETERMINE THEIR IDEOLOGICAL
ORIENTATION AND HOW BOTH DECISIONS DEPEND ON EACH OTHER.
QUITE NATURALLY DISSEMINATION OF INFORMATION PLAYS AN
IMPORTANT ROLE. THE MODEL IS SET UP AS A TWO-STAGE GAME.
BECAUSE ELEMENTS OF HORIZONTAL AS WELL AS VERTICAL PRODUCT
DIFFERENTIATION ARE PRESENT IN THIS MODEL LOCATION PATTERNS
IN IDEOLOGY SPACE EXHIBIT IN GENERAL NEITHER MAXIMAL NOR
MINIMAL DIFFERENTIATION. FURTHERMORE, THE MODEL SHOWS BY WAY
OF EXAMPLE THAT ECONOMIC THEORY CAN BE A USEFUL TOOL TO
INVESTIGATE ISSUES WHICH ARE CENTRAL TO COMMUNICATION
SCIENCE.

08089 SCHUSSHEIM, M.J.
HOUSING POLICY FOR NOW AND LATER
CRS REVEIN, 10(9) (OCT 89), 24-26.
PRODUCTION SUBSIDIES AND A LARGER ROLE FOR STATE AND
LOCAL GOVERNMENTS AND NONPROFIT GROUPS ARE BEING CONSIDERED
BY CONGRESSIONAL POLICYMAKERS GRAPPLING WITH THE PROBLEM OF
PROVIDING LOW-INCOME HOUSING. EMERGING LEGISLATION IS
COMPLICATED BY THE FEDERAL BUDGET DEFICIT AND INSTANCES OF
MISMANAGEMENT AND POLITICAL FAVORITISM AT HUD.

08090 SCHUTT, R.
OBJECTIVITY VERSUS OUTRAGE
SOCIETY, 26(4) (MAY 89), 14-15.
THE ARTICLE EXAMINES SOME OF THE POSSIBLE CAUSES OF AND
SOLUTIONS TO THE HOMELESS PROBLEM. ALTHOUGH THE PROBLEM IS
WIDESPREAD AND INCREASING, THE LOW STATUS AND MINIMAL
RESOURCES OF HOMELESS PERSONS MAKE INDEIFFERENCE, EVEN
HOSTILITY, TO THEIR PLIGHT AN EASY COURSE OF ACTION.
CURRENTLY, THE PLIGHT OF HOMELESS INDIVIDUALS AND FAMILIES
IN AMERICA HAS NOT EVOKED A GREAT DEAL OF MORAL OUTRAGE AND
THE PREVAILING OPINION OS LIKELY TO CONTINUE WITHOUT
EFFECTIVE ADVOCACY EFFORTS.

08091 SCHWARTZ, H.
FOREIGN CREDITORS AND THE POLITICS OF DEVELOPMENT IN
AUSTRALIA AND ARGENTINA, 1880-1913
INTERNATIONAL STUDIES QUARTERLY, 33(3) (SEP 89), 281-302.
MOST COMPARATIVE STUDIES OF AUSTRALIA AND ARGENTINA
ARGUE THAT THE ECONOMIC EFFECTS OF CONCENTRATED LANDHOLDING
IMPEDE DEVELOPMENT, AND THAT AUSTRALIA'S GREATER DEVELOPMENT
IS THUS ATTRIBUTABLE TO LANDHOLDERS' POLITICAL DEFEAT AT
LABOR'S HANDS. IN CONTRAST, THIS PAPER ARGUES FIRST THAT
AUSTRALIAN LARGEHOLDERS WERE PRIMARILY DESTROYED BY THEIR
CREDITORS, NOT LABOR; AND SECOND THAT ARGENTINA AND
AUSTRALIAN LANDHOLDERS BEHAVED LIKE PRODUCTIVE CAPITALISTS,
NOT RENTIERS. LANDHOLDERS' POLITICAL BEHAVIOR, NOT THEIR
ECONOMIC BEHAVIOR, AFFECTED THE LATER DEVELOPMENT OF
AGRICULTURE AND INDUSTRY, FOR LARGE LANDHOLDERS DID MAKE
PRODUCTIVITY-ENHANCING INVESTMENTS. BUT IN AUSTRALIA,
LANDHOLDERS' POLITICAL WEAKNESS ALLOWED INVESTMENT MARKETS
TO BE DISTORTED IN FAVOR OF INDUSTRY, ACCELERATING
INDUSTRIAL DEVELOPMENT. THE AUSTRALIAN AND ARGENTINE
EXPERIENCES SUGGEST THAT A BALANCE OF MARKET-LED AND MARKET-
DISTORTING POLICIES ARE NEEDED TO RESOLVE THE CURRENT THIRD
WORLD DEBT CRISIS.

08092 SCHWARTZ, V.
BEIJING JOURNAL: MEMORY, COMMEMORATION, AND THE PLIGHT OF
CHINA'S INTELLECTUALS
WILSON QUARTERLY, XIII(4) (AUT 89), 120-129.
THE USE AND ABUSE OF THE PAST HAS LONG BEEN A PROBLEM IN
CHINA, ESPECIALLY FOR CHINESE INTELLECTUALS. TODAY, CHINA IS
IN GRAVE DANGER OF LOSING ITS PAST. THE MASS MOVEMENT FOR
DEMOCRACY IN THE SPRING OF 1989 IS ALREADY BEING FORGOTTEN.
THE GOVERNMENT CLAIMS IT WAS NOTHING MORE THAN COUNTER-
REVOLUTIONARY TURMOIL INSTIGATED BY A HANDFUL OF HOOLIGANS.
THE STUDENTS AND ORDINARY CITIZENS KILLED IN BEIJING MAY NOT
BE MOURNED PUBLICLY. REMEMBRANCE OF THE DEAD IS CRUSHED
UNDER THE WEIGHT OF OFFICIALLY MANDATED AMNESIA.

08093 SCHWARZ, A.
CALL FOR CONSTRAINTS
FAR EASTERN ECONOMIC REVIEW, 142(52) (DEC 89), 55.
THE INDONESIAN CHAMBER OF COMMERCE AND INDUSTRY HAS
CALLED UPON THE GOVERNMENT TO DRAW UP ANTI-TRUST LEGISLATION
TO STEM THE GROWTH OF CONGLOMERATES. ALTHOUGH THE CALL
APPEARS TO REFLECT SPECIFIC CONCERNS IN THE BUSINESS
COMMUNITY, IT ALSO IMPLIES A DEBATE ABOUT BROADER ISSUES:
THE RELATIVE ROLES OF THE STATE AND PRIVATE SECTORS,
INDIGENOUS AND NON-INDIGENOUS CAPITAL, AND THE RELATIVE
IMPORTANCE OF FREE MARKETS AND WEALTH DISTRIBUTION. DESPITE
THE RISING SENTIMENT AGAINST CONGLOMERATES, THE GOVERNMENT
HAS SHOWN LITTLE INCLINATION TO CURTAIL THEIR GROWTH. THEIR

REASONS FOR LACK OF ACTION INCLUDE: BELIEF THAT COMPANIES
MUST ENJOY ECONOMIES OF SCALE IF THEY ARE TO COMPETE IN
FOREIGN MARKETS, AND A DISLIKE FOR THE ADDED BUREAUCRACY
ANTI-TRUST LEGISLATION WOULD GENERATE.

08094 SCHWARZ, A.; BUTLER, V.; DAWSON, K.
    INDONESIA
    SOUTH, (109) (SEP 89), 63-69.
        ALTHOUGH THE 1980'S WERE A ROLLER-COASTER DECADE FOR
    INDONESIA, THE GOVERNMENT ADOPTED SUCCESSFUL MACROECONOMIC
    REFORMS THAT ARE PAYING OFF. THE DECADE BEGAN WITH A
    CONTINUATION OF THE STATIST, IMPORT-SUBSTITUTING POLICIES OF
    THE 1970'S, FUELLED BY RISING OIL PRICES AND GENEROUS LOANS
    FROM INTERNATIONAL BANKS. WHEN OIL PRICES COLLAPSED,
    INDONESIA WAS FORCED TO CHANGE COURSE AND SHIFT ITS EMPHASIS
    TO EXPORTS, PARTICULARLY NON-OIL MANUFACTURES. A STEADY
    STREAM OF DEREGULATION PACKAGES REMOVED MANY RESTRICTIONS OF
    FINANCE, TRADE, AND INVESTMENT.

08095 SCHWEITZER, G.E.
    CHANGING CONCEPTS OF MILITARY POWER AND NATIONAL SECURITY;
    TECHNO-DIPOMACY
    PLENUM PRESS, NEW YORK, LONDON, 1989, 23-60.
        THIS CHAPTER DEALS WITH SOVIET AND AMERICAN ASSESSMENTS
    WHICH INCREASINGLY RECOGNIZE THAT MILITARY STABILITY IN THE
    SUPERPOWER RELATIONSHIP CAN BE MAINTAINED WITH MUCH LOWER
    LEVELS OF NUCLEAR AND CONVENTIONAL FORCES ON EACH SIDE. IT
    ADVOCATES AN EVENTUAL REDUCTION OF THE NUCLEAR FORCE LEVELS
    OF BOTH COUNTRIES BY 75%. IT ALSO ADVOCATES THAT THE TWO
    COUNTRIES SHOULD RELY MORE AND MORE ON UNILATERAL ACTIONS TO
    REDUCE THEIR ARMAMENTS WHILE AWAITING THE COMPLETION OF
    COMPLICATED FORMAL AGREEMENTS TO CODIFY SUCH ACTIONS

08096 SCHWEITZER, G.E.
    CHANGING THE COURSE THROUGH PERESTROIKA; TECHNO-DIPLOMACY
    PLENUM PRESS, NEW/YORK. LONDON, 1989, 101-130.
        THIS CHAPTER EXAMINES THE SOVIET MODEL FOR FUTURE CHANGE
    AND INDUSTRIAL GROWTH, WHICH WILL BE DESIGNED TO ENSURE THE
    CONTINUATION OF THE USSR AS A WORLD POWER INCLUDING ECONOMIC
    PROSPERITY AT HOME AS WELL AS MILITARY STRENGTH IT. DETAILED
    ARE PLANS FOR CHANGE IN THE AREAS OF AGRICULTURE, INDUSTRY,
    MILITARY, EDUCATION, RESEARCH, CONSUMER GOODS AND SCIENCE.
    THE SOVIET MODEL WILL BE UNIQUE TO THE USSR IS THE
    CONCLUSION.

08097 SCHWEITZER, G.E.
    PERESTROIKA, TECHNOLOGY, AND THE UNCERTAIN SOVIET-AMERICAN
    RELATIONSHIP; TECHNO-DIPLOMACY
    PLENUM PRESS, NEW YORK, LONDON, 1989, 1-22.
        THIS CHAPTER EXAMINES THE RECENT CHANGES IN SOVIET
    POLITICAL AND ECONOMIC POLICY. AS PERESTROIKA IS EXPLORED SO
    IS THE NEED TO BROADEN THE TRADITIONAL SOVIET CONCEPT OF
    NATIONAL SECURITY FROM SOLE RELIANCE ON MILITARY STRENGTH.
    IT DETAILS GORBACHEV'S PROGRAM OF REFORM AS TO BETTER USE OF
    SCIENCE AND TECHNOLOGY. IT DETAILS THE NEED FOR SHAPING NEW
    U.S. POLICIES IN RESPONSE TO THE CHANGES IN THE USSR.
    EXPLORED IS THE UNCERTAIN SUPERPOWER RELATIONSHIP WHICH IS
    CRITICAL TO GLOBAL SURVIVAL.

08098 SCHWEITZER, G.E.
    SCIENTISTS MARCH TO THE DIPLOMATS' DRUMS; TECHNO-DIPLOMACY
    PLENUM PRESS, NEW YORK, LONDON, 1989, 131-158.
        THIS CHAPTER DEALS WITH THE FACT THAT SINCE APPLICATIONS
    OF SCIENCE AND TECHNOLOGY PROVIDE MUCH OF THE BASIS FOR THE
    EAST-WEST MILITARY CONFRONTATION, COOPERATION IN SCIENCE AND
    TECHNOLOGY ASSUMES A SPECIAL SYMBOLIC IMPORTANCE IN THE
    RELATIONSHIP BETWEEN THE TWO SUPERPOWERS. USING PERSONAL
    EXPERIENCES OF THE AUTHOR THIS CHAPTER EXPLORES THE
    PAINSTAKING ASPECTS OF NEGOTIATING FORMAL AGREEMENTS BETWEEN
    THE TWO GOVERNMENTS. IT EXPLORES HOW FOREIGN POLICY SHAPES
    AND CONSTRAINS SCIENTIFIC COOPERATION.

08099 SCHWEITZER, G.E.
    SOVIET SCIENCE AND TECHNOLOGY FALL BEHIND; TECHNO -
    DIPLOMACY
    PLENUM PRESS, NEW YORK, LONDON, 1989, 61-100.
        THIS CHAPTER DETAILS THE DECLINE IN SOVIET SCIENCE. IT
    TRACES THE SLOWLY DEVELOPING SOVIET SCIENCE BACK TO 1724AND
    BRINGS IT TO THE PRESENT AND CHERNOBYL. IT DESCRIBES THE
    ECONOMICS, GOVERNMENT DIRECTION AND CONTROL AND THE STIFLING
    EFFECT OF THE CLOSED NATURE OF SOVIET SOCIETY. COMPUTERS AND
    MILITARY SYSTEMS ARE EXPLORED AS WELL AS THE PROS AND CONS
    OF TECHNOLOGY TRANSFER WITH THE WEST.

08100 SCHWEITZER, G.E.
    TECHNO-DIPLOMACY
    PLENUM PRESS, NEW YORK, LONDON, 1989, 1-300.
        THIS BOOK IS ABOUT POWER-MILITARY, ECONOMIC,
    ENVIRONMENTAL. IT EQUATES, ALSO, SCIENCE AND TECHNOLOGY WITH
    POWER. AS IT ADDRESSES THE QUESTION OF WHETHER OR NOT THE U.
    S. SHOULD HELP GORBACHEV SUCCEED, TECHNO-DIPLOMACY IS
    DEFINED AS THE ART AND PRACTICE OF NEGOTIATING BETWEEN
    COUNTRIES THAT HOLD CONFLICTING INTERESTS. IT RETHINKS THE
    TRADITIONAL VIEW OF MILITARY BUILD-UPS, THE SHARING OF

TECHNOLOGICAL INFORMATION, AND DIPLOMATIC AGREEMENTS AMONG
THE SUPERPOWERS. THE DISCUSSION OF TECHNOLOGICAL COMPETITION
BETWEEN EAST AND WEST IS ROUNDED OUT WITH COMMENTARIES ON
THE ACTIVITIES OF THE FOREIGN INTELLIGENCE SERVICES AND THE
INTERNAL SECURITY AGENCIES OF THE US AND THE USSR. THE BOOK
IS COMPLETE WITH PERSONAL EXPERIENCES OF THE AUTHOR.

08101 SCHWEITZER, G.E.
    TRADE, COOPERATION, AND THE TECHNO-BANDITS; TECHNO-
    DIPLOMACY
    PLENUM PRESS, NEW YORK, LONDON, 1989, 191-228.
        THE CHAPTER DEALS WITH WESTERN EFFORTS TO PROTECT HIGH
    TECHNOLOGIES FROM TECHNO-BANDITS, IT EXPLORES HOW THE SOVIET
    TECHNOLOGY COLLECTION PROCESS OPERATES AND HOW THE UNITED
    STATES HAS RESPONDED BY RESTRICTING SOVIET ACCESS TO
    AMERICAN SCIENTIFIC AND TECHNOLOGICAL ACCOMPLISHMENTS. IT
    CONCLUDES THAT THE UNITED STATES SHOULD CONCENTRATE ON
    PRESERVING TECHNOLOGICAL LEAD TIMES FOR PRODUCING MILITARY
    SYSTEMS AND COMPONENTS WHICH COULD MAKE A DIFFERENCE IN
    MILITARY BALANCE.

08102 SCHWEITZER, M.
    A NEW LOOK AT ECONOMIC CAUSES OF THE CONSTITUTION:
    MONETARY AND TRADE POLICY IN MARYLAND, PENNSYLVANIA, AND
    VIRGINIA
    SOCIAL SCIENCE JOURNAL. 26(1) (1989), 15-26.
        BY CONTRAST TO CHARLES BEARD'S 1913 ECONOMIC
    INTERPRETATION OF THE CONSTITUTION, THIS ARTICLE MAINTAINS
    THAT THE KEY IS THE ECONOMIC POLICIES OF THE VARIOUS
    COLONIAL (LATER STATE) LEGISLATURES. PRIOR TO INDEPENDENCE
    THE COLONIES HAD STRONG AND AUTONOMOUS ECONOMIC POLICIES
    WHICH THEY DEFENDED VIGOROUSLY AGAINST THE BRITISH
    GOVERNMENT. ALTHOUGH THEY RESENTED REGULATION FROM LONDON,
    THEY ALSO BENEFITED BECAUSE LONDON KEPT THEIR NEIGHBORING
    COLONIES IN LINE. AFTER INDEPENDENCE, THIS RESTRAINT WAS
    GONE. IF THEY WANTED THE BENEFITS OF COOPERATION, THEY HAD
    TO NEGOTIATE IT THEMSELVES. MARYLAND, PENNSYLVANIA, AND
    VIRGINIA FACED THESE PROBLEMS AND SOUGHT A SOLUTION IN A
    STRONG CONSTITUTION.

08103 SCIABARRA, C.M.
    TOWARD A RADICAL CRITIQUE OF UTOPIANISM: DIALECTICS AND
    DUALISM IN THE WORKS OF FRIEDRICH HAYEK, MURRAY ROTHBARD,
    AND KARL MARX
    DISSERTATION ABSTRACTS INTERNATIONAL, 49(9) (MAR 89),
    2797-A.
        THE AUTHOR DEVELOPS A RADICAL CRITIQUE OF UTOPIAN
    THINKING BY EXAMINING THE DIALECTICAL AND DUALISTIC
    METHODOLOGICAL ELEMENTS IN HAYEKIAN, ROTHBARDIAN, AND
    MARXIAN THEORY.

08104 SCICCHITANO, M.J.; HEDGE, D.; METZ, P.
    THE STATES AND DEREGULATION: THE CASE OF SURFACE MINING
    POLICY STUDIES REVIEW, 9(1) (AUT 89), 120-131.
        THE SURFACE MINING CONTROL AND RECLAMATION ACT OF 1977
    (SMCRA), PASSED TO CORRECT THE ABUSES OF SURFACE MINING,
    ASSIGNED KEY IMPLEMENTATION ROLES TO THE STATES. WHILE THE
    FEDERAL GOVERNMENT ORIGINALLY ENFORCED SMCRA, STATES COULD
    OPERATE THE PROGRAM THEMSELVES. ONCE STATES DECIDED TO RUN
    THEIR OWN PROGRAM THE FEDERAL GOVERNMENT WOULD OVERSEE THEM
    TO INSURE THEY PROPERLY ENFORCE THE ACT. THIS RESEARCH
    EXAMINES THE ENFORCEMENT BEHAVIOR OF STATES IN THE 1980S.
    THE RESULTS INDICATE THAT EARLY IN THE REAGAN ADMINISTRATION
    EASTERN STATES ENFORCED THE SMCRA LESS STRINGENTLY THAN
    OTHER STATES. EASTERN STATES INCREASED THEIR LEVEL OF
    ENFORCEMENT LATER IN THE 1980S IN RESPONSE TO PRESSURES FOR
    INCREASED FEDERAL OVERSIGHT FROM CONGRESS, INTEREST GROUPS
    AND OTHERS.

08105 SCICLUNA, J.
    MALTA: IN A SQUEEZE
    THIRD WORLD WEEK, 7(9) (JAN 89), 76-77.
        FOR THE GOVERNMENT OF MALTA, THE LATEST DISPUTE BETWEEN
    THE UNITED STATES AND LIBYA HAS DEEPENED A DILEMMA THAT
    WON'T GO AWAY. ON THE ONE HAND, THE NATIONALIST GOVERNMENT
    WANTS AND NEEDS CLOSER RELATIONS WITH THE WEST, INCLUDING
    THE USA. ON THE OTHER, IT WANTS AND NEEDS CONTINUED
    FRIENDSHIP WITH LIBYA. MALTA FINDS ITSELF IN THE MIDDLE AS
    LIBYA AND THE USA CONTINUE TO SPAR OVER SUCH ISSUES AS
    LIBYA'S CHEMICAL WEAPONS FACTORY.

08106 SCIME, J.A.
    GOVERNMENT POLICY, WORKING WOMEN, AND FEMINISM IN THE
    GREAT DEPRESSION: SECTION 213 OF THE 1932 ECONOMY ACT
    DISSERTATION ABSTRACTS INTERNATIONAL, 48(10) (APR 88),
    2713-A.
        THE STUDY ANALYZES SECTION 213 OF THE 1932 ECONOMY ACT
    WHICH IS WIDELY BELIEVED TO BE AIMED AT THE RESTRICTION OF
    MARRIED WORKING WOMEN. THE STUDY EXAMINES THE LAW'S
    INTENTIONS AND IMPLEMENTATION AND THE VARIOUS REACTIONS OF
    FEMINIST GROUPS WITH REGARDS TO THE LAW. IT CONCLUDES THAT
    SECTION 213 REPRESENTED POLICYMAKERS' ATTEMPTS TO REGULATE
    THE RELATIONSHIP BETWEEN THE FAMILY AND THE ECONOMY BY
    DETERMINING WHO IN A FAMILY WOULD BE EMPLOYED, AND THAT

WOMEN'S GROUPS PROVED THEMSELVES EFFECTIVE AGENTS OF CHANGE IN THEIR EFFORTS TO CHANGE OR REPEAL THE LAW.

08107 SCOTT, D.S.; DORN, A.W.
MAKING ARMS CONTROL TREATIES STRONGER
INTERNATIONAL PERSPECTIVES, XVIII(1) (JAN 89), 13-17.
THE AUTHORS ARGUE THAT ARMS CONTROL CALLS FOR A FULL-SCOPE VERIFICATION SYSTEM: INSPECTION, SURVEILLANCE, EVALUATION, AND RESPONSE. THIS SYSTEM HAS NOT BEEN DEVELOPED BECAUSE OF THE ADAMANT OPPOSITION OF THAT WAS SUBSTANTIALLY RELAXED IN 1988. IT IS IMPORTANT FOR CANADA AND THE OTHER MIDDLE-SIZED POWERS TO MAKE A GREATER CONTRIBUTION TO THE PROCESS OF DESIGNING A SYSTEM AND NOT TO ALLOW THE SUPERPOWERS TO MONOPOLIZE IT. THE NEGOTIATIONS FOR THE CHEMICAL WEAPONS CONVENTION ARE EXAMINED IN THIS

08108 SCOTT, I.
ADMINISTRATION IN A SMALL CAPITALIST STATE: THE HONG KONG EXPERIENCE
PUBLIC ADMINISTRATION AND DEVELOPMENT, 9(2) (APR 89), 185-200.
ALTHOUGH HONG KONG HAS OFTEN BEEN TAKEN AS THE EPITOME OF THE BENEFITS THAT CAN BE DERIVED FROM KEEPING GOVERNMENT UT OF THE ECONOMY, THE BUREAUCRACY HAS IN FACT PLAYED A CRITICAL ROLE IN THE SUPPORT OF ECONOMIC GROWTH. THE ARTICLE EXAMINES THE FEATURES OF HONG KONG'S BURAUCRATIC PRACTICE WHICH APPEAR TO HAVE BEEN IMPORTANT IN THE DEFINITION OF THE BUREAUCRACY'S TASKS IN THE ECONOMIC GROWTH PROCESS. THEY ARE 'VALUE FOR MONEY' AND THE CONSTANT NEED TO JUSTIFY GOVERNMENT EXPENDITURE, EFFECTIVE LINE IMPLEMENTATION, AND THE ABILITY TO MANAGE CRISES. THESE MINIMAL ESSENTIAL REQUIREMENTS FOR SUCH GOVERNMENTS MAY PROVE TO BE A USEFUL CRITERIA FOR OTHER SMALL OR MICRO-STATES WHICH DESIRE HIGHER LEVELS OF ECONOMIC GROWTH.

08109 SCOTT, J.
TRANSBORDER COOPERATION, REGIONAL INITIAVES, AND SOVEREIGNTY CONFLICTS IN WESTERN EUROPE: THE CASE OF THE UPPER RHINE VALLEY
PUBLIUS: THE JOURNAL OF FEDERALISM, 19(1) (WIN 89), 139-156.
TRANSBORDER COOPERATION IN WESTERN EUROPE HAS MADE CONSIDERABLE PROGRESS. PRIMARILY BECAUSE OF THE ACTIVITIES OF LOCAL GROUPS, SUCH AS THE REGIO BASILIENSIS, AND THE SUPPORT OF INTERNATIONAL ORGANIZATIONS, SUCH AS THE COUNCIL OF EUROPE, THE UPPER RHINE VALLEY AND OTHER EUROPEAN BORDER REGIONS HAVE SUCCEEDED IN VOICING THEIR INTERESTS IN A FAIRLY COHESIVE MANNER. HOWEVER, THE CONTINUED EMPHASIS OF NATIONAL GOVERNMENTS ON SOVEREIGNTY AND NATIONAL INTERESTS HAS PREVENTED INTERNATIONAL BORDER REGIONS FROM ACHIEVING SUCH BASIC GOALS AS INFRASTRUCTURE INTEGRATION AND HARMONIZATION OF ENVIRONMENTAL POLICY. PRESENT FORMS OF TRANSBORDER POLITICAL ACTIVITY HAVE BEEN INSUFFICIENT TO OVERCOME CONFLICTS BETWEEN REGIONAL NEEDS AND NATIONAL INTERESTS. FOR THIS AND OTHER REASONS, EUROPEAN BORDER REGIONS HAVE RESORTED TO NEW LOCAL ECONOMIC AND POLITICAL INITIIATIVES TO ARGUE MORE FORCEFULLY FOR BORDER REGION DEMANDS. IN POOLING THE COMBINED RESOURCES OF ITS SWISS, FRENCH, AND GERMAN PARTICIPANTS, THE UPPER RHINE PROGRAM OF INNOVATION MIGHT WELL SERVE AS A MODEL FOR THIS KIND OF REGIONAL INITIATIVE. PERHAPS SETTING A PRECEDENT FOR FUTURE FORMS OF TRANSBORDER POLITICAL ACTIVITY.

08110 SCULLY, G.; SLOTTJE, D.
THE PARADOX OF POLITICS AND POLICY IN REDISTRIBUTING INCOME
PUBLIC CHOICE, 60(1) (JAN 89), 55-70.
THE AUTHORS STUDY THE LINK BETWEEN ELECTORAL OUTCOMES AND INCOME DISTRIBUTION. THEY ATTEMPT TO TEST THE HYPOTHESIS THAT VOTER CHOICE ON THE LIBERAL-CONSERVATIVE CONTINUUM AFFECTS INCOME DISTRIBUTION. THEY FIND SOME EVIDENCE THAT PERIODS IN WHICH CONSERVATIVE STRENGTH IS HIGH IN CONGRESS ARE ASSOCIATED WITH INCREASED INEQUALITY. THEY ALSO ATTEMPT TO RECONCILE THESE FINDINGS WITH THE FAILURE TO OBSERVE A TREND IN INCOME INEQUALITY IN THE AMERICAN ECONOMY.

08111 SCULLY, G.W.
THE SIZE OF THE STATE, ECONOMIC GROWTH AND THE EFFICIENT UTILIZATION OF NATIONAL RESOURCES
PUBLIC CHOICE, 63(2) (NOV 89), 149-164.
THIS PAPER EXPLORES A SEGMENT OF THE QUESTION OF SUBSTITUTION OF PUBLIC CHOICE OVER PRIVATE CHOICE, EVIDENCE IS OFFERED ON THE EFFECT OF THE SIZE OF THE FISCAL SECTOR, NET OF RESOURCE GROWTH, ON ECONOMIC GROWTH AND THE EFFECIENCY OF RESOURCE ALLOCATION FOR 115 MARKET ECONOMIES FOR THE PERIOD 1960-1980. THE OVERALL CONCLUSION IS THAT FOR THESE CRITERIA AT LEAST THE GROWTH IN THE SIZE OF THE STATE HAS BEEN HARMFUL.

08112 SEABORG, G.T.
SCIENCE ADVICE TO THE PRESIDENT: DURING AND IMMEDIATELY AFTER WORLD WAR II
AVAILABLE FROM NTIS. NO. DE89008154/GAR, JAN 89, 27.
AT THE TIME OF THE OUTBREAK OF WORLD WAR II THE UNITED STATES HAD LITTLE CAPACITY FOR SCIENCE ADVICE TO THE

PRESIDENT OR THE ORGANIZATION OF AMERICAN SCIENCE FOR WAR. THE NATIONAL ACADEMY OF SCIENCES, CREATED BY AN ACT OF CONGRESS IN 1863, AND THE NATIONAL RESEARCH COUNCIL, CREATED BY AN EXECUTIVE ORDER IN 1918, WERE IN THE POSITION TO BE HELPFUL, BUT THEY WERE NOT GOVERNMENT AGENCIES SUPPORTED BY THE CONGRESS AND REPORTING DIRECTLY TO THE PRESIDENT AND WERE, THEREFORE, NOT DESIGNED TO FOCUS ATTENTION ON SUCH RELATIVELY NARROW PORTIONS OF THE FIELD OF SCIENCE AS THOSE CONCERNED WITH THE INSTRUMENTALITIES OF WAR. A MORE EFFECTIVE ORGANIZATION WAS THE NATIONAL ADVISORY COMMITTEE FOR AERONAUTICS (NACA), ESTABLISHED BY CONGRESS IN 1915 "TO SUPERVISE AND DIRECT THE SCIENTIFIC STUDY OF THE PROBLEMS OF FLIGHT." PRESIDENT ROOSEVELT, IN JUNE 1939, DIRECTED THE NACA TO BECOME A CONSULTING AND RESEARCH AGENCY FOR THE JOINT ARMY AND NAVY AERONAUTICAL BOARD AT THE OUTBREAK OF A NATIONAL EMERGENCY. FOR SOME YEARS PRIOR TO THE OUTBREAK OF THE WAR, THE MEMBERS OF THE NACA HAD BECOME ACUTELY CONSCIOUS THAT THEY WERE LIVING IN A PRE-WAR PERIOD. VANNEVAR BUSH BECAME CHAIRMAN OF THE NACA IN 1939. AFTER THE OUTBREAK OF WAR IN EUROPE, BUSH'S THOUGHTS TURNED MORE AND MORE TO THE NEED FOR AN OVERALL ORGANIZATION OF SCIENCE FOR WAR. IT WAS AT HIS INITIATIVE MORE THAN ANYONE ELSE'S THAT AN APPARATUS FOR SCIENCE ADVICE TO THE PRESIDENT AND THE GEARING OF SCIENCE FOR AID TO THE WAR EFFORT TOOK PLACE.

08113 SEARS, D.O.
THE ECOLOGICAL NICHE OF POLITICAL PSYCHOLOGY
POLITICAL PSYCHOLOGY, 10(3) (SEP 89), 501-506.
THIS PAPER ELABORATES ON A PAPER BY ROBERT JARVIS ON ONE KEY POINT. IT ANALYSES INTELLECTUAL FADS AND FASHIONS AND TWO STYLES OF SCHOLARSHIP AND LISTS FOUR DIFFERENCES TO THE UNDERSTANDING OF POLITICAL LIFE BETWEEN PSYCHOLOGISTS AND ECONOMISTS. IT CONCLUDES THAT POLITICAL PSYCHOLOGY IS INDISPENSABLE TO OUR ACADEMIC ECOLOGY.

08114 SEAWARD, N.
PRINCELY OPPOSITION
FAR EASTERN ECONOMIC REVIEW, 141(39) (SEP 88), 18.
THIRTEEN OF MALAYSIAN PRIME MINISTER DATUK SERI MAHATHIR MOHAMAD'S MOST BITTER RIVALS HAVE DECLARED THEMSELVES TO BE INDEPENDENT MEMBERS OF PARLIAMENT AND WILL SIT IN THE OPPOSITION BENCH AT THE NEXT SITTING OF PARLIAMENT. THEY WERE LED BY TUNKU RAZALEIGH HAMZAH, A KELANTAN PRINCE WHO NARROWLY LOST TO MAHATHIR IN A BATTLE FOR THE PRESIDENCY OF THE UNITED MALAYS' NATIONAL ORGANIZATION LAST YEAR. THE CROSSOVER WAS NOT UNEXPECTED BY MANY OBSERVERS.

08115 SEAWARD, N.
THE DAIM STEWARDSHIP
FAR EASTERN ECONOMIC REVIEW, 141(35) (SEP 88), 52-54.
THE REVIEW ANALYZES THE TENURE OF MALAYSIA'S FINANCE MINISTER DAIM ZAINUDDIN. IT CONCLUDES THAT THE ALMOST CONTINUAL ALLEGATIONS OF CONFLICT OF INTEREST AND NEPOTISM AS WELL AS A GENERAL PERCEPTION OF UNPLEASANTNESS HAVE MASKED HIS VERY SUCCESSFUL EFFORTS TO REJUVENATE THE MALAYSIAN ECONOMY. THE TWO-YEAR TURNAROUND FROM RECESSION TO SOLID GROWTH IS A RESULT OF ONE OF THE MOST RAPID AND SUCCESSFUL STRUCTURAL ADJUSTMENTS AMONG DEVELOPING ECONOMIES, AND DAIM WAS LARGELY RESPONSIBLE FOR THE CHANGES.

08116 SECREST, S.M.
MINORS' RIGHTS TO ABORTION - ARE PARENTAL NOTICE AND CONSENT LAWS JUSTIFIED?
UNIVERSITY OF DETROIT LAW REVIEW, 66(4) (SUM 89), 691-712.
THIS NOTE PRESENTS THE EVOLUTION OF THE LAW REGARDING MINORS' ABORTION RIGHTS BY EXAMINING SUPREME COURT CASES DEALING WITH THESE RIGHTS. THE AUTHOR THEN REVIEWS CURRENT STATISTICAL AND SOCIAL SCIENCE DATA REGARDING MINORS' DECISIONS WHETHER OR NOT TO HAVE ABORTIONS IN ORDER TO DETERMINE WHETHER OR NOT PARENTAL NOTICE OR CONSENT STATUTES DO, IN FACT, SERVE THE STATE INTERESTS OF PROTECTING MINORS AND PROMOTING PARENTAL INVOLVEMENT. IN PARTICULAR, THIS NOTE FOCUSES UPON FINDINGS IN MASSACHUSETTS AND MINNESOTA, WHOSE STATUTES RESTRICTING A MINOR'S RIGHT TO AN ABORTION HAVE BEEN CHALLENGED AS UNCONSTITUTIONAL IN THEIR APPLICATION. THE NOTE ARGUES, BASED UPON A CRITICAL ANALYSIS OF SOCIAL SCIENCE DATA, THAT A STATUTE WHICH REQUIRED NOTICE OR CONSENT OF ONE PARENT, ALONG WITH A JUDICIAL BYPASS PROCEDURE, WOULD SERVE THE ASSERTED STATE INTERESTS. THE AUTHOR CONCLUDES BY ASSESSING THE LIKELIHOOD OF THE SUPREME COURT OVERRULING ESTABLISHED LEGAL PRINCIPLES CONCERNING MINORS' ABORTION RIGHTS IN LIGHT OF CURRENTLY AVAILABLE EVIDENCE.

08117 SECRET, P.; WELCH, S.
SEX, RACE, AND PARTICIPATION: AN ANALYSIS OF THE 1980 AND 1984 ELECTIONS
WOMEN AND POLITICS, 9(4) (1989), 57-68.
HAS THE RATE OF ELECTORAL PARTICIPATION BY WOMEN AND BLACKS INCREASED RELATIVE TO THAT OF WHITE MALES OVER THE PAST DECADE? THIS NOTE UPDATES AN EARLIER WORK REPORTING COMPARATIVE RATES OF PARTICIPATION OF BLACK AND WHITE MALES AND FEMALES. THIS UPDATE INDICATES THAT THE GENDER AND RACIAL GAPS FOUND IN THE 1960S AND 1970S HAVE ALMOST

DISAPPEARED IN THE 1980S. WHAT DIFFERENCES THAT REMAIN
BETWEEN BLACKS AND WHITES ARE LARGELY ACCOUNTED FOR BY CLASS
DIFFERENCES.

08118 SEDUNARY, E.
THE MINISTER'S NEXT DOMINO: TOWARDS A NATIONAL CURRICULUM
ARENA, 86 (FAL 89), 23-28.
THE DECISION OF AUSTRALIA'S MINISTER DAWKINS TO
RADICALLY EXPAND COMMONWEALTH INVOLVEMENT IN SCHOOLS BY
VENTURING INTO THE HEARTLAND OF CURRICULUM, ASSESSMENT AND
TEACHING PRACTICES, BY FRAMING CONDITIONS BY WHICH SCHOOLS
WILL RETAIN PUPILS LONGER AND BECOME MORE ACCOUNTABLE TO THE
COMMUNITY, AND BY STREAMLINING THE PRODUCTION OF EDUCATIONAL
OUTCOMES, LENDS POLITICAL DEFINITION TO AN EARLIER CHANGE IN
EMPHASIS. WHEREAS PRIOR COMMONWEALTH INTEREST IN SCHOOLING
WAS CONCERNED MORE WITH ITS IDEOLOGICAL OR SOCIAL
INTEGRATIVE FUNCTIONS THAN WITH ITS ACTUAL CONTENT, THE
DAWKINS INITIATIVE MAY BE SEEN AS THE POLITICAL EXPRESSION
OF A SHIFT IN THE FORM OF SOCIAL MANAGEMENT TO BE ACHIEVED
NOW WITH THE HELP OF SCHOOLING. AUSTRALIAN SCHOOLS ARE TO
JOIN THEIR TERTIARY COUNTERPARTS IN THE SERVICE OF A SOCIAL
FUTURE PIVOTED ON ECONOMIC DEVELOPMENT.

08119 SEGAL, G.
CHINA, THE PACIFIC, AND THE BALANCE OF POWER
JERUSALEM JOURNAL OF INTERNATIONAL RELATIONS, 11(3) (SEP
89), 121-138.
AS THE TWENTY-FIRST CENTURY APPROACHES, CHINA IS
BUILDING ITS STATUS AS A "WEAK SUPERPOWER." ITS INCREASING
MILITARY POWER AND REACH WILL ENABLE IT TO PROJECT ITS
INFLUENCE IN CONFLICTS THROUGHOUT THE GLOBE. CLOSER TO HOME,
HOWEVER, THE RISE OF JAPANESE POWER POSES PROBLEMS AND
UNCERTAINTIES FOR CHINA.

08120 SEGAL, G.
TAKING SINO-SOVIET DETENTE SERIOUSLY
WASHINGTON QUARTERLY, 12(3) (SUM 89), 53-64.
THE ARTICLE ANALYZES THE "SECOND MOST IMPORTANT
STRATEGIC RELATIONSHIP" BETWEEN THE SOVIET UNION AND CHINA.
IT ARGUES THAT MOST WESTERN NATIONS DO NOT TAKE THE ONGOING
SINO-SOVIET DETENTE SERIOUSLY ENOUGH. IT EXAMINES THE EFFECT
THAT WARMING RELATIONS WILL HAVE ON BOTH NATIONS'
EXPERIMENTAL REFORMS OF COMMUNISM. IT ALSO ANALYZES THE
GEOPOLITICAL EFFECT THAT SINO-SOVIET DETENTE WILL HAVE ON
THE NORTHEAST ASIAN ARENA WITH EMPHASIS ON THE KOREAN
PENINSULA, AND ALSO IN SOUTHEAST ASIA WHERE SINO-SOVIET
COOPERATION PLAYED A LARGE ROLE IN THE WINDING DOWN OF THE
KAMPUCHEAN CONFLICT. IT ALSO EXAMINES THE OVERALL EFFECT ON
THE "GREAT POWER TRIANGLE." IT CONCLUDES THAT ALTHOUGH THE
FORMATION OF A GEOPOLITICAL SITUATION ADVERSE TO THE
INTERESTS OF THE US IS POSSIBLE, SINO-SOVIET DETENTE IS MORE
LIKELY TO CREATE A WORLD OF "CONSULTATION AND COOPERATION"
WHERE THE US MAY NOT BE PREDOMINANT, BUT PEACE WILL BE MORE
LIKELY.

08121 SEGAL, G.
THE NEW BALANCES OF POWER
WORLD POLICY JOURNAL, 6(4) (FAL 89), 731-757.
THIS ARTICLE EXPLORES GREAT CHANGES THAT TAKE PLACE ON
THE "MARGINS" OF INTERNATIONAL RELATIONS, AND THE RESULTANT
MULTIPOLARITY AND INTERDEPENDENCE. IT FOCUSES ON THE NEW
BALANCES OF POWER AND INTERDEPENDENCE IN EAST ASIA, AND ALSO
THE RISKS OF FUTURE INSTABILITY. QUESTIONS RAISED ARE: ARE
THE SUPERPOWERS AS LIKELY TO RESTRAIN CONFLICT IF THEY ARE
NO LONGER AS POWERFUL: HOW THE U.S. JAPANESE RELATIONSHIP
WILL EVOLVE AND: HOW THE SMALLER ECONOMIC POWERS WILL ADAPT
TO THE INEVITABLE CHANGES.

08122 SEGAL, G.
THE USSR AND AISA IN 1988: ACHIEVEMENTS AND RISKS
ASIAN SURVEY, XXIX(1) (JAN 89), 101-111.
1988 IS HAILED AS A "YEAR OF REWARD" FOR THE USSR WITH
REGARDS TO ASIA. MIKHAIL GORBACHEV AND THE SOVIET'S WERE
ABLE TO CONVINCE NATIONS THAT THEY WERE SERIOUS ABOUT THEIR
PROCLAIMED REFORMS AND WERE ABLE TO THAW PREVIOUSLY FROZEN
RELATIONS WITH CHINA, JAPAN, AND EVEN THE NEWLY
INDUSTIALIZED COUNTRIES (NICS). SOVIET OVERTURES TO THESE
NATIONS CORRESPONDED WITH A DRIFTING AWAY FROM ERSTWHILE
ALLIES SUCH AS VIETNAM AND AFGHANISTAN. ALL OF THESE CHANGES
ARE PART OF THE OVERALL SOVIET STRATEGY FOR ECONOMIC
DEVELOPMENT OF THE FAR EAST.

08123 SEGAL, J.
A FOREIGN POLICY FOR THE STATE OF PALESTINE
JOURNAL OF PALESTINE STUDIES, XVIII(2) (WIN 89), 16-28.
THE ARTICLE DISCUSSES THE ISSUE OF THE RECENTLY DECLARED
STATE OF PALESTINE'S NEED FOR FOREIGN POLICY. IT OUTLINES
THE GEOPOLITICAL CONTEXT THAT THE STATE FINDS ITSELF IN AND
ATTEMPTS TO OUTLINE SOME OBJECTIVES FOR CONSODERATION IN
FOREIGN POLICY. THESE OBJECTIVES INCLUDE: PREVENTING THE
EXPULSION OF THE POPULATION FROM THE WEST BANK, AND BRINGING
ABOUT AN ISRAELI TROOP WITHDRAWAL. ONCE THESE ALL-IMPORTANT
ISSUES ARE RESOLVED, THE NEWLY CREATED STATE WILL ALSO HAVE
TO DEAL WITH ISSUES SUCH AS: NEGOTIATIONS WITH ISRAEL,

DEMILITARIZATION OF THE PAEESTINIAN STATE, THE STATUS OF THE
PLO COVENANT, THE VARIOUS COMMANDO GROUPS THAT CLAIM TO
REPRESENT PALESTINE, AND THE RIGHT TO RETURN.

08124 SEGAL, J. M.
THE MEANING OF THE PNC IN ALGIERS
TIKKUN, 4(1) (JAN 89), 41-43, 92-94.
FROM A HISTORICAL PERSPECTIVE, THE MEETINGS OF THE PNC
IN NOVEMBER 1988 WERE REVOLUTIONARY, GIVING A NEW DEFINITION
TO PALESTINIAN NATIONALISM. FROM THE POLITICAL PERSPECTIVE,
THE MEETINGS WERE POSITIVE BUT SOME WHAT DISAPPOINTING. BUT
THE HISTORICAL BREAKTHROUGH SET THE STAGE FOR FURTHER
ADVANCES ON THE POLITICAL LEVEL IN THE NEAR FUTURE.

08125 SEGAL, J.A.; COVER, A.D.
IDEOLOGICAL VALUES AND THE VOTES OF U.S. SUPREME COURT
JUSTICES
AMERICAN POLITICAL SCIENCE REVIEW, 83(2) (JUN 89), 557-566.
IT IS COMMONLY ASSUMED THAT THE VOTES OF SUPREME COURT
JUSTICES LARGELY REFLECT THEIR ATTITUDES, VALUES, AND
PERSONAL POLICY PREFERENCES. BUT THIS ASSUMPTION HAS NEVER
BEEN ADEQUATELY TESTED WITH INDEPENDENT MEASURES OF THE
IDEOLOGICAL VALUES OF JUSTICES. USING CONTENT ANALYTIC
TECHNIQUES, THE AUTHORS DERIVE INDEPENDENT, RELIABLE
MEASURES OF THE VALUES OF ALL SUPREME COURT JUSTICES FROM
EARL WARREN TO ANTHONY KENNEDY.

08126 SEGAL, L.
SLOW CHANGE OR NO CHANGE? FEMINISM, SOCIALISM, AND THE
PROBLEM OF MEN
FEMINIST REVIEW, (31) (SPR 89), 5-21.
THE AUTHOR LOOKS AT THE RELATIONSHIP BETWEEN FEMINISM
AND SOCIALISM AND THE QUESTION OF WHETHER THE WOMEN'S
MOVEMENT HAS ACTUALLY CHANGED THE TRADITIONAL MALE
DOMINATION OF SOCIETY.

08127 SEGEV, S.
THE IRANIAN TRIANGLE: THE UNTOLD STORY OF ISRAEL'S ROLE IN
THE IRAN-CONTRA AFFAIR
THE FREE PRESS, NEW YORK, NY, 1988, .
THE AUTHOR PROBES ISRAEL'S CRUCIAL ROLE IN THE IRAN ARMS
DEAL AND THE NEGOTIATIONS FOR THE RELEASE OF THE HOSTAGES IN
LEBANON. HE TRACES HOW THE CLANDESTINE RELATIONSHIP BETWEEN
ISRAEL AND IRAN BEGAN, HOW THE USA SUPPORTED ISRAEL'S PLANS
TO SUPPLY ARMS FOR AN IRANIAN COUP ATTEMPT, AND HOW ISRAEL
BECAME A LIAISON BETWEEN THE AMERICANS AND THE KHOMEINI
REGIME.

08128 SEIDENFADEN, T.
HOW THE DANES VIEW NATO
SCANDINAVIAN REVIEW, 77(1) (SPR 89), 5-12.
DENMARK WAS A FOUNDING MEMBER OF NATO AND HAS
PARTICIPATED IN THE INTEGRATED MILITARY DEFENSE ORGANIZATION.
LARGE MAJORITIES OF THE DANES SUPPORT MEMBERSHIP IN THE
ALLIANCE AND HAVE DONE SO CONSISTENTLY FOR NEARLY FORTY
YEARS. IT WOULD SEEM THAT THESE FACTS PROVIDE A SOLID
FOUNDATION FOR A STABLE, UNDRAMATIC RELATIONSHIP BETWEEN
DENMARK AND NATO. THIS, HOWEVER, IS NOT THE CASE. IN 1988, A
MAJORITY OF THE DANISH PARLIAMENT TOOK A POSITION ON THE
ISSUE OF VISITS BY ALLIED WARSHIPS TO DANISH PORTS THAT
SEEMED TO BE A DIRECT CHALLENGE TO MAJOR NATO ALLIES,
ESPECIALLY THE UNITED STATES AND THE UNITED KINGDOM.

08129 SEIFERT, E.K.
SCHMOLLER ON JUSTICE -- TODAY
INTERNATIONAL JOURNAL OF SOCIAL ECONOMICS, 16(9-11) (1989),
69-92.
SCHMOLLER CLAIMED THAT THE BASIC PRINCIPLE OF SOCIAL
REFORM HAS A CONTEMPORARY VERSION OF ARISTOTELIAN "JUSTICE".
ON THE ONE HAND SCHMOLLER DEFENDS THE NECESSITY FOR SOCIAL
REFORM AGAINST CONSERVATIVE ATTACKS WHILST AT THE SAME TIME
DENYING THE LEGITIMACY OF SOCIALIST DEMANDS FOR INCOME
DISTRIBUTION. THE SCHMOLLER APPROACH TO JUSTICE IS RE-
EXAMINED NOT ONLY AS AN IMPORTANT CONTRIBUTION TO THE
HISTORY OF ECONOMICS, BUT OF SURPRISING CONTEMPORARY
RELEVANCY.

08130 SEIFFERT, W.
ENTERING INTO OFFICIAL RELATIONS BETWEEN THE EEC AND
COMECON - ASPECT OF INTERNATIONAL LAW
PEACE AND THE SCIENCES, 1 (1989), 10-23.
BY ESTABLISHING OFFICIAL RELATIONS BETWEEN THE EEC AND
CMEA A LONG-STANDING POLITICAL PROCESS CAME TO A CONCLUSION
BASED ON THE JURIDICAL EQUAL STATUS OF THE LEGAL SYSTEMS OF
THE EEC AND CMEA SUCH AS THEY ARE. IN THE BEGINNING, THE
COMECON COUNTRIES HAD CONSIDERED THE EEC AS AN "ECONOMIC
BASIS OF NATO", LATER THEY ARGUED WHETHER THE DIFFERENT
COMPETENCES OF THE TWO INTERNATIONAL ORGANIZATIONS PERMITTED
TAKING UP OFFICIAL RELATIONS IN ANY WAY AND/OR IF THE CMEA-
STATES CONSIDERED THE SUPRA-NATIONAL COMPETENCES OF THE EEC
CONTRARY TO INTERNATIONAL LAW.

08131 SEITZ, R.
AMERICAN SECURITY POLICIES: THE NEW PERSPECTIVES

RUSI JOURNAL, 134(1) (SPR 89), 5-8.
THE AUTHOR ENUMERATES FOUR ELEMENTS THAT WILL SHAPE THE EUROPEAN AGENDA FOR THE BUSH ADMINISTRATION: THE EUROPEAN COMMUNITY AND 1992, THE AMERICAN PRESENCE IN EUROPE, THE CONDITION OF GERMANY, AND THE NUCLEAR DEBATE.

08132 SEIZABURO, S.
THE RECRUIT AFFAIR: CRITIZING THE CRITICS
JAPAN ECHO, XVI(3) (AUT 89), 40-46.
IN ORDER TO UNDERSTAND THE SIGNIFICANCE OF THE RECRUIT SCANDAL, IT IS NECESSARY TO CLASSIFY THE ACTIONS OF THE POLITICIANS WHO BOUGHT SHARES FROM RECRUIT COSMOS OR ACCEPTED POLITICAL DONATIONS FROM RECRUIT INTO THREE CATEGORIES: (1) ACTS THAT VIOLATED EXISTING LAWS, (2) ACTS THAT WERE NOT TECHNICALLY ILLEGAL BUT WERE IMPROPER FOR POLITICIANS, AND (3) ACTS THAT WERE NOT WRONG IN ANY WAY. ONLY THEN CAN THE PUBLIC DEMAND THAT THE POLITICIANS BE PUNISHED FOR ILLEGAL OR INAPPROPRIATE BEHAVIOR. BUT, IN FACT, THE SCANDAL HAS TURNED INTO A WITCH HUNT, PURE AND SIMPLE. STARTING FROM THE ASSUMPTION THAT THE RECRUIT GROUP IS BAD, OBSERVERS HAVE JUMPED TO THE CONCLUSION THAT ANYONE WHO RECEIVED RECRUIT MONEY MUST ALSO BE BAD AND THEY ARE DEMANDING THAT ALL IMPLICATED OFFICIALS RESIGN. THIS REACTION IS THOUGHTLESS AND HYPOCRITICAL.

08133 SEIZABURO, S.
THE UPPER HOUSE ELECTION: MOBOCRACY TRIUMPHANT
JAPAN ECHO, XVI(4) (WIN 89), 30-35.
GIVEN THE COMPLEXITY AND SCALE OF MODERN SOCIETY, IT IS UNREALISTIC TO EXPECT ALL VOTERS TO HAVE A THOROUGH GRASP OF EACH POLICY ISSUE FROM THE OUTSET. IT IS THE JOB OF POLITICIANS AND POLITICAL PARTIES TO EXPLAIN THE NATURE OF EACH ISSUE, OUTLINE POSSIBLE RESPONSES, AND ARGUE THE PROS AND CONS OF EACH OPTION IN CLEAR, COMPREHENSIBLE TERMS. SINCERE, OPEN DEBATE BETWEEN OPPOSING SIDES ON A GIVEN QUESTION IS THE ONLY WAY TO ENHANCE PUBLIC AWARENESS AND UNDERSTANDING AND PROVIDE VOTERS WITH THE KNOWLEDGE THEY NEED TO MAKE DEMOCRACY WORK. WHEN THE PROCESS BREAKS DOWN, DEMOCRACY IS IN DANGER OF BECOMING MOB RULE. IN THIS ESSAY, THE AUTHOR CONSIDERS THE 1989 JAPANESE UPPER HOUSE ELECTION IN LIGHT OF THESE PRINCIPLES.

08134 SEKLEJ, L.
THE COMMUNIST LEAGUE OF YUGOSLAVIA: ELITE OF POWER OR CONSCIOUSNESS
SOCIALISM AND DEMOCRACY, (6) (SPR 89), 115-134.
THROUGHOUT THE HISTORY OF THE LABOR MOVEMENT, THERE HAS NEVER BEEN AGREEMENT ABOUT THE TYPE OF ORGANIZATIONAL VEHICLE NEEDED TO FULFILL THE SOCIAL GOALS FOR WHICH WORKERS' ORGANIZATIONS ARE FORMED. THE ARTICLE DEALS WITH THIS PROBLEM OF ORGANIZATION WITH EMPHASIS ON THE RELATIONSHIP BETWEEN ONE TYPE OF WORKERS' ORGANIZATION, THE COMMUNIST, AND THE CLASS WHOSE INTERESTS DEFINE THE GOALS THE ORGANIZATION IS PRESUMABLY DESIGNED TO FULFILL, NAMELY THE WORKING CLASS. IT EXPLORES VARIOUS MODELS OF ORGANIZATION AND EXAMINES THE OPERATIONALIZATIONS OF THESE MODELS IN THE PROGRAM OF THE LEAGUE OF YUGOSLAVIAN COMMUNISTS.

08135 SEKULA, I.; RZEMIENIECKI, K.
WE INTEND TO TURN POLAND INTO A COUNTRY FOR ENTERPRISING PEOPLE
CONTEMPORARY POLAND, XXII(3) (1989), 50-59.
POLAND'S DEPUTY PRIME MINISTER IRENEUSZ SEKULA ANSWERS QUESTIONS ABOUT REFORMS IN POLAND AND THE PROGRESS OF ECONOMIC CHANGE.

08136 SELBY, A.
ARE NEGOTIATIONS POSSIBLE?
SECHABA, 23(9) (SEP 89), 22-23.
THE ARTICLE EXPLORES THE POSSIBILITY OF NEGOTIATIONS FROM AN AFRICAN NATIONAL CONGRESS POINT OF VIEW. ESSENTIAL PRECONDITIONS TO NEGOTIATIONS INCLUDE: A SPIRIT OF GOOD FAITH; A GENUINE EFFORT TO REACH A SATISFACTORY AGREEMENT; THE NEGOTIATING PARTIES SPEAKING ONLY FOR THEMSELVES; SOLID SUPPORT OF THE REGIME BY THE MAJORITY OF WHITE SOUTH AFRICANS; AND A LACK OF OUTSIDE INTERFERENCE. THE ANC POSITION ON NEGOTIATIONS ACKNOWLEDGES THE FEASIBILITY AND EVEN DESIRABILITY OF NEGOTIATIONS, WHILE AT THE SAME TIME DOES NOT ABANDON THE NEED FOR ARMED AGGRESSION.

08137 SELBYG, A.
WHY ARE WOMEN IN POWER IN THE NORDIC COUNTRIES BUT NOT IN THE UNITED STATES?
SCANDINAVIAN REVIEW, 77(4) (WIN 89), 20-25.
THE AUTHOR TRACES THE DEVELOPMENT OF WOMEN'S RIGHTS MOVEMENTS IN SCANDINAVIA AND COMPARES THE SCANDINAVIAN EXPERIENCE, WHICH HAS LED TO LARGE NUMBERS OF WOMEN HOLDING POWERFUL POLITICAL OFFICES, TO THAT OF FEMINISTS IN THE UNITED STATES.

08138 SELCHER, W.A.
A NEW START TOWARD A MORE DECENTRALIZED FEDERALISM IN BRAZIL?

PUBLIUS: THE JOURNAL OF FEDERALISM, 19(3) (SUM 89), 167-184.
BRAZIL'S POLITICAL HISTORY CAN BE READ AS A CYCLICAL ALTERNATION BETWEEN CENTRALIZATION AND DECENTRALIZATION--A CONTEST BETWEEN THE CENTER AND THE PERIPHERY. CENTRALIZING TENDENCIES REACHED ONE HEIGHT UNDER THE "ESTADO NOVO" OF GETULIO VARGAS (1937-1945) AND PEAKED AGAIN UNDER A SERIES OF MILITARY GOVERNMENTS FROM 1964 TO 1985. FORCES FAVORING REGIONALISM AND MORE STATE AND LOCAL AUTONOMY HAVE BEEN GIVEN IMPETUS DURING THE 1980S BY TRENDS OF REGIONAL DIFFERENTIATION, POPULAR MOBILIZATION, RETURN TO CIVILIAN GOVERNMENT IN 1985, SEVERAL KEY ELECTIONS, AND STATE AND LOCAL FINANCIAL CRISES. THE CONSTITUTION PROMULGATED IN OCTOBER 1988 FEATURES DECENTRALIZING FISCAL PROVISIONS THAT GIVE REASON TO BELIEVE THAT FEDERALISM MAY BE REVITALIZED IN THE NEXT SEVERAL YEARS IN RESPONSE TO GRASSROOTS DEMANDS FROM STATE AND LOCAL GOVERNMENTS. HOWEVER, THESE FEDERALISM REFORMS MAY BE THREATENED BY THE NATIONAL GOVERNMENT'S ATTEMPTS TO THWART THE CONSTITUTION'S DECENTRALIZATION PROVISIONS AND BY NATIONAL ECONOMIC AND POLITICAL INSTABILITY.

08139 SELGIN, G.
KEYNE'S SPECIAL THEORY
CRITICAL REVIEW, 3(3) (SUM 89), 411-434.
KEYNES'S ANALYSIS OF THE POSSIBILITY OF UNDERCONSUMPTION IN CAPITALIST ECONOMIES IS NOT A GENERAL THEORY OF MARKET ECONOMIES, BUT RATHER IS RELEVANT, AT BEST, TO ECONOMIES WITH CENTRAL BANKING SYSTEMS. THIS ARTICLE DEMONSTRATES THAT BY CONTRAST, COMPETITION IN MONEY PRODUCTION CAN LINK SAVING AND INVESTMENT, THUS AVOIDING KEYNES'S CRITIQUE. IN ADDITION, THIS ARGUMENT PROVIDES A FRAMEWORK TO UNDERSTAND CENTRAL BANKING'S INABILITY TO ACHIEVE ITS INTENDED RESULTS. MANY OF THE MACROECONOMIC PROBLEMS IN HISTORICAL CAPITALISM CAN THUS BE TRACED TO INTERFERENCE WITH FINANCIAL MARKETS, RATHER THAN TO MARKET FAILURES.

08140 SELIUNIN, V.
A PROFOUND REFORM OR THE REVENGE OF THE BUREAUCRACY?
SOVIET REVIEW, 30(3) (MAY 89), 3-25.
THE AUTHOR OUTLINES WHAT HE SEES AS FATAL FLAWS IN THE GORBACHEV ECONOMIC REFORM PROGRAM THROUGH 1988 AND PREDICTS THAT RECESSION MAY GIVE WAY TO ECONOMIC COLLAPSE UNLESS A PROFOUND ECONOMIC REFORM IS INITIATED IN 1989-90.

08141 SELMON, M.L.
ENGENDERING DRAMA: CARYL CHURCHILL AND THE STAGES OF REFORM
DISSERTATION ABSTRACTS INTERNATIONAL, 49(9) (MAR 89), 2836-A.
CARYL CHURCHILL HAS EMERGED AS A LEADING PLAYWRIGHT WHOSE WORKS ARE ACCLAIMED BOTH FOR THE INTEGRITY OF THEIR POLITICS AND FOR THE ORIGINALITY OF THEIR TECHNIQUE. HER DRAMA PRESUMES THAT THE AESTHETIC AND THE POLITICAL ARE INTRINSICALLY LINKED AND THAT CHANGE IN ONE REALM CAN LEAD TO RETHINKING CONVENTIONS IN THE OTHER. CONSEQUENTLY, SHE USES TRANSGRESSIONS OF SOCIAL, LINGUISTIC, AND GENERIC FORM TO ENCOURAGE POLITICAL REFORM.

08142 SELTSOVSKI, V.
THE STRUCTURE OF THE USSR'S FOREIGN TRADE AND WAYS TO IMPROVE IT
FOREIGN TRADE, 11 (1988), 10-12.
FOREIGN ECONOMIC TIES HAVE ALWAYS BEEN IMPORTANT FOR ACCOMPLISHING POLITICAL AND ECONOMIC TASKS IN ALL STAGES OF SOVIET HISTORY. THIS ARTICLE EXAMINES MAJOR OBSTACLES WHICH PREVENT THE GROWTH OF SOVIET PRODUCT EXPORTS AND CALLS FOR URGENT IMPROVEMENT OF THE EXPORT AND IMPORT STRUCTURE.

08143 SEMIN, N.
PREREQUISITES FOR THE CMEA COUNTRIES GREATER COOPERATION
FOREIGN TRADE, 1 (1989), 7-11.
THIS ESSAY REVIEWS THE ACTIVITIES OF AND RESULTS ACCOMPLISHED BY THE COUNCIL FOR MUTUAL ECONOMIC ASSISTANCE. THIS COUNCIL WAS FORMED IN 1946 TO COORDINATE ECONOMIC PROGRAMS AMONG THE EASTERN EUROPEAN COUNTRIES INCLUDING THE SOVIET UNION. ONE RECENT TREND HAS BEEN THE EFFECTING OF AGREEMENTS BETWEEN THE COUNTRIES CONCERNED WITHOUT DIRECTIONS OR APPROVAL FROM HIGHER AUTHORITIES.

08144 SEN, A.
FOOD AND FREEDOM
WORLD DEVELOPMENT, 17(6) (JUN 89), 769-781.
THE LINKS BETWEEN FOOD AND FREEDOM MAY AT FIRST SIGHT APPEAR TO BE RATHER REMOTE TO POLICY MAKING AND FAR FROM CENTRAL TO PRACTICAL CONCERNS. BUT THE ROLE OF FOOD IN FOSTERING FREEDOM CAN BE AN EXTREMELY IMPORTANT ONE. MOREOVER, FREEDOM MAY CAUSALLY INFLUENCE THE SUCCESS OF THE PURSUIT OF FOOD FOR ALL. INSOFAR AS PUBLIC POLICY TO COMBAT HUNGER AND STARVATION MAY DEPEND ON THE EXISTENCE AND EFFICIENCY OF POLITICAL PRESSURE GROUPS TO INDUCE GOVERNMENTS TO ACT, POLITICAL FREEDOM MAY HAVE A CLOSE CONNECTION WITH THE DISTRIBUTION OF RELIEF AND FOOD TO VULNERABLE GROUPS.

08145 SENGUPTA, U.
    HIMALAYAN CRISIS
    INDIA TODAY, XIV(8) (MAY 89), 48-55.
        THERE ARE UNMISTAKABLE SIGNS OF A CRISIS IN NEPAL SINCE
    THE LAPSE OF CRUCIAL TRADE AND TRANSIT TREATIES WITH INDIA
    LAPSED ON MARCH 23, 1989, LEADING TO SEVERE SHORTAGES OF
    ESSENTIAL COMMODITIES. ANTI-INDIAN SENTIMENT IS PERILOUSLY
    CLOSE TO MASS HYSTERIA, DESPITE GOVERNMENT EFFORTS TO
    CONTROL IT.

08146 SENGUPTA, U.
    POLL BONANZA
    INDIA TODAY, (JUL 89), 36-37.
        THIS ARTICLE REPORTS ON UPCOMING ELECTIONS IN BIHAR
    WHERE THE PARTY IN POWER HOPES TO CONTINUE. IT EXAMINES A
    PROMISED ECONOMIC PACKAGE AND DETAILS THE PROPOSED PROJECTS.
    IT CONCLUDES WITH A REPORT ON PRIME MINISTER, RAJIV GANDHI'S
    CAMPAIGN STRATEGIES AND PONDERS THE EFFECT THAT DAMAGE
    CAUSED BY THE MONSOON SEASON WILL HAVE ON THE ELECTION.

08147 SENIGALLIA, S.
    ITALIAN JUSTICE ON THE RUN
    NEW LEADER, LXXII(13) (SEP 89), 10-11.
        THE ARTICLE EXAMINES THE POLICIES AND PRACTICES OF THE
    ITALIAN MAFIA. THE LONG REGARDED AS A GROUP OF SICILIAN
    ROBIN HOODS WHO ROBBED THE RICH, HELPED THE POOR, AND DEFIED
    AUTHORITY. HOWEVER, THE FACE OF THE ORGANIZATION HAS CHANGED
    IN RECENT DECADES; ITALIAN MAFIA FAMILIES ARE NOW HEAVILY
    INTO POLITICS AND DRUG SMUGGLING. THE NUMBER OF DEATHS IN
    THE DRUG WAR BETWEEN MAFIA AND GOVERNMENT HAS EXCEEDED 500
    IN THE FIRST HALF OF 1989 AND CONTINUES TO ESCALATE.
    GOVERNMENT AUTHORITIES SPEAK OF THE NEED FOR HARSHER
    MEASURES, BUT SEEM UNABLE TO ENACT THEM.

08148 SENIGALLIA, S.
    ITALY WATCHES AN EMPIRE STUMBLE
    NEW LEADER, LXXII(16) (OCT 89), 10-11.
        THE ARTICLE EXAMINES THE REACTION OF THE ITALIAN
    GOVERNMENT AND PRESS TOWARDS THE SWEEPING CHANGES TAKING
    PLACE IN THE USSR AND EASTERN EUROPE. THE PRESS GENERALLY
    PRAISES THE REFORMS OF THE EAST AND CRITICIZES THE SLUGGISH
    RESPONSE OF THE US. ALTHOUGH THE "AVERAGE" ITALIAN SEEMS TO
    BE IN FAVOR OF THE ONGOING CHANGES, THEY REMAIN COMMITTED TO
    A LEVEL-HEADED PRAGMATISM WITH REGARDS TO FOREIGN POLICY.

08149 SENIGALLIA, S.F.
    ONE EUROPE INDIVISIBLE?
    NEW LEADER, LXXII(2) (JAN 89). 5-6.
        DESPITE ITALY'S SEMINAL ROLE AS A CO-FOUNDER OF THE
    EUROPEAN COMMUNITY, IT HAS SO FAR BEEN A RATHER TEPID
    SUPPORTER OF THE 1992 INTEGRATION PROJECT.

08150 SERAFIMOV, K., B.
    ACHIEVING WORLDWIDE COOPERATION IN SPACE
    SPACE POLICY, 5(2) (MAY 89), 111-116.
        ALTHOUGH COOPERATION AMONG THE SPACEFARING NATIONS IS
    WELL ESTABLISHED, THE POSSIBILITIES FOR THE PARTICIPATION OF
    OTHER, PARTICULARLY DEVELOPING, COUNTRIES IN SPACE
    ACTIVITIES REMAIN SEVERELY LIMITED BY ECONOMIC AND TECHNICAL
    CONSTRAINTS. THE AUTHOR DEMONSTRATES THE NEED FOR GREATER
    GLOBAL COOPERATION IN THE FIELD OF SPACE, AFTER EXAMINING
    EXISTING MECHANISMS, HE OFFERS A NUMBER OF SUGGESTIONS FOR
    THE ESTABLISHMENT OF A WORLD SPACE ORGANIZATION AND MAKES
    SOME PROPOSALS AS TO ITS ACTIVITIES.

08151 SERAFINO, N.M.
    COSTA RICA: OUR UNEASY ALLY
    CRS REVEIW, 10(2) (FEB 89), 22-23.
        PRESIDENT OSCAR ARIAS AND THE REGIONAL PEACE ACCORD HAVE
    BEEN INFLUENTIAL IN SHAPING INTERNATIONAL AND CONGRESSIONAL
    ATTITUDES CONCERNING THE MEANS TO RESOLVE CONFLICT IN
    CENTRAL AMERICA. DESPITE THE RESULTING TENSIONS IN RELATIONS
    WITH THE UNITED STATES, COSTA RICA CONTINUES TO LOOK TO THE
    UNITED STATES FOR SUPPORT.

08152 SERAFINO, N.M.
    NICARAGUA: POSSIBILITIES FOR MUTUAL ACCOMMODATION?
    CRS REVEIW, 10(2) (FEB 89), 11-13.
        THE ADVENT OF A NEW ADMINISTRATION, THE PAST RELUCTANCE
    OF THE CONGRESS TO CONTINUE FUNDING A CONTRA WAR, AND
    MANAGUA'S DESPERATE NEED TO STABILIZE A DETERIORATING
    ECONOMY HAVE SET THE SCENE FOR POSSIBLE NEW ATTEMPTS TO
    RESOLVE THE DECADE-LONG DIFFERENCES BETWEEN THE UNITED
    STATES AND NICARAGUA. THESE DIFFERENCES HAVE CENTERED ON THE
    THREAT THE UNITED STATES PERCEIVES BOTH FROM THE
    SANDINISTAS' SOVIET BLOC TIES, EXTERNAL REVOLUTIONARY
    ACTIVITY, AND MILITARY BUILDUP, AND FROM THE REPRESSION OF
    THEIR DOMESTIC OPPOSITION.

08153 SERAFINO, N.M.
    OVERVIEW: CENTRAL AMERICAN DILEMMAS AND U.S. POLICY
    CRS REVEIW, 10(2) (FEB 89), 1-4.
        SINCE THE EARLY 1980S U.S. POLICY HAS SOUGHT TO ISOLATE
    LEFTIST NICARAGUA, FRUSTRATE IT MILITARY, AND PROTECT ITS

NEIGHBORS AGAINST SIMILAR LEFTIST REVOLUTIONS. THIS HAS
DEEPLY ENMESHED THE UNITED STATES IN THE AFFAIRS OF THE
CENTRAL AMERICAN COUNTTRIES. THE FOUR U.S. ALLIES IN THE
REGION INITIALLY SUPPORTED U.S. POLICY TO VARYING DEGREES
AND SHARED U.S. CONCERNS. BUT THEY HAVE RECENTLY TO RESOLVE
THE CRISIS CAUSED BY NICARAGUA, BUT ALSO HAS CREATED NEW
PROBLEMS FOR THEM. THEY HAVE ATTEMPTED TO DEAL WITH
NICARAGUA AND OTHER PROBLEMS ON THEIR OWN, BUT THESE EFFORTS
THUS FAR HAVE FOUNDERED BECAUSE OF DIFFERENCES AMONG THEM
AND OTHER REASONS.

08154 SERAFINO. N.M.
    U.S. INTERESTS IN CENTRAL AMERICA
    CRS REVEIW, 10(2) (FEB 89), 5-7.
        EVENTS IN PANAMA AND NICARAGUA IN THE 1970S ABRUPTLY
    DREW THE ATTENTION OF THE UNITED STATES TO THE SMALL STATES
    OF CENTRAL AMERICA. SOVIET BLOC ASSISTANCE TO THE NICARAGUAN
    GOVERNMENT AND TO LEFTIST INSURGENTS IN THE AREA HAS
    PROVOKED CONTINUING CONGRESSIONAL CONCERN AND CONTROVERSY
    OVER THE BEST MEANS TO PROTECT U.S. INTEREST THERE.

08155 SEROKA, J.
    ECONOMIC STABILIZATION AND COMMUNAL POLITICS IN YUGOSLAVIA
    JOURNAL OF COMMUNIST STUDIES, 5(2) (JUN 89), 131-147.
        THE YUGOSLAV COMMUNE IS THE MOST IMPORTANT GENERAL
    PURPOSE UNIT OF LOCAL GOVERNMENT IN THE COUNTRY. AS SUCH, IT
    SHARES SOME OF THE BLAME FOR THE FAILURE OF MANY OF
    YUGOSLAVIA'S ATTEMPTED ECONOMIC REFORMS. THE ARTICLE REVIEWS
    THE ECONOMIC DIFFICULTIES FACED BY THE COMMUNE. IT OUTLINES
    THE INSTITUTIONAL ROLE OF THE COMMUNE AND DISCUSSES INTER-
    COMMUNAL VARIATION WITHIN THE CONTEXT OF ECONOMIC REFORM. IT
    ALSO EXAMINES THE EVAPORATION OF POLITICAL LEGITIMACY WITHIN
    THE COMMUNE AND ITS IMPACT ON YUGOSLAVIA'S NATIONAL ECONOMIC
    STABILIZATION POLICY. IT CONCLUDES WITH AN ANALYSIS OF THE
    EMERGENCE OF AN ALTERNATE FORM OF POLITICAL AUTHORITY WITHIN
    THE COMMUNE, STIMULATED, IN PART, BY THE FAILURE OF THE
    ECONOMIC STABILIZATION POLICY.

08156 SERRY-KAMAL, M.
    THE DEFENSE SPENDING DECISION-MAKING PROCESS IN THE UNITED
    STATES: 1945 TO 1987
    DISSERTATION ABSTRACTS INTERNATIONAL, 49(10) (APR 89),
    3152-A.
        THE AUTHOR EXAMINES A NUMBER OF GENERAL PROPOSITIONS:
    THAT DEFENSE SPENDING IS BASED MORE ON ECONOMIC AND
    POLITICAL CONSIDERATIONS THAN ON PRACTICAL NATIONAL SECURITY
    REASONS; THAT THE DOMESTIC ECONOMIC IMPACT OF INCREASED
    DEFENSE SPENDING IS NEGATIVE; AND THAT, AS A RESULT, CERTAIN
    PUBLIC MEASURES ARE NECESSARY TO ALTER THE STRUCTURE AND THE
    PROCESS OF DEFENSE SPENDING.

08157 SETON-WATSON, C.
    1919 AND THE PERSISTENCE OF NATIONALIST ASPIRATIONS
    REVIEW OF INTERNATIONAL STUDIES, 15(4) (OCT 89), 309-318.
        IN THIS ARTICLE THE AUTHOR SHOWS HOW THE PEACE
    SETTLEMENT OF 1919 IS NOT ONLY STILL WITH US, BUT ALSO ONLY
    NOW BEGINNING TO YIELD ITS FRUIT IN WESTERN EUROPE AND THE
    SOVIET UNION ITSELF, IT EXAMINES THE GERMAN QUESTION AND THE
    PROBLEMS CONFRONTED BY ITALY, RUSSIA AND EAST-CENTRAL
    DISSATISFIED MINORITIES.

08158 SEUTOVA, S.
    GLASNOST AND THE CRIMEAN TATARS
    GLASNOST, (16-18) (JAN 89), 56.
        THE QUESTION OF THE CRIMEAN TATARS RETURNING TO THEIR
    HOMELAND REMAINS UNDECIDED. THE INTERESTS OF THE RUSSIANS
    AND UKRAINIANS WHO NOW LIVE IN THE CRIMEA COMPLICATE THE
    SITUATION. MEANWHILE, THE CRIMEAN TATARS REGRET THAT THEY
    ARE UNABLE TO PRESERVE THEIR CULTURE AND LANGUAGE DUE TO
    THEIR DISPERSAL THROUGHOUT THE SOVIET UNION.

08159 SEVE, L.
    MARX AND HUMAN RIGHTS
    COMMUNIST VIEWPOINT, 21(1) (SPR 89), 9-13.
        AN EVALUATION OF MARX AND HUMAN RIGHTS IS THAT THE
    MARXIST DOES NOT WANT ANY RIGHTS OF MAN, AND WHAT IS MORE,
    WANTS TOO MANY OF THEM. THIS ARTICLE ATTEMPTS TO HELP
    CLARIFY TO WHAT EXTENT THIS IS A FAIR EVALUATION OF MARX'S
    ATTITUDE AND THAT OF CONTEMPORARY MARXISTS WITH REGARD TO
    THE RIGHTS OF MAN. THE WRITER TIES THIS QUESTION TO THE
    FRENCH REVOLUTION AND FINALLY CONCLUDES THAT FOR MARX "THE
    RIGHTS OF MAN ARE INTEGRATED INTO A PROCESS OF DEVELOPMENT
    WHERE THEY ARE IN NO WAY WIPED OUT BUT ARE TRANSCENDED."

08160 SEVERGIN, S.
    USSR-DPRK: NEW FORMS OF COOPERATION
    FOREIGN TRADE, 4 (1988), 16-19.
        THIS ARTICLE EXAMINES THE TRADE AND ECONOMIC RELATIONS
    BETWEEN THE USSR AND NORTH KOREA. WHICH ARE GROWING IN A
    POSITIVE DIRECTION. REPORTED ARE THE RESULTS OF THE MEETING
    OF GORBACHEV AND KIM II SUNG IN OCTOBER OF 1986. DETAILED IS
    THE CONTENT OF A DRAFT LONG-TERM PROGRAM FOR THE DEVELOPMENT
    OF ECONOMIC, SCIENTIFIC AND TECHNICAL COOPERATION BETWEEN
    THE USSR AND DPRK OVER THE PERIOD UP TO YEAR 2000.

08161 SEYMOUR-URE, C.
PRIME MINISTERS, POLITICAL NEWS, AND POLITICAL PLACES
CANADIAN PUBLIC ADMINISTRATION, 32(2) (SUM 89), 311-319.
TELEVISION HAS ENLARGED THE RANGE OF POSSIBLE LOCATIONS
FOR INFORMAL NEWS CONFERENCES, OR "SCRUMS," WITH THE
CANADIAN PRIME MINISTER. AT FIRST GLANCE, THIS MIGHT SEEM TO
BE MOST ADVANTAGEOUS TO THE PRIME MINISTER, BECAUSE IT
INCREASES THE SCOPE FOR PROJECTING HIMSELF AS HE WISHES. BUT
ONCE THE PRIME MINISTER IS FREED FROM HIS PARLIAMENTARY
PUBLICITY BASE, HE BECOMES INVOLVED IN A PROCESS OF
NEGOTIATING OR JOCKEYING WITH THE MEDIA FOR CONTROL--FIRST,
OVER WHAT LOCATIONS ARE CHOSEN FOR NEWSGATHERING AND,
SECONDLY, OVER THE TERMS ON WHICH THE EXCHANGE TAKES PLACE.

08162 SEYMOUR-URE, C.
PRIME MINISTERS' REACTIONS TO TELEVISION: BRITAIN,
AUSTRALIA, AND CANADA
MEDIA, CULTURE, AND SOCIETY, 11(2) (APR 89), 307-325.
PRIME MINISTERS HAVE ENCOUNTERED TELEVISION IN THREE
ROLES: AS PERFORMERS, AS NEWS MANAGERS, AND AS MEDIA POLICY-
MAKERS. IN THIS PAPER, THE AUTHOR STUDIES THE PRIME
MINISTERS OF BRITAIN, AUSTRALIA, AND CANADA AS THEY HAVE
REACTED TO TELEVISION SINCE THE BEGINNINGS OF THE MEDIUM IN
THE 1940'S AND 1950'S. HE DIVIDES THE PRIME MINISTERS INTO
FOUR GROUPS: THOSE HOLDING OFFICE AS THE INAUGURATORS OF TV;
THOSE SERVING DURING A PERIOD OF INITIATIVE, EXPERIMENT, AND
ADJUSTMENT; THOSE SERVING DURING TELEVISION'S POLITICAL
COMING OF AGE; AND THOSE HOLDING OFFICE DURING TELEVISION'S
ASCENDANCY.

08163 SEYMOUR, J.D.
CADRE ACCOUNTABILITY TO THE LAW
AUSTRALIAN JOURNAL OF CHINESE AFFAIRS, (21) (JAN 89), 1-27.
TO SOME CHINESE "POLITICAL MODERNIZATION" MEANS
DEMOCRACY, BUT THERE HAS BEEN LITTLE DEMOCRATIZATION.
HOWEVER, THERE HAS BEEN A MAJOR EFFORT TO IMPROVE THE LEGAL
SYSTEM AND TO EDUCATE THE POPULATION ABOUT THE MEANING AND
IMPORTANCE OF LAW. WHILE THIS HAS HAS SOME SUCCESS, THE IDEA
THAT THOSE HOLDING POLITICAL POWER ARE THEMSELVES
ACCOUNTABLE TO THE LAW HAS YET TO TAKE ROOT AND LAWLESSNESS
AMONG CADRES IS WIDELY VIEWED AS A SERIOUS PROBLEM.

08164 SEYMOUR, JAMES D.
TAIWAN IN 1988: NO MORE BANDITS
ASIAN SURVEY, XXIX(1) (JAN 89), 54-63.
THE ARTICLE EXAMINES THE POLITICAL, ECONOMIC, AND
INTERNATIONAL CHANGES AFFECTING TAIWAN IN 1988. CHIEF AMONG
THESE WAS THE DEATH OF CHAING CHING-KUO, LEADER OF THE
RULING KUOMINTANG (KMT), AND THE ENSUING GROWTH OF
OPPOSITION PARTIES. TAIWAN ENJOYED CONTINUED ECONOMIC GROWTH,
THOUGH NOT AT THE STUNNING RATE OF 1987. THE MOST
SIGNIFICANT CHANGE IN EXTERNAL RELATIONS WAS A TENTATIVE
AGREEMENT TO TRADE WITH THE PEOPLE'S REPUBLIC OF CHINA VIA
HONG KONG.

08165 SEZER, D.
TURKEY'S SECURITY POLICY: CHALLENGES OF ADAPTATION TO THE
POST INF-ERA
RUSI JOURNAL, 134(4) (WIN 89), 47-54.
IN THE PAST FOUR DECADES, TURKEY HAS BEEN INTIMATELY
TIED TO THE WEST. HOWEVER, AS DOMINANT FORCES AND
RELATIONSHIPS OF THE INTERNATIONAL SYSTEM ARE CAUGHT IN A
PROCESS OF PROFOUND CHANGE, TURKEY FINDS HERSELF COMPELLED
TO TAKE A HARD LOOK AT THE CORE ASSUMPTIONS AND EQUATIONS OF
HER SECURITY POLICY IN ORDER TO AVOID POLICY IRRELEVANCE AND
REDUNDANCY. THE ARTICLE EXAMINES SEVERAL CRITICAL QUESTIONS
IN LIGHT OF TURKEY'S UNIQUE GEOGRAPHIC, POLITICAL, AND
ETHNIC POSITION. THESE QUESTIONS INCLUDE: WHETHER THE
FLOWERING EAST-WEST MILITARY-POLITICAL STABILITY SIGNALS THE
BEGINNING OF THE END OF THE ATLANTIC ALLIANCE; WHETHER THE
NEW STABILITY WILL RESULT IN DEFINITIVE DISENGAGEMENT OF THE
US FROM WEST EUROPEAN SECURITY CONCERNS AND COMMITMENTS; AND
WHAT IS THE ULTIMATE NATURE, SCOPE, AND INSTITUTIONAL
EXPRESSION OF THE PRESENT TRENDS AMONG WEST EUROPEANS.

08166 SHA'ATH, N.
KEYNOTE SPEECH
NEW OUTLOOK, 32(3-4 (289-290)) (MAR 89), 13-15.
THE PLO AND THE PALESTINIAN PEOPLE ARE COMMITTED TO A
PEACE PLAN BASED ON THE FOLLOWING: THE PARTITION OF
PALESTINE INTO A JEWISH STATE AND AN INDEPENDENT PALESTINIAN
STATE; ACCEPTANCE OF UN RESOLUTIONS 242 AND 338; THE RIGHT
OF THE PALESTINIAN AND ISRAELI STATES TO EXIST IN PEACE,
WITH SECURE BORDERS; A DEFINITE COMMITMENT TO ENDING
TERRORISM; AN IMMEDIATE END TO THE OCCUPATION OF THE
PALESTINIAN TERRITORY; AND A NEGOTIATED SETTLEMENT TO EFFECT
A FINAL, CONTRACTUAL, NEGOTIATED PEACE IN THE CONTEXT OF AN
INTERNATIONAL CONFERENCE. THIS PEACE PROPOSAL COULD NOT HAVE
BEEN OFFERED WITHOUT THE INTIFADA IN THE OCCUPIED
TERRITORIES. THE INTIFADA IS THE MOTHER OF THE PEACE PLAN
AND WILL PROVE TO BE THE MOTHER OF PEACE IN THE MIDEAST.

08167 SHACKNOVE, A.E.
THE AMERICAN RESPONSE TO HAITIAN REFUGEE MIGRATION
DISSERTATION ABSTRACTS INTERNATIONAL, 48(10) (APR 88),
2724-A.
THE STUDY EXAMINES THE POLITICAL, ECONOMIC, AND MORAL
DIMENSIONS OF THE AMERICAN RESPONSE TO HATIAN REFUGEE
MIGRATION. IT ASKS AND ATTEMPTS TO ANSWER THE QUESTIONS:
"WHO IS A REFUGEE?" AND "WHAT ARE THE SCOPE AND LIMITS OF
AMERICAN DUTIES TO REFUGEES?". AN ALTERNATIVE POLICY WHICH
SEEKS TO IMPROVE THE ABILITY OF HOST STATES TO ENFORCE THEIR
IMMIGRATION LAWS AND AT THE SAME TIME MEET THE FUNDAMENTAL
NEEDS OF GENUINE REFUGEES IS PROPOSED.

08168 SHADID, A.
US AND PALESTINIAN UNIVERSITY LINKS
MIDDLE EAST INTERNATIONAL, (360) (OCT 89), 15.
THE MOVEMENT AMONG AMERICAN UNIVERSITIES TO ESTABLISH
LINKS WITH PALESTINIAN UNIVERSITIES IS GROWING. SUCH DIVERSE
UNIVERSITIES AS THE UNIVERSITY OF WISCONSIN, MICHIGAN, IOWA,
RUTGERS UNIVERSITY, AND SAN FRANCISCO STATE UNIVERSITY ARE
ALL WORKING TO ESTABLISH SISTER UNIVERSITIES IN THE OCCUPIED
TERRITORIES. THE INVOLVEMENT OF STUDENTS IS ONE OF THE GOALS
OF PALESTINIAN ACTIVISTS IN AMERICA.

08169 SHAFAEDDIN, S.
SOME CAUSE OF WORSENING OF INCOME INEQUALITY IN IRAN
DURING THE OIL BOOM OF THE MID 1970'S: A KALECKI-RIACH
APPROACH
SCANDINAVIAN JOURNAL OF DEVELOPMENT ALTERNATIVES, VIII(2)
(JUN 89), 123-141.
THE ARTICLE PRESENTS A HISTORICAL REVIEW OF INCOME
INEQUALITY IN IRAN IN GENERAL AND IN URBAN AREAS IN
PARTICULAR. IT UTILIZES THE KALECKI-RIACH HYPOTHESIS TO
ANALYZE TRENDS IN INCOME INEQUALITY AND CONCLUDE THAT
GOVERNMENT EMPLOYEES AND PROFIT EARNERS, AS OPPOSED TO WAGE
EARNERS, WERE FAVORED IN INCOME DISTRIBUTION. THE OIL BOOM
AND GOVERNMENT REDISTRIBUTION POLICIES ARE VIEWED AS PRIMARY
CAUSES OF THIS PHENOMENON.

08170 SHAFER, B.
THE ELECTION OF 1988 AND THE STRUCTURE OF AMERICAN POLITICS
ELECTORAL STUDIES, 8(1) (APR 89), 5-22.
THE AMERICAN ELECTIONS OF 1988, DISMISSED AS UNEVENTFUL
ON THEIR FACE, REVEAL AN UNDERLYING ELECTORAL PATTERN, WHICH
HAS BEEN IN EXISTENCE FOR MORE THAN A GENERATION. EXAMPLES
FROM THE CURRENT CAMPAIGN, ALONG WITH BROADER HISTORICAL
DEVELOPMENTS, SUGGEST THAT THIS PATTERN IS THE PRODUCT OF AN
INSTITUTIONALIZED 'ELECTORAL ORDER' -- COMBINING ISSUE
DIVISIONS, SOCIAL CLEAVAGES, AND GOVERNMENTAL REINFORCEMENT
IN ORDER TO PRODUCE RECURRING ELECTION OUTCOMES. TACTICAL
ADJUSTMENTS BY INDIVIDUAL CANDIDATES ARE COMPARATIVELY
INCONSEQUENTIAL WHEN CONFRONTED BY THIS CONTINUING STRUCTURE,
BUT OTHER SOURCES OF POSSIBLE, FURTHER EVOLUTION DO EXIST.

08171 SHAFER, B.E.
"EXCEPTIONALISM" IN AMERICAN POLITICS?
PS: POLITICAL SCIENCE AND POLITICS, XXII(3) (SEP 89),
588-594.
IF THERE IS AN EXCEPTIONALISM TO AMERICAN POLITICS, IT
MUST BY DEFINITION BE FOUND IN ONE OR MORE OF THREE AREAS:
(1) THE PUBLIC ATTITUDES AT THE BASE OF THAT POLITICS, (2)
THE KEY ORGANIZATIONS IN THE MIDDLE OF THAT POLITICS, AND
(3) THE INSTITUTIONS OF GOVERNMENT AT THE TOP.

08172 SHAFFER, W.R.
RATING THE PERFORMANCE OF THE ADA IN THE U.S. CONGRESS.
WESTERN POLITICAL QUARTERLY, 42(1) (MAR 89), 33-52.
MANY INTEREST GROUPS COMPUTE RATINGS OF CONGRESSMEN AND
SENATORS BASED ON A NUMBER OF "KEY" ROLL-CALL VOTES. WHILE
SOME STUDIES HAVE ATTEMPTED TO EVALUATE SEVERAL OF THE
COMPOSITE INDICES, NONE HAS SOUGHT TO ASSESS THE RELIABILITY
AND VALIDITY OF ANY GIVEN MEASURE ON THE BASIS OF THE
SEPARATE INDICATORS WHICH CONSTITUTE THAT RATING. IN THIS
PAPER THE MAJOR LIBERAL/CONSERVATIVE DIMENSION TAPPED BY THE
ADA'S LIBERALISM QUOTIENT IS EXAMINED FOR RELIABILITY AND
VALIDITY FOR THE U.S. SENATE AND HOUSE OF REPRESENTATIVES
FROM 1969 THROUGH 1986. THE CHIEF ANALYTICAL TECHNIQUE
UTILIZED FOR THIS PURPOSE IS PRINCIPAL COMPONENTS ANALYSIS.
WHILE SOME SPECIFIC ROLL-CALL VOTES ARE WEAK INDICATORS OF
THE "LIBERALISM" FACTOR, THIS MAJOR COMPONENT DOES APPEAR TO
BE BOTH RELIABLE AND VALID. MOREOVER, SINCE FACTOR SCORES
FOR THE "LIBERALISM" DIMENSION CORRELATE HIGHLY WITH THE
SIMPLE ADA RATING, THE LATTER MEASURE CAN BE USED FOR MOST
RESEARCH PURPOSES.

08173 SHAFIR, M.
XENOPHOBIC COMMUNISM: THE CASE OF BULGARIA AND ROMANIA
WORLD TODAY, 45(12) (DEC 89), 208-212.
THE AUTHOR LOOKS AT HOW THE CHANGES IN THE SOVIET UNION
AND THE SOVIETS' REDUCED INTERVENTION IN INTERNAL AFFAIRS IN
EASTERN EUROPE HAS AFFECTED THE BRAND OF COMMUNISM PRACTISED
IN BULGARIA AND ROMANIA.

08174 SHAFROTH, F.
TAX-EXEMPT BONDS VITAL FOR FUTURE
AMERICAN CITY AND COUNTY, 104(11) (NOV 89), 8.
WHILE THE FEDERAL GOVERNMENT HAS INCREASED ITS BORROWING
TO UNPRECEDENTED LEVELS, IT HAS IMPOSED MORE RESTRICTIONS
AND LIMITATIONS ON THE ABILITY AND AUTHORITY OF CITIES AND
TOWNS TO GENERATE FUNDS. FIRST, IT HAS LIMITED THE USE FOR
WHICH CITIES MAY ISSUE TAX-EXEMPT BONDS, THEREBY USURPING
THE RIGHT OF LOCAL TAXPAYERS TO DETERMINE THE PUBLIC
INTEREST. SECONDLY, THE FEDERAL GOVERNMENT HAS LIMITED THE
TOTAL AMOUNT OF TAX-EXEMPT MUNICIPAL BOND FINANCING,
NOTWITHSTANDING EVEN THE FEDERAL DEFINITIONS OF LEGITIMATE
PUBLIC NEEDS. FINALLY, NUMEROUS COSTLY MANDATES HAVE BEEN
PLACED ON THE ABILITY TO EVEN ISSUE TAX-EXEMPT BONDS.

08175 SHAH, S.
DEVELOPING BHUTAN'S ECONOMY: LIMITED OPTIONS, SENSIBLE
CHOICES
ASIAN SURVEY, 29(8) (AUG 89), 816-831.
THE PURPOSE OF THIS ARTICLE IS TO REVIEW BHUTAN'S
DEVELOPMENT EXPERIENCE DURING THE PAST 25 YEARS. IT FOCUSES
ON THOSE PARTICULAR ASPECTS OF THE EXPERIENCE THAT CONTAIN
USEFUL LESSONS FOR OTHER COUNTRIES SIMILARLY PLACED. THE
FIRST SECTION REVIEWS BHUTAN'S FIRST FOUR DEVELOPMENT PLANS
EMPHASIZING INFRASTRUCTURE AND INSTITUTION BUILDING. THE
FOLLOWING SECTIONS DISCUSS THE ESSENTIALS OF BHUTAN'S
DEVELOPMENT STRATEGY THAT BEGAN IN FORCE IN 1981. FINANCIAL
ASPECTS OF ECONOMIC DEVELOPMENT ARE THEN DISCUSSED.

08176 SHAH, S.M.C.
LOK SABHA SECRETARIAT REACHES HISTORIC MILESTONE
PARLIAMENTARIAN, 70(2) (APR 89), 83-89.
THE AUTHOR DISCUSSES THE CELEBRATION, BY THE LOK SABHA
SECRETARIAT OF THE SIXTIETH ANNIVERSARY OF THE CREATION OF A
SEPARATE INDIAN SECRETARIAT, INDEPENDENT OF THE EXECUTIVE
CALLED THE LEGISLATIVE ASSEMBLY DEPARTMENT, WHICH WAS MADE
MEMBERS OF BOTH THE OPPOSITION AND RULING PARTY ARE QUOTED
ON THE TOPIC OF THE ACHIEVEMENTS THAT THE ASSEMBLY HAS
WITNESSED TOWARDS PRESERVING PARLIAMENTARY PRINCIPLES. THE
MAINTENANCE OF HIGH STANDARDS IN DEMOCRACY IS SUPPORTED AS
IT APPLIES TO INDIA IN PARTICULAR, WHICH IS A COUNTRY OF
DIVERSE CULTURES, ETHNIC ASPIRATIONS, CASTE, AND RELIGIONS.

08177 SHAHAK, I.
A HISTORY OF THE CONCEPT OF "TRANSFER" IN ZIONISM
JOURNAL OF PALESTINE STUDIES, XVIII(3) (SPR 89), 22-37.
SINCE EARLY SUMMER 1987, A MOVEMENT HAS BEEN GROWING IN
ISRAELIJEWISH SOCIETY WHICH SUPPORTS THE IDEA OF EXPELLING
ALL PALESTINIANS FROM THE WEST BANK AND GAZA STRIP TO
NEIGHBORING ARAB COUNTRIES OR, PREFERABLY, BEYOND. THE
PRESENT PLANS RESEMBLE OLDER ZIONIST ATTEMPTS OR PLANS FOR
THE EXPULSION OF PALESTINIANS, REFERRED TO EUPHEMISTICALLY
AS "TRANSFER" PLANS. THE EXISTENCE OF A VERY STRONG MINORITY
THAT ADVOCATES THIS IDEA, COMBINED WITH THE SUPPORT OR AT
VERY LEAST THE LACK OF OPPOSITION FROM INFLUENTIAL
PERSONALITIES, MAKES THIS IDEA OF "TRANSFER" A POTENTIALLY
VERY DANGEROUS ONE. INDEED, A SIGNIFICANT MINORITY OF
ISRAELI JEWS TAKES THIS OPTION SERIOUSLY. THIS ARTICLE
EXAMINES THE ROOTS AND CONSEQUENCES OF THE CONCEPT OF
"TRANSFER" OR PALESTINIAN EXPULSION.

08178 SHAHAK, I.
DIPLOMACY MUST NOT OBSCURE THE REALITIES OF ISRAELI
OCCUPATION
MIDDLE EAST INTERNATIONAL, (351) (MAY 89), 16.
THE ARTICLE DISCUSSES SOME OF THE "REALITIES" OF THE
ISRAELI OCCUPATION OF THE WEST BANK. IT CONCENTRATES ON
ISRAELI THEFT OF WATER, AND THE DAILY HUMILIATION,
INDIGNITIES AND INCONVENIENCES THAT PALESTINIANS SUFFER AT
THE HAND OF THE ISRAELI OCCUPYING FORCES.

08179 SHAHAK, I.
INTERVIEW WITH ISRAEL SHAHAK
AMERICAN-ARAB AFFAIRS, (29) (SUM 89), 56-64.
THIS IS AN INTERVIEW WITH DR. SHAHAK, PROFESSOR OF
CHEMISTRY AT HEBREW UNIVERSITY AND CHAIRPERSON OF THE
ISRAELI LEAGUE FOR HUMAN AND CIVIL RIGHTS. SHAHAK TELLS HOW
HIS RELENTLESS CRITICISM OF ZIONISM AND ISRAELI POLICY
DEVELOPED. HE EXPLORES THE IMPACT OF THE INTIFADA AND THE
RACIST BASE OF THE ARGUMENT THAT ISRAEL WOULD BE IMPERILED
BY A PALESTINIAN STATE. U.S. POLICY IN THE MIDDLE EAST,
HUMAN RIGHTS, CIVIL WAR, AMERICAN ORGANIZED JEWISH GROUPS,
AND THE PLO ARE, EACH IN TURN, DETAILED BY DR. SHAHAK.

08180 SHAHAK, I.
THE IMPACT OF THE INTIFADA ON THE ISRAELI ARMY
MIDDLE EAST INTERNATIONAL, (354) (JUL 89), 16.
THE ARTICLE EXAMINES THE EFFECT OF THE PALESTINIAN
UPRISING ON THE PERFORMANCE AND EFFECTIVENESS OF THE ISRAELI
ARMY. IT CONCLUDES THAT TRAINING AND DISCIPLINE ARE
SUFFERING AS THE INTIFADA DRAGS ON. DISAFFECTION AMONG HIGH,
ELITE MEMBERS OF THE ARMED FORCES IS ALSO ON THE RISE. IF
CURRENT TRENDS CONTINUE, ISRAEL'S OVERALL MILITARY
EFFECTIVENESS WILL BE SEVERELY HAMPERED.

08181 SHAHANE, C.; GEORGE, M.K.
HOME THOUGHTS FROM ABROAD
SOUTH, (100) (FEB 89), 28-29.
NEW DELHI'S EFFORTS TO WOO INVESTMENTS FROM INDIANS
LIVING ABROAD HAVE MET WITH LITTLE SUCCESS. DISENCHANTED NON-
RESIDENT INDIANS BLAME THE GOVERNMENT'S INEFFICIENT
BUREAUCRACY AND ACCUSE NEW DELHI OF QUIETLY CHANGING ITS
STRATEGY TO ATTRACT CAPITAL FROM WESTERN INVESTORS INSTEAD.
BUT THE INDIAN GOVERNMENT CLAIMS TO BE COMMITTED TO
INDIGENOUS SELF-RELIANCE.

08182 SHAIN, Y.
CASE STUDY: THE WAR OF GOVERNMENTS AGAINST THEIR
OPPOSITION IN EXILE
GOVERNMENT AND OPPOSITION, 24(3) (SUM 89), 341-356.
THE ACTIVITIES OF POLITICAL EXILES HAVE LONG BEEN A
SOURCE OF UNEASINESS FOR GOVERNMENTS. OPERATING FROM OUTSIDE
THEIR RESPECTIVE STATES AND OFTEN UNDER THE SHELTER OF
SYMPATHETIC GOVERNMENTS, EXILE GROUPS SOMETIMES HAVE A
BETTER OPPORTUNITY THAN AN INTERNALLY-BASED OPPOSITION TO
CARRY ON A FORCEFUL CAMPAIGN AGAINST THE HOME REGIME.

08183 SHAIN, Y.
IN SEARCH OF LOYALTY AND RECOGNITION: THE POLITICAL
ACTIVITY OF EXILES
DISSERTATION ABSTRACTS INTERNATIONAL, 50(5) (NOV 89),
1426-A.
THE AUTHOR SURVEYS THE POLITICAL ACTIVITY OF EXILES FROM
A BROAD CROSS-NATIONAL AND TRANS-HISTORICAL PERSPECTIVE,
CONCERNTRATING ON POLITICAL EXILES WHO STRIVE TO OVERPOWER A
HOME NATIVE REGIME. HE FOCUSES ON FIVE MAJOR ASPECTS OF
EXILE ACTIVITY: THE EXILE'S RELATIONS WITH THE DOMESTIC
OPPOSITION TO THE HOME REGIME; THE EXILE'S ATTEMPTS TO
ENLIST THE SUPPORT OF HIS FELLOW NATIONALS ABROAD; THE
EXILE'S INTERACTION WITH THE INTERNATIONAL COMMUNITY; THE
HOME REGIME'S RESPONSE TO THE CHALLENGE POSED BY POLITICAL
EXILES; AND INTRA- AND INTER-EXILE ORGANIZATIONAL RELATIONS.

08184 SHAKHNAZAROV, O.
ON THE CLASS STRUGGLE
INTERNATIONAL AFFAIRS (MOSCOW), (12) (DEC 89), 81-92.
THE AUTHOR CONSIDERS THE IMPORTANCE OF THE WORKING CLASS
IN THE SOVIET UNION AND HOW THE 1989 SOVIET MINERS' STRIKE
EXEMPLIFIES THE ATTITUDES OF SOVIET WORKERS.

08185 SHALKIN, O.
PACIFIC ANOMALY
REPRINTS FROM THE SOVIET PRESS, 49(11 12) (DEC 89), 41-44.
THIS ARTICLE EXPLORES THE WARMING TREND OF THE
INTERNATIONAL POLITICAL CLIMATE, AS WELL AS THE OBSTACLES
AND BARRIERS STILL IN THE WAY TO A WORLD WITHOUT NUCLEAR
WEAPONS AND MILITARY THREAT. IT THEN ANALYZES THE
INCONSISTENCIES IN U.S. POLICY AND WELL AS THE USA'S PACIFIC
ANOMALY WHICH REFLECTS ITS STAND ON SEA-BASED CRUISE
MISSILES. THE HOPE OF THE USSR IS THAT THEY ARE CLOSE TO THE
TIME WHEN THE RIVALRY COMPLEX IN THE ASIA-PACIFIC REGION IS
ELIMINATED.

08186 SHAMBAUGH, D.L.
CHINA'S AMERICA WATCHERS' IMAGES OF THE UNITED STATES,
1972-1986
DISSERTATION ABSTRACTS INTERNATIONAL, 50(6) (DEC 89),
1796-A.
THE AUTHOR TRACES THE EVOLUTION OF CHINESE VIEWS OF THE
UNITED STATES AS ARTICULATED BY CHINA'S AMERICA WATCHERS. HE
FINDS THAT THESE IMAGES CLUSTER INTO MARXIST AND NON-MARXIST
CATEGORIES, HAVE EVOLVED FROM THE FORMER TO THE LATTER, AND
VARY PRIMARILY ACCORDING TO THE SOCIALIZATION OF EACH
AMERICA WATCHER.

08187 SHAMBAUGH, D.L.
THE FOURTH AND FIFTH PLENARY SESSIONS OF THE 13TH CCP
CENTRAL COMMITTEE
CHINA QUARTERLY, (120) (DEC 89), 852-862.
THE FOURTH AND FIFTH PLENARY SESSIONS OF THE 13TH
CENTRAL COMMITTEE WERE THE FIRST COMPREHENSIVE CENTRAL PARTY
MEETINGS TO BE CONVENED IN THE AFTERMATH OF THE TIANANMEN
SQUARE RIOTS IN JUNE 1989. ALTHOUGH THE AGENDAS OF THE TWO
PLENUMS VARIED, BOTH DEALT WITH THE IMPACT OF THE MOMENTOUS
EVENTS OF THE SPRING, PARTICULARLY THEIR EFFECT ON
LEADERSHIP PERSONNEL, PUBLIC SECURITY, IDEOLOGY AND
PROPAGANDA, ECONOMIC POLICY, CIVIL-MILITARY RELATIONS, AND
FOREIGN AFFAIRS. THEY WERE ALSO SIGNIFICANT IN THE LONG-TERM
SUCCESSION STRUGGLE OVER WHO WILL SUCCEED DENG XIAOPING,
WHICH HAS BEEN UNDERWAY SINCE HU YAOBANG'S DISMISSAL AS CCP
GENERAL SECRETARY.

08188 SHAMES, G.
ISRAEL: THE DISSENTERS
THIRD WORLD WEEK, 7(12) (FEB 89), 89-90.
THREE JOURNALISTS WORKING FOR A MARXIST, PRO-ARAB
NEWSPAPER HAVE BEEN PROSECUTED IN ISRAEL ON CHARGES OF
MEMBERSHIP IN A TERRORIST ORGANIZATION AND SUPPLYING

SERVICES TO AN ILLEGAL ORGANIZATION. AN ISRAELI OFFICIAL DESCRIBED THE INCIDENT AS THE FIRST IN WHICH "JEWISH ISRAELI CITIZENS JOINED AN ARAB TERRORIST GROUP." THE JOURNALISTS WERE KNOWN TO HAVE ACCEPTED FUNDS FROM THE DEMOCRATIC FRONT FOR THE LIBERATION OF PALESTINE, WHICH HAS BEEN ACCUSED OF TERRORIST ACTS.

08189 SHAMES, G.W.
ISRAEL: HARMONY PROVES ELUSIVE
THIRD WORLD WEEK, 7(9) (JAN 89), 68-69.
ISRAEL HAS MORE THAN SIXTY SMALL GRASSROOTS ORGANIZATIONS WORKING FOR BETTER RELATIONS BETWEEN THE NATION'S ARABS AND JEWS. UNDERSTAFFED AND OVERWORKED, THESE ORGANIZATIONS FACE AN UPHILL STRUGGLE, WHICH HAS BEEN COMPLICATED BY THE INTIFADAH. BEFORE THE UPRISING, COEXISTENCE ACTIVISTS RECEIVED LUKEWARM RESPONSES FROM MOST ISRAELIS. NOW THEY MEET CYNICISM, CONTEMPT, OR DESPAIR.

08190 SHAMES, G.W.
ISRAEL: WOMEN WARRIORS
THIRD WORLD WEEK, 8(10) (MAY 89), 73-74.
SINCE THE START OF THE INTIFADA, THOUSANDS OF PALESTINIAN WOMEN HAVE BEEN CATAPULTED TO VITAL, VISIBLE ROLES IN THE WORKPLACE AND ON THE BARRICADES. WHILE STATISTICS SHOW THAT THE ISRAELIS HAVE KILLED OR ARRESTED FAR FEWER WOMEN THAN MEN, THE NUMBERS PROVE THAT WOMEN ARE RISKING THEIR LIVES IN THE PALESTINIAN STRUGGLE. WOMEN HAVE PROVED TO BE EFFECTIVE COMMUNITY ORGANIZERS, FORMED CENTRAL COMMITTEES TO HELP PALESTINIAN FAMILIES. WITHIN THESE ORGANIZATIONS, THE STRUGGLE FOR PALESTINIAN NATIONAL LIBERATION HAS ECLIPSED THE FIGHT FOR WOMEN'S EQUALITY.

08191 SHAMPANSKY, J.R.
CONGRESSIONAL INVESTIGATORY POWER
CRS REVEIW, 10(3) (MAR 89), 28-30.
CHALLENGES TO CONGRESSIONAL PROBES HAVE RAISED QUESTIONS ABOUT THE SCOPE OF THE INVESTIGATORY POWER AND THE ROLE OF THE COURTS AND CRIMINAL LAW IN INFORMATION-ACCESS DISPUTES BETWEEN THE CONGRESS, ON THE ONE HAND, AND THE EXECUTIVE BRANCH AND PRIVATE PARTIES, ON THE OTHER.

08192 SHAN, S.; NING, L.
CUBA ADJUSTS ITS FOREIGN POLICY
BEIJING REVIEW, 32(21) (MAY 89), 15-16.
SINCE ITS REVOLUTION, CUBA HAS MAINTAINED CLOSE RELATIONS WITH THE SOVIET UNION. ALTHOUGH THE SOVIET UNION'S REFORM POLICIES HAVE SUBTLY CHANGED ITS RELATIONS WITH CUBA, THE TWO COUNTRIES HAVE STRESSED THAT THEIR RELATIONS ARE SOLID AND WILL NOT BE GREATLY AFFECTED BY TEMPORARY FLUCTUATIONS. CUBA IS SEEKING TO IMPROVE ITS RELATIONS WITH OTHER LATIN AMERICAN COUNTRIES AND HAS MADE SOME CONCESSIONS TOWARD RELAXING TENSIONS WITH THE USA.

08193 SHANDRO, A., M.
A MARXIST THEORY OF JUSTICE?
CANADIAN JOURNAL OF POLITICAL SCIENCE, XXII(1) (MAR 89), 27-48.
ABSTRACT. SOME RECENT MARXOLOGISTS (NOTABLY ALLEN BUCHANAN, RICHARD MILLER AND ALLEN WOOD) HAVE DENIED THAT THE IDEA OF JUSTICE CAN PLAY ANY SIGNIFICANT ROLE WITHIN MARXIST THOUGHT. THIS ARTICLE MAINTAINS, ON THE CONTRARY, THAT THE VERY LOGIC OF HISTORICAL MATERIALISM, NOTABLY THE CONCEPT OF THE HISTORICAL DEVELOPMENT OF HUMAN NEEDS, NECESSITATES A CONCEPT OF JUSTICE EVEN IN THE HIGHER PHASE OF COMMUNISM. FURTHERMORE, THE "ANTI-JURIDICAL" INTERPRETATION OF MARX FAILS TO PROVIDE AN ADEQUATE ACCOUNT OF THE CONNECTION BETWEEN THE COMMUNIST VALUES OF SELF-REALIZATION AND COMMUNITY. IT THEREFORE OBSCURES THE CONCERNS ADDRESSED BY A NOTION OF JUSTICE. THE EARLY MARX'S CONCEPT OF SPECIES-BEING (GATTUNGSWESEN) EXPRESSES THE RELATION BETWEEN SELF-REALIZATION AND COMMUNITY IN HISTORICAL TERMS. THUS IT PROVIDES AN APPROPRIATE CONTEXT FOR A MARXIST THEORY OF JUSTICE.

08194 SHANGQUAN, G.
CHINA'S ECONOMY AFTER TEN YEARS OF REFORM
CHINA RECONSTRUCTS, XXXVIII(1) (JAN 89), 13-14.
AFTER TEN YEARS OF ECONOMIC REFORM, CHINA HAS ENTERED A CRITICAL PERIOD OF TRANSITION FROM THE OLD SYSTEM TO THE NEW. VARIOUS ADJUSTMENTS ARE BEING MADE TO THE ECONOMIC STRUCTURE. THESE DO NOT REPRESENT A REJECTION OF THE REFORM PROCESS BUT ARE STRENGTHENING AND DEEPENING IT.

08195 SHANIN, T.
ETHNICITY IN THE SOVIET UNION: ANALYTICAL PERCEPTIONS AND POLITICAL STRATEGIES
COMPARATIVE STUDIES IN SOCIETY AND HISTORY, 31(3) (JUL 89), 409-424.
A MAJOR NEW UNDERSTANDING AND STRATEGY MUST BE RAPIDLY DEVELOPED IF THE ETHNIC DIVISIONS OF THE SOVIET UNION ARE TO BE ADDRESSED THROUGH THE POLITICAL PROCESS, RATHER THAN THROUGH BRUTE FORCE, WHICH WOULD FLY IN THE FACE OF EVERYTHING GORBACHEV IS TRYING TO ACHIEVE. IT IS CLEAR BY NOW THAT A MAJOR NEW PERCEPTION AND POLITICAL STRATEGY WILL

BE NECESSARY TO MEET THE SEVERITY OF THE ISSUE. IT CANNOT SIMPLY BE AN EPIPHENOMENON OF GENERAL ECONOMIC STRATEGIES AND SOCIAL REFORMS. A GENERAL FORMULA WILL NOT BE ENOUGH. THE DIVERSE CONDITIONS IN DIFFERENT REPUBLICS MUST BE ADDRESSED BOTH MATERIALLY AND COGNITIVELY. NOT ONLY MUST THE CENTRIFUGAL PRESSURES IN NON-RUSSIAN REPUBLICS BE TAKEN INTO ACCOUNT BUT ALSO THE SWELLING OF RUSSIAN NATIONALISM--THE FEELING OF "BEING DONE OUT OF ONE'S RIGHTS," WHICH IS POTENTIALLY MORE POWERFUL WHEN LINKED TO THE PERCEPTION OF THE UPSIDE-DOWN DEPENDENCY MODEL.

08196 SHANIN, T.
SOVIET ECONOMIC CRISIS: THE MOST IMMEDIATE STUMBLING BLOCK AND THE NEXT STEP
MONTHLY REVIEW, 41(5) (OCT 89), 18-21.
THIS ARTICLE EXPLORES THE FOUNDATION LAID FOR PERESTROIKA AND THE ORIGINAL VISION AND EXPECTED TRANSITIONAL PERIOD OF THE NEW ECONOMY. IT DESCRIBES THE ATTEMPTS OF THE SOVIET GOVERNMENT INEXPERIENCED IN THE HANDLING OF "OPEN MARKET" ECONOMICS TO REPAIR THE COLLAPSE OF THE MARKET FOR CONSUMER GOODS, THE POWER OF THE SOVIET MONOPOLISTIC MINISTRIES IS IDENTIFIED AS THE ANTI-PERESTROIKA OBSTACLE AND THE NEED TO ABOLISH THEM IS ADDRESSED.

08197 SHANKER, A.
VOUCHERS FOR THE AYATOLLAH?
CHURCH AND STATE, 42(6) (JUN 89), 20 (140)-21 (141).
RECENTLY BRITISH MUSLIMS HAVE APPLIED FOR GOVERNMENT AID TO THEIR SCHOOLS IN GREAT BRITAIN. BECAUSE OF THE SALMAN RUSHDIE AFFAIR, THEIR APPLICATION HAS RAISED A DIFFICULT ISSUE: SHOULD PUBLIC FUNDS GO TO PRIVATE SCHOOLS THAT MIGHT TEACH VALUES THAT CLASH WITH THE FUNDAMENTAL VALUES OF THE NATION?

08198 SHANNON, J.M.; DIETZ, C.K.
LICENSING HEALTH PROFESSIONALS: QUALITY, COMPETITIVE HEALTH CARE
JOURNAL OF STATE GOVERNMENT, 62(3) (MAY 89), 121-123.
PROFESSIONAL AND OCCUPATIONAL LICENSURE IN THE HEALTH CARE SYSTEM IS AWASH IN CONTROVERSY. CRITICS ARGUE THAT LICENSING FAILS TO PROTECT THE PUBLIC FROM INCOMPETENT PRACTITIONERS AND CREATES CONDITIONS ANTITHETICAL TO CONSUMERS' INTERESTS. PROPONENTS INSIST THAT SOCIETY BENEFITS FROM STATE REGULATION OF OCCUPATIONS. THE ISSUE CENTERS ON WHO IS MOST LIKELY TO BE PROTECTED, THE PUBLIC OR THE LICENSED PROFESSION, AND AT WHAT SOCIAL COST. IN LICENSING, STATES NEED TO PROTECT THE PUBLIC FROM UNQUALIFIED PRACTITIONERS WITHOUT LIMITING PRICE COMPETITION OR CONSUMER FREEDOM.

08199 SHANOR, D.
THE CHOICE FOR EAST GERMANY
NEW LEADER, LXXII(16) (OCT 89), 3-4.
EAST GERMANY'S RULING COMMUNIST PARTY IS FACING SOME DIFFICULT CHOICES. THE CONTINUING DECLINE OF THE ECONOMY, THE EXODUS OF THE CREAM OF THE CROP TO THE WEST, THE GROWING OPPOSITION, AND FREQUENT BLUNDERS SUCH AS THE OUTSPOKEN APPROVAL FOR THE POLICE REPRESSION OF DEMONSTRATORS IN CHINA ALL INDICATE THAT THE COMMUNIST MONOLITH IS CRACKING AT THE FOUNDATIONS. THE REPLACEMENT OF AGING LEADER ERICH HONECKER BY EGON KRENZ WILL PROBABLY NOT QUELL THE SMOULDERING RESENTMENT; KRENZ IS TOO READILY IDENTIFIED WITH THE POLICIES OF HIS PREDECESSOR. ADOPTING THE OPPOSITION'S PLATFORM OF DEMOCRACY, DIALOGUE, AND JUSTICE IS RAPIDLY BECOMING THE ONLY PRESCRIPTION FOR SURVIVAL OF THE COMMUNISTS.

08200 SHANOR, D. R.
FIGHTING HONECKER'S STAGNATION
NEW LEADER, LXXII(6) (MAR 89), 8-9.
SOVIET-STYLE REFORMS HAVE BEEN FAIRLY EFFECTIVELY BLOCKED IN EAST GERMANY BY PRESIDENT ERICH HONECKER AND HIS AGING LIEUTENANTS. BUT THERE ARE SIGNS THAT PERESTROIKA IS CAUSING STRAIN IN THE RULING SOCIALIST UNION PARTY, WITH YOUNGER AND MORE PRAGMATIC OFFICIALS URGING LIBERALIZATION. MEANWHILE, DISSIDENT PEACE ACTIVISTS ARE TAKING ADVANTAGE OF THIS STRESS WITHIN THE PARTY.

08201 SHAO, I.F.
CAN AFRICA FEED ITSELF: FACTORS OF FOOD INSECURITY
WORLD MARXIST REVIEW, 32(9) (SEP 89), 75-76.
THIS ARTICLE EXAMINES THE EXISTING FOOD SUPPLY IN TANZANIA. IT TRACES DIFFICULTIES SINCE INDEPENDENCE IN THE EARLY 1970S. THE REASONS FOR FOOD INSECURITY IN A COUNTRY ENDOWED WITH ABUNDANT HUMAN AND NATURAL RESOURCES ARE EXPLORED AND CALLED TO BE, NOT THE WEATHER, BUT ECONOMIC PLANNING AND MANAGEMENT FAILURES. THE INTERPLAY OF A CONGLOMERATE OF CLIMATIC, ECOLOGICAL, SOCIAL, ECONOMIC, CULTURAL, POLITICAL, AND ADMINISTRATIVE FACTORS ARE DETAILED.

08202 SHAOHUA, Y.
POLITICAL CRISIS IN SOUTH KOREA
BEIJING REVIEW, 32(44) (OCT 89), 14-16.

THE DEMANDS IN SOUTH KOREA FOR ROH TAE WOO'S RESIGNATION
HAVE NEVER STOPPED SINCE HE TOOK POWER. IN THE COMING YEARS,
ROH WILL FACE A STILL MORE DIFFICULT SITUATION AND WHETHER
HE CAN SURVIVE WILL BE DECIDED BY HOW HE DEALS WITH THE
PRESENT PROBLEMS AND THOSE WHICH ARISE IN THE FUTURE.

08203 SHAPIRA, A.
    LABOUR ZIONISM AND THE OCTOBER REVOLUTION
    JOURNAL OF CONTEMPORARY HISTORY, 24(4) (OCT 89), 623-656.
    PROBABLY NO SINGLE EVENT THAT OCCURRED OUTSIDE PALESTINE
EVOKED A RESPONSE QUITE AS IMPASSIONED OR AS VEHEMENT (BOTH
PRO AND CON) AS DID THE OCTOBER REVOLUTION. THE CENTRALITY
OF THE REVOLUTION IN THE CULTURAL AND IDEOLOGICAL FABRIC OF
JEWISH PALESTINE IS PARTICULARLY STRIKING WHEN ONE SURVEYS
THE MAINSTREAM CENTRE OF THE LABOR MOVEMENT IN PALESTINE,
WHICH ALWAYS STRESSED ITS INDEPENDENCE FROM THE SOVIET
REVOLUTION. THE LEADING TRIUMVIRATE OF THE AHDUT HA-AVODAH
PARTY (BERL KATZNELSON, DAVID BEN-GURION, AND YITZHAK
TABENKIN) EXEMPLIFY THE WAYS IN WHICH THE MAINSTREAM SOUGHT
TO COPE WITH THE REVOLUTION.

08204 SHAPIRO, A.
    CARLOS MENEM IN THE DRIVER'S SEAT
    NEW LEADER, LXXII(11) (JUL 89), 10-11.
    ARGENTINA'S PRESIDENT-ELECT CARLOS SAUL MENEM HAS
ELECTED INTO OFFICE BY AN ELECTORAL LANDSLIDE. ALTHOUGH BOTH
MILITARY AND LABOR GROUPS SEEM WILLING TO GIVE HIM A LITTLE
TIME AND SPACE TO ATTEMPT TO IMPLEMENT REFORMS, HE FACES
SIGNIFICANT CHALLENGES. THE MERE THREAT OF HIS ELECTION
CAUSED THE ARGENTINE ECONOMY TO FALL APART. MENEM ALSO FACES
THE THORNY ISSUE OF AMNESTY FOR MILITARY MEN CONVICTED OF
HUMAN RIGHTS ABUSES IN THE 1970'S. MOST OBSERVERS FEEL THE
CHANCE OF AN OUTRIGHT COUP IS SMALL, BUT A VIRTUAL COUP IN
MENEM'S NAME WHICH WOULD REDUCE THE PRESIDENT TO ALMOST
CAPTIVITY IS MUCH MORE LIKELY.

08205 SHAPIRO, A.
    MENEM'S DANGEROUS MANEUVERS
    NEW LEADER, LXXII(17) (NOV 89), 12-14.
    JUAN PERON WOULD HAVE DIFFICULTY RECOGNIZING THE FOUR-
MONTH-OLD "PERONIST" GOVERNMENT OF CARLOS SAUL MENEM. MENEM
HAS ATTEMPTED TO IMPLEMENT THE VERY ECONOMIC REFORMS THAT
WERE BLOCKED BY PERONISM THROUGHOUT THE SIX YEARS OF RAUL
ALFONSIN'S PRESIDENCY. MENEM HAS ALSO PARDONED MANY
POLITICAL PRISONERS, A MOVE THAT IS INTERPRETED DIFFERENTLY
BY DIFFERENT GROUPS; SOME VIEW IT AS A GENUINE ABANDONING OF
PAST TACTICS, WHILE OTHERS SEE IT AS A TRANSPARENT PLOY TO
GAIN SUPPORT OF THE ARMED FORCES. WHATEVER THE CASE, MENEM
IS TREADING ON THIN ICE AS MILITARY, LABOR, AND OTHER
FACTIONS JOCKEY FOR POWER.

08206 SHAPIRO, A.M.
    ARGENTINA AFTER VILLA MARTELLI
    NEW LEADER, LXXII(1) (JAN 89), 11-12.
    PRESIDENT RAUL ALFONSIN'S HANDLING OF THE VILLA MARTELLI
REBELLION WAS LESS THAN SATISFYING TO THE MOST FERVENT
DEFENDERS OF ARGENTINA'S CONSTITUTION, BUT IT WAS PROBABLY
THE BEST THAT COULD BE EXPECTED. SURPRISINGLY, THE EPISODE
SEEMS TO HAVE HAD SCANT IMPACT ON THE COURSE OF THE
PRESIDENTIAL CAMPAIGN.

08207 SHAPIRO, A.M.
    PRIVATIZING ARGENTINA
    NEW LEADER, LXXII(2) (JAN 89), 7-8.
    BIG GOVERNMENT AND BIG SPENDING HAVE BECOME A MAJOR
CAMPAIGN ISSUE IN ARGENTINA. DUE TO THE GROWING MILITANCY
AND POPULIST APPEALS OF THE PERONISTS, THE RADICALS ARE MORE
AND MORE PROCLAIMING THEMSELVES FISCAL CONSERVATIVES AND
ATTEMPTING VARIOUS INITIATIVES TO PRIVATIZE ELEMENTS OF THE
ECONOMY THAT HAVE LONG BEEN UNDER STATE CONTROL.

08208 SHAPIRO, A.M.
    WHY THE LEFT RUNS LAST IN ARGENTINA
    NEW LEADER, LXXII(3) (FEB 89), 10-12.
    ALTHOUGH ARGENTINA WOULD SEEM TO BE A GOOD BREEDING
GROUND FOR THE LEFT, IT IS NOT. EVEN LESS THAN AMERICANS,
ARGENTINES DO NOT PERCEIVE THE LEFT AS OFFERING VIABLE
SOLUTIONS TO THE NATION'S WOES. THE TRADITIONAL EXPLANATION
FOR THIS IS THAT THE LEFT'S APPEAL TO THE WORKERS HAS
THOROUGHLY COOPTED BY THE PERSONS.

08209 SHAPIRO, I.
    GROSS CONCEPTS IN POLITICAL ARGUMENT
    POLITICAL THEORY, 17(1) (FEB 89), 51-76.
    THE AUTHOR ARGUES THAT POLITICAL THEORISTS FREQUENTLY
THINK IN TERMS OF GROSS CONCEPTS: THEY REDUCE WHAT ARE
ACTUALLY RELATIONAL CLAIMS TO CLAIMS ABOUT ONE OR ANOTHER OF
THE COMPONENTS OF THE RELATION. THIS NOT ONLY OBSCURES THE
PHENOMENA THEY WISH TO ANALYZE, IT ALSO GENERATES DEBATES
THAT CAN NEVER BE RESOLVED BECAUSE THE ALTERNATIVES THAT ARE
OPPOSED TO ONE ANOTHER ARE VULNERABLE WITHIN THEIR OWN TERMS.
THE AUTHOR OFFERS A PAIR OF EXPLANATIONS FOR WHY GROSS
CONCEPTS PERSIST IN POLITICAL THEORY, AND SUGGESTS A WAY FOR
AVOIDING THEIR TRAP.

08210 SHAPIRO, I.
    THE DISPUTE OVER THE MINIMUM WAGE
    DISSENT, (WIN 89), 18-20.
    THE AUTHOR EVALUATES TWO ARGUMENTS--ONE OLD AND ONE NEW--
THAT HAVE BEEN RAISED IN OPPOSITION TO AN INCREASE IN THE
MINIMUM WAGE. THE OLD ARGUMENT IS THAT BY ARTIFICIALLY
RAISING THE COST OF LABOR, A MINIMUM-WAGE INCREASE WOULD
PRICE MANY WORKERS OUT OF JOBS. THE NEW ARGUMENT STATES THAT
IN LIEU OF A MINIMUM-WAGE INCREASE, ADJUSTMENTS IN THE TAX
CODE COULD TARGET ASSISTANCE TO LOW-WAGE WORKERS WITHOUT JOB
LOSSES.

08211 SHAPIRO, M.J.
    POLITICIZING ULYSSES: RATIONALISTIC, CRITICAL, AND
    GENEOLOGICAL COMMENTARIES
    POLITICAL THEORY, 17(1) (FEB 89), 9-32.
    HOMER'S ODYSSEY CONTINUES TO ATTRACT REWORKINGS, AND A
RECENT ONE BY A POLITICAL THEORIST, JON ELSTER, IS
PARTICULARLY INTERESTING BECAUSE IT EXEMPLIFIES BOTH A MAJOR
GENRE OF SOCIAL AND POLITICAL THOUGHT AND ONE OF MODERNITY'S
DOMINANT MODES FOR CONSTRUCTING THE PROBLEMATIC OF THE SELF
AND THE ORDER. ELSTER'S ANALYSIS IN HIS ULYSSES AND THE
SIRENS, TREATS ULYSSES AS A RATIONAL DECISION MAKER.
ALTHOUGH ELSTER'S COMMENTARY IS AIMED AT PROVIDING A
POLITICAL PEDAGOGY, THE APPROACH IS ULTIMATELY
DEPOLITICIZING, FOR AS IS ARGUED HERE, THE RATIONALITY
PROBLEMATIC, AS A MODE FOR THINKING THE SELF AND THE ORDER,
FAILS TO PROMOTE QUESTIONS ABOUT THE DISTRIBUTIONS OF THOSE
SPACES THAT ARE DEEMED ACCESSIBLE AND PROBLEMATIC ENOUGH TO
CALL FOR "DECISIONS," "POLICYMAKING," AND SO ON, AND IT
FAILS, IN ADDITION, TO RAISE QUESTIONS ABOUT THE IDENTITIES
OF THE SELVES GIVEN ELIGIBILITY TO OPERATE IN THESE SPACES.

08212 SHAPIRO, R.Y.; YOUNG, J.T.
    PUBLIC OPINION AND THE WELFARE STATE: THE UNITED STATES IN
    COMPARATIVE PERSPECTIVE
    POLITICAL SCIENCE QUARTERLY, 104(1) (SPR 89), 59-90.
    TO WHAT EXTENT DO CITIZENS OF THE USA AND OTHER
COUNTRIES PREFER PARTICULAR SOCIAL WELFARE POLICIES? HOW
HAVE THESE OPINIONS CHANGED OVER THE LAST 20 YEARS? WHAT
HAVE BEEN THE EFFECTS OF THESE PREFERENCES ON GOVERNMENT
POLICIES? THIS ARTICLE REVIEWS SOME OF THE EMPIRICAL ENGLISH
LANGUAGE LITERATURE THAT HAS DIRECTLY OR INDIRECTLY
CONSIDERED THESE MATTERS AND EXAMINES NATIONAL-LEVEL SURVEY
DATA.

08213 SHAPOURI, S.; ROSEN, S.
    EXPORT PERFORMANCE IN AFRICA
    AVAILABLE FROM NTIS, NO. PB89-194393/GAR, MAY 89, 39.
    AS THE SCARCITY OF FOREIGN EXCHANGE CONTINUES, AFRICA'S
EXPORT SECTOR MUST PLAY THE KEY ROLE IN GENERATING
INVESTMENT INCOME FOR AFRICA'S FINANCIAL RECOVERY. THE
AVERAGE ANNUAL INCREASE IN REAL EXPORT EARNINGS FOR THE
COUNTRIES INCLUDED IN THE STUDY WAS LESS THAN 1 PERCENT FROM
1980 TO 1986. ALONG WITH SLOW GROWTH, THE INSTABILITY OF
EXPORT EARNINGS HAS A DESTABILIZING EFFECT ON IMPORT
CAPACITY AND ECONOMIC GROWTH. THE COEFFICIENTS OF VARIATION
OF EXPORT EARNINGS AVERAGED ABOUT 26 PERCENT; AN INDEX OF
EXPORT SHORTFALLS AVERAGED ABOUT 10 PERCENT. COMMODITY
DIVERSIFICATION WAS FOUND TO BE A SIGNIFICANT FACTOR IN
IMPROVING EXPORT EARNINGS GROWTH AND REDUCING EXPORT
INSTABILITY. GIVEN THE SLOW MOVEMENT TOWARD DIVERSIFICATION,
THE PERFORMANCE OF PRIMARY COMMODITIES, ESPECIALLY PRICES,
AND IMPROVED GOVERNMENT INCENTIVES WILL REMAIN THE KEY
FACTORS IN AFRICA'S EXPORT AND ECONOMIC RECOVERY.

08214 SHARABI, H.
    THE INTIFADA AND THE DIASPORA
    MIDDLE EAST INTERNATIONAL, (365) (DEC 89), 20-21.
    THE ARTICLE ANALYZES THE EFFECT THAT THE INTIFADA HAS
HAD ON THE PALESTINIAN DIASPORA: PALESTINIANS LIVING OUTSIDE
OF THEIR TRADITIONAL HOMELAND. PERHAPS THE MOST SIGNIFICANT
EFFECT HAS BEEN THE TRANSFORMATION OF THE PLO FROM A SMALL,
ANNOYING, TERRORIST ORGANIZATION TO THE LEADER OF A PEOPLE
ENGAGED IN A HEROIC NATIONAL STRUGGLE. HOWEVER, AFTER THE
INTIAL, LANDMARK ANNOUNCEMENTS OF RECOGNITION OF ISREAL'S
RIGHT TO EXISTS AND RENUNCIATION OF TERRORISM, THE PLO HAS
NOT MADE ANY SIGNIFICANT PROGRESS. AS THE SECOND ANNIVERSARY
OF THE INTIFADA DREW NEAR, IT BECAME CLEAR THAT FRUSTRATION
AND ANGER, BOTH WITH THE US AND ISRAEL, AND THE PLO WAS ON
THE INCREASE.

08215 SHARKANSKY, I.
    ISRAELI CIVIL SERVICE OPEN TO POLITICAL APPOINTMENTS
    INTERNATIONAL JOURNAL OF PUBLIC ADMINISTRATION, 12(5)
    (1989), 731-748.
    THE INCIDENCE OF CIVIL SERVICE POSITIONS OPEN TO
POLITICAL APPOINTMENT IN ISRAEL IS HIGH BY THE STANDARDS OF
OTHER WESTERN DEMOCRACIES. MOREOVER, THERE MAY HAVE BEEN AN
INCREASE IN THE CRUDER FORMS OF PATRONAGE DURING THE CURRENT
NATIONAL UNITY GOVERNMENT. WITHOUT AN EFFECTIVE OPPOSITION,
BOTH MAJOR PARTIES MAY BE SHARING THE SPOILS. AMONG THE
FACTORS THAT MAY EXPLAIN THE GENERALLY HIGH INCIDENCE OF

ISRAELI CIVIL SERVICE POSITIONS OPEN TO POLITICAL
APPOINTMENT ARE: THE FAILURE TO HAVE DEVELOPED STRONG NORMS
OF NON-PARTISAN PROFESSIONALISM IN THE 40 YEARS OF
INDEPENDENCE: THE IMPORTANCE OF GOVERNMENT POSITIONS IN THE
NATIONAL ECONOMY; AND THE LACK OF A STRONG MAJORITY PARTY.

08216 SHARMA, B.; JAIN, H.C.
STRATEGIES FOR MANAGEMENT OF INDUSTRIAL RELATIONS IN INDIA
AND INDONESIA
ASIAN PROFILE, 17(6) (DEC 89), 523-532.
ONE OF THE MAJOR OBJECTIVES OF POLICY-MAKERS IN
DEVELOPING COUNTRIES HAS BEEN TO DEVELOP INDUSTRIAL
RELATIONS STRATEGIES TO FACILITATE INDUSTRIALIZATION AND
ECONOMIC DEVELOPMENT. SINCE SOCIAL PEACE IS A PREREQUISITE
FOR STIMULATING INVESTMENT AND GROWTH, THE MANAGEMENT OF
INDUSTRIAL CONFLICTS IS IMPORTANT IN THE THIRD WORLD.
AVOIDING OR RESOLVING CONFLICTS THROUGH APPROPRIATE
INSTITUTIONAL ARRANGEMENTS IS A MAJOR THRUST OF PUBLIC
POLICY IN MANY DEVELOPING COUNTRIES. BUT GOVERNMENTS VARY IN
THEIR ABILITY AND WILLINGNESS TO INSTITUTE INNOVATIVE
METHODS AND MECHANISMS FOR THE MANAGEMENT OF INDUSTRIAL
RELATIONS. THIS PAPER EXAMINES SUCH VARIATIONS, WITH SPECIAL
REFERENCE TO THE POLICIES OF INDIA AND INDONESIA.

08217 SHARMA, K.
OPENNESS, TRANSPARENCY, AND CONFIDENCE-BUILDING MEASURES
DISARMAMENT, XII(3) (AUT 89), 28-34.
THE TRADITIONAL DEFINITION OF CONFIDENCE-BUILDING
MEASURES HAS BEEN ENLARGED TO ENVISAGE THEM IN TERMS NOT OF
POTENTIAL DAMAGE CONTAINMENT ALONE BUT TO INCLUDE THE
PRINCIPLES OF HEALTHY RELATIONS BETWEEN STATES. IN THIS
ARTICLE, THE AUTHOR SURVEYS THE EVOLUTION OF THE DEFINITION
OF CONFIDENCE-BUILDING MEASURES AND THEIR IMPORTANCE IN
INTERNATIONAL RELATIONS.

08218 SHARMA, P.
NATION BUILDING IN SOUTH ASIA: THE CASE OF NEPAL
SOUTH ASIA JOURNAL, 2(3) (JAN 89), 251-270.
THE AUTHOR ATTEMPTS TO SEE HOW THE NATION-STATES IN
SOUTH ASIA ARE INSPIRED BY AND DERIVED FROM CONCEPTS OF
WESTERN NATION-STATES. IT FOCUSES ON NEPAL AND INDO-NEPAL
RELATIONS TO STUDY THE "LIFE-HISTORY" OF THE STATES IN SOUTH
ASIA. IT STUDIES THE FAIRLY DISTINCT PHASES OF THE INCEPTION
AT COLONIZATION, THE CARREER AS INCIPIENT NATION-STATES, AND
THE LATER TENDENCY TO SETTLE DOWN INTO WHAT MAY BE CALLED
"STATISM".

08219 SHARMA, R.N.
MAO'S CONCEPTS OF POWER, AUTHORITY AND LEGITIMACY
CHINA REPORT, 25(2) (APR 89), 135-145.
THIS ARTICLE DEALS WITH AN EPISTEMOLOGICAL EXAMINATION
OF MAO'S OBSERVATIONS REGARDING POWER, STRENGTH, FORCE,
MIGHT, AUTHORITY AND VIOLENCE. IT EXPLORES THE MARXIAN
CONCEPT OF POWER AND SHOWS A BLENDING OF POWER AND FORCE IN
MAO'S THOUGHT. IT EXAMINES MAO'S USE OF MASS ORIENTATION AND
THE POWER OF IDEAS. IT WRAPS UP WITH MAO'S CRITERIA OF
LEGITIMACY.

08220 SHARMA, T.R.
RAWLSIAN JUSTICE: DISJUNCTION BETWEEN CHOICE AND OBSERVANCE
INDIAN JOURNAL OF POLITICAL SCIENCE, L(1) (JAN 89), 28-48.
THE AUTHOR ENDEAVORS TO ASSESS THE EMPIRICAL VALIDITY OF
THE RAWLSIAN THEORY OF JUSTICE. HE CONSIDERS WHETHER IT IS
POSSIBLE TO BRING THE RAWLSIAN JUST SOCIETY INTO EXISTENCE
AND TO WHAT EXTENT EXISTING SOCIETIES CONFORM TO RAWLS'
SCHEME.

08221 SHARP, A.
WHAT BASIS DOES THE TREATY OF WAITANGI PROVIDE FOR
REASONING ABOUT JUSTICE IN NEW ZEALAND?
POLITICAL SCIENCE, 41(2) (DEC 89), 69-84.
THE TREATY OF WAITANGI IMPARTS A UNIQUE AND INDELIBLE
COLOR TO MORAL, LEGAL, AND POLITICAL REASONING IN
CONTEMPORARY NEW ZEALAND. MOST OBVIOUSLY, IT HAS COME TO
DOMINATE THE PRACTICE OF ARGUMENT AS TO JUSTICE BETWEEN
MAORI AND PAKEHA AND BETWEEN TE IWI MAORI AND THE GOVERNMENT.
IN ADDITION, CERTAIN OF THE EXTENSIVE INTERPRETATIONS OF
THE MEANING OF ITS PRINCIPLES HAVE FOUND APPLICATION WELL
BEYOND THAT LIMITED REALM AND ARE BEING APPLIED TO LARGER,
NATIONAL ISSUES.

08222 SHARP, G.
THE INTIFADAH AND NONVIOLENT STRUGGLE
JOURNAL OF PALESTINE STUDIES, 19(1) (FAL 89), 3-13.
THE INTIFIDAH HAS THUS FAR BEEN DISTINGUISHED ON THE
PALESTINIAN SIDE BY PREDOMINANTLY NONVIOLENT FORMS OF
STRUGGLE, AS WELL AS THE USE OF DEVELOPING SELF-RELIANT,
EDUCATIONAL, SOCIAL, ECONOMIC, AND POLITICAL INSTITUTIONS.
THIS ARTICLE STUDIES THE INTIFIDAH AND THE PALESTINIAN GOALS,
USING NONVIOLENCE AS A STRATEGY. THE PRESENT DANGERS OF
ESCALATION IN THE "LIMITED VIOLENCE" COMPONENT IS ANALYZED
AND THE NEED FOR A NEW APPROACH IS PRESENTED. IT CONCLUDES
THAT BY MAKING THE STRUGGLE 100 PERCENT NONVIOLENT, THE
PALESTINIANS WOULD BOTH REMOVE THE "JUSTIFICATION" FOR
ISRAELI REPRESSION AND INCREASE THEIR ACTUAL AND RELATIVE
POWER CAPACITY IN THE CONFLICT.

08223 SHAVER, S.
GENDER, CLASS AND THE WELFARE STATE: INCOME SECURITY IN
AUSTRALIA
SOCIALISM AND DEMOCRACY, (8) (SPR 89), 143-172.
THIS IS A STUDY OF THE SOCIALIZING PROCESS IN THE
INSTITUTIONAL LIFE OF AUSTRALIA. THE AUTHOR USES A
RIGOROUSLY SOCIOLOGICAL METHODOLOGY TO EVALUATE THE
RELATIONSHIP BETWEEN THE STRUGGLE FOR INCOME SECURITY AND
THE ADVANCEMENT OF SOCIALISM IN AUSTRALIA. THIS STUDY
PROVIDES A MODEL FOR STUDYING SOCIALIZING OTHER SOCIETY AS
WELL. THE STUDY CLAIMS THAT MORE THAN CLASS FACTORS PLAY A
ROLE IN MINIMAL SOCIALIZATIONS OF CAPITALIST INSTITUTIONS.

08224 SHAVER, S.
GENDER, CLASS, AND THE WELFARE STATE: THE CASE OF INCOME
SECURITY IN AUSTRALIA
FEMINIST REVIEW, (32) (SUM 89), 90-110.
WHEN FEMINISM HAS RAISED QUESTIONS ABOUT THE STATE,
THESE HAVE INVARIABLY ALSO RAISED QUESTIONS ABOUT CLASS AND
THE RELATIONSHIP BETWEEN GENDER AND CLASS. THE TRILOGY OF
TERMS INVOKES A TRIANGLE OF CONCEPTUAL RELATIONSHIPS. FOR
MOST OF ITS HISTORY, DISCUSSION OF THE WELFARE STATE HAS
PRIVILEGED THE RELATIONSHIP BETWEEN STATE AND CLASS. IT IS
ONLY IN THE LAST DECADE THAT FEMINISTS HAVE FORCED
RECOGNITION THAT THE WELFARE STATE IS ALSO DEEPLY IMPLICATED
IN A POLITICS OF GENDER. THERE HAVE BEEN RELATIVELY FEW
ATTEMPTS TO THEORIZE GENDER AND STATE INDEPENDENTLY OF CLASS;
FOR THE WELFARE STATE AT LEAST, THE POLITICS OF CLASS ARE
TOO SALIENT TO BE IGNORED. BUT NEITHER CAN GENDER SIMPLY BE
GRAFTED ONTO AN INDEPENDENTLY CONSTRUCTED ANALYSIS OF CLASS
AND STATE. THE TRILOGY OF CONCEPTS MUST BE REWORKED TOGETHER.
USING INCOME SECURITY IN AUSTRALIA AS AN ILLUSTRATIVE CASE,
THE AUTHOR OF THIS PAPER ATTEMPTS TO REWORK THE TRILOGY AND
APPLY HER FRAMEWORK TO THE CASE.

08225 SHAH, E.
THE LABOUR PARTY AND THE MILITANT TENDENCY
PARLIAMENTARY AFFAIRS, 42(2) (APR 89), 180-196.
THE ARTICLE EXAMINES THE EFFORTS OF THE TROTSKYIST
MILITANT TENDENCY TO USE THE TACTIC OF ENTRYISM TO GAIN
CONTROL OF AND "REVOLUTIONIZE" THE LABOUR PARTY. IT EXPLORES
THE ATTEMPTS OF THE LABOUR PARTY TO COMBAT THE GROUP AND
EXAMINES THE CONSTRAINTS UNDER WHICH THE LABOUR LEADERSHIP
OPERATED AND WHICH SO DRASTICALLY RESTRICTED ITS MARGIN OF
MANEUVER. IT ALSO CONSIDERS THE FACTORS THAT MADE THE SECOND
DRIVE AGAINST MILITANT MORE SUCCESSFUL THAN THE FIRST.

08226 SHAW, T.M.
THE REVIVAL OF REGIONALISM IN AFRICA: CURE FOR CRISIS OR
PRESCRIPTION FOR CONFLICT?
JERUSALEM JOURNAL OF INTERNATIONAL RELATIONS, 11(4) (DEC
89), 79-105.
THE POSITION AND PROSPECTS OF AFRICA IN AN UNEQUAL WORLD
ORDER POSE PROBLEMS FOR BOTH ANALYSIS AND ACTION, PERCEPTION
AND PREDICTION. THIS ARTICLE IS CONCERNED, THEREFORE, NOT
ONLY WITH THE COMPARATIVE STUDY OF TWO AFRICAN REGIONS, BUT
ALSO WITH ALTERNATIVE APPROACHES TO ANALYSIS AS WELL AS
ALTERNATIVE DEVELOPMENT STRATEGIES. IN PARTICULAR, IT WILL
CONSIDER AND CONTRAST BOTH THE MORE "ORTHODOX" AND "RADICAL"
MODES OF ANALYSIS AND MODES OF PRODUCTION, TAKING INTO
ACCOUNT THE INTERRELATIONSHIP BETWEEN THEORY AND POLICY. THE
PARADOXES AND DILEMMAS OF AFRICA'S ROLE IN THE WORLD SYSTEM
ARE RELEVANT TO THE COMPARATIVE ANALYSIS OF REGIONALISM, TO
COMPARATIVE EXPLANATIONS OF INTEGRATION, AND TO COMPARATIVE
POLICY CHOICES. THEY ALSO INFORM CONTRASTS BETWEEN ECOWAS
AND SADCC AS CASE STUDIES.

08227 SHE, Z.
IN MEMORY OF HU YAOBANG
CHINA RECONSTRUCTS, XXXVIII(7) (JUL 89), 24-29.
THE AUTHOR EULOGIZES CHINESE LEADER HU YAOBANG, WHO DIED
ON APRIL 15, 1989. HU PARTICIPATED IN THE EARLY STRUGGLES OF
THE CHINESE COMMUNIST PARTY AND WAS PART OF THE RED ARMY'S
FAMOUS LONG MARCH IN 1934. FROM 1982 TO 1987 HE WAS
COMMUNIST PARTY GENERAL SECRETARY.

08228 SHEARER, S.B.
THE DOMESTIC ECONOMICS AND INTERNATIONAL POLITICS OF
POSTWAR U.S. TRADE POLICY, 1945-1980. CASE STUDY: JAPAN
DISSERTATION ABSTRACTS INTERNATIONAL, 49(9) (MAR 89),
2797-A.
THE AUTHOR PROBES AMERICAN TRADE POLICY FORMULATION IN
THE POSTWAR PERIOD, FOCUSING ON HOW IT WAS AFFECTED BY THE
STRATEGIC ENVIRONMENT, AMERICA'S ECONOMIC STATUS, PROBLEMS
OF POLICY-MAKING, AND INTEREST GROUP NEEDS. CONGRESSIONAL
AND EXECUTIVE RESPONSES TO THE CHANGING TRADE ENVIRONMENT
ARE EXAMINED. US-JAPANESE TRADE IS USED AS A CASE STUDY.

08229 SHEARMAN, P.
GORBACHEV AND THE RESTRUCTURING OF SOVIET-CUBAN RELATIONS
JOURNAL OF COMMUNIST STUDIES, 5(4) (DEC 89), 63-82.

THE SOVIET UNION AND CUBA HAVE DEVELOPED CLOSE TIES
DURING THE PAST 30 YEARS. HOWEVER, AT TIMES BILATERAL
RELATIONS HAVE BEEN TENSE DUE TO DIFFERENT PERSPECTIVES ON
IMPORTANT INTERNATIONAL ISSUES. THE RELATIONSHIP IS
DETERMINED BY A MIXTURE OF INTERNATIONAL FACTORS, IDEOLOGY
AND DOMESTIC POLICIES. AT A TIME OF UNPRECEDENTED AND
RADICAL CHANGES IN OVERALL INTERNATIONAL SYSTEMIC STABILITY
AND SOVIET IDEOLOGY, AND WITH THE RESTRUCTURING OF THE
SOVIET ECONOMY AND POLITICAL SYSTEM FOLLOWING THE EMERGENCE
OF A NEW LEADERSHIP IN THE KREMLIN, SOVIET-CUBAN RELATIONS
HAVE ENTERED A NEW PHASE. SOVIET REFORMISM HAS UNLEASHED A
WAVE OF CHANGE THROUGHOUT THE COMMUNIST WORLD. AS PART OF
THIS WORLD, CUBA TOO IS AFFECTED, BUT THERE IS STRONG CUBAN
ANTIPATHY TO MANY OF THE IDEAS AND POLICIES CURRENTLY BEING
ARTICULATED AND ENACTED IN THE USSR.

08230 SHEATE, W.R.; MACRORY, R.B.
    AGRICULTURE AND THE EC ENVIRONMENTAL ASSESSMENT DIRECTIVE:
    LESSONS FOR COMMUNITY POLICY-MAKING
    JOURNAL OF COMMON MARKET STUDIES, XXVIII(1) (SEP 89),
    68-81.
    THE 1985 EC DIRECTIVE ON ENVIRONMENTAL ASSESSMENT
INTRODUCES A COMMON SET OF DECISION-MAKING PROCEDURES
THROUGHOUT THE COMMUNITY FOR AUTHORIZING SPECIFIED CLASSES
OF LAND-USE PROJECTS. DURING THE DEVELOPMENT OF THE
DIRECTIVE, PROJECTS INVOLVING AGRICULTURAL INTENSIFICATION
RECEIVED A HIGH PROFILE BUT WERE MARGINALIZED IN THE FINAL
TEXT, IN NO SMALL PART DUE TO OPPOSITION BY THE UNITED
KINGDOM. EVEN THEN, IMPLEMENTATION OF THE DIRECTIVE IN THE
UNITED KINGDOM IN RESPECT OF AGRICULTURE HAS PROVED
PECULIARLY TROUBLESOME, NOT LEAST BECAUSE OF PRESUMPTIONS
FIRMLY ENTRENCHED IN THE COUNTRY'S LONG-ESTABLISHED LAND-USE
PLANNING SYSTEM. THE HISTORY OF THE DIRECTIVE AND ITS EFFECT
IN ONE COUNTRY HAS WIDER IMPLICATIONS FOR THE FUTURE
DEVELOPMENT OF COMMUNITY ENVIRONMENTAL POLICY, PARTICULARLY
IN THE LIGHT OF CURRENT CONCERNS TO SECURE MORE EFFECTIVE
POLICY INTEGRATION IN AREAS HITHERTO LARGELY UNAFFECTED BY
SUCH CONSIDERATIONS.

08231 SHEEHAN, K.P.
    PREPARING FOR AN IMAGINARY WAR? EXAMINING PEACETIME
    FUNCTIONS AND CHANGES OF ARMY DOCTRINE
    DISSERTATION ABSTRACTS INTERNATIONAL, 49(10) (APR 89),
    3144-A.
    IN RECENT TIMES, THE U.S. ARMY HAS CHANGED ITS
OPERATIONAL AND TACTICAL DOCTRINE ON A NUMBER OF OCCASIONS--
MOST NOTABLY IN THE CASES OF THE PENTOMIC DIVISION CONCEPT
(1956), THE ACTIVE DEFENSE (1976), AND THE AIR-LAND BATTLE
(1982). THIS DISSERTATION EXAMINES THE PROCESS OF DOCTRINAL
CHANGE IN EACH OF THESE THREE CASES ALONG WITH THE FAILURE
OF THE U.S. ARMY TO ADOPT METHODS COMPATIBLE WITH THE
PHILOSOPHY OF CLASSIC COUNTERINSURGENCY DURING THE VIETNAM
CONFLICT. DOCTRINAL CHANGES MAY BE THE RESULT OF CHANGES IN
THE ARMY AS AN ORGANIZATION. CHANGES IN MILITARY REALITIES,
THE INTERVENTION OF CIVILIAN POLICY MAKERS, OR
ORGANIZATIONAL DETERMINISM.

08232 SHEEHAN, M.
    THE PLACE OF THE BALANCER IN BALANCE OF POWER THEORY
    REVIEW OF INTERNATIONAL STUDIES, 15(2) (APR 89), 123-134.
    THE BASIC FUNCTION OF THE BALANCER IS TO PREVENT THE
OCCURRENCE OF A PERMANENT DISEQUILIBRIUM IN THE
INTERNATIONAL SYSTEM, THAT IS THE EXISTENCE OF A SITUATION
IN WHICH ONE STATE OR ALLIANCE IS ABLE TO EXERCISE A
HEGEMONY OVER THE OTHERS, OR EVEN TO ESTABLISH AN IMPERIUM.
ALL VARIATIONS OF THE BALANCE OF POWER SYSTEM HAVE THIS
BASIC FUNCTION, THAT IS, THE PRESERVATION OF A SYSTEM BASED
UPON NUMEROUS SOVEREIGN STATES. THE PRESENCE OF A 'BALANCER',
THAT IS A STATE OR GROUP OF STATES SPECIFICALLY COMMITTED
TO THE MAINTENANCE OF SUCH A BALANCE, IS SIMPLY ONE OF
SEVERAL MEANS TO THAT PARTICULAR END. THE AIM OF THIS PAPER
THEREFORE IS TO TRY TO CLARIFY THE NATURE AND FUNCTION OF
THE BALANCER BY SYNTHESIZING THE VIEWS OF ANALYSTS OF THE
ROLE OVER THE PAST THREE CENTURIES TO PRODUCE A PARADIGM OF,
THE BALANCER STRATEGY.

08233 SHEEHAN, M.A.
    COMPARATIVE COUNTERINSURGENCY STRATEGIES: GUATEMALA AND EL
    SALVADOR
    CONFLICT, 9(2) (1989), 127-154.
    THE AUTHOR REVIEWS THE COUNTERINSURGENCY EXPERIENCES OF
GUATEMALA AND EL SALVADOR IN THE 1980S. PART I LOOKS AT
THEIR UNIQUE GEOGRAPHICAL, ETHNIC, AND INSTITUTIONAL
VARIANCES IN THE CONTEXT OF INSURGENCY. PART II ASSESSES THE
DIFFERENT COUNTERINSURGENCY STRATEGIES EMPLOYED BY EACH. EL
SALVADOR DEVELOPED A PREDOMINANTLY MILITARY STRATEGY FOUNDED
ON COMBAT FIREPOWER AND "MANEUVER," WHILE GUATEMALA OPTED
FOR A STRATEGY OF "POSITION" THAT SPREAD COUNTERINSURGENCY
UNITS THROUGHOUT THE COUNTRYSIDE, SUPPORTED BY AN INTEGRATED
PLAN OF CIVIC ACTION, CIVIL DEFENSE, AND PSYCHOLOGICAL
OPERATIONS. SUGGESTIONS ARE PRESENTED FOR THE REEVALUATION
OF SALVADORAN COUNTERINSURGENCY STRATEGY, AND THE CONTINUING
CHALLENGE OF INSTABILITY IN GUATEMALA IS PROJECTED.

08234 SHEFF, D.
    AN INTERVIEW WITH DANIEL ELLSBERG: U.S. FOREIGN POLICY IN
    VIETNAM AND NOW
    BULLETIN OF CONCERNED ASIAN SCHOLARS, 21(2-4) (APR 89),
    94-99.
    THIS INTERVIEW TOOK PLACE IN DECEMBER 1987 AND MR.
ELLSBERG PROVIDED AN AFTERWARD WRITTEN IN JULY 1989 TO TOUCH
ON SOME OF THE DEVELOPMENTS SINCE THEN. THE EDITORS FEEL
THAT THE BASIC POINTS MADE IN THE INTERVIEW ARE AS VALID
TODAY AS THEY WERE TWO YEARS AGO. MR. ELLSBERG MAKES THE
FOLLOWING POINTS: 1) THAT THE AMERICANS WERE THE ENEMY IN
THE VIETNAM WAR AND IS DOING THE SAME THING TODAY IN CENTRAL
AMERICA. 2) HOW THINGS HAVE CHANGED SINCE THE PENTAGON
PAPERS WERE RELEASED, 3) NICARAGUA IS A REPEAT OF VIETNAM 4)
THE U.S. GOVERNMENT IS ORGANIZING AN OPERATION RESPONSIBLE
FOR A HUGE PERCENTAGE OF ALL THE DRUGS COMING IN FROM
CENTRAL AMERICA, 5) THE REASONS FOR HIS CHANGE IN THINKING
ABOUT THE U.S. AND VIETNAM.

08235 SHELL, D.
    THE BRITISH CONSTITUTION IN 1988
    PARLIAMENTARY AFFAIRS, 42(3) (JUL 89), 287-301.
    IN GREAT BRITAIN THE ANNIVERSARY OF THE 1688-89
"GLORIOUS REVOLUTION" WAS CELEBRATED DURING 1988 IN A MUTED
MANNER BECAUSE OF CONTINUING CONTROVERSY OVER THE GROWTH OF
AN AUTHORITARIAN GOVERNMENT. IN SOME CASES MINISTERS CAN
DEFEND AT LEAST PART OF WHAT THEY ARE DOING ON LIBERAL
GROUNDS, BUT TAKEN AS A WHOLE THE LEGISLATION ON OFFICIAL
SECRECY AND SECURITY SERVICES, ALONG WITH NUMEROUS OTHER
DECISIONS OF GOVERNMENT, HAS A PROFOUNDLY ILLIBERAL TONE, AS
EVEN A PERFUNCTORY ANALYSIS INDICATES. THIS ARTICLE EXAMINES
OFFICIAL SECRECY, HOW THE PRIME MINISTER'S TEAM IS CHOSEN
AND MANAGED, THE OPPOSITION PARTIES AND TELEVISING THE
COMMONS.

08236 SHELLEY, F.M.; ARCHER, J.C.
    SECTIONALISM AND PRESIDENTIAL POLITICS: VOTING PATTERNS IN
    ILLINOIS, INDIANA, AND OHIO
    JOURNAL OF INTERDISCIPLINARY HISTORY, XX(2) (AUT 89),
    227-255.
    THE AUTHORS EXAMINE PRESIDENTIAL ELECTION RETURNS AT THE
COUNTY LEVEL FOR ILLINOIS, INDIANA, AND OHIO FROM 1868 TO
1984. TIME-SERIES FACTOR ANALYSIS IS USED TO STUDY SUCH
QUESTIONS AS: ARE PRESIDENTIAL POLITICS IN THESE THREE
STATES CHARACTERIZED BY SECTIONAL DISTINCTIONS? TO WHAT
EXTENT HAVE THE NINETEENTH-CENTURY SECTIONAL CLEAVAGES
CHANGED? HOW CLOSELY DO THESE CHANGES PARALLEL CHANGES IN
ELECTORAL PATTERNS THAT HAVE OCCURRED ON A NATIONAL SCALE?

08237 SHELLEY, L.I.
    HUMAN RIGHTS AS AN INTERNATIONAL ISSUE
    PHILADELPHIA: ANLS OF AMER ACHY OF POLITICAL AND SOC
    SCIENCE, (506) (NOV 89), 42-56.
    THIS ARTICLE FOCUSES ON THE CHANGE IN THE
CONCEPTUALIZATION OF HUMAN RIGHTS IN LATIN AMERICA AND THE
SOVIET UNION AND THE CURRENT PRIORITY GIVEN IN THESE AREAS
TO THE ISSUE OF HUMAN RIGHTS. IT ALSO FOCUSES ON THE UTILITY
OF THE HUMAN RIGHTS ISSUE FOR THESE COUNTRIES. THE DYNAMICS
IN THE HUMAN RIGHTS ARENA HAVE CHANGED IN THE 1980S, BUT
THERE IS NO GUARANTEE THAT THE PRESENT CONDITIONS WILL
CONTINUE.

08238 SHEMELIN, Y.; SREVYRKOVA, O.
    NON-TRADITIONAL FORMS OF TRADE AND ECONOMIC TIES WITH PERU:
    DEVELOPMENT TRENDS.
    FOREIGN TRADE, 10 (1988), 34-36.
    THIS ARTICLE EXAMINES SOVIET-PERUVIAN TRADE AND ECONOMIC
RELATIONS WHICH HAVE BEEN DEVELOPING SINCE THE LATE 1960S.
IT TRACES ITS GROWTH DURING THE SEVENTIES AND EARLY EIGHTIES
AND THEN EXPLORES THE DECLINE OF TRADE SINCE THE MID-1980S.
THE NECESSITY OF CHANGE TO NON-TRADITIONAL FORMS OF
COOPERATION IS DETAILED.

08239 SHENZHI, L.
    REALITY, NOT DOGMA
    WORLD MARXIST REVIEW, 32(8) (AUG 89), 23-25.
    THIS ARTICLE IS A REPORT ON THE FIRST SOVIET-CHINESE
SUMMIT MEETING IN 30 YEARS. THE EXCHANGE OF VIEWS BETWEEN
LEADERS ARE IN CONCERT WITH THE LONG TERM INTERESTS OF BOTH
PEOPLES, AND THEY PROMOTE UNIVERSAL PEACE AND SECURITY.
EXPLORED ARE SINO-SOVIET RELATIONS, MARXIST-LENINIST
IDEOLOGY, THE PERIOD OF THE FOUR MODERNISATIONS IN CHINA,
AND THE OBJECTIVES OF CHINA'S POLITICAL REFORMS.

08240 SHEPARD, W. E.
    ISLAM AS A "SYSTEM" IN THE LATER WRITINGS OF SAYYID ZUTB
    MIDDLE EASTERN STUDIES, 25(1) (JAN 89), 31-50.
    IN THIS ARTICLE THE AUTHOR DEALS WITH AN INFLUENTIAL
REPRESENTATIVE OF ISLAMIC FUNDAMENTALISM, THE EGYPTIAN
WRITER SAYYID QUTB, WHOSE LATER WRITINGS PRESENT VIEWS
SIMILAR TO THOSE OF MAWDUDI AND ARE, INDEED, INFLUENCED BY
HIM, AND IN WHICH THE IDEA OF ISLAM AS A SYSTEM IS NO LESS
PROMINENT. THE AUTHOR SPELLS OUT IN JUST WHAT SENSE LUTB
CONSIDERS ISLAM A SYSTEM AND SHOWS HOW THIS IDEA UNDERGIRDS

AND ILLUMINES CERTAIN OTHER ASPECTS OF HIS THOUGHT, SUCH AS HIS PARTICULAR COMBINATION OF RIGIDITY AND FLEXIBILITY, AND HOW IT MAY HELP TO EVALUATE THE RELATION BETWEEN 'TRADITION' AND 'MODERNITY' IN HIS THINKING. THE AUTHOR ALSO TO ILLUSTRATES SOME OF THE REASONS WHY LUTB'S THINKING HAS CONSIDERABLE APPEAL AMONG MUSLIMS TODAY.

08241 SHEPERD, R.
SOCIOECONOMIC CHANGE IN FAR-WEST NEPAL: A TOWN IN THE DOTI VALLEY
ASIAN SURVEY, XXIX(6) (JUN 89), 573-579.
THE ARTICLE BRIEFLY EXAMINES THE ECONOMIC AND SOCIAL IMPACT UPON LOCAL SOCIETY BROUGHT ABOUT BY THE OPENING OF A SEASONAL ROAD LINK IN THE FAR-WEST DEVELOPMENT REGION OF NEPAL. SINCE THE OPENING OF THE ROAD, THE TOWN HAS BECOME THE MOST IMPORTANT TRADING CENTER IN THE FAR-WEST DISTRICT, BUT THE ARTICLE CONCLUDES THAT THE CITIZENS OF THE AREA HAVE YET TO BENEFIT FROM THE NEW ECONOMIC ACTIVITY AND MAY HAVE BEEN NEGATIVELY AFFECTED.

08242 SHEPHARD, R.; GOLDMAN, C.
P.W. BOTHA'S FOREIGN POLICY
NATIONAL INTEREST, (15) (SPR 89), 68-78.
THE ARTICLE FOCUSES ON THE FOREIGN POLICY OF SOUTH AFRICAN PRESIDENT R. W. BOTHA. IT GIVES AS BACKGROUND THE FACTORS THAT LED TO THE ASCENDANCY OF BOTHA AND DEMONSTRATES HOW HE CONSOLIDATED HIS POWER BASE ONCE HE REACHED OFFICE. IT ALSO ANALYZES HIS POLICY WITH REGARDS TO REGIONAL ISSUES SUCH AS THE AFRICAN HOMELANDS AND RELATIONS WITH NEIGHBORING MOZAMBIQUE, NAMIBIA AND ZIMBABWE. HIS RESPONSE TO INTERNATIONAL PRESSURE MAINFESTED IN THE FORM OF TRADE SANCTIONS IS ALSO EXAMINED. BOTHA WAS ABLE TO SUCCESSFULLY PLAY OFF STATE'S INTERESTS AGAINST EACH OTHER TO MAINTAIN AND EXPAND SOUTH AFRICAN TRADE. THE ARTICLE INCLUDES THAT ALTHOUGH SOME OF BOTHA'S POLICIES WERE EXTREME BY ANY STANDARD, HE HAS DEALT WITH SOUTH AFRICA'S UNIQUE CIRCUMSTANCES AS WELL AS COULD BE EXPECTED.

08243 SHEPHERD, J.
FOOD AID AS AN INSTRUMENT OF U.S. FOREIGN POLICY: THE CASE OF ETHIOPIA, 1982-1984 (VOLUME 1 OF 2)
DISSERTATION ABSTRACTS INTERNATIONAL, 49(11) (MAY 89), 3499-A.
UNITED STATES' FOOD AID IS INHERENTLY POLITICAL, NOT HUMANITARIAN, AND IS USED TO FURTHER THE POLITICAL INTERESTS OF THE STATE. USING ETHIOPIA AS A CASE STUDY, THIS DISSERTATION EXPLORES THE POLITICAL HISTORY OF THE USE OF FOOD AS AN INSTRUMENT OF AMERICAN FOREIGN POLICY.

08244 SHER, G.
THREE GRADES OF SOCIAL INVOLVEMENT
PHILOSOPHY AND PUBLIC AFFAIRS, 18(2) (SPR 89), 133-157.
ONE MAY AGREE THAT SHARED EXPERIENCE AND FRATERNAL CONCERN ARE VALUABLE WHILE STILL MAINTAINING A RECOGNIZABLY INDIVIDUALISTIC STANCE. TO DO SO, ONE NEED ONLY INSIST THAT THE REASON SHARED EXPERIENCE AND FRATERNITY ARE VALUABLE IS THAT THEY ENRICH THE LIVES OF INDIVIDUALS. GIVEN THIS POSSIBILITY, THE DEEPER ISSUE EVIDENTLY CONCERNS THE NATURE OF THE BASIC MORAL UNIT--OF THE TYPE OF ENTITY WITH WHICH MORALITY IS ULTIMATELY CONCERNED. ACCORDING TO ONE FAMILIAR TRADITION, SUCH ENTITIES ARE THE PHYSICALLY DISCRETE, PSYCHOLOGICALLY CONTINUOUS PERSONS WHO REASON AND ACT. BUT OTHERS REGARD THE INDIVIDUAL AS FAR TOO DEEPLY IMPLICATED IN HIS SOCIAL AND CULTURAL ENVIRONMENT TO BE MORALLY BASIC. ACCORDING TO THESE THINKERS, SOCIETY IS IN SOME SENSE MORALLY PRIOR TO ITS MEMBERS. THIS ARTICLE EXAMINES WHAT SEEM THE MOST IMPORTANT OF THE ANTI-INDIVIDUALIST ARGUMENTS. THESE ARGUMENTS, THE AUTHOR CONTENDS ARE UNIFORMLY UNSUCCESSFUL.

08245 SHERMAN, A.
ALGERIA: AN INTELLECTUAL FASHION REVISITED
WORLD TODAY, 45(1) (JAN 89), 8-10.
THE RECENT RIOTS IN ALGERIA MARK A TURNING POINT IN THAT COUNTRY'S EVOLUTION AFTER A QUARTER-CENTURY OF INDEPENDENCE. THEY ALSO CALL INTO QUESTION THE INTELLECTUAL FASHIONS OF THE 1960'S AND 1970'S, WHICH PLAYED A LARGE PART IN THE CREATION OF AN INDEPENDENT MOSLEM ALGERIA. THEY THROW NEW LIGHT ON THE UNDERLYING ASSUMPTIONS OF "THIRD WORLDISM" AND INDICATE THE NEED FOR AN ASSESSMENT OF THE ROLE OF ISLAMIC POLITICAL CULTURE IN THE EVOLUTION OF MOSLEM STATES.

08246 SHERMAN, H.
THEORIES OF ECONOMIC CRISIS: DEMAND-SIDE, SUPPLY-SIDE AND PROFIT SQUEEZE.
SCIENCE AND SOCIETY, 53(1) (SPR 89), 62-70.
THE ARTICLE ANALYZES A RECENT SERIES OF ARTICLES, SOME WHICH UTILIZE A SUPPLY-SIDE APPROACH TO ECONOMICS, SOME A DEMANDSIDE APPROACH. IT EXPLAINS AND CRITICIZES EACH THEORY AND PRESENTS A THIRD, ALTERNATE THEORY OF PROFIT SQUEEZE TO EXPLAIN THE COMPLEX ECONOMIC INTERACTIONS THAT THE SIMPLISTIC THEORIES OF SUPPLY-SIDE AND DEMAND-SIDE MARXISM TEND TO OBSCURE.

08247 SHERMAN, S.
ISRAEL IN THE DOCK
MIDDLE EAST INTERNATIONAL, 356 (AUG 89), 10-11.
AS THE INTIFADA CONTINUES IN OCCUPIED PALESTINE AMID EVER MORE REPRESSIVE ISRAELI MEASURES TO CONTROL IT, A GATHERING OF INTERNATIONAL LAWYERS, POLITICIANS AND OTHER MIDDLE EAST EXPERTS TOOK PLACE IN LONDON ON 25 JULY. THE SYMPOSIUM SOUGHT PRACTICAL OPTIONS WITHIN THE BRITISH LEGAL AND POLITICAL CONTEXT FOR ENFORCING THE APPLICATION OF THE FOURTH GENEVA CONVENTION BY ISRAEL IN THE OCCUPIED TERRITORIES. THIS ARTICLE DETAILS THE RESULTS OF THIS SYMPOSIUM.

08248 SHERMAN, S.
THATCHER NOT SATISFIED
MIDDLE EAST INTERNATIONAL, (351) (MAY 89), 8.
ISRAELI PRIME MINISTER SHAMIR'S ATTEMPTS TO CONVINCE THE BRITISH GOVERNMENT OF THE BENEFICIAL NATURE OF HIS PEACE PROPOSALS BORE NO FRUIT DESPITE A PERSONAL VISIT TO LONDON. BOTH PRIME MINISTER MARGARET THATCHER AND FOREIGN MINISTER SIR GEOFFREY HOWE EXPRESSED THEIR "DISSATISFACTION" WITH THE PROPOSALS AND THEIR UNWILLINGNESS TO ENDORSE THEM WITHOUT FURTHER CLARIFICATION.

08249 SHERMAN, S.; HAERI, S.; JABER, N.
THE SATANIC VERSES: KHOMEINI'S "FATWA" AND THE WEST
MIDDLE EAST INTERNATIONAL, (345) (MAR 89), 9-11.
THE AUTHOR LOOKS AT THE INTERNATIONAL CONSEQUENCES OF THE AYATOLLAH KHOMEINI'S ATTACK ON SALMON RUSHDIE AND THE SEVERING OF BRITISH-IRANIAN DIPLOMATIC RELATIONS.

08250 SHERMAN, S.; HAERI, S.
THE SLAYING OF ABD AL-RAHMAN QASSEMLOU
MIDDLE EAST INTERNATIONAL, 355 (JUL 89), 12.
ABD AL-RAHMAN QASSEMLOU, LEADER OF THE KURDISTAN DEMOCRATIC PARTY OF IRAN (KDPI), WAS SHOT DEAD IN VIENNA ON 14 JULY. MYSTERY SURROUNDS QASSEMLOU'S DEATH. HIS ASSASSINS, IT APPEARS, BURST IN ON A MEETING BETWEEN THE KDPI AND A REPRESENTATIVE OF THE IRANIAN GOVERNMENT, PRESUMABLY DISCUSSING FURTHER MOVES TOWARDS RECONCILIATION. SUBSEQUENTLY, THE KILLINGS WERE BLAMED ON IRAN BY BOTH THE MUJAHIDEEN AND THE KDPI.

08251 SHESTACK, J.J.
HUMAN RIGHTS, THE NATIONAL INTEREST, AND U.S. FOREIGN POLICY
PHILADELPHIA: ANLS OF AMER ACMY OF POLITICAL AND SOC SCIENCE, (506) (NOV 89), 17-29.
FOREIGN POLICY DECISIONS ARE DRIVEN BY CONCEPTIONS OF THE NATIONAL INTEREST. IT SERVES THE NATIONAL INTEREST OF THE UNITED STATES TO PURSUE HUMAN RIGHTS GOALS BECAUSE THEY ADVANCE OUR SECURITY INTERESTS; HELP ESTABLISH A SYSTEM OF WORLD ORDER BASED ON THE ASPIRATIONS OF PEOPLE AND ON THE RULE OF LAW; ARE GEOPOLITICALLY ADVANTAGEOUS BY FURTHERING PEACEFUL EVOLUTIONARY DEMOCRATIZATION OF STATES; AND COMMAND POPULAR SUPPORT, AS THEY REFLECT FUNDAMENTAL VALUES OF THE AMERICAN PEOPLE. NONETHELESS, HUMAN RIGHTS HAD VIRTUALLY NO ROLE IN U.S. FOREIGN POLICY UNTIL THE CARTER ADMINISTRATION. PRESIDENT CARTER MADE HUMAN RIGHTS A KEY FOCUS OF U.S. FOREIGN POLICY. WHEN THE REAGAN ADMINISTRATION BEGAN, IT DENIGRATED HUMAN RIGHTS POLICY, SUPPORTING MANY REPRESSIVE AUTHORITARIAN STATES. GRADUALLY, THE REAGAN ADMINISTRATION TOOK A MORE POSITIVE STANCE TOWARD HUMAN RIGHTS, LARGELY ACCEPTING THE CARTER ADMINISTRATION'S HUMAN RIGHTS POLICIES BY THE END OF THE REAGAN YEARS.

08252 SHETH, D.L.
NATION-BUILDING IN MULTI-ETHNIC SOCIETIES: THE EXPERIENCE OF SOUTH ASIA
ALTERNATIVES, 14(4) (OCT 89), 379-388.
THIS ARTICLE DEFINES "MODERN STATE" AS A POLITICAL AUTHORITY WHICH DERIVES ITS LEGITIMACY BY WORKING FOR A WELL-DEFINED TERRITORIAL ENTITY, WHICH IS ALSO SUPPOSED TO BE A SOCIALLY AND CULTURALLY COHERENT ENTITY CALLED NATION. IT EXPLORES NATION-BUILDING AND THE THEORY OF COMPARATIVE POLITICAL DEVELOPMENT AND THEN, NATION-BUILDING IN SOUTH ASIAN SOCIETIES. IT CONCLUDES, AFTER STUDYING PAKISTAN, SRI LANKA, AND INDIA, THAT A STATE WITHIN AND IN COMMAND OF CIVIL SOCIETY SEEMS TO BE AN APPROPRIATE STATE FORM FOR MULTI-ETHNIC SOCIETIES OF THE THIRD WORLD.

08253 SHEVARDNADZE, E.
EDUARD SHEVARNADZE'S ADDRESS IN VIENNA
REPRINTS FROM THE SOVIET PRESS, 48(8) (APR 89), 21-28.
IN AN ADDRESS IN VIENNA, EDUARD SHEVARNADZE DISCUSSES THE UNILATERAL TROOP WITHDRAWALS MADE THE USSR. HE SPEAKS OF THE NEED FOR NEGOTIATIONS THAT WOULD RESULT IN THE EVENTUAL REDUCTION OF ARMS, TROOPS, AND WEAPONS SYSTEMS TO AN ACCEPTABLE DEFENSE-ONLY LEVEL. HE OUTLINES THREE PHASES TO SUCH A PLAN AND ATTEMPTS TO RESOLVE CONFLICTS OVER CONFLICTING DATA ON THE SIZE AND STRUCTURE OF ARMED FORCES.

08254 SHEVARDNADZE, E.
OUR GOAL IS TO GUARANTEE HUMAN RIGHTS

REPRINTS FROM THE SOVIET PRESS, 49(3) (AUG 89), 23-33.
IN THIS SPEECH AT THE PARIS HUMANITARIAN CONFERENCE THE
SOVIET FOREIGN MINISTER FOCUSES ON THE NEW SOVIET PARLIAMENT
WHICH HAS BEFORE IT SOME 50 IMPORTANT DOCUMENTS, INCLUDING
THE BILLS ON FREEDOM OF CONSCIENCE, ON THE PRESS, ON PUBLIC
ORGANIZATIONS AND ON ENTRY IN AND EXIT FROM THE COUNTRY.
THEY ARE DESIGNED TO CONSOLIDATE EQUALITY AND FREEDOMS --
SOCIAL, CIVIL AND NATIONAL -- IN THE USSR.

08255 SHEVARDNADZE, E.
THE IMPORTANT LINE OF SOVIET DIPLOMACY
INTERNATIONAL AFFAIRS (MOSCOW), (3) (MAR 89), 3-16.
ON DEC. 28, 1988, USSR MINISTER OF FOREIGN AFFAIRS
EDUARD SHEVARDNADZE DELIVERED A REPORT TO THE CONFERENCE OF
CONSULAR OFFICERS OF THE MINISTRY OF FOREIGN AFFAIRS. THE
REPORT DISCUSSED THE ROLE OF THE CONSULAR ADMINISTRATION IN
FORMULATING SOVIET FOREIGN POLICY AND CHANGES IN THE OVERALL
THRUST OF SOVIET DIPLOMACY.

08256 SHEVARDNADZE, E.
THE LEVEL OF RESPONSIBILITY
REPRINTS FROM THE SOVIET PRESS, 48(10) (MAY 89), 27-36.
THERE CAN BE NO ABSOLUTE OPENNESS IN DIPLOMACY AND MANY
OTHER PROFESSIONS. PROFESSIONAL SECRETS ARE NOT A WHIMSICAL
CREATION OF THE PROFESSIONALS, SUCH AS DOCTORS, LAWYERS,
TEACHERS OF JOURNALISTS. THESE SECRETS ARE OFTEN REQUIRED BY
THE MORAL PRINCIPLES OF A TRADE, WHICH DICTATE RATHER STRICT
NORMS OF CONDUCT. THE PRESS SHOULD KNOW AND UNDERSTAND THE
PROFESSIONAL PRIORITIES OF DIPLOMACY, WHILE DIPLOMATS SHOULD
KNOW AND UNDERSTAND JOURNALISTS' PROFESSIONAL PRIORITIES. IN
OTHER WORDS, HE SHOULD MUTUALLY TAKE INTO ACCOUNT THE
BALANCE OF INTERESTS, BUT WITH THE UNDOUBTED PRIMACY OF THE
INTERESTS OF THE COUNTRY AND THE PEOPLE. HE SHOULD COOPERATE.
THE TASK HAS TWO ASPECTS: TO IMPART PLURALISM OF OPINIONS
AND ASSESSMENTS TO JOURNALISM DEALING WITH INTERNATIONAL
TOPICS, AND TO IMPART JOURNALISTS' IDEAS, PASSION, VISION
AND ERUDITION TO FOREIGN POLICY.

08257 SHIBIN, S.
ECONOMIC REFORM BOOSTS NIGERIA'S ECONOMY
BEIJING REVIEW, 32(30) (JUL 89), 14-15.
NIGERIA HAS ENTERED THE THIRD YEAR OF ITS ECONOMIC
ADJUSTMENT PROGRAM, WHICH HAS HALTED THE DECLINE IN ITS
GROSS DOMESTIC PRODUCT AND BROUGHT A SLIGHT INCREASE IN 1988.
NIGERIA'S ECONOMIC REFORM PLAN INCLUDES REORGANIZING ITS
ECONOMIC STRUCTURE, DIVERSIFYING PRODUCTION AND INCREASING
THE DOMESTIC SUPPLY OF RAW MATERIALS, ENDING EXCESSIVE
RELIANCE ON OIL AND IMPORTED MATERIALS, LIBERALIZING TRADE,
AND DEVELOPING THE FOREIGN-ORIENTED SECTORS OF THE ECONOMY.

08258 SHIELDS, J.
BARRE, CHIRAC, LE PEN ET AL; FRANCE'S FRAGMENTED RIGHT
CONTEMPORARY REVIEW, 254(1476) (JAN 89), 1-6.
THE ARTICLE EXAMINES THE SUCCESSIVE POLITICAL FAILURES
OF THE FRENCH RIGHT. THE MAJOR PARTIES OF THE RIGHT, THE NEO-
GAULLIST "RASSEMBLEMENT POUR LA REPUBLIQUE (RPR) AND THE
CENTER-RIGHT UNION POUR LA DEMOCRATIE FRANCAISE (UDF), HAVE
BEEN PLAGUED WITH INFIGHTING AND FACTIONALISM. THE THREE
MAIN LEADERS OF THE RIGHT, JACQUES CHIRAC, RAYMOND BARRE,
AND JEAN-MARIE LE PEN HAVE OVERSEEN FRAGMENTATION THAT MAKES
THE FRENCH SOCIALIST PARTY, WHICH IS WELL KNOWN FOR ITS
FACTIONALISM, SEEM HOMOGENEOUS. THE FUTURE FOR THE RIGHT IS
NOT MUCH BRIGHTER; THE ARTICLE CONCLUDES THAT THEIR
POLITICAL FORTUNES WILL CONTINUE TO SLIDE FOR SOME YEARS TO
COME.

08259 SHIELDS, T.
STARVING THE SOUTH
AFRICA REPORT, 34(1) (JAN 89), 63-65.
ALTHOUGH SOME PROGRESS HAS BEEN ACHIEVED TOWARD A PEACE
PLAN BETWEEN THE SUDANESE GOVERNMENT AND THE SPLA, BOTH
PARTIES CONTINUE TO IMPEDE THE DELIVERY OF EMERGENCY FOOD
SUPPLIES TO TO SOUTHERN SUDAN. THE REBEL SPLA SEIZES CROPS
AND BURIES LAND MINES TO MAKE THE FOOD-PRODUCING LAND
USELESS. AT THE SAME TIME, THE KHARTOUM GOVERNMENT
DELIBERATELY DENIES FOOD TO THE SOUTH IN A BID TO DEPOPULATE
THE REBELLIOUS REGION.

08260 SHIGERU, I.
JAPAN'S RESURGENT SOCIALISTS: WHERE TO FROM HERE?
JAPAN ECHO, XVI(4) (WIN 89), 36-43.
IN THIS INTERVIEW, THE CHAIRMAN OF THE JAPANESE
SOCIALIST PARTY POLICY BOARD DISCUSSES THE FUTURE OF HIS
PARTY FOLLOWING ITS SUCCESS IN THE JULY 1989 HOUSE OF
COUNCILLORS ELECTION.

08261 SHIH, C.
FACE DIPLOMACY: THE PSYCHO-CULTURAL CYBERNETIC MODEL OF
CHINESE FOREIGN POLICY BEHAVIOR
DISSERTATION ABSTRACTS INTERNATIONAL, 50(6) (DEC 89),
1979-A.
THE AUTHOR PROPOSES A PSYCHO-CULTURAL CYBERNETIC MODEL
OF FOREIGN POLICY BEHAVIOR THAT ACCOMMODATES THE FACTOR OF
MOTIVATION, IN ORDER TO ASSIST IN UNDERSTANDING DIPLOMACY BY

READING THE PSYCHOLOGICAL DRIVE OF STATESMEN. THEN HE
ENDEAVORS TO INTERPRET CHINESE DIPLOMATIC HISTORY FROM THE
PSYCHO-CULTURAL CYBERNETIC PERSPECTIVE.

08262 SHILON, D.
AN INDEPENDENT PALESTINIAN STATE DOESN'T FRIGHTEN ME
NEW OUTLOOK, 32(3-4 (289-290)) (MAR 89), 36-37.
ISRAEL'S FORMER FOREIGN MINISTER ABBA EBAN BELIEVES THAT
ISRAEL SHOULD NEGOTIATE WITH THE PLO AND JORDAN IN THE
CONTEXT OF AN INTERNATIONAL CONFERENCE UNDER THE AUSPICES OF
THE SUPERPOWERS. HE REJECTS YITZHAK RABIN'S DEMAND FOR A
PERIOD OF CALM IN THE OCCUPIED TERRITORIES BEFORE AGREEING
TO NEGOTIATIONS WITH THE PALESTINIANS AND PREDICTS THAT
RABIN'S PROPOSED POLITICAL SOLUTION WILL BE FRUITLESS.

08263 SHILS, E.
THE LIMITS ON THE CAPACITIES OF GOVERNMENT
GOVERNMENT AND OPPOSITION, 24(4) (AUT 89), 441-457.
THE MANHATTAN PROJECT APPEARED TO DEMONSTRATE THAT THE
POWERS OF GOVERNMENT, SUPPORTED BY AND SUPPORTING THE GROWTH
OF SCIENTIFIC KNOWLEDGE, HAD NO BOUNDARIES. THE CONSTRUCTION
OF THE ATOMIC BOMB STRENGTHENED THE BELIEFS PROMULGATED BY
BACON AND COMTE. THE ALLIANCE OF GOVERNMENT AND SCIENCE
SEEMED TO BE CONFIRMED, AND TOGETHER THEIR POWERS WERE
LIMITLESS. BUT, IN RECENT YEARS, SOME UNEASINESS ABOUT EACH
OF THE PARTIES TO THIS ALLIANCE HAS ARISEN.

08264 SHIM, J.
WINDS OF COMPROMISE
FAR EASTERN ECONOMIC REVIEW, 142(52) (DEC 89), 8-9.
SOUTH KOREAN PRESIDENT ROH TAE WOO AND THE THREE MAIN
OPPOSITION LEADERS ABANDONED THEIR CONFRONTATIONAL TACTICS
AND HAVE AGREED ON A FRAMEWORK FOR PUTTING BEHIND THEM
DIVISIVE ISSUES LEFT OVER FROM THE ADMINISTRATION OF FORMER
PRESIDENT CHUN DOO HWAN AND FOR FURTHER POLITICAL REFORMS.
ROH GAVE IN TO OPPOSITION DEMANDS THAT CHUN AND OTHERS PAY
FOR THEIR CORRUPT PRACTICES, PARTICULARLY THE USE OF THE
ARMY TO QUELL A CIVILIAN UPRISING IN KWANGJU IN WHICH SOME
200 CIVILIANS WERE KILLED. IN RETURN, THE OPPOSITION AGREED
TO SUPPORT THE NATIONAL BUDGET AND SEVERAL OTHER DEMOCRATIC
REFORMS. THE SPIRIT OF COMPROMISE, RARE IN SOUTH KOREA'S
POLITICAL TRADITION, BODES WELL FOR THE COUNTRY'S LONG-TERM
FUTURE.

08265 SHIN, D.C.; CHEY, M.; KIM, K.
CULTURAL ORIGINS OF PUBLIC SUPPORT FOR DEMOCRACY IN KOREA
AN EMPIRICAL TEST OF THE DOUGLAS-WILDAVSKY THEORY OF
CULTURE
COMPARATIVE POLITICAL STUDIES, 22(2) (JUL 89), 217-238.
ANTHROPOLOGIST MARY DOUGLAS AND POLITICAL SCIENTIST
AARON WILDAVSKY HAVE PROPOSED A THEORY THAT PEOPLE'S
POLITICAL PREFERENCES ARE SHAPED LARGELY BY THE CULTURE IN
WHICH THEY PREFER TO LIVE. THIS STUDY TESTS THEIR THEORY
WITH PUBLIC OPINION DATA RECENTLY COLLECTED FROM THE
REPUBLIC OF KOREA. SECONDARY ANALYSIS OF THE DATA REVEALS
THAT UPHOLDERS OF AN INDIVIDUALIST CULTURE ARE MOST
SUPPORTIVE OF DEMOCRATIC POLITICS, WHEREAS THOSE OF A
HIERARCHICAL CULTURE ARE LEAST SUPPORTIVE OF IT. MOREOVER,
THE ANALYSIS REVEALS THAT GENERAL LEVELS OF PUBLIC SUPPORT
IN KOREA DEPEND FAR MORE ON THE TYPE OF CULTURE THAN ON ANY
SOCIOECONOMIC AND DEMOGRAPHIC CHARACTERISTICS. ON THE BASIS
OF THESE FINDINGS IT IS ARGUED THAT CULTURE SHOULD BE
CONSIDERED AS A PROMISING RIVAL THEORY OF POLITICAL
PREFERENCES.

08266 SHIN, M.
DEMOCRATIZATION IN KOREAN POLITICS: PRESIDENTIAL AND
PARLIAMENTARY ASPECTS
KOREA OBSERVER, XX(1) (SPR 89), 111-125.
SINCE 1948, FEW OPPORTUNITIES FOR DEMOCRATIC
EXPERIMENTATION HAVE EXISTED IN SOUTH KOREA. IN 1960, UNDER
THE LEADERSHIP OF CHANG MYON OF THE DEMOCRATIC PARTY,
LIBERAL DEMOCRACY HAS ATTEMPTED BUT WAS OVERTHROWN BY THE
MILITARY COUP OF GENERAL PARK CHUNG HEE. IN 1980, KOREA HAD
ANOTHER CHANCE TO ACHIEVE DEMOCRACY AFTER THE FALL OF PARK'S
AUTHORITARIAN REGIME. BUT GENERAL CHUN DOO HWAN SEIZED POWER.
KOREA IS PRESENTLY UNDERGOING A THIRD ATTEMPT AT
DEMOCRATIZATION. WHETHER THE SIXTH REPUBLIC WILL
SUCCESSFULLY COMPLETE THE DEMOCRATIZATION PROCESS DEPENDS TO
A LARGE EXTENT ON THE PERFORMANCE OF PRESIDENT ROH TAE WOO
AND HIS ABILITY TO HURDLE THE MANY DIFFICULT CHALLENGES ON
THE ROAD TO DEMOCRACY.

08267 SHINGLES, R.D.
CLASS, STATUS, AND SUPPORT FOR GOVERNMENT AID TO
DISADVANTAGED GROUPS
THE JOURNAL OF POLITICS, 51(4) (NOV 89), 933-964.
THE LITERATURE DESCRIBING IDEOLOGICAL ORIENTATIONS OF
AMERICANS IS COMPLEX AND ENIGMATIC. IT IS LARGELY ORGANIZED
AROUND TWO, SEEMINGLY INCOMPATIBLE THEORIES. MUCH OF THE
CONTROVERSY PERTAINS TO PEOPLE IN THE HIGHEST STRATUM. THE
"CLASS POLARIZATION" THESIS DESCRIBES THEM AS ECONOMICALLY
CONSERVATIVE. THE "CLASS INVERSION" THESIS MAINTAINS THEY
ARE LIBERAL. THE DEBATE IS HIGHLY INFLUENCED BY THE CHOICE

OF DEFINITIONS AND INDICATORS. MOST PRIOR RESEARCH FAILS TO
DISTINGUISH BETWEEN TYPES OF STRATA (CLASS AND STATUS) AND
BETWEEN DIFFERENT TYPES OF LIBERAL-CONSERVATIVE BELIEFS.
THIS PAPER SHOWS SEEMINGLY CONTRADICTORY THEORIES CAN BE
MADE COMPATIBLE BY BASING ONE THEORY ON CLASS AND THE OTHER
ON STATUS. POOLED DATA FROM THE 1976, 1980, AND 1984 NES
SURVEYS IS USED TO ESTIMATE THE EFFECTS OF CLASS AND STATUS
ON ATTITUDES TOWARD GENERAL WELFARE AND AID TO MINORITIES.
CONTROLS ARE PROVIDED FOR RACE, PARTY IDENTIFICATION, AND
TYPE OF OCCUPATION. TOGETHER CLASS AND STATUS PROVIDE A MORE
COMPREHENSIVE EXPLANATION OF ISSUE POSITIONS THAN DOES
EITHER CONCEPT ALONE. HOWEVER, THE VARIABLES EXPLAIN ONLY A
SMALL PROPORTION OF THE IDEOLOGICAL DIVISION BETWEEN
REPUBLICANS AND DEMOCRATS.

08268 SHINJI, O.
THE FSX CONTROVERSY REVIVED
JAPAN QUARTERLY, XXXVI(4) (OCT 89), 433-443.
THE AUTHOR DISCUSSES AN IRRITANT TO US-JAPANESE
BILATERAL RELATIONS, THE DISPUTE OVER THE DEVELOPMENT OF THE
JAPANESE AIR SELF-DEFENSE FORCE'S NEXT GENERATION SUPPORT
FIGHTER (FSX). HE CONSIDERS TWO BASIC QUESTIONS: WHY DID THE
USA REOPEN NEGOTIATIONS ON A JOINT DEVELOPMENT AGREEMENT
AFTER THE JAPANESE CONSIDERED THE ISSUE CLOSED? HOW DID THE
JAPANESE PEOPLE REACT TO THIS UNPRECEDENTED AMERICAN DEMAND
TO FUNDAMENTALLY CHANGE THE SUBSTANCE OF AN AGREEMENT THAT
HAD ALREADY BEEN OFFICIALLY CONCLUDED?

08269 SHINSAKU, K.
CHANGING VALUES IN JAPANESE POLITICS
JAPAN ECHO, XVI(4) (WIN 89), 23-29.
SINCE THE MEIJI RESTORATION, WHEN JAPAN BEGAN TO IMPOSE
THE MODERN LAWS AND INSTITUTIONS OF THE WEST ON THE
INDIGENOUS TRADITIONS OF VILLAGE LIFE, JAPANESE SOCIETY HAS
HAD A DUALISTIC STRUCTURE. ORIGINALLY THE JAPANESE VILLAGE
WAS A COMMUNAL BODY SERVING TO SECURE EVERYONE'S COOPERATION
IN THE MAINTENANCE OF THE IRRIGATION FACILITIES THAT ARE
INDISPENSABLE FOR RICE CULTIVATION. FOR THE SAKE OF COMMUNAL
UNITY, THE VILLAGE RESIDENTS STROVE TO BLEND SMOOTHLY AND TO
SUPPRESS THEIR INDIVIDUALITY. AFTER JAPAN EMBARKED ON
MODERNIZATION, THE VILLAGE PRINCIPLES CONTINUED TO EXERT A
PERVASIVE INFLUENCE BUT CAME INTO CONFLICT WITH MODERN LAWS
AND INSTITUTIONS, WHICH ARE PREMISED ON INDIVIDUALISM AND
HORIZONTAL INTERPERSONAL RELATIONS. RECENT JAPANESE HISTORY
HAS WITNESSED PENDULAR SWINGS BETWEEN THE TWO OPPOSING
SOCIAL SYSTEMS THAT HAVE AFFECTED ALL ASPECTS OF NATIONAL
LIFE, INCLUDING POLITICS.

08270 SHINTARO, I.
FROM BAD TO WORSE IN THE FSX PROJECT
JAPAN ECHO, XVI(3) (AUT 89), 59-65.
THE CONTROVERSY OVER THE FSX SUPPORT FIGHTER FOR THE
JAPANESE AIR FORCE IS FAR MORE IMPORTANT THAN MOST
POLITICIANS REALIZE. IF IT HAD BEEN HANDLED PROPERLY, IT HAD
THE POTENTIAL TO ALTER THE ATTITUDES THE JAPANESE HAVE
FORMED TOWARD POLITICS AND OTHER AREAS OF ACTIVITY SINCE
WORLD WAR II. THE MOST CURIOUS ASPECT OF THE HANDLING OF THE
FSX AFFAIR ON THE AMERICAN SIDE HAS BEEN THE EXTRAORDINARY
MOVE ON THE PART OF THE BUSH ADMINISTRATION TO ALTER THE
CONTENT OF THE FSX ACCORD REACHED BY THE REAGAN
ADMINISTRATION. THE MOST CURIOUS ASPECT ON THE JAPANESE SIDE
HAS BEEN THE ABRUPT DECISION TO ABANDON THE PRINCIPLE THAT
THE FSX BE DEVELOPED ENTIRELY IN JAPAN AND TO ALLOW IT TO
PROCEED AS A JOINT DEVELOPMENT PROJECT WITH THE USA.

08271 SHIPING, C.
"INTERNATIONALIZATION" OF HONG KONG GETS NOWHERE
BEIJING REVIEW, 32(50) (DEC 89), 14-15.
SINCE THE CHINESE GOVERNMENT QUELLED THE COUNTER-
REVOLUTIONARY REBELLION IN BEIJING, SOME LEADING BRITISH
GOVERNMENT OFFICIALS HAVE EXPRESSED CONCERN OVER THE FATE OF
HONG KONG. THEY HAVE PROPAGATED A "CONFIDENCE CRISIS" IN
HONG KONG AND ADVOCATED "INTERNATIONALIZING" THE HONG KONG
ISSUE. THEY ARGUE THAT THE SINO-BRITISH JOINT DECLARATION ON
THE QUESTION OF HONG KONG SOLVED ONLY THE SOVEREIGNTY ISSUE
AND FAILED TO COMPLETELY DEFINE CITY'S FUTURE.

08272 SHIPLER, D.
ON THE HUMAN RIGHTS TRACK
FOREIGN POLICY, (75) (SUM 89), 164-181.
ONE OF THE MOST REMARKABLE CHANGES IN THE USSR HAS BEEN
IN THE AREA OF HUMAN RIGHTS. RECENTLY, THE KREMLIN HAS
ADDRESSED POSITIVELY EVERY MAJOR HUMAN RIGHTS GRIEVANCE ON
THE AMERICAN AGENDA, AND THE VAST MAJORITY OF INDIVIDUAL
CASES CITED BY AMERICAN RIGHTS CAMPAIGNERS HAVE BEEN
RESOLVED UNDER GORBACHEV. THE ABRUPT TURNAROUND BY THE
SOVIETS PRESENT NEW CHALLENGES TO US POLICYMAKERS: HUMAN
RIGHTS COULD EASILY SLIP OUT OF THE SPOTLIGHT NOW THAT SOME
OF THE MAJOR ABUSES ARE NO LONGER OCCURRING. THE US ALSO IS
FACED WITH THE DILEMMA OF SANCTIONS IMPOSED AGAINST THE USSR;
MANY POLICYMAKERS ARE ABOUT TO DISCOVER THAT IT IS MUCH
EASIER TO PUNISH THAN TO STOP PUNISHING.

08273 SHIPLER, D.K.
FUTURE DOMESTIC AND INTERNATIONAL TERRORISM: MEDIA
PERSPECTIVE
TERRORISM, 11(6) (1988), 543-545.
THIS IS A TALK GIVEN AT A CONFERENCE ON TERRORISM BY
DAVID SHIPLER, SENIOR ASSOCIATE OF THE CARNAGIE ENDOWMENT
FOR INTERNATIONAL PEACE. HE SUGGESTS THAT IN DEALING WITH
TERRORISM, THAT THE MOST CHALLENGING TASK FOR AN OPEN
SOCIETY IS GOING TO BE HOW TO MAINTAIN THE PRINCIPLES OF
OPENNESS AND DEMOCRATIC PLURALISM IN THE FACE OF THE THREATS
OF TERRORISM. HE USES ISRAEL AS AN EXAMPLE OF A DEMOCRATIC
OPEN SOCIETY WHO IS ABUSING THE RIGHTS OF THE ARABS WHO LIVE
IN THE WEST BANK AND THE GAZA STRIP. HE CONCLUDES THAT THERE
IS TOO LITTLE DISCUSSION ABOUT THE NEED TO PROTECT DEMOCRACY
AND CIVIL LIBERTIES WHILE COMBATING TERRORISM AND THAT IF
THIS CONTINUES, THE TERRORISTS WILL SCORE A VICTORY OVER THE
U.S. WITH U.S. HELP.

08274 SHIPLEY, P.
HOSTILE ACTION: THE KGB AND SECRET SOVIET OPERATIONS IN
BRITAIN
JOHN SPIERS PUBLISHING, BRIGHTON, SUSSEX, GB, 1989, 280.
THE AUTHOR SURVEYS THE TOTALITY OF SECRET SOVIET
ACTIVITY AGAINST BRITAIN FROM 1917 TO THE PRESENT. HE
REVIEWS EFFORTS TO INFLUENCE SPECIFIC POLITICIANS AND TO
PENETRATE BRITISH INSTITUTIONS, INCLUDING THE FOREIGN OFFICE,
THE UNIVERSITIES, AND THE SECURITY AUTHORITIES. HE ALSO
CONSIDERS THE PROSPECTS FOR CHANGE IN SOVIET BEHAVIOR UNDER
GORBACHEV.

08275 SHISHKOV, Y.
DIFFERENCES BETWEEN INTEGRATION IN EASTERN AND WESTERN
EUROPE: ECONOMIC AND POLITICAL CAUSES
GOVERNMENT AND OPPOSITION, 24(3) (SUM 89), 327-340.
NEW TRENDS IN THE DEVELOPMENT OF ECONOMIC MECHANISMS IN
THE CMEA AND THE EC WILL OPEN THE WAY TO MORE MUTUALLY-
BENEFICIAL COOPERATION BETWEEN THE COUNTRIES OF EASTERN AND
WESTERN EUROPE. A CERTAIN RAPPROCHEMENT OF ECONOMIC METHODS
BASED ON WORLD MARKET LAWS WILL REMOVE MANY ARTIFICIAL
OBSTACLES THAT HAVE FOR DECADES HAMPERED THE PROCESS. THE
NEW ECONOMIC AND POLITICAL CLIMATE IN EUROPE HAS MADE IT
POSSIBLE TO LAY THE FOUNDATION FOR FUTURE JURIDICAL
RELATIONS BETWEEN THE INTEGRATION GROUPS OF EASTERN AND
WESTERN EUROPE.

08276 SHIU-HING, L.
ASPECTS OF POLITICAL DEVELOPMENT IN MACAO
CHINA QUARTERLY, (120) (DEC 89), 837-851.
THE AUTHOR SURVEYS IMPORTANT ASPECTS OF MACAO'S
POLITICAL DEVELOPMENT SINCE THE PORTUGUESE REVOLUTION IN
1974 AND THE FUTURE VIABILITY OF MACAO UNDER THE SINO-
PORTUGUESE AGREEMENT THAT STIPULATES THAT THE COUNTRY WILL
BECOME A CHINESE SPECIAL ADMINISTRATIVE REGION IN 1999.

08277 SHIVE, G.
ACADEMIC ANGUISH
FAR EASTERN ECONOMIC REVIEW, 142(52) (DEC 89), 17.
FOLLOWING A DECADE OF OPEN DOOR POLICY, THE SINO-
AMERICAN ACADEMIC EXCHANGE PROCESS HAS BEEN UPENDED BY THE
CRACKDOWN ON PRO-DEMOCRACY PROTESTS IN BEIJING, AND ITS
BASIC PREMISES HAVE BEEN CHALLENGED IN ANGER BY BOTH SIDES.
HOWEVER, THE FUNDAMENTAL INTERESTS OF CHINA AND ITS MANPOWER
DEVELOPMENT SYSTEMS REQUIRE CONTINUED EXCHANGES WITH THE
ADVANCED COUNTRIES OF THE WEST. ALTHOUGH U.S. ATTENTION IS
LIKELY TO TURN AWAY FROM CHINA AS CHINA'S IMPORTANCE AS A
COUNTERWEIGHT TO SOVIET AGGRESSION DIMINISHES, SIGNIFICANT U.
S. INTERESTS ARE STILL MET BY CONTINUED ACADEMIC EXCHANGE.
THE FUTURE IS NOW IN THE HANDS OF U.S. AND CHINESE
POLITICIANS.

08278 SHKLAR, J.
ROUSSEAU AND THE REPUBLICAN PROJECT
FRENCH POLITICS AND SOCIETY, 7(2) (SPR 89), 42-49.
ROUSSEAU'S SELF-IMPOSED TASK WAS TO FIND A RELEVANT
PLACE FOR EGALITARIAN REPUBLICANISM IN MODERN POLITICAL
THEORY. MONTESQUIEU'S HISTORICAL SCIENCE WAS NOT ENTIRELY
UNWELCOME TO ROUSSEAU. IT PERMITTED HIM TO USE THE DAMNING
MEMORY OF REPUBLICAN VIRTUE TO EXCORIATE MODERNITY IN ALL
ITS ASPECTS. MOREOVER, AS A DESPAIRING AND PROFOUND
PSYCHOLOGIST, HE COULD USE THE DECLINE AND FAILURES OF
REPUBLICS TO CAST A HARSH LIGHT UPON THE UNIVERSAL CONFLICT
BETWEEN NATURE AND CULTURE. IT WAS ONLY IN HIS INTERMITTENT
SPECULATIONS ABOUT THE POSSIBLE APPLICATIONS OF
REPUBLICANISM TO POLITICAL ETHICS IN GENERAL THAT HE FOUND
MONTESQUIEU AN OBSTACLE. OF ALL THE POLITICAL IMPEDIMENTS TO
A REVIVED REPUBLIC, NONE LOOMED LARGER IN THE EYES OF
ROUSSEAU'S CONTEMPORARIES THAN SHEER SIZE.

08279 SHMAGIN, Y.; BRATCHIKOV, I.
PERESTROIKA IN THE USSR FOREIGN MINISTRY
INTERNATIONAL AFFAIRS (MOSCOW), (3) (MAR 89), 42-53.
THE AUTHORS SURVEY THE FORMER IMAGE AND HISTORY OF THE
SOVIET DIPLOMATIC SERVICE AND DISCUSS THE CHANGES SINCE
PERESTROIKA.

08280 SHMELEV, N.; HEWETT, E.A.
A PRAGMATIST'S APPROACH TO THE SOVIET ECONOMY
BROOKINGS REVIEW, 8(1) (WIN 90), 27-32.
THE AUTHORS, BOTH OF WHOM ARE EXPERTS ON THE ECONOMIC
SITUATION IN THE SOVIET UNION, DISCUSS THE CURRENT SOVIET
ECONOMIC PROBLEMS AND STRATEGIES FOR SOVIET ECONOMIC
RECOVERY.

08281 SHOEMAKER, C.C.
THE NSC STAFF: REBUILDING THE POLICY CRUCIBLE
PARAMETERS, XIX(3) (SEP 89), 35-45.
THE IRAN-CONTRA AFFAIR PUT A SPOTLIGHT ON THE NATIONAL
SECURITY COUNCIL, SUBJECTING IT TO SCRUTINY UNPARALLELED IN
ITS FORTY-YEAR HISTORY. THE AFFAIR REVEALED THE DEEP PROBLEM
THAT HAS PLAGUED EVERY ADMINISTRATION SINCE TRUMAN--THE
ABSENCE OF CLEARLY DEFINED AND FUNCTIONALLY ADEQUATE
RESPONSIBILITIES FOR THE ASSISTANT TO THE PRESIDENT FOR
NATIONAL SECURITY AFFAIRS AND THE NATIONAL SECURITY COUNCIL
STAFF.

08282 SHOEMAKER, S.T.
THE INFANT WELFARE MOVEMENT IN LIVERPOOL AND PHILADELPHIA,
1890-1918
DISSERTATION ABSTRACTS INTERNATIONAL, 49(12) (JUN 89),
3868-A.
INFANT WELFARE BECAME A MAJOR TOPIC OF CONCERN IN
INDUSTRIALIZED NATIONS FROM 1890 TO 1918. THIS STUDY
ANALYZES THE INFANT WELFARE MOVEMENT AS IT DEVELOPED IN
LIVERPOOL, U.K., AND PHILADELPHIA, PENNSYLVANIA, U.S.A.,
PROVIDING A PERSPECTIVE ON THE TYPES OF REFORMS UNDERTAKEN
INTERNATIONALLY AS WELL AS ON THE PARTICIPATION OF GROUPS AT
THE LOCAL LEVEL WHERE THE FIRST SIGNIFICANT PROGRAMS WERE
INITIATED.

08283 SHOMRON, D.
THE IDF PERSPECTIVE
IDF JOURNAL, (17) (SUM 89), 3-5.
THIS ARTICLE FOCUSES ON THE IDF PERSPECTIVE FOR THE
1990S AND THE ISRAEL MILITARY INDUSTRY. EXAMINED ARE BOTH
THE INTERNAL AND EXTERNAL THREAT TO ISRAEL'S SECURITY.
ADDRESSED ARE THE STRATEGIC FORCAST, THE SECURITY DOCTRINE,
DEFENSE AND ATTACK, BUILDING THE IDF AND FORCAST FOR THE
FUTURE. ISRAEL IS CONFIDENT THAT THEY WILL WIN A WAR FROM
THE EASTERN FRONT AND THAT POLITICAL ADVANTAGE WILL BE IN
THEIR HANDS.

08284 SHORT, T.
HOMOPHOBIAPHOBIA
NATIONAL REVIEW, XLI(15) (AUG 89), 19-20.
BLACK STUDIES, WOMEN'S STUDIES, AND MINORITY STUDIES
CLAIM TO REPRESENT SOCIETY'S VICTIMS, HITHERTO "EXCLUDED"
FROM THE LIBERAL ARTS. THIS VICTIM-BASED CURRICULUM IS
NECESSARILY TENDENTIOUS, FOR ITS VERY RATIONALE IS AN
IMPLICIT CONDEMNATION OF AMERICAN SOCIETY. AND SINCE ITS AIM
IS POLITICAL, NOT INTELLECTUAL, IT SPURNS ACADEMIC STANDARDS,
CONTRIBUTING TO THE GENERAL DECLINE OF SOCALLED HIGHER
EDUCATION. VICTIM STATUS, HOWEVER, MAKES THESE COURSES AND
THOSE WHO PROPOSE THEM SACROSANCT.

08285 SHOU-NAN, H.
"BAFFLED, SORROWFUL, PAINED, AND HOPEFUL"
FREE CHINA REVIEW, 39(8) (AUG 89), 24.
IN THIS INTERVIEW, A TAIWANESE REPORTER WHO WAS SHOT IN
TIENANMEN SQUARE DURING THE ARMED SUPPRESSION OF THE
PROTESTS THERE IN JUNE 1989 DESCRIBES THE SCENE IN THE
SQUARE.

08286 SHOUMIKHIN, A. U.
SOVIET PERCEPTIONS OF US MIDDLE EAST POLICY
MIDDLE EAST JOURNAL, 43(1) (WIN 89), 16-19.
A STRONG DESIRE TO ACHIEVE EQUAL STATUS WITH THE UNITED
STATES, WHICH CHRONOLOGICALLY ACCOMPANIED ACTIVE SOVIET
POLICY IN THE REGION, BEGAN TO IMPLY ESTABLISHING ONE'S OWN
PRESENCE, RAISING THE LEVEL OF INVOLVEMENT IN REGIONAL
CONFLICTS, AND ACQUIRING NEW ALLIES, AMONG OTHER FACTORS. AS
A RESULT, THE WORLD DRIFTED INTO THE MOST UNFORTUNATE AND
DANGEROUS SITUATION OF THE SUPERPOWER "ZERO-SUM GAME" IN THE
MIDDLE EAST, CONSTANTLY EXACERBATED BY BILATERAL RIVALRIES
AND THE POSSIBLITY THAT SOME OF THE COUNTRIES WOULD USE
GREAT POWER COMPETITION TO THEIR ADVANTAGE. IN DESCRIBING
SOVIET PERCEPTIONS OF CERTAIN AMERICAN APPROACHES TO THE
MIDDLE EAST, THIS AUTHOR FOCUSES ON THE ANXIETY CAUSED BY
THE AMERICAN EMPHASIS ON THE "SOVIET THREAT" AS A
JUSTIFICATION FOR AMERICA'S OWN ACTIONS.

08287 SHOUP, P.
LEADERSHIP DRIFT IN THE SOVIET UNION AND YUGOSLAVIA
STUDIES IN COMPARATIVE COMMUNISM, XXII(1) (SPR 89), 43-55.
THIS ARTICLE EXAMINES THE PHENOMENON OF LEADERSHIP DRIFT
IN THE SOVIET UNION AND YUGOSLAVIA THE AUTHOR ARGUES THAT AN
ANALYSIS OF LEADERSHIP DRIFT IN THESE TWO CASES CAN BE USED
AS A STARTING POINT FOR UNDERSTANDING LEADERSHIP BEHAVIOR IN
EASTERN EUROPE AND THE SOVIET UNION IN THE 1980'S AND BEYOND.

FOCUS IS ON THE "NEW POLITICS" - THAT IS, THE POLITICS OF
COMMUNIST STATES WHICH HAVE ADOPTED THE RHETORIC OF REFORM
BUT ARE FINDING IT DIFFICULT TO FOLLOW THROUGH WITH
SUBSTANTIVE REFORM MEASURES.

08288 SHOUP, P.
NATIONAL COMMUNISM IN EASTERN EUROPE REVISITED
CANADIAN REVIEW OF STUDIES IN NATIONALISM, XVI(1-2) (1989),
251-262.
THE AUTHOR ADDRESSES THE ISSUE OF NATIONAL COMMUNISM:
ITS DEFINITION AND USE AS A TOOL OF COMPARATIVE ANALYSIS TO
DISTINGUISH AMONG ONE-PARTY TYPE SYSTEMS AND ITS POSSIBLE
EMERGENCE AS A TRANSITIONAL TYPE OF REGIME BETWEEN A
REVOLUTIONARY AND A NATIONAL ONE-PARTY SYSTEM.

08289 SHREFFLER, R.
THE DEFENSE OF WESTERN EUROPE: AN INDICTMENT OF NATO'S
POSTURE OF FLEXIBLE RESPONSE AND WHAT CAN BE DONE ABOUT IT
JOURNAL OF SOCIAL, POLITICAL AND ECONOMIC STUDIES, 13(4)
(WIN 89), 351-369.
THE AUTHOR EXAMINES THE SHORTCOMINGS IN THE CURRENT NATO
POSTURE OF FLEXIBLE RESPONSE. HE THEN LISTS CONSTRAINTS THAT
MUST BE CONSIDERED IN THE FORMULATION OF ANY RATIONAL
POSTURE. FINALLY, HE PROPOSES A NEW POSTURE FOR NATO AND
SPECULATES ABOUT THE CONSEQUENCES OF ITS DEPLOYMENT.

08290 SHREITEH, T.
GAZANS DEFEAT THE MAGNETIC CARDS
MIDDLE EAST INTERNATIONAL, 355 (JUL 89), 11.
THE ISRAELI MILITARY AUTHORITIES' LATEST POLICY OF
FORCING GAZAN WORKERS TO CARRY MAGNETIC IDENTITY CARDS IN
ORDER TO ENTER ISRAEL SEEMS TO BE FACING MAJOR PROBLEMS.
PALESTINIAN ACTIVISTS ARE MAKING SURE THAT WORKERS WILL NOT
EVEN BE TEMPTED TO USE THEM. MASKED YOUTHS, REPRESENTING
LOCAL NATIONALIST COMMITTEES, ARE MAKING THE ROUNDS EVERY
NIGHT CONFISCATING THE CARDS BEFORE THE WORKERS EVEN HAVE A
CHANCE TO USE THEM. IN THE PREVIOUS 12 MONTHS, PALESTINIANS
HAD NOT BEEN SUCCESSFUL IN STOPPING THE ISRAELIS FROM
CHANGING THE REGULAR ID CARDS OF ALL GAZANS. BUT THIS TIME,
THEY SEEM TO HAVE SUCCEEDED. THE QUESTION REMAINS - WHO HAS
MORE ENDURANCE? AT ANY RATE, THE RELATIVE SUCCESS OF
PALESTINIANS IN DEFEATING THE MAGNETIC CARDS WILL PROBABLY
RESULT IN THE ISRAELIS ABANDONING THE INTRODUCTION OF A
SIMILAR SCHEME IN THE WEST BANK.

08291 SHUBIK, M.; VERKERKE, J.H.
OPEN QUESTIONS IN DEFENSE ECONOMICS AND ECONOMIC WARFARE
JOURNAL OF CONFLICT RESOLUTION, 33(3) (SEP 89), 480-499.
A DISTINCTION IS MADE CONCERNING FIVE DISTINCT WAR
SCENARIOS, AND A DISCUSSION IS GIVEN OF THE DIFFERENT
ECONOMIC REQUIREMENTS FOR EACH OF THESE SCENARIOS. THESE
REQUIREMENTS POSE A CONSIDERABLE NUMBER OF NEW ECONOMIC
PROBLEMS THAT WERE NOT PRESENT IN DEFENSE ECONOMICS PRIOR TO
WORLD WAR II. THE FIVE WAR SCENARIOS ARE: 1) COLD WAR, 2)
CLIENT WAR, 3) LIMITED WAR, 4) FULL CONVENTIONAL WAR, AND,
5) NUCLEAR WAR. BUDGETING AND COSTS, MEASUREMENT PROBLEMS,
AND THE SPECIAL PROBLEMS OF NUCLEAR WAR ARE ADDRESSED.

08292 SHUBIK, M.; VERKERKE, J.H.
OPEN QUESTIONS IN DEFENSE ECONOMICS AND ECONOMIC WARFARE
JOURNAL OF CONFLICT RESOLUTION, 33(3) (SEP 89), 480-499.
A DISTINCTION IS MADE CONCERNING FIVE DISTINCT WAR
SCENARIOS, AND A DISCUSSION IS GIVEN OF THE DIFFERENT
ECONOMIC REQUIREMENTS FOR EACH OF THESE SCENARIOS. THESE
REQUIREMENTS POSE A CONSIDERABLE NUMBER OF NEW ECONOMIC
PROBLEMS THAT WERE NOT PRESENT IN DEFENSE ECONOMICS PRIOR TO
WORLD WAR II.

08293 SHUDUO, G.
CHINESE REVOLUTION AND CULTURE
CHINA REPORT, 25(1) (JAN 89), 67-84.
THE PAPER DEALS WITH THE RELATIONSHIP BETWEEN CHINA'S
CULTURE AND THE TWO REVOLUTIONS THAT HAVE TAKEN PLACE IN
CHINA. IT EXAMINES THE DEMOCRATIC REVOLUTION OF SUN YAT-SEN
AND OTHERS AND ANALYZES THE CONFLICT BETWEEN THE OLD
IMPERIAL ORDER OF AUTOCRATIC, CENTRALIZED GOVERNMENT AND THE
NEW REPUBLICANISM BROUGHT IN BY THE REVOLUTION. IT ALSO
EXAMINES THE ENTRANCE OF MARXIST-LENINIST CULTURE ON THE
CHINESE SCENE AND THE EFFECTS THAT IT HAD IN A TIME OF
NATIONAL TURMOIL. MARXISM-LENINISM REMAINS THE SOLE SURVIVOR
ON THE FIELD THAT WAS ONCE FILLED WITH "ISMS". HOWEVER,
CHINESE CULTURE STILL INTERACTS AND SOMETIMES CONFLICTS WITH
THE MARXIST-LENINIST CULTURE.

08294 SHUGART, M.F.S.
DUVERGER'S RULE, DISTRICT MAGNITUDE, AND PRESIDENTIALISM
DISSERTATION ABSTRACTS INTERNATIONAL, 50(1) (JUL 89),
248-A.
DUVERGER'S RULE POSITS THAT ONE-SEAT DISTRICTS TEND TO
REDUCE THE NUMBER OF PARTIES TO TWO WHILE MULTI-SEAT
DISTRICTS WITH PROPORTIONAL REPRESENTATION (PR) TEND TO
ENCOURAGE MULTIPARTY SYSTEMS. MOST PREVIOUS ANALYSES OF
DUVERGER'S RULE HAVE FOCUSED ON NATIONWIDE OUTCOMES OF
ELECTIONS IN PARLIAMENTARY SYSTEMS. HOWEVER, THE UNDERLYING

CAUSES OPERATE MAINLY AT THE LEVEL OF THE ELECTORAL DISTRICT,
WHERE VOTERS ACTUALLY MAKE THE DECISION ON WHAT PARTY TO
VOTE FOR AND WHERE, IN MOST SYSTEMS, ALL OR MOST OF THE
SEATS ARE ALLOCATED. FURTHERMORE, IN PRESIDENTIAL SYSTEMS
THE NATIONWIDE ELECTION OF THE PRESIDENT IMPOSES A ONESEAT
DISTRICT OVER THE LEGISLATIVE DISTRICTS, EVEN THOUGH THE
LATTER MAY BE MULTI-SEAT DISTRICTS USING PR.

08295 SHUGER, S.
WHAT AMERICA HASN'T LEARNED FROM ITS GREATEST PEACEKEEPING
DISASTER
WASHINGTON MONTHLY, 21(9) (OCT 89), 40.
THE AUTHOR EXAMINES THE EVENTS THAT LED TO THE DEATH OF
241 US MARINES IN LEBANON AND THE DEMISE OF THE US
PEACEKEEPING OPERATION. US ACTIONS FAVORED LEBANESE
CHRISTIANS AND ALIENATED THE ARAB POPULATION, MANY OF WHO
WERE NEUTRAL BEFORE THE ARRIVAL OF THE MARINES. US
RHETORICAL SUPPORT FOR THE PHALANGE CHRISTIANS, US NAVAL
PRESENCE OFF THE COAST OF LEBANON, AND THE ABANDONING OF ANY
PRETENSE OF BIPARTISANSHIP OR EVEN SELF-DEFENSE, SEALED THE
FATE OF THE MARINES. THE AUTHOR CONCLUDES THAT THE ACTIONS
OF SECRETARY OF STATE SHULTZ AND PRESIDENTIAL ENVOY ROBERT
MCFARLANE EXACERBATED THE TENSION CONSIDERABLY AND DIRECTLY
LED TO THE BOMBING.

08296 SHUKEIR, M.
PALESTINE: THE WAY TO PEACE
WORLD MARXIST REVIEW, 32(11) (NOV 89), 64-65.
THE ORGANIC COMBINATION OF TWO NEW ELEMENTS - THE
INTIFADA AND THE PALESTINIAN PEACE SLAN - EXPLAINS MANY
POLITICAL SHIFTS THAT HAVE RECENTLY OCCURRED IN THE PLO.
THIS ARTICLE DESCRIBES HOW THE PLO IS CONTINUING ITS
DIALOGUE WITH THE UNITED STATES, GUIDED THE CLEAN-CUT
DIRECTIVES OF THE PALESTINE NATIONAL COUNCIL'S 19TH SESSION
AND OF THE CONVICTION THAT IN AN INTERDEPENDENT WORLD IT IS
INCREASINGLY DIFFICULT TO UPHOLD A POLICY HAMPERING THE
ATTAINMENT OF A JUST AND LASTING SETTLEMENT IN THE MIDDLE
EAST.

08297 SHUKLA, S.K.
AFGHANISTAN: A STUDY OF THE TURBULENT 70'S AND 80'S
ASIAN PROFILE, 17(5) (OCT 89), 455-468.
THE EARLY 1970'S IN AFGHANISTAN SAW TECHNOLOGICAL
DEVELOPMENT, THE EMERGENCE OF A NEW ELITE, AND THE
CRYSTALLIZATION OF POLITICAL PARTIES. THE TURBULENT POLITICS
IN AFGHANISTAN MAY BE ATTRIBUTED TO A MIX OF INTERNAL AND
EXTERNAL FACTORS. AMONG THE INTERNAL CAUSES WAS THE
TECHNOLOGICAL DEVELOPMENT WITH THE RESULTANT EMERGENCE OF A
NEW ELITE ALONG WITH NEW LEVELS OF INEQUALITY. WHAT BEGAN AS
INTERNAL POLITICAL WRANGLES SOON BECAME ENMESHED IN THE
SUPERPOWER NET.

08298 SHUKR, A.
THE FOUNDATIONS FOR ACCORD
WORLD MARXIST REVIEW, 32(9) (SEP 89), 53-54.
THIS ARTICLE IS INCLUDED BECAUSE WMR INTENDS TO PROVIDE
READERS WITH BROADER COVERAGE OF THE EXPERIENCE OF VARIOUS
LEFT-WING PARTIES AND ORGANISATIONS IN THE BELIEF THAT THEIR
ACTIVITY CONTAINS MUCH OF INTEREST TO COMMUNISTS AND OTHER
ACTIVISTS IN THE WORKING-CLASS AND DEMOCRATIC MOVEMENTS. IT
IS FROM THE LEFT FORCES' EXPERIENCE OF THE NATIONAL
PROGRESSIVE UNIONIST PARTY. IT GIVES THE HISTORY AND
BACKGROUND OF THE PARTY AND DETAILS ITS MOST RECENT CONGRESS,
IT STRIVES FOR UNITY ON A DEMOCRATIC BASIS.

08299 SHULIN, D.
SOUNDING THE ALARM ON POPULATION GROWTH
CHINA RECONSTRUCTS, XXXVIII(7) (JUL 89), 30-33.
ALTHOUGH CHINA HAS MOUNTED A MASSIVE FAMILY-PLANNING
CAMPAIGN OVER THE PAST TWO DECADES, THE POPULATION GROWTH
RATE STILL REMAINS A FORMIDABLE OBSTACLE TO NATIONAL SOCIAL
AND ECONOMIC PROGRESS. UNLESS THE COUNTRY'S FAMILY-PLANNING
POLICY IS PROMOTED MORE VIGOROUSLY, CHINA WILL NOT BE ABLE
TO ACHIEVE ITS TARGET OF A POPULATION OF LESS THAN 1.2
BILLION BY THE END OF THIS CENTURY. SINCE 1979, NATIONAL
POLICY HAS ENCOURAGED EACH COUPLE TO HAVE ONLY ONE CHILD. IN
ADDITION TO PUBLICITY AND EDUCATIONAL CAMPAIGNS, FINANCIAL
INCENTIVES ARE USED TO ENFORCE THE POLICY, WITH BENEFITS FOR
ONE-CHILD FAMILIES AND FINES FOR EXTRA BIRTHS.

08300 SHULL, S.; RINGELSTEIN, A.
PRESIDENTIAL ATTENTION, SUPPORT, AND SYMBOLISM IN CIVIL
RIGHTS, 1953-1984
SOCIAL SCIENCE JOURNAL, 26(1) (1989), 45-49.
PUBLIC STATEMENTS OF SEVEN RECENT AMERICAN PRESIDENTS ON
CIVIL RIGHTS VARY IN THE EXTENT TO WHICH THEY TRULY SUPPORT
INCREASED RIGHTS FOR BLACKS OR ARE MERELY SYMBOLIC. THESE
SEVEN PRESIDENTS ALSO VARY IN THE ATTENTION THEY PAY TO
CIVIL RIGHTS. THE AUTHORS ANALYZE THE CONTENT OF ALL
PRESIDENTIAL SPEECHES, PRESS CONFERENCES, LETTERS, AND OTHER
PUBLIC MESSAGES IN THE PUBLIC PAPERS OF THE PRESIDENTS FROM
1953 THROUGH 1984. THE PRESIDENTS ARE EISENHOWER, KENNEDY,
JOHNSON, NIXON, FORD, CARTER, AND REAGAN.

08301 SHULL, S.A.
PRESIDENTIAL INFLUENCE VERSUS BUREAUCRATIC DISCRETION:
PRESIDENT-AGENCY RELATIONS IN CIVIL RIGHTS POLICY
AMERICAN REVIEW OF PUBLIC ADMINISTRATION, 19(3) (SEP 89),
197-216.
THIS RESEARCH EXAMINES PRESIDENTS' ADMINISTRATIVE
ACTIONS IN CIVIL RIGHTS POLICY AND AGENCY RESPONSES TO THOSE
ACTIONS. IT CONSIDERS THE FREQUENT DEBATE BETWEEN
PRESIDENTIAL INFLUENCE OVER THE BUREAUCRACY VERSUS THE MORE
COMMONLY POSITED MODEL OF BUREAUCRATIC DISCRETION. RESULTS
SUGGEST THAT ASSERTIVE PRESIDENTS LIKE JOHNSON AND REAGAN
CAN INFLUENCE AGENCY ACTIONS IN CIVIL RIGHTS POLICY; THEY
OBTAIN CLOSER CORRESPONDENCE WITH THEIR PREFERRED POLICIES
THAN DO LESS ASSERTIVE PRESIDENTS. OVERALL, HOWEVER, ONLY
LIMITED CORRESPONDENCE BETWEEN PRESIDENTIAL AND AGENCY
ACTIONS APPEARS BECAUSE AGENCIES HAVE CONSIDERABLE
DISCRETION IN THEIR IMPLEMENTING ACTIONS. THUS NEITHER
PRESIDENTIAL INFLUENCE NOR BUREAUCRATIC DISCRETION FULLY
EXPLAINS THE RELATIONSHIP.

08302 SHULMAN, D.
TELEVISION AND CIVIC EDUCATION: AN INTERVIEW WITH PATRICK
WATSON
NATIONAL CIVIC REVIEW, 78(4) (JUL 89), 286-295.
PATRICK WATSON IS THE CREATOR AND HOST OF "THE STRUGGLE
FOR DEMOCRACY," A PBS SERIES BROADCAST THROUGHOUT THE UNITED
STATES. IN THIS INTERVIEW, WATSON DISCUSSES THE PROSPECTS
FOR AN EXPANDED MEDIA ROLE IN THE DEVELOPMENT OF RESPONSIBLE
CITIZENSHIP AND THE ASSURANCE OF A BETTER INFORMED, MORE
INVOLVED ELECTORATE.

08303 SHULMAN, G.
METAPHOR AND MODERNIZATION IN THE POLITICAL THOUGHT OF
THOMAS HOBBES
POLITICAL THEORY, 17(3) (AUG 89), 392-416.
THIS READING EXPLORES THE SENSES AND WAYS IN WHICH
HOBBES WRITES THE SCIPT PEOPLE HAVE FOLLOWED AS THEY HAVE
AUTHORIZED MODERNITY. IT IS NOT JUST THAT HOBBES DEPICTS
MANY OF THE INSTITUTIONS AND NORMS THAT HAVE CHARACTERIZED
CAPITALIST MODERNIZATION AND LIBERAL POLITICS. HOBBES
ANTICIPATES MODERNITY IN A FAR DEEPER WAY: HE IS CONCERNED
NOT SO MUCH WITH ESTABLISHING PARTICULAR INSTITUTIONS, AS
WITH ANALYZING THE PROBLEM OF CONVENTIONALITY PER SE, AS
SIGNIFIED BY THE POLITICS AND LANGUAGE THAT GENERATE THE
STATE AND BY CONSTITUTIVE POWER TO CONSTRUCT ANY SOCIAL
RELATIONSHIPS. HOBBES'S ARGUMENTS, WITH THEIR TECHNICAL
DIFFICULTIES, ARE READ IN LIGHT OF THEIR HISTORICAL
PRESCIENCE.

08304 SHULTZ, G.
EFFORTS FOR PEACE IN AFRICA
DEPARTMENT OF STATE BULLETIN (US FOREIGN POLICY), 88(2141)
(DEC 88), 20-22.
IN A SPEECH AT A RECEPTION IN HONOR OF THE ORGANIZATION
OF AFRICAN UNITY (OAU) SECRETARY OF STATE GEORGE SHULTZ
DISCUSSED SEVERAL OF THE REGIONAL CONFLICTS IN AFRICA AND
THE EFFORTS OF THE US AND THE OAU TO SOLVE THEM. THEY
INCLUDE THE CHAD-LIBYA CONFLICT AND THE CONTINUED FIGHTING
IN ANGOLA AND NAMBIA. SHULTZ ALSO DISCUSSED APARTHEID AND
THE ENORMOUS ECONOMIC PROBLEMS THAT MANY AFRICANS NATIONS
FACE.

08305 SHULTZ, G.
KEY TO THE FUTURE: ENLIGHTENED ENGAGEMENT
DEPARTMENT OF STATE BULLETIN (US FOREIGN POLICY), 88(2141)
(DEC 88), 16-19.
SECRETARY OF STATE GEORGE SHULTZ DISCUSSES GLOBAL AND US
ACHIEVEMENTS OF THE PAST FEW YEARS AND THE IMPLICATIONS OF
THE INCREASINGLY INTERDEPENDENT WORLD ECONOMY. HE OUTLINES
POTENTIAL FUTURE DEVELOPMENTS AND CONCENTRATES ON SOME KEY
ISSUES THAT WILL DETERMINE THE ABILITY OF THE US TO COPE
WITH AND KEEP UP WITH A RAPIDLY CHANGING WORLD. THESE
INCLUDE: REGIONAL ECONOMIC COOPERATION AND PROSPERITY, US
DEFICITS, DEBT AND DEVELOPMENT IN THE THIRD WORLD, AND
INTERNATIONAL INSTITUTIONS SUCH AS THE WORLD BANK, THE IMF,
AND GATT.

08306 SHULTZ, G.; BURNS, W.F.
PROHIBITION OF CHEMICAL WEAPONS CONFERENCE HELD IN PARIS
DEPARTMENT OF STATE BULLETIN (US FOREIGN POLICY), 89(2144)
(MAR 89), 4-10.
THE CONFERENCE ON THE PROHIBITION OF CHEMICAL WEAPONS
WAS HELD IN PARIS IN JANUARY 1989. THIS REPORT CONTAINS THE
SECRETARY OF STATE'S ADDRESS AT THE CONFERENCE, THE TEXT OF
THE FINAL DECLARATION, AND A STATEMENT BY THE HEAD OF THE US
DELEGATION AND DIRECTOR OF THE ARMS CONTROL AND DISARMAMENT
AGENCY.

08307 SHULTZ, G.
PROMOTING PEACE AND PROSPERITY IN THE SOUTH ASIAN REGION
DEPARTMENT OF STATE BULLETIN (US FOREIGN POLICY), 88(2141)
(DEC 88), 19-20.
IN AN ADDRESS BEFORE THE SOUTH ASIAN ASSOCIATION FOR
REGIONAL COOPERATION (SAARC) SECRETARY OF STATE SHULTZ

PRAISED THE ORGANIZATION FOR ITS RECENT CONVENTION ON
TERRORISM AND THEIR EFFORTS TO STEM NARCOTICS TRAFFICKING
AND ABUSE. HE ALSO DISCUSSED NUCLEAR PROLIFERATION AND
AFGHANISTAN AND FUTURE CHALLENGES THAT THE SAARC WILL FACE.

08308 SHULTZ, G.
PUBLIC SERVICE IN AMERICA
DEPARTMENT OF STATE BULLETIN (US FOREIGN POLICY), 89(2144)
(MAR 89), 1-4.
PUBLIC SERVICE RESTS ON THREE PRECEPTS: (1) VOLUNTARISM,
(2) DIVERSITY, AND (3) THE DEMOCRATIC TRUST IN THE ABILITY
OF THE PEOPLE TO SELECT THEIR GOVERNMENT, TRUST THAT THE
PEOPLE'S WILL WILL BE SERVED, AND TRUST THAT PEOPLE WILL
DEAL WITH EACH OTHER HONESTLY.

08309 SHULTZ, G.
SECURITY AWARENESS, MEASURES, AND MANAGEMENT
DEPARTMENT OF STATE BULLETIN (US FOREIGN POLICY), 89(2142)
(JAN 89), 4-5.
IN THIS SPEECH BEFORE THE OVERSEAS SECURITY ADVISORY
COUNCIL, SECRETARY OF STATE SHULTZ DISCUSSED THE PROBLEM OF
INTERNATIONAL TERRORISM AND THE MEASURES THE USA HAS TAKEN
TO DEFEND AGAINST TERRORISTS.

08310 SHULTZ, G.
THE ADMINISTRATION'S APPROACH TO MIDDLE EAST PEACEMAKING
DEPARTMENT OF STATE BULLETIN (US FOREIGN POLICY), 88(2140)
(NOV 88), 10-11.
SECRETARY OF STATE GEORGE SHULTZ GIVES AN OVERVIEW OF
THE CURRENT MIDDLE EASTERN SITUATION AND OUTLINES SOME OF
THE PRINCIPLES THAT GUIDE US FOREIGN POLICY THERE. HE
CONCENTRATES ON THE ARAB-ISRAELI CONFLICT AND THE
POSSIBILITY OF DEFUSING AND SOLVING THE CONFLICT THROUGH
NEGOTIATIONS. HE DEMONSTRATES THE US STAND ON VARIOUS ISSUES
THAT WOULD BE CENTRAL TO ANY PEACE NEGOTIATION SUCH AS THE
SECURITY OF ISREAL, PALESTINIAN POLITICAL RIGHTS AND THE
IMPORTANCE OF PARTICIPATION OF ALL PARTIES INVOLVED.

08311 SHULTZ, G.
THE ECOLOGY OF INTERNATIONAL CHANGE
DEPARTMENT OF STATE BULLETIN (US FOREIGN POLICY), 89(2142)
(JAN 89), 6-10.
THERE ARE THREE AREAS WHERE NEW DEVELOPMENTS WILL
OUTSTRIP OLD APPROACHES UNLESS AMERICAN POLICY-MAKERS
IDENTIFY WHAT IS HAPPENING AND DEAL MORE FLEXIBLY WITH THE
SITUATIONS. (1) IN THE FUTURE, THE SOVIET-AMERICAN
RELATIONSHIP WILL NOT BE THE SAME KIND OF RIVALRY. (2) OLD-
STYLE DIPLOMACY WILL NOT BE SUFFICIENT TO MEET THE NEW
THREATS TO WORLD SECURITY THAT HAVE ALREADY BEGUN TO EMERGE.
(3) THE NATURE OF NATIONS, THEIR PEOPLES, AND THEIR
ASSOCIATIONS ARE CHANGING THE INTERNATIONAL ENVIRONMENT IN
WAYS NOT FELT SINCE THE BIRTH OF THE NATION-STATE AT THE END
OF THE MIDDLE AGES.

08312 SHULTZ, G.
THE FUTURE AGENDA IN ARMS CONTROL
DEPARTMENT OF STATE BULLETIN (US FOREIGN POLICY), 89(2142)
(JAN 89), 1-4.
IN THIS ADDRESS TO THE AMERICAN AND EUROPEAN NUCLEAR
SOCIETIES AND THE NUCLEAR ENERGY FORUM, US SECRETARY OF
STATE SHULTZ DISCUSSED THE IMPACT OF THE NUCLEAR ERA AND THE
NEED FOR NUCLEAR NONPROLIFERATION.

08313 SHULTZ, G.
THE INF TREATY: ADVANCING U.S. SECURITY INTERESTS
DEPARTMENT OF STATE BULLETIN (US FOREIGN POLICY), 88(2134)
(MAY 88), 18-20.
IN DEFENSE OF THE INF TREATY, SECRETARY OF STATE GEORGE
SHULTZ ADDRESSES THE SENATE FOREIGN RELATIONS COMMITTEE. HE
EXAMINES THE BENEFITS OF THE TREATY AND THE NEGOTIATING
PROCESS AND LOOKS FORWARD TO OTHER NEGOTIATIONS REGARDING
CONVENTIONAL ARMS CONTROL. HE OUTLINES SOME OF THE CONCERNS
THAT MEMBERS OF THE COMMITTEE HAD WITH REGARDS TO THE INF
TREATY AND DEMONSTRATES THAT THE TREATY CAN STAND ON ITS OWN
MERITS AND WILL NOT HAMPER NATO EFFORTS TO MAINTAIN A
CREDIBLE DETERRENT.

08314 SHULTZ, G.
THE INTER-AMERICAN SYSTEM: INTO THE NEXT CENTURY
DEPARTMENT OF STATE BULLETIN (US FOREIGN POLICY), 89(2142)
(JAN 89), 10-13.
THE CHALLENGES CONFRONTING THE ORGANIZATION OF AMERICAN
STATES ARE BECOMING MORE ACUTE. CHANGES IN GLOBAL POLITICAL
AND ECONOMIC RELATIONS PORTEND NEW FORMS OF COOPERATION AND
PEACEFUL COMPETITION. THE OAS MUST PREPARE ITSELF AND ITS
PEOPLES FOR THE NEXT CENTURY BY DEALING SUCCESSFULLY WITH
TODAY'S PROBLEMS, SUCH AS DRUGS AND THE DEBT CRISIS.

08315 SHULTZ, G.
U.S., CHINA CELEBRATE DECADE OF DIPLOMATIC RELATIONS
DEPARTMENT OF STATE BULLETIN (US FOREIGN POLICY), 89(2143)
(FEB 89), 25-26.
IN THIS SPEECH, US SECRETARY OF STATE SHULTZ RECALLS
SIGNIFICANT EVENTS IN SINO-AMERICAN RELATIONS, INCLUDING THE

SHANGHAI COMMUNIQUE OF 1972 AND THE JOINT COMMUNIQUE OF
AUGUST 17, 1982. HE ALSO ENUMERATES CHALLENGES TO FUTURE
RELATIONS: UNRESOLVED REGIONAL DISPUTES, THE PROFILERATION
OF ADVANCED WEAPONRY, AND OPEN INTERNATIONAL TRADE.

08316 SHULTZ, R.H. JR.
DISCRIMINATE DETERRENCE AND LOW-INTENSITY CONFLICT: THE
UNINTENTIONAL LEGACY OF THE REAGAN ADMINISTRATION
CONFLICT, 9(1) (1989), 21-44.
ALMOST IMMEDIATELY UPON ASSUMING OFFICE, THE REAGAN
ADMINISTRATION WARNED THAT LOW-INTENSITY CONFLICT (LIC),
MOST NOTABLY GUERRILLA INSURGENCY AND INTERNATIONAL
TERRORISM, POSED A SERIOUS AND LONG-TERM CHALLENGE TO THE
UNITED STATES. TO MEET THE THREAT IT STATED IT WOULD DEVELOP
AN INTEGRATED POLICY AND THE APPROPRIATE STRATEGY AND
CAPABILITIES. THIS ARTICLE ARGUES THAT, DESPITE THE
APPROPRIATION OF APPROXIMATELY TWO TRILLION DOLLARS FOR
DEFENSE, THE U.S. ABILITY TO RESPOND TO LOW-INTENSITY
CHALLENGES HAS IMPROVED ONLY MARGINALLY SINCE 1981.
FURTHERMORE, SEVERAL ENDURING PROBLEMS HAVE YET TO BE
RESOLVED. THESE INCLUDE: (1) INSUFFICIENT COORDINATION AMONG
AGENCIES AND DEPARTMENTS OF THE EXECUTIVE BRANCH INVOLVED IN
THIS ASPECT OF NATIONAL SECURITY POLICY; (2) A LACK OF
UNIFYING GUIDELINES FOR ACTION; (3) NO CONSENSUS ON STRATEGY;
AND (4) THE ABSENCE OF A NATIONAL DOCTRINE FOR LOW-
INTENSITY CONFLICT. AS PRESIDENT BUSH ENTERS OFFICE, HE
FACES MANY OF THE SAME PROBLEMS AND CHALLENGES THAT
CONFOUNDED THE REAGAN ADMINISTRATION IN THE LIC AREAS OF
COUNTERINSURGENCY, SUPPORT FOR RESISTANCE MOVEMENTS, AND
COUNTERTERRORISM. GIVEN THE TRENDS AND DEVELOPMENTS
DISCUSSED IN THE ARTICLE, THERE IS LITTLE TO SUGGEST THAT
THE NEW ADMINISTRATION WILL BE ABLE TO AVOID THE ISSUE OF
LOW-INTENSITY CONFLICT. IN FACT, IT IS LIKELY TO BE FACED
WITH DIVERSE, URGENT, AND COMPLEX CHALLENGES IN THIS AREA OF
NATIONAL SECURITY POLICY. CONSEQUENTLY, THE NEW
ADMINISTRATION WILL NEED TO FORMULATE A NATIONAL STRATEGY
FOR LOW-INTENSITY CONFLICT, AND DEVELOP AN ORGANIZATIONAL
STRUCTURE THAT WILL APPROACH LIC IN A MANNER THAT IS NEITHER
DISJOINTED NOR AD HOC. THE ARTICLE CONCLUDES WITH A SERIES
OF RECOMMENDATIONS TO ACCOMPLISH THESE OBJECTIVES.

08317 SHUMILKINA, N.
CHAUVINISM AND LOATHING IN ALMA-ATA
GLASNOST, (16-18) (JAN 89), 62.
CONFLICTS IN ALMA-ATA AND IN OTHER REGIONS OF KAZAKHSTAN
HAD OCCURRED INTERMITTENTLY, BUT IN DECEMBER 1986 THEY
ASSUMED AN UNPRECEDENTED SCOPE. THE ADMINISTRATION OF
DINMUKHAMED KUNAEV HAD RAVAGED KAZAKHSTAN AND ROBBED THE
PEOPLE BLIND. UNDER KUNAEV'S LEADERSHIP, KAZAKH NATIONALISM
AND CHAUVINISM BLOSSOMED MARKEDLY, ATTAINING ITS FULLEST
EXPRESSION THUS FAR IN THE EVENTS OF 1986.

08318 SHUMON, M.
THE EMPEROR
JAPAN ECHO, XVI(1) (SPR 89), 44-45.
DURING THE FOUR MONTHS THAT ELAPSED BETWEEN THE ONSET OF
THE LATE EMPEROR HIROHITO'S SERIOUS ILLNESS AND HIS DEATH,
THE JAPANESE PEOPLE DISPLAYED A REVERENCE FOR THE MONARCHY
THAT FANNED FEARS OF RESURGENT ULTRANATIONALISM IN SOME
QUARTERS. IN THIS ESSAY, THE AUTHOR EXAMINES THIS REVERENCE
FOR THE JAPANESE EMPEROR AND EXPLAINS ITS SIGNIFICANCE.

08319 SHUMON, M.
THE JAPANESE MONARCHY
JAPAN ECHO, XVI(2) (SUM 89), 6-7.
THE EMPEROR WAS THE FORCE THAT SUCCEEDED IN CUTTING
ACROSS AND SUBSUMING THE LOCAL AFFILIATIONS AND LOYALTIES
THAT DOMINATED THE PRE-MODERN ERA IN JAPAN. UNDER THE
UNIFYING FORCE OF THE MONARCHY, THE VERTICAL DIVISIONS OF
CLASS AND THE HORIZONTAL REGIONAL BOUNDARIES THAT SEGMENTED
JAPANESE SOCIETY FADED AS THE PEOPLE PROCLAIMED THEMSELVES,
ONE AND ALL, EQUAL SUBJECTS OF THE EMPEROR.

08320 SHUNPEI, U.; TAKESHI, U.; TORU, Y.
THE IMPERIAL INSTITUTION IN JAPANESE HISTORY
JAPAN ECHO, XVI(1) (SPR 89), 46-52.
THE AUTHORS REVIEW THE ROLE OF THE IMPERIAL INSTITUTION
IN JAPANESE HISTORY, FOCUSING ON THE SHOWA ERA AND EMPEROR
HIROHITO.

08321 SHUPE, A.
THE RECONSTRUCTIONIST MOVEMENT ON THE NEW CHRISTIAN RIGHT
THE CHRISTIAN CENTURY, 106(28) (OCT 89), 880-881.
IN THIS ARTICLE, THE ANTIPLURALISTIC CHRISTIAN
RECONSTRUCTIONIST MOVEMENT AND THE DRASTIC CHANGES IT SEEKS
IN AMERICAN SOCIETY ARE SCRUTINIZED BY ANSON SHUPE, CHAIR OF
THE DEPARTMENT OF SOCIOLOGY AND ANTHROPOLOGY AT INDIANA-
PURDUE UNIVERSITY. IT EXPLORES THE BELIEF OF
RECONSTRUCTIONISTS THAT MOSAIC LAW OFFERS A PERFECT
BLUEPRINT FOR REBUILDING MODERN SOCIETY, AND ANALYZES THE
PRICE THAT WOULD BE REQUIRED TO MAKE THE CHANGE.

08322 SHUR, C.
THE BATTLE FOR HERUT

NEW OUTLOOK, 32(8 (294)) (AUG 89), 5.
IN THE LIFE AND DEATH STRUGGLE FOR THE LEADERSHIP OF HERUT, ARIEL SHARON HAS CURRIED THE SUPPORT OF THE EASILY AROUSED UNDERDOGS IN ISRAELI SOCIETY, A CONSTITUENCY THAT IS SWAYED MORE BY EMOTIONS AND HATRED FOR ARABS THAN BY ANY COHERENT POLITICAL RATIONALE. AND IT IS A CONSTITUENCY THAT IS NOT PARTICULARLY ATTRACTIVE TO THE PRESENT LEADERSHIP OF HERUT, DESPITE THE FACT THAT IT PLAYED A SIGNIFICANT ROLE IN BRINGING THE PARTY TO POWER. UNDER THE LEADERSHIP OF YITZHAK SHAMIR, THE PRESENT RULING ELITE IN HERUT HAS DECIDED TO TRANSFORM IT INTO A RESPECTABLE, PRAGMATIC, CENTRIST PARTY THAT WILL BE ABLE TO ENTRENCH ITSELF IN POWER FOR YEARS TO COME. IN ORDER TO DO SO, HERUT MUST PENETRATE TRADITIONAL LABOR PARTY STRONGHOLDS, INCLUDING THE UPPER MIDDLE CLASS, BUSINESSMEN, AND ACADEMICS.

08323 SHUTIAN, G.; CHUNBIN, L.
A PROBE INTO URBANIZATION IN RURAL AREAS
BEIJING REVIEW, 32(21) (MAY 89), 26-30.
GOVERNMENT POLICIES HAVE KEPT URBANIZATION AT A LOW LEVEL IN CHINA. IN THE RURAL AREAS, EFFORTS HAVE CONCENTRATED ON DEVELOPING SMALL TOWNS IN ORDER TO ACCOMMODATE THE LOCAL SURPLUS LABOR. BUT THIS ROAD TO RURAL URBANIZATION IS NOT IDEAL BECAUSE IT IS COSTLY, PRODUCES POOR RESULTS, AND HAS SERIOUS SIDE-EFFECTS. THE GOVERNMENT SHOULD GIVE FREE REIN TO THE DEVELOPMENT OF MEDIUM-SIZED CITIES TO SPEED UP THE PROGRESS OF URBANIZATION.

08324 SHUTTLEWORTH, G.
POLICIES IN TRANSITION: LESSONS FROM MADAGASCAR
WORLD DEVELOPMENT, 17(3) (MAR 89), 397-408.
TRANSITIONAL PROBLEMS IN THE PROCESS OF AGRICULTURAL POLICY LIBERALIZATION ARE USUALLY REGARDED BY POLICY MAKERS AND ANALYSTS AS POLITICAL CONSTRAINTS, WHICH MERELY DELAY THE PROCESS. IN SOME CASES, IT IS RECOGNIZED THAT SOCIAL PRESSURES CAN PREVENT LIBERALIZATION. THESE CONSTRAINTS ON THE PROCESS TEND TO BE REGARDED AS AN UNAVOIDABLE NUISANCE BY REFORMERS--WHETHER THE REFORMERS ARE PART OF THE NATIONAL GOVERNMENT OR COME FROM AID DONOR INSTITUTIONS. SUCH PROBLEMS ARE COMMONLY DEALT WITH BY MODIFYING THE ULTIMATE GOAL OF THE LIBERALIZATION. BUT RECENT EXPERIENCE IN AFRICAN COUNTRIES SUGGESTS THAT SOME TRANSITIONAL PROBLEMS ARISE NOT SO MUCH FROM THE NEW POLICIES THEMSELVES AS FROM THE DIFFICULTY GOVERNMENTS FACE IN IMPLEMENTING ANY SET OF DESIRED REFORMS. THIS PAPER EXAMINES THE EXPERIENCE OF MADAGASCAR, WHERE THE PROCESS OF TRANSITION IN FOOD POLICIES HAS PROVEN TRAUMATIC.

08325 SHUYU, W.
U.S. DIFFERS WITH WEST GERMANY ON MAJOR DEFENCE ISSUES
BEIJING REVIEW, 32(34) (AUG 89), 8-10.
AT THE NATO SUMMIT MEETING IN MAY 1989, THE UNITED STATES REACHED A COMPROMISE WITH WEST GERMANY AND OTHER NATO MEMBERS ON THE SHORT-RANGE MISSILE ISSUE. WASHINGTON HAD INSISTED THAT THE MISSILES DEPLOYED IN WEST GERMANY BE MODERNIZED IMMEDIATELY, WHILE THE WEST GERMANS FELT THIS WAS UNNECESSARY. IN THE END, THE UNITED STATES AGREED TO POSTPONE MODERNIZATION UNTIL 1992, WHILE WEST GERMANY AND ITS SUPPORTERS AGREED THAT NEGOTIATIONS MUST PROCEED CONDITIONALLY, AFTER THE CONVENTIONAL FORCES OF THE WARSAW PACT AND NATO HAVE REACHED A BALANCE. THE DISAGREEMENT WITHIN NATO REFLECTS DIFFERING ASSESSEMENTS OF THE OVERALL SECURITY SITUATION IN EUROPE.

08326 SIAZON, D.L.
UNIDO'S CONCERNS
INTERNATIONAL AFFAIRS (MOSCOW), (12) (DEC 89), 21-26.
THE NEW CONSTITUTION OF THE UNITED NATIONS INDUSTRIAL DEVELOPMENT ORGANIZATION GOES BEYOND THE PROMOTION AND ACCELERATION OF THE DEVELOPMENT OF THE MANUFACTURING SECTORS OF THE DEVELOPING COUNTRIES TO ENCOMPASS THE PROMOTION OF INDUSTRIAL DEVELOPMENT AND COOPERATION ON GLOBAL, REGIONAL, AND NATIONAL LEVELS. AS A RESULT, UNIDO HAS BEGUN PLAYING A MORE VIGOROUS, CATALYTIC ROLE IN DEVELOPMENT. IT HAS BEEN MOBILIZING THE FLOW OF TECHNICAL, MANAGERIAL, AND FINANCIAL RESOURCES FROM THE INDUSTRIALIZED COUNTRIES TO THE DEVELOPING COUNTRIES.

08327 SICK, G.
TRIAL BY ERROR: REFLECTIONS ON THE IRAN-IRAQ WAR
MIDDLE EAST JOURNAL, 43(2) (SPR 89), 230-246.
THE AUTHOR OBSERVES SEVERAL KEY TURNING POINTS OF THE IRAN-IRAQ WAR, EACH INVOLVING ONE OR MORE ERRORS OF JUDGEMENT OR EXECUTION BY ONE OR MORE PARTIES. HE ALSO EXAMINES THE ORIGINS OF THE CONFLICT AND ANALYZES THE ROLE THAT THE US AND THE UNITED NATIONS PLAYED IN THE CONFLICT. HE CONCLUDES BY OUTLINING THE IMPLICATIONS FOR FUTURE POLICYMAKING, ESPECIALLY WITH REGARDS TO THE US.

08328 SIDANIUS, J.; LAU, R.
POLITICAL SOPHISTICATION AND POLITICAL DEVIANCE: A MATTER OF CONTEXT
POLITICAL PSYCHOLOGY, 10(1) (MAR 89), 85-110.
THE IMPLICATIONS OF THE CONTEXT HYPOTHESIS CONCERNING THE RELATIONSHIPS BETWEEN INDICES OF POLITICAL SOPHISTICATION, SELF-ESTEEM, RACISM, AND IDEOLOGICAL DEVIANCE FROM VARIOUS POLITICAL CONTEXTS ARE TESTED USING THREE SAMPLES. THE RESULTS SHOW THAT MOST OF THE PREDICTIONS OF THE CONTEXT HYPOTHESIS ARE CONFIRMED: (1) THERE ARE LINEAR RELATIONSHIPS BETWEEN RACISM AND INTELLECTUAL AND POLITICAL SOPHISTICATION, INDICATING THAT THE GREATER AN INDIVIDUAL'S LEVEL OF RACISM, THE LOWER HIS OR HER COGNITIVE AND POLITICAL SOPHISTICATION; (2) QUADRATIC RELATIONSHIPS ARE FOUND BETWEEN POLITICAL-ECONOMIC CONSERVATISM AND POLITICAL SOPHISTICATION; INDICATING THAT THE MORE INDIVIDUALS DEVIATE FROM THE CENTER OF POLITICAL-ECONOMIC ISSUE SPACE, THE HIGHER THEIR OBSERVED LEVELS OF POLITICAL SOPHISTICATION; AND (3) LISREL STRUCTURAL EQUATION ANALYSES DISCLOSE THAT THE CAUSAL ASSUMPTIONS UNDERLYING THE CONTEXT HYPOTHESIS RELATING POLITICAL SOPHISTICATION, SELF-ESTEEM, VARIOUS INDICES OF POLITICAL DEVIANCE AND RACISM ARE, IN LARGE PART, CONSISTENT WITH THE EMPIRICAL DATA. THE THEORETICAL IMPLICATIONS OF THE FINDINGS ARE DISCUSSED.

08329 SIEDLECKI, M.
TIME FOR POSITIVE ACTION
EAST EUROPEAN REPORTER, 3(4) (SPR 89), 35.
THE ARTICLE EXAMINES HOW SOME OF POLAND'S MORE RADICAL OPPOSITION PARTIES REGARD THE RECENT ROUND TABLE TALKS BETWEEN THE MORE MODERATE OPPOSITION AND THE RULING COMMUNIST GOVERNMENT. THE RADICALS ARGUE THAT THE WILLINGNESS TO NEGOTIATE OF LECH WALESA AND OTHERS IS A SIGN OF DIMINISHING POLITICAL POWER. THE RADICALS ADVOCATE THE FORMATION OF A HARD-LINE ANTI-COMMUNIST FRONT WITH THE ULTIMATE GOAL OF COMPLETE INDEPENDENCE.

08330 SIEFF, M.
A DUMA BY ANY OTHER NAME
NATIONAL REVIEW, XLI(12) (JUN 89), 40-41.
THE RED ARMY COMMANDERS ARE NOT IN FAVOR OF THE NEW DUMA -- SUPREME SOVIET. DO NOT EXPECT THE CHAIRMAN OF THE KGB, THE SENIOR GENERALS OF THE GENERAL STAFF, OR POLITBURO MEMBERS YEGOR LIGACHEV AND VIKTOR CHEBRIKOV TO RECANT THEIR LIFETIMES OF ERROR AND BECOME ZEALOUS APOSTLES OF THE GOSPEL ACCORDING TO JAMES MADISON. EXPECT THE LION TO LIE DOWN WITH THE LAMB FIRST. WE STILL LIVE IN A WORLD WHERE LIONS EAT LAMBS-AND KGB CHIEFS AND MARSHALS OF THE SOVIET UNION EAT DUMAS FOR BREAKFAST.

08331 SIEGEL, F.
WHAT LIBERALS HAVEN'T LEARNED AND WHY
COMMONWEAL, CXVI(1) (JAN 89), 16-20.
THE AUTHOR ANALYZES MICHEAL DUKAKIS' FAILURE IN THE 1988 PRESIDENTIAL ELECTION.

08332 SIGELMAN, L.; GANT, M.
ANTICANDIDATE VOTING IN THE 1984 PRESIDENTIAL ELECTION
POLITICAL BEHAVIOR, 11(1) (MAR 89), 81-92.
DATA FROM A NATIONAL SURVEY CONDUCTED IN 1984 FORM THE BASIS FOR A NEW ANALYSIS OF ANTICANDIDATE VOTING IN PRESIDENTIAL ELECTIONS, I.E., VOTING FOCUSED MORE ON A CANDIDATE ONE OPPOSES THAN ON A CANDIDATE ONE PREFERS. ANTICANDIDATE VOTING IS VIEWED AS THE END PRODUCT OF A PROCESS WHEREBY VOTERS ATTEMPT TO REDUCE DISCOMFORT THAT CROSS-PRESSURES GENERATE WITHIN THEIR DECISION FRAMEWORKS. IN 1984, NEARLY A THIRD OF ALL LIKELY VOTERS SAID THEY WERE PRIMARILY MOTIVATED BY A DESIRE TO VOTE AGAINST ONE OF THE TWO PRESIDENTIAL CANDIDATES, A RATE OF ANTICANDIDATE VOTING SIMILAR TO THAT OBSERVED IN THE JOHNSONGOLDWATER ELECTION OF 1964 BUT WELL BELOW THAT OF THE 1980 REAGAN-CARTER ELECTION. HOWEVER, FACTORS RELATED TO ANTICANDIDATE VOTING IN THE PAST WERE NOT CONSISTENTLY LINKED TO ANTICANDIDATE VOTING IN 1984. THE AUTHORS CONCLUDE THAT THE PRESENCE OF RONALD REAGAN EXERTED SUCH A STRONG INFLUENCE ON THE 1984 CAMPAIGN THAT PROCESSES THAT WOULD NORMALLY BE OBSERVABLE, SUCH AS ANTICANDIDATE VOTING, WERE OVERRIDDEN.

08333 SIGELMAN, L.
THE 1988 PRESIDENTIAL NOMINATIONS: WHATEVER HAPPENED TO MOMENTUM?
PS: POLITICAL SCIENCE AND POLITICS, XXII(1) (MAR 89), 35-39.
THE AUTHOR EXPLORES HOW THE CONCEPT OF MOMENTUM CAN HELP TO EXPLAIN WHAT HAPPENED IN THE 1988 DEMOCRATIC AND REPUBLICAN PRESIDENTIAL NOMINATION CAMPAIGNS.

08334 SIGELMAN, L.
VOTING IN GUBERNATORIAL SUCCESSION RERERENDA
THE JOURNAL OF POLITICS, 51(4) (NOV 89), 869-885.
THIS PAPER EXAMINES THE PROPOSITION THAT THE ROLE PLAYED BY THE INCUMBENT GOVERNOR IS A KEY FACTOR SHAPING PUBLIC SUPPORT OR OPPOSITION IN CONSTITUTIONAL REFERENDA ON THE RIGHT OF GOVERNORS TO SUCCEED THEMSELVES IN OFFICE. TO THE EXTENT THAT THE INCUMBENT GOVERNOR HAS PLAYED A LEADING ROLE IN THE REFERENDUM CAMPAIGN, MANY VOTERS SHOULD SUPPORT A SUCCESSION AMENDMENT IN ORDER TO KEEP THE GOVERNOR IN OFFICE WHILE MANY OTHERS SHOULD OPPOSE A SUCCESSION AMENDMENT IN ORDER TO DRIVE THE GOVERNOR OUT OF OFFICE. IF THE GOVERNOR'S

ROLE IN THE REFERENDUM CAMPAIGN HAS BEEN LESS VISIBLE, APPRAISALS OF THE GOVERNOR SHOULD HAVE A LESSER IMPACT ON THE VOTERS. SURVEY DATA FROM KENTUCKY, NORTH CAROLINA, AND MISSISSIPPI ARE USED TO TEST THIS INTERPRETATION WHICH PERFORMS QUITE WELL.

08335 SIGLER, J.
CONFLICT IN THE MIDDLE EAST; CANADA AND REGIONAL CONFLICTS 1988-1989
ETUDES STRATEGIQUES ET MILITARES, MONTREAL, QUEBEC, 1989, 71-109.
THE ARTICLE EXAMINES RECENT CHANGES IN SEVERAL CONFLICTS AND SITUATIONS IN THE MIDDLE EATS. THESE INCLUDE: THE IRAN-IRAQ CONFLICT; THE PALESTINE QUESTION; LEBANON; THE LIBYA-U. S. CONFLICT; AND THE WESTERN SAHARA CONFLICT. IT ALSO EXAMINES CANADA'S ROLE IN THESE CONFLICTS AS WELL AS THE EFFECT THAT CHANGE IN THE MIDDLE EAST HAS HAD ON CANADA'S DOMESTIC AND FOREIGN POLICIES.

08336 SIGLER, J.
THE STATE OF STRATEGIC STUDIES: THE HEDGEHOGS AND THE FOXES
ETUDES INTERNATIONALES, 20(3) (SEP 89), 519-532.
WESTERN WRITERS AND THINKERS CAN BE DIVIDED INTO TWO CATEGORIES: THOSE WHO ARE HEDGEHOGS AND EMPHASIZE ONE CENTRAL VISION AND UNITY OF THE WORLD, AND THOSE WHO ARE FOXES WHO EMPHASIZE DIVERSITY, SEPARATENESS AND UNIQUENESS. THE ARGUMENT IN THIS ARTICLE IS THAT MUCH OF THE DEBATE ABOUT THE PROPER PLACE OF STRATEGIC STUDIES IN THE LARGER FIELD OF INTENATIONAL RELATIONS STEMS FROM THIS MAJOR DISTINCTION. THE STRATEGISTS TEND TO BE HEDGEHOGS WHO TAKE ONE PARADIGM, ONE SET OF APPLICATIONS AND ONE SET OF POLITICAL COMMITMENTS AND MAKE A GREAT DEAL OUT OF IT WILL ARGUE THAT THERE IS ALSO MERIT TO UNDERSTANDING THAT THERE ARE FOXES AS WELL, WHO WOULD PLACE THE CENTRAL VISION OF THE STRATEGISTS IN A LARGER CONTEXT OF OTHER TRUTHS, OTHER APPLICATIONS, AND BROADER COMMITMENTS.

08337 SIGLER, J. (ED.)
CANADA AND REGIONAL CONFLICTS 1988-1989
ETUDES STRATEGIQUES ET MILITAIRES, MONTREAL, QUEBEC, 1989, 200.
THE BOOK IS A COLLECTION OF ESSAYS ON GEOPOLITICAL CHANGES IN THE WORLD AND THEIR EFFECT ON CANADA. TOPICS DISCUSSED INCLUDE: EAST-WEST RELATIONS AND ARMS NEGOTIATIONS; SOCIAL AND POLITICAL CHANGE IN THE SOVIET UNION; THE MIDDLE EAST; SUB-SAHARAN AFRICA; ASIA; AND LATIN AMERICAN AND THE CARIBBEAN. THIS REVIEW OF CANADIAN FOREIGN POLICY IN TERMS OF CONFLICT IN THE WORLD'S REGIONS DEMONSTRATES THE ACCURACY OF THE STATEMENT THAT 1988-89 WAS A TIME OF TRANSITION.

08338 SIGUR, G.J. JR.
CURRENT REFLECTIONS ON US-JAPAN RELATIONS
DEPARTMENT OF STATE BULLETIN (US FOREIGN POLICY), 88(2134) (MAY 88), 31-33.
ASSISTANT SECRETARY FOR EAST ASIAN AND PACIFIC AFFAIRS GASTON SIGUR REFLECTS ON CURRENT US-JAPANESE RELATIONS. HE EXAMINES THE DEFENSE RELATIONSHIP, DEVELOPMENT AID AND FOREIGN POLICY COOPERATION, THE ECONOMIC RELATIONSHIP, AND US TRADE POLICY TOWARD JAPAN. HE CONCLUDES THAT ALTHOUGH THERE HAVE BEEN AND CONTINUE TO BE PROBLEMS THE US AND JAPAN WILL BE ABLE TO SOLVE THEIR PROBLEMS IN A WAY THAT WILL CONTRIBUTE TO THE PROSPERITY AND WELL-BEING OF BOTH NATIONS.

08339 SIGUR, G.J. JR.
PROPOSED SALE OF AEGIS WEAPONS SYSTEM TO JAPAN
DEPARTMENT OF STATE BULLETIN (US FOREIGN POLICY), 88(2138) (SEP 88), 13-15.
THE ARTICLE DISCUSSES THE PROPOSED SALE OF AEGIS--AN INTEGRATED AIR DEFENSE SYSTEM DESIGNED TO TRACK, SELECT, AND FIRE UPON MULTIPLE INCOMING TARGETS--TO JAPAN. IT ARGUES THAT THE SALE IS IMPORTANT FOR MILITARY. ECONOMIC, AND POLITICAL REASONS. IT DISCUSSES THE IMPORTANT ISSUE OF THE SECURITY OF THE SYSTEM AND THE FINANCIAL BENEFITS THAT WOULD RESULT FROM THE SALE.

08340 SIK, O.
ECONOMIC REFORM: CZECHOSLOVAKIA 1968, USSR 1989
FREEDOM AT ISSUE, (111) (NOV 89), 37-40.
THE MAIN FEATURES OF ECONOMIC REFORM IN CZECHOSLOVAKIA IN THE LATE 1960'S HERE AS FOLLOWS: (1) THE ECONOMISTS GRADUALLY AND WITH EXTREME DIFFICULTY OVERCAME UNREALISTIC DOGMAS AND (2) RULERS AND THE BUREAUCRACY TRIED TO IMPEDE THE DEVELOPMENT OF ECONOMIC REFORM. TO COMPARE THIS SITUATION WITH THE PRESENT REFORM IN CZECHOSLOVAKIA IS VERY REVEALING NOT ONLY ABOUT CZECHOSLOVAKIA BUT ALSO ABOUT SOVIET PERESTROIKA AND THE PROBLEMS IT FACES.

08341 SIKHAKREANE, J.
BLACK BUSINESSMEN DEFEND CAPITALISM
NEW AFRICAN, (MAR 88), 46-47.
THIS ARTICLE DESCRIBES BLACK BUSINESS IN SOUTH AFRICA BEING ENGAGED IN A BATTLE TO DEFEND CAPITALISM AND TO SECURE A FUTURE FOR ITSELF IN A POST-APARTHEID AFRICA. IT DESCRIBES COURSES OF ACTIONS TAKEN TO BRING THIS TO PASS, AS WELL AS

THE LEGAL AND ECONOMIC IMPLICATIONS INFLUENCING THIS EFFORT.

08342 SIKKINK, K.A.
DEVELOPMENTALISM AND DEMOCRACY: IDEAS, INSTITUTIONS, AND ECONOMIC POLICY MAKING IN BRAZIL AND ARGENTINA (1954-1962)
DISSERTATION ABSTRACTS INTERNATIONAL, 49(12) (JUN 89), 3839-A.
FOCUSING ON THE GOVERNMENTS OF JUSCELINO KUBITSCHEK AND ARTURO FRONDIZI, THE AUTHOR SURVEYS THE ADOPTION, IMPLEMENTATION, AND CONSOLIDATION OF A DEVELOPMENTALIST ECONOMIC MODEL IN BRAZIL AND ARGENTINA IN 1954 TO 1962. DEVELOPMENTALISM IS CONTRASTED WITH TWO MAIN ALTERNATIVE ECONOMIC MODELS: NATIONAL POPULISM AND LIBERALISM.

08343 SIKORSKI, R.
AFGHAN SITZKRIEG
NATIONAL REVIEW, XLI(7) (APR 89), 37-38.
ALTHOUGH MANY PREDICATED A SPEEDY FALL OF AFGHANISTAN"S CAPITAL, KABUL AFTER THE SOVIET TROOP WITHDRAWAL, A MUJAHADIN VICTORY IS NOT A FORGONE CONCLUSION. THE REBELS ARE STILL PLAGUED WITH DISUNITY AND ARE FACING A STILL FORMIDABLE COMMUNIST REGIME IN KABUL. THE VICTORY OF THE MUJAHEDIN, IF IT HAPPENS AT ALL, WILL COME AFTER A LONG AND BITTER STRUGGLE.

08344 SIKORSKI, R.
AFRICA'S NEXT BASKET CASE?
NATIONAL REVIEW, XLI(17) (SEP 89), 21-27.
THE BEST HOPE FOR NAMIBIA LIES IN SOUTH AFRICA'S CONTINUED INTEREST IN ITS FORMER COLONY. SOUTH AFRICA ALONE HAS THE LEVERAGE TO TAME THE SWAPO GOVERNMENT, AND UNLESS IT DOES, INDEPENDENT NAMIBIA COULD LOSE ITS TECHNICAL ELITE, FOREIGN INVESTMENT, AND RULE OF LAW.

08345 SIKORSKI, R.
NOBODY HERE BUT US DEMOCRATS
NATIONAL REVIEW, XLI(18) (SEP 89), 40-43.
THE COMMUNIST PARTY HAS LOST ITS LEADING ROLE IN POLAND AND NOW, UNDER A SOLIDARITY MINISTER, IT IS BEING PUSHED OUT OF WORKPLACE POLITICS AS WELL. BUT THE POLISH PEOPLE'S REPUBLIC HAS GONE BUST NOW, IN THE WAKE OF DEPOSED COMMUNIST RULE AND SOLIDARITY MANAGEMENT MUST TRY TO SALVAGE WHAT IT CAN FROM A SHOCKINGLY RIGID CLASS SYSTEM, A 150 PERCENT INFLATION RATE AND AN UNTRUDED INDUSTRIAL BASE.

08346 SIKORSKI, R.
POLAND'S GOOD OLD DAYS (NOW)
NATIONAL REVIEW, 61(24) (DEC 89), 23-24.
IN THIS ARTICLE, THE WRITER SUSPECTS THAT INTELLECTUALS IN POLAND AND OTHER SOON-TO-BE BOURGEOIS NATIONS MAY COME TO FEEL A CERTAIN NOSTALGIA FOR THE DAYS OF EVIL AND HEROISM. HE LIKENS GETTING RID OF COMMUNISM NOT TO CASTING OFF CHAINS AND SUDDENLY WALKING FREE AGAIN BUT RATHER LIKE DROPPING SOME HEIGHT OUT OF A HEAVY RUCKSACK ON A LONG SLOG TOWARD ELUSIVE HIGHLANDS, HE ANALYSES THE FUTURE AND CONCLUDES THAT POLAND, INDEED, WILL BE BETTER OFF WITHOUT COMMUNISM

08347 SIKORSKI, R.; GRENIER, R.; LLOYD, J.
THE COMING CRACK-UP OF COMMUNISM
NATIONAL REVIEW, XLI(1) (JAN 89), 28-32.
WHATEVER THE THEORETICAL ARGUMENTS ABOUT GORBACHEV'S CHANCES OF SUCCESS, THE FACT IS THAT SERIOUS RESTRUCTURING HAS NOT EVEN BEGUN IN THE SOVIET UNION. AND THE CHANCES FOR FUNDAMENTAL REFORM ARE SLIM.

08348 SIKORSKI, R.
THE LAST BATTLE?
NATIONAL REVIEW, XLI(14) (AUG 89), 19-20.
IN THIS ARTICLE THE AUTHOR EXPLAINS WHY THE COMMUNISTS IN ANGOLA FINALLY RECOGNIZED SAVIMBIS FREEDOM-FIGHTERS. THE MPLA DECISION TO TALK TO UNITA, WHICH ADVOCATED NEGOTIATIONS FOR YEARS, SHOWS A NEW REALISM IN LUANDA. HERE THE OFFENSIVE TO FAIL, THE MPLA POLITBURO NO DOUBT SPECULATED, THE CLOCK WOULD BEGIN TO TICK IN UNITA'S FAVOR. AFTER THE CUBAN WITHDRAWAL FROM SOUTHERN ANGOLA, UNITA MIGHT WELL HAVE CAPTURED A PROVINCIAL CAPITAL OR TWO.

08349 SIKORSKI, R.
THE MYSTIQUE OF SAVIMBI
NATIONAL REVIEW, XLI(15) (AUG 89), 34-37.
FRESH FROM THE LAST BATTLE IN ANGOLA, THE AUTHOR REPORTS THAT UNITA IS TACTICALLY COMPETENT AND STRATEGICALLY WELL SITUATED TO PREVENT COMMUNIST CONTROL OF THIS CRUCIAL AFRICAN NATION. HOWEVER, THE AUTHOR QUESTIONS WHETHER, AFTER THIRTY YEARS AS NEAR-ABSOLUTE LEADER OF HIS PARTY, JONAS SAVIMBI IS THE MAN TO LEAD THE NATION TO FULL FREEDOM.

08350 SILBERMAYR, W.
AUSTRIA: PRESSING DOMESTIC POLICY ISSUES
INFORMATION BULLETIN, 27 (MAR 89), 5-7.
THE AUTHOR CONSIDERS AUSTRIA'S ECONOMIC SITUATION, ITS ENTRY INTO THE EEC, AND THE NEED FOR A REDISTRIBUTION OF THE NATIONAL INCOME.

08351 SILBEY, J.H.
AFTER "THE FIRST NORTHERN VICTORY": THE REPUBLICAN PARTY
COMES TO CONGRESS, 1855-1856
JOURNAL OF INTERDISCIPLINARY HISTORY, XX(1) (SUM 89), 1-24.
BETWEEN ITS FIRST ELECTORAL VICTORIES IN THE
CONGRESSIONAL RACES OF 1854 AND ABRAHAM LINCOLN'S TRIUMPH IN
THE PRESIDENTIAL CONTEST SIX YEARS LATER, THE REPUBLICAN
PARTY GREW FROM ONE FACTION AMONG SEVERAL OPPOSING THE
DOMINANT DEMOCRATS TO A MAJORITY POSITION WITHIN THE
NORTHERN ELECTORATE. ACCOUNTS OF ITS RISE TO POLITICAL
PROMINENCE OFTEN HAVE THE QUALITY OF AN AMERICAN MORALITY
PLAY. DETERMINED TO RESIST THE FURTHER EXPANSION OF SLAVERY
ON THE AMERICAN CONTINENT, THE REPUBLICANS PROVED ABLE TO
OVERCOME THE HESITATIONS AND RESISTANCE OF THE INDIFFERENT,
THE HOSTILE, AND THOSE WITH OTHER AGENDA. ALTHOUGH
REPUBLICANS THEMSELVES DISAGREED ABOUT TIMING AND THE REACH
OF THEIR FUTURE POLICIES, THERE WAS NO QUESTION THAT WITH
THEIR VICTORY IN 1860, AT A MINIMUM, THE FURTHER EXPANSION
OF SLAVERY HAD BEEN CHECKED, A SITUATION WHICH SOUTHERN
SECESSIONISTS READ CLEARLY, TO THEIR ULTIMATE SORROW.

08352 SILVA. K.P.
A STEP TOWARDS SETTLING THE CONFLICT
WORLD MARXIST REVIEW, 31(1) (JAN 88), 120-127.
REGIONAL SIGNIFICANCE OF THE INDO-SRI LANKA ACCORD LIES
IN THE FACT THAT IT REPRESENTS A TREMENDOUS BLOW TO THE US
POLICY IN THE REGION AND, IN PARTICULAR, TO THE ATTEMPT BY
US IMPERIALISM TO INVOLVE SRI LANKA IN DESTABILISING INDIA
WHICH PURSUES AN INDEPENDENT AND PEACEFUL FOREIGN POLICY. IT
THUS STRENGTHENS THE SECURITY OF THE NEIGHBOURING STATES AND
THAT OF THE REGION AS A WHOLE.

08353 SILVA, K.P.
IN THE SPIRIT OF OPENNESS, GLASNOST, AND REALISM
WORLD MARXIST REVIEW, 32(1) (JAN 89), 26-28.
THE AUTHOR, WHO IS GENERAL SECRETARY OF THE COMMUNIST
PARTY OF SRI LANKA, DISCUSSES THE PRESENT STAGE IN THE
DEVELOPMENT OF THE INTERNATIONAL COMMUNIST MOVEMENT, THE
SIGNIFICANCE OF THE NEW POLITICAL THINKING, AND WHY
BOURGEOIS PARTIES ARE MORE POPULAR THAN COMMUNIST PARTIES IN
MANY ASIAN COUNTRIES.

08354 SILVER, G.D.
FRIENDSHIP, COMMERCE AND NAVIGATION TREATIES AND UNITED
STATES DISCRIMINATION LAW: THE RIGHT OF BRANCHES OF
FOREIGN COMPANIES TO HIRE EXECUTIVES "OF THEIR CHOICE
FORDHAM LAW REVIEW, 57(5) (APR 89), 765-784.
THIS NOTE ADDRESSES THE PROPER SCOPE OF THE EMPLOYER
CHOICE PROVISION. PART I DETAILS THE BACKGROUND AND PURPOSE
OF FCN TREATIES IN GENERAL, AND THEN FOCUSES ON THE EMPLOYER
CHOICE PROVISION. PART II DESCRIBES THE DIFFERING VIEWS ON
THE PROPER INTERPRETATION OF THE EMPLOYER CHOICE PROVISION.
PART III EMPLOYS STANDARD METHODS OF TREATY CONSTRUCTION TO
DETERMINE THE PROPER INTERPRETATION OF THE PROVISION. THIS
NOTE CONCLUDES THAT A LIBERAL CONSTRUCTION OF THE PROVISION
COMPORTS WITH THE INTENT OF THE PARTIES AND THUS SHOULD BE
OBSERVED.

08355 SILVERSTEIN, J.
HAS THE WORLD FORGOTTEN BURMA?
CULTURAL SURVIVAL QUARTERLY, 13(4) (1989), 2.
MORE THAN A YEAR HAS PASSED SINCE REVOLUTION ERUPTED IN
BURMA IN 1988. THE TWO STRUGGLES--OF THE ETHNIC MINORITY
INSURGENTS AND THE PRO-DEMOCRACY STUDENTS--CONTINUE, WITH
VARYING RESULTS. BUT IT IS RARE TO FIND A STRAY ARTICLE ON
BURMA IN THE PRESS, LET ALONE AN IN-DEPTH REPORT ON THE
CIVIL WAR OR THE REVOLUTION AND THE REPRESSION.

08356 SILVERSTEIN, K.
THE SELLING OF ARENA
NACLA REPORT ON THE AMERICAS, 22(6) (MAR 89), 7.
THE NATIONALIST REPUBLICAN ALLIANCE (ARENA) OF EL
SALVADOR IS SEEKING TO IMPROVE ITS IMAGE ON CAPITOL HILL.
LONG TARNISHED BY RUMORS OF SPONSORSHIP OF DEATH SQUADS,
ARENA IS GAINING FRIENDS AND ADMIRATION IN WASHINGTON
LARGELY DUE TO THE EFFORTS OF THE NEW ARENA EXECUTIVE
COMMITTEE PRESIDENT, ALFREDO CRISTIANI. ALTHOUGH THE US
STILL BACKS ARENA'S CHRISTIAN DEMOCRATIC OPPONENTS, THE
GROUNDWORK IS BEING LAID FOR A SMOOTH TRANSITIONS OF
PERCEPTIONS IN WASHINGTON IF, AS EXPECTED, ARENA WINS THE
UPCOMING ELECTIONS.

08357 SILVESTRI. S.
WESTERN EUROPEAN SECURITY BETWEEN NUCLEAR AND CONVENTIONAL
INTERNATIONAL SPECTATOR, XXIII(2) (APR 88), 63-73.
ALTHOUGH THE DISMANTLING OF SOVIET INF'S AND SRINF'S
DOES NOT ELIMINATE THE NUCLEAR THREAT TO EUROPE NOR THE NEED
FOR A STRATEGY OF DETERRENCE, IT DOES CONSIDERABLY REDUCE
THE SOVIET NUCLEAR, CONVENTIONAL, AND CHEMICAL THREATS TO
EUROPEAN TERRITORY. THE REAL PROBLEM LIES IN UNDERSTANDING
WHETHER, AND TO WHAT EXTENT, DETERRENCE WILL BE MODIFIED BY
ELIMINATION OF AMERICAN NUCLEAR WEAPONS FROM EUROPE.

08358 SIMIAN, G.
"NEW POLITICAL THINKING" AND THE SOVIET UNION'S
READJUSTMENT OF ITS ASIAN PACIFIC POLICY
COMPARATIVE STRATEGY, 8(2) (1989), 139-148.
IN SOVIET GLOBAL STRATEGY, THE ASIAN-PACIFIC REGION
PLAYS AN IMPORTANT ROLE, NEXT ONLY TO EUROPE. UNDER THE
GUIDANCE OF GORBACHEV'S "NEW POLITICAL THINKING," SOVIET
ASIAN-PACIFIC POLICY IS ALSO BEING REEXAMINED AND READJUSTED.
THIS PAPER GIVES AN ANALYSIS OF THE ECONOMIC AND POLITICAL
BACKGROUND FOR RECENT CHANGES IN THE SOVIET ASIAN-PACIFIC
POLICY SINCE 1985 AND AN ASSESSMENT OF THE NEW GESTURES AND
ACTIONS, AS WELL AS SOME RESTRAINING FACTORS TO THE
IMPLEMENTATION OF NEW POLICY TOWARD THIS REGION.

08359 SIMMONS, A.
LOCKE'S STATE OF NATURE
POLITICAL THEORY, 17(3) (AUG 89), 449-470.
THIS ARTICLE ATTEMPTS TO PRESENT A CLEAR ACCOUNT OF AND
DEFINITION OF LOCKE'S STATE OF NATURE. IT CLAIMS THAT THE
STATE OF NATURE IS MOST MISUNDERSTOOD IDEA IN LOCKE'S
POLITICAL PHILOSOPHY. THE AUTHOR STATES THAT HE WILL POINT TO
WHAT HE BELIEVES ARE LOCKE'S TRUE CONFUSIONS ABOUT THE STATE
OF NATURE, WHICH LIE IN RATHER DIFFERENT AREAS THAN IS
GENERALLY SUPPOSED. ALSO, HE HOPES TO CAST SOME LIGHT ON THE
POINT AND THE VIRTUES OF THE PARTICULAR CONCEPT OF THE STATE
OF NATURE LOCKE EMPLOYS IN HIS TWO TREATISES.

08360 SIMON, D.
PRESIDENTS, GOVERNORS, AND ELECTORAL ACCOUNTABILITY
THE JOURNAL OF POLITICS, 51(2) (MAY 89), 286-304.
THIS PAPER IS DESIGNED TO DEMONSTRATE THAT CITIZEN
EVALUATIONS OF PRESIDENTIAL PERFORMANCE OPERATE AS AN
INFLUENCE ON VOTING IN GUBERNATORIAL ELECTIONS. THE
DISCUSSION FIRST HIGHLIGHTS THE DEBATE OVER THE IMPACT OF
PRESIDENTIAL SUPPORT IN NATIONAL ELECTIONS AND PRESENTS
AGGREGATE-LEVEL EVIDENCE SUGGESTING THAT THIS IMPACT EXTENDS
TO GUBERNATORIAL CONTESTS. NEXT, AN INDIVIDUAL-LEVEL MODEL
OF THE GUBERNATORIAL VOTE IS ESTIMATED USING A POOLED DATA
SET FROM THE ELECTION YEAR SURVEYS CONDUCTED BY THE CENTER
FOR POLITICAL STUDIES FROM 1972 THROUGH 1986. THE ESTIMATED
MODEL REVEALS THAT EVALUATIONS OF THE PRESIDENT OPERATE AS
AN INFLUENCE ON THE VOTING PREFERENCES OF CITIZENS. A SERIES
OF DIAGNOSTIC EXERCISES SHOWS THAT THIS INFLUENCE IS NOT AN
ARTIFACT OF A PARTICULAR SURVEY, TYPE OF ELECTION, OR
PRESIDENTIAL ADMINISTRATION. A SERIES OF SIMULATIONS REVEALS
THAT THE IMPACT OF THESE EVALUATIONS IS SIZABLE ENOUGH TO
ALTER BOTH VOTING OF INDIVIDUALS AND THE OUTCOMES OF
GUBERNATORIAL CONTESTS. THE DISCUSSION CONCLUDES BY USING
THESE RESULTS TO REFLECT UPON THE CHARACTER OF ELECTORAL
ACCOUNTABILITY IN UNITED STATES.

08361 SIMON, D.F.
CHINA'S DRIVE TO CLOSE THE TECHNOLOGICAL GAP: S-T REFORM
AND THE IMPERATIVE TO CATCH UP
CHINA QUARTERLY, (119) (SEP 89), 598-630.
IT IS DIFFICULT TO UNDERSTAND THE COMPLEXITIES OF
CHINESE AFFAIRS WITHIN THE POLITICAL, ECONOMIC, AND MILITARY
SPHERES WITHOUT DIRECT REFERENCE TO CHINA'S RESEARCH AND
DEVELOPMENT SYSTEM AND ITS EDUCATIONAL PROGRAM. CHINA'S
PERSISTENT STRUGGLE TO ACHIEVE RAPID, SUSTAINED ECONOMIC
GROWTH HAS BEEN CHARACTERIZED BY THE CRITICAL IMPORTANCE
ATTACHED TO THE MODERNIZATION OF SCIENCE AND TECHNOLOGY. IN
SPITE OF PERIODIC DIFFERENCES BETWEEN VARIOUS LEADERSHIP
FACTIONS REGARDING THE APPROPRIATE SCIENCE AND TECHNOLOGY
DEVELOPMENT STRATEGY FOR CHINA, IT HAS CONSISTENTLY BEEN
VIEWED AS A MEANS TO CATAPULT THE COUNTRY AHEAD, BOTH
ECONOMICALLY AND MILITARILY. WHILE THERE HAS BEEN AGREEMENT
ON THE IMPORTANCE OF SCIENCE AND TECHNOLOGY, THE MEANS FOR
ADVANCING IT HAVE BEEN CAUGHT UP IN DISPUTES OVER POLITICS,
INVESTMENT OPTIONS, AND ECONOMIC PRIORITIES.

08362 SIMON, D.M.; OSTROM, C.W. JR.
THE IMPACT OF TELEVISED SPEECHES AND FOREIGN TRAVEL ON
PRESIDENTIAL APPROVAL
PUBLIC OPINION QUARTERLY, 53(1) (SPR 89), 58-82.
CONSIDERABLE ATTENTION HAS BEEN DEVOTED IN RECENT YEARS
TO THE USE OF POLITICAL DRAMA BY THE PRESIDENT, WITH THE
MOST DISCRETIONARY FORMS OF DRAMA--SPEECHES AND FOREIGN
TRAVEL-RECEIVING MUCH SCRUTINY. IN FACT, THERE HAS ARISEN A
CONVENTIONAL WISDOM WHICH ASSERTS THAT TELEVISED SPEECHES
AND FOREIGN TRAVEL BY THE PRESIDENT (1) HAVE INCREASED OVER
TIME. (2) EXERT A UNIFORMLY POSITIVE IMPACT ON PUBLIC
EVALUATIONS OF THE PRESIDENT'S PERFORMANCE, AND (3) CAN
THEREFORE BE USED AS A STRATEGY FOR INFLUENCING THE
PRESIDENT'S APPROVAL RATINGS, A VITAL RESOURCE FOR THE
MODERN PRESIDENT. THE PURPOSE OF THIS PAPER IS TO EVALUATE
THIS CONVENTIONAL WISDOM AND THUS ASSESS THE VALUE OF
TELEVISED SPEECHES AND FOREIGN TRAVEL AS INFLUENCES ON
PRESIDENTIAL APPROVAL. THE PAPER FIRST DEFINES POLITICAL
DRAMA AND CASTS THE CONVENTIONAL WISDOM IN THE FORM OF THREE
PROPOSITIONS. IT NEXT DEVELOPS A RESEARCH STRATEGY FOR
EVALUATING THESE PROPOSITIONS IN AN APPROPRIATE MANNER.
FINALLY, THE PAPER TESTS THE PROPOSITIONS.

08363 SIMON, J.
      ARC WITHOUT COVENANT
      NATIONAL REVIEW, XLI(8) (MAY 89), 30-32.
         THE AUTHOR CONSIDERS ISSUES INVOLVED IN BUYING ART FOR
      PUBLIC PLACES WITH PUBLIC FUNDS. HE FOCUSES ON THE "TILTED
      ARC" LITIGATION, WHICH DEFENDED AN UNPOPULAR SCULPTURE ON
      THE GROUNDS THAT IT WAS PROTECTED BY THE FIRST AND FIFTH
      AMENDMENTS.

08364 SIMON, J.L.
      LEBENSRAUM: PARADOXICALLY, POPULATION GROWTH MAY
      EVENTUALLY END WARS
      JOURNAL OF CONFLICT RESOLUTION, 33(1) (MAR 89), 164-180.
         POPULATION GROWTH MAY PROGRESSIVELY REDUCE ONE OF THE
      MOTIVES FOR MAKING WAR. NAMELY, POPULATION GROWTH THREATENS
      SHORTAGES OF RESOURCES, AND ESPECIALLY LAND. IMPENDING
      SHORTAGES CAUSE A SEARCH FOR WAYS TO MITIGATE THE SHORTAGES.
      THE DISCOVERIES EVENTUALLY PRODUCE GREATER AVAILABILITY OF
      RESOURCES THAN IF POPULATION GROWTH AND PRESSURE ON
      RESOURCES HAD NEVER OCCURRED. THE ARGUMENT RUNS AS FOLLOWS:
      (1) RHETORIC ABOUT RESOURCE SCARCITY INDUCED BY POPULATION
      DENSITY HAS OFTEN CONTRIBUTED TO INTERNATIONAL CONFLICT,
      EVEN IF ECONOMICS HAS NOT BEEN THE MAIN MOTIVE IN MAKING WAR.
      (2) IN THE PRE-MODERN ERA, WAR TO OBTAIN LAND AND OTHER
      NATURAL RESOURCES MAY SOMETIMES HAVE BEEN AN ECONOMICALLY
      SOUND POLICY. (3) POLITICIANS AND OTHERS IN INDUSTRIALLY
      DEVELOPED NATIONS BELIEVE RESOURCES MAY STILL BE A CASUS
      BELLI. (4) LAND AND OTHER PRODUCTIVE RESOURCES ARE NO LONGER
      WORTH ACQUIRING AT THE COST OF WAR.

08365 SIMON, J.L.
      ROBINSON CRUSOE WAS NOT MAINLY A RESOURCE ALLOCATOR
      SOCIAL SCIENCE QUARTERLY, 70(2) (JUN 89), 471-478.
         COUNTLESS ECONOMIC EXPOSITIONS ILLUSTRATE ECONOMIC
      ACTIVITY WITH ROBINSON CRUSOE AS AN EXAMPLE BECAUSE OF THE
      APPARENT ONE-PERSON SIMPLICITY OF HIS "ECONOMY." BUT
      CONTRARY TO STANDARD DISCUSSION, THE MOST IMPORTANT ECONOMIC
      ACTIVITY FOR CRUSOE HAS NOT SKILLFUL ALLOCATION OF KNOWN AND
      EXISTING RESOURCES. RATHER, CREATING NEW WAYS OF DEALING
      WITH HIS ENVIRONMENT KEPT HIM ALIVE AND EVENTUALLY
      COMFORTABLE. SUCH CREATION IS A PROPER MODEL FOR THE
      ECONOMIC HISTORY AND FUTURE OF HUMANKIND; ALLOCATION IS ONLY
      ITS HANDMAIDEN.

08366 SIMON, L.
      THE VOCABULARY OF BUSINESS SPEAKS TO BOTH BRANCHES
      STATE LEGISLATURES, 15(3) (MAR 89), 10-13.
         ECONOMIC DEVELOPMENT HAS BECOME ONE OF THE MOST
      IMPORTANT FUNCTIONS OF A GOVERNOR. AND THE BUSINESS OF
      ECONOMIC DEVELOPMENT MAY ALTER THE INTERACTIONS BETWEEN
      LEGISLATURES AND GOVERNORS WHEN LEGISLATURES TAKE SERIOUSLY
      THE CHALLENGE OF BEING A CO-EQUAL BRANCH OF GOVERNMENT.

08367 SIMON, P.
      THE FUTURE OF SDI
      JOURNAL OF LEGISLATION, 15(2) (1989), 89-92.
         SENATOR PAUL SIMON EXAMINES SOME MYTHS THAT SURROUND SDI
      SUCH AS THE INVINCIBILITY MYTH, THE AFFORDABILITY MYTH, AND
      THE MYTH THAT SDI WILL BRING ABOUT ARMS REDUCTIONS. HE
      CONCLUDES THAT THESE MYTHS ARE NOTHING MORE THAN MYTHS AND
      THAT FURTHER US SPENDING ON SDI IS HIGHLY UNWARRANTED.

08368 SIMON, R.J.
      ASSESSING ISRAEL'S RECORD ON HUMAN RIGHTS
      PHILADELPHIA: ANLS OF AMER ACMY OF POLITICAL AND SOC
      SCIENCE, (506) (NOV 89), 115-128.
         USING PUBLIC OPINION DATA, THIS ARTICLE EXAMINES ISRAELI
      JEWISH AND ARAB ATTITUDES TOWARD AND SUPPORT FOR VARIOUS
      ASPECTS OF CIVIL LIBERTIES IT ALSO CONTRASTS PUBLIC
      ATTITUDES WITH THE ISRAELI SYSTEM OF LAW AND JUSTICE AND
      WITH ISRAELI RESPONSES TO THE UPRISING IN THE OCCUPIED
      TERRITORIES OF THE WEST BANK AND GAZA. THE PUBLIC OPINION
      DATA SHOW ISRAELIS TO BE SIMILAR TO AMERICANS IN THEIR
      ATTITUDES TOWARD MANY CIVIL LIBERTY ISSUES. THE DATA ALSO
      SHOW DIFFERENCES BETWEEN JEWISH AND ARAB RESPONSES IN THEIR
      SATISFACTION WITH THE WAY DEMOCRACY WORKS IN ISRAEL. CURRENT
      ISRAELI PRACTICES ON THE WEST BANK AND IN GAZA INVOLVING
      VIOLATIONS OF HUMAN RIGHTS JUXTAPOSED WITH THE PUBLIC
      OPINION DATA. THE AUTHOR CONCLUDES THAT DUE PROCESS,
      ADHERENCE TO THE RULE OF LAW, AND TOLERANCE FOR UNPOPULAR
      IDEAS ARE NOT USUALLY HONORED WHEN A SOCIETY BELIEVES IT
      MUST RESPOND TO EXTERNAL THREATS TO ITS SECURITY.

08369 SIMON, R.J.; AMIR, M.; LANDIS, J.M.
      PUBLIC SUPPORT FOR CIVIL LIBERTIES IN ISRAEL
      MIDDLE EAST REVIEW, XXI(4) (SUM 89), 2-8.
         ISRAEL'S GOVERNMENTAL STRUCTURE IS MODELED AFTER THE
      BRITISH GOVERNMENT AND, LIKE GREAT BRITAIN, ISRAEL HAS NO
      CONSTITUTION. OVER THE YEARS, ISRAEL'S LACK OF A
      CONSTITUTION OR ANY SIMILAR AUTHORITATIVE DECLARATION OF
      INDIVIDUAL CIVIL LIBERTIES HAS GENERATED A CONTINUING PUBLIC
      AND PARLIAMENTARY DEBATE OVER ESTABLISHING A STRONGER LEGAL
      BASIS FOR THE PROTECTION OF SUCH LIBERTIES.

08370 SIMON, S. W.
      ASEAN SECURITY IN THE 1990'S
      ASIAN SURVEY, XXIX(6) (JUN 89), 580-600.
         THE 1990'S PROMISE TO BRING SIGNIFICANT CHANGES IN
      SOUTHEAST ASIA. THE MAJOR POWERS' ROLE IN THE REGION IS
      DECREASING, A TREND WHICH NECESSITATES GREATER INVOLVEMENT
      ON THE PART OF THE NATIONS IN THE REGION. THE ARTICLE
      ASSESSES THE MAJOR UNRESOLVED SECURITY ISSUES IN SOUTHEAST
      ASIA AND THE PROSPECTS FOR THEIR RESOLUTION IN THE FUTURE.
      THE ROLE OF THE SUPERPOWERS AS WELL AS THE INDIGENOUS
      CAPACITIES OF THE ASEAN STATES ARE ANALYZED. THE POSSIBILITY
      FOR A REGIONAL NEUTRALIZATION SCHEME--THE ZONE OF THE PEACE
      FREEDOM AND NEUTRALITY--IS ALSO EXPLORED.

08371 SIMON, S.W.
      THE SINO-SOVIET FUTURE: SOME PRC PERSPECTIVES
      THIRD WORLD QUARTERLY, 11(3) (JUL 89), 85-106.
         THIS ARTICLE ATTEMPTS TO PROJECT THE PRC'S POLICIES
      TOWARDS THE USSR INTO THE EARLY 1990'S AND TO ASSESS THE
      EFFECTS OF SINO-SOVIET RELATIONS ON OTHER MAJOR TARGETS OF
      PRC FOREIGN POLICY, INCLUDING THE USA, JAPAN, AND SUCH
      IMPORTANT NEIGHBOURS AS INDOCHINA AND THE KOREAS. IT FOCUSES
      PRIMARILY ON THE DIMENSION OF POLITICAL SECURITY AS IT
      AFFECTS CHINA'S POLICY TOWARDS THE USSR UNDER DENG XIAOPING
      AND THE MODERNISERS. THIS POLICY IS SEEN AS SUBORDINATE TO
      AND SERVING THE ENDS OF LONG-TERM DOMESTIC ECONOMIC
      MODERNISATION.

08372 SINDI, T.A.
      WORK AND ACHIEVEMENT ORIENTATION AMONG SELECTED SAUDI
      PUBLIC OFFICIALS
      DISSERTATION ABSTRACTS INTERNATIONAL, 50(6) (DEC 89),
      1801-A.
         THE AUTHOR INVESTIGATES THE PROBLEM OF ADMINISTRATIVE
      COMPETENCE AND EFFICIENCY AMONG SAUDI PUBLIC OFFICIALS IN
      TERMS OF THE DIVERSE WORK, AUTHORITY, AND SKILL REQUIREMENTS.
      THE ANALYSIS IS BASED ON TWO SETS OF DATA: (1) GOVERNMENT
      DOCUMENTS, COMMISSION REPORTS, HISTORICAL RECORDS, AND
      SOCIOLOGICAL REPORTS, AND (2) A SURVEY OF INDIVIDUAL
      PERCEPTIONS OF SKILL, AUTHORITY, AND WORK ORIENTATION USING
      A SELECTED SAMPLE OF SAUDI BUREAUCRATS.

08373 SINEDUBSKY, V.
      SOVIET-MONGOLIAN FIRST JOINT VENTURE
      FOREIGN TRADE, 1 (1989), 12-13.
         THIS INTERVIEW WITH AN OFFICIAL OF THE USSR MINISTRY OF
      RAILWAYS DESCRIBES THE OPERATION OF THE ULAN BATOR RAILWAY,
      FORMED IN 1949 BY A JOINT VENTURE BETWEEN MONGOLIA AND THE
      USSR. DETAILED ARE THE MANY WAYS THE RAILROAD'S MANAGEMENT
      HAS IMPROVED ITS EFFICIENCY, WITH EMPHASIS GIVEN TO THE
      GREATER FREEDOM OF ACTION GIVEN TO MANAGEMENT IN RECENT
      YEARS.

08374 SINGER, B.C.J.
      VIOLENCE IN THE FRENCH REVOLUTION: FORMS OF
      INGESTION/FORMS OF EXPULSION
      SOCIAL RESEARCH, 56(1) (SPR 89), 263-293.
         THE AUTHOR EXAMINES THE CHARACTER OF VIOLENCE AS PART OF
      AN EFFORT TO FORMULATE A SOCIOLOGY OF VIOLENCE. THE BEGINS
      HIS ESSAY WITH A BRIEF ANALYSIS OF GEORGE RUDE'S WORK ON
      POPULAR VIOLENCE, "THE CROWD IN THE FRENCH REVOLUTION." HE
      SUGGESTS THAT ELABORATING A SOCIOLOGY OF VIOLENCE RESTORES
      VIOLENCE ITS CHARACTER AS INSTITUTION AND ENABLES ONE TO
      UNDERSTAND IT AS FORM. IT ALSO ENTAILES EXAMINING VIOLENCE
      AS INSTITUTED IN DIFFERENT SOCIETIES AS REVEALING SOMETHING
      ABOUT THAT SOCIETY, AS EXPRESSIVE OF THAT SOCIETY AND ITS
      SELF-UNDERSTANDING.

08375 SINGER, D.
      ON REVOLUTION
      MONTHLY REVIEW, 41(2) (JUN 89), 33-36.
         THE AUTHOR ARGUES THAT THE LEADERS OF THE WESTERN WORLD
      ARE MEETING IN FRANCE IN JULY TO CELEBRATE THE END OF
      REVOLUTION; IN OTHER WORDS, THE AGE OF REVOLUTION IS OVER
      AND THE REIGN OF CAPITAL IS ETERNAL. HOWEVER, REVOLUTIONARY
      THOUGHT AND SPIRIT IS ALIVE AND WELL IN THE WORLD, AND THE
      REJOICING OF THE WEST MAY BE PREMATURE.

08376 SINGER, D.
      THE GREENING OF DANY THE RED
      NEW POLITICS, 11(2) (WIN 89), 38-.
         DANY COHN - BENDIT, ONE OF THE KEY FIGURES IN THE MAY
      1968 MOVEMENT IN FRANCE, OFFERS HIS THOUGHTS ON THE IMPACT
      OF THE FRENCH MAY AND ON EUROPEAN REFORM MOVEMENT OF TODAY,
      INCLUDING THE WEST GERMAN GREENS AND THE WORKERS' UPRISINGS
      IN POLAND AND CZECHOSLOVAKIA.

08377 SINGER, D.
      WHITHER THE SOVIET UNION
      MONTHLY REVIEW, 41(3) (JUL 89), 1-8.
         THIS ARTICLE ADDRESSES THE QUESTION, "CAN RADICAL
      REFORMS FROM ABOVE PREVENT A REVOLUTION FROM BELOW?"
      CONSIDERED ARE THE FIELD OF INTERNATIONAL RELATIONS, THE
      NATIONAL QUESTION, AND THE IMPACT OF CHANGES IN THE CENTER

ON THE PERIPHERY. IT CONCLUDES BY ANSWERING THE ORIGINAL
QUESTION.

08378 SINGER, M.
    JUSTICE FOR THE PALESTINIANS
    NATIONAL REVIEW, XLI(19) (OCT 89), 40-42.
        IT IS NOT ISRAEL THAT IS RESPONSIBLE FOR THE INJUSTICE
    OF THE PALESTINIAN SITUATION. ISRAEL AND PALESTINE ARE BOTH
    VICTIMS OF THE ARAB STATES' ENMITY TOWARD ISRAEL. THE WAY TO
    PURSUE PEACE IS TO EXPOSE AND COUNTER THE ARAB STRATEGY OF
    PRETENDING THAT THE WAR AGAINST ISRAEL IS A PALESTINIAN WAR.
    PALESTINE IS JUST THE "FRONT MAN".

08379 SINGH, A.L.; HASHMI, S.N.I.
    LAND RECLAMATION AND RURAL TRANSFORMATION IN ALIGARH
    DISTRICT: SOME PROJECTIONS
    ASIAN PROFILE, 17(5) (OCT 89), 425-436.
        THE GREEN REVOLUTION, INTRODUCED IN 1964-65, SEEMED TO
    BE THE ANSWER TO THE PROBLEM OF FEEDING INDIA'S ENORMOUS
    POPULATION. THE TECHNOLOGICAL PACKAGE FOR AGRICULTURAL
    DEVELOPMENT WAS ENTHUSIASTICALLY ACCEPTED BY PLANNERS AND
    FARMERS ALIKE AS THE LASTING SOLUTION TO THE PERENNIAL
    PROBLEMS OF RURAL POVERTY AND HUNGER. BUT, FAR FROM
    ALLEVIATING POVERTY, THE GREEN REVOLUTION HAS ACTUALLY
    INCREASED IT AND HAS WIDENED THE GAP BETWEEN THE RURAL RICH
    AND THE RURAL POOR. WITH FUTURE INCREASES IN POPULATION, THE
    SKEWED LANDHOLDINGS WILL BECOME MORE ACUTE AND THE POTENTIAL
    FOR INCREASED AGRICULTURAL PRODUCTION WILL REACH A
    SATURATION POINT DESPITE CROPPING PATTERNS, FERTILIZER USE,
    IMPROVED SEEDS, AND INCREASED WET AREA UNDER CULTIVATION.

08380 SINGH, B.
    ASEAN'S ARMS INDUSTRIES: POTENTIAL AND LIMITS
    COMPARATIVE STRATEGY, 8(2) (1989), 249-264.
        THE ARTICLE EXAMINES THE INDIGENOUS ARMS INDUSTRIES OF
    THE ASEAN NATIONS, NAMELY INDONESIA, MALAYSIA, THAILAND,
    SINGAPORE, THE PHILIPPINES, AND BRUNEI. IT OUTLINES THE
    ORGANIZATION AND DIMENSIONS OF THEIR ARMS PRODUCTION
    ORGANIZATION AND DIMENSIONS OF THEIR ARMS PRODUCTION
    CAPABILITIES AND ALSO THE MOTIVES IMPELLING THESE NATIONS TO
    PRODUCE THEIR OWN WEAPONS. IT CONCLUDES WITH AN ANALYSIS OF
    THE FUTURE OF ARMS PRODUCTION IN THESE ASEAN NATIONS.

08381 SINGH, E.
    THE APARTHEID STATE AND THE CHURCHES
    SECHABA, 23(10) (OCT 89), 20.
        THIS ARTICLE REPORTS ON THE STRONG RESISTANCE TO
    APARTHEID BY THE CHURCHES AND THE ACTION THREATED AGAINST
    THEM BY THE GOVERNMENT. IT INTERVIEWS FATHER MICHAEL LAPSLEY,
    A MEMBER OF THE RELIGIOUS DEPARTMENT OF THE AFRICAN
    NATIONAL CONGRESS, ABOUT THE SITUATION.

08382 SINGH, H.; NARAYANAN, S.
    CHANGING DIMENSIONS IN MALAYSIAN POLITICS: THE JOHORE BARU
    BY-ELECTION
    ASIAN SURVEY, 29(5) (MAY 89), 514-529.
        THIS ARTICLE EXAMINES THE SIGNIFICANCE OF AN INDEPENDENT
    CANDIDATE WINNING A MALAYSIAN ELECTION AND THE SYMBOLIC
    IMPLICATIONS OF THE GOVERNMENT LOSING JOHORE BARU TO THE
    OPPOSITION. IT CONSIDERS WHAT THE RESULTS SIGNAL FOR THE
    MALAYSIAN PRIME MINISTER AND ARGUES THAT THE JOHORE BARU
    ELECTION MAY PROVE TO BE A WATERSHED IN MALAYSIAN POLITICS.

08383 SINGH, K.
    OIL POLITICS IN VENEZUELA DURING THE LOPEZ CONTRERAS
    ADMINISTRATION (1936-1941)
    JOURNAL OF LATIN AMERICAN STUDIES, 21(1) (FEB 89), 89-104.
        WHEN THE VENEZUELAN DICTATOR JUAN VINCENTE GOMEZ DIED IN
    DECEMBER 1935, AFTER RULING VENEZUELA WITH AN IRON FIST FOR
    27 YEARS, AN OUTBURST OF POPULAR UNREST AND NATIONALISTIC
    FERVOR WAS UNLEASHED AGAINST THE FOREIGN OIL COMPANIES
    OPERATING ON VENZUELAN SOIL. IN THE MIDST OF THE RESULTING
    POLITICAL CRISIS, GOMEZ'S MINISTER OF WAR AND THE NAVY,
    ELEAZAR LOPEZ CONTREARAS, WAS NOMINATED BY A GOMECISTA
    EXECUTIVE COMMITTEE AS INTERIM PRESIDENT. IN APRIL 1936,
    LOPEZ CONTRERAS WAS CONFIRMED AS PRESIDENT AND A NEW
    CONSTITUTION, WHICH PROVED TO BE A BITTER DISAPPOINTMENT TO
    ALL THOSE WHO HOPED FOR A GENUINE OPENING UP OF THE
    POLITICAL SYSTEM, WAS PASSED.

08384 SINGH, K.
    THE NARMADA ISSUE: AN OVERVIEW
    CULTURAL SURVIVAL QUARTERLY, 13(2) (1989), 12-16.
        THE NARMADA VALLEY PROJECT IS MADE UP OF PLANS TO BUILD
    MORE THAN 3,000 DAMS OVER THE NEXT 25 YEARS. THE SARDAR
    SAROVAR PROJECT (SSP) IN GUJARAT AND THE NARMADA SAGAR
    PROJECT (NSP) IN MADHYA PRADESH ARE MAJOR COMPONENTS OF THE
    NARMADA VALLEY PLANS. THE INDIAN GOVERNMENT RECENTLY GAVE
    CLEARANCE FOR THE SSP AND THE NSP, EVEN THOUGH VERY FEW
    DISPUTE THE FACT THAT THE ECOLOGICAL IMPACTS OF THESE
    PROJECTS HAVE NOT BEEN PROPERLY STUDIED. BOTH
    ENVIRONMENTALISTS AND SOCIAL ACTIVISTS HAVE RAISED SERIOUS
    QUESTIONS ABOUT THE PROJECTS.

08385 SINGH, M.
    POPULATION PROJECTIONS FOR INDIA: 1981-2016
    ASIAN PROFILE, 17(6) (DEC 89), 533-552.
        THE AUTHOR REVIEWS INDIA'S PREVIOUS POPULATION
    PROJECTIONS, FRAMES BASE-LINE ASSUMPTIONS, AND DISCUSSES THE
    FINDINGS OF THESE PROJECTIONS IN LIGHT OF NATIONAL
    POPULATION POLICY AND PLANNING. HE ALSO PROJECTS THE SIZE OF
    RURAL AND URBAN POPULATIONS FOR EACH TENTH YEAR DURING THE
    PROJECTION PERIOD. THE DOUBLING TIME OF THE POPULATION IS
    CALCULATED, WITH A VIEW TO ASSESSING THE POSSIBILITY FOR
    STABILIZATION OF INDIA'S POPULATION IN THE FUTURE.

08386 SINGH, N.
    MADHYA PRADESH: SIMMERING CRISIS
    INDIA TODAY, XIV(7) (APR 89), 50-51.
        IN THE CENTRAL INDIAN FORESTS, THE TENDU LEAF HAS COME
    TO STMBOLIZE POLITICAL ONE UPMANSHIP. IT HAS BEEN THE CENTER
    OF AN ONGOING CONFLICT BETWEEN MINISTERS AND BUSINESSMEN WHO
    ARE FIGHTING FOR CONTROL OF PRODUCTION OF THE LEAF. EVERY
    POLITICAL CHANGE IN THE STATE BRINGS A NEW POLICY WITH
    REGARDS TO THE TENDU AND ITS TENDERS, THE TRIBES THAT
    INHABIT THE FORESTS. THE CONFLICT SHOWS NO SIGN OF SLOWING
    AND A CONCRETE RESOLUTION SEEMS INLIKELY.

08387 SINGH, N.K.
    ARJUN SINGH: FIGHTING BACK
    INDIA TODAY, XIV(10) (MAY 89), 28.
        THIS ARTICLE DESCRIBES HOW ARJUN SINGH, ONCE UNCROWRED
    KING OF MADHYA PRADESH, HAS LAUNCHED A GRAND DESIGN TO
    ESTABLISH HIMSELF AT THE CENTER OF STATE POLITICS.

08388 SINGH, N.K.
    BATTLE LINES DRAWN
    INDIA TODAY, XIV(2) (JAN 89), 34-36.
        LESS THAN A YEAR AFTER HIS TRIUMPHANT RETURN TO MADHYA
    PRADESH AS CHIEF MINISTER, ARJUN SINGH IS UNDER ATTACK FROM
    A GALAXY OF PARTY LEADERS HEADED BY UNION MINISTERS MOTILAL
    VORA AND MADHAVRAO SCINDIA. SINGH IS FIGHTING BACK, BUT HIS
    OPPONENTS SEEM TO HAVE THE TACIT SUPPORT OF THE CENTRE.

08389 SINGH, N.K.
    COLLAPSE OF A KINGPIN
    INDIA TODAY, XIV(3) (FEB 89), 27-29.
        FOLLOWING A COURT JUDGMENT THAT THE CHURAT LOTTERY RUN
    BY ARJUN SINGH'S SON WAS GUILTY OF LEGAL VIOLATIONS, SINGH
    WAS FORCED TO RESIGN AS MADHYA PRADESH'S CHIEF MINISTER. AS
    SINGH LICKED HIS WOUNDS, HIS ARCH-ENEMY, MOTILAL VORA, WAS
    SWORN IN AS CHIEF MINISTER.

08390 SINGH, N.K.
    INJUDICIOUS ACTIONS
    INDIA TODAY, XIV(12) (JUN 89), 52-53.
        UNLESS THE CURRENT FLAWED PROCEDURE OF SELECTION,
    APPOINTMENT, PROMOTIONS AND TRANSFERS OF JUDGES IS REVIEWED
    AND RADICALLY ALTERED, THE EXECUTIVE WILL CONTINUE TO
    INTERFERE - AND INFLUENCE - THE COURSE OF JUSTICE IN INDIA.

08391 SINGH, N.K.
    IRDP LOANS: A METHODICAL FRAUD
    INDIA TODAY, XIV(5) (MAY 89), 74-77.
        THE INTEGRATED RURAL DEVELOPMENT PROGRAM HAS AIMED AT
    UPLIFTING THE POOR. BUT IN MADHYA PRADESH A SYSTEMATIC
    FUDGING OF RECORDS, IRREGULARITIES, AND MALPRACTICES HAVE
    ENSURED THAT THE BENEFITS DO NOT REACH THEM. THIS ARTICLE
    EXAMINES THE DETAILS OF THIS FINANCIAL SCANDAL.

08392 SINGH, N.K.
    MADHYA PRADESH: FORCED PEACE
    INDIA TODAY, XIV(11) (JUN 89), 28-29.
        THE POLITICAL NUANCES DISCERNIBLE AT THE MLA'S DELHI
    JAMBOREE SUGGESTED THAT EFFORTS TO RECONCILE OPPOSING
    FACTIONS OF MADHYA PRADESH MAY FOUNDER AT ANY TIME GIVEN THE
    DEEP-ROOTED BIASES, SUSPICIONS AND THE UNENDING GAME OF
    POLITICAL ONE-UPMARSLIP THAT MAKES FOR MADHYA PRADESH'S
    POLITICAL PASTICLE.

08393 SINGH, R.
    PATRIARCH'S PROBLEMS
    INDIA TODAY, XIV(1) (JAN 89), 33-34.
        HARYANA CHIEF MINISTER DEVI LAL HAS BEEN UNDER FIRE FOR
    THE BEHAVIOR OF HIS SONS. THE MISBEHAVIOR OF DEVI LAL'S
    CHILDREN HAS PROVIDED FODDER FOR THE CONGRESS (I)
    POLITICIANS WHO WISH TO DISCREDIT HIM BECAUSE HE HAS BECOME
    THE LYNCH PIN OF OPPOSITION UNITY EFFORTS.

08394 SINGH, R.; AWASTHI, D.; SENGUPTA, U.
    TOWARDS ESTRANGEMENT
    INDIA TODAY, XIV(8) (APR 89), 70-72.
        INDIA-NEPALESE RELATIONS HAVE BEEN LOCKED IN AN IMPASSE
    SINCE THE EXPIRATION OF THE BILATERAL TREATIES ON TRADE AND
    TRANSIT. NEPAL HAS SUGGESTED THAT A MEETING OF THE INDIA-
    NEPAL JOINT COMMISSION BE CONVENED TO DISCUSS THE RELEVANT
    ISSUES. MEANWHILE, BOTH ISLAMABAD AND DACCA HAVE SENT
    MESSAGES OF SYMPATHY AND POSSIBLE SUPPORT TO NEPAL IN ITS

CONFRONTATION WITH INDIA.

08395 SINGH, R.; KAKARIA, A.
    UNION CARBIDE CASE: UNSETTLING VERDICT
    INDIA TODAY, XIV(5) (MAR 89), 42-46.
        THE SUPREME COURT ORDER ASKING UNION CARBIDE TO PAY $470
    MILLION AS COMPENSATION FOR THE BHOPAL GAS VICTIMS RAISED
    PROTESTS THAT THE COMPANY HAD BEEN LET OFF LIGHTLY. EVEN
    MORE DISTURBING WAS THE COURT'S DECISION TO QUASH ALL
    PROCEEDINGS, PRESENT AND FUTURE AGAINST THE MULTINATIONAL.
    THE CONTROVERSIES SURROUNDING THE CASE AND THE JUDGEMENT
    WILL CONTINUE. THEY WILL RECEDE INTO THE BACKGROUND ONLY IF
    ADEQUATE MONETARY RELIEF AND MEDICAL AID REACHES THE GAS
    VICTIMS AND SETS THEM BACK ON THEIR FEET.

08396 SINGH, S.N.
    RESPONSIBILITY OF THE PRESS
    INDIA TODAY, XIV(1) (JAN 89), 92.
        SINCE REVELATIONS ARE THE STOCK IN TRADE OF THE INDIAN
    PRESS, MEDIA RESPONSIBILITY HAS BECOME A MAJOR ISSUE. THE
    COUNTRY'S POLITICAL CULTURE IS IN AN ERA OF TRANSITION, AND
    MAKING EXTRAVAGANT CHARGES AGAINST LEADERS HAS BECOME AN
    ACCEPTED METHOD OF PLAYING POLITICS, THE MORE THE PRESS
    SEEMS IRRESPONSIBLE IN REPORTING THESE CHARGES, THE GREATER
    WILL BE THE GOVERNMENT'S SUCCESS IN CONVINCING THE PUBLIC
    THAT THE MEDIA SHOULD BE RESTRICTED.

08397 SINNOTT, D.H.
    DSTO'S RADAR RESEARCH STRENGTHENS AUSTRALIA'S SECURITY
    PACIFIC DEFENCE REPORTER, 15(9) (MAR 89), 49, 52.
        AUSTRALIA'S DEFENCE SCIENCE AND TECHNOLOGY ORGANIZATION
    (DSTO) HAS BEEN ACTIVE IN RADAR RESEARCH AND DEVELOPMENT FOR
    MANY YEARS. THIS ARTICLE DESCRIBES AUSTRALIA'S WORK IN THE
    AREAS OF CONVENTIONAL LINE-OF-SIGHT RADARS AND THE
    INNOVATIVE OVER-THE-HORIZON RADAR. THE LATTER, KNOWN AS
    JINDALEE, IS PLANNED AS A CORNERSTONE OF AUSTRALIA'S LONG-
    RANGE DEFENCE SURVEILLANCE FOR THE 1990'S AND BEYOND.

08398 SINNOTT, R.
    LOCATING PARTIES, FACTIONS, AND MINISTERS IN A POLICY
    SPACE: A CONTRIBUTION TO UNDERSTANDING THE PARTY-POLICY
    LINK
    EUROPEAN JOURNAL OF POLITICAL RESEARCH, 17(6) (NOV 89),
    689-705.
        COMPARATIVE RESEARCH ON THE LINKS BETWEEN PARTIES AND
    POLICY SPANS THREE DISTINCT FIELDS: THE WIDE RANGE OF
    STUDIES WHICH SEEK TO LINK PARTY COMPLEXION OF GOVERNMENT TO
    POLICY OUTCOMES; RESEARCH ON COALITION BEHAVIOUR; AND
    RESEARCH ON THE POLICY IMPACT OF PARTY MANIFESTOS. DESPITE
    THE FACT THAT THE THREE APPROACHES STEM FROM WIDELY
    DIFFERING THEORETICAL ORIENTATIONS, TWO ASSUMPTIONS HAVE
    DOMINATED VIRTUALLY ALL THE RESEARCH IN QUESTION (WITH ONE
    IMPORTANT EXCEPTION). THESE ARE THAT POLITICAL CONFLICT IS
    UNIDIMENSIONAL AND THAT PARTIES CAN BE TREATED AS UNITARY
    ACTORS. THIS PAPER ARGUES THAT BOTH SHOULD BE TREATED AS
    MATTERS TO BE DETERMINED EMPIRICALLY AND ADVOCATES A
    DISAGGREGATIVE APPROACH TO THE ISSUE.

08399 SIRISOMBOONWECH, S.
    THE IMPACT OF THE NEW LAW OF THE SEA ON THAILAND'S FISHERY
    DEVELOPMENT: A LEGAL CASE STUDY
    DISSERTATION ABSTRACTS INTERNATIONAL, 50(6) (DEC 89),
    1797-A.
        FOR THAILAND, THE PROBLEM OF ACCESS TO FISHERY RESOURCES
    IS URGENT AND NEEDS TO BE RESOLVED. THAILAND'S LEGAL
    ARGUMENTS FOR OBTAINING ACCESS TO THE EXCLUSIVE ECONOMIC
    ZONES (EEZ) OF NEIGHBORING STATES UNDER THE LAW OF THE SEA
    ARE (1) ITS GEOGRAPHICAL DISADVANTAGED STATUS, (2) ITS
    STATUS AS A DEVELOPING STATE THAT WISHES TO HARVEST PART OF
    ANY SURPLUS IN THE REGION, AND (3) THE NEED TO MINIMIZE
    ECONOMIC DISLOCATION OF ITS FISHERMEN WHO HAVE HABITUALLY
    FISHED IN THE ZONE. BUT AN EXAMINATION OF THE RELEVANT
    PROVISIONS OF THE LAW OF THE SEA CONVENTION SUGGESTS THAT
    THAILAND MAY NOT BE ABLE TO GAIN ANY BENEFIT FROM THESE
    LEGAL REMEDIES.

08400 SISO, G.S.
    CRUSADER AGAINST CORRUPTION
    NEW AFRICAN, (257) (FEB 89), 33-34.
        GEOFF NYAROTA, THE EDITOR OF A ZIMBABWEAN NEWSPAPER, HAS
    BEEN CARRYING OUT A FEARLESS CAMPAIGN AGAINST CORRUPTION,
    EXPOSING TOP MINISTERS AND PARTY LEADERS. AS A RESULT,
    PRESIDENT MUGABE HAS ESTABLISHED A COMMISSION TO DETERMINE
    HOW SERIOUS THE CORRUPTION IS AND TO REVEAL THE NAMES OF
    THOSE INVOLVED.

08401 SISO, G.S.
    FALL OUT FROM MANDELA AFFAIR
    NEW AFRICAN, (259) (APR 89), 39.
        THE ARTICLE EXAMINES THE AFTERMATH OF THE "MANDELA
    AFFAIR" IN WHICH A YOUTH WAS KILLED BY THE MANDELA UNITED
    FOOTBALL CLUB. IT CONCLUDES THAT THE AFFAIR IS NOT DEAD AND
    THAT TIT FOR TAT KILLINGS CONTINUE IN THE TOWNSHIPS BETWEEN
    OPPONENTS AND SUPPORTERS OF THE MANDELA "FOOTBALL CLUB",

WHILE AN INCREASING NUMBER OF THOSE INVOLVED ARE APPEARING
IN COURT. THE ANTI-APARTHEID MOVEMENTS ARE NOW TRYING TO
REPAIR THE DAMAGE AND STOP ANY FURTHER ESCALATION.

08402 SISO, G.S.
    ROW OVER ZIMBABWE LANDLESS
    NEW AFRICAN, (OCT 89), 32.
        THIS ARTICLE ANALYSES THE CURRENT SITUATION IN ZIMBABWE
    INVOLVING THE MANY LANDLESS PEASANTS AS THE STOCK OF LAND
    AVAILABLE TO THEM DRIES UP UNDER THE EXISTING SYSTEM. THE
    DEBATE AS TO WHETHER THE WHITES SHOULD BE FORCED TO GIVE UP
    SOME OF THEIR LAND TO THE PEASANTS IS DETAILED. GOVERNMENT
    SOLUTION TO THE PROBLEM REMAINS UNKNOWN.

08403 SISO, G.S.
    SOUTH AFRICAN BLACKS DEMAND ECONOMIC EMPOWERMENT
    NEW AFRICAN, (OCT 89), 31.
        THIS ARTICLE REPORTS ON A NEW ASPECT OF SOUTH AFRICAN'S
    BLACK RESISTENCE TO APARTHEID. IT EXAMINES THE DISCOVERY BY
    THE BLACK POPULATION OF THE VALUE OF ECONOMIC STRENGTH.
    EXPLORED IS THE RECENT DISCOVERY OF ECONOMIC EMPOWERMENT AS
    BLACKS BOYCOTT WHITE SHOPS AND SET UP THEIR OWN BUSINESSES.

08404 SISO, G.S.
    THE RISE AND FALL OF ENOS NKALA
    NEW AFRICAN, (260) (MAY 89), 22.
        THE RESIGNATION OF ZIMBABWE'S ONCE POWERFUL DEFENSE
    MINISTER ENOS NKALA COULD HERALD A FRESH START FOR ZIMBABWE.
    NKALA, WHO FINALLY ADMITTED HIS GUILT IN THE WILLOGATE
    SCANDAL, SHOWED LITTLE REGARD FOR THE HUMAN SIDE OF
    SOCIALISM ESPOUSED BY THE PARTY AND GOVERNMENT OF PRESIDENT
    ROBERT MUGABE.

08405 SISO, G.S.
    TOP MEN FACE INQUIRY
    NEW AFRICAN, (258) (MAR 89), 21-23.
        FOLLOWING PRESS ALLEGATIONS ABOUT MISDEEDS AMONG
    GOVERNMENT OFFICIALS, PRESIDENT MUGABE SET UP A COMMISSION
    OF INQUIRY TO INVESTIGATE ALLEGATIONS OF CORRUPTION AMONG
    HIS TOP MEN.

08406 SISO, G.S.
    USHEWOKUNZE HOISTED BY HIS OWN PETARD
    NEW AFRICAN, (OCT 89), 23.
        THIS ARTICLE DESCRIBES CORRUPTION AND WRONGDOING AMONGST
    TOP PERSONNEL IN THE ZIMBABWE GOVERNMENT. IN PARTICULAR, DR.
    HERBERT USHEWOKUNZE IS CRITICIZED FOR HIS ACTIONS FOLLOWING
    HIS BEING SIDELINED FROM THE CABINET.

08407 SISS, S.
    ESTONIA AND THE JOYS OF TRIUMPHANT SOCIALISM
    GLASNOST, II(4) (SEP 89), 28-31.
        THE AUTHOR COMPARES LIFE IN INDEPENDENT ESTONIA BEFORE
    1940 WITH LIFE IN ESTONIA AFTER IT WAS ANNEXED BY THE SOVIET
    UNION. HIS VIEW DIFFERS GREATLY FROM THE OFFICIAL SOVIET
    PICTURE.

08408 SITA, S.Y.
    THE TRADITION OF DEMOCRACY IN THE SHAN STATE
    CULTURAL SURVIVAL QUARTERLY, 13(4) (1989), 10-12.
        THE SHAN STATE JOINED NEIGHBORING BURMA IN 1948 TO FORM
    AN INDEPENDENT FEDERAL REPUBLIC CALLED THE UNION OF BURMA,
    WHICH ENJOYED PARLIAMENTARY DEMOCRACY UNTIL 1962 WHEN THE
    ELECTED GOVERNMENT WAS OVERTHROWN BY GENERAL NE WIN, WHO HAS
    EXERCISED ABSOLUTE CONTROL OVER THE COUNTRY EVER SINCE. THE
    PRESENT REGIME IS FOREIGN TO SHAN, WHICH HAS A RICH
    TRADITION OF DEMOCRACY AND COMMUNAL VILLAGE CULTURE.

08409 SIVAN, E.
    ISRAEL'S DECOLONIZATION CRISIS
    NEW OUTLOOK, 32(11-12 (297-298)) (NOV 89), 16-19.
        ISRAEL'S DECOLONIZATION CRISIS ERUPTED IN THE FALL OF
    1987. TERRORIST ACTS BY THE ISLAMIC UNDERGROUND IN GAZA LED
    TO A VICIOUS CYCLE OF REPRESSION AND COUNTER-TERROR, WHICH
    CREATED TENSION AND REBELLION AMONG THE LOCAL POPULATION. IN
    THIS EXPLOSIVE ATMOSPHERE, A ROAD ACCIDENT IN WHICH THREE
    PALESTINIANS WERE KILLED SERVED AS THE MATCH THAT IGNITED
    THE BLAZE. THE BEHAVIOR PATTERNS OF THE LOCAL POPULATION AND
    THE ISRAELI RESPONSE DEVELOPED RAPIDLY--WITHOUT PLANNING AND
    THROUGH TRIAL AND ERROR, AS IN OTHER DECOLONIZATION CRISES.
    BUT THE COST OF THE OCCUPATION TO ISRAELI SOCIETY IS STILL
    NOT HIGH, DESPITE THE INTIFADA. ISRAEL IS AT A RELATIVELY
    EARLY STAGE IN ITS DECOLONIZATION CRISIS, AND DIFFICULT
    CONCESSIONS AWAIT BOTH SIDES.

08410 SIVAN, E.
    SUNNI RADICALISM IN THE MIDDLE EAST AND THE IRANIAN
    REVOLUTION
    INTERNATIONAL JOURNAL OF MIDDLE EAST STUDIES, 21(1) (FEB
    89), 1-30.
        SUNNI RADICALISM SURFACED BEFORE THE IRANIAN REVOLUTION
    OF 1978, ARISING FROM CONDITIONS SPECIFIC TO ARAB COUNTRIES
    AND THE MANNER IN WHICH THOSE FAITHFUL TO THE SUNNA REACTED
    TO THOSE CONDITIONS. IN THIS ESSAY, THE AUTHOR TRACES THE

ORIGINS OF SUNNI RADICALISM AND ITS RELATIONSHIP TO IRANIAN
ISLAM.

08411 SIVARAMAKRISHNA, P.
FIGHTING FOR THE FOREST: A GODAVARI EXPERIENCE
CULTURAL SURVIVAL QUARTERLY, 13(2) (1989), 23-25.
AS A MATTER OF POLICY, INDIA'S FOREST DEPARTMENTS HAVE
BEEN SYSTEMATICALLY CUTTING DOWN THE NATURAL FOREST IN THE
RESERVED AREAS FOR PURELY COMMERCIAL GAINS, UNDER THE
AUSPICES OF "SCIENTIFIC MANAGEMENT" OF THE FORESTS. THIS
POLICY WHICH WAS BORN WHEN THE BRITISH DECLARED THEMSELVES
THE SOLE PROPRIETORS OF THE FORESTS, HAS MADE THE TRIBALS
ALIENS ON THEIR OWN SOIL, SUBJECTING THEM TO VARIOUS TYPES
OF RESTRICTIONS ON THEIR FREEDOM OF MOVEMENT AND LIVELIHOOD.
THE COMMERCIAL EXPLOITATION OF THE FORESTS, SPECIFICALLY THE
LARGE-SCALE FELLING OF TREES, HAS HAD DISASTROUS RESULTS.
REGRETTABLY, THE GOVERNMENT OF INDEPENDENT INDIA HAS
CONTINUED THIS POLICY. IT HAS REDUCED THE FOREST COVER FROM
AROUND 23 PERCENT AT THE TIME OF INDEPENDENCE TO A
PRECARIOUS 11 PERCENT TODAY. THE MEASLY AFFORSTATION
PROGRAMS HAVE, BY AND LARGE, BEEN REDUCED TO MONOCULTURE
PLANTATIONS OF TEAK AND EUCALYPTUS.

08412 SIVARAMAKRISHNAN, A.
SOCIAL SCIENCE, PROFESSIONAL AUTHORITY, AND CITIZENSHIP
DISSERTATION ABSTRACTS INTERNATIONAL, 49(10) (APR 89),
3144-A.
THE AUTHOR PROBES THE NATURE OF POLITICAL ASSOCIATION
VIA AN EXAMINATION OF QUESTIONS RAISED BY SOCIAL WORK,
PSYCHOANALYSIS AND PSYCHIATRY, AND PUNISHMENT. HE BEGINS BY
CONSIDERING THE POSSIBILITY THAT THE ONLY RESPONSE TO
CONDITIONS OF MORAL AND POLITICAL PLURALISM IS ONE BASED ON
TECHNICAL THEORIES OF HUMAN NATURE DRAWN FROM THE SOCIAL
SCIENCES. THEN HE EXAMINES THE CLAIMS TO KNOWLEDGE THAT ARE
ENTERED BY PROFESSIONALS IN SOCIAL WORK, PSYCHOANALYSIS, AND
PSYCHIATRY. HE ARGUES THAT THE ISSUES OVER WHICH THE
RELEVANT PROFESSIONS ATTEMPT TO CLAIM AUTHORITATIVE
JUDGEMENT ARE INEXTRICABLY MORAL AND POLITICAL IN NATURE AND
THAT THE GIVEN PROFESSIONS ARE THEREFORE ENTERING UNTENABLE
CLAIMS TO MORAL AND POLITICAL AUTHORITY.

08413 SIVERSON, R.M.; STARR, H.
ALLIANCE AND BORDER EFFECTS ON THE WAR BEHAVIOR OF THE
STATES: REFINING THE INTERACTION OPPORTUNITY MODEL
CONFLICT MANAGEMENT AND PEACE SCIENCE, 10(2) (SPR 89),
21-46.
THE AUTHORS INVESTIGATE THE EXPECTATIONS GENERATED BY
THE "INTERACTION OPPORTUNITY" MODEL INITIALLY DEVELOPED BY
MOST AND STARR FOR THE STUDY OF DIFFUSION. THE IMPACT THAT
BORDERS AND ALLIANCES HAVE AS "TREATMENTS" ON THE OVERALL
WAR BEHAVIOR OF STATES IS THE FOCUS OF STUDY, LOOKING AT
BOTH INDIVIDUAL AND INTERACTIVE EFFECTS. USING THE WAR
BEHAVIOR OF ALL STATES IN THE SYSTEM FROM 1815-1965, THE
ANALYSES SUPPORT THE EXPECTATIONS GENERATED BY THE
INTERACTION OPPORTUNITY MODEL. THE TREATMENTS OF WARRING
BORDER NATIONS AND WARRING ALLIANCE PARTNERS, OF VARIOUS
TYPES AND COMBINATIONS, PREDISPOSE STATES TO BE AT WAR.

08414 SIWICKI, F.; REPEROWICZ, S.
CHANGES IN THE POLISH ARMY
CONTEMPORARY POLAND, XXII(2) (1989), 1-7.
IN THIS INTERVIEW, POLISH GENERAL AND MINISTER OF
NATIONAL DEFENSE FLORIAN SIWICKI ANSWERS QUESTIONS ABOUT
POLAND'S ARMED FORCES, ITS DEFENSE STRATEGY, CONFIDENCE-
BUILDING MEASURES, AND RELATED ISSUES.

08415 SIZHI, H.
ROADBLOCKS TO MIDDLE EAST PEACE PROCESS
BEIJING REVIEW, 32(46) (NOV 89), 14-15.
THE AUTHOR REVIEWS RECENT DEVELOPMENTS IN THE MIDEAST,
INCLUDING THE PLO CONCESSIONS, YITZHAK SHAMIR'S PROPOSAL FOR
ELECTIONS IN THE OCCUPIED TERRITORIES, AND EGYPTIAN
PRESIDENT MUBARAK'S TEN-POINT PROPOSAL FOR SOLVING THE
MIDEAST PROBLEM.

08416 SKAK, M.
EXTERNAL DYNAMICS OF THE KOREAN CONFLICT: THE PRESENT
SOVIET POLICY REORIENTATION
COOPERATION & CONFLICT: NORDIC JOURNAL OF INTERNATIONAL
POLITICS, XXIV(1) (1989), 19-33.
GREAT POWER POLICY DYNAMICS ARE DECISIVE DETERMINANTS
FOR DEVELOPMENTS WITHIN THE KOREAN CONFLICT, AND THIS
CONTRIBUTION FOCUSES UPON SOVIET KOREAN POLICY IN THE
FRAMEWORK OF THE PRESENT OVERALL POLICY REORIENTATION OF TH
SOVIET UNION. THE 1984 RAPPROCHEMENT BETWEEN THE USSR AND
NORTH KOREA SERVES AS THE POINT OF DEPARTURE, BECAUSE
OBSERVERS SAW THIS AS AN OMINOUS SIGN. I.E. AS A STIMULUS
FOR NORTH KOREAN AND/OR SOVIET MILITANCY. THE POINT IS,
HOWEVER, THAT NORTH KOREA IS DEPENDENT UPON THE USSR, AND
THE ANALYSIS OF THE NEW SOVIET LEADERSHIP'S INTEREST
PERCEPTION AND ACTUAL POLICY IN RELATION TO KOREA SUGGESTS
SERIOUS STRAINS IN THE SOVIET-NORTH KOREAN RELATIONSHIP.
SOVIET CONDUCT IN CONNECTION WITH THE SEOUL OLYMPICS AND
SOVIET-SOUTH KOREAN ECONOMIC CONTACTS ARE OBVIOUS SIGNS OF

THIS, AS IS THE NON-MILITANT SOVIET APPROACH TO REGIONAL
CONFLICTS. NONE OF THE GREAT POWERS HAVE A SIGNIFICANT
INTEREST IN A NEW WAR BETWEEN THE TWO KOREAS, NOT EVEN IN A
PEACEFUL REUNIFICATION OF KOREA (WITH THE POSSIBLE EXCEPTION
OF CHINA). ALL OF THEM CAN BE ASSUMED TO HAVE A VITAL
INTEREST IN AN INTER-KOREAN DETENTE (GERMANIZATION), WHICH
IS AN ARGUMENT THAT THE WISE REUNIFICATION POLICY OF THE
KOREAN NATION IS THE TACTICAL AND INCREMENTAL ONE.

08417 SKALIN, O.
SOUTH SEAS: NEW CALEDONIA
CURRENT DIGEST OF THE SOVIET PRESS, XL(19) (JUN 88), 19.
THE FRENCH ARE MANAGING WITH GREAT DIFFICULTY TO CONTAIN
THE GROWING UNREST IN NEW CALEDONIA. THE KANAK SOCIALIST
NATIONAL LIBERATION FRONT HAS BEEN DEPRIVED OF THE GAINS IT
ACHIEVED DURING YEARS OF PERSISTENT, NONVIOLENT STRUGGLE AND
HAS TURNED TO USING FORCE.

08418 SKALSKI, E.
AMERYKA MY AMERICA
NEW LEADER, LXXII(17) (NOV 89), 8-9.
THE AUTHOR ANALYZES THE TENACIOUS, ALMOST NAIVE FAITH
THAT MANY POLES HAVE FOR THE UNITED STATES. ALTHOUGH POLISH
EXPECTATIONS HAVE SOMETIMES BEEN EXAGGERATED, AMERICA HAS
FULFILLED TWO FUNDAMENTAL ONES; FREEDOM AND BREAD. COMMUNIST
AUTHORITIES HAVE ATTEMPTED TO TARNISH AMERICA'S REPUTATION
IN A VARIETY OF WAYS, BUT TO NO AVAIL. THE PICTURES AND
DOLLARS THAT COME BACK TO THE HOMELAND FROM IMMIGRANTS SPEAK
LOUDER THAN ANY PROPAGANDA EFFORT.

08419 SKALSKI, E.
POLAND TURNS TO THE POLLS
NEW LEADER, LXXII(7) (APR 89), 5-7.
THE AUTHOR DISCUSSES THE IMPLICATIONS OF THE RECENT
ROUND TABLE TALKS OF THE POLISH GOVERNMENT AND SOLIDARITY.
HE FOCUSES PARTICULARLY ON THE ELECTIONS THAT ARE ONE OF THE
RESULTS OF THE NEGOTIATIONS. HE OUTLINES THE CHALLENGES THAT
SOLIDARITY AND OTHER OPPOSITION GROUPS FACE IN THE COMING
ELECTIONS.

08420 SKELTON, I.
WHAT NEXT FOR U.S. POLICY IN CENTRAL AMERICA?
ARMY, 39(1) (JAN 89), 18-22, 24.
THE AUTHOR BEGINS WITH A QUICK REVIEW OF RECENT AMERICAN
HISTORY, DRAWING PARALLELS BETWEEN VIETNAM AND CENTRAL
AMERICA. HE THEN LOOKS AT AMERICAN FOREIGN POLICY IN CENTRAL
AMERICA, PARTICULARLY RONALD REAGAN'S APPROACH TO NICARAGUA.

08421 SKERRY, P.
BORDERS AND QUOTAS: IMMIGRATION AND THE AFFIRMATIVE-ACTION
STATE
PUBLIC INTEREST, (96) (SUM 89), 86-102.
IN TODAY'S POST-CIVIL RIGHTS POLITICAL CULTURE, MANY
GROUPS HAVE ENORMOUS INCENTIVES TO DEPICT THEMSELVES AS
SUFFERING FROM RACIAL OPPRESSION. NEW IMMIGRANT GROUPS ARE
ENCOURAGED TO DO SO BY THE BREADTH OF THE CIVIL-RIGHTS
LEGISLATION PASSED BEFORE THE GREAT UPSURGE OF IMMIGRATION
AFTER 1965 AND BEFORE ITS SOURCES SHIFTED FROM EUROPE TO
ASIA AND LATIN AMERICA. BESTOWING BENEFITS INTENDED FOR
BLACK CITIZENS UPON NEWLY-ARRIVED IMMIGRANTS HAS LED TO
CONFUSION IN SEVERAL AREAS OF PUBLIC POLICY. IN THIS ESSAY,
THE AUTHOR DISCUSSES FIVE POLICY AREAS WHERE THIS PROBLEM IS
EVIDENT.

08422 SKIDELSKY, R.; JENKINS, P.; KAVANAGH, D.; PIMLOTT, B.
THE AUDIT OF THATCHERISM 1979-89
CONTEMPORARY RECORD, 3(1) (FAL 89), 12-17.
TO MARK THE TENTH ANNIVERSARY IN MAY 1989 OF MRS.
THATCHER'S ARRIVAL AT NUMBER 10 A SEMINAR AT THE LONDON
SCHOOL OF ECONOMICS WAS ORGANIZED. TWO HISTORIANS, A
POLITICAL SCIENTIST, AND A POLITICAL COMMENTATOR WERE
INVITED TO OFFER DIFFERENT PERSPECTIVES ON THOSE TEN YEARS.
THEY COVER: THE ORIGINS OF THATCHERISM; THE UNIMPORTANCE OF
'THATCHERISM'; MRS. THATCHER IN EUROPE: AND THE LEGACY OF
THATCHER.

08423 SKIDMORE, D.G. II
THE CARTER ADMINISTRATION AND HEGEMONIC DECLINE:
CONSTRAINTS ON POLICY ADJUSTMENT
DISSERTATION ABSTRACTS INTERNATIONAL, 50(6) (DEC 89),
1797-A.
THE 1970'S WERE A PERIOD OF ABORTED CHANGE IN U.S.
FOREIGN POLICY. HEGEMONIC POWER ABROAD FREED THE UNITED
STATES OF NORMAL INTERNATIONAL CONSTRAINTS WHILE STATE
WEAKNESS AT HOME FED A PREOCCUPATION WITH DOMESTIC
LEGITIMACY. THIS COMBINATION LED TO A RELATIVE INSENSITIVITY
TOWARD INTERNATIONAL CHANGE AND THE RIGIDIFICATION OF
DOMESTIC STRUCTURES THAT LATER IMPEDED POLICY ADJUSTMENT
UNDER CARTER. A SPORADIC MODEL OF POLICY CHANGE, WHICH
PREDICTS LAGS IN ADJUSTMENT, FITS THE U.S. CASE BETTER THAN
THE EVOLUTIONARY MODEL IMPLIED BY REALIST THEORY.

08424 SKINNER, C.
MEXICO: THE CARDENISTA CHALLENGE AND PROSPECTS FOR THE LEFT

NEW POLITICS, 11(3) (SUM 89), 67-74.
    MEXICO'S POLITICAL OUTLOOK IS MIXED. CARDENAS'S POWERFUL
CHALLENGE TO THE PRI'S ONE-PARTY RULE HAS OPENED IMPORTANT
NEW POLITICAL TERRAIN AND THE REJUVENATED POPULAR MOVEMENTS
ARE SPOILING TO BATTLE SALINAS'S ECONOMIC AUSTERITY POLICIES.
THE SHIFT IN THE POLITICAL CORRELATION OF FORCES IS SUCH
THAT SHARP POPULAR CONFRONTATIONS WITH THE GOVERNMENT ARE
INEVITABLE DURING SALINAS'S TERM, NO MATTER WHAT COMPRISES
CARDENAS MAY MAKE WITH THE PRI. LESS CERTAIN IS WHETHER THIS
BROAD POPULAR AROUSAL CAN BE CHANNELED INTO A COHERENT
POLITICAL MOVEMENT CAPABLE OF LAUNCHING AN EFFECTIVE
CAMPAIGN FOR FUNDAMENTAL SOCIAL CHANGE IN THE YEARS BEFORE
THE 1994 MEXICAN PRESIDENTIAL ELECTIONS. A CRITICAL FACTOR
WILL BE THE LEFT'S ABILITY TO CONFRONT AND TRANSCEND THE
EMPTY AND OUTMODED NATIONALISM THAT CARDENAS REPRESENTS.
POL/PARTY

08425 SKJOSTAO, O.V.
    U.S. MARITIME STRATEGY AND ITS EFFECTS ON U.S. - NORWEGIAN
    RELATIONS AND SECURITY
    AVAILABLE FROM NTIS, NO. AD-A209 807/7/GAR, MAY 89, 34.
    WHILE THE UNITED STATES MARITIME STRATEGY HAS A GLOBAL
PERSPECTIVE, THIS STUDY FOCUSES ON OPERATIONAL CONSEQUENCE
OF THE MARITIME STRATEGY IN THE NORWEGIAN SEA. IT ADDRESSES
BOTH PRESENT PATTERNS OF U.S. NAVAL OPERATIONS AND POSSIBLE
CONSEQUENCES OF THE MARITIME STRATEGY IN CRISIS AND WARTIME.
THE STUDY RECOGNIZES AN INCREASED INTERDEPENDENCE BETWEEN U.
S. NAVAL OPERATIONS AND THE DEFENSE OF NORTH NORWAY AND
POINTS OUT MILITARY STRENGTHS AND WEAKNESSES AS WELL AS
POLITICAL LIMITATIONS IN CONNECTION TO THESE OPERATIONS. THE
CONCLUSION GIVES ADVICE TO U.S. STRATEGIC PLANNERS BOTH ON
THE MILITARY AND POLITICAL FIELDS. KEYWORDS: MILITARY
STRATEGY; NAVAL OPERATIONS; NAVAL WARFARE; INTERNATIONAL
POLITICS.

08426 SKOCPOL, T.
    RECONSIDERING THE FRENCH REVOLUTION IN WORLD-HISTORICAL
    PERSPECTIVE
    SOCIAL RESEARCH, 56(1) (SPR 89), 53-70.
    MODERN SOCIAL REVOLUTIONS HAVE BEEN TIED TOGETHER IN
BOTH PRACTICAL POLITICS AND ACADEMIC SCHOLARSHIP. IN
PRACTICAL POLITICS, THE ACTORS IN THE SOCIAL REVOLUTIONS
THAT FOLLOWED THE FRENCH REVOLUTION OFTEN UNDERSTOOD THEIR
OWN ROLES BY REFERENCE TO WHAT HAD HAPPENED IN FRANCE.
SIMILARLY, THE FRENCH REVOLUTION HAS SERVED AS A PROTOTYPE
FOR THE ACADEMIC ANALYSIS OF SUCCEEDING REVOLUTIONS. IN THIS
ESSAY. THE AUTHOR RE-EXAMINES THE FRENCH REVOLUTION WITHIN A
WORLD-HISTORICAL PERSPECTIVE.

08427 SKOK, J.E.
    TOWARD A DEFINITION OF STRATEGIC MANAGEMENT FOR THE PUBLIC
    SECTOR
    AMERICAN REVIEW OF PUBLIC ADMINISTRATION, 19(2) (JUN 89),
    133-148.
    THE AUTHOR SUGGESTS THE FOLLOWING VISION OF PUBLIC
SECTOR STRATEGIC MANAGEMENT: AGENCIES COMPETE WITHIN A
PLURALIST POLITICAL UNIVERSE COMPOSED OF DYNAMIC PUBLIC
POLICY SUBSYSTEMS WHOSE MEMBERS ACCUMULATE AND USE RESOURCES
TO ADVANCE THE POWER AND POLICY PREFERENCES OF THEIR
AGENCIES. COMPETITION AMONG PUBLIC AGENCIES IS SEEN AS
OFFENSIVE (PIRATING) OR DEFENSIVE (TURF-PROTECTING) AND AS
INTRASUBSYSTEM OR INTERSUBSYSTEM IN NATURE. PUBLIC POLICY
SUBSYSTEMS ARE SEEN AS BEING DISTRIBUTIVE, REDISTRIBUTIVE,
OR REGULATORY IN ACCORDANCE WITH THE TYPOLOGY DEVELOPED BY
RIPLEY AND FRANKLIN (1984) AND OTHERS. RESOURCES, VARYING IN
THE DEGREE OF LIQUIDITY, ARE SEEN AS GROWING OUT OF
KNOWLEDGE AND POLITICAL SUPPORT AS SUGGESTED BY ROURKE
(1984), MEIER (1987), AND OTHERS.

08428 SKOLNIKOFF, E.B.
    TECHNOLOGY AND THE WORLD TOMORROW
    CURRENT HISTORY, 88(534) (JAN 89), 5-8, 42-46.
    THE AUTHOR CONSIDERS THE RELATIONSHIP BETWEEN TECHNOLOGY
AND PUBLIC POLICY. HE WARNS THAT, ALTHOUGH THE DRAMATIC
CHANGES PRODUCED BY THE RAPID DEVELOPMENT OF SCIENCE AND
TECHNOLOGY HAVE CREATED HOPE THAT THEY CAN SOLVE ALL
MANKIND'S PROBLEMS, EXPERIENCE HAS SHOWN THAT THEY ARE NOT
PANACEAS.

08429 SKOWRONSKI, A.
    THE COMMON EUROPEAN HOME: A POLISH POINT OF VIEW
    CONTEMPORARY POLAND, XXII(7) (1989), 1-2.
    THE SPECIFIC CHARACTER OF EUROPE HAS TRADITIONALLY BEEN
EXPRESSED IN ITS INTELLECTUAL AND MATERIAL ACCOMPLISHMENTS.
BUT TODAY IT IS DETERMINED PRIMARILY BY THE EVER-MORE
UNIVERSAL FEELING OF THE COMMUNITY OF HISTORICAL FATES, THE
INDIVISIBILITY OF THREATS, AND THE COLLECTIVE RESPONSIBILITY
FOR THE FURTHER DEVELOPMENT OF THE WHOLE CONTINENT WHILE
MAINTAINING THE FREEDOM OF SELECTION OF INDIVIDUAL NATIONAL
DEVELOPMENT, NATIONAL ATTITUDES, AND OPTIONS. UNIVERSAL
MORAL VALUES SHAPED BY NATIONS THROUGHOUT THE CENTURIES ARE
INCREASINGLY BECOMING THE COMMON DENOMINATOR OF THAT
SELECTION.

08430 SKUTEL, H. J.
    ISRAEL'S ORTHODOX RIGHT AND THE KILLING OF NON-JEWS
    MIDDLE EAST INTERNATIONAL, 353 (JUN 89), 17-19.
    IT IS A BASIC ASSUMPTION OF THE HALACHA, ORTHODOX JEWISH
LAW, THAT THE KILLING OF A NON-JEW DOES NOT CONSTITUTE
"MURDER". WHILE IT IS REGARDED AS A SIN, IT IS DEEMED OF
LITTLE ENOUGH CONSEQUENCE TO BE LEFT TO GOD ALONE TO PASS
JUDGEMENT AND IS EXEMPT FROM ANY PUNITIVE ACTION BY TEMPORAL
JEWISH AUTHORITY. IN SHORT, THE TRADITIONAL WESTERN RACISM
WHICH HAS ALWAYS CHARACTERISED ISRAELI ATTITUDES TOWARDS THE
ARABS, HAS, SINCE 1967 ESPECIALLY, BEEN COMPOUNDED BY
INHUMANE, EVEN GENOCIDAL TEACHINGS PROPAGATED BY THE
ORTHODOX RIGHT. AS LONG AS THESE DOCTRINES ARE ESPOUSED BY
AN IMPORTANT SEGMENT OF THE OCCUPYING CIVILIAN AND MILITARY
POPULATION, WHO PERCEIVE THEIR MESSIANIC DREAM GROWING DAILY
MORE THREATENED, THE LIVES OF PALESTINIANS IN THE
TERRITORIES BECOME EVER MORE PRECARIOUS.

08431 SKUTEL, H.J.
    EGYPT'S ISLOMIC FUNDAMENTALISTS
    INTERNATIONAL PERSPECTIVES, XVIII(3) (MAY 89), 11-14.
    BESET BY A HOST OF SEEMINGLY INSURMOUNTABLE SOCIAL AND
ECONOMIC PROBLEMS AND OUTRAGED BY THEIR GOVERNMENT'S FAILURE
TO SEVER RELATIONS WITH ISRAEL, EGYPTIANS, IN INCREASING
NUMBERS AND FROM ALL STATIONS IN SOCIETY, ARE LOOKING TO
ISLAMIC FUNDAMENTALISM FOR SOLUTIONS. IT IS IMPERATIVE,
THEREFORE, THAT THE WESTERN DEMOCRACIES (INCLUDING JAPAN),
WHOSE ECONOMIC AND INDUSTRIAL VITALITY IS DEPENDENT ON
MAINTAINING AMICABLE DIPLOMATIC AND COMMERCIAL RELATIONS
WITH THE MIDDLE EAST (REPOSITORY OF OVER 50 PERCENT OF THE
WORLD'S PROVEN OIL RESERVES), DEVELOP A SOUND APPRECIATION
FOR THE GRIEVANCES THAT GIVE IMPETUS TO THE FUNDAMENTALIST
PHENOMENON. ONLY THEN CAN THEY HOPE TO MODERATE, MUCH LESS
REDIRECT, A POWERFUL RELIGIO-POLITICAL CURRENT WHOSE
EXTREMIST ELEMENTS CALL FOR THE ERADICATION OF ALL WESTERN
AND "ATHEISTIC" SOVIET INFLUENCES FROM THE ISLAMIC WORLD.

08432 SLABBERT, F.
    QUEST FOR A NEW STATE
    SOUTH AFRICA FOUNDATION REVIEW, 15(7) (JUL 89), 2.
    TWO CURRENT DEVELOPMENTS UNDERSCORE SOUTH AFRICA'S
MOVEMENT TOWARDS THE CREATION OF A ONE-NATION STATE. THESE
ARE THE STAGNATION AND DECLINE OF THE SOUTH AFRICAN ECONOMY,
AND THE INTERNATIONAL COMMITMENT TO A POLITICAL SOLUTION IN
SOUTH AFRICA, AS EXEMPLIFIED BY THE USSR, U.S, BRITAIN AND
ITS EUROPEAN COMMUNITY PARTNERS. FUTURE ACTIONS BY PARTIES
BOTH WITHIN AND OUTSIDE OF SOUTH AFRICA WILL DETERMINE THE
NATURE OF THE NATION-STATE; THE BATTLE FOR A NON-RACIAL,
DEMOCRATIC STATE HAS NOT YET BEEN WON.

08433 SLATER, D.
    TERRITORIAL POWER AND THE PERIPHERAL STATE: THE ISSUE OF
    DECENTRALIZATION
    DEVELOPMENT AND CHANGE, 20(3) (JUL 89), 501-531.
    THE AUTHOR STRUCTURES HIS STUDY OF DECENTRALIZATION INTO
THREE INTERRELATED COMPONENTS. FIRST, HE CONNECTS THE THEME
OF THE DECENTRALIZATION OF THE STATE TO A SERIES OF MORE
GENERAL THEORETICAL CONCERNS RELATING TO DEVELOPMENT,
DEMOCRACY, SOCIAL STRUGGLE, AND STATE POWER. THEN HE
DISCUSSES THE VARIED PERCEPTIONS AND ATTRIBUTED MEANINGS OF
DECENTRALIZATION IN TERMS OF THEIR IDEOLOGICAL SIGNIFICANCE.
FINALLY, HE CRITICALLY EXAMINES A RECENT PAPER BY RONDINELLI
ET AL. AS ONE EXAMPLE OF THE NEWLY EMERGING OFFICIAL
DISCOURSE OF DECENTRALIZATION FOR DEVELOPING COUNTRIES.

08434 SLATER, J.
    ISRAELI-SOVIET LINKS
    MIDDLE EAST INTERNATIONAL, (360) (OCT 89), 17-18.
    THE RENEWAL OF DIPLOMATIC LINKS BETWEEN HUNGARY AND
ISRAEL INCREASED SPECULATION THAT DIPLOMATIC RELATIONS
BETWEEN ISRAEL AND THE SOVIET UNION MIGHT NOT BE FAR BEHIND.
ALTHOUGH THE SOVIETS REMAIN GUARDED ABOUT THIS POSSIBILITY,
THE TWO NATIONS ARE DEFINITELY INCREASING CONTACTS. SOVIET
FOREIGN MINISTER EDUARD SHEVARDNADZE HAS MET HIS ISRAELI
COUNTERPART, MOSHE ARENS THREE TIMES IN ONE YEAR. LOW LEVEL
EXCHANGES ARE ON THE INCREASE AS ARE PLANS TO COOPERATE IN
ECONOMIC AND BUSINESS VENTURES. HOWEVER, THE PROSPECT OF
NORMALIZED RELATIONS HAS RESULTED IN SOME INTERNAL CONFLICT
IN BOTH NATIONS.

08435 SLATER, J.
    THE SOVIET MEDIA LOOKS AT ISRAEL
    MIDDLE EAST INTERNATIONAL, (362) (NOV 89), 16-17.
    THE ARTICLE EXAMINES RECENT CHANGES IN SOVIET ATTITUDES
TOWARDS ISRAEL AS REFLECTED IN THE SOVIET MEDIA. AS
PROMINENT SOVIET PERSONALITIES HAVE BEGUN TO VISIT ISRAEL
AND REPORT ON IT, THERE HAS BEEN A GENERAL INCREASE IN
AWARENESS OF ISRAEL, AND A RETREAT FROM THE TRADITIONAL ANTI-
ISRAELI STANCE. A PROBLEM TROUBLING SOVIET JOURNALISTS IS
THAT OBJECTIVELY REPORTING ON ISRAEL HAS BEEN TABOO FOR SO
LONG, THEY DON'T KNOW THE RIGHT QUESTIONS TO ASK.

08436 SLATER, R.; WATSON, J.
    DEMOCRATIC DECENTRALIZATION OR POLITICAL CONSOLIDATION:

THE CASE OF LOCAL GOVERNMENT REFORM IN KARNATAKA
PUBLIC ADMINISTRATION AND DEVELOPMENT, 9(2) (APR 89),
147-158.
THE ARTICLE EXAMINES THE REFORMS IMPLEMENTED BY THE
INDIAN STATE OF KARNATAKA KNOWN AS "PANCHAYAT REFORM"
LEGISLATION. THE LEGISLATION ATTEMPTS TO DECENTRALIZE
POLITICAL POWER BY ALLOWING LOCAL UNITS A GREATER AMOUNT OF
AUTONOMY. THE ARTICLE CONSIDERS THE QUESTION OF WHETHER
STRONGER LOCAL GOVERNMENT IN INDIA INCREASES THE STATE'S
AUTONOMY WITHIN THE FEDERATION. IT ALSO OUTLINES SOME OF THE
SIGNIFICANT DIFFERENCES IN THE REFORMS ENACTED IN KARNATAKA
FROM THE REFORMS ENACTED IN OTHER STATES.

08437 SLEEPER, J.
ED KOCH AND THE END OF THE LIBERAL JEWISH COMMUNITY IN NEW
YORK
TIKKUN, 4(3) (MAY 89), 20-22, 116-118.
ED KOCH'S IDEOLOGICAL, POLITICAL, AND PERSONAL FAILURE
IS A LOST OPPORTUNITY OF HUGE DIMENSIONS FOR THE JEWISH
COMMUNITY AND FOR THE VISION OF NEW YORK CITY TO WHICH IT
HAS COMMITTED. WHILE KOCH TRIED VALIANTLY TO DEFEND THE
BASIC PREMISES BEHIND THE CITY'S CULTURE OF PROGRESSIVE
INSTITUTIONS, HE STRUCK DEVIL'S BARGAINS WITH POWERFUL
FORCES INIMICAL TO THE SURVIVAL OF THE CITY'S PROGRESSIVE
CULTURE.

08438 SLIWINSKI, M.
AFGHANISTAN: THE DECIMATION OF A PEOPLE
ORBIS, 33(1) (WIN 89), 39-56.
IN THE DECADE SINCE APRIL 1978, WHEN A COUP D'ETAT
ESTABLISHED A COMMUNIST REGIME IN AFGHANISTAN, THE AFGHANS
HAVE SUFFERED A TRAUMA. BY THE END OF 1987, APPROXIMATELY 9
PERCENT OF THE POPULATION HAD BEEN KILLED BY WAR, A FIGURE
THAT RANKS AMONG THE HIGHEST IN RECENT HISTORY, SURPASSING
EVEN THE 8.6 PERCENT DEATH RATE SUFFERED BY THE SOVIET UNION
DURING WORLD WAR II. PROJECTING THIS DEATH RATE ON A TOTAL
PREWAR POPULATION OF BETWEEN 12 AND 15.5 MILLION, THE NUMBER
OF AFGHANS KILLED BY THE WAR IS PROBABLY CLOSE TO 1.25
MILLION, ALTHOUGH IT MAY BE AS HIGH AS 1.5 MILLION OR AS LOW
AS 1 MILLION.2 IN THE ORIGINAL AND LITERAL SENSE OF THE TERM,
AFGHANISTAN HAS BEEN DECIMATED. THIS ARTICLE DESCRIBES THE
SOCIAL, DEMOGRAPHIC, AND ECOLOGICAL CONSEQUENCES OF THE WAR
IN AFGHANISTAN.

08439 SLOAN, F.A.; BOVBJERG; MERGENHAGEN, P.M.
EFFECTS OF TORT REFORMS ON THE VALUE OF CLOSED MEDICAL
MALPRACTICE CLAIMS: A MICROANALYSIS
JOURNAL OF HEALTH POLITICS, POLICY AND LAW, 14(4) (WIN 89),
663-690.
TORT REFORMS ENACTED BY STATE LEGISLATURES MAINLY SEEK
TO REDUCE THE RATE OF INCREASE IN MEDICAL MALPRACTICE
INSURANCE PREMIUMS AND OTHER COSTS OF THE PROFESSIONAL
LIABILITY SYSTEM, SUCH AS "DEFENSIVE MEDICINE." THIS ARTICLE
EXAMINES THE EFFECTS TORT REFORMS ENACTED DURING THE 1970S
HAVE HAD ON THE PROBABILITY THAT A CLAIM WILL BE PAID, THE
AMOUNT OF PAYMENT, AND THE SPEED WITH WHICH THE CLAIM IS
RESOLVED. CLAIMS FREQUENCY IS NOT USED AS A VARIABLE IN THIS
ANALYSIS, BUT FINDINGS FROM OTHER STUDIES PERTAINING TO
FREQUENCY ARE NOTED. THIS STUDY USES TWO CLOSED CLAIMS
DATABASES -- ONE FROM THE NATIONAL ASSOCIATION OF INSURANCE
COMMISSIONERS, AND ONE FROM THE U.S. GENERAL ACCOUNTING
OFFICE. THE TWO DATA SETS ARE MERGED FOR PURPOSES OF THIS
ANALYSIS. THE OBSERVATIONAL UNIT WAS THE INDIVIDUAL CLAIM.
DATA ON TORT REFORMS CAME FROM THE AUTHORS OWN ANALYSIS OF
STATUTORY CHANGES BY STATE. DOLLAR CEILINGS ON RECOVERIES
("CAPS") ARE SHOWN TO BE THE STRONGEST REFORMS IN TERMS OF
THEIR IMPACT ON PAID CLAIM SIZE. MOST CAPS LIMIT RECOVERY
FOR NONECONOMIC LOSS, THOUGH SOME LIMIT DOLLAR AWARDS. OTHER
REFORMS THAT REDUCED PAYMENTS PER CLAIM WERE COSTS AWARDABLE
PROVISIONS AND MANDATORY COLLATERAL OFFSETS.

08440 SLOAN, J.W.
EISENHOWER, HUMPHREY, AND NEUSTADT: A NOTE ON THE BATTLE
OF THE BUDGET FOR FY 1958
WESTERN POLITICAL QUARTERLY, 42(4) (DEC 89), 691-699.
IN "PRESIDENTIAL POWER" RICHARD NEUSTADT CONCLUDES THAT
THE PRESIDENCY IS NO PLACE FOR AMATEURS. TO DEMONSTRATE THE
INEFFECTIVENESS OF AN AMATEUR, NEUSTADT PRESENTS A CASE
STUDY BASED ON TREASURY SECRETARY GEORGE HUMPHREY'S
CRITICISM OF PRESIDENT EISENHOWER'S FY58 BUDGET. IN
NEUSTADT'S ANALYSIS, ONLY AN AMATEUR IN POLITICS WOULD HAVE
ALLOWED SUCH A BLUNDER, WHICH SQUANDERED THE BARGAINING
ADVANTAGES EARNED FROM EISENHOWER'S 1956 LANDSLIDE ELECTORAL
VICTORY. THIS STUDY REPLICATES NEUSTADT'S CASE STUDY USING
EVIDENCE FROM THE EISENHOWER LIBRARY. IT INDICATES THAT
EISENHOWER'S STAFF PROCEDURES SERVED HIM BETTER THAN
NEUSTADT REALIZED. IT ALSO DEMONSTRATES THAT IN THIS
CONTROVERSY EISENHOWER WAS NEITHER AN AMATEUR NOR A "HIDDEN
HAND" POLITICAL GENIUS. EISENHOWER'S MISTAKE WAS NOT DUE TO
POLITICAL AMATEURISM; IT WAS DUE TO HIS FRUSTRATION WITH THE
BUDGET. FINALLY, THE PRESIDENT DID NOT ASK NEUSTADT'S
CLARIFYING EXPERIENCE, BUT HE DID GO THROUGH A CLARIFYING
EXPERIENCE. IN FIGHTING THE BATTLE OF THE BUDGET, EISENHOWER
DISCOVERED THAT HIS CONSERVATIVE VALUES WERE STRONGER THAN

HIS LIBERAL ONES. THIS ALLOWED THE NEW EISENHOWER TO EMERGE
IN 1959.

08441 SLOAN, S.R.
NATO AT FORTY: CHALLENGES AND OPPORTUNITIES
CRS REVEIH, 10(4) (APR 89), 1-3.
NATO HAS SERVED U.S., CANADIAN, AND WEST EUROPEAN
INTEREST WELL SINCE ITS FOUNDING, PROVIDING A RESPONSE TO
SOVIET MILITARY POWER IN CENTRAL EUROPE AND A FRAMEWORK FOR
STABILIZING RELATIONS AMONG THE WEST EUROPEAN NATIONS AFTER
WORLD WAR II. TODAY, AS THE ALLIANCE CELEBRATES ITS SUCCESS,
IT FACES NEW CHALLENGES AND OPPORTUNITIES.

08442 SLOAN, S.R.
NATO NUCLEAR POSTURE AFTER THE INF TREATY
CRS REVEIH, 10(4) (APR 89), 13-15.
THE CONTROVERSY OVER INTERMEDIATE-RANGE NUCLEAR MISSILES
THAT DISRUPTED NATO UNITY UNTIL THE USA AND THE USSR AGREED
TO ELIMINATE THE MISSILES HAS BEEN FOLLOWED BY A NEW DEBATE
OVER SHORT-RANGE NUCLEAR SYSTEMS. SHORT-RANGE NUCLEAR
ARTILLERY, DUAL-CAPABLE ATTACK AIRCRAFT, AND THE AGING LANCE
MISSILE WILL BE THE PRIMARY REMAINING U.S. NUCLEAR SYSTEMS
IN EUROPE WHEN ALL INF MISSILES HAVE BEEN REMOVED.

08443 SLOAN, S.R.
NEW CONVENTIONAL ARMS NEGOTIATIONS
CRS REVEIH, 10(4) (APR 89), 11-12.
NEW NEGOTIATIONS ON CONVENTIONAL ARMED FORCES IN EUROPE
COULD REVOLUTIONIZE POLITICAL AND MILITARY RELATIONS IN
EUROPE IF THEY ELIMINATE IMBALANCES IN IMPORTANT WEAPONS
SYSTEMS, REDUCE FORCE LEVELS SUBSTANTIALLY, AND RESTRUCTURE
FORCES TOWARD DEFENSIVE POSTURES.

08444 SLUGA, H.
METADISCOURSE: GERMAN PHILOSOPHY AND NATIONAL SOCIALISM
SOCIAL RESEARCH, 56(4) (WIN 89), 795-818.
THE AUTHOR STUDIES HEIDEGGER IN RELATION TO THE
PHILOSOPHICAL FIELD IN WHICH HE OPERATED--A FIELD COMPOSED
OF A DIVERSITY OF SCHOOLS OF PHILOSOPHY, ALL INFLUENCED BY
NAZISM. METHODOLOGICALLY, THE AUTHOR CONSIDERS THE ATTEMPTS
OF MEMBERS OF THESE SCHOOLS TO ESTABLISH THEIR WORK AS THE
APPROPRIATE PHILOSOPHY OF THE NEW SYSTEM (THAT IS, TO STATE
THE CONNECTION BETWEEN THE PHILOSOPHICAL AND POLITICAL
REALMS) AS NEITHER PLAINLY PHILOSOPHICAL NOR SIMPLY
POLITICAL, BUT AS METADISCURSIVE.

08445 SMALEC, T.
A LAW AGAINST LYING
CAMPAIGNS AND ELECTIONS, 10(2) (AUG 89), 49.
THE AUTHOR LOOKS AT SOME STATE, "FAIR CAMPAIGN
PRACTICES" LAWS AND SPECULATES ABOUT WHETHER SUCH LAWS COULD
STOP THE TYPE OF NEGATIVE CAMPAIGNING PREVALENT IN THE 1988
PRESIDENTIAL ELECTION CAMPAIGN.

08446 SMALL, A.H.
RESEARCH MONOGRAPH ON FEDERAL INTERNATIONAL ECONOMIC
EMERGENCY PLANNING
AVAILABLE FROM NTIS, NO. AD-A207 469/8/GAR, OCT 85, 140.
IN FOCUSING ON INTERNATIONAL ECONOMIC EMERGENCY PLANNING,
THIS STUDY DISTINGUISHES BETWEEN INTERNATIONAL EMERGENCIES
WHICH ARE BASICALLY ECONOMIC IN NATURE AND THE ECONOMIC
ASPECTS OF PLANNING FOR 'TOTAL' EMERGENCIES (I.E., RECOVERY
FROM ALL-OUT NUCLEAR ATTACK). IT IS THE FORMER WITH WHICH
THIS STUDY DEALS. IN REVIEWING THE CONCEPTS 'ECONOMIC'
'INTERNATIONAL' 'EMERGENCY' AND 'PREPAREDNESS' IT IS POINTED
OUT THAT INTERNATIONAL ECONOMIC EMERGENCIES COULD BE NON-
ADVERSARIAL IN NATURE, FOR EXAMPLE A MAJOR NATURAL DISASTER
REQUIRING CONTROLS ON IMPORTS AND EXPORTS. HOWEVER ACTUAL
INTERNATIONAL ECONOMIC EMERGENCIES HAVE ALL BEEN OF AN
ADVERSARIAL NATURE. LIKE THE ARAB OIL EMBARGO OF 1973, THEY
HAVE ALSO ALL HAD POLITICAL ASPECTS. BUT WHILE THE OIL
EMBARGO WAS FOREIGN 'AUTONOMOUS' IN NATURE (NOT ARISING
THROUGH U.S. ACTION) OTHER EMERGENCIES HAVE REPRESENTED U.S.
POLICY RESPONSES TO INTERNATIONAL SITUATIONS. PROPOSED U.S.
ECONOMIC ACTION AGAINST SOUTH AFRICA WOULD BE A POLICY
RESPONSE TO EVENTS IN THE NATION. A MAJOR REASON FOR BEING
CONCERNED WITH INTERNATIONAL ECONOMIC EMERGENCIES IS THE
INCREASING EXPOSURE OF THE U.S. ECONOMY TO INTERNATIONAL
INFLUENCES. IMPORTS AMOUNT TO ALMOST 10% OF GNP, AND
PRODUCTION OF SOME TYPES OF GOODS IN THE UNITED STATES HAS
CEASED. THE U.S. TECHNOLOGICAL LEAD MAY BE DIMINISHING. AND
FOREIGN INVESTMENT IN THE UNITED STATES HAS REACHED THE
POINT IN MID-1985 WHERE WE HAVE BECOME A DEBTOR NATION.

08447 SMALL, D.
NEW CALEDONIA: WILL THE ROCARD PLAN LAST THE DISTANCE?
NEW ZEALAND INTERNATIONAL REVIEW, 14(3) (MAY 89), 24-25.
THE AUTHOR DISCUSSES THE POLITICAL SITUATION IN NEW
CALEDONIA, A FRENCH TERRITORY WHICH IS NOW UNDER A STATUTE
CALLED THE ROCARD PLAN, SINCE VOTING IN FRANCE IN NOVEMBER
1988. THE PLAN ESTABLISHES A TEN-YEAR PROGRAM OF REGIONAL
DEVELOPMENT AND MANAGEMENT TRAINING FOR KANAKS WITHIN THE
FRAMEWORK OF A TERRITORIAL ADMINISTRATION BASED ON THREE
SEMI-AUTONOMOUS PROVINCES, AND CULMINATING IN INDEPENDENCE

IN 1998. VOTER TURNOUT IN FRANCE CN THIS MOVEMENT IS
REPORTED AS LOW, AND CHALLENGES BY POTENTIALLY NEW PRIME
MINISTER CHIRAC ARE DISCUSSED. REFERENDUM RESULTS FROM NEW
CALEDONIA ARE ALSO ANALYZED. KANAK POLITICAL PRISONERS, THE
MATIGNON ACCORS (WHICH WERE THE CHANNEL FOR ROCARD),
PARTICIPATION BY FLNKS AND RPCR ARE ALSO TOPICS WHICH ARE
EXPLORED.

08448 SMALLER, J.T.
    NUCLEAR RIVALRY AND BOUNDED VISION: AN INVESTIGATION OF
    CONFLICT RESOLUTION TECHNIQUE AND A DEVELOPMENT OF
    COGNITIVE MAPPING IN RELATION TO THE PROBLEM OF DISARMAMENT
    DISSERTATION ABSTRACTS INTERNATIONAL, 49(7) (JAN 89),
    1953-A.
        THIS THESIS DETAILS THE HISTORY AND CONTEXT OF NUCLEAR
    WEAPONS AND ALSO THE ENSUING NEGOTIATIONS ON THE PROBLEMS OF
    THEIR CONTROL AND ASSOCIATED ISSUES. THE DEVELOPMENT OF
    TECHNIQUES FOR THE RESOLUTION OF CONFLICTS IS EXAMINED AND A
    CONTRIBUTION TO THE AVAILABLE TECHNIQUES IS MADE TOGETHER
    WITH A VIEW OF FUTURE POSSIBLE APPLICATIONS.

08449 SMART, I.
    LIFE ON A REFRACTORY PLANET: THE QUEST FOR STABILITY
    INTERNATIONAL JOURNAL, XLIV(4) (AUG 89), 743-771.
        THE AUTHOR CONSIDERS QUESTIONS OF POLITICAL STABILITY;
    POLITICAL INSTABILITY; STABILITY VERSUS RIGIDITY; THE LINKS
    BETWEEN PHYSICAL, SOCIAL, AND POLITICAL EQUILIBRIA;
    MODERNIZING POLITICS AND STABILITY, SUCH AS IN THE SOVIET
    UNION UNDER GORBACHEV; AND INTERNATIONAL STABILITY.

08450 SMART, P.; MOREY, T.
    REMEMBERING THE WAFFLE
    CANADIAN FORUM, LXVIII(784) (DEC 89), 2.
        ON THE TWENTIETH ANNIVERSARY OF THE "WAFFLE MANIFESTO,"
    TWO "WAFFLES" RECALL THEIR ATTEMPTS TO REMAKE CANADA'S NEW
    DEMOCRATIC PARTY. BRANDED AS A BUNCH OF "RADICALS AND KIDS,"
    THE WAFFLES SET OUT TO UNITE STUDENTS, CHRISTIAN SOCIALISTS,
    ACADEMICS, MEDIA PEOPLE, AND UNIONISTS INTO A COHESIVE UNIT.
    IT TOOK YEARS FOR THE MOVEMENT TO COME BACK TO EARTH, BUT
    THE AUTHORS ENJOYED THE EUPHORIC IDEALISM WHILE IT LASTED.

08451 SMARYL, O.L.
    STALIN'S REVOLUTION
    ENCOUNTER, LXXII(3) (MAR 89), 34-36.
        THE AUTHOR DISCUSSES TWO BOOKS DEALING WITH THE
    DECIMATION OF THE POLITBURO AND THE CONGRESS OF THE
    COMMUNIST PARTY DURING THE TIME OF STALIN'S MASS POLITICAL
    TRIALS. ARTHUR KOESTLER'S "DARKNESS AT NOON" AND RYBAKOV'S
    "THE CHILDREN OF ARBAT" DESCRIBE SOVIET LIFE IN THE 1930'S.
    BOTH HAVE ONLY RECENTLY BECOME AVAILABLE IN THE SOVIET UNION.

08452 SMIL, V.
    CHINA'S ENVIRONMENTAL MORASS
    CURRENT HISTORY, 88(539) (SEP 89), 277-280, 287-288.
        IN CHINA, THE WORLD'S MOST POPULOUS NATION,
    ENVIRONMENTAL CONCERNS HAVE BEEN OVERSHADOWED BY THE
    CREEPING TROUBLES OF AN INCREASINGLY DISJOINTED ECONOMY AND
    BY THE EVENTS OF SPRING, 1989. AND YET THERE CAN BE LITTLE
    DOUBT THAT, IN THE COMING YEARS, THE PARTICULARS OF
    SOCIOPOLITICAL ARRANGEMENT WILL BE LESS IMPORTANT IN
    DETERMINING CHINA'S FATE THAN THE COUNTRY'S TREATMENT OF ITS
    BADLY DETERIORATING ENVIRONMENT. OF COURSE, ONE CAN HOPE FOR
    THE EVENTUAL TRANSITION FROM ONE-PARTY DICTATORSHIP TO
    GENUINE DEMOCRACY-BUT THIS EVOLUTION MAY BRING LITTLE RELIEF
    TO CHINA'S ENVIRONMENTAL ILLS.

08453 SMIST, F.J.
    CONGRESS OVERSEES THE UNITED STATES INTELLIGENCE COMMUNITY:
    1947-1984
    DISSERTATION ABSTRACTS INTERNATIONAL, 49(10) (APR 89),
    3144-A.
        THE AUTHOR EXAMINES THE INTERACTION OF THE EXECUTIVE AND
    LEGISLATIVE BRANCHES IN THE AREA OF INTELLIGENCE POLICY. HE
    SUGGESTS THAT THE CONGRESSIONAL COMMITTEE IS THE APPROPRIATE
    INSTITUTION FOR STUDYING AND EXPLAINING CONGRESSIONAL
    ACTIVITY IN THIS AREA. UTILIZING A COMMITTEE MODEL DEVELOPED
    BY RICARD FENNO, THE AUTHOR STUDIES THE STRUCTURE OF THE
    CONGRESSIONAL INTELLIGENCE COMMITTEES.

08454 SMITH, A.
    KANAKS, CALDOCHES, AND METIS, PART 2: NEW CALEDONIA AND
    THE 1988 FRENCH ELECTIONS
    CONTEMPORARY REVIEW, 254(1477) (FEB 89), 69-76.
        NEW CALEDONIA'S HISTORY SINCE 1853 HAS BEEN ONE OF
    SUSTAINED RESISTANCE TO FRENCH RULE BY AN INDIGENOUS BUT
    SHRINKING MELANESIAN COMMUNITY-THE KANAKS. THE EUROPEANS, OR
    CALOCHES NOW MAKE UP AROUND 40 PER CENT OF NEW CALEDONIA'S
    146,000 INHABITANTS, THE VAST MAJORITY OF THEM STILL
    CONCENTRATED ON THE WESTERN COASTAL STRIP, AND IN THE
    CAPITAL OF OF NOUMEA. A FURTHER 20 PER CENT OF THE
    POPULATION COMPRISES IMPORTED LABOUR AND REFUGEES FROM SOUTH-
    EAST ASIA, NOTABLY INDONESIA AND SOUTH VIETNAM, OR FROM
    FRANCE'S OTHER PACIFIC TERRITORIES. FEARFUL THAT
    INDEPENDENCE COULD BRING EXPULSION OR SECOND-CLASS

CITIZENSHIP, THE ASIANS, AND IRONICALLY, THE POLYNESIANS,
VOTE SOLIDLY WITH THE CALDOCHES IN FAVOUR OF REMAINING
FRENCH. REDUCED TO A MINORITY IN THEIR OWN COUNTRY THE
KANAKS HAVE LITTLE CHANCE OF CONTROLLING THE TERRITORIAL
ASSEMBLY, OF SECURING REPRESENTATION IN THE NATIONAL
ASSEMBLY AND, MOST CRUCIALLY, OF WINNING ANY REFERENDUM ON
SELF-DETERMINATION.

08455 SMITH, C.
    CRAFTY COMEBACK
    FAR EASTERN ECONOMIC REVIEW, 142(50) (DEC 89), 23.
        JAPAN'S BATTERED LIBERAL DEMOCRATIC PARTY (LDP) HAS
    MANAGED TO REGAIN MUCH OF THE SUPPORT IT LOST IN THE JULY
    ELECTIONS TO PARLIAMENT'S UPPER HOUSE. THE LDP HAS ALSO
    WORKER OUT AN ARRANGEMENT WITH THE KOMEI (CLEAN GOVERNMENT)
    PARTY WHICH ALLOWS IT TO RETAIN A WORKING PARLIAMENTARY
    MAJORITY AND REDUCE THE SOCIALIST PARTIES' ABILITY TO FORM
    AN EFFECTIVE OPPOSITION COALITION. THE DEAL WITH KOMEI DOES
    NOT MEAN THAT THE LDP HAS RECOUPED ALL OF ITS LOSSES. THE
    PARTY IS STILL LIKELY TO LOSE SEATS IN THE FORTHCOMING HOUSE
    ELECTION, PERHAPS ONLY BARELY MAINTAINING ITS MAJORITY OVER
    THE COMBINED OPPOSITION GROUPS.

08456 SMITH, C.
    FACTIONS TO THE FORE
    FAR EASTERN ECONOMIC REVIEW, 141(28) (JUL 88), 36-37.
        JAPAN'S RULING LIBERAL DEMOCRATIC PARTY (LDP) HAS GROWN
    IN POWER ON THE NATIONAL LEVEL TO THE POINT THAT THE IDEA OF
    AN OPPOSITION COALITION GAINING POWER SEEMS UNLIKELY.
    HOWEVER THERE HAS BEEN AN INCREASE OF INTRA-PARTY STRIFE ON
    THE LOCAL AND PROVINCIAL LEVEL. DISAGREEMENT OVER THE CHOICE
    FOR THE CANDIDATE FOR THE PREFECTURAL GOVERNOR HAS RESULTED
    IN STRIFE THAT HAS SPILLED OVER TO OTHER AREAS AND EVEN HAS
    EFFECTED TOP PARTY OFFICIALS.

08457 SMITH, C.
    FOUR BONES OF CONTENTION
    FAR EASTERN ECONOMIC REVIEW, 141(33) (AUG 88), 24-25.
        A VISIT TO THE SOVIET UNION BY FORMER PRIME MINISTER
    YASUHIRO NAKASONE BROUGHT AN UNEXPECTED BENEFIT FOR THE
    JAPANESE. THE ISSUE OF JAPAN'S SO-CALLED NORTHERN
    TERRITORIES--THE FOUR ISLANDS LYING NORTHEAST OF HOKKAIDO,
    WHICH THE USSR OCCUPIED AFTER THE END OF WORLD WAR II WAS
    DISCUSSED BY SOVIET LEADER MIKHAIL GORBACHEV. TRADITIONALLY,
    THE SOVIET STANCE HAS BEEN TO REFUSE TO ACKNOWLEDGE THE
    EXISTENCE OF A TERRITORIAL ISSUE; THEREFORE, THE ADMISSION
    OF THE ISSUE IS VIEWED BY JAPANESE AS AN IMPORTANT FIRST
    STEP IN THE RESOLUTION OF THE CONFLICT.

08458 SMITH, C.
    LOW KEY, BUT EFFECTIVE
    FAR EASTERN ECONOMIC REVIEW, 141(34) (AUG 88), 22-24.
        ALTHOUGH HE HAD LITTLE FOREIGN EXPERIENCE WHEN HE TOOK
    OFFICE, JAPAN'S PRIME MINISTER NOBORU TAKESHITA HAS
    SURPRISED THE WORLD WITH HIS SUCCESSES AND IS NOW A FORCE TO
    BE RECKONED WITH IN THE FIELD OF FOREIGN AFFAIRS. PART OF
    HIS SUCCESS IS ATTRIBUTED TO HIS PERSONAL STYLE WHICH IS
    VASTLY DIFFERENT FROM HIS PREDECESSOR YASUHIRO NAKASONE, BUT
    HE HAS ALSO PROVEN TO BE TECHNICALLY ADEPT. A TOP OFFICIAL
    NOTED THAT TAKESHITA "HABITUALLY CHOOSES THE RIGHT MOMENT TO
    SAY WHAT HE MEANT TO SAY."

08459 SMITH, C.
    RED-FACED RECRUITS
    FAR EASTERN ECONOMIC REVIEW, 141(29) (JUL 88), 17-18.
        JAPANESE PRIME MINISTER NOBORU TAKESHITA HAS SAID THAT
    HE WILL STAKE HIS POLITICAL LIFE ON A TAX-REFORM PACKAGE
    WHICH INCLUDES A NEW CONTROVERSIAL SALES TAX. FOLLOWING A
    SERIES OF REVELATIONS ABOUT SHARE PROFITEERING BY PEOPLE
    CLOSE TO TOP POLITICIANS, INCLUDING A SECRETARY OF TAKESHITA
    HIMSELF, HE MAY NOW WISH HE HAD NOT GONE QUITE SO FAR. THE
    SHARE SCAM MAY HAVE TILTED PUBLIC OPINION AGAINST THE TAX
    REFORM.

08460 SMITH, C.
    RENGO STAR RISES
    FAR EASTERN ECONOMIC REVIEW, 142(49) (DEC 89), 27.
        JAPAN'S LONG-DIVIDED LABOR MOVEMENT PASSED A MILESTONE
    ON 21 NOVEMBER, WHEN THE TWO LARGEST CONFEDERATIONS OF NON-
    COMMUNIST UNIONS, SOHYP (THE GENERAL COUNCIL OF TRADE
    UNIONS) AND RENGO (THE JAPAN PRIVATE TRADE UNION COUNCIL)
    MERGED TO FORM A SINGLE, 8 MILLION-STRONG BODY. THE NEW
    FLAGSHIP GROUP, SHIN-RENGO, OR THE JAPAN TRADE UNION
    CONFEDERATION, IS PLAGUED WITH PROBLEMS THAT BELIE ITS SIZE.
    THESE INCLUDE LACK OF GRASSROOTS STRENGTH, INSUFFICIENT
    POLITICAL MUSCLE, AND FINANCIAL PROBLEMS. UNTIL THESE
    PROBLEMS ARE RESOLVED, SHIN-RENGO WILL HAVE TO ACT AS A
    CHANNEL OF COMMUNICATIONS BETWEEN ORGANIZED LABOR AND THE
    RULING LIBERAL DEMOCRATIC PARTY, RATHER THAN AS A CANTER OF
    POWER IN ITS OWN RIGHT.

08461 SMITH, C.
    THE TAXING BY-ELECTIONS
    FAR EASTERN ECONOMIC REVIEW, 141(37) (SEP 88), 30.

THE RULING LIBERAL DEMOCRATIC PARTY (LDP) WON TWO BY-ELECTIONS IN THE FUKUSHIMA PREFEDTURE IN A CRUCIAL PHASE IN THE PARTY'S MOVES ON A CONTROVERSIAL TAX REFORM PACKAGE. VICTORY IN FUKUSHIMA MAY NOT ENSURE SUCCESS FOR THE TAX PACKAGE, BUT AT THE VERY LEAST, IT DOES SEEM TO HAVE CLEARED THE WAY FOR AN ALL-OUT EFFORT BY THE GOVERNMENT TO ENACT ITS PROGRAM.

08462 SMITH, C.
WHY LATIN AMERICA MATTERS
FAR EASTERN ECONOMIC REVIEW, 142(50) (DEC 89), 101.
ALTHOUGH DISCUSSIONS OF ECONOMIC RELATIONS BETWEEN LATIN AMERICA AND JAPAN USUALLY FOCUS ON LATIN AMERICA'S NEED FOR JAPANESE INVESTMENT. HOWEVER, JAPAN ALSO WOULD BENEFIT FROM A ECONOMIC REVIVAL BECAUSE IT WOULD EASE JAPAN-U.S. TRADE FRICTION BY HELPING TO INCREASE MARKETS FOR U.S. EXPORTS. A POLICY OF CONSCIOUS ASSISTANCE AND ADVICE WOULD BE MUTUALLY BENEFICIAL FOR BOTH JAPAN AND LATIN AMERICA.

08463 SMITH, C.E.
UNITED STATES MAGISTRATES: SUBORDINATE JUDGES IN THE FEDERAL COURTS
DISSERTATION ABSTRACTS INTERNATIONAL, 49(12) (JUN 89), 3859-A.
THE AUTHOR EXAMINES THE SELECTION, ACTIVITIES, ROLES, AND CONSEQUENCES OF THE FEDERAL COURTS' AUTHORITATIVE, SUBORDINATE JUDGES. A DETAILED ANALYSIS OF FOUR ILLUSTRATIVE DISTRICTS PROVIDES THE BASIS FOR A TYPOLOGY OF EIGHT MODEL MAGISTRATE ROLES.

08464 SMITH, D.
DIPLOMACY OF FEAR: CANADA AND THE COLD WAR
UNIVERSITY OF TORONTO PRESS, TORONTO, ONTARIO, CA, 1988, 300.
THE WARTIME ALLIANCE OF THE USSR WITH BRITAIN, THE UNITED STATES, AND CANADA UNRAVELLED VERY QUICKLY AFTER THE WAR. IN THIS BOOK, THE AUTHOR RECOUNTS HOW MUTUAL CONFLICT AND MISUNDERSTANDING LED TO THE DISINTEGRATION OF THE WARTIME ALLIANCE AND HOW CANADA CHOSE ITS PLACE AS A SECONDARY MEMBER OF THE EMERGING AMERICAN ALLIANCE.

08465 SMITH, D.
MEMBER STATE REPORT: PORTUGAL
EUROPE, (289) (SEP 89), 34-37.
MEMBERSHIP IN THE EUROPEAN COMMUNITY HAS BEEN A BOON FOR PORTUGAL. THE SUPPORT FUNDS AND LONG-TERM EUROPEAN INVESTMENT BANK LOANS HAVE FUELED A MODERNIZATION MOVEMENT THAT IS TRANSFORMING AND REVITALIZING THE ENTIRE NATION. MASS TRANSIT, PUBLIC SANITATION, INDUSTRY, AND AGRICULTURE ARE AMONG THE AREAS THAT HAVE BENEFITED FROM THE INFLUX OF FUNDS AND THE ACCOMPANYING RISE IN SPIRITS.

08466 SMITH, D.A.; VODDEN, K.
GLOBAL ENVIRONMENTAL POLICY: THE CASE OF OZONE DEPLETION
CANADIAN REVIEW OF SOCIOLOGY AND ANTHROPOLOGY, 15(4) (DEC 89), 413-424.
THE MONTREAL PROTOCOL IS AN INTERNATIONAL AGREEMENT TO REDUCE CONSUMPTION OF SUBSTANCES THAT DEPLETE THE OZONE LAYER. THIS PAPER PROVIDES A QUANTITATIVE ASSESSMENT OF THE COSTS AND BENEFITS FOR CANADA OF THE PROTOCOL. BENEFITS ARE ESTIMATED THROUGH THE USE OF A HEALTH EFFECTS IMPACT MODEL. COSTS ARE ASSESSED IN AN ADJUSTMENT COST MODEL THAT IS TRIGGERED BY INCREASES IN THE PRICES OF THE CONTROLLED CHEMICALS. THE ENVIRONMENTAL POLICY ASPECTS OF THE PROTOCOL ARE NOTEWORTHY. CANADIAN IMPLEMENTATION OF THE PROTOCOL DIVERGES FROM MANY TRADITIONAL POLICIES FOR LOCAL POLLUTION THAT MANDATE CONTROLS WITHOUT REGARD TO DIFFERENCES AMONG POLLUTERS IN CONTROL COSTS. THE MARKET-ORIENTED APPROACH TO REDUCING CONSUMPTION OF OZONE-DEPLETING SUBSTANCES INCREASES THE LIKELIHOOD THAT REDUCTIONS WILL BE UNDERTAKEN WHERE CONTROLS COSTS ARE LOWEST.

08467 SMITH, D.C.; STONE, W.F.
PEACE AND HUMAN RIGHTS: H.G. WELLS AND THE UNIVERSAL DECLARATION
PEACE RESEARCH, 21(1) (JAN 89), 21-26.
THROUGHOUT THE FIRST HALF OF THE TWENTIETH CENTURY, IDEALISTIC, EVEN UTOPIAN SCHEMES FOR A NEW WORLD ORDER WITH PEACE AND JUSTICE FOR ALL PEOPLES CONTINUED TO BE PROPOSED AND DISCUSSED. THAT ERA CULMINATED IN THE PRESENTATION, IN 1948, BY U.S. AMBASSADOR ELEANOR ROOSEVELT, OF THE UNIVERSAL DECLARATION OF HUMAN RIGHTS TO THE GENERAL ASSEMBLY OF THE UNITED NATIONS AND ITS ADOPTION BY THAT INTERNATIONAL BODY. THIS PAPER EXAMINES THE ORIGINS OF THE UNIVERSAL DECLARATION TO TRY TO UNDERSTAND ITS INSPIRATION AS WELL AS THE DIMMING OF THE GREAT HOPES REPRESENTED IN THAT DOCUMENT. THE PRESENT PAPER ATTEMPTS TO SKETCH THE INFLUENCE OF HERBERT GEORGE WELLS ON THE CONTENT OF THE DECLARATION AND TO EXPLORE HIS ROLE IN REFLECTING AND SHAPING THE WORLDWIDE CONCERNS THAT LED TO ITS ACCEPTANCE.

08468 SMITH, D.E.
FEMINIST REFLECTIONS ON POLITICAL ECONOMY
STUDIES IN POLITICAL ECONOMY: A SOCIALIST REVIEW, (30)

(FAL 89), 37-60.
THIS ARTICLE PRESENTS REFLECTIONS ON FEMINISM AND POLITICAL ECONOMY WHICH ORIGINATED IN THE WRITER'S EXPERIENCE AS ACTIVIST AND ACADEMIC IN THE WOMAN'S MOVEMENT. THEY ARISE FROM HER EFFORTS TO TRANSLATE INTO PRACTICE THE DISCOVERIES OF THE POWER RELATIONS. ORGANIZING THE PERSONAL AND DOMESTIC AS FEMINISTS HAVE EXPERIENCED AND ANALYSED THEM. SHE EXPLORES THE RELATIONS AND APPARATUSES OF RULING; CLASS IN THE COMMUNIST MANIFESTO AND IN CONTEMPORARY MARXIST THEORY; FEMINISM, POLITICAL ECONOMY AND THE 'MAIN BUSINESS' OF RULING; AND CONCLUDES WITH A STANDPOINT OUTSIDE THE RELATIONS OF RULING.

08469 SMITH, G.
CORE PERSISTENCE: SYSTEM CHANGE AND THE 'PEOPLE'S PARTY'
WEST EUROPEAN POLITICS, 12(4) (OCT 89), 157-168.
THE QUESTION OF PARTY CONTINUITY CAN BE TREATED FROM A NUMBER OF PERSPECTIVES AND THIS ARTICLE IS CONCERNED IS WITH WHAT MAY BE TERMED STRUCTURAL CONTINUITIES. ONE OF THESE REFERS TO A SPECIFIC KIND OF PARTY, AND THE OTHER IS A CHARACTERISTIC OF PARTY SYSTEMS: THE ALMOST UBIQUITOUS 'PEOPLE'S PARTY' AND THE 'CORE' ELEMENT IN PARTY SYSTEMS. THESE TWO FEATURES ARE STRONGLY RELATED, AND AN ANALYSIS OF THEIR PERSISTENCE SERVES TO CLARIFY SOME OF THE PROBLEMS MET IN DISCUSSING SYSTEM CHANGE. THE ARTICLE EXAMINES THE NATURE OF A PEOPLE'S PARTY AND SIMPLE CORES AS WELL AS THE SPLIT SYSTEM.

08470 SMITH, G.
GORBACHEV'S GREATEST CHALLENGE: PERESTROIKA AND THE NATIONAL QUESTION
POLITICAL GEOGRAPHY QUARTERLY, 8(1) (JAN 89), 7-20.
ABSTRACT. THE 'NATIONAL QUESTION' IN THE SOVIET UNION HAS EMERGED AS A MAJOR THREAT TO THE SUCCESS OF PERESTROIKA. THIS PAPER EXAMINES THE NATURE OF THE NATIONALITIES PROBLEM NOW FACING THE GORBACHEV ADMINISTRATION AND HOW IT DIFFERS FROM THE BREZHNEV ERA. PARTICULAR ATTENTION IS PAID TO EXAMINING IMPORTANT DEVELOPMENTS OCCURRING WITHIN THE NON-RUSSIAN UNION REPUBLICS DURING THE 1960S AND 1970S WHICH SHED LIGHT ON THE CURRENT PROBLEM. AS A PRECONDITION TO DECENTRALIZATION AND TO THE SUCCESSFUL IMPLEMENTATION OF 'REFORM FROM ABOVE', THE GORBACHEV ADMINISTRATION HAD FIRST TO RETAKE CONTROL OF THE REGIONS. THE CONSEQUENCES THAT THIS HAS HAD FOR THE NON-RUSSIAN UNION REPUBLICS IN COMBINATION WITH THE UPHEAVALS NOW BEGINNING TO ARISE OUT OF PERESTROIKA ARE ALSO EXAMINED. IT IS CONCLUDED THAT ONE OF THE MAJOR ISSUES NOW FACING THE STATE IS WHETHER REFORM FROM ABOVE AND ETHNO-REGIONAL INTERESTS CAN ACCOMMODATE ONE ANOTHER.

08471 SMITH, G.; MAIR, P.
HOW ARE WEST EUROPEAN PARTY SYSTEMS CHANGING?
WEST EUROPEAN POLITICS, 12(4) (OCT 89), 1-2.
THIS IS AN INTRODUCTION TO A SPECIAL ISSUE ON UNDERSTANDING PARTY SYSTEM CHANGE IN WESTERN EUROPE, IT ADDRESSES QUESTIONS SUCH AS: WHAT DOES THE EVIDENCE OF AN APPARENT 'ELECTORAL FLUX' MEAN FOR THE FUTURE DEVELOPMENT OF WEST EUROPEAN PARTY SYSTEM; AND IS ONE EUROPEAN-WIDE PATTERN EMERGING OR ARE THEIR SEVERAL? IT OBSERVES THAT IN ORDER TO UNDERSTAND HOW WEST EUROPEAN PARTY SYSTEMS ARE CHANGING, ONE NEEDS TO APPRECIATE HOW INDIVIDUAL PARTY SYSTEMS ARE HANDLING THE PROBLEMS OF ELECTORAL CHANGE.

08472 SMITH, G.C.; COBBAN, H.
A BLIND EYE TO NUCLEAR PROLIFERATION
FOREIGN AFFAIRS, 68(3) (SUM 89), 53-70.
THE AMERICAN GOVERNMENT SHOULD UNDERTAKE A FRESH ASSESSMENT OF THE STATUS OF THE INTERNATIONAL NONPROLIFERATION EFFORT, INCLUDING THE US CONTRIBUTION. AMERICAN ACTIONS HAVE BEEN CONTRADICTORY, SOMETIMES ENCOURAGING NONPROLIFERATION AND SOMETIMES IGNORING IT. IN PARTICULAR, THE USA HAS ADOPTED A PERMISSIVE ATTITUDE TOWARD NUCLEAR DEVELOPMENT IN ISRAEL AND PAKISTAN.

08473 SMITH, G.H.
THE ANTECEDENTS AND CONSEQUENCES OF PARTY ORGANIZATIONAL STRENGTH
DISSERTATION ABSTRACTS INTERNATIONAL, 49(12) (JUN 89), 3859-A.
THE AUTHOR CONCEPTUALIZES PARTY ORGANIZATIONAL STRENGTH AS BEING MULTI-DIMENSIONAL AND CONSISTING OF PERMANENT ORGANIZATION, CAMPAIGN ACTIVITY, AND PRIMARY ELECTION INVOLVEMENT. HE EXAMINES PARTY ORGANIZATION AS BOTH AN INDEPENDENT AND A DEPENDENT VARIABLE, USING COUNTY POLITICAL PARTIES IN MICHIGAN.

08474 SMITH, H.
FOREIGN-POLICY MAKING IN WASHINGTON
INTERNATIONAL AFFAIRS (MOSCOW), (1) (JAN 89), 61-70.
AN ENDURING MYTH OF AMERICAN POLITICS IS THAT FOREIGN POLICY IS RUN--AND IS SUPPOSED TO BE RUN--BY THE SECRETARY OF STATE. IT IS A PRESIDENTIAL CAMPAIGN RITUAL FOR CHALLENGERS TO DENOUNCE THE DISARRAY OF THE EXISTING FOREIGN POLICY TEAM AND TO PROMISE REFORM THAT WILL BRING UNITY AND CLARITY. THIS PROMISE HAS BEEN MADE BY EVERY AMERICAN

PRESIDENT SINCE JOHN KENNEDY AND HAS THEN BEEN BROKEN BY ALL
OF THEM, WITH THE EXCEPTION OF GERALD FORD.

08475 SMITH, J.L.
DEBT AND DEMOCRACY IN THE PHILIPPINES
MULTINATIONAL MONITOR, 10(6) (JUN 89), 22-25.
PHILIPPINE PRESIDENT CORAZON AQUINO WANTS THE PHILIPPINE
PEOPLE TO BELIEVE THAT THE FOREIGN DEBT CRISIS IS A
COMPLICATED FINANCIAL PROBLEM THAT ONLY HER FINANCE
SECRETARY AND THE CENTRAL BANK GOVERNOR CAN UNDERSTAND AND
RESOLVE. BUT A GROWING NUMBER OF PEOPLE IN THE PHILIPPINES
UNDERSTAND THAT THE SITUATION IS REALLY QUITE SIMPLE: THE
COUNTRY WILL NEVER BE ABLE TO REPAY ALL THE BILLIONS OWED TO
FOREIGN CREDITORS AND, THEREFORE, GOVERNMENT AND CREDITOR
POLICIES MUST CHANGE. THE GOVERNMENT'S DEBT POLICIES ARE
IMPINGING UPON DEMOCRATIC INSTITUTIONS AND REVEAL PRESIDENT
AQUINO'S WILLINGNESS TO SACRIFICE ECONOMIC AND POLITICAL
SOVEREIGNTY TO PLACATE FOREIGN CREDITORS.

08476 SMITH, K.F.
DETERMINANTS OF SUCCESS IN THE DESIGN &
INSTITUTIONALIZATION OF MANAGEMENT INFORMATION SYSTEMS FOR
DEVELOPMENT ADMINISTRATION: LESSONS FROM THE PHILIPPINE
"MASAGANA 99" EXPERIENCE
DISSERTATION ABSTRACTS INTERNATIONAL, 49(7) (JAN 89),
1960-A.
IN THIS STUDY, 12 VARIABLES WERE HYPOTHESIZED AS
"NECESSARY, IF NOT SUFFICIENT" FOR SUCCESSFUL DEVELOPMENT
MANAGEMENT INFORMATION SYSTEMS DESIGN AND
INSTITUTIONALIZATION. A RELATIVELY SUCCESSFUL MANAGEMENT
INFORMATION SYSTEMS APPLICATION TO MONITOR AND MANAGE
MASAGANA 99 (A PHILIPPINE NATIONAL RICE PRODUCTION PROGRAM)
WAS THEN EXAMINED AS A PROTOTYPE DMIS.

08477 SMITH, K.V.
THE RESURRECTION OF EVAN MECHAM
NATIONAL REVIEW, XLI(9) (MAY 89), 42-43.
DESPITE HIS REMOVAL FROM THE ARIZONA GOVERNOR'S OFFICE
BY A STATE SENATE COURT OF IMPEACHMENT, EVAN MECHAM HAS
DECLARED HIS INTENTION TO RETURN TO THAT OFFICE IN 1990 AND
HE'S THE FAVORITE TO WIN THE REPUBLICAN PRIMARY.

08478 SMITH, M.
BURMA AND WORLD WAR II
CULTURAL SURVIVAL QUARTERLY, 13(4) (1989), 4-6.
BURMA WAS ONE OF THE MOST VIOLENT THEATERS OF CONFLICT
IN THE ENTIRE HISTORY OF WORLD WAR II. IT WITNESSED SCENES
OF THE MOST APPALLING DEATH AND DESTRUCTION AS TROOPS FROM
JAPAN, BRITAIN, CHINA, AND THE UNITED STATES FOUGHT THEIR
WAY BACK AND FORTH ACROSS THE LANDSCAPE. OTHER COUNTRIES
HAVE LONG SINCE TRIED TO PUT THE TRAGIC MEMORIES OF THOSE
DARK DAYS BEHIND THEM. BUT IN BURMA THE WAR LEFT DEEP
PHYSICAL AND PSYCHOLOGICAL SCARS THAT HAVE NEVER REALLY BEEN
ERASED. IN ANY ANALYSIS OF BURMA'S ECONOMIC MALAISE,
POLITICAL ISOLATIONISM, AND ETHNIC CONFLICT, THE HAVOC
WROUGHT BY WORLD WAR II IS A VITAL STARTING POINT.

08479 SMITH, M.
BURMA'S MUSLIM BORDERLAND: SOLD DOWN THE RIVER
CULTURAL SURVIVAL QUARTERLY, 13(4) (1989), 27-29.
ARAKAN (RAKHINE) STATE, GUIDED BY THE UNIQUE BURMESE WAY
TO SOCIALISM OF GENERAL NE WIN, IS IN MANY WAYS PRESENT-DAY
BURMA IN MICROCOSM: A LARGELY RURAL RICE-GROWING POPULATION,
A STAGNANT ECONOMY, A THRIVING BLACK MARKET, ETHNIC
DISCONTENT, AND INSURGENTS IN THE MOUNTAINS. FOR LOCAL
VILLAGERS, BLACK MARKET TRADING HAS BECOME ALMOST A WAY OF
LIFE. UNDER ITS CURIOUS BLEND OF MARXIST AND BUDDHIST
PRINCIPLES, THE BURMESE WAY TO SOCIALISM REQUIRES FARMERS TO
SELL THEIR HARVEST TO THE GOVERNMENT AT FIXED PRICES. BUT
SELLING CROPS TO BANGLADESH ON THE BLACK MARKET BRINGS
HIGHER PRICES AND ENABLES MANY FAMILIES TO BUY A VARIETY OF
ILLICIT GOODS. ARAKAN CROPS ARE NOT THE ONLY THING TO LEAVE
BURMA FOR BANGLADESH. A STEADY STREAM OF MUSLIMS ALSO
FILTERS THROUGH THE BORDER TO THE OUTSIDE WORLD.

08480 SMITH, M. J.
THE ANNUAL REVIEW: THE EMERGENCE OF A CORPORATIST
INSTITUTION?
POLITICAL STUDIES, XXXVII(1) (MAR 89), 81-96.
OF THE MANY THEORIES OF CORPORATION THE MOST ADEQUATE IS
THAT WHICH SEES THE RELATIONSHIP AS A FORM OF INTEREST GROUP
INTERMEDIATION AND POLICY IMPLEMENTATION. IT HAS BEEN ARGUED
THAT THE ANNUAL REVIEW OF AGRICULTURE IS ONE OF THE BEST
EXAMPLES OF A CORPORATIST INSTITUTION. THIS PAPER EXAMINES
THE ANNUAL REVIEW AND DEMONSTRATES THAT, ALTHOUGH IT HAS
FEATURES OF CORPORATISM, THE RELATIONSHIP BETWEEN THE
MINISTRY OF AGRICULTURE AND THE NATIONAL FARMERS' UNION IS
NOT CORPORATIST. THE PAPER THEN EXAMINES THE POLICY
COMMUNITY APPROACH AND BY LOOKING AT THE FORMATION AND
OPERATION OF THE ANNUAL REVIEW ARGUES THAT THIS IS A MUCH
BETTER DESCRIPTION OF THE RELATIONSHIP BETWEEN THE MINISTRY
AND THE UNION.

08481 SMITH, M.R.
A SOCIOLOGICAL APPRAISAL OF THE FREE TRADE AGREEMENT
CANADIAN PUBLIC POLICY--ANALYSE DE POLITIQUES, XV(1) (MAR
89), 57-71.
CANADIAN SOCIOLOGISTS ARE LIKELY TO BE ATTRACTED TO SOME
OR ALL OF THE FOLLOWING KINDS OF OBJECTIONS TO THE FREE
TRADE AGREEMENT: 1/ THAT IT WILL TEND TO INCREASE INEQUALITY
WITHIN CANADA; 2/ THAT IT DRAMATICALLY INFRINGES UPON
CANADIAN SOVEREIGNTY; AND 3/ THAT IT FORECLOSES THE OPTION
OF A SET OF INTERVENTIST POLICIES IN THE FUTURE, INCLUDING A
RELATIVELY AMBITIOUS INDUSTRIAL POLICY. THE FIRST OBJECTION
IS NOT WELL-FOUNDED, THE SECOND IS EASILY EXAGGERATED, AND
THE THIRD DEPENDS HEAVILY ON A PESSIMISTIC APPRAISAL OF THE
SUBSIDY CODE THAT HAS YET TO BE NEGOTIATED AND ON A
COMMITMENT TO A SET OF INTERVENTIONIST POLICIES, MANY OF
WHICH HAVE NOT BEEN ADEQUATELY AND ANALYSED BY THEIR
PROTAGONISTS.

08482 SMITH, R. C.
FINANCING BLACK POLITICS: A STUDY OF CONGRESSIONAL
ELECTIONS
REVIEW OF BLACK POLITICAL ECOMOMY, 17(1) (SUM 88), 5-30.
THE PURPOSE OF THIS ARTICLE IS TO PRESENT A
COMPREHENSIVE ANAYLSIS (FOCUSING ON EXPENDITURES AS WELL AS
RECEIPTS) OF CAMPAIGN FINANCE AND THE ELECTION OF BLACKS TO
CONGRESS. POLITICAL RESOURCES AS A MEANS BY WHICH ONE PERSON
CAN INFLUENCE THE BEHAVIOR OF OTHER PERSONS ARE EXAMINED

08483 SMITH, S.
HEGELIANISM AND THE THREE CRISES OF RATIONALITY
SOCIAL RESEARCH, 56(4) (WIN 89), 943-973.
THE AUTHOR CONFRONTS THE BASIC PROBLEM OF POLITICS AND
RATIONALITY IN TERMS OF THREE HISTORICAL CHANGES IN THE
CONCEPTION OF RATIONALITY ITSELF. THE CENTRAL SECTION OF THE
ESSAY IS CONCERNED WITH KOJEVE'S MARXIAN READING OF HEGEL
AND THE CRITICISM OF THAT READING BY LEO STRAUSS. THE DEBATE
TURNS ON THE NOTIONS OF RECOGNITION, EQUALITY, DIGNITY, AND
THE END OF HISTORY. TO KOJEVE, THE ACHIEVEMENT OF A RATIONAL
SOCIETY MEANS NOT ONLY THE END OF HISTORY BUT ALSO THE END
OF ALIENATION AND THE SUBJECT-OBJECT DICHOTOMY, THE END OF
MAN, AND, IN THE ABSOLUTE KNOWLEDGE OF THE PHILOSOPHER, THE
END OF PHILOSOPHY. TO STRAUSS, A RATIONAL SOCIETY OR UTOPIA
IS NOT IN ACCORD WITH POLITICAL REALITY, HENCE NOT FEASIBLE
NOR EVEN DESIRABLE, SINCE IF IT WERE THE GOAL OF HISTORY,
THEN HISTORY IS A TRAGEDY WITHOUT THE POSSIBILITY OF HUMAN
HAPPINESS.

08484 SMITH, S.B.
HEGEL AND THE FRENCH REVOLUTION: AN EPITAPH FOR
REPUBLICANISM
SOCIAL RESEARCH, 56(1) (SPR 89), 233-262.
THE AUTHOR ANALYZES HEGEL'S PERSPECTIVE ON THE FRENCH
REVOLUTIONARY EXPERIENCE. HEGEL NEITHER WANTED TO EMPHASIZE
THE ABSOLUTELY UNPRECEDENTED CHARACTER OF THE FRENCH
REVOLUTION, AS BURKE DID, NOR DID HE WANT TO MINIMIZE ITS
SPECIFICITY BY DISSOLVING IT INTO A KIND OF LONGUE DUREE, AS
TOCQUEVILLE DID. HEGEL WANTED TO CELEBRATE THE REVOLUTION,
BUT ONLY AFTER IT HAD BEEN FIRMLY LOCATED AND ENSNARED
WITHIN HIS OWN PHILOSOPHY OF HISTORY. ONCE HE HAD DONE THIS,
IT BECAME POSSIBLE TO HONOR THE MEMORY OF THE REVOLUTION
PRECISELY BECAUSE AND TO THE DEGREE THAT IT NO LONGER
REPRESENTED A THREAT. HENCEFORTH, THE FRENCH REVOLUTION
COULD BE REGARDED NOT AS AN ISOLATED OR DISCRETE HAPPENING
BUT AS PART OF THE WORLDWIDE STRUGGLE FOR FREEDOM.

08485 SMITH, S.B.
WHAT IS RIGHT IN HEGEL'S PHILOSOPHY OF RIGHT?
AMERICAN POLITICAL SCIENCE REVIEW, 83(1) (MAR 89), 3-18.
THE AUTHOR PROVIDES A THEMATIC RECONSTRUCTION OF HEGEL'S
POSITIVE CONCEPT OF RIGHT. AGAINST THOSE WHO CHARGE THAT
HEGEL DENIES ANY ROLE TO SUBSTANTIVE POLITICAL EVALUATION,
HE ARGUES THAT THE "PHILOSOPHY OF RIGHT" ARTICULATES A
NOTION OF THE RIGHT TO RECOGNITION AS THE CENTRAL FEATURE OF
THE MODERN STATE. THE CONCEPT OF RECOGNITION REQUIRES NOT
JUST TOLERATION OF OTHERS BUT A MORE ROBUST NOTION OF
RESPECT FOR THE "FREE PERSONALITY" THAT IS THE PHILOSOPHICAL
GROUND OF RIGHT. THE RIGHT TO RECOGNITION IS, FURTHERMORE,
INTENDED TO PROVIDE THE FOUNDATION OF A NEW FORM OF ETHICAL
LIFE, HEGEL'S MODERN ANALOGUE TO CLASSICAL CONCEPTIONS OF
CIVIC VIRTURE. THE AUTHOR ALSO BRIEFLY EXAMINES TWO
OBJECTIONS THAT STAND IN THE WAY OF A CONTEMPORARY
REHABILITATION OF HEGELIAN POLITICAL PHILOSOPHY.

08486 SMITH, S.S.; FLATHMAN, M.
MANAGING THE SENATE FLOOR: COMPLEX UNANIMOUS CONSENT
AGREEMENTS SINCE THE 1950S
LEGISLATIVE STUDIES QUARTERLY, 14(3) (AUG 89), 349-374.
AS THE SENATE MOVED FROM A COMMUNITARIAN TO A MORE
INDIVIDUALISTIC ENVIRONMENT, INCREASING AND OFTEN COMPETING
DEMANDS ON FLOOR LEADERS PRODUCED INNOVATIONS IN THE USE AND
CONTENT OF UNANIMOUS CONSENT AGREEMENTS. THIS PAPER
DEMONSTRATES 1) THAT SINCE THE MID-1950S LEADERS HAVE RELIED
ON UNANIMOUS CONSENT AGREEMENT MORE FREQUENTLY AND THAT
AGREEMENTS (2) INCREASINGLY CONTAINED AMENDMENT-SPECIFIC

DEBATE LIMITS AND INCREASINGLY SPECIFIED CERTAIN TIMES FOR
VOTES ON MEASURES AND AMENDMENTS, (3) DECREASINGLY
RESTRICTED NONGERMANE AMENDMENTS, (4) INCREASINGLY CONTAINED
PROVISIONS AFFECTING INDIVIDUAL AMENDMENTS AND INDIVIDUAL
SENATORS, AND (5) INCREASINGLY GOVERNED THE ENTIRE DEBATE ON
MEASURES BUT ALSO INCREASINGLY REQUIRED MIDDEBATE ADJUSTMENT.
TO GENERALIZE, AS THE SENATE EVOLVED FROM A COMMUNITARIAN
TO AN INDIVIDUALISTIC LEGISLATIVE BODY, UNANIMOUS CONSENT
AGREEMENTS BECAME MORE TACTICAL, COMPLEX, INDIVIDUALIZED,
AND AD HOC. LEADERSHIP STRATEGY IN MANAGING THE FLOOR BECAME
MORE FLEXIBLE AND CREATIVE.

08487 SMITH, W.S.
    WASHINGTON'S QUARREL WITH CASTRO
    SAIS REVIEW, 9(2) (SUM 89), 165-183.
       THE AUTHOR APPLIES THE LESSONS OF A TWENTY NINE YEAR
    BATTLE FOR INFLUENCE IN THE WESTERN HEMISPHERE TO THE
    EXPLOSIVE ATMOSPHERE OF LATIN AMERICAN RELATIONS. THE
    ARTICLE PUTS INTO PERSPECTIVE CASTRO'S POSITION WITH REGARD
    TO SUPERPOWER INFLUENCE.

08488 SMITH, W.H.
    THE CULTURAL SURVIVAL TIBET PROJECT
    CULTURAL SURVIVAL QUARTERLY, 13(1) (1989), 49-51.
       IT HAS BEEN 38 YEARS SINCE THE CHINESE INVASION OF TIBET
    AND 30 YEARS SINCE THE FLIGHT OF THE DALAI LAMA AND MANY
    REFUGEES TO INDIA. DURING THAT TIME, THE TIBETAN CULTURE HAS
    BEEN SUBJECTED TO EVERY TECHNIQUE OF TRANSFORMATION KNOWN TO
    SOCIALIST IDEOLOGY AND VIRTUALLY EVERY TECHNIQUE FOR
    ERADICATING A DISTINCT CULTURAL IDENTITY KNOWN TO CHINESE
    ASSIMILATIONIST IMPERIALISM. THE TIBETANS HAVE, NEVERTHELESS,
    NOT BEEN SUBSUMED WITHIN THE CHINESE MASSES NOR, IN THE
    DIASPORA, ASSUMED THE USUAL HELPLESSNESS OF THE REFUGEES.
    RECENT EVENTS IN TIBET HAVE STRENGTHENED THE CAUSE OF
    TIBETAN NATIONALISM, GIVING IT NEW, MORE SOPHISTICATED FORMS.
    AT THE SAME TIME, ETHNIC AND NATIONAL CAUSES HAVE BECOME
    MORE VISIBLE WORLDWIDE.

08489 SMOLLA, R.A.
    WHY DOES LIBEL LAW NEED REFORM?
    SOCIETY, 26(5) (JUL 89), 67-70.
       LIBEL SUITS TEND TO DRAG ON INTERMINABLY. FIRST
    AMENDMENT PROTECTIONS HAVE THE UNINTENDED SIDE EFFECT OF
    COMPLICATING LIBEL CASES. EVEN MANY JUDGES WITH LONG
    EXPERIENCE HAVE DIFFICULTY SORTING THROUGH ALL THE RULES.
    THIS ARTICLE EXAMINES THE PROPOSED LIBEL REFORM ACT WHICH
    INTRODUCES A NEW PREMISE OF LIBEL LAW: THAT ITS ULTIMATE
    PURPOSE IS THE TIMELY DISSEMINATION OF TRUTH. THIS ACT SETS
    FORTH A THREE-STAGE PROCESS IN WHICH BOTH SIDES ARE
    ENCOURAGED TO CAREFULLY ASSESS THEIR OWN POSITIONS AND TO
    SOLVE THEIR DISPUTES WITHOUT RESORTING TO SUITS FOR MONEY
    DAMAGES.

08490 SMYTH, D.; DUA, P.
    THE PUBLIC'S INDIFFERENCE MAP BETWEEN INFLATION AND
    UNEMPLOYMENT: EMPIRICAL EVIDENCE FOR THE NIXON, FORD,
    CARTER, AND REAGAN PRESIDENCIES
    PUBLIC CHOICE, 60(1) (JAN 89), 71-86.
       THE AUTHORS EXAMINE THE ASSUMPTION THAT SOCIETY HAS AN
    INDIFFERENCE MAP BETWEEN INFLATION AND UNEMPLOYMENT. THEY
    EXAMINE THE DRAWBACKS TO THE PRESIDENTIAL POPULARITY MEASURE
    USED IN EARLIER STUDIES AND PRESENT AN ALTERNATE MEASURE.
    THIS ALTERNATE MEASURE ATTEMPTS TO OVERCOME TWO IMPORTANT
    DEFICIENCIES: THE USE OF AN UNSATISFACTORY MEASURE OF PUBLIC
    SATISFACTION OR DISSATISFACTION AND THE A PRIORI ASSUMPTION
    OF LINEAR INDIFFERENCE CURVES.

08491 SMYTH, F.H.
    RELIGION AND SCOIALISM
    MONTHLY REVIEW, 40(9) (FEB 89), 35-44.
       THE RELIGIOUS APPROACH TO THE ECONOMIC AND SOCIAL
    PROBLEMS PRESENTED BY DEVELOPED CAPITALISM IS NOT SO MUCH
    IMMEDIATELY ONE OF MORAL LEADERSHIP AND OF PROPHETIC
    EXHORTATION (ALTHOUGH THESE CAN CERTAINLY NOT BE ABSENT), AS
    IT IS ONE OF SCIENTIFIC GUIDANCE AND OF SOCIAL ENGINEERING
    FOR THE ACHIEVEMENT OF AN ORDER SUCH THAT RELIGIOUS
    PRINCIPLES CAN, AT LEAST, BE PUT INTO PRACTICE IN EVERY
    DEPARTMENT OF LIFE BY ALL WHO ARE DETERMINED TO DO SO. THIS
    DOES NOT, OF COURSE, MEAN THAT ALL MEN WITHOUT EXCEPTION
    MUST BE MOTIVATED BY RELIGIOUS CONVICTION. BUT IT DOES MEAN
    THAT THOSE WHO ARE SO MOTIVATED MUST NOT BE FLATLY IMPEDED,
    AS THEY ARE NOW, BY THE OBJECTIVE REALITIES OF CONTEMPORARY
    CAPITALIST SOCIETY.

08492 SMYTH, J.
    STRETCHING THE BOUNDARIES: THE CONTROL OF DISSENT IN
    NORTHERN IRELAND
    TERRORISM, 11(4) (1988), 275-288.
       THE ARTICLE EXAMINES THE "IRISH PROBLEM" AND THE LESSONS
    THAT CAN BE LEARNED ABOUT THE NATURE OF STATE POWER AND THE
    GENERAL RESPONSE TO DISSENT IN TIMES OF SOCIAL CONFLICT. IT
    ARGUES THAT MANY ELEMENTS OF THE IRISH CONTEXT ARE SHARED BY
    OTHER REAL AND POTENTIAL CONFLICT SITUATIONS IN EUROPE AND
    ELSEWHERE. IT CONCLUDES THAT THE LESSONS OF THE IRISH

SITUATION ARE AMBIGUOUS AND CONTRADICTORY BUT SHOW THAT
ALTHOUGH A STATE CAN CONTROL AND CONTAIN A VERY HIGH LEVEL
OF DISSENT, THERE IS A HIGH COST TO PAY IN TERMS OF
ESTABLISHED DEMOCRATIC PRACTICES AND THE ROLE OF
INSTITUTIONS SUCH AS THE MEDIA AND PRESSURE GROUPS.

08493 SNAPE, R.H.
    IS NON-DISCRIMINATION REALLY DEAD?
    WORLD ECONOMY, 11(1) (MAR 88), 1-18.
       THIS ARTICLE REVIEWS TRENDS IN TRADE POLICY,
    PARTICULARLY THOSE OF THE U.S., AND CONSIDERS RECENT
    DEVELOPMENTS AND THEIR IMPLICATIONS FOR THE INTERNATIONAL
    TRADING SYSTEM. IT REMINDS THAT TRADE POLICY IS FOREING
    POLICY AS WELL AS THE PRODUCT OF DOMESTIC INDUSTRY POLICY
    AND PRESSURES. TRADE POLICY IS ALSO THE PRODUCT OF THE
    BALANCE BETWEEN DIFFERENT ARMS OF GOVERNMENT. THE FOCUS OF
    THIS ARTICLE IS ON THE IMPACT ON THE INTERNATIONAL TRADING
    SYSTEM PER SE AS THE CRITERION BY WHICH TO MEASURE TRADE
    POLICY.

08494 SNAVELY, K.
    WHAT'S NEW AND USED IN STATE TAX ADMINISTRATION. HOW TOP
    OFFICIALS RATE INNOVATIONS
    STATE AND LOCAL GOVERNMENT REVIEW, 21(2) (SPR 89), 60-65.
       OVER THE PRESENT DECADE, STATE AGENCIES RESPONSIBLE FOR
    THE ADMINISTRATION AND ENFORCEMENT OF STATE TAX LAWS HAVE
    ADOPTED A NUMBER OF NEW FUNCTIONS ACROSS THE COERCIVE,
    TAXPAYER SERVICE, AND VALUES-DEVELOPMENT DIMENSIONS OF TAX
    ADMINISTRATION. EVIDENCE GATHERED FROM A SURVEY REVEALS THAT
    TOP ADMINISTRTORS PERCEIVE COERCIVE (AUDITING AND
    COLLECTIONS) POLICIES TO BE THE MOST IMPORTANT OF RECENT
    INNOVATIONS. THOSE PERCEPTIONS, EXPRESSED IN RESPONSE TO A
    SURVEY QUESTIONNAIRE, ARE COMPARED WITH SURVEY DATA ON STATE
    TAX ADMINISTRATION PRACTICES.

08495 SNIDERMAN, P.M.; FLETCHER, J.F.; RUSSELL, P.H.; TETLOCK,
    P.E.
    POLITICAL CULTURE AND THE PROBLEM OF DOUBLE STANDARDS:
    MASS AND ELITE ATTITUDES TOWARD LANGUAGE RIGHTS IN THE
    CANADIAN CHARATER OF RIGHTS AND FREEDOMS
    CANADIAN JOURNAL OF POLITICAL SCIENCE, XXII(2) (JUN 89),
    259-284.
       LANGUAGE RIGHTS REPRESENT CLAIMS OF ENTITLEMENT NOT ONLY
    ON BEHALF OF INDIVIDUALS, BUT ALSO ON BEHALF OF LINGUISTIC
    COMMUNITIES. AS SUCH, THEY RAISE DEEP QUESTIONS OF IDENTITY
    AND AFFINITY FOR CANADIANS. THIS STUDY, THE FIRST REPORT OF
    THE CHARTER PROJECT, INVESTIGATES MASS AND ELITE ATTITUDES
    TOWARD LANGUAGE RIGHTS IN CANADA. BEGINNING WITH THE PROBLEM
    OF DOUBLE STANDARDS—WHETHER ANGLOPHONES AND FRANCOPHONES
    WANT TO AFFIRM CERTAIN RIGHTS FOR THEIR OWN GROUP BUT NOT
    FOR THE OTHER—THIS STUDY FINDS THAT ATTITUDES TOWARD
    LANGUAGE RIGHTS ARE SHAPED BY AN INTERPLAY BETWEEN CORE
    VALUES TO WHICH CITIZENS SUBSCRIBE AND THEIR CONCERN FOR THE
    STATUS OF THE GROUPS, BOTH LINGUISTIC AND PARTISAN, WITH
    WHICH THEY IDENTIFY.

08496 SNIDERMAN, P.M.; GLASER, J.M.; GREEN, D.P.; HOUT, M.;
    TETLOCK, P.E.
    PRINCIPLED TOLERANCE AND THE AMERICAN MASS PUBLIC
    BRITISH JOURNAL OF POLITICAL SCIENCE, 19(1) (JAN 89),
    25-45.
       AMERICANS APPEAR TO BE MORE TOLERANT OF DEVIANT OPINIONS
    AND LIFESTYLES NOW THAN THEY WERE A GENERATION AGO. BUT
    RECENT RESEARCH SUGGESTS THAT THIS CHANGE IS LARGELY
    ILLUSORY: A PRODUCT NOT OF AN INCREASE IN PRINCIPLED SUPPORT
    FOR TOLERANCE, BUT RATHER OF SHIFTS IN PUBLIC DISLIKE FOR,
    AND HENCE INTOLERANCE OF, PARTICULAR POLITICAL GROUPS. THIS
    ESSAY PROPOSES AN ALTERNATIVE ACCOUNT OF TOLERANCE, WHICH
    SHOWS THAT PUBLIC ATTITUDES ON ISSUES OF TOLERANCE ARE
    REMARKABLY CONSISTENT. THE BROADER IMPLICATIONS OF THIS FOR
    THE STUDY OF PUBLIC OPINION AND DEMOCRATIC THEORY ARE NOTED.

08497 SNIR, R.
    TWO EGYPTIAN WRITERS IN THE SERVICE OF PEACE
    MIDDLE EAST REVIEW, XXI(2) (WIN 89), 41-46.
       LONG BEFORE THE EGYPT-ISRAEL PEACE TREATY, EGYPTIAN
    DRAMATIST TAHFIQ AL-HAKIM AND NOVELIST NAJIB MAHFUZ CALLED
    FOR AN END TO THE CONFLICT BETWEEN ISRAEL AND THE ARAB
    COUNTRIES. NEITHER SAW ISRAEL'S EXISTENCE AS THE CENTRAL
    PROBLEM OF THE ARAB WORLD. THE POSITION THAT THESE WRITERS
    ESPOUSED ON THE MIDDLE EAST SITUATION WAS PART OF THEIR
    HIGHLY DEVELOPED SOCIAL AND POLITICAL CONSCIOUSNESS.
    POINTING TO THE PRESSING DEVELOPMENTAL PROBLEMS OF EGYPTIAN
    SOCIETY AND OF THE ARAB WORLD IN GENERAL, THEY WARNED THAT
    IF THE ARABS DID NOT MAKE WISE USE OF THE MASSIVE INCOME
    FROM THEIR OIL EXPORTS, THEY WOULD FALL BACK TO THEIR AGE-
    OLD STATUS AS CAMEL HERDERS AND PENNILESS NOMADS.

08498 SNOEK, H.
    PROBLEMS OF BANK SUPERVISION IN LDCS
    FINANCE AND DEVELOPMENT, 26(4) (DEC 89), 14-16.
       THIS ARTICLE FOCUSES ON THE INCREASING EMPHASIS THAT IS
    BEING GIVEN TO THE IMPROVING OF AND STRENGTHENING OF
    SUPERVISION OF BANKS IN DEVELOPING COUNTRIES. THE PROBLEMS

DISCUSSED ARE FACED BY A LARGE NUMBERS OF THESE COUNTRIES AS WELL AS DEVELOPED COUNTRIES. THE SOLUTIONS OFFERED ARE OF A GENERAL NATURE AND FOR AN INDIVIDUAL COUNTRY NEED TO BE ADAPT TO ITS SPECIFIC CIRCUMSTANCES AND ITS INSTITUTIONAL STRUCTURE. IT SUGGESTS THAT BANK SUPERVISORS WILL BE MORE EFFECTIVE IF THEY ASSUME THE ROLE OF PARTNERSHIP WITH THE BANKS.

08499 SNOOK, D.A.
WHAT IT TAKES TO WIN: THE POLITICAL STYLE OF STATE LEGISLATORS AS CANDIDATES FOR STATE-WIDE OFFICE
DISSERTATION ABSTRACTS INTERNATIONAL, 49(12) (JUN 89), 3860-A.
WITHIN THE GENERAL FRAMEWORK OF ALBERT BANDURA'S SOCIAL LEARNING THEORY, THIS STUDY DEVELOPS THE CONCEPT OF CANDIDATE PERSONAL CAMPAIGN STYLE AS AN ANALYTIC DEVICE TO EXAMINE WAYS IN WHICH EXPERIENCE IN THE SMALL CAMPAIGN SETTING PREPARES, OR FAILS TO PREPARE, CANDIDATES FOR WINNING STATE-WIDE ELECTIONS. USING INFORMATION GATHERED THROUGH QUESTIONNAIRES MAILED TO LEGISLATORS IN COLORADO, KANSAS, IOWA, AND WISCONSIN. THE AUTHOR IDENTIFIES SIXTEEN "STYLE POINTS." HE CONCLUDES THAT CANDIDATE CAMPAIGN STYLE APPEARS TO BE AN IMPORTANT FACTOR IN THE ELECTORAL SUCCESS OF THE CANDIDATES HE STUDIED.

08500 SOBARZO, A.
PEACE IS RESPECT FOR THE RIGHTS OF OTHERS
WORLD MARXIST REVIEW, 32(6) (JUN 89), 72-75.
THE INSTITUTIONAL REVOLUTIONARY PARTY (PRI) HAS NOW BEEN IN POWER IN MEXICO FOR 60 YEARS, AND ITS FOREIGN POLICY HAS WON INTERNATIONAL RECOGNITION. ALEJANDRO SOBARZO, A LEADING FIGURE IN THE PRI IS INTERVIEWED AND DESCRIBES THE MAIN FEATURES OF MEXICO'S INTERNATIONAL STAND. JUAREZ'S MAXIM IS APPLIED IN THE HISTORY OF MEXICO'S FOREIGN POLICY, PLURALISM, DICTATORSHIPS, IMMIGRATION, AND DIPLOMATIC RELATIONS ARE ANALYZED.

08501 SOBEL, R.
PUBLIC OPINION ABOUT UNITED STATES INTERVENTION IN EL SALVADOR AND NICARAGUA
PUBLIC OPINION QUARTERLY, 53(1) (SPR 89), 114-128.
SINCE THE START OF THE REAGAN ADMINISTRATION, THE NATIONAL MEDIA AND POLLS HAVE DEVOTED SUBSTANTIAL ATTENTION TO UNITED STATES INVOLVEMENT IN CENTRAL AMERICA. IN THE EARLY 1980S POLLING QUESTIONS FOCUSED ON OPINION ABOUT THE CONFLICT IN EL SALVADOR BETWEEN OPPOSITION FORCES AND THE GOVERNMENT. IN THE MIDDLE 1980S THE FOCUS TURNED TO NICARAGUA AND QUESTIONS ABOUT SUPPORT FOR OR OPPOSITION TO AID FOR THE CONTRAS OPPOSING THE SANDINISTA GOVERNMENT. A REVIEW OF THE POLLS INDICATES THAT MOST PEOPLE IN THE U.S. ARE AWARE BUT NOT VERY KNOWLEDGEABLE OR INTENSELY CONCERNED ABOUT THESE SITUATIONS IN CENTRAL AMERICA. AND, THOUGH PERCEIVING COMMUNISM AS A THREAT IN CENTRAL AMERICA, MOST AMERICANS OPPOSE U.S. INTERVENTION THERE.

08502 SOBOLEV, G.
POWERS INHERENT IN EARTH'S ENTRAIL
REPRINTS FROM THE SOVIET PRESS, 48(10) (MAY 89), 37-42.
IN THIS ARTICLE, THE AUTHOR, WHO IS CHIEF OF A SOVIET RESEARCH GROUP TRYING TO PREDICT EARTHQUAKES, DESCRIBES THE LOCATION OF EARTHQUAKE ZONES IN THE SOVIET UNION, EXAMINES THE COUNTRY'S PREPAREDNESS TO MEET A NATURAL EARTHQUAKE DISASTER AND COMMENTS ON THE LOCATION AND STRUCTURAL SOUNDNESS OF NUCLEAR POWER PLANTS NEAR KNOWN EARTHQUAKE ZONES.

08503 SOBRINO, J.
DEATH IN EL SALVADOR
COMMONWEAL, CXVI(22) (DEC 89), 693-695.
AMERICANS SHOULD UNDERSTAND THAT THE PROBLEM IN EL SALVADOR IS NOT POLITICAL. IT GOES MUCH DEEPER; IT IS A PROBLEM OF POVERTY. THE KILLING IN EL SALVADOR WILL GO ON, AS IT WILL THROUGHOUT LATIN AMERICA, BECAUSE THE SITUATION IS GETTING WORSE. THE EXTREME RIGHT, THE OLIGARCHY, THE DEATH SQUADS, AND SOME MEMBERS OF THE ARMY ARE IN CONTROL OF THE COUNTRY. THEY HAVE CONTEMPT FOR CHRISTIANS AND CHURCH WORKERS BECAUSE THEY WANT THE POOR TO ACCEPT CONDITIONS AS THEY ARE AND NOT TO QUESTION THEIR LOT IN LIFE.

08504 SOCHOR, E.
CONFLICTS IN INTERNATIONAL CIVIL AVIATION: SAFEGUARDING THE AIR ROUTES
CONFLICT, 8(4) (1988), 271-284.
THE INTERNATIONAL CIVIL AVIATION ORGANIZATION (ICAO) HAS BEEN SPARED THE BITTER CONFRONTATIONS AND ACRIMONIES THAT HAVE REVERBERATED IN THE UNITED NATIONS AND OTHER AGENCIES OVER THE YEARS. SINCE ALL NATIONS, BIG OR SMALL, HAVE A VESTED INTEREST IN THE SAFE AND ORDERLY DEVELOPMENT OF AIR TRANSPORT WHICH ARE ICAO'S MAJOR OBJECTIVES, IT WOULD BE AGAINST THE INTEREST OF ANY NATION TO JEOPARDIZE ITS OWN ACCESS TO INTERNATIONAL AIRWAYS. THE SOLID CONFIDENCE ALL STATES HAVE PLACED IN THE ORGANIZATION FROM ITS EARLIEST DAYS HAS HELPED CREATE AN ENVIRONMENT CONDUCTIVE TO COMPROMISE. NONETHELESS, THIS CONCILIATORY INCLINATION HAS

BEEN TESTED TO THE LIMIT AS INTERNATIONAL AND REGIONAL CONFLICTS HAVE DRAWN THE ORGANIZATION INTO POLITICAL ISSUES OUTSIDE ITS TRADITIONAL COMPETENCE. THIS CHALLENGE HAS BEEN TO RECONCILE THE SOVEREIGNTY PRINCIPLE OVER THE AIRSPACE WITH THE OBLIGATION OF STATES TO ASSURE THE SECURITY OF COMMERCIAL AIR TRAVEL AND THE SAFETY OF AIR ROUTES.

08505 SOELDNER, T.; HEXHAM, I.; POEWE-HEXHAM, K.
CHARISMATIC CHURCHES AND THE STRUGGLE AGAINST APARTHEID: A DISPUTE
THE CHRISTIAN CENTURY, 106(1) (JAN 89), 16, 18-21.
THE AUTHORS DISCUSS THE SOUTH AFRICAN COUNCIL OF CHURCHES, CHARISMATIC CHURCHES, AND THE USE OF VIOLENCE AND ECONOMIC SANCTIONS IN SOUTH AFRICA.

08506 SOFAER, A.D.
THE WAR POWERS RESOLUTION
DEPARTMENT OF STATE BULLETIN (US FOREIGN POLICY), 88(2140) (NOV 88), 36-39.
THE US GOVERNMENT HAS DEBATED ON THE RELATIVE POWERS OF THE POLITICAL BRANCHES OVER FOREIGN POLICY AND WAR SINCE ITS FORMATION AND THE DEBATE AND CONTROVERSY SURROUNDING THE WAR POWERS RESOLUTION IS NO EXCEPTION. THE ARTICLE EXAMINES THE RESOLUTION AS A WHOLE AS WELL AS SPECIFIC PROVISIONS OF THE LEGISLATION. THE AUTHOR CONCLUDES THAT THE WAR POWERS RESOLUTION HAS NOT MADE A POSITIVE CONTRIBUTION TO EXECUTIVE-CONGRESSIONAL COOPERATION THAT WOULD JUSTIFY THE CONTROVERSY AND UNCERTAINTY IT HAS CAUSED AND SEEMS CERTAIN TO CAUSE IN THE FUTURE. HE ADVOCATES A REPEAL OF THE RESOLUTION ALTOGETHER.

08507 SOHNG, S.
THE SOUTH KOREAN MODEL FOR INDUSTRIALIZATION: THEORY AND REALITY
ASIAN PROFILE, 17(6) (DEC 89), 513-522.
IN SPITE OF THE GOVERNMENT'S ASSERTION THAT SOUTH KOREA HAS ACHIEVED ECONOMIC GROWTH WITH EQUITY, KOREAN INDUSTRIALIZATION HAS CAUSED MANY PROBLEMS THAT HAVE NOT RECEIVED SUFFICIENT ATTENTION. INCREASING INEQUALITY IS ONE OF THE MOST PRESSING PROBLEMS. THIS ESSAY EXAMINES THE KOREAN INDUSTRIALIZATION PROCESS AND ITS CONSEQUENCES, WITH SPECIAL REFERENCE TO SECTORAL IMBALANCES AND INEQUALITY.

08508 SOIFER, S.D.
ELECTORAL POLITICS AND SOCIAL CHANGE: THE CASE OF BURLINGTON, VERMONT
DISSERTATION ABSTRACTS INTERNATIONAL, 49(8) (FEB 89), 2420-A.
MAYOR BERNARD SANDERS OF BURLINGTON, VERMONT, IS THE ONLY SELF-PROCLAIMED SOCIALIST MAYOR IN THE USA. THIS DISSERTATION STUDIES SANDERS' ADMINISTRATION, INCLUDING HOW IT CAME TO BE ELECTED AND HOW IT HAS HANDLED IMPORTANT ISSUES. THE STUDY ALSO CONTAINS A BRIEF HISTORY OF MUNICIPAL SOCIALISM IN THE USA.

08509 SOKOLEWICZ, W.
NEW POLITICAL ORDER
POLISH PERSPECTIVES, XXXII(2) (1989), 8-11.
THE CHANGES IN POLISH POLITICAL LIFE SHOULD BE SEEN AS THE FIRST STEPS TOWARD DEVELOPING NEW PRINCIPLES AND MODES OF GOVERNMENT. THE FINAL POLITICAL MODEL IS STILL UNKNOWN, BUT IT WILL GO FORWARD ACCORDING TO THE NEW RULES AGREED UPON AT THE ROUND TABLE NEGOTIATIONS AND ENACTED BY PARLIAMENT. THE FUNDAMENTAL FEATURE OF THE REFORM IS THE OPENING OF THE POLITICAL SYSTEM TO OPPOSITION GROUPS. NEW LEGISLATION HAS LAID DOWN RULES FOR A PERIOD OF TRANSITION, OR CONSTITUTIONAL INTERIM, AS THE FINAL SHAPE OF THE NEW POLITICAL SYSTEM TAKES FORM.

08510 SOKOLEWICZ, W.; KROL, M.; MADEJ, Z.; WINCZOREK, P.
VIEWPOINT
POLISH PERSPECTIVES, XXXII(1) (1989), 48-55.
CHANGES IN THE POLISH POLITICAL SYSTEM ARE EXPECTED IN THE IMMEDIATE FUTURE. THIS ARTICLE LOOKS AT SOME AREAS THAT WILL BE AFFECTED BY THE REFORMS, INCLUDING THE POWER STRUCTURE, POLITICAL PARTIES, AND THE OPPOSITION.

08511 SOKOLOW, A.D.
LEGISLATORS WITHOUT AMBITION: WHY SMALL-TOWN CITIZENS SEEK PUBLIC OFFICE
STATE AND LOCAL GOVERNMENT REVIEW, 21(1) (WIN 89), 23-30.
WITH LIMITED OPPORTUNITIES TO CLIMB THE POLITICAL CAREER LADDER, WHAT MOTIVATES CITIZENS TO SEEK ELECTED OFFICE IN LOCAL GOVERNMENT? THIS ARTICLE FINDS THAT PERSONAL AND POLICY INCENTIVES, MORE THAN APPEALS TO CIVIC OBLIGATION, DOMINATED THE RECRUITMENT DECISIONS AND ACTIONS OF OFFICEHOLDERS IN A SAMPLE OF 12 SMALL MUNICIPAL AND COUNTY GOVERNMENTS IN CALIFORNIA AND ILLINOIS. EVEN WHEN RECRUITED BY OTHERS, OR APPOINTED TO OFFICE, RESPONDENTS WERE GENERALLY ENTHUSIASTIC ABOUT ENTERING PUBLIC LIFE--A FINDING AT ODDS WITH THE CONVENTIONAL IMAGE OF THE RELUCTANT CANDIDATE IN RURAL POLITICS. SINCE THE GREAT MAJORITY OF ELECTED POSITIONS IN THE AMERICAN POLITICAL SYSTEM ARE IN LOCAL GOVERNMENT, THE ARTICLE SUGGESTS THAT THE THEORY OF

POLITICAL AMBITION NEEDS REVISION TO CAPTURE MORE OF THE
ESSENCE OF OFFICEHOLDING AT THIS LEVEL.

08512 SOKOLOW, A.D.
SMALL LOCAL GOVERNMENTS AS COMMUNITY BUILDERS
NATIONAL CIVIC REVIEW, 78(5) (SEP 89), 362-370.
WHILE SMALL LOCAL GOVERNMENTS LACK THE ADVANTAGES OF
REVENUE BASE, ADEQUATE STAFF, AND PROFESSIONALIZATION, THE
LIMITATIONS OF SMALL SIZE ARE REPLACED BY ITS ADVANTAGES:
PROXIMITY TO CONSTITUENCY, RESPONSIVENESS, AND FLEXIBILITY.
THE EXTERNAL (FEDERAL) ASSISTANCE OF THE 1970S HELPED BRING
ABOUT SUBSTANTIAL LOCAL IMPROVEMENTS AND SURELY AIDED
COMMUNITYBUILDING EFFORTS. NONETHELESS, MAJOR SMALL TOWN
PROJECTS CONTINUE TO BE DRIVEN BY LOCAL PRIORITIES AND VIEW;
SUCCESS OF SUCH EFFORTS DEPENDS ON THE QUALITY OF LOCAL
LEADERSHIP AND THE LEADERSHIP AGENDA ITSELF, VOLUNTEER
ACTION, MULTIPLE ASSIGNMENTS TO PUBLIC EMPLOYEES, AND AD HOC-
-BUT EFFECTIVE--ADMINISTRATION

08513 SOKOLSKY, J.J.
A SEAT AT THE TABLE: CANADA AND ITS ALLIANCES
ARMED FORCES AND SOCIETY, 16(1) (FAL 89), 11-35.
CANADA'S ALLIANCE RELATIONSHIPS -- THE NORTH ATLANTIC
TREATY ORGANIZATION AND THE NORTH AMERICAN AEROSPACE DEFENSE
COMMAND -- CONSTITUTE NEARLY THE SUM TOTAL OF CANADIAN
DEFENSE POLICY. SINCE BOTH NATO AND NORAD ARE AMERICAN-LED
PACTS, CANADIAN DEFENSE POLICY COMPLEMENTS AND IS CLOSELY
COORDINATED WITH U.S. GLOBAL STRATEGIC INTERESTS AND
POSTURES. APART FROM ITS OWN NATIONAL INTEREST IN SUPPORTING
COLLECTIVE DEFENSE, CANADA HAS JOINED AND ACTIVELY
PARTICIPATES IN THESE ALLIANCES AS PART OF A GLOBAL FOREIGN
POLICY.

08514 SOLINGER, D.J.
CAPITALIST MEASURES WITH CHINESE CHARACTERISTICS
PROBLEMS OF COMMUNISM, XXXVIII(1) (JAN 89), 19-33.
IN THE MID-1980'S, CHINA APPEARED TO BE UNDERTAKING
MEASURES THAT AUGURED A STARTLING RESHAPING OF THE STRUCTURE
OF THE URBAN ECONOMY: INDUSTRIAL FIRMS BEGAN SELLING OFF
THEIR STATE-OWNED ASSETS AS SHARES; BIGGER, MORE SUCCESSFUL,
ENTERPRISES STARTED TAKING OVER FAILING ONES IN A MANNER
SUGGESTIVE OF MERGERS IN THE WEST; A TINY HANDFUL OF HAPLESS
PLANTS EVEN WENT BANKRUPT, A VIRTUALLY UNPRECEDENTED
PHENOMENON IN A SOCIALIST ECONOMY. THESE MOST CAPITALIST OF
PRACTICES HAVE NOT, HOWEVER, BEEN SANCTIONED BY THE CHINESE
LEADERSHIP OUT OF AN URGE TO REORIENT THE ECONOMY AWAY FROM
STATE OWNERSHIP AND TOWARD PRIVATIZATION. IN THE EYES OF
CHINA'S LEADERS, THESE REFORMS ARE A WAY TO MANAGE THE
STATE'S MACRO-FINANCES, WHILE PRESERVING STATE/PUBLIC
OWNERSHIP--THE IMPULSES BEHIND THEM HAVE A STATIST RATIONALE
AND A STATIST ORGANIZATION. WHAT MIGHT BE MISTAKEN FOR A
CHINESE LURCH TOWARD CAPITALISM IS ACTUALLY A FLESHING OUT
OF THE VAGUE CONCEPT OF "SOCIALISM WITH CHINESE
CHARACTERISTICS."

08515 SOLINGER, D.J.
DEMOCRACY WITH CHINESE CHARACTERISTICS
WORLD POLICY JOURNAL, 6(4) (FAL 89), 621-632.
THIS ARTICLE IDENTIFIES THE RECURRING THEMES IN MASS
BEHAVIOR AND POLITICAL CONSCIOUSNESS IN CHINA WHICH ARE
IMPORTANT FOR UNDERSTANDING WHICH COURSE THE LEADERSHIP AND
THE DISSENTERS MIGHT TAKE IN THE PEOPLES REPUBLIC OF CHINA.
IT EXPLORES THE DEMOCRACY MOVEMENT IN LIGHT OF PARALLELS
WITH PAST PROTEST IN CHINA, TO BETTER PREDICT THE COURSE
DISSENT MIGHT TAKE AFTER THE JUNE MASSACRE. IT CONCLUDES
THAT THE ATMOSPHERE REMAINS RIPE FOR FUTURE OUTBURSTS SINCE
MASS PROTESTS USUALLY TAKE PLACE WHEN THE GOVERNMENT IS WEAK,
AND PERCEIVED AS ILLEGITIMATE.

08516 SOLINGER, D.J.
URBAN REFORM AND RELATIONAL CONTRACTING IN POST-MAO CHINA:
AN INTERPRETATION OF THE TRANSITION FROM PLAN TO MARKET
STUDIES IN COMPARATIVE COMMUNISM, 22(2/3) (SUM 89),
171-186.
THIS ARTICLE ASSESSES THE IMPACT OF CHINA'S 1984 URBAN
REFORMS ON COMMERCIAL BEHAVIOR OF INDUSTRIAL ENTERPRISES IN
THE STATEOWNED SECTOR. IT FINDS THAT THUS FAR IT FAILS TO
BECOME A FREE MARKET EXCHANGE. THIS IS ATTRIBUTED TO THREE
WEAKNESSES IN THE ECONOMY: 1) SCARCITY, 2) LACK OF DESIGN
STANDARDIZATION, AND 3) INFORMATIONAL UNCERTAINTY. DUE TO
THESE THREE PROBLEMS THE TRANSITION COSTS TO OPERATE ON THE
OPEN MARKET ARE EXCESSIVELY HIGH. THE RESULT IS THAT THE
ECONOMIC BEHAVIOR OF STATE -OWNED FIRMS IN TH E URBAN SECTOR
HAS BEEN FAR LESS MARKET-ORIENTED THAN ANTICIPATED.

08517 SOLLIE, F.
THE POLITICAL AND STRATEGIC IMPORTANCE OF THE ARCTIC: A
ETUDES INTERNATIONALES, XX(1) (MAR 89), 71-96.
NORWEGIAN PERSPECTIVE DEVELOPMENTS IN MANY FIELDS, AND
ESPECIALLY IN TECHNOLOGY AND ECONOMICS, IN INTERNATIONAL
POLITICS AND IN MILITARY STRATEGY, HAVE COMBINED TO GIVE THE
ARCTIC A MORE IMPORTANT ROLE IN INTERNATIONAL AFFAIRS. BY
GEOGRAPHICAL LOCATION, WITH ITS MAINLAND AND ISLANDS
STRETCHING FAR TO THE NORTH AND FRAMING THE MARITIME LINK

BETWEEN THE ATLANTIC AND THE ARCTIC, NORWAY HAS A STRATEGIC
POSITION AT THE MAIN GATEWAY TO AND FROM THE ARCTIC BASIN.
WITH THE SOVIET UNION EMERGING AS THE MAJOR MILITARY POWER
IN EUROPE AT THE END OF THE SECOND WORLD WAR AND
CONCENTRATING ITS NEW AND GLOBAL NAVAL FORCES IN NORTHERN
BASES ON THE KOLA PENINSULA, THE NORTHERN WATERS BETWEEN
NORWAY'S COASTS HAVE BECOME A STRATEGIC CORE AREA FOR ANY
CONTEST FOR MARITIME CONTROL OF ATLANTIC SUPPLY LINES, AS
WELL ·AS FOR THE STRATEGIC NUCLEAR BALANCE BETWEEN THE TWO
SUPERPOWERS AND FOR A NEW NUCLEAR THREAT AGAINST EUROPE. IN
SUM, THE BROAD DEVELOPMENTS IN THE ARCTIC AND THE SPECIFIC
STRATEGIC INTERESTS IN ARCTIC RELATIONS NOW FOCUSING ON THE
NORWEGIAN ARCTIC, THE NORWEGIAN NORTH HAS BEEN TURNED INTO A
CENTER STAGE OF INTERNATIONAL POLITICAL AND MILITARY
INTEREST AND CONCERN. NOTE: ARTICLE IS IN FRENCH

08518 SOLLIS, P.
THE ATLANTIC COAST OF NICARAGUA: DEVELOPMENT AND AUTONOMY
JOURNAL OF LATIN AMERICAN STUDIES, 21(3) (OCT 89), 481-520.
IN RESPONSE TO THE ETHNIC DIVERSITY OF THE ATLANTIC
COAST, THE NICARAGUAN REVOLUTION HAS UNDERTAKEN A PROCESS OF
GRANTING AUTONOMY TO THE DIFFERENT ETHNIC GROUPS WHILE, AT
THE SAME TIME, ENGAGING IN A REAPPRAISAL OF NATIONAL
IDENTITY ITSELF. THIS ARTICLE DISCUSSES THE DISTINCT
HISTORICAL PHASES IN THE DEVELOPMENT OF THE NICARAGUAN
ATLANTIC COAST AS THE ESSENTIAL BACKGROUND TO AN ANALYSIS OF
THE PROCESS OF AUTONOMY CURRENTLY UNFOLDING THERE. IT
IDENTIFIES THREE MAIN PERIODS: ENGLISH COLONIAL RULE,
ENCLAVE ECONOMY WHEN U.S. COMPANIES WERE INVOLVED IN A
NUMBER OF EXTRACTIVE ENTERPRISES, AND CONTROL BY THE
SANDINISTAS SINCE 1979.

08519 SOLO, P.
A NEW PEACE POLITICS
SOJOURNERS, 18(2) (FEB 89), 18, 20.
COMMON SECURITY IS BOTH A NEW WAY OF THINKING ABOUT THE
CONDUCT OF INTERNATIONAL RELATIONS AND A POLITICAL PROGRAM.
IT RECOGNIZES THE FUNDAMENTAL REALITIES OF A WORLD WEARY OF
WAR: NO NATION CAN ACHIEVE SECURITY AT THE EXPENSE OF
ANOTHER. COMMON SECURITY DEMANDS REAL PROGRESS IN
DISARMAMENT, DEVELOPMENT, AND THE RESOLUTION OF REGIONAL
CONFLICTS. THE CHALLENGE NOW IS TO CONVINCE CYNICAL
POLITICIANS THAT THE PUBLIC IS READY FOR A PRINCIPLED AND
COMMON SENSE APPROACH TO FOREIGN POLICY.

08520 SOLOMATIN, A.
SOVIET-DANISH ECONOMIC RELATIONS
FOREIGN TRADE, 1 (1988), 32-33.
THIS ARTICLE EXAMINES THE UNSATISFACTORY TRADE BETWEEN
USSA AND DENMARK - 1987-1988. IT REPORTS ON THE 16TH SESSION
OF THE INTERGOVERNMENTAL SOVIET-DANISH COMMISSION FOR
ECONOMIC, SCIENTIFIC AND TECHNICAL COOPERATION HELD IN
MOSCOW, OCTOBER 1987. IT CONCLUDES THAT PROSPECTS ARE GOOD
FOR THE FURTHER DEVELOPMENT OF SOVIET-DANISH RELATIONS.

08521 SOLOMON, R.
SOVIET-U.S. COOPERATION IN A TIME OF GLOBAL CHANGE
INTERNATIONAL AFFAIRS (MOSCOW), (2) (FEB 89), 48-54.
THE AUTHOR CONSIDERS TWO FUTURE-ORIENTED ASPECTS OF U.S.-
SOVIET DIALOGUE: THE AMERICAN ASSESSMENT OF THE GLOBAL
TRENDS THAT REQUIRE BOTH COUNTRIES TO ADJUST TO A NEW FUTURE
AND THE KIND OF AGENDA FOR U.S.-SOVIET RELATIONS THAT COULD
MOVE THE COUNTRIES AWAY FROM CONFRONTATION AND TOWARD MORE
COOPERATION.

08522 SOLOMON, R.H.
AN AGENDA FOR US-SOVIET COOPERATION
DEPARTMENT OF STATE BULLETIN (US FOREIGN POLICY), 89(2143)
(FEB 89), 38-42.
THE U.S. POLICY PLANNING STAFF HAS AN AGENDA ORIENTED TO
THE PROFOUND SCIENTIFIC, ECONOMIC, AND POLITICAL CHANGES
THAT ARE TRANSFORMING THE GLOBAL SYSTEM. U.S.-SOVIET
DIALOGUE REQUIRES BOTH COUNTRIES TO ADJUST TO A NEW FUTURE
AND TO MOVE AWAY FROM CONFRONTATION TOWARD INCREASING
COOPERATION IN SUCH AREAS AS HUMAN RIGHTS, ARMS CONTROL, AND
REGIONAL CONFLICTS.

08523 SOLOMON, R.H.
CAMBODIA AND VIETNAM: TRAPPED IN AN EDDY OF HISTORY?
DEPARTMENT OF STATE BULLETIN (US FOREIGN POLICY), 89(2152)
(NOV 89), 47-51.
THE AUTHOR, WHO IS ASSISTANT SECRETARY OF STATE FOR EAST
ASIAN AND PACIFIC AFFAIRS, DISCUSSES ASIA AFTER VIETNAM, U.S.
OBJECTIVES IN THE REGION, CAMBODIAN PEACE EFFORTS, AND THE
PARIS CONFERENCE ON CAMBODIA.

08524 SOLOMON, R.H.
PACIFIC DEVELOPMENT AND THE NEW INTERNATIONALISM
DEPARTMENT OF STATE BULLETIN (US FOREIGN POLICY), 88(2134)
(MAY 88), 33-36.
MANY PEOPLE FIND THE WORDS "PACIFIC" AND "FUTURE" TO BE
NEARLY SYNONYMOUS. THE ARTICLE ANALYZES THE CHALLENGES THAT
THE US WILL WILL FACE WITH REGARDS TO THE PACIFIC IN THE
COMING YEARS. THEY INCLUDE ECONOMIC CHALLENGES SUCH AS

AGRICULTURAL PRODUCTION, THE EMERGENCE OF GLOBAL FINANCIAL
MARKETS AND TRADE ISSUES. STRENGTHENING DEMOCRACY AND
DEALING WITH REGIONAL CHALLENGES WILL ALSO BE OF IMPORTANCE
TO FUTURE POLICYMAKERS IN THE US AS WILL BE SECURITY
CHALLENGES FROM SOURCES BOTH OLD AND NEW. THERE IS A GREAT
POTENTIAL FOR DISRUPTION IN THE YEARS AHEAD, BUT, AS
SECRETARY OF STATE SHULTZ STATED: "IF WE FACE UP TO OUR
RESPONSIBILITIES AS WELL AS OUR OPPORTUNITIES, IT IS CLEAR
THAT THE DEMOCRACIES OF THE PACIFIC HOLD THE WINNING HAND."

08525 SOLOMON, R.H.
    THE PROMISE OF PACIFIC ECONOMIC COOPERATION
    DEPARTMENT OF STATE BULLETIN (US FOREIGN POLICY), 89(2153)
    (DEC 89), 34-36.
        U.S. SECRETARY OF STATE JAMES BAKER HAS CALLED FOR A NEW
    PACIFIC PARTNERSHIP, WITH PACIFIC RIM COOPERATION AS AN
    IMPORTANT ELEMENT. IN ASIA, AS IN EUROPE, A NEW
    INTERNATIONAL ERA IS DAWNING. THE DOMINANT TRENDS OF THIS
    NEW ERA ARE AN INCREASINGLY INTEGRATED GLOBAL ECONOMY
    SPARKED BY SPECTACULAR TECHNOLOGICAL CHANGE, THE BANKRUPTCY
    OF COMMUNISM AS AN ECONOMIC AND POLITICAL ALTERNATIVE, AND A
    WORLDWIDE MOVEMENT TOWARD DEMOCRACY AND FREE ENTERPRISE. THE
    UNITED STATES' CHALLENGE IS TO GIVE INSTITUTIONAL FORM TO
    THESE TRENDS IN A MANNER CONSISTENT WITH AMERICAN INTERESTS
    AND TO THE BENEFIT OF ALLIES AND FRIENDS. THE NEW ERA WILL
    OFFER ENHANCED OPPORTUNITIES FOR ECONOMIC COOPERATION AMONG
    THE NATIONS OF THE PACIFIC RIM.

08526 SOLOMOS, J.
    EQUAL OPPORTUNITIES POLICIES AND RACIAL INEQUALITY: THE
    ROLE OF PUBLIC POLICY
    PUBLIC ADMINISTRATION, 67(1) (SPR 89), 79-94.
        THIS ARTICLE EXAMINES THE SEEMING CONTRADICTION BETWEEN
    THE PUBLICLY STATED OBJECTIVE OF SUCCESSIVE GOVERNMENTS TO
    PROMOTE GREATER EQUALITY OF OPPORTUNITY FOR RACIAL
    MINORITIES AND THE LIMITED IMPACT OF SUCCESSIVE POLICIES AND
    PROGRAMMES ON PROCESSES OF RACIAL DISCRIMNATION AND
    EXCLUSION IN BRITISH SOCIETY. THE ARTICLE BEGINS BY
    OUTLINING THE DIFFERENT CONCEPTUAL APPROACHES USED TO
    ANALYSE THE DEVELOPMENT OF PUBLIC POLICIES ON RACIAL
    INEQUALITY. IT THEN ANALYSES THE MAIN ASPECTS OF NATIONAL
    POLICY CHANGE IN THIS AREA OVER THE PAST TWO DECADES, AND
    MORE RECENT INITIATIVES WHICH HAVE SOUGHT TO USE LOCAL
    GOVERNMENT AS A VEHICLE FOR PROMOTING RACIAL EQUALITY. THIS
    ANALYSIS OFFERS A CRITICAL REVIEW OF THE ACHIEVEMENTS AND
    LIMITATIONS OF BOTH PAST AND PRESENT POLICIES. THE
    CONCLUDING SECTION TAKES UP THE QUESTION OF THE PROSPECTS OF
    CHANGE IN THE FUTURE.

08527 SOMARATNE, G.P.V.
    RENEWAL OF TIES BETWEEN SRI LANKA AND ISRAEL
    JERUSALEM JOURNAL OF INTERNATIONAL RELATIONS, 11(1) (MAR
    89), 74-86.
        ISRAELI-SRI LANKAN RELATIONS HAVE SEEN WIDE FLUCTUATIONS
    OVER THE YEARS, FROM ESTABLISHMENT OF FULL DIPLOMATIC
    RELATIONS IN 1957 TO A COOLING IN THE SIXTIES AND A FREEZE
    IN THE SEVENTIES AND EARLY EIGHTIES, TO THE MORE RECENT
    PARTIAL RESUMPTION OF TIES. THIS ARTICLE EXAMINES THE
    REASONS FOR THAT PARTIAL RESUMPTION, AND ASSESSES THE
    CURRENT SITUATION AND THE LIKELY FUTURE COURSE OF THESE
    RELATIONS.

08528 SOMERSET, H.
    BY ANTI-NUCLEAR UNITY - TOWARDS PEOPLE'S UNITY
    WORLD MARXIST REVIEW, 31(2) (FEB 88), 142-146.
        IN NORTHERN IRELAND ONE OF THE MAJOR QUESTIONS IS THE
    RELATIONSHIP BETWEEN THE PROLONGED CONFLICT OF SUCCESSIVE
    BRITISH GOVERNMENTS WITH THE NATIONAL ASPIRATION, GIVEN ALL
    ITS PRESENT-DAY RAMIFICATIONS AND BITTER DIVISIONS, AND THE
    CARDINAL ISSUES OF WORLD PEACE AND THE ENDING OF THE NUCLEAR
    THREAT. THIS ARTICLE EXAMINES HOW THESE LATTER ARE TO BE
    ADDRESSED IN A SOCIETY BLEEDING EMOTIONALLY AND PHYSICALLY
    FROM THE LONG YEARS OF INVECTIVE AND DISCRIMINATION, OF
    BOMBING AND SHOOTING.

08529 SOMERVILLE, K.
    ELECTORAL APATHY
    NEW AFRICAN, (JAN 88), 27-28.
        THIS ARTICLE REPORTS ON THE LACK OF ENTHUSIASM FOR
    ELECTIONS TO BE HELD UNDER RAWLINGS FOR DISTRICT ASSEMBLIES.
    IT DESCRIBES OBSTRUCTION, DELAYING REGISTRATION BY SOME
    ANTIGOVERNMENT ELEMENTS, PLUS APATHY AND TRADITIONAL
    OPPOSITION.

08530 SONENSHEIN, R.J.
    THE DYNAMICS OF BIRACIAL COALITIONS: CROSSOVER POLITICS IN
    LOS ANGELES
    WESTERN POLITICAL QUARTERLY, 42(2) (JUN 89), 333-354.
        BIRACIAL COALITIONS BETWEEN BLACKS AND WHITE LIBERALS,
    ONCE WIDELY ADMIRED, HAVE BEEN SEVERELY CRITICIZED IN RECENT
    DECADES. THE POLARIZATION MODEL OF RACIAL POLITICS, IN WHICH
    BLACK POWER DERIVES LARGELY FROM BLACK MOBILIZATION IN THE
    FACE OF WHITE HOSTILITY, HAS BECOME A DOMINANT VIEW. LESS
    ATTENTION HAS BEEN PAID TO A CROSSOVER MODEL IN WHICH BLACK

MOBILIZATION IS STRONGLY LINKED TO WHITE LIBERALISM. THE
CONDITIONS IN WESTERN STATES MAY BE AMENDABLE TO CROSSOVER
POLITICS. IN LOS ANGELES, A PROTOTYPICAL WESTERN CITY,
CROSSOVER POLITICS HAS ALLOWED A SMALL BLACK POPULATION TO
GAIN SUBSTANTIAL POLITICAL INCORPORATION IN COMBINATION WITH
LIBERAL REFORMERS. AT THE ELITE LEVEL, THIS COALITION HAS
BEEN DIRECTED BY A TIGHTLY KNIT ALLIANCE OF BLACKS AND
JEWISH LIBERALS. WHILE THE BIRACIAL RELATIONSHIP HAS AT
TIMES FACED INTEREST AND IDEOLOGICAL CONFLICTS, THIS
RESEARCH ADDS TO THE EVIDENCE THAT BLACK-LIBERAL COALITIONS
MAY HAVE BEEN PREMATURELY DECLARED DEAD.

08531 SONG, K.
    PRESIDENTIAL-CONGRESSIONAL-MEDIA RELATIONS IN THE SOCIAL
    WELFARE POLICY AGENDA BUILDING PROCESS
    DISSERTATION ABSTRACTS INTERNATIONAL, 48(10) (APR 88),
    2726-A.
        THE RESEARCH ATTEMPTS TO REVEAL THE DYNAMIC STRUCTURE OF
    THE AGENDA BUILDING PROCESS IN THE FIELD OF SOCIAL WELFARE
    POLICY BY BUILDING PROPER MODELS OF THE INTERACTIONS AMONG
    THE PRESIDENT, CONGRESS, AND THE MEDIA DURING THE PERIOD
    FROM JANUARY 1961 TO JANUARY 1977.

08532 SONG, L.
    SUMMIT AGREEMENT PROMOTES PEACE PROCESS
    BEIJING REVIEW, 32(36) (SEP 89), 18.
        ON AUGUST 7, 1989, THE PRESIDENTS OF NICARAGUA, HONDURAS,
    GUATEMALA, COSTA RICA, AND EL SALVADOR ENDED THEIR FIFTH
    SUMMIT WITH A PLAN TO DISSOLVE THE NICARAGUA CONTRA FORCES.
    THE PLAN SHOULD HELP TO EASE THE TENSION AMONG THE CENTRAL
    AMERICAN COUNTRIES, ESPECIALLY BETWEEN HONDURAS AND
    NICARAGUA. THE FIVE CENTRAL AMERICAN PRESIDENTS ALSO CALLED
    ON GUERRILLAS IN EL SALVADOR AND GUATAMELA TO HOLD TALKS
    WITH THE AUTHORITIES TO SEEK WAYS TO SOLVE THEIR INTERNAL
    CONFLICTS. THE SUMMIT SHOWS THAT CENTRAL AMERICAN COUNTRIES
    HAVE THE ABILITY TO REMOVE FOREIGN INTERVENTION AND SOLVE
    REGIONAL PROBLEMS BY THEMSELVES, EVEN THOUGH THE USA HAS
    ALWAYS TRIED TO PREVENT THIS.

08533 SONG, Y.B.
    THE PEOPLES REPUBLIC OF CHINA AND THE NEW OCEAN REGIME: A
    A STUDY IN THE LAW OF THE SEA AND MARINE POLICY
    DISSERTATION ABSTRACTS INTERNATIONAL, 49(10) (APR 89),
    3148-A.
        RECOGNIZING THAT CHINA IS EMERGING AS A MAJOR MARITIME
    POWER, THE AUTHOR EXAMINES ITS ATTITUDES TOWARD THE NEW
    OCEAN REGIME AND MARINE POLICY. HE SUGGESTS THAT CHINA'S
    MARINE POLICY IS DETERMINED BY EXTERNAL AND INTERNAL INPUTS.
    EXTERNAL FACTORS INCLUDE TRENDS IN THE INTERNATIONAL SYSTEM,
    CHANGES IN THE INTERNATIONAL POWER STRUCTURE, AND THE OCEAN
    POLICIES OF OTHER STATES. INTERNAL FACTORS INCLUDE
    GEOGRAPHICAL FEATURES, ECONOMIC DEVELOPMENT, CHANGES IN
    POLITICAL LEADERSHIP, AND NATIONAL SECURITY CONCERNS.

08534 SONG, Y.H.
    CHINA'S OCEAN POLICY: EEZ AND MARINE FISHERIES
    ASIAN SURVEY, 29(10) (OCT 89), 983-998.
        THIS ARTICLE EXAMINES CHINA'S OCEAN POLICY BY FOCUSING
    ON ISSUES CONCERNING THE EXCLUSIVE ECONOMIC ZONE (EEZ) AND
    MARINE FISHERIES. IT FIRST DISCUSSES THE DEVELOPMENT OF THE
    LEGAL REGIME OF THE EEZ, CHINA'S POSITION ON IT, AND THE
    REASONS FOR CHINA'S RELUCTANCE TO DECLARE A 200-MILE
    ECONOMIC ZONE. THEN, RELATIONS WITH NEIGHBORING COUNTRIES
    SPECIFICALLY REGARDING FISHING ACTIVITIES WILL BE REVIEWED,
    FOLLOWED BY A LOOK AT THE DEVELOPMENT OF CHINA'S MARINE
    FISHING POLICY, AND FINALLY, A DISCUSSION OF PROBLEMS AND
    PROSPECTS FOR CHINA'S OCEAN POLICY.

08535 SONTAG, F.
    LIBERATION THEOLOGY AND ITS VIEW OF POLITICAL VIOLENCE
    JOURNAL OF CHURCH & STATE, 31(2) (SPR 89), 269-286.
        THE ISSUE OF USING VIOLENCE TO FREE HUMANS FROM BONDAGE
    TAKES ON A NEW URGENCY TODAY DUE TO TWO SIGNIFICANT CHANGES:
    MOST COMMUNIST PROPOSALS HAVE MILITANTLY ASSERTED THE
    NECESSITY TO USE FORCE AND LIBERATION THEOLOGY HAS BEEN
    ESPOUSED BY SOME CHRISTIAN THEOLOGIANS EVEN THOUGH THE
    ADOPTION OF PACIFISM OR THE ABHORRENCE OF VIOLENCE IS
    ASSOCIATED WITH MOST CHRISTIAN GROUPS. THE QUESTION OF
    RELIGION'S INTRUSION INTO THE POLITICAL REALM IS PROBLEM
    ENOUGH AND THE USE OF VIOLENCE ADDS INTENSITY TO THE ISSUE.

08536 SORENSEN, V.
    ECONOMIC RECOVERY VERSUS CONTAINMENT: THE ANGLO-AMERICAN
    CONTROVERSY OVER EAST-WEST TRADE, 1947-51
    COOPERATION & CONFLICT: NORDIC JOURNAL OF INTERNATIONAL
    POLITICS, XXIV(2) (JUN 89), 69-98.
        THE ARTICLE EXAMINES THE ANGLO-AMERICAN CONTROVERSY OVER
    ECONOMIC WARFARE BETWEEN 1947 AND 1951, AND AIMS TO SHOW
    THAT BRITAIN'S REJECTION OF ECONIMIC WARFARE AS STRATEGY FOR
    THE CONTAINMENT IF THE SOVIET UNION HAS DIRECTLY CONNECTED
    TO THE BRITISH ECONOMY'S DEPENDENCY ON EAST-WEST TRADE AND
    THAT THE ACCEPTANCE OF ECONOMIC WARFARE IN 1950/51 WAS NOT
    PART OF THE CHANGED SECURITY PREFERENCES WHICH LED TO
    BRITISH REARMAMENT IN AUGUST 1950, BUT A CONSEQUENCE OF THE

AMERICAN CONGRESS'S DECISION IN 1951 TO LINK MILITARY AID
DIRECTLY TO EAST-WEST TRADE. AS SUCH, THE ARTICLE'S
CONCLUSIONS TEND TO SUPPORT ADLER-KARLSSON'S CLASSICAL
ARGUMENT THAT CONSIDERATIONS FOR ECONOMIC AND MILITARY AID
DETERMINED WESTERN EUROPE'S ACCEPTANCE OF ECONOMIC WARFARE
BETWEEN 1950 AND 1953/54. HOWEVER, THE ARTICLE ALSO SHOWS
THAT THE US ADMINISTRATION'S LEVERAGE WITH RESPECT TO
BRITIAN AND WESTERN EUROPE WAS SIGNIFICANTLY CONSTRAINED BY
CONSIDERATIONS FOR THE NATO ALLIANCE AND THE US
INTERNATIONAL ECONOMIC REGIME AND THAT IT WAS THE
ADMINISTRATION'S ATTEMPT TO DEFEND ITS DISCRETIONARY POWERS
OVER FOREIGN AID AGAINST AND INCREASINGLY HOSTILE CONGRESS
WHICH WAS RESPONSIBLE FOR THE ADMINISTRATION'S COERCION OF
ITS MOST IMPORTANT NATO PARTNER IN 1951.

08537 SORENSON, L.
THE FEDERALIST PAPERS ON THE CONSTITUTIONALITY OF
EXECUTIVE PREROGATIVE
PRESIDENTIAL STUDIES QUARTERLY, XIX(2) (SPR 89), 267-284.
AN ATTEMPT TO CLARIFY AND RESOLVE THE CURRENT DEBATE
AMONG SCHOLARS ON THE ISSUE OF CONSTITUTIONALITY OF
EXECUTIVE PREOGATIVE, ACCORDING TO THE FEDERALIST PAPERS.
AMONG THOSE WHO ADMIT PREROGATIVE, SOME CLAIM THAT IT IS AN
EXTRA-CONSTITUTIONAL NOT A CONSTITUTIONAL POWER AND SOME
AMONG THESE ASSERT THAT IT IS A LEGISLATIVE NOT EXECUTIVE
POWER. BOTH POSITIONS ARE IN ERROR DUE TO A PARTIAL
UNDERSTANDING OF PUBLIUS SO-CALLED DOCTERINE OF
PROPORTIONATE MEANS BUT MISTAKENLY CONCLUDES THAT THE POWER
OF PREROGATIVE IS NOT THE CULMINATION OF THAT TEACHING. THE
LATTER POSITION ADMITS THAT THE DOCTRINE OF PROPORTIONATE
MEANS CULMINATES THE POWER OF PREROGATIVE BUT FAILS TO NOTE
THE EVIDENCE FOR BOTH IT'S CONSTITUTIONLITY AND ITS
APPLICABILITY TO THE EXECUTIVE AS WELL AS THE LEGISLATURE.

08538 SORENSON, L.R.
THE LIMITS OF CONSTITUTIONAL GOVERNMENT: REFLECTIONS
TOWARD THE CONCLUSION OF THE BICENTENNIAL CELEBRATION OF
OUR CONSTITUTION
REVIEW OF POLITICS, 51(4) (FAL 89), 551-580.
THERE IS VAST DISAGREEMENT ON THE PRECISE MEANING OF
FUNDAMENTAL MARK OF LIMITED GOVERNMENT AS ESTABLISHED IN THE
U.S. CONSTITUTION. IN THIS ESSAY, THE AUTHOR IDENTIFIES THE
VARIOUS DEFINITIONS AND DEFENSES OF LIMITED GOVERNMENT THAT
CAN BE DERIVED FROM THE CONSTITUTION AND UNVEILS THEIR
CONTRADICTORY ASSUMPTIONS AND IMPLICATIONS. THEN HE PRESENTS
THE ORIGINAL FUNDAMENTAL DEFINITION AND DEFENSE OF LIMITED
GOVERNMENT AS PROPOSED BY PUBLIUS IN THE "FEDERALIST PAPERS"
AND EXPLORES TWO QUESTIONS: IS THAT DEFINITION COMPATIBLE
WITH THE OTHER LIMITING FEATURES OF THE CONSTITUTION? CAN
THAT DEFINITION RENDER THOSE DIVERSE LIMITING FEATURES
MUTUALLY COHERENT?

08539 SOROKIN, K.
NATO: NO BREAKTHROUGH YET?
REPRINTS FROM THE SOVIET PRESS, 49(9) (NOV 89), 19-22.
THIS ARTICLE EXAMINES THE CLAIMS OF THE WEST THAT NATO
HAS CHANGED ITS DOCTRINE. IT CONCLUDES THAT NATO HAS BEGUN A
GRADUAL REASSESSMENT OF VALUES AND ITS EMPHASIS ON POLITICAL
METHODS HAS BECOME MORE PRONOUNCED BUT THAT IT IS TOO EARLY
TO SAY THAT NATO HAS ADOPTED AN ENTIRELY NEW DOCTRINE, FREE
FROM THE VESTIGES OF THE PAST.

08540 SORRENTINO, E.M.A.
PROPERTY RIGHTS AND HOSPITAL BEHAVIOR UNDER DRGS: AN
EXAMINATION OF NONPROFIT, GOVERNMENT, AND FOR-PROFIT
SECTORS
DISSERTATION ABSTRACTS INTERNATIONAL, 50(5) (NOV 89),
1434-A.
PROPERTY RIGHTS ARE DEFINED AS RIGHTS TO RESIDUAL
PROFITS IN FOR-PROFIT HOSPITALS AND THE TAX-EXEMPTION STATUS
IN NONPROFIT AND GOVERNMENT HOSPITALS WITH OBLIGATIONS TO
SERVE CHARITABLE PURPOSES IN THE PUBLIC INTEREST. THIS
DISSERTATION DERIVES AND TESTS IMPLICATIONS ABOUT
DIFFERENCES IN BEHAVIOR IN THE CONTEXT OF EFFICIENCY, EQUITY,
AND THE QUALITY OF CARE DELIVERED IN NONPROFIT, GOVERNMENT,
AND FOR-PROFIT HOSPITALS IN SOUTH FLORIDA.

08541 SOULE, J.W.
ISSUE CONFLICT IN NORTHERN IRELAND: THE DEATH OF
LEGISLATURE
POLITICAL PSYCHOLOGY, 10(4) (DEC 89), 725-744.
THIS STUDY IS BASED UPON ATTITUDE SURVEYS OF (1) A
SAMPLE OF THE GENERAL PUBLIC, AND (2) A SAMPLE OF MEMBERS OF
THE LEGISLATIVE ASSEMBLY OF NORTHERN IRELAND. THE SAME
QUESTIONS WERE USED FOR EACH SURVEY, ENABLING US TO EVALUATE
ISSUE CONFLICT AND CONSENSUS AMONG CITIZENS AND ELITES.
SEVENTEEN YEARS OF CIVIL VIOLENCE PRODUCED A MARKED DEGREE
OF POLARIZATION BETWEEN POLITICAL PARTIES AS WELL AS AN
HOMOGENIZATION OF ATTITUDES WITHIN PARTIES. FINDINGS
INDICATE THE NATURE OF DISAGREEMENT BETWEEN CITIZENS AND
PARTY LEADERS, AND HELP US TO UNDERSTAND WHY SOME
LEGISLATIVE SYSTEMS COLLAPSE.

08542 SOULE, J.W.
PROBLEMS IN APPLYING COUNTERTERRORISM TO PREVENT TERRORISM:
TWO DECADES OF VIOLENCE IN NORTHERN IRELAND RECONSIDERED
TERRORISM, 12(1) (1989), 31-46.
REVOLUTIONARIES AND AUTHORITIES IN MANY PLACES AND AT
MANY TIMES ENTER INTO A RECIPROCAL
TERRORIST/COUNTERTERRORIST RELATIONSHIP THAT OVER TIME CAN
BECOME RITUALISTIC IN NATURE. THE RECIPROCITY BETWEEN THE
PROVISIONAL IRISH REPUBLICAN ARMY (PIRA) AND THE BRITISH
AUTHORITIES IS ANALYZED AS A CASE IN POINT TO ILLUSTRATE HOW
EACH SIDE CAN ADAPT OR RECIPROCATE TO EACH MOVE OR
COUNTERMOVE. THE GOALS, ORGANIZATIONAL STRUCTURE,
RECRUITMENT, FINANCE, WEAPONS PROCUREMENT, AND COMMUNITY
SUPPORT OF THE PIRA ARE EXAMINED OVER A 20-YEAR PERIOD. IN
EACH CATEGORY THE PIRA HAS SYSTEMATICALLY EVOLVED IN
REACTION TO COUNTERTERRORIST POLICIES PURSUED BY THE
AUTHORITIES. LIKEWISE, THE AUTHORITIES HAVE LEARNED AND
ADOPTED NEW COUNTERTERRORIST TECHNIQUES. RATHER THAN
MILITARILY DEFEATING ONE ANOTHER, WHICH IS THE GOAL OF BOTH
TERRORIST AND COUNTERTERRORIST, THE TWO SIDES SEEM LOCKED IN
A RITUALISTIC DANCE OF DEATH THAT CAN NEVER END, BECAUSE THE
ADAPTIVE CAPACITIES OF EACH APPEAR INEXHAUSTIBLE.

08543 SOUPIOS, M.A.
MACHIAVELLI'S HOMEOPATHIC THEORY OF STATE
DISSERTATION ABSTRACTS INTERNATIONAL, 49(12) (JUN 89),
3860-A.
MACHIAVELLI PROPOSES TAKING THE PSYCHOLOGICAL "GIVENS"
OF HUMAN NATURE--THE ILLS THAT TYPICALLY FOSTER CHAOS IN THE
POLITICAL DOMAIN--AND CONVERTING THESE INTO METHODS OF STATE.
JUST AS INDIVIDUAL MEN ARE MANIPULATIVE, VIOLENT,
DISSIMULATIVE, AND SELF-SERVING, SO IS THE STATE PROPOSED BY
MACHIAVELLI. THE STATE BECOMES THE INDIVIDUAL "WRIT LARGE,"
AND MACHIAVELLI'S NEW ORDER IS IN FACT A SOCIO-POLITICAL
ICON OF HUMAN PSYCHOLOGY.

08544 SOUTER, D.
THE CYPRUS CONUNDRUM: THE CHALLENGE OF THE INTERCOMMUNAL
TALKS
THIRD WORLD QUARTERLY, 11(2) (APR 89), 76-91.
TALKS TO SOLVE THE CYPRUS PROBLEM HAVE BEEN SPONSORED BY
THE UNITED NATIONS FOR ALMOST A QUARTER OF A CENTURY. THIS
ARTICLE EXAMINES THE REASONS FOR RENEWED OPTIMISM ABOUT THE
PROSPECTS FOR A RESOLUTION AND DESCRIBES THE ISSUES UNDER
NEGOTIATION.

08545 SOUTHWELL, P.L.
STRATEGIC VOTING IN THE 1984 DEMOCRATIC PRESIDENTIAL
PRIMARIES
SOCIAL SCIENCE JOURNAL, 26(4) (1989), 445-454.
WHEN CASTING THEIR BALLOTS IN PRIMARY ELECTIONS, VOTERS
USUALLY VOTE IN A STRAIGHTFORWARD MANNER FOR THE CANDIDATE
OF THEIR PREFERENCE. BUT SOMETIMES SOPHISTICATED VOTERS VOTE
FOR A SECOND OR THIRD CHOICE WHO HAS A BETTER CHANCE OF
WINNING IN THE GENERAL ELECTION OR EVEN CROSS OVER TO THE
OPPOSITION PARTY TO VOTE FOR A CANDIDATE WHO WILL BE EASIER
TO DEFEAT IN THE GENERAL ELECTION. THIS ARTICLE ASSESSES THE
AMOUNT AND IMPORTANCE OF SUCH STRATEGIC VOTING IN DEMOCRATIC
PRESIDENTIAL PRIMARIES IN 1984 USING DISCRIMINATE ANALYSIS.

08546 SOUZA, R. D.
REASON VS. VIOLENCE
WORLD MARXIST REVIEW, 32(9) (SEP 89), 7-10.
THE LEADER OF PANAMANIAN COMMUNISTS GIVES HIS VIEWS ON
HOW TO AVOID A NUCLEAR CATASTROPHE AND LAY THE FOUNDATIONS
OF A NON-VIOLENT AND SECURE WORLD. HE ALSO ADDRESSES THE
RELATION BETWEEN GLOBAL HUMAN PROBLEMS AND THE PROLETARIAT'S
CLASS INTERESTS AND THE STRUGGLE FOR NATIONAL LIBERATION AND
SOCIAL EMANCIPATION. THE PROSPECT OF LATIN AMERICA PULLING
OUT OF THE EXTERNAL DEBT CRISIS, THE PRESENT STATE OF
AFFAIRS IN THE CENTRAL AMERICAN SUBREGION; AND THE
UNDERLYING CAUSES OF THE CONFLICT BETWEEN THE UNITED STATES
AND PANAMA ARE EACH EXAMINED.

08547 SOWELL, T.
"AFFIRMATIVE ACTION": A WORLDWIDE DISASTER
COMMENTARY, 88(6) (DEC 89), 21-41.
THIS ARTICLE DEMANDS RECOGNITION THAT "AFFIRMATIVE
ACTION" HAS BEEN A FAILURE IN THE UNITED STATES AND A
DISASTER IN OTHER COUNTRIES THAT HAVE HAD SUCH POLICIES
LONGER. IT EXPLORES FOUR AREAS OF THE ISSUE. FIRST: THE
ASSUMPTIONS OF "AFFIRMATIVE ACTION". SECOND: THE ILLUSION OF
COMPENSATION. THREE: REPLACING ILLUSIONS. FOUR: INCENTIVES
VERSUS HOPES. IT CONCLUDES THAT A GROWING POLARIZATION OF
UGLY RACIAL INCIDENTS MAY BE WARNINGS THAT WE MAY BE MOVING
FROM THE STAGE OF MERE FAILURE TO THE STAGE OF SOCIAL
DISASTER.

08548 SOWERBY, N.
ECCENTRIC ELECTIONS
NEW AFRICAN, (FEB 88), 26-27.
THIS ARTICLE REPORTS ON RECENT ELECTIONS IN SWAZILAND
WHICH RESULTED IN NOT A SINGLE MEMBER OF THE OLD HOUSE BEING
RE-ELECTED. IT ALSO DESCRIBES A SITUATION WHERE UNSPECTING

VOTERS FOUND THEMSELVES AS A CANDIDATE UNKNOWN TO THEMSELVES.
THE ROLE OF THE ELDERS WHO SELECT CANDIDATES IS EXAMINED.

08549 SPAKES, P.
A FEMINIST CASE AGAINST NATIONAL FAMILY POLICY: VIEW TO
THE FUTURE
POLICY STUDIES REVIEW, 8(3) (SPR 89), 610-621.
THIS PAPER EXAMINES THE GOALS OF CURRENT FAMILY POLICY
PROPOSALS FROM A FEMINIST PRESPECTIVE. IT REVEALS THE
FUNDAMENTAL PRONATALIST VALUES THAT ARE INHERENT IN SUCH
PROPOSALS. IT REVIEWS RECENT RESEARCH THAT RAISES QUESTIONS
REGARDING THE ACTUAL IMPACT OF SCANDINAVIAN FAMILY POLICIES
(WHICH ARE OFTEN USED AS A MODEL), IN TERMS OF ACTUALLY
ACHIEVING THE STATED OBJECTIVE OF ENHANCING EQUALITY BETWEEN
THE SEXES. IT BRIEFLY EXPLORES THE FAMILY POLICY THAT
ALREADY EXISTS IN THE UNITED STATES, HAVING BEEN JUDICIALLY
ENACTED BY THE SUPREME COURT, AND FINALLY, IT SHOWS HOW MOST
CURRENT FAMILY BASED POLICY PROPOSALS SERVE TO MAINTAIN
INEQUALITY RATHER THAN TO PROMOTE EQUALITY, BOTH IN SOCIETY
AND THE HOME.

08550 SPARKS, S.
A CHALLENGE TO THE ONE PARTY STATE: THE NEED FOR A LABOR
PARTY?
MULTINATIONAL MONITOR, 11(11) (NOV 89), 28-31.
LABOR ACTIVIST TONY MAZZOCHI IS AMONG THOSE ADVOCATING
THE FORMATION OF A NEW, ALTERNATIVE WORKERS' PARTY IN THE
UNITED STATES. MAZZOCHI BELIEVES THAT THE NEW PARTY SHOULD
NOT BEGIN BY NOMINATING CANDIDATES TO RUN FOR OFFICE.
INSTEAD, IT SHOULD WORK TO CREATE A STRONG MOVEMENT,
NURTURING A NEW KIND OF POLITICAL THOUGHT THAT WOULD
CHALLENGE ESTABLISHMENT POLITICS, INCLUDING BOTH BIG
BUSINESS AND THE LABOR BUREAUCRACY ITSELF.

08551 SPARKS, S.
BRADY'S HALL OF MIRRORS
SOUTH, (103) (MAY 89), 29-30.
THE LATEST US PROPOSALS FOR DEALING WITH THE THIRD WORLD
DEBT PROBLEM HAVE RAISED EXPECTATIONS AMONG THE FINANCE
MINISTERS OF THE SOUTH. BUT AS THE DETAILS ARE HAMMERED OUT,
THE PLAN IS SHRINKING IN SCALE. FOR DEBTORS WHO ARE NOT ON
WASHINGTON'S PRIORITY LIST, LITTLE IS LIKELY TO CHANGE.

08552 SPARKS, S.
BRITISH LABOR'S NEW START
MULTINATIONAL MONITOR, 10(6) (JUN 89), 26-27.
GREAT BRITAIN FACES THE PROSPECT OF LABOR UNREST, WITH
DEMANDS FOR HIGHER WAGES AT THE HEART OF MOST OF THE LABOR-
MANAGEMENT DISPUTES. THE PAY PINCH IS DUE TO WORSENING MACRO-
ECONOMIC CONDITIONS. LIKE OTHER WESTERN INDUSTRIAL NATIONS,
BRITAIN APPEARS TO BE STUCK IN A PERIOD OF SLOWER GROWTH AND
HIGHER INFLATION. FOR SOME WORKERS, PAY RAISES ARE SYMBOLIC
OF WHAT THEY PERCEIVE TO BE MANAGEMENT ATTEMPTS TO
RESTRUCTURE WORKING CONDITIONS FUNDAMENTALLY AND ADVERSELY.

08553 SPARKS, S.; ISLAM, S.
NEW PUSH IN A DIRTY WAR
SOUTH, (102) (APR 89), 20-23.
AN OMINOUS AND SUBTLE NEW FORM OF PROTECTIONISM IS
THREATENING TO CHOKE OFF EXPORTS FROM DEVELOPING COUNTRIES.
THE DEVICES USED ARE ANTI-DUMPING AND ANTI-SUBSIDY SUITS,
ORIGINALLY INTENDED TO PROTECT DOMESTIC PRODUCERS FROM
PREDATORY PRICING BY OVERSEAS SUPPLIERS. BUT THE USA, THE
EUROPEAN COMMUNITY, AND OTHER INDUSTRIALIZED COUNTRIES ARE
FASHIONING THESE INSTRUMENTS INTO POWERFUL WEAPONS TO HARASS
FOREIGN RIVALS WITH WHICH THEY CAN NO LONGER COMPETE.

08554 SPARKS, S.
RISKING THE LIFEBOAT
SOUTH, (108) (OCT 89), 21-23.
HAVING BATTLED TO KEEP THIRD WORLD DEBTORS AFLOAT DURING
SEVEN YEARS OF CRISIS, THE WORLD BANK AND THE IMF ARE
BEGINNING TO FIND THAT THEY HAVE AN INCIPIENT DEBT PROBLEM
OF THEIR OWN. ARREARS ON LOANS MADE BY THE TWO INSTITUTIONS
ARE RISING SHARPLY, PROVOKING MOUNTING CONCERN THAT THE BANK
AND THE FUND MAY HAVE TO CONSIDER RESCHEDULING THE DEBTS
OWED TO THEM OR, MORE LIKELY, CONCOCT AN ALTERNATIVE
REFINANCING SCHEME TO GET THEM OFF THE HOOK.

08555 SPARKS, S.
STAND BY FOR THE CHARGE
SOUTH, (104) (JUN 89), 19-21.
A TOUGH, NEW PROVISION OF THE 1988 TRADE ACT IS THE
LATEST, MOST POTENT WEAPON IN THE GROWING ARSENAL OF
AMERICAN STRATEGIES TO REDUCE ITS TRADE DEFICIT. ORIGINALLY
DRAFTED WITH JAPAN IN MIND, THE PROVISION MAY ALSO STRIKE
OTHER TARGETS, SUCH AS SOUTH KOREA, BRAZIL, INDIA, AND EVEN
THE EUROPEAN COMMUNITY. PARTICULARLY VULNERABLE ARE
COUNTRIES THAT HAVE NOT SIGNED BILATERAL TRADE ACCORDS WITH
WASHINGTON.

08556 SPASSKY, N.
NATIONAL SECURITY: REAL AND ILLUSORY
INTERNATIONAL AFFAIRS (MOSCOW), (7) (JUL 89), 3-13.

ONE OF THE MOST SERIOUS DISTORTIONS OF STALINISM IN THE
FOREIGN POLICY SPHERE WAS THE DEVALUATION OF THE ROLE OF
POLITICAL MEANS IN ENSURING THE NATION'S SECURITY. THE
PREVAILING THEORY PRESCRIBED VIEWING ALL SOVIET TIES AND
DEALINGS WITH OTHER STATES THROUGH THE PRISM OF POTENTIAL
MILITARY CONFRONTATION. THE DOMINATION OF THE MILITARY
COMPONENT WAS MOST PATENTLY MANIFEST IN SOVIET-AMERICAN
RELATIONS. TODAY, THE NATIONAL SECURITY EMPHASIS IS SHIFTING
FROM THE SPHERE OF MILITARY DEVELOPMENT TO THAT OF POLITICAL
COOPERATION AMONG STATES. IN THE DISTANT FUTURE, THE
MILITARY ELEMENT MAY GRADUALLY DISAPPEAR FROM SOVIET-
AMERICAN RELATIONS.

08557 SPAULDING, W.
SOVIET-LINE FRONTS IN 1988
PROBLEMS OF COMMUNISM, XXXVIII(1) (JAN 89), 69-75.
IN 1988, THE USSR EASED CONTROLS OVER SOVIET-LINE TRADE-
UNION AND JOURNALIST ORGANIZATIONS, WHILE STRENGTHENING
CONTROLS OVER THE SOVIET-LINE PEACE MOVEMENT. AS IN PREVIOUS
YEARS, THESE AND OTHER SOVIET-LINE FRONTS ORCHESTRATED
SUPPORT FOR THE USSR'S FOREIGN POLICIES. THUS, DOMINANT
FRONT THEMES WERE PEACE, SECURITY, AND DISARMAMENT; SOCIO-
ECONOMIC DEVELOPMENT; HUMAN RIGHTS; THE ENVIRONMENT; AND
CULTURE AND EDUCATION FOR PEACE. THE ASIA-PACIFIC REGION WAS
AN IMPORTANT FOCUS OF FRONT ACTIVITY, AGAIN REFLECTING A
MAJOR SOVIET FOREIGN POLICY CONCERN. FINALLY, INDIA AND EAST
GERMANY—A SOVIET ALLY AND A SOVIET CLIENT RESPECTIVELY —
WERE THE SITES OF IMPORTANT FRONT MEETINGS.

08558 SPEAR, R.K.
RATED MUNICIPAL BONDS: AN ANALYSIS, CLASSIFICATION, AND
EXTENSION
DISSERTATION ABSTRACTS INTERNATIONAL, 50(3) (SEP 89),
790-A.
THE AUTHOR ENDEAVORS TO (1) IDENTIFY THE VARIABLES
IMPORTANT TO ANALYZING A GENERAL OBLIGATION MUNICIPAL BOND'S
INVESTMENT QUALITY USING IMPROVED STATISTICAL TECHNIQUES,
(2) DEVELOP MODELS THAT ACCURATELY CLASSIFY MUNICIPAL BONDS
INTO INVESTMENT QUALITY VERSUS NONINVESTMENT QUALITY, USING
VARIABLES IDENTIFIED BY THE LITERATURE AND PRACTITIONERS,
AND (3) EVALUATE THE STABILITY OF THE VARIABLES IN
PREDICTING INVESTMENT QUALITY OVER TIME.

08559 SPECHLER, M.C.
THE ECONOMIC ADVANTAGES OF BEING PERIPHERAL; SUBORDINATE
NATIONS IN MULTINATIONAL EMPIRES
EASTERN EUROPEAN POLITICS AND SOCIETIES, 3(3) (FAL 89),
448-464.
THIS ESSAY BEGINS BY INTERPRETING THE POSTWAR
DISCUSSIONS IN TERMS OF THE THREE PERSPECTIVES AND BY
PRESENTING SOME THEORETICAL BENEFITS OF SUBORDINATION WITHIN
A LARGER EMPIRE. IT THEN POINTS TO A DIVERSE
"ANTINATIONALIST" HISTORIOGRAPHY WHICH HAS ARISEN IN A
NUMBER OF FORMERLY SUBJECT NATIONS, INCLUDING IRELAND,
HUNGARY, FINLAND, AND THE UKRAINE UNDER THE TSARIST EMPIRE.
HISTORIANS FROM THESE ONCE-SUBORDINATE NATIONS HAVE BEGUN TO
ACKNOWLEDGE SOME MATERIAL BENEFITS OF INCLUSION IN
MULTINATIONAL EMPIRES. THE CONCLUDING SECTION APPLIES THE
FINDINGS TO THE EXPLANATION OF BOURGEOIS NATIONALISM ON THE
PERIPHERY.

08560 SPECTOR, D.
A NO ORDINARY AND TIMELY CONFERENCE
INFORMATION BULLETIN, 27(3-4) (FEB 89), 31.
THIS BRIEF REPORT DESCRIBES THE TOPICS AND PARTICIPANTS
AT A CONFERENCE ON THE HISTORY AND CONSEQUENCES OF ANTI-
COMMUNISM IN THE UNITED STATES HELD AT HARVARD UNIVERSITY IN
NOVEMBER 1988. IN REMARKS PREPARED FOR A PANEL ENTITLED "ARE
THERE NEW OPPORTUNITIES FOR INDEPENDENT POLITICS?" COMMUNIST
PARTY LEADER HALL CALLED THE CONFERENCE "MOST UNUSUAL AND
TIMELY." HE SAID THE DIVERSITY OF THE GATHERING "TESTIFIES
TO THE LEVEL OF INTEREST AND CONCERN THIS SUBJECT AROUSES IN
OUR COUNTRY TODAY."

08561 SPEER, J.A.
AN EXAMINATION OF THE INFLUENCE OF BAPTIST BELIEF ON THE
GOVERNING STYLE OF PRESIDENT JIMMY CARTER: 1977-1980
DISSERTATION ABSTRACTS INTERNATIONAL, 50(6) (DEC 89),
1790-A.
THE AUTHOR HYPOTHESIZES THAT THE BAPTIST INFLUENCE WOULD
INHIBIT EMBRACING THE BARGAINING DIMENSIONS OF PRESIDENTIAL
POWER. HIS STUDY OF THE CARTER PRESIDENCY REVEALS THAT ONLY
RELUCTANTLY DID JIMMY CARTER EMBRACE PRESIDENTIAL BARGAINING.
THOUGH AVOWEDLY OPPOSED TO "TRADING" AT THE OUTSET OF HIS
TERM, THERE IS SOME EVIDENCE THAT CARTER EARLY ON USED TACIT
BARGAINING. LATER HE MILDLY EMBRACED CERTAIN KINDS OF NON-
INTEGRAL BARGAINING AND TOWARD THE END OF HIS TERM MORE
OPENLY EMBRACED EXPLICIT BARGAINING.

08562 SPEIER, H.
MANNHEIM AS A SOCIOLOGIST OF KNOWLEDGE
INTERNATIONAL JOURNAL OF POLITICS, CULTURE AND SOCIETY,
2(1) (FAL 88), 81-94.
THIS ARTICLE EXPLORES THE RELATIONSHIP BETWEEN THE

SOCIOLOGY OF KNOWLEDGE AND PHILOSOPHY, ASSERTING THAT TRUTH
CANNOT BE ATTAINED BY A PHILOSOPHICALLY UNINFORMED SOCIOLOGY.
THE CRISIS OF MODERN CONSCIOUSNESS DOES NOT CONSIST IN THE
TOTAL SUSPICION OF IDEOLOGIES, BUT IN THE CLAIM OF
POLITICIANS, SOCIOLOGISTS, AND PSYCHOLOGISTS TO DO AWAY WITH
PHILOSOPHY. AN ALLEGEDLY SOCIALLY FREE FLOATING
INTELLIGENTSIA IS NOT GOING TO SHOW US THE WAY OUT OF THE
CRISIS. RATHER, THIS TASK BELONGS TO THE SPIRITUALLY FREE
MAN WHO CHERISHES SPIRITUAL FREEDOM.

08563 SPELLER, P.
POLITICAL MEDIATION ON THE PIONEER FRONTIER: THE ROLE OF
LAW, BUREAUCRACY, AND VIOLENCE IN THE AMAZON REGION OF
BRAZIL
DISSERTATION ABSTRACTS INTERNATIONAL, 50(2) (AUG 89),
538-A.
THE AUTHOR EXAMINES THE INTERVENTION OF STATE
INSTITUTIONS TO PREVENT THE OCCURRENCE OF POTENTIAL
CONFLICTS OR TO CONTAIN AND RESOLVE ACTUAL DISPUTES ON THE
CONTEMPORARY FRONTIER IN AMAZONIA. THE DISSERTATION IS
ORGANIZED INTO TWO PARTS. THE FIRST INCLUDES AN HISTORICAL
ANALYSIS OF THE ROLE OF THE STATE BUREAUCRACY IN THE
EXPANSION OF THE PIONEER FRONTIER AFTER 1930. THE SECOND
DEALS WITH CHARACTERISTIC FORMS OF THE MILITARY REGIME'S
MEDIATION IN NORTHERN MATO GROSSO.

08564 SPENCE, J.E.
A DEAL FOR SOUTHERN AFRICA?
WORLD TODAY, 45(5) (MAY 89), 80-83.
THE SIGNING OF THE ANGOLA-NAMIBIA ACCORDS IN DECEMBER
1988 ENDED A BITTER CONFLICT IN A REGION THAT HITHERTO HAD
OFFERED LITTLE, IF ANY, SCOPE FOR A "PARTIAL SOLUTION" OF
THE KIND FAVORED BY MIKHAIL GORBACHEV. THE AGREEMENT WAS
MADE POSSIBLE BY THE COMBINATION OF SUPERPOWER MIDWIFERY AND
THE DISCOVERY OF NEW AND UNEXPECTED INCENTIVES BY THE LOCAL
PROTAGONISTS: ANGOLA, CUBA, AND SOUTH AFRICA.

08565 SPENCE, J.T.
AMERICAN INDIVIDUALISM: CHALLENGES FOR THE 21ST CENTURY
INTERNATIONAL SOCIAL SCIENCE REVIEW, 64(4) (AUG 89),
147-152.
CONCERNS HAVE BEEN RISING AMONG AMERICANS ABOUT THE
NATION'S DECLINING ABILITY TO COMPETE WITH OTHER COUNTRIES,
ESPECIALLY JAPAN, AND SELF-DOUBTS ABOUT THEMSELVES AS A
PEOPLE. SOLUTIONS TO THE COUNTRY'S PROBLEMS DEMAND
UNDERSTANDING OF ITS OWN HISTORY AND THE FORCES THAT SHAPE
THE AMERICAN CHARACTER. AMERICAN ATTITUDES TOWARD
ACHIEVEMENT ARE ROOTED IN THE CONCEPT OF INDIVIDUALISM AND A
SECULAR VERSION OF THE PROTESTANT WORK ETHIC. ALTHOUGH THESE
VALUES HAVE SERVED THE NATION WELL, THEY LEAVE US VULNERABLE
TO EXCESSIVE SELF-CONCERN AND SELF-GRATIFICATION. THE
CHALLENGE TO AMERICAN SOCIETY IS TO RECONCILE FREEDOM AND
EXERCISE OF SENSE OF SELF WITH OBLIGATIONS TO SOCIETY AND
COMMITMENT TO OTHERS.

08566 SPENCER, L.P.
CHURCH AND STATE IN COLONIAL AFRICA: INFLUENCES GOVERNING
THE POLITICAL ACTIVITY OF CHRISTIAN MISSIONS IN KENYA
JOURNAL OF CHURCH & STATE, 31(1) (WIN 89), 115.
IN THE WESTERN TRADITION, MUCH OF THE CHURCH-STATE
DEBATE FOCUSED UPON STRUCTURAL ASPECTS OF SOCIETY AND ITS
GOVERNANCE, UPON THE DEMOCRATIZATION OF WESTERN SOCIETIES,
AND UPON THE APPROPRIATE ROLE OF THE CHURCH IN SOCIETIES OF
DIVERSE PRIORITIES AND EXPRESSIONS. THE CHURCH-STATE DEBATE
IN COLONIAL AFRICA SHARED ELEMENTS OF THESE FOCI BUT, DURING
THE COLONIAL PERIOD, CHRISTIAN MISSIONS AND THE AFRICAN
CHURCH ALSO HAD TO COPE WITH IMPERIAL NUANCES THAT LED THE
COLONIAL AUTOCRACY TO STUDY THOSE ISSUES ANEW.

08567 SPERO, J.E.
THE MID-LIFE CRISIS OF AMERICAN TRADE POLICY
WORLD TODAY, 45(1) (JAN 89), 10-14.
TWO RECENT EVENTS PROVIDE SOME CLUES AS TO THE DIRECTION
AMERICAN TRADE POLICY IS TAKING: THE PASSAGE OF THE OMNIBUS
TRADE AND COMPETITIVENESS ACT OF 1988 AND THE UNITED STATES-
CANADA TREE TRADE AGREEMENT. SOME OBSERVERS SEE THESE STEPS
AS MOVEMENT IN THE WRONG DIRECTION, BUT OTHERS VIEW THEM
DIFFERENTLY.

08568 SPERO, R.
SHOWDOWN ON MIDDLE NECK ROAD
PRESENT TENSE, 16(4) (MAY 89), 18-28.
THE ARTICLE DESCRIBES THE SOCIAL AND CULTURAL UPHEAVAL
WHICH OCCURRED IN GREAT NECK, NEW YORK WHEN THOUSANDS OF
IRANIANS, FLEEING THE REGIME OF THE AYATOLLAH KHOMEINI,
SEEMED TO SNAP UP EXPENSIVE HOMES OVERNIGHT IN NEIGHBORHOODS
IT HAD TAKEN THE AMERICAN YEARS OF HARD WORK TO AFFORD TO
LIVE IN.

08569 SPIEGEL, S.L.
THE U.S.-ISRAEL RELATIONSHIP: A FRAMEWORK FOR ASSESSING
AMERICAN POLICY
MIDDLE EAST REVIEW, XXII(1) (FAL 89), 2-9.
THIS ASSESSMENT OF US-ISRAELI RELATIONS IS OFFERED AS A

GUIDE FOR JUDGMENT--A SERIES OF BENCHMARKS BY WHICH TO
ASSESS THE CHANGING ENVIRONMENT. THE AUTHOR CONSIDERS
POSSIBLE CHANGES FROM THE PERSPECTIVE OF THE U.S.
PRESIDENTIAL ELITE, THE STRATEGIC AND ECONOMIC ENVIRONMENTS,
ETHNIC GROUPS, THE CONGRESS, PUBLIC OPINION, AND THE MEDIA.

08570 SPIELMANN, J.
A BALDER RESPENSE TO THE CHALLENGES OF THE TIMES
WORLD MARXIST REVIEW, 32(12) (DEC 89), 3-8.
IN THIS ARTICLE, THE GENERAL SECRETARY OF THE SWISS
PARTY OF LABOUR EXAMINES THE EFFECTS OF REAGANESM,
THATILEUSM AND REOLILERSLISM ON THE DEVELOPMENT OF SOCIALIST
COUNTRIES. VIEWING THE STATE AND THE PROSPECTS OF THE
COMMUNIST MOVEMENT FROM THE ANGLE OF THE "NEW THINKING", THE
AUTHOR CONCLUDES THAT MARXISM-TENINISM CAN SURVIVE ONLY IF
IT ADAPTS IN AN INNOVATIVE MATTER TO THE ECONOMIES, CULTURES
AND POLITICAL SITUATIONS OF INDIVIDUAL COUNTRIES.

08571 SPIERINGS, J.
AN EXACTING SCIENCE: THE UNIVERSITY AND THE BEGINNINGS OF
ARENA, 86 (FAL 89), 122-135.
ECONOMIC POLICY MAKING THE AUTHOR SUGGESTS THAT WHILE WE
ARE PRESENTLY WITNESSING THE MOST RADICAL EXPRESSION OF SO-
CALLED RATIONAL VALUES, THE RELATIONSHIP OF THE UNIVERSITY
TO THE ECONOMY AND CULTURE HAS ALWAYS BEEN TENSE AND COMPLEX.
BY EXAMINING THE PARTICULAR EXAMPLE OF THE COMMERCE SCHOOL
OF THE UNIVERSITY OF MELBOURNE IN A DIFFERENT PERIOD, AT A
DISTANT TIME, THE AUTHOR SLOWS THE POWER OF THE LOGIC OF THE
MARKETPLACE TO CONTINUALLY TRANSFORM THE NATURE OF THE
ACADEMY.

08572 SPINARDI, G.
THE DEVELOPMENT OF U.S. FLEET BALLISTIC MISSILE TECHNOLOGY:
POLARIS TO TRIDENT
DISSERTATION ABSTRACTS INTERNATIONAL, 50(2) (AUG 89),
541-A.
THE AUTHOR DOCUMENTS THE DEVELOPMENT OF U.S. FLEET
BALLISTIC MISSILE TECHNOLOGY FROM ITS BEGINNINGS THROUGH
TRIDENT II D5. THIS HISTORICAL STUDY IS FRAMED BY A
PERSPECTIVE THAT EMPHASIZES HOW TECHNOLOGY EVOLVES AND WHAT
THE RELATIONSHIP IS BETWEEN TECHNOLOGY AND STRATEGY OR
TECHNOLOGY AND POLITICS. THE EXTREME CHARACTERIZATIONS OF
THE RELATIONSHIP BETWEEN TECHNOLOGY AND POLITICS (EITHER
THAT TECHNOLOGY IS SIMPLY THE TOOL OF POLITICAL WILL OR THAT
TECHNOLOGY IS OUT-OF-CONTROL) ARE INADEQUATE. INSTEAD, THE
BUREAUCRATIC POLITICS APPROACH CAPTURES MUCH OF THE RICH
COMPLEXITY OF THE PROCESS OF TECHNOLOGICAL CHANGE. BUT EVEN
THIS APPROACH FAILS TO FULLY CAPTURE THE COMPLEX
INTERRELATIONS OF TECHNOLOGY AND POLITICS.

08573 SPINELLI, L.
SAILING INTO DRY DOCK: THE HARDING ADMINISTRATION'S
SHIPPING POLICY AND NATIONAL PROHIBITION
PRESIDENTIAL STUDIES QUARTERLY, 19(4) (FAL 89), 747-768.
THIS ARTICLE ILLUSTRATES THE THEME, "HUMAN RIGHTS AND
POLITICAL ALIGNMENT." IT EXAMINES PRESIDENT HARDING'S GOAL
FOR A STRONG MERCHANG MARINE AS IT WAS CONFOUNDED BY THE
MORALIST PROHIBITIONIST FORCES IN THE NATION. THE QUESTION
WAS, DID THE 18TH AMENDMENT PRECLUDE AMERICAN PASSENGER
SHIPS FROM SELLING LIQUOR ON THE HIGH SEAS? IT CONCLUDES
THAT "THE DRYS" WERE TOO STRONG, EVEN AFTER THE SUPREME
COURT RULED THAT AMERICAN SHIPS COULD SELL LIQUORS BEYOND
THE THREE MILE LIMIT, AND THAT THE 18TH AMENDMENT
UNEXPECTEDLY REFLECTED THE NEW INTERNATIONAL STATURE OF THE
US. HARDING TOOK THIS DEFEAT, AS HE DID WITH SO MANY ISSUES,
TO HIS GRAVE.

08574 SPINKS, P.
EUROPE SECRETLY TRADES IN SOUTH AFRICAN COAL
AFRICAN BUSINESS, (JAN 89), 10-13.
THIS REPORT DESCRIBES HOW SOUTH AFRICAN COAL IS SHIPPED
BY DUTCH AND BRITISH COMPANIES, IN SPITE OF THEIR
GOVERNMENTS' OFFICIAL SUPPORT OF SANCTIONS AGAINST SUCH
TRADE. THE AUTHOR LISTS BY NAME MANY OF THE COMPANIES
INVOLVED, AND MAKES REFERENCE TO THE DOCUMENTS WHICH SUPPORT
THE REPORT'S CONCLUSIONS.

08575 SPIRO, D.E.
POLICY COORDINATION IN THE INTERNATIONAL POLITICAL ECONOMY:
THE POLITICS OF RECYCLING PETRODOLLARS
DISSERTATION ABSTRACTS INTERNATIONAL, 50(4) (OCT 89),
1084-A.
DATA ON CREDIT, CAPITAL FLOWS, INVESTMENT, AND
INTERNATIONAL TRADE REVEAL THAT MARKET FORCES HAD LITTLE TO
DO WITH RECYCLING PETRODOLLARS DURING THE PERIOD 1973-1981.
THE PRIMARY MECHANISM WAS THROUGH U.S. GOVERNMENT
OBLIGATIONS. SOON AFTER THE FIRST OIL SHOCK, THE AMERICAN
GOVERNMENT CONVINCED SAUDI ARABIA TO INVEST MUCH OF ITS
SURPLUS CAPITAL IN TREASURY OBLIGATIONS THAT WERE HELD BY
THE NEW YORK FEDERAL RESERVE BANK. IN ADDITION, U.S. POLICY-
MAKERS CONVINCED THE SAUDIS TO KEEP OIL PRICED IN DOLLARS.
THESE AND OTHER POLICIES GAVE THE USA AN ECONOMIC ADVANTAGE
AND VIOLATED THE MULTILATERAL NORMS OF LEGITIMATE POLICY
COODINATION.

08576 SPIRO, P.; MIRUISH, D.
    WHOSE NO-FAULT IS IT, ANYWAY?
    WASHINGTON MONTHLY, 21(9) (OCT 89), 24-29.
        THIS ARTICLE ADDRESSES THE NEED FOR AUTOMOBILE INSURANCE
    REFORM IN THE UNITED STATES. IT DESCRIBES THE CURRENT TORT
    SYSTEM AS ROUTINELY UNDERCOMPENSATING PEOPLE SERIOUSLY
    INJURED IN AUTO ACCIDENTS, AND OVERCOMPENSATING THOSE WITH
    MINOR INJURIES. IN A NUMBER OF STATES THE DEMAND FOR AUTO
    INSURANCE REFORM HAS EMERGED AS A PIVOTAL POLITICAL ISSUE.
    IT SUGGESTS THAT THE SOLUTION IS "CHEAP, QUICK, AND FAIR" --
    NO-FAULT INSURANCE. IT SUGGESTS THAT THE TRIAL LAWYERS AND
    RALPH NADER HAVE BEEN SO SUCCESSFUL IN MISLEADING THE PUBLIC
    ABOUT NO-FAULT INSURANCE THAT NO STATE HAS ENACTED A NO-
    FAULT MEASURE SINCE 1983, BUT THAT THE NEED FOR IT WILL MAKE
    NO-FAULT ALMOST INEVITABLE.

08577 SPITZER, N.
    A SECRET CITY
    WILSON QUARTERLY, XIII(1) (JAN 89), 102-115.
        THE CITY OF WASHINGTON, D.C., REPRESENTS A PECULIAR
    POLITICAL ANOMALY. FOR A CENTURY, CONGRESS, IN EFFECT,
    GOVERNED IT THROUGH PRESIDENTIALLY APPOINTED OFFICIALS. NOW,
    RESIDENTS ELECT THE MAYOR, THE CITY COUNCIL, AND THE SCHOOL
    BOARD. BUT THERE ARE STILL VESTIGES OF COLONIAL RULE.
    CONGRESS MUST STILL APPROVE THE CITY BUDGET AND MAY VETO
    LOCAL LEGISLATION. DISTRICT RESIDENTS OCCASIONALLY HAVE THE
    FEELING THAT THEY ARE NOT U.S. CITZENS BUT SUBJECTS OF A
    FOREIGN POWER. ON THE OTHER HAND, SOME CRITICS COMPARE THE
    DISTRICT'S LOCAL GOVERNMENT TO A LACKLUSTER POST-COLONIAL
    REGIME IN AFRICA.

08578 SPRINZAK, E.
    THE EMERGENCE OF THE ISRAELI RADICAL RIGHT
    COMPARATIVE POLITICS, 21(2) (JAN 89), 171-192.
        THE AUTHOR REVIEWS THE SEQUENCE OF EVENTS THAT PRODUCED
    THE ISRAELI RADICAL RIGHT, PORTRAYS IT AS A POLITICAL
    CULTURE, AND ASSESSES ITS POLITICS AND PUBLIC IMPACT.

08579 SQUIRE, P.
    CHALLENGERS IN U.S. SENATE ELECTIONS
    LEGISLATIVE STUDIES QUARTERLY, 14(4) (NOV 89), 531-548.
        THE LEVEL OF COMPETITION IN HOUSE ELECTIONS HAVE BEEN
    SHOWN TO RESULT PRIMARILY FROM THE QUALITY OF THE CHALLENGER.
    THIS PAPER DEMONSTRATES THAT THE SAME DYNAMIC FUNCTIONS IN
    SENATE ELECTIONS. THE QUALITY OF SENATE CHALLENGERS VARIES,
    AND THE HIGHER THE QUALITY OF A CHALLENGER THE MORE VOTES HE
    OR SHE RECEIVES AND THE MORE LIKELY THE CHALLENGER IS TO
    DEFEAT AN INCUMBENT. HIGHER QUALITY CHALLENGERS ARE MORE
    LIKELY TO RUN IN STATES WHERE THE POOL OF SUCH CANDIDATES IS
    LARGE; THEIR APPEARANCE IN A CONTEST IS NOT DUE TO ANY
    PERSONAL OR POLITICAL CHARACTERISTICS OF THE INCUMBENT.
    CHALLENGER QUALITY MATTERS, IN PART, BECAUSE HIGHER LEVELS
    TRANSLATE INTO MORE CAMPAIGN MONEY, BUT QUALITY ALSO
    INDICATES OTHER SKILLS THAT PRODUCE ADDITIONAL VOTES.

08580 SQUIRE, P.
    COMPETITION AND UNCONTESTED SEATS IN U.S HOUSE ELECTIONS
    LEGISLATIVE STUDIES QUARTERLY, 15(2) (MAY 89), 281-296.
        MOST THEORIES OF DEMOCRACY ASSUME THAT VOTERS ARE
    OFFERED PARTIES, CANDIDATES, OR ISSUE POSITIONS AMONG WHICH
    TO CHOOSE IN AN ELECTION. BETWEEN 1978 AND 1988, 14% OF
    RACES FOR THE U.S. HOUSE OF REPRESENTATIVES WERE UNCONTESTED,
    ALTHOUGH THIS NUMBER REPRESENTS A DROP FROM THE HIGHER
    FIGURES OF TWO DECADES AGO, IT STILL SUGGESTS A SIGNIFICANT
    VIOLATION OF DEMOCRATIC PRINCIPLES. PROBIT ANALYSIS OF DATA
    COLLECTED ON THE 1978 TO 1984 ELECTIONS REVEALS THAT
    UNCONTESTED RACES ARE MORE LIKELY TO OCCUR IN DISTRICTS
    WHERE THE INCUMBENT RECEIVED A HIGH PERCENTAGE OF THE VOTE
    IN THE PREVIOUS ELECTION WHERE THE INCUMBENT IS A DEMOCRAT,
    AND IN THE SOUTH. A MAJORITY OF REPRESENTATIVES WHO ARE
    UNCHALLENGED IN ONE ELECTION, HOWEVER, ARE OPPOSED IN THE
    NEXT CAMPAIGN. BECAUSE THE VAST MAJORITY OF HOUSE MEMBERS
    WILL FACE A CHALLENGER IN SOME FUTURE ELECTION, THE
    INCENTIVE FOR REPRESENTATION PROVIDED BY POTENTIAL
    OPPOSITION AND DEFEAT IS MAINTAINED.

08581 SREEDHAR
    TREATY RELATIONS BETWEEN NEPAL AND TIBET
    CHINA REPORT, 24(3) (JUL 88), 243-288.
        THIS ARTICLE DESCRIBES TRADE AGREEMENTS BETWEEN NEPAL
    AND TIBET, STARTING WITH THE FIRST AGREEMENT OF KUTI (1615-
    20 AD) UP TO THE AGREEMENT ON BARTER TRADE, 1896. THE AUTHOR
    SHOWS HOW TRADE BETWEEN NEPAL AND TIBET DURING THE LAST
    THREE CENTURIES HAS BEEN CONCENTRATED IN THE HANDS OF THE
    NIWARS FROM KATMANDU VALLEY.

08582 SRICHARATCHANYA, P.
    A HARD ACT TO FOLLOW
    FAR EASTERN ECONOMIC REVIEW, 141(32) (AUG 88), 10-11.
        THE ANNOUNCEMENT OF NON-PARTISAN PRIME MINISTER PREM
    TINSULANOND THAT HE WOULD NOT ACCEPT A NOMINATION FOR A
    FOURTH TERM WILL LIKELY RESULT IN INCREASED UNCERTAINTY AND
    INTER-PARTY RIVALRY IN THAILAND'S FUTURE. FOR 12 YEARS, PREM

MAINTAINED A DIFFICULT BALANCING ACT BETWEEN THE POLITICAL
PARTIES AND THE POWERFUL MILITARY FACTIONS AND WAS ABLE TO
SUSTAIN THE DEMOCRATIC PROCESS AND FOR THE MOST PART, ALLOW
FREE EXPRESSION. FORMER DEPUTY PRIME MINISTER CHATICHAI
CHOONHAVAN WHO IS THE MOST LIKELY REPLACEMENT FOR PREM WILL
FACE SIGNIFICANT CHALLENGES.

08583 SRICHARATCHANYA, P.
    A KITCHEN CABINET
    FAR EASTERN ECONOMIC REVIEW, 141(35) (SEP 88), 27.
        THAILAND PRIME MINISTER CHATICHAI CHOONHAVAN HAS
    ESTABLISHED A THINK-TANK OF SIX ACADEMIC AND OTHER
    SPECIALISTS WHO WILL ADVISE HIM ON A RANGE OF KEY SUBJECTS,
    INCLUDING FOREIGN POLICY AND INTERNATIONAL-TRADE LAW. THE
    THINK-TANK WILL GIVE A NEEDED BOOST THE THE NEW
    ADMISTRATION'S IMAGE OF POLITICAL INSTABILITY AND
    INCOMPETENCE.

08584 SRICHARATCHANYA, P.
    A LACK-LUSTRE LINE-UP
    FAR EASTERN ECONOMIC REVIEW, 141(33) (AUG 88), 22-25.
        THE 45 MEMBER CABINET SELECTED BY PRIME MINISTER
    CHATICHAI CHOONHAVAN LEAVES MUCH TO BE DESIRED IN THE EYES
    OF MANY OBSERVERS IN THAILAND. APPARENTLY, LITTLE REGARD HAS
    GIVEN TO QUALIFICATIONS OR COMPETENCE, RATHER, IMAGE SEEMED
    TO BE THE DETERMINING FACTOR IN THE SELECTION. IF CHATICHAI
    IS TO MAINTAIN THE POPULARITY HE HAS GAINED THROUGH A SERIES
    OF CLEVER POLITICAL MOVES, THE CABINET MUST FACE THE
    CHALLENGES AHEAD IN A WAY TO PROVE THEIR DETRACTORS WRONG.

08585 SRICHARATCHANYA, P.
    CAMPUSES COME TO LIFE
    FAR EASTERN ECONOMIC REVIEW, 141(35) (SEP 88), 27.
        IN THE MID-1970'S STUDENT MOVEMENT WERE RESPONSIBLE FOR
    SPEARHEADING A POPULAR UPRISING THAT TOPPLED A LONG
    SUCCESSION OF MILITARY DICTATORSHIPS IN THAILAND. WITH THE
    REPRESSION OF THE BRIEF PERIOD OF DEMOCRACY BY YET ANOTHER
    MILITARY COUP, THE STUDENT MOVEMENT ENTERED A LONG PERIOD OF
    REPRESSION AND APATHY. HOWEVER, A RECENT RESURGENCE OF
    CAMPUS ACTIVITY HAS TURNED THAILAND'S LONG DORMANT STUDENT
    BODY INTO A POTENT POLITICAL FORCE. ALTHOUGH NOT ON THE
    SCALE OF THE MOVEMENT IN THE 1970'S, STUDENT GROUPS ARE ONCE
    AGAIN EXERCSING THEIR POLITICAL CLOUT.

08586 SRICHARATCHANYA, P.
    CHAMLONG COULD CLEAN UP
    FAR EASTERN ECONOMIC REVIEW, 141(29) (JUL 88), 26-27.
        IN THAILAND, POLITICAL PARTIES TEND TO BE LOOSELY
    STRUCTURED AT THE TOP RATHER THAN RELYING ON GRASS ROOTS
    SUPPORT FROM BELOW. BANGKOK GOVERNOR CHAMLONG SIRMUANG'S
    BRAND-NEW PALANG DHARME (FORCE OF SPIRITUAL RIGHTEOUSNESS)
    PARTY SEEMS TO BE A NOTABLE EXCEPTION. THE APPEAL OF THE
    PARTY IS BUILT ALMOST SOLELY AROUND THE POPULAR CHAMLONG AND
    HIS FIRM ANTI-CORRUPTION STANCE. IF HE CONTINUES IN HIS
    COURSE OF APPEALING TO THE OTHERWISE SILENT MIDDLE CLASS,
    THE BANGKOK ELECTORAL LANDSCAPE COULD BE VASTLY ALTERED.

08587 SRICHARATCHANYA, P.
    CREATING A HUMAN FENCE
    FAR EASTERN ECONOMIC REVIEW, 141(32) (AUG 88), 27.
        AFTER 10 YEARS OF A COSTLY BORDER DEFENSE OPERATION,
    THAILAND IS TRYING A DIFFERENT STRATEGY. THEY ARE SETTING UP
    A "HUMAN FENCE" COMPRISING STRATEGIC BORDER-DEFENCE HAMLETS
    THAT COULD SERVE AS A PERMANENT SECURITY BUFFER ON THE
    THAILAND-CAMBODIA BORDER. THE NUMBER OF TROOPS ON THE BORDER
    HAS DECREASED FROM 18,000 TO 7,000 AS 11 OF THE PROPOSED 20
    HAMLETS ARE ALREADY IN PLACE.

08588 SRICHARATCHANYA, P.
    DRAWING A BEAD
    FAR EASTERN ECONOMIC REVIEW, 141(29) (JUL 88), 24-25.
        WITH THE BOOMING ECONOMY ROBBING IT OF ITS 1986 ELECTION
    ISSUE OF FINANCIAL STRAITS, THE CAMPAIGN FOR THE THAI
    GENERAL ELECTION HAS FOCUSED ON THE POSITION OF SOMEONE WHO
    IS NOT EVEN STANDING FOR ELECTION--PRIME MINISTER PREM
    TINSULANOND WHO IS NEITHER A MEMBER OF A POLITICAL PARTY NOR
    AN ELECTED MEMBER OF PARLIMENT. AN INFORMAL ANTI-PREM
    ALLAINCE HAS FORMED ON THE ISSUE THAT PREM SHOULD NOT BE
    GIVEN A FOURTH TERM AS PRIME MINISTER. AFTER THREE TERMS OF
    SERVICE, SOME WANT TO SEE A NEW FACE MERELY FOR CHANGE'S
    SAKE.

08589 SRICHARATCHANYA, P.
    ON THE OFFENSIVE AGAIN
    FAR EASTERN ECONOMIC REVIEW, 141(38) (SEP 88), 23.
        THE COMMUNIST KHMER ROUGE, THE MOST POWERFUL OF THE
    THREE ANTI-VIETNAM FACTIONS IN CAMBODIA HAS MOUNTED A
    MILITARY CAMPAIGN TO REGAIN LOST TERRITORY AND LOST
    PRESTIDGE. THEY PLANNED TO FILL THE VACUUM LEFT BY THE
    RECENT REDEPLOYMENT OF VIETNAMESE TROOPS AWAY FROM THE THAI
    BORDER. THE KHMER ROUGE ALSO ENGAGED IN A CIVIL AFFAIRS
    CAMPIAGN WITH GIFTS OF MONEY AND RICE TO PEASANTS BEHIND
    ENEMY LINES IN AN ATTEMPT TO SECURE "LIBERATED" AREAS IN
    CAMBODIA IN PREPARATION FOR THE DAY WHEN ITS TROOPS AND

CIVILIANS UNDER ITS CONTROL HAVE TO LEAVE SANCTUARIES ACROSS
THE BORDER IN THAILAND.

08590 SRICHARATCHANYA, P.
PERENNIAL PREM AGAIN
FAR EASTERN ECONOMIC REVIEW, 141(31) (AUG 88), 16-17.
DESPITE OPPOSITION EFFORTS TO NOMINATE A RIVAL CONTENDER
AND THREATS OF A STUDENT PROTEST, NON-PARTISAN PRIME
MINISTER PREM TINSULANOND LOOKED SET TO SERVE A FOURTH TERM
IN OFFICE FOLLOWING THE GENERAL ELECTION. THE FOUR MAJOR
PARTIES WHICH COMPRISED THE PREVIOUS COALITION STRUCK AN
UNOFFICIAL UNDERSTANDING TO BACK PREM FOR ANOTHER TERM. PREM
WAS OPPOSED BY POLITICIANS AND STUDENTS BECAUSE OF HIS CLOSE
MILITARY TIES, BUT THE GENERAL POPULACE AND THE BUSINES
LEADERS WHO SUPPORT MANY OF THAILAND'S POLITICAL PARTIES
SEEM UNWILLING TO CHANGE THE STATUS QUO; THE YEAR OF 1988
WAS A GOLDEN ONE FOR THE THAI ECONOMY.

08591 SRICHARATCHANYA, P.
PUT POLITICS ASIDE
FAR EASTERN ECONOMIC REVIEW, 141(36) (SEP 88), 27-28.
LOCAL HUMAN RIGHTS AND STUDENT GROUPS ARE LOOKING TO
PRIME MINISTER CHATICHAI CHOONHAVAN FOR A MORE SYMPATHETIC
HEARING ON HUMAN RIGHTS ISSUES THAN FROM HIS PREDECESSOR,
PREM TINSULANOND. THEY ARE SEEKING A GENERAL AMNESTY FOR ALL
POLITICAL PRISONERS. ALTHOUGH CHATICHAI LOOKED UPON THE
PROPOSAL FAVORABLY, IT IS UNLIKELY THAT PARLIAMENT, WHICH IS
CONCERNED WITH THE FISCAL 1989 BUDGET, WILL PAY MUCH
ATTENTION TO THE PROPOSAL IN THE NEAR FUTURE.

08592 SRICHARATCHANYA, P.
SPARKS FROM THE STRIKES
FAR EASTERN ECONOMIC REVIEW, 141(27) (JUL 88), 12-13.
AN OUTBURST OF LABOR UNREST IN LATE JUNE WHICH DISRUPTED
SOME KEY PUBLIC UTILITIES HAS CAST A SHADOW OVER THAILAND'S
POLITICAL SCENE. ONLY A MONTH BEFORE THE GENERAL ELECTION,
THE UNREST WAS ALLEGEDLY MANIPULATED BY GROUPS PLANNING A
MILITARY COUP. PROTESTING WORKERS WENT BACK ON THE JOB WITH
ASSURANCES THAT THEIR DEMANDS WOULD BE CONSIDERED, BUT LABOR
RESENTMENT IS LIKELY TO CONTINUE.

08593 SRICHARATCHANYA, P.
THE PRINCE DOES IT AGAIN
FAR EASTERN ECONOMIC REVIEW, 141(29) (JUL 88), 22.
THE RESIGNATION OF PRINCE NORODOM SIHANOUK FROM THE
PRESIDENCY OF THE ANTI-HANOI CAMBODIAN RESISTANCE COALITION
PUT THE SUCCESS OF THE UPCOMING JAKARTA INFORMAL MEETING
(JIM) IN SERIOUS DOUBT. THE MEETING INTENDED TO BRING
RESISTANCE LEADERS AND REPRESENTATIVES OF THE VIETNAMESE-
BACKED HENG SAMRIN REGIME TOGETHER IN AN "ICE-BREAKING"
SESSION TO SET THE STAGE FOR FUTURE TALKS. HOWEVER
SIHANOUK'S ABSCENCE WILL REDUCE THE MEANING OF THE MEETING.
AS OF YET, THE REASONS FOR THE PRINCE'S RESIGNATION ARE
UNKNOWN.

08594 SRIVASTAVA, M.P.
ASSESSING POLITICAL RISKS AND OPPORTUNITIES IN
INTERNATIONAL BUSINESS: A CASE STUDY IN INDIA
DISSERTATION ABSTRACTS INTERNATIONAL, 49(11) (MAY 89),
3500-A.
USING HAN S. PARK'S PARADIGM OF HUMAN NEEDS AND
POLITICAL DEVELOPMENT, THE AUTHOR FORMULATES A FRAMEWORK FOR
ASSESSING POLITICAL RISKS AND OPPORTUNITIES. HE CONCLUDES
THAT THE FRAMEWORK IS USEFUL IN OFFERING A GENERAL GUIDELINE
FOR INTERNATIONAL BUSINESS TO ASSESS OPPORTUNITIES AND
POLITICAL RISKS BY IDENTIFYING THE UNDERLYING PROCESS OF
POLITICAL CHANGE. HE APPLIES THE FRAMEWORK TO INDIA IN THE
PERIOD 1950-1984.

08595 SRIVASTAVA, R.
TENACY CONTRACTS DURING TRANSITION: A STUDY BASED ON FIELD
WORK IN UTTAR PRADESH (INDIA)
JOURNAL OF PEASANT STUDIES, 16(3) (APR 89), 339-395.
THIS ARTICLE ATTEMPTS TO SITUATE THE NATURE OF AND
CHANGES IN TENANCY CONTRACTS IN THE CONTEXT OF AGRARIAN
TRANSITION IN DEVELOPING COUNTRIES SUCH AS INDIA. INTER- AND
INTRA-VILLAGE VARIATIONS IN TENANCY CONTRACTS ARE EXAMINED
IN DETAIL FOR THREE CONTRASTED VILLAGES IN UTTAR PRADESH
(INDIA), WITH THE AIM OF BRINGING OUT THE SYSTEMATIC BASIS
OF SUCH VARIATIONS. IT IS ARGUED THAT MARXIST ANALYSIS,
BASED ON THE NATURE OF CLASS RELATIONS, OFFERS A MORE
CREDIBLE EXPLANATION OF THE NATURE AND UNEVENNESS OF CHANGE,
THAN NEO-CLASSICAL ANALYSIS. MOREOVER, SUCH ANALYSIS ALSO
OFFERS A SATISFACTORY EXPLANATION OF THE IMPACT OF TENANCY
ON SEVERAL COMMONLY STUDIED VARIABLES.

08596 SRP, K.
WE TOO ARE RESPONSIBLE FOR CIBULKA'S CRIME
EAST EUROPEAN REPORTER, 3(4) (SPR 89), 59-60.
THE ARTICLE EXAMINES THE ACTIVITIES OF PETR CIBULKA, A
MUSICIAN IN CZECHOSLOVAKIA. CIBULKA HAS BEEN REPEATEDLY
IMPRISONED FOR THE ILLEGAL DISTRIBUTION OF RECORDS AND
CASSETTES. THE AUTHOR ARGUES THAT CIBULKA'S MOTIVE WAS NOT
PROFIT, BUT THE FURTHERING OF CZECHOSLOVAKIAN ART AND

CULTURE. THE VERDICT OF CIBULKA'S MOST RECENT TRIAL IS STILL
PENDING.

08597 STAAR, R.F.
CHECKLIST OF COMMUNIST PARTIES IN 1988
PROBLEMS OF COMMUNISM, XXXVIII(1) (JAN 89), 47-68.
THE WORLD REVOLUTIONARY MOVEMENT AS PERCEIVED BY MOSCOW
WAS ALIVE IN 1988, BUT NO LONGER WELL, ACCORDING TO THE
LATEST VERSION OF THE CHECKLIST PUBLISHED BY PROBLEMS OF
COMMUNISM IN CONJUNCTION WITH THE HOOVER INSTITUTION ON WAR,
REVOLUTION AND PEACE (STANFORD, CA). REFORM IN THE SOVIET
UNION HAS STIMULATED DIVISION IN COMMUNIST PARTIES,
ESPECIALLY RULING ONES, WITH SOME OPPOSED TO EMULATING
MOSCOW. THE COMMUNIST PARTIES OF CHINA, THE USSR, ROMANIA,
AND POLAND REPORTED SUBSTANTIAL MEMBERSHIP INCREASES, BUT
SIGNIFICANT LOSSES WERE NOTED IN YUGOSLAVIA AND HUNGARY.
SEVERAL NONRULING PARTIES CLAIMED GAINS, BUT THE ONCE STRONG
ITALIAN PARTY SHOWED MEMBERSHIP FALLING FAR BELOW PREVIOUS
LEVELS. DURING THE YEAR, THE LEADERSHIP OF A NUMBER OF
PARTIES CHANGES AS A RESULT OF RETIREMENT, FACTIONAL
STRUGGLE, OR UNIFICATION OF DISPARATE MOVEMENTS.

08598 STAAR, R.F.
POLAND: RENEWAL OR STAGNATION?
CURRENT HISTORY, 88(541) (NOV 89), 373-376, 405-407.
POLAND IS FACED WITH A BASIC DECISION, TO CHOOSE RENEWAL
OR STAGNATION. FUTURE PROGRESS WILL DEPEND LESS ON FOREIGN
ECONOMIC AID THAN ON THE WILLINGNESS OF THE POPULATION TO
ACCEPT AUSTERITY AND TO IMPLEMENT LONG-RANGE ECONOMIC REFORM.

08599 STAATS, E. B.
PUBLIC SERVICE AND THE PUBLIC INTEREST
PUBLIC ADMINISTRATION REVIEW, 48(2) (MAR 88), 601-605.
THIS ARTICLE EXPRESSES THE VALUES AND DISCIPLINES WHICH
HAVE BEEN FOUNDATIONS OF THEIR VITAL SERVICE TO AMERICAN
CONSTITUTIONAL GOVERNMENT. IT IS AN INFORMED URGENT CALL FOR
PUBLIC SERVICE RENWAL. THE ROLE OF THE PRESIDENT AS CHIEF
EXECUTIVE IS EXPLORED AS WELL AS PUBLIC AND PRIVATE
INTERDEPENDENCE. RELIANCE ON NONGOVERNMENTAL ENTITIES AND
THE EROSION OF THE CAREER SERVICE ARE EXAMINED.

08600 STABER, U.
ORGANIZATIONAL FOUNDINGS IN THE COOPERATIVE SECTOR OF
ATLANTIC CANADA: AN ECOLOGICAL PERSPECTIVE
ORGANIZATION STUDIES, 10(3) (1989), 381-404.
THIS PAPER EXAMINES, FROM AN ECOLOGICAL PERSPECTIVE, THE
FOUNDING FREQUENCIES OF THREE ORGANIZATIONAL FORMS OF
COOPERATIVES IN ATLANTIC CANADA FROM 1940 TO 1987: WORKER
COOPERATIVES, CONSUMER COOPERATIVES AND MARKETING
COOPERATIVES. THE FINDINGS SHOW THAT COOPERATIVE FOUNDINGS
ARE SENSITIVE TO INSTITUTIONAL CHANGE AS WELL AS TO THE
LEVEL OF PRIOR FOUNDINGS, DEATHS, AND POPULATION DENSITY.
THE PATTERN OF THESE EFFECTS, HOWEVER, VARIES ACROSS
ORGANIZATIONAL FORMS, SUGGESTING SUBSTANTIAL DIFFERENCES IN
THE ECOLOGIES OF POPULATIONS OF COOPERATIVES.

08601 STACKHOUSE, M.L.
THE THEOLOGICAL CHALLENGE OF GLOBALIZATION
THE CHRISTIAN CENTURY, 106(15) (MAY 89), 468-471.
THE AUTHOR CONSIDERS THREE DIMENSIONS OF GLOBALIZATION:
THE EXPERIENCE OF DEPROVINCIALIZATION, THE FACT OF
INTERNATIONALIZATION, AND THE SEARCH FOR UNIVERSALITY.
INTERNATIONALIZATION POSES THE QUESTION OF WHETHER THE USA
AS A NATION HAS THE DEPTH OF CHARACTER TO MODEL AND GUIDE
WHAT IS LIKELY TO BE, AT LEAST TEMPORARILY, A GLOBAL PAX
AMERICANA.

08602 STACKHOUSE, S.B.
UPHOLDING JUSTICE IN AN UNJUST WORLD: A PRACTITIONER'S
VIEW OF PUBLIC ADMINISTRATION ETHICS
INTERNATIONAL JOURNAL OF PUBLIC ADMINISTRATION, 12(6) (NOV
89), 889-912.
THIS ARTICLE PRESENTS THE AUTHOR'S APPROACH TO
PROFESSIONAL ETHICS AS A PRACTITIONER OF PUBLIC
ADMINISTRATION. PUBLIC ADMINISTRATORS ARE HELD TO BE
PERSONALLY RESPONSIBLE FOR THEIR ACTIONS. THEREFORE,
PROFESSIONAL ETHICAL STANDARDS ARE BOTH POSSIBLE AND
NECESSARY, NOT ONLY TO PREVENT WRONGDOING BUT ALSO TO GUIDE
AND PROMOTE RIGHT BEHAVIOR. AN IDEALLY JUST REGIME IS FIRST
HYPOTHESIZED, BASED ON THE PRINCIPLES OF JUSTICE DEVELOPED
IN JOHN RAWLS'S A THEORY OF JUSTICE. A NORMATIVE ETHICAL
STANDARD OF NEUTRAL COMPETENCE IS THEN POSTULATED FOR AGENTS
OF SUCH A HYPOTHETICAL REGIME. THE AUTHOR THEN ADDRESSES THE
IMPLICATIONS OF REAL-WORLD INJUSTICE, AND DISCUSSES THE
EXCEPTIONS TO NEUTRAL COMPETENCE WHICH ARE JUSTIFIABLE WHEN
CONFRONTED BY INJUSTICE. THE SUGGESTED APPROACH ESTABLISHES
A HIGH ETHICAL STANDARD, PROVIDING JUSTIFICATION FOR NOT
ONLY AVOIDING WRONGDOING, BUT ALSO FOR DOING RIGHT. THIS
APPROACH ALSO PROVIDES PRACTICAL AND REALISTIC GUIDANCE FOR
ETHICAL DECISION-MAKING. BOTH JUSTIFIABILITY AND
APPLICABILITY ARE HELD TO BE NECESSARY IF SUCH AN ETHICAL
SYSTEM IS TO BE FOLLOWED BY PUBIC ADMINISTRATORS.

08603 STAGGENBORG, S.
   STABILITY AND INNOVATION IN THE WOMEN'S MOVEMENT: A
   COMPARISON OF TWO MOVEMENT ORGANIZATIONS
   SOCIAL PROBLEMS, 36(1) (FEB 89), 75-92.
      THIS PAPER EXAMINES THE EFFECTS OF ORGANIZATIONAL
   STRUCTURE AND IDEOLOGY ON THE MOBILIZATION AND TACTICS OF
   SOCIAL MOVEMENT ORGANIZATIONS (SMOS). DOCUMENTARY AND
   INTERVIEW DATA ON TWO LOCAL MOVEMENT ORGANIZATIONS, THE
   CHICAGO WOMEN'S LIBERATION UNION (CWLU) AND THE CHICAGO
   CHAPTER OF THE NATIONAL ORGANIZATION FOR WOMEN (CHICAGO NOW),
   ARE USED TO PROVIDE A DETAILED ACCOUNT OF THE WAYS IN WHICH
   SMOS DEAL WITH ORGANIZATIONAL PROBLEMS. THE INFORMAL,
   DECENTRALIZED STRUCTURE OF THE NOW DEFUNCT CWLU, TOGETHER
   WITH ITS IDEOLOGICAL APPROACH, ENCOURAGED STRATEGIC AND
   TACTICAL INNOVATION BUT UNDERMINED ORGANIZATIONAL
   MAINTENANCE. CHICAGO NOW'S MORE FORMALIZED AND CENTRALIZED
   STRUCTURE FACILITATED ORGANIZATIONAL MAINTENANCE BUT LED TO
   A NARROWING OF STRATEGIES AND TACTICS. SUCCESSFUL SOCIAL
   MOVEMENTS ARE LIKELY TO INCLUDE BOTH TYPES OF ORGANIZATIONAL
   STRUCTURES.

08604 STALLWORTHY, M.
   CENTRAL GOVERNMENT AND LOCAL GOVERNMENT: THE USES AND
   ABUSES OF A CONSTITUTIONAL HEGEMONY
   POLITICAL QUARTERLY (THE), 60(1) (JAN 89), 22-37.
      THE PAST DECADE HAS SEEN A SIGNIFICANT ALTERATION IN THE
   STATUS OF LOCAL GOVERNMENT AND IN ITS RELATIONSHIP WITH THE
   CENTRE. A CONSTITUTIONAL SETTLEMENT WHICH IS RESISTANT TO
   DIALOGUE AND WHICH CONFERS AN UNCONDITIONAL LEGITIMACY UPON
   IMPOSED CENTRAL SOLUTIONS IS ANTITHETICAL TO REASONABLE
   EXPECTATIONS WITHIN A PURPORTED LIBERAL DEMOCRACY. WHILST
   CORPORATIST VALUES MAY BE IN DECLINE, REFORM STILL REQUIRES
   A CENTRAL RECOGNITION OF THE IMPERATIVE NEED FOR LIMITED
   GOVERNMENT. IT IS A MEASURE OF THE IMPOTENCE OF THE
   PRINCIPLES AND PROCESSES OF PUBLIC LAW THAT IT IS TO THE
   CLOSED SPHERES OF CENTRAL GOVERNMENT THAT WE MUST LOOK FOR
   SOLUTIONS.

08605 STAM, A.
   MARXIST ETHNIC VIEWS AND POLICIES - AN ESSAY IN
   COMPARATIVE HISTORY
   PLURAL SOCIETIES, 18(2) (MAR 89), 45-86.
      INTER-ETHNIC RELATIONS IN THE COMMUNIST WORLD ARE A
   DECISIVE TEST FOR MARXISM-LENINISM IN GENERAL AND ESPECIALLY
   FOR ITS TEACHINGS ON "PROLETARIAN IN THIS ARTICLE THE RATHER
   VARIEGATED AND SOMETIMES CONTRADICTIONARY VIEWS OF MARX AND
   ENGELS CONCERNING ETHNICITY ARE BRIEFLY TRACE. NEWTONIAN
   EMPHASIZES THOSE PARTS OF THEIR WRITINGS, THAT LATER ON
   ACQUIRED MUCH SIGNIFICANCE FOR THEIR MARXIST-LENINIST
   SUCCESSORS.

08606 STAMPER, N.H.
   EXECUTIVE LEADERSHIP AND EXECUTIVE MANAGEMENT IN BIG CITY
   POLICE DEPARMENTS: THE PROFESSED VALUES VS. THE OBSERVED
   BEHAVIOR OF AMERICAN POLICE CHIEFS
   DISSERTATION ABSTRACTS INTERNATIONAL, 50(1) (JUL 89),
   258-A.
      THE AUTHOR INVESTIGATES THE PROFESSED VALUES AND THE
   EXECUTIVE BEHAVIOR OF AMERICA'S BIG-CITY POLICE CHIEFS TO
   DETERMINE TO WHAT EXTENT, IF ANY, THEY DRAW A DISTINCTION
   BETWEEN THEIR EXECUTIVE LEADERSHIP FUNCTIONS AND THEIR
   EXECUTIVE MANAGEMENT FUNCTIONS. HE FINDS THAT THE CHIEFS
   PLACE A SIGNIFICANTLY HIGHER VALUE ON THEIR LEADERSHIP
   FUNCTIONS THAN THEY DO THEIR MANAGERIAL FUNCTIONS, ALTHOUGH
   THEY PLACE A HIGH VALUE ON BOTH.

08607 STANFIELD, J.
   VEBLENIAN AND NEO-MARXISM PERSPECTIVES ON THE CULTURAL
   CRISIS OF LATE CAPITALISM
   JOURNAL OF ECONOMIC ISSUES, XXIII(3) (SEP 89), 689-716.
      THE ARTICLE REVIEWS THE PERSPECTIVE OF THORSTEIN VEBLEN
   AND THE INSTITUTIONALISTS AND OF RECENT US NEO-MARXIAN
   ECONOMISTS ON ECONOMIC CRISES AND THE PATHOLOGY OF LATE
   CAPITALISM. IT SEEKS TO DRAW ATTENTION TO THE PSYCHOCULTURAL
   CONSEQUENCES OF THE SYSTEMIC LATE CAPITALIST RESPONSE TO
   ECONOMIC CRISES AND TO THE NEED FOR RESEARCH AGENDA TO
   DELINEATE AND EVALUATE THESE CONSEQUENCES.

08608 STANISCHEV, D.
   KHRISTIAN RAKOVSKY: HIS LIFE AND WORK
   INTERNATIONAL AFFAIRS (MOSCOW), (1) (JAN 89), 90-95.
      ON FEBRUARY 4, 1988, THE USSR SUPREME COURT EXONERATED
   THE DEFENDANTS PROSECUTED IN THE THIRD MOSCOW TRIAL OF THE
   ANTI-SOVIET RIGHT-WING TROTSKYITE BLOC. AMONG THOSE
   EXONERATED HERE NIKOLAI BUKHARIN, ALEXEI RYKOV, ARKADY
   ROZENGOLTS, NIKOLAI KRESTINSKY, AND KHRISTIAN RAKOVSKY. THIS
   ARTICLE REVIEWS THE LIFE AND POLITICAL HISTORY OF RAKOVSKY.

08609 STANKOVSKY, J.
   WORLD TRADE IS EXPANDING STRONGLY
   AUSTRIA TODAY, (1) (1989), 14-15.
      CONTINUING HIGH RATES OF GROWTH MADE 1988 THE BEST YEAR
   IN MORE THAN A DECADE FOR THE WORLD ECONOMY. AUSTRIA HAD A
   HIGHER GROWTH RATE THAN ITS MOST IMPORTANT TRADING PARTNERS

AND EXPERIENCED BOTH RISING HOURLY PRODUCTIVITY AND FALLING
LABOR COSTS. THE PROSPECTS FOR CONTINUING GROWTH ARE
FAVORABLE IN AUSTRIA, AND FORECASTS INDICATE IT WILL
EXPERIENCE ECONOMIC EXPANSION IN LINE WITH THE WESTERN
EUROPEAN AVERAGE DURING THE NEXT FEW YEARS. INVESTMENT
ACTIVITY IS LIKELY TO REMAIN LIVELY, DUE TO THE EUROPEAN
COMMUNITY'S INTERNAL MARKET PROGRAM.

08610 STANKOVSKY, S.
   JAPAN'S FOREIGN ECONOMIC POLICY: PROSPECTS OF SOVIET-
   JAPANESE COOPERATION
   FOREIGN TRADE. 1 (1988), 34-38.
      THIS ARTICLE EXAMINES JAPAN'S FOREIGN ECONOMIC POLICY
   AND TRACES ITS GROWTH THROUGH THE 1960S AND EARLY 1970S. IT
   COMMENTS ON U.S. COOPERATION WITH JAPAN, THE YEN, AND
   ANALYSES NEW PROBLEMS THAT THE JAPANESE GOVERNMENT FACE.
   PROSPECTS OF SOVIET-JAPANESE COOPERATION ARE EXPLORED.

08611 STANLEY, J.R.
   GENDER DISCRIMINATION IN A STATE BUREAUCRACY: THE
   PERCEPTIONS OF TEXAS PUBLIC ADMINISTRATORS
   JOURNAL OF POLITICAL SCIENCE, 17(1-2) (1989), 86-98.
      THE AUTHOR REPORTS ON A STUDY OF HIGH-LEVEL PUBLIC
   ADMINISTRATORS IN TEXAS DESIGNED TO IDENTIFY BARRIERS TO THE
   ADVANCEMENT OF WOMEN. FINDINGS INDICATE THAT GENDER
   SEGREGATION AND DISCRIMINATION PERSIST AT THE TOP LEVELS OF
   ADMINISTRATORS AS A RESULT OF BOTH INSTITUTIONAL AND INTER-
   PERSONAL PRACTICES. BUT MOST TEXAS ADMINISTRATORS, BOTH MALE
   AND FEMALE, WERE FOUND TO SUPPORT REFORMS TO ADDRESS CERTAIN
   DOMESTIC AND INSTITUTIONAL CONSTRAINTS THAT IMPEDE FEMALE
   ADVANCEMENT.

08612 STAPLES, C. L.
   THE POLITICS OF EMPLOYMENT-BASED INSURANCE IN THE UNITED
   STATES
   INTERNATIONAL JOURNAL OF HEALTH SERVICES, 19(3) (1989),
   415-432.
      ANALYSES OF THE CORPORATIZATION OF US HEALTH CARE
   TYPICALLY FOCUS ON THE POLITICAL STRUGGLE BETWEEN
   CORPORATIONS AND TRADITIONAL HEALTH CARE PROVIDERS. THE
   PAPER FOCUSES ON A NEGLECTED AREA OF STUDY: THE STRUGGLE
   BETWEEN CORPORATIONS AND THEIR EMPLOYEES OVER THE EMPLOYMENT-
   BASED HEALTH INSURANCE SYSTEM. THE PAPER ARGUES THAT THE
   EMPLOYMENT-BASED HEALTH INSURANCE SYSTEM HAS A PART OF A
   POLITICAL COMPROMISE BETWEEN CAPITAL AND LABOR THAT EMERGED
   AFTER WORLD WAR II. IN EXCHANGE FOR CONTROL OVER PRODUCTION
   AND INCREASED WORKER PRODUCTIVITY, CORPORATIONS AGREED TO
   PROVIDE WORKERS WITH STEADY WAGE INCREASES AND AN EXPANDED
   SYSTEM OF FRINGE BENEFITS, OR "CORPORATE WELFARE." THE PAPER
   ARGUES THAT THIS SYSTEM OF "CORPORATE WELFARE" HAS MADE THE
   US WORKING CLASS MORE VULNERABLE TO CORPORATE POWER.

08613 STAPLES, W.G.
   CASTLES OF OUR CONSCIENCE: THE POLITICAL ECONOMY OF
   INSTITUTIONAL CARE AND CONTROL IN THE UNITED STATES, 1850-
   1985
   DISSERTATION ABSTRACTS INTERNATIONAL, 49(7) (JAN 89),
   1988-A.
      THE CENTRAL CONCERN OF THIS STUDY IS TO UNDERSTAND HOW
   THE STRUCTURAL CONDITIONS, MECHANISMS AND CONTRADICTIONS OF
   THE POLITICAL STATE SHAPE THE CHARACTER OF EMERGENT SOCIAL
   POLICIES. THE FIRST TASK OF THE PROJECT IS TO DERIVE A
   THEORETICAL FRAMEWORK FOR UNDERSTANDING THE STRUCTURAL
   CONDITIONS AND MECHANISMS WHICH SHAPE THE FORM AND CAPACITY
   OF STATE POLICY-MAKING AND ADMINISTRATION. THE SECOND IS TO
   UTILIZE THIS THEORETICAL MODEL TO PROVIDE A HISTORICAL
   INTERPRETATION OF THE CHANGING PRACTICES AND POLICIES OF HOW
   WE, AS A SOCIETY, RESPOND TO MATTERS OF DEVIANCE, ILLNESS,
   CRIME, AND POVERTY.

08614 STAPLETON, J.
   THE NATIONAL CHARACTER OF ERNEST BARKER'S POLITICAL SCIENCE
   POLITICAL STUDIES, XXXVII(2) (JUN 89), 171-187.
      THIS ARTICLE CONSIDERS THE WRITINGS OF SIR ERNEST BARKER
   (1874-1960), ONE OF THE FIRST PROFESSIONAL POLITICAL
   SCIENTISTS IN BRITAIN. IT EXAMINES HIS BACKGROUND IN LITERAE
   HUMANIORES AND MODERN HISTORY AT LATE-VICTORIAN OXFORD,
   DISCIPLINES WHICH RESPECTIVELY IMPARTED THE IDEALIST AND
   WHIG FRAMEWORK OF HIS LATER THOUGHT. IT IS ARGUED THAT
   BARKER'S FUSION OF THESE TWO RIVAL DISCOURSES - TOGETHER
   WITH THE CONCERNS OF EARLY TWENTIETH-CENTURY PLURALISM -
   REINFORCED POWERFUL CULTURAL MOTIFS. AS A CONSEQUENCE, THE
   SIGNIFICANCE OF POLITICAL SCIENCE SEEMS TO HAVE OUTSTRETCHED
   THE ACADEMIC BOUNDARIES IN WHICH IT INCREASINGLY BECAME
   CONFINED AFTER HIS DEATH.

08615 STARGARDT, A.W.
   THE EMERGENCE OF THE ASIAN SYSTEM OF POWERS
   MODERN ASIAN STUDIES, 23(3) (JUL 89), 561-596.
      THIS ARTICLE EXPLORES THE RESULTS OF THE 'DOWNWARD
   SWEEP' OF JAPAN AFTER PEARL HARBOR WHICH HAS BEEN WIDELY
   NOTED FOR ITS LONG-TERM EFFECTS IN SOUTHEAST ASIA. JAPANESE
   RULE PLUS THE INDEPENDENCE IN INDIA ARE EXAMINED AS CAUSES
   WHICH VITIATED THE ATTEMPTS AT COLONIAL RESTORATION BY THE

BRITISH. THE ATTAINMENT OF INDEPENDENCE OF INDIA, PAKISTAN, CEYLON AND BERMA WAS ACHIEVED BY A PROCESS OF NEGOTIATIONS, AGREEMENTS AND ACTS OF PARLIAMENT WHICH STAND WITHOUT HISTORICAL PARALLEL AND ARE DETAILED BY THE AUTHOR.

08616 STARK, A.
CANADIAN CONUNDRUMS: NATIONALISM, SOCIALISM, AND FREE TRADE
AMERICAN SPECTATOR, 22(4) (APR 89), 20-22.
THE AUTHOR DISCUSSES CANADIAN NATIONALISM, ANTI-AMERICANISM, SOCIALISM, AND HOW THEY RELATE TO THE FREE TRADE ISSUE.

08617 STARR, S.F.
A PECULIAR PATTERN
WILSON QUARTERLY, XIII(2) (SPR 89), 37-50.
SOME WESTERN SCHOLARS BELIEVE THAT GORBACHEV MUST OVERCOME NOT ONLY THE LEGACY OF JOSEPH STALIN, BUT ALSO A THOUSAND YEARS OF RUSSIAN HISTORY, IF PERESTROIKA IS TO SUCCEED. IN THIS ARTICLE, THE AUTHOR COMPARES THE CURRENT BEWILDERING UPHEAVAL TO PAST ATTEMPTS AT REFORM IN RUSSIA. HE FINDS SOME STRONG SIMILARITIES BETWEEN PAST AND PRESENT.

08618 STASSEN, G.
SCHOOLING FOR DEMOCRACY
THE CHRISTIAN CENTURY, 106(39) (DEC 89), 1199-1201.
THE ARTICLE EXAMINES THE ROLE THAT CHURCHES PLAYED IN ACHIEVING THE REMARKABLE BREAKTHROUGHS IN EAST GERMANY. IT CONCLUDES THAT THE CHURCHES WERE THE ONE PLACE WHERE OPPOSITION GROUPS COULD MEET, DISCUSS AND ORGANIZE. IN ADDITION, THE CHURCHES ALSO CLARIFIED THE PEOPLE'S DEMANDS AND THUS PUT WELL-DEFINED PRESSURE ON THE GOVERNMENT. THE VISIBLE AND SIGNIFICANT ROLE THAT CHURCHES PLAYED IN THE ONGOING DRAMA OF DEMOCRACY HAS WON THEM NEW CREDIBILITY AND TRUST..

08619 STATION, E.
BRAZIL: CONFRONTING AN "INVISIBLE" ISSUE
NACLA REPORT ON THE AMERICAS, XXIII(2) (JUL 89), 10-12.
WOMEN'S POLICE STATIONS WHICH SERVE THE VICTIMS OF BRAZIL'S ALARMING RATES OF DOMESTIC VIOLENCE AND RAPE MAY BE NO PANACEA. BUT THE STATIONS, RUN AND STAFFED BY FEMALE OFFICERS, HAVE BROUGHT THE ISSUE OF VIOLENCE AGAINST WOMEN TO PUBLIC ATTENTION.

08620 STAVIS, B.
THE POLITICAL ECONOMY OF INFLATION IN CHINA
STUDIES IN COMPARATIVE COMMUNISM, 22(2/3) (SUM 89), 235-250.
THIS ARTICLE EXAMINES THE CAUSES AND CONSEQUENCES OF INFLATION IN CHINA. THREE CAUSES OF THIS INFLATION ARE EXAMINED: 1) PARTIAL DECONTROL OF FOOD PRICES, 2) RUNAWAY MONEY SUPPLY, AND 3) RELAXATION OF CONTROLS OVER CAPITAL INVESTMENT AND INSTITUTIONAL CONSUMPTION. FINAL ANALYSES CONCLUDES THAT THE INFLATION WAS CAUSED BY A WEAKENED GOVERNMENT, AND THAT IT WILL BE DIFFICULT TO MAINTAIN COMPLETE GOVERNMENT CONTROL IN TODAYS CHINA.

08621 STEACT, A.; BEHN, S.
SYMBOLIC FLAMES
MACLEAN'S (CANADA'S NEWS MAGAZINE), 102(30) (JUL 89), 37.
KENYAN PRESIDENT DANIEL ARAP MOI LIT A BONFIRE MADE OF SOME $3.6 MILLION WORTH OF ELEPHANT TUSKS CONFISTICATED FROM POACHERS IN AN EFFORT TO SPARK WORLDWIDE INTEREST IN PROTECTING THE INCREASINGLY ENDANGERED AFRICAN ELEPHANT. ALTHOUGH ANTI-POACHING SENTIMENT IN THE US THE EUROPEAN COMMUNITY IS FAIRLY HIGH, A NUMBER OF AFRICAN NATIONS INCLUDING SOUTH AFRICA, ZIMBABWE, AND BOTSWANA OPPOSE AN INTERNATION BAN ON IVORY. THEY CLAIM THAT THEY ARE WORKING TO CONSERVE AND EVEN INCREASE THEIR ELEPHANT HERDS AND NEED THE IVORY TRADE TO AID THEIR FALTERING ECONOMICS. IF THEY REFUSE TO COOPERATE, THE ENTIRE EFFOR TO SAVE THE ELEPHANT COULD FALTER.

08622 STEDMAN, S.J.
PEACEMAKING IN REVOLUTIONARY SITUATIONS
DISSERTATION ABSTRACTS INTERNATIONAL, 49(12) (JUN 89), 3863-A.
THIS THESIS EXAMINES THE PROBLEM OF NEGOTIATING A SETTLEMENT OF A REVOLUTIONARY SITUATION (DEFINED AS AN INSTANCE OF MULTIPLE SOVEREIGNTY WITHIN A COUNTRY) WITH THE PRESENCE OF AN OPPOSITION FACTION THAT CALLS FOR THE COMPLETE TRANSFORMATION OF THE COUNTRY'S SOCIAL, ECONOMIC, AND POLITICAL VALUES AND INSTITUTIONS. THE AUTHOR COMPARES FOUR DIFFERENT INTERNATIONAL EFFORTS TO RESOLVE THE ZIMBABHEAN REVOLUTIONARY WAR OF THE 1970'S. HE BUILDS ON THE WORK OF WILLIAM ZARTMAN, WHO HAS ARGUED THAT THERE ARE MOMENTS WITHIN A CONFLICT WHEN THE DISPUTE IS RIPE FOR RESOLUTION.

08623 STEEL, B.; SODEN, D.
ACID RAIN POLICY IN CANADA AND THE UNITED STATES: ATTITUDES OF CITIZENS, ENVIRONMENTAL ACTIVISTS, AND LEGISLATORS
SOCIAL SCIENCE JOURNAL, 26(1) (1989), 27-44.

ACID RAIN IS AN INTERNATIONAL PROBLEM FOR CANADA AND THE UNITED STATES. ACID FROM FACTORIES AND ELECTRIC GENERATING PLANTS IN MICHIGAN FALLS ON ONTARIO, KILLING FISH IN ITS LAKES. THIS ARTICLE EVALUATES THE ATTITUDES OF ORDINARY CITIZENS, ENVIRONMENTAL ACTIVISTS AND STATE OR PROVINCIAL LEGISLATORS IN MICHIGAN AND ONTARIO. BASED ON A SURVEY OF 1076 CITIZENS, 1238 ACTIVISTS, AND OVER A HUNDRED LEGISLATORS, IT FINDS THAT ALL GROUPS FAVORED FORCEFUL GOVERNMENT ACTION TO CONTROL THE ACID RAIN. CANADIANS WERE MORE SUPPORTIVE THAN MICHIGANDERS.

08624 STEEL, B.S.; LOURICH, N.P.; SODEN, D.L.
A COMPARISON OF MUNICIPAL RESPONSES TO THE ELIMINATION OF FEDERAL GENERAL REVENUE SHARING IN FLORIDA, MICHIGAN AND WASHINGTON
STATE AND LOCAL GOVERNMENT REVIEW, 21(3) (FAL 89), 106-115.
AFTER SEVERAL YEARS OF CHALLENGES TO FEDFRAL GENERAL REVENUE SHARING (GRS) IN CONGRESS, THE PROGRAM WAS TERMINATED IN 1986. THE OUTCOME OF THIS TERMINATION UPON MUNICIPAL BUDGETS HAS BEEN DEBATED BOTH IN ACADEMIC AND POLITICAL CIRCLES. IT HAS BEEN ARGUED THAT THE EFFECTS OF TERMINATION DEPEND UPON A VARIETY OF POLITICAL, ECONOMIC, AND ADMINISTRATIVE FACTORS. THIS STUDY ATTEMPTS TO ASSESS THE VARIOUS RESULTS OF THE ELIMINATION OF GRS AND TO IDENTIFY THOSE FACTORS THAT ADVERSELY AFFECT A CITY'S ABILITY TO MINIMIZE THE LOSS OF THESE FUNDS, UTILIZING DATA FROM 326 CITIES IN FLORIDA, MICHIGAN, AND WASHINGTON. FINDINGS SUGGEST THAT THE DEMISE OF GRS HAD A DRAMATIC IMPACT UPON MUNICIPAL BUDGETS IN THOSE AREAS OF THE COUNTRY WHICH CAN LEAST AFFORD IT.

08625 STEEL, R.
NATO'S LAST MISSION
FOREIGN POLICY, (76) (FAL 89), 83-95.
THIS PAPER STUDIES THE HISTORY OF NATO, HOW IT CAME INTO BEING, WHAT IT HAS AND HAS NOT ACCOMPLISHED AND WHAT IS FUTURE MAY BE. IT ANALYSES THE U.S., THE USSR, AND THE EUROPEAN PRESENT DAY SITUATION. IT PRESENTS A DIFFERENT WORLD SITUATION TODAY THAN EXISTED WHEN NATO WAS FORMED. IT PREDICTS THAT THE GREAT POWERS NOW HAVE AN OPPORTUNITY TO END, ON TERMS THAT PROTECT THEIR COMMON INTERESTS AND EUROPEAN STABILITY, THE GREAT CONFRONTATION THAT HAS DIVIDED THE CONTINENT.

08626 STEELE, J.
THE POST-ELECTION STRUGGLE FOR POLITICAL INDEPENDENCE
POLITICAL AFFAIRS, LXVIII(3) (MAR 89), 25-33, 45.
THE 1989 AND 1990 ELECTIONS CAN HAVE A PIVOTAL IMPACT ON THE POLITICAL BALANCE OF FORCES IN THE USA. THE RESULTS OF THESE ELECTIONS AND THE CUMULATIVE EFFECT WILL HELP DETERMINE THE RELATIVE STRENGTH OR WEAKNESS OF THE BUSH ADMINISTRATION. THE MUNICIPAL ELECTIONS ARE ESPECIALLY SIGNIFICANT IN THAT THEY CAN STRENGTHEN THE CONFIDENCE OF THE PEOPLE AND STIMULATE A UNITED MOBILIZATION.

08627 STEELE, M.
FROM CUSTOM TO RIGHT: THE POLITICIZATION OF THE VILLAGE IN EARLY MEIJI JAPAN
MODERN ASIAN STUDIES, 23(4) (OCT 89), 729-748.
JAPAN'S MEIJI RESTORATION RESULTED IN THE DESTRUCTION OF EXISTING POLITICAL NORMS AND STRUCTURES AT ALL LEVELS OF SOCIETY. AN IMPORTANT CHANGE WAS THAT THE MEIJI RESTORATION MADE EVERYONE EQUALLY CITIZENS OF THE STATE. THROUGHOUT THE EARLY MEIJI PERIOFD, VILLAGES AND OTHER LOCAL UNITS ATTEMPTED TO PROTECT AND ENHANCE THE CUSTOMS ASSOCIATED WITH LOCAL AUTONOMY INHERITED FROM THE OLD REGIME. THIS SOMETIMES TOOK THE FORM OF VIOLENT PROTEST AND EVEN CIVIL WAR, BUT, MORE GENERALLY, IT INVOLVED THE "POLITICALIZATION" OF THE VILLAGE. THE ARTICLE SETS OUT TO CLARIFY WHAT IS MEANT BY "POLITICALIZATION." IT EXAMINES THE TRANSITION FORM POLITICAL CUSTOM TO POLITICAL RIGHTS IN TOCHIGI PREFECTURE, CONCENTRATING ON ARGUMENTS FOR THE ESTABLISHMENT OF VILLAGE ASSEMBLIES BETWEEN 1874 AND 1884.

08628 STEFFEN, M.
PRIVATIZATION IN FRENCH HEALTH POLITICS: FEW PROJECTS AND LITTLE OUTCOME
INTERNATIONAL JOURNAL OF HEALTH SERVICES, 19(4) (1989), 651-662.
THE AUTHOR PRESENTS THE MAIN FEATURES OF THE ORGANIZATION OF THE FRENCH HEALTH CARE SYSTEM, REVEALING AN IMPORTANT MIXTURE OF PUBLIC AND PRIVATE ACTORS AND INSTITUTIONS AND A LARGE NUMBER OF POLITICAL RESTRAINTS THAT OPPOSE RESISTANCE TO PRIVATIZATION. IN SPITE OF TRADITIONAL REFERENCES TO "LIBERAL MEDICINE" AND RECURRENT DEBATES OPPOSING PUBLIC AND PRIVATE INTERVENTION, NEITHER THE DOCTORS NOR THE POLITICAL DECISION MAKERS HAVE REALLY SUPPORTED THE FEW PROJECTS THAT HAVE BEEN PROPOSED FOR PRIVATIZATION OR LIBERALIZATION OF HEALTH CARE. ON THE CONTRARY, THE COST-CONTROL POLICY INTRODUCED GROWING STATE INTERVENTION AND NEW MANAGEMENT METHODS INTO THE HEALTH CARE SECTOR, WHOSE ACTORS WERE NOT USED TO IT. THE PRIVATIZATION AND LIBERALIZATION DEBATES APPEAR AS A RHETORIC NECESSARY TO ACCOMMODATE THESE DIFFICULT CHANGES.

08629 STEGEMANN, K.
POLICY RIVALRY AMONG INDUSTRIAL STATES: WHAT WE LEARN FROM
MODELS OF STRATEGIC TRADE POLICY?
INTERNATIONAL ORGANIZATION, 43(1) (WIN 89), 73-100.
THE ECONOMIC THEORY OF INTERNATIONAL TRADE HAS CHANGED
DRAMATICALLY OVER THE LAST DECADE BY ADMITTING INTO ITS
MAINSTREAM A BODY OF LITERATURE THAT FOCUSES ON THE
IMPLICATIONS OF MONOPOLISTIC AND OLIGOPOLISTIC ELEMENTS IN
INTERNATIONAL MARKETS. BY APPLYING THE TOOLS OF THE "NEW"
INDUSTRIAL ORGANIZATION IN AN INTERNATIONAL CONTEXT, TWO NEW
CLASSES OF MODELS HAVE EMERGED: MODELS OF INTRA-INDUSTRY
TRADE AND MODELS OF STRATEGIC TRADE POLICY. THE POLICY
IMPLICATIONS OF MODELS OF STRATEGIC TRADE POLICY WERE QUITE
DISTURBING FOR THE ECONOMICS PROFESSION, SINCE THESE MODELS
DEMONSTRATED THAT THE CLASSICAL HARMONY BETWEEN NATIONAL AND
COSMOPOLITAN WELFARE MAXIMIZATION DOES NOT EXIST IF ONE
ASSUMES OPPORTUNITIES FOR STRATEGIC MANIPULATION OF
OLIGOPOLISTIC INTERNATIONAL INDUSTRIES. THIS ARTICLE REVIEWS
TWO PROMINENT MODELS OF STRATEGIC TRADE POLICY -- THE
BRANDER-SPENCER MODEL AND THE KRUGMAN MODEL -AND RELATES
THEM TO MORE FAMILIAR EARLIER CONCEPTS, SUCH AS
STACKELBERG'S ASYMMETRICAL DUOPOLY SOLUTION AND THE
VENERABLE INFANT-INDUSTRY ARGUMENT FOR GOVERNMENT
INTERVENTION. THE PRIMARY PURPOSE OF THIS ARTICLE, HOWEVER,
IS TO PROVIDE A SYNOPSIS OF THE LARGE LITERATURE ADDRESSING
THE QUESTION OF WHETHER MODELS OF STRATEGIC TRADE POLICY CAN
GIVE GUIDANCE FOR GOVERNMENT POLICY.

08630 STEGER, M.A.E.; WITT, S.L.
GENDER DIFFERENCES IN ENVIRONMENTAL ORIENTATIONS: A
COMPARISON OF PUBLICS AND ACTIVISTS IN CANADA AND THE U.S.
WESTERN POLITICAL QUARTERLY, 42(4) (DEC 89), 627-650.
THE STUDY ANALYZES DIFFERENCES IN THE ENVIRONMENTAL
ORIENTATIONS AND POLICY PREFERENCES OF MALE AND FEMALE
PUBLICS AND ENVIRONMENTAL ACTIVISTS IN TWO RESEARCH SITESTHE
CANADIAN PROVINCE OF ONTARIO AND THE STATE OF MICHIGAN.
WOMEN TO A GREATER DEGREE THAN MEN HELD BELIEFS THAT
REFLECTED A NURTURING AND PROTECTIVE ATTITUDE TOWARD THE
ENVIRONMENT, PERCEIVED HIGH RISKS FROM ACID RAIN POLLUTION,
SUPPORTED THE BELIEFS OF THE NEW ENVIRONMENTAL PARADIGM, AND
BACKED A MORATORIUM ON ACID RAIN-CAUSING ACTIVITIES. WOMEN
ALSO EXPRESSED HIGHER LEVELS OF PERCEIVED POLICY INFLUENCE
AND POLITICAL PARTICIPATION THAN MEN, BUT MEN HAD ACQUIRED
MORE ISSUE SPECIFIC INFORMATION ON THE SOURCES OF ACID RAIN
AND ABATEMENT TECHNOLOGIES THAN THEIR FEMALE COUNTERPARTS.
ALTHOUGH THESE GENDER SENSITIVE PATTERNS VARIED SOMEWHAT
CROSS-NATIONALLY, RELATIONSHIPS BETWEEN THE PERSON'S SEX AND
ENVIRONMENTAL ORIENTATIONS PERSISTED WHEN CONTROLS WERE
IMPOSED FOR PUBLIC VERSUS ACTIVIST AND COUNTRY EFFECTS.

08631 STEGER, M.E.; LOURICH, N.P.; PIERCE, J.C.; STEEL, B.S.
POLITICAL CULTURE, POSTMATERIAL VALUES, AND THE NEW
ENVIRONMENTAL PARADIGM: A COMPARATIVE ANALYSIS OF CANADA
AND THE UNITED STATES
POLITICAL BEHAVIOR, 11(3) (SEP 89), 233-254.
THIS STUDY INVESTIGATES THE RELATIONSHIP BETWEEN
POSTMATERIAL VALUES AND THE NEW ENVIRONMENTAL PARADIGM IN
CANADA (ONTARIO) AND THE UNITED STATES (MICHIGAN). BASED ON
SURVEY DATA COLLECTED AMONG BOTH CITIZENS AND ENVIRONMENTAL
ACTIVISTS, IT IS EVIDENT THAT AMONG BOTH CANADIAN AND
AMERICAN RESPONDENTS OF BOTH CITIZEN AND ACTIVIST TYPE THE
TWO VALUE DIMENSIONS ARE SIMILARLY MULTIDIMENSIONAL AND
SEPARATE. RATHER THAN REFLECTING A SINGLE LARGER DIMENSION
OF VALUE ORIENTATION, AS CLAIMED BY SOME, IT IS CLEAR THAT
THE INGLEHART POSTMATERIALIST VALUE MEASURE AND THE DUNLAP
AND VAN LIERE NEP INDEX ARE SEPARATE CONSTRUCTS IN THE
THINKING OF THE CANADIANS AND AMERICANS SURVEYED. WHILE
THESE FINDINGS WERE PARALLEL IN THE CANADIAN AND AMERICAN
SETTINGS, A NUMBER OF CROSS-NATIONAL DIFFERENCES IN HOW
THESE VALUES INFLUENCE ATTITUDES AND BEHAVIORS ARE REPORTED.
IN GENERAL, THESE FINDINGS UNDERSCORE THE NEED TO CONTINUE
TO FOCUS ON VARIATIONS IN THE CULTURAL CONTEXT OF CITIZEN
RESPONSES TO POSTINDUSTRIAL CHANGE.

08632 STEHR, H.
THE LESSONS OF A STRIKE
WORLD MARXIST REVIEW, 32(12) (DEC 89), 78-80.
THE SUCCESSFUL STRIKE BY THE WEST GERMAN PRINTWORKERS IN
THE SPRING OF 1989 HAS CLEARLY DEMONSTRATED THE
CONTRADICTIONS EXISTING BETWEEN LABOUR AND CAPITAL,
PARTICULARLY IN CONNECTION WITH PREPARATIONS FOR THE
ESTABLISHMENT OF A SINGLE INTERNAL MARKET WITHIN THE EEC, A
CIRCUMSTANCE WHICH DICTATES CERTAIN CONCLUSIONS FOR THE
TRADE UNION AND POLITICAL WORKING-CLASS MOVEMENTS.
COOPERATION AND PERSISTENT EFFORTS ARE NEEDED TO MAINTAIN
THE SOLIDARITY OF THE TRADE UNIONS IN THE FACE OF THIS MAJOR
CAPITALIST PUSH.

08633 STEIBEL, G.L.
AGAINST THE GRAIN: THE LIMITS OF TOLERANCE
FREEDOM AT ISSUE, (108) (MAY 89), 4.
WHEN THE AYATOLLAH KHOMEINI ISSUED HIS ASSASSINATION
EDICT AGAINST SALMAN RUSHDIE, WESTERN INTELLECTUALS

EXPRESSED ALARM AND EMPHASIZED THEIR RIGHT TO FREE SPEECH,
BUT THEY STOPPED WELL SHORT OF THE REAL ISSUE: THE HUGE GULF
IN VALUES BETWEEN KHOMEINI'S CULTURE AND WESTERN CULTURE AND
THE QUESTION OF WHICH VALUES ARE SUPERIOR. THAT ISSUE RUNS
UP AGAINST DEEP AND WELL-FOUNDED INHIBITIONS AGAINST
DENOUNCING SOMEONE ELSE'S CULTURAL BELIEFS AND RELIGIOUS
CONVICTIONS, BUT THE AYATOLLAH'S ACTION HAS MADE IT
IMPOSSIBLE TO CONTINUE IGNORING THE DIFFERENCES AND THE
THREAT THEY POSE.

08634 STEIBEL, G.L.
AGAINST THE GRAIN: TRANSPLANTING DEMOCRACY
FREEDOM AT ISSUE, (110) (SEP 89), 16.
FOR THOSE WHO LIKE THEIR POLITICS WITH A DASH OF IRONY,
AMERICA'S BATTLE WITH ITSELF OVER CHINA IS A TREAT. LIBERALS
ARE DEMANDING THE HARSHEST OF SANCTIONS AGAINST THE CHINESE
COMMUNIST TYRANTS, IN LANGUAGE THAT WOULD DELIGHT THE OLD
CHINA LOBBY. CONSERVATIVES ARE THE ACCOMMODATORS, DECRYING
THE BORN-AGAIN COLD WAR RHETORIC, COMPLAINING ABOUT IDEOLOGY
GETTING OUT OF HAND.

08635 STEIF, W.
A SAVINGS AND LOAN CRISIS, FUNDAMENTALIST STYLE
MULTINATIONAL MONITOR, 10(3) (MAR 89), 6.
ONE OF THE TRICKIEST PROBLEMS FACING THE GOVERNMENT OF
EGYPTIAN PRESIDENT HOSNI MUBARAK IS HOW TO HANDLE THE
PHENOMENON OF ISLAMIC INVESTMENT COMPANIES. THESE COMPANIES
BEGAN TO APPEAR ABOUT A DECADE AGO AS EGYPTIAN SAVINGS GREW,
SWELLED BY CONTRIBUTIONS FROM EXPATRIATES WORKING IN THE OIL-
RICH NATIONS OF THE ARAB WORLD. THE COMPANIES PROMISE TO
INVEST FUNDS DEPOSITED WITH THEM IN ACCORDANCE WITH ISLAMIC
STRICTURES AGAINST PAYMENT OF INTEREST. BUT THEY ARE
UNREGULATED AND ARE RUMORED TO BE CONDUITS FOR BLACK
MARKETEERING, EXPORT OF CAPITAL, MONEY LAUNDERING, AND
PYRAMID SCHEMES THAT SKIM OFF NEW DEPOSITORS' FUNDS TO REPAY
OLD DEPOSITORS.

08636 STEIF, W.
PARAGUAY IN TRANSITION
MULTINATIONAL MONITOR, 10(7-8) (JUL 89), 25-27.
THE AUTHOR LOOKS AT THE RULE OF GENERAL ALFREDO
STROESSNER IN PARAGUAY, AT HIS OUSTER IN FEBRUARY 1989, AND
AT THE ARCHITECT OF STROESSNER'S DOWNFALL.

08637 STEIF, W.
PERONISM IN A TROUBLED ECONOMY
MULTINATIONAL MONITOR, 10(7-8) (JUL 89), 22-24.
IN JUNE 1989, ARGENTINE PRESIDENT RAUL ALFONSIN STEPPED
DOWN, SIX MONTHS BEFORE HIS TERM OFFICIALLY ENDED. WHEN HE
WAS ELECTED IN 1983, ALFONSIN WAS EXPECTED TO HEAL NATIONAL
WOUNDS, PUT ARGENTINA ON A DEMOCRATIC FOOTING, AND LEAD THE
COUNTRY TO PROSPERITY. HIS ADMINISTRATION DID MAKE PROGRESS
IN RECTIFYING SOME OF THE MILITARY'S ABUSES, BUT HE ACHIEVED
LITTLE IN THE ECONOMIC SECTOR. THE 1989 VICTORY OF THE
PERONIST PARTY'S PRESIDENTIAL CANDIDATE, CARLOS SAUL MENEM
REPUDIATED ALFONSIN'S POLICIES. IT WAS ALSO SEEN AS EVIDENCE
THAT A FOLKLORIC FASCISM AND A DEEP ANTAGONISM TO THE UNITED
STATES LIVE ON IN ARGENTINA.

08638 STEIF, W.
URUGUAY'S ECONOMIC MALAISE
MULTINATIONAL MONITOR, 11(10) (OCT 89), 21-23.
URUGUAY'S DEPENDENCE ON ITS NEIGHBORS, ESPECIALLY
ARGENTINA, IS ONE OF THE MAJOR PROBLEMS FACING URUGUAYAN
PRESIDENT JULIO MARIA SANGUINETTI. SINCE TAKING OFFICE IN
1985, SANGUINETTI HAS STRIVED TO DIVERSIFY THE COUNTRY'S
INTERNATIONAL TRADE TO LESSEN ITS ECONOMIC DEPENDENCE ON ITS
NEIGHBORS. BUT ENTRY INTO THE WIDER WORLD MARKET HAS HAD
SOME ADVERSE EFFECTS. REDUCING TARIFFS HAS CAUSED SOME
AMERICAN INVESTMENT TO PULL OUT, AND OPENING THE ECONOMY HAS
HURT URUGUAYAN PRODUCTION OF CONSUMER PRODUCTS, SUCH AS SOAP
AND COOKING OIL. AFTER IMPROVING DURING THE FIRST YEARS OF
SANGUINETTI'S ADMINISTRATION, THE ECONOMY NOW FACES SERIOUS
PROBLEMS.

08639 STEIGERWALD, R.
THE DIALECTICS OF NEW THINKING AND ACTION
WORLD MARXIST REVIEW, 31(11) (NOV 88), 87-92.
THE GAP BETWEEN TECHNOLOGICAL AND SOCIAL PROGRESS IS THE
SOURCE OF NUMEROUS GLOBAL PROBLEMS WHICH CAN ONLY BE
RESOLVED THROUGH JOINT EFFORT. THE THREAT TO HUMAN SURVIVAL
DEMANDS THAT WE TACKLE THEM WITHOUT WAITING FOR THE
WORLDWIDE VICTORY OF SOCIALISM. IT FOLLOWS THAT THE
COMPETITION BETWEEN CAPITALIST AND SOCIALIST COUNTRIES MAKES
IT IMPERATIVE FOR THE TWO SYSTEMS TO COOPERATE.

08640 STEIN, H.
GOVERNING THE $5 TRILLION ECONOMY
BROOKINGS REVIEW, 7(2) (SPR 89), 16-23.
DISCUSSION OF FEDERAL BUDGET POLICY IN THE USA HAS
FALLEN TO AN ABYSMALLY LOW LEVEL. FEW PLANS FOR DEALING WITH
THE DEFICIT TAKE INTO ACCOUNT THE BUDGET'S EFFECT ON
NATIONAL OBJECTIVES. IN THIS ESSAY, THE AUTHOR PROPOSES THAT
THE $5 TRILLION GNP SHOULD BE BUDGETED BEFORE BUDGETING THE

$1 TRILLION THAT THE FEDERAL GOVERNMENT SPENDS.

08641 STEIN, H.
PROBLEMS AND NON-PROBLEMS IN THE AMERICAN ECONOMY
PUBLIC INTEREST, (97) (FAL 89), 56-70.
ALTHOUGH MANY LEADERS BELIEVE THE "TWIN DEFICITS" ARE
THE MOST PRESSING PROBLEMS OF THE AMERICAN ECONOMY, THE
AUTHOR ARGUES THAT THE EMPHASIS ON THEM IS A MISTAKE. THE
BUDGET DEFICIT IS BEST REGARDED AS PART OF A LARGER PROBLEM,
WHICH IS THAT THE USA DOES NOT WISELY ALLOCATE ITS LARGE
NATIONAL INCOME AMONG COMPETING USES. SPECIFICALLY, IT
ALLOCATES TOO LITTLE TO PROVIDING FOR THE FUTURE AND TOO
MUCH TO PRESENT CONSUMPTION. THE TRADE DEFICIT IS NOT A
PROBLEM, EVEN THOUGH IT DRIVES A GOOD DEAL OF THINKING ABOUT
POLICY IN THE USA AND ALSO SEEMS TO GREATLY AFFECT THE
ATTITUDE OF THE REST OF THE WORLD.

08642 STEIN, J.G.
GETTING TO THE TABLE: PROCESSES OF INTERNATIONAL
PRENEGOTIATION
INTERNATIONAL JOURNAL, XLIV(2) (SPR 89), 231-236.
THE PROCESS OF PRENEGOTIATION BEGINS WHEN ONE OR MORE
PARTIES CONSIDERS NEGOTIATION AS A POLICY OPTION AND
COMMUNICATES THIS INTENTION TO OTHER PARTIES. PRENEGOTIATION
ENDS WHEN THE PARTIES AGREE TO FORMAL NEGOTIATIONS OR WHEN
ONE PARTY ABANDONS THE CONSIDERATION OF NEGOTIATION AS A
POLICY OPTION. PRENEGOTIATION DEFINES THE BOUNDARIES, SHAPES
THE AGENDA, AND AFFECTS THE OUTCOME OF NEGOTIATION. IT MAY
HAVE IMPORTANT CONSEQUENCES EVEN IF THE PARTICIPANTS DO NOT
GET AS FAR AS THE BARGAINING TABLE.

08643 STEIN, J.G.
GETTING TO THE TABLE: THE TRIGGERS, STAGES, FUNCTIONS, AND
CONSEQUENCES OF PRENEGOTIATION
INTERNATIONAL JOURNAL, XLIV(2) (SPR 89), 475-504.
COMPARATIVE EXAMINATION OF SEVERAL CASES OF
PRENEGOTIATION ISOLATES A NUMBER OF IMPORTANT ATTRIBUTES IN
THE PROCESS OF GETTING TO THE TABLE. IN THIS PAPER, THE
AUTHOR FIRST CONSIDERS THE FACTORS THAT TRIGGER ACTIVE
CONSIDERATION OF NEGOTIATION AS ONE AMONG AN ARRAY OF
OPTIONS. THEN SHE EXPLORES THE PATTERN OF PROGRESS THROUGH
THE STAGES OF PRENEGOTIATION AS LEADERS APPROACH AND AVOID
THE BARGAINING TABLE. NEXT SHE TURNS TO THE FUNCTIONS THAT A
PROCESS OF PRENEGOTIATION PERFORMS. BY COMPARING CASES, SHE
ATTEMPTS TO IDENTIFY THE CONDITIONS FOR GETTING TO THE TABLE.
FINALLY, SHE EXPLORES THE LARGER SIGNIFICANCE OF
PRENEGOTIATION AS A PROCESS OF LEARNING AND CONFLICT
MANAGEMENT.

08644 STEIN, J.G.
PRENEGOTIATION IN THE ARAB-ISRAELI CONFLICT: THE PARADOXES
OF SUCCESS AND FAILURE
INTERNATIONAL JOURNAL, XLIV(2) (SPR 89), 410-441.
PRENEGOTIATION HAS BEEN EXTRAORDINARILY IMPORTANT IN THE
ARAB-ISRAELI CONFLICT. THROUGHOUT MUCH OF ITS HISTORY,
DIRECT CONTACT BETWEEN THE PRINCIPAL PARTIES HAS BEEN
IMPOSSIBLE AND FORMAL NEGOTIATION VERY DIFFICULT, EVEN WHEN
DONE THROUGH INTERMEDIARIES. THIS STUDY REVIEWS TWO CASES OF
PRENEGOTIATION THAT WERE BRIEFLY INTERRUPTED BY A PERIOD OF
NEGOTIATION. THE FIRST INVOLVED THE USA, ISRAEL, EGYPT,
JORDAN, SAUDI ARABIA, SYRIA, THE PLO, AND THE USSR FROM
JANUARY TO NOVEMBER 1977. THE SECOND BEGAN IN JANUARY 1978
AMONG THE USA, EGYPT, ISRAEL, JORDAN, AND SAUDI ARABIA AND
TERMINATED IN AUGUST 1978.

08645 STEIN, K.W.
THE PALESTINIAN UPRISING AND THE SHULTZ INITIATIVE
MIDDLE EAST REVIEW, XXI(2) (WIN 89), 13-20.
IN EARLY 1988, THE REAGAN ADMINISTRATION REACTED TO
EVENTS IN THE MIDDLE EAST BY PROPOSING THAT THE STALLED ARAB-
ISRAELI NEGOTIATING PROCESS BE REACTIVATED. THE PALESTINIAN
UPRISING HAD PROMPTED THE OTHERWISE RELUCTANT ADMINISTRATION
TO TRY TO REVIVE ACTIVE DIPLOMACY AS THE ROAD TO PEACE. THE
SHULTZ INITIATIVE WAS EXCEPTIONAL BECAUSE THE REAGAN
ADMINISTRATION HAD PREVIOUSLY OPERATED ON THE PREMISE THAT
IT WOULD STUDIOUSLY AVOID INVOLVEMENT IN THE NEGOTIATING
PROCESS UNTIL IT FOUND THE REGIONAL ACTORS SERIOUSLY READY
TO ENGAGE ON ISSUES OF SUBSTANCE.

08646 STEIN, R.M.
MARKET MAXIMIZATION OF INDIVIDUAL PREFERENCES AND
METROPOLITAN MUNICIPAL SERVICE RESPONSIBILITY
URBAN AFFAIRS QUARTERLY, 25(1) (SEP 89), 86-116.
THE ASSIGNMENT OF FUNCTIONAL RESPONSIBILITY IN THE
AMERICAN FEDERAL SYSTEM IS EXAMINED FROM THE PERSPECTIVE OF
THE MUNICIPAL GOVERNMENT. TIEBOUT'S MODEL OF MARKET
MAXIMIZATION OF INDIVIDUAL PREFERENCES IS CONTRASTED WITH
THE MORE RECENT THEORIES OF BUCHANAN, PETERSON, AND MILLER.
THE EXPLANATION THAT THE HISTORICAL ORIGINS OF THE CITY AND
THE PERMEABILITY OF ITS BORDERS STRUCTURE THE SCOPE AND
LEVEL OF ITS SERVICE RESPONSIBILITIES IS TESTED. THE
FINDINGS HAVE SIGNIFICANT IMPLICATIONS FOR THE MODE OF
MUNICIPAL SERVICE PROVISION AND THE POTENTIAL FOR MUNICIPAL
GOVERNMENTS TO OPERATE OUTSIDE OF THE CONSTRAINTS IMPOSED ON
THEM BY THEIR POSITION IN THE AMERICAN FEDERAL SYSTEM.

08647 STEINBERG, D.I.
CRISIS IN BURMA
CURRENT HISTORY, 88(537) (APR 89), 185-188, 196-198.
BURMA'S CRISIS IS NEITHER WHOLLY POLITICAL NOR MERELY
ECONOMIC. IT IS THE RESULT OF POOR POLICIES, INSENSITIVITY
TO DOMESTIC NEEDS, VIOLENCE, POLITICAL ARROGANCE, AND DECEIT.
ITS ROOTS CAN BE TRACED TO THE ADVENT OF MILITARY POWER IN
BURMA, TO TRADITIONAL ECONOMIC POLICIES AND PROBLEMS, AND TO
BURMESE INSECURITY IN A WORLD VIEWED AS POLITICALLY AND
ECONOMICALLY HOSTILE.

08648 STEINBERG, G.M.
THE 1988 ISRAELI ELECTIONS: THE DEADLOCK CONTINUES
MIDSTREAM, XXXV(1) (JAN 89), 3-7.
FOR ALMOST A DECADE, THE ISRAELI ELECTORATE HAS BEEN
EVENLY DIVIDED, AND THE 1988 ELECTIONS DID NOT RESULT IN A
SIGNIFICANT CHANGE. THE DIFFERENCE BETWEEN LABOR AND LIKUD
WAS A SINGLE PERCENTAGE POINT AND, WITH THEIR RESPECTIVE
ALLIED PARTIES, THE RIGHT WING AND LEFT WING BLOCS WERE
STILL EVENLY MATCHED. EFFORTS, PARTICULARLY BY LABOR, TO
BREAK THIS DEADLOCK BY STRESSING POLICY DIFFERENCES WITH THE
LIKUD REGARDING THE PEACE PROCESS FAILED TO ALTER THE
STRUCTURE OF THE ISRAELI POLITICAL DIVISION.

08649 STEINBERG, M.
CHANGE DESPITE DUALITY
NEW OUTLOOK, 32(1 (287)) (JAN 89), 15-17.
THE PLO'S DECISION TO DECLARE A PALESTINIAN STATE MARKED
A CHANGE IN THE ORGANIZATION'S PRIORITIES. SINCE 1974, THE
PLO HAS ARGUED THAT THE PALESTINIAN STATE MUST RESULT FROM
THE ISRAELI WITHDRAWAL FROM THE WEST BANK AND GAZA STRIP.
THE DECISION TO ESTABLISH A STATE WHILE ISRAEL IS STILL IN
THE TERRITORIES INDICATES THE PLO'S INTENTION OF USING THE
DECLARATION OF STATEHOOD TO PROMPT ISRAEL'S WITHDRAWAL.
THERE CAN BE NO DOUBT THAT THE UPRISING IN THE TERRITORIES
WAS CRUCIAL IN THE DECISION TO ADVANCE THE TIMETABLE.

08650 STEINBERG, M.
THE DEMOGRAPHIC DIMENSION OF THE STRUGGLE WITH ISRAEL --
AS SEEN BY THE PLO
JERUSALEM JOURNAL OF INTERNATIONAL RELATIONS, 11(4) (DEC
89), 27-51.
THE PLO HAS COME TO ASSUME THAT ITS ADVERSARY'S
ACKNOWLEDGEMENT OF ITS DEMOGRAPHIC PREDICAMENT SIGNIFIES A
POTENTIAL STRONG POINT FOR THE PLO CAUSE, WITHIN THE PLO,
HOWEVER, THERE IS UNCERTAINTY ABOUT THE MATTER, AND HOPES
ARE MIXED WITH FEARS. THIS ARTICLE EXPLORES THE HISTORICAL
CONTEXT: THE ORIGINAL FEAR OF ZIONIST DEMOGRAPHY, AND THEN
THE REVERSAL: AN AWARENESS OF THE POTENTIAL ADVANTAGES OF
PALESTINIAN DEMOGRAPHY. IT THEN EXPLORES THE DEMOGRAPHIC
FACTOR UNDER THE TEST OF REALITY

08651 STEINBERG, M.
THE PRAGMATIC STREAM OF THOUGHT WITHIN THE PLO ACCORDING
TO KHALID AL-HASAN
JERUSALEM JOURNAL OF INTERNATIONAL RELATIONS, 11(1) (MAR
89), 37-57.
KHALID AL-HASAN IS THE FORMULATOR OF THE PRAGMATIC
STREAM OF THOUGHT IN THE PLO. AT THE BASE OF HIS CONCEPTION
LIES THE AWARENESS THAT POLITICS IS ALWAYS THE MAKING OF
CHOICES IN THE CONTEXT OF CONSTRAINTS AND THAT IN EXCHANGE
FOR OBTAINING PART OF PALESTINE THE PALESTINIANS WILL HAVE
TO CONCEDE ANOTHER PART.

08652 STEINBERG, S.
THE UNDERCLASS: A CASE OF COLORBLINDNESS
NEW POLITICS, 11(3) (SUM 89), 42-60.
BY VIRTUE OF THEIR UNIQUE OPPRESSION, BLACKS HAVE
HISTORICAL AND MORAL CLAIM TO HAVE THEIR GRIEVANCES
REDRESSED BEFORE THOSE OF OTHER GROUPS. BLACKS SHOULD NOT
HAVE TO QUEUE UP WITH THE OTHER DISPLACED WORKERS IN THE
NATION'S RUST BELT. FOR THEIR UNDERCLASS STATUS IS NOT
MERELY RESULT OF PLANT SHUTDOWNS. IT IS THE END PRODUCT OF
THREE CENTURIES OF RACIAL OPPRESSION. THE BLACK UNDERCLASS
REPRESENTS NOT JUST ECONOMIC DISLOCATION, INCOME
MALDISTRIBUTION, AND SOCIAL INJUSTICE; IT REPRESENTS ALL
THAT, AND RACISM. THE BLACK UNDERCLASS IS THE PRESENTDAY
MANIFESTATION OF AMERICA'S GREATEST CRIME, AND IS A BLOT ON
AMERICAN DEMOCRACY. AT STAKE IS NOT JUST SOCIAL AND ECONOMIC
JUSTICE, BUT THE VERY SOUL OF THE NATION.

08653 STEINBERGER, P.J.
A FALLACY IN RAWLS'S THEORY OF JUSTICE
REVIEW OF POLITICS, 51(1) (WIN 89), 55-69.
AN IMPORTANT FEATURE OF RAWLS'S THEORY OF JUSTICE IS THE
PUTATIVE SEPARATION OF JUSTICE AND DESERT. IT IS SHOWN THAT
RAWLS IN FACT PRESUPPOSES A QUITE STRONG THEORY OF DESERT
WHICH PROVIDES THE KEY JUSTIFICATION FOR THE ORIGINAL
POSITION. IT IS FURTHER ARGUED THAT THE THEORY OF DESERT HAS
IMPLICATIONS FOR DISTRIBUTIVE SHARES WHICH CONTRADICT THOSE
OF RAWLSIAN JUSTICE IN GENERAL AND THE DIFFERENCE PRINCIPLE
IN PARTICULAR. FINALLY, IT IS CLAIMED THAT THIS

CONTRADICTION SEEMS TO RESIST ANY KIND OF EASY RESOLUTION SINCE THE THEORY OF JUSTICE RESTS UPON, HENCE REQUIRES, THE THEORY OF DESERT.

08654 STEINBERGER, P.J.
RULING: GUARDIANS AND PHILOSOPHER-KINGS
AMERICAN POLITICAL SCIENCE REVIEW, 83(4) (DEC 89), 1027-1226.
ACCORDING TO SOME ACCOUNTS, PLATO VIEWS RULING AS A PHILOSOPHICAL ACTIVITY; ACCORDING TO OTHERS, HE UNDERSTANDS IT TO BE A CRAFT. GIVEN THE APPARENT DISCREPANCY BETWEEN PHILOSOPHICAL AND TECHNICAL ANDEAVOR, IT SEEMS THAT THE TWO INTERPRETATIONS CANNOT BOTH BE CORRECT. THE ISSUE IS EXPLORED IN LIGHT OF THE RELATIONSHIP BETWEEN GUARDIANS AND PHILOSOPHER-KINGS AS IT MANIFESTS ITSELF IN THE BASIC STRUCTURE OF THE REPUBLIC AND ALSO WITH RESPECT TO QUESTIONS OF EDUCATION, CHARACTER, AND DECEIT.

08655 STEINBRUNER, J.D.
THE PROSPECT OF COOPERATIVE SECURITY
BROOKINGS REVIEW, 7(1) (WIN 89), 53-68.
PRESSURES IN BOTH THE UNITED STATES AND THE SOVIET UNION ARE PUSHING THE TWO NATIONS TOWARDS CONSIDERATION OF COOPERATIVE SECURITY MEASURES. REDUCING AND STABILIZING STRATEGIC AND CONVENTIONAL FORCES WOULD BE ONE STEP ON THE WAY TO A MORE SECURE WORLD.

08656 STEINHOFF, P.G.
HIHACKERS, BOMBERS, AND BANK ROBBERS: MANAGERIAL STYLE IN THE JAPANESE RED ARMY
JOURNAL OF ASIAN STUDIES, 48(4) (NOV 89), 724-740.
THIS STUDY EXAMINES THE ORGANIZATIONAL DEVELOPMENT OF SEKIGUN (RED ARMY), A GROUP WHOSE MEMBERS CAME OUT OF THE MAINSTREAM OF JAPANESE YOUTH BUT PLACED THEMSELVES IN CONFLICT WITH BOTH STATE AND SOCIETY. THIS ANALYSIS OF SEKIGUN IS BASED ON A WIDE RANGE OF WRITTEN DOCUMENTS PRODUCED BY THE ORGANIZATION, AUTOBIOGRAPHICAL ACCOUNTS AND THEORETICAL WORKS PUBLISHED BY SEKIGUN MEMBERS, TRIAL DOCUMENTS STEMMING FROM THE ARREST AND PROSECUTION OF SEKIGUN MEMBERS, POLICE REPORTS, SECONDARY WORKS BY JOURNALISTS AND OTHER OBSERVERS, AND INTERVIEWS WITH SEKIGUN MEMBERS AND ASSOCIATES CONDUCTED BY THE AUTHOR FROM 1983 TO 1989.

08657 STELZER, I. M.
THIRD WORLD DEADBEATS
AMERICAN SPECTATOR, 22(4) (APR 89), 34-35.
LATIN AMERICA'S DEBT PROBLEMS RESULT FROM POOR ECONOMIC POLICIES THAT PRODUCE BLOATED WELFARE STATES DOMINATED BY INEFFICIENT STATE-OWNED ENTERPRISES AND CORRUPT BUREAUCRACIES. IT WOULD BE FOOLISH FOR THE USA TO FLING GOOD MONEY AFTER BAD BY FORGIVING PAST THIRD WORLD DEBT.

08658 STELZER, I.M.
CORPORATISM OUSTS REAGANOMICS
AMERICAN SPECTATOR, 22(5) (MAY 89), 31-34.
THE UNITED STATES IS SEEING THE DEVELOPMENT OF AN "INDUSTRIAL POLICY," A LONGLOVED LIBERAL EUPHEMISM FOR ECONOMIC PLANNING. JUST WHEN MIKHAIL GORBACHEV IS ADMITTING THAT HIS BUREAUCRATS AREN'T SMART ENOUGH TO DIRECT THE FLOW OF RESEARCH AND INVESTMENT FUNDS EFFICIENTLY, PRESIDENT BUSH IS PERMITTING THEIR AMERICAN COUNTERPARTS TO UNDERTAKE JUST SUCH A ROLE. MOST LIKELY, GOVERNMENT-FINANCED CONSORTIUMS WILL EMERGE, INJECTING GOVERNMENT INTO THE HIGH-TECH BUSINESS. THIS WILL BRING TO POWER A NEW SET OF DECISION-MAKERS: THE BUREAUCRATS AND POLITICIANS WHO HAVE DEMONSTRATED THEIR MANAGEMENT SKILLS BY RUNNING THE BUSINESS THEY ARE SUPPOSED TO KNOW SOMETHING ABOUT - GOVERNMENT - AT A $170 BILLION ANNUAL LOSS.

08659 STENT, A.
FRANCO-SOVIET RELATIONS FROM DEGAULLE TO MITTERAND
FRENCH POLITICS AND SOCIETY, 7(1) (WIN 89), 14-27.
SOVIET TIES WITH FRANCE, MORE THAN THOSE WITH ANY OTHER COUNTRY IN THE POSTWAR ERA, HAVE BEEN INFLUENCED BY THE VISION OF ONE INDIVIDUAL-GENERAL CHARLES DE GAULLE. HE ESTABLISHED THE STRUCTURE OF POSTWAR FRANCO-SOVIET RELATIONS, AND HIS APPROCH AND SUCCESSES BECAME THE STANDARD AGAINST WHICH SUBSEQUENT RELATIONS WOULD BE JUDGED. OF COURSE, THE KREMLIN HAS ALSO INFLUENCED THE DEVELOPMENT OF RELATIONS BETWEEN MOSCOW AND PARIS. BUT FRANCE IS ONLY ONE OF SEVERAL WEST EUROPEAN COUNTRIES OF SIGNIFICANCE TO THE USSR, AND IT HAS BY NO MEANS ALWAYS BEEN THE MOST IMPORTANT ONE. BY CONTRAST, THE SOVIET UNION HAS PLAYED A MAJOR ROLE IN THE RESTORATION OF FRENCH CREDIBILITY AND INFLUENCE IN THE WORLD AFTER 1945.

08660 STEPAN-NORRIS, J.; ZEITLIN, M.
"WHO GETS THE BIRD?" OR, HOW THE COMMUNISTS WON POWER AND TRUST IN AMERICA'S UNIONS: THE RELATIVE AUTONOMY OF INTRACLASS POLITICAL STRUGGLES
AMERICAN SOCIOLOGICAL REVIEW, 54(4) (AUG 89), 503-523.
DO INTRACLASS STRUGGLES SHAPE THE POLITICAL TERRAIN ON WHICH ENSUING STRUGGLES, WITHIN AND BETWEEN CLASSES, ARE

FOUGHT AND RESOLVED? THE ATTEMPT TO ANSWER THIS QUESTION FOCUSES ON THE RIVALRY AMONG THE FACTIONS AND PARTIES INVOLVED IN ORGANIZING AMERICAN INDUSTRIAL WORKERS FROM THE LATE 1930S FORWARD, THE POLITICAL PRACTICES OF THE COMMUNISTS AND THEIR RIVALS DETERMINED WHICH POLITICAL CAMP WON POWER IN THE NEW CIO UNIONS. A LOGIT MODEL SHOWS THAT TWO ENSEMBLES OF POLITICAL PRACTICES "LOADED THE HISTORICAL DICE" IN FAVOR OF THE COMMUNISTS. THE CHANCES THAT COMMUNISTS WOULD WIN UNION LEADERSHIP WERE FAR HIGHER: FIRST, IF THE UNION HAD SECEDED FROM THE AFL AND JOINED THE CIO FROM BELOW, IN AN INSURGENT WORKERS' MOVEMENT, RATHER THAN FROM ABOVE, IN A REVOLT OF ITS TOP OFFICERS; AND SECOND, IF THE UNION HAD BEEN ORGANIZED INDEPENDENTLY, RATHER THAN BY A CIO "ORGANIZING COMMITTEE." TWO OTHER POLITICAL PRACTICES INDIRECTLY FAVORED THE COMMUNISTS: EARLIER RED UNION ORGANIZING IN THE INDUSTRY (ALTHOUGH ITS EFFECTS WERE CONTRADICTORY) AND FORMING THE UNION AS AN AMALGAMATED RATHER THAN AS A UNITARY ORGANIZATION.

08661 STEPHENS, E.H.
CAPITALIST DEVELOPMENT AND DEMOCRACY IN SOUTH AMERICA
POLITICS AND SOCIETY, 17(3) (SEP 89), 281-352.
THE AUTHOR ENDEAVORS TO ANALYZE THE EMERGENCE AND DECLINE OF DEMOCRACY IN SOUTH AMERICA. HER ANALYSIS DIFFERS FROM OTHERS IN THAT SHE DRAWS ON THE EXPERIENCE OF ALL 10 MAJOR SOUTH AMERICAN COUNTRIES SINCE INDEPENDENCE AND USES THE SORT OF COMPARATIVE HISTORICAL FRAMEWORK USUALLY RESERVED FOR CASE STUDIES. SHE ALSO INTEGRATES THE ANALYSIS OF STRUCTURAL VARIABLES WITH THAT OF POLITICAL INSTITUTIONS, STUDYING THEIR INTERACTION RATHER THAN ASSIGNING PRIMACY TO ONE OR THE OTHER. A BROAD RANGE OF VARIABLES IS CONSIDERED, INCLUDING THE PROCESS OF CONSOLIDATION OF STATE POWER, THE ROLE OF THE STATE IN SHAPING CIVIL SOCIETY, AND THE NATURE OF POLITICAL PARTY SYSTEMS.

08662 STEPHENS, G.
21ST CENTURY CRIME NEEDS PROACTIVE POLICIES
AMERICAN CITY AND COUNTY, 104(9) (SEP 89), 38, 40, 42.
THE UNITED STATES COULD ENTER THE 21ST CENTURY WITH A REVITALIZED, RELATIVELY CRIME-FREE SOCIETY IF LEADERS MAKE THE BEST CHOICES AND TAKE ADVANTAGE OF THE MOST PROMISING OPPORTUNITIES TO CREATE A SAFE, SANE SOCIETY. BUT THE REACTIVE, RETRIBUTIONIST PHILOSOPHY OF TODAY'S CRIMINAL JUSTICE SYSTEM MUST CHANGE BEFORE THERE CAN BE ANY HOPE FOR A NEW AGE. WAITING FOR CRIME TO OCCUR AND THEN TRYING TO CAPTURE AND PUNISH THE OFFENDER IS INEFFICIENT, INEFFECTIVE, AND WASTEFUL. WHAT IS NEEDED IS A PROACTIVE APPROACH THAT PERMEATES THE SYSTEM FROM LAW TO ENFORCEMENT TO ADJUDICATION TO CORRECTIONS.

08663 STEPHENS, G.R.; PARSONS, K.T.
RICH STATES, POOR STATES: AN ADDENDUM
STATE AND LOCAL GOVERNMENT REVIEW, 21(2) (SPR 89), 50-59.
A PERENNIAL PROBLEM IN FEDERAL SYSTEMS IS THE MALDISTRIBUTION OF TAXABLE RESOURCES WHICH DENIES SOME STATES THE ABILITY TO FINANCE A BASIC LEVEL OF PUBLIC SERVICES. FEDERAL EXPENDITURES IN THE UNITED STATES CONSTITUTE ONE-FOURTH OF GNP; DEFENSE AND GRANTS EXPLAIN MORE THAN FOUR-FIFTHS OF INTERSTATE VARIATION BOTH IN PER CAPITA FEDERAL SPENDING AND IN STATE AND LOCAL TAX CAPACITY AND REVENUES. THE FEDERAL GOVERNMENT SPENDS MORE MONEY IN TAX-RICH STATES AND THIS SPENDING IS DIRECTLY RELATED TO INTERSTATE VARIATION IN BUSINESS TAX CAPACITY WHICH, IN TURN, IS A MAJOR DETERMINANT OF DIFFERENCES IN OVERALL STATE TAX CAPACITY AND REVENUE COLLECTION. LACKING A REDISTRIBUTIVE GRANT SYSTEM THAT PLACES A FLOOR UNDER THE TAX CAPACITY OF POORER STATES, FEDERAL SPENDING PATTERNS ONLY EXACERBATE THESE DIFFERENCES-THE RICH GET RICHER AND THE POOR, POORER.

08664 STEPHENS, G.R.
THE LEAST GLORIOUS, MOST LOCAL, MOST TRIVIAL, HOMELY, PROVINCIAL, AND MOST IGNORED FORM OF LOCAL GOVERNMENT
URBAN AFFAIRS QUARTERLY, 24(4) (JUN 89), 501-512.
SCHOLARS IN THE AREA OF STATE AND LOCAL GOVERNMENT, FOR THE MOST PART, IGNORE LOCAL GOVERNMENTS CALLED TOWNS AND TOWNSHIPS, WRITE THEM OFF AS INSIGNIFICANT, ASSUME THEY WILL WITHER AWAY AND DISAPPEAR OVER THE NEXT FEW YEARS. YET, THESE PRESUMABLY INSIGNIFICANT LOCAL GOVERNMENTS SERVE 51 MILLION RESIDENTS, NEARLY HALF THE POPULATION OF TOWNSHIP STATES, AND ARE OF INCREASING IMPORTANCE AS LOCAL GOVERNING BODIES IN URBAN AND SUBURBAN AREAS. THE ACTIVITIES OF TOWNSHIP GOVERNMENTS RANGE FROM PROVIDING VERY LIMITED SERVICE TO ACTING AS FULL-SCALE MUNICIPAL CORPORATIONS THAT PROVIDE ALL LOCAL PUBLIC SCHOOLS AND EVEN COUNTY-TYPE SERVICES.

08665 STEPHENS, J.D.
DEMOCRATIC TRANSITION AND BREAKDOWN IN WESTERN EUROPE, 1870-1939: A TEST OF THE MOORE THESIS
AMERICAN JOURNAL OF SOCIOLOGY, 94(5) (MAR 89), 1019-1077.
BARRINGTON MOORE'S "SOCIAL ORIGINS OF DICTATORSHIP AND DEMOCRACY" IS WIDELY REGARDED AS A CONTEMPORARY CLASSIC, YET THERE HAVE BEEN FEW ATTEMPTS TO EVALUATE THE VALIDITY OF HIS ARGUMENT ON A LARGE NUMBER OF COMPARABLE CASES. THIS ARTICLE

MAKES SUCH AN ATTEMPT WITH ALL WESTERN EUROPEAN COUNTRIES EXPERIENCING DEMOCRATIC RULE BETWEEN 1870 AND 1939. IT SEEKS (1) TO EXPLAIN WHAT STRUCTURAL AND HISTORICAL FEATURES DISTINGUISH THE BREAKDOWN CASES FROM THOSE THAT REMAINED DEMOCRATIC AND (2) TO TRACE THE PROCESS OF CLASS COALITION FORMATION IN THE TRANSITION TO DEMOCRACY AND THE SUBSEQUENT BREAKDOWN. MOORE'S THESIS DOES FIT, WITH SOME MODIFICATION.

08666 STERN, M.
    JOHN F. KENNEDY AND CIVIL RIGHTS: FROM CONGRESS TO THE
        PRESIDENCY
    PRESIDENTIAL STUDIES QUARTERLY, 19(4) (FAL 89), 797-824.
        THIS ESSAY EXAMINES KENNEDY'S RECORD IN REGARDS TO CIVIL
    RIGHTS. IT EXPLORES HIS FAILURE TO JOIN THE 1954 CENSURE OF
    JOSEPH MCCARTHY WHICH PUT HIM AT ODDS WITH THE LIBERALS; HIS
    OPPOSITION TO THE EISENHOWER SUPPORTED CIVIL RIGHTS ACT; AND
    THE INCIDENTAL CALL TO CORETTA KING TO EXPRESS EMPATHY FOR
    HER JAILED HUSBAND, WHICH SHIFTED THE BLACK VOTE INTO THE
    DEMOCRATIC COLUMN. IN MAY 1961 KENNEDY DID NOT THINK IT
    NECESSARY TO ENACT CIVIL RIGHTS LEGISLATION AND THE ESSAY
    CONCLUDES THAT KENNEDY'S PUBLIC POSITION ON CIVIL RIGHTS WAS,
    ALMOST ALWAYS, SIMPLY A REFLECTION OF HIS PERCEPTION OF ITS
    STRATEGIC VALUE TO HIM IN HIS PURSUIT OF OFFICE.

08667 STERN, M.
    PRESIDENTIAL STRATEGIES AND CIVIL RIGHTS: EISENHOWER, THE
        EARLY YEARS, 1952-54
    PRESIDENTIAL STUDIES QUARTERLY, 19(4) (FAL 89), 769-796.
        THIS ESSAY REGARDING CIVIL RIGHTS PRESENTS A DISCERNING
    PORTRAYAL OF THE CONSIDERATIONS WHICH PROMPTED EISENHOWER'S
    DECISION TO RUN FOR THE PRESIDENCY IN 1952. IT THAT
    EISENHOWER BECAME THE MOST SKILLED POLITICALLY OF THE MODERN
    PRESIDENTS WITH THE POSSIBLE EXCEPTION OF FDR. IT EXAMINES
    THE SKILL WITH WHICH HE ACCOMPLISHED MUCH IN THE CIVIL
    RIGHTS AREA. FAR MORE THAN HE IS GIVEN CREDIT FOR, AND GIVES
    SPECIFIC EXMPLES. IT CONCLUDES THAT EISENHOWER'S STEWARDSHIP
    AS PARTY LEADER AND PRESIDENT WAS A VERY SUCCESSFUL AND WELL
    CRAFTED BALANCING ACT OF PARTY BUILDING AND POLICY
    LEADERSHIP.

08668 STERN, P.
    ANTIFOUNDATIONALISM AND PLATO'S PHAEDO
    REVIEW OF POLITICS, 51(2) (SPR 89), 190-217.
        THE CLAIM MADE BY ANTIFOUNDATIONALIST THINKERS SUCH AS
    NIETZSCHE, HEIDEGGER, AND MORE RECENTLY RICHARD RORTY IS
    THAT THE SEARCH FOR A STANDARD OR FOUNDATION FOR OUR MORAL
    AND POLITICAL JUDGMENTS INEVITABLY ARRIVES AT A DISTORTING
    REDUCTIVISM. THIS RADICAL CLAIM, IF TRUE, MAKES DUBIOUS THE
    VERY POSSIBILITY OF POLITICAL PHILOSOPHY UNDERSTOOD AS THE
    RATIONAL INVESTIGATION OF HUMAN AFFAIRS. A RESPONSE TO THIS
    CLAIM WHICH MERELY ADDUCES THE POTENTIALLY HARMFUL
    CONSEQUENCES OF SUCH A VIEW IS INADEQUATE; OUR MANIFEST NEED
    FOR SUCH A STANDARD IN NO WAY GUARANTEES THE EXISTENCE OF
    SUCH A STANDARD. AN ADEQUATE RESPONSE REQUIRES THAT WE MEET
    THE PREMISE OF THE ANTIFOUNDATIONALIST VIEW. THAT PREMISE
    RESIDES IN A CERTAIN UNDERSTANDING OF PLATONIC THOUGHT, AN
    UNDERSTANDING WHICH IS MISTAKEN. SOCRATES' FAMOUS REVOLUTION
    IN THOUGHT HAS UNDERTAKEN PRECISELY TO AVOID THE DOGMATISM
    WHICH THINKERS SUCH AS RORTY ATTRIBUTE TO PLATO, THUS MAKING
    DUBIOUS THE PREMISE OF THE ANTIFOUNDATIONALIST VIEW. THIS
    REVOLUTION, TAKEN BY THE TRADITION TO BE THE ORIGIN OF
    POLITICAL PHILOSOPHY, RESULTS IN A MODE OF INQUIRY WHICH IS
    NOT ONLY NONDOGMATIC BUT NONARBITRARY, FINDING ITS GROUND IN
    A CLEAR UNDERSTANDING OF THE PROBLEMATIC BUT PERSISTENT
    HUMAN SITUATION.

08669 STERN, P.
    U.S. - SOVIET TRADE: THE QUESTION OF LEVERAGE
    WASHINGTON QUARTERLY, 12(4) (FAL 89), 183-200.
        THIS ARTICLE DEFINES ECONOMIC LEVERAGE AS THE USE OF
    ECONOMIC MUSCLE TO ADVANCE POLITICAL ENDS, AND THEN EXAMINES
    THE CHARACTERISTICS OF U.S. - SOVIET TRADE WHICH LIMITS U.S.
    LEVERAGE. WHILE PAST ATTEMPTS BY THE UNITED STATES TO
    EXERCISE ECONOMIC LEVERAGE GENERALLY HAVE BEEN DISAPPOINTING,
    A REVIEW OF HISTORICAL PATTERNS AND BENCHMARKS CAN GUIDE
    POLICYMAKERS AROUND FUTURE PITFALLS. A BRIEF HISTORICAL SCAN
    HIGHLIGHTS HOW MOST-FAVOREDNATION (MFN) TARIFF TREATMENT,
    FINANCIAL CREDITS, EXPORT LICENSES, DEBT RESETTLEMENT, AND
    GRAIN SALES HAVE BEEN USED AS INSTRUMENTS OF TRADE POLITICS.
    CERTAINLY THERE ARE LESSONS HERE FOR THE 1990S ABOUT HOW TO
    PROCEED WITH DEFINING AN EAST-WEST TRADE AGENDA IN THE AGE
    OF PERESTROIKA.

08670 STERNBERG, E.
    INCREMENTAL VERSUS METHODOLOGICAL POLICYMAKING IN THE
        LIBERAL STATE
    ADMINISTRATION AND SOCIETY, 21(1) (MAY 89), 54-77.
        DISJOINTED INCREMENTALISM BECAME A FEASIBLE PARADIGM FOR
    AMERICAN ADMINISTRATIVE DECISION MAKING DURING THE GROWTH OF
    INTEREST-GROUP LIBERALISM. OVER THE SAME TIME, METHODS OF
    QUANTITATIVE RATIONALISM GAINED THEIR EFFICACY FOR
    ADMINISTRATIVE DECISION MAKING AMID THE RISE OF A
    TECHNOCRATIC LIBERALISM. AND AMID SOCIAL TRANSFORMATIONS
    THAT MADE PUBLIC LIFE MORE SYSTEMATIC, ENUMERABLE, AND

QUANTIFIABLE. HOW COULD BOTH THESE FORMS OF REASONING COME TO BE PLAUSIBLE WAYS OF RESPONDING TO THE WORLD, DESPITE THEIR SEEMING INCOMPATIBILITY? HOW COULD THE TWO PARADIGMS COEXIST IN AMERICAN ADMINISTRATION DURING THE LIBERAL ERA? IN VIEW OF THE APPARENT FAILINGS OF INCREMENTALISM, DID METHODOLOGICAL POLICYMAKING FARE BETTER? THIS ARTICLE ARGUES THAT INCREMENTALISM AND METHODOLOGY EACH DEPENDED FOR ITS POLICYMAKING EFFICACY ON HISTORICALLY DERIVED STRUCTURAL CONDITIONS. SINCE HISTORY NEVER FULFILLED THE REQUISITES OF ANY RATIONALIST DECISION PARADIGM, THE PARADIGMS PROVIDED INADEQUATE PRINCIPLES FOR PUBLIC DECISIONS.

08671 STEVENS, C.G.
    GERMAN REUNIFICATION: A SOVIET OPPORTUNITY
    AVAILABLE FROM NTIS, NO. AD-A208 041/4/GAR, MAR 89, 37.
        THE INTER-GERMAN BORDER (IGB) HAS BEEN THE FOCUS OF
    CONSISTENT NATO/WARSAW PACT CONFRONTATION AND THE GERMAN
    QUESTION, THE QUESTION OF GERMAN REUNIFICATION, HAS BEEN AT
    THE ROOT OF EAST/WEST RELATIONS IN EUROPE SINCE THE END OF
    WORLD WAR II. THERE IS A CONSENSUS THAT NO SOLUTION TO THE
    CHALLENGE OF EAST/WEST CONFRONTATION EXISTS WHICH DOES NOT
    INCLUDE RESOLUTION OF THE GERMAN QUESTION. THIS STUDY USES
    THE MEDIUM OF A FICTIONAL STATE MEMORANDUM FROM GENERAL
    SECRETARY GORBACHEV TO FOREIGN MINISTER SCHEVARDNADZE LAYING
    OUT A SCENARIO IN WHICH RESOLUTION OF THE PROBLEM OF THE
    SEPARATE GERMANIES IS PROPOSED BY THE SOVIETS AND EXPLOITED
    TO THEIR ADVANTAGE. IT CONSIDERS HOW SUCH A SCENARIO MIGHT
    BE ORCHESTRATED TO MEET CURRENT AND FUTURE NEEDS IN THE
    SOVIET UNION FOR ECONOMIC DEVELOPMENT ASSISTANCE, ACCESS TO
    WESTERN TECHNOLOGY AND MOST IMPORTANTLY AS A GUARANTEE FOR
    THE NATION'S SECURITY. FINALLY, IT EXPLORES THE LACK OF
    PREPAREDNESS ON THE PART OF THE UNITED STATES TO DEAL WITH
    SUCH A SOVIET INITIATIVE. THE SCENARIO DETAILS A SERIES OF
    EVENTS WHICH, IF THEY OCCURRED, COULD RESULT IN MAJOR
    CHANGES IN THE WORLD BALANCE OF POWER.

08672 STEVENS, S.A.
    PREFERENTIAL PROCUREMENT IN CANADA: ECONOMIC COST FOR
        POLITICAL BENEFIT?
    DISSERTATION ABSTRACTS INTERNATIONAL, 50(2) (AUG 89),
        538-A.
        THE AUTHOR UTILIZES A MODEL OF POLICY BEHAVIOR TO TEST
    THE INFLUENCE OF POLITICAL AND ECONOMIC VARIABLES ON THE
    ALLOCATION OF THE DEPARTMENT OF SUPPLY AND SERVICES
    CONTRACTS BY FEDERAL ELECTORAL DISTRICTS. SHE TESTS TWO
    HYPOTHESES. FIRST, CONTRACT ALLOCATION REFLECTS A VOTE-
    SEEKING STRATEGY RESPONDING TO COMPETITION IN ELECTORAL
    DISTRICTS. SECOND, CONTRACT ALLOCATION REWARDS POLITICAL
    SUPPORTERS.

08673 STEVENSON, M.
    FIJI: A SECOND GRENADA?
    AMERICAN SPECTATOR, 22(7) (JUL 89), 21-25.
        IT IS CLEAR THAT THE ANTI-NUCLEAR, NEUTROLIST GOVERNMENT
    OVERTHROWN IN FIJI IN 1987 WAS PLAYING DIRECTLY INTO THE
    HANDS OF THE SOVIETS AND THEIR PLANS FOR THE SOUTH PACIFIC
    THIS ARTICLE EXAMINES U.S. COMPLICITY IN THE COUP.

08674 STEWART, C. III
    A SEQUENTIAL MODEL OF U.S. SENATE ELECTIONS
    LEGISLATIVE STUDIES QUARTERLY, 14(4) (NOV 89), 567-602.
        THIS PAPER EXTENDS THE LITERATURE ON CAMPAIGNS AND
    ELECTIONS FOR THE UNITED STATES SENATE BY DISAGGREGATING THE
    PROCESS THAT LEADS TO THE CASTING OF VOTES ON ELECTION DAY.
    THE EMPIRICAL ANALYSIS UTILIZES A DATA SET ON CONTESTS FOR
    SENATE SEATS INVOLVING INCUMBENTS AND CHALLENGERS BETWEEN
    1974 AND 1988. THE EMPHASES OF THE RESEARCH ARE ON
    PREDICTING THE POLITICAL QUALITY OF THE CHALLENGER, THE FUND-
    RAISING EFFORT OF BOTH CANDIDATES, AND THE NUMBER OF VOTES
    RECEIVED BY EACH CANDIDATE ON ELECTION DAY. SPECIAL
    ATTENTION IS PAID TO THE ROLE THAT EXPECTATIONS PLAY IN THE
    DYNAMICS OF SENATE ELECTIONS.

08675 STEWART, J. JR.; ENGLAND, R.E.; MEIER, K.J.
    BLACK REPRESENTATION IN URBAN SCHOOL DISTRICTS: FROM
        SCHOOL BOARD TO OFFICE TO CLASSROOM
    WESTERN POLITICAL QUARTERLY, 42(2) (JUN 89), 287-306.
        STUDIES OF PASSIVE REPRESENTATION OF MINORITIES IN URBAN
    EDUCATIONAL SYSTEMS ARE INFREQUENT AND GENERALLY LIMITED TO
    LOOKING AT BLACKS ON SCHOOL BOARDS OR ON FACULTIES. THIS
    ANALYSIS, USING DATA DRAWN FROM A SURVEY OF LARGE, URBAN U.S.
    SCHOOL DISTRICTS AND FROM SCHOOL DISTRICT-LEVEL CENSUS
    FILES, EXAMINES THE LEVELS AND DETERMINANTS OF BLACK
    REPRESENTATION AMONG SCHOOL BOARD MEMBERS, SCHOOL
    ADMINISTRATORS, AND TEACHERS. INSIGHTS ARE GAINED ON THE
    POLITICS OF BLACK REPRESENTATIONAL EQUITY IN THESE IMPORTANT
    POSITIONS. THE FINDINGS SUGGEST THE POLITICAL IMPORTANCE OF
    THE REPRESENTATIVENESS OF ELITES, ESPECIALLY IN URBAN SCHOOL
    DISTRICTS, AND STIMULATE THINKING ABOUT PATHS TO MORE
    SUCCESSFUL AFFIRMATIVE ACTION PLANS.

08676 STEWART, P.D.; HERMANN, C.F.; HERMANN, M.G.
    MODELING THE 1973 SOVIET DECISION TO SUPPORT EGYPT
    AMERICAN POLITICAL SCIENCE REVIEW, 83(1) (MAR 89), 35-60.

THE AUTHORS PRESENT A CONTINGENCY MODEL OF SOVIET
FOREIGN POLICY MAKING THAT FOCUSES ON DECISION MAKING IN THE
POLITBURO. THE MODEL IS DESIGNED AROUND THREE QUESTIONS AND
SHOWS HOW THE ANSWERS TO THESE QUESTIONS DETERMINE THE
LIKELY NATURE OF THE DECISION THE POLITBURO WILL REACH AT
ANY POINT IN TIME. THE QUESTIONS ARE (1) WHOSE POSITIONS ON
THE POLITBURO ARE CRITICAL TO MAKING A DECISION? (2) WHAT
ARE THE POSITIONS OR PREFERENCES OF THOSE WHO COUNT ON THE
ISSUE UNDER CONSIDERATION? (3) HOW ARE DISAGREEMENTS AMONG
THESE INDIVIDUALS HANDLED? THE MODEL IS ILLUSTRATED BY
EXAMINING THE SOVIET DECISION TO INCREASE SIGNIFICANTLY THE
NUMBERS AND TYPES OF WEAPONS DELIVERED TO EGYPT IN EARLY
1973. OF INTEREST IN THIS CASE IS ACCOUNTING FOR THE SHIFT
IN SOVIET POLICY FROM REFUSING EGYPT OFFENSIVE WEAPONS TO
PROVIDING THEM.

08677 STEWER, P.P.
IN COLLUSION WITH THE NATION: A CASE STUDY OF GROUP
DYNAMICS AT A STRATEGIC NUCLEAR POLICYMAKING MEETING
POLITICAL PSYCHOLOGY, 10(4) (DEC 89), 647-674.
GROUP DYNAMICS ARE SHOWN TO HAVE NARROWED A POLICY
DISCUSSION ON THE PREVENTION AND MANAGEMENT OF NUCLEAR WAR.
THE DISCUSSION TOOK PLACE AT THE 1981 NATIONAL SECURITY
ISSUES SYMPOSIUM, "STRATEGIC NUCLEAR POLICIES, WEAPONS AND
THE C3 CONNECTION," CO-SPONSORED BY THE U.S. AIR FORCE
ELECTRONIC SYSTEMS DIVISION AND THE MITRE CORPORATION. IN
ADDITION TO THE PRECONSCIOUS INFLUENCE OF THE GROUP DYNAMICS
OF THE SYMPOSIUM ITSELF, GROUP DYNAMIC INFLUENCES FROM THE
DEFENSE COMMUNITY, THE AMERICAN PEOPLE, AND THE GENERIC
FAMILY OF ORIGIN ARE DISCUSSED. IF DECISION-MAKERS WERE
AWARE OF GROUP DYNAMICS IN POLICY DISCUSSIONS, THEY COULD BE
FREED FOR FRESH THINKING.

08678 STIDHAM, R.; CARP, R.A.
SUPPORT FOR LABOR AND ECONOMIC REGULATION AMONG REAGAN AND
CARTER APPOINTEES TO THE FEDERAL COURTS
SOCIAL SCIENCE JOURNAL, 26(4) (1989), 433-444.
APPOINTMENT OF FEDERAL JUDGES HAS BECOME HIGHLY
POLITICIZED OVER THE PAST 25 YEARS AS PRESIDENTS AND
POLITICAL PARTIES HAVE BECOME MORE INTENT ON APPOINTING
JUDGES WHO AGREE WITH THEIR POLITICAL IDEOLOGY AND PERHAPS
EVEN SPECIFIC POLICY GOALS. THIS STUDY OF 3700 OPINIONS
ASSESSES THE EXTENT TO WHICH PRESIDENTS CARTER AND REAGAN
SUCCEEDED IN INFLUENCING THE POLICY DECISIONS OF THEIR
APPOINTEES IN LABOR AND ECONOMIC REGULATION CASES. ANALYSIS
SHOWS THAT REAGAN JUDGES ARE SIMILAR TO JUDGES APPOINTED BY
OTHER REPUBLICAN PRESIDENTS AND THAT CARTER JUDGES ARE
SIMILAR TO JUDGES APPOINTED BY OTHER DEMOCRATIC PRESIDENTS.

08679 STOBART, J.; EARLE, J.
ITALY
SOUTH, (104) (JUN 89), 53-63.
AT PRESENT, ITALY IS THE WORLD'S FIFTH BIGGEST DONOR TO
THE THIRD WORLD. THIS YEAR'S PLANNED FUNDS FOR AID HAVE
NEARLY DOUBLED AS A PERCENTAGE OF GNP TO REACH 0.7 PER CENT -
DESPITE THE PENNY-PINCHING AT HOME. SUB-SAHARAN AFRICA IS
THE MAIN BENEFICIARY, WITH THE EMPHASIS ON AGRICULTURAL,
HEALTH AND TELECOMMUNICATIONS PROJECTS USING LOCAL LABOUR
AND RESOURCES. IN TRADE, ITALY HAS ESTABLISHED NEW MARKETS
IN SOUTHEAST ASIA AND IN CHINA, WHERE ITALIAN INDUSTRALISTS
ARE KEEN TO SET UP JOINT VENTURES.

08680 STODDARD, E.R.
AMNESTY: FUNCTIONAL MODIFICATIONS OF A CONGRESSIONAL
MANDATE
JOURNAL OF BORDERLAND STUDIES, IV(2) (FAL 89), 26-58.
POLICIES CREATED BY WASHINGTON BUREAUCRACIES ARE OFTEN
UNREALISTIC AND DYSFUNCTIONAL WHEN IMPLEMENTED ALONG THE U.S.
-MEXICAN BORDER. THIS ESSAY FOCUSES ON SOME OF THE CHANGES
THAT WERE NECESSARY TO CONVERT AMNESTY PROVISIONS OF THE
IMMIGRATION REFORM AND CONTROL ACT OF 1986 TO A REALISTIC
AND OPERATIONAL PROGRAM. THIS ANALYSIS SHOWS HOW POLITICAL
IDEOLOGY THAT REFLECTS ONLY THE CONCERNS OF CENTRALIZED
NATIONAL ISSUES ARE DYSFUNCTIONAL TO AREAS OF THE NATION'S
PERIPHERY AND TO THE TOTALITY OF AMERICAN SOCIETY.

08681 STOECKER, R.R.
FROM CONCRETE TO GRASS ROOTS: A CASE STUDY OF SUCCESSFUL
URBAN INSURGENCY IN CEDAR-RIVERSIDE
DISSERTATION ABSTRACTS INTERNATIONAL, 49(8) (FEB 89),
2421-A.
THE AUTHOR EXPLORES THE SOURCES OF SOCIAL MOVEMENT
SUCCESS BY ANALYZING THE CEDAR-RIVERSIDE NEIGHBORHOOD
MOVEMENT IN MINNEAPOLIS, MINNESOTA. HE USES A THEORETICAL
MODEL THAT PLACES SOCIAL MOVEMENTS IN POLITICAL-ECONOMIC
CONTEXTS.

08682 STOEVER, W.A.
FOREIGN COLLABORATIONS POLICY IN INDIA: A REVIEW
JOURNAL OF DEVELOPING AREAS, 23(4) (JUL 89), 485-504.
THE INDIAN GOVERNMENT HAS EVOLVED A HIGHLY ELABORATE SET
OF POLICIES AND PROCEDURES FOR SCREENING AND REGULATING
FOREIGN INVESTMENTS ("FOREIGN COLLABORATIONS" IN INDIAN
TERMINOLOGY), PARTICULARLY IN MANUFACTURING. THESE POLICIES

AND PROCEDURES ARE INTENDED TO PROMOTE CERTAIN NATIONAL GOAL
WHICH THE GOVERNMENT CONSIDERS IMPORTANT FOR THE COUNTRY'S
DEVELOPMENT. IN PRACTICE, HOWEVER, THE SCREENING AND
REGULATING MECHANISMS HAVE PROVEN TO BE BURDENSOME,
DISCOURAGING, AND EVEN COUNTERPRODUCTIVE TO THE PROFESSED
GOALS. THIS PAPER FIRST DESCRIBES THE GOVERNMENT'S POLICIES,
THEN EVALUATES THEM, AND FINALLY DRAWS SOME CONCLUSIONS AND
RECOMMENDATIONS.

08683 STOGA, A.J.
THE UNITED STATES IN A GLOBAL ECONOMY: RISKS AND CHALLENGES
FLETCHER FORUM, 13(1) (WIN 89), 1-8.
CONSENSUS ON AMERICA'S ECONOMIC STATUS IS GROWING.
CONTINUED DEPENDENCE ON FOREIGN CAPITAL AND FOREIGN ENERGY,
ARGUES ALAN STOGA, WILL ERODE US INFLUENCE. AN AGGRESSIVE
GOVERNMENT STRATEGY, HOWEVER, CAN AVERT ECONOMIC DISASTER
AND ENSURE AMERICA'S INTERNATIONAL POSITION.

08684 STOKER, R.P.
A REGIME FRAMEWORK FOR IMPLEMENTATION ANALYSIS:
COOPERATION AND RECONCILIATION OF FEDERALIST IMPERATIVES
POLICY STUDIES REVIEW, 9(1) (AUT 89), 29-49.
THE DIFFUSION OF AUTHORITY CHARACTERISTIC OF FEDERAL
GOVERNANCE CHALLENGES NATIONAL LEADERSHIP AND COMPLICATES
EVEN THE IMPLEMENTATION OF POLICY THAT PROMISES MUTUAL GAINS.
TO EXPLORE THE PROBLEMS OF IMPLEMENTING NATIONAL POLICY IN
A FEDERALIST CONTEXT, THIS PAPER PROPOSES A NEW APPROACH TO
ANALYSIS, THE IMPLEMENTATION REGIME FRAMEWORK. FROM THE
REGIME PERSPECTIVE, THE ESSENTIAL TASK OF THE IMPLEMENTATION
PROCESS IS TO CREATE A CONTEXT IN WHICH IMPLEMENTORS ARE
LIKELY TO COOPERATE TO ACHIEVE POLICY GOALS DESPITE THE
ABSENCE OF DOMINATING AUTHORITY. DRAWING UPON THE LITERATURE
ON INTERNATIONAL COOPERATION, THE REGIME FRAMEWORK OUTLINES
THE CONTEXTUAL CONDITIONS AND ELEMENTS OF POLICY DESIGN THAT
ARE LIKELY TO LEAD TO COOPERATION IN COLLECTIVE DECISION
MAKING.

08685 STOKES, E.
MACROECONOMIC IMPACT OF THE CANADA-US FREE TRADE AGREEMENT
JOURNAL OF POLICY MODELING, 11(2) (SUM 89), 225-245.
THE ARTICLE IS CONCERNED WITH MODELING THE MACROECONOMIC
IMPACT OF THE RECENT CANADA-U.S. FREE TRADE AGREEMENT (FTA)
FROM A CANADIAN PERSPECTIVE. THE RESULTS OF THE ARTICLE
ILLUSTRATE THE DIFFICULTY OF EXAMINING THE IMPACT OF THE FTA
AND THE IMPORTANCE OF THE ASSUMPTIONS AND MODEL USED IN THE
ANALYSIS. AN INTERESTING RESULT OF THE ARTICLE IS OBTAINED
FROM THE USE OF A "CONSISTENT EXPECTATIONS" ASSUMPTION FOR
THE MODEL. THE LATTER ILLUSTRATES HOW THE FTA MAY ALREADY BE
HAVING AN IMPACT ON THE CANADIAN ECONOMY. THE RESULTS IN
GENERAL INDICATE THAT THE FTA WILL HAVE A POSITIVE SHORT- TO
MEDIUM-TERM MACROECONOMIC IMPACT.

08686 STOKES, S.C.
CONFRONTATION AND ACCOMODATION: POLITICAL CONSCIOUSNESS
AND BEHAVIOR IN URBAN LOWER CLASS PERU
DISSERTATION ABSTRACTS INTERNATIONAL, 49(12) (JUN 89),
3860-A.
THE AUTHOR STUDIES THE POLITICAL ATTITUDES AND BEHAVIOR
OF SHANTYTOWN RESIDENTS IN CONTEMPORARY LIMA, PERU. HE FINDS
THAT ONE SET OF RESIDENTS IS IDEOLOGICALLY CONSERVATIVE OR
NOT GIVEN TO ABSTRACT FORMULATIONS ABOUT THEIR SOCIETY OR
POLITICAL SYSTEM. THEY PREFER FRIENDLY, FACE-TO-FACE
NEGOTIATIONS TO SECURE CONCRETE BENEFITS FOR A
GEOGRAPHICALLY-DEFINED COMMUNITY. A SECOND SET OF
CONFRONTATIONAL LEADERS AND ACTIVISTS IS IDEOLOGICALLY
RADICAL AND PREFERS STREET PROTESTS. THESE INDIVIDUALS SEE
THEMSELVES AS PART OF A BROAD SOCIAL MOVEMENT LEADING TO
DEEP TRANSFORMATIONS.

08687 STONE, A.
DEBT PROBLEMS MOUNT
AFRICAN BUSINESS, (JAN 88), 19-20.
THIS ARTICLE EXAMINES THE ECONOMIC SITUATION IN LIBERIA.
IT DISCUSSES THE DECISION OF THE WORLD BANK AND THE IMF TO
CLOSE DOWN THEIR OFFICES IN THAT COUNTRY, WHILE THE EEC WILL
STILL OFFER ECONOMIC AID TO LIBERIA. IT DISCUSSES THE
INTERIM MEASURES WHICH MUST BE TAKEN TO STABILIZE THE
ECONOMY AS WELL AS THE NEED TO REDUCE ARREARS BY THE
CONCERTED EFFORTS OF EVERY LIBERIAN, THE PRIVATE SECTOR, THE
INTERNATIONAL ORGANIZATIONS AND BILATERAL DONOR INSTITUTIONS.

08688 STONE, A.
IN THE SHADOW OF THE CONSTITUTIONAL COUNCIL: THE
JURIDICISATION OF THE LEGISLATIVE PROCESS IN FRANCE
WEST EUROPEAN POLITICS, 12(2) (APR 89), 12-34.
THIS STUDY EXAMINES, FIRST, WHY AND HOW THE FRENCH
PARLIAMENT WAS 'JURIDICISED', THAT, IS, GRADUALLY PLACED
UNDER THE TUTELAGE OF THE CONSTITUTIONAL COUNCIL, AND,
SECONDLY, THE INFLUENCE OF PAST COUNCIL JURISPRUDENCE AND
THE THREAT OF FUTURE CENSURE ON THE LEGISLATION OF THE 1986
PARLIAMENTARY SESSIONS. THIS INFLUENCE IS GREATER THAN HAS
BEEN HERETOFORE ACKNOWLEDGED - INDEED, ONE SIMPLY CANNOT
ASSESS THE LEGISLATIVE PROCESS WITHOUT UNDERSTANDING THE
ROLE, DIRECT AND INDIRECT, OF THE COUNCIL. ASSESSMENT OF THE

LEGISLATIVE EFFECTS OF COUNCIL CONTROL OF LEGISLATION SHOWS
THAT THE CONTROVERSY SURROUNDING THE LEGITIMACY OF JUDICIAL
REVIEW IN FRANCE, AND THE EXTENT TO WHICH THE COUNCIL
FUNCTIONS AS A GOUVERNEMENT DES JUGES, IS UNDERSTANDABLE AND
PROBABLY PERMANENT.

08689 STONE, C.
THE JAMAICAN GENERAL ELECTION OF 1989
ELECTORAL STUDIES, 8(2) (AUG 89), 175-182.
ON 9 FEBRUARY 1989 JAMAICA, A SMALL BRITISH COMMONWEALTH
ISLAND STATE WITH 2.3 MILLION PEOPLE, HELD ITS ELEVENTH POST-
WAR PARLIAMENTARY ELECTION AND ITS SIXTH SUCH ELECTION SINCE
INDEPENDENCE IN AUGUST 1962. THE PEOPLES NATIONAL PARTY
(PNP) LED BY PARTY PRESIDENT MICHAEL MANLEY RECORDED A
LANDSLIDE VICTORY AT THE POLLS ON 9 DECEMBER 1989 TO TAKE
POWER FROM THE JAMAICA LABOUR PARTY (JLP) LED BY EDWARD
SEAGA. THE PNP WON 45 OF THE 60 SEATS AND 57 PER CENT OF THE
POPULAR VOTE. THE ELECTION REAFFIRMED THE COUNTRY'S TWO-
PARTY TRADITION IN WHICH THE TWO MAJOR PARTIES HAVE SHARED
POWER EQUALLY, WITH PARTY GOVERNMENTS CHANGING AT TWO TERM
INTERVALS. THE JLP CAME TO POWER IN 1980 AND WAS RE-ELECTED
IN 1983 IN AN UNPRECEDENTED UNCONTESTED ELECTION.

08690 STONE, D.A.
AT RISK IN THE WELFARE STATE
SOCIAL RESEARCH, 56(3) (AUT 89), 591-634.
THE NEW SOCIOMEDICAL TECHNOLOGIES HAVE SEVERAL
DISTURBING IMPLICATIONS. IN MANY RESPECTS, THEY REPRODUCE
OLDER FORMS OF CHARACTER ASSESSMENT AS A MODE OF PREVENTING
POVERTY, BUT THEY ARE MORE POWERFUL AND AFFECT PEOPLE'S
LIVES MORE PROFOUNDLY. THEY ARE MORE POWERFUL BECAUSE THEY
ARE INVESTED WITH THE ENORMOUS CULTURAL AND POLITICAL
LEGITIMACY OF MEDICAL AUTHORITY AND BECAUSE, TO A LARGE
EXTENT, THEY ARE PROMOTED, FUNDED, AND DISSEMINATED BY THE
GOVERNMENT. ANY FORM OF PREVENTION, HOWEVER SENSIBLE AND
WELL MEANING, IS LIKELY TO TAKE ON A DIFFERENT CAST WHEN IT
IS CONDUCTED BY AND IN A STATE WHOSE WELFARE POLICY
EMPHASIZES INDIVIDUALISM, RESPONSIBILITY FOR ONESELF, AND
DETERRENCE.

08691 STONE, D.A.
CAUSAL STORIES AND THE FORMATION OF POLICY AGENDAS
POLITICAL SCIENCE QUARTERLY, 104(2) (SUM 89), 281-300.
THE AUTHOR ANALYZES HOW SITUATIONS COME TO BE SEEN AS
CAUSED BY HUMAN ACTIONS AND, THEREFORE, AMENABLE TO HUMAN
INTERVENTION. SHE ARGUES THAT CAUSAL IDEAS ARE THE CORE
SUBSTANCE OF THE TRANSFORMATION OF DIFFICULTIES INTO
POLITICAL PROBLEMS. POLITICAL ACTORS COMPOSE STORIES THAT
DESCRIBE HARMS AND DIFFICULTIES, ATTRIBUTE THEM TO THE
ACTIONS OF OTHER INDIVIDUALS OR ORGANIZATIONS, AND THEREBY
CLAIM THE RIGHT TO INVOKE GOVERNMENT POWER TO STOP THE HARM.

08692 STONE, I.F.
THE RIGHTS OF GORBACHEV
NEW POLITICS, 11(3) (SUM 89), 108-118.
THE OLD AND ANACHRONISTIC DOGMA OF ABSOLUTE NATIONAL
SOVEREIGNTY AND NONINTERFERENCE IN SO-CALLED DOMESTIC
AFFAIRS HAS ALWAYS BEEN THE SOVIET RESPONSE TO HUMAN RIGHTS
CRITICISM, AND REMAINS THE BASIC ARGUMENT OF ALL
AUTHORITARIAN REGIMES ACCUSED OF VIOLATING THE RIGHTS AND
LIBERTIES OF THEIR SUBJECTS. GORBACHEV WOULD TURN THE
STRUGGLE FOR HUMAN RIGHTS UPSIDE DOWN. ALTHOUGH HE AND OTHER
SOVIET OFFICIALS SPEAK WITH SEVERAL VOICES, THE MAIN
EMPHASIS IN HIS STATEMENTS IS ON GUARANTEEING NOT THE RIGHT
OF INDIVIDUALS AGAINST STATE OPPRESSION BUT THE RIGHT OF
EACH STATE TO TREAT ITS SUBJECTS AS IT DEEMS FIT.

08693 STONE, J.
POWER AND INFLUENCE OF INTELLECTUALS IN POLITICS: THE
FRENCH COMMUNIST PARTY AS A CASE STUDY
DISSERTATION ABSTRACTS INTERNATIONAL, 49(7) (JAN 89),
1946-A.
THE AUTHOR ARGUES THAT INTELLECTUALS IN THE FRENCH
COMMUNIST PARTY HAVE BEEN DENIED INFLUENCE AND POWER, FOR
THREE REASONS. (1) HISTORICAL AND CULTURAL FACTORS HAVE
LIMITED PARTICIPATION. (2) THE ORGANIZATIONAL CONCEPTS AND
THE PARTY'S HIERARCHICAL NATURE LIMIT DISCUSSION AND CURTAIL
DISSENTING VIEWS. (3) INTELLECTUALS HAVE BEEN UNABLE TO
DEVELOP A COMMUNITY WITHIN THE PARTY DUE TO DISUNIFYING
FEATURES.

08694 STONE, N.
A CONFLICT OF INTEREST: THE WARREN COMMISSION, THE FBI,
AND THE CIA
DISSERTATION ABSTRACTS INTERNATIONAL, 49(11) (MAY 89),
3495-A.
THE WARREN COMMISSION DIFFERED FROM OTHER PRESIDENTIAL
ADVISORY COMMISSIONS IN THREE SIGNIFICANT ASPECTS: (1)
MANDATE; (2) DEGREE OF INDEPENDENCE; AND (3) PROBLEMS OF
INTERNAL DYNAMICS AND DECISION-MAKING. ITS WORK WAS
INFLUENCED BY PROBLEMS OF COORDINATION AMONG AGENCIES,
BUREAUCRATIC RIVALRIES, CONFLICTING PRIORITIES, AND THE
EXTREME COMPARTMENTALIZATION OF KNOWLEDGE.

08695 STONECASH, J.M.
POLITICAL CLEAVAGE IN GUBERNATORIAL AND LEGISLATIVE
ELECTIONS: PARTY COMPETITION IN NEW YORK, 1970-1982
WESTERN POLITICAL QUARTERLY, 42(1) (MAR 89), 69-82.
THIS STUDY EXAMINES FOUR STATE ELECTIONS IN NEW YORK
FROM 1970 TO 1982 AND FINDS THAT GUBERNATORIAL CHOICES HAVE
A SIGNIFICANT IMPACT ON THE SIMILARITY AND STABILITY OF
PARTY ELECTORAL BASES. THE IMPLICATION IS THAT ASSESSMENTS
OF INTERPARTY COMPETITION (ITS EXISTENCE, THE BASES
UNDERLYING IT, AND THE "MEANING" OF ELECTIONS) MUST BE
DERIVED FROM SPECIFIC ANALYSES OF ELECTORAL COMPETITION AND
NOT JUST FROM AGGREGATE PROPORTIONS.

08696 STOPER, E.
THE GENDER GAP CONCEALED AND REVEALED: 1936-1984
JOURNAL OF POLITICAL SCIENCE, 17(1-2) (1989), 50-62.
THE AUTHOR QUESTIONS WHY SOME WOMEN VOTE SO MUCH LIKE
MEN IN PRESIDENTIAL ELECTIONS EVEN THOUGH THEY HAVE
SIGNIFICANTLY DIFFERENT ATTITUDES FROM MEN OVER THE LONG
TERM. SHE ARGUES THAT IN AT LEAST THREE ISSUE AREAS, ALL OF
WHICH EMERGED DURING THE SUFFRAGE BATTLE, WOMEN HAVE VOTED
DIFFERENTLY IN REFERENDA AND DIFFERENTLY IN POLLS AND
SURVEYS. HOWEVER, UNTIL THE 1980'S, THESE DIFFERENCES WERE
ONLY RARELY TRANSLATED INTO DIFFERENT CANDIDATE VOTES OR
PARTISAN AFFILIATIONS, DUE TO PECULIARITIES OF THE AMERICAN
POLITICAL SYSTEM. THE THREE ISSUE AREAS ARE POLITICAL
CORRUPTION, WAR AND PEACE, AND SUMPTUARY LEGISLATION.

08697 STORK, J.; WENGER, M.
POLITICAL ASPECTS OF HEALTH
MIDDLE EAST REPORT, 19(6) (NOV 89), 4-11.
THIS ARTICLE ADDRESSES THE POLITICAL ASPECTS OF HEALTH
IN THE MIDDLE EAST. AFTER EXPLORING THE ECONOMIC RESOURCES
AVAILABLE, IT CONTINUES ON TO THE PRIMARY CARE STRATEGY. IT
DETAILS POLITICS AND MEDICINE IN HISTORY AND TODAY AS WELL
AS ANALYSING THE EFFECTS OF "DEVELOPMENT" WHICH IN MANY
INSTANCES HAS COMPLICATED, RATHER THAN ALLEVIATED HEALTH
PROBLEMS.

08698 STORRS, K.L.
CENTRAL AMERICA'S ECONOMIC DEVELOPMENT: OPTIONS FOR U.S.
ASSISTANCE
CRS REVIEW, 10(2) (FEB 89), 8-10.
AFTER FIVE YEARS OF EXTRAORDINARY U.S. ASSISTANCE TO
CENTRAL AMERICA, AS RECOMMENDED BY THE "KISSINGER COMMISSION,
" THE ECONOMIC RECOVERY OF THE REGION STILL SEEMS REMOTE. IN
1989 THE CONGRESS WILL HAVE TO DECIDE HOW TO DEAL WITH THE
CONTINUING CRISIS AND HOW TO RELATE TO SEVERAL EMERGING
MULTILATERAL APPROACHES.

08699 STORRS, K.L.
EL SALVADOR: NEW CHALLENGES FOR U.S. POLICY
CRS REVEIW, 10(2) (FEB 89), 14-16.
AFTER NINE YEARS OF LARGE-SCALE U.S. ASSISTANCE, EL
SALVADOR MAY BE RETURNING TO A PATTERN OF INTENSE
POLARIZATION AND VIOLENCE. RESURGENT GUERRILLA ATTACKS,
REVIVED DEATH SQUAD ACTIVITY, AND THE EXPECTED RIGHTIST
VICTORY IN THE 1989 PRESIDENTIAL ELECTIONS POSE CHALLENGES
FOR THE CONGRESS AND THE ADMINISTRATION.

08700 STOVALL, D.O.
A PARTICIPANT'S VIEW OF ON-SITE INSPECTIONS
PARAMETERS, XIX(2) (JUN 89), 2-17.
THE AUTHOR LED THE FIRST CDE ON-SITE INSPECTION OF A
SOVIET GROUND FORCE EXERCISE IN BELORUSSIA IN AUGUST 1987.
IN THIS ARTICLE, HE DISCUSSES THE BACKGROUND TO THE
STOCKHOLM DOCUMENT VERIFICATION AGREEMENT AND HIS OWN
EXPERIENCE WITH THE INSPECTION PROCESS.

08701 STOVALL, T.
FRENCH COMMUNISM AND SUBURBAN DEVELOPMENT: THE RISE OF THE
PARIS RED BELT
JOURNAL OF CONTEMPORARY HISTORY, 24(3) (JUL 89), 437-460.
FRENCH COMMUNISM IS IMPORTANT BECAUSE IT IS A MASS-BASED
PARTY IN AN ADVANCED CAPITALIST COUNTRY. IT IS NECESSARY FOR
HISTORIANS OF THE PCF TO ADOPT THE TECHNIQUES OF SOCIAL
HISTORY IN ORDER TO EXPLAIN WHY SO MANY FRENCH WORKERS HAVE
VOTED COMMUNIST SINCE 1920. THIS ARTICLE ENDEAVORS TO MAKE A
CONTRIBUTION TO THE HISTORY OF THE PCF BY ANALYZING THE
GROWTH OF A COMMUNIST POLITICAL CONSENSUS IN THE PARISIAN
SUBURB OF BOBIGNY DURING THE INTER-WAR YEARS.

08702 STOWE, W.M. JR.
WILLIE RAINACH AND THE DEFENSE OF SEGREGATION IN LOUISIANA,
1954-59
DISSERTATION ABSTRACTS INTERNATIONAL, 50(6) (DEC 89),
1784-A.
THIS STUDY OF WILLIE RAINACH'S LEADERSHIP OF THE
SEGREGATIONIST FORCES IN LOUISIANA EXPLORES HIS MOTIVES,
STRATEGIES, AND ACTIVITIES IN ATTEMPTING TO DEFEAT
INTEGRATION. USING RAINACH'S PERSONAL PAPERS, THE AUTHOR
FINDS THAT RAINACH RECOGNIZED THAT DEFIANCE ALONE WOULD NOT
STOP INTEGRATION. THEREFORE, HE ADOPTED A THREE-PART
STRATEGY TO DELAY INTEGRATION, ORGANIZE THE OPPOSITION TO

INTEGRATION, AND PROSELYTIZE SEGREGATION TO WHITE AMERICA.

08703 STRAFFORD, P.
AUSTRALIAN TROOPS' IMPORTANT ROLE
PACIFIC DEFENCE REPORTER, 16(9) (MAR 90), 8-10.
THE YEAR-LONG NAMBIA INDEPENDENCE PROCESS OVERSEEN BY
THE UNITED NATIONS TRANSITION ASSISTANCE GROUP (UNTAG) WILL
END WHEN AFRICA'S LAST COLONY ACHIEVES INDEPENDENCE SHORTLY.
THIS ARTICLE EXAMINES AUSTRALIA'S IMPORTANT ROLE IN EACH
STEP OF THIS OFTEN DIFFICULT TRANSITION PROCESS. MUCH OF THE
WORK OF THE AUSTRALIAN CONTINGENT HAS INVOLVED THE
CONSTRUCTION, RENOVATION AND REPAIR OF UNTAG MILITARY AND
CIVILIAN OFFICES AND ACCOMMODATION THROUGHOUT NAMIBIA. THE
CONTINGENT HAS ALSO BEEN RESPONSIBLE FOR THE CONSTRUCTION OF
ROADS, CULVERTS, LIGHT AIRCRAFT STRIPS AND OBSERVATION POSTS.
THROUGH FORCE OF CIRCUMSTANCE AND BECAUSE OF ITS VARIED
SKILLS, THE CONTINGENT HAS ALSO BEEN INVOLVED IN MOST OF
UNTAG'S MORE IMPORTANT AND SENSITIVE OPERATIONS.

08704 STRAHAN, R.
MEMBERS' GOALS AND COALITION-BUILDING STRATEGIES IN THE U.
S. HOUSE: THE CASE OF TAX REFORM
THE JOURNAL OF POLITICS, 51(2) (MAY 89), 373-384.
AN IMPORTANT ISSUE RAISED BY RECENT WORK WHICH VIEWS
MEMBERS OF THE U.S. CONGRESS AS PURPOSIVE ACTORS IS HOW TO
CONCEPTUALIZE MEMBERS' GOALS. THIS NOT PROPOSES THAT
COALITION-BUILDING STRATEGIES EMPLOYED BY CONGRESSIONAL
LEADERS MAY PROVIDE EMPIRICAL EVIDENCE BEARING ON THIS
QUESTION. UNLIKE OTHER SOURCES OF EVIDENCE ON MEMBERS' GOALS,
APPEALS MADE DIRECTLY BY LEADERS TO RANK-AND-FILE
LEGISLATORS ARE NOT EASILY DISCOUNTED AS POSTURING OR
"POSITION-TAKING." AN ANALYSIS OF THE COMMITTEE COALITION-
BUILDING STRATEGY EMPLOYED BY HOUSE WAYS AND MEANS COMMITTEE
CHAIRMAN DAN ROSTENKOWSKI (D-ILLINOIS) ON THE ISSUE OF TAX
REFORM IN 1985 SUPPORTS EARLIER FINDINGS ON THE IMPORTANCE
OF PRESTIGE AND POLICY GOALS FOR MEMBERS OF THIS COMMITTEE
AND PROVIDES SOME ADDITIONAL EMPIRICAL GROUNDING FOR A
CONCEPTUALIZATION OF MEMBERS' GOALS OF THE TYPE ADVANCED BY
RICHARD F. FENNO, JR.

08705 STRAIT, R.S.; JUDD, B.R.
VERIFYING ARMS CONTROL TREATIES TO DETER VIOLATIONS
AVAILABLE FROM NTIS, NO. DE88014 181/GAR, JUN 23 88, 29.
VERIFICATION HAS DEVELOPED INTO A VERY IMPORTANT ARMS
CONTROL ISSUE. AS EVIDENCED BY THE RECENT SENATE DEBATES
CONCERNING RATIFICATION OF THE INF TREATY, VERIFICATION CAN
BE A VERY CONTROVERSIAL AND EMOTIONAL TOPIC. IN ADDITION,
VERIFICATION'S IMPORTANCE WILL SURELY CONTINUE FOR THE
FORESEEABLE FUTURE. IT IS A MAJOR ISSUE IN THE NEGOTIATIONS
TOWARD LARGE REDUCTIONS IN STRATEGIC WEAPONS AND WILL GAIN
EVEN GREATER IMPORTANCE SHOULD DEEPER CUTS BE CONSIDERED. 34
REFS., 7 FIGS.

08706 STRATE, J.M.; ELDER, C.D.; FORD, C. III; PARRISH, C.J.
LIFE SPAN CIVIC DEVELOPMENT AND VOTING PARTICIPATION ..
AMERICAN POLITICAL SCIENCE REVIEW, 83(2) (JUN 89), 443-464.
THE AUTHORS POSIT A THEORY OF CIVIC DEVELOPMENT THAT
FOCUSES ON THE NATURE AND CAUSES OF AGE-RELATED CHANGES IN
LEVELS OF POLITICAL PARTICIPATION. BECAUSE OF THESE CHANGES,
PARTICIPATION AMONG OLDER PERSONS IS HIGHER THAN WOULD
OTHERWISE BE EXPECTED. ALTHOUGH THEY BELIEVE THIS WOULD
APPLY TO MOST CONVENTIONAL MODES OF POLITICAL PARTICIPATION,
THEY FOCUS ON VOTING PARTICIPATION AND TEST THE THEORY
THROUGH A SECONDARY ANALYSIS OF SURVEY DATA FROM NINE
PRESIDENTIAL ELECTION SURVEYS OF THE U.S. NATIONAL ELECTION
STUDIES (NES).

08707 STREETEN, P.P.
GLOBAL INSTITUTIONS FOR AN INTERDEPENDENT WORLD
WORLD DEVELOPMENT, 17(9) (SEP 89), 1349-1359.
AFTER A BRIEF DISCUSSION OF SOME NECESSARY CONDITIONS
FOR AN INTERNATIONAL ORDER CONCERNED WITH DEVELOPMENT, A
DISTINCTION IS DRAWN BETWEEN THE EXCHANGE SYSTEM, THE THREAT
SYSTEM AND THE INTEGRATIVE SYSTEM. IT PAYS ONE COUNTRY TO
PUT UP PROTECTIONIST BARRIERS, WHETHER OTHERS DO SO OR NOT;
IT PAYS ONE COUNTRY TO BUILD UP ARMS, WHETHER OTHERS DO SO
OR NOT; IT PAYS ONE COUNTRY TO POLLUTE THE GLOBAL AIR AND
OCEANS, WHETHER OTHERS DO SO OR NOT. THESE TYPICAL
PRISONER'S DILEMMA SITUATIONS CALL FOR GLOBAL REFORMS. THERE
IS A LAG BETWEEN TECHNOLOGICAL ADVANCE THAT HAS UNIFIED THE
GLOBE AND THE INSTITUTION OF THE NATION STATE. SUGGESTIONS
ARE MADE AS TO HOW TO OVERCOME THIS LAG, WHEN THE WORLD NO
LONGER HAS A DOMINANT POWER THAT PROVIDES THE GLOBAL PUBLIC
GOODS AND AVOIDS THE GLOBAL PUBLIC BADS.

08708 STREIKER, L.D.
BRAINWASHED OR CONVERTED
THE CHRISTIAN CENTURY, 106(23) (AUG 89), 721-723.
IN ITS ZEAL TO GUARD SOCIETY AGAINST THE CONTROVERSIAL
METHODS OF A MALIGNED CHURCH THE UNIFICATION CHURCH - THE
CALIFORNIA SUPREME COURT HAS ENDANGERED AMERICA'S BASIC
FREEDOMS. COURTS DO NOT HAVE THE AUTHORITY TO DETERMINE
WHETHER ONE'S RELIGIONS EXPERIENCES ARE BASED ON CONVERSION
OR BRAINWASHING.

08709 STRICKLAND, J.Z.
WAR MAKING AND STATE BUILDING: THE DYNAMICS OF AMERICAN
INSTITUTIONAL DEVELOPMENT, 1917-1935
DISSERTATION ABSTRACTS INTERNATIONAL, 49(10) (APR 89),
3149-A.
THIS STATE-CENTRIC STUDY ANALYZES THE IMPACT OF NATIONAL
CRISES ON THE DEVELOPMENT AND OUTCOMES OF AMERICAN NATIONAL
PUBLIC POLICY AND POLITICAL INSTITUTIONS IN LABOR POLICY AND
INDUSTRIAL POLICY DURING WORLD WAR I (1917-1918) AND THE
EARLY NEW DEAL (1933-1935). THE DISSERTATION IS CONCERNED
WITH EXPLAINING HOW AND WHY THE POLICY AND INSTITUTIONAL
OUTCOMES DURING WORLD WAR I IN BOTH LABOR AND INDUSTRIAL
POLICY WERE SUCCESSFUL RESPONSES TO THE EXIGENCIES OF THAT
CRISIS, WHILE SUCH OUTCOMES IN THE NEW DEAL WERE SUCCESSFUL
ONLY IN LABOR POLICY.

08710 STROM, K.; LIEPART, J.Y.
IDEOLOGY, STRATEGY, AND PARTY COMPETITION IN POSTWAR NORWAY
EUROPEAN JOURNAL OF POLITICAL RESEARCH, 17(3) (MAY 89),
26-288.
ELECTORAL MANIFESTOS ARE A KEY INSTRUMENT OF DEMOCRATIC
POLITICAL PARTIES IN THEIR QUEST FOR POPULAR SUPPORT. THIS
ARTICLE INVESTIGATES THE CONTENTS OF POSTWAR NORWEGIAN PARTY
MANIFESTOS. THE ANALYSIS BUILDS ON THE SALIENCY THEROY OF
PARTY COMPETITION. METHODOLOGICALLY, IT REPLICATES THE
FACTOR ANALYSIS OF BUDGE, ROBERTSON, AND HEARL (1987). FOUR
FACTORS ARE UNCOVERED. TWO OF THESE CAN BE IDENTIFIED WITH
THE LEFT-RIGHT DIMENSION, ONE WITH THE MORAL-RELIGIOUS AXIS,
AND ONE WITH MATERIAL CENTRE-PERIPHERY CONFLICTS. A HIGH
DEGREE OF INTERPARTY CONSENSUS AND COVERAGE IS EVIDENT,
PARTICULARLY PRIOR TO 1970. THE RESULTS ARE GENERALLY
CONSISTENT WITH PREVIOUS RESEARECH ON NORWEGIAN MASS AND
PARTY POLITICS.

08711 STROM, K.
PARTY COMPETITION AND THE POLITICS OF ECONOMIC OPENNESS
AND GROWTH
EUROPEAN JOURNAL OF POLITICAL RESEARCH, 17(1) (JAN 89),
1-16.
THE POLITICAL EFFECTS OF ECONOMIC OPENNESS HAVE RECENTLY
ATTRACTED CONSIDERABLE SCHOLARLY ATTENTION. THIS PAPER
ANALYZES THE RELATIONSHIPS BETWEEN OPENNESS OF TRADE, PARTY
COMPETITION, AND ECONOMIC PERFORMANCE IN 15 ADVANCE WESTERN
DEMOCRACIES. RESTRAINTS ON PARTY COMPETITION ARE FOUND TO
DEPEND MORE ON DOMESTIC SOCIAL PLURALISM THAN ON OPENNESS OF
TRADE. ECONOMIC GROWTH IS PROMOTED BOTH BY ECONOMIC EXPOSURE
AND BY PARTYSYSTEM COMPETITION. THE RESULTS SUGGEST THAT
RESTRAINTS ON POLITICAL COMPETITION MAY BE LESS BENEFICIAL
IN PARTY SYSTEMS THAN IN INTEREST GROUP SYSTEMS.

08712 STROMSETH, J.
UNEQUAL ALLIES: NEGOTIATIONS OVER U.S. BASES IN THE
PHILIPPINES
JOURNAL OF INTERNATIONAL AFFAIRS, 43(1) (SUM 89), 161-184.
DURING THE PAST THREE DECADES, THE UNITED STATES AND THE
PHILIPPINES HAVE ENGAGED IN PROTRACTED AND AT TIMES
ACRIMONIOUS NEGOTIATIONS OVER THE STATUS OF U.S. BASES ON
PHILIPPINE TERRITORY. MORE NEGOTIATIONS ARE EXPECTED TO
OCCUR BETWEEN NOW AND 1991, WHEN THE CURRENT MILITARY BASES
AGREEMENT (MBA) EXPIRES. THIS ARTICLE ANALYZES THE ISSUE BY
APPLYING A THEORY OF ASYMMETRICAL NEGOTIATIONS TO THE TWO
ROUNDS OF NEGOTIATIONS THAT OCCURRED IN THE 1970S. BY TAKING
THIS THEORETICAL APPROACH, IT ATTEMPTS TO EXPLAIN THE
DYNAMICS BEHIND THESE NEGOTIATIONS AND EXPLORES THE LARGER
QUESTION OF BARGAINING POWER BETWEEN LARGE AND SMALL ALLIES.
THIS APPROACH ALSO MAY PROVIDE SOME TOOLS FOR ANALYZING THE
LATEST ROUND OF NEGOTIATIONS, WHICH WERE CONCLUDED IN
OCTOBER 1988, AS WELL AS THOSE LIKELY TO UNFOLD OVER THE
NEXT TWO YEARS.

08713 STRONG, M.
THE UNITED NATIONS IN AN INTERDEPENDENT WORLD
INTERNATIONAL AFFAIRS (MOSCOW), (1) (JAN 89), 11-21.
THE UNITED NATIONS IS THE SOLE MULTILATERAL ORGANIZATION
THAT IS GLOBAL IN SCOPE, UNIVERSAL IN MEMBERSHIP, AND
MANDATED BY THE NATIONS OF THE WORLD THROUGH THE UNITED
NATIONS CHARTER TO BE THE INSTRUMENT THROUGH WHICH THE WORLD
COMMUNITY ADDRESSES ISSUES OF FUNDAMENTAL SECURITY. THE
WORLD HAS CHANGED IMMENSELY SINCE THE FOUNDING OF THE U.N.
AND THE ISSUES OF GLOBAL SECURITY HAVE BECOME MUCH MORE
COMPLEX AND INTER-RELATED. EVEN THE STRONGEST SUPPORTERS OF
THE UNITED NATIONS RECOGNIZE THAT SIGNIFICANT CHANGES ARE
REQUIRED TO STRENGTHEN ITS CAPACITY TO PERFORM ITS ROLE.

08714 STROTHER,R
NO MORE MANANA
NATIONAL REVIEW, 62(22) (NOV 89), 21 - 22.
THIS ARTICLE REPORTS ON EFFORTS OF MEXICO PRESIDENT,
CAROLS SALINAS DE GORTARI, TO IMPLEMENT HIS PLANS OF REFORM
AND GIVE MEXICO A REAL FREE-MARKET DEMOCRACY AND A SOUND
CURRENCY, IT DESCRIBES THE OPPOSITION OF THE ESTABLISHMENT
WHO FEEL THAT THEIR JOBS AND LIFE STYLE ARE THREATENED. HIS
SUCCESS WOULD MEAN THAT MEXICO COULD WIN ITS PLACE AS ONE OF

THE SUCCESSFUL NATIONS OF THE FREE WORLD.

08715 STRUM, P.
WOMEN AND THE POLITICS OF RELIGION IN ISRAEL
HUMAN RIGHTS QUARTERLY, 11(4) (NOV 89), 483-503.
THIS PAPER ANALYZES THE IMPACT OF RELIGION IN POLITICS
ONLY UPON JEWISH ISRAELI WOMEN. THE RELIGIOUS LIVES OF THE
JEWISH, MOSLEM, AND CHRISTIAN COMMUNITIES ARE SEPARATE AND
MUST BE DISCUSSED AS SUCH. TO THE EXTENT THAT ISRAELI ARAB
WOMEN, MOST OF WHOM ARE MOSLEMS, HAVE BEEN "LIBERATED" FROM
TRADITIONAL ROLES BY THE JEWISH ISRAELI MODEL, HOWEVER, THE
LIMITATIONS ON THE LATTER NECESSARILY MINIMIZE THE FORMER.
THE ARTICLE EXAMINES THE RABBINICAL COURTS AND EMPLOYMENT AS
WELL AS WOMEN'S RIGHTS IN THE JEWISH SYSTEM. IT CONCLUDES
THAT EFFECTIVE IMPLEMENTATION OF THE RIGHT NOT TO BE
DISCRIMINATED AGAINST HAS BEEN IGNORED.

08716 STRYKER, J.
IV DRUG USE AND AIDS: PUBLIC POLICY AND DIRTY NEEDLES
JOURNAL OF HEALTH POLITICS, POLICY AND LAW, 14(4) (WIN 89),
719-740.
USERS OF INTRAVENOUS HEROIN, COCAINE, AND AMPHETAMINES
RISK THE TRANSMISSION OF HUMAN IMMUNODEFICIENCY VIRUS (HIV)
THROUGH THE SHARING OF CONTAMINATED INJECTION EQUIPMENT.
ALTHOUGH MOST USERS ARE AWARE OF THIS RISK, THE SCARCITY OF
STERILE NEEDLES AND SYRINGES, COMBINED WITH VARIOUS SOCIAL
AND CULTURAL FACTORS, FOSTERS DANGEROUS SHARING PRACTICES.
THIS PAPER EXAMINES THE LEGAL AND POLITICAL CONTEXTS OF
PROPOSALS TO EASE ACCESS TO STERILE NEEDLES AND INJECTION
EQUIPMENT. THE AUTHOR SEEKS AN EXPLANATION FOR THE CONTINUED
RELUCTANCE TO INSTITUTE SUCH PROGRAMS IN THE UNITED STATES,
WHILE SIMILAR PROGRAMS HAVE BEEN INSTITUTED IN OTHER
COUNTRIES WHERE INTRAVENOUS DRUG USE HAS ALSO CONTRIBUTED TO
THE SPREAD OF HIV INFECTION AND AIDS.

08717 STUART - FOX, MARTIN
LAOS IN 1988: THE PURSUIT OF NEW DIRECTIONS
ASIAN SURVEY, XXIX(1) (JAN 89), 81-88.
1988 SAW SURPRISING AND SOMETIMES SIGNIFICANT CHANGES IN
THE LAO PEOPLE'S DEMOCRATIC REPUBLIC. THE NATION EXPERIENCED
THE FIRST ELECTIC SINCE THE REGIME TOOK POWER IN 1975.
SEEKING PRIVATE INVESTMENT, TRANSFER OF TECHNOLOGY, AND
TRADE, LAOS ALSO ATTEMPTED TO IMPROVE RELATIONS WITH
THAILAND, THE US, AND OTHER WESTERN NATIONS. THE LEADERS OF
THE LDPR ALSO HAVE ENGAGED IN "ECONOMIC RESTRUCTURING" AND
DECENTRALIZATION. ALL IN ALL, LAOS TOOK A LONG STEP IN 1988
DOWN THE ROAD OF ECONOMIC REFORM AT HOME AND OPENNESS ABROAD.

08718 STUBBS, J.
CUBA
MONTHLY REVIEW PRESS, NEW YORK, NY, 1989, 150.
THE AUTHOR ANALYZES CUBA'S DEVELOPMENT STRATEGIES. SHE
DISCUSSES ECONOMIC DEPENDENCY AND THE POSSIBILITIES FOR
DIVERSIFICATION, ECONOMIC REFORM WITHIN THE FRAMEWORK OF
CENTRAL PLANNING, THE NATURE OF THE SINGLE-PARTY STATE,
CIVIL AND HUMAN RIGHTS, SOCIALIST EGALITARIANISM, AND CUBA'S
ROLE IN INTERNATIONAL AFFAIRS.

08719 STUBBS, R.
GEOPOLITICS AND THE POLITICAL ECONOMY OF SOUTHEAST ASIA
INTERNATIONAL JOURNAL, XLIV(3) (SUM 89), 517-540.
THE AUTHOR FOCUSES ON THREE SETS OF EVENTS THAT WERE
PRECIPITATED BY THE GEOPOLITICAL OR STRATEGIC CONFIGURATION
OF THE ASIA-PACIFIC REGION: THE KOREAN WAR, THE VIETNAM WAR,
AND JAPANESE INVESTMENT AND AID IN THE REGION. THESE EVENTS
AFFECTED TWO INTERRELATED FACTORS WIDELY REGARDED AS CRUCIAL
TO ECONOMIC DEVELOPMENT. THE FIRST IS THE ACCUMULATION OF
CAPITAL, EITHER DOMESTIC OR FOREIGN, WHICH IS THEN DEPLOYED
THROUGH EITHER PUBLIC OR PRIVATE CHANNELS TO ADVANCE
ECONOMIC GROWTH. THE SECOND IS ABSORPTIVE CAPACITY, THAT
COMBINATION OF FACTORS WHICH INCLUDES THE ABILITY OF THE
STATE TO MANAGE EFFECTIVELY AND TO DIRECT DOMESTIC AND
FOREIGN CAPITAL AND THE EXTENT TO WHICH THE ECONOMIC
INFRASTRUCTURE AND THE SOCIAL INFRASTRUCTURE ARE DEVELOPED
ENOUGH TO SUPPORT ECONOMIC EXPANSION.

08720 STUDNICKI-GIZBERT, K. W.
HARD-NOSED IDEALISM
POLICY OPTIONS, 10(3) (APR 89), 23-25.
AS CANADA HEADS INTO YET ANOTHER PERIODIC REEXAMINATION
OF FOREIGN AID, IT OUGHT TO CONSIDER BOTH THE ADVANTAGES OF
BILATERAL, AS OPPOSED TO MULTILATERAL, AID PROGRAMS AND THE
ADVANTAGES OF A PRAGMATIC RATHER THAN IDEALISTIC APPROACH.
AID WHICH IS TIED TO TRADE OR SHOWS OTHER OBVIOUS BENEFITS
FOR THE DONOR COUNTRY IS NOT SELFISH BUT MAY IN THE LONG RUN
BE THE BEST FORM OF AID, SINCE IT IS MOST LIKELY TO WORK FOR
BOTH SIDES CANADA, IN DEVELOPING BILATERAL AID, SHOULD
CONCENTRATE ON AREA WHERE IT ALREADY HAS ESTABLISHED
EXPERTISE, SUCH AS RESOURCE MANAGEMENT AND THE DEVELOPMENT
OF MIXED ENTERPRISE, RATHER THAN ATTEMPT TOOAMBITIOUS OR
VAGUE APPROACHES THAT MAY FAIL.

08721 STUPISHIN, V.
THE STEREOTYPES WE ABANDON
INTERNATIONAL AFFAIRS (MOSCOW), (7) (JUL 89), 26-34.
THE SURVIVAL OF THE EARTH'S CIVILIZATION DEMANDS A NEW
THEORY OF INTERNATIONAL RELATIONS. WITHOUT A SCIENTIFICALLY-
GROUNDED THEORY, THERE CAN BE NO SERIOUS POLICY--ONLY
IMPROVISATION INCAPABLE OF YIELDING LONG-TERM RESULTS.
FORMULATING THIS THEORY REQUIRES A CRITICAL ANALYSIS OF BOTH
PAST AND PRESENT FOREIGN POLICY.

08722 STUPISHIN, V.
WHO HAS POWER IN A RULE-OF-LAW STATE
INTERNATIONAL AFFAIRS (MOSCOW), (12) (DEC 89), 27-40.
THE AUTHOR DEFINES THE LENINIST MODEL OF A TRULY
DEMOCRATIC STATE COMMITTED TO THE RULE OF LAW AND COMPARES
IT TO THE ACTUAL SITUATION IN THE SOVIET UNION.

08723 STURM, R.
THE ROLE OF THE BUNDESBANK IN GERMAN POLITICS
WEST EUROPEAN POLITICS, 12(2) (APR 89), 1-11.
THE BUNDESBANK PLAYS A CENTRAL ROLE IN GERMAN POLITICS.
IT'S STRONG POSITION IS MAINLY THE RESULT OF ITS
INDEPENDENCE FROM THE NATIONAL GOVERNMENT. THIS INDEPENDENCE
IS GUARANTEED BY THE BUNDESBANK ACT AND HAS BEEN DEFENDED
TIME AFTER TIME EVEN AT THE PRICE OF OPEN CONFLICT WITH THE
CENTRAL GOVERNMENT. THE IMPORTANCE OF THE INDEPENDENCE OF
THE CENTRAL BANK IS ALSO THE BASIS OF THE ATTITUDE OF THE
BUNDESBANK TOWARDS EUROPEAN MONETARY INTEGRATION. TODAY, THE
INDEPENDENCE OF THE BUNDESBANK IS THREATENED BY PARTY-
POLITICAL INFLUENCE ON THE SELECTION OF ITS BOARD MEMBERS,
BY THE PUBLIC REACTION AGAINST THE BANK'S VIEWS ON MATTERS
OTHER THAN MONETARY, CREDIT AND EXCHANGE-RATE POLICIES, AND
BY RECENT EFFORTS AT THE EUROPEAN LEVEL TO EXTEND THE EMS.

08724 SUAN, H.
MULTI-POLAR TENDENCY IN THE WORLD ECONOMY
BEIJING REVIEW, 32(35) (AUG 89), 15-18.
THE MULTI-POLAR DEVELOPMENT OF THE WORLD ECONOMY IS
TRANSFORMING THE BIPOLAR ECONOMIC SYSTEM THAT DEVELOPED
AFTER WORLD WAR II. THE MULTI-POLAR DEVELOPMENT IS REFLECTED
IN THE BREAK-UP OF THE WESTERN UNIFIED DOMAIN UNDER THE
LEADERSHIP OF THE UNITED STATES TO ONE IN WHICH THE USA,
EUROPE, AND JAPAN ARE CONFRONTING ONE ANOTHER. THE TENDENCY
OF THE WORLD ECONOMY TO DEVELOP INTO REGIONAL GROUPS IS
ACCELERATING AND BECOMING STRONGER. THE LEADERSHIP OF THE
USA IN DECIDING ISSUES IMPORTANT TO THE WEST IS DECLINING
AND A PROCESS OF CONSULTATIONS AMONG WESTERN COUNTRIES IS
REPLACING U.S. DOMINANCE.

08725 SUBTELNY, M.E.
THE CULT OF HOLY PLACES: RELIGIOUS PRACTICES AMONG SOVIET
MUSUMS
MIDDLE EAST JOURNAL, 43(4) (FAL 89), 593-604.
THE AUTHOR EXAMINES THE PERSISTENCE AND SIGNIFICANCE OF
THE CULT OF HOLY PLACES, A HIGHLY VISIBLE FEATURE OF ISLAM
IN THE MUSLIM AREAS OF THE SOVIET UNION. SHE POINTS OUT THAT
THESE ARE NOT JUST SHRINES TO LONG DEAD SAINTS, THEY ARE A
PART OF A WAY OF LIFE AND MAY COME TO PLAY AN INSTRUMENTAL
ROLE IN TODAY'S POLITICS.

08726 SUEC, M.
EAST EUROPEAN DIVIDES
FOREIGN POLICY, (77) (WIN 89), 41-63.
THIS ARTICLE PRESENTS AN ANALYSIS OF HOW EASTERN EUROPE
OFFERS VALUABLE CLUES TO PRESENT AND FUTURE SOVIET POLICY AS
WELL AS TO PROPER WESTERN RESPONSES IT EXAMINES CLASS
STRUGGLE, HUMAN RIGHTS, AND THE POLISH AND HUNGARIAN REFORM.
ARGUMENTS FAVOURING A HIGH-PROFILE U.S. COMMITMENT TO
DEMOCRACY AND FREE MARKETS IN EASTERN EUROPE ARE GIVEN.

08727 SUGARMAN, J.
LETHARGY AT LABOR
MULTINATIONAL MONITOR, 10(7-8) (JUL 89), 38-40.
IN RESPONSE TO DEMANDS FROM CONGRESS, LABOR UNIONS, AND
INDUSTRY TRADE ASSOCIATIONS, THE DEPARTMENT OF LABOR IS
TAKING A MORE AGGRESSIVE STANCE IN ITS EFFORTS TO PROMOTE
WORKER RIGHTS. AWAKENING AFTER EIGHT YEARS OF THE REAGAN
REIGN, THE LABOR DEPARTMENT HAS ANNOUNCED SEVERAL NEW
PROJECTS SINCE PRESIDENT BUSH'S INAUGURATION. THESE INCLUDE
SETTING NEW LEVELS FOR PERMISSIBLE EXPOSURE TO TOXIC
CHEMICALS, RESTRUCTURING THE JOB TRAINING PARTNERSHIP ACT,
AND ISSUING FINAL REGULATIONS ON THE NOTIFICATION OF PLANT
CLOSINGS AS WELL AS HOLDING HEARINGS ON A VARIETY OF OTHER
REGULATIONS.

08728 SUH, J.J.
CAPITALIST CLASS FORMATION AND THE LIMITS OF CLASS POWER
IN KOREA
DISSERTATION ABSTRACTS INTERNATIONAL, 49(7) (JAN 89),
1990-A.
THIS STUDY IS BASED ON THE CONCEPTUALIZATION OF THE
KOREAN BIG BUSINESS GROUPS, OR CHAEBOL, AS "THE CAPITALIST
CLASS". IT HAS ELABORATED THE CONCEPT OF SOCIAL CLASS INTO
FOUR DIMENSIONS (ORGANIZATIONAL, ECONOMIC, SOCIAL NETWORK,
AND IDEOLOGICAL) AND THEN CONSTRUCTED A FRAMEWORK OF
CAPITALIST CLASS FORMATION IN TERMS OF CLASS ACTIVITY AND

ITS INTERPLAY WITH OBJECTIVE CONDITIONS (POLITICAL REGIME, STATE, WORLD SYSTEM, CLASS STRUCTURE).

08729 SUKATIPAN, S.
THE MEDIA AND POLITICS: A STUDY OF RADIO BROADCASTING IN THAILAND
DISSERTATION ABSTRACTS INTERNATIONAL, 49(7) (JAN 89), 1947-A.
THIS STUDY ATTEMPTS TO SEEK AN ALTERNATIVE UNDERSTANDING OF THE CONTINUITY OF THE BUREAUCRATIC POLITY OF THE THAI STATE BY FOCUSING ON THE IDEOLOGICAL ROLE OF MEDIA PRACTICES IN THE PROCESS OF LEGITIMATION. THE CENTRAL THESIS IS THAT THE DOMINANT CLASS FRACTION, THE CAPITALISTBUREAUCRAT ALLIANCE, MAINTAINS ITS RULE WITH POPULAR CONSENT NOT MERELY THROUGH COERCIVE APPARATUSES OF THE STATE BUT ALSO VIA THE APPARATUSES FOR MAINTENANCE OF HEGEMONY WHICH BRING THE MASS OF THE PEOPLE INTO CONFORMITY WITH THE PREVAILING SOCIAL ORDER.

08730 SUKHOTIN, I.; DEMENT'EV, V.
ECONOMIC REFORM AND THE FORCES OF INHIBITION
SOVIET REVIEW, 30(2) (MAR 89), 3-9.
UNLIKE UNSUCCESSFUL PAST ATTEMPTS TO REFORM THE ECONOMIC MECHANISM IN THE SOVIET UNION, THE CURRENT RESTRUCTURING IS CHARACTERIZED BY A SERIOUS ATTITUDE TOWARD THE CONSERVATIVE FORCES CAPABLE OF PUTTING A DAMPER ON THE REFORMS. SUCCESSFUL REFORM CALLS FOR A PERVASIVE DEMOCRATIZATION OF DECISION-MAKING IN SOVIET SOCIETY AND FOR EXTENDING THE PRINCIPLE OF ENTERPRISE SELF-MANAGEMENT TO SOCIAL SELF-GOVERNMENT. THIS POLITICAL REFORM TO ACCOMPANY THE ECONOMIC RESTRUCTURING SHOULD INCLUDE REFERENDUMS AND ELECTION AND RECALL OF HIGHER-LEVEL PUBLIC OFFICIALS.

08731 SUKHOV, M.
E.P. THOMPSON AND THE PRACTICE OF THEORY: SOVEREIGNTY, DEMOCRACY AND INTERNATIONALISM
SOCIALISM AND DEMOCRACY, (FAL 89), 105-140.
THIS PAPER IS INTENDED AS AN ANALYSIS OF SOME OF E.P. THOMPSON'S WRITINGS ON NUCLEAR DISARMAMENT AND THE EUROPEAN PEACE MOVEMENT. ITS FOCUS IS THE DEVELOPMENT OF THREE KEY CONCEPTUAL THEMES WHICH INFORM HIS CONTINUING ANALYSES OF (1) THE POLITICAL CRISIS OCCASIONED BY THE NATO DECISION OF DECEMBER 12, 1979 TO DEPLOY A NEW GENERATION OF INTERMEDIATE RANGE MISSILES IN WESTERN EUROPE; AND (2) THE CHARACTER AND DYNAMICS OF THE PEACE MOVEMENT WHICH EMERGED AS A CONCRETE EXPRESSION OF, AS WELL AS RESPONSE TO, THIS CRISIS.

08732 SULLIVAN, B.A.
AFRICAN-AMERICAN POLITICAL EMPOWERMENT IN THE REALIGMENT ERA: A CASE STUDY OF THE NORTH CAROLINA GENERAL ASSEMBLY
DISSERTATION ABSTRACTS INTERNATIONAL, 49(8) (FEB 89), 2379-A.
THE AUTHOR PROVIDES A CASE STUDY OF BLACK POLITICAL EFFECTIVENESS WITHIN STATE LEGISLATIVE STRUCTURES. SHE EXAMINES THE DEVELOPMENT OF A BLACK LEGISLATIVE BASE DURING AN ERA OF EMERGING CONTROL BY THE REPUBLICAN PARTY IN NORTH CAROLINA.

08733 SULLIVAN, G.
A STUDY OF POLITICAL CAMPAIGNS OF DISCRIMINATION AGAINST GAY PEOPLE IN THE UNITED STATES, 1950-1978
DISSERTATION ABSTRACTS INTERNATIONAL, 48(10) (APR 88), 2731-A.
THE RESEARCH EXAMINES EIGHT CAMPAIGNS OF DISCRIMINATION AGAINST GAY PEOPLE IN THE US BETWEEN 1950 AND 1978. THE EFFECT ON THE GAY COMMUNITY AND THE RESPONSE IT MADE TO THE CAMPAIGNS ARE EXAMINED. A THEORETICAL FRAMEWORK IS ESTABLISHED TO ANALYZE TO PHENOMENON OF SOCIAL MOVEMENTS AND LABELING AND THEIR ROLE IN THE CAMPAIGNS.

08734 SULLIVAN, K.
THE BATTLE'S STILL ON IN RHODE ISLAND
STATE LEGISLATURES, 15(4) (APR 89), 19-21.
DURING THE 1989 RHODE ISLAND LEGISLATIVE SESSION, A NARROW 22-19 VICTORY FOR SENATE MAJORITY LEADER RESULTED IN UPHEAVAL. THE LOSER, WITH SUPPORT FROM MOST OF THE MINORITY PARTY, PUNISHED THE LEADER BY PASSING RULES CHANGES THAT STRIPPED HIM OF MOST OF HIS POWER.

08735 SULLIVAN, L., JR.
MAJOR DEFENSE OPTIONS
WASHINGTON QUARTERLY, 12(2) (SPR 89), 97-114.
FAILING THE ABILITY TO GENERATE BETTER ACCOMODATION WITH BOTH U.S. ALLIES AND POTENTIAL ADVERSARIES, THE UNITED STATES PROBABLY SHOULD ESCHEW THE QUEST FOR CHEAPER DEFENSE POLICY OPTIONS. INSTEAD, POLICYMAKERS SHOULD BE LOOKING MORE CLOSELY AT THE READILY AVAILABLE FEDERAL REVENUE OPTIONS TO RESTORE AND SUSTAIN DEFENSE SPENDING AT A PERMANENT LEVEL APPROACHING 6.5 PERCENT OF U.S GNP-INDEFINITELY.

08736 SULLIVAN, M.P.
HONDURAS: THE REGIONAL MIDDLEMAN
CRS REVEIW, 10(2) (FEB 89), 17-19.
HONDURANS EXPRESS FRUSTRATION OVER THEIR ROLE AS

REGIONAL MIDDLEMEN IN U.S. POLICY TOWARD CENTRAL AMERICA. THE UNITED STATES FACES SEVERAL ISSUES IN U.S.-HONDURAN RELATIONS: WHAT TO DO ABOUT THE CONTRAS, WHETHER TO CONTINUE OR EXPAND THE U.S. MILITARY PRESENCE, AND HOW U.S. POLICY WILL AFFECT DEMOCRACY AND HUMAN RIGHTS IN HONDURAS.

08737 SULLIVAN, M.P.
PANAMA: DILEMMA FOR U.S. POLICY
CRS REVEIW, 10(2) (FEB 89), 24-26.
DESPITE STRONG U.S. ACTION TO OUST GENERAL MANUEL ANTONIO NORIEGA FROM POWER, HE RETAINS FIRM CONTROL OF THE PANAMANIAN POLITICAL SYSTEM. THE UNITED STATES MUST NOW DECIDE WHETHER TO CONTINUE ECONOMIC SANCTIONS AGAINST PANAMA AND NONRECOGNITION OF THE NORIEGA REGIME OR TO SEEK AN ALTERNATIVE POLICY.

08738 SULLIVAN, P.
ISSUES IN THE INTERNATIONAL ECONOMICS OF INDUSTRIAL MOBILIZATION AND SURGE FOR CRISIS IN AN INTERDEPENDENT WORLD
AVAILABLE FROM NTIS, NO. DE89008627/GAR, 1989, 61.
THE PURPOSE OF THIS PAPER IS TO PRESENT ASPECTS OF INTENATIONAL TRADE WHICH ARE IMPORTANT FOR INDUSTRIAL MOBILIZATION IN TIME OF CRISIS, SUCH AS WAR, FAMINE AND NATURAL DISASTERS, IN AN INTERDEPENDENT WORLD. WE WILL FIRST PRESENT AN OVERVIEW OF THE INTERNATIONAL TRADE OF THE UNITED STATES IN TERMS OF OVERALL IMPORTS AND EXPORTS, IMPORTS AND EXPORTS BY MAJOR GEOGRAPHICAL REGIONS, AND TRADE BALANCE OF INDUSTRIES IMPORTANT TO DEFENSE. WE WILL THEN LOOK AT SPECIFIC CHARACTERISTICS OF THE INTERNATIONAL ARMS TRADE INCLUDING SOME MAJOR VULNERABILITIES AND DEPENDENCIES FACING THE US. WE WILL ANALYZE THE RELATIVE IMPORTANCE OF THE USSR, THE USA, THE COUNTRIES OF WESTERN EUROPE AND THE THIRD WORLD IN THE INTERNATIONAL ARMS TRADE. WE WILL THEN INTRODUCE AND EXPLAIN SOME OF THE MOST IMPORTANT CONCEPTS OF INTERNATIONAL TRADE AND MOBILIZATION INCLUDING: COMPARATIVE ADVANTAGE, ABSOLUTE ADVANTAGE, DYNAMIC COMPARATIVE ADVANTAGE, STRATEGIC COMPARATIVE ADVANTAGE AND DYNAMIC STRATEGIC COMPARATIVE ADVANTAGE. WHILE THESE CONCEPTS ARE BEING INTRODUCED EXAMPLES OF HOW THEY CAN BE APPLIED TO EXPLAIN THE STATE OF INTERNATIONAL TRADE AND MOBILIZATION WILL BE GIVEN.

08739 SUN, L.; GE, M.; ZHANG, S.
PROSPECTS OF CHINESE WAGE REFORM: A SYNERGY OF MARKET AND PLANNING SYSTEMS
INTERNATIONAL JOURNAL OF SOCIAL ECONOMICS, 16(8) (1989), 26-34.
WAGE REFORM IS AN IMPORTANT ASPECT OF CHINESE ECONOMIC REFORM. THE SUCCESS OF WAGE REFORM IS LIKELY TO DEPEND UPON THE FOLLOWING UNDERSTANDING: NEITHER USE OF THE EFFICIENCY-ORIENTED MARKET WAGE SYSTEM NOR USE OF THE EQUITY-ORIENTED PLANNED WAGE SYSTEM CAN SOLVE THE DUAL PROBLEM OF ECONOMIC GROWTH AND INCOME DISTRIBUTION. A SYNERGY OF THE TWO SYSTEMS WILL THEREFORE BE NEEDED. SUCH A SYNERGETIC WAGE SYSTEM, WHICH SIMULTANEOUSLY SOLVES THE DUAL PROBLEM OF PRODUCTION AND DISTRIBUTION, CAN EXPEDITE THE RISE OF SOCIAL PRODUCTIVITY -- THE FUNDAMENTAL MISSION IN THE PRELIMINARY STAGE OF CHINESE SOCIALISM. IN OTHER WORDS, WAGES SHOULD BE DIFFERENTIATED, AND THE DIFFERENCES SHOULD BE RELATED TO WORKERS' EFFORT AND SOCIETY'S DEMAND FOR THEM. THESE DIFFERENCES, HOWEVER, NEED NOT BE VERY LARGE.

08740 SUN, Y.
DIPLOMACY OF ILLUSION: CHINA'S QUEST FOR ANTI-JAPANESE ALLIANCES, 1931-1941
DISSERTATION ABSTRACTS INTERNATIONAL, 49(7) (JAN 89), 1929-A.
THE KEY TO UNDERSTANDING CHINESE ATTITUDES TOWARD THE IMPERIALIST POWERS DURING 1931-1941 WAS THE WIDESPREAD IDEA THAT CHINA SHOULD FORM INTERNATIONAL ALLIANCES TO CHECK JAPAN'S EXPANSIONISM ON THE ASIAN CONTINENT. JAPAN WAS PERCEIVED AS A THREAT TO CHINA'S NATIONAL SURVIVAL AND JAPAN'S AGGRESSIVE POLICIES RAN COUNTER TO THE INTERESTS OF THE OTHER IMPERIALIST POWERS.

08741 SUNDARAM, J.K.
MALAYSIA'S NEW ECONOMIC POLICY AND NATIONAL UNITY
THIRD WORLD QUARTERLY, 11(4) (OCT 89), 36-53.
THIS ARTICLE EXPLORES MALAYSIA'S NEW ECONOMIC POLICY AND NATIONAL UNITY AS THEIR SOCIETY AND CULTURE IS DOMINATED BY RACIAL AND ETHNIC PREOCCUPATIONS. THE DETERIORATION IN INTERETHNIC RELATIONS IS EXPLORED ON ECONOMIC, CULTURAL AND POLITICAL FRONTS POLITICAL CONTRADICTIONS AND PAST PERFORMANCE OF THE MALAYSIAN ECONOMIC POLICY ARE DETAILED. PROSPECTS FOR GROWTH ARE ANALYSED.

08742 SUNDEEN, R.A.
VOLUNTEER PARTICIPATION IN LOCAL GOVERNMENT AGENCIES
JOURNAL OF URBAN AFFAIRS, 11(2) (1989), 155-168.
USING DATA COLLECTED IN A NATIONAL SURVEY OF 1,638 INDIVIDUALS REGARDING VOLUNTEER BEHAVIOR, THIS ARTICLE EXAMINES FACTORS RELATED TO VOLUNTEER PARTICIPATION IN LOCAL GOVERNMENT ACTIVITIES. THE FINDINGS SUGGEST THAT AMONG ALL VOLUNTEERS (REGARDLESS OF SECTOR), THOSE INDIVIDUALS

RESIDING IN CITIES WITH POPULATIONS OF UNDER 100,000, IN
CENTRAL CITIES, AND IN STATES WHERE LIMITATIONS ON LOCAL TAX
REVENUES HAVE BEEN IMPOSED ARE MOST LIKELY TO VOLUNTEER TO
PERFORM ACTIVITIES UNDER THE AUSPICES OF A PUBLIC
JURISDICTION. FURTHERMORE, NONE OF THE OTHER
SOCIODEMOGRAPHIC VARIABLES ARE RELATED TO VOLUNTEERING TO
PUBLIC JURISDICTIONS. THE STUDY ALSO REVEALED THAT AMONG
THOSE WHO VOLUNTEER TO PUBLIC JURISDICTIONS, DIFFERENT
COMBINATIONS OF SOCIODEMOGRAPHIC AND ENVIRONMENTAL VARIABLES
ARE ASSOCIATED WITH DIFFERENT TYPES OF VOLUNTEER ACTIVITIES.

08743 SUNDELIUS, B.
      DAS PRIMAT DER NEUTRALITATSPOLITIK: BUILDING REGIMES AT
      HOME
      COOPERATION & CONFLICT: NORDIC JOURNAL OF INTERNATIONAL
      POLITICS, XXIV(3-4) (DEC 89), 163-178.
      IN THIS ARTICLE THE STRATEGIES USED BY THE TRADITIONAL
      FOREIGN POLICY CHIEF TO CONTROL THE PASSAGEWAY BETWEEN THE
      FOREIGN AND DOMESTIC ARENAS OF PUBLIC ACTIVITY ARE DISCUSSED.
      THE PAPER FOCUSES ON THE DOMESTIC STRUGGLE OVER THE CONDUCT
      OF FOREIGN POLICY. DRAWING ON THE WORKS OF CHARLES KEGLEY
      AND ROBERT KEOHANE, IT IS ARGUED THAT THE CONTINUED
      PROMINENCE OF THE SWEDISH FOREIGN MINISTRY IN THIS SECTOR
      CAN BE UNDERSTOOD IN THE CONTEXT OF THE PERSISTENCE OF A
      WELL-ENTRENCHED DECISION REGIME BUILT AROUND THE CONCEPT OF
      NEUTRALITY. THE APPARENT ABILITY OF THIS TRADITIONAL
      GATEKEEPER TO DOMINATE THIS INTERNAL MANAGEMENT PROCESS ALSO
      IN THE FACE OF THE DECENTRALIZING PRESSURES ASSOCIATED WITH
      INTERDEPENDENCE ARE EXPLAINED IN TERMS OF THE DECISION
      REGIME CONCEPT. THE STUDY CONTRIBUTES TO AN UNDERSTANDING OF
      HOW INTERNATIONAL DEVELOPMENTS AFFECT THE INTERNAL
      ORGANIZATIONAL LIFE OF A STATE.

08744 SUNDQUIST, J.L.
      CAN DIVIDED GOVERNMENT BE MADE TO WORK?
      BROOKINGS REVIEW, 7(2) (SPR 89), 14-15.
      POLITICAL PARTIES ARE ORGANIZED NOT FOR COLLABORATION
      BUT FOR COMBAT. THEY ARE FORMED BECAUSE PEOPLE HAVE DEEP-
      SEATED DIFFERENCES OF OPINION ABOUT THE GOALS AND POLICIES
      OF GOVERNMENT. PARTY RIVALRY IS HEALTHY, INDEED ESSENTIAL,
      FOR A DEMOCRACY. BUT WHEN EACH OF THE MAJOR PARTIES CONTROL
      ITS OWN BRANCH OF GOVERNMENT, AS HAS HAPPENED OFTEN IN
      RECENT AMERICAN HISTORY, THE INSTITUTIONS OF GOVERNMENT
      THEMSELVES ARE THROWN INTO CONFLICT, IMPELLED BY THE
      DYNAMICS OF PARTY COMPETITION TO ATTEMPT TO DISCREDIT AND
      DEFEAT EACH OTHER.

08745 SUNDQUIST, J.L.
      NEEDED: A POLITICAL THEORY FOR THE NEW ERA OF COALITION
      GOVERNMENT IN THE UNITED STATES
      POLITICAL SCIENCE QUARTERLY, 103(4) (WIN 89), 585-612.
      IN NOVEMBER 1988, WHEN THE AMERICAN VOTERS ELECTED A
      REPUBLICAN PRESIDENT AND A DEMOCRATIC CONGRESS, IT WAS THE
      SIXTH TIME IN NINE PRESIDENTIAL ELECTIONS THAT THE
      GOVERNMENT HAS SPLIT BETWEEN THE PARTIES, CREATING A UNIQUE
      VERSION OF COALITION GOVERNMENT. THE ADVENT OF THIS NEW ERA
      HAS RENDERED OBSOLETE MUCH OF THE POLITICAL THEORY DEVELOPED
      TO EXPLAIN HOW THE UNITED STATES GOVERNMENT CAN AND SHOULD
      WORK. THIS ARTICLE REVIEWS THE ANTI-PARTY DOCTRINE THE
      FRAMERS WROTE INTO THE CONSTITUTION BUT PROMPTLY ABANDONED.
      THEN IT PRESENTS THE THEORY OF PARTY GOVERNMENT AND
      PRESIDENTIAL LEADERSHIP AS IT WAS FORMULATED IN THE ERA THAT
      ENDED IN THE MID-1950'S. FINALLY, IT DISCUSSES THE
      OBSOLESENCE OF THAT THEORY DURING THE PAST THREE DECADES.

08746 SUNG-JOO, HAN
      SOUTH KOREA IN 1988: A REVOLUTION IN THE MAKING
      ASIAN SURVEY, XXIX(1) (JAN 89), 29-38.
      THE ARTICLE EXAMINES 1988, A YEAR OF BLOODLESS,
      NONVIOLENT "REVOLUTION" FOR SOUTH KOREA. NOT ONLY DID SOUTH
      KOREA GAIN INTERNATIONAL ATTENTION AND ACCLAIM BY HOSTING
      THE 1988 SUMMER OLYMPIC GAMES, BUT THE NATION ALSO UNDERWENT
      SIGNIFICANT SOCIOPOLITCAL CHANGES. THE ARTICLE BRIEFLY
      OUTLINES THE GENERAL TREND TOWARDS INCREASING
      DEMOCRATIZATION IN POLITICS AS WELL AS TOWARDS AN INCREASED
      INTERNATIONAL STANDING AMONG BOTH CAPITALIST AND SOCIALIST
      NATIONS.

08747 SUNIC, T.
      HISTORICAL DYNAMICS OF LIBERALISM: FROM TOTAL MARKET TO
      TOTAL STATE?
      JOURNAL OF SOCIAL, POLITICAL AND ECONOMIC STUDIES, 13(4)
      (WIN 88), 455-471.
      THE PURPOSE OF THIS ESSAY IS TO CRITICALLY EXAMINE THE
      HISTORICAL DYNAMICS OF LIBERALISM AND ITS IMPACT ON
      CONTEMPORARY WESTERN POLITIES. THIS ESSAY ARGUES (A) THAT
      LIBERALISM TODAY PROVIDES A COMFORTABLE IDEOLOGICAL
      "RETREAT" FOR MEMBERS OF THE INTELLECTUAL ELITE AND DECISION
      MAKERS TIRED OF THE THEOLOGICAL AND IDEOLOGICAL DISPUTES
      THAT ROCKED WESTERN POLITICS FOR CENTURIES; (B) THAT
      LIBERALISM CAN MAKE COMPROMISES WITH VARIOUS BRANDS OF
      SOCIALISM ON PRACTICALLY ALL ISSUES EXCEPT THE FREEDOM OF
      THE MARKET PLACE; (C) THAT LIBERALISM THRIVES BY EXPANDING
      THE ECONOMIC ARENA INTO ALL ASPECTS OF LIFE AND ALL CORNERS

OF THE WORLD, THEREBY GRADUALLY ERASING THE SENSE OF
NATIONAL AND HISTORICAL COMMUNITY WHICH HAD FORMERLY
PROVIDED THE INDIVIDUAL WITH A BASIC SENSE OF IDENTITY AND
PSYCHOLOGICAL SECURITY. THIS ESSAY ALSO QUESTIONS WHETHER
LIBERALISM, DESPITE ITS REMARKABLE SUCCESS IN THE REALM OF
THE ECONOMY, PROVIDES AN ADEQUATE BULWARK AGAINST NON-
DEMOCRATIC IDEOLOGIES OR WHETHER UNDER SOME CONDITIONS IT
MAY ACTUALLY STIMULATE THEIR GROWTH.

08748 SUNIC, T.
      THE EUROPEAN NEW RIGHT AND THE CRISIS OF MODERN POLITY
      DISSERTATION ABSTRACTS INTERNATIONAL, 49(12) (JUN 89),
      3860-A.
      THE AUTHOR SURVEYS THE CULTURAL AND POLITICAL IMPACT OF
      A DISTINCT BRAND OF CONTINENTAL EUROPEAN CONSERVATIVES, WHO
      ARE CALLED "NEUE KULTUR," "THULE SEMINAR," AND "G.R.E.C.E."
      THE GOAL OF THESE GROUPS IS TO RESTORE THE CREDIBILITY OF
      SOME EARLIER, PROMINENT ANTI-LIBERAL AND ANTI-COMMUNIST
      THINKERS AND ALSO TO INQUIRE INTO THE ROOTS OF THE
      CONTEMPORARY POLITICAL AND SOCIAL CRISIS IN BOTH EASTERN AND
      WESTERN EUROPE.

08749 SUNKEL, O.
      STRUCTURALISM, DEPENDENCY AND INSTITUTIONALISM: AN
      EXPLORATION OF COMMON GROUND AND DISPARITIES
      JOURNAL OF ECONOMIC ISSUES, XXIII(2) (JUN 89), 519-533.
      BY FOCUSING EXPLICITLY ON STOCKS, THEIR DYNAMICS, THE
      RELATIONS AMONG THEM, THE WAYS IN WHICH THEY GENERATE FLOWS,
      AND THE FEED-BACK OF FLOWS ON STOCKS, STRUCTURALISTS AND
      INSTITUTIONALISTS HAVE COMMON GROUND TO SUPPORT A JOINT
      INTELLECTUAL EFFORT AIMED AT A BETTER UNDERSTANDING OF
      ECONOMIC DEVELOPMENT AND OF THE STRATEGIES AND POLICIES THAT
      MIGHT BRING IT ABOUT AND CONTRIBUTE ESPECIALLY TO THE
      IMPROVEMENT OF THE LIVING CONDITIONS OF THE POOR.

08750 SUNUNU, J.
      RESTORING THE BALANCE
      JOURNAL OF STATE GOVERNMENT, 62(1) (JAN 89), 25-27.
      TWO HUNDRED YEARS AGO, THE FOUNDING FATHERS WORKED HARD
      TO ESTABLISH AN EFFECTIVE AND APPROPRIATE CONSTITUTIONAL
      BALANCE BETWEEN THE STATES AND THE NATIONAL GOVERNMENT.
      ALTHOUGH THE U.S. CONSTITUTION PROVIDES A STRONG FOUNDATION
      FOR GOVERNMENT, IN RECENT DECADES THE STRUCTURE THAT RESTS
      ON IT HAS BEGUN TO LEAN PERILOUSLY AWAY FROM THE STATES
      TOWARD WASHINGTON, D.C. UNLESS BALANCE IS RESTORED, THE
      UNITED STATES RUNS THE RISK OF LETTING ITS FEDERAL STRUCTURE
      LEAN SO FAR THAT IT MIGHT EVENTUALLY TOPPLE.

08751 SUPINA, P.D.
      CHINA'S COMING AGRICULTURAL CRISIS
      INTERNATIONAL SOCIAL SCIENCE REVIEW, 64(2) (SPR 89), 67-75.
      THE ARTICLE DISCUSSES THE AGRARIAN REFORMS OF DENG
      XIAOPING AND THE 11TH PARTY CONGRESS OF 1978. WHILE
      RECOGNIZING SOME OF THE BENEFITS AND VAST IMPROVEMENTS WHICH
      HAVE OCCURRED SINCE THEN, IT ALSO RECOGNIZES SOME OF THE
      MAJOR PROBLEMS AND DANGERS THOSE VERY REFORMS HAVE CREATED.
      MOST OF ALL, THERE HAS BEEN A SHARP DECLINE IN RURAL
      AGRICULTURAL INVESTMENT ON THE PART OF BOTH FARMERS AND
      COLLECTIVES, AND, AT THE SAME TIME, THERE HAS BEEN AN UPTURN
      IN THE BIRTH RATE. THE ARTICLE WARNS OF THE DANGERS OF
      INFLATION AND OF PUTTING TOO MUCH HOPE IN THE RECLAMATION
      AND DEVELOPMENT OF UNUSED LANDS. FINALLY, IT DOES MAKE SOME
      LONG-TERM RECOMMENDATIONS THAT ARE ABSOLUTELY ESSENTIAL IF
      CHINA IS TO AVOID ITS IMPENDING AGRICULTURAL CRISIS.

08752 SURIYAKUMARAN, C.
      THE ANATOMY OF NATIONAL IDENTITY IN SRI LANKA
      SCANDINAVIAN JOURNAL OF DEVELOPMENT ALTERNATIVES, 8(3)
      (SEP 89), 95-110.
      THIS ARTICLE WAS WRITTEN AMIDST THE EVENTS AND SENSE OF
      GROPING ARISING AFTER THE EVENTS OF 1983 IN SRI LANKA. THE
      PREMISE IS THAT WHEN SECURITY IS HIGH IN A SOCIETY AND WHEN
      EXPECTATIONS OF EMPLOYMENT AND ECONOMIC SECURITY ARE ALSO
      HIGH, ITS PEOPLE, EVEN IF MIXED, TEND TO THINK OF THEMSELVES
      EASILY AS AN ENTITY WITHIN THEIR COUNTRY. HOWEVER, WHEN A
      NON-TRADITIONAL POPULATION INCREASES BEYOND A CERTAIN NUMBER
      IN AN AREA, IT SEEMS THE TRADITIONAL POPULATION BEGINS TO
      GET UNCOMFORTABLE. WHEN THE CRITICAL MASS WILL BE REACHED IS
      DETERMINED BY MANY FACTORS WHICH ARE DETAILED AND THEN THESE
      FACTORS ARE EXAMINED AGAIN FROM THE POINT OF VIEW OF THEIR
      USE AS LEVERAGES IN NATIONAL UNITY. UNIFICATION TRAUMAS ARE
      DESCRIBED. THE ARTICLE CONCLUDES WITH THE TEXT OF A SPEECH
      DELIVERED IN 1854 BY RED INDIAN CHIEF SEATTLE IN RESPONSE TO
      A DEMAND THAT HE SELL HIS PEOPLE LAND.

08753 SURJEET, H.S.
      THE CONCEPT, ITS PLUSES AND MINUSES
      WORLD MARXIST REVIEW, 31(11) (NOV 88), 46-47.
      THIS ARTICLE DESCRIBES WHAT THE AUTHOR, A MEMBER OF THE
      COMMUNIST PARTY OF INDIA, CONSIDERS TO BE THE MAJOR
      SHORTCOMINGS OF THE CONCEPT OF NUCLEAR-WEAPON-FREE ZONES.

08754 SURLIS, P.
      THE SAG HARBOR INITIAVE: THE TOWN MEETING AS MODEL

MONTHLY REVIEW, 40(11) (APR 89), 27-36.
THE ARTICLE EXAMINES THE "TOWN MEETINGS" AT SAG, HARBOR, NEW YORK. THE MEETINGS WERE HELD BY A GROUP OF ARTISTS, WRITERS, SOCIAL WORKERS, TEACHERS, AND OTHER CONCERNED CITIZENS AND IMPORTANT SOCIAL ISSUES SUCH AS POVERTY, CRIME DISCRIMINATION, AND APATHY WERE DISCUSSED. THE MEETINGS GAINED SOME REKNOWN FOR THEIR CANDOR AND WILLINGNESS TO DISCUSS THE "UNSPOKEN ISSUES"--ISSUES THAT WERE RARELY HEARD IN THE PRESIDENTIAL CAMPAIGN.

08755 SUSSER, B.
"PARLIADENTIAL POLITICS": A PROPOSED CONSTITUTION FOR ISRAEL
PARLIAMENTARY AFFAIRS. 42(1) (JAN 89), 112-122.
THE ARTICLE EXAMINES THE EFFORTS OF A GROUP OF ISRAELI JURISTS AND POLITICAL SCIENTISTS WHO, MOVED BY ISRAEL'S LACK OF CONSTITUTION AND ALARMED BY THE UNSATISFACTORY FUNCTION OF ITS POLITICAL INSTITUTIONS, ATTEMPTED TO DRAFT AN "UNSOLICITED CONSTITUTION. THE ARTICLE CONCENTRATES ON ONE PARTICULAR FEATURE: A TRUE SYNTHESIS BETWEEN PARLIAMENTARY AND PRESIDENTIAL ARRANGEMENTS, A "PARLIADENTIAL" SYSTEM OF GOVERNMENT. THE CONSTITUTION COMBINES THE LEADERSHIP POTENTIALITIES OF PRESIDENCY WITH THE RESPONSIVENESS OF PARLIAMENTARY POLITICS. THE ARTICLE DISCUSSES THE IMPLICATIONS OF SUCH A SYSTEM FOR NOT ONLY ISRAEL, BUT OTHER NATIONS AS WELL.

08756 SUSSMAN, L.R.
NEWS FLOWS SUFFER WHEN JOURNALISTS BECOME VICTIMS
FREEDOM AT ISSUE, (106) (JAN 89), 39-45.
THE AUTHOR CATEGORIZES PRESS FREEDOM IN 159 COUNTRIES IN 1988 AND FINDS THAT 36 PERCENT BELONG IN THE MOST-FREE CATEGORY, 52 PERCENT ARE AMONG THE LEAST FREE, AND 12 PERCENT FALL INTO AN INTERMEDIARY GROUP. THE UNITED KINGDOM AND ISRAEL WERE INCLUDED IN THE FREEST CATEGORY, EVEN THOUGH THEY BOTH HAVE REPEATEDLY RESTRICTED PRESS COVERAGE. AMONG THE LEAST-FREE NATIONS, SIGNS OF GREATER DIVERSITY HAVE RECENTLY BEEN APPARENT IN THE USSR AND COMMUNIST CHINA.

08757 SUSSMAN, L.R.
THE INFORMATION REVOLUTION
ENCOUNTER, LXXIII(4) (NOV 89), 60-65.
IN THE 1990'S AND THE CENTURY BEYOND, THE TECHNOLOGIES OF COMMUNICATION WILL SERVE TO ENLARGE HUMAN FREEDOM EVERYWHERE, TO CREATE A COUNSEL OF THE PEOPLE. NEW COMMUNICATIONS TECHNOLOGIES WILL INDUCE THE HUMAN MIND TO THINK MORE CLEARLY, TO TEST NEW POSSIBILITIES, AND TO GAIN CONFIDENCE FROM THE PROCESS OF IDEA-DISCOVERY. WHETHER THIS WILL SERVE TO CREATE A PARLIAMENT OF THE PEOPLE, AS WOODROW WILSON ENVISIONED, WILL REMAIN A POLITICAL DETERMINATION. BUT SO PERVASIVE WILL COMMUNICATIONS BECOME, THAT THE TECHNOLOGY WILL TEND TO OVERCOME MANY POLITICAL RESTRICTIONS.

08758 SUSSMAN, L.R.
WHO CONTROLS INFORMATION?
FREEDOM AT ISSUE, (109) (JUL 89), 20-25.
THE AUTHOR REVIEWS THE MONTH-LONG INFORMATION FORUM HELD IN LONDON IN MAY 1989. THE CONVENING OF THE MEETING UNDER EAST-WEST AUSPICES UNDERSCORED THE FACT THAT NEWS AND INFORMATION HAVE BECOME CRUCIAL COMPONENTS OF NATIONAL AND INTERNATIONAL RELATIONSHIPS, INCLUDING THE PROMOTION OF PEACE. THE IMPORTANCE OF THE MEETING WAS NOT LIMITED TO THIS ONE FORUM, BECAUSE IT IS PART OF THE CONTINUING HELSINKI PROCESS BEGUN IN 1975. A MAJOR ISSUE AT THE FORUM WAS WHETHER THE SOVIET UNION WILL PERMIT THE FULL DEMOCRATIZATION OF INTERNAL AND EXTERNAL INFORMATION FLOWS-- A VITAL QUESTION FOR GLOBAL RELATIONS.

08759 SUSUMU, N.
DEFENDING THE DIGNITY OF THE SYMBOLIC EMPEROR
JAPAN ECHO, XVI(2) (SUM 89), 22-27.
IN THE TUMULTUOUS PERIOD FROM SEPTEMBER 1988, WHEN THE SHOWA EMPEROR BECAME SERIOUSLY ILL, TO JANUARY 1989, WHEN THE NEW EMPEROR ACCEDED TO THE THRONE, REPORTERS, COMMENTATORS, AND CRITICS FLOODED THE JAPANESE MEDIA WITH AN UNENDING STREAM OF MATERIAL PERTAINING TO THE AILING EMPEROR, HIS HEIR, AND THE IMPERIAL HOUSEHOLD. IN THIS ESSAY, THE AUTHOR ATTEMPTS TO PROVIDE A COMPREHENSIVE ASSESSMENT OF THE VIEWS AND ATTITUDES CONVEYED BY THE MEDIA. HE ALSO OFFERS HIS OWN IDEAS ON THE NATURE AND ROLE OF THE IMPERIAL INSTITUTION IN JAPAN.

08760 SUSUMU, O.
RECRUIT AND THE CHANGING POPULAR MOOD
JAPAN ECHO, XVI(3) (AUT 89), 51-56.
A SOMBER STATE OF MIND ENVELOPED JAPAN IN THE EARLY MONTHS OF 1989, BROUGHT ON BY THE DEATH OF THE EMPEROR, THE DEEPENDING RECRUIT SCANDAL, AND A RASH OF CHILD KIDNAPPINGS AND MURDERS IN TOKYO. THIS CHANGE IN MOOD WAS APPARENT IN THE STYLE OF POLITICAL LEADERSHIP. IN CONTRAST TO THE CHARISMATIC NAKASONE YASUHIRO, PRIME MINISTER TAKESHITA NOBORU IS A PRACTICAL, BUSINESSLIKE ADMINISTRATOR CONCERNED MORE WITH THE MACHINERY OF POLITICS THAN THE VENEER. TAKESHITA'S PROMISE TO WORK FOR THE CREATION OF A HOMETOWN

ATMOSPHERE SIGNALED A MORE DOWN-TO-EARTH BRAND OF LEADERSHIP THAN NAKASONE'S.

08761 SUTER, K.D.
REFORMING THE UNITED NATIONS
CONTEMPORARY REVIEW, 254(1477) (FEB 89), 57-62.
THE IMMEDIATE NEED FOR REFORM HAS BEEN FORCED UPON THE UN THROUGH ITS CURRENT FINANCIAL CRISIS - LARGELY, BUT NOT SOLELY, INITIATED BY THE UNITED STATES. THE UN OBTAINS ITS FUNDS BY ASSESSING EACH MEMBER-NATION FOR A CERTAIN PERCENTAGE OF THE TOTAL BUDGET FIGURE DECIDED BY THE GENERAL ASSEMBLY. THESE ASSESSED CONTRIBUTIONS ARE PAYABLE AT THE START OF THE CALENDAR YEAR (WHICH IS ALSO THE UN'S FINANCIAL YEAR). DIFFERENCES BETWEEN THE BUDGETARY CYCLES OF SOME MEMBER NATIONS AND THE UN NECESSITATED THE CREATION OF A RESERVE FUND TO GIVE THE UN SUFFICIENT OPERATING CAPITAL TO CONTINUE OPERATIONS WHILE AWAITING PAYMENT OF THESE CONTRIBUTIONS. THE UNITED STATES, WHICH IS THE MAJOR CONTRIBUTOR, DOES NOT PAY ITS BILL UNTIL THE LAST QUARTER OF THE YEAR. DESPITE NUMEROUS EFFORTS SINCE THE MID-1960S TO REMEDY THE SITUATION LATE PAYMENT OF ASSESSED CONTRIBUTIONS HAS BECOME AN INCREASING PROBLEM FOR THE UN. THE PROBLEM HAS BEEN EXACERBATED IN THE LAST DECADE BY THE DOWNTURN IN THE INTERNATIONAL ECONOMY.

08762 SUTER, K.D.
THE IVORY COAST
CONTEMPORARY REVIEW, 255(1485) (OCT 89), 173-177.
THE OBJECT OF THIS ARTICLE IS TO PROVIDE SOME BACKGROUND INFORMATION ON THE IVORY COAST. IT DEALS WITH FRENCH COLONIAL POLICY, THE SIGNIFICANT ROLE OF THE IVORY COAST'S SOLE PRESIDENT, THE CONTINUING IMPORTANCE OF FRANCE TO THE IVORY COAST AND THE IVORY COAST'S COMPARATIVE ECONOMIC SUCCESS AND POLITICAL STABILITY. IT CONCLUDES, HOWEVER, WITH THREE WARNINGS ABOUT THE NATION'S FUTURE.

08763 SUTHERLAND, M.E.
INDIVIDUAL DIFFERENCES IN RESPONSE TO THE STRUGGLE FOR THE LIBERATION OF PEOPLE OF AFRICAN DESCENT.
JOURNAL OF BLACK STUDIES, 20(1) (SEP 89), 40-59.
THIS ARTICLE ACKNOWLEDGES THE CONTRIBUTIONS OF AUTHORS OF AN AFRICAN PSYCHOLOGY AND RECOGNIZES THE USEFULNESS OF AFFIRMING AFRICAN PEOPLE'S POSITIVE PSYCHOLOGICAL ASPECTS. THEN CONTENDS THAT THOSE VERY STUDIES IS PROACTIVE FOR BLACK LIBERATION. FIVE ORIENTATIONS ARE PRESENTED WITH A PHENOMENOLOGICAL PERSPECTIVE. THE SEMINAL VIEWS OF THE OPPRESSOR-OPPRESSED RELATIONSHIP ARE INTERWOVEN IN THE DISCUSSION. IT IS ARGUED THAT OPPRESSION REMAINS A FORCE IN THE LIVES OF BLACKS AND THAT THEIR PATTERNS OF BEHAVING PLAY SOME ROLE IN THE MAINTENANCE OF THAT OPPRESSION.

08764 SUTTMEIER, R.P.
REFORM, MODERNIZATION, AND THE CHANGING CONSTITUTION OF SCIENCE IN CHINA
ASIAN SURVEY, 29(10) (OCT 89), 999-1015.
PRIOR TO THE SUPPRESSION OF STUDENT DEMONSTRATIONS IN JUNE 1989, MOST OBSERVERS OF CONTEMPORARY CHINA SAW THE NATION'S REFORM PROGRAMS AS HAVING ENTERED A NEW AND UNQUESTIONABLY MORE COMPLEX STAGE. THE "EASY" REFORMS HAD BEEN MADE, AND THE RELATIONSHIPS BETWEEN POLITICAL AND ECONOMIC REFORMS HAD BECOME MORE PROMINENT. HOPES FOR ELITE CONSENSUS SEEMED TO BE FADING AS THE STRESSES OF THIS NEW STAGE BECAME MORE ACUTE. WITH THE CRACKDOWN ON THE DEMONSTRATORS AND THE PURGE OF ZHAO ZIYANG AND THOSE REFORMERS CLOSE TO HIM, THE FUTURE HAS BECOME EVEN MORE UNCERTAIN. THIS ARTICLE EXPLORES THE DYNAMICS OF REFORM IN A CRITICAL AREA OF MODERNIZATION--THE DEVELOPMENT OF SCIENCE AND TECHNOLOGY--WITH AN EYE TOWARD UNDERSTANDING THE SYSTEMIC FORCES THAT, ALONG WITH ELITE POLITICS, ARE LIKELY TO SHAPE THE REFORM AGENDA IN THE NEAR- TO MEDIUM-TERM FUTURE.

08765 SUTTON, M.
THE ROSE GARDEN AND THE EAST WIND
ENCOUNTER, LXXIII(3) (SEP 89), 50-57.
SINCE THE EARLY 1980'S, THE VIRTUALITIES OF THE FRANCO-GERMAN ALLIANCE HAVE LESSENED IN THEIR RELATIVE IMPORTANCE FOR BONN. FIRST, AS THE PRIVILEGED RELATION EMBODIED IN THE SCHMIDT-GISCARD PARTNERSHIP CAME TO AN END, WITH BRITAIN'S PRESENCE MORE STRONGLY ASSERTED IN EUROPE, THERE WAS NO LONGER THE SAME SCOPE FOR A FRANCO-GERMANY DIRECTORY AT THE EUROPEAN COMMUNITY LEVEL. THEN, FROM THE MIDDLE OF THE DECADE ON, AS BONN LOOKED INCREASINGLY EASTWARDS WITH A REINVIGORATED OSTPOLITIK, ATTENTION BECAME MORE FOCUSED ON THE ELBE THAN ON THE RHINE.

08766 SUYEHIRO, S.
NUCLEAR TEST BAN AND VERIFICATION
DISARMAMENT, XII(3) (AUT 89), 24-27.
THE VERIFICATION OF UNDERGROUND NUCLEAR TESTING HAS BECOME A MAJOR ISSUE IN CONNECTION WITH THE PROPOSED TOTAL BAN ON NUCLEAR TESTS. GLOBAL SEISMIC OBSERVATION HAS BEEN INTERNATIONALLY ACCEPTED AS THE MOST PROMISING MEANS OF VERIFYING A BAN ON UNDERGROUND NUCLEAR TESTS. A GLOBAL

NETWORK OF ABOUT FIFTY SENSITIVE, WELL-EQUIPPED SEISMIC
STATIONS WOULD BE NEEDED. THE DATA FROM THESE STATIONS WOULD
HAVE TO BE EXCHANGED OPENLY AND EXPEDITIOUSLY. A PRACTICAL
SYSTEM IS NOW UNDER STUDY, MAKING FULL USE OF MODERN
COMPUTER AND COMMUNICATIONS TECHNOLOGY. BUT THERE ARE STILL
A NUMBER OF PROBLEMS TO BE SOLVED, REQUIRING POLITICAL AND
ADMINISTRATIVE DECISIONS.

08767 SVARA, J.H.
IS THERE A FUTURE FOR CITY MANAGERS? THE EVOLVING ROLES OF
OFFICIALS IN COUNCIL-MANAGER GOVERNMENT
INTERNATIONAL JOURNAL OF PUBLIC ADMINISTRATION, 12(2)
(1989), 179-212.
CHANGES IN THE ROLES OF ELECTED OFFICIALS IN
COUNCILMANAGER GOVERNMENT HAVE IMPORTANT IMPLICATIONS FOR
THE POSITION OF THE MANAGER AS A PROFESSIONAL PUBLIC
ADMINISTRATOR. THE FORM OF GOVERNMENT ITSELF WILL BE
THREATENED IF MAYORS TAKE ON EXECUTIVE TASKS AND IF THE
COUNCIL CARRIES ACTIVISM AND CONSTITUENCY SERVICE TO THE
POINT OF UNDERMINING THE PROFESSIONALISM OF THE MANAGER AND
STAFF. THESE NEGATIVE CONSEQUENCES ARE NOT NECESSARY
OUTCOMES OF CURRENT TRENDS. THE ROLE OF THE MANAGER WILL
CONTINUE TO BE TRANSFORMED BUT NEED NOT BE UNDERMINED BY THE
EXPANDING CONTRIBUTIONS OF ELECTED OFFICIALS. COMPLEMENTARY
ROLES MAY BE IDENTIFIED FOR THE MAYOR, COUNCIL MEMBERS, AND
MANAGER WHICH REPRESENT A BLENDING OF GREATER PARTS OF BOTH
POLITICAL AND PROFESSIONAL LEADERSHIP IN CITY GOVERNMENT.

08768 SVARA, J.H.
PROGRESSIVE ROOTS OF THE MODEL CHARTER AND THE MANAGER
PROFESSION: A POSITIVE HERITAGE
NATIONAL CIVIC REVIEW, 78(5) (SEP 89), 339-355.
THE MODEL CITY CHARTER'S VISION OF A FORM OF GOVERNMENT
WITH COMPLEMENTARY AND COOPERATIVE RELATIONSHIPS BETWEEN
OFFICIALS WHO REFLECT DEMOCRATIC ACCOUNTABILITY (COUNCIL
MEMBERS) AND ADMINISTRATIVE PROFESSIONALISM (THE MANAGER) IS
THE CONTRIBUTION OF THE PROGRESSIVE REFORM ERA TO THE
AMERICAN POLITICAL TRADITION. CITIES BENEFIT FROM A
GOVERNMENTAL ARRANGEMENT THAT PLACES EXPERTS IN A POSITION
TO SERVE THE PUBLIC BETTER THAN ANY ALTERNATIVE FORM OF
GOVERNMENT. WITH PERIODIC MODIFICATION THE COUNCIL-MANAGER
PLAN WILL CONTINUE TO BE THE BASIS AND MODEL FOR RESPONSIVE
AND EFFECTIVE LOCAL GOVERNMENT.

08769 SVEJNAR, J.
MODELS OF MODERN-SECTOR LABOR MARKET INSTITUTIONS IN
DEVELOPING COUNTRIES
WORLD DEVELOPMENT, 17(9) (SEP 89), 1409-1415.
THE PAPER ARGUES THAT POLICY CONCLUSIONS DERIVED FROM
EXISTING THEORIES OF ECONOMIC DEVELOPMENT MAY BE SERIOUSLY
FLAWED BECAUSE THE THEORIES DO NOT MODEL CORRECTLY THE
MODERN-SECTOR LABOR MARKET. THE PAPER FIRST PRESENTS
EVIDENCE THAT TRADE UNIONS AND GOVERNMENTS FREQUENTLY EXERT
POSITIVE INFLUENCE NOT ONLY ON FIRMS' WAGES BUT ALSO ON
THEIR EMPLOYMENT LEVELS. IT THEN PRESENTS MODELS THAT
CAPTURE THIS PHENOMENON AND PERMIT ONE TO DETERMINE WHETHER
THE OBSERVED LEVELS OF EMPLOYMENT ARE INSUFFICIENT, OPTIMAL,
OR EXCESSIVE FROM THE PRIVATE AND SOCIAL STANDPOINTS. THE
PAPER CONCLUDES WITH A DISCUSSION OF HOW THE ANALYSIS COULD
BE IMPLEMENTED IN EMPIRICAL STUDIES AND IN PRACTICAL POLICY
WORK.

08770 SVENNSON, L.
A DEMOCRATIC STRATEGY FOR ORGANIZATIONAL CHANGE
INTERNATIONAL JOURNAL OF HEALTH SERVICES, 19(2) (1989),
319-334.
THIS ARTICLE PRESENTS A MODEL OF DEMOCRATIC WORK
ORGANIZATION BASED ON CONCRETE EXAMPLES FROM SWEDEN. IT
FOCUSES ON HOW DEMOCRATIC WORK ORGANIZATIONS CAN COME ABOUT;
HOW THEY CAN BE INTRODUCED, DEVELOPED, AND PROTECTED; AND,
IN GENERAL, HOW THEIR GROWTH CAN BE ENCOURAGED. IN THE FINAL
SECTION THE PERSPECTIVE IS BROADENED. THE POSSIBILITIES OF
CREATING AN INDUSTRIAL DEMOCRACY ARE DISCUSSED FROM A
SOCIETAL PERSPECTIVE. WOMEN IN THE PUBLIC SECTOR ARE SEEN AS
A POSSIBLE "AVANT-GARDE" IN A UNION-BASED STRUGGLE FOR THE
DEMOCRATIC ORGANIZATION OF WORK.

08771 SVERSTYUK, Y.
A PROBLEM THAT SHOULD NOT EXIST
GLASNOST, (16-18) (JAN 89), 82.
THE PROBLEM OF THE CRIMEAN TARTARS SHOULD NOT STILL
EXIST. AND IT WOULD NOT IF THE SOCIALIST DEMOCRACY AND
NATIONAL RIGHTS PROCLAIMED BY THE GOVERNMENT WERE GUARANTEED
BY THE DIGNITY OF THE STATE. BY NOW, THE CRIMEAN TARTARS
SHOULD HAVE RETURNED TO THE LAND OF THEIR FOREFATHERS,
SHOULD HAVE BECOME MASTERS OF THEIR OWN HOMES, AND SHOULD
HAVE FORGOTTEN THE PAIN CAUSED THEM IN THE WAR BY BOTH A
CRUEL INVADER AND A CRUEL LIBERATOR.

08772 SHADDLE, K.; HEATH. A.
OFFICIAL AND REPORTED TURNOUT IN THE BRITISH GENERAL
ELECTION OF 1987
BRITISH JOURNAL OF POLITICAL SCIENCE, 19(4) (OCT 89),
537-551.

THE OFFICIAL VOTER TURNOUT FOR GREAT BRITAIN IN 1987 WAS
ABOUT 75 PERCENT. BUT THE BRITISH GENERAL ELECTION STUDY
(BGES) INDICATES A VOTER TURNOUT OF 86 PERCENT. IN THIS
ESSAY, THE AUTHORS EXPLORE THE DISCREPANCY BETWEEN THE
OFFICIAL AND THE BGES ESTIMATE OF TURNOUT. THEN THEY ASSESS
HOW REPRESENTATIVE THE SURVEY RESPONDENTS ARE OF VOTERS AND
NONVOTERS AND REASSESS SURVEY-BASED RESEARCH ON THE
DETERMINANTS OF NON-VOTING.

08773 SWAIN, N.
HUNGARY'S SOCIALIST PROJECT IN CRISIS
NEW LEFT REVIEW, (176) (JUL 89), 3-30.
THE AUTHOR SURVEYS THE POLITICAL ARENA IN CONTEMPORARY
HUNGARY, WHICH APPEARS TO BE A LABORATORY OF CHANGE IN THE
EASTERN BLOC. HIS ACCOUNT PAINTS A PICTURE OF A FAST-MOVING
POLITICAL CRISIS AND OF THE IDEAS THAT HAVE DEVELOPED WITHIN
AND OUTSIDE THE COMMUNIST MOVEMENT TO ADDRESS IT.

08774 SWAN, W. L.
THAI-JAPAN MONETARY RELATIONS AT THE START OF THE PACIFIC
WAR
MODERN ASIAN STUDIES, 23(2) (MAY 89), 313-347.
THE POINT MADE IN THIS ARTICLE IS THAT THAILAND'S PLACE
IN JAPAN'S MONETARY POLICY WAS DISTINCTLY DIFFERENT FROM AND
PREFERABLE TO THOSE AREAS TAKEN OVER DIRECTLY BY THE
JAPANESE. THAILAND WAS NOT INCORPORATED INTO THE JAPANESE
MILITARY SCRIP SYSTEM INTRODUCED INTO SOUTHEAST ASIA, A FACT
CRUCIAL TO THAILAND'S WARTIME EXPERIENCE. IT MEANT THAT
THAILAND'S MONETARY SYSTEM REMAINED IN THAI HANDS AND BEYOND
THE CONTROL OF THE JAPANESE MILITARY. IT MEANT THAT THE
THAIS COULD KEEP TRACK OF THEIR FINANCIAL AFFAIRS THUS
ALLOWING THEM TO PURSUE ACTIVE POLICIES TO REMEDY THEIR
ECONOMIC AND MONETARY PROBLEMS BROUGHT ON BY THE WAR. IN
JAPAN'S NAMPO POLICY, THAILAND'S SOVEREIGNTY AND NATIONHOOD
WERE NEVER DENIED; THAI-JAPAN RELATIONS WERE ON A GOVERNMENT-
TO-GOVERNMENT BASIS AND WORKED OUT THROUGH THE NEGOTIATION
PROCESS, THINGS DENIED TO THE AREAS DIRECTLY ADMINISTERED BY
JAPAN.

08775 SHANEY, J.A.; EVERS, M.A.
THE SOCIAL COST CONCEPTS OF K. WILLIAM KAPP AND KARL
POLANYI
JOURNAL OF ECONOMIC ISSUES, 23(1) (MAR 89), 7-34.
THIS ARTICLE EXPLORES THE SOCIAL COST CONCEPT WITH THREE
OBJECTIVES: 1) TO DRAW ATTENTION TO KNAPP'S INSTITUTIONALISM,
2) TO PROMOTE POLANYI'S FUNDAMENTAL CONTRIBUTION TO THE
ANALYSIS OF SOCIAL COSTS, AND 3) TO RECAST THE SOCIAL COST
CONCEPT ITSELF IN THE CONTEXT OF THE PERVASIVE CONSEQUENCES
OF ECONOMIC ACTIVITIES ON INDIVIDUALS, SOCIOSYSTEMS AND
ECOSYSTEMS. IT CONCLUDES WITH A DEMONSTRATION OF
RECIPROCALITY AND OFFERS SUGGESTIONS FOR PURSUING ECOLOGICAL
ECONOMICS.

08776 SHANKEY, B.
1919 WINNIPEG GENERAL STRIKE
COMMUNIST VIEWPOINT, 20(4) (WIN 88), 11-15.
THIS PAPER DETAILS THE 1919 WINNIPEG GENERAL STRIKE AS
TO IMMEDIATE CAUSES, ITS VETERAN SUPPORT, ITS SUPPORT FOR
THE RUSSIAN REVOLUTION AND THE CITIZEN COMMITTEE OF 1,000.
IT EXPLORES THE ARREST AND TRIAL OF STRIKE LEADERS AND THE
ROLE OF SOCIALISTS AS LABOR TURNS TO POLITICAL STRUGGLE. IT
CONCLUDES WITH LESSONS OF THE STRIKE.

08777 SHANN, R.
CHEMICAL WEAPONS: LIBYA INTO THE BACKGROUND
MIDDLE EAST INTERNATIONAL, (342) (JAN 89), 10.
IN JANUARY 1989, 80 FOREIGN MINISTERS MET IN PARIS FOR A
CONFERENCE ON THE BANNING OF CHEMICAL WEAPONS. THE MEETING
UNDERLINED THE CONVERGENT POLICY OF THE TWO SUPERPOWERS ON
THE CHEMICAL WARFARE ISSUE AND THE DIFFERENT ATTITUDE OF THE
THIRD WORLD, PARTICULARLY THE ARAB STATES. FOR NATIONS
POSSESSING LARGE STOCKS OF THE WEAPONS, THE ISSUE IS
NONPROLIFERATION. OTHER NATIONS, PARTICULARLY THE ARAB BLOC,
CALLED FOR A LINK BETWEEN CHEMICAL AND NUCLEAR DISARMAMENT.

08778 SHANN, R.
FRANCE INTERVENES
MIDDLE EAST INTERNATIONAL, (357) (AUG 89), 6.
AFTER INCREASED MILITARY PRESENCE NEARLY RESULTED IN
DISASTER IN APRIL, 1989, FRANCE SEEMS WILLING TO TRY AGAIN
IN LEBANON. FRENCH NAVAL FORCES HAVE INCREASED SIGNIFICANTLY
OFF OF THE COAST OF LEBANON TO INCLUDE AN AIRCRAFT CARRIER
AND A FRIGATE. ALTHOUGH FRANCE'S MOTIVES MAY SEEM OBSCURE TO
THE OUTSIDE OBSERVER (FRANCE OBVIOUSLY DOES NOT DESIRE FULL-
SCALE MILITARY INTERVENTION), THE DEEP ROMANTIC ATTACHMENT
TO LEBANON CONTINUES TO COMPEL FRANCE TO TAKE SOME SORT OF
ACTION.

08779 SHANN, R.
MITTERAND PROPOSES A CONFERENCE
MIDDLE EAST INTERNATIONAL, (362) (NOV 89), 7-8.
FRANCOIS MITTERAND'S CALL FOR A CONFERENCE OF THE
EUROPEAN ECONOMIC COMMUNITY AND THE 22 ARAB MEMBER-STATES OF
THE ARAB LEAGUE WAS NOT A LARGE SURPRISE; HE WAS MERELY

FULFILLING A PREVIOUS AGREEMENT. HOWEVER, HIS
UNPRECEDENTEDLY STRAIGHTFORWARD LANGUAGE WAS SHOCKING TO
SOME. HE FLATLY STATED, "WHAT IS HAPPENING ON THE WEST BANK
HAS GONE ON LONG ENOUGH." MITTERAND'S MOVE WAS CRITICIZED IN
FRANCE, BUT MANY IN INTERNATIONAL CIRCLES VIEW IT AS NEW
LIFE IN A SLUGGISH PEACE PROCESS.

08780 SWANN, R.
THE EURO-ARAB DIALOGUE: FRANCE'S HEADSCARF ROW
MIDDLE EAST INTERNATIONAL, (365) (DEC 89), 11.
FRANCE IS ASSUMING AN INCREASING ACTIVE AND VISIBLE ROLE
IN THE MIDEAST PEACE PROCESS. FRANCOIS MITTERAND SPONSORED A
HIGH-LEVEL CONFERENCE OF MIDEAST LEADERS IN PARIS. FRANCE
HAS ALSO EXPANDED ITS INTEREST IN RESOLVING THE LEBANESE
CONFLICT. THESE ACTIONS HAVE SOMEWHAT ANGERED FRANCE'S EC
NEIGHBORS--NOTABLY BRITIAN--WHO STATE THAT FRANCE IS MAKING
TOO MUCH OF ITS SPECIAL EC STATUS.

08781 SWANSINGER, A.J.
THE MAGIC CARPET: LEND-LEASE IN THE MIDDLE EAST, 1940-1944
DISSERTATION ABSTRACTS INTERNATIONAL, 49(10) (APR 89),
3149-A.
THE AUTHOR EXAMINES THE NATURE OF THE ANGLO-AMERICAN
COALITION IN THE MIDDLE EAST DURING THE WAR YEARS AND THE
DEVELOPMENT OF AMERICAN-MIDDLE EASTERN RELATIONS. THE ANGLO-
AMERICAN MILITARY ALLIANCE, WHICH WAS CREATED IN A SPIRIT OF
COOPERATION AND IN SUPPORT OF BRITAIN'S WAR EFFORT, WAS
QUICKLY TRANSFORMED BY THE RAPID ESCALATION OF AMERICAN AID.
WASHINGTON'S INVOLVEMENT GREW AT A RAPID PACE AND WITH IT
GREW A PRONOUNCED AMBIVALENCE REGARDING ITS ROLE AS ALLY AND
SUPPORTER OF BRITAIN'S IMPERIAL POLICIES.

08782 SHARTZ, P.
FLOATING BASES: MOVING OUT TO SEA?
NATO'S SIXTEEN NATIONS, 34(2) (APR 89), 65-68, 71.
THE AMERICAN GOVERNMENT IS COMING TO GRIPS WITH ITS
DOMESTIC BASE CLOSURE PROBLEM FOR THE FIRST TIME IN OVER A
DECADE, WHILE MILITARY, POLITICAL, AND ECONOMIC PRESSURES AT
HOME AND OVERSEAS HAVE PROMPTED REASSESSMENTS OF AMERICA'S
FOREIGN BASE SYSTEM. SINCE OVERSEAS BASES ARE NOT ON HOME
TERRITORY, POLITICAL AND ECONOMIC PROBLEMS CAN NULLIFY THEIR
PURPOSE. ALTERNATIVES INCLUDE HOME-BASED FORCES WITH RAPID
AND POWERFUL TRANSPORT FACILITIES AND LONG-RANGE WEAPON
SYSTEMS. OTHER OPTIONS, SUCH AS BASING IN SPACE, IN THE AIR,
OR PERMANENTLY ON THE HIGH SEAS, CAN BE EFFECTIVE BUT COSTLY.

08783 SWEET, D.C.
BUILDING UNIVERSITY-COMMUNITY PARTNERSHIPS: INCREASING
URBAN COMPETITIVENESS
NATIONAL CIVIC REVIEW, 78(1) (JAN 89), 25-36.
UNIVERSITIES, IN COOPERATION WITH THE PRIVATE AND PUBLIC
SECTORS, CAN MAKE SIGNIFICANT CONTRIBUTIONS TO ADDRESSING
BOTH THE SOCIAL AND SERVICE-DELIVERY PROBLEMS OF A REGION,
WHILE CREATING AND REINFORCING A REGIONAL CULTURE OF
COMPETITIVENESS AND PREPAREDNESS FOR A CHALLENGING WORLD
ECONOMY. IN THE EARLY YEARS OF PUBLIC HIGHER EDUCATION,
FORMAL PATTERN OF EDUCATIONAL-AGRICULTURAL COOPERATION WERE
COMMON. TODAY'S URBAN, INFORMATION-BASED ECONOMY CAN BENEFIT
MUCH FROM THE EDUCATIONAL AND TECHNOLOGICAL RESOURCES OF
COLLEGES AND UNIVERSITIES.

08784 SWEEZY, P.
SOCIALISM AND ECOLOGY
MONTHLY REVIEW, 41(4) (SEP 89), 1-8.
THIS ARTICLE ADDRESSES THE FAILURE OF SOCIALISM IN THE
USSR AND THE PROBLEM OF WHERE TO GO FROM THERE, AS WELL AS
THE COMPANION FAILURE OF CAPITALISM. THE MAIN FOCUS, HOWEVER,
IS ON THE SPECULATIVE, LONGER RUN PROSPECTS OF THE TWO
SYSTEMS WHICH ARE ANALYSED. THE PROTECTION AND PRESERVATION
OF THE ENVIRONMENT AS A PRIORITY ISSUE IS IGNORED BY BOTH
IDEALOGIES, BUT SOCIALISM OFFERS THE BEST HOPE FOR OUR
SURVIVAL IS THE CONCLUSION

08785 SWEEZY, P.M.
U.S. IMPERIALISM IN THE 1990S
MONTHLY REVIEW, 41(5) (OCT 89), 1-17.
THIS ARTICLE ARGUES FIVE PROPOSITIONS: 1) THE U.S.
EMPIRE ACHIEVED DOMINANCE IN THE LATE 1940S AND EARLY 1950S,
2) SYMPTOMS OF DECLINE BEGAN TO APPEAR IN THE EARLY 1960S,
3) DECLINE CONTINUED IN THE SECOND HALF OF THE 1970S, 4) THE
REAGAN ERA ENDED IN FURTHER DECLINE, AND, 5) THE 1990S WILL
WITNESS THE DISINTEGRATION OF THE WORLDWIDE U.S. EMPIRE AND
ITS POSSIBLE REPLACEMENT BY A SYSTEM OF COMPETING TRADE-AND-
CURRENCY BLOCS, COMMENT IS MADE ON EACH OF THE SUB-PERIODS,
BUT NO ATTEMPT AT A COMPREHENSIVE ANALYSIS.

08786 SWENSON, P.A.
BEYOND THE WAGE STRUGGLE: POLITICS, COLLECTIVE BARGAINING,
AND THE EGALITARIAN DILEMMAS OF SOCIAL DEMOCRATIC TRADE
UNIONISM IN GERMANY AND SWEDEN
DISSERTATION ABSTRACTS INTERNATIONAL, 48(10) (APR 88),
2720-A.
THE DISSERTATION ANALYZES THE IMPACT OF COLLECTIVE
BARGAINING ON THE POLITICS AND TRADE UNIONS AND SOCIAL

DEMOCRATIC PARTIES IN GERMANY AND SWEEDEN. IT COMPARES THE
SWEEDISH LABOR CONFEDERATION AND THE GERMAN LABOR
CONFEDERATION WITH EMPHASIS ON THE LATTER'S METALWORKERS'
UNION AND SHOWS HOW EACH ORGANIZATION FACED THE "TRILEMMA"
OF WAGE SHARE MAXIMIZATION, WAGE LEVELLING, AND FULL
EMPLOYMENT.

08787 SHICK, T.
ROMANIA, ROMANIA
COMMONWEAL, CXVI(9) (MAY 89), 263-264.
ROMANIA PROVES THE OLD POLITICAL AXIOM THAT PEOPLE TRULY
OPPRESSED DO NOT REVOLT. THE COUNTRY'S VIRTUAL INTERNATIONAL
INVISIBILITY CAN BE ATTRIBUTED TO THE NATURE OF ITS PRESENT
HORROR-PRODUCING REGIME, WHICH CULTIVATES AN ATMOSPHERE OF
SECRECY, SURVEILLANCE, AND UNRELENTING OPPRESSION.

08788 SWIECICKI, M.
THE ECONOMY: PRIVATIZE WITH CARE
POLISH PERSPECTIVES, XXXII(2) (1989), 57-63.
IN THIS INTERVIEW, THE GENERAL SECRETARY OF THE POLISH
ECONOMIC CONSULTATIVE COUNCIL DISCUSSES THE STATE OF THE
POLISH ECONOMY, HOW PAST REFORM EFFORTS HAVE IMPACTED IT,
AND THE PROSPECTS FOR FUTURE REFORMS, INCLUDING
PRIVATIZATION.

08789 SHIFT, E. K.
RECONSTITUTIVE CHANGE IN THE U.S. CONGRESS: THE EARLY
SENATE, 1789-1841
LEGISLATIVE STUDIES QUARTERLY, 15(2) (MAY 89), 175-204.
RECONSTITUTIVE CONGRESSIONAL CHANGE IS A MARKED AND
ENDURING SHIFT IN THE FUNDAMENTAL DIMENSIONS OF A CHAMBER:
ITS COMMITTEES, PARTIES, RULES, MEMBERS, AND LEADERS, AS
WELL AS ITS RELATIONS WITH THE EXECUTIVE, THE CONSTITUENCY,
AND THE OTHER CHAMBER. THE OCCURRENCE OF SUCH CHANGE DEPENDS
ON THE CONFLUENCE OF FIVE FACTORS: THE CONGRESSIONAL AGENDA,
THE ELECTORATE, THE POLITICAL PARTIES CONGRESS, THE
INSTITUTION'S VERSION OR BELIEFS ABOUT WHAT ROLE CONGRESS
SHOULD PLAY IN GOVERNMENT, AND THE EXISTENCE OF A GROUP OF
MEMBERS WHO SPEARHEAD RECONSTITUTION. THIS ARTICLE
ELABORATES ON THE CONCEPT AND THEORY OF RECONSTITUTIVE
CHANGE BY APPLYING THEM TO THE FIRST CASE OF CONGRESSIONAL
RECOSTITUTION, THE EARLY SENATE.

08790 SHINBANK, A.
THE COMMON AGRICULTURAL POLICY AND THE POLITICS OF
EUROPEAN DECISION-MAKING
JOURNAL OF COMMON MARKET STUDIES, XXVII(4) (JUN 89),
303-322.
MANY CASUAL OBSERVERS OF THE COMMON AGRICULTURAL POLICY
(CAP) FIND THE EC'S DECISION-MAKING PROCESS BAFFLING.
SIMILARLY, TO SOME, THE POLICIES ACTUALLY ADOPTED CAN APPEAR
COUNTER-INTUITIVE. IN PART THIS REFLECTS THE COMPLEX, AND
OFTEN CONFLICTING, POLICY OBJECTIVES THAT THE CAP, EITHER
IMPLICITLY OR EXPLICITLY, IS DESIGNED TO ACHIEVE AND IN PART
THE TRADEOFFS AND COMPROMISES THAT INEVITABLY ARISE WHEN
HARD DECISIONS MUST BE MADE IN A MULTI-COUNTRY GROUPING.
THIS ARTICLE. DOES NOT SEEK TO EXPLAIN THE DECISIONS OF THE
EC'S COUNCIL OF AGRICULTURE MINISTERS NOR EVEN TO DELINEATE
THE EC'S DECISION-MAKING PROCESS; IT MERELY ATTEMPTS TO
SKETCH THE FRAMEWORK WITHIN WHICH DECISIONS ARE REACHED.

08791 SYCREOV, V.
CMEA: RADICAL CHANGES TO THE COOPERATION MECHANISM
FOREIGN TRADE, 5 (1988), 2-5.
THIS ARTICLE REPORTS ON THE 43RD CMEA SESSION WHICH
FOCUSED ON THE PRINCIPAL AIMS AND DIRECTIONS OF MEMBER
NATIONS ON THE COUNCIL. RESTRUCTURING PROCESSES WERE
OUTLINED. IT EXAMINES THE ADOPTED MEASURES AS A MEANS OF
SHIFTING EMPHASIS FROM MUTUAL TRADE TO MORE MUTUAL SCIENCE
AND PRODUCTION.

08792 SYED, A.H.
FACTIONAL CONFLICT IN THE PUNJAB MUSLIM LEAGUE, 1947-1955
POLAND, 22(1) (FAL 89), 49-74.
POLITICAL PARTIES IN PAKISTAN HAVE BEEN UNABLE TO GIVE
STABILITY AND ORDER TO THAT NATION'S POLITICAL SYSTEM, IN
PART BECAUSE THEY HAVE BEEN RIDDLED WITH FACTIONS. THIS
ARTICLE EXAMINES FACTIONAL CONFLICT WITHIN THE MUSLIM LEAGUE,
THE OLDEST PARTY IN THE COUNTRY, AND FINDS IT ROOTED IN THE
POLITICAL CULTURE OF THE LANDLORDS WHO DOMINATE PARTY
COUNCILS AND LEGISLATIVE ASSEMBLIES. THIS FACTIONALISM IS
ENCOURAGED BY THE HIGHER LEVELS OF BUREAUCRACY, WHICH
EXERCISE EFFECTIVE POWER IN THE STATE, SO AS TO KEEP THE
POLITICAL PARTIES FROM CHALLENGING THE BUREAUCRACY'S
PREPONDERANCE IN GOVERNMENT. THIS PATTERN HAS CHARACTERIZED
PAKISTAN'S EXPERIENCE WITH DEMOCRATIC POLITICS AND IS
UNLIKELY TO CHANGE, THE AUTHOR CONCLUDES, UNLESS THE
ECONOMIC BASIS OF THE LANDLORD CULTURE CHANGES.

08793 SYKES, P.
THE PRESIDENT AS LEGISLATOR; A "SUPEREPRESENATOR"
PRESIDENTIAL STUDIES QUARTERLY, XIX(2) (SPR 89), 301-316.
POLITICAL SCIENTISTS WHO STUDY PRESIDENTIAL POWER TEND
TO NEGLECT THE IMPLICATIONS OF INCREASED EXECUTIVE AUTHORITY

FOR DEMOCRATIC ACCOUNTABILITY. PLACING THE PRESIDENTIAL
POWER IN THE CONTEXT OF DEMOCRATIC THEORY, THIS RESEARCH
EXPLORES THE RELATIONSHIPS AMONG THE PEOPLE, THEIR
REPRESENTATIVES IN CONGRESS, AND THE PRESIDENT - AS
PRESIDENTS THEMSELVES HAVE UNDERSTOOD AND SHAPED THOSE
RELATIONSHIPS. IN PARTICULAR, THE AUTHOR EXAMINES
JUSTIFICATIONS FOR EXPANDING THE EXECUTIVE'S POLICY-MAKING
POWER, A PROCESS IN WHICH THE PEOPLE PLAY A CRUCIAL ROLE.
THIS STUDY CONCLUDES BY EVALUATING THE CONSEQUENCES OF A
"SUPEREPRESENATOR" - A PRESIDENT WHO IS SUPERIOR TO
REPRESENTATIVE AND SENATOR - FOR ACCOUNTABILITY AND
LEGITIMACY. THIS ARTICLE INCLUDES SKETCHES OF FOUR
"PRESIDENTIAL PERSPECTIVES" DERIVED FROM JAMES MADISON,
ANDREW JACKSON, THEODORE ROOSEVELT, AND FRANKLIN D.
ROOSEVELT.

08794 SYLVERS, M.
     AMERICAN COMMUNISTS IN THE POPULAR FRONT PERID:
     REORGANIZATION OR DISORGANIZATION?
     JOURNAL OF AMERICAN STUDIES, 23(3) (DEC 89), 375-393.
       THE COMMUNIST PARTY'S ORGANIZATIONAL STRUCTURE AND ITS
     INTERNAL EDUCATIONAL PROGRAM VIVIDLY DEMONSTRATE HOW THE
     PARTY CHANGED DURING THE POPULAR FRONT PERIOD. CLOSE
     ATTENTION TO THE CHANGES SUGGESTS THAT THE PARTY--THOUGH
     APPARENTLY STRONGER IN TERMS OF MEMBERSHIP, INFLUENCE, AND
     ACCEPTABILITY--ACTUALLY UNDERWENT TRANSFORMATIONS THAT
     ULTIMATELY WEAKENED ITS ABILITY TO CONFRONT COLD WAR
     REPRESSION AND THE LATER COMPLEX UPHEAVALS IN THE SOVIET
     WORLD.

08795 SYMONS, T. H.
     CULTURE IN THE COMMONWEALTH
     POLICY OPTIONS, 10(2) (MAR 89), 11-13.
       CULTURAL DIVERSITY AND PLURALISM IN CANADA AND MANY
     OTHER COMMONWEALTH COUNTRIES OFFER ENORMOUS ADVANTAGES, AND
     THE CHANCE TO BUILD A SOCIETY ENRICHED BY A MULTITUDE OF
     HERITAGES. CANADA OUGHT TO CELEBRATE AND BUILD ON DIVERSITY,
     AND OUGHT TO PAY FAR MORE CONSCIOUS ATTENTION TO THE STUDY
     OF VARIOUS CULTURES IN THE EDUCATIONAL SYSTEM. IT IS, FOR
     EXAMPLE, TIME TO PAY FAR MORE ATTENTION TO THE CULTURE,
     HERITAGE AND RIGHTS OF ABORIGINAL PEOPLES IN ALL
     COMMONWEALTH COUNTRIES, AND TIME TO BRING THE STUDY OF FINE
     AND PERFORMING ARTS FROM THE PERIPHERY OF ACADEMIC PROGRAMS
     MUCH CLOSER TO THE CENTRE OF THE CURRICULUM IN POST-
     SECONDARY INSTITUTIONS.

08796 SYRKIN, M.
     1992: READ THEIR SLIPS!
     MIDSTREAM, XXXV(2) (FEB 89), 12-15.
       THE AUTHOR REVIEWS THE REASONS FOR THE REPUBLICAN
     VICTORY IN THE 1988 PRESIDENTIAL ELECTION AND CONSIDERS THE
     LESSONS THAT THE CAMPAIGN HOLDS FOR THE FUTURE.

08797 SZAJKOWSKI, B.
     ETHIOPIA: A WEAKENING SOVIET CONNECTION?
     WORLD TODAY, 45(8-9) (AUG 89), 153-156.
       THE ETHIOPIAN GOVERNMENT HAS FUNDAMENTAL PROBLEMS IN
     FOUR PRINCIPAL AREAS: ITS LEGITIMACY, THE CONTINUOS WAR IN
     ERITREA AND TIGRE, RELATIONS WITH THE SOVIET UNION, AND THE
     NATIONAL ECONOMY. DUE TO THE NEW POLITICAL SITUATION IN THE
     USSR, THE SOVIET INVOLVEMENT IN ETHIOPIA IS VIEWED AS A
     PRODUCT OF BREZHNEV'S "YEARS OF STAGNATION," THE PERIOD AND
     POLICIES BEING REPUDIATED BY THE NEW LEADERSHIP. AS TENSION
     BETWEEN THE USSR AND THE USA RELAXES AND IS INCREASINGLY
     REPLACED BY COOPERATION, THE SOVIET LEADERSHIP HAS EMBARKED
     ON THE FORMULATION OF NEW FOREIGN POLICIES, WHICH HAVE MAJOR
     CONSEQUENCES FOR ETHIOPIA.

08798 SZALLI, E.
     THE NEW ELITE
     ACROSS FRONTIERS, 5(3) (FAL 89), 25-31.
       THIS ARTICLE EXPLORES CONCERNS RELATING TO THE
     TRANSITION TO A MULTIPARTY SYSTEM IN HUNGARY. ONE CONCERN IS
     WHAT WILL HAPPEN IF THERE IS NO RETRENCHMENT? IT FEARS THAT
     MEMBERS OF THE BUREAUCRACY ARE CONVERTING THEIR POWER AND
     PRIVILEGES FROM THE OLD SYSTEM INTO THE NEW SYSTEM. IT
     EXPLORES THE DIFFERENCES AND SIMILARITIES OF THE NEW ELITE
     FROM THE OLD, AND WHAT CAN BE EXPECTED FROM THE NEW. IT
     FEARS THAT INDEPENDENT ORGANIZATIONS ARE AT THE CROSS ROADS.

08799 SZAMUELY, G.
     THE INTELLECTUAL AND THE COLD WAR
     COMMENTARY, 88(6) (DEC 89), 54-56.
       THE ARTICLE EXAMINES THE ROLE THAT LIBERAL ANTI-
     COMMUNIST INTELLECTUALS HAVE PLAYED IN THE COLD WAR. IT
     REVIEWS PETER COLEMAN'S NEW HISTORY OF THE CONGRESS FOR
     CULTURAL FREEDOM, "THE LIBERAL CONSPIRACY." HE QUALIFIES THE
     BASIC HALLMARK OF THE CONGRESS'S ANTI-COMMUNISM WHICH WAS
     THAT IT FELT ITSELF TO BE OF THE LEFT AND ON THE LEFT. IT
     ALSO EXPLORES SIDNEY HOOK MEMOIRS IN RELATION TO THE
     CONGRESS. IT CONCLUDES THAT IF THE CONGRESS'S DAY HAS COME
     AND GONE. IT HAS GONE FOR REASONS MORE COMPLICATED AND
     RATHER LESS ADMIRABLE THAN ITS HISTORIAN'S VERDICT OF
     SUCCESS WOULD LEAD ONE TO BELIEVE.

08800 SZAMUELY, G.
     THE POLITICS OF 1992
     COMMENTARY, 88(4) (OCT 89), 42-45.
       THIS ARTICLE EXPLORES PLANS FOR EUROPE IN AREAS OF
     ECONOMICS, TRADE, AND POLITICS IN THE NEAR FUTURE, IT
     ANALYSES THE SINGLE EUROPEAN ACT OF 1985 WHICH HAS THREE
     GOALS: EUROPEAN UNION, SOCIAL DIMENTION, AND EUROPEAN
     EXTERNAL IDENTITY. THE U.S. 1992 PRESIDENTIAL ELECTIONS
     WHICH WILL TAKE PLACE A FEW WEEKS BEFORE THE DEADLINE THAT
     THE EUROPEAN COMMISSION HAS SET FOR THE FALL OF THE LAST OF
     THE NON-TARIFF TRADE BARRIES AMONG MEMBER NATIONS OF THE
     COMMUNITY WILL BE IMPACTED BY EVENTS IN EUROPE AND THIS
     ARTICLE EXPLORES THE ISSUES.

08801 SZASZ, T.
     WHOSE COMPETENCE?
     NATIONAL REVIEW, XLI(17) (SEP 89), 38.
       IF AMERICANS ARE TRULY INTERESTED IN GUARANTEEING A
     DEFENDANT'S RIGHT TO A FAIR AND SPEEDY TRIAL, WE SHOULD
     APPLY THE "MENTAL COMPETEXCY" STANDARD TO ALL THE PLAYERS -
     JUDGE, LAWYERS, JURORS - NOT TO JUST THE DEFENDANT, OR WE
     SHOULD DROP THE ISSUE ENTIRELY.

08802 SZEGEDY-MASZAK, M.
     RISE AND FALL OF THE WASHINGTON PEACE INDUSTRY
     BULLETIN OF THE ATOMIC SCIENTISTS, 45(1) (JAN 89), 18-23.
       THIS PAPER REVIEWS THE ACTIVITIES OF VARIOUS PEACE AND
     ARMS CONTROL GROUPS DURING THE REAGAN PRESIDENTIAL TERMS.
     THESE GROUP MOVEMENTS WERE FORMED AND OPERATED IN DIFFERENT
     WAYS TO OPPOSE THE POLITICAL FORCES SUPPORTING MILITARY
     STRENGTH IN THE UNITED STATES.

08803 SZELACHOWSKI, T.
     AMENDMENT OF THE POLISH CONSTITUTION
     CONTEMPORARY POLAND, XXII(5) (1989), 24-29.
       THE AUTHOR, WHO IS A SEJM DEPUTY, EXPLAINS THE PROPOSED
     CHANGES AND AMENDMENTS TO THE BILL OF RIGHTS OF THE
     CONSTITUTION OF THE POLISH PEOPLE'S REPUBLIC. HE STATES THAT
     THE PRESENT POLISH CONSTITUTION DOES NOT MEET THE
     REQUIREMENTS FOR POLAND'S POLITICAL TRANSFORMATION TO A
     SOCIETY WHERE THE PEOPLE ENJOY FULL FRANCHISE AND EXERT REAL
     INFLUENCE ON THE COURSE OF PUBLIC LIFE.

08804 SZOKAI, I.; TABAJDI, C.
     CHANGE OF HUNGARIAN SOCIAL MODEL-CHANGE OF ORIENTATION IN
     HUNGARIAN FOREIGN POLICY?
     WORLD AFFAIRS, 151(4) (1989), 208-219.
       THE ARTICLE EXAMINES THE FUTURE OF HUNGARY'S FOREIGN
     POLICY. IT ANALYZES WHETHER THE SHIFT AWAY FROM THE
     STALINIST MODEL OF SOCIALISM WILL NECESSITATE A TURNING AWAY
     FROM THE USSR AND OTHER SOCIALIST COUNTRIES. IT CONCLUDES
     THAT HUNGARY WILL NEED OUTSIDE HELP TO SOLVE FUTURE PROBLEMS
     AND THAT A WHOLESALE ABANDONING OF THE EAST IS NOT PRUDENT.
     INSTEAD, HUNGARY SHOULD DEVELOP A FOREIGN POLICY ORIENTATION
     THAT EMPHASIZES THE LINKAGE OF DEMOCRACY AND NATIONAL
     INTERESTS. TRADE AND RELATIONS WITH BOTH EAST AND WEST CAN
     BE CONDUCTED WITHIN A FRAMEWORK OF THIS HUNGARIAN SELF-
     DEFINITION.

08805 SZOKE, M.
     THE ECONOMIC POLICY BACKGROUND AND THE MAIN FEATURES OF
     ITALO-HUNGARIAN ECONOMIC RELATIONS
     INTERNATIONAL SPECTATOR, XXIII(3) (JUL 88), 186-195.
       ITALY IS HUNGARY'S THIRD BIGGEST TRADING PARTNER AMONG
     MARKET ECONOMIES, BUT ECONOMIC RELATIONS WITH HUNGARY ARE OF
     MARGINAL IMPORTANCE TO ITALY. THE DISPARITY IN THE WEIGHT OF
     MUTUAL ECONOMIC RELATIONS, THE ASYMMETRY OF INTERESTS IN
     THEIR DEVELOPMENT, AND THE SIMILARITY WITH SOME GENERAL
     CHARACTERISTICS OF EAST-WEST TRADE INDICATE THAT THE ROOTS
     OF THE PROBLEM MUST BE NOT SO MUCH IN THE MUTUAL RELATIONS
     THEMSELVES AS IN THEIR ECONOMIC BACKGROUND AND THE DIVERSE
     ECONOMIC DEVELOPMENT OF THE TWO COUNTRIES.

08806 SZORCSIK, S.
     HUNGARY: A SOCIALIST PARTY IS BORN
     WORLD MARXIST REVIEW, 32(12) (DEC 89), 37-40.
       AS A PARTICIPANT IN THE EUROPEAN LEFT, THE HUNGARIAN
     SOCIALIST PARTY HAS STATED ITS READINESS TO COOPERATE WITH
     ALL THE FORCES WHICH RECOGNISE THEIR RESPONSIBILITY FOR THE
     FUTURE OF EUROPE, PRIMARILY WITH THOSE WHO ADVOCATE REFORMS
     IN THE COMMUNIST, SOCIALIST, SOCIAL DEMOCRATIC AND OTHER
     LEFT MOVEMENTS, WITH THOSE WHO DESIRE THE SUCCESSFUL
     ACCOMPLISHMENT OF THE PARTY'S HISTORICAL MISSION, WITH
     VARIOUS NEW MOVEMENTS FOR ENVIRONMENTAL PROTECTION AND PEACE,
     AND WITH YOUTH AND WOMEN'S ORGANISATIONS.

08807 SZPORLUK, R.
     DILEMMAS OF RUSSIAN NATIONALISM
     PROBLEMS OF COMMUNISM, XXXVIII(4) (JUL 89), 15-35.
       AMIDST THE GROWING ASSERTIVENESS OF THE NON-RUSSIAN
     NATIONS IN THE SOVIET UNION AGAINST THE CENTRALIZED COMMAND-
     ADMINISTRATIVE SYSTEM, THE RUSSIAN NATION MUST DECIDE
     WHETHER TO CONTINUE IDENTIFYING ITSELF WITH SOVIET IMPERIAL

POWER OR TO SEEK TO DEVELOP ITS NATIONAL IDENTITY IN A
RUSSIAN HOMELAND, THE RSFSR. ALTHOUGH THE "IMPERIAL"
MENTALITY STILL PREDOMINATES AMONG RUSSIANS, A GROWING
NUMBER OF THEM IS DEMANDING THAT THE RSFSR BE ALLOWED TO
ESTABLISH A COMPLETE SET OF INSTITUTIONS SEPARATE FROM THOSE
OF THE USSR, AND EVEN HAVE A SEPARATE CAPITAL. THE
RELATIONSHIP BETWEEN THE RUSSIAN PEOPLE AND THE SOVIET STATE
CAN BE TERMED THE CENTRAL NATIONAL PROBLEM IN THE USSR TODAY.
NOT LEAST BECAUSE THE AGENDA OF THE NON-RUSSIANS IS LARGELY
DETERMINED BY THEIR PERCEPTION OF THE POSITION OF THE
RUSSIANS IN THE SOVIET POLITY.

08808 SZULC, T.
BREAKTHROUGH IN THE MIDDLE EAST: SWEDEN'S ROLE AS MIDDLEMAN
SCANDINAVIAN REVIEW, 77(3) (AUT 89), 14-17.
IN THE WORLD OF FLASHY SHUTTLE DIPLOMACY AND PUBLIC
POSTURING, SWEDEN HAS CHOSEN ANOTHER PATH, APPLYING
DIPLOMATIC TECHNIQUES THAT HAVE BEEN DISCARDED BY OTHER
NATIONS. IN THE SPRING OF 1987, SWEDISH FOREIGN MINISTER
STEN STURE ANDERSSON CAME TO THE CONCLUSION THAT THE
INCREASINGLY LETHAL DEADLOCK BETWEEN ISRAEL AND THE
PALESTINIANS IN THE OCCUPIED TERRITORIES HAD BECOME
INTOLERABLE FOR THE PARTIES DIRECTLY INVOLVED AND COULD
BECOME INTOLERABLE FOR THE REST OF THE WORLD. HE RECOGNIZED
THAT THE TIME WAS RIPE FOR OUTSIDE MEDIATION. HE SET UP A
SPECIAL TASK FORCE IN THE FOREIGN MINISTRY AND CAUTIOUSLY
PROCEEDED ON HIS MISSION. WHAT HE ACHIEVED MAY PROVE
MONUMENTAL BECAUSE THE USA AND THE PLO HAVE BEEN BROUGHT
TOGETHER FOR THEIR FIRST DIALOGUE.

08809 SZYMANDERSKI, J.
POLAND'S "MYTH OF THE MILITARY"
ACROSS FRONTIERS, 5(2) (SUM 89), 22-49.
THIS ARTICLE IS BY A POLISH PRESS SPOKESMAN FOR WIP
(WOLNOSC I POKOJ, OR "FREEDOM AND PEACE") IN WARSAW. HE
EXPLAINS WIP'S STRATEGY AND OBJECTIVES IN MAKING
CONSCIENTIOUS OBJECTION AND ALTERNATE CIVILIAN SERVICE ITS
FIRST PRIORITY AS AN INDEPENDENT MOVEMENT. HE ALSO DISCUSSES
THE REASONS FOR THE GREAT RESPECT FOR THE MILITARY WHICH HE
CLAIMS IT DOESN'T DESERVE.

08810 SZYMANDERSKI, J.; WINIECKI, J.
THE GORBACHEV CHALLENGE, II: A VIEW FROM THE EAST
WORLD TODAY, 45(8-9) (AUG 89), 145-149.
THE AUTHORS ENDEAVOR TO ANSWER SEVERAL IMPORTANT
QUESTIONS ABOUT THE SITUATION IN THE EAST: IS IT A MOMENTOUS
CHANGE OR MERELY ANOTHER THAW IN THE SEEMINGLY ENDLESS CYCLE
OF RELAXATION AND REPRESSION? IF IT IS A MOMENTOUS CHANGE,
WHAT SHOULD WESTERN ATTITUDES AND POLICIES BE? IS GORBACHEV
PUTTING THE WEST ON THE SPOT? DOES THE WEST POSSESS ANY
LEVERAGE WITH WHICH TO PROD THE SOVIET UNION IN THE DESIRED
DIRECTION?

08811 TAAGEPERA, M.
THE ECOLOGICAL AND POLITICAL PROBLEMS OF PHOSPHORITE
MINING IN ESTONIA
JOURNAL OF BALTIC STUDIES, XX(2) (SUM 89), 165-174.
THE PROPOSED MINING OF PHOSPHORITE RESERVES IN
NORTHEASTERN ESTONIA HAS TAKEN ON MANY DIMENSIONS BEYOND
MINING. DUE TO PUBLIC OUTCRY IN 1987, THE SCHEDULED START-UP
OF A TRIAL MINE IN KABALA WAS POSTPONED UNTIL THE END OF
1989. THE CASE OFFERS INTERESTING INSIGHTS INTO THE SHIFTING
POWER STRUCTURE OF THE SOVIET UNION AND RAISES THE
POSSIBILITY THAT GLASNOST IS FACILITATING PUBLIC EXPRESSION
THAT IS MAKING A DIFFERENCE.

08812 TAAGEPERA, R.; SHUGART, M.
DESIGNING ELECTORAL SYSTEMS
ELECTORAL STUDIES, 8(1) (APR 89), 49-58.
THE PAPER OUTLINES THE INSIGHTS GAINED FROM A BOOK-
LENGTH STUDY OF ELECTORAL SYSTEMS IN THE WORLD AND APPLY THE
INSIGHTS TO EVALUATE EXISTING ELECTORAL SYSTEMS AND SUGGEST
GUIDELINES FOR CHANGES. IT CONCLUDES THAT ALTHOUGH SOME
ELECTORAL REFORM MAY APPEAR TO BE WORTHWHILE MAY ULTIMATELY
BE COUNTERPRODUCTIVE DUE TO THE INCREASED INSTABILITY THAT
ANY NEW SYSTEM WILL CAUSE. THE EXISTING SYSTEM MAY CONTAIN
FAULTS, BUT GENERALLY THE POLITICAL FORCES THAT ARE
DISADVANTAGED BY THE EXISTING RULES LEARN TO LIVE WITH THEM
AND GRADUALLY DEVISE STRATEGIES THAT MINIMIZE THEIR
DISADVANTAGES. STABILITY IS AN IMPORTANT FACTOR IN
DETERMINING EXPECTATIONS.

08813 TAAGEPERA, R.
EMPIRICAL THRESHOLD OF REPRESENTATION
ELECTORAL STUDIES, 8(2) (AUG 89), 105-116.
AN OPERATIONAL METHOD USING DATA FROM PREVIOUS ELECTIONS
IS PROPOSED FOR DETERMINING THE VOTE SHARE A SMALL PARTY
NEEDS TO HAVE A FIFTY-FIFTY CHANCE OF WINNING ITS FIRST SEAT.
THE RESULTING MEDIAN VALUE OF 23 ELECTORAL SYSTEMS IS 1.0
PER CENT OF THE NATION-WIDE VOTE, WITH A RANGE FROM 0.1 TO 8
PER CENT. THIS EMPIRICAL THRESHOLD OF REPRESENTATION IS
AFFECTED BY ASSEMBLY SIZE, LEGAL REPRESENTATION THRESHOLD
(IF ANY EXISTS), AND GEOGRAPHICAL CONCENTRATION OF SMALL
PARTY VOTES. IN TURN, THIS THRESHOLD AFFECTS THE NUMBER OF

SEAT-WINNING PARTIES AND THE EFFECTIVE NUMBER OF PARTIES IN
THE SYSTEM. EMPIRICAL THRESHOLDS CAN ALSO BE CALCULATED ON
THE DISTRICT LEVEL. THEY CAN THEN BE COMPARED WITH
THEORETICAL THRESHOLDS OF REPRESENTATION, AND UNANTICIPATED
DISCREPANCIES OCCUR, BECAUSE APPARENTLY MINOR ASPECTS OF
ELECTORAL RULES CAN ALTER THE OUTCOME.

08814 TAAGEPERA, R.
ESTONIA IN SEPTEMBER 1988: STALINISTS, CENTRISTS, AND
RESTORATIONISTS
JOURNAL OF BALTIC STUDIES, XX(2) (SUM 89), 175-190.
THREE BASIC POLITICAL CURRENTS TOOK SHAPE IN ESTONIA IN
1987 AND ARE LIKELY TO CONTINUE THROUGHOUT FURTHER
LIBERALIZATION OR EVEN A CRACKDOWN. BROADLY PUT, THE THREE
FORCES VYING FOR PROMINENCE IN ESTONIA ARE STALINISTS WHO
WANT TO KEEP THE SOVIET EMPIRE INTACT, PERESTROIKA-MINDED
CENTRISTS WHO WANT ESTONIA'S SOVEREIGNTY WITHIN A LOOSE
SOVIET CONFEDERATION, AND RESTORATIONISTS WHO WANT TO RE-
ESTABLISH THE PRE-WAR REPUBLIC OF ESTONIA.

08815 TAAGEPERA, R.
ESTONIA'S ROAD TO INDEPENDENCE
PROBLEMS OF COMMUNISM, XXXVIII(6) (NOV 89), 11-26.
EMERGING TRENDS IN THE SOVIET UNION INDICATE THAT THE
SOVIET OCCUPATION OF ESTONIA WILL END SOMETIME IN THE 1990'S.
A NUMBER OF GRASSROOTS ORGANIZATIONS, INCLUDING THE POPULAR
FRONT OF ESTONIA, HAVE EMERGED TO PUSH FOR FUNDAMENTAL
POLITICAL AND ECONOMIC CHANGES. THE LEADERSHIP OF THE
COMMUNIST PARTY OF ESTONIA HAS ALSO RESPONDED TO POPULAR
DEMANDS FOR REFORM. THESE EFFORTS HAVE ELICITED ORGANIZED
RESISTANCE FROM RUSSIAN-SPEAKERS IN THE REPUBLIC AND
VEHEMENT CRITICISM FROM THE KREMLIN. IN RESPONSE, POPULAR
DEMANDS HAVE BECOME MORE AND MORE RADICAL. THE POPULAR FRONT
OF ESTONIA HAS ADVOCATED FULL INDEPENDENCE, BUT IT DIFFERS
WITH OTHER GROUPS, SUCH AS THE ESTONIAN NATIONAL
INDEPENDENCE PARTY, ON HOW THAT GOAL SHOULD BE ATTAINED.

08816 TABAN, T.
INSIDE LIBERATED TIGRE: JOURNEY INTO WOLLO
NEW AFRICAN, (OCT 89), 40-41.
THIS ARTICLE CHRONICLES A 25 DAY WALK INTO THE REMOTE
AREAS OF ETHIOPIA, CONTROLLED BY THE ETHIOPIAN PEOPLE'S
DEMOCRATIC MOVEMENT, BY CORRESPONDENT ALFRED TABAN, HE
RECORDS THAT HE FOUND A PEOPLE WITH LITTLE FOOD, WATER, NOR
THE MOST BASIC NECESSITIES OF LIFE. ALSO DOCUMENTED IS A
SITUATION WHERE THERE IS NO DOCTOR, NO MEDICAL SUPPLIES AND
FREQUENT BOMBINGS, PARTICULARLY ON MARKET DAYS, BY ETHIOPIAN
PLANES. TABAN FOUND THAT, REMARKABLY, THE SPIRIT OF THE
PEOPLE SURVIVES

08817 TABONE, V.
WE BELIEVE IN NEUTRALITY
WORLD MARXIST REVIEW, 32(7) (JUL 89), 13-15.
THIS ARTICLE IS AN INTERVIEW WITH VINCENT, TABONE,
PRESIDENT OF THE REPUBLIC OF MALTA. HE APPLAUDS THE
RAPPROCHMENT BETWEEN THE TWO SUPERPOWERS AND ALSO THE CALL
FOR NEW POLITICAL THINKING IN THE NUCLEAR AGE. HIS
PRINCIPLES OF FOREIGN POLICY ARE EXAMINED, AS WELL AS HIS
CONCEPT OF THE ROLE FOR SMALL COUNTRIES IN BIG POLITICS. HE
CONCLUDES WITH A SUMMARY OF THE PERMANENT INTERESTS OF MALTA.

08818 TAFT-MORALES, M.
GUATEMALA: DEVELOPMENT OF DEMOCRACY AND U.S. INFLUENCE
CRS REVEIW, 10(2) (FEB 89), 19-21.
THE CIVILIAN GOVERNMENT OF PRESIDENT VINICIO CEREZO HAS
FACED STRONG OPPOSITION SINCE HIS ELECTION IN 1985. ALTHOUGH
CEREZO'S EFFORTS TO INITIATE DEMOCRATIC REFORMS ARE WIDELY
SUPPORTED, MANY QUESTION HOW MUCH HE CAN ACCOMPLISH, DUE TO
OPPOSITION FROM SMALL BUT POLITICALLY POWERFUL GROUPS AND
GUATEMALA'S ANTI-DEMOCRATIC LEGACY. WHEN THE U.S. CONGRESS
CONSIDERS ASSISTANCE TO GUATEMALA, MEMBERS MUST DECIDE HOW
BEST TO SUPPORT THE COUNTRY'S FRAGILE DEMOCRACY AND HOW TO
INFLUENCE GUATEMALA ON SUCH ISSUES AS IMPROVED HUMAN RIGHTS.

08819 TAFT, R.
ATTITUDES OF THE ORIENTAL JEWISH ELITE IN ISRAEL TOWARD
THE ARAB-ISRAELI CONFLICT
DISSERTATION ABSTRACTS INTERNATIONAL, 50(6) (DEC 89),
1790-A.
THE AUTHOR EXPLORES THE ATTITUDES OF THE ORIENTAL JEWISH
ELITE TOWARD THE ARAB-ISRAELI CONFLICT. IT IS ASSUMED THAT
MEMBERS OF THE ORIENTAL JEWISH ELITE REFLECT THE SAME VIEWS
TOWARD THE ARAB-ISRAELI CONFLICT AS OTHER JEWISH MEMBERS OF
ISRAELI SOCIETY AND CANNOT BE LABELED AS "HAWKS" SIMPLY
BECAUSE THEY COME FROM MIDDLE EASTERN COUNTRIES.

08820 TAGGERT, W.A.
A NOTE ON TESTING MODELS OF SPENDING IN THE AMERICAN
STATES: THE CASE OF PUBLIC EXPENDITURES FOR CORRECTIONS
WESTERN POLITICAL QUARTERLY, 42(4) (DEC 89), 679-690.
THIS RESEARCH NOTE EXTENDS THE WORK OF LOWERY, KONDA,
AND GARAND (1984) BY EXAMINING THE ABSOLUTE AND RELATIVE
USEFULNESS OF FIVE MODELS OF THE SPENDING PROCESS IN THE
AREA OF STATE EXPENDITURES FOR CORRECTIONS. EMPLOYING TIME

SERIES EXPENDITURE DATA IN 48 STATES FOR THE YEARS 1945 TO 1984, THE ANALYSIS SUPPORTS THE CONCLUSION REACHED BY LOWERY AND HIS COLLEAGUES THAT THE AUTOREGRESSIVE SPECIFICATION IS THE STRONGEST BIVARIATE MODEL FOR EXPLAINING STATE LEVEL SPENDING OVER TIME. IN ADDITION, THE NOTE ASSESSES THE OVERALL PERFORMANCE OF THE AUTOREGRESSIVE MODEL AND FINDS THAT IT MEETS SEVERAL REQUIREMENTS WITH ONE EXCEPTION. AS OTHER STUDIES HAVE REPORTED, THE AUTOREGRESSIVE OR INCREMENTAL SPECIFICATION FAILS TO CAPTURE THE HIGH DEGREE OF CHANGE IN ANNUAL EXPENDITURES WHICH WAS EVIDENT ACROSS THE AMERICAN STATES DURING THIS PERIOD.

08821 TAGUIEFF, P.A.
THE DOCTRINE OF THE NATIONAL FRONT IN FRANCE (1972-1989): A "REVOLUTIONARY" PROGRAMME? IDEOLOGICAL ASPECTS OF A NATIONAL-POPULIST MOBILIZATION
NEW POLITICAL SCIENCE, (FAL 89), 29-70.
THE AUTHOR REVIEWS THE MAIN POINTS OF THE DOCTRINE OF THE NATIONAL FRONT IN FRANCE, BY OUTLINING THE CULTURAL AND POLITICAL ORIGINS. THE FUNCTIONAL COHERENCE OF THE MOVEMENT IS DEMONSTATED, WHILE THE AUTHOR INDICATES THE LATENT INTERNAL CONTRADICTIONS, ON A THEORETICAL LEVEL. THESE THESES ARE DEVELOPED IN LIGHT OF ATTACKS FROM JOURNALISTS AND MILITANTS ON J.M. LE PEN, WHO HAS BEEN TARGETED AS BEING DANGEROUS TO THE IDEALS OF A PLURALIST DEMOCRACY. THE AUTHOR ATTEMPTS TO DELINEATE LE PEN'S PURPOSES AND IDEALS IN CONTRAST WITH THE PURSUIT OF NATIONAL FRONT'S IDEALS AND GOALS.

08822 TAI-CHU, C.
THE TIENANMEN LESSON
ASIAN OUTLOOK, 25(1) (NOV 89), 11-12.
THE TIENANMEN SQUARE MASSACRE HAS AROUSED GREAT ANTIPATHY AROUND THE WORLD AND HIGHLIGHTED TWO IMPORTANT FACTS. ONE IS THE UNPRECEDENTED SCOPE AND VIOLENCE OF THE CHINESE PEOPLE'S RESENTMENT AGAINST THE COMMUNIST REGIME. THEIR DISILLUSIONMENT WITH COMMUNIST IDEOLOGY AND THEIR COURAGE, RESOLUTION, AND LONGING FOR DEMOCRACY CANNOT BE DENIED. THE OTHER IS THE DEGREE OF BARBARISM EXERCISED BY THE MILITARY AGAINST INNOCENT PEOPLE, THUS DISPELLING THE ILLUSION THAT THE CHINESE COMMUNIST REGIME HAS LIBERALIZED ITS DOMESTIC POLICIES.

08823 TAIFA, Y.
A NEGLECTED DIMENSION OF THE SINO-U.S. CULTURAL RELATIONSHIP: CULTURAL EXCHANGES, CULTURAL DIPLOMACY, AND CULTURAL INTERACTION
DISSERTATION ABSTRACTS INTERNATIONAL, 49(10) (APR 89), 3150-A.
CHINA'S CULTURAL RELATIONSHIP WITH THE UNITED STATES WAS RESUMED ON A SMALL SCALE IN 1972 AND HAS EXPANDED IN 1979, WHEN CHINA SOUGHT AMERICAN ASSISTANCE IN TRAINING CHINESE STUDENTS AS PART OF ITS EFFORTS TO MODERNIZE ITS ECONOMY. CHINA'S DECISION TO EXPAND CULTURAL EXCHANGES ON A MASSIVE SCALE HAS EPOCH-MAKING IT LIGHT OF ITS DEEP-ROOTED FEAR OF AMERICAN CULTURAL INFLUENCES AND ITS SUSPICION THAT THE UNITED STATES WANTS TO TRANSFORM CHINESE SOCIETY BY INSTILLING ITS CULTURE, VALUES, AND IDEAS INTO THE CHINESE PEOPLE.

08824 TAJALLI-TEHRANI, M.H.
A COMPARATIVE ANALYSIS OF THE MOTIVATIONAL INFLUENCES OF MANAGEMENT BY OBJECTIVES ON PUBLIC EMPLOYEES
DISSERTATION ABSTRACTS INTERNATIONAL, 50(6) (DEC 89), 1801-A.
THE AUTHOR ENDEAVORS TO DETERMINE THE MOTIVATIONAL INFLUENCE OF MANAGEMENT BY OBJECTIVES (MBO) ON PUBLIC EMPLOYEES BY COMPARING MBO-USING AND NON-MBO AGENCIES IN TEXAS. THE STUDY MEASURES AND ANALYZES THE AMOUNT OF EFFORT INDIVIDUALS INVEST IN THEIR JOB, THE DEGREE TO WHICH THEY ARE INTERNALLY MOTIVATED TO PERFORM THEIR DUTIES, AND THEIR ATTITUDES TOWARD THEIR JOB AND THE ORGANIZATION.

08825 TAKAO, I.; KENZO, U.; KIMIHIRO, M.; SEIZABURO, S.
THE LDP IN CRISIS
JAPAN ECHO, XVI(3) (AUT 89), 14-21.
THE AUTHORS DISCUSS THE RECRUIT SCANDAL AND THE STATUS OF THE LIBERAL DEMOCRATIC PARTY IN THE WAKE OF THE INVESTIGATION OF OFFICIAL CORRUPTION.

08826 TAKESHI, I.
ANIMOSITY OR GROWING PAINS: THE US-JAPAN RELATIONSHIP
JAPAN QUARTERLY, XXXVI(1) (JAN 89), 11-17.
THE AUTHOR CONSIDERS THE PRESENT STATUS AND DIRECTIONS OF US-JAPANESE TIES FROM THE JAPANESE POINT-OF-VIEW. HE CONCLUDES THAT THE PROBLEMS THE UNITED STATES FACES AT HOME AND ABROAD, # INCLUDING THE TWIN DEFICITS IN TRADE AND THE FEDERAL BUDGET, CANNOT FAIL TO HAVE A SERIOUS IMPACT ON THE US-JAPANESE RELATIONSHIP.

08827 TAKESHI, M.
THE EMPEROR AS PRIEST-KING
JAPAN ECHO, XVI(1) (SPR 89), 53-59.
THE AUTHOR EXAMINES THE EXALTED POSITION OF THE JAPANESE

EMPEROR SINCE THE MEIJI RESTORATION IN 1868, WHEN THE EMPEROR AUTHORIZED AN ANNOUNCEMENT PROCLAIMING THE END OF THE SHOGUNATE RULE AND THE REINSTATEMENT OF IMPERIAL RULE AS AT THE TIME OF THE FIRST EMPEROR JINMU.

08828 TAKESHI, S.
THE LDP TEETERS IN THE POLITICAL BALANCE
JAPAN QUARTERLY, XXXVI(4) (OCT 89), 375-380.
THE YEAR 1989 HAS MARKED THE LOWEST EBB IN THE FORTUNES OF JAPN'S LIBERAL DEMOCRATIC PARTY SINCE ITS FOUNDING IN 1955. THE PARTY'S DEFEAT IN THREE MAJOR ELECTIONS IN THE FIRST HALF OF 1989 FORESHADOWED ITS LOSS IN THE HOUSE OF COUNCILORS TRIENNIAL ELECTION. IN THAT CONTEST, THE LDP LOST ITS MAJORITY IN THE UPPER HOUSE OF THE DIET, WHILE THE JAPAN SOCIALIST PARTY SCORED A MAJOR TRIUMPH BY WINNING 46 SEATS.

08829 TAKESHIGE, K.
UNO SOSUKE AND THE WINDFALL OF CRISIS
JAPAN QUARTERLY, XXXVI(3) (JUL 89), 252-255.
IN JUNE 1989, UNO SOSUKE BECAME THE PRESIDENT OF JAPAN'S RULING LIBERAL DEMOCRATIC PARTY AND PRIME MINISTER, FORMING A NEW CABINET IN THE WAKE OF THE SCANDAL-TAINTED ADMINISTRATION OF TAKESHITA NOBORU. UNO, WHO WAS FOREIGN MINISTER AT THE TIME OF HIS NOMINATION, EMERGED FROM THE MIDDLE ECHELON OF THE PARTY, RESPONDING TO THE INVITATION TO FILL THE COUNTRY'S TOP POST WHEN IT BECAME EVIDENT THAT HE WAS THE MOST INNOCUOUS CHOICE.

08830 TAKHSHID, M.R.
THE ULAMA OF IRAN: FLUCTUATIONS IN POWER, 1796-1941
DISSERTATION ABSTRACTS INTERNATIONAL, 49(9) (MAR 89), 2800-A.
THE AUTHOR OUTLINES THE HISTORY OF IRAN FROM THE LATE 18TH CENTURY THROUGH THE REIGN OF REZA SHAH TO IDENTIFY THE FACTORS THAT CONTRIBUTED TO THE FLUCTUATIONS IN THE ULAMA'S INFLUENCE ON IRANIAN POLITICS. HE ALSO INCLUDES A BRIEF DESCRIPTION OF THE ISLAMIC REVOLUTION OF 1979 AND SPECULATES ABOUT THE FUTURE OF THE ULAMA'S ROLE IN IRANIAN POLITICS.

08831 TALAL, E.H.B.
JORDON AND THE PEACE IMPERATIVE
AMERICAN-ARAB AFFAIRS, (30) (FAL 89), 10-17.
HIS ROYAL HIGHNESS, THE CROWN PRINCE OF THE HASHEMITE KINGDOM OF JORDON DELIVERED THIS ADDRESS AT HARVARD UNIVERSITY, ON SEPTEMBER 14, 1989. HE TALKED ABOUT THE MIDDLE EAST - ITS POLITICAL AND ECONOMIC PROBLEMS, ITS DESIRE FOR PROGRESS AND STABILITY, AND THEIR CONTINUOUS SEARCH FOR THE ELUSIVE PEACE. HE EXPLAINED THE SITUATION FROM THE VANTAGE POINT OF A CROWN PRINCE. HE INCLUDES POINTS ABOUT PRINCIPLES OF PEACE AND JORDON'S CONTRIBUTION, AND OUTLINES THE MUBARAK PROPOSAL.

08832 TAM, N.D.
COMMITMENT TO REVOLUTION THROUGH PRACTICE
WORLD MARXIST REVIEW, 31(10) (OCT 88), 63-69.
DELEGATES TO THE SIXTH CONGRESS OF THE COMMUNIST PARTY OF VIETNAM (DECEMBER 1986) NOTED THE COUNTRY'S IMPORTANT ACHIEVEMENTS IN BUILDING SOCIALISM BUT AT THE SAME TIME THOROUGHLY ANALYSED MISTAKES IN THE SOCIOECONOMIC SPHERE AND FRANKLY IDENTIFIED THEIR MAIN CAUSES, NAMELY, SHORTCOMINGS IN THE PARTY'S IDEOLOGICAL, ORGANISATIONAL AND CADRE WORK. ENERGETIC EFFORTS HAVE NOW BEEN LAUNCHED ACROSS THE COUNTRY TO IMPLEMENT THE IMPORTANT DECISIONS OF THE JUNE 1988 PLENARY MEETING, TO PROMOTE THE PARTY'S VANGUARD ROLE IN SOCIETY AND TO RECTIFY MISTAKES AND SHORTCOMINGS IN PARTY DEVELOPMENT. IT IS ONLY IN THIS WAY THAT THE COMMUNIST PARTY OF VIETNAM WILL FULFIL ITS MISSION COMPREHENSIVELY AND THUS MEET THE ASPIRATIONS OF THE ENTIRE VIETNAMESE PEOPLE.

08833 TAMBO, O.
JANUARY 8TH STATEMENT: MASS ACTION FOR PEOPLE'S POWER
SECHABA, 23(2) (FEB 89), 2-13.
AFRICAN NATIONAL CONGRESS PRESIDENT, O. R. TAMBO ADDRESSES SOME OF THE VICTORIES AND FAILURES OF THE MOVEMENT FOR FREEDOM AND DEMOCRACY IN SOUTH AFRICA. HE RECOUNTS THE INCREASINGLY BRUTAL REPRESSION OF ANC AND OTHER GROUP EFFORTS TO PUSH FOR RACIAL EQUALITY. HE PRAISES ACTIVISTS FOR THEIR ROLE IN THE BOYCOTT OF LOCAL ELECTIONS AND PRAISES FREEDOM FIGHTERS IN NAMIBIA, A COUNTRY THAT HE STATES IS ON THE "THRESHOLD OF FREEDOM." HE DECLARES 1989 TO BE THE "YEAR OF MASS ACTION FOR PEOPLE'S POWER" AND CALLS FOR AN INTENSIFICATION OF UNITED OPPOSITION TO PRETORIA IN ALL SECTORS INCLUDING ARMED STRUGGLE.

08834 TAMBS, L.A.
INTERNATIONAL COOPERATION IN ILLICIT NARCOTICS AND ILLEGAL IMMIGRATION--A GRAND ILLUSION?
COMPARATIVE STRATEGY, 8(1) (1989), 11-19.
PRIVATE GREED, MILITANT MARXIST-LENINISM, AND WESTERN SOCIETY'S SUICIDAL SELF-INDULGENCE OF ILLICIT NARCOTICS HAVE COMBINED TO FREE COMMUNIST INSURGENTS IN COLOMBIA AND PERU FROM SOVIET SUPPORT. THESE NARCO-GUERRILLAS ARE NOT ONLY ATTACKING DEMOCRATIC GOVERNMENTS, BUT ARE ALSO ACCELERATING RURAL MIGRATION TO THE URBAN AREAS ON AN INTER-AMERICAN

SCALE. OPULENCE ATTRACTS MISERY. THUS, ARGENTINA, VENEZUELA, AND THE U.S. ARE PARTICULARLY AFFECTED. MOREOVER, SOME NATIONS, PROFITING FROM ILLICIT NARCOTICS TRAFFICKING, WILL NOT FULLY COOPERATE IN INTERNATIONAL NARCOTICS OR IMMIGRATION CONTROL, SINCE THEY PERCEIVE IT TO BE TO THEIR ADVANTAGE TO WEAKEN THE WEST.

08835 TAMBURRANO, G.
ITALIAN SOCIALIST PARTY: ITS POLICY AND FAILURE TO UNITE WITH WITH THE COMMUNIST PARTY
ITALIAN JOURNAL, III(4) (1989), 13-18.
THE AUTHOR REVIEWS EFFORTS TO UNITE THE ITALIAN SOCIALIST AND COMMUNIST PARTIES AND EXPLAINS WHY THEY FAILED.

08836 TAMBURRANO, G.
THE OBJECTIVES OF THE ITALIAN SOCIALISTS
WORLD MARXIST REVIEW, 32(11) (NOV 89), 50-52.
FOR ALL THE DIFFICULTIES AND CONVOLUTED ENTANGLEMENTS OF ITALIAN POLITICAL LIFE, THERE IS EVIDENCE OF A GENERAL TREND TOWARDS GREATER UNITY ON THE LEFT: IN POLITICS, IN CULTURE AND IN THE TRADE UNIONS. THIS ARTICLE DESCRIBES THE SPECTRUM OF POLITICAL FORCES IN ITALY WHICH IS CREATING MOVEMENTS IN ECOLOGY, DISARMAMENT, AND WORKER REFORMS.

08837 TAMMISOLA, H.
THE CONSCIENCE OF SOCIETY
WORLD MARXIST REVIEW, 32(11) (NOV 89), 9-12.
THE GROWING DIVERSIFICATION OF SOCIETY AND THE FRAGMENTATION OF THE ONCE MONOLITHIC CLASSES HAVE SUBVERTED THE TRADITIONAL SOCIAL BASE OF THE COMMUNIST PARTIES, WHILE DIVERGING INTERESTS WITHIN INDIVIDUAL CLASSES HAVE WEAKENED WORKERS' SOLIDARITY. THE OBJECTIVE CONDITIONS FOR WORK AMONGST THE PEOPLE ON THE BASIS OF CLASS PRINCIPLES HAVE BECOME MORE COMPLEX. THESE AND OTHER FACTORS EXPLAIN THE SHRINKING SUPPORT FOR COMMUNISTS IN THE CAPITALIST WORLD. THIS ARTICLE ANALYZES SOME OF THE PROBLEMS EXISTING IN THE PRESENT COMMUNIST SYSTEM FROM THE FINNISH PERSPECTIVE.

08838 TANADA, W.E.
FREEDOM FROM NUCLEAR WEAPONS
WORLD MARXIST REVIEW, 31(10) (OCT 88), 38-42.
THE AUTHOR, A SENATOR IN THE REPUBLIC OF THE PHILIPPINES ARGUES THAT THE US BASES ARE THE MOST POTENT INSTRUMENTS OF COLONIALISM AND NEOCOLONIALISM. SO LONG AS THEY EXIST IN THE PHILIPPINES, WASHINGTON WILL BE ABLE TO INTERFERE IN PHILIPPINE ECONOMY AND POLITICS.

08839 TANCHEV, P.
INTERNATIONAL TIES OF THE BULGARIAN AGRARIAN PEOPLE'S UNION
INTERNATIONAL AFFAIRS (MOSCOW), (2) (FEB 89), 20-26.
FOR MORE THAN THIRTY YEARS, THE BULGARIAN AGRARIAN PEOPLE'S UNION HAS BEEN ENGAGED IN EXTENSIVE INTERNATIONAL ACTIVITY CLOSELY ASSOCIATED WITH THE FOREIGN POLICY OF THE PEOPLE'S REPUBLIC OF BULGARIA. IT MAINTAINS TIES WITH MORE THAN 130 PARTIES AND ORGANIZATIONS IN APPROXIMATELY EIGHTY COUNTRIES. MOST OF THESE PARTIES ARE AGRARIAN, CENTRIST, LEFT-RADICAL, LIBERAL, OR DEMOCRATIC. ABOUT HALF OF THE PARTIES ARE IN POWER OR BELONG TO GOVERNMENT COALITIONS. THE BAPU'S TIES SERVE THE INTERESTS OF COOPERATION, CLOSER INTERNATIONAL RELATIONS, AND ECONOMIC INTEGRATION IN THE CONTEXT OF RENEWAL AND RESTRUCTURING.

08840 TANGREDI, S.J.
NEGOTIATION FROM WEAKNESS: CONCEPT, MODEL, AND APPLICATION TO STRATEGIC NEGOTIATIONS
DISSERTATION ABSTRACTS INTERNATIONAL, 50(5) (NOV 89), 1429-A.
THE AUTHOR DEVELOPS A MODEL CONSISTING OF FIVE NEGOTIATING STRATEGIES AND TWELVE CORRESPONDING TACTICS USED BY STRATEGICALLY-INFERIOR STATES. STRATEGIES INCLUDE CONCEDING, CONCEDING BUT ATTEMPTING TO DEVELOP A NEW RELATIONSHIP, OBTAINING CONCESSIONS THAT INCREASE STRENGTH, PROLONGING NEGOTIATIONS WHILE BUILDING STRENGTH, AND ENGAGING IN DIPLOMATIC DECEPTION. HE APPLIES THE MODEL TO ARMS CONTROL NEGOTIATIONS BETWEEN THE USA AND THE USSR FROM 1962 TO 1972.

08841 TANNER, L.D.
SHARED CONCERNS, COMMON OBJECTIVES
BUREAUCRAT, 18(3) (FAL 89), 17-20.
DURING THE PAST DECADE, THE FEDERAL WORK FORCE HAS BEEN BELEAGUERED BY A SERIES OF ABUSES. PAY AND BENEFIT LEVELS HAVE BEEN SERIOUSLY ERODED AND, MORE IMPORTANTLY, PUBLIC SERVICE AS A CARREER HAS BEEN DEVALUED BY THE AMERICAN PEOPLE. THESE DEVELOPMENTS ARE INFLICTING GRAVE CONSEQUENCES ON THE GOVERNMENT'S ABILITY TO OPERATE EFFICIENTLY AND TO CARRY OUT THE PEOPLE'S MANDATES. A NUMBER OF ORGANIZATIONS WITHIN GOVERNMENT AND FEDERAL EMPLOYEES ARE ATTEMPTING TO ALERT THE ADMINISTRATION AND CONGRESS TO THE URGENCY OF THE PROBLEM AND TO REVERSE THE DECLINE.

08842 TARAKI, L.
THE ISLAMIC RESISTANCE MOVEMENT IN THE PALESTINIAN UPRISING
MIDDLE EAST REPORT, 19(156) (JAN 89), 30-32.

THE ISLAMIC RESISTANCE MOVEMENT (KNOWN AS "HAMAS") APPEARS TO BE ENGAGED IN A RACE WITH THE UNIFIED NATIONAL LEADERSHIP OF THE UPRISING TO DETERMINE WHO WILL DIRECT THE DAILY STRUGGLE OF THE PEOPLE OF THE OCCUPIED TERRITORIES. IN THIS ARTICLE, THE AUTHOR REVIEWS THE RECENT HISTORY OF HAMAS AND WHAT THE MOVEMENT OFFERS THE PALESTINIANS.

08843 TARASCIO, V.J.
ECONOMIC AND WAR CYCLES
HISTORY OF POLITICAL ECONOMY, 21(1) (SPR 89), 91-102.
THE AUTHOR RE-EXAMINES THE NATURE OF THE RELATIONSHIP BETWEEN ECONOMIC AND WAR CYCLES AS REFLECTED IN THE WORKS OF KONDRATIEFF AND HAROLD T. DAVIS. HE ARGUES THAT THEIR INDIVIDUAL CONTRIBUTIONS TAKE ON A NEW RELEVANCE WHEN THEY ARE SYNTHESIZED, REFINED, UPDATED, AND APPLIED TO THE UNITED STATES' EXPERIENCE.

08844 TARCOV, N.
IF THIS LONG WAR IS OVER
NATIONAL INTEREST, (18) (WIN 89), 50-53.
THIS ARTICLE IS A ANSWER TO THE SERIES QUESTION: WHAT SHOULD AMERICA'S PURPOSE BE IN THE CONDITIONS LIKELY TO PREVAIL DURING THE REST OF THIS CENTURY NOW THAT THE COLD WAR IS CHANGING ITS CHARACTER IN RADICAL WAYS, THIS WRITER BEGINS WITH A LIST OF HYPOTHETICAL CONDITIONS AND SUGGESTS THAT REMAINING FAITHFUL TO THE POSITIVE AND GLOBAL CHARACTER OF AMERICAN OBJECTIVES AFTER THE COLD WAR SHOULD NOT INVOLVE DOCTRINAIRE CRUSADING OR RECKLESS DISREGARD FOR THE VALUE OF AMERICAN RESOURCES, THE COSTS AND RISKS OF PARTICULAR POLICIES, AND THE CHOICES OF OTHER PEOPLES, HE BELIEVES THAT COMPETITION WITH THE SOVIET UNION WILL CONTINUE.

08845 TARTE, S.
REGIONALISM AND GLOBALISM IN THE SOUTH PACIFIC
DEVELOPMENT AND CHANGE, 20(2) (APR 89), 181-201.
THIS PAPER ARGUES THAT THE FUTURE OF REGIONALISM IN THE SOUTH PACIFIC WILL BE LARGELY DETERMINED BY THE STRATEGIC AND ECONOMIC INTERESTS OF THE WESTERN DEVELOPED STATES, WHO WILL PLAY AN INCREASINGLY SIGNIFICANT ROLE IN THE REGION. THESE INCLUDE THE UNITED STATES, FRANCE, AUSTRALIA, NEW ZEALAND AND JAPAN. MEANWHILE LEADERS OF VULNERABLE AND INTERNALLY UNSTABLE ISLAND STATES WILL BE MOTIVATED IN THEIR SUPPORT OF REGIONALISM BY THE OPPORTUNITIES IT PROVIDES FOR MEETING POLITICAL AND ECONOMIC OBJECTIVES, RELATIVE TO OTHER INTERNATIONAL STRATEGIES.

08846 TARVER, H.
LANGUAGE AND POLITICS IN THE 1980'S: THE STORY OF U.S. ENGLISH
POLITICS AND SOCIETY, 17(2) (JUN 89), 225-245.
THE EFFORT TO CODIFY ENGLISH AS THE OFFICIAL LANGUAGE OF THE UNITED STATES WAS ONE OF THE MORE SUCCESSFUL, IF LESSER KNOWN, MOVEMENTS OF THE REAGAN ERA. THE SO-CALLED "OFFICIAL ENGLISH MOVEMENT" BEGAN IN 1983 AS A HANDFUL OF CONSERVATIVE ACTIVISTS COMMITTED TO RESTRICTIVE NATIONAL LANGUAGE POLICY AND HAS EXPANDED INTO A LARGE, WELL-FINANCED, AND RELATIVELY EFFECTIVE NATIONAL EFFORT WHOSE SUPPORT CUTS ACROSS PARTY, CLASS, AND RACIAL LINES. ALTHOUGH IT IS FUNDAMENTALLY CONSERVATIVE IN ITS POLITICAL MOTIVATIONS AND ITS CORE ELITE BACKING, IT HAS SUCCEEDED IN ATTRACTING WIDESPREAD SUPPORT THAT EXTENDS WELL BEYOND ITS NATURAL CONSTITUENCY.

08847 TASA, C. E.
SOME ARE MORE EQUAL THAN OTHERS: A CROSS-CULTURAL STUDY OF THE EVOLUTION OF SOCIAL STRATIFICATION AND THE STATE
DISSERTATION ABSTRACTS INTERNATIONAL, 49(9) (MAR 89), 2710-A.
SOCIAL STRATIFICATION IS A COMMON FEATURE OF STATE LEVEL SOCIETIES. TWO GRAND THEORIES, CONFLICT THEORY AND FUNCTIONAL/INTEGRATIVE THEORY, ATTEMPT TO EXPLAIN THE EVOLUTION OF SYSTEMS OF SOCIAL STRATIFICATION AND THE DEVELOPMENT OF THE STATE. NUMEROUS HYPOTHESES IDENTIFY SPECIFIC VARIABLES AS CAUSES OR EFFECTS OF SOCIAL STRATIFICATION AND POLITICAL DEVELOPMENT. THE VARIABLES EXAMINED IN THIS STUDY INCLUDE POPULATION PRESSURE, HEALTH ACCUMULATION, DEVELOPMENT OF FORMAL LEADERSHIP, WARFARE, AND GROWTH OF THE MILITARY.

08848 TASHAN, S.
TURKEY ON THE THRESHOLD OF ASIA
NATO'S SIXTEEN NATIONS, 34(2) (APR 89), 90-93.
TURKEY HAS A SPECIAL POSITION IN NATO BECAUSE IT IS THE ONLY ALLIANCE COUNTRY WHOSE TERRITORY LIES IN BOTH EUROPE AND ASIA. THROUGHOUT ITS HISTORY, THIS HAS LED TO A UNIQUE POLITICAL CULTURE AND TO SPECIAL CONCERNS IN FOREIGN POLICY AND DEFENSE.

08849 TASKER, R.
KEEPING THE KEYS
FAR EASTERN ECONOMIC REVIEW, 141(32) (AUG 88), 12-13.
SINGAPORE IS ABOUT TO CHANGE ITS POLITICAL STRUCTURE TO INSTALL A DIRECTLY ELECTED PRESIDENT WHO WILL BE NEITHER A FULLY EXECUTIVE PRESIDENT, NOR A LARGELY CEREMONIAL FIGURE LIKE THE REPUBLIC'S CURRENT HEAD OF STATE. THE PRESIDENT

WILL HAVE POWERS TO BLOCK ANY ATTEMPT BY THE GOVERNMENT TO SQUANDER RESERVES THAT IT HAS NOT ACCUMULATED, AND TO APPROVE KEY MEMBERS OF THE PUBLIC SERVICE. THE MOST LIKELY CANDIDATE FOR THE FIRST SIX-YEAR TERM IS PRIME MINISTER LEE KUAN YEW.

08850 TASKER, R.
PLAYING IT SAFE
FAR EASTERN ECONOMIC REVIEW, 141(37) (SEP 88), 14-15.
ALTHOUGH SINGAPORE'S RULING PEOPLE'S ACTION PARTY (PAP) WON 69 OF THE CONTESTED 70 PARLIAMENTARY SEATS AND PICKED UP ANOTHER 11 WHERE THERE WAS NO OPPOSITION CHALLENGE, THE RESULTS OF THE ELECTION ARE A CAUSE FOR CONCERN AMONG PAP LEADERS. THE OPPOSITION PARTIES LOST SEVERAL SEATS ON VERY NARROW MARGINS AND INCREASED THEIR SHARE OF THE POPULAR VOTE. THE PAP'S LONG RUN OF 70%-PLUS MAJORITIES COULD BE A THING OF THE PAST.

08851 TASKER, R.
PRINCE ON THE LOOSE
FAR EASTERN ECONOMIC REVIEW, 141(34) (AUG 88), 25-26.
IT APPEARS AS IF ASEAN WILL HAVE TO DO SOME DIPLOMATIC FOOTWORK TO KEEP INTERNATIONAL SUPPORT FOR THE CAMBODIAN RESISTANCE. THE THREE FACTIONS WERE DIVIDED FURTHER BY STATEMENTS OF FORMER COALITION LEADER PRINCE NORODOM SIHANOUK. THE PRINCE'S STRIDENT ANTI-KHMER ROUGE RHETORIC HAS EMBARRASSED HIS ALLIES IN ASEAN AND ELSEWHERE. MANY FEEL THAT ALTHOUGH THE EVIL DEEDS OF THE KHMER ROUGE ARE UNDENIABLE, ATTENTION SHOULD NOT BE DRAWN TO THEM AT THIS TIME WHEN NEGOTIATIONS WITH VIETNAM SEEM A DISTINCT POSSIBILITY.

08852 TASKER, R.
STRIKING WHILE IT'S HOT
FAR EASTERN ECONOMIC REVIEW, 141(35) (SEP 88), 20-21.
THE ANNOUNCEMENT OF GENERAL ELECTIONS IN SINGAPORE DEMONSTRATES PRIME MINISTER LEE KUAN YEW'S ATTEMPTS TO TAKE ADVANTAGE OF A BOOMING ECONOMY AND AN OPPOSITION THAT IS IN DISARRAY. IT ALSO ALLOWS THE RULING PEOPLE'S ACTION PARTY TO BEGIN A GENERATIONAL CHANGE AS 14 OF ITS MPS ANNOUNCED THEIR RETIREMENT TO MAKE WAY FOR NEW BLOOD. LEE HIMSELF INDICATED THAT HE WILL RELINQUISH THE PRIME MINISTERSHIP SOON.

08853 TASKER, R.
TAKING UP THE GAUNTLET
FAR EASTERN ECONOMIC REVIEW, 141(32) (AUG 88), 14.
AFTER 72 DAYS OF DETENTION AND INTERROGATION FOR ALLEGEDLY COLLABORATING WITH US DIPLOMATS, FORMER SOLICITOR-GENERAL FRANCIS SEOW SAYS HE PLANS TO RUN IN SINGAPORE'S NEXT GENERAL ELECTION. HE RECOUNTS THE INTENSE INTERROGATION THAT HE UNDERWENT WHICH AGGRAVATED HIS HEART CONDITION. HE CLAIMS THAT NONE OF THE GOVERNMENT'S CLAIMS WERE SUBSTANTIATED THROUGH THE INTERROGATION.

08854 TASKER, R.
THE NOT-SO-SILENT MAJORITY
FAR EASTERN ECONOMIC REVIEW, 141(38) (SEP 88), 36-37.
UNDER A CONSTITUTIONAL AMMENDMENT, OPPOSITION PARTIES WERE ABLE TO HAVE A MAXIMUM OF THREE MPS, EVEN IF FEWER THAN THAT NUMBER WERE ELECTED. THE SEPTEMBER ELECTION LEFT ONLY ONE ELECTED OPPOSITION MP, AND AFTER SOME AGONIZING, THE WORKERS PARTY IS GRUDINGLY ALLOWING THE NEXT BIGGEST OPPOSITION VOTE GETTERS, FRANCIS SEOW, AND LEE SIEW CHOH TO GO TO PARLIAMENT.

08855 TASKER, R.; VATIKIOTIS, M.
THE PRINCE OFFSTAGE
FAR EASTERN ECONOMIC REVIEW, 141(31) (AUG 88), 13-14.
ALTHOUGH IT MAY BE ONLY A FIRST STEP ON THE LONG ROAD TO PEACE, THE JAKARTA INFORMAL MEETING WAS HISTORIC IN THAT IT BROUGHT ALL FOUR WARRING CAMBODIAN FACTIONS TOGETHER FOR THE FIRST TIME. A NOTABLE ABSCENCE WAS THAT OF PRINCE SIHANOUK, WHO RESIGNED AS PRESIDENT OF THE RESISTANCE COALITION A WEEK PREVIOUSLY. SIHANOUK HAS AGREED TO SOME POINTS OF A SEVEN-POINT PEACE PROPOSAL OFFERED BY VIETNAMESE REPRESENTATIVE HUN SEN.

08856 TASSIN, J.
INTERNATIONAL CIVIL SERVICE--COMPENSATION
INTERNATIONAL REVIEW OF ADMINISTRATIVE SCIENCES, 55(1) (MAR 89), 85-94.
THE ARTICLE EXAMINES THE LEVEL OF COMPENSATION OF INTERNATIONAL CIVIL SERVANTS IN WORLD ORGANIZATIONS SUCH AS THE UN AND ITS SPECIALIZED AGENCIES OR IN MORE REGIONAL ORGANIZATIONS SUCH AS THE EUROPEAN COMMUNITY. IT FOCUSES ON THE UN SYSTEM AND ESTABLISHES THE NEED FOR A COMPREHENSIVE REVIEW OF THE UN COMMON SYSTEM DUE TO CHANGING EXCHANGE RATES AND AN INCREASING NUMBER OF "NATIONAL PROFESSIONAL OFFICERS."

08857 TATE, C.N.; SITTIWONG, P.
DECISION MAKING IN THE CANADIAN SUPREME COURT: EXTENDING THE PERSONAL ATTRIBUTES MODEL ACROSS NATIONS
THE JOURNAL OF POLITICS, 51(4) (NOV 89), 900-916.

THEORY-BASED PERSONAL ATTRIBUTES MODELS OF THE CIVIL RIGHTS AND LIBERTIES AND ECONOMICS DECISION MAKING OF THE CANADIAN SUPREME COURT JUSTICES SERVING FROM 1949-1985 ARE DEVELOPED FROM LIPSET AND ROKKAN'S (1967) APPROACH TO EXPLAINING MASS POLITICAL BEHAVIOR. THE MODELS SHOW BOTH BEHAVIORS TO BE INFLUENCED BY QUEBEC/NON-QUEBEC REGIONAL ORIGINS AND RELIGIOUS AFFILIATION. POLITICAL PARTY, BEING APPOINTED BY THE LAST LAISSEZ FAIRE LIBERAL PRIME MINISTER, KING, AND HAVING JUDICIAL AND POLITICAL EXPERIENCE. THE MODELS ARE REASONABLY POTENT, STATISTICALLY. THEIR MOST IMPORTANT ATTRIBUTES CAPTURE CRUCIAL DIMENSIONS IN CONTEMPORARY CANADIAN POLITICS, REGION, AND PARTY, AND ALSO HAVE IMPLICATIONS FOR THE CROSS-NATIONAL STUDY OF JUDICIAL BEHAVIOR.

08858 TATE, K.
BLACK POLITICS AS A COLLECTIVE STRUGGLE: THE IMPACT OF RACE AND CLASS IN 1984
DISSERTATION ABSTRACTS INTERNATIONAL, 50(6) (DEC 89), 1790-A.
USING DATA DRAWN FROM A NATIONAL SURVEY OF BLACK AMERICANS IN 1984, THE AUTHOR PROBES THE ISSUE OF RACE VERSUS CLASS IN THE FORMATION OF BLACK PUBLIC OPINION. SHE DEVELOPS STRUCTURAL EQUATION MODELS THAT INCORPORATE THE PSYCHOLOGICAL COMPONENT OF GROUP IDENTITIES TO ASSESS THE RELATIONSHIP BETWEEN SOCIOECONOMIC STATUS AND RACE/CLASS IDENTITIES, AS WELL AS THEIR RELATIVE EFFECTS ON BLACK POLITICAL ATTITUDES.

08859 TATUM, J.S.
ENERGY AND SOCIETY: BEYOND THE BOUNDS OF CONVENTIONAL ANALYSIS
DISSERTATION ABSTRACTS INTERNATIONAL, 49(11) (MAY 89), 3495-A.
THE AUTHOR CONSIDERS THE SELECTIVITY OF ATTENTION IMPLICIT IN DOMESTIC ENERGY POLICY IN THE USA AND THE EFFECTS OF THAT SELECTIVITY ON THE NATION'S FUTURE, BOTH MATERIALLY AND IN TERMS OF IMPLIED SOCIAL RELATIONSHIPS. HE STUDIES TWO CASES OF ALTERNATIVE ENERGY ACTIVITY: ONE BY LOCAL GOVERNMENTS IN CALIFORNIA AND THE OTHER BY A COMMUNITY ACTION GROUP. THESE CASES HIGHLIGHT SERIOUS OVERSIGHTS IN CONVENTIONAL POLICY PERSPECTIVES AND SUGGEST A BROAD, RELATIVELY UNTAPPED RANGE OF TECHNICAL AND SOCIO-CULTURAL POSSIBILITIES FOR THE FUTURE.

08860 TAUBER, E.
SAYYID TALIB AND THE YOUNG TURKS IN BASRA
MIDDLE EASTERN STUDIES, 25(1) (JAN 89), 3-22.
THE STORY OF THE ANTI-TURKISH REFORM MOVEMENT IN BASRA AT THAT TIME IS COMPLETELY DIFFERENT FROM THE STORY OF THE REFORM AND DECENTRALIZATION MOVEMENTS WHICH AROSE IN THE OTHER ARAB PROVINCES OF THE OTTOMAN EMPIRE. THE STORY OF THIS MOVEMENT IS IN EFFECT THE STORY OF ONE INDIVIDUAL: SAYYID TALIB AL-NAQIB, THE 'STRONG MAN' OF BASRA, WHOSE HOMETOWN WAS TRANSFORMED BY HIM INTO THE 'WILD SOUTH' OF IRAQ. THIS ARTICLE CHRONICLES TALIB'S RISE TO POWER AND HIS INFLUENCE OVER THE DIRECTION AND POLITICAL INTEGRATION OF THE OTTOMAN EMPIRE.

08861 TAVAREZ, R.
OUR CONCEPT OF POPULAR POWER
WORLD MARXIST REVIEW, 32(11) (NOV 89), 43-46.
THIS ARTICLE DETAILS HOW THE 4TH CONGRESS OF THE DOMINICAN COMMUNIST PARTY (PCD), HELD IN SANTO DOMINGO FROM MARCH 16 TO 19 THIS YEAR, CONSIDERED THE PROBLEMS OF RENEWING AND CONSOLIDATING THE PARTY, STRENGTHENING THE UNITY OF THE LEFT REVOLUTIONARY FORCES, AND EVENTUALLY SETTING UP A BROAD FRONT OR MOVEMENT FOR A POPULAR NATIONAL ALTERNATIVE, FOR THE DEFEAT OF THE OLIGARCHY AND IMPERIALISM, AND FOR THE ESTABLISHMENT OF POPULAR POWER.

08862 TAVERS, A.
RATIONAL COMMON GROUND IN THE SOCIOLOGY OF KNOWLEDGE
PHILOSOPHY OF THE SOCIAL SCIENCES, 19(3) (SEP 89), 273-290.
THIS ARTICLE EXPLORES THE COMMON THEME OF RELATIVISM IN THE SOCIOLOGY OF KNOWLEDGE. THE CONCERN IS THE APPLICATION OF THIS THEME TO THE STANDARDS OF COGNITIVE SUCCESS: THE CRITERIA OF TRUTH, VALIDITY, AND RATIONALITY. IT ARGUES AGAINST THE VERSION OF RELATIVISM WHICH PROPOSES THAT ALL BELIEFS ARE ON A PAR WITH RESPECT TO THE CAUSES OF THEIR CREDIBILITY. IT EXPLORES THE COMMON GROUND IN THE CRITERIA FOR WHAT IS TO COUNT AS A SET OF BELIEFS AND IN THE ROLE THEY PLAY IN THE EXPLANATION OF ACTION.

08863 TAYLOR-GOOBY, P.
THE POLITICS OF WELFARE PRIVATIZATION: THE BRITISH EXPERIENCE
INTERNATIONAL JOURNAL OF HEALTH SERVICES, 19(2) (1989), 209-220.
THE 1980S CONSERVATIVE GOVERNMENT IN BRITAIN IS COMMITTED TO POLICIES OF WELFARE PRIVATIZATION FOR PRACTICAL AND IDEOLOGICAL REASONS-TO FACILITATE TAX CUTS AND TO ROLL BACK THE STATE. ONE PROBLEM THIS POLICY FACES IS THAT THE MOST EXPENSIVE AND INTERVENTIONIST SERVICES ARE HIGHLY

POPULAR WITH VOTERS FROM ALL PARTIES. IN THIS ARTICLE, THE AUTHOR EXAMINES THE EXTENT TO WHICH RECENT PRIVATIZATION POLICIES IN WELFARE ARE INFLUENCED BY CONFLICT BETWEEN THE GOALS OF ACHIEVING TAX CUTS AND OF MAINTAINING ELECTORAL SUPPORT, SO THAT THE OUTCOME IS A CHANGE IN THE FORM OF STATE INTERVENTIONISM, RATHER THAN A ROLLING BACK OF THE WELFARE STATE. IT ALSO CONSIDERS THE IMPACT OF NEW POLICIES DESIGNED TO UNDERMINE THE CONSENSUS ACROSS SOCIAL GROUPS AND POLITICAL PARTIES OF SUPPORT FOR BIG-SPENDING STATE SERVICES, WHICH MAY FACILITATE REDUCTIONS IN THE OVERALL SCOPE OF WELFARE PROVISION IN FUTURE YEARS.

08864 TAYLOR, G.
A BITTERSWEET VICTORY
MACLEAN'S (CANADA'S NEWS MAGAZINE), 102(29) (JUL 89), 18.
THE SUPREME COURT RULING ALLOWING BARBARA DODD TO HAVE AN ABORTION IS A PART OF CANADA'S LARGER STRUGGLE TO DEFINE THE RULES AND LIMITS FOR ABORTION. THE RULING, WHICH TURNED ASIDE AN EARLIER INJUCTION WHICH HAD TEMPORARILY PREVENTED DODD FROM HAVING AN ABORTION, IS CONSIDERED A VICTORY FOR THE PRO-CHOICE ACTIVISTS, BUT THE BATTLE IS DESTINED TO RAGE ON.

08865 TAYLOR, G.; BROSNAHAN, M.
A PARALLEL ACCORD
MACLEAN'S (CANADA'S NEWS MAGAZINE), 102(29) (JUL 89), 15, 17.
AFTER MONTHS OF UNCERTAINTY, THE GOALS OF THE MEECH LAKE CONSTITUTIONAL ACCORD SEEM MORE LIKELY TO BE MET. MANITOBAN POLITICIANS HAVE HAMMERED OUT A COMPROMISE SOLUTION THAT IS ACCEPTABLE TO ALL INVOLVED. NOW ONLY NEW BRUNSWICK'S RATIFICATION REMAINS NECESSARY.

08866 TAYLOR, G.; WALLACE, B.
SEEKING ANSWERS
MACLEAN'S (CANADA'S NEWS MAGAZINE), 102(30) (JUL 89), 10-12.
A SERIES OF AIR DISASTERS AND THE RESULTING CONFUSION AND DEBATE OVER THEIR CAUSES HAVE INCREASED PUBLIC UNCERTAINTY ABOUT THE GOVERNMENT'S ABILITY TO PREVENT THEM IN THE FUTURE. PUBLIC CONFIDENCE HAS BEEN FURTHER SHAKEN BY INFIGHTING AMONG THE NINE-MEMBER CANADIAN AVIATION SAFETY BOARD. GOVERNMENT OFFICIALS PLAN SWEEPING CHANGES IN THE WAY IN WHICH FUTURE AIR DISASTERS ARE INVESTIGATED IN HOPES THAT PUBLIC CONFIDENCE CAN BE RESTORED. RESTORED.

08867 TAYLOR, I.
HILLSBOROUGH, 15 APRIL 1989: SOME PERSONAL CONTEMPLATIONS
NEW LEFT REVIEW, (177) (SEP 89), 89-110.
THE RECENT SERIES OF DISASTERS IN BRITAIN ARE TESTIMONY TO THE CONSEQUENCES OF A CORROSION OF PUBLIC SPACE BY THE VALUES OF FREE-MARKET CAPITALISM, PARTICULARLY IN A COUNTRY WITH AN AGEING, OFTEN DECREPIT SOCIAL INFRASTRUCTURE. THE TRAGEDY AT HILLSBOROUGH FOOTBALL STADIUM, IN WHICH 95 PEOPLE DIED, POINTS TO THE DEADLY EFFECTS OF A CLASS STRATEGY OF CONTAINING THE POPULATION AT POINTS OF TENSION AND EFFERVESCENCE.

08868 TAYLOR, R.
CHINESE HIERACHY IN COMPARATIVE PERSPECTIVE
JOURNAL OF ASIAN STUDIES, 48(3) (AUG 89), 490-511.
THIS ARTICLE ON CHINA ATTEMPTS TO ADAPT LOUIS DUMONT'S GENERAL THEORY OF HIERARCHY TO CHINESE SOCIAL HISTORY. DUMONT PLACES INDIGENOUS IDEOLOGY AT THE CENTER OF HIS ANALYSIS AND SUBORDINATES ECONOMICS AND POLITICS TO IT. WORKING IN AN INDOLOGICAL CONTEXT, HE ARGUES THAT THE SOCIAL WHOLE SHOULD BE UNDERSTOOD IN TERMS OF ITS DOMINANT IDEOLOGY, WHICH STRUCTURES SOCIETY HIERCHICALLY AND ENDOWS IT WITH MEANING FOR ITS PARTICIPANTS. TAYLOR ANALYZES CHINESE HIERCHY IN SIMILAR TERMS AND PLACES IT IN A LONG-TERM CHINESE HISTORICAL CONTEXT.

08869 TAYLOR, S.E.
CONGRESS AND PUBLIC HEALTH POLICY
CRS REVEIW, 10(3) (MAR 89), 4-5.
THE CONGRESS PLAYS A CENTRAL ROLE IN WEIGHING PUBLIC HEALTH CONCERNS AGAINST COMPETING INTERESTS AND IN FINDING A BALANCE IN THE FORMULATION OF NATIONAL PUBLIC HEALTH POLICY. THE PROCESS OF PUBLIC HEALTH POLICY FORMATION IN THE CONGRESS INVOLVES THREE PHASES: IDENTIFICATION OF A PROBLEM AS A HEALTH CONCERN THAT MIGHT BE IMPROVED THROUGH PUBLIC HEALTH INTERVENTION; THE SELECTIVE FORMULATION OF PUBLIC POLICIES TO SERVE AS THE BASES OF PUBLIC HEALTH INTERVENTION; AND THE EXECUTION OF THE PUBLIC HEALTH POLICIES SELECTED.

08870 TAYLOR, S.E.
PUBLIC HEALTH AND POLITICS
CRS REVEIW, 10(3) (MAR 89), 1-3.
CONTEMPORARY PUBLIC HEALTH POLICY IS DEFINED LESS BY WHAT HEALTH PROFESSIONALS KNOW HOW TO DO THAN BY WHAT THE POLITICAL SYSTEM DECIDES IS APPROPRIATE OR FEASIBLE, ACCORDING TO A REPORT BY THE INSTITUTE OF MEDICINE OF THE NATIONAL ACADEMY OF SCIENCES. THE STUDY ALSO STATES THAT THE USA HAS SLACKENED ITS PUBLIC HEALTH VIGILANCE AND THAT THE

HEALTH OF THE PUBLIC IS UNNECESSARILY THREATENED AS A RESULT. PUBLIC HEALTH IS A VITAL FUNCTION THAT IS IN TROUBLE BECAUSE MANY PUBLIC HEALTH ISSUES HAVE BECOME POLITICIZED.

08871 TAYLOR, S.E.; SMITH-COLEMAN, I.
TRANSLATING SCIENCE INTO PUBLIC HEALTH PROMOTION
CRS REVEIW, 10(3) (MAR 89), 14-22.
THE ROAD TO PUBLIC POLICY IS OFTEN AN UNCHARTED ONE, WITH MANY OBSTACLES ALONG THE WAY. SCIENCE HELPS IDENTIFY HEALTH PROBLEMS, SUGGEST AVENUES TO CONTROL THEM, AND HELPS MEASURE THE RESULTS OF THE CHOICES MADE. HOWEVER, THE PROCESS BY WHICH WHAT IS "KNOWN" IS TRANSLATED INTO PUBLIC HEALTH POLICIES IS NOT A SCIENTIFIC ONE, BUT ONE THAT MINGLES SCIENCE AND POLITICS. PUBLIC HEALTH POLICIES EMERGE GRADUALLY AND OFTEN THROUGH OVERLAPPING PHASES: BUILDING SCIENTIFIC CONSENSUS, CHOOSING A POLICY COURSE, AND IMPLEMENTING, EVALUATING, AND REVISING THE POLICIES SELECTED.

08872 TAYLOR, T.
CONVENTIONAL ARMS CONTROL: A THREAT TO ARMS PROCUREMENT
WORLD TODAY, 45(7) (JUL 89), 121-124.
ALTHOUGH ARMS CONTROL EFFORTS HAVE AFFECTED NUCLEAR STRATEGY AND EQUIPMENT, THEY HAVE NOT HAD AN IMPACT ON CONVENTIONAL ARMS PROCUREMENT OR ON THE WIDER DEFENSE PLANNING ASSOCIATED WITH PROCUREMENT. THE OPENING OF THE CONVENTIONAL FORCES IN EUROPE NEGOTIATIONS IN MARCH 1989 MARKED THE END OF THIS ISOLATION OF DEFENSE PROCUREMENT FROM ARMS CONTROL. THIS ARTICLE EXPLORES THE CONSEQUENCES OF PROCUREMENT THAT WILL RESULT FROM THIS NEW ARMS CONTROL LINK.

08873 TAYLOR, V.
SOCIAL MOVEMENT CONTINUITY: THE WOMEN'S MOVEMENT IN ABEYANCE
AMERICAN SOCIOLOGICAL REVIEW, 54(5) (OCT 89), 761-775.
THIS ARTICLE USES SOCIAL MOVEMENT AND ORGANIZATION THEORY TO DEVELOP A SET OF CONCEPTS THAT HELP EXPLAIN SOCIAL MOVEMENT CONTINUITY. THE THEORY IS GROUNDED IN NEW DATA ON WOMEN'S RIGHTS ACTIVISM FROM 1945 TO THE 1960S THAT CHALLENGE THE TRADITIONAL VIEW THAT THE AMERICAN WOMEN'S MOVEMENT DIED AFTER THE SUFFRAGE VICTORY IN 1920 AND WAS REBORN IN THE 1960S. THIS CASE DELINEATES A PROCESS IN SOCIAL MOVEMENTS THAT ALLOWS CHALLENGING GROUPS TO CONTINUE IN NONRECEPTIVE POLITICAL CLIMATES THROUGH SOCIAL MOVEMENT ABEYANCE STRUCTURES. FIVE CHARACTERISTICS OF MOVEMENT ABEYANCE STRUCTURES ARE IDENTIFIED AND ELABORATED: TEMPORALITY, PURPOSIVE COMMITMENT, EXCLUSIVENESS, CENTRALIZATION, AND CULTURE. THUS, SOCIAL MOVEMENT ABEYANCE STRUCTURES PROVIDE ORGANIZATIONAL AND IDEOLOGICAL BRIDGES BETWEEN DIFFERENT UPSURGES OF ACTIVISM BY THE SAME CHALLENGING GROUP.

08874 TE'AN, C.
THATCHER RESHUFFLES CABINET FOR NEW IMAGE
BEIJING REVIEW, 32(33) (AUG 89), 17.
THE MID-1989 BRITISH CABINET RESHUFFLE WAS THE BIGGEST IN MARGARET THATCHER'S TEN-YEAR PREMIERSHIP. IT APPEARED TO BE AN ATTEMPT TO HALT THE MID-TERM SLIDE IN THE GOVERNMENT'S POPULARITY AND PUT A NEW FACE ON HER ADMINISTRATION IN THE RUN-UP TO THE NEXT ELECTION. THE RESHUFFLE, INCLUDING SENIOR OFFICIALS OF NON-CABINET RANK, INVOLVED HALF OF THATCHER'S ADMINISTRATIVE ELITE.

08875 TEAN, C.
A CHALLENGE FOR COMMONWEALTH
BEIJING REVIEW, 32(46) (NOV 89), 16-17.
THE 1989 COMMONWEALTH SUMMIT IN KUALA LUMPUR HAS CONSIDERED A SUCCESS, DESPITE A BITTER QUARREL OVER WHETHER TO INCREASE ECONOMIC SANCTIONS AGAINST SOUTH AFRICA. WHILE HAILING IMPROVED EAST-WEST RELATIONS, THE SUMMIT COMMUNIQUE EMPHASIZED THE NEED TO HELP THE FINANCIALLY-STRAPPED DEVELOPING WORLD AND CALLED FOR GLOBAL EFFORTS TO OVERCOME THE PROBLEMS OF DRUG TRAFFICKING, REFUGEES, TERRORISM, REGIONAL DISPUTES, AND ENVIRONMENTAL POLLUTION.

08876 TEBBEN, C.L.
A CONCEPTUAL FRAMEWORK FOR THE JUDICIAL RESOLUTION OF FEDERALISM CASES
DISSERTATION ABSTRACTS INTERNATIONAL, 49(7) (JAN 89), 1943-A.
THE US SUPREME COURT HAS RELEGATED THE FEDERALISM ISSUE TO CONGRESS FOR RESOLUTION. TO CONGRESS FOR RESOLUTION. THIS PAPER EXAMINES THE THESIS THAT STATE POWER IS ADEQUATELY PROTECTED IN THE NATIONAL POLITICAL PROCESS, ARGUING THAT STATE DECISION-MAKING POWER IS NOT SUFFICIENTLY PROTECTED IN THE NATIONAL POLITICAL PROCESS AND THAT FEDERALISM ISSUES OUGHT TO BE JUSTIFIABLE.

08877 TEDESCO, T.; KALHLA, P.
COMBAT IN ONTARIO
MACLEAN'S (CANADA'S NEWS MAGAZINE), 102(5) (JAN 30), 14-15.
DAVID PETERSON, THE PREMIER OF ONTARIO, SURPRISED POLITICAL ANALYSTS BY LEADING THE LIBERAL PARTY INTO POWER IN 1987. HOWEVER, HE IS FACING SIGNIFICANT CHALLENGES ON BOTH PROVINCIAL AND NATIONAL FRONTS THAT WILL TAX HIS

POLITICAL ABILITY TO THE LIMIT. THESE CHALLENGES INCLUDE:
THE RISING COST AND DETERIORATING QUALITY OF BOTH HEALTH
CARE AND EDUCATION, A CRISIS OVER THE SOARING COST OF
HOUSING IN THE CITIES, ALLEGATIONS OF POLICE RACISM,
STRAINED RELATIONS WITH BRIAN MULRONEY'S FEDERAL GOVERNMENT
OVER THE US-CANADA FREE TRADE AGREEMENT, AND PRESSURE FORM
OTHER PREMIERS TO REOPEN THE 1987 MEECH LAKE ACCORD ON
CONSTITUTIONAL REFORM.

08878 TEDESCO, T.; MACKENZIE, H.; WALMSLEY, A.
FREE TRADE'S SELLING POINTS
MACLEAN'S (CANADA'S NEWS MAGAZINE), 102(26) (JUL 89),
66-67.
THE PASSAGE OF THE US-CANANDA FREE TRADE AGREEMENT HAS
BROUGHT ABOUT THE CREATION OF A NEW BREED OF BUSINESSMAN:
THE FREE TRADE MIDDLEMAN. REQUESTS FOR INFORMATION ABOUT THE
AGREEMENT AND ITS IMPLICATIONS HAVE INCREASED DRAMATICALLY
AND ASTUTE CONSULTANTS HAVE JUMPED IN TO FILL THE NEED AND
TURN A GOOD PROFIT IN THE PROCESS. THESE MIDDLEMEN ARE
VIEWED AS AN INTEGRAL FIRST STEP IN THE GRADUAL PROCESS OF
EXPANDING TRADE BETWEEN THE US AND CANADA THAT IS EXPECTED
TO TAKE PLACE OVER THE NEXT DECADE AS MAJOR REMAINING
DISPUTES ARE MET WITH.

08879 TEDESCO, T.; LOWTHER, W.
IN REAGAN'S FOOTSTEPS
MACLEAN'S (CANADA'S NEWS MAGAZINE), 102(6) (FEB 89), 14.
THE PROMPT VISIT OF GEORGE BUSH TO CANADA INSPIRED MANY
CANADIANS TO HOPE THAT THE US WILL GIVE CANADIAN CONCERNS
HIGHER PRIORITY THAN IN THE PAST. BUSH AND CANADIAN PRIME
MINISTER, BRIAN MULRONEY, DISCUSSED TRADE ISSUES, ACID RAIN,
AND INTERNATIONAL ISSUES THAT AFFECT BOTH NATIONS IN AN
INFORMAL MEETING. BUSH ANNOUNCED THAT HE WOULD CONTINUE THE
ANNUAL US-CANADA SUMMITS THAT WERE STARTED BY HIS
PREDECESSOR, RONALD REAGAN.

08880 TEDESCO, T.; CLARK, M.; MACKENZIE, H.
OPENING WITH A BANG
MACLEAN'S (CANADA'S NEWS MAGAZINE), 102(3) (JAN 89), 15.
SCANT DAYS AFTER THE PASSAGE OF THE CANADA U.S. FREE
TRADE ACT, DISPUTES OVER PLYWOOD AND WOOL PROVIDE THE FIRST
TEST OF HOW WELL THE ACT WILL FUNCTION TO SERVE BOTH
NATIONS' INTEREST. OTHER POTENTIAL POINTS OF DISPUTE INCLUDE
CANADIAN PORK SUBSIDIES, SUGAR EXPORTS, AND WINE PRICES.
UNDER THE DISPUTE-SETTLEMENT TERMS OF THE FREE TRADE
AGREEMENT TRADE EXPERTS WOULD BE CALLED UPON TO SIT ON
PANELS MADE UP OF TWO CANADIANS, TWO AMERICANS AND A FIFTH
MEMBER ACCEPTABLE TO BOTH SIDES. THE ACTUAL MAKE-UP OF THESE
PANELS IS ALSO A POINT OF DISPUTE. HOW BOTH NATIONS HANDLE
THESE EARLY CHALLENGES MAY LARGELY DETERMINE HOW CANADA WILL
FARE IN THE NEW ERA OF FREE TRADE.

08881 TEDESCO, T.
REVISITING MEECH LAKE
MACLEAN'S (CANADA'S NEWS MAGAZINE), 102(28) (JUL 89), 16.
PRESSURE TO AMMEND THE MEECH LAKE ACCORD HAS INCREASED
STEADILY IN CANADA. SEVERAL PROVINCIAL PREMIERS EXPRESSED
DOUBT ABOUT THE CURRENT AGREEMENT--WHICH WOULD RECOGNIZE
QUEBEC AS A DISTINCT SOCIETY WITHIN CANADA--AND ITS ABILITY
TO PROTECT MINORITY RIGHTS. ALTHOUGH THE GOVERNMENT HAS YET
TO ACKNOWLEDGE THE GROWING UNREST ABOUT MEECH LAKE, THEY
ARE CURRENTLY IN A MINORITY CAMP OF ONTARIO, QUEBEC, AND
ALBERTA. SINCE THE ACCORD MUST BE RATIFIED BY ALL 10
PROVINCES TO BECOME A PART OF CANADA'S CONSTITUTION, SOME
SORT OF COMPROMISE SEEMS INEVITABLE.

08882 TEH-FU, H.
GRASSROOTS ORGANIZERS
FREE CHINA REVIEW, 39(12) (DEC 89), 24-29.
LOCAL FACTIONS HAVE PLAYED A SIGNIFICANT ROLE IN
TAIWAN'S CENTRAL AND LOCAL POLITICS SINCE 1947, WHEN THE
FIRST LOCAL ELECTION WAS HELD FOLLOWING THE ISLAND'S RETURN
TO CHINA. LOCAL FACTIONS HAVE MONOPOLIZED LOCAL POLITICAL
AND ECONOMIC PRIVILEGES THROUGH A PATRONAGE SYSTEM, WITHOUT
CHALLENGING EITHE THE KUOMINTANG'S POLITICAL LEGITIMACY OR
ITS DOMINATION OF THE POLITICAL SCENE. IN FACT, THE KMT HAS
FOR DECADES BEEN ABLE TO CONSOLIDATE ITS RULE WITH THE
SUPPORT OF THESE LOCAL FACTIONS.

08883 TEITELBOIM, V.
COMMUNISTS, CULTURE, AND REVOLUTION
POLITICAL AFFAIRS, LXVIII(5) (MAY 89), 33-39.
THE PROCESS OF INTELLECTUALIZATION EMBRACES NOT JUST THE
INTELLIGENTSIA BUT EVERYBODY, ESPECIALLY NOW IN THE MIDST OF
A SCIENTIFIC AND TECHNOLOGICAL REVOLUTION, WITH THE WORLD OF
LABOR AND MATERIAL PRODUCTION ADVANCING NUMEROUS INNOVATIONS
THAT REQUIRE HIGH-LEVEL TRAINING. IN THIS SENSE ONE HAS
EVERY RIGHT TO SAY THAT HUMANKIND ITSELF IS BECOMING MORE
AND MORE INTELLECTUAL. THE SAME HOLDS TRUE FOR THE COMMUNIST
PARTY. THE TALK IS NOT OF A SPECIAL PARTY OF THE
INTELLEGENTSIA BUT OF THE COLLECTIVE INTELLECT OF THE PARTY
INTELLIGENTSIA, WHICH ARE TWO VERY DIFFERENT THINGS.

08884 TEITELBOIM, V.
THE REKINDLING OF OCTOBER
WORLD MARXIST REVIEW, 32(11) (NOV 89), 3-8.
IN THIS ARTICLE, THE LEADER OF THE CHILEAN COMMUNISTS
REASSESSES THE IMPORTANCE OF THE GREAT OCTOBER SOCIALIST
REVOLUTION, ITS EXPERIENCE AND ITS LESSONS. HE ENVISIONS THE
PRESENT COMMUNIST MOVEMENT AS A SEQUEL TO OCTOBER; AND HE
ACKNOWLEDGES THAT THE WORKING CLASS HAS EVOLVED IN WAYS
WHICH MUST BE MATCHED BY THE EVOLUTION OF THE PARTY. ONLY IN
THIS WAY CAN THE COMMUNIST MOVEMENT BEGIN TO TRANSFORM
SOCIETY IN A DEMOCRATIC WAY, USING TOOLS NOT ENVISIONED AT
THE OCTOBER REVOLUTION.

08885 TEIWES, F.C.
MAO AND HIS LIEUTENANTS
AUSTRALIAN JOURNAL OF CHINESE AFFAIRS, (19-20) (JAN 88),
1-80.
MANY DIFFERENT VIEWS OF MAO AS LEADER HAVE BEEN ADVANCED
BOTH INSIDE AND OUTSIDE CHINA. ONE PICTURES MAO AS THE GREAT
REVOLUTIONARY UNIFIER WHO WELDED THE DIVERSE ELEMENTS OF THE
CCP INTO A POWERFUL ORGANIZATION CAPABLE OF SEIZING VICTORY
AGAINST THE ODDS AND WHO KEPT PARTY SOLIDARITY AT A HIGH
LEVEL AFTER THE VICTORY. ANOTHER PRESENTS HIM AS A
MANIPULATIVE POLITICIAN WHO REPEATEDLY PLAYED OFF HIS
LEADERSHIP COLLEAGUES WITH SHREWD DIVIDE-AND-RULE TACTICS. A
THIRD FOCUSES ON MAO'S DESPOTIC WAYS, PORTRAYING HIM AS AN
ESPECIALLY VINDICTIVE TYRANT. THIS ESSAY ASSESSES THE
ACCURACY OF THESE VIEWS OF MAO AND EXAMINES HIS ATTITUDES
TOWARD POWER.

08886 TEIXEIRA, F.B.
DEMOCRACY IS ACTION
WORLD MARXIST REVIEW, 32(11) (NOV 89), 46-48.
THE EXPERIENCE OF THE PORTUGUESE COMMUNIST PARTY SHOWS
THAT, IRRESPECTIVE OF THE SIZE OF A CELL, ITS SPHERE OF
ACTIVITIES, WHETHER AT AN ENTERPRISE OR IN THE COMMUNITY, IS
WIDE ENOUGH AND CAPABLE ENOUGH OF MOBILISING THE ENERGIES OF
ITS MEMBERS AND ESTABLISHING GROUPS TO TACKLE THE MOST
DIVERSE PROBLEMS. ON THE OTHER HAND, THE RICHNESS OF THIS
SPHERE IS ALSO A PRODUCT OF THE INITIATIVE AND ACTIVITY OF
THE PARTY ORGANISATION.

08887 TEKIE, A.
ETHIOPIA ON THE WRONG TRACK
NEW AFRICAN, (258) (MAR 89), 37.
THE AMHARA-DOMINATED REGIME OF ETHIOPIA IS TRYING TO
IMPOSE ITS WILL ON MINORITIES AND NATIONALITIES IN THE
INTEREST OF NATIONAL SECURITY. BUT ATTEMPTS BY THE RULING
DERGUE HAVE FAILED BECAUSE THE MAJORITY OF THE ETHIOPIAN
PEOPLE-INCLUDING THE OROMOS, ERITREANS; AND TIGRAYANS-WILL
NOT ACCEPT CENTRALIZED, IMPERIAL RULE.

08888 TELLING, D.C.
SCIENCE IN POLITICS: EUGENICS, STERILIZATION, AND GENETIC
SCREENING
DISSERTATION ABSTRACTS INTERNATIONAL, 49(12) (JUN 89),
3860-A.
THE AUTHOR PROBES THE USE OF GENETIC KNOWLEDGE FOR
POLITICAL PURPOSES. THE CENTRAL CONCERN IS THE CAPABILITY OF
THE POLITICAL SYSTEM TO ENSURE THAT TECHNOLOGICAL
APPLICATIONS SERVE ENDS CONSONANT WITH THE DEMOCRATIC AND
MORAL VALUES OF THE AMERICAN POLITICAL SYSTEM.

08889 TELTSCHIK, H.
GORBACHEV'S REFORM POLICY AND THE OUTLOOK FOR EAST-WEST
RELATIONS
AUSSEN POLITIK, 40(3) (1989), 201-214.
THIS PAPER DESCRIBES THE ESSENTIAL CHARACTERISTICS OF
SOVIET LEADER, GORBACHEV'S REFORM POLICY, AS WELL AS THE
CONSEQUENCES OF GLASTNOST AND PERESTROIKA AND
DEMOCRATIZATION OF POLITICS AND SOCIETY. THE REORIENTATION
OF SOVIET FOREIGN POLICY AND CHANGES IN INTERNATIONAL
STRUCTURE PROVIDES THE BACKGROUND FOR THE COALITION WITH
EUROPE AND THE KEY ROLE OF THE FEDERAL REPUBLIC OF GERMANY.
THE CENTRAL ROLE OF GERMAN-SOVIET RELATIONS IS EMPHASISED
WHILE THE SUMMIT MEETING BETWEEN LEADERS OF STATE IN BOTH
COUNTRIES RESULTING IN A JOINT DECLARATION IS EXAMINED.

08890 TENG-HUI, L.
TIENANMEN: ACTIONS JUDGED BY HISTORY
FREE CHINA REVIEW, 39(8) (AUG 89), 18.
THE CHINESE COMMUNISTS USURPED THE CHINESE MAINLAND WITH
VIOLENCE AND LIES, BUT THERE HAVE BEEN CONSTANT INTERNAL
STRUGGLES AND SUPPRESSION OF THE PEOPLE OVER THE PAST 40
YEARS. THE INHUMANE ACTIONS OF THE CHINESE COMMUNISTS ARE
CERTAIN TO BE JUDGED BY HISTORY, EVOKE EVER STRONGER
INTERNAL OPPOSITION, AND HASTEN THE DEMISE OF COMMUNISM ON
THE MAINLAND.

08891 TENOFSKY, E.
THE WAR MEASURES AND EMERGENCIES ACTS: IMPLICATIONS FOR
CANADIAN CIVIL RIGHTS AND LIBERTIES
AMERICAN REVIEW OF CANADIAN STUDIES, 29(3) (FAL 89),
293-306.

THE CANADIAN PARLIAMENT FIRST PASSED THE WAR MEASURES ACT IN 1914 IN ORDER TO DEAL WITH THE EMERGENCY OF WORLD WAR I. IT REMAINED ON THE BOOKS AFTER THE EMERGENCY WAS OVER AND ALLOWED THE GOVERNMENT TO TAKE CONTROL OF PROPERTY AND CIVIL RIGHTS. THIS ARTICLE DETAILS THE EMERGENCY ACT AND QUESTIONS WHETHER THERE REMAIN PROBLEMS WITH THE LAW. IT CONCLUDES THAT THE GOVERNMENT, GIVEN ANY POWER, NEEDS TO BE WATCHED.

08892 TEP, N.
THE COMMUNISTS AND BUDDHISTS IN KAMPUCHEA
WORLD MARXIST REVIEW, 32(4) (APR 89), 61-62.
PRACTICE SHOWS THAT A MARXIST-LENINIST PARTY COMING TO POWER CANNOT DISREGARD THE CHURCH, WHICH IS A REAL SOCIOPOLITICAL FORCE. THE SUCCESS OF THE COMMUNISTS' POLICY WILL DEPEND IN LARGE MEASURE ON HOW THEY SHAPE THEIR RELATIONS WITH BELIEVERS. THIS ARTICLE EXAMINES THE SOCIO-POLITICAL NATURE OF RELIGION IN KAMPUCHEA.

08893 TERCHEK, R.J.; BRUBAKER, S.C.
PUNISHING LIBERALS OR REHABILITATING LIBERALISM?
AMERICAN POLITICAL SCIENCE REVIEW, 83(4) (DEC 89), 1309-1316.
IN THIS ARTICLE, RONALD TERCHEK DENIES THAT LIBERALISM IS CRIPPLED BY MORAL RELATIVISM OR INCAPACITATED FOR PUNISHMENT. BUT STANLEY C. BRUBAKER ARGUES THAT LIBERALS STRIVE FOR NEUTRALITY CONCERNING HOW PEOPLE SHOULD LIVE AND "NO" IS THE ANSWER TO THE QUESTION: CAN LIBERALS PUNISH?

08894 TERRELL, K.
AN ANALYSIS OF THE WAGE STRUCTURE IN GUATEMALA CITY
JOURNAL OF DEVELOPING AREAS, 23(3) (APR 89), 405-424.
THIS STUDY CONTRIBUTE TO THE LITERATURE ON WAGE DETERMINATION IN URBAN AREAS OF LDC'S BY ANALYZING THE DETERMINANTS OF INDIVIDUAL WORKERS' INCOMES THROUGH DIFFERENCES IN THEIR PERSONAL CHARACTERISTICS, AS WELL AS DIFFERENCES IN THE OCCUPATION AND INDUSTRY WHERE THEY ARE EMPLOYED. SEVERAL HYPOTHESES ARE TESTED CONCERNING THE RELATIVE IMPORTANCE OF VARIOUS FORCES ON EARNINGS. SPECIAL ATTENTION IS GIVEN TO TESTING FOR GENDERRELATED WAGE DISCRIMINATION AND DIFFERENCES IN THE LEVEL AND DETERMINANTS OF WAGES IN THE FORMAL AND INFORMAL SECTORS OF THE ECONOMY.

08895 TERRILL, W.A.
THE LESSONS OF UNTSO AND THE FUTURE OF UN TRUCE SUPERVISION
CONFLICT, 9(2) (1989), 197-208.
UNITED NATIONS TRUCE OBSERVATION FORCES HAVE PLAYED AN IMPORTANT ROLE IN UN EFFORTS TO CONTAIN CONFLICT. THE UN TRUCE SUPERVISION ORGANIZATION (UNTSO) WAS THE EARLIEST AND IS AMONG THE MOST IMPORTANT OF THESE TYPES OF FORCES. UNTSO OPERATIONS HAVE DISPLAYED A NUMBER OF SHORTCOMINGS BUT HAVE ALSO CONTRIBUTED TO CONTAINING AND MODERATING THE LEVEL OF CONFLICT IN THE MIDDLE EAST. THE LESSONS OFFERED BY UNTSO DURING THE YEARS WHEN IT WAS MOST ACTIVE ARE THEREFORE OF CONSIDERABLE VALUE. IT IS ESPECIALLY IMPORTANT TO UNDERSTAND UNTSO FAILURES AND SUCCESSES TO GAIN A FULLER UNDERSTANDING OF THE POTENTIAL FOR TRUCE SUPERVISION FORCES TO CONTROL CONFLICT. THE IMPORTANCE OF UNDERSTANDING THESE LESSONS IS NOW BECOMING ESPECIALLY SIGNIFICANT WITH THE CREATION OF ADDITIONAL TRUCE SUPERVISION FORCES SUCH AS THE UN IRANIRAQ MILITARY OBSERVERS FORCE.

08896 TERRY, J.
THE BODY INVADED: MEDICAL SURVEILLANCE OF WOMEN AS REPRODUCERS
SOCIALIST REVIEW, (MAR 89), 13-44.
THIS ARTICLE DESCRIBES THE SITUATION IN WHICH WOMEN OF CHILDBEARING AGE AND PREGNANT WOMEN IN PARTICULAR ARE SUBJECT TO INTENSIFIED SCRUTINY BY BOTH STATE AND CIVIL SOCIETY. IT EXAMINES HOW AIDS AND DRUG USE ALLOW FOR THE EMERGENCE OF DISCOURSES AND PRACTICES THAT PLACE THESE WOMEN IN PARTICULAR JEOPARDY. IT EXPLORES HOW NEW TECHNOLOGIES ARE CHANGING THE TERMS OF THE REPRODUCTIVE RIGHTS DEBATE.

08897 TERRY, J.L.
THE POLITICAL ECONOMY OF MIGRANT FARM LABOR AND THE FARMWORKER MOVEMENT IN THE MIDWEST
DISSERTATION ABSTRACTS INTERNATIONAL, 49(9) (MAR 89), 2832-A.
THE AUTHOR STUDIES THE MIGRANT FARMWORKER MOVEMENT IN THE MIDWEST, WHICH WAS ORGANIZED BY THE FARM LABOR ORGANIZING COMMITTEE, IN THE CONTEXT OF THE POLITICAL ECONOMIC STRUCTURE OF MIDWESTERN AGRICULTURAL PRODUCTION. THE POLITICAL ECONOMIC FORCES THAT CREATED AND PERPETUATED A MIGRANT LABOR POOL AND THE ORGANIZATION OF SPECIALTY CROP AGRICULTURAL PRODUCTION THAT UTILIZED THESE WORKERS ARE EXAMINED.

08898 TERRY, L.D.
A THEORY OF ADMINISTRATIVE CONSERVATORSHIP
DISSERTATION ABSTRACTS INTERNATIONAL, 50(4) (OCT 89), 1087-A.
TRANSFORMATIONAL LEADERS ARE DEEMED EXTREMELY IMPORTANT BECAUSE THEY ARE CAPABLE OF REVITALIZING INSTITUTIONS THROUGH THE RADICAL TRANSFORMATION OF THE TECHNICAL,

POLITICAL, AND CULTURAL SYSTEMS. BUT, IN FACT, THE TRANSFORMATIONAL VIEW POSES A SERIOUS THREAT TO VALUABLE INSTITUTIONS AND THE PROVEN LEADERSHIP PRACTICES THAT HAVE SUSTAINED THEM. INSTEAD OF RADICALLY TRANSFORMING AMERICAN GOVERNMENTAL INSTITUTIONS, IT IS IMPORTANT TO CONSERVE THEM, BECAUSE THEY ARE THE REPOSITORY OF VALUES EMBODIED IN THE CONSTITUTION OF THE UNITED STATES.

08899 TERUMASA, N.
JAPAN AS NUMBER TWO
JAPAN ECHO, XVI(2) (SUM 89), 66-68.
IT IS EVIDENT THAT THE JAPANESE-AMERICAN PARTNERSHIP IS IN TRANSITION. IF THE EXISTING WORLD ORDER HAS REACHED THE BEGINNING OF THE END, THE JAPAN-U.S. RELATIONSHIP HAS REACHED THE END OF THE BEGINNING. ONE SIGN OF CHANGE IN THE RELATIONSHIP IS THE HEATED DEBATE ON NEW ISSUES, SUCH AS HIGH TECHNOLOGY. THERE ARE ALSO COMPLAINTS FROM SOME JAPANESE THAT JAPAN HAS LITTLE SAY IN CURRENCY AFFAIRS AND THE MAKING OF INTERNATIONAL MONETARY POLICY AND THAT IT SHOULD BE GIVEN MORE VOTING POWER IN MULTILATERAL BODIES LIKE THE INTERNATIONAL MONETARY FUND AND THE WORLD BANK. FORMERLY, THE BILATERAL CONFLICTS BETWEEN TOKYO AND WASHINGTON CENTERED AROUND SUCH ISSUES AS TRADE SURPLUSES AND DEFICITS. IN THE NEAR FUTURE, DISPUTES CAN BE EXPECTED OVER LEADERSHIP IN FOREIGN AID, CURRENCY MANAGEMENT, AND TECHNOLOGICAL DEVELOPMENT.

08900 TESKE, P.E.
IMPLEMENTING DEREGULATION: THE POLITICAL ECONOMY OF STATE TELECOMMUNICATIONS REGULATION AFTER DIVESTITURE
DISSERTATION ABSTRACTS INTERNATIONAL, 50(5) (NOV 89), 1434-A.
THIS DISSERTATION PRESENTS AN ANALYSIS OF U.S. STATE TELECOMMUNICATIONS REGULATORY DECISIONS AFTER THE AT&T DIVESTITURE AND SUBSEQUENT FEDERAL COMMUNICATIONS COMMISSION DEREGULATION. ON A THEORETICAL LEVEL, THE ANALYSIS IS USED TO TEST POLITICAL ECONOMY THEORIES OF POLICY CHOICE, PARTICULARLY THE INTEREST GROUP AND INSTITUTIONAL MODELS. FOR THE PURPOSES OF POLICY ANALYSIS, THE DISSERTATION EXPLAINS THE DIFFERENCES IN STATE CHOICES ABOUT THE PRICING OF TELECOMMUNICATIONS SERVICES AND ALLOWING COMPETITIVE ENTRY INTO LOCAL MARKETS. IT UTILIZES BOTH QUANTITATIVE ANALYSES AND CASE STUDIES TO TEST THESE THEORIES AND TO EXPLAIN STATE REGULATORY CHOICES IN TELECOMMUNICATIONS.

08901 TESSLER, M.
ARABS IN ISRAEL; ISRAEL, EGYPT AND THE PALESTINIANS: FROM CAMP DAVID TO INTIFADA
INDIANA UNIVERSITY PRESS BLOOMINGTON, INDIANA, 1989, 89-124.
THE AUTHOR POINTS OUT THAT IF ISRAEL REGARDS ITS PARTIAL PEACE WITH EGYPT AS A RESPITE FROM INTERNATIONAL PRESSURE AND CONCLUDES THAT IT THEREFORE HAS LESS NEED TO ADDRESS THE GRIEVANCES OF ITS ARAB CITIZENS, FRUSTRATION AND ANGER WILL MOUNT ON ALL SIDES, INTENSIFYING RATHER THAN DEFUSING TENSION BETWEEN ARABS AND JEWS IN ISRAEL.

08902 TESSLER, M.
CENTER AND PERIPHERY WITHIN REGIONAL INTERNATIONAL SYSTEMS: THE CASE OF THE ARAB WORLD
JERUSALEM JOURNAL OF INTERNATIONAL RELATIONS, 11(3) (SEP 89), 74-89.
BASED ON AN IMPRESSIONISTIC ANALYSIS, THIS ARTICLE ASSIGNS CENTRALITY IN THE ARAB WORLD TO EGYPT, SYRIA, IRAQ, AND SAUDI ARABIA IN THE EAST AND TO TUNISIA, ALGERIA, AND MOROCCO IN THE WEST. IT SUGGESTS REASONS FOR THE CENTRALITY OF THE RESPECTIVE COUNTRIES AND DISCUSSES WAYS IN WHICH CENTRALITY, BOTH IN THE ARAB WORLD AND ELSEWHERE, MIGHT BE MORE RIGOROUSLY DEFINED AND ANALYZED.

08903 TESSLER, M.; LESCH, A. M.
ISRAEL'S DRIVE INTO THE WEST BANK AND GAZA; ISRAEL, EGYPT AND THE PALESTINIANS: FROM CAMP DAVID TO INTIFADA
INDIANA UNIVERSITY PRESS BLOOMINGTON, INDIANA, 1989, 194-222.
MANY BELIEVE THAT IF THE GOVERNMENT OF PRIME MINISTER MENACHEM BEGIN SUCCEEDS IN ITS ATTEMPT TO LAY A FOUNDATION FOR THE EXERCISE OF ISRAELI SOVEREIGNTY OVER WEST BANK & GAZA TERRITORIES, THEN MOVEMENT TOWARD PEACE WILL END AND PROSPECTS FOR ARAB-ISRAELI ACCOMMODATION WILL BE DEALT A BLOW FROM WHICH THEY WILL NOT RECOVER FOR A DECADE OR MORE. THIS WAS THE ASSUMPTION UNDERLYING THE PEACE INITIATIVE LAUNCHED BY PRESIDENT RONALD REAGAN ON SEPTEMBER 1, 1982. THE PRESIDENT EXPRESSED THE VIEW THAT THE MOMENTUM OF PEACE MUST BE REVIVED BEFORE ISRAEL'S CREEPING ANNEXATION ON THE WEST BANK AND IN GAZA REACHES THE POINT OF NO RETURN. THIS ARTICLE EXAMINES WHETHER ISRAEL CAN BE PERSUADED TO REDEFINE ITS THINKING ABOUT THESE TERRITORIES AND WHETHER THE PRESENT GOVERNMENT POLICIES IN THIS MATTER CAN BE HALTED.

08904 TESSLER, M.
ISRAELI POLITICS AND THE PALESTINIANS AFTER CAMP DAVID; ISRAEL, EGYPT AND THE PALESTINIAN PROBLEM AFTER CAMP DAVID
INDIANA UNIVERSITY PRESS BLOOMINGTON, INDIANA, 1989,

140-173.
THIS ARTICLE DESCRIBES THE THREE CATEGORIES OF ISSUES
WHICH SEPARATED THE EGYPTIANS AND THE ISRAELIS OVER
IMPLEMENTATION OF THE PROVISIONS OF CAMP DAVID. FIRST, THE
TWO COUNTRIES HAD RADICALLY DIFFERENT AND INCOMPATIBLE
POSITIONS REGARDING THE MEANING OF PALESTINIAN "AUTONOMY"
AND "SELF-DETERMINATION". SECOND, THERE WAS INTENSE
DISAGREEMENT ABOUT THE LEGALITY AND DESIRABITY OF ISRAELI
EFFORTS TO ESTABLISH JEWISH SETTLEMENTS IN WEST BANK AND
GAZA. THIRD, THE TWO COUNTRIES DIFFERED OVER HOW THE
PALESTINIANS SHOULD BE REPRESENTED AND OVER THE INVOLVEMENT
OF THE PLO.

08905 TESSLER, M.
POST-SINAI PRESSURES IN ISRAEL AND EGYPT; ISRAEL, EGYPT
AND THE PALESTINIANS: FROM CAMP DAVID TO INTIFADA
INDIANA UNIVERSITY PRESS BLOOMINGTON, INDIANA, 1989, 23-42.
THE PROSPECTS FOR EGYPT'S RECONCILIATION WITH THE REST
OF THE ARAB WOULD IMPROVED DURING THE SUMMER OF 1982 AND
THIS HELD OUT THE PROSPECT OF INCREASED POPULARITY AT HOME
FOR THE REGIME OF HOSNI MUBARAK. MORE GENERALLY, HOWEVER, AS
THIS ESSAY DESCRIBES, MOST OF THE CHALLENGES FACING CAIRO
REMAINED AS SERIOUS AS EVER. THE EXODUS OF THE ISRAELIS FROM
THE SINAI HAD NOT BROUGHT CALM AND STABILITY; IT HAD REMOVED
AN ISSUE WHICH TENDED TO DEVERT ATTENTION FROM OTHER
PROBLEMS. THE PROBLEMS BEGAN TO RESURFACE, FOR BOTH ISRAEL
AND EGYPT.

08906 TESSLER, M.
SECULARISM AND NATIONALISM IN THE ISRAELI PALESTINIAN
CONFLICT; ISRAEL, EGYPT AND THE PALESTINIANS: FROM CAMP
DAVID TO INTIFADA
INDIANA UNIVERSITY PRESS BLOOMINGTON, INDIANA, 1989,
174-193.
THREE INTERRELATED ASSUMPTIONS GUIDE THIS ANALYSIS OF
HISTORICAL, IDEOLOGICAL, AND POLITICAL FACTORS BEARING ON A
TWO-STATE SOLUTION TO THE ISRAELI-PALESTINIAN CONFLICT.
FIRST, BOTH JEWS AND ARABS HAVE LEGITIMATE RIGHTS IN
PALESTINE. SECOND, JEWS AND PALESTINIAN ARABS MUST BE
PERMITTED TO DEFINE FOR THEMSELVES THE CHARACTER OF THEIR
RESPECTIVE COMMUNAL IDENTITIES AND PATHS TO SELF-
DETERMINATION. THIRD, THE ISRAELIPALESTINIAN CONFLICT MUST
NOT BE SEEN AS A ZERO-SUM GAME; MORE IMPORTANT THAN
PREPARING A BALANCE SHEET OF THE VALIDITY OF EACH SIDE'S
CLAIMS AND COUNTERCLAIMS IS THE SEARCH FOR A BASIS FOR
COMPROMISE AND RECONCILIATION.

08907 TESSLER, M.
THE CAMP DAVID ACCORDS AND THE PALESTINIAN PROBLEM; ISRAEL,
EGYPT, AND THE PALESTINIANS: FROM CAMP DAVID TO INTIFADA
INDIANA UNIVERSITY PRESS BLOOMINGTON, INDIANA, 1989, 3-22.
THIS ESSAY TAKES A DETAILED LOOK AT THE CAMP DAVID
AGREEMENT AND THE PROBLEMS OF IMPLEMENTATION FROM BOTH THE
EGYPTIAN AND THE ISRAELI PERSPECTIVES. THE AUTHOR DESCRIBES
HOW IT HAS BEEN THE BROADER ISSUES OF PALESTINIAN AUTONOMY
AND SELF-DETERMINATION, OF THE ISRAELI PUSH TO SETTLE THE
OCCUPIED TERRITORIES AND OF PALESTINIAN REPRESENTATION THAT
HAVE FRUSTRATED THE ASPIRATIONS OF CAMP DAVID AND KEPT
EGYPTIANISRAELI RELATIONS FROM DEVELOPING MORE SUBSTANCE.

08908 TESSLER, M.
THINKING ABOUT TERRITORIAL COMPROMISE IN ISRAEL; ISRAEL,
EGYPT AND THE PALESTINIANS: FROM COMP DAVID TO INTIFADA
INDIANA UNIVERSITY PRESS BLOOMINGTON, INDIANA, 1989,
272-284.
IT IS TOO EARLY TO TELL HOW THE POLITICAL EQUATION
INSIDE ISRAEL WILL BE AFFECTED BY THE INTIFADA. IN THE SHORT
RUN, PUBLIC OPINION HAS TENDED TO MOVE TO THE RIGHT; THERE
IS WIDESPREAD SUPPORT FOR RABIN'S TOUGH LINE AND GENERAL
AGREEMENT THAT ORDER MUST BE RESTORED BEFORE UNDERLYING
PROBLEMS CAN BE ADDRESSED. YET MANY OBSERVERS AND ANALYSTS,
PROMINENT ISRAELIS AMONG THEM, BELIEVE THE PROBLEM OF THE
TERRITORIES HAS ENTERED THE ISRAELI POLITICAL CONSCIOUSNESS
IN A WAY THAT IS SHAKING THE ASSUMPTIONS ON WHICH CURRENT
ISRAELI POLICIES ARE BASED. WHATEVER ITS EVENTUAL OUTCOME,
THE UPRISING THAT BEGAN ON DECEMBER 9, 1987, HAS MADE IT
INCREASINGLY DIFFICULT FOR ISRAELIS TO TAKE SERIOUSLY THE
CLAIM OF PRIME MINISTER YITZHAK SHAMIR AND THE LIKUD UNION
THAT THE INHABITANTS OF THE WEST BANK AND GAZA WILL ACCEPT
OCCUPATION ONCE THEY REALIZE THAT ISRAEL HAS NO INTENTION OF
WITHDRAWING FROM ANY PART OF THE TERRITORY AND THAT THE
"ADMINISTERED AREAS" CAN THEREFORE BE RETAINED, AND
EVENTUALLY ANNEXED, WITH NO SIGNIFICANT COST TO THE JEWISH
STATE.

08909 TETHER, C.G.
THE "VISION" COLLIDES WITH THE "GRAND DESIGN"
CONTEMPORARY REVIEW, 254(1479) (APR 89), 177-183.
IT MAY BE THAT THE DIFFERENCES OF OPINION BETWEEN
BRITISH AND OTHER MEMBERS OF THE COMMUNITY ON WHAT THE
IMPLEMENTATION OF THE SINGLE MARKET SHOULD MEAN WILL BE
RESOLVED IN A MANNER THAT MRS THATCHER CONSIDERS ACCEPTABLE -
ONE, THAT IS, THAT WILL NOT REQUIRE BRITISH INVOLVEMENT IN
THE BRUSSELS BUREAUCRACY OR IN EEC ECONOMIC AND MONETARY

TOGETHERNESS ON A SCALE CALCULATED TO COMPROMISE THE
PROGRESS OF THE 'GRAND DESIGN' AT HOME. HOWEVER, IT IS
ALREADY APPARENT THAT THERE IS LITTLE OR NO CHANCE OF THE
'IRON LADY' ALTERING HER STANCE IN SIGNIFICANT DEGREE. FROM
WHICH IT FOLLOWS THAT THERE WILL EITHER HAVE TO BE A MAJOR
CLIMB-DOWN ON THE OTHER SIDE OF THE CHANNEL OR THE 1992
EXERCISE WILL BRING ABOUT A PARTING OF THE WAYS.

08910 TETLOCK, P.E.; BOETTGER, R.
COGNITIVE AND RHETORICAL STYLES OF TRADITIONALIST AND
REFORMIST SOVIET POLITICIANS: A CONTENT ANALYSIS STUDY
POLITICAL PSYCHOLOGY, 10(2) (JUN 89), 209-232.
PREVIOUS RESEARCH ON DEMOCRATIC POLITICAL LEADERS HAS
REVEALED SYSTEMATIC RELATIONSHIPS BETWEEN THE CONTENT
(IDEOLOGICAL ORIENTATION) AND STRUCTURE (INTEGRATIVELY
COMPLEXITY) OF POLITICAL THOUGHT. CONSERVATIVES TEND TO BE
LESS INTEGRATIVELY COMPLEX THAN LIBERALS AND MODERATE
SOCIALISTS -ALTHOUGH THIS EFFECT IS QUALIFIED BY THE
EXISTENCE OF ROLE-BY-IDEOLOGY AND ISSUE-BY-IDEOLOGY
INTERACTIONS. THE PRESENT STUDY EXPLORES THE RELATIONSHIP
BETWEEN IDEOLOGY AND INTEGRATIVE COMPLEXITY IN A VERY
DIFFERENT POLITICAL AND CULTURAL CONTEXT: THE SOVIET UNION
IN THE MID-1980S. SYSTEMATIC CODING OF POLITCY STATEMENTS OF
KEY SOVIET LEADERS REVEALED A NUMBER OF EFFECTS: (A)
COMMUNIST PARTY LEADERS CLASSIFIED AS REFORMERS (PRO-
GORBACHEV) HAD MORE INTEGRATIVELY COMPLEX STYLES OF POLICY
REASONING THAN TRADITIONALISTS; (B) THIS DIFFERENCE WAS
SIGNIFICANT IN BOTH TIME PERIODS EXAMINED (THE LAST SIX
MONTHS OF CHERNENKO'S TENURE IN OFFICE AND THE FIRST SIX
MONTHS OF GORBACHEV'S) AND WAS MUCH MORE PRONOUNCED IN THE
GORBACHEV PERIOD. THE ARTICLE CONCLUDES BY NOTING PARALLELS
BETWEEN THE DATA ON SOVIET AND WESTERN POLITICAL LEADERS AND
BY CONSIDERING ALTERNATIVE COGNITIVE, IMPRESSION MANAGEMENT,
AND INSTITUTIONAL EXPLANATIONS FOR THESE DATA.

08911 TETSUHISA, M.
ELECTORAL REFORM: A FLAWED LDP INITIATIVE
JAPAN ECHO, XVI(3) (AUT 89), 25-30.
SOME LEADING VOICES IN THE RULING LIBERAL DEMOCRATIC
PARTY HAVE CALLED FOR A SHIFT FROM MULTI-SEAT TO SINGLE-SEAT
ELECTORAL DISTRICTS IN JAPAN'S HOUSE OF REPRESENTATIVES.
THIS PROPOSAL APPEARS TO BE AN ATTEMPT BY THE HARD-PRESSED
LDP TO GRAB THE INITIATIVE IN THE REFORM DEBATE. AS SUCH, IT
MAY BE NO MORE THAN A TRIAL BALLOON FLOATED TO CAPTURE A FEW
HEADLINES. HOWEVER, GIVEN THE STRONG APPEAL THAT THE SINGLE-
SEAT CONCEPT HAS FOR SOME MEMBERS OF THE RULING PARTY, THE
PROPOSAL COULD MOVE QUICKLY TOWARD IMPLEMENTATION IF THE
OPPOSITION PROVES AMENABLE. THIS PROPOSAL SHOULD NOT BE
ENACTED WITHOUT CAREFUL CONSIDERATION BECAUSE THE PRESENT
SYSTEM WAS INSTITUTED IN 1928 AND ITS DURABILITY HAS PROVED
THAT IT IS WELL SUITED TO CONDITIONS IN JAPAN.

08912 TEUNE, H.
GROWTH
SAGE PUBLICATIONS, NEWBURY PARK, CA, 1988, 144.
THE AUTHOR PRESENTS A CONCEPTUAL AND THEORETICAL
ANALYSIS OF GROWTH PHENOMENA IN AN ATTEMPT TO PREDICT THE
FUTURE OF GROWTH. HE ANALYZES GROWTH AS A SOCIAL CONCEPT,
LOOKS AT MEASUREMENTS OF GROWTH, AND CONSIDERS THE
CONSEQUENCES OF GROWTH IN POLITICAL, ECONOMIC, AND SOCIAL
AREAS. HE ALSO DISCUSSES GROWTH AS BENEFIT OR DETRIMENT, THE
COSTS OF GROWTH, AND THE POSSIBILITIES OF OVERCOMING THE
LIMITS OF GROWTH.

08913 TEVETH, S.
CHARGING ISRAEL WITH ORIGINAL SIN
COMMENTARY, 88(3) (SEP 89), 24-33.
THIS ARTICLE EXPLORES THE RECENT TREND TO REWRITE
HISTORY OF THE FOUNDING OF THE JEWISH STATE. IT EXAMINES
EXTENSIVELY THE WRITINGS OF AVI SHLAIM AND BENNY MORRIS ON
THE SUBJECT. IT CONCLUDES THAT THEIR WRITINGS ARE DISTORTED,
AND INCLUDE OMISSIONS, TENDENTIOUS READINGS AND OUTRIGHT
FALSIFICATIONS, AND THAT IT IS OBVIOUS THAT THEY WILL FAIL
IN THEIR INTENTION TO UNDERMINE IF NOT THOROUGHLY DEMOLISH
THE OLD HISTORY.

08914 THAKUR, R.
CREATION OF THE NUCLEAR-FREE NEW ZEALAND MYTH:
BRINKMANSHIP WITHOUT A BRINK
ASIAN SURVEY, 29(10) (OCT 89), 919-939.
THE PRIMARY OBJECTIVE OF THIS ARTICLE IS TO SUGGEST THAT
THE CONVENTIONAL WISDOM IS A GROSS OVERSIMPLIFICATION ON ALL
COUNTS: THE LABOUR GOVERNMENT DID NOT SEEK TO TRANSFORM A
PRONUCLEAR POLICY INTO AN ANTINUCLEAR ONE; IT DID DEPART
CRUCIALLY FROM THE PRECEDENTS OF DENMARK AND THE 1972-75
LABOUR GOVERNMENT OF NEW ZEALAND; IT HAS NOT SUBORDINATED
POLITICAL EXPEDIENCY TO MORAL COMPULSIONS: ITS POLITICAL
COURAGE IS NOT ABOVE SUSPICION; AND ITS DEMOCRATIC MANDATE
CAN BE VARIOUSLY INTERPRETED. A MEMBER OF THE 1986 DEFENCE
COMMITTEE OF ENQUIRY HAS REFERRED TO THE "ANTI-NUCLEAR
ORTHODOXY" OF NEW ZEALAND. ONE OF THE VIRTUES OF AMERICAN
SOCIETY IS THE WILLINGNESS OF ACADEMICS AND INTELLECTUALS TO
CHALLENGE ORTHODOXIES. LAMENTING THE ABSENCE OF THEIR
COUNTERPARTS IN NEW ZEALAND. THE SECOND OBJECTIVE IN THIS

ESSAY IS TO INTRODUCE INTELLECTUAL HETERODOXY INTO THE
DEFENSE DEBATE IN THE COUNTRY, AND TO SUGGEST THAT THE
ORTHODOXY IS BASED ON THE APPLICATION OF DOUBLE STANDARDS,
FIRST, TO THE RELATIVE MERITS OF NEW ZEALAND AND THE UNITED
STATES IN THE BILATERAL INTERNATIONAL DISPUTE. AND SECOND,
TO THE DEFENSE POLICIES OF THE TWO MAJOR PARTIES IN NEW
ZEALAND DOMESTIC POLITICS.

08915 THAKURTA, P.; MENON, S.; PRATAP, A.; TRIPATHI, S.
      NRI ENTERPRENUES: A MIXED HOMECOMING
      INDIA TODAY, XIV(14) (JUL 89), 52-55.
        THE ARTICLE EXAMINES THE EXPERIENCES OF NON-RESIDENT
      INDIANS (NRI) AS THEY RESPOND TO ECONOMIC INCENTIVES TO
      LOCATE IN INDIA. THE INCENTIVES OFFERED ARE ATTRACTIVE, BUT
      UNFAMILLIAR CONDITIONS AND BUREAUCRATIC DELAYS OFTEN RESULT
      IN STAGNATION AND FAILURE. A FEW SUCCESSES EXIST, BUT THE
      OVERALL PICTURE IS GRIM.

08916 THAKURTA, P.G.
      OPERATION COVER-UP
      INDIA TODAY, XIV(11) (JUN 89), 22-24.
        THE CONGRESS (I) MEMBERS OF INDIA'S PUBLIC ACCOUNTS
      COMMITTEE HAVE ASKED FOR CHANGES IN ITS DRAFT REPORT ON THE
      HDW SUBMARINE. THAT REQUEST HAS SERVED AS A STALL TACTIC TO
      DELAY THE PUBLICATION OF THE REPORT WHICH SEEKS TO INDICT
      THE GOVERNMENT. THIS ARTICLE EXAMINES THE SEQUENCE OF EVENTS
      WHICH LEAD TO THE PURCHASE OF THE SUBMARINE AND WHICH
      SUGGEST THAT IT IS NOT AS STRAIGHTFORWARD AS THE GOVERNMENT
      CLAIMS IT TO HAVE BEEN.

08917 THANAWALA, K.
      SOCIAL ECONOMIC ASPECTS OF INDIA'S DEVELOPMENT
      INTERNATIONAL JOURNAL OF SOCIAL ECONOMICS, 16(7) (1989),
      34-47.
        INDIA WAS A COLONY OF GREAT BRITAIN UNTIL 1947 WHEN THE
      SUBCONTINENT WAS PARTITIONED INTO TWO POLITICALLY SEPARATE
      AND INDEPENDENT COUNTRIES: INDIA AND PAKISTAN. THE PARTITION
      RESULTED IN A MAJOR POLITICAL AND ECONOMIC UPHEAVAL IN THE
      SUBCONTINENT. IN 1950, A PLANNING COMMISSION WAS SET UP TO
      DETERMINE PRIORITIES AND CO-ORDINATE INDIAN ECONOMIC
      DEVELOPMENT. THE SYSTEM HAS BEEN CALLED A "MIXED ECONOMY" AS
      OPPOSED TO EITHER A CENTRALLY PLANNED ECONOMY OR AN
      ESSENTIALLY FREE MARKET-DRIVEN SYSTEM. OVER THE YEARS, THE
      PRINCIPAL OBJECTIVES OF PLANNED DEVELOPMENT HAVE BEEN TO
      BUILD UP WITHIN A DEMOCRATIC CONTEXT: (1) A RAPIDLY
      EXPANDING AND TECHNOLOGICALLY PROGRESSIVE ECONOMY AND (2) A
      SOCIAL ORDER BASED ON JUSTICE AND OFFERING EQUAL OPPORTUNITY
      TO EVERY PERSON. SEVERAL OF THE ACHIEVEMENTS AND THE
      PROBLEMS FACED IN THE COURSE OF THE DEVELOPMENT EFFORT ARE
      DISCUSSED.

08918 THARAMANGALAM, J.
      RELIGIOUS PLURALISM AND THE THEORY AND PRACTICE OF
      SECULARISM: REFLECTIONS ON THE INDIAN EXPERIENCE
      JOURNAL OF ASIAN AND AFRICAN STUDIES, XXIV(3-4) (JUL 89),
      199-212.
        DESPITE INDIA'S LONG HISTORY OF RELIGIOUS PLURALISM AND
      RELATIVISTIC PATTERNS OF THOUGHT AND ITS DECLARED POLICY OF
      CREATING A SECULAR AND DEMOCRATIC SOCIETY, RELIGIOUS STRIFE
      HAS CHARACTERISED ALL THE MAJOR SOCIAL UPHEAVALS IN MODERN
      INDIA. THIS PAPER EXAMINES THE NATURE OF INDIAN PLURALISM
      AND SECULARISM WITH A VIEW TO UNDERSTANDING WHY AND HOW THE
      TWO ARE NOT AS CONGRUENT AS THEY ARE HELD TO BE IN THE WEST.
      IT FOCUSES SPECIAL ATTENTION ON HIERARCHY AS THE SPECIFIC
      MODALITY OF INDIA'S TRADITIONAL PLURALISM, LEGITIMATED
      WITHIN THE FRAMEWORK OF A RELIGIOUSLY SANCTIONED IDEOLOGY.
      IT ARGUES THAT THE PRESENT CRISIS IN INDIA'S SECULARISM IS
      AT ONCE A CRISIS IN INDIA'S HIERARCHICAL STRUCTURE AND A
      CRISIS IN ITS RELIGIOUS CULTURE. A GENUINELY DEMOCRATIC AND
      SOCIALIST INDIA REQUIRES A SECULARISM THAT TRANSCENDS THE
      TRADITIONAL INDIAN THEORY AND PRACTICE OF TOLERANT
      HIERARCHICAL PLURALISM AND EMBRACES A MORE UNIVERSALISTIC,
      RATIONAL, HUMANISTIC, AND NONRELIGIOUS CULTURE.

08919 THAYER, N.B.
      BEYOND SECURITY: U.S.-JAPANESE RELATIONS IN THE 1990S
      JOURNAL OF INTERNATIONAL AFFAIRS, 43(1) (SUM 89), 57-68.
        THIS ARTICLE EXAMINES THE SECURITY TREATY BETWEEN THE U.
      S. AND JAPAN, IT EXPLORES THE FUTURE OF THE TREATY IF SOVIET
      THREAT DIMINISHES, IF ECONOMIC TENSIONS BETWEEN JAPAN AND
      THE U.S. HEIGHTEN, AND IF JAPAN COMES TO ASSUME A GREATER
      POLITICAL PRESENCE IN THE INTERNATIONAL ORDER OF EAST ASIA.
      THE FOUR FUNCTIONS OF THE SECURITY TREATY ARE EXAMINED IN
      LIGHT OF THESE DEVELOPMENTS.

08920 THEAKSTON, K.; FRY, G.
      BRITAIN'S ADMINISTRATIVE ELITE: PERMANENT SECRETARIES 1900-
      1986
      PUBLIC ADMINISTRATION, 67(2) (SUM 89), 129-148.
        THIS ARTICLE IS BASED UPON ANALYSIS OF BIOGRAPHICAL DATA
      OF THOSE MEN AND WOMEN WHO REACHED THE RANK OF PERMANENT
      SECRETARY IN THE CAREER CIVIL SERVICE BETWEEN 1900 AND 1986.
      AMONG OTHER MATTERS, THE ARTICLE GIVES DETAILS OF THE
      SCHOOLS AND UNIVERSITIES ATTENDED BY PERMANENT SECRETARIES,

THEIR AGE ON, AND MODE OF, ENTRY TO THE CIVIL SERVICE, AND
THEIR CAREER PATTERN WITHIN THAT SERVICE, INCLUDING THE
NUMBER OF DEPARTMENTS SERVED IN, THE AGE OF APPOINTMENT TO
THE RANK OF PERMANENT SECRETARY, AND THE LENGTH OF TENURE IN
THAT ROLE. THE EVIDENCE SHOWS THAT FOR THE PRESENT CADRE OF
PERMANENT SECRETARIES THE ROUTE TO THE TOP HAS BEEN
CHARACTERIZED BY INTER-DEPARTMENTAL MOBILITY, PRIVATE OFFICE
SERVICE, AND EXPERIENCE IN THE KEY CENTRAL DEPARTMENTS OF
THE TREASURY AND THE CABINET OFFICE.

08921 THEAKSTON, K.
      THE CIVIL SERVICE
      CONTEMPORARY RECORD, 2(6) (SUM 89), 16-17.
        A SERIES OF RADICAL PROPOSALS RELATING TO THE WAY IN
      WHICH WHITEHALL IS ORGANISED AND WORKS MARK 1988 AS A
      POTENTIALLY CRUCIAL YEAR IN THE HISTORY OF THE BRITISH CIVIL
      SERVICE. IT MAY WELL BE THAT THE WRITING IS ON THE WALL FOR
      THE NORTHCOTE- TREVELYAN-FISHER INHERITANCE OF A UNIFIED
      CAREER CIVIL SERVICE, TIGHTLY CONTROLLED FROM THE CENTRE BY
      THE TREASURY AND RESPONSIBLE THROUGH MINISTERS TO PARLIAMENT.

08922 THEILMANN, J.; WILHITE, A.
      THE DETERMINANTS OF INDIVIDUALS' CAMPAIGN CONTRIBUTIONS TO
      CONGRESSIONAL CAMPAIGNS
      AMERICAN POLITICS QUARTERLY, 17(3) (JUL 89), 312-331.
        USING DATA OBTAINED FROM THE FEC, AN EXPLORATORY
      EMPIRICAL SKETCH OF THE DETERMINANTS OF INDIVIDUALS'
      CONTRIBUTIONS TO CONGRESSIONAL CANDIDATES FOR THE 1980 AND
      1982 ELECTION CYCLES IS CONSTRUCTED. THERE APPEAR TO BE
      IMPORTANT DIFFERENCES BETWEEN INDIVIDUAL AND INSTITUTIONAL
      (PAC AND PARTY) CAMPAIGN CONTRIBUTIONS. INDIVIDUAL
      CONTRIBUTIONS MAKE UP A MUCH LARGER SHARE OF THE
      CHALLENGERS' FINANCES THAN THE INCUMBENTS' FINANCES AND
      BECAUSE INDIVIDUAL CONTRIBUTIONS REQUIRE MORE TIME AND
      EFFORT TO ACQUIRE, CHALLENGERS FACE A CRUEL COROLLARY TO THE
      INCUMBENT ADVANTAGE. CHALLENGERS HAVE TO WORK HARDER TO
      RECEIVE LESS MONEY. IN ADDITION, THE DATA SUGGEST INDIVIDUAL
      CONTRIBUTORS ARE NOT SWAYED BY THE RACE AND SEX OF THE
      CANDIDATE, WHICH MAY NOT BE TRUE FOR INSTITUTIONAL
      CONTRIBUTORS. FINALLY, THIS WORK QUESTIONS THE VALIDITY OF
      THE CLASSICAL ASSUMPTION THAT CHALLENGERS' FUND-RAISING
      EFFORTS ARE UNAFFECTED BY THE SIZE OF THE INCUMBENTS'
      CAMPAIGN CHEST.

08923 THELEN, D.
      REMEMBERING THE DISCOVERY OF THE WATERGATE TAPES
      JOURNAL OF AMERICAN HISTORY, 75(4) (MAR 89), 1222-1227.
        THE AUTHOR RECOUNTS THE AFTERNOON OF JULY 13, 1973, WHEN
      THE EXISTENCE OF THE WATERGATE TAPES WAS DISCOVERED BY
      WATERGATE COMMITTEE STAFFERS.

08924 THEODORACOPULOS, T.
      GREEK FARCE
      NATIONAL REVIEW, 61(20) (OCT 89), 25-26.
        THIS ARTICLE REPORTS ON THE POLITICAL STATUS OF GREECE.
      IT TRACES THE VICTORY OF PASOK IN 1981 WITH ANDREAS
      PAPANDREOU AT ITS HEAD AND EXPLORES THE NEW POLICIES
      IMPLEMENTED BY HIM. IT DETAILS THE UPROAR THAT GREECE HAS
      BEEN EVER SINCE PAVLOS BAKOYANNIS, MEMBER OF PARLIAMENT, AND
      PRESS OFFICER FOR THE NEW DEMOCRATIC PARTY WAS SHOT BY
      TERRORISTS IN SEPTEMBER OF 89.

08925 THEODORE, K.
      GOVERNMENT INFLUENCE IN AN ENCLAVE ECONOMY: AN EXERCISE IN
      MODELLING
      SOCIAL AND ECONOMIC STUDIES, 38(1) (MAR 89), 37-59.
        THIS PAPER ATTEMPTS TO EXPLORE THE SIGNIFICANCE OF
      GOVERNMENT BEHAVIOUR ON AN ECONOMY WHICH IS A DOMINATED
      ENCLAVE SECTOR. REFERRING TO SUCH A SYSTEM AS "AN ENCLAVE
      ECONOMY", THE PAPER ANALYSES THE BEHAVIOUR OF THE THREE KEY
      AGENTS IN SUCH A SYSTEM. ALTHOUGH AN APPARENT GENERAL
      EQUILIBRIUM IS ARRIVED AT, IT IS ARGUED THAT THE PROPERTIES
      OF THE EQUILIBRIUM ARE NONTRADITIONAL AND ESSENTIALLY
      POLITICAL. BECAUSE OF THIS, IT IS CONCLUDED THAT IN THE
      CONTEXT OF WESTERN DEMOCRATIC FORMS, GOVERNMENT BEHAVIOUR
      POSSESSES NO PARTICULAR BIAS TOWARDS DEALING WITH THE
      CHRONIC PROBLEMS OF THE ECONOMY, FOR EXAMPLE THE PROBLEM OF
      UNEMPLOYMENT. WHAT REALLY MATTERS IS THE KIND OF CONSENSUS
      STRUCK BETWEEN THE GOVERNMENT AND THE OTHER AGENTS IN THE
      SYSTEM. THE ECONOMY OF TRINIDAD AND TOBAGO IS USED AS AN
      EXAMPLE.

08926 THEVENIN, M.
      FRANCE'S ROLE IN US-ALLIED DEFENCE INDUSTRY COOPERATION
      NATO'S SIXTEEN NATIONS, 34(6) (OCT 89), 23-24, 26, 29
      (SPECIAL SECTION).
        FRANCE HAS BEEN CONVINCED FOR MANY YEARS OF THE NEED FOR
      COOPERATION IN ARMAMENTS PRODUCTION. IT HAS A PROVEN RECORD
      OF BI-LATERAL AND MULTI-LATERAL PROJECTS WITH EUROPEAN AND
      AMERICAN PARTNERS, AS WELL AS OF WHOLEHEARTED PARTICIPATION
      IN NATO GROUPS AND PROGRAMMES. HOWEVER, INTERNAL BUDGET SLOW-
      DOWN AND EXPORT DECLINE ON THE ONE HAND AND THE SURGE OF
      TECHNOLOGY ON THE OTHER CHALLENGES THE FRENCH DEFENCE
      INDUSTRY TO RESTRUCTURE AND TO LOOK FOR INCREASED

COOPERATION. VARIOUS ARRANGEMENTS BETWEEN INDUSTRIES AND
GOVERNMENTS ARE BEING APPLIED AND, IF THE POLITICAL AND
INDUSTRIAL WILL IS THERE, WILL SUCCEED. OBSTACLES SUCH AS
TECHNOLOGY TRANSFER RESTRICTIONS AND EXCLUSIVENESS ON BOTH
SIDES OF THE ATLANTIC MUST STILL BE OVERCOME.

08927 THIEL, E.
    CONFLICT AND COOPERATION: US-EUROPEAN ECONOMIC RELATIONS
    AUSSEN POLITIK, 40(3) (1989), 264-276.
    THE SINGLE EUROPEAN MARKET IS BASED ON FREE-MARKET
CONCEPTS. INASMUCH AS IT IS AIMED AT ENHANCING THE
INTERNATIONAL COMPETITIVENESS OF THE EC, IT IS DIRECTED
OUTWARD. BY REMOVING INTERNAL TRADE BARRIERS, THE COMMUNITY
IS EXPOSING ITSELF TO INCREASED INTERNATIONAL COMPETITION.
SUCH STATEMENTS BY DR. ELKE THIEL OF THE STIFTUNG
WISSENSCHAFT UND POLITIK, EBENHAUSEN, RUN COUNTER TO US
FEARS THAT THE FURTHER ECONOMIC INTEGRATION OF WESTERN
EUROPE ON THE ROAD TO 1992 COULD RESULT IN A DISENGAGEMENT
OF THE REGION FROM WORLD TRADE THAT MIGHT THEN EXTEND BEYOND
COMMUNITY BORDERS TO INCLUDE THE COUNTRIES OF EASTERN EUROPE.
    THERE IS NO DOUBT THAT THE UNITED STATES HAS LOST SOME
FREEDOM OF ACTION, AND IT WILL NOT REGAIN THE HEGEMONIC
POSITION IN THE WORLD ECONOMY IT ASSUMED AFTER WORLD WAR II.
WITH AMERICA'S LARGE FOREIGN DEBT AND DEFICITS IN ITS
FEDERAL BUDGET, IN FOREIGN TRADE AND IN THE BALANCE OF
CURRENT ACCOUNTS ON THE ONE HAND, AND THE RISE OF NEW
PLAYERS AND COMPETITORS - JAPAN, THE NEWLY INDUSTRIALIZED
ASIAN COUNTRIES AND THE EUROPEAN COMMUNITY - ON THE OTHER, A
PICTURE EMERGES OF AN INTERNATIONAL ECONOMY MOVING FROM A
HEGEMONIC REGIME TO A MULTIPOLAR ONE. CONSEQUENTLY, THE US
IS FACED WITH THE NECESSITY OF HAVING TO ADJUST TO A NEW
ECONOMIC ORDER. IT WOULD BE WRONG IF THE THREE ECONOMIC
BLOCS MENTIONED - NORTH AMERICA, WESTERN EUROPE AND
JAPANASIA - WITHDREW INTO REGIONALISM. JAPAN UNDOUBTEDLY
WANTS TO FREE ITSELF FROM THE BILATERALISM THAT HAS
CHARACTERISED ITS RELATIONS WITH THE US, AND IT IS READY TO
SHOW A MORE INDEPENDENT POLITICAL PROFILE. AND WITH ITS
PROGRAMME FOR THE SINGLE INTERNAL MARKET, THE EUROPEAN
COMMUNITY WANTS TO INJECT NEW DYNAMISM INTO ITS
COMPETITIVENESS. IT DOES NOT WANT TO BE A "FORTRESS EUROPE",
HOWEVER, BUT A PARTNER IN AN OPEN, COOPERATIVE WORLD ECONOMY.

08928 THIEL, E.
    FROM THE INTERNAL MARKET TO AN ECONOMIC AND MONETARY UNION
    AUSSEN POLITIK, 40(1) (JAN 89), 66-75.
    THE ARTICLE TRACES THE PROGRESS OF THE EUROPEAN
COMMUNITY AS IT MOVES TOWARDS FULL MONETARY INTEGRATION AND
THE ESTABLISHMENT OF A EUROPEAN CENTRAL BANK SYSTEM.
MONETARY INTEGRATION IS ALREADY MAKING GREAT HEADWAY IN THE
COMMUNITY WITH GREAT BRITAIN AS A NOTABLE EXCEPTION. THE
ARTICLE EXPLORES THE LOGIC BEHIND THE ONE MONEY SYSTEM AND
THE ARGUEMENTS AGAINST IT.

08929 THIELEMANN, G.S.
    THE REALITY OF REALIGNMENT IN THE POST WORLD WAR II SOUTH
    DISSERTATION ABSTRACTS INTERNATIONAL, 49(10) (APR 89),
    3144-A.
    THE HISTORICAL-CULTURAL EXPLANATIONS OF SOUTHERN
POLITICS DESCRIBE A SOCIETY AND POLITICAL STRUCTURE THAT WAS,
AND STILL IS, DOMINATED BY THE INDIVIDUAL. GIVEN THE
HISTORY OF THIS ONE-PARTY REGION, THE COMPETITION THAT HAS
EMERGED SINCE WORLD WAR II IS ONE OF FACTIONALISM DOMINATED
BY INDIVIDUALS. EVEN RECENT REPUBLICAN PARTY GAINS REFLECT
THE EVEN RECENT REPUBLICAN PARTY GAINS REFLECT THE POWER OF
INDIVIDUALS IN SOUTHERN ELECTIONS. THUS, THE HYPOTHESIS THAT
THE SOUTH IS UNDERGOING A PROCESS OF PARTISAN REALIGNMENT IS
MISTAKEN.

08930 THIES, J.
    WEST GERMANY: THE RISKS AHEAD
    WORLD TODAY, 45(5) (MAY 89), 76-79.
    THE CLOSE ASSOCIATION OF THE FEDERAL REPUBLIC WITH THE
WEST APPEARS LESS CLEARLY DEFINED THAN A FEW YEARS AGO.
THERE IS A WEAKENING OF THE COMMITMENT TO A COMMON WESTERN
DEFENSE EFFORT. THE GAP BETWEEN WEST GERMANY AND THE USA
SEEMS TO BE WIDENING. THE GENERATION OF POLITICIANS WHOSE
ATTITUDES WERE FORMED BY PERSONAL CONTACTS WITH THE
AMERICANS IN THE IMMEDIATE POST-WAR YEARS IS BEGINNING TO
HAND OVER POWER TO A NEW GENERATION OF LEADERS WITH
DIFFERENT POLITICAL AND SOCIAL ATTITUDES. ALL THESE
DEVELOPMENTS ARE OCCURRING AMID DRAMITIC CHANGES IN EAST-
WEST RELATIONS THAT CALL FOR A NEW PERSPECTIVE ON, AND A
REASSESSMENT OF, WEST GERMAN FOREIGN AND DEFENSE POLICY.

08931 THIES, W.J.
    CRISES AND THE STUDY OF ALLIANCE POLITICS
    ARMED FORCES AND SOCIETY, 15(3) (SPR 89), 349-369.
    THE HISTORY OF THE ATLANTIC ALLIANCE IS ONE OF RECURRENT
"CRISES" AMONG ITS MEMBERS. PARTICIPANTS AND OBSERVERS ALIKE
HAVE BEEN PRONE TO USE THE NOTION OF AN "ALLIANCE CRISIS" AS
A FORM OF POLITICAL SHORTHAND TO INDICATE THE PRESENCE OF
GREATER-THAN-NORMAL TENSIONS AND STRAINS. AN EXCESSIVE
RELIANCE ON THIS KIND OF SHORTHAND, HOWEVER, CAN OBSCURE FAR
MORE THAN IT REVEALS; IT CAN ALSO SERVE AS AN IMPEDIMENT

RATHER THAN AS AN AID TO THEORY CONSTRUCTION. A BETTER
APPROACH WOULD BE TO DEVELOP A STRUCTURAL THEORY OF ALLIANCE
BEHAVIOR-ONE THAT MIGHT PROVIDE INSIGHTS INTO THE NATURE OF
ALLIANCE RELATIONSHIPS.

08932 THIESSEN, G. G.
    FOREIGN EXCHANGE MARKETS VIEWED FROM A MACRO-POLICY
    PERSPECTIVE
    CANADIAN PUBLIC POLICY--ANALYSE DE POLITIQUES, XV (FEB 89),
    67-70.
    THE RECENT SWINGS IN EXCHANGE RATES AND THE ASSOCIATED
TRADE AND PAYMENTS IMBALANCES HAVE COMPLICATED THE OPERATION
OF MACRO-POLICY IN INDUSTRIAL COUNTRIES. THE RELATIVELY
UNPREDICTABLE TIMING OF CHANGES IN TRADE FLOWS IN RESPONSE
TO EXCHANGE RATE MOVEMENTS HAVE IN SOME INSTANCES
CONTRIBUTED TO VARIATIONS IN OVERALL AGGREGATE DEMAND THAT
HAVE PRESENTED DIFFICULTIES FOR POLICY. COUNTRIES WITH
DEPRECIATING CURRENCIES HAVE IN SOME CASES FELT THAT THEY
HAD TO KEEP THEIR POLICIES MORE RESTRICTIVE THAN THEY WOULD
OTHERWISE HAVE WANTED TO ENSURE THAT THE ASSOCIATED PRICE
LEVEL EFFECTS FROM THE DEPRECIATION DID NOT GET TRANSLATED
INTO INFLATION RATE INCREASES. AND VOLATILE EXCHANGE MARKETS
TEND TO NARROW THE SHORT-RUN ROOM FOR POLICY MANOEUVRE OF A
CENTRAL BANK, PARTICULARLY IF CONFIDENCE IN THE EXTERNAL
VALUE OF ITS CURRENCY IS AT ALL LACKING. WHILE ANY SHARP
SLOWDOWN IN WORLD EXPANSION INVOLVES SUBSTANTIAL ECONOMIC
COSTS, SUCH COSTS WOULD BE PARTICULARLY BURDENSOME IN
CURRENT CIRCUMSTANCES FOR HEAVILY INDEBTED DEVELOPING
COUNTRIES AND THEIR CREDITOR FINANCIAL INSTITUTIONS.

08933 THIGPEN, R.B.; DOWNING, L.A.
    LIBERAL AND COMMUNITARIAN APPROACHES TO JUSTIFICATION
    REVIEW OF POLITICS, 51(4) (FAL 89), 533-550.
    LIBERALS AND COMMUNITARIANS DIFFER MOST BASICALLY ON THE
JUSTIFICATION OF VALUES, A DISAGREEMENT THAT LEADS TO
ALTERNATIVE APPROACHES TO SOCIAL CRITICISM. LIBERALS INSIST
ON COSMOPOLITAN JUSTIFICATION, WHICH HAS UNIVERSALISTIC
CRITERIA, WHILE COMMUNITARIANS ARE COMMITTED TO LOCAL
JUSTIFICATION BASED ON THE SHARED VALUES OF PARTICULAR
SOCIETIES. ALTHOUGH COMMUNITARIANS CORRECTLY BELIEVE THAT
JUSTIFICATION CANNOT BE FOUNDATIONALIST, THE UNIVERSALISM OF
COSMOPOLITAN JUSTIFICATION IS ESSENTIAL TO THE DEFENSE OF
VALUES LIKE FREEDOM THAT ARE SUPPORTED BY BOTH
COMMUNITARIANS AND LIBERALS. MOREOVER, COSMOPOLITIAN
JUSTIFICATION IS POSSIBE WHEN UNDERSTOOD IN CONTEXTUAL TERMS.
AN EXPLORATION OF THE POLITICAL IMPLICATIONS OF THE HUMAN
CAPACITIES OF RATIONALITY AND MORAL AGENCY CAN DERIVE
UNIVERSAL PRINCIPLES AS CRITERIA FOR SOCIAL CRITICISM.

08934 THIMMAYYA, C.M.
    SOURCES OF EXTERNAL DEPENDENCE IN THE ORGANIZATION FOR
    ECONOMIC COOPERATION AND DEVELOPMENT
    DISSERTATION ABSTRACTS INTERNATIONAL, 48(10) (APR 88),
    2724-A.
    THE PURPOSE OF THE STUDY WAS TO EXAMINE THE REASONS FOR
THE CONTINUED PARTICIPATION OF INDUSTRIAL NATIONS IN THE
INTERNATIONAL POLITICAL ECONOMY EVEN THOUGH PARTICIPATION
RESULTED IN NEGATIVE EFFECTS ON THE DOMESTIC POLITICAL
ECONOMY. THE FINDINGS OF EXTENSIVE STUDY SUGGEST THAT
GOVERNMENTS IN DEMOCRATIC SOCIETIES ARE LIMITED IN THEIR
POLICY CHOICES TO CONTAIN EXTERNAL DEPENDENCE AND ITS IMPACT
ON DOMESTIC INSTITUTIONS.

08935 THIREAU, I.
    RECENT CHANGE IN A GUANGDONG VILLAGE
    AUSTRALIAN JOURNAL OF CHINESE AFFAIRS, (19-20) (JAN 88),
    289-310.
    THE CONSEQUENCES OF CHINA'S RECENT RURAL
DECOLLECTIVIZATION ON SOCIETY REMAIN OBSCURE. THIS PAPER
ENDEAVORS TO IDENTIFY HOW THE REFORM HAS AFFECTED FAMILY AND
VILLAGE SOCIETY. IT ALSO CONSIDERS HOW THE CHANGES IN THE
ECONOMIC AND POLITICAL STRUCTURES HAVE CONTRIBUTED TO THE
EMERGENCE OF NEW VALUES AND BEHAVIORAL NORMS. A VILLAGE IN
NANHAI COUNTY, GUANGDONG PROVINCE, IS USED AS A CASE STUDY.
NANHAI COUNTY HAS BEEN CITED BY THE GOVERNMENT AS A
"NATIONAL PACE-SETTER IN ACHIEVING RAPID ECONOMIC GROWTH
UNDER THE POLICY OF REFORM AND OPENING TO THE OUTSIDE WORLD."

08936 THIREAU, I.
    THE CHINESE FAMILY IN TRANSITION
    CHINA NEWS ANALYSIS, (1381) (MAR 89), 1-9.
    THE POLITICAL AND ECONOMIC CHANGES THAT HAVE SHAKEN
CHINESE SOCIETY IN THE PAST DECADE HAVE NOT SPARED THE
FAMILY AS AN INSTITUTION. BIRTH CONTROL POLICIES AND THE ONE-
CHILD CAMPAIGN HAVE BROUGHT A REDUCTION IN THE SIZE OF
HOUSEHOLDS AS WELL AS A NEW TYPE OF RELATIONSHIP BETWEEN
PARENTS AND CHILDREN. THROUGH LAND REDISTRIBUTION AND THE
RETURN OF PRIVATE INITIATIVE, MOST CHINESE FAMILIES HAVE
ONCE AGAIN BECOME PRODUCTION UNITS. INCREASED
RESPONSIBILITIES WEIGHT ON THE HOUSEHOLDS, FOR WHOM COHESION
AND UNITY OFTEN GO ALONG WITH PROSPERITY.

08937 THISEN, J.K.
    THE PRIVATE VERSUS THE SOCIAL MAN

INTERNATIONAL JOURNAL OF SOCIAL ECONOMICS, 16(3) (1989), 35-48.
HOWEVER, THOUGH EVERY INDIVIDUAL TENDS TO FOLLOW THE PATTERNS AND DIRECTIONS OF HIS (HER) SOCIETY'S WAY OF LIVING, HE OR SHE OFTEN CONSERVES SOME PECULIARITIES WHICH CAN BE IDENTIFIED WITH HIS OR HER PERSONALITY. INDIVIDUAL AND SOCIAL BEHAVIOURS ARE TODAY BECOMING SO INTERDEPENDENT THAT IT IS DIFFICULT TO DEMARCATE BETWEEN "PRIVACY" AND "SOCIALITY". THIS IS PARTICULARLY TRUE IN AN ADVANCED AND COMPLEX SOCIETY IN WHICH CONFLICT BETWEEN PRIVATE AND SOCIAL INTERESTS IS APPARENT. IT IS PROPOSED THAT WITH EFFORT THIS CONFLICT CAN BE REMOVED OR AT LEAST ATTENUATED BY ADOPTING A MORE PRAGMATIC APPROACH TO THE HUMANISTIC ECONOMIC SYSTEM IN WHICH BOTH PRIVATE AND SOCIAL INTERESTS ARE ALLOWED TO BE TRADED OFF WITHOUT ONE NECESSARILY IMPINGING ON THE OTHER. IT IS ARGUED THAT, AS THE WORLD ECONOMY PROGRESSES AND THE MEANS OF TRANSPORTATION AND COMMUNICATION BECOME INCREASINGLY AVAILABLE, THE INTERDEPENDENCE AMONG MEANS AND WAYS OF LIFE ALSO BECOMES INEVITABLE AND HUMAN RELATIONS TIGHTEN ACCORDINGLY.

08938 THOEMMES, E.H.
WESTERN THREAT PERCEPTIONS: IMPLICATIONS FOR NATO NUCLEAR PLANNING
DISSERTATION ABSTRACTS INTERNATIONAL, 49(12) (JUN 89), 3863-A.
THIS DISSERTATION EXAMINES THE RELATIONSHIP BETWEEN NATO'S PERCEPTION OF THE SOVIET THREAT AND ITS MILITARY STRATEGY AND NUCLEAR PLANNING. IN PARTICULAR, TWO MUTUALLY INTERACTIVE RELATIONSHIPS ARE ASSESSED: FIRST, THE EXTENT TO WHICH NATO STRATEGY AND NUCLEAR PLANNING HAVE BEEN SHAPED BY THE OBJECTIVE SOVIET THREAT, AS OPPOSED TO SUBJECTIVE AND INTERNAL FACTORS; AND SECOND, THE EXTENT TO WHICH NATO'S PERCEPTION AND DEFINITION OF THAT THREAT HAS BEEN DETERMINED OR INFLUENCED BY WESTERN PREFERENCES AND CONSTRAINTS

08939 THOMAS, A.
SCHOOLS BRIEF: POLITICAL PARTIES
CONTEMPORARY RECORD, 3(2) (NOV 89), 28-30.
THIS IS THE SECOND OF A SERIES DESIGNED TO BRING A-LEVEL STUDENTS FULLY UP-TO-DATE ON MAINSTREAM TOPICS. IT IS A SURVEY OF POLITICAL PARTIES AND EXPLORES WHY PARTIES ARE NECESSARY, WHAT THEY DO, AND THE BACK GROUND AND THE FUTURE OF THE BRITISH PARTY SYSTEM.

08940 THOMAS, C.M.
CANADA'S MARITIME FORCE: THE WAY AHEAD
NATO'S SIXTEEN NATIONS, 34(5) (SEP 89), 29-30, 32.
ECONOMIC SOUNDNESS IS AN ESSENTIAL PART OF THE STRENGTH OF ANY COUNTRY. CANADA HAS THEREFORE EMBARKED ON AN AUSTERITY PROGRAMME WHICH NECESSARILY ALSO AFFECTS ITS DEFENCE FORCES. NEVERTHELESS, CLEAR THINKING, RATIONALIZATION, AND GOOD WILL ARE EXPECTED TO PRODUCE A MARITIME FORCE WHICH, ALTHOUGH LEANER, WILL BE HIGHLY EFFECTIVE. IT WILL ALSO ACHIEVE CANADA'S REVISED STRATEGIC OBJECTIVE.

08941 THOMAS, D.N.
GEORGE BUSH AND THE PROBLEM OF DIVIDED GOVERNMENT
CONTEMPORARY REVIEW, 255(1484) (SEP 89), 113-117.
THIS ARTICLE EXPLORES PROBLEMS ENCOUNTERED BY THE BUSH ADMINISTRATION CAUSED BY DIVIDED GOVERNMENT. THE TRANSITION IN PRESIDENTIAL LEADERSHIP WAS ANTICIPATED TO RUN SMOOTHLY, BUT DID NOT. THE STANDARD OF CRITERIA FOR ACCEPTING OR REJECTING PRESIDENTAL CABINET APPOINTEES BY THE U.S. SENATE IS EXAMINED. CONCLUDED IS THAT BUSH IS THE FIRST PRESIDENT ELECTED AMID PROSPECTS OF AN INDEFINITE PERIOD OF DIVIDED GOVERNMENT; THAT DIVIDED GOVERNMENT POSES A RISK OF POLITICAL DEADLOCK NEVER ENVISAGED BY THE DRAFTERS OF THE AMERICAN CONSTITUTION; AND THAT BUSH NOW FACES THE HISTORIC PROBLEM OF SETTING HIS OWN COURSE WITHOUT RUNNING AGROUND.

08942 THOMAS, P.
ACCOUNTING FOR BUREAUCRATS
POLICY OPTIONS, 10(1) (JAN 89), 33-34.
IN RECENT YEARS, CANADIANS HAVE BEEN INCREASINGLY CONCERNED OVER THE POWER EXERCISED BY THE BUREAUCRACY. AS THOMAS POINTS OUT, BUREAUCRACIES ARE SELDOM PASSIVE AND THE NEED TO HOLD THEM ACCOUNTABLE IS A REAL ONE. OTHERWISE, THERE IS A DANGER THAT THEY WILL RIDE ROUGHSHOD OVER INDIVIDUAL RIGHTS. HOWEVER, HE ARGUES, THERE IS A STRONG ELEMENT OF EXAGGERATION IN CHARGES THAT BUREAUCRACIES ARE SYSTEMATICALLY AND CONSISTENTLY IRRESPONSIBLE. WHILE CABINET MINISTERS NO LONGER AUTOMATICALLY RESIGN OVER BUREAUCRATIC BLUNDERS, PARLIAMENT AND THE COURTS BOTH HOLD STRONG POWERS TO ENFORCE RESPONSIBILITY. IN ADDITION, A NUMBER OF BODIES SUCH AS THE PRIVACY COMMISSION AND THE HUMAN RIGHTS COMMISSION HAVE BEEN CREATED IN RECENT YEARS TO RESTORE THE BALANCE. IN FACT, THE NUMBER AND STRENGTH OF ACCOUNTABILITY MECHANISMS HAS GROWN, IRONICALLY, ALONG WITH THE CLAIM THAT GOVERNMENTS AND THEIR SERVANTS ARE LESS ACCOUNTABLE.

08943 THOMAS, S.
VOTING PATTERNS IN THE CALIFORNIA ASSEMBLY: THE ROLE OF

GENDER
WOMEN AND POLITICS, 9(4) (1989), 43-56.
THE LITERATURE ON ROLL CALL VOTING BEHAVIOR IN THE UNITED STATES CONGRESS POINTS TO SMALL, BUT SIGNIFICANT, DIFFERENCES IN THE IDEOLOGICAL PROCLIVITIES AND VOTING DECISIONS OF MALE AND FEMALE LEGISLATORS. HOWEVER, COMPARABLE STUDIES HAVE NOT BEEN DONE ON THE STATE LEVEL. THIS ARTICLE EXPLORES GENDER DIFFERENCES IN ROLL CALL VOTING BEHAVIOR IN THE CALIFORNIA ASSEMBLY ON TWO MEASURES, LIBERALISM AND SUPPORT FOR WOMEN'S ISSUES. THE FINDINGS SUGGEST, IN CONTRAST TO STUDIES OF WOMEN IN CONGRESS, THAT FEMALE ASSEMBLYMEMBERS ARE NOT MORE LIBERAL THAN THEIR MALE COUNTERPARTS; THEY ARE, IN FACT, LESS SO. HOWEVER, A GENDER DIFFERENCE IN THE PREDICTED DIRECTION IS MANIFESTED ON THE WOMEN'S RIGHTS INDEX. SPECIFICALLY, WHEN PARTY IS CONTROLLED, REPUBLICAN WOMEN TEND TO BE MUCH MORE SUPPORTIVE OF WOMEN'S RIGHTS ISSUES THAN REPUBLICAN MEN WHILE DEMOCRATIC WOMEN ARE SLIGHTLY MORE SUPPORTIVE THAN DEMOCRATIC MEN.

08944 THOMAS, S.J.
DO INCUMBENT CAMPAIGN EXPENDITURES MATTER?
THE JOURNAL OF POLITICS, 51(4) (NOV 89), 965-976.
PREVIOUS RESEARCH REACHED THE PUZZLING CONCLUSION THAT AN INCUMBENT CANNOT INCREASE HIS VOTE BY INCREASING HIS CAMPAIGN EXPENDITURES. THIS PAPER REEXAMINES THE FINDING BY DEVELOPING A THEORY OF CAMPAIGN EXPENDITURES. THE THEORY IS THEN USED TO SPECIFY AN ECONOMETRIC MODEL; PREVIOUS STUDIES DID NOT DEVELOP A THEORY PRIOR TO SPECIFYING THEIR ECONOMETRIC MODELS. THE NEW EMPIRICAL RESULTS DEMONSTRATE THAT, IN MOST RACES, INCUMBENT EXPENDITURES DO MATTER.

08945 THOMASSEN, J.; VAN DETH, J.
HOW NEW IS DUTCH POLITICS?
WEST EUROPEAN POLITICS, 12(1) (JAN 89), 61-78.
THE DUTCH POLITICAL SYSTEM IS OFTEN DEPICTED AS AN IMPORTANT EXAMPLE OF THE RISE AND SPREAD OF 'NEW POLITICS' IN THE LAST FEW DECADES. ALTHOUGH A NOT INSUBSTANTIAL NUMBER OF DUTCH CITIZENS FAVOUR ELEMENTS OF THE CONCEPT OF 'NEW POLITICS', THE EMPIRICAL EVIDENCE HARDLY INDICATES A SUBSTANTIVE CHANGE IN THIS DIRECTION. DUTCH CULTURE HAS CHANGED IN THE LAST FEW DECADES, AND CHANGES STILL CONTINUE. THESE CHANGES, HOWEVER, ARE PRIMARILY LOCATED IN THE FIELD OF PRIVATE AFFAIRS AND MORAL ISSUES. EXPECTATIONS ABOUT CHANGES IN POLITICAL VALUES, POLITICAL INTEREST, POLITICAL PARTICIPATION AND THE PARTY SYSTEM DO NOT SURVIVE CAREFUL EMPIRICAL TESTING.

08946 THOMPSON, F.
WHY AMERICA'S MILITARY BASE STRUCTURE CANNOT BE REDUCED
PUBLIC ADMINISTRATION REVIEW, 48(1) (JAN 88), 557-563.
THIS ARTICLE EXAMINES THE TWO KINDS OF COSTS OPPORTUNITY COSTS. AND EXCESS OPERATING COSTS WHICH THE CURRENT MILITARY BASE STRUCTURE IMPOSES ON THE AMERICAN PUBLIC. SELF-INTEREST ON THE PART OF CONGRESS OR THE BUREAUCRACY WHICH IS OFTEN ATTRIBUTED TO THE FEDERAL GOVERNMENT'S INABILITY TO CLOSE UNNECESSARY MILITARY BASES IS EVALUATED IN ORDER TO REDUCE THE U.S. BASE STRUCTURE AND END THE WASTE OF MILLIONS OF ACRES.

08947 THOMPSON, G.
FLEXIBLE SPECIALISATION, INDUSTRIAL DISTRICTS, REGIONAL ECONOMIES: STRATEGIES FOR SOCIALISTS?
ECONOMY AND SOCIETY, 18(4) (NOV 89), 527-545.
THE ISSUE OF MASS PRODUCTION VERSUS FLEXIBLE SPECIALISATION AS THE TWO MAIN CONTEMPORARY FORMS OF PROCESS TECHNOLOGY AND ENTERPRISE STRATEGY UNDER MODERN CAPITALISM IS A CONCERN OF CONTEMPORARY SOCIALISTS. IN THIS PAPER, THE AUTHOR ARGUES THAT THERE MAY BE LESS CONNECTION BETWEEN LOCAL INDUSTRIAL STRATEGIES AND SOCIALISM THAN MANY ON THE LEFT MIGHT LIKE TO BELIEVE. BUT THAT IS NO REASON FOR SOCIALISTS TO BE UNINTERESTED IN THIS AREA NOR FOR THEM TO SUPPORT THINGS THAT MAY HAVE LITTLE TO DO WITH TRADITIONAL NOTIONS OF SOCIALISM OR, INDEED, MUCH TO DO WITH SOCIALISM AT ALL. AFTER ALL, LENIN HAD AN UNCANNY POLITICAL KNACK OF FINDING THE MOST ADVANCED ELEMENTS WITHIN CAPITALISM THAT SOCIALISM COULD EXPLOIT. THIS IS THE FRAME OF MIND IN WHICH SOCIALISTS MIGHT APPROACH THE TREND TOWARDS FLEXIBLE SPECIALISATION, IF INDEED THERE IS SUCH A TREND.

08948 THOMPSON, J.
CRACKDOWN ON RADICALS
NEW AFRICAN, (266) (NOV 89), 30-31.
THIS ARTICLE EXAMINES THE CASE OF CHIEF GANI FAWEHINMI AS NIGERIA'S MILITARY GOVERNMENT DRAWS TIGHT PARAMETERS FOR THE RETURN TO CIVILIAN RULE, IT REPORTS ON THE REDUCTION OF PARTIES TO ONLY TWO; STOPPING THE VOICE OF DISSENT AND CRITICISM; AND CRACKING DOWN ON RADICALS IN TEACHING, UNIVERSITIES, AND THE PROFESSIONS.

08949 THOMPSON, J.
ELECTORAL GUESSING GAME
NEW AFRICAN, 261 (JUN 89), 18.
THE MORE NIGERIAN POLITICIANS PLOT AND PLAN, THE MORE THE FEDERAL GOVERNMENT RAISES FRESH ELECTORAL OBSTRUCTIONS

AND OBJECTIONS. THIS ARTICLE DESCRIBES HOW ONLY THE ARMED
FORCES RULING COUNCIL WITH PRESIDENT BABANGIDA AS CHAIRMAN
DECIDES WHICH POLITICAL GROUPS VYING FOR ELECTORAL
CREDIBILITY WILL PASS THE TEST FOR POLITICAL EXISTENCE.

08950 THOMPSON, J.
    IS THE GOVERNMENT SINCERE?
    NEW AFRICAN, (264) (SEP 89), 12-13.
        THIS ARTICLE EXPLORES THE NIGERIAN GOVERNMENT'S POSITION
    WHICH IS BEING QUESTIONED BY SOME. ITS SUPPORTERS ARGUE THAT
    THE GOVERNMENT HAS IMPOSED ITS TOUGH STRUCTURAL ADJUSTMENT
    PROGRAM (SAP) IN ORDER TO GET THE ECONOMY RIGHT BEFORE
    HANDLING TO CIVILIAN RULE CRITICS SAY THAT IT IS ONLY MAKING
    POLITICAL PROMISES IN ORDER TO DIVERT ATTENTION FROM ITS OWN
    ECONOMIC FAILURE AND THE HARSHNESS OF SAP. THE GOALS AND
    ACTIONS OF PRESIDENT BABANGIDA ARE EXAMINED IN CONTEXT OF
    THE CONTROVERSY.

08951 THOMPSON, J.
    NIGERIA: US TRADE RIFT STRAINS RELATIONS
    AFRICAN BUSINESS, (JAN 89), 17-18.
        THE AUTHOR REPORTS ON TRADE CONFLICTS BETWEEN NIGERIA
    AND THE UNITED STATES. NIGERIA HAS BANNED PURCHASE OF FOOD
    PRODUCTS FROM THE UNITED STATES TO SUPPORT LOCAL AGRICULTURE.
    THE UNITED STATES, IN TURN, HAS THREATENED SANCTIONS TO
    DISCOURAGE THIS PRACTICE. THE ARTICLE REVIEWS THE ISSUES
    INVOLVED IN THIS TRADE DISAGREEMENT.

08952 THOMPSON, J.L.P.
    DEPRIVATION AND POLITICAL VIOLENCE IN NORTHERN IRELAND,
    1922-1985
    JOURNAL OF CONFLICT RESOLUTION, 33(4) (DEC 89), 676-699.
        TERRORIST MOVEMENTS ARE DISCUSSED UNDER THE RUBRIC OF
    SOCIAL MOVEMENTS THAT GENERATE COLLECTIVE VIOLENCE.
    DEPRIVATION THEORY IS TESTED WITH MULTIVARIATE TIME-SERIES
    REGRESSION MODELS, WITH CONTROLS FOR SECURITY FORCE LEVELS
    AND INDUSTRIAL PRODUCTION. FINDINGS ARE: (1) ALTHOUGH
    NORTHERN IRELAND SUFFERS FROM HIGH UNEMPLOYMENT, INCREASES
    IN FATAL VIOLENCE ARE NOT RELATED TO RISES IN UNEMPLOYMENT;
    (2) THE VIOLENCE HAS A TENDENCY TO PERPETUATE ITSELF,
    INDEPENDENTLY OF ITS STIMULI; (3) THE CONFLICT IS
    UNREPRESENTATIVE OF CLASHES BETWEEN STATE AND INSURGENT
    FORCES IN THAT MOST OF THE FATALITIES IN IT ARE NOT
    ATTRIBUTABLE TO THE SECURITY FORCES; AND (4) FURTHER
    EXPLANATIONS SHOULD INCORPORATE BOTH POLITICAL FACTORS AND
    MECHANISMS THAT CONTRIBUTE TO THE ESCALATION PROCESS.
    SEVERAL POSSIBILITIES ARE EXPLORED.

08953 THOMPSON, P.
    TOWARD PEACE IN THE MIDDLE EAST?
    EUROPE, 287 (JUN 89), 26-27.
        IT IS NOW OVER 20 YEARS SINCE THE UNITED NATIONS' (U.N.)
    SECURITY COUNCIL RESOLUTION 242 LAID DOWN THE FORMULA OF
    "TERRITORY IN RETURN FOR PEACE" AS THE INTERNATIONAL
    COMMUNITY'S APPROACH TO RESOLVING THE PROTRACTED MIDDLE EAST
    CONFLICT. YASSER ARAFAT, LEADER OF THE PALESTINE LIBERATION
    ORGANIZATION (PLO), REMOVED THE LAST AMBIGUITIES BY
    AFFIRMING THAT THE PLO ACCEPTED RESOLUTIONS 242 AND 338
    WITHOUT QUALIFICATION, RECOGNIZED ISRAEL'S RIGHT TO EXIST
    AND UNEQUIVOCALLY RENONCED THE USE OF TERRORISM. AFTER 13
    YEARS, THE WAY HAS THUS OPENED FOR THE UNITED STATES TO
    RESUME A DIALOGUE WITH THE PLO, AND FOR THE EUROPEAN
    COMMUNITY TO EMBARK ON AN AMBITIOUS DIPLOMATIC QUEST FOR A
    PEACE SETTLEMENT. AT LONG LAST, MAJOR PIECES OF THIS
    INTRICATE JIGSAW SEEM TO BE FALLING INTO PLACE.

08954 THOMPSON, R.N.
    A PRAGMATIC VIEW OF GLASNOST/PERESTROIKA
    ASIAN OUTLOOK, 24(2) (MAR 89), 18.
        UNTIL THERE ARE SOME BASIC CHANGES IN THE SOVIET SYSTEM,
    ONE CAN ONLY REMAIN SKEPTICAL ABOUT THE ULTIMATE RESULT OF
    GLASNOST AND PERESTROIKA. GORBACHEV HAS YET TO RENOUNCE
    MARXIST-LENINISM. AND POLITICAL COMMUNISM DOES NOT RECOGNIZE
    THE CAPITALIST SYSTEM'S RIGHT TO EXIST. MOREOVER, COMMUNIST
    WARFARE IS NOT MERELY MATERIALISTIC OR PHYSICAL. IT IS ALSO
    SPIRITUAL, OPPOSED TO EVERYTHING CHRISTIANITY STANDS FOR. AS
    LONG AS CHRISTIANS IN THE SOVIET UNION REMAIN IN PRISON
    WITHOUT HAVING COMMITTED ANY CRIME EXCEPT TO PROFESS THEIR
    FAITH, IT IS OBVIOUS THAT GLASNOST HAS NOT CHANGED THE INNER
    IMAGE OF SOVIET COMMUNISM.

08955 THOMPSON, W.C.
    WESTERN EUROPE: SHIFTING FREEDOMS, SHIFTING THREATS
    FREEDOM AT ISSUE, (106) (JAN 89), 32-37.
        THE AUTHOR DISCUSSES NATO REACTIONS TO GORBACHEV'S ARMS
    CONTROL OVERTURES, THE THATCHER REVOLUTION, POLITICAL
    STABILITY IN ITALY, AND FRANCE'S MINORITY GOVERNMENT
    POLITICAL COALITION.

08956 THOMPSON, W.H.
    EVOLUTION OF SOVIET POLICY: REAL CHARGE ON MORE OF THE SAME
    AVAILABLE FROM NTIS. NO. AD-A209 578/4/GAR, MAR 13 89, 27.
        THE EVOLUTION OF SOVIET POLICY UNDER MIKHAIL GORBACHEV
    HAS CAUSED CONTINUING CONTROVERSY IN THE WEST. HIS

SUPPORTERS BELIEVE THAT HE IS TRULY OPENING UP (GLASNOST)
AND RE-STRUCTURING (PERESTROIKA) THE SOVIET UNION, WHEREAS
HIS DETRACTORS CLAIM THAT HE IS JUST ANOTHER COMMUNIST,
CHANGING HIS MEANS, BUT IMPLACABLE ABOUT THE GOAL OF SOVIET
DOMINATION. THE PURPOSE OF THIS PAPER IS TO COMPARE
GORBACHEV'S KEY POLICIES WITH THOSE OF PREVIOUS SOVIET
LEADERS, TO ANALYZE THESE COMPARISONS, AND TO FORMULATE
CONCLUSIONS ON THE EVOLUTION OF SOVIET POLICY--TO ANSWER THE
QUESTION: IS GORBACHEV MERELY DEVISING NEW AND MORE CLEVER
MEANS FOR CONTINUING THE OCTOBER REVOLUTION AND EXPANDING
SOVIET HEGEMONY, OR IS HE MAKING REAL CHANGES IN BOTH THE
MEANS AND ENDS OF SOVIET POLICY. THE CONCLUSIONS OF THIS
PAPER ANSWER THIS QUESTION IN THE KEY SOVIET POLICY AREAS OF
GLASNOST, ECONOMICS, DEFENSE, AND FOREIGN AFFAIRS, WITH
SPECIAL EMPHASIS ON THE 'GERMAN QUESTION.' KEYWORDS: FOREIGN
GOVERNMENTS; USSR LEADERSHIP POLICIES.

08957 THOMPSON, W.S.
    CORY'S COUP
    NATIONAL REVIEW, 61(25) (DEC 89), 18-19.
        THIS ARTICLE ANALYZES THE LATEST COUP ATTEMPT IN THE
    PHILIPPINES AND CONCLUDES THAT MRS. AQUINO HAS NO ONE BUT
    HERSELF TO BLAME FOR IT. IT CLAIMS THAT THE OBVIOUS POINT
    ABOUT THE COUP IN ITS CRITICAL FIRST HALF-DAY, WAS THE
    FEEBLE MILITARY RESPONSE BY THE ARMED FORCES. IT REPORTS
    THAT THE REBELS EXPECTED TO WIN AND CONSIDERED THAT THE
    AMERICAN INTERVENTION CHEATED THEM OF THEIR VICTORY. THE
    SURPRISE IS THAT THE COUP WAS SO HARD FOUGHT AND WENT ON SO
    LONG.

08958 THOMSON, J.A.
    IMPLICATIONS OF THE GORBACHEV FORCE CUTS
    AVAILABLE FROM NTIS, NO. AD-A205 399/9/GAR, FEB 89, 13.
        THIS TESTIMONY WILL DISCUSS THE MILITARY AND POLITICAL
    IMPLICATIONS OF THE UNILATERAL FORCE REDUCTIONS RECENTLY
    ANNOUNCED BY THE SOVIET UNION AND EAST EUROPEAN COUNTRIES.
    IN THE MAIN, IT WILL COVER THE MILITARY IMPLICATIONS,
    TOUCHING BRIEFLY ON THE POLITICAL IMPLICATIONS AT THE END.
    THESE CUTS WILL BE IMPORTANT WHEN THEY ARE CARRIED OUT.
    HOWEVER, A NUMBER OF QUESTIONS REMAIN ABOUT DETAILS THAT
    LEAVE LARGE UNCERTAINTIES ABOUT THEIR ULTIMATE MILITARY
    EFFECT. THE POLITICAL EFFECT, HOWEVER, IS ALREADY
    SUBSTANTIAL. (JHD)

08959 THOMSON, J.E.
    THE STATE, SOVEREIGNTY AND INTERNATIONAL VIOLENCE: THE
    INSTITUTIONAL AND NORMATIVE BASIS OF STATE CONTROL OVER
    EXTERNAL VIOLENCE
    DISSERTATION ABSTRACTS INTERNATIONAL, 49(12) (JUN 89),
    3864-A.
        THE AUTHOR STUDIES THE EVOLUTION OF STATE CONTROL OVER
    EXTERNAL VIOLENCE. USING CASE STUDIES OF MERCENARIES,
    PRIVATEERS AND PIRATES, MERCANTILE COMPANIES, AND
    FILIBUSTERS, SHE CHARTS CROSS-SECTIONAL AND DIACHRONIC
    VARIATIONS IN STATE CONTROL OVER VARIOUS ASPECTS OF
    INTERNATIONAL VIOLENCE FROM THE 17TH TO THE 20TH CENTURY.
    SHE ARGUES THAT THE PROXIMATE CAUSE IN THE DECLINE OF NON-
    STATE VIOLENCE WAS THE ASSERTION OF NEW STATE AUTHORITY
    CLAIMS THAT MARKED THE INSTITUTIONALIZATION OF NEW NORMS OF
    SOVEREIGNTY. THESE CLAIMS, IN TURN, REFECTED BOTH THE
    STATE'S GROWING CAPACITY TO CONTROL NON-STATE VIOLENCE AND
    ITS GROWING RESPONSIBILITY FOR ITS CITIZEN'S ACTIVITIES
    BEYOND ITS BORDERS.

08960 THOMSON, J.R.
    HOLIDAY IN CAMBODIA
    NATIONAL REVIEW, XLI(19) (OCT 89), 26-27.
        THE UNITED STATES SHOULD OPENLY ENDORSE AND AID THE TWO
    NON-COMMUNIST FREEDOM - FIGHTING FACTIONS IN CAMBODIA -- THE
    ANS AND THE KPNLF -WHILE SETTING CLEAR GROUND RULES FOR THEM
    TO FOLLOW. IN THIS WAY THERE IS A CHANCE THAT THE KHMER
    PEOPLE WILL RETAIN A NATIONAL IDENTIFY IN A GOVERNING FORMAT
    WHICH TRULY REPRESENTS THEM.

08961 THOMSON, R.
    CONSTITUTIONAL APPLICATIONS TO THE MILITARY CRIMINAL
    DEFENDANT
    UNIVERSITY OF DETROIT LAW REVIEW, 66(2) (WIN 89), 221-238.
        THE UNITED STATES ARMY REPRESENTS A UNIQUE SOCIETY, AS
    AN ORGANIZATION WHOSE PRIMARY FUNCTION IS TO FIGHT WAR, THE
    RELAXATION OF SELECT CONSTITUTIONAL PROTECTIONS IS AN
    ABSOLUTE REQUIREMENT TO MAINTAIN GOOD DISIPLINE. THIS
    ANALYSIS OF DISTINCTIONS BETWEEN MILITARY AND CIVILIAN LAW
    DEMONSTRATES THAT MILITARY PERSONNEL LOSE PROTECTIONS IN
    SOME AREAS, AND ENHANCED PROTECTIONS IN OTHERS. MILITARY
    CRIMINAL DEFENDANTS ARE NOT DEPRIVED OF BASIC DUE PROCESS
    AND THEY CAN A SUBSTANTIALLY FAIRER TRIAL THAN AN INDIVIDUAL
    FACING ADJUDICATION IN THE CIVIL COURTS.

08962 THORBECKE, E.; MORRISSON, C.
    INSTITUTIONS, POLICIES, AND AGRICULTURAL PERFORMANCE: A
    COMPARATIVE ANALYSIS
    WORLD DEVELOPMENT, 17(9) (SEP 89), 1485-1498.
        THIS PAPER PROVIDES A SYNTHESIS OF A LARGE-SCALE OECD

DEVELOPMENT CENTER PROJECT ON THE EFFECTS OF INSTITUTIONS ON
AGRICULTURAL PERFORMANCE, BASED ON A COMPARATIVE ANALYSIS OF
SIX INDIVIDUAL CASE STUDIES OF POOR DEVELOPING COUNTRIES
(MALI, BURKINA FASO, KENYA, TANZANIA, NEPAL, AND SRI LANKA)
OVER THE PERIOD 1960-85. A NUMBER OF POLICY INFERENCES AND
GENERALIZATIONS ARE DRAWN FROM THE COMPARATIVE EXPERIENCE OF
THESE SIX COUNTRIES. THE UNDERLYING METHODOLOGY IS PRESENTED
IN SECTION 1. THE RELATION BETWEEN INSTITUTIONS, POLICIES
AND PERFORMANCE IS ANALYZED IN SECTIONS 2 AND 3, WHILE
SECTION 4 FOCUSES ON THE INSTITUTIONAL ROLE OF THE STATE IN
AGRICULTURE.

08963 THORMOND, S.
COMMENTS ON THE JUDICIAL SELECTION PROCESS
JOURNAL OF LAW & POLITICS, VI(1) (FAL 89), 31-34.
IN THE ESSAY, SENATOR STROM THURMOND DISCUSSES ONE
ASPECT OF MADISON'S CONSTITUTIONAL PLAN, THE REQUIREMENT
ESTABLISHED IN ARTICLE II, SECTION 2, OF THE CONSTITUTION
THAT THE SENATE OF THE UNITED STATES PROVIDE "ADVICE AND
CONSENT" TO THE APPOINTMENT OF FEDERAL JUDGES. HE HOPES TO
PROVOKE DISCUSSION REGARDING HOW THE SENATE JUDICIARY
COMMITTEE FUNCTIONS, WHAT QUALIFICATIONS ITS MEMBERS SHOULD
LOOK FOR IN JUDICIAL NOMINEES, HOW IT HAS HANDLED APPOINTEES
IN THE PAST, AND WHAT THE PROSPECTS ARE FOR THE FUTURE. HE
CONCLUDES THAT THE SENATE, AND THE JUDICIARY COMMITTEE CAN
MAKE A USEFUL CONTRIBUTION TO JUDICIAL SELECTION, PROVIDED
THAT ITS ROLE IS EXERCISED WITH THE HIGHEST RESPONSIBILITY
AND A COMMITMENT TO SERVE THE PUBLIC.

08964 THORN, J.
DESIGNS ON THE MARKET
SOUTH, (110) (DEC 89), 39.
A GOVERNMENT-BACKED PACKAGE TO BOOST THE COMPETITIVE
EDGE OF SINGAPORE'S EXPORTS PUTS DESIGN CENTER-STAGE. THE
DESIGN VENTURES PROGRAM OFFERS SUBSIDIES TO COMPANIES
LOOKING FOR A NEW IMAGE FOR THEIR PRODUCTS, AND THE
GOVERNMENT IS BACKING THE TRADE DEVELOPMENT BOARD'S
AGGRESSIVE DESIGN PROMOTION CAMPAIGN.

08965 THORNDIKE, T.
THE FUTURE OF THE BRITISH CARIBBEAN DEPENDENCIES
JOURNAL OF INTERAMERICAN STUDIES AND WORLD AFFAIRS, 31(3)
(FAL 89), 117-1.
THIS ARTICLE EXPLORES THE ISSUES INVOLVED IN
INDEPENDENCE FOR BRITISH DEPENDENT TERRITORIES IN THE
CARRIBEAN: ANGUILLA, BERMUDA, BVL, CAYMAN ISLANDS,
MONSTERRAT AND THE TURKS AND CAICOS ISLANDS. THE ISSUE OF
POPULAR OPPOSITION TO INDEPENDENCE IS DETAILED AS WELL AS A
DISCUSSION OF THE ECONOMIES AND PROSPECTS OF THE DIFFERENT
TERRITORIES. THEN, IDENTIFICATION AND ANALYSIS OF
ALTERNATIVES ARE EXAMINED.

08966 THORNE, L.
IN CONVERSATION WITH SERGEI GRIGORYANTS
FREEDOM AT ISSUE, (110) (SEP 89), 17-23.
IN THIS INTERVIEW, THE EDITOR OF "GLASNOST" ANSWERS
QUESTIONS ABOUT THE PRESS IN THE SOVIET UNION AND ABOUT HIS
OWN INDEPENDENT, OPPOSITION MAGAZINE.

08967 THORNTON, T.P.
THE NEW PHASE IN US-PAKISTANI RELATIONS
FOREIGN AFFAIRS, 68(3) (SUM 89), 142-159.
RECENT POLITICAL DEVELOPMENTS IN PAKISTAN HAVE ALTERED
NOT ONLY THE INTERNAL SCENE BUT ALSO THE CONTEXT IN WHICH
PAKISTAN RELATES TO ITS NEIGHBORS AND THE REST OF THE WORLD,
INCLUDING THE USA.

08968 THORNTON, T.P.
THE REGIONAL INFLUENTIALS: PRECEPTION AND REALITY
SAIS REVIEW, 9(2) (SUM 89), 247-260.
AN APPROPRIATE FRAMEWORK FOR U.S. POLICY IS TO BE FOUND
IN THE EMERGING REGIONAL FRAMEWORKS IN VARIOUS PARTS OF THE
THIRD WORLD. IN SOUTHEAST ASIA, SOUTH ASIA, THE PERSIAN GULF,
SOUTHERN AFRICA, CENTRAL AMERICA, AND ELSEWHERE, ONE CAN
SEE SIGNIFICANT ATTEMPTS BY GROUPINGS OF REGIONAL STATES TO
ADDRESS THEIR MUTUAL PROBLEMS IN WAYS THAT GIVE THEM GREATER
CONTROL OVER THE OUTCOMES, RATHER THAN LEAVING THEM
VULNERABLE TO OUTSIDE INTERVENTION. THESE GROUPINGS ARE IN
EARLY STAGES AND SOME ARE WEAK REEDS. THEY DO, HOWEVER,
REPRESENT A CERTAIN REALITY WHICH THE UNITED STATES SHOULD
RECOGNIZE AND FOSTER -- NOT BECAUSE THEY WILL ACT IN OUR
INTERESTS, BUT BECAUSE WE ARE INTERESTED IN SEEING REGIONAL
FORCES ASSUME MORE RESPONSIBILITY FOR SECURITY MAINTENANCE.
MOST OF THE GROUPINGS CONTAIN A REGIONAL INFLUENTIAL AND
MOST ARE CONCERNED WITH THE PROBLEM OF INTEGRATING THAT
COUNTRY BETTER INTO THEIR SUBSYSTEM, A GOAL WHICH THE UNITED
STATES GENERALLY SUPPORTS.

08969 THORPE, A.
THE RELIGIOUS OPIUM OF LIBERATION: REDEMPTION POLITICISED?
INTERNATIONAL JOURNAL OF SOCIAL ECONOMICS, 16(12) (1989),
14-25.
IN CONSIDERING THE HISTORIC WRITINGS OF MARX, THE
ARTICLE SEEKS TO SHOW THAT AS RELIGION HAS BECOME

INSTITUTIONALISED IN THE FORM OF THE CATHOLIC CHURCH IT
BECOMES SIMPLY ANOTHER COMPONENT OF THE EDIFICE OF THE
SUPERSTRUCTURE. THIS POSITION IS CHALLENGED CHIEFLY THROUGH
THE EMERGENCE OF THE LIBERATION CHURCHES. THE ROOTS,
INSTITUTIONALISATION, AND ESTABLISHMENT OF THE PRESENT-DAY
CHURCH ARE DESCRIBED. THE ROLE OF THE LIBERATION CHURCHES IN
SERVING THOSE SUFFERING OPPRESSION IS ALSO DISCUSSED IN
COMPARISON WITH MARXIST THOUGHT, AND IN SOME AREAS THE TWO
VIEWS ARE SEEN TO BE IRRECONCILABLE.

08970 THOUMI, F.E.
BILATERAL TRADE FLOWS AND ECONOMIC INTEGRATION IN LATIN
AMERICA AND THE CARIBBEAN
WORLD DEVELOPMENT, 17(3) (MAR 89), 421-429.
A GRAVITY EQUATION IS USED TO ANALYZE INTRA-LATIN
AMERICAN AND CARIBBEAN TRADE, WHICH IS SHOWN TO DEPEND
MAINLY ON THE EXPORTERS' GNP AND DISTANCE. IMPORTERS' GNP
AND EXPORTER GOVERNMENT POLICIES ARE ALSO RELEVANT VARIABLES.
RICHER COUNTRIES IMPORT MORE NATURAL RESOURCE-BASED
PRODUCTS THAN MANUFACTURES FROM POORER ONES. THUS, LARGER
AND RICHER COUNTRIES ENJOY LARGE TRADE SURPLUSES,
PARTICULARLY IN MANUFACTURES. INTEGRATION SYSTEMS HAVE HAD
MIXED RESULTS. THE CENTRAL AMERICAN COMMON MARKET AND
CARICOM HAVE CONTRIBUTED SUBSTANTIALLY TO MANUFACTURING
TRADE, LAFTA HAS ACHIEVED MODERATE RESULTS, WHILE THE ANDEAN
GROUP'S IMPACT HAS BEEN POOR.

08971 THOUMI, F.E.
THWARTED COMPARATIVE ADVANTAGE: ECONOMIC POLICY AND
INDUSTRIALIZATION IN THE DOMINICAN REPUBLIC AND TRINIDAD
AND TOBAGO
JOURNAL OF INTERAMERICAN STUDIES AND WORLD AFFAIRS, 31(1,
2) (SPR 89), 147-168.
THIS ARTICLE EXAMINES THE PARADIGM OF THWARTED
COMPARATIVE-ADVANTAGE INDUSTRIALIZATION AS ILLUSTRATED BY
THE CASES OF THE DOMINICAN REPUBLIC AND TRINIDAD AND TOBAGO.
IT DESCRIBES THE DILEMMAS FACED BY PUBLIC POLICYMAKERS WHERE
EXPORT-ORIENTED INDUSTRIAL ACTIVITIES ARE SUBJECT TO EXTREME
BOOM-AND-BUST CYCLES, AND WHEN DOMESTIC MARKETS ARE TOO
SMALL TO PURSUE AN EFFICIENT, IMPORT-SUBSTITUTING
INDUSTRIALIZATION POLICY. IT CONCLUDES THAT THE PRESENCE OF
RENT SEEKING ELITES MAKES A SOCIALLY BENEVOLENT PUBLIC
POLICY EVEN MORE DIFFICULT.

08972 THOUMI, F.E.
TRADE FLOWS AND ECONOMIC INTEGRATION AMONG THE LDC'S OF
THE CARIBBEAN BASIN
SOCIAL AND ECONOMIC STUDIES, 38(2) (JUN 89), 215-233.
IN THIS ESSAY, A GRAVITY EQUATION IS USED TO ANALYZE THE
PATTERN OF THE CARIBBEAN BASIN TRADE FLOWS. ECONOMICS
INTEGRATION IN THE CARIBBEAN BASIN HAS BEEN VIEWED AS A WAY
OF ENLARGING DOMESTIC MARKETS, OF DIVERSITYING THE
PRODUCTIVE BASE OF THE COUNTRIES AND, THUS, LOWERING THEIR
VULNERABILITY TO THE FLUCTUATIONS ON PRIMARY PRODUCT PRICES.
THIS STUDY DOES NOT ATTEMPT TO DEVELOP A MODEL FROM WHICH
THE GRAVITY EQUATION IS DERIVED. THE AIM IS TO USE THE
GRAVITY EQUATION TO EXPLORE THE STRUCTURE OF INTRA-REGIONAL
TRADE AMONG THE LDC'S OF THE CARIBBEAN BASIN AND TO IDENTIFY
SOME OF ITS CHARACTERISTICS WHICH MAKE CERTAIN TYPES OF
ECONOMIC INTEGRATION MORE LIKELY TO SUCCEED IN GENERATING
TRADE. THOSE THAT LOWERED TRADE BARRIERS APPEAR TO BE
RELATIVELY MORE SUCCESSFUL. THE CACM AND CARICOM APPEAR TO
HAVE HAD A SUBSTANTIAL IMPACT ON INTRA-BASIN EXPORTS WHILE
LAFTA HAS FAILED TO PROMOTE TRADE SIGNIFICANTLY IN THIS SUB-
REGION.

08973 THROGMORTON, J.A.
SYNTHESIZING POLITICS, RATIONALITY, AND ADVOCACY: ENERGY
POLICY ANALYSIS FOR MINORITY GROUPS
POLICY STUDIES REVIEW, 8(2) (WIN 89), 300-321.
THIS PAPER EXPLORES THE INTERACTION BETWEEN THREE
PRIMARY ACTIVITIES (POLITICAL INFLUENCE, SCIENTIFIC ANALYSIS,
AND ADVOCACY) IN THE PRACTICE OF POLICY ANALYSIS. AFTER
ARGUING THAT SUCCESSFUL PRACTICE DEPENDS ON THE ABILITY OF
POLICY ANALYSTS TO SYNTHESIZE THOSE THREE ACTIVITIES, THE
PAPER DESCRIBES AND CRITIQUES ONE ANALYTICAL TEAM'S RECENT
EFFORTS TO DEFINE THE IMPACTS OF FEDERAL ENERGY POLICY AND
PROGRAMS ON MINORITY GROUPS. IT REPORTS THAT THE ANALYTICAL
TEAM FAILED TO MAINTAIN CRITICAL DISTANCE FROM ITS CLIENT
AND TO COMMUNICATE EFFECTIVELY WITH ITS LAY CONSTITUENCY;
ACTING AS A "CLIENT ADVOCATE." THE TEAM UNINTENTIONALLY BUT
SYSTEMATICALLY DISTORTED KNOWLEDGE CONCERNING MINORITIES AND
ENERGY. THE PAPER CONCLUDES BY URGING ANALYSTS TO RECOGNIZE
THAT THEY HAVE THREE DISTINCT AUDIENCES (CLIENTS, TECHNICAL
PEERS, AND LAY CONSTITUENCIES) AND THAT SUCCESSFUL ANALYSIS
DEPENDS ON COMMUNICATING HONESTLY AND OPENLY WITH EACH OF
THEM.

08974 THUROW, L.C.
AMERICAN MIRAGE: A POST-INDUSTRIAL ECONOMY?
CURRENT HISTORY, 88(534) (JAN 89), 13-14, 53.
THIS PAPER REVIEWS THE RECENT HISTORY IN EMPLOYMENT AND
PRODUCTIVITY IN THE UNITED STATES AND FORECASTS WHAT CHANGES
ARE EXPECTED. THE RECENT RAPID RISE OF SERVICE EMPLOYMENT

WILL BE LESSENED IN THE FUTURE, AND THE PAST REDUCTIONS IN
MANUFACTURING JOBS WILL BE REVERSED IN THE COMING YEARS,
ACCORDING TO THE AUTHOR.

08975 THYGESEN, N.
    THE DELORS REPORT AND EUROPEAN ECONOMIC AND MONETARY UNION
    INTERNATIONAL AFFAIRS, (FAL 89), 637-652.
        THIS ARTICLE SURVEYS WHAT THE DELORS REPORTS CONTAINS
    AND IN WHAT SENSE IT MAY BE REGARDED AS CONTROVERSIAL. IT
    REVIEWS WHAT ECONOMIC AND MONETARY UNION WOULD INVOLVE, IT
    DISCUSSES THE PROPOSED THREE-STAGE APPROACH TO UNION, AND
    ASSESSES WHETHER AFTER THE CONTROVERSY AND AFTER THE MADRID
    SUMMIT, THE EUROPEAN COMMUNITY HAS COME ANY CLOSER TO
    ECONOMIC AND MONETARY UNION.

08976 TIANSHEN, H.
    THE OPEN POLICY REVITALIZES THE ECONOMY
    CHINA RECONSTRUCTS, XXXVIII(12) (DEC 89), 61-68.
        ACCORDING TO GOVERNOR WU GUANZHENG, JIANGXI PROVINCE HAS
    EXPERIENCED RAPID ECONOMIC DEVELOPMENT DURING THE 1980'S.
    BASICALLY AN AGRICULTURAL PROVINCE IN THE PAST, IT HAS TAKEN
    GREAT STRIDES FORWARD, BOTH IN AGRICULTURAL PRODUCTION AND
    IN INDUSTRIALIZATION. DURING THE PAST TEN YEARS, THE
    PROVINCIAL GOVERNMENT HAS RATIFIED A TOTAL OF 416 FOREIGN
    JOINT VENTURES AND COOPERATIVE CONTRACTS. THE GOVERNOR PLANS
    TO CONTINUE THE POLICY OF OPENING TO THE OUTSIDE WORLD AND
    WELCOMING FOREIGN INVESTMENT.

08977 TIEN, H.
    ECONOMIC DEVELOPMENT AND SOCIAL CHANGE; THE GREAT
    TRANSITION: POLITICAL AND SOCIAL CHANGE IN THE REPUBLIC OF
    CHINA
    HOOVER INSTITUTION PRESS, STANFORD, CA, 1989, 17-42.
        THE CHAPTER ANALYZES THE PATTERN OF DEVELOPMENT AND
    CURRENT PROGRESS OF TAIWAN'S SOCIOECONOMIC MODERNIZATION.
    MODERNIZATION EXPANDS ECONOMIC OPPORTUNITIES AND LEADS TO
    SOCIAL PLURALISM, URBANIZATION, MASS EXPOSURE TO THE MEDIA,
    RISING EXPECTATIONS, POPULAR DEMANDS FOR MORE CIVIL
    LIBERTIES AND POLITICAL PARTICIPATION, ORGANIZED POLITICAL
    OPPOSITION, AND GROWING DIFFERENTIATION OF THE ELITE
    STRUCTURE. ALL OF THESE CHANGES CONFLICT WITH INSTITUTIONAL
    AND POLICY CONSTRAINTS THAT DETER DEVELOPMENT TO A POLITICAL
    DEMOCRACY.

08978 TIEN, H.
    ELECTORAL POLITICS; THE GREAT TRANSITION: POLITICAL AND
    SOCIAL CHANGE IN THE REPUBLIC OF CHINA
    HOOVER INSTITUTION PRESS, STANFORD, CA, 1989, 162-194.
        THE CHAPTER DISCUSSES THE ELECTORAL PROCESS IN TAIWAN
    AND THE ROLES OF THE KMT AND THE OPPOSITION. AS MORE PUBLIC
    OFFICIALS ARE SUBJECT TO POPULAR ELECTIONS, THE ELECTORAL
    PROCESS HAS GAINED IMPORTANCE IN THE OVERALL POLITICAL
    PROCESS. BY THE TIME LOCAL ELECTIONS WERE INSTITUTED BY THE
    ROC THE PRINCIPLE OF UNIVERSAL SUFFRAGE HAD ALREADY BEEN
    IMPLEMENTED. HOWEVER, THE ISSUE OF WHICH PUBLIC OFFICIALS
    ARE TO BE ELECTED HAS BEEN A MATTER OF PUBLIC DEBATE AND
    POLITICAL CONFLICT. THE CHAPTER ALSO ANALYZES THE VARIOUS
    FACTIONS THAT EXIST IN TAIWAN AS WELL AS THE PROCESS BY
    WHICH CANDIDATES ARE SELECTED, CAMPAIGNS ARE RUN, AND VOTING
    RESULTS ARE ESTABLISHED.

08979 TIEN, H.
    FOREING RELATIONS AND INTERNATIONAL STATUS: CHALLENGES AND
    CONSTRAINTS; THE GREAT TRANSITION: POLITICS AND SOCIAL
    CHANGE IN THE REPUBLIC OF CHINA
    HOOVER INSTITUTION PRESS, STANFORD, CA, 1989, 216-249.
        THE CHAPTER EXAMINES THE RECENT HISTORY OF THE REPUBLIC
    OF CHINA'S EXTERNAL RELATIONS AND THE DILEMMA POSED BY ITS
    DIPLOMATIC ISOLATION. IT FOCUSES ON THREE MAJOR ISSUES: THE
    CHANGING STATUS OF THE ROC IN INTERNATIONAL ORGANIZATIONS,
    BOTH GOVERNMENTAL AND NONGOVERNMENTAL, AND IN BILATERAL
    DIPLOMACY; RELATIONS WITH THE UNITED STATES; AND THE
    CHALLENGE OF THE PEOPLE'S REPUBLIC OF CHINA'S UNIFICATION
    CAMPIAGNS.

08980 TIEN, H.
    INTEREST GROUPS; THE GREAT TRANSITION: POLITICAL AND
    SOCIAL CHANGE IN THE REPUBLIC OF CHINA
    HOOVER INSTITUTION PRESS, STANFORD, CA, 1989, 43-63.
        THE CHAPTER ANALYZES THE PROLIFERATING INTEREST GROUPS
    IN TAIWAN. AS THE SOCIETY BECOMES MORE COMPLEX, ORGANIZED
    GROUPS ARE GROWING IN NUMBER AND DIVERSITY. SINCE THE RULING
    KMT STILL PLAYS A CRITICAL ROLE IN SOCIAL CONTROL, TAIWAN'S
    INTEREST GROUPS HAVE YET TO ACHIEVE THE AUTONOMY COMMONLY
    SEEN IN WESTERN PLURALISTIC DEMOCRACIES. BY AND LARGE THE
    PARTY STILL DOMINATES THE SELECTION OF GROUP LEADERS.
    NEVERTHELESS, THE IMPACT OF TAIWAN'S EVOLVING SOCIAL
    PLURALISM ON THE POLITICAL PROCESS CAN BE SEEN IN THE
    GROWING AUTONOMY OF CERTAIN SOCIO-ECONOMIC GROUPS,
    PARTICULARLY SINCE THE 1986-1988 POLITICAL REFORMS.

08981 TIEN, H.
    REPRESENTATIVE INSTITUTIONS; THE GREAT TRANSITION:
    POLITICAL AND SOCIAL CHANGE IN THE REPUBLIC OF CHINA

HOOVER INSTITUTION PRESS, STANFORD, CA, 1989, 139-161.
    THE CHAPTER DEALS WITH LEGISLATURES, PARTICULARLY AT THE
NATIONAL AND PROVINCIAL LEVELS. ALTHOUGH THE LEGISLATURES
REMAIN RELATIVELY IMPOTENT IN LAWMAKING AND IN THE BUDGETARY
PROCESS, THEY HAVE LATELY PROVIDED LAWMAKERS WITH A CRUCIAL
FORUM FOR POLICY DEBATE AND INTERROGATION. IN ADDITION,
TAIWAN'S INTEREST GROUPS HAVE FOCUSED MORE OF THEIR
ATTENTION ON THE LEGISLATORS RATHER THAN JUST ON THE KMT AND
GOVERNMENT OFFICIALS. THEIR PRESSURE IS CERTAINLY FELT IN
THE LEGISLATIV YUAN, WHICH UNTIL THE 1970S HAD NO MEANINGFUL
CONNECTION WITH ELECTORAL POLITICS OR ORGANIZED POLITICAL
PRESSURE. THE STRUCTURE AND MAKEUP OF THE LEGISLATIVE YUAN,
THE CONTROL YUAN, THE NATIONAL ASSEMBLY, AND THE TAIWAN
PROVINCIAL ASSEMBLY ARE EXAMINED.

08982 TIEN, H.
    THE GOVERNMENT; THE GREAT TRANSITION: POLITICAL AND SOCIAL
    CHANGE IN THE REPUBLIC OF CHINA
    HOOVER INSTITUTION PRESS, STANFORD, CA, 1989, 105-138.
        THE CHAPTER ANALYZES THE GOVERNMENTAL STRUCTURE OF THE
    ROC. IT OUTLINES THE FEATURES OF THE CONSTITUTIONAL ORDER
    AND ASSESSES HOW THE IMPOSITION OF MARTIAL LAW AND OTHER
    "TEMPORARY PROVISIONS" HAVE AFFECTED THE CONSTITUTIONAL
    STRUCTURE. IT ALSO OUTLINES THE FEATURES AND
    RESPONSIBILITIES OF THE PRESIDENCY, THE EXECUTIVE YUAN, AND
    PROVINCIAL AND LOCAL GOVERNMENTS.

08983 TIEN, H.
    THE GREAT TRANSITION POLITICS AND SOCIAL CHANGE IN THE
    REPUBLIC OF CHINA
    HOOVER INSTITUTION PRESS, STANFORD, CA, 1989, 324.
        THE BOOK CONCERNS GOVERNMENT AND POLITICS IN TAIWAN
    UNDER THE RULE OF THE CHINESE NATIONALIST PARTY, OR
    KUOMINTANG (KMT). THE KMT REGIME HAS EXERCISED AUTHORITARIAN
    RULE OVER THE ISLAND STATE AND HAS CLAIMED SOVEREIGN
    JURISDICTION OVER THE MAINLAND FOR ALMOST FOUR DECADES. THE
    BOOK FOCUSES ON THE POLITICAL TRANSITION THAT HAS BEEN
    UNDERWAY SINCE 1986. IF IT SUCCEEDS, TAIWAN WILL BE HAILED
    AS A MODEL OF NOT ONLY OF INDUSTRIALIZATION AND ECONOMIC
    GROWTH BUT ALSO OF POLITICAL DEVELOPMENT. THE AUTHOR
    ANALYZES THE PROSPECTS OF A SUCCESSFUL TRANSITION AND
    DISCUSSES THE SOCIAL, ECONOMIC AND POLITICAL TRANSFORMATION
    THAT HAS OCCURRED OVER THE PAST FOUR DECADES.

08984 TIEN, H.
    THE MASS MEDIA; THE GREAT TRANSITION: POLITICAL AND SOCIAL
    CHANGE IN THE REPUBLIC OF CHINA
    HOOVER INSTITUTION PRESS, STANFORD, CA, 1989, 195-215.
        THE CHAPTER OUTLINES THE VARIOUS TYPES OF MASS MEDIA IN
    TAIWAN, THEIR SIZE, ROLE, AND INFLUENCE. IT ANALYZES THE
    RELATIONSHIP BETWEEN THE KUOMINTANG AND THE MEDIA AND
    ILLUSTRATES SOME OF THE LAWS AND REGULATIONS USED BY THE KMT
    TO CONTROL THE MEDIA. IT CONCLUDES THAT AS TAIWAN BECOMES
    MORE AFFLUENT AND MORE PEOPLE GAIN ACCESS TO MASS MEDIA THE
    INDEPENDENCE OF THE MEDIA WILL INCREASE. THESE CHANGES ARE
    DEMONSTRATED BY THE SUBSTANTIALLY LIBERALIZED REGULATIONS
    THAT TOOK EFFECT IN JANUARY OF 1988.

08985 TIEN, H.
    THE NATIONALIST REGIME PERSPECTIVE; THE GREAT TRANSITION:
    POLITICAL AND SOCIAL CHANGE IN THE REPUBLIC OF CHINA
    HOOVER INSTITUTION PRESS, STANFORD, CA, 1989, 1-16.
        THE CHAPTER GIVES A BRIEF BACKGROUND OF EVENTS THAT LED
    TO THE CREATION OF THE REPUBLIC OF CHINA. IT OUTLINES THE
    RETREAT OF THE KUOMINTANG TO TAIWAN AND THEIR EVENTUAL
    DEFEAT ON THE MAINLAND. IT ANALYZES THE POLITICAL SYSTEM
    THAT EXISTED ON TAIWAN FOR NEARLY FOUR DECADES AND CONCLUDES
    THAT THE ROC POLITY IS ESSENTIALLY A MODERNIZING
    AUTHORITARIAN REGIME WITH STRONG CHARACTERISTICS OF A
    ONEPARTY PLURALISTIC SYSTEM IN TRANSITION TOWARD A
    DOMINANTPARTY SYSTEM. IT SETS THE SCENE FOR THE FOLLOWING
    CHAPTERS WHICH CONCENTRATE ON RECENT CHANGES AND DEVELOPMENT
    IN THE ROC.

08986 TIEN, H.
    THE PARTY SYSTEM: THE KMT AND THE OPPOSITION; THE GREAT
    TRANSITION: POLITICAL AND SOCIAL CHANGE IN THE REPUBLIC OF
    CHINA
    HOOVER INSTITUTION PRESS, STANFORD, CA, 1989, 64-104.
        THE CHAPTER ANALYZES THE DEVELOPMENT OF THE KMT SINCE
    ITS REFORMS IN 1950-1952. OVER THE YEARS THE PARTY HAS
    MOVED FROM A PREDOMINANTLY MAINLANDER ORIENTATION TO ITS
    PRESENT MAKEUP, WITH A SUBSTANTIAL NUMBER OF TAIWANESE IN
    HIGH POSTS AND A TAIWANESE MAJORITY IN OVERALL MEMBERSHIP.
    THE PARTY'S INTEGRATIVE FUNCTION IS REFLECTED IN THE GRADUAL
    CONVERGENCE OF ELITE INTERESTS AMONG THE MAJOR ETHNIC GROUPS:
    THE MAINLANDERS, THE FUKIEN-TAIWANESE, AND THE HAKKAS. AS
    THE KMT EXPANDED ITS ORGANIZATIONAL NETWORK INTO THE MOST
    REMOTE CORNERS OF RURAL TAIWAN, IT FOSTERED SOCIAL CONTROL
    AND PROVIDED SOCIAL SERVICES, BOTH OF WHICH HAVE BECOME
    ESSENTIAL TO THE PARTY'S CONTINUING ELECTORAL SUCCESS. THE
    CHAPTER ALSO OUTLINES THE DEVELOPMENT OF THE POLITICAL
    OPPOSITION AND ITS RELATION TO THE RULING PARTY.

08987 TIKHOMIROV, V.I.
THE USSR AND SOUTH AFRICA: AN END TO THE "TOTAL ONSLAUGHT"?
AFRICA REPORT, 34(6) (NOV 89), 58-61.
THE SOVIETS' NEW POLITICAL THINKING HAS REMOVED
IDEOLOGICAL CONCERNS FROM GLOBAL POLITICS AND HAS ELIMINATED
SOUTH AFRICA AS AN ARENA FOR EAST-WEST CONFRONTATION. THIS
ARTICLE EXPLAINS THE CHANGES IN SOVIET ATTITUDES TOWARD THE
SOLUTION OF THE SOUTH AFRICAN CRISIS, INCLUDING ITS SUPPORT
FOR A NEGOTIATED SETTLEMENT TO GUARANTEE A TRULY DEMOCRATIC
FUTURE.

08988 TILAK, J.B.G.
THE RECESSION AND PUBLIC INVESTMENT IN EDUCATION IN LATIN
AMERICA
JOURNAL OF INTERAMERICAN STUDIES AND WORLD AFFAIRS, 31(1,
2) (SPR 89), 125-146.
WITH THE HELP OF LATIN AMERICAN AND CARRIBEAN CROSS-
COUNTRY DATA ON A SET OF ECONOMIC AND EDUCATIONAL INDICATORS,
THIS ARTICLE EXAMINES THE HYPOTHESIS THAT WHILE UNDER
NORMAL ECONOMIC CONDITIONS PUBLIC SPENDING ON EDUCATION MAY
NOT BE SIGNIFICANTLY INFLUENCED BY ECONOMIC FACTORS-
DETERIORATION IN ECONOMIC ENVIRONMENT DOES NOT ADVERSELY
INFLUENCE LEVELS IN EDUCATION. IT CONCLUDES THAT PUBLIC
SPENDING ON EDUCATION IS MORE INFLUENCED BY ECONOMIC POLICY
THAN PURELY ECONOMIC FACTORS.

08989 TILLANDER, S.
THE CHIEF EXECUTIVE'S POWER IN FEDERAL SYSTEMS: A
COMPARATIVE STUDY OF WEST GERMANY AND THE UNITED STATES
DISSERTATION ABSTRACTS INTERNATIONAL, 49(7) (JAN 89),
1947-A.
THIS DISSERTATION EXAMINES THE POWERS OF THE POLITICAL
CHIEF EXECUTIVE IN WEST GERMANY AND THE UNITED STATES.
PRESIDENT RONALD REAGAN'S "REVOLUTION" AND CHANCELLOR HELMUT
KOHL'S WENDE (TURNAROUND) ARE USED TO ILLUSTRATE THE IMPACT
OF FEDERALISM ON THE POLITICAL PROCESS.

08990 TILLOTSON, A.R.
OPEN STATES AND OPEN ECONOMIES: DENMARK'S CONTRIBUTION TO
A STATIST THEORY OF DEVELOPMENT
COMPARATIVE POLITICS, 21(3) (APR 89), 339-354.
THE RECENT RESURGENCE OF INTEREST IN SMALL STATES HAS
DRAWN ATTENTION TO SOME UNIQUE FEATURES OF DANISH POLITICAL
AND ECONOMIC DEVELOPMENT: THE EARLY LIBERATION OF THE SERFS,
THE PRESERVATION OF AN INDEPENDENT PEASANTRY, AND AN
ADJUSTMENT STRATEGY THAT MET THE GREAT DEPRESSION OF 1873-96
WITH AGRICULTURAL INNOVATION AND ECONOMIC LIBERALISM RATHER
THAN WITH TRADE PROTECTION. BUT EXISTING ATTEMPTS TO ACCOUNT
FOR DIFFERENCES IN THE PACE, SECTORAL EMPHASIS, AND
POLITICAL CONSEQUENCES OF MODERNIZATION AND
INDUSTRIALIZATION EXPLAIN ONLY PIECES OF THE DANISH STORY.
THE LOGIC THAT INFORMS THESE EXISTING EXPLANATIONS FAILS
WHEN APPLIED TO THE FULL RANGE OF DANISH POLITICAL AND
ECONOMIC HISTORY AS IT PLAYED OUT DURING THE TRANSITION FROM
FEUDALISM TO INDUSTRIALIZATION.

08991 TILLY, C.
STATE AND COUNTERREVOLUTION IN FRANCE
SOCIAL RESEARCH, 56(1) (SPR 89), 71-98.
THIS ESSAY (1) EXAMINES RELATIONS BETWEEN THE FRENCH
REVOLUTION AND THE LONG-TERM MUTATION OF THE FRENCH STATE,
(2) UNDERSCORES THE CRITICAL PART PLAYED BY REVOLUTIONARY
AND NAPOLEONIC FRANCE IN THE TRANSFORMATION OF EUROPEAN
STATES (ESPECIALLY THE TRANSITION FROM INDIRECT TO DIRECT
RULE), AND (3) EMPHASIZES THE CONNECTION BETWEEN RESISTANCE
TO THE REVOLUTION AND EFFORTS OF REVOLUTIONARY LEADERS TO
IMPROVISE NEW FORMS OF GOVERNMENT IN PLACE OF THE ONES THEY
AND THEIR SUPPORTERS HAD DESTROYED. IN THE PROCESS, IT ALSO
GIVES REASONS FOR THINKING THAT IN THE SPHERE OF THE STATE
SOMETHING LIKE A BOURGEOIS REVOLUTION DID, DESPITE ALL
RECENT DOUBTS, ACTUALLY OCCUR.

08992 TIMBERG, B.
PICTURES OF THE MIND: A PERSONAL ACCOUNT OF THE ISRAELI-
PALESTINIAN CONFLICT AS A HISTORY OF IMAGES
NEW OUTLOOK, 32(1 (287)) (JAN 89), 36-37.
THE AUTHOR DESCRIBES HOW HIS IMAGES OF ISRAEL AND
ISRAELI SOCIETY WERE SHATTERED BY THE INTIFADA. UNTIL THE
UPRISING, HIS MENTAL PICTURES OF ISRAELI SOCIETY WERE
MONOPOLIZED BY POSITIVE IMAGES EVOKED BY LEON URIS' "EXODUS"
AND SIMILAR LITERARY WORKS. HE REFUSED TO BELIEVE AMNESTY
INTERNATIONAL REPORTS OF BRUTALITY, TORTURE, AND OTHER HUMAN
RIGHTS VIOLATIONS BY ISRAELIS TOWARD PALESTINIAN PRISONERS.
BUT THE DETAILED ACCOUNTS OF ISRAEL'S POLICY OF FORCE AND
BEATINGS IN RESPONSE TO THE PALESTINIAN UPRISING REPLACED
THE OLD, ROMATICIZED IMAGES OF ISRAEL.

08993 TIMMERMANN, H.
IS GORBACHEV A BUKHARINIST? MOSCOW'S REAPPRAISAL OF THE
NEP PERIOD
JOURNAL OF COMMUNIST STUDIES, 5(1) (MAR 89), 1-17.
A REAPPRAISAL OF THE HISTORICAL ROLE OF BUKHARIN IS
UNDER WAY IN THE SOVIET UNION. THE REOPENING OF SOVIET
HISTORY THAT THIS INVOLVES CONSTITUTES AN ATTEMPT BY THE

REFORMING SOVIET LEADERSHIP TO SHOW THAT STALIN'S REVOLUTION
FROM ABOVE WAS NOT THE ONLY COURSE ACCEPTABLE AS SOCIALIST,
AND INDEED CERTAIN THEORISTS NOW BELIEVE BUKHARIN TO HAVE
BEEN RIGHT AND STALIN WRONG IN THE 'GREAT DEBATE' OF THE
1920S. LESS NOTED IN THE WEST IS THE INTERNATIONAL DIMENSION
OF THIS REAPPRAISAL OF BUKHARIN. THE LATTER'S VIEW THAT
FASCISM AND NOT SOCIAL DEMOCRACY WAS THE CHIEF DANGER AT THE
TIME OF THE COMINTERN'S SIXTH CONGRESS IN 1928 HAS A CLEAR
RELEVANCE TO THE EUROPEAN POLICIES OF THE GORBACHEV
LEADERSHIP. ON BOTH THE INTERNAL AND THE INTERNATIONAL
LEVELS, BUKHARIN'S VIEWS ARE NOT MERELY TO BE TOLERATED:
THEY ACTUALLY SUPPORT THE INTERNAL PERESTROIKA AND THE
INTERNATIONAL 'NEW THINKING'.

08994 TIMMERMANN, H.
THE COMMUNIST PARTY OF THE SOVIET UNION'S REASSESSMENT OF
INTERNATIONAL SOCIAL DEMOCRACY: DIMENSIONS AND TRENDS
JOURNAL OF COMMUNIST STUDIES, 5(2) (JUN 89), 173-184.
THE ARTICLE EXAMINES THE SOCIAL DEMOCRATIC PARTIES OF
THE WEST AS SOURCES OF IDEAS FOR SOVIET "NEW THINKING."
SOVIET THEORISTS ARE CLOSELY EXAMINING THE ONCE CRITICIZED
SOCIAL DEMOCRATS AND ARE ATTEMPTING TO INCORPORATE IDEAS AND
CONCEPTS INTO THEIR OWN PROGRAMS OF PERESTROIKA. ALTHOUGH
THIS REAPPRAISAL SEEMS SOMEWHAT SENSATIONAL, A FULL-SCALE
CONVERGENCE WITH SOCIAL DEMOCRACY IS NOT LIKELY. INSTEAD,
THE MARKET AND ITS LAWS ARE SEEN AS NEUTRAL AND SYSTEM-
INDEPENDENT. THE ARTICLE CONCLUDES THAT THIS RETHINKING
OFFERS OPPORTUNITIES TO THE WEST FOR CONTACTS AND DIALOGUES
THAT GO BEYOND FOREIGN AND SECURITY POLICY ISSUES. MOSCOW'S
INTEREST IN THE SWEDISH "MODEL" ILLUSTRATES THE FUTURE
POSSIBILITIES

08995 TIMMERMANN, H.
THE CPSU AND THE INTERNATIONAL COMMUNIST PARTY SYSTEMS-A
CHANGE OF PARADIGMS IN MOSCOW
STUDIES IN COMPARATIVE COMMUNISM, 22(2/3) (SUM 89),
265-278.
THIS ARTICLE EXAMINES THE PROCESS OF PERESTROIKA IN THE
INTERNATIONAL COMMUNIST MOVEMENT AND ITS MEMBERS. IT
COMPARES MOSCOW AND THE WORLD SOCIALIST SYSTEM AND DESCRIBES
THE CONTROVERSY WITH THE TRADITIONALISTS. AN APPRAISAL IS
MADE OF WESTERN SYSTEMS AND ITS CONSEQUENCES FOR RELATIONS
WITH WESTERN COMMUNISTS AS WELL AS A DESCRIPTION GIVEN OF
SPECIAL RELATIONS WITH THE REFORM-ORIENTED LEFT. THE
CONCLUSION IS THAT ONE CAN AS YET HARDLY OBTAIN AN OVERVIEW
OF THE PROFOUND AND EXTENSIVE IMPLICATIONS ALL THIS POSES
FOR THE CHANGE IN ITS RELATIONS WITH INTERNATIONAL COMMUNISM.

08996 TIMMERMANN, H.
WHEN HISTORY IS POLITICS: PERESTROIKA AND THE GERMAN
DEMOCRATIC REPUBLIC
JOURNAL OF COMMUNIST STUDIES, 5(3) (SEP 89), 355-357.
THIS ARTICLE EXPLORES HOW PUBLIC OPINION IN THE GDR HAS
REACTED TO THE WAY IN WHICH THE LEADERSHIP HAS CLEARLY
DISTANCED ITSELF FROM MOSCOW'S INTERNAL PERESTROIKA. THERE
HAVE BEEN SHARP CONTROVERSIES ABOUT THE THOROUGH-GOING
REVISION OF HISTORY IN MOSCOW-A RESULT OF MOSCOW'S REFORMERS
REALIZING THAT THE USSR'S FUTURE CANNOT BE SUCCESSFUL
WITHOUT COMING TO TERMS WITH ITS PAST. AFTER ANALYZING THE
USSR DILEMMA THE GDR MUST ANALYZE ITS OWN HISTORY WHICH THE
LEADERSHIP OF THE SED CONTINUES TO RESIST IS CONCLUDED.

08997 TINDEMANS, L.
THE BELGIAN SEGMENT OF EUROPEAN POLITICS
INTERNATIONAL AFFAIRS (MOSCOW), (9) (SEP 89), 80-86.
THE AUTHOR, WHO IS A FORMER PRIME MINISTER OF BELGIUM,
DISCUSSES HIS COUNTRY'S TRADITIONAL ROLE IN THE POLITICS OF
EUROPE.

08998 TINDIGARUKAYO, J.K.
THE VIABLITY OF FEDERALISM AND CONSOCIATONALISM IN
CULTURAL PLURAL SOCIETIES OF POST-COLONIAL STATES
PLURAL SOCIETIES, 19(1) (SEP 89), 41-54.
THE THESIS THAT THE INSTITUTIONAL DEVICES OF FEDERALISM
AND CONSOCIATIONALISM ARE CAPABLE OF PROMOTING ORDER AND
COHESION IN PLURAL SOCIETIES IS CRITICALLY EXAMINED IN THE
CONTEXT OF POSTCOLONIAL PLURAL STATES. THE CONTENTION OF THE
ARTICLE IS THAT THE VIABILITY OF THESE DEVICES IN SUCH
STATES DEPENDS ON (I) A REALIZATION AMONG POLITICAL ELITES
THAT PEACEFUL INSTITUTIONAL CHANGES WITHIN THEIR STATES
REQUIRE A FEDERAL AND/OR CONSOCIATIONAL PATTERN OF DECISION-
MAKING; (II) LEADERS' RESPECT FOR RULES AND PROCEDURES OF
SUCH INSTITUTIONAL CHANGES; A SPIRIT OF COMPROMISE, TRUST,
AND GOOD WILL AMONG SEGMENTAL LEADERS; AND AN ABILITY, ON
THE PART OF POLITICAL LEADERS, TO ACQUIRE LEGITIMACY TO RULE.

08999 TISHKON, V.
GLASTNOST AND NATIONALITIES WITHIN THE SOVIET UNION
THIRD WORLD QUARTERLY, 11(4) (OCT 89), 191-207.
THIS ARTICLE EXPLORES THE MULTI-ETHNIC COMPOSITION OF
THE POPULATION OF THE USSR, THE LEGACY OF EMPIRE AND NEW
HISTORICAL CHALLENGES; ALSO THE PHENOMENON OF 'ETHNIC
REVIVAL' IN RUSSIA. A NEW CONCEPTION OF THE RIGHTS OF
PEOPLES AND A CONSTITUTION IS PROPOSED AND THE IMPERATIVES

OF A MULTI-ETHNIC STATE IS STUDIED.

09000 TISHKOV, V.
GLASNOST AND THE NATIONALITIES WITHIN THE SOVIET UNION
THIRD WORLD QUARTERLY, 11(4) (OCT 89), 191-207.
THE PROCESSES OF DEMOCRATIZATION IN SOVIET SOCIETY HAVE
CREATED BOTH AN INCREASE IN INTER-ETHNIC STRIFE AND A CRISIS
IN OVERALL NATIONALITY POLICY. THIS SITUATION THREATENS THE
VERY EXISTENCE OF THE USSR, WHICH ENCOMPASSES APPROXIMATELY
128 ETHNIC GROUPS, AS A SINGLE UNIT.

09001 TISMANEANU, V.
BULLDOZER SOCIALISM
EAST EUROPEAN REPORTER, 3(4) (SPR 89), 21.
THE ARTICLE OUTLINES THE EFFORTS OF ROMANIAN DICTATOR
CEAUSESCU TO "SYSTEMIZE" THE ROMANIAN POPULACE BY RAZING
NEARLY HALF OF THE COUNTRY'S VILLAGES AND RESETTLING THE
POPULACE IN "URBAN COMPLEXES." IT ALSO CONTAINS A LETTER OF
PROTEST WRITTEN AND SIGNED BY ROMANIAN HUMAN RIGHTS
ACTIVISTS.

09002 TISMANEANU, V.
CIVIL SOCIETY: AN IDEA THAT BECAME THE STORY
DEADLINE, IV(5) (NOV 89), 9-12.
THE SWEEPING CHANGES TAKING PLACE IN POLAND AND HUNGARY
HAVE TAKEN MANY US JOURNALISTS BY SURPRISE. THESE CHANGES
ARE NOT AN OVERNIGHT RESULT OF MAGNANIMOUS LEADERS GIVING
CONCESSIONS, BUT TO AN EXTENSIVE AND GROWING "CIVIL
SOCIETIES." THE CONCEPT OF CIVIL SOCIETY REFERS TO AN ARENA
OUTSIDE GOVERNMENT CONTROL WHERE INDIVIDUALS COME TOGETHER
TO PURSUE PROJECTS OF THEIR OWN CHOOSING AND DESIGN. THESE
GROUPS INCLUDE SUCH DIVERSE ELEMENTS AS INDEPENDENT UNIONS.
PRESENCE IS OBIQUITOUS AND ACCEPTED, CIVIL SOCIETIES ARE
RELATIVELY NEW TO COMMUNIST EASTERN EUROPE AND HAVE BEEN A
SIGNIFICANT CATALYSTS FOR REFORM.

09003 TISMANEANU, V.
NASCENT CIVIL SOCIETY IN THE GERMAN DEMOCRATIC REPUBLIC
PROBLEMS OF COMMUNISM, XXXVIII(2-3) (MAR 89), 90-111.
THE OPPOSITION MOVEMENT OF THE 1980'S IN THE GERMAN
DEMOCRATIC REPUBLIC BEGAN AS PACIFISM SUPPORTED BY THE
EVANGELICAL CHURCH. SINCE THE MID-1980'S, IT HAS NOT ONLY
BECOME INCREASINGLY CONCERNED WITH THE MILITARIZATION OF
PUBLIC LIFE INTERNALLY AND THE THREAT OF NUCLEAR
ANNIHILATION BUT HAS ALSO INSISTED THAT TRUE PEACE BOTH
DOMESTICALLY AND INTERNATIONALLY REQUIRES THE OBSERVANCE OF
HUMAN RIGHTS, INCLUDING POLITICAL RIGHTS, ON THE PART OF THE
EAST GERMAN REGIME. TOGETHER, THE VARIOUS PACIFIST,
ECOLOGICAL, AND OTHER GROUPS REPRESENT A NASCENT CIVIL
SOCIETY.

09004 TISMANEANU, V.
PERSONAL POWER AND POLITICAL CRISIS IN ROMANIA
GOVERNMENT AND OPPOSITION, 24(2) (SPR 89), 177-198.
ROMANIA SUFFERS FROM A DEEP AND POTENTIALLY EXPLOSIVE
SOCIAL, POLITICAL, AND ECONOMIC CRISIS DUE TO ITS HYPER-
CENTRALIZED MODEL OF LEADERSHIP BASED ON CLAN INSTEAD OF
PARTY DICTATORSHIP; AN OBEDIENT, CORRUPT, AND STRIKINGLY
INCOMPETENT POLITICAL CLASS; A MARKED PREFERENCE FOR
COERCIVE RATHER THAN PERSUASIVE METHODS OF DOMINATION; AND
STUBBORN OPPOSITION TO REFORMS. THE PRICE FOR THIS UNABATED
COMMITMENT TO THE STALINIST MODEL HAS BEEN A GRADUAL
INSTITUTIONAL EROSION, THE GROWING DETERIORATION OF THE
SOCIAL FABRIC, THE HEIGHTENING OF ECONOMIC TENSIONS, AND
INTELLECTUAL ASPHYXIATION. THE CONFLICT HAS BEEN EXACERBATED
BY PRESIDENT NICOLAE CEAUSESCU'S WILFUL AND INCREASINGLY
IDIOSYNCRATIC BEHAVIOR.

09005 TISMANEANU, V.
THE REBELLION OF THE OLD GUARD
EAST EUROPEAN REPORTER, 3(4) (SPR 89), 23-24.
THE ARTICLE EXAMINES THE RECENT LETTER WRITTEN BY SIX
MEMBERS OF THE ROMANIAN "OLD GUARD" CRITICIZING THE
CEAUCSECU REGIME FOR HAVING DISCREDITED THE IMAGE OF
SOCIALISM AND FOR VIOLATING BASIC HUMAN RIGHTS. THE SIX
SIGNATORIES HAVE IMPRESSIVE COMMUNIST PEDIGREES AND
UNDENIABLE LOYALTY, A FACT WHICH CLEARLY REVEALS THE DEFUNCT
NATURE OF THE CEAUSECU REGIME. THE ARTICLE BRIEFLY OUTLINES
THE BACKGROUND OF EACH SIGNATORY AND CONTAINS A COPY OF THE
LETTER.

09006 TISMANEANU, V.
THE TRAGICOMEDY OF ROMANIAN COMMUNISM
EASTERN EUROPEAN POLITICS AND SOCIETIES, 3(2) (SPR 89),
329-375.
IN AN EASTER EUROPE THAT IS INCREASINGLY DESTABILIZED BY
GORBACHEV'S GLASNOST. ROMANIA REMAINS TRUE TO ITS HARD-LINE,
STALINIST ROOTS. THE AUTHOR SEEKS TO GRASP BOTH THE UNIQUE
AND UNIVERSAL, NATIONAL AND INTERNATIONAL ATTRIBUTES OF THE
ROMANIAN COMMUNIST PEDAGOGY IN ORDER TO UNDERSTAND THE RISE
TO POWER OF THE CEAUSESCU REGIME AND ITS TENACITY IN
REMAINING IN POWER.

09007 TIWARI, A.
TERRORISM: STUNNING BLOW
INDIA TODAY, XIV(14) (JUL 89), 40.
IN THE NEVER ENDING WAR BETWEEN POLICE AND TERRORISTS,
THE POLICE STRUCK A MAJOR BLOW BY KILLING TWO NOTORIOUS AND
WANTED CRIMINALS AND CAPTURING ANOTHER. THE CAPTURE OF
PRADUMAN SINGH SIGNALS THE END OF THE KHALISTAN LIBERATION
ORGANIZATION, BU THE WAR TERROR IS DESTINED TO CONTINUE.

09008 TLEMCANI, R.; HANSEN, W.W.
DEVELOPMENT AND THE STATE IN POST-COLONIAL ALGERIA
JOURNAL OF ASIAN AND AFRICAN STUDIES, XXIV(1-2) (1989),
114-133.
THIS ARTICLE ANALYSES THE ROLE OF ALGERIAN BUREAUCRACY
IN DEVELOPMENT. IT SHOWS THAT THE ALGERIAN STATE OWNS THE
SIGNIFICANT MEANS OF PRODUCTION AND HAS USED THE BUREAUCRACY
TO IMPLEMENT ITS STATIST MODEL OF DEVELOPMENT. IN DOING SO
IT HAS EMPHASIZED THE DEVELOPMENT OF HEAVY INDUSTRY AND THE
USE OF THE MOST ADVANCED TECHNOLOGY AVAILABLE TO PROMOTE IT.
IT WAS HOPED THAT WITH THIS MODEL OF DEVELOPMENT AND THE
HELP OF A SKILLED AND TRAINED BUREAUCRACY, RAPID INDUSTRIAL
GROWTH WOULD TRANSFORM THE COUNTRY'S SOCIO-ECONOMIC
STRUCTURE SUFFICIENTLY TO ABSORB THE MASSES OF PEASANT
LABOUR AND ALLOW ALGERIA TO PRODUCE ANYTHING IT CHOOSES.
THIS MODEL, HOWEVER, FAILED TO CREATE JOBS FOR THE BULK OF
THE ALGERIAN POPULATION, LED TO HEAVY RELIANCE ON FOREIGN
CAPITAL, AND CREATED LARGE POOLS OF UNEMPLOYED AND UNDER-
EMPLOYED. FOR TWO DECADES THESE PROBLEMS WERE STAVED OFF
WHEN HIGH OIL PRICES SHAPED THE RELATIONSHIP BETWEEN
BUREAUCRACY AND DEVELOPMENT. WHEN OIL PRICES WENT DOWN
DRASTICALLY IN THE 1980S, THEY CAUSED UNREST AND TURMOIL IN
ALGERIA AND CREATED AN ECONOMIC CRISIS WHICH THE STATE AND
ITS BUREAUCRACY ARE CURRENTLY TRYING TO MANAGE.

09009 TOENSING, V.
FUTURE U.S. POLICY AND ACTION: THE JUSTICE DEPARTMENT'S
APPROACH TO TERRORISM
TERRORISM, 11(6) (1988), 553-557.
THIS IS A TALK GIVEN AT A CONFERENCE ON TERRORISM GIVEN
BY VICTORIA TOENSING, FORMER DEPUTY ASSISTANT ATTORNEY
GENERAL, CRIMINAL DIVISION, DEPARTMENT OF JUSTICE. SHE
ADDRESSES WHERE THE DEPARTMENT OF JUSTICE IS GOING IN THE
FUTURE LEGALLY WITH TERRORISM. IN DOING THIS SHE TALKS ABOUT
THREE MAIN AREAS: THE LAW, PARTICULARLY LAWS THAT HAVE BEEN
PASSED RECENTLY; A LAW TO EXPEDITE THE PROCESS TO HAVE
ILLEGAL ALIENS REMOVED; AND EXTRADITION.

09010 TOKES, R.
HUNGARY ON THE WAY TO DEMOCRACY
NEW LEADER, LXXII(14) (SEP 89), 9-11.
THE YEAR 1989 HAS BEEN ONE OF DISINTEGRATION OF THE
RULING HUNGARIAN SOCIALIST WORKERS PARTY (HSWP) AND ITS
LEADER JANOS KADAR. ALTHOUGH HUNGARY SEEMS TO BE ON THE ROAD
TO A PEACEFUL TRANSITION TO DEMOCRACY, THE VIEWS OF
HUNGARY'S "SILENT MAJORITY" ARE DIFFICULT TO FATHOM. THE
ONLY THING THEY SEEM UNIFIED ON IS THEIR DISTRUST OF THE
HSWP. ALTHOUGH MANY DIVERSE OPPOSITION PARTIES ARE VYING FOR
POWER, NO SINGLE GROUP HAS RECEIVED A MANDATE FROM THE
PEOPLE.

09011 TOKES, R.
HUNGARY'S HAZY FUTURE
NEW LEADER, LXXII(16) (OCT 89), 5-7.
THE BIRTH OF THE HUNGARIAN SOCIALIST PARTY (HSP) SIGNALS
THE END OF THE DICTATORSHIP OF THE PROLETARIAT IN HUNGARY.
THE NEW HSP REFLECTS THE GROWING DISSATISFACTION WITH OLD
PARTIES AND OLD MODELS. HOWEVER, IT SEEMS THAT FOR MANY
MEMBERS OF THE NOW DEFUNCT HUNGARIAN SOCIALIST WORKER'S
PARTY (HSWP) THE CHANGE IS NOT ENOUGH; BARELY FOUR PER CENT
OF THE COUNTRY'S 725,000 PARTY MEMBERS JOINED THE NEW HSP.
OPPOSITION GROUPS, LOOSELY GROUPED INTO THE "OPPOSITION
ROUND TABLE" AND OTHER MASS ORGANIZATIONS HAVE ATTEMPTED TO
SEIZE THE INITIATIVE AND FILL THE VACUUM LEFT BY THE
SOCIALISTS.

09012 TOKMAN, V.
ECONOMIC DEVELOPMENT AND LABOR MARKET SEGMENTATION IN THE
LATIN AMERICAN PERIPHERY
JOURNAL OF INTERAMERICAN STUDIES AND WORLD AFFAIRS, 31(1,
2) (SPR 89), 23-47.
THIS ARTICLE ESPOUSES AND EXPANDS THE STRUCTURALIST,
DEPENDENCY, CENTER - PERIPHERY HYPOTHESIS THAT EXTERNAL
FACTORS ARE PRIMARILY RESPONSIBLE FOR THE UNFORTUNATE
PREDICAMENT OF LATIN AMERICAN LABOR MARKET SEGMENTATION,
ACCORDING TO THE AUTHOR, THE CENTER-PERIPHERY FRAMEWORK OF
PREBISCH AND THE RELATED CONCEPTS OF DEPENDENCY,
HETEROGENEITY, AND EXCLUSION ARE ALIVE AND WELL AND PERMIT A
BETTER UNDERSTANDING OF THE EMPLOYMENT SITUATION WHICH
PRESENTLY PREVAILS.

09013 TOKMAN, V.E.
POLICIES FOR A HETEROGENEOUS INFORMAL SECTOR IN LATIN
AMERICA
WORLD DEVELOPMENT, 17(7) (JUL 89), 1067-1076.

THE CONCEPT OF THE "INFORMAL SECTOR" HAS GAINED
INCREASING ACCEPTANCE IN LATIN AMERICA. SOME 30 MILLION
PERSONS NOW WORK OUTSIDE THE MODERN ECONOMY IN LOW-
PRODUCTIVITY JOBS WITH MARGINAL INCOMES; MANY OF THEM ARE
LIVING IN POVERTY. INTERNATIONAL AND NATIONAL POLICY MAKERS
HAVE BECOME AWARE OF THE POLITICAL AND ECONOMIC CONSEQUENCES
OF THIS PHENOMENON AND ARE SEEKING WAYS TO IMPROVE RETURNS
AND INCOMES. THE SECTOR, HOWEVER, IS COMPOSED OF DIFFERENT
KINDS OF ACTIVITIES, EACH WITH ITS OWN PROBLEMS, WHICH NEED
TO BE ADDRESSED IN DIFFERENT WAYS. POLICY PLANNERS SHOULD
BEAR THIS IN MIND AS THEY SEEK SOLUTIONS. THE PAPER
RECOMMENDS THREE TYPES OF MEASURES: PROVIDING PRODUCTIVE
ASSISTANCE TO INFORMAL ENTERPRISES, SUPPORTING INFORMAL
SECTOR WORKERS, AND REVISING REGULATIONS THAT GOVERN
INFORMAL SECTOR ACTIVITIES.

09014 TOLBA, M.K.
ECOLOGICAL SECURITY THROUGH COOPERATION
WORLD MARXIST REVIEW, 32(10) (OCT 89), 35-36.
THIS ARTICLE IS THE FIRST IN A SERIES OF PUBLICATIONS
SEARCHING FOR SOLUTIONS TO FORMIDABLE GLOBAL PROBLEMS. THIS
ONE IS IMMEDIATELY CONCERNED WITH ECOLOGICAL SECURITY. IT
SUGGESTS THAT ENVIRONMENTAL SECURITY SHOULD BE EQUITABLE FOR
STATES AND THAT POLITIO-MILITARY, ENVIRONMENTAL, ECONOMIC
AND SOCIAL PROBLEMS ARE ARE ALL INTERCONNECTED, THUS IT
MAKES SENSE TO INCLUDE ALL OF THEM IN THE CONCEPT OF
COMPREHENSIVE INTERNATIONAL SECURITY. IT ALSO SUGGESTS THAT
DETERRENCE COULD BE TRANSCENDED IN A VARIETY OF WAYS. UNEP
(U.N. ENVIRONMENT PROGRAMME) IS DEFINED AND EXPLAINED.

09015 TOLLEY, H.
POPULAR SOVEREIGNTY AND INTERNATIONAL LAW: ICJ STRATEGIES
FOR HUMAN RIGHTS STANDARD SETTING
HUMAN RIGHTS QUARTERLY, 11(4) (NOV 89), 561-585.
HOW DOES A NONGOVERNMENTAL ORGANIZATION (NGO) INFLUENCE
GOVERNMENTS TO ADOPT INTERNATIONAL LAWS AND PROCEDURES
LIMITING STATE POWER? THIS ARTICLE ASSESSES HOW A LEADING
NGO, THE INTERNATIONAL COMMISSION OF JURISTS (ICJ) HAS
PROMOTED NEW HUMAN RIGHTS LAWS AND INSTITUTIONS AT THE
GLOBAL, REGIONAL, AND NATIONAL LEVELS, IT EXPLORES NGO
LEADERSHIP/COLLABORATION, EXPERT DRAFTING/CONSULTATION,
CONTACTS WITH GOVERNMENT LEADERS AND ADMINISTRATIVE FOLLOW-
UP/IMPLEMENTATION.

09016 TOMA, M.
WILL BOUNTY - HUNTING REVENUE AGENTS INCREASE ENFORCEMENT?
PUBLIC CHOICE, 61(3) (JUN 89), 247-260.
WHILE THE FINAL VERSION OF THE 1986 TAX REFORM ACT
RETAINED BUDGET FUNDING OF THE IRS, THE SENATE PROPOSAL TO
FINANCE SPENDING FROM AUDIT REVENUES REPRESENTED A SERIOUSLY
DEBATED ALTERNATIVE THAT CONTINUES TO RECEIVE ATTENTION AS A
METHOD FOR INCREASING ENFORCEMENT. AT ONE LEVEL, THE
ULTIMATE FAILURE OF THE PROPOSAL IS PUZZLING. GIVEN
CONGRESS'S UNWILLINGNESS TO RAISE TAX RATES TO COVER
SPENDING, THE BUDGET DEFICITS OF THE 1980S MUST BE FINANCED
FROM SOME OTHER SOURCE - INFLATION, BORROWING OR INCREASED
ENFORCEMENT. TURNING THE IRS INTO A BOUNTY-HUNTING AGENCY
WOULD SEEM TO BE A STRAIGHTFORWARD WAY OF PRODUCING EXTRA
REVENUE. HOWEVER, THIS POPULAR VIEW REVEALS A BASIC
CONFUSION ABOUT THE BEHAVIOR OF BOUNTYHUNTING AGENTS. IT
IMPLICITLY ASSUMES THAT A BOUNTY-HUNTING AGENCY WOULD BEHAVE
AS A GENERAL REVENUE-MAXIMIZING LEVIATHAN AND AUTOMATICALLY
INCREASE ENFORCEMENT ABOVE THE STATUS QUO BUDGETARY LEVEL IN
PURSUIT OF ADDITIONAL REVENUE. BUT BOUNTY HUNTERS WANT TO
MAXIMIZE NET AUDIT REVENUES - NOT NET GENERAL REVENUES. AS
THE AUTHOR EMPHASIZES, TOO THOROUGH A HUNT WILL REDUCE THE
BOUNTY.

09017 TOMLIN, B.H.
THE STAGES OF PRENEGOTIATION: THE DECISION TO NEGOTIATE
NORTH AMERICAN FREE TRADE
INTERNATIONAL JOURNAL, XLIV(2) (SPR 89), 254-279.
AN ADEQUATE UNDERSTANDING OF THE U.S.-CANADIAN FREE
TRADE NEGOTIATIONS MUST INCLUDE AN ANALYSIS OF THE DECISIONS
AND INTERACTIONS THAT PRECEDED THE START OF FORMAL
NEGOTIATION IN 1986. THE DYNAMICS OF THE PRENEGOTIATION
PROCESS CONTRIBUTES TO THE ESTABLISHMENT OF THE PARAMETERS
IN WHICH FORMAL NEGOTIATION SUBSEQUENTLY UNFOLDS. THESE
PARAMETERS MAY BE MORE OR LESS PRECISELY DEFINED AND THEY
ARE NOT IMMUTABLE ONCE NEGOTIATION STARTS, BUT THE INITIAL
DEFINITION OF THEIR SCOPE MAY HAVE IMPORTANT EFFECTS ON BOTH
THE PROCESS AND OUTCOMES OF NEGOTIATION.

09018 TOMLINSON, J.
LABOUR'S MANAGEMENT OF THE NATIONAL ECONOMY 1945-51:
SURVEY AND SPECULATIONS
ECONOMY AND SOCIETY, 18(1) (FEB 89), 1-24.
THE LABOUR GOVERNMENT 1945-51 PLAYED A CRUCIAL PART IN
SETTING THE PATTERN OF POST-WAR BRITISH ECONOMIC POLICY.
THIS ARTICLE SURVEYS THE RECORD OF THAT GOVERNMENT. IT DEALS
WITH BOTH THE MACROECONOMIC AND INDUSTRIAL POLICY ASPECTS OF
POLICY. ON THE FIRST IT ARGUES THAT THE POLICIES WERE
SUCCESSFUL IN ACHIEVING A ROUGH 'BALANCE' BY 1950,
ESPECIALLY ON THE VITAL BALANCE OF PAYMENTS FRONT. ON THE

SECOND ASPECT THE RECORD IS LES CLEAR, BUT THE BROAD THRUST
OF THE ARGUMENT IS THAT THE POLITICS OF THE GOVERNMENT
INHIBITED IT FROM MAKING AN 'ALL OUT' ATTACK ON THE PROBLEMS
OF INDUSTRIAL STRUCTURE AND MANAGERIAL INCOMPETENCE WHICH
LAY AT THE HEART OF BRITIAN'S POOR PRODUCTIVITY RECORD.

09019 TONELSON, A.
A MANIFESTO FOR DEMOCRATS
NATIONAL INTEREST, 16 (SUM 89), 36-48.
TO PASS POLITICAL TESTS AND TO COPE WITH THE FOREIGN
POLICY AGENDA OF THE 1990S AND BEYOND, THE DEMOCRATS NEED A
COMPLETE OVERHAUL IN THEIR FOREIGN POLICY THINKING.
SPECIFICALLY, THEY ARE GOING TO HAVE TO ABANDON
INTERNATIONALISM AND ITS NO LONGER AFFORDABLE STRATEGY OF
GROUNDING AMERICAN SECURITY AND PROSPERITY IN A CONGENIAL
WORLD ENVIRONMENT OF LIBERAL DEMOCRACIES, COLLECTIVE
SECURITY, AND FREE TRADE. INSTEAD, THE PARTY NEEDS AN
APPROACH THAT EMPHASIZES THE RESTORATION OF U.S. MILITARY
AND ECONOMIC STRENGTH; THAT IS MORE DISCRIMINATING ABOUT
FOREIGN MILITARY COMMITMENTS AND MORE WILLING TO USE FORCE
UNILATERALLY TO SECURE TRULY IMPORTANT INTERESTS; THAT
ADVOCATES TOUGHER TRADE POLICIES WITH THE COUNTRY'S LEADING
ECONOMIC PARTNERS; AND THAT SEEKS GREATER SELF-SUFFICIENCY
IN STRATEGICALLY IMPORTANT RESOURCES AND MANUFACTURES. WHAT
THE DEMOCRATS NEED IS A NEW NATIONALISM.

09020 TONELSON, A.
AMERICA IN A MULTIPOLAR WORLD - WHATEVER THAT IS
SAIS REVIEW, 9(2) (SUM 89), 45-59.
THE AUTHOR HERE PROPOSES AN INTEREST-BASED RATES THAN AN
ANALYSIS-BASED FOREIGN POLICY. HE SPECIFICALLY POINTS TO THE
ABSURDITIES THAT COME OUT OF "CRYSTAL-BALL GAZING" ABOUT
FUTURE EVENTS. THE AUTHOR ARTICULATES THE IDEA THAT THE
PASSAGE OF TIME FOR ADVOCATES OF CHANGE - WHETHER GOVERNMENT
OFFICIALS ON ACADEMICS - RUNS ON A SUBSTANTIALLY ACCELERATED
CLOCK COMPARED TO THE REALITY OF GLOBAL EVENTS.

09021 TONELSON, A.
THE DEMOCRATIC PARTY AND FOREIGN POLICY: A PROPOSED
MANIFESTO
CURRENT, (317) (NOV 89), 25-34.
THE DEMOCRATS NEED A COMPLETE OVERHAUL IN THEIR FOREIGN
POLICY THINKING. SPECIFICALLY, THEY MUST ABANDON
INTERNATIONALISM AND THE STRATEGY OF GROUNDING AMERICAN
SECURITY AND PROSPERITY IN A CONGENIAL WORLD ENVIRONMENT OF
LIBERAL DEMOCRACIES, COLLECTIVE SECURITY, AND FREE TRADE.
INSTEAD, THE PARTY NEEDS AN APPROACH THAT EMPHASIZES THE
RESTORATION OF U.S. MILITARY AND ECONOMIC STRENGTH; THAT IS
MORE DISCRIMINATING ABOUT FOREIGN MILITARY COMMITMENTS AND
MORE WILLING TO USE FORCE UNILATERALLY TO SECURE TRULY
IMPORTANT INTERESTS; THAT ADVOCATES TOUGHER TRADE POLICIES
WITH THE COUNTRY'S LEADING ECONOMIC PARTNERS; AND THAT SEEKS
GREATER SELF-SUFFICIENCY IN STRATEGICALLY IMPORTANT
RESOURCES AND MANUFACTURES.

09022 TONG, G.C.
A MINORITY RIGHT-ENSURING MULTI-RACIAL REPRESENTATION IN
THE SINGAPORE PARLIAMENT
PARLIAMENTARIAN, 70(1) (JAN 89), 6-11.
THE AUTHOR DISCUSSES HIS INTRODUCTION OF TWO BILLS INTO
SINGAPORE'S PARLIAMENT WHICH MAY HELP SINGAPORE AVOID
COMMUNAL POLITICS BY LINKING CANDIDATES FROM DIFFERENT RACES
IN CONSTITUENCY TEAMS. THE BILLS WHICH HE INTRODUCED WERE
THE CONSTITUTION OF THE REPUBLIC OF SINGAPORE AMENDMENT BILL
AND THE PARLIAMENTARY ELECTIONS AMENDMENT BILL, WHICH ARE
THE RESULT OF SIX YEARS OF GOVERNMENT DISCUSSION. THE AUTHOR
EXAMINES THE INADEQUECY OF THE WESTMINISTER MODEL IN MULTI-
RACIAL SOCIETIES IN GENERAL, USING SPECIFIC REALITIES ABOUT
SINGAPORE'S ETHNICITY AND RELIGIOUS COMPLEXITIES TO SUPPORT
HIS ARGUMENTS. DISCUSSIONS WHICH OCCURRED BEFORE THESE BILLS
WERE PASSED BY PARLIAMENT IN 1988 ARE ALSO SUMMARIZED.

09023 TONG, J.
FISCAL REFORM, ELITE TURNOVER, AND CENTRAL-PROVINCIAL
RELATIONS IN POST-MAO CHINA
AUSTRALIAN JOURNAL OF CHINESE AFFAIRS, (22) (JUL 89), 1-28.
SINCE MAO'S DEATH AND THE DEMISE OF THE RADICALS IN LATE
1976, THE FISCAL SYSTEM IN CHINA HAS UNDERGONE MAJOR
STRUCTURAL CHANGES. THIS PAPER EXAMINES THE EFFECTS OF THESE
REFORMS ON CENTRAL-PROVINCIAL RELATIONS, IN PARTICULAR THE
DEGREE OF A) PROVINCIAL COMPLIANCE WITH CENTRAL FISCAL
TARGETS; B) INTERPROVINCIAL EQUALITY IN THE PROVISION OF
SOCIAL SERVICES; AND C) CENTRAL-PROVINCIAL POLITICAL
CONFLICT. ANALYSING PROVINCIAL DATA ON REVENUES AND
EXPENDITURES, PUBLIC HEALTH AS WELL AS EDUCATION SERVICES,
AND ELITE TURN-OVER FROM 1979-86, PRELIMINARY FINDINGS
SUGGEST THAT THESE MAJOR REFORMS HAVE ENHANCED PROVINCIAL
FISCAL EFFORT AND REDUCED THE LEVEL OF CENTRAL-PROVINCIAL
ELITE CONFLICT, WITHOUT SIGNIFICANTLY INCREASING THE LEVEL
OF INTERPROVINCIAL VARIATIONS IN SOCIAL SERVICE OUTPUTS.

09024 TOO, C.
MALAYSIA'S COMMUNIST THREAT
FAR EASTERN ECONOMIC REVIEW, 142(49) (DEC 89), 29-33.

THE AUTHOR EXAMINES THE LONG HISTORY OF THE ARMED
STRUGGLE BETWEEN THE MALAYSIAN GOVERNMENT AND COMMUNIST
REVOLUTIONARIES. HE OUTLINES THE VARIOUS STRATEGIES ENGAGED
BY THE COMMUNIST PARTY OF MALAYSIA RANGING FROM THE
ESTABLISHMENT OF SCORES OF LABOR, WOMEN'S SHOPKEEPER'S,
BARBER'S, AND OTHER UNIONS IN AN ATTEMPT TO TAKE CONTROL OF
THE NATION'S ECONOMY, TO GUERRILLA WARFARE FROM JUNGLE BASES.
THE AUTHOR CONCLUDES THAT GOVERNMENT AUTHORITIES NEED TO
RECEIVE WITH CAUTION THE PROPOSAL OF THE REMNANTS OF THE
COMMUNIST PARTY FOR AMNESTY AND A RETURN TO CIVILIAN LIFE IN
EXCHANGE FOR A CESSATION OF HOSTILITIES. IF HISTORY IS ANY
GUIDE, THE OVERTURES BY THE COMMUNISTS MAY BE YET ANOTHER
PLOY TO INFILTRATE LEGITIMATE PUBLIC ORGANIZATIONS.

09025 TOO, C.
    ROUT OF THE REDS
    FAR EASTERN ECONOMIC REVIEW, 142(50) (DEC 89), 26-27.
    THE ARTICLE EXAMINES THE DESPERATE STRATEGY OF
SINGAPORE'S RULING PEOPLE'S ACTION PARTY (PAP) LEADER, LEE
KUAN YEH, DESIGNED TO SAVE SINGAPORE FROM COMMUNIST TAKEOVER
IN 1962. LEE WAS FACED WITH THE DILEMMA OF SELLING THE IDEA
OF MERGER WITH THE FEDERATION OF MALAYA TO SINGAPORE'S
CHINESE MAJORITY, WHILE AT THE SAME TIME DEALING WITH
COMMUNIST SUBVERSIVES WHO WERE ALSO PREDOMINANTLY CHINESE.
IN THE END, REFERENDUM RESULTS INDICATED SUPPORT FOR THE
MERGER, WHICH GAVE LEE, AS WELL AS HIS BRITISH AND MALAYSIAN
ALLIES, A FREE HAND TO IMPLEMENT A POLICY OF MASS ARRESTS OF
SUSPECTED COMMUNISTS. ONCE AGAIN, THE COMMUNISTS WERE
DEFEATED.

09026 TOPOUZIS, D.
    A CHARTER FOR HUMAN RIGHTS
    AFRICA REPORT, 34(4) (JUL 89), 31-33.
    EARLY IN THE HISTORY OF THE OAU, THE QUESTION OF
PROTECTING HUMAN RIGHTS WAS SECONDARY TO AFRICA'S STRUGGLE
FOR SELF-DETERMINATION. WITH THE RECENT OPENING OF THE
HEADQUARTERS OF THE AFRICAN COMMISSION ON HUMAN AND PEOPLE'S
RIGHTS IN BANJUL, HOWEVER, A NEW FOCUS ON THE RIGHTS OF THE
CONTINENT'S CITIZENS IS A STEP FORWARD IN THE PROMOTION OF
DEMOCRATIC PRACTICE.

09027 TOPOUZIS, D.
    CONTE'S CHALLENGES
    AFRICA REPORT, 34(6) (NOV 89), 38-41.
    THE TERROR OF SEKOU TOURE'S RULE LEFT MORE THAN JUST A
HAUNTING MEMORY FOR GUINEA; IT LEFT A DILAPIDATED ECONOMY
AND A DISILLUSIONED POPULACE. PRESIDENT LANSANA CONTE'S
AMBITIOUS STRUCTURAL ADJUSTMENT REFORMS HAVE JUMP-STARTED
THE ECONOMY AND THERE ARE PLANS TO DEMOCRATIZE THE POLITICAL
SYSTEM, BUT DAUNTING CHALLENGES LIE AHEAD.

09028 TOPOUZIS, D.
    DETERMINED TO DEVELOP
    AFRICA REPORT, 34(5) (SEP 89), 52-54.
    A NATION LACKING IN NATURAL RESOURCES AND STRUGGLING
AGAINST ARDUOUS CLIMATIC CONDITIONS, CAPE VERDE HAS
NONETHELESS RECORDED IMPRESSIVE MACRO-ECONOMIC INDICATORS
AND CONSIDERABLE SOCIAL ADVANCEMENT. ALTHOUGH DEPENDENT ON
AID INFLOWS AND REMITTANCES FROM ABROAD, THE NATION HAS
GAINED A REPUTATION FOR EFFICIENT AND CREATIVE UTILIZATION
OF ITS MEAGER RESOURCES.

09029 TOPOUZIS, D.
    SHIFTING COURSE
    AFRICA REPORT, 34(5) (SEP 89), 49-51.
    ONCE REGARDED AS A MODEL OF REVOLUTIONARY SOCIALISM,
GUINEA-BISSAU HAS REVERSED ITS ECONOMIC COURSE, ADOPTING A
TOUGH STRUCTURAL ADJUSTMENT PROGRAM AND INTRODUCING MAJOR
FISCAL REFORMS. NEAR ECONOMIC COLLAPSE PROMPTED THE ABOUT-
FACE, BUT NEW WORRIES HAVE ARISEN CONCERNING THE COUNTRY'S
GROWING DEPENDENCE ON FOREIGN AID.

09030 TORRES, C.A.
    THE MEXICAN STATE AND DEMOCRACY: THE AMBRIGIUTIES OF
    CORPORATISM
    INTERNATIONAL JOURNAL OF POLITICS, CULTURE AND SOCIETY,
    2(4) (SUM 89), 563-586.
    RESEARCHERS HAVE ARGUED THAT THE CENTRAL FEATURE OF THE
STATE IN MEXICO IS ITS AUTHORITARIANISM--HENCE MAKING IT
COMPARABLE WITH OTHER STATES IN THE REGION. THE DOMINANT
EXPLANATION OF WHAT HAS BEEN CALLED THE AUTHORITARIAN STATE
FORMS PREVAILING IN LATIN AMERICA IN THE SEVENTIES AND EARLY
EIGHTIES IS GUILLERMO O'DONNELL'S BUREAUCRATIC-AUTHORITARIAN
STATE APPROACH, WHICH HAS BEEN APPLIED IN AN ATTEMPT TO
UNDERSTAND THE MEXICAN STATE. THIS ARTICLE EXAMINES THE
BUREAUCRATIC-AUTHORITARIAN STATE APPROACH. I.E. ITS MAIN
ANALYTICAL DIMENSIONS, HYPOTHESES AND THEORETICAL
UNDERPINNINGS, THE FEASIBILITY OF APPLYING THIS MODEL TO THE
MEXICAN CASE, AND ITS EVENTUAL UTILITY FOR EXPLAINING THE
PROCESS OF POLICY-MAKING IN MEXICO.

09031 TORREZ, L.
    CHICANO-MEXICAN EQUALITY AND QUESTIONS OF IDEOLOGY
    POLITICAL AFFAIRS, LXVIII(8) (AUG 89), 30-33.

THE ARTICLE EXAMINES ISSUES THAT ARE OF PARTICULAR
IMPORTANCE TO THE CHICANO-MEXICAN WORKING CLASS. THE AUTHOR
ATTEMPTS TO SEARCH FOR "COMMON GROUND," "COMMON ISSUES," AND
"COMMON DEMOCRATIC RIGHTS" THAT ARE SHARED BY ALL MEMBERS OF
THE WORKING CLASS. IT CONCLUDES THAT ALTHOUGH MANY
SIGNIFICANT OBSTACLES ARE FACED, FULL EQUALITY CAN BE
ACHIEVED.

09032 TORUMTAY, N.
    DEFENCE INDUSTRY IN TURKEY
    NATO'S SIXTEEN NATIONS, 34(2) (APR 89), 49-52.
    AFTER VARIOUS ATTEMPTS TO ESTABLISH A NATIONAL DEFENCE
INDUSTRY IN THE PRIVATE AND PUBLIC SECTORS, TURKEY IS NOW
FORGING AHEAD WITH AN INTEGRATED NATIONALIZED INDUSTRY. IT
IS ORGANIZED UNDER A LEGALLY CONSTITUTED DIRECTORY WHICH
CONTROLS THE DIFFERENT CATEGORIES OF MANUFACTURERS. WITH
OUTSIDE INVESTMENT, ALLIED SUPPORT AND CONSIDERABLE NATIVE
EFFORT THIS INDUSTRY IS ALREADY SUPPLYING A LARGE PART OF
THE NEEDS OF THE TURKISH ARMED FORCES AND IS BEGINNING TO
EXPORT SOME OF ITS PRODUCTS.

09033 TOTTERDILL, P.
    LOCAL ECONOMIC STRATEGIES AS INDUSTRIAL POLICY: A CRITICAL
    REVIEW OF BRITISH DEVELOPMENTS IN THE 1980'S
    ECONOMY AND SOCIETY, 18(4) (NOV 89), 478-526.
    THE PROLIFERATION OF INTERVENTIONIST LOCAL AUTHORITY
STRATEGIES FOR EMPLOYMENT AND ECONOMIC DEVELOPMENT HAS BEEN
WIDESPREAD IN BRITAIN SINCE THE EARLY 1980s. BUT MUCH OF THE
RADICAL PROMISE OF THESE STRATEGIES HAS BEEN SLOW TO
MATERIALISE, DUE IN PART TO THE ABOLITION OF THE
METROPOLITAN AUTHORITIES AND TO THE ELECTION OF A THIRD
THATCHER GOVERNMENT. MOREOVER NEW AND TRADITIONAL FORMS OF
POLICY PRODUCTION HAVE CO-EXISTED IN AN UNEASY RELATIONSHIP
WITHIN LOCAL AUTHORITIES, AND THIS THREATENS THE STRATEGIC
CAPACITY OF INTERVENTION. IT IS ARGUED THAT THE REGENERATION
OF STRATEGIC PERSPECTIVES SHOULD BE A PRIORITY FOR LOCAL
AUTHORITIES; AT THE SAME TIME FLEXIBLE SPECIALISATION IN
MANUFACTURING OFFERS NEW POLITICAL AND TACTICAL
OPPORTUNITIES FOR STRATEGIC INTERVENTION IN PURSUIT OF BOTH
REGENERATION AND ACCOUNTABILITY IN THE ECONOMIC SPHERE.

09034 TOULMIN, L. M.
    THE TREASURE HUNT: BUDGET SEARCH BEHAVIOR BY PUBLIC
    EMPLOYEE UNIONS
    PUBLIC ADMINISTRATION REVIEW, 48(2) (MAR 88), 620-630.
    THIS ARTICLE DESCRIBES THE IMPORTANT ROLE THAT MANY
NATIONAL UNIONS PLAY IN ASSISTING THEIR LOCALS IN THE SEARCH
FOR HIDDEN MONEY. THE UNIONS INVOLVED IN THIS ACTIVITY AND
HOW THEY PROCESS BUDGET DATA ARE DESCRIBED. IT LISTS THE
SOURCES OF INFORMATION THE UNIONS DREW UPON, DESCRIBES
ANALYSIS TECHNIQUES USED, ECONOMETRIC TECHNIQUES USED AND
DISCUSSES THE EFFECTIVENESS OF THE UNION TECHNIQUES.

09035 TOULOUSE, M.G.
    PAT ROBERTSON: APOCALYPTIC THEOLOGY AND AMERICAN FOREIGN
    POLICY
    JOURNAL OF CHURCH & STATE, 31(1) (WIN 89), 73-100.
    PAT ROBERTSON'S 1988 CANDIDACY FOR THE PRESIDENT RAISED
ANEW OLD QUESTIONS OF THE SEPARATION OF CHURCH AND STATE. IT
IS CERTAIN THAT ROBERTSON'S POLITICS MIXES RELIGION AND
POLICY, BUT DID HIS CANDIDACY ACTUALLY THREATEN SEPARATION
OF CHURCH AND STATE? HOW DO HIS BELIEFS INFLUENCE HIS VIEW
OF THE UNITED STATES' POSITION IN THE WORLD ORDER AND
AMERICAN FOREIGN POLICY?

09036 TOW, W.T.
    THE ANZUS DISPUTE: TESTING U.S. EXTENDED DETERRENCE IN
    ALLIANCE POLITICS
    POLITICAL SCIENCE QUARTERLY, 104(1) (SPR 89), 117-150.
    THIRTY-FIVE YEARS AFTER ITS FOUNDING, THE ANZUS ALLIANCE
HAS BECOME THE LATEST VICTIM IN THE STEADY DISSOLUTION OF
WASHINGTON'S POSTWAR COLLECTIVE DEFENSE FRAMEWORK. THIS
ESSAY REVIEWS THE HISTORY OF ANZUS AND THE REASONS FOR ITS
REDUCED ROLE IN PACIFIC SECURITY.

09037 TOWNSHEND, J.
    REASSESSING KAUTSKY'S MARXISM
    POLITICAL STUDIES, XXXVII(4) (DEC 89), 659-664.
    RECENT INTERPRETATIONS AND EXTRACTS OF KAUTSKY'S
WRITINGS ARE BEGINNING TO CHALLENGE, EXPLICITY OR IMPLICITLY,
AND IN VARYING DEGREES, THE NEO-HEGELIAN INTERPRETATION,
WHICH HAS BECOME A WIDELY HELD ORTHODOX AMONGST MARIXISTS
AND NON-MARXISTS ALIKE. THIS ARTICLE EXAMINES AND SUPPORTS
THE REASONS WHY THE NEO-HEGELIAN POSITION THAT KAUTSKY'S
SCIENTISM AND DETERMINATION LED HIM TO DIVORCE THEORY AND
PRACTICE, IS DUBIOUS.

09038 TOYNE, P.
    TWO LAWS IN ONE TERRITORY
    ARENA, (88) (SPR 89), 37-40.
    THIS REPORT FROM AUSTRALIA EXPLAINS THE DIFFICULTIES
CONFRONTING THE COUNTRY LIBERAL PARTY GOVERNMENT WHICH IS
ACTIVELY PROMOTING THE DRIVE TOWARDS STATEHOOD FOR THE
NORTHERN TERRITORY. THE PROBLEM FOR CONSTITUTION MAKERS IS

THAT WHILE PART OF THE POPULATION-THOSE WHO HAVE MIGRATED IN
FROM OTHER PARTS OF THE COUNTRY ACCEPT AND EXPECT A CERTAIN
DEFINITION OF RIGHTS, WHILE ANOTHER PART, THE ABORIGINAL
POPULATION, KNOWS ITS RIGHTS BY ANOTHER PROCESS WHICH IS
OFTEN A CONTRADICTORY ONE, THE WARLPIRI PEOPLE SEE THE
DEVELOPMENT OF A STATE CONSTITUTION AND THE PASSAGE OF THE
NORTHERN TERRITORY TO STATEHOOD AS A MAJOR NEW THREAT TO
THEIR SOVERNIGNTY OVER THEIR COUNTRY AND AFFAIRS, THIS
ARTICLE EXPLORES THE RELATIONSHIP OF THE PEOPLE TO THE LAND
WHICH IS THE CORE PROBLEM.

09039 TRACHTENBERG, M.
    STRATEGIC THOUGHT IN AMERICA, 1952-1966
    POLITICAL SCIENCE QUARTERLY, 104(2) (SUM 89), 301-334.
    IN THE 1950'S, STRATEGY EMERGED IN THE UNITED STATES AS
A NEW FIELD WITH A DISTINCT INTELLECTUAL PERSONALITY. THIS
ESSAY LOOKS AT HOW THIS INTELLECTUAL TRADITION TOOK SHAPE,
WHAT CAUSED IT TO EMERGE, HOW THE CENTRAL IDEAS DEVELOPED,
AND WHY IT SEEMED TO HAVE PLAYED ITSELF OUT BY AROUND 1966.

09040 TRAIN, J.
    PONDERING PERESTROIKA
    AMERICAN SPECTATOR, 22(2) (FEB 89), 30-31.
    THE SOVIET EMPIRE, LIKE THE ROMAN EMPIRE OR THE OTTOMAN
EMPIRE OR INDEED ALL PREVIOUS EMPIRES, IS IN A STATE OF
IRRETRIEVABLE DECAY. IT IS BLOTED AND HERETOGENEOUS, WHICH
MEANS A HUGH DEFENSE ESTABLISHMENT, AT CRIPPLING EXPENSE,TO
HOLD IT DOWN. A ROUGH FIGURE FOR THE PART OF SOVIET GNP THAT
GOES TO MAINTAINING THEIR PRODIGIOUS AND GROWING MILITARY
ESTABLISHMENT IS 20 PERCENT - THREE TIMES THE U. S.,
PROPORTION. BUT THAT'S OF AN ECONOMY HALF AS LARGE AND MUCH
LESS EFFICIENT, WITH VERY LITTLE TO SPARE. SO IT'S A KILLING
BURDEN, WHICH STIFLES EVERYTHING, AT THE SAME TIME THAT THE
PRODUCTIVITY OF A DEMORALIZED POPULATION IS DECLINING.
PERHAPS A PARALLEL TO GORBACHEV IS DIOCLETIAN, WHOSE ENDLESS
REORGANIZATION AN REFORMS COULD NOT FORSTALL HIS EMPIRE'S
DECAY.

09041 TRAINER, F.E.
    RECONSTRUCTING RADICAL DEVELOPMENT THEORY
    ALTERNATIVES, 14(4) (OCT 89), 481-516.
    THE FIRST MAJOR CONCERN IN THIS ESSAY IS TO SUMMARIZE
THE NOW OVERWHELMING CASE AGAINST THE CONVENTIONAL GROWTH OR
MODERNIZATION THEORY AND PRACTICE OF DEVELOPMENT. THE SECOND
IS TO ARGUE FOR EXCHANGE RELATIONS OR MARKET FORCES AND
APPROPRIATENESS AS THE FOUNDATION CONCEPTS ON WHICH RADICAL
DEVELOPMENT THEORY SHOULD BE BUILT. IT ARUGES THAT RADICAL
DEVELOPMENT HAS BEEN MISTAKEN AS CONNENTIONAL DEVELOPMENT
THOUGHT. FINALLY, THE IMPLICATIONS FOR NEW DIRECTION IN
DEVELOPMENT THEORY AND PRACTICE ARE DRAWN.

09042 TRAUB, P.J.
    SPEAKERS DU JOUR IN INDIANA
    STATE LEGISLATURES, 15(6) (JUL 89), 16-22.
    ALTHOUGH THE 1988 ELECTION IN INDIANA WAS ANOTHER STEP
IN THE DEMOCRATIC RESURGENCE THERE, VOTERS ELECTED 50
REPUBLICANS AND 50 DEMOCRATS TO THE HOUSE OF REPRESENTATIVES.
FOLLOWING DAYS OF NEGOTIATIONS, TWO MEN BECAME SPEAKER OF
THE HOUSE OF REPRESENTATIVES. ONE WAS REPUBLICAN PAUL S.
MANNWEILER; THE OTHER, DEMOCRAT MICHAEL K. PHILLIPS.

09043 TRAUGOTT, M. W.
    CANDIDATE APPEAL IN THE 1988 PRESIDENTIAL CAMPAIGN
    ECONOMIC OUTLOOK USA, 15(2) (FAL 88), 3-7.
    WRITTEN MIDWAY THROUGH THE 1988 PRESIDENTIAL CAMPAIGN,
THIS ARTICLE ANALYSES THE CONTEST THUS FAR AND PREDICTS THAT
THE RACE WILL BE CLOSE, THE CANDIDATES ARE EVALUATED, AS
WELL AS THE MOOD OF THE ELECTORATE. THE ROLE OF ISSUES IN
THE CAMPAIGN IS EXPLORED.

09044 TRAUT, C.A.
    VOLUNTEERING AND POLITICS: A STUDY OF VOLUNTEERS AND THEIR
    ATTITUDES ON THE POLITICAL WORLD
    DISSERTATION ABSTRACTS INTERNATIONAL, 49(10) (APR 89),
    3144-A.
    VOLUNTEERISM IS CLEARLY A PUBLIC ACT THAT REALLOCATES
RESOURCES IN SOCIETY AND AFFECTS HOW GOVERNMENT AND OTHER
INSTITUTIONS RESPOND TO SOCIAL PROBLEMS. THIS STUDY FOCUSES
ON VOLUNTEERING IN THE SOCIAL SERVICES AND EXAMINES THE
INTERPRETATIONS THAT INDIVIDUALS THEMSELVES GIVE TO THEIR
VOLUNTEERISM. INTERVIEWS WITH VOLUNTEERS REVEAL THAT THEY
SEE THEIR ACTIVITIES AS NON-POLITICAL BECAUSE THEY GIVE
POLITICS A NARROW, NEGATIVE DEFINITION INVOLVING SELF-
INTEREST AND CONFLICT.

09045 TREADAWAY, D.
    IS RECYCLING THE ANSWER?
    AMERICAN CITY AND COUNTY, 104(5) (MAY 89), 40-54.
    THE U.S. ENVIRONMENTAL PROTECTION AGENCY HAS SET A
RECYCLING AND WASTE REDUCTION GOAL OF 25 PERCENT OF THE
NATION'S WASTE STREAM BY 1992. A HANDFUL OF STATES HAVE
INITIATED MANDATORY RECYCLING LAWS TO HELP MEET THIS GOAL.
ALTHOUGH RECYCLING HAS BEEN SLOW TO CATCH ON IN MANY SMALL
COMMUNITIES, RISING DISPOSAL COSTS AND SHRINKING LANDFILL

SPACE MAY PROMPT LARGE NUMBERS OF AMERICAN CITIES AND
COUNTRIES TO RECYCLE MORE OF THEIR GARBAGE IN THE NEXT
DECADE.

09046 TREADAWAY, D.
    THE BUSH AGENDA
    AMERICAN CITY AND COUNTY, 104(1) (JAN 89), 57-59.
    PRESIDENT BUSH WILL HAVE TO DO A GREAT DEAL OF FENCE
MENDING WITH LOCAL GOVERNMENT OFFICIALS. AFTER EIGHT YEARS
OF SEVERE FUNDING CUTBACKS TO LOCAL GOVERNMENTS UNDER REAGAN,
BUSH MAY HAVE A DIFFICULT TIME WOOING BACK AMERICA'S LOCAL
LEADERS. CONDITIONS UNDER REAGAN HAVE LED TO AN ATTITUDE OF
RESENTMENT AND DISTRUST TOWARD THE FEDERAL GOVERNMENT THAT
MAY BE VERY DIFFICULT TO CHANGE. BUT SOME OBSERVERS BELIEVE
THAT BUSH HAS A GOOD UNDERSTANDING OF THE PROBLEMS FACING
LOCAL LEADERS AND THAT HE WILL BE VERY WILLING TO TRY TO
REBUILD THE FEDERAL PARTNERSHIP WITH LOCAL GOVERNMENT.

09047 TREBING, H.M.
    RESTORING PURPOSEFUL GOVERNMENT: THE GALBRAITHIAN
    CONTRIBUTION
    JOURNAL OF ECONOMIC ISSUES, XXIII(2) (JUN 89), 393-411.
    THIS ARTICLE EXAMINES THE CONSEQUENCES OF TRANSPORT AND
TELECOMMUNICATIONS DEREGULATION, BENIGN NEGLECT IN ANTITRUST,
POTENTIAL FAILURES IN FINANCIAL MARKETS, AND NEGLECTED
DIMENSIONS OF SOCIAL COSTS. IN TOTAL, THESE SHORTCOMINGS
STRONGLY SUGGEST A RETURN TO MORE PURPOSEFUL GOVERNMENT
INTERVENTION. IN LIGHT OF THIS, PROFESSOR GALBRAITH'S
CONCEPTUAL FRAMEWORK, WHICH INTEGRATES GOVERNMENT IN THE
CONTEXT OF AN INDUSTRY STRUCTURE CHARACTERIZED BY GREAT
CONCENTRATIONS OF ECONOMIC POWER, BECOMES PARTICULARLY
MEANINGFUL.

09048 TRELAWNEY, C.
    VUYISILE MINI: TRADE UNIONIST, PATRIOT AND HERO
    SECHABA, 23(12) (DEC 89), 16-17.
    VUYISILE MINI, WILSON KHAYINGO AND ZINAKILE MKABA WERE
THE FIRST AFRICAN NATIONAL CONGRESS PATRIOTS TO BE HANGED BY
THE APARTHEID REGIME, NOVEMBER 6TH 1989 MARKED THE 25TH
ANNIVERSARY OF THEIR DEATHS. THIS ARTICLE IS A TRIBUTE TO
MINI AND A CALL FOR REDEDICATION TO THE STRUGGLE FOR WHICH
THESE MEN DIED.

09049 TREPCZYNSKI, S.
    WITHOUT ILLUSIONS
    POLISH PERSPECTIVES, XXXII(1) (1989), 26-28.
    THE AUTHOR LOOKS AT THE ILLUSIONS AND MYTHS THAT ARE
PRESENT IN THE FIRST DAYS OF A WAR. HE REMEMBERS THE
ILLUSIONS OF THE POLISH PEOPLE AND HOW THE TENDENCY TO BRUSH
ASIDE REALITIES BECAME A PERMANENT FEATURE OF POLISH
POLITICAL THINKING IN WORLD WAR II.

09050 TREPTOW, K.W.
    THE WINTER OF DESPAIR: JAN PALACH AND THE COLLAPSE OF THE
    PRAGUE SPRING
    UKRAINIAN QUARTERLY, XLV(1) (SPR 89), 30-47.
    ONE OF THE EVENTS THAT MARKED A TURNING POINT IN THE
PRAGUE SPRING WAS THE TRAGIC SELF-IMMOLATION OF JAN PALACH.
HIS ACT OF SELF-SACRIFICE SHOCKED THE NATION AND THE WORLD.
PALACH RESORTED TO THIS DESPERATE FORM OF POLITICAL PROTEST
IN RESPONSE TO THE GRADUAL COLLAPSE OF THE PRAGUE SPRING
FOLLOWING THE INVASION OF CZECHOSLOVAKIA BY SOVIET AND
WARSAW PACT TROOPS. HIS SUICIDE EXPRESSED THE FUTILITY OF
THE HEROIC EFFORTS OF THE CZECHOSLOVAK PEOPLE TO MAINTAIN
THEIR POLITICAL SOVEREIGNTY IN THE FACE OF FOREIGN
INTERVENTION.

09051 TRESCOTT, P.B.
    SCOTTISH POLITICAL ECONOMY COMES TO THE FAR EAST: THE
    BURTON-CHAMBERS "POLITICAL ECONOMY" AND THE INTRODUCTION
    OF WESTERN ECONOMIC IDEAS INTO JAPAN AND CHINA
    HISTORY OF POLITICAL ECONOMY, 21(3) (FAL 89), 481-502.
    A RELATIVELY UNKNOWN TEXTBOOK ON POLITICAL ECONOMY,
ORIGINALLY PUBLISHED IN EDINBURGH IN 1852, HAS ONE OF THE
FIRST WESTERN WORKS ON SOCIAL SCIENCE TRANSLATED INTO
JAPANESE AND CHINESE. IT WAS RECEIVED WITH ENTHUSIASM BY
IMPORTANT INTELLECTUALS IN BOTH COUNTRIES, WHERE IT WAS
PROBABLY MORE WIDELY READ THAN IN THE ENGLISH-SPEAKING WORLD.
THE BOOK WAS "POLITICAL ECONOMY FOR USE IN SCHOOLS AND FOR
PRIVATE INSTRUCTION," WRITTEN BY JOHN HILL BURTON AND
PUBLISHED BY WILLIAM AND ROBERT CHAMBERS.

09052 TREVOR-ROPER, H.; URBAN, G.
    AFTERMATHS OF EMPIRE: THE LESSONS OF UPHEAVALS AND
    DESTABILISATION
    ENCOUNTER, LXXIII(5) (DEC 89), 3-16.
    NO REVOLUTIONARY IDEOLOGY PRESERVES ITS FULL VIGOR FOR
LONG BECAUSE THE ESSENTIAL UNIT IN HISTORICAL CHANGE IS THE
GENERATION. THE GENERATION THAT HAS BEEN THROUGH AN
IDEOLOGICAL CRUSADE, BUILDING AN EMPIRE ON A REVOLUTIONARY
BASIS, HAS A DIFFERENT ATTITUDE TOWARDS THE WORLD THAN THE
NEXT GENERATION, # WHICH TENDS TO LOSE THE REVOLUTIONARY
PASSION. SO THE PRESENT EVAPORATION OF THE SOVIET
IDEOLOGICAL COMMITMENT TO COMMUNISM IS NOT SURPRISING. THE

DIFFICULTY IS FORECASTING WHAT WILL HAPPEN NEXT AND IF THE WEST SHOULD HASTEN THE DISINTEGRATION IN THE EAST BECAUSE IT ENCOURAGES FREEDOM OR IMPEDE IT BECAUSE IT ENCOURAGES INSTABILITY.

09053 TREZISE, P.H.
JAPAN, THE ENEMY?
BROOKINGS REVIEW, 8(1) (WIN 90), 3-13.
ON ANY RATIONAL CALCULATION, ECONOMIC COMPETITION FROM JAPAN DOES NOT THREATEN AMERICA'S NATIONAL SECURITY. IF JAPANESE GOVERNMENT AND INDUSTRY ENGAGE IN CONDUCT CONTRARY TO INTERNATIONAL RULES OR NORMS, AMPLE LEGAL, ADMINISTRATIVE, AND ECONOMIC REMEDIES ARE AVAILABLE. JAPAN'S DEMOCRACY HAS ITS WARTS, BUT IT FUNCTIONS EFFECTIVELY IN A SOCIETY THAT IS IN ALL FUNDAMENTALS FREE. "CONTAINING" JAPAN IS THE IDEA OF A JOURNALIST WHO SEES AMERICAN VULNERABILITIES THAT DO NOT EXIST. ANOTHER PACIFIC WAR? MORE REMOTE EVENTUALITIES CAN BE IMAGINED, BUT NOT READILY.

09054 TRIGGER, B.G.
HYPERRELATIVISM, RESPONSIBILITY, AND THE SOCIAL SCIENCES
CANADIAN REVIEW OF SOCIOLOGY AND ANTHROPOLOGY, 26(5) (NOV 89), 776-797.
THIS PAPER EXAMINES THE CURRENT CONTROVERSY BETWEEN POSITIVISM AND RELATIVISM IN THE SOCIAL SCIENCES, WITH SPECIAL REFERENCE TO HISTORY AND ARCHAEOLOGY. THE INFLUENCES THAT THE SOCIAL MILIEU EXERTS UPON RESEARCHERS RULE OUT TOTAL OBJECTIVITY IN THE INTERPRETATION OF DATA RELATING TO HUMAN HISTORY AND HUMAN BEHAVIOR. EVEN THE BASIC CATEGORIZATION OF DATA IS INFLUENCED BY THE PRESUPPOSITIONS OF RESEARCHERS. YET THE CONSTRAINTS IMPOSED BY EVIDENCE CREATED INDEPENDENTLY OF THE WILL OF THE RESEARCHER OFFER HOPE THAT IN THE LONG RUN THE SOCIAL SCIENCES CAN CONTRIBUTE TO THE MORE OBJECTIVE UNDERSTANDING OF HUMAN BEHAVIOR.

09055 TRIMARCHI, A.
PEKING'S LATEST SABOTAGE: "THE 10,000 BOAT ATTACK"
ASIAN OUTLOOK, 24(3) (MAY 89), 23-24.
ON APRIL 29, 1989, THE TAIWANESE DEFENSE MINISTRY ANNOUNCED THAT ITS INTELLIGENCE SOURCES HAD FINALLY OBTAINED CONCRETE EVIDENCE OF THE MAINLAND COMMUNISTS' STRATEGY TO SABOTAGE THE ISLAND. A CLASSIFIED CHINESE COMMUNIST MILITARY DOCUMENT ACQUIRED BY TAIWAN REVEALED PEKING'S PLANS TO LAUNCH A "HUMAN WAVE" OF ARMED FISHING BOATS AGAINST TAIWAN AND ITS ADJACENT ISLANDS.

09056 TRIMARCHI, A.G.
A TRIUMPH OF PERSEVERANCE! DALAI LAMA WINS NOBEL PEACE PRIZE
ASIAN OUTLOOK, 25(1) (NOV 89), 20-28.
DESPITE PEKING'S ATTEMPT TO DEPICT THE DALAI LAMA AS A POLITICAL GANGSTER, THE TIBETAN SPIRITUAL LEADER IS REVERED AS A LIVING GOD BY HIS FOLLOWERS. HIS PERSISTENT NONVIOLENT STRUGGLE AGAINST CHINESE OPPRESSION AND BRUTALITY IN HIS HOMELAND, WHERE THOUSANDS OF INNOCENT TIBETANS HAVE BEEN KILLED BY COMMUNIST TROOPS IN THE LAST FOUR DECADES, HAVE BEEN INSTRUMENTAL IN EARNING HIM A HIGH DEGREE OF RESPECT IN INTERNATIONAL CIRCLES.

09057 TRIMARCHI, A.G.
MOSCOW-PEKING RAPPROCHEMENT
ASIAN OUTLOOK, 24(1) (JAN 89), 10-11, 16.
THE SOVIET UNION AND COMMUNIST CHINA HAVE MUCH TO GAIN FROM A NORMALIZATION THAT INEVITABLY WILL TRANSCEND THE PALE OF PHILOSOPHICAL FRIENDSHIP AND IDEOLOGICAL COMMITMENT TO MARXISM AND LENINISM. THEIR COMMON INTERESTS INCLUDE REGIONAL TENSIONS, SECURITY OF THE COMMUNIST FLANKS, GREATER UNITED NATIONS COOPERATION, TECHNOLOGY TRANSFERS, AND COOPERATION IN ESPIONAGE.

09058 TRIMARCHI, A.G.
PEKING MASSACRE: COLD TERROR AT TIENANMEN
ASIAN OUTLOOK, 24(2) (MAR 89), 4-6.
THE AUTHOR DESCRIBES EVENTS IN TIENANMEN SQUARE FOLLOWING THE EMERGENCE OF LI PENG AS THE VICTOR IN THE STRUGGLE WITHIN THE TOP CHINESE LEADERSHIP AND THE IMPOSITION OF MARTIAL LAW IN THE SPRING OF 1989.

09059 TRIMARCHI, A.G.
TIENANMEN: BLAME THE VICTIMS?
ASIAN OUTLOOK, 24(4) (JUL 89), 20-24.
SOME WESTERN OBSERVERS HAVE EMBRACED THE "BLAME THE VICTIM" SYNDROME AND ARE ARGUING THAT THE STUDENTS THEMSELVES WERE LARGELY TO BLAME FOR THE TIENANMEN SQUARE MASSACRE IN JUNE 1989.

09060 TRIPATHI, D.
INDIA AND NEPAL AT LOGGERHEADS
WORLD TODAY, 45(6) (JUN 89), 91-92.
INDIA AND NEPAL ARE EMBROILED IN A DISPUTE OVER TRADE AND TRANSIT ARRANGEMENTS, BUT THE DISAGREEMENT IS NOT EXCLUSIVELY ABOUT COMMERCE. SEVERAL UNDERLYING FACTORS ARE RESPONSIBLE FOR THE SERIOUS BREAKDOWN IN THE RELATIONSHIP BETWEEN THE TWO COUNTRIES. THE INDIANS SEEM TO BE MOST

ANNOYED ABOUT A 1988 ARMS DEAL BETWEEN NEPAL AND CHINA, WHICH SOLD THE SMALL HIMALAYAN KINGDOM A NUMBER OF ANTI-AIRCRAFT GUNS, RIFLES, AND MISSILES. INDIA CLAIMS THAT THE ARMS SALE AND OTHER NEPALESE ACTIONS HAVE VIOLATED THE PEACE AND FRIENDSHIP TREATY BETWEEN THE TWO.

09061 TRIPATHI, D.
INDIA'S MALDIVES MISSION AND AFTER
WORLD TODAY, 45(1) (JAN 89), 3-4.
THE ATTEMPTED TAKE-OVER BY ARMED INVADERS OF THE TINY REPUBLIC OF MALDIVES IN NOVEMBER 1988 AND INDIA'S DECISION TO SEND ITS TROOPS TO FOIL THE BID HAVE RAISED SEVERAL IMPORTANT ISSUES. THE EPISODE HIGHLIGTED THE SECURITY CONCERNS OF SMALL, VULNERABLE STATES. IT ALSO SERVED TO INCREASE THE AWARENESS OF HOW EASILY THE STABILITY CAN BE DISTURBED IN AN AREA OF INTENSE REGIONAL AND SUPERPOWER RIVALRIES. IT SHOWED HOW UNREST IN ONE COUNTRY CAN SPILL OVER INTO ANOTHER, BECAUSE THE MERCENARY INVADERS CAME FROM SRI LANKA. MOREOVER, THE EPISODE RENEWED THE DEBATE OVER INDIA'S ROLE AS THE REGIONAL SUPERPOWER.

09062 TROFIMENKO, H.
LONG-TERM TRENDS IN THE ASIA-PACIFIC REGION: A SOVIET EVALUATION
ASIAN SURVEY, XXIX(3) (MAR 89), 237-251.
THE ARTICLE ANALYZES MANY OF THE CHANGES THAT WILL AFFECT ASIA AND THE WORLD AS IT INTERACTS WITH ASIA ON AN INCREASINGLY LARGER SCALE. SOME OF THE CHANGES AND CONDITIONS INCLUDE: THE ASIA-PACIFIC REGION IS STEADILY BECOMING THE MOST IMPORTANT ZONE IN THE WORLD; IT IS THE MOST RAPIDLY DEVELOPING REGION IN TODAY'S WORLD, IT IS LEADING THE REST OF THE WORLD IN TECHNOLOGY, IT IS THE ZONE WHERE FOUR OUT OF THE FIVE MAJOR POWER CENTERS OF THE WORLD FACE EACH OTHER, IT IS A REGION OF HIGH POPULATION GROWTH, AND ARMS RACES. MILITARY CONFLICTS, AND TENSIONS BASED ON ECONOMIC AND MILITARY IMBALANCES ALL ARE HAPPENING IN THE REGION. THE ARTICLE ALSO ANALYZES SOME OF THE SOVIET UNION'S PLANS FOR THE FUTURE OF THE REGION INCLUDING PLANS TO INCREASE TRADE AND INTERDEPENCE, INCREASE STABILITY, AND ACCELERATE THE DEVELOPMENT OF SIBERIA AND THE MARITIME PROVINCES.

09063 TROMP, B.
PARTY STRATEGIES AND SYSTEM CHANGE IN THE NETHERLANDS
WEST EUROPEAN POLITICS, 12(4) (OCT 89), 82-97.
THIS ARTICLE EXPLORES THE PERSISTANCE, OR CHANGE, OF POLITICAL PARTY SYSTEMS BY TURNING TO THE TWO GROUPS OF DETERMINANTS OF A PARTY SYSTEM. IT SUGGESTS THAT IN ORDER TO EXPLAIN SHIFTS IN THE BALANCE OF POWER, ONE MUST LOOK TO THE STRATEGIES OF STATES AND IS DETAILS THE ADVANTAGES OF DOING SO THIS ARTICLE SKETCHES THE BROAD OUTLINES AND THE GENERAL TREND OF PARTY STRATEGIES IN THE NETHERLANDS.

09064 TROYANO, T.S.
U.S. STRATEGIC FORCES UNDER A START AGREEMENT
COMPARATIVE STRATEGY, 8(2) (1989), 221-240.
THE EMERGING START AGREEMENT WILL REQUIRE REDUCTIONS IN US STRATEGIC NUCLEAR FORCES AND LIMITATIONS IN US MODERNIZATION OPTIONS. THE ARTICLE SEEKS TO ESTABLISH AN ANALYTICAL FRAMEWORK FOR ASSESSING STRATEGIC FORCE OPTIONS UNDER A START AGREEMENT. IT ANALYZES VARIOUS FORCE POSTURES AND MEASURES THEIR ABILITY TO MEET ESTABLISHED FORCE PLANNING CRITERIA. THIS CRITERIA IS COMPRISED OF ISSUES OF SURVIVABILITY, TIMING AND CONTROL, ABILITY TO PENETRATE SOVIET DEFENSES, AND THE ABILITY TO DESTROY DESIGNATED TARGETS.

09065 TRUELSON, J.A.
IMPLICATIONS FOR WHISTLEBLOWING FOR PUBLIC ADMINISTRATION EDUCATION
POLICY STUDIES REVIEW, 8(4) (SUM 89), 871-876.
WHISTLEBLOWING, OR GOING PUBLIC, IS AN ISSUE WHICH HAS RECEIVED A GREAT DEAL OF MEDIA ATTENTION AND SCHOLARLY CONSIDERATION. THE AUTHOR OF THIS ARTICLE DIVIDES WHISTLEBLOWING INTO INDIVIDUAL, ORGANIZATION, AND ENVIRONMENTAL LEVELS OF ANALYSIS. EACH LEVEL HAS ITS OWN UNIQUE CONSIDERATIONS WHICH MUST BE UNDERSTOOD SEPARATELY BEFORE THEY CAN BE UNDERSTOOD COMPREHENSIVELY. MOREOVER, THE AUTHOR ASSERTS THAT THE STUDY OF WHISTLEBLOWING FOSTERS AWARENESS OF ETHICS, PROVIDES THE SKILLS NEEDED TO EFFECTIVELY COPE WITH DISSENT, AND IMPARTS LEGAL KNOWLEDGE ABOUT THE DISCIPLINE OF PUBLIC ADMINISTRATION TO STUDENTS.

09066 TRUETT, D.B.; TRUETT, L.J.
LEVEL OF DEVELOPMENT AND THE U.S. GENERALISED SYSTEM OF PREFERENCES: MALAYSIA AND MEXICO
JOURNAL OF DEVELOPMENT STUDIES, 25(2) (JAN 89), 226-239.
THIS ARTICLE EXAMINES THE EFFECTS OF THE UNITED STATES GENERALISED SYSTEM OF PREFERENCES (GSP) ON THE EXPORTS OF MEXICO AND MALAYSIA. MEXICO AND MALAYSIA WERE SELECTED BECAUSE DIFFERENCES IN INDUSTRIALISATION BETWEEN THEM WOULD HIGHLIGHT POSSIBLE PROBLEMS CONNECTED WITH THE COMPETITIVE NEED PROVISIONS OF THE US GSP PROGRAMME. THE FINDINGS ARE GENERALLY CONSISTENT WITH OTHER GSP STUDIES THAT COVERED

DIFFERENT COUNTRIES, COMMODITIES, AND TIME PERIODS AND EMPLOYED VARIOUS EMPIRICAL MODELS. HOWEVER, THE RESULTS FOR MEXICO DO NOT LEND SUPPORT TO THE RECENTLY ADVANCED PROPOSITION THAT HIGH-INCOME LDCS ARE THE PRIMARY BENEFICIARIES OF THE US GSP.

09067 TRYMAN, M.
WAS JESSE JACKSON A THIRD PARTY CANDIDATE IN 1988?
BLACK SCHOLAR, 20(1) (JAN 89), 19-29.
THE PURPOSE OF THE PAPER IS TO DEVELOP THE THESIS THAT JESSE JACKSON'S 1984 AND 1988 CAMPAIGNS WERE ESSENTIALLY THOSE OF A THIRD PARTY CANDIDATE ATTEMPTING TO GAIN LEGITIMACY INSIDE THE DEMOCRATIC PARTY. IT DEMONSTRATES HOW THE RAINBOW COALITION TOOK ON AND STILL HAVE MANY OF THE ASPECTS OF A THIRD PARTY, PARTICULARLY WITH REGARDS TO THE ISSUES OF 1988. IT ALSO EXAMINES LITERATURE ON THIRD PARTIES AND PRESIDENTIAL ELECTIONS IN US POLITICS AND THEIR CHARACTERISTICS.

09068 TSAL, W.H.
SOCIAL CHANGES UNDER THE IMPACTS OF ECONOMIC TRANSFORMATION IN TAIWAN: FROM INDUSTRIALIZATION TO MODERNIZATION DURING THE POST-WORLD WAR II ERA
SOUTHERN CALIFORNIA LAW REVIEW, 24(2) (SUM 89), 24-41.
THIS ARTICLE EXAMINES THE PROCESS OF CHANGE IN TAIWAN DURING THE PAST FORTY YEARS UNDER RAPID INDUSTRIALIZATION AND ECONOMIC GROWTH. DISTINCTIONS AMONG THE THREE CONCEPTS OF INDUSTRIALIZATION, ECONOMIC GROWTH, AND MODERNIZATION ARE OUTLINED. CHANGES IN TAIWAN'S ECONOMY, DEMOGRAPHY, CLASS STRUCTURE, HEALTH CARE, EDUCATION, WELFARE SYSTEM, AND POLITICAL PARTICIPATION ARE DISCUSSED. BASED ON TAIWAN'S EXPERIENCE, A MODEL OF INTERLOCKING RELATIONSHIPS BETWEEN MACRO AND MICRO LEVELS OF CHANGE IS PRESENTED.

09069 TSAREVSKI, N.
THE BALKANS - A ZONE FREE OF NUCLEAR AND CHEMICAL ARMS
PEACE AND THE SCIENCES, 1 (1989), 61-67.
THE IDEA FOR A NUCLEAR-FREE BALKANS HAS SUPPORTED AND APPROVED BY THE USSR AND THE REST OF THE MEMBER COUNTRIES OF THE WARSAH TREATY AS WELL AS BY A NUMBER OF OTHER COUNTRIES, PEACE MOVEMENTS, PUBLIC FIGURES AND CHAMPIONS OF PEACE FROM ALL OVER THE WORLD. THE UNITED STATES AND NATO, HOWEVER, WHO WISH TO RETAIN THEIR NUCLEAR ARMS AND BASES IN THIS REGION HAVE DECLARED THEIR OPPOSITION TO THE ABOVE IDEA. FROM THE BALKAN COUNTRIES BULGARIA, ROMANIA AND GREECE ARE TAKING AN ACTIVE PART IN THE PROCESS TO CREATE THE ZONE. JUGOSLAVIA SUPPORTS IN ESSENCE THE IDEA FOR A NUCLEAR-FREE BALKANS. TURKEY IS STILL IGNORING THE QUESTION OF CREATING A NUCLEAR-FREE ZONE ON THE BALKANS, CONSIDERING IT ALL BUT OUTSIDE THE COMPETENCE OF THE BALKAN COUNTRIES AND RELATED TO THE SOLUTION OF THE PROBLEM GLOBALLY.

09070 TSEBELIS, G.
THE ABUSE OF PROBABILITY IN POLITICAL ANALYSIS: THE ROBINSON CRUSOE FALLACY
AMERICAN POLITICAL SCIENCE REVIEW, 83(1) (MAR 89), 77-92.
THE DECISION TO STAY AT HOME WHEN YOU HAVE NO UMBRELLA AND RAIN IS PROBABLE IS AN APPROPRIATE PROBLEM FOR DECISION THEORY. THE DECISION TO SPEED WHEN YOU ARE IN A HURRY AND THE POLICE MIGHT BE PATROLLING IS A GAME AGAINST A RATIONAL OPPONENT. TREATING THE LATTER LIKE A PROBLEM FOR DECISION THEORY IS THE ROBINSON CRUSOE FALLACY. IT IS QUITE COMMON AND LEADS TO INCORRECT CONCLUSIONS. IF THE GAME HAS NO PURE STRATEGY EQUILIBRIUM, CHANGES IN THE PAYOFFS TO A PLAYER AFFECT NOT THAT PLAYER'S STRATEGY BUT THE STRATEGY OF THE OPPONENT IN EQUILIBRIUM. FOR EXAMPLE, MODIFYING THE SIZE OF THE PENALTY DOES NOT AFFECT THE FREQUENCY OF CRIME COMMITMENT AT EQUILIBRIUM, BUT RATHER THE FREQUENCY OF LAW ENFORCEMENT. EXAMPLES OF THIS FALLACY OCCUR IN REGULATION, INTERNATIONAL ECONOMIC SANCTIONS, AND ORGANIZATION THEORY AND STEM FROM INAPPROPRIATE USE OF THE CONCEPT OF PROBABILITY.

09071 TSENG, O.
PRAGMATIC AND FLEXIBLE
FREE CHINA REVIEW, 39(7) (JUL 89), 63-65.
TAIWAN'S PARTICIPATION IN THE 1989 ASIAN DEVELOPMENT BANK MEETING WAS A REFLECTION OF ITS WILLINGNESS TO BE MORE FLEXIBLE IN CONDUCTING ITS FOREIGN RELATIONS. FOLLOWING LENGTHY DEBATES, THE GOVERNMENT DECIDED TO SEND A DELEGATION TO THE MEETING IN PEKING, EVEN THOUGH IT MIGHT BE INTERPRETED BY SOME AS VIOLATING THE OFFICIAL "THERE NO'S" POLICY TOWARD COMMUNIST CHINA: NO CONTACT, NO NEGOTIATION, AND NO COMPROMISE.

09072 TSENG, O.
SAVE THAT OZONE!
FREE CHINA REVIEW, 39(6) (JUN 89), 57-59.
IN RESPONSE TO GROWING CONCERN OVER THE EROSION OF UPPER ATMOSPHERIC OZONE, TAIWAN IS MOVING TO CONTROL THE EMISSIONS OF CHLOROFLUOROCARBONS AND HALONS AND TO EVENTUALLY PHASE OUT THE USE OF THESE CHEMICALS. IN ADDITION, TAIWAN IS SEEKING TO BECOME A PARTY TO THE MONTREAL PROTOCOL ON SUBSTANCES THAT DEPLETE THE OZONE LAYER.

09073 TSENG, O.
TIME FOR NEW BANKS
FREE CHINA REVIEW, 39(11) (NOV 89), 44-47.
MANY TAIWAN INVESTORS WHO HAVE LONG PLANNED ON ENTERING THE BANKING BUSINESS AS SOON AS A LIBERALIZED BANKING LAW WAS ENACTED NOW FACE THE POSSIBILITY OF HAVING THEIR DREAMS DASHED BY SEVERE QUALIFICATION REQUIREMENTS SET BY THE MINISTRY OF FINANCE. THE REVISED BANKING LAW, PASSED IN JULY 1989, WILL LIBERALIZE THE INDUSTRY IN SEVERAL IMPORTANT WAYS. BUT THE REQUIREMENTS OF THE NEW LAW ENCOUNTERED VEHEMENT CRITICISM DURING A SERIES OF PUBLIC HEARINGS HELD IN THE SUMMER OF 1989.

09074 TSENG, O.
UPGRADING THE BANKS
FREE CHINA REVIEW, 39(1) (JAN 89), 12-17.
THE GOVERNMENT OF TAIWAN IS TRYING TO LIBERALIZE ITS BANKING INDUSTRY BY OPENING IT TO PRIVATE INVESTMENT AND BY PROVIDING NATIONAL TREATMENT FOR FOREIGN BANKS OPERATING IN TAIWAN. THE GOVERNMENT HOPES TO INJECT NEEDED COMPETITION INTO THIS SECTOR AND THUS MAKE BANKING SERVICES MORE EFFICIENT AND DIVERSE. BUT IMPLEMENTING CHANGE AND ENSURING EFFICIENCY ARE DIFFICULT. WHILE THERE IS CAUSE FOR OPTIMISM ABOUT THE EVENTUAL SUCCESS OF BANKING LIBERALIZATION, THE PROCESS PROMISES TO BE COMPLEX.

09075 TSENG, O.
URGENT ISSUES AT HAND
FREE CHINA REVIEW, 39(8) (AUG 89), 26-29.
THE AUTHOR DISCUSSES THE MAJOR ISSUES CONFRONTING TAIWAN'S NEWLY-APPOINTED PREMIER, LEE HUAN.

09076 TSU-YI, C.
A LEGACY OF VIRTUE AND DETERMINATION
FREE CHINA REVIEW, 39(2) (FEB 89), 8-13.
THE AUTHOR, WHO WAS DEPUTY SECRETARY-GENERAL TO TAIWAN'S PRESIDENT CHIANG CHING-KUO, ASSESSES SOME OF THE LATE PRESIDENT'S PERSONAL AND POLITICAL ACHIEVEMENTS.

09077 TSUGUIO, I.
POLITICAL CORRUPTION AND THE BUSINESS ESTABLISHMENT
JAPAN ECHO, XVI(3) (AUT 89), 47-50.
DURING THE PAST YEAR, THE RECRUIT COMPANY HAS COME UNDER ATTACK FOR PROVIDING POLITICAL FUNDS ON A GRAND SCALE. AT THE HEART OF THE AFFAIR ARE THE HUGE AMOUNTS OF FUNDING JAPANESE POLITICIANS NEED TO SUPPORT THEIR ACTIVITIES. THE BEST WAY TO PREVENT THIS TYPE OF SCANDAL WOULD BE TO SLASH THE COST OF CAMPAIGNING AND OTHER POLITICAL ACTIVITIES, THEREBY ELIMINATING THE DEMAND FOR MASSIVE DONATIONS. BUT REFORM OF THIS NATURE IS DIFFICULT TO IMPLEMENT. GIVEN THAT COSTLY POLITICKING AND ELECTIONEERING IS LIKELY TO REMAIN A FACT OF LIFE FOR SOME TIME TO COME, WAYS FOR POLITICIANS TO RAISE FUNDS WITHOUT OPENING THE DOOR TO CORRUPTION ARE URGENTLY NEEDED.

09078 TSUNEKAWA, K.
DEPENDENCY AND LABOR POLICY: THE CASE OF THE MEXICAN AUTOMOTIVE INDUSTRY
DISSERTATION ABSTRACTS INTERNATIONAL, 50(3) (SEP 89), 785-A.
THE AUTHOR EXAMINES INTERACTIONS AMONG TRANSNATIONAL CORPORATIONS, GOVERNMENT, AND LABOR IN THE MEXICAN AUTOMOTIVE INDUSTRY DURING 1964 TO 1988. THE CONTRAST BETWEEN THE AUTOMOTIVE INDUSTRY CORPORATIONS' OBJECTIVES AND THEIR ACTUAL ACHIEVEMENTS REVEALS THAT THEIR POWER DID NOT ALWAYS LEAD TO THE REALIZATION OF THEIR GOALS. IN ORDER TO UNDERSTAND THIS PUZZLING PHENOMENON, THE AUTHOR INTRODUCES THE CONCEPT OF STATE STRUCTURE, WHICH INCLUDES (1) THE RULING COALITION AND ITS BASIC POLICY GOALS, (2) ORGANIZATIONAL CONFIGURATIONS OF GOVERNMENT INSTITUTIONS, AND (3) PATTERNS OF GOVERNMENT-SOCIETY INTERACTIONS.

09079 TSURUMI, Y.
U.S.-JAPANESE RELATIONS: FROM BRINKMANSHIP TO STATESMANSHIP
WORLD POLICY JOURNAL, 7(1) (WIN 89), 1-33.
THIS ARTICLE EXAMINES THE RELATIONSHIP BETWEEN THE UNITED STATES AND JAPAN AND DISCUSSES THE POSSIBILITY THAT THE GROWING NEONATIONALIST SENTIMENT ON BOTH SIDES OF THE PACIFIC COULD PUSH U.S.-JAPANESE RELATIONS ONTO A CONFRONTATIONAL PATH. REVISIONISM WHICH HAS HELPED TO CREATE THE IMAGE THAT AMERICA'S TRADE PROBLEMS ARE LARGELY OF JAPANESE MAKING IS LABELED AS WRONG-HEADED THINKING, THE TWO SIDES ARE NOW APPROACHING THE POINT WHERE ECONOMIC BRINKMANSHIP SUBSTITUTES FOR CAREFULLY PLANNED POLICY COORDINATION. THIS PAPER SUGGESTS AN AGENDA FOR STRENGTHENING THE INTERNATIONALIST AND DEMOCRATIC FORCES IN JAPAN BY REDUCING THE POTENTIAL FOR EMOTIONALLY LADEN BILATERAL DISPUTES AND BY PUTTING U.S.-JAPANESE RELATIONS INTO A LARGER GLOBAL CONTEXT THAT ALLOWS BOTH SIDES TO RECOGNIZE THEIR COMMON INTERESTS AND SUPPRESS THEIR WORST FEARS OF EACH OTHER.

09080 TUBBESING, C.
    CALLING ON CONGRESS IN '89
    STATE LEGISLATURES, 15(1) (JAN 89), 24-26.
        IN 1989, THE PRESSURES BUILDING TO REDUCE THE FEDERAL
    BUDGET DEFICIT ARE INVITING FURTHER INVASIONS OF STATE
    REVENUE SOURCES AND MORE DETERMINED ATTACKS ON FUNDING OF
    IMPORTANT STATE AND LOCAL PROGRAMS. FOR THE LONG-TERM,
    FISCAL ISSUES WILL HAVE THE MOST CRITICAL IMPACT ON STATE-
    FEDERAL RELATIONS.

09081 TUCKER, H.J.
    LEGISLATIVE CALENDARS AND WORKLOAD MANAGEMENT IN TEXAS
    THE JOURNAL OF POLITICS, 51(3) (AUG 89), 631-645.
        THERE IS A WELL-DEVELOPED NORMATIVE MODEL OF HOW STATE
    LEGISLATURES OUGHT TO USE CALENDARS TO MAKE THE MANAGEMENT
    OF THEIR WORKLOADS MORE EFFICIENT. STATE LEGISLATURES THAT
    FOLLOW THE NORMATIVE MODEL IDENTIFY MORE AND LESS IMPORTANT
    BILLS. PRESUMABLY, MAJOR AND MINOR BILLS ARE TREATED
    DIFFERENTLY--BUT ARE THEY? THIS STUDY DESEGREGATES THE
    AGENDA OF THE TEXAS LEGISLATURE INTO UNIMPORTANT, LESS
    IMPORTANT, AND MORE IMPORTANT BILLS AS DEFINED BY BILL
    PLACEMENT ON CALENDARS. THERE ARE SYSTEMATIC DIFFERENCES IN
    THE WAY BILLS OF VARYING IMPORTANCE ARE TREATED. MOREOVER,
    THE DIFFERENCES ARE CONSISTENT WITH THE CONTENTION THAT
    CALENDARS CAN FACILITATE THE MORE EFFICIENT MANAGEMENT OF
    LEGISLATIVE WORKLOADS.

09082 TUCKER, W.
    THE ECONOMICS OF PUBLIC HOUSING.
    AMERICAN SPECTATOR, (NOV 89), 26-29.
        THIS ARTICLE EXAMINES THE PRESENT APPROACH TO GOVERNMENT
    MANAGEMENT OF FUNDS FOR PUBLIC HOUSING. IT POINTS OUT THE
    PROBLEMS CAUSED BY MISUSE OF FUNDS, LOCATION OF PUBLIC
    HOUSING, (A LOCAL PROBLEM), AND THE FAILURE OF PAST PROGRAMS
    OF URBAN RENEWAL. IT ADVOCATES GETTING THE COUNTRY OUT OF
    THE EXPENSIVE, LONG-TERM BUSINESS OF BUILDING HOUSING AND
    INTO THE FAR MORE SENSIBLE STRATEGY OF ISSUING RENT VOUCHERS.

09083 TUDORAN, D.
    TESTIMONY BEFORE THE HOUSE BY DORIN TUDORAN
    EAST EUROPEAN REPORTER, 4(1) (WIN 89), 57.
        DORIN TUDORAN, A ROMANIAN JOURNALIST, SPEAKS OF THE
    DECLINE OF ROMANIA AND THE CONTINUING ATROCITIES COMMITTED
    BY THE CEAUSESCU REGIME. HE OUTLINES THE UBIQUITOUS POWER OF
    THE SECRET POLICE, THE MUZZLING OF THE PRESS, THE DECLINE OF
    ROMANIAN CULTURE, AND INFRINGEMENTS ON RELIGIOUS LIFE. HE
    CONCLUDES BY CALLING ON THE WEST TO "ISOLATE CEAUSESCU, BUT
    NOT THE ROMANIANS."

09084 TULIN, M.
    LOVE AND LITIGATION
    SOJOURNERS, 18(10) (NOV 89), 19.
        THE WEBSTER DECISION OF THE US SUPREME COURT CAUSED
    IMMEDIATE EUPHORIA FOR SUPPORTERS OF THE PRO-LIFE MOVEMENT.
    HOWEVER, THE AFTERMATH OF THE DECISION PRESENTS PRO-LIFERS
    WITH A SERIES OF SIGNIFICANT CHALLENGES. NOT THE LEAST OF
    THESE IS THE SIMPLE FACT THAT THE BATTLE FOR LIFE WILL NEVER
    BE COMPLETELY WON THROUGH LITIGATION; EVEN IF A HUMAN LIFE
    AMENDMENT WERE PASSED, ABORTIONS WOULD STILL OCCUR. CHANGE
    MUST COME IN THE CONDITIONS THAT LEAD SO MANY
    DISENFRANCHISED WOMEN TO SEEK ABORTIONS.

09085 TULIS, J. K.
    THE RHETORICAL PRESIDENCY
    PRINCETON UNIVERSITY PRESS, LAWRENCEVILLE, NJ, 1988, 208.
        MODERN PRESIDENTS REGULARLY APPEAL "OVER THE HEADS" OF
    CONGRESS TO THE PUBLIC AT LARGE TO GENERATE SUPPORT FOR
    PUBLIC POLICIES. TWENTIETH-CENTURY PRESIDENTS SPEAK DIRECTLY
    TO THE PEOPLE MORE OFTEN THAN DID THEIR NINETEENTHCENTURY
    PREDECESSORS AND DEFEND THEMSELVES PUBLICLY AND PROMOTE
    POLICY INITIATIVES NATIONWIDE. JEFFREY TULIS CONTENDS THAT
    THIS COMMONLY RECOGNIZED SHIFT TO A "RHETORICAL PRESIDENCY"
    IS MUCH MORE SIGNIFICANT THAN PREVIOUSLY SUPPOSED. HE ARGUES
    THAT POPULAR LEADERSHIP BY PRESIDENTS IS NOT SIMPLY A
    LOGICAL CONSTITUTIONAL DEVELOPMENT BUT IS INSTEAD A
    FUNDAMENTAL TRANSFORMATION OF THE CONSTITUTIONAL ORDER AND
    OF THE ENTIRE POLITICAL SYSTEM.

09086 TULLIO, G.
    SMITH AND RICARDO ON THE LONG-RUN EFFECTS OF THE GROWTH OF
    GOVERNMENT EXPENDITURE, TAXATION, AND DEBT: IS THEIR
    THEORY RELEVANT TODAY?
    HISTORY OF POLITICAL ECONOMY, 21(4) (WIN 89), 723-736.
        WHAT SMITH AND RICARDO HAD TO SAY ABOUT THE INFLUENCE OF
    TAXATION ON WAGES AND ABOUT THE CONSEQUENCE OF THE GROWTH OF
    GOVERNMENT EXPENDITURE ON PROFIT RATE, CAPITAL ACCUMULATION,
    AND EMPLOYMENT HAS ATTRACTED LITTLE ATTENTION. THEIR THEORY
    AND THE CONCLUSIONS DERIVED FROM IT ARE DISMISSED TODAY ON
    THE GROUNDS THAT SOME OF THEIR ASSUMPTIONS ARE NO LONGER
    VALID. HOWEVER, THIS PAPER ARGUES THAT THEIR CONTRIBUTION
    CONTAINS A NUMBER OF ELEMENTS THAT ARE STILL RELEVANT IN
    UNDERSTANDING THE CONSEQUENCES OF THE GROWTH OF GOVERNMENT
    EXPENDITURE THAT HAS OCCURRED IN EUROPE IN RECENT DECADES
    AND THAT THEIR MAIN CONCLUSION IS STILL VALID.

09087 TULLY, J.
    WITTGENSTEIN AND POLITICAL PHILOSOPHY: UNDERSTANDING
    PRACTICES OF CRITICAL REFLECTION
    POLITICAL THEORY, 17(2) (MAY 89), 172-204.
        THE AIM OF THE ARTICLE IS TO DRAW ATTENTION TO A
    WIDESPREAD, BUT MISTAKEN CONVENTION OF CONTEMPORARY
    POLITICAL THOUGHT: THAT OUR WAY OF POLITICAL LIFE IS FREE
    AND RATIONAL ONLY IF IT IS FOUNDED ON SOME FORM OF CRITICAL
    REFLECTION. IT SEEKS TO ACCOMPLISH ITS AIM BY A SURVEY OF
    TWO WELL-KNOWN PRACTICES OF CRITICAL REFLECTION. IT
    CONCLUDES THAT OFTEN DISCUSSION ABOUT WHICH SORT OF CRITICAL
    REFLECTION IS ESSENTIAL TO POLITICAL FREEDOM AND REASON
    NEGLECTS THE UNDERLYING QUESTION OF WHETHER SOME FORM OF
    CRITICAL REFLECTION IS NECESSARY AT ALL.

09088 TUOBIN, Z.
    CHINA'S FOREIGN TRADE POLICY
    BEIJING REVIEW, 32(42) (OCT 89), 13-16.
        CHINA HAS ALWAYS UPHELD A FOREIGN TRADE POLICY BASED ON
    EQUALITY AND MUTUAL BENEFIT. IN LIGHT OF DOMESTIC AND
    INTERNATIONAL CIRCUMSTANCES, CHINA HAS DEVELOPED A SET OF
    PRINCIPLES TO PROMOTE ITS FOREIGN TRADE. ESPECIALLY SINCE
    THE THIRD PLENARY SESSION OF THE ELEVENTH CENTRAL COMMITTEE
    OF THE CPC IN 1978, CHINA HAS STRESSED ITS EAGERNESS TO
    DEVELOP ECONOMIC COOPERATION WITH ALL COUNTRIES, IN
    ACCORDANCE WITH THIS POLICY.

09089 TURIANSKY, L.C.
    MIDDLE EAST: NEW YEAR IN THE OCCUPIED PALESTINIAN
    TERRITORIES
    WORLD TRADE UNION MOVEMENT, 3 (1988), 17-20.
        THIS ARTICLE EXAMINES THE SITUATION OF THE OCCUPIED
    PALESTINIAN TERRITORIES. A VISIT TO THE REFUGEE CAMPS
    DETAILS THE MISERABLE LIVING CONDITIONS OF CAMPS THAT HAVE
    EXISTED SINCE 1948. THE IMPACT OF THE DELIBERATE POLICY OF
    STRANGULATION OF THE ARAB ECONOMY BY THE ISRAELI GOVERNMENT
    IS DESCRIBED AS WELL AS THE ARBITRARINESS OF THE MILITARY
    COURTS FOR THE DETAINEES, INTERNATIONAL SOLIDARITY IS CALLED
    FOR.

09090 TURITS, M.
    FREEDOM AND CIVILITY: NORBERTO BOBBIO'S POLITICAL ETHICS
    SOCIALISM AND DEMOCRACY, (FAL 89), 49-80.
        THIS ARTICLE EXAMINES THE WRITING AND PHILOSOPHY OF
    NORBERTO BOBBIO, ITALY'S MOST INFLUENTIAL LIVING POLITICAL
    THEORIST. IT ATTEMPTS TO SHOW, FIRST BY OUTLINING THE
    LIBERAL SOCIALIST PROGRAM BOBBIO ELABORATES IN "WHICH
    SOCIALISM?" AND "THE FUTURE OF DEMOCRACY", AND SECOND, BY
    TRACING HIS STRATEGIES FOR AVOIDING THE PROBLEM OF FREEDOM
    IN KANT AND ROUSSEAU, IS THAT IT IS PRECISELY BOBBIO'S NEO-
    MODERATE IMPASS THAT HAS LED HIM TO ELABORATE A POST-
    POLITICAL "ETHICS" OF PUBLIC LIFE, A METHODOLOGY FOR THOUGHT
    AND ACTION AFTER THE DISAPPOINTMENTS OF REFORMIST AS WELL AS
    REVOLUTIONARY POLITICS.

09091 TURNER, G.
    THE INTERNAL EUROPEAN MARKET AND ITS IMPACT ON SCIENCE AND
    RESEARCH
    AUSSEN POLITIK, 40(2) (1989), 173-181.
        THE DYNAMISM OF INDUSTRY DEPENDS ON THE QUALITY AND
    QUANTITY OF SCIENCE, ON THE UNIVERSITIES' TURNING OUT TOP
    EXECUTIVES, AND ON RESEARCH AND DEVELOPMENT. BY 1992 THE
    INTERNAL EUROPEAN MARKET IS TO BECOME REALITY. WITH THE
    SINGLE EUROPEAN ACT THE ROLES OF EDUCATION, SCIENCE AND
    RESEARCH WERE DEALT WITH FOR THE FIRST TIME; THE TREATIES OF
    ROME HAD MADE NO REFERENCE TO THEM. THE MINISTERS-PRESIDENT
    OF THE STATES OF THE FEDERAL REPUBLIC OF GERMANY, HOWEVER,
    CITING FEDERALISM, HAVE SOUGHT CONSTRAINTS ON THE EUROPEAN
    COMMUNITY IN THE CULTURAL AND EDUCATIONAL SPHERE. THE AUTHOR
    HERE ADVOCATES COOPERATION BETWEEN EUROPEAN SCIENCE AND
    INDUSTRY IN THE AREA OF RESEARCH AND DEVELOPMENT. IT IS
    CLEAR THAT THE FACT OF EUROPEAN UNITY COMPELS COOPERATION,
    AND THE DYNAMISM OF SCIENCE AND INDUSTRY WILL DEMAND
    CONCESSIONS OF THE POLITICIANS.

09092 TURNER, R.S.
    LAND USE POLITICS IN FLORIDA COMMUNITIES: A POLITICAL
    ECONOMY ANALYSIS
    DISSERTATION ABSTRACTS INTERNATIONAL, 50(4) (OCT 89),
    1080-A.
        INTEREST GROUPS, SUCH AS BUSINESSES AND RESIDENTIAL
    INTERESTS, COMPETE FOR THE ATTENTION OF GOVERNMENT IN ORDER
    TO AFFECT LOCAL LAND USE AND PLANNING POLICIES. BASED ON A
    COMPARATIVE STUDY OF URBAN AREAS IN FLORIDA, THIS
    DISSERTATION CONCLUDES THAT COMMUNITIES MOST OFTEN ADOPT
    TRADITIONAL DEVELOPMENTAL LAND USE POLICIES AND ADOPT MORE
    POLITICALLY-RISKY POLICIES ONLY IN SITUATIONS OF INTEREST
    GROUP COMPETITION. COMMUNITIES DOMINATED BY BUSINESS/PRO-
    GROWTH INTERESTS RELY ON TRADITIONAL LAND USE POLICIES AND
    DO NOT EMBRACE INNOVATIVE APPROACHES THAT TEND TO RESTRICT
    GROWTH.

09093 TURNER, T.
   KAYAPO PLAN MEETING TO DISCUSS DAMS
   CULTURAL SURVIVAL QUARTERLY, 13(1) (1989), 20-22.
      AN UNPRECEDENTED ATTEMPT BY AMAZONIAN INDIANS TO USE
   PEACEFUL LEGAL AND POLITICAL MEANS TO RESIST THE DESTRUCTION
   OF THEIR FOREST HABITAT AND THE EXPROPRIATION OF THEIR
   TRADITIONAL LANDS IS UNDER WAY IN CENTRAL BRAZIL. THE
   INDIANS PLAN TO FORM A PERMANENT ORGANIZATION THAT WILL WORK
   WITH BRAZILIAN AND FOREIGN SUPPORTERS COMMITTED TO SAVING
   THE FOREST, ITS ANIMALS, AND ITS NATIVE PEOPLES.

09094 TUROK, I.
   EVALUATION AND UNDERSTANDING IN LOCAL ECONOMIC POLICY
   URBAN STUDIES, 26(6) (DEC 89), 587-606.
      RECENT EVALUATIVE STUDIES OF LOCAL ECONOMIC POLICY HAVE
   EMPHASISED THE MEASUREMENT OF POLICY IMPACTS AND
   COSTEFFECTIVENESS ABOVE ALL ELSE. MORE EFFORT COULD USEFULLY
   BE MADE TO UNDERSTAND THE MECHANISMS BY WHICH POLICY EFFECTS
   ARE PRODUCED AND THE CIRCUMSTANCES WHICH CONDITION THEIR
   EFFECTIVENESS. THE PAPER OUTLINES A SIMPLE CONCEPTUAL
   FRAMEWORK TO HELP EXPLAIN IN BROAD TERMS WHY LOCAL
   INDUSTRIAL POLICIES ARE OR ARE NOT EFFECTIVE AT CREATING
   EMPLOYMENT. THE FRAMEWORK IS ILLUSTRATED WITH EXAMPLES DRAWN
   FROM AN INITIATIVE IN LONDON. THIS INVOLVED THE PROVISION OF
   FINANCIAL ASSISTANCE TO LOCAL FIRMS, BUT DID NOT PROVE VERY
   SUCCESSFUL AT CREATING OR SECURING JOBS, PARTLY BECAUSE
   CIRCUMSTANCES WERE UNFAVOURABLE AND THE PROBLEMS DEEP-SEATED.
   THE IMPLICATION IS THAT FOR LOCAL POLICIES TO BE EFFECTIVE
   IN THESE CONDITIONS WIDER-RANGING AND MORE CAREFULLY
   TARGETED INTERVENTIONS ARE REQUIRED.

09095 TUSHNET, M.
   RIGHTS: AN ESSAY IN INFORMAL POLITICAL THEORY
   POLITICS AND SOCIETY, 17(4) (DEC 89), 403-452.
      THIS ESSAY OFFERS A PERSPECTIVE ON QUESTIONS OF HUMAN
   RIGHTS, DRAWING FROM SOCIOLOGY, LAW, AND POLITICAL THEORY.
   THE AUTHOR DISCUSSES THE ORIGINS OF THE MODERN CONCEPT OF
   RIGHTS, AS WELL AS WHAT HAS BEEN CALLED THE " CRITIQUE OF
   RIGHTS," A MOVEMENT WITHIN CRITICAL LEGAL STUDIES THAT
   CHALLENGES THE EFFICACY OF APPEALS TO RIGHTS BY SUBORDINATE
   GROUPS. THEN HE RESPONDS TO MINORITY AND FEMINIST CRITIQUES
   OF THE CRITIQUE OF RIGHTS AND CONSIDERS A POSSIBLE
   RECONSTRUCTION OF THE IDEA OF RIGHTS THAT DEVELOPS THE
   CONCEPT OF GROUP RIGHTS TO PROVIDE A CONCEPTUAL FOUNDATION
   FOR A PROGRAM OF POLITICAL AND ECONOMIC DECENTRALIZATION.

09096 TUTUY, J.
   THE DRUG TRAFFICKERS' BID FOR POWER
   WORLD MARXIST REVIEW, 32(11) (NOV 89), 71-75.
      IT APPEARS THAT THE PROLIFERATION OF NARCOTICS CANNOT BE
   CHECKED IF THE UNITED STATES FAILS TO REVISE ITS CURRENT
   TWOFACED AND UNPRINCIPLED POLICY AND TO ADMIT ITS SHARE OF
   THE BLAME FOR THE PRESENT SITUATION. PRESIDENT BUSH IS
   CONSIDERING THE "OPTION OF SENDING THE GREEN BERETS TO
   CONFRONT NARCO-TRAFFICKERS IN THE ANDEAN COUNTRIES". HOWEVER,
   ONE CANNOT REMAIN CAPTIVE TO OBSOLETE THOUGHT PATTERNS AND
   THE DOGMA OF THE CONSERVATIVE RIGHT, WHICH SEES THE ROOT OF
   ALL DOMESTIC PROBLEMS IN THE PLOTS "DIABOLICAL FORCES" ARE
   HATCHING SOMEWHERE OUTSIDE THE UNITED STATES.

09097 TUTUY, J.
   THE MILITARY AND DEMOCRACY
   WORLD MARXIST REVIEW, 32(8) (AUG 89), 76-78.
      THIS ARTICLE DISCUSSES THE ROLE OF THE ARMED FORCES IN
   THE COUNTRIES OF THE LATIN AMERICAN CONTINENT. THE PERUVIAN
   EXPERIENCE FROM 1968-1975 IS EXPLORED. THE RESULTS OF
   PENTAGON INTERVENTION ARE EXAMINED AND A CALL IS MADE TO GET
   THE ARMY OUT OF ITS "GHETTO."

09098 THIGHT, C.
   THE POLITICAL ECONOMY OF THE NATIONAL DEFENSE STOCKPILE
   POLICY STUDIES REVIEW, 8(4) (SUM 89), 774-799.
      FEW GOVERNMENT PROGRAMS DISPLAY BOTH THE POLITICAL
   SALABILITY AND THE VULNERABILITY TO POLITICAL MANIPULATION
   THAT CHARACTERIZE THE NATIONAL DEFENSE STOCKPILE. THIS
   ARTICLE ANALYZES THE WAYS IN WHICH CHANGING INSTITUTIONAL
   CONSTRAINTS HAVE SHAPED THE NATURE AND EXTENT OF PAROCHIAL
   MANIPULATION OF THE NATIONAL DEFENSE STOCKPILE OVER MORE
   THAN HALF A CENTURY OF U.S. STOCKPILING EXPERIENCE. FOCUSING
   ON THE ROLES OF CONGRESS AND THE EXECUTIVE BRANCH IN
   ESTABLISHING THE RELEVANT INSTITUTIONAL RULES AND
   ACCOMMODATING CONSTITUENT PRESSURES WITHIN THE FRAMEWORK OF
   THOSE RULES, THIS ARTICLE EXAMINES THE USE AND PERPETUATION
   OF THE STRATEGIC MATERIALS STOCKPILE FOR PERSONAL POLITICAL
   GAIN.

09099 THINAM, J.W.
   CONTROVERSIAL ARMS SALES TO SAUDI ARABIA: AN AMERICAN
   TRAGEDY IN POSSIBLY FOUR ACTS
   AMERICAN-ARAB AFFAIRS, (29) (SUM 89), 47-55.
      THIS ARTICLE EXPLORES THE POSSIBILITY OF PRESIDENT BUSH
   PROPOSING TO CONGRESS AN ARMS SALE TO SAUDI ARABIA WHICH
   WILL HAVE BEEN TARGETED AS CONTROVERSIAL. IT EXAMINES THE
   CONGRESSIONAL SUPPORT OF A STRONG U.S. SECURITY-ASSISTANCE

ROLE IN SAUDI ARABIA, AND ALSO FOLLOWS THE HISTORY OF THE
CONTROVERSY STARTING IN 1976. REPERCUSSIONS OF THIS
ASSISTANCE ON U.S. ISRAELI RELATIONS IS DETAILED. THE
ARTICLE EXAMINES THE RECORD, THE HOUSE FACTOR, THE SENATE,
AND IDENTIFIES THE OPPOSITION, THE SUPPORT BASE, AND THE
TARGET GROUP. IT CONCLUDES THAT IF THE SALE OF ARMS IS
CONTROVERSIAL THEN THERE WILL BE NO WINNERS, WHATEVER THE
OUTCOME.

09100 TWINING, C.H.
   SITUATION IN CAMBODIA
   DEPARTMENT OF STATE BULLETIN (US FOREIGN POLICY), 88(2141)
   (DEC 88), 31-33.
      DIRECTOR OF THE OFFICE OF VIETNAM, LAOS AND CAMBODIA
   AFFAIRS CHARLES TWINING DISCUSSES THE CONTINUED VIETNAMESE
   OCCUPATION OF CAMBODIA AND THE DIPLOMATIC EFFORTS TO RESOLVE
   THE SITUATION. VIETNAM HAS RECENTLY ANNOUNCED THAT THEY WILL
   WITHDRAW 50,000 TROOPS FROM CAMBODIA, BUT TWINING URGES A
   CAUTIOUS APPRACH TO ENSURE THAT THE KHMER ROUGE DOES NOT
   REGAIN POWER IN CAMBODIA. HE OUTLINES POLICY OBJECTIVES FOR
   THE US, ASEAN, AND THE NATIONS INVOLVED TO ENSURE A PEACEFUL
   TRANSITION TO A FREE AND INDEPENDENT CAMBODIA.

09101 TWINING, D.C.
   THE POLITICS OF HEALTH CARE REFORM: HEALTH PLANNING FOR
   THE POOR IN CLEVELAND, 1960-1982
   DISSERTATION ABSTRACTS INTERNATIONAL, 49(7) (JAN 89),
   1925-A.
      DESPITE THE GOOD INTENTIONS OF GREAT SOCIETY LEGISLATION
   TO ASSIST PEOPLE BY ENCOURAGING AND FINANCIALLY SUPPORTING
   LOCAL PLANNING AND CONTROL OF SOCIAL PROGRAMS, WHAT ACTUALLY
   HAPPENED WAS THE FURTHER ADVANCE OF A SYSTEM OF REGIONAL
   HIERARCHIES UNDER WHICH HEALTH CARE IN AN AREA MOVED UP
   THROUGH A HIERARCHY TO A MEDICAL SCHOOL AT THE APEX, MAKING
   IT THE MOST SIGNIFICANT FORCE IN ATTEMPTING TO PATTERN A
   HEALTH CARE SYSTEM FOR THE POOR. WITHOUT STRUCTURAL CHANGE
   IN THE DELIVERY SYSTEM, THERE COULD BE NO REAL IMPROVEMENT
   IN THE HAPHAZARD WAY WE CARE FOR THE HEALTH NEEDS OF THE
   POOR.

09102 THOMEY, M.J.
   THE DEBT CRISIS AND LATIN AMERICAN AGRICULTURE
   JOURNAL OF DEVELOPING AREAS, 23(4) (JUL 89), 545-566.
      TO WHAT DEGREE DID SHORTFALLS IN AGRICULTURAL PRODUCTION
   AND EXPORTS CAUSE THE CURRENT DEBT CRISIS IN LATIN AMERICA,
   AND BY HOW MUCH HAS AGRICULTURE'S RECENT PERFORMANCE HELPED
   RESOLVE THAT CRISIS? THIS PAPER WILL ATTEMPT TO ANSWER THESE
   QUESTIONS BY INVESTIGATING THE DEBT PROBLEM'S MACROECONOMIC
   CONTEXT AND ITS RELATIONSHIP WITH THE AGRICULTURAL SECTOR.
   IT WILL ARGUE THAT AGRICULTURE'S ROLE IN CAUSING THE CRISIS
   WAS DISTINCTLY SECONDARY, GIVEN THE OVERALL STRENGTH OF LONG-
   TERM PRODUCTION TRENDS. MORE IMPORTANTLY, IN SPITE OF
   EXCHANGE RATE DEVALUATIONS AND OTHER EFFORTS AT CHANGING
   INCENTIVES TO PRODUCTIVE ACTIVITIES, AGRICULTURE, ALONG WITH
   OTHER KEY SECTORS, HAS LANGUISHED SINCE THE ONSLAUGHT OF THE
   CRISIS. THIS PAPER'S EXPLANATION FOR THAT SITUATION MOVES
   BEYOND THE FAMILIAR CULPRIT OF LOW SUPPLY ELASTICITIES, TO
   HIGHLIGHT FOUR OTHER EXPLANATORY FACTORS. FIRST, THE
   AUSTERITY PROGRAMS HAVE REDUCED THE AVAILABILITY OF CREDIT
   (IN REAL TERMS) AND IMPORTANT AGRICULTURAL INPUTS SUCH AS
   FERTILIZERS. SECOND, THE DECLINE IN GOVERNMENT SUBSIDIES HAS
   FURTHER REDUCED THE SECTOR'S OUTPUT. THIRD, AGRICULTURAL
   PRICES FELL SIGNIFICANTLY ON WORLD MARKETS, A FACT THAT
   LESSENED THE EFFECT OF THE POSITIVE PRODUCTION INCENTIVES
   FROM DEVALUATIONS. FINALLY, THE INCREASE IN INFLATION IN THE
   REGION HAS SIGNIFICANTLY ADDED TO UNCERTAINTY, WHILE TENDING
   TO BLUR RELATIVE PRICE CHANGES. THE ANALYSIS ALSO CAUTIONS
   THAT THE LONG-TERM EFFICIENCY GAINS FROM "GETTING THE PRICES
   RIGHT" RISK BEING OVERWHELMED BY THE APPARENT REDUCTION IN
   INVESTMENT IN THE REGION'S AGRICULTURE.

09103 TYERS, R.; ANDERSON, K.
   PRICE ELASTICITIES IN INTERNATIONAL FOOD TRADE: SYNTHETIC
   ESTIMATES FROM A GLOBAL MODEL
   JOURNAL OF POLICY MODELING, 11(3) (FAL 89), 315-344.
      GOVERNMENT INTERVENTION, PARTICULARLY IN AGRICULTURAL
   COMMODITY MARKETS, IS FREQUENTLY JUSTIFIED ON THE GROUNDS
   THAT IT FAVORABLY AFFECTS THE TERMS OF TRADE. IN THIS PAPER
   AN ESTABLISHED DYNAMIC SIMULATION MODEL OF SEVEN FOOD
   COMMODITY MARKETS IS USED TO PROVIDE SYNTHETIC ESTIMATES OF
   THE ELASTICITIES OF NET EXPORT DEMAND AND IMPORT SUPPLY ON
   WHICH SUCH JUSTIFICATIONS REST. ESTIMATES ARE PRESENTED FOR
   BOTH THE SHORT AND LONG RUNS, AND THE EFFECTS OF MARKET-
   INSULATING AGRICULTURAL POLICIES ON THESE ELASTICITIES ARE
   INVESTIGATED. THE RESULTS CAST DOUBT ON THE PROPOSITION THAT
   ANY INDIVIDUAL ECONOMY HAS STRONG MONOPOLY OR MONOPSONY
   POWER IN INTERNATIONAL FOOD MARKETS IN ANYTHING OTHER THAN
   THE VERY SHORT RUN. BUT EFFECTIVE COOPERATION BY GROUPS OF
   EXPORTING COUNTRIES, SUCH AS THE CAIRNS GROUP OF
   "NONSUBSIDIZING" AGRICULTURAL EXPORTERS, ALONG WITH THE
   UNITED STATES OR EVEN THE EC, COULD YIELD SUBSTANTIAL MARKET
   POWER TO THOSE GROUPS IN BOTH THE SHORT AND LONG RUNS.
   NEVERTHELESS, THE MAJOR PART OF THE POWER SUCH GROUPS MIGHT
   WIELD STEMS FROM SELF-IMPOSED DOMESTIC-MARKET-INSULATING

AGRICULTURAL POLICIES IN THE REST OF THE WORLD.

09104 TYLER, T.R.; CASPER, J.D.; FISHER, B.
MAINTAINING ALLEGIANCE TOWARD POLITICAL AUTHORITIES: THE
ROLE OF PRIOR ATTITUDES AND THE FAIR USE OF PROCEDURES
AMERICAN JOURNAL OF POLITICAL SCIENCE, 33(3) (AUG 89),
629-652.
THIS STUDY EXAMINES THE IMPACT OF EXPERIENCE WITH THE
CRIMINAL JUSTICE SYSTEM ON DEFENDANT ATTITUDES TOWARDS LEGAL
AUTHORITIES, LAW, AND GOVERNMENT. THE FOCUS IS ON THE EXTENT
TO WHICH PARTICULAR EXPERIENCES AFFECT MORE GENERAL
ATTITUDES TOWARD THE POLITICAL SYSTEM IN WHICH COURTS ARE
EMBEDDED. THE DATA COME FROM A PANEL STUDY OF FELONY
DEFENDANTS IN THREE CITIES. THE CONCLUSION IS THAT THE
FAIRNESS OF THE EXPERIENCE HAS A SUBSTANTIAL INFLUENCE ON
THE LESSONS CITIZENS LEARN FROM THEIR ENCOUNTERS WITH
GOVERNMENT INSTITUTIONS.

09105 TYLER, W. P. N.
THE BEISAN LANDS ISSUE IN MANDATORY PALESTINE
MIDDLE EASTERN STUDIES, 25(2) (APR 89), 123-162.
THIS ARTICLE FOCUSES ON THE BEISAN LANDS WHERE JEWISH
INTERESTS WERE AGAIN DISAPPOINTED DESPITE HAVING BEEN
ENCOURAGED BY GOVERNMENT TO BELIEVE THAT, AFTER THE NEEDS OF
THE EXISTING OCCUPANTS HAD BEEN MET, EXTENSIVE AREAS WOULD
BE MADE AVAILABLE FOR JEWISH UTILIZATION. IT CASTS
CONSIDERABLE LIGHT ON BRITAIN'S VIEW OF ITS OBLIGATIONS
REGARDING LAND, ON BRITISH PRIORITIES AND ATTITUDES TO
DEVELOPMENT, AND ALSO HIGHLIGHTS THE CONTRASTS INVOLVED IN
THE CLASH OF ARAB AND JEWISH CULTURES, ASPIRATIONS,
LIFESTYLES AND ATTITUDES TOWARD LAND AND ITS UTILIZATION. IT
FURTHER PERMITS AN EVALUATION OF THE ZIONIST OPINION
REGARDING THE ALLOCATION OF THE BEISAN LANDS.

09106 TYN, M.
FREE THE ECONOMY AND BRING BACK DEMOCRACY
FAR EASTERN ECONOMIC REVIEW, 141(34) (AUG 88), 19.
TYN MYINT-U, A SENIOR UN OFFICIAL GIVES POLICY
SUGGESTIONS FOR BURMA'S UNCERTAIN FUTURE. HE STATES THAT
UNLESS STEPS ARE TAKEN IMMEDIATELY TO TRANSFER POWER TO A
REPRESENTATIVE AND RESPONSIBLE GOVERNMENT AND REVERSE THE
ECONOMIC AND POLITICAL SITUATION, PRESENT CONDITIONS COULD
LEAD TO WIDESPREAD FAMINE, TOTAL CIVIL WAR, AND THE
UNDERMINING OF THE NATIONAL SECURITY OF BURMA. HE OUTLINES
POLITICAL AND ECONOMIC REFORMS DEEMED NECESSARY TO REVERSE
THE TREND.

09107 TYNES, S.R.
TURNING POINTS IN SOCIAL SECURITY: EXPLAINING LEGISLATIVE
CHANGE, 1935-1985
DISSERTATION ABSTRACTS INTERNATIONAL, 49(9) (MAR 89),
2833-A.
THE AUTHOR USES ARCHIVAL DOCUMENTS, THE CONGRESSIONAL
RECORD, CONGRESSIONAL HEARINGS REPORTS, AND SECONDARY
SOURCES TO PIECE TOGETHER THE SOCIAL AND POLITICAL HISTORY
OF THE SOCIAL SECURITY PROGRAM. THEN SHE ASSESSES THE
HISTORICAL RECORD IN LIGHT OF THE PLURALIST, NEO-MARXIST,
AND NEO-WEBERIAN THEORETICAL FRAMEWORKS TYPICALLY UTILIZED
TO STUDY POLITICAL CHANGE.

09108 TZE-CHI, C.
WACL/APACL PRESIDENT ADDRESSES PALAU CONFERENCE
ASIAN OUTLOOK, 25(1) (NOV 89), 1-2.
RECENT COMMUNIST ATTEMPTS AT REFORM HAVE LED TO MORE
CHAOS THAN STABILITY. THE FAILURES OF SOVIET PERESTROIKA AND
CHINESE REFORM REFLECT THE TREMENDOUS CRISES FACING ALL
COMMUNIST REGIMES. THE REASONS FOR THE FAILURE LIE IN BASIC
POLITICAL AND ECONOMIC FLAWS IN THE SYSTEM.

09109 UEKI, Y.
POLITICS OF ISSUE LINKAGE AND DELINKAGE: AN ANALYSIS
JAPANESE-SOVIET NEGOTIATIONS
DISSERTATION ABSTRACTS INTERNATIONAL, 49(10) (APR 89),
3149-A.
THE AUTHOR STUDIES ISSUE LINKAGE AND DELINKAGE IN THREE
CASES OF DIRECT NEGOTIATION BETWEEN JAPAN AND THE SOVIET
UNION: THE NORMALIZATION OF DIPLOMATIC RELATIONS IN 1955-56
(THE SOVIET FISHERY-POLITICAL LINKAGE), THE SUMMIT
NEGOTIATIONS OF 1973 (THE JAPANESE TERRITORIAL-ECONOMIC
LINKAGE), AND THE FISHERIES NEGOTIATIONS OF 1977 (THE SOVIET
FISHERY-TERRITORIAL LINKAGE AND JAPANESE DELINKAGE ATTEMPTS).

09110 UGURU, J.
MILITARY MAD DOGS RULE
NEW AFRICAN, (APR 88), 9-10.
THIS ARTICLE REPORTS ON MILITARY ABUSE IN YORUBALAND. IT
FOCUSES ON THE ARBITUARY ARREST AND DETENTION OF CHIEF
ABIOLA'S FAMILY AS A SPOTLIGHT OF PUBLICITY ON A WHOLE RANGE
OF CASES IN WHICH THE MILITARY ABUSE THE RULE OF LAW AND
BROWBEAT INNOCENT CIVILIANS SIMPLY BECAUSE THEY HAVE THE
POWER AND WEAPONS TO DO SO, EXAMPLES OF ABUSE ARE GIVEN.

09111 UGURU, J.
NIGERIA: UNDER THE "DEMOCRATIC" CARPET

NEW AFRICAN, (259) (APR 89), 40.
THE ARTICLE BRIEFLY OUTLINES THE ONGOING ATROCITIES
COMMITTED BY NIGERIAN POLICE AND THE EFFORTS OF THE CIVIL
LIBERTIES ORGANIZATION (CLO) AND OTHER GROUPS TO STOP
ILLEGALITIES. CONDITIONS IN NIGERIAN PRISONS ARE TERRIBLE
YET THE POLICE OFTEN MOUNT RAIDS TO ARREST PEOPLE ON
VAGRANCY CHARGES SO THEY CAN EXTORT MONEY FROM THEM. THOSE
WITH MONEY BUY THEIR FREEDOM, WHILE THE POOR ARE GIVEN
TRUMPED UP CHARGESM DUMPED INTO PRISONS AND FORGOTTEN. THE
CLO AND OTHER ORGANIZATIONS ARE FIGHTING TO END THESE ABUSES,
BUT CORRUPTION IS HIGH AND LITTLE PROGRESS IS BEING MADE.

09112 UGURU, J.
ONLY MILLIONAIRES NEED APPLY
NEW AFRICAN, (264) (SEP 89), 10-12.
THIS ARTICLE EXPLORES EVIDENCE THAT NIGERIA IS RETURNING
TO THE OLD SYSTEM WHERE WEALTH BUYS VOTES AND THE POOR ARE
ELIMINATED. THE REGISTRATION OF NIGERIA'S PARTIES WHICH WILL
BE ALLOWED TO CAMPAIGN FOR CIVILIAN RULE IS FOUND TO BE A
BUREAUCRATIC NIGHTMARE. IT EXAMINES THE REQUIREMENTS OF THE
NATIONAL ELECTION COMMISSION WHICH ARE SO COMPLEX THAT ALL
BUT THE WEALTHIEST PARTIES WILL BE ELIMINATED.

09113 UGURU, J.
OUR OWN ROBBEN ISLAND
NEW AFRICAN, (256) (JAN 89), 16.
TWO MONTHS AFTER NIGERIA'S ITA-OKO, A SECRET DETENTION
CAMP, WAS OFFICIALLY ANNOUNCED CLOSED, SECURITY ACTIVITIES
AROUND THE PENAL ENCLAVE FUELED SPECULATION THAT IT HAD BEEN
REOPENED.

09114 UHLANER, C.
RATIONAL TURNOUT: THE NEGLECTED ROLE OF GROUPS
AMERICAN JOURNAL OF POLITICAL SCIENCE, 33(2) (MAY 89),
390-422.
THE ARTICLE EXAMINES A PROBLEM THAT HAS PLAGUED RATIONAL
CHOICE THEORIES: ACCOUNTING FOR INDIVIDUAL PARTICIPATION IN
COLLECTIVE ACTION. THE AUTHOR ARGUES THAT VOTERS ACT NOT IN
ISOLATION BUT AS A PART OF GROUPS WITH SHARED INTERESTS.
WHILE INDIVIDUALS STILL VOTE BECAUSE OF CONSUMPTION BENEFITS
ARISING FROM THE ACT OF VOTING, SOME OF THESE CONSUMPTION
BENEFITS ARE PROVIDED BY GROUP LEADERS OUT OF COLLECTIVE
BENEFITS RECEIVED BY THE GROUP IN RETURN FOR ITS VOTES. DATA
FROM RECENT OFF-YEAR ELECTIONS ARE SHOWN TO BE CONSISTENT
WITH THE MODEL.

09115 UHLANER, C.
TURNOUT IN RECENT AMERICAN PRESIDENTIAL ELECTIONS
POLITICAL BEHAVIOR, 11(1) (MAR 89), 57-80.
THE WELL-NOTED DECLINE IN THE PARTICIPATION OF AMERICANS
IN PRESIDENTIAL ELECTIONS SINCE THE EARLY SIXTIES REVERSED
IN THE 1984 ELECTION, ALTHOUGH ONLY SLIGHTLY. AN IMPROVED
"NATIONAL MOOD" APPEARS TO HAVE CONTRIBUTED LITTLE TO
INCREASING TURNOUT. HOWEVER, THE GAP IN PARTICIPATION
BETWEEN THE WEALTHIER AND POORER WIDENED, WHILE THAT BETWEEN
MEN AND WOMEN NARROWED AND REVERSED DIRECTION, AND BELONGING
TO A GROUP ASSOCIATED WITH AN IDENTITY AFFECTED
PARTICIPATION MORE POWERFULLY. TAKEN TOGETHER, THESE
FINDINGS INDICATE SHIFTS IN PATTERNS OF TURNOUT
CORRESPONDING TO SHIFTS IN THE LINES OF POLITICIZED
INTERESTS. ANALYSIS OF THE PARTICIPATION OF BLACKS FINDS
LITTLE EVIDENCE FOR ELECTORAL MOBILIZATION BY THE RAINBOW
COALITION IN 1984.

09116 UHLANER, C.J.
"RELATIONAL GOODS" AND PARTICIPATION: INCORPORATING
SOCIABILITY INTO A THEORY OF RATIONAL ACTION
PUBLIC CHOICE, 62(3) (SEP 89), 253-286.
THEORETICAL EXPLANATIONS OF WHY RATIONAL INDIVIDUALS
WOULD PARTICIPATE IN POLITICS REMAIN UNSATISFACTORY. THIS
ADDRESSES THE PROBLEM BY DEVELOPING AND ANALYZING MODELS
WHICH INCLUDE AMONG CITIZENS' PAYOFFS "RELATIONAL GOODS,"
OBJECTIVES WHICH DEPEND UPON INTERACTIONS AMONG PERSONS. THE
MODELS PREDICT MORE PARTICIPATION THAN DO THE STANDARD
APPROACHES. FOR EXAMPLE, UNDER SOME CIRCUMSTANCES PERSONS
WILL BE MORE LIKELY TO ACT IF THEY BELIEVE OTHERS WILL ACT,
CONTRARY TO FREE-RIDER LOGIC. MORE IMPORTANTLY, CONDITIONS
ARE IDENTIFIED UNDER WHICH LEADERS COULD INCREASE MASS
ACTIVITY. THUS, A MODEL IS PROVIDED OF "MOBILIZATION" IN
TERMS OF THE PREFERENCES AND DECISIONS OF A RATIONAL
INDIVIDUAL.

09117 UHLANER, C.J.; CAIN, B.E.; KIEWIET, D.R.
POLITICAL PARTICIPATION OF ETHNIC MINORITIES IN THE 1980S
POLITICAL BEHAVIOR, 11(3) (SEP 89), 195-232.
CURRENTLY POLITICAL PARTICIPATION, ESPECIALLY VOTER
REGISTRATION AND TURNOUT, VARIES SUBSTANTIALLY WITH
ETHNICITY. BLACKS AND NON-HISPANIC WHITES PARTICIPATE AT
ROUGHLY EQUAL RATES, WHILE LATINOS AND ASIAN-AMERICANS ARE
SUBSTANTIALLY LESS ACTIVE. THIS VARIATION MAY BE THE DIRECT
PRODUCT OF CULTURAL FACTORS, OR IT MAY REFLECT DIFFERENCES
IN THE DISTRIBUTION OF VARIOUS DETERMINANTS OF PARTICIPATION,
MOST NOTABLY EDUCATION, CITIZENSHIP, AND AGE. USING DATA
COLLECTED IN 1984 ON SAMPLES OF CALIFORNIA'S BLACK, LATINO,

ASIAN-AMERICAN, AND NON-HISPANIC WHITE POPULATIONS, HE CONCLUDE THAT SUCH VARIABLES FULLY ACCOUNT FOR LOWER LATINO PARTICIPATION RATES. EVEN WITH THESE CONTROLS, HOWEVER, ASIAN-AMERICANS REMAIN LESS LIKELY TO VOTE. BECAUSE ETHNIC GROUP CONSCIOUSNESS IS ONE OF THE VARIABLES RELATED TO ACTIVITY, IT CONCLUDES THAT ETHNICITY DOES HAVE AN INDIRECT EFFECT ON PARTICIPATION AS A BASIS FOR MOBILIZATION. IN ADDITION, IT ESTABLISHS THAT NONCITIZENS ENGAGE IN NONELECTORAL ACTIVITIES, AND HE PROJECT FUTURE POLITICAL PARTICIPATION RATES OF LZTINOS AND ASIANAMERICANS UNDER SEVERAL SCENARIOS.

09118 ULC, O.
CZECHOSLOVAKIA: REALISTIC SOCIALISM?
CURRENT HISTORY, 541 (NOV 89), 389-392, 401-404.
CZECHOSLOVAKIA HAS BECOME AN ANACHRONIS. IT IS A POST-TOTALITARIAN HOLDOVER SURROUNDED BY THREE MODERNIZING ONE-PARTY STATES AND TWO PLURALISTIC DEMOCRACIES. BUT IT IS UNLIKELY THAT CZECHOSLOVAKIA, WITH ITS DEMOCRATIC TRADITION, WILL REMAIN OUT OF STEP FOR VERY LONG

09119 ULLMAN, R.
THE COVERT FRENCH CONNECTION
FOREIGN POLICY, (75) (SUM 89), 3-33.
THE ARTICLE EXAMINES THE US-FRENCH MILITARY RELATIONSHIP. ON THE SURFACE, THERE WAS LITTLE OR NO COOPERATION BETWEEN THE TWO NATIONS WITH REGARDS TO NUCLEAR WEAPONS; HOWEVER, THERE WAS A SIGNIFICANT AMOUNT OF COVERT COOPERATION ON A VARIETY OF ISSUES RANGING FROM TESTING TO MINUTARIZATION. THE ARTICLE EXPLORES THE DEVELOPMENT OF THESE COVERT RELATIONS AND ANALYZES THEIR IMPLICATIONS WHICH INCLUDE THE FRENCH AGREEMENT TO PLACE THEIR NUCLEAR WEAPONS UNDER NATO COMMAND IN EVENT OF WAR.

09120 UM, KHATHARYA
CAMBODIA IN 1988: THE CURVED ROAD TO SETTLEMENT
ASIAN SURVEY, XXIX(1) (JAN 80), 73-80.
THE ARTICLE EXAMINES THE CURVED, OFTEN SERPENTINE ROAD TO RESOLUTION OF THE DECADE-OLD CONFLICT IN CAMBODIA. 1988 SAW SIGNIFICANT MEETINGS BETWEEN THE RESISTANCE COALITION IN CAMBODIA, VIETNAM, AND OTHER NATIONS. BOTH MOSCOW AND BEIJING HAVE STEPPED UP THEIR EFFORTS TO ENCOURAGE A RESOLUTION OF THE CONFLICT. THE MAIN IMPEDIMENT TO PROGRESS REMAINS THE ROLE OF CAMBODIA'S ERSTWHILE LEADERS, THE KHMER ROUGE. THE UN, MOST ASEAN NATIONS, VIETNAM, AND THE LEADER OF THE LARGEST RESISTANCE FACTION, PRINCE SIHANOUK, HAVE ALL STRIDENTLY DEMANDED THE DISBANDMENT OF THE KHMER ROUGE AS A VITAL PRECONDITION TO CONFLICT RESOLUTION. THE KHMER ROUGE, INCREASINGLY SQUEEZED OUT OF THE DIPLOMATIC SCENE HAVE RETALIATED BY TAKING CONTROL OF SIZABLE PORTIONS OF THE COUNTRYSIDE. 1988 SAW SOME PROGRESS TOWARDS PEACE, BUT MUCH REMAINS TO BE DONE.

09121 UMPLEBY, S.A.
STRATEGIES FOR REGULATING THE GLOBAL ECONOMY
FUTURES, 21(6) (DEC 89), 585-592.
RECENT WORK IN THE SCIENCE OF CYBERNETICS HAS IDENTIFIED FOUR SEPARATE STRATEGIES FOR REGULATING COMPLEX SYSTEMS COMPOSED OF THINKING PARTICIPANTS. USING THESE STRATEGIES AS A FOUNDATION, THIS ARTICLE REVIEWS THE HISTORY OF GLOBAL DEVELOPMENT, SUMMARIZES CURRENT CONCERNS, AND THEN IDENTIFIES SEVERAL POSSIBLE COURSES OF ACTION FOR REGULATING A GLOBAL ECONOMY.

09122 UNDERWOOD, J.
THE WORLD BANK'S RESPONSE TO THE DEVELOPING COUNTRY DEBT CRISIS
CONTEMPORARY POLICY ISSUES, VII(2) (APR 89), 50-65.
THE WORLD BANK HAS RESPONDED TO WHAT IT HAS PERCEIVED AS TWO DEBT CRISES. THE FIRST IS THE HIGHLY PUBLICIZED CRISIS IN THE MIDDLE-INCOME, HEAVILY INDEBTED COUNTRIES--MAINLY THOSE IN LATIN AMERICA. THE SECOND HAS AFFECTED A SET OF ABOUT TWENTY MUCH POORER AFRICAN COUNTRIES. IN THE CASE OF THE HEAVILY INDEBTED, MIDDLE INCOME COUNTRIES, THE WORLD BANK FIRST RESPONDED WITH ITS SPECIAL PROGRAM OF ACTION IN 1983. UNDER THE 1985 BAKER PLAN, THE WORLD BANK HAS ALMOST MET ITS GOAL OF INCREASING ITS GROSS DISBURSEMENTS TO THESE COUNTRIES BY FIFTY PERCENT. THE BANK HAS RESPONDED TO THE SECOND CRISIS THROUGH ITS SPECIAL PROGRAM OF ACTION FOR AFRICA AND HAS COORDINATED ITS OWN CONCESSIONAL INTERNATIONAL DEVELOPMENT AGENCY LENDING WITH AID FROM OTHER OFFICIAL CREDITORS AND DONORS.

09123 UNGAR, S. J.
PRESSING FOR A FREE PRESS
FOREIGN POLICY, (77) (WIN 89), 132-153.
THIS ARTICLE SUGGESTS THAT THE U.S. GOVERNMENT HAS OFTEN FAILED TO RECOGNIZE THE FUNDAMENTAL ROLE OF A FREE PRESS IN BUILDING AND SUSTAINING DEMOCRACIES ELSEWHERE IN THE WORLD. IT ALSO SUGGESTS THAT A FREE PRESS MAY BE MORE EFFECTIVE IN ACHIEVING CHANGE IN AN OPPRESSIVE SYSTEM THAN AN OPPOSITION PARTY. IT ILLUSTRATES THIS WITH EXAMPLES FROM AFRICA, PANAMA, NICARAGUA, KENYA, CHILE, IRAN AND POLAND. IT URGES THE U.S. AND IT'S ALLIES TO AVOID HYPOCRISY IN THIS AREA, AND ALSO TO

RAISE ISSUES OF PRESS FREEDOM ROUTINELY IN INTERNATIONAL FORUMS AND TO BE A STRONG FACTOR IN AMERICAN FOREIGN POLICY

09124 UNGERER, H.
THE EUROPEAN MONETARY SYSTEM AND THE INTERNATIONAL MONETARY SYSTEM
JOURNAL OF COMMON MARKET STUDIES, XXVII(3) (MAR 89), 231-248.
THE AUTHOR REVIEWS THE EUROPEAN MONETARY SYSTEM (EMS) EXPERIENCE AND QUESTIONS WHETHER IT CAN BE APPLIED TO THE INTERNATIONAL MONETARY SYSTEM. HE ALSO DISCUSSES THE RELATIONSHIP BETWEEN THE EMS EXCHANGE-RATE-MECHANISM CURRENCIES AND THE U.S. DOLLAR. HE CONCLUDES THAT THE ACHIEVEMENTS OF THE EMS DO NOT SUGGEST THAT A SYSTEM OF STABILIZED EXCHANGE RATES WOULD WORK SATISFACTORILY ON A WORLDWIDE SCALE. A HIGH DEGREE OF ECONOMIC POLICY COORDINATION, ALONG WITH MONETARY POLICY COORDINATION, WOULD BE NEEDED ON AN INTERNATIONAL LEVEL.

09125 UPDIKE, J.
ON NOT BEING A DOVE
COMMENTARY, 87(3) (MAR 89), 22-30.
THE AUTHOR RECALLS THE REACTIONS OF A FEW AMERICAN AUTHORS TO US INVOLVEMENT IN VIETNAM AND WHY HE FELT THE USA COULD NOT ABDICATE ITS RESPONSIBILITY THERE.

09126 UPTON, G.
THE COMPONENTS OF VOTING CHANGE IN ENGLAND 1983-1987
ELECTORAL STUDIES, 8(1) (APR 89), 59-74.
THE PAPER PRESENTS AN ANALYSIS OF THE CHANGES IN THE VOTING PATTERNS OF 512 ENGLISH CONSTITUENCIES BETWEEN THE GENERAL ELECTIONS OF 1983 AND 1987. THE AIM OF THE ANALYSIS IS TO OBTAIN REASONABLY ACCURATE ESTIMATES OF THE VARIOUS COMPONENTS OF CHANGE. THESE COMPONENTS INCLUDE: NATIONAL CHANGE, PREVIOUS ELECTION EFFECT, GEOGRAPHICAL EFFECT, INTERVENING BY-ELECTION EFFECT, INCUMBENCY EFFECT, GENDER EFFECT, AND LOCAL EFFECT. GEOGRAPHY, INCUMBENCE, BY-ELECTIONS AND GENDER WERE ALL SHOWN TO HAVE A STATISTICALLY SIGNIFICANT EFFECT ON CONSTITUENCY CHANGE.

09127 UPTON, G.H.
THE CONCEPT OF PUBLIC SERVICE ETHIC AS A DIFFERENTIATING FACTOR BETWEEN PUBLIC AND PRIVATE PROFESSIONALS: CONSTRUCT DEVELOPMENT AND APPLICATION
DISSERTATION ABSTRACTS INTERNATIONAL, 50(6) (DEC 89), 1801-A.
THE AUTHOR DEFINES PUBLIC SERVICE ETHIC AS A VALUE SYSTEM THAT REPRESENTS A PERSON'S DEDICATION TO SERVICE, TO SOCIETY, AND TO A BELIEF IN THE REGIME VALUES OF EQUALITY, EQUITY, AND JUSTICE. HE TESTS THIS DEFINITION THROUGH A SURVEY THAT MEASURES CAREER IDEALS, PERSONAL VALUES, AND ETHICS; VIEW OF THE WORLD AND VIEW OF SELF; PROFESSIONALISM; OCCUPATIONAL VALUES; AND A BELIEF IN REGIME VALUES. THE TEST SAMPLE CONSISTED OF MPA AND MBA STUDENTS ENROLLED IN TEN UNIVERSITIES IN TEXAS.

09128 URBAN, G.
THE PARADOX OF TRUTH-TELLING
ENCOUNTER, LXXIII(4) (NOV 89), 31-33.
GLASNOST IS HAVING SOME INTRIGUING SIDE EFFECTS. THE FIRST CASUALTY HAS BEEN SOVIET PROPAGANDA. THE SECOND IS THE SOVIET AND EAST EUROPEAN PUBLIC'S IMAGE OF THE WESTERN WORLD. FORMERLY, MANY CITIZENS IN COMMUNIST COUNTRIES BELIEVED THAT THE WEST WAS A KIND OF "CELESTIAL CITY" WHERE LIFE WAS HEAVENLY COMPARED TO THEIR OWN CITIES. BUT NOW THE AVERAGE COMMUNIST CITIZEN REALIZES THAT IMAGES OF A CRIME-RIDDEN NEW YORK CITY, A SLUMMY GLASGOW, OR A RACIST FRANCE CAN NO LONGER BE ASCRIBED TO COMMUNIST PROPAGANDA ALONE.

09129 URBAN, G.R. (ED.)
CAN THE SOVIET SYSTEM SURVIVE REFORM?
JOHN SPIERS PUBLISHING, BRIGHTON, SUSSEX, GB, 1988, 320.
THIS VOLUME BY A PANEL OF SEVEN EXPERTS EXAMINES TWO CRUCIAL QUESTIONS: (1) IS THE SOVIET SYSTEM OPEN TO FUNDAMENTAL REFORM AND (2) ARE GORBACHEV AND HIS COLLEAGUES GENUINE REFORMERS?

09130 URBAN, L.K.
AUTONOMY UNDER SOVIET INSTITUTIONAL CONSTRAINTS: EXTERNAL INFLUENCES ON HUNGARIAN AND EAST GERMAN ECONOMIC IDEAS AND PERFORMANCE
DISSERTATION ABSTRACTS INTERNATIONAL, 49(10) (APR 89), 3149-A.
THE AUTHOR EXPLORES THE QUESTION OF IF AND HOW NATIONAL AUTONOMY AND ECONOMIC PERFORMANCE AFFECT EACH OTHER. HE COMPARES HUNGARY'S MARKET-BASED ECONOMIC MECHANISM AND ITS EXPOSURE TO GLOBAL INFLUENCES WITH EAST GERMANY'S CONTINUED RELIANCE ON A CENTRALIZED PLANNING SYSTEM THAT IS SYNCHRONIZED WITH INTRA-BLOC ECONOMIC INTEGRATION. THE YEARS 1980-85 ARE USED FOR THE COMPARISON.

09131 URBAN, M.E.
CENTRALIZATION AND ELITE CIRCULATION IN A SOVIET REPUBLIC
BRITISH JOURNAL OF POLITICAL SCIENCE, 19(1) (JAN 89), 1-23.

CENTRAL CONTROL OVER PERSONNEL PLACEMENT IN THE CENTRAL
CONTROL OVER PERSONNEL PLACEMENT IN THE SOVIET UNION ARE
REASONABLY ACCURATE FOR THE FULL DATA SET BUT FIT THE DATA
SOVIET UNION (THE NOMEKLATURA SYSTEM) IS WIDELY (THE
NOMENKLATURA SYSTEM) IS REGARDED AS THE COMPLEMENT TO THE
CENTRALIZATION OF SUBSTANTIVE POLICY MAKING AND
IMPLEMENTATION. SOME RECENT STUDIES, HOWEVER, ARGUE THAT THE
CENTRAL WIDELY REGARDED AS THE COMPLEMENT TO THE
CENTRALIZATION OF AUHTORITIES HAVE USED THEIR APPOINTMENTS
POWERS TO RATIFY RATHER THAN ALTER RESULTS OF THE
CIRCULATION SUBSTANTIVE POLICY MAKING AND IMPLEPROCESS
SPECIFIC TO LOCALITIES. IN ORDER TO ADVANCE MORE FROM THE
INTERACTION BETWEEN NATIONAL AND REPUBLIC TERMS OF
DISCUSSION. THE PRESENT STUDY EMPLOYSA SYSTEMIC MODELS OF
CIRCULATION. HERE CIRCULATION IS CENTRAL AUTHORITIES HAVE
USED THEIR REGARDED AS A MARKOV PROCESS INVOLVING MOVEMENT
OF VACANCIES ACROSS A STRATIFIED HIERARCHY OF 2,034 CO-
ORDINATED CADRES POLICIES IN EITHER MOSCOW OR MINSK. THREE
POSITIONS IN BELORUSSIAN REPUBLIC, AND ALL-UNION JOBS
OCCUPIED BY BELORUSSIAN POLITICIANS, OVER AUXILIARY TESTS
ALSO SUPPORT THE THE PERIOD 1966-86. THE MODEL'S PREDICTIONS
ARE REASONABLY ACCURATE FOR FULL DATA SET BUT FIT THE
CONCLUSIONS DERIVED FROM THE MARKOV ANALYSIS. DATA
ESPECIALLY WELL WHEN ALL-UNION POSITIONS ARE EXCLUDED
INDICATING MARGINAL CENTRALIZING INFLUENCE ON ELITE
CIRCULATION THAT RESULTS MORE FROM INTERTHE PRESENT STUDY
EMPLOYS A SYSTEMIC ACTION BETWEEN NATIONAL & REPUBLIC
PERSONNEL SYSTEM MODEL OF CIRCULATION. HERE, CIRCULATION IS
REGARDED AS A MARKOV PROCESS INVOLVING THE MOVEMENT THAN
FROM CENTRALLY CO-ORDINATED CADRES POLICIES IN EITHER MOSCOW
OR MINSK. THREE AUXILIARY TESTS ALSO OF VACANCIES ACROSS A
STRATIFIED HIERARCHY OF 2,034 POSITIONS IN THE BELORUSSIAN
REPUBLIC, AND ALLSUPPORT CONCLUSIONS DERIVED FROM MARKOV
ANALYSIS. UNION JOBS OCCUPIED BY BELORUSSIAN POLITICANS,
OVER THE PERIOD

09132 URDANG, S.
AND STILL THEY DANCE: WOMEN, WAR, AND THE STRUGGLE FOR
CHANGE IN MOZAMBIQUE
MONTHLY REVIEH PRESS, NEW YORK, NY, 1989, 320.
THE AUTHOR DEPICTS THE STATUS OF MOZAMBICAN WOMEN AS
THEY STRUGGLE BOTH FOR SURVIVAL AND LIBERATION IN THE MIDST
OF WAR.

09133 URQUHART, B.
PROBLEMS AND PROSPECTS OF THE UNITED NATIONS
INTERNATIONAL JOURNAL, XLIV(4) (AUG 89), 803-822.
THE AUTHOR REVIEWS THE PAST ACHIEVEMENTS OF THE UNITED
NATIONS AND SPECULATES ABOUT ITS ROLE IN THE WORLD ORDER OF
THE FUTURE.

09134 URQUHART, B.
THE FUTURE OF PEACEKEEPING
REGULATION, 5(1) (JAN 89), 25-31.
THE ESSENCE OF PEACEKEEPING IS THE USE OF SOLDIERS AS
THE CATALYST FOR PEACE RATHER THAN AS INSTRUMENTS OF WAR.
THIS ARTICLE DESCRIBES THE PEACEKEEPING OPERATIONS OF THE
UNITED NATIONS SECURITY COUNCIL WHICH HAVE PREVENTED
REGIONAL CONFLICTS FROM ESCALATING INTO A CONFRONTATION
BETWEEN EAST AND WEST.

09135 URQUHART, B.
THE UNITED NATIONS SYSTEM AND THE FUTURE
INTERNATIONAL AFFAIRS, 65(2) (SPR 89), 225-232.
THE EXTRAORDINARY CHANGE IN THE TWO CONDITIONS THAT
DETERMINE THE EFFECTIVENESS OF THE UNITED NATIONS: THE
INTERNATIONAL CLIMATE AND THE WAYS GOVERNMENTS CHOOSE TO USE
THE ORGANIZATION, NECESSITATE A LOOK TO THE FUTURE OF THE
ORGANIZATION. THE ARTICLE BRIEFLY EXAMINES THE PAST
SUCCESSES AND FAILURES OF THE UN AND ANALYZES THE FUTURE
ECONOMIC AND ENVIRONMENTAL PROBLEMS THAT THE UN WILL FACE.
IT ADVOCATES UPDATING THE UN MACHINERY AND GIVES SOME
SUGGESTIONS AS TO HOW THE TASK COULD BE ACCOMPLISHED.

09136 URQUHART, I.T.
INTERDEPENDENCE, STATE COMPETITION, AND NATIONAL POLICY:
REGULATING THE BRITISH COLUMBIA AND WASHINGTON PACIFIC
SALMON FISHERIES, 1957-1984
DISSERTATION ABSTRACTS INTERNATIONAL, 49(7) (JAN 89),
1961-A.
THIS STUDY EXPLORES THE POLITICS OF REGULATING THE
BRITISH COLUMBIA AND WASHINGTON COMMERCIAL SALMON FISHERIES
BETWEEN 1957 AND 1984. THE PRINCIPAL FOCUS IS UPON ONE
PARTICULARLY STRIKING EXCEPTION TO THE TENDENCY OF
REGULATORS TO TIGHTEN COMMERCIAL SALMON FISHING RESTRICTIONS
OVER TIME - THE PERSISTENCE OF LIBERAL OFFSHORE TROLLING
REGULATIONS. THE DISSERTATION ARGUES THAT THE ANOMALOUS
TREATMENT OF THE OFFSHORE TROLL FISHERY DURING THIS PERIOD
MAY BE ASCRIBED TO THE COMPETITION BETWEEN STATES FOR THE
RIGHT TO HARVEST SALMON - A COMMON PROPERTY RESOURCE.

09137 URQUIDI, V.L.
CONSTRAINTS TO GROWTH IN THE DEVELOPING WORLD: CURRENT
EXPERIENCE IN LATIN AMERICA

INTERNATIONAL SOCIAL SCIENCE JOURNAL, (120) (MAY 89),
203-210.
THE AUTHOR EXAMINES ISSUES AFFECTING THE DEVELOPING
COUNTRIES DURING THE 1970'S THAT HAVE CONTRIBUTED TO THE
EXTERNAL DEBT SERVICE PROBLEM OF THE 1980'S THEN HE
EVALUATES THE OUTLOOK FOR GROWTH AND DEVELOPMENT AFTER YEARS
OF VIRTUAL STAGNATION, WITH SPECIAL REFERENCE TO LATIN
AMERICA.

09138 URRIOLA, O.
A DIALOGUE WITH THE ARMY
WORLD MARXIST REVIEW, 31(12) (DEC 88), 118-123.
AN ANALYSIS OF THE MAJOR COUPS D'ETAT IN LATIN AMERICA
REVEALS A POWERFUL NATIONALISTIC TREND FOR THE PROTECTION OF
NATURAL RESOURCES FROM THE RAPACITY OF IMPERIALIST
CORPORATIONS. THIS TREND APPEARED DESPITE THE ARMED FORCES'
ACCEPTANCE OF THE PENTAGON'S NATIONAL SECURITY DOCTRINE, AND
DESPITE THEIR PARTICIPATION IN THE INTER-AMERICAN TREATY OF
RECIPROCAL ASSISTANCE. THE CRISIS IN LATIN AMERICA IS THE
RESULT OF THE STAGNATION IN THE TRADITIONAL SECTORS OF THE
ECONOMY AND THE DEEPENING CONTRADICTION BETWEEN THE MODERN
PRODUCTIVE FORCES AND THE RELATIONS OF PRODUCTION THAT HAVE
BEEN IMPOSED BY IMPERIALISM. THE ONLY WAY OUT OF THE CRISIS
IS GENUINE NATIONAL LIBERATION LEADING TO A RESTRUCTURING OF
THE RELATIONS OF PRODUCTION IN ACCORDANCE WITH THE
REQUIREMENTS OF THE PRODUCTIVE FORCES, WHICH HAVE BEEN
DEVELOPING RAPIDLY UNDER THE IMPACT OF SCIENTIFIC AND
TECHNOLOGICAL PROGRESS.

09139 USEEM, M.
THE REVOLT OF THE CORPORATE OWNERS AND THE DEMOBILIZATION
OF BUSINESS POLITICAL ACTION
CRITICAL SOCIOLOGY, 16(2-3) (SUM 89), 7-25.
AFTER HALF A CENTURY OF CONSOLIDATION, MANAGERIAL
CONTROL OF MANY LARGE CORPORATIONS CAME UNDER INCREASING
ATTACK DURING THE 1980S. SPEARHEADED BY MANAGEMENT BUYOUTS
AND HOSTILE TAKEOVERS, OWNERSHIP GROUPS AND INTERESTS CAME
TO EXERCISE GREATER INFLUENCE ON COMPANY POLICIES AND
PRACTICES. DRAWING ON A RANGE OF SOURCES, THIS ARTICLE
ARGUES THAT THE REEMERGENCE OF OWNERSHIP POWER AND THE
DEMAND FOR ENHANCED SHAREHOLDER VALUE IS REDIRECTING COMPANY
POLITICAL ACTION TOWARD MORE NARROWLY DEFINED ISSUES OF
SPECIFIC COMPANY INTEREST. THE TURNOVER IN OWNERSHIP IS ALSO
SERVING TO UNDERCUT GENERAL BUSINESS CONSENSUS AND TO
DEMOBILIZE AGGREGATE POLITICAL ACTION. CONTINUED TURBULENCE
IN THE MARKET FOR CORPORATE CONTROL IS REDUCING ACTION IN
THE MARKET FOR POLITICAL CONTROL.

09140 USLANDER, E.M.
LOOKING FORWARD AND LOOKING BACKWARD: PROSPECTIVE AND
RETROSPECTIVE VOTING IN THE 1980 FEDERAL ELECTIONS IN
CANADA
BRITISH JOURNAL OF POLITICAL SCIENCE, 19(4) (OCT 89),
495-513.
THEORIES OF VOTING HAVE DISTINGUISHED BETWEEN
PROSPECTIVE AND RESTROSPECTIVE EVALUATIONS OF POLITICAL
PARTIES. HOWEVER, NOT ONLY MAY BOTH FACTORS BE AT WORK IN AN
ELECTION, BUT THEY MAY ALSO BE COMPLEMENTARY. THE 1980
CANADIAN FEDERAL ELECTIONS WERE, ACCORDING TO MOST ACCOUNTS,
BOTH A RETROSPECTIVE AND A PROSPECTIVE REFERENDUM ON THE
ENERGY ISSUE. HOWEVER, PREVIOUS EXAMINATIONS OF THIS
ELECTION HAVE FAILED TO SHOW ANY MANDATE EMERGING FROM THE
CONTEST. THIS RE-ANALYSIS OF ELECTION DATA FROM THAT CONTEST,
SHOWS THAT BOTH PROSPECTIVE AND RETROSPECTIVE EVALUATIONS
MATTERED, ABOVE AND BEYOND THE QUALITY OF LEADERSHIP IN THE
COUNTRY. MOREOVER, THE PATTERN OF VOTING STRONGLY SUGGESTS
AN ELITE-LED PATTERN OF ISSUE CONCERNS AKIN TO THAT
SUGGESTED BY THE 'TWOSTEP FLOW OF COMMUNICATIONS'. THOSE
WITH THE STRONGEST PATTERN OF ISSUE CONCERNS VOTED
PROSPECTIVELY, WHILE LESS COMMITTED PARTISANS CAST THEIR
BALLOTS RESTROSPECTIVELY.

09141 USLANER, E.M.
MULTIPLE PARTY IDENTIFIERS IN CANADA: PARTICIPATION AND
AFFECT
THE JOURNAL OF POLITICS, 51(4) (NOV 89), 993-1006.
MANY CANADIANS IDENTIFY WITH ONE PARTY AT THE FEDERAL
LEVEL AND ANOTHER IN PROVINCIAL POLITICS. SPLIT-LEVEL
PARTISANSHIP IS FAR LESS FREQUENT IN THE UNITED STATES.
NEVERTHELESS, IT IS AN OPEN QUESTION WHETHER SUCH DUAL
PARTISANSHIP IS TRACEABLE TO THE SAME DETERMINANTS IN BOTH
COUNTRIES. FOLLOWING NIEMI ET AL. (1987), THIS PAPER
EXAMINES WHETHER SPLIT-LEVEL IDENTIFIERS ARE LESS LIKELY TO
PARTICIPATE IN POLITICS, AS WELL AS TO HAVE LOWER LEVELS OF
EFFICACY THAN PEOPLE WHO IDENTIFY WITH ONE PARTY (EITHER
BEING FULLY CONSISTENT OR PARTIALLY CONSISTENT). NO SUPPORT
FOR EITHER HYPOTHESIS IS FOUND. SPLIT-LEVEL IDENTIFIERS
PARTICIPATE JUST AS MUCH AS FULLY CONSISTENT AND PARTIALLY
CONSISTENT PARTISANS. THEIR EFFICACY IS GENERALLY EQUAL TO
THAT OF OTHER GROUPS AS WELL. THE ONLY EXCEPTIONS SUGGEST
THAT SPLIT-LEVEL PARTISANSHIP REFLECTS CITIZENS' POLITICAL
ENVIRONMENTS. IF PEOPLE FACE TWO VERY DIFFERENT PARTY
SYSTEMS AT THE FEDERAL AND PROVINCIAL TIERS, THEY ARE LIKELY
TO HAVE DIFFERENT PATTERNS OF IDENTIFICATION REGARDLESS OF

THEIR LEVELS OF PARTICIPATION AND EFFICACY.

09142 UWAH, G.
MITTERAND'S SECOND TERM: THE ELECTION OF A MONARCH
CONTEMPORARY REVIEW, 254(1478) (MAR 89), 122-126.
THE ARTICLE EXAMINES THE POLITICAL RISE OF FRANCOIS
MITTERRAND AND THE CONTRADICTIONS THAT MAKE HIM SO APPEALING
TO THE FRENCH PEOPLE. IT EXPLORES THE VAGUE LONGINGS OF THE
FRENCH PEOPLE FOR A "MONARCH" OF SORTS AND HOW MITTERAND
FITS THE IMAGE.

09143 VACS, A.C.
A DELICATE BALANCE: CONFRONTATION AND COOPERATION BETWEEN
ARGENTINA AND THE UNITED STATES IN THE 1980S
JOURNAL OF INTERAMERICAN STUDIES AND WORLD AFFAIRS, 31(4)
(WIN 89), 23-59.
THIS ARTICLE IS FOCUSED ON THOSE ASPECTS OF THE
BILATERAL RELATIONSHIP BETWEEN THE U.S. AND ARGENTINA THAT
HELP TO EXPLAIN RECENT DEVELOPMENTS, AS WELL AS TO
ANTICIPATE THE MOST LIKELY DIRECTIONS IN WHICH RELATIONS
WILL MOVE IN THE 1990S. IT EXPLORES ECONOMIC, POLITICAL,
STRATEGIC, CULTURAL, DOMESTIC AND INTERNATIONAL FACTORS THAT
INFLUENCE THE BILATERAL RELATIONSHIP AND THE MOST LIKELY
PROSPECTS FOR BILATERAL RELATIONS IN THE FUTURE.

09144 VAJIRAKACHORN, S.
THE INFLUENCE OF BUDDHISM IN THAI ADMINISTRATIVE BEHAVIOR:
A Q TECHNIQUE STUDY OF THAI BUREAUCRACY
DISSERTATION ABSTRACTS INTERNATIONAL, 50(4) (OCT 89),
1088-A.
FOCUSING ON THE IMPACT OF THE BUDDHIST RELIGION AND
MODERN BUREAUCRATIC IDEAS ON THE THAI BUREAUCRACY, THE
AUTHOR INVESTIGATES THE ADMINISTRATIVE PATTERN OF THAI
PUBLIC OFFICIALS. STEPHENSON'S Q-METHODOLOGY IS EMPLOYED TO
ANALYZE AND COMPARE THE EFFECT OF THESE TWO CULTURALLY
DIFFERENT IDEAS. THE AUTHOR CONCLUDES THAT THE THAI
BUREAUCRACY IS IN THE PROCESS OF CHANGE FROM TRADITIONAL TO
MODERN ADMINISTRATION.

09145 VALDES, R.M.
THE COLLAPSE OF CORPORATISM: FINANCIAL REFORM AND
POLITICAL CHANGE IN EL SALVADOR
DISSERTATION ABSTRACTS INTERNATIONAL, 50(1) (JUL 89),
248-A.
DURING THE DICTATORSHIP OF GENERAL MAXIMILIANO HERNANDEZ-
MARTINEZ, A CORPORATIST REGIME WAS ESTABLISHED IN EL
SALVADOR, SUPPLANTING THE LIBERAL-OLIGARCHIC ONE THAT
COLLAPSED DURING THE GREAT DEPRESSION. THIS DICTATORSHIP
CREATED VARIOUS NATIONAL ECONOMIC INSTITUTIONS THAT WERE
BOTH AN IMPORTANT RESULT OF, AND A MEANS FOR, THE
ESTABLISHMENT OF A CORPORATIST POLITICAL SYSTEM. AFTER WORLD
WAR II, THE CORPORATIST EDIFICE WAS CHALLENGED FROM MANY
QUARTERS AND IT WAS STEADILY UNDERMINED, LEADING TO THE
CRISIS AND COLLAPSE IN THE 1980'S. POSTWAR FINANCIAL REFORMS
WERE PART AND PARCEL OF THIS CHANGE.

09146 VALE, C.A.
TIES THAT BIND: PART ONE: BRITISH SOUTH AFRICAN RELATIONS
INTO THE NINETIES
CONTEMPORARY REVIEW, 255(1483) (AUG 89), 57-62.
THE POLITICAL HISTORY OF SOUTH AFRICA IS MADE UP OF A
FEW ENDURING STRANDS. IN ORDER TO UNDERSTAND THE TIME IN
WHICH ONE LIVES, IT IS OFTEN NECESSARY TO RECOGNISE AND COME
TO TERMS, WITH THE PAST, THAT SOUTH AFRICA IS WESTERN
BECAUSE WHITES WERE INSTALLED AS THE COLONIAL INHERITORS HAS
HAD A PROFOUND INFLUENCE ON THE FATE OF THAT COUNTRY. THIS
ARTICLE ARGUES THAT THE BRITISH CONNECTION, AS A SUBJECT OF
POLITICAL DEBATE, HAS MOVED OUT OF DOMESTIC POLITICS ALMOST
ENTIRELY. IT THEN EXPLORES THREE IMPORTANT DIMENSIONS TO
CONSIDER WHICH AFFECT FOREIGN RELATIONS. THEY ARE: THE
CAMPAIGN TO ISOLATE AND DESTROY SOUTH AFRICA; THE SOUTH
AFRICAN REGIONAL INITIATIVE, AND THE SEARCH FOR
INTERNATIONAL ACCEPTANCE OF THE SOUTH AFRICAN REFORM
INITIATIVE.

09147 VALE, C.A.
TIES THAT BIND: PART 2: BRITISH SOUTH AFRICAN RELATIONS
INTO THE NINETIES
CONTEMPORARY REVIEW, 255(1484) (SEP 89), 124-129.
THIS ARTICLE CONSIDERS TWO OPINIONS ABOUT THE NATURE OF
AFRIKANER NATIONALISM. ONE IS THAT IT IS ISOLATIONIST AND
EXHIBITS A LAAGER MENTALITY. THE OTHER IS THAT AFRIKANER
NATIONALISM IS FUNDAMENTALLY EXPANSIONIST. IT THEN SUGGESTS
THAT THE APPARENT CONTRADICTION CAN BE CLEARED UP BY
CONSIDERING THE SITUATION IN THE LIGHT OF THE HISTORY OF
BRITISH INTERVENTION IN THE REGION. IT EXPLORES THE TWO
RIVAL GROUPINGS IN A SUBCONTINENT WHICH CAN BARELY SUSTAIN
ONE, WHO INSTEAD OF WORKING JOINTLY, EXPEND THEIR LIMITED
RESOURCES IN OPPOSING ONE ANOTHER. ALSO EXPLORED IS THE
COMMON CONCERN WITH THE PROMOTION OF DEVELOPMENT IN SOUTH
AFRICA SHARED BY BRITAIN AND SOUTH AFRICA.

09148 VALENTA, J.; CUNNINGHAM, J.
HOW MOSCOW VOTES IN U.S. PRESIDENTIAL ELECTIONS

ORBIS, 33(1) (WIN 89), 3-20.
SOVIET LEADERS FOLLOW THE U.S. ELECTION POLLS
ASSIDUOUSLY, PARTICULARLY IN THE FINAL WEEKS OF A CAMPAIGN.
DURING A CLOSE RACE, THEY APPEAR TO WEIGH CAREFULLY THE
EFFECTS OF THEIR PUBLIC PRONOUNCEMENTS AND COMMENTS; AT
TIMES (1960, 1968), THEY EVEN APPEAR TO BELIEVE THAT THEY
HAVE SUFFICIENT LEVERAGE TO INFLUENCE THE OUTCOME IN FAVOR
OF THEIR PREFERRED CANDIDATE. AT OTHER TIMES, WHEN THEIR
PREFERRED CANDIDATE APPEARS TO HAVE A SUBSTANTIAL LEAD,
MOSCOW WANTS TO BE SEEN LEANING CAUTIOUSLY TOWARD HIM (1964,
1972, 1988), APPARENTLY BELIEVING THAT IS A PLUS AMONG THE
AMERICAN VOTERS. SINCE WORLD WAR II, THE SOVIET LEADERS HAVE
SHOWN AN INCREASING ABILITY TO DISTINGUISH AMONG AMERICAN
PRESIDENTIAL CANDIDATES. THEIR IDEAL PRESIDENT IS ONE WHO,
IN THEIR TERMS, IS REALISTIC, PREDICTABLE, AND SOBER-MINDED.
THOUGH THEY HAVE AN IDEOLOGICAL PREFERENCE FOR LIBERAL
DEMOCRATIC CANDIDATES LIKE JOHN KENNEDY AND GARY HART, THEY
MOST FREQUENTLY CAST A PRAGMATIC VOTE FOR REPUBLICANS FROM
THE CENTER OR CENTER-LEFT SECTORS OF THE GOP, SUCH AS DWIGHT
EISENHOWER, THE SECOND-TERM RICHARD NIXON, GERALD FORD, AND
GEORGE BUSH.

09149 VALENZUELA, A.; CONSTABLE, P.
THE CHILEAN PLEBISCITE: DEFEAT OF A DICTATOR
CURRENT HISTORY, 88(536) (MAR 89), 129-132, 152-153.
THE AUTHOR DISCUSSES THE IMPACT OF THE 1988 PLEBISCITE
IN CHILE.

09150 VALENZUELA, J.S.
LABOR MOVEMENTS IN TRANSITIONS TO DEMOCRACY: A FRAMEWORK
FOR ANALYSIS
COMPARATIVE POLITICS, 21(4) (JUL 89), 445-472.
THE AUTHOR PROBES THE SPECIAL RELATIONSHIP BETWEEN LABOR
MOVEMENTS AND PROCESSES OF REDEMOCRATIZATION, BOTH IN TERMS
OF LABOR'S REACTIONS TO THE OVERALL CHANGE AND THE LATTER'S
EFFECTS ON IT. HE CONSIDERS THE CASES OF REDEMOCRATIZATION
THAT HAVE OCCURRED SINCE THE MID-1970'S INCLUDING THOSE IN
ARGENTINA, BRAZIL, GREECE, PERU, THE PHILIPPINES, SPAIN, AND
PORTUGAL.

09151 VALIVNAS, A.
THE RAPE OF POLAND AND THE DEATH OF HOPE
AMERICAN SPECTATOR, 22(9) (SEP 89), 17-18.
LESS THAN ONE POLISH JEW IN TEN MANAGED TO GET THROUGH
WORLD WAR II ALIVE. THOSE WHO SURVIVED COULD NEVER HOPE TO
REMAKE THE WORLD THEY HAD ONCE KNOWN. THE STRUGGLE OF THE
POLISH PEOPLE TO REGAIN FREEDOM ON THEIR OWN HAS BEEN AT
ONCE AMONG THE MOST PITIABLE AND THE MOST THRILLING
SPECTACLES OF THE POSTWAR WORLD. YET THE WEST ONCE AGAIN
OFFERS THE EAST LITTLE BUT ITS HOPE THAT THE TYRANT, WEARY
OF TYRANNY, WILL AT LAST TURN OUT TO BE LIBERTY'S TRUE
CHAMPION; AND ONE CANNOT BUT THINK THAT WHATEVER MIGHT
BECOME OF TODAY'S HOPE, CERTAIN LESSONS HISTORY HAS TO TEACH
ARE LIKELY NEVER TO BE LEARNED.

09152 VALLADARES, A.
CUBA'S HUMAN RIGHTS ABUSES UNDER THE UN SPOTLIGHT
DEPARTMENT OF STATE BULLETIN (US FOREIGN POLICY), 89(2153)
(DEC 89), 54-55.
THE UN COMMISSION FOR HUMAN RIGHTS VISITED CUBA TO
COLLECT FIRST-HAND EVIDENCE OF THE SWEEPING HUMAN RIGHTS
ABUSES THAT ROUTINELY OCCUR THERE. BECAUSE HE WAS IN THE UN
SPOTLIGHT, FIDEL CASTRO COOPERATED WITH THE INTERNATIONAL
HUMAN RIGHTS MONITORS AND RELEASED MANY POLITICAL PRISONERS.
AT THE END OF THE INVESTIGATION, THE UN GROUP RELEASED A
LENGTHY REPORT BUT DREW NO CONCLUSIONS ABOUT THE HUMAN
RIGHTS SITUATION IN CUBA.

09153 VALLS-RUSSELL, J.
EUROPE'S BUMPY ROAD TO '92
NEW LEADER, LXXII(13) (SEP 89), 8-9.
THE ARTICLE EXAMINES THE PROGRESS OF THE EUROPEAN
COMMUNITY TOWARDS ITS GOAL OF EUROPEAN INTEGRATION IN 1992.
ALTHOUGH GREAT STRIDES ARE BEING MADE, RESISTANCE FROM
BRITAIN'S MARGARET THATCHER, DISAGREEMENT OVER A PROPOSED
SOCIAL CHARTER OF WORKERS' RIGHTS, AND CONFLICT OVER
ENVIRONMENTAL DEGRADATION COMBINE TO ENSURE THAT THE ROAD TO
INTEGRATION WILL BE A BUMPY ONE.

09154 VALLS-RUSSELL, J.
ISLAM IN ENGLAND AND FRANCE
NEW LEADER, LXXII(12) (AUG 89), 5-6.
THE ARTICLE EXAMINES THE SIZABLE MUSLIM COMMUNITIES ON
BRITAIN AND FRANCE. ALTHOUGH MUSLIMS IN EUROPE ARE A RACIAL
AND CULTURAL MOSAIC AND COME FROM A VARIETY OF NATIONS, SOME
GENRALIZATIONS ABOUT BRITISH AND FRENCH MUSLIMS CAN BE MADE.
MUSLIMS IN FRENCH ARE GENERALLY OF NORTH AFRICAN ORIGIN AND
ARE USUALLY ASSIMILATED INTO THE FRENCH CULTURE VIA FRANCE'S
SECULAR EDUCATION PROGRAMS. BRITISH MUSLIMS GENERALLY HAIL
FROM ASIA AND MAINTAIN A SEPARATE, MORE MILITANT IDENTITY.
THEREFORE, RECENT ATTEMPTS TO RALLY MUSLIMS OF ALL ORIGINS
AGAINST THE PUBLICATION OF SALMAN RUSHDIE'S THE SATANIC
VERSES, WAS FAIRLY SUCCESSFUL IN ENGLAND, BUT LARGELY FAILED
IN FRANCE.

09155 VALLS-RUSSELL, J.
SHIFTING POLITICS IN SPAIN
NEW LEADER, 72(18) (NOV 89), 9-10.
THIS ARTICLE EXPLORES A CHANGE IN THE POLITICAL CLIMATE
IN SPAIN ILLUSTRATED BY THE RESULTS OF THE GENERAL ELECTION
IN OCT. IT PREDICTS THAT THE SPANISH PARLIAMENT SHOULD NOW
BECOME A BRIGHTER PLACE. REGIONALIST PARTY SUCCESSES ARE
EVALUATED AND THE REASONS FOR THE LABOR - PSOE DIVORCE ARE
DETAILED. ECONOMIC POLICY AND GROWTH ARE EXAMINED.

09156 VALLS-RUSSELL, J.
SPAIN TIGHTENS UP ITS EUROPEAN TIES
NEW LEADER, LXXII(8) (MAY 89), 7-8.
THAT SPAIN BELONGS TO EUROPE MAY SEEM GEOGRAPHICALLY
OBVIOUS. BUT TO SPANIARDS THE RELATIONSHIP MEANS MUCH MORE
THAN PHYSICAL PROXIMITY. IT IMPLIES A CHOICE. AND THE WORD
"EUROPEAN" HOLDS SUCH A WEALTH OF POLITICAL, SOCIAL,
HISTORICAL, AND ETHICAL CONNOTATIONS HERE THAT INDIVIDUALS
STILL DISAGREE ON HOW IT APPLIES IN THEIR PARTICULAR CASE.
OPINION POLLS HAVE STEADILY SHOWN THAT THE SPANISH PEOPLE
FAVOR EC MEMBERSHIP--IN CONTRAST WITH THEIR DOUBTS ABOUT
NATO, WHICH SPAIN JOINED IN 1982. ADMISSION TO THE WESTERN
EUROPEAN UNION, LOOKED UPON HERE AS A MILITARY COUNTERPART
TO THE EC. WAS WELCOMED BY COMMUNISTS AND CONSERVATIVES
ALIKE. MOST SPANIARDS WOULD AGREE THAT MAKING SURE THE
SPANISH COACH IS WELL HITCHED TO THE EUROPEAN TRAIN IS WHAT
MATTERS.

09157 VAN DEN HAAG, E.
ABORTION: THE MORALITY: IS THERE A MIDDLE GROUND
NATIONAL REVIEW, 61(24) (DEC 89), 29.
MR. VAN DEN HAAG BELIEVES THAT THE MAJORITY OF THE
AMERICAN PEOPLE ARE IN FAVOR OF ABORTION ON DEMAND DURING
THE FIRST TRIMESTER OF PREGNANCY. HE STRESSES THAT THE
SECULARIZATION OF OUR CULTURE MAKES IT PROGRESSIVELY MORE
DIFFICULT TO URGE SANCTIONS THAT ARE PRIMARILY RELIGIOUS IN
PROVENANCE UPON THOSE WHO DO NOT ACCEPT RELIGIOUS INSIGHTS
AND COMMANDMENTS; OR WHO, EVEN IF THEY DO, WISH TO BE LEFT
FREE TO TRADUCE THEM. HE CONTENDS THAT THE INCONSISTENCY OF
THE FACT THAT ALTHOUGH THE MAJORITY OF AMERICANS ARE OF THE
JUDAEO-CHRISTIAN TRADITION, YET DO NOT BELIEVE THAT ABORTION
SHOULD BE A CRIME WILL ASSURE CONTINUATION OF THE DEBATE.

09158 VAN DEN HAAG, E.
COMRADE, CAN YOU SPARE A DIME?
NATIONAL REVIEW, XLI(5) (MAR 89), 35-37.
THE AUTHOR HERE CONTENDS THAT SINCE THE SOVIETS COULD
NEVER REPAY ALL THE CASH THEY'D LIKE TO BORROW, THE UNITED
STATES SHOULD OFFER GIFTS TO THE SOVIET PEOPLE. CONSUMER
GOODS WOULD HELP THE SOVIETS RAISE THEIR LIVING STANDARD.
THEY WOULD ALSO BE HIGHLY VISIBLE: SOVIET CITIZENS WOULD BE
AWARE OF RECEIVING AMERICAN GIFTS, WHICH SHOULD BE
DISTRIBUTED RANDOMLY RATHER THAN SOLD OR USED AS REWARDS. IT
WILL MAKE FOR GOOD WILL AND, PERHAPS, IT WILL HELP PEACE IN
THE FUTURE-MORE CERTAINLY THAN LOANS, WHICH CANNOT BE REPAID,
LEAVE A SOUR TASTE, AND STRENGTHEN THE SOVIETS MILITARILY.

09159 VAN DEN HAAG, E.
THE END OF COMMUNISM IN ITALY
NATIONAL REVIEW, 61(23) (DEC 89), 21-22.
THIS ARTICLE EXAMINES THE PRESENT STATUS OF COMMUNISM
(PRO-SOVIET) AS A POLITICAL FORCE IN NON-COMMUNIST COUNTRIES.
IT SUGGESTS THAT WE MAY BE SEEING THE END OF COMMUNISM AS
WE KNOW IT. HOWEVER, IT STUDIES THE ONE EXCEPTION TO THE
DEMISE OF COMMUNIST PARTIES IN WESTERN EUROPE AND THAT IS
THE ITALIAN COMMUNIST PARTY (PCI). THE NATURE OF THE PARTY
HAS CHANGED, AND THE ARTICLE SUGGESTS THAT THE U.S. LEAVE
ITALIAN POLITICS TO THE ITALIAN POLITICIANS.

09160 VAN DEN HAAG, E.
THE WAR BETWEEN PALEOS AND NEOS
NATIONAL REVIEW, XLI(3) (FEB 89), 21-23.
THE AUTHOR DIFFERENTIATES BETWEEN PALEO-CONSERVATIVES
AND NEO-CONSERVATIVES.

09161 VAN DER EIJK, C.
THE NETHERLANDS
ELECTORAL STUDIES, 8(3) (DEC 89), 305-312.
THIS ARTICLE EXAMINES THE 1989 EUROPEAN ELECTIONS IN THE
NETHERLANDS, THE NATURE AND SIGNIFICANCE OF WHICH SHIFTED
CONSIDERABLY DURING THE SPRING OF THAT YEAR. THE CONTEXT OF
THE ELECTIONS, THE CAMPAIGN AND RESULTS ARE EXPLORED AS WELL
AS THE TURNOUT, AND PARTY CHOICE IN EUROPEAN AND NATIONAL
ELECTIONS, WHEN THE ELECTIONS WERE OVER, IT WAS EVIDENT THAT
THE REVISED EXPECTATIONS OF MAY HAD NOT BEEN BORNE OUT, AND
THAT THE ELECTION HAD BEEN EVEN MORE OF A NON-EVENT THAN HAD
BEEN FORESEEN EARLIER IN THE SPRING.

09162 VAN DER KROEF, J.
AQUINO AND THE COMMUNISTS: A PHILIPPINE STRATEGIC
STALEMATE?
WORLD AFFAIRS, 151(3) (WIN 89), 117-130.
THE ARTICLE EXTENSIVELY ANALYZES THE CLAIMS BY THE
COMMUNIST PARTY OF THE PHILIPPINES (CPP) THAT THEY ARE
MOVING INTO THE SECOND STAGE OF "PROTRACTED WAR": STRATEGIC
STALEMATE. IT CONCLUDES THAT THE CPP, ITS GUERRILLA FORCE,
AND FRONT COMPLEX EVEN NOW FORM AN INDESTRUCTIBLE DE FACTO
COUNTERGOVERNMENT THAT THE CONSTITUTIONAL AUTHORITY WILL
HAVE TO LIVE FOR AN INDEFINITE TIME TO COME. VICTORY FOR THE
GOVERNMENT WILL NOT COME THROUGH A SIMPLE MILITARY VICTORY
OVER THE NPA, THE COMMUNIST MOVEMENT'S MILITARY ARM, BUT
RATHER IN THE SUCCESSFUL DEVELOPMENT OF A PUBLIC CONSENSUS
ON NATIONAL INSTITUTIONS OF DEMOCRATIC GOVERANCE, AND A
BROAD POPULAR DETERMINATION TO SUSTAIN THEM.

09163 VAN DER PLOEG, F.
DISPOSABLE INCOME, UNEMPLOYMENT, INFLATION AND STATE
SPENDING IN A DYNAMIC POLITICAL-ECONOMIC MODEL
PUBLIC CHOICE, 60(3) (MAR 89), 211-240.
ABSTRACT. THIS PAPER FORMULATES A MEDIUM-TERM
MACROECONOMIC MODEL OF DISPOSABLE INCOME, UNEMPLOYMENT,
INFLATION AND STATE SPENDING, PROPOSES A THEORY OF
QUALITATIVE CHOICE TO EXPLAIN ELECTORAL POPULARITY IN TERMS
OF THESE VARIABLES AND DEVELOPS THREE APPROACHES TO THE
FORMULATION OF POLITICAL-ECONOMIC POLICY. THE FIRST APPROACH
IS STATIC, SETS THE TAX RATE TO RECONCILE THE INTERESTS OF
VARIOUS PRESSURE GROUPS AND YIELDS A POLITICAL TRADE-OFF
BETWEEN THE PRIVATE AND PUBLIC SECTOR. THE SECOND APPROACH
RELIES ON MAXIMIZING THE PROBABILITY OF WINNING THE NEXT
ELECTION AND GIVES RISE TO A POLITICAL BUSINESS CYCLE UNLESS
THE ELECTORATE VOTES STRATEGICALLY. THE IMPLICATIONS OF
CROWDING OUT OF PRIVATE INVESTMENT UNDER ALTERNATIVE
MONETARY RULES, AUTOMONOMOUS BEHAVIOUR OF THE STATE
BUREAUCRACY AND TAX-INDEXATION FOR THE POLITICAL BUSINESS
CYCLE ARE ALSO EXAMINED. THE THIRD APPROACH ANALYZES THE
OBJECTIVE OF MAXIMIZING THE UNINTERRUPTED LENGTH IN OFFICE.
IT YIELDS A SHORTRUN POLITICAL CYCLE SUPERIMPOSED ON A
LONGER CYCLE.

09164 VAN DOREN, P.
SHOULD CONGRESS LISTEN TO ECONOMISTS?
THE JOURNAL OF POLITICS, 51(2) (MAY 89), 319-336.
ECONOMISTS PRESCRIBE WELL-KNOWN REMEDIES FOR THOSE
SITUATIONS WHERE PRIVATE BEHAVIOR DOES NOT MAXIMIZE
ALLOCATIONAL EFFICIENCY. LEGISLATURES, HOWEVER, RARELY ENACT
MICROECONOMIC POLICIES WITHOUT SUBSTANTIALLY ALTERING
ECONOMISTS' SOLUTIONS. THOSE WHO DEFEND ELECTED OFFICIALS'
ALTERATIONS OFFER THREE CATEGORIES OF JUSTIFICATION -
WINDFALL LOSSES OF INCOME NEGATE EFFICIENCY IMPROVEMENTS;
INDIRECT REDISTRIBUTION, THOUGH INEFFICIENT, SERVES
PROGRESSIVE GOALS WITHOUT GENERALLY REPUDIATING MARKET
INCOMES; COMMAND-AND-CONTROL REGULATION PRODUCES VALUABLE
SYMBOLIC OUTPUTS. ONLY THE FIRST LINE OF ARGUMENT HAS MERIT.
POLICY PRESCRIPTIONS OFTEN ARE INSENSITIVE TO THE HEALTH
LOSSES THEY CREATE AND CAN BE IMPROVED THROUGH CONGRESSIONAL
ATTENTION TO DISTRIBUTIONAL ISSUES. FOR THE MOST PART,
HOWEVER, NO NORMATIVE GOAL IS WELL SERVED WHEN CONGRESS
IGNORES ECONOMIC EFFICIENCY IN THE DESIGN OF POLICIES.

09165 VAN DUREN, E.; MARTIN, L.
THE ROLE OF ECONOMIC ANALYSIS IN COUNTERVAILING DUTY
DISPUTES: CASES INVOLVING AGRICULTURE
CANADIAN PUBLIC POLICY--ANALYSE DE POLITIQUES, XV(2) (JUN
89), 162-174.
SEVERAL RECENT COUNTERVAILING DUTY CASES INVOLVING
AGRICULTURAL PRODUCTS HAVE RESULTED IN LIVELY DEBATE, AND IN
SOME CASES, ADDITIONAL POLITICAL OR LEGAL ACTION. THIS
ARTICLE EXAMINES WHETHER SEVERAL RECENT DECISIONS INVOLVING
AGRICULTURAL PRODUCTS MADE UNDER CANADIAN AND US
COUNTERVAILING DUTY LAW WERE CONSISTENT WITH ECONOMIC THEORY,
THE GATT SUBSIDIES CODE AND THE RELEVANT NATIONAL LAW. ON
THE BASIS OF THE ANALYSIS THE ARTICLE CONCLUDES THAT
NATIONAL TRADE LAWS, BOTH IN THE US AND CANADA, COULD BE
IMPROVED BY EXPLICITLY INCORPORATING AN ECONOMIC DEFINITION
OF A TRADE DISTORTING DOMESTIC PRODUCTION SUBSIDY, AND AN
ECONOMIC TEST FOR THE CAUSAL LINK BETWEEN A FOREIGN SUBSIDY
AND INJURY TO A DOMESTIC INDUSTRY.

09166 VAN EEKELEN, W.F.
NEW POSSIBILITIES IN EAST-WEST RELATIONS.
PLURAL SOCIETIES, 18(2) (MAR 89), 23-29.
UNTIL RECENTLY CHANGE IN EASTERN EUROPE CAME FROM THE
BOTTOM UP. IT WAS PRIMARILY ECONOMIC AND INCHED FORWARD IN
CREATING MARKET-CONDITIONS, ACCEPTABLE TO THE COMMUNIST
PARTY LEADERSHIP. THIS ARTICLE DESCRIBES THE CONCERN OF MAY
EASTERN EUROPEAN LEADERS ABOUT THE EFFECTS OF GLASNOST AND
PERESTROIKA ON THEIR OWN POSITION.

09167 VAN REE, E.
THE LIMITS OF "JUCHE": NORTH KOREA'S DEPENDENCE ON SOVIET
INDUSTRIAL AID, 1953-76
JOURNAL OF COMMUNIST STUDIES, 5(1) (MAR 89), 50-73.
THE ARTICLE EXPLORES THE CONCEPT OF "JUCHE" OR SELF-
RELIANCE THAT WAS INITIATED BY NORTH KOREAN COMMUNIST LEADER
KIM IL-SUNG. IT IMPLIES, AMONG OTHER THINGS, A REJECTION OF
SERVILE IMITATION OF FOREIGN EXAMPLES, UTILIZING INSTEAD A
GENUINE KOREAN MODEL OF COMMUNISM. THE ARTICLE EXAMINES SOME

OF KIM IL SUNG'S POLICIES IN THE EARLIER PART OF HIS CARREER IN WHICH MANY ACTIONS WHICH APPEAR TO BE INDEPENDENT AND ANTI-SOVIET ARE, IN REALITY, NOT SO WHEN VIEWED IN THE CONTEXT OF DEVELOPMENTS WITHIN THE COMMUNIST BLOC AS A WHOLE. THE ARTICLE CONCENTRATES ON THE ECONOMIC ASPECT OF JUCHE AND ARGUES THAT JUCHE IN ITS ECONOMIC SENSE IS A PARADOXICAL CONCEPT WHICH, IF PURSUED TOO SINGLE-MINDEDLY, PRODUCES RELATIONS OF DEPENDENCE.

09168 VAN STADEN, A.
THE CHANGING ROLE OF THE NETHERLANDS IN THE ATLANTIC ALLIANCE
WEST EUROPEAN POLITICS, 12(1) (JAN 89), 99-111.
THE ARTICLE ANALYZES THE EVOLUTION OF THE DUTCH POSITION IN NATO FROM A PERSPECTIVE OF THE LINKAGE BETWEEN FOREIGN POLICY AND DOMESTIC POLITICS. THE AUTHOR ARGUES THAT THE CHANGING OF THE NETHERLANDS FROM A FAITHFUL ALLY OF THE 60'S WAS NOT DUE TO THE RE-EMERGING OF PREWAR NEUTRALIST IMPULSES, BUT RATHER THE OPENNES OF THE DUTCH POLITICAL SYSTEM TO ORGANIZED AND DETERMINED SINGLE INTEREST GROUPS. THE ARTICLE EXAMINES CURRENT DEVELOPMENTS AND EVENTS WHICH SHOW A TENDENCY OF RETURNING TO OLD, FAMILIAR PATTERNS.

09169 VANAGGELEN, J.G.C.
CONFLICTING CLAIMS TO SOVEREIGNTY OVER THE WEST BANK: AN IN-DEPTH ANALYSIS OF THE HISTORICAL ROOTS AND FEASIBLE OPTIONS IN THE FRAMEWORK OF A FUTURE SETTLEMENT OF THE DISPUTE
DISSERTATION ABSTRACTS INTERNATIONAL, 50(4) (OCT 89), 1074-A.
THE AUTHOR BEGINS BY TRACING THE ORIGINS OF THE CONFLICTING CLAIMS TO SOVEREIGNTY OVER THE AREA NOW CALLED "THE WEST BANK." THEN HE STUDIES THE CONSTITUENT ELEMENTS FOR THE LEGALITY OR ILLEGALITY OF THE SOVEREIGNTY CLAIMS INVOKED BY THE PARTIES CONCERNED. HE ANALYZES ISRAEL'S POSITION AS A BELLIGERENT OCCUPANT SINCE 1967 AND DISCUSSES PROPOSALS TO SOLVE THE CONFLICTING CLAIMS TO SOVEREIGNTY.

09170 VANALSTYNE, R.W.
THE UNITED STATES AND RUSSIA IN WORLD WAR II
CURRENT HISTORY, 88(534) (JAN 89), 26-29, 52-53.
THE AUTHOR REVIEWS THE WAR-TIME RELATIONSHIP BETWEEN THE USA AND THE USSR, THE FAMOUS AGREEMENTS AT YALTA AND POTSDAM, AND THE FAILURE OF AMERICAN FOREIGN POLICY--THREE FACTORS THAT SHAPED THE POSTWAR WORLD AND LED TO THE COLD WAR ERA.

09171 VANBRABANT, J.M.
THE SOVIET UNION IN THE GATT? A PLEA FOR REFORM
INTERNATIONAL SPECTATOR, XXIV(2) (APR 89), 72-93.
SOVIET LEADERS HAVE LEFT NO DOUBT THAT THEY WILL BE SUBMITTING A REQUEST FOR FULL ACCESSION TO THE GENERAL AGREEMENT ON THE BASIS OF ORTHODOX COMMERCIAL POLICY PRINCIPLES AS SOON AS THEY SUCCEED IN EMBARKING ON THEIR COMPREHENSIVE PRICE REFORM, PERHAPS IN 1991. BARRING ANY RADICAL MOVEMENT TOWARD UNDOING PERESTROIKA, AT SOME POINT IN THE NOT TOO DISTANT FUTURE, THE ISSUE OF SOVIET PARTICIPATION IN INTERNATIONAL ECONOMIC ORGANIZATIONS WILL BECOME PREGNANT WITH A HOST OF DIPLOMATIC, ORGANIZATIONAL, POLITICAL, FINANCIAL, MONETARY, AND COMMERCIAL PROBLEMS.

09172 VANDEEMEN, A.M.A.
DOMINANT PLAYERS AND MINIMUM-SIZE COALITIONS
EUROPEAN JOURNAL OF POLITICAL RESEARCH, 17(3) (MAY 89), 313-322.
THE AUTHOR EXAMINES PELEG'S THEORY OF COALITION FORMATION IN DOMINATED SIMPLE GAMES. HE ALSO ESTABLISHES A CONNECTION BETWEEN PELEG'S THEORY AND RIKER'S MINIMUM-SIZE THEORY. THIS CONNECTION LEADS TO A NEW THEORY OF COALITION FORMATION IN SIMPLE GAMES.

09173 VANDEMARK, B.
LYNDON JOHNSON AND THE ESCALATION OF THE VIETNAM WAR, 1964-65
DISSERTATION ABSTRACTS INTERNATIONAL, 49(9) (MAR 89), 487.
DOMESTIC POLITICAL CONSIDERATIONS, ESPECIALLY CONCERN ABOUT CONSERVATIVE OPPOSITION TO THE GREAT SOCIETY, HEAVILY INFLUENCED LYNDON JOHNSON'S APPROACH TO THE VIETNAM WAR. IN THIS STUDY, THE AUTHOR ANALYZES JOHNSON'S DECISION-MAKING ON VIETNAM DURING A PERIOD OF ESCALATING AMERICAN INVOLVEMENT, NOVEMBER 1964 THROUGH JULY 1965.

09174 VANDER KROEF, J.M.
AQUINO AND THE COMMUNISTS: A PHILLIPINE STRATEGIC STALEMATE?
WORLD AFFAIRS, 151(3) (WIN 88), 117-130.
THIS PAPER EXAMINES THE ANTICIPATED STRATEGIC STALEMATE PREDICTED IN EARLY 1988 IN THE PHILLIPINES. IT DEFINES THE MEANING OF "STRATEGIC STALEMATE" THE QUESTION OF HOW CLOSE IN ITS CONFRONTATION OF THE CPP-NPA IS THE PHILLIPINES OF AQUINO NOW, OR LIKELY TO BE TO THE STATIC CONDITION OF BEING STRATEGICALLY "STALEMATED"? IS EXPLORED, AND SEVERAL CRITERIA ARE CONSIDERED IN EVALUATING THAT QUESTION. IT EXPLORES THE LEVEL OF VIOLENCE ENGENDERED BY THE COMMUNIST INSURGENCY YEAR AFTER YEAR AND ALSO THE COMMUNIST MOVEMENTS

FINANCIAL RESOURCES. IT CONCLUDES THAT THE STRATEGIC STALEMENT BETWEEN THE PHILLIPINE GOVERNMENT AND PHILLIPINE COMMUNISM IS ALREADY HERE AND THAT A BROAD POPULAR DETERMINATION TO SUSTAIN IT IS REQUIRED.

09175 VANDERGIESSEN, H.
THE DETERMINANTS OF HEALTH SERVICES POLICY: A MODEL AND TWO CASE STUDIES
DISSERTATION ABSTRACTS INTERNATIONAL, 50(1) (JUL 89), 248-A.
THIS STUDY INVESTIGATES THE RELATIONSHIP BETWEEN THE STRUCTURE OF AN ELECTORAL SYSTEM, A POLITICAL PARTY SYSTEM, AND A PUBLIC POLICY SECTOR. IT HYPOTHESIZES THAT THE MANNER IN WHICH DEMANDS ARE PROCESSED BY THE POLITICAL SYSTEM IS STRONGLY INFLUENCED BY THE STRUCTURE OF THE ELECTORAL SYSTEM, AND THAT THIS IN TURN STRONGLY INFLUENCES THE STRUCTURE OF THE (HEALTH) POLICY SECTOR. TO DEMONSTRATE THESE RELATIONSHIPS BELGIUM AND THE NETHERLANDS, TWO NATIONS THAT ARE SOCIO-ECONOMICALLY SIMILAR BUT WITH DIFFERENT ELECTORAL SYSTEMS AND HEALTH POLICY SECTORS, ARE CHOSEN. THE DEPENDENT VARIABLE IS HEALTH POLICY, AND THE ELECTORAL SYSTEM DIFFERENCES ARE THE EXPLANATORY VARIABLES.

09176 VANDERLEEUW, J.M.
A CITY IN TRANSITION: THE IMPACT OF CHANGING RACIAL COMPOSITION ON VOTING BEHAVIOR
DISSERTATION ABSTRACTS INTERNATIONAL, 49(11) (MAY 89), 3495-A.
THE AUTHOR EXAMINES VOTING BEHAVIOR IN MAYORAL AND COUNCILMANIC ELECTIONS FROM 1965 TO 1986 IN THE CITY OF NEW ORLEANS. THE ANALYSIS PRODUCES A MODEL OF VOTING BEHAVIOR IN WHICH THE DIFFERENCE BETWEEN BLACK AND WHITE VOTER PREFERENCE BECOMES MORE PRONOUNCED AS THE BLACK PERCENTAGE OF THE ELECTORATE NEARS PARITY WITH THAT OF WHITES AND THEN DECLINES AS BLACKS BECOME THE MAJORITY.

09177 VANDETH, J.W.; GEURTS, P.A.T.M.
VALUE ORIENTATION, LEFT-RIGHT PLACEMENT, AND VOTING
EUROPEAN JOURNAL OF POLITICAL RESEARCH, 17(1) (JAN 89), 17-34.
THE AUTHORS DISENTANGLE THE CONSTRAINTS BETWEEN TRADITIONAL LINES OF POLITICAL POLARIZATION (LEFT-RIGHT PLACEMENT) AND NEWER DISTINCTIONS (MATERIALIST/POSTMATERIALIST VALUES) AMONG MASS PUBLICS. IT IS SHOWN THAT VOTING OR PARTY PREFERENCE IS MOST CLEARLY RELATED TO THE LEFT-RIGHT PLACEMENT OF THE RESPONDENTS. HOWEVER, THIS PLACEMENT IS DIRECTLY AND STRONGLY DEPENDENT ON THE MATERIALIST/POSTMATERIALIST ORIENTATION, WHILE BACKGROUND VARIABLES LIKE EDUCATION, INCOME AND AGE ARE LINKED TO VOTING VIA THIS VALUE ORIENTATION. THE MATERIALIST/POSTMATERIALIST ORIENTATION APPEARS TO BE THE PRESENT-DAY INTERPRETATION OF THE DOMINANT POLITICAL CONFLICT IN ADVANCED INDUSTRIAL SOCIETY. ALTHOUGH ALIGNMENTS AND ORIENTATIONS COUNT FOR A SUBSTANTIVE PART OF THE VARIANCE IN VOTING. THE POWER OF THESE MODELS TO PREDICT THE ACTUAL VOTE OF PEOPLE TURNS OUT TO BE RATHER POOR.

09178 VANDEVELDE, J.R.
150 JAPAN'S EMERGENCE INTO WESTERN SECURITY DOCTRINE: U.S.-JAPAN DEFENSE COOPERATION, 1976-1986
DISSERTATION ABSTRACTS INTERNATIONAL, 49(11) (MAY 89), 3500-A.
THE AUTHOR TRACES JAPANESE SECURITY POLICY, NUCLEAR STRATEGY, DEFENSE POLICY-MAKING, AND DEFENSE TECHNOLOGY-SHARING FROM 1976 TO 1986. SUBJECTS INCLUDE JAPAN'S POSTWAR CONSTITUTION AS IT APPLIES TO DEFENSE POLICY, SOVIET SECURITY POLICY TOWARD JAPAN, AMERICAN-JAPANESE DEFENSE CONSULTATION AND COOPERATION, JAPAN'S NUCLEAR STRATEGY, AND THE JAPANESE POLICY-MAKING STRUCTURE.

09179 VANDEVEN, H.J.
THE FOUNDING OF THE CHINESE COMMUNIST PARTY AND THE SEARCH FOR A NEW POLITICAL ORDER, 1920-1927
DISSERTATION ABSTRACTS INTERNATIONAL, 49(7) (JAN 89), 1930-A.
FOR THE CHINESE COMMUNIST PARTY TO BECOME A CENTRALIZED MASS PARTY ASSERTING AN IDEOLOGY, MANY CHANGES WERE NEEDED IN THE BEHAVIOR OF EARLY CCP MEMBERS, MOSTLY INTELLECTUALS. FROM INDIVIDUALISTIC PUBLICISTS THEY NEEDED TO BE MOLDED INTO REVOLUTIONARIES ABLE TO ORGANIZE UPRISINGS, TO BATTLE OUT DIFFERENCES OF OPINION IN COMMITTEES, AND WILLING TO ACCEPT THE IDEOLOGICAL AND POLITICAL AUTHORITY OF A SMALL GROUP OF LEADERS. THIS THESIS ARGUES THAT THE PROCESS LASTED FROM 1920 TO 1927 AND INVOLVED OVERCOMING TRADITIONAL MODES OF POLITICAL BEHAVIOR.

09180 VANDEWALLE, N.
PRIVATIZATION IN DEVELOPING COUNTRIES: A REVIEW OF THE ISSUES
WORLD DEVELOPMENT, 17(5) (MAY 89), 601-615.
PRIVATIZATION HAS BEEN SPURRED BY WIDESPREAD DISSATISFACTION WITH THE PERFORMANCE OF PUBLIC ENTERPRISES AND THE NEED TO CUT GOVERNMENT EXPENDITURES. UNLESS IT IS ACCOMPANIED BY LIBERALIZATION MEASURES, PRIVATIZATION OF

09181 VANGEYT, L.
CAN WE SURMOUNT OUR CRISIS?
WORLD MARXIST REVIEW, 32(2) (FEB 89), 36-39.
A CLOSE LOOK SHOWS THAT TODAY, AT THE END OF THE 1980S,
A SUFFICIENTLY BROAD AND DIVERSE SPECTRUM OF SOCIAL FORCES
CAPABLE OR QUESTIONING THE HEGEMONY OF FINANCIAL CAPITAL IN
THE WEST EUROPEAN COUNTRIES CAN HARDLY BE MOBILISED BY
APPEALING TO A SOCIALISTTYPE PERSPECTIVE, SINCE A MAJORITY
OF THE POPULATION STILL REGARDS FINANCE CAPITAL AS THE
"VEHICLE OF SCIENTIFIC AND TECHNOLOGICAL PROGRESS AND OF
MODERNITY". TODAY IT'S RATHER A MATTER OF ISOLATING, AS FAR
AS POSSIBLE, THOSE SOCIAL GROUPS AND STRATA, IN CAPITALIST
SOCIETY, INCLUDING WESTERN EUROPE, WHICH ARE AN OBSTACLE TO
RE-ORIENTING THE SCIENTIFIC AND TECHNOLOGICAL REVOLUTION FOR
THE BENEFIT OF THE WORKING CLASS AND THE POPULAR MAJORITY,
AND WHICH HAMPER DEVELOPMENT IN THE SPIRIT OF PEACEFUL
COOPERATION.

09182 VANGEYT, L.
REAWAKENING HOPE
WORLD MARXIST REVIEW, 31(2) (FEB 88), 22-30.
IN THE PAST FEW YEARS TRANSNATIONAL FINANCIAL CAPITAL
AND ITS POLITICAL PLACEMEN. USING IN THEIR INTERESTS THE
WORLD CAPITALIST CRISIS AND THE RESULTS OF PUTTING INTO
EFFECT LATEST SCIENTIFIC AND TECHNOLOGICAL ACHIEVEMENTS,
MANAGED TO LAUNCH AN OFFENSIVE IN PRACTICALLY ALL AREAS.
THIS ARTICLE EXAMINES THE DIALECTICAL RELATIONSHIP BETWEEN
SOCIO-POLITICAL STRUGGLE IN THE WORLD OF CAPITAL
(PARTICULARLY IN THE DEVELOPED WEST EUROPEAN COUNTRIES) AND
CHANGES IN THE WORLD OF SOCIALISM.

09183 VANHANEN, T.
DEVELOPMENT STRATEGY OF INDIA
SOUTH ASIA JOURNAL, 2(3) (JAN 89), 295-310.
THE ARTICLE EXAMINES THE ECONOMIC POLICIES OF INDIA
BEGINING WITH THE PRINCIPLES OF ECONOMIC DEVELOPMENT MOLDED
BY JAWAJARLAL NEHRU. IT TRACES THE DEVELOPMENT OF NEHRU'S
POLICIES AND THAT OF HIS SUCCESSORS. THE VISIONS OF INDIA'S
NATIONAL LEADERS HAVE BEEN QUITE DIFFERENT, BUT WERE OFTEN
NOT FULLY IMPLEMENTED. THE STRATEGIES OF RAJIV GANDHI ARE
EXAMINED, AND THE AUTHOR CONCLUDES THAT GANDHI IS HAVING
DIFFICULTY DISCARDING THE OUTDATED POLICIES OF THE PAST.

09184 VANHEAR, N.
NIGERIA LOSES ZEST FOR REFORM
SOUTH, (106) (AUG 89), 23.
NIGERIA'S EXPERIENCE WITH AGRICULTURAL MARKETING REFORM,
INCLUDING SCRAPPING THE STATE MARKETING BOARDS AND
INTRODUCING MARKET FORCES, IS PROVIDING A LITMUS TEST FOR
WORLD BANK-INSPIRED AGRICULTURAL REFORMS IN AFRICA. GHANA'S
MORE MODEST EXPERIMENT IN REDUCING STATE CONTROL HAS BOOSTED
COCOA EXPORTS AND REDUCED SMUGGLING. BUT NIGERIA'S PROBLEMS
ARE NOT OVER AND SOME OBSERVERS BELIEVE A RETURN TO SOME
FORM OF GOVERNMENT-REGULATED MARKETING IS NEEDED. THIS VIEW,
WHICH IS GROWING AS FREE-MARKET EUPHORIA FADES, IS GIVEN
WEIGHT BY THE EXPERIENCE OF OTHER AFRICAN COUNTRIES THAT
HAVE LIBERLIZED MARKETING WHILE RETAINING SOME STATE
INTERVENTION.

09185 VANHEAR, N.
UNIONS SHAPE UP FOR THE SHAKEDOWN
SOUTH, (103) (MAY 89), 42.
THE NIGERIAN LABOUR CONGRESS IS SHAPING UP FOR RENEWED
CONFRONTATION WITH THE GOVERNMENT OVER ECONOMIC ADJUSTMENT
POLICIES BACKED BY THE IMF AND THE WORLD BANK. THE LABOUR
MOVEMENT IS SET TO CONTINUE TO CHALLENGE THOSE POLICIES,
WHICH ELIMINATED MORE THAN 10,000 PUBLIC SECTOR JOBS IN 1988
AND HAVE ALMOST DOUBLED FOOD PRICES.

09186 VANHEERDEN, D.
F.W. DEKLERK: A SEA CHANGE
SOUTH AFRICA FOUNDATION REVIEW, 15(4) (APR 89), 3-8.
THE AUTHOR LOOKS AT SOUTH AFRICAN LEADER F.W. DEKLERK
AND SPECULATES ABOUT THE CHALLENGES THAT WILL CONFRONT HIS
ADMINISTRATION.

09187 VANPRAAGH, D.
THAILAND'S DEMOCRATIC COMEBACK
FREEDOM AT ISSUE, (111) (NOV 89), 31-34.
DEMOCRACY IN THAILAND HAS COME BACK IN ITS OWN WAY IN
RECENT YEARS, ALTHOUGH IT IS NOT YET FULLY ESTABLISHED AND
IS STILL VULNERABLE. THERE IS SOME TRUTH TO THE CHARGE THAT
THE UNITED STATES HURT THAILAND'S CHANCES FOR DEMOCRACY BY

SUPPORTING CORRUPT GENERALS, BUT THERE IS MORE EVIDENCE THAT
THE UNINTENTIONAL RESULT OF THE AMERICAN PRESENCE IN
THAILAND HAD JUST THE OPPOSITE EFFECT. BY MAKING THE RULING
GENERALS DEPENDENT ON OUTSIDE SUPPORT AND BY PROVIDING
ECONOMIC AID THAT BEGAN TO TRANSFORM THE LARGELY-FEUDAL
SOCIETY, U.S. POLICY LED TO THE DEMOCRATIC REVOLUTION OF
1973.

09188 VANROON, G.
GREAT BRITAIN AND THE OSLO STATES
JOURNAL OF CONTEMPORARY HISTORY, 24(4) (OCT 89), 657-664.
THE HISTORY OF THE ECONOMIC AND POLITICAL COOPERATION
AMONG THE OSLO STATES (NORWAY, SWEDEN, DENMARK, BELGIUM,
LUXEMBOURG, FINLAND, AND THE NETHERLANDS) BETWEEN 1930 AND
1940 IS A SUBJECT ALMOST IGNORED IN THE LITERATURE OF THE
INTER-WAR PERIOD. THE COOPERATION BEGAN WITH THE SIGNING OF
A TRADE AGREEMENT IN OSLO IN 1930. THE CONVENTION OF OSLO
WAS DRAWN UP ON THE INITIATIVE OF SOME SMALLER COUNTRIES IN
ORDER TO REDUCE TRADE BARRIERS AND SUPPORT EFFORTS BY THE
LEAGUE OF NATIONS TO COMBAT THE EFFECTS OF THE ECONOMIC
DEPRESSION.

09189 VANSANT, J.; BARCLAY, H.; TZAVARAS, A.
OPPORTUNITIES AND RISKS FOR U.S. PRIVATE VOLUNTARY
ORGANIZATIONS AS AGENTS OF LDC POLICY CHANGE
AVAILABLE FROM NTIS, NO. PB89-204309/GAR, JUN 87, 20.
GIVEN THE TREMENDOUS IMPACT OF HOST GOVERNMENT POLICIES
ON DEVELOPMENT PROJECTS, PRIVATE VOLUNTARY ORGANIZATIONS
(PVOS) ARE BECOMING MORE AND MORE INVOLVED IN POLICY
DIALOGUE. THE STUDY EXAMINES THE POTENTIAL FOR SUCCESSFUL
PVO INVOLVEMENT IN ESTABLISHING NATIONAL AND REGIONAL
GOVERNMENTAL POLICIES. SPECIFIC EXAMPLES OF SUCCESSFUL PVO
INVOLVEMENT IN POLICYMAKING ARE DISCUSSED, TOGETHER WITH THE
ADVANTAGES AND POTENTIAL PITFALLS OF ENGAGING HOST
GOVERNMENTS IN POLICY DIALOGUE. PVOS HAVE NOT TRADITIONALLY
FOSTERED THE DATA COLLECTION AND ANALYSIS CAPABILITIES
REQUIRED IN POLICY ANALYSIS, AND TEND TO BE ISOLATED FROM
DONOR AND HOST GOVERNMENT BUREAUCRACIES. DEVELOPING SUCH
CAPABILITIES MAY BE DIFFICULT. THE STUDY CONCLUDES THAT THE
DECISION TO MOVE DIRECTLY INTO POLICY INTERVENTION POSES
HARD CHOICES TO PVOS. THOSE WITH SIGNIFICANT SUCCESS IN THIS
AREA TEND TO BE WELL ESTABLISHED IN THE HOST COUNTRY, WITH
RECOGNIZED TECHNICAL EXPERTISE AND EFFECTIVE LINKAGES TO
RELEVANT SECTOR INSTITUTIONS.

09190 VANSLYCK, P.
THE U.S.: DIVISIVE CAMPAIGNS AND NEEDED CONSENSUS
FREEDOM AT ISSUE, (106) (JAN 89), 20-22.
THE PROTRACTED, PROFLIGATE, AND RANCOROUS 1988
PRESIDENTIAL ELECTION CAMPAIGN LEFT MANY AMERICANS ANNOYED
WITH THE INTERMINABLE NOMINATING PROCESS, APPALLED AT THE
LEVEL OF CAMPAIGN SPENDING, AND DISAPPOINTED BY THE
TRIVIALITY AND MEANNESS OF THE CAMPAIGN RHETORIC. THE
TRANSITION PERIOD BETWEEN ADMINISTRATIONS WAS CHARACTERIZED
BY WIDESPREAD UNEASE ABOUT THE PROSPECTS FOR EFFECTIVE
GOVERNANCE BY A GOVERNMENT THAT IS DIVIDED BY PARTISANSHIP,
IDEOLOGY, AND BITTERNESS.

09191 VANVOREN, R.
CHANGES EXPECTED IN SOVIET PSYCHIATRY
GLASNOST, (16-18) (JAN 89), 36-38.
A REPORT IN "IZVESTIA" AND A SUDDEN INCREASE IN THE
NUMBER OF PATIENTS RELEASED FROM PSYCHIATRIC HOSPITALS
INDICATE THAT THE SOVIET AUTHORITIES HAVE CHANGED THEIR
ATTITUDE TOWARD THE IMPRISONMENT OF DISSIDENTS IN
PSYCHIATRIC INSTITUTIONS. RECENT DEVELOPMENTS INDICATE THAT
SOVIET OFFICIALS ARE SERIOUS ABOUT IMPROVING THEIR BAD
REPUTATION BEFORE THE EIGHTH WORLD CONGRESS OF THE WORLD
PSYCHIATRIC ASSOCIATION MEETS IN 1989.

09192 VARAS, A.
MOSCOW AND LATIN AMERICA
HEMISPHERE, 1(3) (SUM 89), 36-37.
GLASNOST, PERESTROIKA, THE RELAXATION OF EAST-WEST
TENSIONS, AND THE DEMILITARIZATION OF INTERNATIONAL POLITICS
HAVE TRANSFORMED SOVIET POLICY TOWARD LATIN AMERICA.
ALTHOUGH THE DETAILS HAVE YET TO BE DEFINED, THE OUTLINES OF
WHAT HAS BEEN CALLED THE "RESTRUCTURING" OF SOVIET-LATIN
AMERICAN RELATIONS ARE ALREADY EVIDENT.

09193 VARAS, A.
THE TRANSFER OF MILITARY TECHNOLOGY TO LATIN AMERICA
DISARMAMENT, XII(3) (AUT 89), 95-109.
ARGENTINA, CHILE, CUBA, EL SALVADOR, HONDURAS, NICARAGUA,
GUYANA, PANAMA, PERU, AND URUGUAY ARE COUNTRIES IN WHICH A
GREATER SHARE OF RESOURCES IS BEING DIVERTED TO DEFENSE
PURPOSES, BOTH INTERNALLY AND EXTERNALLY, THAN THE
RESPECTIVE ECONOMICS CAN AFFORD. ON THE OTHER HAND, BRAZIL,
COSTA RICA, GUATEMALA, MEXICO, COLOMBIA, AND BOLIVIA ARE
ALLOCATING A SMALLER PART OF THEIR GROSS NATIONAL PRODUCT TO
DEFENSE AS A RESULT OF THE ARMED FORCES' RELATIVELY SMALLER
PART IN DECISION-MAKING AT THE GOVERNMENTAL LEVEL. MILITARY
EXPENDITURES ARE BASICALLY DEPENDENT UPON THE POSITION OF
THE ARMED FORCES IN THE STATE. THUS, THE ABILITY TO CURB

MILITARY EXPENDITURES AND ARMS SUPPLIES IN LATIN AMERICA
WILL DEPEND UPON THE STATE AND THE DEVELOPMENT OF MORE
SIGNIFICANT CIVILIAN CONTROL OVER THE MILITARY.

09194 VARDYS, V.S.
  LITHUANIAN NATIONAL POLITICS
  PROBLEMS OF COMMUNISM, XXXVIII(4) (JUL 89), 53-76.
    GLASNOST' IN THE SOVIET UNION HAS PERMITTED THE RISE OF
  THE LITHUANIAN REFORM MOVEMENT (SAJUDIS), AS WELL AS SMALLER
  INDEPENDENT GROUPS PROMOTING RADICAL CHANGES IN LITHUANIA.
  INITIALLY CLOSE TO THE GORBACHEV PROGRAM OF PERESTROYKA, THE
  SAJUDIS AGENDA HAS. IN REACTION TO RESISTANCE BY REPUBLIC
  AUTHORITIES, MOVED TO ADVOCATE LITHUANIA'S COMPLETE
  INDEPENDENCE FROM THE USSR. SAJUDIS'S MASSIVE SUCCESS
  SPURRED A COUNTER-MOVEMENT OF THE REPUBLIC'S RUSSIANS AND
  POLES SEEKING TO STEM THE TIDE OF NATIONALISM AND REFORM.
  HOWEVER, AFTER A RESOUNDING ELECTORAL DEFEAT IN THE MARCH
  1989 ELECTIONS, THE COMMUNIST PARTY OF LITHUANIA ITSELF HAS
  BEGUN TO PROMOTE LITHUANIAN AUTONOMY AND HAS EVEN PROMISED
  TO WORK FOR LITHUANIA'S INDEPENDENCE, ALTHOUGH NOT AT THE
  RAPID PACE ADVOCATED BY SAJUDIS.

09195 VARKONYI, P.
  HUNGARY: RECENT POLITICAL AND ECONOMIC DEVELOPMENTS
  WORLD TODAY, 45(5) (MAY 89), 83-85.
    HUNGARY IS EXPERIENCING A PERIOD OF PROFOUND SOCIAL,
  POLITICAL, AND ECONOMIC REFORMS. IN MAY 1988, THE HUNGARIAN
  SOCIALIST WORKERS' PARTY CONCLUDED THAT THE COUNTRY'S SOCIAL
  PRACTICE OF 40 YEARS HAD EXHAUSTED ITS POSSIBILITIES OF
  DEVELOPMENT. THIS LED TO THE DECISION TO PRESS ON WITH THE
  PROCESS OF PROFOUND RENEWAL. THE RADICAL REFORM OF BOTH THE
  POLITICAL AND THE ECONOMIC SYSTEMS REPRESENTS THE ONLY
  GUARANTEE THAT THE NEGATIVE TRENDS THAT GATHERED STRENGTH IN
  THE 1980'S WILL BE ARRESTED AND THAT THE DEVELOPMENT OF
  HUNGARIAN SOCIETY WILL RECEIVE A FRESH IMPETUS.

09196 VARON, B.W.
  THE MAGIC OF THREE YESES
  MIDSTREAM, XXXV(2) (FEB 89), 30-33.
    YASIR ARAFAT HAS FINALLY UTTERED THE "THREE YESES"
  DEMANDED BY THE UNITED STATES. ONE DOES NOT HAVE TO BE A
  CYNIC TO CONSIDER ARAFAT'S RENUNCIATION OF TERRORISM,
  INCLUDING STATE TERRORISM, AS THE WEAKEST OF HIS THREE
  AFFIRMATIONS. FIRST OF ALL, THE INTIFADA IS CLEARLY EXEMPT
  FROM THIS RENUNCIATION. SECONDLY, THE PLO HAS MANY FACTIONS,
  SOME THAT ARAFAT CONTROLS AND SOME THAT DO NOT FOLLOW HIS
  LEAD.

09197 VARSHNEY, A.
  IDEAS, INTEREST, AND INSTITUTIONS IN POLICY CHANGE:
  TRANSFORMATION OF INDIA'S AGRICULTURAL STRATEGY IN THE MID-
  1960'S
  POLICY SCIENCES, 22(3-4) (1989), 289-323.
    POLICY CHANGE IN THE THIRD WORLD HAS BECOME A MATTER OF
  CONSIDERABLE INTELLECTUAL AND PRACTICAL IMPORTANCE. FOR THE
  THEORETICALLY INCLINED, HOW ONE EXPLAINS CHANGES IN THE
  BEHAVIOR OF THE STATE IS THE MAIN ISSUE. BOTH MARXIAN AND
  LIBERAL ORTHODOXIES HAD A TENDENCY TO 'READ OFF' STATE
  BAHAVIOR FROM THE POWER RELATIONSHIPS AT THE LEVEL OF THE
  SOCIETY, THOUGH DIFFERING IN THE WAY THEY CONCEPTUALIZED
  POWER. THE RETURN OF INSTITUTIONAL AND STATECENTRIC
  EXPLANATIONS OVER THE LAST DECADE HAS ATTEMPTED TO REVERSE
  THIS BIAS BY LOOKING MORE CLOSELY AT THE POWER STRUGGLES
  WITHIN THE STATE INSTITUTIONS. FOR THE PRACTICALLY INCLINED,
  THE POWERFUL INTELLECTUAL RATIONALE BEHIND SO MANY POLICY
  RECOMMENDATIONS HAS OFTEN BEEN PUZZLINGLY LOST IN THE MAZE
  OF POLITICS. WHAT INTERESTS IMPEDE THE IMPLEMENTATION OF
  GOOD 'IDEAS', WHAT 'INSTITUTIONS' BLOCK GETTING POLICIES
  RIGHT' THESE ARE SOME OF THE KEY QUESTIONS ON THE AGENDA OF
  INTERNATIONAL DEVELOPMENT INSTITUTIONS. RESPONDING TO THESE
  VARIED CONCERNS, THIS PAPER ANALYZES A PARTICULARLY
  SUCCESSFUL CASE OF POLICY CHANGE. WHILE MOST OF THIRD WORLD
  WAS STILL EXPERIMENTING WITH LAND REFORMS AND COOPERATIVES
  AS THE WAYS TO DEVELOP AGRICULTURE, INDIA SWITCHED TO
  PRODUCER PRICE INCENTIVES AND INVESTMENTS IN NEW TECHNOLOGY,
  A CHANGE THAT IS WIDELY BELIEVED TO HAVE TURNED INDIA FROM A
  FOOD-DEFICIT SURPLUS COUNTRY.

09198 VARTANOV, I.
  THE STEAM HAS ESCAPED
  GLASNOST, (16-18) (JAN 89), 72-73.
    FOR MORE THAN FIFTY YEARS, ENORMOUS EFFORTS HAVE BEEN
  EXERTED TO DENY THE SOVIET NATIONALITIES PROBLEM AND PRETEND
  THAT IT DOES NOT EXIST. ALTHOUGH THE AUTHORITIES HAVE TRIED
  VERY HARD, THEY CANNOT KEEP UP THE CHARADE. THE DOMINANT
  IDEOLOGY CONSIGNS CONCRETE NATIONAL PROBLEMS TO AN
  ARTIFICIAL OBLIVION AND SIMULTANEOUSLY ATTEMPTS TO INSTILL
  THE ABSTRACTION OF INTERNATIONALISM INTO THE PUBLIC
  CONSCIOUSNESS. BUT THE INCREASING NUMBER OF ETHNIC CONFLICTS
  BELIES ALL THE GOVERNMENT'S EFFORTS TO WISH THE
  NATIONALITIES PROBLEM AWAY.

09199 VASCONCELOS, A.
  VIEW FROM LISBON

NATO'S SIXTEEN NATIONS, 34(5) (SEP 89), 14.
    PORTUGAL IS NOW CLOSER TO THE OTHER COUNTRIES OF WESTERN
  EUROPE, DEMOCRACY BEING FIRMLY IN PLACE AND MAJOR GOALS
  BEING MORE OF LESS THE SAME: PROGRESS AND ECONOMIC
  LIBERALIZATION, WITH BROAD SOCIAL RESPONSIBILITIES RESTING
  UPON THE GOVERNMENT. THE GROWING CONSUMER DEMAND AND
  INFLATION INDICATE THAT THE PORTUGUESE GOVERNMENT OVER THE
  NEXT FEW YEARS WILL FACE THE STRENUOUS TASK OF RECONCILING
  THE PUBLIC'S ENORMOUS EXPECTATIONS FOR IMPROVED LIVING
  STANDARDS WITH THE URGENT NEED TO INCREASE THE PACE OF
  ECONOMIC MODERNIZATION, RESTRUCTURE THE PUBLIC SECTOR AND
  STATE BUREAUCRACY, AND SIGNIFICANTLY IMPROVE EDUCATION.

09200 VASETSKY, N.
  OUTLINING TROTSKY'S POLITICAL PROFILE
  WORLD MARXIST REVIEW, 32(12) (DEC 89), 50-54.
    THIS ARTICLE PROVIDES A BRIEF BIOGRAPHICAL PROFILE OF
  LEV (LEON) TROTSKY, THEN PROCEEDS TO "OPEN UP" TROTSKY'S
  POLITICAL RESUME IN A WAY NOT POSSIBLE BEFORE THE ERA OF
  "GLASNOST" AND "PERESTROIKA". THE BITTER PERSONAL RIVALRY
  BETWEEN STALIN AND TROTSKY HAS CLOUDED UNDERSTANDING OF
  TROTSKY'S CONTRIBUTION TO THE PARTY. THOUGH MAKING SERIOUS
  MISTAKES AND MISCALCULATIONS, TROTSKY ACTED AS A RESOLUTE
  AND PURPOSEFUL LEADER CAPABLE OF MOBILIZING PEOPLE TO TACKLE
  VERY DIFFICULT TASKS.

09201 VASUKI, S. N.
  SANJAY KHAN: TRYING TIMES
  INDIA TODAY, XIV(5) (MAR 89), 28-29.
    THIS ARTICLE EXAMINES THE DETAILS OF A NEGLIGENCE SUIT
  BROUGHT AGAINST DIRECTOR/ACTOR SANJAY KHAN FOR HIS
  INVOLVEMENT WITH A PRODUCTION FIRE WHICH KILLED 42 ACTORS
  AND TECHNICIANS ON THE SET, AND INJURED MANY MORE.

09202 VASUKI, S.N.; THAKURTA, P.G.
  A SMART NEW BREED
  INDIA TODAY, 14(15) (AUG 89), 62-64.
    THIS ARTICLE REPORTS ON THE FACT THAT THE OLD-TIME TRADE
  UNION BOSSES WHO HELD UNQUESTIONED SWAY OVER THE COUNTRY'S
  WORKERS ARE SLOWLY GIVING WAY TO A NEW BREED - MORE
  PRAGMATIC, BETTER AWARE OF TECHNOLOGY, AND OFTEN, WORKERS
  THEMSELVES. IT PROVIDES SKETCHES OF A NUMBER OF YOUNGER
  UNION LEADERS TO ILLUSTRATE THE CHANGE THAT IS TAKING PLACE.

09203 VATIKIOTIS, M.
  CHANGING THE GUARDS
  FAR EASTERN ECONOMIC REVIEW, 142(52) (DEC 89), 11.
    ALMOST ONE YEAR AFTER EAST TIMOR WAS DECLARED AN OPEN
  PROVINCE ON 1 JANUARY 1989, REPORTS FROM THE CAPITAL DILI
  INDICATE THAT TENSION BETWEEN THE LOCAL POPULATION AND THE
  INDONESIAN MILITARY AUTHORITIES HAS WORSENED RATHER THAN
  IMPROVED. FEARS OF GROWING URBAN UNREST HAS PROMPTED A
  CONCILIATORY MOVE BY THE AUTHORITIES TO REORGANIZE THE LOCAL
  MILITARY COMMAND STRUCTURE.

09204 VATIKIOTIS, M.
  FAITH IN TEACHING
  FAR EASTERN ECONOMIC REVIEW, 141(30) (JUL 88), 25.
    THE PRESENTATION OF A DRAFT LAW ON EDUCATION TO THE
  INDONESIAN PARLIAMENT HAS UPSET MUSLIMS AND RAISED THE
  SENSITIVE ISSUE OF THE ROLE OF THE MAJORITY RELIGION IN THE
  STATE. MUSLIMS FEEL THAT THE NEW LAW WOULD DOWNPLAY THE ROLE
  OF RELIGIOUS INSTRUCTION IN THE SCHOOLS. THE UNDERLYING
  ISSUE, HOWEVER, IS THE GROWING SENTIMENT AMONG MUSLIMS THAT
  THE GOVERNMENT IS ATTEMPTING TO ERODE THE ROLE OF ISLAM.

09205 VATIKIOTIS, M.
  MISSION COMPLETED
  FAR EASTERN ECONOMIC REVIEW, 141(38) (SEP 88), 18.
    IN INDONESIA, THE PRESIDENT REMOVED THE ARMED FORCES'
  MOST PERVASIVE AND VISIBLE SECURITY ROLE BY ABOLISHING
  KOPKAMTIB, THE OPERATIONAL COMMAND FOR RESTORING SECURITY
  AND ORDER. THE MOVE SEEMS TO BE ONE OF THE MOST SWEEPING
  CHNAGES TO THE STRUCTURE OF THE NEW ORDER GOVERNMENT SINCE
  IT WAS ESTABLISHED 22 YEARS AGO. IT WILL AFFECT THE ROLE OF
  THE ARMED FORCES IN GENERAL AND THE BALANCE OF POWER BETWEEN
  THE MILITARY AND THE BUREAUCRACY AT THE CENTER. MANY FEEL
  THAT THE ABOLITION OF KOPKAMTIB REPRESENTS A MOVE TOWARDS A
  MORE OPEN SOCIETY SEEING THAT WHILE IT EXISTED, THE
  ACCEPTABLE PARAMETERS OF MILITARY INTERVENTION IN SOCIETY
  WERE UNDEFINED AND THAT THE KOPKAMTIB WAS ASSOCIATED WITH
  MANY "MYSTERIOUS KILLING" AND ARRESTS.

09206 VATIKIOTIS, M.
  ONE CODE FOR ALL COURTS
  FAR EASTERN ECONOMIC REVIEW, 141(38) (SEP 88), 28-30.
    XX A NEW CODIFICATION OF ISLAMIC SHARIAH LAW IS DUE TO
  BE ENACTED IN INDONESIA, COVERING MARRIAGE, DIVORCE AND
  INHERITACE. THE NEW LEGAL CODE IS AN ATTEMPT TO UNIFY THE
  COURT SYSTEM WHICH HAS OPERATED QUITE DIFFERENTLY IN THE
  PAST. IT IS AN ATTEMPT TO FORGE A PRAGMATIC APPRACH TO ISLAM
  THAT IS THE ONLY WAY TO RECONCIL ISLAMIC TRADITION WITH THE
  REALITIES OF MODERN INDONESIA. SO FAR, ALL PARTIES INVOLVED
  HAVE EXPRESSED APPROVAL FOR THE CHANGES.

09207 VATIKIOTIS, M.
OPENING THE DOOR
FAR EASTERN ECONOMIC REVIEW, 141(27) (JUL 88), 15-16.
ARGUING THAT THE PROVINCE'S CLOSED STATUS WAS HAMPERING
DEVELOPMENT, THE GOVERNOR OF EAST TIMOR CALLED FOR THE
RELAXATION OF THE PROVINCE'S STATUS AS A CLOSED AREA. MANY
ANALYSTS FEEL THAT THE POINTED NATURE OF THE APPEAL WAS AN
INDICATION THAT THERE WAS SIGNIFICANT REASON TO BELIEVE THAT
THE PROPOSAL WOULD BE WELL RECEIVED. THE DECISION IS NOW UP
TO THE INDONESIAN GOVERNMENT, AND MORE SPECIFICALLY THE
ARMED FORCES WHO EXERCISE JURISDICTION OVER EAST TIMOR.

09208 VATIKIOTIS, M.
OUT OF THE SHADOWS
FAR EASTERN ECONOMIC REVIEW, 141(36) (SEP 88), 41-42.
AFTER 12 YEARS, INDONESIA SEEMS FINALLY READY TO BEGIN
TO SCALE DOWN ITS REPRESSION IN THE FORMER PORTUGESE COLONY
OF EAST TIMOR. INDONESIAN AUTHORITIES HAVE DECLARED THEIR
INTENT TO DECLARE THE PROVIDENCE TO BE "OPEN" BY THE END OF
1988. ALTHOUGH THE MILITARY STILL ADMITS TO "LOW-LEVEL"
INSURGENCY IN THE FORM OF 300-400 FRETILIN GUERRILLAS, TUMOR
IS FOR THE MOST PART STABLE.

09209 VATIKIOTIS, M.
RESTLESS ON CIVVY STREET
FAR EASTERN ECONOMIC REVIEW, 141(32) (AUG 88), 22.
IN AN EFFORT TO RAISE THEIR PROFILE BEFORE THE PARTY'S
NATIONAL CONGRESS, SEVERAL YOUNGER MEMBERS OF THE GOVERNMENT
PARTY, GOLKAR, HAVE STRONGLY SPOKEN OUT AGAINST THE
GOVERNMENT-BACKED LOTTERY. THEIR UNDERLYING AIM IS TO SECURE
FOR "CIVILIAN POLITICIANS" A LARGER ROLE IN THE ARMED FORCES
DOMINATED GOLKAR.

09210 VATIKIOTIS, M.
SMILES AND SOFT WORDS
FAR EASTERN ECONOMIC REVIEW, 141(32) (AUG 88), 28-29.
THE MEETING OF THE FOUR WARRING FACTIONS IN CAMBODIA AND
"OTHER INTERESTED PARTIES" AT THE "JAKARTA INFORMAL MEETING"
HAS BROUGHT A MIXED REACTION. ALTHOUGH ALL AGREE ON THE
IMPORTANCE OF HAVING ALL THE INVOLVED FACTIONS SIT DOWN
TOGETHER FOR THE FIRST TIME, MANY FEEL THAT NO REAL PROGRESS
WAS MADE; OLD POSITIONS WERE SIMPLY PRESENTED IN NEW CLOTHES.
A MAJOR FACTOR THAT RESULTED IN THE MEETING'S ONLY MARGINAL
SUCCES WAS THE REFUSAL OF EITHER VIETNAM OR THE KHMER ROUGE
TO ALTER THEIR POSITIONS.

09211 VAUGHAN, M.B.; MUSGRAVE, F.W.; THOMAS, H.L.
THE EVOLVING HEALTH CARE SYSTEM: ECONOMIC INTEGRATION
THROUGH RECIPROCITY
JOURNAL OF ECONOMIC ISSUES, XXIII(2) (JUN 89), 493-502.
POLANYI VIEWED RECIPROCITY AS ONE OF THREE KEY ELEMENTS
FOR ECONOMIC INTEGRATION. THIS ARTICLE EXAMINES RECIPROCAL
RELATIONSHIPS IN THE HEALTH CARE SECTOR AND SHOWS THAT THE
ALLOCATION OF MUCH MODERN BIOTECHNOLOGY IS GOVERNED BY
RECIPROCITY. IN THE ARENA OF RECIPROCAL HEALTH CARE
ARRANGEMENTS, THE ALLOCATIVE DECISIONS OF PHYSICIANS ARE
CRITICAL. THIS SUGGESTS THAT RECIPROCITY MAY SERVE AS A
DEVICE FOR PERPETUATING PHYSICIAN AUTONOMY. IT ALSO POINTS
TO THE NEED FOR FUTURE RESEARCH TO EXPLORE BOTH THE GENERAL
EXTENT OF PHYSICIAN CONTROL AND THE COMPLEX CRITERIA THAT
PHYSICIANS USE TO GUIDE NON-MARKET ALLOCATIONS.

09212 VAXBERG, A.I.
CIVIL RIGHTS IN THE SOVIET UNION
PHILADELPHIA: ANLS OF AMER ACMY OF POLITICAL AND SOC
SCIENCE, (506) (NOV 89), 109-114.
CIVIL RIGHTS IN THE SOVIET UNION ARE DISCUSSED AGAINST
THE BACKDROP OF CHANGES OCCURRING IN THE SOVIET LEGAL SYSTEM.
THE SOVIET UNION IS SET ON A COURSE TO CREATE A LAW-BASED
STATE. WITH THE SIGNING OF THE VIENNA CONCLUDING DOCUMENT,
THE SOVIET UNION RECOGNIZED THE PRIORITY OF INTERNATIONAL
LAW OVER DOMESTIC SOVIET LAW, WITH THE CONSEQUENCE THAT
EFFORTS ARE BEING MADE TO BRING DOMESTIC SOVIET LEGISLATION
INTO CONFORMITY WITH INTERNATIONAL LAW. NOW PERMITTED, EVEN
ENCOURAGED, IS THE CREATION OF VOLUNTARY ORGANIZATIONS THAT
MONITOR THE IMPLEMENTATION OF THE HELSINKI ACCORD.
FURTHERMORE, A PROGRAM IS BEING CARRIED OUT TO EDUCATE THE
PUBLIC ON THE INTERNATIONAL AGREEMENTS ON HUMAN RIGHTS THAT
THE USSR HAS SIGNED.

09213 VAYRYNEN, P.
THE FINNISH CENTRE PARTY: A UNIQUE PARTY
INTERNATIONAL AFFAIRS (MOSCOW), (11) (NOV 89), 49-57.
THE SPECTRUM OF FINNISH POLITICAL PARTIES IS SIMILAR TO
THAT OF MANY WEST EUROPEAN COUNTRIES, INCLUDING THE FINNISH
SOCIAL DEMOCRATIC PARTY AND THE NATIONAL COALITION PARTY.
THE FINNISH CENTRE PARTY, WHICH IS A STRONG PEASANT PARTY,
ALSO PLAYS AN IMPORTANT ROLE. POLITICAL PARTIES LIKE THE
FINNISH CENTRE EXIST ONLY IN THE NORDIC COUNTRIES, BUT THE
CENTRIST PARTIES OF SWEDEN AND NORWAY ARE RELATIVELY WEAK.
THE DISTINCTIVE POLITICAL CONDITIONS OF THE NORDIC COUNTRIES
EXPLAIN THE EXISTENCE OF THE CENTRIST PARTIES.

09214 VAYRYNEN, R.
FROM A PARTIAL TO A COMPREHENSIVE TEST BAN
DISARMAMENT, XII(1) (WIN 89), 17-24.
SINCE WORLD WAR II, A BAN ON ALL NUCLEAR TESTS HAS BEEN
ONE OF THE MAJOR DEMANDS OF THOSE OPPOSING THE PROLIFERATION
OF NUCLEAR WEAPONS. THE PRIMARY DEMAND HAS BEEN FOR A
COMPREHENSIVE BAN ON NUCLEAR TESTS, BUT THE ACTUAL TREATY
REALIZED IN 1963 FELL SHORT OF THIS OBJECTIVE. INSTEAD OF A
COMPREHENSIVE BAN, IT PROHIBITS TESTS IN THREE ENVIRONMENTS:
THE ATMOSPHERE, OUTER SPACE, AND UNDERWATER. THE FAILURE TO
ACHIEVE A BAN ON UNDERGROUND TESTING ASSURED THAT THE ISSUE
WOULD REMAIN ON THE INTERNATIONAL ARMS CONTROL AGENDA.

09215 VEASEY, R.
DEVOLUTIONARY FEDERALISM AND ELAZAR'S TYPOLOGY: THE
ARKANSAS RESPONSE TO REAGAN'S NEW FEDERALISM
PUBLIUS: THE JOURNAL OF FEDERALISM, 18(1) (WIN 88), 61-78.
THE ARTICLE EXAMINES THE RELATIONSHIP BETWEEN THE
FEDERAL AND STATE GOVERNMENTS WITH REGARD TO THE REAGAN
ADMINISTRATION'S NEW FEDERALISM. THE UNDERLYING CONCERN
CENTERS ON THE FINANCIAL RELATIONSHIP AMONG GOVERNMENTS
PORTRAYED BY ELAZAR'S TYPOLOGY OF FEDERAL AID. THE FOCUS OF
THIS INVESTIGATION IS DIRECTED TOWARD THE ADJUSTMENTS BEING
MADE BY THE STATES TO ACCOMMODATE THE FINANCIAL AND
ADMINISTRATIVE CHANGES OCCURING ON THE NATIONAL LEVEL, AS
ILLUSTRATED BY THE CASE OF ARKANSAS. THE ANALYSIS CENTERS ON
TWO QUESTIONS: 1) HAS THE NEW FEDERALISM INITIATIVE ACHIEVED
REAGAN'S GOALS OF DECENTRALIZING GOVERNMENTAL AUTHORITY BACK
TO THE STATES? 2) HAS A MAJOR REDIRECTION IN THE FEDERAL
SYSTEM BEEN ACHIEVED BY REDUCING THE FEDERAL FINANCIAL
OBLIGATION IN THE INTERGOVERNMENTAL SYSTEM? THE CHANGES
BEING MADE IN THE FEDERAL SYSTEM, AS REFLECTED BY THE
ADJUSTMENTS OCCURING AMONG THE STATES, MAY SIGNAL AN
IMPORTANT REALIGNMENT OF FEDERALISM.

09216 VEDLITZ, A.
A QUESTION OF VALUES: CONSERVATIVES AND THE CULTURE OF
POVERTY
SOCIAL JUSTICE RESEARCH, 2(4) (DEC 88), 235-248.
EVERY SOCIETY HAS WITHIN IT SOME INDIVIDUALS AND GROUPS
WHO ARE SUCCESSFUL AND SOME WHO ARE LESS SUCCESSFUL.
EXPLANATIONS FOR THESE DIFFERENCES RANGE FROM THE POLITICAL
TO THE ECONOMIC AND FROM THE CULTURAL TO THE RELIGIOUS. FOR
AMERICAN CONSERVATIVES, THE DIFFERENCES IN INDIVIDUAL LEVELS
OF ACHIEVEMENT CAN BE EXPLAINED PRIMARILY IN CULTURAL TERMS.
THE CONSERVATIVE MYTHOLOGY ARGUES THAT THERE ARE CLEARLY
SUPERIOR AND CLEARLY INFERIOR CULTURAL VALUES AND THAT GOOD
VALUES PRODUCE SUCCESSFUL INDIVIDUALS. THIS ARTICLE DEALS
WITH THE FUNDAMENTALLY TAUTOLOGICAL NATURE OF THIS ARGUMENT:
WHY IS SO-AND-SO SUCCESSFUL? BECAUSE HE OR SHE HAS BETTER
VALUES. HOW DO WE KNOW HE OR SHE HAS BETTER VALUES? BECAUSE
HE OR SHE IS SUCCESSFUL. AFTER ELABORATING THIS INTELLECTUAL
PROBLEM, AN EMPIRICAL TEST IS MADE OF THE EXISTENCE OF
DIFFERENT VALUES AMONG AMERICA'S SOCIAL GROUPS. USING CENSUS
DATA AND NATIONAL SURVEY DATA, THE PERSONAL GOALS AND
ATTITUDES OF VARIOUS SOCIETAL GROUPS AND THEIR RELATIVE
ECONOMIC ACCOMPLISHMENTS ARE PRESENTED AND COMPARED. THIS
ANALYSIS DEMONSTRATES THAT FEW OF THE CULTURE-BASED
DIFFERENCES WHICH ARE ASSERTED BY CONSERVATIVES CAN BE
VALIDATED EMPIRICALLY.

09217 VEENSTRA, J.
THEORY AND PRACTICE OF FOREIGN ASSISTANCE TO REGIONAL
DEVELOPMENT PLANNING: THE CASE OF PERIPHERAL RURAL AREAS
IN ACEH, INDONESIA
PUBLIC ADMINISTRATION AND DEVELOPMENT, 9(5) (NOV 89),
523-542.
THIS PAPER DEALS WITH THE PILOT CASE OF DUTCH TECHNICAL
AND FINANCIAL ASSISTANCE TO THE PROVINCIAL PLANNING BOARD IN
INDONESIA'S MOST WESTERN SPECIAL TERRITORY OF ACEH. WITH
SPECIFIC REFERENCE TO THE TWO DISTRICTS OF ACEH UTARA AND
ACEH TENGAH, THE PICTURE OF DEPENDENCY RELATIONSHIPS IS
SKETCHED FOR RURAL PERIPHERIES IN THE THIRD WORLD.
DEVELOPMENT PLANNING EFFORTS HAVE NOT SUCCESSFULLY ADDRESSED
PERSISTENT PROBLEMS, EITHER BECAUSE THEY WERE BASED UPON
URBAN-BIASED POLICY PRESCRIPTIONS WRONGLY TRANSFERRED FROM
THE NORTHERN HEMISPHERE, OR BECAUSE RATIONALCOMPREHENSIVE
PLANNING PROCEDURES WERE TOO ARBITRARILY BLUEPRINTED.
FOCUSING UPON THE LATTER MISAPPLICATION, THE PAPER PRESENTS
A PRACTICAL WORKING PROCEDURE FOR MANAGING, THROUGH FIVE
STAGES, A MULTI-ANNUAL AND RATIONALIZING EXERCISE, SUCH AS
DUTCH ASSISTANCE TO IMPROVING REGIONAL PLANNING METHODS
EMPLOYED BY LOW-LEVEL ADMINISTRATIVE UNITS IN PERIPHERAL
RURAL REGIONS. THERE FOLLOWS A CRITICAL REVIEW OF NINE YEARS
OF DUTCH REGIONAL PLANNING ASSISTANCE BY COMPARING THEORY
AND PRACTICE OF THREE APPROACHES APPLIED TO THE TWO
DISTRICTS OF ACEH UTARA/TENGAH. THE DUTCH LESSONS LEARNED
UNDERLINE INTER-SECTORAL PROGRAMME PREPARATION,
INSTITUTIONALIZATION AND TRAINING COMPONENTS. A 6-7 YEARS
WORKING PROCEDURE FOR FUTURE FOREIGN-ASSISTED DISTRICT
PLANNING PROJECTS IS PROPOSED.

09218 VELAZQUEZ, D.
FROM NEIGHBORHOOD TO NATION

NACLA REPORT ON THE AMERICAS, XXIII(4) (NOV 89), 22-27.
OVER 600,000 SQUATTER FAMILIES ARE ORGANIZED NATION-WIDE
IN MEXICO'S "URBAN PEOPLES' MOVEMENT," WHICH HAS GROWN FROM
A COLLECTION OF LOCAL STRUGGLES TO BECOME A FORCE CAPABLE OF
CHALLENGING THE REGIME. WHILE RESISTING CO-OPTATION BY THE
RULING PARTY, AND INSISTING ON AUTONOMY FROM THE OPPOSITION,
THE MOVEMENT HAS SHOWN THAT DEMOCRATIC COMMUNITY
PARTICIPATION NOT ONLY CAN SOLVE SOME OF THE DRASTIC
PROBLEMS FACED BY THE POOR MAJORITY, IT CAN BE A VEHICLE FOR
REVOLUTIONARY CHANGE.

09219 VELYAMINOV, G.
WHAT KIND OF A UNITED MARKET?
INTERNATIONAL AFFAIRS (MOSCOW), (2) (FEB 89), 72-77.
ECONOMIC ISOLATION, WITH INDUSTRY AND AGRICULTURE GEARED
TO SUPPLYING ONLY THE NATIONAL MARKET, SPELLS STAGNATION AND
LOSS OF THE ECONOMY'S COMPETITIVE CAPACITY. BY CONTRAST,
ACCESS TO AN INTEGRATED MULTINATIONAL MARKET PROVIDES
SUBSTANTIAL ECONOMIC BENEFITS. THE NEED TO CREATE A SINGLE
MARKET OF SOCIALIST COUNTRIES IS GAINING URGENCY. AS FAR AS
THE CMEA COUNTRIES ARE CONCERNED, THIS IS AN IMPORTANT,
URGENT TASK. DECISIONS OF THE 43RD (EXTRAORDINARY) AND 44TH
SESSIONS OF THE CMEA DEFINED IT AS A GENERAL GUIDELINE FOR
THE MEMBER STATES.

09220 VENKATRAMAN, A.
PROPOSED CONSTITUTIONAL AMENDMENT ON PANCHAYATI RAJ: SOME
REFLECTIONS
INDIAN JOURNAL OF POLITICAL SCIENCE, L(3) (JUL 89),
402-408.
THE PROPOSED 64TH AMENDMENT TO THE CONSTITUTION OF INDIA
ON PANCHAYATI RAJ HAS ATTRACTED VOCIFEROUS POLITICAL
REACTION. PREDICTABLY, THE NON-CONGRESS (I) STATE
GOVERNMENTS VIEW THE PROPOSAL WITH SUSPICION AND DISTRUST,
SEEING IT AS YET ANOTHER UNION INFRINGEMENT ON STATE
GOVERNMENT AUTONOMY. THE MAJOR POLITICAL PARTIES ARE
CAPITALIZING ON THE ISSUE, EITHER SUPPORTING OR OPPOSING THE
EFFORT TO AMEND THE CONSTITUTIONAL PROVISIONS ON THE
ORGANIZATION OF PANCHAYATS AS UNITS OF LOCAL SELF-GOVERNMENT.

09221 VENTER, A.J.
THE SOUTH AFRICAN PLURAL SOCIETY: REFLECTIONS AND MUSINGS
TOWARDS ITS UNDERSTANDING....
PLURAL SOCIETIES, 19(1) (SEP 89), 1-20.
THE AUTHOR EXPLAINS THE CONTEXT OF THE COMPLEX
PHENOMENOM NAMED SOUTH AFRICAN POLITICS. IN ATTEMPTING TO
GEAR THIS ANALYSIS TO A READERSHIP WHICH MAY ONLY BE
BEGINNING THE EXPLORATION, HE WRITES FROM A HIGH LEVEL OF
GENERALIZATION AND CONCEPTUALIZATION, WHILE TRYING TO AVOID
BEING REDUCTIONIST. THE APPROACH IS THEORETICAL, EMPIRICAL
AND REFLECTIVE, FROM A BASIC PREMISE THAT THERE IS NO ONE
SOUTH AFRICAN SOCIETY, THAT IT IS MARKED BY THE ABSENCE OF A
SOCIAL AND POLITICAL ORDER SHARING COMMON VALUES, TRADITIONS,
LANGUAGE, CULTURE, POLITICAL LOYALTY, RELIGION, MYTHS, OR
OTHER USUAL FORMS AND MANIFESTATIONS OF SOCIAL COHESION.

09222 VENTER, D.
IMPLICATIONS OF THE 1992 EUROPEAN COMMUNITY SINGLE MARKET
FOR SOUTH AFRICA
SOUTH AFRICA FOUNDATION REVIEW, 15(7) (JUL 89), 6.
THE ARTICLE EXAMINES THE IMPLICATIONS OF THE 1992
EUROPEAN COMMUNITY SINGLE MARKET FOR SOUTH AFRICA; IT
DIVIDES THE RAMIFICATIONS INTO THREE AREAS: EUROPEAN
ECONOMIC UNION AND PROTECTIONISM; EUROPEAN COMMUNITY
POLITICAL UNION; AND EUROPEAN COMMUNITY ECONOMIC SANCTIONS
AGAINST SOUTH AFRICA. THE ARTICLE WARNS AGAINST THE DANGERS
OF A "FORTRESS EUROPE" AND THE POSSIBILITY OF INCREASED
ECONOMIC SANCTIONS. CORPORATE PLANING AND THE ASSUMPTION OF
A EUROPEAN IDENTITY BY SOUTH AFRICAN COUNTRIES ARE ADVOCATED
AS IMPORTANT MEASURES DESIGNED TO PREPARE SOUTH AFRICA FOR
1992.

09223 VENTRISS, C.
THE INTERNATIONALIZATION OF PUBLIC ADMINISTRATION AND
PUBLIC POLICY: IMPLICATIONS FOR TEACHING
POLICY STUDIES REVIEW, 8(4) (SUM 89), 898-903.
INCREASINGLY, THE NATIONS OF THE WORLD ARE BECOMING MORE
INTERDEPENDENT THIS IS TRUE NOT ONLY IN AN ECONOMIC SENSE,
BUT IN A POLITICAL SENSE AS WELL. THE FIELD OF PUBLIC
ADMINISTRATION HAS BECOME INTERNATIONALIZED, PRESENTING A
NEW CHALLENGE TO BOTH TEACHERS AND STUDENTS OF THE
DISCIPLINE. THE ARTICLE ARGUES THAT SPECIAL ATTENTION SHOULD
BE GIVEN TO TEACHING STUDENTS HOW TO MANAGE POLICY
INTERDEPENDENCY. FURTHERMORE, THE INTERDISCIPLINARY APPROACH
IS ADVOCATED AS A METHOD OF BROADENING STUDENTS'
PERSPECTIVES IN PUBLIC ADMINISTRATION. IN CONCLUDING THE
ARTICLE, THE AUTHOR OFFERS SEVERAL RECOMMENDATIONS FOR
IMPROVING PUBLIC ADMINISTRATION PROGRAMS.

09224 VENTURONI, G.
EMERGING TECHNOLOGIES FOR NAVAL WARFARE AND MARITIME FORCES
INTERNATIONAL SPECTATOR, XXIII(1) (JAN 89), 53-59.
TECHNOLOGY OFFERS A VARIETY OF OPTIONS AND OPPORTUNITIES
THAT CAN CONSIDERABLY ENHANCE OPERATIONAL CAPABILITIES AND

REMARKABLY INFLUENCE WARFARE CONCEPTS. IN THIS ESSAY, THE
AUTHOR SURVEYS THE TRENDS AND IMPLICATIONS OF EMERGING
TECHNOLOGIES FOR CONVENTIONAL FORCES IN THE PREVAILING
CONTEXT OF A NATO SCENARIO REFERRING TO THE SOUTHERN REGION
AND, IN PARTICULAR, TO ITALY.

09225 VERBAAN, M.
BORN IN BLOOD
AFRICA REPORT, 34(5) (SEP 89), 27-29.
AS THE FINAL COUNT-DOWN TO ELECTIONS IN NAMIBIA BEGINS,
POLITICAL VIOLENCE AND INTIMIDATION CONTINUE TO MAR THE
PROCESS LEADING TO THE NATION'S INDEPENDENCE. ALTHOUGH VOTER
REGISTRATION WAS COMPLETED AND CAMPAIGNING IS UNDERWAY, THE
BRUTAL MURDER OF SWAPO MEMBER ANTON LUBOWSKI HAS SIGNALLED
THAT NAMIBIA'S BIRTH WILL BE FAR FROM PAINLESS.

09226 VERBAAN, M.
NAMIBIA: SOUTH AFRICA RULES
NEW AFRICAN, (262) (JUL 89), 21.
THIS ARTICLE EXPLORES THE TENUOUS WORKING RELATIONSHIP
BETWEEN SOUTH AFRICA AND THE UN IN NAMBIA. THOUGH BOTH
SHOULD BE ADMINISTERING THE INDEPENDENCE PROCESS, SOUTH
AFRICA IS RUNNING THE SHOW AND MAINTAINS AN OFFENSIVE POLICY
IN ITS DEALINGS WITH THE UN. ARRANGEMENTS ARE BEING RIGGED
AGAINST SWAPO, THE ARMED WING OF THE OPPOSITION GROUP;
POLITICAL PRISONERS ARE STILL DETAINED AND INCIDENTS OF
INTIMIDATION ESCALATE AS THE UN IS FORCED INTO A DEFENSIVE
POSITION.

09227 VERBAAN, M.
PEACE ON PRETORIA'S TERMS?
AFRICA REPORT, 34(3) (MAY 89), 13-16.
THE APRIL 1, 1989, MOVEMENT OF SWAPO FIGHTERS FROM BASES
IN ANGOLA INTO NORTHERN NAMIBIA HAS RAISED QUESTIONS
REGARDING THE ROLE OF THE UNITED NATIONS TRANSITION
ASSISTANCE GROUP, AS WELL AS PROVIDING PRETORIA WITH
JUSTIFICATIONS TO DELAY THE PEACE PROCESS. INTIMIDATION AND
VIOLENCE CONTINUE TO JEOPARDIZE PROSPECTS FOR NAMIBIA'S
INDEPENDENCE.

09228 VERBAAN, M.
THE ROAD TO INDEPENDENCE
AFRICA REPORT, 34(6) (NOV 89), 13-16.
FOLLOWING ITS LANDSLIDE VICTORY IN THE NOVEMBER ELECTION,
SWAPO'S FIRST FORMIDABLE TEST WILL BE WRITING A
CONSTITUTION FOR AN INDEPENDENT NAMIBIA. SWAPO MUST FIND
SOME COMMON GROUND WITH ITS ELECTORAL OPPONENTS IN THE
NATION'S NEW CONSTITUENT ASSEMBLY BECAUSE IT WILL NEED SEVEN
ADDITIONAL VOTES TO GET ITS CONSTITUTION ADOPTED.

09229 VERBAAN, M.
VIEW FROM NAMIBIA
NEW AFRICAN, (257) (FEB 89), 12-14.
CONFUSION AND DOUBT PERVADE VIRTUALLY EVERY LEVEL OF
NAMIBIAN SOCIETY FROM THE SOUTH AFRICAN-APPOINTED INTERIM
GOVERNMENT MINISTERS TO THE MANY THOUSANDS LIVING IN THE
NORTHERN WAR ZONE. NAMBIBIANS ARE FINDING THAT THE SITUATION
HAS BECOME A HARD ONE TO MONITOR AND ANALYZE NOW THAT THE
MATTER OF NAMIBIA'S INDEPENDENCE SEEMS TO HAVE DRIFTED OUT
OF THE HANDS OF POLITICIANS AND INTO THE REALM OF THE HARD-
CORE BUREAUCRACY WHERE VITAL DECISIONS MUST STILL BE MADE BY
THE FIVE PERMANENT MEMBERS OF THE UN SECURITY COUNCIL.

09230 VEREBELYI, I.
CHANGES AND CONTRADICTIONS IN HUNGARIAN PUBLIC
ADMINISTRATION
INTERNATIONAL REVIEW OF ADMINISTRATIVE SCIENCES, 55(1)
(MAR 89), 15-24.
THE ARTICLE EXAMINES PUBLIC ADMINISTRATION IN HUNGARY
WHICH THE AUTHOR IDENTIFIES AS "THE PUBLIC ADMINISTRATION OF
A SOCIALIST SYSTEM BUILT ON THE INTER-RELATION OF CENTRAL
PLANNING AND A MARKET ECONOMY, AND IS CHARACTERIZED BY AN
IMPLEMENTED DECENTRALIZATION AND BY A RECENT INCREASE IN
DEMOCRATIZATION." THE ARTICLE EXPLORES THE CHANING ROLE OF
PUBLIC ADMINISTRATION INCLUDING THE TRANSFORMATION OF PUBLIC
ADMINISTRATION'S ORGANIZATION AND STAFF AND EFFORTS TO
REDUCE BUREAUCRACY.

09231 VERHEYEN, T.F.
FOREIGN POLICY CULTURES: GERMANY AND THE UNITED STATES IN
HISTORICAL AND COMPARATIVE PERSPECTIVE
DISSERTATION ABSTRACTS INTERNATIONAL, 49(11) (MAY 89),
3500-A.
THIS DISSERTATION OFFERS A COMPARATIVE ANALYSIS OF WEST
GERMAN AND AMERICAN FOREIGN POLICY CULTURE. THE AUTHOR SEEKS
TO IDENTIFY THOSE SUBJECTIVE, OFTEN INTANGIBLE, PSYCHO-
CULTURAL INGREDIENTS THAT MAKE THE USA AND WEST GERMANY
"TICK." AMERICAN FOREIGN POLICY CULTURE HAS BEEN INFLUENCED
BY LIBERALISM, PURITANISM, THE FRONTIER, OPTIMISM, SELF-
CONFIDENCE, AND OTHER FACTORS. AMONG THE WEST GERMAN
INFLUENCES ARE AN ILLIBERAL POLITICAL TRADITION, AN ANTI-
WESTERN CULTURAL LEGACY, PROBLEMS OF IDENTITY, A TROUBLED
PAST, AND SO FORTH.

09232 VERIASKIN, V.G.
ON THE PERSONALITY FACTOR IN THE HISTORY OF THE CPSU
SOVIET REVIEW, 30(3) (MAY 89), 40-51.
THE AUTHOR DISCUSSES A METHODOLOGICAL SEMINAR HELD TO
CONSIDER THE ROLE OF COMMUNIST HISTORIANS IN OVERCOMING THE
STAGNATION IN SOVIET SOCIETY. HISTORICAL EVENTS ARE THE
RESULT OF THE ACTIONS OF THE WORKING MASSES AND THE
COMMUNIST PARTY. BUT SOVIET HISTORIANS OFTEN FAIL TO SHOW
THE ROLE OF SPECIFIC INDIVIDUALS IN CONCRETE CIRCUMSTANCES,
THEIR FATES, SUCCESSES, CONFUSION, AND ERRORS, THEREBY
DEPERSONALIZING HISTORY AND DEPRIVING IT OF ITS HEROIC AND
DRAMATIC QUALITY. BUT MARXISM-LENINISM RECOGNIZES THE MASSES
AS THE DECISIVE FORCE IN HISTORICAL PROGRESS AND DOES NOT
DENY OR UNDERESTIMATE THE ROLE OF INDIVIDUALS IN HISTORY.

09233 VERKHOUSKLL, A.
WORKERS CLUBS ON THE EVE OF KUZBASS
ACROSS FRONTIERS, 5(3) (FAL 89), 9.
THIS IS A REPORT ON THE STATUS OF WORKERS CLUBS IN THE
USSR. IT DESCRIBES THE INTER-CITY WORKERS' CLUB (MRK) AND
ANALYZES ITS GROWTH, THE JULY CONFERENCE OF WORKERS' CLUBS
IS EVALUATED BY DELEGATES AND GUESTS.

09234 VERMAAT, J.A.E.
MIRAGE IN THE MIDDLE EAST
MIDSTREAM, XXXV(2) (FEB 89), 26-29.
AFTER HECTIC DEBATES AT A MEETING OF THE PALESTINE
NATIONAL COUNCIL IN NOVEMBER 1988, YASIR ARAFAT PROCLAIMED
THE ESTABLISHMENT OF THE STATE OF PALESTINE ON PALESTINIAN
TERRITORY, WITH ITS CAPITAL JERUSALEM. THIS DECLARATION
ELEVATED POLITICAL BANALITY TO THE LEVEL OF OBSCURANTIST
INTERNATIONAL DIPLOMACY. IT ALSO REVEALED THE CAPACITY OF
THE PLO AND THE VARIOUS PALESTINIAN POLITICAL FACTIONS TO
CREATE MIRAGES IN THE MIDDLE EAST.

09235 VERMAAT, J.A.E.
SHOULD HERR HONECKER VISIT THE U.S.?
FREEDOM AT ISSUE, (109) (JUL 89), 5-8.
THE GREAT BULK OF THE POPULATION OF EAST GERMANY IS NOT
COMMUNIST. IN FACT, RESENTMENT TOWARD COMMUNISM AND THE
COMMUNIST PARTY REGIME IN EAST GERMANY HAS GROWN IN RECENT
YEARS AND THE REGIME FEELS INCREASINGLY INSECURE. WITH
POLAND AND HUNGARY TAKING THE LEAD IN LIBERALIZATION AND
SOVIET GLASNOST KNOCKING AT THE DOOR, THERE IS VERY LITTLE
FOR THE BREZHNEVITES OR STALINISTS TO CLING TO. THE ONLY
THING THEY HAVE LEFT IS THEIR "ANTI-FASCIST PROTECTION WALL,
" AND THOSE WHO BUILT IT--ERICH HONECKER ABOVE ALL--ARE MORE
LIKE PRISON WARDENS THAN STATESMEN.

09236 VERNEY, D. V.
FROM EXECUTIVE TO LEGISLATIVE FEDERALISM? THE
TRANSFORMATION OF THE POLITICAL SYSTEM IN CANADA AND INDIA
REVIEW OF POLITICS, 51(2) (SPR 89), 241-263.
CANADA AND INDIA HAVE HYBRID SYSTEMS OF GOVERNMENT. BOTH
EXPERIENCED CONSTITUTIONAL CRISES IN THE 1970'S. THESE
CRISES HAVE USUALLY BEEN TREATED AS SUI GENERIS. IT IS THE
HYPOTHESIS OF THIS ARTICLE THAT THE CRISES RAISE FUNDAMENTAL
QUESTIONS REGARDING THE VERY NATURE OF SUCH SYSTEMS, WHICH
ARE BASED ON "PARLIAMENTARY FEDERALISM," A POLITICAL SYSTEM
INVENTED IN CANADA TO PROVIDE STRONG CENTRAL GOVERNMENT.
THIS HYBRID SYSTEM COMBINES TWO CLASSICAL MODELS: BRITISH
TRADITION, BASED ON PARLIAMENTARY SUPREMACY AND CONVENTIONS,
AND AMERICAN PRINCIPLES, WHICH REQUIRE A WRITTEN
CONSTITUTION, THE SEPARATION OF POWERS AND JUDICIAL REVIEW.
THE TWO MODELS ARE CONTRADICTORY, SINCE PARLIAMENTARY
SUPREMACY AND CONSTITUTIONAL SUPREMACY ARE INCOMPATIBLE.
NEITHER CANADA NOR INDIA CAN PROPERLY BE COMPARED TO THE
CLASSICAL MODELS. THEY WERE NEVER WHOLLY BRITISH BECAUSE
THEY ADOPTED THE FEDERAL PRINCIPLE, AND THEY COULD NEVER
BECOME WHOLLY AMERICAN BECAUSE THEY RETAINED THE
PARLIAMENTARY TRADITION. AS HYBRIDS THEY HAVE EACH EVOLVED
INTO SOMETHING QUITE DIFFERENT. THE SYSTEMS MAY NOW BE IN A
PERIOD OF TRANSITION FROM EXECUTIVE TO LEGISLATIVE
FEDERALISM.

09237 VERNON-WORTZEL, H.; WORTZEL, L.H.
PRIVATIZATION: NOT THE ONLY ANSWER
WORLD DEVELOPMENT, 17(5) (MAY 89), 633-641.
GOVERNMENTS IN MANY DEVELOPING COUNTRIES CREATED STATE-
OWNED ENTERPRISES (SOE'S) TO PRODUCE GOODS OR PROVIDE
SERVICES THE PRIVATE SECTOR SEEMED UNWILLING OR UNABLE TO
OFFER. IN MANY CASES, SOE'S HAVE TURNED OUT TO BE PROBLEM
CHILDREN - AT BEST, INEFFICIENT AND, AT WORST, UNABLE TO
FULFILL THEIR ORIGINAL FUNCTIONS. NOW THE RECOMMENDED
SOLUTION TO THE PROBLEM OF STATE-OWNED ENTERPRISES IS
PRIVATIZATION. BUT PRIVATIZATION IS NO MORE A SOLUTION TO
THE PROBLEMS OF SOE'S THAN SOE'S WERE A SOLUTION TO THE
PROBLEMS THEY WERE CREATED TO SOLVE. THE PROBLEM OF SOE'S IS
NOT OWNERSHIP, BUT RATHER A LACK OF EXPLICIT GOALS AND
OBJECTIVES AND AN ABSENCE OF ORGANIZATION CULTURES AND
SYSTEMS THAT SUPPORT AND ENCOURAGE FULFILLMENT OF AN
ENTERPRISE'S GOALS AND OBJECTIVES BECAUSE OF THE CULTURE AND
SYSTEMS IT FOSTERS; IN OTHER CASES NOT.

09238 VERNON, G.D.
THE ROLE OF THE THIRD WORLD IN US-SOVIET RELATIONS
DISSERTATION ABSTRACTS INTERNATIONAL, 49(7) (JAN 89),
1953-A.
THE AUTHOR EXAMINES THE DETERMINANTS OF SOVIET FOREIGN
POLICY, WITH SPECIAL EMPHASIS ON THE ROLE OF SOVIET IDEOLOGY
TOWARD THE THIRD WORLD. HE USES CASE STUDIES OF THE VIETNAM
WAR, THE 1973 OCTOBER WAR, AND THE ANGOLA CRISIS TO
DETERMINE HOW THE SOVIET UNION HAS BALANCED ITS THIRD WORLD
GOALS AND US-SOVIET RELATIONS IN THE RECENT PAST.

09239 VERNON, R.; SPAR, D.L.
BEYOND GLOBALISM: REMAKING AMERICAN FOREIGN ECONOMIC POLICY
THE FREE PRESS, NEW YORK, NY, 1988,
AMERICAN INTERNATIONAL ECONOMIC POLICY, THOUGH
FORMULATED BY A PROCESS OF STRUGGLE AMONG COMPETING
INTERESTS, HAS BEEN GUIDED BY CERTAIN GENERALLY ACCEPTED
VALUES. AS A RESULT OF TRYING TO ADHERE TO THESE VALUES, THE
ACTIONS OF THE PRESIDENT AND CONGRESS ON TRADE, INVESTMENT,
AND FOREIGN AID ISSUES HAVE OFTEN SEEMED WAVERING AND
INCONSISTENT. TODAY, A NEW INTERNATIONAL ECONOMIC ORDER IS
EMERGING AND AMERICA MUST REASSESS ITS FOREIGN ECONOMIC
OBJECTIVES. THIS REFORMULATION, HOWEVER, MUST RECOGNIZE THAT
THE VALUES TO WHICH AMERICA CLINGS WILL INEVITABLY CONFLICT,
GENERATING A PATTERN THAT WILL OFTEN SEEM VACILLATING.
NEVERTHELESS, THE U.S. STILL HAS THE POWER TO INCREASE ITS
EFFECTIVENESS IN MEETING THE CHALLENGES OF THE NEW
INTERNATIONAL ENVIRONMENT.

09240 VERSI, A.
HOPES SHATTERED
NEW AFRICAN, (257) (FEB 89), 15-16.
THE PEACE AGREEMENT BETWEEN THE DEMOCRATIC UNIONIST
PARTY AND THE SOUTHERN PEOPLES LIBERATION ARMY IS IN TATTERS.
THE DUP HAS RESIGNED FROM THE COALITION GOVERNMENT,
DEMONSTRATIONS AND STRIKES HAVE INFLICTED HEAVY BLOWS ON AN
ALREADY BELEAGURED ECONOMY, A COUP WAS ATTEMPTED, AND A
STATE OF EMERGENCY IS IN FORCE.

09241 VERYHA, W.
UKRAINIAN SETTLEMENT IN YUGOSLAVIA (C. 1700-1980)
UKRANIAN QUARTERLY, XLV(2) (SUM 89), 195-208.
THE UKRAINIAN MINORITY IN YUGOSLAVIA CONSISTS OF
ESSENTIALLY TWO DIFFERENT GROUPS OF IMMIGRANTS DISTINGUISHED
BY THE TIME OF THEIR ARRIVAL AND ALSO BY THE REGION OF THEIR
ORIGIN. THE UKRAINIAN SETTLERS IN YUGOSLAVIA FORMED
COMMUNITIES OF THEIR OWN WHERE THEY HAVE PRESERVED THEIR
LANGUAGE, THE GREEK CATHOLIC-BYZANTINE RITE FAITH, AND
NATIONAL TRADITIONS CHARACTERISTIC OF THE REGION OF THEIR
ORIGIN. GEOGRAPHICALLY, AND SUBSEQUENTLY POLITICALLY, THEY
ARE REPRESENTED IN FOUR DIFFERENT PROVINCES BELONGING TO
THREE DIFFERENT YUGOSLAV REPUBLICS. NOTWITHSTANDING THE FACT
THAT THE UKRAINIANS OF YUGOSLAVIA ARE NOT NUMEROUS AND ARE
DIVIDED GEOGRAPHICALLY, THEY HAVE THEIR OWN GEOGRAPHICAL,
SOCIOPOLITICAL, HISTORICAL, AND CULTURAL CHARACTERISTICS.

09242 VERYHA, W.
UKRAINIAN SETTLEMENT IN YUGOSLAVIA (C. 1700-1980): PART II
UKRANIAN QUARTERLY, XLV(3) (FAL 89), 289-317.
THE AUTHOR OFFERS A BRIEF HISTORICAL SURVEY OF THE
UKRAINIAN MIGRATION TO YUGOSLAVIA, UKRAINIAN EFFORTS TO KEEP
THEIR IDENTITY AND CULTURE ALIVE IN YUGOSLAVIA, AND THE
UKRAINIAN CONTRIBUTION TO PUBLIC LIFE.

09243 VESTA U.
HOW GOVERNMENTS FILTER RESEARCH. THE CASE OF THE
RELATIONSHIP BETWEEN DISARMAMENT AND DEVELOPMENT
CURRENT RESEARCH ON PEACE AND VIOLENCE, 11(4) (1988),
169-176.
THE INTERNATIONAL CONFERENCE ON THE RELATIONSHIP BETWEEN
DISARMAMENT AND DEVELOPMENT WAS HELD IN THE UN HEADQUARTERS
IN 1987. THE OUTCOME WAS THE FINAL DOCUMENT ADOPTED BY
CONSENSUS. THIS ARTICLE LOOKS AT THE FINAL DOCUMENT FROM THE
PERSPECTIVE OF PEACE RESEARCH, AND MORE SPECIFICALLY,
SCRUTINIZES HOW A GOVERNMENTAL CONFERENCE FILTERS RESEARCH,
I.E. HOW GOVERNMENTS PERCEIVE, SELECT, MOLD RESEARCH RESULTS
AND TURN THEM TO ACTION-PROGRAMS. IT CONCLUDES THAT A BETTER-
INFORMED INTERESTED PUBLIC OPINION CAN HELP TO CREATE
POLITICAL WILL AT THE GOVERNMENTAL LEVEL.

09244 VESTAL, T.
FEDERAL ADMINISTRATION OF THE SURFACE MINING CONTROL AND
RECLAMATION ACT OF 1977 IN OKLAHOMA
PUBLIUS: THE JOURNAL OF FEDERALISM, 18(1) (WIN 88), 45-60.
THE ARTICLE STUDIES THE INTERACTION OF THE COAL INDUSTRY
AND THE STATE AND FEDERAL REGUATORY AGENCIES. SPECIAL
EMPHASIS IS PLACED ON THE SURFACE MINING CONTROL AND
RECLAMATION ACT OF 1977. THE STUDY CONCLUDES THAT THE
INTERACTION HAS BEEN BENEFICIAL FOR OKLAHOMA AND THAT A NEW.
AND MORE "COOPERATIVE FEDERALISM" IS DEVELOPING IN THE
REGULATION OF COAL MINING.

09245 VESTAL, T.M.
THE SURFACE MINING CONTROL AND RECLAMATION ACT OF 1977 IN

OKLAHOMA: STATE AND FEDERAL COHABITATION
POLICY STUDIES REVIEW, 9(1) (AUT 89), 143-151.
THE ENFORCEMENT OF THE SMCRA IN OKLAHOMA HAS LED TO
IMPROVEMENTS AND TRANSFORMATIONS IN THE COAL INDUSTRY, STATE
AND FEDERAL REGULATORY AGENCIES, AND THE PUBLIC. THE
CATALYST FOR THESE CHANGES WAS THE FEDERAL TAKEOVER OF
INSPECTION AND ENFORCEMENT OF THE SMCRA IN OKLAHOMA WITH THE
STATE CARRYING ON ALL OTHER MINING REGULATORY ACTIVITIES
FROM 1984 THROUGH 1987. THIS PATTERN OF COHABITATION
DIFFERED FROM THAT IN TENNESSEE WHERE OSM TOOK OVER ALL
ENFORCEMENT OF THE SMCRA OR THAT IN STATES THAT ENTER INTO
COOPERATIVE AGREEMENTS TO PROVIDE STATE REGULATION OF COAL
MINING ON FEDERAL LANDS WITHIN THE STATE. COHABITATION IN
OKLAHOMA PRODUCED A NEW, MORE POSITIVE ATTITUDE TOWARD
COOPERATIVE FEDERALISM BY BOTH FEDERAL AND STATE REGULATORY
BODIES THAT MIGHT SERVE AS A MODEL FOR OTHER STATES.

09246 VETSCHERA, H.
REDUCTION OF CONVENTIONAL ARMED FORCES IN EUROPE: PROBLEMS
AND PROSPECTS
DISARMAMENT, XII(2) (SUM 89), 70-71.
THE AUTHOR LOOKS AT THE BACKGROUND OF THE CONFERENCE ON
SECURITY AND COOPERATION IN EUROPE (CSCE) AND THE TALKS ON
MUTUAL REDUCTION OF FORCES AND ARMAMENTS AND ASSOCIATED
MEASURES IN CENTRAL EUROPE (MURFAAMCE). HE ALSO DISCUSSES
THE PROBLEMS CONFRONTING THE NEGOTIATORS AND THE PROSPECTS
FOR SUCCESS.

09247 VIALET, J.C.
IMMIGRATION REFORM IN THE 1980'S
CRS REVEIW, 10(6) (JUL 89), 24-25.
DURING THE 1980S THE CONGRESS HAS BEEN REVIEWING AND
REVISING ALL ASPECTS OF IMMIGRATION POLICY. LEGISLATION
PROVIDING FOR FLEXIBILITY IN RESPONSE TO REFUGEES WITHIN THE
FRAMEWORK OF THE BASIC IMMIGRATION LAW WAS ENACTED IN 1980.
AFTER LENGTHY AND INTENSIVE DEBATE, LEGISLATION AIMED AT
CONTROLLING ILLEGAL IMMIGRATION WAS ENACTED IN 1986.
CONGRESS IS CURRENTLY REAPPRAISING THE REGULATION OF LEGAL
IMMIGRATION. AT THE SAME TIME, LARGELY UNANTICIPATED
INTERNATIONAL EVENTS ARE FORCING A REEVALUATION OF THE 1980
REFUGEE LEGISLATION.

09248 VIASUVANNA, N.
AN ANALYSIS OF RECRUITMENT AND SELECTION PROCESSES OF
PUBLIC ENTERPRISES IN THAILAND
DISSERTATION ABSTRACTS INTERNATIONAL, 50(3) (SEP 89),
790-A.
THE AUTHOR PROBES THE RELATIONSHIP BETWEEN THE LEVEL OF
TECHNOLOGY USED IN THAI PUBLIC ENTERPRISE AND THE
RECRUITMENT AND SELECTION BEHAVIOR OF ENTERPRISE PERSONNEL.
HIS MAJOR HYPOTHESIS IS THAT THE HIGHER THE LEVEL OF
TECHNOLOGY USED IN THE ENTERPRISE, THE HIGHER THE
TECHNOLOGICAL QUALIFICATIONS OF THE EMPLOYEES AND THE HIGHER
THE UNIVERALISTIC CHARACTERISTIC OF THE RECRUITMENT AND
SELECTION PROCESS.

09249 VICKERS, G.D.
THE VIETNAM ANTIWAR MOVEMENT IN PERSPECTIVE
BULLETIN OF CONCERNED ASIAN SCHOLARS, 21(2-4) (APR 89),
100-110.
THIS ARTICLE EXAMINES THE THREE MAIN TYPES OF ASSERTIONS
ABOUT THE IMPACT AND SIGNIFICANCE OF THE VIETNAM ANTWAR
MOVEMENT. IT THEN DETAILS FIVE PRINCIPAL ARGUMENTS FOR
JUSTIFICATION BY THE ADMINISTRATION FOR U.S. INTERVENTION.
IT FOLLOWS PROGRESS OF THE MOVEMENT FROM PROTEST TO
RESISTANCE, DESCRIBES WINS AND LOSSES AND THE ANTIWAR
MOVEMENT AS A SOCIAL MOVEMENT. IT DETAILS THE LESSONS OF
VIETNAM AND SUGGESTS HISTORICAL RESPONSIBILITY OF THE
ANTIWAR MOVEMENT.

09250 VICKERY, M.
CAMBODIA (KAMPUCHEA) HISTORY, TRAGEDY, AND UNCERTAIN FUTURE
BULLETIN OF CONCERNED ASIAN SCHOLARS, 21(2-4) (APR 89),
35-58.
THIS IS A HISTORICAL SKETCH TO HELP ILLUSTRATE IMPORTANT
FEATURES OF CAMBODIA'S HISTORICAL, GEOGRAPHICAL, AND
INTERNATIONAL SITUATION THAT ARE RELEVANT FOR UNDERSTANDING
BOTH THE PAST AND THE PRESENT. IT DETAILS THE RISE AND FALL
OF PARTY POLITICS, ROYAL SOCIALIST DICTATORSHIP, THE
CAMBODIAN WAR AND THE LATER POLITICAL ECONOMY. THE PRK AND
THE INTERNATIONAL COMMUNITY IS EXPLORED

09251 VIDAL-HALL, J.
A STRANGE KIND OF PEACE
SOUTH, (100) (FEB 89), 10-14.
THE GENEVA ACCORDS BETWEEN PAKISTAN AND THE AFGHAN
GOVERNMENT IN KABUL, DESIGNED TO USHER IN A POLITICAL
SETTLEMENT OF THE AFGHAN STALEMATE, HAVE PRODUCED A STRANGE
KIND OF PEACE. AFGHANS ARE PREDICTING THE RETURN OF CIVIL
WAR, WITH THE USA FINDING ITSELF IN THE HOT SEAT RECENTLY
VACATED BY THE USSR.

09252 VIDAL-HALL, J.
ROOTS OF THEOCRACY

SOUTH, (100) (FEB 89), 32-33.
AS THE PRICE FOR SUPPORTING YITZHAK SHAMIR'S LIKUD,
WHICH WAS UNABLE TO FORM A GOVERNMENT ON ITS OWN, ISRAEL'S
ULTRA-RELIGIOUS PARTIES DEMANDED THE IMPLEMENTATION OF WHAT
MANY CALL "A TYRANNY OF THE MINORITY." THEY ARE ATTEMPTING
TO MOVE ISRAEL CLOSER TO THE THEOCRACY THAT LIBERAL,
WESTERNIZED JEWS OPPOSE.

09253 VIDAL-HALL, J.
THE YEAR OF LETTING GO
SOUTH, (99) (JAN 89), 28-30.
WITH DETENTE GATHERING MOMENTUM AMONG THE SUPERPOWERS,
1989 WILL BE THE YEAR WHEN EUROPE BEGINS TO REASSEMBLE THE
PIECES FRAGMENTED IN THE AFTHERMATH OF WORLD WAR II. THE
YEAR 1989 MAY WELL SEE FURTHER REDUCTIONS IN NUCLEAR WEAPONS,
A BREAKTHROUGH IN NEGOTIATIONS ON THE WITHDRAWAL OF
CONVENTIONAL FORCES IN EUROPE, AND PROGRESS ON THE STRATEGIC
ARMS REDUCTION AGREEMENT. BUT THERE IS LESS REASON FOR
OPTIMISM ABOUT NORTH-SOUTH DIALOGUE AND THE SOLUTION OF
REGIONAL CONFLICTS.

09254 VIDAL-HALL, J.
WELLSPRINGS OF CONFLICT
SOUTH, (103) (MAY 89), 23-25.
URBANIZATION, POPULATION GROWTH, INDUSTRIALIZATION, AND
AGRICULTURAL DEVELOPMENT ARE DEPLETING THE ONCE-ABUNDANT
WATER RESOURCES OF THE MIDDLE EAST. FROM TURKEY TO EGYPT,
ALL THE STATES IN THE REGION SHARE THE WATER FROM THREE
RIVER SYSTEMS. WITH SO MUCH DEPENDENCE ON SO LITTLE WATER,
IT COULD REPLACE OIL AS THE PRECIOUS COMMODITY OF THE FUTURE.

09255 VIDAL, A.C.; KOMIVES, B.
COMMUNITY DEVELOPMENT CORPORATIONS: A NATIONAL PERSPECTIVE
NATIONAL CIVIC REVIEW, 78(3) (MAY 89), 168-177.
INCREASINGLY, COMMUNITY DEVELOPMENT CORPORATIONS ARE
BEING RECOGNIZED AS MAJOR AGENTS OF IMPROVEMENT IN
DETERIORATED NEIGHBORHOODS AND STAGNATED ECONOMIES. THE
NUMBER OF SUCH OF GROUPS AND THEIR TOTAL FUNDING CONTINUES
TO GROW. THE EXTENT AND NATURE OF THIS SUPPORT WILL DEFINE
THEIR FUTURE ROLE IN COMMUNITY DEVELOPMENT.

09256 VIDIC, D.
WHAT ARE THE UNSETTLED QUESTIONS IN THE BALKANS?
REVIEW OF INTERNATIONAL AFFAIRS, (JAN 88), 7-8.
THIS ARTICLE EXAMINES THE EXTENT TO WHICH UNSETTLED
QUESTIONS IN BILATERAL RELATIONS AMONG BALKAN COUNTRIES
INFLUENCE THE REALIZATION OF MULTILATERAL ACTIVITIES AMONG
THEM. THE AUTHOR CONCLUDES THAT THE FACT THAT ALL
GOVERNMENTS OF THE BALKAN COUNTRIES REPLIED IN THE
AFFIRMATIVE TO THE YUGOSLAV INITIATIVE FOR HOLDING A FOREIGN
MINISTERS' CONFERENCE IS A POSITIVE STEP TOWARD FURTHER
COOPERATION.

09257 VIDICH, A.J.; HUGHEY, M.W.
FRATERNIZATION AND RATIONALITY IN GLOBAL PERSPECTIVE
INTERNATIONAL JOURNAL OF POLITICS, CULTURE AND SOCIETY,
2(2) (WIN 88), 242-256.
IN ECOLOGICAL TERMS, THE EARTH MAY BE A GLOBAL VILLAGE,
BUT IT IS NOT A COMMUNITY. YET, IN THIS VILLAGE, THE
POSSIBILITIES FOR FRATERNIZATION ACROSS ETHNIC, RACIAL,
SEXUAL, GENDER, RELIGIOUS, COMMERCIAL, POLITICAL, AND
ELECTRONIC LINES ARE BOTH COMMONPLACE AND UNLIMITED. THE
UNITED STATES, THE MOST DEEPLY SECULARIZED AND INNER-WORDLY
OF ALL THE NATIONS OF THE WORLD, BEARS THE BURDEN OF PROVING
THAT CIVILIZED FRATERNIZATION ACROSS ALL SOCIAL BOUNDARIES
IS POSSIBLE.

09258 VIDICH, A.J.
STATE, SOCIETY AND CALVINISM: PARSONS AND MERTON AS SEEN
FROM ABROAD
INTERNATIONAL JOURNAL OF POLITICS, CULTURE AND SOCIETY,
2(1) (FAL 88), 109-125.
SINCE WORLD WAR II, THE DOMINANT SOCIOLOGICAL
ORIENTATIONS IN THE UNITED STATES HAVE BEEN STRUCTURAL-
FUNCTIONALISM AND SYSTEMS THEORY. IN THIS ESSAY THE
IDEOLOGICAL SOURCES OF THESE SOCIAL THEORIES ARE SHOWN TO BE
IN PROTESTANT THOUGHT, A POINT STRESSED IN THE RECENT
EVALUATIONS OF THE WORKS OF PARSONS, BUT OVERLOOKED IN A
RECENT ASSESSMENT OF THE SOCIOLOGY OF ROBERT MERTON.

09259 VIDYADHARAN, A
THE ENEMY WITHIN: INDIA'S SEPARATIST MOVEMENTS
CULTURAL SURVIVAL QUARTERLY, 13(2) (1989), 43-52.
ALL OVER THE WORLD SEPARATIST MOVEMENTS ARE SEEKING
INDEPENDENCE FROM STATE AUTHORITY. INDIA IS NO EXCEPTION TO
THIS PHENOMENON; ITS DIVERSE TRIBAL POPULATIONS AND THE
POLITICAL STRUGGLES CARRIED OVER FROM INDEPENDENCE MAKE IT
PARTICULARLY VULNERABLE TO INTERIOR STRIFE. ON THE ONE HAND,
REGIONAL GROUPS ARE CLAMORING FOR STATEHOOD: GORKHALAND,
KOLHANISTAN, JHARKHAND. ON THE OTHER, INSURGENTS ARE FIGHTING
FOR INDEPENDENCE: THE TRIPURA NATIONAL VOLUNTEERS, THE
UNITED LIBERATION FRONT OF ASSAM, THE NATIONAL SOCIALIST
COUNCIL OF NAGALAND. THIS ARTICLE PROVIDE A BRIEF OVERVIEW
OF SOME OF THE TENSION POINTS AROUND THE COUNTRY.

09260 VIEIRA, G.
COLUMBIA: "WE WILL CONTINUE TO RESPOND TO THE DEATH SQUADS WITH MASS MOBILIZATIONS, STRIKES AND SELF-DEFENSE" INFORMATION BULLETIN, 26(23-24) (DEC 88), 14-15.
IN THIS ARTICLE, THE AUTHOR DESCRIBES HIS YEARS AS GENERAL SECRETARY OF THE COLUMBIA COMMUNIST PARTY AND OFFERS AN EVALUATION OF CURRENT PEACE PROCESS IN COLUMBIA. SINCE COLUMBIA'S VARIOUS GUERRILLA MOVEMENTS HAVE UNITED AND FORMED THE SIMON BOLIVAR NATIONAL COORDINATING COMMISSION, THESE HAS BEEN A CLEAR WILLINGNESS TO RESUME TALKS WITH THE GOVERNMENT. IT IS UP TO THE GOVERNMENT TO RESPOND AND EASE THE TENSION.

09261 VIGLIETTA, R.
U.S. PRESENCE IN THE MEDITERRANEAN SEA AS A RESULT OF NATIONAL INTERESTS IN THE AREA AND NATO INVOLVEMENT AVAILABLE FROM NTIS, NO. AD-A209 068/6/GAR. MAR 89, 71.
IN THE MEDITERRANEAN AREA AND ITS PROXIMITIES (MIDDLE EAST AND NORTH AFRICA) THERE ARE SEVERAL CONTRASTS AND ELEMENTS OF TENSION DUE TO: DIFFERENT POLITICAL REGIMES, RELIGION AND CULTURAL BACKGROUND; TERRITORIAL CLAIMS; NO UNIFORM DISTRIBUTION OF POPULATION; AND INEQUITIES IN ECONOMIC RESOURCES (OIL AND OTHER RAW MATERIAL). THE AREA HAS ALSO SEEN A LONGSTANDING CONFRONTATION BETWEEN NATO AND THE USSR. AS MOSCOW HAS TRIED TO ESTABLISH AND THEN EXPAND ITS MILITARY PRESENCE AND INFLUENCE IN THE MEDITERRANEAN AREA AND EVEN MORE IN THE MIDDLE EAST. IN THIS TROUBLED AREA, THE UNITED STATES HAS A SIGNIFICANT MILITARY PRESENCE AND DECLARED POLITICAL AND ECONOMIC INTERESTS. THIS ESSAY ANALYZES THE SITUATION IN THE AREA, FOCUSING ON THE ELEMENTS OF TENSION, AND EXAMINES THE POSSIBILITY THAT A CONFLICT COULD ARISE FOR THE U.S. BETWEEN NATO DEFENSE NEEDS AND U.S. NATIONAL INTERESTS. THE ANALYSIS CONCLUDES THAT, EVEN WITH PERIODIC DISAGREEMENTS WITH ITS ALLIES, THE U.S. CAN ACHIEVE ITS OBJECTIVES WHILE THE NATO COUNTRIES OF THE AREA WILL CONTINUE TO RECEIVE FULL BENEFIT FROM THE U.S. PRESENCE AND ACTIONS. THE UNITED STATES SHOULD WORK TO IMPROVE ITS COORDINATION AND CONSULTATION WITH ITS PARTNERS, WITHIN THE NATO ORGANIZATION AND ON A BILATERAL BASIS. THE EUROPEAN NATO COUNTRIES, AT THE SAME TIME, ARE INVITED TO COOPERATE MORE AND COORDINATE THEIR INVOLVEMENT TO HELP THE U.S. IN RESOLVING THE VARIOUS CONFLICTS IN THE REGION.

09262 VILE, J.
ANN DIAMOND ON AN UNLIMITED CONSTITUTIONAL CONVENTION PUBLIUS: THE JOURNAL OF FEDERALISM, 19(1) (WIN 89), 177-184.
ANN DIAMOND HAS ARGUED THAT. UNLESS IT IS CALLED BY ALL THE STATES, A CONVENTION HELD UNDER ARTICLE V OF THE CONSTITUTION OF THE UNITED STATES WOULD BE LIMITED TO PROPOSING PIECEMEAL CHANGES. DIAMOND'S ARGUMENTS ARE FLAWED. THE POWER OF THE STATES TO CALL A CONVENTION TO PROPOSE AMENDMENTS IS COEQUAL WITH THE POWER OF CONGRESS TO PROPOSE AMENDMENTS AND IS SUBJECT TO ONLY ONE EXPLICIT LIMITATION. THE CONVENTION OF 1787 WAS NOT ATTENDED BY ALL THE STATES, AND IT DID NOT DELIMIT TWO TYPES OF FUTURE CONVENTIONS. DIAMOND'S ANALYSIS REFLECTS EXTREME NOTIONS OF INDIVIDUAL STATE SOVEREIGNTY THAT LACK HISTORICAL SUPPORT AND WOULD, IN ANY EVENT, UNDULY HOBBLE THE STATES AS A WHOLE.

09263 VILE, J.R.; FOSHEE, A.W.
DOMESTIC POLITICS IN THE BOOK OF JUDGES
JOURNAL OF POLITICAL SCIENCE, 16(1-2) (1988), 33-42.
THE AUTHORS LOOK AT CONTEMPORARY AMERICAN POLITICAL PROBLEMS THROUGH THE BIBLICAL CASE STUDY OF GIBEAH IN THE BOOK OF JUDGES. THEY ARGUE THAT THIS CASE STUDY ILLUSTRATES THE NEED FOR A MORE REGULARIZED SYSTEM OF LEADERSHIP AND FAR-SIGHTED FEDERALISM AS WELL AS FOR BETTER APPLICATION OF JUSTICE AND VIRTUE IN THE HEBREW SENSE.

09264 VILLAFRANKA, A.M.
THE VENEZUELAN ELECTIONS OF 1988
ELECTORAL STUDIES, 8(2) (AUG 89), 183-188.
IN THE ELECTIONS OF 4 DECEMBER 1988 THE SUPREME ELECTORAL COMMISSIONS (CSE) OF VENEZUELA DECLARED CARLOS ANDRES PEREZ OF ACCION DEMOCRATICA (AD) ELECTED FOR A FIVE YEAR TERM, SUCCEEDING JAIME LUSINCHI (ALSO OF AD) TO THE PRESIDENCY. HOWEVER, AD LOST ITS ABSOLUTE MAJORITY IN THE CONGRESS. CARLOS ANDRES PEREZ TOOK POSSESSION OF THE POST FOR THE SECOND TIME ON 4 FEBRUARY 1989, WITHOUT DOUBT A HISTORIC ACT. PRINCIPALLY BECAUSE ONCE MORE, SINCE THE START OF VENEZUELA'S DEMOCRATIC PERIOD IN 1958, THE SYSTEM HAS BEEN STRENGTHENED BY THE CHOICE OF INCUMBENT THROUGH THE FREE WILL OF THE PEOPLE. FURTHER, SINCE FOR THE FIRST TIME A VENEZUELAN WHO HAD ALREADY HELD THE HIGHEST OFFICE IN THE LAND, FROM 1973-78, WILL SERVE A SECOND TERM OF OFFICE, 1988-93. THIS ELECTION IS ALSO THE FIRST TIME SINCE 1968 THAT THE PRESIDENCY WILL STAY IN THE HANDS OF THE SAME PARTY FOR TWO CONSECUTIVE TERMS.

09265 VILLALOBOS, J.
A DEMOCRATIC REVOLUTION FOR EL SALVADOR
FOREIGN POLICY, (74) (SPR 89), 103-122.

THE AUTHOR ATTEMPTS TO DEMONSTRATE THE NECESSITY OF THE REFORMS ADVOCATED BY THE "REVOLUTIONARY" FARABUNDO MARTI NATIONAL LIBERATION FRONT (FMLN) IN EL SALVADOR. HE ARGUES THAT THE US-BACKED CHRISTIAN DEMOCRATIC GOVERNMENT HAS COLLAPSED AND THAT A NEGOTIATED POLITICAL SETTLEMENT IS A PRECONDITION TO SOLVING THE CURRENT CONFLICT. HE FOCUSES ON THE DIFFERENCES BETWEEN THE FMLN AND OTHER LEFT-WING REVOLUTIONARY MOVEMENTS AND ARGUES THAT THE FMLN'S ADAPTABILITY AND ITS ABILITY TO FORM PLURALISTIC COALITIONS WITH OTHER MOVEMENTS MAKES IT A VITAL COMPONENT TO PEACE AND LASTING STABILITY IN EL SALVADOR. HE ALSO ANALYSES THE IMPLICATIONS OF NEGOTIATED SETTLEMENT FOR THE US AND CENTRAL AMERICA AND CONCLUDES THAT SETTLEMENT WOULD RESULT IN PEACE AND EQUILIBRIUM IN ALL OF CENTRAL AMERICA, A GOAL THAT THE US OSTENSIBLY SUPPORTS.

09266 VILLALOBOS, J.
POPULAR INSURRECTION: DESIRE OR REALITY?
LATIN AMERICAN PERSPECTIVES, 16(3) (SUM 89), 5-37.
THIS ARTICLE ASSESSES THE SITUATION IN EL SALVADOR AND EXPLAINS THE STRATEGY OF THE FARABUNDO MARTI NATIONAL LIBERATION (FMLN). THE AUTHOR ANALYZES THE DEMISE OF THE CHRISTIAN DEMOCRATS AS A SETBACK FOR THE UNITED STATES COUNTERINSURGENCY. PROJECT, ANTICIPATES THE NEW ARENA REGIME AND OUTLINES WHY THE FMLN BELIEVES THE STAGE IS SET FOR A PROCESS OF POPULAR INSURRECTION.

09267 VILLALOBOS, J.
THE PROSPECT OF A REVOLUTIONARY VICTORY
CENTRAL AMERICA BULLETIN, 8(7-8) (JUN 89), 1-8.
AT THIS STAGE IN THE EL SALVADORAN CONFLICT, IT IS HARDLY REASONABLE TO DISMISS THE FMLN'S PROGNOSIS OF A REVOLUTIONARY VICTORY BASED ON THE PROCESS OF MASS INSURRECTION AS EITHER A SIMPLE IDEOLOGICAL DELUSION OR BELLICOSE GRANDSTANDING. WHEN THE POSSIBILITY OF MASS SOCIAL UPHEAVAL IS RAISED, IT BECOMES A QUESTION NOT ONLY OF THE FMLN'S WILLINGNESS TO ACT BUT ALSO OF THE EVIDENT OBJECTIVE REALITY WITHIN WHICH THE FMLN ACTS. FAILING TO ACT WOULD NOT ONLY CONSTITUTE A STRATEGIC POLITICAL ERROR, IT WOULD PAVE THE WAY FOR THE RESURGENCE OF THE ECONOMIC AND POLITICAL MODEL OF DOMINATION THAT LED TO THE WAR AND TO U.S. INTERVENTION.

09268 VINCENT, R.
ARMS CONTROL AND FUTURE MILITARY CONCEPTS
RUSI JOURNAL, 134(4) (WIN 89), 5-9.
GENERAL SIR RICHARD VINCENT EXAMINES THE FUTURE OF WESTERN MILITARY STRATEGY IN LIEU OF THE SWEEPING POLITICAL CHANGES TAKING PLACE IN EASTERN EUROPE AND THE USSR. HE ARGUES THAT THE CURRENT CHANGES ARE A DIRECT RESULT OF THE WESTERN POLICY OF MAINTAINING ADEQUATE MILITARY MIGHT WHILE REMAINING WILLING TO NEGOTIATE. HOWEVER, THE WESTERN MILITARY POLICY IS BECOMING A VICTIM OF ITS OWN SUCCESS: MANY NOW QUESTION THE CONTINUING RELEVANCE OF SOME ASPECTS OF THE BVERY STRATEGY THAT FACILITATED THE CHANGES IN THE EAST IN THE FIRST PLACE. VINCENT ASSESSES THE POSSIBILITY OF ARMS REDUCTION IN EUROPE AND ANALYZES THE IMPLICATIONS OF (ONGOING NEGOTIATIONS.

09269 VINING, D.R. JR.
THE 'DEMOGRAPHIC PROBLEM' IN ISRAEL
MANKIND QUARTERLY, 33(1,2) (FAL 89), 65-70.
THE 'DEMOGRAPHIC PROBLEM' IS SIMPLY THE FOLLOWING: THE PERCENTAGE OF THE POPULATION OF ISRAEL THAT IS NONJEWISH IS GROWING. THERE HAS BEEN SOME DISPUTE THIS. SOME VIEW THAT THIS PROPORTION IS GROWING AND SOME OTHERS VIEW THAT IT IS NOT, THE PURPOSE OF THIS PAPER IS SIMPLY TO INVESTIGATE THIS PROBLEM, USING THE OFFICIAL STATISTICS OF THE CENTRAL BUREAU OF STATISTICS IN ISRAEL.

09270 VINOD, M.J.
IMAGES OF INDIA IN THE UNITED STATES: RETROSPECT AND PROSPECT
INDIAN JOURNAL OF POLITICAL SCIENCE, L(3) (JUL 89), 376-388.
A MAJOR REASON FOR THE OFTEN-UNSATISFACTORY RELATIONS BETWEEN NEW DELHI AND WASHINGTON LIES WITH THE UNREALISTIC IMAGES AND PERCEPTIONS OF INDIA COMMON IN THE UNITED STATES. A MAJOR HURDLE IN U.S.-INDIA RELATIONS IS AMERICAN INDIFFERENCE, IN SPITE OF RECENT EFFORTS TO PROJECT A FRESH LOOK AT INDIA. TWO MAJOR REASONS LIE BEHIND THIS DIFFERENCE: (1) THE LOW PRIORITY ACCORDED TO THE SOUTH ASIAN REGION IN GENERAL AND INDIA IN PARTICULAR IN THE U.S. STRATEGIC SCHEME AND (2) THE AVERAGE AMERICAN'S IGNORANCE ABOUT INDIA, ITS SOCIETY, CULTURE, AND POLITICAL DEVELOPMENT. A STUDY OF POPULARLY-HELD U.S. IMAGES OF INDIA PRESENTS A FASCINATING EXERCISE.

09271 VINOGRADOV, V.
THE DIPLOMACY OF RUSSIA
INTERNATIONAL AFFAIRS (MOSCOW), (2) (FEB 89), 55-61.
THOUGH THE PROCESS OF PERESTROIKA HAS BEGUN ONLY A FEW YEARS AGO, SOVIET FOREIGN POLICY HAS ALREADY BEGAINED ITS LOST DYNAMISM AND INITIATIVE. IT HAS BECOME MORE EFFICIENT

AND APPEALING TO LARGE SECTIONS OF THE PUBLIC IN OTHER
COUNTRIES AND TO OTHER GOVERNMENTS. IT IS DISCARDING
STEREOTYPED APPROACHES TO INTERNATIONAL PROBLEMS AND
RELATIONS. THE FUNCTIONING OF THE SOVIET FOREIGN MINISTRY,
THE MAIN AGENCY IMPLEMENTING SOVIET FOREIGN POLICY, IS BEING
IMPROVED. THE MINISTRY IS SHOWING GREATER MOBILITY AND
FLEXIBILITY, WITH INCREASING SENSITIVITY TO THE CHANGING
EXTERNAL CONDITIONS.

09272 VIPOND, R.
     1787 AND 1867: THE FEDERAL PRINCIPLE AND CANADIAN
     CONFEDERATION RECONSIDERED
     CANADIAN JOURNAL OF POLITICAL SCIENCE, XXII(1) (MAR 89),
     3-26.
          ABSTRACT. THIS ARTICLE CHALLENGES THE CONVENTIONAL
     INTERPRETATION OF THE INTELLECTUAL ORIGINS OF CANADIAN
     FEDERALISM. THE ARTICLE ARGUES THAT THE DEBATE OVER
     CONFEDERATION CAN BE INTERPRETED AS A DEBATE OVER THE
     MEANING OF SOVEREIGNTY. IT ARGUES CENTRALLY THAT CERTAIN OF
     THE MOST PROMINENT SUPPORTERS OF CONFEDERATION WERE MORE
     POWERFULLY ATTRACTED TO THE CONCEPTION OF CLASSICAL
     FEDERALISM AND CO-ORDINATE SOVEREIGNTY THAN IS USUALLY
     ASSUMED, THUS CREATING A STRIKING PARALLEL TO UNITED STATES
     FEDERALISM THAT IS NOT TYPICALLY RECOGNIZED. IT CONCLUDES BY
     SHOWING HOW THIS UNDERSTANDING OF CLASSICAL FEDERALISM HAS
     USED WITH GREAT SUCCESS IN OPPOSING THE POST-CONFEDERATION
     CENTRALISM OF JOHN A. MACDONALD.

09273 VIROLI, M.
     REPUBLIC AND POLITICS IN MACHIAVELLI AND ROUSSEAU
     HISTORY OF POLITICAL THOUGHT, X(3) (FAL 89), 405-420.
          THE PURPOSE OF THE PAPER IS TO COMPARE THE POLITICAL
     LANGUAGE OF MACHIAVELLI AND ROUSSEAU AND TO ILLUMINATE THE
     DIFFERENT USES THEY MADE OF THE REPUBLICAN VOCABULARY. THE
     AUTHOR ARGUES THAT THE TWO PHILOSOPHERS PRESENT TWO FACES OF
     REPUBLICANISM AND REVEAL THE DILEMMAS OF REPUBLICAN POLITICS.
     THE AUTHOR ALSO FOCUSES ON THE FACT THAT ROUSSEAU PRESENTED
     HIMSELF AS AN ADMIRER AND, TO A CERTAIN EXTENT, A DISCIPLE
     OF MICHAVELLI; THE AUTHOR EXPLORES VARIOUS MOTIVES AND
     MEANINGS FOUND IN THIS SELF-COMPARISON. ALTHOUGH THE
     SIMILARITY BETWEEN THE TWO POLITICAL MASTERS' WORKS ARE
     PRESENT, THE AUTHOR ALSO EXPLORES SIGNIFICANT DIFFERENCES,
     INCLUDING ROUSSEAU'S IDEA THAT THE REPUBLIC IS NO LONGER A
     POLITICAL PROBLEM TO BE SETTLED WITHIN CONCRETE HISTORICAL
     CONDITIONS, AS IT WAS FOR MACHIAVELLI; RATHER IT IS A
     NORMATIVE IDEAL, AN "IDEA OF REASON."

09274 VISHNEVSKII, A.T.
     ARE THINGS MOVING? ON DEMOGRAPHIC PROCESSES AND SOCIAL
     POLICY
     SOVIET REVIEW, 30(1) (JAN 89), 3-19.
          BEFORE PERESTORIKA, THERE WAS CONCERN OVER THE SOVIET
     POPULATION BECAUSE LIFE EXPECTANCY IN THE USSR HAS BEEN
     DECLINING AND THE BIRTH RATE HAS DROPPED IN MANY AREAS. BUT
     THE SOVIET UNION IS BEGINNING TO EMERGE FROM ITS DEMOGRAPHIC
     STAGNATION. IN THIS ESSAY, THE AUTHOR LOOKS AT SOVIET
     EFFORTS TO REDUCE ITS MORTALITY INDICES AND EVEN OUT BIRTH
     RATES IN DIFFERENT POPULATION GROUPS. HE ALSO CONSIDERS THE
     APPROPRIATENESS OF VARIOUS METHODS OF STATE INTERVENTION IN
     DEMOGRAPHIC PROCESSES.

09275 VITALE, R.
     CASTRO'S CHAMPIONS
     SOUTH, (104) (JUN 89), 90.
          THE SPORTS ARENA HAS PROVIDED AN IDEAL SETTING FOR CUBA
     TO MANIFEST THE RESULTS OF FIDEL CASTRO'S SOCIAL AND
     ECONOMIC REFORMS. CASTRO ESTABLISHED A COMPREHENSIVE
     SPORTING PROGRAM AND A NETWORK OF SPORTS SCHOOLS IN THE
     1960'S. EARLY SELECTION POLICIES, SPECIALIST TRAINING, AND
     THE DEVELOPMENT OF AN ADVANCED SPORTS MEDICINE UNIT HAVE LED
     TO CUBA'S PRESENT SPORTING SUCCESSES. FINANCED BY THE
     GOVERNMENT, THE SPORTS PROGRAM HAS PROVED THAT CUBA IS
     CAPABLE OF PERFORMING AT THE HIGHEST LEVEL, IN CONTRAST TO
     THE PRE-REVOLUTION ERA.

09276 VITAS, R.A.
     U.S. NONRECOGNITION OF THE SOVIET OCCUPATION OF LITHUANIA
     DISSERTATION ABSTRACTS INTERNATIONAL, 50(4) (OCT 89),
     1080-A.
          THE AUTHOR STUDIES THE OFFICIAL U.S. POLICY OF
     NONRECOGNITION OF THE SOVIET OCCUPATION OF LITHUANIA. THE
     POLICY IS A MANIFESTATION OF THE TRADITIONAL MORALISTIC
     ASPECT OF AMERICAN FOREIGN POLICY. IT IS ALSO AN ACTIVE
     INTERVENTION IN THE LITHUANIAN SITUATION WITH DEFINITE LEGAL,
     POLITICAL, AND FINANCIAL CONSEQUENCES. ITS PRACTICAL
     ASPECTS HAVE BEEN CONTINUALLY DEBATED IN OFFICIAL CIRCLES
     SINCE WORLD WAR II.

09277 VIVIAN, J.
     THE LAST TAX-EXEMPT PRESIDENT
     PRESIDENTIAL STUDIES QUARTERLY, XIX(1) (WIN 89), 107-116.
          DURING THE ERA OF ROOSEVELT AND WILSON, THE US UNDERWENT
     A FUNDAMENTAL CHANGE IN THE WAY IT FINANCED THE OPERATIONS
     OF THE FEDERAL GOVERNMENT. THE INCOME TAX, OPENED A NEW WAY

AND LARGER SOURCE FOR FUNDING GOVERNMENT ACTIONS. HOWEVER
THERE HAS SOME CONTROVERSY SURROUNDING THE EXEMPTIONS,
ALLOWED BY THE INITIAL TAX STATUTES, OF THE INCUMBENT
PRESIDENT, THE FEDERAL JUDGES, AND STATE EMPLOYEES. THE
ARTICLE TRACES THE DEVELOPMENT OF TAX LAW WITH REGARDS TO
PUBLIC SERVANTS AND EXAMINES THE CONFLICT THAT SURROUNDED
THIS ISSUE. IT TRACES THE CHANGES IN LAW TO THE POINT WHERE
PRESIDENT WARREN G. HARDING DECIDED IN 1921 TO PAY HIS TAXES
LIKE ANY OTHER CITIZEN.

09278 VOGAN, C.S.
     WAR POWERS RESOLUTION OF 1973: A SIGN OF THE TIMES
     AVAILABLE FROM NTIS, NO. AD-A202 846/2/GAR, MAY 88, 68.
          REVIEWS THE HISTORY OF THE DEBATE REGARDING THE 'SHARED
     POWERS' BETWEEN THE CONGRESS AND THE PRESIDENT FOR THE USE
     OF MILITARY POWER IN SUPPORT OF FOREIGN POLICY. THE PURPOSE
     OF THE PAPER IS TO EXAMINE THE ORIGINS OF THE WAR POWERS
     RESOLUTION AND THE INTERACTIONS OF THE CONGRESS AND THE
     COMMANDER IN CHIEF OVER THE USE OF UNITED STATES ARMED
     FORCES SINCE ITS ENACTMENT. THIS EXAMINATION IS A PRECURSOR
     TO ASCERTAINING WHETHER THE WAR POWERS RESOLUTION IS VIABLE
     AS A BONA FIDE CONSTITUTIONAL MANDATE, OR IS IT MORE
     ACCURATELY A BUILDING CATALYST FOR CHANGE. THE INABILITY OF
     THE CONGRESS TO HOLD THE COMMANDER IN CHIEF ACCOUNTABLE TO
     THE REQUIREMENTS OF THE RESOLUTION APPEARS TO RENDER IT AN
     ISSUE MORE TIED TO THE SUCCESS ACHIEVED BY THE MILITARY OR
     THE POPULARITY OF THE ACTION UNDERTAKEN. THE NECESSITY OF A
     RE-EXAMINATION OF THE CURRENT MILITARY FOCUS TOWARDS ITS
     FUTURE UTILITY IN SUPPORT OF UNITED STATES FOREIGN POLICY IS
     DISCUSSED.

09279 VOGEL, D.
     AIDS AND THE POLITICS OF DRUG LAG
     PUBLIC INTEREST, (96) (SUM 89), 73-85.
          OVER THE PAST TWO YEARS, THE POLITICS OF AMERICAN DRUG
     REGULATION HAS BEEN TRANSFORMED. AS A RESULT OF THE AIDS
     CRISIS, FOR THE FIRST TIME THE FOOD AND DRUG ADMINISTRATION
     IS BEING CHALLENGED POLITICALLY BY A GROUP OF ARTICULATE AND
     WELL-ORGANIZED PEOPLE WHO WANT TO FACILITATE THE APPROVAL OF
     NEW DRUGS. BECAUSE OF THE POLITICAL MOBILIZATION OF
     POTENTIAL CONSUMERS OF CURRENTLY UNAVAILABLE DRUGS, THE
     ADVOCATES OF STRICT DRUG-APPROVAL STANDARDS NOW FIND
     THEMSELVES ON THE DEFENSIVE FOR THE FIRST TIME IN THREE
     DECADES.

09280 VOGEL, H.
     THE GORBACHEV CHALLENGE, I: TO HELP OR NOT TO HELP
     WORLD TODAY, 45(8-9) (AUG 89), 142-145.
          THE GORBACHEV CHALLENGE IS POLITICAL RATHER THAN
     ECONOMIC BECAUSE THE USSR IS NOT A GREAT ECONOMIC POWER. TO
     DEVELOP A NEW APPROACH IN RESPONSE TO THE GORBACHEV
     CHALLENGE IS A TASK FOR THOSE WHO SHAPE WESTERN POLICIES,
     ESPECIALLY THOSE CONCERNED WITH WESTERN DEFENSE. THEY,
     HOWEVER, EITHER TOTALLY DENY ANY NEED TO REASSESS THE
     SITUATION OR, ALTERNATIVELY, THEY PLUNGE HEADLONG INTO THE
     "TO HELP OR NOT TO HELP" DEBATE WITHOUT ARTICULATING EITHER
     THEIR PREMISES OR THEIR BELIEFS.

09281 VOGEL, H.
     THE POLITICAL DIMENSION OF THE EUROPEAN SINGLE MARKET
     INTERNATIONAL SPECTATOR, XXIV(1) (JAN 89), 3-7.
          THE GERMAN SOCIAL DEMOCRATS SUPPORT THE SWIFT ENACTMENT
     OF THE EUROPEAN SINGLE MARKET, NOT ONLY FOR ECONOMIC BUT
     ALSO FOR POLITICAL REASON. EUROPE WILL NEED THE SINGLE
     MARKET TO FACE THE COMPETITION FROM OTHER IMPORTANT WORLD
     TRADE PARTNERS. BUT MORE IMPORTANTLY, ONLY THROUGH THE
     SINGLE MARKET WILL EUROPE BE ABLE TO INCREASE ITS STRENGTH
     AS AN INTERNATIONAL POWER AND ITS CAPACITY FOR SELF-
     ASSERTION.

09282 VOGEL, R.K.; SWANSON, B.E.
     THE GROWTH MACHINE VERSUS THE ANTI-GROWTH COALITION: THE
     BATTLE FOR OUR COMMUNITIES
     URBAN AFFAIRS QUARTERLY, 25(1) (SEP 89), 63-85.
          IN 1987, IN "URBAN FORTUNE: THE POLITICAL ECONOMY OF
     PLACE," LOGAN AND MOLOTCH ARGUED THAT GROWTH IS NOT USUALLY
     IN THE COMMUNITY INTEREST. THEY PROPOSED A STRATEGY TO ALTER
     THE ABILITY OF BUSINESS TO FORCE CITIES TO COMPETE FOR
     CAPITAL. THIS STRATEGY DEPENDS UPON THE ANTIGROWTH COALITION
     WINNING ITS STRUGGLE AGAINST THE GROWTH MACHINE IN
     INDIVIDUAL COMMUNITIES. BUT THE ISSUE OF GROWTH IS MORE
     COMPLEX THAN SUGGESTED BY A GROWTH/NO GROWTH DICHOTOMY. THE
     REAL ISSUE FACING LOCALITIES IS HOW TO ATTRACT, DIRECT, OR
     REPEL GROWTH TO SERVE THE COMMUNITY INTEREST. THIS ARTICLE
     CONSIDERS (1) WHETHER GROWTH MANAGEMENT CAN RESOLVE THE
     POWER STRUGGLE BETWEEN PRO-AND ANTIGROWTH FORCES AND (2)
     WHETHER GROWTH MANAGEMENT CAN ENCOURAGE COMMUNITIES TO
     UNDERTAKE A SEARCH FOR THE PUBLIC INTEREST.

09283 VOGELE. W.B.
     TOUGH BARGAINING AND ARMS CONTROL: LESSONS FROM THE INF
     TREATY
     JOURNAL OF STRATEGIC STUDIES, 12(3) (SEP 89), 257-272.
          THE AUTHOR ARGUES THAT THE CASE FOR A TOUGH BARGAINING

STRATEGY IN ARMS NEGOTIATIONS IS NOT AS STRONG AS IT APPEARS. THE FINAL MONTHS OF SOVIET CONCESSIONS IN 1987 DID NOT PRODUCE DELIGHT WITHIN THE RANKS OF AMERICAN POLICY-MAKERS OR WITHIN THE WESTERN ALLIANCE. INSTEAD, DEEP CONCERNS EMERGED ABOUT THE CONSEQUENCES OF ACHIEVING THE ORIGINAL "ZERO OPTION." THE NEGOTIATIONS' ENDGAME HIGHLIGHTED ALLIANCE DILEMMAS AND UNCERTAINTIES. ONE SOURCE FOR THESE DILEMMAS CAN BE FOUND IN THE PATTERN OF BARGAINING. POLICY SHIFTS AND COMPROMISES BY BOTH THE USA AND THE USSR SHOW LESS CONSISTENCY THAN THE TOUGH STRATEGY ARGUMENT ASSUMES. MOREOVER, UNDERSTANDING CHANGES IN SOVIET POSITIONS REQUIRES ANALYSIS OF CHANGES IN SOVIET LEADERSHIP AND MILITARY DOCTRINE. DOMESTIC POLITICAL ANALYSIS IS A NECESSARY SUPPLEMENT TO AN ANALYSIS OF BARGAINING STRATEGIES AND TACTICS.

09284 VOGELGESANG, S.L.
FY 1990 ASSISTANCE REQUEST FOR ORGANIZATIONS AND PROGRAMS
DEPARTMENT OF STATE BULLETIN (US FOREIGN POLICY), 89(2146)
(MAY 89), 81-84.
THE AUTHOR SUMMARIZES PRESIDENT BUSH'S FY 1990 BUDGET REQUEST FOR THE INTERNATIONAL ORGANIZATIONS AND PROGRAMS ACCOUNT. THE $209 MILLION REQUEST FUNDS THE US GOVERNMENT'S VOLUNTARY CONTRIBUTIONS FOR DEVELOPMENT, HUMANITARIAN, AND SCIENTIFIC ASSISTANCE PROGRAMS AND ACTIVITIES UNDERTAKEN BY THE UNITED NATIONS AND THE ORGANIZATION OF AMERICAN STATES.

09285 VOGELGESANG, S.L.
U.S. OPPOSES PLO ADMISSION TO UN AGENCIES
DEPARTMENT OF STATE BULLETIN (US FOREIGN POLICY), 89(2148)
(JUL 89), 65-66.
THE BUSH ADMINISTRATION OPPOSES PLO MEMBERSHIP IN THE WORLD HEALTH ORGANIZATION AND OTHER UN AGENCIES BECAUSE IT WOULD POLITICIZE THESE SPECIALIZED AGENCIES, COMPLICATING THEIR ESSENTIAL TECHNICAL WORK, AND WOULD ALSO BE SERIOUSLY DETRIMENTAL TO THE SEARCH FOR PEACE IN THE MIDDLE EAST.

09286 VOIGI, R.
FINANCING THE GERMAN FEDERAL SYSTEM IN THE 1980S
PUBLIUS: THE JOURNAL OF FEDERALISM, 19(4) (FAL 89), 99-114.
THIS ARTICLE EXAMINES PUBLIC FINANCE, A CRUCIAL ISSUE IN ANY FEDERATION. IN THE SYSTEM OF SHARED PUBLIC FINANCING IN GERMANY, NO UNIT OF GOVERNMENT IS FISCALLY DEPENDENT ON THE OTHER. THE FEDERAL AND LAND GOVERNMENTS SHARE THE PERSONAL INCOME TAX, THE CORPORATION TAX, AND THE VALUE-ADDED SALES TAX. BECAUSE THE BUNDESRAT APPROVES OF THE SHARES OF THESE TAX YIELDS GRANTED THE FEDERAL AND LAND GOVERNMENTS, THE LANDER ARE DEEPLY INVOLVED IN THE PUBLIC FINANCE SYSTEM. FISCAL EQUALIZATION OCCURS BOTH VERTICALLY AND HORIZONTALLY. THE FEDERAL GOVERNMENT PROVIDES THE LANDER WITH GRANTSIN-AID, AND ALSO SHARES THE FINANCING OF A NUMBER OF "JOINT TASKS." THE LANDER SHARE THEIR TAX YIELDS WITH THEIR LOCAL GOVERNMENTS. FISCAL TRANSFERS ALSO TAKE PLACE AMONG THE RICHER AND POORER LANDER AND AMONG THE MUNICIPALITIES WITHIN THE BOUNDARIES OF INDIVIDUAL COUNTIES. CONTROVERSY EXISTS OVER THE SHARES TO BE GIVEN THE RESPECTIVE GOVERNMENTS FROM THE VALUE-ADDED TAX AND OVER FISCAL EQUALIZATION BETWEEN THE RICHER (SOUTH) AND POORER (NORTH) LANDER.

09287 VOINOVICH, V.
THE BALD AND THE HAIRY
ENCOUNTER, LXXII(2) (FEB 89), 41-42.
BALD AND HAIRY LEADERS HAVE ALTERNATED IN THE KREMLIN WITH AMAZING REGULARITY. ALL THE BALD LEADERS (LENIN, KHRUSCHEV, ANDROPOV, AND GORBACHEV) HAVE BEEN REVOLUTIONARIES OR, AT LEAST, REFORMERS. ALL THE HAIRY ONES (STALIN, BREZHNEV, CHERNENKO) HAVE BEEN REACTIONARIES. ALL THE BALD ONES HAVE HAD UTOPIAN GOALS AND ULTIMATELY SUFFERED DEFEAT. THE HAIRY, HOWEVER, HAVE ALWAYS ACHIEVED WHAT THEY WANTED.

09288 VOLCANSEK, M.L.
IMPACT OF JUDICIAL POLICIES IN THE EUROPEAN COMMUNITY: THE ITALIAN CONSTITUTIONAL COURT AND EUROPEAN COMMUNITY LAW
WESTERN POLITICAL QUARTERLY, 42(4) (DEC 89), 569-586.
THIS PAPER IS A STUDY OF JUDICIAL POLICY IMPLEMENTATION INVOLVING THE LEGAL NORMS OF THE EUROPEAN COMMUNITY. THE FOCUS OF THE PAPER IS IMPLEMENTATION OF THESE NORMS BY THE ITALIAN CONSTITUTIONAL COURT, AND, MORE SPECIFICALLY, HOW ONE NATIONAL CONSTITUTIONAL COURT EVOLVED A MEANS OF RECONCILING THE COMPETING NORMS OF TWO SEPARATE LEGAL AND POLITICAL CULTURES. THE CONCLUSION IS THAT INSTITUTIONAL LEGITIMACY, THE ELEMENT THAT UNDERLIES ALL THEORIES OF JUDICIAL IMPLEMENTATION AND IMPACT, EXPLAINS BOTH THE INITIAL RELUCTANCE OF THE ITALIAN CONSTITUTIONAL COURT TO IMPLEMENT COMMUNITY RULES AND THE EVOLUTION OF A PREDISPOSITION BY THAT COURT TO VIGOROUSLY ENFORCE COMMUNITY LAW, EVEN IN THE FACE OF CONTRADICTORY NATIONAL LAW.

09289 VOLGT, K.D.
TOWARDS PARTNERSHIP ON GLOBAL SECURITY
WORLD MARXIST REVIEW, 31(11) (NOV 88), 45-46.
IT IS OBVIOUS THAT THE GREATER THE SCALE ON WHICH NUCLEAR WEAPONS ARE ELIMINATED, THE MORE SIGNIFICANT

CONVENTIONAL ARMS WILL BECOME. THIS PARTICULARLY APPLIES TO CENTRAL EUROPE AND BORDER AREAS. GENERAL STABILITY, ON A LOWER LEVEL OF ARMAMENTS FROM THE ATLANTIC TO THE URALS, CAN ONLY BE ACHIEVED BY SUBSTANTIAL CUTS IN MILITARY FORCES AND THE ELIMINATION OF ANY SUPERIORITY IN CONVENTIONAL ARMS.

09290 VOLGYES, I.
HUNGARY: DANCING IN THE SHACKLES OF THE PAST
CURRENT HISTORY, 88(541) (NOV 89), 381-384, 399-400.
THE HUNGARIAN STATE HAS BEEN DRIVEN TO THE BRINK OF ECONOMIC DISASTER. THE TRANSFORMATION INTO A WESTERN, MARKET-BASED, DEMOCRATIC, PLURALIST ECONOMIC AND POLITICAL SYSTEM REMAINS THE ONLY HOPE OF AVOIDING COLLAPSE. BUT MOST HUNGARIANS ARE NOT CONVINCED THAT THEY SHOULD PLACE THEIR HOPES IN SUCH A TRANSFORMATION.

09291 VOLGYES, I.
LEADERSHIP DRIFT IN HUNGARY: EMPIRICAL OBSERVATION ON A NORMATIVE CONCEPT
STUDIES IN COMPARATIVE COMMUNISM, XXII(1) (SPR 89), 23-41.
THE PRESENT ARTICLE DEALS WITH THE CONTRADICTION BETWEEN THE PRINCIPLE OF ACTIVE COMMUNIST LEADERSHIP AS JUSTIFIED IN MARXIST-LENINIST IDEOLOGY, AND THE REALITY OF THE POLITICAL DRIFT IN HUNGARY, A POLITICAL DRIFT THAT CONTINUES EVEN AFTER THE DRAMATIC PERSONNEL CHANGES OF MAY 1988. THUS, IT MATCHES A NORMATIVE CONCEPT, E.G. CENTRALLY CONTROLLED AND DIRECTED RULE, AGAINST AN EMPIRICAL REALITY, E.G. THE DRIFT SO CLEARLY OBSERVABLE AMONG THE TOP ELITES IN CONTEMPORARY HUNGARY. PART 1 OF THIS ARTICLE DEALS WITH THE THEORY OF CENTRALIZED LEADERSHIP IN COMMUNIST IDEOLOGY AND THE RESULTANT PRAXIS; PART 2 ANALYZES THE EMERGENCE AND SOURCES OF LEADERSHIP DRIFT IN THE TWILIGHT OF THE KADAR ERA; PART 3 EXAMINES THE TYPES OF DRIFTS OBSERVABLE IN CONTEMPORARY HUNGARY; PART 4 ANALYZES THE INFLUENCE OF THE USSR ON THE DRIFTS AND CLEAVAGES; WHILE PART 5 DELINEATES THE CLEAVAGES THAT ARE NOTABLE AMONG THE LEADERSHIP. THE FINAL PART OF THIS STUDY OFFERS SOME CONCLUSIONS CONCERNING THE POSSIBLE AND POTENTIAL CONSEQUENCES OF THE EXISTENCE OF THESE DRIFTS.

09292 VOLGYES, I.
THE GERMAN QUESTION IN HUNGARY
EAST EUROPEAN QUARTERLY, XXIII(2) (JUN 89), 145-157.
THE AUTHOR (1) ANALYZES THE HISTORICAL ANTECEDENTS OF THE EMERGENCE OF THE GERMAN QUESTION IN HUNGARY, (2) EXAMINES THE IDEOLOGICAL-POLICY ORIENTATIONS OF RECENT YEARS, (3) DISCUSSES THE DIVERGENT IMPLICATIONS RESULTING FROM THE RISE OF EAST GERMANY, AND (4) EXPLAINS THE PROBLEMS RESULTING FROM THE INTERPRETATION OF THE GERMAN QUESTION IN THE CONTEMPORARY POLITICAL-IDEOLOGICAL, ECONOMIC, AND CULTURAL REALMS.

09293 VOLGYES, I.
THE WARSAW PACT: CHANGES IN STRUCTURE AND FUNCTIONS
ARMED FORCES AND SOCIETY, 15(4) (SUM 89), 551-570.
THE ARTICLE TRACES THE EVOLUTION OF THE VARIOUS INSTRUMENTS USED BY THE SOVIET MILITARY AND POLITICAL LEADERSHIP TO CONTROL THE ARMED FORCES OF THE WARSAW PACT STATES. IT CONCLUDES THAT THE SOVIET LEADERSHIP AT FIRST TRIED TO USE SOVIET MILITARY ADVISERS TO CONTROL PACT FORCES. THIS TOOL PROVED TO BE UNSUCCESSFUL AND WAS LATER REPLACED WITH THE CONCEPT OF INTEGRATION OF THESE UNITS INTO A MULTINATIONAL SOCIALIST ARMY. WHEN IN THE EARLY 1980S THIS INSTRUMENT ALSO PROVED TO BE INADEQUATE, THE SOVIET ELITE BEGAN THE INCORPORATION OF THESE UNITS INTO THE SOVIET ARMY THROUGH THEIR DIRECT SUBORDINATION TO SOVIET COMMANDS AND OPERATIONAL DESIDERATA. THROUGH A CASE STUDY OF THE BULGARIAN AND HUNGARIAN ARMED FORCES, THE ARTICLE THEN PROCEEDS TO EXAMINE THE CONCEPT OF RELIABILITY OF WARSAW PACT ARMIES AND EVALUATES THE EXTENT OF THEIR RELIABILITY IN TERMS OF THE DUAL INSTRUMENTS OF INTEGRATION AND SUBORDINATION TO SOVIET MILITARY NEEDS.

09294 VOLKAN, V.D.
CYPRUS: ETHNIC CONFLICTS AND TENSIONS
INTERNATIONAL JOURNAL OF GROUP TENSIONS, 19(4) (WIN 89), 297-316.
THE AUTHOR DESCRIBES THE CONFLICT BETWEEN TURKISH AND GREEK ETHNIC GROUPS ON CYPRUS FROM THE PERSPECTIVE OF A PSYCHANALYST AND POLITICAL PSYCHOLOGIST. HE CONCLUDES THAT THE ESTABLISHMENT OF THE REPUBLIC OF CYPRUS, FOR WHICH THE POPULATION HAD NOT BEEN PSYCHOLOGICALLY PREPARED, THREATENED THE PSYCHOLOGICAL BALANCE THAT HAD EXISTED BETWEEN CYPRIOT TURKS AND CYPRIOT GREEKS. THE FORCED "TOGETHERNESS" WAS AN INTRUSION INTO THE PSYCHOLOGICAL GAP BETWEEN THE TWO PARTIES, AND PLAYFUL, PEACEFUL RITUALS AND RITUALISTIC POSTURES WERE NO LONGER ENOUGH FOR THE ISSUES OF SAMENESS AND DISTANCING. IN THIS SITUATION, AND WITH THE DEPARTURE OF THE BRITISH, GREATER AGGRESSION APPEARED AND HISTORICAL GRIEVANCES WERE RECALLED.

09295 VOLKOV, N.
COOPERATION WITH THE THIRD WORLD
INTERNATIONAL AFFAIRS (MOSCOW), (9) (SEP 89), 103-110.
THE AUTHOR LOOKS AT THE DEVELOPMENT OF SOVIET ECONOMIC

TIES WITH THE THIRD WORLD SINCE WORLD WAR II AND DISCUSSES
THE PROSPECTS FOR FUTURE ECONOMIC RELATIONS.

09296 VOLOSINOV, V.
    POLITICS AND THE LINGUISTIC SIGN: VOLOSINOV'S PHILOSOPHY OF
    LANGUAGE
    CRITICAL REVIEW, 3(3) (SUM 89), 568-578.
        THE CONTRIBUTIONS OF VOLOSINOV'S THEORIES OF LANGUAGE
    ARE ASSESSED AND ARE CONTRASTED TO TRADITIONAL MARXIST
    PHILOSOPHY, SAUSSUREAN LINGUISTICS AND RECENT DEVELOPMENTS
    IN TRANSFORMATIONAL GRAMMAR AND SOCIOLINGUISTICS. STUDYING
    CONNECTIONS BETWEEN LANGUAGE AND POLITICS IN THE 1920S,
    VOLOSINOV EXPLORED THE WAYS SOCIAL REALITY ENTERS VERBAL
    SIGNS AND THEIR USAGE, ANTICIPATING MANY OF THE DEBATES
    WITHIN MODERN LINGUISTICS.

09297 VOLSKY, A.
    DIFFICULT PROBLEMS OF KARABAKH
    REPRINTS FROM THE SOVIET PRESS, 48(8) (APR 89), 33-38.
        THE ARTICLE DISCUSSES THE ETHNIC STRIFE THAT HAS TAKEN
    PLACE IN THE PROVINCE OF NAGORNY KARABAKH. IT EXAMINES ITS
    ORIGINS, BOTH ETHNIC; AND ECONOMIC, AND OUTLINES THE EFFORTS
    BEING MADE BY THE CENTRAL GOVERNMENT AND THE "SPECIAL FORM
    OF GOVERNMENT" TO RESOLVE THE SITUATION.

09298 VON DER ROPP, K.F.
    PEACE INITIATIVES IN SOUTH WEST AFRICA
    AUSSEN POLITIK, 40(2) (1989), 182-194.
        FOLLOWING POSITIVE DEVELOPMENTS TOWARD THE SETTLEMENT OF
    CONFLICTS IN AND AROUND AFGHANISTAN AND CAMBODIA THERE IS
    NOW HOPE THAT THE ARMED CONFLICTS IN NAMIBIA AND ANGOLA CAN
    BE ENDED AS WELL, WITH THE RESULT THAT NAMIBIA IS GIVEN
    INDEPENDENCE. IN ALL THREE INSTANCES THERE HAS BEEN A DE-
    INTERNATIONALISATION OF THE CONFLICTS, A DISENTANGLEMENT
    FROM OUTSIDE PARTICIPATION AND INFLUENCE. ACCORDINGLY, THE
    TREATY SIGNED IN NEW YORK DOES NOT IMPINGE ON THE INNER-
    ANGOLAN CIVIL WAR. THE AUTHOR FOCUSES HERE ON THE FACTORS
    THAT LAST YEAR LED TO THE SUCCESS OF CAREFULLY CONTRIVED
    SECRET DIPLOMACY.

09299 VON KUEHNELT-LEDDIHN, E.
    REFLECTIONS ON THE TERROR
    NATIONAL REVIEW, XLI(13) (JUL 89), 38-40.
        THE FRENCH REVOLUTION WAS THE OVERTURE TO OUR "AGE OF
    THE GS"--GUILLOTINES, GALLOWS, THE GESTAPO. GAS CHAMBERS,
    GULAGS. THE GUILLOTINE MARKS THE FIRST STEP TOWARD A
    MECHANICAL/TECHNOLOGICAL MASS EXTERMINATION, TOWARD GENOCIDE.

09300 VON KUEHNELT-LEDDIHN, E.
    RUSTING IRON CURTAIN
    NATIONAL REVIEW, 110(21) (NOV 89), 25.
        THIS ARTICLE EXPLORES THE EAST GERMAN STORY. IT EXPLAINS
    THE EAST GERMANS AS A MOSTLY PROGRESSIVE, ENLIGHTENED, LAW
    ABIDING PROTESTANT PEOPLE WITH GREAT RESPECT FOR THE PRINTED
    WORD BELIEVING IN EVOLUTION RATHER THAN REVOLUTION. IT
    EXAMINES SOCIALISM, COMMUNISM, GLASTNOST AND PERESTROIKA AND
    RECENT EVENTS AND DEVELOPMENTS WITHIN THE GDR.

09301 VON LUCIUS, R.
    NAMBIA AT THE CROSSROADS: AFRICA'S LAST COLONY
    SOUTH AFRICA INTERNATIONAL, 20(1) (JUL 89), 34-41.
        THIS ARTICLE PROVIDES A SOMBER REVIEW OF NAMBIA'S
    PROSPECTS. IT SPECULATES WHAT NAMBIA WILL LOOK LIKE IN FIVE
    OR TEN YEARS TIME, AND ASKS: WILL IT BE A PROSPEROUS AN
    RESPECTED STATE THAT HONORS HUMAN RIGHTS, DEMOCRACY AND A
    FREE ECONOMY, OR WILL IT HAVE DECLINED INTO POLITICAL AND
    ECONOMIC DIRIGISME, INTOLERANT OF POLITICAL DISSIDENCE AND
    INDIVIDUAL ENTERPRISE. IT THEN EXAMINES THE PROBABILITY OF
    EACH.

09302 VON MEYENFELDT, M.H.
    EUROPE NEEDS A CHURCHILL OF PEACE
    WORLD MARXIST REVIEW, 31(11) (NOV 88), 43-45.
        THE IDEA OF DENUCLEARISATION SHOULD NOT BE REDUCED TO
    THE MERE DESIRE TO SURVIVE, TO ESCAPE THE CONSEQUENCES OF A
    POSSIBLE NUCLEAR CONFLICT, BECAUSE THERE IS NO PROTECTION
    AGAINST SUCH A CATASTROPHE. IT RECOGNISES NO FRONTIERS.
    RATHER, IT IS THE PREVENTIVE ASPECT THAT ASSUMES GREATEST
    IMPORTANCE. DENUCLEARISATION AS A CONCEPT HAS BECOME AN
    INDISPENSABLE ELEMENT OF A STRATEGY DESIGNED TO GRADUALLY
    DECREASE AND FINALLY RULE OUT THE POSSIBILITY OF NUCLEAR WAR.

09303 VON SCHIRNDING, K.
    THE IMPACT OF CURRENT INTERNATIONAL DEVELOPMENTS ON SOUTH
    AFRICA
    SOUTH AFRICA FOUNDATION REVIEW, 15(6) (JUN 89), 1-2, 8.
        THE ARTICLE EXAMINES SEVERAL OF THE CHANGES IN THE
    INTERNATIONAL SCENE THAT WILL HAVE A SIGNIFICANT EFFECT ON
    SOUTH AFRICA. THESE INCLUDE: THE INCREASING PRAGMATISM IN
    SOVIET FOREIGN POLICY, THE EUROPEAN MOVE TOWARDS A SINGLE
    MARKET IN 1992, IMPORVING US-SOVIET RELATIONS, AND CHANGES
    IN REGIONAL CONFLICTS AND TENSIONS. MANY OF THE SHIFTS SEEM
    TO INDICATE THAT SOUTH AFRICA WILL BE SUBJECT TO MORE
    OUTSIDE PRESSURES TO ELIMINATE OR REFORM APARTHEID IN THE

FUTURE. THE FUTURE OF THE NATION AS A WHOLE WILL DEPEND ON
HOW IT HANDLES THESE INCREASING PRESSURES.

09304 VON SCHIRNDING, K.R.S.
    SUPERPOWER DIPLOMACY: THE UN AS AN INSTRUMENT OF
    IDEOLOGICAL PROPAGANDA
    SOUTH AFRICA INTERNATIONAL, 20(1) (JUL 89), 1-7.
        THE DIRECTOR GENERAL OF THE SOUTH AFRICAN FOUNDATION
    EXAMINES THE UNITED NATIONS FROM A SOUTH AFRICAN PERSPECTIVE
    IN THE LIGHT OF RECENT DEVELOPMENTS IN SUPERPOWER
    RAPPROCHEMENT. HE CONCLUDES THAT THE US-SOVIET CO-OPERATION
    HAS THE POTENTIAL TO INCREASE THE SIGNIFICANCE OF THE UN
    GREATLY, AND OUTLINES THE POSSIBLE IMPLICATIONS OF THIS FOR
    SOUTH AFRICA'S HANDLING OF ITS INTERNATIONAL RELATIONS.

09305 VON STADEN, B.
    PRESIDENT GEORGE BUSH'S AGENDA
    AUSSEN POLITIK, 40(1) (JAN 89), 3-14.
        THE ARTICLE BEGINS WITH THE FORMATIVE ELEMENTS THAT
    SHAPED THE PERSONALITY OF THE NEW PRESIDENT AND MADE HIM A
    MODERATELY CONSERVATIVE PATRIOT OF A MARKEDLY PRAGMATIC BENT,
    AND WITH THE EXPERIENCE DRAWN FROM MANY YEARS OF PUBLIC
    SERVICE AS A CONGRESSMAN, AMBASSADOR TO CHINA, DIRECTOR OF
    THE CIA AND. ABOVE ALL, AS VICE PRESIDENT. IT ALSO ANALYZES
    THE CHALLENGES THAT BUSH FACES IN AN INCREASINGLY POWERFUL
    DEMOCRATIC CONGRESS, ENORMOUS DEBT, AND AN UNBALANCED
    INTERNATIONAL ECONOMY. HE ALSO FACES FOREIGN POLICY
    CHALLENGES IN ARMS REDUCTION, RESPONSE TO SOVIET CHANGES AND
    THE SOLUTION OF REGIONAL CONFLICTS.

09306 VONBRATT, G.C.
    AN EVALUATION OF THE CURRENT SOUTH AFRICAN POLITICAL ORDER
    AS A BASIS FOR FUTURE DEVELOPMENT WITH SPECIAL REFERENCE
    TO THE REVIEW FUNCTION OF THE JUDICIARY
    DISSERTATION ABSTRACTS INTERNATIONAL, 49(11) (MAY 89),
    3487-A.
        THE PRESENT SOUTH AFRICAN CONSTITUTIONAL DISPENSATION
    LACKS SUFFICIENT CONTROL MECHANISMS FOR THE IMPLEMENTATION
    OF GOVERNMENTAL AUTHORITY. THE INADEQUATE CONSTITUTIONAL
    MECHANISMS FOR LIMITING AND CONTROLLING GOVERNMENTAL
    AUTHORITY MUST BE VIEWED WITH GRAVE CONCERN. A SPECIALIST
    COURT ENDOWED WITH MATERIAL TESTING POWERS SHOULD BE
    INTRODUCED AND CAST MORE OR LESS IN THE SAME MOULD AS THE
    WEST GERMAN "BUNDESVERFASSUNGSGERICHT." THIS WOULD BE AN
    ESSENTIAL FIRST STEP IN THE LONG PROCESS OF NORMALIZING THE
    EXERCISE OF GOVERNMENTAL AUTHORITY AND WOULD ALSO OFFER THE
    OPPORTUNITY FOR A RE-EVALUATION OF THE POSITION OF THE
    CITIZENS OF THE SOUTH AFRICAN STATE.

09307 VRAALSEN, T.
    NON-PROLIFERATION OF NUCLEAR, CHEMICAL AND OTHER WEAPONS
    DISARMAMENT, XII(3) (AUT 89), 3-15.
        IN ADDITION TO DISCOURAGING NUCLEAR WEAPONS DEVELOPMENT
    AND THE RELIANCE ON SUCH WEAPONS IN THE CONTEXT OF
    DETERRENCE THROUGH THE PROMOTION OF DETENTE AND PEACEFUL
    COEXISTENCE IN INTERNATIONAL RELATIONS, NUCLEAR
    NONPROLIFERATION REQUIRES; (1) REAL PROGRESS URGENT
    CONCLUSION OF A COMPREHENSIVE TEST-BAN TREATY; (3)
    STRENGTHENING OF THE INTERNATIONAL ATOMIC ENERGY AGENCY AND
    APPLICATION OF FULL-SCOPE SAFEGUARDS IN ALL NON-NUCLEAR
    WEAPON STATES; AND (4) ESTABLISHMENT OF A RIGID TRADE SYSTEM
    FOR SUPPLY OF NUCLEAR MATERIAL AND EQUIPMENT.

09308 VRANITZKY, F.
    EUROPEAN INTEGRATION, GLOBAL COMPETITION, AND AUSTRIA'S
    POSITION
    AUSTRIA TODAY, (2) (1989), 8-11.
        AFTER LONG CONSIDERATION. THE AUSTRIAN PARLIAMENT HAS
    GIVEN THE GOVERNMENT THE GREEN LIGHT TO APPLY FOR MEMBERSHIP
    IN THE EUROPEAN COMMUNITY. THE ESSENTIAL CONDITION IS THAT
    THE COUNTRY'S PERMANENT NEUTRALITY MUST NOT BE IMPAIRED. IN
    THIS ARTICLE, AUSTRIAN FEDERAL CHANCELLOR FRANZ VRANITZKY
    PUTS AUSTRIA'S INTERNATIONAL TRADE AMBITIONS IN GLOBAL
    PERSPECTIVE.

09309 VRANITZKY, F.
    NEUTRALITY AND GOOD-NEIGHBOURLINESS
    INTERNATIONAL AFFAIRS (MOSCOW), (7) (JUL 89), 14-25.
        IN THIS CENTURY, AUSTRIA HAS UNDERGONE MORE MARKED
    CHANGES THAN ANY OTHER EUROPEAN COUNTRY. IN LESS THAN FIVE
    DECADES, IT CHANGED FROM A EUROPEAN POWER TO A SMALL STATE,
    FROM A SMALL STATE TO THE OSTMARK (EASTERN TERRITORY) OF AN
    EMPIRE THAT HAD GROWN IN SIZE THROUGH A WAR OF CONQUEST AND
    VIOLENCE, AND FROM OSTMARK TO A COUNTRY COMPOSED OF FOUR
    OCCUPATION ZONES UNTIL IT FINALLY ASSUMED ITS PRESENT FORM.
    AUSTRIAN FOREIGN POLICY HAS, LIKEWISE, UNDERGONE CHANGES
    REFLECTING ITS ALTERED STATUS.

09310 VUKADINOVIC, R.
    NORMAL COMMUNICATION AMONG NEIGHBOURS.
    REVIEW OF INTERNATIONAL AFFAIRS, (JAN 88), 8-10.
        INTENSIFIED BALKAN COOPERATION RESULTING FROM A SOBER
    PERCEPTION OF PRESENT REALITIES AND THE NEEDS OF BALKAN
    COUNTRIES MUST BE THE BEGINNING FOR A GRADUAL TRANSCENDENCE

OF ALL OTHER PROBLEMS ASSOCIATED WITH QUESTIONS OF SECURITY
AND COOPERATION IN THE BALKANS. SECURITY AND COOPERATION ARE
INTERTWINED SO THAT GREATER COOPERATION IN THE BALKANS WOULD
AUTOMATICALLY MEAN GREATER SECURITY, WHILE GREATER SECURITY
WOULD PAVE THE WAY FOR STRENGTHENING MUTUALLY USEFUL AND
COMPREHENSIVE COOPERATION AMONG BALKAN PEOPLES AND STATES.

09311 WACHBROIT, R.
WHO IS THE PATIENT?
REPORT FROM THE INSTITUTE FOR PHILOSOPHY AND PUBLIC POLICY,
9(4) (FAL 89), 9-11.
THE AUTHOR CONSIDERS THE PHYSICIAN'S DUTY OF
CONFIDENTIALITY TO HIS PATIENT IN THE CONTEXT OF A PRIVATE
HEALTH MODEL, A PUBLIC HEALTH MODEL, AND A FAMILY HEALTH
MODEL. IN THE PUBLIC HEALTH MODEL, CONCEPTS SUCH AS AUTONOMY
OR INFORMED CONSENT MUST BE UNDERSTOOD IN TERMS OF THE
POLITICAL WILL AND THE DECISION-MAKING PROCESS OF THE PUBLIC.
IN THIS MODEL, THERE IS NO DUTY OF CONFIDENTIALITY TO THE
INDIVIDUAL PATIENT BECAUSE THE PHYSICIAN'S MISSION IS TO
PROMOTE THE PUBLIC'S HEALTH. BECAUSE THE PUBLIC'S WILL DOES
NOT ALWAYS REFLECT A CONSENSUS, THE MISSION OF THE PUBLIC
HEALTH MODEL MAY AT TIMES CONFLICT WITH A RESPECT FOR THE
AUTONOMY OF SOME INDIVIDUALS.

09312 WACHTEL, P.
WHAT'S GOING ON HERE? -- WHO MAKES ECONOMIC POLICY AND WHY?
ECONOMIC OUTLOOK USA, 15(1) (SUM 88), 10-16.
THIS ARTICLE EXAMINES THE INSTITUTIONS THAT MAKE POLICY
AND SEES HOW THEY ARE RESPONDING TO THE ISSUES OF THE LATE
1980S. BOTH MONETARY AND FISCAL POLICY AS WELL AS POLICY
PROSPECTS ARE DISCUSSED. THE HISTORY OF THE FEDERAL RESERVE
SYSTEM IS TRACED.

09313 WACQUANT, L.J.D.; WILSON, W.J.
THE COST OF RACIAL AND CLASS EXCLUSION IN THE INNER CITY
PHILADELPHIA: ANLS OF AMER ACMY OF POLITICAL AND SOC
SCIENCE, (501) (JAN 89), 8-25.
DISCUSSIONS OF INNER-CITY SOCIAL DISLOCATIONS ARE OFTEN
SEVERED FROM THE STRUGGLES AND STRUCTURAL CHANGES IN THE
LARGER SOCIETY, ECONOMY, AND POLITY THAT IN FACT DETERMINE
THEM, RESULTING IN UNDUE EMPHASIS ON THE INDIVIDUAL
ATTRIBUTES OF GHETTO RESIDENTS AND ON THE ALLEGED GRIP OF
THE SO-CALLED CULTURE OF POVERTY. THIS ARTICLE PROVIDES A
DIFFERENT PERSPECTIVE BY DRAWING ATTENTION TO THE SPECIFIC
FEATURES OF THE PROXIMATE SOCIAL STRUCTURE IN WHICH GHETTO
RESIDENTS EVOLVE AND TRY TO SURVIVE. THIS IS DONE BY
CONTRASTING THE CLASS COMPOSITION, WELFARE TRAJECTORIES,
ECONOMIC AND FINANCIAL ASSETS, AND SOCIAL CAPITAL OF BLACKS
WHO LIVE IN CHICAGO'S GHETTO NEIGHBORHOODS WITH THOSE WHO
RESIDE IN THIS CITY'S LOW-POVERTY AREAS. THE CENTRAL
ARGUMENT IS THAT THE INTERRELATED SET OF PHENOMENA CAPTURED
BY THE TERM "UNDERCLASS" IS PRIMARILY SOCIAL-STRUCTURAL AND
THAT THE INNER CITY IS EXPERIENCING A CRISIS BECAUSE THE
DRAMATIC GROWTH IN JOBLESSNESS AND ECONOMIC EXCLUSION
ASSOCIATED WITH THE ONGOING SPATIAL AND INDUSTRIAL
RESTRUCTURING OF AMERICAN CAPITALISM HAS TRIGGERED A PROCESS
OF HYPERGHETTOIZATION.

09314 WADDOCK, S.A.
UNDERSTANDING SOCIAL PARTNERSHIPS AN EVOLUTIONARY MODEL OF
PARTNERSHIP ORGANIZATIONS
ADMINISTRATION AND SOCIETY, 21(1) (MAY 89), 78-100.
A MODEL OF THE EVOLUTIONARY PROCESS OF DEVELOPING SOCIAL
PARTNERSHIPS IS PRESENTED. THE MODEL FOCUSES ON THE
INTERORGANIZATIONAL CONTEXT OUT OF WHICH PARTNERSHIPS
ORIGINATE AND PROPOSES THAT SIX TYPES OF FORCES IN THE
ENVIRONMENT FOSTER INTERACTION. NEXT, PROCESSES OF ISSUE
CRYSTALLIZATION, COALITION BUILDING, AND PURPOSE FORMULATION,
WHICH ORIGINATE IN AN "INITIATION" STAGE AND FOCUS THE
CONTENT OF THE PARTNERSHIP, ARE DESCRIBED. THE EVOLUTIONARY
STAGES OF SOCIAL PARTNERSHIP ARE IDENTIFIED AS (1) A CONTEXT
OF FORCES GENERATING A RECOGNITION OF THE NEED/USE OF
PARTNERSHIP, (2) INITIATION OF THE PARTNERSHIP (ENCOMPASSING
ISSUE CRYSTALLIZATION, COALITION BUILDING, AND PURPOSE
FORMULATION), (3) ESTABLISHMENT, AND (4) MATURITY. PROCESSES
ARE SEEN TO BE REPETITIVE AND CYCLICAL, AND PURPOSE IN
SUCCESSFUL PARTNERSHIPS TENDS TO BROADEN OVER TIME. A CASE
EXAMPLE IS USED TO ILLUSTRATE THE MODEL.

09315 WADE, L.L.
THE INFLUENCE OF SECTIONS AND PERIODS ON ECONOMIC VOTING
IN AMERICAN PRESIDENTIAL ELECTIONS: 1828-1984
POLITICAL GEOGRAPHY QUARTERLY, 8(3) (JUL 89), 271-288.
THE STUDY SEEKS TO PROVIDE A NEW PERSPECTIVE ON THE
STUDY OF THE HISTORICAL EFFECT OF ECONOMIC FLUCTUATIONS ON
VOTING IN US NATIONAL ELECTIONS. ITS PURPOSE IS TO
ILLUMINATE A MATTER OF SOME SUBSTANTIVE IMPORTANCE IN
AMERICAN POLITICAL AND ECONOMIC HISTORY, AND TO DEMONSTRATE
THAT THE APPROACH AND FINDINGS MAY HAVE RELEVANCE FOR
SCHOLARS INTERESTED IN EXTENDING THE ECONOMIC THEORY OF
VOTING IN OTHER SETTINGS. IT CONCLUDES THAT SHORT-TERM
ECONOMIC EVENTS HAVE INFLUENCED PRESIDENTIAL VOTING MORE IN
SOME GEOGRAPHICAL SECTIONS AND HISTORICAL PERIODS (E.G. THE
NORTH IN 1828-1940) THAN IN OTHERS.

09316 WADE, R.
WHAT CAN ECONOMICS LEARN FROM EAST ASIAN SUCCESS?
PHILADELPHIA: ANLS OF AMER ACMY OF POLITICAL AND SOC
SCIENCE, (505) (SEP 89), 68-79.
MOST ECONOMICS LITERATURE ON EAST ASIAN
INDUSTRIALIZATION FALLS VICTIM TO THE ASSUMPTION THAT ONLY
THOSE FEATURES OF ECONOMIC POLICY CONSISTENT WITH
NEOCLASSICAL PRINCIPLES COULD HAVE CONTRIBUTED TO GOOD
ECONOMIC PERFORMANCE. EXPLANATIONS OF GOOD PERFORMANCE
ACCORDINGLY IGNORE NONEOCLASSICAL FEATURES. THIS ARTICLE
SUGGESTS THAT NEW INSIGHTS CAN BE GAINED BY CAREFULLY
EXAMINING WHAT THESE GOVERNMENTS ACTUALLY DID. MUCH OF WHAT
THEY DID IS CONSISTENT WITH THE PRINCIPLES OF OLD-STYLE PRE-
1970 DEVELOPMENT ECONOMICS. IN PARTICULAR, THEY GAVE CENTRAL
ATTENTION TO WAYS OF AUGMENTING AND DIRECTING THE
COMPOSITION OF INVESTMENT AND MUCH LESS ATTENTION TO WAYS OF
INCREASING EFFICIENCY OF RESOURCE USE. THEY USED PROTECTION
AS AN INSTRUMENT TO ENHANCE INNOVATION AND INTERNATIONAL
COMPETITIVENESS. IN IMPORTANT INDUSTRIES THEY REGULATED BOTH
QUANTITIES AND PRICES SO AS TO ACHIEVE GOVERNMENT-SELECTED
GOALS, PREVENTING THOSE PARTS OF THE ECONOMY FROM BEING
GUIDED BY INTERNATIONAL PRICES.

09317 WADEKIN, K.
THE RE-EMERGENCE OF THE KOLKHOZ PRINCIPLE
SOVIET STUDIES, XLI(1) (JAN 89), 20-38.
THE REALIZATION BY SOVIET LEADERS THAT THEIR OVER-
FORMALIZED CUMBERSOME WAGE SYSTEM APPLIED IN OVER-SIZED
ENTERPRISES, WAS ANYTHING BUT AN EFFECTIVE INCENTIVE
PROVIDED IMPETUS FOR SOVIET AGRICULTURAL REFORM. THE CHANGES
SPANNED NOT ONLY RENUMERATION, BUT THE ACTUAL ORGANIZATION
IN SOVIET FARMING. THE PAPER ANALYZES THESE DEVELOPMENTS
WITH A VIEW TO THE IMPLIED RETURN TO EARLY KOLKHOZ
PRINCIPLES AND TO THE SIMULATANEOUS CHANGE TOWARDS SMALLER
PRODUCTION UNITS WITHIN THE BIG FARMS, COMBINED WITH NEW,
AND REDUCED FUNCTIONS FOR THE LATTER.

09318 WAGER, S.J.
A REPOLITICIZED MILITARY?
HEMISPHERE, 1(2) (WIN 89), 50-51.
ALTHOUGH THE MEXICAN MILITARY HAS ENJOYED HEIGHTENED
VISIBILITY IN THE LAST FEW YEARS, IT IS ERRONEOUS TO EQUATE
THIS WITH HEIGHTENED POLITICAL INFLUENCE. THE MILITARY
REMAINS INSUFFICIENTLY TRAINED TO TAKE OVER THE REINS OF
GOVERNMENT, AND THERE IS EVIDENCE THAT THE MEXICAN MILITARY
LEADERSHIP WELCOMES THE OPPORTUNITY TO AVOID THE POLITICAL
LIMELIGHT.

09319 WAGNER, D.
RADICAL MOVEMENTS IN THE SOCIAL SERVICES: A THEORETICAL
FRAMEWORK
SOCIAL SERVICE REVIEW, 63(2) (JUN 89), 264-284.
THIS ARTICLE, BASED ON RESEARCH OF A POPULATION OF
RADICAL SOCIAL WORKERS ACTIVE IN THE LAST DECADES, DEVELOPS
A THEORETICAL FRAMEWORK FOR ASSESSING RADICAL MOVEMENTS
AMONG SOCIAL SERVICE WORKERS. IN COMPARING THESE RECENT
MOVEMENTS WITH THOSE OF THE 1930S AND 1940S, THE AUTHOR
SUGGESTS A THREE-STAGE PROGRESSION IN WHICH SOCIAL UNREST
LED BY CLIENT GROUPS STIMULATES GROUPS OF SOCIAL SERVICE
WORKERS TO ALLY WITH PROTESTERS; A SECOND PERIOD
CHARACTERIZED AS "MILITANT PROFESSIONALISM" IN WHICH RADICAL
SOCIAL WORKERS DEVELOP STRONG CRITIQUES OF PROFESSIONAL
LEADERSHIP; AND FINALLY A PERIOD OF "ABSORBED" RADICALISM IN
WHICH RELATIVE PEACE IS ESTABLISHED WITH THE MAINSTREAM OF
THE PROFESSION. THE AUTHOR EMPHASIZES KEY SOCIAL AND
ECONOMIC FACTORS RELATED TO THE RISE AND FALL OF SOCIAL
WORKER RADICALISM.

09320 WAGNER, D.H.
POLITICAL IDEOLOGY AND PROFESSIONAL CAREERS: A STUDY OF
RADICAL SOCIAL SERVICE WORKERS
DISSERTATION ABSTRACTS INTERNATIONAL, 49(8) (FEB 89),
2398-A.
THE AUTHOR PROBES THE RELATIONSHIP BETWEEN UPWARD
MOBILITY, PROFESSIONALIZATION, AND PERSISTENCE OF RADICAL
POLITICAL IDEOLOGY BY STUDYING MEMBERS OF A LEFTIST
COLLECTIVE OF HUMAN SERVICE WORKERS. HE FOLLOWS A POPULATION
OF RADICALS OVER TIME TO EXPLORE WHAT CONSTITUTES A RADICAL
CAREER, WHETHER RADICAL POLITICAL IDEOLOGY IS COMPLIMENTARY
TO PROFESSIONAL LOYALTY, AND TO WHAT DEGREE MILITANT SOCIAL
ACTION IS CONSTRAINED OR ENCOURAGED BY PROFESSIONAL
ADVANCEMENT.

09321 WAGNER, E.H.
LIBERAL ESTABLISHMENT ON TORY ROW
NATIONAL REVIEW, 61(25) (DEC 89), 19-21.
THIS ARTICLE CATCHES THE UPPERCRUST OF CAMBRIDGE, MASS.,
IN AN ACT OF RACISM. AS SOON AS THE COMMONWEALTH DAY SCHOOL
(90 PERCENT BLACK) BOUGHT THE PROPERTY, THE LOCAL RESIDENTS
HAD PUT ON A FULL-COURT PRESS TO RID THEMSELVES OF THIS
UNWANTED NEIGHBOR. PUBLIC REACTION TO THESE SUCCESSFUL
EFFORTS ARE REPORTED. IT WAS SUGGESTED THAT THE WHOLE
CONTROVERSY WAS A MATTER OF "CLASS WAR."

STEMMING FROM PERESTROIKA.

09322 WAGNER, P.
SOCIAL SCIENCE AND THE STATE IN CONTINENTAL WESTERN EUROPE:
THE POLITICAL STRUCTURATION OF DISCIPLINARY DISCOURSE
INTERNATIONAL SOCIAL SCIENCE JOURNAL, (122) (NOV 89),
509-528.
THE EMERGENCE OF SOCIAL SCIENCE IS OFTEN TOO EASILY
RELATED TO THE MODERNIZATION OF SOCIETY IN GENERAL, AS IN
THE FOLLOWING STATEMENT: "THERE IS CLEARLY A CLOSE
CONNECTION BETWEEN THE SCIENTIFIC STUDY OF SOCIAL CONDITIONS,
INDUSTRIALIZATION, AND INTENSIFIED URBANIZATION." THOUGH
THIS STATEMENT IS CLEARLY NOT FALSE, IT SUGGESTS A SMOOTH,
OBVIOUS, AND INEVITABLE PROCESS FOR WHAT IN REALITY HAS
FUNDAMENTALLY PROBLEMATIC IN THREE MAJOR RESPECTS: COGNITIVE,
INSTITUTIONAL, AND POLITICAL.

09323 WAHBY, M.
THE ARAB COOPERATION COUNCIL AND THE ARAB POLITICAL ORDER
AMERICAN-ARAB AFFAIRS, (28) (SPR 89), 60-67.
THE ESSAY EXAMINES THE NEWLY FOUNDED ARAB COOPERATION
COUNCIL AND ITS IMPLICATIONS FOR THE ARAB POLITICLA ORDER.
IT OUTLINES EARLIER ATTEMPTS AT ARAB UNITY SUCH AS THE ARAB
LEAGUE, THE GULF COOPERATION COUNCIL, AND THE UNITED ARAB
REPUBLIC AND COMPARES THESE PREVIOUS ORGANIZATIONS WITH THE
ACC. IT CONCLUDES THAT ALTHOUGH THE CHALLENGES FACED BY THE
ACC ARE MANY AND ARE NOT TO BE UNDERESTIMATED, THE ACC BY
ITS VERY INTERNAL COMPOSITION, INTERNAL COMPULSIONS AND
POLITICAL ORIENTATION WILL INCREASE THE PROSPECTS FOR ORDER
AND LONG-TERM SUCCESS.

09324 WAHEEDUZZAMAN, M.
TOWARDS A SYSTEMATIC APPROACH TO PUBLIC ADMINISTRATION
TRAINING IN BANGLADESH
DISSERTATION ABSTRACTS INTERNATIONAL, 50(3) (SEP 89),
791-A.
THE AUTHOR ASSESSES THE STATE OF PUBLIC ADMINISTRATION
TRAINING IN BANGLADESH, IN LIGHT OF THE DEFICIENCIES ALLEGED
IN A NUMBER OF GOVERNMENT DOCUMENTS AND INDEPENDENT STUDIES.
HE USES THE SYSTEMATIC TRAINING MODEL PROPOSED BY IRWIN L.
GOLDSTEIN AS THE CONCEPTUAL FRAMEWORK FOR THE STUDY.

09325 WAISMAN, C.
COUNTERREVOLUTION AND STRUCTURAL CHANGE: THE CASE OF
ARGENTINA
INTERNATIONAL POLITICAL SCIENCE REVIEW, 10(2) (APR 89),
159-174.
ABSTRACT. THIS ARTICLE DISCUSSES THE REVERSAL OF
DEVELOPMENT IN ARGENTINA. IT ARGUES THAT THIS COUNTRY
SWITCHED DEVELOPMENTAL TRACKS: FROM BEING A "LAND OF RECENT
SETTLEMENT," IT BECAME AN UNDERDEVELOPED SOCIETY. THIS SHIFT
WAS THE UNINTENDED CONSEQUENCE OF TWO POLICIES THAT WERE
INSTITUTIONALIZED IN THE POSTWAR PERIOD: AUTARKIC
INDUSTRIALIZATION, AND A CORPORATIST SYSTEM OF LABOR
RELATIONS. THE AUTHOR CLAIMS THAT THESE POLICIES WERE A
RESPONSE BY THE STATE ELITE TO A PERCEIVED REVOLUTIONARY
THREAT, THAT THIS FEAR OF REVOLUTION WAS UNREALISTIC, AND
THAT THESE POLICIES HAD THE EFFECTS THEY DID BECAUSE OF THE
"MODERN" CHARACTERISTICS OF ARGENTINA. THE PECULIAR PATTERN
OF ARGENTINE DEVELOPMENT COULD NOT HAVE BEEN UNDERSTOOD BY
EITHER MODERNIZATION AND DEPENDENCY APPROACHES, AND THUS
THIS CASE CALLS INTO QUESTION THE BASIC ASSUMPTIONS OF THESE
THEORIES OF DEVELOPMENT.

09326 WAITT, G.R.
INTERNATIONAL SPECIALISATION OF MANUFACTURING ACTIVITY AND
ECONOMIC INTEGRATION WITHIN THE EUROPEAN ECONOMIC COMMUNITY
DISSERTATION ABSTRACTS INTERNATIONAL, 50(2) (AUG 89),
538-A.
SINCE 1974, THE NATURE OF EEC TRADE FOR TOTAL
MANUFACTURED TRADE HAS BEEN INCREASINGLY CHARACTERIZED BY
INTRA-INDUSTRY TRADE--THAT IS, TRADE IN A CLOSELY
DIFFERENTIATED PRODUCT RATHER THAN INTER-INDUSTRY
SPECIALIZATION. THE PATTERN OF TRADE IN TERMS OF INTEGRATION
FOR TOTAL MANUFACTURED TRADE IS ALSO INCREASING. THIS TREND
TOWARDS INTEGRATION IN MANUFACTURED PRODUCTS INDICATES THAT
INTRA-INDUSTRY SPECIALIZATION MAY PARTIALLY ACCOUNT FOR
INTRA-INDUSTRY TRADE. CONFIRMATION OF THIS TREND IS FOUND IN
EMPIRICAL ANALYSIS FOR SELECTED INDUSTRIES (PULP AND PAPER,
IRON AND STEEL, TEXTILES AND BASE METALS) AT A DISAGGREGATE
LEVEL OF DATA.

09327 WAKIL, A.
AFGHANISTAN SOLUTION, "THE FIRST TRACK"
ORIENT, 30(3) (SEP 89). 359-378.
THE GENEVA ACCORD, REFERRED TO AS THE "FIRST TRACK OF
THE AFGHAN SOLUTION," TOOK SIX FULL YEARS AND TWELVE FULL
ROUNDS OF INTENSE NEGOTIATIONS. THE PAPER ATTEMPTS TO ASSESS
THE PROCESS WHICH CULMINATED IN THE GENEVA ACCORD AS THE
"FIRST TRACK" POLITICAL SOLUTION OF THE AFGHAN DILEMMA. IT
FOCUSES SPECIAL ATTENTION ON SOME BACKGROUND DETAILS AS WELL
AS THOSE ASPECTS OF THE CRISIS WHICH COULD HAVE A BEARING ON
THE SHAPING OF AFGHANISTAN'S FUTURE. TOPICS COVERED INCLUDE:
VARIOUS SOVIET INITIATIVES RANGING FROM BABRAK KARMAL'S
DEMANDS, THROUGH BREZHNEV'S GULF PLAN, TO THE CHANGES

09328 WALD, P.
RANDOM THOUGHTS ON A RANDOM PROCESS: SELECTING APPELLATE
JUDGES
JOURNAL OF LAW & POLITICS, VI(1) (FAL 89), 15-24.
THE HONORABLE PATRICIA M. WALD, A CHIEF U.S. CIRCUIT
COURT JUDGE, REFLECTS ON THE PROCESS OF FEDERAL JUDGE
SELECTION. SHE CONCLUDES THAT THE BEST HOPE FOR IMPROVEMENT
LIES IN THE COURAGE AND VISION OF THE APPOINTING AND
CONFIRMING OFFICIALS OF THE GOVERNMENT I WHOM THE FRAMERS OF
THE CONSTITUTION ENTRUSTED THEIR HOPES FOR AN INDEPENDENT
AND IMPARTIAL JUDICIARY. SHE ADVOCATES THE FIRMER ADOPTION
OF THE CONCEPT THAT FEDERAL JUDGES ARE LONG-TERM INVESTMENTS
FOR ALL THE NATION'S CITIZENS, NOT SHORT-TERM POLITICAL
ALLIES FOR THE PARTY IN POWER.

09329 HALDEGRAVE, W.
THE PARTIAL TEST-BAN TREATY: A BRITISH VIEW
DISARMAMENT, XII(1) (WIN 89), 1-16.
THE AUTHOR REVIEWS THE BACKGROUND TO THE PARTIAL NUCLEAR
TEST-BAN TREATY OF 1963, FOCUSING ON THE BRITISH ROLE IN
FORMULATING AND IMPLEMENTING IT.

09330 WALDEN, G.
OUR MORALISTIC MEDIA
ENCOUNTER, LXXII(2) (FEB 89), 13-18.
THE AVERAGE ELECTOR, IF HE IS INTERESTED AT ALL, HAS
SIMPLE INSTINCTS ON FOREIGN POLICY. BUT IF THESE ARE TO BE
TRANSLATED INTO A HEALTHY INFLUENCE ON GOVERNMENT, SOMETHING
MORE IS REQUIRED. IT HELPS TO KNOW THE FACTS. A SIMPLE
SOLUTION IS TO LEAVE THE INSTINCTS TO THE PEOPLE AND FOR
THOSE IN POWER TO KEEP THE FACTS TO THEMSELVES. FOR BOTH
SIDES, THIS CAN BE A CONVENIENT DIVISION OF RESPONSIBILITY,
BUT IT IS A HIGHLY DANGEROUS ONE. IF DEMOCRATIC STATES ARE
TO FUNCTION DEMOCRATICALLY IN FOREIGN AS WELL AS DOMESTIC
AFFAIRS, THE PUBLIC MUST BE INFORMED AND ITS MATURE OPINIONS
RELAYED AND REFLECTED IN THE MEDIA AND ELSEWHERE FOR THE
EDIFICATION OF ELECTED OFFICIALS.

09331 WALDEN, G.
PEACEFUL CO-AMNESIA
ENCOUNTER, LXXIII(2) (JUL 89), 3-9.
THE AUTHOR CONSIDERS TWO THEMES: THE MORAL BANKRUPTCY OF
THE EAST, DEMONSTRATED BY THE DISINTEGRATION OF COMMUNISM,
AND THE MORAL INSTABILITY OF THE WEST, REFLECTED IN ITS
EDUCATIONAL VALUES. HE WARNS THAT THE WORLD IS NOT
WITNESSING A MORAL REBIRTH OF NATIONS BUT THE TRIUMPH OF THE
MANAGERIAL ETHIC. IN THE EAST, THE MOTIVATION, AS WELL AS
THE OUTCOME, OF THE REFORMS IS UNCERTAIN. IF WESTERN WAYS
HAVE WON, IT IS BY A TECHNICAL, NOT A MORAL, KNOCKOUT. THUS,
THE WEST'S TRIUMPH IS FULLY COMPATIBLE WITH ITS DECLINE.

09332 WALDER, A.
BEYOND THE DENG ERA: CHINA'S POLITICAL DILEMMA
ASIAN AFFAIRS, AN AMERICAN REVIEW, 16(2) (SUM 89), 83-92.
CHINA MADE SURPRISINGLY GREAT STRIDES IN THE 1980S UNDER
DENGISM, A DOCTRINALLY ILL-DEFINED KIND OF PRAGMATISM THAT
INITIALLY APPEALED TO BOTH OLD-TIME PARTY LOYALISTS AS A
STRATEGY FOR STRENGTHENING AND SURVIVAL AND TO FREETHINKING
REFORMERS BENT ON PROFOUND REDEFINITION OF CHINESE SOCIALISM.
DENGISM ENDORSED A SOCIALIST ECONOMY, RECONSTRUCTION OF
POPULAR TRUST IN GOVERNMENT, AND OPEN ENDED EXPLORATION OF A
NEW ORGANIZATION. AS THE 1980S DREW TO A CLOSE, THIS OPEN-
ENDED APPROACH BECAME ONE OF THE PROMINENT WEAKNESSES IN THE
SYSTEM. CHINA IS NOW IN AN ECONOMIC SITUATION VERY DIFFERENT
FROM THAT OF THE EARLY MID-1980S. INDUSTRIAL INVESTMENT HAS
SURGED OUT OF CONTROL, CONSUMER INFLATION HAS HIT HARD, AND
CORRUPTED GROWS UNCHECKED. CHINA'S DILEMMA IS WHETHER TO
MAINTAIN STABILITY OR TO SUCUMB TO THE PEOPLE'S DEMAND FOR
REFORM.

09333 WALDER, A.G.
THE POLITICAL SOCIOLOGY OF THE BEIJING UPHEAVAL OF 1989
PROBLEMS OF COMMUNISM, XXXVIII(5) (SEP 89), 30-40.
BEIJING'S 1989 POPULAR REBELLION PRESENTS TWO PUZZLES.
WHY DID THE 1989 STUDENT PROTESTS TOUCH OFF THE LARGEST
POPULAR CHALLENGE TO PARTY RULE IN THE HISTORY OF THE
PEOPLE'S REPUBLIC OF CHINA WHEN SIMILAR CAMPAIGNS IN THE
PAST FOUND LITTLE POPULAR RESPONSE AND WERE EASILY
SUPPRESSED? AND GIVEN THE APPARENT LACK OF AN ORGANIZED
FOUNDATION WITHIN FACTORIES AND OTHER WORKPLACES, HOW COULD
SUCH A NONVIOLENT MOVEMENT LEAD SO QUICKLY TO THE PARALYSIS
AND POLITICAL CRISIS OF MAY 1989?

09334 WALDRON, J.
JOHN LOCKE: SOCIAL CONTRACT VERSUS POLITICAL ANTHROPOLOGY
REVIEW OF POLITICS, 51(1) (WIN 89), 3-28.
IN THE SECOND TREATISE, JOHN LOCKE PRESENTS TWO STORIES
ABOUT THE DEVELOPMENT OF POLITICAL SOCIETY: (1) THE DRAMATIC
STORY OF THE STATE OF NATURE AND SOCIAL CONTRACT AND (2) A
MORE GRADUALIST ACCOUNT OF THE EVOLUTION OF POLITICAL
SOCIETY "BY AN INSENSIBLE CHANGE" OUT OF THE FAMILY GROUP.
THE RELATION BETWEEN THESE TWO ACCOUNTS IS ANALYZED IN ORDER

TO DEAL WITH FAMILIAR OBJECTIONS ABOUT THE HISTORICAL TRUTH AND INTERNAL CONSISTENCY OF CONTRACT THEORY. IT IS ARGUED THAT LOCKE REGARDED STORY (2) AS THE HISTORICALLY ACCURATE ONE, BUT THAT HE BELIEVED HISTORICAL EVENTS NEEDED MORAL INTERPRETATION. STORY (1) REPRESENTS A MORAL FRAMEWORK OR TEMPLATE TO BE USED AS A BASIS FOR UNDERSTANDING THE IMPLICATIONS -- FOR POLITICAL OBLIGATION AND POLITICAL LEGITIMACY -- OF STORY (2). EVEN IF THE WHOLE COURSE OF THE EVOLUTION OF POLITICAL INSTITUTIONS OUT OF PREPOLITICAL SOCIETY CANNOT BE SEEN AS A SINGLE INTENTIONAL OR CONSENSUAL PROCESS, STILL INDIVIDUAL STEPS IN THAT PROCESS CAN BE ANALYZED AND EVALUATED IN CONTRACTUALIST TERMS. THE TASK OF POLITICAL JUDGMENT IS TO INFER THE RIGHTS AND OBLIGATIONS OF POLITICS FROM THIS REPRESENTATION OF POLITICAL DEVELOPMENT AS AN OVERLAPPING SERIES OF CONSENSUAL EVENTS.

09335 WALI, A.
IN EASTERN PANAMA, LAND IS THE KEY TO SURVIVAL
CULTURAL SURVIVAL QUARTERLY, 13(3) (1989), 25-29.
THE PANAMANIAN GOVERNMENT BEGAN CONSTRUCTION OF THE BAYANO DAM AND THE EXTENSION OF THE PAN-AMERICAN HIGHWAY TO EXPAND ITS CONTROL OF ENERGY RESOURCES AND STIMULATE ECONOMIC DEVELOPMENT IN EASTERN PANAMA. ALTHOUGH PLANS EXISTED ON PAPER TO PROTECT THE REGION'S FRAGILE ECOLOGY AND PROVIDE EQUITABLE COMPENSATION TO ITS RESIDENTS FOR THEIR LOSS OF LAND AND LIVELIHOOD, THE GOVERNMENT HAS LARGELY FAILED TO IMPLEMENT THEM. INSTEAD, MORE THAN 12 YEARS AFTER THE DAM'S COMPLETION, THE REGION CONTINUES TO FEEL ITS NEGATIVE IMPACT.

09336 WALKER, D.
LOCAL GOVERNMENT: 1988/89
CONTEMPORARY RECORD, 3(1) (FAL 89), 29.
THIS ARTICLE EXPLORES THE RELATIONSHIP BETWEEN NATIONAL AND LOCAL GOVERNMENT IN GREAT BRITAIN. IT SUGGESTS THAT, WITH OR WITHOUT MRS. THATCHER. THE ROLE OF GOVERNMENT RELATIVE TO THE OPERATION OF PRIVATE MARKETS, THE ARCHECTURE OF THE STATE, MIGHT WELL HAVE CHANGED IN THE 1980S... AND THE ORGANIZATION OF LOCAL GOVERNMENT WITH IT. IT SUGGESTS, ALSO, THE NEED FOR REINVIGORATION OF LOCAL AUTHORITIES AS VITAL CENTERS OF POLITICAL DEBATE.

09337 WALKER, D.B.
AMERICAN FEDERALISM: PAST, PRESENT, AND FUTURE
JOURNAL OF STATE GOVERNMENT, 62(1) (JAN 89), 3-11.
THE STUDY OF FEDERAL SYSTEMS IN THE UNITED STATES AND OTHER COUNTRIES REVEALS THAT THREE FACTORS HAVE UNDERMINED THE FUNDAMENTAL BASES OF A GENUINE FEDERALIST REGIME. THESE FACTORS, OR CONDITIONERS, ARE: (1) THE REPRESENTATIONAL AND INDIRECTLY THE POLITICAL, (2) THE FUNCTIONAL OR OPERATIONAL, AND (3) THE JUDICIAL AND JURISDICTIONAL. ALL THREE ARE INCORPORATED IN CONSTITUTIONS PURPORTING TO ESTABLISH A FEDERAL SYSTEM OF FREE GOVERNMENT. UNDERSTANDING HOW THESE FORMAL FEATURES OF GOVERNMENT HAVE SHAPED AND BEEN SHAPED BY SOCIO-CULTURAL, ECONOMIC, TECHNOLOGICAL, AND INTERNATIONAL CHALLENGES OVER THE LAST TWO CENTURIES IS A PREREQUISITE FOR GRAPPLING WITH CURRENT FEDERAL-STATE-LOCAL ISSUES IN THE USA.

09338 WALKER, E.S.; BURLEIGH, A.P.
FY 1990 ASSISTANCE REQUEST FOR THE MIDDLE EAST
DEPARTMENT OF STATE BULLETIN (US FOREIGN POLICY), 89(2146) (MAY 89), 61-68.
THIS ARTICLE CONTAINS STATEMENTS, BY THE DEPUTY ASSISTANT SECRETARIES FOR NEAR EAST AND SOUTH ASIAN AFFAIRS, THAT WERE PRESENTED TO THE SUBCOMMITTEE ON EUROPE AND THE MIDDLE EAST OF THE HOUSE FOREIGN AFFAIRS COMMITTEE. THE DEPUTY ASSISTANT SECRETARIES REVIEWED AMERICAN POLICY IN THE MIDDLE EAST AND EXPLAINED THE BUSH ADMINISTRATION'S BUDGET REQUESTS FOR AID TO THE REGION.

09339 WALKER, I.
SOCIALISM AND DEMOCRACY: CHILE IN COMPARATIVE PERSPECTIVE
DISSERTATION ABSTRACTS INTERNATIONAL, 50(1) (JUL 89), 249-A.
THE AUTHOR COMPARES SUCCESSFUL AND UNSUCCESSFUL DEMOCRATIC SOCIALIST EXPERIENCES. HE BEGINS WITH A STUDY OF WESTERN EUROPEAN SOCIALISM BASED ON THREE CASES: THE GERMAN SOCIAL DEMOCRATIC PARTY, THE FRENCH SOCIALIST PARTY, AND THE ITALIAN COMMUNIST PARTY. THEN HE CONSIDERS THE UNSUCCESSFUL CASE OF CHILEAN SOCIALISM, ESPECIALLY IN THE PERIOD PRIOR TO THE 1973 MILITARY COUP.

09340 WALKER, J.
RED CARPET TREATMENT
MIDDLE EAST INTERNATIONAL, (343) (FEB 89), 10-11.
THE EUROPEAN COMMUNITY HAS A FUNDAMENTAL ROLE TO PLAY IN ACHIEVING PEACE IN THE MIDDLE EAST, ACCORDING TO YASSER ARAFAT. ARAFAT, ON AN OFFICIAL VISIT TO SPAIN IN JANUARY 1989, WAS GREETED WITH HONORS NORMALLY RESERVED FOR A HEAD-OF-STATE. BUT HE FAILED IN HIS BASIC GOAL OF PERSUADING EUROPEANS, EITHER AS A GROUP OR AS INDIVIDUAL NATIONS, TO RECOGNIZE THE STATE OF PALESTINE.

09341 WALKER, J.L.
POLICY COMMUNITIES AS A GLOBAL PHENOMENA
GOVERNANCE, 2(1) (JAN 89), 1-4.
POLICY SPECIALISTS HAVE MORE INFLUENCE ON THE COURSE OF PUBLIC POLICY WHEN ISSUES ARE SEEN AS MAINLY TECHNICAL MATTERS WHICH DO NOT CHALLENGE THE INTERESTS OR IDEOLOGY OF THE COUNTRY'S ESTABLISHED POLITICAL OR ECONOMIC INTERESTS. AT THE SAME TIME, THIS DOES NOT MEAN THAT POLICY SPECIALISTS ARE POWERLESS TO INFLUENCE THE THINKING OF LEADERS ABOUT THE FUNDAMENTAL TENETS OF THEIR POLITICAL FAITHS. ORGANIZED POLICY PROFESSIONALS HAVE LITTLE POWER IN THE CONVENTIONAL SENSE OF THE WORD - THEY DO NOT CONTROL LARGE VOTING BLOCS NOR CAN THEY MOBILIZE THE FINANCIAL RESOURCES POLITICIANS IN DEMOCRATIC SYSTEMS NEED TO INSURE THEIR REELECTION. YET BY BROADCASTING PERSUASIVE JUSTIFICATIONS FOR CHANGE, THEY ARE ABLE TO EXERT A STEADY, COERCIVE INFLUENCE ON POLICY FORMULATION, SOMETIMES OVERCOMING THE BEST EFFORTS OF ORGANIZED ECONOMIC OR SOCIAL GROUPS WHO ARE RESISTING CHANGES IN THE STATUS QUO.

09342 WALKER, K.
THE STATE IN ENVIRONMENTAL MANAGEMENT: THE ECOLOGICAL DIMENSION
POLITICAL STUDIES, XXXVII(1) (MAR 89), 25-38.
THE ARTICLE EXAMINES AN AGE-OLD CONFLICT THAT THE STATE MUST DEAL WITH: THE NEED FOR CREATION AND MAINTENANCE OF ECONOMIC GROWTH VERSUS THE NECESSITY OF MAINTAINING THE ECOLOGICAL BALANCE AND CONSERVATION OF RESOURCES. IT TRACES THE DEVELOPMENT OF THE STATE FROM ANCIENT TIME TO THE PRESENT AND EXAMINES HOW VARIOUS STATES HAVE DEALT WITH THIS CONFLICT. IT CONCLUDES THAT ALTHOUGH THE EXPRESSION OF INTERSTATE COMPETITION GENERALLY EXPRESSED THROUGH WAR HAS EXISTED FOR MILLENNIA, THE TECHNICALLY ADVANCED SOCIETY OF TODAY PRESENTS UNIQUE AND AWESOME CHALLENGES TO THE ENVIRONMENT. ECOLOGICAL CRISES ARE LIKELY TO PRESENT SIGNIFICANT ADAPTIVE CHALLENGES TO MODERN STATE. ONE OF THE MOST IMPORTANT CHALLENGES IS THE CURBING OF THE "WRONG" KINDS OF ECONOMIC GROWTH AND INTERSTATE COMPETITION.

09343 WALKER, K.R.
FORTY YEARS ON: PROVINCIAL CONTRASTS IN CHINA'S RURAL ECONOMIC DEVELOPMENT
CHINA QUARTERLY, (119) (SEP 89), 448-480.
THIS PAPER IS DIVIDED INTO FIVE SECTIONS. THE FIRST CLASSIFIES CHINESE PROVINCES ACCORDING TO THEIR RURAL ECONOMIC STRUCTURE AND LEVEL OF OUTPUT. THE SECOND CONSIDERS THE PROVINCIAL PATTERN OF AGRICULTURAL (AS OPPOSED TO RURAL) DEVELOPMENT AND MODERNIZATION, WHILE THE THIRD EXAMINES DEVELOPMENT AS MEASURED BY INCOMES AND FOOD CONSUMPTION. SECTION FOUR SUMMARIZES THE FINDINGS OF THE FIRST THREE SECTIONS, AND THE FINAL SECTION SPECULATES ABOUT FUTURE PROSPECTS IN LIGHT OF THE CURRENT STAGE OF RURAL DEVELOPMENT.

09344 WALKER, L.
WOODROW WILSON, PROGRESSIVE REFORM, AND PUBLIC ADMINISTRATION
POLITICAL SCIENCE QUARTERLY, 104(3) (FAL 89), 509-525.
LARRY WALKER OFFERS A BROAD REVIEW OF WOODROW WILSON'S INFLUENCE ON TWENTIETH-CENTURY ADMINISTRATION. THROUGH EXAMINATION OF WILSON'S ROLE IN ACADEMIC AND POLITICAL REFORM MOVEMENTS OF HIS DAY AND OF HIS PRESIDENCY, WALKER ARGUES THAT WILSON HAD A SUBSTANTIAL ROLE IN THE SHAPING OF AMERICAN PUBLIC ADMINISTRATION AND POLITICAL SCIENCE.

09345 WALKER, M.
NATIONAL SOCIALISM AND GERMAN PHYSICS
JOURNAL OF CONTEMPORARY HISTORY, 24(1) (JAN 89), 63-89.
TRADITIONALLY, THE DEUTSCHE PHYSIK MOVEMENT HAS BEEN REGARDED AS THE ONLY EXAMPLE OF THE PERVERSION OF PHYSICS TO THE SUPPORT OF THE NATIONAL SOCIALIST REGIME. BUT THIS ARTICLE TAKES A DIFFERENT APPROACH WITH RESPECT TO THE CASE OF GERMAN PHYSICS AND PHYSICISTS DURING THE THIRD REICH. THE STRIDENT CALLS FOR A MORE ARYAN, LESS JEWISH SCIENCE WERE NOT THE ONLY EXAMPLES OF THE PENETRATION OF NATIONAL SOCIALIST IDEOLOGY INTO THE PRACTICE OF PHYSICS. THE RELATIONSHIPS BETWEEN DEUTSCHE PHYSIK, NATIONAL SOCIALISM, AND THE GERMAN PHYSICS COMMUNITY PROVIDE A FASCINATING EXAMPLE OF THE IMPACT THAT AN IDEOLOGY CAN HAVE ON SCIENCE AS WELL AS OF HOW SCIENCE AND SCIENTISTS CAN, IN TURN, INFLUENCE AN IDEOLOGY.

09346 WALKER, R.
CLAUDE LEFORT ON THE DIALECTIC OF TWENTIETH-CENTURY POLITICS
JOURNAL OF COMMUNIST STUDIES, 5(1) (MAR 89), 98-102.
THE ARTICLE IS A REVIEW OF THE POLITICAL FORMS OF MODERN SOCIETY: BUREAUCRACY, DEMOCRACY, TOTALITARIANISM, BY CLAUDE LEFORT. THE BOOK PROVIDES AN INTERESTING INSIGHT INTO THE PERSONAL ODYSSEY OF A CRITICAL MARXIST AND PRACTICING MEMBER OF THE FRENCH LEFT WHO HAS CONSISTENTLY ENDEAVOURED TO CONFRONT BOTH THE SHIBBOLETHS OF THE MARXIST TRADITION AND THE REALITIES OF COMMUNIST (AND TROTSKYIST) PARTY PRACTICE FROM WITHIN THE FRAMEWORK OF A MARXIST CRITIQUE.

09347 WALKER, R.
    MARXISM-LENINISM AS DISCOURSE: THE POLITICS OF THE EMPTY
    SIGNIFIER AND THE DOUBLE BIND
    BRITISH JOURNAL OF POLITICAL SCIENCE, 19(2) (APR 89),
    161-189.
        THIS ARTICLE EMPLOYS A SEMIOTIC APPROACH TO INVESTIGATE
    THE MEANING OF 'MARXISM-LENINISM' WITH A VIEW TO CLARIFYING
    OUR UNDERSTANDING OF THIS TERM. CONTRARY TO CONVENTIONAL
    INTERPRETATIONS IT DEMONSTRATES THAT 'MARXISM LENINISM' IS
    AN EMPTY SIGNIFIER WHICH IS SUBJECT TO DEFINITION ON A
    CONTEMPORARY BASIS BY THE CPSU ITSELF. HOWEVER, IT ALSO
    DEMONSTRATES THAT 'MARXISM-LENINISM' IS THE CENTRAL ELEMENT
    IN A MECHANISM OF CONTROL WHICH BEARS ALL THE HALLMARKS OF A
    CLASSIC LINGUISTIC DOUBLE BIND. IT THEREFORE CONCLUDES THAT
    WHILE 'MARXISM-LENINISM' IS REFERENTIALLY OPEN TO RE-
    DEFINITION IT IS CONNOTATIVELY ATTACHED TO THE PRACTICES OF
    THE CPSU. IT IS BOTH FIXED AND NOT FIXED IN MEANING. THE
    RESULTING ANALYSIS LEADS TO A CRITIQUE OF TERMS WHICH ARE
    CONVENTIONALLY TAKEN FOR GRANTED BY SOVIETOLOGISTS AND
    INTRODUCES A NEW METHODOLOGICAL APPROACH TO THE STUDY OF
    'MARXISMLENINISM'.

09348 WALKER, R.; LAWTON, D.
    THE SOCIAL FUND AS AN EXERCISE IN RESOURCE ALLOCATION
    PUBLIC ADMINISTRATION, 67(3) (FAL 89), 295 - 318.
        THE SOCIAL FUND IS THE LATEST ATTEMPT TO COPE WITH THE
    EXCEPTIONAL NEEDS SOMETIMES EXPERIENCED BY PEOPLE IN RECEIPT
    OF SOCIAL ASSISTANCE. IT IS ALSO THE FIRST OCCASION WHEN
    RESOURCE ALLOCATION DECISIONS HAVE BEEN LOCATED CENTRE-STAGE
    IN A POLICY AREA THAT HITHERTO, HAS BEEN PRIMARILY DEMAND-
    LED. THE SOCIAL FUND, WHICH IS EVENTUALLY TO BE CASH LIMITED,
    IS ALLOCATED BETWEEN OVER 400 DEPARTMENT OF SOCIAL SECURITY
    (DSS; FORMERLY DEPARTMENT OF HEALTH AND SOCIAL SECURITY,
    DHSS) LOCAL OFFICES. THE ARTICLE DESCRIBES HOW THE 1988/9
    BUDGET WAS FIXED AND ALLOCATED BETWEEN LOCAL OFFICES,
    CONSIDERS SOME OF THE PROBLEMS THAT POLICYMAKERS FACED WHEN
    DEVISING THE ALLOCATION CRITERIA AND EXAMINES THE
    TERRITORIAL REDISTRIBUTION INHERENT IN THE CHOSEN STRATEGY
    AND WHICH MAY OR MAY NOT HAVE BEEN INTENDED.

09349 WALKER, S.G.; WATSON, G.L.
    GROUPTHINK AND INTEGRATIVE COMPLEXITY IN BRITISH FOREIGN
    POLICY-MAKING: THE MUNICH CASE
    COOPERATION & CONFLICT: NORDIC JOURNAL OF INTERNATIONAL
    POLITICS, XXIV(3-4) (DEC 89), 199-212.
        THE AUTHORS FOCUS UPON THE GROUPTHINK CONSTRUCT AS A
    PARTIAL EXPLANATION FOR THE FLAWED DECISION-MAKING BY
    BRITISH LEADERS IN MANAGING THE MUNICH CRISIS WITH GERMANY.
    IN ORDER TO ASSESS ITS EXPLANATORY POWER, THEY FOLLOW THE
    PRECEDENT ESTABLISHED IN PREVIOUS CASE STUDIES, WHICH
    EXPLORE THE LINK BETWEEN GROUPTHINK AND THE LEVELS OF
    INTEGRATIVE COMPLEXITY EXHIBITED BY DECISION-MAKERS. THE
    HYPOTHESIS LINKING THE TWO PHENOMENA IS THAT IN CASES WHERE
    GROUPTHINK IS PRESENT, THE LEVEL OF INTEGRATIVE COMPLEXITY
    WILL BE SIGNIFICANTLY LOWER THAN IN CASES WHERE IT IS ABSENT.
    THE MUNICH CASE IS A PARTICULARLY APPROPRIATE CASE FOR
    REPLICATING THE TEST OF THIS HYPOTHESIS BECAUSE, UNLIKE
    OTHER GROUPTHINK CASES, IT DID NOT LEAD TO UNSUCCESSFUL
    MILITARY INTERVENTIONS OR ESCALATIONS. THE RESULTS INDICATE
    THAT: (1) GROUPTHINK EXISTED IN THE MUNICH CASE; HOWEVER, IT
    DID NOT PERSIST THROUGHOUT THE ENTIRE CRISIS. (2) ITS
    PRESENCE AND ABSENCE FLUCTUATED CONSISTENTLY WITH THE
    EXPECTATIONS ASSOCIATED WITH THE THEORY WHICH ACCOUNTS FOR
    ITS DYNAMICS. (3) THE INTEGRATIVE COMPLEXITY EXHIBITED BY
    PRIME MINISTER CHAMBERLAIN AND FOREIGN SECRETARY HALIFAX
    VARIED AS PREDICTED.

09350 WALKER, W.; GUMMETT, P.
    BRITAIN AND THE EUROPEAN ARMAMENTS MARKET
    INTERNATIONAL AFFAIRS, 65(3) (SUM 89), 419-442.
        THE ARTICLE ATTEMPTS TO GIVE A PANORAMIC VIEW OF THE
    EUROPEAN ARMAMENTS MARKET AND BRITAIN'S RELATIONSHIP WITH IT.
    THE MAIN THEME IS THAT VARIOUS FACTORS ARE TENDING TO PLACE
    GREATER MARKET POWER IN THE HANDS OF THE LARGE EUROPEAN
    DEFENCE CONTRACTORS - WHICH ARE ACTING INCREASINGLY IN
    CONCERT WITH EACH OTHER - WITHOUT ANY ASSURANCE THAT
    ECONOMIES OF SCALE OR OTHER ECONOMIC BENEFITS WILL RESULT.
    THE ARTICLE EXAMINES BRITISH DEFENCE PROCUREMENT REFORM, THE
    SHIFT TOWARDS EUROPE, THE EMERGING STRUCTURE OF THE DEFENCE
    INDUSTRY IN EUROPE AND THE POLICIES OF MARKET LIBERALIZATION
    BEING APPLIED IN BRITAIN.

09351 HALL, J.
    FEAR SHIFTS, TROUBLE FLOATS AS THE COLD WAR ENDS
    THE CHRISTIAN CENTURY, 106(39) (DEC 89), 1190-1191.
        ALTHOUGH NOT OFFICIALLY DECLARED, THE COLD EAR IS OVER.
    HOWEVER, THE FEAR THAT ACCOMPANIED TENSION BETWEEN THE
    SUPERPOWERS WILL NOT DISAPPEAR. INSTEAD, THE OBJECT OF FEAR
    WILL SHIFT. WEST GERMANS NO LONGER FEAR AN ARMED
    CONFRONTATION WITH EAST GERMANS, BUT THEY DO FEAR THE
    ECONOMIC CONSEQUENCES OF LARGE POPULATIONS OF "POOR
    RELATIVES" COMING TO VISIT.

09352 WALLACE, B.; LAVER, R.; VAN DUSEN, L.
    WAR OVER WORDS
    MACLEAN'S (CANADA'S NEWS MAGAZINE), 102(1) (JAN 89), 38-41.
        IN CANADA, THE ALWAYS SIMMERING LANGUAGE CONTROVERSY
    FLARED UP AGAIN AS POLITICIANS IN QUEBEC CONSIDERED
    LEGISLATION THAT WOULD RESTRICT THE USE OF ENGLISH SIGNS.
    THREE MINISTERS IN PREMIER ROBERT BOURASSA'S CABINET
    RESIGNED IN A WIDENING CONTROVERSY OVER THE RIGHTS OF
    CANADA'S LINGUISTIC MINORITIES. THE INVOCATION OF THE SO-
    CALLED NOTWITHSTANDING PROVISION THAT ALLOWS PROVINCES TO
    ENFORCE LAWS THAT CONTRAVENE THE CONSTITUTION FOR PERIODS UP
    TO FIVE YEARS CAUSED THE CONTROVERSY TO BECOME EVEN MORE
    WIDESPREAD. PRIME MINISTER MULRONEY'S CHERISHED MEECH LAKE
    ACCORD IS IN DANGER AS MANITOBA'S PREMIER DECIDED TO
    WITHDRAW SUPPORT IN PROTEST OVER QUEBEC'S ACTIONS.

09353 WALLACE, H.
    THE EXTERNAL IMPLICATIONS OF 1992, II: AUSTRIA IN THE WINGS
    WORLD TODAY, 45(2) (FEB 89), 31-32.
        THE LUXEMBOURG DECLARATION OF 1984 COMMITTED BOTH THE
    EUROPEAN COMMUNITY AND THE EUROPEAN FREE TRADE ASSOCIATION
    TO A DEEPER RELATIONSHIP AND TO THE CREATION OF A EUROPEAN
    ECONOMIC SPHERE. AT A TECHNICAL LEVEL AND OCCASIONALLY AT A
    POLITICAL LEVEL, THE EUROPEAN COMMISSION AND THE EFTA HAVE
    BEEN PAINSTAKINGLY AT WORK TO REMOVE BARRIERS, TO REDUCE
    DISCRIMINATION, AND TO OPEN NEW AREAS OF COOPERATION. THESE
    NEGOTIATIONS ARE SLOWLY BEARING FRUIT, ALTHOUGH IT IS
    DIFFICULT FOR THEM TO KEEP PACE WITH THE MOVEMENT TO CREATE
    A SINGLE EUROPEAN MARKET BY 1992. WITHIN THIS CONTEXT,
    AUSTRIA, ALREADY A MEMBER OF THE EFTA, IS EXPECTED TO APPLY
    FOR MEMBERSHIP IN THE EUROPEAN COMMUNITY.

09354 WALLACE, S.; ESTES, C.
    HEALTH POLICY FOR THE ELDERLY
    SOCIETY, 26(6) (SEP 89), 66-75.
        HEALTH CARE FOR THE ELDERLY IS BECOMING AN INCREASINGLY
    SIGNIFICANT POLICY ISSUE. DEMOGRAPHIC TRENDS ENSURE THAT THE
    NUMBER OF ELDERLY WILL DRAMATICALLY INCREASE IN THE FUTURE.
    THE ARTICLE EXAMINES SEVERAL STRATEGIES DESIGNED TO RESPOND
    TO THE GROWING NUMBER FOR THE ELDERLY AND THEIR UNIQUE
    DEMANDS AND PROBLEMS. IT CONCENTRATES ON TWO MAIN MODELS:
    MARKET COMPETITION, AND GOVERNMENT REGULATION. IT CONCLUDES
    THAT THE REAGAN ADMINISTRATION HAS REDIRECTED THE COURSE OF
    HEALTH POLICY FOR THE ELDERLY, AND IF CURRENT TRENDS
    CONTINUE, HEALTH CARE FOR THE AGED WILL BECOME INCREASINGLY
    MEDICALIZED, COMMODIFIED, AND PROVIDED BY CORPORATIONS.

09355 WALLER, H.
    CANADA TACKLES ITS DEFICIT
    NEW LEADER, LXXII(15) (OCT 89), 8-9.
        CANADIAN CITIZENS HAVE RESISTED ANY ATTEMPTS AT REDUCING
    THE BENEFITS OF THEIR "WOMB-TO-TOMB" COVERAGE PROVIDED BY
    THE GOVERNMENT. THE RESULTING $28 BILLION DEFICIT HAS CAUSED
    THE MULRONEY GOVERNMENT TO SCRAMBLE FOR ALTERNATE SOURCES OF
    GOVERNMENT REVENUE. THE LATEST IDEA IS THE GOODS AND
    SERVICES TAX (GST), A VALUE-ADDED TAX THAT COVERS SUCH
    DIVERSE ITEMS AS HAIRCUTS, ENERGY, HOTEL ROOMS, AND
    PRACTICALLY ALL CONSUMER PRODUCTS. THE GOVERNMENT'S
    RATIONALE IS THAT THE GST WILL REPLACE THE MUCH CRITICIZED
    MANUFACTURER SALES TAX AND WILL GENERATE MORE REVENUE AT
    LITTLE ADDITIONAL COST TO THE AVERAGE CANADIAN.

09356 WALLER, H.M.
    THE 1988 ISRAELI ELECTION: PROPORTIONAL REPRESENTATION
    WITH A VENGEANCE
    MIDDLE EAST REVIEW, XXI(4) (SUM 89), 9-17.
        THE 1988 ISRAELIS ELECTION APPEARS TO HAVE BEEN A WASTED
    OPPORTUNITY. ALTHOUGH MOMENTOUS ISSUES OF FUNDAMENTAL
    IMPORTANCE TO ISRAEL WERE DEVELOPING, THE COUNTRY'S
    POLITICAL LEADERS AND VOTERS DID NOT FOCUS CLEARLY ON THE
    CENTRAL ISSUES DURING MOST OF THE ELECTION CAMPAIGN.
    AFTERWARDS, THEY CONCENTRATED ON TANGENTIAL ONES.
    UNDERSTANDABLY, THE SPECTACLE OF THE POST-ELECTION
    BARGAINING PROCESS, COUPLED WITH THE FACT THAT THIS WAS
    ISRAEL'S SECOND CONSECUTIVE ELECTION WITHOUT A DECISIVE
    VICTOR, ENCOURAGED SERIOUS THINKING ABOUT REFORMING THE
    SYSTEM. WHAT HAS EMERGED IS A GROWING FEELING THAT PARALYSIS
    OF ISRAEL'S ELECTORAL SYSTEM, EITHER DURING THE FORMATION OF
    A GOVERNMENT OR AFTER THE ACHIEVEMENT OF A COALITION, IS A
    LUXURY THAT ISRAEL CAN ILL AFFORD.

09357 WALLER, M.
    COMMUNIST PARTIES AND THE GREENS IN THE EUROPEAN ELECTIONS
    OF 1989
    JOURNAL OF COMMUNIST STUDIES, 5(4) (DEC 89), 189-194.
        THIS ARTICLE REPORTS ON THE FACT THAT AS THE COMMUNIST
    PARTIES OF THE EUROPEAN COMMUNITY COUNTRIES PREPARED FOR THE
    JUNE ELECTIONS TO THE EUROPEAN PARLIAMENT THEY HAD A NUMBER
    OF REASONS FOR CONCERN. IT EXPLORES THESE REASONS AND
    CONTINUES ON TO THE ONE CONSOLING FACTOR WHICH HELPED TO
    OFFSET THE REASONS. IN THIS ANALYSIS OF THE EUROPEAN
    ELECTIONS THE RESULTS ARE FIRST TREATED, AFTER WHICH THE NEW
    EUROPEAN ALIGNMENTS WILL BE EXAMINED

09358 WALLER, M.
THE ECOLOGY ISSUE IN EASTERN EUROPE: PROTEST AND MOVEMENTS
JOURNAL OF COMMUNIST STUDIES. 5(3) (SEP 89), 303-328.
AN AWARENESS OF THE SEVERE ENVIRONMENTAL PROBLEMS THAT
AFFECT THE REGION HAS DEVELOPED IN EASTERN EUROPE, BUT THE
POSSIBILITIES OF ORGANIZING COUNTERVAILING POLITICAL ACTION
REMAIN RESTRICTED BY THE EXISTING SYSTEM OF POLITICS. TWO
DEVELOPMENTS, HOWEVER, HAVE FAVOURED THE EMERGENCE OF AN
ECOLOGY MOVEMENT. THE FIRST IS A SHIFT IN THE STRATEGY OF
THE MAJOR DISSENTING GROUPS IN THE REGION, WHICH HAVE
BROADENED THEIR EMPHASIS ON HUMAN RIGHTS TO INCLUDE ECOLOGY
AND PEACE ISSUES. THE SECOND, WHICH AFFECTS HUNGARY AND
POLAND IN PARTICULAR, IS THE NEW POSSIBILITIES FOR
AUTONOMOUS ORGANIZATION THAT HAVE OPENED UP IN THE WAKE OF
GORBACHEV'S REFORMS IN THE SOVIET UNION. IN THESE TWO CASES
THE MIDDLE GROUND OF THE POLITICAL SYSTEM IS COMING TO
FEATURE A PROCESS OF ORGANIZED GROUP FORMATION. DESPITE
THESE IMPORTANT CHANGES THAT ARE TAKING PLACE, THE
EFFECTIVENESS OF PROTEST OVER ENVIRONMENTAL ISSUES REMAINS
LIMITED. ONLY IN THE MOST DIFFUSE SENSE CAN IT BE SAID THAT
THERE IS AN ECOLOGY MOVEMENT IN EASTERN EUROPE.

09359 WALLER, M.
THE RADICAL SOURCES OF THE CRISIS IN WEST EUROPEAN
COMMUNIST PARTIES
POLITICAL STUDIES, XXXVII(1) (MAR 89), 39-61.
THE ARTICLE OFFERS AN ANALYSIS OF THE WAVE OF RADICALISM
THAT SWEPT THROUGH EUROPEAN COMMUNIST PARTIES IN THE 1960'S
AND 1970'S. IT SEEKS TO IDENTIFY THE SOURCES OF RADICALISM
AS BEING A PUSH FOR MODERNIZATION AND AN INFUSION OF
MILITANT "NEW MEMBERS." IT ALSO ANALYZES THE IMPLICATIONS OF
THE RADICAL SURGE FOR THE EUROCOMMUNIST MOVEMENT. THE
RADICAL MOVEMENT RAISED THE FORTUNES OF THE COMMUNISTS
PARTIES DURING THE '70S, BUT ALSO BROUGHT ABOUT THE CRISIS
AT THE END OF THE DECADE.

09360 WALLER, W.
THE IMPOSSIBILITY OF FISCAL POLICY
JOURNAL OF ECONOMIC ISSUES, 23(4) (DEC 89), 1047-1058.
THIS ARTICLE EXPLORES THE RELATIONSHIP BETWEEN FISCAL
POLICY AND TRANSFER PROGRAMS. IT EXPLORES THE POSITIONS OF
ECONOMISTS WHO HAVE RESISTED THE USE OF FISCAL POLICY AS
WELL AS GIVING A RADICAL INSTITUTIONALIST APPROACH TO FISCAL
POLICY. IT CONCLUDES THAT IF FISCAL POLICY IS TO BE USED
AFTER THE REAGAN ERA, WE MUST REJECT THE CONVENTIONAL WISDOM.
IT GIVES AN INSTITUTIONALIST ANALYSIS SUGGESTING A
MINIMALIST WAY TO ATTEMPT TO SOLVE GENUINE ECONOMIC PROBLEMS
AND REHABILITATE FISCAL POLICY.

09361 WALLERSTEIN, I.
THE CAPITALIST WORLD-ECONOMY: MIDDLE-RUN PROSPECTS
ALTERNATIVES, 64(3) (JUL 89), 279-288.
IN THE SHORT RUN, THE CAPITALIST WORLD-ECONOMY IS IN
SOME DIFFICULTIES WHICH MAY SOON GET WORSE. IN THE LONG RUN,
IT IS DESTINED TO COME TO AN END IN ONE WAY OR ANOTHER. THIS
ARTICLE ADDRESSES THE MIDDLE RUN AND SUGGESTS WHAT MAY
POSSIBLY HAPPEN IN THE PERIOD 2000-2050. IT STARTS WITH A
REVIEW OF THE MAJOR DEVELOPMENTS IN THE WORLD-SYSTEM SINCE
1945; IT THEN PROJECTS THE SHORT-RUN PROSPECTS (TO THE YEAR
2000); AND CONCLUDES WITH THE MIDDLE RUN FUTURE, THE
AUTHOR'S PREDICTIONS INCLUDE FOUR POSSIBLE VECTORS.

09362 WALLERSTEIN, I.
THE FRENCH REVOLUTION AS A WORLD-HISTORICAL EVENT
SOCIAL RESEARCH, 56(1) (SPR 89), 33-52.
THE SIGNIFICANCE OF THE FRENCH REVOLUTION HAS USUALLY
BEEN ANALYZED IN ONE OF TWO WAYS: AS AN "EVENT" IN FRENCH
HISTORY WHICH HAD ITS COURSE AND CONSEQUENCES OR AS A
PHENOMENON THAT HAD A SPECIFIC INFLUENCE ON THE HISTORY OF
OTHER COUNTRIES. BUT THIS ESSAY VIEWS THE FRENCH REVOLUTION
AS A WORLD-HISTORICAL EVENT IN THE VERY SPECIFIC SENSE OF
ITS SIGNIFICANCE AND IMPORTANCE IN THE HISTORY OF THE MODERN
WORLD-SYSTEM AS A WORLD-SYSTEM.

09363 WALLERSTEIN, I.
THE MYRDAL LEGACY: RACISM AND UNDERDEVELOPMENT AS DILEMMAS
COOPERATION & CONFLICT: NORDIC JOURNAL OF INTERNATIONAL
POLITICS, XXIV(1) (MAR 89), 1-18.
THE LEGACY OF GUNNAR MYRDAL IS IN HIS HAVING POSED IN
VERY IMPORTANT WAYS TWO CENTRAL QUESTIONS: THE EXPLANATIONS
OF, AND PRACTICAL SOLUTIONS FOR, RACISM AND UNDERDEVELOPMENT;
THE RELATIONSHIP BETWEEN THE SCIENTIST AND HIS VALUATIONS
AND THE OBJECTS OF SCIENTIFIC ENQUIRY. IT IS ARGUED HERE
THAT RACISM AND UNDERDEVELOPMENT ARE CONSTITUTIVE OF THE
CAPITALIST WORLD-ECONOMY AS AN HISTORICAL SYSTEM AND ARE NOT
CURABLE MALADIES WITHIN THE SYSTEM. IT IS FURTHER ARGUED
THAT SOCIAL SCIENTIFIC IS GOING THROUGH A GREAT SEA-CHANGE
AT PRESENT, ALONG WITH THE THEORY OF PHYSICAL SCIENCE WHICH
IS IN THE PROCESS OF REJECTING ITS PREVIOUS NEWTONIAN PREMIS
MYRDAL'S VIEWS ARE AS PERTINENT AS EVER.

09364 WALLERSTEIN, M.
UNION ORGANIZATION IN ADVANCED INDUSTRIAL DEMOCRACIES
AMERICAN POLITICAL SCIENCE REVIEW, 83(2) (JUN 89), 481-502.

THE AUTHOR SUGGESTS A NEW EXPLANATION OF CROSS-NATIONAL
DIFFERENCES IN UNIONIZATION RATES: THE SIZE OF THE LABOR
FORCE. SIZE MATTERS BECAUSE THE GAINS UNIONS ARE ABLE TO
ACHIEVE IN COLLECTIVE BARGAINING DEPEND ON THE PROPORTION OF
SUBSTITUTABLE WORKERS WHO ARE ORGANIZED, WHILE THE COSTS OF
ORGANIZING DEPEND IN PART ON THE ABSOLUTE NUMBER TO BE
RECRUITED. THE COMPARISON OF THE COSTS AND BENEFITS OF
ORGANIZING NEW WORKERS YIELDS THE CONCLUSION THAT UNIONS IN
LARGER LABOR MARKETS WILL ACCEPT LOWER LEVELS OF
UNIONIZATION. STATISTICAL ANALYSIS OF CROSS-NATIONAL
DIFFERENCES IN UNIONIZATION RATES AMONG ADVANCED INDUSTRIAL
SOCIETIES IN THE LATE 1970S INDICATES THAT THE SIZE OF THE
LABOR FORCE AND THE CUMULATIVE PARTICIPATION OF LEFTIST
PARTIES IN GOVERNMENT EXPLAIN MOST OF THE VARIANCE.

09365 WALLIS, D.
THE TORY BUDGET, TRANSNATIONALS AND NEOCONSERVATISM
COMMUNIST VIEWPOINT, 20(4) (WIN 88), 1-5.
THE PURPOSE OF THIS ARTICLE IS TO SHOW THE DIRECT
CONNECTION BETWEEN THE RISE IN NEO-CONSERVATISM AND THE
GROWING INFLUENCE OF THE TRANSNATIONALS OVER BOTH CANADIAN
AND WORLD ECONOMIES. NOTED IS THE INCREASED USE OF THE STATE
IN STRENGTHENING THE TRANSNATIONALS. EXAMINED ARE THE RISE
IN MONOPOLIES, THE BUDGET, WAGES, AND UNEMPLOYMENT INSURANCE,
SOME SOLUTIONS ARE OFFERED.

09366 WALLIS, J.
DIALOGUE AND DISSENT
SOJOURNERS, 18(2) (FEB 89), 26-31.
IN THE SOVIET UNION, A VIRTUAL CORNUCOPIA OF NEW
POLITICAL GROUPS AND INITIATIVES HAVE SPRUNG UP, ALL BORN
UNDER GLASNOST AND PERESTROIKA. WHILE THEY SEEM TO RUN THE
ENTIRE IDEOLOGICAL SPECTRUM, THEY ALL WANT THE SAME THING: A
MORE DEMOCRATIC, PLURALISTIC, AND OPEN POLITICAL SYSTEM AND
SOCIETY.

09367 WALLIS, J.; KIMBALL, C.
THE CLOCK IS TICKING
SOJOURNERS, 18(10) (NOV 89), 30-32.
THE ARTICLE EXAMINES THE EFFECTS OF 21 MONTHS OF
INTIFADA IN PALESTINE. THE COLLECTIVE UPRISING HAS BEEN A
CATALYST ENABLING THE PLO TO TAKE THE STEPS OF RECOGNIZING
ISRAEL AND RENOUNCING TERRORISM. HOWEVER, ATTEMPTS AT
ISRAELI-PALESTINIAN DIALOGUE HAVE NOT BEEN MET WITH MUCH
SUCCESS. THE ARTICLE CONCLUDES THAT IF VISIBLE PROGRESS IS
NOT MADE SOON, THE OPTIMISM HELD BY THE PALESTINIANS AND THE
INTERNATIONAL COMMUNITY WILL FADE AND THE STALEMATE WILL
CONTINUE. IF NEGOTIATIONS ARE NOT PURSUED, ESCALATING
VIOLENCE SEEMS A LIKELY FUTURE.

09368 WALLIS, J.
THE ESSENCE OF POLITICAL LEADERSHIP
SOJOURNERS, 18(2) (FEB 89), 23-24.
THE PRESIDENTIAL CONTEST WAGED BETWEEN GEORGE BUSH AND
MICHAEL DUKAKIS HAS BEEN CRITICIZED AS DIRTY, EMPTY, BORING,
EMBARRASSING, AND DISGUSTING. AS TRUE AS ALL THAT IS, THE
FAILURE OF THE CANDIDATES AND THEIR CAMPAIGNS GOES MUCH
DEEPER. THIS ELECTION WAS DECIDED WITHOUT EVER COMING TO
GRIPS WITH THE THE TWO THINGS THE NATION MOST NEEDS --AN HONEST
FACING-UP TO PRESSING SOCIAL REALITIES AND A COURAGEOUS
OFFERING OF MORAL VISION. SOCIAL REALITY AND MORAL VISION
WERE THE MOST AVOIDED TOPICS IN THIS MOST DISMAL CAMPAIGN.

09369 WALLIS, J.
US CHURCHES AND THE CONTRA WAR
SOJOURNERS, 18(5) (MAY 89), 4.
WHEN THE REAGAN ADMINISTRATION LOST ITS FINAL SHOWDOWN
VOTE ON MILITARY AID TO THE CONTRAS, IT BLAMED THE US
CHURCHES FOR THE FAILURE. THE ARTICLE EXPLORES THE ACTIONS
OF US CHURCHES SUCH AS THEIR WITNESS FOR PEACE AND THE
PLEDGE OF RESISTANCE PROGRAMS THAT DID HAVE A GREAT DEAL TO
DO WITH RISING PUBLIC RESISTANCE TO FURTHER AID TO THE
CONTRAS. IT ALSO EXPLORES THE FUTURE ROLE OF CHURCHES IN
NICARAGUA AS THE NATIONS SEEKS TO HEAL WAR TORN WOUNDS.

09370 WALLIS, W.A.
AMERICAN LEADERSHIP IN INTERNATIONAL TRADE
DEPARTMENT OF STATE BULLETIN (US FOREIGN POLICY), 89(2143)
(FEB 89), 30-31.
THE AUTHOR, WHO IS US UNDER-SECRETARY FOR ECONOMIC
AFFAIRS AND AGRICULTURE, OUTLINES THE REAGAN
ADMINISTRATION'S VIEW OF THE FUTURE OF INTERNATIONAL TRADE,
WITH SPECIAL ATTENTION TO THE EUROPEAN COMMUNITY'S PLANS FOR
INTEGRATING THEIR MARKETS BY 1992. HE ALSO DISCUSSES THE
INTERNATIONAL TRADE DEFICIT PICTURE AND THE FOREIGN DEBT
PROBLEM.

09371 WALLIS, W.A.
OVERVIEW OF U.S. TRADE POLICY
DEPARTMENT OF STATE BULLETIN (US FOREIGN POLICY), 88(2141)
(DEC 88), 33-34.
UNDER SECRETARY FOR ECONOMIC AFFAIRS AND AGRICULTURE W.
ALLEN WALLIS GOVES AN OVERVIEW OF US TRADE POLICY AND POINTS
OUT THAT THE REMARKABLE SUCCES OF THE US ECONOMY IS THE

FOUNDATION FOR HEALTHY WORLD TRADE, THAT THE MULTILATERAL TRADE NEGOTIATIONS ARE GOING WELL, AND THAT THE US TRADE BILL NEED NOT BE THE HARBINGER OF PROTECTIONISM. HE CONCLUDES THAT THE FUTURE OF INTERNATIONAL TRADE IS BRIGHT.

09372 WALMSEY, A.
A CHANGE OF HEART
MACLEAN'S (CANADA'S NEWS MAGAZINE), 102(30) (JUL 89), 18-19.
AFTER A BITTERLY FOUGHT COURT BATTLE WHICH GRANTED BARBARA DODD THE RIGHT TO HAVE AN ABORTION, BARBARA DODD SURPRISED BOTH THE PROCHOICE AND PROLIFE FACTIONS BY DECLARING A CHANGE OF HEART. SHE ANNOUNCED THAT SHE REGRETTED HER CHOICE AND STATES THAT WOMEN SHOULDN'T ACCEPT ABORTION. VARIOUS OBSERVERS BELIEVE THAT DODD WAS MANIPULATED BY HER BOYFRIEND, GREGORY MURPHY. OTHERS ASSUME THAT IT ID DODD'S INSATIABLE DESIRE FOR ATTENTION THAT PROMPTED HER DECISION. WHATEVER THE CAUSE, THE DECISION SHOCKED AND SURPRISED ALL THOSE INVOLVED.

09373 WALMSLEY, A.
UNEASY OVER NEWCOMERS
MACLEAN'S (CANADA'S NEWS MAGAZINE), 102(1) (JAN 89), 28-29.
CANADA'S MULTICULTURALISM ACT ENSURES LEGAL PROTECTION FOR THE DIVERSITY OF CULTURES AND LANGUAGES IN CANADA. CANADIANS HAVE HISTORICALLY WELCOMED IMMIGRANTS FROM ANYWHERE IN THE WORLD REGARDLESS OF COUNTRY OF ORIGIN. HOWEVER, A RECENT POLL INDICATES THAT A MAJORITY OF RESPONDENTS WERE DEEPLY UNEASY ABOUT THE DEVELOPMENT OF CANADA AS A CULTURAL MOSAIC AS OPPOSED TO THE AMERICAN MELTING POT TO THE SOUTH. FULLY 58 PER CENT SAID THAT THEY WANTED NEW IMMIGRANTS TO "INTEGRATE WITH THE CANADIAN CULTURE" RATHER THAN MAINTAIN THEIR DISTINCT CULTURES WHEN THEY ARRIVE. THIS SCHIZOPHRENIC FORM OF RACISM CONCERNS MANY OBSERVERS AS AN INDICATION OF FURTHER RACIAL AND ETHNIC TENSION.

09374 WALT, S.
HEGEL ON WAR: ANOTHER LOOK
HISTORY OF POLITICAL THOUGHT, X(1) (SPR 89), 113-124 113-124.
HEGEL'S BRIEF AND NOTORIOUS STATEMENTS ABOUT WAR HAVE BEEN SUBJECT TO DISPARATE INTERPRETATIONS RANGING FROM THE VIEW THAT HEGEL GLORIFIES WAR AND CONSIDERS IT "GOOD IN ITSELF" TO THE VIEW THAT HEGEL CONDEMS WAR PER SE AND HOLDS THAT WARS ARE NEVER MORALLY JUSTIFIABLE. THE AUTHOR SUGGESTS THAT HEGEL HAS TWO INDEPENDENT ARGUEMENTS FOR THE NECESSITY OF WAR: AN ARGUEMENT FROM THE ETHICAL RELATION OF THE INDIVIDUAL TO THE STATE AND AN ARGUEMENT FROM THE NATURE AND RELATIONS BETWEEN NATION STATES. THE AUTHOR TAKES THE "MIDDLE VIEW" THAT HEGEL DOES FIND A PHILISOPHICAL JUSTIFICATION FOR WAR, BUT DOES NOT GLORIFY IT OR FIND IT "GOOD IN ITSELF."

09375 WALT, S.
THE CASE FOR FINITE CONTAINMENT: ANALYZING U.S. GRAND STRATEGY
INTERNATIONAL SECURITY, 14(1) (SUM 89), 5-49.
THE AUTHOR ARGUES THAT FOUR CRITICAL ISSUES MUST BE ADDRESSED IN FORMULATING GRAND STRATEGY: IDENTIFYING KEY AREAS OF VITAL INTEREST; THE BALANCE OF OFFENSE AND DEFENSE; SOVIET INTENTIONS; AND THE CAUSES OF ALIGNMENT. HE CONCLUDES THAT THE MOST APPROPRIATE GRAND STRATEGY FOR THE UNITED STATES IS FINITE CONTAINMENT: SIMILAR TO THE STRATEGIES OUTLINED BY WALTER LIPPMANN AND GEORGE KENNAN IN THE 1940S, IT WOULD EMPHASIZE CONTAINING SOVIET EXPANSION ON THE EURASIAN LANDMASS. THE UNITED STATES WOULD PRESERVE ITS PRESENT ALLIANCES WITH WESTERN EUROPE, JAPAN, AND KOREA, AND PROTECT WESTERN ACCESS TO PERSIAN GULF OIL. IT WOULD NOT, HOWEVER, DEVELOP FORCES FOR LARGE-SCALE INTERVENTIONS IN THE THIRD WORLD OR MOUNT A GLOBAL CRUSADE AGAINST MARXISM.

09376 WALT, S.M.
ALLIANCES IN THEORY AND PRACTICE: WHAT LIES AHEAD?
JOURNAL OF INTERNATIONAL AFFAIRS, 43(1) (SUM 89), 1-18.
THIS ARTICLE EXAMINES THE COLD WAR BETWEEN THE UNITED STATES AND THE SOVIET UNION AS A COMPETITION FOR ALLIES. IT DETAILS THE LONGEVITY OF THE ALLIANCE NETWORKS OF EACH SUPERPOWER AND THE RESULTANT FACT THAT THESE ALLIANCE SYSTEMS HAVE MADE WAR LESS LIKELY, IT CONCLUDES THAT A DURABLE SOVIET-AMERICAN DETENTE COULD HAVE FAR REACHING EFFECTS ON A WIDE RANGE OF INTERNATIONAL POLITICAL RELATIONSHIPS.

09377 WALTER, H.
APPEASEMENT IN OUR TIME
NATIONAL REVIEW, XLI(10) (JUN 89), 26-28, 30-31.
THE AUTHOR PROFILES WEST GERMANY'S FOREIGN MINISTER, HANS-DIETRICH GENSCHER, WHO HAS ENDORSED GORBACHEV'S CONCEPT OF A "COMMON EUROPEAN HOME."

09378 WALTERS, J.
RENEGOTIATING DEPENDENCY: THE CASE OF THE SOUTHERN AFRICAN CUSTOMS UNION
JOURNAL OF COMMON MARKET STUDIES, XXVIII(1) (SEP 89), 29-52.
THE SOUTHERN AFRICAN CUSTOMS UNION AGREEMENT (SACUA) BETWEEN BOTSWANA, LESOTHO AND SWAZILAND (BLS) AND SOUTH AFRICA HAS GENERATED A CONSIDERABLE LITERATURE. THE PRESENT ARTICLE SEEKS TO EXTEND THE DEBATE BY CLARIFYING SOME OF THE CONCEPTS UNDERLYING THE AGREEMENT AND BY EXAMINING SOME KEY FEATURES OF THE ACTUAL WORKINGS OF THE CUSTOMS UNION. IN THE CONTEXT OF THE CURRENT RENEGOTIATION OF SACUA SEVERAL PROPOSALS FOR MODIFICATION ARE MADE. PARTICULAR ATTENTION IS PAID TO (I) THE POLITICAL BACKGROUND TO SACUA; (II) PROTECTION OF INFANT INDUSTRIES; (III) AGRICULTURAL PROTECTION; (IV) THE IMPLICATIONS FOR BLS OF SOUTH AFRICA'S IMPORT POLICIES; (V) SOUTH AFRICA'S REGIONAL POLICY AND BLS; (VI) FISCAL HARMONIZATION; (VII) REVENUE SHARING; (VIII) ALTERNATIVES TO FISCAL COMPENSATION.

09379 WALUCNOW, W.
THE EVOLUTION OF RIGHTS IN LIBERAL THEORY
PHILOSOPHY OF THE SOCIAL SCIENCES, 19(4) (DEC 89), 501-506.
THE ARTICLE IS A REVIEW OF THE EVOLUTION OF RIGHTS IN LIBERAL THEORY BY IAN SHAPIRO. SHAPIRO'S MAIN GOAL IS TO SHOW HOW MODERN LIBERALS, NOTABLY RAWLS AND NOZICK, HAVE FRAGMENTED OLDER TRADITION BY APPROPRIATING PARTS OF IT WHILE LEAVING BEHIND CRUCIAL PREMISES THAT GAVE THOSE PARTS THEIR UNDERLYING COHERENCE. RAWLS AND NOZICK USE OF THESE ARGUMENTS CONSTITUTE A "LETHAL MUTATION OF THE EARLIER ARGUMENTS OF HOBBES AND LOCKE." PHILOSOPHERS FREED FROM THESE BLINDING MUTATIONS WILL BE ABLE TO DEVELOP THEORIES MORE ATTUNE TO THE EMPIRICAL AND SOCIOECONOMIC CONTINGENCIES OF OUR DAY.

09380 WALZER, M.
THE STATE OF POLITICAL THEORY
DISSENT, (SUM 89), 337.
MORE PEOPLE ARE WORKING AT POLITICAL THEORY IN THE ACADEMIC WORLD THAN EVER BEFORE. THE FIELD IS THRIVING, PERHAPS BECAUSE THERE IS SO LITTLE SERIOUS THINKING AND ARGUING ABOUT POLITICS OUTSIDE THE ACADEMY. THE NEOCONSERVATIVE THINK TANKS OF THE 1970S AND EARLY 1980S PROVIDE THE ONLY RECENT EXAMPLE OF THE UNITY OF THEORY AND PRACTICE. LEFTIST AND EVEN LIBERAL ARGUMENTS THESE DAYS ARE LARGELY THEORETICAL IN CHARACTER: PROFESSORS WRITING FOR OTHER PROFESSORS. WITHOUT RESONANCE, POLITICAL THEORY IS A KIND OF ALIENATED POLITICS, AN ENTERPRISE CARRIED ON AT SOME DISTANCE FROM THE ACTIVITIES TO WHICH IT REFERS. THE RESULT VERY OFTEN IS ENDLESS REFINEMENT, ESOTERIC JARGON, ROMANTIC POSTURING, AND FIERCE INTRAMURAL POLEMIC. NONETHELESS, INTERESTING WORK GETS DONE AND IT IS STILL POSSIBLE TO DETECT CERTAIN TENDENCIES THAT MAY ONE DAY HAVE PRACTICAL IMPACT.

09381 WALZER, M.
WHAT KIND OF STATE IS A JEWISH STATE?
TIKKUN, 4(4) (JUL 89), 34-37, 126-128.
THE AUTHOR ANALYZES SOME OF THE VARIOUS APPROACHES TO THE "JEWISH STATE", INCLUDING A STATE WHERE "JEWISH" IS A STRONG OR AUTHORITATIVE MODIFIER, AND WHERE "JEWISH" IS MERELY A WEAK DESCRIPTOR. THE PROBLEMS OF "WHO IS A JEW?" AND OF THE INDIGENIOUS ARAB POPULATION ARE ALSO DISCUSSED. ALTHOUGH SEVERAL POSSIBLITIES ARE DISCUSSED, THE AUTHOR CONCLUDES THAT THE BEST (AND ONLY) ANSWER TO THE QUESTION IS "WAIT AND SEE."

09382 WANANDI, J.
ARMED, YES, BUT MUST IT BE TO THE TEETH?
FAR EASTERN ECONOMIC REVIEW, 141(28) (JUL 88), 32-33.
THE ARTICLE EXAMINES THE GROWTH OF THE JAPANESE SELFDEFENSE FORCE IN RECENT YEARS. THE SDF CONTINUES TO ACQUIRE HIGH TECH WEAPONS FROM THE US. PRIME MINISTER NOBORU TAKESHITA STATED THAT JAPAN SHOULD DEVELOP A DEFENSE CAPABILITY PROPORTIONATE TO ITS NATIONAL POWER. SOME FEAR A RESURGENCE OF MILITARISM IN JAPAN, BUT THE MAJORITY OF OBSERVERS ARE COMFORTABLE WITH THE CURRENT JAPANESE DEFENSE STARTEGY AND SECURITY ROLE AS WELL AS WITH THE LEVEL OF ITS DEFENSE CAPABILITIES.

09383 WANDLING, R.A.
THE URBAN DEVELOPMENT GRANT PROGRAM IN OHIO
DISSERTATION ABSTRACTS INTERNATIONAL, 49(7) (JAN 89), 1961-A.
THIS STUDY EXAMINES FEDERAL AGENCY NAGATIVE ASSESSMENTS OF LOCAL GOVERNMENT ECONOMIC DEVELOPMENT CAPACITY AND APPLIES AN ANALYTICAL FRAMEWORK THAT SPECIFIES FIVE DIMENSIONS OF LOCAL GOVERNMENT ABILITIES IMPORTANT IN ECONOMIC DEVELOPMENT. THE DIMENSIONS OF THE ANALYTICAL FRAMEWORK ARE: (1) PROJECT PLANNING AND ANALYSIS, (2) COMPLIANCE WITH PROCEDURAL REQUIREMENTS, (3) PROJECT IMPLEMENTATION MANAGEMENTS, (4) COMMITMENT TO EQUITY GOALS, AND (5) INTERGOVERNMENT COORDINATION SKILLS.

09384 WANG, A.
CARIBBEAN LINKS
FREE CHINA REVIEW, 39(3) (MAR 89), 4-6.

IN JANUARY 1989, TAIWANESE PREMIER YU KUO-HWA AND PRIME MINISTER LYNDEN PINDLING OF THE BAHAMAS SIGNED A DIPLOMATIC RELATIONS PACT. THE AGREEMENT, WHICH IS PART OF TAIWAN'S EFFORTS TO EXPAND ITS DIPLOMATIC PRESENCE IN THE CARIBBEAN, IS DESIGNED TO PROMOTE RELATIONS IN TRADE, TECHNOLOGY, CULTURE, EDUCATION, AND SPORTS. IT RECOGNIZES THE TWO COUNTRIES' BROAD COMMON INTERESTS AND ORIENTATION TOWARD NATIONAL DEVELOPMENT AND WORLD TRADE.

09385 WANG, A.
    CHANGING ATTITUDES
    FREE CHINA REVIEW, 39(11) (NOV 89), 8-9.
    TAIWAN'S MIDDLE CLASS HAS BEEN TRAINED TO BE CONSERVATIVE. BUT BECAUSE MIDDLE CLASS CITIZENS ARE BETTER EDUCATED AND TEND TO MOVE UPWARD SOCIALLY, THEY ALSO DEMAND REFORM. IN MANY CASES, THE MIDDLE CLASS EXHIBITS A DUAL PERSONALITY. IF A STREET DEMONSTRATION OR REFORM MOVEMENT BENEFITS THE MIDDLE CLASS, THEN MEMBERS WILL SUPPORT THE MOVEMENT FROM BEHIND THE SCENES BUT WILL NOT ACTUALLY JOIN.

09386 WANG, B.
    ENTERING A DARK PERIOD
    FREE CHINA REVIEW, 39(8) (AUG 89), 25.
    IN THIS INTERVIEW, A REPORTER DESCRIBES EVENTS IN TIENANMEN SQUARE DURING THE MASSACRE AND IN THE DAYS IMMEDIATELY FOLLOWING IT.

09387 WANG, B.
    GROWING VEGETABLES ON STONES
    FREE CHINA REVIEW, 39(10) (OCT 89), 50-53.
    IN THIS INTERVIEW, JOURNALIST ANTONIO CHIANG DISCUSSES THE POLITICAL SITUATION IN MAINLAND CHINA FOLLOWING THE SUPPRESSION OF STUDENT DEMONSTRATIONS IN TIENANMEN SQUARE IN JUNE 1989.

09388 WANG, B.
    INEQUITIES FUELED BY SPECULATION
    FREE CHINA REVIEW, 39(11) (NOV 89), 26-29.
    DURING THE 1960'S AND 1970'S, GOVERNMENT POLICIES LED TO STEADY IMPROVEMENT IN INCOME DISTRIBUTION IN TAIWAN. BUT TAIWAN'S MIDDLE CLASS CITIZENS ARE NOW ANGRY OVER THE UNEVEN DISTRIBUTION OF INCOME, AND ALL INDICATORS SUGGEST THE PROBLEM WILL WORSEN. IT IS FEARED THAT IMPROVEMENT WILL NOT OCCUR UNTIL TAIWAN'S FINANCIAL MARKET AND BANKING SYSTEMS ARE REFORMED AND ADOPT INTERNATIONAL STANDARDS THAT WILL ENCOURAGE MORE CONSTRUCTIVE LINES OF INVESTMENT.

09389 WANG, B.
    SMALL ISLAND, BIG PROBLEMS
    FREE CHINA REVIEW, 39(6) (JUN 89), 4-11.
    IN TAIWAN, GOVERNMENT CONCERN ABOUT CONSERVATION DID NOT BEGIN IN EARNEST UNTIL THE 1970'S. SINCE THEN, LEGISLATIVE INTERPELLATIONS HAVE COVERED WILDLIFE PROTECTION, MAINTENANCE OF ECOSYSTEMS, CONSERVATION OF MOUNTAIN SLOPES AND FORESTS, PROTECTION OF MANGROVES, THE ABUSE OF PESTICIDES, AND PROBLEMS CAUSED BY NUCLEAR POWER PLANTS. NEW LAWS AND REVISIONS OF EXISTING LAWS HAVE BEEN PASSED TO PROTECT THE ENVIRONMENT IN THE 1980'S.

09390 WANG, B.
    TAX REFORM IS FOREVER
    FREE CHINA REVIEW, 39(1) (JAN 89), 26-29.
    THE AUTHOR REVIEWS THE HISTORY OF TAXATION IN CHINA AND THE CURRENT TAX SITUATION IN TAIWAN.

09391 WANG, H.
    ENERGY POLICY IN THE REPUBLIC OF CHINA AND JAPAN, 1970-1985: A COMPARATIVE EXAMINATION OF ENERGY POLITICS AND POLICIES
    DISSERTATION ABSTRACTS INTERNATIONAL, 48(8) (FEB 88), 2159-A.
    THE DISSERTATION EXAMINES AND COMPARES THE ENERGY POLITICS AND POLICY PROCESSES IN THE REPUBLIC OF CHINA AND JAPAN DURING THE PERIOD 1970-1985. IT FOCUSES ON THE POLITICS OF ENERGY POLICIES, USING A POLICY ANALYSIS OR SYSTEMS FRAMEWORK FOR EXAMINING THE POLICY PROCESSES IN THE TWO COUNTRIES. A COMPARISON IS MADE OF ENERGY ENVIRONMENTS, THE POLITICAL ACTORS, THE INSTITUTIONS AND THE SUBSTANCE OF ENERGY POLICY.

09392 WANG, J.
    POLITICAL MOVEMENTS AGAINST THE STATE: THE TRANSITION OF TAIWAN'S AUTHORITARIAN RULE
    DISSERTATION ABSTRACTS INTERNATIONAL, 49(9) (MAR 89), 2836-A.
    USING CASE STUDIES OF OPPOSITION/REGIME RELATIONS IN TAIWAN OVER THE PAST 38 YEARS, THE AUTHOR EXPLORES THE ROLE OF THE OPPOSITION IN THE PROCESS OF REGIME TRANSFORMATION. HE ARGUES THAT THE OPPOSITION BY ITSELF IS NOT CAPABLE OF PRESSURING THE REGIME TO REFORM. ALSO NECESSARY ARE THE STATE'S WEAKNESS OR EROSION OF AUTHORITY AND THE RISE OF THE MASSES.

09393 WANG, R.P.
    PROBLEMS IN EVALUATING ECONOMIC DEVELOPMENT POLITICS: AN URBAN PERSPECTIVE
    INTERNATIONAL JOURNAL OF PUBLIC ADMINISTRATION, 12(2) (1989), 305-329.
    THE CENTRAL CONCERN IN THIS PAPER IS WITH THE WAY WE THINK ABOUT ECONOMIC DEVELOPMENT AT THE LOCAL LEVEL. THE AUTHOR FIRST LOOKS AT THE LOCAL CONTEXT OF ECONOMIC DEVELOPMENT POLICYMAKING, THEN TO THE STRATEGY DERIVED FROM THIS CONTEXT AND THE RESULTANT "POLITICS OF GROWTH". FINALLY, REFOCUS ON THE NEED FOR A THEORETICALLY GROUNDED MODEL TO EVALUATE THE ECONOMIC DEVELOPMENT EFFORTS OF LOCAL PUBLIC OFFICIALS. MAYORS AND SCHOLARS ALIKE MUST BEGIN THE TASK OF BUILDING SUCH A MODEL BY FIRST RECOGNIZING THE IMPORTANCE OF CONDUCTING THEIR WORK WITHIN A THEORETICAL FRAMEWORK WHICH PLACES THE CITY WITHIN THE LARGER POLITICAL, SOCIAL, AND ECONOMIC CONTEXT WHICH DEFINES IT. THE CENTRAL REALITY OF THAT WIDER CONTEXT IS THAT THE BUSINESS COMMUNITY DOMINATES ECONOMIC DEVELOPMENT POLITICS: BUSINESSMEN ISSUE COMMANDS (AS A CONDITION OF INVESTING IN THE LOCAL ECONOMY) AND POLITICIANS OFFER INDUCEMENTS (IN COMPETITION WITH OTHER POLITICIANS FOR THAT INVESTMENT).

09394 WANG, Y.C.
    THE JEWISH AUTONOMOUS REGION OF BIROBIDJAN
    PLURAL SOCIETIES, 19(1) (SEP 89), 73-90.
    IT WAS THE PARTITION OF POLAND THAT FORCED JEWS, FORMALLY, TO BE EMERGED INTO RUSSIA AS A MINORITY. THE PALE OF SETTLEMENT WAS THE NEW POLICY OF THE RUSSIAN GOVERNMENT TO SETTLE ITS NEW JEWISH SUBJECTS. THIS ARTICLE EXAMINES THE PROJECT OF JEWISH AUTONOMY AND THE ESTABLISHMENT OF BIROBIDJAN AS THE PLACE FOR JEWISH SETTLEMENT.

09395 WARD, H.
    TESTING THE WATERS: TAKING RISKS TO GAIN REASSURANCE IN PUBLIC GOODS GAMES
    JOURNAL OF CONFLICT RESOLUTION, 33(2) (JUN 89), 274-308.
    INDIVIDUALS OFTEN FAIL TO COOPERATE BECAUSE THEY ARE NOT SUFFICIENTLY REASSURED THAT OTHERS INVOLVED SHARE THEIR DESIRE FOR RECIPROCAL COOPERATION. SUCH SITUATIONS MAY BE SEEN AS ASSURANCE GAMES. THE EXISTING LITERATURE FAILS TO EXAMINE THE PROBLEMS POSED BY LACK OF INFORMATION ABOUT OTHERS' PREFERENCES, EITHER ASSUMING THAT INFORMATION IS PERFECT, OR THAT IT MAY BE MADE PERFECT BY MUTUAL VERBAL REASSURANCES. THIS ARTICLE SHOWS THAT IN SEQUENTIAL PUBLIC GOODS SUPERGAMES, PLAYERS WITH ASSURANCE PREFERENCES MAY GATHER INFORMATION ABOUT OTHERS' PREFERENCES FROM THEIR GAME MOVES, AND THAT IT MAY PAY THEM TO TAKE RISKS OF SHORT-TERM LOSSES IN ORDER TO DO SO. THE MOST EFFICIENT INFORMATION-GATHERING FOR SUCH A PLAYER IS COOPERATION. THE MODEL HELPS US UNDERSTAND WHY PLAYERS OF ASSURANCE OFTEN APPEAR TO TAKE RISKS IN ORDER TO "TEST THE WATERS" WITH COOPERATIVE MOVES, AND WHY THE PROBLEM POSED FOR COLLECTIVE ACTION IS SOMETIMES SUCCESSFULLY RESOLVED.

09396 WARD, J.D.
    CONTRACTING OUT MUNICIPAL SERVICES: A REGIONAL COMPARISON
    DISSERTATION ABSTRACTS INTERNATIONAL, 49(11) (MAY 89), 3503-A.
    BASED ON THE EXPERIENCES OF FOUR CITIES IN OHIO AND FOUR IN MISSISSIPPI, THE AUTHOR IDENTIFIES THE POLITICAL, ECONOMIC, AND ORGANIZATIONAL FACTORS THAT IMPACT CONTRACTING OUT IN SMALL CITIES. HE FINDS THAT CONTRACTING OUT IS MORE PERVASIVE IN OHIO THAN MISSISSIPPI DUE TO THE HIGHER LEVEL OF AFFLUENCE IN OHIO AND A POLITICAL CULTURE MORE ATTUNED TO THE QUALITY OF PUBLIC SERVICES THAN TO CREATING PUBLIC SECTOR EMPLOYMENT BY PROVIDING SERVICES.

09397 WARD, J.R.
    VIETNAM: INSURGENCY OR WAR?
    MILITARY REVIEW, LXIX(1) (JAN 89), 14-23.
    THE AUTHOR POSES THE QUESTION OF WHETHER THE CONFLICT IN VIETNAM WAS AN INSURGENCY OR A CONVENTIONAL WAR. HE FINDS THAT IT WAS BOTH, AND THAT US LEADERS FAILED TO RECOGNIZE THIS DUAL NATURE OF THE CONFLICT. THE RESULTS WERE AN INAPPROPRIATE STRATEGY AND A MISDIRECTED MILITARY EFFORT. IN HINDSIGHT, THE AUTHOR OFFERS FOUR STEPS WHICH COULD HAVE PRODUCED DRAMATICALLY DIFFERENT RESULTS.

09398 WARD, M.D.
    THINGS FALL APART: A LOGICAL ANALYSIS OF CRISIS RESOLUTION DYNAMICS
    INTERNATIONAL INTERACTIONS, 15(1) (1988), 65-79.
    THE TRANSITION FROM AN INTERNATIONAL CRISIS TO A STATE OF CONFLICT IS EXAMINED FROM THE PERSPECTIVE OF A GENERAL THEORY OF ADAPTIVE RESPONSE MECHANISMS. THE DYNAMICAL LOGICAL STRUCTURES OF CRISES ARE EXAMINED IN DETAIL, AND IMPLICATIONS DRAWN ABOUT THE ABILITY OF A SYSTEM TO RESPOND TO FOREIGN POLICY CRISES. IT IS SHOWN THAT NOT ONLY CAN THE CRISIS RESPONSE MECHANISM BE "IMMUNIZED" AGAINST SUBSEQUENT CRISES, BUT IT ALSO CAN BE PARALYZED AGAINST FURTHER EFFECTIVE ACTIONS.

09399 WARDE, I.A.
OLIGOPOLISTIC STRUCTURES AND THE EVOLUTION OF POLITICAL
ECONOMY: U.S. RESPONSES TO DECLINE
DISSERTATION ABSTRACTS INTERNATIONAL, 49(11) (MAY 89),
3495-A.
IN RESPONSE TO DECLINE, IDEOLOGY, COALITIONS, AND POLICY
GOALS BECOME MEDIATING VARIABLES ON WHICH THE FOLLOWING SETS
OF STRUCTURES HAVE A MAJOR IMPACT: (1) THE NATIONAL SECURITY
STRUCTURE, (2) THE INTERNATIONAL ECONOMIC STRUCTURE, AND (3)
SECTORAL STRUCTURES. IN MOST SECTORS IN THE USA, THE
COMPETITIVE PATTERN HAS SHIFTED FROM AN ALL-AMERICAN STABLE
OLIGOPOLY TO AN INTERNATIONAL, POLITICIZED, AND UNSTABLE
OLIGOPOLY.

09400 WARE, A.
PARTIES, ELECTORAL COMPETITION AND DEMOCRACY
PARLIAMENTARY AFFAIRS, 42(1) (JAN 89), 1-22.
THE ARTICLE EXAMINES THE COMPLEX AND OFTEN CONFUSING
ISSUE OF ELECTORAL COMPETITION. IT EXAMINES PARALLELS
BETWEEN ELECTORAL COMPETITION AND MARKETS; IT ALSO DEALS
WITH THE ISSUE OF VOTER CHOICE: THE ISSUE OF WHETHER VOTING
IS AN ACTUAL CHOICE OR MERELY A RITUALISTIC REAFFIRMATION OF
THE EXISTING REGIME. THE ARTICLE CONCLUDES THAT THERE ARE
SOME CLEAR PARALLELS BETWEEN POLITICAL AND ECONOMIC
COMPETITION AND THAT, IN A VARIETY OF WAYS, LIBERAL
DEMOCRACIES CAN OFTEN BE CONCEIVED AS SYSTEMS IN WHICH
VOTERS CHOOSE. HOWEVER, IT WARNS AGAINST OVERSIMPLIFYING THE
NATURE OF POLITICAL COMPETITION AND ACKNOWLEDGES THE
EXISTENCE OF SIGNIFICANT EXCEPTIONS TO THESE GENERAL
CONCLUSIONS.

09401 WARE, L.
TOWARD A EURO-AMERICAN POLICY FOR THE ARAB MAGHREB
AMERICAN-ARAB AFFAIRS, (28) (SPR 89), 49-59.
THE ARAB MAGHREB UNION (AMU) POSES NEW CHALLENGES TO THE
GOVERNMENTS OF EUROPE AND AMERICA. THE ARTICLE DISCUSSES THE
NEED FOR A CREATIVE AND INNOVATIVE APPROACH TO THE AMU THAT
APPRECIATES THE ROLE THAT THE AMU CAN PLAY IN REGIONAL
SECURITY AND ECONOMIC INTERESTS. IT EXAMINES RECENT MAGHREBI
ECONOMIC AND SOCIO-POLITICAL INITIATIVES AND THEIR
IMPLICATIONS AS WELL AS THEIR RELATION TO SPECIFIC ISSUES
SUCH AS NATO SECURITY AND EEC POLITICS. IT CONCLUDES BY
INVESTIGATING THE CONDITIONS UNDER WHICH A MUTUALLY
BENEFICIAL RELATIONSHIP CAN BE PUT INTO POLICY.

09402 WAREN, H.T.
MINORITY SET-ASIDE PROGRAMS: WHAT FUTURE AFTER RICHMOND VS.
CROSON?
STATE LEGISLATURES, 15(6) (JUL 89), 32-36.
THE HOLDING IN RICHMOND VS. CROSON, IN ESSENCE, IS THAT
RACE-CONSCIOUS MEASURES IN MINIORITY BUSINESS PROGRAMS WILL
BE SUBJECT TO STRICT SCRUTING. SUCH MEA SURES MUST BE
JUSTIFIED WITH A DETAILED, EVIDENTIARY RECORD INDENTIFYING
PAST DISCRIMINATION, AND PLANS MUST BE NARROWLY TAILORED FOR
PURPOSES OF REMEDYING SUCH DISCRIMINATION.

09403 WARFORD, J.; PARTOW, Z.
EVOLUTION OF THE WORLD BANK'S ENVIRONMENTAL POLICY
FINANCE AND DEVELOPMENT, 26(4) (NOV 89), 5-8.
THIS ARTICLE EXAMINES INTENSIFIED EFFORTS BY THE WORLD
BANK TO INTEGRATE ENVIRONMENTAL CONSIDERATIONS INTO ITS DAY-
TO-DAY WORK, AS ENVIRONMENTAL DEGRATION INCREASINGLY
THREATENS ECONOMIC DEVELOPMENT. IT ANALYSES COUNTY
ENVIRONMENTAL STUDIES AND DETERMINES HOW TO INTEGRATE THE
RESULTS. IT ALSO STUDIES THE UNADDRESSED STRATEGIC ISSUES
AND THE POLITICAL CONSTRAINTS INVOLVED.

09404 WARIAVWALLA, BHARAT
INDIA IN 1988: DRIFT, DISARRAY, OR PATTERN?
ASIAN SURVEY, XXIX(2) (FEB 89), 189-198.
THE ARTICLE EXAMINES THE POLITICAL CHANGES THAT HAVE
TAKEN PLACE IN INDIA IN 1988. THE YEAR WAS CHARACTERIZED BY
A DISAPPEARANCE OF PUBLIC PROPRIETY, GROWING COERCIVE POWER
OF THE STATE OVER THE CITIZEN, AND CORRUPTION. THE RULING
CONGRESS (I) PARTY LED BY RAJIV GANDHI SUFFERED SIGNIFICANT
LOSSES IN BY-ELECTIONS AND EVEN MORE SIGNIFICANT LOSS OF
TRUST DUE TO SCANDAL AND CORRUPTION. OPPOSITION COALITIONS
ARE LOOKING TO OVERCOME THEIR FACTIONAL DIFFERENCES AND
ASSUME POWER IN THE NEAR FUTURE. INDIA'S FOREIGN POLICY WAS
AFFECTED MOST BY MIKHAIL GORBACHEV AND THE CHANGES IN THE
USSR. INDIA IS SEEKING TO SHIFT FROM A COLD-WAR ORIENTATION
TO ONE THAT EMPHASIZES GLOBAL INTERDEPENDENCE. TAKING CUES
FROM GORBACHEV, INDIA IS SEEKING BETTER RELATIONS WITH THE
PEOPLE'S REPUBLIC OF CHINA AS WELL.

09405 WARK, M.
THE NEWS FROM BEIJING
ARENA, (88) (SPR 89), 50-62.
THIS IS AN EVALUATION OF THE RESULTS OF THE STUDENT
DEMONSTRATIONS AT TIANANMEN SQUARE. DENG XIAOPING IS QUOTED
AS SAYING THAT "THEY WOULD HAVE NO EFFECT ON THE FOUNDATIONS
OF OUR STATE OR ON THE POLICIES WE HAVE ESTABLISHED,"
HOWEVER, IN THE OPINION OF THE AUTHOR, THE DEMONSTRATIONS
MANAGED TO TURN THE GOVERNMENT POWER SHOWN AT TIANANMEN

SQUARE AND THE MORAL FORCE OF COMMUNIST IDEOLOGY AGAINST
ITSELF, AND MANAGED TO PLUG THE STAGING OF THEIR
DEMONSTRATIONS INTO THE GLOBAL MEDIA AT A LEVEL
UNPRECEDENTED FOR A POPULAR MOVEMENT IN A SOCIALIST STATE.
THIS IS THE POLITICS OF 'DETOURNEMENT' OF TURNING A SPACE
AND AN IDEOLOGY AGAINST ITSELF. THIS ARTICLE EXAMINES THE
POSSIBILITY OF DETOURNEMENT BEING INACTED AS WHAT OFFICIAL
HISTORY SUBLIMATES OR EXCLUDES: THE POSSIBILITY OF ITS OWN
NEGATION.

09406 WARNER, D.
BOUGAINVILLE NEEDS COUNTER-INSURGENCY EXPERT
PACIFIC DEFENCE REPORTER, 16(3) (SEP 89), 50.
IT IS HIGHLY IMPROBABLE THAT PAPUA NEW GUINEA'S
INTELLIGENCE IN BOUGAINVILLE HAS REACHED AN EFFECTIVE STAGE
ALTHOUGH THE INSURGENTS ARE VERY FEW IN NUMBER. IT MIGHT
SEEM AN EASY MATTER TO ELIMINATE THE 60 OR SO, OR WHATEVER
THE NUMBER MAY BE, BUT AN ILL-DIRECTED EFFORT TO DO SO COULD
BE DANGEROUSLY COUNTER-PRODUCTIVE, SINCE PART OF THE
INSURGENTS' PLAN WILL BE TO PROVOKE RETALIATORY ACTION IN
WHICH INNOCENT BOUGAINVILLEANS ARE SHOT AT AND KILLED.
BOUGAINVILLE NEEDS GOOD INTELLIGENCE.

09407 WARNER, D.
CHINA STUMBLES AS THE WORLD MOVES ON
PACIFIC DEFENCE REPORTER, 16(6) (DEC 89), 3-6.
WHILE PROFESSING THAT THE ECONOMIC DOOR REMAINS OPEN,
THE BREAKING OF THE STUDENTS' "DEMOCRACY" MOVEMENT IN TIAN
AN MEN SQUARE HERALDED A RETREAT BY CHINA INTO THE PUNITIVE
AND REPRESSIVE YEARS OF THE STALINIST '50S. ALTHOUGH THE
POWER STRUGGLE IS NOT YET ENDED, AGING DESPOTS WITH PROVEN
REVOLUTIONARY RECORDS, BUT FEW OF THE SKILLS DEMANDED FOR
ECONOMIC DEVELOPMENT, ARE ONCE AGAIN IN CONTROL. CHINA'S
IMMEDIATE FUTURE, AND FUTURE BEHAVIOR, ARE IN DOUBT, A
SITUATION THAT IS A LEGITIMATE CAUSE FOR UNEASE ACROSS THE
TAIWAN STRIAT AND IN SOUTH-EAST ASIA, WHILE DEEP CLOUDS OF
CONCERN HANG OVER THE PEAK IN HONG KONG.

09408 WARNER, D.
LIMITS TO SINO-SOVIET REAPPROCHEMENT
PACIFIC DEFENCE REPORTER, 16(1) (JUL 89), 24-25.
THIS ARTICLE IS THE TEXT OF AN INTERVIEW WITH SINGAPORE
PRIME MINISTER LEE KUAN YEW ON THE SUBJECT OF THE SINO-
SOVIET SUMMIT AND ITS REGIONAL IMPACT. MR. LEE SEES IT AS A
LIMITED RAPPROCHEMENT WHICH DOES NOT NECESSARILY MEAN
IMPROVED ACCESS TO THE REGION FOR THE SOVIET UNION.

09409 WARNER, D.
MORESBY'S PLAN FOR PRESERVING PEACE
PACIFIC DEFENCE REPORTER, 16(2) (AUG 89), 34-35.
THE ASIA-PACIFIC NATIONS, ALTHOUGH BASKING IN THE GLOW
OF REDUCED INTERNATIONAL TENSION ON THE SUPERPOWER LEVEL,
SEE LITTLE REASON TO REDUCE THEIR OWN CAPACITIES TO DETER
AGGRESSION. THIS ARTICLE DESCRIBES EFFORTS OF ASIAN-PACIFIC
NATIONS, SPECIFICALLY AUSTRALIA AND NEW ZEALAND, TO MAINTAIN
STABILITY IN THE AREA.

09410 WARNER, D.
THE DENG ENIGMA
PACIFIC DEFENCE REPORTER, 16(1) (JUL 89), 17.
FOR THE PAST DECADE DENG HAS BEEN IDENTIFIED WITH
ECONOMIC REFORM. MORE THAN ANY OTHER, HE HELPED CHINA TO
JOIN THE 20TH CENTURY. WHY HE COULD BE SO FAR SIGHTED AND
ALSO SO SHORT SIGHTED IS AN ENIGMA IN WHICH THE EXPRESSION
"COUNTER REVOLUTIONARY" MAY HOLD THE ANSWER. WHAT HE DOES
NOT SEEM TO HAVE UNDERSTOOD IS THAT CHINA HAS CHANGED BEYOND
RECOGNITION IN INTERVENING YEARS. "OFFER AN ASIAN A CHOICE
BETWEEN A LOAF OF BREAD AND A GOOD SLOGAN LIKE 'LIBERTY,
EQUALITY AND FRATERNITY' AND HE'LL TAKE THE SLOGAN EVERY
TIME," BURMA'S MAW USED TO SAY. DENG OFFERED BREAD. THE
PEOPLE OF BEIJING PREFERRED LIBERTY. AND DENG, AS HE HAD IN
THE PAST, TURNED TO THE GUN.

09411 WARNER, P.D.
ALTERNATIVE STRATEGIES FOR ECONOMIC DEVELOPMENT: EVIDENCE
FROM SOUTHERN METROPOLITAN AREAS
URBAN AFFAIRS QUARTERLY, 24(3) (MAR 89), 389-411.
IN RECENT YEARS, PRESSURES HAVE MOUNTED ON LOCAL
OFFICIALS TO DEVELOP POLICIES THAT STIMULATE ECONOMIC GROWTH.
THE TRADITIONAL APPROACH, WHICH CALLS FOR ATTRACTING
MANUFACTURING PLANTS THROUGH THE USE OF COST-CUTTING
INDUCEMENTS, HAS BEEN BROUGHT INTO QUESTION, AND THE SEARCH
FOR ALTERNATIVE APPROACHES LED TO A HUMAN CAPITAL STRATEGY
THAT FOCUSES ON ATTRACTING, RETAINING, AND DEVELOPING
SKILLED LABOR. EMPIRICAL TESTS OF TWO MODELS, ONE
REPRESENTING HUMAN CAPITAL DEVELOPMENT AND THE OTHER BASED
ON FIRM COSTS IN THE LOCAL ECONOMY, ARE DESCRIBED. THE
EVIDENCE SUGGESTS THAT A STRATEGY FOCUSING ON HUMAN CAPITAL
WOULD HAVE BEEN MORE EFFECTIVE AT STIMULATING PER CAPITA
INCOME GROWTH THAN ONE DESIGNED TO REDUCE FIRM COSTS.

09412 WARNER, R.L.; LOVRICH, N.P.; STEEL, B.S.
CONDITIONS ASSOCIATED WITH THE ADVENT OF REPRESENTATIVE
BUREAUCRACY: THE CASE OF WOMEN IN POLICING

SOCIAL SCIENCE QUARTERLY, 70(3) (SEP 89), 562-578.
WITH THE PASSAGE OF THE EQUAL EMPLOYMENT OPPORTUNITY ACT
OF 1972, TITLE VII PROVISIONS OF FEDERAL LAW PROHIBITING
DISCRIMINATION IN PERSONNEL PRACTICES WERE EXTENDED TO STATE
AND LOCAL GOVERNMENTS. WHILE WOMEN HAVE MADE NOTABLE
PROGRESS IN ATTAINING EMPLOYMENT AND ASCENDING TO MANAGERIAL
STATUS WITHIN SOME AREAS OF GOVERNMENTAL EMPLOYMENT, LESS
PROGRESS HAS BEEN SEEN IN MUNICIPAL POLICE DEPARTMENTS--
PARTICULARLY AMONG THE RANKS OF COMMISSIONED OFFICERS. THE
RESEARCH REPORTED IN THIS ARTICLE, BASED ON SURVEYS OF 281 U.
S. CITIES IN 1984 AND AGAIN IN 1987, INDICATES THAT THE
VARIATION AMONG CITIES WITH RESPECT TO THE LEVEL OF
UTILIZATION OF WOMEN AS POLICE OFFICERS IS PROBABLY DUE TO A
COMBINATION OF ECONOMIC CONDITIONS, LOCAL-LEVEL
REPRESENTATION OF WOMEN IN PUBLIC OFFICES, AND EXPLICIT
ADMINISTRATIVE MECHANISMS ESTABLISHED FOR HIRING WOMEN. IT
IS SUGGESTED THAT PROGRESS TOWARD SOCIAL EQUITY FOR WOMEN IN
SUCH MALE-DOMINATED OCCUPATIONS AS POLICING IS HIGHLY
DEPENDENT UPON A FORMAL ADMINISTRATIVE STRUCTURE ESTABLISHED
SPECIFICALLY TO ACHIEVE THIS GOAL.

09413 HARNKE, P.C.
CAN NATO SURVIVE SUCCESS?
JOURNAL OF INTERNATIONAL AFFAIRS, 43(1) (SUM 89), 47-56.
THIS ARTICLE EXAMINES THE INITIATIVES TAKEN BY GORBACHEV
IN REDUCING THE SOVIET MILITARY THREAT TO WESTERN EUROPE, AS
THE THREAT IS PERCEIVED TO BE RECEDING THE ARTICLE ADDRESSES
TWO MAJOR QUESTIONS. THE FIRST IS WHETHER NATO CAN SURVIVE.
THE SECOND IS WHETHER NATO SHOULD SURVIVE? RECIPROCAL
RESTRAINTS FOR IMPLEMENTING UNILATERAL INITIATIVES ARE
EXPLORED.

09414 HARNOCK, J.
LAMBS TO THE SLAUGHTER
CANADIAN FORUM, 68(783) (NOV 89), 10-13.
THIS ARTICLE ANALYSES NEW ZEALAND'S EXPERIMENT IN NEO-
CONSERVATISM AND EXAMINES THE REAL NATURE OF NEO-
CONSERVATISM THERE, IT EXPLORES KEYNESIANISM AND THE 1982
RECESSION AND THE FOURTH LABOR GOVERNMENT, AS WELL AS THE
GOODS AND SERVICE TAX AND THE EFFECT ON LABOR.

09415 HARNOCK, J. H.
THE THREAT TO THE REGIONS
POLICY OPTIONS, 10(3) (APR 89), 33-34.
EXPERIENCE HAS SHOWN THAT THE U.S. GOVERNMENT IS
DETERMINED TO INVOKE ITS OWN TRADE LAWS AGAINST ANY STEPS
CANADIAN GOVERNMENTS TAKE TO EVEN OUT DIFFERENCES AMONG THE
CANADIAN REGIONS BY WAY OF SUBSIDY OR OTHER AID. IT WAS
CONCERN IN THIS AREA THAT LED THE PROVINCIAL PREMIERS TO
DEMAND A BINDING MECHANISM FOR SOLVING TRADE DISPUTES AS
PART OF A FREE TRADE AGREEMENT. HOWEVER, NO SUCH MECHANISM
WAS PROVIDED; INSTEAD, THERE IS A WORKING GROUP TO TRY TO
DEVELOP A NEW SET OF RULES ON SUBSIDIES WITHIN THE NEXT
SEVEN YEARS.

09416 HARR, P.
EXPORT PROCESSING ZONES AND TRADE POLICY
FINANCE AND DEVELOPMENT, 26(2) (JUN 89), 34-36.
SINCE THE MID 1960'S, MANY DEVELOPING COUNTRIES HAVE
INITIATED POLICES DESIGNED TO STIMULATE EXPORTS OF
NONTRADITIONAL MANUFACTURED GOODS. ONE FORM OF SUCH EXPORT
PROMOTION EFFORTS HAS BEEN THE ESTABLISHMENT OF EXPORT
PROCESSING ZONES (EPZ). THE ARTICLE ASSESSES THE RECORD OF
EPZS TO DATE, DRAWING PARTLY ON A DETAILED STUDY OF EPZS IN
FOUR ASIAN COUNTRIES: INDONESIA, THE REPUBLIC OF KOREA,
MALAYSIA, AND THE PHILIPPINES. IT CONCLUDES THAT EPZS CAN
MAKE A LIMITED CONTRIBUTION TO THE GROWTH OF EXPORTS,
ESPECIALLY IN THE EARLY STAGES OF INDUSTRIALIZATION. HOWEVER,
A MUCH MORE EFFECTIVE STRATEGY IS TO CREATE A LIBERAL
ECONOMIC ENVIRONMENT CONDUCIVE TO EXPORT-OREINTED
DEVELOPMENT.

09417 WARREN, M.E.
WHAT IS POLITICAL THEORY/PHILOSOPHY?
PS: POLITICAL SCIENCE AND POLITICS, XXII(3) (SEP 89),
606-612.
THE SUBDISCIPLINE OF POLITICAL THEORY AND POLITICAL
PHILOSOPHY CONTINUES TO SUFFER SOME MISUNDERSTANDING WITHIN
POLITICAL SCIENCE AS A WHOLE. NOTWITHSTANDING ITS
RENAISSANCE IN THE LAST DECADE, POLITICAL THEORY/PHILOSOPHY
IS STILL TOO OFTEN CHARACTERIZED IN TERMS THAT OBSCURE ITS
ROLES AND FUNCTIONS WITHIN THE DISCIPLINE.

09418 WARREN,M.
LIBERAL CONSTITUTIONALISM AS IDEOLOGY: MARX AND HABERMAS
POLITICAL THEORY, 17(4) (NOV 89), 511-534.
IT IS COMMON AMONG THOSE OF STRONGLY DEMOCRATIC, MARXIST,
AND NEO-MARXIST PERSUASIONS TO SEE LIBERAL
CONSTITUTIONALISM AS HAVING AN IDEOLOGICAL DIMENSION, THIS
CLAIM IS INVESTIGATED IN THIS ARTICLE. LIBERAL
CONSTITUTIONALISM IS ASSESSED, IN A LARGE PART VIA MARX AND
HAVERMAS, IN A WAY THAT DISTINGUISHES ITS DEMOCRATIC
POTENTIALS FROM ITS IDEOLOGICAL EFFECTS. ONE DIMENSION OF
THIS CRITIQUE INVOLVES SHOWING HOW A GIVEN SET OF POLITICAL

PRACTICES FAILS TO ACHIEVE THE POTENTIALS EXPRESSED BY THE
NORMS THAT LEGITIMATE THESE PRACTICES. THIS "UNMASKING"
LEADS TO THE SECOND DIMENSION DISCUSSED HERE: IDENTIFYING
CONDITIONS UNDER WHICH NORMATIVE POTENTIALS MIGHT BE
REALISED. FINALLY, IDENTIFYING CONDITIONS OF POSSIBILITY
ALSO SHOWS HOW SOME KINDS OF IDEOLOGIES WORK BY
DISSIMULATING OR MASKING THESE CONDITIONS. MECHANISMS FOR
THIS DISSIMULATING ARE DISCUSSED.

09419 HARSZAWSKI, D.
DIFFERENT THINGS TO DIFFERENT PEOPLE: POLAND, MARCH '68
NEW POLITICS, 11(2) (WIN 89), 49-54.
THE MARCH '68 CAMPAIGN BROKE THE BACK OF THE TRADITIONAL
ANTI-SEMITISM OF LARGE SEGMENTS OF THE POLISH INTELLIGENTSIA
AND OF THE CHURCH. THE SOLIDARITY OF THE PERSUCUTED
INTELLECTUALS AND JEWS ALONG WITH THE CHURCH'S MORAL
REFLECTION ON THE ROOTS OF SOCIAL EVIL CREATED A NEW
ATTITUDE. THAT DEVELOPMENT WAS RESPONSIBLE FOR HEIGHTENED
INTEREST AND SYMPATHY FOR ALL THINGS JEWISH, FACILIATING
POLAND'S "JEWISH REVIVAL" OF THE SEVENTIES AND EIGHTIES. IT
BECAME PARTICULARLY IMPORTANT DURING THE "SOLIDARNOSC"
PERIOD WHEN ALL KINDS OF SUPPRESSED SOCIAL
ATTITUDESINCLUDING RESIDUAL ANTI-SEMITISM--CAME OUT INTO THE
OPEN.

09420 HARSZAWSKI, D.
SOLIDARITY MAKES A CHOICE
NEW LEADER, LXXII(13) (SEP 89), 3-4.
THE DECISION OF SOLIDARITY TO TAKE OVER THE REINS OF
GOVERNMENT WITHOUT HAVING FULL CONTROL WAS A DIFFICULT ONE
FOR THE MOVEMENT. TADEUSZ MAZOWIECKI, THE FIRST NON-
COMMUNIST PRIME MINISTER TO BE APPOINTED IN OVER 40 YEARS,
NOW FACES THE DAUNTING TASK OF REFORMING POLAND'S ECONOMY
USING BASICALLY THE SAME PEOPLE THAT BROUGHT THE NATION TO
ITS CURRENT STATE OF ECONOMIC TURMOIL. ONLY WIDESPREAD GRASS
ROOTS SUPPORT WILL GIVE THE SOLIDARITY PRIME MINISTER A
FIGHTING CHANCE.

09421 HARSZAWSKI, D.
THE CONVENT AND SOLIDARITY
TIKKUN, 4(6) (NOV 89), 29-32, 92-93.
RECENT CONTROVERSY OVER A CARMELITE CONVENT IN AUSCHWITZ
AND A SPEECH BY POLAND'S CARDINAL JOZEF GLEMP HAS REVEALED
THAT ANTI-SEMITISM IS ALIVE AND WELL IN POLAND. FEW POLES
REMEMBER THAT THREE MILLION JEWS LIVED IN POLAND BARELY A
HALF CENTURY AGO, AND MANY SEEM MORE THAN WILLING TO LISTEN
TO AND BELIEVE ANTI-SEMITIC STATEMENTS SUCH AS GLEMP'S.
ALTHOUGH THE SPECIFIC POINTS OF CONTROVERSY MAY BE SETTLED,
IT IS UNLIKELY THAT ANTI-SEMITISM WILL DISAPPEAR OVERNIGHT.

09422 HARSZAWSKI, D.
TOO LITTLE, TOO LATE
NEW POLITICS, 11(3) (SUM 89), 129-136.
IT IS HARD TO PREVENT A REVOLUTION IN A POOR AND
DESPERATE COUNTRY. FOR ALL THE LAST-DITCH EFFORTS OF WELL-
INTENTIONED POLITICAL ELITES, FOR ALL THE RELUCTANCE OF THE
POLISH PEOPLE TO FACE THE TURMOIL - AND POSSIBLE DEFEAT AS
THEY DID IN '81, IT SEEMS THAT THE ROUND TABLE HAS PRODUCED
A TRANSIENT CONTRACT, AT BEST, ONE THAT WILL MAKE IT
POSSIBLE FOR THE REAL POLITICAL FORCES TO FINALLY EMERGE,
BUT AT THE SAME TIME WILL BE UNABLE TO CONTAIN THEM. THE
ECONOMIC CRISIS CAN ONLY DEEPEN IN THE IMMEDIATE FUTURE, AND
IT IS CLEAR FROM HISTORY. WHAT HAPPENS WHEN ASPIRATIONS ARE
AROUSED, AND NOT MET.

09423 WASHINGTON, A. J.
AN EXAMINATION OF FACTORS WHICH CONTRIBUTE TO ERRORS AND
OMISSIONS IN THE POLLING PLACE ON ELECTION DAY
DISSERTATION ABSTRACTS INTERNATIONAL, 49(8) (FEB 89),
2379-A.
THE AUTHOR STUDIED FACTORS THAT CONTRIBUTE TO ERRORS AND
OMISSIONS IN THE POLLING PLACE, IN THREE PHASES: (1) A
COMPARISON OF SUBJECT-FORMATTING AND TIME-FORMATTING; (2) AN
EXAMINATION OF DEMOGRAPHIC FACTORS THAT COULD CONTRIBUTE TO
ERRORS AND OMISSIONS; AND (3) AN INVESTIGATION OF OVERALL
MANAGEMENT AT THE POLLING PLACE.

09424 WASHINGTON, C.A.
IMPLEMENTING SITE AND SERVICE PROGRAMS IN ZAMBIA: 1965-1980
DISSERTATION ABSTRACTS INTERNATIONAL, 50(4) (OCT 89),
1088-A.
THE AUTHOR REVIEWS THE EFFORTS OF THE ZAMBIAN GOVERNMENT
TO IMPLEMENT SELF-HELP HOUSING (SITE AND SERVICE) AND
SQUATTER UPGRADING POLICIES OVER A FIFTEEN-YEAR PERIOD, AS A
MEANS OF COPING WITH THEIR URBAN HOUSING SHORTAGE. SITE AND
SERVICE IMPLEMENTATION HAS A DYNAMIC, EVOLUTIONARY PROCESS
IN WHICH THE POLICY, THE IMPLEMENTING INSTITUTIONS, AND
FACTORS IN THE ENVIRONMENT WERE CAUGHT IN A WEB OF MUTUAL
CAUSALITY AND CHANGE. SITE AND SERVICE POLICY AND LOCAL
GOVERNMENT CAPACITY PROVED TO BE INTERDEPENDENT.
UNFORTUNATELY, SITE AND SERVICE WAS NEEDED MOST WHERE LOCAL
GOVERNMENTS WERE WEAKEST, BUT THE SUCCESS OF THE POLICY
DEPENDED LARGELY ON THE STRENGTH OF LOCAL GOVERNMENT.

09425 WASILEWSKI, A.
CULTURE: OBJECTIVE AND INDISPENSABLE CONDITION
WORLD MARXIST REVIEW, 31(1) (JAN 88), 27-34.
ACCESS TO CULTURAL ACHIEVEMENTS AND PARTICIPATION IN
AUGMENTING ITS RICHES IS AN INALIENABLE RIGHT OF THE WORKING
PEOPLE GUARANTEED BY THE POLISH CONSTITUTION. THROUGHOUT THE
HISTORY OF PEOPLE'S POLAND THIS POLICY HAS BEEN YIELDING
TANGIBLE RESULTS. CULTURE HAS BECOME AN IMPORTANT FACTOR OF
THE PEOPLE'S GROWING SELF-CONSCIOUSNESS AND OF SOCIAL
TRANSFORMATION IN THE COUNTRY. THE MORE VALUABLE FRUITS OF
THOUGHT AND CREATIVE ACTIVITY ARE NOW WITHIN THE REACH OF
ALL AND EVERYONE.

09426 WASLEKAR, S.
THE MAKING OF A PROBLEM DEBTOR
SOUTH, (100) (FEB 89), 29.
INDIA, THE THIRD WORLD'S SIXTH BIGGEST BORROWER, IS
HEADING FOR TROUBLE IN THE 1990'S. THE WORLD BANK EXPECTS
INDIA'S COMMERCIAL BORROWINGS TO DOUBLE DURING THE 1989-94
PERIOD. THE MOST SERIOUS PROBLEM IS THE STEADY RISE IN
DOMESTIC GOVERNMENT DEFICITS, FROM US$10 BILLION IN 1978-79
TO US$70 BILLION IN 1988-89.

09427 WASSERMAN, I.M.
PROHIBITION AND ETHNOCULTURAL CONFLICT: THE MISSOURI
PROHIBITION REFERENDUM OF 1918
SOCIAL SCIENCE QUARTERLY, 70(4) (DEC 89), 886-901.
THE PAPER EXAMINES ALTERNATE EXPLANATIONS OF THE SOCIAL
SOURCES OF THE PROHIBITION MOVEMENT. DATA FROM THE
PROHIBITION REFERENDUM IN MISSOURI ARE UTILIZED TO TEST THE
DIFFERENT HYPOTHESES. A MULTIVARIATE ANALYSIS OF THE STATE
DATA AT THE COUNTY LEVEL SUGGESTS THAT ETHNIC, RECENT
IMMIGRANT, AND OLDER STOCK POPULATION CONCENTRATIONS WERE
SIGNIFICANT FOR EXPLANING VARIATIONS IN THE PROHIBITION VOTE.
THE OUTCOME OF THE VOTE INFLUENCED INTERPARTY STRUGGLES AT
THE STATE AND NATIONAL LEVELS THROUGHOUT THE 1920S.

09428 WASZCZUK, E.
POLAND-EEC
CONTEMPORARY POLAND, XXII(4) (1989), 5-7.
THE THAW IN INTERNATIONAL POLITICAL RELATIONS HAS BEEN
FOLLOWED BY A WARMING TREND ON THE ECONOMIC FRONT. ON JUNE
25, 1988, THE FIRST STEP WAS TAKEN TO DISMANTLE THE ECONOMIC
BARRIERS DIVIDING EUROPE, WITH THE SIGNING OF A JOINT
DECLARATION CONCERNING THE ESTABLISHMENT OF OFFICIAL
RELATIONS BETWEEN THE COUNCIL FOR MUTUAL ECONOMIC ASSISTANCE
AND THE EUROPEAN ECONOMIC COMMUNITY. POLAND IS ESPECIALLY
ANXIOUS TO RELAX EUROPEAN TRADE BARRIERS BECAUSE ITS EXPORTS
HAVE BEEN SUBJECTED TO PARTICULARLY HARSH RESTRICTIONS SINCE
THE INTRODUCTION OF MARTIAL LAW IN 1981.

09429 WATARU, K.
MAKING PEACE WITH HIROHITO AND A MILITARISTIC PAST
JAPAN QUARTERLY, XXXVI(2) (APR 89), 186-192.
DEPENDING ON WHETHER THEY WERE EDUCATED BEFORE OR AFTER
WORLD WAR II, THE JAPANESE GENERALLY HOLD ONE OF TWO
ATTITUDES TOWARD HIROHITO AND THE EMPEROR SYSTEM. PEOPLE
OVER 50 YEARS OLD WERE TAUGHT TOO MUCH ABOUT THE EMPEROR.
THOSE UNDER 50 HAVE NOT BEEN TAUGHT ENOUGH. THE RESULT IS
WIDESPREAD AMBIVALENCE ABOUT THE IMPERIAL INSTITUTION. THIS
HAS PREVENTED JAPAN FROM PASSING JUDGMENT ON THE ERA OF
MILITARISM AND EMPEROR WORSHIP AND PUTTING IT TO REST.

09430 WATCHER, BURMA
BURMA IN 1988: THERE CAME A WHIRLWIND
ASIAN SURVEY, XXIX(2) (FEB 89), 174-180.
1988 WAS BURMA'S MOST TURBULENT AND VIOLENT SINCE 1962.
AFTER 26 YEARS OF RULE, GENERAL NE WIN RESIGNED FROM HIS
POLITICAL POSTS BUT RETAINED POWER BEHIND THE SCENES, WHILE
THE BURMESE PEOPLE ENDURED POLITICAL TURBULENCE, ECONOMIC
DISINTEGRATION, AND BRUTAL REPRESSION DURING A HEADY PERIOD
OF POLITICAL HOPE FOR A BETTER WAY OF LIFE. THE BRUTAL
VIOLENCE OVERSHADOWED THE NORMAL POLITICAL AND ECONOMIC
DEVELOPMENTS.

09431 WATERMAN, P.
FOR THE LIBERATION OF INTERNATIONALISM: A LONG MARCH
THROUGH THE LITERATURES
ALTERNATIVES, XIV(1) (JAN 89), 5-47.
THE CREATION OF A NEW LABOUR INTERNATIONALISM REQUIRES
AN UNDERSTAND ING OF THE RELATIVE FAILURE OF THE OLD "CLASS"
ONE AND THE RELATIVE SUCCESS OF THE NEW "DEMOCRATIC"
INTERNATIONALISMS. IN THE PROCESS OF TRYING UNDERSTAND AND
ADVANCE A NEW KIND OF LABOUR INTERNATIONALISM, THE AUTHOR
EXAMINES A RANGE OF VERY DIFFERENT CONTEMPORARY LITERATURES
THAT DEAL WITH ONE ASPECT OR ANOTHER OF INTERNATIONALIZATION
AND INTERNATIONALISM, EXPLICITY OR IMPLICITY. THE PURPOSE OF
THE REVIEW IS TO REMOVE OBSTACLES TO A CONTEMPORARY
UNDERSTANDING OF INTERNATIONALISM, TO INDICATE POSSIBLE
OPENINGS AND TO IDENTIFY SOME OF THE REMAINING LACUNAE

09432 WATERS, E.
RESTRUCTURING THE "WOMAN QUESTION": PERESTROIKA AND
PROSTITUTION
FEMINIST REVIEW, (33) (AUT 89), 3-19.
THUS FAR, GLASNOST HAS BEEN SELECTIVE IN ITS CHOICE OF
SUITABLE SUBJECTS FOR TREATMENT. THE SOVIET GOVERNMENT HAS
ADOPTED A FLEXIBLE APPROACH TO MATTERS OF IDEOLOGY AND
ADMINISTRATION AND IS PREPARED TO ADAPT OR DISCARD SLOGANS
AND POLICIES THAT NO LONGER SEEM APPROPRIATE, HOWEVER
CENTRAL THEY WERE TO THE SOCIALIST CANNON IN THE PAST. THERE
HAS BEEN MUCH TALK OF PRIVATE ENTERPRISE AND UNEMPLOYMENT,
BUT VERY LITTLE OF FEMALE EMANCIPATION. THE "WOMAN QUESTION"
DOES NOT FIGURE IN THE GOVERNMENT'S LIST OF POLITICAL
PRIORITIES. WOMEN'S SECONDARY POSITION IN THE LABOR FORCE
AND THEIR SOCIAL SUBORDINATION ARE NOT RECOGNIZED AS URGENT
ISSUES. ONE CLUE TO THE OFFICIAL VIEW OF WOMEN IS SEEN IN
THE ATTITUDE TOWARD PROSTITUTION. THE GOVERNMENT HAS NOW
ADMITTED THAT PROSTITUTION EXISTS AND HAS ATTRIBUTED IT TO
MORAL FAILINGS FOR WHICH THE WOMEN MUST TAKE THE MAIN SHARE
OF THE BLAME.

09433 WATERS, M.
COLLEGIALITY, BUREAUCRATIZATION, AND PROFESSIONALIZATION:
A WEBERIAN ANALYSIS
AMERICAN JOURNAL OF SOCIOLOGY, 94(5) (MAY 89), 945-972.
THIS ARTICLE ANALYZES WEBER'S WRITING ON THE TOPIC OF
COLLEGIALITY IN ECONOMY AND SOCIETY IN ORDER TO REINTEGRATE
THE CONCEPT OF COLLEGIALITY WITH HIS OTHER CONCEPTS OF
LEGITIMATE DOMINATION, STATUS GROUP CLOSURE, BUREAUCRACY,
AND LEGAL FORMALISM. AN IDEAL-TYPE OF COLLEGIATE
ORGANIZATION IS IDENTIFIED, AND THE CONSEQUENCES OF THE
EMERGENCE OF COLLEGIAL SOCIAL STRUCTURE OF THIS FORM IN
PROFESSIONAL CONTEXTS ARE EXAMINED. THESE ARGUMENTS PROVIDE
A CRITIQUE OF THE PREDOMINANT UNDERSTANDINGS OF THE
RELATIONSHIP BETWEEN PROFESSIONALIZATION AND
BUREAUCRATIZATION, IN WHICH PROFESSIONAL IDEOLOGY IS
CONCEIVED OF AS ETHICAL COMMITMENT. THE ARTICLE CALLS FOR A
RESTORATION OF WEBERIAN UNDERSTANDINGS OF THE
RATIONALIZATION OF MODERN LIFE AS THE OUTCOME OF A CONTEST
FOR DOMINATION BETWEEN INTEREST GROUPS RATHER THAN AS THE
INSTITUTIONALIZATION OF TRANSCENDENT NORMATIVE STRUCTURES.

09434 WATERS, W. R.
SOCIAL ECONOMICS A SOLIDARIST PERSPECTIVE
REVIEW OF SOCIAL ECONOMY, 46(2) (OCT 88), 113-143.
THIS PAPER IS ONE SOCIAL ECONOMIST'S SKETCH OF THE THREE
COMPONENTS OF SOCIAL ECONOMICS. IT STARTS WITH AN
INTRODUCTION TO THE PHILOSOPHICAL BASE. THEN CONTINUES WITH
AN OUTLINE OF THE SIGNIFICANT CORE OF THE ECONOMIC SYSTEM,
CONTENDING THAT IT DIFFERS FROM THE EMPIRICAL BASE ROUTINELY
OFFERED BY ECONOMISTS IN PRINCIPLES COURSES AND OTHERWISE.
FINALLY, IT REFERS TO SOCIAL ECONOMIC POLICY, THE SOCIAL
ARCHITECTONIC DIMENSION NEEDED FOR HUMAN SOCIAL ECONOMIC
DEVELOPMENT.

09435 WATHEN, T.A.
BURMA: WHAT COMES NEXT
MULTINATIONAL MONITOR, 10(3) (MAR 89), 9-12.
WHILE MULTI-NATIONAL CORPORATIONS HAVE GREATLY EXPANDED
THEIR PRESENCE THROUGHOUT ASIA, BURMA'S GOVERNMENT HAS
CHOSEN A PATH OF ECONOMIC AND POLITICAL ISOLATION. FOR
ALMOST 30 YEARS, NE WIN AND HIS SUPPORTERS RULED UNDER THE
BANNER OF THE BURMA SOCIALIST PROGRAM PARTY. HE SUCCEEDED IN
DEVELOPING A SELF-CONTAINED ECONOMY, BUT BURMESE SOCIALISM
HAS BEEN DISASTROUS. SHOULD A POPULAR UPRISING SUCCEED IN
OVERTHROWING THE CURRENT REGIME AND INSTALLING A GOVERNMENT
THAT OPENS THE COUNTRY TO FOREIGN TRADE, ONE OF THE WORLD'S
RICHEST SOURCES OF NATURAL RESOURCES COULD BE UP FOR GRABS.

09436 WATSON, A.
FROM A EUROPEAN TO A GLOBAL INTERNATIONAL SOCIETY: CHANGES
AND CONTRADICTIONS IN THE STATES SYSTEM
JERUSALEM JOURNAL OF INTERNATIONAL RELATIONS, 11(2) (JUN
89), 17-26.
SINCE WORLD WAR II, THE PROCESSES OF DECOLONIZATION,
MULTIPLICATION OF INDEPENDENCES, AND CULTURAL REJECTION OF
EUROPEAN (INCLUDING NORTH AMERICAN AND RUSSIAN) DOMINANCE
HAVE MADE FOR A LOOSER, ANTIHEGEMONIAL WORLD. THE NEWER OR
WEAKER STATES, HOWEVER, WHILE COMMITTED TO LIBERATIONIST
THEORY, REMAIN ECONOMICALLY DEPENDENT ON THE POWERS. THIS
SITUATION IS ROOTED IN, AND BEST UNDERSTOOD IN THE LIGHT OF,
THE LEGACY OF THE RISE AND PARTIAL DECLINE OF EUROPEAN
DOMINANCE.

09437 WATSON, A.
INVESTMENT ISSUES IN THE CHINESE COUNTRYSIDE
AUSTRALIAN JOURNAL OF CHINESE AFFAIRS, (22) (JUL 89),
85-126.
SOME OBSERVERS ARGUE THAT THE MAIN ACHIEVEMENT OF
CHINA'S AGRICULTURAL REFORMS HAS TO REALIZE THE FULL
POTENTIAL OF THE INVESTMENTS IN LAND, WATER, AND TECHNOLOGY
THAT HAD BEEN MADE UNDER THE COMMUNE SYSTEM. THE
INEFFICIENCIES IN COMMUNE MANAGEMENT, THE LACK OF INCENTIVES
FOR LABOR, AND THE LOW PRICES HAD HINDERED THE PROPER
EXPLOITATION OF THOSE COMMUNAL INVESTMENTS. ONCE THE REFORMS
REMOVED THE CONSTRAINTS, THE POTENTIAL WAS REALIZED. THE
RAPID DEVELOPMENT OF 1978-1984 WAS BASED ON THE EXPLOITATION

OF HITHERTO UNDER-UTILIZED RESOURCES AND THE RATES OF GROWTH, ONCE THE SLACK HAS BEEN TAKEN UP, COULD NOT BE MAINTAINED. IT WAS INEVITABLE THAT RURAL AREAS WOULD AGAIN SHIFT TOWARD A MORE "NORMAL" RATE OF GROWTH. OTHER OBSERVERS AGREE WITH SOME OF THESE BASIC ASSUMPTIONS BUT ARGUE THAT THERE IS STILL POTENTIAL FOR DEVELOPMENT BY EXPLOITING EXISTING INVESTMENT AND TECHNOLOGY AND ADOPTING NEW STRUCTURAL REFORMS.

09438 HATSON, C.
A PLACE TO GIVE PEACE A CHANCE
SOUTH, (103) (MAY 89), 11.
IN UGANDA, THOUSANDS OF FORMER SOLDIERS AND REBELS HAVE TURNED THEMSELVES IN SINCE YOWERI MUSEVENI'S NATIONAL RESISTANCE ARMY TOOK POWER THREE YEARS AGO. RECONCILIATION CAMPS, SET UP AS A HALFWAY POINT TO HELP REINTEGRATE REBELS, ARE HELPING TO MAKE THE COUNTRY MORE SECURE AS THE FORMER MILITARY MEN ADJUST TO A MORE PEACEFUL LIFESTYLE.

09439 HATSON, C.
AFTER THE MASSACRE
AFRICA REPORT, 34(1) (JAN 89), 51-55.
IN AUGUST 1988, THE HORST VIOLENCE BETWEEN TUTSI AND HUTU SINCE 1972 FLARED IN BURUNDI, LEAVING THOUSANDS DEAD, MANY MORE DISPLACED, AND A NATION RIVEN ALONG ETHNIC LINES. ALTHOUGH PRESIDENT BUYOYA HAS SINCE ADOPTED A SERIES OF REFORMS, INCLUDING INCREASED HUTU REPRESENTATION IN HIS GOVERNMENT, TENSIONS ARE LIKELY TO SIMMER BENEATH THE SURFACE FOR SOME TIME TO COME.

09440 HATSON, G.
THE DISINVITATION OF NOLTE
ENCOUNTER, LXXII(1) (JAN 89), 34-36.
IN OCTOBER 1988, PROFESSOR ERNST NOLTE OF THE FREE UNIVERSITY OF BERLIN HAS DISINVITED FROM LECTURING AT HOLFSON COLLEGE, OXFORD, BECAUSE HE HOLDS HETERODOX VIEWS ABOUT HITLER'S SOCIALISM AND HIS PRIVATELY-CONFESSED DEBT TO MARXISM--ESPECIALLY THE VIEWS OF MARX AND ENGELS ABOUT GENOCIDE. NOLTE HAS STATED THAT HITLER'S IDEAS ON EXTERMINATION COULD ONLY HAVE COME FROM MARX. THE WRITINGS OF BOTH MARX AND ENGELS ABOUND IN RACIAL ANALYSIS AND RACIAL ABUSE.

09441 HATSON, M.
DRUG USE AND POLICY IN POLAND IN THE 1980'S
INTERNATIONAL JOURNAL OF HEALTH SERVICES, 19(3) (1989), 443-456.
IN THIS ARTICLE, THE AUTHOR DESCRIBES THE RECENT CHANGES IN PATTERNS OF DRUG USE IN POLAND IN THE LIGHT OF AVAILABLE DATA. A MUCH HIGHER INCIDENCE OF USE HAS BEEN SEEN IN THE 1980S, AND THERE ARE INDICATIONS THAT THIS CAN BE ACCOUNTED FOR BY INCREASED USE AMONG YOUNG PEOPLE FROM THE MANUAL WORKING CLASS. SOCIAL DEPRIVATION MAY PLAY A PART IN THE ETIOLOGY OF THE 1980S "EPIDEMIC," AND EVIDENCE IS PUT FORWARD IN SUPPORT OF THIS VIEW. BOTH PATTERNS OF USE AND THE POLICIES THAT HAVE BEEN INTRODUCED TO DEAL WITH THEM ARE VIEWED IN TERMS OF THE POLITICAL, ECONOMIC, AND SOCIAL CONTEXT OF POST-SOLIDARITY PERESTROIKA.

09442 HATSON, S.S.
DECENTRALIZATION, THE CDBG PROGRAM, AND LOCAL SPENDING PRIORITIES: A STUDY OF OKLAHOMA SMALL CITIES
DISSERTATION ABSTRACTS INTERNATIONAL, 50(6) (DEC 89), 1790-A.
THE AUTHOR SURVEYS THE SPENDING PRIORITIES OF CDBG GRANT RECIPIENTS IN THE STATE OF OKLAHOMA TO DETERMINE IF FUNDS ARE USED MOSTLY FOR REDISTRIBUTIVE PROJECTS OR FOR ACTIVITIES THAT PROMOTE THE ECONOMIC INTERESTS OF SMALL CITIES. SHE ALSO ENDEAVORS TO IDENTIFY VARIOUS SOCIAL, ECONOMIC, AND POLITICAL FORCES PRESENT IN SMALL COMMUNITIES THAT SERVE TO DIRECT THE USE AND THE BENEFITS OF CDBG FUNDS.

09443 HATT, D.C.
1939 REVISITED: ON THEORIES OF THE ORIGINS OF WARS
INTERNATIONAL AFFAIRS, 65(4) (FAL 89), 685-692.
THIS ARTICLE EXAMINES THE LEGACY OF THE FIRST WORLD WAR AS A MODEL OF WAR BY ESCALATION AND AGGRESSION. IT THEN ADDRESSES THE MODEL AFTER THE SECOND WORLD WAR AND THE CONSPIRACY TO INSTIGATE AN AGGRESSIVE WAR AS IT DETAILS THE TRIALS ON WAR CRIMES. IT ATTEMPTS TO FIT STALIN TO THE HITLER MODEL AND EXPLORES STRATEGIC BARGAINING AND THE RETURN OF THE 'OLD DIPLOMACY.'

09444 HATT, V.
OUR KIND OF SELF: AUTOBIOGRAPHY AND AMERICAN PROGRESSIVES
DISSERTATION ABSTRACTS INTERNATIONAL, 49(8) (FEB 89), 2283-A.
USING AUTOBIOGRAPHIES WRITTEN BY EARLY THENTIETH CENTURY AMERICAN PROGRESSIVES, THIS THESIS LOOKS AT THE NATURE OF THE RELATIONSHIP BETWEEN PROGRESSIVISM AND AUTOBIOGRAPHY, EXAMINES THE VARIOUS FORMS OF THE SELF-IMAGE THAT THE PROGRESSIVES PRESENTED IN THEIR AUTOBIOGRAPHIES, AND CONSIDERS HOH THESE HELP TO ILLUMINATE PROGRESSIVISM.

09445 HATTS, H.
PRESIDENT BUSH: WHAT LIES AHEAD?
JAPAN QUARTERLY, XXXVI(1) (JAN 89), 4-10.
THE AUTHOR REVIEWS THE STRATEGY OF THE 1988 PRESIDENTIAL ELECTION CAMPAIGN AND SPECULATES ABOUT THE FUTURE OF THE BUSH ADMINISTRATION

09446 HAUGH, H.
STATES, COUNTIES, AND THE QUESTIONS OF TRUST AND CAPACITY
PUBLIUS: THE JOURNAL OF FEDERALISM, 18(1) (WIN 88), 189-198.
THIS STUDY INDICATES THAT THERE IS A HIGH LEVEL OF CONFIDENCE AMONG COUNTY REPRESENTATIVES THAT STATE OFFICIALS HILL BE RESPONSIVE TO LOCAL NEEDS, BUT LESS CONFIDENCE IN STATE WILLINGNESS TO PROVIDE FISCAL SUPPORT FOR PROGRAMS. THE PREFERENCE FOR CONTINUED FEDERAL FUNDING OF PROGRAMS IS STRONGLY EVIDENT. COUNTY REPRESENTATIVES FEEL THAT THEIR POLICYMAKING AND ADMINISTRATIVE RESPONSIBILITIES ARE INCREASING BUT THAT THEIR FISCAL (TAXING AND BORROWING) CAPACITIES ARE NOT BEING EXPANDED AS QUICKLY. THE HIGHEST LEVELS OF TRUST IN STATE OFFICIALS HERE FOUND AMONG THOSE COUNTY REPRESENTATIVES WHO PERCEIVED THE GREATEST INCREASES IN LOCAL GOVERNMENT CAPACITIES TO RESPOND TO LOCAL PROBLEMS.

09447 HAUGH, H.L., JR.
INFORMING POLICY AND ADMINISTRATION: A COMPARATIVE PERSPECTIVE ON TERRORISM
INTERNATIONAL JOURNAL OF PUBLIC ADMINISTRATION, 12(3) (1989), 477-499.
THE CLICHE THAT "ONE MAN'S TERRORIST IS ANOTHER MAN'S FREEDOM FIGHTER" REPRESENTS THE MAJOR DILEMA OF ANTI-TERRORISM POLICYMAKERS AND ADMINISTRATORS. THE CONCEPTUAL CONFUSION IS FURTHER COMPLICATED BY THE IDEOLOGICAL ORIENTATIONS AND POLICY INTERESTS OF THE OBSERVERS. THE COMPARATIVE STUDY OF TERRORISM, HOWEVER, HAS PROVIDED A CONCEPTUAL UNDERPINNING AND DOES PROVIDE THE TOOLS FOR SORTING OUT THE BIASES. THIS ARTICLE COMPARES THE SIX PRINCIPAL MODELS OF POLITICAL TERRORISM AND SUGGESTS THAT EACH IN FACT DESCRIBES A DISTINCT FORM OF POLITICAL VIOLENCE DEPENDING UPON THE PERSPECTIVE OF THE OBSERVER. EACH OF THE FORMS OF TERRORISM, MOREOVER, MAY REQUIRE A UNIQUE SET OF REMEDIES. USING THE HIDELY PUBLICIZED THA HIJACKING DURING THE SUMMER OF 1985 AS AN EXAMPLE, THE ANALYSIS EXAMINES THE DIFFERENCES IN THE AMERICAN, ISRAELI, AND LEBANESE GOVERNMENT PERSPECTIVES AND HOW THOSE DIFFERENCES INFLUENCED POLICYMAKING.

09448 HAY, F.
RELIGIOUS DISPUTATION AND THE CIVIL COURTS: QUASI-ESTABLISHMENT AND SECULAR PRINCIPLES
WESTERN POLITICAL QUARTERLY, 42(4) (DEC 89), 523-544.
IN A STUDY OF 271 CHURCH PROPERTY DISPUTE CASES FROM 1800 THROUGH 1981 CIVIL COURTS FREQUENTLY ACTED AS QUASI-ECCLESIASTICAL COURTS; DISPUTED PROPERTY HAS OFTEN AWARDED UNDER A RULE WHICH FAVORED RELIGIOUS ORTHODOXY. THE STATE COURTS THAT ADOPTED THIS APPROACH INITIALLY STRESSED THE NEED FOR CHRISTIAN HARMONY AND CONTINUITY IN CHURCH DOCTRINE AND POLITY. UNTIL THE UNITED STATES SUPREME COURT HANDED DOWN A SERIES OF OPINIONS BEGINNING IN 1969, THE QUESTION OF SEPARATION OF CHURCH AND STATE WAS RARELY RAISED EITHER BY THE LITIGANTS OR BY THE COURTS. THE FAILURE OF STATE COURTS TO CONSIDER THE CONSTITUTIONAL IMPLICATIONS OF THEIR RULINGS IN THSE DISPUTES IS PART OF A BROADER PICTURE IN WHICH STATE COURTS IN THE NINETEENTH CENTURY WERE SLOW TO PERCEIVE ANY NEED FOR STATE NEUTRALITY IN RELIGIOUS AFFAIRS. ALTHOUGH THE RULE HAS MODIFIED OVER THE YEARS, NONETHELESS THE RULE SUVIVED EVEN IN THE FACE OF SUBSTANTIAL EVIDENCE THAT IT HAS DYSFUNCTIONAL. THE DEGREE OF RULE DETERMINACY REPORTED HERE SUGGESTS THAT UNDER CERTAIN CONDITIONS INSTITUTIONAL AUTONOMY RATHER THAN RULE FUNCTIONALISM IS THE IMPORTANT INDEPENDENT VARIABLE.

09449 HAYNBERG, L.M.
THE ILLUSION OF INDEPENDENCE: NARCISSISTIC ASPECTS OF ROUSSEAU'S POLITICAL THEORY
DISSERTATION ABSTRACTS INTERNATIONAL, 49(8) (FEB 89), 2379-A.
UNLIKE OTHER ATTEMPTS TO INTERPRET ROUSSEAU'S POLITICAL THEORY, THIS STUDY FOCUSES ON THE PROBLEM OF PERSONAL DEPENDENCE. THE THEORY OF NARCISSISM HELPS TO EXPLAIN WHY ROUSSEAU BELIEVED THAT THIS IS A PROBLEM MOST PEOPLE FACE. HIS POLITICAL THEORY IMPOSED ON THE MAJORITY A SOLUTION TO A PROBLEM THAT IN REALITY AFFECTS ONLY THOSE FEW WHO SUFFER FROM NARCISSISTIC PERSONALITY DISORDERS.

09450 HEATHERFORD, M.S.; KUKUI, H.
DOMESTIC ADJUSTMENT TO INTERNATIONAL SHOCKS IN JAPAN AND THE UNITED STATES
INTERNATIONAL ORGANIZATION, 43(4) (FAL 89), 585-624.
THIS ARTICLE SEEKS TO EXPLAIN HOW POLICYMAKERS IN THE WORLD'S TWO MAJOR ECONOMIES RESPONDED TO EXTERNAL ECONOMIC SHOCKS. THE ANALYSIS SUCCESSIVELY EMPLOYS THREE VANTAGE POINT-SYSTEM, SOCIETY, AND STATE-IN TRACING THE SOURCES OF DOMESTIC ADJUSTMENT POLICIES. IT FOCUSES SPECIFICALLY ON THE

EXTENT TO WHICH POLICIES ACCOMMODATED OR EXTINGUISHED EACH
SHOCK'S INFLATIONARY IMPULSES AND ON THE COHERENCE AND
CONSISTENCY WITH WHICH THE EXECUTIVE IN EACH GOVERNMENT
FORMULATED AND PURSUED PARTICULAR POLICY GOALS. A COMPARISON
OF THESE FOUR CASES ILLUSTRATES THE STRENGTHS AND WEAKNESSES
OF INCREASINGLY DETAILED THEORETICAL FRAMEWORKS FOR
EXPLAINING POLICY CHOICE. ALTHOUGH THE RESEARCH DOES NOT
CONTRADICT THE DEPICTION OF THE UNITED STATES AND JAPAN IN
TERMS OF STATE STRENGTH, IT DOES UNDERSCORE THE IMPORTANCE
OF LOOKING BEYOND FORMAL INSTITUTIONAL ARRANGEMENTS TO
CONSIDER HOW ELITE POLICY PREFERENCES, AMBITIONS, AND
CAPACITIES CAN DEFINE THE WAY CONSTRAINTS INFLUENCE POLICY.

09451 WEAVER, P.H.
A TOKYO TOCQUEVILLE
REASON, 21(7) (DEC 89), 37-40.
THIS ARTICLE IS A REVIEW OF. "THE ENIGMA OF JAPANESE
POWER," BY KAREL VAN WOLFEREN. THIS BOOK RANGES WIDELY
THROUGH JAPANESE HISTORY, CULTURE AND POSTWAR POLITICS, AND
IS A WORK OF HIGH SOCIAL THEORY. THE AUTHOR WRITES IN PART
TO WARN THE WEST THAT JAPAN REALLY IS DIFFERENT, THAT JAPAN
IS CAPABLE OF UNDERTAKING THE ECONOMIC EQUIVALENT OF PEARL
HARBOR BY CONTINUING TO EXPAND EXPORTS BUT NOT IMPORTS,
WOLFEREN ARGUES THAT JAPAN, BEHIND A FACADE OF
CONSTITUTIONAL DEMOCRACY AND FREE MARKETS, IS ACTUALLY AN
OLIGARCHY.

09452 WEAVER, R.K.; HARRIS, C.H.
WHO'S IN CHARGE HERE? CONGRESS AND THE NATION'S CAPITAL
BROOKINGS REVIEW, 7(3) (SUM 89), 39-46.
INCREASING FEDERAL GOVERNMENT INVOLVEMENT IN THE
DISTRICT OF COLUMBIA'S LOCAL GOVERNMENT SHOULD NOT BE TAKEN
LIGHTLY. RESIDENTS OF THE DISTRICT HAVE JUST AS MUCH RIGHT
TO GOVERN THEMSELVES AS OTHER CITIZENS OF THE UNITED STATES
DO. IF THE FEDERAL GOVERNMENT DOES DECIDE TO INTERVENE, IT
SHOULD DO SO ONLY WHEN THE LEGITIMATE FEDERAL INTEREST IN
PRESERVING THE CITY'S ABILITY TO FUNCTION AS A NATIONAL
CAPITAL CLEARLY OUTWEIGHS THE RIGHT OF LOCAL RESIDENTS TO
SELF-GOVERNANCE AND WHEN FEDERAL INTERVENTION IS LIKELY TO
PRODUCE A MAJOR IMPROVEMENT.

09453 WEBB, A.J.; FIGUEROA, E.E.; MCCALLA, A.F.; WECKER, H.E.
IMPACT OF THE SOVIET GRAIN EMBARGO: A COMPARISON OF METHODS
JOURNAL OF POLICY MODELING, 11(3) (FAL 89), 361-389.
EMBARGOES ON AMERICAN AGRICULTURAL EXPORTS HAVE BEEN
USED WITH SOME FREQUENCY. NONE WAS MORE PROMINENT THAN
PRESIDENT CARTER'S EMBARGO OF GRAIN EXPORTS TO THE SOVIET
UNION IN 1980-81. IN THIS ESSAY, THE AUTHORS ANALYZE THE
EMBARGO'S EFFECTS, USING THREE METHODOLOGIES. TIME SERIES
METHODS SHOW WHAT PRICES AND TRADE FLOWS WOULD HAVE BEEN IF
PRE-EMBARGO TRENDS HAD PERSISTED. A QUARTERLY ARMINGTON
MODEL SIMULATES EMBARGO EFFECTS HOLDING OTHER STRUCTURAL
CHANGES CONSTANT. DESCRIPTIVE STATISTICS REVEAL WHAT
ACTUALLY HAPPENED. ALL THREE APPROACHES CONFIRM THAT THE
EMBARGO HAD LITTLE EFFECT ON GLOBAL TRADE OR PRICES.

09454 WEBB, K.W.
ARE OVERSEAS BASES WORTH THE BUCKS? AN APPROACH TO
ASSESSING OPERATIONAL VALUE AND AN APPLICATION TO THE
PHILIPPINES
DISSERTATION ABSTRACTS INTERNATIONAL, 49(10) (APR 89),
3153-A.
THIS STUDY DESCRIBES AND APPLIES A METHODOLOGY TO
ADDRESS ONE ASPECT OF THE PROBLEM OF EVALUATING U.S.
OVERSEAS MILITARY BASES AND THEIR IMPORTANCE TO THE OVERALL
U.S. DEFENSE POSTURE. IT ESTIMATES THE COST OF REPLACING A
BASE'S CAPABILITIES, USING ALTERNATIVE LOCATIONS AND MEANS.
THE METHODOLOGY IS APPLIED TO U.S. FACILITIES IN THE
PHILIPPINES.

09455 WEBB, M. C.; KRASNER, S. D.
HEGEMONIC STABILITY THEORY: AN EMPIRICAL ASSESSMENT
REVIEW OF INTERNATIONAL STUDIES, 15(2) (APR 89), 183-198.
THE BASIC CONTENTION OF THE HEGEMONIC STABILITY THESIS
IS THAT THE DISTRIBUTION OF POWER AMONG STATES IS THE
PRIMARY DETERMINANT OF THE CHARACTER OF THE INTERNATIONAL
ECONOMIC SYSTEM. A HEGEMONIC DISTRIBUTION OF POWER, DEFINED
AS ONE IN WHICH A SINGLE STATE HAS A PREDOMINANCE OF POWER,
IS MOST CONDUCIVE TO THE ESTABLISHMENT OF A STABLE, OPEN
INTERNATIONAL ECONOMIC SYSTEM. THIS PAPER IS AN ATTEMPT TO
ASSESS THE EMPIRICAL VALIDITY OF THE HEGEMONIC STABILITY
THESIS AS AN EXPLANATION FOR TRENDS IN THE INTERNATIONAL
POLITICAL ECONOMY SINCE 1945.

09456 WEBB, S.
UNCHANGING MISSION OF THE WORKING CLASS
POLITICAL AFFAIRS, LXVIII(6) (JUN 89), 22-25.
THE ARTICLE DEALS WITH MANY OF THE ARGUEMENTS
PERPETUATED BY THE SUPER-RICH OF CORPORATE AMERICA THAT THE
WORKING CLASS IS NO LONGER A VIABLE FORCE IN THE US. IT
ATTEMPTS TO ANSWER AGRUEMENTS RANGING FROM THOSE OF MARCUSE
AND OTHERS THAT THE WORKING CLASS HAS BEEN ABSORBED INTO THE
MIDDLE CLASS AND NOW HAVE A STAKE IN IMPERIAL EXPLOITATION,
TO ARGUMENTS THAT STATE THAT THE WORKING CLASS HAS

DIMINISHED TO THE POINT THAT IT IS RELATIVELY POWERLESS TO
INITIATE OR SUPPORT SOCIAL CHANGE. IT CONCLUDES THAT
ALTHOUGH THE WORKING CLASS REMAINS A SOLID FOUNDATION FOR
ANY MOVE TOWARDS SOCIALISM, TO CONTINUE THE MOMENTUM WILL
REQUIRE SKILL, FLEXIBILITY, AND COMPROMISE.

09457 WEBBER, C.
PLUCKING THE GOOSE
WILSON QUARTERLY, XIII(2) (SPR 89), 75-85.
THROUGHOUT HISTORY, DEBATES OVER TAXES HAVE TRIGGERED
LARGER CONTROVERSIES NOT ONLY OVER THE SIZE OF GOVERNMENT
BUT ALSO OVER ITS PURPOSES. IN THIS ARTICLE, THE AUTHOR
REVIEWS HIGHLIGHTS OF THE HISTORY OF TAXATION. SHE NOTES
THAT NEW TAXES IMPOSED BETWEEN THE 13TH AND 18TH CENTURIES
HELPED EUROPEAN MONARCHS FORGE THE MODERN NATION AND WAGE
WARS. TODAY, AMERICAN AND WESTERN EUROPEAN TAXES FINANCE
WELFARE STATES.

09458 WEBBER, D.
DIMENSIONS OF FEDERALISM IN US SENATE VOTING 1981-1982
PUBLIUS: THE JOURNAL OF FEDERALISM, 19(1) (WIN 89),
185-192.
THE CONCEPT OF FEDERALISM IS IMPORTANT IN POLITICAL
SCIENCE; YET IT HAS PROVEN DIFFICULT TO CLARIFY AND TO USE
IN EMPIRICAL ANALYSES OF AMERICAN POLITICAL INSTITUTIONS.
THIS ANALYSIS DEMONSTRATES THAT THE CONGRESSIONAL FEDERALISM
SCORES REPORTED IN PUBLIUS ARE NOT UNIDIMENSIONAL AND THAT A
BETTER MEASURE OF FEDERALISM CAN RESULT IN IMPROVED
EXPLANATORY POWER OF EMPIRICAL ANALYSIS OF THE DETERMINANTS
OF CONGRESSIONAL ATTITUDES TOWARD FEDERALISM. A PROCEDURE
FOR CONSTRUCTING A BETTER MEASURE OF FEDERALISM IS SUGGESTED.

09459 WEBER, E.
ACTING WITH VIGOR AND PURPOSE
INFORMATION BULLETIN, 27 (JAN 89), 9-10.
THE AUTHOR, WHO IS DEPUTY CHAIR OF THE GERMAN COMMUNIST
PARTY, SURVEYS THREE INITIATIVES LAUNCHED RECENTLY BY
VARIOUS CONTINGENTS WITHIN THE PEACE MOVEMENT.

09460 WEBER, P.J.
STRICT NEUTRALITY: THE NEXT STEP IN FIRST AMENDMENT
INTERPRETATION
JOURNAL OF POLITICAL SCIENCE, 16(1-2) (1988), 70-78.
THE AUTHOR TRACES THE EVOLUTION OF THE STRICT NEUTRALITY
CONCEPT AS APPLIED TO THE INTERPRETATION OF THE FIRST
AMENDMENT'S RELIGION CLAUSES. HE CONSIDERS BOTH THE ASSETS
AND LIABILITIES OF THIS INTERPRETATION. HE ARGUES THAT
STRICT NEUTRALITY COULD BE THE NEXT STAGE IN RESOLVING FIRST
AMENDMENT ISSUES CONCERNING RELIGION.

09461 WEBER, S.
COOPERATION AND DISCORD IN SECURITY RELATIONSHIPS: TOWARD
A THEORY OF U.S.-SOVIET ARMS CONTROL
DISSERTATION ABSTRACTS INTERNATIONAL, 50(2) (AUG 89),
539-A.
USING THE METHOD OF STRUCTURED, FOCUSED COMPARISON OF
CASE STUDIES, THE AUTHOR BUILDS UPON A STRUCTURAL LEVEL
ANALYSIS OF NECESSARY CONDITIONS TO IDENTIFY CONDITIONS
SUFFICIENT FOR COOPERATION IN THE U.S.-SOVIET ARMS CONTROL
RELATIONSHIP. HE STUDIES THREE CASES: ANTIBALLISTIC MISSILE
SYSTEMS, MULTIPLE INDEPENDENTLY TARGETABLE RE-ENTRY VEHICLES,
AND ANTI-SATELLITE WEAPONS. HE ARGUES THAT, ALTHOUGH EACH
CASE FULFILLS THE CONDITIONS FOR COOPERATION IDENTIFIED BY
DEDUCTIVE THEORY, THE OUTCOMES OF THE THREE CASES ARE
FUNDAMENTALLY DIFFERENT IN CHARACTER AND IN LONG-TERM
IMPLICATIONS FOR U.S.-SOVIET RELATIONS.

09462 WEBSTER, G.R.
PARTISANSHIP IN AMERICAN PRESIDENTIAL, SENATORIAL AND
GUBERNATORIAL ELECTIONS IN TEN WESTERN STATES
POLITICAL GEOGRAPHY QUARTERLY, 8(2) (APR 89), 161-180.
THERE IS A SIZEABLE BODY OF RECENT LITERATURE WHICH
CONCLUDES THAT THE STRENGTH OF ELECTORAL PARTISANSHIP IN THE
UNITED STATES HAS WANED IN THE POST WORLD WAR II PERIOD.
ALTHOUGH THERE IS AMPLE EVIDENCE THAT PARTISAN DEALIGNMENT
HAS OCCURRED AT THE NATIONAL LEVEL, THERE IS LITTLE BASIS ON
WHICH TO CONFIRM THAT THE IMPACTS OF DEALIGNMENT ARE
SPATIALLY UNIFORM AND WELL ADVANCED IN ALL AREAS OF THE
COUNTRY. THE PURPOSE OF THIS PAPER IS TO EXAMINE THE
DEALIGNMENT HYPOTHESIS IN THE CONTEXT OF A SINGLE ELECTORAL
REGION. COUNTY-LEVEL VOTING RETURNS FOR PRESIDENTIAL,
SENATORIAL AND GUBERNATORIAL ELECTIONS IN TEN WESTERN STATES
ARE EXAMINED USING PRINCIPAL COMPONENTS AND CORRELATION
ANALYSES TO GAUGE THE IMPACT OF DEALIGNMENT ON THIS REGION.
THE RESULTS OF THIS RESEARCH CONTRADICT MUCH OF THE
LITERATURE ON PARTISAN DEALIGNMENT. THIS STUDY FOUND NO
EVIDENCE OF PARTISAN DEALIGNMENT IN PRESIDENTIAL ELECTIONS
AND ONLY LIMITED TENTATIVE SUPPORT FOR THE INFLUENCE OF
DEALIGNMENT ON THE REGION'S VOTING CHOICES IN GUBERNATORIAL
AND SENATORIAL ELECTIONS.

09463 WEBSTER, P.
VIEW FROM LONDON
NATO'S SIXTEEN NATIONS, 34(4) (AUG 89), 13.

THE BRITISH LABOR PARTY'S SUCCESS IN THE EUROPEAN
ELECTIONS AND ITS SURGE IN THE OPINION POLLS HAVE LED TO A
NEW OPTIMISM AMONG ITS LEADERS. THE SUCCESSFUL LAUNCH OF A
NEW PACKAGE OF POLICIES HAS BEEN THE SPUR FOR LABOR'S
ADVANCE. FOLLOWING A TWO-YEAR REVIEW OF THE PLATFORM ON
WHICH THEY HAD FOUGHT AND LOST SEVERAL ELECTIONS, THE PARTY
THREW OFF SOME OF ITS POLICY MILLSTONES--MOST NOTABLY ITS
COMMITMENT TO UNILATERAL NUCLEAR DISARMAMENT.

09464 WEED, C.P.
AN EXAMINATION OF MINORITY PARTY DYNAMICS DURING PERIODS
OF POLITICAL REALIGNMENT: THE CASE OF THE REPUBLIC PARTY,
1932-38
DISSERTATION ABSTRACTS INTERNATIONAL, 49(3) (SEP 88),
611-A.
THE CHANGES AND ADJUSTMENTS OF THE REPUBLICAN PARTY
DURING THE PERIOD 1932-1938 ARE STUDIED. THE PARTY WENT
THROUGH STAGES OF PARALYSIS AND HESITANCY DURING THE FIRST
TWO YEARS OF THE NEW DEAL, FOLLOWED BY A PERIOD OF
ADJUSTMENT AND EVENTUALLY A MILD RESTORATION.

09465 WEED, C.P.
WHAT HAPPENED TO THE REPUBLICANS IN THE 1930S: MINORITY
PARTY DYNAMICS DURING POLITICAL REALIGNMENT
POLITY, 22(1) (FAL 89), 5-24.
LOSERS HAVE NOT DRAWN MUCH ATTENTION IN POLITICAL
SCIENCE; THE FOCUS IS ALMOST ENTIRELY ON THE WINNERS. THIS
IS CERTAINLY TRUE IN THE STUDY OF PARTISAN REALIGNMENT,
WHERE ANALYSIS HAS CENTERED MAINLY ON EXPLAINING THE
EMERGENCE OF A NEW MAJORITY PARTY. BUT TO WHAT EXTENT DO THE
MACHINATIONS OF THE FALLEN MAJORITY PARTY CONTRIBUTE TO
SECURING THE POLITICAL STATUS OF THE NEW MAJORITY? THIS
ARTICLE EXAMINES THAT QUESTION BY EXPLORING WHAT HAPPENED TO
THE REPUBLICANS IN THE 1930S. THE AUTHOR ARGUES THAT THE GOP
RESPONSE TO THE NEW DEAL LIES IN THE PERCEPTIONS (OR
MISPERCEPTIONS) OF REPUBLICAN ELITES AND THE EFFECTS THAT
RAPID POLICY TRANSFORMATION CAN HAVE ON INTEREST GROUPS
WITHIN PARTY COALITIONS.

09466 WEED, S. L.
LOW-INTENSITY CONFLICT: AN AMERICAN DILEMMA
DISSERTATION ABSTRACTS INTERNATIONAL, 49(8) (FEB 89),
2384-A.
THIS STUDY BEGINS WITH AN OVERVIEW OF THE AMERICAN
EXPERIENCE WITH LOW INTENSITY CONFLICT. THEN IT ADDRESSES
THE DEFITIONAL PROBLEM, LACK OF UNDERSTANDING REGARDING WHAT
THIS TYPE OF WARFARE ENTAILS, MILITARY INTER-SERVICE RIVALRY,
COMMAND AND CONTROL PROBLEMS, AND THE VIETNAM SYNDROME.

09467 WEEDE, E.
DEMOCRACY AND INCOME RECONSIDERED
AMERICAN SOCIOLOGICAL REVIEW, 54(5) (OCT 89), 865-868.
WHILE CROSS-NATIONAL STUDIES ON THE RELATIONSHIP BETWEEN
THE LEVEL OF DEMOCRACY AND INCOME INEQUALITY HAVE PRODUCED
CONTRADICTORY RESULTS, IT HAS BEEN RECENTLY ARGUED THAT
THERE IS A THEORETICALLY AND STATISTICALLY SIGNIFICANT
RELATIONSHIP BETWEEN THE AGE OF DEMOCRACY AND INCOME
REDISTRIBUTION. IN THIS ESSAY, THE AUTHOR DEMONSTRATES THAT
THIS FINDING IS NOT SUSTAINABLE WHEN A SINGLE CASE IS ADDED
TO SOME EQUATIONS OR WHEN LITERACY RATES ARE CONTROLLED FOR.

09468 WEEKLY, T.M.
PROLIFERATION OF CHEMICAL WARFARE: CHALLENGE TO
TRADITIONAL RESTRAINTS
PARAMETERS, XIX(4) (DEC 89), 51-66.
THIS ARTICLE SURVEYS THE CIRCUMSTANCES SURROUNDING THE
INITIATION OF CHEMICAL WARFARE IN WORLD WAR I AND THE
SUBSEQUENT INTERNATIONAL RESPONSE. IT THEN VIEWS THE
RESTRAINTS THAT WORKED SUCCESSFULLY AGAINST CHEMICAL WARFARE
DURING WORLD WAR II IN RELATION TO THE CURRENT WORLD
SITUATION TO DETERMINE HOW AND WHY THESE RESTRAINTS HAVE
BEEN CHALLENGED IN RECENT YEARS.

09469 WEEKS, J.; ZIMBALIST, A.
THE FAILURE OF INTERVENTION IN PANAMA: HUMILIATION IN THE
BACKYARD
THIRD WORLD QUARTERLY, 11(1) (JAN 89), 1-27.
THE AUTHORS ANALYZE THE FAILURE OF U.S. FOREIGN POLICY
IN PANAMA UNDER GENERAL MANUEL NORIEGA. THEY BEGIN BY
PROVIDING A BRIEF HISTORICAL BACKGROUND INTENDED TO OUTLINE
THE DEVELOPMENT OF BILATERAL RELATIONS BETWEEN THE USA AND
PANAMA, WITH EMPHASIS ON U.S. STRATEGIC AND ECONOMIC
INTERESTS. THEN THEY IDENTIFY THE SALIENT CHARACTERISTICS OF
PANAMA'S INTERNAL POLITICS. THEY CONSIDER A MOST PERPLEXING
ASPECT OF THE NORIEGA AFFAIR: WHY DID THE REAGAN
ADMINISTRATION TURN AGAINST A LEADER WHO, BY ALL ACCOUNTS,
HAD SERVED THE U.S. GOVERNMENT WELL FOR MORE THAN FIFTEEN
YEARS. FINALLY, THEY ANALYZE REAGAN'S CAMPAIGN TO OUST
NORIEGA, EXPLAIN WHY IT FAILED, AND DRAW CONCLUSIONS.

09470 WEHLING, H.G,
THE BUNDESRAT
PUBLIUS: THE JOURNAL OF FEDERALISM, 19(4) (FAL 89), 53-64.
THE ARTICLE DISCUSSES IN DETAIL THE PARTICIPATION OF THE

BUNDESRAT IN THE NATIONAL LEGISLATIVE PROCESS, IT
DISTINGUISHES BETWEEN THE ABSOLUTE VETO AND THE SUSPENSIVE
VETO OF THE BUNDESRAT OVER LAWS PASSED BY THE POPULARLY
ELECTED PARLIAMENT, THE BUNDESTAG. IT NOTES THAT THE
BUNDESRAT WAS NOT DESIGNED AS A PARTISAN INSTITUTION; BUT
ADMITS THAT PARTISAN POLITICS CAN AND DO ENTER THE
BUNDESRAT'S DECISIONMAKING. IT CONCLUDES THAT LAND INTERESTS
AND THE VIEWS OF THAT LAND BUREAUCRACY ARE GENERALLY OF
GREATER IMPORTANCE THAN PARTISAN CONSIDERATIONS.

09471 WEI, H.; JIANGUO, Y.
CAMPUSES AFTER DISTURBANCE
BEIJING REVIEW, 32(46) (NOV 89), 23-26.
BEIJING UNIVERSITY, WHERE THE STUDENT MOVEMENT IN
BEIJING BEGAN, RESUMED CLASSES IN OCTOBER 1989. BEFORE THE
DEMONSTRATIONS IN MAY AND JUNE, BIG POSTERS ATTACKING THE
COMMUNIST PARTY AND THE GOVERNMENT WERE HUNG AROUND CAMPUS
AND PEOPLE FREQUENTLY GAVE AGITATING SPEECHES. FOLLOWING THE
RESUMPTION OF CLASSES, MOST STUDENTS RETURNED QUIETLY TO
THEIR STUDIES. MANY STUDENTS ARE MORE MATURE, DUE TO THE
POLITICAL DISORDER, AND UNDERSTAND THAT THEY DIDN'T KNOW HOW
TO BEST PROMOTE DEMOCRACY, EVEN THOUGH THAT WAS THEIR GOAL.

09472 WEI, J.
FRUIT OF THE OPEN POLICY
BEIJING REVIEW, 32(34) (AUG 89), 11-13.
SHENZHEN IN GUANGDONG PROVINCE WAS THE FIRST SPECIAL
ECONOMIC ZONE ESTABLISHED IN CHINA. IT HAS BEEN A TESTING
GROUND FOR CHINA'S ECONOMIC REFORM AND ITS POLICY OF OPENING
TO THE OUTSIDE WORLD SINCE THE EARLY 1980'S. THIS ARTICLE
SURVEYS THE GROWTH IN SHENZHEN'S INDUSTRY AND FOREIGN
INVESTMENT.

09473 WEI, J.
OVERSTRETCHED: TAIWAN'S "ELASTIC DIPLOMACY"
BEIJING REVIEW, 32(14) (APR 89), 7.
IN RECENT MONTHS, THE TAIWANESE AUTHORITIES HAVE
ENTHUSIASTICALLY PROMOTED A POLICY THAT THEY CALL "ELASTIC
DIPLOMACY." FOLLOWING THE ESTABLISHMENT OF DIPLOMATIC
RELATIONS BETWEEN THE UNITED STATES AND THE PEOPLE'S
REPUBLIC OF CHINA, THE TAIWANESE INTRODUCED THE CONCEPT OF
"SUBSTANTIAL DIPLOMACY," INVOLVING THE IDEA OF DEVELOPING
SUBSTANTIAL RELATIONS WITH COUNTRIES WITHOUT DIPLOMATIC
RELATIONS. THE FAILURE OF SUBSTANTIAL DIPLOMACY LED TO A NEW
CALL FOR ELASTIC DIPLOMACY. UNDER THIS POLICY, THE TAIWANESE
GOVERNMENT NO LONGER SUPPORTS THE PRINCIPLE OF ONE CHINA BUT
IS PREPARED TO TOLERATE DUAL RECOGNITION FROM COUNTRIES THAT
WISH TO ESTABLISH DIPLOMATIC RELATIONS WITH BOTH THE ISLAND
AND THE MAINLAND.

09474 WEI, S.
WHAT HAS HAPPENED IN BEIJING?
BEIJING REVIEW, 32(26) (JUN 89), 15-19.
THE AUTHOR OFFERS AN ACCOUNT OF THE EVENTS IN BEIJING
DURING THE FIRST WEEK IN JUNE 1989 AND EXPLAINS THE
NECESSITY FOR USING MARTIAL LAW AND FORCE TO QUELL THE
COUNTER-REVOLUTIONARY REVOLT.

09475 WEI, S.
WHY IMPOSE MARTIAL LAW IN BEIJING?
BEIJING REVIEW, 32(26) (JUN 89), 20-25.
THE AUTHOR EXPLAINS THE NECESSITY OF USING THE PEOPLE'S
LIBERATION ARMY TO END THE POLITICAL TURMOIL IN BEIJING IN
LATE MAY AND EARLY JUNE 1989.

09476 WEI, W.
VIEWS FROM TAIWAN: RECOMMENDATIONS FOR THE FUTURE
ASIAN AFFAIRS, AN AMERICAN REVIEW, 16(2) (SUM 89), 93-97.
TAIWAN'S INITIAL REACTION TO THE TIANANMEN SQUARE
TRADGEDY IN CHINA WAS ONE OF TEMENDOUS ANGER. HOW COULD THE
PEOPLE'S LOBERATION ARMY ATTACK UNARMED CIVILIANS? TAIWAN'S
GOVERNMENT WERE SHOCKED AT THE EVENTS IN BEIJING. THEY HAVE
MADE MANY OBSERVATIONS AND RECOMMENDATIONS. THE LEADERS OF
MAINLAND CHINA MUST RECOGNIZE THE PRESENT ECONOMIC REALITY
AND EMPHASIZE CARRYING OUT SUCH POLICIES AS THE DEVELOPMENT
OF AGRICULTURE TO BE THE FOUNDATION FOR ECONOMIC DEVELOPMENT;
THE INDUSTRIALIZATION UP THE NATION TO BUILD UP ITS STRENGH;
AND THE ESTABLISHMENT OF BUSINESSES TO BUILD THE NATION'S
WEALTH. HOWEVER THE TIANAMEN SQUARE INCIDENT HAS SERIOUSLY
DAMAGED ITS IMAGE IN THE INTERNATIONAL COMMUNITY, AND IT
WILL NOT BE EASY FOR CHINA TO OVERCOME THIS PROBLEM AND
IMPROVE ITS IMAGE.

09477 WEICHENG, G.
MEXICO BENEFITS FROM DEBT ACCORD
BEIJING REVIEW, 32(36) (SEP 89), 17-18.
IN JULY 1989, THE MEXICAN GOVERNMENT AND ITS CREDITOR
BANKS AGREED ON THREE OPTIONS FOR DEALING WITH MEXICO'S
FOREIGN BANK DEBT, INCLUDING A SUBSTANTIAL DISCOUNT ON
PRINCIPAL AND A REDUCTION OF INTEREST RATES. THE AGREEMENT
MARKED THE FIRST SIGNIFICANT CONCESSION THAT THE CREDITOR
BANKS HAVE MADE SINCE THE START OF THE WORLDWIDE DEBT CRISIS.
MEXICAN PRESIDENT CARLOS SALINAS SAID THAT THE ACCORD HAS
CREATED CONDITIONS FOR MEXICO'S ECONOMIC DEVELOPMENT IN THE

NEXT FIVE YEARS. BUT IT DOES NOT MEAN THAT A GENERAL
SOLUTION HAS BEEN FOUND FOR THE COUNTRY'S ECONOMIC WOES.

09478 WEIDENBAUM, M.
FACING REALITY IN THE GEORGE BUSH ERA
SOCIETY, 26(3) (MAR 89), 25-28.
THE ARTICLE EXPLORES THE ECONOMIC LEGACY LEFT BY RONALD
REAGAN AND THE CHALLENGES THAT THE BUSH ADMINSTRATION WILL
FACE IN THE COMING YEARS. THE CHIEF CHALLENGE WILL BE THE
BUDGET DEFICIT AND NATIONAL DEBT, BUT IT IS MERELY A
REFLECTION OF THE UNDERLYING "SPEND NOW, PAY LATER" ATTITUDE
THAT SEEMS TO PERVADE IN CINGRESS AND TO SOME EXTENT
THROUGHOUT THE AMERICAN PEOPLE. THE ARTICLE PREDICTS A NEW
POLICY CLIMATE WHICH WILL BE MUCH LESS HOSPITABLE TO
BUSINESS THAN THE CLIMATE THAT EXISTED UNDER THE REAGAN
ADMINISTRATION. IT ALSO EXPLORES TRENDS IN EDUCATION,
FOREIGN INVESTMENT, ENVIRONMENTAL PROTECTION, AND CORPORATE
MERGERS.

09479 WEIDENBAUM, M.
PROTECTING THE ENVIRONMENT
SOCIETY, 27(1) (NOV 89), 49-56.
THE ARTICLE EXAMINES THE THORNY PROBLEM OF ENVIRONMENTAL
PROTECTION IN THE US. ALTHOUGH A HUGE MAJORITY OF US
CITIZENS SUPPORT ADDITIONAL EFFORTS TO CLEAN UP THE
ENVIRONMENT, MOST ARE SUBJECT TO THE "NOT IN MY BACKYARD"
SYNDROME AS WELL AS A GENERAL RELUCTANCE TO PROVIDE
ADDITIONAL FUNDING FOR CLEAN-UP MEASURES. IN ADDITION, THE
HUGE, LUMBERING, BUREAUCRACY FACES NEARLY INSURMOUNTABLE
CHALLENGES IN OVERCOMING RED TAPE AND LITIGATION. THE
ARTICLE ADVOCATES A "POLLUTER PAYS" SYSTEM SIMILAR TO ONES
FOUND IN EUROPE TO FUND ADDITIONAL CLEAN-UP EFFORTS.

09480 WEIDENBAUM, M.
WHY DEFENSE SPENDING DOESN'T MATTER
NATIONAL INTEREST, 16 (SUM 89), 91-96.
THE U.S. MILITARY BUDGET COULD VARY OVER A CONSIDERABLE
RANGE WITHOUT RAISING THE SPECTER OF ECONOMIC HARM OR
NATIONAL DECLINE. THIS IS NOT A PLEA FOR ADOPTING THE HIGH
END OF THAT RANGE, OR FOR OTHERWISE ASSAYING THE DESIRABLE
SIZE OF THE MILITARY BUDGET. BUT THE AMOUNT OF RESOURCES
THAT THE UNITED STATES DEVOTES TO DEFENSE PROGRAMS SHOULD BE
DETERMINED PRIMARILY ON NON-ECONOMIC, AND ESSENTIALLY
POLITICAL--THAT IS, NATIONAL SECURITY-GROUNDS, WITH LITTLE
FEAR OF UNDERMINING THIS NATION'S POSITION IN THE WORLD.

09481 WEIDIG, R.
NEW FEATURES IN THE SOCIAL STRUCTURE
WORLD MARXIST REVIEW, 32(5) (MAY 89), 17-20.
WE CANNOT VIEW THE PERFECTION OF THE SOCIAL STRUCTURE
MERELY AS A MERE ECONOMIC FACTOR OR AN ELEMENT IN THE LABOUR
PROCESS. WE CAN'T ASSESS ITS LEVEL ONLY BY THE EFFECTIVENESS
OF MATERIAL AND SPIRITUAL PRODUCTION. HERE WE MUST KEEP A
CONSTANT EYE ON POLITICAL ASPECTS, AND WITH GOOD REASON--THE
STABILITY OF SOCIALISM AS A WHOLE LARGELY DEPENDS ON THE
STABILITY OF SOCIAL, AND PARTICULARLY CLASS STRUCTURE.
WITHOUT DETRACTING FROM THE SIGNIFICANCE OF OTHER SOCIAL
FACTORS, IT IS ESSENTIALLY A QUESTION OF DEVELOPING AND
FOSTERING STRUCTURES WHICH, FIRSTLY, CORRESPOND TO THE
SOCIAL GOALS, VALUES AND POSSIBILITIES OF SOCIALISM, AND,
SECONDLY, MEET THE REQUIREMENTS OF ECONOMIC GROWTH AND THE
AFFIRMATION OF A NEW QUALITY OF THE PRODUCTIVE FORCES. THE
EXPERIENCE OF THE POLICY OF ALLIANCES, AND OF THE UNITY OF
SED ECONOMIC AND SOCIAL POLICIES, HAVE PUT THESE TWO CLOSELY
INTERRELATED CRITERIA ON THE AGENDA IN OUR REPUBLIC. THEY
BOTH AIM AT ACTIVATING THE WORKING CLASSES AND SOCIAL STRATA
AS THE SUBJECT OF THE IMPROVEMENT OF PRODUCTIVE FORCES.

09482 WEIFEN, N.
NEW TREND IN AMERICAN PROTECTIONISM
BEIJING REVIEW, 32(35) (AUG 89), 32-33.
OVER THE PAST TEN YEARS, DUE TO THE INCREASE IN THE
UNITED STATES' TRADE DEFICIT, PROTECTIONISM HAS GROWN WHILE
MANAGED TRADE AND THE ADVOCACY OF FAIR TRADE HAVE REPLACED
FREE TRADE. BILATERAL AND REGIONAL TRADE ARE ALSO PLAYING A
MORE IMPORTANT ROLE IN INTERNATIONAL TRANSACTIONS. THE
AMERICAN GENERAL TRADE ACT PASSED IN 1988 SHOWS STRONG
PROTECTIONIST TENDENCIES.

09483 WEIGE, Z.
FEDERAL GERMANY'S POLICY TOWARDS THE EAST
BEIJING REVIEW, 32(29) (JUL 89), 14-18.
WITH THE WORLD SITUATION CHANGING, THE FEDERAL REPUBLIC
OF GERMANY IS USING THIS "HISTORICAL OPPORTUNITY" TO
STRENGTHEN ITS INTERNATIONAL POSITION AND ATTAIN THE
REUNIFICATION OF THE TWO GERMAN STATES. HOWEVER, WESTERN
COUNTRIES ARE ADOPTING DIFFERENT WAYS TO HALT THIS
ADJUSTMENT IN BONN'S POLICY WHILE MOSCOW IS PLANNING BOTH TO
USE AND RESTRICT ITS APPLICATION.

09484 WEIGEL, G.
CATHOLICISM AND DEMOCRACY: THE OTHER TWENTIETH-CENTURY
REVOLUTION
WASHINGTON QUARTERLY, 12(4) (FAL 89), 5-28.

THIS PAPER EXPLORES THE TRANSFORMATION OF THE CATHOLIC
CHURCH FROM A BASTION OF THE ANCIEN REGIME INTO PERHAPS THE
WORLD'S FOREMOST INSTITUTIONAL DEFENDER OF HUMAN RIGHTS. THE
SHIFT IN OFFICIAL CATHOLIC TEACHING IN THE PERIOD 1864-1965
IS ANALYZED AS WELL AS THE SECOND VATICAN COUNCIL'S
DECLARATIONS ON CHURCH AND STATE. ISSUES FOR THE FUTURE ARE
LISTED AND EXAMINED. THE CONCLUSION IS THAT THE NEW OFFICIAL
SUPPORT FOR DEMOCRACY RAISES AS MANY QUESTIONS AS IT ANSWERS
FOR POLITICAL THEORY AND ACTION.

09485 WEIGERT, K.M.
PEACE STUDIES AS EDUCATION FOR NONVIOLENT SOCIAL CHANGE
PHILADELPHIA: ANLS OF AMER ACMY OF POLITICAL AND SOC
SCIENCE, (504) (JUL 89), 37-47.
ONE OF THE GOALS OF PEACE STUDIES IS TO NOURISH A
COMMITMENT TO NONVIOLENT SOCIAL CHANGE. TO ACCOMPLISH THIS,
IT IS IMPERATIVE THAT TEACHERS EDUCATE ACCORDINGLY, BOTH IN
WHAT THEY TEACH AND IN HOW THEY TEACH. THIS ARTICLE EXPLORES
THAT IDEA BY EXAMINING THE KEY TERMS: "EDUCATION,"
"NONVIOLENCE," AND "SOCIAL CHANGE." FIRST, DEFINITIONS OF
THE WORD "EDUCATION" ARE EXAMINED, AND IT IS ARGUED THAT
PEACE STUDIES IS EDUCATION THAT IS LIBERAL AND LIBERATING.
THIS LEADS TO A DISCUSSION OF THE CONCEPT OF NONVIOLENCE,
WHICH IS PRESENTED IN TERMS OF THREE ISSUES: VIOLENCE AND
HUMAN NATURE, STRUCTURAL VIOLENCE, AND PERSONAL COMMITMENT
TO NONVIOLENCE. FINALLY, THE CONCEPT OF SOCIAL CHANGE IS
EXAMINED IN ITS RELATIONSHIP TO THE NOTION OF POWER, TO THE
IMPORTANCE OF ENVISIONING A BETTER WORLD, AND TO THE
IMPORTANCE OF GROUP ACTION. TWO MODELS OF SOCIAL CHANGE ARE
OFFERED. FINALLY, CLASSROOM EXAMPLES ARE PROVIDED THAT
ILLUSTRATE WAYS IN WHICH BOTH CONTENT AND PEDAGOGY CAN
CONTRIBUTE TO THE GOAL OF EDUCATION FOR NONVIOLENT SOCIAL
CHANGE.

09486 WEIHER, G.R.
PUBLIC POLICY AND PATTERNS OF RESIDENTIAL SEGREGATION
WESTERN POLITICAL QUARTERLY, 42(4) (DEC 89), 651-678.
IN THE POST-WORLD-WAR-TWO PERIOD, THE FEDERAL COURTS
HAVE DEVELOPED TWO PARALLEL LINES OF POLICY. ONE IS
COMPRISED OF DECISIONS WHICH STRIKE DOWN DISCRIMINATORY
MECHANISMS WITHIN JURISDICTIONS-SEGREGATED SCHOOL ATTENDANCE
ZONES, RESTRICTIVE COVENANTS. THE OTHER IS COMPRISED OF
DECISIONS WHICH RECOGNIZE RIGHTS OF LOCAL JURISDICTIONAL
AUTONOMY OVER EDUCATION AND LAND USE, THUS STRENGTHENING
MECHANISMS WHICH HAVE TENDED TO SEGREGATE RACIAL AND
SOCIOECONOMIC GROUPS ACROSS JURISDICTIONS. THIS PAPER ARGUES
THAT SUCH POLICY DEVELOPMENTS SHOULD RESULT IN A SHIFT IN
GEOGRAPHIC PATTERNS OF SEGREGATION. IT OFFERS EVIDENCE FROM
LOS ANGELES COUNTY, CALIFORNIA, AND COOK COUNTY, ILLINOIS,
THAT SUCH A SHIFT HAS TAKEN PLACE. FINALLY, THE PAPER
SUGGESTS PROCESSES WHICH LINK THE SHIFT IN POLICY WITH THE
SHIFT IN PATTERNS OF SEGREGATION.

09487 WEIL, F.D.
THE SOURCES AND STRUCTURE OF LEGITIMATION IN WESTERN
DEMOCRACIES: A CONSOLIDATED MODEL TESTED WITH TIME-SERIES
DATA IN SIX COUNTRIES SINCE WORLD WAR II
AMERICAN SOCIOLOGICAL REVIEW, 54(5) (OCT 89), 682-706.
BOTH NEW-LEFT AND NEO-CONSERVATIVE THEORISTS ARGUE THAT
POOR STATE PERFORMANCE CAN LEAD TO A LEGITIMATION CRISIS,
BUT THEY NEGLECT DISTINCTIONS AMONG DIFFERENT FORMS OF
POLITICAL SUPPORT AND OBJECTIVE CONDITIONS. THE AUTHOR
PROPOSES A THEORETICAL MODEL THAT DISTINGUISHES BETWEEN (A)
CONFIDENCE IN INSTITUTIONS AND LEGITIMATION OF DEMOCRACY AND
(B) STATE PERFORMANCE AND THE STRUCTURE OF OPPOSITION. HE
TESTS THE MODEL WITH DATA FROM SIX WESTERN COUNTRIES. THE
RESULTS SHOW THAT POOR STATE PERFORMANCE LEADS TO A DECLINE
OF CONFIDENCE BUT NOT TO A SOFTENING OF SUPPORT FOR
DEMOCRACY. PROBLEMS IN THE STRUCTURE OF OPPOSITION LEAD TO A
DECLINE OF BOTH CONFIDENCE AND SUPPORT FOR DEMOCRACY.

09488 WEIL, R.
"A COMMUNIST NAMED SALVADOR ALLENDE": THE TEACHING AND
UNTEACHING OF SOCIALISM IN U.S. HIGH SCHOOL AND MIDDLE
SCHOOL TEXTS
SOCIALISM AND DEMOCRACY, (8) (SPR 89), 89-118.
THIS IS A STUDY OF THE SOCIALIZING PROCESS IN THE
INSTITUTIONAL LIFE OF THE UNITED STATES. IT IS A PRELIMINARY
ANALYSIS FOR A LARGER STUDY ON THIS SUBJECT WHICH ZEROS IN
ON THE WAY SOCIALISM IS TAUGHT IN U.S. SCHOOLS. IT ADVOCATES
THE NEED FOR FURTHER STUDY OF WHAT IS BEING TAUGHT AND FOR
EFFORTS TO REDESIGN THE CURRICULUM TO ACHIEVE A MORE
BALANCED AND APPRECIATIVE AWARENESS OF SOCIALISM.

09489 WEIL, R.
BUREAUCRATIZATION: THE PROBLEM WITHOUT A "CLASS" NAME
SOCIALISM AND DEMOCRACY, 6 (SPR 89), 57-88.
THE ARTICLE EXAMINES THE PROCESS IN WHICH THE "POLITICAL
KNOWLEDGE" ACCUMULATED IN THE REVOLUTIONARY PROCESS ITSELF
LAYS THE BASIS FOR THE SPECIFIC CHARACTERISTICS OF THE
"SOCIALIST BUREAUCRACY." IN CONSOLIDATING THEIR OWN HOLD ON
POWER, THESE "PROFESSIONAL COMMUNISTS" CANNOT HELP BUT
REVISE THE ORIGINAL PROLETARIAN CONCEPTS ON WHICH THEIR
LEGITIMACY RESTED. IN THE PROCESS THEY ALTER THEIR RELATION

WITH THE WORKING CLASS. IN THE END, THE WORKING CLASS WILL
HAVE TO CONFRONT ALL THOSE WHO, IN ITS NAME, REALLY ASSERT
ONLY THEIR OWN CLASS INTERESTS.

09490 HEILER, R.
THE ETHICAL APPROACH TO MILITARY DOCTRINES
PEACE AND THE SCIENCES, 1 (1989), 31-38.
THIS ARTICLE DESCRIBES HOW THE GROWING REFERENCE TO
ETHICAL ISSUES, TOGETHER WITH THE INSIGHT THAT THE OUTBREAK
OF AN ALL-OUT NUCLEAR WAR WOULD MAKE VICTORY MEANINGLESS,
FINALLY, FOR, POLITICAL REASONS, LED TO THE MILITARY
DOCTRINE DECLARATION OF THE WARSAW TREATY IN SPRING 1987.
THE DOCTRINE IS PRESENTED WITH PURELY DEFENSIVE INTENTIONS
HOWEVER, THE POTENTIALS INVOLVED APPEAR TO BE INDICATIVE OF
AN OFFENSIVE CONCEPT IN CASE OF WAR.

09491 HEIMANN, G.; BROSIUS, H.B.
THE PREDICTABILITY OF INTERNATIONAL TERRORISM: A TIME-
SERIES ANALYSIS
TERRORISM, 11(6) (1988), 491-502.
THE STUDY EXAMINES THE PREDICTABILITY OF INTERNATIONAL
TERRORISM IN TERMS OF THE EXISTENCE OF TRENDS, SEASONALITY,
AND PERIODICITY OF TERRORIST EVENTS. THE DATA BASE USED WAS
THE RAND CORPORATION'S CHRONOLOGY OF INTERNATIONAL TERRORISM.
IT CONTAINS THE ATTRIBUTES OF EVERY CASE OF INTERNATIONAL
TERRORISM FROM 1968 TO 1986 (N = 5,589). THE AUTHORS APPLIED
BOX-JENKINS MODELS FOR A TIME-SERIES ANALYSIS OF THE
OCCURRENCE OF TERRORIST EVENTS AS WELL AS THEIR
VICTIMIZATION RATES. THE ANALYSIS REVEALED THAT OCCURRENCE
OF TERRORIST EVENTS IS FAR FROM BEING RANDOM: THERE IS A
CLEAR TREND AND AN ALMOST CONSTANT PERIODICITY OF ONE MONTH
THAT CAN BE BEST DESCRIBED BY A FIRST-ORDER MOVING AVERAGE
MODEL. THE FIT OF THIS MODEL WAS TESTED BOTH BY STATISTICAL
DIAGNOSTICS AND THE ACCURACY OF PREDICTIONS BASED ON THIS
MODEL COMPARED TO ACTUAL OCCURRENCE. HOWEVER, THE SERIES OF
VICTIMIZATION RATES DID NOT REVEAL ANY PREDICTABILITY ASIDE
FROM THE OVERALL TREND OF AN INCREASING LEVEL OF
VICTIMIZATION. THE FINDINGS OF THE STUDY ARE DISCUSSED BY
TWO APPROACHES: THE CONTAGIOUSNESS OF TERRORISM AND THE
CONCEPT OF MEDIA-ORIENTED TERRORISM. THESE TWO CONCEPTS,
SEPARATELY OR COMBINED, MAY EXPLAIN SOME OF THE PATTERNS
REVEALED IN THE OCCURRENCE OF TERRORIST EVENTS. HOWEVER,
THEY BOTH HIGHLIGHT THE PART PLAYED BY THE MASS MEDIA,
EITHER AS A TARGET FOR PUBLICITYSEEKING TERRORISTS OR AS AN
INFLUENTIAL FACTOR IN THE PROCESS OF CONTAGION.

09492 WEINBAUM, M.
THE POLITICS OF AFGHAN RESETTLEMENT AND REHABILITATION
ASIAN SURVEY, XXIX(3) (MAR 89), 287-307.
THE ESSAY IS CONCERNED WITH THE POLITICAL ECONOMY OF
AFGHAN RESETTLEMENT AND REHABILITATION, IN PARTICULAR AS IT
AFFECTS THE LARGEST NUMBER OF REFUGEES--THE MORE THAN THREE
MILLION THAT FLED TO PAKISTAN. IT ANALYZES THE VARIOUS
FACTORS WHICH WILL CONTRIBUTE TO THE FUTURE STATUS OF THE
REFUGEES AND WILL DETERMINE THE PRINCIPLE PARAMETERS FOR
INTERNATIONAL AND BILATERAL ASSISTANCE. IT ALSO EXAMINES THE
CHALLENGES THAT AFGHANISTAN FACES AS IT ATTEMPTS TO BALANCE
ITS DEPENDENCIES AND AVOID HEAVY POLITICAL INDEBTEDNESS. A
FURTHER SECTION OF ANALYSIS FOCUSES ON THE EFFECT THAT
ASSISTANCE FOR RESETTLEMENT AND REHABILITATION WILL HAVE ON
DETERMINING THE POWER STRUCTURES IN AFGHANISTAN.

09493 WEINBERG, G.L.
THE NAZI-SOVIET PACTS: A HALF-CENTURY LATER
FOREIGN AFFAIRS, 68(4) (FAL 89), 175-189.
THE AUTHOR REVIEWS THE TERMS OF THE NAZI-SOVIET NON-
AGRESSION PACTS OF AUGUST AND SEPTEMBER 1939 AND THEIR
IMPACT ON WORLD AFFAIRS.

09494 WEINGAST, B.R.
FLOOR BEHAVIOR IN THE U.S. CONGRESS: COMMITTEE POWER UNDER
THE OPEN RULE
AMERICAN POLITICAL SCIENCE REVIEW, 83(3) (SEP 89), 795-816.
THE OPEN RULE IN THE HOUSE IS A COMPLEX SET OF
RESTRICTIONS, LIMITING, FOR EXAMPLE, THE NUMBER OF MOTIONS
AND THE ORDER OF RECOGNITION. BY INCORPORATING CONSTRAINTS
BASED ON THE ACTUAL SET OF RULES INTO A MODEL, THE AUTHOR
SHOWS THAT LEGISLATIVE OUTCOMES APPEAR MORE PREDICTABLE THAN
WAS PREVIOUSLY THOUGHT. THESE RULES NEARLY ALWAYS ALLOW THE
PROPONENTS OF LEGISLATION TO RESPOND TO AN OPPONENT'S
AMENDMENT, MITIGATING THE POTENTIAL DAMAGE OF THE LATTER. AN
ADVANTAGE OF APPROACH IS THAT IT PROVIDES A NEW
INTERPRETATION OF THE CHANGES IN FLOOR ACTIVITY OBSERVED IN
THE POSTREFORM PERIOD.

09495 WEINGROD, D.
THE POLITICS OF CORPORATE TAX REDUCTIONS: A HISTORY OF THE
WISCONSIN MANUFACTURER'S MACHINERY AND EQUIPMENT EXEMPTION
DISSERTATION ABSTRACTS INTERNATIONAL, 49(8) (FEB 89),
2421-A.
THREE MARXIAN THEORIES (INSTRUMENTATION, STRUCTURALISM,
AND POLITICAL/STRUCTURALISM) ARE USED IN THIS CASE STUDY OF
HOW BUSINESS INFLUENCE OPERATES IN POLICY ARENAS. BY
FOCUSING ON THE INITIATION, PASSAGE, AND AFTERMATH OF

WISCONSIN'S MANUFACTURER'S MACHINERY AND EQUIPMENT EXEMPTION,
THE AUTHOR ANALYZES THE RELATIONSHIP BETWEEN BUSINESS AND
THE STATE.

09496 HEINROD, H.B.
SOVIET "NEW THINKING" AND U.S. FOREIGN POLICY
WORLD AFFAIRS, 151(2) (FAL 88), 59-65.
THERE ARE SIGNS OF A RETHINKING OF IDEOLOGY IN THE USSR.
PERHAPS WE ARE ON THE VERGE OF CHANGES OF TRULY HISTORICAL
SIGNIFICANCE. BUT FOR U.S. POLICY TO CHANGE SIGNIFICANTLY,
THERE MUST BE NEW SOVIET BEHAVIOR AS WELL AS NEW THINKING.
THE CAUTIONARY FACTORS DISCUSSED IN THIS ARTICLE PROVIDE
MORE THAN REASONABLE GROUNDS FOR CAUTION, BUT THEY DO NOT
CALL FOR RIGIDITY. U.S. POLICY MUST BE IMAGINATIVE AND
FLEXIBLE, AND IT MUST BE READY TO SEIZE ANY OPPORTUNITIES
WHICH PRESENT THEMSELVES TO ENCOURAGE GENUINE AND LONG-
LASTING CHANGE IN ITS U.S.-SOVIET RELATIONSHIP. WHILE THE
PRINCIPAL DETERMINANTS OF SOVIET DEVELOPMENTS ARE WITHIN THE
USSR, THE UNITED STATES AND OTHER NATIONS CAN HAVE AN
IMPORTANT INFLUENCE AT THE MARGINS, THE UNITED STATES AND
ITS FRIENDS SHOULD WORK FOR A FUTURE IN WHICH THIRD WORLD
NATIONS CAN DETERMINE THEIR OWN DESTINY AND IN WHICH THE U.S.
-SOVIET RIVALRY IS PLAYED OUT THROUGH PEACEFUL POLITICAL,
ECONOMIC, AND CULTURAL COMPETITION.

09497 WEINSTEIN-MOUSLI, T.
STRATEGIES OF PROTEST: THE CASE OF THE PEACE MOVEMENT IN
ISRAEL: 1978-1985
DISSERTATION ABSTRACTS INTERNATIONAL, 50(1) (JUL 89),
249-A.
THE RESOURCE MOBILIZATION THEORY CONTENDS THAT EFFECTIVE
SOCIAL MOVEMENT ORGANIZATIONS RECRUIT THROUGH PRE-EXISTING
GROUPS AND, AS A RESULT OF THEIR WEAK COMMITMENTS AND LARGE
CONSTITUENCIES, ENGAGE IN LARGE-SCALE, SHORT-TERM PROTEST.
THIS THESIS SUGGESTS THAT, IN ADDITION TO THE STANDARD
PATTERN, ORGANIZATIONS CAN HAVE EITHER AN "EPISODIC" OR A
"MARGINAL" PATTERN. TO STUDY THESE ORGANIZATIONAL PATTERNS,
THIS DISSERTATION EXAMINES THE RECUIRTMENT PRACTICES,
COLLECTIVE ACTION, AND POLITICAL IMPACT OF PEACE NOW,
PARENTS AGAINST SILENCE, AND EAST TO PEACE-THREE
ORGANIZATIONS WITHIN A BROADER PEACE MOVEMENT THAT HAS
EVOLVED IN ISRAEL DURING THE LAST DECADE.

09498 WEIR, A.
ALGERIA: HUMAN RIGHTS RIVALRY
MIDDLE EAST INTERNATIONAL, 353 (JUN 89), 13.
ALTHOUGH ALGERIA HAS PUT MUCH OF ITS REPRESSIVE PAST
BEHIND IT, THE HUMAN RIGHTS ORGANISATIONS WILL STILL HAVE
MUCH TO DO. NEWS RECENTLY EMERGED ABOUT THE ALLEGED BEATING-
UP BY SECURITY FORCES OF A NUMBER OF WORKERS ON HUNGER
STRIKE AT A PUBLICLY OWNED FACTORY, AND FEARS HAVE BEEN
EXPRESSED ABOUT A POSSIBLE RETURN TO THE BRUTAL METHODS USED
DURING OCTOBER. TWO HUMAN RIGHTS ORGANIZATIONS VIE FOR
SANCTION AS THE OFFICIAL WATCHDOG FOR HUMAN RIGHTS
VIOLATIONS IN THAT COUNTRY.

09499 WEIR, F.
THE SOVIET REVOLUTION SHAKING THE WORLD AGAIN
COMMUNIST VIEWPOINT, 20(4) (WIN 88), 16-20.
THIS ARTICLE DISCUSSES THE PROCESS OF PERESTROIKA NOW
UNDER WAY IN THE SOVIET UNION, IT EXAMINES THE ATTEMPT TO RE-
FOCUS SOCIALIST VISION TO RECONSTRUCT SOCIETY IN A NEW MODEL
WHICH IS NOT A CAPITALIST PROJECT. IT WARNS OF THE DANGERS
AND CONCERN IN CRISIS.

09500 WEIR, M. (ED.); ORLOFF, A. S. (ED.); SKOCPOL, T. (ED.)
THE POLITICS OF SOCIAL POLICY IN THE UNITED STATES
PRINCETON UNIVERSITY PRESS, LAWERENCEVILLE, NJ, 1988, 478.
THIS VOLUME PLACES THE WELFARE DEBATES OF THE 1980S IN
THE CONTEXT OF PAST PATTERNS OF U.S. POLICY, SUCH AS THE
SOCIAL SECURITY ACT OF 1935, THE FAILURE OF EFFORTS IN THE
1940S TO EXTEND NATIONAL SOCIAL BENEFITS AND ECONOMIC
PLANNING, AND THE BACKLASHES AGAINST "BIG GOVERNMENT" THAT
FOLLOWED REFORMS OF THE 1960S AND EARLY 1970S. HISTORICAL
ANALYSIS REVEALS THAT CERTAIN SOCIAL POLICIES HAVE
FLOURISHED IN THE UNITED STATES: THOSE THAT HAVE APPEALED
SIMULTANEOUSLY TO MIDDLECLASS AND LOWER-INCOME PEOPLE, WHILE
NOT INVOLVING DIRECT BUREAUCRATIC INTERVENTIONS INTO LOCAL
COMMUNITIES. THE EDITORS SUGGEST HOW NEW FAMILY AND
EMPLOYMENT POLICIES, DEVISED ALONG THESE LINES, MIGHT
REVITALIZE BROAD POLITICAL COALITIONS AND FURTHER BASIC
NATIONAL VALUES.

09501 WEIR, S.
MAGGIE'S POWER
NEW POLITICS, 11(3) (SUM 89), 96-100.
MRS. THATCHER IS THE MOST UNPOPULAR BRITISH PREMIER
SINCE THE WAR. SHE IS PROFOUNDLY OPPOSED TO THE BETTER
INSTINCTS OF GREAT MAJORITIES OF THE BRITISH PEOPLE (AS
REVEALED THROUGH OPINION POLLS). BUT SHE ALSO SPEAKS
DIRECTLY TO THEIR WORST INSTINCTS: TO CHAUVINISM, RACISM,
AND ALL MANNER OF REACTIONARY PREJUDICES, AND IN DOING SO,
SHE HAS THE FULL-BLOODED BACKING OF THE MOST DISGUSTING
POPULAR PRESS IN THE WEST. AND THE ABSENCE OF SAFEGUARDS,

THE ABSENCE OF THE NEED TO BARGAIN AND COMPROMISE WITH OTHER
PARTIES AND INTEREST GROUPS, WHICH IS THE WAY OF A MODERN
PLURALISTIC DEMOCRACY, ALLOWS HER NOT SIMPLY TO APPEAR
POWERFUL; CRAZILY, IT MAKES HER POWERFUL, IT ENHANCES THE
VERY IMAGE SHE SEEKS, IT UNDERMINES THE ESSENCE OF DEMOCRACY.

09502 WEIR, S.J.
LONG-TERM CARE REFORM: CONFLICT AND CONSENSUS AMONG POLICY
INFLUENTIALS
DISSERTATION ABSTRACTS INTERNATIONAL, 49(8) (FEB 89),
2379-A.
THE AUTHOR ASSESSES THE PROSPECT FOR REFORM OF FEDERAL
LONG-TERM CARE POLICY FOR THE ELDERLY BY ANALYZING THE
ATTITUDES AND PREFERENCES OF A GROUP OF PROFESSIONALS
WORKING IN THE FIELD OF AGING. THE EVALUATION IS DIVIDED
INTO THREE PARTS, AND THE APPROACH EMPHASIZES POLITICAL
IDEOLOGY, PERSONAL EXPERIENCE, AND INSTITUTIONAL ROLE.

09503 WEISS, C.
IMPORTED STRATEGIES: WOMEN AND DEVELOPMENT
MULTINATIONAL MONITOR, 10(9) (SEP 89), 24-26.
THE NOTION THAT "DEVELOPED" COUNTRIES TEACH
"UNDEVELOPED" COUNTRIES STILL PERSISTS, BUT SOME PROFOUND
CHANGES ARE TAKING PLACE IN THE UNITED STATES. WOMEN'S
ORGANIZATIONS ARE BEGINNING TO MOVE AWAY FROM THE
DEVELOPED/DEVELOPING DISTINCTION. AS THEY RECOGNIZE MORE
CROSS-CULTURAL PARALLELS. IN DEVELOPING NEW PROGRAMS AND
CREATING NEW STRATEGIES, AMERICAN WOMEN'S ORGANIZATIONS ARE
BEGINNING TO STUDY RESEARCH, ANALYSIS, AND PROJECT
DEVELOPMENT IN THIRD WORLD COUNTRIES.

09504 WEISS, J.
ASIA PREPARES FOR 1992
EUROPE, (290) (OCT 89), 22-24.
THE ARTICLE EXAMINES THE RELATIONSHIP BETWEEN THE
EUROPEAN COMMUNITY (EC) AND THE NATIONS OF THE FAR EAST:
JAPAN AND THE "FOUR TIGERS": KOREA, HONG KONG, TAIWAN, AND
SINGAPORE. HISTORIC, ECONOMIC, AND CULTURAL TIES BETWEEN THE
EC AND EAST ASIA HAVE CREATED THE POTENTIAL FOR HARMONY AND
FOR COMPETITION. BOTH SIDES WILL HAVE TO MOVE CAREFULLY TO
ENSURE MUTUALLY BENEFICIAL GROWTH AND TO AVOID TRADE
CONFLICTS.

09505 WEISS, J.A.
THE POWERS OF PROBLEM DEFINITION: THE CASE OF GOVERNMENT
PAPERWORK
POLICY SCIENCES, 22(2) (MAY 89), 97-121.
PROBLEM DEFINITION IS A PACKAGE OF IDEAS THAT INCLUDES,
AT LEAST IMPLICITLY, AN ACCOUNT OF THE CAUSES AND
CONSEQUENCES OF UNDESIRABLE CIRCUMSTANCES AND A THEORY ABOUT
HOW TO IMPROVE THEM. AS SUCH, IT SERVES AS THE OVERTURE TO
POLICYMAKING, AS AN INTEGRAL PART OF THE PROCESS OF
POLICYMAKING, AND AS A POLICY OUTCOME. IN EACH OF THESE
ROLES IT SEEMS TO EXERT INFLUENCE ON GOVERNMENT ACTION.
DISTINGUISHING AMONG THE ROLES CLARIFIES THE NATURE OF THAT
INFLUENCE. A CASE STUDY EXAMINES THE TRANSITION FROM ONE
PROBLEM DEFINITION TO ANOTHER IN THE DOMAIN OF INFORMATION
COLLECTION BY THE FEDERAL GOVERNMENT. THE RISE OF THE
PAPERWORK REDUCTION DEFINITION ILLUSTRATES THE VARIETY OF
WAYS IN WHICH PROBLEM DEFINITION HAS POWERFUL CONSEQUENCES.

09506 WEISS, K.G.
THROWING DOWN THE GAUNTLET: THE SOVIET CHALLENGE IN THE
PACIFIC
COMPARATIVE STRATEGY, 8(2) (1989), 149-180.
THE ARTICLE ANALYZES US AND SOVIET INTERESTS IN THE ASIA-
PACIFIC REGION. IT PAYS SPECIAL ATTENTION TO THE GROWING
SOVIET EFFORTS TO UNDERMINE POLITICAL, MILITARY, AND
ECONOMIC CONNECTIONS BETWEEN THE US AND ITS FRIENDS AND
ALLIES IN THE PACIFIC. MIKHAIL GORBACHEV'S SPEECH IN
VLADIVOSTOK IN 1986 IS VIEWED AS AN ATTEMPT TO PORTRAY THE
SOVIETS AS "PEACEMAKERS" BY DRAWING ATTENTION AWAY FROM THE
SOVIET MILITARY PRESENCE IN THE REGION. THE ARTICLE ALSO
OUTLINES HOW US NAVAL FORCES COULD HELP COUNTER SOVIET
POLICY.

09507 HEISSBERG, R.
POLITICAL CENSORSHIP: A DIFFERENT VIEW
PS: POLITICAL SCIENCE AND POLITICS, XXII(1) (MAR 89),
47-51.
THE AUTHOR DISCUSSES THE ROLE OF POLITICAL CENSORSHIP IN
WRITING AND EDITING TEXTBOOKS.

09508 WEISSMAN, R.
CORRUPTING SCIENCE
MULTINATIONAL MONITOR, 11(12) (DEC 89), 7-8.
CAPITULATING TO INTENSE PRESSURE FROM UNIVERSITIES AND
THE BIOMEDICAL INDUSTRY, U.S. SECRETARY OF HEALTH AND HUMAN
SERVICES LOUIS SULLIVAN HAS QUASHED CONFLICT OF INTEREST
GUIDELINES PROPOSED BY THE NATIONAL INSTITURES OF HEALTH
(NIH). THE PROPOSED GUIDELINES RECOMMENDED THAT RECIPIENTS
OF FUNDING FROM NIH OR THE ALCOHOL, DRUG ABUSE, AND MENTAL
HEALTH ADMINISTRATION DISCLOSE THEIR FINANCIAL HOLDINGS AND
DIVEST THEIR STOCK HOLDINGS IN COMPANIES WHOSE PRODUCTS THEY

TEST.

09509 WEIHEN, Z.
INDIA: DEVELOPING ECONOMIC DIPLOMACY FOR THE 1990'S
BEIJING REVIEW, 32(47) (NOV 89), 13-14.
INDIA HAS EMBARKED ON A POLICY TO INCREASE ITS ROLE IN
THE INTERNATIONAL MARKET, GIVING PRIORITY TO THE DEVELOPMENT
OF EXPORTS AND ECONOMIC DIPLOMACY. ITS TWO PRIMARY GOALS ARE:
(1) TO CONSOLIDATE ITS ECONOMIC RELATIONS WITH WESTERN
EUROPE TO AVOID A FINANCIAL BEATING IN 1992 WHEN THE
EUROPEAN COMMUNITY'S UNIFIED MARKET IS ESTABLISHED AND (2)
TO DEVELOP ITS ECONOMIC RELATIONS WITH THE USA AND THE ASIA-
PACIFIC REGION.

09510 WELBORN, D.
CONJOINT FEDERALISM AND ENVIRONMENTAL REGULATION IN THE
UNITED STATES
PUBLIUS: THE JOURNAL OF FEDERALISM, 18(1) (WIN 88), 27-44.
THE ARTICLE EXPLORES MANY OF THE ENVIRONMENTAL LAWS
ENACTED BY CONGRESS WHICH EMPLOY A DISTINCTIVE BLEND OF
NATIONAL AND STATE AUTHORITY. IN THESE CONJOINT AGREEMENTS,
STATE AUTHORITY IS NOT TOTALLY PREEMPTED, BUT IS
SUBORDINATED TO NATIONAL AUTHORITY IF STATES WISH TO
PARTICIPATE IN ENVIRONMENTAL REGULATION. IT EXPLORES THE
ORIGIN OF SUCH CONJOINT ARRANGEMENTS AND THE DIFFERENT WAYS
IN WHICH THEY ARE IMPLEMENTED. IT CONCLUDES WITH AN ANALYSIS
OF FUTURE DIRECTIONS OF SUCH POLICIES.

09511 WELBORN, D.M.; LYONS, W.; THOMAS, L.W.
THE FEDERAL GOVERNMENT IN THE SUNSHINE ACT AND AGENCY
DECISION MAKING
ADMINISTRATION AND SOCIETY, 20(4) (FEB 89), 465-485.
CONGRESS PASSED THE GOVERNMENT IN THE SUNSHINE ACT IN
1976, REGULATING THE MEETING PROCEDURES OF MORE THAN 50
AGENCIES HEADED BY COLLEGIAL BODIES HENCEFORTH THE MAJOR
FEDERAL REGULATORY COMMISSIONS AND MANY OTHER AGENCIES
WERE REQUIRED TO HOLD MEETINGS IN PUBLIC UNLESS EXEMPT
INFORMATION WAS INVOLVED. THIS STUDY EXAMINES THE EFFECTS OF
THE LAW ON AGENCY DECISION-MAKING PROCESSES. IT FINDS THAT
PERHAPS THE MOST IMPORTANT EFFECT OF THE SUNSHINE LAW IS TO
DIMINISH THE COLLEGIAL CHARACTER OF THOSE PROCESSES.

09512 WELCH, D.A.
CRISIS DECISION-MAKING RECONSIDERED
JOURNAL OF CONFLICT RESOLUTION, 33(3) (SEP 89), 430-445.
SERIOUS PROBLEMS MAY BE FOUND IN HEREK, JANIS, AND
HUTH'S 1987 STUDY OF THE RELATIONSHIP BETWEEN THE QUALITY OF
THE DECISION-MAKING PROCESS IN AN INTERNATIONAL CRISIS AND
THE DESIRABILITY OF ITS OUTCOME. A CLOSER LOOK AT THE BEST
UNDERSTOOD AND MOST THOROUGHLY DOCUMENTED CASE USED IN THEIR
STUDY (THE CUBAN MISSILE CRISIS OF 1962) REVEALS THE CHIEF
CAUSE OF THOSE PROBLEMS TO BE THE USE OF SOURCES THAT APPEAR
TO BE INCOMPLETE IN THE LIGHT OF NEW EVIDENCE. BOTH THE
CONCLUSIONS OF THE HEREK, JANIS, AND HUTH STUDY AND THE
CRITERIA WITH WHICH THEY ASSESS THE QUALITY OF A DECISION-
MAKING PROCESS ARE CALLED INTO QUESTION.

09513 WELCH, S.; SIGELMAN, L.
A BLACK GENDER GAP?
SOCIAL SCIENCE QUARTERLY, 70(1) (MAR 89), 120-133.
THIS NOTE LOOKS TOWARD BLACK AMERICANS FOR EVIDENCE OF A
"GENDER GAP" OF THE TYPE PREVIOUSLY DOCUMENTED AMONG WHITE
AMERICANS AND IN SEVERAL OTHER WESTERN DEMOCRACIES. SUCH
EVIDENCE PROVES, FOR THE MOST PART, TO BE LACKING.

09514 HELFELD, I.
POOR TENANTS, POOR LANDLORDS, POOR POLICY
PUBLIC INTEREST, 92 (SUM 88), 110-120.
THIS ARTICLE EXAMINES THE NEGATIVE IMAGE OF A TYPICAL
LANDLORD AND THE UNFAIRNESS OF THE STEREOTYPE. HIS ESSENTIAL
ROLE IN AMERICA'S HOUSING SYSTEM IS EXPLORED. THE ECONOMICS
OF RENTAL PROPERTY AND THE PROBLEMS OF THE POOR ARE
ADDRESSED.

09515 WELLHOFER, E.S.
CORE AND PERIPHERY: TERRITORIAL DIMENSIONS IN POLITICS
URBAN STUDIES, 26(3) (JUN 89), 340-355.
THE ESSAY REVIEWS DEVELOPMENTS OF THE CORE-PERIPHERY
PARADIGM. TWO VARIANTS OF THE PARADIGM ARE ISOLATED. BOTH
VARIANTS DEFINE CORE-PERIPHERY RELATIONS BY THREE FEATURES:
CHARACTERISTICS DISTINGUISHING CORE FROM PERIPHERY, THE
GOODS EXCHANGED, AND THE NATURE OF THE EXCHANGE AND THE
PATTERN OF CORE-PERIPHERY RELATIONS. THESE FEATURES FORM THE
EXPLANATORY VARIABLES IN THE EXAMINATION OF THREE CENTRAL
PROBLEMS IN SOCIAL SCIENCE: THE RISE OF THE STATE, THE
DEVELOPMENT OF IMPERIALISM AND COLONIALISM AND REGIONAL
SOCIAL MOVEMENTS. HOWEVER, THE DISTINGUISHING FEATURE OF
CORE-PERIPHERY ANALYSIS IS THE SPATIAL REPRESENTATION OF
THESE DYNAMICS. YET SPATIAL REPRESENTATIONS IN CORE-
PERIPHERY PARADIGMS ARE LATENT AND POORLY DEVELOPED. SEVERAL
ALTERNATIVE SPATIAL REPRESENTATIONS ARE MORE EFFECTIVE IN
DISPLAYING CORE-PERIPHERY DYNAMICS, PERMITTING SIMPLER
ASSUMPTIONS, INTRODUCING TEMPORAL DYNAMICS AND MULTI-LINEAR
MODELS.

09516 WELLHOFER, E.S.
    THE COMPARATIVE METHOD AND THE STUDY OF DEVELOPMENT,
    DIFFUSION, AND SOCIAL CHANGE
    COMPARATIVE POLITICAL STUDIES, 22(3) (OCT 89), 315-342.
        THE RESEARCH INVESTIGATES SUBSTANTIVE AND METHODOLOGICAL
    CONCERNS IN COMPARATIVE RESEARCH, PARTICULARLY THE
    CONFOUNDING INFLUENCES OF WITHIN-SYSTEM DEVELOPMENTAL OR
    CASUAL DYNAMICS, ACROSS-TIME OR WITHIN-SYSTEM DIFFUSION, AND
    ACROSS-SYSTEM OR SPATIAL DIFFUSION. THE ARTICLE ARGUES THAT
    EXTRA-SYSTEM INFLUENCES REPRESENT A SPECIAL CASE OF THE
    UNMEASURED RELEVANT VARIABLE PROBLEM RESULTING IN MODEL
    SPECIFICATION ERROR AND THAT PROPER MODEL SPECIFICATION CAN
    MITIGATE THE PROBLEM. STRUCTURAL EQUATION MODELING IS
    ADVOCATED AS A SIGNIFICANT ADVANCE IN SUCH SPECIFICATIONS.
    THE ARGUMENT IS ELABORATED WITH TIME-SERIES DATA ON
    ARGENTINA FROM 1908 TO 1946 TO TEST THE DEVELOPMENT
    RELATIONSHIP BETWEEN INDUSTRIALIZATION AND POLITICAL
    BEHAVIOR.

09517 WELLS, F.J.
    BANKS AND THRIFTS: RESTRUCTURING AND SOLVENCY
    CRS REVEIW, 10(9) (OCT 89), 1-2.
        THE INTERACTION BETWEEN MARKET FORCES AND REGULATION HAS
    BEEN MOST EVIDENT IN RECENT YEARS IN DEVELOPMENTS AFFECTING
    THE NATION'S SAVINGS INSTITUTIONS AND THE FEDERAL SAVINGS
    AND LOAN INSURANCE CORPORATION (FSLIC). THE FINANCIAL
    INSTUIONS REFORM, RECOVERY, AND ENFORCEMENT ACT OF 1989
    (FIRREA) IS INTENDED TO ADDRESS THE FINANCIAL PROBLEMS OF
    SAVINGS INSTITUTIONS AND THE FSLIC. THE FEDERAL DEPOSIT
    INSURANCE FUND THAT HAD BEEN INSURING DEPOSITS AT MOST OF
    THESE INSTITUTIONS. FIRREA CHANGES THE STRUCTURE FOR
    DEPOSITORY INSTITUTIONS AND THE FEDERAL FINANCIAL REGULATORY
    AGENCIES IN THIS COUNTRY. OF PARTICULAR INTEREST ARE THE
    STRONGER ENFORCEMENT POWERS THE REGULATORY AGENCIES HAVE
    BEEN GIVEN, THE NEW HOUSING FINANCE SYSTEM THAT SHOULD
    EMERGE FROM THE LEGISLATION, AND THE LONG-TERM QUESTIONS
    ABOUT DEPOSIT INSURANCE THAT ARE TO BE STUDIED.

09518 WELLS, S.F. JR.
    A NEW TRANSATLANTIC BARGAIN
    WASHINGTON QUARTERLY, 12(4) (FAL 89), 53-60.
        THIS ARTICLE SUGGESTS THAT THE TIME HAS COME FOR THE U.S.
    TO BEGIN THE PROCESS OF NEGOTIATING A NEW BALANCE OF
    RESPONSIBILITIES WITH ITS EUROPEAN ALLIES, ALSO, THAT THE
    PROBLEMS BEFORE NATO AT THIS MOMENT ARE THE PROBLEMS OF
    SUCCESS. IT DEFINES THE CHALLENGE FOR THE ALLIANCE AS
    MIKHAIL GORBACHEV AND THE ACTUAL RESULTS OF HIS REFORM
    POLICIES. IT ASSESSES GORBACHEV AND EASTERN EUROPE'S
    DELICATE BALANCE AS WELL AS OTHER CHANGES IN THE EAST AND
    WEST.

09519 WELSH, D.
    THE DEMOCRATIC PARTY: PRINCIPLES AND PROSPECTS
    SOUTH AFRICA FOUNDATION REVIEW, 15(4) (APR 89), 1-2.
        NEWLY-MERGED PARTIES INVARIABLY HAVE TO FACE THE
    PROSPECT OF A SOMEWHAT BUMPY ROAD AS THEIR STRUCTURES,
    MEMBERSHIPS, AND LEADERSHIPS INTEGRATE. THE MERGER OF SOUTH
    AFRICA'S INDEPENDENT PARTY, THE NATIONAL DEMOCRATIC MOVEMENT,
    AND THE PROGRESSIVE FEDERAL PARTY OFFERS THE OPPORTUNITY TO
    COMBINE THE STRENGTHS OF THE THREE GROUPS AND FULFILL AN
    IMPORTANT CATALYTIC ROLE IN THE COUNTRY'S POLITICS.

09520 WELTMAN, J.
    THE SHORT, UNHAPPY LIFE OF THE MARITIME STRATEGY
    NATIONAL INTEREST, (15) (SPR 89), 79-86.
        THE ARTICLE EXAMINES THE MARITIME STRATEGY IN THE
    CONTEXT OF THE VIEW OF THE REAGAN ADMINISTRATION THAT
    HORIZONTAL ESCALATION AND "PROTRACTED WAR" WERE THE NEW WAY
    TO DETER SOVIET CONVENTIONAL FORCES. THE ARTICLE ANALYZES
    SOME OF THE STRATEGIC PRINCIPLES THAT UNDERPIN THE MARITIME
    STRATEGY AND EXAMINES THE ONGOING DEBATE OF SPECIFIC
    STRATEGY AND TACTICS. THE ARTICLE CONCLUDES THAT BUDGETARY
    CONSIDERATIONS WILL LIMIT THE NAVY'S ABILITY TO FLEXIBLY
    RESPOND TO SOVIET THREATS AND THAT THE MARITIME STRATEGY
    WILL LIKELY BE REPLACED WITH A STRATEGY EMPHASIZING
    DEFENSIVE SEA CONTROL IN SUPPORT OF THE LAND BATTLE.

09521 WELZ, W.
    FROM OHIO TO BRUSSELS: THE US STATES ENTER THE
    INTERNATIONAL MARKETPLACE
    EUROPE, (291) (NOV 89), 14-15.
        FACED WITH DOUBLE DIGIT INFLATION AND MAJOR FEDERAL
    CUTBACKS, US STATES ENTERED THE REALM OF ECONOMIC
    DEVELOPMENT. ALTHOUGH THE EMPHASIS HAS. THUS FAR. BEEN ON
    THE FAR EAST, THE COVERAGE OF "EUROPE 1992" IN THE AMERICAN
    MEDIA HAS INCREASED STATES' RECOGNITION OF THE IMPORTANCE OF
    THE EUROPEAN COMMUNITY. STATE GOVERNMENTS ARE INCREASINGLY
    SERVING AS BROKERS AND PUBLIC RELATIONS AGENTS FOR THEIR
    HOME-STATE BUSINESSES AND HAVE BECOME A DRIVING FORCE IN US
    INTERNATIONAL ECONOMIC POLICY.

09522 WEN-CHENG, W.; I-HSIN, C.
    CONSTRUCTIVE CONTROVERSIES

FREE CHINA REVIEW, 39(12) (DEC 89), 38-45.
    TAIWAN'S RULING KUOMINTANG AND THE MAJOR OPPOSITION
DEMOCRATIC PROGRESSIVE PARTY HELD THEIR FIRST PRIMARIES IN
JULY 1989 TO CHOOSE THEIR CANDIDATES FOR THE UPCOMING
PARLIAMENTARY AND LOCAL ELECTIONS. THE KMT PRIMARY WAS
VIEWED AS A MAJOR BREAKTHROUGH IN THE POLITICS OF TAIWAN. IN
FACT, BOTH PRIMARIES WERE WIDELY REGARDED AS SIGNS OF
GREATER DEMOCRACY IN THE POLITICAL PROCESS. EVEN THOUGH THE
ISLAND'S OTHER POLITICAL PARTIES DID NOT FOLLOW SUIT, THERE
WAS NO QUESTION THAT THE TWO PRIMARIES WERE IN TUNE WITH THE
TAIWANESE PUBLIC'S DEMANDS FOR GREATER DEMOCRATIZATION.

09523 WEN-CHENG, W.; I-HSIN, C.
    ENTERING THE AGE OF PARTY POLITICS
    FREE CHINA REVIEW, 39(4) (APR 89), 52-57.
        IN 1989, TAIWAN'S LEGISLATIVE YUAN PASSED A REVISED
    CIVIC ORGANIZATIONS LAW, A REVISED LAW OF ELECTION AND
    RECALL OF PUBLIC OFFICIALS, AND A BILL ON VOLUNTARY
    RETIREMENT OF SENIOR PARLIAMENTARIANS. IN THIS ESSAY, THE
    AUTHORS CONSIDER THE SOCIAL AND POLITICAL BACKGROUNDS OF
    THESE BILLS, THE MAIN DIFFERENCES BETWEEN THE OLD LAWS AND
    THE REVISIONS, HOW THE RETIREMENT LAW WILL PERMIT MORE
    TAIWAN-ELECTED PARLIAMENTARIANS TO REPLACE THE AGED MAINLAND
    CHINA-ELECTED DEPUTIES, AND THE MAIN CONTROVERSIES
    SURROUNDING THE BILLS DESIGNED TO CREATE AN ENVIRONMENT FOR
    COMPETITIVE POLITICAL PARTIES.

09524 WEN-TSUNG, C.; VUYLSTEKE, R.R.
    DEMOCRATIZATION IN THE ROC
    FREE CHINA REVIEW, 39(3) (MAR 89), 46-56.
        IN JANUARY 1989, TWENTY POLITICAL SCIENTISTS FROM THE
    USA AND 160 TAIWANESE SCHOLARS MET TO EXAMINE IN DEPTH THE
    POLITICAL DEVELOPMENT OF TAIWAN DURING THE PAST FOUR DECADES.
    THE MAIN GOAL OF THE CONFERENCE WAS TO DETERMINE THE
    IMPLICATIONS OF THAT EXPERIENCE FOR GENERAL DEVELOPMENT
    THEORY IN POLITICAL SCIENCE.

09525 WEN-TSUNG, C.
    FINDING THE BEST AND THE BRIGHTEST
    FREE CHINA REVIEW, 39(9) (SEP 89), 4-14.
        THE AUTHOR EXAMINES THE TESTING AND PLACEMENT METHODS
    USED IN THE TAIWANESE CIVIL SERVICE.

09526 WEN-TSUNG, C.
    MODIFICATIONS FOR EFFECTIVENESS
    FREE CHINA REVIEW, 39(1) (JAN 89), 18-19.
        IN THIS INTERVIEW, TAIWAN'S DIRECTOR OF THE DEPARTMENT
    OF MONETARY AFFAIRS DISCUSSES THE ISLAND'S EFFORTS TO
    INTERNATIONALIZE AND LIBERALIZE ITS FINANCIAL SYSTEM. THE
    MOMENTUM FOR CHANGE IN TAIWANESE FINANCIAL INSTITUTIONS HAS
    BEEN BUILDING OVER THE PAST THREE YEARS, WITH MAJOR
    RESTRUCTURING OF BASIC LAWS AND REGULATIONS ALREADY WELL
    UNDERWAY.

09527 WEN-TSUNG, C.
    TESTING FOR TALENT
    FREE CHINA REVIEW, 39(9) (SEP 89), 15-17.
        SINCE ITS FOUNDING IN 1930, THE EXAMINATION YUAN HAS
    PLAYED A MAJOR ROLE IN TAIWAN'S FIVE-POWER CONSTITUTIONAL
    GOVERNMENT. THE EXAMINATION SYSTEM HAS DEEP HISTORICAL ROOTS
    IN CHINA, BUT THE PACE OF CHANGE IN RECENT YEARS HAS PLACED
    NEW PRESSURES ON THE CIVIL SERVICE SYSTEM. BOTH GENERAL
    ADMINISTRATIVE SKILLS AND SPECIALIZED EXPERIENCE ARE IN
    GREATER DEMAND TO MEET GOVERNMENT REQUIREMENTS.

09528 HENDT, E.A.
    U.S. EXPORT CONTROL POLICY: ITS PRESENT AND FUTURE COURSE
    DEPARTMENT OF STATE BULLETIN (US FOREIGN POLICY), 88(2139)
    (OCT 88), 46-48.
        THE ARTICLE EXAMINES SEVERAL FACTORS THAT WILL INFLUENCE
    FUTURE US EXPORT CONTROL POLICY. THEY INCLUDE THE TRANSFER
    OF US TECHNOLOGY TO THE EASTERN BLOC, THE TOSHIBA/KNOGSBERG
    AFFAIR WHERE A JAPANESE AND NORWEGIAN FIRM ILLEGALLY SOLD
    MULTIAXIS MILLING MACHINES TO THE USSR, AND THE
    REVITALIZATION OF THE COORDINATING COMMITTEE ON MULTILATERAL
    EXPORT CONTROLS (COOCOM). IT OUTLINES SEVERAL CHALLENGES
    THAT THE US WILL FACE IN ORDER TO MEET ITS POLICY OBJECTIVES.

09529 HENDT, E.A.
    U.S. STANCE TOWARD THE SOVIET UNION ON TRADE AND TECHNOLOGY
    DEPARTMENT OF STATE BULLETIN (US FOREIGN POLICY), 89(2142)
    (JAN 89), 20-23.
        AMERICAN POLICY ON TRADE AND TECHNOLOGY WITH THE USSR IS
    AN ISSUE OF GREAT IMPORTANCE BECAUSE IT HAS SIGNIFICANT
    IMPACT ON NATIONAL SECURITY AND ON THE UNITED STATES'
    POLITICAL AND ECONOMIC RELATIONSHIPS WITH THE SOVIET UNION
    AND EASTERN EUROPE. CONTROLS ON TRADE AND TECHNOLOGY
    TRANSFER TO THE USSR ARE APPLIED BECAUSE OF NATIONAL
    SECURITY, FOREIGN POLICY, AND SHORT SUPPLY.

09530 WENXIAN, Z.; XIAORONG, J.
    THE TRANSFORMATION OF AGRICULTURAL POPULATION AND THE
    URBANISATION PROCESS IN CHINA
    INTERNATIONAL JOURNAL OF SOCIAL ECONOMICS, 16(1) (1989),

40-51.
NINE CAUSES FOR THE OCCURRENCE OF SURPLUS AGRICULTURAL
LABOUR WITH THE MODERNISATION OF AGRICULTURE HAVE BEEN
IDENTIFIED. SEVERAL SOLUTIONS TO THIS PROBLEM ARE PRESENTED.
URBANISATION OF THE AGRICULTURAL POPULATION IN A WAY SUITED
TO CHINA'S CHARACTERISTICS IS NECESSARY, IMPORTANT AND
POSSIBLE.

09531 WEPENER, W. J.
BEELD INTERVIEWS THATCHER
SOUTH AFRICA FOUNDATION REVIEW, 15(4) (APR 89), 4-5.
IN THIS INTERVIEW, PRIME MINISTER MARGARET THATCHER
EXPLAINS HER VIEWS ON ECONOMIC SANCTIONS, TERRORISM, THE
DIFFERENCE BETWEEN THE IRA AND THE ANC, AND THE IMPORTANCE
OF NEGOTIATIONS IN SOLVING SOUTH AFRICA'S PROBLEMS.

09532 HERLIN, H.
CONTINGENCY THEORY: THE WRONG DOOR
INTERNATIONAL REVIEW OF ADMINISTRATIVE SCIENCES, 55(1)
(MAR 89), 117-132.
THE AUTHOR ANALYZES CONTINGENCY THEORY (CT) IN LIGHT OF
A RECENT PUBLICATION: ORGANIZATIONAL CHANGE AS A DEVELOPMENT
STRATEGY: MODELS AND TACTICS FOR IMPROVING THIRD WORLD
ORGANIZATIONS BY HAGE AND FINSTERBUSCH. HE EXPLORES THE
ROOTS OF CONTINGENCY THEORY AND POINTS OUT SOME OF THE
DEFECTS THAT HE FINDS IN THE THEORY AND IN THE PUBLICATION.
HE CONCLUDES WITH AN ALTERNATIVE APPROACH DESIGNED TO
OVERCOME THE SHORTCOMINGS INHERRENT IN CURRENT THEORY.

09533 WERNER, C.
JAMES BALDWIN: POLITICS AND THE GOSPEL IMPULSE
NEW POLITICS. 11(2) (WIN 89), 106-124.
BY THE END OF HIS LIFE, JAMES BALDWIN HAD FALLEN OUT OF
INTELLECTUAL FASHION. THE PRIMARY REASON LIES IN HIS
UNFLAGGING CONCERN WITH THE POSSIBILITY OF SALVATION, A TERM
NEARLY MEANINGLESS IN THE VOCABULARIES OF LATE
THWENTIETHCENTURY INTELLECTUAL CULTURE. THE CONFUSION AND
FRAGMENTATION OF POTENTIALLY LIBERATING MOVEMENTS IN AFRO-
AMERICAN CULTURE, HAS CONSIGNED BALDWIN TO THE MARGINS,
THEREBY DECREASING THE IMPACT OF WHAT COULD BE MAJOR VOICE
IN SHAPING THE COMMON FUTURE.

09534 WERNER, P.
ATHLETES FOR PEACE
WORLD MARXIST REVIEW, 32(12) (DEC 89), 22-23.
THIS ARTICLE EXAMINES THE INTERNATIONAL MOVEMENT OF
ATHLETES FOR PEACE AND DESCRIBES A 3,000 KILOMETER TREK FROM
PARIS TO MOSCOW OF MORE THAN 120 ATHLETES CONCERNED WITH
PEACE AND DISARMOMENT.

09535 HERTMAN, P.A.
THE "BRADY PLAN": A NEW DIRECTION IN THIRD WORLD DEBT
STRATEGY
CRS REVEIW, 10(9) (OCT 89), 22-23.
ON MARCH 10, 1989, U.S. SECRETARY OF THE TREASURY
NICHOLAS F. BRADY ANNOUNCED A NEW APPROACH TO THE
INTERNATIONAL DEBT PROBLEM, BASED ON VOLUNTARY DEBT
REDUCTION. A PROPOSAL FOR STUDYING THE ADVISABILITY AND
FEASIBILITY OF ESTABLISHING A DEBT MANAGEMENT AUTHORITY TO
DISCOUNT THIRD WORLD DEBT HAD BEEN ENACTED BY CONGRESS AS
PART OF THE OMNIBUS TRADE AND COMPETITIVENESS ACT OF 1988.
WHILE REJECTING THE PROPOSAL TO ESTABLISH A DEBT MANAGEMENT
AUTHORITY, THE BRADY PLAN ACCEPTED ITS BASIC PREMISE. DEBT
STRATEGY, PREVIOUSLY BASED ON NEW FINANCING, WOULD NOW BE
BASED ON A REDUCTION OF CAPITAL OUTFLOWS.

09536 WESLEY-SMITH, T.
NEW DEVELOPMENTS IN PACIFIC ISLANDS REGIONALISM
NEW ZEALAND INTERNATIONAL REVIEW, 14(3) (MAY 89), 21-23.
THE AUTHOR REVIEWS THE OUTCOME OF THE 28TH PACIFIC
CONFERENCE HELD AT RAROTONGA, COOK ISLANDS IN OCTOBER 1988.
THE THEME WAS "HEALTH—A CAUSE FOR CONCERN", BUT OTHER
CRITICAL TOPICS SURFACED, INCLUDING THE CHARGING OF
ALLEGATIONS OF MALFEASANCE AT THE SOUTH PACIFIC COMMISSION'S
TOP OFFICIAL, SECRETARY GENERAL AFIOGA PULEFA'ASISINA P.M.
TUIASOSOPO, WHO RESIGNED AFTER THE CONFERENCE.

09537 WESSELS, J.S.
DISCIPLINING OF PERSONNEL WITH SPECIFIC REFERENCES TO THE
SOUTH AFRICAN CIVIL SERVICE
DISSERTATION ABSTRACTS INTERNATIONAL, 49(11) (MAY 89),
3503-A.
THE AIM OF DISCIPLINARY MEASURES IN THE SOUTH AFRICAN
PUBLIC SERVICE IS TO ENSURE THAT THE OFFICIAL CONDUCT OF
CIVIL SERVANTS CORRESPONDS TO THE VALUES OF THE SOCIETY. THE
MAIN NORMS ON WHICH THE ETHICAL CONDUCT OF SOUTH AFRICAN
CIVIL SERVANTS ARE BASED ARE DERIVED FROM CHRISTIAN ETHICS,
THE PRINCIPLES OF DEMOCRACY, ADMINISTRATIVE EXCELLENCE, AND
THE RULES OF ADMINISTRATIVE LAW THAT PROMOTE FAIRNESS AND
REASONABLENESS. DISCIPLINARY MEASURES ENSURE THAT OFFICIAL
CONDUCT BY BUREAUCRATS CONFORMS TO THE RULES OF CONDUCT
APPROVED BY PARLIAMENT.

09538 WEST, E.G.
NONPROFIT ORGANIZATIONS: REVISED THEORY AND NEW EVIDENCE
PUBLIC CHOICE. 63(2) (NOV 89), 165-174.
THE MAIN FOCUS OF THIS ARTICE IS ON THE AFFECTS AND
SIGNIFICANCE OF THE COSTS OF GOVERNMENT MISALLOCATION AS
WELL AS OF ADMINISTRATION. SECTION 2 EXAMINES THE TRUST
ARGUMENT FOR THE NEED FOR NONPROFIT ORGANIZATIONS WHILE
SECTION 3 PROBES THE QUESTION WHETHER NONPROFIT EMPLOYEES
ARE "DIFFERENT". THE FAVORABLE TAX TREATMENT OF NONPROFIT
OVER FOR-PROFIT FIRMS RECEIVES ATTENTION IN SECTION 4. THE
ISSUE OF COMPETITION BETWEEN NONPROFITS AND FOR-PROFITS IS
ANALYZED IN SECTION 5 IN THE CONTEXT OF NEW EMPIRICAL
EVIDENCE. FINALLY SECTION 6 OFFERS AN ELEMENTARY PUBLIC
CHOICE EXPLANATION OF SOME OF THE PHENOMENA EXAMINED IN THE
PREVIOUS SECTIONS.

09539 WEST, J.
GORBACHEV AT THE UN: A TRULY EPOCHAL ADDRESS
POLITICAL AFFAIRS, LXVIII(2) (FEB 89), 10-13.
THE AUTHOR ENUMERATES STEPS ADVOCATED BY MIKHAIL
GORBACHEV AS NECESSARY FOR WORLD PEACE AND SURVEYS AMERICAN
REACTION TO GORBACHEV'S ADDRESS TO THE UNITED NATIONS ON DEC.
7, 1988.

09540 WEST, J.
THE STRUGGLE TO PRESERVE AND EXPAND DEMOCRACY
POLITICAL AFFAIRS, LXVIII(7) (JUL 89), 20-24.
THE CHIEF STIMULUS TOWARD DEMOCRATIC DEVELOPMENT COMES
FROM THE SOVIET UNION WHICH IS SETTING NEW STANDARDS OF REAL,
PEOPLEBASED DEMOCRACY AND HUMAN RIGHTS. THIS INCREASINGLY
PUTS CAPITALISM ON THE MORAL AND POLITICAL DEFENSIVE. IT IS
A POWERFUL ASSIST TO THE STRUGGLE FOR MORE DEMOCRACY IN THE
UNITED STATES. THE DEMOCRATIC CURRENT IN AMERICAN LIFE IS
ROOTED IN THE MAJORITY. IT IS IMPORTANT TO REALLY KNOW AND
UNDERSTAND THIS IF THE STRUGGLE AGAINST RABID REACTION AND
FOR PRESERVING AND EXPANDING DEMOCRACY IS TO BE WON. IT IS
NECESSARY TO OVERCOME A TENDENCY TO WRITE OFF WHITE, WORKING
CLASS AREAS AS BEING RACIST. THIS IS A PRETEXT FOR NOT
OPPOSING RACISM AND BETRAYS A LACK OF CONFIDENCE IN THE FACT
THAT WHITE WORKERS ARE BASICALLY DEMOCRATIC AND CAN BE WON
FOR THE STRUGGLE AGAINST RACISM; THAT THE CLASS SELF-
INTERESTS OF WORKERS PROVIDE THE MOTIVATION FOR THEIR BEING
A SOLID BASTION OF DEMOCRACY.

09541 HESTING, A.H.
CHEMICAL AND BIOLOGICAL WARFARE: THE ROAD NOT TAKEN
PEACE RESEARCH, 21(1) (JAN 89), 17-20.
THIS ARTICLE REVIEWS THE HALF-DOZEN AUTHENTICATED CASES
OF CHEMICAL WARFARE IN THE TWENTIETH CENTURY, AS WELL AS THE
NUMEROUS UNSUBSTANTIATED ACCUSATIONS. THE SIX DOCUMENTED
CASES HERE ARE: WORLD WAR 1; STALO-ETHOPIAN WAR OF 1935-36;
THE SECOND SIRO - JAPANESE WAR 1937-45; THE MALAYAN
INSURGENCY OF 1948-1960; THE SECOND INDOCHIRA WAR OF 1961-
1975; AND, THE IRAN-IRAQ WAR OF 1980-1988

09542 HESTLAKE, M.
AFRICA'S LAST CHANCE
SOUTH, (110) (DEC 89), 10-11.
A WORLD BANK REPORT ON THE FUTURE OF AFRICA SAYS THAT
AFRICANS THEMSELVES MUST AVERT THE HUMAN AND ECOLOGICAL
CATASTROPHE THAT THREATENS TO ENGULF THEIR CONTINENT IN THE
1990'S. HELP WILL BE NEEDED FROM THE INTERNATIONAL COMMUNITY
ON A SUBSTANTIAL SCALE, BUT POLITICAL RENEWAL AND THE
FOSTERING OF POPULAR, ACCOUNTABLE INSTITUTIONS MUST COME
FROM WITHIN EACH COUNTRY. THE REPORT IMPLIES THAT THOSE
COUNTRIES WHERE POLITICAL REPRESSION, CORRUPTION, AND
EXTREME INEQUALITY GO UNCHECKED CAN EXPECT TO SEE
INTERNATIONAL SUPPORT WITHDRAWN.

09543 HESTLAKE, M.
ALL THE PRESIDENT'S GHOSTS
SOUTH, (101) (MAR 89), 15.
PRESIDENT BUSH HAS BECOME SO ALARMED BY THE WORSENING
PLIGHT OF THIRD WORLD DEBTORS THAT HE HAS ANNOUNCED A TOP-TO-
BOTTOM REVIEW OF US POLICY ON THE ISSUE. THE INCREASINGLY
PREVALENT VIEW IN WASHINGTON IS THAT THIRD WORLD DEBT HAS
BECOME A VITAL NATIONAL SECURITY ISSUE. SIGNIFICANTLY, THE
NATIONAL SECURITY COUNCIL AND THE STATE DEPARTMENT WILL BE
INVOLVED IN THE REVIEW, ALONG WITH THE TREASURY.

09544 HESTLAKE, M.
BUDGETS, BRIDGES, AND GEORGE BUSH
SOUTH, (104) (JUN 89), 18.
THE ASSESSMENT OF THE US BUDGET PICTURE BY STAFF
ECONOMISTS AT THE IMF SUGGESTS THAT THE US BUDGET DEFICIT
WILL RISE TO ALMOST US$170 BILLION IN 1989 AND, UNLESS
POLICIES CHANGE, WILL STILL EXCEED US$100 BILLION IN 1993.
THIS IS THE YEAR WHEN, UNDER THE AMENDED GRAMM-RUDMAN
LEGISLATION, IT IS SUPPOSED TO BE WIPED OUT ALTOGETHER. THE
US FOREIGN TRADE POSITION, WHICH HAS SHOWN SOME IMPROVEMENT,
WILL WORSEN AGAIN WHILE JAPANESE AND WEST GERMAN TRADE
SURPLUSES ARE PROJECTED TO HIT NEW PEAKS IN 1990.

09545 WESTLAKE, M.
    DIGEST WITH A PINCH OF SALT
    SOUTH, (103) (MAY 89), 19.
        A NEW STUDY BY THE WORLD BANK CLAIMS THAT ITS PRESCRIBED
    POLICY REFORMS ARE WORKING IN AFRICA. THE BANK HAS STAKED SO
    MUCH ON ITS ADJUSTMENT LENDING THAT IT MUST DEMONSTRATE THAT
    ITS APPROACH IS WORKING, PARTICULARLY IN SUB-SAHARAN AFRICA.
    BUT THE REPORT IS FLAWED AND ITS CASE UNPROVEN.

09546 WESTLAKE, M.
    INTO THE COLD LIGHT OF DAWN
    SOUTH, (99) (JAN 89), 6-10.
        RONALD REAGAN'S LEGACY TO HIS SUCCESSOR COULD HARDLY BE
    LESS BENEFICENT. GEORGE BUSH HAS INHERITED AN ECONOMY IN THE
    MATURE STAGES OF EXPANSION, WITH A BOTHERSOME UPTURN IN
    INFLATION AND A FOREIGN DEBT THAT IS STEAMING TOWARDS A
    TRILLION DOLLARS. A RECESSION IS A CERTAINTY UNDER BUSH. IT
    WILL BRING TO THE FOREFRONT MANY NEGLECTED ISSUES, INCLUDING
    THE BUDGET AND TRADE DEFICITS AND AMERICAN AND THIRD WORLD
    DEBT. MEANWHILE, WORRIES THAT THE USA IS SLIPPING BEHIND
    JAPAN IN MANY INDUSTRIES ARE LEADING TO MORE INTERVENTIONIST
    POLICIES AND ACCELERATING THE DRIFT TO PROTECTIONISM. THE
    IMPLICATIONS FOR CAPITAL FLOWS, DEBT MARKETS, AND DEVELOPING
    REGIONS SUGGEST THAT ECONOMIC PROSPECTS ARE NOT BRIGHT FOR
    MUCH OF THE SOUTH, WITH THE EXCEPTION OF ASIA.

09547 WESTLAKE, M.
    SEEDS OF A BITTER HARVEST
    SOUTH, (100) (FEB 89), 18.
        THE URUGUAY ROUND TRADE TALKS MAY BE IN TROUBLE, BUT
    NEGOTIATIONS ARE NOT SCHEDULED TO END UNTIL LATE 1990. TRADE
    DIPLOMATS BELIEVE THEY STILL HAVE TIME TO ARRANGE A HAPPY
    ENDING. THEIR FIRST TASK IS TO PICK UP THE PIECES LEFT BY
    THE FAILURE OF THE TRADE MINISTERS' MEETING IN MONTREAL IN
    DECEMBER 1988.

09548 WESTLAKE, M.
    THE BUCK STOPS AT THE BANK
    SOUTH, (108) (OCT 89), 18.
        US TREASURY SECRETARY NICK BRADY'S PLAN FOR REDUCING
    THIRD WORLD DEBT AND INTEREST PAYMENTS WILL INVOLVE
    INCREASED RISK FOR THE WORLD BANK AND THE IMF. MOST LIKELY,
    THEIR EXPOSURE TO THE HIGHLY INDEBTED COUNTRIES WILL RISE AS
    THE COMMERCIAL BANKS' EXPOSURE IS REDUCED. ACCORDING TO SOME
    CALCULATIONS, THE TYPICAL INDEBTED COUNTRY PARTICIPATING IN
    THE SCHEME COULD FIND HALF OF ITS ANNUAL DEBT SERVICE
    PAYMENTS GOING TO THE WORLD BANK AND THE IMF, COMPARED WITH
    ABOUT ONE-QUARTER NOW.

09549 WESTLAKE, M.
    THE GOSPEL SPREADS
    SOUTH, (106) (AUG 89), 19-21.
        ALTHOUGH WESTERN INDUSTRIALIZED COUNTRIES ARE FORCEFUL
    ADVOCATES OF OPEN AND LIBERAL TRADE, THEY ARE, IN FACT,
    BECOMING MORE PROTECTIONIST. MEANWHILE, THE SOUTH IS SHOWING
    SIGNS OF TRADE LIBERALIZATION AND OPENING UP. SOME
    INDUSTRIALISTS AND TRADE UNIONS IN DEVELOPED COUNTRIES ARE
    FEARFUL THAT THE NORTH WILL BE OBLIGED TO DISMANTLE ITS
    TRADE BARRIERS IN RETURN FOR MARKET-OPENING MEASURES BY THE
    DEVELOPING WORLD. AT A TIME WHEN ATTEMPTS TO RESTRICT
    COMPETITION AND PRESERVE JOBS IN EUROPE AND THE USA COMMAND
    RISING PUBLIC SUPPORT, NORTHERN GOVERNMENTS MAY BE RELUCTANT
    TO GIVE UP THEIR PROTECTIONIST STANCE.

09550 WESTLAKE, M.
    THE GUNS OF NEVERLAND
    SOUTH, (106) (AUG 89), 18.
        DEVELOPING COUNTRIES HAVE MORE THAN QUINTRUPLED THEIR
    MILITARY SPENDING IN REAL TERMS SINCE THE 1960'S, ALMOST
    TRIPLING THEIR SHARE OF WORLDWIDE MILITARY EXPENDITURES.
    THIS SPENDING HAS OFTEN AFFECTED SIGNIFICANTLY BOTH THE
    BALANCE OF PAYMENTS AND THE GOVERNMENT BUDGET.

09551 WESTLAKE, M.
    THE RUB OF THE GREEN
    SOUTH, (110) (DEC 89), 17.
        THE AUTHOR DISCUSSES THE ECONOMIC PROPOSALS OF THE
    EUROPEAN GREEN PARTIES AND THE CONSEQUENCES THE GREEN
    ECONOMIC POLICIES WOULD HAVE ON THE THIRD WORLD.

09552 WESTLAKE, M.; FERIA, M.; MELLY, P.; SPARKS, S.; WOLF, J.
    THE US$50 BILLION HUSTLE
    SOUTH, (103) (MAY 89), 12-18.
        DEVELOPMENT PROJECTS IN THE THIRD WORLD GENERATE
    THOUSANDS OF CONTRACTS WORTH MORE THAN $50 BILLION EVERY
    YEAR. THIS PROCUREMENT MARKET WAS ONCE THE EXCLUSIVE
    PRESERVE OF THE INDUSTRIALIZED COUNTRIES. NOW DEVELOPING
    COUNTRIES HAVE LEARNED THE RULES OF THE GAME AND ARE MAKING
    SIZEABLE INROADS INTO THE PROCUREMENT BUSINESS. STILL, MUCH
    BILATERAL FOREIGN AID IS TIED TO THE PROCUREMENT PROCESS, IN
    ORDER TO LOCK OUT FOREIGN COMPETITION FOR THE MONEY.

09553 WESTLAKE, M.
    WHEN THE RIGHT MAKES A WRONG

SOUTH, (105) (JUL 89), 17.
        CENTRAL TO THE ECONOMIC POLICY SHIFTS IN THE
    INDUSTRIALIZED COUNTRIES DURING THE 1980'S WAS A NEW CONCERN
    WITH THE SUPPLY SIDE OF THE ECONOMY. WHAT WAS NEW ABOUT THE
    APPROACH WAS THE MECHANISMS THAT GOVERNMENTS CHOSE TO
    IMPLEMENT IT. BUT, DESPITE THE RHETORIC, THE IMPLEMENTATION
    OF SUPPLY-SIDE MEASURES IN THE MAJOR INDUSTRIALIZED COUNTRIES
    HAS BEEN PATCHY. AND THE RESULTS SHOW LITTLE SIGN OF LIVING
    UP TO ALL THE PROMISES.

09554 WETHERALL, W.
    NATURALLY SPEAKING
    JAPAN QUARTERLY, XXXVI(1) (JAN 89), 45-49.
        IN JAPAN, THE LAST DAYS OF EMPEROR HIROHITO STIRRED A
    VARIETY OF FEELINGS ABOUT BOTH THE MAN AND THE EMPEROR
    SYSTEM. THE MOST STRIKING POINT ABOUT THE MOSAIC OF REACTION
    WAS THE CONTRAST BETWEEN THE ILLUSIONARY AND EVEN DISHONEST
    ATTEMPTS OF ESTABLISHMENT INTELLECTUALS TO ROMANTICIZE THE
    EMPEROR SYSTEM, IF NOT GLORIFY HIROHITO, AND THE MORE CANDID
    VOICES OF APATHY, AMUSEMENT, CONCERN, DISCONTENT, AND EVEN
    OPEN RAGE TOWARD BOTH THE SYSTEM AND THE DYING MAN.

09555 WETTENHALL, R.
    THE EMERGENCE OF PUBLIC ENTERPRISE PEAK ORGANIZATIONS:
    FILLING A GAP IN GOVERNMENT ENTERPRISE RELATIONS
    INTERNATIONAL REVIEW OF ADMINISTRATIVE SCIENCES, 55(3)
    (SEP 89), 381-400.
        THIS ARTICLE FOCUSES ON BOARD MEMBERS AND CHIEF
    EXECUTIVES OF CORPORATE BODIES CREATED TO MANAGE PUBLIC
    ENTERPRISES. ITS PRIMARY CONCERN IS TO EXPLAIN WHY SUCH
    PUBLIC ENTERPRISE LEADERS IN SEVERAL CONTRIES HAVE FELT THE
    NEED TO "GET TOGETHER," AND TO DESCRIBE THE PEAK
    ORGINIZATIONS THEY HAVE ESTABLISHED TO HELP THEM MANAGE
    THEIR OFTEN PROBLEMATIC RELATIONSHIPS WITH POLITICIANS AND
    ADMINISTRATORS IN CENTRAL GOVERNMENT. THE PAPER OUTLINES SIX
    CONCLUSIONS OF POSSIBLE PROPOSITIONS. IT CONCLUDES WITH
    STATING THAT IT IS TIME FOR POLITICAL AND ADMINISTRATIVE
    SCIENCE TO TAKE MORE NOTICE OF PUBLIC ENTERPRISE MANAGERS AS
    ANOTHER GROUP OF "PARTNERS" IN THE ACTIVITY OF GOVERNING.

09556 WETTIG, G.
    DETERRENCE, MISSILES AND NATO IN SOVIET FOREIGN POLICY
    AUSSEN POLITIK, 40(4) (1989), 321-331.
        THIS ARTICLE EXAMINES THE KEYSTONE OF NATO POLICY WHICH
    IS NUCLEAR DETERRENCE, DR. GERHARD WETTIG, EXPLAINS THE ROLE
    OF THIS CONCEPT IN THE FORCEFUL WITH WHICH GORBACHEV AGAIN
    PRESSED FOR THE ELIMINATIN OF SHORT RANGE NUCLEAR MISSILES
    AS THE NEXT STEP TOWARD THE DENUCLEARIZATION OF EUROPE
    DURING HIS VISITS TO BONN AND PARIS. POLITICAL IMPLICATIONS
    ARE DISCUSSED AS WELL AS THE PIVOTAL ROLE OF NUCLEAR
    DETERRENCE IN EUROPEAN RELATIONS.

09557 WHARTON, A.S.
    GENDER SEGREGATION IN PRIVATE-SECTOR, PUBLIC-SECTOR, AND
    SELF-EMPLOYED OCCUPATIONS, 1950-1981
    SOCIAL SCIENCE QUARTERLY, 70(4) (DEC 89), 923-940.
        THIS STUDY ANALYZES U.S. CENSUS AND CURRENT POPULATION
    SURVEY DATA TO EXAMINE HOW GENDER SEGREGATION BY OCCUPATION
    VARIES ACCORDING TO THE TYPE OF OWNERSHIP OF THE EMPLOYING
    ORGANIZATION. THE AGGREGATE LEVELS AND TRENDS IN
    OCCUPATIONAL SEGREGATION IN THE PRIVATE SECTOR, IN THE
    PUBLIC SECTOR, AND AMONG THE SELF-EMPLOYED ARE COMPARED FOR
    THE POST-WORLD WAR II ERA (1950-81). THE POSTWAR LEVELS AND
    TRENDS IN SEGREGATION WITHIN OCCUPATIONAL GROUPS IN EACH
    SECTOR ARE ALSO DESCRIBED. THE RESULTS SUGGEST THAT GENDER
    SEGREGATION HAS DECLINED MORE RAPIDLY IN THE PUBLIC SECTOR
    THAN THE PRIVATE SECTOR, WHILE SEGREGATION AMONG THE SELF-
    EMPLOYED HAS REMAINED RELATIVELY STABLE OVER THE POSTWAR ERA.

09558 WHEELER, J.
    THE CRITICAL ROLE FOR OFFICIAL DEVELOPMENT ASSISTANCE IN
    THE 1990S
    FINANCE AND DEVELOPMENT, 26(3) (SEP 89), 38-40.
        THE TURN OF THE DECADE FINDS THE DONOR COMMUNITY TAKING
    STOCK. THIS ARTICLE ANALYZES WHAT HAS BEEN ACCOMPLISHED,
    WHAT IS THE RIGHT JOB FOR THE 1990S, IF THEY ARE DOING
    ENOUGH, AND IF THEY ARE USING THE RIGHT INSTRUMENTS IT
    STUDIES HOW THE MEMBERS OF THE DEVELOPMENT ASSISTANCE
    COMMITTEE OF THE OECD ANNUALLY JUSTIFY THEIR REQUESTS FOR
    OFFICIAL DEVELOPMENT ASSISTANCE (ODA) TO THEIR PARLIAMENTS,
    AND DEFINES SOME OF THE KEY AREAS WHERE ODA CAN PLAY AN
    IMPORTANT ROLE IN THE 1990S. IT CONCLUDES THAT THE URGENCY
    AND IMPORTANCE OF THE DEVELOPMENT AGENDA AND THE FACT THAT
    THERE ARE MANY STRONG DEVELOPING COUNTRY EFFORTS DESERVING
    EXTERNAL SUPPORT JUSTIFY GROWING LEVELS OF OFFICIAL
    DEVELOPMENT ASSISTANCE.

09559 WHEELER, N.J.
    THE ROLES PLAYED BY THE BRITISH CHIEFS OF STAFF COMMITTEE
    IN THE EVOLUTION OF BRITAIN'S NUCLEAR WEAPON PLANNING AND
    POLICY-MAKING, 1945-1955
    DISSERTATION ABSTRACTS INTERNATIONAL, 49(12) (JUN 89),
    3861-A.
        THE AUTHOR UTILIZES RECENTLY-RELEASED OFFICIAL RECORDS

TO ASSESS THE CONTRIBUTION OF THE BRITISH CHIEFS OF STAFF TO BRITAIN'S DEVELOPMENT AS A NUCLEAR STATE. HE CONSIDERS THREE MAJOR ASPECTS OF THE SUBJECT: (1) THE MERITS OF THE CONVENTIONAL WISDOM CONCERNING BRITAIN'S DEFENSE POLICY-MAKING PROCESS, WHICH PORTRAYS THE CHIEFS OF STAFF COMMITTEE AS PREY TO PAROCHIAL SERVICE INTERESTS; (2) THE VALUE OF THE THEORETICAL LITERATURE ON INTER-SERVICE RIVALRY AND DEFENSE POLICY-MAKING; AND (3) THE APPLICABILITY OF THE BUREAUCRATIC POLITICS MODEL IN ANALYZING BRITAIN'S EVOLUTION AS A NUCLEAR WEAPONS STATE.

09560 WHICKER, M.L.; ARESON, T.W.
THE MALENESS OF THE AMERICAN PRESIDENCY
JOURNAL OF POLITICAL SCIENCE, 17(1-2) (1989), 63-73.
THE AUTHORS IDENTIFY FOUR FACTORS THAT ACCOUNT FOR THE BUMPY PRESIDENTIAL "PLAYING FIELD" CONFRONTING FEMALE CANDIDATES: THE PRESIDENTIAL ELECTION SYSTEM, THE PAUCITY OF WOMEN WITH EXPERIENCE IN THE PRESIDENTIAL "LAUNCHING ROLES," THE DIFFICULTY WOMEN FACE IN SECURING CAMPAIGN FUNDING, AND THE LONGSTANDING PUBLIC PERCEPTION OF A CONFLICT BETWEEN FAMILIAL AND POLITICAL ROLES FOR WOMEN BUT NOT FOR MEN.

09561 WHIDDON, B.; MARTIN, P.Y.
ORGANIZATIONAL DEMOCRACY AND WORK QUALITY IN A STATE WELFARE AGENCY
SOCIAL SCIENCE QUARTERLY, 70(3) (SEP 89), 667-686.
WORK QUALITY IS STUDIED IN RELATION TO DISCRETION AND PARTICIPATION AMONG 180 SERVICE WORKERS AND 55 FIRST-LINE SUPERVISORS IN A LARGE STATE WELFARE AGENCY. RESULTS FOR WORKERS SHOW THAT (A) GREATER DISCRETION AND PARTICIPATION FOSTER HIGH-QUALITY WORK, WITH DISCRETION MORE INFLUENTIAL; (B) WORKERS DESIRE MORE DISCRETION AND PARTICIPATION THAN THEY HAVE, ESPECIALLY PARTICIPATION; (C) INCONGRUENCE (ACTUAL NET DIFFERENCES BETWEEN REPORTED AND DESIRED DISCRETION AND PARTICIPATION) IS UNABLE TO ACCOUNT FOR WORK QUALITY; AND (D) GENDER PREDICTS WORK QUALITY (WOMEN REPORT A HIGHER QUALITY). THE UNANTICIPATED GENDER EFFECTS, THE FAILURE OF DEMOCRACY TO ACCOUNT FOR SUPERVISORS' WORK QUALITY, AND THE MEASUREMENT OF WORK QUALITY AS PERCEPTIONS ARE DISCUSSED.

09562 WHITAKER, R.
NO LAMENTS FOR THE NATION: FREE TRADE AND THE ELECTION OF 1988
CANADIAN FORUM, LXVIII(779) (MAR 89), 9-13.
THE CANADIAN NATIONAL ELECTION OF 1988 WAS ACTUALLY TWO DIFFERENT CONTESTS. ITS FORM WAS A FIGHT AMONG THREE PARTIES FOR THE CONTROL OF PARLIAMENT, WHICH WAS WON BY THE TORIES. ITS SUBSTANCE WAS A REFERENDUM ON FREE TRADE AND WAS WON BY THE OPPONENTS OF FREE TRADE. BUT SUBSTANCE LOST OUT TO FORM.

09563 WHITBECK, J.
PALESTINE EXISTS: THE CRITERIA FOR STATEHOOD
MIDDLE EAST INTERNATIONAL, (351) (MAY 89), 18.
EFFORTS TO DISMISS PALESTINIAN STATEHOOD ON TECHNICAL LEGAL GROUNDS ARE ILL-PLACED. THE ARTICLE OUTLINES THE FOUR CUSTOMARY CRITERIA FOR SOVERIGN STATEHOOD AND DEMONSTRATES HOW THE CRITERIA IS MET IN PALESTINE. IN SOME CASES, PALESTINE MEETS THE CRITERIA FOR STATEHOOD MORE CLEARLY THAN MANY OTHER NATIONS WHOSE SOVEREIGNTY HAS NOT BEEN LEGALLY DISPUTED FOR YEARS.

09564 WHITBECK, J.
SHARING THE HOLY LAND
MIDDLE EAST INTERNATIONAL, (362) (NOV 89), 20-21.
THE ARTICLE EXAMINES THE CURRENT SNAIL'S PACE OF NEGOTIATIONS BETWEEN ISRAEL AND PALESTINE. IT CONCLUDES THAT, CONTRARY TO POPULAR OPINION, SHARING THE HOLY LAND IS NOT A ZERO-SUM SOLUTION. IT OUTLINES A PROPOSAL IN WHICH POLITICAL AND VOTING RIGHTS ARE SEVERED FROM ECONOMIC AND SOCIAL RIGHTS; PALESTINE WOULD BE A SINGLE ECONOMIC AND SOCIAL UNIT ENCOMPASSING TWO SOVEREIGN STATES AND JERUSALEM WOULD FORM AN UNDIVIDED PART OF BOTH STATES. SUCH A SOLUTION WOULD REQUIRE A MORAL, SPIRITUAL, AND PSYCHOLOGICAL TRANSFORMATION FROM BOTH ISRAELIS AND PALESTINIANS; HOWEVER, THE AUTHOR ARGUES THAT THE SAME CONDITIONS ARE NECESSARY FOR ANY SETTLEMENT.

09565 WHITBECK, J.
THE ROAD TO PEACE STARTS IN JERUSALEM
MIDDLE EAST INTERNATIONAL, (348) (APR 89), 15-16.
THE ARTICLE ARGUES THAT SOME SORT OF SOLUTION TO THE "JERUSALEM PROBLEM" WILL HAVE TO BE REACHED BEFORE A LASTING SOLUTION TO THE GENERAL PROBLEM OF THE OCCUPIED TERRITORIES CAN BE REACHED. IT PROPOSES THAT JERUSALEM BE GIVEN THE STATUS AS BOTH THE CAPITAL OF ISRAEL AND THE CAPITAL OF PALESTINE AND BE RULED BY AN AUTONOMOUS MUNICIPAL GOVERNMENT. SUCH A PROPOSAL WOULD ASSUAGE THE FEARS AND DEMANDS OF BOTH SIDES AND MAY BE THE CRITICAL FIRST STEP THAT WOULD LEAD TO SUBSTANTIVE NEGOTIATIONS BETWEEN ISRAEL AND THE PLO.

09566 WHITBECK, J. V.
A WAY TO SOOTHE ISRAELI FEARS
MIDDLE EAST INTERNATIONAL, 355 (JUL 89), 18-19.

TO BURST THE PSYCHOLOGICAL BARRIERS BLOCKING PROGRESS TOWARD PEACE, THE UNITED STATES SHOULD PROMPTLY GRANT TO ALL CURRENT ISRAELI CITIZENS WHAT HONG KONG'S PEOPLE ARE SEEKING FROM BRITAIN - A RIGHT TO LIVE AND WORK IN AMERICA AND, IN DUE COURSE, TO BECOME AMERICAN CITIZENS. AS IN THE HONG KONG CASE, SUCH A RIGHT WOULD HAVE BOTH PRACTICAL AND HUMANITARIAN BENEFITS. IT WOULD BOTH ENCOURAGE ISRAELIS TO TAKE RISKS FOR PEACE IN THE HOLY LAND AND AT THE SAME TIME PROVIDE THOSE WHO HAVE HAD ENOUGH WITH A REFUGE AND A NEW START IN LIFE. GIVEN THE "COMMON VALUES" WHICH ISRAELIS AND AMERICANS ARE COMMONLY HELD TO HOLD, ISRAELI IMMIGRANTS SHOULD BE EASILY ASSIMILABLE AND AN ASSET TO AMERICAN SOCIETY. INDEED THOUSANDS OF ISRAELIS ARE ALREADY LIVING AND WORKING IN THE US.

09567 WHITE, D.
REFLECTIONS ON THE TERROR OF TIANANMEN SQUARE
ARENA, (88) (SPR 89), 5-11.
THIS ARTICLE SUGGESTS THAT THE MILITARY TERROR LAUNCHED BY THE GOVERNMENT OF CHINA AGAINST ITS OPPOSITION IN TIANANMEN SQUARE MEANT THE END OF THAT GOVERNMENT AS A LEGITIMATE RULER OF THE PEOPLE. HOWEVER, IN RESPONSE TO THOSE WHO ASSERT THAT COLLECTIVISM IS DEFEATED, IT CONTENDS THAT CHINA, UNDER THE LEADERSHIP OF DENG XIAOPING IN REALITY PROVIDES NO EVIDENCE AT ALL FOR A DECLINE OF SOCIALISM, QUITE THE CONTRARY. ENTREPRENEURSHIP AND THE DEMOCRACY MOVEMENT ARE EXPLORED AS WELL AS THE USE OF TERROR BY THE CHINESE GOVERNMENT. IT CONCLUDES THAT "A BAD THING CAN BE TURNED INTO A GOOD THING" IF THE EVENTS IN CHINA LEAD TO THE RETHINKING OF MARXIST THEORY AND THE REWORKING OF SOCIAL PRACTICE.

09568 WHITE, E.L.
IN SEARCH OF A UNITED STATES NATIONAL SECURITY STRATEGY: REPUBLIC OF SOUTH AFRICA
AVAILABLE FROM NTIS, NO. AD-A202 040/2/GAR, MAY 88, 33.
THIS RESEARCH REPORT IS AN ANALYSIS AND ASSESSMENT OF THE ESSENTIAL CHARACTERISTICS AND QUALITIES OF U.S. NATIONAL SECURITY POLICY TOWARD SOUTH AFRICA. THE CONSTRUCTIVE ENGAGEMENT POLICY STRATEGY OF THE U.S. DOES NOT PROVIDE A MEASUREMENT CRITERIA TO DETERMINE ITS IMPACT ON APARTHEID AND WHETHER OR NOT POLICY OBJECTIVES HAVE BEEN ACHIEVED. THE EXTENT OF CURRENT SOVIET INFLUENCE IN THE SOUTHERN AFRICAN REGION DOES NOT WARRANT THE EAST-WEST CONFLICT AS THE DOMINANT FACTOR UNDERLYING U.S. POLICY. U.S. POLICY HAS HAD MINIMUM IMPACT IN ALLEVIATING REGIONAL INSTABILITY AND U.S. ECONOMIC INTERESTS HAVE BEEN ADVERSELY AFFECTED. THE REALITIES OF U.S. POLICY HAVE NOT SIGNIFICANTLY ADVANCED THE CAUSE OF HUMAN RIGHTS AND BASIC AMERICAN VALUE CONCEPTS. SOME U.S. POLICY MODIFICATIONS ARE RECOMMENDED TO PROMOTE LONG-TERM U.S. NATIONAL INTERESTS.

09569 WHITE, E.T. JR.
SCORPIONS, SNAPPERS, AND ARMADILLOS
DISSERTATION ABSTRACTS INTERNATIONAL, 49(10) (APR 89), 3153-A.
THE AUTHOR EXAMINES THE STRATEGIC DEFENSE INITIATIVE WITHIN THE CONTEXT OF NUCLEAR THEORY, DOCTRINE, STRATEGY, AND FORCE STRUCTURE TO DETERMINE THE OVERALL OBJECTIVE FOR STRATEGIC DEFENSE AND HOW TO ACHIEVE IT.

09570 WHITE, G.
THE ONTARIO LEGISLATURE: A POLITICAL ANALYSIS
UNIVERSITY OF TORONTO PRESS, TORONTO, ONTARIO, CA, 1989, 320.
IN THIS STUDY OF THE ONTARIO LEGISLATURE, GRAHAM WHITE EXPLORES THE STRUCTURE, OPERATIONS, AND POLITICS OF THIS POWERFUL BODY. ALTHOUGH HE DEALS WITH IMPORTANT DEVELOPMENTS THROUGH THE 1970S, HE CONCENTRATES ON MORE RECENT HISTORY; HIS ANALYSIS EXTENDS THROUGH THE TIME OF THE LIBERAL-NDP' ACCORD' INTO THE MASSIVE LIBERAL MAJORITY FOLLOWING THE 1987 ELECTION. HIS UNDERLYING CONCERN IS THE POLITICAL AND POLICY INFLUENCE THAT CAN BE EXERCISED BY MEMBERS OF A MODERN PARLIAMENT OF THE WESTMINSTER MODEL.

09571 WHITE, J.; WILDAVSKY, A.
HOW TO FIX THE DEFICIT--REALLY
PUBLIC INTEREST, (94) (WIN 89), 3-24.
THERE IS NO ECONOMIC NECESSITY TO BALANCE THE BUDGET WITHIN THE NEXT FIVE YEARS BECAUSE MAINSTREAM ECONOMICS PROVIDES NO REASON FOR BELIEVING THAT DEFICITS OF ONE OR TWO PERCENT OF GNP SHOULD CAUSE PANIC. THE DEFICIT PERSISTS NOT BECAUSE OF A LACK OF POLITICAL COURAGE BUT BECAUSE POLITICIANS AND THE PUBLIC CORRECTLY JUDGE THAT SERIOUS EFFORTS TO REDUCE IT, WHETHER THROUGH TAX HIKES OR DRASTIC SPENDING CUTS, WOULD THEMSELVES SERIOUSLY HARM THE GENERAL WELFARE. THE POLITICAL STRATEGIES FOLLOWED BY THE MOST VOCAL ADVOCATES OF "RESPONSIBLE" BUDGETING ARE MISGUIDED AND SELF-DEFEATING. TO RELIEVE THE WORRIES OF THE INTERNATIONAL FINANCIAL MARKETS AND THE FINANCE MINISTRIES AND CENTRAL BANKS OF OUR MAJOR TRADING PARTNERS, THE AMERICAN GOVERNMENT NEED NOT BALANCE THE BUDGET. IT WILL BE SUFFICIENT TO REDUCE THE DEFICIT TO A TOLERABLE LEVEL.

09572 WHITE, J.L. JR.
URBAN-RURAL COOPERATION IN THE 1990'S
NATIONAL CIVIC REVIEW, 78(1) (JAN 89), 47-57.
IN THIS ADAPTATION OF HIS PLENARY REMARKS TO THE 94TH
NATIONAL CONFERENCE ON GOVERNMENT, JESSE L. WHITE, JR.,
EXECUTIVE DIRECTOR OF THE SOUTHERN GROWTH POLICIES BOARD,
IDENTIFIES THE UNIQUE ECONOMIC DEVELOPMENT CHALLENGES OF THE
SOUTH; PROJECTS THE SOCIAL, DEMOGRAPHIC AND ECONOMIC TRENDS
THAT WILL IMPACT ON THAT REGION'S WORK FORCE DURING THE NEXT
DECADE; AND CALLS FOR AN URBAN AGENDA THAT WILL ALSO ADDRESS
THE NEEDS OF THE RURAL, SMALL TOWN SOUTH INTO THE NEXT
CENTURY.

09573 WHITE, L.C.
THE COURT OF JUSTICE: THE E.C.'S LAWMAKER
EUROPE, 287 (JUN 89), 41-42.
THE EUROPEAN COMMUNITY IS MORE THAN AN INTERNATIONAL
ORGANIZATION, BUT IT IS NOT YET A FEDERAL ENTITY. ITS
ORIGINS LIE NOT IN FORCE BUT IN LAW, AND ITS FURTHER GROWTH
WILL OWE MUCH TO THE DEVELOPMENT OF ITS LAWS. IT IS
THEREFORE NO WONDER THAT THE EUROPEAN COURT OF JUSTICE HAS
ASSUMED SUCH AN IMPORTANT ROLE AMONG THE COMMUNITY'S
INSTITUTIONS. THE EUROPEAN COURT'S DECISIONS ARE BASED ON
THE TREATIES OF PARIS AND ROME (WHICH, RESPECTIVELY,
ESTABLISHED THE EUROPEAN COAL AND STEEL COMMUNITY, AND THE E.
C. COMMISSION) AND THE SINGLE EUROPEAN ACT (WHICH, IN 1987,
AMENDED THE TREATY OF ROME), WHICH ALL OF THE MEMBER STATES
HAVE ACCEPTED.

09574 WHITE, N.D.
THE UNITED NATIONS AND THE MAINTENANCE OF INTERNATIONAL
PEACE AND SECURITY
DISSERTATION ABSTRACTS INTERNATIONAL, 49(12) (JUN 89),
3864-A.
THE AUTHOR REVIEWS THE POWERS, PRACTICE, AND
EFFECTIVENESS OF THE UNITED NATIONS IN THE MAINTENANCE OF
INTERNATIONAL PEACE AND SECURITY SINCE ITS INCEPTION. HIS
FOCUS IS ON THE SECURITY COUNCIL, THE GENERAL ASSEMBLY, AND
THE SIGNIFICANT POLITICAL FACTORS THAT LIMIT THE AMBIT AND
EFFECTIVENESS OF THEIR POWERS.

09575 WHITE, O.K. JR.
MORMONISM AND THE EQUAL RIGHTS AMENDMENT
JOURNAL OF CHURCH & STATE, 31(2) (SPR 89), 249-268.
IN THE EARLY 1980'S, THE MORMON CHURCH'S AGGRESSIVE
CAMPAIGN AGAINST RATIFICATION OF THE EQUAL RIGHTS AMENDMENT
BECAME AN OBJECT OF PUBLIC SCRUTINY. THE NOTORIETY
ASSOCIATED WITH THE ANTI-ERA ACTIVITIES RAISED THE SPECTER
OF MORMON POLITICAL POWER. THIS ESSAY EXAMINES THE MORMON-
ERA CONTROVERSY BY DESCRIBING AN INCIPIENT MORMON FEMINISM,
THE CHURCH'S ANTI-ERA CAMPAIGN, THE ORGANIZED RESPONSE OF
PRO-ERA MORMONS, AND BROADER MORMON ATTITUDES.

09576 WHITE, R. W.
FROM PEACEFUL PROTEST TO GUERRILLA WAR: MICROMOBILIZATION
OF THE PROVISIONAL IRISH REPUBLICAN ARMY
AMERICAN JOURNAL OF SOCIOLOGY, 94(6) (MAY 89), 1277-1302.
CONCENTRATING ON THE DEVELOPMENT OF ONE POLITICALLY
VIOLENT ORGANIZATION, THE PROVISIONAL IRISH REPUBLICAN ARMY
(IRA), LEADS TO CONCLUSIONS THAT DIFFER FROM MORE AGGREGATE
APPROACHES. A QUANTITATIVE EXAMINATION OF THE DEVELOPMENT OF
IRA VIOLENCE IN A COMMUNITY MOBILIZED FOR PEACEFUL PROTESTS
SHOWS THAT STATE REPRESSION, NOT ECONOMIC DEPRIVATION, WAS
THE MAJOR DETERMINANT OF THIS VIOLENCE. INTENSIVE INTERVIEWS
WITH IRA SUPPORTERS HELP TO INTERPRET THESE QUANTITATIVE
RESULTS BY SHOWING THAT, BEFORE ENDORSING POLITICAL VIOLENCE,
VICTIMS OF REPRESSION MUST (1) VIEW THE AUTHORITY
REPRESSING THEM AS ILLEGITIMATE, (2) VIEW PEACEFUL PROTEST
IN THE FACE OF REPRESSION AS INEFFECTIVE, AND (3) CONSIDER
THE REACTIONS TO REPRESSION OF PEOPLE WITH WHOM THEY HAVE
CLOSE TIES. THESE RESPONSES TO REPRESSION APPEAR TO BE
CONDITIONED BY SOCIAL PLACEMENT; THAT IS, IN CONTRAST TO
MEMBERS OF THE MIDDLE CLASS, MEMBERS OF THE WORKING CLASS
AND STUDENT ACTIVISTS ARE MORE LIKELY TO EXPERIENCE
REPRESSION, TO BE AVAILABLE FOR COSTLY VIOLENT PROTEST, AND
TO EXPERIENCE THE EFFICACY OF POLITICAL VIOLENCE.

09577 WHITE, R.E.
COMPROMISE OR LOSE
COMMONWEAL, CXVI(13) (JUL 89), 390-391.
IN CONCERT WITH CONGRESS AND THE DEMOCRATIC LEADERS OF
LATIN AMERICA, THE BUSH ADMINISTRATION HAS MOVED TO WORK OUT
POLITICAL SOLUTIONS TO THE CRISES THERE. IN EL SALVADOR, THE
COMMITMENT TO NEGOTIATION AND COMPROMISE WILL MEET ITS
TOUGHEST TEST. THE NEAR-TOTAL BREAKDOWN OF THE CENTRIST,
RULING CHRISTAIN DEMOCRATIC PARTY HAS DEALT A MAJOR SHOCK TO
A POLICY THAT ALREADY LACKED COHERENCE AND DIRECTION.

09578 WHITE, S.; WIGHTMAN, G.
GORBACHEV'S REFORMS: THE SOVIET ELECTIONS OF 1989
PARLIAMENTARY AFFAIRS, 42(4) (OCT 89), 560-581.
ELECTIONS HAVE NOT TRADITIONALLY BEEN AN IMPORTANT FORM
OF LINKAGE BETWEEN REGIME AND PUBLIC IN THE USSR. THIS
ARTICLE EXPLORES THE ACCESSION OF MIKHAIL GORBACHEV WHICH
HAS LED TO A SERIES OF REFORMS WHICH PROBABLY REPRESENT THE
MOST RADICAL RECONSTRUCTION OF THE SOVIET POLITICAL SYSTEM
SINCE THE REVOLUTION ITSELF. EXAMINED ARE: ELECTORAL REFORM,
CANDIDATE SELECTION, THE FIRST RESULTS, THE LATER ROUNDS AND
THE CONGRESS OF THE USSR PEOPLE'S DEPUTIES. IT CONCLUDES
THAT A MORE CONSIDERED JUDGMENT ON THE EFFECTS OF THE
POLITICAL SYSTEM MUST BE DEFERRED UNTIL MORE TIME HAS PASSED.

09579 WHITEHEAD, J.
THE DEPARTMENT OF STATE: REQUIREMENTS FOR AN EFFECTIVE
FOREIGN POLICY IN THE 1990S
PRESIDENTIAL STUDIES QUARTERLY, XIX(1) (WIN 89), 11-24.
THE ARTICLE EXAMINES THE REAGAN ADMINISTRATION'S SUCCESS
IN PROMOTING US OBJECTIVES IN THE INCREASINGLY COMPLEX AND
AMBIGUOUS ARENA OF INTERNATIONAL RELATIONS. IT OUTLINES THE
KEY ELEMENTS FOR AN EFFECTIVE FOREIGN POLICY AS AMERICA
ENTERS THE FINAL DECADE OF THIS CENTURY. THESE ELEMENTS
INCLUDE: PROVIDING LEADERSHIP IN A COMPLEX WORLD; MAKING
CLEAR TO THE AMERICAN PUBLIC AND TO US ALLIES AMERICA'S
POLICY GOALS; MAINTAINING PERSISTENCE IN THE PURSUIT OF
THOSE GOALS; UNDERSTANDING THE RELATIONSHIP BETWEEN POWER
AND DIPLOMACY; RECOGNIZING AND PROMOTING FAVORABLE TRENDS;
MAINTAINING CONTINUITY; AND ADAPTING THE STATE DEPARTMENT
FOR THE DEMANDS OF DIPLOMACY IN THE 21ST CENTURY.

09580 WHITEHEAD, J. W.
POLITICAL PHILOSOPHY AND PUBLIC CHOICE THEORY: ECONOMIC
MYTH AND POLITICAL REALITY
DISSERTATION ABSTRACTS INTERNATIONAL, 49(7) (JAN 89),
1947-A.
ALTHOUGH PUBLIC CHOICE THEORY IS GENERALLY CONSIDERED A
POSITIVE BODY OF WORK AIMED AT EXPLAINING ACTUAL POLITICAL
ACTIVITY, THE WORK ALSO CONTAINS A NORMATIVE THEORY OF
POLITICS THAT HAS NOT BEEN ADEQUATELY RECOGNIZED OR
CRITIQUED BY POLITICAL THEORISTS. THE PURPOSE OF THIS
DISSERTATION IS TO PROVIDE SUCH A CRITIQUE.

09581 WHITEHEAD, J.C.
GLOBAL ECONOMIC INTEGRATION
DEPARTMENT OF STATE BULLETIN (US FOREIGN POLICY), 89(2142)
(JAN 89), 18-20.
THE AUTHOR DISCUSSES THE FOLLOWING ASPECTS OF GLOBAL
ECONOMIC INTEGRATION: THE BASIC FORCES PROMOTING FREER TRADE
AND ECONOMIC INTEGRATION SINCE WORLD WAR II, THE DAMAGE
NATIONAL GOVERNMENTS DO WHEN THEY TRY TO FRUSTRATE ECONOMIC
INTEGRATION, THE CURRENT CHALLENGES TO INTEGRATION AND
GLOBAL PROSPERITY, AND THE POSITION OF THE USA IN THE WORLD
ECONOMY.

09582 WHITEHEAD, J.C.
HUMAN RIGHTS AND CHANGE IN EASTERN EUROPE
DEPARTMENT OF STATE BULLETIN (US FOREIGN POLICY), 88(2134)
(MAY 89), 54-56.
DEPUTY SECRETARY OF STATE JOHN WHITEHEAD EXAMINES THE
HUMAN RIGHTS SITUATION IN EASTERN EUROPE. HE ANALYZES THE
EFFECT THAT BILATERAL RELATIONS WITH THE US HAS HAD ON
VARIOUS NATIONS' HUMAN RIGHTS POLICIES AND OUTLINES THE US'
EFFORTS TO USE TRADE RELATIONS TO INFLUENCE HUMAN RIGHTS
POLICIES. HE ALSO TAKES A DETAILED CASE-BY-CASE LOOK AT
SEVERAL EASTERN EUROPEAN NATIONS SUCH AS POLAND, BULGARIA,
ROMANIA, AND CZECHOSLAVAKIA.

09583 WHITEHEAD, J.C.
OPENNESS: THE ONLY PATH TO PROGRESS
DEPARTMENT OF STATE BULLETIN (US FOREIGN POLICY), 88(2138)
(SEP 88), 33-36.
DUE TO MIKHAIL GORBACHEV'S POLICY OF GLASNOST, THE TERM
"OPENNESS" HAS APPEARED IN THE WEST WITH REGULARITY. THE
ARTICLE EXAMINES OPENNESS AS BEING INDISPENSIBLE TO SECURITY.
IT OUTLINES THREE AREAS: ARMS CONTROL, ECONOMICS, AND HUMAN
RIGHTS, WHERE OPENNESS IS A VITAL PRECONDITON TO PROGRESS.

09584 WHITEHEAD, J.C.
THE PLACE OF THE UNITED STATES IN THE WORLD TODAY
PRESIDENTIAL STUDIES QUARTERLY, 19(4) (FAL 89), 703-704.
THIS ARTICLE IS A RECOUNTING OF REMARKS MADE BY MR.
WHITEHEAD AT AN 1989 AWARDS DINNER OF THE CENTER FOR THE
STUDY OF THE PRESIDENCY. HE CONTRASTS THE STEADY STREAM OF
BAD NEWS ON TV TO THE VERY POSITIVE SEA OF CHANGE THAT IS
TAKING PLACE. HE DETAILS THE POSITIVE ACTIONS THAT THE USSR
IS TAKING IN THE AREAS OF ARMS REDUCTION AND IN REDUCING
REGIONAL TENSIONS AROUND THE WORLD. HE STATES THE THE
SOVIETS WERE FORCED TO DO THIS BECAUSE OF THE FAILURE OF
THEIR SYSTEM. WHILE THE SOVIET PROBLEM WAS YESTERDAY'S
PROBLEM, TODAYS CHALLENGES MUST BE MET AND THEY REQUIRE
MULTINATIONAL SOLUTIONS.

09585 WHITEHEAD, L.
LATIN AMERICAN DEBT: AN INTERNATIONAL BARGAINING
PERSPECTIVE
REVIEW OF INTERNATIONAL STUDIES, 15(3) (JUL 89), 231-249.
THIS ARTICLE FOCUSES ON A FEW ISSUES WHICH FREQUENTLY
ARISE IN INTERNATIONAL RELATIONS, AND WHICH REAPPEAR IN A
DISTINCTIVE GUISE IN DISCUSSIONS OF LATIN AMERICAN DEBT. THE

BRIEF HISTORICAL SURVEY LOOKS PARTICULARLY AT THE
RELATIONSHIP BETWEEN PRIVATE CREDITORS AND THE US GOVERNMENT,
TO IDENTIFY THE CIRCUMSTANCES IN WHICH THE POWER OF
WASHINGTON MAY BE ENLISTED IN THE CAUSE OF SOVEREIGN DEBT
COLLECTION. IN THE 1980S THE REAGAN ADMINISTRATION RESISTED
DEMANDS FOR OVERT GOVERNMENT INVOLVEMENT, AND THE BARGAINING
PROCESS LARGELY INVOLVED THE PRIVATE BANKS AND MULTILATERAL
FINANCIAL INSTITUTIONS DEALING 'CASE BY CASE' WITH
INDIVIDUAL DEBTOR NATIONS (ALTHOUGH NO DOUBT THERE WAS
ORCHESTRATION BY CREDITOR GOVERNMENTS IN THE BACKGROUND).
THE NEXT SECTION SHOWS THAT THE RESULT HAS NOT BEEN THE
RESTORATION OF VOLUNTARY CAPITAL FLOWS, BUT A PROTRACTED
DEADLOCK IN WHICH THE DEVELOPMENT OBJECTIVES OF THE DEBTORS
HAVE BEEN SACRIFICED, AND THE CREDITOR BANKS HAVE RUN OUT OF
CONCESSIONS TO OFFER, WHILE BROADER AMERICAN FOREIGN POLICY
INTERESTS HAVE BEEN NEGLECTED. SECTIONS 4 AND 5 CONSIDER
SEVERAL FACETS OF THIS OUTCOME, DISCUSSING THE UNDERLYING
STRUCTURAL ASYMMETRIES BETWEEN THE TWO SIDES, AND OFFERING
AN INTERPRETATION OF DEBTOR DISUNITY.

09586 WHITEHEAD, L.
TIGERS IN LATIN AMERICA?
PHILADELPHIA: ANLS OF AMER ACMY OF POLITICAL AND SOC
SCIENCE, (505) (SEP 89), 142-151.
THIS ARTICLE DISCUSSES THE CONTRASTING TRADE
ORIENTATIONS OF THE EAST ASIAN NEWLY INDUSTRIALIZING
ECONOMIES-THE FOUR TIGERS-AND LATIN AMERICA. IT QUESTIONS
SOME MYTHS ABOUT THE INGREDIENTS OF EAST ASIAN POLICY
SUCCESS AND DRAWS ATTENTION TO THE UNDERLYING GEOPOLITICAL
FACTORS THAT HELP TO ACCOUNT FOR THE CONTRASTING TRADE
PERFORMANCE OF THE TWO REGIONS. IT CONCLUDES THAT THE EAST
ASIAN EXPERIENCE IS AT LEAST AS ABERRANT AS THAT OF LATIN
AMERICA AND THAT TO CALL THE FORMER A MODEL IS A MISNOMER
SINCE THE MOST ESSENTIAL INGREDIENTS ARE NOT TRANSFERABLE.

09587 WHITEHOUSE, C.S.
FUTURE U.S. POLICY AND ACTION: DEFENSE DEPARTMENT
PERSPECTIVE
TERRORISM, 11(6) (1988), 546-549.
THIS IS A TALK GIVEN AT A CONFERENCE ON TERRORISM BY
CHARLES WHITEHOUSE, ASSISTANT SECRETARY OF DEFENSE FOR
SPECIAL OPERATIONS, U.S. DEPARTMENT OF DEFENSE. HE ADDRESSES
INTERNATIONAL TERRORISM AND ITS IMPACT ON U.S. RELATIONS
WITH OTHER COUNTRIES. HE EXAMINES THE PLO AND ITS OBJECTIVES
AND SUGGESTS THAT INTERNATIONAL TERRORISM IS GOING TO
CONTINUE. TO COMBAT IT, HE SUGGESTS THAT THE GAP BETWEEN
COMMANDER AND COMMANDER-IN-CHIEF MUST BE A SMALL ONE. HE
ADDRESSES: INTERNATIONAL COOPERATION; TERRORISM; INSURGENCY;
NARCOTICS TRAFFICKING; INTERPLAY BETWEEN MILITARY
ESTABLISHMENTS; THE PROBLEM OF TELEVISION COVERAGE; AND
COUNTERTERRORISM AND ANTITERRORISM,

09588 WHITEMAN, K.
REFLECTIONS ON LOME
AFRICA REPORT, 34(1) (JAN 89), 40-42.
A TRADE AND AID TREATY BETWEEN THE EUROPEAN COMMUNITY
AND THE AFRICAN, CARIBBEAN, AND PACIFIC, THE LOME CONVENTION
IN ITS THIRD RENEGOTIATION IS RUNNING INTO SNAGS AS A
CHANGING EUROPEAN ENVIRONMENT AND AFRICA'S MOUNTING ECONOMIC
PROBLEMS ARE THREATENING THE VERY BASIS OF THE AGREEMENT.
"CONDITIONALITY" HAS MOVED TO THE CENTER OF THE DISCUSSIONS,
POTENTIALLY UNDERMINING THE LOME PHILOSOPHY.

09589 WHOLSTETTER, P.
THE POLITICS OF LEGISLATIVE OVERSIGHT: MONITORING
EDUCATIONAL REFORM IN SIX STATES
POLICY STUDIES REVIEW, 9(1) (AUT 89), 50-65.
THE MAJOR THEME OF THIS PAPER IS THAT OVERSIGHT IS BEST
UNDERSTOOD AS AN INTEGRAL PART OF LEGISLATIVE-ADMINISTRATIVE
POLITICS. BY EXAMINING HOW SIX STATES MONITORED RECENT
EDUCATIONAL REFORMS, THE AUTHOR FINDS THAT LEGISLATORS
CONDUCTED OVERSIGHT IN WAYS THAT MINIMIZED TIME COMMITMENTS
AND MAXIMIZED POLITICAL BENEFITS. THE PAPER CONCLUDES THAT
LEGISLATIVE INTEREST IN CONTROLLING IMPLEMENTATION OFTEN HAS
SECONDARY TO POLITICAL CONSIDERATIONS. OVERSIGHT, THEREFORE,
MAY NOT REALLY BE EFFECTIVE AS AN ACCOUNTABILITY TOOL.

09590 WIARDA, H.J.
POLITICAL CULTURE AND THE ATTRACTION OF MARXISM-LENNINISM:
NATIONAL INFERIORITY COMPLEXES AS AN EXPLANATORY FACTOR
WORLD AFFAIRS, 151(3) (WIN 88), 143-150.
THIS PAPER EXAMINES THE PRESENT CRISIS OF MARXISM-
LENINISM AND ALSO THE APPEALS OF THAT IDEOLOGY. IT EXPLORES
THE RELATIONSHIP BETWEEN NATIONAL INFERIORITY COMPLEXES AND
THE APPEAL OF "ADVANCED IDEOLOGIES" USING LATIN AMERICA AS
ONE EXAMPLE. IT SUGGESTS THAT IN EXPLAINING REVOLUTIONS,
SOCIAL SCIENCE HAS TENDED TO FOCUS ON SOCIOECONOMIC FACTORS
RATHER THAN ON POLITICAL CULTURAL EXPLANATIONS AND OFFERS
RESEARCH SUGGESTIONS FOR FURTHER STUDY ON THE SUBJECT.

09591 WIARDA, H.J.; WIARDA, I.S.
THE UNITED STATES AND SOUTH AMERICA: THE CHALLENGE OF
FRAGILE DEMOCRACY
CURRENT HISTORY, 88(536) (MAR 89), 113-117, 151-152.

THE BASIC CHALLENGE TO INTER-AMERICAN RELATIONS IS THE
CONTINUING ECONOMIC CRISIS AND THE UNRAVELING OF DEMOCRATIC
PROCESSES IN SOUTH AMERICA. DEMOCRACY IN LATIN AMERICA IS
FRAGILE AT BEST; AT WORST, IT MAY NOT SURVIVE THROUGH THE
BUSH ADMINISTRATION.

09592 WIATR, J. J.
WHY DO WE REPENT? THE RESPONSIBILITY OF MARXISTS
SOCIALISM AND DEMOCRACY, (FAL 89), 27-33.
THIS TEXT IS BASED ON A TALK GIVEN AT THE PLENARY
SESSION OF THE THIRD THEORETICAL AND IDEOLOGICAL CONFERENCE
OF THE POLISH UNITED WORKERS PARTY, FEBRUARY 2, 1989. IT
ARRIVES FROM WITHIN THE STRUGGLE FOR A REDEFINITION OF THE
SOCIALIST PROJECT IN POLAND AND OFFERS SOME NEW THINKING ON
THE SUBJECTS OF REFORM, CIVIL SOCIETY, AND MARXISM. IT
CONCENTRATES ON THE THEORETICAL FOUNDATIONS OF THE POLICY
THAT AIMS AT THE FORMATION OR REFORMATION OF SOCIALIST CIVIL
SOCIETY. IT CONCLUDES THAT THE NEW, DIFFERENT, AND BETTER
SOCIALISM REQUIRES AN ACCURATE, WISE POLICY, GUIDED BY
REALISM.

09593 WICE, J.
TAKING THE COUNT TO COURT
CAMPAIGNS AND ELECTIONS, 10(2) (AUG 89), 47.
THE U.S. CENSUS CONTINUES TO BE PLAGUED BY SIGNIFICANT
INACCURACIES, COMMONLY KNOWN AS THE "UNDERCOUNT." A LAWSUIT
HAS BEEN FILED TO FORCE THE CENSUS BUREAU TO CHANGE ITS
PROCEDURES TO MITIGATE THE EFFECTS OF THE UNDERCOUNT, WHICH
IS MOST PRONOUNCED IN THE INNER CITIES. THE FEDERAL
GOVERNMENT IS THE DEFENDANT IN THE CASE, WHICH IS BEING
PURSUED BY NEW YORK, CALIFORNIA, NEW YORK CITY, LOS ANGELES,
AND CHICAGO.

09594 WICK, C.
THE FUTURE OF PUBLIC DIPLOMACY
PRESIDENTIAL STUDIES QUARTERLY, XIX(1) (WIN 89), 25-30.
THE AUTHOR DISCUSSES THE FUTURE OF DIPLOMACY AND
CONCENTRATES ON US-USSR RELATIONS. HE OUTLINES THE
INCREASING AVAILABILITY OF INFORMATION WORLDWIDE AND
CHRONICLES THE IMPACT OF THE INFORMATION REVOLUTION ON
DIPLOMACY. HE ARGUES THAT THE INFORMATION AGE IS BEING FELT
EVEN IN AUTHORITARIAN REGIMES, AND THE VISION OF A "GLOBAL
COTTAGE" WHERE WORLD PUBLIC OPINION DETERMINE WORLD POLICY
IS RAPIDLY BECOMING A REALITY.

09595 WICK, C. Z.
U.S.-SOVIET RELATIONS: THE GLOBAL VILLAGE AND THE FREE
FLOW OF INFORMATION
POLITICAL COMMUNICATION AND PERSUASION, 5(3) (1988),
217-223.
THE FULL AND POWERFUL SWEEP OF THE INFORMATION
REVOLUTION IS STILL UNFOLDING. ITS FORCE -- WHICH BEGAN AS
THE MEDIEVAL SCRIBES WERE REPLACED BY GUTENBERG'S MECHANICAL
PRINTING PRESS -- HAS GATHERED MOMENTUM AND IS NOW SHAKING
THE SOCIAL, ECONOMIC, POLITICAL, AND IDEOLOGICAL FOUNDATIONS
OF OUR WORLD. TODAY, A HIGH-TECH "WAR OF IDEAS" HAS SHIFTED
TO CENTER STAGE IN GLOBAL POLITICS. A WAR OF IDEAS THAT
RESPECTS NEITHER TIME NOR SPACE, A GLOBAL TELEVISED WAR OF
IDEAS THAT IS FOUGHT IN LIVING ROOMS AND PLACES OF WORK, IN
CITIES AND IN COUNTRYSIDES IN EVERY HEMISPHERE.

09596 WICKENS, B.; LOWTHER, W.; NIXON, D.
A CALL FOR ACTION
MACLEAN'S (CANADA'S NEWS MAGAZINE), 102(28) (JUL 89),
38-39.
AS SCIENTIST CONTINUE TO ARGUE OVER THE "GREENHOUSE
EFFECT" THERE IS INCREASING PRESSURE FOR OTTAWA TO PUT ITS
ENVIRONMENTAL AFFAIRS IN ORDER. CANADA HAS EMERGED AS A
WORLD LEADER IN EFFORTS AT ENVIRONMENTAL PROTECTION. HOWEVER,
CRITICS INSIDE OF CANADA ARE BLASTING THE GOVERNMENT FOR
ENCOURAGING OTHER NATIONS TO REDUCE FOSSIL FUEL CONSUMPTION
WHILE, AT THE SAME TIME, ENCOURAGING THE DEVELOPMENT OF
PETROLUEM MEGAPROJECTS.

09597 WICKENS, B.; ABRAMSON, G.; JANSSEN, B.
TWO SHOWDOWNS WITH SOCIALISM
MACLEAN'S (CANADA'S NEWS MAGAZINE), 102(1) (JAN 89), 53-54.
WORKERS IN SPAIN AND FRANCE STAGE SIGNIFICANT STRIKES IN
PROTEST OF THEIR SOCIALIST GOVERNMENT'S WAGE POLICIES. IN
FRANCE, PUBLIC SERVICE STRIKES CRIPPLED MASS TRANSIT IN
PARIS, SLOWED MAIL DELIVERY NATIONWIDE, AND INTERRUPTED
HOSPITAL SERVICES. IN SPAIN, AN ESTIMATED EIGHT MILLION
WORKERS STAGED THE MOST WIDESPREAD WORK STOPPAGE IN 54 YEARS.
THE SOCIALIST GOVERNMENTS IN BOTH NATIONS STILL ENJOY
MAJORITY SUPPORT; THEIR CREDIBILITY AS GOOD MONEY MANAGERS
MAY BE STRONG ENOUGH TO ALLOW THEM TO GIVE LITTLE OR NO
CONCESSIONS TO LABOR.

09598 WICKHAM-CROWLEY, T.P.
UNDERSTANDING FAILED REVOLUTION IN EL SALVADOR: A
COMPARATIVE ANALYSIS OF REGIME TYPES AND SOCIAL STRUCTURES
POLITICS AND SOCIETY, 17(4) (DEC 89), 511.
THE AUTHOR UTILIZES JOHN STUART MILL'S METHOD OF
DIFFERENCE TO ANALYZE THE CONDITIONS IN NICARAGUA AND EL

SALVADOR THAT LED TO DISPARATE REVOLUTIONARY OUTCOMES. HE
ALSO CONSIDERS THE "IMPERIAL PROP" THESIS: THAT THE UNITED
STATES WITHDREW SUPPORT FROM SOMOZA AND HE FELL TO A POPULAR
INSURGENCY, BUT THE USA THREW ALL ITS ECONOMIC AND MILITARY
WEIGHT BEHIND THE SALVADORAN REGIME, ENABLING THE GOVERNMENT
TO WITHSTAND THE POPULAR INSURGENCY BUT NOT DESTROY IT. HE
ARGUES THAT THE CASE OF GUATEMALA, A FAILED INSURGENCY IN
SPITE OF WITHDRAWN US SUPPORT, CASTS STRONG DOUBT ON US
SUPPORT AS THE SINGLE, DECISIVE CAUSE OF FAILURE OR SUCCESS
IN CENTRAL AMERICAN REVOLUTIONS.

09599 WIDGREN, J.
ASYLUM SEEKERS IN EUROPE IN THE CONTEXT OF SOUTH-NORTH
MOVEMENTS
INTERNATIONAL MIGRATION REVIEW, 23(3) (FAL 89), 599-605.
THIS ARTICLE WILL ELUCIDATE THE THREAT TOWARDS THE
ESTABLISHED SYSTEM FOR ASYLUM IN EUROPE WHICH ORIGINATES
FROM THE INCREASE OF ASYLUM SEEKERS WITH VERY WEAK OR NO
GENUINE CLAIMS AT ALL. THIS INCREASE MIGHT BE THE EARLY SIGN
OF NEW INTERCONTINENTAL MOVEMENTS OF MIGRATION. IT EXPLORES
NEW INTERCONTINENTAL MOVEMENTS, THE CHALLENGE PRESENTED BY
THESE PATTERNS AND OFFERS SOLUTIONS TO THE NEW ASYLUM
SITUATION.

09600 WIDLANSKI, M.
ISRAEL MOVES RIGHT
NATIONAL REVIEW, XLI(12) (JUN 89), 24-25.
THE CENTER OF ISRAELI POLITICS HAS MOVED SOLIDY TO THE
RIGHT ON ECONOMIC MATTERS AS WELL AS SECURITY ISSUES, WHILE
THE SOCIALIST LABOR PARTY, UNDER SHIMON PERES, MAY BE
HEADING THE WAY OF BRITAIN'S LABOUR PARTY AND THE U.S.
DEMOCRATIC PARTY ON A NATIONAL LEVEL: PERMANENT MINORITY
STATUS.

09601 WIDMAIER, U.
DEMOGRAPHIC CHANGE, LABOUR FORCE DYNAMICS, AND EMPLOYMENT;
NEW PROBLEMS AND OLD POLITICS?
EUROPEAN JOURNAL OF POLITICAL RESEARCH, 17(4) (JUL 89),
501-531.
THE PAPER EXAMINES THE PROBLEMS FOR SOCIAL PROCTECTION
AND ECONOMIC GROWTH THAT RISE FROM THE DEVELOPMENT OF A
DUALISTIC LABOR FORCE - DIVIDED INTO A PRIVILEGED CORE AND A
DISADVANTAGED PERIPHERY - CREATED BY THE DYNAMIC INTERACTION
OF LABOR SUPPLY RIGIDITIES AND RAPID TECHNOLOGICAL GROWTH.
IT CONCLUDES THAT REFORMS LABORS MARKET INSTITUTIONS HAVE TO
BE INTRODUCED IN ORDER TO SOLVE THE EXISTING PROBLEMS.

09602 WIECHERS, M.
THE LAW COMMISSION'S BILL OF RIGHTS REPORT
SOUTH AFRICA FOUNDATION REVIEW, 15(7) (JUL 89), 4,8.
THE ARTICLE EXAMINES THE WORKING PAPER OF SOUTH AFRICA'S
LAW COMMISSION ON THE POSSIBILITY OF, AND THEORETICAL AND
LEGAL FRAMEWORK FOR, A BILL OF RIGHTS. THE AUTHOR OUTLINES
THE UNDERLYING THEORIES OF HUMAN RIGHTS AND THE RECOGNITION
OF GROUP VALUES (NOT BASED ON RACE), AND DECLARES THE REPORT
TO BE A "DOCUMENT OF UTMOST CONSTITUTIONAL IMPORTANCE."
ALTHOUGH THE LAW COMMISSION HAS NO EXECUTIVE POWERS AND
CANNOT ASSUME ANY GOVERNMENT FUNCTIONS, THE PAPER IS
UNLIKELY TO BE COMPLETELY IGNORED. THE AUTHOR CONCLUDES THAT
A BILL OF RIGHTS IS NOT A CURE-ALL FOR SOUTH AFRICA'S
SOCIETAL ILLS, BUT IT IS AN IMPORTANT FIRST STEP IN THE
DIRECTION OF DEMOCRACY AND EQUALITY

09603 WIECHERS, M.
THE LAW COMMONS BILL OF RIGHTS REPORT: A NEW DAWN FOR
HUMAN RIGHTS IN SA
SOUTH AFRICA INTERNATIONAL, 20(1) (JUL 89), 24-33.
THIS ARTICLE IS AN ASSESSMENT OF THE RECENT LAW
COMMISSION'S BILL OF RIGHTS REPORT WHICH IS A HISTORIC
LANDMARK FOR SOUTH AFRICA. THIS WORKING PAPER RESTORES HUMAN
RIGHTS PROTECTION AS A CENTRAL ELEMENT IN NEW CONSTITUTIONAL
DISPOSITION. THE NATURE, THE BACKGROUND, CONTENTS AND
IMPLICATIONS AND FUTURE OF THE REPORT IS GIVEN.

09604 WIESELTIER, L.
SPOILERS AT THE PARTY
NATIONAL INTEREST, (17) (FAL 89), 12-16.
THIS ARTICLE PUTS TWO FENCES AROUND FUKUYAMA'S END OF
HISTORY ARGUMENT. THE FIRST IS HISTORICAL -THAT THE DEFEAT
OF COMMUNISM IS NOT QUITE THE SAME THING AS THE VICTORY OF
LIBERALISM. THE SECOND IS PHILOSOPHICAL - THAT IT IS AN
INSULT TO LIBERALISM TO DESCRIBE ITS SUCCESS AS AN END OF
HISTORY. THE SOURCES OF CONFLICT AFTER THE END OF HISTORY
WILL CONTINUE TO BE IDEATIONAL OR IDEOLOGICAL. IT OFFERS
FIVE SUCH SPOILERS OF FUKUYAMA'S PARTY - LIBERALISM ITSELF,
INCOMPLETE LIBERALISM, NUCLEAR LIBERALISM, NATIONALISM, AND
RELIGION.

09605 WIGHTMAN, G.
CZECHOSLOVAKIA UNDER MILOS JAKES
JOURNAL OF COMMUNIST STUDIES, 5(3) (SEP 89), 349-354.
THIS ARTICLE NOTES THAT IN THE 16 MONTHS SINCE MILOS
JAKES BECAME GENERAL SECRETARY OF THE COMMUNIST PARTY OF
CZECHOSLOVAKIA THERE HAVE BEEN NO DRAMATIC POWER SHIFTS. IT

ANALYZES THE SEVERAL CHANGES IN DIRECTION REGARDING ECONOMIC
REFORM AND POLITICAL DEMOCRATIZATION. IT ALSO NOTES THAT
THERE ARE SIGNS OF CHANGE IN FUTURE PARTY LEADERSHIP AND IN
THE FEDERAL GOVERNMENT, AS WELL AS THE ESTABLISHMENT OF A
NEW COMMITTEE FOR PARTY WORK. IT DETAILS THESE CHANGES AND
ANALYZES THE POSSIBILITIES OF FUTURE REFORM.

09606 WIGHTMAN, G.
NO PROSPECT FOR REFORM IN CZECHOSLOVAKIA?
CONTEMPORARY REVIEW, 254(1477) (FEB 89), 63-68.
ECONOMIC NECESSITY AND A DESIRE TO STAY IN LINE WITH THE
BROAD THRUST OF POLICY IN THE SOVIET UNION HAVE COMBINED TO
PLACE ECONOMIC REFORM BACK ON THE AGENDA IN PRAGUE. IT
REMAINS TO BE SEEN WHAT THE LONGER-TERM CONSEQUENCES IN THE
POLITICAL SPHERE OF THE ECONOMIC CHANGES WILL BE, OR WHETHER
THE MINIMAL MODIFICATIONS THAT HAVE BEEN MADE TO POLITICAL
PRACTICE WILL LEAD TO DEEPER CHANGES, BUT IN THE MEANTIME IT
WOULD BE A MISTAKE TO OVERSIMPLIFY THE CASE AND REGARD
CZECHOSLOVAKIA IN 1989 AS A BASTION OF UNSWERVING OPPOSITION
TO PERESTROIKA IN ANY SHAPE OR FORM. AT LEAST IN THE ECONOMY
THAT IS NOT THE CASE. ECO/POLICY EUROPE/E

09607 WIJEWEERA, B.S.
POLICY DEVELOPMENTS AND ADMINISTRATION CHANGES IN SRI
LANKA: 1948-1987
PUBLIC ADMINISTRATION AND DEVELOPMENT, 9(3) (JUN 89),
271-286.
IN ITS STUDY OF ADMINISTRATIVE CHANGE AND REFORM IN SRI
LANKA, THE ARTICLE CONCENTRATES ON TWO MAJOR STRANDS OF
ADMINISTRATIVE CHANGE: THE FIRST DERIVES FROM THE "IMPERIAL
HERITAGE" FLOWING MAINLY FROM BRITISH COLONIAL RULE; THE
SECOND RELATES TO POST-INDEPENDENT POLICY DEVELOPMENTS
BEARING ON ADMINISTRATIVE STYLES AND STRUCTURES. THE ARTICLE
PAYS CLOSE ATTENTION TO HOW THE TWO STRANDS ARE INTERWOVEN
OVER THE PAST FOUR DECADES. IT CONCLUDES WITH A PROGNOSIS OF
THE EMERGING ADMINISTRATIVE STRUCTURE, STYLE, AND
ENVIRONMENT OF PUBLIC ADMINISTRATION IN SRI LANKA'S FUTURE.

09608 WIJKMAN, P.M.
PATTERNS OF TRADE IN THE EUROPEAN ECONOMIC SPACE
INTERNATIONAL SPECTATOR, XXIV(1) (JAN 89), 30-38.
THE UNITY OF THE EUORPEAN ECONOMIC SPACE IS SOMETIMES
OBSCURED BY ITS INSTITUTIONAL DIVISION INTO TWO TRADE
GROUPINGS: THE EUORPEAN COMUNITY AND THE EUROPEAN FREE TRADE
ASSOCIATION. THIS ESSAY EXPLORES SOME ASPECTS OF THIS
ECONOMIC SPACE, INCLUDING ITS HISTORY AND ITS CURRENT
STRUCTURE. FACTORS THAT CALL FOR INSTITUTIONAL DIVERSITY AND
INNOVATION IN THE EES ARE IDENTIFIED.

09609 WILCOX, C.; COOK, E.A.
EVANGELICAL WOMEN AND FEMINISM: SOME ADDITIONAL EVIDENCE
WOMEN AND POLITICS, 9(2) (1989), 27-49.
ALTHOUGH A NUMBER OF STUDIES HAVE DEMONSTRATED THAT
EVANGELICAL WOMEN ARE MORE LIKELY THAN OTHER WOMEN TO TAKE
ANTIFEMINIST POSITIONS, RECENT RESEARCH SUGGESTS THAT THERE
MIGHT BE SUBSTANTIAL SUPPORT AMONG EVANGELICALS FOR CERTAIN
FEMINIST POSITIONS. IN ADDITION, THIS RESEARCH SUGGESTS THAT
COGNITIVE STRUCTURING MAY PLAY AN IMPORTANT ROLE IN
DETERMINING THE POSITIONS OF EVANGELICAL WOMEN: THOSE WHO
ARE ABLE TO SEPARATE THE RELIGIOUS AND POLITICAL DOMAINS ARE
MORE LIKELY TO TAKE FEMINIST POSITIONS. USING DATA FROM THE
1984 AMERICAN NATIONAL ELECTION STUDY, THE AUTHORS FIND THAT
EVANGELICAL WOMEN ARE INDEED MORE ANTIFEMINIST THAN OTHER
WOMEN, BUT THAT A SIZABLE MINORITY TAKE FEMINIST POSITIONS
ON A NUMBER OF ISSUES. APPROXIMATELY ONE IN SIX CAN BE
CLASSIFIED AS HAVING A POLITICIZED FEMINIST CONSCIOUSNESS,
WHILE AN ADDITIONAL QUARTER ARE POTENTIAL CONVERTS TO THE
FEMINIST CAUSE. THESE POTENTIAL FEMINISTS ARE FAIRLY
NEGATIVE TOWARD THE FEMINIST MOVEMENT, HOWEVER. THIS IS DUE
IN PART TO THE ASSOCIATION BY MANY EVANGELICAL WOMEN BETWEEN
THE WOMEN'S MOVEMENT, LESBIAN RIGHTS, AND ABORTION.

09610 WILCOX, C.
FEMINISM AND ANTI-FEMINISM AMONG EVANGELICAL WOMEN
WESTERN POLITICAL QUARTERLY, 42(1) (MAR 89), 147-160.
ALTHOUGH MUCH RESEARCH HAS SUGGESTED A LINK BETWEEN
EVANGELICAL RELIGION AND ANTI-FEMINIST POSITIONS, FOWLER HAS
REPORTED THAT EVANGELICAL ELITES HAVE BEEN SPLIT ON FEMINIST
ISSUES. OTHER RESEARCH HAS SUGGESTED THAT THERE IS SOME
VARIATION AMONG EVANGELICAL AND FUNDAMENTALIST WOMEN IN
THEIR ATTITUDES ON FEMINIST ISSUES, BUT TO DATE THERE HAS
BEEN NO ATTEMPT FULLY TO EXAMINE SUPPORT FOR FEMINIST AND
ANTI-FEMINIST POSITIONS AND ORGANIZATIONS. USING DATA FROM A
NATIONAL SURVEY OF EVANGELICALS IN 1983, EVANGELICAL WOMEN
ARE INDEED DIVIDED ON FEMINIST ISSUES, WITH APPROXIMATELY
EQUAL NUMBERS FALLING INTO FEMINIST AND ANTI-FEMINIST CAMPS.
MOREOVER, WHEN THE POTENTIAL FOR FURTHER MOBILIZATION BY
FEMINIST AND ANTI-FEMINIST GROUPS IS TAKEN INTO ACCOUNT,
SUPPORT FOR FEMINIST AND ANTI-FEMINIST ORGANIZATIONS IS
STILL ROUGHLY EQUAL.

09611 WILCOX, C.
ORGANIZATIONAL VARIABLES AND CONTRIBUTION BEHAVIOR OF
LARGE PACS: A LONGITUDINAL ANALYSIS

POLITICAL BEHAVIOR, 11(2) (JUN 89), 157-173.
ALTHOUGH THERE HAS BEEN A GOOD DEAL OF RESEARCH ON PAC
CONTRIBUTION BEHAVIOR, TO DATE THERE HAS BEEN NO EFFORT TO
SYSTEMATICALLY EVALUATE THE IMPACT OF VARIOUS ORGANIZATIONAL
CHARACTERISTICS OF PACS ON THEIR CONTRIBUTION BEHAVIOUR OVER
TIME. USING DATA FROM A NEWLY RELEASED LONGITUDINAL FILE
FROM THE FEDERAL ELECTION COMMISSION, THE AUTHOR EXAMINES
THE IMPACT OF ORGANIZATIONAL VARIABLES ON THE CONTRIBUTION
BEHAVIOR OF LARGE PACS IN THREE ELECTION CYCLES, AND ON
CHANGES IN CONTRIBUTION BEHAVIOR BETWEEN THESE ELECTIONS. HE
FINDS THAT PAC TYPE, SIZE, AGE. AND THE PRESENCE OF A
WASHINGTON OFFICE ARE ALL IMPORTANT DETERMINANTS OF PAC
CONTRIBUTIONS. CHANGES IN ORGANIZATIONAL CHARACTERISTICS,
PARTICULARLY GROWTH IN REVENUES, ARE WEAKLY RELATED TO
CHANGE IN CONTRIBUTION BEHAVIOR, WHICH SEEMS TO BE PRIMARILY
A RESPONSE TO CHANGES IN THE STRATEGIC ENVIRONMENT.

09612 WILCOX, C.
POLITICAL ACTION COMMITTEES AND ABORTION: A LONGITUDINAL
ANALYSIS
WOMEN AND POLITICS, 9(1) (1989), 1-19.
MOST RESEARCH ON ABORTION HAS FOCUSED ON THE
DETERMINANTS OF ATTITUDES AMONG THE PUBLIC OR ELITES, OR ON
THE TACTICS OF ACTIVISTS ON BOTH SIDES OF THE ISSUE. TO DATE,
HOWEVER, THERE HAS BEEN LITTLE ATTENTION TO THE FORMATION
AND BEHAVIOR OF PRO-LIFE AND PROCHOICE ORGANIZATIONS. THIS
PAPER ADDRESSES THESE LATTER QUESTIONS AND COMPARES THE
RESOURCES AND STRATEGIES OF PACS ON BOTH SIDES OF THE
ABORTION ISSUE. PRO-LIFE PACS OUTNUMBER THEIR PRO-CHOICE
COUNTERPARTS BY A WIDE MARGIN AND RAISE CONSIDERABLY MORE
MONEY AS WELL. PRO-CHOICE GROUPS ARE MORE PARTISAN, GIVING
HEAVILY TO DEMOCRATS, AND ALSO GIVE HIGHER PROPORTIONS OF
THEIR CONTRIBUTIONS TO INCUMBENTS. MANY PROF-LIFE GROUPS
HAVE ENGAGED IN INDEPENDENT EXPENDITURES, A PRACTICE NOT
COMMON IN PRO-CHOICE PACS.

09613 WILCOX, C.
SHARE THE WEALTH
AMERICAN POLITICS QUARTERLY, 17(4) (OCT 89), 386-408.
ALTHOUGH HE NOW KNOW A GOOD DEAL ABOUT THE CONTRIBUTION
STRATEGIES OF INDIVIDUALS, PARTIES, AND POLITICAL ACTION
COMMITTEES (PACS), WE KNOW CONSIDERABLY LESS ABOUT
CONTRIBUTIONS MADE BY INCUMBENT MEMBERS OF CONGRESS TO OTHER
CANDIDATES. SUCH CONTRIBUTIONS ARE SOMETIMES MADE THROUGH
PACS ESTABLISHED BY THE INCUMBENT, BUT MANY MORE MEMBERS
CONTRIBUTE THROUGH THEIR CAMPAIGN COMMITTEES. THIS ARTICLE
EXPLORES INCUMBENTS' CONTRIBUTIONS DURING THE 1983-84
ELECTION CYCLE. THOSE CONTRIBUTORS WHO GIVE LARGE AMOUNTS
OFTEN DO SO FOR INSTRUMENTAL PURPOSES-TO FURTHER THEIR
ELECTION, POWER, OR POLICY ENDS. THE VAST MAJORITY OF
CONTRIBUTORS, HOWEVER, SEEM TO CHANNEL THEIR SURPLUS
CAMPAIGN FUNDS TO CANDIDATES IN NEED-PARTICULARLY THOSE
IDENTIFIED BY THEIR PARTIES' CAMPAIGN COMMITTEES AS LIKELY
TO BE INVOLVED IN A CLOSE ELECTION.

09614 WILDE, M.D.
A HOBSON'S CHOICE FOR MISKITS REFUGEES
THE CHRISTIAN CENTURY, 106(23) (AUG 89), 726-728.
THIS ARTICLE DETAILS THE DILEMMAS FACING NICARAGUA'S
MISKITO INDIANS. THOUGH SIGNIFICANT PROGRESS HAS BEEN MADE
TOWARD PEACEFULLY RESOLVING INDIAN GRIEVANCES IN NICARAGUA,
IT IS AN UNSTABLE PEACE, MARRED BY SPORADIC CONFLICTS AND
DEEPENING ECONOMIC HARDSHIP-PARTLY THE FAULT OF CONTINUING
U.S. PRESSURES ON NICARAGUA. SOME REFUGEES MAY NEVER GO HOME,
DESPITE THE URGING OF THE UNHCR AND THE HONDURAN GOVERNMENT.
THESE REFUGEES NEED HELP IN THE SHORT RUN, WHILE U.S. AID
IS BEING WITHDRAWN AND HONDURAS GRAPPLES WITH THE REGIONAL
RECESSION. FORCED TO CHOOSE BETWEEN AN UNSTABLE REPATRIATION
AND PERMANENT RESETTLEMENT, THE INDIANS ARE CAUGHT IN A
HOBSON'S CHOICE.

09615 WILDS, L.J.
ORGANIZATIONAL BEHAVIOR IN THE IMPLEMENTATION OF
ENVIRONMENTAL WATER POLICY
DISSERTATION ABSTRACTS INTERNATIONAL, 49(8) (FEB 89),
2379-A.
THE APPLICATION OF ENVIRONMENTAL REGULATORY POLICY TO
SITE-SPECIFIC WATER RESOURCE PROJECTS IN THE USA OCCURS IN A
CLIMATE OF INTER-ORGANIZATIONAL, INTER-GOVERNMENTAL
BARGAINING. OFTEN, THE IMPLEMENTATION PROCESS BREAKS DOWN
BECAUSE INDIVIDUALS FIND IT DIFFICULT TO UNDERSTAND THE
PROCESS ITSELF OR THE OTHER ORGANIZATIONS INVOLVED. TOOLS
ARE NEEDED TO HELP INDIVIDUALS INVOLVED IN THE PROCESS AT
THE BOTTOM LEVEL. THIS DISSERTATION DEVELOPS THE LEGAL-
INSTITUTIONAL ANALYSIS MODEL TO SERVE AS ONE OF THOSE TOOLS.

09616 WILEY, J.
THE ISLAMIC POLITICAL MOVEMENT OF IRAQ
DISSERTATION ABSTRACTS INTERNATIONAL, 49(7) (JAN 89),
1953-A.
WITH RELIGION PROVIDING THE WITH RELIGION PROVIDING THE
NECESSARY COHESION, IRAQI SOCIAL GROUPS DISADVANTAGED BY
GOVERNMENT POLICIES HAVE BANDED TOGETHER. THE ULTIMATE GOAL
OF THEIR MOVEMENT IS TO ESTABLISH ISLAMIC GOVERNMENT AND A

MODERN ISLAMIC SOCIETY UNDER THE LEADERSHIP OF MUSLIM
ACTIVISTS.

09617 WILEY, S.L.
DIMENSIONS OF CANDIDATE EVALUATION: US PRESIDENTIAL
ELECTIONS
DISSERTATION ABSTRACTS INTERNATIONAL, 49(3) (SEP 88),
611-A.
THE RESEARCH CONSIDERS AMERICAN PRESIDENTIAL ELECTIONS
WHERE THE AGENDA IS SET BY THE NOMINATING PROCESS WHICH
EFFECTIVELY FORCES A MAJORITY WINNER BY RESTRICTING THE
CHOICE TO TWO CANDIDATES IN THE GENERAL ELECTION. ANALYSIS
OF SURVEY DATA WAS CONDUCTED TO DETERMINE WHETHER THERE WAS
A PRE-NOMINATION CANDIDATE WHO COULD DEFEAT ALL OTHER
CANDIDATES AND WHETHER THERE WAS EVIDENCE OF MULTIPLE
EVALUATION DIMENSIONS IN ANY OR ALL OF THE ELECTION YEARS.

09618 WILF, C.
THE HISTORY AND POLITICS OF THE MOVEMENT FROM JUDICIAL TO
CONGRESSIONAL PREEMPTION OF STATE AUTHORITY WITH SPECIAL
REFERENCE TO HAZARDOUS WASTE MANAGEMENT
DISSERTATION ABSTRACTS INTERNATIONAL, 50(6) (DEC 89),
1791-A.
AS MANAGEMENT OF HAZARDOUS WASTE BECOMES AN INCREASINGLY
URGENT PRIORITY, THE UNITED STATES FINDS ITSELF CONFRONTED
WITH A DILEMMA. THE CONGRESS IS REGULARLY RELYING ON
PREEMPTORY IMPLEMENTATION SCHEMES TO CARRY OUT BROAD
ENVIRONMENTAL GOALS, ALTHOUGH THE HISTORY OF PREEMPTION
INDICATES THAT IT RETARDS STATE ACTION AND PREVENTS STATES
FROM FILLING IN REGULATORY GAPS. THIS DISSERTATION EXPLORES
THE CONSTITUTIONAL ROOTS OF PREEMPTION AND THE HISTORY OF
PREEMPTION AS A POLITICAL TACTIC. THEN, #EMPLOYING THE CASE
STUDY METHOD, THE CONGRESSIONALLY-CENTERED REGULATORY
APPROACH FOSTERED BY INTERESTS SEEKING FEDERAL PREEMPTION OF
STATE REGULATORY AUTHORITY IS INVESTIGATED.

09619 WILKINS, S.C.
LEADERSHIP AND PERFORMANCE IN A RULE-GOVERNED ORGANIZATION:
IS EXCELLENCE ATTAINABLE?
DISSERTATION ABSTRACTS INTERNATIONAL, 49(9) (MAR 89),
2805-A.
THE AUTHOR LOOKS AT THE ROLE OF TODAY'S PUBLIC SECTOR
MANAGERS AND CONCLUDES THAT THEY LAG BEHIND THE POWER CURVE
IN THE APPLICATION OF LEADERSHIP AND MANAGERIAL SKILLS. THE
MAJORITY OF PUBLIC SECTOR MANAGERS RELY TOO HEAVILY ON THE
AUTHORITY OF THEIR POSITION AND THE RULES OF THE
ORGANIZATION TO ACCOMPLISH TASKS. THE DISSERTATION INCLUDES
LEADERSHIP STRATEGIES FOR IMPROVING ORGANIZATIONAL
PERFORMANCE.

09620 WILKINSON, B.
THE SASKATCHEWAN POTASH INDUSTRY AND THE 1987 US
ANTIDUMPING ACTION
CANADIAN PUBLIC POLICY--ANALYSE DE POLITIQUES, XV(2) (JUN
89), 145-161.
THIS PAPER EXAMINES THE US ANTIDUMPING ALLEGATIONS
AGAINST THE SASKATCHEWAN POTASH INDUSTRY. IT CONCLUDES THAT
THE US 'FAIR TRADE' LAWS AND THE ADMINISTRATION OF THEM WERE
ESSENTIALLY USED TO PROTECT THE US INDUSTRY AS IT CONTINUES
ITS LONG RUN DECLINE DUE TO EXHAUSTION OF RESERVES. IT THEN
CONSIDERS WHETHER THE RECENT CANADA-US COMPREHENSIVE TRADE
AGREEMENT WILL GRANT ANY RELIEF TO CANADIAN INDUSTRIES FROM
SUCH ACTIONS IN THE FUTURE AND CONCLUDES THAT IT LIKELY WILL
NOT. IT ALSO BRIEFLY CONSIDERS WHY IT TOOK ANTIDUMPING
CHARGES BY THE US TO STIMULATE THE SASKATCHEWAN POTASH
INDUSTRY TO TAKE ACTION IN ITS OWN SELF INTEREST AND
EXERCISE ITS MONOPOLY POWER.

09621 WILKS, S.
GOVERNMENT-INDUSTRY RELATIONS; PROGRESS AND FINDINGS OF
THE ESRC RESEARCH INITIATIVE
PUBLIC ADMINISTRATION, 67(3) (FAL 89), 329-338.
THIS ARTICLE PROVIDES A PERSPECTIVE ON THE ECONOMIC AND
SOCIAL RESEARCH COUNCIL'S (ESRC) RESEARCH INITIATIVE ON
GOVERNMENT INDUSTRY RELATIONS. IT TAKES AN ANALYTIC APPROACH
TO THE STUDY, REPORTS ON THE GENERAL PROGRESS OF THE
RESEARCH BEING DONE, PROBLEMS COMMON TO THE INIATIVE AND
SHARES THE EARLY RESULTS OF THE STUDIES.

09622 WILL, J.
MUST WALLS OF HOSTILITY CONTINUE TO DIVIDE?
THE CHRISTIAN CENTURY, 106(39) (DEC 89), 1191-1192.
AS THE BERLIN WALL CRUMBLES, MANY NATIONALISTS AND
IDEOLOGUES ARE SHIFT TO TAKE CREDIT FOR THE "DEMISE OF
COMMUNISM." THEIR DECLARATIONS THAT CAPITALISM HAS
DEMONSTRATED ITS SUPERIORITY OR THAT THE HARD-LINE MILITARY
STANCE OF THE WEST FORCED EASTERN CONCESSIONS REVEALS THAT
THERE STILL IS A LARGE AMOUNT OF ANIMOSITY TOWARDS THE EAST
IN THE HEARTS OF CITIZENS OF THE WEST. THE AUTHOR CALLS FOR
THE DEMOLITION OF ALL "WALLS OF HOSTILITY," BOTH VISIBLE AND
UNSEEN.

09623 WILL, J.E.
THE POLITICS OF RELIGION IN THE MIDDLE EAST PEACE PROCESS:

MANIPULATED IDEOLOGY OR GENUINE RELIGION?
AMERICAN-ARAB AFFAIRS, (30) (FAL 89), 77-80.
THE SPEAKER EXPLAINS THE ISSUES OF THE POLITICS OF
RELIGION WHICH ARE MESHED WITH THE ISSUES OF THE RELATION OF
RELIGION AND CULTURE FROM THE PERSPECTIVE OF THE SITUATION
IN ZIMBABWE. HE THEN MOVES ANALOGICALLY FROM SOUTHERN AFRICA
TO THE MIDDLE EAST AND OFFERS THREE SUGGESTIONS OF HEURISTIC
VALUE. FIRST, HE EXPLORES A "THEOLOGY OF SILENCE;" SECOND,
HE SUGGESTS THAT THE SILENCE IN AMERICAN CHURCHES ABOUT
PEACE AND JUSTICE ISSUES IN THE MIDDLE EAST DERIVES FROM
CONFUSION OR IGNORANCE, THIRD HE OBSERVES THAT THE TOP
PRIORITY FOR RELIGIONS IS NOT PERSONAL CONVERSIONS BUT FOR A
JUST PEACE BETWEEN SOCIETIES WITH DIFFERING WORD RELIGIONS.
HE CONCLUDES THAT CHURCHES MUST FIND WAYS TO CREATE A MORE
GENUINELY RELIGIOUS BASIS FOR THEIR PRAXIS IN THE MIDDLE
EAST PROCESS.

09624 WILL, W.M.
DEMOCRACY, ELECTIONS AND PUBLIC POLICY IN THE EASTERN
CARIBBEAN: THE CASE OF BARBADOS
JOURNAL OF COMMONWEALTH AND COMPARATIVE POLITICS, XXVII(3)
(NOV 89), 321-346.
THIS ARTICLE EXAMINES THE POTENTIAL FOR MULTI-TERM
REGIME RETENTION FOLLOWING THE IMPORTANT 1986 ELECTION AND
WHETHER THE SUCCESSION OF ERSKINE SANDIFORD TO THE OFFICE OF
PRIME MINISTER IN 1987, PLUS THE IMPACT OF THE LESS-THAN-
ROBUST ECONOMY, WILL RESTRICT THAT POTENTIAL. THERE IS ALSO
AN ATTEMPT TO ASSESS THE IMPACT OF THE ELECTION AND THE POST-
ELECTION CHANGE IN LEADERSHIP ON PUBLIC POLICY. IT IS
HYPOTHESISED THAT CHANGES WILL BE RELATIVELY SMALL AND
WITHIN THE CONTEXT OF BARBADOS' LONG-ESTABLISHED
CONSERVATIVE YET CHANGE-ORIENTED CULTURE.

09625 WILLERS, D.
THATCHERISM FOR SOUTH AFRICA
SOUTH AFRICA FOUNDATION REVIEW, 15(3) (MAR 89), 6-7.
PRIME MINISTER THATCHER HAS ADVOCATED POLITICAL REFORM
AS THE ROAD TO ECONOMIC PROGRESS IN POLAND AND SOUTH AFRICA.
THE POLISH EXPERIENCE IS A CLASSIC EXAMPLE OF A COUNTRY
RESPONDING TO THE THATCHER DICTUM THAT MARKET FORCES SHOULD
BE THE ARBITER OF INTERNATIONAL RELATIONS AND DOMESTIC
REGENERATION.

09626 WILLERS, D.
1988: A YEAR OF CONTRADICTION
SOUTH AFRICA FOUNDATION REVIEW, 15(1) (JAN 89), 8.
THE AUTHOR SURVEYS BRITISH REACTIONS TO EVENTS IN SOUTH
AFRICA IN 1988.

09627 WILLERTON, J.P. JR.
EVOLVING CENTER-PERIPHERY RELATIONS IN THE SOVIET POLITY
PROBLEMS OF COMMUNISM, XXXVIII(6) (NOV 89), 70-77.
WESTERN SCHOLARSHIP ON RELATIONS BETWEEN THE CENTER AND
THE PERIPHERY IN THE SOVIET POLITICAL SYSTEM REVEALS A RICH
MOSAIC IN WHICH THE CENTER CONTINUES TO DOMINATE EVEN AS
LOCAL ACTORS ATTEMPT, THROUGH ELABORATE INSTITUTIONAL
ARRANGEMENTS, TO INFLUENCE CENTRALLY-DETERMINED DECISIONS.
SINCE THE 1950'S, LOCAL AND REGIONAL GOVERNMENTS HAVE BEEN
ACQUIRING AN EXPANDED SHARE OF TOTAL BUDGETARY RESOURCES.
BUT THIS HAS NOT BEEN SUFFICIENT TO COVER THE EVEN BROADER
RANGE OF POLICY IMPLEMENTATION TASKS DEVOLVED TO THEM NOR
HAVE THEY BEEN GRANTED A FREE HAND IN SUCH IMPORTANT AREAS
AS HOUSING. ONLY THE MOST FAR-REACHING REFORMS COULD
SIGNIFICANTLY TRANSFORM THE PROCLIVITY OF THE SOVIET SYSTEM
TOWARD POLICY RIGIDITY AND INCREMENTALISM.

09628 WILLIAMS, A.
ACCESS AND ACCOMODATION IN THE CANADIAN WELFARE STATE: THE
POLITICAL SIGNIFICANCE OF CONTACTS BETWEEN STATE, LABOR,
AND BUSINESS LEADERS.
CANADIAN REVIEW OF SOCIOLOGY AND ANTHROPOLOGY, 26(2) (MAY
89), 217-239.
THIS PAPER USES DATA FROM A 1977 SURVEY OF 600 SENIOR
DECISION-MAKERS IN CANADIAN GOVERNMENT, BUSINESS AND LABOR
FIRST, TO EXAMINE PATTERNS OF REPORTED CONTACTS BETWEEN
ELITES, AND SECOND, TO ESTIMATE THE POLITICAL SIGNIFICANCE
OF SUCH PATTERNS IN TERMS OF THEIR ASSOCIATION WITH LEVELS
OF ELITE SUPPORT FOR OR OPPOSITION TO SOCIAL POLICY
ALTERNATIVES. PERSONAL CONTACTS BETWEEN ELITES, AND
PARTICULARLY THOSE WITH STATE OFFICIALS, ARE ADDRESSED AS A
TERRAIN FOR POLITICAL CONFLICT ON WHICH BUSINESS, LABOR AND
OTHER SECTORAL ELITES ATTEMPT TO IMPRESS THEIR INTERESTS ON
ONE ANOTHER AND ON STATE POLICIES. IN THIS CONNECTION, THE
DATA FAIL TO CONFIRM THAT THERE IS A MONOLITHIC ELITE
STRUCTURE IN CANADA, ALTHOUGH THEY SUGGEST THAT SENIOR
BUSINESSMEN HAVE MORE EXTENSIVE ACCESS TO THE STATE AND TO
OTHER SECTORAL ELITES THAN DO LABOR LEADERS. BUT MORE
IMPORTANTLY THE ANALYSIS SHOWS THAT STATE CONTACTS WITH
BUSINESS ARE MORE SIGNIFICANT POLITICALLY THAN THOSE WITH
LABOR, SINCE THE FORMER PREDICT THE SOCIAL POLICY POSITIONS
OF STATE OFFICIALS WHEREAS THE LATTER NEITHER PRODUCE, NOR
ARE THE PRODUCT OF, SUPPORT FOR LABOR'S POSITIONS WITHIN THE
SENIOR OFFICES OF THE CANADIAN STATE.

09629 WILLIAMS, C.
STRATEGIC SPENDING CHOICES
INTERNATIONAL SECURITY, 13(4) (SPR 89), 25-35.
THE ARTICLE EXAMINES THE OPTIONS THAT THE NEW
ADMINISTRATION HAS FOR SETTING DEFENSE PRIORITIES IN AN ERA
OF FISCAL RESTRAINT. IT EXPLORES THE DILEMMA OF STRATEGIC
VERSUS OTHER DEFENSE SPENDING AND CONSIDERS THE FACTORS THAT
WILL AFFECT THE SPENDING PRIORITES THAT WILL BE ESTABLISHED.
IT ALSO SEEKS TO DISPEL SOME NATIONAL MYTHS ABOUT DEFENSE
AND MILITARY POLICY ESPECIALLY WITH REGARDS TO US NUCLEAR
FORCES AND SDI.

09630 WILLIAMS, D.N.
CHRISTIAN SCIENCE AND THE CARE OF CHILDREN: THE
CONSTITUTIONAL ISSUES
CHURCH AND STATE, 42(8) (SEP 89), 19 (187)-20 (188).
SHOULD SPIRITUAL HEALING AS CHRISTIAN SCIENTISTS
PRACTICE IT BE ACCOMMODATED IN STATE LAW, OR SHOULD THAT
PRACTICE BE RESTRICTED BY STATE STATUTE AND SHOULD PARENTS
WHO HAVE LOST CHILDREN UNDER SPIRITUAL TREATMENT BE SUBJECT
TO CRIMINAL PROSECUTION? THE CONSTITUTIONAL ISSUE IN THE
DEBATE OVER SPIRITUAL HEALING FOR CHILDREN REVOLVES AROUND
THE FREE EXERCISE AND ESTABLISHMENT CLAUSES OF THE FIRST
AMENDMENT. BUT NO ONE, INCLUDING CHRISTIAN SCIENTISTS, IS
SAYING THAT A PARENT'S RELIGIOUS FREEDOM SUPERVENES A
CHILD'S RIGHT TO LIVE OR THAT THE FIRST AMENDMENT OR ANY
OTHER LEGAL OR RELIGIOUS PRINCIPLE ENTITLES A PARENT TO
MARTYR A CHILD ON THE ALTAR OF RELIGIOUS BELIEF.

09631 WILLIAMS, F.
WORRYING BLOCKADES
FAR EASTERN ECONOMIC REVIEW, 141(30) (JUL 88), 88-89.
THERE IS A RISING ANXIETY AMONG ASIAN EXPORTERS OVER THE
GROWING NUMBER OF REGIONAL AND BILATERAL DEALS BETWEEN THE
WORLD'S TRADING NATIONS. THE US-CANADA FREE TRADE AGREEMENT
IS ONLY THE LATEST IN A LIST OF ABOUT 40 SUCH AGREEMENTS
NOTIFIED TO THE GENERAL'AGREEMENT ON TARIFFS AND TRADE. A
NUMBER OF COUNTRIES INCLUDING JAPAN, SOUTH KOREA, AND NDIA
ARE PRESSING FOR A RE-EXAMINATION OF GATT RULES ON FREE
TRADE AGREEMENTS. HOWEVER, A TIGHTENING OF RESTRICTIONS ON
FTA'S WOULD NOT BE IN THE INTEREST OF THE US OR THE EUROPEAN
COMMUNITY WHO ARE THE TWO MOST POWERFUL BLOCS IN GATT. AN
IMPASSE IN THE FUTURE ON THIS ISSUE MAY RESULT IN INCREASED
ECONOMIC INTEGRATION OF THE ASIAN NATIONS.

09632 WILLIAMS, G.I.
THE POLITICS OF JOINT CUSTODY
DISSERTATION ABSTRACTS INTERNATIONAL, 50(5) (NOV 89),
1426-A.
A STUDY OF THREE STATES (MASSACHUSETTS, MISSOURI, AND
NEW JERSEY) REVEALS THAT THE POLITICS AND DISCOURSE
SURROUNDING THE JOINT CUSTODY ISSUE HAVE BEEN SIMILAR IN
EACH STATE. MEN'S RIGHTS GROUPS HAVE BEEN THE INITIATORS OF
JOINT CUSTODY LEGISLATION, FEMINIST ORGANIZATIONS HAVE
OPPOSED SUCH BILLS, AND ATTORNEYS' ASSOCIATIONS HAVE USUALLY
WORKED FOR LEGISLATIVE COMPROMISES THAT WOULD ALLOW JOINT
CUSTODY BUT WOULD NOT MAKE IT A JUDICIAL PRESUMPTION.

09633 WILLIAMS, J.W.
CARLOS MARIGHELA: THE FATHER OF URBAN GUERRILLA WARFARE
TERRORISM, 12(1) (1989), 1-20.
TWO DECADES AGO CARLOS MARIGHELA, THE BRAZILIAN
REVOLUTIONARY, WAS KILLED BY BRAZILIAN SECURITY FORCES.
KNOWN AS "THE FATHER OF URBAN GUERRILLA WARFARE," MARIGHELA
LAID OUT HIS THEORIES IN HIS MINIMANUAL OF THE URBAN
GUERILLA. HE IS NOTED FOR ESPOUSING URBAN-BASED REVOLUTION
OVER A "RURAL FOCO," MILITARIZATION OF THE POLITICAL PROCESS,
AND MANIPULATION OF THE MEDIA. HE BROKE WITH THE BRAZILIAN
COMMUNIST PARTY, WHICH HISTORICALLY WAVERED BETWEEN
COOPERATION WITH THE GOVERNMENT AND RURAL-BASED GUERRILLA
WARFARE. WITH THE FAILURE TO TRANSPLANT A CUBAN-STYLE
REVOLUTION IN SOUTH AMERICA, MARIGHELA TURNED HIS ATTENTION
TO THE GROWING URBANIZATION OF THE CONTINENT. FOR HIM, THE
CITY WOULD BE THE PRIMARY BATTLEGROUND. IN HIS MINIMANUAL,
MARIGHELA ARGUED FOR THE MILITARIZATION OF THE POLITICAL
PROCESS. AS VIOLENCE WAS ESCALATED, THE FORCES OF LAW AND
ORDER WOULD BE FORCED TO BECOME MORE REPRESSIVE. THE "SOFT
CENTER" WOULD BE ELIMINATED AS THE SIDES WERE POLARIZED.
EVENTUALLY, THE MASSES WOULD JOIN THE REVOLUTIONARIES IN
REACTION TO THE OPPRESSION OF THE GOVERNMENT. MARIGHELA ALSO
ARGUED FOR MANIPULATION OF THE MEDIA, BOTH AS A VEHICLE TO
REACH THE URBAN MASSES AND AS A TOOL TO GOOD THE GOVERNMENT
INTO ESCALATION. AS EVIDENCE OF HIS BELIEF, HE TRIED TO PUT
HIS PRECEPTS INTO PRACTICE - RAIDING BANKS AND PAYROLLS,
KIDNAPPING A U.S. AMBASSADOR, AND SIEZING RADIO STATIONS.
HOWEVER, HIS STRUGGLE WAS FOR NAUGHT. MARIGHELA DIED HAVING
FAILED TO FOMENT AN URBAN REVOLUTION, AND IT APPEARS THAT
HIS TACTICS HAVE FAILED TO BRING SUCCESS TO ANYONE ELSE.

09634 WILLIAMS, M.; MOOMAW, R.L.
CAPITAL AND LABOUR EFFICIENCIES: A REGIONAL ANALYSIS
URBAN STUDIES, 26(6) (DEC 89), 573-586.
FOR THIS ARTICLE THE AUTHORS USE SATO'S FACTOR-
AUGMENTING TECHNICAL PROGRESS APPROACH TO CALCULATE RATES OF

GROWTH OF CAPITAL EFFICIENCY, LABOUR EFFICIENCY, AND
EFFICIENCY-BASED TOTAL FACTOR PRODUCTIVITY GROWTH IN
MANUFACTURING BY STATE. CAPITAL EFFICIENCY GAINS, BUT NOT
LABOUR EFFICIENCY GAINS, HAVE ACCOMPANIED THE RAPID OUTPUT
GROWTH OF SOUTHERN AND WESTERN STATES. REGRESSION ANALYSIS
INDICATES THAT VARIABLES MEASURING SCALE EFFECTS, EDUCATION,
URBANISATION, CAPITAL INTENSITY, AND RESEARCH AND
DEVELOPMENT ACTIVITY ARE DIRECTLY ASSOCIATED WITH
PRODUCTIVITY AND/OR INPUT-EFFICIENCY GROWTH AND THAT
VARIABLES MEASURING REGULATION, INTEREST-GROUP EFFECTS, AND
UNIONISATION EFFECTS ARE INVERSELY ASSOCIATED.

09635 WILLIAMS, M.
    CHINA AND THE WORLD AFTER TIAN AN MEN
    WORLD TODAY, 45(8-9) (AUG 89), 127-128.
        THE BRUTALITY OF EVENTS IN TIAN AN MEN SQUARE HAS LAID
    BARE THE EXTRAORDINARY AUTHORITARIAN NATURE OF THE CURRENT
    POLITICAL REGIME IN CHINA. THE MOST OBVIOUS FOREIGN POLICY
    CONSEQUENCE OF THIS HAS BEEN THAT RELATIONS BETWEEN CHINA
    AND THE WEST HAVE BEEN PLACED UNDER CONSIDERABLE STRAIN.
    ALTHOUGH THERE HAVE BEEN EFFORTS BY THE BUSH ADMINISTRATION
    AND OTHER WESTERN GOVERNMENTS TO PREVENT A COMPLETE
    BREAKDOWN IN THEIR RELATIONSHIP WITH CHINA, THE CHILL
    BETWEEN PEKING AND THE WEST IS UNLIKELY TO BE TEMPORARY.
    BARRING A MAJOR AND UNLIKELY REVERSAL OF THE CURRENT
    POLICIES OF REPRESSION, THE INTIMACY THAT PREVAILED IN
    RELATIONS BETWEEN CHINA AND THE WEST OVER THE LAST DECADE
    APPEARS TO BE IRRETRIEVABLY LOST.

09636 WILLIAMS, M.
    REGULATION OF FINANCIAL INSTITUTIONS IN THE CARIBBEAN:
    IMPLICATIONS FOR GROWTH AND DEVELOPMENT
    SOCIAL AND ECONOMIC STUDIES, 38(4) (DEC 89), 181-199.
        THIS PAPER EXAMINES REGULATIONS GOVERNING FINANCIAL
    INSTITUTIONS IN THE CARIBBEAN AND THEIR IMPACT ON THE GROWTH,
    DEVELOPMENT AND STABILITY OF THE FINANCIAL SYSTEMS. THE
    ARGUMENT FOR 'STABILITY' IS PREMISED ON THE INTERPRETATION
    OF THE CONCEPT AS A STATE IN WHICH CHANGES TAKE PLACE IN
    SUCH A WAY AS TO INSPIRE CONFIDENCE IN THE FINANCIAL SYSTEMS.
    CONFIDENCE CREATION, IN TURN, IS ESSENTIAL IF SYSTEMS ARE
    TO BE INNOVATIVE AND GROW. OTHER FACTORS CRITICAL TO THE
    DEVELOPMENT OF FINANCIAL SYSTEMS ARE, FOR EXAMPLE, THE RATE
    OF ECONOMIC GROWTH AND OF FINANCIAL SAVINGS. REGULATORY
    ARRANGEMENTS WILL THEREFORE NEED TO KEEP PACE AND BE
    REVIEWED CONSTANTLY.

09637 WILLIAMS, P.
    NATO CRISIS MANAGEMENT: DILEMMAS AND TRADE-OFFS
    WASHINGTON QUARTERLY, 12(2) (SPR 89), 29-39.
        DECISION MAKERS CAN FOLLOW SEVERAL BROAD STRATEGIES IN
    RESPONSE TO THE KINDS OF DILEMMAS AND TRADE-OFFS THAT
    CHARACTERIZE CRISES. THE FIRST IS TO IGNORE THE PROBLEM OF
    INCOMPATIBLE OBJECTIVES AND SIMPLY OPT FOR ONE SET OF
    OBJECTIVES RATHER THAN ANOTHER. AN ALTERNATIVE APPROACH TO
    THESE DILEMMAS IS TO REGARD THEM AS INESCAPABLE. ONE COULD
    EFFECTIVELY ABROGATE RESPONSIBILITY FOR DEALING WITH THEM AT
    AN ANALYTICAL AND PROBLEM-SOLVING LEVEL BY FOCUSING INSTEAD
    ON THE POLITICAL DIMENSIONS OF THE ISSUE. THE THIRD APPROACH,
    THEREFORE, IS EXPLICITLY TO ACKNOWLEDGE THE EXISTENCE OF
    DILEMMAS AND THE NEED FOR TRADE-OFFS AND ATTEMPT TO DEVISE
    OPTIONS THAT MEET THE COMPETING REQUIREMENTS. THIS IS THE
    MOST EFFETIVE OF THE ALTERNATIVES AND AT LEST ATTEMPTS TO
    DEAL WITH THE PROBLEMS IN ANALYTICAL, PROBLEM-SOLVING TERMS.

09638 WILLIAMS, P.
    US-SOVIET RELATIONS: BEYOND THE COLD WAR?
    INTERNATIONAL AFFAIRS, 65(2) (SPR 89), 273-288.
        THE ARTICLE AIMS TO ANSWER THE QUESTION WHETHER THE
    DETENTE OF THE 1980'S AND THE 1990'S IS QUALITATIVELY
    DIFFERENT FROM EARLIER POSTWAR CYCLES OF DETENTE FOLLOWED BY
    TENSION. IT ANALYZES THE NATURE OF THE SUPERPOWER
    RELATIONSHIP SINCE THE SECOND WORLD WAR AND THE DETENTE OF
    THE 1970'S AND EXPLAINS HOW AND WHY THIS DETENTE ENDED IN
    DISILLUSION AND RENEWED SUPERPOWER TENSION. IT ALSO COMPARES
    THE CURRENT WARMING OF SUPERPOWER RELATIONS WITH THE
    EXPERIENCE OF THE 1970'S AND HIGHLIGHTS WHAT IS NEW ABOUT
    THE DEVELOPMENTS OF THE 1980'S.

09639 WILLIAMS, R.
    POLITICAL DECISIONS WHERE THE TECHNICAL COMPONENT IS
    SUBSTANTIAL
    GOVERNMENT AND OPPOSITION, 24(4) (AUT 89), 458-472.
        THE INTRODUCTION OF SYSTEMATIC RESEARCH, DEVELOPMENT,
    AND INNOVATION INTO INDUSTRIAL SOCIETIES IS A BENCHMARK TO
    WHICH POLITICAL SYSTEMS, AND ABOVE ALL THE INTERNATIONAL
    SYSTEM, HAVE YET TO FULLY ACCOMMODATE THEMSELVES. THERE IS
    EVERY REASON TO ASSUME THAT TECHNO-POLITICAL QUESTIONS WILL
    GROW IN NUMBER AS WELL AS SIGNIFICANCE. THE EVENTS OF THE
    20TH CENTURY HAVE ESTABLISHED BEYOND DOUBT THAT THE
    TECHNICAL ALMOST ALWAYS HAS FAR-REACHING IMPLICATIONS FOR
    THE POLITICAL.

09640 WILLIAMS, R.
    THE EC'S TECHNOLOGY POLICY AS AN ENGINE FOR INTEGRATION

GOVERNMENT AND OPPOSITION, 24(2) (SPR 89), 158-176.
    THE AUTHOR EXAMINES THE CONCEPT OF A TECHNOLOGY GAP
BETWEEN NATIONS AND BETWEEN REGIONS OF THE WORLD. THEN HE
LOOKS AT THE IDEA THAT THE EUROPEAN COMMUNITY'S TECHNOLOGY
POLICY FUNCTIONS AS AN ENGINE FOR INTEGRATION.

09641 WILLIAMS, R.E.
    INTENT, IMPACT, AND PUBLIC POLICY CONSEQUENCES OF
    INCREASED CONGRESSIONAL CONTROL OF DEPARTMENT OF THE NAVY
    BUDGET EXECUTION
    AVAILABLE FROM NTIS, NO. AD-A207 381/5/GAR, DEC 88, 77.
        THIS THESIS (I) REVIEWS CONSTITUTIONAL AND LEGISLATIVE
    FOUNDATIONS FOR CONGRESSIONAL CONTROL AND OVERSIGHT OVER DOD,
    (II) DISCUSSES METHODS OF CONTROL AND OVERSIGHT, (III)
    DOCUMENTS A TREND TOWARD INCREASING CONTROL AND OVERSIGHT,
    (IV) EVALUATES POTENTIAL EXPLANATIONS FOR THIS TREND, (V)
    INVESTIGATES THE INTENT OF LINE ITEM SPECIFICATION AND
    RESTRICTIVE LANGUAGE IN AUTHORIZATION BILLS, APPROPRIATIONS
    BILLS, AND COMMITTEE REPORTS, AND (VI) EXAMINES THEIR IMPACT
    ON DON BUDGET EXECUTION. IT CONCENTRATES ON DON PROCUREMENT
    ACCOUNTS FOR 1980BB AND AIRCRAFT PROCUREMENT, NAVY (APN) FOR
    1988. IT CONCLUDES THAT (I) THE INTENT OF INCREASED
    OVERSIGHT AND CONTROL IS TO ENSURE THAT THE WILL OF CONGRESS
    IS CARRIED OUT BY THE EXECUTIVE BRANCH, (II) CONGRESSIONAL
    BUDGETARY DECISIONS MAY IMPEDE DON BUDGET EXECUTION
    EFFICIENCY AND EFFECTIVENESS, AND (III) THE FULL IMPACT OF
    THESE CONTROLS DID NOT OCCUR IN APN IN 1988 BECAUSE NEGATIVE
    AND UNINTENDED CONSEQUENCES WERE POINTED OUT TO CONGRESS BY
    DON AND THE CONTROLS WERE PARTIALLY RESCINDED.

09642 WILLIAMS, R.E.
    THE EVOLUTION OF DISARMAMENT AND ARMS CONTROL THOUGHT,
    1945-1963
    DISSERTATION ABSTRACTS INTERNATIONAL, 49(11) (MAY 89),
    3500-A.
        THE ONSET OF THE COLD WAR AND THE TOTAL FAILURE OF
    NUCLEAR DISARMAMENT EFFORTS AT THE UNITED NATIONS WERE ONLY
    THE MOST OBVIOUS OF SEVERAL FACTORS PROMPTING A RE-
    EXAMINATION OF DISARMAMENT THEORY IN THE EARLY 1950'S. TO
    REPLACE DISARMAMENT, THE STRATEGY COMMUNITY DEVELOPED THE
    ARMS CONTROL APPROACH, WHICH HAS BEEN THE BASIS OF AMERICAN
    POLICY ON THE REGULATION OF NUCLEAR WEAPONS SINCE THE
    KENNEDY ADMINISTRATION.

09643 WILLIAMS, R.H.
    CULTURAL POWER: RELIGION AND POLITICS IN AN AMERICAN CITY
    DISSERTATION ABSTRACTS INTERNATIONAL, 49(8) (FEB 89),
    2422-A.
        THIS IS AN EXAMINATION OF THE INFLUENCE OF RELIGION AND
    RELIGIOUS ORGANIZATION ON POLITICAL POWER IN SPRINGFIELD, MA.
    THE GOAL OF STUDY IS THOFOLD: FIRST, TO ADVANCE A
    CONCEPTUAL MODEL OF POWER THAT IS SUBTLE ENOUGH TO CAPTURE
    THE WAYS CULTURE AND CULTURAL PRODUCTS SHAPE PUBLIC POLITICS;
    AND SECOND, TO ANCHOR THIS FRAMEWORK IN THE PRACTICES AND
    HISTORY OF AN EMPIRICAL SETTING.

09644 WILLIAMS, R.L.
    U.S. RESPONSE TO CHANGES IN CHINA
    DEPARTMENT OF STATE BULLETIN (US FOREIGN POLICY), 89(2151)
    (OCT 89), 27-30.
        THE AUTHOR DISCUSSES THE POLICY IMPLICATIONS FOR THE
    UNITED STATES OF THE DEVELOPMENTS IN CHINA REGARDING THE
    DEMONSTRATIONS IN TIANANMEN SQUARE AND THE STEPS THE USA
    TOOK IN RESPONSE TO THE CHINESE SUPPRESSION OF THE PROTESTS.
    HE ALSO BRIEFLY DESCRIBES THE FUNDAMENTAL ELEMENTS OF SINO-
    AMERICAN RELATIONS AS THEY HAVE EVOLVED OVER THE PAST TWO
    DECADES.

09645 WILLIAMS, S.
    THE NEW AUTHORITARIANISM
    POLITICAL QUARTERLY (THE), 60(1) (JAN 89), 4-9.
        THE EROSION OF BRITIAN'S DEMOCRACY, AND OF THE LIBERTIES
    OF ITS CITIZENS, IS LIKELY TO CONTINUE AND EVEN ACCELERATE
    UNLESS THERE IS RADICAL CONSTITUTIONAL REFORM. MASKED BY THE
    EFFECTIVENESS OF OPPOSITION AND THE SELF-RESTRAINT OF
    MINISTERS, BRITAIN'S UNWRITTEN CONSTITUTION HAS ACCEPTED AS
    AN ADEQUATE FOUNDATION FOR DEMOCRATIC POLITICAL SYSTEM. BUT
    THE INHERENT AUTHORITARIANISM OF A CONSTITUTION BASED ON
    UNFETTERED PARLIAMENTARY SOVEREIGNTY, ONCE THE EXECUTIVE
    CONTROLS PARLIAMENT ITSELF, HAS BECOME INCREASINGLY APPARENT
    IN THE LAST TWENTY YEARS UNDER GOVERNMENTS OF BOTH PARTIES,
    AND IS NOW PLAIN FOR ANYONE WHO CARES TO SEE. THAT IS WHAT
    MAKES CONSTITUTIONAL REFORM BOTH ESSENTIAL AND URGENT.

09646 WILLIAMS, W.
    CENTRAL GOVERNMENT CAPACITY AND THE BRITISH DISEASE
    PARLIAMENTARY AFFAIRS, 42(2) (APR 89), 250-264.
        THE ARTICLE EXAMINES THE EVIDENCE TO DETERMINE WHETHER
    THE "BRITISH DISEASE" IS IN REMISSION OR NOT. FOR MANY YEARS,
    BRITAIN WAS PORTRAYED AS THE "SICK MAN" IN THE WESTERN
    EUROPEAN ECONOMY, BUT SOME ANALYSTS NOW FEEL THAT "MRS
    THATCHER'S ECONOMIC RENAISSANCE" HAS REVOVED BRITAIN. THE
    AUTHOR CONCLUDES THAT THERE IS NO OVERWHELMING EVIDENCE THAT
    THE BRITISH DISEASE IS IN REMISSION; ALTHOUGH THE EVIDENCE

IS MIXED AND OFTEN CONFLICTING, ON BALANCE THE AVAILABLE
EVIDENCE AT THE END OF TWO THATCHER GOVERNMENTS SUMS UP TO
FAILURE.

09647 WILLIAMS, H. E.; SELIGMAN, D.
RACE, SCHOLARSHIP, AND AFFIRMATIVE ACTION
NATIONAL REVIEW, XLI(8) (MAY 89), 36-40.
THE AUTHOR ARGUES THAT THE VICTIMS OF AFFIRMATIVE ACTION
ARE WHITE AND ASIAN STUDENTS, INDEPENDENT-MINDED SCHOLARS,
AND THE MINORITY STUDENTS WHO ARE ITS SUPPOSED BENEFICIARIES.

09648 WILLIAMSON, C.J.
A ONE-COUNTRY, TWO-SYSTEM FORMULA IN THE CHINA OF 1999
INTERNATIONAL SOCIAL SCIENCE REVIEW, 64(4) (AUG 89),
153-157.
THIS PAPER IS CONCERNED WITH THE THEORETICAL PROBLEMS,
AS WELL AS THE PRACTICAL DIFFICULTIES OF A ONE-COUNTRY, TWO-
SYSTEM FORMULA UNDER WHICH HONG KONG AND MACAU WILL RETURN
TO THE PEOPLE'S REPUBLIC OF CHINA BY THE END OF THE PRESENT
CENTURY. IT PAINTS A BRIEF PICTURE OF THE CONDITIONS UNDER
WHICH MACAU AND HONG KONG HAVE AGREED TO THIS ARRANGEMENT
AND THE POSSIBLE VENUES OPEN TO THE PEOPLES OF THESE TWO
COLONIES IN EAST ASIA. IT IS, THEREFORE, A CONTRIBUTION TO
THE STUDY OF DEVELOPMENTS IN POLITICAL THEORY, ON THE ONE
HAND, AND AN EXAMINATION OF THE GLOBAL SCENARIO UNDER WHICH
A UNIQUE EXPERIMENT IN INTERNATIONAL RELATIONS IS BEING
CONDUCTED, ON THE OTHER. THE PAPER DOES NOT TAKE ANY
POSITION BUT POINTS OUT PRECISELY UNDER WHAT CONDITIONS THIS
EXPERIMENT WITH SOVEREIGNTY IS LIKELY TO SUCCEED.

09649 WILLIAMSON, R.S.
ADVANCING U.S. OBJECTIVES IN THE UNITED NATIONS
DEPARTMENT OF STATE BULLETIN (US FOREIGN POLICY), 88(2138)
(SEP 88), 67-69.
DESPITE AN INCREASING FRUSTRATION FELT BY MANY AMERICANS
WITH REGARDS TO THE UN DUE TO DOUBLE STANDARDS, INEFFICIENCY,
AND HOSTILITY TO US VALUES, THE US STAND ON THE UN IS THAT
"THE UN MATTERS." MANY OF THE SPECIALIZED AGENCIES PROVIDE
IMPORTANT SERVICES FOR NATIONS AND PEOPLES WORLDWIDE AND
ACTIONS BY THE SECURITY COUNCIL AND GENERAL ASSEMBLY HAVE--
AT TIMES--ENCOURAGED PEACE. THE US IS OFFERING A GROUP OF 18
RECOMMENDATIONS REGARDING REFORM OF THE UN TO INCREASE ITS
EFFICIENCY AND ITS EFFECTIVENESS.

09650 WILLIAMSON, R.S.
DEVELOPMENTS IN THE UN SYSTEM
DEPARTMENT OF STATE BULLETIN (US FOREIGN POLICY), 88(2138)
(SEP 88), 62-64.
THE ARTICLE EXAMINES SEVERAL MAJOR EVENTS AND ACTIVITIES
IN THE UN SYSTEM INCLUDING INVESTIGATION OF THE CUBAN HUMAN
RIGHTS SITUATION, AND EFFORTS TO END THE CONFLICT IN
AFGHANISTAN AND IRAN-IRAQ; THE UN ACTION WITH REGARDS TO
ETHIOPIAN FAMINE IS RECOUNTED AS ARE THE ACTIVITIES OF THE
UN SECURITY COUNCIL AND SEVERAL SPECIALIZED AGENCIES SUCH AS
WHO AND THE ILO. THE ARTICLE CONCLUDES WITH AN ANALYSIS OF
THE FUTURE PROBLEMS AND CHALLENGES THAT THE UN WILL FACE.

09651 WILLIAMSON, R.S.
SERPENTS IN THE U.N.
MIDSTREAM, XXXV(1) (JAN 89), 8-10.
ON NOVEMBER 10, 1975, THE UNITED NATIONS GENERAL
ASSEMBLY ADOPTED RESOLUTION 3379, WHICH EQUATES ZIONISM WITH
RACISM. THIS CONDEMNATION OF ZIONISM IN THE FACE OF OPEN AND
FERVENT SUPPORT FOR OTHER NATIONAL LIBERATION MOVEMENTS
DEMONSTRATES BLATANT HYPOCRISY BY THE U.N. GENERAL ASSEMBLY.
THE ZIONISM EQUALS RACISM PROPOSITION ATTEMPTS TO DEPRIVE
ISRAEL OF ETHICAL LEGITIMACY. IT IS PART OF AN EFFORT TO
DEFAME ISRAEL, DEPRIVE IT OF LEGITIMACY, AND ULTIMATELY
EXPEL IT FROM THE U.N.

09652 WILLIAMSON, R.S.
THE UNITED NATIONS AND DISARMAMENT
DEPARTMENT OF STATE BULLETIN (US FOREIGN POLICY), 88(2138)
(SEP 88), 65-66.
AMBASSADOR RICHARD S WILLIAMSON ADDRESSES THE ROLE THAT
THE UNITED NATIONS HAS PLAYED IN ENCOURAGING DISARMAMENT. HE
OUTLINES THE BILATERAL AND MULTILATERAL EFFORTS TO REDUCE
ORELIMINATE ARMAMENTS THAT THE US HAS PARTICIPATED IN AND
DEMONSTRATES THE ROLE OF THE UN IN INITIATING AND
MAINTAINING SOME OF THESE INITIAVES. HE POINTS OUT THAT THE
UN IS DOING TOO LITTLE AND IN SOME CASES IS EVEN
COUNTERPRODUCTIVE TO ARMS REDUCTION EFFORTS. HE OUTLINES
SOME POSSIBLE METHODS OF REMEDY FOR THE SITUATION.

09653 WILLIAMSON, R.S.
THE UNITED NATIONS: PROGRESS IN THE 1980'S
DEPARTMENT OF STATE BULLETIN (US FOREIGN POLICY), 89(2143)
(FEB 89), 68-71.
IN RECENT DAYS THERE HAS BEEN A RESURGENCE OF ENTHUSIASM
FOR THE UNITED NATIONS IN SOME QUARTERS. THREE DISTINCT AND
SEPARATE ELEMENTS HAVE CONTRIBUTED TO THIS: PRESIDENT
REAGAN'S POLICIES IN THE UN AND ELSEWHERE HAVE HAD A
SALUTORY IMPACT; THE THIRD WORLD IS PLAYING AN INCREASINGLY
CONSTRUCTIVE ROLE WITHIN THE UNITED NATIONS; THE POSITIVE

DEVELOPMENTS IN US-SOVIET RELATIONS HAVE INCREASED THE
OPPORTUNITIES FOR THE UN TO PLAY A MEANINGFUL ROLE.

09654 WILLIAMSON, R.S.
TOWARD THE 21ST CENTURY: THE FUTURE FOR MULTILATERAL
DIPLOMACY
DEPARTMENT OF STATE BULLETIN (US FOREIGN POLICY), 88(2141)
(DEC 88), 53-56.
THE 21ST CENTURY WILL SEE EVERY NATION FACING A VARIETY
OF EMERGING PROBLEMS OF GREAT URGENCY WHICH TRANSCEND THE
NATIONAL BORDERS. THE CHANGING GLOBAL CONDITIONS NECESSITATE
AN INCREASE IN MULTILATERAL NEGOTIATIONS AND DIPLOMACY. THE
ARTICLE EXAMINES THE IMPORTANCE OF POLITICAL GROUPINGS AND
THE INCREASING IMPORTANCE OF SMALL-POWER DIPLOMACY. IT
ASSESSES THE ROLE OF THE UNITED NATIONS IN PROVIDING REFUGEE
ASSISTANCE, THE GURANTEE OF HUMAN RIGHTS, AND IN CONFLICT
RESOLUTION.

09655 WILLIE
PUERTO RICAN EQUALITY AND PUERTO RICAN INDEPENDENCE
POLITICAL AFFAIRS, LXVIII(6) (JUN 89), 26-27.
THE ARTICLE DISCUSSES SOME OF THE MISPERCEPTIONS HELD BY
THE WHITE MAJORITY OF THE US ABOUT PUERTO RICO AND PUERTO
RICANS IN THE US. IT DISCUSSES THE NEED TO COMBAT THESE
MISPERCEPTION AND HIGHLIGHT THE IMPERIALISTIC EXPLOITATION
OF PUERTO RICO BY THE US. IT EXAMINES THE MOVEMENT FOR
INDEPENDENCE AND OUTLINES MEASURES THAT THE COMMUNIST PARTY,
USA CAN TAKE TO AID THE MOVEMENT FOR INDEPEDENCE AND
EQUALITY.

09656 WILLOUGHBY, R.K.
EUROPEAN MISSILE DEFENSE
DISSERTATION ABSTRACTS INTERNATIONAL, 50(5) (NOV 89),
1426-A.
THE AUTHOR SUMMARIZES THE CONTROVERSY OVER MISSILE
DEFENSES IN EUROPE. HE SKETCHES EIGHT PERSPECTIVES CENTRAL
TO THE DEBATE, DISCUSSES HOW U.S. THINKING ON EUROPEAN
MISSILE DEFENSE HAS BEEN COLORED BY SDI, AND CONSIDERS THE
EUROPEAN ADVOCACY OF EXTENDED AIR DEFENSE. HE CONCLUDES THAT
THERE IS SUBSTANTIAL SUPPORT FOR NUCLEAR DISARMAMENT AND
MARGINAL SUPPORT FOR NUCLEAR FIGHTING IN EUROPE. THIS IS
ATTRIBUTED TO A MODEST RESOURCE BASE AND AN INTERNAL
ALLIANCE DYNAMIC THAT ENCOURAGES DISASSOCIATION FROM U.S.
POLICIES.

09657 HILLS, G.
IN THE SHADOW OF A SPYMASTER PRESIDENT
SOJOURNERS, 18(2) (FEB 89), 16-17.
THE AUTHOR FINDS THE 1988 PRESIDENTIAL ELECTION CAMPAIGN
LACKING IN A MORAL VISION FOR AMERICA. HE ALSO SPECULATES
ABOUT HOW GEORGE BUSH'S CIA BACKGROUND MAY AFFECT HIS
PRESIDENCY.

09658 HILLS, G.
RIGHT WING RELIGIOSITY
SOJOURNERS, 18(7) (JUL 89), 24-26.
THERE COULD NOT BE A MORE VIVID SYMBOL OF THE CULTURAL-
RELIGIOUS CHANGES IN RECENT TIMES THAN RELIANCE ON A NEW
LOWCHURCH ESTABLISHMENT BY A SCION OF THE HIGHCHURCH
TRADITION. AND THIS COULD NEVER HAVE TAKEN PLACE WITHOUT THE
INCREASED POLITICAL ACTIVISM OF EVANGELICALS,
FUNDAMENTALISTS, AND OTHERS WHO ONCE THOUGHT OF RELIGION AS
AN ESSENTIALLY PRIVATE MATTER, WITHOUT SOCIAL CONSEQUENCES.
WE ARE LOOKING AT A LARGER, BROADER, MORE IMPORTANT CHANGE
IN THE UNITED STATES THAN HAS BEEN INDICATED BY MOST STUDIES
OF THE RELIGIOUS RIGHT AS A SEPARATE PHENOMENON THE
RELIGIOUS RIGHT WAS NEVER THE "MORAL MAJORITY" IT CLAIMED TO
BE, AND IT HAS ALWAYS BEEN MISREPRESENTED WHEN IT WAS
TREATED AS A SEPARATE THREAT. THIS IS THE PROBLEM PAT
ROBERTSON UNDERSTOOD AND TRIED TO OBVIATE BY TURNING HIMSELF
FROM TELEVANGELIST INTO CEO.

09659 WILSON-SMITH, A.
A NEW SOVIET DEMOCRACY
MACLEAN'S (CANADA'S NEWS MAGAZINE), 102(13) (MAR 89),
18-19.
THE SOVIET UNION IS EXPERIMENTING IN DEMOCRATIC
ELECTIONS FOR THE FIRST TIME. VOTERS ARE GIVEN THE
UNPRECEDENTED OPPORTUNITY TO CHOOSE--BY SECRET BALLOT--
BETWEEN TWO RIVAL CANDIDATES. THE RESULT IS OFTEN
CONTROVERSIAL, BUT EXCITING. MAVERICK CANDIDATE BORIS
YELTSIN HAS ATTRACTED MUCH ATTENTION IN HIS MOSCOW RACE AND
HAS GIVEN PARTY CONSERVATIVES MUCH CAUSE FOR WORRY. THESE
DEVELOPMENTS, ALTHOUGH ENCOURAGING FROM A WESTERN POINT OF
VIEW, ARE A FAR CRY FROM FULL SCALE WESTERN-STYLE DEMOCRACY.

09660 WILSON-SMITH, A.
GOOD NEIGHBOURS AGAIN
MACLEAN'S (CANADA'S NEWS MAGAZINE), 102(26) (JUL 89), 19.
AFTER 10 YEARS OF SEPARATION, THE SOVIET UNION AND IRAN
ARE ON A COURSE OF RECONCILIATION. SPEAKER OF PARLIAMENT
RAFSANJANI MET WITH SOVIET LEADER MIKHAIL GORBACHEV AND
SIGNED AGREEMENTS ON SUCH DIVERSE SUBJECTS AS RAILWAY LINES,
JOINT SPACE VENTURES, AND DEFENSE COOPERATION.

09661 HILSON-SMITH, A.; NEMETH, M.
RISING FEAR IN KABUL
MACLEAN'S (CANADA'S NEWS MAGAZINE), 102(7) (FEB 89), 22-23.
AS SOVIET TROOPS STEP UP THEIR PACE OF WITHDRAWAL FROM
AFGHANISTAN, THE REBEL MUJAHEDEEN GUERRILLAS ARE MOVING IN
FOR THE KILL. REBEL LEADERS ARE CONFIDENT THAT THE
NAIJBULLAH REGIME WILL FALL WITHIN WEEKS OF THE FINAL SOVIET
WITHDRAWAL. CITIZENS OF KABUL, THE NATION'S CAPITAL ARE
STOCKING UP ON NECESSITIES AND EXPECTING A PROTRACTED
CONFLICT. FOR THE MOST PART, THE SOVIETS ARE RELIEVED TO
LEAVE AND WILL TRY TO FORGET THE ENTIRE CONFLICT.

09662 HILSON-SMITH, A.
SOVIET PROFITS
MACLEAN'S (CANADA'S NEWS MAGAZINE), 102(28) (JUL 89),
24-25.
THE INTRODUCTION OF PROFIT-ORIENTED COOPERATIVES IN THE
SOVIET UNION HAS BEEN ONE OF THE MOST CONTROVERSIAL ASPECTS
OF MIKHAIL GORBACHEV"S POLICIES OF PERESTROIKA. TWO YEARS
AFTER THEIR CREATION, MANY COOPERATIVES ARE FLOURISHING;
THE AVERAGE CO-OP WORKER MAKES MORE THAN TWICE THE NATIONAL
AVERAGE WAGE. HOWEVER, MANY ACCUSE THE COOPERATIVES OF
ENGAGING IN SPECULATION AND CHARGING EXTREMELY HIGH PRICES
FOR BASIC GOODS AND SERVICES. THE SUPPORTERS OF THE CO-OP
MOVEMENT MUST CONVINCE THEIR FELLOW CITIZENS OF THE
BENEFICIAL AND USEFUL NATURE OF THE CO-OPS IF THEY ARE TO
SURVIVE.

09663 HILSON-SMITH, A.
SUMMER OF DISCONTENT
MACLEAN'S (CANADA'S NEWS MAGAZINE), 102(30) (JUL 89), 29.
THE SOVIET GOVERNMENT IS FACING SIGNIFICANT PROBLEMS IN
THE SUMMER HEAT. COAL MINERS IN SIBERIA AND THE UKRAINE
SPARKED THE LARGEST LABOR DISTURBANCE IN SOVIET HISTORY WITH
MORE THEN 150,000 MINERS JOINING THE RANKS OF THE STRIKERS.
ETHNIC UNREST ALSO SWEPT ACROSS THE AUTONOMOUS REGION OF
ABKHAZIA, LOCATED IN THE SOUTHERN REPUBLIC OF GEORGIA
LEAVING AT LEAST 18 DEAD AND MORE THAN 100 INJURED. CONSUMER
GOODS SUCH AS MEAT, SOAP, SUGAR, AND TOILET PAPER WERE IN
SHORT SUPPLY AND INCREASING DISSATISFACTION AND IMPATIENCE
WITH THE GOVERNMENT'S REFORMS IS BECOMING INCREASINGLY
APPARENT.

09664 HILSON-SMITH, P.
EUROPEAN BANKING: A HIVE OF CROSS-BORDER ACTIVITY
EUROPE, 287 (JUN 89), 31-32.
THE STRATEGIES THAT BANKS ARE ADOPTING IN PREPARATION
FOR 1992 VARY GREATLY. HOWEVER, MUCH OF THE ACTIVITY
HAPPENING IN EUROPEAN BANKING NOW HAS A DEFENSIVE FLAVOR AS
BANKS PREPARE FOR GREATER COMPETITION FROM ABROAD. THIS IS
PARTICULARLY THE CASE IN BOTH SPAIN AND ITALY, TWO EUROPEAN
MARKETS LIKELY TO SEE PROFOUND CHANGES.

09665 WILSON, D.
TOWARDS A REVISED URBAN MANAGERIALISM: LOCAL MANAGERS AND
COMMUNITY DEVELOPMENT BLOCK GRANTS
POLITICAL GEOGRAPHY QUARTERLY, 8(1) (JAN 89), 21-42.
ABSTRACT. GEOGRAPHERS HAVE RECENTLY NOTED THE NEED FOR A
THEORETICALLY INFORMED INSTITUTIONALIST ANALYSIS. IN
RESPONSE TO THIS CALL, THIS PAPER BEGINS TO RESUSCITATE THE
URBAN MANAGERIALIST THEORETICAL PERSPECTIVE BY RECASTING THE
CONCEPT WITHIN A FRAMEWORK WHICH INCORPORATES
STRUCTURE/AGENCY INFLUENCES. THIS IS ACCOMPLISHED BY
EXTENDING THE SOCIAL CONSTRUCTIONIST THESIS OF MICKEY LAURIA
AND LAWRENCE KNOPP TO THE REALM OF MANAGERIAL INQUIRY. WITH
A FOCUS ON THE COMMUNITY DEVELOPMENT BLOCK GRANT PROGRAM IN
1985, THE PAPER DEMONSTRATES THAT STRUCTURAL PROPERTIES
EMBEDDED IN INSTITUTIONS ARE BOTH END PRODUCTS AND SHAPERS
OF EVERYDAY MANAGERIAL PRACTICES. THE RESULTS SUGGEST THAT
MANAGERS CONSTANTLY REPRODUCE/REARRANGE INSTITUTIONAL
STRUCTURE, THE RESULT OF EVOLVING MANAGERIAL VALUES MEETING
STRUCTURAL RULES AND RESOURCES. FAR FROM BEING FIXED OR
PERMANENT, INSTITUTIONAL STRUCTURE REFLECTS THE ONGOING
INTERACTION OF ORGANIZATIONAL ARRANGEMENTS AND INDIVIDUAL
PRACTICES.

09666 WILSON, D.A.
CONSEQUENTIAL CONTROVERSIES
PHILADELPHIA: ANLS OF AMER ACMY OF POLITICAL AND SOC
SCIENCE, (502) (MAR 89), 40-57.
ACADEMIC SCIENCE IN CERTAIN DISCIPLINES AND THE MILITARY
HAVE HAD A CURIOUS QUASI PARTNERSHIP FOR MORE THAN FORTY
YEARS. WHILE THE OPERATORS OF THIS PARTNERSHIP SHARE
ELEMENTS OF A SCIENTIFIC ETHOS, THEIR INSTITUTIONAL
FRAMEWORKS ARE RADICALLY DIFFERENT. A NUMBER OF
CONTROVERSIES RELATED TO THE RELATIONSHIP BETWEEN THE
MILITARY AND THE UNIVERSITY THAT HAVE AFFECTED THE
UNIVERSITIES, THE SCIENCE PROGRAMS OF THE MILITARY
DEPARTMENTS, AND THE CONDITIONS OF RESEARCH ARE EXPLORED.
STILL THE PARTNERSHIP PERSISTS.

09667 WILSON, H.
CALLING THE TUNE IN VIENNA

NATIONAL INTEREST, 16 (SUM 89), 83-90.
THE GREATEST MISTAKE THAT THE WEST COULD MAKE IN THE
FACE OF CHANGING SOVIET POLICIES WOULD BE TO FAIL TO
ARTICULATE AND DEFEND OUR OWN VIEW OF THE EUROPE WE WOULD
WISH. IN THE FACE OF SOVIET RHETORIC ABOUT A COMMON EUROPEAN
HOME, ARMS CONTROL TECHNOCRATS MUST NOT BE LEFT BY WESTERN
POLITICAL LEADERS TO EXPLAIN TO UNINTERESTED JOURNALISTS WHY
TANKS CANNOT BE TRADED FOR ARTILLERY. LONG STAGNANT--INDEED,
LONG STAGNANT BY DESIGN--EASTERN EUROPE IS MOVING. THE WEST
MUST TAKE ADVANTAGE OF THE FORUM CREATED BY THE CFE
NEGOTIATION TO SHAPE THE POLITICAL FUTURE OF EUROPE.

09668 WILSON. M.; LYNXWILER, J.
ABORTION CLINIC VIOLENCE AS TERRORISM
TERRORISM, 11(4) (1988), 263-274.
THE ARTICLE EXAMINES INSTANCES OF ABORTION CLINIC
VIOLENCE FOR 1982-1987 IN ORDER TO DETERMINE WHETHER THERE
IS A CORRESPONDENCE BETWEEN THESE INCIDENTS AND DEFINITIONS
OR MODELS OF TERRORISM. IT CONCLUDES THAT, ALTHOUGH THE FBI
DENIES THAT THESE ACTIONS ARE TERRORISM, THEY FIT THE
CLASSIFICATION OF "LIMITED POLITICAL" OR "SUBREVOLUTIONARY"
TERRORISM. THE ARTICLE ANALYZES POSSIBLE REASONS WHY THE FBI
HAS MADE THE DECISION NOT TO INCLUDE THESE ACTS AS FORMS OF
TERRORISM. THESE INCLUDE: PRESSURE FROM ANTI-ABORTION GROUPS,
AND A DEFINITIONAL NARROWING DUE TO INTERNATIONAL
PROMINENCE OF CERTAIN TYPES OF TERRORISM.

09669 WILSON, R.; JILLSON, C.
LEADERSHIP PATTERNS IN THE CONTINENTAL CONGRESS: 1774-1789
LEGISLATIVE STUDIES QUARTERLY, XIV(1) (FEB 89), 5-38.
THE PAPER INVESTIGATES PATTERNS OF LEADERSHIP IN THE US
CONTINENTAL CONGRESSES OF 1174 TO 1789/. ITS FINDINGS SHOW
THAT TRADITIONAL BASES OF LEADERSHIP POWER WERE LARGELY
ABSENT IN THE CONTINENTAL CONGRESS. IT TRACES THE ORIGINS OF
THESE LEADERSHIP DEFICIENCIES TO A SERIES OF DECISIONS
CONCERNING INSTITUTIONAL STRUCTURE THAT WERE TAKEN ON THE
OPENING DAY OF THE CONGRESS'S FIRST SESSION AND
SUBSTANTIALLY MAINTAINED OVER THE 15-YEAR COURSE OF ITS
HISTORY. UTILIZING THE KNOWLEDGE OF THE INSTITUTIONAL FLAWS,
THE AUTHORS SPECULATE ON THE GENERAL IMPORTANCE OF SECURELY
GROUNDED INSTITUTIONAL POWERS FOR SUSTAINING LEADERSHIP IN
LEGISLATIVE BODIES.

09670 WILSON, S. Y.
POVERTY AND PROTECTIONISM
REVIEW OF BLACK POLITICAL ECOMOMY, 16(3) (WIN 88), 25-52.
THIS ARTICLE ASSESSES THE IMPORTANCE OF TRADE TO THE
EMPLOYMENT OF THE U.S. POOR; EVALUATES THE CONSUMER COSTS OF
PROTECTIONISM; EXAMINES WHICH JOBS HAVE BEEN SAVED BY
PROTECTIONISM; AND SUGGESTS POLICY DIRECTIONS THAT WOULD
MORE DIRECTLY AND MORE EFFECTIVELY GET AT THE PROBLEM OF
PROVIDING EMPLOYMENT OPPORTUNITIES TO THE POOR WHILE
SAFEGUARDING THE CONSUMER BENEFITS OF OPEN TRADE.

09671 WILTGEN, R.
THE EVOLUTION OF MARX'S PERSPECTIVE OF MERCANTILISM
INTERNATIONAL JOURNAL OF SOCIAL ECONOMICS, 16(7) (1989),
48-56.
MARX, LIKE ORTHODOX POLITICAL ECONOMISTS, DEVELOPED A
CONCEPT OF HISTORICAL AND ECONOMIC CHANGE THAT CORRESPONDS
TO THE PERIOD AND MODE OF THOUGHT AND POLICY THAT IS TODAY
CALLED "MERCANTILISM". MARX'S TREATMENT OF THE SUBJECT WAS
VARIED AND UNEVEN AND DID NOT ACHIEVE A FULLY DEVELOPED
STATE UNTIL HIS CONCEPTION OF VALUE AND CAPITALISM WAS WELL
DEFINED AND HE COULD APPLY THE NOTION OF MERCANTILISM TO HIS
ANALYSIS OF ECONOMIC DEVELOPMENT. IN HIS EARLY WRITINGS,
MARX ADDRESSED MERCANTILISM DOCTRINE WHILE MAINLY IGNORING
ECONOMIC DEVELOPMENTS TAKING PLACE IN THE MERCANTILIST ERA.
IN THE SECOND PERIOD, MARX AND ENGEL'S EMPHASIS WAS SHIFTED
TO HISTORICAL DEVELOPMENT. IT WAS DURING THE THIRD PERIOD
WHEN MARX DEVELOPED HIS THEORY OF SURPLUS VALUE THAT HIS
CONCEPTION OF MERCANTILISM BECAME GROUNDED IN ECONOMIC
DEVELOPMENT AND ATTAINED MATURITY. ONLY WHEN MARX'S CONCEPT
OF MERCANTILISM HAD PRACTICAL SIGNIFICANCE COULD ITS
SIGNIFICANCE BE FULLY DEVELOPED.

09672 WINCZOREK, P.
TOWARD PLURALISTIC PARLIAMENTARY DEMOCRACY
CONTEMPORARY POLAND, XXII(11-12) (1989), 1-5.
THE NEED FOR MAKING SWEEPING POLITICAL REFORMS HAS BEEN
GROWING IN POLAND FOR MANY YEARS. PART OF THE GOVERNMENT
ELITE AND BROAD CIRCLES OF SOCIETY HAVE BECOME INCREASINGLY
AWARE THAT POLAND'S MARCH TO CIVILIZATION CANNOT BE ACHIEVED
WITHOUT ABANDONING THE EXISTING, ANACHRONISTIC POLITICAL
STRUCTURES. USING A LIFE-SUPPORT SYSTEM TO KEEP OUTDATED
MECHANSIMS OF GOVERNMENT WORKING HAS BEEN THE MAJOR REASON
FOR THE ECONOMIC CRISIS. THE ECONOMIC AND POLITICAL CRISES
ARE TWO PARALLEL BUT CLOSELY INTERCONNECTED SOCIAL PROCESSES.

09673 WINEBRENNER. D.
A WORKING CLASS COMMUNITY CONFRONTS RACISM
POLITICAL AFFAIRS, LXVIII(2) (FEB 89), 35-37.
RACIST ATTACKS ON A BLACK CHURCH IN LORAIN COUNTY, OHIO,
MIRRORED THE RACISM, ANTI-SEMITISM, AND RED-BAITING USED BY

REPUBLICANS IN THE BUSH-QUAYLE CAMPAIGN AND THE CAMPAIGN
AGAINST OHIO SENATOR HOWARD METZENBAUM. BUT, ON THE POSITIVE
SIDE, THE ATTACKS GAVE LOCAL UNIONS AN OPPORTUNITY TO SHOW
THEIR SUPPORT FOR THE CHURCH AND FOR UNITY WITHIN THE
WORKING CLASS.

09674 HINGLEE, P.
   AGRICULTURAL TRADE POLICIES OF INDUSTRIAL COUNTRIES
   FINANCE AND DEVELOPMENT, 26(1) (MAR 89), 9-11.
     THE AUTHOR REVIEWS SOME OF THE AGRICULTURAL SUPPORT
   POLICIES OF THE INDUSTRIALIZED COUNTRIES AND DISCUSSES THE
   BENEFITS OF LIBERALIZATION FOR THESE COUNTRIES AND OTHERS.

09675 HINHAM, G.R.
   THE PRENEGOTIATION PHASE OF THE URUGUAY ROUND
   INTERNATIONAL JOURNAL, XLIV(2) (SPR 89), 280-303.
     THE PATH TO THE URUGUAY DECLARATION OF 1986 WAS TORTUOUS.
   THE TOKYO ROUND OF THE GATT MULTILATERAL NEGOTIATIONS,
   CONCLUDED IN 1979, HAD MADE CONSIDERABLE PROGRESS IN
   REDUCING PROTECTIONISM FROM NON-TARIFF BARRIERS. SHORTLY
   AFTER 1979, PRESSURE BEGAN TO BUILD TO EXPAND THE GATT
   REGIME TO INCLUDE NEW ISSUES LIKE SERVICES AND INVESTMENT.
   THE ENTIRE MOVEMENT TOWARDS THE URUGUAY DECLARATION FALLS
   WITHIN THE DEFINITION OF A PRENEGOTIATION PROCESS.

09676 HINIK, J.
   RESTORING BIPARTISANSHIP
   WASHINGTON QUARTERLY, 12(1) (WIN 89), 109-122.
     AMERICANS MUST RECONCILE THE DOMESTIC DEBATE THAT
   CONTINUES TO TEAR THE COUNTRY APART AND TAKE BIPARTISANSHIP
   BEYOND THE LOWEST COMMON DENOMINATOR WHICH DESCRIBES ITS
   POSITION TODAY. THEY WILL ACCOMPLISH THIS ONLY IF THEY
   ADDRESS CONCEPTS AND PHILOSOPHY RATHER THAN GIMMICKS AND
   POLEMICS.

09677 HINKEL, E.A.
   THE ONTOLOGICAL STATUS OF POLITICS IN ISLAM AND THE
   EPISTEMOLOGY OF ISLAMIC REVIVAL
   DISSERTATION ABSTRACTS INTERNATIONAL, 49(7) (JAN 89),
   1953-A.
     MYSTIC ATTEMPTS IN ISLAM TO REMOVE THE VEIL CORRESPOND
   TO THE REDUCTION OF EPISTEMOLOGICALLY DISTORTING INTERESTS
   IN POST-MODERN CRITICISM. BY COOPTING THE TOOLS OF THE POST-
   MODERN CRITIC WHILE REMAINING IN THE "WELTANSCHAUUNG" OF
   ISLAMIC REVIVALISTS, IT IS POSSIBLE TO: (1) ACHIEVE A FULL
   UNDERSTANDING AND APPRECIATION OF ISLAMIC REVIVAL AND (2)
   ARRIVE AT A LOGICAL, SYSTEMATIC, AND PERSUASIVE CRITIQUE OF
   POST-MODERNISM.

09678 HINKEL, R.J.
   SOVIET STRATEGIC NUCLEAR DOCTRINE UNDER GORBACHEV
   AVAILABLE FROM NTIS, NO. AD-A209 795/4/GAR, APR 89, 24.
     THIS PAPER EXAMINES SOVIET OFFENSIVE STRATEGIC NUCLEAR
   DOCTRINE UNDER GENERAL SECRETARY AND PRESIDENT MIKAIL S.
   GORBACHEV. THE DEVELOPMENT OF SOVIET NUCLEAR DOCTRINE
   STARTING WITH THE STALIN ERA IS REVIEWED. A DOES LOOK AT
   THOSE PIECES OF GORBACHEV'S NEW THINKING THAT PERTAIN TO
   NUCLEAR WEAPONS DOCTRINE ARE PRESENTED. IMPLICATIONS FOR U.S.
   STRATEGY ARE OFFERED. ARMS CONTROL.

09679 HINKLER, C.
   PRESIDENTS HELD HOSTAGE: THE RHETORIC OF JIMMY CARTER AND
   RONALD REAGAN
   TERRORISM, 12(1) (1989), 21-30.
     HOSTAGE CRISES HAVE HAD NEGATIVE EFFECTS ON THE LAST TWO
   PRESIDENTS, CRIPPLING REELECTION BIDS AND EXECUTIVE
   EFFECTIVENESS. THE PUBLIC NEVER FORGAVE JIMMY CARTER, BUT
   ALLOWED RONALD REAGAN TO LEAVE OFFICE THE MOST POPULAR
   PRESIDENT SINCE FRANKLIN ROOSEVELT. THIS ANALYSIS ARGUES
   THAT PRESIDENTIAL RHETORIC IS A KEY VARIABLE WHICH EXPLAINS
   THE PUBLIC'S DISCREPANT RESPONSE. RECOGNIZING THE
   CONSTRAINING EFFECT OF PRESIDENTIAL RHETORIC ON FUTURE WORDS
   AND ACTIONS, THIS STUDY POSITS THAT CARTER'S EARLY
   RHETORICAL CHOICES PLACED HIM IN AN UNTENABLE POSTURE WITH
   THE PUBLIC, WHILE REAGAN'S EARLY CHOICES ALLOWED HIM
   SUFFICIENT FLEXIBILITY TO RETAIN A SUCCESSFUL IMAGE. THE
   STUDY CONCLUDES THAT CARTER'S RHETORIC HEIGHTENED THE SENSE
   OF CRISIS, ASSOCIATED HIM WITH REPEATED FAILURES, INTIMATED
   THAT HE HAD NO OTHER SOLUTIONS, AND PRECLUDED TRADITIONAL
   ARGUMENTS FOR ALLAYING PUBLIC CONCERN. REAGAN'S RHETORIC
   DISCOURAGED PUBLIC SCRUTINY, PRESERVED ARGUMENTATIVE OPTIONS
   FOR DIFFUSING PUBLIC FRUSTRATION, AND MAINTAINED CONSISTENCY
   WITH HIS PROMISE TO BRING CRIMINALS TO JUSTICE.

09680 HINN, M.
   BLACK ADMINISTRATORS AND RACIAL ROADBLOCKS IN PUBLIC
   ORGANIZATIONS: PROBLEMS AND RECOURSE
   INTERNATIONAL JOURNAL OF PUBLIC ADMINISTRATION, 12(5)
   (1989), 797-820.
     DISCUSSIONS IN THE REPRESENTATIVE BUREAUCRACY LITERATURE
   HAVE TACITLY ASSIGNED THE RESPONSIBILITY OF REPRESENTING THE
   INTERESTS OF BLACKS TO INDIVIDUAL BLACK ADMINISTRATORS.
   RELYING ON BLACK EMPLOYEE GROUPS (OR SOLIDARITY GROUPS) TO
   REPRESENT THE INTERESTS OF BLACKS IS IGNORED. THE

POSSIBILITY THAT BLACK MEMBERS OF ORGANIZATIONS HAVE A GROUP
INTEREST TO BE REPRESENTED IS NOT CONSIDERED IN THE
LITERATURE. ASSIGNING THE REPRESENTATION RESPONSIBILITY TO
INDIVIDUAL BLACK ADMINISTRATORS IS REJECTED BECAUSE OF
BARRIERS THAT CAN BE CREATED BY RACIAL ROADBLOCKS (TOKENISM
AND DIFFERENT PERCEPTIONS OF RACE RELATIONS). IT IS ARGUED
THAT SOLIDARITY GROUPS ARE A MORE EFFECTIVE MEANS OF
REPRESENTING THE INTERESTS OF BLACKS.

09681 WINN, M.
   ETHICS IN ORGANIZATIONS: A PERSPECTIVE ON RECIPROCATION
   INTERNATIONAL JOURNAL OF PUBLIC ADMINISTRATION, 12(6) (NOV
   89), 867-888.
     SOME SCHOLARS HAVE ASSIGNED THE RESPONSIBILITY FOR
   ETHICAL CONDUCT IN THE PUBLIC SECTOR TO INDIVIDUAL
   ADMINISTRATORS. SUPPORTERS OF THIS PERSPECTIVE CONTEND THAT
   INDIVIDUALS ARE ABLE TO INTRODUCE ETHICS INTO THE
   ADMINISTRATIVE PROCESS BY ASSUMING PERSONAL RESPONSIBILITY
   FOR ETHICAL ACTION. THE INFERENCE IS THAT ORGANIZATIONS
   CANNOT BE EXPECTED TO ASSUME RESPONSIBILITY FOR ETHICAL
   CONDUCT. CONVERSELY THE CONTENTION THAT INDIVIDUAL ETHICS
   ARE INADEQUATE IN ORGANIZATIONS IS POSED AS A COUNTER
   ARGUMENT. SUPPORTERS OF THIS CONTENTION ARGUE THAT
   INDIVIDUAL INTEGRITY DOES NOT MEAN THAT ORGANIZATIONS WILL
   ACT ETHICALLY. THEY ARGUE THAT ORGANIZATIONAL ETHICS ARE
   INDEPENDENT OF INDIVIDUAL ETHICS. HENCE, THEY ARE TREATED AS
   SEPARATE ENTITIES THAT DO NOT COMPLIMENT EACH OTHER. AN
   ARGUMENT THAT ORGANIZATIONS AND INDIVIDUALS ENGAGE IN
   COMPLIMENTARY ACTIONS WHICH LEAD TO ETHICAL CONDUCT IS
   LARGELY ABSENT IN THE LITERATURE. I ARGUE THAT THERE IS A
   RECIPROCAL RELATIONSHIP BETWEEN INDIVIDUALS AND
   ORGANIZATIONS. THUS, INDIVIDUAL AND ORGANIZATIONAL ETHICS
   ARE NOT SEPARATE BUT INTERACTIVE ENTITIES.

09682 WINSLOW, D.
   FRANCE'S DEVELOPMENT PLANS FOR NEW CALEDONIA
   CULTURAL SURVIVAL QUARTERLY, 13(2) (1989), 69-70.
     IN 1988, FRANCE AND MAJOR FACTIONS IN NEW CALEDONIA
   NEGOTIATED THE MATIGNON ACCORDS TO STOP THE FIGHTING AND
   PREVENT A REAL CIVIL WAR IN THE FRENCH COLONY. UNDER THE
   ACCORDS, DEVELOPMENT PROJECTS WILL BE INSTITUTED, AND
   BUREAUCRATIC STRUCTURES AND GOVERNMENT SERVICES WILL BE
   DECENTRALIZED TO BETTER SERVE THE MORE REMOTE NORTHERN AND
   ISLANDS REGIONS. BUT THE ACCORDS DO NOT ADEQUATELY ADDRESS
   THE SOCIAL AND ECONOMIC INEQUALITIES IN NEW CALEDONIA. THIS
   DISCRIMINATION IS A PRODUCT OF COLONIALISM. BECAUSE THE
   ACCORDS DO NOT DISSOLVE THE COLONIAL STRUCTURES, THEY CANNOT
   HOPE TO REMEDY THE INEQUALITY. IN FACT, THEY RISK
   REINFORCING THE VERY STRUCTURES THAT HANDICAP NATIVE
   DEVELOPMENT.

09683 WINSOR, C. JR.
   TREATING THE SYMPTOM OR THE ILLNESS?
   MEXICO-UNITED STATES REPORT, II(7) (APR 89), 1-2.
     THE AUTHOR DISCUSSES THE BRADY PLAN, WHICH IS RECEIVING
   MUCH ATTENTION AS A CURE FOR THE THIRD WORLD'S DEBT PROBLEMS.
   IT ASSUMES THAT THE LACK OF ECONOMIC GROWTH IN MANY
   COUNTRIES IS THE RESULT OF FOREIGN DEBT REPAYMENT AND
   PROPOSES TO TRIM THEIR FOREIGN DEBT BY AT LEAST 20 PERCENT.
   MEXICO IS BEING TOUTED AS THE "TEST CASE" FOR THE BRADY PLAN.

09684 HINSTON, F.
   IDEOLOGY AND WOMEN'S EQUALITY
   POLITICAL AFFAIRS, LXVIII(6) (JUN 89), 31-32.
     THE ARTICLE STUDIES SOME OF THE PROBLEMS THAT WOMEN ARE
   CONFRONTING IN THEIR FIGHT FOR EQUALITY. THESE INCLUDE A
   BARRAGE OF FIERCE IDEOLOGICAL ATTACKS FROM THE ULTRA-RIGHT,
   INCREASING DOMESTIC VIOLENCE, AND A GROWING INSECURITY AND
   DESPAIR. IT ALSO EXAMINES THE CURRENT "WAGES FOR HOUSEWORK"
   MOVEMENT AND CONCLUDES THAT THE MOVEMENT IS
   COUNTERPRODUCTIVE TO THE OVERALL MOVEMENT FOR EQUALITY. THE
   ARTICLE CONCLUDES BY CALLING ON THE COMMUNIST PARTY TO
   INCREASE ITS EFFORTS TO UNITE THE WOMEN'S MOVEMENT WITH THE
   OTHER MOVEMENTS OF THE WORKING CLASS.

09685 HINSTON, F.
   THE MALIGN NEGLECT OF WELFARE REFORM
   POLITICAL AFFAIRS, LXVIII(3) (MAR 89), 40-43.
     THE AUTHOR DISCUSSES WELFARE REFORM IN THE USA AND
   REVIEWS THE PROVISIONS OF THE FAMILY SECURITY ACT OF 1987.

09686 HINSTON, H.
   FROM ANTI-SLAVERY TO THE ANTI-MONOPOLY STRATEGY
   POLITICAL AFFAIRS, LXVIII(2) (FEB 89), 2-9.
     THE AUTHOR EXAMINES THE RELATIONSHIP BETWEEN MARXISM AND
   THE BLACK CIVIL RIGHTS STRUGGLE AS REVEALED BY THE WORK OF
   MARTIN LUTHER KING JR. FREDERICK DOUGLAS, KARL MARX, AND
   PAUL ROBESON.

09687 HINTERFORD, D.
   ASSESSING THE SOVIET NAVAL BUILD-UP IN SOUTHEAST ASIA:
   THREATS TO REGIONAL SECURITY
   AVAILABLE FROM NTIS, NO. AD-A201291/2/GAR, SEP 88, 36.
     THIS REPORT ANALYZES THE STARK SECURITY CHALLENGES

CONFRONTING ASEAN AND CHINA AS A RESULT OF THE SUBSTANTIAL
AND CONTINUOUS STRENGTHENING OF SOVIET NAVAL CAPABILITY IN
THE ASIA-PACIFIC. THE REPORT DISCUSSES THE COMMANDING
COERCIVE BENEFITS ACCRUING TO MOSCOW FROM THE SOVIET UNION'S
SUCCESSFUL GEO-STRATEGIC LEAPFROG TO NAVAL AND AIR
FACILITIES AT CAM RANH BAY AND DA NANG IN VIETNAM. OVERALL,
THIS ANALYSIS CONCLUDES THAT THE MAJOR OBJECTIVES OF THE
SOVIET NAVAL BUILDUP IN THE REGION ARE TO COMPEL SOUTHEAST
ASIA GOVERNMENTS TO ACCOMMODATE SOVIET FOREIGN POLICY GOALS
AND TO RAISE CONCERNS IN THE REGION ABOUT THE WISDOM OF
CLOSE ASSOCIATION WITH THE U.S. THE REPORT CALLS FOR
ENHANCED NAVAL COOPERATION AND DEFENSE-SHARING BETWEEN THE U.
S. AND ASEAN IN ORDER TO PROVIDE THE REQUISITE REGIONAL
MARITIME SECURITY TO COUNTER SOVIET THREATS.

09688 WINTERFORD, D.
    SINO-SOVIET DETENTE: NEW CHALLENGE TO AMERICAN INTERESTS
    IN ASIA
    AVAILABLE FROM NTIS, NO. AD-A207 071/2/GAR, MAR 89, 45.
    THIS REPORT ANALYZES THE INTENSIFYING CHALLENGES THAT
SINO-SOVIET DETENTE POSES FOR AMERICAN INTERESTS AND
POLICIES IN THE ASIA-PACIFIC. IT ADDRESSES AND EVALUATES
SOVIET PRESIDENT GORBACHEV'S SUCCESSFUL EFFORTS AT MAKING
CHINA THE CENTERPIECE OF HIS ASIAN STRATEGY. ALTHOUGH BOTH
BEIJING AND MOSCOW DISINGENUOUSLY ARGUE THAT SINO-SOVIET
DETENTE WILL NOT AFFECT THEIR RELATIONS WITH THE U.S. THIS
REPORT INDICATES THAT SUBSTANTIAL HARM HAS ALREADY OCCURRED
TO U.S. INTERESTS IN ASIA AS A RESULT OF SOVIET AND CHINESE
RAPPROACHEMENT. THE REPORT EXAMINES THE WIDENING AND
DEEPENING RANGE OF SINO-SOVIET POLITICAL AND ECONOMIC TIES,
AND STATES THAT PROSPECTIVE COOPERATIVE MILITARY EXCHANGES
BETWEEN THE TWO ASIAN COMMUNIST STATES MUST NOW BE
CONSIDERED LIKELY. THIS ASSESSMENT OF SINO-SOVIET DETENTE
GIVEN IN THIS REPORT INDICATES THAT THE BALANCE OF POWER MAY
BE SHIFTING IN ASIA IN WAYS UNFAVORABLE TO THE U.S. FINALLY,
THE REPORT CALLS FOR A RECOGNITION BY U.S. DECISION-MAKERS
THAT THE APPARENT ANTI-SOVIET COALITION FORGED BY THE U.S.
IN ASIA, CONSISTING OF THE U.S. JAPAN, AND CHINA, HAS NOW
BEEN BROKEN. NOT ONLY IS THIS PART OF THE SHIFT IN THE
BALANCE OF POWER, BUT SINOSOVIET DETENTE PROVIDES THE SOVIET
UNION WITH A FREEDOM IT HAS NOT YET ENJOYED FOR DECADES TO
CONDUCT ITS ASIA-PACIFIC POLICY

09689 WINTHROP, S.V.
    DEBT-FOR-NATURE SWAPS: DEBT RELIEF AND BIOSPHERE
    PRESENATION?
    SAIS REVIEW, 9(2) (SUM 89), 129-149.
    THIS ARTICLE TRACES THE DEVELOPMENT AND STATUS OF A
UNIQUE APPROACH TO KILLING TWO BIRDS WITH ONE STONE. THE
IDEA OF PRESERVING THE LATIN AMERICAN ENVIRONMENT BY SELLING
OFF DEBT TO INTERNATIONAL ENVIRONMENTAL ORGANIZATION AFFECTS
A NUMBER OF INTEREST GROUPS - LATIN AMERICAN GOVERNMENTS,
THE GLOBAL BANKING SYSTEM, DRUG TRAFFICKERS, AND
ENVIRONMENTAL OFFICIALS. THIS ARTICLE EXAMINES WHAT EACH
INTEREST GROUP HAS AT STAKE IN THE WAKE OF SUCH DEVELOPMENTS.

09690 WIRLS, D.J.
    DEFENSE AS DOMESTIC POLITICS: NATIONAL SECURITY POLICY AND
    POLITICAL POWER IN THE 1980'S
    DISSERTATION ABSTRACTS INTERNATIONAL, 49(10) (APR 89),
    3145-A.
    THE POLITICS OF NATIONAL SECURITY IN THE REAGAN ERA
DERIVED FROM THE CONFLICTS AMONG THREE FORCES THAT SOUGHT TO
SHAPE AMERICAN MILITARY POLICY IN THE 1980'S: THE NUCLEAR
PEACE MOVEMENT, THE NEW COLD WAR COALITION, AND THE MILITARY
REFORM MOVEMENT. THE FIRST HALF OF THIS DISSERTATION
CONCENTRATES ON THE ORIGINS, ORGANIZATION, CONSTITUENCIES,
AND POLICY AGENDAS BEHIND THE THREE MOVEMENTS. THE SECOND
HALF USES CASE STUDIES OF THREE POLICY INNOVATIONS TO PROBE
THE POLITICAL COMPETITION AMONG THE INSTITUTIONS AND
COALITIONS.

09691 WIRTH, D.
    CLIMATE CHAOS
    FOREIGN POLICY, (74) (SPR 89), 1-22.
    THE ARTICLE EXAMINES THE GROWING ENVIRONMENTAL MENACE OF
GLOBAL WARMING. IT OUTLINES THE EXTENT OF THE PROBLEM AND
ANALYZES FUTURE TRENDS AND EXPLORES ALTERNATIVES DESIGNED TO
ARREST AND REVERSE THE WARMING TREND. THE AUTHOR ARGUES THAT
THE "GREENHOUSE EFFECT" IS A DANGER OF EPIC PROPORTIONS THAT
GOVERNMENTS ARE ILL-EQUIPPED TO COMBAT. HE EXAMINES THE ROLE
THAT GOVERNMENTS OF BOTH DEVELOPED AND DEVELOPING NATIONS
CAN PLAY IN REDUCING THE RISK. HE ADVOCATES ELIMINATION OF
CHLOROFLOUROCARBONS AND HALONS, REFORESTATION, AND
EXPLORATION OF CO2 FREE ENERGY SOURCES.

09692 WISENSALE, S.
    FAMILY POLICY IN THE STATE LEGISLATURE: THE CONNECTICUT
    AGENDA
    POLICY STUDIES REVIEW, 8(3) (SPR 89), 622-637.
    IN 1987 THE CONNECTICUT GENERAL ASSEMBLY MADE THE FIRST
ATTEMPT IN THE NATION'S HISTORY TO PASS A COMPREHENSIVE
FAMILY POLICY. A TOTAL OF 16 OF 26 PROPOSED BILLS WERE
APPROVED AT A TOTAL COST OF NEARLY $35 MILLION. INCLUDED IN

THE PACKAGE WAS A PARENTAL AND MEDICAL LEAVE BILL FOR STATE
EMPLOYEES, A PILOT PROGRAM FOR DISPLACED HOMEMAKERS, AND A
BILL TO IMPROVE ACCESS TO CHILD DAY CARE. THIS STUDY
EMPHASIZES THE IMPORTANCE OF STRONG PARTY LEADERSHIP, THE
NEED FOR COMPREHENSIVE PROPOSALS THAT APPEAL TO A VARIETY OF
CONSTITUENCIES, AND THE IMPORTANCE OF THE RIGHT POLITICAL
AND ECONOMIC TIMING IN ENACTING FAMILY-ORIENTED LEGISLATION.

09693 WISTRICH, R.
    FUNDAMENTALISTS ON THE RISE
    ENCOUNTER, LXXII(3) (MAR 89), 56-60.
    THE NEW ANTI-SEMITISM IN THE MIDDLE EAST CANNOT BE
DIVORCED FROM THE ARAB-ISRAELI CONFLICT. IN EGYPT, SYRIA,
AND OTHER ARAB COUNTRIES, ANTI-JEWISH ATTITUDES ARE AN
INTEGRAL PART OF THE EFFORT TO DE-LEGITIMIZE ISRAEL NOT ON
THE BASIS OF ITS POLICIES BUT RATHER BECAUSE IT EMBODIES AN
INTRINSICALLY EVIL OR DEMONIC ESSENCE. THE ARABS MAKE NO
REAL DISTINCTION BETWEEN ISRAEL AND THE JEWS, BETWEEN
THEOLOGY AND POLITICS. THERE IS A PLETHORA OF MATERIAL IN
CLASSICAL MUSLIM SOURCES THAT CAN BE USED TO VINDICATE THE
CURRENT IMAGE OF THE JEW AS AN ENEMY OF ISLAM AND AN AGENT
OF THE DARKEST FORCES OF EVIL.

09694 WISTRICH, R. S.
    GORBACHEV'S RUSSIA
    PRESENT TENSE, 16(2) (JAN 89), 20-24.
    THE AUTHOR DISCUSSES HOW GORBACHEV'S NEW POLICIES ARE
AFFECTING RUSSIAN JEWRY AND SOVIET ATTITUDES TOWARD ISRAEL.

09695 WISZNIEWSKI, A.
    SOLIDARITY: TRADE UNION OR FACADE?
    EAST EUROPEAN REPORTER, 4(1) (WIN 89), 61-62.
    THE ARTICLE ANALYZES THE METAMORPHOSIS OF POLAND'S
SOLIDARITY FROM A DEMOCRATIC TRADE UNION TO A HUGE POLITICAL
ORGANIZATION. ALTHOUGH MARTIAL LAW AND THE LACK OF ANY OTHER
SIGNIFICANT OPPOSITION FORCED SOLIDARITY TO "TREAD ON THE
GROUND OF BIG POLITICS," THE RESULT IS A SOLIDARITY THAT IS
"CREASED AND CRACKED." THE AUTHOR CRITICIZES THE LOSS OF
DEMOCRACY IN THE ORGANIZATION AND BLAMES BOTH THE UNION'S
MEMBERS AND LEADERS FOR THE SHIFT AWAY FROM THE TRADE
UNION'S ORIGINAL PURE GOALS AND PRACTICES.

09696 WITT, U.
    THE EVOLUTION OF ECONOMIC INSTITUTIONS AS A PROPAGATION
    PROCESS
    PUBLIC CHOICE, 62(2) (AUG 89), 155-172.
    BASED ON SOME NOTIONS FROM RECENT GAME THEORETIC
APPROACHES TO EXPLAIN THE EMERGENCE OF INSTITUTIONS, A MODEL
IS PUT FORWARD WHICH IMPLIES SOME GENERALIZATIONS AND
EXTENSIONS. THE EVOLUTION OF INSTITUTIONS IS INTERPRETED AS
A DIFFUSION PROCESS. THIS PROVIDES A GENERAL FORMAL
FRAMEWORK TO COVER BOTH, THE CASE OF THE STRATEGIC AND THAT
OF NON-STRATEGIC INTERACTION. THEN, DIFFERENT FORMS OF
INTERDEPENDENCY EFFECTS BETWEEN THE INDIVIDUALS INVOLVED ARE
IDENTIFIED AS MAKING THE CRUTIAL DIFFERENCE BETWEEN THE CASE
WHERE INSTITUTIONS EMERGE SPONTANEOUSLY IN AN UNORGANIZED
FORM AND THE CASE WHERE THEY DO NOT.

09697 WITTLIN, F.M.
    SWISS INDUSTRY PARTICIPATION IN FOREIGN ARMS PROCUREMENT
    NATO'S SIXTEEN NATIONS, 34(6) (OCT 89), 71-73 (SPECIAL
    SECTION).
    ALTHOUGH IT HAS NOT BEEN INVOLVED IN A MILITARY CONFLICT
SINCE 1815 AND IS A NEUTRAL COUNTRY, SWITZERLAND HAS A LARGE,
WELL-TRAINED MILITIA WITH MODERN EQUIPMENT. ITS ARMED
FORCES ARE DESIGNED FOR VERY POWERFUL DEFENSIVE OPERATIONS
AND HAVE A "STRUCTURAL INABILITY TO ATTACK." THE ARMED
FORCES' PRIMARY TASK IS TO DETER POTENTIAL AGGRESSORS AND,
FAILING THAT, MAINTAIN THE COUNTRY'S INDEPENDENCE THROUGH
PERSISTENT, LENGTHY RESISTANCE THAT INFLICTS MAXIMUM LOSSES
ON THE ENEMY. SWITZERLAND'S ARMS TRADE IS NORMALLY CONDUCTED
ON A STRICTLY COMMERCIAL BASIS, AND THE USA IS ITS MAIN
FOREIGN SUPPLIER.

09698 WITTMAN, D.
    ARMS CONTROL VERIFICATION AND OTHER GAMES INVOLVING
    IMPERFECT DETECTION
    AMERICAN POLITICAL SCIENCE REVIEW, 83(3) (SEP 89), 923-948.
    THIS ARTICLE PRESENTS AN ANALYSIS OF THE STRATEGIC
BEHAVIOR OF COUNTRIES WHEN THERE IS IMPERFECT VERIFICATION
OF AN ARMS CONTROL AGREEMENT. IT PROVIDES A FRAMEWORK FOR
DETERMINING WHETHER AN ARMS CONTROL AGREEMENT IS DESIRABLE,
SHOWS WHICH FACTORS ARE NEEDED FOR THE AGREEMENT TO BE
MAINTAINED IN THE ABSENCE OF THIRDPARTY ENFORCERS, AND
DEVELOPS PROPOSITIONS RELATING CHANGES IN VERIFICATION
CAPABILITIES TO CHANGES IN THE LIKELIHOOD OF CHEATING AND
THE USE OF VERIFICATION TECHNOLOGY. THESE PROPOSITION YIELD
SEVERAL PARADOXES OF INFORMATION (FOR EXAMPLE, THE BETTER
THE VERFICATION TECHNOLOGY, THE LESS OFTEN IT WILL BE
EMPLOYED). SINCE THE ANALYSIS INCORPORATES BOTH SIMULTANEOUS
AND SEQUENTIAL MOVES BY THE PLAYERS, IT PROVIDES NEW
INSIGHTS INTO OTHER APPLIED AREAS AS WELL AS GAME THEORY.

09699 WITTROCK, B.
SOCIAL SCIENCE AND STATE DEVELOPMENT: TRANSFORMATIONS OF
THE DISCOURSE OF MODERNITY
INTERNATIONAL SOCIAL SCIENCE JOURNAL, (122) (NOV 89),
497-507.
SOCIAL SCIENCE DOES NOT PRIMARILY PROVIDE WELL-DEFINED
INPUTS INTO SMOOTH DECISION AND PROGRAMMING PROCESSES. NOR
IS ITS ROLE LIMITED TO SERVING AS A DISTANT DISCOURSE FOR
THE TRAINING OF PROFESSIONALS TO OPERATE THE APPARATUS OF
MODERN PUBLIC AND PRIVATE ADMINISTRATION. RATHER, IT IS THE
PRE-EMINENT FORM OF INSTITUTIONALLY BASED AND DISCURSIVELY
REPRODUCED INQUIRY ABOUT SOCIETAL PHENOMENA. IT EMERGED AND
EVOLVED IN CLOSE INTERACTION WITH THE EVOLUTION OF THE
MODERN STATE AND OF THE SECULAR TRANSFORMATION OF EUROPEAN
SOCIETIES FROM PRE-INDUSTRIAL TO INDUSTRIAL, FROM RURAL TO
URBAN, FROM TRADITIONAL TO MODERN. THUS, SOCIAL SCIENCE IS
THE DISCURSIVE CONCOMITANT TO THE VAST INCREASE IN
ADMINISTRATIVE AND COMMUNICATIVE CAPACITIES THAT
CHARACTERIZED THE NEW TYPE OF STATE FORMATION OF LATE
NINETEENTH-AND EARLY TWENTIETH-CENTURY EUROPE AND NORTH
AMERICA.

09700 WLECH, S.
POLITICAL CULTURE AND COMMUNISM: DEFINITION AND USE
JOURNAL OF COMMUNIST STUDIES, 5(1) (MAR 89), 92-97.
IN AN ANALYSIS OF SOME CURRENT LITERATURE ON THE SUBJECT,
THE ARTICLE EXAMINES THE QUESTION OF WHETHER IT IS BETTER
TO VIEW POLITICAL CULTURE AS THE "SUBJECTIVE ORIENTATION TO
POLITICS", OR AS THE "ATTITUDNAL AND BEHAVORIAL MATRIX
WITHIN WHICH THE POLITICAL SYSTEM IS LOCATED." IT ALSO
ANALYZES THE QUESTION OF USE. IT CONCLUDES THAT BOTH
INTERPRETATIONS ARE VALID UNDER CERTAIN CIRCUMSTANCES AND
THAT FURTHER DEBATE OVER DEFINITIONS IS NOT LIKELY TO BE OF
GREAT UTILITY.

09701 WOERNER, F. F.
THE STRATEGIC IMPERATIVES FOR THE UNITED STATES IN LATIN
MILITARY REVIEW, LXIX(2) (FEB 89), 18-28.
AMERICA AMERICA'S CORE INTERESTS ARE FULLY ENGAGED IN
LATIN AMERICA. GEOGRAPHIC PROXIMITY, INCREASING HEMISPHERIC
ECONOMIC INTERDEPENDENCE AND COMMON DEMOCRATIC ASPIRATIONS
FOR AN INTERNATIONAL ORDER FREE OF VIOLENCE AND MILITARY OR
POLITICAL DOMINANCE BY HOSTILE INTERESTS ALL BESTOW A
SPECIAL IMPORTANCE TO THE REGION. STRATEGIC PLANNING FOR
LATIN AMERICA MUST CONSIDER THE DEVELOPMENT OF CERTAIN
ACTIVITIES. THESE INCLUDE SUPPORT FOR THE DEMOCRATIC PROCESS
AND PROFESSIONALIZATION OF HOST NATION MILITARIES AND
LEGITIMIZATION OF THEIR ROLE IN DEMOCRATIC PROCESSES.

09702 WOLDEGABRIEL, B.
WHO ELSE IS TALKING PEACE
NEW AFRICAN, (262) (JUL 89), 13.
THE FIRST OPEN ETHIO-ERITREAN PEACE DIALOGUE HELD IN 27
YEARS WAS CONCLUDED ON 4 APRIL IN KHARTOUM, BUT IT ONLY
INVOLVED THE MINOR PARTIES, NOT THE EPLF. (ERITREAN PEOPLE'S
LIBERATION FRONT). THE POLITICAL GROUPINGS HERE: ELF-RC
(REVOLUTIONARY COUNCIL OF AHMED MOHAMMED NASSER); ELF-UO
(UNITED ORGANIGATION OF OMAR BURUGE); ELF-NC (NATIONAL
COUNCIL OF ABDELGADIR JEILANI); ELF-PLF-UO (POPULAR
LIBERATION FORCES OF MOHAMMEDS MAUD). THE PROBABILITY OF
FUTURE TALKS IS EXPLORED

09703 WOLF, J.B.
ANTITERRORIST INITIATIVES
PLENUM PRESS, NEW YORK, NY, 1989, 204.
THIS BOOK OFFERS AN IN SIGHTFUL ACCOUNT OF THE OFTEN
FUTILE EFFORTS OF VARIOUS COUNTRIES TO ERADICATE THEIR
TERRORIST OPPONENTS. POINTING OUT THAT "NICE GUYS FINISH
LAST" WOLF--AN EXPERT ON NATIONAL AND INTERNATIONAL
ANTITERRORISM--REVIEWS THE SHORTCOMINGS AND PROGRESS OF
VARIOUS ANTITERRORIST OPERATIONS THROUGHOUT THE WORLD. HE
EXAMINES POLITICAL ASSASSINATION FROM THE PERSPECTIVES OF
BOTH THE TERRORIST AND ANTITERRORIST AND THE JUDEO-CHRISTIAN
ETHIC; THE ACTIVITIES OF "HIT TEAMS," PARTICULARLY THOSE
SQUADS UNLEASHED BY IRAN AND LIBYA; AND CUBA'S INVOLVEMENT
IN THE NARCOTICS TRADE AND TERRORISM. HE ALSO DISCUSSES THE
INABILITY OF THE UNITED STATES--PRIMARILY ITS ARMED FORCES
AND INTELLIGENCE AGENCIES--TO COPE WITH STATESPONSORED
TERRORISM IN THE MIDDLE EAST AND ELSEWHERE. WOLF DETAILS
EFFORTS TO REDRESS THIS PROBLEM DURING THE REAGAN
ADMINISTRATION, PARTICULARLY THE UPGRADING OF INTELLIGENCE
OPERATIONS AND STEPS TO PROTECT ITS FOREIGN EMBASSY NETWORK.
IN ADDITION, HE CRITICALLY EXAMINES BRITISH ANTITERRORIST
INITIATIVES IN NORTHERN IRELAND AND SIMILAR EFFORTS BY THE
GOVERNMENTS OF FRANCE, THE PHILIPPINES, AND SRI LANKA TO
CONTROL TERRORISM IN THE PACIFIC BASIC AND INDIAN OCEAN
REGIONS.

09704 WOLF, J.B.
CHAPTER 1: THE DEADLY MASQUERADE: IS POLITICAL
ASSASSINATION AN INTELLIGENCE TASK?; ANTITERROR INITIATIVES
PLENUM PRESS, NEW YORK, NY, 1989, --.
CHAPTER ONE, IN ANSWERING THE TITLE QUESTION EXAMINES:
"EXECUTIVE ACTION," ASSASSINATIONS: SOVIET STYLE, THE

PROPAGANDA COVERUP, THE SOVIET COMMITTEE FOR SECURITY (K.G.B.
), THE MURDER OF RICHARD S. WELCH, THE C.I.A. AND POLITICAL
ASSASSINATION, AND, SPECIAL OPERATIONS IN FICTION AND FACT.
THIS CHAPTER ALSO EXPLORES PHILOSOPHICAL AND MORAL
CONSIDERATIONS, REAGAN'S EXECUTIVE ORDER, PROACTIVE
ANTITERRORIST POLICY, AS WELL AS THE CASE FOR "ACTIVE
MEASURES."

09705 WOLF, J.B.
CHAPTER 3: PROPAGANDA: ACTIVITIES AND ANALYSIS; ANTITERROR
INITIATIVES
PLENUM PRESS, NEW YORK, NY, 1989, 41-54.
THIS CHAPTER EXAMINES THE ELEMENTS OF PROPAGANDA AND
ANALYSES PRESS RELEASES BY OTHER COUNTRIES THAN THE US -
IRAN AND CUBA. IT DESCRIBES TECHNIQUES USED IN ECUDOR,
BOLIVIA, INDIA, USSR, AND PAN AMERICA. IT DISCUSSES THE
COLLAPSE OF THE PUBLIC SAFETY PROGRAM.

09706 WOLF, J.B.
CHAPTER 6: CLANDESTINE CHANNELS AND NETWORKS; ANTITERROR
INITIATIVES
PLENUM PRESS, NEW YORK, NY, 1989, 89-106.
THIS CHAPTER EXAMINES CLANDESTINE CHANNELS AND NETWORKS
AS A TOOL OF TERRORISM. "NARCO-TERRORISM" IS DESCRIBED AS
WELL AS CUBAN MAYOMBERO BANDIDOS FROM MARIEL. THE INFLUENCE
OF SANTERIA (SAINT WORSHIP) IS EXPLORED. ALSO DISCUSSED ARE:
NICARAGUA AND WEAPONS TRAFFIC; I.R.A. WEAPONS CHANNELS;
OPERATION SHAMROCK; IRISH NORTHERN AID COMMITTEE AND THE
AMERICAN-MADE "STINGER" MISSILE.

09707 WOLF, J.B.
CHAPTER 8: TERRORISM IN THE PACIFIC REGIONS; ANTITERROR
INITIATIVES
PLENUM PRESS, NEW YORK, NY, 1989, 133-156.
THIS CHAPTER EXAMINES TERRORISM IN THE PACIFIC REGIONS.
IT BEGINS WITH A DISCUSSION ON LIBERATION THEOLOGY, THE
NICARAGUAN CLERICS, AND VATICAN ANALYSIS. IT EXPLORES
PHILLIPINE PRESIDENT, CORAZON AQUINO'S ALLIANCE WITH THE
CATHOLIC CHURCH IN MANILLA, AS WELL AS MANY AREAS OF
PHILLIPINE INVOLVEMENT IN TERRORIST AND ANTITERRORIST
ACTIVITIES, ALSO EXPLORED IS LIBYA'S ROLE IN THE SOUTH WEST
PACIFIC, ACTIVITIES IN NEW CALDONIA AND SRI LANKA.

09708 WOLFE, D.
THE CANADIAN STATE IN COMPARATIVE PERSPECTIVE
CANADIAN REVIEW OF SOCIOLOGY AND ANTHROPOLOGY, 26(1) (FEB
89), 95-126.
RECENT DEBATES ABOUT THE NATURE OF THE STATE IN
CAPITALIST SOCIETY HAVE TENDED TO POLARIZE AROUND STATE-
CENTRED VERSUS SOCIETY-CENTRED EXPLANATIONS. THIS ARTICLE
ATTEMPTS TO OVERCOME THAT DICHOTOMY BY ANALYSING THE
CANADIAN STATE IN TERMS OF THE INTERSECTION OF THE CHANGING
BALANCE OF POLITICAL FORCES IN CANADIAN SOCIETY WITH THE
ENSEMBLE OF INSTITUTIONS THAT COMPOSE THE STATE. THE
ANALYSIS OF THE RELATIVE BALANCE OF POLITICAL FORCES IN
CANADA IS SITUATED IN A COMPARATIVE CONTEXT AND THE POSTWAR
PATTERN OF STATE INTERVENTION IN CANADA IS INTERPRETED IN
COMPARISON WITH THE EXPERIENCE OF OTHER INDUSTRIALIZED
DEMOCRACIES. A CRITICAL FACTOR CONSTRAINING THE CHOICE OF
POLICY OPTIONS THROUGHOUT THIS PERIOD HAS BEEN THE
PARTICULAR POINT OF INSERTION OF THE CANADIAN IN THE GLOBAL
ECONOMYESPECIALLY ITS PRIVILEGED RELATIONSHIP WITH THE
PRINCIPAL HEGEMON OF THE TWENTIETH CENTURY, THE UNITED
STATES. THE DECLINE OF U.S. HEGEMONY POSES SPECIAL PROBLEMS
FOR THE CANADIAN STATE AND THE SOLUTIONS ADOPTED TO THOSE
PROBLEMS MAY FUNDAMENTALLY ALTER THE ROLE THAT THE STATE HAS
COME TO PLAY OVER THE PAST FOUR DECADES.

09709 WOLFE, E.E.
U.S. RESPONSIBILITIES IN INTERNATIONAL FISHERIES MATTERS
DEPARTMENT OF STATE BULLETIN (US FOREIGN POLICY), 89(2148)
(JUL 89), 56-58.
SINCE 1980, THE PRINCIPAL FISHERIES POLICY THAT THE
UNITED STATES HAS PURSUED HAS BEEN THE "AMERICANIZATION" OF
FISHERIES IN THE UNITED STATES EXCLUSIVES ECONOMIC ZONE.
CONSISTENT WITH THIS POLICY, THE DEPARTMENT OF STATE AND THE
DEPARTMENT OF COMMERCE HAVE FOLLOWED THE ALLOCATION CRITERIA
SPECIFIED IN THE MAGNUSON FISHERIES CONSERVATION AND
MANAGEMENT ACT. THE PRINCIPAL ROLE OF THE STATE DEPARTMENT
HAS BEEN TO NEGOTIATE GOVERNING AGREEMENTS WITH FOREIGN
NATIONS DESIRING TO OPERATE OFF THE U.S. COAST AND TO
ALLOCATE SURPLUS AMERICAN FISHERIES RESOURCES O FISHERMEN
FROM COUNTRIES WITH WHICH THE USA HAS GOVERNING AGREEMENTS

09710 WOLFF, M.
SAY IT AIN'T SO, JOE!
CAMPAIGNS AND ELECTIONS, 10(3) (OCT 89), 32-34.
FROM 1970 TO 1985, THE NUMBER OF ALL-ROCK RADIO STATIONS
NEARLY QUADRUPLED. IN SOME MARKETS, WHERE THERE PREVIOUSLY
HAD BEEN ONE OR TWO ROCK STATIONS, THERE ARE NOW AS MANY AS
FIFTEEN. JOE SLADE WHITE, AN AUTHORITY ON POLITICAL RADIO
ADVERTISING, SAYS THAT THIS PROLIFERATION OF STATIONS HAS
CONFUSED THE TARGETING OF POLITICAL ADVERTISING. LISTENERS
ARE NO LONGER CLEARLY SPLIT ALONG DEMOGRAPHIC LINES, MAKING

IT HARDER TO TARGET A SPECIFIC GROUP OF RADIO LISTENERS.

09711 HOLFSON, M.; FARRELL, J.P.
FOUNDATIONS OF A THEORY OF ECONOMIC WARFARE AND ARMS
CONTROL
CONFLICT MANAGEMENT AND PEACE SCIENCE, 10(2) (SPR 89),
47-75.
WAR IS CARRIED OUT EVEN IN "PEACETIME" BY EXERTING
ECONOMIC PRESSURE IN THE FORM OF FORCED DETERRING
EXPENDITURE AS WELL AS BY MILITARY THREAT. PEACE CAN
ACHIEVED ONLY BY CONSIDERING BOTH ECONOMIC AND MILITARY ARMS
CONTROL. IN THIS PAPER, DISARMAMENT AND ITS VERIFICATION BY
FISCAL CONTROL ARE STUDIED AS A MEANS OF NEGOTIATING A
REDUCTION AND ELIMINATION OF BOTH DIMENSIONS OF WAR. THIS IS
FIRST DONE UNDER SIMPLIFYING ASSUMPTIONS, BUT THEN IS
FOLLOWED BY AN ANALYSIS OF THE COMPLETE THEORY OF ECONOMIC
AND MILITARY INTERACTIONS.

09712 HOLINETZ, S.
SOCIO-ECONOMIC BARGAINING IN THE NETHERLANDS: REDEFINING
THE POST-WAR POLICY COALITION
WEST EUROPEAN POLITICS, 12(1) (JAN 89), 79-98.
THE ACCOUNT EXAMINES THE CHANGING CONTOURS OF DEMOCRATIC
CORPORATISM IN THE NETHERLANDS IN LIGHT OF THE INITIAL
BARGAINS AND COMPROMISES WHICH LED TO THE ESTABLISHMENT OF
CORPORATIST STRUCTURES IN THE AFTERMATH OF THE SECOND WORLD
WAR AND THE WAYS IN WHICH THESE WERE RENEGOTIATED IN THE
1960S, 1970S, AND 1980S. CONTARY TO THE ARGUMENTS OF PETER
KATZENSTEIN, CHANGING ECONOMIC AND POLITICAL CONDITIONS
ALLOWED WIDE SCOPE FOR THE ESTABLISHMENT OF ALTERNATIVE
POLITICAL COALITIONS. SOCIAL PARTNERSHIP DID NOT SERVE AS A
DEVICE FOR FACILITATING ADJUSTMENT TO TRENDS IN THE
INTERNATIONAL ECONOMY. INSTEAD, THE DUTCH GOVERNMENT IMPOSED
CHANGES WITHOUT THE CONSENT OF THE TRADE UNIONS.

09713 HOLIVER, L.
THE DEFLECTIVE POWER OF REPRODUCTIVE TECHNOLOGIES: THE
IMPACT ON WOMEN
WOMEN AND POLITICS, 9(3) (1989), 17-48.
ADVANCES IN REPRODUCTIVE TECHNOLOGIES ARE ALTERING
WOMEN'S EXPERIENCE OF MATERNITY AND CHILDBIRTH. THEY
INCREASE MEDICAL INTERVENTION WHILE DECREASING WOMEN'S
OPTIONS AND CONTROL OVER MATERNITY. ALTHOUGH PRESENTED AS
INCREASING INDIVIDUAL CHOICES FOR WOMEN, THEIR POTENTIAL IS
TO RESTRICT CHOICES FOR WOMEN AS A GROUP. THE BABY M CASE
ILLUSTRATES THAT WOMEN'S EXPERIENCE OF MATERNITY IS
BELITTLED EVEN IN THE LEAST TECHNOLOGICALLY DEPENDENT
ARRANGEMENT OF SURROGACY. THESE TECHNOLOGIES DEFLECT
PRESSURES FOR SOCIAL REFORMS BY PROMISING TECHNOLOGICAL
FIXES FOR REPRODUCTIVE DIFFICULTIES. OFTEN THESE PROBLEMS
HAVE SOCIAL CAUSES. WOMEN DELAY MOTHERHOOD AND INCREASE
REPRODUCTIVE RISKS, FOR EXAMPLE, TO CONFORM TO MALE CAREER
TIMETABLES. REFORMING EMPLOYMENT POLICIES IS BLUNTED, THOUGH,
BY THE TECHNOLOGICAL TURN. THESE TECHNOLOGIES SHOULD NOT BE
ALLOWED TO DEFLECT THE WOMEN'S MOVEMENT FROM PRESSURING FOR
SOCIAL CHANGE.

09714 HOLL, J.
FRUITS OF GLASNOST
DISSENT, (WIN 89), 25-38.
THE AUTHOR REPRINTS A SAMPLING OF EXCERPTS FROM THE
SOVIET PRESS THAT SUGGESTS THE RANGE OF SUBJECTS, DEGREES OF
PASSIONS, AND POINTS OF VIEW REPRESENTED ON RUSSIAN AND
SOVIET HISTORY SINCE GLASNOST HAS PERMITTED MORE TRUTHFUL
AND CRITICAL HISTORICAL INQUIRY.

09715 HOLL, J.
GLASNOST AND SOVIET CULTURE
PROBLEMS OF COMMUNISM, XXXVIII(6) (NOV 89), 40-50.
THE POLICY OF GLASNOST WAS FIRST INTRODUCED IN THE AREA
OF SOVIET CULTURE AND HAS BEEN MOST EXTENSIVELY APPLIED IN
THAT SPHERE. NOT ONLY HAVE LONG-SUPPRESSED WORKS BEEN SHOWN
ON STAGE AND SCREEN, BUT THERE HAS BEEN A VIRTUAL EXPLOSION
OF BOOKS BY PREVIOUSLY FORBIDDEN WRITERS. THE NEW POLICY HAS
POLARIZED THE CREATIVE INTELLIGENTSIA BETWEEN "LIBERALS" AND
"CONSERVATIVES," AND THE LITERARY JOURNALS HAVE TAKEN SIDES.
THE RESULTING DIALOGUE BETWEEN THE OPPOSING CAMPS HAS
ENGAGED SOVIET READERS, LISTENERS, AND VIEWERS IN THE
DYNAMIC PROCESS OF GLASNOST.

09716 HOLLEMBORG, L.J.
ITALY, THE MIDEAST, AND WESTERN TIES
FREEDOM AT ISSUE, (111) (NOV 89), 35-36.
RECENT DEVELOPMENTS AND PROSPECTS HAVE REVIVED THE
DEBATE ON WHETHER ITALY IS THE MOST MEDITERRANEAN OF THE
EUROPEAN NATIONS OR THE MOST EUROPEAN OF THE MEDITERRANEAN
COUNTRIES. BOTH DEFINITIONS ARE CORRECT, BUT THE EMPHASIS ON
ONE OR THE OTHER HAS LONG DETERMINED ITALY'S INTERNATIONAL
POSTURE AS WELL AS THE INTERPLAY BETWEEN HER FOREIGN POLICY
AND HER DOMESTIC POLICIES; IT HAS BEEN THE MAIN POTENTIAL
SOURCE OF DISSENT FROM HER PARTNERS IN THE WEST, NOTABLY THE
UNITED STATES.

09717 HOLLEMBORG, L.J.
REFORMS AND REGRESS IN ITALY
FREEDOM AT ISSUE, (108) (MAY 89), 15-17.
IN RECENT YEARS, ITALY'S ECONOMIC GROWTH HAS ENABLED IT
TO SIGNIFICANTLY NARROW THE GAP BETWEEN ITSELF AND OTHER
LEADING INDUSTRIAL DEMOCRACIES. BUT THIS ACHIEVEMENT HAS NOT
BEEN MATCHED BY A COMPARABLE ADVANCE IN PUBLIC SERVICES AND
INSTITUTIONS, INCLUDING THE POLITICAL SYSTEM. THE CONSEQUENT
IMBALANCE COULD ENDANGER THE RESULTS ACHIEVED IN THE
ECONOMIC SECTOR, ESPECIALLY AFTER EUROPEAN ECONOMIC
INTEGRATION IN 1992. MOREOVER, FAILURE TO CORRECT THE
PROBLEMS WOULD MAKE IT INCREASINGLY DIFFICULT, IF NOT
IMPOSSIBLE, TO ATTACK THE BUDGET DEFICIT AND THE PUBLIC DEBT,
THE BACKWARDNESS OF MANY SOUTHERN AREAS, AND THE HIGH
LEVELS OF UNEMPLOYMENT AND UNDER-EMPLOYMENT.

09718 HOLLMANN, H.
POLICY ANALYSIS IN WEST GERMANY'S FEDERAL GOVERNMENT: A
CASE OF UNFINISHED GOVERNMENTAL AND ADMINISTRATIVE
MODERNIZATION?
GOVERNANCE, 2(3) (JUL 89), 233-266.
THIS ARTICLE DOCUMENTS THE "INSTITUTIONALIZATION" OF
POLICY ANALYSIS AS IT HAS OCCURRED HISTORICALLY IN GERMANY,
BUT ESPECIALLY THE FEDERAL REPUBLIC OF GERMANY AFTER WW II.
POLICY ANALYSIS IS HERE DEFINED AS GOVERNMENTALLY ORGANIZED
OR SPONSORED WORK TO COLLECT AND PRODUCE INFORMATION AND
KNOWLEDGE FOR THE USE OF POLICY-MAKING AND ADMINISTRATION
(MELTSNER 1976, 18). FOR THE PURPOSE OF THIS ARTICLE, THE
QUESTIONS OF WHY AND HOW THE COLLECTED KNOWLEDGE AND
INFORMATION ARE USED ARE NOT PERTINENT; RATHER, THIS ARTICLE
CONCENTRATES ON THE GRADUAL AWARENESS OF GERMAN GOVERNMENTS
OF THEIR NEED FOR THE POLICY-ANALYSIS TOOL AND THE
INSTITUTIONALIZATION OF THIS RESOURCE. PARTICULARLY, THE
ARTICLE ADDRESSES DEVELOPMENTS AT THE CENTRAL (FEDERAL)
LEVEL OF GOVERNMENT RATHER THAN THE STATE (LAENDER) OR LOCAL
LEVEL.

09719 HOLNICKI, M.J.
INSTEAD OF REVOLUTION
COMMONWEAL, CXVI(10) (MAY 89), 293-294.
OBSERVERS OF THE POLISH COMPROMISE WONDER: WHO HAS WON?
WHICH SIDE HAS SHOWN MORE POLITICAL AND TACTICAL FORESIGHT?
SOLIDARITY CANDIDATES ARE AWARE THAT COOPERATION WITH THE
GOVERNMENT WILL COST THEM THE SUPPORT OF THE OPPOSITION LEFT
AND RADICAL UNION FACTIONS. BUT ACCEPTING ELECTORAL
CHALLENGE IS EVEN RISKIER FOR THE COMMUNIST PARTY. TOKEN
OPPOSITION PARTIES, COMBINED WITH SOLIDARITY, WILL LEAVE
EMBARRASSINGLY FEW SEATS FOR COMMUNISTS IN THE SENATE.

09720 WOLOCH, I.
THE REPUBLIC WITHOUT THE GUILLOTINE
FRENCH POLITICS AND SOCIETY, 7(3) (SUM 89), 110-119.
THE DIRECTORY REGIME GAVE FRENCH REPUBLICANISM A SECOND
CHANCE. THIS ESSAY EXAMINES THE VALUES, THE COMMITMENTS, THE
STRENGTHS, AND THE WEAKNESSES OF THE DIRECTORIAL REPUBLIC.

09721 HOLSBORN, K.G.
POLITICAL PARTICIPATION IN THE US: MORE THAN AN ELECTORATE
RESPONSIVE
DISSERTATION ABSTRACTS INTERNATIONAL, 49(7) (JAN 89),
1947-A.
THE OBJECTIVES OF THIS STUDY ARE TWOFOLD: (A) TO PROPOSE
AN INTEGRATED CONCEPTUAL FRAMEWORK OF POLITICAL
PARTICIPATION THAT IS BOTH EXHAUSTIVE OF THE RANGE OF
PARTICIPATORY BEHAVIORS AND THEORETICALLY USEFUL; AND (B) TO
EMPIRICALLY EXPLORE ONE COMPONENT OF THE FRAMEWORK--
ELECTORAL PARTICIPATION--USING REMOTE DEMOGRAPHIC AND
DECISION-PROXIMATE INDEPENDENT VARIABLES.

09722 HONG, J.
INTEGRATION OF CHINA INTO THE ASIAN-PACIFIC REGION
WORLD ECONOMY, 11(3) (SEP 88), 327-354.
WITH THE ADVENT OF INTERNATIONAL DETENTE, CHINA STARTED
TO MODIFY THE ORIENTATION OF HER ECONOMY WITH A VIEW TO
INTERACTING MORE FULLY WITH THE WORLD ECONOMY. THIS ARTICLE
DISCUSSES THE GROWING INTEGRATION OF CHINESE ECONOMY INTO
THE ASIAN-PACIFIC REGION IN PARTICULAR, AND TRACES THE
ECONOMIC HISTORY OF EACH OF THE FOUR COMPONENTS OF THIS
REGION.

09723 HONG, K.K.
POLICY MAKING IN THE AMERICAN STATES: TYPOLOGY, PROCESS,
AND INSTITUTIONS
POLICY STUDIES REVIEW, 8(3) (SPR 89), 527-548.
THE THREE LEVELS OF GOVERNMENT IN THE U.S. FEDERAL
SYSTEM MAINTAIN A DIFFERENT SET OF POLICY PRIORITIES BECAUSE
THEY OPERATE UNDER VARYING ENVIRONMENTAL CONSTRAINTS AND
RESOURCES. EFFORTS TO CATEGORIZE AND SPECIFY THE POLITICS IN
TERMS OF POLICY TYPES HAVE BEEN PARTICULARLY FRUITFUL AT
BOTH THE FEDERAL AND THE LOCAL LEVELS. AT THE STATE LEVEL,
HOWEVER, THE TYPOLOGY PERSPECTIVE HAS YET TO BE MORE FULLY
DEVELOPED. THIS PAPER MAKES A PRELIMINARY EFFORT TO
CONSTRUCT A TYPOLOGY FRAMEWORK IN UNDERSTANDING STATE
POLITICS AND POLICY. FIRST, POLITICS CAN BE DIFFERENTIATED

BETWEEN GROWTH AND REDISTRIBUTION IN THE STRUCTURAL ECONOMIC CONTEXT. WHILE REDISTRIBUTIVE POLITICS ARE LARGELY STRUCTURED BY CLASS-ORIENTED ISSUES, GROWTH POLITICS ARE PREDOMINANTLY SHAPED BY TERRITORIAL CONCERNS THAT TEMPER CLASS AND IDEOLOGICAL DIFFERENCES. EQUALLY IMPORTANT, THE GROWTHREDISTRIBUTION DISTINCTION CAN BE SUPPLEMENTED BY THE POLITICS OF ROUTINE SERVICES, SUCH AS PUBLIC EDUCATION. THE LATTER REMAINS DOMINATED BY SERVICEPROVIDER GROUPS. MOREOVER, BASED ON AN EMPIRICAL ANALYSIS OF HUNDREDS OF BILLS IN ONE STATE LEGISLATURE, THESE POLITICAL DIFFERENCES ARE FOUND TO HAVE CONTRIBUTED TO VARIATIONS IN POLICY CONSENSUS AMONG LAWMAKERS AS WELL AS INTEREST GROUP REPRESENTATION IN AGENDA SETTING AND LEGITIMATION ACROSS POLICY ARENAS. THE FINDINGS ALSO SUGGEST LIMITATIONS TO THE TYPOLOGY FRAMEWORK.

09724 WONGTRANGAN, C.
THAT ELITE STRUGGLE IN THE 1932 REVOLUTION
DISSERTATION ABSTRACTS INTERNATIONAL, 49(7) (JAN 89), 1991-A.
THE AUTHOR BEGINS WITH AN INVESTIGATION OF THE EFFECT OF THE WORLD CAPITALIST SYSTEM ON THAI SOCIETY AND ITS ELITE STRUGGLE. THAN HE ANALYZES THE ROLE OF CULTURE IN THE THAI ELITE STRUGGLE. HE EXPLAINS WHY AND HOW THE 1932 REVOLUTION OCCURRED AS WELL AS ITS IMPACT ON THAI SOCIETY. REVLOUTION CAPITALISM CULTURE

09725 WOOD, B.
NAMIBIA'S HARD ROAD
SOUTH, (109) (NOV 89), 10-11.
AS NAMBIANS PREPARE FOR THEIR FIRST NATIONAL ELECTION WITH UNIVERSAL SUFFRAGE, THE SIGNS INDICATE THAT PRETORIA WILL MAKE THE ROAD TO INDEPENDENCE AS BUMPY AS POSSIBLE. VARIOUS LEGAL, SECURITY, AND ECONOMIC OBSTACLES HAVE BEEN DELIBERATELY ERECTED TO COMPOUND THE ALREADY DAUNTING POLITICAL PROBLEMS FACING NAMIBIA.

09726 WOOD, C.; ALLEN, G.; DUSEN, L.; HOWSE, J.; OGSTEN, L.; WOLFF, D.
POLICE UNDER FIRE
MACLEAN'S (CANADA'S NEWS MAGAZINE), 102(2) (JAN 89), 30-33.
A RECENT SHOOTING OF A 17-YEAR OLD BLACK MAN WAS THE LATEST OF A LIST OF TRAGEDIES THAT HAS FORCED A PAINFUL REASSESSMENT OF RELATIONS BETWEEN CANADIAN POLICE AND THE COMMUNITIES THEY ARE SWORN TO SERVE. AMONG SOME CANADIANS-- ESPECIALLY THE EXPANDING COMMUNITIES OF VISIBLE MINORITIES-- THERE IS VOCAL SUSPICION THAT POLICE FORCES ARE, AT BEST, OUT OF TOUCH WITH A CHANGING SOCIETY AND, AT WORST, RACIST. THE POLICE RESPOND THAT IT HAS BECOME MORE DIFFICULT AND DANGEROUS TO KEEP THE PEACE AND ENFORCE THE LAW. EDUCATIONAL PROGRAMS, TRAINING PROGRAMS WHICH EMPHASIZE PSYCHOLOGY AND COMMUNICATION SKILLS, AND ACTIVE RECRUITING AMONG MINORITIES ARE SOME OF THE STEPS BEING TAKEN TO ALLEVIATE THE PROBLEM. HOWEVER, THE HIGH LEVEL OF EMOTION AND TENSION VIRTUALLY GUARANTEE THAT SOLUTIONS WILL NOT COME EASILY.

09727 WOOD, E.M.
OLIGARHIC "DEMOCRACY"
MONTHLY REVIEW, 41(3) (JUL 89), 42-51.
THIS ARTICLE REVIEWS A BOOK BY ARTHUR D. KAHN CALLED," THE EDUCATION OF JULIUS CAESAR: A BIOGRAPHY, A RECONSTRUCTION." HE PAINTS A VIVID PICTURE OF OLIGARCHIC CONFLICT AND CORRUPTION. HE REVEALS THE EXTORTIONATE PRACTICES OF CRASSUS; DESCRIBES ELECTION CORRUPTION BY CICERO; AND THE MANEUVERING FOR POLITICAL POWER AND MILITARY POSITION BY POMPEIUS AND CAESAR. HE DESCRIBES CAESAR AS ONE WHO WISHED TO SAVE ROME AND ACHIEVE IMERIAL UNITY. THE DECLINING YEARS OF THE ROMAN REPUBLIC ARE ADDRESSED.

09728 WOOD, E.M.
RATIONAL CHOICE MARXISM: IS THE GAME WORTH THE CANDLE?
NEW LEFT REVIEW, (177) (SEP 89), 41-88.
SOME ANALYTICAL MARXISTS HAVE CONSTRUCTED A NEW PARADIGM, "RATIONAL CHOICE MARXISM." IN THIS PAPER, THE AUTHOR EXAMINES THE CLAIMS MADE FOR THE RATIONAL CHOICE APPROACH, QUESTIONS ITS EXPLANATORY POWER, AND ARGUES THAT ITS FORMALISM WEAKENS ITS CRITIQUE OF CAPITALISM AT A TIME WHEN A CREATIVE DEVELOPMENT OF THIS CRITIQUE IS ONE OF THE PRINCIPAL TASKS FOR THE LEFT.

09729 WOOD, G.Y.
AESTHETIC REGULATION: A STUDY OF GOVERNMENTAL EFFORTS TO REGULATE THE PHYSICAL BEAUTY OF THE CITY
DISSERTATION ABSTRACTS INTERNATIONAL, 50(2) (AUG 89), 542-A.
"AESTHETIC REGULATION" REFERS TO THE METHODS MUNICIPAL GOVERNMENTS USE TO PURPOSEFULLY GUIDE THE FUTURE DEVELOPMENT AND CURRENT USE OF URBAN LAND, WITH AN EYE TOWARD ITS POTENTIAL IMPACT ON COMMUNITY APPEARANCE. THIS DISSERTATION DEVELOPS A MEASURE OF POLICY STRICTNESS AND LEVEL OF ENFORCEMENT VIGOR. THEN VARIATIONS AMONG CITIES ARE ANALYZED WITH REGARD TO THESE DEPENDENT VARIABLES.

09730 WOOD, J.E. JR.
MAKING A NATION'S FLAG A SACRED SYMBOL

JOURNAL OF CHURCH & STATE, 31(3) (AUT 89), 375-380.
IN JUNE 1989, THE UNITED STATES SUPREME COURT RULED THAT THE ACT OF BURNING THE AMERICAN FLAG DURING A PROTEST RALLY IS AN ACT OF POLITICAL EXPRESSION PROTECTED BY THE FIRST AMENDMENT. THE RESPONSE TO THE COURT'S DECISION WAS IMMEDIATE AND OVERWHELMINGLY VOCIFEROUS IN ITS DENUNCIATION. PRESIDENT BUSH PROPOSED A CONSTITUTIONAL AMENDMENT TO THE BILL OF RIGHTS. OTHERS, INCLUDING SOME LEADING MEMBERS OF CONGRESS, PROPOSED THAT THE COURT'S DECISION BE OVERTURNED BY A STATUTE THAT WOULD EXPLICITLY PROHIBIT ANY FORM OF PHYSICAL DESECRATION OF THE FLAG.

09731 WOOD, J.E. JR.
RELIGIOUS PLURALISM AND RELIGIOUS FREEDOM
JOURNAL OF CHURCH & STATE, 31(1) (WIN 89), 7-14.
RELIGIOUS PLURALISM IS INCREASINGLY A FEATURE OF CONTEMPORARY SOCIETY THROUGHOUT MOST OF THE WORLD. THE EMERGENCE AND SPREAD OF THE NEW RELIGIONS HAVE PROFOUNDLY INFLUENCED CONTEMPORARY SOCIETY AND RAISED FUNDAMENTAL QUESTIONS WITH RESPECT TO THE RELATIONSHIP OF RELIGION AND THE STATE AND RELIGIOUS LIBERTY.

09732 WOOD, J.E. JR.
SEPARATION VIS-A-VIS ACCOMMODATION: A NEW DIRECTION IN AMERICAN CHURCH-STATE RELATIONS?
JOURNAL OF CHURCH & STATE, 31(2) (SPR 89), 197-206.
FOR MANY AMERICANS, THE CONCEPT OF THE SEPARATION OF CHURCH AND STATE HAS COME TO BE VIEWED AS INHERENTLY IN CONFLICT WITH THE SOCIAL BENEFITS OF RELIGION AND IN CONTENTION WITH THE CONSTITUTIONAL GUARANTEE OF THE FREE EXERCISE OF RELIGION. INCREASINGLY THE CONCEPT OF THE SECULAR STATE HAS COME TO BE HELD IN DISFAVOR BY MANY AMERICANS WHO ASSOCIATE THE SECULAR STATE WITH A STATE COMMITTED TO SECULARISM AND A SOCIETY WITHOUT MORAL OR RELIGIOUS VALUES. SOME ARGUE THAT "SEPARATION" IS NEITHER AN APPROPRIATE TERM NOR THE KEY TO AMERICAN CHURCH-STATE RELATIONS. IN ITS PLACE, "ACCOMMODATION" IS ESPOUSED AS THE MORE ACCURATE AND MORE APPROPRIATE DESCRIPTION OF BOTH THE ORIGINAL INTENT OF THE FOUNDING FATHERS AND THE TRUE MEANING OF THE RELIGION CLAUSES OF THE FIRST AMENDMENT.

09733 WOOD, N.
CICERO'S SOCIAL AND POLITICAL THOUGHT: AN INTRODUCTION
UNIVERSITY OF CALIFORNIA PRESS, BERKELEY, CA, 1988, 270.
THE AUTHOR ANALYZES CICERO'S SOCIAL AND POLITICAL THOUGHT AND DEFINES ITS CRUCIAL IMPORTANCE BY A SYSTEMATIC SURVEY OF HIS IDEAS WITHIN THEIR HISTORICAL CONTEXT. HE FOCUSES ON CICERO'S CONCEPTS OF STATE AND GOVERNMENT, SHOWING THAT CICERO IS THE FATHER OF CONSTITUTIONALISM, THE ARCHETYPE OF THE POLITICALLY CONSERVATIVE MIND, AND THE FIRST TO REFLECT EXTENSIVELY ON POLITICS AS AN ACTIVITY.

09734 WOOD, P.J.
MARXISM AND MARITIMES: ON THE DETERMINANTS OF REGIONAL CAPITALIST DEVELOPMENT
STUDIES IN POLITICAL ECONOMY: A SOCIALIST REVIEW, 29 (SUM 89), 123-153.
IN THIS ARTICLE, TWO CONTENDING MARXIST APPROACHES TO REGIONAL CAPITALIST DEVELOPMENT, ONE DETERMINIST, THE OTHER VOLUNTARIST, ARE IDENTIFIED; THEIR IMPLICATIONS FOR THE STUDY OF THE MARITIMES ARE ASSESSED AND CRITICZED FROM THE PERSPECTIVE OF HISTORICAL MATERIALISM. ALSO, AN HISTORICAL MATERIALIST FRAMEWORK FOR UNDERSTANDING REGIONAL CAPITALIST DEVELOPMENT WHICH AVOIDS THE LIMITATIONS OF THE ABOVE, PROVIDING A MORE USEFUL BLEND OF HISTORICAL CONTINGENCY AND THEORETICAL SOCIAL DETERMINATION, IS SET FORTH. FINALLY, AN ATTEMPT IS MADE TO USE THIS FRAMEWORK TO INVESTIGATE HISTORICAL REGIONAL VARIATIONS IN PRODUCTIVE RELATIONS AND PATTERNS OF EXPLOTATION DURING THE CRUCIAL (AND MOST SUCCESSFUL) FORMATIVE PERIOD OF MARITIME INDUSTRIALIZATION.

09735 WOOD, R.
STRATEGIC CHOICES, GEOPOLITICS, AND RESOURCE CONSTRAINTS
WASHINGTON QUARTERLY, 12(3) (SUM 89), 139-156.
THE ARTICLE EXPLORES THE REASONS THAT HAS CAUSED THE US TO ADOPT AN ATTITUDE OF RELATIVE DETACHMENT WITH REGARDS TO ITS INTERNATIONAL ROLE. THIS IS PARTIALLY DUE TO US GEOGRAPHY AND RELATIVE MATERIAL INVULNERABILITY TO EXTERNAL HARM. THE ARTICLE OUTLINES THE DEVELOPMENT OF THE US AS A "MARITIME POWER" SIMILAR IN FASHION TO THE UNITED KINGDOM AND JAPAN AND STUDIES THE EFFECT THAT CHANGES IN TECHNOLOGY, THE GENERAL CONFIGURATION OF THE RELATION OF FORCES, AND IN THE CHARACTER OF THE POLITICAL ECONOMY HAVE HAD ON US INTERNATIONAL POLICY. IT CONCLUDES BY ANALYZING FUTURE OPTIONS OF THE US IN AN EVER CHANGING GEOPOLITICAL SITUATION

09736 WOOD, W.B.; DEMKO, G.J.; MOFSON, P.
ECOPOLITICS IN THE GLOBAL GREENHOUSE
ENVIRONMENT, 31(7) (SEP 89), 12-17; 32-34.
AS THE POLITICAL SPOTLIGHT SHIFTS FROM LOCAL TO GLOBAL ENVIRONMENTAL PROBLEMS, THE NUMBER OF PLAYERS, JURISDICTIONS, AND ECOLOGICAL INTERACTIONS INVOLVED ESCALATES QUICKLY. THE RESULTING COMPLEXITY DEMANDS NEW APPROACHES FOR RESOLVING THE ISSUES, BUT THIS ARTICLE ASKS: IS A NEW SUPRANATIONAL

AUTHORITY NEEDED? THE MOST INFLUENTIAL SUPRANATIONAL
AGENCIES ON THE ENVIRONMENTAL FRONT ARE EXPLORED AS WELL AS
HYBRID INSTITUTIONS THAT CAN CREATIVELY TACKLE INTERNATIONAL
ENVIRONMENTAL PROGRAMS.

09737 WOOD, W.B.
    POLITICAL GEOGRAPHY OF CONTEMPORARY EVENTS XI: THE
    POLITICAL GEOGRAPHY OF ASYLUM: TWO MODELS AND A CASE STUDY.
    POLITICAL GEOGRAPHY QUARTERLY, 8(2) (APR 89), 161-180.
    THIRD-WORLD ASYLUM-SEEKERS ARE INTERNATIONAL MIGRANTS
CAUGHT UP IN AN EVER-TIGHTENING CYCLE OF RESTRICTIONS ON
THEIR ENTRY INTO WESTERN EUROPEAN AND NORTH AMERICAN
COUNTRIES AND ON GOVERNMENT PROTECTION OF THEM ONCE THEY
HAVE GAINED ENTRANCE. THIS PAPER PRESENTS TWO MODELS: ONE
DIAGRAMING THE MIGRATION CHANNELS USED BY A GROUP OF TAMIL
ASYLUM-SEEKERS AND THE OTHER PREDICTING THE IMPLICATIONS OF
THEIR MIGRATION, AS WELL AS OTHER ASYLUM-SEEKERS, ON
NATIONAL ASYLUM POLICIES. THE FOCUS HERE IS ON MIGRATION
'PULL' FACTORS AT POTENTIAL DESTINATIONS AND 'INTERVENING
OBSTACLES' BETWEEN ALTERNATIVE DESTINATIONS. THE CURRENT
CONFLICTS AMONG ASYLUM-SEEKERS, NATIONAL ASYLUM POLICIES,
AND ATTEMPTS AT INTERNATIONAL COOPERATION IN MANAGING
MIGRATION STREAMS AND RESETTLEMENT MAY GREATLY AFFECT FUTURE
GENERATIONS OF ASYLUM-SEEKERS AND REFUGEES.

09738 WOOD, W.P.
    A COMPARISON OF THE POLITICAL PHILOSOPHIES OF JOHN
    WINTHROP AND JOHN WISE
    DISSERTATION ABSTRACTS INTERNATIONAL, 50(6) (DEC 89),
    1791-A.
    THE AUTHOR COMPARES AND CONTRASTS THE POLITICAL VIEWS OF
JOHN WINTHROP AND JOHN WISE, TWO MASSACHUSETTS PURITANS.

09739 WOODLEY, O. L.
    THE CASE FOR A GUARANTEED INCOME
    POLICY OPTIONS, 10(2) (MAR 89), 6-10.
    IN THIS PAPER, THE AUTHOR ARGUES FOR THE INTRODUCTION IN
CANADA OF A FORM OF UNIVERSAL MINIMUM GUARANTEED INCOME PLAN
AS SOON AS POSSIBLE. SHE BASES HER ARGUMENT ON AN ASSESSMENT
OF THE CURRENT ECONOMIC SITUATION IN CANADA AND AROUND THE
WORLD, WHICH SHE FINDS PERILOUS, AND WHICH SHE BLAMES ON THE
VALUES AND MYTHS ATTENDANT ON THE DEVELOPMENT OF A
FREEMARKET ECONOMY. FROM HERE, SHE MOVES TO CONSIDERATION OF
THE DEVELOPMENT OF SOCIAL SECURITY PROGRAMS, FIRST ABROAD
AND THEN IN CANADA, WITHIN THE CONTEXT OF THIS SYSTEM AND
ITS MYTHS, AND CONCLUDES THAT A SYSTEM BASED ON NEED RATHER
THAN GREED OUGHT TO PREVAIL. THIS LEADS TO THE ARGUMENT THAT
A MINIMUM GUARANTEED INCOME PLAN, WHICH SHE DESCRIBES, WOULD
PROVE AN ECONOMIC, AS WELL AS A SOCIAL BENEFIT, AND PROVIDE
A MORE STABLE BASE FOR THE FUTURE THAN THE PRESENT
UNCERTAINTY IS LIKELY TO DO.

09740 WOODMAN, S.
    ROOTS OF CHINESE RACIST FURY
    NEW AFRICAN, (257) (FEB 89), 39-41.
    DESPITE RACIST ATTACKS BY THE CHINESE ON AFRICAN
STUDENTS LIVING IN COMMUNIST CHINA, AUTHORITIES IN BEIJING
CONTINUE TO INSIST THAT RACIAL PREJUDICE DOES NOT EXIST IN
THEIR COUNTRY. BUT THE RHETORIC OF THIRD WORLD UNITY, WHICH
HAS BEEN A PART OF CHINESE FOREIGN POLICY SINCE THE BANDING
CONFERENCE OF 1955, IS BEING IGNORED IN THE UNIVERSITIES AND
THE STREETS.

09741 WOODS, A.
    DEVELOPMENT AND THE NATIONAL INTEREST: US ECONOMIC
    ASSISTANCE INTO THE 21ST CENTURY
    AVAILABLE FROM NTIS, NO. PB89-203160/GAR, FEB 17 89, 157.
    DRAMATIC CHANGES IN THE ECONOMIC ENVIRONMENT HAVE
CREATED THE NEED FOR NEW APPROACHES TO DEVELOPMENT
ASSISTANCE. THE REPORT EXAMINES THE CURRENT DIRECTION OF U.S.
DEVELOPMENT POLICY AS IT RELATES TO EMERGING GLOBAL ISSUES
AND NATIONAL INTERESTS. CHAPTER I TRACES THE ORIGINS AND
EVOLUTION OF U.S. FOREIGN AID EFFORTS. WAYS IN WHICH
DEVELOPMENT ASSISTANCE HAS RAISED DEVELOPING COUNTRY
ECONOMIC AND SOCIAL STANDARDS ARE EXAMINED IN CHAPTER II.
CHAPTER III EXAMINES THE HISTORICAL INTERRELATIONSHIPS
BETWEEN ECONOMIC GROWTH AND GOVERNMENT POLICIES. CHAPTER IV
DESCRIBES CONTRIBUTIONS MADE BY PRIVATE U.S. VOLUNTARY,
CHARITABLE, RELIGIOUS, AND EDUCATIONAL ORGANIZATIONS.
CHAPTER V SURVEYS THE IMPACT OF THE U.S. BUSINESS COMMUNITY
AND U.S. TRADE, INVESTMENT, AND ECONOMIC POLICY ON
DEVELOPING COUNTRIES. CHAPTER VI OUTLINES DEVELOPMENT
PROSPECTS FOR THE DECADES AHEAD. THE FINAL SECTION CALLS FOR
A COMPREHENSIVE REVIEW OF U.S. DEVELOPMENT POLICY TO RESHAPE
CURRENTLY OUTDATED DEVELOPMENT AID STRUCTURES AND CONCEPTS.

09742 WOODS, R.B.
    F.D.R. AND THE TRIUMPS OF AMERICAN NATIONALISM
    PRESIDENTIAL STUDIES QUARTERLY, XIX(3) (SUM 89), 567-581.
    WHILE FRANKLIN D. ROOSEVELT EMBRACED THE PRINCIPLES
EXPRESSED IN THE ATLANTIC CHARTER, HE PROVED DIPLOMATICALLY
AND POLITICALLY INCAPABLE OF ACHIEVING THEM DURING THE
PERIOD FROM 1941-1945. HE HOPED, THROUGH A POLICY OF
REALPOLITIK, TO MAINTAIN A BALANCE OF POWER IN EUROPE,

REASSURING THE INSECURE VICTIMS OF AXIS AGGRESSION AND
ENCOURAGING THE OPPRESSED TO ACHIEVE NATIONAL SELF-
DETERMINATION, BUT F.D.R. FAILED TO CONTAIN SOVIET
EXPANSIONISM BY REFUSING TO PARTICIPATE IN SPHERES-OF-
INTEREST AGREEMENTS PRIOR TO THE END OF WORLD WAR II.
MOREOVER, HE APPROVED POLICIES IN THE ECONOMIC SPHERE THAT
WEAKENED GREAT BRITAIN, A NATION THAT WOULD CERTAINLY BE
AMERICA'S STAUNCHEST EUROPEAN ALLY IN THE POST-WAR ERA.
THESE FAILURES STEMMED FROM THE PRESIDENT'S INABILITY TO
CONFRONT AND DEFEAT THE FORCES OF ISOLATIONISM AND ECONOMIC
NATIONALISM WITHIN CONGRESS AND AMONG THE AMERICAN PEOPLE,
FORCES THAT BY HIS DEATH CONSTITUTED THE DOMINANT STRAINS IN
THE FOREIGN POLICY OF THE UNITED STATES.

09743 WOODSIDE, A.
    HISTORY, STRUCTURE, AND REVOLUTION IN VIETNAM
    INTERNATIONAL POLITICAL SCIENCE REVIEW, 10(2) (APR 89),
    143-158.
    ABSTRACT. THE SINGULARITY OF THE VIETNAMESE REVOLUTION
CANNOT BE EXPLAINED ENTIRELY BY FACTORS SUCH AS A RACIALLY
DISCRIMINATING COLONIALISM OR OPPRESSIVE LANDLORDISM. THESE
FACTORS ARE TO BE FOUND IN MANY ASIAN AND AFRICAN COUNTRIES
WHICH DID NOT PRODUCE A HO CHI MINH OR A VO NGUYEN GIAP.
VIETNAM'S CONFUCIAN PAST IS CRITICALLY IMPORTANT. IT WAS
DISTINGUISHED BY (1) AN INCOMPLETELY CENTRALIZED MONARCHY
WHICH GENERATED BOTH POLITICAL AND MORAL EXPECTATIONS THAT
IT COULD NEVER SATISFY; (2) A PECULIARLY BIPOLAR POLITICAL
SYSTEM IN WHICH THE MONARCHY HAD TO SHARE POWER WITH A
PROVINCIAL INTELLIGENTSIA WHICH LIVED CLOSE TO THE PEASANTRY;
 AND (3) A TRANSCENDENTAL NEOCONFUCIAN PHILOSOPHY, DIFFUSED
THROUGH CIVIL SERVICE EXAMINATIONS, WHICH STRESSED THE
WRITINGS OF THE IDEALIST PHILOSOPHER MENCIUS. LARGE PEASANT
REBELLIONS, OFTEN ADVISED BY CONFUCIAN SCHOLARS, AND BENT ON
PUNISHING RULERS WHO DID NOT EXEMPLIFY THE PROPER COSMIC
PRINCIPLES THROUGH "BENEVOLENT GOVERNMENT," RECURRED IN
VIETNAM BEFORE FRENCH COLONIALISM. HO CHI MINH AND MANY OF
HIS ASSOCIATES WERE DESCENDANTS OF THE PROVINCIAL SCHOLAR
CLASS WHO MIGHT BE SO INVOLVED.

09744 WOODWARD, C.
    SOUTH AFRICA AS AN ISSUE IN AMERICAN PRESIDENTIAL CAMPAIGNS
    SOUTH AFRICA INTERNATIONAL, 19(3) (JAN 89), 152-161.
    THE ARTICLE EXAMINES THE EFFECT THAT SOUTH AFRICA HAS
HAD ON US FOREIGN POLICY AND PRESIDENTIAL ELECTIONS. IT
OVERVIEWS THE FIRST STIRRINGS OF ANTI-APARTHEID MOVEMENTS IN
THE 1960'S AND THE GROWING OF THE MOVEMENT THROUGH THE
ENSUING DECADES TO THE HIGH-WATER POINT OF 1986. HOWEVER,
THE ANTI-APARTHEID AND PRO-SANCTIONS MOVEMENT HAS BECOME
MORE POLITICIZED AS POLITICIANS BEGAN TO USE THE PLATFORM AS
A METHOD OF GAINING RECOGNITION AND POLITICAL POWER, AND
LIKE MANY COALITIONS, MAINTAINING THE MOMENTUM WAS DIFFICULT.
THE RESULT WAS THAT SOUTH AFRICA BECAME ALMOST A NON-ISSUE
IN THE CAMPAIGNS OF DUKAKIS AND BUSH.

09745 WOODWARD, G.T.
    THE DILEMMA OF DEPOSIT INSURANCE
    CRS REVEIW, 10(9) (OCT 89), 6-7.
    GOVERNMENT LOAN GUARANTEES IN THE FORM OF DEPOSIT
INSURANCE HIGHLIGHT A PROBLEM THAT HAS YET TO BE RESOLVED BY
THE FINANCIAL INSTITUTIONS REFORM, RECOVERY, AND ENFORCEMENT
ACT OF 1989: HOW TO ACHIEVE THE GOALS OF DEPOSIT INSURANCE
WITHOUT CREATING INCENTIVES FOR FINANCIAL INSTITUTIONS TO
ENGAGE IN RISKY LENDING PRACTICES.

09746 WOODWARD, J.
    STIRRINGS IN BULGARIA
    EAST EUROPEAN REPORTER, 3(4) (SPR 89), 26.
    THE ARTICLE EXPLORES THE LEVEL OF DISSIDENT ACTIVITY IN
BULGARIA. APPARENTLY TAKING THEIR CUE FROM THE DEVELOPMENTS
IN OTHER EASTERN EUROPEAN STATES, ORGANIZATIONS SUCH AS THE
ASSOCIATION FOR THE DEFENSE OF HUMAN RIGHTS, AND THE
DISCUSSION CLUB FOR THE SUPPORT OF PERESTROIKA, HAVE BEGUN
THE FIRST HESITANT ATTACKS ON TODOR ZHIVKOV"S RULING
GOVERNMENT. THEY HAVE MET WITH REPRESSION, BUT THEIR EFFORTS
HAVE NOT DIMINISHED.

09747 WOODWARD, M.C.
    THE POLITICAL ECONOMY OF STEEL IN MEXICO AND BRAZIL
    DISSERTATION ABSTRACTS INTERNATIONAL, 50(4) (OCT 89),
    1081-A.
    THE MEXICAN STEEL INDUSTRY HAS CLEARLY DECLINED RELATIVE
TO ITS BRAZILIAN COUNTERPART. CONVENTIONAL ECONOMIC ANALYSIS
CANNOT ADEQUATELY EXPLAIN THIS BECAUSE THE FACTOR ENDOWMENTS
OF THE TWO COUNTRIES ARE NOT SIGNIFICANTLY DIFFERENT AND
BOTH STATES HAVE INTERVENED EXTENSIVELY IN THE INDUSTRY.
THEREFORE, POLITICAL AND INSTITUTIONAL FACTORS MUST ALSO BE
CONSIDERED.

09748 WOOLCOCK, S.; KELLY, J.
    GATT: THE PRICE OF FALSE EXPECTATIONS
    WORLD TODAY, 45(3) (MAR 89), 50-53.
    THE MID-TERM REVIEW MEETING OF THE URUGUAY ROUND OF THE
GENERAL AGREEMENT ON TARIFFS AND TRADE TOOK PLACE IN
MONTREAL IN DECEMBER 1988. THE NEGOTIATIONS COLLAPSED DUE TO

THE INABILITY OF THE UNITED STATES AND THE EUROPEAN
COMMUNITY TO SETTLE THEIR DIFFERENCES ON AGRICULTURAL POLICY.
IF THE DISPUTE CAN BE RESOLVED BEFORE THE MINISTERS MEET
AGAIN, THEN THE DAMAGE WILL BE LIMITED. IF NOT,
INTERNATIONAL SUPPORT FOR THE ROUND COULD WEAKEN. THIS, IN
TURN, MIGHT JEOPARDIZE THE CHANCES OF AGREEMENT ON THE NEW
ISSUES IN THE URUGUAY ROUND.

09749 WOOLF, S.
STATISTICS AND THE MODERN STATE
COMPARATIVE STUDIES IN SOCIETY AND HISTORY, 31(3) (JUL 89),
588-604.
IN THE HISTORY OF STATISTICS SINCE THE SEVENTEENTH AND
EIGHTEENTH CENTURIES, IT IS EVIDENT THAT OVER THE LONG-TERM
NATIONAL DIFFERENCES GAVE WAY TO SIMILARITIES AND
CONVERGENCES IN THE ADOPTION AND DIFFUSION OF STATISTICAL
APPROACHES. AN EARLY AND FUNDAMENTAL DISTINCTION CAN BE MADE
BETWEEN LIBERAL OR DEMOCRATIC COUNTRIES, SUCH AS ENGLAND AND
THE UNITED STATES, AND THOSE WITH A STRONG STATE TRADITION,
LIKE FRANCE OR PRUSSIA. IN THE FORMER, EDUCATED ELITES IN
SOCIETY FORCED THE PACE, FORMED PRESSURE GROUPS (LIKE THE
STATISTCAL SOCIETIES) TO MAKE THEIR RESPECTIVE
ADMINISTRATIONS EXTEND THEIR STATISCAL ACTIVITIES, AND
INSISTED ON PUBLICATION OF THE RESULTS. IN THE LATTER,
WHATEVER THE CONTRIBUTIONS OF INDIVIDUALS OR SPECIFIC GROUPS
(LIKE MEDICAL SOCIETIES), THE STATE WAS ALWAYS THE MAJOR
SPONSOR AND AGENT OF STATISTICAL METHODS AND USUALLY REFUSED
TO RENDER THE INFORMATION PUBLIC.

09750 WOOLLEY, J.T.; LELOUP, L.T.
THE ADEQUACY OF THE ELECTORAL MOTIVE IN EXPLAINING
LEGISLATIVE ATTENTION TO MONETARY POLICY: A COMPARATIVE
STUDY
COMPARATIVE POLITICS, 22(1) (OCT 89), 63-82.
THE AUTHORS CONSIDER EVIDENCE CONCERNING LEGISLATORS'
OVERSIGHT OF MONETARY POLICY IN THE USA, BRITAIN, FRANCE,
AND GERMANY. THEY ARGUE THAT THE HYPOTHESIS OF ELECTORAL
MOTIVATION ALONE IS INADEQUATE IN UNDERSTANDING RECENT
POLICY OVERSIGHT BEHAVIOR IN THE USA. IN THE EUROPEAN
SETTINGS, THE ELECTORAL MOTIVATION ASSUMPTION IS FAR MORE
USEFUL.

09751 WOOLSEY, R.J.
U.S. STRATEGIC FORCE DECISIONS FOR THE 1990'S
WASHINGTON QUARTERLY, 12(1) (WIN 89), 69-83.
THE AUTHOR'S ANALYSIS OF THE SURVIVALITY AND ABILITY TO
EMPLOY U.S. STRATEGIC FORCES PROCEEDS FROM THE FOLLOWING
CONVICTIONS. FIRST, THE UNITED STATES STRATEGIC FORCES ARE
REASONABLY SURVIVABLE TODAY. EMERGENCY STEPS ARE NOT NEEDED
TO HELP THEM MAINTAIN THEIR ABILITY TO DETER. SECOND, U.S.
STRATEGIC FORCES MUST BE AFFORDABLE AND MUST BE ASSESSED IN
THE CONTEXT OF PLAUSIBLE ARMS-CONTROL AGREEMENTS. THIRD,
DETERRING GENERAL WAR BETWEEN EAST AND WEST IS THE MOST
IMPORTANT UNDERTAKING OF THE UNITED STATES' OR ANY
GOVERNMENT. THE CONTINUED SUCCESS OF THE UNITED STATES IN
THIS UNDERTAKING WILL REQUIRE, FOR THE FORESEEABLE FUTURE,
CONTINUED EFFORT AND CARE IN THE MODERNIZATIONS OF ITS
STRATEGIC NUCLEAR FORCES.

09752 WOOSTER, M.M.
BLOOD AND DEMOCRATIC GUTS
REASON, 20(11) (APR 89), 42-43.
THE AUTHOR REVIEWS JOURNALISTIC REACTIONS TO GEORGE
BUSH'S VICTORY OVER MICHAEL DUKAKIS.

09753 WOOTTEN, J.P.
NATO OUT-OF-AREA PROBLEMS AND INTERNATIONAL TERRORISM
CRS REVEIH, 10(4) (APR 89), 21-22.
THROUGHOUT THE PAST FORTY YEARS, SECURITY ISSUES ARISING
OUTSIDE NATO'S GEOGRAPHIC AREA HAVE SOMETIMES THREATENED
ALLIED POLITICAL COHESION. TODAY, AN INCREASINGLY
SOPHISTICATED TERRORIST THREAT PRESENTS A NEW OUT-OF-AREA
CHALLENGE TO THE ALLIANCE.

09754 WORCESTER, K.
TEN YEARS OF THATCHERISM
WORLD POLICY JOURNAL, VI(2) (SPR 89), 297-320.
THE ARTICLE ASSESES THE TEN YEARS OF MARGARET THATCHER'S
TENURE AS PRIME MINISTER OF BRITAIN AND THE REFORMS AND
CHANGES THAT THE CONSERVATIVES HAVE IMPLEMENTED. THE
THATCHER LEGACY INCLUDES THE MOVE FROM "POSTWAR SETTLEMENT
TO THE ENETERPRISE CULTURE." SHE SIMULTANEOUSLY ENCOURAGED A
FREE, CAPITALISTIC MARKET AND A STRONG CENTRALIZED STATE.
THE ARTICLE SEEKS TO EXPLAIN THE DEVELOPMENT OF THESE
AFFAIRS AND DISCUSSES THE EFFORTS OF OPPOSITION PARTIES AND
THE VIABILITY OF THE RADICAL DEMOCRATIC ALTERNATIVE TO
CONTINUED ADHERENCE TO THATCHER'S POLICIES.

09755 WORCESTER, R.M.
PUBLIC OPINION POLLING: PROBLEMS AND PROSPECTS
CONTEMPORARY RECORD, 3(2) (NOV 89), 15-18.
THIS IS THE CONCLUSION OF A TWO-PART SURVEY BY ROBERT
WORCESTER. THE FIRST REVIEWED PUBLIC OPINION POLLING IN
BRITAIN SINCE ITS INCEPTION IN THE MID-THIRTIES AND FOCUSSED

ON THE MOST RECENT, 1987 GENERAL ELECTION. IN THIS ISSUE HE
CONCLUDES WITH AN EXAMINATION OF RECENT EFFORTS TO GAIN
WIDER UNDERSTANDING OF THE USES AND LIMITATIONS OF PUBLIC
OPINION POLLS AND LOOKS AT THEIR LIKELY FUTURE IN THIS
COUNTRY AND ABROAD, HE EXPLORES THE PROBLEMS WITH POLLING,
TELEPHONE POLLS, AND THE USE OF COMPUTERS.

09756 WORRE, T.
DENMARK
ELECTORAL STUDIES, 8(3) (DEC 89), 237-245.
IN MOST EC COUNTRIES THE INTRODUCTION OF DIRECT POPULAR
ELECTIONS TO THE EUROPEAN PARLIAMENT IN 1979 PRODUCED NO
DEVIATION FROM THE TRADITIONAL NATIONAL PARTY SYSTEM. BUT IN
DENMARK IT GAVE RISE TO A PECULIAR EURO-PARTY SYSTEM, THE
STRUCTURE OF WHICH DEVIATED CONSIDERABLY FROM THE USUAL
PATTERN. THE DEVIANT PATTERN WAS REPLICATED IN THE
SUBSEQUENT ELECTION OF 1984. MANY OBSERVERS HAD EXPECTED
THAT THE ELECTION OF 1989 WOULD BREAK THIS PECULIAR PATTERN
OF VOTER BEHAVIOR, BUT WHEN THE VOTES WERE COUNTED, IT
PROVED ON THE WHOLE TO BE INTACT.

09757 WOZNIUK, V.
A NOTE ON THE POLITICS OF COLLABORATIONISM
CONFLICT, 8(4) (1988), 285-294.
DEFINITIONS OF COLLABORATIONSM ARE NOT CONCEPTUALLY
RIGOROUS. THE PHENOMENON OF COLLABORATIONISM IS OFTEN SIMPLY
EQUATED WITH BETRAYAL AND TREASON. ALTHOUGH TREASON AND
COLLABORATIONISM ARE BOTH SUBCATEGORIES OF BETRAYAL,
IMPORTANT DIFFERENCES EXIST BETWEEN THE TWO. BECAUSE
EXISTING DEFINITIONS ARE VAGUE AND CONTRIBUTE LITTLE TO
CONCEPTUAL CLARITY, THIS PAPER SEEKS PRIMARILY TO DEFINE
THIS PHENOMENON MORE PRECISELY. SECONDARILY, IT STRIVES FOR
A SYNTHESIS OF COMMON ATTRIBUTES AMONG COLLABORATIONIST
EXPERIENCES THAT CAN PROVIDE A CONCEPTUAL FRAMEWORK FOR A
CLEARER UNDERSTANDING OF THE POLITICS OF COLLABORATIONISM.

09758 WRAY, L.R.
A KEYNESIAN PRESENTATION OF THE RELATIONS AMONG GOVERNMENT
DEFICITS, INVESTMENT, SAVING, AND GROWTH
JOURNAL OF ECONOMIC ISSUES, 24(4) (DEC 89), 977-1002.
RECENTLY, BOTH THE COUNCIL OF ECONOMIC ADVISORS AND THE
CHAIRMAN OF THE BOARD OF GOVERNORS OF THE FEDERAL RESERVE
SYSTEM PRESENTED THEIR VIEWS OF THE IMPACT GOVERNMENT
DEFICITS AND SAVING HAVE ON INVESTMENT AND ECONOMIC GROWTH.
THIS ARTICLE SUMMARIZES THEIR VIEWS, PRESENTS THE KEYNESIAN
ALTERNATIVE, AND EXAMINES THE EMPIRICAL EVIDENCE, IT ARGUES
THAT ANY DEFICIT SPENDING CREATES SURPLUS INCOME THAT CAN BE
USED TO PURCHASE THE BONDS ISSUED BY DEFICIT UNITS. IT SHOWS
THAT MUCH OF THE RECENT GROWTH OF INCOME IS EXPLAINED BY
GOVERNMENT DEFICIT SPENDING. IT ALSO PRESENTS EVIDENCE THAT
THE GROWTH OF BANK BALANCE SHEETS HAS MORE THAN KEPT PACE
WITH THE GROWTH OF GOVERNMENT DEBT.

09759 WRIGGINS, H.
INTERESTS OF THE MAJOR POWERS IN THE INDIAN OCEAN
DISARMAMENT, XII(3) (AUT 89), 140-149.
THE AUTHOR DISCUSSES THE SECURITY INTERESTS OF THE
UNITED STATES, THE SOVIET UNION, CHINA, THE UNITED KINGDOM,
AND FRANCE IN THE INDIAN OCEAN REGION.

09760 WRIGHT, E.O.
DEMOCRATIC DEMANDS AND RADICAL RIGHTS
SOCIALIST REVIEW, 19(4) (OCT 89), 35-56.
THIS ARTICLE ADDRESSES THE KINDS OF RADICAL DEMOCRATIC
STRUGGLES WHICH INSPIRED THE NEW LEFT. IT IDENTIFIES THE
POSITION THAT THE WRITERS TAKE ON THESE ISSUES AND THEN
CRITIQUES THE WRITINGS OF JOHN ROEMER AND MICHAEL BURAWAY.
THREE IMPORTANT POINTS OF CONTENTION APPEAR IN ROEMER'S AND
BURAWAY'S ESSAYS: THE UNDERSTANDING OF CLASS CONFLICT IN
PRODUCTION; THE ANALYSIS OF THE RADICAL POTENTIAL OF
DEMOCRATIC REFORMS WON THROUGH THE EXPANSION OF CITIZEN
RIGHTS; AND THE ADVOCACY OF ECONOMIC DEMOCRACY. THE ARTICLE
EXPLORES EACH OF THESE IN TURN.

09761 WRIGHT, E.O.
WOMEN IN THE CLASS STRUCTURE
POLITICS AND SOCIETY, 17(1) (MAR 89), 35-66.
THE AUTHOR CONSIDERS THE PROBLEM OF "CROSS-CLASS"
HOUSEHOLD COMPOSITIONS IN WHICH THE OCCUPATION OF ONE SPOUSE
PLACES THE FAMILY IN A HIGHER OR LOWER CLASS THAN THE OTHER
SPOUSE'S OCCUPATION. (FOR EXAMPLE, A DOCTOR MARRIED TO A
CARPENTER IS A CROSS-CLASS COUPLE.) IN THIS PAPER, THE
AUTHOR ENDEAVORS TO PROVIDE A COHERENT CONCEPTUAL SOLUTION
TO THE PROBLEM OF INDENTIFYING THE CLASS LOCATION OF MARRIED
WOMEN IN THE LABOR FORCE. THEN HE DEPLOYS THIS SOLUTION IN
AN EMPIRICAL ANALYSIS OF THE RELATIONSHIP BETWEEN CLASS
LOCATION AND SUBJECTIVE CLASS IDENTITY IN SWEDEN AND THE USA.

09762 WRIGHT, G.C.
LEVEL-OF-ANALYSIS EFFECTS ON EXPLANATIONS OF VOTING: THE
CASE OF THE 1982 US SENATE ELECTIONS
BRITISH JOURNAL OF POLITICAL SCIENCE, 19(3) (JUL 89),
381-398.
THE AVAILABILITY OF RICH SURVEY DATA AND CONCERNS OVER

THE ECOLOGICAL FALLACY HAVE LED VOTING RESEARCHERS TO FOCUS
ON THE EXPLANATION OF INDIVIDUAL VOTING DECISIONS AT THE
EXPENSE OF ACCOUNTING FOR PATTERNS OF AGGREGATE ELECTION
OUTCOMES. THIS HAS SKEWED OUR UNDERSTANDING OF THE RELATIVE
IMPORTANCE OF VARIOUS FACTORS IN THE ELECTORAL PROCESS. A
FRAMEWORK FOR ANALYSIS OF ELECTIONS AT MULTIPLE LEVELS IS
DEVELOPED AND APPLIED USING DATA FROM TWENTY-THREE EXIT
POLLS FROM THE US SENATE ELECTIONS. COMPARABLE PARAMETERS
FOR A SIMPLE VOTING MODEL ARE ESTIMATED FOR INDIVIDUAL
VOTING AND FOR ELECTION OUTCOMES. ELECTION-LEVEL FACTORS,
ESPECIALLY CANDIDATES' ISSUE STRATEGIES AND INCUMBENCY, ARE
SUBSTANTIALLY MORE IMPORTANT IN ACCOUNTING FOR ELECTION
OUTCOMES THAN IN EXPLAINING INDIVIDUAL VOTING DECISIONS.
FINALLY, WORKING WITH ELECTION OUTCOMES PERMITS AN ESTIMATE
OF A PATH MODEL OF SENATE ELECTION OUTCOMES THAT SHOWS KEY
RELATIONSHIPS THAT ARE NOT ACCESSIBLE FROM INDIVIDUAL LEVEL
DATA.

09763 WRIGHT, G.C.
PInteractions VOTING IN THE U.S. SENATE: WHO IS REPRESENTED?
LEGISLATIVE STUDIES QUARTERLY, 14(4) (NOV 89), 465-486.
THIS STUDY DEVELOPS NEW STATE-LEVEL MEASURES OF MASS AND
PARTY ELITE IDEOLOGY TO ASSESS SENATORIAL RESPONSIVENESS TO
DIFFERENT CONSTITUENCIES. THE IDEOLOGICAL PREFERENCES OF TWO
GROUPS-INDEPENDENT IDENTIFIRES AND SENATORS' STATE PARTY
ELITES-PROVE IMPORTANT IN ACCOUNTING FOR SENATORIAL
CONSERVATIVE COALITION SCORES (1981-84), WHILE THE
PREFERENCES OF STATE PARTISANS HAVE NO DIRECT EFFECT ON ROLL-
CALL VOTING. THE OFTEN NOTED IDEOLOGICAL DIFFERENCES BETWEEN
SAME-STATE SENATORS FROM DIFFERENT PARTIES ARE EXPLAINED BY
THE DIFFERING VALUES OF THEIR RESPECTIVE STATE PARTY ELITES.
CHALLENGERS, IN CONTRAST TO INCUMBENTS, ARE UNRESPONSIVE TO
INDEPENDENTS; THEIR CAMPAIGN ISSUE STANCES ARE CONSISTENT
WITH THE MORE EXTREME VALUES OF THEIR STATE PARTY ELITES. AS
A RESULT SENATE ELECTIONS TEND TO BE CONTESTS BETWEEN
RELATIVELY MODERATE INCUMBENTS AND IDEOLOGICALLY EXTREME
CHALLENGERS.

09764 WRIGHT, J.
ADDRESS UNKNOWN: HOMELESSNESS IN CONTEMPORARY AMERICA
SOCIETY, 26(6) (SEP 89), 45-53.
THE HOMELESS PROBLEM IN AMERICA HAS RISEN SHARPLY IN THE
PAST DECADE. THE HOMELESS ARE A DIVERSE, HETEROGENEOUS LOT.
NO SINGLE CATCH PHRASE OR STEREOTYPE CAN POSSIBLY DESCRIBE
THEM ALL. TO DISTINGUISH BETWEEN THE LITERALLY HOMELESS, THE
MARGINALLY HOUSED, AND THE POTENTIALLY HOMELESS, IS HELPFUL.
THE CAUSE OF THE HOMELESS PROBLEM IS AN OBVIOUS ALTHOUGH
OFTEN OVERLOOKED POINT: HOMELESS PEOPLE ARE PEOPLE WITHOUT
HOUSING, AND THUS, THE ULTIMATE CAUSE OF THE PROBLEM IS AN
INSUFFICIENT SUPPLY OF HOUSING SUITABLE TO THE NEEDS OF
HOMELESS PEOPLE. BASED ON THIS ANALYSIS, THE SOLUTION HAS
TWO ESSENTIAL STEPS: THE FEDERAL GOVERNMENT MUST MASSIVELY
INTERVENE IN THE PRIVATE HOUSING MARKET, TO HALT THE LOSS OF
ADDITIONAL LOW-INCOME UNITS AND TO UNDERWRITE THE
CONSTRUCTION OF MANY MORE; AND THE BENEFITS PAID TO THE
WELFARE-DEPENDENT POPULATION MUST APPROXIMATELY DOUBLE.

09765 WRIGHT, J.R.
PAC CONTRIBUTIONS, LOBBYING, AND REPRESENTATION
THE JOURNAL OF POLITICS, 51(3) (AUG 89), 713-729.
IT IS OFTEN BELIEVED THAT ORGANIZED INTERESTS PURCHASE
ACCESS--AND, CONSEQUENTLY, REPRESENTATION--TO MEMBERS OF
CONGRESS THROUGH PAC CONTRIBUTIONS. BY CONTRIBUTING TO
REPRESENTATIVES FROM DISTRICTS WHERE THEY HAVE LITTLE OR NO
ORGANIZATIONAL STRENGTH, GROUPS MAY SHIFT THE
REPRESENTATIONAL FOCUS OF ELECTED OFFICIALS AWAY FROM
GEOGRAPHIC CONSTITUENCIES TO BROADER, FUNCTIONAL
CONSTITUENCIES BASED ON OCCUPATIONAL, INDUSTRIAL, AND
PROFESSIONAL GROUPINGS. THIS PAPER EXAMINES THIS POSSIBILITY
BY ASSESSING THE EXTENT TO WHICH GROUPS' CAMPAIGN
CONTRIBUTIONS AND LOBBYING EFFORTS ARE DIRECTED TO
REPRESENTATIVES FROM DISTRICTS WHERE GROUPS HAVE LITTLE OR
NO ORGANIZATIONAL PRESENCE. THE EMPIRICAL ANALYSIS IS BASED
ON DATA FROM A SURVEY OF PROFESSIONAL LOBBYISTS WITH
ORGANIZATIONS THAT SPONSORED POLITICAL ACTION COMMITTEES
DURING THE 1983-1984 ELECTION CYCLE. RESULTS OF THE ANALYSIS
INDICATE THAT ORGANIZED INTERESTS SELDOM CONTRIBUTE TO AND
LOBBY MEMBERS OF THE U.S. HOUSE OF REPRESENTATIVES IN THE
ABSENCE OF GEOGRAPHIC TIES TO THEIR DISTRICTS.

09766 WRIGHT, L.E.
THE POLITICAL THOUGHT OF ELIJAH MUHAMMAD: INNOVATION AND
CONTINUITY IN WESTERN TRADITION
DISSERTATION ABSTRACTS INTERNATIONAL, 49(3) (SEP 88),
611-A.
THE STUDY IDENTIFIES THE THOUGHT OF ELIJAH MUHAMMAD,
LEADER OF THE NATION OF ISLAM (1933-1975) AS A RESPONSE TO
THE AMERICAN SOCIAL AND POLITICAL MILIEU AND AS AN OUTGROWTH
OF THEOLOGICAL AND POLITICAL THINKING AMONG AFRICAN
AMERICANS. ITS BASIC THESIS IS THAT MUHAMMAD'S FORMULATIONS
CONSTITUTE A UNIFIED SYSTEM OF THOUGHT AND PRESENT A
SIGNIFICANT CRITIQUE OF DEMOCRATIC FREEDOM IN AMERICA AND
WESTERN TRADITION.

09767 WRIGHT, M.
THE BALANCE OF POWER - CONTROVERSIAL BUT INDISPENSIBLE
REVIEW OF INTERNATIONAL STUDIES, 15(2) (APR 89), 211-214.
THE CONTROVERSIES SURROUNDING THE BALANCE OF POWER ARE
BOTH ANCIENT AND ENDURING. THIS BRIEF NOTE HIGHLIGHTS SOME
OF THE CONVERGENCES AND DIFFERENCES IN THEIR APPROACHES TO
THESE CONTROVERSIES. THE CHOICE OF THEMES FOR THIS ANALYSIS
IS PERSONAL AND SELECTIVE, BUT IT DOES REFLECT THE CENTRAL
ISSUES OF BALANCE OF POWER THEORY AND PRACTICE.

09768 WRIGHT, M.J.
SIR JOSEPH WARD AND NEW ZEALAND'S NAVAL DEFENSE POLICY,
1907-12
POLITICAL SCIENCE, 41(1) (JUL 89), 45-58.
MUCH REMAINS ENIGMATIC ABOUT THE POLITICAL CHARACTER AND
POLICIES OF SIR JOSEPH WARD, NEW ZEALAND'S PRIME MINISTER
FROM 1906 UNTIL 1912. HIS ACTIONS IN DEFENSE HAVE LONG BEEN
CONSIDERED TO HAVE BEEN CHARACTERIZED BY THE SAME KING OF
IMPULSIVE BEHAVIOR THAT MANY ANALYSTS HAVE IDENTIFIED IN HIS
APPROACH TO OTHER AREAS OF GOVERNMENTAL POLICY DEVELOPMENT.
BUT SUCH ASSESSMENTS DO NOT TAKE FULL ACCOUNT OF THE
COMPLEXITY OF THE SITUATION IN WHICH WARD FOUND HIMSELF. FAR
FROM BEING A WEAK BUT AMBITIOUS PATRIOT, EAGER TO LEAP ON
ANY CONVENIENT BANDWAGON THAT MIGHT BENEFIT THE EMPIRE, WARD
DISPLAYED CONSIDERABLE SKILL AND POLITICAL CUNNING.

09769 WRIGHT, N.E.
THE UN'S ENVIRONMENTAL PROJECT
MULTINATIONAL MONITOR, 10(7-8) (JUL 89), 15-17.
HAVING SUCCESSFULLY PUT INTO FORCE A TREATY DESIGNED TO
LIMIT THE PRODUCTION AND USE OF CHLOROFLOUROCARBONS AND
PREVENT FURTHER DAMAGE TO THE OZONE LAYER, THE UNITED
NATIONS ENVIRONMENTAL PROGRAM IS CONFRONTING THE NEXT MAJOR
ENVIRONMENTAL CHALLENGE TO THE ATMOSPHERE: GLOBAL WARMING.
THE OZONE TREATY REPRESENTS A UNIQUE CONVERGENCE BECAUSE THE
NEGOTIATIONS INCLUDED PUBLIC AND PRIVATE SECTORS AS WELL AS
THE SCIENTIFIC COMMUNITY CONCERNED ABOUT THE POTENTIALLY
HARMFUL EFFECTS OF CFC'S ON THE EARTH'S ATMOSPHERE.

09770 WRIGHT, S.G.
VOTES TURNOUT IN RUNOFF ELECTION
THE JOURNAL OF POLITICS, 51(2) (MAY 89), 385-396.
THIS ARTICLE EXAMINES THE EXTENT TO WHICH VOTER TURNOUT
TENDS TO DROP FROM THE PRIMARY TO THE RUNOFF ELECTION.
RESULTS INDICATE THAT TURNOUT DECLINED IN ALMOST 77% OF ALL
DEMOCRATIC GUBERNATORIAL, SENATORIAL, AND CONGRESSIONAL
RUNOFFS HELD FROM 1956 TO 1984. THE EXTENT OF DECLINE IS
GREATER IN CONGRESSIONAL AND SENATORIAL RUNOFFS THAN IN
GUBERNATORIAL RUNOFFS AND IS ESPECIALLY PRONOUNCED IN
CONGRESSIONAL RUNOFFS UNACCOMPANIED BY GUBERNATORIAL OR
SENATORIAL RUNOFFS. THE AUTHOR EXPLORE SEVERAL OTHER
DETERMINANTS OF TURNOUT DECLINE, INCLUDING BOTH CONTEXTUAL
AND PROCEDURAL VARIABLES. ESPECIALLY IMPORTANT IS THE DEGREE
OF REPUBLICAN OPPOSITION: AS THE LEVEL OF REPUBLICAN
VIABILITY IN A STATE OR CONSTITUENCY INCREASES, SO DOES THE
RELATIVE LEVEL OF RUNOFF ABSTENTION.

09771 WRIGHTSON, M.T.
THE ROAD TO SOUTH CAROLINA: INTERGOVERNMENTAL TAX IMMUNITY
AND THE CONSTITUTIONAL STATUS OF FEDERALISM
PUBLIUS: THE JOURNAL OF FEDERALISM, 19(3) (SUM 89), 39-56.
IN SOUTH CAROLINA V. BAKER THE SUPREME COURT STRUCK A
POWERFUL BLOW AT CONSTITUTIONAL FEDERALISM. AS A RESULT OF
THIS LANDMARK CASE, THE QUESTION OF WHETHER ISSUING TAX
EXEMPT BONDS IS A SOVEREIGN RIGHT OF THE STATES OR A
PRIVILEGE THEY ARE ACCORDED BY THE NATIONAL GOVERNMENT HAS
BEEN SETTLED. RELYING IN PART ON PRECEDENT FROM GARCIA, THE
COURT DETERMINED THAT IMMUNITY IS NOT A RIGHT UNDER THE
TENTH AMENDMENT. IN ADDITION, SOUTH CAROLINA ESTABLISHED A
NEW DOCTRINE OF INTERGOVERNMENTAL TAX IMMUNITY WHICH
FORMALLY ACCORDS SUPERIOR POWERS TO THE NATIONAL GOVERNMENT.
TAKEN TOGETHER, THESE RESULTS HAVE IMPLICATIONS FOR THE
FUTURE COURSE OF INTERGOVERNMENTAL FISCAL POLICY AS WELL AS
THE BASIC CHARACTER OF THE RELATIONSHIP BETWEEN THE NATIONAL
AND STATE AND LOCAL GOVERNMENTS.

09772 WROBLESKI, A.B.
GLOBAL NARCOTICS COOPERATION AND PRESIDENTIAL CERTIFICATION
DEPARTMENT OF STATE BULLETIN (US FOREIGN POLICY), 89(2151)
(OCT 89), 49-59.
THE AUTHOR, WHO IS THE STATE DEPARTMENT'S ASSISTANT
SECRETARY FOR INTERNATIONAL NARCOTICS MATTERS, REVIEWS THE
BUSH ADMINISTRATION'S 1989-90 DRUG AGENDA, SURVEYS THE SCOPE
OF INTERNATIONAL COOPERATION IN COMBATING DRUG TRAFFIC, AND
OFFERS A COUNTRY-BY-COUNTRY REPORT ON THE DRUG PROBLEM.

09773 WROBLEWSKI, A.; RZEMIENIECKI, K.
POLAND'S MONETARY-FINANCIAL PROBLEMS
CONTEMPORARY POLAND, XXII(4) (1989), 1-4.
IN THIS INTERVIEW, POLAND'S MINISTER OF FINANCE
DISCUSSES POLAND'S ECONOMIC SITUATION AND TRENDS, INCLUDING
INFLATION AND DEBT-TO-EQUITY CONVERSION.

09774 WROBLEWSKI, A.; JEZIORANSKI, T.
THE MONEY GAME
CONTEMPORARY POLAND, XXII(1) (1989), 4-13.
IN THIS INTERVIEW, POLAND'S MINSTER OF FINANCE ANDRZEJ
WROBLEWSKI DISCUSSES HIS ROLE AS THE PERSON CHARGED WITH
BRINGING A SEMBLANCE OF ORDER TO POLISH FINANCIAL POLICY AND
RATIONALIZING ITS RULES AND MECHANISMS WHILE SUBORDINATING
THE WHOLE SHOW TO GENERAL ECONOMIC INTERESTS.

09775 WRONG, D.
THE WANING OF THE COLD WAR
DISSENT, (SPR 89), 192-197.
GORBACHEV'S REFORMISM HAS CREATED REASONABLE
EXPECTATIONS OF FAR-REACHING CHANGES BEYOND A RENEWED AND
MORE LASTING DETENTE, EVEN IF VISIONS OF TOTAL NUCLEAR
DISARMAMENT ARE UNREALISTIC. BUT PREOCCUPATION WITH HOPEFUL
POSSIBILITIES WITHIN THE SOVIET UNION SHOULD NOT DISTRACT
ATTENTION FROM BROADER AND LESS REVERSIBLE CHANGES IN WORLD
POLITICS THAT MAKE A RETURN TO COLD WAS UNLIKELY, EVEN IF
GORBACHEV WERE TO BE REPLACED BY A LEADER IN THE BREZHNEV
MOLD. TODAY, BOTH THE USA AND THE USSR HAVE A WARY INTEREST
IN MAINTAINING THE EXISTING BALANCE OF POWER, NOT ONLY DUE
TO FEARS OF A SUICIDAL NUCLEAR WAR BUT BECAUSE OF
APPREHENSIONS THAT THE OTHER SIDE WILL MAKE POLITICAL AND
ECONOMIC GAINS THAT WILL MAKE IT THE DOMINANT WORLD POWER.

09776 HRONSKI, S.
THE GREAT BEGINNING IS NO ILLUSION
WORLD MARXIST REVIEW, 32(9) (SEP 89), 19-21.
THIS ARTICLE, BY A MEMBER OF THE POLISH UNITED WORKERS
PARTY (PZPR), ANALYSES THE PAST EXPERIENCES AND THE PRESENT
PROGRESS BEING MADE IN THE EFFORT TO SPREAD SOCIALISM
THROUGHOUT THE WORLD. IT DELVES DEEPLY INTO THE MEANINGS OF
LENIN'S WRITINGS WITH ATTENTION GIVEN TO THE EFFECT THAT
VOLLINTARY LABOR IN THE FORM OF SUBBOTNIKS HAD IN BUILDING
SOCIALISM. EXAMPLES FROM POLAND'S EXPERIENCE OF BENEFITTING
FROM CIVIC VOLUNTEER LABOR IN PEACE TIME ARE GIVEN. THE
WRITER DRAWS UPON HIS PERSONAL EXPERIENCES IN THE EARLY DAYS
OF SOCIALISM IN THE USSR AND DETAILS THE HILLING SUFFERING
OF THE MASSES FOR THE CAUSE, HE CONCLUDES THAT THE GREAT
BEGINNING OF SOCIALISM IS NO ILLUSION, BUT REAL, AND READY
TO SUCCEED.

09777 WU, H.
THE KUOMINTANG AND POLITICAL DEVELOPMENT IN TAIWAN SINCE
1968
DISSERTATION ABSTRACTS INTERNATIONAL, 49(3) (SEP 88),
611-A.
THE DISSERTATION FOCUSES ON THE KUOMINTANG (OR
NATIONALIST PARTY) IN TAIWAN AND ITS CHANGES IN RESPONSE TO
POLITICAL, SOCIO-ECONOMIC, AND INTERNATIONAL CONDITIONS. THE
CENTRAL THESIS IS THAT THE KUOMINTANG GRADUALLY CHANGED FROM
A REVOLUTIONARY AND EXCLUSIONARY PARTY TO A PRAGMATIC AND
INCLUSIONARY ONE.

09778 WU, Y.
MARKETIZATION OF POLITICS: THE TAIWAN EXPERIENCE
ASIAN SURVEY, XXIX(4) (APR 89), 382-400.
IN THE PAST, TAIWAN WAS CHARACTERIZED AS A SYSTEM OF
POLITICAL STAGNATION AND ECONOMIC DYNAMICS, AND ONLY QUITE
RECENTLY DID SCHOLARS REALIZE THAT THE RULE OF THE
KUOMINTANG (KMT) HAD BEEN TRANSFORMED FROM "HARD" TO "SOFT"
AUTHORITARIANISM. BUT THEN THEY NOTED THAT REALITY HAD EVEN
OUTPACED THIS MODIFIED THEORETICAL FORMAT. IN THIS SWIFTLY
CHANGING CONTEXT, TWO POLITICAL TRENDS HAVE EMERGED THAT
DESERVE SPECIAL ATTENTION: THE SURFACING OF INTERSECTING
SOCIAL CLEAVAGES AND THE MARKETIZATION OF THE KMT. THESE TWO
TRENDS FORM A PICTURE OF A POLITICAL REGIME EXPERIENCING
INTERNAL TRANSFORMATION AT THE SAME TIME THAT AUTHORITY
RELATIONS BETWEEN THE STATE AND THE SOCIETY ARE BEING
REDEFINED. THIS ARTICLE IS AN ANALYSIS OF THE BACKGROUND,
PROCESSES, AND REPERCUSSIONS OF THE DRAMATIC CHANGES THAT
HAVE TAKEN PLACE SINCE THE MID-1980S.

09779 HUFFLE, A.; FELD, S.; GROFMAN, B.; OWEN, G.
FINAGLE'S LAW AND THE FINAGLE POINT, A NEW SOLUTION
CONCEPT FOR TWO-CANDIDATE COMPETITION IN SPATIAL VOTING
GAMES WITHOUT A CORE
AMERICAN JOURNAL OF POLITICAL SCIENCE, 33(2) (MAY 89),
348-375.
THE AUTHORS INVESTIGATE THE GEOMETRY UNDERLYING
FINAGLE'S LAW WHICH STATES, "NO MATTER WHAT HAPPENS, YOU CAN
COME OUT AHEAD IF YOU KNOW JUST HOW TO FINAGLE." THEY
INTRODUCE A NEW SOLUTION CONCEPT FOR TWO-CANDIDATE
SEQUENTIAL SPATIAL VOTING GAMES, THE "FINAGLE POINT." FROM
THE FINAGLE POINT A CANDIDATE CAN, WITH A MINIMUM OF CHANGES
IN INITIAL POLICY LOCATION, FIND A RESPONSE TO ANY
CHALLENGER THAT WILL DEFEAT THE CHALLENGER.

09780 WUNNICKE, P.
THE ACCIDENTAL EMPIRE
STATE LEGISLATURES, 15(9) (OCT 89), 18-25.
THE USA HAS BECOME THE PROTECTOR AND DEFENDER OF A
NUMBER OF TROPICAL ISLANDS, MANY OF THEM UNKNOWN TO MOST
AMERICANS, WHOSE RESIDENTS ARE TORN BETWEEN THE NEED FOR
FINANCIAL AID AND THE DESIRE TO BE INDEPENDENT. ALTHOUGH
SOME ISLANDERS CHAFE WITH RESENTMENT AGAINST AMERICAN
DOMINANCE, THE MATERIAL BENEFITS OF BEING A PROTECTORATE ARE
ENOUGH TO INHIBIT ALL BUT A FEW PROPONENTS OF TOTAL
INDEPENDENCE.

09781 WUNSCH, J.C.
PARENTAL RECOVERY FOR LOSS OF SOCIETY OF THE UNBORN: THE
PLAINTIFF'S PERSPECTIVE
ILLINOIS BAR JOURNAL, 77(10) (JUN 89), 538-545.
LAWSUITS FOR THE WRONGFUL DEATH OF UNBORN CHILDREN HAVE
RAISED THE QUESTION OF WHETHER PARENTS MAY RECOVER FOR LOSS
OF AN UNBORN CHILD'S SOCIETY. THIS ARTICLE CRITICIZES A
RECENT CASE WHICH DENIED SUCH RECOVERY AND SUGGESTS A
DIFFERENT APPROACH.

09782 WURFEL, D.
THE PHILIPPINES' PRECARIOUS DEMOCRACY: COPING WITH FOREIGN
AND DOMESTIC PRESSURES UNDER AQUINO
INTERNATIONAL JOURNAL, XLIV(3) (SUM 89), 676-697.
CORAZON AQUINO TOOK OFFICE WITH A NATIONAL SURGE OF
SUPPORT GREATER THAN THAT ENJOYED BY ANY PREVIOUS PRESIDENT
OF THE PHILIPPINES. "PEOPLE POWER" PUT HER IN OFFICE. THIS
ARTICLE EXAMINES HOW AQUINO HAS USED HER POWER, HOW SHE HAS
DEALT WITH THE NATION'S PROBLEMS, AND WHETHER THE CRITICISM
OF HER IN THE MEDIA AND IN POLITICAL CIRCLES IS JUSTIFIED.

09783 WURTH, A. H. JR.
POLICY ANALYSIS AS ORGANIZING: PUBLIC GOODS, INFORMATION,
AND ORGANIZATION
DISSERTATION ABSTRACTS INTERNATIONAL, 49(8) (FEB 89),
2380-A.
THE MISUNDERSTANDING OF THE SCOPE OF POLICY ORIGINATES
IN THE ARTIFICIAL SEPARATION OF POLITICS AND ECONOMICS IN
THE ECONOMIC MODEL OF POLICY AS GOVERNMENTAL RESPONSE TO
MARKET FAILURE. THIS SEPARATION IMPLIES A DENIAL OF POLITICS,
INHIBITING BOTH GOOD POLICY AND GOOD CITIZENSHIP AND
NEGLECTING IMPORTANT POLITICAL CONCEPTS IN POLICY ANALYSIS.
THE LINKS BETWEEN POLITICS AND ECONOMICS ARE UNCOVERED UNDER
THE RUBRICS OF ORGANIZATION AND INFORMATION.

09784 WYCKOFF, P. G.
BUREAUCRACY AND THE 'PUBLICNESS' OF LOCAL PUBLIC GOODS: A
REPLY TO GONZALEZ, FOLSOM, AND MEHAY
PUBLIC CHOICE, 62(1) (JUL 89), 79-82.
THE AUTHOR RESPONDS TO A CRITIQUE OF HIS EARLIER WORK ON
BUREAUCRACY, AND LOCAL GOVERNMENT SPENDING. HE ARGUES THAT
HIS CONCLUSIONS ARE SIMILAR TO THOSE OF HIS DETRACTORS: THAT
LOCAL PUBLIC GOODS ARE REALLY PRIVATE GOODS HE ARGUES THAT
THE EFFECT OF BUREAUCRACY IS TO BIAS THE RESULTS OF
EXPERIMENTS TOWRD THE CONCLUSION THAT LOCAL PUBLIC GOODS ARE
PUBLIC IN NATURE.

09785 WYMAN, H. JR.
THE NATION'S PULSE/SLIM GOP PICKIN'S IN DIXIE
AMERICAN SPECTATOR, (AUG 89), 30-31.
THIS ARTICLE TRACES THE RECENT HISTORY OF GOP LOSSES IN
THE SOUTH. IT ANALYSES FACTORS AFFECTING THIS SITUATION AND
EXPLAINS REASONS FOR OPTOMISISM FOR THE REPUBLICAN PARTY
INSPITE OF CURRENT LOSSES.

09786 WYNIA, G.W.
CAMPAIGNING FOR FOR PRESIDENT IN ARGENTINA
CURRENT HISTORY, 88(536) (MAR 89), 133-136, 144-145.
ARGENTINA'S ECONOMIC PROBLEMS, ESPECIALLY INFLATION,
HERE A MAJOR FACTOR AS THE COUNTRY LOOKED FORWARD TO THE
1989 PRESIDENTIAL ELECTION.

09787 WYNNE, B.
THE TOXIC WASTE TRADE: INTERNATIONAL REGULATORY ISSUES AND
OPTIONS
THIRD WORLD QUARTERLY, 11(3) (JUL 89), 102-146.
THE AUTHOR REVIEWS SOME CASES OF INTERNATIONAL WASTE-
TRADING AND OUTLINES SYSTEMATIC PATTERNS IN THIS ACTIVITY.
CURRENT REGULATORY INITIATIVES ARE DESCRIBED AND ANALYZED.
THEN HE SUGGESTS THAT WHEN THE SCALE AND QUALITY OF THE
UNCERTAINTIES IN HAZARDOUS WASTE LIFE-CYCLES ARE TAKEN INTO
ACCOUNT, THE ONLY VIABLE REGULATORY STRATEGY IS ONE THAT
FOCUSES MORE ATTENTION ON THE POINT OF PRODUCTION OF THE
WASTES AND ON BETTER ORDERING THE BADLY-DEFINED
ORGANIZATIONAL MILIEUX THAT MAKE UP WASTE LIFE-CYCLES AND
THEIR RISKS. ATTEMPTING TO CONTROL WASTES BY RELYING ALMOST
TOTALLY UPON DOCUMENTARY NOTIFICATION SYSTEMS IS UNREALISTIC
BECAUSE SUCH A POLICY DOES NOT RECOGNIZE THE INSUPERABLE
INDETERMINACIES IN DEFINING HAZARDOUS WASTES AND IS BASED
UPON NAIVELY SIMPLE MODELS OF ACTUAL LIFE-CYCLES.

09788 WYSZOMIRSKI, M.J.
ADMINISTRATIVE AGENTS, POLICY PARTNERS, AND POLITICAL
CATALYSTS: A STRUCTURAL PERSPECTIVE ON THE INTERACTIONS OF
GOVERNMENTAL AND NONPROFIT ORGANIZATIONS
TEACHING POLITICAL SCIENCE, 16(3) (SPR 89), 122-130.
TRADITIONALLY, POLITICAL SCIENCE HAS BEEN CONCERNED WITH

THE INSTITUTIONS, PROCESSES, AND PERFORMANCE OF GOVERNMENT. LESS APPARENT BUT NONETHELESS PERSISTENT AND GROWING HAS BEEN THE INTERACTION BETWEEN THE PUBLIC AND NONPROFIT SECTORS. THIS INTERACTION IS NOT RESTRICTED TO THE IMPLEMENTATION OF PUBLIC POLICY. THIS ARTICLE EXPLORES A VARIETY OF PARTNERSHIPS ENGAGED IN: DEVELOPING POLICY OPTIONS, DEFINING PUBLIC ISSUES, MOBILIZING PUBLIC OPINION, AND GENERATING RESOURCES NECESSARY TO ADDRESS COMMON GOALS. IT EXPLORES THE NATURE AND IMPLICATIONS OF THE BLURRING OF BOUNDARIES BETWEEN THE PUBLIC AND PRIVATE SECTORS.

09789 XANDERS, E.L.
A HANDYMAN'S GUIDE TO FIXING NATIONAL SECURITY LEAKS: AN ANALYTICAL FRAMEWORK FOR EVALUATING PROPOSALS TO CURB UNAUTHORIZED PUBLICATION OF CLASSIFIED INFORMATION
JOURNAL OF LAW & POLITICS, 5(4) (SUM 89), 759-826.
THE PURPOSE OF THIS NOTE, IS TO PROVIDE A FRAMEWORK OF ANALYSIS FOR REVIEWING ANY PROPOSAL TO CURB LEAKS, WHETHER THE MEASURES ARE COMPREHENSIVE OR LIMITED IN SCOPE. ACCORDINGLY, THIS NOTE WILL DISCUSS THE EXTENT TO WHICH LEAKS ACTUALLY ENDANGER NATIONAL SECURITY AND WILL PROVIDE THE GENERAL CONSIDERATIONS AND GOALS THAT ANY LEAKPLUGGING PROPOSAL SHOULD TAKE INTO ACCOUNT. IN EFFECT, THIS NOTE WILL ANSWER THE FOLLOWING QUESTIONS: (1) ARE ALL LEAKS HARMFUL TO NATIONAL SECURITY? AND IF NOT, WHAT TYPES OF LEAKS, I.E., THE DISCLOSURES OF WHAT TYPES OF INFORMATION, ACTUALLY ARE HARMFUL?; (2) SHOULD LEAK-PLUGGING MEASURES TREAT ALIKE THE GOVERNMENT OFFICIAL WHO LEAKS INFORMATION AND THE MEDIA THAT EVENTUALLY PROVIDES PUBLICATION?; AND (3) IN LIGHT OF SEPARATION OF POWERS' CONCERNS, WHAT ROLES SHOULD THE THREE SEPARATE BRANCHES OF GOVERNMENT PLAY IN THE INTRODUCTION OF LEAK-PLUGGING REFORMS?

09790 XIAN, Z.W.
ON THE SOCIALIST MARKET SYSTEM AND ITS MODEL
INTERNATIONAL JOURNAL OF SOCIAL ECONOMICS, 16(2) (1989), 54-58.
IT IS ARGUED THAT A UNIFIED SOCIALIST MARKET SHOULD BE A SOLID, FULL-VIEW MARKET, AND THAT WHETHER THE MARKET SYSTEM IS COMPLETE OR NOT HAS AN IMPORTANT EFFECT ON THE DEVELOPMENT OF A COMMODITY ECONOMY. THUS THE SOCIALIST COMMODITY ECONOMY IN ORDER TO PROMOTE A COMPLETE MARKET SYSTEM IS REQUIRED TO INCLUDE COMMODITIES, FUNDS, TECHNOLOGY, INFORMATION AND LABOUR, AND THIS MODEL SHOULD BE REFLECTED IN ALL ITS ASPECTS. THE CONCEPT OF MARKET FROM A SOCIAL AND AN ECONOMIC VIEW IS DISCUSSED.

09791 XIANG, H.
RELATIVE DETENTE BEFALLS THE WORLD
BEIJING REVIEW, 32(1) (JAN 89), 15-19.
WITH THE RELAXING OF SOVIET-U.S. RELATIONS, SOME DIFFICULT PROBLEMS, INCLUDING REGIONAL CONFLICTS, HAVE SHOWN SIGNS OF YIELDING TO POLITICAL SOLUTIONS. THE SUPERPOWERS HAVE BEGUN TO SHIFT THE FOCUS OF THEIR COMPETITIVE STRATEGIES FROM ARMS TO COMPREHENSIVE NATIONAL STRENGTH. AS THE WORLD IS BECOMING MULTIPOLAR, INTERNATIONAL DETENTE WILL REMAIN AN IMPORTANT PRIORITY.

09792 XIANGANG, G.
U.S. ADJUSTS POLICY ON KAMPUCHEA
BEIJING REVIEW, 32(50) (DEC 89), 16-18.
IN A MAJOR DEPARTURE FROM ITS OLD POLICY ON KAMPUCHEA, WASHINGTON IS NOW PROVIDING MILITARY ASSISTANCE TO TWO FACTIONS OF THE RESISTANCE FORCES LED BY PRINCE NORODOM SIHANOUK AND SON SANN, PRIME MINISTER OF THE COALITION GOVERNMENT OF DEMOCRATIC KAMPUCHEA. IF A POLITICAL SOLUTION SEEMS LIKELY AFTER THE VIETNAMESE TROOP PULLOUT, U.S. MILITARY AID CAN CONSOLIDATE THE POSITION OF THE NON-COMMUNIST FORCES IN THE NEGOTIATIONS. ON THE OTHER HAND, IF A CIVIL WAR BREAKS OUT, U.S. WEAPONS AND EQUIPMENT CAN STRENGTHEN THE SIHANOUK AND SON SANN FACTIONS IN THEIR MILITARY CONFRONTATION WITH THE HENG SAMRIN REGIME AND THE KHMER ROUGE. IN EITHER CASE, THE UNITED STATES CAN EXPECT TO EXPAND ITS INFLUENCE IN KAMPUCHEA.

09793 XIANGDONG, L.
CHINA'S FOREIGN ECONOMIC RELATIONS AND TRADE: 1988-89
BEIJING REVIEW, 32(10) (MAR 89), 20-23.
DURING 1988, CHINA OPENED ITS DOORS STILL WIDER TO THE WORLD. IT EXPANDED ECONOMIC DEVELOPMENT OF ITS COASTAL AREAS AND FURTHER DEEPENED THE REFORM OF ITS FOREIGN TRADE SYSTEM, IMPLEMENTING A CONTRACT RESPONSIBILITY SYSTEM AND DELEGATING RIGHTS TO MANAGE FOREIGN TRADE DOWNWARDS. AS A RESULT, IMPORTS AND EXPORTS BOTH GREW SUBSTANTIALLY, AS DID INVESTMENT AND BORROWING FROM ABROAD, AND CONTRACTS FOR OVERSEAS PROJECTS AND LABOR SERVICES. FOR 1989, CHINA PLANS TO CONTINUE TO SEEK FOREIGN CAPITAL, ESPECIALLY FOR TRANSPORT AND COMMUNICATIONS, TECOMMUNICATIONS AND THE DEVELOPMENT OF ITS ENERGY AND RAW MATERIAL RESOURCES.

09794 XIANGZHI, G.
THE TAIWAN ISSUE
CHINA RECONSTRUCTS, XXXVIII(2) (FEB 89), 27-30.
AT VIRTUALLY EVERY MEETING BETWEEN CHINESE AND AMERICAN DIPLOMATS, THE TAIWAN ISSUE OCCUPIES A PROMINENT PLACE ON THE AGENDA. THE CHINESE SIDE INVARIABLY REMINDS U.S. REPRESENTATIVES OF THE PRINCIPLES AGREED UPON IN SUCH DOCUMENTS AS THE SHANGHAI COMMUNIQUE OF 1972 AND THE 1979 COMMUNIQUE ON THE ESTABLISHMENT OF DIPLOMATIC RELATIONS. IN CHINA'S VIEW, THE AMERICAN GOVERNMENT INITIATIVES COULD PLAY AN ACTIVE ROLE IN SPEEDING UP THE PEACEFUL REUNIFICATION OF TAIWAN WITH THE MAINLAND.

09795 XIAOBIN, Y.; RONGXIA, L.
PREMIER LI ON INTERNAL, EXTERNAL POLICIES
BEIJING REVIEW, 32(16) (APR 89), 14-19.
THIS ARTICLE INCLUDES QUESTIONS AND ANSWERS AT A NEWS CONFERENCE GIVEN BY CHINESE PREMIER LI PEN AND THREE OF HIS VICE-PREMIERS ON APRIL 3, 1989. TOPICS INCLUDE CHINA'S REFORM POLICIES, THE SINO-SOVIET SUMMIT, THE PREMIER'S VISIT TO JAPAN, AND THE THREE GORGES PROJECT.

09796 XIAOBING, Y.; WEI, Z.
A VILLAGE BY THE LHASA RIVER (V)
BEIJING REVIEW, 32(15) (APR 89), 29-31.
THE CHINESE GOVERNMENT'S POLICY OF PROMOTING RELIGIOUS FREEDOM HAS BEEN WARMLY WELCOMED IN XIANGGA, A TYPICAL TIBETAN VILLAGE. NOW THAT THE VILLAGE HAS BECOME MORE AFFLUENT UNDER THE NEW ECONOMIC POLICIES, THE CITIZENS USE THEIR NEW PROSPERITY TO ENJOY RELIGIOUS RITES AND CEREMONIES ON A MORE LAVISH SCALE.

09797 XIAOBING, Y.
CHINA'S BATTLE AGAINST CORRUPTION
BEIJING REVIEW, 32(3) (JAN 89), 20-24.
CHINA'S STRUGGLE AGAINST CORRUPTION ENJOYS WIDESPREAD POPULAR SUPPORT. BUT THE MOST IMPORTANT STEP TAKEN IN THE LAST COUPLE OF YEARS TO "PURIFY GOVERNMENT" HAS BEEN THE ESTABLISHMENT OF AN ADMINISTRATIVE SUPERVISORY NETWORK ACROSS THE COUNTRY. ALREADY IT HAS PROVED SUCCESSFUL IN FERRETING OUT SERIOUS CASES OF ILLEGAL ECONOMIC DEALINGS IN OVERSEAS TRADE, AS WELL AS SERIOUS CRIMES AND DISCIPLINARY BREACHES COMMITTED BY ADMINISTRATIVE ORGANS.

09798 XIAOBING, Y.
CIVILIANS CAN SUE OFFICIALS
BEIJING REVIEW, 32(19) (MAY 89), 7.
THE ADMINISTRATIVE PROCEDURE LAW OF THE PEOPLE'S REPUBLIC OF CHINA WILL GO INTO EFFECT ON OCTOBER 1, 1990. THIS WILL BE A MAJOR EVENT IN THE REFORM OF CHINA'S LEGAL SYSTEM AS WELL AS AN IMPORTANT STEP TOWARDS POLITICAL DEMOCRACY. THE NEW LAW WILL PLACE ADMINISTRATORS UNDER THE PEOPLE'S SUPERVISION AND WILL ALLOW ORDINARY CITIZENS TO SUE GOVERNMENT OFFICIALS.

09799 XIAOJUN, L.
POLITICS, LAW, AND CULTURE; HISTORICAL DIFFERENCE BETWEEN CHINA AND WEST
BEIJING REVIEW, 32(28) (JUL 89), 34-37.
THE GREAT DIFFERENCE BETWEEN CHINESE AND WESTERN POLITICS, LAW, AND CULTURE HAS BEEN ESTABLISHED BEFORE THE BEGINNING OF CLASS SOCIETY. IN THE WEST, THE SLAVE SOCIETIES OF ANCIENT GREECE ARE REGARDED AS THE CRADLE OF EUROPEAN CIVILIZATION. THUS, THE HISTORY OF WESTERN POLITICS, LEGAL SYSTEMS, AND CULTURE IS TRACED TO THE POLITICAL CIVILIZATION OF ANCIENT GREECE. IN CHINA, POLITICS, LAW, AND CULTURE ORIGINATED AT THE TRANSITION FROM PRIMITIVE CLAN COMMUNES TO CLASS SOCIETY AND FORMED SOME OF THE IMPORTANT CHARACTERISTICS DURING THE PERIOD OF SLAVERY.

09800 XIAOPING, D.
MARXISM-LENINISM NEEDS TO BE INTEGRATED WITH CHINA'S REALITY
BEIJING REVIEW, 32(38) (SEP 89), 18-19.
IN THIS EXCERPT FROM "SELECTED WORKS OF DENG XIAOPING," THE CHINESE LEADER ANSWERS TWO QUESTIONS: WHAT ARE THE IMPLICATIONS OF MEMBERSHIP IN THE COMMUNIST PARTY OF CHINA? WHO IS TO DECIDE WHICH OF THE INTERNATIONAL CLASSICAL COMMUNIST PRINCIPLES ARE APPLICABLE TO CHINA?

09801 XIAOPING, D.
THE COMMUNIST PARTY MUST ACCEPT SUPERVISION
BEIJING REVIEW, 32(39) (SEP 89), 20, 24-26.
THIS EXCERPT FROM "SELECTED WORKS OF DENG XIAOPING" STRESSES THE NEED FOR THE CHINESE COMMUNIST PARTY TO OVERCOME SUBJECTIVISM, BUREAUCRATISM, AND SECTARIANISM. IT ALSO EMPHASIZES THE NECESSITY OF ACCEPTING SUPERVISION AND EXPANDING DEMOCRACY WITHIN THE PARTY AND THE STATE, IN ORDER TO EXERCISE EFFECTIVE LEADERSHIP.

09802 XIAOZENG, L.
ASEAN COUNTRIES: ADJUSTING FOREIGN POLCIES
BEIJING REVIEW, 32(52) (DEC 89), 20-22.
IN THE PAST, COLD WAR CONFRONTATIONS INFLUENCED THE FOREIGN POLICY OF ASEAN MEMBERS. ASEAN NATIONS TENDED TO DEVELOP CLOSE RELATIONS WITH WESTERN COUNTRIES AND PURSUED PRO-WESTERN FOREIGN POLICIES BECAUSE THEY DEPENDED ON WESTERN SUPPORT TO SAFEGUARD THEIR INDEPENDENCE AND SECURITY.

NOW THAT EAST-WEST TENSIONS ARE RELAXING, ASEAN MEMBERS ARE BEGINNING TO GRADUALLY BREAK AWAY FROM COLD WAR INFLUENCES AND DISTANCE THEMSELVES FROM THE UNITED STATES WHILE SIMULTANEOUSLY DEVELOPING RELATIONS WITH THE SOVIET UNION.

09803 XICHENG, H.
AFGHANISTAN: SITUATION AND PROSPECTS
BEIJING REVIEW, 32(17) (APR 89), 18-19.
AS THE DUST SETTLES AFTER THE SOVIET PULLOUT FROM AFGHANISTAN, IT HAS BECOME APPARENT THAT THE CHIEF TASK IS THE UNITY OF THE AFGHAN RESISTANCE FORCES. THE RESISTANCE FORCES INCLUDE MANY FACTIONS WITH DIFFERENT NATIONAL, RELIGIOUS, TRIBAL, AND LANGUAGE HERITAGES AND VARYING POLITICAL VIEWS. THERE ARE REPORTS THAT THE SOVIET UNION AND THE KABUL REGIME ARE ATTEMPTING TO EXPLOIT THESE DIFFERENCES IN ORDER TO DESTABILIZE THE RESISTANCE.

09804 XIN, H.
YUAN MU ON FRANCE'S RECENT ATTITUDE
BEIJING REVIEW, 32(45) (NOV 89), 17.
IN A NEWS CONFERENCE ON OCTOBER 25, 1989, STATE COUNCIL SPOKESMAN YUAN MU SAID THAT CHINA WELCOMES FRANCE'S STATEMENT THAT IT WILL NOT ALLOW POLITICAL EXILES TO ENGAGE IN POLITICAL ACTIVITIES ON FRENCH TERRITORY AGAINST GOVERNMENTS WITH WHOM IT HAS DIPLOMATIC RELATIONS. YUAN MU ALSO STATED THAT MARTIAL LAW IN BEIJING IS A TEMPORARY SITUATION AND THAT THE CHINESE PEOPLE WILL NEVER YIELD TO THE PRESSURE FROM FOREIGN GOVERNMENTS THAT WISH TO USE THE MARTIAL LAW ISSUE TO INTERFERE IN CHINA'S INTERNAL AFFAIRS.

09805 XIN, R.
KAMPUCHEAN SETTLEMENT SEES GOOD BEGINNING
BEIJING REVIEW, 32(34) (AUG 89), 7-8.
THE 1989 PARIS INTERNATIONAL CONFERENCE ON KAMPUCHEA ADOPTED THE CONCEPT OF A COMPREHENSIVE RATHER THAN A PARTIAL SETTLEMENT OF THE KAMPUCHEAN ISSUE, THUS OPENING A GOOD BEGINNING FOR A FINAL SOLUTION.

09806 XIN, W.
FROM SAPLING TO FLOURISHING TREE
CHINA RECONSTRUCTS, XXXVIII(3) (MAR 89), 28-31.
THE AUTHOR BRIEFLY REVIEWS THE HIGHLIGHTS OF US-SINO DIPLOMATIC RELATIONS FROM 1949 TO THE PRESENT.

09807 XIN, W.
SINO-U.S. HANDS ACROSS THE OCEAN
CHINA RECONSTRUCTS, XXXVIII(5) (MAY 89), 55-56.
THE AUTHOR REVIEWS THE FLOWERING OF DIPLOMATIC RELATIONS AND CULTURAL EXCHANGES BETWEEN CHINA AND THE UNITED STATES, BEGINNING WITH PRESIDENT NIXON'S TRIP TO CHINA IN 1972 AND RESTORATION OF FULL DIPLOMATIC RELATIONS IN 1979.

09808 XIN, W.
STRIKES SPARK POLITICAL CRISIS
BEIJING REVIEW, 32(22) (MAY 89), 11-13.
IN APRIL AND MAY 1989, MILLIONS OF CHINESE YEARNING FOR DEMOCRACY TOOK TO THE STREETS WITH UNPRECEDENTED BOLDNESS. THE DEMONSTRATIONS WERE TRIGGERED BY THE DEATH OF HU YAOBANG ON APRIL 15. THE MOURNING ACTIVITIES SOON DEVELOPED INTO PRO-DEMOCRACY DEMONSTRATIONS, WHICH WERE DISAPPROVED OF AN OBSTRUCTED BY THE CHINESE AUTHORITIES.

09809 XING, F.
WHAT WE KNOW OF WEI JINGSHENG
BEIJING REVIEW, 32(18) (MAY 89), 27-29.
WHENEVER CHINA'S HUMAN RIGHTS PROBLEM IS MENTIONED, THE CASE OF WEI JINGSHENG, WHO WAS IMPRISONED TEN YEARS AGO, SEEMS TO COME UP FOR DISCUSSION. WESTERNERS BELIEVE THAT WEI IS A POLITICAL OR IDEOLOGICAL PRISONER. BUT THE CHINESE GOVERNMENT CLAIMS THAT HE PASSED MILITARY INFORMATION TO FOREIGNERS AND THAT HE WROTE ARTICLES ATTACKING THE CHINESE POLITICAL SYSTEM AS A "FEUDAL MONARCHY IN THE GARB OF SOCIALISM."

09810 XINGHAO, D.
CHINA'S POLICY ON A MULTIPOLAR WORLD
BEIJING REVIEW, 32(14) (APR 89), 14.
THE REASONS BEHIND POLITICAL MULTI-POLARIZATION HAVE BEEN THAT THE NEWLY EMERGING COUNTRIES HAVE BECOME STRONGER WHILE THE POLITICAL AND ECONOMIC STRENGTH OF THE WESTERN AND EASTERN BLOCS HAS DECLINED. THIS PROCESS HAS CHECKED THE BEHAVIOR OF BOTH THE SOVIET UNION AND THE UNITED STATES. THE NEW MULTIPOLAR WORLD OFFERS OPPORTUNITIES FOR EVERY COUNTRY, AND NATIONS THAT ATTUNE THEIR FOREIGN POLICY TO THIS GLOBAL TREND WILL GAIN THE INITIATIVE. THE READJUSTMENT OF SOVIET-AMERICAN RELATIONS AND THE DIVERSIFICATION OF THE INTERNATIONAL SITUATION MAKE IT ESSENTIAL FOR CHINA TO DEFINE ITS FOREIGN POLICY PRIORITIES.

09811 XINGWU, W.
THE CRYING NEED FOR PRESS REFORM
BEIJING REVIEW, 32(21) (MAY 89), 7.
SINCE THE LATE 1970'S A NATIONWIDE EFFORT HAS BEEN MADE TO REFORM THE CHINESE PRESS. ONE OF THE MAJOR GOALS HAS BEEN

TO CHANGE THE POOR IMAGE THE MEDIA INHERITED FROM THE CHAOTIC YEARS OF THE CULTURAL REVOLUTION. AS A RESULT, THERE HAS BEEN MUCH IMPROVEMENT. TRUTHFUL, BALANCED REPORTING IS NOW STRESSED AND PROMOTED; THE COVERAGE OF DISASTERS, CORRUPTION, AND SOCIAL EVILS IS NO LONGER TABOO. BUT THERE IS NO DENYING THAT PROBLEMS STILL ABOUND. PARTY LEADERSHIP OVER THE PRESS IS, OF COURSE, NECESSARY. BUT FEW JOURNALISTS ARE HAPPY WITH THE PRESENT SYSTEM AND METHODS OF LEADERSHIP. THE DISCONTENT AMONG CHINESE JOURNALISTS IS EXPECTED TO HASTEN THE PACE OF PRESS REFORM AND THE REFORM OF THE ENTIRE POLITICAL STRUCTURE.

09812 XIONGCHENG, W.
THE INTERNATIONAL CLIMATE AND THE JUNE REBELLION
BEIJING REVIEW, 32(37) (SEP 89), 13-16.
THE JUNE 1989 COUNTER-REVOLUTIONARY REBELLION WAS ORCHESTRATED BY A SMALL NUMBER OF PEOPLE BOTH INSIDE AND OUTSIDE THE CPC WHO STUBBORNLY CLUNG TO THEIR BOURGEOIS STAND AND ENGAGED IN POLITICAL CONSPIRACY IN COLLABORATION WITH ANTI-COMMUNIST AND ANTI-SOCIALIST FORCES IN THE WEST, TAIWAN, AND HONG KONG. THEIR GOAL WAS TO OVERTHROW THE LEADERSHIP OF THE CPC, SUBVERT THE SOCIALIST PEOPLE'S REPUBLIC OF CHINA, AND ESTABLISH A COMPLETELY WESTERNIZED BOURGEOIS REPUBLIC IN CHINA.

09813 XITONG, C.
REPORT ON CHECKING THE TURMOIL AND QUELLING THE COUNTER-REVOLUTIONARY REBELLION
BEIJING REVIEW, 32(29) (JUL 89), I-XX.
THE AUTHOR, WHO IS THE MAYOR OF BEIJING AND A STATE COUNCILLOR, OFFERS AN OFFICIAL VERSION OF THE EVENTS SURROUNDING THE POLITICAL TURMOIL IN BEIJING IN 1989. HE IDENTIFIES ZHAO ZIYANG'S SPEECH ON MAY 4 AS THE EVENT THAT ESCALATED THE CONFLICT, AND HE VINDICATES MARTIAL LAW AS BEING THE ONLY ALTERNATIVE FOR THE GOVERNMENT IN BEIJING.

09814 XU, H.
CURRENT DEVELOPMENTS IN CHINA AND CHINA-U.S. RELATIONS
BEIJING REVIEW, 32(38) (SEP 89), 30-33.
THE AUTHOR, WHO FORMERLY SERVED AS THE CHINESE AMBASSADOR TO THE UNITED STATES, DISCUSSES THE COUNTER-REVOLUTIONARY REVOLT OF 1989 AND ITS IMPACT ON SINO-AMERICAN RELATIONS.

09815 XUELING, Z.
SISTER CITY RELATIONSHIPS GROW
BEIJING REVIEW, 32(4) (JAN 89), 36-37.
THE ESTABLISHMENT OF SINO-US DIPLOMATIC RELATIONS IN 1979 MADE IT POSSIBLE FOR THE PEOPLE TO ESTABLISH AND DEVELOP SISTER CITY RELATIONSHIPS, AS WELL AS SISTER PROVINCES AND SISTER STATES. THE RELATIONSHIPS HAVE PROMOTED MUTUAL UNDERSTANDING, LOCAL EXCHANGES, AND COOPERATION BASED ON EQUALITY AND MUTUAL BENEFIT. THESE SISTER CITY RELATIONS HAVE BECOME AN INDISPENSABLE PART OF THE CONTACTS BETWEEN THE TWO COUNTRIES.

09816 XUEQUN, Z.
BEIJING: THE OPEN POLICY FLOURISHES
CHINA RECONSTRUCTS, XXXVIII(9) (SEP 89), 40-42.
FOLLOWING THE TURBULENCE IN BEIJING IN THE SPRING OF 1989, THE SITUATION IN THE CAPITAL HAS QUICKLY STABILIZED. REFORM AND THE OPEN POLICY REMAINED VERY MUCH IN EFFECT. THIS FACT WAS STRESSED A NUMBER OF TIMES DURING THE MONTH OF JUNE BY DENG XIAOPING AND OTHER TOP LEADERS. THE FOURTH PLENARY SESSION OF THE 13TH CENTRAL COMMITTEE OF THE CHINESE COMMUNIST PARTY ALSO REAFFIRMED THE COMMITMENT TO CONTINUING REFORM AND OPENING TO THE OUTSIDE WORLD.

09817 YA-LI, L.
ELECTIONS RECAST
FREE CHINA REVIEW, 39(12) (DEC 89), 6-8.
THE DECEMBER 1989 ELECTION WILL BE ONE OF THE MOST IMPORTANT IN TAIWAN'S POLITICAL HISTORY BECAUSE IT WILL BE THE FIRST FOLLOWING A SERIES OF MAJOR REFORMS. RESTRICTIONS ON FREE EXPRESSION HAVE BEEN VIRTUALLY ELIMINATED AND THERE ARE HARDLY ANY TABOOS AS FAR AS EXPRESSION OF POLITICAL OPINION IS CONCERNED, WHICH WILL GIVE ALL THE CANDIDATES FREE REIGN TO PROPAGATE THEIR VIEWS. UNLIKE PREVIOUS ELECTIONS, WHICH WERE DOMINATED BY THE RULING KUOMINTANG, A NUMBER OF PARTIES WILL RUN CANDIDATES AND THIS WILL BE TAIWAN'S FIRST ELECTION CONTESTED BY POLITICAL PARTIES INSTEAD OF INDIVIDUALS.

09818 YACHIR, F.
CRISIS AND ADJUSTMENT POLICIES IN ARAB COUNTRIES
INTERNATIONAL SOCIAL SCIENCE JOURNAL, (120) (MAY 89), 223-234.
BY MASKING A GROWING THREEFOLD IMBALANCE IN THE AREAS OF FOOD, TECHNOLOGY, AND FINANCE, ARAB DEPENDENCE ON TRANSFER INCOME NURTURED A LATENT CRISIS, WHICH BECAME APPARENT AS SOON AS THE RECESSION IN THE WEST BROUGHT ABOUT A DRASTIC FALL IN TRANSFER INCOME. THE CRISIS AND THE POLICIES ADOPTED IN REACTION TO IT ARE FACTORS OF CONVERGENCE AMONG ALL THE ARAB COUNTRIES.

09819 YADAV, S. S.
CHANCES FOR PEACE IN AFGHANISTAN
INTERNATIONAL PERSPECTIVES, XVIII(1) (JAN 89), 22-23.
CHANCES ARE SLIM FOR A NEGOTIATED AGREEMENT THAT WILL
ESTABLISH A STABLE POLITICAL ORDER IN AFGHANISTAN. PAPER
AGREEMENTS DO NOT CHANGE AFGHAN REGIMES; VIOLENCE DOES.
AFGHANISTAN'S GEOPOLITICAL SIGNIFICANCE WILL PROBABLY ASSURE
ITS CONTINUED INTEREST TO THE SUPER POWERS, BUT THEIR
DECLINING POWER MAY DIMINISH THIS THREAT TO AFGHANISTAN'S
INTERNAL STABILITY.

09820 YADLIN, R.
THE EGYPTIAN OPPOSITION AND THE BOUNDARIES OF NATIONAL
CONSENSUS
MIDDLE EAST REVIEW, XXI(4) (SUM 89), 18-26.
THE EGYPTIAN OPPOSITION UNDER MUBARAK STILL HAS NOT BEEN
GRANTED THE MAIN FUNCTION OF A REAL OPPOSITION--THE ABILITY
TO PRESENT AN ALTERNATIVE TO THE REGIME--BUT FREEDOM OF THE
PRESS HAS BEEN EXPANDED TO AN EXTENT UNKNOWN SINCE THE
REVOLUTION. NOT ONLY ARE MORE OPPOSITION ORGANS BEING
PUBLISHED, BUT OPPOSITION PERSONALITIES ARE BEING GIVEN
ENTRE INTO THE ESTABLISHMENT PRESS AND TOPICS THAT WOULD
HAVE FORMERLY LANDED THEIR AUTHORS IN JAIL ARE BEING
BROACHED. HOWEVER, BECAUSE OF THE PARAMETERS SET BY
CENSORSHIP, ONE MAY ASSUME THAT WHATEVER IS SPOKEN AND
PUBLISHED IS WITHIN THE SCOPE OF THE ACCEPTABLE. DUE TO THE
OPPOSITION'S NEWNESS. IT STILL LACKS SOLID LEGITIMIZATION.
DUE TO THE IGNORANCE OR INDIFFERENCE OF THE ELECTORATE, IT
NEEDS A GREAT DEAL OF APPEAL.

09821 YAGODKIN, Y.
DIPLOMACY AND CULTURE
INTERNATIONAL AFFAIRS (MOSCOW), (7) (JUL 89), 76-82.
CIRCUMSTANCES OFTEN COMPEL DIPLOMATS TO ASSUME THE ROLE
OF HISTORIANS, ECONOMICS, OR LAWYERS. EXPERT KNOWLEDGE OF
THESE FIELDS UNDERLIES PROFESSIONAL COMPETENCE AND IS OFTEN
CONSIDERED INDISPENSABLE. IT HAS LONG BEEN CUSTOMARY FOR
CULTURAL PROBLEMS (MEANING NOT ONLY CULTURAL RELATIONS BUT
CULTURE AS THE BASIS FOR CLOSER TIES BETWEEN PEOPLE AND
COUNTRIES AND ALSO AS AN ATTRIBUTE OF DIPLOMACY) TO HOLD AN
EQUAL, AND OFTEN EVEN LARGE, PLACE IN DIPLOMATIC WORK.
INDEED, A COUNTRY'S CULTURAL HERITAGE LARGELY DETERMINES THE
INTELLECTUAL CHARACTER, VITALITY, AND REAL MERITS OF
DIPLOMACY. DIPLOMATIC SKILL FADES UNLESS IT DRAWS ON
NATIONAL AND UNIVERSAL CULTURE.

09822 YAHUDA, M.B.
THE PEOPLE'S REPUBLIC OF CHINA AT FORTY: FOREIGN RELATIONS
CHINA QUARTERLY, (119) (SEP 89), 519-539.
THE EXTENT TO WHICH CHINA WILL BE ABLE TO EXPLOIT ITS
NEW OPPORTUNITIES AND COPE WITH POTENTIAL PROBLEMS DEPENDS,
AT LEAST IN PART, UPON ITS INTERNATIONAL STANDING AND HEIGHT
IN INTERNATIONAL AFFAIRS. THIS ARTICLE FIRST ADDRESSES THAT
ISSUE BEFORE EXAMINING CHINA'S RELATIONS WITH THE
SUPERPOWERS AND THE NORMALIZATION OF SINO-SOVIET RELATIONS.
THE ARTICLE ALSO ASSESSES THE IMPACT ON CHINA'S FOREIGN
RELATIONS PRODUCED BY THE GROWING INTERDEPENDENCY OF ITS
DOMESTIC SOCIETY WITH THE OUTSIDE WORLD AND THE IMPLICATIONS
THIS MAY HAVE FOR THE PROCESS OF FOREIGN POLICY DECISION-
MAKING.

09823 YAKOVLEV, A.
THE HUMANISTIC CHOICE OF PERESTROIKA
WORLD MARXIST REVIEW, 32(2) (FEB 89), 8-13.
FOR THE FIRST TIME, THE RECORD OF SOCIALIST
TRANSFORMATIONS HAS MADE IT POSSIBLE TO SEE THE DEEPER
MECHANISMS THAT PRESERVE AND DEVELOP THE SOCIAL FABRIC, AS
WELL AS TO SEPARATE THE GENUINE FOUNDATIONS AND LAWS OF
SOCIAL REALITY FROM IMAGINARY ONES. THE EXPERIENCE
ACCUMULATED BY THE WORLD SOCIALIST SYSTEM HAS MADE IT
POSSIBLE TO SEE UNITY AND DIALECTICAL INTERCONNECTION IN
THINGS THAT WERE PREVIOUSLY REGARDED AS ABSOLUTELY
INCOMPATIBLE AND ESSENTIALLY ANTAGONISTIC. THE PAINFULLY
CRYSTALLISING ABILITY TO SEE OURAS WE ARE, UNDERSTAND THE
REAL MEANING OF FACTS AND EVENTS AND REALISE THAT WORTHY
IDEALS CAN BE TRANSLATED INTO REALITY INSTEAD OF REMAINING
HOPELESS ILLUSIONS IS THE IMPORTANT MORAL AND INTELLECTUAL
ACCOMPLISHMENT OF PERESTROIKA.

09824 YAKUNIN, G.
THE MOSCOW PATRIARCHATE AND STALIN'S CULT OF PERSONALITY
GLASNOST, II(2) (MAR 89), 8-15.
NEVER HAS THE CLIMATE IN THE SOVIET UNION BEEN SO
FAVORABLE FOR THE LEADERS OF THE RUSSIAN ORTHODOX CHURCH TO
TELL THE TRUTH ABOUT STALIN'S CULT OF PERSONALITY, TO
APOLOGIZE FOR THEIR COMPLICITY IN PROMOTING AND SERVING THE
CULT, AND TO REPENT. BY CONDEMING THE CULT OF STALIN, THE
CHURCH COULD EXPRESS SUPPORT FOR THE NEW POLICY OF
PERESTROIKA. APPARENTLY, THE MAIN REASON THAT THE CHURCH HAS
NOT YET CONDEMNED THE STALIN CULT IS THAT CONSERVATIVE
FORCES HOSTILE TO PERESTROIKA STILL GOVERN THE MOSCOW
PATRIARCHATE.

09825 YAKUSHIJI, T.
POLITICAL FACTORS IN SHAPING JAPAN'S FOREIGN ECONOMIC
POLICY
INTERNATIONAL SPECTATOR, XXIV(3-4) (JUL 89), 208-213.
NUMEROUS CONTRADICTIONS AND DILEMMAS SURROUND JAPANESE
ATTEMPTS AT INTERNATIONAL COOPERATION. WITH THIS IN MIND,
THIS PAPER POSES TWO QUESTIONS. THE FIRST IS WHETHER JAPAN'S
POSITION IN THE ARENA OF INTERNATIONAL RELATIONS IS SOMEHOW
UNIQUE AMONG NATIONS. THE SECOND QUESTION, WHICH INVOLVES
JAPANESE POLITICS, IS WHETHER THE JAPANESE GOVERNMENT CAN BE
PLACED IN THE SAME CATEGORY AS ITS WESTERN COUNTERPARTS WITH
RESPECT TO SUFFICIENT POLITICAL POWER IN POLICY-MAKING.
SINCE THE LIBERAL DEMOCRATIC PARTY HAS ENJOYED A CONTINUOUS
HOLD ON POWER SINCE 1955, THE CORE OF JAPAN'S PROBLEMS IN
INTERNATIONAL COOPERATION MIGHT RESULT FROM INTERNAL POWER
DIVERSIFICATION WITHIN THE PARTY.

09826 YAMPOLSKY, A.
USSR-VIETNAM: IMPROVEMENT OF TRADE AND ECONOMIC TIES
FOREIGN TRADE, 5 (1988), 5-9.
THE DYNAMICS OF SOVIET-VIETNAMESE TRADE AS WELL AS ITS
35 YEAR OLD HISTORY ARE EXPLORED IN THIS ARTICLE, VIETNAM'S
ECONOMIC DEVELOPMENT PROBLEMS ARE DETAILED AS WELL AS ITS
DETERIORATING FOREIGN RELATIONS IN THE LATE 1970S. WITH
RUSSIA AS VIETNAM'S MAIN TRADING PARTNER, SOVIET PLANS TO
INTENSIFY TRADE AND ECONOMIC TIES BECOME MORE PROMISING AS
TIME GOES ON.

09827 YANG, B.
COMPLEXITY AND REASONABILITY: REASSESSMENT OF THE LI LISAN
ADVENTURE
AUSTRALIAN JOURNAL OF CHINESE AFFAIRS, (21) (JAN 89),
111-141.
THE FIRST PART OF THIS STUDY PROVIDES A CHRONOLOGICAL
ACCOUNT OF THE DEVELOPMENT AND EXECUTION OF THE LI LISAN
LINE WITH EMPHASIS ON THE RELATIONSHIPS BETWEEN THE
COMINTERN AND THE CCP AND BETWEEN LI LISAN AND ZHOU ENLAI
WITHIN THE CCP CENTRE. THE SECOND SECTION OFFERS AN
ASSESSMENT OF THE PRACTICAL CONSEQUENCES OF THE LI LISAN
LEADERSHIP IN VIEW OF THE OVERALL COMMUNIST MOVEMENT. THE
FINAL SECTION EXAMINES THE INVOLVEMENT OF THE LI LISAN
CENTRE WITH MAO ZEDONG.

09828 YANG, D.H.
THE MILITARY AND THE POLITICS OF DEMOCRATIZATION IN SOUTH
AMERICA: A COMPARATIVE STUDY
DISSERTATION ABSTRACTS INTERNATIONAL, 50(6) (DEC 89),
1792-A.
THE AUTHOR DEFINES THE FUNDAMENTAL CONDITIONS FOR THE
INSTALLATION OF DEMOCRACY, EXPLAINS THE PROCESS OF
LIBERALIZATION, CONSIDERS THE RELATIONSHIP BETWEEN THE
MILITARY AND THE FORM OF GOVERNMENT, AND EVALUATES THE
PROSPECTS FOR DEMOCRACY IN BRAZIL AND ARGENTINA.

09829 YANG, H.I.
FEDERAL DECENTRALIZATION AND DEREGULATION, URBAN
CONDITIONS, AND LOCAL DECISION-MAKING FOR RESOURCE
ALLOCATION: THE CASE OF THE COMMUNITY DEVELOPMENT BLOCK
GRANT
DISSERTATION ABSTRACTS INTERNATIONAL, 50(5) (NOV 89),
1435-A.
THE AUTHOR DISCUSSES HOW FEDERAL DECENTRALIZATION AND
DEREGULATION AFFECT LOCAL RESOURCE ALLOCATION DECISIONS IN
IMPLEMENTING AN INTERGOVERNMENTAL GRANT PROGRAM. HE ALSO
EXAMINES HOW THE LOCAL GOVERNMENT'S FINANCIAL BEHAVIOR IN
RESPONDING TO FEDERAL POLICY CHANGES IS ASSOCIATED WITH
LOCAL SOCIOECONOMIC CONDITIONS. THE COMMUNITY DEVELOPMENT
BLOCK GRANT PROGRAM IS USED AS A CASE STUDY.

09830 YANG, M.M.
BETWEEN STATE AND SOCIETY: THE CONSTRUCTION OF
CORPORATENESS IN A CHINESE SOCIALIST FACTORY
AUSTRALIAN JOURNAL OF CHINESE AFFAIRS, (22) (JUL 89),
31-60.
THE AUTHOR CONSIDERS THE ROLE OF CHINESE SOCIALIST
FACTORY WORK UNITS AND HOW THESE CORPORATE GROUPS FIT INTO
THE LARGER URBAN SOCIAL STRUCTURE THAT WAS INSTITUTED WITH
THE STATE'S RADICAL RECONSTRUCTION OF SOCIETY AFTER 1949. HE
ALSO LOOKS AT THE KINDS OF STRUCTURAL TENSIONS BEING FELT IN
SMALL URBAN INDUSTRIAL ENTERPRISES DURING THE CURRENT
ECONOMIC REFORM AND HOW WORKER-MANAGEMENT STRUGGLES SHOULD
BE INTERPRETED IN A STATE SOCIALIST SYSTEM WHERE THE UNIT OF
PRODUCTION AND THE UNIT OF APPROPRIATION OF SURPLUS DO NOT
COINCIDE.

09831 YANG, M.M.
THE GIFT ECONOMY AND STATE POWER IN CHINA
COMPARATIVE STUDIES IN SOCIETY AND HISTORY, 31(1) (JAN 89),
25-54.
THE STATE APPARATUS IN CHINA TODAY HAS TAKEN UPON ITSELF
ALMOST TOTAL RESPONSIBILITY FOR ADMINISTERING THE SOCIAL AND
ECONOMIC DOMAIN. THE WELFARE AND CONTROL OF THE POPULATION,
THE ORGANIZATION OF PRODUCTION, PLANNING ALL SOCIAL
ACTIVITIES, AND THE DISTRIBUTION OF THE MEANS OF SUBSISTENCE

HAVE BECOME PRIMARY CONCERNS OF ORGANS OF THE STATE. THE
TYPES OF POWER RELATIONSHIPS AND THEIR SOCIAL AND SYMBOLIC
EXPRESSIONS, WHICH HAVE CRYSTALLIZED AROUND THE DISTRIBUTION
AND CIRCULATION OF DESIRABLES IN SUCH A POLITICAL ECONOMY,
ARE THE SUBJECT OF THE PRESENT STUDY. THE STUDY ALSO
EXAMINES HOW CERTAIN COUNTERTECHNIQUES OF POWER DEVIATE FROM
THE LARGER STRATEGY OF POWER EXERCISED THROUGH THE STATE
SOCIALIST POLITICAL ECONOMY, FORMING POCKETS OF
INTRANSIGENCE FROM WITHIN.

09832 YANG, S.
THE ROLE OF MASS MEDIA IN IMMIGRANTS' POLITICAL
SOCIALIZATION:
DISSERTATION ABSTRACTS INTERNATIONAL, 49(9) (MAR 89),
2439-A.
A STUDY OF KOREAN IMMIGRANTS IN NORTHERN CALIFORNIA THIS
STUDY EXAMINES THE RELATIONSHIP BETWEEN IMMIGRANTS' MASS
MEDIA USE AND THEIR POLITICAL SOCIALIZATION. MORE
SPECIFICALLY, THE STUDY FOCUSES ON (A) THE STRUCTURE OF
IMMIGRANTS' CULTURALLY HETEROGENEOUS MEDIA USE, (B) CULTURE-
BOUND EFFECTS OF THE MASS MEDIA IN IMMIGRANTS' POLITICAL
SOCIALIZATION, (C) CONTINGENT EFFECTS OF THE MASS MEDIA
UNDER CERTAIN CONDITIONS, AND (D) MEDIA EFFECTS ON
IMMIGRANTS' PERCEPTIONS OF THE MEDIA-GOVERNMENT RELATIONSHIP.

09833 YANIV, A.
ISRAEL COMES OF AGE
CURRENT HISTORY, 88(535) (FEB 89), 69-72, 100-102.
IN 1988, ISRAEL SUFFERED NO MAJOR UPHEAVALS ON THE
ECONOMIC FRONT AND MADE SOME VERY IMPORTANT STRIDES IN
FOREIGN RELATIONS. BUT THESE WERE OFFSET BY THE PAINFUL
REPERCUSSIONS OF THE INTIFADA, BY CONTINUING INSTABILITY AND
BLOODSHED IN SOUTH LEBANON, AND BY THE DEBILITATING
TRANSFORMATION OF THE PARLIAMENTARY SCENE AS A RESULT OF THE
KNESSET ELECTIONS.

09834 YANKELOVICH, D.; SMOKE, R.
CHANGING COLD WAR ATTITUDES: AMERICA'S "NEW THINKING"
CURRENT, (309) (JAN 89) 32-41.
THE AMERICAN PUBLIC IS WILLING TO EXPERIMENT WITH
WINDING DOWN THE COLD WAR. BUT THIS "NEW THINKING" IN
AMERICA DIFFERS IN AT LEAST ONE IMPORTANT RESPECT FROM
MIKHAIL GORBACHEV'S "NEW THINKING" ABOUT SOVIETAMERICAN
RELATIONS. GORBACHEV SEEMS TO WANT TO MAKE CHANGES SWIFTLY.
AMERICANS INSIST UPON PROCEEDING CAUTIOUSLY, TESTING SOVIET
GOOD FAITH AT EACH STEP. THE AVERAGE AMERICAN WANTS TO
EXPLORE NEW POSSIBILITIES BUT CANNOT EASILY BRUSH ASIDE
FORTY YEARS OF HOSTILITY AND MISTRUST.

09835 YANNIAN, D.
CAN INFLATION BE CURBED?
BEIJING REVIEW, 32(7-8) (FEB 89), 7, 9.
CURTAILING INFLATION INVOLVES A SERIES OF COMPLEX AND
RELATED STEPS. FIRST, IT IS NECESSARY TO UNDERSTAND WHY
INFLATION NEEDS CONTROLLING. THEN ITS CAUSES MUST BE
ANALYZED AND, FINALLY, EFFECTIVE MEASURES MUST BE INSTITUTED
TO CHECK IT.

09836 YANNIAN, D.
ENCOURAGING CLEAN GOVERNMENT, COMBATING CORRUPTION
BEIJING REVIEW, 32(33) (AUG 89), 7.
THE CPC CENTRAL COMMITTEE AND STATE COUNCIL HAVE ACTED
TO MAINTAIN AND PROMOTE THE TRADITION OF HARD WORK AND
HONEST PERFORMANCE OF DUTIES AMONG PUBLIC OFFICIALS. THE
ANTI-CORRUPTION PROGRAM DOES NOT CONSIST MERELY OF EMPTY
SLOGANS. IT ENUMERATES SEVEN STEPS, INCLUDING PROHIBITING
THE CHILDREN OF HIGH-RANKING OFFICIALS FROM ENGAGING IN
COMMERCE, CANCELLING THE "SPECIAL SUPPLY" OF CERTAIN
FOODSTUFFS TO LEADING CADRES, AND PROVIDING OFFICIAL MOTOR
VEHICLES ONLY ACCORDING TO REGULATIONS. LEADING CADRES WILL
BE REQUIRED TO PLAY AN EXEMPLARY ROLE AND FOLLOW THE ANTI-
CORRUPTION RULES CAREFULLY.

09837 YANNIAN, D.
PATRIOTISM, SCIENCE, AND DEMOCRACY
BEIJING REVIEW, 32(18) (MAY 89), 7,9.
THE MAY FOURTH MOVEMENT OPENED A PATH FOR THE
DISSEMINATION OF MARXISM IN CHINA AND HELPED IT QUICKLY
INTEGRATED WITH THE CHINESE WORKERS' MOVEMENT. THE SPIRIT OF
PATRIOTISM, SCIENCE, AND DEMOCRACY DEMONSTRATED BY THE MAY
FOURTH MOVEMENT IS STILL NEEDED IN CHINA TODAY.

09838 YANNIAN, D.
THE ROAD TO STRENGTH AND PROSPERITY
BEIJING REVIEW, 32(32) (AUG 89), 8.
CHINA HAS STRESSED THE SPIRIT OF SELF-RELIANCE IN THE
FACE OF SANCTIONS IMPOSED BY SOME WESTERN COUNTRIES. THIS
EVOKES THE QUESTION WHETHER OR NOT CHINA WILL REVERT TO A
CLOSEDDOOR POLICY. THE ANSWER IS "NO" BECAUSE THE POLICY OF
REFORM AND OPENING TO THE OUTSIDE WORLD HAS PROVED IN
PRACTICE AN EFFECTIVE MEANS TO ACHIEVE STRENGTH AND
PROSPERITY. CHINA, THEREFORE, WILL CONTINUE STEADFASTLY TO
IMPLEMENT THIS POLICY.

09839 YANNOPOULOS, G.N.
THE MANAGEMENT OF TRADE-INDUCED STRUCTURAL ADJUSTMENT: AN
EVALUATION OF THE EC'S INTEGRATED MEDITERRANEAN PROGRAMMES
JOURNAL OF COMMON MARKET STUDIES, XXVII(4) (JUN 89),
283-302.
FROM THE VERY BEGINNING OF THE NEGOTIATIONS FOR THE
LATEST ENLARGEMENT OF THE EUROPEAN COMMUNITY, FRANCE, ITALY,
AND GREECE EXPRESSED FEARS THAT THEIR AGRICULTURAL REGIONS
WOULD BE ADVERSELY AFFECTED BY COMPETITION FROM THE TWO
IBERIAN NEWCOMERS. AFTER PROTRACTED TALKS, THE COUNCIL OF
MINISTERS REACHED A COMMON POSITION ON A PACKAGE OF
ADJUSTMENT MEASURES UNDER THE TITLE "INTEGRATED
MEDITERRANEAN PROGRAMMES." IN THIS ARTICLE, THE AUTHOR
ENDEAVORS TO EVALUATE THE EFFECTIVENESS OF THE IMP'S AS
ADJUSTMENT POLICY MEASURES.

09840 YANOMAMI, D.P.
LETTER TO ALL THE PEOPLES OF THE EARTH
CULTURAL SURVIVAL QUARTERLY, 13(4) (1989), 68-69.
THE AUTHOR, WHO IS A YANOMAMI INDIAN, ARGUES THAT THE
BRAZILIAN GOVERNMENT DOES NOT RESPECT THE RIGHTS OF HIS
PEOPLE AND TREATS THE INDIANS LIKE ANIMALS. HE STATES THAT
THE GOVERNMENT DOESN'T UNDERSTAND INDIAN CUSTOMS OR IDEAS.
HE ACCUSES BRAZILIAN PRESIDENT JOSE SARNEY OF ALLOWING OTHER
NATIONS TO DESTROY YANOMAMI LAND, BUILD ROADS THROUGH INDIAN
TERRITORY, AND MINE INDIAN PROPERTY.

09841 YANOV, A.
NEW THINKING AND AMERICAN "BREZHEVISM"
INTERNATIONAL AFFAIRS (MOSCOW), (3) (MAR 89), 34-41.
THE AUTHOR REVIEWS HOW VARIOUS SCHOOLS OF AMERICAN
POLITICAL THOUGHT HAVE RESPONDED TO PERESTROIKA IN THE
SOVIET UNION. HIS CATEGORIES INCLUDE RICARD NIXON'S
ORWELLIAN WORLD, BRZEZINSKI'S POLITICAL REALISM, THE HARVARD
SCHOOL OF NONINTERVENTION, AND THE PRINCETON SCHOOL OF
DEMILITARIZING THE RIVALRY.

09842 YANOV, A.
NEW THINKING AND AMERICAN "BREZHNEVISM"
INTERNATIONAL AFFAIRS (MOSCOW), (2) (FEB 89), 27-33.
THE AUTHOR SURVEYS THE MAIN SCHOOLS OF AMERICAN FOREIGN
POLITICAL THOUGHT TO SHOW THAT NOT ONE OF THEM IS PREPARED
TO ACCEPT SOVIET "NEW THINKING" WITHOUT QUALIFICATION. THUS,
THERE IS A NEED FOR A WELL THOUGHT OUT AND PRECISELY
DIFFERENTIATED STRATEGY IF NEW THINKING IS TO ENTER THE
INTERNATIONAL ARENA.

09843 YANSHI, Z.
MEDITATION AFTER THE DISTURBANCE
BEIJING REVIEW, 32(32) (AUG 89), 27-31.
NOW THAT CHINA HAS RETURNED TO POLITICAL STABILITY AFTER
THE COUNTER-REVOLUTION REVOLT IN JUNE 1989, THE PEOPLE
HAVE BEGUN TO DRAW LESSONS FROM THEIR BITTER EXPERIENCES.
THEY ARE REALIZING THAT THE DISTURBANCE WAS THE RESULT OF
THE MACRO-INTERNATIONAL CLIMATE AND CHINA'S OWN MICRO-
CLIMATE, WITH COMPLICATED FORCES AT WORK. THESE INCLUDED NOT
ONLY VARIOUS POLITICAL FORCES AT HOME AND ABROAD BUT ALSO
SOME CONSPIRATORIAL REACTIONARIES WHO MANOEUVRED BOTH ON THE
PUBLIC STAGE AND BEHIND THE SCENES.

09844 YAO, Y.
GENDER DIFFERENCES IN ORGANIZATIONAL COMMITMENT AMONG
PUBLIC EMPLOYEES: THE CASE OF TAIWAN, REPUBLIC OF CHINA
DISSERTATION ABSTRACTS INTERNATIONAL, 49(11) (MAY 89),
3504-A.
THE AUTHOR STUDIES THE RELATIONSHIP BETWEEN GENDER AND
ORGANIZATIONAL COMMITMENT AMONG PUBLIC EMPLOYEES IN TAIWAN.
FINDINGS SHOW THAT (1) GENDER IS NOT A CRUCIAL FACTOR
LEADING TO DIFFERENCES IN ORGANIZATIONAL COMMITMENT, (2)
ORGANIZATIONAL COMMITMENT AMONG MEN AND WOMEN IS BASED
ESSENTIALLY ON THE SAME SET OF DETERMINANTS BUT THE
DETERMINANTS VARY IN THE INTENSITY OF THEIR EFFECTS, AND (3)
MANY OTHER PERSONAL AND SITUATIONAL FACTORS ARE STRONGER
PREDICTORS OF ORGANIZATIONAL COMMITMENT THAN IS GENDER.

09845 YAO, Z.
THE EVOLUTION OF SOCIALISM
BEIJING REVIEW, 32(2) (JAN 89), 22-24.
THE SOVIET MODEL OF SOCIALISM WHICH WAS LATER ADOPTED BY
CHINA AND OTHER SOCIALIST COUNTRIES, FOR A CONSIDERABLE
PERIOD, PLAYED A VALUABLE ROLE IN AIDING INDUSTRIAL AND
ECONOMIC DEVELOPMENT. SINCE THEN, HOWEVER, ITS MANY
DRAWBACKS HAVE GROWN EVER MORE APPARENT. AND NOW, IT IS
RAPIDLY BEING TRANSFORMED INTO A MULTIPLICITY OF MODERN
VARIANTS, REFLECTING THE SPECIFIC NATIONAL CONDITIONS OF
INDIVIDUAL COUNTRIES.

09846 YAOBANG, C.
CHINA'S AGRICULTURE AFTER TEN YEARS OF REFORM
CHINA RECONSTRUCTS, XXXVIII(2) (FEB 89), 8-11.
THE REFORMS OF THE PAST DECADE HAVE BROUGHT TREMENDOUS
CHANGES IN CHINESE AGRICULTURE. THE CHRONIC SHORTAGE OF
STAPLE FOOD CROPS HAS BEEN SOLVED AND THE COUNTRY NOW FEEDS
NEARLY ONE-FIFTH OF THE WORLD'S POPULATION. BUT SOME NAGGING

PROBLEMS REMAIN AND MUST BE SOLVED IF CHINA IS TO MEET THE CHALLENGE OF FEEDING 1.25 BILLION PEOPLE BY THE YEAR 2000.

09847 YAOHUA, Z.
MOSCOW'S NEW JAPAN POLICY
BEIJING REVIEW, 32(18) (MAY 89), 17-19.
SINCE MIKHAIL GORBACHEV TOOK OFFICE, THE SOVIET UNION'S POLICY AND ATTITUDE TOWARDS JAPAN HAVE CHANGED, LEADING TO IMPROVEMENTS IN DIPLOMATIC RELATIONS BETWEEN THE TWO COUNTRIES. JAPAN IS TAKING ADVANTAGE OF THIS OPPORTUNITY TO PRESSURE THE SOVIETS TO RETURN THE KURILES, FOUR ISLANDS OFF JAPAN'S HOKAIDO ISLAND OCCUPIED BY THE SOVIET UNION SINCE WORLD WAR II.

09848 YAOPING, X.
THROUGH A GLASS, LIGHTLY
CHINA RECONSTRUCTS, XXXVIII(5) (MAY 89), 40-43.
THE CONCEPT OF "UNDERSTANDING" IS AN IMPORTANT ONE IN CONTEMPORARY CHINA. THE COUNTRY IS EXPERIENCING A PERIOD OF COLLISION BETWEEN THE OLD AND THE NEW, BETWEEN CONSERVATIVE AND LIBERAL. MOST CHINESE LOOK FOR A COMMON GROUND ON THE MAJOR ISSUES WHILE TRYING TO RESERVE THEIR DIFFERENCES ON THE MINOR ONES. IN LARGE COMPANIES, WHERE MISUNDERSTANDINGS AND DISAGREEMENTS CAN HAPPEN ALL TOO EASILY, UNDERSTANDING HAS BECOME PART OF THE CORPORATE CULTURE, A KIND OF FORMAL POLICY AIMED AT KEEPING THINGS RUNNING WITH A MINIMUM OF FRICTION.

09849 YARNOLD, B.M.
UNITED STATES REFUGEE AND ASYLUM POLICY: FACTORS THAT IMPACT LEGISLATIVE, ADMINISTRATIVE, AND JUDICIAL DECISIONS
DISSERTATION ABSTRACTS INTERNATIONAL, 49(10) (APR 89), 3145-A.
THE AUTHOR STUDIES FACTORS THAT HAVE IMPACTED THE UNITED STATES' REFUGEE AND ASYLUM POLICY SINCE 1980. HE CONSIDERS THE INFLUENCE OF SUCH FACTORS AS STATE AND LOCAL ORGANIZATIONS, PUBLIC INTEREST GROUPS, CONGRESSMEN, AND ADMINISTRATIVE DECISION-MAKERS. THE ANALYSIS EXTENDS TO DECISION-MAKING BY THE JUDICIAL BRANCH, INCLUDING FEDERAL DISTRICT COURTS AND COURTS OF APPEAL.

09850 YASUO, T.
EMERGING ECONOMIC INEQUITIES
JAPAN ECHO, XVI(2) (SUM 89), 45-46.
STATISTICS TELL US THAT JAPAN IS AN EXCEPTIONALLY HEALTHY COUNTRY. ITS EXTERNAL ASSETS ARE THE WORLD'S LARGEST AND ITS WAGES ARE AMONG THE WORLD'S HIGHEST. BUT THE MAJORITY OF JAPANESE DO NOT FEEL ESPECIALLY RICH, PARTIALLY DUE TO THE INADEQUACIES IN THE GOVERNMENT'S APPROACH TO HEALTH REDISTRIBUTION.

09851 YASUO, T.
RECRUIT IN REVIEW
JAPAN ECHO, XVI(3) (AUT 89), 38-39.
THE RECRUIT SCANDAL FORCED 43 JAPANESE POLITICIANS AND OFFICIALS, INCLUDING PRIME MINISTER TAKESHITA NOBORU AND FINANCE MINISTER MIYAZAWA KIICHI, TO RESIGN THEIR POSITIONS. IN THIS ARTICLE, THE AUTHOR BRIEFLY REVIEWS THE SCANDAL AND ITS CONSEQUENCES.

09852 YATES, I.
MARKET FORCES AND THE DEFENSE INDUSTRIES
RUSI JOURNAL, 134(4) (WIN 89), 58-62.
THE ARTICLE DEVELOPS THE CONCEPT THAT A NATION'S MILITARY STRENGTH IS DEFINED IN TERMS OF ITS ECONOMIC POTENTIAL, ESPECIALLY THE BASIC WEALTH CREATING SECTORS. THE ARTICLE SPECIFICALLY EXAMINES GREAT BRITAIN WHERE THE RELATIVE DECLINE IN MANUFACTURING OUTSIDE THE DEFENSE INDUSTRIAL BASE MAY TEND TO UNDERMINE THE COUNTRY'S ECONOMIC AND NATIONAL SECURITY. AFTER AN ANALYSIS OF THE HISTORICAL TRENDS THAT LED TO THE CURRENT PROBLEMS, THE ARTICLE CONCLUDES THAT REMEDIAL MEASURES, PARTICULARLY SUBSTANTIAL INCREASES IN RESEARCH AND DEVELOPMENT SPENDING, ARE NECESSARY TO IMPROVE THE TECHNOLOGICAL COMPETITIVENESS OF UK DEFENSE INDUSTRIES.

09853 YATES, L. A.
FROM SMALL WARS TO COUNTERINSURGENCY: US MILITARY INTERVENTIONS IN LATIN AMERICA SINCE 1898
MILITARY REVIEW, LXIX(2) (FEB 89), 74-86.
THE RECENT FLURRY OF ACTIVITY IN DOCTRINE DEVELOPMENT AND PUBLIC DEBATE IN THE BROADENING ARENA OF LOWINTENSITY CONFLICT (LIC) AT TIMES APPEARS TO TREAT THE SUBJECT AS A NEW OR MODERN PHENOMENA. THE AUTHOR REMINDS US THAT THE US MILITARY HAS FREQUENTLY BEEN REQUIRED TO ENTER INTO ACTIONS ABROAD THAT WOULD NOW BE INCLUDED IN OUR LIC DEFINITIONS. HE REVIEWS AND LOOKS FOR LESSONS IN SEVERAL OF WHAT WAS THEN CALLED "SMALL WARS" AROUND THE TURN OF THE CENTURY.

09854 YATES, L.A.
MOUNTING AN INTERVENTION: THE DOMINICAN REPUBLIC, 1965
MILITARY REVIEW, LXIX(3) (MAR 89), 50-61.
IN TERMS OF ACCOMPLISHING ITS MISSIONS, THE JOINT CONTINGENCY/PEACEKEEPING OPERATION LAUNCHED BY THE UNITED STATES IN THE DOMINICAN REPUBLIC WAS A SUCCESS. BUT DESPITE THIS SUCCESS, THE MILITARY RECOGNIZED THAT THE PROCESS OF PREPARING AND MOUNTING THE OPERATION HAD NOT GONE SMOOTHLY IN SUCH CRITICAL AREAS AS COMMAND AND CONTROL, PLANNING, COORDINATION, COMMUNICATION, INTELLIGENCE, DEPLOYMENT AND SUPPORT. A SENSE OF HISTORY AND A CRYSTAL BALL WOULD HAVE REVEALED THAT A PERFECT CONFLUENCE BETWEEN DOCTRINE AND PRACTICE, PLAN AND EXECUTION, NEED AND AVAILABILITY HAS NEVER BEEN AND NEVER WILL BE ACHIEVED IN JOINT (OR ANY OTHER KIND OF MILITARY) OPERATIONS HAD US TROOPS IN THE DOMINICAN REPUBLIC FACED A WELL-ORGANIZED, WELL-ARMED, WELL-TRAINED, HIGHLY DISCIPLINED OPPONENT, THE PROBLEMS EXPERIENCED IN MOUNTING THE INTERVENTION COULD HAVE BEEN COSTLY. TIME WAS ON THE SIDE OF THE UNITED STATES IN THE DOMINICAN INTERVENTION AND IT ALLOWED THE SYSTEM TO RESPOND SLOWLY TO THE UNEXPECTED DEMANDS PLACED ON IT.

09855 YAZOV, D.
IN THE INTERESTS OF UNIVERSAL SECURITY AND PEACE
REPRINTS FROM THE SOVIET PRESS, 48(8) (APR 89), 16-20.
IN AN INTERVIEW WITH THE NEWSPAPER IZVESTIA, DEFENSE MINISTER DIMITRI YAZOV DISCUSSES THE UNILATERAL TROOP REDUCTIONS BY THE USSR IN EUROPE AND ASIA. HE EMPHASIZED THE UNILATERAL NATURE OF THE REDUCTIONS BUT STATED THAT ANY CORRESPONDING MOVE BY THE WEST WAS WELCOME. HE ALSO EMPHASIZED THAT THE TROOPS WERE BEING REDUCED AND NOT MERELY REDEPLOYED.

09856 YE, R.
THE GRADUAL APPROACH TO PRICE REFORM
CHINA RECONSTRUCTS, XXXVIII(2) (FEB 89), 16-19.
THE DUAL PRICING SYSTEM PERMEATES EVERY ASPECT OF EVERYDAY CHINESE LIFE. COMMODITIES ARE AVAILABLE IN STATE-OWNED SHOPS AT HEAVILY SUBSIDIZED RATES AND ARE ALSO AVAILABLE ON THE OPEN MARKET AT DOUBLE OR TRIPLE THE STATE PRICE. THIS PRICING SYSTEM, TOGETHER WITH INFLATION, HAS CAUSED WIDESPREAD DISSATISFACTION AMONG THE PEOPLE. THE DUAL PRICING SYSTEM HAS BEEN IN OPERATION SINCE 1984 AND IS OFTEN VIEWED AS A NECESSARY TRANSITIONAL MEASURE IN THE PROCESS OF REFORM.

09857 YEAGER, R.
DEMOCRATIC PLURALISM AND ECOLOGICAL CRISIS IN BOTSWANA
JOURNAL OF DEVELOPING AREAS, 23(3) (APR 89), 385-404.
THIS ARTICLE EXAMINES THE POLITICS OF CATTLE, NATURAL RESOURCES AND ENVIRONMENT IN MODERN BOTSWANA. THE NATIONAL CONSERVATION STRATEGY MAY AFFORD THE NECESSARY POLICY GUIDANCE FOR ECOLOGICAL REFORM IF IT ESCAPES BEING COOPTED IN THE SAME MANNER AS THE TRIBAL GRAZING LAND POLICY. DISTRICT COUNCILS AND LAND BOARDS MAY SERVE CONSERVATION GOALS IF THEY ARE SUPPLIED WITH STAFF TRAINED NOT ONLY TO OFFER TECHNICAL EXPERTISE BUT ALSO TO TEMPORIZE WITH HEGEMONIC MINISTRIES AND CATTLE HUNGRY CHIEFS ON BEHALF OF BROAD-BASED RURAL DEVELOPMENT. BOTSWANA'S PLURALIST DEMOCRACY AND ECOLOGICAL SURVIVAL DEPENDS ON THESE CONTINGENCIES.

09858 YEFREMOV, A.
THE FIRST STEP TOWARDS A NUCLEAR-FREE WORLD
WORLD TRADE UNION MOVEMENT, 2 (1988), 10-13.
THIS ARTICLE EXAMINES THE RESULTS OF THE SOVIET AMERICAN SUMMIT MEETING WHERE AN AGREEMENT TO BEGIN TO DE-ESCALATE THE NUCLEAR ARMS RACE WAS SIGNED. EXPLORED IS WHAT THIS AGREEMENT MEANS TO THE WORKERS OF THE WORLD. THE EFFECT OF THE ARMS RACE ON THE DEVELOPING COUNTRIES AND HOW THE FREED RESOURCES COULD RAISE THE STANDARD OF LIVING IN BOTH CAPITALIST AND SOCIALIST COUNTRIES ARE STUDIED. THE PROCESS OF CONVERSION PLANS FOR MILITARY INDUSTRIES IS ADDRESSED. POSSIBILITIES FOR JOINT TRADE UNION ACTIVITIES OF EAST-WEST ARE EXAMINED.

09859 YEH, M.D.
TIENANMEN: CRUSHING A GODDESS
FREE CHINA REVIEW, 39(8) (AUG 89), 15-17.
PEKING'S BIGGEST MASS PROTEST IN THE POST-MAO PERIOD WAS NOT TOTALLY UNEXPECTED. NUMEROUS FACTORS CONTRIBUTED TO THE MOMENTUM OF THE EVENTS, FROM THE DEATH OF HU YAO-PANG ON APRIL 15, 1989, UNTIL THE SOUND OF AUTOMATIC WEAPON FIRE ON JUNE 4 AWAKENED THE WORLD TO THE REALITY OF POLITICAL SUPPRESSION IN MAINLAND CHINA.

09860 YELDAN, A.E.
STRUCTURAL ADJUSTMENT AND TRADE IN TURKEY: INVESTIGATING THE ALTERNATIVES "BEYOND EXPORT-LED GROWTH"
JOURNAL OF POLICY MODELING, 11(2) (SUM 89), 273-296.
THE ARTICLE SEARCHES FOR A VIABLE ALTERNATIVE FOR TURKEY'S ECONOMY TO RESOLVE ITS CURRENT CONFRONTATION WITH THE DILEMMA OF STABILIZATION AND GROWTH. WITH THE AID OF A DYNAMIC, COMPUTABLE, GENERAL EQUILIBRIUM MODEL, IT IS ARGUED THAT AN INTEGRATED, INDUSTRIALIZATION STRATEGY THAT COMBINES A DOMESTIC-DEMAND-BASED, WAGE-GOODS-ORIENTED PUBLIC INVESTMENT PROGRAM WITH A SELECTIVE EXPORT-PROMOTION SCHEME PROMISES TO BE THE MOST APPROPRIATE ONE SERVING TURKEY'S LONG-TERM INDUSTRIALIZATION INTERESTS. THE MODEL RESULTS

FURTHER EMPHASIZE THE PRESSING NEED FOR THE REVITALIZATION OF THE DOMESTIC DEMAND AND THE IMPORTANCE OF THE AGRICULTURAL PRODUCTIVITY GROWTH IN PROMOTING TURKEY'S OVERALL OBJECTIVES OF INDUSTRIALIZATION, INCOME EQUITY, AND FOREIGN TRADE OVER THE FIFTH AND SIXTH PLAN PERIODS.

09861 YEN-LIN, K.
THE FEMINIST MOVEMENT IN TAIWAN, 1972-87
BULLETIN OF CONCERNED ASIAN SCHOLARS, 21(1) (JAN 89), 12-23.
THE ARTICLE EXPLORES THE DEVELOPMENT AND GROWTH OF THE FEMINIST MOVEMENT IN TAIWAN. IT EXAMINES THE SOCIAL CONTEXT AND ORIGINS OF THE MOVEMENT INCLUDING THE IMPOSITION OF MARTIAL LAW AND THE RULING PARTY'S POLICY ON WOMEN. IT ALSO OUTLINES THE STAGES OF DEVELOPMENT OF THE MOVEMENT BEGINING WITH THE PIONEERING PERIOD, MOVING TO THE PERIOD OF AWAKENING, AND ON THE POST-MARTIAL LAW PERIOD.

09862 YEOM, J.
A BUREAUCRATIC ORGANIZATION IN A NETWORK SETTING: MITI AND JAPANESE INDUSTRIAL POLICY FOR HIGH TECHNOLOGY
DISSERTATION ABSTRACTS INTERNATIONAL, 50(6) (DEC 89), 1801-A.
THE AUTHOR EXAMINES THE CHARACTERISTICS OF JAPANESE INDUSTRIAL POLICY AND THE POLICY-MAKING PROCESS. HE EXPLORES TWO PERSPECTIVES: THE BUREAUCRATIC ORGANIZATIONAL PERSPECTIVE AND THE NETWORK RELATIONS PERSPECTIVE. TWO RESEARCH METHODS ARE UTILIZED: A CASE STUDY OF THE POLICY-MAKING PROCESS OF THE VERY LARGE SCALE INTEGRATED CIRCUIT PROJECT AND AN ANALYSIS OF MITI EVALUATIONS OF THE INDUSTRIAL POLICY-MAKING PROCESS BY INTERVIEW METHODS.

09863 YEUNG, I.
MANAGING A SHIFTING POPULATION
FREE CHINA REVIEW, 39(10) (OCT 89), 22-31.
THE AUTHOR LOOKS AT SOME OF THE IMPLICATIONS OF TAIWAN'S EXPANDING POPULATION FOR GOVERNMENT PLANNING AND POPULATION POLICY.

09864 YEUNG, I.
SPECIAL INTEREST ACTIVISTS
FREE CHINA REVIEW, 39(12) (DEC 89), 46-52.
SINCE TAIWAN LIFTED MARTIAL LAW AND PASSED THE CIVIC ORGANIZATIONS LAW, STREET DEMONSTRATIONS HAVE BECOME AN ALMOST DAILY EVENT IN TAIPEI. THEY ARE ORGANIZED BY SELF-HELP GROUPS OR SPECIAL INTEREST GROUPS AND CIVIC ORGANIZATIONS FORMED BY THE GENERAL PUBLIC. THEY REFLECT THE IMMENSE WAVE OF SOCIAL CHANGE THAT IS SWEEPING TAIWAN. POLITICAL DEMOCRATIZATION HAS OPENED THE DOOR FOR THESE NEW SOCIAL GROUPINGS, BUT MANY OF THEM STILL HAVE FLUID OR UNCLEAR GOALS AND ORGANIZATIONAL METHODS.

09865 YEVDOKIMOV, A.
USSR-PORTUGAL: A NEW IMPETUS TO TRADE AND ECONOMIC RELATIONS.
FOREIGN TRADE, 4 (1988), 31-32.
THIS ARTICLE EXAMINES THE TURN ABOUT IN TRADE BETWEEN USSR AND PORTUGAL AFTER 1986. IT EXPLORES THE OBJECTIVE REASONS FOR THE EARLIER DECREASE IN MUTUAL TRADE, AS WELL AS THE CAUSE FOR A MORE POSITIVE SHIFT. VISITS MADE AND AGREEMENTS SIGNED ARE DETAILED. TRADE SEMINARS ARE REPORTED.

09866 YI-MING, C.
CAMPAIGN STRATEGIST
FREE CHINA REVIEW, 39(12) (DEC 89), 32-33.
WANG SHU-CHING IS THE CHIEF COMMISSIONER OF THE KMT TAIPEI CITY COMMITTEE. IN THIS INTERVIEW, HE DISCUSSES TAIWAN'S DECEMBER 1989 ELECTIONS AND SOME OF THE CAMPAIGN STRATEGIES UTILIZED BY THE RULING PARTY TO CULTIVATE THE ELECTORATE.

09867 YI-MING, C.
CULTIVATING IMAGES
FREE CHINA REVIEW, 39(12) (DEC 89), 24-29.
ALTHOUGH TAIWAN'S OFFICIAL CAMPAIGN PERIOD DOES NOT BEGIN UNTIL 15 DAYS BEFORE THE ELECTION, CANDIDATES SPEND MONTHS PURSUING ACTIVITIES GUARANTEED TO KEEP THEM IN THE PUBLIC EYE. THEY PLACE "NON-POLITICAL" ADS IN NEWSPAPERS AND APPEAR ON TELEVISION TALK SHOWS, GAME SHOWS, AND DISCUSSION PANELS. SOME CAMPAIGN PUBLICITY TACTICS USED IN TAIWAN ARE IDENTICAL TO THOSE IN THE WEST WHILE OTHER CAMPAIGN METHODS HAVE A DISTINCTLY ORIENTAL FLAVOR.

09868 YI-MING, C.
NO LONGER THE SILENT MAJORITY
FREE CHINA REVIEW, 39(11) (NOV 89), 20-25.
IN THIS ARTICLE, TWO REPORTERS AND AN ATTORNEY DISCUSS THE IMAGE OF TAIWAN'S MIDDLE CLASS AS THE "SILENT MAJORITY" AND GIVE THEIR OPINIONS ON HOW WELL THE GOVERNMENT RESPONDS TO THE CONCERNS OF THE MIDDLE CLASS.

09869 YI-MING, C.
POST-MASSACRE TREMORS
FREE CHINA REVIEW, 39(10) (OCT 89), 44-46.

IN THIS INTERVIEW, CHAO CHUN-SHAN ASSESSES THE CONSEQUENCES OF THE TIENANMEN SQUARE MASSACRE, BOTH INSIDE AND OUTSIDE MAINLAND CHINA.

09870 YI, Z.
THE U.S. CONGRESS AND SINO-U.S. RELATIONS
BEIJING REVIEW, 32(20) (MAY 89), 32-35.
TEN YEARS HAVE PASSED SINCE THE ESTABLISHMENT OF SINO-AMERICAN DIPLOMATIC RELATIONS. THIS ARTICLE LOOKS AT THE ROLE OF CONGRESS, WHICH ON THE WHOLE HAS PLAYED A POSITIVE ROLE IN PROMOTING THE DEVELOPMENT OF RELATIONS BETWEEN THE USA AND COMMUNIST CHINA.

09871 YICK, J.K.S.
THE URBAN STRATEGY OF THE CHINESE COMMUNIST PARTY: THE CASE OF BEIPING-TIANJIN, 1945-49
DISSERTATION ABSTRACTS INTERNATIONAL, 50(2) (AUG 89), 536-A.
THE URBAN AND RURAL STRATEGIES OF THE CHINESE COMMUNIST PARTY WERE TWO MAJOR FACTORS IN THE COMMUNIST CONQUEST OF CHINA. THIS DISSERTATION STUDIES THE COMMUNIST URBAN STRATEGY IN A SPECIFIC AREA IN NORTH CHINA, WHICH WAS THE BASIC SOURCE OF STRENGTH FOR THE PARTY, USING A POLITICAL-ADMINISTRATIVE APPROACH STRENGTHENED BY AN IDEOLOGICAL FRAMEWORK.

09872 YILIN, Y.
REPORT ON THE DRAFT 1989 PLAN FOR NATIONAL ECONOMIC AND SOCIAL DEVELOPMENT
BEIJING REVIEW, 32(18) (MAY 89), I-X.
THE AUTHOR, WHO IS VICE-PREMIER OF THE CHINESE STATE COUNCIL AND MINISTER IN CHARGE OF THE STATE PLANNING COMMISSION, REVIEWS THE PROGRESS MADE BY CHINA IN ITS MODERNIZATION DRIVE IN 1988. THEN HE DISCUSSES THE PROPOSED PLAN FOR NATIONAL ECONOMIC AND SOCIAL DEVELOPMENT FOR 1989.

09873 YIN, L.
CHINESE WOMEN IN POLITICS
CHINA RECONSTRUCTS, XXXVIII(9) (SEP 89), 16-18.
IN PRE-COMMUNIST CHINA, WOMEN DID NOT ENJOY EQUALITY WITH MEN, THE RIGHT TO VOTE, OR THE PRIVILEGE OF HOLDING OFFICE. SINCE 1949, THE COMMUNIST GOVERNMENT HAS RECRUITED AND TRAINED AS MANY WOMEN AS POSSIBLE FOR RESPONSIBLE POSITIONS AT ALL LEVELS. THE RESULT HAS BEEN A STEADY RISE IN THE NUMBER OF FEMALE OFFICIALS, ALTHOUGH CERTAIN PROBLEMS PERSIST IN INTEGRATING WOMEN INTO POLITICAL LIFE.

09874 YIN, N.
REJUVENATING THE FINANCIAL SYSTEM
FREE CHINA REVIEW, 39(1) (JAN 89), 4-7.
MAKING SUBSTANTIAL CHANGES IN NATIONAL FINANCIAL POLICY ENTAILS CONSIDERABLE RISKS, BUT THE TAIWANESE GOVERNMENT RECENTLY HAS EXPERIENCED MOUNTING DOMESTIC AND INTERNATIONAL PRESSURE FOR CHANGE IN THE ISLAND'S FINANCIAL SYSTEM. THE LEGACY OF THE PAST RECOMMENDS CAUTION AND THE EXERCISE OF WISDOM, WHILE THE CURRENT PACE OF ECONOMIC GROWTH AND FOREIGN EXCHANGE ACQUISITION DICTATES IMMEDIATE ACTION. AT PRESENT, THE PROCESS OF FORMULATING NEW FINANCIAL POLICIES IS STILL IN PROGRESS IN TAIWAN.

09875 YITRI, M.
THE CRISIS IN BURMA: BACK FROM THE HEART OF DARKNESS?
ASIAN SURVEY, XXIX(6) (JUN 89), 543-558.
THE ARTICLE RECOUNTS THE EVENTS THAT ROCKED BURMA IN 1988. THESE EVENTS INCLUDE RIOTS, MASS ARRESTS, BRUTAL KILLINGS, THE FALL OF THREE PRESIDENTS AND A MILITARY COUP. IT SEEKS TO ANALYZE THE UNDERLYING POLITICAL, ECONOMIC AND SOCIAL CAUSES FOR THE PLUNGE INTO NEAR-ANARCHY. IT CONCLUDES THAT THE ONE-PARTY GOVERNMENT BECAME INCREASINGLY OUT OF TOUCH WITH THE PEOPLE IT LED AND EVENTUALLY HAD TO RELY UPON THE "MANDATE OF THE GUN" TO REMAIN IN POWER. BURMA'S CRUMBLING ECONOMY AND TEARING SOCIAL FABRIC WILL REQUIRE EXTENSIVE AND FUNDAMENTAL REFORMS TO REPAIR.

09876 YIXIAN, X.
CHINA'S FOREIGN POLICY: A 1980'S TUNE-UP
BEIJING REVIEW, 32(7-8) (FEB 89), 16-21.
CHINA'S FOREIGN POLICY WENT THROUGH A SERIES OF ADJUSTMENTS IN THE 1980'S. IT WAS TRANSFORMED BY EXTERNAL CHANGES IN INTERNATIONAL SITUATIONS AND INTERPRETATIONS REGARDING SUPERPOWER POLICY AND RELATIONS. DEVELOPMENTS REGARDING U.S.-SOVIET RELATIONS WERE PARTICULARLY INFLUENTIAL IN FORMULATING CHINESE FOREIGN POLICY.

09877 YOCHELSON, J.; HUNTER, R.
1992 WILL CHANGE THE TRANS-ATLANTIC RELATIONSHIP
EUROPE, (285) (APR 89), 14-15, 47.
AS THE EUROPEAN NATIONS MOVE TOWARDS INCREASED INTEGRATION IN 1992, A SYSTEMATIC RETHINKING OF THE RELATIONSHIP BETWEEN THE US AND EUROPE IS NECESSARY. THE ARTICLE OUTLINES IMPLICATIONS FOR THE US OF EUROPEAN INTEGRATION IN THE INCREASINGLY INTERCONNECTED AREAS OF BOTH COMMERCIAL AND SECURITY RELATED ISSUES. THE TRILLION DOLLAR COMMERCIAL RELATIONSHIP IS ANALYZED AS WELL AS IMPACT ON

OVERALL GLOBAL TRADE; THE ISSUES OF POLITICS AND SECURITY
ARE ALSO EXAMINED.

09878 YOICHI, M.
FOCUS ON FOREIGN AID
JAPAN ECHO, XVI(1) (SPR 89), 6-7.
CHANGES IN THE GLOBAL ECONOMY HAVE NATURALLY LED THE
WORLD TO EXPECT MORE OF JAPAN. PEOPLE EVERYWHERE ARE CALLING
ON JAPAN TO PLAY A LARGER ROLE IN INTERNATIONAL AFFAIRS. THE
UNITED STATES WANTS JAPAN AND WESTERN EUROPE TO SHOULDER
MORE OF THE GLOBAL BURDEN. BUT JAPAN'S ANTI-WAR CONSTITUTION
LIMITS THE COUNTRY'S ABILITY TO ASSIST IN THE MILITARY
SPHERE. THIS ACCOUNTS FOR THE JAPANESE FOCUS ON ECONOMIC
COOPERATION, AND ESPECIALLY FOREIGN AID TO DEVELOPING
COUNTRIES, AS A WAY OF DOING ITS PART FOR THE REST OF THE
WORLD.

09879 YOICHI, M.
ONE-PARTY RULE ON TRIAL
JAPAN ECHO, XVI(3) (AUT 89), 5-6.
THE OUTLOOK HAS TURNED CLOUDY FOR THE CONTINUED REIGN OF
THE LIBERAL DEMOCRATIC PARTY. THE PARTY'S PROBLEMS ARE THREE-
FOLD. ONE PROBLEM IS THE UPROAR OVER THE RECRUIT GROUP'S
STOCK DEALS AND POLITICAL CONTRIBUTIONS, WHICH HAVE ERODED
PUBLIC TRUST IN THE POLITICIANS WHO BENEFITED FROM THEM.
ANOTHER IS THE CONSUMPTION TAX, WHICH IS HIGHLY UNPOPULAR
BECAUSE IT ADDS THREE PERCENT TO THE PRICE OF MOST CONSUMER
GOODS. THE THIRD PROBLEM IS RURAL DISCONTENT WITH THE
GOVERNMENT'S EFFORTS TO LIBERALIZE THE AGRICULTURAL SECTOR.

09880 YOICHI, M.; EIICHI, N.; KEIZO, O.; TOSHIFUMI, T.
POLITICS IN TRANSITION: THREE LEADERS SPEAK OUT
JAPAN ECHO, XVI(3) (AUT 89), 31-37.
THE AUTHORS CONSIDER THE DILEMMAS FACING THE LIBERAL
DEMOCRATIC PARTY, WHICH HAS RULED JAPAN FOR NEARLY FOUR
DECADES. AFTER FORTY YEARS IN POWER, MANY OF THE PARTY'S
ORIGINAL GOALS HAVE BEEN ACHIEVED AND IT FACES A TIME OF
TRANSITION WHEN IT MUST MOVE ON TO A NEW VISION WHILE
HOLDING ONTO ITS BASIC COMMITMENTS TO PRINCIPLES LIKE
LIBERALISM AND DEMOCRACY.

09881 YOICHI, M.
THE FSX FIGHTER FLAP
JAPAN ECHO, XVI(3) (AUT 89), 57-58.
INITIALLY INTENDED TO BE AN INDEPENDENT JAPANESE PROJECT,
THE DEVELOPMENT AND PRODUCTION OF THE FSX PLANE BECAME A
JOINT JAPANESE-AMERICAN UNDERTAKING AT U.S. INSISTENCE.
REPRESENTATIVES OF THE TWO GOVERNMENTS THRASHED OUT AN
AGREEMENT ON THE JOINT PROJECT, WHICH WAS FORMALIZED ON
NOVEMBER 29, 1988. ALTHOUGH SOME MEMBERS OF JAPAN'S DEFENSE
ESTABLISHMENT WERE UNHAPPY WITH THE ACCORD BECAUSE THEY
BELIEVED IT WAS AN EXCESSIVE SACRIFICE OF JAPANESE SECURITY
INTERESTS, THE GOVERNMENT AS A WHOLE FELT THAT THE
CONCESSIONS WERE NECESSARY FOR THE SAKE OF A HEALTHY
BILATERAL RELATIONSHIP. MUCH TO THE JAPANESE GOVERNMENT'S
SURPRISE, THE AGREEMENT HAS COME UNDER ATTACK WITHIN THE
UNITED STATES.

09882 YONGXING, X.
ELECTION FEVER BEGINS IN BRITAIN
BEIJING REVIEW, 32(45) (NOV 89), 16-17.
THE RACE IS ALREADY ON BETWEEN BRITAIN'S RULING
CONSERVATIVES AND THE OPPOSITION LABOR PARTY FOR THE NEXT
GENERAL ELECTION IN 1992. LABOUR HAS ENTERED THE RACE AS A
SLIGHT FAVORITE BECAUSE THE GOVERNMENT OF PRIME MINISTER
THATCHER IS CURRENTLY BESET WITH A SERIES OF ECONOMIC
PROBLEMS AND RISING DISCONTENT OVER ITS RADICAL SOCIAL
REFORM PROGRAMS.

09883 YONGYAO, W.
OPENING NEW DOORS TO DEVELOPMENT
CHINA RECONSTRUCTS, XXXVIII(3) (MAR 89), 8-12.
THIS IS A PROFILE OF GOVERNOR HE ZHIQIANG OF YUNNAN
PROVINCE. THE AUTHOR REVIEWS THE GOVERNOR'S ACHIEVEMENTS AND
HIS PLANS FOR THE CONTINUED FUTURE DEVELOPMENT OF THE
PROVINCE.

09884 YORKE, V.
HUSSEIN AND HASHEMITE LEGITIMACY
MIDDLE EAST INTERNATIONAL, (363) (NOV 89), 17-19.
THE ARTICLE EXAMINES JORDAN'S KING HUSSEIN'S CALL FOR
PARLIAMENTARY ELECTIONS. IT CONCLUDES THAT HUSSEIN HAS NO
INTENTIONS TO ABANDON THE POWER HE HAS HELD FOR 37 YEARS.
INSTEAD, THE REFORMS SHOULD BE VIEWED AS A MECHANISM
DESIGNED TO LEGITIMIZE HASHEMITE RULE IN THE EYES OF BOTH
TRANSJORDANIANS AND EAST BANK PALESTINIANS. HUSSEIN SHREWDLY
REALIZES THAT THE JORDANIAN GOVERNMENT WILL BE FORCED TO
MAKE SOME UNPOPULAR ECONOMIC DECISIONS IN THE NEAR FUTURE;
AN INCREASED IN PARLIAMENTARY PARTICIPATION WOULD DISTANCE
HUSSEIN AND THE THRONE FROM THESE UNPOPULAR DECISIONS.

09885 YOSHIKAZU, K.
PRIVATIZATION IN GLOBAL PERSPECTIVE
JAPAN ECHO, XVI(1) (SPR 89), 37-43.

SINCE SERVICES THAT HAD TRADITIONALLY BEEN REGARDED AS
THE EXCLUSIVE PRESERVE OF GOVERNMENT ARE NOW BEING PLACED IN
PRIVATE HANDS, SOME OF THE ACCEPTED CONCEPTS ON WHICH MODERN
SOCIETY IS BASED ARE BEGINNING TO BREAK DOWN. THIS ARTICLE
SURVEYS SOME OF THE MAJOR PRIVATIZATION PROJECTS IN EUROPE
AND THE UNITED STATES AND DISCUSSES SOME OF THE
PRIVATIZATION OPTIONS OPEN TO JAPAN.

09886 YOSHITOMI, M.
YEN APPRECIATION, STRUCTURAL REFORMS, AND EXTERNAL
IMBALANCES: INTERNATIONAL AND DOMESTIC FACTORS IN JAPAN'S
ECONOMIC ADJUSTMENT
INTERNATIONAL SPECTATOR, XXIV(3-4) (JUL 89), 198-207.
THIS PAPER EXAMINES RECENT ECONOMIC DEVELOPMENTS IN
JAPAN, FOCUSING ON THE FOLLOWING: THE NATURE OF STRUCTURAL
REFORMS AND THEIR RELEVANCE TO A MACROECONOMIC EXCESS OF
SAVINGS OVER INVESTMENT IN JAPAN; DRIVING FORCES BEHIND
STRUCTURAL REFORMS AND INTERNATIONAL POLICY COORDINATION;
AND CHARACTERISTICS OF THE CURRENT RESTRUCTURING OF THE
JAPANESE ECONOMY.

09887 YOTOPOULOS, P.A.
THE (RIP) TIDE OF PRIVATIZATION: LESSONS FROM CHILE
WORLD DEVELOPMENT, 17(5) (MAY 89), 683-702.
CHILE IS ONE OF THE RARE EXCEPTIONS WHERE THE VOLUBLE
ENTHUSIASM FOR PRIVATIZATION HAS BEEN PUT INTO EFFECT. OF
THE 500 COMPANIES THAT WERE UNDER STATE OWNERSHIP IN THE
EARLY 1970S, ONLY 19 REMAINED UNDER PUBLIC CONTROL AT THE
END OF THE DECADE. PRIVATIZATION INDISPUTABLY INCREASED THE
ECONOMIC POWER OF A NUMBER OF CONGLOMERATES AND FOSTERED THE
CONCENTRATION OF ASSETS. HOWEVER, THE COMPLEXITY OF THE
LIBERALIZATION PACKAGE THAT ACCOMPANIED PRIVATIZATION MAKES
IT DIFFICULT TO ESTABLISH STRICT CAUSALITY FOR THE ECONOMIC
COLLAPSE THAT FOLLOWED IN THE EARLY 1980S. THE CHILEAN
EXPERIENCE WITH PRIVATIZATION REVEALS SOME INTERESTING
LESSONS THAT OTHER COUNTRIES MAY WISH TO CONSIDER.

09888 YOUNG, D.G.
HUNGARY: DEBT VERSUS REFORM
WORLD TODAY, 45(10) (OCT 89), 171-175.
THE LEGACY OF STALINIST ECONOMIC DEVELOPMENT AND HALF-
HEATED REFORM UNDER JANOS KADAR HAVE LEFT HUNGARY WITH AN
ECONOMY THAT IS NEITHER CENTRALLY-PLANNED NOR MARKET-
ORIENTED. IT IS PLAGUED BY IMBALANCE, UNCERTAINTY AND
STAGNATION, WHILE ITS PRODUCTS ARE BECOMING LESS AND LESS
COMPETITIVE ON WESTERN MARKETS, MAKING ANY REDUCTION IN THE
HIGH LEVEL OF DEBT UNLIKELY IN THE FORESEEABLE FUTURE. THE
EXPORT SECTOR IS TORN BETWEEN THE NEED TO COMPETE IN TOUGH
WESTERN MARKETS AND THE EASY OPTION OF EXPORTING LOW-QUALITY,
LOW-TECH GOODS TO THE COMECON COUNTRIES. SO HUNGARY FACES A
DIFFICULT DILEMMA. ON ONE HAND, IT MUST MAINTAIN STABILITY
ON THE CURRENT ACCOUNT. ON THE OTHER, THE ECONOMY MUST BE
RADICALLY REFORMED. MARKET FORCES MUST BE INTRODUCED,
INDUSTRY RESTRUCTURED, AND THE INFRASTRUCTURE IMPROVED. YET
CARE MUST BE TAKEN TO INSURE THAT GOODS FLOW, INFLATION IS
CONTROLLED, AND THE STANDARD OF LIVING DOES NOT WORSEN.

09889 YOUNG, F. E.; NORRIS, J. A.
LEADERSHIP CHANGE AND ACTION PLANNING: A CASE STUDY
PUBLIC ADMINISTRATION REVIEW, 48(1) (JAN 88), 564-570.
THIS ARTICLE DOCUMENTS HOW THE U.S. FOOD AND DRUG
ADMINISTRATION (FDA) COMBINED A NEW PLANNING TECHNIQUE WITH
ITS LONG STANDING TRADITION OF ORGANIZATIONAL PLANNING TO
EASE THE PRESSURE, SMOOTH THE TRANSITION, AND AT THE SAME
TIME PREPARE THE AGENCY FOR THE FUTURE. A CASE STUDY IS
WHERE THE SOLUTION WAS AN ACTION PLANNING PROCESS UNDERTAKEN
BY THE FDA'S NEW LEADERSHIP AND THE AGENCY'S CAREER
EMPLOYEES.

09890 YOUNG, G.
POLITICAL CRISIS IN CHINA
ARENA, (88) (SPR 89), 63-71.
THIS ARTICLE EXAMINES THE LESSONS THAT STUDENTS OF
CHINESE POLITICS HAVE RELEARNED THROUGH THE BRUTAL EVENTS IN
BEIJING. IT FINDS IT USEFUL TO REFLECT UPON THE BACKGROUND
OF WHAT IS HAPPENING IN CHINA TO AID IN UNDERSTANDING WHY IT
HAS OCCURRED. IT WILL FOCUS ON THE LONG TERM DEVELOPMENT OF
THE PRECONDITIONS FOR FUNDAMENTAL POLITICAL CRISIS IN CHINA.
IT EXAMINES ECONOMIC DEVELOPMENT, POLITICAL REFORM,
POLITICAL CLEAVAGES, THE APPEAL TO SOCIALISM AND THE WAY
THIS HAS BEEN UNDERMINED OVER THE LAST DECADE.

09891 YOUNG, J.T.
THE NATIONAL AGRICULTURAL BARGAINING ACT OF 1979: AMERICAN
ARGRICULTURE'S CONTINUING PURSUIT OF COUNTERVAILING POWER
DISSERTATION ABSTRACTS INTERNATIONAL, 50(3) (SEP 89),
785-A.
THE AUTHOR STUDIES AMERICAN POLITICS AT ITS MOST
ELEMENTAL LEVEL--THE INTEREST GROUP AND POLICY--OVER AN
EXTENDED PERIOD IN THE AGRICULTURAL SECTOR. HE CONCLUDES
THAT A POLICY'S SUPPORTERS AND GOALS ARE THE KEY VARIABLES
AND PREDICTORS OF THE FATE OF LEGISLATION.

09892 YOUNG, J.W.
    TOTALITARIAN LANGUAGE: ORWELL'S NEWSPEAK AND ITS NAZI AND
    COMMUNIST PREDECESSORS
    DISSERTATION ABSTRACTS INTERNATIONAL, 49(11) (MAY 89),
    3495-A.
        "NEWSPEAK" REFLECTS GEORGE ORWELL'S BELIEF THAT LANGUAGE
    AND POLITICS ARE CLOSELY CONNECTED AND THAT POLITICS CAN
    ADVERSELY AFFECT LANGUAGE, WHILE LANGUAGE CAN CONTRIBUTE TO
    POLITICAL DECAY. THROUGH HIS DESCRIPTION OF THE LANGUAGE OF
    OCEANIA, ORWELL PROVIDES A MODEL OF TOTALITARIAN LANGUAGE.
    THE MAJOR COMPONENTS ARE (1) INTENT OF THE RULERS TO CONTROL
    THOUGHT AND ACTION THROUGH LANGUAGE, (2) EXALTATION OF THE
    STATE OVER THE INDIVIDUAL, (3) VIOLENCE AND VILIFICATION,
    (4) EUPHEMISM, (5) SPECIAL POLITICAL TERMINOLOGY, AND (6)
    THE FAILURE OF WORDS TO REFLECT REALITY.

09893 YOUNG, L.
    ELECTRONICS AND COMPUTING
    PHILADELPHIA: ANLS OF AMER ACMY OF POLITICAL AND SOC
    SCIENCE, (502) (MAR 89), 82-93.
        ELECTRONICS AND COMPUTING ARE AMONG THE FASTEST-MOVING
    AREAS OF SCIENCE AND ENGINEERING. THE UNIVERSITIES HAVE
    PLAYED AND WILL CONTINUE TO PLAY A MAJOR ROLE IN ADVANCING
    THE STATE OF THE ART. NOWHERE IS IT MORE IMPORTANT TO BE AT
    THE CUTTING EDGE OF TECHNOLOGY FROM THE POINT OF VIEW OF
    DEFENSE, AND NOWHERE IS ACADEMIC RESEARCH MORE REWARDING.
    THESE AREAS ILLUSTRATE WELL THE COOPERATION THAT IS POSSIBLE
    BETWEEN THE DEPARTMENT OF DEFENSE AND THE UNIVERSITIES WHEN
    THEIR INTERESTS COINCIDE.

09894 YOUNG, M.A.; HOLMES, M.
    HEATH'S GOVERNMENT REASSESSED
    CONTEMPORARY RECORD, 3(2) (NOV 89), 24-27.
        THE SUBJECT OF THIS DEBATE IS THE CONSERVATIVE
    GOVERNMENT OF EDWARD HEATH WHICH HAS GENERALLY BEEN WRITTEN
    OFF, BY RIGHT AND LEFT, AS A PERIOD OF WEAK GOVERNMENT WITH
    FEW CONCRETE ACHIEVEMENTS. IN A SYMPATHIC RE-EVALUATION,
    MICHAEL YOUNG ATTEMPTS TO DEFEND THE RECORD OF THE
    GOVERNMENT, IN IN PARTICULAR, MR. HEATH HIMSELF. YOUNG'S
    ARTICLE IS THEN SUBJECTED TO A CRITICAL COMMENTARY BY A WELL-
    KNOWN HEATH DETRACTOR, MARTIN HOLMES.

09895 YOUNG, O.
    INTERNATIONAL POLITICS IN THE ARCTIC: AN AMERICAN
    PERSPECTIVE
    ETUDES INTERNATIONALES, XX(1) (MAR 89), 97-114.
        THE ARCTIC IS EMERGING TODAY AS AN INTERNATIONAL REGION
    WHOSE IMPORTANCE IN POLITICAL, ECONOMIC, AND ENVIRONMENTAL
    TERMS RIVALS THAT OF THE WORLD'S OTHER MAJOR REGIONS. WHAT
    REMAINS IN DOUBT, AT THIS JUNCTURE, IS HOW THE ARCTIC STATES
    NOT TO MENTION OTHERS - WILL RESPOND TO THIS DEVELOPMENT IN
    POLICY TERMS. ARE THESE STATES LIKELY TO UPGRADE THEIR
    CAPACITY TO HANDLE ARCTIC ISSUES BY ADDING SUBSTANTIAL
    ARCTIC EXPERTISE TO THEIR POLICY PLANNING STAFFS; CREATING
    BUREAUX OF ARCTIC OR NORTHERN AFFAIRS IN THEIR FOREIGN
    MINISTRIES; ESTABLISHING EFFECTIVE INTERAGENCY COORDINATING
    MECHANISMS TO HANDLE COMPLEX ARCTIC ISSUES, OR DEVISING NEW
    ARCTIC POLICIES TO REPLACE THE POLICIES OF BENIGN NEGLECT
    THEY HAVE LONG RELIED ON IN DEALING WITH ARCTIC MATTERS?
    THESE ARE SERIOUS CONCERNS WHOSE RESOLUTION WILL TAKE TIME
    AND MAY DIFFER FROM STATE TO STATE. JUST AS THE RECOGNITION
    OF THE ARCTIC AS A DISTINCTIVE INTERNATIONAL REGION HAS BEEN
    A MAJOR DEVELOPMENT OF THE 1980S, THE FORMULATION OF
    APPROPRIATE PUBLIC RESPONSES TO THIS DEVELOPMENT SEEMS
    LIKELY TO BECOME A CENTRAL ARCTIC CONCERN OF THE 1990S. NOTE:
    ARTICLE IS PRINTED IN FRENCH

09896 YOUNG, O. R.
    THE POLITICS OF INTERNATIONAL REGIME FORMATION: MANAGING
    NATURAL RESOURCES AND THE ENVIRONMENT
    INTERNATIONAL ORGANIZATION, 43(3) (SUM 89), 349-376.
        WHY DO ACTORS IN INTERNATIONAL SOCIETY SUCCEED IN
    FORMING INSTITUTIONAL ARRANGEMENTS OR REGIMES TO COPE WITH
    SOME TRANSBOUNDARY PROBLEMS BUT FAIL TO DO SO IN CONNECTION
    WITH OTHER, SEEMINGLY SIMILAR, PROBLEMS? THIS ARTICLE
    EMPLOYS A THREEFOLD STRATEGY TO MAKE PROGRESS TOWARD
    ANSWERING THIS QUESTION. THE FIRST SECTION PREPARES THE
    GROUND BY IDENTIFYING AND CRITIQUING THE PRINCIPAL MODELS
    EMBEDDED IN THE EXISTING LITERATURE ON REGIME FORMATION, AND
    THE SECOND SECTION ARTICULATES AN ALTERNATIVE MODEL, CALLED
    INSTITUTIONAL BARGAINING. THE THIRD SECTION EMPLOYS THIS
    ALTERNATIVE MODEL TO DERIVE SOME HYPOTHESES ABOUT THE
    DETERMINANTS OF SUCCESS IN INSTITUTIONAL BARGAINING AND USES
    THESE HYPOTHESES, IN A PRELIMINARY WAY, TO ILLUMINATE THE
    PROCESS OF REGIME FORMATION IN INTERNATIONAL SOCIETY. TO
    LEND EMPIRICAL CONTENT TO THE ARGUMENT, THE ARTICLE FOCUSES
    THROUGHOUT ON PROBLEMS RELATING TO NATURAL RESOURCES AND THE
    ENVIRONMENT.

09897 YOUNG, P.
    FAIRNESS IN TAXATION
    REPORT FROM THE INSTITUTE FOR PHILOSOPHY AND PUBLIC POLICY,
    9(1) (WIN 89), 12-15.
        DEBATE ABOUT INCOME TAX POLICY USUALLY CENTERS AROUND

THE QUESTION OF FAIRNESS--THAT IS, WHO OUGHT TO PAY HOW MUCH
AND WHY. SIMPLE AS THIS QUESTION MAY SEEM, ATTEMPTS TO
TRANSLATE FAIRNESS INTO PRACTICAL POLICY RAISE A HOST OF
ADDITIONAL ISSUES. THE QUESTION THAT EVOKES THE MOST
CONTROVERSY CONCERNS FAIRNESS IN THE WAY THAT TAXATION IS
DISTRIBUTED ACROSS INCOME BRACKETS. HOW MUCH OF THE BURDEN
SHOULD FALL ON THE POOR AND THE MIDDLE CLASS? HOW MUCH OF
THE BURDEN SHOULD THE RICH BEAR?

09898 YOUNG, R.A.
    POLITICAL SCIENTISTS, ECONOMISTS, AND THE CANADA-US FREE
    TRADE AGREEMENT
    CANADIAN PUBLIC POLICY--ANALYSE DE POLITIQUES, XV(1) (MAR
    89), 49-56.
        WHEN MOST CANADIAN ECONOMISTS SUPPORT THE CANADA-US
    TRADE DEAL, WHY DO MOST POLITICAL SCIENTISTS APPOSE IT? THIS
    QUESTION IS APPROACHED FROM THE POLITICAL SCIENCE SIDE. THE
    TREATMENT CONCENTRATES ON THREE TOPICS WHICH ARE CENTRAL TO
    POLITICS-THE STATE, IDEOLOGY, AND POWER. ANALYSING THE TRADE
    DEAL IN THESE TERMS SHOWS THAT POLITICAL SCIENTISTS TEND TO
    OPPOSE IT BECAUSE IT WOULD RESTRICT THE SCOPE OF "POLITICAL
    EXCHANGE," BECAUSE MUCH SUPPORT FOR IT IS CLEARLY
    IDEOLOGICAL, AND BECAUSE IT WOULD CONFER ON THE AMERICAN
    AUTHORITIES GREATER LEVERAGE OVER CANADIAN POLICIES.

09899 YOUNG, S.
    POLICY, PRACTICE, AND THE PRIVATE SECTOR IN CHINA
    AUSTRALIAN JOURNAL OF CHINESE AFFAIRS, (21) (JAN 89),
    57-80.
        WHEN PRIVATE BUSINESS WAS FIRST REVIVED IN COMMUNIST
    CHINA, THERE WAS MUCH DISAGREEMENT OVER THE PROPRIETY OF
    EVEN SMALL PRIVATE BUSINESSES UNDER SOCIALISM. NOW CHINA'S
    CONSTITUTION HAS BEEN ALTERED TO ALLOW BOTH SMALL AND LARGE
    PRIVATE BUSINESSES, IN RECOGNITION OF THE ENORMOUS GROWTH OF
    THE PRIVATE SECTOR SINCE 1978. BUT OFFICIAL RECOGNITION MUST
    BE FOLLOWED BY MORE CONCRETE POLICIES AND REGULATIONS, AND
    IT IS HERE THAT THE QUESTION OF THE PRIVATE SECTOR UNDER
    SOCIALISM BECOMES VERY COMPLICATED. WHILE THE PRIVATE SECTOR
    HAS GROWN RAPIDLY, THE THEORETICAL RESPONSE HAS BEEN SLOWER,
    CONSTRAINED AS IT IS BY POLITICAL CONSIDERATIONS AND THE
    WEIGHT OF SOCIALIST TRADITION.

09900 YOUNG, T.
    RESTRUCTURING THE STATE IN SOUTH AFRICA: NEW STRATEGIES OF
    INCORPORATION AND CONTROL
    POLITICAL STUDIES, XXXVII(1) (MAR 89), 62-80.
        ALTHOUGH IT IS NOW WIDELY CONCEDED THAT THERE HAVE BEEN
    MANY CHANGES IN SOUTH AFRICA IN RECENT YEARS, NOT LEAST IN
    THE POLITICAL SPHERE, THE NATURE AND SIGNIFICANCE OF THESE
    CHANGES REMAIN HOTLY CONTESTED. AFTER SKETCHING THE PRE-
    REFORM SYSTEM, THIS ARTICLE PRESENTS A BROAD AND
    COMPREHENSIVE ACCOUNT OF THE INSTUTIONAL REORGANIZATION OF
    THE SOUTH AFRICAN STATE AND THE OFFICIAL JUSTIFICATION FOR
    IT. ACKNOWLEDGING THAT AT THE MOMENT ONLY TENTATIVE
    INTERPRETATIONS OF THESE DEVELOPMENTS ARE POSSIBLE, IT POSES
    QUESTIONS ABOUT THE ADEQUACY OF OFFICIAL EXPLANATIONS AND
    SUGGESTS THAT A DEEPER MOTIVATION FOR THE CHANGES LIES IN A
    COMMITMENT TO BOTH ORDER AND REFORM, THE OUTLINES OF WHICH
    ARE MUCH CLEARER AT THE LOCAL THAN AT THE NATIONAL LEVEL.

09901 YOUNG, T.
    THE AUSTRALIAN-UNITED STATES STRATEGIC RELATIONSHIP:
    MERELY AN ISSUE OF SUITABLE REAL ESTATE?
    COMPARATIVE STRATEGY, 8(1) (1989), 125-138.
        SINCE THE EARLY 1960S, THE BILATERAL AUSTRALIAN-UNITED
    STATES SECURITY RELATIONSHIP HAS INCLUDED COOPERATION AT THE
    STRATEGIC LEVEL BY VIRTUE OF THE JOINT FACILITIES LOCATED IN
    AUSTRALIA. THE JOINT FACILITIES APPARENTLY PLAY AN INTEGRAL
    ROLE IN, INTER ALIA, U.S. STRATEGIC RECONNAISSANCE AND
    SURVEILLANCE OF THE SOVIET UNION AND THE PEOPLE'S REPUBLIC
    OF CHINA. THESE STATIONS HAVE COME UNDER POLITICAL FIRE IN
    AUSTRALIA SINCE THEIR ESTABLISHMENT OVER THE ISSUE THAT THEY
    WOULD BE A LIKELY TARGET FOR SOVIET STRATEGIC PLANNERS IN A
    SUPERPOWER NUCLEAR EXCHANGE. IN CONSEQUENCE, IT IS CLAIMED
    BY SOME THAT ARE INIMICAL TO AUSTRALIAN INTERESTS. WHAT
    THESE CRITICS OF THE JOINT FACILITIES FAIL TO UNDERSTAND,
    HOWEVER, IS THAT THEY MUST BE ASSESSED IN RELATION TO TWO
    LONG-STANDING AUSTRALIAN POST WAR SECURITY OBJECTIVES. THESE
    ARE: (1) OBTAINING DETAILED INFORMATION OF U.S. WAR PLANS
    AND (2) EFFECTING AN ONGOING CONSULTING RELATIONSHIP WITH
    HIGH U.S. DEFENSE OFFICIALS. BY VIRTUE OF TWO LITTLE-KNOWN
    BILATERAL AGREEMENTS BETWEEN CANBERRA AND WASHINGTON SIGNED
    IN THE 1970S, THESE TWO ESSENTIAL AUSTRALIAN SECURITY
    INTERESTS WITH THE UNITED STATES HAVE BEEN ACHIEVED.
    THEREFORE, THE CONTINUED OPERATION OF THE JOINT FACILITIES
    WILL REMAIN A CORNERSTONE IN AUSTRALIAN DEFENSE RELATIONS
    WITH THE UNITED STATES AND IS NOT AT VARIANCE WITH
    CANBERRA'S SECURITY INTERESTS.

09902 YOUNG, T.D.
    ANZUS: REQUIESCAT IN PACE?
    CONFLICT, 9(1) (1989), 45-58.
        IT IS THE ASSUMPTION OF SOME THAT ONCE THE NEW ZEALAND
    GOVERNMENT CHANGES ITS ANTINUCLEAR POLICIES, IT CAN THEN

RETURN TO ITS PREVIOUS FULL MEMBERSHIP IN THE ANZUS SECURITY
ALLIANCE WITH THE UNITED STATES. THE PROBLEM WITH THIS
POSITION IS THAT IT FAILS TO CONSIDER FUNDAMENTAL CHANGES
WHICH HAVE TAKEN PLACE IN NEW ZEALAND DOMESTIC AND DEFENSE
POLICIES. AT THE POLITICAL LEVEL, THE COUNTRY HAS MOVED AWAY
FROM ITS STRICT ADHERENCE TO THE BROAD SECURITY OBJECTIVES
OF THE WESTERN ALLIANCE. DESPITE THE RECENT IMPROVEMENTS IN
THE CAPABILITIES OF THE SMALL NEW ZEALAND DEFENCE FORCES,
THEIR PREVIOUS MODEST CONTRIBUTIONS TO WESTERN SECURITY HAVE
PROVED TO BE EASILY REPLACED BY AUSTRALIA AND THE UNITED
STATES. FUNDAMENTALLY, THE PREVAILING VIEW IN WASHINGTON IS
THAT WELLINGTON HAS RECEIVING MORE FROM THE RELATIONSHIP
THAN IT HAS CONTRIBUTING IN RETURN. FINALLY, OPPOSITION TO
THE REESTABLISHMENT OF THE STATUS QUO ANTE CAN BE EXPECTED
FROM AUSTRALIA, WHICH IS NOW IN A POSITION OF DOMINATION
OVER NEW ZEALAND IN BILATERAL DEFENSE MATTERS. THUS, BY
FORCING THE NUCLEAR ISSUE WITH THE UNITED STATES IN 1985 AND
1986, NEW ZEALAND HAS PROVED TO ITS TRADITIONAL ALLIES HOW
UNIMPORTANT IT TRULY IS FOR WESTERN SECURITY WHEN COMPARED
WITH ITS PREVIOUS MODEST CONTRIBUTIONS.

09903 YOUSEFFI, K.
THE ALLIANCE OF SOCIAL FORCES IN THE IRANIAN REVOLUTION
DISSERTATION ABSTRACTS INTERNATIONAL, 49(7) (JAN 89),
1937-A.
THE AUTHOR ANALYZES THE ALLIANCE OF THE VARIOUS
POLITICAL AND SOCIAL GROUPS THAT FORMED THE OPPOSITION TO
IRAN'S PAHLAVI REGIME, USING A RESOURCE MOBILIZATION
APPROACH. THE SHIITE POLITICAL CULTURE AND THE EFFECTIVE USE
OF SYMBOLIC LANGUAGE WERE IMPORTANT IN MOBILIZING THE
DISSENTERS INTO A POLITICAL FORCE, AND ISLAMIC RELIGIOUS
LEADERS EMERGED AS REVOLUTIONARY LEADERS ALSO, TOWARD THE
END.

09904 YU-MING, S.
TIENANMEN: PROCLAIMING STEADFAST SUPPORT
FREE CHINA REVIEW, 39(8) (AUG 89), 19.
IN THIS STATEMENT DELIVERED BY SHAW YU-MING ON MAY 21,
1989, THE TAIWANESE GOVERNMENT VOWED "TO ACT AS THE REAR
GUARD" IN THE CHINESE DISSIDENTS' MOVEMENT FOR FREEDOM AND
DEMOCRACY. TAIWAN ALSO CALLED ON THE CHINESE COMMUNIST
REGIME TO STOP THE USE OF MILITARY FORCE AGAINST THE
PEOPLE'S MOVEMENT, TO RESTORE THE RIGHTS OF JOURNALISTS, TO
ABANDON ITS TYRANNICAL MEASURES, AND TO MARCH TOWARD
POLITICAL DEMOCRATIZATION, ECONOMIC LIBERALIZATION, SOCIAL
PLURALISM, AND THE RENAISSANCE OF CHINESE CULTURE.

09905 YU, P.K.
DANGER IN MOUNTING PRESSURE FOR TWO CHINA POLICY
PACIFIC DEFENCE REPORTER, 16(4) (OCT 89), 31-32.
THE ABILITY OF THE REPUBLIC OF CHINA (ROC) ON TAIWAN TO
DETER ITS ENEMY, THE PEOPLE'S REPUBLIC OF CHINA (PRC), IS
CLOSELY RELATED TO ITS ADHERENCE TO THE ONE CHINA POLICY IN
WORDS AND DEEDS. IN OCTOBER 1985, THE CARIBBEAN COMMONWEALTH
OF GRENADA RECOGNIZED THE PRC AFTER 11 YEARS OF INDEPENDENCE.
ON JULY 21 IT BECAME THE 24TH COUNTRY TO RECOGNIZE THE ROC.
TO MANY PEOPLE ON TAIWAN, THIS IS CALLED DUAL RECOGNITION
AND HAS MADE ROOM FOR TAIPEI TO BE RECOGNIZED BY OTHER
COUNTRIES. BUT, ACCORDING TO THE AUTHOR, AFTER THE JUNE 4
POGROM AT THE TIEN AN MEN SQUARE IN BEIJING, THERE IS
CONSIDERABLE DOUBT ABOUT THE BENEFIT DERIVED FROM DUAL
RECOGNITION BECAUSE, SHOULD OTHER COUNTRIES, BIG OR SMALL,
FOLLOW THE FOOTSTEP OF ST GEORGE'S IN RECOGNIZING BOTH
CHINAS FOR ONE REASON OR ANOTHER, AND TAIPEI ENCOURAGES IT,
BEIJING MAY WELL USE FORCE TO SETTLE ITS INTERNAL PROBLEM -
TAIWAN - ONCE AND FOR ALL.

09906 YU, P.K.
PENETRATING THE PARTY-SYSTEM OF MAINLAND CHINA: CAN THE
KUOMINTANG DO IT?
CHINA REPORT, 25(3) (JUL 89), 249-258.
DEPENDING ON THE PARTY WHICH IS DOING THE ACT,
PENETRATION, IN OUR STUDY, COULD HAVE EITHER A POSITIVE OR A
NEGATIVE EFFECT UPON A SYSTEM. FOR A POLITICAL PARTY LIKE
THE KUOMINTANG (KMT), PENETRATING THE EXISTING PARTY-SYSTEM
IN MAINLAND CHINA WOULD PRODUCE A NEGATIVE EFFECT, BECAUSE
THE VERY ACT WOULD DISRUPT, OR EVEN BRING ABOUT THE COLLAPSE
OF THAT PARTY-SYSTEM, FOR REASONS SEEN LATER. BUT FOR A
PARTY WHICH IDENTIFIES WITH OR WANTS TO BE PART OF THAT
SYSTEM, PENETRATION WOULD HAVE A POSITIVE EFFECT. FIRST,
THIS ARTICLE ATTEMPTS TO BRIEFLY DESCRIBE THE EXISTING PARTY-
SYSTEM IN MAINLAND CHINA; SECOND, MATHEMATICALLY AND
VERBALLY EXPLAIN WHY IT IS POSSIBLE FOR THE KMT TO PENETRATE
MAINLAND CHINA'S PARTY-SYSTEM; AND THIRD, OBJECTIVELY
ANALYSE WHETHER THE KMT CAN PENETRATE THE PARTY-SYSTEM OF
MAINLAND CHINA.

09907 YU. P.K.H.
CORRUPTION IN MAINLAND CHINA
ASIAN OUTLOOK, 24(1) (JAN 89), 11-12.
MANY CHINESE BELIEVE THAT CORRUPTION HAS BECOME PUBLIC
ENEMY NUMBER ONE, SUPERSEDING DOUBLE-DIGIT INFLATION AS THE
COUNTRY'S MOST URGENT PROBLEM. IN THIS ARTICLE, THE AUTHOR
SUMMARIZES SOME OF THE CAUSES AND EFFECTS OF CORRUPTION IN

COMMUNIST CHINA.

09908 YU, R.
EASTERN POWERS THAW LINES TO SOUTH KOREA
BEIJING REVIEW, 32(2) (JAN 89), 19-20.
AS WORLD TENSIONS ARE TENDING TO EASE UP, THE RELATIONS
BETWEEN SOUTH KOREA AND THE SOVIET UNION AND EAST EUROPEAN
COUNTRIES HAVE BEGUN TO THAW. THIS WILL HAVE AN IMPACT ON
THE KOREAN PENINSULA'S SITUATION. KUWAIT'S POLITICAL CULTURE
CREATES A

09909 YU, S.
THE WEST'S PEACEFUL EVOLUTION EXAMINED
BEIJING REVIEW, 32(43) (OCT 89), 13-14.
PEACEFUL EVOLUTION REFERS TO THE CAPITALIST COUNTRIES'
PROMOTION OF CHANGE FROM THE INSIDE IN THE CHARACTER OF
POLITICAL POWER IN SOCIALIST COUNTRIES THROUGH PEACEFUL
MEANS. PEACEFUL EVOLUTION IS AN ATTEMPT TO SUBVERT THE
SOCIALIST SYSTEM AND RESTORE CAPITALISM IN SOCIALIST
COUNTRIES. WHILE CHINA IS PURSUING ITS OWN POLICIES OF
REFORM AND OPENING TO THE OUTSIDE WORLD, IT MUST ALSO
STRUGGLE AGAINST THE FORCES OF PEACEFUL EVOLUTION.

09910 YU, X.
EL SALVADOR AND CENTRAL AMERICAN PEACE
BEIJING REVIEW, 32(48) (NOV 89), 13-15.
ALFREDO CRISTIANA WAS SWORN IN AS PRESIDENT OF EL
SALVADOR ON JUNE 1, 1989. HIS ELECTION HAS AROUSED WIDE
CONCERN OVER POSSIBLE CHANGES IN EL SALVADOR AND WHETHER THE
CENTRAL AMERICAN PEACE PROCESS WILL BE AFFECTED. CRISTIANI
HAS INHERITED A TURBULENT POLITICAL SITUATION IN EL SALVADOR
AND MUST SHOULD ER TWO TREMENDOUS BURDENS--A CIVIL WAR AND
ECONOMIC DIFFICULTIES. HE MUST ALSO CONFRONT PROBLEMS HIS
OWN PARTY, THE NATIONALIST REPUBLIC ALLIANCE, HAS CREATED.

09911 YUAN-LI, W.
INTERNATIONALIZATION: THE TAIWAN ECONOMY
ASIAN OUTLOOK, 25(1) (NOV 89), 29-31.
FOR SEVERAL YEARS, "INTERNATIONALIZATION" HAS BEEN A
CATCH WORD IN THE CONCEPTUAL FRAMEWORK OF TAIWAN'S ECONOMIC
DEVELOPMENT. BUT RARELY HAS THE TERM BEEN FULLY DEFINED. IN
THIS ARTICLE, THE AUTHOR CONSIDERS WHAT INTERNATIONALIZATION
MEANS IN THE CONTEXT OF THE TAIWANESE ECONOMY.

09912 YUAN, L.
BEIJING DIARY
NEW LEFT REVIEW, (177) (SEP 89), 3-26.
AN EYEWITNESS DESCRIBES EVENTS IN BEIJING AS THE POPULAR
MOBILIZATION HAS FIRST VILIFIED AND THEN BRUTALLY SURPRESSED
IN MAY AND JUNE 1989. SHE INTERWEAVES A DAY-BY-DAY ANALYSIS
OF MAJOR POLITICAL EVENTS WITH AN EVOCATIVE ACCOUNT OF THEIR
IMPACT ON FAMILY AND SOCIAL RELATIONSHIPS.

09913 YUANZHENG, L.
STRUCTURAL REFORM AND ECONOMIC DEVELOPMENT IN CHINA
INTERNATIONAL SOCIAL SCIENCE JOURNAL, (120) (MAY 89),
189-202.
THE AUTHOR SURVEYS CHINA'S FIRST DECADE OF STRUCTURAL
ECONOMIC REFORM AND THE ACCOMPANYING PROGRESS IN
INDUSTRIALIZATION AND MODERNIZATION

09914 YUBO, S.
MOSCOW PLUGS NEW EASTERN EUROPE DEAL
BEIJING REVIEW, 32(17) (APR 89), 15-17.
SINCE SOVIET LEADER MIKHAIL GORBACHEV TOOK OFFICE, HE
HAS RESHAPED MOSCOW'S POLICY TOWARDS THE EAST EUROPEAN
COUNTRIES. THE NEW GORBACHEV VISION PROMISES A NEW DEAL FOR
EASTERN EUROPE BASED ON MUTUAL RESPECT AND TRUST. UNDER
GORBACHEV, THE SOVIET UNION ADVOCATES POLITICAL EQUALITY
AMONG THE SOCIALIST COUNTRIES AND NO LONGER REGARDS ITSELF
AS THE HEAD OF "ONE BIG FAMILY."

09915 YUGUO, D.
KEEPING UP THE PROMISE
BEIJING REVIEW, 32(1) (JAN 89), 33-35.
IN DECEMBER 1988, 200 CHINESE AND AMERICAN EXPERTS AND
SCHOLARS GATHERED IN BEIJING FOR A SYMPOSIUM ON SINO-
AMERICAN RELATIONS. THE PARTICIPANTS REVIEWED THE PROGRESS
IN SINO-US RELATIONS DURING THE LAST DECADE AND MADE
RECOMMENDATIONS FOR THE FUTURE.

09916 YUH-JIUN, L.
MAINLAND TRADE ASSESSMENTS
FREE CHINA REVIEW, 39(4) (APR 89), 28-32.
THE AUTHOR SUGGESTS A BASIC METHODOLOGICAL APPROACH TO
ANALYZING THE POTENTIAL IMPACT OF STRENGTHENED TAIWAN-
MAINLAND CHINA TRADE ON THE ECONOMIC AND POLITICAL SECURITY
OF TAIWAN. SHE FOCUSES ON THE FIRST THREE STAGES OF INDIRECT
TRADE BETWEEN TAIWAN AND THE MAINLAND VIA HONG KONG FROM
1978 TO 1986 BEFORE CONSIDERING THE PRESENT, OR FOURTH,
STAGE.

09917 YUJUN, R.
TALKS BODE WELL FOR SOUTH ASIA

BEIJING REVIEW, 32(4) (JAN 89), 13-16.
PAKISTANI-INDIAN RELATIONS HAVE HAD A CHEQUERED HISTORY
OF PROGRESS AND SETBACKS. UNDER RAJIV GANDHI AND BENAZIR
BHUTTO RELATIONS ONCE AGAIN ARE SHOWING SIGNS OF IMPROVEMENT.
IN DECEMBER 1988, GANDHI AND BHUTTO SIGNED THREE AGREEMENTS
CONSENTING TO KEEP THEIR HANDS OFF THE OTHER'S NUCLEAR
INSTALLATIONS, TO END DOUBLE TAXATION BETWEEN THE TWO
COUNTRIES, AND TO ENCOURAGE CULTURAL EXCHANGES.

09918 YUJUN, R.
VISIT PROMOTES BILATERAL RELATIONS
BEIJING REVIEW, 32(32) (AUG 89), 18-19.
INDIAN PRIME MINISTER RAJIV GANDHI, WHO IS PURSUING A
STEP-BY-STEP RAPPROCHEMENT WITH PAKISTAN, VISITED THE
NEIGHBORING COUNTRY IN JULY 1989. ALTHOUGH NO SUBSTANTIVE
ACHIEVEMENTS RESULTED, INDIA AND PAKISTAN PLEDGED TO STRIVE
FOR A SOLUTION TO THE PROBLEM OF THE DISPUTED SIACHEN
GLACIER, WHICH SEPARATES THE NATIONS, ON THE CONDITION THAT
TROOPS FIRST BE WITHDRAWN TO AVOID A MILITARY CONFLICT THERE.

09919 YUJUN, R.
WILL NEPAL-INDIA RELATIONS IMPROVE?
BEIJING REVIEW, 32(30) (JUL 89), 15-16.
ON MARCH 23, 1989, AFTER THE EXPIRATION OF THE NEPALESE-
INDIAN TRADE AND TRANSIT TREATIES, INDIA STOPPED THE SUPPLY
OF PETROLEUM PRODUCTS AND ESSENTIAL COMMODITIES TO NEPAL.
THE NEPALESE GOVERNMENT HAS PROPOSED TALKS TO END THE
DISPUTE AND INDIA HAS SAID THAT IT IS WILLING, BUT THERE IS
NO INDICATION THAT INDIA IS ACTUALLY PLANNING TO TAKE
POSITIVE STEPS TO REMEDY THE SITUATION. INDIA WANTS AN
AGREEMENT THAT WILL LINK NEPAL'S TRANSIT RIGHTS TO THEIR
BILATERAL TRADE. BUT NEPAL INSISTS THAT THESE TWO ISSUES
SHOULD BE SEPARATE BECAUSE TRANSIT IS A RIGHT ENJOYED BY
LANDLOCKED COUNTRIES UNDER INTENATIONAL LAW.

09920 YUKSEL, M.
THE DETERMINANTS OF AGRICULTURAL POLICY IN MODERN TURKEY:
A COMPARATIVE PERSPECTIVE
DISSERTATION ABSTRACTS INTERNATIONAL, 49(10) (APR 89),
3145-A.
THE AUTHOR IDENTIFIES THE VARIATIONS OF GOVERNMENT
PRIORITIES TOWARDS AGRICULTURE. IN THE FIRST SECTION OF THE
DISSERTATION, AGGREGATE CROSS-NATIONAL DATA FOR 34 COUNTRIES
DURING THE PAST THREE DECADES ARE ANALYZED. IN THE SECOND
SECTION, AGGREGATE TIME-SERIES DATA ARE STUDIED FOR TURKEY,
A DEVIANT CASE DUE TO ITS RELATIVELY FAVORABLE RESOURCES AND
CONTINUAL (BUT NOT CONTINUOUS) DEMOCRATIZATION PROCESS. THE
AUTHOR FOCUSES ON THE CAUSAL ANTECEDENTS OF AGRICULTURE
POLICY FROM THE PERSPECTIVE OF STRUCTURAL IMPEDIMENTS.

09921 YUN-HAN, C.
THE SEARCH FOR COMMON GROUND
FREE CHINA REVIEW, 39(11) (NOV 89), 12-29.
THE MIDDLE CLASS IS BEGINNING TO PLAY A CRITICAL ROLE IN
TAIWAN'S POLITICAL DEVELOPMENT. THE DEGREE OF POLITICAL
SOPHISTICATION AND ACTIVISM DEMONSTRATED BY THE MIDDLE CLASS
IN THE NEXT FEW YEARS WILL HAVE A SIGNIFICANT IMPACT ON THE
SPEED AND DIRECTION OF DEMOCRATIC REFORMS, THE QUALITY OF
REPRESENTATIVE DEMOCRACY, AND THE PUBLIC POLICY AGENDA.

09922 YUN, L.
ATTACKING FROM THE FUNNY SIDE
BEIJING REVIEW, 32(3) (JAN 89), 24-25.
DING CONG IS ONE OF CHINA'S LEADING POLITICAL
CARTOONISTS. HIS RECENT EFFORTS HAVE CONCENTRATED ON
SATIRIZING THE WIDESPREAD CORRUPTION IN THE CHINESE
BUREAUCRACY AND SUPPORTING ECONOMIC REFORM POLICIES.

09923 YUN, L.
FOLLOWING IN THE FOOTSTEPS OF CONFUCIUS
BEIJING REVIEW, 32(24-25) (JUN 89), 23.
KONG LINGREN, A DESCENDANT OF CONFUCIUS, IS CONTINUING
HER FAMOUS ANCESTOR'S PRACTICE OF COMBINING SOCIAL AND
POLITICAL THOUGHT SO AS TO BENEFIT SOCIETY. KONG HEADS ONE
OF THE STATE'S KEY EDUCATIONAL PROJECTS FOR THE SEVENTH FIVE-
YEAR PLAN PERIOD AND ALSO LEADS A GROUP OF ACADEMICS
RESEARCHING ANOTHER KEY PROJECT CONCERNING THE ECONOMIC
HISTORY OF MODERN CHINA. THIS PROJECT HAS BROKEN WITH THE
TRADITIONAL METHOD OF BASING ECONOMIC HISTORY SOLELY ON
CLASS STRUGGLE AND POLITICAL EVENTS. INSTEAD, IT STRESSES
CHANGES IN ECONOMIC RELATIONS AND ECONOMIC STRUCTURE AND
ANALYZES HOW ECONOMICS AND POLITICS ARE RELATED.

09924 YUN, L.
GOVERNMENT FUNCTIONARY DISCUSSES RELIGION
BEIJING REVIEW, 32(33) (AUG 89), 22-27.
IN THIS INTERVIEW, THE DEPUTY DIRECTOR OF CHINA'S STATE
COUNCIL RELIGIOUS AFFAIRS BUREAU EXPLAINS THE OFFICIAL
CHINESE POLICY ON FREEDOM OF RELIGIOUS BELIEF. HE ALSO
SHARES HIS OPINIONS ON SINO-VATICAN RELATIONS AND CHINA'S
ATTITUDE TOWARD THE RELIGIOUS COMMUNITIES IN HONG KONG AND
MACAO.

09925 YUN, L.
STATE AID TO POOR COUNTRIES OF NATIONAL MINORITIES
BEIJING REVIEW, 32(52) (DEC 89), 33-37.
AFTER TEN YEARS OF ECONOMIC REFORMS, A GROWING NUMBER OF
CHINA'S ONCE-POOR RURAL RESIDENTS HAVE ENOUGH FOOD AND
CLOTHING. MANY PEOPLE, PARTICULARLY IN EASTERN AND CENTRAL
CHINA, HAVE MADE REMARKABLE IMPROVEMENTS IN THEIR LIVES.
THOSE STILL LIVING IN RURAL POVERTY ARE FOUND MAINLY IN THE
WESTERN AREAS OF CHINA, WHERE THERE ARE HIGHLY COMPACT
MINORITY COMMUNITIES. IN AUGUST 1989, THE STATE COUNCIL
ISSUED A DOCUMENT STATING THAT THE FOCUS OF THE COUNTRY'S
AID-THE-POOR WORK WOULD BE SHIFTED TO THE MINORITY
NATIONALITY AREAS.

09926 YUNDT,K.
THE ORGANIZATION OF AMERICAN STATES AND LEGAL PROTECTION
TO POLITICAL REFUGEES IN CENTRAL AMERICA
INTERNATIONAL MIGRATION REVIEW, XXIII(2) (SUM 89), 201-218.
SINCE 1978, MASSIVE INFLUXES OF ASYLUM SEEKERS HAVE
PLACED GREAT STRAIN UPON RECIPIENT STATES IN CENTRAL AMERICA.
AT THE GLOBAL LEVEL, PROTECTION AND ASSISTANCE TO REFUGEES
IS ENTRUSTED TO THE UNITED NATIONS HIGH COMMISSIONER FOR
REFUGEES (UNHCR). AT THE REGIONAL LEVEL, ONE WOULD EXPECT
INVOLVEMENT BY THE ORGANIZATION OF AMERICAN STATES WITH
CENTRAL AMERICA REFUGEES; EITHER TO SUPPLEMENT UNHCR
ACTIVITIES OR TO ENFORCE INDEPENDENT INTER-AMERICAN
STANDARDS. THIS ARTICLE REVIEWS INTER-AMERICAN STANDARDS AND
AGENCIES OF CONCERN FOR ASYLUM SEEKERS AND REFUGEES. SPECIAL
ATTENTION IS GIVEN TO THE INTER-AMERICAN HUMAN RIGHTS REGIME
AS THE MECHANISM BEST SUITED TO SUPPLEMENT OR COMPLEMENT
UNHCR ACTIVITIES IN CENTRAL AMERICA.

09927 YUNKER, J.A.
AN ECONOMIC MODEL OF THE EAST-WEST CONFRONTATION
CONFLICT MANAGEMENT AND PEACE SCIENCE, 10(2) (SPR 89),
1-20.
THIS PAPER DEVELOPS A COMPREHENSIVE ANALYTICAL
PERSPECTIVE ON THE CONTEMPORARY CONFLICT BETWEEN THE UNITED
STATES AND THE SOVIET UNION, BASED UPON STANDARD CONCEPTS
AND METHODOLOGIES IN CONTEMPORARY ECONOMIC THINKING. THE
PAPER, BASED UPON RESULTS OBTAINED FROM ITS USE OF STATIC -
MODEL SPECIFICATION, DOES NOT NECESSARILY SUPPORT THE
WIDESPREAD CONTEMPORARY PRESUMPTION THAT THE INVENTION AND
DISSEMINATION OF NUCLEAR WEAPONS HAS REDUCED THE PROBABILITY
OF TOTAL WAR.

09928 YUNQI, L.
CHINA'S INFLATION: CAUSES, EFFECTS, AND SOLUTIONS
ASIAN SURVEY, 29(7) (JUL 89), 655-668.
THIS ARTICLE EXAMINES PRIMARY CAUSES OF INFLATION IN
CHINA AND WHETHER CHINA CAN MAKE USE OF INFLATION. IT OFFERS
TWO WAYS TO REDUCE EXCESS AGGREGATE DEMAND AND BRING DOWN
INFLATIONARY PRESSURES AND OUTLINES POSSIBLE TEMPORARY
POLICIES. IT OFFERS FUNDAMENTAL SOLUTIONS, WHICH IF PURSUED
IN THE CONTEXT OF APPROPRIATE MONETARY POLICY, SHOULD ENABLE
CHINA TO FUNDAMENTALLY ELIMINATE INFLATION.

09929 YUSHENG, Y.
MAJOR CONTROVERSIES IN CHINA'S U.S. HISTORY RESEARCH
BEIJING REVIEW, 32(46) (NOV 89), 32-34.
FOR NEARLY 40 YEARS, A LEGION OF CHINESE HISTORIANS AND
SCHOLARS IN OTHER FIELDS HAS DEVOTED ITSELF TO THE STUDY OF
AMERICAN HISTORY. THEIR WORK HAS DEEPENED CHINESE
UNDERSTANDING OF THE UNITED STATES, PROVIDING A FIRMER
FOUNDATION FOR CHINESE FOREIGN POLICY TOWARDS AMERICA. THIS
ARTICLE REVIEWS THE CHINESE VIEW OF SOME IMPORTANT EVENTS
AND FIGURES IN AMERICAN HISTORY, INCLUDING ALEXANDER
HAMILTON, THE MONROE DOCTRINE, ABRAHAM LINCOLN, AND SOUTHERN
RECONSTRUCTION FOLLOWING THE CIVIL WAR.

09930 ZAFFARONI, E.R.
THE RIGHT TO LIFE AND LATIN AMERICAN PENAL SYSTEMS
PHILADELPHIA: ANLS OF AMER ACMY OF POLITICAL AND SOC
SCIENCE, (506) (NOV 89), 57-67.
DEATHS AT THE HANDS OF THE STATE IN LATIN AMERICA,
THROUGH THE PENAL SYSTEM, ARE A SERIOUS MENANCE TO DEMOCRACY
IN THE REGION. ACCORDING TO THE PUBLIC PORTRAYAL OF THESE
DEATHS, IT SEEMS NECESSARY TO PROJECT A CONTINUOUS WAR,
SOMETIMES AS A POLITICAL WAR AND SOMETIMES AS A WAR AGAINST
COMMON DELINQUENCY. HUMAN RIGHTS ORGANIZATIONS ARE USUALLY
WORRIED ABOUT THE FIRST PHENOMENON AND ITS DEATHS, BUT THEY
DO NOT PERCEIVE THE ENORMOUS IMPORTANCE OF THE DEATHS
PRODUCED BY THE WAR AGAINST CRIMINALITY, WHICH IS PUBLICIZED
BY THE POLICE AGENCIES TO JUSTIFY THE USE OF THEIR ILLEGAL
POWER. SOCIAL CONTAMINATION WITH COMMON DELINQUENCY, AND
WITH MARGINALIZATION IN GENERAL, IS THE TOOL USED TO INHIBIT
THE PUBLIC DENUNCIATION OF THESE DEATHS-THE NUMBER OF WHICH
IS FREQUENTLY HIGHER THAN THE NUMBER OF DEATHS CAUSED IN
CASES OF OPEN POLITICAL VIOLENCE.

09931 ZAIDI, S. A.
RELIGIOUS MINORITIES IN PAKISTAN TODAY
JOURNAL OF CONTEMPORARY ASIA, 18(4) (1988), 444-457.
THE ROLE OF THE BELIEVERS OF CHRISTIANITY, HINDUISM AND

AHMADISM IS ONE IN WHICH THEY SHOULD IDENTIFY THEMSELVES
WITH THOSE FORCES WHICH ARE GENIUNELY DEMOCRATIC AND THUS
WORK WITH ALL THE OPPRESSED PEOPLE OF PAKISTAN AND STRIVE
FOR A DEMOCRATIC PAKISTAN. THE ONLY WAY THEY CAN GAIN THEIR
OWN FREEDOM IS TO ALIGN THEMSELVES WITH OTHER FREEDOM
FIGHTERS AND THUS TRY TO ESTABLISH THE FREEDOM OF ALL THE
EXPLOITED PEOPLE IN PAKISTAN. THE MORE THESE RELIGIOUS
GROUPS IDENTIFY THEMSELVES WITH THOSE STRUGGLING FOR
DEMOCRACY, THE MORE PROTECTION WILL THEY RECEIVE FROM THOSE
WHO BELIEVE IN THE SAME CAUSE. RIGHT-REACTIONARY FORCES WILL
FEEL THREATENED WHEN THEY FIND MORE AND MORE PEOPLE
SUPPORTING THE STRUGGLE FOR DEMOCRACY AND WILL THUS THINK
TWICE BEFORE THEY BURN ANY OTHER CHURCHES OR MANDIRS. THUS,
ANY ATTEMPT TO DIVIDE THE VARIOUS MINORITIES, AS IS BEING
DONE AT PRESENT, SHOULD BE ANSWERED WITH A SHOW OF STRENGTH,
NOT ONLY OF THE MINORITIES, BUT IN UNITY WITH ALL THEIR
FELLOW SUFFERERS WHO ARE WORKING TOWARDS A FREER, DEMOCRATIC
AND SECULAR PAKISTAN.

09932 ZALESKI, P.A.
THE DETERMINANTS AND EFFECTS OF CAMPAIGN CONTRIBUTIONS
FROM CORPORATE PAC'S
DISSERTATION ABSTRACTS INTERNATIONAL, 49(9) (MAR 89),
2740-A.
USING A STATE PREFERENCE MODEL, THE AUTHOR ANALYZES THE
DETERMINANTS AND EFFECTS OF POLITICAL CAMPAIGN CONTRIBUTIONS
FROM CORPORATE POLITICAL ACTION COMMITTEES. HE FINDS THAT
FIRMS MAKE POLITICAL CAMPAIGN CONTRIBUTIONS TO EXTRACT RENTS.
ONCE A FIRM ATTAINS POLITICAL ACCESS, AN INCREASE IN THE
FIRM'S SIZE WILL NOT LEAD TO A PROPORTIONATE INCREASE IN
CAMPAIGN CONTRIBUTIONS BECAUSE THE FIRM CANNOT EXPECT TO
OBTAIN PROPORTIONATELY MORE POLITICAL ACCESS.

09933 ZALKIN, M.
AGRARIAN CLASS STRUCTURE IN NICARAGUA IN 1980: A NEW
INTERPRETATION AND SOME IMPLICATIONS
JOURNAL OF PEASANT STUDIES, 16(4) (JUL 89), 575-605.
THE NICARAGUAN GOVERNMENT HOPES TO REDUCE ECONOMIC
EXPLOITATION BY ALTERING AGRARIAN CLASS STRUCTURE. ITS
EFFORTS DEPEND, IN PART, ON THE AVAILABILITY OF DATA TO
ANALYZE THE NATURE OF THE EXISTING CLASS STRUCTURE. IN THIS
ESSAY, A FAMILY RURAL SURVEY THAT COVERED MORE THAN 50,000
FAMILIES IS USED TO REINTERPRET NICARAGUAN AGRARIAN CLASS
STRUCTURE IN 1980. THE AUTHOR CONTRASTS HIS RESULTS WITH
THOSE OF A PRIOR PROCESSING AND THE CONCLUSIONS OF OTHER
ANALYSTS. HE CONCLUDES BY CONSIDERING THE IMPLICATIONS OF
THE WORK FOR THE PRESENT AGRARIAN CLASS STRUCTURE AND FOR
SOCIAL AND ECONOMIC POLICIES IN AGRICULTURE.

09934 ZAMAN, M. Q.
THE SOCIOECONOMIC AND POLITICAL DYNAMICS OF ADJUSTMENT TO
RIVERBANK EROSION HAZARD AND POPULATION RESETTLEMENT IN
THE BRAHMAPUTRA-JAMUNA FLOODPLAIN
DISSERTATION ABSTRACTS INTERNATIONAL, 49(9) (MAR 89),
2710-A.
THE AUTHOR DESCRIBES AND EXPLAINS HUMAN RESPONSES AND
ADJUSTMENT TO RIVERBANK EROSION DISPLACEMENT IN THE
BRAHMAPUTRA-JAMUNA FLOODPLAIN IN THE CONTEXT OF THE MICRO-
LEVEL SOCIAL, ECONOMIC, AND POLITICAL ENVIRONMENT THAT
SHAPES LOCAL ADJUSTMENT STRATEGIES AND RESETTLEMENT OPTIONS.
THE FIERCE BATTLES FOR CHANGING LAND RESOURCES PERMEATE ALL
SOCIAL AND POLITICAL RELATIONSHIPS BETWEEN PATRONS AND
DEPENDENT CLIENTS BECAUSE OWNERSHIP OR USE OF LAND IS THE
PRIME FACTOR OF ADJUSTMENT.

09935 ZAMOYSKI, A.
STATES OF MIND
ENCOUNTER, LXXIII(2) (JUL 89), 21-25.
THE EFFECT OF IMAGE AND MYTH ON NATIONS AND THEIR
LEADERS CAN BE IMMENSE BUT IS SELDOM BENEFICIAL. IT OFTEN
PRODUCES COMIC SITUATIONS BUT CAN ALSO LEAD TO TRAGEDY. IN
THIS ESSAY, THE AUTHOR CONSIDERS THE ATTITUDES THAT HAVE
HELPED SHAPE THE STATES OF IRELAND AND POLAND.

09936 ZAMYATIN, L.
THATCHERISM
INTERNATIONAL AFFAIRS (MOSCOW), (8) (AUG 89), 50-59.
DESPITE THE CONTRADICTORY NATURE OF THE DEVELOPMENTS OF
THE PAST DECADE, BRITAIN HAS MANAGED TO BREAK OUT OF A
SERIOUS SOCIO-ECONOMIC CRISIS, TO CONSOLIDATE ITS STANDING
AMONG THE MOST INDUSTRIALIZED COUNTRIES OF THE WORLD, AND TO
ENHANCE ITS PRESTIGE AND ROLE IN INTERNATIONAL AFFAIRS.
THESE RESULTS ARE LINKED WITH THE WORK OF PRIME MINISTER
THATCHER AND WITH THE CONSERVATIVE POLITICS THAT SHE
REPRESENTS. THE TERM "THATCHERISM" HAS BECOME FIRMLY
ENTRENCHED IN BRITISH POLITICAL LIFE. IT IS USED TO DESCRIBE
THE POLITICAL, IDEOLOGICAL, AND MORAL GOALS PURSUED BY
THATHCHER AND ALSO HER STYLE OF LEADERSHIP.

09937 ZANIEWSKI, K.
HOUSING INEQUALITIES UNDER SOCIALISM: A GEOGRAPHIC
PERSPECTIVE
STUDIES IN COMPARATIVE COMMUNISM, XXII(4) (WIN 89),
291-306.

HOUSING SHORTAGE IS ONE OF THE MOST SEVERE AND SENSITIVE
ISSUES IN SOVIET BLOC COUNTRIES. THE ARTICLE EXAMINES
HOUSING CONDITIONS IN THE SOVIET UNION, POLAND, AND OTHER
EAST EUROPEAN COUNTRIES. REASONS FOR HOUSING INEQUALITY
INCLUDE: A BIAS SLANTED TOWARDS CITIES AND PEOPLE THAT
FURTHER GOALS OF NATIONAL INDUSTRIALIZATION; STATE
INVESTMENT POLICY; LOW RENTS; AND EXCESSIVE STATE
INTERFERENCE IN HOUSING ALLOCATION.

09938 ZANINOVICH, M.G.
A PROGNOSIS FOR YUGOSLAVIA
CURRENT HISTORY, 88(541) (NOV 89), 393-396, 404-405.
THE YUGOSLAV POLITICAL SYSTEM INCREASINGLY PROJECTS AN
IMAGE TO WHICH THE DEMOCRATIC WEST CAN RELATE. THERE ARE
SIGNS THAT THE YUGOSLAV REGIME WANTS TO RECEIVE THE FIRST
WORLD'S STAMP OF APPROVAL AND WALK HAND-IN-HAND POLITICALLY
AND ECONOMICALLY WITH THE INDUSTRIAL CORE RATHER THAN REMAIN
ON THE PERIPHERY.

09939 ZAPRUDNIK, J.
BELORUSSIAN REAWAKENING
PROBLEMS OF COMMUNISM, XXXVIII(4) (JUL 89), 36-52.
SINCE THE ADVENT OF REFORM EFFORTS IN THE SOVIET UNION,
A NATIONAL MOVEMENT OF INTELLECTUALS AND YOUNG PEOPLE HAS
EMERGED IN THE REPUBLIC OF BELORUSSIA. THIS MOVEMENT HAS
PRESSED FOR PUBLICIZING THE TRUTH ABOUT THE STALINIST TERROR
IN THE REPUBLIC AND ABOUT EFFORTS OF THE REGIME TO RUSSIFY
BELORUSSIA. THE NATIONAL MOVEMENT HAS SOUGHT TO PERSUADE THE
REPUBLIC'S AUTHORITIES TO IMPLEMENT POLICIES PROMOTING THE
BELORUSSIAN LANGUAGE AND CULTURE, ALTHOUGH MORE RADICAL
POLITICAL DEMANDS HAVE ALSO BEEN ADVANCED. MOSCOW HAS LENT
SOME SUPPORT TO THE INDEPENDENT GROUPS. THE REPUBLIC PARTY
AND GOVERNMENT HAVE STRONGLY RESISTED THE DEMANDS OF THE
NATIONAL MOVEMENT, ALTHOUGH RECENTLY THEY HAVE MADE SOME
CONCESSIONS IN THE CULTURAL SPHERE.

09940 ZARDKOOHI, A,; PUSTAY, M.
DOES TRANSFERABILITY AFFECT THE SOCIAL COSTS OF LICENSING?
PUBLIC CHOICE, 62(2) (AUG 89), 187-190.
THE PURPOSE OF THIS NOTE IS TO ARGUE THAT THE SIZE OF
THE TOTAL SOCIAL COSTS ASSOCIATED WITH LICENSING ARE
INDEPENDENT OF TRANSFERABILITY, ALTHOUGH TRANSFERABILITY
DOES AFFECT THE COMPOSITION OF THESE SOCIAL COSTS BOTH
TRANSFERABLE AND NONTRANSFERABLE LICENSES ARE EXAMINED RENT-
SEEKING IS EXPLORED.

09941 ZARET, D.
RELIGION AND THE RISE OF LIBERAL-DEMOCRATIC IDEOLOGY IN
17TH-CENTURY ENGLAND
AMERICAN SOCIOLOGICAL REVIEW, 54(2) (APR 89), 163-179.
THIS CASE STUDY PROVIDES AN ANALYSIS THAT EMPHASIZES THE
PROBLEM OF RELIGIOUS CONFLICT AND RADICALISM IN EARLY
LIBERAL-DEMOCRATIC IDEOLOGY. PROPONENTS OF THE NEW IDEOLOGY
REJECTED KEY TENETS OF THEIR PURITAN HERITAGE, ADOPTING
DEISTIC BELIEFS THAT LEGITIMATED PLURALISM AND TOLERANCE AND
OPPOSED THE OLDER PURITAN IDEAL OF GODLY POLITICS. BUILDING
ON RECENT WORK IN THE SOCIOLOGY OF CULTURE, THE PAPER
OUTLINES AN ANALYTIC STRATEGY FOR EXPLAINING CHANGE IN
IDEOLOGICAL SYSTEMS. IDEOLOGICAL CHANGE EMERGES OUT OF THE
INTERACTION OF CONTEXTUAL PRESSURES AND INTELLECTUAL
PRECEDENTS, AS A COLLECTIVE RESPONSE BY IDEOLOGICAL
INNOVATORS TO PROBLEMS OF AUTHORITY. THE ANALYSIS IN THIS
STUDY SHOWS HOW HISTORICAL EVENTS CAN FORM AN EPISODIC
CONTEXT WHICH STRUCTURES THIS PROBLEM OF AUTHORITY.

09942 ZARETSKY, E.
THESES ON LIBERALISM
TIKKUN, 4(2) (MAR 89), 72-75.
THE AUTHOR TRACES THE HISTORY OF THE CONCEPT OF
LIBERALISM AND HOW CONTEMPORARY LIBERALISM LOST ITS MANDATE.

09943 ZARISKI, R.
ETHNIC EXTREMISM AMONG ETHNOTERRITORIAL MINORITIES IN
WESTERN EUROPE: DIMENSIONS, CAUSES, AND INSTITUTIONAL
RESPONSES
COMPARATIVE POLITICS, 21(3) (APR 89), 253-272.
THE PURPOSE OF THIS PAPER IS TO EXAMINE THE CONCEPT OF
EXTREMISM AS APPLIED TO ETHNOTERRITORIAL MINORITIES IN
WESTERN EUROPE. FIRST, SOME SUGGESTED DIMENSIONS OF ETHNIC
EXTREMISM ARE IDENTIFIED. SECOND, SOME FACTORS ALLEGEDLY
CONTRIBUTING TO ETHNIC EXTREMISM ARE REVIEWED AND BRIEFLY
DISCUSSED: WHY DO SOME ETHNIC MINORITIES WITHIN A GIVEN
STATE ADOPT AN EXTREMIST POSTURE, WHEREAS OTHER ETHNIC
MINORITIES DO NOT? AND FINALLY, SOME ATTENTION IS PAID TO
THE EFFICACY OF INSTITUTIONAL RESPONSES TO ETHNIC EXTREMIST
PRESSURES, IN ORDER TO HIGHLIGHT THE NEED FOR ASSESSING THE
RELATIVE EFFECTIVENESS OF VARIOUS INSTITUTIONAL DEVICES FOR
DEALING WITH THE PROBLEM OF ETHNIC ASPIRATIONS.

09944 ZARTMAN, I.W.
PRENEGOTIATION: PHASES AND FUNCTIONS
INTERNATIONAL JOURNAL, XLIV(2) (SPR 89), 237-253.
THE AUTHOR REVIEWS THE SCHOLARSHIP ON THE PHASES AND
FUNCTIONS OF PRENEGOTIATION AS HE SEEKS TO DEFINE AND

DESCRIBE THESE TWO ELEMENTS OF THE EARLY BARGAINING PROCESS
THAT BRINGS NATIONS TO THE NEGOTIATING TABLE.

09945 ZASLAVSKAIA, T.
THE FUNDAMENTAL QUESTION OF RESTRUCTURING
SOVIET REVIEW, 30(6) (NOV 89), 3-11.
PERESTROIKA HAS PRODUCED LITTLE CHANGE IN THE PRACTICAL
REALMS OF LIFE, AND THE PROBLEM IS POLITICAL. AS LONG AS
POWER REMAINS CONCENTRATED IN THE HANDS OF A SMALL PARTY-
STATE ELITE AND ITS ADMINISTRATIVE APPARATUS, NO PROFOUND
CHANGE ENTAILING A REDISTRIBUTION OF POWER AND RESOURCES CAN
OCCUR.

09946 ZASLAVSKAYA, T.
THE TIME OF BIG CHANGES
REPRINTS FROM THE SOVIET PRESS, 48(8) (APR 89), 39-45.
ACADEMICIAN TATYANA ZASLAVSKAYA ANSWERS A SERIES OF
QUESTIONS ON A WIDE VARIETY OF SUBJECTS RANGING FROM THE
FUTURE OF PERESTROIKA TO THE DEPOPULATION OF VILLAGES. THE
MAJORITY OF THE QUESTIONS DEALT WITH SPECIFIC ASPECTS OF
PERESTROIKA AND ECONOMIC REFORM; TOPICS SUCH AS UNEMPLOYMENT,
PRICE REGULATION, AND LABOR STRIKES WERE DISCUSSED.

09947 ZAX, J.S.
INITIATIVES AND GOVERNMENT EXPENDITURES
PUBLIC CHOICE, 63(3) (DEC 89), 267-278.
THIS PAPER DEMONSTRATES THAT PROVISIONS FOR INITIATIVES
HAVE IMPORTANT EFFECTS ON GOVERNMENT SPENDING. PROVISIONS
FOR INITIATIVES ENCOURAGE LEGISLATURES TO APPROVE ANY
PROPOSAL WHICH MIGHT ATTRACT SUBSTANTIAL POPULAR SUPPORT. IF
THESE PROPOSALS ARE MORE LIKELY TO ADVOCATE INCREASES THAN
REDUCTIONS IN EXPENDITURES, THE PRESENCE OF INITIATIVE
PROVISIONS WILL INCREASE TOTAL EXPENDITURES. DIRECT
GOVERNMENT EXPENDITURES PER CAPITA ARE SIGNIFICANTLY HIGHER
IN BOTH STATES AND MUNICIPALITIES WHICH PERMIT INITIATIVES.

09948 ZAYA DIN, Y.
WE WANT ARAB UNITY
WORLD MARXIST REVIEW, 32(4) (APR 89), 17-19.
ARAB UNITY CAN BE ATTAINED IN TWO WAYS. FIRSTLY,
STRUGGLE ON THE GENERAL ARAB LEVEL, AND SECONDLY, ON THE
LEVEL OF EACH INDIVIDUAL COUNTRY. IT IS OUR VIEW THAT THE
LATTER IS THE ONLY TRUE WAY, NOT BECAUSE IT IS A MATTER OF
PREFERENCE: IT IS SIMPLY MORE SCIENTIFIC. REGRETTABLY, MANY
ARAB REVOLUTIONARIES IGNORE LOCAL REALITIES AND STRIVE FOR
GENERAL ARAB UNITY, FORGETTING THAT THERE CAN BE NO GENERAL
BATTLE WITHOUT LOCAL BATTLES AND SOCIAL STRUGGLES IN THE
INDIVIDUAL COUNTRIES.

09949 ZEALEY, L.
PLANNERS MAKE AMENDS WITH THE IMF
AFRICAN BUSINESS, (MAR 88), 13-14.
THIS ARTICLE EXAMINES THE ECONOMIC SITUATION IN TOGO AND
THE ATTEMPTS AT STABILIZATION. IT DISCUSSES THE PRIORITIES
OF THE GOVERNMENT'S ECONOMIC PROGRAM ALONG WITH PRATICAL
DEVELOPMENT AND LONG TERM PLANS OF DEBT REPAYMENTS. IT
EXPLORES THE OPTIMISTIC OUTLOOK OF SMOOTH RELATIONS WITH THE
IMF AND THE WORLD BANK.

09950 ZEFFANE, R.M.
CENTRALIZATION OR FORMALIZATION? INDIFFERENCE CURVES FOR
STRATEGIES OF CONTROL
ORGANIZATION STUDIES, 10(3) (1989), 327-352.
DRAWING ON PREVIOUS RESEARCH ON PATTERNS OF ORGANIZATION
STRUCTURES, THIS PAPER EXAMINES THE QUESTION OF STRATEGIC
STRUCTURAL CHOICE BETWEEN CENTRALIZED AND FORMALIZED MEANS
OF CONTROL. AN ALTERNATIVE APPROACH IN CONCEIVING AND
OPERATIONALIZING THE PROBLEM OF CHOICE IS SUGGESTED. THIS
USES THE 'INDIFFERENCE CURVES' POSTULATE AS PUT FORWARD IN
NEO-CLASSICAL ECONOMIC THEORY. AN OPERATIONAL MODEL
FEATURING 'TRADE-OFFS' BETWEEN CENTRALIZED AND FORMALIZED
CONTROL IS PROPOSED. THE CONCLUSIONS ARE THAT THE FRAMEWORK
BASED ON THE NOTION OF 'INDIFFERENCE' PROVIDES REASONABLE
THEORETICAL STRENGTH IN PORTRAYING AND EXPLAINING TRADE-OFFS
IN STRUCTURAL CHOICES. THEORETICALLY INFINITE TRADE-OFFS IN
CHOICES BETWEEN MEANS OF CONTROL FIND LIMITS IN THE
PURPOSIVE SEARCH FOR EQUILIBRIUM (OPTIMUM CHOICE), FOR
EXAMPLE IN MATCHING THE AMOUNT/TYPE OF STRUCTURING WITH
CONSTRAINTS SUCH AS SIZE.

09951 ZEMIN, J.
ELIMINATE UNFAIR INCOME DISTRIBUTION
BEIJING REVIEW, 32(35) (AUG 89), 19-24.
THE AUTHOR OFFERS A DETAILED ANALYSIS OF THE SENSITIVE
PROBLEM OF UNFAIR INCOME DISTRIBUTION IN CHINA, OUTLINING
ITS MANIFESTATIONS AND CAUSES AS WELL AS EFFECTIVE WAYS TO
REMEDY THE SITUATION.

09952 ZEMIN, J.
SPEECH AT THE MEETING IN CELEBRATION OF THE 40TH
ANNIVERSARY OF THE FOUNDING OF THE PEOPLE'S REPUBLIC OF
CHINA
BEIJING REVIEW, 32(41) (OCT 89), 11-24.
COMMUNIST PARTY GENERAL SECRETARY JIANG ZEMIN HAS
DECLARED THAT SOCIALISM CALLS FOR CONSTANT DEVELOPMENT AND
PERFECTION OF ITSELF. HE HAS OUTLINED TEN MAJOR PROBLEMS
FACING THE CHINESE PEOPLE AND THE GOVERNMENT, INCLUDING
ECONOMIC POLICY ISSUES, SOCIAL DISTRIBUTION, STRENGTHENING
AGRICULTURE AND BASIC INDUSTRIES, BUILDING A SOCIALIST
CULTURE AND ETHICS, AND STRENGTHENING THE PARTY.

09953 ZENGQUAN, Z.
THE ECONOMIC REVITALIZATION OF TURKEY
BEIJING REVIEW, 32(43) (OCT 89), 15-17.
TURKEY WAS CAUGHT IN A MAJOR POLITICAL AND ECONOMIC
CRISIS DURING THE YEARS FROM 1978 TO 1980. AFTER TAKING
POWER IN 1980, THE MILITARY GOVERNMENT LED BY KENAN EVREN
BEGAN PURSUING AN ECONOMIC DEVELOPMENT STRATEGY WORKED OUT
BY LEADING ECONOMIST TURGUT OZAL, WHICH HELPED THE ECONOMY
RECOVER. OVER SEVERAL YEARS, TURKEY'S ECONOMY REVIVED, WITH
ITS PRODUCTIVITY AND INDUSTRIAL EXPORTS INCREASING AND ITS
SPEED OF DEVELOPMENT ACCELERATING. TURKEY'S ECONOMIC
ACHIEVEMENTS WERE WON IN THE 1980S WHEN THE ECONOMIES OF
MOST MIDDLE EAST COUNTRIES WERE IN DIFFICULTIES.

09954 ZHANG, X.
COMMUNITY IN TRANSITION: ECONOMIC REFORM IN SUBEI VILLAGE
1981-85
DISSERTATION ABSTRACTS INTERNATIONAL, 49(7) (JAN 89),
1991-A.
SUBEI VILLAGE UNDERWENT A DRAMATIC CHANGE IN SOCIAL
STRUCTURE DURING THE NATIONWIDE ECONOMIC REFORM OF THE EARLY
1980S IN CHINA. BASED ON A QUALITATIVE FIELD STUDY, THIS
PAPER INQUIRES INTO THE DYNAMICS OF THE STRUCTURAL
TRANSFORMATION, WHEREBY A TENSION REDUCTION MODEL--A REVISED
PROBLEM-SOLVING SCHEME--IS GENERATED FOR THEORETICAL
EXPLANATION.

09955 ZHAO, J.Q.
"INFORMAL PLURALISM" AND JAPANESE POLITICS: SINO-JAPANESE
RAPPROCHMENT REVISITED
JOURNAL OF NORTHEAST ASIAN STUDIES, 8(2) (SUM 89), 65-83.
THIS STUDY ATTEMPTS TO TAKE THE 1972 SINO-JAPANESE
RAPPROCHEMENT AS A CASE STUDY TESTING THE HYPOTHESES THAT
EMERGED FROM RECENT RESEARCH ON THE PLURALISTIC NATURE OF
JAPANESE POLITICS. IT CONCENTRATES ON "INFORMAL PLURALISM,"
AN IMPORTANT CHARACTERISTIC OF JAPANESE POLITICAL LIFE.
INTERNAL MANEUVERS OF JAPANESE POLITICS DURING THE
NORMALIZATION PROCESS HAVE BEEN CLOSELY EXAMINED. THESE
INTERNAL ELEMENTS INCLUDE: THE LIBERAL DEMOCRATIC PARTY--
INFORMAL ORGANIZATIONS IN ACTION, THE RULING
PARTY/BUREACRACY APPARATUS--INFORMAL CHANNELS, OPPOSITION
PARTIES DIPLOMACY--INFORMAL STYLES, AND INTELLECTUALS--
INFORMAL ADVISORY GROUPS. THERE ARE AT LEAST THREE WAYS TO
ANALYZE JAPAN'S "INFORMAL PLURALISM": THE STRUCTURE OF THE
SYSTEM, THE PHENOMENON OF LEADERFOLLOWER FACTIONS AND
INFORMAL ORGANIZATIONS, AND THE WORKING STYLE. ONE CAN STATE
THAT THIS IS INDEED JAPAN'S OWN PATTERN FOR DEVELOPMENT; ONE
CAN ALSO VIEW THIS CHARACTER AS A REFLECTION OF JAPANESE
CULTURE. COMPARED TO PLURALISM IN THE UNITED STATES,
"INFORMAL PLURALISM" IS LESS INSTITUTIONALIZED, MORE
IRREGULAR AND AMBIGUOUS. THE DIFFERENCES BETWEEN THE TWO,
THEREFORE, ARE MAINLY IN STYLE AND METHOD, AS WELL AS THE
PLURALISTIC DEGREE OF THE SOCIETY.

09956 ZHAO, W.
PEOPLE COMMENT ON THE RIOT IN BEIJING
BEIJING REVIEW, 32(28) (JUL 89), 25-30.
THIS ESSAY INCLUDES EDITED ARTICLES PUBLISHED IN CHINESE
NEWSPAPERS AND MAGAZINES FOLLOWING THE 1989 RIOTS IN BEIJING.
THE COMMENTS REVIEW THE DEMANDS OF THE PROTESTORS, THE ROLE
OF STUDENT RADIO BROADCASTS IN THE TURMOIL, AND THE ROLE OF
LIU XIAOBO, A LECTURER AT BEIJING TEACHERS' UNIVERSITY WHO
WAS A LEADER OF THE REVOLT.

09957 ZHEN, Z.
MARXISM-LENINISM IS THE BANNER OF OUR TIMES (I)
BEIJING REVIEW, 32(48) (NOV 89), 17-19.
MARXISM-LENINISM IS THE REVOLUTIONARY THEORY BORN OF THE
STRUGGLE BETWEEN THE INTERNATIONAL WORKING CLASS AND THE
INTERNATIONAL CAPITALIST CLASS. MARXISM-LENINISM. WHICH
GUIDED THE CHINESE REVOLUTION TO VICTORY, WILL REMAIN THE
FUNDAMENTAL IDEOLOGY GUIDING CHINESE COMMUNISM IN THE FUTURE.
EXPONENTS OF BOURGEOIS LIBERALIZATION SAY THAT MARXISM-
LENINISM IS OUTDATED, BUT IN ACTUALITY IT REMAINS THE BANNER
OF THE MODERN ERA.

09958 ZHEN, Z.
MARXISM-LENINISM IS THE BANNER OF OUR TIMES (II)
BEIJING REVIEW, 32(49) (DEC 89), 27-28.
THOSE WHO ADVOCATE BOURGEOIS LIBERALIZATION HAVE
ADVANCED THE THEORY THAT MARXISM-LENINISM IS HARMFUL. THEY
SAY THAT MARXISM-LENINISM IS NOT SUITED TO CHINA'S NATIONAL
CONDITIONS AND IS THE SOURCE OF CHINA'S PROLONGED
BACKWARDNESS. THIS IS AN ABUSE OF TRUTH AND A DISTORTION OF
HISTORY. IT WAS THE INTRODUCTION OF MARXISM-LENINISM TO
CHINA AND THE SUBSEQUENT INTEGRATION OF MARXISM THE THEORY AND THE
WORKERS' MOVEMENT THAT GAVE BIRTH TO THE COMMUNIST PARTY OF

CHINA. MOREOVER, MARXISM-LENINISM HELPED THE CHINESE PEOPLE DEVELOP A SCIENTIFIC WORLD OUTLOOK AND METHODOLOGY ALONG WITH THE CORRECT VISION OF CHINA'S DESTINY.

09959 ZHENQIANG, P.
CHINA'S SECURITY OPTIONS IN THE 1990'S
NATO'S SIXTEEN NATIONS, 34(2) (APR 89), 13-16.
THE REMARKABLE ECONOMIC UPSURGE OF MOST ASIAN COUNTRIES ALSO HAS MAJOR SOCIAL AND POLITICAL CONSEQUENCES WITH SECURITY IMPLICATIONS. THE CHINESE LEADERSHIP IS DETERMINED TO BASE THE COUNTRY'S SECURITY ON A STRONG ECONOMY AND, AS A FIRST PRIORITY, HAS INITIATED A PLAN TO TRANSFORM IT INTO AN ADVANCED STATE OVER A 50-YEAR PERIOD. THIS WILL INCLUDE SOME MODERNIZATION OF THE PEOPLE'S LIBERATION ARMY BUT PUTS THE EMPHASIS ON ECONOMIC DEVELOPMENT, COOPERATION AND DISARMAMENT.

09960 ZHENQIANG, P.
SEEKING A BETTER APPROACH TO END THE NUCLEAR ARMS RACE: A RETROSPECTIVE ON THE PARTIAL TEST-BAN TREATY
DISARMAMENT, XII(1) (WIN 89), 25-33.
THE AUTHOR REVIEWS THE HISTORY OF THE 1963 PARTIAL TEST BAN TREATY AND ITS IMPACT ON ARMS CONTROL OVER THE PAST TWENTY-FIVE YEARS. HE CONCLUDES THAT, ALTHOUGH THE TREATY DID NOT PREVENT CHINA FROM BECOMING A NUCLEAR STATE, THE ORIGINAL PURPOSES OF THE SUPERPOWERS HAVE LARGELY BEEN ACHIEVED BY THE PARTIAL TEST BAN TREATY.

09961 ZHI, X.
CAMPUS INCIDENT IN NANJING
BEIJING REVIEW, 32(4) (JAN 89), 7,9.
A CHRISTMAS EVE BRAWL IN NANJING INVOLVING AFRICAN STUDENTS AND CHINESE STAFF AT HEHAI UNIVERSITY HAS RE CEIVED WIDESPREAD ATTENTION AROUND THE WORLD. UNFORTUNATELY, MANY OF THE REPORTS HAVE EITHER BEEN SEVERELY DISTORTED OR ENTIRELY UNTRUE: THE EVENT WAS AN ISOLATED INCIDENT BEREFT OF ANY OF THE POLITICAL OVERTONES ATTRIBUTED TO IT BY THE WESTERN MEDIA. THE CHINESE AUTHORITIES HAVE NOW TAKEN MEASURES TO RESTORE ORDER ON THE CAMPUS, AND AFRICAN DIPLOMATS HAVE SAID THE EVENT WILL NOT AFFECT THE FRIENDSHIP AND CO-OPERATION BETWEEN THEIR COUNTRIES AND CHINA.

09962 ZHIGANG, W.; MINHUI, Y.
EDUCATION: OPENING AND IMPROVEMENT
BEIJING REVIEW, 32(39) (SEP 89), 35-36.
FOLLOWING THE JUNE 1989 POLITICAL TURMOIL IN BEIJING, MANY CHINESE CITIZENS EXPRESSED THEIR CONCERN ABOUT CHINA'S EDUCATIONAL POLICIES. SOME OF THEM SHARPLY CRITIZED THE GOVERNMENT'S PRACTICE OF SENDING STUDENTS ABROAD, BECAUSE THEY BELIEVE IT WAS ONE OF THE DIRECT CAUSES OF THE UNREST. BUT THE VICE MINISTER OF THE STATE EDUCATION COMMISSION HAS DECLARED THAT THE FUNDAMENTAL POLICY OF OPENING UP TO THE WORLD WILL NOT CHANGE AND THAT THE PRACTICE OF SENDING CHINESE YOUTH TO STUDY ABROAD WILL NOT STOP.

09963 ZHIGUO, A.
ON THE EVENTS IN BEIJING
BEIJING REVIEW, 32(26) (JUN 89), 7,9.
DURING THE SPRING OF 1989, THE SITUATION IN BEIJING DEVELOPED FROM CAMPUS UPHEAVAL TO TURMOIL AND FINALLY TO A COUNTER-REVOLUTIONARY REVOLT. AFTER THE CHINESE GOVERNMENT TOOK DRASTIC MEASURES, THE REVOLT WAS QUICKLY QUELLED, SOCIAL ORDER WAS RESTORED, AND THE POLITICAL SITUATION STABILIZED. BUT THE TURMOIL IS NOT A SIGN THAT THERE IS SOMETHING WRONG WITH THE PARTY'S LINE, PRINCIPLES OR POLICIES. THE PARTY'S ADHERENCE TO THE FOUR CARDINAL PRINCIPLES REMAINS THE CORRECT COURSE FOR CHINA.

09964 ZHONGLIN, R.
DEVELOPMENT AND ROLE OF THE PRIVATE ECONOMY
BEIJING REVIEW, 32(19) (MAY 89), 22-25.
THE PRIVATE ECONOMY IS ONE COMPONENT OF CHINA'S OWNERSHIP STRUCTURE, WITH PUBLIC OWNERSHIP AS THE MAIN BODY. CHINA'S PRIVATE ECONOMIC SECTOR IS STILL IN ITS EARLY STAGES OF GROWTH. FOSTERING THIS PRIVATE ECONOMY IS NOT A MEASURE OF EXPEDIENCY BUT A LONG-TERM PRINCIPLE OF THE COMMUNIST PARTY IN THE PRIMARY STAGE OF SOCIALISM. IT IS IMPORTANT TO UNDERSTAND THE NATURE, STATUS, AND ROLE OF THE PRIVATE ECONOMY AS WELL AS OF THE PARTY'S AND GOVERNMENT'S POLICIES REGARDING IT.

09965 ZHONGQING, T.
LOOKING BACK: SOUTHEAST ASIA IN 1988
BEIJING REVIEW, 32(2) (JAN 89), 15-18.
MOST OF SOUTHEAST ASIA WAS POLITICALLY ABUZZ IN 1988 AND WITNESSED NOTABLE ECONOMIC ACHIEVEMENTS. INDONESIA, SINGAPORE, AND THAILAND ENDURED INTENSE ELECTION CAMPAIGNS, WHILE BURMA EXPERIENCED SIGNIFICANT POLITICAL UNREST. THE KAMPUCHEAN ISSUE REMAINED AN IMPORTANT, UNSOLVED REGIONAL PROBLEM. BUT 1988 WELCOMED CORDIAL RELATIONS AND CLOSER BONDS BETWEEN MANY SOUTHEAST ASIAN COUNTRIES AND THE REPUBLIC OF CHINA.

09966 ZHOU, T.X.
AFTER THE CHINESE MASSACRE: TO MY AMERICAN FRIENDS
FREEDOM AT ISSUE, (110) (SEP 89), 14-15.
WHILE UNANIMOUSLY DENOUNCING THE CHINESE GOVERNMENT FOR ITS BARBAROUS BEHAVIOR, PUBLIC OPINION IN THE UNITED STATES IS NATURALLY DIVIDED ON THE ISSUE OF AMERICAN POLICY TOWARD CHINA FOLLOWING THE JUNE 1989 MASSACRE. IN THIS ARTICLE, THE AUTHOR CONSIDERS SOME OF THE COMMON REASONS ADVANCED TO JUSTIFY A CONTINUED U.S. RAPPROCHEMENT WITH THE DENG XIAOPING REGIME.

09967 ZHUKOV, Y.
SOVIET DIPLOMACY: DISARMAMENT EFFORT IN LENIN'S LIFETIME AND AFTER
REPRINTS FROM THE SOVIET PRESS, 48(2) (JAN 89), 29-32.
THE PAINSTAKING AND RESOURCEFUL DISARMAMENT EFFORT BY SOVIET DIPLOMATS IN 1922-1934 STRENGTHENED PROGRESSIVE FORCES ABROAD AS IT EXPOSED THE RED DANGER ALLEGATIONS AND OFFERED THE PROSPECT OF A WORLD FREE OF WARS AND WEAPONS. NOW, EVERY DAY MAKES IT CLEARER THAT THE MIGHT-IS-RIGHT PRINCIPLE DOESN'T WORK, THAT POLITICAL MATTERS CAN NO LONGER BE SETTLED BY FORCE OF ARMS. IDEAS OF PEACE AND DISARMAMENT GAIN AN EVER FIRMER FOOTING. THE WORLD GIVES HEED TO THEM.

09968 ZHUOYE, L.
FIRST AMBASSADOR TO U.S. REMINSCES
BEIJING REVIEW, 32(4) (JAN 89), 31-34.
BASED ON REMINISCES BY CHAI ZEMIN, WHO SERVED AS THE FIRST AMBASSADOR FROM THE PEOPLE'S REPUBLIC OF CHINA TO THE UNITED STATES, THE AUTHOR REVIEWS THE NEGOTIATIONS THAT PRECEDED THE OFFICIAL ESTABLISHMENT OF DIPLOMATIC RELATIONS AND THE OPENING OF THE NEW EMBASSY.

09969 ZI, H.
THE DEPLORABLE ACTIONS OF THE NOBEL COMMITTEE
BEIJING REVIEW, 32(49) (DEC 89), 7.
THE NOBEL PEACE PRIZE COMMITTEE HAS ANNOUNCED THAT THE 1989 PEACE PRIZE WILL BE GIVEN TO THE DALAI LAMA. THIS MISGUIDED DECISION, WHICH IS TAINTED WITH A STRONG POLITICAL HUE, HAS ELICITED CONDEMNATION AND PROTESTS FROM THE MAINLAND CHINESE PEOPLE AND FROM PATRIOTIC OVERSEAS CHINESE. AT A FORUM IN LHASA, PUBLIC FIGURES OF THE TIBET AUTONOMOUS REGION UNANIMOUSLY AGREED THAT THE COMMITTEE'S ACTION WAS WANTON INTERFERENCE IN CHINA'S INTERNAL AFFAIRS AND OPEN SUPPORT FOR SECESSIONISTS.

09970 ZIEGLER, J.; WEBER, A.
COMMUNISTS AND SOCIAL DEMOCRATS: A TIME TO GATHER STONES TOGETHER
WORLD MARXIST REVIEW, 36(8) (AUG 89), 51-58.
THIS ARTICLE ANALYSES THE EFFORTS TO FIND A COMMON GROUND AND ALSO THE PERIODS OF ACUTE CONFRONTATION, PRIMARILY IN RELATIONS BETWEEN COMMUNISTS AND SOCIAL DEMOCRATS AS REPRESENTATIVES OF THE TWO MAJOR CURRENTS OF THE WORKING CLASS MOVEMENT. TODAY, MUTUAL RECRIMINATIONS AND BIASED ASSESSMENTS ARE YIELDING INCREASINGLY TO A CIVILIZED DIALOGUE IN WHICH VIEWS ARE OPENLY EXPRESSED AND EACH SIDE LISTENS TO WHAT THE OTHERS HAVE TO SAY. A REPRESENTATIVE FROM SWITZERLAND AND THE USSR SHARE THEIR VIEWS ON THE CURRENT STATE OF COOPERATION BETWEEN COMMUNISTS AND SOCIAL DEMOCRATS AND PROSPECTS FOR IT.

09971 ZIELINSKI, A.
A HOME FOR EVERY FAMILY
CONTEMPORARY POLAND, XXII(2) (1989), 8-12.
ONE OF THE MOST ACUTE AND COMPLEX PROBLEMS FACING POLAND TODAY IS THE HOUSING SHORTAGE. IT IS NOT SURPRISING THAT THE RAKOWSKI GOVERNMENT HAS SINGLED IT OUT AS ONE OF THE THREE TOP PRIORITY PROBLEMS THAT MUST BE SOLVED. THE SLOGAN "A HOME FOR EVERY FAMILY," LAUNCHED IN THE MID-1970'S BUT NEVER IMPLEMENTED, HAS NOW BECOME OFFICIAL POLICY. THE MAJOR MISTAKE IN DRAFTING PAST POLICY HAS BEEN TO SEE HOUSING NEEDS IN TERMS OF VOLUME WHILE DISREGARDING THE WHOLE RANGE OF ISSUES AND PROBLEMS RELATED TO IT.

09972 ZIELINSKI, A.
BREAKTHROUGH IN THE OFFING?
CONTEMPORARY POLAND, XXII(3) (1989), 6-9.
DOUBTS PERSIST ABOUT REFORM IN POLAND BECAUSE NONE OF THE PAST DEVELOPMENT PLANS HAS YIELDED THE EXPECTED EFFECTS. NO WONDER THAT THE LATEST PROJECT, THE PROPOSED ECONOMIC CONSOLIDATION PLAN COVERING 1989-1990, HAS PROVOKED HEATED, EMOTIONAL DEBATE. THE PLAN CALLS FOR SUBORDINATING ALL ACTIONS IN THE SPHERES OF SOCIAL AND ECONOMIC POLICY TO THE FOLLOWING OBJECTIVES: SPEEDING UP DEVELOPMENT OF THE FIELDS THAT DIRECTLY INFLUENCE THE QUALITY OF LIFE (FOODSTUFFS, HOUSING, ENVIRONMENT) AND MODERNIZING THE ECONOMIC STRUCTURE WHILE EXPANDING ITS CAPACITY FOR BALANCED GROWTH, ESPECIALLY BY PROMOTING PROFITABLE EXPORTS AND ENCOURAGING NEW TECHNOLOGIES.

09973 ZIELINSKI, A.
NEW ROLE OF THE BANKS
CONTEMPORARY POLAND, XXII(7) (1989), 6-9.

MONEY DID NOT PLAY A SIGNIFICANT ROLE IN POLAND'S POST-
WAR ECONOMY UNTIL RECENT YEARS, WHEN THE ADVENT OF ECONOMIC
REFORM ASSIGNED MONEY A MORE ACTIVE ROLE AND BANKS GAINED IN
STATURE. STILL, CREATION OF CREDIT WAS MORE AKIN TO
DISTRIBUTION THAN A COMMERCIAL PROPOSITION. THE BANKING
REFORM LAUNCHED IN 1989 WAS THE FIRST TO SHAPE AN
ENVIRONMENT WHERE CREDIT BECAME A COMMODITY AND WAS
PROFFERED ON A COMMERCIAL BASIS.

09974 ZIEM, K.
    AN INTERIM REPORT ON THE SITUATION IN AFGHANISTAN
    AUSSEN POLITIK, 40(1) (JAN 89), 41-54.
        THE ARTICLE EXAMINES AFGHANISTAN IN LIGHT OF THE 1988
    GENEVA ACCORDS. IT CONCLUDES THAT THE ACCORDS SET ASIDE TOO
    MANY PROBLEMS FOR LONG TERM PEACE TO BE REACHED. ALTHOUGH
    THE SOVIET TROOPS WILL UNDOUBTABLY COMPLETE THEIR WITHDRAWAL,
    THERE IS NO SIGN OF EITHER AN END TO THE CIVIL WAR OR A
    CLEAR POLITICAL SOLUTION ON THE BASIS OF A SETTLEMENT
    BETWEEN ALL CONCERNED. THE USSR WILL PROBABLY CONTINUE TO
    SUPPLY AND SUPPORT PRESIDENT NAJIBULLAH AND THE US WILL
    CONTINUE TO AID THE REBELS. IT SEEMS CLEAR THAT NO-ONE IN
    AFGHANISTAN WILL BE IN A POSITION TO SET UP A NEW REGIME AND
    DETERMINE THE COURSE OF POLITICS ON HIS OWN. THE EXISTENCE
    OF ROUGHLY ONE-THIRD OF THE POPULATION OF AFGHANISTAN IN
    PAKISTAN AND IRAN ALSO COMPOUNDS THE PROBLEM.

09975 ZIHUI, Y.
    POPULATION STUDIES GET PRIORITY
    BEIJING REVIEW, 32(17) (APR 89), 32-37.
        IN THE 1950'S, CHINA WHOLLY ACCEPTED THE SOVIET THEORY
    THAT POPULATION GROWTH WAS A PARTICULAR PATTERN OF SOCIALISM
    AND A REFLECTION OF SOCIALIST ADVANTAGES. CHINA EMULATED THE
    SOVIETS BOTH IN THEORY AND IN PRACTICE BY REWARDING WOMEN
    WHO GAVE BIRTH TO SEVERAL CHILDREN. IN 1978, CHINA'S
    READJUSTED POPULATION POLICY BROKE THE TRAMMELS OF THE
    MISTAKEN THEORY. CHINESE POPULATION EXPERTS BEGAN TO STUDY
    THE PROBLEM PRACTICALLY AND REALISTICALLY. IMPROVED
    RELATIONS WITH THE WEST, ESPECIALLY THE UNITED STATES, HAVE
    ENABLED CHINESE POPULATION EXPERTS TO EXCHANGE INFORMATION
    AND LEARN ADVANCED RESEARCH METHODS.

09976 ZIMBALIST, A.
    CUBA'S REVOLUTIONARY ECONOMY
    MULTINATIONAL MONITOR, 10(4) (APR 89), 7-9.
        CUBAN ECONOMIC PERFORMANCE IS IN THE EYE OF THE BEHOLDER.
    DESPITE THE FACT THAT BETWEEN 1980 AND 1987 NATIONAL PER
    CAPITA INCOME IN CUBA GREW AT A REAL ANNUAL RATE OF 4.4
    PERCENT WHILE IT FELL IN THE REST OF LATIN AMERICA, U.S.
    MAINSTREAM OPINION HAS NEVER REFLECTED THAT PROGRESS. VIEWS
    OF THE CUBAN ECONOMY HAVE BEEN DIVIDED BETWEEN "IT'S AN
    ECONOMIC MESS" AND "ONLY THROUGH MASSIVE SOVIET AID IS
    ANYTHING ACHIEVED." BUT THE REAL STORY OF CUBAN ECONOMIC
    DEVELOPMENT OVER THE PAST THIRTY YEARS IS OBSCURED BY
    EXCLUSIVE FOCUS ON ALLOCATIONAL AND MANAGEMENT DEFICIENCIES.
    THE LONG-RUN GROWTH, THE SUCCESSFUL STRUCTURAL CHANGE, AND
    THE VIRTUALLY UNIVERSAL PROVISION OF BASIC NEEDS PROVIDE A
    MORE REVEALING PICTURE.

09977 ZIMMERMAN, C.
    FEDS EYE VALUE-ADDED TAX
    STATE LEGISLATURES, 15(1) (JAN 89), 10-13.
        DISCUSSION ABOUT THE POSSIBLE INTRODUCTION OF A VAT IN
    THE UNITED STATES HAS, IN SOME QUARTERS, RECENTLY TAKEN ON A
    SERIOUS TONE. MANY IN GOVERNMENT AND BUSINESS HAVE BEGUN FOR
    THE FIRST TIME TO CONSIDER THE POTENTIAL CONSEQUENCES OF
    SUCH A NEW TAX SYSTEM FOR THE AMERICAN ECONOMY AND FOR
    AMERICAN FEDERALISM. THE REASON THAT THE VAT IS NOW BEING
    TAKEN SERIOUSLY, BOTH BY ADVOCATES AND OPPONENTS, IS THE
    LARGE AND CONTINUING FEDERAL BUDGET DEFICIT.

09978 ZIMMERMAN, J.F.
    CHARTER REFORM IN THE 1990'S
    NATIONAL CIVIC REVIEW, 78(5) (SEP 89), 329-338.
        RECENT RELEASE OF THE NEW SEVENTH EDITION OF THE MODEL
    CITY CHARTER BY THE NATIONAL CIVIC LEAGUE HAS HEIGHTENED
    AWARENESS OF THE NEED FOR SUBSTANTIVE CHARTER REVIEW IN MANY
    MUNICIPALITIES. THE NEW MODEL--WITH ITS EMPHASIS ON
    SIMPLICITY AND BREVITY--IS TRULY A CHARTER FOR THE 1990S, IN
    THAT IT FOSTERS CITIZEN UNDERSTANDING OF LOCAL GOVERNMENT
    STRUCTURE AND (ULTIMATELY) BROADER PARTICIPATION IN LOCAL
    GOVERNANCE. ADMINISTRATIVE SPECIFICS ON WHICH THE CHARTER IS
    SILENT CAN READILY BE PROVIDED THROUGH LEGISLATIVE ORDINANCE
    APPROPRIATE ATE FOR UNIQUE LOCAL CONDITIONS.

09979 ZIMMERMAN, S.L.
    MYTHS ABOUT PUBLIC WELFARE: POVERTY, FAMILY INSTABILITY,
    AND TEEN ILLEGITIMACY
    POLICY STUDIES REVIEW, 8(3) (SPR 89), 674-688.
        TO RATIONALIZE FEDERAL CUTBACKS IN SPENDING FOR PUBLIC
    WELFARE, PRESIDENT REAGAN CHARGED THAT PUBLIC WELFARE
    PROGRAMS ARE RESPONSIBLE FOR LEADING TO A "NATIONAL TRAGEDY
    INVOLVING FAMILY BREAKDOWN, TEEN-AGE ILLEGITIMACY AND
    WORSENING PROVERTY." YET ANALYSIS OF 1980 AND 1982 CENSUS
    DATA FOR THE 50 STATES SUGGESTS THAT IF THIS IS SO, IT IS

BECAUSE OF LOW, NOT NOT HIGH, SPENDING FOR PUBLIC WELFARE.
WHILE LOW STATE SPENDING FOR PUBLIC WELFARE IS PREDICTIVE OF
HIGH TEEN ILLEGITIMACY RATES AND DIRECTLY LINKED TO HIGH
STATE POVERTY AND DIVORCE RATES, HIGHER STATE SPENDING FOR
PUBLIC WELFARE IS PREDICTIVE OF LOWER TEEN BIRTH RATES, AND
LINKED TO LOWER RATES OF FAMILY BREAKUP AND POVERTY. DESPITE
LIMITATIONS INHERENT IN THE ANALYSIS, THE FINDINGS CHALLENGE
THE CONTENTION THAT SPENDING FOR PUBLIC WELFARE CONTRIBUTES
TO FAMILY BREAKUP, TEEN ILLEGITIMACY AND POVERTY.

09980 ZIMMERMANN, E.
    POLITICAL UNREST IN WESTERN EUROPE: TRENDS AND PROSPECTS
    WEST EUROPEAN POLITICS, 12(3) (JUL 89), 179-196.
        EMPIRICAL EVIDENCE IS PRESENTED ON THE DEVELOPMENT OF
    (VIOLENT) POLITICAL CONFLICT IN 19 WEST EUROPEAN COUNTRIES
    DURING THE 1970S, THE EARLY 1980S AND THE ENTIRE POST-SECOND
    WORLD WAR PERIOD. IT IS POSSIBLE TO IDENTIFY THREE TYPES OF
    NATION-GROUPS: 'NOISYPARTICIPATORY' STATES SUCH AS THE
    UNITED KINGDOM, FRANCE, ITALY, AND MORE RECENTLY SPAIN AND
    PORTUGAL - AND GREECE IF TAKEN ON A PER CAPITA BASE. THE
    GROUP OF RATHER 'QUIET' DEMOCRACIES CONSISTS OF THE
    SCANDINAVIAN COUNTRIES, SWITZERLAND AND LUXEMBOURG, WITH THE
    REMAINING COUNTRIES FORMING THE MIDDLE, LESS CLEARLY
    DELINEATED GROUP. THERE ARE TWO DIMENSIONS OF POLITICAL
    CONFLICT: COLLECTIVE PROTEST, MADE UP OF VARIABLES SUCH AS
    PROTEST DEMONSTRATIONS, POLITICAL STRIKES AND RIOTS, AND
    INTERNAL WAR, CHARACTERISED BY THE BREAKDOWN OF THE STATE
    MONOPOLY OF VIOLENCE AND THE ORGANISED USE OF VIOLENCE BY
    ANTI-SYSTEM GROUPS. A CAUSAL MODEL OF POLITICAL PROTEST IS
    PRESENTED AND CONFRONTED WITH RIVAL EXPLANATIONS. EMPIRICAL
    EVIDENCE AND THEORETICAL ARGUMENTS LEAD TO SCEPTICISM ABOUT
    ACCURATE PREDICTIONS OF POLITICAL VIOLENCE AND POLITICAL
    INSTABILITY.

09981 ZINNER, P.E.
    FRENCH ATTITUDES CONCERNING MAJOR CONTEMPORARY ISSUES
    AFFECTING EUROPEAN SECURITY
    AVAILABLE FROM NTIS, NO. DE89005949/GAR, OCT 88, 7.
        WHILE IN EUROPE THIS PAST SUMMER, PROF. ZINNER HAD AN
    INTERESTING OPPORTUNITY TO MEET IN PARIS WITH A NUMBER OF
    HIGHLY PLACED FRENCH OFFICIALS CONCERNED WITH NATIONAL
    SECURITY AFFAIRS. THEIR VIEWS SEEMED TO BE OF SUFFICIENT
    INTEREST AND DIFFERENT IN SUCH SIGNIFICANT WAYS FROM THOSE
    EXPRESSED BY FRG OFFICIALS TO PREPARE A BRIEF SUMMARY. THIS
    PAPER DOES JUST THAT AND SPEAKS FOR ITSELF. THIS PAPER IS
    PART OF A CONTINUING PROGRAM OF STUDIES FUNDED BY THE OFFICE
    OF ARMS CONTROL/DP/DOE AND CONDUCTED BY D DIVISION.

09982 ZINSMEISTER, K.
    PLOWING UNDER SUBSIDIES
    REASON, 21(5) (OCT 89), 30-37.
        CONTRARY TO BOTH POPULAR BELIEF AND TO THE OPINION ON
    CAPITOL HILL, A SIZABLE PORTION OF US FARMERS ARE OPPOSED TO
    GOVERNMENT SUBSIDIES OF ANY KIND. THEY VIEW THEM AS
    COUNTERPRODUCTIVE AND RESPONSIBLE FOR THE PROLIFRATION THE
    US DEPENDENCE ON OVERSEAS PRODUCE. THE ARTICLE EXPLORES
    SEVERAL FARMERS' EXPERIENCE WITH GOVERMEN SUBSIDIES AND
    THEIR OPINIONS ABOUT THE SUBJECT

09983 ZIRAKZADEH, C.E.
    ECONOMIC CHANGES AND SURGES IN MICRO-NATIONALIST VOTING IN
    SCOTLAND AND THE BASQUE REGION OF SPAIN
    COMPARATIVE STUDIES IN SOCIETY AND HISTORY, 31(2) (APR 89),
    318-339.
        THE DATA IN THIS PAPER SUGGEST THAT THE STRIKING
    ECONOMIC CHANGES OF THE 1970S IN SCOTLAND AND IN THE BASQUE
    REGION (AND IN THE NORTH ATLANTIC AREA IN GENERAL) WERE ONE
    COMMON AND IDENTIFIABLE CONDITION THAT HELPED BRING ABOUT
    MAJOR ELECTORAL CHANGES IN BOTH PLACES. WITH THE DATA
    COLLECTED IN THIS PAPER, ONE CAN SERIOUSLY ENTERTAIN THE
    HYPOTHESIS THAT ECONOMIC CHANGES IN SCOTLAND AND THE BASQUE
    REGION HERE TO A SIGNIFICANT EXTENT CONNECTED TO SUDDEN
    CHANGES IN LOCAL ELECTORAL BEHAVIOR. THE SURGES IN
    NATIONALIST VOTING IN SCOTLAND AND THE BASQUE REGION APPEAR
    TO BE ASPECTS NOT SO MUCH OF PERSISTENT, REGIONAL
    "ETHNONATIONALISMS," AS OF HISTORICALLY RISING AND FALLING
    "ECO-NATIONALISMS."

09984 ZIRAKZADEH, C.E.
    TRADITIONS OF PROTEST AND THE HIGH-SCHOOL STUDENT
    MOVEMENTS IN
    WEST EUROPEAN POLITICS, 12(3) (JUL 89), 220-237.
        SPAIN AND FRANCE IN 1986-87 THIS ARTICLE EXPLORES THE
    SOCIAL CIRCUMSTANCES THAT NURTURE SOCIAL MOVEMENTS IN
    ADVANCED CAPITALIST SOCIETIES BY EXAMINING THE SPANISH AND
    FRENCH HIGH-SCHOOL STUDENT MOVEMENTS OF 1986-87. ATTENTION
    IS GIVEN TO THE INFLUENCE OF UNEMPLOYMENT, OUTSIDE
    ORGANISERS, THE POLITICAL EDUCATION OF COMMUNITY LEADERS,
    AND PAST PROTESTS THAT PROVIDED EXAMPLES FOR MOVEMENT
    PARTICIPANTS. THE ARTICLE PROPOSES THAT FUTURE RESEARCH ON
    EUROPEAN SOCIAL MOVEMENTS FOCUS, FIRST, ON ORGANISATIONAL
    PREREQUISITES, AND, SECOND, ON THE SOCIAL AND PSYCHOLOGICAL
    PROCESSES BY WHICH PEOPLE DERIVE LESSONS FROM PAST POLITICAL
    EVENTS.

09985 ZIVANOV, S.
RESTRUCTURING IS A TRAJECTORY OF RENEWAL
WORLD MARXIST REVIEW, 32(6) (JUN 89), 14-17.
THIS ARTICLE EXPLORES THE PRESENT NEED FOR RESTRUCTURING
IN THE FACE OF GLOBAL ENVIRONMENTAL THREAT AND THE DECLINE
OF ECONOMIC GROWTH RATES IN SOCIALIST COUNTRIES. IT REVEALS
THE POTENTIAL FOR RENEWAL OF THE WORLD IN GENERAL AND OF
SOCIALISM IN PARTICULAR. THE CURRENT PRE-CRISIS SITUATION
FOR SOCIALISM IS EXAMINED. IDEAS AND THEIR IMPLEMENTATION
ARE DISCUSSED AND THE FACT THAT THE SOCIALIST COUNTRIES ARE
NOW EMBARKED ON A RESTRUCTURING EFFORT AND ARE NOW AT A
DECISIVE, CRUTIAL JUNCTURE IN THEIR REFORMS IS ANALYZED.

09986 ZIYANG, Z.
CHINA: EQUIPPING THE PARTY WITH THE THEORY OF THE 13TH
CONGRESS
INFORMATION BULLETIN, 27 (MAR 89), 24.
IN THIS SPEECH, ZHAO ZIYANG EXTOLLED THE SIGNIFICANCE OF
THE THIRD PLENARY MEETING OF THE 11TH CPCCC BECAUSE IT
RESTORED MARXISM AS THE PARTY'S IDEOLOGICAL COURSE. THAT
MEETING PAVED THE WAY FOR REFORM AND PROVIDED THE IMPETUS
FOR THE GRADUAL DEVELOPMENT OF THE THEORY GUIDING THE
REFORMS AND RECONSTRUCTION.

09987 ZMELNOVA, Y.
TASKS OF THE ECONOMIC REFORM IN POLAND
FOREIGN TRADE, 4 (1988), 20-21.
THIS ARTICLE REPORTS ON ACTIVITIES OF THE POLISH FOREIGN
TRADE CHAMBER TO PROMOTE THE DEVELOPMENT OF POLISH
ENTERPRISES' TIES WITH THEIR FOREIGN TRADE PARTNERS.
ANALYSED IS HOW THE CHAMBER IS RESPONDING TO THE ON-GOING
CHANGES IN THE MANAGEMENT OF THE ECONOMY, STIMULI FOR
ENCOURAGING EXPORTER MANUFACTURERS, THE IMPACT OF POLISH
CLUBS OF POLISH-SOVIET COOPERATION ON THE DEVELOPMENT OF
TRADE WITH THE USSR, AND THE CHAMBER'S FLEXIBILITY TO CHANGE
DUE TO NEW DEMANDS.

09988 ZOGBY, J.
A WAY TOWARDS THE SAVING OF LEBANON
MIDDLE EAST INTERNATIONAL, 353 (JUN 89), 19-20.
PEEL AWAY THE MANY LAYERS THAT HAVE ACCUMULATED SINCE
THE LEBANESE CONFLICT BEGAN AND IT REMAINS, AT ITS CORE, ONE
ARISING OUT OF THE POLITICAL AND ECONOMIC INEQUITIES OF AN
OUTMODED SYSTEM OF GOVERNANCE, THAT GAVE PREFERENCE TO THE
ELITES OF THE CHRISTIAN AND MUSLIN SECTS. AS THE INJUSTICES
OF THIS SYSTEM INTENSIFIED, THE DISENFRANCHISED REBELLED AND
THOSE WITH POWER FOUGHT TO MAINTAIN THEIR HEGEMONY, LEADING
ULTIMATELY TO A BREAKDOWN IN NATIONAL COHESION. WHILE THE
INITIAL ROUNDS OF FIGHTING HAD AN IDEOLOGICAL AND POLITICAL
CHARACTER, INCREASINGLY THE SECTARIAN LOYALTIES HAVE COME TO
DOMINATE. THE SIMPLE FACT IS THAT THERE CAN BE NO MILITARY
SOLUTION TO LEBANON'S POLITICAL PROBLEMS. THOSE ON ALL SIDES
WHO HAVE CHOSEN KILLING AS A WAY OF SAVING LEBANON ARE
PRODUCING THE OPPOSITE RESULT - THEY ARE, IN FACT, KILLING
LEBANON.

09989 ZOLBERG, A.R.
THE NEXT WAVES: MIGRATION THEORY FOR A CHANGING WORLD
INTERNATIONAL MIGRATION REVIEW, 23(3) (FAL 89), 403-430.
IN THE LAST QUARTER OF A CENTURY, MIGRATION THEORY HAS
UNDERGONE FUNDAMENTAL CHANGE, MOVING FROM THE CLASSIC
"INDIVIDUAL RELOCATION" GENRE INITIATED BY RAVENSTEIN A
CENTURY AGO, TO A VARIETY OF NEW APPROACHES WHICH
NEVERTHELESS SHARE IMPORTANT ELEMENTS: THEY TEND TO BE
HISTORICAL, STRUCTURAL, GLOBALIST AND CRITICAL.
HISTORICIZATION IMPLIES A CONSTANT MODIFICATION OF
THEORETICAL CONCERNS AND EMPHASES IN THE LIGHT OF CHANGING
SOCIAL REALITIES, AND COMMITMENT TO A CRITICAL APPROACH
ENTAILS A VIEW OF RESEARCH AS ONE ELEMENT IN A BROADER
PROJECT CONCERNED WITH THE ELUCIDATION OF SOCIAL AND
POLITICAL CONDITIONS. THE ARTICLE USES ELEMENTS FROM TWO
MAJOR THEORETICAL TRADITIONS - A MODIFIED WORLD-SYSTEMS
APPROACH AND STATE THEORY - TO PROJECT CURRENT TRENDS.
GLOBAL INEQUALITY IS CONSIDERED AS A STRUCTURAL GIVEN. THE
ARTICLE THEN REVIEWS MAJOR TOPICS, INCLUDING THE PERSISTENCE
OF RESTRICTIVE IMMIGRATION POLICIES AS BARRIERS TO MOVEMENT,
CHANGING PATTERNS OF EXPLOITATION OF FOREIGN LABOR,
LIBERALIZATION OF EXIT FROM THE SOCIALIST WORLD AND THE
REFUGEE CRISIS IN THE DEVELOPING WORLD. IT CONCLUDES WITH A
BRIEF CONSIDERATION OF THE NORMATIVE IMPLICATIONS OF THESE
TRENDS.

09990 ZOTOV, G.; SABELNIKOV, L.
ECONOMIC OUTLOOK AND TRADE POLICY OF THE CAPITALIST
COUNTRIES IN 1987 AND EARLY 1988
FOREIGN TRADE, 6 (1988), 14-18.
THIS ARTICLE INSPECTS THE GENERAL ECONOMIC OUTLOOK OF
THE CAPITALIST WORLD AND ANALYSES VARIOUS FACTORS
CONTRIBUTING TO THE DECLINE IN ECONOMIC GROWTH RATES. THE
ECONOMIES OF THE USA, JAPAN, WEST GERMANY, BRITAIN AND ITALY
ARE TRACED. CONSUMER DEMAND IS EXPLORED. MEASURES TAKEN BY
INDIVIDUAL COUNTRIES TO ACCELERATE ECONOMIC GROWTH ARE
DESCRIBED. VARIOUS CONFERENCES HELD ON AREAS OF ECONOMIC

GROWTH AND TRADE RELATIONS ARE CAPSULIZED.

09991 ZUBOK, V.M.
OVERCOMING STEREOTYPES
SOVIET REVIEW, 30(5) (SEP 89), 36-50.
AFTER A SEVEN-YEAR INTERRUPTION, THE SOVIET-AMERICAN
COMMISSION MET IN NOVEMBER 1987 TO EXCHANGE OPINIONS AND
RECOMMENDATIONS ON THE TEACHING OF SOVIET HISTORY IN
AMERICAN SCHOOLS AND ON THE WAY U.S. HISTORY IS PRESENTED IN
SOVIET SECONDARY SCHOOLS. THE GOAL IS TO COLLABORATE TO
PRODUCE SCHOOL TEXTBOOKS THAT PRESENT HISTORY OBJECTIVELY,
WITHOUT DISTORTIONS PRODUCED BY IDEOLOGY.

09992 ZUCKER, D.
JUST LEGAL: HUMAN RIGHTS IN THE TERRITORIES
TIKKUN, 4(5) (SEP 89), 49-51.
THIS ARTICLE EXAMINES THE PATHOLOGY OF THE OCCUPATION.
FOR THE FIRST TIME SINCE 1967, THE TOPIC OF HUMAN RIGHTS HAS
BECOME A MAJOR THEME IN ISRAELI PUBLIC DEBATE. THE VICIOUS
CIRCLE OF ABUSE, REBELLION AND FURTHER ABUSE IS THREATENING
THE MORAL FOUNDATIONS OF ISRAELI SOCIETY. THIS PAPER
PROVIDES A SOBER EXAMINATION OF THE HUMAN RIGHTS IN THE
TERRITORIES IN THE HOPE THAT THIS WILL INCREASE
UNDERSTANDING OF THE AXIS ON WHICH THIS VICIOUS CIRCLE TURNS.

09993 ZUCKERT, M. P.
"BRINGING PHILOSOPHY DOWN FROM THE HEAVENS": NATURAL RIGHT
IN THE ROMAN LAW
REVIEW OF POLITICS, 50(1) (WIN 89), 70-85.
THE TREATMENT OF THE NATURAL LAW IN THE ROMAN LAW IS
PUZZLING BECAUSE THE RELATIONSHIP BETWEEN JUS NATURALE AND
THE TWO OTHER FORMS OF LAW, JUS GENTIUM AND JUS CIVILE, IS
FAR FROM CLEAR IN THE TEXTS. MOREOVER, THE JUS NATURALE DOES
NOT APPEAR TO HAVE THE DIGNITY MOST READERS EXPECT IT TO
HAVE. THIS ARTICLE ATTEMPTS TO SORT OUT THE RELATIONSHIPS
AMONG THE THREE TYPES OF JUS BY SHOWING THAT THE VARIOUS
CLASSIFICATIONS THE JURISTS USE ARE BASED ON THEIR
PERCEPTIONS OF THE COMPLEXITIES OF NATURE AS A SOURCE OF
RIGHT AND ON THE ATTEMPT TO WORK OUT A POLITICAL EMBODIMENT
OF NATURAL RIGHT.

09994 ZUMA, T.
VENDA: TEN YEARS OF REPRESSION
SECHABA, 23(7) (JUL 89), 8-12.
THE TEN YEARS OF INDEPENDENCE IN VENDA HAVE SEEN
INCREASED SUFFERING AMONG THE PEOPLE. INDEPENDENCE HAS BEEN
OF NO BENEFIT TO THE PEOPLE AT ALL; ONLY TO THE PUPPETS OF
THE APARTHEID STATE. THERE IS NOTHING FOR THE PEOPLE TO
CELEBRATE, AND THE MOOD OF THE PEOPLE WAS CLEARLY
DEMONSTRATED IN THE GENERAL STRIKE OF AUGUST 1988. PEOPLE
HAVE TO WORK TOWARDS REMOVING THE RAVELE REGIME. THERE IS A
NEED TO PUT FORWARD CONTINUALLY THE PERSPECTIVE OF A UNITED,
DEMOCRATIC AND NONRACIAL SOUTH AFRICA. THROUGH STRUGGLE, THE
REPRESSIVE BANTUSTAN REGIMES CAN BE REMOVED, AS PART OF THE
FORWARD MARCH TO PEOPLE'S POWER IN A UNITED SOUTH AFRICA.

09995 ZVEREV, A.
THE MONETARY MECHANISM IN THE FOREIGN TRADE ACTIVITY OF
INDUSTRIAL ENTERPRISES
FOREIGN TRADE, 7 (1988), 37-41.
THIS ARTICLE ADDRESSES QUESTIONS WHICH ARE RAISED BY THE
RESTRUCTURING OF THE PLANNING AND MANAGEMENT MECHANISM FOR
THE USSR'S EXTERNAL ECONOMIC TIES, EXAMINED IS THE
FUNCTIONING OF THE DOMESTIC CURRENCY MECHANISM. IT CONSIDERS
THE INTERCONNECTION BETWEEN THE RESULTS OF THE ECONOMIC AND
FOREIGN TRADE ACTIVITY OF INTERPRISES, AS WELL AS BETWEEN
THE STATE BUDGET AND THE BALANCE OF PAYMENTS.

09996 ZVEREV, A.
THE PERMANENT REVOLUTIONARY? TROTSKY'S TRAGEDY HAS TO BE
REAPED BY THE DICTATORSHIP THAT HE SOWED
GLASNOST, II(3) (MAY 89), 40-43.
THE AUTHOR OFFERS A BRIEF PROFILE OF THE IDEAS OF LEON
TROTSKY AND DISCUSSES TROTSKY'S PLACE IN THE HISTORY OF
COMMUNISM.

09997 ZVESPER, J.
THE AMERICAN FOUNDERS AND CLASSICAL POLITICAL THOUGHT
HISTORY OF POLITICAL THOUGHT, X(4) (WIN 89), 701-718.
THE AUTHOR ARGUES THAT THE LOGICAL COMPATIBILITY OF THE
FOUNDERS' CLASSICAL REPUBLICANISM WITH THEIR MODERN
LIBERALISM - THEIR BALANCE BETWEEN THE DEMANDS OF THE
POLITICAL COMMUNITY AND THOSE OF HUMAN INDIVIDUALITY -
DEPENDS ON THEIR REFERENCE TO UNIVERSAL NATURAL STANDARDS.
HOWEVER MUCH THEIR SENSIBLE LIBERAL DEMOCRATIC PRINCIPLES
MAY HAVE BEEN DEGRADED INTO NINETEENTH-AND TWENTIETH-CENTURY
LIBERTARIANISM AND PROGRESSIVISM, IN ALL HONESTY WE SHOULD
ACKNOWLEDGE THAT THEY WOULD HAVE DETECTED THIS DEGRADATION,
AND THAT THEY WOULD HAVE RESISTED IT BY APPEALING TO THE
PRINCIPLES OF NATURAL RIGHT THAT THEY SHARED WITH THE
CLASSICS.

09998 ZVEZDA, K.
IS A STAR WAR WINNABLE?

REPRINTS FROM THE SOVIET PRESS, 49(9) (NOV 89), 14-18.
    THIS IS AN INTERVIEW WITH GHERMAN TITOU, COLONEL-GENERAL
(AIR FORCE), A COSMONAUT OF THE USSR, HERO OF THE SOVIET
UNION. IT DISCUSSES THE STRATEGIC DEFENSE INIATIVE, ITS
ENORMOUS COST, ITS PURPOSE, ITS WEAKNESSES AND THE FACT THAT
THE US MILITARY CONTINUES TESTING SPACE-BASED WEAPONS.

09999 ZWEIG, D.
    PEASANTS AND POLITICS
    WORLD POLICY JOURNAL, 6(4) (FAL 89), 633-645.
    THIS ARTICLE REPORTS THAT RURAL CHINESE RESIDENT'S VIEWS
DIFFERED SIGNIFICANTLY FROM THOSE OF URBAN RESIDENTS. RURAL
INHABITANTS WERE FAR LESS ENTHUSIASTIC ABOUT THE DEMOCRACY
MOVEMENT BECAUSE IT HAD LITTLE IMPACT ON THEIR DAILY LIVES,
THEY GENERALLY ACCEPTED THE GOVERNMENT'S EXPLANATION FOR THE
CRACKDOWN, AND THEIR CONCERN FOR STABILITY MADE THEM MORE
SUPPORTIVE OF THE USE OF FORCE AGAINST DEMONSTRATORS IT
DESCRIBES, HOWEVER, RURAL SUPPORT FOR THE CENTRAL GOVERNMENT
AS TENUOUS AT BEST. IT CONCLUDES THAT RURAL PROBLEMS WILL BE
THE CAUSE OF RURAL UNREST.

10000 ZWICK, P.
    NEW THINKING AND NEW FOREIGN POLICY UNDER GORBACHEV
    PS: POLITICAL SCIENCE AND POLITICS, XXII(2) (JUN 89),
    215-224.
    NEW THINKING (NOVOYE MYSHLENIYE) HAS RAISED QUESTIONS
ABOUT THE SOVIET APPROACH TO INTERNATIONAL RELATIONS AND THE
PLACE OF THE SOVIET UNION IN THE INTERNATIONAL ORDER IT IS
AN EVOLVING DOCTRINE AND GORBACHEV INITIATES NEW FOREIGN
POLICY AS HE GOES ALONG.

MIX
Papier aus verantwortungsvollen Quellen
Paper from responsible sources
FSC® C105338

Printed by Books on Demand, Germany